# Editorial Advisory Board

**Susan A. Cady**
Associate Director
of Technical Services
Linderman Library
Lehigh University Libraries

**Mary Elizabeth Clack**
Serial Records Librarian
Harvard College Library

**Genevieve Clay**
Head, Central Serials
Eastern Kentucky University
Crabbe Library

**Claude Daris**
Head of Serials Department
Universite Libre de Bruxelles
Belgium

**Kenneth E. Dowlin**
Director, San Francisco Public Library
City Librarian
Main Library Civic Center

**Ludo Holans**
Librarian
Campus Bibliotheekdienst
Katholieke Universiteit Leuven
Belgium

**Sul H. Lee**
Dean, University Libraries
University of Oklahoma

**Lois N. Upham**
Uncle Remus Regional Library
Madison, Georgia

---

The 9th Edition of *The Serials Directory: An International Reference Book* was compiled and published by EBSCO Publishing, division of EBSCO Industries, Inc.

J.T. Stephens, President-EBSCO Industries, Inc.
Tim Collins, Vice President, Division General Manager-EBSCO Publishing
Mary Beth Vanderpoorten, M.S.L.S., Vice President-EBSCO Subscription Services, General Manager-Title Information

## EDITORIAL / PRODUCTION

Leanne Wofford, Editorial Manager
Jill Hinds, Special Projects Editor
Stefanie Letanosky, Titles Editor

Jean Bowick, Editorial Assistant
Joe B. Crowe, Editorial Assistant
Kathy Entrekin, Editorial Assistant

Loyd McIntosh, Editorial Assistant
Mona Powell, Editorial Assistant
Kelly Rogers, Editorial Assistant

Database and publishing software
provided by Syscomp, Inc., Atlanta, Georgia, using Advanced Revelation®

Typesetting software provided by
Laser Solutions, Inc., Atlanta, Georgia using FrameMaker®

# AN INTERNATIONAL REFERENCE BOOK

## NINTH EDITION 1995
## VOLUME III

## M-Z

Division of EBSCO Industries Inc., Birmingham, Alabama

Published by EBSCO Publishing
division of EBSCO Industries, Inc.
P.O. Box 1943, Birmingham, AL 35201-1943   USA

Copyright © 1995 by EBSCO Industries, Inc.
Printed and bound in the United States of America.

All rights reserved. Reproduction of this Directory, in whole or in part, by any method, without prior written permission of the publisher is prohibited.

Direct all editorial inquiries to EBSCO Publishing, P.O. Box 1943, Birmingham, AL 35201-1943.

Direct all other inquiries to EBSCO Publishing, 83 Pine Street, PO Box 2250, Peabody, MA 01960-7250

International Standard Book Number (5-Volume Set) 0-913956-86-4
International Standard Book Number (Volume-1) 0-913956-81-3
International Standard Book Number (Volume-2) 0-913956-82-1
International Standard Book Number (Volume-3) 0-913956-83-X
International Standard Book Number (Volume-4) 0-913956-84-8
International Standard Book Number (Volume-5) 0-913956-85-6

International Standard Serial Number 0886-4179

Every effort has been made to ensure the accuracy of information in *The Serials Directory* and since no payment has been made for the inclusion of any entries, the publisher cannot accept liability for errors or omissions, regardless of the cause.

# CONTENTS

Preface . . . . . . . . . . . . . . . . . . . . . . . . . . . . . . . . . . . . . . . . . . . . . . . . . . . . . vii
User's Guide . . . . . . . . . . . . . . . . . . . . . . . . . . . . . . . . . . . . . . . . . . . . . . . . .ix
Filing Rules. . . . . . . . . . . . . . . . . . . . . . . . . . . . . . . . . . . . . . . . . . . . . . . . xvi
Subject Headings. . . . . . . . . . . . . . . . . . . . . . . . . . . . . . . . . . . . . . . . . . . xvii
Subject Cross References . . . . . . . . . . . . . . . . . . . . . . . . . . . . . . . . . . . . . xxi
Tables . . . . . . . . . . . . . . . . . . . . . . . . . . . . . . . . . . . . . . . . . . . . . . . . . . xxxvii
    Frequency. . . . . . . . . . . . . . . . . . . . . . . . . . . . . . . . . . . . . . . . . . xxxviii
    Document Delivery . . . . . . . . . . . . . . . . . . . . . . . . . . . . . . . . . . . xxxviii
    Wire Services . . . . . . . . . . . . . . . . . . . . . . . . . . . . . . . . . . . . . . . . .xxxix
    Country of Publication by Code. . . . . . . . . . . . . . . . . . . . . . . . . . . . .xl
    Country of Publication by Country . . . . . . . . . . . . . . . . . . . . . . . . . xli
    Unit of Currency . . . . . . . . . . . . . . . . . . . . . . . . . . . . . . . . . . . . . . . xlii
    Indexes/Abstracts. . . . . . . . . . . . . . . . . . . . . . . . . . . . . . . . . . . . . . .xliii

**Volume 1**
    Serial Listings (A–Em) . . . . . . . . . . . . . . . . . . . . . . . . . . . . . . . . . . . . . 3
**Volume 2**
    Serial Listings (En-L). . . . . . . . . . . . . . . . . . . . . . . . . . . . . . . . . . . . 1923
**Volume 3**
    Serial Listings (M-Z) . . . . . . . . . . . . . . . . . . . . . . . . . . . . . . . . . . . . 3475
**Volume 4**
    Newspapers
        US Newspapers. . . . . . . . . . . . . . . . . . . . . . . . . . . . . . . . . . . . . . 5625
        International Newspapers . . . . . . . . . . . . . . . . . . . . . . . . . . . . . 5777
    Alphabetical Title Index. . . . . . . . . . . . . . . . . . . . . . . . . . . . . . . . . . 5815
**Volume 5**
    ISSN Index. . . . . . . . . . . . . . . . . . . . . . . . . . . . . . . . . . . . . . . . . . . . 7607
    Peer Reviewed Index . . . . . . . . . . . . . . . . . . . . . . . . . . . . . . . . . . . . 7987
    Serials on CD-ROM Index. . . . . . . . . . . . . . . . . . . . . . . . . . . . . . . . 8051
    Serials Online Index. . . . . . . . . . . . . . . . . . . . . . . . . . . . . . . . . . . . . 8075
    Book Review Index . . . . . . . . . . . . . . . . . . . . . . . . . . . . . . . . . . . . . 8113
    Advertising Accepted Index. . . . . . . . . . . . . . . . . . . . . . . . . . . . . . . 8275
    Controlled Circulation Index . . . . . . . . . . . . . . . . . . . . . . . . . . . . . . 8465
    Copyright Clearance Center Index. . . . . . . . . . . . . . . . . . . . . . . . . . 8601
    New Title Index . . . . . . . . . . . . . . . . . . . . . . . . . . . . . . . . . . . . . . . . 8675

# PREFACE

At EBSCO Publishing it is our goal to produce the primary serial reference source available. We have directed our energies toward obtaining the most up-to-date and accurate information on every title -- from the most familiar to the most obscure. In working toward this goal, several additions and changes have been made to the newest edition of *The Serials Directory: An International Reference Book*.

Eight new bibliographic elements are included in this edition to provide information professionals with a means for quick and easy serial research. In the newspaper section, Full and Half-page ad rates are now listed along with Publication Size, Wire Service Affiliations, and a notation for the inclusion of Photographs. Also included is data on document delivery availability/vendors, "Acid Free" notations and both Internet and E-mail addresses when provided by the publisher.

This edition of *The Serials Directory* contains approximately 151,000 serial titles with up to 60 bibliographic elements available for each one. Included in Volumes I, II and III are over 6,500 new titles, 2,800 titles available on CD-ROM or an online database, 10,600 titles registered with the Copyright Clearance Center, 24,000 serials publishing book reviews, and over 27,000 serials accepting advertising. This Edition contains verified information for over 100,000 serial titles representing approximately 65,000 publishers worldwide.

EBSCO Publishing is a sister division to EBSCO Subscription Services; therefore, gaining access to serial information on an ongoing basis is more simplified. EBSCO remains in constant contact with publishers throughout the world ensuring the accuracy of title and publisher information as well as providing the latest pricing and subscription data.

Information found in *The Serials Directory* is maintained through four sources.

First, through the internal EBSCO Subscription Services database, updated daily as a result of continuous contact with publishers worldwide. The second source is The Library of Congress' CONSER file of which EBSCO is an affiliate member. The CONSER file is maintained by the National Serials Data Program, National Library of Canada, National Library of Medicine, Chemical Abstracts Service, and the National Agricultural Library. The third source is The ISSN Register (formerly ISDS) which provides extensive coverage of international serials. The fourth source for data is direct correspondence with thousands of publishers throughout the world.

With this edition, you will receive two cumulative Updates throughout 1995 to keep you abreast of changes in title status, publisher and subscription addresses, format changes or additions, price and frequency changes, as well as information on new titles. With a subscription to *The Serials Directory: EBSCO CD-ROM*, you will receive four quarterly updated discs containing all historical serial data that may not be included in the print version.

Our other international offering is *The Index and Abstract Directory: An International Guide to Services and Serials Coverage*. This valuable reference tool, which is now contained in two volumes, consists of information on over 950 "active" Indexing/Abstracting services and includes bibliographic information on the more than 56,000 serials that are monitored by each.

You will also find that we go beyond just providing reference products alone. As always, we will continue to offer free serials research to any of our customers needing assistance in locating the more ambiguous serial publications. We receive thousands of calls each year and have proven very successful in pinpointing the answers to a variety of serials questions.

At EBSCO Publishing, we continue to grow -- to change -- to improve. *The Serials Directory* and the *Index and Abstract Directory* reflect this growth and, combined with EBSCO's valued reputation within the library community, provide the highest standard of quality available in serials reference.

Leanne Wofford
Editorial Manager

EBSCO Publishing, PO Box 1943, Birmingham, AL 35201-1943 USA
(800)826-3024 / (205)980-2773 / FAX (205)995-1582

# USER'S GUIDE

# USER'S GUIDE

## How to Use The Serials Directory.
*Twelve sections comprise The Serials Directory. Each of these sections allows the user to access information easily. The following is a brief explanation of each section.*

- **Serial Listings (Subjects A-Z)**
  (Volumes I, II and III)
- **Newspaper Listings**
  (Volume IV)
- **Alphabetical Title Index**
  (Volume IV)
- **ISSN Index**
  (Volume V)
- **Peer Reviewed Index**
  (Volume V)
- **Serials Available on CD-ROM Index**
  (Volume V)
- **Serials Available Online Index**
  (Volume V)
- **Book Review Index**
  (Volume V)
- **Advertising Accepted Index**
  (Volume V)
- **Controlled Circulation Index**
  (Volume V)
- **Copyright Clearance Center Index**
  (Volume V)
- **New Title Index**
  (Volume V)

### ● Serial Listings—
The Serial Listings are arranged alphabetically by subject category. Titles given under each subject heading are in alphabetical order (See Filing Rules—page xvi). The Serial Listing arrangement enables the user to quickly locate the relevant subject area and to review all serial titles relating to that subject. There are over 18,000 "see notes" throughout the 146 major subject headings and 330 subheadings in the Serial Listings. These notes refer the user from related subject areas to the primary subject heading under which the full title listing appears. See pages xvii-xxxvi for a list of subject headings and subject cross references.

### ● Newspaper Listings—
This section lists all US and international newspapers included in our database. US newspapers will be listed alphabetically by state. International titles will follow and are arranged alphabetically, by country. Newspaper listings can be found in the Alphabetical Title Index as well as the ISSN Index along with the regular listings in Volume IV.

### ● Alphabetical Title Index—
Arranged alphabetically by title, this index lists the primary title, along with Country of Publication/ISSN, and MARC control number, when available.

### The following notations are made in the Alphabetical Title Index:

**1. New Titles—** Titles are denoted with a bullet "●". Bullets will appear in both the Serial Listing, as well as the Alphabetical Title Index. This edition includes over 6,500 new titles which began publication after 1992 and were active at the time data was secured for publication.

**2. Ceased Titles—** Titles that have ceased publication and do not have a "succeeding entry." Ceased titles are denoted with "*CEASED*" in bold italics, following the primary title in the Serial Listing, as well as the Alphabetical Title Index. Ceased titles are included in the Directory for two consecutive editions after EBSCO is notified of the status change. This edition contains over 4,700 cessations.

**3. Title Changes—** Titles which have a succeeding entry, MARC field 785. These entries are included in the Alphabetical Title Index with a reference to the current title(s). Title changes are included in the Directory for two consecutive editions based on the "ending date of publication," MARC field 008/11-14. This edition contains over 4,840 title changes. See the User's Guide/Sample Listing for more information.

**4. Suspended Titles—** Titles for which EBSCO has received notification of suspension. Suspended titles are denoted in both the Serial Listing and the index with "*SUSPENDED*" in bold italics, following the primary title. These titles will remain suspended until EBSCO is notified otherwise.

**5. Preceding Entries—** Preceding entries print with a "see" note to the primary title provided the primary title has a MARC publication start date (008/7-10) later than 1992. Preceding entries will remain in the Directory for two consecutive editions with a reference to the newer title(s).

**6. Main Entry - Corporate Name—** A corporate name used as a main entry, this element prints in the Alphabetical Title Index as another access point to the publication in question. To further aid the user, the Main Entry-Corporate Name is listed with a "see" note to the primary title in the Serial Listings. Over 24,000 Main Entry-Corporate Names are included in the Directory.

# USER'S GUIDE

● **ISSN Index—**
The ISSN Index contains current as well as preceding ISSN's, arranged in numerical order. The ISSN will be followed by a "see" note giving the title under which the ISSN will appear. The preceding ISSN is included with a "see" note to the primary title provided the MARC publication start date (field 008/7-10) is later than 1992. Preceding ISSN will appear in italicized typeface in order to distinguish it from the current ISSN. The page number for which the Serial Listing appears prints in boldface. There are over 100,400 titles included in the ISSN Index.

● **Peer Reviewed Index—**
Arranged alphabetically by title, the Peer Reviewed Index lists all active serials found in Volumes I, II and III which contain peer reviewed articles. Country of Publication/ISSN and MARC control number are provided, when available. The page number for which the Serial Listing appears prints in boldface. There are over 8,800 titles included in the Peer Reviewed Index.

● **Serials Available on CD-ROM Index—**
Arranged alphabetically by title, this index lists all active serial titles in Volumes I, II and III that are available on CD-ROM, either as the primary format, or as an "additional" available format. Included in this index are the Country of Publication/ISSN and publisher address/telephone number(s) when available. The page number for which the Serial Listing appears prints in boldface. There are over 1,300 titles included in the Serials Available on CD-ROM Index.

● **Serials Available Online Index—**
Arranged alphabetically by title, this index lists all active serials found in Volumes I, II and III that are available online, either as the primary format, or as an "additional" available format. Included in this index are the Country of Publication/ISSN and publisher address/telephone number(s) when available. The page number for which the Serial Listing appears prints in boldface. There are over 2,500 titles included in the Serials Available Online Index.

● **Book Review Index—**
Arranged alphabetically by title, this index lists all active serials found in Volumes I, II and III that contain book reviews. Included in this index are Country of Publication/ISSN and the quantity of book reviews published "per year" (unless otherwise specified). The page number for which the Serial Listing appears prints in boldface. There are over 24,000 titles included in the Book Review Index.

● **Advertising Accepted Index—**
Arranged alphabetically by title, this index contains all active serials found in Volumes I, II and III that accept advertising. The Country of Publication/ISSN and advertising manager/telephone number(s) are also provided, when supplied by the publisher. The page number for which the Serial Listing appears prints in boldface. There are over 27,000 titles included in the Advertising Accepted Index.

● **Controlled Circulation Index—**
Arranged alphabetically by title, this index lists all active titles in the Directory that have a controlled circulation. The Country of Publication/ISSN and circulation figures [printing in brackets] are provided when available. The page number for which the Serial Listing appears prints in boldface. There are over 19,000 titles included in the Controlled Circulation Index.

● **Copyright Clearance Center Index—**
Arranged alphabetically by title, this index lists all active serials found in Volumes I, II and III that are registered with the Copyright Clearance Center (CCC). The Country of Publication/ISSN are provided when available. The page number for which the Serial Listing appears prints in boldface. There are over 10,600 titles included in the Copyright Clearance Center Index.

● **New Title Index—**
Arranged by subject, then alphabetically by title, this index consists of all active titles that have a MARC "beginning date" of "1992" or greater, as well as, "non-MARC" titles where the start date has been verified by the publisher. Country of Publication/ISSN follow the title, with the page number on which the Serial Listing appears. There are over 6,500 titles included in the New Title Index.

# USER'S GUIDE/SAMPLE LISTING

## SAMPLE LISTING

Country of Publication/ISSN
● **KEY TITLE.** *CEASED/SUSPENDED.* (TITLE STATEMENT). [Abbreviated Title]. **Main/Conf** Main Entry—Meeting. **Main/Corp** Main Entry—Corporate Name. **Added/Corp** Added Entry—Corporate Name. **Series/Conf** Series Statement—Meeting Name. **VFOAT** Varying Form of a Title. **VAT** Variant Access Title. Date of Publication. Type of Serial. Language(s). Frequency. Price. Publisher Name & Address. **Tel** Telephone/Telex Number/Fax/Internet Address/Email Address. (subscription address:) **ED** Editor. **LC** Library of Congress Classification. **DD** Dewey Decimal Classification. **UDC** Universal Decimal Classification. **NLM** National Library of Medicine Classification. **CODEN** CODEN Designation. **[CCC]** Copyright Clearance Center. Index Availability. cum. index (Cumulative Index Availability). **Bk Rev** (Book reviews published), (Qty: Quantity Published). **Photos** [Photographs published]. **Ad Acc** (Advertising accepted), **Adv. Mgr**: Advertising Manager. **Tel** Telephone. Full Page (B&W) - Full page black and white ad rates. Half Page (B&W) - Half page black and white ad rates. Full Page (Color) - Full page color ad rates. Half Page (Color) - Half page color ad rates. **Pub. Size** [Publication trim size]. **Wire Svcs** [Newspaper wire services]. **Pr Rev.** (Peer Reviewed or Refereed). **Acid Free** [Acid free paper]. Circulation. (ctrl) - Controlled circulation. Document Delivery Available. Additional Physical Forms Available. *Preceding Entry-Title, Preceding Entry-ISSN. Succeeding Entry-Title, Succeeding Entry-ISSN.*

**Desc:** Descriptive listing.

**Ind/Abst** Indexes/Abstracts. Dates of Coverage. Full Text. Full/Selective Coverage

## SERIAL LISTING CONTENTS

For the purpose of defining a serial, the definition as given in the USMARC Bibliographic Format is used: a bibliographic item issued in successive parts bearing numerical or chronological designations and intended to be continued indefinitely. Serials include periodicals; newspapers; annuals (reports, yearbooks, etc.); the journals, memoirs, proceedings, transactions, etc., of societies; and numbered monographic series, etc.

The following data elements (when available) are shown in order of appearance within a listing. Some definitions are taken in part from USMARC Formats Bibliographic Data.

**Country of Publication.** A two letter code indicating the place of publication, production, or execution. See Country of Publication Table, Page xxxvi for additions/changes.

**ISSN.** International Standard Serial Number, a unique identification number assigned to a serial title by national centers under the auspices of the ISSN Register (formerly ISDS).

●Denotes new titles beginning after 1992, that were active at the time data was secured for publication.

**Key Title.** Key Title is assigned by various national centers under the auspices of the ISSN Register (formerly International Serials Data System /ISDS). It is formed from title information transcribed from a piece of the serial and is constructed with qualifiers to make it unique when necessary. Since serial titles are taken from both the CONSER and ISSN Register databases, the primary title has not been altered to differentiate the alternative format from the original. In cases where CONSER or the ISSN Register has included a notation for the alternative format within the primary title, the primary title will reflect that notation. Serials in an alternative format (microfiche, microfilm, CD-ROM, etc.) are included in the Directory. Also in cases where multiple language entries appear, the user must refer to the primary language of the publication to ensure that the correct title is located. These titles may appear to be identical with the primary language being the only unique qualifier.

**Ceased.** This element is present only when a title has ceased publication. This does not include titles that have a succeeding entry or have had a title change. The word *"CEASED"* in bold italics, follows the primary title in the Serial Listing. Ceased titles are included in the Directory for two consecutive editions after the actual date of cessation. This edition contains over 4,700 cessations.

**Suspended.** Denotes temporary suspension of a title. The word *"SUSPENDED"* in bold italics, follows the primary title in the Serial Listing to denote suspended titles. These titles remain suspended in the database until the publisher notifies EBSCO otherwise.

**Title Statement.** Title Statement is present only when it differs from Key Title in any way, other than initial articles and prepositions. It consists of the title proper (including short title and alternative title, the numerical designation of a part/section and the name of a part/section) and may also contain the medium, remainder of title, other title information, and the statement of responsibility/remainder of title page transcription. Title Statement will follow Key Title in uppercase and will be enclosed in parentheses.

**Abbreviated Title.** Assigned by the ISSN Register (formerly ISDS), in accordance with ISO 4-1984, Documentation - Rules for the Abbreviation of Title Words and Titles of Publications and List of Serial Title Word Abbreviations. The Abbreviated Title is based on the Key Title and files in [brackets].

# USER'S GUIDE/SAMPLE LISTING

**Main Entry-Meeting.** A meeting or conference name used as a main entry. Main entry under a meeting name is assigned to works that contain proceedings, reports, etc. Main Entry-Meeting will be preceded by the prefix "**Main/Conf**" in boldface.

**Main Entry-Corporate Name.** A corporate name used as a main entry. Main entry under corporate name is assigned to works that represent the collective thought of a body, including conference and meeting names that are entered subordinately to a corporate body. Main Entry-Corporate Name is preceded by the prefix "**Main/Corp**" in boldface.

**Added Entry-Corporate Name.** Contains a corporate heading used as main entry. A corporate body is identified by a name that acts or may act as an entity. Included in this definition are: associations, institutions, business firms, governments and their agencies, ships, churches and programs. The Added Entry-Corporate Name will be preceded by a prefix of "**Added/Corp**" in boldface.

**Series Statement-Meeting Name.** Series statement entered under a named conference or meeting. Series Statement-Meeting is preceded by "**Series/Conf**" in boldface.

**Varying Form of a Title.** Titles which may appear on different parts of a serial, or consisting of portions of the title proper or alternative forms of titles. Varying Form of a Title differs substantially from Key Title/Title Statement and contributes to the further identification of the serial. It is preceded by the prefix "**VFOAT**" in boldface. Additional titles are separated by commas.

**Variant Access Title.** A variant form of the title that does not appear on the serial. It is used when the title contains an initialism, non-roman alphabet character, etc. It provides additional access for searching purposes when access is not provided by any other title. Variant Access Title is preceded by the prefix of "**VAT**" in boldface. Additional titles are separated by commas.

**Dates of Publication and Volume Information.** Beginning (and ending) dates of publication and volume designation. The date may consist of the year, month, or day; month or season and year; or year alone, depending upon the frequency of publication and the usage of the publisher. Dates may appear in the vernacular and/or may be abbreviated.

**Type of Serial.** Indicates if the serial is a periodical, monographic series, or newspaper. When available, more specific types will be used such as bibliography, catalog, bulletin, directory, government publication, newsletter, proceedings, trade publication, consumer publication, corporate report, academic scholarly publication and abstracting/indexing publication.

**Language(s).** If the serial is published in more than one language, the predominant language will appear first and any additional languages will follow in parentheses (including languages for translations, summaries, tables of contents, etc.) with appropriate explanation if necessary.

**Frequency.** Indicated by a two letter code - see Frequency Table, page xxxviii. Exceptions to frequency are noted and in parentheses following code.

**Price.** The current annual subscription price at the time information was secured for publication. Prices are usually given in US dollars and currency of Country of Publication, if other than US. Exceptions are noted and explained.

**Publisher Name and Address/Telecommunications Numbers.** The complete name and address of the publisher when available. Telephone, telex and/or facsimile number as well as Internet and E-mail addresses are given for serials. Preceded by a prefix of "**Tel**" in boldface.

**Subscription Address.** The complete name and subscription/fulfillment address. Telecommunication numbers are listed when available.

**Editor(s).** Name, address and telephone number(s), when available. Preceded by a prefix of "**ED**" in boldface.

**Library of Congress Classification.** Contains an LC class/call number, shelf number, or pseudo-call-number assigned by The Library of Congress or one of its authorized agencies. Preceded by a prefix of "**LC**" in boldface.

**Dewey Decimal Classification.** Assigned according to the Dewey Decimal schedules maintained by The Library of Congress. Preceded by a prefix of "**DD**" in boldface.

**Universal Decimal Classification.** Derived from the Dewey Decimal Classification, the UDC differs in arrangement and philosophy. The UDC is distinguished from the DDC by its extensive expansions. Preceded by a prefix of "**UDC**" in boldface.

**National Library of Medicine Classification.** Contains either a complete NLM call number or an NLM classification number. Preceded by a prefix of "**NLM**" in boldface.

**CODEN Designation.** Abbreviation for periodical titles, which is assigned by the CODEN section of Chemical Abstracts Service. It is a unique identifier for scientific and technical publications. Preceded by a prefix of "**CODEN**" in boldface.

**Copyright Clearance Center.** [CCC] indicates titles registered with the Copyright Clearance Center. The Copyright Clearance Center has been authorized to give photocopy permission and to collect any pre-set royalty fees set by the publisher.

**Index Availability.** Shows the existence of an index, or a table of contents issued as an index, and the method of acquisition.

**Cumulative Index Availability.** Specifies if a cumulative index, or a table of contents issued as a cumulative index, is published.

# USER'S GUIDE/SAMPLE LISTING

Appears in abbreviated form as "cum. index."

**Book Reviews.** If book reviews are published, "**Bk Rev**" will appear in the Serial Listing.

**Book Review Quantity.** Quantity of book reviews published "per year," unless otherwise specified. Quantity is preceded by "**Qty:**" and prints in parentheses.

**Photos.** If photographs are included within the serial, "**Photos**" will appear in the listing.

**Advertising.** If advertising is accepted in a serial, the abbreviation "**Ad Acc**" will appear in boldface.

**Advertising Manager/Telephone.** Lists the name and telephone number of the Advertising Manager, when available. Advertising Manager name is preceded by "**Adv Mgr:**" in boldface. Telephone is preceded by the prefix "**Tel**" in boldface.

**Advertising Rates.** Advertising rates for full and half-page ads. (B&W) designates rates for ads in black and white. (Color) designates ads printed in color.

**Publication Size.** The trim size of the serial or newspaper. Preceded by the abbreviation **Pub. Size**. Common publication sizes include Tabloid, Standard and Broadsheet.

**Wire Services.** Lists the news and photograph wire services affiliated with any given newspaper. These are preceded by a prefix of "**Wire Svcs**" in boldface. A chart of abbreviations used can be found on page xxxix.

**Peer Reviewed.** If a journal is peer reviewed or refereed, the abbreviation "**Pr Rev**" will appear.

**Acid Free.** If a publication is available on acid free paper, "**Acid Free**" will be seen in boldface.

**Circulation.** Annual circulation of publication, unless noted otherwise. Multiple circulation figures are separated by a comma.

**Controlled Circulation.** If circulation of a serial is controlled by the publisher, the abbreviation "ctrl" in parentheses follows the circulation figures. If no circulation figures are given, but the publisher has notified us that circulation is controlled, "ctrl circ" will appear.

**Document Delivery.** Indicates the availability of that serial for document delivery through the specified service(s). Refer to the chart on page xxxviii.

**Additional Physical Forms Available.** Additional media in which a serial is published, other than its original or conventional form.

**Preceding Entry - Title/Preceding Entry - ISSN.** The immediate predecessor(s) for the title, along with ISSN, appears in italics. Depending on indicators taken from the CONSER 780 field, a title's preceding entry will be preceded by one of the following: Continues, Continues in part, Supersedes, Supersedes in part, Formed by the union of... and..., Absorbed, Absorbed in part, or Separated from. If the title Continues in part, another title which is current, both titles will then be listed. Additional titles and ISSN are separated by semicolons and are preceded by one of the above, in boldface.

**Succeeding Entry Title/Succeeding Entry - ISSN.** The immediate successor(s) for the serial title (along with corresponding ISSN) will be listed. Multiple titles and ISSN are separated by semicolons, and preceded by a prefix of one of the following: Continued by, Continued in part by, Superseded by, Superseded in part by, Absorbed by, Absorbed in part by, Split into... and..., Merged with... to form..., Merged into, or Changed back to. In cases where CONSER did not give an ending date or a title was only continued "in part" both titles will be listed.

**Descriptive Listing.** Description of content submitted by publisher or by CONSER. Descriptions may have been edited for clarity. Description is preceded by "**Desc:**" in boldface.

**Indexes/Abstracts.** Specifies the publication(s) in which a serial has been indexed and/or abstracted. These are preceded by a prefix of "**Ind/Abst**" in boldface. Over 920 "active" Indexing/Abstracting services are used for the purposes of this Directory and can be found within the Serial Listings. See Indexes/Abstracts Abbreviations Table on page xliii.

**Dates of Coverage.** Dates of coverage are included for each index or abstract, when available. Dates are enclosed in parentheses and follow the abbreviation as used in the Serial Listing for each Indexing/Abstracting service. If no dates are provided by the Indexing/Abstracting service publisher, and we have been notified that a serial is no longer covered by a particular service, question marks will be used to notify the user that coverage of the particular serial by the service has been discontinued.

**Full Text.** Specifies if a journal is covered by an Indexing/Abstracting service in "Full Text." Full Text coverage indicates that all articles in the journal are indexed/abstracted completely, with any pertinent graphics, charts etc. For the purposes of this Directory, "Full Text" and "Full Image" are treated as if they were the same. These will be coded in the Serial Listing as [Full Txt.]. This notation will follow the dates of coverage in the Serial Listing.

**Full/Selective Coverage** — Full coverage indicates that journals are indexed/abstracted cover to cover. Selective coverage specifies serials in which the Indexing / Abstracting service selects only articles relevant to their publication. These will be coded in the Serial Listing as [Full Cov.] or [Select. Cov.]. This notation will follow the dates of coverage, when available, or will precede the Index or Abstract abbreviation when no dates of coverage are noted in the Serial Listing.

# FILING RULES

**A. General Rules—** Filing is word for word with exceptions noted below. The order of characters applies the principle "nothing files before something," with numerals before letters, file A to Z.

**1. Spaces, hyphens, diagonal slashes, and periods** are filed as blanks:

> AAG-AAG
> 
> AAG Directory / Association of American Geographers
> 
> AAG Newsletter
> 
> AAHA Directory of Membership

**2. Variant spellings** are filed as written:

> Ageing and Society
> 
> Aging and Aging Disorders

**B. Special Rules and Exceptions.**

**1. Modified letters and diacritics—** Modified letters are written as their plain English alphabet equivalents.

**2. Punctuation—** Punctuation and non-alphabetic symbols (except those noted in A above) are ignored for filing purposes:

> "A" Magazine
> 
> A Magyar Talalkozo Kronikaja
> 
> A.N.A. Audiologia Protesica

**3. Abbreviations—** Filed exactly as written.

> Dr. McBirnie's Newsletter
> 
> St. Louis Review
> 
> U.N. Observer & International Report
> 
> U.S. Census Report

**4. Numerals—** Filed character by character according to the numeric value of each string of characters.
**Numerals precede letters:**

> 33 Metal Producing
> 
> 35/70; Journal of the Feature Film Industry
> 
> 35MM Photography London England : 1983)
> 
> 36 Cities : Real Estate Forecast and Review

**5. Initials, initialisms, acronyms—** Those in which each letter is separated by a space, dash, hyphen, period, or diagonal slash are regarded as a series of separate words. Those in which characters are separated by other marks or symbols, or which are not separated in any way, are regarded as single words:

> A. C. C. L. Union List of Serials
> 
> A C E Q-A C G R Information
> 
> A/C Flyer, The
> 
> A.C.G.C.-Information : Bulletin d'Information de l'Association des Cadres et Gerants des Colleges du Quebec
> 
> A C I S
> 
> A. C. L. : Agence Cambodge Laos

**6. Initial Articles—** The following words are ignored when they appear at the beginning of an entry.

| | | | |
|---|---|---|---|
| A | Eine | Hio | 'n |
| al | Eit | Hin | Na |
| An | el- | Hinar | Nje |
| As | El | Hinir | Nji |
| Az | Els | Hinn | O |
| Bir | En | Ho | Os |
| Das | Et | Hoi | 't |
| De | Ett | I | Ta |
| Dei | Gl' | Il | The |
| Den | Gli | Ka | To |
| Der | ha- | Ke | Um |
| Di | Hai | L' | Uma |
| Die | He | La | Un |
| Dos | he- | Las | Un' |
| Een | Heis | Le | Una |
| Eene | Hen | Les | Une |
| Egy | Hena | Lo | Uno |
| Ei | Henas | Los | Y |
| Ein | Het | Mia | Yr |

**Exceptions—** Titles composed entirely of words on the list above are filed as written, as well as place names.
**Hence:**

> A Tavola
> 
> A to Z of Who is Who in Australia's History, The
> 
> A Traverso

**7. Names and prefixes—** A prefix that is part of the name of a person or place is treated as a separate word unless it is joined to the rest of the name:

> De Paul Law Review
> 
> McCall's Book for Brides
> 
> Van Buren Register

# SUBJECT HEADINGS

*The following section lists the subject headings used throughout the Directory. The list is arranged alphabetically, by subject, with the major subject (printing in boldface) followed by specific subheadings within the same category.*

# CROSS REFERENCES

*This section combines all subject headings into one alphabetical list, regardless of whether it is a general, main subject or specific, subordinate subject. Cross references from a subject or topic not used in the Directory are made to that which is used. "See also" notes from one subject to a similar subject are included as well.*

# SUBJECT HEADINGS

**Aeronautics, Astronautics** ............ 3
**Agriculture** ........................ 42
   Agricultural Equipment ............ 158
   Crop Production and Soil ......... 161
   Dairy Industry ................... 191
   Feed Grain and Milling ........... 199
   Livestock and Poultry ............ 204
**Animal Welfare** ................... 225
**Anthropology** ..................... 227
**Antiques** ......................... 248
**Archaeology** ...................... 253
**Architecture** ..................... 286
**Arts, The** ........................ 311
   Art ............................ 335
   Crafts and Decorative Arts ....... 369
   Graphic Arts .................... 376
   Performing Arts ................. 383
**Astrology** ........................ 389
**Astronomy** ........................ 391
**Beauty and Cosmetics** ............. 402
**Bibliographies** ................... 406
**Bicycles and Bicycling** ........... 427
**Biographies** ...................... 429
**Biology** .......................... 439
   Biochemistry .................... 479
   Biophysics ...................... 494
   Botany .......................... 496
   Cytology and Histology .......... 531
   Embryology ...................... 541
   Genetics ........................ 541
   Marine Biology .................. 552
   Microbiology .................... 558
   Microscopy ...................... 572
   Mycology ........................ 574
   Physiology ...................... 577
**Birth Control** .................... 587
**Boats and Boating** ................ 591
**Building and Construction** ........ 597
   Carpentry and Woodwork .......... 633
**Business** ......................... 636
   Accounting ...................... 735
   Advertising and Public Relations ... 753
   Banking and Finance ............. 768
   Chamber of Commerce ............. 817
   Commerce ........................ 821
   General Management .............. 858
   Investments ..................... 890
   Marketing ....................... 920
   Personnel Management ............ 938
   Purchasing ...................... 948
   Retail .......................... 952
**Chemistry** ........................ 958
   Analytical Chemistry ............ 1012
   Chemical Technology ............. 1020
   Crystallography ................. 1031
   Electrochemistry ................ 1033
   Inorganic Chemistry ............. 1035
   Organic Chemistry ............... 1038
   Physical and Theoretical Chemistry . 1049
**Children and Youth Interests** ..... 1059
**Civil Defense** .................... 1072
**Classical Studies** ................ 1073
**Clothing Industry and Fashion** .... 1081
**College and School Publications** .. 1088
   Alumni .......................... 1096

**Communication** .................... 1103
   Broadcasting .................... 1125
   Postal Communications ........... 1144
   Telecommunications .............. 1148
**Computers** ........................ 1169
   Artificial Intelligence ......... 1210
   Automation ...................... 1217
   Computer Assisted Instruction ... 1222
   Computer Crimes and Security .... 1225
   Computer Engineering ............ 1227
   Computer Games .................. 1230
   Computer Graphics and Design .... 1231
   Computer Industry and Industry
     Directories .................. 1235
   Computer Music .................. 1240
   Computer Networks ............... 1240
   Computer Sales, Service
     and Supply ................... 1244
   Computer Systems ................ 1246
   Cybernetics ..................... 1250
   Data Base Management ............ 1252
   Data Processing ................. 1255
   Desktop Publishing .............. 1263
   Hardware ........................ 1264
   Microcomputers, Personal
     Computers .................... 1265
   Minicomputers ................... 1273
   Online Computing and
     Information .................. 1274
   Optical Storage, CD-ROM
     Applications ................. 1276
   Programs and Programming ........ 1277
   Simulation ...................... 1282
   Software ........................ 1283
   Word Processing ................. 1292
**Consumer Interests** ............... 1293
**Copyright, Intellectual Property** . 1300
**Dance** ............................ 1310
**Dentistry** ........................ 1314
**Drug Abuse and Alcoholism** ........ 1338
**Earth Sciences** ................... 1351
   Geology ......................... 1364
   Geophysics ...................... 1402
   Hydrology ....................... 1412
   Meteorology ..................... 1419
   Mineralogy ...................... 1437
   Oceanography .................... 1445
   Petrology ....................... 1458
**Economics** ........................ 1459
   Cooperatives .................... 1541
   Economic History, Conditions .... 1544
   Economic Theory ................. 1589
   Industry and Production ......... 1596
   International Economics ......... 1632
   Labor ........................... 1642
**Education** ........................ 1720
   Adult and Continuing Education .. 1799
   Early Childhood and
     Primary Education ............ 1802
   Higher Education ................ 1806
   Physical Education and
     Training ..................... 1854
   School Organization and
     Administration ............... 1859
   Special Education and
     Rehabilitation ............... 1874
   Teaching and Curriculum ......... 1887
   Vocational Education ............ 1909

**Emigration and Immigration** ....... 1918
**Encyclopedias and General
   Reference Books** ............... 1923
**Energy** ........................... 1930
**Engineering** ...................... 1963
   Chemical Engineering ............ 2007
   Civil Engineering ............... 2018
   Electricity, Electrical
     Engineering, Electronics ..... 2034
   Hydraulic Engineering ........... 2087
   Industrial Engineering
     and Design ................... 2096
   Materials Engineering and
     Mechanics .................... 2100
   Mechanical Engineering and
     Machinery .................... 2108
   Mines and Mining Engineering .... 2132
   Nuclear Engineering ............. 2153
**Environmental Issues** ............. 2159
   Conservation and Natural
     Resources .................... 2185
   Ecology ......................... 2210
   Pollution and Waste
     Management ................... 2222
**Ethics** ........................... 2248
**Ethnic Interests** ................. 2253
**Family and Marriage** .............. 2276
**Fire Prevention** .................. 2287
**Fish and Fisheries** ............... 2293
**Folklore** ......................... 2318
**Food and Food Industry** ........... 2325
   Beverage Industry ............... 2363
**Forestry** ......................... 2373
   Lumber and Wood ................. 2399
**Funeral Service** .................. 2406
**Gardening and Horticulture** ....... 2407
   Florist Trade ................... 2434
**Genealogy and Heraldry** ........... 2436
   Archives ........................ 2478
**General Interest** ................. 2484
   General Interest-Africa ......... 2497
   General Interest-Asia ........... 2501
   General Interest-Australia
     and Oceania .................. 2510
   General Interest-Central
     America ...................... 2511
   General Interest-Europe ......... 2513
   General Interest-Middle East ....
   General Interest-North America .. 2526
   General Interest-South America .. 2551
**Geography** ........................ 2553
   Cartography ..................... 2580
**Gifts, Toys** ...................... 2583
**Glass and Ceramics** ............... 2585
**Health and Personal Fitness** ...... 2595
**Heating, Plumbing, and
   Refrigeration** ................. 2602
**History(General)** ................. 2609
   History of Africa ............... 2636
   History of Asia ................. 2644
   History of Australia and
     Oceania ...................... 2668
   History of Europe ............... 2671
   History of North, South, and
     Central America .............. 2717
   History of the Middle East ...... 2767

# SUBJECT HEADINGS

Hobbies............................2770
   Numismatics....................2779
   Philately......................2784
Home Economics....................2788
Homosexuality.....................2793
Horses and Horsemanship...........2796
Hotels/Motels.....................2803
Household Hardware
   and Appliances.................2810
Housing and Urban Development.....2812
Humanities........................2841
Hypnosis..........................2857
Industrial Health and Safety......2858
Insurance.........................2872
Interior Design...................2898
   Home Furnishings...............2904
International Assistance and
   Development....................2907
Jewelry...........................2913
   Clocks and Watches.............2916
Journalism........................2917
Law...............................2926
   Banking Law....................3084
   Civil Law......................3088
   Constitutional Law.............3091
   Corporate Law..................3094
   Criminal Law...................3104
   Environmental Law..............3109
   Estate Planning................3117
   Family Law.....................3119
   International Law..............3122
   Judicial Systems...............3138
   Labor Law......................3143
   Law Enforcement and
      Criminology.................3156
   Legal Aid......................3179
   Maritime Law...................3180
   Military Law...................3182
Leather and Fur Industry..........3183
Library and Information Sciences..3186
Linguistics.......................3260
Literary and Political Reviews....3337
Literature........................3357
   Poetry.........................3459
Manufacturing.....................3475
Mathematics.......................3490
Medical Science and Technology....3543
   Allergy and Immunology.........3662
   Anatomy........................3678
   Anesthesiology.................3680
   Biotechnology..................3685
   Cardiology.....................3697
   Communicable Diseases..........3711
   Dermatology....................3717
   Emergency Medicine.............3723
   Endocrinology..................3726
   Epidemiology...................3733
   Family Practice................3736
   Forensic Medicine, Medical
      Jurisprudence...............3739
   Gastroenterology...............3743
   Geriatrics.....................3748
   Gynecology and Obstetrics......3755
   Hematology.....................3769
   Homeopathy.....................3774

   Hospital Administration and
      Medical Centers.............3775
   Internal Medicine..............3794
   Musculoskeletal System.........3802
   Neoplasma, Neoplastic..........3808
   Neurology......................3825
   Nuclear Medicine...............3847
   Nursing........................3849
   Ophthalmology..................3871
   Orthopedics....................3880
   Otorhinolaryngology............3885
   Pathology......................3891
   Pediatrics.....................3899
   Physicians and Medical
      Personnel...................3912
   Podiatry.......................3917
   Psychiatry.....................3918
   Radiology......................3938
   Respiratory System.............3947
   Sports Medicine................3953
   Surgery........................3957
   Toxicology.....................3978
   Tropical Medicine..............3985
   Urology and Nephrology.........3987
Men's Interests...................3994
Metals and Metallurgy.............3996
   Welding........................4026
Metrology and Standardization.....4029
Military and Defense..............4033
Motion Picture....................4062
Motorcycles.......................4080
Museums and Galleries.............4083
Music.............................4098
Natural History...................4161
Naval Science, Navigation.........4174
New Age Publications..............4185
Newspapers........................5625
Nutrition and Dietetics...........4186
Occupations and Careers...........4201
Office Equipment and Services.....4210
Optometry.........................4214
Packaging.........................4217
Paints and Painting...............4222
Paleontology......................4226
Paper and Pulp Industry...........4232
Parapsychology and
   Occultism......................4240
Pest Control......................4243
Petroleum and Natural Gas.........4248
Pets..............................4285
Pharmacy and Pharmacology.........4288
Philanthropy......................4334
Philosophy........................4339
Photography and Video.............4366
Physical Therapy..................4378
Physically Impaired...............4382
Physics...........................4395
   Analytic and Experimental
      Mechanics...................4427
   Heat...........................4430
   Light, Optics, Radiation.......4432
   Magnetism......................4443
   Nuclear Physics................4445
   Sound..........................4451

Plastics..........................4453
Political Science.................4461
   Civil Rights...................4503
   International Relations........4514
   Socialism, Communism,
      Anarchism, Utopianism.......4539
Population Studies................4549
Printing Industry.................4563
Psychology........................4570
Public Administration.............4623
   Civil Service..................4701
   Parks and Recreation...........4705
   Public Finance and Taxation....4708
   Public Utilities...............4759
Public Health and Safety..........4763
Publishing........................4811
   Books and Bookmaking...........4822
Real Estate.......................4833
Recreation, Leisure...............4848
   Games and Amusements...........4856
   Outdoor Life...................4868
   Sports.........................4881
Religion and Theology.............4931
   Bible..........................5013
   Buddhism.......................5020
   Catholicism....................5022
   Eastern Christian Churches.....5039
   Hinduism.......................5040
   Islam, Bahaism, Theosophy......5041
   Judaism........................5045
   Protestantism..................5054
Restaurants.......................5070
Romance and Adventure.............5073
Rubber............................5075
Science and Technology............5078
Security Systems and Alarms.......5176
Senior Citizens...................5177
Sewing and Needlework.............5182
Sexual Life.......................5186
Social Sciences...................5189
Societies and Clubs...............5228
Sociology.........................5237
   Manners and Customs............5267
   Social Services and Welfare....5269
Sound Recordings and
   Systems........................5315
Statistics........................5320
Textiles..........................5347
Theater...........................5361
Tobacco...........................5372
Transportation....................5375
   Automobiles....................5403
   Railroads......................5429
   Roads and Traffic..............5438
   Ships and Shipping.............5447
Travel and Tourism................5458
Veterinary Sciences...............5501
Water Resources...................5528
Women's Interests.................5550
Zoology...........................5572
   Entomology.....................5604
   Ornithology....................5614

# SUBJECT HEADINGS

*The 117 subject headings listed below all contain a sub-heading for "Abstracting, Bibliographies, and Statistics." This sub-heading, which follows the major heading in the Serial Listing, contains serials which abstract and/or index publications in the applicable subject area. Bibliographies and statistical publications pertaining to each subject are also included.*

| Subject | Page |
|---|---|
| Aeronautics, Astronautics | 3 |
| Agriculture | 42 |
| Anthropology | 227 |
| Antiques | 248 |
| Archaeology | 253 |
| Architecture | 286 |
| Arts, The | 311 |
| Astronomy | 391 |
| Bicycles and Bicycling | 427 |
| Biographies | 429 |
| Biology | 439 |
| Birth Control | 587 |
| Boats and Boating | 591 |
| Building and Construction | 597 |
| Business | 636 |
| Chemistry | 958 |
| Children and Youth Interests | 1059 |
| Classical Studies | 1073 |
| Clothing Industry and Fashion | 1081 |
| Communication | 1103 |
| Computers | 1169 |
| Consumer Interests | 1293 |
| Copyright, Intellectual Property | 1300 |
| Dance | 1310 |
| Dentistry | 1314 |
| Drug Abuse and Alcoholism | 1338 |
| Earth Sciences | 1351 |
| Economics | 1459 |
| Education | 1720 |
| Encyclopedias and General Reference Books | 1923 |
| Energy | 1930 |
| Engineering | 1963 |
| Environmental Issues | 2159 |
| Ethnic Interests | 2253 |
| Family and Marriage | 2276 |
| Fire Prevention | 2287 |
| Fish and Fisheries | 2293 |
| Folklore | 2318 |
| Food and Food Industry | 2325 |
| Forestry | 2373 |
| Gardening and Horticulture | 2407 |
| Genealogy and Heraldry | 2436 |
| General Interest | 2484 |
| Geography | 2553 |
| Glass and Ceramics | 2585 |
| Health and Personal Fitness | 2595 |
| History (General) | 2609 |
| Hobbies | 2770 |
| Homosexuality | 2793 |
| Horses and Horsemanship | 2796 |
| Hotels/Motels | 2803 |
| Household Hardware and Appliances | 2810 |
| Housing and Urban Development | 2812 |
| Humanities | 2841 |
| Industrial Health and Safety | 2858 |
| Insurance | 2872 |
| International Assistance and Development | 2907 |
| Journalism | 2917 |
| Law | 2926 |
| Library and Information Sciences | 3186 |
| Linguistics | 3260 |
| Literary and Political Reviews | 3337 |
| Literature | 3357 |
| Manufacturing | 3475 |
| Mathematics | 3490 |
| Medical Science and Technology | 3543 |
| Metals and Metallurgy | 3996 |
| Metrology and Standardization | 4029 |
| Military and Defense | 4033 |
| Motion Picture | 4062 |
| Motorcycles | 4080 |
| Museums and Galleries | 4083 |
| Music | 4098 |
| Natural History | 4161 |
| Naval Science, Navigation | 4174 |
| New Age Publications | 4185 |
| Newspapers | 5625 |
| Nutrition and Dietetics | 4186 |
| Occupations and Careers | 4201 |
| Packaging | 4217 |
| Paints and Painting | 4222 |
| Paleontology | 4226 |
| Paper and Pulp Industry | 4232 |
| Parapsychology and Occultism | 4240 |
| Pest Control | 4243 |
| Petroleum and Natural Gas | 4248 |
| Pharmacy and Pharmacology | 4288 |
| Philosophy | 4339 |
| Photography and Video | 4366 |
| Physically Impaired | 4382 |
| Physics | 4395 |
| Plastics | 4453 |
| Political Science | 4461 |
| Population Studies | 4549 |
| Printing Industry | 4563 |
| Psychology | 4570 |
| Public Administration | 4623 |
| Public Health and Safety | 4763 |
| Publishing | 4811 |
| Real Estate | 4833 |
| Recreation, Leisure | 4848 |
| Religion and Theology | 4931 |
| Restaurants | 5070 |
| Rubber | 5075 |
| Science and Technology | 5078 |
| Social Sciences | 5189 |
| Sociology | 5237 |
| Sound Recordings and Systems | 5315 |
| Textiles | 5347 |
| Theater | 5361 |
| Tobacco | 5372 |
| Transportation | 5375 |
| Travel and Tourism | 5458 |
| Veterinary Sciences | 5501 |
| Water Resources | 5528 |
| Women's Interests | 5550 |
| Zoology | 5572 |

# SUBJECT CROSS REFERENCES

Abortion –See **Medical Science and Technology -- Gynecology and Obstetrics** pg 3755

Abrasives –See **Metals and Metallurgy** pg 3996

Accessories –See **Clothing Industry and Fashion** pg 1081

Accident Prevention –See **Industrial Health and Safety** pg 2858; **Public Health and Safety** pg 4763; **Transportation -- Roads and Traffic** pg 5438

**Accounting** –pg 735; see also Law pg 2926; Public Administration -- Public Finance and Taxation pg 4708

Acoustics –See **Physics -- Sound** pg 4451

Acquired Immune Deficiency Syndrome (AIDS) –See **Medical Science and Technology -- Allergy and Immunology** pg 3662; see also Medical Science and Technology -- Communicable Diseases pg 3711; Public Health and Safety pg 4763

Acting –See **Motion Picture** pg 4062; **The Arts -- Performing Arts** pg 383; **Theater** pg 5361

Actuarial Science –See **Insurance** pg 2872

Acupuncture –See **Medical Science and Technology** pg 3543

Addictions –See **Drug Abuse and Alcoholism** pg 1338; see also Psychology pg 4570

Adhesives –See **Chemistry -- Physical and Theoretical Chemistry** pg 1049; see also Chemistry -- Chemical Technology pg 1020; Engineering -- Chemical Engineering pg 2007; Engineering -- Materials Engineering and Mechanics pg 2100; Metals and Metallurgy -- Welding pg 4026; Paints and Painting pg 4222; Plastics pg 4453

Administrative Law –See **Law -- Constitutional Law** pg 3091

Adoption –See **Sociology -- Social Services and Welfare** pg 5269

**Adult and Continuing Education** –pg 1799

Adventure –See **Romance and Adventure** pg 5073

Advertising –See **Business -- Advertising and Public Relations** pg 753

**Advertising and Public Relations** –pg 753

Aerobics –See **Health and Personal Fitness** pg 2595

Aerodynamics –See **Aeronautics, Astronautics** pg 3

**Aeronautics, Astronautics** –pg 3; see also Military and Defense pg 4033; Transportation pg 5375

Aerospace Medicine –See **Aeronautics, Astronautics** pg 3; **Medical Science and Technology** pg 3543

Aesthetics –See **The Arts -- Art** pg 335; see also Philosophy pg 4339

Africa –See **General Interest -- General Interest-Africa** pg 2497; **History(General) -- History of Africa** pg 2636

African Studies –See **History(General) -- History of Africa** pg 2636; **Literature** pg 3357

Aging –See **Medical Science and Technology -- Geriatrics** pg 3748; **Sociology -- Social Services and Welfare** pg 5269; see also Senior Citizens pg 5177

Agricultural Aviation –See **Aeronautics, Astronautics** pg 3; see also Agriculture pg 42

Agricultural Chemistry –See **Agriculture** pg 42; see also Chemistry pg 958

Agricultural Economics –See **Agriculture** pg 42; see also Economics pg 1459

Agricultural Engineering –See **Agriculture** pg 42; see also Engineering pg 1963

**Agricultural Equipment** –pg 157

Agricultural Marketing –See **Agriculture** pg 42; see also Business -- Marketing pg 920

Agricultural Meteorology –See **Earth Sciences -- Meteorology** pg 1419; see also Agriculture pg 42

**Agriculture** –pg 42; see also Food and Food Industry pg 2325; Gardening and Horticulture pg 2407

Agronomy –See **Agriculture** pg 42; see also Agriculture -- Crop Production and Soil pg 161

AIDS –See **Medical Science and Technology -- Allergy and Immunology** pg 3662; see also Medical Science and Technology -- Communicable Diseases pg 3711; Public Health and Safety pg 4763

Air Cargo –See **Transportation** pg 5375; see also Aeronautics, Astronautics pg 3

Air Conditioning –See **Heating, Plumbing, and Refrigeration** pg 2810

Air Force –See **Aeronautics, Astronautics** pg 3; **Military and Defense** pg 4033

Air Pollution –See **Environmental Issues -- Pollution and Waste Management** pg 2222

Air Travel –See **Aeronautics, Astronautics** pg 3; **Travel and Tourism** pg 5458

Airplanes –See **Aeronautics, Astronautics** pg 3

Airports –See **Aeronautics, Astronautics** pg 3

Alarm/Security Systems –See **Engineering -- Electricity, Electrical Engineering, Electronics** pg 2034

Alcoholic Beverages –See **Food and Food Industry -- Beverage Industry** pg 2363

Alcoholism –See **Drug Abuse and Alcoholism** pg 1338

Alimony –See **Law -- Family Law** pg 3119

**Allergy and Immunology** –pg 3662

Almanacs –See **Encyclopedias and General Reference Books** pg 1923

**Alumni** –pg 1096

Amateur Radio –See **Communication -- Broadcasting** pg 1125; see also Communication pg 1103

American Studies –See **History(General) -- History of North, South, and Central America** pg 2717

Amusements –See **Recreation, Leisure -- Games and Amusements** pg 4856

**Analytic and Experimental Mechanics** –pg 4427

**Analytical Chemistry** –pg 1012

Anarchism –See **Political Science -- Socialism, Communism, Anarchism, Utopianism** pg 4539

Anatomy –See **Medical Science and Technology -- Anatomy** pg 3543; see also Biology -- Embryology pg 541; Medical Science and Technology -- Pathology pg 3891

Anesthesia –See **Medical Science and Technology -- Anesthesiology** pg 3680; see also Medical Science and Technology -- Surgery pg 3957; Pharmacy and Pharmacology pg 4288

**Anesthesiology** –pg 3680; see also Medical Science and Technology -- Surgery pg 3957

Angiology –See **Medical Science and Technology -- Cardiology** pg 3697

Anglo-Saxon Studies –See **History(General) -- History of Europe** pg 2671; **Literature** pg 3357

Animal Husbandry –See **Agriculture** pg 42; **Veterinary Sciences** pg 5501

Animal Science –See **Veterinary Sciences** pg 5501; see also Zoology pg 5572

# SUBJECT CROSS REFERENCES

**Animal Welfare** –pg 225; see also Ethics pg 2248

**Animals** –See **Horses and Horsemanship** pg 2796; **Pets** pg 4285; see also Veterinary Sciences pg 5501; Zoology pg 5572

**Anthropology** –pg 227; see also Archaeology pg 253; Paleontology pg 4226; Sociology pg 5237

Antibiotics –See **Medical Science and Technology** pg 3543; **Pharmacy and Pharmacology** pg 4288; see also Chemistry pg 958

**Antiques** –pg 248; see also Hobbies pg 2770; Museums and Galleries pg 4083

Antitrust Law –See **Law -- Corporate Law** pg 3094

Anxiety –See **Medical Science and Technology -- Psychiatry** pg 3918; see also Psychology pg 4570

Apartments –See **Housing and Urban Development** pg 2812

Apparel –See **Clothing Industry and Fashion** pg 1081; see also Business -- Retail pg 952; Textiles pg 5347

Appliances –See **Household Hardware and Appliances** pg 2810

Applied Mechanics –See **Engineering -- Materials Engineering and Mechanics** pg 2100; **Physics -- Analytic and Experimental Mechanics** pg 4427; see also Engineering -- Mechanical Engineering and Machinery pg 2108

Apprenticeship –See **Economics -- Labor** pg 1642

Aquaculture –See **Fish and Fisheries** pg 2293; see also Biology pg 439; Biology -- Marine Biology pg 552

**Archaeology** –pg 253; see also Anthropology pg 227; History(General) pg 2609; Paleontology pg 4226

Archery –See **Recreation, Leisure -- Sports** pg 4881

**Architecture** –pg 286; see also Building and Construction pg 597; Engineering pg 1963; Interior Design pg 2898

**Archives** –pg 2478; see also History(General) pg 2609; Library and Information Sciences pg 3186

Army –See **Military and Defense** pg 4033

Aromatherapy –See **Beauty and Cosmetics** pg 402

**Art** –pg 335; see also Humanities pg 2841

Art Galleries –See **Museums and Galleries** pg 4083; see also The Arts -- Art pg 335

Art History –See **The Arts -- Art** pg 335; see also Humanities pg 2841; Museums and Galleries pg 4083; The Arts pg 311

Arthritis –See **Medical Science and Technology -- Musculoskeletal System** pg 3802

**Artificial Intelligence** –pg 1210; see also Computers -- Automation pg 1217; Science and Technology pg 5078

Arts and Sciences –See **The Arts** pg 311; see also Humanities pg 2841; Social Sciences pg

Asbestos –See **Building and Construction** pg 597; **Engineering -- Mines and Mining Engineering** pg 2132; see also Public Health and Safety pg 4763

Asia –See **General Interest -- General Interest-Asia** pg 2501; **History(General) -- History of Asia** pg 2644

Asian Studies –See **History(General) -- History of Asia** pg 2644; **Literature** pg 3357

Associations –See **Societies and Clubs** pg 5228

Asthma –See **Medical Science and Technology -- Respiratory System** pg 3947

**Astrology** –pg 389

Astronautics –See **Aeronautics, Astronautics** pg 3

**Astronomy** –pg 391

Atheism –See **Philosophy** pg 4339

Athletic Clubs –See **Health and Personal Fitness** pg 2595; see also Recreation, Leisure -- Sports pg 4881

Athletics –See **Recreation, Leisure -- Sports** pg 4881; see also Health and Personal Fitness pg 2595

Atlas –See **Geography** pg 2553

Atmospheric Science –See **Earth Sciences -- Meteorology** pg 1419; see also Science and Technology pg 5078

Atomic Energy –See **Energy** pg 1930; **Engineering -- Nuclear Engineering** pg 2153

Attorney General –See **Law -- Judicial Systems** pg 3138

Audio-Visual Education –See **Education -- Teaching and Curriculum** pg 1887

Audiology –See **Medical Science and Technology -- Otorhinolaryngology** pg 3885

Auditing –See **Business -- Accounting** pg 735; see also Public Administration -- Public Finance and Taxation** pg 4708

Audubon Society –See **Environmental Issues -- Conservation and Natural Resources** pg 2185; see also Natural History pg 4161

Australia –See **General Interest -- General Interest-Australia and Oceania** pg 2510; **History(General) -- History of Australia and Oceania** pg 2668

Authors –See **Biographies** pg 429; **Literature** pg 3357; see also Literature -- Poetry pg 3459; Publishing pg 4811

**Automation** –pg 1217

Automobile Racing –See **Recreation, Leisure -- Sports** pg 4881

**Automobiles** –pg 5403

Aviation –See **Aeronautics, Astronautics** pg 3

Bacteriology –See **Biology** pg 439; **Biology -- Microbiology** pg 558

Badminton –See **Recreation, Leisure -- Sports** pg 4881

Bahaism –See **Religion and Theology -- Islam, Bahaism, Theosophy** pg 5041

Bakers and Bakeries –See **Food and Food Industry** pg 2325

Balkan Studies –See **History(General) -- History of Europe** pg 2671

Banking –See **Business -- Banking and Finance** pg 768

**Banking and Finance** –pg 768; see also Business -- Cooperatives pg 1541; Business -- Investments pg 890; Economics pg 1459; Public Administration -- Public Finance pg 4708

**Banking Law** –pg 3084; see also Business -- Banking and Finance pg 768; Law -- Corporate Law pg 3094

Bankruptcy –See **Law -- Banking Law** pg 3084; see also Business -- Banking and Finance pg 768

Baptist –See **Religion and Theology -- Protestantism** pg 5054

Baseball –See **Recreation, Leisure -- Sports** pg 4881

Baseball Cards –See **Hobbies** pg 2770; **Recreation, Leisure -- Sports** pg 4881

**Beauty and Cosmetics** –pg 402

Beekeeping –See **Agriculture** pg 42

Behavior Therapy –See **Psychology** pg 4570

Behavioral Science –See **Medical Science and Technology -- Psychiatry** pg 3918; **Psychology** pg 4570; see also Sociology pg 5237

# SUBJECT CROSS REFERENCES

**Belizean Studies** –See **History(General) -- History of North, South, and Central America** pg 2717

**Beverage Industry** –pg 2363

**Bible** –pg 5013

**Bibliographies** –pg 406; see also Library and Information Sciences pg 3186

**Bicycles and Bicycling** –pg 427

**Bilingual** –See **Education -- Special Education and Rehabilitation** pg 1874; **Linguistics** pg 3260; see also Education pg 1720

**Biochemistry** –pg 479

**Bioengineering** –See **Medical Science and Technology -- Biotechnology** pg 3685

**Biofeedback** –See **Psychology** pg 4570; see also Biology -- Physiology pg 577; Medical Science and Technology pg 3543

**Biographies** –pg 429

**Biology** –pg 439; see also Medical Science and Technology pg 3543; Zoology 5572

**Biomechanics** –See **Medical Science and Technology -- Biotechnology** pg 3685

**Biomedical Engineering** –See **Medical Science and Technology -- Biotechnology** pg 3685

**Biomedicine** –See **Medical Science and Technology -- Biotechnology** pg 3685

**Biophysics** –pg 494

**Biotechnology** –pg 3685

**Birds** –See **Zoology -- Ornithology** pg 5614; see also Environmental Issues -- Conservation and Natural Resources pg 2185; Natural History pg 4161

**Birth Control** –pg 587; see also Population Studies pg 4549

**Blind** –See **Physically Impaired** pg 4382; see also Education -- Special Education and Rehabilitation pg 1874; Medical Science and Technology -- Ophthalmology pg 3871; Sociology -- Social Services and Welfare pg 5269

**Blood** –See **Medical Science and Technology -- Hematology** pg 3769

**Blood Groups** –See **Medical Science and Technology -- Hematology** pg 3769

**Blood Preservation** –See **Medical Science and Technology -- Hematology** pg 3769

**Blood Transfusions** –See **Medical Science and Technology -- Hematology** pg 3769; see also Medical Science and Technology pg 3543; Medical Science and Technology -- Internal Medicine pg 3794; Medical Science and Technology -- Surgery pg 3957

**Boats and Boating** –pg 591

**Bodybuilding** –See **Health and Personal Fitness** pg 2595; see also Recreation, Leisure -- Sports pg 4881

**Books and Bookmaking** –pg 4822

**Booksellers** –See **Publishing -- Books and Bookmaking** pg 4822; see also Publishing pg 4811

**Botany** –pg 496; see also Agriculture -- Crop Production and Soil pg 161; Gardening and Horticulture pg 2407

**Bowling** –See **Recreation, Leisure -- Sports** pg 4881

**Boxing** –See **Recreation, Leisure -- Sports** pg 4881

**Brahmanism** –See **Hinduism** pg 5040

**Braille** –See **Physically Impaired** pg 4382; see also Education -- Special Education and Rehabilitation pg 1874

**Breast-feeding** –See **Medical Science and Technology -- Gynecology and Obstetrics** pg 3755; see also Medical Science and Technology -- Pediatrics pg 3899

**Breweries** –See **Food and Food Industry -- Beverage Industry** pg 2363

**Bricks** –See **Building and Construction** pg 597

**Bride** –See **Family and Marriage** pg 2276

**Bridges** –See **Transportation** pg 5375; see also Engineering -- Civil Engineering pg 2018; Transportation -- Roads and Traffic pg 5438

**British Studies** –See **History(General) -- History of Europe** pg 2671; **Literature** pg 3357

**Broadcasting** –pg 1125

**Buddhism** –pg 5020

**Budget** –See **Public Administration -- Public Finance and Taxation** pg 4708; see also Business -- Banking and Finance pg 768

**Building and Construction** –pg 597; see also Engineering -- Civil Engineering pg 2018; Housing and Urban Development pg 2812

**Burns** –See **Medical Science and Technology** pg 3543

**Buses** –See **Transportation** pg 5375

**Business** –pg 636

**Business Education** –See **Business** pg 636; see also Education pg 1720

**Business Law** –See **Business** pg 636; **Law -- Corporate Law** pg 3094; see also Law -- International Law pg 3122

**Buying** –See **Business -- Purchasing** pg 948

**Cable Television** –See **Communication -- Broadcasting** pg 1125

**CAD/CAM** –See **Computers -- Computer Graphics and Design** pg 1231; see also Computers -- Computer Engineering pg 1227

**Calligraphy** –See **The Arts -- Graphic Arts** pg 376

**Cameras** –See **Photography and Video** pg 4366; see also Hobbies pg 2770; Motion Picture pg 4062

**Camping** –See **Recreation, Leisure -- Outdoor Life** pg 4868

**Canadian Studies** –See **History(General) -- History of North, South, and Central America** pg 2717

**Cancer** –See **Medical Science and Technology -- Neoplasma, Neoplastic** pg 3808

**Candy** –See **Food and Food Industry** pg 2325

**Canning and Preserving** –See **Food and Food Industry** pg 2325; see also Gardening and Horticulture pg 2407

**Canoeing** –See **Boats and Boating** pg 591

**Canon Law** –See **Religion and Theology** pg 4931

**Cardiology** –pg 3697; see also Medical Science and Technology -- Hematology pg 3769

**Careers** –See **Occupations and Careers** pg 4201

**Cargo** –See **Transportation** pg 5375

**Caribbean Studies** –See **History(General) -- History of North, South, and Central America** pg 2717

**Carpentry and Woodwork** –pg 633; see also Hobbies pg 2770; Interior Design -- Home Furnishings pg 2904

**Carpet, Rugs** –See **Interior Design -- Home Furnishings** pg 2904

**Cartography** –pg 2580

**Cartoons** –See **The Arts -- Graphic Arts** pg 376; see also Recreation, Leisure -- Games and Amusements pg 4856

**Catalogues** –See **Bibliographies** pg 406

**Catalysis** –See **Chemistry -- Physical and Theoretical Chemistry** pg 1049

# SUBJECT CROSS REFERENCES

Catalysts –See **Chemistry -- Physical and Theoretical Chemistry** pg 1049

Catering –See **Food and Food Industry** pg 2325; **Hotels/Motels** pg 2803; **Restaurants** pg 5070

**Catholicism** –pg 5022

Cattle –See **Agriculture -- Livestock and Poultry** pg 204; see also Agriculture pg 42; Agriculture -- Dairy Industry pg 191; Veterinary Sciences pg 5501

Caves –See **Earth Sciences -- Geophysics** pg 1402; see also Earth Sciences -- Geology pg 1364

CD-ROM –See **Computers -- Optical Storage, CD-ROM Applications** pg 1276

Celebrity Interests –See **General Interest** pg 2484; see also Motion Picture pg 4062

Celtic Studies –See **History(General) -- History of Europe** pg 2671; **Literature** pg 3357

Cement –See **Building and Construction** pg 597; **Chemistry -- Chemical Technology** pg 1020; see also Engineering -- Civil Engineering pg 2018; Industry and Production pg 1596

Cemeteries –See **Funeral Service** pg 2406

Central America –See **General Interest -- General Interest-Central America** pg 2511; **History(General) -- History of North, South, and Central America** pg 2717

Ceramics –See **Glass and Ceramics** pg 2585

Cereals –See **Agriculture -- Feed Grain and Milling** pg 199; see also Food and Food Industry pg 2325

Cerebral Palsy –See **Medical Science and Technology -- Neurology** pg 3825

**Chamber of Commerce** –pg 817

Charities –See **Philanthropy** pg 4334; see also Sociology -- Social Services and Welfare pg 5269

**Chemical Engineering** –pg 2007; see also Chemistry pg 958; Chemistry -- Chemical Technology pg 1020

**Chemical Technology** –pg 1020; see also Chemistry pg 958; Engineering -- Chemical Engineering pg 2007; Medical Science and Technology -- Biotechnology pg 3685

**Chemistry** –pg 958; see also Engineering -- Chemical Engineering pg 2007

Chemotherapy –See **Medical Science and Technology -- Neoplasma, Neoplastic** pg 3808; see also Pharmacy and Pharmacology pg 4288

Chess –See **Recreation, Leisure -- Games and Amusements** pg 4856

Child Development –See **Education -- Early Childhood and Primary Education** pg 1802

Child Psychology –See **Psychology** pg 4570

Child Welfare –See **Sociology -- Social Services and Welfare** pg 5269

**Children and Youth Interests** –pg 1059

China, Tableware –See **Glass and Ceramics** pg 2585; see also Gifts, Toys pg 2583

Chinese Studies –See **History(General) -- History of Asia** pg 2644; **Literature** pg 3357

Chiropractor –See **Medical Science and Technology -- Musculoskeletal System** pg 3802; **Physical Therapy** pg 4378

Christianity –See **Religion and Theology** pg 4931

Chromatography –See **Chemistry -- Analytical Chemistry** pg 1012; see also Chemistry pg 958

Churches –See **Religion and Theology** pg 4931; see also Religion and Theology -- Eastern Christian Churches pg 5039; Religion and Theology -- Protestantism pg 5054

Cinema –See **Motion Picture** pg 4062

Cinematography –See **Photography and Video** pg 4366; see also Motion Picture pg 4062

Citrus Industry –See **Agriculture -- Crop Production and Soil** pg 161; **Food and Food Industry** pg 2325; **Gardening and Horticulture** pg 2407

City Directory –See **Geography** pg 2553

City Planning –See **Housing and Urban Development** pg 2812

**Civil Defense** –pg 1072

**Civil Engineering** –pg 2018

**Civil Law** –pg 3088

**Civil Rights** –pg 4503

**Civil Service** –pg 4701; see also Public Administration pg 4623

**Classical Studies** –pg 1073; see also Archaeology pg 253; History(General) pg 2609; Linguistics pg 3260; Literature pg 3357

Climatology –See **Earth Sciences -- Meteorology** pg 1419

Clinical Medicine –See **Medical Science and Technology** pg 3543; **Medical Science and Technology** pg 3543

Clocks –See **Jewelry -- Clocks and Watches** pg 2916

**Clocks and Watches** –pg 2916

**Clothing Industry and Fashion** –pg 1081; see also Leather and Fur Industry pg 3183; Textiles pg 5347

Clubs –See **Societies and Clubs** pg 5228

Coaching –See **Recreation, Leisure -- Sports** pg 4881

Coal –See **Earth Science -- Mineralogy** pg 1437; see also Energy pg 1930; Engineering -- Mines and Mining Engineering pg 2132

Coast Guard –See **Naval Science, Navigation** pg 4174

Coins –See **Hobbies -- Numismatics** pg 2779

Collectors and Collecting –See **Antiques** pg 248; see also Hobbies pg 2770

**College and School Publications** –pg 1088; see also Education -- Higher Education pg 1806

Colleges and Universities –See **Education -- Higher Education** pg 1806; see also College and School Publications pg 1088

Combustion –See **Chemistry -- Physical and Theoretical Chemistry** pg 1049; **Energy** pg 1930; **Engineering** pg 1963

Comics –See **Recreation, Leisure -- Games and Amusements** pg 4856

**Commerce** –pg 821

Commercial Art –See **The Arts -- Graphic Arts** pg 376

Commercial Law –See **Law -- Corporate Law** pg 3094

Commodities –See **Business -- Commerce** pg 821

Common Law –See **Law -- Civil Law** pg 3088

**Communicable Diseases** –pg 3711; See also **Medical Science and Technology -- Epidemiology** pg 3733; Public Health and Safety pg 248

**Communication** –pg 1103

Communism –See **Political Science -- Socialism, Communism, Anarchism, Utopianism** pg 4539

Community Affairs –See **Public Administration** pg 4623

# SUBJECT CROSS REFERENCES

Community Development –See **Housing and Urban Development** pg 2812

Compact Disc –See **Computers -- Optical Storage, CD-ROM Applications** pg 1276

Company Law –See **Law -- Corporate Law** pg 3094

Comparative Law –See **Law -- International Law** pg 3122

Composite Materials –See **Engineering -- Materials Engineering and Mechanics** pg 2100

Computer Architecture –See **Computers -- Computer Graphics and Design** pg 1231

**Computer Assisted Instruction** –pg 1222; see also Education -- Teaching and Curriculum pg 1887

Computer Crimes –See **Computers -- Computer Crimes and Security** pg 1225

**Computer Crimes and Security** –pg 1225

Computer Directories –See **Computers -- Computer Industry and Industry Directories** pg 1235

**Computer Engineering** –pg 1227

**Computer Games** – pg 1230; see also Recreation, Leisure -- Games and Amusements pg 4856

**Computer Graphics and Design** –pg 1231

Computer Industry –See **Computers -- Computer Industry and Industry Directories** pg 1235

**Computer Industry and Industry Directories** –pg 1235; see also Computers -- Computer Sales, Service and Supply pg 1244

**Computer Music** –pg 1240; see also Music pg 4098

**Computer Networks** –pg 1240

Computer Products –See **Computers -- Computer Sales, Service and Supply** pg 1244

**Computer Sales, Service and Supply** –pg 1244

Computer Science –See **Computers** pg 1169

Computer Simulation –See **Computers -- Simulation** pg 1282

**Computer Systems** –pg 1246

**Computers** –pg 1169

Confectioners –See **Food and Food Industry** pg 2325

Congress –See **Public Administration** pg 4623

**Conservation and Natural Resources** –pg 2185; see also Environmental Issues -- Ecology pg 2210; Natural History pg 4161; Public Administration -- Parks and Recreation pg 4705; Water Resources pg 5528

**Constitutional Law** –pg 3091

Construction –See **Building and Construction** pg 597; see also Engineering -- Civil Engineering pg 2018

**Consumer Interests** –pg 1293; see also Economics pg 1459

Consumer Protection –See **Consumer Interests** pg 1293; see also Law -- Corporate Law pg 3094

Contact Lenses –See **Medical Science and Technology -- Ophthalmology** pg 3871; **Optometry** pg 4214

Continuing Education –See **Education -- Adult and Continuing Education** pg 1799

Contraception –See **Birth Control** pg 587

Contractors –See **Building and Construction** pg 597; **Engineering -- Civil Engineering** pg 2018; see also Architecture pg 286

Conventions –See **Business -- Advertising and Public Relations** pg 753; **Science and Technology** pg 5078

Cookbooks, Cooking –See **Home Economics** pg 2788

**Cooperatives** –pg 1541; see also Agriculture pg 42; Business -- Banking and Finance pg 768

**Copyright, Intellectual Property** –pg 1300

**Corporate Law** –pg 3094

Corporation Law –See **Law -- Corporate Law** pg 3094

Corrosion –See **Engineering -- Chemical Engineering** pg 2007; see also Metals and Metallurgy pg 3996

Cosmetic Surgery –See **Medical Science and Technology -- Surgery** pg 3957

Cosmetics –See **Beauty and Cosmetics** pg 402

Cotton –See **Agriculture -- Crop Production and Soil** pg 161; see also Textiles pg 5347

Counseling –See **Psychology** pg 4570; see also Family and Marriage pg 2276; Religion and Theology pg 4931; Sociology -- Social Services and Welfare pg 5269

Court Rules –See **Law -- Judicial Systems** pg 3138

Courts –See **Law -- Judicial Systems** pg 3138

**Crafts and Decorative Arts** –pg 369; see also Gifts, Toys pg 2583; Glass and Ceramics pg 2585; Hobbies pg 2770; Sewing and Needlework pg 5182

Credit Unions –See **Business -- Banking and Finance** pg 768

Crime Prevention –See **Law -- Law Enforcement and Criminology** pg 3156

Crime Statistics –See **Law -- Law Enforcement and Criminology** pg 3156; see also Statistics pg 5320

Criminal Justice –See **Law -- Law Enforcement and Criminology** pg 3156; see also Law -- Criminal Law pg 3104

**Criminal Law** –pg 3104; see also Law -- Law Enforcement and Criminology pg 3156

Criminal Procedure –See **Law -- Judicial Systems** pg 3138; **Law -- Law Enforcement and Criminology** pg 3156; see also Law -- Criminal Law pg 3104

Criminology –See **Law -- Law Enforcement and Criminology** pg 3156

Croatian Studies –See **History(General) -- History of Europe** pg 2671

**Crop Production and Soil** –pg 161

**Crystallography** –pg 1031

Currency –See **Business -- Banking and Finance** pg 768; **Business -- Investments** pg 890; see also Economics -- International Economics pg 1632

Curriculum –See **Education -- Teaching and Curriculum** pg 1887

Customs –See **Sociology -- Manners and Customs** pg 5267

Customs and Excise –See **Public Administration -- Public Finance and Taxation** pg 4708; see also Law pg 2926

**Cybernetics** –pg 1250

Cystic Fibrosis –See **Medical Science and Technology -- Musculoskeletal System** pg 3802

Cytology –See **Biology -- Cytology and Histology** pg 531

**Cytology and Histology** –pg 531

**Dairy Industry** –pg 191

**Dance** –pg 1310; see also The Arts -- Performing Arts pg 383

**Data Base Management** –pg 1252

**Data Processing** –pg 1255

Data Protection –See **Computers -- Computer Crimes and Security** pg 1225

Daycare –See **Sociology -- Social Services and Welfare** pg 5269

# SUBJECT CROSS REFERENCES

Deaf –See **Physically Impaired** pg 4382; see also Medical Science and Technology -- Otorhinolaryngology pg 3885

Decorative Arts –See **The Arts -- Crafts and Decorative Arts** pg 369

Defense –See **Military and Defense** pg 4033; see also Civil Defense pg 1072

Demography –See **Population Studies** pg 4549; see also Statistics pg 5320

**Dentistry** –pg 1314

Department Stores –See **Business -- Retail** pg 952; see also Business -- Marketing pg 920

**Dermatology** –pg 3717

**Desktop Publishing** –pg 1263; see also Publishing pg 4811

Diabetes –See **Endocrinology** pg 3726

Diagnostic Imaging –See **Medical Science and Technology -- Radiology** pg 3938

Dialysis –See **Medical Science and Technology -- Urology and Nephrology** pg 3987; see also Medical Science and Technology pg 3543; Medical Science and Technology -- Internal Medicine pg 3794

Dictionaries –See **Encyclopedias and General Reference Books** pg 1923

Dietetics –See **Nutrition and Dietetics** pg 4186

Directories –See **Encyclopedias and General Reference Books** pg 1923

Disarmament –See **Military and Defense** pg 4033; see also Law -- International Law pg 3122

Divorce –See **Family and Marriage** pg 2276; **Law -- Family Law** pg 3119

Doctrinal Theology –See **Religion and Theology** pg 4931

Dog Racing –See **Recreation, Leisure -- Sports** pg 4881

Domestic Relations –See **Law -- Family Law** pg 3119

Drama –See **Theater** pg 5361; see also The Arts -- Performing Arts pg 383

Drink –See **Food and Food Industry -- Beverage Industry** pg 2363

**Drug Abuse and Alcoholism** –pg 1338

Dyes and Dyeing –See **Chemistry -- Chemical Technology** pg 1020; **Textiles** pg 5347; see also The Arts -- Crafts and Decorative Arts pg 369

**Early Childhood and Primary Education** –pg 1802

Early Childhood Education –See **Education -- Early Childhood and Primary Education** pg 1802

**Earth Sciences** –pg 1351

**Eastern Christian Churches** –pg 5039

**Ecology** –pg 2210; see also Natural History pg 4161

Economic Conditions –See **Economics -- Economic History, Conditions** pg 1544

Economic History –See **Economics -- Economic History, Conditions** pg 1544

**Economic History, Conditions** –pg 1544

**Economic Theory** –pg 1589

**Economics** –pg 1459

Editing –See **Publishing** pg 4811; see also Journalism pg 2917; Literature pg 3357

**Education** –pg 1720

Educational Psychology –See **Education -- Teaching and Curriculum** pg 1887; **Psychology** pg 4570; see also Education pg 1720; Education -- Special Education and Rehabilitation pg 1874

Elections –See **Political Science** pg 4461; see also Public Administration pg 4623

Electric Power –See **Engineering -- Electricity, Electrical Engineering and Electronic** pg 2034

**Electricity, Electrical Engineering, Electronics** –pg 2034; see also Energy pg 1930; Heating, Plumbing and Refrigeration pg 2602; Public Administration -- Public Utilities pg 4759; Sound Recordings and Systems pg 5315

**Electrochemistry** –pg 1033; see also Chemistry -- Analytical Chemistry pg 1012; Chemistry -- Physical and Theoretical Chemistry pg 1049

Electronic Publishing –See **Desktop Publishing** pg 1263

Electronics –See **Engineering -- Electricity, Electrical Engineering, Electronics** pg 2034

Embroidery –See **Sewing and Needlework** pg 5182

**Embryology** –pg 541; see also Medical Science and Technology -- Anatomy pg 3678

Emergencies –See **Medical Science and Technology -- Emergency Medicine** pg 3723

Emergency Health Services –See **Medical Science and Technology -- Emergency Medicine** pg 3723

**Emergency Medicine** –pg 3723

**Emigration and Immigration** –pg 1918

Employment Law –See **Law -- Labor Law** pg 3143

**Encyclopedias and General Reference Books** –pg 1923

**Endocrinology** –pg 3726

**Energy** –pg 1930; see also Engineering -- Electricity, Electrical Engineering, Electronics pg 2034; Engineering -- Nuclear Engineering pg 2153; Petroleum and Natural Gas pg 4248; Physics -- Nuclear Physics pg 4445; Public Administration -- Public Utilities pg 4759

**Engineering** –pg 1963; see also Computers -- Artificial Intelligence pg 1210

**Entomology** –pg 5604

Environmental Health –See **Environmental Issues** pg 2159; see also Public Health and Safety pg 4763

**Environmental Issues** –pg 2159

**Environmental Law** –pg 3109; see also Environmental Issues pg 2159

Environmental Protection –See **Environmental Issues** pg 2159; see also Environmental Issues -- Pollution and Waste Management pg 2222

Environmental Studies –See **Environmental Issues** pg 2159; see also Environmental Issues -- Conservation and Natural Resources pg 2185; Environmental Issues -- Ecology pg 2210; Environmental Issues -- Pollution and Waste Management pg 2222

Environmental Technology –See **Environmental Issues** pg 2159; see also Science and Technology pg 5078

Environmental Waste Management –See **Environmental Issues** pg 2159

Enzymes –See **Biology -- Biochemistry** pg 479

**Epidemiology** –pg 3733; see also Medical Science and Technology -- Epidemiology pg 3711; Public Health and Safety pg 4763

Epilepsy –See **Medical Science and Technology -- Neurology** pg 3825

Episcopal –See **Religion and Theology -- Protestantism** pg 5054

Ergonomics –See **Engineering -- Mechanical Engineering and Machinery** pg 2108; see also Computers -- Cybernetics pg 1250

Esperanto –See **Linguistics** pg 3260; see also Education -- Teaching and Curriculum pg 1887

# SUBJECT CROSS REFERENCES

**Estate Planning** –pg 3117; see also **Business -- Banking and Finance** pg 768; **Business -- Investments** pg 890

**Ethics** –pg 2248

**Ethnic Interests** –pg 2253

**Ethnology** –See **Anthropology** pg 227

**Europe** –See **General Interest-Europe** pg 2513; **History(General) -- History of Europe** pg 2671

**European Studies** –See **History(General) -- History of Europe** pg 2671; **Literature** pg 3357

**Evangelism** –See **Religion and Theology** pg 4931

**Exceptional Children** –See **Education -- Special Education and Rehabilitation** pg 1874

**Exercise** –See **Health and Personal Fitness** pg 2595

**Exhibits/Exhibitions** –See **Business -- Advertising and Public Relations** pg 753; **Science and Technology** pg 5078

**Experimental Mechanics** –See **Physics -- Analytic and Experimental Mechanics** pg 4427

**Expert Systems** –See **Computers -- Artificial Intelligence** pg 1210

**Expositions** –See **Business -- Advertising and Public Relations** pg 753; **Recreation, Leisure -- Games and Amusements** pg 4856; **Science and Technology** pg 5078

**Fabric** –See **Textiles** pg 5347; see also Clothing Industry and Fashion pg 1081; Sewing and Needlework pg 5182

**Fairs** –See **Recreation, Leisure -- Games and Amusements** pg 4856

**Family and Marriage** –pg 2276; see also Home Economics pg 2788

**Family Law** –pg 3119

**Family Medicine** –See **Medical Science and Technology -- Family Practice** pg 3736

**Family Physicians** –See **Medical Science and Technology -- Family Practice** pg 3736; see also Medical Science and Technology -- Physicians and Medical Personnel pg 3912

**Family Planning** –See **Birth Control** pg 587; **Family and Marriage** pg 2276

**Family Practice** –pg 3736

**Fashion** –See **Clothing Industry and Fashion** pg 1081

**Federal Aid to Education** –See **Education -- Higher Education** pg 1806; see also Education -- School Organization and Administration pg 1859

**Federal Employees** –See **Public Administration -- Civil Service** pg 4701

**Federal Government** –See **Public Administration** pg 4623; see also Political Science pg 4461

**Feed Grain and Milling** –pg 199

**Feminism** –See **Women's Interests** pg 5550

**Fencing** –See **Recreation, Leisure -- Sports** pg 4881

**Fertility** –See **Birth Control** pg 587; **Population Studies** pg 4549; see also Biology -- Physiology pg 577; Medical Science and Technology -- Gynecology and Obstetrics pg 3755

**Fertilizers** –See **Agriculture -- Crop Production and Soil** pg 161; **Chemistry -- Chemical Technology** pg 1020

**Fiber Optics** –See **Communication -- Telecommunications** pg 1148; **Physics -- Light, Optics, Radiation** pg 4432

**Fiction** –See **Literature** pg 3357; see also Literary and Political Reviews pg 3337

**Films and Filmmaking** –See **Motion Picture** pg 4062; see also Photography and Video pg 4366

**Finance** –See **Business -- Banking and Finance** pg 768; **Public Administration -- Public Finance and Taxation** pg 4708

**Fire Prevention** –pg 2287

**Fish and Fisheries** –pg 2293

**Fishing** –See **Fish and Fisheries** pg 2293

**Floor Coverings** –See **Building and Construction** pg 597; **Interior Design -- Home Furnishings** pg 2904

**Florist Trade** –pg 2434

**Flowers** –See **Gardening and Horticulture -- Florist Trade** pg 2434

**Fluid Mechanics** –See **Engineering -- Hydraulic Engineering** pg 2087; **Physics -- Analytic and Experimental Mechanics** pg 4427

**Folk Music** –See **Folklore** pg 2318; **Music** pg 4098

**Folklore** –pg 2318; see also History(General) pg 2609; Literature pg 3357; Sociology -- Manners and Customs pg 5267

**Food and Food Industry** –pg 2325; see also Agriculture pg 42; Home Economics pg 2788; Restaurants pg 5070

**Food Production** –See **Agriculture -- Crop Production and Soil** pg 3475; see also Food and Food Industry pg 2325

**Football** –See **Recreation, Leisure -- Sports** pg 4881

**Footwear** –See **Clothing Industry and Fashion** pg 1081; see also Leather and Fur Industry pg 3183

**Foreign Affairs** –See **International Relations** pg 4514; see also Law -- International Law pg 3122

**Foreign Trade** –See **Business -- Commerce** pg 821; see also Economics -- International Economics pg 1632

**Forensic Medicine** –See **Medical Science and Technology -- Forensic Medicine, Medical Jurisprudence** pg 3739

**Forensic Medicine, Medical Jurisprudence** –pg 3739

**Forestry** –pg 2373; see also Environmental Issues -- Conservation and Natural Resources pg 2185; Gardening and Horticulture pg 2407; Paper and Pulp Industry pg 4232

**Franchises** –See **Business** pg 636

**Fraternities** –See **Societies and Clubs** pg 5228

**Freight** –See **Transportation** pg 5375; see also Aeronautics, Astronautics pg 3; Business -- Commerce pg 821; Transportation - Ships and Shipping pg 5447; Transportation -- Railroads pg 5429

**French Studies** –See **History(General) History of Europe** pg 2671; **Literature** pg 3357

**Frozen Foods** –See **Food and Food Industry** pg 2325

**Fruit** –See **Agriculture -- Crop Production and Soil** pg 161; **Food and Food Industry** pg 2325; **Gardening and Horticulture** pg 2407

**Fuel** –See **Petroleum and Natural Gas** pg 4248; see also Energy pg 1930; Engineering -- Electricity, Electrical Engineering, Electronics pg 2034

**Fund Raising** –See **Philanthropy** pg 4334; see also Sociology -- Social Services and Welfare pg 5269

**Funeral Service** –pg 2406

**Fungi** –See **Biology -- Mycology** pg 574

**Fur** –See **Leather and Fur Industry** pg 3183

**Furniture** –See **Interior Design -- Home Furnishings** pg 2904; see also Antiques pg 248; Building and Construction -- Carpentry and Woodwork pg 633; Interior Design pg 2898

**Galleries** –See **Museums and Galleries** pg 4083

# SUBJECT CROSS REFERENCES

Gambling –See **Recreation, Leisure -- Games and Amusements** pg 4856; see also Psychology pg 4570; Public Administration pg 4623

**Games and Amusements** –pg 4856; see also Children and Youth Interests pg 1059

**Gardening and Horticulture** –pg 2407

**Gastroenterology** –pg 3743

Gay/Lesbian –See **Homosexuality** pg 2793

**Genealogy and Heraldry** –pg 2436; see also History(General) pg 2609

**General Interest** –pg 2484

**General Interest-Africa** –pg 2497

**General Interest-Asia** –pg 2501

**General Interest-Australia and Oceania** –pg 2510

**General Interest-Central America** –pg 2511

**General Interest-Europe** –pg 2513

**General Interest-Middle East** –pg 2525

**General Interest-North America** –pg 2526

**General Interest-South America** –pg 2551

**General Management** –pg 858

General Management and Administration –See **Business -- General Management** pg 858

General Practice –See **Medical Science and Technology -- Family Practice** pg 3736

General Reference Books –See **Encyclopedias and General Reference Books** pg 1923

Genetic Engineering –See **Medical Science and Technology -- Biotechnology** pg 3685; see also Biology -- Genetics pg 541

**Genetics** –pg 541

Geochemistry –See **Chemistry** pg 958

Geodesy –See **Earth Sciences -- Geophysics** pg 1402; **Geography** pg 2553

**Geography** –pg 2553; see also Travel and Tourism pg 5458

**Geology** –pg 1364

**Geophysics** –pg 1402

**Geriatrics** –pg 3748; see also Senior Citizens pg 5177

Germanic Studies –See **History(General) -- History of Europe** pg 2671; **Literature** pg 3357

Gifted Children –See **Education -- Special Education and Rehabilitation** pg 1874

**Gifts, Toys** –pg 2583; see also Glass and Ceramics pg 2585; Recreation, Leisure -- Games and Amusements pg 4856; The Arts -- Crafts and Decorative Arts pg 369

**Glass and Ceramics** –pg 2585; see also The Arts -- Crafts and Decorative Arts pg 369

Golf –See **Recreation, Leisure -- Sports** pg 4881

Government –See **Public Administration** pg 4623; see also Political Science pg 4461

Government Employees –See **Public Administration -- Civil Service** pg 4701

**Graphic Arts** –pg 376; see also Printing Industry pg 4563

Grocery Trade –See **Food and Food Industry** pg 2325

Guns –See **Recreation, Leisure -- Sports** pg 4881; see also Military and Defense pg 4033

Gymnastics –See **Recreation, Leisure -- Sports** pg 4881

**Gynecology and Obstetrics** –pg 3755

Handicrafts –See **The Arts -- Crafts and Decorative Arts** pg 369

**Hardware** –pg 1264; **Household Hardware and Appliances** pg 2810; see also Building and Construction pg 597

Hazardous Waste –See **Environmental Issues -- Pollution and Waste Management** pg 2222; see also Environmental Issues pg 2159

**Health and Personal Fitness** –pg 2595; see also Physical Education and Training pg 1854; Recreation, Leisure -- Sports pg 4881

Hearing Disorders –See **Medical Science and Technology -- Otorhinolaryngology** pg 3885; **Physically Impaired** pg 4382

**Heat** –pg 4430

**Heating, Plumbing, and Refrigeration** –pg 2602; see also Electricity, Electrical Engineering, Electronics pg 2034; Household Hardware and Appliances pg 2810

Helicopters –See **Aeronautics, Astronautics** pg 3

Helminthology –See **Zoology** pg 5572

Hematologic Diseases –See **Medical Science and Technology -- Hematology** pg 3769

**Hematology** –pg 3769; see also Biology -- Physiology pg 577; Medical Science and Technology -- Cardiology pg 3697; Medical Science and Technology -- Internal Medicine pg 3794

Hemodialysis –See **Medical Science and Technology -- Hematology** pg 3769

Heraldry –See **Genealogy and Heraldry** pg 2436

Herbs and Spices –See **Food and Food Industry** pg 2325; see also Gardening and Horticulture pg 2407

Heredity –See **Biology -- Genetics** pg 541

**Higher Education** –pg 1806

**Hinduism** –pg 5040

Histology –See **Biology -- Cytology and Histology** pg 531

**History of Africa** –pg 2636

**History of Asia** –pg 2644

**History of Australia and Oceania** –pg 2668

**History of Europe** –pg 2671

**History of North, South, and Central America** –pg 2717

**History of the Middle East** –pg 2767

**History(General)** –pg 2609

**Hobbies** –pg 2770; see also Recreation, Leisure -- Sports pg 4881; Sewing and Needlework pg 5182; The Arts -- Crafts and Decorative Arts pg 369

Hockey –See **Recreation, Leisure -- Sports** pg 4881

Home and Gardening Publications –See **Gardening and Horticulture** pg 2407

Home Computing –See **Computers -- Microcomputers, Personal Computers** pg 1265

**Home Economics** –pg 2788; see also Family and Marriage pg 2276

**Home Furnishings** –pg 2904; see also Building and Construction -- Carpentry and Woodwork pg 633; Interior Design pg 2898

**Homeopathy** –pg 3774

**Homosexuality** –pg 2793

Hormones –See **Endocrinology** pg 3726; see also Biology -- Biochemistry pg 479; Biology -- Physiology pg 577

Horse Racing –See **Horses and Horsemanship** pg 2796; see also Recreation, Leisure -- Sports pg 4881

**Horses and Horsemanship** –pg 2796; see also Recreation, Leisure -- Sports pg 4881

Horticulture –See **Gardening and Horticulture** pg 2407; see also Agriculture -- Crop Production and Soil pg 161; Biology -- Botany pg 496; Forestry pg 2373

# SUBJECT CROSS REFERENCES

Hospital Administration –See **Medical Science and Technology -- Hospital Administration and Medical Centers** pg 3775

**Hospital Administration and Medical Centers** –pg 3775

Hospitals –See **Medical Science and Technology -- Hospital Administration and Medical Centers** pg 3775

**Hotels/Motels** –pg 2803; see also Travel and Tourism pg 5458; see also Restaurants pg 5070

**Household Hardware and Appliances** –pg 2810; see also Electricity, Electrical Engineering, Electronics pg 2034; Heating, Plumbing, and Refrigeration pg 2602

**Housing and Urban Development** –pg 2812; see also Building and Construction pg 597; Real Estate pg 4833

Human Sexuality –See **Sexual Life** pg 5186

Humane Society –See **Animal Welfare** pg 225

**Humanities** –pg 2841; see also Social Sciences pg 5189; The Arts pg 311

Hunting –See **Recreation, Leisure -- Outdoor Life** pg 4868

**Hydraulic Engineering** –pg 2087; see also Earth Sciences -- Hydrology pg 1412; Energy pg 1930; Water Resources pg 5528

Hydrobiology –See **Biology -- Marine Biology** pg 552; see also Earth Sciences -- Oceanography pg 1445

**Hydrology** –pg 1412; see also Engineering -- Hydraulic Engineering pg 2087; Water Resources pg 5528

Hygiene –See **Industrial Health and Safety** pg 2858; **Public Health and Safety** pg 4763

Hypertension –See **Medical Science and Technology -- Cardiology** pg 3697; see also Medical Science and Technology -- Internal Medicine pg 3794

**Hypnosis** –pg 2857

Immigration –See **Emigration and Immigration** pg 1918

Immunology –See **Medical Science and Technology -- Allergy and Immunology** pg 3662

Imports/Exports –See **Business -- Commerce** pg 821

Income Tax –See **Public Administration -- Public Finance and Taxation** pg 4708; see also Business -- Accounting pg 735

Industrial Arts –See **Education -- Vocational Education** pg 1909; see also Science and Technology pg 5078

Industrial Design –See **Engineering -- Industrial Engineering and Design** pg 2096; see also Manufacturing pg 3475

**Industrial Engineering and Design** –pg 2096

**Industrial Health and Safety** –pg 2858

Industrial Medicine –See **Industrial Health and Safety** pg 2858

Industry –See **Economics -- Industry and Production** pg 1596

**Industry and Production** –pg 1596

Infectious Diseases –See **Medical Science and Technology -- Communicable Diseases** pg 3711; see also Medical Science and Technology -- Epidemiology pg 3733; Public Health and Safety pg 4763

Information Retrieval –See **Library and Information Sciences** pg 3186

Information Science –See **Library and Information Sciences** pg 3186

Inheritance –See **Law -- Estate Planning** pg 3117

**Inorganic Chemistry** –pg 1035

Insecticide –See **Pest Control** pg 4243

Insects –See **Zoology -- Entomology** pg 5604; see also Pest Control pg 4243

Insulation –See **Building and Construction** pg 597; see also Engineering -- Electricity, Electrical Engineering, Electronics pg 2034

**Insurance** –pg 2872

Insurance Law –See **Insurance** pg 2872; **Law -- Corporate Law** pg 3094

Integrated Circuits –See **Engineering -- Electricity, Electrical Engineering, Electronics** pg 2034

Intellectual Property –See **Copyright, Intellectual Property** pg 1300

Intensive Care –See **Medical Science and Technology** pg 3543; see also Medical Science and Technology -- Nursing pg 3849

**Interior Design** –pg 2898; see also Architecture pg 286

**Internal Medicine** –pg 3794

**International Assistance and Development** –pg 2907; see also Economics -- International Economics pg 1632; Sociology -- Social Services and Welfare pg 5269

**International Economics** –pg 1632

**International Law** –pg 3122; see also Political Science -- International Relations pg 4514

**International Relations** –pg 4514; see also History(General) pg 2609; Law -- International Law pg 3122; Military and Defense pg 4033

Invertebrates/Vertebrates –See **Zoology** pg 5572

Investing –See **Business -- Investments** pg 890

**Investments** –pg 890; see also Business -- Banking and Finance pg 768

Irish Slavonic Studies –See **History(General) -- History of Europe** pg 2671; **Literature** pg 3357

Irish Studies –See **History(General) -- History of Europe** pg 2671; **Literature** pg 3357

Irrigation –See **Engineering -- Hydraulic Engineering** pg 2087; see also Agriculture -- Crop Production and Soil pg 161

Islam –See **Religion and Theology -- Islam, Bahaism, Theosophy** pg 5041

**Islam, Bahaism, Theosophy** –pg 5041

Jails –See **Law -- Law Enforcement and Criminology** pg 3156

**Jewelry** –pg 2913

**Journalism** –pg 2917; see also Communication -- Broadcasting pg 1125; Publishing pg 4811

**Judaism** –pg 5045; see also Ethnic Interests pg 2253

Judges –See **Law -- Judicial Systems** pg 3138

Judicial Ethics –See **Law -- Judicial Systems** pg 3138

Judicial Statistics –See **Law -- Judicial Systems** pg 3138

**Judicial Systems** –pg 3138

Judo/Karate –See **Recreation, Leisure -- Sports** pg 4881; see also Health and Personal Fitness pg 2595

Juvenile Delinquency –See **Law -- Law Enforcement and Criminology** pg 3156; see also Sociology -- Social Services and Welfare pg 5269

Kidneys –See **Medical Science and Technology -- Urology and Nephrology** pg 3987

Kindergarten –See **Education -- Early Childhood and Primary Education** pg 1802

Knitting –See **Sewing and Needlework** pg 5182; see also Textiles pg 5347

# SUBJECT CROSS REFERENCES

Korean Studies –See **History(General) -- History of Asia** pg 2644; see also Literature pg 3357

Labels/Labelling –See **Packaging** pg 4217

**Labor** –pg 1642; see also Business -- Personnel Management pg 938; Industrial Health and Safety pg 2858

**Labor Law** –pg 3143; see also Law pg 2926; see also Economics -- Labor pg 1642

Labor Unions –See **Economics -- Labor** pg 1642

LAN (Local Area Networks) –See **Computers -- Computer Networks** pg 1240

Land –See **Economics** pg 1459; **Environmental Issues -- Conservation and Natural Resources** pg 2185; **Public Administration** pg 4623; **Real Estate** pg 4833; see also Geography pg 2553

Landscape Architecture –See **Gardening and Horticulture** pg 2407

Language –See **Linguistics** pg 3260

Lasers –See **Physics -- Light, Optics, Radiation** pg 4432; see also Chemistry pg 958; Engineering pg 1963; Medical Science and Technology -- Surgery pg 3957; Physics pg 4395

Latin American Studies –See **History(General) -- History of North, South, and Central America** pg 2717; see also Literature pg 3357

Laundry –See **Chemistry -- Chemical Technology** pg 1020; see also Textiles pg 5347

**Law** –pg 2926; see also Public Administration pg 4623

Law Enforcement –See **Law -- Law Enforcement and Criminology** pg 2926

**Law Enforcement and Criminology** –pg 3156

Law Offices –See **Law** pg 2926; see also Business -- General Management pg 858

Learning Disabilities –See **Education -- Special Education and Rehabilitation** pg 1874

**Leather and Fur Industry** –pg 3183; see also Clothing Industry and Fashion pg 1081

**Legal Aid** –pg 3179

Legislation –See **Law** pg 2926; see also Public Administration pg 4623

Leisure –See **Recreation, Leisure** pg 4848

Leukemia –See **Medical Science and Technology -- Neoplasma, Neoplastic** pg 3808; see also Medical Science and Technology -- Internal Medicine pg 3794

**Library and Information Sciences** –pg 3186; see also Archives pg 2478; Bibliographies pg 406

Life/Death –See **Philosophy** pg 4339

**Light, Optics, Radiation** –pg 4432

**Linguistics** –pg 3260; see also Literature pg 3357

Liquor –See **Food and Food Industry -- Beverage Industry** pg 2363

Literacy –See **Education -- Special Education and Rehabilitation** pg 1874

**Literary and Political Reviews** –pg 3337; see also Literature pg 3357

Literary Criticism –See **Literary and Political Reviews** pg 3337

Literary Theory –See **Literary and Political Reviews** pg 3337

**Literature** –pg 3357; see also Linguistics pg 3260; Literary and Political Reviews pg 3337; Romance and Adventure pg 5073

**Livestock and Poultry** –pg 204

Local Area Networks –See **Computers -- Computer Networks** pg 1240

Local Government –See **Political Science** pg 4461; **Public Administration** pg 4623; **Public Administration** pg 4708

Lotteries –See **Public Administration** pg 4623

**Lumber and Wood** –pg 2399; see also Paper and Pulp Industry pg 4232

Lutheran –See **Religion and Theology -- Protestantism** pg 5054

Machinery –See **Engineering -- Mechanical Engineering and Machinery** pg 2108

Macroeconomics –See **Economics -- Economic Theory** pg 1589; see also Economics pg 1459; Economics -- International Economics pg 1632

Magic –See **Recreation, Leisure -- Games and Amusements** pg 4856; see also Parapsychology and Occultism pg 4240

Magnetic Resonance Imaging –See **Medical Science and Technology -- Radiology** pg 3938

**Magnetism** –pg 4443

Mainframe Computing –See **Computers -- Data Processing** pg 1255

**Manners and Customs** –pg 5267

**Manufacturing** –pg 3475; see also Industry and Production pg 1596

Maps and Mapmaking –See **Geography -- Cartography** pg 2580

**Marine Biology** –pg 552; see also Earth Sciences -- Oceanography pg 1445; Zoology pg 5572

Marine Engineering –See **Engineering** pg 1963

Marine Pollution –See **Environmental Issues -- Pollution and Waste Management** pg 2222

Marine Toxins –See **Biology -- Marine Biology** pg 552

Marines –See **Naval Science, Navigation** pg 4174

**Maritime Law** –pg 3180

**Marketing** –pg 920

Marriage –See **Family and Marriage** pg 2276

Marriage Law –See **Law -- Family Law** pg 3119

Martial Arts –See **Health and Personal Fitness** pg 2595

Marxism –See **Political Science -- Socialism, Communism, Anarchism, Utopianism** pg 4539; see also Sociology pg 5237

Masonry –See **Building and Construction** pg 597

**Materials Engineering and Mechanics** –pg 2100

Mathematical Geography –See **Geography** pg 2553

**Mathematics** –pg 3490

Matrimonial Actions –See **Law -- Family Law** pg 3119

Meat –See **Food and Food Industry** pg 2325; see also Agriculture -- Livestock and Poultry pg 204

**Mechanical Engineering and Machinery** –pg 2108

Media –See **Communication** pg 1103; see also Journalism pg 2917

Medical Centers –See **Medical Science and Technology -- Hospital Administration and Medical Centers** pg 3775

Medical Jurisprudence –See **Medical Science and Technology -- Forensic Medicine, Medical Jurisprudence** pg 3739

Medical Malpractice –See **Law** pg 2926; see also Medical Science and Technology pg 3543

Medical Personnel –See **Medical Science and Technology -- Physicians and Medical Personnel** pg 3912

**Medical Science and Technology** –pg 3543; see also Public Health and Safety pg 4763

xxx

# SUBJECT CROSS REFERENCES

Medieval Studies –See **History(General) -- History of Europe** pg 2671; see also Classical Studies pg 1073

Meetings –See **Business** pg 636

Memory –See **Psychology** pg 4570

**Men's Interests** –pg 3994

Mental Health –See **Medical Science and Technology -- Psychiatry** pg 3918; **Psychology** pg 4570; **Public Health and Safety** pg 4763; **Sociology -- Social Services and Welfare** pg 5269

Mentally Disabled –See **Education -- Special Education and Rehabilitation** pg 1874; see also Medical Science and Technology -- Psychiatry pg 3918; Psychology pg 4570

Mergers/Acquisitions –See **Business** pg 636

Metabolic Diseases –See **Medical Science and Technology -- Allergy and Immunology** pg 3662

Metallurgy –See **Metals and Metallurgy** pg 3996

**Metals and Metallurgy** –pg 3996; see also Mines and Mining Engineering pg 2132

**Meteorology** –pg 1419

Methodist –See **Religion and Theology -- Protestantism** pg 5054

**Metrology and Standardization** –pg 4029

**Microbiology** –pg 558

Microcomputers –See **Computers -- Microcomputers, Personal Computers** pg 1265

**Microcomputers, Personal Computers** –pg 1265

**Microscopy** –pg 572

Midwifery –See **Medical Science and Technology -- Gynecology and Obstetrics** pg 3755

Migration –See **Emigration and Immigration** pg 1918; **Population Studies** pg 4549; see also Economics -- Labor pg 1642; Zoology pg 5572

Military Administration –See **Military and Defense** pg 4033

**Military and Defense** –pg 4033; see also Political Science -- International Relations pg 4514

Military History –See **Military and Defense** pg 4033

**Military Law** –pg 3182

Military Medicine –See **Medical Science and Technology** pg 3543; see also Military and Defense pg 4033

Milling –See **Agriculture -- Feed Grain and Milling** pg 199

**Mineralogy** –pg 1437

**Mines and Mining Engineering** –pg 2132; see also Earth Sciences -- Mineralogy pg 1437; Metals and Metallurgy pg 4026; Petroleum and Natural Gas pg 4248

**Minicomputers** –pg 1273; see also Computers -- Microcomputers, Personal Computers pg 1265

Mobile Homes –See **Building and Construction** pg 597; **Housing and Urban Development** pg 2812; **Transportation** pg 5375

Money –See **Business -- Banking and Finance** pg 768; **Economics** pg 1459

Monuments –See **History(General)** pg 2609; see also Architecture pg 286; The Arts -- Art pg 335

Mormons –See **Religion and Theology** pg 4931

Morphology –See **Biology -- Botany** pg 496

Motels –See **Hotels/Motels** pg 2803

**Motion Picture** –pg 4062

**Motorcycles** –pg 4080

Mountain Climbing –See **Recreation, Leisure -- Outdoor Life** pg 4868; see also Recreation, Leisure -- Sports pg 4881

Movies –See **Motion Picture** pg 4062

Multiple Sclerosis –See **Medical Science and Technology -- Neurology** pg 3825

Muscular Dystrophy –See **Medical Science and Technology -- Musculoskeletal System** pg 3802; see also Medical Science and Technology -- Neurology pg 3825

**Musculoskeletal System** –pg 3802

**Museums and Galleries** –pg 4083; see also Natural History pg 4161; The Arts -- Art pg 335

**Music** –pg 4098; see also Computers -- Computer Music pg 1240; Sound Recordings and Systems pg 5315; The Arts -- Performing Arts pg 383

Music Therapy –See **Medical Science and Technology** pg 3543; **Music** pg 4098; see also Psychology pg 4570

Mutual Funds –See **Business -- Investments** pg 890; see also Business -- Banking and Finance pg 768

**Mycology** –pg 574; see also Biology -- Botany pg 496

Mysticism –See **Parapsychology and Occultism** pg 4240; see also Literature pg 3357; Religion and Theology pg 4931

Mythology –See **Folklore** pg 2318

Narcotics –See **Drug Abuse and Alcoholism** pg 1338; see also Law -- Law Enforcement and Criminology pg 3156; Pharmacy and Pharmacology pg 4288

Natural Gas –See **Petroleum and Natural Gas** pg 4248

**Natural History** –pg 4161; see also Biology pg 4570; Environmental Issues -- Conservation and Natural Resources pg 2185; Environmental Issues -- Ecology pg 2185

Natural Resources –See **Environmental Issues -- Conservation and Natural Resources** pg 2185

Naturalist –See **Natural History** pg 4161; see also Environmental Issues -- Ecology pg 2210

Naval Architecture –See **Architecture** pg 286; **Naval Science and Navigation** pg 4174

**Naval Science, Navigation** –pg 4174; see also Transportation -- Ships and Shipping pg 5447

Navigation –See **Naval Science, Navigation** pg 4174

Navy –See **Naval Science, Navigation** pg 4174

Needlework –See **Sewing and Needlework** pg 5182

Neoplasma –See **Medical Science and Technology -- Neoplasma, Neoplastic** pg 3808

**Neoplasma, Neoplastic** –pg 3808; see also Medical Science and Technology -- Radiology pg 3938

Neoplastic –See **Medical Science and Technology -- Neoplasma, Neoplastic** pg 3808

Nephrology –See **Medical Science and Technology -- Urology and Nephrology** pg 3987

Neural Networks –See **Computers -- Artificial Intelligence** pg 1210

**Neurology** –pg 3825; see also Medical Science and Technology -- Psychiatry pg 3918; Psychology pg 4570

**New Age Publications** –pg 4185

**Newspapers** –pg 5625

Noise Control –See **Environmental Issues** pg 2159

North America –See **General Interest -- General Interest-North America** pg 2526; **History(General) -- History of North, South, and Central America** pg 2717

**Nuclear Engineering** –pg 2153

Nuclear Medicine –See **Medical Science and Technology -- Internal Medicine** pg 3794; Medical Science and Technology -- Radiology pg 3938

# SUBJECT CROSS REFERENCES

**Nuclear Physics** –pg 4445

Nuclear Waste –See **Environmental Issues -- Pollution and Waste Management** pg 2222

**Numismatics** –pg 2779

**Nursing** –pg 3849; see also Medical Science and Technology -- Surgery pg 3849

Nursing Homes –See **Medical Science and Technology -- Hospital Administration and Medical Centers** pg 3775; see also Sociology -- Social Services and Welfare pg 5269

**Nutrition and Dietetics** –pg 4186; see also Food and Food Industry pg 2325

Nutritional Disorders –See **Nutrition and Dietetics** pg 4186

Obstetrics –See **Medical Science and Technology -- Gynecology and Obstetrics** pg 3755

Occultism –See **Parapsychology and Occultism** pg 4240

Occupational Health –See **Industrial Health and Safety** pg 2858

Occupational Therapy –See **Industrial Health and Safety** pg 2858; see also Education -- Special Education and Rehabilitation pg 1874; Medical Science and Technology -- Psychiatry pg 3918

**Occupations and Careers** –pg 4201; see also Economics -- Labor pg 1642; Education -- Special Aspects of Education pg 1874

Ocean Engineering –See **Engineering -- Hydraulic Engineering** pg 2087; see also Earth Sciences -- Oceanography pg 1445

Oceania –See **General Interest -- General Interest-Australia and Oceania** pg 2510; see also History(General) -- History of Australia and Oceania pg 2668

**Oceanography** –pg 1445

**Office Equipment and Services** –pg 4210; see also Computers pg 1169

Oil –See **Petroleum and Natural Gas** pg 4248

Oncology –See **Medical Science and Technology -- Neoplasma, Neoplastic** pg 3808

**Online Computing and Information** –pg 1274

Opera –See **The Arts -- Performing Arts** pg 383; see also Music pg 4098

**Ophthalmology** –pg 3871

**Optical Storage, CD-ROM Applications** –pg 1276

Optics –See **Physics -- Light, Optics, Radiation** pg 4432

**Optometry** –pg 4214

Oral Surgery –See **Medical Science and Technology -- Surgery** pg 3957; see also Dentistry pg 1314

**Organic Chemistry** –pg 1038

Oriental Studies –See **History(General) -- History of Asia** pg 2644; see also Literature pg 3357

**Ornithology** –pg 5614; see also Natural History pg 4161

Orthodontics –See **Dentistry** pg 1314

**Orthopedics** –pg 3880

**Otorhinolaryngology** –pg 3885

**Outdoor Life** –pg 4868; see also Environmental Issues -- Conservation and Natural Resources pg 2185; Fish and Fisheries pg 2293; Recreation, Leisure -- Sports pg 4881

Pacific Studies –See **History(General) -- History of Australia and Oceania** pg 2671; see also Literature pg 3357

**Packaging** –pg 4217

Pain –See **Medical Science and Technology -- Neurology** pg 3825

**Paints and Painting** –pg 4222

**Paleontology** –pg 4226

**Paper and Pulp Industry** –pg 4232

Parachuting –See **Recreation, Leisure -- Sports** pg 4881

Paramedics –See **Medical Science and Technology -- Emergency Medicine** pg 3723

**Parapsychology and Occultism** –pg 4240

Parenting –See **Family and Marriage** pg 2276

Parks –See **Environmental Issues -- Conservation and Natural Resources** pg 2185; Recreation, Leisure pg 4848

**Parks and Recreation** –pg 4705; see also Environmental Issues -- Conservation and Natural Resources pg 2185

Parliament/House of Commons –See **Public Administration** pg 4623; see also Political Science pg 4461

Patents –See **Copyright, Intellectual Property** pg 1300

**Pathology** –pg 3891; see also Medical Science and Technology -- Anatomy pg 3678

Pediatric Surgery –See **Medical Science and Technology -- Pediatrics** pg 3899; see also Medical Science and Technology -- Surgery pg 3957

**Pediatrics** –pg 3899

Penology –See **Law -- Law Enforcement and Criminology** pg 3156

Pensions –See **Business -- Investments** pg 890; see also Economics -- Labor pg 1642; Insurance pg 2872

**Performing Arts** –pg 383; see also Motion Picture pg 4062; Music pg 4098; The Arts -- Dance pg 1310; Theater pg 5361

Perfumes –See **Beauty and Cosmetics** pg 402; see also Chemistry -- Chemical Technology pg 1020

Perinatology –See **Medical Science and Technology -- Gynecology and Obstetrics** pg 3755; see also Medical Science and Technology -- Pediatrics pg 3899

Personal Computers –See **Computers -- Microcomputers, Personal Computers** pg 1265

Personal Hygiene –See **Health and Personal Fitness** pg 2595

**Personnel Management** –pg 938; see also Economics -- Labor pg 1642

**Pest Control** –pg 4243

**Petroleum and Natural Gas** –pg 4248; see also Energy pg 1930; Engineering -- Mines and Mining Engineering pg 2132

**Petrology** –pg 1458

**Pets** –pg 4285

Pharmaceutical Industry –See **Pharmacy and Pharmacology** pg 4288

**Pharmacy and Pharmacology** –pg 4288; see also Medical Science and Technology -- Toxicology pg 3978

**Philanthropy** –pg 4334; see also Sociology -- Social Services and Welfare pg 5269

**Philately** –pg 2784

Philology –See **Linguistics** pg 3260; see also Classical Studies pg 1073

**Philosophy** –pg 4339

Phonetics –See **Linguistics** pg 3260

**Photography and Video** –pg 4366

**Physical and Theoretical Chemistry** –pg 1049

Physical Education –See **Education -- Physical Education and Training** pg 2595; **Education -- Physical Education and Training** pg 1854; see also Health and Personal Fitness pg 2595

**Physical Education and Training** –pg 1854

Physical Fitness –See **Health and Personal Fitness** pg 2595

**Physical Therapy** –pg 4378

Physical Training –See **Education -- Physical Education and Training** pg 1854

# SUBJECT CROSS REFERENCES

**Physically Impaired** –pg 4382; see also Education -- Special Education and Rehabilitation pg 1874; Sociology -- Social Services and Welfare pg 5269

Physician's Assistants –See **Medical Science and Technology -- Physicians and Medical Personnel** pg 3912

Physicians –See **Medical Science and Technology -- Physicians and Medical Personnel** pg 3912; see also Medical Science and Technology -- Family Practice pg 3736

**Physicians and Medical Personnel** –pg 3912

**Physics** –pg 4395

**Physiology** –pg 577

Phytopathology –See **Biology -- Botany** pg 496; **Gardening and Horticulture** pg 2407

Planned Parenthood –See **Birth Control** pg 587; see also Family and Marriage pg 2276

Plant Breeding –See **Biology -- Botany** pg 496; see also Agriculture -- Crop Production and Soil pg 161; Gardening and Horticulture pg 2407

Plant Culture –See **Gardening and Horticulture** pg 2407

Plastic Surgery –See **Medical Science and Technology -- Surgery** pg 3957

**Plastics** –pg 4453; see also Engineering -- Materials Engineering and Mechanics pg 2100

Plays –See **Literature** pg 3357; **The Arts -- Performing Arts** pg 383; **Theater** pg 5361

Plumbing –See **Heating, Plumbing, and Refrigeration** pg 2602

**Podiatry** –pg 3917

**Poetry** –pg 3459; see also Literary and Political Reviews pg 3337

Political Reviews –See **Literary and Political Reviews** pg 3337

**Political Science** –pg 4461; see also Military and Defense pg 4033; Public Administration pg 4623

Polling –See **Public Administration** pg 4623; see also Sociology pg 5237; Statistics pg 5320

**Pollution and Waste Management** –pg 2222; see also Earth Sciences -- Ecology pg 2210; Environmental Issues -- Ecology pg 2210

Polymers –See **Chemistry -- Organic Chemistry** pg 1038; see also Paints and Painting pg 4222; Plastics pg 4453

**Population Studies** –pg 4549; see also Birth Control pg 587; Statistics pg 5320

Portable Computers –See **Computers -- Microcomputers, Personal Computers** pg 1265

Postage Stamps –See **Hobbies -- Philately** pg 2784

**Postal Communications** –pg 1144; see also Public Administration -- Civil Service pg 4701

Pottery –See **Glass and Ceramics** pg 2585

Poultry –See **Agriculture -- Livestock and Poultry** pg 204

Poverty –See **Sociology -- Social Services and Welfare** pg 5269; see also International Assistance and Development pg 2907

Power –See **Engineering -- Electricity, Electrical Engineering, Electronics** pg 2034

Powerlifting –See **Health and Personal Fitness** pg 2595; see also Recreation, Leisure -- Sports pg 4881

Practical Theology –See **Religion and Theology** pg 4931

Presbyterian –See **Religion and Theology -- Protestantism** pg 5054

Preschool Education –See **Education -- Early Childhood and Primary Education** pg 1802

Preventive Medicine –See **Medical Science and Technology** pg 3543; see also Public Health and Safety pg 4763

Primary Care –See **Medical Science and Technology -- Family Practice** pg 3736

Primary Education –See **Education -- Early Childhood and Primary Education** pg 1802

**Printing Industry** –pg 4563; see also The Arts -- Graphic Arts pg 376

Prisons –See **Law -- Law Enforcement and Criminology** pg 3156

Private Schools –See **Education** pg 1720

Probation –See **Law -- Law Enforcement and Criminology** pg 3156

Production –See **Economics -- Industry and Production** pg 1596

**Programs and Programming** –pg 1277; see also Computers -- Software pg 1283

**Protestantism** –pg 5054

**Psychiatry** –pg 3918; see also Medical Science and Technology -- Neurology pg 3825; Psychology pg 4570

Psychoanalysis –See **Medical Science and Technology -- Psychiatry** pg 3918; **Psychology** pg 4570

**Psychology** –pg 4570; see also Medical Science and Technology -- Psychiatry pg 3918; Sociology pg 5237

Psychopathology –See **Medical Science and Technology -- Psychiatry** pg 3918

Psychosomatic Medicine –See **Medical Science and Technology** pg 3543; **Psychology** pg 4570

Psychotherapy –See **Medical Science and Technology -- Psychiatry** pg 3918; see also Family and Marriage pg 2276; Psychology pg 4570

PTA –See **Education -- School Organization and Administration** pg 1859

**Public Administration** –pg 4623; see also Political Science pg 4461

Public Affairs –See **Public Administration** pg 4623

**Public Finance and Taxation** –pg 4708; see also Law pg 2926

**Public Health and Safety** –pg 4763; see also Environmental Issues -- Pollution and Waste Management pg 2222; Medical Science and Technology -- Communicable Diseases pg 3711; Medical Science and Technology -- Epidemiology pg 3733

Public Opinion –See **Sociology** pg 5237

Public Relations –See **Business -- Advertising and Public Relations** pg 753

Public Transportation –See **Transportation** pg 5375; see also Public Administration pg 4623

**Public Utilities** –pg 4759

Publishing –See **Computers -- Desktop Publishing** pg 1263; Journalism pg 2917

Pulp Industry –See **Paper and Pulp Industry** pg 4232

Puppetry –See **The Arts -- Performing Arts** pg 383

**Purchasing** –pg 948

Puzzles –See **Recreation, Leisure -- Games and Amusements** pg 4856

Quarries –See **Engineering -- Mines and Mining Engineering** pg 2132; see also Industrial Health and Safety pg 2858

Race Relations –See **Sociology** pg 5237; see also Ethnic Interests pg 2253

Radiation –See **Physics -- Light, Optics, Radiation** pg 4432

Radio –See **Communication -- Broadcasting** pg 1125

# SUBJECT CROSS REFERENCES

**Radiology** –pg 3938; see also Medical Science and Technology -- Neoplasma, Neoplastic pg 3808; Medical Science and Technology -- Nuclear Medicine pg 3847

**Railroads** –pg 5429

Rationalism –See **Philosophy** pg 4339

**Real Estate** –pg 4833; see also Housing and Urban Development pg 2812

Record Industry –See **Music** pg 4098; see also Communication -- Broadcasting pg 1125; Sound Recordings and Systems pg 5315

**Recreation, Leisure** –pg 4848; see also Hobbies pg 2770; Travel and Tourism pg 5458

Recreational Vehicles –See **Transportation** pg 5375; see also Recreation, Leisure pg 4848

Recycling –See **Environmental Issues -- Pollution and Waste Management** pg 2222

Red Cross –See **Sociology -- Social Services and Welfare** pg 5269; see also Medical Science and Technology pg 3543

Reformed Church –See **Religion and Theology -- Protestantism** pg 5054

Refrigeration –See **Heating, Plumbing, and Refrigeration** pg 2602

Regional Planning –See **Housing and Urban Development** pg 2812

Rehabilitation –See **Education -- Special Education and Rehabilitation** pg 1874; **Physically Impaired** pg 4382; see also Drug Abuse and Alcoholism pg 1338; Physical Therapy pg 4378; Sociology -- Social Services and Welfare pg 5269

**Religion and Theology** –pg 4931

Religious Education –See **Religion and Theology** pg 4931

Religious Music –See **Music** pg 4098

Research –See **Science and Technology** pg 5078; see also Education -- Higher Education pg 1806

Residential Homes –See **Housing and Urban Development** pg 2812

Resorts –See **Hotels/Motels** pg 2803; **Travel and Tourism** pg 5458

**Respiratory System** –pg 3947

**Restaurants** –pg 5070; see also Food and Food Industry pg 2325; Hotels/Motels pg 2803

**Retail** –pg 952

Rheumatology –See **Medical Science and Technology -- Musculoskeletal System** pg 3802; see also Pharmacy and Pharmacology pg 4288

**Roads and Traffic** –pg 5438

Robotics –See **Computers -- Artificial Intelligence** pg 1210; see also Computers -- Automation pg 1217

Roman Catholic Church –See **Religion and Theology -- Catholicism** pg 5022

**Romance and Adventure** –pg 5073; see also Literature pg 3357

**Rubber** –pg 5075

Rugby –See **Recreation, Leisure -- Sports** pg 4881

Running –See **Health and Personal Fitness** pg 2595

Safety –See **Industrial Health and Safety** pg 2858; see also Public Health and Safety pg 4763

Safety Engineering –See **Engineering -- Industrial Engineering and Design** pg 2096

Sailing –See **Boats and Boating** pg 591

Salary/Wages –See **Economics** pg 1459; **Economics -- Labor** pg 1642

Sanitation/Municipal Engineering –See **Environmental Issues -- Pollution and Waste Management** pg 2222; **Public Health and Safety** pg 4763; see also Environmental Issues -- Conservation and Natural Resources pg 2185; Environmental Issues -- Ecology pg 2210

Scholarships –See **Education -- Higher Education** pg 1806

School Counseling –See **Education -- Special Education and Rehabilitation** pg 1874

School Law/Legislation –See **Education -- School Organization and Administration** pg 1859

**School Organization and Administration** –pg 1859

Science –See **Science and Technology** pg 5078

**Science and Technology** –pg 5078; see also Chemistry -- Chemical Technology pg 1020; Engineering pg 1963

Science Fiction –See **Literature** pg 3357; see also Literary and Political Reviews pg 3337

Scuba Diving –See **Recreation, Leisure -- Sports** pg 4881

Sculpture –See **The Arts -- Art** pg 335; see also Architecture pg 286

Secondary Education –See **Education** pg 1720

Securities Law –See **Law -- Corporate Law** pg 3094

Security –See **Computers -- Computer Crimes and Security** pg 1225

**Security Systems and Alarms** –pg 5176; see also Engineering -- Electricity, Electrical Engineering, Electronics pg 2034

Sedimentology –See **Earth Sciences -- Geology** pg 1364; see also Earth Sciences -- Geophysics pg 1402

Seismology –See **Earth Sciences -- Geophysics** pg 1402

Semantics –See **Linguistics** pg 3260

**Senior Citizens** –pg 5177; see also Medical Science and Technology -- Geriatrics pg 3748; Sociology -- Social Services and Welfare pg 5269

Sewage –See **Environmental Issues -- Pollution and Waste Management** pg 2222; see also Water Resources pg 5528

**Sewing and Needlework** –pg 5182; see also Hobbies pg 2770; The Arts -- Crafts and Decorative Arts pg 369

**Sexual Life** –pg 5186

Sexually Transmitted Diseases –See **Medical Science and Technology -- Communicable Diseases** pg 3711; **Public Health and Safety** pg 4763

Ship Design –See **Engineering** pg 1459; **Naval Science, Navigation** pg 4174; see also Transportation -- Ships and Shipping pg 5447

Shipbuilding –See **Naval Science, Navigation** pg 4174; **Transportation -- Ships and Shipping** pg 5447

**Ships and Shipping** –pg 5447; see also Business -- Commerce pg 821; Naval Science, Navigation pg 4174

Shoes –See **Clothing Industry and Fashion** pg 1081

**Simulation** –pg 1282

Skiing –See **Recreation, Leisure -- Sports** pg 4881

Slavery –See **Civil Rights** pg 4503

Slavic Studies –See **History(General) -- History of Europe** pg 2671; **Literature** pg 3357

Small Business –See **Business** pg 636; see also Economics pg 1459

Smoking –See **Public Health and Safety** pg 4763; **Tobacco** pg 5372

Soap Operas –See **General Interest** pg 2484

Soccer –See **Recreation, Leisure -- Sports** pg 4881

**Social Sciences** –pg 5189; see also Humanities pg 2841

# SUBJECT CROSS REFERENCES

Social Security –See **Sociology -- Social Services and Welfare** pg 5269; see also Economics -- Labor pg 1642; Insurance pg 2872

Social Services –See **Sociology -- Social Services and Welfare** pg 5269

**Social Services and Welfare** –pg 5269

Socialism –See **Political Science -- Socialism, Communism, Anarchism, Utopianism** pg 1589

**Socialism, Communism, Anarchism, Utopianism** –pg 4539

**Societies and Clubs** –pg 5228

**Sociology** –pg 5237

**Software** –pg 1283; see also Computer Industry and Industry Directories pg 1235; Programs and Programming pg 1277

Soil –See **Agriculture -- Crop Production and Soil** pg 161

Solar Energy –See **Energy** pg 1930; see also Engineering -- Mechanical Engineering and Machinery pg 2108

**Sound** –pg 4451

**Sound Recordings and Systems** –pg 5315; see also Engineering -- Electricity, Electrical Engineering, Electronics pg 2034; Music pg 4098

South America –See **General Interest -- General Interest-South America** pg 2551; History(General) -- History of North, South, and Central America pg 2717

Special Education –See **Education -- Special Education and Rehabilitation** pg 1874

**Special Education and Rehabilitation** –pg 1874

Spectroscopy –See **Physics -- Light, Optics, Radiation** pg 4432

Speech Disorders –See **Medical Science and Technology -- Otorhinolaryngology** pg 3885; see also Education -- Special Education and Rehabilitation pg 1874; Physically Impaired pg 4382

Speech Pathology –See **Physically Impaired** pg 4382; see also Education -- Special Education and Rehabilitation pg 1874

Speleology –See **Earth Sciences -- Geophysics** pg 1402

**Sports** –pg 4881; see also Recreation, Leisure -- Games and Amusements pg 4856; Recreation, Leisure -- Health and Personal Fitness pg 2595; Recreation, Leisure -- Outdoor Life pg 4868

**Sports Medicine** –pg 3953

Stained Glass –See **Glass and Ceramics** pg 2585

Standardization –See **Metrology and Standardization** pg 4029

State Government –See **Public Administration** pg 4623; see also Public Administration -- Public Finance and Taxation pg 4708

**Statistics** –pg 5320

Stomatology –See **Dentistry** pg 1314

Stress –See **Medical Science and Technology** pg 3543; **Psychology** pg 4570

Sugar –See **Agriculture -- Crop Production and Soil** pg 161; see also Food and Food Industry pg 2325

Surface Chemistry –See **Chemistry -- Physical and Theoretical Chemistry** pg 1049

Surgeons –See **Medical Science and Technology -- Physicians and Medical Personnel** pg 3912

**Surgery** –pg 3957

Surveying –See **Engineering -- Civil Engineering** pg 2018; **Geography** pg 2553

Swimming –See **Recreation, Leisure -- Sports** pg 4881

Tax Planning –See **Law -- Estate Planning** pg 3117

Taxation –See **Public Administration -- Public Finance and Taxation** pg 4708; see also Business -- Accounting pg 735; Law -- Estate Planning pg 3117

Taxidermy –See **Hobbies** pg 2770

Tea –See **Food and Food Industry -- Beverage Industry** pg 2363; see also Agriculture pg 42

**Teaching and Curriculum** –pg 1887

Teaching Materials –See **Education -- Teaching and Curriculum** pg 1887

Technical Education –See **Education -- Vocational Education** pg 1909

Technology –See **Science and Technology** pg 5078

**Telecommunications** –pg 1148

Telegraph –See **Communication -- Telecommunications** pg 1148

Telephone –See **Communication -- Telecommunications** pg 1148

Telephone Directories –See **Communication -- Telecommunications** pg 1148

Television –See **Communication -- Broadcasting** pg 1125

Tennis –See **Recreation, Leisure -- Sports** pg 4881

Textbooks –See **Education** pg 1720

**Textiles** –pg 5347; see also Clothing Industry and Fashion pg 1081

**The Arts** –pg 311

**Theater** –pg 5361; see also The Arts -- Performing Arts pg 383

Theology –See **Religion and Theology** pg 4931

Theoretical Chemistry –See **Chemistry -- Physical and Theoretical Chemistry** pg 1049

Theosophy –See **Religion and Theology -- Islam, Bahaism, Theosophy** pg 5041

Thrombosis –See **Medical Science and Technology -- Internal Medicine** pg 3794; see also Medical Science and Technology -- Cardiology pg 3697; Medical Science and Technology -- Hematology pg 3769; Medical Science and Technology -- Pathology pg 3891

**Tobacco** –pg 5372

Total Quality Management –See **Business -- General Management** pg 858; **Business -- Personnel Management** pg 938

Tourism –See **Travel and Tourism** pg 5458

**Toxicology** –pg 3978; see also Pharmacy and Pharmacology pg 4288

Toys –See **Gifts, Toys** pg 2583

Track and Field –See **Recreation, Leisure -- Sports** pg 4881

Trade –See **Business -- Commerce** pg 821

Trade Regulation –See **Business -- Commerce** pg 821; see also Law -- Corporate Law pg 3094

Trade Schools –See **Education -- Vocational Education** pg 1909

Trade Shows –See **Business -- Advertising and Public Relations** pg 753

Trade Unions –See **Economics -- Labor** pg 1642

Trademarks –See **Copyright, Intellectual Property** pg 1300

Traffic –See **Transportation -- Roads and Traffic** pg 5438

**Transportation** –pg 5375; see also Business -- Commerce pg 821

**Travel and Tourism** –pg 5458; see also Geography pg 2553; Recreation, Leisure pg 4848

Trees –See **Gardening and Horticulture** pg 2407; see also Forestry pg 2373

Tropical Diseases –See **Medical Science and Technology -- Tropical Medicine** pg 3985

**Tropical Medicine** –pg 3985

Trucks and Trucking –See **Transportation** pg 5375

Trustees –See **Law -- Estate Planning** pg 3117

# SUBJECT CROSS REFERENCES

Trusts –See **Law -- Estate Planning** pg 3117

Ukrainian Studies –See **History(General) -- History of Europe** pg 2671; see also Literature pg 3357

Ultrafication –See **Medical Science and Technology -- Hematology** pg 3769

Ultrasonic Therapy –See **Medical Science and Technology -- Radiology** pg 3938

Ultrasound –See **Medical Science and Technology -- Radiology** pg 3938

Unemployment –See **Economics -- Labor** pg 1642; see also Law pg 2926

Unions –See **Economics -- Labor** pg 1642

Universities and Colleges –See **Education -- Higher Education** pg 1806; see also College and School Publications pg 1088

Urban Development –See **Housing and Urban Development** pg 2812

Urinary Tract –See **Medical Science and Technology -- Urology and Nephrology** pg 3987

Urology –See **Medical Science and Technology -- Urology and Nephrology** pg 3987

**Urology and Nephrology** –pg 3987

Utopianism –See **Political Science -- Socialism, Communism, Anarchism, Utopianism** pg 4539

Vacations –See **Travel and Tourism** pg 5458; see also Recreation,Leisure pg 4848

Veterans –See **Military and Defense** pg 4033; see also Naval Science, Navigation pg 4174

**Veterinary Sciences** –pg 5501; see also Zoology pg 5572

Video –See **Communication -- Broadcasting** pg 1125; **Photography and Video** pg 4366; see also Motion Picture pg 4062

Video Games/Arcades –See **Recreation, Leisure -- Games and Amusements** pg 4856

Virology –See **Biology -- Microbiology** pg 558

Virtual Reality –See **Computers -- Artificial Intelligence** pg 1210; see also Computers -- Automation pg 1217

Visual Arts –See **The Arts -- Art** pg 335

Vitamins –See **Nutrition and Dietetics** pg 4186

**Vocational Education** –pg 1909

Vocational Guidance –See **Education -- Vocational Education** pg 1909; see also Occupations and Careers pg 4201

Volcanoes –See **Earth Sciences -- Geophysics** pg 1402

Volunteer Work –See **Philanthropy** pg 4334

Voting –See **Political Science** pg 4461; see also Public Administration pg 4623

WAN (Wide Area Networks) –See **Computer** pg 1240

War –See **History(General)** pg 2609; see also Political Science pg 4461

Waste Management –See **Environmental Issues -- Pollution and Waste Management** pg 2222

Watches –See **Jewelry -- Clocks and Watches** pg 2916

Water Pollution –See **Environmental Issues -- Pollution and Waste Management** pg 2222; see also Water Resources pg 5528

**Water Resources** –pg 5528; see also Earth Sciences -- Hydrology pg 1412; Engineering -- Hydraulic Engineering pg 2087; Environmental Issues -- Conservation and Natural Resources pg 2185

Water Utilities –See **Public Administration -- Public Utilities** pg 4759; see also Water Resources pg 5528

Weaponry –See **Military and Defense** pg 4033

Weather –See **Earth Sciences -- Meteorology** pg 1419

Weightlifting –See **Health and Personal Fitness** pg 2595; see also Recreation, Leisure -- Sports pg 4881

Weights and Measures –See **Metrology and Standardization** pg 4029

**Welding** –pg 4026

Welfare –See **Sociology -- Social Services and Welfare** pg 5269

Western Australian Studies –See **History(General) -- History of Australia and Oceania** pg 2668

Who's Who –See **Biographies** pg 429

Wide Area Networks –See **Computers -- Computer Networks** pg 1240

Wildlife –See **Environmental Issues -- Conservation and Natural Resources** pg 2185; see also Environmental Issues -- Ecology pg 2210; Recreation, Leisure -- Outdoor Life pg 4868

Wills –See **Law -- Estate Planning** pg 3117

Wine –See **Food and Food Industry -- Beverage Industry** pg 2363

**Women's Interests** –pg 5550

Wood –See **Forestry -- Lumber and Wood** pg 2399

Woodwork –See **Building and Construction -- Carpentry and Woodwork** pg 633

**Word Processing** –pg 1292

Workmen's Compensation –See **Economics -- Labor** pg 1642; see also Insurance pg 2872

World Politics –See **Political Science** pg 4461

Wrestling –See **Recreation, Leisure -- Sports** pg 4881

Writing –See **Journalism** pg 2917; see also Literature pg 3357

Yachts and Yachting –See **Boats and Boating** pg 591; see also Travel and Tourism pg 5458

Yearbooks –See **Encyclopedias and General Reference Books** pg 1923

Youth –See **Children and Youth Interests** pg 1059

Zoning –See **Housing and Urban Development** pg 2812; **Law** pg 2926; see also Real Estate pg 4833

**Zoology** –pg 5572; see also Veterinary Sciences pg 5501

# TABLES

*Frequency*
*Document Delivery*
*Wire Services*
*Country of Publication*
*Unit of Currency*
*Indexes/Abstracts*

# FREQUENCY TABLE

| | | | |
|---|---|---|---|
| an | Annual | sa | Semiannual |
| be | Biennial | sm | Semimonthly |
| bm | Bimonthly | sw | Semiweekly |
| bw | Biweekly | te | Triennial |
| da | Daily | tm | Three times a month |
| ir | Irregular | tq | Tri-quarterly |
| mo | Monthly | tw | Three times a week |
| qt | Quarterly | wk | Weekly |

Additional frequencies may appear in the Serial Listing when provided by the publisher.

# DOCUMENT DELIVERY

*The following document supplier notations, when noted in a Serial Listing, indicate the availability of that serial for document delivery through the specified service. Permission has been granted by the copyright owner and is subject to change without notice. Only the portion in boldface will appear in the listing.*

**ADONIS™**
ADONIS B.V.
Spuistraat 112D
1012VA Amsterdam, The Netherlands

**Article Express International**
Engineering Information Inc.
469 Union Avenue
Westbury, New York 11590

**Ask*IEEE**
(in cooperation with EBSCOdoc™)
1722 Gilbreth Road
Burlingame, CA 94010

**BIOSIS Document Express™**
(in cooperation with EBSCOdoc™)
1722 Gilbreth Road
Burlingame, CA 94010

**BLDSC**
British Library Document Supply Centre - Customer Services
Boston Spa, Wetherby
LS23 7BQ, United Kingdom

**CASDDS** ®
Chemical Abstracts Service Document Delivery Service
PO Box 3012
Columbus, Ohio 43210-0012

**Documents on Demand**
Congressional Information Service
4520 East-West Highway
Bethesda, MD 20814-3389

**FAXON Xpress**
FAXON Research Services, Inc.
15 Southwest Park
Westwood, MA 02090

**Haworth Document Delivery Service**
The Haworth Press, Inc.
10 Alice Street
Binghamton, New York 13904-1580

**Magazine Collection™**
Information Access Company
362 Lakeside Drive
Foster City, CA 94404

**Petroleum Abstracts Document Delivery Service**
University of Tulsa
600 South College
Tulsa, OK 74104-3189

**Quick Copies**
Williams and Wilkins Company
428 East Preston Street
Baltimore, MD 21202-3993

**SWETSCAN-SWETDOC**
Swets & Zeitlinger bv
Heereweg 347, PO Box 830
2160 SZ Lisse, The Netherlands

**The Genuine Article**®
Institute for Scientific Information
3501 Market Street
Philadelphia, PA 19104

**The Uncover Company**
3801 East Florida Avenue
Suite 200
Denver, CO 80210

**UMI Article Clearinghouse**
300 North Zeeb Road
PO Box 1346
Ann Arbor, MI 48106-1346

# WIRE SERVICES

*The following abbreviations represent the news and photograph wire services found in the Directory. Each code is followed by the complete name of the service.*

| CODE: | SERVICE: |
|---|---|
| AF | Agence France Presse |
| AN | Alternet |
| AP | Associated Press |
| API | Associated Press International |
| BU | British United Press |
| CA | Canadian Press |
| CH | Chicago Tribune - New York |
| CN | Capital News |
| CM | Christian Science Monitor |
| CO | Copley News Service |
| CP | Colorado Press |
| CQ | Congressional Quarterly |
| CS | Catholic News Service |
| CT | Chicago Sun Times |
| CP | China and Taiwan News Age |
| CU | Canadian United Press |
| DJ | Dow Jones |
| EI | Empire Information Service |
| ER | Editorial Research Service |
| FN | Federation News Service |
| GN | Gannett News Service |
| GP | Georgia Press Association |
| HH | Hearst Headline Service |
| HN | Harris News Service |
| IT | Independent Television Network |
| IM | Iowa Medialink |
| JT | Jewish Telegraphic Agency |
| KF | King Features |
| KN | Knight News Service |
| KR | Knight-Ridder |
| LA | Los Angeles Times |
| LO | London Daily News |
| LT | Times of London |
| MG | Manchester Guardian |
| ML | MediaLink |
| MN | Morris News Service |
| MP | Montana Press Association |
| NC | NEWSCOM |
| NE | Newspaper Enterprises Association |
| NF | Newsfinder |
| NM | Notimex |
| NN | Newhouse News Service |
| NP | NNAP |
| NU | News USA |
| NW | National Weather Service |
| NY | New York Times |
| ON | Ottawa News Service |
| PN | Pacific News Service |
| RN | Reuters News Service |
| SH | Scripps-Howard Newspaper Alliance-Scripps Howard News Service |
| SS | SportsStats |
| WN | World News |
| WP | Washington Post Writer's Guild |
| WS | Women's News Service |
| WW | Women's Wear Daily |

# COUNTRY OF PUBLICATION TABLE

*The following lists of country codes have been taken directly from the USMARC Bibliographic Format, with the exception being that the United States and Canada state and province codes have been grouped under their respective countries, rather than being listed individually.*

## COUNTRY OF PUBLICATION BY CODE

| Code | Country | Code | Country | Code | Country |
|---|---|---|---|---|---|
| AA | Albania | GS | Georgia (Republic) | PY | Paraguay |
| AE | Algeria | GT | Guatemala | QA | Qatar |
| AF | Afghanistan | GU | Guam | RE | Reunion |
| AG | Argentina | GV | Guinea | RH | Zimbabwe |
| AI | Armenia | GW | Germany | RM | Romania |
| AJ | Azerbaijan | GY | Guyana | RW | Rwanda |
| AM | Anguilla | GZ | Gaza Strip | RU | Russia (Republic) |
| AN | Andorra | HK | Hong Kong | SA | South Africa |
| AO | Angola | HM | Heard and McDonald Islands | SE | Seychelles |
| AQ | Antigua and Barbuda | HO | Honduras | SF | Sao Tome and Principe |
| AS | American Samoa | HT | Haiti | SG | Senegal |
| AT | Australia | HU | Hungary | SH | Spanish North Africa |
| AU | Austria | IC | Iceland | SI | Singapore |
| AW | Aruba | IE | Ireland | SJ | Sudan |
| AY | Antarctica | II | India | SL | Sierra Leone |
| BA | Bahrain | IO | Indonesia | SM | San Marino |
| BB | Barbados | IQ | Iraq | SO | Somalia |
| BD | Burundi | IR | Iran | SP | Spain |
| BE | Belgium | IS | Israel | SQ | Swaziland |
| BF | Bahamas | IT | Italy | SR | Surinam |
| BG | Bangladesh | IV | Ivory Coast | SS | Western Sahara |
| BH | Belize | IY | Iraq-Saudi Arabia Neutral Zone | SU | Saudi Arabia |
| BI | British Indian Ocean Territory | | | SW | Sweden |
| BL | Brazil | JA | Japan | SX | Namibia |
| BM | Bermuda Islands | JI | Johnson Atoll | SY | Syria |
| BN | Bosnia Hercegovina | JM | Jamaica | SZ | Switzerland |
| BO | Bolivia | JO | Jordan | TA | Tajikstan |
| BP | Solomon Islands | KE | Kenya | TC | Turks and Caicos Islands |
| BR | Burma | KG | Kyrgyzstan | TG | Togo |
| BS | Botswana | KN | Korea (North) | TH | Thailand |
| BT | Bhutan | KO | Korea (South) | TI | Tunisia |
| BU | Bulgaria | KU | Kuwait | TK | Turkmenistan |
| BV | Bouvet Island | KZ | Kazakhstan | TL | Tokelau Islands |
| BW | Byelarus | LB | Liberia | TO | Tonga |
| BX | Brunei | LE | Lebanon | TR | Trinidad and Tobago |
| CB | Cambodia | LH | Liechtenstein | TS | Trucial States (United Arab Emirates) |
| CC | China | LI | Lithuania | | |
| CD | Chad | LO | Lesotho | TU | Turkey |
| CE | Sri Lanka | LS | Laos | TZ | Tanzania |
| CF | Congo (Brazzaville) | LU | Luxembourg | UA | Egypt |
| CG | Zaire | LV | Latvia | UC | United States Misc. Caribbean Islands |
| CH | China (Republic: 1949) | LY | Libya | | |
| CI | Croatia | MC | Monaco | UG | Uganda |
| CJ | Cayman Islands | MF | Mauritius | UK | United Kingdom (Including Scotland) |
| CK | Colombia | MG | Madagascar | | |
| CL | Chile | MH | Macao | UN | Ukraine |
| CM | Cameroon | MJ | Montserrat | UP | United States Misc. Pacific Islands |
| CN | Canada | MK | Oman | | |
| CP | Canton and Enderbury Islands | ML | Mali | UR | USSR |
| CQ | Comorus | MM | Malta | US | United States |
| CR | Costa Rica | MP | Mongolia | UV | Burkina Faso |
| CS | Czechoslovakia | MQ | Martinique | UY | Uruguay |
| CU | Cuba | MR | Morocco | UZ | Uzbekistan |
| CV | Cape Verde | MU | Mauritania | VB | Virgin Islands (British V.I.) |
| CW | Cook Islands | MV | Moldova | VC | Vatican City |
| CX | Central African Republic | MW | Malawi | VE | Venezuela |
| CY | Cyprus | MX | Mexico | VI | Virgin Islands (U.S.) |
| DK | Denmark | MY | Malaysia | VM | Vietnam |
| DM | Benin | MZ | Mozambique | WF | Wallis and Futuna |
| DQ | Dominica | NA | Netherlands Antilles | WJ | West Bank of the Jordan River |
| DR | Dominican Republic | NE | Netherlands | WK | Wake Island |
| EC | Ecuador | NG | Niger | WS | Western Samoa |
| EG | Equatorial Guinea | NL | New Caledonia | XA | Christmas Island (Indian Ocean) |
| ER | Estonia | NN | Vanuatu | | |
| ES | El Salvador | NO | Norway | XB | Cocos (Keeling) Islands |
| ET | Ethiopia | NP | Nepal | XC | Maldives |
| FA | Faroe Islands | NQ | Nicaragua | XD | Saint Kitts-Nevis |
| FG | French Guiana | NR | Nigeria | XE | Marshall Islands |
| FI | Finland | NU | Nauru | XF | Midway Island |
| FJ | Fiji | NW | Northern Mariana Islands | XH | Niue |
| FM | Micronesia (Federated States) | NX | Norfolk Island | XJ | Saint Helena |
| FP | French Polynesia | NZ | New Zealand | XK | Saint Lucia |
| FR | France | OT | Mayotte | XL | Saint Pierre and Miquelon |
| FS | Terres Australes et Antarctiques Francaises | PC | Pitcairn Island | XM | Saint Vincent and the Grenadines |
| | | PE | Peru | | |
| FT | Djibouti | PF | Paracel Islands | XN | Macedonia |
| GB | Kiribati | PG | Guinea-Bissau | XO | Slovakia |
| GD | Grenada | PH | Philippines | XP | Spratly Islands |
| GH | Ghana | PK | Pakistan | XR | Czech Republic |
| GI | Gibralter | PL | Poland | XS | Falkland Islands |
| GL | Greenland | PN | Panama | XV | Slovenia |
| GM | Gambia | PO | Portugal | YE | Yemen |
| GO | Gabon | PP | Papua New Guinea | YU | Yugoslavia |
| GP | Guadeloupe | PR | Puerto Rico | ZA | Zambia |
| GR | Greece | PW | Palau | | |

# COUNTRY OF PUBLICATION TABLE

## COUNTRY OF PUBLICATION BY COUNTRY

| Country | Code | Country | Code | Country | Code |
|---|---|---|---|---|---|
| Afghanistan | AF | Greenland | GL | Paracel Islands | PF |
| Albania | AA | Grenada | GD | Paraguay | PY |
| Algeria | AE | Guadeloupe | GP | Peru | PE |
| American Samoa | AS | Guam | GU | Philippines | PH |
| Andorra | AN | Guatemala | GT | Pitcairn Island | PC |
| Angola | AO | Guinea | GV | Poland | PL |
| Anguilla | AM | Guinea-Bissau | PG | Portugal | PO |
| Antarctica | AY | Guyana | GY | Puerto Rico | PR |
| Antigua and Barbuda | AQ | Haiti | HT | Qatar | QA |
| Argentina | AG | Heard and McDonald Islands | HM | Reunion | RE |
| Armenia | AI | Honduras | HO | Romania | RM |
| Aruba | AW | Hong Kong | HK | Russia (Republic) | RU |
| Australia | AT | Hungary | HU | Rwanda | RW |
| Austria | AU | Iceland | IC | Saint Helena | XJ |
| Azerbaijan | AJ | India | II | Saint Kitts-Nevis | XD |
| Bahamas | BF | Indonesia | IO | Saint Lucia | XK |
| Bahrain | BA | Iran | IR | Saint Pierre and Miquelon | XL |
| Bangladesh | BG | Iraq | IQ | Saint Vincent and the Grenadines | XM |
| Barbados | BB | Iraq-Saudi Arabia Neutral Zone | IY | San Marino | SM |
| Belgium | BE | Ireland | IE | Sao Tome and Principe | SF |
| Belize | BH | Israel | IS | Saudi Arabia | SU |
| Benin | DM | Italy | IT | Senegal | SG |
| Bermuda Islands | BM | Ivory Coast | IV | Seychelles | SE |
| Bhutan | BT | Jamaica | JM | Sierra Leone | SL |
| Bolivia | BO | Japan | JA | Singapore | SI |
| Bosnia Hercegovina | BN | Johnson Atoll | JI | Slovakia | XO |
| Botswana | BS | Jordan | JO | Slovenia | XV |
| Bouvet Island | BV | Kazakhstan | KZ | Solomon Islands | BP |
| Brazil | BL | Kenya | KE | Somalia | SO |
| British Indian Ocean Territory | BI | Kiribati | GB | South Africa | SA |
| Brunei | BX | Korea (North) | KN | Spain | SP |
| Bulgaria | BU | Korea (South) | KO | Spanish North Africa | SH |
| Burkina Faso | UV | Kuwait | KU | Spratly Island | XP |
| Burma | BR | Kyrgyzstan | KG | Sri Lanka | CE |
| Burundi | BD | Laos | LS | Sudan | SJ |
| Byelarus | BW | Latvia | LV | Surinam | SR |
| Cambodia | CB | Lebanon | LE | Swaziland | SQ |
| Cameroon | CM | Lesotho | LO | Sweden | SW |
| Canada | CN | Liberia | LB | Switzerland | SZ |
| Canton and Enderbury Islands | CP | Libya | LY | Syria | SY |
| Cape Verde | CV | Liechtenstein | LH | Tajikistan | TA |
| Cayman Islands | CJ | Lithuania | LI | Tanzania | TZ |
| Central African Republic | CX | Luxembourg | LU | Terres Australes et Antarctiques Francaises | FS |
| Chad | CD | Macao | MH | | |
| Chile | CL | Macedonia | XN | Thailand | TH |
| China | CC | Madagascar | MG | Togo | TG |
| China (Republic: 1949) | CH | Malawi | MW | Tokelau Islands | TL |
| Christmas Island (Indian Ocean) | XA | Malaysia | MY | Tonga | TO |
| Cocos (Keeling) Islands | XB | Maldives | XC | Trinidad and Tobago | TR |
| Colombia | CK | Mali | ML | Trucial States (United Arab Emirates) | TS |
| Comoros | CQ | Malta | MM | | |
| Congo (Brazzaville) | CF | Marshall Islands | XE | Tunisia | TI |
| Cook Islands | CW | Martinique | MQ | Turkey | TU |
| Costa Rica | CR | Mauritania | MU | Turkmenistan | TK |
| Croatia | CI | Mauritius | MF | Turks and Caicos Islands | TC |
| Cuba | CU | Mayotte | OT | Uganda | UG |
| Cyprus | CY | Mexico | MX | Ukraine | UN |
| Czech Republic | XR | Micronesia (Federated States) | FM | United Kingdom (Including Scotland) | UK |
| Czechoslovakia | CS | Midway Island | XF | | |
| Denmark | DK | Moldova | MV | United States | US |
| Djibouti | FT | Monaco | MC | United States (Misc. Caribbean Islands) | UC |
| Dominica | DQ | Mongolia | MP | | |
| Dominican Republic | DR | Montserrat | MJ | United States (Misc. Pacific Islands) | UP |
| Ecuador | EC | Morocco | MR | Uruguay | UY |
| Egypt | UA | Mozambique | MZ | USSR | UR |
| El Salvador | ES | Namibia | SX | Uzbekistan | UZ |
| Equatorial Guinea | EG | Nauru | NU | Vanuatu | NN |
| Estonia | ER | Nepal | NP | Vatican City | VC |
| Ethiopia | ET | Netherlands | NE | Venezuela | VE |
| Falkland Islands | XS | Netherlands Antilles | NA | Vietnam | VM |
| Faroe Islands | FA | New Caledonia | NL | Virgin Islands (British V.I.) | VB |
| Fiji | FJ | New Zealand | NZ | Virgin Islands (U.S.) | VI |
| Finland | FI | Nicaragua | NQ | Wake Island | WK |
| France | FR | Niger | NG | Wallis and Futuna | WF |
| French Guiana | FG | Nigeria | NR | West Bank of the Jordan River | WJ |
| French Polynesia | FP | Niue | XH | Western Sahara | SS |
| Gabon | GO | Norfolk Island | NX | Western Samoa | WS |
| Gambia | GM | Northern Mariana Islands | NW | Yemen | YE |
| Gaza Strip | GZ | Norway | NO | Yugoslavia | YU |
| Georgia (Republic) | GS | Oman | MK | Zaire | CG |
| Germany | GW | Pakistan | PK | Zambia | ZA |
| Ghana | GH | Palau | PW | Zimbabwe | RH |
| Gibralter | GI | Panama | PN | | |
| Greece | GR | Papua New Guinea | PP | | |

# UNIT OF CURRENCY TABLE

*In the Serial Listing, prices are given in country of publication currency and are one-year library subscription rates, unless designated otherwise.*

| Country | Currency | Country | Currency | Country | Currency |
|---|---|---|---|---|---|
| Afghanistan | afghanin | Greece | Greek drachma | Papua New Guinea | kina |
| Albania | lek | Guadeloupe | French franc | Paraguay | guarani |
| Algeria | Algerian dinar | Guatemala | quetzal | Peru | sole |
| Angola | kwanza | Guyana | Guyana dollar | Philippines | peso |
| Antigua and Barbuda | East Caribbean dollar | Haiti | gourde | Papua New Guinea | kina |
| | | Honduras | lempira | Paraguay | guarani |
| Argentina | peso argentino | Hong Kong | Hong Kong dollar | Peru | sole |
| Australia | Australian dollar | Hungary | forint | Philippines | peso |
| Austria | schilling | Iceland | krona | Poland | zloty |
| Bahamas | Bahamian dollar | India | rupee | Portugal | escudo |
| Bangladesh | taka | Indonesia | rupiah | Qatar | Qatar riyal |
| Barbados | Barbados dollar | Iran | rial | Reunion | French franc |
| Belgium | Belgian franc | Iraq | Iraqi dinar | Romania | lei |
| Bermuda Islands | Bermuda dollar | Ireland | Irish pound | Rwanda | Rwanda franc |
| Bolivia | peso | Israel | shekel | San Marino | Italian lira |
| Botswana | pula | Italy | lira | Saudi Arabia | Saudi riyal |
| Brazil | cruzeiro | Ivory Coast | CFA franc | Senegal | CFA franc |
| Belize | Belize dollar | Jamaica | Jamaican dollar | Sierra Leone | leone |
| Benin | CFA franc | Japan | yen | Singapore | Singapore dollar |
| Bulgaria | lev | Jordan | Jordanian dinar | Somalia | Somali shilling |
| Burkina Faso | CFA franc | Kenya | Kenya shilling | South Africa | South African rand |
| Burma | kyat | Korea (North) | won | Southern Yemen | dinar |
| Cameroon | CFA franc | Korea (South) | won | Spain | pesata |
| Canada | Canadian dollar | Kuwait | Kuwaiti dinar | Sri Lanka | rupee |
| Cayman Islands | cordoba/dollar | Lebanon | Lebanese pound | Sudan | Sudanese pound |
| Central African Republic | CFA franc | Liberia | U.S. dollar | Surinam | Surinam guilder |
| | | Libya | Libyan dinar | Swaziland | emalangeni |
| Chad | CFA franc | Liechtenstein | Swiss franc | Sweden | krona |
| Chile | peso | Luxembourg | Luxembourg franc | Switzerland | franc |
| China | renminbi yuan | Madagascar | Malagasy franc | Syria | Syrian pound |
| China (Republic: 1949) | New Taiwan dollar | Malawi | Malawi kwacha | Tanzania | Tanzanian shilling |
| | | Malaysia | ringgit | Thailand | baht |
| Colombia | peso | Mali | CFA franc | Togo | CFA franc |
| Cook Islands | New Zealand dollar | Malta | Maltese pound | Trinidad and Tobago | Trinidad and Tobago dollar |
| Costa Rica | colon | Martinique | French franc | | |
| Cuba | peso | Mauritius | Mauritian rupee | Tunisia | Tunisian dinar |
| Cyprus | Cyprus pound | Mexico | peso | Turkey | Turkish lira |
| Czechoslovakia | korona | Monaco | French franc | Uganda | Uganda shilling |
| Benin | CFA franc | Morocco | dirham | United Kingdom | pound sterling |
| Denmark | krone | Mozambique | meticais | United States | U.S. dollar |
| Djibouti | Djibouti franc | Nauru | Australian dollar | Uruguay | new peso |
| Dominican Republic | peso | Nepal | Nepalese rupee | USSR | ruble |
| Ecuador | sucre | Netherlands | guilder | Vatican City | lira |
| Egypt | Egyptian pound | New Caledonia | CFP franc | Venezuela | bolivare |
| El Salvador | colon | New Zealand | New Zealand dollar | Vietnam | dong |
| Ethiopia | Ethiopian birr | Nicaragua | cordoba | Yemen (Yemen (Sana)) | riyal |
| Fiji | Fiji dollar | Niger | CFA franc | | |
| Finland | fim (finnmark) | Nigeria | naira | Yugoslavia | dinar |
| France | French franc | Norway | krone | Zaire | CFA franc |
| Gambia | dalasi | Oman | rial | Zambia | Zambian kwacha |
| Germany | mark | Pakistan | rupee | Zimbabwe | Zimbabwean dollar |
| Ghana | cedi | Panama | balboa | | |

# INDEXES/ABSTRACTS TABLE

*The following is a list of all publications which may index, or contain an abstract of, titles in the Directory. The Abbreviated Title in boldface is the abbreviation of the index or abstract as used in the Serial Listing. The complete title of the index or abstract follows. Succeeding information or a Ceased/Suspended indicator will follow the complete title for those serials where it applies. For services that share the same journal source list, a reference will be made to that service which will appear in the Serial Listing. This table includes over 1,300 Indexing/Abstracting services, 921 of which are active.*

**A.I.D. RES. DEV. ABSTR.**
[US/0096-1507]
A.I.D. RESEARCH AND DEVELOPMENT ABSTRACTS.
(**Continues** A.I.D. Reference Center. A.I.D. Research Abstracts.)

**ABC POL SCI**
[US/0001-0456]
ABC POL SCI. ADVANCE BIBLIOGRAPHY OF CONTENTS: POLITICAL SCIENCE & GOVERNMENT.

**ABI/INFORM ONDISC**
[US/1062-5127]
ABI/INFORM ONDISC.

**ABI/INFORM ONDISC: EXPR. ED.**
[US]
ABI/INFORM ONDISC: EXPRESS EDITION [COMPUTER FILE].

**ABI/INFORM GLOB. ED.**
[US]
ABI/INFORM GLOBAL EDITION [COMPUTER FILE].

**ABR. CATHOL. PERIOD. LIT. INDEX**
[US/0737-3457]
ABRIDGED CATHOLIC PERIODICAL AND LITERATURE INDEX, THE.

**ABR. INDEX MED.**
[US/0001-3331]
ABRIDGED INDEX MEDICUS.
(**Continues** American Medical Association. Abridged Index Medicus.)

**ABR. READ. GUIDE PERIOD. LIT.**
[US/0001-334X]
ABRIDGED READERS' GUIDE TO PERIODICAL LITERATURE.

**ABS INT. GUIDE CLASSICAL STUD.**
[US]
ABS INTERNATIONAL GUIDE TO CLASSICAL STUDIES.
(**Continued by** International Guide to Classical Studies (1966).)

**ABSTR. ABSTR. BOOK REV. CUR. LEG. PERIOD.**
[US]
ABSTRACTS : ABSTRACTS OF BOOK REVIEWS IN CURRENT LEGAL PERIODICALS.
(**Continues** Abstracts of Book Reviews in Current Legal Periodicals.)

**ABSTR. AIT REP. PUBL. ENERGY**
[TH/0857-6181]
ABSTRACTS OF AIT REPORTS AND PUBLICATIONS ON ENERGY.
(**Continues** Abstracts of AIT Reports and Publications on Renewable Energy Resources.)

**ABSTR. ANTHROPOL.**
[US/0001-3455]
ABSTRACTS IN ANTHROPOLOGY.

**ABSTR. BIOCOMMER.**
[UK/0263-6778]
ABSTRACTS IN BIOCOMMERCE.

**ABSTR. BOOK REV. CURR. LEG. PERIOD.**
[US/0362-1065]
ABSTRACTS OF BOOK REVIEWS IN CURRENT LEGAL PERIODICALS.
(**Continued by** Abstracts : Abstracts of Book Reviews in Current Legal Periodicals.)

**ABSTR. BULL. INST. PAP. SCI. TECH.**
[US/1047-2088]
ABSTRACT BULLETIN OF THE INSTITUTE OF PAPER SCIENCE AND TECHNOLOGY.
(**Continues** Institute of Paper Chemistry (Appleton, Wis.) Abstract Bulletin of the Institute of Paper Chemistry.)

**ABSTR. BULL. INST. PAPER CHEM.**
[US]
ABSTRACT BULLETIN OF THE INSTITUTE OF PAPER CHEMISTRY.
(**Continued by** Abstract Bulletin of the Institute of Paper Science and Technology.)

**ABSTR. CLIN. CARE GUIDEL.**
[US/1042-4423]
ABSTRACTS OF CLINICAL CARE GUIDELINES.

**ABSTR. CRIMINOL. PENOL.**
[NE/0001-3684]
ABSTRACTS ON CRIMINOLOGY AND PENOLOGY.
(**Continued by** Criminology & Penology Abstracts.)

**ABSTR. ENGL. STUD.**
[US/0001-3560]
ABSTRACTS OF ENGLISH STUDIES.
(Suspended)

**ABSTR. ENTOMOL.**
[US/0001-3579]
ABSTRACTS OF ENTOMOLOGY.
***Refer to Biological Abstracts for complete source list.

**ABSTR. FOLK. STUD.**
[US/0001-3587]
ABSTRACTS OF FOLKLORE STUDIES.
(Ceased)

**ABSTR. GRAPHIC ARTS TECH. FOUND.**
[US]
ABSTRACTS (GRAPHIC ARTS TECHNICAL FOUNDATION).
(**Continues** Graphic Arts Abstracts (Pittsburgh, PA. : 1968).)

**ABSTR. HEALTH CARE MANAGE. STUD.**
[US/0194-4908]
ABSTRACTS OF HEALTH CARE MANAGEMENT STUDIES.
(**Continues** Abstracts of Hospital Management Studies.)

**ABSTR. HEALTH ENVIRON. POLLUTANTS**
[US/0044-5819]
ABSTRACTS ON HEALTH EFFECTS OF ENVIRONMENTAL POLLUTANTS.
(Ceased)

**ABSTR. HOSPIT. MANAGE. STUD.**
[US/0001-3595]
ABSTRACTS OF HOSPITAL MANAGEMENT STUDIES.
(**Continued by** Abstracts of Health Care Management Studies.)

**ABSTR. HUM. COMPUT. INTERACT.**
[US/1042-0193]
ABSTRACTS IN HUMAN-COMPUTER INTERACTION.
(Suspended)

**ABSTR. HYG.**
[UK/0001-3692]
ABSTRACTS ON HYGIENE.
(**Continued by** Abstracts on Hygiene and Communicable Diseases.)

**ABSTR. HYG. COMMUN. DIS.**
[UK/0260-5511]
ABSTRACTS ON HYGIENE AND COMMUNICABLE DISEASES.
(**Continues** Abstracts on Hygiene.)
***Refer to Tropical Diseases Bulletin for complete source list.

**ABSTR. J. EARTHQ. ENG.**
[US/0363-5732]
ABSTRACT JOURNAL IN EARTHQUAKE ENGINEERING.

**ABSTR. MIL. BIBLIOGR.**
[AG]
ABSTRACTS OF MILITARY BIBLIOGRAPHY.
(**Continues** Resumenes Analiticos Sobre Defensa y Seguridad Nacional.)

**ABSTR. NEW WORLD ARCHAEOL.**
[US]
ABSTRACTS OF NEW WORLD ARCHAEOLOGY.
(Ceased)

**ABSTR. NORTH AM. GEOL.**
[US/0001-3625]
ABSTRACTS OF NORTH AMERICAN GEOLOGY.
(Ceased)

**ABSTR. OF MYCOL.**
[US/0001-3617]
ABSTRACTS OF MYCOLOGY.
***Refer to Biological Abstracts for complete source list.

**ABSTR. PHOTOGR. SCI. ENG. LIT.**
[US/0001-3633]
ABSTRACTS OF PHOTOGRAPHIC SCIENCE & ENGINEERING LITERATURE.
(**Continues** Monthly Abstract Bulletin from the Kodak Research Laboratories; ANSCO Abstracts.)

**ABSTR. POP. CULT.**
[US/0147-2615]
ABSTRACTS OF POPULAR CULTURE.
(Ceased)

**ABSTR. RES. PASTOR. CARE COUNS.**
[US/0733-2599]
ABSTRACTS OF RESEARCH IN PASTORAL CARE AND COUNSELING.
(**Continues** Pastoral Care and Counseling Abstracts.)

# INDEXES/ABSTRACTS TABLE

**ABSTR. SOC. GERONTOL.**
[US/1047-4862]
ABSTRACTS IN SOCIAL GERONTOLOGY.
(*Continues* Current Literature on Aging.)

**ABSTR. SOC. WORK.**
[US/0001-3412]
ABSTRACTS FOR SOCIAL WORKERS.
(*Continued by* Social Work Research & Abstracts.)

**ABSTR. TROP. AGRIC.**
[NE/0304-5951]
ABSTRACTS ON TROPICAL AGRICULTURE.
(*Supersedes* Tropical Abstracts.)

**ABSTR. WORLD MED.**
[UK]
ABSTRACTS OF WORLD MEDICINE.
(*Absorbed* Abstracts of World Surgery, Obstetrics and Gynaecology.)

**ACAD. ABSTR.**
[US/1056-7496]
ACADEMIC ABSTRACTS.

**ACAD. ABSTR. FULL TEXT ELITE**
[US/1060-6750]
ACADEMIC ABSTRACTS FULL TEXT ELITE.

**ACAD. IND. [COMPUTER FILE]**
[US]
ACADEMIC INDEX. [COMPUTER FILE].

**ACAD. SEARCH**
[US/1071-2720]
ACADEMIC SEARCH.

**ACCESS**
[US/0095-5698]
ACCESS (SYRACUSE).
(*Absorbed* Monthly Periodical Index.)

**ACCESS INDEX LITTLE MAG.**
[US/0363-065X]
ACCESS INDEX TO LITTLE MAGAZINES.
**(Ceased)**

**ACCOUNT. ART.**
[US]
ACCOUNTING ARTICLES.

**ACCOUNT. DATA PROCESS. ABSTR.**
[UK/0001-4796]
ACCOUNTING + DATA PROCESSING ABSTRACTS.
(*Continued by* Accounting + Finance Abstracts.)

**ACCOUNT. INDEX**
[US]
ACCOUNTANTS INDEX.
(*Continued by* Accounting & Tax Index.)

**ACCOUNT. INDEX SUPPL.**
[US/0748-7975]
ACCOUNTANTS' INDEX. SUPPLEMENT.
(*Continued by* Accounting & Tax Index.)

**ACCOUNT. TAX DATAB.**
[US]
ACCOUNTING AND TAX DATABASE [ONLINE DATABASE].

**ACCOUNT. TAX INDEX**
[US/1063-0287]
ACCOUNTING AND TAX INDEX.
(*Continues* Accountants' Index. Supplement.)
\*\*\*Refer to Accounting and Tax Database for complete source list.

**ACCUMU. VET. INDEX**
[US/0567-7033]
ACCUMULATIVE VETERINARY INDEX.
**(Ceased)**

**ACID RAIN ABSTR.**
[US/0882-1402]
ACID RAIN ABSTRACTS.
(*Absorbed by* Environment Abstracts.)

**ACM GUIDE COMPUT. LIT.**
[US/0149-1199]
ACM GUIDE TO COMPUTING LITERATURE.
(*Continues* Computing Reviews. Bibliography and Subject Index of Current Computing Literature.)

**ACOUST. ABSTR.**
[UK/0001-4974]
ACOUSTICS ABSTRACTS.

**ADOLESC. MENT. HEALTH ABSTR.**
[US]
ADOLESCENT MENTAL HEALTH ABSTRACTS.
**(Ceased)**

**ADONIS**
[NE]
ADONIS CD-ROM.

**AERO. DEF. MARK. TECHNOL.**
[US/0885-2286]
AEROSPACE/DEFENSE MARKETS & TECHNOLOGY.
(*Continues* Defense Markets & Technology.)

**AESIS Q.**
[AT/0313-704x]
AESIS QUARTERLY.

**AFR. ABSTR.**
[UK/0568-1200]
AFRICAN ABSTRACTS.
**(Ceased)**

**AGBIOTECH NEWS INF.**
[UK/0954-9897]
AGBIOTECH NEWS AND INFORMATION.

**AGRIC. ENG. ABSTR.**
[UK/0308-8863]
AGRICULTURAL ENGINEERING ABSTRACTS.

**AGRIC. ENVIRON. BIOTECHNOL. ABSTR.**
[US/1063-1151]
AGRICULTURAL & ENVIRONMENTAL BIOTECHNOLOGY ABSTRACTS.
(*Continues in part* Biotechnology Research Abstracts.)
\*\*\*Refer to Biotechnology Research Abstracts for complete source list.

**AGRIC. INDEX**
[US/0196-5883]
AGRICULTURAL INDEX.
(*Continued by* Biological & Agricultural Index.)

**AGRICOLA**
[US/1050-6810]
AGRICOLA.

**AGRINDEX**
[IT/0254-8801]
AGRINDEX.

**AGROFOR. ABSTR.**
[UK/0952-1453]
AGROFORESTRY ABSTRACTS.

**AIDS ABSTR.**
[US/1066-1107]
AIDS ABSTRACTS (ATLANTA, GA.).

**AIR POLLUT. TITLES**
[US/0002-2497]
AIR POLLUTION TITLES.
**(Ceased)**

**AIR UNIV. LIBR. INDEX MIL. PERIOD.**
[US/0002-2586]
AIR UNIVERSITY LIBRARY INDEX TO MILITARY PERIODICALS.
(*Continues* Air University Periodical Index.)

**AIR UNIV. PERIOD. INDEX**
[US]
AIR UNIVERSITY PERIODICAL INDEX.
(*Continued by* Air University Library Index to Military Periodicals.)

**ALCOHOL CLIN. UPDATE**
[US/0740-1035]
ALCOHOL CLINICAL UPDATE.
**(Ceased)**

**ALCOHOL. DIG.**
[US/0093-7010]
ALCOHOLISM DIGEST.
**(Ceased)**

**ALTERN. PRESS INDEX**
[US/0002-662X]
ALTERNATIVE PRESS INDEX.

**ALUM. IND. ABSTR.**
[US/1066-0623]
ALUMINIUM INDUSTRY ABSTRACTS.
(*Continues* World Aluminum Abstracts.)

**AM. BIBLIOGR. SLAVIC EAST EUROP. STUD.**
[US/0094-3770]
AMERICAN BIBLIOGRAPHY OF SLAVIC AND EAST EUROPEAN STUDIES.
(*Continues* American Bibliography of Russian and East European Studies.)

**AM. HIST. LIFE**
[US/0002-7065]
AMERICA, HISTORY AND LIFE (SANTA BARBARA, CALIF. : 1989).
(*Formed by the union of* America, History and Life. Part A, Article Abstracts and Citations **and** America, History and Life. Part B, Index to Book Reviews America, History and Life. Part C, American History Bibliography, Books, Articles and Dissertations America, History and Life. Part D, Annual Index.)

**AM. HIST. LIFE PART B**
[US/0002-7065]
AMERICA: HISTORY AND LIFE. PART B: INDEX TO BOOK REVIEWS.
(*Merged with* America, History and Life. Part A, Article Abstracts and Citations; America, History and Life. Part C, American History Bibliography, Books, Articles and Dissertations **and** America, History and Life. Part D, Annual Index **to form** America, History and Life.)

**AM. HUMANIT. INDEX**
[US/0361-0144]
AMERICAN HUMANITIES INDEX, THE.

**AM. INDIAN INDEX**
[US/0569-5244]
AMERICAN INDIAN INDEX.
**(Ceased)**

**AM. STAT. INDEX**
[US/0091-1658]
AMERICAN STATISTICS INDEX.

**ANAL. ABSTR.**
[UK/0003-2689]
ANALYTICAL ABSTRACTS.
(*Continues* British Abstracts. Section C, Analysis and Apparatus.)

# INDEXES/ABSTRACTS TABLE

**ANBAR ACCOUNT. FINAN. ABSTR.**
[UK/0961-2742]
ANBAR ACCOUNTING & FINANCE ABSTRACTS.
(*Continues* Accounting + Data Processing Abstracts.)

**ANBAR MANAG. SERV. ABSTR.**
[UK]
ANBAR MANAGEMENT SERVICES ABSTRACTS.
(*Superseded in part by* Accounting + Data Processing Abstracts; Marketing + Distribution Abstracts; Personnel + Training Abstracts *and* Top Management Abstracts.)

**ANBAR MARK. DISTR. ABSTR.**
[UK/0305-0661]
ANBAR MARKETING & DISTRIBUTION ABSTRACTS.
(*Continues* Marketing + Distribution Abstracts.)

**ANBAR TOP MANAG. ABSTR.**
[UK]
ANBAR TOP MANAGEMENT ABSTRACTS.
(*Continues* Top Management Abstracts.)

**ANIM. BEHAV. ABSTR.**
[US/0301-8695]
ANIMAL BEHAVIOR ABSTRACTS.
(*Continues* Animal Behaviour Abstracts.)

**ANIM. BREED. ABSTR.**
[UK/0003-3499]
ANIMAL BREEDING ABSTRACTS.
(*Formed by the union of* Imperial Bureau of Animal Breeding and Genetics. Quarterly Bulletin *and* Imperial Bureau of Animal References to Literature Contained in Periodicals Received.)

**ANIM. DISEASE OCCURR.**
[UK/0144-3879]
ANIMAL DISEASE OCCURRENCE.
**(Ceased)**

**ANNALS BEHAV. MED.**
[US/0883-6612]
ANNALS OF BEHAVIORAL MEDICINE.
(*Continues* Behavioral Medicine Update; *Absorbed* Behavioral Medicine Abstracts.)

**ANNOT. BIBLIOGR. ECON. GEOL.**
[US/0003-5076]
ANNOTATED BIBLIOGRAPHY OF ECONOMIC GEOLOGY.
**(Ceased)**

**ANNU. BIBLIOGR. ENGL. LANG. LIT.**
[UK/0066-3786]
ANNUAL BIBLIOGRAPHY OF ENGLISH LANGUAGE AND LITERATURE.
(*Continues* Bibliography of English Language and Literature.)

**ANNU. INDEX POP. MUSIC REC. REV.**
[US/0092-3486]
ANNUAL INDEX TO POPULAR MUSIC RECORD REVIEWS.
(*Continues* Annual Index to Popular Music Record Reviews.)

**ANNU. LEG. BIBLIOGR.**
[US/0073-0793]
ANNUAL LEGAL BIBLIOGRAPHY.
**(Ceased)**

**ANTHROPOL. INDEX**
[UK/0003-5467]
ANTHROPOLOGICAL INDEX TO CURRENT PERIODICALS IN THE LIBRARY OF THE ROYAL ANTHROPOLOGICAL INSTITUTE.
(*Continues* Anthropological Index to Current Periodicals in the Museum of Mankind (Library Incorporating the Royal Anthropological Institute Library).)

**ANTHROPOL. LIT.**
[US/0190-3373]
ANTHROPOLOGICAL LITERATURE.
(*Continues* Anthropological Literature (Cambridge, Mass. : 1984).)

**ANTHROPOL. LIT. MICRO.**
[US/0190-3373]
ANTHROPOLOGICAL LITERATURE.
(*Continued by* Anthropological Literature (Cambridge, Mass. : 1989).)

**APAIS, AUST. PUBLIC AFF. INF. SER.**
[AT/0727-8926]
APAIS. AUSTRALIAN PUBLIC AFFAIRS INFORMATION SERVICE.

**API ABSTR. HEALTH ENVIRON.**
[US]
API ABSTRACTS. HEALTH & ENVIRONMENT.
(*Continued by* Literature Abstracts. Health & Environment.)

**API ABSTR. OIL. CHEM.**
[US]
API ABSTRACTS : OILFIELD CHEMICALS.
(*Continued by* Literature & Patent Abstracts. Oilfield Chemicals.)

**APIBIZ**
[US]
APIBIZ [ONLINE DATABASE].
***Refer to Petroleum/Energy Business News Index for complete source list.

**APIC. ABSTR.**
[UK/0003-648X]
APICULTURAL ABSTRACTS.

**APILIT**
[US]
APILIT [ONLINE DATABASE].
***Refer to Literature & Patent Abstracts Oilfield Chemicals for a complete source list.

**APPL. ECOL. ABSTR.**
[UK/0305-3040]
APPLIED ECOLOGY ABSTRACTS.
(*Continued by* Ecology Abstracts.)

**APPL. MECH. REV.**
[US/0003-6900]
APPLIED MECHANICS REVIEWS.

**APPL. SCI. TECHNOL. INDEX**
[US/0003-6986]
APPLIED SCIENCE & TECHNOLOGY INDEX.
(*Continues in part* Industrial Arts Index.)

**APPL. SOC. SCI. INDEX ABSTR.**
[UK/0950-2238]
ASSIA. APPLIED SOCIAL SCIENCES INDEX & ABSTRACTS.

**AQUALINE ABSTR.**
[UK/0263-5534]
AQUALINE ABSTRACTS.
(*Continues* Water Research Centre (Great Britain). WRC Information.)

**AQUAREF**
[CN]
AQUAREF.
(*Continues* Canadian Environment; Environnement.)

**AQUAT. SCI. FISH. ABSTR.**
[UK/0044-8516]
AQUATIC SCIENCES & FISHERIES ABSTRACTS.
(*Split into* Aquatic Sciences and Fisheries Abstracts. Part 1, Biological Sciences and Living Resources *and* Aquatic Sciences and Fisheries Abstracts. Part 2, Ocean Technology, Policy and Non-Living Resources.)

**AQUAT. SCI. FISH. ABSTR. (COMPUTER FILE)**
[US/1064-0460]
AQUATIC SCIENCES & FISHERIES ABSTRACTS (CD-ROM ED.).

**AQUAT. SCI. FISH. ABSTR. PART 1**
[US/0140-5373]
AQUATIC SCIENCES AND FISHERIES ABSTRACTS. PART 1 : BIOLOGICAL SCIENCES AND LIVING RESOURCES.
(*Continued in part by* Aquatic Sciences and Fisheries Abstracts. Part 3, Aquatic Pollution and Environmental Quality.)
***Refer to Aquatic Science & Fisheries Abstracts [Computer File]: ASFA / Cambridge Scientific Abstracts for complete source list.

**AQUAT. SCI. FISH. ABSTR. 2, OCEAN TECHNOL. POLICY NON-LIVING RESOUR.**
[US/0140-5381]
AQUATIC SCIENCES AND FISHERIES ABSTRACTS. PART 2 : OCEAN TECHNOLOGY, POLICY AND NON-LIVING RESOURCES.
(*Continued in part by* Aquatic Sciences and Fisheries Abstracts. Part 3, Aquatic Pollution and Environmental Quality.)
***Refer to Aquatic Sciences & Fisheries Abstracts [Computer File] : ASFA / Cambridge Scientific Abstracts for complete source list.

**AQUAT. SCI. FISHER. ABSTR. 3, AQUAT. POLLUT. ENVIRO. QUAL.**
[US/1045-6031]
AQUATIC SCIENCES AND FISHERIES ABSTRACTS. PART 3 : AQUATIC POLLUTION AND ENVIRONMENTAL QUALITY.
(*Continues in part* Aquatic Sciences and Fisheries Abstracts. Part 1, Biological Sciences & Living Resources *and* Aquatic Sciences and Fisheries Abstracts. Part 2, Ocean Technology, Policy and Non-Living Resources.)
***Refer to Aquatic Sciences & Fisheries Abstracts [Computer File] : ASFA / Cambridge Scientific Abstracts for complete source list.

**ARCHIT. PERIOD. INDEX**
[UK/0266-4380]
API. ARCHITECTURAL PERIODICALS INDEX.
(*Supersedes* Royal Institute of British Architects. RIBA Library Bulletin; Royal Institute of British Architects. RIBA Annual Review of Periodical Articles.)

**ARCT. BIBLIOGR.**
[CN/0066-6947]
ARCTIC BIBLIOGRAPHY.
**(Ceased)**

**ARECO Q. INDEX PERIOD. LIT. AGING**
[US/0734-5569]
ARECO'S QUARTERLY INDEX TO PERIODICAL LITERATURE ON AGING.
(*Continued by* Index to Periodical Literature on Aging.)

**ART ARCHAEOL. TECH. ABSTR.**
[US/0004-2994]
ART AND ARCHAEOLOGY TECHNICAL ABSTRACTS.
(*Continues* I.I.C. Abstracts.)

**ART DES. PHOTO**
[UK/0306-817X]
ART, DESIGN, PHOTO.
**(Ceased)**

**ART INDEX**
[US/0004-3222]
ART INDEX.

# INDEXES/ABSTRACTS TABLE

**ART INTELL. ABSTR.**
[US/0882-1410]
ARTIFICIAL INTELLIGENCE ABSTRACTS.
**(Ceased)**

**ARTBIBLIOGR. CURR. TITLES**
[UK/0307-9961]
ARTBIBLIOGRAPHIES. CURRENT TITLES.

**ARTBIBLIOGR. MOD.**
[UK/0300-466X]
ARTBIBLIOGRAPHIES MODERN.
(*Continues* LOMA; Literature on Modern Art.)

**ARTS HUMANIT. CITATION INDEX**
[US/0162-8445]
ARTS & HUMANITIES CITATION INDEX (PRINT ED.).

**ASCATOPICS**
[US/0730-8574]
ASCATOPICS.
(*Continued by* Research Alert.)

**ASCE**
[US/0730-3149]
ASCE.
(*Continued by* ASCE Annual Combined Index.)

**ASCE ANNU. COMB. INDEX**
[US/0742-1753]
ASCE ANNUAL COMBINED INDEX.
(*Continues* American Society of Civil Engineers. ASCE.)

**ASCE PUBL. INF.**
[US/0734-1962]
ASCE PUBLICATIONS INFORMATION.
(*Continues* ASCE Publications Abstracts.)

**ASIA.-PAC. ECON. LIT.**
[UK/0818-9935]
ASIAN-PACIFIC ECONOMIC LITERATURE.

**ASSIA PLUS**
[UK]
ASSIA PLUS [COMPUTER FILE].
***Refer to Applied Social Sciences Index & Abstracts for complete source list.

**ASTIS BIBLIOGR.**
[CN/0226-1685]
ASTIS BIBLIOGRAPHY.

**ASTIS CURR. AWARE. BULL.**
[CN/0705-8454]
A S T I S CURRENT AWARENESS BULLETIN.
(*Continues* Arctic Institute of North America. Library Accessions.)

**ASTRON. ASTROPHYS. ABSTR.**
[GW/0067-0022]
ASTRONOMY AND ASTROPHYSICS ABSTRACTS.
(*Continues* Astronomischer Jahresbericht.)

**AUST. EDUC. INDEX**
[AT/0004-9026]
AUSTRALIAN EDUCATION INDEX.

**AUST. LEG. MON. DIG.**
[AT/0004-9646]
AUSTRALIAN LEGAL MONTHLY DIGEST.

**AUST. LIBR. INF. SCI. ABSTR.**
[AT/0810-9265]
ALISA. AUSTRALIAN LIBRARY AND INFORMATION SCIENCE ABSTRACTS.

**AUST. SCI. INDEX**
[AT/0005-0229]
AUSTRALIAN SCIENCE INDEX.
(*Continues* C.S.I.R.O. Science Abstracts.)

**AUTOM. SUBJ. CITATION ALERT**
[US]
AUTOMATIC SUBJECT CITATION ALERT.
(*Continued by* Research Alert.)

**AVERY INDEX ARCHIT. PERIOD. SUPPL.**
[US/0588-540X]
AVERY INDEX TO ARCHITECTURAL PERIODICALS. SUPPLEMENT.
(*Continued by* Avery Index to Architectural Periodicals. Supplement / Columbia University.)

**AVERY INDEX ARCHIT. PERIOD. SUPPL. COLUM. UNIV.**
[US/0196-0008]
AVERY INDEX TO ARCHITECTURAL PERIODICALS. SECOND EDITION. REVISED AND ENLARGED. SUPPLEMENT.
(*Continues* Avery Library. Avery Index to Architectural Periodicals. Supplement.)

**AVIAT. TRADESCAN**
[US/0899-1928]
AVIATION TRADESCAN.

**BEHAV. ABSTR.**
[UK/0262-236X]
BEHAVIOURAL ABSTRACTS.
**(Ceased)**

**BEHAV. MED. ABSTR.**
[US/0197-7717]
BEHAVIORAL MEDICINE ABSTRACTS.
(*Absorbed by* Annals of Behavioral Medicine.)

**BER. BIOCHEM. BIOL.**
[GW/0005-9013]
BERICHTE BIOCHEMIE UND BIOLOGIE.
(*Continues* Berichte uber die Wissenschaftliche Biologie.)

**BHA : BIBLIO. HIST. ART**
[FR/1150-1588]
BIBLIOGRAPHY OF THE HISTORY OF ART : BHA.
(*Formed by the union of* Repertoire International de la Litterature de l'Art *and* Repertoire d'Art et d'Archeologie.)

**BHI PLUS**
[UK/0966-8772]
BHI PLUS [COMPUTER FILE].
***Refer to British Humanities Index for complete source list.

**BIBLIOGR. AGRIC.**
[US/0006-1530]
BIBLIOGRAPHY OF AGRICULTURE.
(*Continues* Bibliography of Agriculture with Subject Index.)
***Refer to AGRICOLA for complete source list.

**BIBLIOGR. BRAS. CIEN. INF.**
[BL/0102-2865]
BIBLIOGRAFIA BRASILEIRA DE CIENCIA DA INFORMACAO.
**(Ceased)**

**BIBLIOGR. BRAS. MED.**
[BL/0067-6675]
BIBLIOGRAFIA BRASILEIRA DE MEDICINA.
(*Continues* Indice-Catalogo Medico Brasileiro.)

**BIBLIOGR. CARTO.**
[GW/0340-0409]
BIBLIOGRAPHIA CARTOGRAPHICA.
(*Supersedes* Bibliotheca Cartographica.)

**BIBLIOGR. ENGL. LIT.**
[UK]
BIBLIOGRAPHY OF ENGLISH LANGUAGE AND LITERATURE.
(*Continued by* Annual Bibliography of English Language and Literature.)

**BIBLIOGR. HIST. MED.**
[US/0067-7280]
BIBLIOGRAPHY OF THE HISTORY OF MEDICINE.
***Refer to Index Medicus for complete source list.

**BIBLIOGR. INDEX GEOL.**
[US/0098-2784]
BIBLIOGRAPHY AND INDEX OF GEOLOGY.
(*Continues* Bibliography and Index of Geology Exclusive of North America; *Absorbed* Bibliography of North American Geology.)
***Refer to GeoRef [Computer File] for complete source list.

**BIBLIOGR. INDEX GEOL. EXCLUS. NORTH AM.**
[US/0376-1673]
BIBLIOGRAPHY AND INDEX OF GEOLOGY EXCLUSIVE OF NORTH AMERICA.
(*Continued by* Bibliography and Index of Geology.)

**BIBLIOGR. INDEX HEALTH EDUC. PERIOD.**
[US/0278-2340]
BIBLIOGRAPHIC INDEX OF HEALTH EDUCATION PERIODICALS : BIHEP.
**(Ceased)**

**BIBLIOGR. INDEX MICROPALEONTOLOGY**
[US/0300-7227]
BIBLIOGRAPHY AND INDEX OF MICROPALEONTOLOGY.
***Refer to GeoRef [Computer File] for complete source list.

**BIBLIOGR. MISSION.**
[IT]
BIBLIOGRAFIA MISSIONARIA.
(*Continued by* Bibliographia Missionaria.)

**BIBLIOGR. MISSION.**
[VC/0394-9869]
BIBLIOGRAPHIA MISSIONARIA / PONTIFICAL MISSIONARY LIBRARY OF THE CONGREGATION FOR THE EVANGELIZATION OF PEOPLES.
(*Continues* Bibliografia Missionaria.)

**BIBLIOGR. NORTH AM. GEOL.**
[US/0740-6347]
BIBLIOGRAPHY OF NORTH AMERICAN GEOLOGY.
(*Absorbed by* Bibliography and Index of Geology.)

**BIOBUSINESS**
[US]
BIOBUSINESS.

**BIOCONT. NEWS INF.**
[UK/0143-1404]
BIOCONTROL NEWS AND INFORMATION.

**BIODETER. ABSTR.**
[UK/0951-0621]
BIODETERIORATION ABSTRACTS.
(*Separated from* International Biodeterioration.)

**BIOENG. ABSTR.**
[US/0093-8378]
BIOENGINEERING ABSTRACTS.
(*Continued by* Engineering Index Bioengineering Abstracts.)

# INDEXES/ABSTRACTS TABLE

**BIOENG. ABSTR.**
[US/1068-5693]
BIOENGINEERING ABSTRACTS (1993).
(*Continues* Engineering Index Bioengineering and Biotechnology Abstracts.)

**BIOGR. INDEX**
[US/0006-3053]
BIOGRAPHY INDEX.

**BIOL. ABSTR. RRM**
[US/0192-6985]
BIOLOGICAL ABSTRACTS / RRM.
(*Continues* Bioresearch Index.)
***Refer to Biological Abstracts for complete source list.

**BIOL. ABSTR.**
[US/0006-3169]
BIOLOGICAL ABSTRACTS.
(*Formed by the union of* Abstracts of Bacteriology *and* Botanical Abstracts.)

**BIOL. ABSTR. ON COMPACT DISC**
[US/1058-4129]
BIOLOGICAL ABSTRACTS ON COMPACT DISC.
***Refer to Biological Abstracts for complete source list.

**BIOL. AGRIC. INDEX**
[US/0006-3177]
BIOLOGICAL & AGRICULTURAL INDEX.
(*Continues* Agricultural Index.)

**BIOL. DIG.**
[US/0095-2958]
BIOLOGY DIGEST.

**BIOSTATISTICA**
[US/1041-7648]
BIOSTATISTICA (DAVENPORT, IOWA).

**BIOTECHNOL. ABSTR.**
[UK/0262-5318]
DERWENT BIOTECHNOLOGY ABSTRACTS.
(*Continued by* Biotechnology Abstracts.)

**BIOTECHNOL. ABSTR.**
[UK]
BIOTECHNOLOGY ABSTRACTS.
(*Continues* Derwent Biotechnology Abstracts.)
***Refer to PESTDOC for complete source list.

**BIOTECHNOL. RES. ABSTR.**
[US/0733-5709]
BIOTECHNOLOGY RESEARCH ABSTRACTS.
(*Continued in part by* Medical & Pharmaceutical Biotechnology Abstracts *and* Agricultural & Environmental Biotechnology Abstracts.)

**BLACK INF. INDEX**
[US/0045-2173]
BLACK INFORMATION INDEX.
**(Ceased)**

**BMT ABSTR.**
[UK/0268-9650]
BMT ABSTRACTS : BRITISH MARITIME TECHNOLOGY ABSTRACTS.
(*Continues* Journal of Abstracts of the British Ship Research Association.)

**BOOK REV. DIGEST**
[US/0006-7326]
BOOK REVIEW DIGEST.
(*Continues* Cumulative Book Review Digest.)

**BOOK REV. INDEX**
[US/0524-0581]
BOOK REVIEW INDEX.

**BOOK REV. MON.**
[US/0006-7342]
BOOK REVIEWS OF THE MONTH.
**(Ceased)**

**BOSTON GLOBE INDEX**
[US/0893-2727]
BOSTON GLOBE INDEX (1987), THE.
(*Continues* Bell & Howell Newspaper Index to the Boston Globe.)

**BOWNE DIG. CORP. SEC. LAWYERS**
[US/0896-906X]
BOWNE DIGEST FOR CORPORATE & SECURITIES LAWYERS.
(*Continues* Abstracts of Legal Periodicals (Corporate & Securities Ed.).)

**BR. ARCHAEOL. ABSTR.**
[UK/0007-0270]
BRITISH ARCHAEOLOGICAL ABSTRACTS.
(*Continued by* British Archaeological Bibliography.)

**BR. ARCHAEOL. BIBLIOGR.**
[UK/0964-7104]
BRITISH ARCHAEOLOGICAL BIBLIOGRAPHY.
(*Continues* British Archaeological Abstracts.)

**BR. CERAM. ABSTR.**
[UK/0300-4570]
BRITISH CERAMIC ABSTRACTS.
(*Continued by* World Ceramics Abstracts.)

**BR. EDUC. INDEX**
[UK/0007-0637]
BRITISH EDUCATION INDEX.

**BR. HUMANIT. INDEX**
[UK/0007-0815]
BRITISH HUMANITIES INDEX.
(*Supersedes in part* Subject Index to Periodicals.)

**BR. TECHNOL. INDEX**
[UK/0007-1889]
BRITISH TECHNOLOGY INDEX.
(*Continued by* Current Technology Index.)

**BULL. ANAL. ENTOMOL. MED. VET.**
[FR/0007-4098]
BULLETIN ANALYTIQUE D'ENTOMOLOGIE MEDICALE ET VETERINAIRE.
**(Ceased)**

**BULL. SIGNAL.**
[FR]
BULLETIN SIGNALETIQUE.
**(Ceased)**

**BUS. ASAP**
[US]
BUSINESS ASAP [COMPUTER FILE].

**BUS. DATELINE**
[US]
BUSINESS DATELINE.

**BUS. EDUC. INDEX**
[US/0068-4414]
BUSINESS EDUCATION INDEX.

**BUS. INDEX**
[US/0273-3684]
BUSINESS INDEX.

**BUS. PERIOD. INDEX**
[US/0007-6961]
BUSINESS PERIODICALS INDEX.
(*Continues in part* Industrial Arts Index.)

**BUS. SOURCE**
[US]
BUSINESS SOURCE. [COMPUTER FILE].

**CA QUICK SEARCH**
[US]
CA QUICK SEARCH [COMPUTER FILE].
***Refer to Concrete Abstracts for complete source list.

**CA SEL., ACID RAIN ACID AIR**
[US/0885-0097]
CA SELECTS: ACID RAIN & ACID AIR.
***Refer to Chemical Abstracts for complete source list.

**CA SEL., ADHESIVES**
[US/0162-7686]
CA SELECTS: ADHESIVES.
***Refer to Chemical Abstracts for complete source list.

**CA SEL., AIDS RELAT. IMMUNODEFIC.**
[US/1040-7111]
CA SELECTS: AIDS & RELATED IMMUNODEFICIENCIES.
***Refer to Chemical Abstracts for complete source list.

**CA SEL., AIR POLLUT. BOOKS REV.**
[US/0895-5980]
CA SELECTS: AIR POLLUTION (BOOKS & REVIEWS).
***Refer to Chemical Abstracts for complete source list.

**CA SEL., ALKYL. CATAL.**
[US/0895-5964]
CA SELECTS: ALKYLATION & CATALYSTS.
***Refer to Chemical Abstracts for complete source list.

**CA SEL., ALUMIN. LITH. ALUMIN. CER. ALLOYS**
[US/1066-1166]
CA SELECTS: ALUMINUM-LITHIUM & ALUMINUM-CERIUM ALLOYS.
***Refer to Chemical Abstracts for complete source list.

**CA SEL., ALZHEIMER'S DIS. RELAT. MEM. DYSFUNC.**
[US/1047-8183]
CA SELECTS: ALZHEIMER'S DISEASE & RELATED MEMORY DYSFUNCTIONS.
***Refer to Chemical Abstracts for complete source list.

**CA SEL., AMINO ACIDS PEP. PROT.**
[US/0275-701X]
CA SELECTS: AMINO ACIDS, PEPTIDES & PROTEINS.
***Refer to Chemical Abstracts for complete source list.

**CA SEL., ANALYT. ELECTROCHEM.**
[US/0160-8959]
CA SELECTS: ANALYTICAL ELECTROCHEMISTRY.
***Refer to Chemical Abstracts for complete source list.

**CA SEL., ANIMAL LONG. AGING**
[US/0162-7694]
CA SELECTS: ANIMAL LONGEVITY & AGING.
***Refer to Chemical Abstracts for complete source list.

**CA SEL., ANTI INFLAM. AGENTS ARTHRIT.**
[US/0148-2394]
CA SELECTS: ANTI-INFLAMMATORY AGENTS & ARTHRITIS.
***Refer to Chemical Abstracts for complete source list.

**CA SEL., ANTIBAC. AGENTS**
[US/1045-8522]
CA SELECTS: ANTIBACTERIAL AGENTS.
(*Continues* CA Selects. Bactericides, Disinfectants & Antiseptics.)
***Refer to Chemical Abstracts for complete source list.

**CA SEL., ANTIOXID.**
[US/0275-7028]
CA SELECTS: ANTIOXIDANTS.
***Refer to Chemical Abstracts for complete source list.

# INDEXES/ABSTRACTS TABLE

**CA SEL., ANTITUMOR AGENTS**
[US/0148-2386]
CA SELECTS: ANTITUMOR AGENTS.
***Refer to Chemical Abstracts for complete source list.

**CA SEL., ARTIF. SWEETEN.**
[US/0890-1813]
CA SELECTS: ARTIFICIAL SWEETENERS.
***Refer to Chemical Abstracts for complete source list.

**CA SEL., ASYMMET. SYNTH. INDUC.**
[US/0890-183X]
CA SELECTS: ASYMMETRIC SYNTHESIS & INDUCTION.
***Refer to Chemical Abstracts for complete source list.

**CA SEL., AT. SPECTROSC.**
[US/0195-4911]
CA SELECTS: ATOMIC SPECTROSCOPY.
***Refer to Chemical Abstracts for complete source list.

**CA SEL., ATHEROSCL. HEART DIS.**
[US/0148-2378]
CA SELECTS: ATHEROSCLEROSIS & HEART DISEASE.
***Refer to Chemical Abstracts for complete source list.

**CA SEL., AUTOM. CHEM. ANAL.**
[US/0740-0683]
CA SELECTS: AUTOMATED CHEMICAL ANALYSIS.
***Refer to Chemical Abstracts for complete source list.

**CA SEL., B-LACTAM ANTIB.**
[US/0148-2459]
CA SELECTS: B-LACTAM ANTIBIOTICS.
***Refer to Chemical Abstracts for complete source list.

**CA SEL., BACTER. DISINFECT. ANTISEP.**
[US/0890-1848]
CA SELECTS: BACTERICIDES, DISINFECTANTS & ANTISEPTICS.
(*Continued by* CA Selects: Antibacterial Agents.)

**CA SEL., BATTER. FUEL CELLS**
[US/0162-7708]
CA SELECTS: BATTERIES & FUEL CELLS.
***Refer to Chemical Abstracts for complete source list.

**CA SEL., BIOGEN. AMINES NERV. SYST.**
[US/0162-7716]
CA SELECTS: BIOGENIC AMINES & THE NERVOUS SYSTEM.
***Refer to Chemical Abstracts for complete source list.

**CA SEL., BIOL. INFO. TRANSF.**
[US/0162-7724]
CA SELECTS: BIOLOGICAL INFORMATION TRANSFER.
**(Ceased)**

**CA SEL., BISMUTH CHEM.**
[US/1061-5342]
CA SELECTS: BISMUTH CHEMISTRY.
***Refer to Chemical Abstracts for complete source list.

**CA SEL., BLOCK GRAFT POLYM.**
[US/0734-8851]
CA SELECTS: BLOCK & GRAFT POLYMERS.
***Refer to Chemical Abstracts for complete source list.

**CA SEL., BLOOD COAG.**
[US/0162-7732]
CA SELECTS: BLOOD COAGULATION.
***Refer to Chemical Abstracts for complete source list.

**CA SEL., CARBOHYDR. (CHEM. ASP.)**
[US/0740-0756]
CA SELECTS: CARBOHYDRATES (CHEMICAL ASPECTS).
***Refer to Chemical Abstracts for complete source list.

**CA SEL., CARBON FIBER COMPOS.**
[US/0895-5956]
CA SELECTS: CARBON FIBER COMPOSITES.
***Refer to Chemical Abstracts for complete source list.

**CA SEL., CARBON GRAPH. FIB.**
[US/0890-1856]
CA SELECTS: CARBON & GRAPHITE FIBERS.
***Refer to Chemical Abstracts for complete source list.

**CA SEL., CARBON HETERO. NMR**
[US/0190-9401]
CA SELECTS: CARBON & HETEROATOM NMR.
(*Continues in part* CA Selects. Nuclear Magnetic Resonance, Chemical Aspects.)
***Refer to Chemical Abstracts for complete source list.

**CA SEL., CARCIN. MUT. TERATO.**
[US/0148-2408]
CA SELECTS: CARCINOGENS, MUTAGENS & TERATOGENS.
***Refer to Chemical Abstracts for complete source list.

**CA SEL., CATAL. (APPL. PHYS. ASP.)**
[US/0146-440X]
CA SELECTS: CATALYSIS (APPLIED AND PHYSICAL ASPECTS).
***Refer to Chemical Abstracts for complete source list.

**CA SEL., CATAL. (ORG. REACT.)**
[US/0146-4396]
CA SELECTS: CATALYSIS (ORGANIC REACTIONS).
***Refer to Chemical Abstracts for complete source list.

**CA SEL., CATAL. KINET. ANAL.**
[US/0890-1864]
CA SELECTS: CATALYTIC & KINETIC ANALYSIS.
***Refer to Chemical Abstracts for complete source list.

**CA SEL., CATAL. REGEN.**
[US/0734-8800]
CA SELECTS: CATALYST REGENERATION.
***Refer to Chemical Abstracts for complete source list.

**CA SEL., CERAM. MATER. J.**
[US/0895-5948]
CA SELECTS: CERAMIC MATERIALS (JOURNALS).
***Refer to Chemical Abstracts for complete source list.

**CA SEL., CERAM. METER. PAT.**
[US/0885-0100]
CA SELECTS: CERAMIC MATERIALS (PATENTS).
***Refer to Chemical Abstracts for complete source list.

**CA SEL., CHELATING AGENTS**
[US/0734-8797]
CA SELECTS: CHELATING AGENTS.
***Refer to Chemical Abstracts for complete source list.

**CA SEL., CHEM. ENG. OPER.**
[US/1040-712X]
CA SELECTS: CHEMICAL ENGINEERING OPERATIONS.
***Refer to Chemical Abstracts for complete source list.

**CA SEL., CHEM. HAZ. HEALTH SAFETY**
[US/0190-9398]
CA SELECTS: CHEMICAL HAZARDS, HEALTH, & SAFETY.
(*Continues* CA Selects. Chemical Hazards.)
***Refer to Chemical Abstracts for complete source list.

**CA SEL., CHEM. INSTRUM.**
[US/0195-4938]
CA SELECTS: CHEMICAL INSTRUMENTATION.
***Refer to Chemical Abstracts for complete source list.

**CA SEL., CHEM. IR OS RH RU**
[US/1040-7146]
CA SELECTS: CHEMISTRY OF IR, OS, RH, & RU.
***Refer to Chemical Abstracts for complete source list.

**CA SEL., CHEM. PROCESS. APPAR.**
[US/0195-4946]
CA SELECTS: CHEMICAL PROCESSING APPARATUS.
***Refer to Chemical Abstracts for complete source list.

**CA SEL., CHEM. VAPOR DEPOS.**
[US/0885-0119]
CA SELECTS. CHEMICAL VAPOR DEPOSITION.
***Refer to Chemical Abstracts for complete source list.

**CA SEL., CHEMILUMIN.**
[US/1040-7138]
CA SELECTS: CHEMILUMINESCENCE.
***Refer to Chemical Abstracts for complete source list.

**CA SEL., COAL SCI. PROC. CHEM.**
[US/0146-4426]
CA SELECTS: COAL SCIENCE & PROCESS CHEMISTRY.
***Refer to Chemical Abstracts for complete source list.

**CA SEL., COAT. INKS REALT. PROD.**
[US/0275-7036]
CA SELECTS: COATINGS, INKS, & RELATED PRODUCTS.
***Refer to Chemical Abstracts for complete source list.

**CA SEL., COLLOIDS (APPL. ASP.)**
[US/0160-8967]
CA SELECTS: COLLOIDS (APPLIED ASPECTS).
(*Continued by* CA Selects. Colloids (Macromolecular Aspects).)

**CA SEL., COLLOIDS (MACROMOL. ASP.)**
[US/0190-9444]
CA SELECTS: COLLOIDS (MACROMOLECULAR ASPECTS).
(*Supersedes in part* CA Selects. Colloids (Applied Aspects).)
***Refer to Chemical Abstracts for complete source list.

**CA SEL., COLLOIDS (PHYSICO. ASP.)**
[US/0160-8975]
CA SELECTS: COLLOIDS (PHYSICOCHEMICAL ASPECTS).
***Refer to Chemical Abstracts for complete source list.

**CA SEL., COLOR SCI.**
[US/0885-0127]
CA SELECTS: COLOR SCIENCE.
***Refer to Chemical Abstracts for complete source list.

**CA SEL., COLOR. DYES**
[US/0734-8789]
CA SELECTS: COLORANTS & DYES.
***Refer to Chemical Abstracts for complete source list.

**CA SEL., COMPOS. MATER. (CERAM.)**
[US/1066-1158]
CA SELECTS: COMPOSITE MATERIALS (CERAMIC).
***Refer to Chemical Abstracts for complete source list.

**CA SEL., COMPOS. MATER. (MET.)**
[US/1066-114X]
CA SELECTS: COMPOSITE MATERIALS (METALLIC).
***Refer to Chemical Abstracts for complete source list.

**CA SEL., COMPOS. MATER. (POLYM.)**
[US/1040-7154]
CA SELECTS: COMPOSITE MATERIALS (POLYMERIC).
***Refer to Chemical Abstracts for complete source list.

**CA SEL., COMPUT. CHEM.**
[US/0160-9025]
CA SELECTS: COMPUTERS IN CHEMISTRY.
***Refer to Chemical Abstracts for complete source list.

# INDEXES/ABSTRACTS TABLE

**CA SEL., CONDUCT. POLYM.**
[US/0885-0135]
CA SELECTS: CONDUCTIVE POLYMERS.
***Refer to Chemical Abstracts for complete source list.

**CA SEL., CONTROL. RELEASE TECHNOL.**
[US/0740-0748]
CA SELECTS: CONTROLLED RELEASE TECHNOLOGY.
***Refer to Chemical Abstracts for complete source list.

**CA SEL., CORROS.**
[US/0146-4434]
CA SELECTS: CORROSION.
***Refer to Chemical Abstracts for complete source list.

**CA SEL., CORROS.-INHIB. COAT.**
[US/0749-7296]
CA SELECTS: CORROSION-INHIBITING COATINGS.
***Refer to Chemical Abstracts for complete source list.

**CA SEL., COSMET. CHEM.**
[US/0275-7044]
CA SELECTS: COSMETIC CHEMICALS.
***Refer to Chemical Abstracts for complete source list.

**CA SEL., COSMOCHEM.**
[US/0195-4954]
CA SELECTS: COSMOCHEMISTRY.
**(Ceased)**

**CA SEL., CROSSLINK. REACT.**
[US/0740-0721]
CA SELECTS: CROSSLINKING REACTIONS.
***Refer to Chemical Abstracts for complete source list.

**CA SEL., CRYS. GROWTH**
[US/0162-7740]
CA SELECTS: CRYSTAL GROWTH.
***Refer to Chemical Abstracts for complete source list.

**CA SEL., DETER. SOAPS, SURFAC.**
[US/0162-7767]
CA SELECTS: DETERGENTS, SOAPS, & SURFACTANTS.
***Refer to Chemical Abstracts for complete source list.

**CA SEL., DISTILL. TECHNOL.**
[US/0275-7052]
CA SELECTS: DISTILLATION TECHNOLOGY.
***Refer to Chemical Abstracts for complete source list.

**CA SEL., DRILL. MUDS**
[US/0749-730X]
CA SELECTS: DRILLING MUDS.
***Refer to Chemical Abstracts for complete source list.

**CA SEL., DRUG COSMET. TOXIC.**
[US/0162-7775]
CA SELECTS: DRUG & COSMETIC TOXICITY.
***Refer to Chemical Abstracts for complete source list.

**CA SEL., DRUG DELIV. SYST. DOS. FORMS**
[US/1040-7162]
CA SELECTS: DRUG DELIVERY SYSTEMS & DOSAGE FORMS.
***Refer to Chemical Abstracts for complete source list.

**CA SEL., ELECT. AUG. SPECTRO.**
[US/0146-4450]
CA SELECTS: ELECTRON & AUGER SPECTROSCOPY.
***Refer to Chemical Abstracts for complete source list.

**CA SEL., ELECT. SPIN RESON. (CHEM. ASP.)**
[US/0146-4469]
CA SELECTS: ELECTRON SPIN RESONANCE (CHEMICAL ASPECTS).
***Refer to Chemical Abstracts for complete source list.

**CA SEL., ELECTR. CONDUCT. ORG.**
[US/0885-0143]
CA SELECTS: ELECTRICALLY CONDUCTIVE ORGANICS.
***Refer to Chemical Abstracts for complete source list.

**CA SEL., ELECTROCHEM. ORG. SYNTH.**
[US/0734-8770]
CA SELECTS: ELECTROCHEMICAL ORGANIC SYNTHESIS.
***Refer to Chemical Abstracts for complete source list.

**CA SEL., ELECTROCHEM. REAC.**
[US/0146-4442]
CA SELECTS: ELECTROCHEMICAL REACTIONS.
***Refer to Chemical Abstracts for complete source list.

**CA SEL., ELECTRODEPOSIT.**
[US/0162-7783]
CA SELECTS: ELECTRODEPOSITION.
***Refer to Chemical Abstracts for complete source list.

**CA SEL., ELECTRON. CHEM. MATER.**
[US/0885-0151]
CA SELECTS: ELECTRONIC CHEMICALS & MATERIALS.
***Refer to Chemical Abstracts for complete source list.

**CA SEL., ELECTROPHOR.**
[US/0195-4962]
CA SELECTS: ELECTROPHORESIS.
***Refer to Chemical Abstracts for complete source list.

**CA SEL., EMULS. POLYM.**
[US/0195-4970]
CA SELECTS: EMULSION POLYMERIZATION.
***Refer to Chemical Abstracts for complete source list.

**CA SEL., EMULSIF. & DEMULSIF.**
[US/0734-8754]
CA SELECTS: EMULSIFIERS & DEMULSIFIERS.
***Refer to Chemical Abstracts for complete source list.

**CA SEL., ENERGY REV. BOOKS**
[US/0162-7791]
CA SELECTS: ENERGY REVIEWS & BOOKS.
***Refer to Chemical Abstracts for complete source list.

**CA SEL., ENGINE EXH.**
[US/0160-9033]
CA SELECTS: ENGINE EXHAUST.
**(Ceased)**

**CA SEL., ENHANC. PETRO. RECOV.**
[US/0734-8746]
CA SELECTS: ENHANCED PETROLEUM RECOVERY.
***Refer to Chemical Abstracts for complete source list.

**CA SEL., ENVIRON. POLLUT.**
[US/0160-9041]
CA SELECTS: ENVIRONMENTAL POLLUTION.
***Refer to Chemical Abstracts for complete source list.

**CA SEL., ENZYM. APPL.**
[US/0895-593X]
CA SELECTS: ENZYME APPLICATIONS.
***Refer to Chemical Abstracts for complete source list.

**CA SEL., ENZYM. ASSAYS**
[US/0895-5808]
CA SELECTS: ENZYME ASSAYS.
***Refer to Chemical Abstracts for complete source list.

**CA SEL., EPOXY RESINS**
[US/0275-7060]
CA SELECTS: EPOXY RESINS.
***Refer to Chemical Abstracts for complete source list.

**CA SEL., FATS OILS**
[US/0275-7079]
CA SELECTS: FATS & OILS.
***Refer to Chemical Abstracts for complete source list.

**CA SEL., FERMENT. CHEM.**
[US/0740-0713]
CA SELECTS: FERMENTATION CHEMICALS.
***Refer to Chemical Abstracts for complete source list.

**CA SEL., FIBER OPT. OPT. COMMUN.**
[US/0890-1872]
CA SELECTS: FIBER OPTICS & OPTICAL COMMUNICATION.
***Refer to Chemical Abstracts for complete source list.

**CA SEL., FIBER-REINFOR. PLAST.**
[US/0734-869X]
CA SELECTS: FIBER-REINFORCED PLASTICS.
***Refer to Chemical Abstracts for complete source list.

**CA SEL., FLAMMABIL.**
[US/0162-7805]
CA SELECTS: FLAMMABILITY.
***Refer to Chemical Abstracts for complete source list.

**CA SEL., FLAV. FRAGR.**
[US/0148-2327]
CA SELECTS: FLAVORS & FRAGRANCES.
***Refer to Chemical Abstracts for complete source list.

**CA SEL., FLUID. SOLIDS TECHNOL.**
[US/0195-4989]
CA SELECTS: FLUIDIZED SOLIDS TECHNOLOGY.
***Refer to Chemical Abstracts for complete source list.

**CA SEL., FLUOROPOLY.**
[US/0895-5921]
CA SELECTS: FLUOROPOLYMERS.
***Refer to Chemical Abstracts for complete source list.

**CA SEL., FOOD DRUGS COSMET.**
[US/1051-3914]
CA SELECTS: FOOD, DRUGS, & COSMETICS.
***Refer to Chemical Abstracts for complete source list.

**CA SEL., FOOD FEED ANAL.**
[US/0895-5913]
CA SELECTS: FOOD & FEED ANALYSIS.
***Refer to Chemical Abstracts for complete source list.

**CA SEL., FOOD TOXIC.**
[US/0162-7813]
CA SELECTS: FOOD TOXICITY.
***Refer to Chemical Abstracts for complete source list.

**CA SEL., FORENS. CHEM.**
[US/0362-9880]
CA SELECTS: FORENSIC CHEMISTRY.
***Refer to Chemical Abstracts for complete source list.

**CA SEL., FORMUL. CHEM.**
[US/0890-1880]
CA SELECTS: FORMULATION CHEMISTRY.
***Refer to Chemical Abstracts for complete source list.

**CA SEL., FREE RADIC.**
[US/0885-016X]
CA SELECTS: FREE RADICALS.
(*Continued by* CA Selects: Free Radicals (Organic Aspects).)

**CA SEL., FREE RADIC. (BIOCHEM. ASP.)**
[US/0895-5905]
CA SELECTS: FREE RADICALS (BIOCHEMICAL ASPECTS).
***Refer to Chemical Abstracts for complete source list.

# INDEXES/ABSTRACTS TABLE

**CA SEL., FREE RADIC. (ORG. ASP.)**
[US/0895-5972]
CA SELECTS: FREE RADICALS (ORGANIC ASPECTS).
(*Continues CA Selects. Free Radicals.*)
\*\*\*Refer to Chemical Abstracts for complete source list.

**CA SEL., FUEL LUBR. ADDIT.**
[US/0195-4997]
CA SELECTS: FUEL & LUBRICANT ADDITIVES.
\*\*\*Refer to Chemical Abstracts for complete source list.

**CA SEL., FUNGICID.**
[US/0160-9068]
CA SELECTS: FUNGICIDES.
\*\*\*Refer to Chemical Abstracts for complete source list.

**CA SEL., GAS CHROMAT.**
[US/0146-4477]
CA SELECTS: GAS CHROMATOGRAPHY.
\*\*\*Refer to Chemical Abstracts for complete source list.

**CA SEL., GAS. WASTE TREAT.**
[US/0160-9076]
CA SELECTS: GASEOUS WASTE TREATMENT.
\*\*\*Refer to Chemical Abstracts for complete source list.

**CA SEL., GEL PERM. CHROMAT.**
[US/0146-4485]
CA SELECTS: GEL PERMEATION CHROMATOGRAPHY.
\*\*\*Refer to Chemical Abstracts for complete source list.

**CA SEL., GEOCHEM.**
[US/1066-5730]
CA SELECTS: GEOCHEMISTRY.
\*\*\*Refer to Chemical Abstracts for complete source list.

**CA SEL., HEAT-RESIST. ABLAT. POLYM.**
[US/0162-7821]
CA SELECTS: HEAT-RESISTANT & ABLATIVE POLYMERS.
\*\*\*Refer to Chemical Abstracts for complete source list.

**CA SEL., HERBIC.**
[US/0160-9084]
CA SELECTS: HERBICIDES.
\*\*\*Refer to Chemical Abstracts for complete source list.

**CA SEL., HIGH PERFORM. LIQ. CHROMATOGR.**
[US/0195-5217]
CA SELECTS: HIGH PERFORMANCE LIQUID CHROMATOGRAPHY.
(*Continues CA Selects. High Speed Liquid Chromatography.*)
\*\*\*Refer to Chemical Abstracts for complete source list.

**CA SEL., HOT-MELT ADHES.**
[US/0895-5891]
CA SELECTS: HOT-MELT ADHESIVES.
\*\*\*Refer to Chemical Abstracts for complete source list.

**CA SEL., HYPERTENS. ANTIHYPERTENS.**
[US/1051-3922]
CA SELECTS: HYPERTENSION & ANTIHYPERTENSIVES.
\*\*\*Refer to Chemical Abstracts for complete source list.

**CA SEL., INFR. SPECTRO. (ORG. ASP.)**
[US/0190-9428]
CA SELECTS: INFRARED SPECTROSCOPY (ORGANIC ASPECTS).
(*Continues in part CA Selects. Infrared Spectroscopy.*)
\*\*\*Refer to Chemical Abstracts for complete source list.

**CA SEL., INFR. SPECTRO. (PHYSICOCHEM. ASP.)**
[US/0190-9436]
CA SELECTS: INFRARED SPECTROSCOPY (PHYSICOCHEMICAL ASPECTS).
(*Continues in part CA Selects. Infrared Spectroscopy.*)
\*\*\*Refer to Chemical Abstracts for complete source list.

**CA SEL., INIT. POLYMER.**
[US/0734-8843]
CA SELECTS: INITIATION OF POLYMERIZATION.
\*\*\*Refer to Chemical Abstracts for complete source list.

**CA SEL., INORG. ANAL. CHEM.**
[US/0275-7087]
CA SELECTS: INORGANIC ANALYTICAL CHEMISTRY.
\*\*\*Refer to Chemical Abstracts for complete source list.

**CA SEL., INORG. CHEM. REACT.**
[US/0275-7095]
CA SELECTS: INORGANIC CHEMICALS & REACTIONS.
\*\*\*Refer to Chemical Abstracts for complete source list.

**CA SEL., INORG. FLOUR. CHEM.**
[US/0195-5004]
CA SELECTS: INORGANIC FLOURINE CHEMISTRY.
**(Ceased)**

**CA SEL., INORG. ORGANOMET. REACT. MECHAN.**
[US/0195-5012]
CA SELECTS: INORGANIC & ORGANOMETALLIC REACTION MECHANISMS.
\*\*\*Refer to Chemical Abstracts for complete source list.

**CA SEL., INSECTIC.**
[US/0160-9092]
CA SELECTS: INSECTICIDES.
\*\*\*Refer to Chemical Abstracts for complete source list.

**CA SEL., ION CHROMATOGR.**
[US/0890-1899]
CA SELECTS: ION CHROMATOGRAPHY.
\*\*\*Refer to Chemical Abstracts for complete source list.

**CA SEL., ION EXCHANGE**
[US/0146-4493]
CA SELECTS: ION EXCHANGE.
\*\*\*Refer to Chemical Abstracts for complete source list.

**CA SEL., ION-CONTAIN. POLYM.**
[US/0195-5020]
CA SELECTS: ION-CONTAINING POLYMERS.
\*\*\*Refer to Chemical Abstracts for complete source list.

**CA SEL., ISOMERI. CATAL.**
[US/0895-5883]
CA SELECTS: ISOMERIZATION & CATALYSTS.
\*\*\*Refer to Chemical Abstracts for complete source list.

**CA SEL., LASER APPL.**
[US/0195-5039]
CA SELECTS: LASER APPLICATIONS.
\*\*\*Refer to Chemical Abstracts for complete source list.

**CA SEL., LASER-INDUC. CHEM REACT.**
[US/0885-0178]
CA SELECTS: LASER-INDUCED CHEMICAL REACTIONS.
\*\*\*Refer to Chemical Abstracts for complete source list.

**CA SEL., LASERS MASERS**
[US/0195-5047]
CA SELECTS: LASERS & MASERS.
**(Ceased)**

**CA SEL., LIQ. CRYST.**
[US/0148-2351]
CA SELECTS: LIQUID CRYSTALS.
\*\*\*Refer to Chemical Abstracts for complete source list.

**CA SEL., LIQ. WASTE TREAT.**
[US/0160-9106]
CA SELECTS: LIQUID WASTE TREATMENT.
\*\*\*Refer to Chemical Abstracts for complete source list.

**CA SEL., LUBR. GREAS. LUBRICAT.**
[US/0734-8738]
CA SELECTS: LUBRICANTS, GREASES & LUBRICATION.
\*\*\*Refer to Chemical Abstracts for complete source list.

**CA SEL., MACROCYCL. ANTIBIOT.**
[US/0195-5055]
CA SELECTS: MACROCYCLIC ANTIBIOTICS.
**(Ceased)**

**CA SEL., MASS SPECTRO.**
[US/0362-9872]
CA SELECTS: MASS SPECTROMETRY.
\*\*\*Refer to Chemical Abstracts for complete source list.

**CA SEL., MEM. REC. DEVICES MATER.**
[US/0890-1821]
CA SELECTS: MEMORY & RECORDING DEVICES & MATERIALS.
\*\*\*Refer to Chemical Abstracts for complete source list.

**CA SEL., MEMBR. SEP.**
[US/1040-7197]
CA SELECTS: MEMBRANE SEPARATION.
\*\*\*Refer to Chemical Abstracts for complete source list.

**CA SEL., METAL. GLASS.**
[US/1062-8681]
CA SELECTS: METALLIC GLASSES.
\*\*\*Refer to Chemical Abstracts for complete source list.

**CA SEL., METALLO ENZ. METALLO COENZ.**
[US/0160-9114]
CA SELECTS: METALLO ENZYMES & METALLO COENZYMES.
\*\*\*Refer to Chemical Abstracts for complete source list.

**CA SEL., MOLEC. MODEL. (BIOCHEM. ASP.)**
[US/1059-2784]
CA SELECTS: MOLECULAR MODELING (BIOCHEMICAL ASPECTS).
\*\*\*Refer to Chemical Abstracts for complete source list.

**CA SEL., NAT. PROD. SYNTH.**
[US/0740-0691]
CA SELECTS: NATURAL PRODUCT SYNTHESIS.
\*\*\*Refer to Chemical Abstracts for complete source list.

**CA SEL., NEW ANTIBIOT.**
[US/0895-5875]
CA SELECTS: NEW ANTIBIOTICS.
\*\*\*Refer to Chemical Abstracts for complete source list.

**CA SEL., NEW BOOKS CHEM.**
[US/0148-2416]
CA SELECTS: NEW BOOKS IN CHEMISTRY.
\*\*\*Refer to Chemical Abstracts for complete source list.

**CA SEL., NEW PLAST.**
[US/0734-8673]
CA SELECTS: NEW PLASTICS.
\*\*\*Refer to Chemical Abstracts for complete source list.

**CA SEL., NITROGEN FIXAT.**
[US/1047-8108]
CA SELECTS: NITROGEN FIXATION.
\*\*\*Refer to Chemical Abstracts for complete source list.

**CA SEL., NONLINEAR OPT. MATER.**
[US/0895-5867]
CA SELECTS: NONLINEAR OPTICAL MATERIALS.
\*\*\*Refer to Chemical Abstracts for complete source list.

# INDEXES/ABSTRACTS TABLE

**CA SEL., NOV. PESTIC. HERBIC.**
[US/0749-7318]
CA SELECTS: NOVEL PESTICIDES & HERBICIDES.
\*\*\*Refer to Chemical Abstracts for complete source list.

**CA SEL., NOVEL NAT. PROD.**
[US/0734-872X]
CA SELECTS: NOVEL NATURAL PRODUCTS.
\*\*\*Refer to Chemical Abstracts for complete source list.

**CA SEL., NOVEL POLYM. PAT.**
[US/0734-8819]
CA SELECTS: NOVEL POLYMERS FROM PATENTS.
\*\*\*Refer to Chemical Abstracts for complete source list.

**CA SEL., NOVEL SULFUR HETEROCYCL.**
[US/0275-7109]
CA SELECTS: NOVEL SULFUR HETEROCYCLES.
\*\*\*Refer to Chemical Abstracts for complete source list.

**CA SEL., OMEGA THREE FAT. ACID. FISH OIL**
[US/1052-1984]
CA SELECTS: OMEGA THREE FATTY ACIDS & FISH OIL.
\*\*\*Refer to Chemical Abstracts for complete source list.

**CA SEL., OPT. PHOTOSENSIT. MATER.**
[US/0195-5063]
CA SELECTS: OPTICAL & PHOTOSENSITIVE MATERIALS.
\*\*\*Refer to Chemical Abstracts for complete source list.

**CA SEL., OPTIMIZ. ORG. REACT.**
[US/0195-5071]
CA SELECTS: OPTIMIZATION OF ORGANIC REACTIONS.
\*\*\*Refer to Chemical Abstracts for complete source list.

**CA SEL., ORAGNOPHOS. CHEM.**
[US/0162-783X]
CA SELECTS: ORGANOPHOSPHORUS CHEMISTRY.
\*\*\*Refer to Chemical Abstracts for complete source list.

**CA SEL., ORG. ANAL. CHEM.**
[US/0275-7117]
CA SELECTS: ORGANIC ANALYTICAL CHEMISTRY.
\*\*\*Refer to Chemical Abstracts for complete source list.

**CA SEL., ORG. OPT. MATER.**
[US/0885-0186]
CA SELECTS: ORGANIC OPTICAL MATERIALS.
\*\*\*Refer to Chemical Abstracts for complete source list.

**CA SEL., ORG. REACT. MECHAN.**
[US/0162-7848]
CA SELECTS: ORGANIC REACTION MECHANISMS.
\*\*\*Refer to Chemical Abstracts for complete source list.

**CA SEL., ORG. STEREOCHEM.**
[US/0195-508X]
CA SELECTS: ORGANIC STEREOCHEMISTRY.
\*\*\*Refer to Chemical Abstracts for complete source list.

**CA SEL., ORG.-TRANS. MET. COMPL.**
[US/0160-9130]
CA SELECTS: ORGANO-TRANSITION METAL COMPLEXES.
\*\*\*Refer to Chemical Abstracts for complete source list.

**CA SEL., ORGANOBOR. CHEM. BORAN.**
[US/0195-5098]
CA SELECTS: ORGANOBORON CHEMISTRY & BORANES.
**(Ceased)**

**CA SEL., ORGANOFLOUR. CHEM.**
[US/0160-905X]
CA SELECTS: ORGANOFLUORINE CHEMISTRY.
\*\*\*Refer to Chemical Abstracts for complete source list.

**CA SEL., ORGANOMET. ORG. SYNTH.**
[US/0895-5859]
CA SELECTS: ORGANOMETALLICS IN ORGANIC SYNTHESIS.
\*\*\*Refer to Chemical Abstracts for complete source list.

**CA SEL., ORGANOSIL. CHEM.**
[US/0362-9899]
CA SELECTS: ORGANOSILICON CHEMISTRY.
\*\*\*Refer to Chemical Abstracts for complete source list.

**CA SEL., ORGANOSUL. CHEM. J.**
[US/1040-7189]
CA SELECTS: ORGANOSULFUR CHEMISTRY (JOURNALS).
\*\*\*Refer to Chemical Abstracts for complete source list.

**CA SEL., ORGANOTIN CHEM.**
[US/0195-5101]
CA SELECTS: ORGANOTIN CHEMISTRY.
\*\*\*Refer to Chemical Abstracts for complete source list.

**CA SEL., OXID. CATAL.**
[US/1040-7170]
CA SELECTS: OXIDATION CATALYSTS.
\*\*\*Refer to Chemical Abstracts for complete source list.

**CA SEL., OXIDE SUPERCOND.**
[US/1040-7219]
CA SELECTS: OXIDE SUPERCONDUCTORS.
\*\*\*Refer to Chemical Abstracts for complete source list.

**CA SEL., PAINT ADDIT.**
[US/0734-8762]
CA SELECTS: PAINT ADDITIVES.
\*\*\*Refer to Chemical Abstracts for complete source list.

**CA SEL., PAP. CHEM.**
[US/1040-7200]
CA SELECTS: PAPER CHEMISTRY.
\*\*\*Refer to Chemical Abstracts for complete source list.

**CA SEL., PAP. THIN-LAY. CHROMATOGR.**
[US/0146-4515]
CA SELECTS: PAPER & THIN-LAYER CHROMATOGRAPHY.
\*\*\*Refer to Chemical Abstracts for complete source list.

**CA SEL., PAPER ADDIT.**
[US/0734-8711]
CA SELECTS: PAPER ADDITIVES.
\*\*\*Refer to Chemical Abstracts for complete source list.

**CA SEL., PHARM. ANAL.**
[US/0890-1902]
CA SELECTS: PHARMACEUTICAL ANALYSIS.
\*\*\*Refer to Chemical Abstracts for complete source list.

**CA SEL., PHARM. CHEM. (PAT.)**
[US/0890-1929]
CA SELECTS: PHARMACEUTICAL CHEMISTRY (PATENTS).
\*\*\*Refer to Chemical Abstracts for complete source list.

**CA SEL., PHARM. CHEM. J.**
[US/0890-1910]
CA SELECTS: PHARMACEUTICAL CHEMISTRY (JOURNALS).
\*\*\*Refer to Chemical Abstracts for complete source list.

**CA SEL., PHASE TRANSF. CATAL.**
[US/0885-0194]
CA SELECTS: PHASE TRANSFER CATALYSIS.
\*\*\*Refer to Chemical Abstracts for complete source list.

**CA SEL., PHOTOBIOCHEM.**
[US/0148-2335]
CA SELECTS: PHOTOBIOCHEMISTRY.
\*\*\*Refer to Chemical Abstracts for complete source list.

**CA SEL., PHOTOCHEM.**
[US/0362-9856]
CA SELECTS: PHOTOCHEMISTRY.
\*\*\*Refer to Chemical Abstracts for complete source list.

**CA SEL., PHOTOCHEM. ORG. SYNTH.**
[US/0885-0208]
CA SELECTS: PHOTOCHEMICAL ORGANIC SYNTHESIS.
\*\*\*Refer to Chemical Abstracts for complete source list.

**CA SEL., PHOTORESIS.**
[US/0885-0216]
CA SELECTS: PHOTORESISTS.
\*\*\*Refer to Chemical Abstracts for complete source list.

**CA SEL., PHOTOSENSIT. POLYM.**
[US/0749-7326]
CA SELECTS: PHOTOSENSITIVE POLYMERS.
\*\*\*Refer to Chemical Abstracts for complete source list.

**CA SEL., PLAS. REACT. ION ETCHING**
[US/0749-7334]
CA SELECTS: PLASMA & REACTIVE ION ETCHING.
\*\*\*Refer to Chemical Abstracts for complete source list.

**CA SEL., PLAST. ADDIT.**
[US/0734-8681]
CA SELECTS: PLASTICS ADDITIVES.
\*\*\*Refer to Chemical Abstracts for complete source list.

**CA SEL., PLAST. FABR. USES**
[US/0275-7125]
CA SELECTS: PLASTICS FABRICATION & USES.
\*\*\*Refer to Chemical Abstracts for complete source list.

**CA SEL., PLAST. FILMS**
[US/0195-511X]
CA SELECTS: PLASTIC FILMS.
\*\*\*Refer to Chemical Abstracts for complete source list.

**CA SEL., PLAST. MANUF. PROCESS.**
[US/0275-7133]
CA SELECTS: PLASTICS MANUFACTURING & PROCESSING.
\*\*\*Refer to Chemical Abstracts for complete source list.

**CA SEL., PLAT. PALLAD. CHEM.**
[US/0890-1937]
CA SELECTS: PLATINUM & PALLADIUM CHEMISTRY.
\*\*\*Refer to Chemical Abstracts for complete source list.

**CA SEL., POLLUT. MONIT.**
[US/0160-9149]
CA SELECTS: POLLUTION MONITORING.
\*\*\*Refer to Chemical Abstracts for complete source list.

**CA SEL., POLYACRYL. J.**
[US/0890-1945]
CA SELECTS: POLYACRYLATES (JOURNALS).
\*\*\*Refer to Chemical Abstracts for complete source list.

**CA SEL., POLYEST.**
[US/0734-8703]
CA SELECTS: POLYESTERS.
\*\*\*Refer to Chemical Abstracts for complete source list.

**CA SEL., POLYIMIDES**
[US/0895-5840]
CA SELECTS: POLYIMIDES.
\*\*\*Refer to Chemical Abstracts for complete source list.

**CA SEL., POLYM. BLENDS**
[US/0734-8827]
CA SELECTS: POLYMER BLENDS.
\*\*\*Refer to Chemical Abstracts for complete source list.

**CA SEL., POLYM. DEGRAD.**
[US/0734-8835]
CA SELECTS: POLYMER DEGRADATION.
\*\*\*Refer to Chemical Abstracts for complete source list.

# INDEXES/ABSTRACTS TABLE

**CA SEL., POLYM. KINET. PROCESS CONTROL**
[US/0885-0224]
CA SELECTS: POLYMERIZATION KINETICS & PROCESS CONTROL.
\*\*\*Refer to Chemical Abstracts for complete source list.

**CA SEL., POLYM. MORPHOL.**
[US/0195-5128]
CA SELECTS: POLYMER MORPHOLOGY.
\*\*\*Refer to Chemical Abstracts for complete source list.

**CA SEL., POLYURETH.**
[US/0740-0705]
CA SELECTS: POLYURETHANES.
\*\*\*Refer to Chemical Abstracts for complete source list.

**CA SEL., PORPHYR.**
[US/0195-5136]
CA SELECTS: PORPHYRINS.
\*\*\*Refer to Chemical Abstracts for complete source list.

**CA SEL., PROSTAGLAND.**
[US/0148-2343]
CA SELECTS: PROSTAGLANDINS.
\*\*\*Refer to Chemical Abstracts for complete source list.

**CA SEL., PROT. MAG. RESON.**
[US/0190-941X]
CA SELECTS: PROTON MAGNETIC RESONANCE.
(*Continues in part* CA Selects. Nuclear Magnetic Resonance, Chemical Aspects.)
\*\*\*Refer to Chemical Abstracts for complete source list.

**CA SEL., PSYCHOBIOCHEM.**
[US/0362-9848]
CA SELECTS: PSYCHOBIOCHEMISTRY.
\*\*\*Refer to Chemical Abstracts for complete source list.

**CA SEL., QUAT. AMMON. COMP.**
[US/0890-1953]
CA SELECTS: QUATERNARY AMMONIUM COMPOUNDS.
\*\*\*Refer to Chemical Abstracts for complete source list.

**CA SEL., RADIAT. CHEM.**
[US/0146-4523]
CA SELECTS: RADIATION CHEMISTRY.
\*\*\*Refer to Chemical Abstracts for complete source list.

**CA SEL., RADIAT. CURING**
[US/0749-7342]
CA SELECTS: RADIATION CURING.
\*\*\*Refer to Chemical Abstracts for complete source list.

**CA SEL., RAMAN SPECTROS.**
[US/0148-2432]
CA SELECTS: RAMAN SPECTROSCOPY.
\*\*\*Refer to Chemical Abstracts for complete source list.

**CA SEL., RECOV. RECYCL. WASTES**
[US/0160-9157]
CA SELECTS: RECOVERY & RECYCLING OF WASTES.
\*\*\*Refer to Chemical Abstracts for complete source list.

**CA SEL., SELEN. TELLUR. CHEM.**
[US/0749-7350]
CA SELECTS: SELENIUM & TELLURIUM CHEMISTRY.
\*\*\*Refer to Chemical Abstracts for complete source list.

**CA SEL., SHAPE MEM. ALLOYS**
[US/1062-869X]
CA SELECTS: SHAPE MEMORY ALLOYS.
\*\*\*Refer to Chemical Abstracts for complete source list.

**CA SEL., SILICAS SILICAT.**
[US/0890-1961]
CA SELECTS: SILICAS & SILICATES.
\*\*\*Refer to Chemical Abstracts for complete source list.

**CA SEL., SILOX. SILIC.**
[US/0895-5832]
CA SELECTS: SILOXANES & SILICONES.
\*\*\*Refer to Chemical Abstracts for complete source list.

**CA SEL., SILVER CHEM.**
[US/0148-2440]
CA SELECTS: SILVER CHEMISTRY.
\*\*\*Refer to Chemical Abstracts for complete source list.

**CA SEL., SOL. ENERGY**
[US/0148-236X]
CA SELECTS: SOLAR ENERGY.
\*\*\*Refer to Chemical Abstracts for complete source list.

**CA SEL., SOLID RADIOACT. WASTE TREAT.**
[US/0160-9165]
CA SELECTS: SOLID & RADIOACTIVE WASTE TREATMENT.
\*\*\*Refer to Chemical Abstracts for complete source list.

**CA SEL., SOLID STATE NMR**
[US/0895-5824]
CA SELECTS: SOLID STATE NMR.
\*\*\*Refer to Chemical Abstracts for complete source list.

**CA SEL., SOLV. EXTRACT.**
[US/0146-4531]
CA SELECTS: SOLVENT EXTRACTION.
\*\*\*Refer to Chemical Abstracts for complete source list.

**CA SEL., SPECTROCHEM. ANAL.**
[US/0885-0232]
CA SELECTS: SPECTROCHEMICAL ANALYSIS.
\*\*\*Refer to Chemical Abstracts for complete source list.

**CA SEL., STEROIDS (BIOCHEM. ASP.)**
[US/0160-9173]
CA SELECTS: STEROIDS (BIOCHEMICAL ASPECTS).
\*\*\*Refer to Chemical Abstracts for complete source list.

**CA SEL., STEROIDS (CHEM. ASP.)**
[US/0160-9181]
CA SELECTS: STEROIDS (CHEMICAL ASPECTS).
\*\*\*Refer to Chemical Abstracts for complete source list.

**CA SEL., STRESS CORROS.-MET.**
[US/1066-1174]
CA SELECTS: STRESS CORROSION - METALS.
\*\*\*Refer to Chemical Abstracts for complete source list.

**CA SEL., STRUCT.-ACT. RELAT.**
[US/0895-5816]
CA SELECTS: STRUCTURE-ACTIVITY RELATIONSHIPS.
\*\*\*Refer to Chemical Abstracts for complete source list.

**CA SEL., SUBSTIT. EFFECTS LIN. FREE ENERGY RELAT.**
[US/0162-7856]
CA SELECTS: SUBSTITUENT EFFECTS & LINEAR FREE ENERGY RELATIONSHIPS.
**(Ceased)**

**CA SEL., SURF. ANAL.**
[US/0195-5152]
CA SELECTS: SURFACE ANALYSIS.
\*\*\*Refer to Chemical Abstracts for complete source list.

**CA SEL., SURF. CHEM. (PHYSICOCHEM. ASP.)**
[US/0146-454X]
CA SELECTS: SURFACE CHEMISTRY (PHYSICOCHEMICAL ASPECTS).
\*\*\*Refer to Chemical Abstracts for complete source list.

**CA SEL., SYNFUELS**
[US/0195-5160]
CA SELECTS: SYNFUELS.
\*\*\*Refer to Chemical Abstracts for complete source list.

**CA SEL., SYNTH. HIGH POLYM.**
[US/0275-7168]
CA SELECTS: SYNTHETIC HIGH POLYMERS.
\*\*\*Refer to Chemical Abstracts for complete source list.

**CA SEL., SYNTH. MACROCY. COMP.**
[US/0195-5179]
CA SELECTS: SYNTHETIC MACROCYCLIC COMPOUNDS.
\*\*\*Refer to Chemical Abstracts for complete source list.

**CA SEL., TECH. CERAM.**
[US/1062-8703]
CA SELECTS: TECHNICAL CERAMICS.
\*\*\*Refer to Chemical Abstracts for complete source list.

**CA SEL., THERM. ANAL.**
[US/0195-5187]
CA SELECTS: THERMAL ANALYSIS.
\*\*\*Refer to Chemical Abstracts for complete source list.

**CA SEL., THERMOCHEM.**
[US/0162-7864]
CA SELECTS: THERMOCHEMISTRY.
\*\*\*Refer to Chemical Abstracts for complete source list.

**CA SEL., TRACE ELEM. ANAL.**
[US/0160-919X]
CA SELECTS: TRACE ELEMENT ANALYSIS.
\*\*\*Refer to Chemical Abstracts for complete source list.

**CA SEL., ULTRAFILTR.**
[US/0195-5195]
CA SELECTS: ULTRAFILTRATION.
\*\*\*Refer to Chemical Abstracts for complete source list.

**CA SEL., ULTRAVIOL. VISI. SPECTRO.**
[US/0195-5209]
CA SELECTS: ULTRAVIOLET & VISIBLE SPECTROSCOPY.
\*\*\*Refer to Chemical Abstracts for complete source list.

**CA SEL., WATER TREAT.**
[US/0740-073X]
CA SELECTS: WATER TREATMENT.
\*\*\*Refer to Chemical Abstracts for complete source list.

**CA SEL., WATER-BASED COAT.**
[US/0749-7369]
CA SELECTS: WATER-BASED COATINGS.
\*\*\*Refer to Chemical Abstracts for complete source list.

**CA SEL., X-RAY ANAL. SPECTRO.**
[US/0162-7872]
CA SELECTS: X-RAY ANALYSIS & SPECTROSCOPY.
\*\*\*Refer to Chemical Abstracts for complete source list.

**CA SEL., ZEOLITES**
[US/0190-4949]
CA SELECTS: ZEOLITES.
\*\*\*Refer to Chemical Abstracts for complete source list.

**CALCIUM CALCIF. TISSUE ABSTR.**
[US/1069-5540]
CALCIUM AND CALCIFIED TISSUE ABSTRACTS.
(*Continues* Calcified Tissue Abstracts.)

**CALIF. PERIOD. INDEX**
[US/0730-1367]
CALIFORNIA PERIODICALS INDEX.
**(Ceased)**

**CALIF. PERIOD. MICROFI.**
[US]
CALIFORNIA PERIODICALS ON MICROFILM.
**(Ceased)**

# INDEXES/ABSTRACTS TABLE

**CAN. BUS. INDEX**
[CN/0227-8669]
CANADIAN BUSINESS INDEX.
(*Merged with* Canadian News Index *and* Canadian Magazine Index (Toronto, Ont.) *to form* Canadian Index (Toronto, Ont.).)

**CAN. BUS. PERIOD. INDEX**
[CN/0318-6717]
CANADIAN BUSINESS PERIODICALS INDEX.
(*Continued by* Canadian Business Index.)

**CAN. CURR. LAW**
[CN/0835-9768]
CANADIAN CURRENT LAW.
(*Split into* Jurisprudence (Scarborough, Ont.); Legislation (Scarborough, Ont.) *and* Canadian Legal Literature.)

**CAN. EDUC. INDEY**
[CN/0008-3453]
CANADIAN EDUCATION INDEX.
(*Absorbed* Directory of Education Studies in Canada.)

**CAN. ENVIRON.**
[CN]
CANADIAN ENVIRONMENT.
(*Continued by* AQUAREF.)

**CAN. ESSAY LIT. INDEX**
[CN/0316-0696]
CANADIAN ESSAY AND LITERATURE INDEX.
(Ceased)

**CAN. INDEX**
[CN/1192-4160]
CANADIAN INDEX (TORONTO).
(*Formed by the union of* Canadian Business Index *and* Canadian News Index Canadian Magazine Index (Toronto, Ont.).)

**CAN. LEGAL LIT.**
[CN/0832-9257]
CANADIAN LEGAL LITERATURE.
(*Continues in part* Canadian Current Law (1988).)

**CAN. LIT. INDEX**
[CN/0838-6021]
CANADIAN LITERATURE INDEX.
(Ceased)

**CAN. MAG. INDEX**
[CN/0829-8777]
CANADIAN MAGAZINE INDEX.
(*Merged with* Canadian Business Index *and* Canadian News Index *to form* Canadian Index (Toronto, Ont.).)

**CAN. NEWS INDEX**
[CN/0225-7459]
CANADIAN NEWS INDEX TORONTO.
(*Merged with* Canadian Business Index *and* Canadian Magazine Index (Toronto, Ont.) *to form* Canadian Index (Toronto, Ont.).)

**CAN. PERIOD. INDEX**
[CN/0008-4719]
CANADIAN PERIODICAL INDEX (1964).
(*Continues* Canadian Index to Periodicals and Documentary Films.)

**CAN., MICROFICHE**
[CN/0225-3216]
CANADIANA. MICROFICHE.
(Ceased)

**CANON LAW ABSTR.**
[UK/0008-5650]
CANON LAW ABSTRACTS.

**CATCH. TRADE NAME INDEX : CATNI**
[UK]
CATCHWORD AND TRADE NAME INDEX : CATNI.
***Refer to Current Technology Index for complete source list.

**CATHOL. PERIOD. INDEX**
[US/0363-6895]
CATHOLIC PERIODICAL INDEX.
(*Continued by* Catholic Periodical and Literature Index.)

**CATHOL. PERIOD. LIT. INDEX**
[US/0008-8285]
CATHOLIC PERIODICAL AND LITERATURE INDEX, THE.
(*Continues* Catholic Periodical Index; *Absorbed* Guide to Catholic Literature.)

**CCLP CONTENTS CURR. LEG. PERIOD.**
[US/0300-7391]
CCLP. CONTENTS OF CURRENT LEGAL PERIODICALS.
(*Continued by* Legal Contents.)

**CERAM. ABSTR.**
[US/0095-9960]
CERAMIC ABSTRACTS.
(*Continues in part* American Ceramic Society. Journal of the American Ceramic Society.)

**CHEM INFORM**
[GW/0931-7597]
CHEM INFORM.
(*Continues* Chemischer Informationsdienst.)

**CHEM. ABSTR.**
[US/0009-2258]
CHEMICAL ABSTRACTS.
(*Supersedes* Review of American Chemical Research.)

**CHEM. BUS. BULL.**
[UK]
CHEMICAL BUSINESS BULLETINS.

**CHEM. BUS. NEWSBASE**
[UK]
CHEMICAL BUSINESS NEWSBASE [ONLINE DATABASE].

**CHEM. BUS. UPDATE**
[UK/0950-6144]
CHEMICAL BUSINESS UPDATE.

**CHEM. ENG. ABSTR.**
[UK/0262-6438]
CHEMICAL ENGINEERING ABSTRACTS.
(*Continued by* Process & Chemical Engineering.)

**CHEM. HAZARDS IND.**
[UK/0265-5721]
CHEMICAL HAZARDS IN INDUSTRY.

**CHEM. IND. NOTES**
[US/0045-639X]
CHEMICAL INDUSTRY NOTES.
(*Supersedes* Plastics Industry Notes.)

**CHEM. INF. DIENST.**
[GW/0009-2975]
CHEMISCHER INFORMATIONSDIENST.
(*Continued by* Chem Inform.)

**CHEM. TITLES**
[US/0009-2711]
CHEMICAL TITLES.

**CHEMORECEPT. ABSTR.**
[US/0300-1261]
CHEMORECEPTION ABSTRACTS.

**CHICAGO PSYCHOANAL. LIT. INDEX**
[US/0009-3661]
CHICAGO PSYCHOANALYTIC LITERATURE INDEX.
(Ceased)

**CHICANO INDEX**
[US/1044-3487]
CHICANO INDEX, THE.
(*Continues* Chicano Periodical index.)

**CHICOREL INDEX MENT. HEALTH BOOK REV.**
[US/0149-4090]
CHICOREL INDEX TO MENTAL HEALTH BOOK REVIEWS.
(*Continues* Mental Health Book Review Index.)

**CHILD DEV. ABSTR. BIBLIOGR.**
[US/0009-3939]
CHILD DEVELOPMENT ABSTRACTS AND BIBLIOGRAPHY.
(*Continues* Selected Child Development Abstracts Currently Published in the Journal of Nervous and Mental Disease, the Wistar Institute Bibliographic Service, American Journal of Diseases of Children, Archives of Neurology and Psychiatry, Psychological Abstracts, Physiological Abstracts, Biological Abstracts, Chemical Abstracts, Endocrinology.)

**CHILD. LIT. ABSTR.**
[UK/0306-2015]
CHILDREN'S LITERATURE ABSTRACTS.

**CHILD. MAG. GUIDE**
[US/0743-9873]
CHILDREN'S MAGAZINE GUIDE.
(*Continues* Subject Index to Children's Magazines.)

**CHRIST. PERIOD. INDEX**
[US/0069-3871]
CHRISTIAN PERIODICAL INDEX.

**CIS ABSTR.**
[US/0302-7651]
CIS ABSTRACTS.
(*Continued by* Safety and Health at Work.)

**CIS INDEX PUBL. U.S. CONGR.**
[US/0007-8514]
CIS INDEX TO PUBLICATIONS OF THE UNITED STATES CONGRESS.

**CIV. STRUCT. ENG. ABSTR.**
[US/1063-7338]
CIVIL AND STRUCTURAL ENGINEERING ABSTRACTS.
(Ceased)

**CLARK'S DIG.-ANNOT.**
[US]
CLARK'S DIGEST-ANNOTATOR.
(*Continued by* New York Law Journal Digest-Annotator.)

**CLASSIFIED ABSTR. ARCH. ALCOHOL LIT.**
[US]
CLASSIFIED ABSTRACT ARCHIVE OF THE ALCOHOL LITERATURE.
(Ceased)

**CLIN. BEHAV. THERAPY REV.**
[US/0162-2269]
CLINICAL BEHAVIOR THERAPY REVIEW.
(Ceased)

**COAL ABSTR.**
[UK/0309-4979]
COAL ABSTRACTS.
(Ceased)

# INDEXES/ABSTRACTS TABLE

**COLL. STUD. PERS. ABSTR.**
[US/0010-1168]
COLLEGE STUDENT PERSONNEL ABSTRACTS.
(*Continued by* Higher Education Abstracts.)

**COMB. CUMUL. INDEX CARDIOL.**
[US/0747-5330]
COMBINED CUMULATIVE INDEX TO CARDIOLOGY.
(**Ceased**)

**COMB. CUMUL. INDEX OB. GYN.**
[US/0884-8092]
COMBINED CUMULATIVE INDEX TO OBSTETRICS AND GYNECOLOGY.

**COMB. CUMUL. INDEX PEDIATR.**
[US/0190-4981]
COMBINED CUMULATIVE INDEX TO PEDIATRICS.

**COMM. FISH. ABSTR.**
[US/0010-2970]
COMMERCIAL FISHERIES ABSTRACTS.
(*Continued by* Marine Fisheries Abstracts.)

**COMMUN. ABSTR.**
[US/0162-2811]
COMMUNICATION ABSTRACTS.

**COMMUNITY DEV. ABSTR.**
[US]
COMMUNITY DEVELOPMENT ABSTRACTS.
(**Ceased**)

**COMMUNITY MENT. HEALTH REV.**
[US/0363-1605]
COMMUNITY MENTAL HEALTH REVIEW.
(*Continued by* Prevention in Human Services.)

**COMPEND. PLUS**
[US/1063-8709]
COMPENDEX PLUS.
\*\*\*Refer to Engineering Index for complete source list.

**COMPUMATH CIT. INDEX**
[US/0730-6199]
COMPUMATH CITATION INDEX : CMCI.

**COMPUT-A-CAL**
[US/0742-5686]
COMPUT-A-CAL.
(**Ceased**)

**COMPUT. ABSTR.**
[UK/0010-4469]
COMPUTER ABSTRACTS.
(*Continues* Computer Bibliography.)

**COMPUT. ASAP**
[US]
COMPUTER ASAP [ONLINE DATABASE].

**COMPUT. BUS.**
[US/0732-8346]
COMPUTER BUSINESS (LOS ANGELES, CALIF.).

**COMPUT. CONTENTS**
[US/0747-0193]
COMPUTER CONTENTS.
(**Ceased**)

**COMPUT. CONTROL ABSTR.**
[UK/0036-8113]
COMPUTER & CONTROL ABSTRACTS.
(*Continues* Control Abstracts.)
\*\*\*Refer to INSPEC [Online Database] for a complete source list.

**COMPUT. DATABASE**
[US]
COMPUTER DATABASE [ONLINE DATABASE].

**COMPUT. IND. UPDATE**
[US/0744-0081]
COMPUTER INDUSTRY UPDATE.

**COMPUT. INF. SYST.**
[US/0010-4507]
COMPUTER & INFORMATION SYSTEMS.
(*Continued by* Computer and Information Systems Abstracts Journal.)

**COMPUT. INF. SYST. ABSTR. J.**
[US/0191-9776]
COMPUTER AND INFORMATION SYSTEMS ABSTRACTS JOURNAL.
(*Continued by* Computer and Information Systems Abstracts.)

**COMPUT. LIT. INDEX**
[US/0270-4846]
COMPUTER LITERATURE INDEX.
(*Continues* Quarterly Bibliography of Computers and Data Processing.)

**COMPUT. REV.**
[US/0010-4884]
COMPUTING REVIEWS.

**COMPUT. REV. INDEX**
[US/1040-5003]
COMPUTER REVIEW INDEX.

**COMPUT. REV., BIBLIOGR. SUBJ. INDEX CURR. COMPUT. LIT.**
[US/0149-1202]
COMPUTING REVIEWS. BIBLIOGRAPHY AND SUBJECT INDEX OF CURRENT COMPUTING LITERATURE.
(*Continued by* ACM Guide to Computing Literature.)

**CONCR. ABSTR.**
[US/0045-8007]
CONCRETE ABSTRACTS.

**CONSTR. INDEX**
[US/0892-2047]
CONSTRUCTION INDEX.

**CONSUM. HEALTH NUTR. INDEX**
[US/0883-1963]
CONSUMER HEALTH & NUTRITION INDEX.

**CONSUM. INDEX PROD. EVAL. INF. SOURCE**
[US/0094-0534]
CONSUMERS INDEX TO PRODUCT EVALUATIONS AND INFORMATION SOURCES.

**CONTENTS CONTEMP. MATH. J.**
[US/0010-759X]
CONTENTS OF CONTEMPORARY MATHEMATICAL JOURNALS.
(*Merged with* New Publications - American Mathematical Society *to form* Contents of Contemporary Mathematical Journals and New Publications.)

**CONTENTS CONTEMP. MATH. J. NEW PUBL.**
[US]
CONTENTS OF CONTEMPORARY MATHEMATICAL JOURNALS AND NEW PUBLICATIONS.
(*Continued by* Current Mathematical Publications.)

**CONTENTS CURR. LEG. PERIOD.**
[US/0300-7391]
CONTENTS OF CURRENT LEGAL PERIODICALS.
(*Continued by* CCLP. Contents of Current Legal Periodicals.)

**CONTENTS PAGES EDUC.**
[UK/0265-9220]
CONTENTS PAGES IN EDUCATION.

**CONTENTS RECENT ECON. J.**
[UK]
CONTENTS OF RECENT ECONOMICS JOURNALS.
(**Ceased**)

**CORROS. ABSTR.**
[US/0010-9339]
CORROSION ABSTRACTS.
(*Supersedes in part* Corrosion.)

**COT. TROP. FIBR. ABSTR. BIBLIOGR.**
[UK]
COTTON AND TROPICAL FIBRES ABSTRACTS BIBLIOGRAPHY.
(*Continues* Cotton and Tropical Fibres Abstracts.)

**CRIM. JUSTICE ABSTR.**
[US/0146-9177]
CRIMINAL JUSTICE ABSTRACTS.
(*Continues* Crime and Delinquency Literature.)

**CRIM. JUSTICE PERIOD. INDEX**
[US/0145-5818]
CRIMINAL JUSTICE PERIODICAL INDEX.

**CRIM. PENOL. POLICE SCI. ABSTR.**
[NE/0928-8759]
CRIMINOLOGY, PENOLOGY AND POLICE SCIENCE ABSTRACTS.
(*Formed by the union of* Criminology & Penology Abstracts *and* Police Science Abstracts.)

**CRIME DELINQ. ABSTR.**
[US/0045-902X]
CRIME AND DELINQUENCY ABSTRACTS.
(*Continues* International Bibliography on Crime and Delinquency.)

**CRIME DELINQ. LIT.**
[US/0037-1327]
CRIME AND DELINQUENCY LITERATURE.
(*Continued by* Criminal Justice Abstracts.)

**CRIMINOL. PENOL. ABSTR.**
[NE/0166-6231]
CRIMINOLOGY & PENOLOGY ABSTRACTS.
(*Merged with* Police Science Abstracts *to form* Criminology, Penology, and Police Science Abstracts.)

**CROP PHYSIOL. ABSTR.**
[UK/0306-7556]
CROP PHYSIOLOGY ABSTRACTS.

**CSA NEURO. ABSTR.**
[US/0141-7711]
CSA NEUROSCIENCES ABSTRACTS.

**CTI PLUS**
[UK]
CTI PLUS [COMPUTER FILE].
\*\*\*Refer to Current Technology Index for complete source list.

**CUMUL. INDEX MED.**
[US/0090-1423]
CUMULATED INDEX MEDICUS.
(*Continues* Quarterly Cumulative Index Medicus.)
\*\*\*Refer to Index Medicus for complete source list.

**CUMUL. INDEX NURS. ALLIED HEALTH LIT.**
[US/0146-5554]
CUMULATIVE INDEX TO NURSING & ALLIED HEALTH LITERATURE.
(*Continued in part by* Nursing and Allied Health Index.)

**CUMUL. INDEX NURS. LIT.**
[US/0011-3018]
CUMULATIVE INDEX TO NURSING LITERATURE.
(*Continued by* Cumulative Index to Nursing & Allied Health Literature.)

# INDEXES/ABSTRACTS TABLE

**CURR. ABSTR. CHEM. INDEX CHEM.**
[US/0161-455X]
CURRENT ABSTRACTS OF CHEMISTRY AND INDEX CHEMICUS.
(*Continued by* Index Chemicus : IC.)

**CURR. ADV. APPL. MICROBIOL. BIOTECHNOL.**
[UK/0964-8712]
CURRENT ADVANCES IN APPLIED MICROBIOLOGY & BIOTECHNOL.
(*Continues* Current Advances in Microbiology.)
\*\*\*Refer to Current Awareness in Biological Sciences : CABS for complete source list.

**CURR. ADV. BIOCHEM.**
[UK/0741-1618]
CURRENT ADVANCES IN BIOCHEMISTRY.
(*Continued by* Current Advances in Protein Biochemistry.)

**CURR. ADV. CANCER RES.**
[UK/0895-9803]
CURRENT ADVANCES IN CANCER RESEARCH.
\*\*\*Refer to Current Awareness in Biological Sciences : CABS for complete source list.

**CURR. ADV. CELL DEV. BIOL.**
[UK/0741-1626]
CURRENT ADVANCES IN CELL AND DEVELOPMENTAL BIOLOGY.
(*Continues in part* Current Awareness in Biological Sciences.)
\*\*\*Refer to Current Awareness in Biological Sciences : CABS for complete source list.

**CURR. ADV. CLIN. CHEM.**
[UK/0885-1980]
CURRENT ADVANCES IN CLINICAL CHEMISTRY.
(*Continues* Current Clinical Chemistry.)
\*\*\*Refer to Current Awareness in Biological Sciences : CABS for complete source list.

**CURR. ADV. ECOL. ENVIRON. SCI.**
[UK/0955-6648]
CURRENT ADVANCES IN ECOLOGICAL & ENVIRONMENTAL SCIENCES.
(*Continues* Current Advances in Ecological Sciences.)
\*\*\*Refer to Current Awareness in Biological Sciences : CABS for complete source list.

**CURR. ADV. ECOL. SCI.**
[UK/0306-3291]
CURRENT ADVANCES IN ECOLOGICAL SCIENCES.
(*Continued by* Current Advances in Ecological & Environmental Sciences.)

**CURR. ADV. ENDOCRIN.**
[UK/0741-1634]
CURRENT ADVANCES IN ENDOCRINOLOGY.
(*Continues in part* Current Awareness in Biological Sciences.)

**CURR. ADV. ENDOCRIN. METAB.**
[UK/0964-8720]
CURRENT ADVANCES IN ENDOCRINOLOGY AND METABOLISM.
(*Continues* Current Advances in Physiology.)
\*\*\*Refer to Current Awareness in Biological Sciences : CABS for complete source list.

**CURR. ADV. GENET. MOL. BIOL.**
[UK/0741-1642]
CURRENT ADVANCES IN GENETICS & MOLECULAR BIOLOGY.
(*Continues* Current Advances in Genetics.)
\*\*\*Refer to Current Awareness in Biological Sciences : CABS for complete source list.

**CURR. ADV. IMMUNOL.**
[UK/0741-1650]
CURRENT ADVANCES IN IMMUNOLOGY.
(*Continued by* Current Advances in Immunology & Infectious Diseases.)

**CURR. ADV. IMMUNOL. INFECT. DISEAS.**
[UK/0964-8747]
CURRENT ADVANCES IN IMMUNOLOGY & INFECTIOUS DISEASES.
(*Continues* Current Advances in Immunology.)
\*\*\*Refer to Current Awareness in Biological Sciences : CABS for complete source list.

**CURR. ADV. MICROBIOL.**
[UK/0741-1669]
CURRENT ADVANCES IN MICROBIOLOGY.
(*Continued by* Current Advances in Applied Microbiology & Biotechnology.)

**CURR. ADV. NEUROSCI.**
[UK/0741-1677]
CURRENT ADVANCES IN NEUROSCIENCE.
(*Continues in part* Current Awareness in Biological Sciences.)
\*\*\*Refer to Current Awareness in Biological Sciences : CABS for complete source list.

**CURR. ADV. PHARMACOL. TOXICOL.**
[UK/0741-1685]
CURRENT ADVANCES IN PHARMACOLOGY & TOXICOLOGY.
(*Continued by* Current Advances in Toxicology.)

**CURR. ADV. PHYSIOL.**
[UK/0741-1693]
CURRENT ADVANCES IN PHYSIOLOGY.
(*Continued by* Current Advances in Endocrinology & Metabolism.)

**CURR. ADV. PLANT SCI.**
[UK/0306-4484]
CURRENT ADVANCES IN PLANT SCIENCE.
\*\*\*Refer to Current Awareness in Biological Sciences : CABS for complete source list.

**CURR. ADV. PROT. BIOCHEM.**
[UK/0965-0504]
CURRENT ADVANCES IN PROTEIN BIOCHEMISTRY.
(*Continues* Current Advances in Biochemistry.)
\*\*\*Refer to Current Awareness in Biological Sciences : CABS for complete source list.

**CURR. ADV. PROT. CHEM.**
[UK/0965-0504]
CURRENT ADVANCES IN PROTEIN CHEMISTRY.
(*Continues* Current Advances in Biochemistry.)
\*\*\*Refer to Current Awareness in Biological Sciences : CABS for complete source list.

**CURR. ADV. TOXICOL.**
[UK/0965-0512]
CURRENT ADVANCES IN TOXICOLOGY.
(*Continues* Current Advances in Pharmacology & Toxicology.)
\*\*\*Refer to Current Awareness in Biological Sciences : CABS for complete source list.

**CURR. AUST. NEW Z. LEG. LIT. INDEX**
[AT]
CURRENT AUSTRALIAN AND NEW ZEALAND LEGAL LITERATURE INDEX.
**(Ceased)**

**CURR. AWARE. BIOL. SCI., CABS**
[UK/0733-4443]
CURRENT AWARENESS IN BIOLOGICAL SCIENCES.
(*Continued in part by* Current Advances in Neuroscience; Current Advances in Cell & Developmental Biology.)

**CURR. AWARENESS LIBR. LIT., CALL**
[US/0091-5270]
CURRENT AWARENESS-LIBRARY LITERATURE : CALL.
**(Ceased)**

**CURR. BIOTECHNOL.**
[UK/0960-5037]
CURRENT BIOTECHNOLOGY.
(*Continues* Current Biotechnology Abstracts.)

**CURR. BIOTECHNOL. ABSTR.**
[UK/0264-3391]
CURRENT BIOTECHNOLOGY ABSTRACTS.
(*Continued by* Current Biotechnology.)

**CURR. BOOK REV. CITATIONS**
[US/0360-1250]
CURRENT BOOK REVIEW CITATIONS.
**(Ceased)**

**CURR. CHEM. REACT.**
[US/0163-6278]
CURRENT CHEMICAL REACTIONS.

**CURR. CONTENTS**
[US/0272-1430]
CURRENT CONTENTS.
(*Continued by* Current Contents of Pharmaceutical Publications.)

**CURR. CONTENTS AFR.**
[UK/0721-5207]
CURRENT CONTENTS AFRICA.
(*Continues* CCA, Current Contents Afrika.)

**CURR. CONTENTS AGRIC. BIOL. ENVIRON. SCI.**
[US/0090-0508]
CURRENT CONTENTS. AGRICULTURE, BIOLOGY, & ENVIRONMENTAL SCIENCES.
(*Continues* Current Contents. Agricultural, Food & Veterinary Sciences.)

**CURR. CONTENTS AGRIC. FOOD VET. SCI.**
[US/0011-3379]
CURRENT CONTENTS : AGRICULTURAL, FOOD AND VETERINARY SCIENCES.
(*Continued by* Current Contents. Agriculture, Biology & Environmental Sciences.)

**CURR. CONTENTS ARTS HUMANIT.**
[US/0163-3155]
CURRENT CONTENTS. ARTS & HUMANITIES.

**CURR. CONTENTS BEHAV. SOC. EDUC. SCI.**
[US/0011-3387]
CURRENT CONTENTS: BEHAVIORAL, SOCIAL & EDUCATIONAL SCIENCES.
(*Continued by* Current Contents. Social & Behavioral Sciences.)

**CURR. CONTENTS BEHAV. SOC. MANAGE. SCI.**
[US/0590-384X]
CURRENT CONTENTS: BEHAVIORAL, SOCIAL & MANAGEMENT SCIENCES.
(*Continued by* Current Contents. Behavioral, Social & Educational Sciences.)

**CURR. CONTENTS CLIN. MED.**
[US/0891-3358]
CURRENT CONTENTS. CLINICAL MEDICINE.
(*Continues* Current Contents. Clinical Practice.)

**CURR. CONTENTS CLIN. PRACT.**
[US/0091-1704]
CURRENT CONTENTS. CLINICAL PRACTICE.
(*Continued by* Current Contents. Clinical Medicine.)

# INDEXES/ABSTRACTS TABLE

**CURR. CONTENTS EDUC.**
[US/0590-3866]
CURRENT CONTENTS. EDUCATION.
(*Absorbed by* Current Contents: Behavioral, Social & Management Sciences.)

**CURR. CONTENTS ENG. TECH. APPL. SCI.**
[US/0095-7917]
CURRENT CONTENTS. ENGINEERING, TECHNOLOGY & APPLIED SCIENCES.
(*Continues* Current Contents: Engineering & Technology.)

**CURR. CONTENTS ENG. TECH.**
[US/0011-3395]
CURRENT CONTENTS: ENGINEERING & TECHNOLOGY.
(*Continued by* Current Contents. Engineering, Technology & Applied Sciences.)

**CURR. CONTENTS LIFE SCI.**
[US/0011-3409]
CURRENT CONTENTS. LIFE SCIENCES.
(*Continues* Current Contents. Your Weekly Guide to the Chemical, Pharmaco-Medical & Life Sciences.)

**CURR. CONTENTS PHARM. PUBL.**
[US/0272-1422]
CURRENT CONTENTS OF PHARMACEUTICAL PUBLICATIONS.
(*Superseded by* Current Contents of Pharmaco-Medical Publications.)

**CURR. CONTENTS PHARM.-MED. PUBL.**
[US/0272-1414]
CURRENT CONTENTS OF PHARMACO-MEDICAL PUBLICATIONS.
(*Continued by* Current Contents: Your Weekly Survey of Chemical, Pharmacological & Clinical Publications.)

**CURR. CONTENTS PHYS. CHEM. EARTH SCI.**
[US/0163-2574]
CURRENT CONTENTS. PHYSICAL, CHEMICAL & EARTH SCIENCES.
(*Continues* Current Contents. Physical and Chemical Sciences.)

**CURR. CONTENTS PHYS. CHEM. SCI.**
[US/0011-3417]
CURRENT CONTENTS. PHYSICAL & CHEMICAL SCIENCES.
(*Continued by* Current Contents. Physical, Chemical & Earth Sciences.)

**CURR. CONTENTS SOC. BEHAV. SCI.**
[US/0092-6361]
CURRENT CONTENTS. SOCIAL & BEHAVIORAL SCIENCES.
(*Continues* Current Contents. Behavioral, Social & Educational Sciences.)

**CURR. CONTENTS YOUR WKLY. GUIDE CHEM. PHARM.-MED. LIFE SCI.**
[US/0272-1503]
CURRENT CONTENTS: YOUR WEEKLY GUIDE OF THE CHEMICAL, PHARMACO-MEDICAL & LIFE SCIENCES.
(*Continued by* Current Contents. Life Sciences.)

**CURR. CONTENTS YOUR WKLY. SURV. CHEM. PHARMACOL. CLIN. PUBL.**
[US/0272-1449]
CURRENT CONTENTS: YOUR WEEKLY SURVEY OF CHEMICAL, PHARMACOLOGICAL & CLINICAL PUBLICATIONS.
(*Continued by* Current Contents. Your Weekly Guide to the Chemical, Pharmaco-Medical & Life Sciences.)

**CURR. DIG. POST SOV. PRESS**
[US/1067-7542]
CURRENT DIGEST OF THE POST-SOVIET PRESS, THE.
(*Continues* Current Digest of the Soviet Press.)

**CURR. GEOGR. PUBL.**
[US/0011-3514]
CURRENT GEOGRAPHICAL PUBLICATIONS.

**CURR. INDEX J. EDUC.**
[US/0011-3565]
CURRENT INDEX TO JOURNALS IN EDUCATION.

**CURR. INDEX STAT.**
[US/0364-1228]
CURRENT INDEX TO STATISTICS.

**CURR. LAW INDEX**
[US/0196-1780]
CURRENT LAW INDEX.

**CURR. LIT. AGING**
[US/0011-3662]
CURRENT LITERATURE ON AGING.
(*Continued by* Abstracts in Social Gerontology.)

**CURR. LIT. BLOOD**
[US/0001-7108]
CURRENT LITERATURE OF BLOOD.
**(Ceased)**

**CURR. LIT. FAM. PLAN.**
[US/0092-6000]
CURRENT LITERATURE IN FAMILY PLANNING.
(*Continues* Acquisitions List - Katharine Dexter McCormick Library.)

**CURR. LIT. SCI. SCI.**
[II]
CURRENT LITERATURE ON SCIENCE OF SCIENCE.
(*Supersedes* Index to Literature on Science of Science.)

**CURR. MATH. PUBL.**
[US/0361-4794]
CURRENT MATHEMATICAL PUBLICATIONS.
(*Continues* Contents of Contemporary Mathematical Journals and New Publications.)
\*\*\*Refer to Mathematical Reviews for complete source list.

**CURR. MIL. POL. LIT.**
[UK/0954-3589]
CURRENT MILITARY & POLITICAL LITERATURE.
(*Continues* Current Military Literature.)

**CURR. PAP. COMPUT. CONTROL**
[UK/0011-3794]
CURRENT PAPERS ON COMPUTERS & CONTROL.
(*Continues* Current Papers on Control.)
\*\*\*Refer to INSPEC [Online Database] for complete source list.

**CURR. PAP. ELECTR. ELECTRON. ENG.**
[UK/0011-3778]
CURRENT PAPERS IN ELECTRICAL & ELECTRONICS ENGINEERING.
(*Continues* Current Papers in Eletrotechnology.)
\*\*\*Refer to INSPEC [Online Database] for complete source list.

**CURR. PAP. PHYS.**
[UK/0011-3786]
CURRENT PAPERS IN PHYSICS.
\*\*\*Refer to INSPEC [Online Database] for complete source list.

**CURR. PHYS. INDEX**
[US/0098-9819]
CURRENT PHYSICS INDEX.

**CURR. PRIMATE REF.**
[US/0590-4102]
CURRENT PRIMATE REFERENCES.
(*Supersedes* Unverified Primate References.)

**CURR. REF. FISH RES.**
[US/0739-540X]
CURRENT REFERENCES IN FISH RESEARCH.

**CURR. TECHNOL. INDEX**
[UK/0260-6593]
CURRENT TECHNOLOGY INDEX : CTI.
(*Continues* British Technology Index.)

**CURR. THOUGHTS TRENDS**
[US/1054-8688]
CURRENT THOUGHTS AND TRENDS.
(*Continues* Current Christian Abstracts.)

**CURR. TITL. DENT.**
[DK/0903-3483]
CURRENT TITLES IN DENTISTRY.

**CURR. TITLES ELECTROCHEM.**
[II/0300-4376]
CURRENT TITLES IN ELECTROCHEMISTRY.
(*Absorbed* Electrochemical News.)

**DAIRY SCI. ABSTR.**
[UK/0011-5681]
DAIRY SCIENCE ABSTRACTS.

**DATA PROCESS. DIG.**
[US/0011-6858]
DATA PROCESSING DIGEST.

**DEEP-SEA OCEANOGR. ABSTR.**
[UK/0011-7471]
DEEP-SEA RESEARCH AND OCEANOGRAPHIC ABSTRACTS.
(*Continued by* Deep-Sea Research.)

**DEEP-SEA RES.**
[UK/0146-6291]
DEEP-SEA RESEARCH.
(*Continued by* Deep-Sea Research. Part A. Oceanographic Research Papers.)

**DEEP-SEA RES., B, OCEANOGR. LIT. REV.**
[UK/0198-0254]
DEEP-SEA RESEARCH. PART B. OCEANOGRAPHIC LITERATURE REVIEW.
(*Continued by* Oceanographic Literature Review.)

**DENT. ABSTR.**
[US/0011-8486]
DENTAL ABSTRACTS (CHICAGO).

**DESALIN. ABSTR.**
[IS/0011-9202]
DESALINATION ABSTRACTS.
(*Continued by* Desalination and Recycling Abstracts.)

**DESALIN. RECYC. ABSTR.**
[IS/0011-9172]
DESALINATION AND RECYCLING ABSTRACTS.
(*Continues* Desalination Abstracts.)

**DEV. DISABIL. ABSTR.**
[US/0191-1600]
DEVELOPMENTAL DISABILITIES ABSTRACTS.
(*Continues* Mental Retardation & Developmental Disabilities Abstracts.)

**DEV. MED. CHILD NEUROL.**
[UK/0012-1622]
DEVELOPMENTAL MEDICINE & CHILD NEUROLOGY.
(*Continued in part by* American Academy For Cerebral Palsy & Developmental Medicine. Meeting. Abstracts.)

# INDEXES/ABSTRACTS TABLE

**DIABETES LIT. INDEX**
[US/0012-1819]
DIABETES LITERATURE INDEX.
(*Supersedes* Diabetes-Related Literature Index.)

**DOANE INF. CENT. INDEX. SYST. SUBJ. INDEX**
[US]
DICIS, DOANE INFORMATION CENTER INDEXING SYSTEM : SUBJECT INDEX.
**(Ceased)**

**DOK. GEFAHRDUNG ALKOHOL, RAUCH., DROGEN, ARZNEIMITTEL**
[GW/0341-8022]
DOKUMENTATION GEFAHRDUNG DURCH ALKOHOL, RAUCHEN, DROGEN, ARZNEIMITTEL.
(*Continues* Dokumentation Drogengefahrdung und Alkoholmissbrauch.)

**DOK. RAUMENTWICKL.**
[GW]
DOKUMENTATION ZUR RAUMENTWICKLUNG.
(*Continues* Documentatio Geographica.)

**DSH ABSTR.**
[US/0011-5150]
DSH ABSTRACTS.
**(Ceased)**

**ECOL. ABSTR.**
[UK/0305-196X]
ECOLOGICAL ABSTRACTS.

**ECOLOGY ABSTR.**
[US/0143-3296]
ECOLOGY ABSTRACTS.
(*Continues* Applied Ecology Abstracts.)

**ECON. LIT. INDEX**
[US]
ECONOMIC LITERATURE INDEX.

**ECONLIT**
[US]
ECONLIT [COMPUTER FILE].
***Refer to Economic Literature Index for a complete source list.

**EDUC. ADM. ABSTR.**
[US/0013-1601]
EDUCATIONAL ADMINISTRATION ABSTRACTS.

**EDUC. INDEX**
[US/0013-1385]
EDUCATION INDEX.

**EDUC. TECHNOL. ABSTR.**
[UK/0266-3368]
EDUCATIONAL TECHNOLOGY ABSTRACTS.

**EI PAGE ONE**
[US]
EI PAGE ONE [COMPUTER FILE].

**ELECT. COMM. ABSTR.**
[US/1069-5303]
ELECTRONICS AND COMMUNICATIONS ABSTRACTS.
(*Continues* Electronics & Communications Abstracts Journal.)

**ELECTR. ELECTRON. ABSTR.**
[UK/0036-8105]
ELECTRICAL & ELECTRONICS ABSTRACTS.
(*Continues* Science Abstracts. Electrical & Electronics Abstracts.)
***Refer to INSPEC [Online Database] for a complete source list.

**ELECTROANAL. ABSTR.**
[SZ/0013-4775]
ELECTROANALYTICAL ABSTRACTS.
(*Continues* Journal of Electroanalytical Chemistry. Abstracts Section.)

**ELECTRON. COMMUN. ABSTR. J.**
[US/0361-3313]
ELECTRONICS AND COMMUNICATIONS ABSTRACTS JOURNAL (RIVERDALE, MD.).
(*Continued by* Electronics and Communications Abstracts.)

**ELECTRON. PUB. ABSTR.**
[UK/0739-2907]
ELECTRONIC PUBLISHING ABSTRACTS.
(*Continued by* World Publishing Monitor.)

**EMBASE LIST J. INDEXED**
[NE]
EMBASE LIST OF JOURNALS INDEXED.
(*Continues* List of Journals Abstracted (1983).)
***Refer to EMBASE [Online Database] for complete source list.

**EMBASE**
[NE]
EMBASE [ONLINE DATABASE].

**EMPLOY. RELAT. ABSTR.**
[US]
EMPLOYMENT RELATIONS ABSTRACTS.
(*Continued by* Work Related Abstracts.)

**ENERGY INDEX**
[US/0094-6281]
ENERGY INDEX.
(*Absorbed by* Energy Information Abstracts Annual.)

**ENERGY INF. ABSTR.**
[US/0147-6521]
ENERGY INFORMATION ABSTRACTS.
**(Ceased)**

**ENERGY INF. ABSTR. ANNU.**
[US/0739-3679]
ENERGY INFORMATION ABSTRACTS ANNUAL.
(*Absorbed* Energy Index.)
***Refer to Energy Information Abstracts for complete source list.

**ENERGY RES. ABSTR.**
[US/0160-3604]
ENERGY RESEARCH ABSTRACTS.
(*Continues* ERDA Energy Research Abstracts.)

**ENG. INDEX**
[US/0739-4624]
ENGINEERING INDEX (1919), THE.
(*Continued by* Engineering Index Annual.)

**ENG. INDEX ANNU.**
[US/0360-8557]
ENGINEERING INDEX ANNUAL.
(*Continues* Engineering Index (New York, N.Y. : 1919).)

**ENG. INDEX BIOENG. ABSTR.**
[US/0736-6213]
ENGINEERING INDEX BIOENGINEERING ABSTRACTS.
(*Continued by* Engineering Index Bioengineering and Biotechnology Abstracts.)

**ENG. INDEX ENERGY ABSTR.**
[US/0093-8408]
ENGINEERING INDEX ENERGY ABSTRACTS.
. ***Refer to Engineering Index Annual for a complete source list.

**ENG. INDEX MON.**
[US/0742-1974]
ENGINEERING INDEX MONTHLY.
(*Continues* Engineering Index Monthly and Author Index.)
***Refer to Engineering Index Annual for a complete source list.

**ENG. INDEX MON. AUTHOR INDEX**
[US/0162-3036]
ENGINEERING INDEX MONTHLY AND AUTHOR INDEX.
(*Continued by* Engineering Index Monthly (1984).)

**ENG. MATER. ABSTR.**
[US/0951-9998]
ENGINEERED MATERIALS ABSTRACTS.

**ENTOMOL. ABSTR.**
[US/0013-8924]
ENTOMOLOGY ABSTRACTS.

**ENVIRO ENERGYLINE PLUS**
[US/1076-6464]
ENVIRO/ENERGYLINE ABSTRACTS PLUS.
(*Continued by* Environment Abstracts.)
***Refer to Environment Abstracts and Energy Infomation Abstracts for complete source list.

**ENVIRON.**
[CN/0709-8847]
ENVIRONNEMENT (MONTREAL).
(*Continues* Journal l'Environnement.)

**ENVIRON. ABSTR.**
[US/0093-3287]
ENVIRONMENT ABSTRACTS.
(*Continues* Environment Information Access; *Absorbed* Acid Rain Abstracts.)

**ENVIRON. ABSTR.**
[US]
ENVIRONMENT ABSTRACTS [COMPUTER FILE].
(*Continues* Enviro/Energyline Abstracts Plus.)
***Refer to Environment Abstracts and Energy Infomation Abstracts for complete source list.

**ENVIRON. ABSTR. ANNU.**
[US/0000-1198]
ENVIRONMENT ABSTRACTS ANNUAL.
(*Absorbed* Environment Index *and* Acid Raid Abstracts Annual.)
***Refer to Environment Abstracts for complete source list.

**ENVIRON. ENG. ABSTR.**
[US/1063-7346]
ENVIRONMENTAL ENGINEERING ABSTRACTS.
**(Ceased)**

**ENVIRON. INDEX**
[US/0090-791X]
ENVIRONMENT INDEX.
(*Absorbed by* Environment Abstracts Annual.)

**ENVIRON. PERIOD. BIBLIOGR.**
[US/0145-3815]
ENVIRONMENTAL PERIODICALS BIBLIOGRAPHY.
(*Continues* Environmental Periodicals.)

**ERGON. ABSTR.**
[UK/0046-2446]
ERGONOMICS ABSTRACTS.
(*Continues* Ergonomics Abstracts (1959).)

**ETHNIC STUD. BIBLIOGR.**
[US/0149-1555]
ETHNIC STUDIES BIBLIOGRAPHY.
**(Ceased)**

# INDEXES/ABSTRACTS TABLE

**ETHNOARTS INDEX**
[US/0893-0120]
ETHNOARTS INDEX.
(*Continues* Tribal Arts Review.)

**EUR. RES.**
[NE/0304-4297]
EUROPEAN RESEARCH.
(*Continued by* Marketing and Research Today.)

**EXCEPT. CHILD EDUC. RESOUR.**
[US/0160-4309]
EXCEPTIONAL CHILD EDUCATION RESOURCES.
(*Continues* Exceptional Child Education Abstracts.)

**EXCEPT. CHILD EDUC. ABSTR.**
[US/0014-4010]
EXCEPTIONAL CHILD EDUCATION ABSTRACTS.
(*Continued by* Exceptional Child Education Resources.)

**EXCEPT. HUM. EXP.**
[US/1053-4768]
EXCEPTIONAL HUMAN EXPERIENCE.
(*Continues* Parapsychology Abstracts International.)

**EXCERPTA MED. LIST J. ABSTR.**
[US]
EXCERPTA MEDICA : LIST OF JOURNALS ABSTRACTED.
(*Continued by* List of Journals Abstracted.)

**EXCERPTA MED., SECT. 06B, ARTHR. RHEUM.**
[NE]
EXCERPTA MEDICA. SECTION 06B. ARTHRITIS AND RHEUMATISM.
**(Ceased)**

**EXCERPTA MEDICA., SECT. 1, ANATOM. ANTHROPOL. EMBRYOL. HISTOL.**
[NE/0014-4053]
EXCERPTA MEDICA. SECTION 1. ANATOMY, ANTHROPOLOGY, EMBRYOLOGY AND HISTOLOGY.
***Refer to EMBASE [Online Database] for complete source list.

**EXCERPTA MED., SECT. 2, PHYSIOL.**
[NE/0367-1089]
EXCERPTA MEDICA. SECTION 2A. PHYSIOLOGY.
(*Continues* Excerpta Medica. Section 2A. Physiology.)
***Refer to EMBASE [Online Database] for complete source list.

**EXCERPTA MED., SECT. 2A, PHYSIOL.**
[NE/0367-1089]
EXCERPTA MEDICA. SECTION 2A. PHYSIOLOGY.
(*Continued by* Excerpta Medica. Section 2. Physiology.)

**EXCERPTA MED., SECT. 3, ENDOCRINOL.**
[NE/0014-407X]
EXCERPTA MEDICA. SECTION 3. ENDOCRINOLOGY.
(*Continues* Excerpta Medica. Section 3. Endocrinology, Experimental and Clinical.)
***Refer to EMBASE [Online Database] for complete source list.

**EXCERPTA MED., SECT. 4, MICROBIOL.**
[NE/0167-4285]
EXCERPTA MEDICA. SECTION 4. MICROBIOLOGY.
(*Continued by* Excerpta Medica. Section 4, Microbiology, Bacteriology, Mycology, Parasitology, and Virology.)

**EXCERPTA MED., SECT. 4, MICROBIOL. BACTERIOL. MYCOL. PARASITOL. VIROL.**
[NE]
EXCERPTA MEDICA. SECTION 4. MICROBIOLOGY, BACTERIOLOGY, MYCOLOGY, PARASITOLOGY, AND VIROLOGY.
(*Continues* Excerpta Medica. Section 4, Microbiology; *Absorbed* Virology.)
***Refer to EMBASE [Online Database] for complete source list.

**EXCERPTA MED., SECT. 5, GEN. PATHOL. PATHOLOGIC. ANAT.**
[NE/0014-4096]
EXCERPTA MEDICA. SECTION 5. GENERAL PATHOLOGY AND PATHOLOGICAL ANATOMY.
***Refer to EMBASE [Online Database] for complete source list.

**EXCERPTA MED., SECT. 6, INTERN. MED.**
[NE/0014-410X]
EXCERPTA MEDICA. SECTION 6. INTERNAL MEDICINE.
***Refer to EMBASE [Online Database] for complete source list.

**EXCERPTA MED., SECT. 7, PEDIATR. PEDIATR. SUR.**
[NE/0373-6512]
EXCERPTA MEDICA. SECTION 7. PEDIATRICS AND PEDIATRIC SURGERY.
(*Continues* Excerpta Medica. Section 7. Pediatrics.)
***Refer to EMBASE [Online Database] for complete source list.

**EXCERPTA MED., SECT. 8, NEUROL. NEUROSURG.**
[NE/0014-4126]
EXCERPTA MEDICA. SECTION 8. NEUROLOGY AND NEUROSURGERY.
(*Continues* Excerpta Medica. Section 8A. Neurology and Neurosurgery.)
***Refer to EMBASE [Online Database] for complete source list.

**EXCERPTA MED., SECT. 8A, NEUROL. NEUROSURG.**
[NE/0014-4126]
EXCERPTA MEDICA. SECTION 8A. NEUROLOGY AND NEUROSURGERY.
(*Continued by* Excerpta Medica. Section 8. Neurology and Neurosurgery.)

**EXCERPTA MED., SECT. 9, SURG.**
[NE/0014-4134]
EXCERPTA MEDICA. SECTION 9. SURGERY.
(*Continued by* Excerpta Medica. Section 28, Urology.)

**EXCERPTA MED., SECT. 9B, ORTHO. TRAUMATOL.**
[NE]
EXCERPTA MEDICA. SECTION 9B. ORTHOPAEDICS AND TRAUMATOLOGY.
(*Continued by* Orthopedic Surgery.)

**EXCERPTA MED., SECT. 10, OBSTETR. GYNECOL.**
[NE/0014-4142]
EXCERPTA MEDICA. SECTION 10. OBSTETRICS AND GYNECOLOGY.
***Refer to EMBASE [Online Database] for complete source list.

**EXCERPTA MED., SECT. 12, OPHTHALMOL.**
[NE/0014-4169]
EXCERPTA MEDICA. SECTION 12. OPHTHALMOLOGY.
***Refer to EMBASE [Online Database] for complete source list.

**EXCERPTA MED., SECT. 13, DERMATOL.**
[NE/0014-4177]
EXCERPTA MEDICA. SECTION 13. DERMATOLOGY AND VENEREOLOGY.
***Refer to EMBASE [Online Database] for complete source list.

**EXCERPTA MED., SECT. 14, RADIOL.**
[NE/0014-4185]
EXCERPTA MEDICA. SECTION 14. RADIOLOGY.
***Refer to EMBASE [Online Database] for complete source list.

**EXCERPTA MED., SECT. 16, CANCER**
[NE/0014-4207]
EXCERPTA MEDICA. SECTION 16. CANCER.
(*Continues* Cancer, Experimental and Clinical.)
***Refer to EMBASE [Online Database] for complete source list.

**EXCERPTA MED., SECT. 17, PUBL. HEALTH SOC. MED EPIDEM.**
[NE]
EXCERPTA MEDICA. SECTION 17. PUBLIC HEALTH, SOCIAL MEDICINE AND EPIDEMIOLOGY.
(*Continues* Excerpta Medica. Section 17, Public Health, Social Medicine and Hygiene.)
***Refer to EMBASE [Online Database] for complete source list.

**EXCERPTA MED., SECT. 17, PUBL. HEALTH SOC. MED. HYG.**
[NE/0014-4215]
EXCERPTA MEDICA. SECTION 17. PUBLIC HEALTH, SOCIAL MEDICINE AND HYGIENE.
(*Continued by* Excerpta Medica. Section 17, Public Health, Social Medicine and Epidemiology.)

**EXCERPTA MED., SECT. 18, CARDIOVASC. DISEAS. CARDIOVASC. SURG.**
[NE/0014-4223]
EXCERPTA MEDICA. SECTION 18. CARDIOVASCULAR DISEASES AND CARDIOVASCULAR SURGERY.
(*Continues* Excerpta Medica. Section 18. Cardiovascular Diseases.)
***Refer to EMBASE [Online Database] for complete source list.

**EXCERPTA MED., SECT. 19, REHABIL. PHYS. MED.**
[NE/0014-4231]
EXCERPTA MEDICA. SECTION 19. REHABILITATION AND PHYSICAL MEDICINE.
(*Continues* Excerpta Medica. Section 19. Rehabilitation.)
***Refer to EMBASE [Online Database] for complete source list.

**EXCERPTA MED., SECT. 20, GERONTOL. GERIATR.**
[NE/0014-424X]
EXCERPTA MEDICA. SECTION 20. GERONTOLOGY AND GERIATRICS.
***Refer to EMBASE [Online Database] for complete source list.

# INDEXES/ABSTRACTS TABLE

**EXCERPTA MED., SECT. 21, DEVELOP. BIOL. TERATOL.**
[NE/0014-4258]
EXCERPTA MEDICA. SECTION 21. DEVELOPMENTAL BIOLOGY AND TERATOLOGY.
(*Continues* Excerpta Medica. Section 21. Human Developmental Biology.)
***Refer to EMBASE [Online Database] for complete source list.

**EXCERPTA MED., SECT. 22, HUMAN GENET.**
[NE/0014-4266]
EXCERPTA MEDICA. SECTION 22. HUMAN GENETICS.
(*Continues* Human Genetics Abstracts.)
***Refer to EMBASE [Online Database] for complete source list.

**EXCERPTA MED., SECT. 23, NUCL. MED.**
[NE/0014-4274]
EXCERPTA MEDICA. SECTION 23. NUCLEAR MEDICINE.
***Refer to EMBASE [Online Database] for complete source list.

**EXCERPTA MED., SECT. 24, ANESTHESIOL.**
[NE/0014-4282]
EXCERPTA MEDICA. SECTION 24. ANESTHESIOLOGY.
***Refer to EMBASE [Online Database] for complete source list.

**EXCERPTA MED., SECT. 25, HEMATOL.**
[NE/0014-4290]
EXCERPTA MEDICA. SECTION 25. HEMATOLOGY.
***Refer to EMBASE [Online Database] for complete source list.

**EXCERPTA MED., SECT. 26, IMMUNOL. SEROL. TRANSPLANT.**
[NE/0014-4304]
EXCERPTA MEDICA. SECTION 26. IMMUNOLOGY, SEROLOGY AND TRANSPLANTATION.
(*Supersedes in part* Excerpta Medica. Section 4, Medical Microbiology, Immunology and Serology.)
***Refer to EMBASE [Online Database] for complete source list.

**EXCERPTA MED., SECT. 27, BIOPHYS. BIOENG. MED. INSTRUMEN.**
[NE/0014-4312]
EXCERPTA MEDICA. SECTION 27. BIOPHYSICS, BIOENGINEERING AND MEDICAL INSTRUMENTATION.
(*Continues* Excerpta Medica. Section 27. Medical Instrumentation.)
***Refer to EMBASE [Online Database] for complete source list.

**EXCERPTA MED., SECT. 28, UROL.**
[NE]
EXCERPTA MEDICA. SECTION 28. UROLOGY.
(*Continued by* Excerpta Medica. Section 28, Urology and Nephrology.)

**EXCERPTA MED., SECT. 28, UROL. NEPHROL.**
[NE/0014-4320]
EXCERPTA MEDICA. SECTION 28. UROLOGY AND NEPHROLOGY.
(*Continues* Excerpta Medica. Section 28, Urology.)
***Refer to EMBASE [Online Database] for complete source list.

**EXCERPTA MED., SECT. 29, CLIN. BIOCHEM.**
[NE/0300-5372]
EXCERPTA MEDICA. SECTION 29. CLINICAL BIOCHEMISTRY.
(*Continues* Excerpta Medica. Section 29. Biochemistry.)
***Refer to EMBASE [Online Database] for complete source list.

**EXCERPTA MED., SECT. 30, CLIN. EXPER. PHARMACOL.**
[NE]
EXCERPTA MEDICA. SECTION 30. CLINICAL AND EXPERIMENTAL PHARMACOLOGY.
(*Formed by the union of* Excerpta Medica. Section 30, Pharmacology *and* Excerpta Medica. Section 130, Clinical Pharmacology.)
***Refer to EMBASE [Online Database] for complete source list.

**EXCERPTA MED., SECT. 30, PHARMACOL.**
[IE/0167-9643]
EXCERPTA MEDICA. SECTION 30. PHARMACOLOGY.
(*Continued in part by* Excerpta Medica. Section 130, Clinical Pharmacology; *Merged into* Excerpta Medica. Section 30. Clinical and Experimental Pharmacology.)
***Refer to EMBASE [Online Database] for complete source list.

**EXCERPTA MED., SECT. 32, PSYCH.**
[NE/0014-4363]
EXCERPTA MEDICA. SECTION 32. PSYCHIATRY.
(*Continues* Excerpta Medica. Section 8B, Psychiatry.)
***Refer to EMBASE [Online Database] for complete source list.

**EXCERPTA MED., SECT. 35, OCCUPAT. HEALTH INDUSTR. MED.**
[NE/0014-4398]
EXCERPTA MEDICA. SECTION 35. OCCUPATIONAL HEALTH AND INDUSTRIAL MEDICINE.
***Refer to EMBASE [Online Database] for complete source list.

**EXCERPTA MED., SECT. 36, HEALTH POLICY ECON. MANAG.**
[NE]
EXCERPTA MEDICA. SECTION 36. HEALTH POLICY, ECONOMICS, AND MANAGEMENT.
(*Continues* Health Economics and Hospital Management.)
***Refer to EMBASE [Online Database] for complete source list.

**EXCERPTA MED., SECT. 37, DRUG LIT. INDEX**
[NE/0167-9171]
EXCERPTA MEDICA. SECTION 37. DRUG LITERATURE INDEX.
(*Continues* Drug Literature Index.)

**EXCERPTA MED., SECT. 38, ADVERSE REACT. TITLES**
[NE/0167-9090]
EXCERPTA MEDICA. SECTION 38. ADVERSE REACTIONS TITLES.
(*Continues* Adverse Reactions Titles.)
***Refer to EMBASE [Online Database] for complete source list.

**EXCERPTA MED., SECT. 40, DRUG DEPEND. ALCOHOL ABUSE ALCOHOL.**
[NE/0304-4041]
EXCERPTA MEDICA. SECTION 40. DRUG DEPENDENCE, ALCOHOL ABUSE, AND ALCOHOLISM.
(*Continues* Excerpta Medica. Section 40, Drug Dependence.)
***Refer to EMBASE [Online Database] for complete source list.

**EXCERPTA MED., SECT. 46, ENVIRON. HEALTH POLLUT. CONT.**
[NE/0300-5194]
EXCERPTA MEDICA. SECTION 46. ENVIRONMENTAL HEALTH AND POLLUTION CONTROL.
(*Continues* Environmental Health and Pollution Control.)
***Refer to EMBASE [Online Database] for complete source list.

**EXCERPTA MED., SECT. 50, EPILEP. ABSTR.**
[NE/0303-8459]
EXCERPTA MEDICA. SECTION 50. EPILEPSY ABSTRACTS.
(*Continues* Epilepsy Abstracts.)
***Refer to EMBASE [Online Database] for complete source list.

**EXCERPTA MED., SECT. 52, TOXICOL.**
[NE/0167-8353]
EXCERPTA MEDICA. SECTION 52. TOXICOLOGY.
(*Continues in part* Excerpta Medica. Section 30, Pharmacology and Toxicology.)
***Refer to EMBASE [Online Database] for complete source list.

**EXCERPTA MED., SECT. 54, AIDS**
[NE/0922-6532]
EXCERPTA MEDICA. SECTION 54. AIDS (ACQUIRED IMMUNE DEFICIENCY SYNDROME).
**(Ceased)**

**EXCERPTA MED., SECT. 65, CANCER IMMUNOL. LIT. INDEX**
[NE/0304-3789]
EXCERPTA MEDICA. SECTION 65. CANCER IMMUNOLOGY. LITERATURE INDEX.
***Refer to EMBASE [Online Database] for complete source list.

**EXCERPTA MED., SECT. 130, CLINIC. PHARMACOL.**
[NE/0921-4496]
EXCERPTA MEDICA. SECTION 130. CLINICAL PHARMACOLOGY.
(*Separated from* Excerpta Medica. Section 30, Pharmacology.)

**EXCERPTA MED., SECT. 151, MYCOBACTER. DISEAS. LEPROSY TUBERCUL. RELATED SUBJ.**
[NE/0168-8944]
EXCERPTA MEDICA. SECTION 151. MYCOBACTERIAL DISEASES--LEPROSY, TUBERCULOSIS, AND RELATED SUBJECTS.
(*Continues* Excerpta Medica. Section 51, Mycobacterial Diseases--Leprosy, Tuberculosis, and Related Subjects.)

**EXPAND. ACAD. INDEX**
[US]
EXPANDED ACADEMIC INDEX [COMPUTER FILE].

# INDEXES/ABSTRACTS TABLE

**F & S INDEX CORP. IND.**
[US/0014-567X]
F & S INDEX OF CORPORATIONS AND INDUSTRIES.
(*Continued by* Predicasts F & S Index United States (Annual Edition).)

**F & S INDEX PLUS TEXT, INT.**
[US/1065-5956]
F & S INDEX PLUS TEXT. INTERNATIONAL.

**F & S INDEX PLUS TEXT, U.S.**
[US/1065-5964]
F & S INDEX PLUS TEXT. UNITED STATES.
\*\*\*Refer to F&S Index Plus Text International for complete source list.

**FABA BEAN ABSTR.**
[UK/0260-8456]
FABA BEAN ABSTRACTS.
**(Ceased)**

**FAMLI, FAM. MED. LIT. INDEX**
[CN/0227-2393]
FAMLI : FAMILY MEDICINE LITERATURE INDEX.
**(Ceased)**

**FARM GARD. INDEX**
[US/0736-9980]
FARM & GARDEN INDEX.
**(Ceased)**

**FDA CLIN. EXP. ABSTR.**
[US/0429-9442]
FDA CLINICAL EXPERIENCE ABSTRACTS.
**(Ceased)**

**FED. PRINT**
[US/0891-2769]
FED IN PRINT.
(*Continued by* Fed in Print: Economics and Banking Topics.)

**FED. PRINT ECON. BANK. TOP.**
[US]
FED IN PRINT: ECONOMICS AND BANKING TOPICS.
(*Continues* Fed in Print: Business and Banking Topics.)

**FED. TAX ARTIC.**
[US]
FEDERAL TAX ARTICLES: INCOME, ESTATE, GIFT, EXCISE, EMPLOYMENT TAXES.

**FERT. ABSTR.**
[US/0015-0290]
FERTILIZER ABSTRACTS.
**(Ceased)**

**FIELD CROP ABSTR.**
[UK/0015-069X]
FIELD CROP ABSTRACTS.

**FILM LIT. INDEX**
[US/0093-6758]
FILM LITERATURE INDEX.

**FISH REV.**
[US/1042-6299]
FISHERIES REVIEW (FORT COLLINS, COLO.).
(*Continues* Sport Fishery Abstracts; **Absorbed** Fish Health News.)

**FLUID ABSTR. CIVIL ENG.**
[UK/0962-7170]
FLUID ABSTRACTS. CIVIL ENGINEERING.
(**Formed by the union of** Civil Engineering Hydraulics Abstracts; Industrial Aerodynamics Abstracts; Offshore Engineering Abstracts **and** World Ports & Harbours Abstracts (Incorporating International Dredging Abstracts).)

**FLUID ABSTR. PROC. ENG.**
[UK/0962-7162]
FLUID ABSTRACTS. PROCESS ENGINEERING.
(**Formed by the union of** Fluid Flow Measurements Abstracts; Fluid Power Abstracts; Fluid Sealing Abstracts; Pipelines Abstracts; Pumps and Other Fluids Machinery Abstracts; Solid-Liquid Flow Abstracts; Computer-Aided Process Control Abstracts **and** Mixing and Separation Technology Abstracts.)

**FLUIDEX**
[UK]
FLUIDEX [ONLINE DATABASE].

**FOOD SCI. TECHNOL. ABSTR.**
[UK/0015-6574]
FOOD SCIENCE AND TECHNOLOGY ABSTRACTS.

**FOODS ADLIBRA**
[US/0146-9304]
FOODS ADLIBRA (1975).

**FOR. ABSTR.**
[UK/0015-7538]
FORESTRY ABSTRACTS.

**FOR. PROD. ABSTR.**
[UK/0140-4784]
FOREST PRODUCTS ABSTRACTS.

**FOREIGN LANG. INDEX**
[US/0048-5810]
FOREIGN LANGUAGE INDEX.
(*Continued by* PAIS Foreign Language Index.)

**FRESH. AQUA. CONTENTS TABLES**
[IT]
FRESHWATER AND AQUACULTURE CONTENTS TABLES. ACTUALITES DES EAUX DOUCES ET DE L'AQUACULTURE.

**FUNK & SCOTT ANNU. INDEX CORP. LIB.**
[US]
FUNK & SCOTT ANNUAL INDEX OF CORPORATIONS & INDUSTRIES, THE.
(**Continued by** F & S Index of Corporations and Industries.)

**FUNK & SCOTT INDEX CORP. IND.**
[US/0532-8705]
FUNK & SCOTT INDEX OF CORPORATIONS AND INDUSTRIES.
(**Continued by** Funk & Scott Annual Index of Corporations & Industries.)

**FUT. SURV.**
[US/0190-3241]
FUTURE SURVEY.
(**Continues** Public Policy Book Forecast.)

**GARDEN LIT.**
[US/1061-3722]
GARDEN LITERATURE.

**GAS ABSTR.**
[US/0016-4844]
GAS ABSTRACTS.

**GASTROENTEROL. ABSTR. CITATIONS**
[US/0016-5093]
GASTROENTEROLOGY: ABSTRACTS & CITATIONS.
**(Ceased)**

**GEN. BUSINESSFILE**
[US]
GENERAL BUSINESSFILE [COMPUTER FILE].

**GEN. PERIOD. INDEX**
[US]
GENERAL PERIODICALS INDEX [COMPUTER FILE].

**GEN. PERIOD. ONDISC**
[US/1064-8380]
GENERAL PERIODICALS ONDISC (RESEARCH 1 ED.).
\*\*\*Refer to Newspaper and Periodical Abstracts for complete source list.

**GEN. SCI. INDEX**
[US/0162-1963]
GENERAL SCIENCE INDEX.

**GEN. SCI. SOURCE**
[US/1073-1954]
GENERAL SCIENCE SOURCE.

**GENEALOGICAL PERIOD. ANNU. INDEX**
[US/0072-0593]
GENEALOGICAL PERIODICAL ANNUAL INDEX.

**GENET. ABSTR.**
[US/0016-674X]
GENETICS ABSTRACTS.

**GEO ABSTR.**
[UK]
GEO ABSTRACTS.
(*Continued by* Geographical Abstracts : Physical Geography; Geographical Abstracts. Human Geography.)

**GEOGR. ABSTR.**
[UK]
GEOGRAPHICAL ABSTRACTS.
(**Continued by** Geo Abstracts.)

**GEOGR. ABSTR. HUMAN GEOGR.**
[UK/0953-9611]
GEOGRAPHICAL ABSTRACTS. HUMAN GEOGRAPHY.
(**Formed by the union of** Geographical Abstracts. C, Economic Geography (1986); Geographical Abstracts. D, Social and Historical Geography **and** Geographical Abstracts. F, Regional and Community Planning.)

**GEOGR. ABSTR. PHYS. GEOGR.**
[UK/0954-0504]
GEOGRAPHICAL ABSTRACTS : PHYSICAL GEOGRAPHY.
(**Formed by the union of** Geographical Abstracts. A, Landforms and the Quaternary; Geographical Abstracts. B, Climatology and Hydrology; Geographical Abstracts. E, Sedimentology **and** Geographical Abstracts. G, Remote Sensing, Photogrammetry, and Cartography.)

**GEOL. ABSTR.**
[UK/0954-0512]
GEOLOGICAL ABSTRACTS.
(**Formed by the union of** Geological Abstracts. Economic Geology; Geological Abstracts. Geophysics & Tectonics Abstracts; Geological Abstracts. Palaeontology & Stratigraphy **and** Geological Abstracts. Sedimentary Geology.)

**GEOL. ABSTR. ECON. GEOL.**
[UK]
GEOLOGICAL ABSTRACTS. ECONOMIC GEOLOGY.
(**Merged with** Geological Abstracts. Geophysics & Tectonics Abstracts; Geological Abstracts. Palaeontology & Stratigraphy **and** Geological Abstracts. Sedimentary Abstracts **to form** Geological Abstracts.)

**GEOL. ABSTR. GEOPHYS. TECTON.**
[UK/0262-0847]
GEOLOGICAL ABSTRACTS. GEOPHYSICS & TECTONICS.
(**Merged with** Geological Abstracts. Economic Geology; Geological Abstracts. Palaeontology & Stratigraphy **and** Geological Abstracts. Sedimentary Geology **to form** Geological Abstracts.)

# INDEXES/ABSTRACTS TABLE

**GEOL. ABSTR. PALAEON. STRAT.**
[UK/0268-8018]
GEOLOGICAL ABSTRACTS. PALAEONTOLOGY & STRATIGRAPHY.
(*Merged with* Geological Abstracts. Economic Geology; Geological Abstracts. Geophysics & Tectonics Abstracts *and* Geological Abstracts. Sedimentary Geology *to form* Geological Abstracts.)

**GEOL. ABSTR. SEDIMEN. GEOL.**
[UK/0268-8026]
GEOLOGICAL ABSTRACTS. SEDIMENTARY GEOLOGY.
(*Merged with* Geological Abstracts. Economic Geology; Geological Abstracts. Geophysics & Tectonics Abstracts *and* Geological Abstracts. Palaeontology & Stratigraphy *to form* Geological Abstracts.)

**GEOPHYS. ABSTR.**
[UK/0309-4332]
GEOPHYSICAL ABSTRACTS.
(*Continued by* Geological Abstracts. Geophysics & Tectonics Abstracts.)

**GEOREF**
[US/0197-7482]
GEOREF (CD-ROM).

**GEOSCI. ABSTR.**
[US/0435-5628]
GEOSCIENCE ABSTRACTS.
(*Supersedes* Geological Abstracts.)

**GEOSCI. DOC.**
[UK/0016-8483]
GEOSCIENCE DOCUMENTATION.

**GEOTECH. ABSTR.**
[US/0016-8491]
GEOTECHNICAL ABSTRACTS.
**(Ceased)**

**GERONTOL. ABSTR.**
[US/0736-4342]
GERONTOLOGICAL ABSTRACTS.
**(Ceased)**

**GRAPH. ARTS ABSTR.**
[US/0017-3282]
GRAPHIC ARTS ABSTRACTS.
(*Continued by* Abstracts (Graphic Arts Technical Foundation).)

**GRAPH. ARTS BULL. INST. PAP. SCI. TECHNOL.**
[US/1064-9638]
GRAPHIC ARTS BULLETIN OF THE INSTITUTE OF PAPER SCIENCE AND TECHNOLOGY.
(*Continues* Graphic Arts Literature Abstracts.)

**GRAPH. ARTS LIT. ABSTR.**
[US/0090-8207]
GRAPHIC ARTS LITERATURE ABSTRACTS.
(*Continued by* Graphic Arts Bulletin of the Institute of Paper Science and Technology.)

**GUIDE PERFORM. ARTS**
[US/0072-873X]
GUIDE TO THE PERFORMING ARTS.
(*Absorbed* Guide to Dance Periodicals.)

**GUIDE REV. BOOKS HISP. AM.**
[US/0716-0348]
GUIDE TO REVIEWS OF BOOKS FROM AND ABOUT HISPANIC AMERICA.
**(Ceased)**

**GUIDE SOC. SCI. RELIG.**
[US/1054-0946]
GUIDE TO SOCIAL SCIENCE AND RELIGION.
(*Continues* Guide to Social Science and Religion in Periodical Literature.)

**GUIDE SOC. SCI. RELIG. PERIOD. LIT.**
[US/0017-5307]
GUIDE TO SOCIAL SCIENCE AND RELIGION IN PERIODICAL LITERATURE.
(*Continued by* Guide to Social Science and Religion.)

**HEALTH DEVICES ALERTS**
[US/0163-0458]
HEALTH DEVICES ALERTS.

**HEALTH INDEX**
[US]
HEALTH INDEX [COMPUTER FILE].

**HEALTH PERIOD. DATABASE**
[US]
HEALTH PERIODICALS DATABASE [ONLINE DATABASE].

**HEALTH PLAN. ADMINIS.**
[US/1065-0679]
HEALTH PLANNING AND ADMINISTRATION.

**HEALTH SAF. SCI. ABSTR.**
[US/0892-9351]
HEALTH AND SAFETY SCIENCE ABSTRACTS.
(*Continues* Safety Science Abstracts Journal.)

**HEALTH SERV. ABSTR.**
[UK/0268-0459]
HEALTH SERVICE ABSTRACTS.
(*Formed by the union of* Current Literature on Health Services; Current Literature on General Medical Practice *and* Hospital Abstracts.)

**HEALTH SOURCE**
[US/1063-9810]
HEALTH SOURCE (PEABODY, MASS.).

**HELMINTHOL. ABSTR.**
[UK/0957-6789]
HELMINTHOLOGICAL ABSTRACTS.
(*Continues* Helminthological Abstracts. Series A, Animal and Human Helminthology.)

**HELMINTHOL. ABSTR. SER. A, ANIM. HUM. HELMINTHOL.**
[UK/0300-8339]
HELMINTHOLOGICAL ABSTRACTS. SERIES A, ANIMAL AND HUMAN HELMINTHOLOGY.
(*Continued by* Helminthological Abstracts.)

**HELMINTHOL. ABSTR. SER. B, PLANT NEMATOLOGY**
[UK/0300-8320]
HELMINTHOLOGICAL ABSTRACTS. SERIES B, PLANT NEMATOLOGY.
(*Continued by* Nematological Abstracts.)

**HERB. ABSTR.**
[UK/0018-0602]
HERBAGE ABSTRACTS.
(*Continued by* Grasslands and Forage Abstracts.)

**HIGH. EDUC. ABSTR.**
[US/0748-4364]
HIGHER EDUCATION ABSTRACTS.
(*Continues* College Student Personnel Abstracts.)

**HIGHW. RES. ABSTR.**
[US/0018-1730]
HIGHWAY RESEARCH ABSTRACTS.
(*Continued by* Transportation Research Abstracts.)

**HIGHW. RES. ABSTR.**
[US/1050-0804]
HIGHWAY RESEARCH ABSTRACTS (1990).
(*Continues* HRIS Abstracts.)

**HILITES**
[US]
HILITES DATABASE [ONLINE DATABASE].

**HISP. AM. PERIOD. INDEX**
[US/0270-8558]
HISPANIC AMERICAN PERIODICALS INDEX (LOS ANGELES, CALIF.).

**HIST. ABSTR.**
[US/0018-2435]
HISTORICAL ABSTRACTS.
(*Split into* Historical Abstracts. Part A, Modern History Abstracts *and* Historical Abstracts. Part B, Twentieth Century Abstracts.)

**HIST. ABSTR., PART A, MOD. HIST. ABSTR.**
[US/0363-2717]
HISTORICAL ABSTRACTS. PART A, MODERN HISTORY ABSTRACTS.
(*Continues in part* Historical Abstracts.)
\*\*\*Refer to America: History and Life for complete source list.

**HIST. ABSTR., PART B, TWENT. CENTURY ABSTR.**
[US/0363-2725]
HISTORICAL ABSTRACTS. PART B, TWENTIETH CENTURY ABSTRACTS.
(*Continues in part* Historical Abstracts.)
\*\*\*Refer to America: History and Life for complete source list.

**HIST. SOURCE**
[US/1063-9799]
HISTORY SOURCE.
(*Merged into* Humanities Source CD-ROM.)

**HORTIC. ABSTR.**
[UK/0018-5280]
HORTICULTURAL ABSTRACTS.

**HOSPIT. ABSTR.**
[UK/0018-5507]
HOSPITAL ABSTRACTS.
(*Merged with* Current Literature on Health Services *and* Current Literature on General Medical Practice *to form* Health Service Abstracts.)

**HOSPIT. HEALTH ADMIN. INDEX**
[US/1077-1719]
HOSPITAL AND HEALTH ADMINISTRATION INDEX.
(*Continues* Hospital Literature Index.)

**HOSPIT. LIT. INDEX**
[US/0018-5736]
HOSPITAL LITERATURE INDEX.
(*Continued by* Hospital and Health Administration Index.)

**HOSPIT. MANAGE. REV.**
[US/0737-903X]
HOSPITAL MANAGEMENT REVIEW.

**HRIS ABSTR.**
[US/0017-6222]
HRIS ABSTRACTS.
(*Continued by* Highway Research Abstracts (Washington, D.C. : 1990).)

**HTFS DIG.**
[UK/0952-2654]
HTFS DIGEST (1987).
(*Continues* Heat Transfer & Fluid Flow Digest; *Absorbed* Fouling Prevention Research Digest.)

# INDEXES/ABSTRACTS TABLE

**HUM. GENOME ABSTR.**
[US/1045-4470]
HUMAN GENOME ABSTRACTS.

**HUM. RESOUR. ABSTR.**
[US/0099-2453]
HUMAN RESOURCES ABSTRACTS.
(*Continues* Poverty and Human Resources Abstracts.)

**HUM. RIGHTS INTERN. REP.**
[US/0275-049X]
HUMAN RIGHTS INTERNET REPORTER.
(*Continues* Human Rights Internet Newsletter.)

**HUMANIT. INDEX**
[US/0095-5981]
HUMANITIES INDEX.
(*Supersedes in part* Social Sciences & Humanities Index.)

**HUMANIT. SOURCE**
[US/1073-1962]
HUMANITIES SOURCE.
(*Absorbed* History Source CD-ROM.)

**HUNGAR. LIBR. INFO. SCI. ABSTR.**
[HU/0046-8304]
HUNGARIAN LIBRARY AND INFORMATION SCIENCE ABSTRACTS.

**IAG, LIT. AUTO.**
[NE/0376-9666]
IAG - LITERATURE ON AUTOMATION.
(*Continued by* New Literature on Automation.)

**IMAGING ABSTR.**
[US/0896-100X]
IMAGING ABSTRACTS.
(*Continues* Photographic Abstracts.)

**IMMUNOL. ABSTR.**
[US/0307-112X]
IMMUNOLOGY ABSTRACTS.

**IND. ARTS INDEX**
[US/0275-1682]
INDUSTRIAL ARTS INDEX.
(*Split into* Business Periodicals Index *and* Applied Science & Technology Index.)

**IND. HYG. DIG.**
[US/0019-8382]
INDUSTRIAL HYGIENE DIGEST.

**INDEX AM. PERIOD. VERSE**
[US/0090-9130]
INDEX OF AMERICAN PERIODICAL VERSE.

**INDEX BLACK PERIOD.**
[US/0899-6253]
INDEX TO BLACK PERIODICALS.
(*Continues* Index to Periodical Articles by and About Blacks.)

**INDEX BOOK REV. HUMANIT.**
[US/0073-5892]
INDEX TO BOOK REVIEWS IN THE HUMANITIES.
**(Ceased)**

**INDEX BOOK REV. RELIG.**
[US/0887-1574]
INDEX TO BOOK REVIEWS IN RELIGION.
(*Continues in part* Religion Index One. Periodicals.)

**INDEX BUS. REPORTS**
[UK]
INDEX TO BUSINESS REPORTS.
(*Continues* Index to Special Reports in UK Newspapers and Selected Periodicals.)

**INDEX CAN. LEG. PERIOD. LIT.**
[CN/0316-8891]
INDEX TO CANADIAN LEGAL PERIODICAL LITERATURE.

**INDEX CHEM.**
[US/0891-6055]
INDEX CHEMICUS (1987).
(*Continues* Current Abstracts of Chemistry and Index Chemicus (Philadelphia, Pa. : 1978).)

**INDEX DENT. LIT.**
[US/0019-3992]
INDEX TO DENTAL LITERATURE.
(*Continues* Index to Dental Literature in the English Language.)

**INDEX ECON. ARTIC. J. COLLECT. VOL.**
[US/0536-647X]
INDEX OF ECONOMIC ARTICLES IN JOURNALS AND COLLECTIVE VOLUMES.
(*Formed by the union of* Index of Economic Journals *and* Index of Economic Articles in Collective Volumes.)
***Refer to Journal of Economic Literature for complete source list.

**INDEX ECON. J.**
[US/0893-9527]
INDEX OF ECONOMIC JOURNALS.
(*Merged with* Index of Economic Articles in Collective Volumes *to form* Index of Economic Articles in Journals and Collective Volumes.)

**INDEX FOREIGN LEG. PER.**
[UK/0019-400X]
INDEX TO FOREIGN LEGAL PERIODICALS.

**INDEX FREE PERIOD.**
[US/0147-5630]
INDEX TO FREE PERIODICALS.
(*Merged into* Matter of Fact.)

**INDEX IEEE PUBL.**
[US/0099-1368]
INDEX TO IEEE PUBLICATIONS.
(*Supersedes* Institute of Electrical and Electronics Engineers. Index to IEEE Periodicals.)

**INDEX INF.**
[US/0073-5930]
INDEX TO HOW TO DO IT INFORMATION.

**INDEX ISLAM.**
[UK]
INDEX ISLAMICUS.
(*Continues* Index Islamicus. Supplement.)

**INDEX ISLAM. LIT.**
[UK]
INDEX OF ISLAMIC LITERATURE.

**INDEX JEW. PERIOD.**
[US/0019-4050]
INDEX TO JEWISH PERIODICALS.

**INDEX LEG. PERIOD.**
[US/0019-4077]
INDEX TO LEGAL PERIODICALS.

**INDEX LIT. AM. INDIAN**
[US/0091-7346]
INDEX TO LITERATURE ON THE AMERICAN INDIAN.
**(Ceased)**

**INDEX MATH. PAP.**
[US/0019-3917]
INDEX OF MATHEMATICAL PAPERS.
**(Ceased)**

**INDEX MED.**
[US/0019-3879]
INDEX MEDICUS (1960).
(*Continues* Current List of Medical Literature; *Absorbed* Monthly Bibliography of Medical Reviews.)

**INDEX NEW Z. PERIOD.**
[NZ]
INDEX TO NEW ZEALAND PERIODICALS.
**(Ceased)**

**INDEX PERIOD. ARTIC. BLACKS**
[US/0161-8245]
INDEX TO PERIODICAL ARTICLES BY AND ABOUT BLACKS.
(*Continued by* Index to Black Periodicals.)

**INDEX PERIOD. ARTIC. NEGROES**
[US/0073-5973]
INDEX TO PERIODICAL ARTICLES BY AND ABOUT NEGROES.
(*Continued by* Index to Periodical Articles by and About Blacks.)

**INDEX PERIOD. ARTIC. RELAT. LAW**
[US/0019-4093]
INDEX TO PERIODICAL ARTICLES RELATED TO LAW.

**INDEX PERIOD. LIT. AGING**
[US/0882-3405]
INDEX TO PERIODICAL LITERATURE ON AGING.
(*Continues* ARECO's Quarterly Index to Periodical Literature on Aging.)

**INDEX PHILIP. PERIOD.**
[PH/0073-599X]
INDEX TO PHILIPPINE PERIODICALS.

**INDEX RELIG. PERIOD. LIT.**
[US/0019-4107]
INDEX TO RELIGIOUS PERIODICAL LITERATURE.
(*Continued by* Religion Index One. Periodicals.)

**INDEX SCI. REV.**
[US/0360-0661]
INDEX TO SCIENTIFIC REVIEWS.

**INDEX U.S. GOV. PERIOD.**
[US/0098-4604]
INDEX TO U.S. GOVERNMENT PERIODICALS.
**(Ceased)**

**INDEX VET.**
[UK/0019-4123]
INDEX VETERINARIUS.

**INDIAN GEOSCI. ABSTR.**
[II]
INDIAN GEOSCIENCE ABSTRACTS.

**INDIAN LIBR. SCI. ABSTR.**
[II/0019-5790]
INDIAN LIBRARY SCIENCE ABSTRACTS.

**INDIAN SCI. ABSTR.**
[II/0019-6339]
INDIAN SCIENCE ABSTRACTS.
(*Continues* Bibliography of Scientific Publications of South and South East Asia.)

**INDICE AGRICOLA AM. LAT. CARIBE**
[CR/0304-0119]
INDICE AGRICOLA DE AMERICA LATINA Y EL CARIBE.
(*Continues* Bibliografia Agricola Latinoamericana y del Caribe.)

**INDICE HIST. ESP.**
[SP/0537-3522]
INDICE HISTORICO ESPANOL.

# INDEXES/ABSTRACTS TABLE

**INDICE MED. ESP.**
[SP]
INDICE MEDICO ESPANOL.

**INF. INSTRUC. TECHNOL.**
[US]
INFORMATION & INSTRUCTION TECHNOLOGIES.

**INF. MANAGE. TECHNOL.**
[UK]
INFORMATION MANAGEMENT & TECHNOLOGY.
(*Continues* Information Media & Technology.)

**INF. SCI. ABSTR.**
[US/0020-0239]
INFORMATION SCIENCE ABSTRACTS.
(*Continues* Documentation Abstracts and Information Science Abstracts.)

**INFO-SOUTH ABSTR.**
[US/1059-5910]
INFO-SOUTH ABSTRACTS.

**INFOBANK**
[IO]
INFOBANK.

**INFOMAT INT. BUS.**
[US]
INFOMAT INTERNATIONAL BUSINESS [ONLINE DATABASE].

**INIS ATOMINDEX**
[AU/0004-7139]
INIS ATOMINDEX.
(*Continued by* INIS Atomindex.)

**INIS ATOMINDEX [MICRO.]**
[AU]
INIS ATOMINDEX [MICROFORM].
(*Continues* INIS Atomindex.)

**INS. PERIOD. INDEX**
[US/0074-073X]
INSURANCE PERIODICALS INDEX.

**INSPEC**
[UK]
INSPEC [ONLINE DATABASE].

**INT. ABSTR. BIOL. SCI.**
[UK/0020-5818]
INTERNATIONAL ABSTRACTS OF BIOLOGICAL SCIENCES.
(*Continued by* Current Awareness in Biological Sciences : CABS.)

**INT. ABSTR. OPER. RES.**
[UK/0020-580X]
INTERNATIONAL ABSTRACTS IN OPERATIONS RESEARCH.

**INT. AEROSP. ABSTR.**
[US/0020-5842]
INTERNATIONAL AEROSPACE ABSTRACTS.
(*Supersedes in part* Aerospace Engineering.)

**INT. BIBLIOGR. BOOK REV.**
[GW]
INTERNATIONAL BIBLIOGRAPHY OF BOOK REVIEWS.
(*Continued by* Internationale Bibliographie der Rezensionen Wissenschaftlicher Literatur (Osnabruck, Germany : 1984).)

**INT. BIBLIOGR. HIST. RELIG.**
[NE/0538-5105]
INTERNATIONAL BIBLIOGRAPHY OF THE HISTORY OF RELIGIONS.
**(Ceased)**

**INT. BIBLIOGR. PERIOD. LIT.**
[GW]
INTERNATIONAL BIBLIOGRAPHY OF PERIODICAL LITERATURE.
(*Continued by* Internationale Bibliographie der Zeitschriftenliteratur aus Allen Gebieten des Wissens (Osnabruck, Germany : 1984).)

**INT. BIBLIOGR. REZEN. WISSEN. LIT.**
[GW/0020-918X]
INTERNATIONALE BIBLIOGRAPHIE DER REZENSIONEN WISSENSCHAFTLICHER LITERATUR.
(*Continues* Internationale Bibliographie der Rezensionen.)

**INT. BIBLIOGR. SOCIOL.**
[UK/0085-2066]
INTERNATIONAL BIBLIOGRAPHY OF SOCIOLOGY.
(*Continues in part* Current Sociology (Paris, France).)

**INT. BIBLIOGR. ZEITSCHRIFTENLITERATUR ALLEN GEBIETEN WISSENS**
[GW]
INTERNATIONALE BIBLIOGRAPHIE DER ZEITSCHRIFTENLITERATUR AUS ALLEN GEBIETEN DES WISSENS.
(*Continues* Internationale Bibliographie der Zeitschriftenliteratur.)

**INT. BUILD. SERV. ABSTR.**
[UK/0140-4237]
INTERNATIONAL BUILDING SERVICES ABSTRACTS.
(*Continues* Thermal Abstracts.)

**INT. CIVIL ENG. ABSTR.**
[IE/0332-4095]
INTERNATIONAL CIVIL ENGINEERING ABSTRACTS.
(*Continues* Institution of Civil Engineers (Great Britain). I.C.E. Abstracts.)

**INT. COPPER INF. BULL.**
[UK/0309-2216]
INTERNATIONAL COPPER INFORMATION BULLETIN.
(*Formed by the union of* Selected Abstracts of Recent Literature on Copper and Copper Alloys *and* Kupfer-Mitteilungen.)

**INT. DEV. ABSTR.**
[UK/0262-0855]
INTERNATIONAL DEVELOPMENT ABSTRACTS.
(*Absorbed* International Development Index.)

**INT. EXEC.**
[US/0020-6652]
INTERNATIONAL EXECUTIVE.

**INT. GUIDE CLASSICAL STUD.**
[US/0020-6849]
INTERNATIONAL GUIDE TO CLASSICAL STUDIES.
(*Continues* ABS International Guide to Classical Studies.)

**INT. INDEX**
[US/0363-0382]
INTERNATIONAL INDEX.
(*Continued by* Social Sciences & Humanities Index.)

**INT. INDEX FILM PERIOD.**
[US/0000-0388]
INTERNATIONAL INDEX TO FILM PERIODICALS.

**INT. INDEX MULTI MEDIA INF.**
[US/0094-6818]
INTERNATIONAL INDEX TO MULTI-MEDIA INFORMATION.
(*Continues* Film Review Index.)

**INT. INDEX PERIOD.**
[US]
INTERNATIONAL INDEX TO PERIODICALS.
(*Continued by* International Index.)

**INT. LABOUR DOC.**
[SZ/0020-7756]
INTERNATIONAL LABOUR DOCUMENTATION.
(*Continues* International Labour Office. Library. International Labour Documentation.)

**INT. NURS. INDEX**
[US/0020-8124]
INTERNATIONAL NURSING INDEX.

**INT. PACKAG. ABSTR.**
[UK/0260-7409]
INTERNATIONAL PACKAGING ABSTRACTS.
(*Continues* PIRA Packaging Abstract.)

**INT. PET. ABSTR.**
[UK/0309-4944]
INTERNATIONAL PETROLEUM ABSTRACTS.
(*Continued by* International Petroleum Abstracts Incorporating Offshore Abstracts.)

**INT. PHARM. ABSTR.**
[US/0020-8264]
INTERNATIONAL PHARMACEUTICAL ABSTRACTS.

**INT. POLIT. SCI. ABSTR.**
[FR/0020-8345]
INTERNATIONAL POLITICAL SCIENCE ABSTRACTS.

**INT. POLYM. SCI. TECH.**
[UK/0307-174X]
INTERNATIONAL POLYMER SCIENCE AND TECHNOLOGY.
(*Formed by the union of* Soviet Plastics *and* Soviet Rubber Technology.)

**INT. RISK CONTROL REV.**
[US/0739-389X]
INTERNATIONAL RISK CONTROL REVIEW.
(*Continued by* International Loss Control Review.)

**INT. ZEITSCHRIFTENSCHAU BIBELWISS. GRENZGEB.**
[GW/0074-9745]
INTERNATIONALE ZEITSCHRIFTENSCHAU FUER BIBELWISSENSCHAFT UND GRENZGEBIETE.

**IOWA DRUG INF. SERV.**
[US]
IOWA DRUG INFORMATION SERVICE.

**IRR. DRAIN. ABSTR.**
[UK/0306-7327]
IRRIGATION AND DRAINAGE ABSTRACTS / COMMONWEALTH AGRICULTURAL BUREAUX.

**ISMEC BULL.**
[US/0306-0039]
ISMEC BULLETIN.
(*Continued by* ISMEC, Mechanical Engineering Abstracts.)

**ISMEC MECH. ENG. ABSTR.**
[US/0896-7113]
ISMEC, MECHANICAL ENGINEERING ABSTRACTS.
(*Continued by* Mechanical Engineering Abstracts.)

**J. ABSTR. ARTIC. INT. EDUC.**
[US/1064-0746]
JOURNAL OF ABSTRACTS (AND ARTICLES) IN INTERNATIONAL EDUCATION.
(*Continues* Journal of Abstracts in International Education.)

# INDEXES/ABSTRACTS TABLE

**J. ABSTR. BR. SHIP RES. ASSOC.**
[UK/0141-903X]
JOURNAL OF ABSTRACTS OF THE BRITISH SHIP RESEARCH ASSOCIATION.
(*Continued by* BMT Abstracts.)

**J. ABSTR. INT. EDUC.**
[US/0094-2383]
JOURNAL OF ABSTRACTS IN INTERNATIONAL EDUCATION.
(*Continued by* Journal of Abstract (and Articles) in International Education.)

**J. CONTENTS QUAN. METHODS**
[UK/0142-5951]
JOURNAL CONTENTS IN QUANTITATIVE METHODS.

**J. ECON. ABSTR.**
[US/0364-281X]
JOURNAL OF ECONOMIC ABSTRACTS.
(*Continued by* Journal of Economic Literature.)

**J. ECON. LIT.**
[US/0022-0515]
JOURNAL OF ECONOMIC LITERATURE.
(*Continues* Journal of Economic Abstracts.)

**J. FERROCEMENT**
[TH/0125-1759]
JOURNAL OF FERROCEMENT.

**J. PLAN. LIT.**
[US/0885-4122]
JOURNAL OF PLANNING LITERATURE.

**J. WATCH**
[US/0896-7210]
JOURNAL WATCH.

**JAZZ INDEX**
[GW/0344-5399]
JAZZ INDEX.
**(Ceased)**

**JMR ABSTR.**
[US/1066-2375]
JMR ABSTRACTS.
(*Absorbed by* MRS Bulletin.)

**JR. HIGH MAG. ABSTR.**
[US/1045-5493]
JUNIOR HIGH MAGAZINE ABSTRACTS.
**(Ceased)**

**KEY ABSTR., ADV. MATER.**
[UK/0950-4753]
KEY ABSTRACTS. ADVANCED MATERIALS.
***Refer to INSPEC [Online Database] for complete source list.

**KEY ABSTR., ANTENNAS PROPAG.**
[UK/0950-4761]
KEY ABSTRACTS. ANTENNAS & PROPAGATION.
(*Continues in part* Key Abstracts. Communication Technology.)
***Refer to INSPEC [Online Database] for complete source list.

**KEY ABSTR., ARTIF. INTELL.**
[UK/0950-477X]
KEY ABSTRACTS. ARTIFICIAL INTELLIGENCE.
(*Continues* Key Abstracts. Systems Theory.)
***Refer to INSPEC [Online Database] for complete source list.

**KEY ABSTR., BUS. AUTOMAT.**
[UK/0954-9153]
KEY ABSTRACTS. BUSINESS AUTOMATION.
(*Continues* IT Focus.)
***Refer to INSPEC [Online Database] for complete source list.

**KEY ABSTR., COMPUT. COMMUN. STOR.**
[UK/0950-4788]
KEY ABSTRACTS. COMPUTER COMMUNICATIONS & STORAGE.
***Refer to INSPEC [Online Database] for complete source list.

**KEY ABSTR., COMPUT. ELECTRON. POWER**
[UK/0950-4796]
KEY ABSTRACTS. COMPUTING IN ELECTRONICS AND POWER.
***Refer to INSPEC [Online Database] for complete source list.

**KEY ABSTR., ELECTR. MEAS. INSTRUM.**
[UK/0307-7977]
KEY ABSTRACTS : ELECTRICAL MEASUREMENTS AND INSTRUMENTATION.
(*Continued by* Key Abstracts. Electronic Instrumentation.)

**KEY ABSTR., ELECTRON. CIRC.**
[UK/0306-557X]
KEY ABSTRACTS. ELECTRONIC CIRCUITS.
***Refer to INSPEC [Online Database] for complete source list.

**KEY ABSTR., ELECTRON. INSTRUM.**
[UK/0950-480X]
KEY ABSTRACTS. ELECTRONIC INSTRUMENTATION.
(*Continues* Key Abstracts. Electrical Measurements and Instrumentation.)
***Refer to INSPEC [Online Database] for complete source list.

**KEY ABSTR., FACTORY AUTOMAT.**
[UK]
KEY ABSTRACTS. FACTORY AUTOMATION.
***Refer to INSPEC [Online Database] for complete source list.

**KEY ABSTR., HIGH-TEMP. SUPERCONDUC.**
[UK/0953-1262]
KEY ABSTRACTS. HIGH-TEMPERATURE SUPERCONDUCTORS.
***Refer to INSPEC [Online Database] for complete source list.

**KEY ABSTR., HUMAN-COMPUT. INTERACT.**
[UK]
KEY ABSTRACTS. HUMAN-COMPUTER INTERACTION.
***Refer to INSPEC [Online Database] for complete source list.

**KEY ABSTR., MACH. VISION**
[UK/0952-7052]
KEY ABSTRACTS. MACHINE VISION.
***Refer to INSPEC [Online Database] for complete source list.

**KEY ABSTR., MEAS. PHYS.**
[UK/0950-4818]
KEY ABSTRACTS. MEASUREMENTS IN PHYSICS.
(*Continues* Key Abstracts. Physical Measurements and Instrumentation.)
***Refer to INSPEC [Online Database] for complete source list.

**KEY ABSTR., MICROELECTRON. PRINT. CIRC.**
[UK/0952-7060]
KEY ABSTRACTS. MICROELECTRONICS AND PRINTED CIRCUITS.
***Refer to INSPEC [Online Database] for complete source list.

**KEY ABSTR., MICROWAVE TECHNOL.**
[UK/0952-7079]
KEY ABSTRACTS. MICROWAVE TECHNOLOGY.
***Refer to INSPEC [Online Database] for complete source list.

**KEY ABSTR., NEUR. NETWORKS**
[UK]
KEY ABSTRACTS. NEURAL NETWORKS.
***Refer to INSPEC [Online Database] for complete source list.

**KEY ABSTR., OPTOELECTRON.**
[UK/0950-4826]
KEY ABSTRACTS. OPTOELECTRONICS.
(*Continues in part* Key Abstracts. Solid State Devices.)
***Refer to INSPEC [Online Database] for complete source list.

**KEY ABSTR., PHYS. MEAS. INSTRUM.**
[UK/0307-7969]
KEY ABSTRACTS : PHYSICAL MEASUREMENTS AND INSTRUMENTATION.
(*Continued by* Key Abstracts. Measurements in Physics.)

**KEY ABSTR., POWER SYST. APPL.**
[UK/0950-4834]
KEY ABSTRACTS. POWER SYSTEMS AND APPLICATIONS.
(*Continues* Key Abstracts. Power Transmission and Distribution.)
***Refer to INSPEC [Online Database] for complete source list.

**KEY ABSTR., ROBOT. CONTROL**
[UK/0950-4842]
KEY ABSTRACTS. ROBOTICS & CONTROL.
(*Continues* Key Abstracts. Industrial Power and Control Systems.)
***Refer to INSPEC [Online Database] for complete source list.

**KEY ABSTR., SEMICOND. DEVICES**
[UK/0950-4850]
KEY ABSTRACTS. SEMICONDUCTOR DEVICES.
(*Continues in part* Key Abstracts. Solid State Devices.)
***Refer to INSPEC [Online Database] for complete source list.

**KEY ABSTR., SOFTW. ENG.**
[UK/0950-4869]
KEY ABSTRACTS. SOFTWARE ENGINEERING.
***Refer to INSPEC [Online Database] for complete source list.

**KEY ABSTR., TELECOM.**
[UK/0950-4877]
KEY ABSTRACTS. TELECOMMUNICATIONS.
(*Continues* Key Abstracts. Communication Technology.)
***Refer to INSPEC [Online Database] for complete source list.

**KEY ECON. SCI.**
[NE]
KEY TO ECONOMIC SCIENCE.
(*Continued by* Key to Economic Science and Managerial Sciences.)

**KEY ECON. SCI. MANAGE. SCI.**
[NE/0165-4748]
KEY TO ECONOMIC SCIENCE AND MANAGERIAL SCIENCES.
(*Continues* Key to Economic Science.)

**KEY WORD INDEX WILDL. RES.**
[SZ]
KEY-WORD-INDEX OF WILDLIFE RESEARCH.

# INDEXES/ABSTRACTS TABLE

**KEY WORD INDEX MED. LIT.**
[US/0145-9716]
KEY-WORD INDEX FOR THE MEDICAL LITERATURE.
(*Continues* Keyword Index in Internal Medicine.)

**KEYWORD INDEX INTERN. MED.**
[US/0097-0220]
KEYWORD INDEX IN INTERNAL MEDICINE.
(*Continued by* Key-Word Index for the Medical Literature.)

**LAB. HAZARDS BULL.**
[UK/0261-2917]
LABORATORY HAZARDS BULLETIN.

**LABORDOC**
[SZ]
LABORDOC [ONLINE DATABASE].

**LANG. LANG. BEHAV. ABSTR.**
[US/0023-8295]
LANGUAGE AND LANGUAGE BEHAVIOR ABSTRACTS : LLBA.
(*Continued by* Linguistics and Language Behavior Abstracts.)

**LANG. TEACH.**
[UK/0261-4448]
LANGUAGE TEACHING.
(*Continues* Language Teaching & Linguistics Abstracts.)

**LANG. TEACH. LINGUIST. ABSTR.**
[UK/0306-6304]
LANGUAGE TEACHING & LINGUISTICS ABSTRACTS.
(*Continued by* Language Teaching.)

**LAW OFFICE INF. SERV.**
[US/0164-5390]
LAW OFFICE INFORMATION SERVICE.
**(Ceased)**

**LEAD ABSTR.**
[US/0023-9569]
LEAD ABSTRACTS.
(*Continued by* Leadscan.)

**LEADSCAN**
[UK/0950-1584]
LEADSCAN.
(*Continues* Lead Abstracts (London, England : 1962).)

**LEFT INDEX**
[US/0733-2998]
LEFT INDEX.

**LEG. CONTENTS, LC**
[US/0279-5787]
LEGAL CONTENTS : LC.
(*Continues* CCLP, Contents of Current Legal Periodicals.)

**LEG. INF. MANAGE. INDEX**
[US/0747-9298]
LEGAL INFORMATION MANAGEMENT INDEX.

**LEG. RESOUR. INDEX**
[US/0272-9296]
LEGAL RESOURCE INDEX.

**LEGALTRAC**
[US]
LEGALTRAC [COMPUTER FILE].

**LEIS. RECREAT. TOUR. ABSTR.**
[UK/0261-1392]
LEISURE, RECREATION, AND TOURISM ABSTRACTS.
(*Continues* Rural Recreation and Tourism Abstracts.)

**LEUKEMIA ABSTR.**
[US/0024-1466]
LEUKEMIA ABSTRACTS.
**(Ceased)**

**LIBR. INF. SCI. ABSTR.**
[UK/0024-2179]
LIBRARY & INFORMATION SCIENCE ABSTRACTS.
(*Supersedes* Library Science Abstracts.)

**LIBR. LIT.**
[US/0024-2373]
LIBRARY LITERATURE.

**LIBR. SCI. ABSTR.**
[UK/0459-262X]
LIBRARY SCIENCE ABSTRACTS.
(*Continued by* Library & Information Science Abstracts.)

**LIFE SCI. COLLECT.**
[US/0891-3889]
PERIODICALS SCANNED AND ABSTRACTED. LIFE SCIENCES COLLECTION.

**LINGUIST. LANG. BEHAV. ABSTR.**
[US/0888-8027]
LINGUISTICS AND LANGUAGE BEHAVIOR ABSTRACTS.
(*Continues* Language and Language Behavior Abstracts; *Absorbed* Reading Abstracts.)

**LISA PLUS**
[UK/0966-8799]
LISA PLUS [COMPUTER FILE].
***Refer to Library and Information Science Abstracts for complete source list.

**LIST J. ABSTR.**
[NE/0923-5582]
LIST OF JOURNALS ABSTRACTED.
(*Continued by* EMBASE List of Journals Indexed.)

**LIT. ABSTR., CATAL. CATAL.**
[US/1065-0539]
LITERATURE ABSTRACTS. CATALYSTS & CATALYSIS.
(*Continued by* Literature Abstracts. Catalysts/Zeolites.)

**LIT. ABSTR., HEALTH ENVIRON.**
[US/1065-0490]
LITERATURE ABSTRACTS. HEALTH & ENVIRONMENT.
(*Continues* API Abstracts. Health & Environment.)

**LIT. ABSTR., PET. REFIN. PETROCHEM.**
[US/1065-0512]
LITERATURE ABSTRACTS. PETROLEUM REFINING & PETROCHEMICALS.
(*Continues* Petroleum Refining and Petrochemicals.)

**LIT. ABSTR., PET. SUBSTIT.**
[US/1065-0504]
LITERATURE ABSTRACTS. PETROLEUM SUBSTITUTES.
(*Continues* Petroleum Substitutes.)

**LIT. ABSTR., TRANSP. STORAGE**
[US/1065-0520]
LITERATURE ABSTRACTS. TRANSPORTATION & STORAGE.
(*Continues* Transportation and Storage.)

**LIT. ANALY. MICROCOMPUT. PUBL.**
[US/0735-9721]
LITERATURE ANALYSIS OF MICROCOMPUTER PUBLICATIONS : LAMP.
**(Ceased)**

**LIT. CRIT. REGIST.**
[US/0733-2165]
LITERARY CRITICISM REGISTER.

**LIT. PAT. ABSTR., OILFIELD CHEM.**
[US/1065-0547]
LITERATURE & PATENT ABSTRACTS. OILFIELD CHEMICALS.
(*Continued in part by* Literature Abstracts. Oilfield Chemicals *and* Patent Abstracts. Oilfield Chemicals.)

**LOMA LIT. MOD. ART**
[US/0090-7235]
LOMA; LITERATURE ON MODERN ART.
(*Continued by* ARTbibliographies Modern.)

**MAG. ARTIC. SUMMAR.**
[US/0895-3376]
MAGAZINE ARTICLE SUMMARIES (PRINT ED.).
(*Continues* Popular Magazine Review.)

**MAG. ARTIC. SUMMAR. CD-ROM**
[US/1041-1151]
MAGAZINE ARTICLE SUMMARIES (CD-ROM ED.).

**MAG. ARTIC. SUMMAR. ELITE**
[US/1060-6769]
MAGAZINE ARTICLE SUMMARIES FULL TEXT ELITE.

**MAG. ARTIC. SUMMAR. SELECT**
[US/1058-0255]
MAGAZINE ARTICLE SUMMARIES FULL TEXT SELECT.

**MAG. ASAP PLUS**
[US]
MAGAZINE ASAP PLUS [COMPUTER FILE].

**MAG. ASAP SEL.**
[US]
MAGAZINE ASAP SELECT [COMPUTER FILE].

**MAG. EXPRESS**
[US]
MAGAZINE EXPRESS [COMPUTER FILE].

**MAG. INDEX**
[US]
MAGAZINE INDEX, THE.

**MAG. INDEX PLUS**
[US]
MAGAZINE INDEX PLUS [COMPUTER FILE].

**MAG. INDEX SEL. MICROFICHE**
[US]
MAGAZINE INDEX SELECT MICROFICHE.

**MAG. INDEX. SEL.**
[US]
MAGAZINE INDEX SELECT [COMPUTER FILE].

**MAG. SEARCH**
[US/1071-2739]
MAGAZINE SEARCH.

**MAGYAR KONYV. SZAK. BIBLIO.**
[HU/0133-736X]
MAGYAR KONYVTARI SZAKIRODALOM BIBLIOGRAFIAJA, A.

**MAIZE ABSTR.**
[UK/0267-2987]
MAIZE ABSTRACTS.
(*Continues* Maize Quality Protein Abstracts.)

**MANAGE. BIBLIOGR. REV.**
[UK/0309-0582]
MANAGEMENT BIBLIOGRAPHIES & REVIEWS.
(*Continues* Business Education.)

**MANAGE. CONTENTS**
[US/0360-2400]
MANAGEMENT CONTENTS.
**(Ceased)**

# INDEXES/ABSTRACTS TABLE

**MANAGE. CONTENTS**
[US]
MANAGEMENT CONTENTS [ONLINE DATABASE].

**MANAGE. INDEX**
[US]
MANAGEMENT INDEX.
**(Ceased)**

**MANAGE. MARKET. ABSTR.**
[UK/0308-2172]
MANAGEMENT AND MARKETING ABSTRACTS.

**MANAGE. RES.**
[US/0099-2224]
MANAGEMENT RESEARCH.
(**Continues** Bi-Monthly Review of Management Research.)

**MANUF. PROCESS ENG. ABSTR.**
[US/1063-7354]
MANUFACTURING AND PROCESS ENGINEERING ABSTRACTS.
**(Ceased)**

**MAR. FISH. ABSTR.**
[US/0735-3782]
MARINE FISHERIES ABSTRACTS.
(**Continues** Commercial Fisheries Abstracts.)

**MAR. SCI. CONTENTS TABLES**
[IT/0025-3308]
MARINE SCIENCE CONTENTS TABLES. ACTUALITES DES SCIENCES DE LA MER. INDICES DE REVISTAS SOBRE CIENCIAS MARINAS.
(**Continues** Current Contents in Marine Sciences; **Continues in part** International Marine Science.)

**MARK. ADVERT. REF. SERV.**
[US]
MARKETING AND ADVERTISING REFERENCE SERVICE [ONLINE DATABASE].

**MARK. DISTR. ABSTR.**
[UK]
MARKETING + DISTRIBUTION ABSTRACTS.
(**Continued by** Anbar Marketing & Distribution Abstracts.)

**MARK. INF. GUIDE**
[US/0025-374X]
MARKETING INFORMATION GUIDE.
(**Continues** Marketing Information Guide (Washington : 1961).)

**MARK. RES. ABSTR.**
[UK/0025-3596]
MARKET RESEARCH ABSTRACTS.

**MARK. RES. TODAY**
[NE/0923-5957]
MARKETING AND RESEARCH TODAY : THE JOURNAL OF THE EUROPEAN SOCIETY FOR OPINION AND MARKETING RESEARCH.
(**Continues** European Research.)

**MASS SPECT. BULL.**
[UK/0025-4738]
MASS SPECTROMETRY BULLETIN.

**MATER. SCI. ENG. ABSTR.**
[US/1063-732X]
MATERIALS SCIENCE AND ENGINEERING ABSTRACTS.
**(Ceased)**

**MATH. REV.**
[US/0025-5629]
MATHEMATICAL REVIEWS.

**MECH. ENG. ABSTR.**
[US/1063-7311]
MECHANICAL ENGINEERING ABSTRACTS.
(**Continues** ISMEC, Mechanical Engineering Abstracts.)

**MED. ABSTR. NEWSL.**
[US/0730-7810]
MEDICAL ABSTRACTS NEWSLETTER.

**MED. ELECTRON. COMMUN. ABSTR.**
[UK/0025-7222]
MEDICAL ELECTRONICS AND COMMUNICATIONS ABSTRACTS.
**(Ceased)**

**MED. PHARM. BIOTECHNOL. ABSTR.**
[US/1063-1178]
MEDICAL & PHARMACEUTICAL BIOTECHNOLOGY ABSTRACTS.
(**Continues in part** Biotechnology Research Abstracts.)
***Refer to Biotechnology Research Abstracts for complete source list.

**MED. REV. DIG.**
[US/0363-7778]
MEDIA REVIEW DIGEST.
(**Continues** Multi Media Reviews Index.)

**MED. SOCIOECON. RES. SOURCE.**
[US/0025-7540]
MEDICAL SOCIOECONOMIC RESEARCH SOURCES.
(**Supersedes** Weekly Bulletin **and** Index to Medical Socioeconomic Literature.)

**MEDOC**
[US/0097-9732]
MEDOC.
**(Ceased)**

**MENT. HEALTH BOOK REV. INDEX**
[US/0076-6445]
MENTAL HEALTH BOOK REVIEW INDEX.
(**Continued by** Chicorel Index to Mental Health Book Reviews.)

**MENT. RETARD. ABSTR.**
[US/0025-9691]
MENTAL RETARDATION ABSTRACTS.
(**Continued by** Mental Retardation & Developmental Disabilities Abstracts.)

**MENT. RETARD. DEV. DISABIL. ABSTR.**
[US/0361-3798]
MENTAL RETARDATION & DEVELOPMENTAL DISABILITIES ABSTRACTS.
(**Continued by** Developmental Disabilities Abstracts.)

**MET. ABSTR.**
[UK/0026-0924]
METALS ABSTRACTS.
(**Formed by the union of** Metallurgical Abstracts **and** Review of Metal Literature.)

**MET. ABSTR. INDEX**
[UK/0026-0932]
METALS ABSTRACTS INDEX.
(**Formed by the union of** Metallurgical Abstracts **and** Review of Metal Literature.)
***Refer to Metals Abstracts for complete source list.

**MET. FINISHING ABSTR.**
[UK/0026-0584]
METAL FINISHING ABSTRACTS.
(**Continued by** Surface Treatment Technology Abstracts.)

**METEOROL. GEOASTROPHYS. ABSTR.**
[US/0026-1130]
METEOROLOGICAL AND GEOASTROPHYSICAL ABSTRACTS.
(**Continues** Meteorological Abstracts and Bibliography.)

**METEOROL. GEOASTROPHYS. ABSTR. [CD-ROM]**
[US/1066-2707]
METEOROLOGICAL & GEOASTROPHYSICAL ABSTRACTS.
***Refer to Meteorological and Geoastrophysical Abstracts for a complete source list.

**METHODIST PERIOD. INDEX**
[US]
METHODIST PERIODICAL INDEX.
(**Continued by** United Methodist Periodical Index.)

**METHODS ORGAN. SYNTH.**
[UK/0265-4245]
METHODS IN ORGANIC SYNTHESIS.

**MICROBIOL. ABSTR. SECT. A**
[US/0300-838X]
MICROBIOLOGY ABSTRACTS. SECTION A : INDUSTRIAL & APPLIED MICROBIOLOGY.
(**Continues** Microbiology Abstracts. Section A. Industrial Microbiology.)

**MICROBIOL. ABSTR. SECT. B**
[US/0300-8398]
MICROBIOLOGY ABSTRACTS. SECTION B, BACTERIOLOGY.
(**Continues** Microbiology Abstracts. Section B: General Microbiology and Bacteriology.)

**MICROBIOL. ABSTR. SECT. C**
[US/0301-2328]
MICROBIOLOGY ABSTRACTS. SECTION C, ALGOLOGY, MYCOLOGY & PROTOZOOLOGY.

**MICROCOMPUT. IND. UPDATE**
[US/0741-6016]
MICROCOMPUTER INDUSTRY UPDATE.

**MICROCOMPUT. INDEX**
[US/8756-7040]
MICROCOMPUTER INDEX.
(**Continued by** Microcomputer Abstracts.)

**MID. SEARCH**
[US/1071-2755]
MIDDLE SEARCH.
(**Continues** Junior Search.)

**MIDDLE EAST ABSTR. INDEX**
[US/0162-766X]
MIDDLE EAST, ABSTRACTS AND INDEX.

**MIDDLE EAST J.**
[US/0026-3141]
MIDDLE EAST JOURNAL, THE.

**MINERAL. ABSTR.**
[UK/0026-4601]
MINERALOGICAL ABSTRACTS.

**MINPROC**
[CN/0828-8461]
MINPROC : MINERAL PROCESSING ABSTRACTS.
**(Ceased)**

**MINTEC, MIN. TECHNOL. ABSTR.**
[CN/0823-0773]
MINTEC : MINING TECHNOLOGY ABSTRACTS.
**(Ceased)**

# INDEXES/ABSTRACTS TABLE

**MISSIONALIA**
[SA/0256-9507]
MISSIONALIA.
(*Formed by the union of* Lux Mundi (Pretoria, South Africa) *and* Missionaria.)

**MLA INT. BIBL. BOOKS ARTIC. MOD. LANG. LIT.**
[US/0024-8215]
MLA INTERNATIONAL BIBLIOGRAPHY OF BOOKS AND ARTICLES ON THE MODERN LANGUAGES AND LITERATURES (COMPLETE ED.).
(*Continues* MLA International Bibliography of Books and Articles on the Modern Languages and Literatures.)

**MOD. MED.**
[US/0026-8070]
MODERN MEDICINE (MINNEAPOLIS).

**MON. PERIOD. INDEX**
[US/0197-6567]
MONTHLY PERIODICAL INDEX.
(*Absorbed by* Access.)

**MOSHER PERIOD. INDEX**
[US/0194-0716]
MOSHER PERIODICAL INDEX.
(*Continues* Subject Index to Select Periodical Literature.)

**MRS BULL.**
[US/0883-7694]
MRS BULLETIN.
(*Absorbed* JMR Abstracts.)

**MULTI MEDIA REV. INDEX**
[US/0091-5858]
MULTI MEDIA REVIEWS INDEX.
(*Continued by* Media Review Digest.)

**MULTICULT. EDUC. ABSTR.**
[UK/0260-9770]
MULTICULTURAL EDUCATION ABSTRACTS.

**MUSCULAR DYSTROPHY ABSTR.**
[US/0027-3732]
MUSCULAR DYSTROPHY ABSTRACTS.
**(Ceased)**

**MUSEUM ABSTR.**
[UK/0267-8594]
MUSEUM ABSTRACTS.

**MUSIC ARTIC. GUIDE**
[US/0027-4240]
MUSIC ARTICLE GUIDE.

**MUSIC INDEX**
[US/0027-4348]
MUSIC INDEX, THE.

**N. Y. LAW J. DIG.-ANNOT.**
[US/0745-4406]
NEW YORK LAW JOURNAL DIGEST-ANNOTATOR.
(*Continues* Clark's Digest-Annotator.)

**NAPRALERT**
[US]
NAPRALERT [ONLINE DATABASE].

**NAT. PROD. UPDATES**
[UK/0950-1711]
NATURAL PRODUCT UPDATES.

**NATL. NEWSP. INDEX**
[US/0273-3676]
NATIONAL NEWSPAPER INDEX.

**NEMATOL. ABSTR.**
[UK/0957-6797]
NEMATOLOGICAL ABSTRACTS.
(*Continues* Helminthological Abstracts. Series B, Plant Nematology.)

**NEW LIT. AUTOMAT.**
[NE]
NEW LITERATURE ON AUTOMATION.
(*Continues* IAG-Literature on Automation.)

**NEW PERIOD. INDEX**
[US/0146-5716]
NEW PERIODICALS INDEX.
**(Ceased)**

**NEW TESTAM. ABSTR.**
[US/0028-6877]
NEW TESTAMENT ABSTRACTS.

**NEWSP. ABSTR.**
[US/1064-993X]
NEWSPAPER ABSTRACTS ONDISC.

**NEWSP. ABSTR.**
[US]
NEWSPAPER ABSTRACTS.

**NEWSP. PERIOD. ABSTR.**
[US]
NEWSPAPER & PERIODICAL ABSTRACTS [ONLINE DATABASE].

**NEXIS**
[US]
NEXIS.

**NONWOVENS ABSTR.**
[UK/9036-1234]
NONWOVENS ABSTRACTS.

**NUCL. ACIDS ABSTR.**
[US/1070-2466]
NUCLEIC ACIDS ABSTRACTS (1994).
(*Continues* Cambridge Scientific Biochemistry Abstracts, Part 2: Nucleic Acids.)

**NUCL. SCI. ABSTR.**
[US/0029-5612]
NUCLEAR SCIENCE ABSTRACTS.
(*Continues* Abstracts of Declassified Documents; Guide to Published Research on Atomic Energy.)

**NUMIS. LIT.**
[US/0029-6031]
NUMISMATIC LITERATURE.

**NURS. ABSTR.**
[US/0195-3354]
NURSING ABSTRACTS.

**NURS. ALLIED HEALTH INDEX**
[US/0744-8732]
NURSING AND ALLIED HEALTH INDEX.
(*Absorbed by* Cumulative Index to Nursing & Allied Health Literature.)

**NURS. DIG.**
[US/0091-4215]
NURSING DIGEST.
(*Continued by* Nursing Dimensions.)

**NURS. DIMEN.**
[US/0164-0232]
NURSING DIMENSIONS.
(*Continues* Nursing Digest.)

**NUTR. ABSTR. REV.**
[UK/0029-6619]
NUTRITION ABSTRACTS AND REVIEWS.
(*Split into* Nutrition Abstracts and Reviews. Series A. Human and Experimental *and* Nutrition Abstracts and Reviews. Series B, Livestock Feeds and Feeding.)

**NUTR. ABSTR. REV., SER. A, HUM. EXP.**
[UK/0309-1295]
NUTRITION ABSTRACTS AND REVIEWS. SERIES A: HUMAN & EXPERIMENTAL.
(*Continues in part* Nutrition Abstracts and Reviews.)

**NUTR. ABSTR. REV., SER. B, LIVE FEEDS AND FEED.**
[UK/0309-135X]
NUTRITION ABSTRACTS AND REVIEWS. SERIES B. LIVESTOCK FEEDS AND FEEDING.
(*Continues in part* Nutrition Abstracts and Reviews.)

**NUTR. RES. NEWSL.**
[US/0736-0037]
NUTRITION RESEARCH NEWSLETTER.

**OCCUP. MENT. HEALTH**
[US/0090-1679]
OCCUPATIONAL MENTAL HEALTH.
(*Supersedes* Occupational Mental Health News.)

**OCCUP. MENT. HEALTH NOTES**
[US/0029-795X]
OCCUPATIONAL MENTAL HEALTH NOTES.
(*Superseded by* Occupational Mental Health.)

**OCEAN. ABSTR.**
[US/0748-1489]
OCEANIC ABSTRACTS (BETHESDA, MD.).
(*Continues* Oceanic Abstracts with Indexes.)

**OCEAN. ABSTR. INDEXES**
[US/0093-6901]
OCEANIC ABSTRACTS WITH INDEXES.
(*Continued by* Oceanic Abstracts (Bethesda, Md.).)

**OCEANIC CIT. J. ABSTR.**
[US]
OCEANIC CITATION JOURNAL WITH ABSTRACTS / OCEANIC RESEARCH INSTITUTE.
(*Merged with* Oceanic Index *to form* Oceanic Abstracts with Indexes.)

**OCEANIC INDEX CIT. J. ABSTR.**
[US]
OCEANIC INDEX CITATION JOURNAL WITH ABSTRACTS.
(*Continued by* Oceanic Citation Journal with Abstracts.)

**OCEANOGR. LIT. REV.**
[UK/0967-0653]
OCEANOGRAPHIC LITERATURE REVIEW.
(*Continues* Deep-Sea Research. Part B, Oceanographic Literature Review.)

**OLD TESTAM. ABSTR.**
[US/0364-8591]
OLD TESTAMENT ABSTRACTS.

**ONCOG. GROWTH FACTORS ABSTR.**
[US/1043-8963]
ONCOGENES AND GROWTH FACTORS ABSTRACTS.

**OPER. PROD. MANAGE. ABSTR.**
[UK]
OPERATIONS & PRODUCTION MANAGEMENT ABSTRACTS.
(*Continues* Management Services and Production Abstracts.)

**OPER. RES. MANAG. SCI.**
[US/0030-3658]
OPERATIONS RESEARCH/MANAGEMENT SCIENCE.

**ORAL RES. ABSTR.**
[US/0030-4212]
ORAL RESEARCH ABSTRACTS.
**(Ceased)**

**ORNAMENTAL HORT.**
[UK/0305-4934]
ORNAMENTAL HORTICULTURE.

# INDEXES/ABSTRACTS TABLE

**ORTHO. SUR.**
[NE/0014-4371]
ORTHOPEDIC SURGERY.
(*Continues* Orthopedics and Traumatology.)
\*\*\*Refer to EMBASE [Online Database] for complete source list.

**OZARK PERIOD. INDEX**
[US/0275-9713]
OZARK PERIODICAL INDEX.

**PAIS BULL.**
[US/0898-2201]
PAIS BULLETIN.
(*Merged with* PAIS Foreign Language Index *to form* PAIS International in Print.)

**PAIS FOREIGN LANG. INDEX**
[US/0896-792X]
PAIS FOREIGN LANGUAGE INDEX.
(*Merged with* PAIS Bulletin *to form* PAIS International in Print.)

**PAIS INT. PRINT**
[US/1051-4015]
PAIS INTERNATIONAL IN PRINT.
(*Formed by the union of* PAIS Bulletin *and* PAIS Foreign Language Index.)

**PAP. BOARD ABSTR.**
[UK/0307-0778]
PAPER & BOARD ABSTRACTS.
(*Continues in part* Kenley Abstracts.)

**PARAPSYCHOL. ABSTR. INT.**
[US/0740-7629]
PARAPSYCHOLOGY ABSTRACTS INTERNATIONAL.
(*Continued by* Exceptional Human Experience.)

**PASTOR. CARE COUNS. ABSTR.**
[US]
PASTORAL CARE AND COUNSELING ABSTRACTS.
(*Continued by* Abstracts of Research in Pastoral Care and Counseling.)

**PEACE RES. ABSTR. J.**
[US/0031-3599]
PEACE RESEARCH ABSTRACTS JOURNAL.

**PERIODEX**
[CN]
PERIODEX: INDEX ANALYTIQUE DE PERIODIQUES DE LANGUE FRANCAISE.
(*Merged with* Radar *to form* Point de Repere.)

**PERSON. MANAGE. ABSTR.**
[US/0031-577X]
PERSONNEL MANAGEMENT ABSTRACTS.

**PERSON. TRAIN. ABSTR.**
[UK/0305-067X]
PERSONNEL + TRAINING ABSTRACTS.
(*Continues in part* Anbar Management Services Abstracts.)

**PESTDOC**
[UK]
PESTDOC.

**PET. ABSTR.**
[US/0031-6423]
PETROLEUM ABSTRACTS (TULSA, OKLA.).

**PET. ENERGY BUS. NEWS INDEX**
[US/0098-7743]
PETROLEUM/ENERGY BUSINESS NEWS INDEX.

**PET. REFIN. PETROCHEM.**
[US]
PETROLEUM REFINING AND PETROCHEMICALS.
(*Continued by* Literature Abstracts. Petroleum Refining & Petrochemicals.)

**PET. SUBS.**
[US]
PETROLEUM SUBSTITUTES.
(*Continued by* Literature Abstracts. Petroleum Substitutes.)

**PHARM. NEWS INDEX**
[US/0362-4439]
PHARMACEUTICAL NEWS INDEX.

**PHILIP. ABSTR.**
[PH/0031-7438]
PHILIPPINE ABSTRACTS.
(*Continued by* Philippine Science & Technology Abstracts.)

**PHILIP. SCI. TECHNOL. ABSTR.**
[PH/0115-8724]
PHILIPPINE SCIENCE & TECHNOLOGY ABSTRACTS.
(*Continues* Philippine Science and Technology Abstract Bibliography.)

**PHILOS. INDEX**
[US/0031-7993]
PHILOSOPHER'S INDEX.

**PHOTOGR. ABSTR.**
[UK/0031-8701]
PHOTOGRAPHIC ABSTRACTS.
(*Continued by* Imaging Abstracts.)

**PHYS. ABSTR.**
[UK/0036-8091]
PHYSICS ABSTRACTS.
(*Continues* Science Abstracts. Physics Abstracts.)
\*\*\*Refer to INSPEC [Online Database] for a complete source list.

**PHYS. BRIEFS**
[UK/0170-7434]
PHYSICS BRIEFS.
(*Supersedes* Physikalische Berichte.)

**PHYS. EDUC. INDEX**
[US/0191-9202]
PHYSICAL EDUCATION INDEX (CAPE GIRARDEAU).

**PHYS. MED. BIOL.**
[UK/0031-9155]
PHYSICS IN MEDICINE & BIOLOGY.

**PHYSIC. MEDLINE PLUS**
[US/1065-6545]
PHYSICIAN'S MEDLINE PLUS.

**PIG NEWS INF.**
[UK/0143-9014]
PIG NEWS AND INFORMATION.

**PINPOINTER**
[AT/0031-9910]
PINPOINTER.
**(Ceased)**

**PLANT BREED. ABSTR.**
[UK/0032-0803]
PLANT BREEDING ABSTRACTS.

**PLANT GROW. REG. ABSTR.**
[UK/0305-9154]
PLANT GROWTH REGULATOR ABSTRACTS.

**POINT REPERE**
[CN/0822-8633]
POINT DE REPERE (MONTREAL).
(*Continued by* Repere.)

**POLICE SCI. ABSTR.**
[NE/0166-6282]
POLICE SCIENCE ABSTRACTS.
(*Merged with* Criminology & Penology Abstracts *to form* Criminology, Penology, and Police Science Abstracts.)

**POLLUT. ABSTR. INDEXES**
[US/0032-3624]
POLLUTION ABSTRACTS WITH INDEXES.

**POLYMER CONTENTS**
[UK/0883-153X]
POLYMER CONTENTS.
(*Continues* PRA Report: Polymer Contents.)

**POP. MAG. REV.**
[US/0740-3763]
POPULAR MAGAZINE REVIEW : PMR.
(*Continued by* Magazine Article Summaries.)

**POP. PERIOD. INDEX**
[US/0092-9727]
POPULAR PERIODICAL INDEX.
**(Ceased)**

**POPUL. INDEX**
[US/0032-4701]
POPULATION INDEX.
(*Continues* Population Literature.)

**POTATO ABSTR.**
[UK/0308-7344]
POTATO ABSTRACTS.

**POULT. ABSTR.**
[UK/0306-1582]
POULTRY ABSTRACTS.

**POVER. HUM. RESOUR.**
[US/0032-5864]
POVERTY & HUMAN RESOURCES.
(*Continued by* Poverty and Human Resources Abstracts.)

**POVER. HUM. RESOUR. ABSTR.**
[US/0094-4394]
POVERTY & HUMAN RESOURCES ABSTRACTS.
(*Continued by* Human Resources Abstracts.)

**PREDICASTS**
[US/0032-7166]
PREDICASTS.
(*Continued by* Predicasts Forecasts.)

**PREDICASTS F & S INDEX INT.**
[US/0270-4528]
PREDICASTS F & S INDEX INTERNATIONAL.
(*Continued by* F&S Index International (Foster City, Calif.).)
\*\*\*Refer to Predicasts Forecasts for a complete source list.

**PREDICASTS F&S INDEX, U. S. ANNU. ED.**
[US/0277-9676]
PREDICASTS F&S INDEX. UNITED STATES ANNUAL EDITION.
(*Continued by* F&S Index United States Annual.)

**PREDICASTS FORECASTS**
[US/0278-0135]
PREDICASTS FORECASTS.
(*Continues* Predicasts.)

**PREV. HUM. SERV.**
[US/0270-3114]
PREVENTION IN HUMAN SERVICES.
(*Continues* Community Mental Health Review.)

**PRIM. SEARCH**
[US/1065-2485]
PRIMARY SEARCH.

**PRINT. ABSTR.**
[UK/0031-109X]
PRINTING ABSTRACTS.

# INDEXES/ABSTRACTS TABLE

**PROC. CHEM. ENG.**
[UK/0960-5045]
PROCESS AND CHEMICAL ENGINEERING.
(*Continues* Chemical Engineering Abstracts.)

**PROMT**
[US/0161-8032]
PROMT / PREDICASTS OVERVIEW OF MARKETS AND TECHNOLOGY.
(*Formed by the union of* Chemical Market Abstracts *and* EMA, Equipment Market Abstracts.)

**PROTOZOOLOG. ABSTR.**
[UK/0309-1287]
PROTOZOOLOGICAL ABSTRACTS.

**PSYCHEDELIC REV.**
[US/0033-2631]
PSYCHEDELIC REVIEW.
**(Ceased)**

**PSYCHOANAL. ABSTR.**
[US/1066-9884]
PSYCHOANALYTIC ABSTRACTS.
(*Continues* Psycscan. Psychoanalysis.)

**PSYCHOL. ABSTR.**
[US/0033-2887]
PSYCHOLOGICAL ABSTRACTS.

**PSYCHOL. READ. GUIDE**
[SZ/0300-0443]
PSYCHOLOGICAL READER'S GUIDE.
**(Ceased)**

**PSYCHOPHARMACOLOGY ABSTR.**
[US/0033-3166]
PSYCHOPHARMACOLOGY ABSTRACTS.
**(Ceased)**

**PSYCINFO**
[US]
PSYCINFO.

**PSYCLIT**
[US]
PSYCLIT DATABASE.

**PSYCSCAN PSYCHOANAL.**
[US/0889-5236]
PSYCSCAN: PSYCHOANALYSIS.
(*Continued by* Psychoanalytic Abstracts.)

**PSYCSCAN: APPL. EXP. ENG. PSYCH.**
[US/0891-0685]
PSYCSCAN: APPLIED EXPERIMENTAL AND ENGINEERING PSYCHOLOGY.

**PSYCSCAN: APPL. PSYCH.**
[US/0271-7506]
PSYCSCAN. APPLIED PSYCHOLOGY.

**PSYCSCAN: CLIN. PSYCH.**
[US/0197-1484]
PSYCSCAN. CLINICAL PSYCHOLOGY.

**PSYCSCAN: DEVELOP. PSYCH.**
[US/0197-1492]
PSYCSCAN. DEVELOPMENTAL PSYCHOLOGY.

**PSYCSCAN: LD/MR**
[US/0730-1928]
PSYCSCAN. LD/MR.

**PSYCSCAN: NEUROPSYCH.**
[US/1058-6660]
PSYCSCAN. NEUROPSYCHOLOGY.

**PTS NEWSL. DATABASE**
[US]
PTS NEWSLETTER DATABASE [ONLINE DATABASE].

**PUBLIC ADM. ABSTR. INDEX ARTIC. INDIA**
[II/0033-331X]
PUBLIC ADMINISTRATION ABSTRACTS AND INDEX OF ARTICLES (INDIA).
**(Ceased)**

**PUBLIC AFF. INF. SERV. BULL.**
[US/0033-3409]
PUBLIC AFFAIRS INFORMATION SERVICE BULLETIN.
(*Continued by* PAIS Bulletin (Annual).)

**Q. BIBLIOGR. COMPUT. DATA PROCESS.**
[US/0048-6132]
QUARTERLY BIBLIOGRAPHY OF COMPUTERS AND DATA PROCESSING.
(*Continued by* Computer Literature Index.)

**Q. INDEX ISLAM.**
[UK/0308-7395]
QUARTERLY INDEX ISLAMICUS.
\*\*\*Refer to Index Islamicus for complete source list.

**QUAL. CONTROL APPL. STAT.**
[US/0033-5207]
QUALITY CONTROL AND APPLIED STATISTICS.

**RAPRA ABSTR.**
[UK/0033-6750]
RAPRA ABSTRACTS.
(*Formed by the union of* Plastics. RAPRA Abstracts *and* Rubbers. RAPRA Abstracts.)

**READ. ABSTR.**
[US/0361-6118]
READING ABSTRACTS.
(*Continued by* Linguistics and Language Behavior Abstracts.)

**READ. GUIDE ABSTR.**
[US/0899-1553]
READERS' GUIDE ABSTRACTS (PRINT EDITION).
(*Continued by* Readers' Guide Abstracts (School and Public Library Ed. : Monthly).)

**READ. GUIDE ABSTR.**
[US/1058-1219]
READERS' GUIDE ABSTRACTS (SCHOOL AND PUBLIC LIBRARY ED.).
(*Continued by* Readers' Guide Abstracts Select Edition.)

**READ. GUIDE ABSTR. SELECT ED.**
[US]
READERS' GUIDE ABSTRACTS SELECT EDITION.
(*Continues* Readers' Guide Abstracts School and Public Library Edition.)

**READ. GUIDE PERIOD. LIT.**
[US/0034-0464]
READERS' GUIDE TO PERIODICAL LITERATURE.
(*Continues* Monthly Cumulative Index to ... Important Periodicals; *Absorbed* Cumulative Index to a Selected List of Periodicals (Annual).)

**RECENT. PUBL. ARTIC.**
[US/0145-5311]
RECENTLY PUBLISHED ARTICLES - AMERICAN HISTORICAL ASSOCIATION.
**(Ceased)**

**RECIPE PERIOD. INDEX**
[US/0743-3484]
RECIPE PERIODICAL INDEX.
**(Ceased)**

**REF. BOOK REV. INDEX**
[US]
REFERENCE BOOK REVIEW INDEX.
**(Ceased)**

**REF. SOURCES**
[US/0163-3546]
REFERENCE SOURCES.
**(Ceased)**

**REF. UPD. BASIC ED.**
[US]
REFERENCE UPDATE BASIC EDITION [COMPUTER FILE].

**REF. UPD. CLINICAL ED.**
[US]
REFERENCE UPDATE CLINICAL EDITION [COMPUTER FILE].

**REF. UPD. DELUXE ED.**
[US]
REFERENCE UPDATE DELUXE EDITION [COMPUTER FILE].

**REFER. Z.**
[RU]
REFERATIVNYI ZHURNAL: ORGANIZATSIIA I BEZOPASNOST DOROZHNOGO DVIZHENIIA.

**REHABIL. LIT.**
[US/0034-3579]
REHABILITATION LITERATURE.
**(Ceased)**

**RELIG. INDEX ONE PERIOD.**
[US/0149-8428]
RELIGION INDEX ONE. PERIODICALS.
(*Continued in part by* Index to Book Reviews in Religion.)

**RELIG. PERIOD. INDEX**
[US/0034-4117]
RELIGIOUS PERIODICALS INDEX.
**(Ceased)**

**RELIG. THEOL. ABSTR.**
[US/0034-4044]
RELIGIOUS AND THEOLOGICAL ABSTRACTS.

**REPERT. ANAL. ARTIC. REV. QUE.**
[CN/0315-2316]
RADAR: REPERTOIRE ANALYTIQUE D'ARTICLES DE REVUES DU QUEBEC.
(*Merged with* Periodex *to form* Point de Repere.)

**RES. ALERT**
[US]
RESEARCH ALERT.
(*Continues* Ascatopics.)

**RES. HIGH. EDUC. ABSTR.**
[UK/0034-5326]
RESEARCH INTO HIGHER EDUCATION ABSTRACTS.

**RESOURCE/ONE ONDISC**
[US]
RESOURCE/ONE ONDISC [COMPUTER FILE].

**REV. AGRIC. ENTOMOL.**
[UK/0957-6762]
REVIEW OF AGRICULTURAL ENTOMOLOGY.
(*Continues* Review of Applied Entomology. Series A, Agricultural.)

**REV. APPL. ENTOMOL. SER. A, AGRIC.**
[UK/0305-0076]
REVIEW OF APPLIED ENTOMOLOGY. SERIES A: AGRICULTURAL.
(*Continued by* Review of Agricultural Entomology.)

# INDEXES/ABSTRACTS TABLE

**REV. APPL. ENTOMOL. SER. B, MED. VET.**
[UK/0305-0084]
REVIEW OF APPLIED ENTOMOLOGY. SERIES B, MEDICAL AND VETERINARY.
(*Continued by* Review of Medical and Veterinary Entomology.)

**REV. MED. VET. ENTOMOL.**
[UK/0957-6770]
REVIEW OF MEDICAL AND VETERINARY ENTOMOLOGY.
(*Continues* Review of Applied Entomology. Series B, Medical and Veterinary.)

**REV. MED. VET. MYCOLOGY**
[UK/0034-6624]
REVIEW OF MEDICAL AND VETERINARY MYCOLOGY.
(*Continues* Annotated Bibliography of Medical Mycology.)

**REV. PLANT PATHOL.**
[UK/0034-6438]
REVIEW OF PLANT PATHOLOGY.
(*Continues* Review of Applied Mycology.)

**RIBA LIB. BULL.**
[UK]
RIBA LIBRARY BULLETIN.
(*Superseded by* Architectural Periodicals Index.)

**RILA, INT. REP. LIT. ART**
[US/0145-5982]
RILA : INTERNATIONAL REPERTORY OF THE LITERATURE OF ART.
(*Merged with* Repertoire d'Art et d'Archeologie **to form** Bibliography of the History of Art.)

**RILM ABSTR.**
[US/0033-6955]
RILM ABSTRACTS.

**RINGDOC**
[UK]
RINGDOC.
***Refer to PESTDOC for complete source list.

**RISK ABSTR.**
[CN/0824-3336]
RISK ABSTRACTS.

**ROBOMATIX REPORT.**
[US/0748-1624]
ROBOMATIX REPORTER.
(*Continued by* Robotics Abstracts.)

**ROBOTICS ABSTR.**
[US/0000-1139]
ROBOTICS ABSTRACTS.
(*Continues* Robomatix Reporter.)

**ROMANT. MOVE.**
[US/0557-2738]
ROMANTIC MOVEMENT.

**ROTHS AM. POETRY ANNUAL**
[US/1040-5461]
ROTH'S AMERICAN POETRY ANNUAL.
(*Formed by the union of* Annual Survey of American Poetry; Annual Index to Poetry in Periodicals **and** American Poetry Index.)

**RURAL EXT. EDUC. TRAIN. ABSTR.**
[UK/0140-4776]
RURAL EXTENSION, EDUCATION AND TRAINING ABSTRACTS.
**(Ceased)**

**RURAL RECREAT. TOUR. ABSTR.**
[UK/0308-0137]
RURAL RECREATION AND TOURISM ABSTRACTS.
(*Continued by* Leisure, Recreation and Tourism Abstracts.)

**SAF. HEALTH WORK**
[SZ/1010-7053]
SAFETY AND HEALTH AT WORK : ILO-CIS BULLETIN.
(*Continues* International Occupational Safety and Health Information Centre. CIS Abstracts.)

**SAF. SCI. ABSTR.**
[US/0092-542X]
SAFETY SCIENCE ABSTRACTS.
(*Continued by* Safety Science Abstracts Journal.)

**SAF. SCI. ABSTR. J.**
[US/0160-1342]
SAFETY SCIENCE ABSTRACTS JOURNAL.
(*Continued by* Health and Safety Science Abstracts.)

**SAGE FAM. STUD. ABSTR.**
[US/0164-0283]
SAGE FAMILY STUDIES ABSTRACTS.

**SAGE PUBLIC ADM. ABSTR.**
[US/0094-6958]
SAGE PUBLIC ADMINISTRATION ABSTRACTS.

**SAGE RACE RELAT. ABSTR.**
[UK/0307-9201]
SAGE RACE RELATIONS ABSTRACTS.
(*Continues* Race Relations Abstracts.)

**SAGE URBAN STUD. ABSTR**
[US/0090-5747]
SAGE URBAN STUDIES ABSTRACTS.

**SCHOOL ORGAN. MANAGE. ABSTR.**
[UK/0261-2755]
SCHOOL ORGANISATION & MANAGEMENT ABSTRACTS.

**SCI. ABSTR. PHYS. ABSTR.**
[UK]
SCIENCE ABSTRACTS. PHYSICS ABSTRACTS.
(*Continued by* Science Abstracts. Series A, Physics Abstracts.)

**SCI. ABSTR. SECT. A. PHYS. ABSTR.**
[UK]
SCIENCE ABSTRACTS. SECTION A, PHYSICS ABSTRACTS / EDITED AND ISSUED MONTHLY BY THE INSTITUTION OF ELECTRICAL ENGINEERS, IN ASSOCIATION WITH THE PHYSICAL SOCIETY, THE AMERICAN PHYSICAL SOCIETY, THE AMERICAN INSTITUTE OF ELECTRICAL ENGINEERS.
(*Continued by* Science Abstracts. Physics Abstracts.)

**SCI. ABSTR. SER. A, PHYS. ABSTR.**
[UK]
SCIENCE ABSTRACTS. SERIES A, PHYSICS ABSTRACTS.
(*Continued by* Physics Abstracts.)

**SCI. CIT. INDEX**
[US/0036-827X]
SCIENCE CITATION INDEX (PRINT ED.).

**SCI. CIT. INDEX ABSTR.**
[US/1061-1290]
SCIENCE CITATION INDEX WITH ABSTRACTS.
***Refer to Science Citation Index (US/0036-827X) for a complete source list.

**SCI. CIT. INDEX [CD-ROM]**
[US/1044-6052]
SCIENCE CITATION INDEX (COMPACT DISC ED.).
***Refer to Science Citation Index (US/0036-827X) for a complete source list.

**SCI. CIT. INDEX, ABR. ED.**
[US/0737-2108]
SCIENCE CITATION INDEX. ABRIDGED EDITION.
**(Ceased)**

**SCI. FICT. FANTASY BOOK REV. INDEX**
[US/1046-1922]
SCIENCE FICTION AND FANTASY BOOK REVIEW INDEX.
(*Continues* Science Fiction Book Review Index.)

**SCI. RES. ABSTR. J.**
[US/0731-0943]
SCIENCE RESEARCH ABSTRACTS JOURNAL.
(*Absorbed by* Solid State Abstracts Journal.)

**SCI. RES. ABSTR. J. PART A.**
[US/0194-7486]
SCIENCE RESEARCH ABSTRACTS JOURNAL. PART A: SUPERCONDUCTIVITY, MAGNETOHYDRODYNAMICS AND PLASMAS, THEORETICAL PHYSICS.
(*Merged with* Science Research Abstracts Journal. Part B: Laser and Electro-Opticreviews, Quantum Electronics and Unconventional Energy Sources **to form** Science Research Abstracts Journal.)

**SCISEARCH**
[US]
SCISEARCH [ONLINE DATABASE].

**SEA ABSTR.**
[PH]
SEA ABSTRACTS.

**SEED ABSTR.**
[UK/0141-0180]
SEED ABSTRACTS.

**SEL. PHILIP. PERIOD. INDEX**
[PH/0037-1335]
SELECTED PHILIPPINE PERIODICAL INDEX.
**(Ceased)**

**SEL. WATER RESOUR. ABSTR.**
[US/0037-136X]
SELECTED WATER RESOURCES ABSTRACTS (WASHINGTON, D.C.).
**(Ceased)**

**SELEC. COOP. INDEX MANAGE. PERIOD.**
[FI/0782-2979]
SCIMP SELECTIVE CO-OPERATIVE INDEX OF MANAGEMENT PERIODICALS.
**(Ceased)**

**SEVENTH-DAY ADVENTIST PERIOD. INDEX**
[US/0270-3599]
SEVENTH-DAY ADVENTIST PERIODICAL INDEX.

**SHIP ABSTR.**
[NO/0346-1025]
SHIP ABSTRACTS.
(*Absorbed by* Journal of Abstracts of the British Ship Research Association.)

**SHOCK VIBR. DIG.**
[US/0583-1024]
SHOCK AND VIBRATION DIGEST, THE.

**SMALL ANIM. ABSTR. BIBLIOGR.**
[UK]
SMALL ANIMAL ABSTRACTS BIBLIOGRAPHY.
(*Continues* Small Animal Abstracts.)

**SOC. PLANN. POLICY DEV. ABSTR.**
[US/1042-8380]
SOCIAL PLANNING, POLICY & DEVELOPMENT ABSTRACTS.
(*Continues* Social Welfare, Social Planning/Policy & Social Development.)

# INDEXES/ABSTRACTS TABLE

**SOC. RES. METHODOL. ABSTR.**
[NE/0167-8477]
SOCIAL RESEARCH METHODOLOGY ABSTRACTS.
(*Continues in part* SRM Abstract Bulletin.)

**SOC. SCI. CIT. INDEX**
[US/0091-3707]
SOCIAL SCIENCES CITATION INDEX (PRINT ED.).

**SOC. SCI. HUMANIT. INDEX**
[US/0037-7899]
SOCIAL SCIENCES & HUMANITIES INDEX.
(*Split into* Social Sciences Index *and* Humanities Index.)

**SOC. SCI. INDEX**
[US/0094-4920]
SOCIAL SCIENCES INDEX.
(*Supersedes in part* Social Sciences & Humanities Index.)

**SOC. SCI. INDEX FULLTEXT**
[US]
SOCIAL SCIENCES INDEX / FULLTEXT.

**SOC. SCI. SOURCE**
[US/1063-9802]
SOCIAL SCIENCE SOURCE.

**SOC. WELF. SOC. PLAN./POLICY SOC. DEV.**
[US/0195-7988]
SOCIAL WELFARE, SOCIAL PLANNING/POLICY & SOCIAL DEVELOPMENT.
(*Continued by* Social Planning, Policy & Development Abstracts.)

**SOC. WORK ABSTR.**
[US/1070-5317]
SOCIAL WORK ABSTRACTS.
(*Continues in part* Social Work Research and Abstracts.)

**SOC. WORK RES.**
[US/1070-5309]
SOCIAL WORK RESEARCH.
(*Continues in part* Social Work Research and Abstracts.)
***Refer to Social Work Abstracts for a complete source list.

**SOC. WORK RES. ABSTR.**
[US/0148-0847]
SOCIAL WORK RESEARCH & ABSTRACTS.
(*Split into* Social Work Abstracts *and* Social Work Research.)

**SOCIOL. ABSTR.**
[US/0038-0202]
SOCIOLOGICAL ABSTRACTS.

**SOCIOL. EDUC. ABSTR.**
[UK/0038-0415]
SOCIOLOGY OF EDUCATION ABSTRACTS.

**SOFT. ABSTR. ENG.**
[IE/0790-150X]
SOFTWARE ABSTRACTS FOR ENGINEERS : SAFE.

**SOILS FERT.**
[UK/0038-0792]
SOILS AND FERTILIZERS.
(*Supersedes* Imperial Bureau of Soil Science. Monthly Letter.)

**SOLID STATE ABSTR. J.**
[US/0038-108X]
SOLID STATE ABSTRACTS JOURNAL.
(*Continued by* Solid State and Superconductivity Abstracts.)

**SOLID STATE SUPERCOND. ABSTR.**
[US/0896-5900]
SOLID STATE AND SUPERCONDUCTIVITY ABSTRACTS.
(*Continues* Solid State Abstracts Journal.)

**SORGHUM MILL. ABSTR.**
[UK/03082970]
SORGHUM AND MILLETS ABSTRACTS.
**(Ceased)**

**SOUTH. BAPTIST PERIOD. INDEX**
[US/0081-3028]
SOUTHERN BAPTIST PERIODICAL INDEX.

**SOYABEAN ABSTR.**
[UK/0141-0172]
SOYABEAN ABSTRACTS.

**SPEC. EDUC. NEEDS ABSTR.**
[UK/0954-0822]
SPECIAL EDUCATIONAL NEEDS ABSTRACTS.

**SPIN**
[US]
SPIN.

**SPORT DISCUS**
[US]
SPORT DISCUS [COMPUTER FILE].

**SPORT FISH. ABSTR.**
[US/0038-786X]
SPORT FISHERY ABSTRACTS.
(*Continued by* Fisheries Review.)

**SPORTSEARCH**
[US/0882-553X]
SPORTSEARCH.

**STAT. REF. INDEX**
[US/0885-6834]
STATISTICAL REFERENCE INDEX.

**STAT. THEORY METHOD ABSTR.**
[UK/0039-0518]
STATISTICAL THEORY AND METHOD ABSTRACTS.
(*Continues* International Journal of Abstracts: Statistical Theory and Method.)

**STUD. WOMEN ABSTR.**
[UK/0262-5644]
STUDIES ON WOMEN ABSTRACTS.

**SUBJ. INDEX CHILD. MAG.**
[US/0039-4351]
SUBJECT INDEX TO CHILDREN'S MAGAZINES.
(*Continued by* Children's Magazine Guide.)

**SUBJ. INDEX PERIOD.**
[UK]
SUBJECT INDEX TO PERIODICALS.
(*Split into* British Humanities Index *and* British Technology Index.)

**SUBJ. INDEX SEL. PERIOD. LIT.**
[US/0194-0708]
SUBJECT INDEX TO SELECT PERIODICAL LITERATURE.
(*Continued by* Mosher Periodical Index.)

**SUG. INDUS. ABSTR.**
[UK/0957-5022]
SUGAR INDUSTRY ABSTRACTS / [CAB INTERNATIONAL, BUREAU OF HORTICULTURE AND PLANTATION CROPS IN ASSOCIATION WITH TATE & LYLE PLC].
(*Continues* Tate & Lyle's Sugar Industry Abstracts.)

**SURF. TREAT. TECHNOL. ABSTR.**
[UK]
SURFACE TREATMENT TECHNOLOGY ABSTRACTS.
(*Continues* Metal Finishing Abstracts.)

**TECH. DATA DIG.**
[US]
TECHNICAL DATA DIGEST.
**(Ceased)**

**TECH. EDUC. ABSTR.**
[UK/0040-0920]
TECHNICAL EDUCATION ABSTRACTS.
(*Continued by* Technical Education & Training Abstracts.)

**TECH. EDUC. TRAIN. ABSTR.**
[UK]
TECHNICAL EDUCATION & TRAINING ABSTRACTS.
(*Continues* Technical Education Abstracts.)

**TELEGEN ABSTR.**
[US/0000-118X]
TELEGEN ABSTRACTS.
(*Continues* Telegen Reporter.)

**TELEGEN REPORT.**
[US/0743-8443]
TELEGEN REPORTER.
(*Continued by* Telegen Abstracts.)

**TERMITE ABSTR.**
[UK/0144-5995]
TERMITE ABSTRACTS.
**(Ceased)**

**TEXT. TECHNOL. DIG.**
[US/0040-5191]
TEXTILE TECHNOLOGY DIGEST.

**THEOL. RELIG. INDEX**
[UK]
THEOLOGICAL AND RELIGIOUS INDEX.
**(Ceased)**

**THEOR. CHEM. ENG.**
[UK/0960-5053]
THEORETICAL CHEMICAL ENGINEERING.
(*Continues* Theoretical Chemical Engineering Abstracts.)

**THEOR. CHEM. ENG. ABSTR.**
[UK/0040-5787]
THEORETICAL CHEMICAL ENGINEERING ABSTRACTS.
(*Continued by* Theoretical Chemical Engineering.)

**TOM GEN. INDEX**
[US]
TOM GENERAL INDEX.

**TOP MANAGE. ABSTR.**
[UK/0049-4100]
TOP MANAGEMENT ABSTRACTS.
(*Continued by* Anbar Top Management Abstracts.)

**TOPICATOR**
[US/0040-9340]
TOPICATOR.

**TOXICOL. ABSTR.**
[US/0140-5365]
TOXICOLOGY ABSTRACTS.

**TRADE IND. ASAP**
[US]
TRADE & INDUSTRY ASAP [ONLINE DATABASE].

**TRADE IND. INDEX**
[US]
TRADE & INDUSTRY INDEX [ONLINE DATABASE].

# INDEXES/ABSTRACTS TABLE

**TRANS. AM. SOC. CIV. ENG.**
[US/0066-0604]
TRANSACTIONS OF THE AMERICAN SOCIETY OF CIVIL ENGINEERS.

**TRANSP. RES. ABSTR.**
[US/0095-2648]
TRANSPORTATION RESEARCH ABSTRACTS.
(*Absorbed in part by* HRIS Abstracts.)

**TRANSP. STORAGE**
[US]
TRANSPORTATION AND STORAGE.
(*Continued by* Literature Abstracts. Transportation & Storage.)

**TROP. ABSTR.**
[NE/0041-3208]
TROPICAL ABSTRACTS.
(*Superseded by* Abstracts on Tropical Agriculture.)

**TROP. DIS. BULL.**
[UK/0041-3240]
TROPICAL DISEASES BULLETIN.
(*Supersedes* Bulletin of the Sleeping Sickness Bureau and the Kala Azar Bulletin.)

**U.S. POLIT. SCI. DOC.**
[US/0148-6063]
UNITED STATES POLITICAL SCIENCE DOCUMENTS.
(*Absorbed* Asian Studies Indexed Journal Reference Guide.)

**UMI ABI/INFORM--BUS. PERIOD. ONDISC**
[US/1064-5381]
UMI ABI/INFORM--BUSINESS PERIODICALS ONDISC.

**UNITED METHODIST PERIOD. INDEX**
[US/0041-7319]
UNITED METHODIST PERIODICAL INDEX.
(*Continues* Methodist Periodical Index.)

**URBAN AFF. ABSTR.**
[US/0300-6859]
URBAN AFFAIRS ABSTRACTS.

**VET. BULL.**
[UK/0042-4854]
VETERINARY BULLETIN (LONDON).
(*Supersedes* Tropical Veterinary Bulletin; *Absorbed* Veterinary Reviews.)

**VETDOC**
[UK]
VETDOC.
***Refer to PESTDOC for complete source list.

**VIROL. ABSTR.**
[US/0042-6830]
VIROLOGY ABSTRACTS.
(*Continued by* Virology and AIDS Abstracts.)

**VIROL. AIDS ABSTR.**
[US/0896-5919]
VIROLOGY & AIDS ABSTRACTS.
(*Continues* Virology Abstracts.)

**VIS. INDEX**
[US/0049-6510]
VISION INDEX.
(Ceased)

**VITIS VITIC. ENOL. ABSTR.**
[GW/0175-8292]
VITIS, VITICULTURE AND ENOLOGY ABSTRACTS.
(*Separated from* Vitis.)

**VOCAT. SEARCH**
[US/1071-2747]
VOCATIONAL SEARCH.

**WALL STREET J. INDEX**
[US/0083-7075]
WALL STREET JOURNAL INDEX.
(Ceased)

**WATER POLLUT. ABSTR.**
[UK/0043-1281]
WATER POLLUTION ABSTRACTS.
(*Merged with* Water Research Association Library List *to form* WRC Information.)

**WEED ABSTR.**
[UK/0043-1729]
WEED ABSTRACTS.

**WEST. HIST. Q.**
[US/0043-3810]
WESTERN HISTORICAL QUARTERLY.

**WHEAT BARLEY TRIT. ABSTR.**
[UK/0265-7880]
WHEAT, BARLEY AND TRITICALE ABSTRACTS.
(*Continues* Triticale Abstracts.)

**WILDL. REV.**
[US/0043-5511]
WILDLIFE REVIEW (FORT COLLINS).

**WILSON BUS. ABSTR.**
[US/1057-6533]
WILSON BUSINESS ABSTRACTS.

**WOMEN MANAG. REV. ABSTR.**
[UK/0955-8357]
WOMEN IN MANAGEMENT REVIEW & ABSTRACTS.
(*Continued by* Women in Management Review.)

**WOMEN MANAGE. REV.**
[UK/0964-9425]
WOMEN IN MANAGEMENT REVIEW.
(*Continues* Women in Management Review & Abstracts.)

**WOMEN STUD. ABSTR.**
[US/0049-7835]
WOMEN STUDIES ABSTRACTS.

**WORK RELAT. ABSTR.**
[US/0273-3234]
WORK RELATED ABSTRACTS.
(*Continues* Employment Relations Abstracts.)

**WORLD AGRIC. ECON. RURAL SOCIOL. ABSTR.**
[UK/0043-8219]
WORLD AGRICULTURAL ECONOMICS AND RURAL SOCIOLOGY ABSTRACTS.

**WORLD ALUM. ABSTR.**
[US/0002-6697]
WORLD ALUMINUM ABSTRACTS.
(*Continued by* Aluminium Industry Abstracts.)

**WORLD CERAM. ABSTR.**
[UK/0957-8897]
WORLD CERAMICS ABSTRACTS.
(*Continues* British Ceramic Abstracts.)

**WORLD FISH. ABSTR.**
[IT/0043-8472]
WORLD FISHERIES ABSTRACTS.
(Ceased)

**WORLD PUBL. MONIT.**
[UK/0960-653X]
WORLD PUBLISHING MONITOR.
(*Continues* Electronic Publishing Abstracts.)

**WORLD SURF. COAT. ABSTR.**
[UK/0043-9088]
WORLD SURFACE COATINGS ABSTRACTS.
(*Continues* Review of Current Literature Relating to the Paint, Colour, Varnish and Allied Industries.)

**WORLD TEXT. ABSTR.**
[UK/0043-9118]
WORLD TEXTILE ABSTRACTS.
(*Supersedes* Textile Abstracts.)

**WRC INF.**
[UK/0306-6649]
WRC INFORMATION.
(*Continued by* Aqualine Abstracts.)

**WRIT. AM. HIST.**
[US/0364-2887]
WRITINGS ON AMERICAN HISTORY.
(Ceased)

**ZENTRALBL. MATH. IHRE GRENZGEB.**
[GW/0044-4235]
ZENTRALBLATT FUER MATHEMATIK UND IHRE GRENZGEBIETE.
(*Superseded in part by* Zentralblatt fuer Mechanik.)

**ZOOL. REC.**
[UK/0144-3607]
ZOOLOGICAL RECORD (LONDON).
(*Continues* Record of Zoological Literature.)

# Manufacturing

# MANUFACTURING

US
**ADVANCE REPORT ON DURABLE GOODS MANUFACTURERS' SHIPMENTS AND ORDERS.** Government Publication. English. mo. US Department of Commerce / Bureau of the Census, Data User Services Division, Customer Services, Washington DC 20233-0800. **Tel** (301)763-4100. **(Subscription address:** Superintendent of Documents, US Government Printing Office, Washington DC 20402.)

US
**AEROSOL RELEASE AND TRANSPORT PROGRAM QUARTERLY PROGRESS REPORT / PREPARED FOR THE U.S. NUCLEAR REGULATORY COMMISSION, OFFICE OF NUCLEAR REGULATORY RESEARCH; PREPARED BY THE OAK RIDGE NATIONAL LABORATORY.** See Packaging.

UK/0568-062X
**AEROSOL REVIEW.** See Packaging.

US/1045-2664
**ALABAMA MANUFACTURERS REGISTER.** [Ala. manuf. regist.]. (1990)-. Directory. English. an $79.00 (print); $495.00 (diskette or CD-ROM). Manufacturers News Inc., 1633 Central Street, Evanston IL 60201-1569. **Tel** (708)864-7000, FAX (708)332-1100. **LC** HF5065.A37; A347. **DD** 338.7/67/029/4761.

GW/0002-4406
**ALAMBRE.** [Alambre]. (1951)-. Academic Scholarly Publication. Spanish (German; translations available in German). Twice a year. DM42.06 Germany, DM45.00 others (surface mail); DM51.80 Germany, DM65.20 others (airmail). Meisenbach GmbH, Postfach 2069, D 96011 Bamberg Germany. **Tel** 011 49 951 861135. **ED** Klaus Ohlwein. **CODEN** ALAMBE. **[CCC].** Index available (Free). **Ad Acc. Circ:** 3,370 (ctrl). Documents available from CASDDS.
**Desc:** Technical journal for the production and manufacturing or wire, steel bars and derivatives and all relating sectors.
**Ind/Abst** Chem. Abstr.

CN/0823-4450
**ALBERTA MANUFACTURERS INDEX.** [Alta. manuf. index]. **Added/Corp** Alberta. Alberta Economic Development. Stategic Planning Branch. No. 1 (1982)-. Directory. English. an (Publishes every two years). Free. Alberta Economic Development, 9940-106th Street, 8th Floor, Edmonton Alberta T5K 2P6 Canada. **Tel** (403)427-0670. **DD** 338.4/025/7123. **Continues** Alberta Business Index, 0227-7972.
**Desc:** A directory of Albertan manufacturing companies.

US/0731-5368
**AMERICAN MACHINIST MANUFACTURING COST ESTIMATING GUIDE.** 1982 Ed.-. English. an. McGraw Hill Publishing Company, Inc., 1221 Avenue of the Americas, New York NY 10020. **Tel** (212)512-6410, (800)525-5003, FAX (212)512-6111. **LC** TS213; .O87. **DD** 671.

●US/1061-219X
**AMERICAN MANUFACTURERS DIRECTORY.** [Am. manuf. dir.]. **Added/Corp** American Business Directories, Inc. (1992)-. English. an (Feb.). $495.00. American Business Directory, 5711 South 86th Circle, Omaha NE 68127. **Tel** (402)593-4600, FAX (402)331-5481. **LC** HD9723; .U27. **DD** 338.7/67/02573. available on CD-ROM. **Continues** U.S. Manufacturers Directory, 1042-1742.

US/0192-5709
**AMERICAN TOOL, DIE & STAMPING NEWS.** **VAT** American Tool, Die and Stamping News. (1973)-. Periodical. English. bm. $9.80 US; $60.00 other. Eagle Publications Circ Dept, 42400 Nine Mile Road, Suite B, Novi MI 48050. **Tel** (313)347-3490. **ED** Bonnie Paschke. **Bk Rev. Ad Acc. Circ:** 22,000.
**Desc:** Information on new products related to the tool and die and metal stamping industries.

US/0890-9970
**AMERICA'S TEXTILES INTERNATIONAL.** See Textiles.

US
**AMR'S CIM STRATEGIES.** English. mo. $395.00. Advance Manufacturing Research, 2 Oliver Street, Fifth Floor, Boston MA 02109. **Tel** (617)542-6600. **Continues** Enterprise Integration Strategies.

UK
**AMTRI LIBRARY BULLETIN.** (19??)-. Bulletin. English. mo. £90.00. Advanced Manufacturing Tech Research Institute, Hulley Road, Macclesfield, Cheshire SK10 2NE England. **Tel** 011 44 625 25421.

AT
**ANNUAL REPORT.** **Main/Corp** Queensland. Dept. of Commercial and Industrial Development. (1972)-. English. Free. The Director / Australia, Box 183, PO North Quay, 4000 Brisbane Australia. **Tel** (07)2242087. **LC** HC631; .A26. **DD** 354/.943/0082. **Circ:** 6,000 (ctrl). **Continues** Queensland. Dept. of Industrial Development. Report of the Director ... for the Year Ending June 30th ...
**Desc:** Contains the summary of industrial development in the state of Queensland during the previous year.

AT
**ANNUAL REPORT / AUSTRALIAN MANUFACTURING COUNCIL.** **Main/Corp** Australian Manufacturing Council. (19??)-. Government Publication. English. an. Australian Government Publishing Service, GPO Box 84, Canberra ACT 2601 Australia. **Tel** 011 61 6 2954411, FAX 011 61 6 2954455.

US
**ANNUAL REPORT - DENNISON MANUFACTURING COMPANY.** **Main/Corp** Dennison Manufacturing Company. 19 -. Corporate Report. English. an. Free. Dennison Manufacturing Company, 300 Howard Street, Framingham MA 01701. **Tel** (617)879-0511, telex 920407. **LC** HD9829.D4. **Circ:** 35,000 (ctrl).
**Desc:** Corporate annual report of public corporations.

US
**ANNUAL SURVEY OF MANUFACTURES. MANUFACTURERS' ALTERNATIVE ENERGY CAPABILITIES.** **VFOAT** Manufacturers' Alternative Energy Capabilities. 1976-. Government Publication. English. an. US Department of Commerce / Bureau of the Census, Data User Services Division, Customer Services, Washington DC 20233-0800. **Tel** (301)763-4100. **(Subscription address:** Superintendent of Documents, US Government Printing Office, Washington DC 20402.)

US
**ANNUAL SURVEY OF MANUFACTURES. STATISTICS FOR STATES, STANDARD METROPOLITAN STATISTICAL AREAS, LARGE INDUSTRIAL COUNTIES, AND SELECTED CITIES.** See Manufacturing-Abstracting, Bibliographies and Statistics.

US
**ANNUAL SURVEY OF MANUFACTURES. VALUE OF MANUFACTURERS' INVENTORIES.** **VFOAT** Value of Manufacturers' Inventories; ASM. Government Publication. English. an. US Department of Commerce / Bureau of the Census, Data User Services Division, Customer Services, Washington DC 20233-0800. **Tel** (301)763-4100. **(Subscription address:** Superintendent of Documents, US Government Printing Office, Washington DC 20402.) **LC** HD9721; .A564. **DD** 338.4/767/0973021.

US
**ANNUAL SURVEY OF MANUFACTURES. VALUE OF PRODUCT SHIPMENTS : ASM.** **Added/Corp** United States. Bureau of the Census. **VFOAT** Value of Product Shipments; ASM. (19??)-. Government Publication. English. ir. Price varies per volume. Superintendent of Documents, US Government Printing Office, Washington DC 20402. **Tel** (202)275-3328, FAX (202)786-2377. **LC** HD9721; .A565. **DD** 381/.4567/0973021.
**Ind/Abst** Predicasts Forecasts.

US/0082-9307
**ANNUAL SURVEY OF MANUFACTURES (WASHINGTON).** (ANNUAL SURVEY OF MANUFACTURES : ASM.). **Added/Corp** United States. Bureau of the Census. Began with (1949-50)-. Government Publication. English. be. US Department of Commerce / Bureau of the Census, Data User Services Division, Customer Services, Washington DC 20233-0800. **Tel** (301)763-4100. **(Subscription address:** Superintendent of Documents, US Government Printing Office, Washington DC 20402.) **LC** HD9724; .A211. **DD** 338.4.
**Desc:** Provides estimates of such statistics as employment, payroll, work hours, value added by manufacture and supplemental labor costs for industry group and industries. The survey also includes fuels and electric energy data by industry group and industry.

US/0744-2270
**ANTIFRICTION BEARINGS.** **Ceased.** (CURRENT INDUSTRIAL REPORTS. MA-35Q, ANTIFRICTION BEARINGS / U.S. DEPARTMENT OF COMMERCE, BUREAU OF THE CENSUS.). **Added/Corp** United States. Bureau of the Census. **VFOAT** Antifriction bearings. (1978)-(199?). Government Publication. English. an. US Department of Commerce, 14th Street & Constitution Avenue NW, Washington DC 20230. **Tel** (202)482-2000, FAX (202)482-3772. **LC** HD9705.5.B433; U63. **DD** 380.1/45621822/0973.
**Desc:** Presents timely data on the production, inventories, and orders of approximately 5,000 products, which represents 40 percent of all US manufacturing.

US/0889-177X
**ANVIL'S RING, THE.** See Metals and Metallurgy.

US/0003-679X
**APPLIANCE MANUFACTURER.** See Household Hardware and Appliances.

US/0742-910X
**AQUA-FIELD SPORTSMAN.** **VFOAT** Colt American Handgunning; Gutmann Knife Journal; Resort Parks International Vacationlife Outdoors; Resort Parks International Vacation Life Outdoors; Scubapro Diving & Snorkeling; Scubapro Diving and Snorkeling. Vol. 1, No. 1 (May 1983)-?. Periodical. English. qt. $2.50 (single issue) US; $2.95 (single issue) Canada. Aqua Field Publications Inc, 66 West Gilbert Street, Shrewsbury NJ 07702. **Tel** (201)842-8300. **LC** TS580; .A68. **DD** 621.9/32/05.
**Continued in part by** Scubapro Diving & Snorkeling.

US/1071-3514
**ARIZONA INDUSTRIAL DIRECTORY.** [Ariz. ind. dir.]. **Added/Corp** Phoenix Metropolitan Chamber of Commerce. (1988)-. Directory. English. an. $85.00. Manufacturers News Inc., 1633 Central Street, Evanston IL 60201-1569. **Tel** (708)864-7000, FAX (708)332-1100. **LC** T12; .A72. **DD** 670/.25/791. **Continues** Arizona Directory of Manufacturers (1982), 0739-974X.

HK/0301-7117
**ASIAN MANUFACTURING.** [Asian manuf.]. Periodical. English. $6.00. Far East Trade Press Ltd, BL C 10 F Seaview E, 2 8 Watson, North Point Hong Kong. **Tel** 011 852 5 5668381. **LC** TS191; .A83. **DD** 670/.5.

HK/0254-1114
**ASIAN SOURCES ELECTRONICS.** See Engineering-Electricity, Electrical Engineering, Electronics.

US/1050-8171
**ASSEMBLY (CAROL STREAM, ILL.).** See Engineering-Mechanical Engineering and Machinery.

AT
**AUSTRALASIAN MANUFACTURER.** **Title Change.** (1916)-(19??). Periodical. English. wk. **Continued by** Australasian Weekly Manufacturer. **Ind/Abst** Ceram. Abstr. (19??-19??).

US
**AUSTRALASIAN WEEKLY MANUFACTURER.** Vol. 1 (1916)-. English. **LC** Microfilm 86/706. **Absorbed** Australasian Engineer.

AT/0004-9719
**AUSTRALIAN MACHINERY AND PRODUCTION ENGINEERING.** See Engineering-Mechanical Engineering and Machinery.

NE/0951-7162
**AUTOMATED MANUFACTURING STRATEGY.** **Title Change.** See Computers-Automation.

GW
**BAKO MAGAZINE.** (19??)-. German. mo. DM99.00. Chmielorz GmbH, Postfach 2229, D 65012 Wiesbaden Germany. **Tel** 011 49 611 360980. **Bk Rev. Ad Acc.** ctrl circ. **Continues** Bako informationen.

GW/0005-3848
**BANDER BLECHE ROHRE.** [Bander, Bleche, Rohre]. Vol. 1, (1960)-. Academic Scholarly Publication. German. Twelve times a year. DM172.00 Germany; DM190.00 other. Vogel Verlag, Postfach 6740, D-97064 Wuerzburg Germany. **Tel** 011 49 931 4182145, 011 49 931 4182483, FAX 011 49 931 4182670, telex 841 680131. **ED** Wil Prolo and Ulrike Gloger. **CODEN** BBROABBBRDAB. **[CCC]. Bk Rev. Ad Acc. Circ:** 5,000 (ctrl). Documents available from Article Express International, CASDDS.
**Desc:** One of a series of technical journals for the manufacture, working and treatment of semi-finished products.
**Ind/Abst** Alum. Ind. Abstr.; Bioeng. Abstr.; Chem. Abstr.; Ei Page One; EMBASE; Energy Res. Abstr.; Eng. Index Annu. [Select. Cov.]; Leadscan; Met. Abstr.; Saf. Health Work.

UK
**BASIC DATA ON SEALANTS IN SELECTED EUROPEAN COUNTRIES.** ir. £150.00. IAL Consultants Ltd, 14 Buckingham Palace Road, London SW1W 0QP United Kingdom. **Tel** 071 828 5036, FAX 071 828 9318, telex 918666 CRECON G. **Bk Rev.**
**Desc:** Brings together published statistics and

# Manufacturing

information about the sealants industry in France, West Germany, the UK, Belgium and the Netherlands. Lists over 150 suppliers of sealants and gives details on types of sealants supplied by about 100 companies.

US/0746-3634
**BLACKPOWDER REPORT, THE.** VFOAT Black Powder Report. Vol. 11, No. 1 (Oct. 1983)-. Periodical. English. mo. The Buckskin Press Inc, PO Box 789, Big Tumber MT 59011. **LC** TS536.6.M8; B76. **DD** 683.4. *Formed by the union of Buckskin Report, 0145-4234 and Black Powder Cartridge Rifles, 0273-6594.*

UK
**BOILER EXPLOSIONS ACTS, 1882 AND 1890, REPORT OF PRELIMINARY INQUIRY.** Title Change. (BOILER EXPLOSIONS ACTS, 1882 AND 1890.). **Main/Corp** Great Britain. Board of Trade. English. *Continues Boiler Explosions Acts, 1882 and 1890. Continued by Great Britain. Ministry of Transport. Boiler Explosions Acts, 1882 and 1890; Report of Preliminary Inquiry.*

CN/0704-6278
**BRITISH COLUMBIA.** (BRITISH COLUMBIA MANUFACTURERS' DIRECTORY). **Added/Corp** British Columbia. Ministry of Industry and Small Business Development. (1975)-. English. an. 28.50Can$. Crown Publications Inc., 521 Fort Street, Victoria, British Columbia, V8W 1E7 Canada. **Tel** (604)386-4636, FAX (604)386-0221. **ED** Krisha Toora. **Circ:** 2,000 (ctrl). available on diskette. *Continues British Columbia Directory, 0381-2197.*

UK
**BULK MATERIALS INTERNATIONAL.** English. mo. $175.00. Loadstar Publications, 77A High Road Willesden Green, London NW10 2SU England. **Tel** 011 44 81 4516578.
**Ind/Abst** Coal Abstr.

SZ/0250-7730
**BULLETIN DES DESSINS ET MODELES INTERNATIONAUX : PUBLICATION MENSUELLE DU BUREAU INTERNATIONAL DE L'ORGANISATION MONDIALE DE LA PROPRIETE INTELLECTUELLE.** VFOAT International Designs Bulletin : Monthly Publication of the International Bureau of the World Intellectual Property Organization; International Designs Bulletin. Bulletin. French (English). mo. 200.00F Switzerland; $135.00 US. Bureau International de l'Organisation Mondiale de la Propriete Intellectuelle, 34 Chemin des Colombettes Case Postale 18, 1211 Geneve 20 Suisse Switzerland. **Tel** 999.111, telex 22376 OMPI. **LC** TS171.A1; B85. **DD** 745.2/027. **Ad Acc.**
**Desc:** Gives deposits under the Hague Agreement concerning the protection of industrial designs.

JA/0916-8311
**BULLETIN OF PRECISION AND INTELLIGENCE LABORATORY.** [Bull. Precis. Intell. Lab.]. **Added/Corp** Tokyo Kogyo Daigaku. Seimitsu Kogaku Kenkyujo. No. 66 (Sept. 1991)-. Bulletin. English. Tokyo Kogyo Daigaku Hikaku Bunka Kenkyukai, 12-2 Ookayana Meguro-ku, Tokyo-To 152 Japan. **Tel** 03-726-1111. *Continues Tokyo Kogyo Daigaku. Seimitsu Kogaku Kenkyujo. Bulletin of Research Laboratory of Precision Machinery and Electronics, 0385-7832.*
**Ind/Abst** Bioeng. Abstr.; Eng. Index Annu.; FLUIDEX; INSPEC; Int. Aerosp. Abstr.; Math. Rev.; Met. Abstr.; World Alum. Abstr.

CN/0319-5902
**C I E N, CANADIAN INDUSTRIAL EQUIPMENT NEWS.** VFOAT Canadian Industrial Equipment News. (1940)-. Periodical. English. mo. 50.00Can$ (one year), 85.00Can$ (two year), 115.00Can$ (three year) Canada; 52.00Can$ (one year), 90.00Can$ (two year), 125.00Can$ (three year) US; 72.00Can$ (one year), 130.00Can$ (two year), 180.00Can$ (three year) other. Southam Information and Technology Group Inc., 1450 Don Mills Road, Don Mills Ontario M3B 2X7 Canada. **Tel** (416)445-6641, (800)668-2374, FAX (416)442-2261. **ED** Olga Markovitch. **Bk Rev. Ad Acc. Circ:** 35,000 (ctrl). *Absorbed Industrial Products and Equipment, 0319-5910.*
**Desc:** Provides up-to-date information on new and improved industrial products and technical literature.

US/1051-7545
**C2C CURRENTS JAPAN. MANUFACTURING.** [C2C curr. Jpn., Manuf.]. VFOAT Manufacturing; C2C Currents. Manufacturing; Scan C2C Currents Japan. Manufacturing. **VAT** Sea to Sea Currents Japan. Manufacturing. Vol. 1, No. 1 (July 1990)-. English. mo. $100.00. SCAN C2C Inc, Attn Carol G Heffernan Marketing Director, 500 E Street Southwest, Suite 800, 8th Floor, Washington DC 20024. **Tel** (202)863-3850, (800)525-3855, FAX (202)863-3855. **DD** 670. available on an online database from ORBIT; and DIALOG.
**Desc:** Previews the abstracts from leading Japanese journals in English in a range of manufacturing areas including industrial engineering, materials handling, production, instrumentation and control, safety engineering, waste management, quality control and manufacturing management.

US/1041-2166
**CABINET MANUFACTURING & FABRICATIONS.** [Cabinet manuf. fabr.]. VFOAT Cabinet Manufacturing and Fabricating; CM&F. Periodical. English. mo. Free. KBC Publications Inc, 2 University Plaza/Suite 11, Hackensack NJ 07601. **DD** 684.

US/0068-5739
**CALIFORNIA MANUFACTURERS REGISTER.** [Calif. manuf. regist.]. **Added/Corp** California Manufacturers Association. (1968)-. English. an (January). $173.50 softcover; $192.00 hardcover. Database Publishing Company, PO Box 7440, Newport Beach CA 92658. **Tel** (714)646-1623, (800)-888-8434, FAX (714)631-8471. **DD** 338. Index available. **Ad Acc, Adv Mgr:** D Pearce. **Circ:** 5,000 (ctrl). available on diskette. *Continues California Manufacturers Annual Register, 0730-5818.*
**Desc:** Contains 32,000 manufacturers, 80,000 executives. Companies listed alphabetically by city and town, by product, geographically, numerically, by SIC key executives, SIC, number of employees, zip codes and telephone numbers.

US
**CALS CE REPORT.** (19??)-. English. Twelve times a year. $295.00 US; $325.00 Canada & Mexico; $395.00 others. Knowledge Base International, 2700 Northwest Central Drive, Suite 160, Houston TX 77092. **Tel** (713)690-7644. *Continues CALS Report, 0897-991X.*

US/0897-991X
**CALS REPORT.** Title Change. [CALS rep.]. **VAT** Computer-Aided Acquisition and Logistics Support Report. Vol. 1 No. 1 (Apr 1988)-(19??). Periodical. English. Twelve times a year. Knowledge Base International, 2700 Northwest Central Drive, Suite 160, Houston TX 77092. **Tel** (713)690-7644. **DD** 670. *Continued by CALS CE Report.*
**Desc:** Covers standards, methodologies, products and policies for DoD's CALS integration initiative.

US
**CAN SHIPMENTS REPORT.** **Added/Corp** Can Manufacturers Institute (U.S.). (1983)-. English. Thirteen times a year. $265.00. Can Manufacturers Institute, 1625 Massachusettes Avenue NW, Washington DC 20036. **Tel** (202)232-4677. *Continues Metal Cans Shipments Report.*
**Ind/Abst** Predicasts Forecasts.

CN
**CANADIAN CONTROLS AND INSTRUMENTATION. BUYERS' GUIDE.** 1971-. Consumer Publication. English. an. Southam Information and Technology Group Inc., 1450 Don Mills Road, Don Mills Ontario M3B 2X7 Canada. **Tel** (416)445-6641, (800)668-2374, FAX (416)442-2261. **ED** Leslie M Burt. **DD** 629.8/025/71. **Ad Acc. Circ:** 40,000 (ctrl). *Supersedes Control/Instrument Buyers' Guide.*
**Desc:** Covers the latest in process control, industrial measurement, instrumentation and manufacturing automation in an editorial mix of articles and new product write-ups.

CN/0382-8069
**CANADIAN MANUFACTURER (1908).** *Ceased.* (CANADIAN MANUFACTURER.). V. -59, 1908-1909; V. 30- 1910-Ceased (Jan. 1990). Periodical. English. mo. Canadian Manufacturers Assn. One Yonge Street/Suite 1400, Toronto Ontario M5E 1J9 Canada. **Tel** (416)363-7261. *Continues Canadian Manufacturer and Industrial World, 0382-8050.*

UK
**CANMAKING & CANNING INTERNATIONAL.** See Packaging.

US
**CAPACITY UTILIZATION, MANUFACTURING AND MATERIALS.** **Added/Corp** Board of Governors of the Federal Reserve System (U.S.). (197?)-. Periodical. English. mo. $15.00. Board of Governors of the Federal Reserve System, Mail Stop 127, Washington DC 20551. **Tel** (202)452-3244 or 3245. Documents available from Documents on Demand. *Continues Capacity Utilization in Manufacturing, 0364-2860.*
**Ind/Abst** Am. Stat. Index.

PR
**CENSO DE INDUSTRIAS MANUFACTURERAS DE PUERTO RICO. CENSUS OF MMANUFACTURING INDUSTRIES OF PUERTO RICO.** **Added/Corp** Puerto Rico. Bureau of Labor Statistics. Employment Statistics Division. Puerto Rico. Bureau of Labor Statistics. VFOAT Census of Manufacturing Industries of Puerto Rico. (1946)-. Spanish (English). **LC** HD5744; .A25.

AT/0157-2156
**CENSUS OF MANUFACTURING ESTABLISHMENTS. DETAILS OF OPERATIONS AND SMALL AREA STATISTICS, TASMANIA / [AUSTRALIAN BUREAU OF STATISTICS, TASMANIA].** See Manufacturing-Abstracting, Bibliographies and Statistics.

FR/0399-0001
**CETIM INFORMATIONS.** See Engineering-Mechanical Engineering and Machinery.

US/0160-4716
**CHATTANOOGA AND TRI-STATE AREA DIRECTORY OF MANUFACTURERS.** VFOAT Manufacturers Directory, Chattanooga and Tri-State Area. Directory. English. $10.00. 819 Broad Street, Chattanooga TN 37402. **LC** T12; .C49. **DD** 338.4/7/67102576882.

US/8755-2523
**CHILTON'S IMPO.** [Chilton's IMPO]. **Added/Corp** Chilton Company. VFOAT Chilton's I.M.P.O.; Industrial Maintenance and Plant Operations; Industrial Maintenance & Plant Operations. **VAT** Chilton's Industrial Maintenance and Plant Operations. (198?)-. Periodical. English. mo. $60.00 US; $79.00 Canada. Chilton Company, 201 King of Prussia Road, Radnor PA 19089. **Tel** (610)964-4122, (800)695-1214, FAX (610)964-4978, telex 6851035 CHILTON UW. **ED** Jerry Steinbrink and James McCanney. **DD** 658. **[CCC].** **Ad Acc. Circ:** 120,000 (ctrl). available on microfilm from University Microfilms International (UMI). *Continues Industrial Maintenance and Plant Operations, 0192-8201.*
**Desc:** Product tabloid covering all aspects of plant engineering and maintenance (replacement, installation, and repair).
**Ind/Abst** Ei Page One.

HK
**CHINAMAC JOURNAL.** Chinese. Three times a year. HK$117.00 Hong Kong; K$33.00 other. Adsale Publishing Company, 14/F Devon House Taikoo Place, 979 King's Road, Quarry Bay, Hong Kong. **Tel** 011 852 811 8897, FAX 011 852 516 5119. **ED** Josephine Gheng. **Ad Acc. Pr Rev. Circ:** 20,000 (ctrl).
**Desc:** A specialized industrial magazine designed to introduce to China advanced foreign technology, foreign trends and products ofthe machine-building and metal-working industry.

KO
**CHONGUK CHUNGSO KWANGGONGOP TONGGYE CHOSA POGOSO.** See Engineering-Mines and Mining Engineering.

CH
**CHUNG-KUO CHIH LIANG KUAN LI / CHUNG-KUO CHIH LIANG KUAN LI HSIEH HUI CHU PAN.** VFOAT China Quality Control. Began with Feb. 15, 1981 issue. Periodical. Chinese. mo. NT$0.35. Pei-Ching Pao Kan Fa Hsing Chu, Beijing, People's Republic of China. **Tel** 483531. **LC** TS156.A1; C48. **DD** 620/.0045/05.

GW/0931-3125
**CIM-PRAXIS.** See Computers-Automation.

US/0748-9250
**CIM STRATEGIES.** Title Change. [CIM strategies]. VFOAT C.I.M. Strategies; Computer-Integrated Manufacturing Strategies; Computer Integrated Manufacturing Strategies. Vol. 1, No. 1 (Aug. 1984)-(1993). Periodical. English. mo. Cutter Information Corporation, 37 Broadway, Arlington MA 02174-5539. **Tel** (617)648-8700, (800)964-5118, FAX (617)648-8707, (617)648-1950, telex 650 100 9891. (**Subscription address:** PO Box 173306, Denver, CO 80217-3306) **DD** 670. **[CCC].** available on an online database (file 636/Full-Text) from DIALOG. *Continued by Enterprise Integration Strategies.*

FR/0397-006X
**CIMENTS, BETONS, PLATRES, CHAUX.** See Building and Construction.

CN/0843-2651
**CIRCUIT INDUSTRIEL.** [Circuit ind.]. Vol. 8, No. 4/No. 5 (Nov./Dec. 1988)-. Periodical. French. Four times a year. Promotions Andre Pageau Inc., 1627 Boulevard St Joseph, Quebec Quebec G2K 1H1 Canada. **Tel** (418)623-3383. **DD** 338.4/7671/09714. *Continues Magazine l'Outilite, 0228-7889.*

US/0069-4525
**CLASSIFIED DIRECTORY OF WISCONSIN MANUFACTURERS.** *Ceased.* **Added/Corp** Wisconsin Manufacturers' Association. Wisconsin Association of Manufacturers & Commerce. 1st Ed. (1936)-(19??). Directory. English. an.

Manufacturers News Inc., 1633 Central Street, Evanston IL 60201-1569. **Tel** (708)864-7000, FAX (708)332-1100. **LC** T12; .C57. **DD** 670/.25/775.
**Desc:** Lists 8,700 manufacturers and processors in five sections: alphabetical, geographical, by product, SIC and computer.

UK/0007-8654
**CMM, CONFECTIONERY MANUFACTURE AND MARKETING.** [CMM. Confect. manuf. mark.]. Vol. 1 (Jan. 1964)-. Periodical. English. Eleven times a year (July/Aug. issue combine). £38.00 UK; £43.00 other. JG Kennedy & Company Ltd, 100 Blackstock Road, Islington, London N4 2DF England. **Tel** 071-226-3423, FAX 071-354-5372, telex 8952838. **ED** Margaret Lang. **CODEN** CMMADZ. **Bk Rev**. **Ad Acc. Circ:** 6,700. available on microfilm from University Microfilms International (UMI). ***Supersedes*** *Confectionery Manufacture.*
**Desc:** The magazine brings international reports to the trade.
**Ind/Abst** Dairy Sci. Abstr.; Food Sci. Technol. Abstr.; Int. Packag. Abstr.

US/0747-3362
**CNC WEST.** **VFOAT** CNC/West; C.N.C. West. (Oct. 1982)-. Trade Publication. English. Six times a year. Free on request. Arnold Publishing Inc., 4111 South Street Suite F, Lakewood CA 90712. **Tel** (310)634-2321, FAX (310)634-2812. **ED** Shawn Arnold. **Ad Acc. Circ:** 22,000.
**Desc:** Metalworking and manufacturing journal.

IT
**COLLANA DEL CENTENARIO.** **VFOAT** Serie di Studi e Testi Loretani. (1979)-. Monographic series. Italian. Price varies per volume.

US/1040-5054
**COMPOSITES IN MANUFACTURING.** (COMPOSITES IN MANUFACTURING / SME.). [Compos. manuf.]. **Added/Corp** Society of Manufacturing Engineers. (19??)-. Periodical. English. qt. $60.00 US, $64.00 Canada and Mexico (business, library and academic institution); $80.00 airmail, other. Society of Manufacturing Engineers, One SME Drive, PO Box 930, Member's Records Dept., Dearborn MI 48121-0930. **Tel** (313)271-1500, FAX (313)271-2861, telex 297742 SME UR (VIA RCA). **DD** 666.

UK/0956-7143
**COMPOSITES MANUFACTURING.** **See** Engineering-Materials Engineering and Mechanics.

UK/0951-5240
**COMPUTER-INTEGRATED MANUFACTURING SYSTEMS.** **See** Computers-Computer Engineering.

US/0746-3405
**COMPUTERIZED MANUFACTURING.** **See** Computers-Computer Industry and Industry Directories.

CN/0708-6199
**CONCRETE PRODUCTS MANUFACTURERS (PRELIMINARY ED.).** (CONCRETE PRODUCTS MANUFACTURERS.). **Main/Corp** Statistics Canada. Manufacturing and Primary Industries Division. **VFOAT** Fabricants de Produits en Beton. **VAT** Fabricants de Produits en Beton (Ed. Provisoire). Began with issue for 1971?. English (French). an. South Carolina Department of Education, 1429 Senate Street, Columbia SC 29201. **Tel** (803)734-8262, FAX (803)734-8624.

US/1063-5432
**CONFERENCE PROCEEDINGS / AUTOFACT.** [Conf. proc. - AUTOFACT]. **Main/Conf** Autofact. **Added/Corp** Society of Manufacturing Engineers. Computer and Automated Systems Association of SME. **VFOAT** Proceedings. (19??)-. Proceedings. English. an. $99.00 (non-member), $94.00 (SME member). Society of Manufacturing Engineers, One SME Drive, PO Box 930, Member's Records Dept., Dearborn MI 48121-0930. **Tel** (313)271-1500, FAX (313)271-2861, telex 297742 SME UR (VIA RCA). **LC** TS155.6; .A865a. **DD** 670/.285.

US/0099-0124
**CONNECTICUT MANUFACTURING DIRECTORY.** Directory. English. $5.00 per copy. Connecticut Labor Department, 200 Folly Brook Boulevard, Wethersfield CT 06109. **Tel** (203)566-4380. **LC** HD9727.C8; A23. **DD** 338/.0025/746. ***Continues*** *Directory of Connecticut Manufacturing and Mechanical Establishments, 0197-3002.*

US/0193-5909
**CONNECTICUT, RHODE ISLAND DIRECTORY OF MANUFACTURERS.** **Added/Corp** Commerce Register, Inc. (1979)-. English. an (Aug.). $76.85 New Jersey; $72.00 others. Commerce Register Inc., 190 Godwin Avenue, Midland Park NJ 07432. **Tel** (201)445-3000, (800)221-2172. **ED** Joel Rosano. **LC** HD9727.C8; C66. **DD** 338.4/025/746. **Ad Acc. Circ:** 3,000.
**Desc:** Detailed listings of all manufacturing companies, including top executives, annual sales, number of employees, address, phone, and more. Available in machine readable format and on mailing lists.

●US/1068-4158
**CONSUMER PRODUCT AND MANUFACTURER RATINGS.** **Added/Corp** Gale Research Inc. (1992)-. English. $395.00. Gale Research Inc., 835 Penobscot Building, Detroit MI 48226. **Tel** (800)877-GALE, (313)961-2242, FAX (313)961-6083, telex TWX 810-221-7086. **ED** David J. Faulds. available on diskette; available on magnetic tape.
**Desc:** Takes a 30-year retrospective look at how the products of thousands of the world's major manufacturers have been rated by independent testing organizations.

US/1071-2240
**CONTINUOUS IMPROVEMENT.** [Contin. improv.]. **VFOAT** Continuous Improvement Newsletter. (19??)-. Periodical. English. Twelve times a year. $150.00. Solutions Specialists, 8460 Dygert Drive, Alto MI 49302. **Tel** (616)891-9114, FAX (616)891-9114. **DD** 658. Index available (Bound in Dec. iss.). cum. index. **Bk Rev**, (Qty: 4). **Circ:** 2,000 (ctrl). available on an online database. ***Continues*** *Manufacturing Success, 0895-6006.*

US/1049-5541
**CONTROL (CHICAGO, ILL.).** (CONTROL.). [Control]. Vol. 1, No. 1 (Oct. 1988)-. Periodical. English. Twelve times a year. $40.00 US; $80.00 (surface mail), $150.00 (airmail) other; $5.00 (single issue). Putnam Publishing Company, 301 East Erie Street, Chicago IL 60611. **Tel** (312)644-2020, FAX (312)644-1131. **LC** TS156.8; .C6747. **DD** 670.42.

US/0887-1930
**CORPORATE TECHNOLOGY DIRECTORY.** [Corp. technol. dir.]. **Added/Corp** Corporate Technology Information Services. (1986)-. Directory. English. an (Feb.). $495.00 (hard cover), $445.00 (soft cover). Corporate Technology Information Services Inc, 12 Alfred Street, Suite 200, Woburn MA 01801-9998. **Tel** (617)932-3939, (800)333-8036, FAX (617)932-6335, telex 497-2961 CRPTECH. **ED** Steven W. Parker. **LC** HG4057; .A16. **DD** 338.7/4/02573. **[CCC]**. Index available. **Bk Rev**. **Ad Acc. Circ:** 3,000. available on CD-ROM from R.R. Bowker; available on diskette; available on an online database.
**Desc:** Directory of over 35,000 U.S. high technology manufacturers. Profiles can be referenced via name, location, products manufactured and parent/subsidiary.

US/0566-5469
**COTTON FIBER AND PROCESSING TEST RESULTS.** **See** Textiles.

US
**CURRENT INDUSTRIAL REPORTS. MA31A, FOOTWEAR.** **VFOAT** Footwear. Began with 1977. Government Publication. English. an. $16.00. US Department of Commerce / Bureau of the Census, Data User Services Division, Customer Services, Washington DC 20233-0800. **Tel** (301)763-4100. **(Subscription address:** Superintendent of Documents, US Government Printing Office, Washington DC 20402.**)** **LC** HD9787.U4; C87. **DD** 338.4/76853F/0973.
**Desc:** Presents timely data on the production, inventories, and orders of approximately 5,000 products, which represents 40 percent of all US manufacturing.

US/0099-1961
**DCAS MANUFACTURING COST CONTROL DIGEST.** **Main/Corp** United States. Defense Contract Administration Services. **Added/Corp** United States. Defense Contract Administration Services. Manufacturing Cost Control Digest. **VFOAT** Manufacturing Cost Control Digest. **VAT** Defense Contract Administration Services Manufacturing Cost Control Digest. Vol. 1 (1975)-. English. an. Defense Supply Agency, Defense Contract Administration Services, Cameron Street, Alexandria VA 22314. **LC** TS165; .U55a. **DD** 658.1/552.

US
**DESIGN FOR MANUFACTURING NEWSLETTER.** (19??)-. Newsletter. English. Six times a year. $42.00 US; $66.00 Canada; $80.00 Canada; $85.00 other. Penton Publishing, 1100 Superior Avenue, Cleveland OH 44114-2543. **Tel** (216)696-7000, FAX (216)696-0836. **(Subscription address:** Penton Publishing, PO Box 96732, Chicago IL 60693.**)**

UK/0266-156X
**DEVELOPMENTS IN PRESSURE VESSEL TECHNOLOGY.** [Dev. press. vessel technol.]. (1979)-. Academic Scholarly Publication. English. ir. Elsevier Science Publishers Ltd, Crown House, Linton Road, Barking Essex IG11 8JU England. **Tel** 011 44 81 5947272, FAX 081-594-5942, telex 896950. **LC** TS283; .D46. **DD** 681/.76041.
**Ind/Abst** Ei Page One.

US/0745-449X
**DIE CASTING MANAGEMENT.** [Die cast. manage.]. **Added/Corp** American Die Casting Institute (Des Plaines, Ill.). Vol. 1, No. 1 (Jan./Feb. 1983)-. Periodical. English. bm. $35.00. C K Publishing Inc, 3110 Pleasant Drive, Box 247, Wonder Lake IL 60097. **Tel** (815)728-0912. **ED** John J Kolar. **LC** TS239; .D515. **DD** 671.2/53. **Bk Rev**. **Ad Acc. Circ:** 3,300 (ctrl).
**Desc:** Edited for management decision makers in the die-casting industry and to contribute to the profitable management of the die-casting business.
**Ind/Abst** Leadscan.

US
**DIEMAKING STAMPING & EDMING.** ***Title Change.*** **See** Engineering-Mechanical Engineering and Machinery.

KO/0376-8449
**DIRECTORY : KOREA ELECTRONICS MANUFACTURERS.** **VFOAT** Directory of Korea Electronics Manufacturers; Korea Electronics Manufacturers. Directory. Multiple languages (English and Korean). Korea Electronics and Manufacturers, Fine Instruments Center, 222-13 Kuro-dong, Seoul Korea. **LC** HD9696.A3; K75.

US/0145-3866
**DIRECTORY - NATIONAL FLUID POWER ASSOCIATION.** **See** Engineering-Mechanical Engineering and Machinery.

US/0084-9898
**DIRECTORY OF COLORADO MANUFACTURERS.** **Added/Corp** Colorado Development Council. University of Colorado (Boulder Campus). Bureau of Business Research. University of Colorado, Boulder. Business Research Division. (19??)-. English. ir (Published every 18 months). $75.00. Business Research Division, Campus Box 420, University of Colorado at Boulder, Boulder CO 80309-0420. **Tel** (303)492-8227, FAX (303)492-3620. **ED** Ginny Sue Hayden. **LC** T12; .C6. **DD** 338.4/767/025788. ***Continues*** *University of Colorado (Boulder Campus). Bureau of Business Research. Colorado Manufacturers Directory.*
**Desc:** Includes address, zip, telephone, year established, officers and number of employees.

US/1052-0031
**DIRECTORY OF FOREIGN MANUFACTURERS IN THE UNITED STATES.** [Dir. foreign manuf. U. S.]. **Added/Corp** Georgia State University. School of Business Administration. Publishing Services Division. Georgia State University. College of Business Administration. Business Publishing Division. Georgia State University. Business Press. **VFOAT** Foreign Manufacturers in the U.S. (1975)-. English. ir. $195.00. Georgia State University Business Press, University Plaza, Atlanta GA 30303. **Tel** (404)651-4253, FAX (404)651-4256. **ED** Jerrey Arpan and David Ricks. **LC** HD9723; .D39. **DD** 338.8/8873/025.
**Desc:** Listing of over 5,000 foreign-owned companies in the U.S. with name, address and parent company listed.

US/0095-4446
**DIRECTORY OF IOWA MANUFACTURERS.** ***Title Change.*** [Dir. Iowa manuf.]. **VFOAT** Iowa Manufacturers. Directory. English. an. Manufacturers News Inc., 1633 Central Street, Evanston IL 60201-1569. **Tel** (708)864-7000, FAX (708)332-1100. **LC** T12; .I684. **DD** 338.4/7/6702577. ***Continues*** *Directory, Iowa Manufacturers, A Buyer's Guide.* ***Continued by*** *Official Iowa Manufacturers Directory, 1056-6872.*
**Desc:** Lists 4,837 manufacturing and processing companies, names and titles of 9,500 officers. Information on annual sales, plant size, number of employees, type of in-house computer and language used.

US/0070-5721
**DIRECTORY OF KANSAS MANUFACTURERS AND THEIR PRODUCTS.** **Added/Corp** Kansas. Dept. of Commerce. Kansas. Industrial Development Division. Kansas. Dept. of Economic Development. Economic Analysis Section. Kansas. Dept. of Economic Development. Research Division. Kansas Industrial Development Commission. Economics Research Division. Kansas Industrial Development Commission. Research Division. **VFOAT** Directory of Kansas Manufacturers and Products; Kansas Manufacturers and Products; Kansas Manufacturers and Their Products; Kansas Directory of Manufacturers and Products. (1957)-. English. an. $42.10 Kansas; $40.00 other. Kansas Department of Commerce, 700 SW Harrison, Suite 1300, Topeka KS 66603. **Tel** (913)296-3479, (913)296-3481. **LC** T12; .K2. **DD** 670.58. ***Continues*** *Made in Kansas, 0415-9586.*

US/0190-3047
**DIRECTORY OF MANUFACTURERS, STATE OF HAWAII.** **Added/Corp** Chamber of Commerce of Hawaii. (1967/68)-. Directory. English. be. $22.00. Chamber of Commerce of Hawaii, 735 Bishop Street, Suite 220, Honolulu HI 96813. **Tel** (808)522-8813. **ED** Tatsuko Horjo. **LC** HD9727.H3; D57. **DD** 338/.0025/969. **Circ:** 500.

**Desc:** Lists manufacturers by SIC classifications, and alphabetically by island; contains trade names of products.

US
**DIRECTORY OF MANUFACTURING INDUSTRIES OF ROCHESTER AND MONROE COUNTY, NEW YORK : INFORMATION AS SUPPLIED BY THE FIRMS LISTED, OR COMPILED FROM AVAILABLE SOURCES.** **Added/Corp** Rochester Area Chamber of Commerce (N.Y.). Business and Economic Development Dept. **VFOAT** Industrial Directory, Rochester and Monroe County, New York. (1979)-. English. Rochester Area Chamber of Commerce, 55 St Paul Street, Rochester NY 14604. ***Continues*** *Industrial Directory of Rochester, N.Y. and Monroe County.*

US/0889-0382
**DIRECTORY OF NEW ENGLAND MANUFACTURERS.** ***Title Change.*** [Dir. N. Engl. manuf.]. **Added/Corp** New England Council. (19??)-(1992). Directory. English. George D. Hall Company, 50 Congress Street, Boston MA 02109. **Tel** (800)446-1215, (617)523-3745. **LC** HD9723; .D45. **DD** 338.4/767/02574 /2 19. ***Continued by*** *George D. Hall's Directory of New England Manufacturers.*

US
**DIRECTORY OF NORTH DAKOTA MANUFACTURERS & FOOD PROCESSORS.** **Added/Corp** North Dakota. Dept. of Economic Development & Finance. **VFOAT** North Dakota Manufacturers & Food Processors; Directory of North Dakota Manufacturers and Food Processors. (1991)-. Directory. English. $70.00. Manufacturers News Inc., 1633 Central Street, Evanston IL 60201-1569. **Tel** (708)864-7000, FAX (708)332-1100. **LC** HD9727.N9; D57. **DD** 338/.0025/784. ***Continues*** *North Dakota Directory of Manufacturers.*

US/0070-6027
**DIRECTORY OF OREGON MANUFACTURERS.** **Added/Corp** Oregon. Dept. of Economic Development. Oregon. Planning and Development Division. Oregon. Economic Development Division. **VFOAT** Oregon, Directory of Oregon Manufacturers. (1966)-. Directory. English. be (Jan.). $128.86 (IL residents, includes 7.75% sales tax); $125.00 (other, includes postage). Oregon Economic Development Department, 775 Summer Street NE, Salem OR 97310. **Tel** (503)373-1205, FAX (503)581-5115. ***Continues*** *Directory of Oregon Manufacturers and Buyer's Guide.*

CN/0845-6208
**DIRECTORY OF PRODUCTS AND MANUFACTURERS, NEW BRUNSWICK, CANADA.** (DIRECTORY OF PRODUCTS AND MANUFACTURERS, NEW BRUNSWICK / REPERTOIRE DES PRODUITS ET FABRICANTS, NOUVEAU-BRUNSWICK.). [Dir. prod. manuf. N.B. Can.]. **Added/Corp** New Brunswick. Dept. of Commerce and Development. New Brunswick. Dept. of Commerce and Technology. **VFOAT** Repertoire des Produits et Fabricants, Nouveau-Brunswick. (1982)-. English (French). an. New Brunswick Department of Commerce and Development, PO Box 6000, Fredericton New Brunswick E3B 5H1 Canada. **Tel** (506)453-2629, FAX (506)453-7904. **DD** 338.7/67/025715. **Circ:** 8,000. ***Continued in part by*** *Repertoire des Produits & Fabricants, Nouveau-Brunswick., 0845-6216.*

CN/0843-2511
**DIRECTORY OF PRODUCTS AND MANUFACTURERS (SAINT JOHN, N.B.).** (DIRECTORY OF PRODUCTS AND MANUFACTURERS.). [Dir. prod. manuf.]. 1989-. Directory. English. an. $5.00. Manufacturers Directory, c/o Fundy Region Development Commission, 57 King Street, Saint John New Brunswick E2L 1G5 Canada. **Tel** (506)658-2918, FAX (506)658-2861. **ED** Patricia McKinney. **DD** 338/.0025/71532. Index available. ***Continues*** *Manufacturers Directory (Saint John, N.B.), 0713-5556.*
**Desc:** A southern New Brunswick directory of manufacturers and processors, providing product/company indexes and a detailed company list.

US/0070-6450
**DIRECTORY OF TENNESSEE MANUFACTURERS.** [Dir. Tenn. manuf.]. (198?)-. Directory. English. an (Apr.). $81.00. Manufacturers News Inc., 1633 Central Street, Evanston IL 60201-1569. **Tel** (708)864-7000, FAX (708)332-1100. **ED** Martha Smith. **LC** T12; .T43. **DD** 338.7/67/025768. **Ad Acc. Circ:** 6,500 (ctrl). ***Continues*** *Tennessee Directory of Manufacturers, 0196-5360.*
**Desc:** Reference guide to over 5,000 manufacturers in Tennessee.

US
**DIRECTORY OF TEXAS MANUFACTURERS / BUREAU OF BUSINESS RESEARCH, UNIVERSITY OF TEXAS.** **Added/Corp** University of Texas. Bureau of Business Research. University of Texas at Austin. Bureau of Business Research. (1932)-. English. Fourteen times a year. $135.00. Bureau of Business Research / Texas, University of Texas at Austin, Box 7459, Austin TX 78713. **Tel** (512)471-1616, FAX (512)471-1063. **ED** Ida Lambeth. **LC** HD9727.T4; D5. **DD** 338.4/767/025764. **Circ:** 5,000.
**Desc:** Directory of manufacturers including chief officers, products, sales figures, addresses and phone numbers. Also indicates type of company and width of goods distribution.

MY/0126-9801
**DIRECTORY - PERSEKUTUAN PEKILAND-PEKILANG MALAYSIA.** **Main/Corp** Persekutuan Pekiland-Pekilang Malaysia. Directory. English. an. $49.00 Malaysian, Singapore; $28.00 Asean countries; $33.00 East Asia; $37.00 other Asian countries; $35.00 Australia; $44.00 UK, US, Canada; $42.00 Europe. Federation of Malaysian Manufacturers, 17th Floor Wisma Sime Darby, Jalan Raja Laut, PO Box 12194, 50770 Kuala Lumpur Malaysia. **Tel** 03-2931244, telex MA 32437 FMM. **LC** T12.5.M4; P47A. **DD** 670/.25/595. Index available. **Ad Acc. Circ:** 2,000 (ctrl). ***Continues*** *Federation of Malaysian Manufacturers' Directory.*
**Desc:** Guide to business opportunities in Malaysia containing updated profiles of 700 leading manufacturers in Malaysia.

●CN/1191-4297
**DISCOVERY NEWS.** [Discov. news]. **Added/Corp** British Columbia. Discovery Foundation. Vol. 1, No. 1 (Winter 1992)-. English. **DD** 670. ***Continues*** *BCdiscovery (British Columbia. Discovery Foundation)., 0842-4500.*

BE/0012-3935
**DISTRIBUTION D'AUJOURD'HUI.** [Distrib. aujourd'hui]. (1968)-. Trade Publication. Multiple languages (French and Dutch). Ten times a year. 9328F Belgium; 9900F other. Comite Belge la Distribution, 34 rue Marianne, 1180 Brussels Belgium. **Tel** 32 2 3459923, FAX 32 2 3460204. **ED** M. Leon and F. Wegner. **UDC** 339.86. Index available. cum. index. **Ad Acc.** ***Continues*** *Revue Belge de la Distribution, 0773-1183.*
**Desc:** Trade magazine for manufacturers and distributors.

US/0737-0105
**DIXIE GUN WORKS BLACKPOWDER ANNUAL.** [Dixie Gun Works blackpowder annu.]. **VFOAT** Blackpowder Annual. Periodical. English. an. $2.95 US; $3.50 Canada. Pioneer Press / Tennessee, PO Box 684 Gunpowder Lane, Union City TN 38261. **Tel** (901)885-0374, FAX (901)885-0440. **ED** George Winter and Sherry Schmidt. **LC** TS536.6.M8; D59. **DD** 683.4/005. Index available. **Ad Acc. Circ:** 80,000.

GW/0303-2507
**DRAHTHERSTELLUNG UND BEARBEITUNG, DRAHTERZEUGNISSE.** [Drahtherstell. -bearbeit., Drahterzeugn.]. **VFOAT** Wire and Wire Products. Multiple languages. bm. VDI Verlag GmbH, Postfach 101054, D 40001 Dusseldorf Germany. **Tel** 011 49 211 6188313, FAX 011 49 211 6188133. **(Subscription address:** Fulfillment Office, PO Box 1831, Birmingham, AL 35201**)** **LC** Z7914.W7; D73.

CN/0226-7748
**E I C, ELECTRONIQUE, INDUSTRIELLE & COMMERCIALE.** **See** Engineering-Electricity, Electrical Engineering, Electronics.

CN/0828-1777
**ELECTRIC LAMPS, LIGHT BULBS, AND TUBES.** [Electr. lamps, Light bulbs tubes.]. **Added/Corp** Statistics Canada. Industry Division. **VFOAT** Electric Lamps; Lampes Electriques, Ampoules et Tubes. Vol. 14, No. 2 (Feb. 1985)-. English (French). mo. 60.00Can$ Canada; $72.00 US; $84.00 other. Statistics Canada, Publications Sales & Services, Main Building Room 1710, Ottawa Ontario K1A 0T6 Canada. **Tel** (613)951-5078, (800)267-6677, FAX (613)951-1584, telex 053-3585. **LC** HD9697.L333; C224. **DD** 338.4/7621322/0971021. ***Continues*** *Electric Lamps, Light Sources., 0705-5536.*
**Desc:** Contains data on manufacturers' sales (including imports) of electric lamps, light bulbs and tubes.

US/0895-3716
**ELECTRICAL MANUFACTURING (LIBERTYVILLE, ILL.).** ***Title Change.*** (ELECTRICAL MANUFACTURING.). [Electr. manuf.]. Vol. 1 No. 1 (Nov. 1987)-(19??). Periodical. English. bm. IHS Publishing Group, 17730 West Peterson Road, Libertyville IL 60048. **Tel** (708)362-8711, FAX (708)362-3484. **ED** Jennifer Rose and Peter Wagner. **LC** TK7869; .E37. **DD** 621.3. **CODEN** ELEMED. **[CCC].** Index available. **Bk Rev. Ad Acc.** ctrl circ. available on microfilm and microfiche from University Microfilms International (UMI). Documents available from Article Express International, Ask*IEEE. ***Continues*** *Electri-Onics (Electrical Manufacturing Ed.), 0895-3724.* ***Continued by*** *Electrical Design & Mfg., 1065-7436.*
**Desc:** The only magazine concentrating exclusively on the manufacturing, design, development, use, and testing of electrical and electromechanical products and products which are electrically powered, operated, or controlled.
**Ind/Abst** Ei Page One; Eng. Index Annu.; INSPEC (Jan. 1988-).

US/1041-052X
**ELECTRO MANUFACTURING.** [Electro manuf.]. (1988)-. Periodical. English. mo. $150.00 North America. WV Publishing Company, PO Box 138, Babson Park, Boston MA 02157. **DD** 338. available on an online database (file 636/Full-Text) from DIALOG.
**Ind/Abst** PTS Newsl. Database [Full Txt.].

US/0735-3316
**ELECTRONIC INDUSTRY MANUFACTURERS REPRESENTATIVES LOCATOR.** **VFOAT** Locator. 1981/82-. English. an. Electronic Representatives Association, 20 East Huron Street, Chicago IL 60611. ***Continues*** *Electronics Industry Directory of Manufacturers Representatives.*

US
**ELECTRONICS IN MANUFACTURING QUARTERLY.** English. qt. $60.00 US, $64.00 Canada and Mexico (business, library and academic institution); $80.00 (airmail), other. Society of Manufacturing Engineers, One SME Drive, PO Box 930, Member's Records Dept., Dearborn MI 48121-0930. **Tel** (313)271-1500, FAX (313)271-2861, telex 297742 SME UR (VIA RCA).

●US/1060-2100
**ELECTRONICS MANUFACTURERS DIRECTORY.** [Electron. manuf. dir.]. **Added/Corp** Harris Publishing Co. (1993)-. English. an. $245.00. Harris Publishing Company, 2057-2 Aurora Road, Twinsburg OH 44087. **Tel** (800)888-5900, (216)425-9000, FAX (216)425-7150, telex 510 601 1740. **LC** HD9696.A3; U6217. **DD** 381/.45621381/02573. available on CD-ROM and diskette. ***Continues*** *U.S. Electronics Industry Directory, 1047-5583.*
**Desc:** Covers over 17,000 U.S. electronics manufacturing firms and nearly 2,000 Canadian electronics manufacturing firms. Written for anyone who provides products or services to the electronics industry.

GW/0170-2033
**ELEKTRISCHE ENERGIE-TECHNIK.** **See** Energy.

US
**ENTERPRISE INTEGRATION STRATEGIES.** ***Title Change.*** English. mo. Advance Manufacturing Research, 2 Oliver Street, Fifth Floor, Boston MA 02109. **Tel** (617)542-6600. ***Continues*** *CIM Strategies, 0748-9250.* ***Continued by*** *AMR's CIM Strategies.*

●UK/1352-8882
**ENVIRONMENT BUSINESS MAGAZINE.** **See** Environmental Issues-Pollution and Waste Management.

GW
**EXPORT TRADE TODAY (ENGINEERING EDITION).** (EXPORT TRADE TODAY.). **VFOAT** Export Markt. Periodical. English. an. DM12.00. Vogel Verlag, Postfach 6740, D-97064 Wuerzburg Germany. **Tel** 011 49 931 4182145, 011 49 931 4182483, FAX 011 49 931 4182670, telex 841 680131. **ED** Arnold Metzner. **LC** HD9735.G3; E95. **DD** 670/.943. Index available. **Ad Acc. Circ:** 20,000 (ctrl).
**Desc:** A product kaleidoscope of dynamic companies.

US/0888-0301
**FABRICATOR (ROCKFORD, ILL.).** (THE FABRICATOR.). **Added/Corp** Fabricators & Manufacturers Association International. (198?)-. Periodical. English. Ten times a year. Free (trade), $30.00 (nontrade) US; $50.00 Canada & Mexico; $125.00 other. Croydon Group Ltd., 833 Featherstone Road, Rockford IL 61107. **Tel** (815)399-8700, FAX (815)399-7279. **ED** Theresa Olmsted. **DD** 338. Index available. cum. index. **Ad Acc, Adv Mgr:** Mike Lacny. **Circ:** 55,000 (ctrl). ***Continues*** *FMA's Journal of the Fabricator, 0192-8066.*
**Desc:** Technical information for sheet metal fabrication.
**Ind/Abst** Alum. Ind. Abstr.; Met. Abstr.

BE/0377-9084
**FABRIMETAL.** [Fabrimetal]. (19??)-. Periodical. French (Dutch). Nine times a year. 1378.00F Belgium; 1500.00F other. Documenta, 21 rue des Drapiers, 1050 Brussels Belgium. **Tel** 011 32 2 5102481, FAX 011 32 2 5102301, telex 21078. **ED** Luc Lambrecht, Dirk Vermeiren, Patrick Gillerot, Katleen de Bosscher. Index available. cum. index. **Bk Rev. Ad Acc. Circ:** 8,100 (ctrl). available with charts; available with illustrations. ***Continues*** *Revue Mensuelle de Fabrimetal Magazine.*

UK/0263-2772
**FACILITIES (BRADFORD, WEST YORKSHIRE, ENGLAND).** (FACILITIES.). (1983)-. Periodical. English. Thirteen times a year. $919.00. MCB University Press, 60 62 Toller Lane, Bradford West Yorkshire BD8 9BX England. **Tel** 011 44 274 499821, FAX 011 44 274 547143, telex 51317 MCBUNI G. **(Subscription address:** MCB University Press / US and Canada Subscriptions, PO Box 10812, Birmingham AL 35201-0812.**)** **ED** Jeremy Melvin and Keith Alexander. **LC** TS177; .F32. **DD** 658.2.
**Desc:** Provides information for facilities managers by supplying information on all aspects of accommodation management.
**Ind/Abst** Oper. Prod. Manage. Abstr. [Full Txt.].

UK/0014-6579
**FACTORY EQUIPMENT NEWS.** (19??)-. English. mo. $159.00 US & Canada; £35.00 UK. Wilmington Publishing Ltd., PO Box 200, Field End Road, Ruislip Middx HA4 OSY England. **Tel** 011 44 81 841 3970, FAX 011 44 81 841 9676.

US/0276-3389
**FINISHED BROADWOVEN FABRIC PRODUCTION.** (CURRENT INDUSTRIAL REPORTS. MA-22S, FINISHED BROADWOVEN FABRIC PRODUCTION / U.S. DEPARTMENT OF COMMERCE, BUREAU OF THE CENSUS.). **Added/Corp** United States. Bureau of the Census. **VFOAT** Finished Broadwoven Fabric Production. (1976)-. Government Publication. English. an. $1.25. US Department of Commerce, 14th Street & Constitution Avenue NW, Washington DC 20230. **Tel** (202)482-2000, FAX (202)482-3772. **(Subscription address:** US Government Bookstore / O'Neil Building, 2023 3rd Avenue North, Birmingham AL 35203.**)** **LC** HD9851; .F56. **DD** 338.4/7677/00973. ***Continues** Broadwoven Fabrics Finished.*
**Desc:** Presents timely data on the production, inventories, and orders of approximately 5,000 products, which represents 40 percent of all US manufacturing.

US/0272-5509
**FINISHED FABRICS. PRODUCTION, INVENTORIES, AND UNFILLED ORDERS.** (CURRENT INDUSTRIAL REPORTS. M22A, FINISHED FABRICS, PRODUCTION, INVENTORIES, AND UNFILLED ORDERS.). Jan. 1980-. Government Publication. English. mo. $15.00. US Department of Commerce, 14th Street & Constitution Avenue NW, Washington DC 20230. **Tel** (202)482-2000, FAX (202)482-3772. **LC** HD9851; .U53B. **DD** 338.4/7677/00973. Documents available from Documents on Demand. ***Continues** Woven Fabrics, Production, Inventories, and Unfilled Orders, 0145-5028.*
**Desc:** Presents timely data on the production, inventories, and orders of approximately 5,000 products, which represents 40 percent of all US manufacturers.
**Ind/Abst** Am. Stat. Index; Text. Technol. Dig.

US
**FINISHING LINE QUARTERLY.** English. qt (Mar., June, Sept., Dec.). $60.00 US, $64.00 Canada and Mexico (business, library and academic institution); $80.00 (airmail), other. Society of Manufacturing Engineers, One SME Drive, PO Box 930, Member's Records Dept., Dearborn MI 48121-0930. **Tel** (313)271-1500, FAX (313)271-2861, telex 297742 SME UR (VIA RCA).

HU/0231-2662
**FINOMMECHANIKA-MIKROTECHNIKA.** [Finommech., mikrotech.]. 12. Vol. - 1973-. Periodical. Hungarian. 72.00ft. Lapkiado Vallalat, Lenin Korut 9-11, 1073 Budapest 7, Hungary. **Tel** 222-408. **LC** TS176; .F55. **CODEN** FNMKAY. Documents available from Ask*IEEE. ***Continues** Finommechanika.*
**Ind/Abst** EMBASE; INSPEC (April 1973-); Int. Aerosp. Abstr.

UK
**FINTECH. ADVANCED MANUFACTURING.** English. sm. £366.00. Financial Times Business Information Ltd., Tower House, Southampton Street, London WC2E 7HA England. **Tel** 011 44 71 353 1040. **(Subscription address:** 30 Epsom Road, Guildford Surrey GU1 3LE England; FAX 0483 302457**)** **ED** John Dwyer. available on microfiche.
**Ind/Abst** PROMT; PTS Newsl. Database [Full Txt.].

US/0882-9438
**FLORIDA MANUFACTURERS REGISTER.** [Fla. manuf. regist.]. 1st Ed. (1986)-. Directory. English. an (Mar.). $112.00 (print); $695.00 (diskette or CD-ROM). Manufacturers News Inc., 1633 Central Street, Evanston IL 60201-1569. **Tel** (708)864-7000, FAX (708)332-1100. **ED** Louise West. **LC** HD9727.F6; F573. **DD** 338.7/67/025759. **Bk Rev. Ad Acc.** ctrl circ.
**Desc:** Lists manufacturers and processing companies; names and titles of officers.

US/0193-5518
**FLUID POWER INDUSTRY OUTLOOK SURVEY.** **Main/Corp** National Fluid Power Association. **VFOAT** Industry Outlook Survey. English. an. $100.00, $50.00 (members). National Fluid Power Association, 3333 North Mayfair Road, Milwaukee WI 53222. **Tel** (414)778-3369, FAX (414)778-3361, telex 704557. **ED** Stephen Latin-Kasper. **LC** HD9705.U6; N27A. **DD** 338.4/7/6817. **Circ:** 350 (ctrl).
**Desc:** Results of annual outlook survey of NFPA member companies. An average of 95 companies participate in the survey, which asks them to estimate calendar year increases in orders and shipments for industrial and mobile hydraulic and pneumatic products, and reveal their "big worries" for the upcoming year. Available with a 35mm slide show.

US/0894-8348
**FURNITURE & CABINET MANUFACTURING.** ***Title Change.*** **See** Interior Design-Home Furnishings.

UK/0306-0519
**FURNITURE MANUFACTURER.** [Furnit. manuf.]. (1975)-. Periodical. English. mo. £42.00 UK and North Ireland; £51.00 (seamail, overseas); £62.00 (airmail) Europe; £69.00 (airmail) other. Publex International Ltd., 110 Station Road East, Oxted Surrey RH8 0QA England. **Tel** 011 44 883 717755, FAX 011 44 883 714554, telex 95359 PUBLEX G. ***Continues** Furniture & Bedding Production.*

US/0743-6858
**GEAR TECHNOLOGY. See** Engineering-Mechanical Engineering and Machinery.

US/0889-0390
**GEORGE D. HALL'S DIRECTORY OF CENTRAL ATLANTIC STATES MANUFACTURERS.** [George D. Hall's dir. cent. Atl. manuf.]. **VFOAT** Central Atlantic States Manufacturers. (1986)-. Directory. English. be. $92.10 (MA residents includes 5% sales tax); $87.95 (other0. George D. Hall Company, 50 Congress Street, Boston MA 02109. **Tel** (800)446-1215, (617)523-3745. **LC** T12; .D485. **DD** 338.7/67/02574. available on diskette. ***Continues** Directory of Central Atlantic States Manufacturers, 0070-5241.*
**Desc:** Covers over 14,000 manufacturing companies listing the company name, address, telephone, SIC numbers, number of employees, key executives by name and function, and product.

US/0196-8270
**GEORGE D. HALL'S DIRECTORY OF CONNECTICUT MANUFACTURERS.** [George D. Hall's dir. Conn. manuf.]. **Main/Corp** Hall, George D., Company, Boston. **VFOAT** Directory of Connecticut Manufacturers. Directory. English. an. $46.00. George D. Hall Company, 50 Congress Street, Boston MA 02109. **Tel** (800)446-1215, (617)523-3745. **LC** HD9727.C8; H34A. **DD** 338/.0025/746.
**Desc:** Manufacturing companies in Connecticut listed alphabetically, geographically, and by product, company name, address, telephone number, number of employees, key executives (by name and title) and product description.

US/0149-6913
**GEORGE D. HALL'S DIRECTORY OF MASSACHUSETTS MANUFACTURERS.** [George D. Hall's dir. Mass. manuf.]. **VFOAT** Directory of Massachusetts Manufacturers. Directory. English. ir (every 18 months). $48.00. George D. Hall Company, 50 Congress Street, Boston MA 02109. **Tel** (800)446-1215, (617)523-3745. **LC** HD9727.M4; G46. **DD** 338.4/7/00025744. **Ad Acc. Circ:** 5,000.
**Desc:** Approximately 22,000 manufacturing companies in New England listed alphabetically, geographically by product, company name, address, telephone number, number of employees, key executive (by name and title), and product description.

●US
**GEORGE D. HALL'S DIRECTORY OF NEW ENGLAND MANUFACTURERS.** **Added/Corp** George D. Hall Company. **VFOAT** Directory of New England Manufacturers. (1994)-. Directory. English. ir (every 16 mos.). $128.00. George D. Hall Company, 50 Congress Street, Boston MA 02109. **Tel** (800)446-1215, (617)523-3745. ***Continues** Directory of New England Manufacturers, 0889-0382.*

●US/1069-5176
**GEORGE D. HALL'S DIRECTORY OF NEW JERSEY MANUFACTURERS.** [George D. Hall's dir. N.J. manuf.]. **Added/Corp** George D. Hall Company. **VFOAT** Directory of New Jersey Manufacturers; Directory of N.J. Manufacturers. (1993)-. Directory. English. $87.90 (MA residents includes 5% sales tax); $83.95 (other). George D. Hall Company, 50 Congress Street, Boston MA 02109. **Tel** (800)446-1215, (617)523-3745. **LC** HD9727.N5; G46. **DD** 338.4/7/000294749. ***Continues** George D. Hall's New Jersey Manufacturers Directory, 0278-9124.*

●US
**GEORGE D. HALL'S DIRECTORY OF NEW YORK MANUFACTURES.** **Added/Corp** George D. Hall Company. **VFOAT** Directory of New York Manufactures; Directory of N.Y. Manufactures. (1993)-. Directory. English. $87.90 (MA residents includes 5% sales tax); $83.95 (other). George D. Hall Company, 50 Congress Street, Boston MA 02109. **Tel** (800)446-1215, (617)523-3745. ***Continues** George D. Hall's New York Manufacturers Directory, 0272-1074.*

US/0892-8282
**GEORGE D. HALL'S DIRECTORY OF NORTH CAROLINA MANUFACTURERS.** [George D. Hall's dir. N.C. manuf.]. **Added/Corp** George D. Hall Company. **VFOAT** Directory of North Carolina Manufacturers. (19??)-. Directory. English. ir. $53.95. George D. Hall Company, 50 Congress Street, Boston MA 02109. **Tel** (800)446-1215, (617)523-3745. **LC** HD9727.N8; G46. **DD** 338.7/67/025756.

US/0278-9124
**GEORGE D. HALL'S NEW JERSEY MANUFACTURERS DIRECTORY.** ***Title Change.*** [George D. Hall's N. J. manuf. dir.]. **Added/Corp** New Jersey Business & Industry Association. George D. Hall Company. **VFOAT** New Jersey Manufacturers Directory. (19??)-(19??). Directory. English. an. George D. Hall Company, 50 Congress Street, Boston MA 02109. **Tel** (800)446-1215, (617)523-3745. **LC** HD9727.N5; G46. **DD** 338.4/7/000294749. **Ad Acc.** ***Continued by** George D. Hall's Directory of New Jersey Manufacturers, 1069-5176.*
**Desc:** 19,000 New Jersey manufacturers listed alphabetically, geographically by product, company name, address, telephone number, number of employees, key personnel by name and title, and product description.

US/0272-1074
**GEORGE D. HALL'S NEW YORK MANUFACTURERS DIRECTORY.** ***Title Change.*** [George D. Hall's N. Y. manuf. dir.]. **Main/Corp** George D. Hall Company. **VFOAT** New York Manufacturers Directory. (19??)-(19??). Directory. English. be. George D. Hall Company, 50 Congress Street, Boston MA 02109. **Tel** (800)446-1215, (617)523-3745. **LC** HD9727.N7; H34a. **DD** 380.1/45/000294747. **Ad Acc.** ***Continued by** George D. Hall's Directory of New York Manufacturers.*
**Desc:** 20,000 New York manufacturers listed alphabetically, geographically and by product, company name, address, telephone number, number of employees, key personnel by name and title and product description.

US/0896-4009
**GEORGIA MANUFACTURERS REGISTER.** **Added/Corp** Manufacturers' News, Inc. (1989)-. Directory. English. an. $89.00 (print); $595.00 (diskette or CD-ROM). Manufacturers News Inc., 1633 Central Street, Evanston IL 60201-1569. **Tel** (708)864-7000, FAX (708)332-1100. **LC** HD9727.G4; G43. **DD** 670/.29/4758.

US/0435-5482
**GEORGIA MANUFACTURING DIRECTORY.** **Added/Corp** Georgia. Dept. of Commerce. Georgia. Dept. of Industry and Trade. Georgia. Bureau of Industry and Trade. (19??)-. Directory. English. an (Spring). $55.00. Georgia Department of Industry and Trade, Directory Service, PO Box 56706, Atlanta GA 30343. **Tel** (404)656-7728, telex 211988. **ED** Deborah Battle (editor's address: P O Box 1776, Atlanta, GA 30301; phone#(404)656-3607).
**Desc:** Lists 9,361 manufacturers throughout Georgia. Information is indexed by company name, county location, product (SIC), and parent company. Listings contain company name, address, phone, key executives, most important to least important product made, market served, parent company, home office location, year established in Georgia, and number of employees.

US/0272-958X
**GLOVES AND MITTENS.** (CURRENT INDUSTRIAL REPORTS. MA-23D, GLOVES AND MITTENS / U.S. DEPARTMENT OF COMMERCE, BUREAU OF THE CENSUS.). **Added/Corp** United States. Bureau of the Census. **VFOAT** Gloves and Mittens. (1965)-. Government Publication. English. an. $1.00. US Department of Commerce / Bureau of the Census, Data User Services Division, Customer Services, Washington DC 20233-0800. **Tel** (301)763-4100. **(Subscription address:** Superintendent of Documents, US Government Printing Office, Washington DC 20402.**)** **LC** HD9947.U6; G48. **DD** 338.4/76854/0973. ***Continues** Current Industrial Reports. M23D, Gloves and Mittens.*
**Desc:** Presents timely data on the production, inventories, and orders of approximately 5,000 products, which represents 40 percent of all US manufacturing.
**Ind/Abst** Text. Technol. Dig. (19??-199?).

US/0196-626X
**GMP LETTER, THE.** [GMP lett.]. **VAT** Good Manufacturing Practices Letter. (Feb. 1980)-. Periodical. English. mo. $407.00 North America; $432.00 other. Washington Business Information Inc., 1117 North 19th Street, Suite 200, Arlington VA 22209. **Tel** (703)247-3433, (800)426-0416, FAX (703)247-3421. **ED** Sam Gilston. **LC** KF3827.M4; A134. **DD** 344.73/042; 347.30442. **[CCC].** available on an online database from DIALOG.

**Desc:** Helps firms cope as federal regulations move into enforcement and actual practice. Also provides detailed and technical help in complying with these crucial rules.

US/1047-6555
**GMP TRENDS.** [GMP trends]. **VAT** Good Manufacturing Practices Trends. No. 1 (1977)-. Periodical. English. sm. $240.00 US and Canada; $270.00 other. GMP Trends, PO Box 8001, Boulder CO 80306. **Tel** (303)443-8716, FAX (303)443-3317. **ED** Rosemary Oliverio. **DD** 338. **Circ:** 1,000.
**Desc:** A unique information dissemination letter publishing significant observations made by FDA Investigators during plant inspections. Edited excerpts form actual FD483 reports are categorized into five sections: Manufacturing Controls; Sterile Product Controls; Packaging/Labeling; Laboratory Controls; and Medical Device/Critical. A publication that helps with interpretation of FDA regulations and policy.

UK
**GRAMPIAN BUSINESS DIRECTORY.** Directory. English. an. £5.00. Grampian Regional Council, Economic Development and Planning Dept, Woodhill House Westburn Road, Aberdeen AB9 2LU Scotland. **Tel** 11 44 224 643322, FAX 0224 697445, telex 739277. **Ad Acc. Circ:** 10,000.
**Desc:** Directory of business contacts for Grampian, Scotland specializing in oil and related industries, professional services and other manufacturing.

AT
**GREAT SOUTHERN MANUFACTURERS DIRECTORY.** Directory. English. an. Department of Industrial Development / Western Australia, 63 Serpentine Road, Albany Western Australia 633 Australia. **LC** HD9738.A83; A423. **DD** 381/.45/0002949412.

US/0890-7242
**GUAYULERO, EL.** [Guayulero]. **Added/Corp** Guayule Rubber Society, Inc. University of California, Riverside. Dept. of Botany and Plant Sciences. Vol. 2 (Fall 1980)-. Periodical. English. sa. $15.00. Guayule Rubber Society, Department of Botany and Plant Science, Riverside CA 92521. **Tel** (714)787-1012. **DD** 678. ***Continues*** *Bulletin of Los Guayuleros.*

CN/0227-2059
**GUIDE TO CANADIAN MANUFACTURERS.** [Guide Can. manuf.]. **Added/Corp** Dun & Bradstreet Canada. (1978)-. English. an. price varies per volume. Dun & Bradstreet Canada Ltd., 5770 Hurontario Street, 10th Floor, Mississauga L5R 365 ONT Canada. **Tel** (905)568-6000. **(Subscription address:** Dun & Bradstreet Information Service, Business Reference Service, 3 Sylvan Way, Parsippany NJ 07054.**)** **LC** HF322.3; .G85. **DD** 338.4/0971.
**Desc:** Contains names, addresses, telephone numbers, sales volume, number of employees, line of business, raw material purchased, capital equipment purchase, and products produced.

US/0073-0211
**HANDLOADER'S DIGEST.** 1st Ed. (1962)-. English. an. $24.00 US; $30.00 other. Comics Journal, 7563 Lake City Way Northeast, Seattle WA 98115. **Tel** (206)524-1967, FAX (206)524-2104. **ED** John T Amber. **LC** TS538; .H3. **DD** 683.4/06/05. **Circ:** 12,000.

●US/1065-4755
**HARRIS GEORGIA MANUFACTURERS DIRECTORY.** [Harris Ga. manuf. dir.]. **Added/Corp** Harris Publishing Co. **VFOAT** Georgia Manufacturers Directory. (1994)-. Directory. English. an (July). $97.00. Harris Publishing Company, 2057-2 Aurora Road, Twinsburg OH 44087. **Tel** (800)888-5900, (216)425-9000, FAX (216)425-7150, telex 510 601 1740. **DD** 338. available on CD-ROM and diskette.
**Desc:** Verified data on over 7,000 Georgia manufacturers.

●US/1061-2025
**HARRIS MANUFACTURERS DIRECTORY (MIDWESTERN ED.), THE.** (THE HARRIS MANUFACTURERS DIRECTORY.). (1992)-. Directory. English. an (January). $199.00. Harris Publishing Company, 2057-2 Aurora Road, Twinsburg OH 44087. **Tel** (800)888-5900, (216)425-9000, FAX (216)425-7150, telex 510 601 1740. available on CD-ROM and diskette.
**Desc:** The top 100 manufacturing business with 100 or more employees organized in a regional directory.

●US/1061-2076
**HARRIS MANUFACTURERS DIRECTORY (NATIONAL ED.).** (HARRIS MANUFACTURERS DIRECTORY.). [Harris manuf. dir.]. **Added/Corp** Harris Publishing Co. (1993)-. English. an (January). $495.00. Harris Publishing Company, 2057-2 Aurora Road, Twinsburg OH 44087. **Tel** (800)888-5900, (216)425-9000, FAX (216)425-7150, telex 510 601 1740. **DD** 338. available on CD-ROM and diskette.
**Desc:** Information on over 37,000 American manufacturers with 100+ employees.

●US/1061-2041
**HARRIS MANUFACTURERS DIRECTORY (NORTHEAST ED.).** (HARRIS MANUFACTURERS DIRECTORY.). [Harris manuf. dir.]. **Added/Corp** Harris Publishing Co. (1993)-. English. an (January). $199.00. Harris Publishing Company, 2057-2 Aurora Road, Twinsburg OH 44087. **Tel** (800)888-5900, (216)425-9000, FAX (216)425-7150, telex 510 601 1740. **LC** HF5041; .H37. **DD** 338.7/67/029474. available on CD-ROM and diskette.
**Desc:** Information on regional manufacturers with 100+ employees.

●US/1061-2033
**HARRIS MANUFACTURERS DIRECTORY (SOUTHEAST ED.).** (HARRIS MANUFACTURERS DIRECTORY.). [Harris manuf. dir.]. **Added/Corp** Harris Publishing Co. (1993)-. English. an (January). $199.00. Harris Publishing Company, 2057-2 Aurora Road, Twinsburg OH 44087. **Tel** (800)888-5900, (216)425-9000, FAX (216)425-7150, telex 510 601 1740. **LC** HF5044; .H37. **DD** 338.7/67/029475. available on CD-ROM and diskette.
**Desc:** Information on regional manufacturers with 100+ employees.

●US/1061-2068
**HARRIS MANUFACTURERS DIRECTORY (SOUTHWEST ED.), THE.** (THE HARRIS MANUFACTURERS DIRECTORY.). (1992)-. English. an (January). $199.00. Harris Publishing Company, 2057-2 Aurora Road, Twinsburg OH 44087. **Tel** (800)888-5900, (216)425-9000, FAX (216)425-7150, telex 510 601 1740. available on CD-ROM and diskette.
**Desc:** Information on regional manufacturers with 100+ employees.

●US/1061-205X
**HARRIS MANUFACTURERS DIRECTORY (WEST & SOUTHWEST ED.).** (HARRIS MANUFACTURERS DIRECTORY.). [Harris manuf. dir.]. **Added/Corp** Harris Publishing Co. (1993)-. English. an (January). $199.00. Harris Publishing Company, 2057-2 Aurora Road, Twinsburg OH 44087. **Tel** (800)888-5900, (216)425-9000, FAX (216)425-7150, telex 510 601 1740. **LC** HF5050; .H37. **DD** 338.7/67/029473. available on CD-ROM and diskette.
**Desc:** Information on regional manufacturers with 100+ employees.

●US/1065-7231
**HARRIS MARYLAND MANUFACTURERS DIRECTORY.** [Harris Md. manuf. dir.]. **Added/Corp** Maryland. Dept. of Economic and Employment Development. (1993)-. English. an (March). $62.00. Harris Publishing Company, 2057-2 Aurora Road, Twinsburg OH 44087. **Tel** (800)888-5900, (216)425-9000, FAX (216)425-7150, telex 510 601 1740. **DD** 338. available on CD-ROM and diskette. ***Continues*** *Harris Maryland Industrial Directory, 1055-5617.*
**Desc:** Verified data on over 4,795 Maryland manufacturers. Information on key executives, new firms, address changes, phone and fax numbers, company name changes and much more.

●US/1065-4720
**HARRIS NORTH CAROLINA MANUFACTURERS DIRECTORY.** (1993)-. Directory. English. an (March). $70.00. Harris Publishing Company, 2057-2 Aurora Road, Twinsburg OH 44087. **Tel** (800)888-5900, (216)425-9000, FAX (216)425-7150, telex 510 601 1740. available on CD-ROM and diskette.
**Desc:** Verified data on over 6,659 North Carolina manufacturers. 15,000 key executives, 628 new firms, address changes, phone and fax numbers and more.

●US/1065-4747
**HARRIS SOUTH CAROLINA MANUFACTURERS DIRECTORY.** (1993)-. Directory. English. an (June). $60.00. Harris Publishing Company, 2057-2 Aurora Road, Twinsburg OH 44087. **Tel** (800)888-5900, (216)425-9000, FAX (216)425-7150, telex 510 601 1740. available on CD-ROM and diskette.
**Desc:** Contains over 3,000 South Carolina manufacturers, key executives, fax numbers statistical charts and more.

US/0887-4247
**HARRIS WEST VIRGINIA MANUFACTURING DIRECTORY.** [Harris West Va. manuf. dir.]. **Added/Corp** Harris Publishing Co. West Virginia Governors Office of Community & Industrial Development. **VFOAT** West Virginia Manufacturing Directory. (1986)-. English. an (September). $49.00. Harris Publishing Company, 2057-2 Aurora Road, Twinsburg OH 44087. **Tel** (800)888-5900, (216)425-9000, FAX (216)425-7150, telex 510 601 1740. **LC** HD9727.W4; W4. **DD** 338.7/67/025754. available on CD-ROM and diskette. ***Continues*** *West Virginia Manufacturing Directory, 0511-6708.*
**Desc:** Verified data on over 2,200 West Virginia manufacturers, new firms, new executives, address changes, phone and fax numbers, company name changes and more.

GW
**HBG-MITTEILUNGEN.** **Main/Corp** Holz-Berfusgenossenschaft. **VFOAT** Ihre Holz-Berufsgenossenschaft Informiert. **VAT** Holz-Berufsgenossenschaft- Mitteilungen. German. qt. Holz-Berufsgenossenschaft, Am Knie 6, W-8000 Munchen 60 Germany. **Tel** (089)88971. **LC** TS810.G3; H64A. **Circ:** 105,000 (ctrl).
**Desc:** Periodical information for members about prevention of accidents in woodworking handicraft and industry.

US/1045-6058
**HIDA MANUFACTURERS DIRECTORY.** **See** Public Health and Safety.

JA
**HINSHITSU.** **VFOAT** Quality, JSQC : Journal of the Japanese Society for Quality Control; Quality, J.S.Q.C.; Journal of the Japanese Society for Quality Control; Quality, JSQC. Japanese (Japanese). Nihon Hinshitsu Kanri Gakkai, c/o Nihon Kagaku Gijutsu Renmei 10-11, Sendagaya 5 Shibuya-ku, Tokyo-to Japan. **LC** TS156.A1; H546.

●US/1056-6155
**I.H.I. GUIDE HOSES.** (I.H.I. INTERNATIONAL HOSE INTERCHANGE GUIDE.). [I.H.I. Int. hose interchange guide]. **VFOAT** I.H.I Guide Hoses; Hoses. **VAT** International Hoses Interchange Guide. (1992)-. English. be. $105.00. Interchange Inc, PO Box 16244, St Louis Park MN 55416. **Tel** (612)929-6669, (800)669-6208, FAX (612)929-0395. **DD** 678.

US/0744-9941
**IAWCM BULLETIN.** [IAWCM bull.]. **VFOAT** I.A.W.C.M. Bulletin. **VAT** International Association of Wiping Cloth Manufacturers Bulletin. Bulletin. English. mo. International Association of Wiping Cloth Manufacturers Bulletin, 300 West Washington Street, Chicago IL 60606. **DD** 677.
**Ind/Abst** Nonwovens Abstr.

UK/0306-2910
**IBCAM.** **See** Transportation-Automobiles.

US/1057-347X
**IDAHO MANUFACTURING DIRECTORY.** (IDAHO MANUFACTURING DIRECTORY / UI--CBDR.). [Ida. manuf. dir.]. **Added/Corp** University of Idaho. Center for Business Development and Research. (198?)-. Directory. English. ir (approximately every 3 years). $50.00. Center for Business Development & Research, University of Idaho, Moscow ID 83843. **Tel** (208)885-6611. **LC** HD9727.I2; M35. **DD** 338.4/025/796. available on CD-ROM. ***Continues*** *High Tech & Manufacturing Directory of Idaho, 1046-2503.*

GW
**IEE PRODUCTRONIC.** **See** Engineering-Electricity, Electrical Engineering, Electronics.

US
**IEEE INDUSTRY APPLICATIONS MAGAZINE.** Periodical. English. bm. $120.00. IEEE, Institution of Electrical and Electronics Engineers, Inc., 345 East 47th Street, New York NY 10017-2394. **Tel** (908)981-1393, FAX (908)981-9667. **(Subscription address:** IEEE / Institute of Electrical and Electronics Engineers, 445 Hoes Lane, PO Box 1331, Piscataway NJ 08855-1331.**)** **ED** John Kasselbaum.
**Desc:** Covers applications in manufacturing operations, with emphasis on petroleum, chemical, rubber, plastic, textile and mining operations. Specific technologies covered include power conversion, drives, lighting, and control.

●US/1070-9886
**IEEE TRANSACTIONS ON COMPONENTS, PACKAGING, AND MANUFACTURING TECHNOLOGY. PART A.** [IEEE trans. compon. packaging manuf. technol., Part A]. **Added/Corp** Institute of Electrical and Electronics Engineers. **VFOAT** Transactions on Components, Packaging, and Manufacturing Technology. Part A. (1994)-. Periodical. English. qt. $250.00. IEEE, Institution of Electrical and Electronics Engineers, Inc., 345 East 47th Street, New York NY 10017-2394. **Tel** (908)981-1393, FAX (908)981-9667. **(Subscription address:** IEEE / Institute of Electrical and Electronics Engineers, 445 Hoes Lane, PO Box 1331, Piscataway NJ 08855-1331.**)** **ED** Paul Slade. **LC** TK7869; .I182. **DD** 621. ***Continues in part*** *IEEE Transactions on Components, Hybrids, and Manufacturing Technology, 0148-6411.*

II/0970-2946
**IEEMA JOURNAL.** (IEEMA JOURNAL : JOURNAL DEVOTED TO ELECTRICAL & ELECTRONICS INDUSTRY TRADE & USERS.). [IEEMA j.]. **Added/Corp** IEEMA (Firm). (19??)-. Periodical. English. mo. $20.00. **(Subscription address:** Prints India, 11 Darya Ganj, New Delhi 110002 India.**)** **CODEN** IJOUEF. ***Continues*** *IEMA Journal.*

US/0160-3302
**ILLINOIS MANUFACTURERS DIRECTORY.** **VFOAT** Where to Buy, Where to Sell. (1976)-. Directory. English. an. $159.00 (print); $795.00 (diskette or CD-ROM). Manufacturers News Inc., 1633 Central Street, Evanston IL 60201-1569. **Tel** (708)864-7000, FAX (708)332-1100. **ED** Louise West. **LC** T12; .W5. **DD** 338.4/767/025773. **Bk Rev. Ad Acc.** ***Continues*** *Directory of Manufacturers of the State of Illinois.*
**Desc:** A guide to major non-manufacturing prospects in Illinois, including wholesalers, jobbers, contractors, retailers, finance, service businesses, etc.

US/0146-0161
**IMP, INDUSTRIAL MODELS & PATTERNS.** **Added/Corp** National Association of Pattern Mfgs. **VFOAT** Industrial Models & Patterns. **VAT** Industrial Models and Patterns. (19??)-. Periodical. English. Four times a year (Mar., June, Sept., Dec.). $18.00 (one year); $21.00 (two years). Pattern Model Plastic Toolbuild, PO Box 7286, Toledo OH 43615. **Tel** (419)826-4465. **ED** Ben J. Imburgia. **Bk Rev. Ad Acc. Circ:** 1,200 (ctrl).
**Desc:** Manufacturers of models, molds, patterns and plastic tooling for industry.

II/0019-476X
**INDIAN FACTORIES JOURNAL, THE.** Vol. 1- 1949/50-. Periodical. English. mo. Laws of India Private Ltd, Thyagarayanagar, Madras 17 India.

II/0019-4891
**INDIAN INDUSTRIES (MADRAS).** (INDIAN INDUSTRIES.). Vol. 1 (1957)-. Periodical. English. an. Price varies. Indian Industries, Madras, India. **(Subscription address:** Prints India, 11 Darya Ganj, New Delhi, 110002 India, (Phone: 011 91 11 3268645)**)** **CODEN** IINDBH.

US
**INDIANA INDUSTRIAL DIRECTORY, THE.** Directory. English. be. $20.00 single copy. Indiana Chamber of Commerce, 1 North Capitol / Suite 200, Indianapolis IN 46204. **Tel** (317)264-3110. **LC** T12; .I63. **DD** 670.9772. Each issue contains an index to its own contents (no volume index)--loose.

US/0735-2417
**INDIANA MANUFACTURERS DIRECTORY.** 1st Ed. (1982)-. Directory. English. an. $102.00 (print); $595.00 (diskette or CD-ROM). Manufacturers News Inc., 1633 Central Street, Evanston IL 60201-1569. **Tel** (708)864-7000, FAX (708)332-1100. **ED** Louise West. **LC** HD9727.I6; I53. **DD** 380.1/029/4772. **Ad Acc.** available on diskette (and lists); available on labels.
**Desc:** Highly detailed profiles of Ohio manufacturers. Includes products, alphabetical, geographical, SIC and computer brand sections.

US/0898-5308
**INDICATOR (SAINT PAUL, MINN. 1985).** **See** Engineering-Mines and Mining Engineering.

UK
**INDUSTRIAL AND SCIENTIFIC INSTRUMENTS.** (19??)-. English. mo. $139.00 US & Canada; £30.00 UK. Wilmington Publishing Ltd., PO Box 200, Field End Road, Ruislip Middx HA4 OSY England. **Tel** 011 44 81 841 3970, FAX 011 44 81 841 9676.

UK/0036-8792
**INDUSTRIAL LUBRICATION AND TRIBOLOGY.** [Ind. lubr. tribol.]. Vol. 19, No. 8; (Aug. 1967)-. Periodical. English. bm. $819.00. MCB University Press, 60 62 Toller Lane, Bradford West Yorkshire BD8 9BX England. **Tel** 011 44 274 499821, FAX 011 44 274 547143, telex 51317 MCBUNI G. **(Subscription address:** MCB University Press / US and Canada Subscriptions, PO Box 10812, Birmingham AL 35201-0812.**)** **ED** Bill Wilson. **LC** TJ1075.A2; S28. **DD** 621.8/9/05. **CODEN** ILTRA7. **Bk Rev. Circ:** 4,250. Documents available from Article Express International. ***Continues*** *Scientific Lubrication.*
**Desc:** Covers the design manufacture operation and maintenance of plant and equipment, requiring efficient lubrication and protection against wear.
**Ind/Abst** Acoust. Abstr.; Bioeng. Abstr.; Curr. Technol. Index; Ei Page One; Eng. Mater. Abstr.; Eng. Index Annu. [Select. Cov.]; Fluid Abstr., Civil Eng.; Fluid Abstr. Proc. Eng.; FLUIDEX (1973-); Lit. Pat. Abstr., Oilfield Chem. (1954-); Lit. Abstr., Catal. Catal.; Lit. Abstr., Health Environ.; Lit. Abstr., Pet. Refin. Petrochem.; Lit. Abstr., Pet. Substit.; Lit. Abstr., Transp. Storage; Shock Vibr. Dig.

US
**INDUSTRIAL MARKET PLACE.** **See** Economics-Industry and Production.

US/0199-2074
**INDUSTRIAL PRODUCT BULLETIN.** [Ind. prod. bull.]. **VFOAT** IPB. (19??)-. Bulletin. English. mo. $60.00 US; $63.00 Canada and Mexico; $72.00 (surface mail), $127.00 (airmail) other. Cahners Publishing Company, 249 West 17th Street, New York NY 10011. **Tel** (212)645-0067, FAX (212)242-6987. **(Subscription address:** Gordon Publications, Inc., Paid Circulation Department, 301 Gibraltar Drive, Box 650, Morris Plains NJ 07950-0650.**)** **ED** Anita La Fond. **DD** 338. **[CCC]. Ad Acc. Circ:** 200,000 (ctrl). available on microfilm from University Microfilms International (UMI). ***Continues*** *Industrial Bulletin, 0019-8021.*
**Desc:** New product tabloid magazine devoted to the manufacturing related areas including product design, production, maintenance, purchasing and management.

CN/0820-6759
**INDUSTRIAL PRODUCT IDEAS!.** [Ind. prod. ideas]. (1978)-. Periodical. English. Eight times a year. Free to Plant subscribers. MacLean Hunter Ltd. Business Publishers / Canada, Box 9100, Station A, Toronto ONT M5W 1A5 Canada. **Tel** (416)946-8420, (800)567-0444. **DD** 670.42/029/4. ***Continues*** *Ideas! in Canada's Manufacturing & Metalworking Industries, 0316-6813.*

CL/0577-7976
**INDUSTRIAS MANUFACTURERAS.** **VFOAT** Anuario de Industrias Manufactureras. Spanish. an. 9.00. Direccion de Estadistica Y Censos, Avenue Bulnes 418, Santiago Chile. **Tel** 6991441. **LC** HD9734.C5; I58. **Circ:** 350 (ctrl). ***Continues*** *Industrias (Chile. Servicio Nacional de Estadistica y Censos).*

GW
**INDUSTRIE SERVICE.** (19??)-. Periodical. German. Ten times a year. DM108.00 Germany; DM204.00 others. Verlag fuer Technik Wirtschaft, Postfach 4026, D 55030 Mainz Germany. **Tel** 011 49 6131 99203. **LC** TS191; .I515. **DD** 681/.767. **Bk Rev. Ad Acc. Circ:** 45,400 (ctrl).
**Desc:** Consists mainly of well-known specialists and high-level executives in all branches of industry with market coverage of over 50 employees.

US
**INDUSTRY WAGE SURVEY. CIGARETTE MANUFACTURING / U.S. DEPARTMENT OF LABOR, BUREAU OF LABOR STATISTICS.** **See** Economics-Labor.

II/0047-0376
**INSTRUMENTS INDIA.** [Instrum. India]. **Added/Corp** All India Instrument Manufacturers & Dealers Association. (1966)-. Academic Scholarly Publication. English. bm. $15.00. Instruments India IMBA, The Editor, A-32 Navyug Niwas 167 Dr D Bhadkamkar Road, Bombay 400-007 India. **(Subscription address:** Prints India, 11 Darya Ganj, New Delhi, 110002 India, (Phone: 011 91 11 3268645)**)** **CODEN** ISIDBS. Documents available from Article Express International, Ask*IEEE, CASDDS. ***Continues*** *IMDA Journal.*
**Ind/Abst** Bioeng. Abstr.; Chem. Abstr.; Ei Page One; Eng. Index Annu.; INSPEC (July 1968-).

US/1055-3274
**INTEGRATED MANUFACTURING (ROCKFORD, ILL.).** (INTEGRATED MANUFACTURING.). **Added/Corp** Numerical Control Society. Integrated Manufacturing Institute. Vol. 4, No. 2 (Mar. 1989)-. Periodical. English. Twelve times a year. Free. Croydon Group Ltd., 833 Featherstone Road, Rockford IL 61107. **Tel** (815)399-8700, FAX (815)399-7279. **DD** 670. ***Continues*** *IM Report (Chicago, Ill.), 0886-1463.*

UK/0268-3768
**INTERNATIONAL JOURNAL, ADVANCED MANUFACTURING TECHNOLOGY, THE.** [Int. j. adv. manuf. technol.]. **VFOAT** Advanced Manufacturing Technology; International Journal of Advanced Manufacturing Technology. Vol. 1, No. 1 (Sept. 1985)-. Periodical. English. Six times a year. £170.00. Springer-Verlag London Ltd., Springer House, 8 Alexandra Road Wimbledon, London SW19 7JZ England. **Tel** 011 44 81 9471280, or 9475885, FAX 011 44 81 9474651, telex 21531 SPRGB G. **(Subscription address:** North America: Springer Verlag, Journal Fulfillment Department, 44 Hartz Way, Secaucus, NJ 07096; Outside North America: Springer Verlag, Postfach 311340, D 10643 Berlin Germany**)** **ED** B J Davies. **LC** TS176; .I65. **CODEN** IJATEA. **[CCC].** Documents available from Article Express International, Ask*IEEE.
**Desc:** Aims to bridge the gap between pure research journals and the more practical publications on factory automation systems.
**Ind/Abst** Ei Page One; Eng. Index Annu.; INSPEC (Sept. 1985-)(1985-); Int. Packag. Abstr.

UK/0951-192X
**INTERNATIONAL JOURNAL OF COMPUTER INTEGRATED MANUFACTURING.** [Int. j. comput. integr. manuf.]. **VFOAT** Computer Integrated Manufacturing. Vol. 1, No. 1 (Jan./March 1988)-. Periodical. English. bm. £179.00 UK; $295.00 other. Taylor & Francis Ltd., Rankine Road, Basingstoke Hampshire, RG24 8PR United Kingdom. **Tel** 011 44 256 840366, FAX 011 44 256 479438, telex 858540. **(Subscription address:** Taylor & Francis Inc., 1900 Frost Road, Suite 101, Bristol PA 19007-1598.**)** **ED** David J. Williams (editor's address: Department of Manufacturing Engineering, University of Technology, Loughborough, LE11 3TU United Kingdom); George Chryssolouris (editor's address: MIT, Laboratory for Manufacturing and Productivity, 77 Massachusetts Avenue, Cambridge, MA 02139); Dr. F. Vernadat (editor's address: INRIA- Lorraine, CESCOM, Tecnopole Metz 2000, 4 Rue Marconi, F57070 Matz, France). **LC** TS155.6; .I593. **DD** 670.42/7. **[CCC].** available on microfilm and microfiche from University Microfilms International (UMI). Documents available from The Genuine Article, Ask*IEEE.
**Desc:** A journal of new knowledge. Reports research and applications, underlining the opportunities and limitations of CIM, and demonstrating how new technology can be developed and used in specific manufacturing situations. The journal has been enthusiastically received by the international manufacturing community, and has become a key forum for academics and industrial researchers to exchange information and ideas.
**Ind/Abst** Abstr. Hum. Comput. Interact.; Compumath Citation Index [Full Cov.]; Curr. Contents Eng. Tech. Appl. Sci.; Ergon. Abstr.; HILITES; INSPEC (Jan./March 1988-);(Jan.-Mar. 1988-); Res. Alert [Full Cov.]; SCISEARCH; Soc. Sci. Cit. Index [Select. Cov.].

●US/1062-6832
**INTERNATIONAL JOURNAL OF ENVIRONMENTALLY CONSCIOUS MANUFACTURING.** (1992)-. Periodical. English. qt. $300.00 (institutions). EMC Press, PO Box 20959, Albuquerque NM 87154-0959.

●US/1064-6345
**INTERNATIONAL JOURNAL OF FLEXIBLE AUTOMATION AND INTEGRATED MANUFACTURING.** [Int. j. flex. autom. integr. manuf.]. **VFOAT** Flexible Automation and Integrated Manufacturing. Vol. 1, Issue 1 (1993)-. Periodical. English. Four times a year. $84.00 (individual); $210.00 (institution). Begell House Inc., PO Box 1109, Pearl River NY 10965. **Tel** (212)725-1999. **ED** Mohammad Munir Ahmad. **DD** 670. **[CCC].**
**Desc:** Presents innovative research and focuses on state-of-the art trends within the general areas of flexible automation, informatin management and integrated manufacturing.

US/0920-6299
**INTERNATIONAL JOURNAL OF FLEXIBLE MANUFACTURING SYSTEMS.** [Int. j. flex. manuf. syst.]. Vol. 1, No. 1 (Sept. 1988)-. Periodical. English. qt. $376.00. Kluwer Academic Publishers / Massachusetts, PO Box 358, Accord Station, Hingham MA 02018. **Tel** (617)871-6600. **ED** Kathryn E. Stecke. **LC** TS155.6; .I587. **DD** 670.42/7. **CODEN** IFMSE5. **[CCC]. Ad Acc. Pr Rev. Acid Free. Circ:** 90. available on microfilm and microfiche from University Microfilms International (UMI). Documents available from Ask*IEEE.
**Desc:** Strives to provide a consolidated forum for the publication of original articles on all topics related to flexible manufacturing.
**Ind/Abst** INSPEC (1990-); Int. Abstr. Oper. Res. [Select. Cov.].

US/1045-2699
**INTERNATIONAL JOURNAL OF HUMAN FACTORS IN MANUFACTURING, THE.** **See** Computers-Automation.

SI/0218-3382
**INTERNATIONAL JOURNAL OF MANUFACTURING SYSTEMS AND DESIGN.** English. Four times a year. $90.00 individuals, $180.00 institutions. World Scientific Publishing Company, PO Box 128, Farrer Road, Singapore 9128 Singapore. **Tel** 011 65 3825663, FAX 011 65 3825919, telex RS 28561 WSPC. **(Subscription address:** US: World Scientific Publishing Co., Inc., 1060 Main Street, River Edge, NJ 07661 Telephone: (201)487-9655, Fax: (201)487-9656; Europe: World Scientific Publishing Co Ltd, 73 Lynton Mead, Totteridge, London N20 8DH United Kingdom Telephone: 011 44 81 4462461, Fax: 011 44 81 4463356; India: World Scientific Publishing Co Pte Ltd, 4911 9th Floor, High Point IV, 45 Palace Road, Bangalore 560 001 India Telephone: (80) 2205972, Fax: (80) 3344593, Telex: 0845-2900 PCO IN; Hong Kong: World Scientific Publishing (HK) Co, PO Box 72482, Kowloon Central Post Office, Hong Kong Telephone: 852-7718791, Fax: 852-7718155**)**

US/0737-7940
**IOWA MANUFACTURERS REGISTER.** [Iowa manuf. reg.]. 1st Ed. (1983)-. Directory. English. an. $64.00 (print); $395.00 (diskette or CD-ROM). Manufacturers News Inc., 1633 Central Street, Evanston IL 60201-1569. **Tel** (708)864-7000, FAX (708)332-1100. **ED** Louise West. **LC** HD9727.I8; I86. **DD** 338.4/767/0294777. **Bk Rev. Ad Acc.** ctrl circ.
**Desc:** Lists 4,924 manufacturers and processing companies; gives names and titles of 10,865 officers.

US/0272-8141
**ISA DIRECTORY OF INSTRUMENTATION (TRADE EDITION).** (ISA DIRECTORY OF INSTRUMENTATION.). [ISA dir. instrum.]. **VFOAT** Directory of Instrumentation. **VAT**

Instrument Society of America Directory of Instrumentation. Began in 1980/81. Directory. English. an. $100.00. Instrument Society of America, 67 Alexander Drive, Research Triangle NC 27709. **Tel** (919)549-8411, FAX (919)549-8288, telex 802 540. **ED** Karen S Hoglund. **LC** HD9706.6.U6; I78. **DD** 681/.2/0294. **[CCC].** Index available. **Ad Acc. Circ:** 45,000. ***Formed by the union of*** *ISA Directory of Instrumentation. International Volume, 0193-7243* ***and*** *ISA Directory of Instrumentation. North American Volume, 0191-9008.*
**Desc:** A reference manual for the control and/or instrumentation engineer. Contents include: an alphabetical listing of products and their manufacturers, specification pages, an alphabetical list of manufacturers with addresses and international offices, sales representatives and their products, service companies arranged by specialty, and other information for buying instrumentation products.

UN/0021-3489
**IZVESTIJA VYSSIH UCEBNYH ZAVEDENIJ. TEHNOLOGIJA LEGKOJ PROMYSLENNOSTI.** ***Ceased.*** (IZVESTIIA VYSSHIKH UCHEBNYKH ZAVEDENII. TEKHNOLOGIIA LEGKOI PROMYSHLENNOSTI.). [Izv. vyss. ucebn. zaved., Teh. legk. prom-ti.]. **Added/Corp** Kyivskyi Tekhnolohichnyi Instytut Lehkoi Promyslovosti. Soviet Union. Ministerstvo Vysshego Obrazovaniia. Soviet Union. Ministerstvo Vysshego i Srednego Spetsialnogo Obrazovaniia. Soviet Union. Gosudarstvennyi Komitet po Narodnomu Obrazovaniiu. **VFOAT** Tekhnologiia Legkoi Promyshlennosti. No. 1 (1958)-(19??). Periodical. Russian (table of contents in English and German). bm. **(Subscription address:** Victor Kamkin, 4956 Boiling Brook Parkway, Rockville MD 20852.**)** **LC** TS940; .R8. **CODEN** IVULAU. Documents available from Ask*IEEE, CASDDS.
**Ind/Abst** Abstr. Bull. Inst. Pap. Sci. Tech.; Chem. Abstr.; INSPEC (1968-).

SP
**JAPANESE NEW MATERIALS IACA SERIES. ADVANCED ALLOYS & METALS.** English. sm. £215.00 UK; $370.00 US. Newmedia International Japan, AV Infanta Carlota 123 5 A, 08029 Barcelona Spain. **Tel** 011 34 3 4195690, FAX 414 42 13. **UDC** 67. available on an online database (files 16,636/Full-Text) from DIALOG.
**Ind/Abst** PROMT [Full Txt.]; PTS Newsl. Database [Full Txt.].

US/0899-0956
**JOURNAL OF APPLIED MANUFACTURING SYSTEMS, THE. See** Economics-Industry and Production.

●US
**JOURNAL OF COST MANAGEMENT. VFOAT** Cost Management. Vol. 6, No. 1 (Spring 1992)-. Periodical. English. qt. $105.00 (US, US possessions, Canada), $136.00 (other). Journal of Cost Management, 210 South Street, Boston MA 02111. **LC** HF5686.M3; J68. ***Continues*** *Journal of Cost Management for the Manufacturing Industry, 0899-5141.*
**Ind/Abst** Acad. Search (July 1993-); Mag. Search.

US/0899-5141
**JOURNAL OF COST MANAGEMENT FOR THE MANUFACTURING INDUSTRY.** ***Title Change.*** **See** Business-General Management.

UK/0962-4694
**JOURNAL OF DESIGN AND MANUFACTURING.** (1991)-. Periodical. English. qt. $245.00 US and Canada; £145.00 Europe; £160.00 other. Chapman & Hall, 2-6 Boundary Row, London SE1 8HN England. **Tel** 011 44 71 865 0066, FAX 011 44 71 522 9623, telex 290164 Chapmag. **(Subscription address:** Chapman & Hall, Cheriton House, North Way, Andover, Hampshire, SP10 5BE England.**)** **ED** Bartholomew O. Nnaji. **CODEN** JDMAEG. **Pr Rev.**
**Desc:** Covers the broad area of contemporary design and manufacturing methodologies. Addresses issues in concurrent or simultaneous engineering, design theory, design for ease of manufacture, assembly and automation, inspection, quality and planning and control in modern manufacturing.
**Ind/Abst** Ergon. Abstr.

US/1041-4673
**JOURNAL OF MANUFACTURING, THE.** ***Ceased.*** [J. manuf.]. (1988)-(1989). Periodical. English. qt. Frost & Sullivan Inc, 106 Fulton Street, Department W, New York NY 10036. **Tel** (315) 472-1224, FAX (315) 472-1235, telex 650 247-7174 (MCI). **DD** 658.

US/0278-6125
**JOURNAL OF MANUFACTURING SYSTEMS.** [J. manuf. syst.]. **Added/Corp** Computer and Automated Systems Association of SME. Society of Manufacturing Engineers. **VFOAT** Manufacturing Systems. Vol. 1, No. 1 (1982)-. Periodical. English. bm (Jan., Mar., May, July, Sept., Nov.). $268.00 (institution/library), $188.00 (non-member individual), $161.00 (SME member individual) US and Canada. Society of Manufacturing Engineers, One SME Drive, PO Box 930, Member's Records Dept., Dearborn MI 48121-0930. **Tel** (313)271-1500, FAX (313)271-2861, telex 297742 SME UR (VIA RCA). **(Subscription address:** Elsevier Science Ltd. Oxford Fulfillment Centre, PO Box 800, Kidlington, Oxford OX5 1DX United Kingdom.**)** **ED** John G. Bollinger. **CODEN** JMSYEB. **[CCC]. Bk Rev. Pr Rev. Circ:** 500. available on microfilm and microfiche from University Microfilms International (UMI). Documents available from Article Express International, The Genuine Article, Ask*IEEE.
**Desc:** Publishes relevant literature for manufacturing industries, research and development organizations and SME members, on the underlying theory and application methodologies of integrating manufacturing processes into systems.
**Ind/Abst** Appl. Sci. Technol. Index (1991-); Curr. Contents Eng. Tech. Appl. Sci.; Ei Page One; Eng. Index Annu.; Fluid Abstr., Civil Eng.; Fluid Abstr. Proc. Eng.; FLUIDEX (19??-); INSPEC (1984-); Oper. Res./Manag. Sci.; Qual. Control Appl. Stat.; Res. Alert [Select. Cov.]; SCISEARCH; Text. Technol. Dig.

●US/1062-0656
**JOURNAL OF MATERIALS MANUFACTURING AND PROCESSING SCIENCE.** [J. mater. process. manuf. sci.]. **VFOAT** Journal of Materials Processing and Manufacturing Science. (1992)-. Periodical. English. qt (Jan., Apr., July and Oct.). $195.00 (one year), $380.00 (two year), $565.00 (three year). Technomic Publishing Company, Inc., 851 New Holland Avenue, Box 3535, Lancaster PA 17604. **Tel** (717)291-5609, (800)233-9936, FAX (717)295-4538. **LC** TS183; .J69. **DD** 670. **CODEN** JPMSEI. **[CCC].**

UK/0959-1524
**JOURNAL OF PROCESS CONTROL.** Vol. 1, No. 1 (Jan. 1991)-. Periodical. English. Six times a year. $358.00 The Americas; £240.00 other. Butterworth Heinemann Publishers, Linacre House, Jordan Hill, Oxford OX2 8DP England. **Tel** 011 44 865 310366. **(Subscription address:** Elsevier Science Ltd. Oxford Fulfillment Centre, PO Box 800, Kidlington, Oxford OX5 1DX United Kingdom.**)** **LC** TS156.8; .J67. **DD** 670.42. **CODEN** JPCOEO. **[CCC].** Index available. **Bk Rev. Ad Acc.** available in microform from University Microfilms International (UMI). Documents available from Ask*IEEE.
**Desc:** Covers the application of control theory, operations research, computer science and engineering principles to the solution of process control problems.
**Ind/Abst** INSPEC (Jan. 1991-).

US/0146-1958
**JOURNAL OF THE FLAGSTAFF INSTITUTE. See** Economics-International Economics.

CN/0712-9262
**JOURNAL / Q.F.M.A. See** Interior Design-Home Furnishings.

IO
**JURNAL PERKEMBANGAN PRODUKSI & TEKHNOLOGI INDUSTRI.** ***Title Change.*** **See** Economics-Industry and Production.

JA/0388-9475
**KAWASAKI STEEL TECHNICAL REPORT (TOKYO. 1980). See** Metals and Metallurgy.

US/0075-5494
**KENTUCKY DIRECTORY OF MANUFACTURERS. Added/Corp** Kentucky. Dept. of Commerce. Kentucky. Dept. of Economic Development. (196?)-. Directory. English. $40.00 (1993 edition). Kentucky Department of Economic Development, 133 Holmes Street, Frankfort KY 40601. **Tel** (502)564-4886, FAX (502)564-4083. ***Continues*** *Kentucky Industrial Directory (Frankfort, Ky. : 1954).*

US/0741-9031
**KENTUCKY MANUFACTURERS REGISTER.** 1st Ed. (1985)-. Directory. English. an (Oct.). $67.00 (print); $395.00 (diskette or CD-ROM). Manufacturers News Inc., 1633 Central Street, Evanston IL 60201-1569. **Tel** (708)864-7000, FAX (708)332-1100. **ED** Louise West. **LC** T12.3.K4; K46. **DD** 670/.25/769. **Bk Rev. Ad Acc.**
**Desc:** Lists manufacturers and processing companies; names and titles of officers.

US
**KEY COMPANY DIRECTORY, U.S. MANUFACTURING.** ***Ceased.*** **Added/Corp** Conference Board. **VFOAT** Key Company Directory, US Manufacturing; Key Company Directory, United States Manufacturing. (March 1980)-(19??). Directory. English. an. Conference Board, 845 Third Avenue, New York NY 10022. **Tel** (212)759-0900 ext. 582, (800)872-6273, FAX (212)980-7014. **ED** Yvonne Burnside. available on magnetic tape. ***Continues*** *Key Company Directory, Manufacturing.*
**Desc:** Guide to overseas and domestic operations of U.S. manufacturing corporations. Includes U.S. and foreign sales, location of facilities, classification of products at 3-digit level.

JA/0387-1053
**KIKAI TO KOGU. See** Engineering-Mechanical Engineering and Machinery.

SZ
**KOMPASS; REGISTER OF INDUSTRY AND COMMERCE OF SWITZERLAND AND LIECHTENSTEIN. VFOAT** Informationswerk fur die Wirtschaft der Schweiz und Liechtenstein; Kompass. Schweiz/Suisse, Liechtenstein. (19??)-. German (English, French, German, Italian and Spanish). an. $445.00. Reed Information Services Ltd., Windsor Court, East Grinstead House, East Grinstead RH19 1BR England. **Tel** 011 44 342 326972, FAX 011 44 342 327100, telex 95127 INFSER G. **(Subscription address:** US/ Cahners Publishing, PO Box 2118, Westport, CT 06880 USA; telephone: (203)454-4147**)**

HU
**KOZERDEKU TAJEKOZTATO ES HIRDETESEK.** Hungarian. Orszagos Anyag-Es Arhivatal, Lapkiado Vallalat, 1073 Lenin Krt 9-11, Budapest Hungary. **LC** TS191.6; .K63.

GW
**LAND- UND FORSTWIRTSCHAFT, FISCHEREI. REIHE 4.3.1 : SCHLACHTTIER- UND FLEISCHBESCHAU. Main/Corp** Germany (Federal Republic, 1949- ). Bundesstelle fur Aussenhandelsinformation. **VFOAT** Fachserie 3. **VAT** Land- und Forstwirtschaft, Fischerei. Reihe Vier.Drei. Zwei: Schlachttier- und Fleischbeschau. 1976-. German. an. DM5.40. **LC** TS1975; .G47A. ***Continues*** *Land- und Forstwirtschaft, Fischerei. Reihe 3: Viehwirtschaft. IV. Schlachttier- und Fleischbeschau.*

CN/0068-8665
**LLOYD'S CANADIAN ENGINEERING & INDUSTRIAL YEAR BOOK. See** Engineering-Industrial Engineering and Design.

US/0882-3618
**LONG ISLAND DIRECTORY OF MANUFACTURERS.** 1981-. Directory. English. an. Macrae's Blue Book Inc., 65 Bleeker Street/Fifth Floor, New York NY 10012. **Tel** (212)673-4700, (800)622-7237, FAX (212)475-1790. **ED** Barry Lee. Each issue contains an index to its own contents (no volume index)--loose. ***Continues*** *Directory of Manufacturers, Suffolk Co., N.Y.*

●US/1053-8992
**LOUISIANA MANUFACTURERS REGISTER.** [La. manuf. regist.]. (1991)-. English. an (May). $65.29 Illinois: $60.95 others. Manufacturers News Inc., 1633 Central Street, Evanston IL 60201-1569. **Tel** (708)864-7000, FAX (708)332-1100. **LC** HF5065.L8; L69. **DD** 338.7/67/0294763.

US
**LOUISVILLE DIRECTORY OF MANUFACTURERS. Added/Corp** Louisville Area Chamber of Commerce. Research Dept. Directory. English. Louisville Chamber of Commerce, 300 West Liberty Street, Louisville KY 40202. **Tel** (502)566-5050. ***Continues*** *Louisville Area Directory of Manufacturers.*

NE/0470-6684
**MAANDSTATISTIEK VAN DE INDUSTRIE. Main/Corp** Netherlands. Centraal Bureau voor de Statistiek. **Added/Corp** Netherlands. Centraal Bureau voor de Statistiek. Monthly Statistical Bulletin of Manufacturing. **VFOAT** Monthly Statistical Bulletin of Manufacturing. Vol. 1 (Jan. 1959)-. Dutch. mo (12 issues). Fl165.00. SDU Uitgeverij, Postbus 20014, Christoffel Plan, 2500 EA Den Haag Netherlands. **Tel** 011 31 70 3789911. **LC** HD9735.N2; A33. ***Supersedes in part*** *Maandstatistiek van de Nijverheid.*

US
**MACHINING TECHNOLOGY QUARTERLY.** English. qt. $60.00 US, $64.00 Canada and Mexico (business, library and academic institution); $80.00 (airmail), other. Society of Manufacturing Engineers, One SME Drive, PO Box 930, Member's Records Dept., Dearborn MI 48121-0930. **Tel** (313)271-1500, FAX (313)271-2861, telex 297742 SME UR (VIA RCA).

US/0749-1093
**MACRAE'S DIRECTORY OF FIRMS MARKETING THROUGH MANUFACTURERS' REPRESENTATIVES.** [MacRAE's dir. firms mark. manuf. represent.]. **VFOAT** Directory of Firms Marketing Through Manufacturers' Representatives. 15th Ed.-. Directory. English. ir. $65.00. Macrae's Blue Book Inc., 65 Bleeker Street/Fifth Floor, New York NY 10012. **Tel** (212)673-4700, (800)622-7237, FAX (212)475-1790. **ED** Barry Lee. **LC** T12; .M36. **DD** 338.4/767/02573.

***Continues*** *Macrae's Manufacturers' Agents' Guide, 0737-4372.*
**Desc:** Nine thousand manufacturers of industrial and consumer products who market through representatives.

US/0740-2929
**MACRAE'S INDUSTRIAL DIRECTORY. MARYLAND, D.C., DELAWARE.** ***Title Change.*** [MacRAE'S ind. dir., Md., D.C., Del.]. **Added/Corp** MacRae's Blue Book Inc. (1984)-(19??). English. an. Macrae's Blue Book Inc., 65 Bleeker Street/Fifth Floor, New York NY 10012. **Tel** (212)673-4700, (800)622-7237, FAX (212)475-1790. **ED** Barry Lee. **LC** T12.3.M3; M32. **DD** 338/.0025/752. **Circ:** 5,000. ***Formed by the union of*** *MacRae's Maryland State Industrial Directory, 0732-9695* ***and*** *MacRae's Delaware State Industrial Directory, 0733-2947.* ***Continued by*** *MacRae's State Industrial Directory. Maryland, DC, Delaware.*

US/0740-2929
**MACRAE'S STATE INDUSTRIAL DIRECTORY. MARYLAND, DISTRICT OF COLUMBIA, DELAWARE.** [MacRAE'S ind. dir., Md., D.C., Del.]. **Added/Corp** MacRae's Blue Book Inc. **VFOAT** Maryland, District of Columbia, Delaware; State Industrial Directory. Maryland, District of Columbia, Delaware. (1987)-. Directory. English. an. Macrae's Blue Book Inc., 65 Bleeker Street/Fifth Floor, New York NY 10012. **Tel** (212)673-4700, (800)622-7237, FAX (212)475-1790. **LC** T12.3.M3; M32. **DD** 338/.0025/752. ***Continues*** *MacRae's Industrial Directory. Maryland, DC, Delaware.*

US/1045-6317
**MAINE MANUFACTURING DIRECTORY.** [Me. manuf. dir.]. 1986-. Directory. English. be. $37.50. Tower Publishing Company, 588 Saco Road, Standish ME 04084. **Tel** (800)969-8693. **LC** HD9727.M2; M34. **DD** 338.7/67/025741. ***Continues*** *Maine Marketing Directory, 0145-9007.*
**Desc:** Contains information on nearly 2000 Maine manufacturing and processing firms. It has been prepared to meet the needs of manufacturers and suppliers, contractors and subcontractors, buyers and sellers, institutions, researchers and industrial reference libraries.

US/0197-1220
**MAINE, VERMONT, NEW HAMPSHIRE DIRECTORY OF MANUFACTURERS.** [Me. Vt. N. H. dir. manuf.]. **Added/Corp** Commerce Register, Inc. (19??)-. English. be. $62.50. Commerce Register Inc., 190 Godwin Avenue, Midland Park NJ 07432. **Tel** (201)445-3000, (800)221-2172. **ED** Joel Rosano. **LC** T12; .M3526. **DD** 338.4/7/0002574. **Ad Acc. Circ:** 3,000. available on labels.
**Desc:** Detailed listings of all manufacturing companies, including top executives, annual sales, number of employees, addresses, phone numbers and more.

UK/0953-2110
**MAINTENANCE FARNHAM.** **See** Engineering.

AT/0158-6335
**MAJOR MANUFACTURING AND MINING INVESTMENT PROJECTS.** [Major manuf. min. invest. proj.]. (1978)-. Periodical. English. sa. Australian Bureau of Statistics, PO Box 10, Belconnen Australian Capital Territory, 2616 Australia. **Tel** 011 61 6 2527911, FAX 011 61 6 2516009. **DD** 338.230994.
**Ind/Abst** AESIS Q.

US/0890-7641
**MANA MEMBERS DIRECTORY OF MANUFACTURERS' SALES AGENCIES.** [MANA memb. dir. manuf. sales agencies]. **Main/Corp** Manufacturers' Agents National Association (U.S.). **VFOAT** Directory of Manufacturers' Sales Agencies; MANA Directory of Members; MANA Directory; Directory of Manufacturers' Agents National Association. **VAT** Manufacturers' Agents National Association Members Directory of Manufacturers' Sales Agencies. (1986)-. English. an. $85.00 U.S.; $105.00 Canada; 117.00 other. Manufacturers' Agents National Association, PO Box 3467, 23016 Mill Creek Road, Laguna Hills CA 92654-3467. **Tel** (714)859-4040, , FAX (7174)855-2973. **LC** HF5421; .M35a. **DD** 658. **Ad Acc. Circ:** 20,000 (ctrl). ***Continues*** *MANA Membership Directory of Manufacturers' Sales Agencies.*
**Desc:** Listings of members, associate members, and manufacturers agents. Also, how-to features.

NZ
**MANUFACTURER NZ.** (19??)-. English. 66.00NZ$ US; 62.59NZ$ Australia and South Pacific; 42.35NZ$ New Zealand; 75.68NZ$ Europe and Africa. New Zealand Manufacturers Federation, PO Box 11, 543 Manners Street, Wellington New Zealand. **Tel** 011 64 4 733000, FAX 011 64 4 733004. **ED** Gilbert Peterson. **Ad Acc, Adv Mgr:** Jill Wood. **Circ:** 2,000.

US/1049-3050
**MANUFACTURERS AND PROCESSORS DIRECTORY, SOUTH DAKOTA.** (MANUFACTURERS AND PROCESSORS DIRECTORY, SOUTH DAKOTA / GOVERNOR'S OFFICE OF ECONOMIC DEVELOPMENT.). **Added/Corp** South Dakota. Governor's Office of Economic Development. **VFOAT** South Dakota Manufacturers and Processors Directory. (1989/1990)-. Directory. English. be. $69.60 Illinois residents; $64.95 other. Manufacturers News Inc., 1633 Central Street, Evanston IL 60201-1569. **Tel** (708)864-7000, FAX (708)332-1100. Index available. **Circ:** 3000 (ctrl). ***Continues*** *Directory of Manufacturers and Processors, 0743-5940.*
**Desc:** Manufacturers directory lists South Dakota Companies assigned SIC Codes 20 through 39. The directory contains SIC Code section, geographic section, alphabetical section, product index and export directory.

CN/0826-7413
**MANUFACTURERS DIRECTORY, WINDSOR-ESSEX COUNTY, ONTARIO, CANADA.** (MANUFACTURERS DIRECTORY.). [Manuf. dir. Windsor-Essex Cty. Ont. Can.]. **VFOAT** Repertoire des Fabricants. 1984-. Directory. English (French). an. 13.00Can$ Canada; $10.00 US. Windsor-Essex County Development Commission, Place Goyeau, 98 Chatham Street East, Windsor Ontario N9A 2W1 Canada. **Tel** (519)255-9200, FAX (519)255-9987, telex 064 77691. **LC** T12.5.C2; W5. **DD** 338.4/025/71332. **Ad Acc. Circ:** 3,000. ***Continues*** *Repertoire des Fabricants, Windsor-Essex, Ontario, Canada, 0822-5036.*
**Desc:** Lists manufacturers in Windsor-Essex, Ontario area, their products and employees. Cross index in back by product. Advertising accepted for yellow pages, manufacturing listing free of charge.

US/0197-2723
**MANUFACTURERS GUIDE : OHIO.** [Manuf. guide, Ohio]. 1st- Ed. English. an. $70.00. State Industrial Directories Corporation, 2 Penn Plaza, New York NY 10001. **LC** HD9727.O3; M36. **DD** 338/.0025/771.

AT/0025-2530
**MANUFACTURERS' MONTHLY.** (1961)-. Periodical. English. mo. 75.00Aus$ Australia; 105.00Aus$ Pacific Region; 125.00Aus$ other. Peter Isaacson Publications, 46-50 Porter Street, Prahran Victoria, 3181 Australia. **Tel** 011 61 3 2457777, FAX 011 61 3 2457605.

CN/0700-0774
**MANUFACTURERS OF ELECTRIC WIRE AND CABLE (PRELIMINARY ED.).** (MANUFACTURERS OF ELECTRIC WIRE AND CABLE. FABRICANTS DE FILS ET DE CABLES ELECTRIQUES.). **Main/Corp** Statistics Canada. Manufacturing and Primary Industries Division. **VFOAT** Fabricants de Fils et de Cables Electriques. **VAT** Fabricants de Fils et de Cables Electriques (Provisoire). (1971)-. English (French). an. 20.00Can$ Canada; 21.00Can$ other. Statistics Canada, Publications Sales & Services, Main Building Room 1710, Ottawa Ontario K1A 0T6 Canada. **Tel** (613)951-5078, (800)267-6677, FAX (613)951-1584, telex 053-3585.

CN
**MANUFACTURERS OF SMALL ELECTRIC APPLIANCES.** **Main/Corp** Statistics Canada. Manufacturing and Primary Industries Division. **VFOAT** Fabricants de Petits Appareils Electriques. 1960-. Periodical. English. mo. $47.00 Canada; $56.00 other. Chief Census of Manufactures, Industry Division, Statistics Canada, J Talon Building/11th Floor, Ottawa Ontario K1A 0T6 Canada. **Tel** (613)951-3523, FAX (613)951- 3522. **ED** L. Vincent. **Circ:** 500. available on microfiche. ***Supersedes in part*** *Canada. Bureau of Statistics. Electrical Apparatus and Supplies Industry.*
**Desc:** Statistics on manufacturing of small electrical appliances.

US/0364-1880
**MANUFACTURERS' SHIPMENTS, INVENTORIES, AND ORDERS.** (CURRENT INDUSTRIAL REPORTS. M3-1, MANUFACTURERS' SHIPMENTS, INVENTORIES, AND ORDERS.). [Manuf. shipm. inventories orders]. Government Publication. English. mo (Advance Summary Issue). $24.00; $1.00 (single issue), $1.00 (Advance Summary Issue) US; $30.00; $1.25 (single issue), $1.25 (Advance Summary Issue) other. US Department of Commerce, 14th Street & Constitution Avenue NW, Washington DC 20230. **Tel** (202)482-2000, FAX (202)482-3772. **LC** HD9724; .U52A. **DD** 380.1/0973. Documents available from Documents on Demand.
**Desc:** Presents timely data on the production, inventories, and orders of approximately 5,000 products, which represents 40 percent of all US manufacturing.
**Ind/Abst** Am. Stat. Index.

US/1060-2712
**MANUFACTURING AUTOMATION.** [Manuf. autom.]. Vol. 1, No. 1 (Oct. 1991)-. Periodical. English. Twelve times a year. $325.00 North America; $345.00 other. Vital Information Publications, 321 Carrera Drive, Mill Valley CA 94941. **Tel** (415)389-8671, (415)345-7018, FAX (415)389-8671, (415)345-7018. **ED** Peter Adrian (editor's address: 899 Bounty Drive, #202 FF, Foster City, CA 94404). **DD** 338. **Bk Rev,** (Qty: 2-3/year). **Ad Acc, Adv Mgr:** Sarah Collings. available on an online database from NEWSNET; and (files 16,636/Full-Text) Predicasts, Inc. ***Formed by the union of*** *Industrial Automation Outlook, 1051-9440; Advanced Manufacturing* ***and*** *Manufacturing Automation News (OCoLC)17273629.*
**Desc:** CADCAM, robotics, material handling, machine tools, systems integration, automation software, and manufacturing management issues.
**Ind/Abst** PROMT [Full Txt.]; PTS Newsl. Database [Full Txt.]; Trade Ind. Index.

UK/0964-2366
**MANUFACTURING BREAKTHROUGH.** ***Title Change.*** Vol. 1, No. 1 (Jan./Feb. 1992)-(1993). Periodical. English. bm. MCB University Press, 60 62 Toller Lane, Bradford West Yorkshire BD8 9BX England. **Tel** 011 44 274 499821, FAX 011 44 274 547143, telex 51317 MCBUNI G. **LC** HF5415.153; .M337. **DD** 658.5/75/05. ***Continued by*** *World Class Design to Manufacture.*

UK/0262-4230
**MANUFACTURING CHEMIST (LONDON: 1981).** **See** Chemistry.

US/0163-4364
**MANUFACTURING CONFECTIONER, THE.** (MC. THE MANUFACTURING CONFECTIONER.). [Manuf. confect.]. **VFOAT** MC. Vol. 36, No. 10 (Oct. 1956)-. Periodical. English. mo. $25.00 US and possessions; $50.00 other. MC - Manufacturing Confectioner Publishing Company Inc, 175 Rock Road, Glen Rock NJ 07452. **Tel** (201)652-2655. **DD** 338. **CODEN** MANCE5. **Ad Acc. Circ:** 4,000. available on microfilm and microfiche from University Microfilms International (UMI). ***Continues*** *Manufacturing Confectioner, 0163-4364.*
**Ind/Abst** BioBusiness; Life Sci. Collect.

US/0361-0853
**MANUFACTURING ENGINEERING.** **See** Engineering.

US/0149-9521
**MANUFACTURING IN MINNESOTA.** **Main/Corp** Minnesota. Dept. of Economic Development. Research Division. English. 480 Cedar Street, St Paul MN 55101. **LC** HD9727.M6; M56A. **DD** 338.4/09776.

CN/0382-4144
**MANUFACTURING INDUSTRIES OF CANADA, NATIONAL AND PROVINCIAL AREAS.** [Manuf. ind. can., Natl. prov. areas]. **Added/Corp** Statistics Canada. Manufacturing and Primary Industries Division. Statistics Canada. Special Projects and Regional Statistics Section. Statistics Canada. Manufacturing and Primary Industries Division. General Statistics Section. Statistics Canada. Regional and Small Business Manufacturing Statistics and Special Services Section. Statistics Canada. Regional and Small Business Statistics Section. Statistics Canada. Information and Classification Services Section. **VFOAT** Industries Manufacturieres du Canada, Niveaux National et Provincial. (1972)-. English (French). an. 66.00Can$ Canada; $80.00 US; $93.00 other. Statistics Canada, Publications Sales & Services, Main Building Room 1710, Ottawa Ontario K1A 0T6 Canada. **Tel** (613)951-5078, (800)267-6677, FAX (613)951-1584, telex 053-3585. **LC** HD9734.C2; C3e. **DD** 338.4/767/0971021. ***Formed by the union of*** *General Review of the Manufacturing Industries of Canada. Volume 1, Industries by Province, 0382-4152; Manufacturing Industries of Canada, Atlantic Provinces, 0527-558X; Manufacturing Industries of Canada, Quebec, 0527-5598; Manufacturing Industries of Canada, Ontario, 0527-5601; Manufacturing Industries of Canada, Prairie Provinces, 0527-561X; Manufacturing Industries of Canada, British Columbia, Yukon and Northwest Territories, 0527-5628* ***and*** *Manufacturing Industries of Canada, Type of Organization and Size of Establishments, 0590-5737.*

CN/0382-4012
**MANUFACTURING INDUSTRIES OF CANADA. SUB-PROVINCIAL AREAS.** ***Ceased.*** (MANUFACTURING INDUSTRIES OF CANADA, SUB-PROVINCIAL AREAS / STATISTICS CANADA, MANUFACTURING AND PRIMARY INDUSTRIES DIVISION.). [Manuf. ind. Can., Sub-prov. areas]. **Added/Corp** Statistics Canada. Manufacturing and Primary Industries Division. Statistics Canada. Special Projects and Regional Statistics Section. Statistics Canada. Manufacturing and Primary Industries Division. General Statistics Section. Statistics Canada. Regional and Small Business Manufacturing Statistics and Special Services Section. Statistics Canada. Regional and Small Business Statistics Section. Statistics Canada. Information and Classification Services Section. **VFOAT** Industries Manufacturieres du Canada, Niveau Infraprovincial. (1972)-(199?). English (French). an. Statistics Canada, Publications Sales & Services, Main Building Room 1710, Ottawa Ontario K1A 0T6 Canada. **Tel** (613)951-5078, (800)267-6677, FAX (613)951-1584, telex 053-3585. **LC** HD9734.C2; C3c. **DD** 338.4/767/0971021. ***Continues*** *Manufacturing Industries of Canada, Geographical Distribution, 0527-5636.*
**Desc:** Detailed small area data. Data totals by industry group and by industry for counties, metropolitan areas and census agglomerations; industry data by industry group for municipalities and economic regions; size distributions of establishments for metropolitan areas and selected municipalities; other tabulations and analysis.

US/0076-4256
**MANUFACTURING MANAGEMENT SERIES.** See Business-General Management.

US/1072-8651
**MANUFACTURING MARKET INSIDER.** [Manuf. mark. insid.]. **VFOAT** MMI. Vol. 1, No. 1 (May 1991)-. Periodical. English. mo. $372.00 North America; $432.00 other. JBT Communications, PO Box 782, Needham Heights MA 02194. **Tel** (617)444-2154, FAX (617)444-2154. **ED** John Tuck. **DD** 621.

CN/0706-0084
**MANUFACTURING + MARKETING OPPORTUNITIES; BULLETIN.** Bulletin. English. mo. Free. Ministry of Industry and Tourism, 900 Bay Street, Queen's Park, Toronto Ontario M7A 2E4 Canada. ctrl circ. ***Continues*** *Ontario Manufacturing & Diversification Opportunities.*

US/0743-023X
**MANUFACTURING OPERATIONS.** [Manuf. oper.]. **VFOAT** Operations. Vol. 1, No. 1 Sept. 1983-. Periodical. English. qt. Hitchcock Publishing Company, 191 South Gary Avenue, Carol Stream IL 60188. **Tel** (708)665-1000.

CN
**MANUFACTURING OPPORTUNITIES.** **Main/Corp** British Columbia. Dept. of Economic Development. English. British Columbia Department of Economic Development, Government of British Columbia, Parliament Buildings, Victoria British Columbia V8V 4R9 Canada. **LC** HF130.B7; B73A. **DD** 338/.09711.

US/0896-1611
**MANUFACTURING REVIEW.** [Manuf. rev.]. **Added/Corp** American Society of Mechanical Engineers. Society for Integrated Manufacturing. Vol. 1, No. 1 (Mar. 1988)-. Periodical. English. Four times a year. $110.00 (non-member), $40.00 (member) US and Canada. American Society of Mechanical Engineers, 22 Law Drive, Fairfield NJ 07007. **Tel** (201)882-1167, (212)705-7722 (editorial). **ED** Philip H. Francis. **DD** 670. **[CCC].** available on microfilm and microfiche from University Microfilms International (UMI). Documents available from Article Express International, Ask*IEEE.
**Desc:** Covers the design and application of discrete goods manufacturing processes and serve as a forum for original work important to the heavy durable goods, electronics, transportation and other manufacturing sectors.
**Ind/Abst** Ei Page One; Eng. Index Annu.; INSPEC (Mar. 1990-).

US/0748-948X
**MANUFACTURING SYSTEMS.** See Economics-Industry and Production.

US/0164-968X
**MANUFACTURING TODAY.** V. 1- Sept. 1978-. Periodical. English. qt. $49.95. Communications Today Ltd, 200 South Main Street, PO Box 2754, High Point NC 27261. **Tel** (919)889-0113, FAX (919)841-8256, telex 910 380 4556. **ED** Gary Evans. **Ad Acc. Circ:** 21,800 (ctrl). available on microfilm from University Microfilms International (UMI).
**Desc:** Covers new materials and technology for residential furniture manufacturing industry.

US/1044-7024
**MANUFACTURING USA.** [Manuf. USA]. **VFOAT** Manufacturing U S A. **VAT** Manufacturing United States of America. (1989)-. English. an. $159.00. Gale Research Inc., 835 Penobscot Building, Detroit MI 48226. **Tel** (800)877-GALE, (313)961-2242, FAX (313)961-6083, telex TWX 810-221-7086. **ED** Arsen J Darnay. **LC** HD9721; .M364. **DD** 338.4/767/0973021.
**Desc:** Profiles and top company rankings for about 450 manufacturing industries. Data in each entry is presented in easy-to-read, information-packed graphs and tables.

●US/1065-2507
**MARYLAND MANUFACTURERS DIRECTORY (EVANSTON, ILL.).** (MARYLAND MANUFACTURERS DIRECTORY.). **Added/Corp** Manufacturers' News, Inc. (1993)-. Directory. English. $69.00. Manufacturer's News Inc., 1633 Central Street, Evanston IL 60201.

RU
**MASHPRIBORINTORG.** **Main/Corp** Vsesoiuznoe Obedinenie Mashpriborintorg. (19??)-. Periodical. English (English). ir. $129.95. V/O Mashpriborintory 121200, Moscow Russia. **LC** TS500; .V75b. **DD** 681/.4/0947.

US/0195-5810
**MASSACHUSETTS DIRECTORY OF MANUFACTURERS.** **Added/Corp** Commerce Register, Inc. (19??)-. English. ir (every 18 months). $72.50. Commerce Register Inc., 190 Godwin Avenue, Midland Park NJ 07432. **Tel** (201)445-3000, (800)221-2172. **ED** Joel Rosano. **LC** HD9727.M4; M45. **DD** 338.4/7/00025744. **Ad Acc. Circ:** 3,000.
**Desc:** Detailed listings of all manufacturing companies, including top executives, annual sales, number of employees, addresses, phone numbers and more. Available in machine readable format and on mailing lists.

US/1042-6914
**MATERIALS AND MANUFACTURING PROCESSES.** [Mater. manuf. process.]. Vol. 4, No. 1 (1989)-. Academic Scholarly Publication. English. bm. $595.00 US; $616.00 other. Marcel Dekker Inc., 270 Madison Avenue, New York NY 10016. **Tel** (212)696-9000, (800)228-1160, FAX (212)685-4540, telex 421419. **(Subscription address:** Marcel Dekker Inc, PO Box 5017, Monticello NY 12701.**) ED** T. S. Sudarshan and T. S. Srivatsan. **LC** TS183; .A38. **DD** 670.42. **CODEN** MMAPET. **[CCC].** Documents available from Article Express International, The Genuine Article, Ask*IEEE, CASDDS. ***Continues*** *Advanced Materials and Manufacturing Processes, 0898-2090.*
**Desc:** Treats such issues as more efficient use of raw materials and energy, integration of design and manufacturing activities requiring the invention of suitable new manufacturing processes, unmanned production dependent on efficient and reliable control of various processes, introduction of new materials in industrial production necessitating new manufacturing process technology, and more. Information is offered in various formats, including research articles, short reports, review articles, conference papers, applied research, book reviews, and entire issues devoted to symposia.
**Ind/Abst** Ceram. Abstr. (19??-); Chem. Abstr. (1990-); Corros. Abstr. (199?-); Ei Page One; Eng. Index Annu.; INSPEC (1990-); Res. Alert [Full Cov.].

US/0276-6418
**MATTRESSES AND FOUNDATIONS.** (CURRENT INDUSTRIAL REPORTS. MA-25E, MATTRESSES AND FOUNDATIONS / U.S. DEPARTMENT OF COMMERCE, BUREAU OF THE CENSUS.). **Added/Corp** United States. Bureau of the Census. **VFOAT** Mattresses and Foundations. (19??)-. Government Publication. English. an. US Department of Commerce / Bureau of the Census, Data User Services Division, Customer Services, Washington DC 20233-0800. **Tel** (301)763-4100. **(Subscription address:** Superintendent of Documents, US Government Printing Office, Washington DC 20402.**) LC** HD9971.5.M383; U63. **DD** 338.4/768415/0973.

US
**MECHANO BUYERS DIRECTORY. NORTHERN CALIFORNIA.** (19??)-. English. an (May). $16.95. Mechano Buyers Directory, PO Box 70460, Sunnyvale CA 94086. **Tel** (408)738-3020. **ED** Gerald Willis. **LC** Discard. **Ad Acc. Circ:** 7,000 (ctrl).
**Desc:** Nationwide listings of manufacturers cross-referenced to Northern California sources for electronic, electrical and mechanical goods and services.

US/0026-055X
**METAL FABRICATING NEWS.** [Met. fabr. news]. (19??)-. Periodical. English. qt (Jan., Apr., July, Oct.). $1.50 US & Canada; $12.00 other. Metal Fabricating Institution Inc, PO Box 1178, Rockford IL 61105. **Tel** (815)965-4031. **ED** Ronald L. Fowler. **Ad Acc. Circ:** 41,713.
**Desc:** Edited for those in the metal fabricating, manufacturing plants, responsible for the plant operations.
**Ind/Abst** Alum. Ind. Abstr.; Eng. Mater. Abstr.; Met. Abstr.

NE
**METALLBEWERKING.** See Metals and Metallurgy.

US/0731-7417
**METRO NEW YORK DIRECTORY OF MANUFACTURERS.** **Added/Corp** Commerce Register, inc. (19??)-. English. ir. price varies per volume. Commerce Register Inc., 190 Godwin Avenue, Midland Park NJ 07432. **Tel** (201)445-3000, (800)221-2172. **ED** Joel Rosano. **LC** HD9728.N4; M47. **DD** 338.4/7/000257471. **Ad Acc. Circ:** 3,000.
**Desc:** Detailed listings of all manufacturing companies, including top executives, annual sales, number of employees, address, phone, and more.

US/0736-2889
**MICHIGAN MANUFACTURERS DIRECTORY.** (1983)-. Directory. English. an (Feb.). $144.00 (print); $795.00 (diskette). Manufacturers News Inc., 1633 Central Street, Evanston IL 60201-1569. **Tel** (708)864-7000, FAX (708)332-1100. **LC** HD9723; .D43. **DD** 338/.0025/774. **[CCC]. Ad Acc. Circ:** 8,000. available on an online database; available on diskette. ***Continues*** *Directory of Michigan Manufacturers.*
**Desc:** Michigan manufacturers by geographic location, alphabet and product. Includes names, addresses, officers, phone sales volume, square footage, date of established employment, import/export, TWX, cable code, telex, affiliations.

US/0193-2047
**MID-AMERICA COMMERCE & INDUSTRY.** See Business-Purchasing.

US
**MINNESOTA DIRECTORY OF MANUFACTURERS.** (1941)-. Directory. English. an. $95.00. K & G Publishing Inc., Box 444058, Eden Prairie MN 55344-0558. **Tel** (612)941-1535, FAX (612)941-2012. **Circ:** 3,500. ***Continues*** *Directory of Minnesota Manufacturers and Guide Book to Minnesota Industry.*

US/0738-1514
**MINNESOTA MANUFACTURERS REGISTER.** (MINNESOTA MANUFACTURERS REGISTER / MNI.). 1st Ed. (1984)-. Directory. English. an (Oct.). $94.00 (print); $595.00 (diskette or CD-ROM). Manufacturers News Inc., 1633 Central Street, Evanston IL 60201-1569. **Tel** (708)864-7000, FAX (708)332-1100. **ED** Louise West. **LC** HD9727.M6; M57. **DD** 338.4/767/0294776. **Bk Rev. Ad Acc.**
**Desc:** Lists information on firms, executives by name and title.

US/0191-4677
**MIRROR NEWS.** Periodical. English. qt. $16.00 US; $22.00 other. Wil Tiller, PO Box 471, Hopkins MN 55343. **Tel** (612)935-3666. **ED** Wil L Tiller. Index available. cum. index. **Bk Rev. Ad Acc. Circ:** 9,700 (ctrl).
**Desc:** Serves management in the manufacture and marketing of mirror products and allied accessories. Coverage includes manufacturing retailing, wholesaling, interior designing and contract installation.

US
**MISSISSIPPI MANUFACTURERS DIRECTORY.** **Added/Corp** Mississippi Research and Development Center. Mississippi Industrial and Technological Research Commission. (1962)-. English. an (June). $50.00. State of Mississippi / Department of Economic Development, PO Box 849, Jackson MS 39205. **Tel** (601)359-3449, FAX (601)359-2832, telex 585489. **Circ:** 8,000. ***Continues*** *Encyclopedia of Mississippi Manufacturers.*
**Desc:** Provides information about 2,580 Mississippi manufacturers and 5,000 executives. Provides address, zip, phone, products manufactured, and home office information.

US/0895-2469
**MISSOURI DIRECTORY OF MANUFACTURERS (1988).** (MISSOURI DIRECTORY OF MANUFACTURERS.). [Mo. dir. manuf.]. **Added/Corp** Harris Publishing Co. Missouri. Dept. of Economic Development. **VFOAT** Harris Missouri Directory of Manufacturers. (1988)-. English. an (August). $97.00. Harris Publishing Company, 2057-2 Aurora Road, Twinsburg OH 44087. **Tel** (800)888-5900, (216)425-9000, FAX (216)425-7150, telex 510 601 1740. **LC** T12; .M57. **DD** 338.7/67/025778. available on CD-ROM and diskette. ***Continues*** *Missouri Directory.*
**Desc:** Verified data on over 8,480 Missouri manufacturers, key executives, new firms, address changes, company name changes, phone and fax numbers and more.

US/0893-2816
**MISSOURI MANUFACTURERS REGISTER.** (MISSOURI MANUFACTURERS REGISTER / MNI.). [Mo. manuf. regist.]. **Added/Corp** Manufacturers' News, Inc. (1988)-. Directory. English. an. $91.00 (print); $595.00 (diskette or CD-ROM). Manufacturers News Inc., 1633 Central Street, Evanston IL 60201-1569. **Tel** (708)864-7000, FAX (708)332-1100. **LC** HD9727.M8; M59. **DD** 338.7/67/025778.

US/0733-6497
**MOBILE/MANUFACTURED HOME BLUE BOOK.** [Mob./manuf. home blue book]. **Added/Corp** National Market Reports, Inc. **VAT** Mobile, Manufactured Home Blue Book. Vol. 46, No. 1 (Jan. 1982)-. Periodical. English. sa. $100.00. MacLean Hunter Publishing Corporation / Chicago, IL, 29 North Wacker Drive, Chicago IL 60606-3298. **Tel** (312)726-2802, FAX (312)726-3091. **(Subscription address:** Maclean Hunter Market Reports, 29 North Wacker Drive, Chicago IL 60606.**) LC** TL297; .M63. **DD** 643/.2. ***Continues*** *Mobile Home Blue Book, 0733-6489.*

US/0277-9951
**MODERN APPLICATIONS NEWS.** See Metals and Metallurgy.

US/0026-8038
**MODERN MATERIALS HANDLING.** [Mod. mater. handl.]. (19??)-. Periodical. English. mo (14 issues). $80.00 US; $118.00 Canada; $110.00 Mexico; $140.00 (surface mail) other. Cahners Publishing Company, 249 West 17th Street, New York NY 10011. **Tel** (212)645-0067, FAX (212)242-6987. **(Subscription address:** Cahners Publishing Company / Colorado, Paid Subscription Service Center, PO Box 7610, Highlands Ranch CO 80126-7610.**) ED** Raymond A. Kulwiec. **LC** TS149; .M63. **DD** 658.7/8/05. **CODEN** MMHHA2. **[CCC].** available on microfilm and microfiche from University Microfilms International (UMI); available on an online database (file 648/Full-Text) from DIALOG. Documents available from Article Express International, UMI Article Clearinghouse, Ask*IEEE. ***Continues*** *Palletizer.*

**Desc:** Published for buyers and specifiers responsible for decisions relating to materials handling and packaging in the manufacturing and distribution industries. It covers industry developments in equipment, transportation, storage, control, safety and management.
**Ind/Abst** ABI/INFORM Glob. Ed.; ABI Inform Ondisc (July 1973-); Acad. Search (Jan. 1994-); Appl. Sci. Technol. Index; Bioeng. Abstr.; Bus. Index (1985-); Comput. Lit. Index; Ei Page One; Energy Inf. Abstr.; Energy Res. Abstr.; Eng. Index Annu.; F&S Index Plus Text, Int. [Select. Cov.]; Gen. BusinessFile (1985-); Gen. Period. Index (1985-); INSPEC (Dec. 1968-); Int. Packag. Abstr.; Mag. Search; Predicasts Forecasts; Trade Ind. ASAP [Full Txt.]; Trade Ind. Index (1981-) [Full Txt.].

●US/1057-6681
**MONTANA MANUFACTURERS DIRECTORY.** [Mont. manuf. dir.]. **Added/Corp** Montana. Small Business Development Center. (1992)-. Directory. English. $20.00. Montana Department of Commerce, 1424 9th Avenue, Helena MT 59620. **Tel** (406)444-3494, FAX (406)444-2903. **DD** 338. ***Continues*** *Montana Manufacturers & Products Directory.*

CN/0840-8238
**MONTHLY SURVEY OF MANUFACTURING.** (MONTHLY SURVEY OF MANUFACTURING / STATISTICS CANADA.). [Mon. surv. manuf.]. **Added/Corp** Statistics Canada. Statistics Canada. Industry Division. **VFOAT** Enquete Mensuelle sur les Industries Manufacturieres. Vol. 42, No. 7 (July 1988)-. Periodical. English (French). mo. 190.00Can$ Canada; $228.00 US; $266.00 other. Statistics Canada, Publications Sales & Services, Main Building Room 1710, Ottawa Ontario K1A 0T6 Canada. **Tel** (613)951-5078, (800)267-6677, FAX (613)951-1584, telex 053-3585. **LC** HD9734.C2; A35. **DD** 338.4/767/0971021. ***Continues*** *Inventories, Shipments & Orders in Manufacturing Industries, 0701-7367.*

US/0146-6143
**MUZZLELOADERS' ANNUAL.** (DIXIE GUN WORKS MUZZLELOADERS' ANNUAL.). **Main/Corp** Dixie Gun Works. English. an. $1.75. Aqua Field Publications Inc, 66 West Gilbert Street, Shrewsbury NJ 07702. **Tel** (201)842-8300. **LC** TS536.6.M8; D58A. **DD** 683/.42.

US/0742-9274
**N.A.D.A. MOBILE HOME MANUFACTURED HOUSING APPRAISAL GUIDE.** ***Title Change.*** [N.A.D.A. mob. home manuf. hous. appraisal guide]. **Added/Corp** National Automobile Dealers Association. **VFOAT** NADA Mobile Home Manufactured Housing Appraisal Guide; Mobile Home Manufactured Housing Appraisal Guide; Mobile Home Manufactured Housing Guide. (Jan./Apr. 1982)-(19??). English. Three times a year. NADA Appraisal Guides, PO Box 7800, Costa Mesa CA 92628. **Tel** (714)556-8511, (800)966-6232, FAX (714)556-8715. **ED** Vince Pulsipher. **LC** HD9715.7.U62; N35a. **DD** 381/.45690879/0973. ***Continues*** *N.A.D.A. Mobile Home Appraisal Guide, 0095-6538.* ***Continued by*** *NADA Manufactured Housing Appraisal Guide.*
**Desc:** Lists used retail values for mobile homes and manufactured housing.

US/0149-032X
**NARROW FABRICS.** (CURRENT INDUSTRIAL REPORTS. MA-22G, NARROW FABRICS.). Began with 1965. Government Publication. English. an. $1.00. US Department of Commerce, 14th Street & Constitution Avenue NW, Washington DC 20230. **Tel** (202)482-2000, FAX (202)482-3772. **LC** HD9851; .N3. **DD** 338.4/7677/0973. ***Continues*** *Current Industrial Reports. M22G, Narrow Fabrics.*
**Desc:** Presents timely data on the production, inventories, and orders of approximately 5,000 products, which represents 40 percent of all US manufacturing.

US
**NATIONAL LUBRICATING GREASE INSTITUTE ANNUAL MEETING PAPERS.** English. $53.00. National Lubricating Grease Institute, 4635 Wyandotte Street, Kansas City MO 64112. **Tel** (816)931-9480, FAX (816)753-5026.

US/0163-2191
**NATIONAL MANUFACTURERS REGISTER.** V. 1- 1977-. English. an. $50.00. 8672 Melrose, Los Angeles CA 90069. **LC** T12; .N29. **DD** 338.4/7/6702573.

GW
**NC FERTIGUNG.** (19??)-. German. Eight times a year. NC Verlag, Goebenstrasse 21, D 42115 Wuppertal Germany. **Tel** 011 49 202 389050.

US/0898-7033
**NEBRASKA DIRECTORY OF MANUFACTURERS AND THEIR PRODUCTS.** (NEBRASKA DIRECTORY OF MANUFACTURERS AND THEIR PRODUCTS / COMPILED AND PUBLISHED BY THE NEBRASKA DEPARTMENT OF ECONOMIC DEVELOPMENT.). [Neb. dir. manuf. prod.]. **Added/Corp** Nebraska. Dept. of Economic Development. **VFOAT** Directory of Manufacturers; Nebraska Directory of Manufacturers; Directory of Nebraska Manufacturers. (1987)-. Directory. English. be (July). $68.52 (IL residents, includes 7.75% sales tax); $69.00 (other, includes postage). Manufacturers News Inc., 1633 Central Street, Evanston IL 60201-1569. **Tel** (708)864-7000, FAX (708)332-1100. **LC** T12; .D62. **DD** 338.7/67/025782. ***Continues*** *Directory of Nebraska Manufacturers and Their Products.*

●US/1059-7727
**NEBRASKA MANUFACTURERS REGISTER.** [Neb. manuf. regist.]. **VFOAT** Manufacturers Register. (1992)-. Directory. English. $59.00 (print); $375.00 (diskette or CD-ROM). Manufacturers News Inc., 1633 Central Street, Evanston IL 60201-1569. **Tel** (708)864-7000, FAX (708)332-1100. **LC** IN PROCESS. **DD** 338.

CN/0028-4971
**NEW EQUIPMENT NEWS.** (1940)-. Periodical. English. mo (10 issues). 44.52Can$ Canada; 55.65Can$ other. Canadian Engineering Publications Ltd., 204 Richmond Street West / Suite 415, Toronto ONT M5V 1V6 Canada. **Tel** (416)599-3737, FAX (416)599-3730. **ED** D. Barrie Lehman (phone: (416)833-4141). **Ad Acc. Circ:** 31,500 (ctrl).
**Desc:** Industrial information source.

US/0195-9352
**NEW JERSEY DIRECTORY OF MANUFACTURERS.** (19??)-. Directory. English. ir. $98.90 residents; $92.50 other. Commerce Register Inc., 190 Godwin Avenue, Midland Park NJ 07432. **Tel** (201)445-3000, (800)221-2172. **ED** Joel Rosano. **LC** HD9727.N5; N38. **DD** 338/.0025/749. **Ad Acc. Circ:** 3,000.
**Desc:** Detailed listings of all manufacturing companies, including top executives, annual sales, number of employees, address, phone, and more.

NZ/1171-5375
**NEW ZEALAND MANUFACTURER 1992.** ***Title Change.*** (NEW ZEALAND MANUFACTURER). [N.Z. manuf.1992]. **VFOAT** Manufacturer. (1992)-(199?). Periodical. English. mo (Except January). New Zealand Manufacturers Federation, PO Box 11, 543 Manners Street, Wellington New Zealand. **Tel** 011 64 4 733000, FAX 011 64 4 733004. **ED** Glibey Pevelson. **DD** _a338.4767099305. ***Continues*** *Manufacturer (Wellington. 1988), 0113-9320.* ***Continued by*** *Manufacturer NZ.*

NZ
**NEW ZEALAND WHOLE EARTH CATALOGUE.** 1st- 1972-. English. $4.95. Alister Taylor Pub, Whole Earth Mail Order Department, Box 10-292, Wellington New Zealand. **LC** TS199; .N5. **DD** 381/.45/6.

SW
**NEWSLETTER ON SURFACE ROUGHNESS.** Newsletter. English. sa. $10.00. Chalmers Univ of Technology, Dept Production Engineering, S-41296 Goteborg Sweden. **Tel** 011 46 31 810100 ext. 1953.

US/0899-0158
**NORTH AMERICAN NEW PRODUCT REPORT, THE.** [North Am. new prod. rep.]. **Added/Corp** Galbraith Associates. IIS/Galbraith. IIS Limited. IIS Publications. Vol. 1 (Sept. 11, 1981)-. Periodical. English. Twenty-six times a year. $525.00 US; $575.00 other. IIS/Galbraith, 1220 Valley Forge Road, PO Box 985, Valley Forge PA 19481. **Tel** (215)935-3944, FAX (215)935-3946. **DD** 658. **CODEN** NANRER.
**Ind/Abst** Foods Adlibra; Infomat Int. Bus.

CN/0381-4912
**NOVA SCOTIA DIRECTORY OF MANUFACTURERS.** **Added/Corp** Nova Scotia. Dept. of Development. (1973)-. Directory. English. be. 5.00Can$. Department of Economic Development / Nova Scotia, 1800 Argyle Street, Halifax NS B3J 2R7 Canada. **Tel** (902)424-8920, FAX (902)424-5793. **DD** 338.4/025/716. ***Continues*** *Nova Scotia Directory of Manufacturing., 0381-4920.*

US
**NTIS ALERT. MANUFACTURING TECHNOLOGY.** **Added/Corp** United States. National Technical Information Service. (19??)-. Periodical. English. Twenty-four times a year. $190.00 US; $265.00 other. National Technical Information Service - NTIS, Room 2027S, 5285 Port Royal Road, Springfield VA 22161. **Tel** (703)487-4630, (703)487-4660, (703)487-4650, FAX (703)321-8547, telex 89-9405. Index available. ***Continues*** *Manufacturing Technology / NTIS, 1043-9897.*
**Desc:** Provides information on CAD/CAM, computer software, domestic commerce, job environment, quality control and reliability, plant design, etc.

US/0147-1333
**OCCUPATIONAL PROFILES OF OREGON'S MANUFACTURING INDUSTRIES.** **See** Economics-Labor.

UK/0306-0381
**OEM DESIGN.** [OEM des.]. **VFOAT** Original Equipment Manufacture. Vol. 1 (Oct. 1971)-. Periodical. English. Eleven times a year. $99.00 US and Canada; £30.00UK. Wilmington Publishing Ltd., PO Box 200, Field End Road, Ruislip Middx HA4 OSY England. **Tel** 011 44 81 841 3970, FAX 011 44 81 841 9676. **LC** TA174; .O2. **CODEN** OEMDAF. **[CCC].** available on an online database (file 771/Full-Text) from DIALOG. Documents available from Ask*IEEE.
**Ind/Abst** BMT Abstr. (19??-); Fluid Abstr., Civil Eng. (19??-); Fluid Abstr. Proc. Eng. (19??-); FLUIDEX (1973-); INSPEC (Oct. 1971-); Leadscan (19??-); Pollut. Abstr. Indexes (19??-).

●US/1072-2580
**OEM INDUSTRY.** [OEM ind.]. **VFOAT** OEM. Vol. 1, No. 1 (Aug./Sept. 1993)-. Trade Publication. English. bm. $50.00 US, Canada and Mexico; $80.00 other. Johnson Hill Press Inc., 1233 Janesville Avenue, PO Box 803, Fort Atkinson WI 53538-0803. **Tel** (414)563-1749, FAX (414)563-1704. **ED** Kay Falk. **LC** HD9705.E7; O35. **DD** 338.4/76218/09405. **Ad Acc.** Full Page (B&W) $4995.00. Full Page (Color) $5995.00 (4-color). **Circ:** 11,011.
**Desc:** Serves the European design and manufacturing sectors of the off-road equipment market. Focuses on providing an editorial curriculum that will help manufacturers compete in a global market.

US/1048-8928
**OEM INTEGRATOR, THE.** (OEM INTEGRATOR : FOR DESIGNERS OF OPEN SYSTEMS.). **VAT** Original Equipment Manufactures Integrator. Vol. 1, No. 1 (Spring 1990)-. Periodical. English. Six times a year (Feb., Apr., June, Aug., Oct., Dec.). $60.00. Transatlantic Publishing, 18 Main Street, Concord MA 01742. **Tel** (617)259-9207. **LC** TK7885.A1; O36. **DD** 621.395.

US/1048-3039
**OEM OFF-HIGHWAY.** [OEM off-highw.]. **VFOAT** OEM Off Highway; OEM. **VAT** Original Equipment Manufacturer Off-Highway. (19??)-. Trade Publication. English. Eight times a year. $40.00 US, Canada and Mexico; $80.00 other. Johnson Hill Press Inc., 1233 Janesville Avenue, PO Box 803, Fort Atkinson WI 53538-0803. **Tel** (414)563-1749, FAX (414)563-1704. **ED** Kay Falk. **LC** WMLC 93/1532. **DD** 681. **Ad Acc.** Full Page (B&W) $2975.00. Full Page (Color) $3870.00 (4-color). **Circ:** 15,007. ***Continues*** *OEM, 0893-5890.*
**Desc:** Serves the design and manufacturing sectors of the off-road equipment market. Provides valuable insight on how OEM's might improve their businesses. Covers manufacturing and industry issues, components and suppliers.

UK/0110-1072
**OFFICE EQUIPMENT NEWS.** (19??)-. English. Eleven times a year. $119.00 US & Canada; £37.00 UK. Wilmington Publishing Ltd., PO Box 200, Field End Road, Ruislip Middx HA4 OSY England. **Tel** 011 44 81 841 3970, FAX 011 44 81 841 9676.

US/1056-6872
**OFFICIAL IOWA MANUFACTURERS DIRECTORY.** [Offic. Iowa manuf. dir.]. **Added/Corp** Iowa. Dept. of Economic Development. **VFOAT** Iowa Manufacturers Directory. (1991)-. Directory. English. an. $73.91 (IL residents, includes 7.75% sales tax); $74.00 (other, includes postage). Manufacturers News Inc., 1633 Central Street, Evanston IL 60201-1569. **Tel** (708)864-7000, FAX (708)332-1100. **ED** Louise West. **LC** T12; .I684. **DD** 670/.29/4777. **Ad Acc, Adv Mgr:** Charles Scherer. ***Continues*** *Directory of Iowa Manufacturers, 0095-4446.*

US/0737-7495
**OHIO MANUFACTURERS DIRECTORY.** [Ohio manuf. dir.]. 1st Ed. (1983)-. Directory. English. an. $141.00 (print); $795.00 (diskette or CD-ROM). Manufacturers News Inc., 1633 Central Street, Evanston IL 60201-1569. **Tel** (708)864-7000, FAX (708)332-1100. **ED** Louise West. **LC** HD9727.O3; O36. **DD** 338.4/7/000294771. **Ad Acc.** available on diskette (and list); available on labels.
**Desc:** Detailed profiles of Ohio manufacturers. Includes products, alphabetical, geographical, SIC and computer brand sections. 27 facts.

US/0884-173X
**OHIO REGISTER OF MANUFACTURERS.** [Ohio regist. manuf.]. **Added/Corp** Commerce Register, inc. (1985/1986)-. Directory. English. ir. $92.50. Commerce Register Inc., 190 Godwin Avenue, Midland Park NJ 07432. **Tel** (201)445-3000, (800)221-2172. **ED** Joel Rosano. **LC** HD9727.O3; O357. **DD** 338.4/7/00025771. **Ad Acc. Circ:** 3,000. ***Continues*** *Ohio Directory of Manufacturers, 0738-3711.*
**Desc:** Detailed listings of all manufacturing companies, including top executives, annual sales, number of employees, address, phone, and more.

US/0275-1887
**OHIO STATE MANUFACTURERS GUIDE, THE.** ***Ceased.*** (1981)-(1984). English. an.

Macrae's Blue Book Inc., 65 Bleeker Street/Fifth Floor, New York NY 10012. **Tel** (212)673-4700, (800)622-7237, FAX (212)475-1790.

●US/1059-4523
**OKLAHOMA MANUFACTURERS REGISTER. See** Economics-Industry and Production.

UN
**OTBOR I OBRABOTKA INFORMATSII / AKADEMIIA NAUK UKRAINSKOI SSR, FIZIKO-MEKANICHESKII INSTITUT IM. G.V. KARPENKO.** Vol. 1 (1988)-. Periodical. Russian. 2.00rub single issue. Fiziko-Mekhanicheskii In-T Im GV Karpenko an USSR, 290047 Lvov 47, Nauchnaia 5A Russia. **LC** PAR. ***Continues*** *Otbor i Peredacha Informatsii, 0474-8662.*
**Ind/Abst** Math. Rev.

CN/0835-0191
**OTHER MANUFACTUREING INDUSTRIES.** (OTHER MANUFACTURING INDUSTRIES / STATISTICS CANADA, INDUSTRY DIVISION, CENSUS OF MANUFACTURES SECTION.). [Other manuf. ind.]. **Added/Corp** Statistics Canada. Census of Manufactures Section. Statistics Canada. Industry Division. Statistics Canada. Annual Survey of Manufactures Section. **VFOAT** Autres Industries Manufacturieres. (1985)-. English (French). an. 38.00Can$ Canada; $46.00 US; $54.00 other. Statistics Canada, Publications Sales & Services, Main Building Room 1710, Ottawa Ontario K1A 0T6 Canada. **Tel** (613)951-5078, (800)267-6677, FAX (613)951-1584, telex 053-3585. **LC** HD9734.C2; O88. **DD** 338.4/767/0971021. Index available. **Circ:** 400. available on microfiche. ***Formed by the union of*** *Jewellery and Precious Metal Industries, 0828-9832; Miscellaneous Manufacturing Industries (Statistics (Canada), 0575-9021; Scientific and Professional Equipment Industries, 0384-4242; Signs and Displays Industry (Final), 0527-6187* ***and*** *Sporting Goods and Toy Industries, 0575-979X.*
**Desc:** Statistics on miscellaneous manufacturing industries including, records, flooring, scientific precision recording instruments, clocks and watches, ophthalmic goods, jewellery and silverware, sporting goods, toys and games.

CN/0384-398X
**OTHER MISCELLANEOUS MANUFACTURING INDUSTRIES. See** Manufacturing-Abstracting, Bibliographies and Statistics.

IT/0391-7487
**OTTAGONO.** (19??)-. Periodical. English (Italian). qt. Rizzoli International Publishing Inc, 300 Park Avenue South, New York NY 10010. **Tel** (212)387-3500, (800)462-2387, FAX (212)982-3866. **LC** NK1390.; O88. **DD** 745.4/442/05. ***Formed by the union of*** *Ottagono* ***and*** *Ottagono. English. Ottagono.*

CN/0701-1687
**P I Q PRODUITS POUR L'INDUSTRIE QUEBECOISE. VFOAT** Products pour l'Industrie Quebecoise. Vol. 1 (Nov. 1976)-. Periodical. French. Six times a year. 35.00Can$ (1 year), 65.00Can$ (2 year) Canada; $55.00 (1 year), $105.00 (2 year) surface mail other; $105.00 airmail other. Action Communications Inc, 135 Spy Ct, Markham Ontario L3R 5H6 Canada. **Tel** (416)477-3222. **ED** D Terhune. **DD** 621.9/009714. **Ad Acc. Circ:** 15,720 (ctrl).
**Desc:** Product news and feature articles of interest to industrial readers, engaged in manufacturing, whose mother-tongue is french.

UK
**PALLET & CASE.** (19??)-. English. qt. £25.00 UK; £35.00 others. TG Scott Subscriber Services, 6 Bourne Enterprise Center, Wrotham Road, Borough Green, Kent TN15 8DG England. **Tel** 011 44 01 732 884023, FAX 011 44 01 732 884034.
**Desc:** Providing news, products, technical and legislation information to the pallet and case making industries. Covers materials, processes, manufacturing and services as well as updating readers on international standards and other legislation.

UK
**PARK WORLD.** (19??)-. Trade Publication. English. Eleven times a year (except Dec.). £68.00 UK; $135.00 Europe; $210.00 Far East; $180.00 Middle East, US and Canada. Worlds Fair Ltd, PO Box 57 / Daltry Street, Oldham OL1 4BB England. **Tel** 011 44 61 624-3687, FAX 011 44 61 665-1260, 011 44 61 628-6921, telex 667352. **ED** Andrew Mellor. Index available. **Bk Rev. Ad Acc, Adv Mgr:** John Slattery, **Tel** same as publisher. **Circ:** 6,500 (ctrl). available on microfiche. Documents available from BLDSC.
**Desc:** Valuable journal for the owners of theme parks and the makers of rides.
**Ind/Abst** Trade Ind. Index.

CN/0710-362X
**PEM : PLANT ENGINEERING AND MAINTENANCE. See** Engineering-Mechanical Engineering and Machinery.

US/0733-5237
**PENNSYLVANIA DIRECTORY OF MANUFACTURERS (HOHOKUS, N.J.).** (PENNSYLVANIA DIRECTORY OF MANUFACTURERS.). (1981)-. English. an. $92.50. Commerce Register Inc., 190 Godwin Avenue, Midland Park NJ 07432. **Tel** (201)445-3000, (800)221-2172. **ED** Joel Rosano. **LC** HD9727.P4; P426. **DD** 338.4/7/00025748. **Ad Acc. Circ:** 3,000. available in machine readable format.
**Desc:** Detailed listings of all manufacturing companies, including top executives, annual sales, number of employees, address, phone, and more.

US/1061-0235
**PENTON'S CONTROLS & SYSTEMS.** ***Title Change.*** [Penton's control. syst.]. **VFOAT** Penton's Controls and Systems; Controls and Systems; Controls & Systems. Vol. 39, No. 1 (Jan. 1992)-(1992). Periodical. English. mo. Penton Publishing, 1100 Superior Avenue, Cleveland OH 44114-2543. **Tel** (216)696-7000, FAX (216)696-0836. **LC** TJ212; .A8. **DD** 670.42. **CODEN** PCTSES. available on microfilm and microfiche from University Microfilms International (UMI); available on an online database (file 15/Full-Text) from DIALOG. Documents available from Ask*IEEE. ***Continues*** *Automation (Cleveland, Ohio: 1987), 0896-6052.* ***Absorbed by*** *Machine Design, 0024-9114.*
**Ind/Abst** Appl. Sci. Technol. Index; Bus. ASAP (1992) [Full Txt.]; Bus. Index (1992-); Comput. Lit. Index; Expand. Acad. Index (1992-); Gen. BusinessFile (1992-); INSPEC (Jan. 1992-); Trade Ind. ASAP [Full Txt.]; Trade Ind. Index [Full Txt.]; UMI ABI/Inform--Bus. Period. Ondisc [Full Txt.].

UK/0955-3894
**PHARMACEUTICAL MANUFACTURING REVIEW.** [Pharm. manuf. rev.]. (1989)-. Periodical. English. qt. £78.20 UK; £100.00, $15.00 other. Argus Press Group, Queensway House, 2 Queensway Redhill, Surrey RH1 1QS England. **Tel** 011 44 737 768611, 011 44 737 761685, FAX 011 44 737 760510, telex 948669 TOPJNL G. **CODEN** PMREEC. available on an online database (file 16/Full-Text) from DIALOG.
**Ind/Abst** BioBusiness (1990-); F&S Index Plus Text, Int. [Full Txt.] [Select. Cov.]; PROMT [Full Txt.].

US/1056-9324
**PHOTONICS EUROPEAN DIRECTORY.** [Photonics Eur. dir.]. (1988)-. English. $98.00 (one year), $176.00 (two year), $218.00 (three year). Laurin Publishing Company Inc, PO Box 4949, Pittsfield MA 01202. **Tel** (413)499-0514, FAX (413)442-3180, telex 232-055 ASAS. **DD** 681. ***Separated from*** *Photonics Spectra, 0731-1230.*

IT/0048-4245
**PITTURE E VERNICI.** [Pitt. vern.]. (19??)-. Academic Scholarly Publication. Italian. mo. L100000.00 Italy; L185000.00 Europe except Italy; L372000.00 other. Onedit, Via Natale Battaglia 19, 20127 Milan Italy. **Tel** 011 39 2 26140708. **CODEN** PIVEAY. Documents available from CASDDS.
**Ind/Abst** Chem. Abstr.; Corros. Abstr. (199?-).

US/0744-3900
**PLANT SYSTEMS & EQUIPMENT. VFOAT** Plant Systems and Equipment. Vol. 1, No. 1 (Jan./Feb. 1982)-. Periodical. English. Six times a year. $20.00. Plant Systems & Equipment, 35 East Wacker Drive, Chicago IL 60601. **Tel** (312)346-3074.

AT/0726-4623
**PLANTLINE.** [Plantline]. (1981)-. Periodical. English. mo ((except Jan.)). 60.00Aus$ Australia; 100.00Aus$ other. Reed Business Publishing Pty Ltd. / Australia, 1 5 Railway Street, Level 12 North Tower, Chatswood W 2067 NSW Australia. **Tel** 011 61 2 3725222, FAX 011 61 2 4197533. **ED** Mr Bruce McEwan. **DD** 670.29494. **Bk Rev**, (Qty: 25). **Ad Acc, Adv Mgr:** Peter Symonds, **Tel** 372-5222. **Circ:** 15,000 (ctrl).
**Desc:** Important news of special interest to manufacturing industry and supplies. New legislation, new products and new processes affecting the manufacturing industry.

US
**PRACTICAL MACHINERY MANAGEMENT FOR PROCESS PLANTS.** Vol. 1 (1982)-. Monographic series. English. ir. Price varies per volume. Gulf Publishing Company / Texas, PO Box 2608, Houston TX 77252. **Tel** (800)231-6275, (713)529-4301, FAX (713)520-4433.

BW/0203-2805
**PRIBOROSTROENIE (MINSK).** (PRIBOROSTROENIE.). [Priborostr.]. **Added/Corp** Belaruski Politekhnichny Instytut. (1978)-. Academic Scholarly Publication. Russian. 1.30rub. **LC** TS500; .P669. **CODEN** PRBRD5. Documents available from CASDDS. ***Continues in part*** *Mashinostroenie i Priborostroenie.*
**Ind/Abst** Chem. Abstr.

US/0892-6727
**PRIVATE LABEL PRODUCT NEWS.** [Priv. label prod. news]. **VFOAT** Private Label; PLPN. Vol. 1, No. 1 (Jan. 1987)-. Periodical. English. bm. $30.00 US; $75.00 (surface mail), $95.00 (airmail) other. Certified Publishers Inc, 459 West 45th Street, New York NY 10036. **Tel** (212)541-5870, FAX (212)541-5916. **ED** Debra Ray. **DD** 680. **Ad Acc. Circ:** 30,000 (ctrl).
**Desc:** Serves the private label industry, including retailers, cooperative, voluntaries, wholesalers, service merchandisers, manufacturers, brokers, and others allied to the field.

US/0096-7963
**PROCEEDINGS - ANNUAL SYMPOSIUM ON INSTRUMENTATION FOR THE PROCESS INDUSTRIES.** (PROCEEDINGS; ANNUAL SYMPOSIUM ON INSTRUMENTATION FOR THE PROCESS INDUSTRIES.). [Proc. - Annu. Symp. Instrum. Process Ind.]. **Added/Corp** Texas A & M University. Dept. of Chemical Engineering. (1946)-. Academic Scholarly Publication. English. Texas A & M University / Engineering, Texas Engineering Experiment Station, College Station TX 77843. **DD** 660. **CODEN** PTIPAB. Documents available from Article Express International, CASDDS.
**Ind/Abst** Bioeng. Abstr.; Chem. Abstr.; Ei Page One; Eng. Index Annu.

US/0737-5921
**PROCEEDINGS OF THE ANNUAL TECHNICAL CONFERENCE.** (PROCEEDINGS OF THE ... ANNUAL TECHNICAL CONFERENCE / SOCIETY OF VACUUM COATERS.). [Proc. annu. tech. conf.]. **Main/Corp** Society of Vacuum Coaters. 25th (1982)-. Academic Scholarly Publication. English. an. **LC** TS695; .S62A. **DD** 671.7/35/05. **CODEN** PASVBF. Documents available from Article Express International, CASDDS. ***Continues*** *Society of Vacuum Coaters. Annual Technical Conference Proceedings, 0731-1699.*
**Ind/Abst** Bioeng. Abstr.; Chem. Abstr.; Ei Page One; Eng. Index Annu.

US
**PROCEEDINGS, SYMPOSIUM ON ADVANCED MANUFACTURING.** Proceedings. English. an. $33.50. OES Publications, University of Kentucky, 226 Anderson Hall, Lexington KY 40506-0046. **Tel** (606)257-3361, FAX (606)257-3342. **Circ:** 100 (ctrl).

UK
**PROCESS EQUIPMENT NEWS.** (19??)-. English. Eleven times a year. $99.00 US & Canada; £30.00 UK. Wilmington Publishing Ltd., PO Box 200, Field End Road, Ruislip Middx HA4 OSY England. **Tel** 011 44 81 841 3970, FAX 011 44 81 841 9676.

SP/0079-5836
**PRODEI.** [Prodei]. (1945)-. Periodical. Spanish. be. $150.00 (surface mail) US. **(Subscription address:** Capel Edit Distribuidora SA, Almirante 21, 28004 Madrid, Spain.) **Ad Acc.** ctrl circ.
**Desc:** A concise and accurate account of the manufacture, exports, and imports of the Spanish market.

CN/0822-8906
**PRODUCT CANADA EXPORT JOURNAL.** [Prod. Can. export j.]. Periodical. English (French). qt. $15.00. Product Canada Export Journal, Suite 601/2050 Mansfield, Montreal Quebec H3A 1Z2 Canada. **Tel** (514)842-5263. **ED** Olaf Silva. **DD** 382.6/0971. **Ad Acc. Circ:** 12,000.
**Desc:** Import-export publication.

UK
**PRODUCTION & INDUSTRIAL EQUIPMENT DIGEST. VFOAT** PED. (19??)-. English. mo. $109.00 US & Canada; £30.00 UK. Wilmington Publishing Ltd., PO Box 200, Field End Road, Ruislip Middx HA4 OSY England. **Tel** 011 44 81 841 3970, FAX 011 44 81 841 9676.

US/0275-8040
**PRODUCTIVITY (STAMFORD, CONN.). See** Business-General Management.

US/0032-9940
**PRODUCTS FINISHING.** [Prod. finish.]. (1936)-. Periodical. English. mo. $36.00. Gardner Publications Inc, 6600 Clough Pike, Cincinnati OH 45244. **Tel** (513)231-8020, (513)231-2818, telex 214132. **ED** G Thomas Robison. **LC** TS200; .P73. **DD** 671.7/05. **CODEN** PRFCAB. **[CCC]**. Index available. **Bk Rev. Ad Acc. Circ:** 46,000 (ctrl). available on microfilm and microfiche from University Microfilms International (UMI). Documents available from Article Express International, CASDDS.
**Desc:** Covers production, engineering, laboratory, management and administrative personnel in plants where metal and plastic products are electroplated, anodized, painted, powder coated, buffed, cleaned, coated, polished, degreased or otherwise surface finished.
**Ind/Abst** Alum. Ind. Abstr.; Bioeng. Abstr.; Ceram. Abstr.; Chem. Abstr.; Curr. Titles Electrochem.; Ei Page One; Eng. Mater. Abstr.; Eng. Index Annu.; Leadscan; Met. Abstr.; Surf. Treat. Technol. Abstr.; World Surf. Coat. Abstr.

CN/0575-9455
**PRODUCTS SHIPPED BY CANADIAN MANUFACTURERS.** (PRODUCTS SHIPPED BY CANADIAN MANUFACTURERS / DOMINION BUREAU OF STATISTICS,). [Prod. shipp. Can. manuf.]. **Added/Corp** Canada. Dominion Bureau of Statistics. Industry Division. Canada. Dominion Bureau of Statistics. Manufacturing and Primary Industries Division. Statistics Canada. Manufacturing and Primary Industries Division. Statistics Canada. Regional and Small Business Manufacturing Statistics and Special Services Section. Statistics Canada. Industry Division. Regional Statistics Section. Statistics Canada. Information and Classification Services Section. **VFOAT** Produits Libres par les Fabricants Canadiens. (1961)-. English (French). an. 65.00Can$ Canada; $78.00 US; $91.00 other. Statistics Canada, Publications Sales & Services, Main Building Room 1710, Ottawa Ontario K1A 0T6 Canada. **Tel** (613)951-5078, (800)267-6677, FAX (613)951-1584, telex 053-3585. **LC** HD9734.C2; P76. **DD** 380.1/4567/0971021.
**Desc:** Total Canadian and provincial shipments of products according to the Industrial Commodity Classification Value and, when available, quantities of shipments.

RU/0131-5560
**PROMYSHLENNYI TRANSPORT.** [Prom. transp.]. **Added/Corp** Soviet Union. Gosudarstvennyi Komitet po Delam Stroitelstva. (1972)-. Periodical. Russian. ir. $294.95. Izdatelstvo Transport, Komsomolskii Prospect, 42, Moscow G-48, Russia. **(Subscription address:** East View Publications Inc., 3020 Harbor Lane North, Suite 110, Minneapolis MN 55447.**)** **LC** TS180; .P75.
**Ind/Abst** Coal Abstr.

SA/0033-1481
**PROSPECT (AFRICAN EXPLOSIVES AND CHEMICAL INDUSTRIES).** (PROSPECT / AECI.). **Added/Corp** African Explosives and Chemical Industries. (19??)-. Periodical. English. qt. AECI Ltd, Carlton Centre, PO Box 1122, JHB Johannesburg South Africa. **Tel** (01127-11)223-9111, FAX 223-1929, telex 48-7048 SA. **ED** F. Putero. Index available. **Circ:** 15,000 (ctrl).
**Desc:** Articles in non-technical style describing interesting uses of AECI products by customers. Covers plastics, chemicals, fertilizers, paints and explosives.

PR/0090-3612
**PUERTO RICO OFFICIAL INDUSTRIAL DIRECTORY.** (1967)-. Directory. Multiple languages (English and Spanish). an. $104.00. Whitney Marketing Inc., Apdo 2631, Old San Juan, Puerto Rico 00903. **Tel** (809)725-7373. **ED** Hugo F. Miranda. **LC** HC157.P8; P596. **DD** 380.1/025/7295. **Circ:** 5,000. ***Continues*** *Puerto Rico Official Industrial & Trade Directory.*
**Desc:** Approximately 8,000 firms listed in four major sections: alphabetical, geographical, SIC, and manufacturers' representative.

US/0163-2418
**QUALITY CONTROL REPORTS.** [Qual. control rep.]. **VFOAT** QC; Gold Sheet. (1967)-. Government Publication. English. mo. $280.00. FDC Reports Inc., 5550 Friendship Boulevard/Suite 1, Chevy Chase MD 20815. **Tel** (301)657-9830. **ED** Bill Paulson. **NLM** W1 GO62. **CODEN** QUCRB6. **[CCC].** Documents available from UMI Article Clearinghouse.
**Desc:** For executives concerned with quality assurance and quality control procedures in the prescription and over-the-counter pharmaceutical, cosmetics, medical device industries.
**Ind/Abst** Pharm. News Index (Dec. 1977-).

US/0033-524X
**QUALITY PROGRESS.** **See** Engineering.

US
**QUARTZ DEVICES DIRECTORY.** Directory. English. Twice a year (Oct. and Mar.). $45.00. Great Southern Marketing, PO Box 24404, Ft. Lauderdale FL 33307. **Tel** (305)563-1338, FAX (305)564-5195. **ED** Lucille Hope. **Bk Rev**, (Qty: 20). **Ad Acc**, **Adv Mgr:** L. Aiken. **Circ:** 3,500 (ctrl).

FI
**RAKENTAMINEN.** **See** Building and Construction.

FR
**RAPPORT D'ACTIVITE / CENTRE DE CREATION INDUSTRIELLE.** **Main/Corp** Centre de Creation Industrielle. French. Centre de Creation Industrielle Service Documentation, Centre George Pompidou, 75191 Paris Cedex 04 France. **LC** TS71; .C46A. **DD** 745.2/07.

US
**RECOGNITION & IDENTIFICATION INDUSTRY BLUE BOOK.** **VFOAT** R & I Blue Book; Recognition and Identification Industry Blue Book; R and I Blue Book. English. an. Engravers Journal, PO Box 318, 26 Summit Street, Brighton MI 48116. **Tel** (313)229-5725, FAX (313( 229-8320. **LC** HD9999.P3953; U57. **DD** 680.

US
**REPORT - NATIONAL ASSOCIATION OF MANUFACTURERS OF THE UNITED STATES OF AMERICA. POSTWAR COMMITTEE.** **Main/Corp** National Association of Manufacturers of the United States of America. Postwar Committee. English. mo. $147.00. National Association of Manufacturers, 1331 Penn Ave NW, 1500 N Lobby, Washington DC 20004. **Tel** (202)637-3082.

US
**REPORT ON SALARIES AND TOTAL PAY IN THE SMALLER MANUFACTURING COMPANY / ECS.** **Added/Corp** Executive Compensation Service (U.S.). (1989/1990)-. English. ECS, Executive Compensation Service, Wyatt Data Services, 218 Route 17 North, Roselle Park NJ 07662-9832. **Tel** (201)843-1177, FAX (201)843-0101. **LC** IN PROCESS.

AT/0812-2660
**RESEARCH REPORT ... / DIVISION OF MANUFACTURING TECHNOLOGY, COMMONWEALTH SCIENTIFIC AND INDUSTRIAL RESEARCH ORGANIZATION.** **Main/Corp** Commonwealth Scientific and Industrial Research Organization (Australia). Division of Manufacturing Technology. (1980/1982)-. English. CSIRO Publications, PO Box 89, 314 Albert Street, East Melborne Victoria 3002 Australia. **Tel** 011 61 3 4187333, 4187217, FAX 011 61 3 4190459, telex AA 30236. **LC** TS183; .C647a. **DD** 670/.5.

FR/0766-5210
**REVUE PRATIQUE DE CONTROLE INDUSTRIEL 1984.** [Rev. prat. controle ind. 1984]. **VFOAT** Revue Pratique de Controle Industriel Qualite; Controle Industriel (Paris). (1984)-. Periodical. French. Eight times a year. 377.00F France; 490.00F other. Group Cepp Editions Ampere, 25 rue Dagorno, 75012 Paris France. **Tel** 011 33 1 43473020, FAX 011 33 1 43473080. **UDC** 658.56. ***Continues*** *Qualite (Paris. 1967), 0033-5142.*

US/0361-5103
**RHODE ISLAND DIRECTORY OF MANUFACTURERS.** [R. I. dir. manuf.]. **Added/Corp** Rhode Island. Dept. of Economic Development. (197?)-. Directory. English. an. $45.00. Manufacturers News Inc., 1633 Central Street, Evanston IL 60201-1569. **Tel** (708)864-7000, FAX (708)332-1100. **DD** 338. ***Continues*** *Rhode Island Directory of Manufacturers and List of Commercial Establishments.*
**Desc:** Lists 2,500 firms by name, location, SIC telephone, total employees, and chief executive officer listed. Includes geographical, alphabetical and SIC sections.

IT
**RIVISTA DI IMPIANTI INDUSTRIALI.** **VFOAT** Impianti Industriali. (Apr. 1968)-. Periodical. Italian. mo. L13330. Dr A Barbieri, Via le Premuda 2, Milan 20129 Italy. **LC** TS155.A1; R47.

US/0736-5845
**ROBOTICS AND COMPUTER-INTEGRATED MANUFACTURING.** **See** Computers-Artificial Intelligence.

US/0279-4616
**ROOFER MAGAZINE, THE.** [Roof. mag.]. Vol. 1, Issue 1 (Sept./Oct. 1981)-. Periodical. English. mo. $25.00 US; $35.00 Canada; $70.00 other. Construction Publications Inc., 12734 Kenwood Lane #73, Fort Myers FL 33907. **Tel** (813)489-2929, FAX (813)489-1747. **ED** Angela Hutto. **LC** TH2391; .R66. **DD** 695/.05. **Ad Acc**, **Adv Mgr:** G. Abrell. **Circ:** 19,857 (ctrl).
**Desc:** Features roofing technology, equipment comparisons, product news, safety, legal and business columns. Format includes contractor interviews and photo essays.
**Ind/Abst** Constr. Index.

NE/0168-4965
**RUBBERVERWERKENDE INDUSTRIE / CENTRAAL BUREAU VOOR DE STATISTIEK, HOOFDAFDELING STATISTIEKEN VAN INDUSTRIE EN BOUWNIJVERHEID.** **VFOAT** Manufacture of Rubber Products. 1981-. Dutch (summaries and/or abstracts in English). an. Fl9.50. Centraal Bureau voor de Statistiek, AFD ALG Zaken, Postbus 959, 2270 AZ Voorburg Netherlands. **Tel** 011 31 70 3373800, FAX 011 31 038 7429, telex 32692 CBS NL. **LC** HD9161.N4; A3. ***Continues*** *Netherlands. Centraal Bureau Voor de Statistiek. Rubberver Werkende Industrie, Produktiestatistieken.*

AU
**SACHGUETERERZEUGUNG SCHNELLBERICHT.** **Main/Corp** Osterreichisches Statistisches Zentralamt. (19??)-. Government Publication. German. qt. S140.00. Osterreichisches Statistisches Zentralamt, Hintere Zollamtsstrasse 2B, Postfach 9000, Vienna 1033 Austria. **Tel** (0222)71128-7628, FAX (0222)71128-7728, telex 0132600. **LC** HC261; .A29a. **DD** 338/.09436. **Circ:** 130 (ctrl). available in Loose-leaf; available on magnetic tape.
**Desc:** Information on manufacturing and produced goods.

US/0273-3447
**SAN DIEGO COUNTY DIRECTORY OF MANUFACTURERS AND INDUSTRIAL DISTRIBUTORS.** **See** Economics-Industry and Production.

CN/0831-9057
**SASKATCHEWAN TRADE DIRECTORY (1986).** (SASKATCHEWAN TRADE DIRECTORY.). [Sask. trade dir.]. 1986-. Directory. English. an. $25.00. Saskatchewan Trade Directory, PO Box 3114, Regina Saskatchewan S4P 3J8 Canada. **Tel** (204)775-0201. **ED** Steve Steigerwald, Herb Krushel, George Gamvrelis, and Alan Cherniak. **DD** 338.4/7/00257124. **Ad Acc. Circ:** 10,500 (ctrl).
**Desc:** Provides an alphabetical listing of manufacturers and distributors. Includes addresses, telephone numbers, head office identification, branches, range of products, names and titles of management personnel, and number of employees.

CN/0831-1854
**SCOTT'S DIRECTORIES, ATLANTIC MANUFACTURERS.** [Scott's dir. Atl. manuf.]. **Added/Corp** Scott's Directories. **VFOAT** Scott's Atlantic; Atlantic Manufacturers; Scott's Directory of Atlantic Manufacturers. (1986)-. Directory. English. ir (every 15 mos.). $115.95. Southam Information and Technology Group Inc., 1450 Don Mills Road, Don Mills Ontario M3B 2X7 Canada. **Tel** (416)445-6641, (800)668-2374, FAX (416)442-2261. **(Subscription address:** Scott's Directories, 1450 Don Mills Road, Don Mills Ontario M3B 2X7 Canada.**)** **DD** 338.4/025/715. ***Continues*** *Scott's Industrial Directory, Atlantic Manufacturers., 0706-5167.*

CN/0830-9272
**SCOTT'S DIRECTORIES. ONTARIO MANUFACTURERS.** [Scott's dir., Ont. manuf.]. **Added/Corp** Scott's Directories. **VFOAT** Directories, Ontario Manufacturers; Ontario Manufacturers; Scott's Ontario ... Ed. **VAT** Scott's Directory of Ontario Manufacturers. (1986)-. Directory. English. be. $215.95. Southam Information and Technology Group Inc., 1450 Don Mills Road, Don Mills Ontario M3B 2X7 Canada. **Tel** (416)445-6641, (800)668-2374, FAX (416)442-2261. **(Subscription address:** Scott's Directories, 1450 Don Mills Road, Don Mills Ontario M3B 2X7 Canada.**)** **LC** HC117.O6; S36. **DD** 338.7/4/025713. ***Continues*** *Scott's Industrial Directory. Ontario Manufacturers, 0316-7879.*

CN/0829-2248
**SCOTT'S DIRECTORIES, WESTERN MANUFACTURERS.** [Scott's dir. west. manuf.]. **VFOAT** Scott's Directory of Western Manufacturers; Scott's Western. 7th Edition (1985/1986)-. English. ir. 225.00Can$. Southam Information and Technology Group Inc., 1450 Don Mills Road, Don Mills Ontario M3B 2X7 Canada. **Tel** (416)445-6641, (800)668-2374, FAX (416)442-2261. **(Subscription address:** Scott's Directories, 1450 Don Mills Road, Don Mills Ontario M3B 2X7 Canada.**)** **ED** Muriel Throop. **DD** 338.4/025/712. **Ad Acc.** available on labels (or 3x5 cards); available on magnetic tape. ***Continues*** *Scott's Industrial Directory. Western Manufacturers, 0317-879X.*

CN/0829-2221
**SCOTT'S REPERTOIRES, FABRICANTS DU QUEBEC.** [Scott's repert. fabr. Que.]. **Added/Corp** Scott's Directories. **VFOAT** Quebec Manufacturers; Fabricants du Quebec; Scott's Directories, Quebec Manufacturers; Scott's Quebec; Repertoires, Fabricants du Quebec; Directories, Quebec Manufacturers. 12th Edition (1984/1985)-. English (French). an (Sept.). 204.95Can$. Southam Information and Technology Group Inc., 1450 Don Mills Road, Don Mills Ontario M3B 2X7 Canada. **Tel** (416)445-6641, (800)668-2374, FAX (416)442-2261. **(Subscription address:** Scott's Directories, 1450 Don Mills Road, Don Mills Ontario M3B 2X7 Canada.**)** **DD** 338.4/025/714. ***Continues*** *Scott's Quebec Industrial Directory, 0582-3080.*

JA
**SEN'I KOBUNSHI ZAIRYO KENKYUJO NENPO.** **Main/Corp** Sen'i Kobunshi Zairyo Kenkyujo (Japan). Began with the issue for I.E. 1949. Japanese. an. Kogyo Gijutsuin Sen'i Kobunshi Zairyo Kenkyujo, (Research Inst. for Polymers & Textiles, Agency of Industrial Scinece & Technology), 1-4, Higashi 1 Chome, Tsukubashi, Ibarakiken 305, Japan. **LC** TS1548.5; .S43. ***Continues*** *Sen'i Kogyo Shikenjo Nenpo.*

US/1060-1902
**SENSOR BUSINESS DIGEST.** [Sens. bus. dig.]. Vol. 1, No. 1 (Oct. 1991)-. Periodical. English. Twelve times a year. $325.00 North America; $345.00 other. Vital Information Publications, 321 Carrera Drive, Mill Valley CA 94941. **Tel** (415)389-8671, (415)345-7018, FAX (415)389-8671, (415)345-7018. **ED** Peter Adrian

(editor's address: 899 Bounty Drive, #202 FF, Foster City, CA 94404). **DD** 338. **Bk Rev**, (Qty: 3-4/year). **Ad Acc**, **Adv Mgr:** Sarah Collings. available on an online database from NEWSNET; and Predicasts, Inc. ***Continues** Measurement Chain, 1051-9432.*
**Desc:** Sensors and instrumentation, process control, monitoring and testing, current and future applications and technologies.
**Ind/Abst** PROMT [Full Txt.]; PTS Newsl. Database [Full Txt.].

US/1042-2757
**SENSORS BUYER'S GUIDE.** [Sens. buy. guide]. (1988)-. English. an. $32.45 US; $33.95 Canada and Mexico; $37.95 other. Helmers Publishing Inc., 174 Concord Street, PO Box 874, Peterborough NH 03458-0874. **Tel** (603)924-9631, FAX (603)924-7408. **LC** TA165; .S4563. **DD** 681/.2. **[CCC]. Ad Acc.** ***Continues** Sensor Directory, 1042-2749.*
**Desc:** Contains a complete listing of all the manufacturers of sensors and transducers including company information, type of sensor, etc. Completely indexed by type of sensor.

JA/0389-2263
**SHIKEN HOKOKU (NIHON SENBAI KOSHA. HIRATSUKA SEIZO SHIKENJO).** (SHIKEN HOKOKU.). Japanese (summaries and/or abstracts in English). Nihon Senbai Kosha Hiratsuka Seizo Shikenjo, 1-31 Kurobegaoka Hiratsuka-shi, Kanagawa-ken Japan. **LC** TS2220; .S48.

US/0275-4533
**SHIPMENTS TO FEDERAL GOVERNMENT AGENCIES.** (CURRENT INDUSTRIAL REPORTS. MA-175, SHIPMENTS TO FEDERAL GOVERNMENT AGENCIES.). [Shipm. fed. gov. agencies]. **Added/Corp** United States. Bureau of the Census. **VFOAT** Shipments to Federal Government Agencies. (1978)-. Government Publication. English. US Department of Commerce / Bureau of the Census, Data User Services Division, Customer Services, Washington DC 20233-0800. **Tel** (301)763-4100. **(Subscription address:** Superintendent of Documents, US Government Printing Office, Washington DC 20402.**) LC** JK1673; .S53. **DD** 353.0071/2. ***Continues** Shipment of Defense-Oriented Industries.*
**Desc:** Presents timely data on the production, inventories, and orders of approximately 5,000 products, which represents 40 percent of all US manufacturing.

SI
**SINGAPORE MANUFACTURERS AND PRODUCTS DIRECTORY. Added/Corp** Singapore. Economic Development Board. (1971)-. Directory. English. Straits Times Press, Press Times House, Kim Seng Road, Singapore 9 Singapore. **LC** HD9736.S54; S49. **DD** 338/.0025/5952.

US/0275-1488
**SITE REPORT, THE.** ***Ceased.*** [Site rep.]. Vol. 1, No. 1 (Jan. 1981)-(199?). Periodical. English. bm. Conway Publishers, 40 Technology Park, Norcross GA 30092. **Tel** (404)446-6996, telex 80-4468. **ED** George Adcock. **[CCC]. Bk Rev. Ad Acc. Circ:** 650 (ctrl).
**Desc:** State by state coverage of new industrial facilities. Also contains comprehensive statistical summaries.

US/0882-7443
**SOFTWHERE. MANUFACTURING. See** Computers-Software.

AT
**SOUTH AUSTRALIAN MAJOR MANUFACTURING, MINING AND DEVELOPMENT PROJECTS. Added/Corp** South Australia. Ministry of Development and Mines. Development Division. **VFOAT** Development. (1974)-. Periodical. English. Twice a year. 13.50Aus$ (latest volume). Major Manufacturing & Mining, 309 Pitt Street, Government Bookshop, Sydney New South Wales 2000 Australia. **Tel** (02)267-8455. ***Continues** South Australian Major Manufacturing and Development Projects.*

US/0277-0733
**SPUN YARN PRODUCTION.** (CURRENT INDUSTRIAL REPORTS. MA-22F.2, SPUN YARN PRODUCTION / U.S. DEPARTMENT OF COMMERCE, BUREAU OF THE CENSUS.). Began in 1959. Government Publication. English. an. $1.25. US Department of Commerce, 14th Street & Constitution Avenue NW, Washington DC 20230. **Tel** (202)482-2000, FAX (202)482-3772. **LC** HD9909.Y3; U633. **DD** 338.4/767702862.
**Desc:** Presents timely data on the production, inventories, and orders of approximately 5,000 products, which represents 40 percent of all US manufacturing.

US
**STATE GUIDE FOR RV MANUFACTURERS. Added/Corp** Recreational Vehicle Industry Association (Chantilly, Va.). **VFOAT** State Guide for R.V. Manufacturers. (19??)-. English. an. $41.50. Recreation Vehicle Industry Association, PO Box 2999, 1896 Preston WH Dr., Reston VA 22090-0999. **Tel** (703)620-6003. **ED** Rvia Staff. **LC** HD9710.37.U6; S74. **DD** 343.73/07862922; 347.3037862922. **Circ:** 1,500.
**Desc:** Meant for information purposes and to serve as a reference for locating appropriate state officials and agencies.

US
**STEEL SHIPPING DRUMS AND PAILS.** [Steel shipp. drums pails]. **Main/Corp** United States. Bureau of the Census. **Added/Corp** United States. Bureau of the Census. **VFOAT** Steel Shipping Drums and Pails. 1st Quarter (1981)-. Government Publication. English. qt. $5.00 domestic; $46.25 other. Superintendent of Documents, US Government Printing Office, Washington DC 20402. **Tel** (202)275-3328, FAX (202)786-2377. **LC** HD9529.B3; U33. **DD** 338.47672. Documents available from Documents on Demand.
**Desc:** Presents tables and statistics based on a survey of manufacturers on the total production, value, shipment, and consumption of various products manufactured by industries in the United States-Steel shipping Drums and Pails.
**Ind/Abst** Am. Stat. Index.

CN/0380-0822
**STEEL WIRE AND SPECIFIED WIRE PRODUCTS.** [Steel wire specif. wire prod.]. **Added/Corp** Canada. Dominion Bureau of Statistics. Mining, Metallurgical & Chemical Section. Canada. Dominion Bureau of Statistics. Canada. Dominion Bureau of Statistics. Metal and Chemical Products Section. Canada. Dominion Bureau of Statistics. Industry and Merchandising Division. Canada. Dominion Bureau of Statistics. Industry Division. Canada. Dominion Bureau of Statistics. Manufacturing and Primary Industries Division. Statistics Canada. Manufacturing and Primary Industries Division. Statistics Canada. Industry Division. **VFOAT** Fil d'Acier et Certains Produits de Fil Metallique. (Apr. 1949)-. Periodical. English (French). mo. 60.00Can$ Canada; $72.00 US; $84.00 other. Statistics Canada, Publications Sales & Services, Main Building Room 1710, Ottawa Ontario K1A 0T6 Canada. **Tel** (613)951-5078, (800)267-6677, FAX (613)951-1584, telex 053-3585. **LC** WMLC L 83/9680. **DD** 338.4/7672/0971. ***Absorbed in part** Steel Wire (1946), 0830-1859; Wire Fencing., 0830-1867; Nails, Tacks and Staples., 0830-1875.*
**Desc:** Provides statistics on production and shipments of steel wire, fabricated wire products, and nails, tacks and staples.

●GW/0941-7583
**STUCK, PUTZ, TROCKENBAU.** [Stuck Putz Trockenbau]. (1992)-. Periodical. German. mo. DM158.00. C Maurer Druck Verlag, Postfach 1361, W-7340 Geislingen Germany. **Tel** 011 49 7331 42011. **UDC** 62. ***Continues** Der Stukkateur (Geislingen), 0177-1477.*

AT/0816-9128
**SURVEY OF MANUFACTURING CONDITIONS AND FUTURE PROSPECTS IN N.S.W.** [Surv. manuf. cond. future prospects N.S.W.]. (1985)-. Periodical. English. Four times a year (Mar., June, Sept., Dec.). 50.00Aus$ Australia; 70.00Aus$ others. Australian Chamber Manufacturers, Private Bag 938, North Sydney NSW 2059 Australia. **Tel** 011 61 2 9637545. **DD** 338.09944021.
**Desc:** A survey that continues private survey of manufacturing in Australia. Covers a representative sample of the small and small to medium sized manufacturers other surveys neglect.

US/0364-7021
**SWEET'S SHOWROOM.** English. $5.00. McGraw Hill Publishing Company, Inc., 1221 Avenue of the Americas, New York NY 10020. **Tel** (212)512-6410, (800)525-5003, FAX (212)512-6111. **LC** TS887; .S95. **DD** 381/.45/684100973.

US/0082-1470
**TAIWAN BUYERS' GUIDE. Added/Corp** Chung-kuo Sheng Ch'an Li Chi Mao i Chung Hsin. (19??)-. Consumer Publication. English (Chinese). an. $120.00. US International Marketing Company, 17057 Bellflower Boulevard, PO Box 428, Bellflower CA 90706. **Tel** (310)925-2918. **ED** R.M. Heaton. **Ad Acc. Circ:** 2,000. ***Continues** Chung Hua Min Kuo Kung Shang Ming Lu.*
**Desc:** Directory listing and illustrating thousands of products. Lists 12,000 Taiwan manufacturers, exporters, and trading firms.

FI/0784-9044
**TALONRAKENNUSYRITYSTEN TILINPAATOSTILASTO.** 1987-. Finnish. an. **LC** HD9715.F5; T35. ***Continues in part** Rakennusyritysten Tilinpaatostilasto, 0784-8463.*

US/0191-085X
**TECHNICAL PAPER - SOCIETY OF MANUFACTURING ENGINEERS (MF).** (TECHNICAL PAPER - SOCIETY OF MANUFACTURING ENGINEERS. MF.). [Tech. pap. - Soc. Manuf. Eng.]. **Main/Corp** Society of Manufacturing Engineers. (1952)-. Academic Scholarly Publication. English. ir. $845.00 (1994 edition). Society of Manufacturing Engineers, One SME Drive, PO Box 930, Member's Records Dept., Dearborn MI 48121-0930. **Tel** (313)271-1500, FAX (313)271-2861, telex 297742 SME UR (VIA RCA). **CODEN** TSMFD7. Documents available from Article Express International, CASDDS.
**Desc:** Conference papers covering the entire spectrum of manufacturing technology.
**Ind/Abst** Bioeng. Abstr.; Chem. Abstr. (1970-1981); Ei Page One; Eng. Index Annu.

FR
**TECHNIQUES INDUSTRIELLES.** French. ir. 48.00. Comite d'Etudes Pedagogiques et Techniques, Sevpen, 29 rue Dulm, 75230 Cachan France. **LC** TS183; .T43. ***Continues** Enseignements Techniques: Technique Industrielles.*

AG
**TECNICA E INDUSTRIA.** (1922)-. Periodical. Spanish. mo (10 issues). Indutec Tecnica & Industria, Rodriguez Pena 486 P10, 1020 Buenos Aires Argentina. **Tel** 011 54 1 490572. **LC** TS1; .T45. **Ad Acc. Circ:** 4,500.
**Desc:** Covers general information, international information, engineering notes, catalogs, and services. Computer devices, telecommunications review, industrial devices, etc.
**Ind/Abst** Surf. Treat. Technol. Abstr.

SP/0040-1838
**TECNICA INDUSTRIAL (MADRID).** (TECNICA INDUSTRIAL.). [Tec. ind. (Madrid)]. **Added/Corp** Asociacion Nacional de Peritos Industriales. Asociacion Nacional de Peritos e Ingenieros Tecnicos Industriales. (1952)-. Academic Scholarly Publication. Spanish. Four times a year. 1200ptas Spain; 1700ptas others. Consejo Ing Tec Indust, Tech Ind Adva Pablo Iglesias, 28003 Madrid Spain. **Tel** 011 34 15 541806. **LC** TS191; .T45. **CODEN** TEINBD. Documents available from CASDDS.
**Ind/Abst** Chem. Abstr.

YU/0494-9846
**TEHNOLOGIJA MESA.** [Tehnol. mesa]. **Added/Corp** Jugoslovenski Institut za Tehnologiju Mesa. Vol. 1 (Aug. 1960)-. Academic Scholarly Publication. Serbo-Croatian (Roman) (English, French and German). mo. $60.00. Tehnologija Mesa, Post Fah 548, 11000 Belgrade Yugoslavia. **Tel** 650-655, telex 12 309 YU INMES. **ED** Nikola Petrovic. **LC** TS1950; .T43. **CODEN** TEMEA5. Index available. cum. index. **Bk Rev. Ad Acc.** ctrl circ. Documents available from CASDDS.
**Ind/Abst** AGRICOLA; Chem. Abstr.; Food Sci. Technol. Abstr.; Pig News Inf.; Rev. Med. Vet. Mycology.

US/0443-5443
**TENTATIVE RECOMMENDED PRACTICE (INSTRUMENT SOCIETY OF AMERICA).** (TENTATIVE RECOMMENDED PRACTICE.). [Tentat. recomm. pract.]. **Main/Corp** Instrument Society of America. English. Instrument Society of America, 67 Alexander Drive, Research Triangle NC 27709. **Tel** (919)549-8411, FAX (919)549-8288, telex 802 540.
**Desc:** The industry's one source and reference guide to standards and practices in instrumentation, design testing, and maintenance.

FI/0300-3124
**TEOLLISUUSSANOMAT.** Periodical. Finnish. mo. Central Statistical Office, PO Box 504, SF-00101 Helsinki Finland. **Tel** 358-0-17347, 1002111 TILASTO SF, FAX 358-0-17342279.

US/0743-1163
**TEXAS MANUFACTURERS REGISTER.** [Tex. manuf. regist.]. 1st Ed. (1985)-. Directory. English. an. $136.00 (print); $795.00 (diskette or CD-ROM). Manufacturers News Inc., 1633 Central Street, Evanston IL 60201-1569. **Tel** (708)864-7000, FAX (708)332-1100. **LC** HD9727.T4; T45. **DD** 338.4/767/0294764. **Bk Rev. Ad Acc.**
**Desc:** Contains information on firms in the state. Lists executives, company addresses and phone numbers, year established, annual sales, plant square footage, model and language of in-house computer.

US/0272-7439
**TEXTURED YARN PRODUCTION.** ***Ceased.*** (CURRENT INDUSTRIAL REPORTS. MA-22F.1, TEXTURED YARN PRODUCTION / U.S. DEPARMENT OF COMMERCE, BUREAU OF THE CENSUS.). [Textured yarn prod.]. **Added/Corp** United States. Bureau of the Census. **VFOAT** Textured Yarn Production. (19??)-(19??). Government Publication. English. an. US Department of Commerce, 14th Street & Constitution Avenue NW, Washington DC 20230. **Tel** (202)482-2000, FAX (202)482-3772. **LC** HD9909.Y3; U63. **DD** 338.4/767702862.
**Desc:** Presents timely data on the production, inventories, and orders of approximately 5,000 products, which represents 40 percent of all US manufacturing.

TH
**THAILAND MANUFACTURERS AND PRODUCTS DIRECTORY.** 1977-. Directory. English. 300.00B. Fareast Media Center, Asvahem Building/Suite 202, 179 Suriwongse Road, Bangkok Thailand. **LC** T12.5.T47; T47. **DD** 338.4/7/67025593.

# Manufacturing —Abstracting, Bibliographies and Statistics

US/0739-8778
**THESAURUS, MANUFACTURING ENGINEERING TERMS.** See Library and Information Sciences.

US/0362-7721
**THOMAS REGISTER OF AMERICAN MANUFACTURERS AND THOMAS REGISTER CATALOG FILE.** 1st Ed. (1906)-. Catalog. English. an (published in March). $225.00 US; $495.00 Central and South America; $395.00 other, except Canada. Thomas Publishing Company, One Penn Plaza, 250 West 34th Street, New York NY 10119. **Tel** (210)290-7277. **(Subscription address:** Business Communications Inc., Five Penn Plaza, New York NY 10001.) **LC** T12; .T6. **DD** 338.7/6/02573. **NLM** T 12 T461. Index available (free). cum. index. available on CD-ROM.

US/0894-4288
**THOMAS REGISTER'S MID-YEAR GUIDE TO FACTORY AUTOMATION PRODUCTS, SYSTEMS, SERVICES.** **Ceased.** See Computers-Computer Graphics and Design.

CN/1183-1448
**THOMPSON-OKANAGAN DEVELOPMENT REGION MANUFACTURERS DIRECTORY.** [Thompson-Okanagan Dev. Reg. manuf. dir.]. **Added/Corp** British Columbia. Ministry of Finance and Corporate Relations. Planning and Statistics Division. Thompson-Okanagan Development Region (B.C.) (1991)-. Directory. English. **DD** 338.4/767/025711. **Continues** Thompson-Okanagan Manufacturers' Directory., 0847-2130.

LH
**TKG : FACHZEITSCHRIFT FUR DIE TECHNIK IN DER KERAMIK, GLAS UND EMAIL INDUSTRIE.** See Glass and Ceramics.

US/1054-1233
**TOTAL PRODUCTIVE MAINTENANCE : TPM.** See Business-General Management.

JA/0041-0144
**TOYO SODA KENKYU HOKOKU.** **VFOAT** Scientific Report of Toyo Soda Manufacturing Company, Ltd. Academic Scholarly Publication. English (Japanese). Tokyo Soda Kogyo, Kabushiki Kaisha 4560, Tonda Shinnanyo-shi, Yamaguchi-ken 746 Japan. **LC** TP245.S7; T62. **CODEN** TSKEAP. Documents available from CASDDS.
**Ind/Abst** Chem. Abstr.

US/0041-0772
**TRAILER/BODY BUILD.** See Transportation.

UK/0263-6263
**TRUCK & BUS BUILDER.** [Truck bus build]. **VFOAT** Truck and Bus Builder. (1978)-. Periodical. English. Twelve times a year. £120.00 UK, £130.00 others; $228.00 US & Canada. Truck and Bus Builder, PO Box 132, Bridgewater Somerset TA5 1YW England. **Tel** 011 44 278 741648, FAX 011 44 278 741641. **DD** 338.4762922405. **Circ:** 1,000.
**Desc:** Developments within the commerical vehicle manufacturing industry on a worldwide basis through the use of concise and easily assimilated news items. Covers statistical information, new products, financial matters, technical and environmental developments, legal changes, take-overs, and company-performance reports.

US/0145-5001
**TRUCK TRAILERS.** **Title Change.** (CURRENT INDUSTRIAL REPORTS. M37L, TRUCK TRAILERS / U.S. DEPARTMENT OF COMMERCE, BUREAU OF THE CENSUS.). [Truck trailers]. **Added/Corp** United States. Bureau of the Census. **VFOAT** Truck Trailers. (19??)-(1992). English. mo (with annual summary). Superintendent of Documents, US Government Printing Office, Washington DC 20402. **Tel** (202)275-3328, FAX (202)786-2377. **LC** HD9710.38.U6; C87. **DD** 338.4/7629224/0973021. Documents available from Documents on Demand. **Continued by** Current Industrial Reports. M37L, Truck Trailers (Computer File).
**Desc:** Presents timely data on the production, inventories, and orders of approximately 5,000 products, which represents 40 percent of all US manufacturing.
**Ind/Abst** Am. Stat. Index.

UK/0263-6794
**TUBE INTERNATIONAL.** See Metals and Metallurgy.

IT
**TUTTONORMEL.** Italian. mo. L120000.00 Italy; L240000.00 other. TNE SRL, CSO Duca Abruzzi 31, 10129 Turin Italy. **Tel** 011 39 11 5819888, FAX 011 39 11 5819304. cum. index. **Circ:** 10,000.

GW/0170-9577
**TZ FUER METALLBEARBEITUNG.** **Ceased.** See Metals and Metallurgy.

US/1056-2052
**UPHOLSTERY DESIGN & MANUFACTURING.** (UPHOLSTERY DESIGN & MANUFACTURING : UDM.). [Upholstery design manuf.]. **VFOAT** Upholstery Design and Manufacturing; UDM. (19??)-. Periodical. English. mo (10 issues). $65.00 US; $96.00 Canada; $90.00 Mexico; $120.00 (surface mail) other. Cahners Publishing Company, 249 West 17th Street, New York NY 10011. **Tel** (212)645-0067, FAX (212)242-6987. **(Subscription address:** Cahners Publishing Company / Colorado, Paid Subscription Service Center, PO Box 7610, Highlands Ranch CO 80126-7610.) **LC** WMLC 93/4406. **DD** 747. **[CCC].** **Ad Acc. Circ:** 16,000 (ctrl).
**Desc:** Edited for producers of upholstered furniture.

US/0732-2860
**UPSTATE NEW YORK DIRECTORY OF MANUFACTURERS.** 1st Ed. (1982-1983)-. Directory. English. ir. $66.25. Commerce Register Inc., 190 Godwin Avenue, Midland Park NJ 07432. **Tel** (201)445-3000, (800)221-2172. **ED** Joel Rosano. **LC** HD9727.N7; U67. **DD** 381/.45/000294747. **Ad Acc. Circ:** 3,000.
**Desc:** Detailed listings of all manufacturing companies, including top executives, annual sales, number of employees, address, phone, etc.

FR
**USINES NOUVELLE TECHNIQUE ET TECHNICIENS.** French. Usine Publications SA, 59 rue du Rocher, 75008 Paris France.

SW
**VENTILEN.** (19??)-. ir. Kr50.00. Ventilen Torstey Kvoon, Stenors Vogen 25, 26141 Landskrona Sweden.

UN/0321-2211
**VESTNIK KIEVSKOGO POLITEKHNICHESKOGO INSTITUTA. SERIIA PRIBOROSTROENIIA.** [Vestn. Kiev. politeh. inst., Ser. priborostr.]. **Main/Corp** Kiev. Politekhnichnyi Instytut. **VFOAT** Seriia Priborostroeniia. (1970)-. Academic Scholarly Publication. Russian (summaries and/or abstracts in English). Izdatelskoe Obedinenie Vyshcha Shkola / Ukraine, Odessa Ostrovskoa 64, Kiev Ukraine. **LC** TS500; .K53a. **CODEN** VKPPDI. Documents available from CASDDS.
**Ind/Abst** Chem. Abstr. (1970-1982).

●US/1065-2493
**VIRGINIA MANUFACTURERS DIRECTORY.** **Added/Corp** Manufacturers' News, Inc. (1992)-. Directory. English. $69.00. Manufacturer's News Inc., 1633 Central Street, Evanston IL 60201.

US
**VISION QUARTERLY.** English. qt. $60.00 US, $64.00 Canada and Mexico (business, library and academic institution); $80.00 (airmail), other. Society of Manufacturing Engineers, One SME Drive, PO Box 930, Member's Records Dept., Dearborn MI 48121-0930. **Tel** (313)271-1500, FAX (313)271-2861, telex 297742 SME UR (VIA RCA).

US/0148-5687
**WASHINGTON MANUFACTURERS REGISTER.** [Wash. manuf. regist.]. **Added/Corp** Washington (State). Dept. of Commerce and Economic Development. Washington (State). Dept. of Trade and Economic Development. (1979)-. Directory. English. an. $99.00 (print); $395.00 (diskette). Manufacturers News Inc., 1633 Central Street, Evanston IL 60201-1569. **Tel** (708)864-7000, FAX (708)332-1100. **LC** T12; .M365. **DD** 338.4/7/67025797. **Ad Acc. Circ:** 2,000. available on diskette. **Continues** Directory of Washington Manufacturers, 0148-3641.
**Desc:** Contains information of 4,000 Washington manufacturing businesses and 12,000 key executives by name and title.

US/0893-2824
**WEST VIRGINIA MANUFACTURERS REGISTER.** (WEST VIRGINIA MANUFACTURERS REGISTER / MNI). [W.V. manuf. regist.]. **Added/Corp** Manufacturers' News, Inc. **VFOAT** MNI West Virginia Manufacturers Register. 1st Ed. (1988)-. Directory. English. an. $50.00 (print); $295.00 (diskette or CD-ROM). Manufacturers News Inc., 1633 Central Street, Evanston IL 60201-1569. **Tel** (708)864-7000, FAX (708)332-1100. **ED** Louise West. **LC** HD9727.W4; W39. **DD** 338.4/767/0294754. Index available. **Ad Acc. Circ:** 1,000 (ctrl).
**Desc:** Detailed profiles of West Virginia's manufacturing establishments.

AT
**WESTERN AUSTRALIAN MANUFACTURERS DIRECTORY.** **Added/Corp** Western Australia. Dept. of Industrial Development. (19??)-. Periodical. English. ir. Department of Industrial Development / Australia, 8th Floor/SGIO Atrium, 170 St Georges Terrace Australia. **LC** HD9738.A83; W46. **DD** 338.4/025/941.

UK
**WHAT'S NEW IN DESIGN.** English. Eight times a year. £60.00 UK and Northern Ireland; $140.00 other. Morgan Grampian, 40 Beresford Street Woolwich, London SE18 6BQ England. **Tel** 011 44 81 855 7777, FAX 011 44 81 855 5548, telex 896238.

US/0740-1809
**WIRE ROPE NEWS & SLING TECHNOLOGY.** [Wire rope news sling technol.]. **Added/Corp** T/A VS Enterprises. **VFOAT** Wire Rope News and Sling Technology. (19??)-. Periodical. English. Six times a year. $20.00 US; $25.00 Canada; $30.00 other. VS Enterprises, PO Box 87, Clark NJ 07066. **Tel** (908)486-3221, FAX (908)396-4215. **ED** Conrad Miller and Barbara McGrath. **Ad Acc, Adv Mgr:** Ed Bluvias. **Circ:** 3,200. **Continues** Wire Rope News.
**Desc:** News and reports describing the manufacture and use of wire, rope and related products.

US/0738-0070
**WISCONSIN MANUFACTURERS REGISTER.** (WISCONSIN MANUFACTURERS REGISTER / MNI.). 1st Ed. (1984)-. Directory. English. an. $100.00 (print); $695.00 (diskette or CD-ROM). Manufacturers News Inc., 1633 Central Street, Evanston IL 60201-1569. **Tel** (708)864-7000, FAX (708)332-1100. **ED** Louise West. **LC** HD9727.W6; W58. **DD** 338.4/767/0294775. **Ad Acc.** available on diskette (and lists); available on labels.
**Desc:** Lists manufacturers and processors. Five sections: alphabetical, geographical, by product, S.I.C. and computer.

●UK/1352-3074
**WORLD CLASS DESIGN TO MANUFACTURE : WCDM.** **VFOAT** WCDM. Vol. 1, No. 1 (1994)-. Periodical. English. bm. $464.00. MCB University Press, 60 62 Toller Lane, Bradford West Yorkshire BD8 9BX England. **Tel** 011 44 274 499821, FAX 011 44 274 547143, telex 51317 MCBUNI G. **(Subscription address:** MCB University Press / US and Canada Subscriptions, PO Box 10812, Birmingham AL 35201-0812.) **Continues** Manufacturing Breakthrough, 0964-2366.

●UK
**WORLD DIRECTORY OF FERTILIZER MANUFACTURERS.** See Agriculture.

US/0085-8307
**WORLD MOTOR VEHICLE DATA.** See Transportation-Automobiles.

US/0511-0289
**WYOMING DIRECTORY OF MANUFACTURING AND MINING.** [Wyo. dir. manuf. min.]. **Added/Corp** Wyoming. Dept. of Economic Planning and Development. University of Wyoming. Division of Business and Economic Research. Wyoming Natural Resource Board. Wyoming. Industrial Development Division. **VFOAT** Wyoming Directory, Manufacturing and Mining. (1956)-. Directory. English. ir. $25.42 IL residents; $23.95 other US; $29.00 other. Manufacturers News Inc., 1633 Central Street, Evanston IL 60201-1569. **Tel** (708)864-7000, FAX (708)332-1100. **LC** HD9727.W8; W95. **DD** 338/.025/787.
**Desc:** Each listing includes firm name, address, chief officer, employee figure, phone, and product and market areas. Alphabetical, geographical and SIC sections.

## ABSTRACTING, BIBLIOGRAPHIES AND STATISTICS

US
**ANNUAL SURVEY OF MANUFACTURES. STATISTICS FOR STATES, STANDARD METROPOLITAN STATISTICAL AREAS, LARGE INDUSTRIAL COUNTIES, AND SELECTED CITIES.** **VFOAT** Statistics for States, Standard Metropolitan Statistical Areas, Large Industrial Counties, and Selected Cities; ASM. Government Publication. English. an. US Department of Commerce / Bureau of the Census, Data User Services Division, Customer Services, Washington DC 20233-0800. **Tel** (301)763-4100. **(Subscription address:** Superintendent of Documents, US Government Printing Office, Washington DC 20402.)

AT/0157-2156
**CENSUS OF MANUFACTURING ESTABLISHMENTS. DETAILS OF OPERATIONS AND SMALL AREA STATISTICS, TASMANIA / [AUSTRALIAN BUREAU OF STATISTICS, TASMANIA].** **Added/Corp** Australian Bureau of Statistics. Tasmanian Office. (19??)-. English. an. Australian Bureau Statistics / Tasmanian Office, Commonwealth Government Centre,

188 Collins Street, Hobart GPO Box 66A, Hobart Tasmania 7001 Australia. **Tel** (002)205889. **LC** HD9738.A83; T382a. **DD** 338.4/767/09946. ***Continues*** *Economic Censuses : Manufacturing Establishments.*
**Desc:** Details of operations by industry class and subdivision, statistical division and local government area - number of establishments, type of employment, average employment, wages and salaries paid, etc.

CN/0384-398X
**OTHER MISCELLANEOUS MANUFACTURING INDUSTRIES.**
**Main/Corp** Statistics Canada. Manufacturing and Primary Industries Division. **VFOAT** Autres Industries Manufacturieres Diverses. Began with issue for 1971. English (French). an. 30.00Can$; $31.50 US. Industry Division Statistics, Canada Publications, Ottawa Ontario K1A 0T6 Canada. **Tel** (613)951-3514. **ED** T R Wright. Index available. **Circ:** 400.
**Desc:** Statistics on miscellaneous manufacturing industries including, records, flooring, fur dressing, brooms, brushes, buttons, buckles, musical instruments, etc.

UK
**WELDASEARCH INDUSTRY NEWS.**
(19??)-. Periodical. English. mo. £390.00. Weldasearch Services, Abington Hall, Abington, Cambridge CB1 6AL England. **Tel** 011 44 223 891162, FAX 011 44 223 892588, telex 81183 WELDEX G.
**Desc:** Business news summaries from the manufacturing industries worldwide.

## MATHEMATICS

GW/0025-5858
**ABHANDLUNGEN AUS DEM MATHEMATISCHEN SEMINAR DER HAMBURGISCHEN UNIVERSITAT.** [Abh. Math. Semin. Univ. Hambg.]. **Added/Corp** Universitat Hamburg. Mathematisches Seminar. Vol. 1, No. 1 (Sept. 1921)-. Periodical. German. an. DM148.00. Vandenhoeck & Ruprecht, Robert Bosch Breite 6, D-37079 Goettingen Germany. **Tel** 011 49 551 695911, FAX 011 49 551 695917, telex 965226 VAN d. **LC** QA1; .H3. **DD** 510.62. **CODEN** AMHAAJ. **[CCC].** cum. index. **Pr Rev.** Documents available from The Genuine Article.
**Ind/Abst** Compumath Citation Index [Full Cov.]; Math. Rev.; Res. Alert [Full Cov.]; SCISEARCH; Stat. Theory Method Abstr. (1961-1963, 1966-1968); Zentralbl. Math. Ihre Grenzgeb.

GW/0341-9843
**ABHANDLUNGEN DER AKADEMIE DER WISSENSCHAFTEN IN GOTTINGEN. MATHEMATISCH-PHYSIKALISCHE KLASSE.** [Abh. Akad. Wiss. Gott. Math. -Phys. Kl.]. **Main/Corp** Akademie der Wissenschaften in Gottingen. (1946)-. Academic Scholarly Publication. Multiple languages (German, French and English). ir. Price varies per volume. Vandenhoeck & Ruprecht, Robert Bosch Breite 6, D-37079 Goettingen Germany. **Tel** 011 49 551 695911, FAX 011 49 551 695917, telex 965226 VAN d. **CODEN** AWGMAI. **Ad Acc.** Documents available from CASDDS. ***Continues*** *Abhandlungen der Gesellschaft der Wissenschaften zu Gottingen. Mathematisch-Physikalische Klasse.*
**Ind/Abst** Chem. Abstr.; GeoRef; Math. Rev.

GW/0002-2993
**ABHANDLUNGEN DER MATHEMATISCH-NATURWISSENSCHAFTLICHEN KLASSE - AKADEMIE DER WISSENSCHAFTEN UND DER LITERATUR.** **See** Science and Technology.

US/0192-5857
**ABSTRACTS OF PAPERS PRESENTED TO THE AMERICAN MATHEMATICAL SOCIETY.** [Abstr. pap. presented Am. Math. Soc.]. **Main/Corp** American Mathematical Society. Vol. 1 (Jan. 1980)-. English. Six times a year. $74.00. American Mathematical Society, PO Box 6248, Providence RI 02940-6248. **Tel** (800)321-4267, (401)455-4000, FAX (401)331-3842, telex 797192. **(Subscription address:** American Mathematical Society, PO Box 5904, Boston MA 02206-5904.**) LC** QA1; .A517. **DD** 510/.5. **[CCC].** Index available. available on microfilm and microfiche from University Microfilms International (UMI).
**Desc:** Contains abstracts in the mathematical sciences of our addresses and papers presented in special sessions and contributed and invited talks presented at AMS meetings.
**Ind/Abst** Math. Rev.; Zentralbl. Math. Ihre Grenzgeb.

US/0098-3500
**ACM TRANSACTIONS ON MATHEMATICAL SOFTWARE.** **See** Computers-Software.

US/1049-3301
**ACM TRANSACTIONS ON MODELING AND COMPUTER SIMULATION : A PUBLICATION OF THE ASSOCIATION FOR COMPUTING MACHINERY.** **See** Computers-Simulation.

FI/0001-5105
**ACTA ACADEMIAE ABOENSIS. SERIES: B, MATHEMATICA ET PHYSICA.** (ACTA ACADEMIAE ABOENSIS. SER. B, MATHEMATICA ET PHYSICA.). [Acta Acad. Abo., B]. **Added/Corp** Abo Akademi (1918- ). Vol. 24, No. 1 (1964)-. Monographic series. English (German and Swedish). ir. Price varies per volume. **(Subscription address:** Tidningsbokhandeln, PO Box 33, SF 21601 Pargas Finland.**) ED** Goran Hognas. **CODEN** AAAMA4. Index available. **Pr Rev. Circ:** 600. Documents available from BIOSIS Document Express. ***Continues*** *Acta Academiae Aboensis. Mathematica et Physica.*
**Desc:** Original work such as theses in science and engineering.
**Ind/Abst** Abstr. Bull. Inst. Pap. Sci. Tech.; Biol. Abstr.; GeoRef; Math. Rev.; Zentralbl. Math. Ihre Grenzgeb.

NE/0167-8019
**ACTA APPLICANDAE MATHEMATICAE.** [Acta appl. math.]. Vol. 1, No. 1 (1983)-. Periodical. English. mo. $1,516.00. Kluwer Academic Publishers, Postbus 322, 3300 AH Dordrecht, The Netherlands. **Tel** 011 (31) 78 524400, FAX 011 31 78 183273, telex 20083. **ED** Michiel Hazewinkel. **LC** QA1; .A158. **DD** 510/.5. **CODEN** AAMADV. **[CCC].** Index available. **Bk Rev. Ad Acc. Pr Rev. Acid Free. Circ:** 500. available on microfilm and microfiche from University Microfilms International (UMI). Documents available from The Genuine Article.
**Desc:** Devoted to the art and techniques of applying mathematics and the development of new applicable mathematical theories.
**Ind/Abst** Appl. Mech. Rev.; Compumath Citation Index [Full Cov.]; Math. Rev.; Res. Alert [Full Cov.]; SCISEARCH; Zentralbl. Math. Ihre Grenzgeb.

PL/0065-1036
**ACTA ARITHMETICA.** [Acta arith.]. **Added/Corp** Uniwersytet Warszawski. Seminarium Matematyczne. Instytut Matematyczny (Polska Akademia Nauk). Vol. 1 (1935/1936)-. Periodical. Polish (English, French and German). ir. $112.00. **(Subscription address:** ARS Polona, PO Box 1001, 00068 Warsaw Poland.**) LC** QA3; .A23. **CODEN** AARIA9. cum. index. **Pr Rev.** Documents available from The Genuine Article.
**Ind/Abst** Compumath Citation Index [Full Cov.]; Curr. Contents Phys. Chem. Earth Sci.; GeoRef; Math. Rev.; Res. Alert [Full Cov.]; Sci. Cit. Index; SCISEARCH; Zentralbl. Math. Ihre Grenzgeb.

II/0970-0455
**ACTA CIENCIA INDICA. MATHEMATICS.** [Acta Cienc. Indica, Math.]. **Added/Corp** Society for the Progress of Science (India). **VFOAT** Mathematics. Vol. 5, No. 1 (1979)-. Periodical. English. qt. $50.00. Pragati Prakashan, PO Box 62, Begum Bridge, 250001 Meerut India. **Tel** 73022. **(Subscription address:** Prints India, 11 Darya Ganj, New Delhi 110002 India.**) ED** V.P. Kudasiya, K.K. Mittal. **LC** QD1; .A3294. **DD** 500.2/05. **UDC** 51. Index available. cum. index. **Bk Rev. Ad Acc. Circ:** 1,000. Documents available from Ask*IEEE. ***Continues in part*** *Acta Ciencia Indica, 0379-5411.*
**Ind/Abst** Energy Res. Abstr. (Aug. 1980-); INSPEC (1979-); Math. Rev.; Zentralbl. Math. Ihre Grenzgeb.

SW/0001-5962
**ACTA MATHEMATICA.** [Acta math.]. Vol. 1 (1882)-. Periodical. English (French and German). Four times a year. $200.00. Institut Mittag-Leffler, Auravagen 17, S-182 62 Djursholm Sweden. **Tel** (08)7551809. **ED** G Ellingsrud, Christer Kiselman, I Madsen and O Martio. **LC** QA1. **DD** 510/.5. **CODEN** ACMAA8. **Pr Rev.** Documents available from The Genuine Article.
**Ind/Abst** Compumath Citation Index [Full Cov.]; Curr. Contents Phys. Chem. Earth Sci.; Energy Res. Abstr. (Jan. 1971-); Math. Rev.; Res. Alert [Full Cov.]; Sci. Cit. Index; SCISEARCH; Stat. Theory Method Abstr. (1959-1963, 1967); Zentralbl. Math. Ihre Grenzgeb.

HU/0236-5294
**ACTA MATHEMATICA HUNGARICA.** [Acta math. Hung.]. **Added/Corp** Magyar Tudomanyos Akademia. **VFOAT** Acta Mathematica. Vol. 41, No. 1-2 (1983)-. Academic Scholarly Publication. English (French, German and Russian). Sixteen times a year. $864.00. Akademiai Kiado, Publishing House of the Hungarian Academy of Sciences, Prielle Kornelia u. 19-35, H-1117 Budapest Hungary. **Tel** 011 36 1 1811991, FAX 011 36 1 1811991, telex 22-6228 AKNYO H. **(Subscription address:** Kluwer Academic Publishers / Netherlands, PO Box 322, 3300 AH Dordrecht Netherlands.**) ED** Karoly Tandori (editor's address: Acta Mathematica Hungarica, PO Box 127, H-1364 Budapest Hungary). **LC** QA1; .A16. **DD** 510/.5. **[CCC].** Index available. **Bk Rev. Ad Acc. Pr Rev. Acid Free. Circ:** 1,000 (ctrl). ***Continues*** *Acta Mathematica Academiae Scientiarum Hungaricae.*
**Desc:** Covers a wide scope in the field of mathematics. It comprises theory of sets, mathematical logic, classical and modern analysis, algebra, number theory, geometry, topology, combinatorics, mathematical statistics, probability theory, as well as information theory. Co-published with Kluwer Academic Publishing Group.
**Ind/Abst** Compumath Citation Index [Full Cov.]; Int. Aerosp. Abstr.; Math. Rev.; SCISEARCH; Zentralbl. Math. Ihre Grenzgeb.

CC/1000-9574
**ACTA MATHEMATICA SINICA. NEW SERIES.** (ACTA MATHEMATICA SINICA.). [Acta math. Sinica, New ser.]. **VFOAT** Chinese Journal of Mathematics. Vol. 1, No. 1 (Feb. 1985)-. Academic Scholarly Publication. English. qt. $250.00. Science Press, 16 Donghuangchenggen North Street, Beijing 100707, People's Republic of China. **Tel** 011 86 1 4019821, 011 86 1 4010642, FAX 011 86 1 4012180, 011 86 1 4019810, telex 210147. **(Subscription address:** VSP International Science Publishers, PO Box 346, 3700 AH Zeist Netherlands.**) ED** Chen Jingrun. **Ad Acc. Circ:** 6,000. Documents available from BLDSC.
**Desc:** Publishes papers from both pure and applied mathematics. The aim is to encourage free discussion between the various schools of thought in mathematics.
**Ind/Abst** Math. Rev. (1985-); Zentralbl. Math. Ihre Grenzgeb.

VM/0251-4184
**ACTA MATHEMATICA VIETNAMICA.** [Acta math. vietnam.]. **Added/Corp** Vien Khoa hoc Viet Nam. Vol. 1, No. 1 (1976)-. Periodical. English (French). ir. $63.00 US & Canada; $53.00 others. Institute of Mathematics Vien Toan Hoc, Box 631 Bo Ho, 10000 Hanoi Vietnam. **Tel** 43303. ***Continues in part*** *Acta Scientiarum Vietnamicarum. Sectio Scientiarum Mathematicarum et Physicarum.*
**Ind/Abst** Math. Rev.; Zentralbl. Math. Ihre Grenzgeb.

CH/0168-9673
**ACTA MATHEMATICAE APPLICATAE SINICA.** **Added/Corp** Chung-Kuo Shu Hsueh Hui. **VFOAT** Ying Yung Shu Hsueh Hsueh Pao. Vol. 1, No. 1 (June 1984)-. Academic Scholarly Publication. English. Four times a year. $395.00. Science Press, 16 Donghuangchenggen North Street, Beijing 100707, People's Republic of China. **Tel** 011 86 1 4019821, 011 86 1 4010642, FAX 011 86 1 4012180, 011 86 1 4019810, telex 210147. **(Subscription address:** Allerton Press Inc., 150 Fifth Avenue, New York NY 10011.**) LC** QA1; .Y5152. **DD** 510/.5. **CODEN** AASIEI. **[CCC].** Index available. **Bk Rev. Ad Acc. Circ:** 6,000.
**Desc:** Published by the Chinese Mathematical Society. Contains information on applied mathematics research in China.
**Ind/Abst** Math. Rev.

●UK/0962-4929
**ACTA NUMERICA.** (1992)-. Academic Scholarly Publication. English. an. $51.00 US, Canada & Mexico; £30.00 other. Cambridge University Press, The Edinburgh Building, Shaftesbury Road, Cambridge CB2 2RU United Kingdom. **Tel** 011 44 223 312393, FAX 011 44 223 325959. **ED** A. Iserles. **LC** QA297; .A327. **DD** 519.4.
**Desc:** Presents survey papers by leading researchers in numerical analysis.

FI/0355-2713
**ACTA POLYTECHNICA SCANDINAVICA. MATHEMATICS AND COMPUTER SCIENCE SERIES. MA.** ***Title Change.*** (ACTA POLYTECHNICA SCANDINAVICA. MATHEMATICS AND COMPUTER SCIENCE SERIES.). [Acta polytech. scand., Math. comput. sci. ser. Ma]. **Added/Corp** Teknillisten Tieteiden Akatemia. **VFOAT** Mathematics and Computer Science Series. No. 26 (1975)-No. 63 (1993). Monographic series. English. ir. The Finnish Academy of Technology, Tekniikantie 12, Fin 02150 Espoo Finland. **Tel** 011 358 0 4554565, FAX 011 358 0 6945041. **LC** QA75; .A18. **CODEN** ASMSD7. Documents available from Ask*IEEE. ***Continues*** *Acta Polytechnica Scandinavica. Mathematics and Computing Machinery Series, 0001-6861.* ***Continued by*** *Acta Polytechnica Scandinavica. Mathematics and Computing in Engineering Series.*
**Ind/Abst** INSPEC (1981-); Int. Aerosp. Abstr.; Math. Rev.

HU/0001-6969
**ACTA SCIENTIARUM MATHEMATICARUM.** **Main/Corp** Szeged, Hungary. Tudomanyegyetem (Founded 1940). **Added/Corp** Magyar Kiralyi Ferenc Jozsef Tudomanyegyetem Baratainak Egyesulete. **VFOAT** A M. Kir. Ferencz Jozsef-Tudomanyegyetem Tudomanyos Kozlemenyei. Mathematikai Tudomanyok. Vol. 1 (1922/1923)-. Academic Scholarly Publication. Multiple languages (English, French and German). qt. $80.00. Akademiai Kiado, Publishing House of the Hungarian Academy of Sciences, Prielle Kornelia u. 19-35, H-1117 Budapest Hungary. **Tel** 011 36 1 1811991, FAX 011 36 1 1811991, telex 22-6228 AKNYO H. **(Subscription address:** Kultura, PO Box 149, H 1389 Budapest 62 Hungary.**) ED** Andras Hajnal and Jozsef Merza (editor's address: J Merza, Managing Editor, H-1053 Budapest, Realtanoda u 13-15 Hungary). **LC** AS142; .S826. **DD** 510.82. **Ad Acc. Circ:** 1,200. available on microfilm and microfiche from University Microfilms International (UMI).
**Desc:** Publishes original research papers on mathematics and its diverse fields of application in

science, technology, economics, etc. Articles on theory of probability, on mathematical statistics, numerical and graphic methods as well as differential equation are also presented.
**Ind/Abst** Math. Rev.; Stat. Theory Method Abstr. (1971-1973, 1977, 1980-1984, 1986); Zentralbl. Math. Ihre Grenzgeb.

XV/0351-580X
**ACTA STEREOLOGICA.** [Acta stereol.]. **Added/Corp** International Society for Stereology. Vol. 1, No. 1 (Jan. 1982)-. Academic Scholarly Publication. English. Twice a year. $30.00. Institute of Histology and Embryology Medical Faculty, University E Kardeljo Ljubljana, Korytkova 2, POB 10, 61105 Ljubljana Slovenia. **Tel** (061)443-642. **ED** Miroslav Kalisnik. **NLM** W1 AC949KH. **CODEN** ASTLDL. Index available. **Bk Rev. Ad Acc. Circ:** 500 (ctrl). Documents available from BIOSIS Document Express, CASDDS. ***Formed by the union of*** *Newsletter in Stereology* ***and*** *Stereologica Iugoslavica, 0350-3062.*
**Desc:** Covers stereology, quantitative, image analysis, morphometry, mathematics, instrumentation materials, and life sciences pattern recognition.
**Ind/Abst** Alum. Ind. Abstr.; Biol. Abstr.; Chem. Abstr.; Coal Abstr.; EMBASE; Eng. Mater. Abstr.; Met. Abstr.; Ref. Z.; Zentralbl. Math. Ihre Grenzgeb.

XR/0001-7140
**ACTA UNIVERSITATIS CAROLINAE. MATHEMATICA ET PHYSICA.** [Acta univ. Carol., Math. phys.]. (1962)-. Periodical. English (German, Russian and French; summaries and/or abstracts in Czech, English and Russian). ir. $24.50. Carolinum Press, Ovochny TRH 5, 11636 Prague 1 Czech Republic. **Tel** 011 42 2 228441. **CODEN** AUMMBZ. ***Continues*** *Acta Universitatis Carolinae. Mathematica.*
**Ind/Abst** Astron. Astrophys. Abstr.; Math. Rev.; Ref. Z.; Zentralbl. Math. Ihre Grenzgeb.

PL/0084-2966
**ACTA UNIVERSITATIS WRATISLAVIENSIS. MATEMATYKA, FIZYKA, ASTRONOMIA.** [Acta Univ. Wratisl., Mat. fiz. astron.]. **Added/Corp** Uniwersytet Wrocawski im. Bolesawa Bieruta. Uniwersytet Wrocawski. **VFOAT** Matematyka, Fizyka, Astronomia. (1962)-. Monographic series. Polish (English, French and German). **(Subscription address:** ARS Polona, PO Box 1001, 00068 Warsaw Poland.**) LC** Q60; .U53a. Documents available from Ask*IEEE, CASDDS. ***Continues*** *Matematyka, Fizyka, Astronomia.*
**Ind/Abst** Chem. Abstr.; INSPEC (1980-).

SP
**ACTAS DE LA 1.- REUNION ANUAL DE MATEMATICOS ESPANOLES. Main/Corp** Universidad Complutense de Madrid. Seccion de Matematica. (1961)-. Spanish. an. Editorial Complutense, Donoso Cortes 65 1RA Planta, 28003 Madrid Spain. **Tel** 011 34 1 3946372.

US
**ACTUARIAL DIGEST, THE. See** Insurance.

SI
**ADVANCED SERIES IN MATHEMATICAL PHYSICS. See** Physics.

US/0884-0016
**ADVANCED STUDIES IN CONTEMPORARY MATHEMATICS.** [Adv. stud. contemp. math.]. Vol. 1 (1986)-. Monographic series. English (translations available in Russian). Gordon & Breach Science Publishers, Inc., PO Box 786, Cooper Station, New York NY 10276. **Tel** (212)206-8900, FAX (212)645-2459. **(Subscription address:** International Publishers Distributor at one of the following addresses: 820 Town Center Drive, Langhorne, PA 19047; or PO Box 90, Reading Berkshire RG1 8JL UK; or Kent Ridge PO Box 1180, Singapore 9111, Republic of Singapore**) DD** 510.
**Ind/Abst** Math. Rev.; Zentralbl. Math. Ihre Grenzgeb.

JA
**ADVANCED STUDIES IN PURE MATHEMATICS (TOKYO, JAPAN).** (1983)-. Monographic series. English. Nagoya Daigaku Kiso Suri Kenkyu Senta, (Research Center for Advanced Mathematics, Nagoya University), Nagoya Daigaku Rigakubu Sugaku Kyoshitsu, Furocho, Chikusaku, Nagoyashi, Aichiken 464 Japan. **LC** UNC.
**Ind/Abst** Math. Rev. (1988-); Zentralbl. Math. Ihre Grenzgeb.

US/0196-8858
**ADVANCES IN APPLIED MATHEMATICS.** [Adv. appl. math.]. Vol. 1 (Mar. 1980)-. Academic Scholarly Publication. English. Four times a year (Mar., June, Sept., Dec.). $198.00 US and Canada; $244.00 other. Academic Press, Inc., 6277 Sea Harbor Drive, Orlando FL 32887. **Tel** (800)543-9534, (407)345-4100, FAX (407)363-9661. **ED** Gian-Carlo Rota. **LC** QA1; .A188. **DD** 510/.5. **[CCC]. Pr Rev.** Documents available from The Genuine Article.
**Desc:** A journal dedicated to the publication of original and expository articles on all aspects of applied mathematics. Features articles on continuum mechanics, mathematical physics, statistics, mathematical biology, mathematical economics, communication theory and computer science.
**Ind/Abst** ACM Guide Comput. Lit.; Compumath Citation Index [Full Cov.]; Comput. Rev.; Curr. Contents Phys. Chem. Earth Sci.; Int. Aerosp. Abstr. (1984-); Math. Rev.; Res. Alert [Full Cov.]; Sci. Cit. Index; SCISEARCH; Soc. Sci. Cit. Index [Select. Cov.]; Zentralbl. Math. Ihre Grenzgeb.

UK/0001-8678
**ADVANCES IN APPLIED PROBABILITY.** [Adv. appl. probab.]. **Added/Corp** Applied Probability Trust. Vol. 1 Spring (1969)-. Periodical. English (French). qt. £99.24. Applied Probability, School of Mathematics and Statistics, Sheffield S3 7RH England. **Tel** 011 44 742 824269, FAX 011 44 742 729782. **ED** C. C. Heyde. **LC** QA273; .A34. **DD** 519/.1/05. **CODEN** AAPBBD. **[CCC].** Index available. cum. index. **Ad Acc. Pr Rev. Circ:** 1,100. Documents available from Article Express International, The Genuine Article, BIOSIS Document Express, UMI Article Clearinghouse, Ask*IEEE.
**Desc:** Review and expository papers in applied probability, also mathematical and scientific papers of interest to probabilists, and letters to the editor.
**Ind/Abst** ABI/INFORM Glob. Ed.; Anim. Breed. Abstr.; Biol. Abstr.; Biostatistica; Compumath Citation Index [Full Cov.]; Comput. Rev.; Curr. Contents Phys. Chem. Earth Sci.; Curr. Index Stat.; Ei Page One; Eng. Index Annu.; GeoRef; INSPEC (Spring 1969-); Int. Abstr. Oper. Res. [Select. Cov.]; Math. Rev.; Oper. Res./Manag. Sci.; Plant Breed. Abstr.; Pollut. Abstr. Indexes; Qual. Control Appl. Stat.; Res. Alert [Full Cov.]; Risk Abstr. (19??-19??); Sci. Cit. Index; SCISEARCH; Soc. Sci. Cit. Index [Select. Cov.]; Stat. Theory Method Abstr. (1971-1984, 1986-1987); Zentralbl. Math. Ihre Grenzgeb.

●NE/1019-7168
**ADVANCES IN COMPUTATIONAL MATHEMATICS.** Vol. 1, No. 1 (May 1993)-. Periodical. English. qt. 292.50F (includes distribution costs). Baltzer Science Publishers BV, Asterweg 1A, 1031 HL Amsterdam Netherlands. **Tel** 011 31 20 6370061, FAX 011 31 20 6323651.

●JA
**ADVANCES IN MATHEMATICAL SCIENCES AND APPLICATIONS.** Vol. 1, No. 1 (1992)-. Periodical. English. sa. $240.00. **(Subscription address:** Maruzen Company Ltd., PO Box 5050, Import & Export Department, Tokyo 100 31 Japan.**)**

US/0001-8708
**ADVANCES IN MATHEMATICS (NEW YORK. 1965).** (ADVANCES IN MATHEMATICS.). [Adv. math.]. Vol. 1 (1965)-. Academic Scholarly Publication. English. Fourteen times a year. $1153.00 US and Canada; $1358.00 other. Academic Press, Inc., 6277 Sea Harbor Drive, Orlando FL 32887. **Tel** (800)543-9534, (407)345-4100, FAX (407)363-9661. **ED** Gian-Carlo Rota. **LC** QA1; .A19. **CODEN** ADMTA4. **[CCC]. Pr Rev.** Documents available from The Genuine Article.
**Desc:** A journal emphasizing contributions that represent significant advances in all areas of pure mathematics, and providing research mathematicians with an effective medium for communicating important recent developments in their areas of specialization to colleagues and to scientists in related disciplines.
**Ind/Abst** Compumath Citation Index [Full Cov.]; Curr. Contents Phys. Chem. Earth Sci.; Math. Rev.; Res. Alert [Full Cov.]; Sci. Cit. Index; SCISEARCH; Zentralbl. Math. Ihre Grenzgeb.

US
**ADVANCES IN MATHEMATICS : SUPPLEMENTARY STUDIES.** ***Ceased.*** Vol. 1 (1978)-Series completed with Vol. 10 (19??). Monographic series. English. be. Academic Press, Inc., 6277 Sea Harbor Drive, Orlando FL 32887. **Tel** (800)543-9534, (407)345-4100, FAX (407)363-9661. **ED** Victor Guillemin.
**Ind/Abst** Math. Rev.; Zentralbl. Math. Ihre Grenzgeb.

IE/0332-3196
**ADVANCES IN NUMERICAL COMPUTATION SERIES.** Began with Vol. 1, (1980)-. Monographic series. English. Boole Press Ltd, 26 Temple Lane, Temple Bar Dublin 2 Ireland. **Tel** 011 353 1 6797655, telex 30547 SHCN E1.
**Ind/Abst** Zentralbl. Math. Ihre Grenzgeb.

JA
**ADVANCES IN NUMERICAL METHODS FOR LARGE SPARSE SETS OF LINEAR EQUATIONS. Added/Corp** Keio Gijuku Daigaku. No. 1 (1986)-. Monographic series. English.
**Ind/Abst** Zentralbl. Math. Ihre Grenzgeb.

US/0065-3217
**ADVANCES IN PROBABILITY AND RELATED TOPICS.** ***Ceased.*** [Adv. probab. relat. top.]. Vol. 1 (1971)-(19??). Monographic series. English. Marcel Dekker Inc., 270 Madison Avenue, New York NY 10016. **Tel** (212)696-9000, (800)228-1160, FAX (212)685-4540, telex 421419. **(Subscription address:** Marcel Dekker Inc, PO Box 5017, Monticello NY 12701.**) ED** P. Ney. **LC** QA273.A1; A4. **DD** 519.2. **[CCC].**
**Desc:** This is an ongoing series. Each title has a different subject.
**Ind/Abst** Math. Rev.; Zentralbl. Math. Ihre Grenzgeb.

US/1051-8037
**ADVANCES IN SOVIET MATHEMATICS.** [Adv. Sov. math.]. **Added/Corp** American Mathematical Society. **VFOAT** Soviet Mathematics. Vol. 1 (1990)-. Periodical. English. qt. American Mathematical Society, PO Box 6248, Providence RI 02940-6248. **Tel** (800)321-4267, (401)455-4000, FAX (401)331-3842, telex 797192. **(Subscription address:** American Mathematical Society, PO Box 5904, Boston MA 02206-5904.**) LC** QA1; .A197. **DD** 510. **[CCC]. Pr Rev.**
**Ind/Abst** Math. Rev.; Zentralbl. Math. Ihre Grenzgeb.

SZ/0001-9054
**AEQUATIONES MATHEMATICAE.** [Aequ. math.]. **Added/Corp** University of Waterloo. Faculty of Mathematics. Vol. 1 (1968)-. Periodical. English (French, German, Italian and Russian). bm. 562.00F Switzerland; 580.40F other. Birkhaeuser Verlag Ag, Klosterberg 23, PO Box 133, CH-4010 Basel Switzerland. **Tel** 011 41 61 2717400, FAX 011 41 0 61 2717666, telex 963475 birk ch. **(Subscription address:** Birkhauser Verlag AG, PO Box 151, CH 4106 Therwil Switzerland; Phone: 011 41 61 7217740**) ED** J. Aczel. **LC** QA1; .A2. **DD** 510/.5. **CODEN** AEMABN. **[CCC].** available on microfilm from University Microfilms International (UMI).
**Desc:** An international journal of pure and applied mathematics, which emphasizes functional equations and combinatorial and numerical analysis. Publishes research papers, reports of meetings, bibliographies, problems and solutions. Also publishes recent developments and research in the field.
**Ind/Abst** Energy Res. Abstr. (Feb. 1982-); Int. Aerosp. Abstr.; Math. Rev.; Ref. Z.; Stat. Theory Method Abstr. (1987); Zentralbl. Math. Ihre Grenzgeb.

CM/1012-9405
**AFRIKA MATHEMATICA.** (AFRIKA MATEMATIKA.). [Afr. math.]. **Added/Corp** African Mathematical Union. Unesco. Association des Universites Partiellement ou Entierement de Langue Francaise. Vol. 1 (1978)-. Periodical. English (French). **LC** QA1; .A215. **DD** 510/.5.
**Ind/Abst** Math. Rev.; Zentralbl. Math. Ihre Grenzgeb.

MX/0188-3054
**AGROCIENCIA. SERIE MATEMATICAS APLICADAS, ESTADISTICA Y COMPUTACION.** [Agrocienc., Ser. mat. apl. estad. comput.]. (1990)-. Periodical. Spanish. Three times a year. $25.00. Colegio de Postgraduados, Gen Lazardo Cardenas 24 La Paz, 56170 Texcoco Mexico. **Tel** 011 52 595 47011. **DD** 630. **Pr Rev.** ***Continues*** *Agrociencia (Montecillo, Edo. Mex.), 0185-0288.*

US/0002-5232
**ALGEBRA AND LOGIC.** [Algebra logic]. Vol. 7 (Jan./Feb. 1968)-. Periodical. English. bm. $915.00 US; $1070.00 other. Consultants Bureau, A Division of Plenum Publishing Corporation, 233 Spring Street, New York NY 10013. **Tel** (212)620-8000, (212)620-8466, FAX (212)463-0742, telex 23/421139. **ED** Yu L. Ershov. **LC** QH150. **CODEN** ALL0A6. **[CCC].** Index available. available on microfilm and microfiche from University Microfilms International (UMI).
**Desc:** This journal reports results of the latest research in the areas of modern general algebra and logic considered primarily from an algebraic viewpoint.
**Ind/Abst** Comput. Rev.; Math. Rev.; Philos. Index; Pollut. Abstr. Indexes; Zentralbl. Math. Ihre Grenzgeb.

GW
**ALGEBRA-BERICHTE. Main/Corp** Munich. Universitat. Mathematisches Institut. (1973)-. German.
**Ind/Abst** Zentralbl. Math. Ihre Grenzgeb.

RU/0234-0852
**ALGEBRA I ANALIZ. Added/Corp** Akademiia Nauk SSSR. Otdelenie Matematiki. **VFOAT** A & A; Algebra i Analiz, A & A. (1989)-. Academic Scholarly Publication. Russian (table of contents in English). bm. $229.95. Izdatelstvo Nauka / Akademiia Nauk, Publishing House of the Russian Academy of Sciences, Leninskii Porspekt 14, 117901 Moscow Russia. **Tel** 011 95 954-21-53, FAX 011 95 938-21-44, telex 411964. **(Subscription address:** East View Publications Inc., 3020 Harbor Lane North, Suite 110, Minneapolis MN 55447.**) [CCC].**
**Desc:** Information on algebra.
**Ind/Abst** Math. Rev.; Zentralbl. Math. Ihre Grenzgeb.

US/1041-5394
**ALGEBRA, LOGIC AND APPLICATIONS.** [Algebra logic appl.]. **VFOAT** Algebra, Logic and Applications Series. Vol. 1 (1989)-. Monographic series. English. Gordon & Breach Science Publishers, Inc., PO Box 786, Cooper Station, New York NY 10276. **Tel** (212)206-8900, FAX (212)645-2459. **(Subscription address:** International Publishers Distributor at one of the following addresses: 820 Town Center Drive, Langhorne, PA 19047; or PO Box 90, Reading Berkshire RG1 8JL UK; or Kent Ridge PO Box 1180, Singapore 9111, Republic of Singapore**) DD** 512.
**Ind/Abst** Zentralbl. Math. Ihre Grenzgeb.

CN/0002-5240
**ALGEBRA UNIVERSALIS.** [Algebra univers.]. **Added/Corp** University of Manitoba. University of Manitoba. Dept. of Mathematics. Vol. 1 (1971)-. Periodical. English. Eight times a year. 963.00F Switzerland; 987.00F other. Birkhaeuser Verlag Ag, Klosterberg 23, PO Box 133, CH-4010 Basel Switzerland. **Tel** 011 41 61 2717400, FAX 011 41 0 61 2717666, telex 963475 birk ch. **(Subscription address:** Birkhauser Verlag AG, PO Box 151, CH 4106 Therwil Switzerland; Phone: 011 41 61 7217740**) ED** G. Birkhoff, G. Gratzer, C. Platt and R. W. Quackenbush. **LC** QA251; .A34. **DD** 512/.005. **CODEN** AGUVA9. **[CCC]. Pr Rev.** available on microfilm and microfiche from University Microfilms International (UMI). Documents available from The Genuine Article.
**Desc:** Welcomes papers from the areas of universal algebra and lattice theory, as well as papers inspired by or having applications to these areas. Also publishes short communications of interest to specialists.
**Ind/Abst** Compumath Citation Index [Full Cov.]; Math. Rev.; Res. Alert [Full Cov.]; SCISEARCH; Zentralbl. Math. Ihre Grenzgeb.

US/0741-9937
**ALGEBRAS, GROUPS, AND GEOMETRIES.** [Algebras groups geom.]. Vol. 1, No. 1 (March 1984)-. Periodical. English. Four times a year. $160.00. Hadronic Press Inc, PO Box 1577, Palm Harbor FL 34682. **Tel** (813)934-9593. **LC** QA150; .A46. **DD** 512/.05.
**Desc:** Devoted to fundamental aspects of pure and applied mathematics in the areas of linear and multinear algebras and matrix theory, nonassociative rings and algebras, linear algebraic and lie groups, differential geometry, and topics related to the above fields. Survey or expository papers on current research in these areas are solicited.
**Ind/Abst** Math. Rev.; Zentralbl. Math. Ihre Grenzgeb.

RU/0373-9252
**ALGERBRA I LOGIKA.** [Algebra log.]. **Added/Corp** Institut Matematiki (Akademiia Nauk SSSR. Sibirskoe Otdelenie). Vol. 6, No. 4 (1967)-. Periodical. Russian. bm. 1.00rub. Institute of Mathematics / Russia, Novosibirsk 90 630090 Russia. **Tel** 383-2-354073. **LC** QA1; .A42. cum. index. ***Continues** Algebra i Logika, Seminar.*
**Ind/Abst** Math. Rev.

GW
**ALGORISMUS. Added/Corp** Institut fur Geschichte der Naturwissenschaften (Munich, Germany). (1988)-. Periodical. German.
**Ind/Abst** Zentralbl. Math. Ihre Grenzgeb.

GW
**ALGORITHMS AND COMBINATORICS.** (1987)-. Monographic series. English. ir. Price varies per volume. Springer-Verlag GmbH & Company KG, Heidelberger Platz 3, D 14197 Berlin Germany. **Tel** 011 49 30 8207223, FAX 011 49 30 8214091, telex 183 319 SPBLN D. **(Subscription address:** Springer Verlag New York Inc. / for North America, 44 Hartz Way, Secaucus NJ 07096.**) ED** R.L. Graham, B. Korte, L. Lovasz.
**Ind/Abst** Math. Rev. (1987-); Zentralbl. Math. Ihre Grenzgeb.

II
**ALIGARH BULLETIN OF MATHEMATICS, THE. Added/Corp** Aligarh Muslim University. Dept. of Mathematics and Statistics. Vol. 1 (1971)-. Bulletin. English. Aligarh Muslim University Department of Mathematics and Statistics, Aligarh, India. **CODEN** ABMAD4.
**Ind/Abst** Math. Rev.; Zentralbl. Math. Ihre Grenzgeb.

HU/0133-3399
**ALKALMAZOTT MATEMATIKAI LAPEK.** [Alkalm. mat. l.]. **Added/Corp** Magyar Tudomanyos Akademia. Matematikai es Fizikai Tudomanyok Osztalya. Vol. 1 (1975)-. Academic Scholarly Publication. Hungarian (summaries and/or abstracts in English and Russian). Four times a year. $12.00. Akademiai Kiado, Publishing House of the Hungarian Academy of Sciences, Prielle Kornelia u. 19-35, H-1117 Budapest Hungary. **Tel** 011 36 1 1811991, FAX 011 36 1 1811991, telex 22-6228 AKNYO H. **(Subscription address:** Kultura, PO Box 149, H 1389 Budapest 62 Hungary.**) ED** A. Prekopa. **LC** QA1; .A475. **CODEN** AMLAD8. **Bk Rev. Ad Acc. Circ:** 500. Documents available from Ask*IEEE. ***Continues** Magyar Tudomanyos Akademia Matematikai es Fizikai Tudomanyok Osztalyanak Kozlemenyai, 0025-035X.*
**Ind/Abst** INSPEC (1975-); Math. Rev.; Zentralbl. Math. Ihre Grenzgeb.

II
**ALLAHABAD MATHEMATICAL SOCIETY LECTURE NOTE SERIES. Added/Corp** Allahabad Mathematical Society. **VFOAT** Lecture Note Series. (1990)-. English. an. $25.00. Allahabad Mathematical Society, 10 C S P Singh Marg, Allahabad 211 001 India. **Tel** 011 91 11 52208. **(Subscription address:** Prints India, 11 Darya Ganj, New Delhi 110002 India.**)**

SP/0211-5239
**ALXEBRA.** [Alxebra]. (1967)-. Monographic series. Spanish. tw. **UDC** 512.
**Ind/Abst** Zentralbl. Math. Ihre Grenzgeb.

US/0740-8404
**AMATYC REVIEW, THE.** [AMATYC rev.]. **Added/Corp** American Mathematical Association of Two-Year Colleges. **VFOAT** American Mathematical Association of Two-Year Colleges Review; A.M.A.T.Y.C. Review; Review. **VAT** American Mathematical Association of Two-Year Colleges Review. (19??)-. Periodical. English. Twice a year (February and September). $25.00 (individual); $170.00 (institution). State Technical Institute, 5983 Macon Cove, c/o Margie Hobbs, Memphis TN 38134. **Tel** (901)377-4110. **LC** QA11.A1; A427. **DD** 510.

US/0196-6324
**AMERICAN JOURNAL OF MATHEMATICAL AND MANAGEMENT SCIENCES.** [Am. j. math. manage. sci.]. Vol. 1, No. 1 (1981)-. Periodical. English. qt. $261.25 (one year), $519.88 (two year), $775.90 (three year). American Sciences Press Inc, 20 Cross Road, Syracuse NY 13224. **Tel** (315)446-1843. **ED** Edward J. Dudewizc, editor's address: Department of Mathematics, Syracuse University, Syracuse, NY 13244. **LC** T55.4; .A52. **DD** 658.4/034. **CODEN** AMMSDX. **[CCC]. Bk Rev**, (Qty: 2). **Ad Acc. Pr Rev.** Documents available from Ask*IEEE.
**Desc:** Brings together new work in the various areas of the mathematical and management sciences. Computer programs are included in articles, which are readable and usable.
**Ind/Abst** Biostatistica; Curr. Index Stat.; Ei Page One; INSPEC (1986-); Int. Abstr. Oper. Res. [Select. Cov.]; Math. Rev.; Oper. Res./Manag. Sci.; Qual. Control Appl. Stat.; Ref. Z.; Stat. Theory Method Abstr. (1982-1984, 1986); Zentralbl. Math. Ihre Grenzgeb.

US/0002-9327
**AMERICAN JOURNAL OF MATHEMATICS.** [Am. j. math.]. **Added/Corp** Johns Hopkins University. American Mathematical Society. Vol. 1 (1878)-. Periodical. English. Six times a year. $175.00 US; $182.50 Canada and Mexico; $197.30 other. Johns Hopkins University Press, 2715 North Charles Street, Baltimore MD 21218-4319. **Tel** (410)516-6987, FAX (410)516-6968. **(Subscription address:** John Hopkins University Press, Journals Publishing Division, PO Box 19966, Baltimore MD 21211.**) ED** Jun-Ichi Igusa and J.H. Sampson. **LC** QA1; .A51. **DD** 510.5. **CODEN** AJMAAN. **[CCC].** cum. index. **Ad Acc. Pr Rev. Circ:** 1,521. available on microfilm and microfiche from University Microfilms International (UMI). Documents available from The Genuine Article, UMI Article Clearinghouse.
**Desc:** Work in applied and pure mathematics; resource for students and scholars.
**Ind/Abst** Compumath Citation Index [Full Cov.]; Curr. Contents Phys. Chem. Earth Sci.; Expand. Acad. Index (1992-); Index Sci. Rev.; Math. Rev.; Newsp. Period. Abstr. (1992-); Pollut. Abstr. Indexes; Res. Alert [Full Cov.]; Sci. Cit. Index; SCISEARCH; Stat. Theory Method Abstr. (1961-1963); Zentralbl. Math. Ihre Grenzgeb.

US/0002-9890
**AMERICAN MATHEMATICAL MONTHLY, THE.** (THE AMERICAN MATHEMATICAL MONTHLY : THE OFFICIAL JOURNAL OF THE MATHEMATICAL ASSOCIATION OF AMERICA.). [Am. math. mon.]. **Added/Corp** Mathematical Association of America. (Jan. 1894)-. Periodical. English. Ten times a year. $165.00. Mathematical Association of America, 1529 18th Street Northwest, Washington DC 20036. **Tel** (202)387-5200, (800)331-1622, FAX (202)265-2384. **ED** Herbert Wilf. **LC** QA1; .A515. **DD** 510/.5. **CODEN** AMMYAE. **[CCC].** Index available (bound in last issue.). **Ad Acc. Pr Rev. Circ:** 20,000. available on microfilm and microfiche from University Microfilms International (UMI). Documents available from The Genuine Article, UMI Article Clearinghouse.
**Desc:** Contains expository articles, covering all parts of mathematics, pure and applied, old and new. Includes mathematical and classroom notes, a section on the teaching of mathematics, elementary and advanced problems and telegraphic and film reviews.
**Ind/Abst** Acad. Ind. [Computer File] (1992-); Acad. Search (July 1993-); ACM Guide Comput. Lit.; Compumath Citation Index [Full Cov.]; Comput. Rev.; Curr. Contents Phys. Chem. Earth Sci.; Curr. Index J. Educ.; Expand. Acad. Index (1989-); Gen. Sci. Index; Gen. Sci. Source (Jul. 1993-); INFO-SOUTH Abstr.; INIS Atomindex [Micro.]; Int. Aerosp. Abstr.; Mag. Search; Math. Rev.; Newsp. Period. Abstr. (1989-); Res. Alert [Full Cov.]; Sci. Cit. Index; SCISEARCH; Stat. Theory Method Abstr. (1967-1969, 1971-1972, 1976-1981); Zentralbl. Math. Ihre Grenzgeb.

US/0883-6221
**AMERICAN SERIES IN MATHEMATICAL AND MANAGEMENT SCIENCES.** [Am. ser. math. manage. sci.]. **VFOAT** American Science Press Series in Mathematical and Management Sciences; Series in Mathematical and Management Sciences. Monographic series. English. Four times a year. Price varies per volume. American Sciences Press Inc, 20 Cross Road, Syracuse NY 13224. **Tel** (315)446-1843. **DD** 515. **UDC** 519.8; 51-74:658. Index available. cum. index. **Bk Rev. Ad Acc. Pr Rev.**
**Desc:** Seeks to bring together new work in the various areas of the mathematical and management sciences.
**Ind/Abst** Math. Rev.

US/1048-1680
**AMYGDALA (SAN CRISTOBAL, N.M.).** (AMYGDALA : A NEWSLETTER OF M--, THE MANDELBROT SET.). (1987)-. Periodical. English. Ten times a year. $15.00. Amygdale, PO Box 219, San Cristobal NM 87564. **Tel** (505)758-7461. **DD** 510.

RM/0041-9109
**ANALELE STIINTIFICE ALE UNIVERSITATII "AL. I. CUZA" DIN IASI. SERIE NOUA. SECTIUNEA 1A, MATEMATICA.** [An. stiint. Univ. "Al. I. Cuza" Iasi, Sect. 1a: Mat.]. **Main/Corp** Jassy. Universitatea. din Iasi. **Added/Corp** Universitatea "Al. I. Cuza" din Iasi. **VFOAT** Analele Stiintifice ale Universitatii "Al. I. Cuza" din Iasi. Sectiunea I, Matematica; Analele Stiintifice ale Universitatii "Al. I. Cuza" din Iasi. Serie Noua, Sectiunea Matematica; Analele Stiintifice ale Universitatii "Al. I. Cuza" din Iasi. Serie Noua, Matematica; Analele Stiintifice ale Universitatii "Al. I. Cuza" din Iasi. Serie Noua, Matematica-Informatica; Analele Stiintifice ale Universitatii "Al. I. Cuza" din Iasi. Matematica; Matematica; Sectiunea Matematica; Matematica-Informatica. Vol. 10 (1964)-. Periodical. Romanian (English, French and Russian). Four times a year. DM461.00. **(Subscription address:** Kubon & Sagner, ABT Zeitschriftenimport, D 80328 Munich Germany.**) LC** QA1; .J47. **CODEN** AUZMAV. ***Continues in part** Analele Stiintifice ale Universitatii "Al. I. Cuza" din Iasi. Serie Noua. Sectiunea 1, Matematica, Fizica, Chimie, 0448-9039.*
**Ind/Abst** Math. Rev.; Stat. Theory Method Abstr. (1969); Zentralbl. Math. Ihre Grenzgeb.

RM
**ANALELE UNIVERSITATI DIN GALATI. FASCICULA II - MATEMATICA, FIZICA, MECANICA TEORETICA.** Bulletin. English (French and German). an. Price varies. Redactia Analelor, 6200 Galati, Str Domneasca Nr. 47 Romania. **Tel** 40 93 413602, FAX 40 93 412328. **ED** Mihai Jascanu. **Bk Rev. Ad Acc. Pr Rev. Circ:** 250 (ctrl).

RM/1010-5433
**ANALELE UNIVERSITATII BUCURESTI. MATEMATICA.** [An. Univ. Bucur., Ser. Mat.]. **Added/Corp** Universitatea din Bucuresti. Facultea de Matematica. **VFOAT** Seria Matematica; Matematica; Matematica-Informatica; Analele Universitatii Bucuresti. Seria Matematica. (1977)-. Romanian (English, French, German, Romany and Russian). Three times a year. DM362.00. **(Subscription address:** Kubon & Sagner, ABT Zeitschriftenimport, D 80328 Munich Germany.**) LC** QA1; .B7658a. **DD** 510. **CODEN** AUBMDG. Documents available from Ask*IEEE. ***Continues in part** Universitatea din Bucuresti. Analele Universitatii Bucuresti. Stiintele Naturii, 0254-8887.*
**Ind/Abst** INSPEC (1981-); Math. Rev.; Zentralbl. Math. Ihre Grenzgeb.

RM/0253-1860
**ANALELE UNIVERSITATII DIN CRAIOVA. MATHEMATICA, FIZICA-CHIMIE.** [An. Univ. Craiova, mat., fiz.-chim.]. **Added/Corp** Universitatea din Craiova. Facultatea de Stiinte ale Naturii. **VFOAT** Analele Universitatii din Craiova. Seria Mathematica, Fizica-Chimie. (19??)-. Academic Scholarly Publication. English (French and German). an. DM164.00. **(Subscription address:** Kubon & Sagner, ABT Zeitschriftenimport, D 80328 Munich Germany.**) LC** QA1; .A5298. **DD** 500.2. **CODEN** ACSFDM. Documents available from CASDDS.
**Ind/Abst** Chem. Abstr. (?-1985); Zentralbl. Math. Ihre Grenzgeb.

RM
**ANALELE UNIVERSITATII DIN TIMISOARA. STIINTE MATEMATICE. Added/Corp** Universitatea din Timisoara. Facultatea de Stiinte ale Naturii. **VFOAT** Stiinte Matematice. Vol. 16, No. 1 (1978)-. Periodical. Romanian (English, French and German). Three times a year. DM362.00. Universitatea din Timisoara, Facultatea de Stiinte ale Naturii, 1900 Timisoara RS Romania. **(Subscription address:** Kubon & Sagner, ABT Zeitschriftenimport, D 80328 Munich Germany.**) LC** QA1; .T553. ***Continues** Analele Universitatii din Timisoara. Seria Stiinte Matematice.*
**Ind/Abst** Zentralbl. Math. Ihre Grenzgeb.

SP/0213-5469
**ANALES DE CIENCIAS - UNIVERSIDAD DE MURCIA.** **See** Chemistry.

MX/0185-0644
**ANALES DEL INSTITUTO DE MATEMATICAS.** [An. inst. mat.]. V. 1- 1961-. English (Spanish, French and German). an. $15.00.

Instituto de Matematicas UNAM, Ciudad Universitaria, Mexico 04510 DF Mexico. **Tel** (5)548 20 07, FAX (5)548 94 99, telex 1760155 CICME. **ED** Carlos Prieto. **LC** QA1. **UDC** 51. Index available. cum. index. **Pr Rev. Circ:** 500 (ctrl).
**Desc:** Original articles of studies on various mathematical topics.
**Ind/Abst** Math. Rev.; Zentralbl. Math. Ihre Grenzgeb.

RU/0130-9412
**ANALIZ NA PROBLEMNYKH SETIAKH / AKADEMIIA NAUK SSSR, INSTITUT MIROVOI EKONOMIKI I MEZHDUNARODNYKH OTNOSHENII.** **Added/Corp** Institut Mirovoi Ekonomiki i Mezhdunarodnykh Otnoshenii (Akademiia Nauk SSSR). Vol. 1 (1980)-. Periodical. Russian. 0.40rub. **LC** QA63; .A5.

RM/1010-3376
**ANALYSE NUMERIQUE ET LA THEORIE DE L'APPROXIMATION, L'.** [Anal. numer. theor. approx.]. **Added/Corp** Academia Republicii Socialiste Romania. Filiala Cluj-Napoca. **VFOAT** Mathematica - Revue d'Analyse Numerique et de Theorie de l'Approximation. Vol. 4 (1975)-. Periodical. English (French, German and Russian). sa. $126.00. **(Subscription address:** Orion Press SRL, SPL Independentei 202-A, Bucharest 6 Romania.**)** **LC** QA297; .R452. **DD** 519.4/05. ***Continues*** *Revue d'Analyse Numerique et de la Theorie de l'Approximation, 0301-9241.*
**Ind/Abst** Math. Rev.

GW
**ANALYSIS.** Vol. 2, No. 1-4 (1982)-. Periodical. English. qt. DM296.00. R Oldenbourg Verlag, Postfach 801360, D 81613 Munich Germany. **Tel** 011 49 89 450190, FAX 011 49 89 45019305. ***Continues*** *Analysis (Wiesbaden).*

HU/0133-3852
**ANALYSIS MATHEMATICA (BUDAPEST).** (ANALYSIS MATHEMATICA.). [Anal. math.]. **Added/Corp** Akademiai Kiado. Akademiia Nauk SSSR. Magyar Tudomanyos Akademia. Vol. 1 (1975)-. Periodical. Multiple languages (English and Russian). qt. $298.00 The Americas; £200.00 other. Pergamon Press, An Imprint of Elsevier Science Ltd., The Boulevard, Langford Lane, Kidlington, Oxford OX5 1GB United Kingdom. **Tel** 011 44 865 843000, 011 44 865 843699, FAX 011 44 865 843010. **(Subscription address:** Elsevier Science Ltd. Oxford Fulfillment Centre, PO Box 800, Kidlington, Oxford OX5 1DX United Kingdom.**)** **ED** Bela Szokefalvi-Nagy (editor's address: Analysis Mathematica, Bolyai Instutte, Aradi Vertanuk tere 1, 6720 Szeged Hungary) and S. M. Nikolsky. **LC** QA300; .A5493. **CODEN** ANMADK. **[CCC]. Bk Rev. Ad Acc.** available on microfilm and microfiche from University Microfilms International (UMI). Documents available from Ask*IEEE.
**Desc:** Dedicated primarily to problems of classical mathematical analysis, such as the differentiation and integration of functions, measure theory, analytic and harmonic functions, Fourier analysis and orthogonal expansions, approximation of functions and quadrature formulae, function spaces, extremal problems, inequalities, etc.
**Ind/Abst** INSPEC (1977-1985); Math. Rev.; Stat. Theory Method Abstr. (1982-1984, 1986); Zentralbl. Math. Ihre Grenzgeb.

FI/0355-0087
**ANNALES ACADEMIAE SCIENTIARUM FENNICAE. SERIES A. I, MATHEMATICA DISSERTATIONES.** [Ann. Acad. sci. Fenn., Ser. A1, Mat., Diss.]. **Added/Corp** Suomalainen Tiedeakatemia. **VFOAT** Mathematica. Dissertationes. Vol. 1 (1975)-. Monographic series. English (German). ir. Price varies per volume. Bookstore Tiedekirja, Kirkkokatu 14, Helsinki 00170 Finland. **Tel** 011 358 0 635177. **ED** Olli Lehto. **LC** UNC. **Circ:** 1,000. ***Continues*** *Annales Academiae Scientiarum Fennicae. Series A. I, Mathematica, 0066-1953.*

FI/0066-1953
**ANNALES ACADEMIAE SCIENTIARUM FENNICAE. SERIES A. I, MATHEMATICA (HELSINKI, FINLAND : 1975).** (ANNALES ACADEMIAE SCIENTIARUM FENNICAE. SERIES A. I, MATHEMATICA.). [Ann. Acad. sci. Fenn., Ser. A1, Math.]. **Added/Corp** Suomalainen Tiedeakatemia. **VFOAT** Mathematica. Vol. 1 (1975)-. Monographic series. English (Finnish and German). ir. Price varies per volume. Suomalainen Tiedeakatemia / Academia Scientiarum Fennica, Mariankatu 5, SF-00170 Helsinki Finland. **(Subscription address:** Bookstore Tiedekirja, Kirkkokatu 14, SF 00170 Helsinki Finland.**)** **ED** Olli Lehto. **LC** QA1; .S88. **DD** 510. **CODEN** AAFMAT. Index available. cum. index. **Pr Rev. Circ:** 1,000. Documents available from The Genuine Article, Ask*IEEE. ***Continues*** *Annales Academiae Scientiarum Fennicae. Series A. I, Mathematica, 0066-1953.*
**Ind/Abst** Compumath Citation Index [Full Cov.]; INSPEC (1975-); Int. Aerosp. Abstr. (1991-); Res. Alert [Full Cov.]; SCISEARCH; Zentralbl. Math. Ihre Grenzgeb.

FR/0240-2963
**ANNALES DE LA FACULTE DES SCIENCES DE TOULOUSE.** (ANNALES DE LA FACULTE DES SCIENCES DE TOULOUSE. MATHEMATIQUES.). [Ann. fac. sci. Toulouse]. Ser. 5, V. 1, Issue 1- = 79E Vol.-. Periodical. French (English). Three times a year. 350F. Annales de la Faculte des Sciences, Universite Paul Sabatier, 31077 Toulouse Cedex France. **LC** Q46; .T75. **DD** 510/.5. **UDC** 51. **CODEN** AFSMDU. Documents available from Ask*IEEE. ***Continues*** *Annales de la Faculte des Sciences de l'Universite de Toulouse.*
**Ind/Abst** INSPEC (1980-); Math. Rev.; Zentralbl. Math. Ihre Grenzgeb.

CG
**ANNALES DE LA FACULTE DES SCIENCES: SECTION MATHEMATIQUE-PHYSIQUE.** **Main/Corp** Universite Nationale du Zaire. Campus de Kinshasa. Faculte des Sciences. Vol. 1 (Juin 1975)-. Periodical. French. sa.
**Ind/Abst** Zentralbl. Math. Ihre Grenzgeb.

FR/0246-0203
**ANNALES DE L'I.H.P. PROBABILITES ET STATISTIQUES.** [Ann. I.H.P. Probab. stat.]. **Added/Corp** Institut Henri Poincare. **VFOAT** Annales de l'IHP. Probabilites et Statistiques; Calcul des Probabilites et Statistique; Probabilites et Statistique; Ann. Inst. Henri Poincare. Section B, Calcul des Probabilites et Statistique. Vol. 19, No. 1 (1983)-. Periodical. English (French). Four times a year. 1240.00F France; 1600.00F other. Gauthier-Villars, 15 rue Gossin, 92543 Montrouge Cedex France. **Tel** 33 1 40 92 65 00, FAX 33 1 40 92 65 97. **(Subscription address:** Centrale des Revues, 11 rue Gossin, 92543 Montrouge Cedex France.**)** **ED** J. Neveu. **LC** QA273.A1; P37. **DD** 519.2/05. **[CCC]. Bk Rev. Ad Acc. Pr Rev. Circ:** 750. Documents available from The Genuine Article. ***Continues*** *Annales de l'Institut Henri Poincare. Section B, Probabilites et Statistiques, 0020-2347.*
**Desc:** Welcomes manuscripts from all areas of the theory of probabilities.
**Ind/Abst** Compumath Citation Index; Math. Rev.; Res. Alert.

FR/0373-0956
**ANNALES DE L'INSTITUT FOURIER.** [Ann. Inst. Fourier.]. **Added/Corp** Institut Fourier. Vol. 1 (1949)-. Periodical. French (English). ir (5 issues). 1410.00F (includes index). Annales de l'Institut Fourier, BP 74, 38402 St. Martin d'Heres France. **Tel** 011 33 76 514657. **LC** Q46; .G75. **DD** 505. **CODEN** AIFUA7. **[CCC].** Index available. cum. index. **Ad Acc. Pr Rev. Circ:** 1,000. Documents available from The Genuine Article. ***Continues*** *Annales de l'Universite de Grenoble. Section des Sciences Mathematiques et Physiques.*
**Desc:** High quality papers in all branches of pure mathematics; main published fields: classical analysis, partial differential equations, differential geometry, theory of singularities and number theory.
**Ind/Abst** Compumath Citation Index [Full Cov.]; Energy Res. Abstr. (July 1980-); Int. Aerosp. Abstr.; Math. Rev.; Res. Alert [Full Cov.]; SCISEARCH; Stat. Theory Method Abstr. (1976-1977, 1979-1984, 1986-1987); Zentralbl. Math. Ihre Grenzgeb.

FR/0294-1449
**ANNALES DE L'INSTITUT HENRI POINCARE. ANALYSE NON LINEAIRE.** [Ann. Inst. Henri Poincare, Anal. non lineaire]. **VFOAT** Analyse Non Lineaire; Nonlinear Analysis. Vol. 1, No. 1 (1984)-. Periodical. French. Six times a year. 1500.00F France; 2000.00F other. Gauthier-Villars, 15 rue Gossin, 92543 Montrouge Cedex France. **Tel** 33 1 40 92 65 00, FAX 33 1 40 92 65 97. **(Subscription address:** Centrale des Revues, 11 rue Gossin, 92543 Montrouge Cedex France.**)** **LC** QA427; .A56. **DD** 515. **UDC** 519.6; 517.9. **[CCC]. Pr Rev.** Documents available from The Genuine Article.
**Ind/Abst** Compumath Citation Index; Curr. Contents Phys. Chem. Earth Sci.; Math. Rev.; Res. Alert; Sci. Cit. Index; SCISEARCH; Zentralbl. Math. Ihre Grenzgeb.

CN/0707-9109
**ANNALES DES SCIENCES MATHEMATIQUES DU QUEBEC.** (LES ANNALES DES SCIENCES MATHEMATIQUES DU QUEBEC.). **Added/Corp** Universite de Montreal. Centre de Recherches Mathematiques. Vol. 1 (Jan. 1977)-. Periodical. French (English). sa. 40.00Can$ institutions; 20.00Can$ individuals. Les Annales des Sciences, University of Montreal, CP 8888 Succ A, Montreal Quebec H3C 3P8 Canada. **Tel** (514)987-7902. **ED** Gilbert Labelle. **LC** QA1; .A543. **DD** 510/.5. Index available. **Pr Rev. Circ:** 300.
**Desc:** Research papers on any subject related to mathematics.
**Ind/Abst** Math. Rev.; Zentralbl. Math. Ihre Grenzgeb.

PL/0066-2216
**ANNALES POLONICI MATHEMATICI.** [Ann. Pol. math.]. **Added/Corp** Instytut Matematyczny (Polska Akademia Nauk). Vol. 1 (1954)-. Periodical. Multiple languages (English, French, German and Multiple languages). ir. $84.00. **(Subscription address:** ARS Polona, PO Box 1001, 00068 Warsaw Poland.**)** **LC** QA1; .A545. **CODEN** APNMA4. cum. index. **Circ:** 1,500 (ctrl). ***Supersedes*** *Annales de la Societe Polonaise de Mathematique.*
**Desc:** Publishes papers concerning analysis and geometry. Particular domain: differential and integral equations theory.
**Ind/Abst** Math. Rev.; Zentralbl. Math. Ihre Grenzgeb.

FR/0012-9593
**ANNALES SCIENTIFIQUES DE L'ECOLE NORMALE SUPERIEURE.** [Ann. sci. Ec. norm. super.]. **Main/Corp** Ecole Normale Superieure (France). Vol. 1-7 (1864)-. Periodical. French (German and English). Six times a year. 1,300.00F France; 1,560.00F other. Gauthier-Villars, 15 rue Gossin, 92543 Montrouge Cedex France. **Tel** 33 1 40 92 65 00, FAX 33 1 40 92 65 97. **(Subscription address:** Centrale des Revues, 11 rue Gossin, 92543 Montrouge Cedex France.**)** **ED** M. Herman. **CODEN** ASENAH. **[CCC].** cum. index. **Ad Acc. Pr Rev. Circ:** 900. Documents available from The Genuine Article.
**Desc:** Leading mathematics journal since 1864.
**Ind/Abst** Compumath Citation Index; Math. Rev.; Res. Alert; SCISEARCH; Stat. Theory Method Abstr. (1959-1963, 1980-1981, 1983, 1987); Zentralbl. Math. Ihre Grenzgeb.

PL/0373-8299
**ANNALES SOCIETATIS MATHEMATICAE POLONAE. COMMENTATIONES MATHEMATICAE.** [Rocz. Pol. Tow. Mat. Ser. 1]. **Main/Corp** Polskie Towarzystwo Matematyczne. **VFOAT** Roczniki Polskiego Towarzystwa Matematycznego. Seria 1.: Prace Matematyczne; Commentationes Mathematicae; Prace Matematyczne. Vol. 14 (1970)-. Polish (English). sa. PAAC Kultury i Nauka, Osrodek Rozpowszechniania Wydawnictw Naukowych Pan, 00-091 Warszawa Poland. **LC** QA1; .P625. ***Continues*** *Roczniki. Seria 1.: Prace Matematyczne.*
**Ind/Abst** Math. Rev.

PL/0365-1029
**ANNALES UNIVERSITATIS MARIAE CURIE-SKODOWSKA. SECTIO A. MATHEMATICA.** [Ann. Univ. Mariae Curie-Skodowska. Sect. A]. **Main/Corp** Uniwersytet Marii Curie-Skodowskiej. **Added/Corp** Uniwersytet Marii Curie-Skodowskiej Roczniki Uniwersytetu Marii Curie-Skodowskiej. Dzial A. Mathematyka. **VFOAT** Roczniki Uniwersytetu Marii Curie-Skodowskiej. Matematyka; Mathematica. Vol. 1 (1946)-. Polish (French; table of contents in Russian). an. Uniwersytet Marii Curie-Sklodowskiej, Pl Marii Curie-Sklodowskiej 5, 20-031 Lublin Poland. **Tel** 37-53-04, telex 0643223. **LC** QA1.L8; A2. **CODEN** ACAMAI.
**Ind/Abst** Math. Rev.; Zentralbl. Math. Ihre Grenzgeb.

GW/0080-5165
**ANNALES UNIVERSITATIS SARAVIENSIS. REIHE : MATHEMATISCH-NATURWISSENSCHAFTLICHE FAKULTAT.** **See** Natural History.

SW
**ANNALES UNIVERSITATIS SARAVIENSIS. SERIES MATHEMATICAE.** **VFOAT** Series Mathematicae. (1986)-. Monographic series. English (German). Price varies per volume.
**Ind/Abst** Math. Rev.; Zentralbl. Math. Ihre Grenzgeb.

HU/0138-9491
**ANNALES UNIVERSITATIS SCIENTIARUM BUDAPESTINENSIS DE ROLANDO EOTVOS NOMINATAE. SECTIO COMPUTATORICA.** [Ann. Univ. Sci. Bp. Rolando Eotvos nom., Sect. comput.]. **Added/Corp** Eotvos Lorand Tudomanyegyetem. (1978)-. English (Russian). an. S20.00. ELTE Department of Computer Algebra, VIII Muzeum krt. 6-8, H-1088 Budapest Hungary. **Tel** 011 36 1 2666428, FAX 011 36 1 2666429. **ED** Dr. L. Lakatos. **LC** QA297 .A63. **DD** 519.4/05. Index available. **Bk Rev. Circ:** 300.
**Desc:** Research and survey papers treating problems from a broad field of applied mathematics. Focuses on classical numerical analysis, modern theories of algorithms of approximation, summation of series, modelling and simulation, theory of automata, and programming languages.
**Ind/Abst** Math. Rev.; Zentralbl. Math. Ihre Grenzgeb.

HU/0524-9007
**ANNALES UNIVERSITATIS SCIENTIARUM BUDAPESTINENSIS DE ROLANDO EOTVOS NOMINATAE. SECTIO MATHEMATICA.** **Main/Corp** Eotvos Lorand Tudomanyegyetem. Vol. 1 (1958)-. English (German, French and Russian). an. Free on request. Eotvos Roland University, V Pesti Barnabas, Budapest U1 Hungary. **Tel** 11 36 1 187396. **LC** QA1; .B766.

IT/0391-173X
**ANNALI DELLA SCUOLA NORMALE SUPERIORE DI PISA, CLASSE DI SCIENZE.** [Ann. Sc. norm. super. Pisa, Cl. sci.]. **Main/Corp** Scuola Normale Superiore (Italy). Classe di Scienze. Vol. 1, (1974)-. Periodical. English (English). Four times a year (Mar., June, Oct., Dec.). $160.00. Scuola Normale Superiore, Piazza Dei Cavalieri 7, I 56126 Pisa Italy. **Tel** 011 39 50509111. **LC** QA1; .P49a. **CODEN** PSNAAI. ***Continues*** *Annali Della Scuola Normale Superiore di Pisa. Scienze Fisiche i Matematiche.*
**Ind/Abst** Math. Rev.; Numis. Lit.; Zentralbl. Math. Ihre Grenzgeb.

IT/0430-3202
**ANNALI DELL'UNIVERSITA DI FERRARA. SEZIONE 7 : SCIENZE MATEMATICHE.** [Ann. Univ. Ferrara, 7]. **Main/Corp** Ferrara. Universita. **VAT** Annali dell'Universita di Ferrarae. Sezione Sette: Scienze Matemati. 1951-. Italian (English, French, Spanish, German and Latin). an. Istituto di Matematica, Via Savonarola 9, 44100 Ferrara Italy. **Tel** 0532-34420. **LC** QA1; .F47A. **DD** 510. **UDC** 51. **CODEN** AUFMAX. **Circ:** 500.
**Ind/Abst** Math. Rev.; Zentralbl. Math. Ihre Grenzgeb.

IT/0373-3114
**ANNALI DI MATEMATICA PURA ED APPLICATA.** [Ann. mat. pura appl.]. Vol. 1 (1858)-Vol. 7 (1865). Periodical. Italian (English, French and German). ir. L50000 per volume. Zanichelli Editore SPA, via Irnerio 34, 40126 Bologna Italy. **Tel** 011 39 51 293263, telex 214885 ZANED I. **ED** B Tortolini and F Brioschi. **UDC** 51. **CODEN** ANLMAE. cum. index. Documents available from The Genuine Article. ***Continues*** *Annali di Scienze, Matematiche e Fisiche.*
**Desc:** Yearbooks of pure and applied mathematics.
**Ind/Abst** Compumath Citation Index [Full Cov.]; Math. Rev.; Res. Alert [Full Cov.]; SCISEARCH; Zentralbl. Math. Ihre Grenzgeb.

US/1050-5164
**ANNALS OF APPLIED PROBABILITY, THE.** (THE ANNALS OF APPLIED PROBABILITY : AN OFFICIAL JOURNAL OF THE INSTITUTE OF MATHEMATICAL STATISTICS.). [Ann. appl. probab.]. **Added/Corp** Institute of Mathematical Statistics. Vol. 1, No. 1 (Feb. 1991)-. Periodical. English. qt. $90.00. Institute of Mathematical Statistics, 3401 Investment Boulevard, Suite 7, Hayward CA 94545-3819. **Tel** (510)783-8141, FAX (510)783-4131. **LC** QA273.A1; A56. **DD** 519.2/05.
**Desc:** Publishes work that develops the interplay of probability and other fields, including computer science, finance, network modeling, and biology.
**Ind/Abst** Curr. Index Stat.; Zentralbl. Math. Ihre Grenzgeb.

CC
**ANNALS OF DIFFERENTIAL EQUATIONS. WEI FEN FANG CHENG NIEN KAN.** **Added/Corp** Fuzhou University. **VFOAT** Wei Fen Fang Cheng Nien Kan. Vol. 1, No. 1 (1985)-. Periodical. English. Four times a year (Mar., June, Sept., Dec.). $200.00. Fuzhou University, Professor Lin Zhensheng, Department of Math, Fuzhou University, Fujian 350002, People's Republic of China.
**Ind/Abst** Math. Rev. (1985-); Zentralbl. Math. Ihre Grenzgeb.

NE/0167-5060
**ANNALS OF DISCRETE MATHEMATICS.** [Ann. discr. math.]. (1977)-. Monographic series. English. ir. Price varies per volume. Elsevier Science Publishers BV, PO Box 211, 1000 AE Amsterdam Netherlands. **Tel** 011 31 20 5803642, FAX 011 31 20 5862696, telex 15682. **(Subscription address:** Elsevier Science Inc. / New York Books, 655 Avenue of the Americas, New York NY 10010.**)** **LC** UNC. **[CCC]. Pr Rev.** Documents available from Ask*IEEE.
**Ind/Abst** INSPEC; Int. Abstr. Oper. Res. [Select. Cov.]; Math. Rev.; Zentralbl. Math. Ihre Grenzgeb.

GW/0232-704X
**ANNALS OF GLOBAL ANALYSIS AND GEOMETRY.** [Ann. glob. anal. geom.]. (1983)-. Periodical. English. qt. $460.00. Kluwer Academic Publishers, Postbus 322, 3300 AH Dordrecht, The Netherlands. **Tel** 011 (31) 78 524400, FAX 011 31 78 183273, telex 20083. **ED** Th. Friedrich and R. Sulanke. **[CCC]. Pr Rev. Acid Free.**
**Desc:** Treats, in particular, global problems of geometry and analysis as well as the interactions between these fields and their application to problems of theoretical physics. These areas include: global analysis, differential geometry, complex manifolds and related results from complex analysis and algebraic geometry, lie groups, lie transformation groups and harmonic analysis, applications of differential geometry and global analysis to problems of theoretical physics.
**Ind/Abst** Math. Rev.; Zentralbl. Math. Ihre Grenzgeb.

US/0003-486X
**ANNALS OF MATHEMATICS.** [Ann. math.]. **Added/Corp** University of Virginia. Harvard University. Princeton University. Institute for Advanced Study (Princeton, N.J.). (Mar. 1884)-. Periodical. English (French and German). Six times a year. $200.00. Princeton University Press, 41 William Street, Princeton NJ 08540. **Tel** (609)258-4900. **(Subscription address:** John Hopkins University Press, Journals Publishing Division, PO Box 19966, Baltimore MD 21211.**)** **ED** Eleanor May. **LC** QA1; .A6. **DD** 510.5. **CODEN** ANMAAH. cum. index. **Pr Rev. Circ:** 1,800. available on microfilm and microfiche from University Microfilms International (UMI). Documents available from The Genuine Article. ***Continues*** *Analyst, 0741-7918.*
**Desc:** Journal of research in pure mathematics.
**Ind/Abst** Compumath Citation Index [Full Cov.]; Curr. Contents Phys. Chem. Earth Sci.; Math. Rev.; Res. Alert [Full Cov.]; Sci. Cit. Index; SCISEARCH; Zentralbl. Math. Ihre Grenzgeb.

NE/1012-2443
**ANNALS OF MATHEMATICS AND OF ARTIFICIAL INTELLIGENCE.** **See** Computers-Artificial Intelligence.

US/0066-2313
**ANNALS OF MATHEMATICS STUDIES.** [Ann. math. stud.]. No. 1 (1940)-. Monographic series. English. ir. Price varies per volume. Princeton University Press, 41 William Street, Princeton NJ 08540. **Tel** (609)258-4900. **(Subscription address:** California Princeton Fulfillment Service, 1445 Lower Ferry Road, Ewing NJ 08618.**)** **CODEN** ANMAA. **Pr Rev.** Documents available from The Genuine Article.
**Ind/Abst** Compumath Citation Index [Full Cov.]; Math. Rev.; Res. Alert [Full Cov.]; SCISEARCH; Zentralbl. Math. Ihre Grenzgeb.

NE
**ANNALS OF NUMERICAL MATHEMATICS.** (19??)-. English. an. 282.50F (includes distribution costs). Baltzer Science Publishers BV, Asterweg 1A, 1031 HL Amsterdam Netherlands. **Tel** 011 31 20 6370061, FAX 011 31 20 6323651.

US/0091-1798
**ANNALS OF PROBABILITY, THE.** [Ann. probab.]. **Added/Corp** Institute of Mathematical Statistics. Vol. 1 (Feb. 1973)-. Periodical. English (French). qt. $130.00. Institute of Mathematical Statistics, 3401 Investment Boulevard, Suite 7, Hayward CA 94545-3819. **Tel** (510)783-8141, FAX (510)783-4131. **ED** Peter Ney. **LC** HA1; .A82. **DD** 519.2/05. **CODEN** APBYAE. **[CCC].** Index available. **Bk Rev. Ad Acc. Pr Rev. Circ:** 3,300. available on microfilm and microfiche from University Microfilms International (UMI). Documents available from The Genuine Article. ***Supersedes in part*** *Annals of Mathematical Statistics, 0003-4851.*
**Desc:** Presents contributions to the theory of probability and its applications.
**Ind/Abst** Biostatistica; Compumath Citation Index [Full Cov.]; Curr. Contents Phys. Chem. Earth Sci.; Curr. Index Stat.; Math. Rev.; Qual. Control Appl. Stat.; Res. Alert [Full Cov.]; Sci. Cit. Index; SCISEARCH; Soc. Sci. Cit. Index [Select. Cov.]; Stat. Theory Method Abstr. (1973-1984, 1986-1987); Zentralbl. Math. Ihre Grenzgeb.

NE/0168-0072
**ANNALS OF PURE AND APPLIED LOGIC.** [Ann. pure appl. logic]. Vol. 24 No. 1 (July 1983)-. Academic Scholarly Publication. English. Eighteen times a year (6 volumes). Fl2400.00. Elsevier Science Publishers BV, PO Box 211, 1000 AE Amsterdam Netherlands. **Tel** 011 31 20 5803642, FAX 011 31 20 5862696, telex 15682. **ED** D van Dalen, Y Gurevich, J Hartmanis, A Nerode, A Prestel, and H Rogers Jr. **LC** QA1; .A585. **DD** 511.3. **CODEN** APALD7. **[CCC]. Ad Acc. Pr Rev.** available on microfilm and microfiche from University Microfilms International (UMI). Documents available from The Genuine Article, Ask*IEEE. ***Continues*** *Annals of Mathematical Logic, 0003-4843.*
**Desc:** A vehicle for fundamental contributions to logic either in its pure form or in its applications to disciplines in mathematics or related subjects.
**Ind/Abst** Compumath Citation Index [Full Cov.]; Curr. Contents Phys. Chem. Earth Sci.; INSPEC (July 1983-); Math. Rev.; Philos. Index; Res. Alert [Full Cov.]; Sci. Cit. Index; SCISEARCH; Zentralbl. Math. Ihre Grenzgeb.

US
**ANNUAL SYMPOSIUM ON FOUNDATIONS OF COMPUTER SCIENCE.** **See** Computers-Cybernetics.

CL
**APORTES MATEMATICOS / UNIVERSIDAD DE TARAPACA, FACULTAD DE CIENCIAS, DEPARTAMENTO DE MATEMATICAS.** Periodical. Spanish. ir. Universidad de Tarapaca / Biblioteca, Direccion de Biblioteca, Campus Velasquez Casilla 747, Arica Chile. **Tel** 32252, telex 221128. **LC** QA1; .A6455. **DD** 510/.5. **UDC** 51. Index available. **Bk Rev. Circ:** 1,987.

GW/0938-1279
**APPLICABLE ALGEBRA IN ENGINEERING, COMMUNICATION AND COMPUTING.** (APPLICABLE ALGEBRA IN ENGINEERING, COMMUNICATION AND COMPUTING : AAECC.). [Appl. algebra eng. commun. comput.]. **VFOAT** AAECC. Vol. 1, No. 1 (July 1990)-. Periodical. English. bm. DM288.00. Springer-Verlag GmbH & Company KG, Heidelberger Platz 3, D 14197 Berlin Germany. **Tel** 011 49 30 8207223, FAX 011 49 30 8214091, telex 183 319 SPBLN D. **(Subscription address:** Springer Verlag New York Inc. / for North America, 44 Hartz Way, Secaucus NJ 07096.**)** **ED** J. Calmet. **CODEN** AAECEW. **[CCC].** available in microform. Documents available from Article Express International, Ask*IEEE.
**Desc:** Publishes mathematically rigorous, original research papers reporting on algebraic methods and techniques relevant to all domains concerned with computers, intelligent systems and communications.
**Ind/Abst** Compumath Citation Index [Full Cov.]; Eng. Index Annu. [Select. Cov.]; INSPEC (1990-); Zentralbl. Math. Ihre Grenzgeb.

US/0003-6811
**APPLICABLE ANALYSIS.** [Appl. anal.]. Vol. 1 (April 1971)-. Periodical. English. mo. $847.00 (academic institutions), $1321.00 (corporate institutions). Gordon & Breach Science Publishers, Inc., PO Box 786, Cooper Station, New York NY 10276. **Tel** (212)206-8900, FAX (212)645-2459. **ED** R. P. Gilbert. **LC** QA300; .A58. **DD** 515/.05. **CODEN** APANCC. **[CCC].** Index available. **Bk Rev. Ad Acc.** Documents available from Ask*IEEE.
**Desc:** Concerned with analyses that have been applied or are potentially applicable to the solution of scientific, technical, engineering and social problems.
**Ind/Abst** INSPEC (April 1971-); Int. Aerosp. Abstr.; Math. Rev.; Pollut. Abstr. Indexes; Zentralbl. Math. Ihre Grenzgeb.

US/0172-4568
**APPLICATIONS OF MATHEMATICS.** [Appl. math.]. (1975)-. Monographic series. English. ir. Price varies per volume. Springer-Verlag New York Inc., 175 5th Avenue, New York NY 10010. **Tel** (212)460-1500, telex 232 235 SPB UR. **(Subscription address:** Springer Verlag New York Inc. / for North America, 44 Hartz Way, Secaucus NJ 07096.**)** **ED** A.V. Balakrishnan, I. Karatzas, M. Yor. **LC** UNC. **CODEN** APMADY. Documents available from Ask*IEEE.
**Desc:** Topics include methods of numerical mathematics, applied functional analysis, and difference methods and their extrapolations.
**Ind/Abst** INSPEC; Math. Rev.; Zentralbl. Math. Ihre Grenzgeb.

XR/0862-7940
**APPLICATIONS OF MATHEMATICS / CZECHOSLOVAK ACADEMY OF SCIENCES.** **Added/Corp** Matematicky Ustav CSAV. Vol. 36, No. 1 (1991)-. Periodical. English. Academia, Publishing House of the Czechoslovak Academy of Sciences, Czech AC SCI, Vodickova 40, PO Box 896, 112 29 Prague 1, Czech Republic. **Tel** 011 42 2 245117. **[CCC].** ***Continues*** *Aplikace Matematiky, 0373-6725.*

XR/0862-7940
**APPLICATIONS OF MATHEMATICS (PRAGUE).** (APPLICATIONS OF MATHEMATICS.). [Appl. math.]. **Added/Corp** Ceskoslovenska Akademie Ved. Matematicky Ustav. No. 1 (1991)-. Periodical. English (German; summaries and/or abstracts in Czech). Six times a year. $515.00 US; $605.00 other. Plenum Press, 233 Spring Street, New York NY 10013-1578. **Tel** (212)620-8000, (800)221-9369, FAX (212)463-0742, (212)807-1047, telex 23/421139. **LC** QA1; .A645. **CODEN** APMTEO. **[CCC].** available on microfilm and microfiche from University Microfilms International (UMI). Documents available from Ask*IEEE. ***Continues*** *Aplikace Matematicky, 0373-6725.*
**Ind/Abst** Ei Page One; INSPEC (1991-); Math. Rev. [Full Cov.].

●US/1063-5203
**APPLIED AND COMPUTATIONAL HARMONIC ANALYSIS.** (1993)-. Academic Scholarly Publication. English. qt (4 issues). $184.00 US and Canada; $221.00 other. Academic Press, Inc., 6277 Sea Harbor Drive, Orlando FL 32887. **Tel** (800)543-9534, (407)345-4100, FAX (407)363-9661. **[CCC].**

NE/0927-2852
**APPLIED CATEGORICAL STRUCTURES.** English. qt. $391.00. Kluwer Academic Publishers, Postbus 322, 3300 AH Dordrecht, The Netherlands. **Tel** 011 (31) 78 524400, FAX 011 31 78 183273, telex 20083. **ED** R. Lowen. **Pr Rev. Acid Free.**
**Desc:** Goal is to promote communication and increase dissemination of new results and ideas among mathematicians and computer scientists who use categorical methods in their research. It focuses on applications of results, techniques and ideas from category theory to mathematics, in particular algebra, analysis, order and topology and computer science.

UK/1350-486X
**APPLIED MATHEMATICAL FINANCE.** (19??)-. Periodical. English. qt. $225.00 US and Canada; £130.00 Europe; £145.00 Other. Chapman & Hall, 2-6 Boundary Row, London SE1 8HN England. **Tel** 011 44 71 865 0066, FAX 011 44 71 522 9623, telex 290164 Chapmag. **(Subscription address:** Chapman & Hall, Cheriton House, North Way, Andover, Hampshire, SP10 5BE England.**)**

UK/0307-904X
**APPLIED MATHEMATICAL MODELLING.** [Appl. math. model.]. Vol. 1 (June 1976)-. Periodical. English. mo. $650.00 US; $750.00 other. Butterworth Heinemann / Woburn, MA, 225 Wildwood Avenue, Unit B, Woburn MA 01801. **Tel** (800)366-2665, FAX (617)928-2620, telex 880052. **(Subscription address:** Elsevier Science Inc. / New York Books, 655 Avenue of the Americas, New York NY 10010.**) ED** Mark Cross (editor's address: Thames Polytechnic, London United Kingdom). **LC** QA1; .A646. **DD** 001.4/24. **CODEN** AMMODL. **[CCC].** Index available. **Bk Rev. Ad Acc. Pr Rev.** available on microfilm and microfiche from University Microfilms International (UMI). Documents available from Article Express International, The Genuine Article, Ask*IEEE, Documents on Demand.
**Desc:** Internationally dedicated to mathematical modelling and the associated numerical techniques and software, charting and influencing the development of the area at a critical time. It remains the primary forum for communication of results, reviews of progress and discussions of topics of interest to those involved in expanding fields.
**Ind/Abst** Abstr. J. Earthq. Eng. (June 1976-); Bioeng. Abstr.; BMT Abstr. (-199?); Coal Abstr.; Compumath Citation Index [Full Cov.]; Comput. Rev.; Curr. Contents Eng. Tech. Appl. Sci.; Ecol. Abstr.; Ei Page One; EMBASE; Eng. Index Annu.; Environ. Abstr.; Fluid Abstr., Civil Eng.; Fluid Abstr. Proc. Eng.; FLUIDEX (1976-); Geogr. Abstr. Phys. Geogr.; Geogr. Abstr. Human Geogr.; Geol. Abstr.; GeoRef; HTFS Dig.; INSPEC (June 1976-); Int. Aerosp. Abstr.; Int. Civil Eng. Abstr.; Int. Dev. Abstr. (?-?); J. Ferrocement; J. Plan. Lit.; Math. Rev. (1976-); Life Sci. Collect.; Res. Alert [Full Cov.]; SCISEARCH; Soc. Plann. Policy Dev. Abstr.; Soc. Sci. Cit. Index [Select. Cov.]; Sociol. Abstr. (?-?); Soft. Abstr. Eng.; Zentralbl. Math. Ihre Grenzgeb.

US/0066-5452
**APPLIED MATHEMATICAL SCIENCES.** [Appl. math. sci.]. Vol. 1 (1971)-. Monographic series. English. ir. Price varies per volume. Springer-Verlag New York Inc., 175 5th Avenue, New York NY 10010. **Tel** (212)460-1500, telex 232 235 SPB UR. **(Subscription address:** Springer Verlag New York Inc. / for North America, 44 Hartz Way, Secaucus NJ 07096.**) ED** F. John, J.E. Marsden, L. Sirovich. **LC** QA1; .A647. **CODEN** AMSCDF. Documents available from Ask*IEEE.
**Desc:** Oriented towards mathematicians interested in the application of their subject. Covers a wide spectrum of current applied mathematics.
**Ind/Abst** Ei Page One; GeoRef; INSPEC; Math. Rev.; Zentralbl. Math. Ihre Grenzgeb.

US/0888-479X
**APPLIED MATHEMATICS.** [Appl. math.]. **VFOAT** Applied Mathematics Series. Vol. 1-. Monographic series. English. ir. Price varies per volume. Gordon & Breach Science Publishers, Inc., PO Box 786, Cooper Station, New York NY 10276. **Tel** (212)206-8900, FAX (212)645-2459. **(Subscription address:** International Publishers Distributor at one of the following addresses: 820 Town Center Drive, Langhorne, PA 19047; or PO Box 90, Reading Berkshire RG1 8JL UK; or Kent Ridge PO Box 1180, Singapore 9111, Republic of Singapore**) DD** 510. **UDC** 519.6.

US/0096-3003
**APPLIED MATHEMATICS AND COMPUTATION.** [Appl. math. comput.]. Vol. 1 (Jan. 1975)-. Academic Scholarly Publication. English. Twenty-one times a year (7 volumes). $1332.00 US; $1415.00 other. Elsevier Science Publishing Company Inc, Madison Square Station, PO Box 882, New York NY 10159-0882. **Tel** (212)633-3950, FAX (212)633-3990. **ED** John Casti and Melvin Scott. **LC** QA1; .A6473. **DD** 519.4/05. **NLM** W1 AP526. **CODEN** AMHCBQ. **[CCC]. Ad Acc. Pr Rev.** available on microfilm and microfiche from University Microfilms International (UMI). Documents available from The Genuine Article, Ask*IEEE.
**Desc:** Focuses on the interplay between mathematics and computation, with emphasis on real-world problems, computational methods such as grid generation and multigrid techniques, and papers on environmental and resource modeling.
**Ind/Abst** ACM Guide Comput. Lit.; Compumath Citation Index [Full Cov.]; Comput. Rev.; Curr. Contents Eng. Tech. Appl. Sci.; Curr. Contents Phys. Chem. Earth Sci.; Ei Page One; GeoRef; HTFS Dig.; INSPEC (Jan. 1981-); Int. Aerosp. Abstr.; Math. Rev.; Pollut. Abstr. Indexes; Res. Alert [Full Cov.]; Sci. Cit. Index; SCISEARCH; Soc. Sci. Cit. Index [Select. Cov.]; Zentralbl. Math. Ihre Grenzgeb.

UK/0950-5903
**APPLIED MATHEMATICS AND ENGINEERING SCIENCE TEXTS.** [Appl. math. eng. sci. texts]. (1987)-. Monographic series. English. ir. Price varies per volume. Blackwell Scientific Publications Ltd, Marston Book Services, PO Box 87, Oxford OX2 0DT UK. **Tel** 011 44 865 791155, FAX 011 44 865 791927, telex 837 515 MARDIS G.
**Ind/Abst** Zentralbl. Math. Ihre Grenzgeb.

US
**APPLIED MATHEMATICS AND MECHANICS. Added/Corp** United States. Dept. of Commerce. Office of Technical Services. (19??)-. English (Russian). **LC** QA801; .P7132. **DD** 531.0822.
**Ind/Abst** Civ. Struct. Eng. Abstr.; Elect. Comm. Abstr.

HK/0253-4827
**APPLIED MATHEMATICS AND MECHANICS.** [Appl. math. mech.]. **VFOAT** Ying Yung Shu Hsueh Ho Li Hsueh. (1980)-. Periodical. English. mo. 831.00F (includes distribution costs). Baltzer Science Publishers BV, Asterweg 1A, 1031 HL Amsterdam Netherlands. **Tel** 011 31 20 6370061, FAX 011 31 20 6323651. **LC** QA1; .Y514. **DD** 620/.0042. **CODEN** AMMEEQ.
**Ind/Abst** Civ. Struct. Eng. Abstr.; Int. Aerosp. Abstr.; Mater. Sci. Eng. Abstr.; Math. Rev.; Mech. Eng. Abstr.; Solid State Supercond. Abstr.; Zentralbl. Math. Ihre Grenzgeb.

US/0095-4616
**APPLIED MATHEMATICS AND OPTIMIZATION.** [Appl. math. optim.]. **VFOAT** Applied Mathematics Optimization. Vol. 1 (1974)-. Periodical. English. Six times a year. $352.00. Springer-Verlag New York Inc., 175 5th Avenue, New York NY 10010. **Tel** (212)460-1500, telex 232 235 SPB UR. **(Subscription address:** Springer Verlag New York Inc. / for North America, 44 Hartz Way, Secaucus NJ 07096.**) ED** G Kallianpur. **LC** QA402.5; .A643. **DD** 519/.05. **CODEN** AMOMBN. **[CCC]. Pr Rev.** available on microfilm and microfiche from University Microfilms International (UMI). Documents available from Article Express International, The Genuine Article, Ask*IEEE.
**Desc:** Publishes original work on mathematical problems of optimization.
**Ind/Abst** Bioeng. Abstr.; Compumath Citation Index [Full Cov.]; Comput. Rev.; Curr. Contents Phys. Chem. Earth Sci.; Ei Page One; Eng. Index Annu. [Select. Cov.]; INSPEC (1974-); Int. Aerosp. Abstr.; Math. Rev.; Res. Alert [Full Cov.]; Sci. Cit. Index; SCISEARCH; Zentralbl. Math. Ihre Grenzgeb.

US/0893-9659
**APPLIED MATHEMATICS LETTERS.** [Appl. math. lett.]. Vol. 1, No. 1 (1988)-. Periodical. English. bm. $470.00 The Americas; £315.00 other. Pergamon Press, An Imprint of Elsevier Science Ltd., The Boulevard, Langford Lane, Kidlington, Oxford OX5 1GB United Kingdom. **Tel** 011 44 865 843000, 011 44 865 843699, FAX 011 44 865 843010. **(Subscription address:** Elsevier Science Ltd. Oxford Fulfillment Centre, PO Box 800, Kidlington, Oxford OX5 1DX United Kingdom.**) ED** Ervin Y. Rodin. **LC** QA1; .A6475. **DD** 510/.5. **CODEN** AMLEEL. **[CCC].** available on microfilm and microfiche from University Microfilms International (UMI). Documents available from The Genuine Article, Ask*IEEE.
**Desc:** Publication for brief applied mathematical papers.
**Ind/Abst** Biostatistica; Compumath Citation Index [Full Cov.]; Comput. Rev.; Ei Page One; INSPEC (1988-1989); Int. Aerosp. Abstr. (1991-); Math. Rev.; Res. Alert [Full Cov.]; SCISEARCH; Soc. Sci. Cit. Index [Select. Cov.]; Zentralbl. Math. Ihre Grenzgeb.

US/1049-4685
**APPLIED MATHEMATICS SERIES.** [Appl. math. ser.]. **Main/Corp** United States. National Bureau of Standards. Began with: 1 in 1948. Government Publication. English. ir. Price varies per volume. US Department of Commerce, 14th Street & Constitution Avenue NW, Washington DC 20230. **Tel** (202)482-2000, FAX (202)482-3772. **LC** QA3; .U5. **DD** 510/.5. **UDC** 519.6.

NE/0168-9274
**APPLIED NUMERICAL MATHEMATICS : TRANSACTIONS OF IMACS.** [Appl. numer. math.]. **Added/Corp** International Association for Mathematics and Computers in Simulation. **VFOAT** Transactions of IMACS. Vol. 1, No. 1 (Jan. 1985)-. Academic Scholarly Publication. English. mo (3 vols.). Fl1710.00; Fl2475.00 combination subscription with Mathematics and Computers in Simulation. Elsevier Science Publishers BV, PO Box 211, 1000 AE Amsterdam Netherlands. **Tel** 011 31 20 5803642, FAX 011 31 20 5862696, telex 15682. **ED** R Stepleman and R Vichnevetsky. **LC** QA297; .A68. **DD** 519.4/05. **[CCC]. Pr Rev.** available on microfilm and microfiche from University Microfilms International (UMI). Documents available from Article Express International, The Genuine Article, Ask*IEEE.
**Desc:** The purpose of the journal is to provide a forum for the publication of research and tutorial papers in computational mathematics. In addition to the traditional issues and problems in numerical analysis, the journal also publishes papers describing relevant applications in such fields as physics, fluid dynamics, engineering and other branches of applied science.
**Ind/Abst** Abstr. J. Earthq. Eng.; ACM Guide Comput. Lit.; Compumath Citation Index [Full Cov.]; Comput. Abstr.; Curr. Contents Phys. Chem. Earth Sci.; Eng. Index Annu. [Select. Cov.]; INSPEC (Jan. 1985-); Int. Abstr. Oper. Res. [Select. Cov.]; Math. Rev.; Res. Alert [Full Cov.]; Sci. Cit. Index; SCISEARCH; Zentralbl. Math. Ihre Grenzgeb.

US/0937-3195
**APPLIED PROBABILITY.** (APPLIED PROBABILITY : A SERIES OF THE APPLIED PROBABILITY TRUST.). [Appl. probab.]. **Added/Corp** Applied Probability Trust. (19??)-. Monographic series. English. ir. Price varies per volume. Springer-Verlag New York Inc., 175 5th Avenue, New York NY 10010. **Tel** (212)460-1500, telex 232 235 SPB UR. **(Subscription address:** Springer Verlag New York Inc. / for North America, 44 Hartz Way, Secaucus NJ 07096.**) ED** J. Gani, C.C. Heyde.
**Ind/Abst** Math. Rev.; Zentralbl. Math. Ihre Grenzgeb.

UK/8755-0024
**APPLIED STOCHASTIC MODELS AND DATA ANALYSIS.** [Appl. stoch. models data anal.]. Vol. 1, No. 1 (July 1985)-. Periodical. English. qt. $425.00. John Wiley & Sons Ltd., Baffins Lane, Chichester West Sussex PO19 1UD England. **Tel** 0243 779777, FAX 0243 776128 BTG:JWP001, telex 86290 WIBOOKG. **(Subscription address:** John Wiley / Philadelphia, PO Box 7247, Philadelphia PA 19170.**) ED** J. Janssen. **LC** QA274.A1; A65. **DD** 519.2. **CODEN** ASMAEM. **[CCC].** available on microfilm and microfiche from University Microfilms International (UMI). Documents available from Article Express International.
**Desc:** Aims to serve as the interface between the theoretical aspects of applied probability and data analysis and their applications in the real world. Compares the various methods available for solving real-life problems and initiates new methods for solving them by analyzing the relevant data.
**Ind/Abst** Biostatistica; Curr. Index Stat.; Eng. Index Annu. [Select. Cov.]; Math. Rev.; Qual. Control Appl. Stat.; Stat. Theory Method Abstr.; Zentralbl. Math. Ihre Grenzgeb.

US
**APPLIED TIME SERIES ANALYSIS.** Vol. 1,(1978)-. Periodical. English.

GW/0937-4051
**APPROXIMATION & OPTIMIZATION.** [Approx. optim.]. **VFOAT** Approximation and Optimization. (1991)-. Monographic series. English. ir. Price varies per volume. Verlag Peter Lang GmbH, Eschborner Landstrasse 42-50, D 60489 Frankfurt Germany. **Tel** 011 49 69 7807050. **UDC** 51.
**Ind/Abst** Zentralbl. Math. Ihre Grenzgeb.

CC/1000-9221
**APPROXIMATION THEORY AND ITS APPLICATIONS.** [Approx. theory its appl.]. **Added/Corp** Hua Chung Kung Hsueh Yuan. (1985)-. Periodical. English. qt (Mar., June, Sep., Dec.). 272.50F (includes distribution costs). Baltzer Science Publishers BV, Asterweg 1A, 1031 HL Amsterdam Netherlands. **Tel** 011 31 20 6370061, FAX 011 31 20 6323651. **LC** WMLC 93/681. ***Continues** Journal of Approximation Theory and its Applications.*
**Ind/Abst** Math. Rev. (1984-); Zentralbl. Math. Ihre Grenzgeb.

IQ
**ARAB JOURNAL OF MATHEMATICS, THE. Added/Corp** Union of Arab Physicists and Mathematicians. Vol. 1, No. 1 (1980)-. Periodical. English. sa.
**Ind/Abst** Math. Rev.

GW/0066-5673
**ARBEITEN ZUR ANGEWANDTEN STATISTIK.** [Arb. angew. Stat.]. No. 16 (1973)-. Monographic series. German. ir. Price varies per volume. Physics-Verlag, Tiergartenstr 17, 6900 Heidelberg Germany. **Tel** (06221)487492. **ED** K A Schaffer, P Schonfeld and W Wetzel. **LC** UNC. **Circ:** 300 (ctrl). ***Continues** Freie Universitat Berlin. Institut fur Statistik und Versicherungsmathematik. Berichte aus dem Institut fur Statistik und Versicherungsmathematik und aus dem Institut fur Angewandte Statistik der Freien Universitat Berlin.*
**Desc:** Monograph series on applied statistics.
**Ind/Abst** Math. Rev.; Zentralbl. Math. Ihre Grenzgeb.

IT/0003-8369
**ARCHIMEDE.** Vol. 1, No. 1 (Feb./Mar. 1949)-. Periodical. Italian. Four times a year. L30400.00 Italy; 54000.00 others. Editoriale Finanz Le Monnier, PB 202, Via Meucci 2, 50015 Grassina Florence Italy. **Tel** 011 39 55 64910. **LC** QA1; .A64795. **DD** 510/.5. **Bk Rev. Ad Acc. Circ:** 5,000. ***Continues** Bollettino di Matematica.*
**Desc:** An outline of different branches of mathematics. Historical development of concepts and theories of elementary mathematics, philosophy and methodology and didactics of mathematics.
**Ind/Abst** Zentralbl. Math. Ihre Grenzgeb.

SW/0003-889X
**ARCHIV DER MATHEMATIK.** [Arch. Math.]. **Added/Corp** Mathematisches Forschungsinstitut Oberwolfach. **VFOAT** Archives of Mathematics; Archives Mathematiques. Vol. 1 (1948)-. Periodical. German (English, French and German). mo. 932.40F Switzerland;

953.80F other. Birkhaeuser Verlag Ag, Klosterberg 23, PO Box 133, CH-4010 Basel Switzerland. **Tel** 011 41 61 2717400, FAX 011 41 0 61 2717666, telex 963475 birk ch. **(Subscription address:** Birkhauser Verlag AG, PO Box 151, CH 4106 Therwil Switzerland; Phone: 011 41 61 7217740**)** **ED** W. Klingenberg, H. W. Knobloch, H. Konig, E. Lamprecht, G. Michler, D Puppe, W. V. Walenfels. **LC** QA1; .A66. **DD** 510.5. **CODEN** ACVMAL. **[CCC]. Pr Rev.** available on microfilm from University Microfilms International (UMI). Documents available from The Genuine Article.
**Desc:** Publishes original contributions from the entire field of mathematics and its applications. Also publishes short but comprehensive authors' summaries of longer works which are not yet published, as well as a limited number of survey articles.
**Ind/Abst** Appl. Mech. Rev.; Compumath Citation Index [Full Cov.]; Curr. Contents Phys. Chem. Earth Sci.; Math. Rev.; Res. Alert [Full Cov.]; SCISEARCH; Stat. Theory Method Abstr. (1959-1963, 1966-1969, 1972-1976, 1979, 1983-1984, 1986-1987); Zentralbl. Math. Ihre Grenzgeb.

GW/0933-5846
**ARCHIVE FOR MATHEMATICAL LOGIC.** [Arch. math. log.]. Vol. 27 No. 1 (Feb. 1988)-. Periodical. English (German). Six times a year. DM598.00. Springer-Verlag GmbH & Company KG, Heidelberger Platz 3, D 14197 Berlin Germany. **Tel** 011 49 30 8207223, FAX 011 49 30 8214091, telex 183 319 SPBLN D. **(Subscription address:** Springer Verlag New York Inc. / for North America, 44 Hartz Way, Secaucus NJ 07096.**)** **ED** H D Ebbinghaus, A Blass, J E Fenstad, J Y Girard, R B Jensen, A Levy, W Maass, P Pudlak, K Schuette, H Schwichtenberg, T A Slaman, E Specker, S S Wainer, and M Ziegler. **LC** QA9.A1; A73. **DD** 511.3. **CODEN** AMLOEH. **[CCC].** available on microfilm and microfiche from University Microfilms International (UMI). Documents available from Ask*IEEE. ***Continues*** *Archiv fur Mathematische Logik und Grundlagenforschung, 0003-9268.*
**Desc:** Publishes research papers and occasionally surveys or expository papers on mathematical logic.
**Ind/Abst** Compumath Citation Index [Full Cov.]; Ei Page One; INSPEC (1988-); Math. Rev. (1988-); Zentralbl. Math. Ihre Grenzgeb.

XR/0044-8753
**ARCHIVUM MATHEMATICUM.** (ARCHIVUM MATHEMATICUM : SCRIPTA FACULTATIS SCIENTIARUM NATURALIUM UNIVERSITATIS PURKYNIANAE BRUNENSIS.). [Arch. math.]. (1965)-. Periodical. English (Russian, German, Czech and French). qt. Archivum Mathematicum, Department of Mathematics, Faculty of Science, Masaryk University, Janackovo Nam 2A 662 95, Brno Czech Republic. **ED** Demeter Krupka. **LC** QA1; .A696. **DD** 510/.5. **UDC** 51. **CODEN** ARVMAO. cum. index. **Circ:** 500 (ctrl).
**Desc:** Publishes mathematical papers in pure and applied mathematics containing new results or original methods in this field.
**Ind/Abst** Math. Rev.; Zentralbl. Math. Ihre Grenzgeb.

CL
**AREA MATEMATICAS.** 1-. Spanish. Direccion de Investigaciones Cientificas y Tecnologicas de la Universidad Tecnica del Estado etc, Avda Ecuador 3469, Santiago Chile. **LC** QA1; .A73. **UDC** 51.

US/0004-136X
**ARITHMETIC TEACHER, THE.** ***Title Change.*** [Arith. teach.]. **Added/Corp** National Council of Teachers of Mathematics. (1954)-(Sept. 1994). Periodical. English. Nine times a year. National Council of Teachers of Mathematics, 1906 Association Drive, Reston VA 22091. **Tel** (703)620-9840, FAX (703)476-2970. **ED** Harry B Tunis. **LC** QA135; .A6. **DD** 510.7. Index available. cum. index. **Bk Rev. Ad Acc. Circ:** 44,000 (ctrl). available on microfilm and microfiche from University Microfilms International (UMI); available on CD-ROM. Documents available from UMI Article Clearinghouse. ***Continued by*** *Teaching Children Mathematics.*
**Desc:** For elementary/middle school mathematics teachers and teacher educators. Articles cover mathematical content and methods of instruction. Reproducible worksheets and selected teaching materials, are featured.
**Ind/Abst** Acad. Abstr. Full Text Elite (July 1989-); Acad. Abstr. (July 1989-); Acad. Ind. [Computer File] (1987-); Acad. Search (July 1989-); Contents Pages Educ.; Curr. Index J. Educ.; Educ. Index; Except. Child Educ. Resour. (19??-19??); Expand. Acad. Index (1987-); INFO-SOUTH Abstr.; Mag. Artic. Summar. Elite (July 1989-May 1994); Mag. Artic. Summar. Select (July 1989-); Mag. Artic. Summar. CD-ROM (July 1989-); Mag. Search; Med. Rev. Dig.; Mid. Search (Jul. 1989-); Newsp. Period. Abstr. (1989-); Prim. Search (Jul. 1989-); Vocat. Search (July 1989-).

FI/0004-1920
**ARKHIMEDES.** [Arkhimedes]. 1949-. Academic Scholarly Publication. Finnish (Swedish; summaries and/or abstracts in English). sa. Fmk73.00. Akakeeminen-Kirjakuppa, PO Box 128, 00101 Helsinki Finland. **Tel** 011/358/0/90/12141, FAX +358 0 121 4441, telex 125080 AKAHE SF. **CODEN** AKMDA5. cum. index. Documents available from CASDDS.
**Ind/Abst** Chem. Abstr.; Energy Res. Abstr.; Math. Rev.; Zentralbl. Math. Ihre Grenzgeb.

SW/0004-2080
**ARKIV FUER MATEMATIK.** [Ark. mat.]. Vol. 1 (1952)-. Periodical. English (French and German). sa. $90.00. Institut Mittag-Leffler, Auravagen 17, S-182 62 Djursholm Sweden. **Tel** (08)7551809. **ED** L Arkeryd, L I Hedberg, J Peetre and U Persson. **LC** QA3; .A7. **UDC** 51. **CODEN** AKMTAJ. **Pr Rev.** Documents available from The Genuine Article, Ask*IEEE. ***Continues in part*** *Arkiv for Matematik, Astronomi Och Fysik, 0365-4133.*
**Ind/Abst** Compumath Citation Index [Full Cov.]; Curr. Contents Phys. Chem. Earth Sci.; INSPEC (1968-1986); Int. Aerosp. Abstr.; Math. Rev.; Res. Alert [Full Cov.]; Sci. Cit. Index; SCISEARCH; Stat. Theory Method Abstr. (1959-1963, 1968-1969, 1971, 1980-1981); Zentralbl. Math. Ihre Grenzgeb.

CN/0381-7032
**ARS COMBINATORIA.** [Ars comb.]. **Added/Corp** University of Waterloo. Dept. of Combinatorics and Optimization. Vol. 1 (June 1976)-. Periodical. English. sa. $76.00. Charles Babbage Research Centre, PO Box 272 St Norbert Postal Station, Winnipeg Manitoba R3V 1L6 Canada. **Tel** (204)474-8313, (204)772-2612. **ED** W L Kocay. **DD** 511/.6/05. **CODEN** ACOMDN. **[CCC]. Pr Rev. Circ:** 400. Documents available from The Genuine Article.
**Ind/Abst** Compumath Citation Index [Full Cov.]; Int. Abstr. Oper. Res. [Select. Cov.]; Math. Rev.; Res. Alert [Full Cov.]; SCISEARCH; Zentralbl. Math. Ihre Grenzgeb.

GW/0179-2148
**ASPECTS OF MATHEMATICS. D.** [Aps. math., D]. **VFOAT** Aspekte der Mathematik. D. (1984)-. Monographic series. German. ir. Price varies per volume. Vieweg Publishing, PO Box 5829, D 65048 Wiesbaden Germany. **Tel** 011 49 611 160230, FAX 011 49 611 160229. **UDC** 51.
**Ind/Abst** Zentralbl. Math. Ihre Grenzgeb.

GW/0179-2156
**ASPECTS OF MATHEMATICS. E.** [Asp. math., E]. **VFOAT** Aspekte der Mathematik. E. Vol. 1 (1981)-. Monographic series. English. ir. Price varies per volume. Vieweg Publishing, PO Box 5829, D 65048 Wiesbaden Germany. **Tel** 011 49 611 160230, FAX 011 49 611 160229. **LC** UNC.
**Ind/Abst** Math. Rev.; Zentralbl. Math. Ihre Grenzgeb.

US/1040-7650
**ASSISTANTSHIPS AND GRADUATE FELLOWSHIPS IN THE MATHEMATICAL SCIENCES.** **See** Education-Higher Education.

FR/0303-1179
**ASTERISQUE.** [Asterisque]. **Added/Corp** Societe Mathematique de France. (1973)-. Monographic series. French (French; summaries and/or abstracts in English). mo. $230.00. Societe Mathematique de France EC Norm Sup Tour L, 1 rue Maurice Arnoux, 92120 Montrouge France. **Tel** 011 33 1 40848054, or 91267464, FAX 011 33 1 40848052, or 91411751. **(Subscription address:** American Mathematical Society, PO Box 5904, Boston MA 02206-5904.**)** **ED** L. Szpino. **LC** UNC. **Pr Rev. Circ:** 900. Documents available from The Genuine Article.
**Desc:** Contains long papers of high quality lecture notes and seminar or conference proceedings, including proceedings of the Bourbaki Seminar.
**Ind/Abst** Compumath Citation Index [Full Cov.]; Math. Rev.; Res. Alert [Full Cov.]; SCISEARCH; Zentralbl. Math. Ihre Grenzgeb.

NE/0921-7134
**ASYMPTOTIC ANALYSIS.** [Asymptot. anal.]. Vol. 1, No. 1 (March 1988)-. Periodical. English. Eight times a year (2 volumes). Fl882.00. IOS Press, Van Diemenstraat 94, 1013 CN Amsterdam Netherlands. **Tel** 011 31 20 6382189, FAX 011 31 20 620 3419. **ED** L S Frank. **CODEN** ASANEZ. Index available. **Ad Acc. Pr Rev. Circ:** 900. available on microfilm and microfiche from University Microfilms International (UMI). Documents available from Ask*IEEE.
**Ind/Abst** INSPEC (Dec. 1989-); Math. Rev. (1988-); Zentralbl. Math. Ihre Grenzgeb.

CN/0705-9078
**ATLANTIC MATHEMATICS BULLETIN.** **Added/Corp** Atlantic Provinces Inter-University Committee on the Sciences. Vol. 1 (May 1977)-. Periodical. English. Limited free distribution. Z Star Mathematics Department, University of New Brunswick, Box 4400, Fredericton New Brunswick E3B 5A3 Canada. **DD** 510/.7/11715. ctrl circ.

IT/1120-6330
**ATTI DELLA ACCADEMIA NAZIONALE DEI LINCEI. RENDICONTI LINCEI. MATEMATICA E APPLICAZIONI.** (RENDICONTI LINCEI. MATEMATICA E APPLICAZIONI.). [Atti Accad. naz. Lincei, Rend. Lincei, Mat. applicazioni]. **Added/Corp** Accademia Nazionale dei Lincei. Classe di Scienze Fisiche, Matematica e Naturali. **VFOAT** Matematica e Applicazioni. Series 9, Vol. 1, No. 1 (1990)-. Periodical. Italian (English). Four times a year. L70000 Italy; L90000 other; Also comes with Rendiconti Lincei Science Fisiche e Naturali. Accademia Nazionale dei Lincei, Via Lungara 10 Uff Diff Pubbl., 00165 Rome Italy. **Tel** 011 39 6 6838831. **(Subscription address:** Bardi Editore, Salita de Crescenzi 16, 00186 Rome Italy.**)** **LC** QA1; .R336; QA1; .R452. **DD** 510/.5. **CODEN** ADAAER. Documents available from Ask*IEEE. ***Continues in part*** *Rendiconti (Accademia Nazionale dei Lincei. Classe di Scienze Fisiche, Matematiche e Naturali), 0392-7881.*
**Ind/Abst** Ei Page One; INSPEC.

IT
**ATTI DELLA SOCIETA DEI NATURALISTI E MATEMATICI DI MODENA.** **See** Science and Technology.

IT/0392-6680
**ATTI - INSTITUTO VENETO DI SCIENZE, LETTRE ED ARTI. CLASSE DI SCIENZE FISICHE, MATEMATICHE E NATURALI.** **See** Science and Technology.

AT/1034-4942
**AUSTRALASIAN JOURNAL OF COMBINATORICS, THE.** **Added/Corp** University of Queensland. Dept. of Mathematics. Vol. 1 (Mar. 1990)-. Periodical. English. sa (March and September). 66.00Aus$. University of Queensland / Mathematics Department, c/o Dr. A. Rahilly, St. Lucia Queensland 4072 Australia. **Tel** 11 61 7 3653277, FAX 11 61 7 8702272.

UK/0950-2815
**AUSTRALIAN MATHEMATICAL SOCIETY LECTURE SERIES.** [Aust. Math. Soc. lec. ser.]. **Added/Corp** Australian Mathematical Society. **VFOAT** Lecture Series. (1985)-. Monographic series. English. Price varies per volume. Cambridge University Press, The Edinburgh Building, Shaftesbury Road, Cambridge CB2 2RU United Kingdom. **Tel** 011 44 223 312393, FAX 011 44 223 325959. **(Subscription address:** Cambridge University Press, 110 Midland Avenue, Port Chester, NY 10573**)** **LC** UNC. **CODEN** AMSSEU. Documents available from BIOSIS Document Express.
**Ind/Abst** Biol. Abstr. (1989-); Math. Rev.; Zentralbl. Math. Ihre Grenzgeb.

AT/0045-0685
**AUSTRALIAN MATHEMATICS TEACHER, THE.** [Aust. math. teach.]. **Added/Corp** Australian Association of Mathematics Teachers. Vol. 1 (1945)-. Periodical. English. Four times a year. 40.00Aus$ Australia; 50.00Aus$ (surface mail), 60.00Aus$ (air mail) other. Australian Association of Math Teachers, GPO Box 1729, Adelaide SA 5001 Australia. **Tel** 11 61 8 3630288, FAX 11 61 8 3629288. **ED** Paul Scott. **Bk Rev. Ad Acc, Adv Mgr Tel** (08)3630288. **Circ:** 4,000.
**Desc:** A magazine type journal with a major focus on teachers of junior secondary mathematics.
**Ind/Abst** Aust. Educ. Index (1978-); Curr. Index J. Educ.

AT
**AUSTRALIAN SENIOR MATHEMATICS JOURNAL.** [Aust. sr. math. j.]. **Added/Corp** Australian Association of Mathematics Teachers. (1987)-. English. sa (May & Oct.). 31.21Aus$ (Australia); 39.01Aus$ (other). Australian Association of Math Teachers, GPO Box 1729, Adelaide SA 5001 Australia. **Tel** 11 61 8 3630288, FAX 11 61 8 3629288.
**Ind/Abst** Aust. Educ. Index (199?-).

PL/0137-6934
**BANACH CENTER PUBLICATIONS.** [Banach Cent. publ.]. **Main/Corp** Stefan Banach International Mathematical Center. Vol. 1 (1976)-. Monographic series. English (Russian). ir. Price varies per volume. **(Subscription address:** ARS Polona, PO Box 1001, 00068 Warsaw Poland.**)**
**Ind/Abst** Math. Rev.; Zentralbl. Math. Ihre Grenzgeb.

US/0362-1413
**BARRON'S REGENTS EXAMS AND ANSWERS, 9TH YEAR MATHEMATICS, ELEMENTARY ALGEBRA.** ***Title Change.*** (BARRON'S REGENTS EXAMS AND ANSWERS: NINTH YEAR MATHEMATICS, ELEMENTARY ALGEBRA.). [Barron's regents exams answ., 9th year math. elem. algebra]. **Main/Corp** Barron's Educational Series, Inc. **Added/Corp** Barron's Educational Series, Inc. Regents Exams and Answers: Ninth Year Mathematics, Elementary Algebra. **VAT** Barron's Regents Exams and Answers, Ninth Year Mathematics, Elementary Algebra. (19??)-(19??). English. Barrons Educational Series, 250 Wireless Boulevard, Hauppauge NY 11788. **Tel** (516)434-3311. **LC** QA157; .E915. **DD** 512.9/042/076. ***Continues*** *Exams and Answers: Elementary Algebra.* ***Continued by*** *Barron's Regents Exams and Answers. Three-year Sequence for High School Mathematics (Course I), 1069-2967.*

US/0191-3425
**BARRON'S REGENTS EXAMS AND ANSWERS: 10TH YEAR MATHEMATICS.** ***Title Change.*** **Main/Corp** Barron's Educational Series, Inc. **Added/Corp** Barron's Educational Series, Inc. Regents Exams and Answers: 10th Year Mathematics. **VFOAT** Regents Exams and Answers: 10th Year Mathematics. **VAT** Barron's Regents

Exams and Answers. Tenth Year Mathematics. (19??)-(19??). English. Barrons Educational Series, 250 Wireless Boulevard, Hauppauge NY 11788. **Tel** (516)434-3311. **LC** QA459; .E95. **DD** 516/.2/076. ***Continues*** *Exams and Answers: Tenth Year Mathematics.* ***Continued by*** *Barron's Regents Exams and Answers. Three-Year Sequence for High School Mathematics (Course II), 1069-2975.*

US/0146-406X
**BARRON'S REGENTS EXAMS AND ANSWERS: 11TH YEAR MATHEMATICS.** ***Title Change.*** [Barron's regents exams answ., 11th year math.]. **Main/Corp** Barron's Educational Series, Inc. **Added/Corp** Barrons's Educational Series, Inc. Regents Exams and Answers: 11th Year Mathematics. **VFOAT** Regents Exams' and Answers. **VAT** Barron's Regents Exams and Answers: Eleventh Year Mathematics. (19??)-(19??). English. Barrons Educational Series, 250 Wireless Boulevard, Hauppauge NY 11788. **Tel** (516)434-3311. **LC** QA43; .B3365a. **DD** 510/.76. ***Continued by*** *Barron's Regents Exams and Answers. Three-Year Sequence for High School Mathematics (Course III), 1069-2983.*

US/0362-0670
**BARRON'S REGENTS EXAMS AND ANSWERS : BUSINESS MATHEMATICS. See** Business.

SZ/1019-6242
**BASLER LEHRBUCHER.** [Basl. Lehrb.]. (199?)-. Monographic series. Multiple languages. ir. Price varies per volume. Birkhaeuser Verlag Ag, Klosterberg 23, PO Box 133, CH-4010 Basel Switzerland. **Tel** 011 41 61 2717400, FAX 011 41 0 61 2717666, telex 963475 birk ch. **UDC** 51.
**Ind/Abst** Zentralbl. Math. Ihre Grenzgeb.

GW/0172-1062
**BAYREUTHER MATHEMATISCHE SCHRIFTEN.** [Bayreuth. math. Schr.]. **Added/Corp** Universitat Bayreuth. (1979)-. Monographic series. German. **LC** QA1; .B154. **DD** 510/.5.
**Ind/Abst** Math. Rev.; Zentralbl. Math. Ihre Grenzgeb.

GW
**BEITRAEGE ZUR ALGEBRA UND GEOMETRIE. Added/Corp** Martin-Luther-Universiteat Halle-Wittenberg. No. 1 (1971)-. Periodical. German. an. 30M. Deutscher Verlag der Wissenschaften, Taubennstrasste 10, D 10117 Berlin Germany. **Tel** 011 49 30 2291146. **ED** O H Keller, O Krotenheerdt, E T Schmidt, and L Stammler. **LC** QA150; .B4. **Bk Rev. Ad Acc.** ctrl circ.
**Desc:** Articles by E Bohme, H Boseck, K Drechsler, U Sterz, B Goldschmidt, O H Keller, G Liebhold, B Renschuch, W Vogel, P Schreiber, B Schultz, L Stammler, G Geise and B Weibbach.
**Ind/Abst** Math. Rev.; Zentralbl. Math. Ihre Grenzgeb.

GW
**BEITRAGE ZUR DIFFERENTIALGEOMETRIE.** Monographic series. German. Price varies per volume. **LC** QA1; .B763 subser. **UDC** 514.7.

GW/0533-9480
**BERICHTE DER GESELLSCHAFT FUER MATHEMATIK UND DATENVERARBEITUNG.** [Ber. Ges. Math. Datenverarb.]. **VFOAT** Bericht - Gesellschaft fuer Mathematik und Datenverarbeitung; GMD-Bericht. (1968)-. Monographic series. Multiple languages. ir. Price varies per volume. R Oldenbourg Verlag, Postfach 801360, D 81613 Munich Germany. **Tel** 011 49 89 450190, FAX 011 49 89 45019305. **UDC** 51.
**Ind/Abst** Zentralbl. Math. Ihre Grenzgeb.

PL/0519-8356
**BIBLIOTEKA MATEMATYCZNA.** [Bibl. mat.]. (1953)-. Monographic series. Polish. Price varies per volume.
**Ind/Abst** Math. Rev.; Zentralbl. Math. Ihre Grenzgeb.

GW/0067-8821
**BIOMATHEMATICS (BERLIN). See** Biology.

GW/0323-3847
**BIOMETRICAL JOURNAL.** (BIOMETRICAL JOURNAL. BIOMETRISCHE ZEITSCHRIFT.). [Biom. j.]. **Added/Corp** Akademie der Wissenschaften der DDR. Zentralinstitut fuer Mathematik und Mechanik. **VFOAT** Biometrische Zeitschrift. Vol. 19, (1977)-. Academic Scholarly Publication. English (German; summaries and/or abstracts in French and Russian). Eight times a year. $580.00. Akademie-Verlag GmbH, Muehlenstrasse 33 34, D 13162 Berlin Germany. **Tel** 011 49 30 47889300, FAX 011 49 30 47889357. **(Subscription address:** VCH Publishers Inc., 303 Northwest 12th Avenue, Journals Department, Deerfield FL 33442.**) LC** QH323.5; .B562. **DD** 574/.072. **NLM** W1 BI858X. **CODEN** BIJODN. **[CCC].** Index Available, published separately, free-automatically sent. Documents available from The Genuine Article, BIOSIS Document Express, CASDDS. ***Continues*** *Biometrische Zeitschrift, 0006-3452.*
**Desc:** A journal of mathematical methods in biosciences. The scope includes new theoretical aspects of mathematics and its application to biological sciences in the widest sense (including biology, medicine agricultural science, forestry) or the application of known mathematical and statistical consideration of electronic data processing.
**Ind/Abst** Biol. Abstr.; Biostatistica; Chem. Abstr.; Compumath Citation Index [Full Cov.]; Curr. Index Stat.; EMBASE; Math. Rev.; Plant Breed. Abstr.; Qual. Control Appl. Stat.; Res. Alert [Full Cov.]; Risk Abstr. (19??-19??); SCISEARCH; Soc. Sci. Cit. Index [Select. Cov.]; Stat. Theory Method Abstr. (1978-1984, 1986-1987); Wheat Barley Trit. Abstr.; Zentralbl. Math. Ihre Grenzgeb.

BE/0006-3436
**BIOMETRIE-PRAXIMETRIE. See** Biology-Abstracting, Bibliographies and Statistics.

PL/0460-2366
**BIULETYN LUBELSKIE TOWARZYSTWA NAUKOWEGO. MATEMATYKA, FIZYKA-CHEMIA.** (BIULETYN. WYDZIA III : MATEMATYKA, FIZYKA-CHEMIA.). [Biul. Lubel. Tow. Nauk., Mat., fiz.-chem.]. **Main/Corp** Lubelskie Towarzystwo Naukowe. **VFOAT** Matematyka, Fizyka-Chemia. Began with Vol. for 1963/64. Polish (summaries and/or abstracts in English). 15.00. Zaklad Narodowy Im Ossolinskch, Ul Szewska 37, Wroclaw Poland. **LC** QA1; .L7813. **UDC** 5. **CODEN** BLTMDK. Documents available from CASDDS. ***Supersedes in part*** *Lubelskie Towarzystwo Naukowe. Biuletyn.*
**Ind/Abst** Chem. Abstr.; Math. Rev.

GW
**BLAETTER DER DEUTSCHEN GESELLSCHAFT FUER VERSICHERUNGSMATHEMATIK.** (19??)-. German. sa (2 issues). Price varies per volume. Konrad Triltsch Druck & Verlagsanstalt, PF 6660, D 97016 Wuerzburg Germany. **Tel** 011 49 931 308030.
**Ind/Abst** Zentralbl. Math. Ihre Grenzgeb.

BL/0100-3569
**BOLETIM DA SOCIEDADE BRASILEIRA DE MATEMATICA.** [Bol. Soc. Bras. Mat.]. **Main/Corp** Sociedade Brasileira de Matematica. **VFOAT** Bulletin. Vol. 1 (1970)-. Bulletin. Portuguese (English, French and Portuguese). sa. $96.00. Springer-Verlag New York Inc., 175 5th Avenue, New York NY 10010. **Tel** (212)460-1500, telex 232 235 SPB UR. **(Subscription address:** Springer Verlag New York Inc. / for North America, 44 Hartz Way, Secaucus NJ 07096.**) ED** J Palis. **LC** QA1; .S56527a. **CODEN** BSBMDD.
**Desc:** Publishes high class papers in mathematics that include such topics as quasi-periodic solutions of non-linear elliptic partial differential equations, polyhedrons and pistable homotopies from 3-manifolds into the plane, and single spaces of matrices and their applications in combinatorics.
**Ind/Abst** Math. Rev.; Stat. Theory Method Abstr. (1959-1963); Zentralbl. Math. Ihre Grenzgeb.

MX/0037-8615
**BOLETIN DE LA SOCIEDAD MATEMATICA MEXICANA.** [Bol. Soc. Mat. Mex.]. **Main/Corp** Sociedad Matematica Mexicana. (Oct. 1943)-. Periodical. Spanish. sa. $40.00. Sociedad Matematica Mexicana, Apartado Postal 14170, Mexico 14 DF Mexico. **LC** QA1; .S5652. **CODEN** BSMXAU.
**Ind/Abst** Math. Rev.; Zentralbl. Math. Ihre Grenzgeb.

IT/0392-4033
**BOLLETTINO DELLA UNIONE MATEMATICA ITALIANA. A.** [Boll. Unione mat. ital., A]. Ser. 5, Vol. 13, No. 1 (Feb. 1976)-. Periodical. English (Italian). Three times a year. Zanichelli Editore Spa, Via Irnerio 34, 40126 Bologna Italy. **Tel** 011 39 51 293263. **LC** QA1; .B67. **DD** 510/.5. **CODEN** BLUMAM. Documents available from The Genuine Article. ***Continues in part*** *Bollettino della Unione Matematica Italiana, 0041-7084.*
**Ind/Abst** Compumath Citation Index [Full Cov.]; Math. Rev.; Res. Alert [Full Cov.]; SCISEARCH.

IT/0392-4432
**BOLLETTINO DI STORIA DELLE SCIENZE MATEMATICHE.** (BOLLETTINO DI STORIA DELLE SCIENZE MATEMATICHE / UNIONE MATEMATICA ITALIANA.). [Boll. stor. sci. mat.]. **Added/Corp** Unione Matematica Italiana. Vol. 1 No. 1 (June 1981)-. Periodical. English (French, German, Italian and Latin). sa. L35000. Unione Matematica Italiana, Piazza Porta S Donato 5, 40127 Bologna, Italy. **Tel** 011 39 51 243190. **(Subscription address:** Editrice Compositori, Via Stalingrado 97 2, 40128 Bologna, Italy.**) ED** Vinicio Villani. **LC** QA21; .B64. **DD** 510/.9. **Bk Rev. Circ:** 1,000 (ctrl).
**Desc:** Publishes correspondence and manuscripts of interest in the history of mathematics, bibliographical essays and original papers concerning the history of mathematical sciences.
**Ind/Abst** Math. Rev.; Zentralbl. Math. Ihre Grenzgeb.

GW/0524-045X
**BONNER MATHEMATISCHE SCHRIFTEN.** [Bonner math. Schr.]. **Added/Corp** Universitat Bonn. Mathematisches Institut. No. 1 (1957)-. Monographic series. German. ir. Price varies per volume. Mathematisches Institut Universitat Library, Wegelerstrasse 10, D 53115 Bonn Germany. **LC** QA1; .B763. **DD** 510/.5.
**Ind/Abst** Math. Rev.; Zentralbl. Math. Ihre Grenzgeb.

US/1053-7422
**BROWN'S DIRECTORY OF INSTRUCTIONAL PROGRAMS (7-12). MATHEMATICS. See** Education-Teaching and Curriculum.

US/1053-7376
**BROWN'S DIRECTORY OF INSTRUCTIONAL PROGRAMS (K-8). MATHEMATICS / PREPARED AND COMPILED BY BROWN PUBLISHING NETWORK. See** Education-Early Childhood and Primary Education.

RM/0254-4385
**BULETINUL UNIVERSITATII DIN GALATI. FASCICULA II, MATEMATICA, FIZICA, MECANICA TEORETICA.** [Bul. Univ. Galati, Fasc. II, mat., fiz., mec. teor.]. **Added/Corp** Universitatea din Galati. (1978)-. Academic Scholarly Publication. English (French and German; summaries and/or abstracts in Romanian). an. Redactia Buletinului, 6200 Galati Str, Republicii Nr 47 Romania. **LC** QA1; .B773. **DD** 510/.5. **CODEN** BUGTD5. Documents available from CASDDS.
**Ind/Abst** Chem. Abstr. (1978-1981); Math. Rev.

CN/0316-8832
**BULLETIN AMQ.** [Bull. AMQ]. **Main/Corp** Association Mathematique du Quebec. Vol. 10 (1968)-. Bulletin. French. qt (Mar., May, Oct., Dec.). 65.00Can$ Canada; 72.00Can$ other. Association Mathematique Quebec, CP 9 Succ Rosemont, Montreal Quebec H1X 3B6 Canada. **Tel** (514)523-5700. **ED** Jean-Marie Labrie. **Bk Rev. Ad Acc. Circ:** 600. ***Continues*** *Association Mathematique du Quebec. Bulletin, 0044-9512.*
**Desc:** Articles on mathematics, class room experience from mathematics teachers, history of mathematic experience from high school, universities in mathematics and computer.
**Ind/Abst** Point Repere (1983-).

FR/0013-4511
**BULLETIN DE LA DIRECTION DES ETUDES ET RECHERCHES, ELECTRICITE DE FRANCE - SERIE C. MATHEMATIQUES, INFORMATIQUE.** (BULLETIN. SERIE C: MATHEMATIQUES, INFORMATIQUE.). [Bull. Dir. etud. rech. - Ser. C, Math., inform.]. **Main/Corp** Electricite de France. Direction des Etudes et Recherches. No. 1 (1968)-. Bulletin. French. sa. Electricite France Direction, Etudes 2 rue Louis Murat, 75784 Paris Cedex 08 France. **Tel** 011 33 1 40423126. **LC** QA1; .E49. **CODEN** EDBCAA. Documents available from Ask*IEEE.
**Ind/Abst** INSPEC (1970-); Int. Civil Eng. Abstr.

BE/0771-1204
**BULLETIN DE LA SOCIETE MATHEMATIQUE DE BELGIQUE. SERIE A.** ***Title Change.*** [Bull. Soc. math. Bel., Ser. A]. **Added/Corp** Societe Mathematique de Belgique. **VFOAT** Tijdschrift van het Belgisch Wiskundig Genootschap. Reeks B. Vol. 29, No. 1 (1977)-(1993). Periodical. English (French). bm. Societe Math Belgique, CP 218, 01 Boulevard du Triomphe, B 1050 Brussels Belgium. **Tel** 011 32 2 6505847, 011 32 2 6505864. **CODEN** BMBEAC. ***Continues in part*** *Bulletin de la Societe Mathematique de Belgique, 0373-2053.* ***Merged with*** *Bulletin de la Societe Mathematique de Belgique. Ser. B; Simon Stevin* ***to form*** *Bulletin of the Belgian Mathematical Society, Simon Stevin.*
**Ind/Abst** Math. Rev. (?-?); Zentralbl. Math. Ihre Grenzgeb. (?-?).

BE/0771-1158
**BULLETIN DE LA SOCIETE MATHEMATIQUE DE BELGIQUE. SERIE B.** ***Title Change.*** [Bull. Soc. math. Bel., Ser. B]. **Added/Corp** Societe Mathematique de Belgique. **VFOAT** Tijdschrift van het Belgisch Wiskundig Genootschap. Reeks B. Vol. 29, No. 1 (1st Quarter 1977)-(1993). Periodical. English (French). sa. Societe Math Belgique, CP 218, 01 Boulevard du Triomphe, B 1050 Brussels Belgium. **Tel** 011 32 2 6505847, 011 32 2 6505864. **CODEN** BMBEAC. ***Continues in part*** *Bulletin de la Societe Mathematique de Belgique, 0373-2053.* ***Merged with*** *Bulletin de la Societe Mathematique de Belgique. Serie A, 0771-1204; Simon Stevin* ***to form*** *Bulletin of the Belgian Mathematical Society, Simon Stevin.*
**Ind/Abst** Math. Rev.; Zentralbl. Math. Ihre Grenzgeb.

FR/0037-9484
**BULLETIN DE LA SOCIETE MATHEMATIQUE DE FRANCE.** [Bull. Soc. math. Fr.]. **Added/Corp** Societe Mathematique de France. Vol. 1 (1873)-. Bulletin. French. Four times a year (plus memoires). 910.00F Europe; 960.00F other. Societe Mathematique de France EC Norm Sup Tour L, 1 rue Maurice Arnoux, 92120 Montrouge France. **Tel** 011 33 1 40848054, or 91267464, FAX 011 33 1 40848052, or 91411751. **(Subscription address:** Centrale des Revues, 11 rue Gossin, 92543 Montrouge Cedex France.**)** **LC** QA1; .S6. **DD** 510/.5. **CODEN** BSMFAA. **[CCC].** cum. index. **Pr Rev.** Documents available from The Genuine Article.
**Ind/Abst** Compumath Citation Index; Energy Res. Abstr.; Math. Rev.; Res. Alert; SCISEARCH; Zentralbl. Math. Ihre Grenzgeb.

FR
**BULLETIN DE L'ASSOCIATION DES PROFESSEURS DE MATHEMATIQUES ET L'ENSEIGNEMENT PUBLIC.** **Main/Corp** Association des Professeurs de Mathematiques de l'Enseignement Public, Paris. No. 1 (1921)-. Periodical. French. Five times a year. 390.00F France; 540.00F other. Association des Professeurs de Mathematiques de L'Enseignement Public, 26 rue Dumeril, 75013 Paris France. **Tel** 33 1 43313405, FAX 33 1 43310732. **ED** N. E. Busser. **Bk Rev**, (Qty: 5). **Ad Acc. Circ:** 7,500 (ctrl).

CN/0848-7510
**BULLETIN DE MATHEMATIQUES ET SCIENCES.** [Bull. math. sci.]. **Added/Corp** Alberta. Student Evaluation and Records. (1989/1990)-. Bulletin. French. **DD** 500.71/27123. ***Continues*** *Mathematiques & Sciences., 0848-7502.*

FR/0007-4497
**BULLETIN DES SCIENCES MATHEMATIQUES.** [Bull. sci. math.]. **Added/Corp** France. Ministere de l'Education Nationale. Series 2, Vol. 9 (1885)-. Bulletin. French. Six times a year. 1160.00F France; 1560.00F other. Gauthier-Villars, 15 rue Gossin, 92543 Montrouge Cedex France. **Tel** 33 1 40 92 65 00, FAX 33 1 40 92 65 97. **(Subscription address:** Centrale des Revues, 11 rue Gossin, 92543 Montrouge Cedex France.**)** **ED** P. Malliavin. **CODEN** BSMQA9. **[CCC]. Ad Acc. Pr Rev. Circ:** 700. Documents available from The Genuine Article. ***Continues*** *Bulletin des Sciences Mathematiques et Astronomiques.*
**Desc:** Journal covering mathematics.
**Ind/Abst** Compumath Citation Index; Curr. Contents Phys. Chem. Earth Sci.; Math. Rev.; Res. Alert; Sci. Cit. Index; SCISEARCH; Zentralbl. Math. Ihre Grenzgeb.

UK/0950-5628
**BULLETIN - INSTITUTE OF MATHEMATICS AND ITS APPLICATIONS.** (BULLETIN.). [Bull. - Inst. Math. Appl.]. **Main/Corp** Institute of Mathematics and Its Applications. **Added/Corp** Institute of Mathematics and Its Applications. Vol. 1, No. 1 (March 1965)-. Bulletin. English. Eight times a year. Free (members); £75.00 (non-members). Institute of Mathematics & Its Applications, 16 Nelson Street, Southend-on-Sea, Essex SS1 1EF England. **Tel** 011 44 702 354020, FAX 011 44 702 354111. **ED** Catherine Richards. **CODEN** IMTABW. Index available. **Bk Rev. Ad Acc. Circ:** 7,000 (ctrl).
**Desc:** Contains articles of wide mathematical and professional interest, book reviews, reports of conferences, reports of meetings and news of members.
**Ind/Abst** Energy Res. Abstr. (Sept. 1980-); Math. Rev.; Stat. Theory Method Abstr. (1973-1975, 1977); Zentralbl. Math. Ihre Grenzgeb.

IE/0790-1690
**BULLETIN / IRISH MATHEMATICAL SOCIETY.** **Added/Corp** Irish Mathematical Society. **VFOAT** Irish Mathematical Society Bulletin. (198?)-. Bulletin. English. tq. ***Continues*** *Newsletter (Irish Mathematical Society), 0790-1690.*
**Ind/Abst** Math. Rev.; Zentralbl. Math. Ihre Grenzgeb.

RM/0373-2908
**BULLETIN MATHEMATIQUE DE LA SOCIETE DES SCIENCES MATHEMATIQUES DE LA REPUBLIQUE SOCIALISTE DE ROUMAINE.** [Bull. math. Soc. sci. math. Repub. Social. Roum.]. **Added/Corp** Societatea de Stiinte Matematice din Republica Socialista Romania. Vol. 8, No. 3/4 (1964)-. Bulletin. French (German and Russian). qt. $126.00. **(Subscription address:** Orion Press SRL, SPL Independentei 202-A, Bucharest 6 Romania.**)** **CODEN** BMSSB4. Documents available from Ask*IEEE. ***Continues*** *Bulletin Mathematique de la Societe des Sciences Mathematiques et Physiques de la Republique Populaire Roumaine.*
**Ind/Abst** INSPEC (1988-); Int. Aerosp. Abstr.; Math. Rev.

US/0273-0979
**BULLETIN (NEW SERIES) OF THE AMERICAN MATHEMATICAL SOCIETY.** [Bull., new ser., Am. Math. Soc.]. **Added/Corp** American Mathematical Society. Vol. 1, No. 1 (Jan. 1979)-. Bulletin. English. qt. $238.00. American Mathematical Society, PO Box 6248, Providence RI 02940-6248. **Tel** (800)321-4267, (401)455-4000, FAX (401)331-3842, telex 797192. **(Subscription address:** American Mathematical Society, PO Box 5904, Boston MA 02206-5904.**)** **LC** QA1; .B84. **DD** 510/.5. **[CCC]. Bk Rev. Pr Rev.** available on microfilm and microfiche from University Microfilms International (UMI). Documents available from The Genuine Article. ***Continues*** *Bulletin of the American Mathematical Society, 0002-9904.*
**Desc:** This journal contains expository articles and research announcements.
**Ind/Abst** Acad. Search (July 1993-); Compumath Citation Index [Full Cov.]; Gen. Sci. Index; Gen. Sci. Source (Jul. 1993-); INFO-SOUTH Abstr.; INIS Atomindex [Micro.]; Math. Rev. (1992-); Res. Alert [Full Cov.]; Sci. Cit. Index; SCISEARCH; Soc. Sci. Cit. Index [Select. Cov.]; Zentralbl. Math. Ihre Grenzgeb.

IR/1018-6301
**BULLETIN OF IRANIAN MATHEMATICAL SOCIETY.** [Bull. Iran. Math. Soc.]. **VFOAT** Bulletin of the Iranian Mathematical Society; BIMS. (1974)-. Periodical. English. Twice a year. $20.00. Iranian Mathematical Society, PO Box 13145 418, Tehran, Iran. **UDC** 51.
**Ind/Abst** Zentralbl. Math. Ihre Grenzgeb.

AG
**BULLETIN OF NUMBER THEORY AND RELATED TOPICS. BOLETIN DE TEORIA DE NUMEROS Y TEMAS CONEXOS.** **VFOAT** Boletin de Teoria de Numeros y Temas Conexos. Vol. 1 (Jan. 1975)-. Bulletin. English (German, Spanish and Italian). tq. $100.00 (airmail) US. Universidad del Salvador, Rodriguez Pena 640, 2 Piso, 1020 Buenos Aires Argentina. **Tel** 40-6645. **ED** Aldo Peretti, Carlos Raitzin, and Werner Nowak. Index available. **Bk Rev. Ad Acc. Circ:** 150.
**Desc:** Specialized publication on number theory.
**Ind/Abst** Math. Rev.; Ref. Z.; Zentralbl. Math. Ihre Grenzgeb.

II/0970-6577
**BULLETIN OF PURE & APPLIED SCIENCES. SEC. E, MATHEMATICS.** **VFOAT** Bulletin of Pure and Applied Sciences. Sec. E, Mathematics; Mathematics. (1985)-. Bulletin. English. an. $24.00. Dr Ajay Kumar Sharma, PO Box 38, Modinagar 201204 India. **(Subscription address:** Prints India, 11 Darya Ganj, New Delhi 110002 India.**)** **ED** A K Sharma. **LC** QA1; .B845. **DD** 510. **Bk Rev. Ad Acc. Pr Rev.** ctrl circ. ***Continues in part*** *Bulletin of Pure & Applied Sciences.*
**Desc:** Publishes research papers and book reviews.

II
**BULLETIN OF THE ALLAHABAD MATHEMATICAL SOCIETY.** **Added/Corp** Allahabad Mathematical Society. Vol. 1 (1986)-. Bulletin. English. an. $50.00. Allahabad Mathematical Society, 10 C S P Singh Marg, Allahabad 211 001 India. **Tel** 011 91 11 52208. **(Subscription address:** Prints India, 11 Darya Ganj, New Delhi 110002 India.**)**
**Ind/Abst** Zentralbl. Math. Ihre Grenzgeb.

AT/0004-9727
**BULLETIN OF THE AUSTRALIAN MATHEMATICAL SOCIETY.** [Bull. Aust. Math. Soc.]. **Added/Corp** Australian Mathematical Society. Vol. 1 (1969)-. Periodical. English. Six times a year (Feb., Apr., June, Aug., Oct., Dec.). 250.00Aus$ Australia; $192.00 US. Australian Mathematical Publishing Association, Department of Mathematics, Australian National University, Canberra ACT 0200 Australia. **Tel** 011 61 6 267 4268, FAX 011 61 6 267 4263. **LC** QA1; .A88. **DD** 510/.5. **CODEN** ALNBAB. **[CCC].** Index available. cum. index. **Bk Rev. Pr Rev. Circ:** 700. Documents available from The Genuine Article, Ask*IEEE.
**Desc:** Aims at the quick publication or original research in all branches of mathematics.
**Ind/Abst** Compumath Citation Index [Full Cov.]; INSPEC (1972-); Math. Rev.; Res. Alert [Full Cov.]; SCISEARCH; Stat. Theory Method Abstr. (1971, 1973, 1975, 1977-1982, 1984); Zentralbl. Math. Ihre Grenzgeb.

●BE
**BULLETIN OF THE BELGIAN MATHEMATICAL SOCIETY, SIMON STEVIN.** **Added/Corp** Societe Mathematique de Belgique. Vol. 1, No. 1 (Jan. 1994)-. Periodical. English (Dutch, French and German). Four times a year. Societe Math Belgique, CP 218, 01 Boulevard du Triomphe, B 1050 Brussels Belgium. **Tel** 011 32 2 6505847, 011 32 2 6505864. **LC** QA1; .B850. ***Formed by the union of*** *Bulletin de la Societe Mathematique de Belgique. Serie A; Bulletin de la Societe Mathematique de Belgique. Ser. B* ***and*** *Simon Stevin.*

II/0008-0659
**BULLETIN OF THE CALCUTTA MATHEMATICAL SOCIETY.** [Bull. Calcutta Math. Soc.]. **Main/Corp** Calcutta Mathematical Society. Vol. 1 (Apr. 1909)-. Bulletin. English. Six times a year. $100.00. University of Central Florida Department of Mathematics, PO Box 161364, Orlando FL 32816-1364. **Tel** (407)823-2754, (407)823-2478, FAX (407)823-3299. **LC** QA1; .C25. **CODEN** BCMSA5. **Bk Rev. Circ:** 800. Documents available from Ask*IEEE.
**Ind/Abst** INSPEC (June 1972-); Int. Aerosp. Abstr.; Math. Rev.; Stat. Theory Method Abstr.; Zentralbl. Math. Ihre Grenzgeb.

JA
**BULLETIN OF THE FACULTY OF SCIENCE, IBARAKI UNIVERSITY. SERIES A : MATHEMATICS.** **Main/Corp** Ibaraki Daigaku. Rigakubu. Sugaku Kyoshitsu. **Added/Corp** Ibaraki Daigaku. Rigakubu. Bulletin of the Faculty of Science, Ibaraki University. Series A: Mathematics. Ibaraki Daigaku. Rigakubu. Ibaraki Daigaku Rigakubu Kiyo. Sugaku. **VFOAT** Ibaraki Daigaku Rigakubu Kiyo (Sugaku). No. 1 (1968)-. Bulletin. English. an. Ibaraki University, Faculty of Science, Department of Mathematics, 1-1 Bunkyo 2-chome Mito-shi, Ibaraki-ken 310 Japan. **Tel** FAX 0292-27-8040. **LC** QA1; .I23. **DD** 510/.5. **CODEN** BFSMD7. **Bk Rev. Circ:** 300 (ctrl).
**Ind/Abst** Math. Rev.; Zentralbl. Math. Ihre Grenzgeb.

CN/1183-1278
**BULLETIN OF THE INSTITUTE OF COMBINATORICS AND ITS APPLICATIONS.** [Bull. Inst. Comb. appl.]. **Added/Corp** Institute of Combinatorics and its Applications. **VFOAT** Bulletin of the ICA. Vol. 1 (Jan. 1991)-. Bulletin. English. Three times a year. $75.00. Institute of Combinatorics and its Applications, 81 Walnut Street, Winnipeg Manitoba R3G 1N9 Canada. **DD** 511/.16.
**Ind/Abst** Math. Rev.

CH/0304-9825
**BULLETIN OF THE INSTITUTE OF MATHEMATICS, ACADEMIA SINICA.** [Bull. Inst. Math., Acad. Sin.]. **Main/Corp** Chung Yang Yen Chiu Yuan. Shu Hsueh Yen Chiu So. **Added/Corp** Chung Yang Yen Chiu Yuan. Shu Hsueh Yen Chiu So. **VFOAT** Shu Hsueh Chi Kan; Chung Yang Yen Chiu Yuan Shu Hsueh Chi Kan. Vol. 1 (June 1973)-. Periodical. English. Four times a year. $60.00. Academia Sinica / Dr. Feng Che Liu, Institute of Mathematics, Nankang Taipei Taiwan. **Tel** 886-2-78512111 ext. 383, FAX 886-2-7827432. **ED** Chii-Ruey Hwang and Ko-Wei Lih. **LC** QA1; .C525a. **DD** 510/.5. **CODEN** BIMSDG. **Circ:** 600.
**Desc:** High standard research articles in pure and applied Mathematics.
**Ind/Abst** Math. Rev.; Stat. Theory Method Abstr. (1978-1979, 1982-1984, 1986-1987); Zentralbl. Math. Ihre Grenzgeb.

KO/1015-8634
**BULLETIN OF THE KOREAN MATHEMATICAL SOCIETY.** [Bull. Korean Math. Soc.]. Periodical. English. qt. Korean Mathematical Society, 538 Dowha dong 706 Sung Ji, Seoul 121 Korea. **Tel** 011 82 2 7178604.
**Ind/Abst** Zentralbl. Math. Ihre Grenzgeb.

UK/0024-6093
**BULLETIN OF THE LONDON MATHEMATICAL SOCIETY, THE.** [Bull. Lond. Math. Soc.]. **Main/Corp** London Mathematical Society. Vol. 1, No. 1 (Mar. 1969)-. Academic Scholarly Publication. English. bm (January, March, May, July, September and November). $276.00 US, Canada & Mexico; £141.75 other. Cambridge University Press, The Edinburgh Building, Shaftesbury Road, Cambridge CB2 2RU United Kingdom. **Tel** 011 44 223 312393, FAX 011 44 223 325959. **(Subscription address:** Cambridge University Press / North America, 110 Midland Avenue, Port Chester NY 10573.**)** **ED** John D. S. Jones and John H. Rawnsley. **LC** QA1; .L496. **DD** 510/.5. **CODEN** LMSBBT. **Bk Rev. Pr Rev.** available on microfilm from University Microfilms International (UMI). Documents available from The Genuine Article.
**Desc:** Publishes short research articles as quickly as possible, with coverage extending across the whole of pure mathematics together with some of the more applied areas of analysis and theoretical computing. Also publishes survey articles and advanced, often very extensive, expositions. Occassional historical and biographical articles are published reviewing the life and mathematical achievements of distinguished mathematicians.
**Ind/Abst** Compumath Citation Index [Full Cov.]; Math. Rev.; Res. Alert [Full Cov.]; Sci. Cit. Index; SCISEARCH; Stat. Theory Method Abstr. (1971, 1973); Zentralbl. Math. Ihre Grenzgeb.

MY/0126-6705
**BULLETIN OF THE MALAYSIAN MATHEMATICAL SOCIETY.** [Bull. Malays. Math. Soc.]. **Main/Corp** Malaysian Mathematical Society. (19??)-. Bulletin. English. sa. $50.00 (institutions), $20.00 (individuals). Malaysian Mathematical Society, University of Malaya, Department of Mathematics, 59100 Kuala Lumpur Malaysia. **ED** S T Chin. **LC** QA1; .M266. **DD** 510/.5. **Pr Rev. Circ:** 1,000 (ctrl).
**Desc:** Publishes original research articles, expository

review papers and abstracts of thesis in all branches of mathematics.
**Ind/Abst** Math. Rev.; Zentralbl. Math. Ihre Grenzgeb.

II/0025-5556
**BULLETIN OF THE MATHEMATICAL ASSOCIATION OF INDIA.** [Bull. Math. Assoc. India]. **Added/Corp** Mathematical Association of India. Vol. 2, Nos. 1-4 (1970)-. Bulletin. English. qt. $15.00. Indian Books and Periodicals, 2429 Tilak Street, Pahar Ganj, New Delhi 110005 India. **(Subscription address:** Prints India, 11 Darya Ganj, New Delhi 110002 India.**)** **LC** QA11.A1; M27. ***Continues*** *Bulletin of Mathematical Association of India.*
**Ind/Abst** Math. Rev.

PL/0239-7269
**BULLETIN OF THE POLISH ACADEMY OF SCIENCES. MATHEMATICS.** [Bull. Pol. Acad. Sci., Math.]. **Added/Corp** Polska Akademia Nauk. **VFOAT** Mathematics. Vol. 31, No. 1/2 (1983)-. Bulletin. English (French, German and Russian). qt. $100.00. **(Subscription address:** ARS Polona, PO Box 1001, 00068 Warsaw Poland.**)** **LC** QA1; .B779. **DD** 510/.5. ***Continues*** *Bulletin de l'Academie Polonaise des Sciences. Serie des Sciences Mathematiques, 0137-639X.*
**Ind/Abst** Alum. Ind. Abstr. (1983-); Math. Rev. (1983-); Met. Abstr. (1983-); Zentralbl. Math. Ihre Grenzgeb. (1983-).

PL
**BULLETIN OF THE SECTION OF LOGIC.** **Added/Corp** Instytut Filozofii i Socjologii (Polska Akademia Nauk). Vol. 1, No. 1 (Feb. 1972)-. Periodical. English. Four times a year. Polish Academy of Sciences, Institute of Philosophy and Sociology, Nowy Swiat, Warsaw Poland. **(Subscription address:** ARS Polona, PO Box 1001, 00068 Warsaw Poland.**)**
**Ind/Abst** Philos. Index.

FR
**BULLETIN SIGNALETIQUE. 110.** **See** Mathematics-Abstracting, Bibliographies and Statistics.

SP/1130-4758
**BUTLLETI DE LES SOCIETATS CATALANES DE FISICA, QUIMICA, MATEMATIQUES I TECNOLOGIA.** **See** Physics.

FR
**CAHIERS DE TOPOLOGIE ET GEOMETRIE DIFFERENTIELLE CATEGORIQUES.** Vol. 25 (1984)-. Periodical. English (French). qt. 400.00F. Madame Ehresmann, UER Mathematique, 33 rue Saint-Leu, 80039 Amiens Cedex France. **Tel** 011 33 22 914722. **ED** Madame Ehresmann. **LC** QA611.A1; T665. **DD** 514/.05. Index available (bound in fourth issue). **Bk Rev**, (Qty: Irregular). **Ad Acc, Adv Mgr:** same as editor. **Pr Rev. Circ:** 450 (ctrl). ***Continues*** *Cahiers de Topologie et Geometrie Differentielle, 0008-0004.*
**Ind/Abst** Math. Rev.; Zentralbl. Math. Ihre Grenzgeb.

FR
**CAHIERS DU SEMINAIRE D'HISTOIRE DES MATHEMATIQUES.** **Added/Corp** Universite Pierre et Marie Curie. Laboratoire de Mathematiques Fondamentales. Ecole Pratique des Hautes Etudes (France). 1ere Section, Sciences Mathematiques. (1980)-. French.
**Ind/Abst** Zentralbl. Math. Ihre Grenzgeb.

IT/0008-0624
**CALCOLO.** [Calcolo]. Began with Jan./Mar. 1964 issue. Periodical. English (French, Italian and German). qt. $100.00. Calcolo, c/o IEI CNR, S Maria 46-56100 Pisa Italy. **Tel** 0039-50-553159, FAX 500342, telex 590305 IEICNRI. **(Subscription address:** Giardini Editorie Stampatori in Pisa, Via S Bibbiana 28, 56100 Pisa Italy**)** **LC** QA75.5; .C32. **DD** 001.6/4/05. **CODEN** CALOBK. cum. index. Documents available from Ask*IEEE.
**Desc:** Numerical analysis, theory of computation, computational complexity and analysis of algorithms.
**Ind/Abst** Comput. Rev.; INSPEC (Jan./March 1973-); Math. Rev.; Stat. Theory Method Abstr. (1967, 1969); Zentralbl. Math. Ihre Grenzgeb.

GW
**CALCULUS OF VARIATIONS AND PARTIAL DIFFERENTIAL EQUATIONS.** (1992)-. qt. DM480.00. Springer-Verlag GmbH & Company KG, Heidelberger Platz 3, D 14197 Berlin Germany. **Tel** 011 49 30 8207223, FAX 011 49 30 8214091, telex 183 319 SPBLN D. **(Subscription address:** Springer Verlag New York Inc. / for North America, 44 Hartz Way, Secaucus NJ 07096.**)**

UK/0950-6330
**CAMBRIDGE STUDIES IN ADVANCED MATHEMATICS.** [Camb. stud. adv. math.]. (1982)-. Monographic series. English. ir. Price varies per volume. Cambridge University Press, The Edinburgh Building, Shaftesbury Road, Cambridge CB2 2RU United Kingdom. **Tel** 011 44 223 312393, FAX 011 44 223 325959. **(Subscription address:** Cambridge University Press / North America, 110 Midland Avenue, Port Chester NY 10573.**)** **LC** UNC.
**Desc:** Series exploring different aspects of mathematics. Contains volumes on subjects such as finite group theory and random series of functions.
**Ind/Abst** Math. Rev.; Zentralbl. Math. Ihre Grenzgeb.

UK/0950-6284
**CAMBRIDGE TRACTS IN MATHEMATICS.** [Camb. tracts math.]. No. 64 (1973)-. Monographic series. English. ir. Price varies per volume. Cambridge University Press, The Edinburgh Building, Shaftesbury Road, Cambridge CB2 2RU United Kingdom. **Tel** 011 44 223 312393, FAX 011 44 223 325959. **(Subscription address:** Cambridge University Press / North America, 110 Midland Avenue, Port Chester NY 10573.**)** ***Continues*** *Cambridge Tracts in Mathematics and Mathematical Physics.*
**Ind/Abst** Math. Rev.; Zentralbl. Math. Ihre Grenzgeb.

US
**CANADIAN APPLIED MATHEMATICS QUARTERLY.** (1993)-. English. Four times a year. $175.00. Arizona State University / Rocky Mountain Mathematics Consortium, Department of Mathematics, Box 871904, Tempe AZ 85287-1904. **Tel** (602)965-3788.

CN/0008-414X
**CANADIAN JOURNAL OF MATHEMATICS.** [Can. j. math.]. **Added/Corp** Canadian Mathematical Congress. Canadian Mathematical Society. Canadian Mathematical Congress (Society). **VFOAT** Journal Canadien de Mathematiques. Vol. 1 (1949)-. Periodical. English (French). bm. 320.00Can$. University of Toronto Press, 5201 Dufferin Street, Downsview Ontario M3H 5T8 Canada. **Tel** (416)667-7781, (416)667-7782, FAX (416)667-7803. **ED** J. Carrell and N. Ghoussoub. **LC** QA1; .C36. **CODEN** CJMAAB. **[CCC].** Index available. **Pr Rev. Circ:** 1,200 (ctrl). available on microfilm and microfiche from University Microfilms International (UMI). Documents available from The Genuine Article.
**Desc:** Companion publication to the Canadian Mathematical Bulletin. It publishes the up to date research in the field of mathematics.
**Ind/Abst** Compumath Citation Index [Full Cov.]; Int. Aerosp. Abstr.; Math. Rev.; Res. Alert [Full Cov.]; SCISEARCH; Stat. Theory Method Abstr. (1967-1969, 1971, 1974-1975); Zentralbl. Math. Ihre Grenzgeb.

CN/0008-4395
**CANADIAN MATHEMATICAL BULLETIN.** [Can. math. bull.]. **Added/Corp** Canadian Mathematical Congress. Canadian Mathematical Congress (Society). Canadian Mathematical Society. **VFOAT** Bulletin Canadien de Mathematiques. Vol. 1 (1958)-. Periodical. English (French). qt. 160.00Can$. University of Toronto Press, 5201 Dufferin Street, Downsview Ontario M3H 5T8 Canada. **Tel** (416)667-7781, (416)667-7782, FAX (416)667-7803. **ED** S. Kochman and T. Salisburg. **CODEN** CMBUA9. **[CCC].** **Pr Rev. Circ:** 1,000 (ctrl). available on microfilm from University Microfilms International (UMI). Documents available from The Genuine Article.
**Desc:** Companion publication to the Canadian Journal of Mathematics. It publishes up to date research in the field of mathematics.
**Ind/Abst** Compumath Citation Index [Full Cov.]; Math. Rev.; Pollut. Abstr. Indexes; Res. Alert [Full Cov.]; SCISEARCH; Stat. Theory Method Abstr. (1967-1975, 1980-1982, 1984, 1986-1987); Zentralbl. Math. Ihre Grenzgeb.

BB/1017-6764
**CARIBBEAN JOURNAL OF MATHEMATICAL AND COMPUTING SCIENCES.** **Added/Corp** University of the West Indies (Cave Hill, Barbados). Vol. 1, No. 1 & 2 (Dec. 1991)-. Periodical. English. an. $40.00. Caribbean Journal of Mathematics, University of West Indies, PO Box 64, Bridgetown Barbados. **Tel** (809)425-1310. ***Continues*** *Caribbean Journal of Mathematics, 0253-3405.*

BB
**CARIBBEAN JOURNAL OF MATHEMATICS.** ***Title Change.*** [Caribb. j. math.]. Vol. 1, No. 1 (May/June 1982)-(19??). Periodical. English. Twice a year. Caribbean Journal of Mathematics, University of West Indies, PO Box 64, Bridgetown Barbados. **Tel** (809)425-1310. Index available. ***Continued by*** *Caribbean Journal of Mathematical and Computing Sciences.*
**Ind/Abst** Math. Rev.; Zentralbl. Math. Ihre Grenzgeb.

CN/0318-6288
**CARLETON MATHEMATICAL LECTURE NOTES.** **Added/Corp** Carleton University. Dept. of Mathematics. Vol. 1 (1972)-. Monographic series. English. Price varies per volume. Carleton University / Department of Mathematics, Colonel by Drive, Ottawa Ontario K1S 5B6 Canada. **Tel** (613)564-5500. **ED** Brian Mortimer. **DD** 510/.8. **Circ:** 120.
**Desc:** Mathematical lectures.

CN/0069-0600
**CARLETON MATHEMATICAL SERIES.** Monographic series. English. ir. Price varies per volume. Carleton University / Department of Mathematics, Colonel by Drive, Ottawa Ontario K1S 5B6 Canada. **Tel** (613)564-5500. **ED** Louis Nel. **DD** 510. **UDC** 51. Index available. **Circ:** 200.
**Desc:** Original research papers and expository surveys.

CN/0827-3669
**CARLETON-OTTAWA MATHEMATICAL LECTURE NOTE SERIES.** [Carlet.-Ott. math. lect. ser.]. **VFOAT** Exposes Mathematiques Carleton-Ottawa. (1984)-. Monographic series. English. ir. Price varie per volume. Carleton University / Department of Mathematics, Colonel by Drive, Ottawa Ontario K1S 5B6 Canada. **Tel** (613)564-5500. **DD** 510.8. ***Continues*** *Carleton Mathematical Lecture Notes, 0318-6288.*
**Ind/Abst** Zentralbl. Math. Ihre Grenzgeb.

US/0069-0813
**CARUS MATHEMATICAL MONOGRAPHS, THE.** (CARUS MATHEMATICAL MONOGRAPHS.). [Carus math. monogr.]. **Added/Corp** Mathematical Association of America. No. 1 (1925)-. Monographic series. English. ir. Price varies per volume. Mathematical Association of America, 1529 18th Street Northwest, Washington DC 20036. **Tel** (202)387-5200, (800)331-1622, FAX (202)265-2384. **CODEN** CAMMDL.
**Desc:** A series of expository books intended to make topics in pure and applied mathematics accessible to teachers, students, nonspecialists and scientific workers.
**Ind/Abst** Math. Rev.; Zentralbl. Math. Ihre Grenzgeb.

UK/0264-3138
**CASTME JOURNAL.** **See** Education-Teaching and Curriculum.

US/0163-9439
**CBMS-NSF REGIONAL CONFERENCE SERIES IN APPLIED MATHEMATICS.** **Main/Corp** Conference Board of the Mathematical Sciences. **Added/Corp** National Science Foundation (U.S.). **VFOAT** Regional Conference Series in Applied Mathematics. **VAT** Conference Board of the Mathematical Sciences-National Science Foundation Regional Conference Series in Applied Mathematics. Vol. 17 (1975)-. Monographic series. English. ir. Price varies per volume. Society for Industrial and Applied Mathematics, 3600 University City Science Center, Philadelphia PA 19104-2688. **Tel** (215)382-9800, (800)447-7426, FAX (215)386-7999, telex 446715. **CODEN** CRCMEN. ***Continues*** *Regional Conference Series in Applied Mathematics, 0097-4455.*
**Ind/Abst** Math. Rev.; Zentralbl. Math. Ihre Grenzgeb.

US/0933-2480
**CHANCE (NEW YORK).** (CHANCE.). [Chance]. Vol. 1, No. 1 (Winter 1988)-. Periodical. English. Four times a year. $22.00. American Statistical Association, 1429 Duke Street, Alexandria VA 22314. **Tel** (703)684-1221, (202)393-3253, FAX (703)684-2037 (orders). **(Subscription address:** North America: Springer Verlag, Journal Fulfillment Department, 44 Hartz Way, Secaucus, NJ 07096; Outside North America: Springer Verlag, Postfach 311340, D 10643 Berlin Germany**)** **ED** W F Eddy and S E Gienberg. **LC** QA276.A1; C45. **DD** 519.5/05. **CODEN** CNDCE4. **[CCC].** Documents available from Ask*IEEE.
**Desc:** Articles on statistical methods, reports of statistical computing programs, and discussions of technical problems. It also features articles of general interest and discussion of new developments in the social, biological, and medical sciences involving the use of statistical ideas. Co-published with Springer-Verlag Inc.
**Ind/Abst** Biostatistica; Curr. Index Stat.; INSPEC (Winter 1988-)(Winter 1988-1991); Qual. Control Appl. Stat.; Zentralbl. Math. Ihre Grenzgeb.

UK/0960-0779
**CHAOS, SOLITONS AND FRACTALS.** [Chaos solitons fractals]. Vol. 1, No. 1 (1991)-. Periodical. English. Twelve times a year. $887.00 The Americas; £595.00 other. Pergamon Press, An Imprint of Elsevier Science Ltd., The Boulevard, Langford Lane, Kidlington, Oxford OX5 1GB United Kingdom. **Tel** 011 44 865 843000, 011 44 865 843699, FAX 011 44 865 843010. **(Subscription address:** Elsevier Science Ltd. Oxford Fulfillment Centre, PO Box 800, Kidlington, Oxford OX5 1DX United Kingdom.**)** **ED** M.S. El Naschie. **LC** Q172.5.C45; C4297. **DD** 003/.7. **[CCC].** Documents available from Article Express International, Ask*IEEE.
**Desc:** Provides a medium for the rapid publication of full length original papers, short communications, reviews and tutorial articles in the following subjects: bifurcation and singularity theory, deterministic chaos and fractals, stability theory, formation of pattern, and more.
**Ind/Abst** Eng. Index Annu.; Fluid Abstr., Civil Eng.; Fluid Abstr. Proc. Eng.; FLUIDEX; INSPEC (1991-); Int. Aerosp. Abstr.; Math. Rev.; Sci. Cit. Index; Zentralbl. Math. Ihre Grenzgeb.

US/0069-3286
**CHICAGO LECTURES IN MATHEMATICS.** [Chicago lect. math.]. **VFOAT** Chicago Lectures in Mathematics Series. (1964)-. Monographic series. English. ir. Price varies per volume. University of Chicago Press / Book Department, 11030 South Langley Avenue, Chicago IL 60628. **Tel**

(800)621-2736, (312)568-1550, FAX (312)753-0811, telex 23933. **LC** UNC.
**Ind/Abst** Math. Rev.

II
**CHILDREN'S WORLD.** (19??)-. Periodical. English. mo. $12.00. Nehru House, 4 Bahadur Shah Zafar Marg, New Delhi India 110002. **(Subscription address:** Prints India, 11 Darya Ganj, New Delhi, 110002 India, (Phone: 011 91 11 3268645))

CC/0252-9599
**CHINESE ANNALS OF MATHEMATICS. SER. B.** [Chin. ann. math., Ser. B]. **VFOAT** Shu Hsueh Nien Kan Ser. B. Vol. 4, No. 1 (March 1983)-. Periodical. English. qt. 477.50F (includes distribution costs). Baltzer Science Publishers BV, Asterweg 1A, 1031 HL Amsterdam Netherlands. **Tel** 011 31 20 6370061, FAX 011 31 20 6323651. **ED** Ke Zhao, Li Daqian, and Li Guoping. **LC** QA1; .C457. **DD** 510/.5. Index available. **Bk Rev. Ad Acc. Pr Rev.** Documents available from The Genuine Article. ***Continues in part*** *Shu Hsueh Nien Kan, 0253-6137.*
**Ind/Abst** Compumath Citation Index [Full Cov.]; Curr. Contents Phys. Chem. Earth Sci.; Math. Rev.; Res. Alert [Full Cov.]; Sci. Cit. Index; SCISEARCH; Zentralbl. Math. Ihre Grenzgeb.

US/0898-5111
**CHINESE JOURNAL OF CONTEMPORARY MATHEMATICS.** [Chin. j. contemp. math.]. Vol. 9, No. 1 (1988)-. Periodical. English (translations available in Chinese). Four times a year. $410.00. Allerton Press, Inc., 150 Fifth Avenue, New York NY 10011. **Tel** (212)924-3950, FAX (212)463-9684, telex 427441 ALPRES. **LC** QA1; .S44723. **DD** 510/.5. **[CCC].**

CH/0379-7570
**CHINESE JOURNAL OF MATHEMATICS.** [Chin. j. math.]. **Added/Corp** Chung-hua Min Kuo Shu Hsueh Hui. Shu Hsueh yen Chiu Chung Hsin. **VFOAT** Chung-kuo Shu Hsueh Tsa Chih. Vol. 1 (June 1973)-. Periodical. English (French). Four times a year. $30.00. National Science Council, Republic of China, Math Res Promotion Center NTU, Taipei Taiwan. **Tel** 011 886 2 3633860. **ED** Huah Chu, Kuo-Shung Cheng, Minking Eie, Chang-Shou Lin, Pei-Yuan Wu, Su-Win Yang. **LC** QA1; .C49. **CODEN** CJMADE. Index available. cum. index. **Circ:** 400.
**Ind/Abst** Math. Rev.; Stat. Theory Method Abstr. (1982); Zentralbl. Math. Ihre Grenzgeb.

US/0899-4358
**CHINESE JOURNAL OF NUMERICAL MATHEMATICS AND APPLICATIONS.** [Chin. j. numer. math. appl.]. **Added/Corp** Academia Sinica. Chinese Academy of Sciences. Computing Center. **VFOAT** Numerical Mathematics and Applications. Vol. 10, No. 1 (1988)-. Academic Scholarly Publication. English (translations available in Chinese). Four times a year. $405.00. Allerton Press, Inc., 150 Fifth Avenue, New York NY 10011. **Tel** (212)924-3950, FAX (212)463-9684, telex 427441 ALPRES. **ED** Feng Kang. **LC** QA297; .C454. **DD** 519.4/05. **[CCC].**
**Desc:** A publication of the Chinese Academy of Sciences devoted to numerical analysis and numerical calculations.
**Ind/Abst** Math. Rev.

AT
**CIRCUIT NEWSLETTER FOR THE CANBERRA MATHEMATICAL ASSOCIATION.** Newsletter. English. Five times a year. Canberra Math Association, O'Connel Educational Centre, Stuart Street, Griffith ACT 2601 Australia.
**Ind/Abst** Aust. Educ. Index (?-?).

●CN/1193-9273
**CMS NOTES.** [CMS notes]. **Added/Corp** Canadian Mathematical Society. **VFOAT** Notes de la SMC. **VAT** Canadian Mathematical Society Notes. Vol. 24, # 1 (Jan./Feb. 1992)-. Periodical. English (summaries and/or abstracts in French). ir. Free to members. $20.00 per year, others. CMS Notes, 577 King Edward Avenue, Ottowa Ontario K1N 6N5 Canada. **DD** 510/.5. ***Continues*** *Canadian Mathematical Society. Notes., 0045-5164.*

SP/0010-0757
**COLLECTANEA MATHEMATICA (BARCELONA).** (COLLECTANEA MATHEMATICA / CONSEJO SUPERIOR DE INVESTIGACIONES CIENTIFICAS [Y] UNIVERSIDAD DE BARCELONA.). [Collect. math. (Barcelona)]. **Added/Corp** Seminario Matematico de Barcelona. Vol. 1, Issue 1 (1948)-. Periodical. English (German and Spanish). Three times a year. $50.00. Universidad de Barcelona / Spain, Gran Via 585 Ciencias Seminario, 08071 Barcelona Spain. **Tel** 011 34 3 3184266 ext. 2328. **ED** Joan Cerda. **LC** QD1; .C788. **CODEN** COLMBA. Index available. cum. index. ctrl circ. available on diskette.
**Ind/Abst** Math. Rev.; Stat. Theory Method Abstr. (1959-1963, 1982); Zentralbl. Math. Ihre Grenzgeb.

US
**COLLECTED ALGORITHMS FROM ACM.** **See** Computers.

US/0746-8342
**COLLEGE MATHEMATICS JOURNAL, THE.** (THE COLLEGE MATHEMATICS JOURNAL : AN OFFICIAL PUBLICATION OF THE MATHEMATICAL ASSOCIATION OF AMERICA.). [Coll. math. j.]. **Added/Corp** Mathematical Association of America. Vol. 15, No. 1 (Jan. 1984)-. Periodical. English. Five times a year. $98.00. Mathematical Association of America, 1529 18th Street Northwest, Washington DC 20036. **Tel** (202)387-5200, (800)331-1622, FAX (202)265-2384. **ED** Warren Page. **LC** QA11.A1; T9. **DD** 510/.071/1. **[CCC]. Bk Rev. Ad Acc. Circ:** 10,500. available on microfilm and microfiche from University Microfilms International (UMI). Documents available from UMI Article Clearinghouse. ***Continues*** *Two-Year College Mathematics Journal, 0049-4925.*
**Desc:** Contains articles of interest to those interested in undergraduate mathematics, problems, and solutions, and computer survey articles.
**Ind/Abst** Acad. Ind. [Computer File] (1992-); Acad. Search (Jan. 1993-); Contents Pages Educ.; Curr. Index J. Educ.; Educ. Index; Expand. Acad. Index (1989-); Gen. Sci. Index; Gen. Sci. Source (Jan. 1993-); Math. Rev. (1984-199?); Newsp. Period. Abstr. (1991-); Vocat. Search (July 1993-).

NE
**COLLOQUIA MATHEMATICA. Main/Corp** Bolyai Janos Matematikai Tarsulat. (19??)-. Monographic series. English. ir. Price varies per volume. Elsevier Science Publishers BV, PO Box 211, 1000 AE Amsterdam Netherlands. **Tel** 011 31 20 5803642, FAX 011 31 20 5862696, telex 15682. **(Subscription address:** Elsevier Science Inc. / New York Books, 655 Avenue of the Americas, New York NY 10010.**)**
**Ind/Abst** Math. Rev.

PL/0010-1354
**COLLOQUIUM MATHEMATICUM.** [Colloq. math.]. **Added/Corp** Instytut Matematyczny (Polska Akademia Nauk). Vol. 1 (1947)-. Periodical. English (French, German and Russian). ir. $84.00. **(Subscription address:** ARS Polona, PO Box 1001, 00068 Warsaw Poland.**) LC** QA1; .C68. cum. index. **Circ:** 2,000 (ctrl).
**Desc:** Publishes communications on new results, survey articles, programs of research, open problems in all fields of mathematics and its applications.
**Ind/Abst** GeoRef; Math. Rev.; Stat. Theory Method Abstr. (1959-1967, 1969, 1976-1983, 1986); Zentralbl. Math. Ihre Grenzgeb.

US/0065-9258
**COLLOQUIUM PUBLICATIONS / AMERICAN MATHEMATICAL SOCIETY.** **Added/Corp** American Mathematical Society. Vol. 6 (1927)-. Monographic series. English. ir. Price varies per volume. American Mathematical Society, PO Box 6248, Providence RI 02940-6248. **Tel** (800)321-4267, (401)455-4000, FAX (401)331-3842, telex 797192. **(Subscription address:** American Mathematical Society, PO Box 5904, Boston MA 02206-5904.**) [CCC].** ***Continues*** *Colloquium Lectures.*
**Ind/Abst** Math. Rev.

NE/0209-9683
**COMBINATORICA (BUDAPEST. 1981).** (COMBINATORICA : AN INTERNATIONAL JOURNAL OF THE JANOS BOLYAI MATHEMATICAL SOCIETY.). [Combinatorica]. Vol. 1 No. 1 (1981)-. Periodical. English. Four times a year. DM448.00. Springer-Verlag GmbH & Company KG, Heidelberger Platz 3, D 14197 Berlin Germany. **Tel** 011 49 30 8207223, FAX 011 49 30 8214091, telex 183 319 SPBLN D. **(Subscription address:** Springer Verlag New York Inc. / for North America, 44 Hartz Way, Secaucus NJ 07096.**) ED** Laszlo Lovasz. **LC** QA164; .C656. **DD** 511/.6/05. **UDC** 519.1. **CODEN** COMBDI. **[CCC]. Pr Rev.** available on microfilm and microfiche from University Microfilms International (UMI). Documents available from The Genuine Article, Ask*IEEE.
**Desc:** Papers from all branches of combinatorics, including: graph theory, hypergraphs, matroids, design, enumeration as well as from adjacent areas of mathematics, including: combinatorial probability, coding theory, combinatorial optimization, and complexity of computation.
**Ind/Abst** Compumath Citation Index [Full Cov.]; Comput. Rev.; INSPEC (1981-); Int. Abstr. Oper. Res. [Select. Cov.]; Math. Rev.; Res. Alert [Full Cov.]; SCISEARCH; Stat. Theory Method Abstr. (1984, 1986); Zentralbl. Math. Ihre Grenzgeb.

●UK/0963-5483
**COMBINATORICS, PROBABILITY & COMPUTING : CPC. VFOAT** Combinatorics, Probability and Computing; CPC. Vol. 1, No. 1 (Mar. 1992)-. Academic Scholarly Publication. English. qt. $176.00 US, Canada & Mexico; £96.00 other. Cambridge University Press, The Edinburgh Building, Shaftesbury Road, Cambridge CB2 2RU United Kingdom. **Tel** 011 44 223 312393, FAX 011 44 223 325959. **(Subscription address:** Cambridge University Press / North America, 110 Midland Avenue, Port Chester NY 10573.**) ED** Bela Bollobas. **LC** QA164; .C665. **DD** 511/.6/05.
**Desc:** Devoted to the three areas of combinatorics, probability theory and theoretical computer science. Topics covered include classical and algebraic graph theory, extremal set theory, matroid theory, probabilistic methods and random combinatorial structures, the theory of algorithms, computational learning theory and optimization.
**Ind/Abst** Math. Rev.

SZ/0010-2571
**COMMENTARII MATHEMATICI HELVETICI.** [Comment. math. Helv.]. **Added/Corp** Schweizerische Mathematische Gesellschaft. Vol. 1, No. 1 (1929)-. Periodical. English (French, German and Italian). Four times a year. 313.50F Switzerland; 326.80F other. Birkhaeuser Verlag Ag, Klosterberg 23, PO Box 133, CH-4010 Basel Switzerland. **Tel** 011 41 61 2717400, FAX 011 41 0 61 2717666, telex 963475 birk ch. **(Subscription address:** Birkhauser Verlag AG, PO Box 151, CH 4106 Therwil Switzerland; Phone: 011 41 61 7217740**) ED** A. Borel, E. Ghys, M. Kervaire, H. Kraft, M. Struwe and C. Weber. **LC** QA1; .C7. **CODEN** COMHAX. **[CCC].** cum. index. **Pr Rev.** available on microfilm from University Microfilms International (UMI). Documents available from The Genuine Article.
**Desc:** Publishes original papers on all aspects of pure mathematics and papers on applied mathematics.
**Ind/Abst** Compumath Citation Index [Full Cov.]; Curr. Contents Phys. Chem. Earth Sci.; Math. Rev.; Res. Alert [Full Cov.]; Sci. Cit. Index; SCISEARCH; Stat. Theory Method Abstr. (1959-1963); Zentralbl. Math. Ihre Grenzgeb.

JA/0010-258X
**COMMENTARII MATHEMATICI UNIVERSITATIS SANCTI PAULI.** [Comment. math. Univ. St. Pauli]. **Added/Corp** Rikkyo Daigaku. **VFOAT** Rikkyo Daigaku Sugaku Zassi. Vol. 1 (Dec. 1, 1952)-. Periodical. English (French and German). sa. $291.00. **(Subscription address:** Kinokuniya Company Ltd., 38-1 Sakuragaoka 5, chome Setagaya-ku, Tokyo 156 Japan.**) ED** T. Shioda. **LC** QA1; .C714. **CODEN** COMAAC.
**Ind/Abst** Math. Rev.; Zentralbl. Math. Ihre Grenzgeb.

XR/0010-2628
**COMMENTATIONES MATHEMATICAE UNIVERSITATIS CAROLINAE.** [Comment. math. Univ. Carolinae]. **Added/Corp** Universita Karlova. Matematicky Ustav. Universita Karlova. Matematicko-Fyzikalni Fakulta. **VFOAT** CMUC. Vol. 1 (1960)-. Periodical. German (English, French, German and Russian). qt. **(Subscription address:** Galloway & Porter Ltd., 30 Sidney Street, Cambridge CB2 3HS United Kingdom.**) LC** QA1; .C715. **CODEN** CMUCAA.
**Ind/Abst** Math. Rev.; Zentralbl. Math. Ihre Grenzgeb.

FI/0788-5717
**COMMENTATIONES PHYSICO-MATHEMATICAE ET CHEMICO-MEDICAE.** **See** Physics.

TU
**COMMUNICATIONS DE LA FACULTE DES SCIENCES DE L'UNIVERSITE D'ANKARA. SERIES AB1S, MATHEMATICS AND STATISTICS. VFOAT** Mathematics and Statistics. Periodical. French (English). sa. Faculty of Sciences, University of Ankara, 06 100, Ankara, Turkey. **Tel** (4)212-6720. **ED** Timur Dogu. ***Continues*** *Communications de la Faculte des Sciences de l'Universite d'Ankara. Serie A1. Mathematique.*

US/0092-7872
**COMMUNICATIONS IN ALGEBRA.** [Commun. Algebra]. Vol. 1 (1974)-. Periodical. English. Fourteen times a year. $1,675.00 US; $1,724.00 other. Marcel Dekker Inc., 270 Madison Avenue, New York NY 10016. **Tel** (212)696-9000, (800)228-1160, FAX (212)685-4540, telex 421419. **(Subscription address:** Marcel Dekker Inc, PO Box 5017, Monticello NY 12701.**) ED** Earl J. Taft. **LC** QA150; .C65. **DD** 512/.005. **CODEN** COALDM. **[CCC]. Bk Rev. Ad Acc. Pr Rev.** ctrl circ. available on microfiche. Documents available from The Genuine Article.
**Desc:** Gives the reader access to the competitively rapid publication of important articles of timely and enduring interest that have made this journal the premier international forum for the exchange of keystone algebraic ideas. Topics covered include nonexistent cycles, comma categories in representation theory, automorphisms of enveloping algebra, Engle margins in metabelian groups, and much more. No personal or institutional mathematics library can afford to be without this consistently superior, undeniably influential, on-going presentation of current interests and activities.
**Ind/Abst** Compumath Citation Index [Full Cov.]; Curr. Contents Phys. Chem. Earth Sci.; Math. Rev.; Phys. Briefs; Res. Alert [Full Cov.]; Sci. Cit. Index; SCISEARCH; Zentralbl. Math. Ihre Grenzgeb.

UK/0748-8025
**COMMUNICATIONS IN APPLIED NUMERICAL METHODS.** ***Title Change.*** [Commun. appl. numer. methods]. **VFOAT** CANM. Vol. 1 No. 1 (Jan. 1985)-(1992). English. bm. John Wiley & Sons Ltd., Baffins Lane, Chichester West Sussex PO19 1UD England. **Tel** 0243 779777, FAX 0243 776128 BTG:JWP001, telex 86290 WIBOOKG. **(Subscription address:** North, South and Central America/ John Wiley & Sons, Inc., PO Box 7247-8491, Philadelphia, PA

19170-8491) **ED** Roland W Lewis and Graham F Carey. **LC** TA335; .C65. **DD** 519.4. **CODEN** CANMER. **[CCC]. Bk Rev. Ad Acc. Pr Rev. Circ:** 1,500. available on microfilm and microfiche from University Microfilms International (UMI). Documents available from Article Express International, The Genuine Article, Ask*IEEE. ***Continued by*** *Communications in Numerical Methods in Engineering, 1069-8299.*
**Desc:** A international journal publishing short, refereed papers describing significant developments in numerical methods and the application of such techniques to the solution of practical engineering problems.
**Ind/Abst** Abstr. J. Earthq. Eng.; Appl. Mech. Rev.; Civ. Struct. Eng. Abstr.; Compumath Citation Index [Full Cov.]; Comput. Inf. Syst. Abstr. J. [Full Cov.]; Curr. Contents Eng. Tech. Appl. Sci.; Ei Page One; Eng. Index Annu.; Fluid Abstr., Civil Eng.; Fluid Abstr. Proc. Eng.; FLUIDEX; Geol. Abstr.; HTFS Dig.; INSPEC (Jan./Feb. 1987-); Int. Aerosp. Abstr.; Int. Civil Eng. Abstr.; Mater. Sci. Eng. Abstr.; Math. Rev.; Mech. Eng. Abstr.; Res. Alert [Full Cov.]; SCISEARCH; Soft. Abstr. Eng.; Zentralbl. Math. Ihre Grenzgeb.

GW/0010-3616
**COMMUNICATIONS IN MATHEMATICAL PHYSICS.** **See** Physics.

●UK/1069-8299
**COMMUNICATIONS IN NUMERICAL METHODS IN ENGINEERING.** [Commun. numer. methods eng.]. **VFOAT** CNME. Vol. 9, No. 1 (Jan. 1993)-. Periodical. English. mo. $595.00; $2,395.00 (combined subscription with International Journal for Numerical Methods in Engineering). John Wiley & Sons Ltd., Baffins Lane, Chichester West Sussex PO19 1UD England. **Tel** 0243 779777, FAX 0243 776128 BTG:JWP001, telex 86290 WIBOOKG. **(Subscription address:** John Wiley / Philadelphia, PO Box 7247, Philadelphia PA 19170.**) ED** R. W. Lewis and G. F. Carey. **LC** TA335; .C65. **DD** 519.4. **CODEN** CANMER. available on microfilm. ***Continues*** *Communications in Applied Numerical Methods, 0748-8025.*
**Desc:** Publishes short contributions describing significant developments in numerical methods and the applications of such techniques to the solution of practical engineering problems.

US/0360-5302
**COMMUNICATIONS IN PARTIAL DIFFERENTIAL EQUATIONS.** [Commun. partial differ. equ.]. Vol. 1 (1976)-. Periodical. English. mo. $895.00 US; $937.00 other. Marcel Dekker Inc., 270 Madison Avenue, New York NY 10016. **Tel** (212)696-9000, (800)228-1160, FAX (212)685-4540, telex 421419. **(Subscription address:** Marcel Dekker Inc, PO Box 5017, Monticello NY 12701.**) ED** M. G. Crandall and J. V. Ralston. **LC** QA377; .C76. **DD** 515/.353/05. **CODEN** CPDIDZCPIDZ. **[CCC]. Bk Rev. Ad Acc. Pr Rev.** ctrl circ. available on microfiche. Documents available from The Genuine Article.
**Desc:** Considers the mathematical aspects of partial differential equations and applications, including the theory of linear and nonlinear equations. These articles advance the study for basic problems of mathematical and scientific interest such as existence, uniqueness, and properties of solutions.
**Ind/Abst** Compumath Citation Index [Full Cov.]; Curr. Contents Phys. Chem. Earth Sci.; INIS Atomindex [Micro.]; Math. Rev.; Res. Alert [Full Cov.]; Sci. Cit. Index; SCISEARCH; Zentralbl. Math. Ihre Grenzgeb.

US/0361-0926
**COMMUNICATIONS IN STATISTICS : THEORY AND METHODS.** [Commun. stat., Theory Methods]. Vol. A5 (1976)-. English. mo. $1,395.00 US; $1,437.00 other; $2,195.00 US, $2,265.00 other (combined with Simulation & Computation and Stochastic Models). Marcel Dekker Inc., 270 Madison Avenue, New York NY 10016. **Tel** (212)696-9000, (800)228-1160, FAX (212)685-4540, telex 421419. **(Subscription address:** Marcel Dekker Inc, PO Box 5017, Monticello NY 12701.**) ED** William B. Smith, W. R. Schucany and A. M. Kshirsagar. **LC** QA276.A1; C66. **DD** 519.5/05. **CODEN** CSTMDC. **[CCC]. Bk Rev. Ad Acc.** available on microfiche. Documents available from The Genuine Article, BIOSIS Document Express, Ask*IEEE. ***Supersedes in part*** *Communications in Statistics, 0090-3272.*
**Desc:** As the first part of the multipart journal 'Communications in Statistics'. Part A focuses primarily on new applications of known statistical methods to actual problems in industry and government, and has a strong mathematical orientation to statistical studies. Additionally, it provides communications discussing practical problems with only ad hoc solutions or none at all; in either case, where there is a difference of opinion on particular techniques, all parties involved vigorously debate the issue with thought-provoking commentary.
**Ind/Abst** Biol. Abstr. (1987-); Biostatistica; Compumath Citation Index [Full Cov.]; Curr. Index Stat.; GeoRef; INSPEC (1976-); Math. Rev.; Oper. Res./Manag. Sci.; Pollut. Abstr. Indexes; Qual. Control Appl. Stat.; Res. Alert [Full Cov.]; Sci. Cit. Index (19??-19??); SCISEARCH; Soc. Sci. Cit. Index [Select. Cov.]; Stat. Theory Method Abstr. (1976-1984, 1986-1987); Zentralbl. Math. Ihre Grenzgeb.

IE/0070-7414
**COMMUNICATIONS OF THE DUBLIN INSTITUTE FOR ADVANCED STUDIES. SERIES A.** [Commun. Dublin Inst. Adv. Stud., Ser. A.]. **Added/Corp** Dublin Institute for Advanced Studies. **VFOAT** Sgribhinni Institiuid Ard-Leiinn Bhaile Atha Cliath. Spaith A. (1943)-. Monographic series. English. ir. Price varies per volume. Dublin Institute for Advanced Studies, 10 Burlington Road, Dublin 4 Ireland. **Tel** 011 353 1 680748. **CODEN** CDIAAH. **Circ:** 500. Documents available from Ask*IEEE.
**Desc:** Reports of research work in mathematics or theoretical physics done in the School of Theoretical Physics of DIAS.
**Ind/Abst** INSPEC (1968-); Math. Rev.; Zentralbl. Math. Ihre Grenzgeb.

US/0010-3640
**COMMUNICATIONS ON PURE AND APPLIED MATHEMATICS.** [Commun. pure appl. math.]. **Added/Corp** New York University. Institute for Mathematics and Mechanics. New York University. Institute of Mathematical Sciences. Courant Institute of Mathematical Sciences. Vol. 2 (1949)-. Periodical. English. Twelve times a year. $1,056.00 US; $1,176.00 Canada and Mexico; $1,221.00 other. John Wiley & Sons, Inc., 605 Third Avenue, New York NY 10158-0012. **Tel** (212)850-6000, (212)850-6645, FAX (212)850-6088, telex 12-7063. **(Subscription address:** John Wiley & Sons / England, Baffins Lane, Chichester, West Sussex PO19 1UD England.**) ED** Natascha A. Brunswick, Louis Nirenberg, and William Klump. **LC** QA1; .C718. **DD** 510. **CODEN** CPMAMV. **[CCC].** Index available in last issue of volume--attached. cum. index. **Ad Acc. Pr Rev. Circ:** 1,400. available on microfilm and microfiche from University Microfilms International (UMI). Documents available from The Genuine Article. ***Continues*** *Communications on Applied Mathematics.*
**Desc:** Recent developments in applied mathematics, mathematical physics, and mathematical analysis.
**Ind/Abst** Appl. Mech. Rev.; Compumath Citation Index [Full Cov.]; Curr. Contents Phys. Chem. Earth Sci.; Int. Aerosp. Abstr.; Math. Rev.; Res. Alert [Full Cov.]; Sci. Cit. Index; SCISEARCH; Stat. Theory Method Abstr. (1968); Zentralbl. Math. Ihre Grenzgeb.

US/0891-2513
**COMPLEX SYSTEMS.** [Complex syst.]. Vol. 1, No. 1 (Feb. 1987)-. Periodical. English. bm (6 issues). $295.00 (institutions), $85.00 (individuals). Complex Systems Publishing Inc, PO Box 6149, Champaign IL 61826. **Tel** (217)398-0700. **LC** QA267.5.C45; C65. **DD** 006.3. Documents available from Ask*IEEE.
**Ind/Abst** Comput. Rev.; INSPEC (Feb. 1987-); Math. Rev.; Zentralbl. Math. Ihre Grenzgeb.

US/0278-1077
**COMPLEX VARIABLES THEORY AND APPLICATION.** [Complex var., theory appl.]. Vol. 1, No. 1 (Sept. 1982)-. Periodical. English. qt (2 volumes). $678.00 (academic institutions), $1057.00 (corporate institutions). Gordon & Breach Science Publishers, Inc., PO Box 786, Cooper Station, New York NY 10276. **Tel** (212)206-8900, FAX (212)645-2459. **ED** Robert P. Gilbert. **LC** QA331; .C6535. **DD** 515.9/05. **CODEN** CVTADV. **[CCC]. Bk Rev. Ad Acc.**
**Ind/Abst** Math. Rev.; Zentralbl. Math. Ihre Grenzgeb.

●US/1076-2787
**COMPLEXITY (NEW YORK, N.Y.).** (COMPLEXITY.). (1993)-. Periodical. English. bm. $195.00 US; $215.25 other. John Wiley & Sons, Inc., 605 Third Avenue, New York NY 10158-0012. **Tel** (212)850-6000, (212)850-6645, FAX (212)850-6088, telex 12-7063. **(Subscription address:** John Wiley & Sons / England, Baffins Lane, Chichester, West Sussex PO19 1UD England.**)**

NE/0010-437X
**COMPOSITIO MATHEMATICA.** [Compos. math.]. Vol. 1 (Jan. 25, 1934)-. Periodical. English (French, German and Italian). ir (Fifteen issues per year). $1,845.00. Kluwer Academic Publishers, Postbus 322, 3300 AH Dordrecht, The Netherlands. **Tel** 011 (31) 78 524400, FAX 011 31 78 183273, telex 20083. **ED** G.M. van der Geer. **LC** QA1; .C73. **DD** 510.5. **CODEN** CMPMAF. **[CCC].** cum. index. **Ad Acc. Pr Rev. Acid Free. Circ:** 650 (ctrl). available on microfilm and microfiche from University Microfilms International (UMI). Documents available from The Genuine Article.
**Desc:** Aims to further the development of mathematics and international mathematical co-operation and communication by the publication of the highest level mathematical papers from all over the world, which have been carefully screened by experts in the field. The journal focuses on papers in the main stream of classical pure mathematics, more exactly the fields of number theory, algebraic and analytic geometry and topology.
**Ind/Abst** Compumath Citation Index [Full Cov.]; Curr. Contents Phys. Chem. Earth Sci.; Math. Rev.; Res. Alert [Full Cov.]; Sci. Cit. Index; SCISEARCH; Stat. Theory Method Abstr. (1959, 1968); Zentralbl. Math. Ihre Grenzgeb.

FR/0764-4442
**COMPTES RENDUS DE L'ACADEMIE DES SCIENCES. SERIE I, MATHEMATIQUE.** [C. r. Acad. sci., Ser. I, Math.]. **Added/Corp** Academie des Sciences (France). **VFOAT** Mathematique. Vol. 298, No. 1 (Jan. 7, 1984)-. Periodical. French (summaries and/or abstracts in English). Twenty-six times a year. 3080.00F France; 4370.00F other. Gauthier-Villars, 15 rue Gossin, 92543 Montrouge Cedex France. **Tel** 33 1 40 92 65 00, FAX 33 1 40 92 65 97. **(Subscription address:** Centrale des Revues, 11 rue Gossin, 92543 Montrouge Cedex France.**) LC** Q2; .A25. **DD** 510/.5. **[CCC].** Documents available from The Genuine Article, Ask*IEEE. ***Continues*** *Comptes Rendus des Seances de l'Academie des Sciences. Serie I, Mathematique, 0249-6291.*
**Ind/Abst** Compumath Citation Index; Curr. Contents Phys. Chem. Earth Sci.; Energy Res. Abstr.; INSPEC (April 1984-); Math. Rev.; Res. Alert; Sci. Cit. Index; SCISEARCH; Zentralbl. Math. Ihre Grenzgeb.

CN/0706-1994
**COMPTES RENDUS MATHEMATIQUES DE L'ACADEMIE DES SCIENCES.** [C.r. math. Acad. sci.]. **Main/Corp** Royal Society of Canada. Academy of Science. **VFOAT** Mathematical Reports of the Academy of Science. Vol. 1, No. 1 (1979)-. Periodical. English (French). Five times a year. 20.00Can$. Mathematical Reports, University of Toronto, Department of Mathematics, Toronto Ontario M5S 1A1 Canada. **Tel** (416)978-4804, FAX (416)978-4107. **ED** G.F.D. Duff. **LC** QA1; .R7a. **DD** 510/.5. Index available. **Pr Rev. Circ:** 300.
**Desc:** Quick publication of short papers summarizing important mathematical research. Also survey papers by fellows of the Royal Society of Canada on their fields of research.
**Ind/Abst** Math. Rev.; Zentralbl. Math. Ihre Grenzgeb.

US/0730-6199
**COMPUMATH CITATION INDEX : CMCI.** **See** Mathematics-Abstracting, Bibliographies and Statistics.

SZ/1016-3328
**COMPUTATIONAL COMPLEXITY.** Vol. 1, No. 1 (1991)-. Periodical. English. Four times a year. 415.50F Switzerland; 428.40F other. Birkhaeuser Verlag Ag, Klosterberg 23, PO Box 133, CH-4010 Basel Switzerland. **Tel** 011 41 61 2717400, FAX 011 41 0 61 2717666, telex 963475 birk ch. **(Subscription address:** Birkhauser Verlag AG, PO Box 151, CH 4106 Therwil Switzerland; Phone: 011 41 61 7217740**) ED** J. von zur Gathen. **LC** QA267; .C732. **CODEN** CPTCEU. **[CCC].** Index available. cum. index. **Bk Rev. Ad Acc, Adv Mgr:** Bavdo Perry. **Circ:** 400 (ctrl). Documents available from Ask*IEEE.
**Desc:** Presents research in computational complexity. Its subject is at the interface between mathematics and theoretical computer science, with a clear mathematical profile and strictly mathematical format.
**Ind/Abst** Comput. Rev.; INSPEC (1991-); Math. Rev.; Ref. Z.; Zentralbl. Math. Ihre Grenzgeb.

NE/0925-7721
**COMPUTATIONAL GEOMETRY.** [Comput. geom.]. Vol. 1 (1991)-. Academic Scholarly Publication. English. Six times a year (1 volume). Fl370.00. Elsevier Science Publishers BV, PO Box 211, 1000 AE Amsterdam Netherlands. **Tel** 011 31 20 5803642, FAX 011 31 20 5862696, telex 15682. **UDC** 681.31 :514. **[CCC].** available on microfilm and microfiche from University Microfilms International (UMI). Documents available from Ask*IEEE.
**Ind/Abst** ACM Guide Comput. Lit.; Comput. Rev.; Ei Page One; INSPEC (July 1991-); Zentralbl. Math. Ihre Grenzgeb.

●UK/0965-5425
**COMPUTATIONAL MATHEMATICS AND MATHEMATICAL PHYSICS.** Vol. 31, No. 1 (1992)-. Periodical. English (translations available in Russian). Twelve times a year. $1416.00 The Americas; £950.00 other. Pergamon Press, An Imprint of Elsevier Science Ltd., The Boulevard, Langford Lane, Kidlington, Oxford OX5 1GB United Kingdom. **Tel** 011 44 865 843000, 011 44 865 843699, FAX 011 44 865 843010. **(Subscription address:** Elsevier Science Ltd. Oxford Fulfillment Centre, PO Box 800, Kidlington, Oxford OX5 1DX United Kingdom.**) ED** AA Dorodnicyn. **LC** QA297; .Z53. **DD** 517.6. **[CCC].** available in microform. Documents available from The Genuine Article, Ask*IEEE. ***Continues*** *U.S.S.R. Computational Mathematics and Mathematical Physics, 0041-5553.*
**Desc:** Publishes papers on mathematical problems arising in all fields of science, e.g. physics, mechanics, computer theory, as well as papers of a purely mathematical nature.
**Ind/Abst** Compumath Citation Index [Full Cov.]; INSPEC; Int. Aerosp. Abstr.; Math. Rev.; Life Sci. Collect.; Res. Alert [Full Cov.]; Sage Race Relat. Abstr.; Soc. Sci. Cit. Index [Select. Cov.].

US/1046-283X
**COMPUTATIONAL MATHEMATICS AND MODELING.** [Comput. math. model.]. **Added/Corp** Consultants Bureau. Vol. 1, No. 1 (Jan.-Mar. 1990)-.

Periodical. English (translations available in Russian). qt. $475.00 US; $555.00 other. Consultants Bureau, A Division of Plenum Publishing Corporation, 233 Spring Street, New York NY 10013. **Tel** (212)620-8000, (212)620-8466, FAX (212)463-0742, telex 23/421139. **ED** W. A. Light and A. N. Tikhonov. **LC** QA76.95; .C63. **DD** 510/.285. **CODEN** CMMOEA. **[CCC].** available on microfilm. Documents available from Ask*IEEE.
**Ind/Abst** INSPEC (Jan.-Mar. 1990-).

NE/0926-6003
**COMPUTATIONAL OPTIMIZATION AND APPLICATIONS.** English. qt. $421.00. Kluwer Academic Publishers / Massachusetts, PO Box 358, Accord Station, Hingham MA 02018. **Tel** (617)871-6600. **(Subscription address:** Kluwer Academic Publishers Group, Journals Department, Distribution Centre, PO Box 322, 3300 AH Dordrecht, The Netherlands (Phone: 31-78-524400, FAX: 31-78-524474)) **ED** William Hager. **Pr Rev. Acid Free.** available on microfilm and microfiche from University Microfilms International (UMI).
**Desc:** It is committed to timely publication of research and tutorial papers on the analysis and development of computational algorithms for optimization. Topics of interest include: large scale optimization, unconstrained linear programming, constrained optimization, integer programming, complexity theory, automatic differentiation, modeling systems, and applications in engineering, finance, optimal control, optimal design, operations research, transportation, economics, communications, manufacturing, and management science and more.
**Ind/Abst** Inf. Sci. Abstr.

●GW
**COMPUTATIONAL STATISTICS. VFOAT** Comp Stat; CompStat. Vol. 7, Issue 1 (1992)-. Periodical. English. Four times a year. DM280.00. Physica-Verlag GmbH & Company, Postfach 105280, D-69042 Heidelberg Germany. **Tel** 06221 487-492, FAX 06221 487177 und 487366, telex 461723 sphdb-d. **(Subscription address:** Springer Verlag New York Inc. / for North America, 44 Hartz Way, Secaucus NJ 07096.**)** **ED** W. Harlde and D. W. Scott. **LC** QA276.4; .C573. **CODEN** CSTAEB. Documents available from Ask*IEEE. ***Continues*** *Computational Statistics Quarterly, 0723-712X.*
**Desc:** Promotes the publication of applications and methodological research in the field of computational statistics.
**Ind/Abst** INSPEC (1992-).

NE/0167-9473
**COMPUTATIONAL STATISTICS & DATA ANALYSIS.** [Comput. stat. data anal.]. **VFOAT** Computational Statistics and Data Analysis. Vol. 1, No. 1 (March 1983)-. Academic Scholarly Publication. English. Twelve times a year (2 volumes). Fl1650.00. Elsevier Science Publishers BV, PO Box 211, 1000 AE Amsterdam Netherlands. **Tel** 011 31 20 5803642, FAX 011 31 20 5862696, telex 15682. **ED** Stanley P Azen. **LC** QA276.A1; C665. **DD** 519.5/05. **CODEN** CSDADW. **[CCC]. Pr Rev.** available on microfilm and microfiche from University Microfilms International (UMI). Documents available from The Genuine Article, Ask*IEEE.
**Desc:** Provides a forum for the rapid dissemination of new research material in computational statistics and the analysis of data.
**Ind/Abst** ACM Guide Comput. Lit.; Biostatistica; Compumath Citation Index [Full Cov.]; Comput. Rev.; Curr. Index Stat.; Ei Page One; INSPEC (March 1983-); Math. Rev. (1983-); Pollut. Abstr. Indexes; Qual. Control Appl. Stat.; Res. Alert [Full Cov.]; SCISEARCH; Soc. Sci. Cit. Index [Select. Cov.]; Stat. Theory Method Abstr. (1983-1984, 1986-1987); Zentralbl. Math. Ihre Grenzgeb.

US
**COMPUTATIONAL TECHNIQUES.** Vol. 1 (1982)-. Monographic series. English. ir. Price varies per volume. Academic Press, Inc., 6277 Sea Harbor Drive, Orlando FL 32887. **Tel** (800)543-9534, (407)345-4100, FAX (407)363-9661.
**Ind/Abst** Zentralbl. Math. Ihre Grenzgeb.

US/0884-2027
**COMPUTER SCIENCE AND APPLIED MATHEMATICS.** ***Title Change.*** [Comput. sci. appl. math.]. Vol. 1 (1968)-(19??). Monographic series. English. ir. Academic Press, Inc., 6277 Sea Harbor Drive, Orlando FL 32887. **Tel** (800)543-9534, (407)345-4100, FAX (407)363-9661. **ED** Peter Lancaster and Miron Tismenetsky. **DD** 519. ***Continued by*** *Computer Science and Scientific Computing.*
**Ind/Abst** Math. Rev.

US/0888-2193
**COMPUTERS AND MATH SERIES.** **See** Computers.

CN/0731-1036
**CONFERENCE PROCEEDINGS / CANADIAN MATHEMATICAL SOCIETY.** [Conf. proc. - Can. Math. Soc.]. **Main/Corp** Canadian Mathematical Society. **Added/Corp** Canadian Mathematical Society. American Mathematical Society. **VFOAT** CMS Conference Proceedings. Vol. 1 (1981)-. Monographic series. English. ir. Price varies per volume. American Mathematical Society, PO Box 6248, Providence RI 02940-6248. **Tel** (800)321-4267, (401)455-4000, FAX (401)331-3842, telex 797192. **(Subscription address:** American Mathematical Society, PO Box 5904, Boston MA 02206-5904.**)** **LC** UNC. **[CCC].**
**Ind/Abst** Math. Rev.

IT/0374-2113
**CONFERENZE DEL SEMINARIO DI MATEMATICA DELL'UNIVERSITA DI BARI.** [Conf. Semin. Mat. Univ. Bari]. **Main/Corp** Universita de Bari. Seminario di Matematica. (1954)-. Monographic series. Italian (English and French). ir. Price varies per volume. Libreria Laterza, Via Sparano 134, 70121 Bari Italy. **Tel** 011 39 80 5211780, FAX 011 39 80 235228, telex 811253. **LC** QA3; .B265. **DD** 510. **CODEN** CSMUAW. Index available. ctrl circ.
**Ind/Abst** Math. Rev.; Zentralbl. Math. Ihre Grenzgeb.

CN/0384-9864
**CONGRESSUS NUMERANTIUM.** [Congr. numer.]. **Added/Corp** Louisiana Conference on Combinatorics, Graph Theory, and Computing. Southeastern Conference on Combinatorics, Graph Theory, and Computing. Manitoba Conference on Numerical Mathematics. Manitoba Conference on Numerical Mathematics and Computing. Canadian Workshop on the Design and Development of Computer Systems. British Combinatorial Conference. Conference on Algebraic Aspects of Combinatorics. Sundance Conference. International Conference on Algol 68 Implementation. West Coast Conference on Combinatorics, Graph Theory, and Computing. (1970)-. Monographic series. English. ir. Price varies per volume. Utilitas Mathematica Publishing Inc., University of Manitoba, Box 7, University Center, Winnipeg Manitoba R3T 2N2 Canada. **Tel** (204)474-8313, (204)474-8675. **LC** QA1; .C76. **DD** 510/.5. **Pr Rev. Circ:** 400. ***Absorbed*** *Southeastern Conference on Combinatorics, Graph Theory, and Computing, 0316-1382.*
**Desc:** A conference journal on numerical themes.
**Ind/Abst** Math. Rev.; Zentralbl. Math. Ihre Grenzgeb.

US/0176-4276
**CONSTRUCTIVE APPROXIMATION.** Vol. 1, No. 1 (1985)-. Periodical. English. qt. $192.00. Springer-Verlag New York Inc., 175 5th Avenue, New York NY 10010. **Tel** (212)460-1500, telex 232 235 SPB UR. **(Subscription address:** Springer Verlag New York Inc. / for North America, 44 Hartz Way, Secaucus NJ 07096.**)** **ED** R A DeVore and E B Staff. **[CCC]. Pr Rev.** available in microform from University Microfilms International (UMI). Documents available from The Genuine Article.
**Desc:** Concerns those aspects of approximation and expansions that relate to work in computation, function theory, interpolation of operators, numerical analysis, orthogonal polynomials, space of functions, special functions and applied areas.
**Ind/Abst** Compumath Citation Index [Full Cov.]; Math. Rev. (1985-); Res. Alert [Full Cov.]; SCISEARCH; Zentralbl. Math. Ihre Grenzgeb.

US/0271-4132
**CONTEMPORARY MATHEMATICS (AMERICAN MATHEMATICAL SOCIETY).** (CONTEMPORARY MATHEMATICS.). [Contemp. math.]. **Added/Corp** American Mathematical Society. Vol. 1 (1980)-. Monographic series. English. ir. Price varies per volume. American Mathematical Society, PO Box 6248, Providence RI 02940-6248. **Tel** (800)321-4267, (401)455-4000, FAX (401)331-3842, telex 797192. **(Subscription address:** American Mathematical Society, PO Box 5904, Boston MA 02206-5904.**)** **LC** UNC. **[CCC].** Documents available from Ask*IEEE.
**Ind/Abst** INSPEC; Math. Rev.; Zentralbl. Math. Ihre Grenzgeb.

IT/0394-0705
**CONTRIBUTI DEL CENTRO LINCEO INTERDISCIPLINAIRE BENIAMINO SEGRE.** [Contrib. Centro linceo interdiscipl. Beniamino Segre]. (1987)-. Monographic series. Italian. ir. Price varies per volume. Accademia Nazionale dei Lincei, Via Lungara 10 Uff Diff Pubbl., 00165 Rome Italy. **Tel** 011 39 6 6838831. **(Subscription address:** Bardi Editore, Salita de Crescenzi 16, 00186 Rome Italy.**)** **UDC** 51. ***Continues*** *Contributi del Centro Linceo Interdisciplinare di Scienze Matematiche e Loro Applicazioni, 0391-8041.*

IT/0391-8041
**CONTRIBUTI DEL CENTRO LINCEO INTERDISCIPLINARE DI SCIENZE E LORO APPLICAZIONI.** ***Title Change.*** [Contrib. Cent. linceo interdiscip. sci. appl.]. **Main/Corp** Accademia Nazionale dei Linceo, Roma. Centro Linceo Interdisciplinare di Scienze Matematiche e Loro Applicazioni. **Added/Corp** Accademia Nazionale dei Lincei. No. 1 (1974)-(19??). Academic Scholarly Publication. Italian. ir. Accademia Nazionale dei Lincei, Via Lungara 10 Uff Diff Pubbl., 00165 Rome Italy. **Tel** 011 39 6 6838831. **CODEN** CCLADS. Documents available from CASDDS. ***Continued by*** *Del Centro Linceo Interdisciplinare Beniamino Segre.*
**Ind/Abst** Chem. Abstr.; Zentralbl. Math. Ihre Grenzgeb.

AU/1011-8918
**CONTRIBUTIONS TO GENERAL ALGEBRA.** [Contrib. gen. algebra]. (1979)-. Periodical. English.
**Ind/Abst** Zentralbl. Math. Ihre Grenzgeb.

US
**CRC STANDARD MATHEMATICAL TABLES AND FORMULAE. Added/Corp** Chemical Rubber Company. **VFOAT** Standard Mathematical Tables and Formulae. **VAT** Chemical Rubber Company Standard Mathematical Tables and Formulae. 29th Ed. (1991)-. English. ir. $39.95. CRC Press Inc., 2000 Corporate Boulevard Northwest, Boca Raton FL 33431. **Tel** (407)994-0555, (800)272-7737, FAX (407)998-9784, telex 568689. **(Subscription address:** CRC Press Inc., PO Box 750, Pearl River NY 10965.**)** **LC** QA47; .M315. **DD** 510/.212. ***Continues*** *CRC Standard Mathematical Tables.*

●US/1065-8599
**CRM MONOGRAPH SERIES / CENTRE DE RECHERCHES MATHEMATIQUES. Added/Corp** American Mathematical Society. Universite de Montreal. Centre de Recherches Mathematiques. (1992)-. Monographic series. English. ir. Price varies per volume. American Mathematical Society, PO Box 6248, Providence RI 02940-6248. **Tel** (800)321-4267, (401)455-4000, FAX (401)331-3842, telex 797192. **(Subscription address:** American Mathematical Society, PO Box 5904, Boston MA 02206-5904.**)** **[CCC].**

●US/1065-8580
**CRM PROCEEDINGS & LECTURE NOTES.** [CRM proc. lect. notes]. **Added/Corp** Universite de Montreal. Centre de Recherches Mathematiques. American Mathematical Society. **VFOAT** CRM Proceedings and Lecture Notes. **VAT** Centre de Recherches Mathematiques Proceedings & Lecture Notes. Vol. 1 (1993)-. Monographic series. English. ir. Price varies per volume. American Mathematical Society, PO Box 6248, Providence RI 02940-6248. **Tel** (800)321-4267, (401)455-4000, FAX (401)331-3842, telex 797192. **(Subscription address:** American Mathematical Society, PO Box 5904, Boston MA 02206-5904.**)** **DD** 510. **[CCC].**

AT
**CROSS SECTION.** (19??)-. English. Eight times a year. 20.00Aus$. Mathematical Association of Western Australia, PO Box 492, Subiaco 6008 Australia. **Tel** 61 09 349-1380. ***Continues*** *Sigma Australia, 0314-7606.*
**Ind/Abst** Aust. Educ. Index (19??-).

CN/0705-0348
**CRUX MATHEMATICORUM. Added/Corp** Carleton-Ottawa Mathematics Association. Algonquin College. Vol. 4 No. 3 (1978)-. Periodical. English (French). mo (10 issues). 50.00Can$. Canadian Mathematical Society, 577 King Edward Avenue, Suite 109, Ottawa Ontario K1N 6N5 Canada. **Tel** (613)564-2223. **DD** 510/.5. **Bk Rev**, (Qty: (varies per year)). **Circ:** 700. ***Continues*** *Eureka, 0700-558X.*
**Ind/Abst** BMT Abstr. (-19??).

US
**CSLI LECTURE NOTES. Added/Corp** Center for the Study of Language and Information (U.S.). No. 1 (1985)-. Monographic series. English. Price varies per volume.
**Ind/Abst** Math. Rev. (1987-); Zentralbl. Math. Ihre Grenzgeb.

SP
**CUADERNOS DE ALGEBRA. Added/Corp** Universidad de Granada. Departmento de Algebra y Fundamentos. No. 1 (Nov. 1984)-. Monographic series. English.
**Ind/Abst** Math. Rev.; Zentralbl. Math. Ihre Grenzgeb.

US/0276-220X
**CURRENT CONTENTS. COMPUMATH.** [Curr. contents. CompuMath]. **Added/Corp** Institute for Scientific Information. **VFOAT** CompuMath; C.C./CompuMath; CC/CompuMath. Vol. 1, No. 1 (July 1981)-. Academic Scholarly Publication. English. mo. Institute for Scientific Information, 3501 Market Street, Philadelphia PA 19104. **Tel** (215)386-0100, (800)523-1850, FAX (215)386-6362, telex 84-5305. **(Subscription address:** Institute for Scientific Information, PO Box 71416, Chicago, IL 60694) **LC** Z6653; .C88; QA1. **DD** 016.51.
**Ind/Abst** Math. Rev.

US/0364-1228
**CURRENT INDEX TO STATISTICS.** **See** Mathematics-Abstracting, Bibliographies and Statistics.

US/0361-4794
**CURRENT MATHEMATICAL PUBLICATIONS.** **See** Mathematics-Abstracting, Bibliographies and Statistics.

NE/0169-4669
**CWI MONOGRAPHS.** (1984)-. Monographic series. English. ir. Price varies per volume. North-Holland

Publishing Company, PO Box 211, Amsterdam The Netherlands. **UDC** 51.
**Ind/Abst** Zentralbl. Math. Ihre Grenzgeb.

NE
**CWI QUARTERLY.** **Added/Corp** Centrum voor Wiskunde en Informatica (Amsterdam, Netherlands). **VFOAT** Quarterly. Vol. 1 No. 3 (Sept. 1988)-. Periodical. English. qt. Fl94.34. Centrum voor Wiskunde en Informatica, PO Box 94079, 1009 GB Amsterdam Netherlands. **Tel** 011 31 20 5929333, FAX 011 31 20 5924199, telex 12571. **LC** WMLC 93/1828. ***Continues*** *Quarterly (Centrum voor Wiskunde en Informatica (Amsterdam, Netherlands)).*

NE
**CWI SYLLABUS.** **Added/Corp** Centrum voor Wiskunde en Informatica (Amsterdam, Netherlands). **VFOAT** C.W.I. Syllabus; CWI Syllabi. (1984)-. Monographic series. English. Price varies per volume.
**Ind/Abst** Math. Rev.; Zentralbl. Math. Ihre Grenzgeb.

NE
**CWI TRACT / CENTRUM VOOR WISKUNDE EN INFORMATICA.** **Added/Corp** Centrum voor Wiskunde en Informatica (Amsterdam, Netherlands). (1984)-. Monographic series. English. ir. Price varies per volume. Centrum voor Wiskunde en Informatica, PO Box 94079, 1009 GB Amsterdam Netherlands. **Tel** 011 31 20 5929333, FAX 011 31 20 5924199, telex 12571. ***Continues*** *Mathematical Centre Tracts.*
**Ind/Abst** Math. Rev.; Zentralbl. Math. Ihre Grenzgeb.

XR/0011-4642
**CZECHOSLOVAK MATHEMATICAL JOURNAL.** [Czech. math. j.]. **Added/Corp** Ceskoslovenska Akademie Ved. Matematicky Ustav. Vol. 19 (1969)-. Periodical. English (French, German and Russian). Four times a year. $610.00 US; $715.00 other. Plenum Press, 233 Spring Street, New York NY 10013-1578. **Tel** (212)620-8000, (800)221-9369, FAX (212)463-0742, (212)807-1047, telex 23/421139. **ED** Miroslav Fiedler. **LC** QA1; .C45. **DD** 510/.5. **[CCC]. Pr Rev.** available on microfilm and microfiche from University Microfilms International (UMI). Documents available from The Genuine Article. ***Continues*** *Chekhoslovatskii Matematicheskii Zhurnal, 0528-9181.*
**Desc:** Publishes original research papers in mathematics.
**Ind/Abst** Compumath Citation Index [Full Cov.]; Comput. Rev.; Int. Aerosp. Abstr.; Math. Rev. (1969-); Res. Alert [Full Cov.]; SCISEARCH; Stat. Theory Method Abstr. (1959-1963, 1968); Zentralbl. Math. Ihre Grenzgeb.

US
**DAIRY, LIVESTOCK, AND POULTRY, U.S. TRADE AND PROSPECTS.** ***Title Change.*** **Added/Corp** United States. Foreign Agricultural Service. Dairy, Livestock, and Poultry Division. United States. World Agricultural Outlook Board. **VFOAT** Dairy, Livestock, and Poultry, US Trade and Prospects. (198?)-(19??). Government Publication. English. mo. US Department of Agriculture / Foreign Agricultural Service, 14th Street & Independence Avenue Southwest, Washington DC 20250. **Tel** (202)720-9445, FAX (202)720-7729. **LC** HD9275.U3; F67. **DD** 382/.416/00973021. Documents available from Documents on Demand. ***Continues*** *Foreign Agriculture Circular. Dairy, Livestock, and Poultry.*; ***Absorbed in part*** *Dairy, Livestock, and Poultry. Meat and Dairy Monthly Imports.* ***Continued by*** *U.S. Trade and Prospects, Dairy, Livestock, and Poultry Products.*
**Ind/Abst** Am. Stat. Index.

PL
**DELTA.** **Added/Corp** Polskie Towarzystwo Matematyczne. Polskie Towarzystwo Fizyczne. (1974)-. Polish. mo. $27.00. **(Subscription address:** ARS Polona, PO Box 1001, 00068 Warsaw Poland.**)** **LC** QA1; .D32.

AT
**DELTA AUSTRALIA.** English. qt. Mathematical Association of Tasmania, PO Box 313, Sandy Bay Tas 7005 Australia.
**Ind/Abst** Aust. Educ. Index.

GR
**DELTION ELLENIKIS MATHEMATIKIS ETAIREIAS.** Greek, Modern. ir. Societe Mathematique de Greece, 34 rue Venizelou, GR-106 79 Athens Greece. **Tel** 30 1 3616532, FAX 3641025. **Circ:** 1,000 (ctrl).
**Desc:** Research articles in mathematics.

GR/0373-1391
**DELTION TES HELLENIKES MATHEMATIKES HETAIREIAS.** **Added/Corp** Hellenike MathematikÂe Hetaireia. **VFOAT** Bulletin de la Societe Mathematique de Grece; Bulletin of the Greek Mathematical Society. (1919)-. Periodical. Greek, Modern (English, French and German). **LC** QA1; .H4.
**Ind/Abst** Zentralbl. Math. Ihre Grenzgeb.

PL/0420-1213
**DEMONSTRATIO MATHEMATICA.** [Demonstr. math.]. **Added/Corp** Politechnika Warszawska. Vol. 1- (1969)-. Polish (English, French and German; summaries and/or abstracts in English, French, German and Russian). ir. **(Subscription address:** ARS Polona, PO Box 1001, 00068 Warsaw Poland.**)** **LC** QA1; .D33. **CODEN** DEMADO.
**Ind/Abst** Int. Aerosp. Abstr.; Math. Rev.; Stat. Theory Method Abstr. (1979, 1982, 1986); Zentralbl. Math. Ihre Grenzgeb.

AU/0379-0207
**DENKSCHRIFTEN - OESTERREICHISCHE AKADEMIE DER WISSENSCHAFTEN, MATHEMATISCH-NATURWISSENSCHAFTLICHE KLASSE.** (DENKSCHRIFTEN / OESTERR. AKADEMIE DER WISSENSCHAFTEN, MATHEMATISCH-NATURWISSENSCHAFTLICHE KLASSE.). [Denkschr. - Oesterr. Akad. Wiss., Math.-Nat.wiss. Kl.]. **Added/Corp** Oesterreichische Akademie der Wissenschaften. Mathematisch-Naturwissenschaftliche Klasse. (194?)-. Monographic series. German. Price varies per volume. Springer-Verlag Wien, Sachsenplatz 4 6, PO Box 89, A-1201 Vienna Austria. **Tel** 011 43 1 3302415. **(Subscription address:** Springer Verlag New York Inc. / for North America, 44 Hartz Way, Secaucus NJ 07096.**)** ***Continues*** *Akademie der Wissenschaften in Wien. Mathematisch-Naturwissenschaftliche Klasse. Denkschriften.*
**Ind/Abst** Math. Rev.; Zentralbl. Math. Ihre Grenzgeb.

UK
**DEVELOPMENTS IN BOUNDARY ELEMENT METHODS.** (1979)-. English. Chapman & Hall, 2-6 Boundary Row, London SE1 8HN England. **Tel** 011 44 71 865 0066, FAX 011 44 71 522 9623, telex 290164 Chapmag. **LC** TA347.B69; D48. **DD** 515/.35.
**Ind/Abst** Zentralbl. Math. Ihre Grenzgeb.

FR/0224-3911
**DIAGRAMMES.** **Added/Corp** Universite de Paris VII. U.E.R. de Mathematiques. Universite de Paris VII. U.F.R. de Mathematiques. Vol. 1 (July 1979)-. Periodical. French (English). qt. 200.00F Europe; 240.00F other. Echec et Compositions, 13 Avenue des Causses, 91940 Les Ulis France. **ED** C Wiedenhoff. **LC** QA169; .D53. **DD** 512/.55. Index available. cum. index. **Bk Rev**, (Qty: 4). **Circ:** 300.
**Desc:** Mathematical publication specializing in theory of categories, universal algebra and model theory as derived from the work of Charles Ehresmann and his school.
**Ind/Abst** Math. Rev.; Trop. Dis. Bull. (?-19??); Zentralbl. Math. Ihre Grenzgeb.

RU/0130-3198
**DIFFERENCIALNAJA GEOMETRIJA.** (DIFFERENTSIALNAIA GEOMETRIIA.). [Differ. geom.]. No. 1 (1974)-. Russian. 0.50rub (single issue). Saratov N.G. Chernyshevskii State University, Astrakhanskaya Ulitsa 83, 410071 Saratov Russia. **Tel** 24-16-96, FAX 24-04-46, telex 241125. **LC** QA641; .D448.
**Ind/Abst** Zentralbl. Math. Ihre Grenzgeb.

US/0893-4983
**DIFFERENTIAL AND INTEGRAL EQUATIONS.** [Diff. integral equ.]. Vol. 1, No. 1 (Jan. 1988)-. Periodical. English. Eight times a year. $530.00 US, Canada & Mexico; $580.00 other. Khayyam Publishing Company Inc., Box 429, Athens OH 45701. **Tel** (614)592-6136, FAX (614)592-1252. **ED** Reza Aftabizadeh. **DD** 515. Index available. **Circ:** 280.
**Ind/Abst** Math. Rev.; Zentralbl. Math. Ihre Grenzgeb.

US/0012-2661
**DIFFERENTIAL EQUATIONS.** [Diff. equ.]. **Added/Corp** Consultants Bureau. Vol. 1 (Jan. 1965)-. Periodical. English (Russian). mo. $1335.00 US; $1560.00 other. Consultants Bureau, A Division of Plenum Publishing Corporation, 233 Spring Street, New York NY 10013. **Tel** (212)620-8000, (212)620-8466, FAX (212)463-0742, telex 23/421139. **ED** E. I. Grundo. **LC** QA371; .D44. **CODEN** DIEQAN. **[CCC].** Index available. **Pr Rev.** available on microfilm and microfiche from University Microfilms International (UMI). Documents available from The Genuine Article.
**Desc:** Devoted exclusively to differential equations and the associated in legal equations. Contents include stability theory, oscillation theory, operational calculus and skill theory.
**Ind/Abst** Appl. Mech. Rev.; Compumath Citation Index [Full Cov.]; Comput. Rev.; Int. Aerosp. Abstr.; Math. Rev.; Pollut. Abstr. Indexes; Res. Alert [Full Cov.]; SCISEARCH; Zentralbl. Math. Ihre Grenzgeb.

US/1053-0517
**DIFFERENTIAL GEOMETRY AND APPLICATIONS.** ***Ceased.*** (1991)-. Periodical. English. qt. Plenum Press, 233 Spring Street, New York NY 10013-1578. **Tel** (212)620-8000, (800)221-9369, FAX (212)463-0742, (212)807-1047, telex 23/421139.
**Ind/Abst** Math. Rev.

NE/0926-2245
**DIFFERENTIAL GEOMETRY AND ITS APPLICATIONS.** Vol. 1, No. 1 (June 1991)-. Academic Scholarly Publication. English. qt (1 volume). Fl380.00. Elsevier Science Publishers BV, PO Box 211, 1000 AE Amsterdam Netherlands. **Tel** 011 31 20 5803642, FAX 011 31 20 5862696, telex 15682. **LC** QA641; .D529. **CODEN** DGAPEO. available on microfilm and microfiche from University Microfilms International (UMI). Documents available from Ask*IEEE.
**Ind/Abst** INSPEC (June 1991-).

RU/0320-104X
**DIFFERENTSIALNYE URAVNENIJA (RJAZAN).** (DIFFERENTSIALNYE URAVNENIIA.). [Differ. uravn.]. **Added/Corp** Ryazan, Russia (City). Gosudarstvennyi Pedagogicheskii Institut. Russia (1917-R.S.F.S.R.). Glavnoe Upravlenie Vysshikh Uchebnykh Zavedenii. No. 1 (1973)-. Russian. mo. $119.95. **(Subscription address:** East View Publications Inc., 3020 Harbor Lane North, Suite 110, Minneapolis MN 55447.**)** **LC** QA371; .D4635.
**Desc:** Information on differential equations.
**Ind/Abst** Math. Rev.; Stat. Theory Method Abstr. (1986); Zentralbl. Math. Ihre Grenzgeb.

RU/0130-318X
**DINAMIKA SISTEM.** (DINAMIKA SISTEM; MEZHVUZOVSKII SBORNIK.). [Din. sist.]. **Added/Corp** Gorki, Russia. Universitet. (1974)-. Periodical. Russian. **LC** QA845; .D56.
**Ind/Abst** Math. Rev.; Zentralbl. Math. Ihre Grenzgeb.

CN/0229-0081
**DIRECTORY OF PROGRAMS IN STATISTICS AND RELATED AREAS IN CANADIAN UNIVERSITIES / STATISTICAL SOCIETY OF CANADA.** [Dir. programs stat. relat. areas Can. univ.]. **VFOAT** Registre de Programmes de Statistique et Sujets Connexes Offerts par les Universites Canadiennes. 1980-. Statistical Publication. English (French). an. Statistical Society of Canada, Montreal Regional Association, PO Box 1433 Station B, Montreal Quebec H38 3L2 Canada. **DD** 519.5/07/1171.

US
**DIRECTORY OF STATISTICAL MICROCOMPUTER SOFTWARE.** **See** Computers-Microcomputers, Personal Computers.

US/0732-5967
**DIRECTORY OF WOMEN IN THE MATHEMATICAL SCIENCES.** [Dir. women math. sci.]. Directory. English. AMS Press Inc., 56 East 13th Street, New York NY 10003. **Tel** (212)777-4700, FAX (212)995-5413, telex 710 581 2302. **LC** QA30; .D57. **DD** 510/.92/2. ***Continues*** *Directory of Women Mathematicians, 0091-7583.*

US
**DISCOURSES IN MATHEMATICS AND ITS APPLICATIONS.** **Added/Corp** Texas A & M University. Dept. of Mathematics. No. 1 (1991)-. English. Texas A & M University / Battalion, The Battalion, Student Publications, College Station TX 77843-1111. **Tel** (409)845-2611, FAX (409)845-5408.
**Ind/Abst** Math. Rev.

US/0179-5376
**DISCRETE & COMPUTATIONAL GEOMETRY.** [Discrete comput. geom.]. **VFOAT** Discrete and Computational Geometry; Geometry. Vol. 1, No. 1 (1986)-. Periodical. English. Eight times a year. $236.00. Springer-Verlag New York Inc., 175 5th Avenue, New York NY 10010. **Tel** (212)460-1500, telex 232 235 SPB UR. **(Subscription address:** Springer Verlag New York Inc. / for North America, 44 Hartz Way, Secaucus NJ 07096.**)** **ED** J E Goodman and R Pollack. **LC** QA440; .D57. **DD** 516/.005. **CODEN** DCGEER. **[CCC]. Pr Rev.** available on microfilm and microfiche from University Microfilms International (UMI). Documents available from The Genuine Article, Ask*IEEE.
**Desc:** Promotes cross-fertilization by covering such fields as: combinatorial geometry, design and analysis of geometric algorithms, convex polytopes, multidimensional searching and sorting, extremal geometric problems, computational topology, geometry of numbers, packing, covering and tiling.
**Ind/Abst** ACM Guide Comput. Lit.; Compumath Citation Index [Full Cov.]; Comput. Rev.; Curr. Contents Eng. Tech. Appl. Sci.; Curr. Contents Phys. Chem. Earth Sci.; INSPEC (1987-); Int. Abstr. Oper. Res. [Select. Cov.]; Math. Rev. (1986-); Res. Alert [Full Cov.]; SCISEARCH; Zentralbl. Math. Ihre Grenzgeb.

NE
**DISCRETE APPLIED MATHEMATICS.** Vol. 21, No. 1 (1988)-. Academic Scholarly Publication. English. Twenty-four times a year (8 volumes). Fl2680.00; Fl6300.00 combination subscription with Discrete Mathematics. Elsevier Science Publishers BV, PO Box 211, 1000 AE Amsterdam Netherlands. **Tel** 011 31 20 5803642, FAX 011 31 20 5862696, telex 15682. **LC** QA1; .D518. **DD** 510/.5. available on microfilm and microfiche from University Microfilms International (UMI).

Documents available from The Genuine Article, Ask*IEEE. ***Continues*** *Discrete Applied Mathematics and Combinatorial Operations Research.*
**Ind/Abst** ACM Guide Comput. Lit.; Bioeng. Abstr.; Compumath Citation Index [Full Cov.]; Comput. Rev.; Curr. Contents Phys. Chem. Earth Sci.; Ei Page One; INSPEC (Sept. 1979-); Int. Abstr. Oper. Res.; Math. Rev. (Sept. 1979-); Pollut. Abstr. Indexes; Res. Alert [Full Cov.]; Sci. Cit. Index; SCISEARCH; Soc. Sci. Cit. Index [Select. Cov.].

NE/0012-365X
**DISCRETE MATHEMATICS.** [Discrete math.]. Vol. 1, No. 1 (May 1971)-. Academic Scholarly Publication. English. Thirty-nine times a year (13 volumes). Fl4355.00; Fl6300.00 combination subscription with Discrete Applied Mathematics. Elsevier Science Publishers BV, PO Box 211, 1000 AE Amsterdam Netherlands. **Tel** 011 31 20 5803642, FAX 011 31 20 5862696, telex 15682. **ED** Peter L Hammer. **LC** QA1; .D52. **DD** 510/.5. **CODEN** DSMHA4. **[CCC].** cum. index. **Ad Acc. Pr Rev.** ctrl circ. available on microfilm and microfiche from University Microfilms International (UMI). Documents available from The Genuine Article, Ask*IEEE.
**Desc:** The aim of the journal is to bring together research papers in different areas of discrete mathematics.
**Ind/Abst** ACM Guide Comput. Lit.; Compumath Citation Index [Full Cov.]; Comput. Rev.; Curr. Contents Phys. Chem. Earth Sci.; Ei Page One; Energy Res. Abstr. (March 1979-); INSPEC (May 1971-); Int. Abstr. Oper. Res. [Select. Cov.]; Int. Aerosp. Abstr.; Math. Rev.; Pollut. Abstr. Indexes; Res. Alert [Full Cov.]; Sci. Cit. Index; SCISEARCH; Soc. Sci. Cit. Index [Select. Cov.]; Zentralbl. Math. Ihre Grenzgeb.

NE/0924-9265
**DISCRETE MATHEMATICS AND APPLICATIONS. VFOAT** Discrete Mathematics and Its Applications. Vol. 1, No. 1 (1991)-. Periodical. English (translations available in Russian). bm. DM900.00. VSP International Science Publishers, Godfried van Seystlaan 47, 3703 BR Zeist Netherlands. **Tel** 011 31 3404 25790, FAX 011 31 3404 32081, telex 40217 USP NL. **(Subscription address:** VSP International Science Publishers, PO Box 346, 3700 AH Zeist Netherlands.**) ED** V. Ya Kozlov. **Pr Rev.**
**Desc:** Covers various subjects such as combinatorial analysis, graph theory, coding, probability problems of discrete mathematics, algorithms and their complexity and the combinatorial and computing problems of number theory and algebra.
**Ind/Abst** Math. Rev.; Zentralbl. Math. Ihre Grenzgeb.

PL
**DISCUSSIONES MATHEMATICAE.** **Added/Corp** Lubuskie Towarzystwo Naukowe. Komisja Matematyki. (19??)-. Polish (English, French, German, Polish and Russian). **LC** QA1; .D523. **DD** 510/.5.
**Ind/Abst** Math. Rev. (1985-); Zentralbl. Math. Ihre Grenzgeb.

HU
**DISQUISITIONES MATHEMATICAE HUNGARICAE. Added/Corp** Magyar Tudomanyos Akademia. Matematikai Bizottsag. (1970)-. Academic Scholarly Publication. Hungarian. ir. Price varies per volume. Akademiai Kiado, Publishing House of the Hungarian Academy of Sciences, Prielle Kornelia u. 19-35, H-1117 Budapest Hungary. **Tel** 011 36 1 1811991, FAX 011 36 1 1811991, telex 22-6228 AKNYO H. **DD** 510.
**Ind/Abst** Math. Rev.; Zentralbl. Math. Ihre Grenzgeb.

FR/0417-8300
**DOCUMENTATION MATHEMATIQUE.** (19??)-. Periodical. French. **DD** 510.
**Ind/Abst** Math. Rev.; Zentralbl. Math. Ihre Grenzgeb.

TA/0002-3469
**DOKLADHOI AKADEMIAI FANHOI RSS TOCIKISTON.** ***Title Change.*** (DOKLADY AKADEMII NAUK TADZHIKSKOI SSR / DOKLADHOI AKADEMIIAI FANHOI RSS TOJIKISTON.). [Dokl. Akad. fanhoi RSS Toc.]. **Added/Corp** Akademiiai Fanhoi RSS Tojikiston. **VFOAT** Dokladhoi Akademiiai Fanhoi RSS Tojikiston. (1951)-(1992). Periodical. Russian (summaries and/or abstracts in Tajik; table of contents in English and Tajik). mo. **LC** AS581; .S8. **NLM** W1 DO64AQ. **CODEN** DANTAL. Documents available from CASDDS. ***Continued by*** *Dokladhoi Akademiiai Ilmhoi Jumhurii Tojikiston.*
**Ind/Abst** Alum. Ind. Abstr.; Chem. Abstr.; Coal Abstr.; GeoRef; Int. Nurs. Index; Math. Rev.; Met. Abstr.

UN
**DOKLADY AKADEMII NAUK UKRAINSKOI SSR. SERIIA A, FIZIKO-MATEMATICHESKIE I TEKHNICHESKIE NAUKI.** ***Title Change.*** **Added/Corp** Akademiia Nauk Ukrainskoi RSR. **VFOAT** Fiziko-Matematicheskie i Tekhnicheskie Nauki. (1975)-(19??). Periodical. Russian (summaries and/or abstracts in English; table of contents in English). mo. **CODEN** DAANEA. ***Merged with*** *Doklady Akademii Nauk Ukrainskoi SSR. Matematika, Estestvoznanie, Tekhnicheskie Nauki, 0868-8044* ***to form*** *Doklady Akademii Nauk Ukrainskoi RSR. Seriia B, Geologicheskie, Khimicheskie i Biologicheskie Nauki, 0201-8454.*

US/1064-5624
**DOKLADY. MATHEMATICS.** ***Title Change.*** (DOKLADY. MATHEMATICS / RUSSIAN ACADEMY OF SCIENCES.). [Dokl., Math.]. **Added/Corp** American Mathematical Society. Rossiiskaia Akademiia Nauk. **VFOAT** Mathematics. Vol. 45, No. 2 (Sept. 1992)-(1994). Periodical. English (translations available in Russian). tq (3 issues). American Mathematical Society, PO Box 6248, Providence RI 02940-6248. **Tel** (800)321-4267, (401)455-4000, FAX (401)331-3842, telex 797192. **(Subscription address:** American Mathematical Society, PO Box 5904, Boston MA 02206-5904.**) LC** QA1; .A3493. **DD** 510. ***Continues*** *Soviet Mathematics - Doklady, 0197-6788.* ***Continued by*** *Doklady Mathematics.*
**Desc:** Contains the entire pure mathematics section of the Doklady Rossiskoi Akademii Nauk, the Reports of the Russian Academy of Sciences.
**Ind/Abst** Math. Rev.

●RU
**DOKLADY MATHEMATICS.** Vol. 340 (1995)-. English. Six times a year. $903.00 US and Canada; $915.00 other. MAIK Nauka / Interperiodica, Ulitsa Profsoyuznaya 90, Moscow 117864 Russia. **(Subscription address:** Interperiodica Publishing, Subscription Office, PO Box 1831, Birmingham AL 35201-1831.**)** ***Continues*** *Doklady. Mathematics. Russian Academy of Sciences, 1064-5624.*

US/0884-4461
**DOLCIANI MATHEMATICAL EXPOSITIONS, THE.** (DOLCIANI MATHEMATICAL EXPOSITIONS.). [Dolciani math. expo.]. **Added/Corp** Mathematical Association of America. **VFOAT** Mathematical Expositions. No. 1 (1973)-. Monographic series. English. ir. Price varies per volume. Mathematical Association of America, 1529 18th Street Northwest, Washington DC 20036. **Tel** (202)387-5200, (800)331-1622, FAX (202)265-2384. **LC** UNC.
**Ind/Abst** Math. Rev.; Zentralbl. Math. Ihre Grenzgeb.

UN
**DOPOVIDI AKADEMII NAUK UKRAINY. MATEMATYKA, PRYRODOZNAVSTVO, TEKHNICHNI NAUKY : NAUKOVYI HURNAL PREZYDII AN UKRAINY.** **Added/Corp** Akademiia Nauk Ukrainy. Prezydium. **VFOAT** Matematyka, Pryrodoznavstvo, Tekhnichni Nauky. (1991)-. Periodical. Ukrainian (summaries and/or abstracts in English and Russian; table of contents in English). mo. Izdatelstvo Naukova Dumka / Ukrainian Academy of Sciences, Vladimirskaia Ulitsa 54, 252601 Kiev Ukraine. **Tel** 225-63-66, telex 131376. ***Continues*** *Dopovidi Akademii Nauk Ukrainskoi RSR. Matematyka, Pryrodoznavstvo, Tekhnichni Nauky, 0868-8052.*

US/0012-7094
**DUKE MATHEMATICAL JOURNAL.** [Duke math. j.]. **Added/Corp** Duke University. Duke University. Mathematics Dept. Vol. 1, No. 1 (Mar. 1935)-. Periodical. English. mo (4 volumes - 12 issues plus 1 supplementary issue). $624.00 (institutions), $312.00 (individuals) US; $660.00 (institutions), $348.00 (individuals) other. Duke University Press, PO Box 90660, Durham NC 27708-0660. **Tel** (919)687-3600, (919)688-5134 (orders), FAX (919)688-4574, telex 802829. **ED** Morris Weisfeld. **LC** QA1; .D8. **DD** 510/.5. **CODEN** DUMJAO. **[CCC].** cum. index. **Bk Rev. Ad Acc. Pr Rev. Circ:** 1,200 (ctrl). available on microfilm and microfiche from University Microfilms International (UMI). Documents available from The Genuine Article.
**Desc:** Published under the auspices of Duke University since 1934, it has long been regarded as one of the leading mathematics journals in the world.
**Ind/Abst** Compumath Citation Index [Full Cov.]; Curr. Contents Phys. Chem. Earth Sci.; Int. Aerosp. Abstr.; Math. Rev.; Res. Alert [Full Cov.]; Sci. Cit. Index; SCISEARCH; Stat. Theory Method Abstr. (1961-1963); Zentralbl. Math. Ihre Grenzgeb.

US/0046-0826
**DUODECIMAL BULLETIN, THE.** Began with Vol. 1, No. 1 (Jan./Mar. 1945). Bulletin. English. sa. Duodecimal Society of America, 9728 Cielo Drive, Huntington Beach CA 92649. **LC** QA141; .D79. **DD** 513/.56. cum. index.

●US/1056-2176
**DYNAMIC SYSTEMS AND APPLICATIONS.** [Dyn. syst. appl.]. **Added/Corp** Clark Atlanta University. Research Center for Science and Technology. Vol. 1, No. 1 (Mar. 1992)-. Periodical. English. qt. $150.00 (institutions), $75.00 (individuals) US and Canada; $166.00 (institutions), $91.00 (individuals) other. Dynamic Publishers, PO Box 48654, Atlanta GA 30362. **Tel** (404)458-7932, FAX (404)451-3616. **ED** M Sambandham (editor's address: Box 287, Clark Atlanta University, Atlanta GA 30314; eitor's phon: (404)880-8596). **LC** QA370; .D96. **DD** 515/.35. **[CCC].** cum. index. **Bk Rev. Ad Acc. Circ:** 100.
**Ind/Abst** Math. Rev.

GW
**DYNAMICS REPORTED.** Vol. 1 (1988)-. English. ir. Price varies per volume. John Wiley & Sons Ltd., Baffins Lane, Chichester West Sussex PO19 1UD England. **Tel** 0243 779777, FAX 0243 776128 BTG:JWP001, telex 86290 WIBOOKG. **(Subscription address:** North America/ John Wiley & Sons, Inc., 1 Wiley Drive, Somerset, NJ 08875; (telephone: (800)225-5945)**) LC** QA614.8; .D95. **DD** 515.3/52.
**Ind/Abst** Math. Rev.; Zentralbl. Math. Ihre Grenzgeb.

NE/0928-0200
**EAST-WEST JOURNAL OF NUMERICAL MATHEMATICS. VFOAT** East West Journal of Numerical Mathermatics. Vol. 1, No. 1 (1993)-. Periodical. English. qt. DM330.00. VSP International Science Publishers, Godfried van Seystlaan 47, 3703 BR Zeist Netherlands. **Tel** 011 31 3404 25790, FAX 011 31 3404 32081, telex 40217 USP NL. **(Subscription address:** VSP International Science Publishers, PO Box 346, 3700 AH Zeist Netherlands.**) ED** Yu A. Kuznetsov. **Pr Rev.**
**Desc:** Promotes the exchange of ideas and results in numerical mathematics between scientists in Eastern Europe and Western countries and familiarizes the world scientific community with the activities of researchers in Russia and other Eastern European countries.

FI/1013-9338
**ECMI NEWSLETTER.** [ECMI newsl.]. **VFOAT** European Consortium for Mathematics in Industry Newsletter. (1987)-. Newsletter. English. sa. **UDC** 51.
**Ind/Abst** Zentralbl. Math. Ihre Grenzgeb.

NE/0013-1954
**EDUCATIONAL STUDIES IN MATHEMATICS.** **See** Education.

TU
**EGE UNIVERSITESI MUHENDISLIK FAKULTESI DERGISI. SERI E, UYGULAMAL ISTATISTIK. VFOAT** Uygulamal Istatistik; E U Muhendislik Fakultesi Dergisi. Vol. 1 (1983)-. Periodical. Turkish (summaries and/or abstracts in English). sa. **LC** QA276.A1; E36.

CS/0013-3027
**EKONOMICKO-MATEMATICKY OBZOR.** ***Ceased.*** **See** Economics-Economic Theory.

RU/0424-7388
**EKONOMIKA I MATEMATICHESKIE METODY.** **See** Economics-Economic Theory.

UN/0204-3572
**ELEKTRONNOE MODELIROVANIE.** **See** Computers-Data Processing.

●US/1058-2754
**ELEMENTARY MODULE SERIES.** **Added/Corp** Consortium for Mathematics and Its Applications (U.S.). **VFOAT** Going Bananas. (1992)-. English. COMAP Inc, 57 Bedford Street, Suite 210, Lexington MA 02173. **Tel** (617)862-7878, FAX (617)863-1202.

SZ/0013-6018
**ELEMENTE DER MATHEMATIK.** [Elem. Math.]. **Added/Corp** Verein Schweizerischer Mathematik- und Physiklehrer. Verein Schweizerischer Mathematiklehrer. **VFOAT** Revue de Mathematiques el Ementaires; Rivista di Matematica Elementare. Vol. 1, No. 1 (Jan. 15, 1946)-. Periodical. German (French and Italian). Four times a year. 87.80F Switzerland; 98.50F other. Birkhaeuser Verlag Ag, Klosterberg 23, PO Box 133, CH-4010 Basel Switzerland. **Tel** 011 41 61 2717400, FAX 011 41 0 61 2717666, telex 963475 birk ch. **(Subscription address:** Birkhauser Verlag AG, PO Box 151, CH 4106 Therwil Switzerland; Phone: 011 41 61 7217740**) ED** Franz Bachmann, Catherine Bandle, Peter Gallin, Henri Joris, Hans Rudolf, Urs Stammbach, John Seinig, Ralph Strebel and Hans Walser. **LC** QA1; .E5. **CODEN** ELMMAF. **[CCC].** Index Available, published separately, free-automatically sent. available on microfilm from University Microfilms International (UMI).
**Desc:** Publishes mathematical articles which are accessible to the nonspecialist. Special emphasis is given to expository papers describing important developments in the field of mathematics and its applications. Special attention is also given to articles that address a particular mathematical question or problem, and to essays giving historical and biographical information relevant to the development of mathematics.
**Ind/Abst** Energy Res. Abstr. (March 1982-); Math. Rev.; Zentralbl. Math. Ihre Grenzgeb.

SZ/0422-9622
**ELEMENTE DER MATHEMATIK VOM HOHEREN STANDPUNKT AUS.** Vol. 1 (1952)-. Monographic series. German. ir. Price varies per volume. Birkhaeuser Verlag Ag, Klosterberg 23, PO Box 133, CH-4010 Basel Switzerland. **Tel** 011 41 61 2717400, FAX 011 41 0 61 2717666, telex 963475 birk ch.

UK/0271-6151
**ELLIS HORWOOD SERIES IN MATHEMATICS & ITS APPLICATIONS.** [Ellis Horwood ser. math. appl.]. **VFOAT** Ellis Horwood Series in Mathematics and Its Applications. Monographic series. English. Price varies per volume. John Wiley & Sons Ltd., Baffins Lane, Chichester West Sussex PO19 1UD England. **Tel** 0243 779777, FAX 0243 776128 BTG:JWP001, telex 86290 WIBOOKG. **(Subscription address:** North, South and Central America/ John Wiley & Sons, Inc., Subscription Department, 605 Third Avenue, New York, NY 10158-0012, USA; telephone: (212)850-6645; FAX: (212)850-6021**)** Documents available from Ask*IEEE.
**Ind/Abst** INSPEC; Math. Rev.

US/0163-3287
**EMPLOYMENT INFORMATION IN THE MATHEMATICAL SCIENCES. See** Economics-Labor.

NE
**ENCYCLOPAEDIA OF MATHEMATICS.** (19??)-. English. ir. Price varies. Kluwer Academic Publishers, Postbus 322, 3300 AH Dordrecht, The Netherlands. **Tel** 011 (31) 78 524400, FAX 011 31 78 183273, telex 20083.

US/0953-4806
**ENCYCLOPEDIA OF MATHEMATICS AND ITS APPLICATIONS.** [Encycl. math. appl.]. **VFOAT** Encyclopedia of Mathematics; Encyclopaedia of Mathematics and its Applications. (1976)-. Monographic series. English. ir. price varies per volume. Addison Wesley Book Express, 1 Jacob Way, Reading MA 01867. **Tel** (617)944-3700. **(Subscription address:** Cambridge University Press / North America, 110 Midland Avenue, Port Chester NY 10573.**) ED** G. C. Rota. **LC** QA5; .E58. Documents available from Ask*IEEE.
**Ind/Abst** INSPEC; Math. Rev.; Zentralbl. Math. Ihre Grenzgeb.

FR/0013-8584
**ENSEIGNEMENT MATHEMATIQUE.** (L'ENSEIGNEMENT MATHEMATIQUE.). [Enseign. math.]. **Added/Corp** International Commission on the Teaching of Mathematics. Universite de Geneve. Institut de Mathematiques. Vol. 1 No. 1 (Jan. 15 1899)-. Periodical. French. Four times a year (2 issues in July and 2 issues in Dec.). 170.00F. Enseignement Mathematique, 2-4 Rue de Lievre, CP 240, CH 1211 Geneva 24 Switzerland. **Tel** 011 41 22 3435060, FAX 011 41 22 3002064. **LC** QA1; .E53. **CODEN** ENMAAR. Index Available, published separately, free-automatically sent. cum. index. **Bk Rev. Ad Acc. Circ:** 900.
**Desc:** Research-expository papers, survey and historical articles in mathematics.
**Ind/Abst** Energy Res. Abstr. (March 1982-); Math. Rev.; Zentralbl. Math. Ihre Grenzgeb.

GW/0071-1136
**ERGEBNISSE DER MATHEMATIK UND IHRER GRENZGEBIETE.** [Ergeb. Math. ihrer Grenzgebiete]. **VFOAT** Series of Modern Surveys of Mathematics. (1932)-. Monographic series. German (English and French). ir. Price varies per volume. Springer-Verlag GmbH & Company KG, Heidelberger Platz 3, D 14197 Berlin Germany. **Tel** 011 49 30 8207223, FAX 011 49 30 8214091, telex 183 319 SPBLN D. **(Subscription address:** Springer Verlag New York Inc. / for North America, 44 Hartz Way, Secaucus NJ 07096.**)**
**Ind/Abst** Energy Res. Abstr. (March 1982-); Math. Rev.; Zentralbl. Math. Ihre Grenzgeb.

UK/0143-3857
**ERGODIC THEORY AND DYNAMICAL SYSTEMS.** [Ergod. theory dyn. syst.]. Vol. 1, Pt. 1 (March 1981)-. Academic Scholarly Publication. English. Six times a year. £228.00. Cambridge University Press, The Edinburgh Building, Shaftesbury Road, Cambridge CB2 2RU United Kingdom. **Tel** 011 44 223 312393, FAX 011 44 223 325959. **(Subscription address:** Cambridge University Press / North America, 110 Midland Avenue, Port Chester NY 10573.**) ED** J. Franks, H. Furstenberg, A. K. Manning and W. Parry. **LC** QA611.5; .E7. **DD** 515.4/2. **[CCC]. Bk Rev. Pr Rev.** available on microfilm from University Microfilms International (UMI). Documents available from The Genuine Article.
**Desc:** Focuses on a variety of research areas which, although diverse, employ as common themes global dynamical methods. Provides a focus for this important and rapidly developing area of mathematics and an opportunity to bring together many major contributions in the field which have previously been scattered over a large number of non-specialist periodicals. The journal acts as a forum for central problems of differential geometry, number theory, operator algebras, topological, differential and symbolic dynamics, and celestial and statistical mechanics. Topics include geodesic and horocycle flows, closed orbit analysis, cohomology for dynamical systems, structural stability, complex dynamics, finitary coding problems and twist maps.
**Ind/Abst** Compumath Citation Index [Full Cov.]; Math. Rev.; Res. Alert [Full Cov.]; SCISEARCH; Zentralbl. Math. Ihre Grenzgeb.

US
**ERIC/SMEAC MATHEMATICS EDUCATION DIGEST / ERIC CLEARINGHOUSE FOR SCIENCE, MATHEMATICS, AND ENVIRONMENTAL EDUCATION. Added/Corp** ERIC Clearinghouse for Science, Mathematics, and Environmental Education. **VFOAT** Mathematics Education Digest; ERIC SMEAC Mathematics Education Digest. No. 1 (1984)-. Periodical. English. Four times a year. $3.00. SMEAC Information Reference Center, 1200 Chambers Road/Room 310, Columbus OH 43212. **Tel** (614)292-6717. ***Continues*** *ERIC/SMEAC Mathematics Education Fact Sheet, 0888-174X.*

US/1057-8390
**ESTIMATION AND TRACKING : PRINCIPLES AND TECHNIQUES.** [Estim. track.]. (1991)-. English. $100.00. Yaakov Bar-Shalom, Box U-157, Storrs CT 06269-3157. **DD** 512.

PO/0251-4230
**ESTUDOS MATEMATICA E INFORMATICA, INSTITUTO GULBENKIAN DE CIENCIA. See** Computers-Data Processing.

NE/0165-0394
**EUCLIDES (GRONINGEN, NETHERLANDS).** (EUCLIDES.). [Euclides]. **Added/Corp** Nederlandse Vereniging van Wiskundeleraren. (1927/28)-. Periodical. Dutch. Nine times a year. 57.75F. Wolters Noordhoff BV, Postbus 567, 9700 AN Groningen Netherlands. **Tel** 011 31 50 226886, FAX 011 31 50 264866. ***Continues*** *Bijvoegsel van net Nieuw Tijdschrift voor Wiskunde Gewijd aan Onderwijsbelangen.*
**Ind/Abst** Math. Rev.; Zentralbl. Math. Ihre Grenzgeb.

UK/0071-2248
**EUREKA : THE ARCHIMEDEANS' JOURNAL. Added/Corp** Cambridge University Mathematical Society. (1939)-. Periodical. English. an (June). £1.50. Cambridge University Math Society, The Arts School, Cambridge CB2 1TD England. **ED** Edward Welbourne. **Ad Acc. Circ:** 1,000 (ctrl).
**Desc:** The appeal of Eureka spans in the mathematical world. Articles vary from a light-hearted approach to serious expositions of new mathematical ideas.

UK/0956-7925
**EUROPEAN JOURNAL OF APPLIED MATHEMATICS. VFOAT** Applied Mathematics. Vol. 1, Pt. 1 (March 1990)-. Academic Scholarly Publication. English. Six times a year. $224.00 US, Canada & Mexico; £124.00 other. Cambridge University Press, The Edinburgh Building, Shaftesbury Road, Cambridge CB2 2RU United Kingdom. **Tel** 011 44 223 312393, FAX 011 44 223 325959. **(Subscription address:** Cambridge University Press / North America, 110 Midland Avenue, Port Chester NY 10573.**) ED** John Ockendon. **LC** QA1; .E95. **DD** 510/.5. available on microfilm and microfiche from University Microfilms International (UMI).
**Desc:** Journal for original work in areas of mathematics in which an understanding of the application requires the use of new and interesting mathematical ideas. Focuses on the burgeoning area of mathematics inspired by real world application, and at the same time fosters the development of theoretical methods with broad areas of applicability.
**Ind/Abst** Math. Rev.; Zentralbl. Math. Ihre Grenzgeb.

UK/0195-6698
**EUROPEAN JOURNAL OF COMBINATORICS.** [Eur. j. comb.]. **VFOAT** Journal Europeen de Combinatoire; Europaische Zeitschrift fur Kombinatorik. Vol. 1 (Mar. 1980)-. Academic Scholarly Publication. English. bm. $380.00. Academic Press Ltd., A Division of Harcourt Brace & Company Ltd., 24-28 Oval Road, London NW1 7DX England. **Tel** 071 267 4466, FAX 071 482 2293, 071 485 4752, telex 25775 ACPRES G. **(Subscription address:** Harcourt Brace & Company, Ltd., Foots Cray, High Street, Sidcup Kent DA14 5HP England.**) ED** M. Deza, M. Las Vergnas and P. Rosenstiehl. **CODEN** EJOCDI. **[CCC]. Pr Rev.** Documents available from The Genuine Article, Ask*IEEE.
**Desc:** An international journal of pure mathematics, specializing in theories arising from combinatorial problems. The journal is primarily open to papers dealing with mathematical structures within combinatorics and/or establishing direct links between combinatorics and other branches of mathematics and the theories of computing. Includes full-length research papers, short notes, and research problems on important topics.
**Ind/Abst** ACM Guide Comput. Lit.; Compumath Citation Index [Full Cov.]; Comput. Rev.; INSPEC (March 1981-); Int. Abstr. Oper. Res. [Select. Cov.]; Math. Rev.; Res. Alert [Full Cov.]; SCISEARCH; Zentralbl. Math. Ihre Grenzgeb.

GW
**EUROPEAN MATHEMATICAL NEWSLETTER.** No. 1 (1981)-. Newsletter. English (French, German and English).

●US/1058-6458
**EXPERIMENTAL MATHEMATICS.** [Exp. math.]. Vol. 1, No. 1 (1992)-. Periodical. English (French and German). Four times a year (Mar., June, Sept., Dec.). $48.00 (members); $150.00 (non-members). A K Peters, Ltd., 289 Linden Street, Wellesley MA 02181. **Tel** (617)235-2210, FAX (617)235-2404. **ED** D. B. A. Epstein and S. Levy. **LC** QA1; .E955. **DD** 519.
**Desc:** Devoted to experimental aspects of mathematical research. Its goal is to make the interplay between mathematical theory and experimentation more fruitful and visible and to aid the development of standards for reporting experimental results in mathematics.

GW/0723-0869
**EXPOSITIONES MATHEMATICAE.** [Expo. math.]. Vol. 1, No. 1 (1983)-. Periodical. English (French and German). Five times a year. DM394.00 Germany; DM401.00 other. Bibliographisches Institut AG, Dudenstrasse 6/PF 100311, W 6800 Mannheim F R Germany. **Tel** 011 49 621 390102, FAX 011 49 621 3901226. **ED** S D Chatterji. **[CCC]. Bk Rev. Ad Acc. Circ:** 300.
**Desc:** International journal of pure and applied mathematics. Original research articles, surveys, expository essays, historical studies, new results, novel points of view.
**Ind/Abst** Math. Rev.; Zentralbl. Math. Ihre Grenzgeb.

YU/0352-9665
**FACTA UNIVERSITATIS. SERIES, MATHEMATICS AND INFORMATICS. Added/Corp** Univerzitet u Nisu. **VFOAT** Facta Universitatis (Nis). Series, Mathematics and Informatics; Series, Mathematics and Informatics; Mathematics and Informatics. (1986)-. English (French, German and Russian; summaries and/or abstracts in Serbo-Croatian (Cyrillic)). University of Nis, TRG Bratstva I Jedinstva 2, PO Box 123, 18000 Nis Yugoslavia. **LC** QA1; .F33. **DD** 510/.5.
**Ind/Abst** Zentralbl. Math. Ihre Grenzgeb.

PL/0044-4413
**FASCICULI MATHEMATICI.** (FASCICULI MATHEMATICI / POLYTECHNICA POSNANIENSIS, INSTITUTUM MATHEMATICUM.). [Fasc. math.]. **Added/Corp** Politechnika Poznanska. Instytut Matematyki. **VFOAT** Zeszyty Matematyczne. (1970)-. Periodical. English (French and Polish; summaries and/or abstracts in Russian). **LC** QA1; .P675. **DD** 510/.5. **CODEN** FMPMDH. ***Continues*** *Zeszyty Matematyczne.*
**Ind/Abst** Math. Rev.; Zentralbl. Math. Ihre Grenzgeb.

US/0015-0517
**FIBONACCI QUARTERLY, THE.** [Fibonacci q.]. **Added/Corp** Fibonacci Association. Vol. 1 (Feb. 1963)-. Periodical. English. Four times a year (Feb., May, Aug., Nov.). $40.00. Fibonacci Association, University of Santa Clara, Santa Clara CA 95053. **Tel** (408)554-4525, (408)378-8577. **ED** G. E. Bergum. **LC** QA1; .F5. **CODEN** FIBQAU. Index available. **Pr Rev. Circ:** 1,000 (ctrl). available on microfilm and microfiche from University Microfilms International (UMI); available in microform from Information Publications International. Documents available from The Genuine Article.
**Desc:** Published by the Fibonacci Association, a nonprofit California corporation, TFQ promotes the study of special numerical sequences, especially recurrent sequences, and, more broadly to special properties of numbers and notions in number theory.
**Ind/Abst** Compumath Citation Index [Full Cov.]; Math. Rev.; Res. Alert [Full Cov.]; SCISEARCH; Zentralbl. Math. Ihre Grenzgeb.

BU/0015-3265
**FIZIKO-MATEMATICHESKO SPISANIE. See** Physics.

US/0731-2040
**FOCUS (MATHEMATICAL ASSOCIATION OF AMERICA).** (FOCUS.). [Focus - Math. Assoc. Am.]. **Added/Corp** Mathematical Association of America. **VFOAT** MAA Focus. Vol. 1, No. 1 (Mar. 1981)-. Periodical. English. Six times a year. comes with membership. Mathematical Association of America, 1529 18th Street Northwest, Washington DC 20036. **Tel** (202)387-5200, (800)331-1622, FAX (202)265-2384. **ED** Keith J. Devlin. **LC** QA1; .M42294. **DD** 510. **Ad Acc. Circ:** 25,000.

US/0272-8893
**FOCUS ON LEARNING PROBLEMS IN MATHEMATICS. See** Education-Special Education and Rehabilitation.

CN/0228-0671
**FOR THE LEARNING OF MATHEMATICS : AN INTERNATIONAL JOURNAL OF MATHEMATICS EDUCATION.** Vol. 1, No. 1 (July 1980)-. Periodical. English. Three times a year. 36.00Can$ (institutions), 24.00Can$ (individuals) Canada; $36.00 (institutions), $24.00 (individuals) other. Flm Publ Assn, 205-1230 Hard Street, Vancouver BC V6E 4J9 Canada. **Tel** (604)536-7205. **ED** David Wheeler. **LC** QA11.A1; F67. **DD** 510/.7. Index available. **Pr Rev. Circ:** 600.
**Desc:** Articles about practices and theories of

mathematics teaching at all levels: for teachers, teacher-trainers, researchers, etc.
**Ind/Abst** Curr. Index J. Educ.

GW/0933-7741
**FORUM MATHEMATICUM.** [Forum math.]. Vol. 1, No. 1 (1989)-. Periodical. English (French). qt. $337.35. Walter de Gruyter Inc., PO Box 303421, D 10728 Berlin Germany. **Tel** 011 49 30 260050, FAX 011 49 30 26005251. **LC** QA1; .F65. **DD** 510/.5. **CODEN** FOMAEF. **[CCC].** Documents available from The Genuine Article.
**Desc:** Devoted entirely to the publication of original research articles in all fields of pure and applied mathematics.
**Ind/Abst** Compumath Citation Index [Full Cov.]; Curr. Contents Phys. Chem. Earth Sci.; Math. Rev.; Res. Alert [Full Cov.]; SCISEARCH; Zentralbl. Math. Ihre Grenzgeb.

●SI/0218-348X
**FRACTALS.** Vol. 1, No. 1 (Mar. 1993)-. Periodical. English. Four times a year. $105.00 individuals, $290.00 institutions. World Scientific Publishing Company, PO Box 128, Farrer Road, Singapore 9128 Singapore. **Tel** 011 65 3825663, FAX 011 65 3825919, telex RS 28561 WSPC. **(Subscription address:** US: World Scientific Publishing Co., Inc., 1060 Main Street, River Edge, NJ 07661 Telephone: (201)487-9655, Fax: (201)487-9656; Europe: World Scientific Publishing Co Ltd, 73 Lynton Mead, Totteridge, London N20 8DH United Kingdom Telephone: 011 44 81 4462461, Fax: 011 44 81 4463356; India: World Scientific Publishing Co Pte Ltd, 4911 9th Floor, High Point IV, 45 Palace Road, Bangalore 560 001 India Telephone: (80) 2205972, Fax: (80) 3344593, Telex: 0845-2900 PCO IN; Hong Kong: World Scientific Publishing (HK) Co, PO Box 72482, Kowloon Central Post Office, Hong Kong Telephone: 852-7718791, Fax: 852-7718155) **LC** IN PROCESS. **CODEN** FRACEG.

US
**FRONTIERS IN APPLIED MATHEMATICS.** **Added/Corp** Society for Industrial and Applied Mathematics. **VFOAT** Frontiers. Vol. 1, (1983)-. Monographic series. English. ir. Society for Industrial and Applied Mathematics, 3600 University City Science Center, Philadelphia PA 19104-2688. **Tel** (215)382-9800, (800)447-7426, FAX (215)386-7999, telex 446715.
**Ind/Abst** Zentralbl. Math. Ihre Grenzgeb.

AT/0313-6825
**FUNCTION.** [Function]. (1977)-. Periodical. English. Five times a year (Feb., Apr., June, Aug., Oct.). 17.00Aus$. Monash University, Department of Mathematics, Clayton Victoria 3168 Australia. **Tel** 011 61 3 5654445, FAX 011 61 3 5654403, telex 23691. **ED** Dr. M. A, B. Deakin. **DD** 510.5. Index available. cum. index. **Bk Rev. Circ:** 500.
**Desc:** This magazine addressed principally to students in the upper forms of secondary schools.

US/0016-2663
**FUNCTIONAL ANALYSIS AND ITS APPLICATIONS.** [Funct. anal. appl.]. **Added/Corp** Consultants Bureau. Vol. 1 (Jan./Mar. 1967)-. Periodical. English (Russian). qt (4 issues). $945.00 US; $1105.00 other. Consultants Bureau, A Division of Plenum Publishing Corporation, 233 Spring Street, New York NY 10013. **Tel** (212)620-8000, (212)620-8466, FAX (212)463-0742, telex 23/421139. **ED** A. K. Kirillov. **CODEN** FAAPBZ. **[CCC].** Index available. **Pr Rev.** available on microfilm and microfiche from University Microfilms International (UMI). Documents available from The Genuine Article.
**Desc:** Devoted to current problems of functional analysis. Covers representation theory, theory of operators, spectral theory, theory of operator equations and theory of normed rings.
**Ind/Abst** Compumath Citation Index [Full Cov.]; Math. Rev.; Res. Alert [Full Cov.]; SCISEARCH; Zentralbl. Math. Ihre Grenzgeb.

PL/0208-6573
**FUNCTIONES ET APPROXIMATIO COMMENTARII MATHEMATICI.** [Funct. approx. comment. math.]. 1-. English (Russian). **(Subscription address:** ARS Polona, PO Box 1001, 00068 Warsaw Poland.) **LC** QA331; .F85.
**Ind/Abst** Math. Rev.; Zentralbl. Math. Ihre Grenzgeb.

CN/0821-2708
**FUNCTIONS.** [Functions]. Vol. 11, No. 2 (Jan. 1982)-. Periodical. English. New Brunswick Teachers' Association, PO Box 752, Fredericton New Brunswick E3B 5R6 Canada. **Tel** (506)452-8921. **ED** John Jewett. **DD** 510/.7/12. **Bk Rev. Ad Acc.** ctrl circ. ***Continues*** *Mathematics (New Brunswick Teachers' Association. Mathematics Council), 0711-1193.*
**Desc:** Articles on puzzles, methodology, and motivation, some computer topics with math applications.

PL/0016-2736
**FUNDAMENTA MATHEMATICAE.** [Fundam. math.]. **Added/Corp** Polska Akademia Nauk. Instytut Matematyczny (Polska Akademia Nauk). (1920)-. Periodical. English (French, German and Italian). ir. $84.00. **(Subscription address:** ARS Polona, PO Box 1001, 00068 Warsaw Poland.) **LC** QA1; .F8. cum. index. **Pr Rev. Circ:** 2,000 (ctrl). Documents available from The Genuine Article.
**Desc:** Publishes papers devoted to set theory, topology, mathematical logic and foundations, real functions, as well as measure and integration and abstract algebra.
**Ind/Abst** Compumath Citation Index [Full Cov.]; Math. Rev.; Res. Alert [Full Cov.]; SCISEARCH; Zentralbl. Math. Ihre Grenzgeb.

JA/0532-8721
**FUNKCIALAJ EKVACIOJ.** (FUNKCIALAJ EKVACIOJ. SERIO INTERNACIA.). [Funkc. ekvacioj]. **Added/Corp** Nihon Sugakkai. Kansu Hoteishiki Bunkakai. (April 1958)-. Multiple languages (English, French, German and Esperanto). Three times a year. $195.00. Nihon Sugakkai Kansu Hoteishiki Bunkakai, (Division of Functional Equations, Mathematical Society of Japan)), c/o Kobe Daigaku Rigakubu Sugaku Kyoshitsu, Rokkodaicho, Nadaku, Kobeshi, Hyogoken 657 Japan. **(Subscription address:** Kinokuniya Company Ltd., 38-1 Sakuragaoka 5, chome Setagaya-ku, Tokyo 156 Japan.) **LC** QA431; .F83. **CODEN** FESIAT.
**Desc:** Provides analysis of mathematics functional equations.
**Ind/Abst** Math. Rev.; Zentralbl. Math. Ihre Grenzgeb.

RU/0374-1990
**FUNKCIONALNYJ ANALIZ I EGO PRILOZENIA.** (FUNKTIONALNYI ANALIZ I EGO PRILOZHENIIA.). [Funkc. anal. i ego priloz.]. **Added/Corp** Akademiia Nauk SSSR. Vol. 1 (Jan./March 1967)-. Academic Scholarly Publication. Russian. qt. $67.00. Izdatelstvo Nauka / Akademiia Nauk, Publishing House of the Russian Academy of Sciences, Leninskii Porspekt 14, 117901 Moscow Russia. **Tel** 011 95 954-21-53, FAX 011 95 938-21-44, telex 411964. **(Subscription address:** Victor Kamkin, 4956 Boiling Brook Parkway, Rockville, MD 20852**)** **DD** 510.
**Desc:** Information on functional analysis.
**Ind/Abst** Math. Rev.; Zentralbl. Math. Ihre Grenzgeb.

RU
**FUNKTSIONAL'NYI ANALIZ. SPEKTRAL'NAIA TEORIIA.** **Added/Corp** Ul'ianovskii Gosudarstvennyi Pedagogicheskii Institut im. I.N. Ul'ianova. **VFOAT** Spektral'naia Teoriia. (19??)-. Russian.
**Ind/Abst** Zentralbl. Math. Ihre Grenzgeb.

NE/0165-0114
**FUZZY SETS AND SYSTEMS.** [Fuzzy sets syst.]. **Added/Corp** International Fuzzy Systems Association. Vol. 1, No. 1 (1978)-. Academic Scholarly Publication. English. Twenty-four times a year (8 volumes). Fl3280.00. Elsevier Science Publishers BV, PO Box 211, 1000 AE Amsterdam Netherlands. **Tel** 011 31 20 5803642, FAX 011 31 20 5862696, telex 15682. **ED** C V Negoita, L A Zadeh and H J Zimmermann. **LC** QA248; .F87. **DD** 511.3/2. **CODEN** FSSYD8. **[CCC]. Pr Rev.** available on microfilm and microfiche from University Microfilms International (UMI). Documents available from Article Express International, The Genuine Article, Ask*IEEE.
**Desc:** The primary purpose is to improve professional communication between scientists and practitioners who are interested in doing research on, or applying fuzzy sets and systems.
**Ind/Abst** ACM Guide Comput. Lit.; Compumath Citation Index [Full Cov.]; Comput. Rev.; Curr. Contents Eng. Tech. Appl. Sci.; Ei Page One; Eng. Index Annu. [Select. Cov.]; GeoRef; INSPEC (1978-); Int. Abstr. Oper. Res. [Select. Cov.]; Math. Rev.; Oper. Res./Manag. Sci.; Qual. Control Appl. Stat.; Res. Alert [Full Cov.]; Sci. Cit. Index; SCISEARCH; Soc. Sci. Cit. Index [Select. Cov.]; Stat. Theory Method Abstr. (1984, 1986); Zentralbl. Math. Ihre Grenzgeb.

SP/0016-3805
**GACETA MATEMATICA.** [Gac. mat.]. Began publication in 1949. Periodical. Spanish. bm (eight no. a year). $10.31. Real Sociedad Matematica Espan. **LC** QA1; .G27.
**Ind/Abst** Math. Rev.; Stat. Theory Method Abstr. (1969, 1980-1982, 1986).

US/0899-8256
**GAMES AND ECONOMIC BEHAVIOR.** [Games econ. behav.]. Vol. 1, No. 1 (Mar. 1989)-. Academic Scholarly Publication. English. Eight times a year. $266.00 US and Canada; $320.00 other. Academic Press, Inc., 6277 Sea Harbor Drive, Orlando FL 32887. **Tel** (800)543-9534, (407)345-4100, FAX (407)363-9661. **ED** Ehud Kalai. **LC** QA269; .G36. **DD** 519.3/05. **CODEN** GEBEEF. **[CCC].** Documents available from The Genuine Article, Ask*IEEE.
**Desc:** Publishes original and survey papers dealing with game-theoretic modeling in the social, biological, and mathematical sciences. Papers published are mathematically rigorous as well as accessible to readers in related fields.
**Ind/Abst** Curr. Contents Soc. Behav. Sci.; Econ. Lit. Index (199?-); INSPEC (Mar. 1990-); J. Econ. Lit. (1989-); Math. Rev.; Res. Alert [Full Cov.]; Soc. Sci. Cit. Index [Full Cov.]; Zentralbl. Math. Ihre Grenzgeb.

BG
**GANIT.** **Added/Corp** Bangladesh Mathematical Society. **VFOAT** Ganita. Vol. 1, No. 1 (1981)-. Periodical. English. sa. Bangladesh Mathematical Society. **LC** QA1; .G279. **DD** 510/.5.
**Ind/Abst** Math. Rev.; Zentralbl. Math. Ihre Grenzgeb.

II/0046-5402
**GANITA.** [Ganita]. **Added/Corp** Bharata Ganita Parisad. Vol. 1 (June 1950)-. English (Hindi). an (Aug.). $25.00. Bharata Ganita Parisad, Mathematics and Astronomy, University of Lucknow, Lucknow India. **Tel** 11 91 11 75944. **(Subscription address:** Prints India, 11 Darya Ganj, New Delhi 110002 India.) **ED** Professor Sunil Datta. **LC** QA1; .G28. **CODEN** GNTAAG. Index available (Bound in next issue). cum. index. **Bk Rev**, (Qty: 1). **Circ:** 500 (ctrl). ***Supersedes*** *Bharata Ganita Parisad. Proceedings.*
**Ind/Abst** Math. Rev.; Zentralbl. Math. Ihre Grenzgeb.

II/0970-0307
**GANITA BHARATI.** [Ganita bharati]. **Added/Corp** Indian Society for History of Mathematics. **VFOAT** Ganita-Bharati. Vol. 1, No. 1-2 (Jan.-June 1979)-. Periodical. English. qt. $50.00. University of Delhi / Ramjas College, Ramjas College, Department of Mathematics, Delhi 110007 India. **(Subscription address:** Prints India, 11 Darya Ganj, New Delhi 110002 India.) **LC** QA21; .G2. **DD** 510/.5. **UDC** 51.
**Ind/Abst** Math. Rev.; Zentralbl. Math. Ihre Grenzgeb.

II/0970-9169
**GANITA SANDESH.** [Ganita Sandesh]. **VFOAT** Ganita Sandesa. (1987)-. Periodical. Multiple languages. sa. **UDC** 510.
**Ind/Abst** Zentralbl. Math. Ihre Grenzgeb.

CC/1000-081X
**GAODENG XUEXIAO JISUAN SHUXUE XUEBAO.** (KAO TENG HSUEH HSIAO CHI SUAN SHU HSUEH HSEUH PAO.). [Gaodeng xuexiao jisuan shuxue xuebao]. **VFOAT** Numerical Mathematics. (1979)-. Periodical. Chinese (summaries and/or abstracts in English). qt. **(Subscription address:** China International Book Trading Corporation, PO Box 399, Library Service Department, Beijing 100044 People's Republic of China.) **LC** QA297; .K36. **DD** 519.4/05. Index available in last issue of volume--attached.
**Ind/Abst** Int. Abstr. Oper. Res. (?-?); Math. Rev.

PO/0373-2681
**GAZETA DE MATEMATICA.** (GAZETA DE MATEMATICA. JORNAL DOS CONCORRENTES DO EXAME DE APTIDAO E DOS ESTUDANTES DE MATEMATICA DAS ESCOLAS SUPERIORES.). [Gaz. mat.]. No. 1- Jan. 1940-. Periodical. Portuguese. qt. Livraria sa da Costa Editora, Rua Garrett 100 102, Lisbon 2 Portugal. **LC** QA1; .G295. **DD** 510.5. **CODEN** GZMTAK. Documents available from Ask*IEEE.
**Ind/Abst** INSPEC (1968-); Math. Rev.; Stat. Theory Method Abstr. (1959-1963).

RM/1010-9943
**GAZETA MATEMATICA (BUCHAREST, ROMANIA : 1974).** ***Ceased.*** (GAZETA MATEMATICA / SOCIETATEA DE STIINTE MATEMATICE.). [Gaz. mat.]. Vol. 79, No. 7 (July 1974-19??). Periodical. Romanian. mo. **LC** QA1; .G2955. **DD** 510/.5. ***Formed by the union of*** *Gazeta Matematica. Seria A* ***and*** *Gazeta Matematica. Seria B.*
**Desc:** Scientific publication on mathematics for youth.
**Ind/Abst** Math. Rev.

AT/0311-0729
**GAZETTE - AUSTRALIAN MATHEMATICAL SOCIETY.** [Gaz. - Aust. Math. Soc.]. **Main/Corp** Australian Mathematical Society. Vol. 1 (1974)-. Periodical. English. Five times a year (Apr., June, Aug., Oct., Dec.). 48.00Aus$ Australia; $37.00 US. Australian Mathematical Publishing Association, Department of Mathematics, Australian National University, Canberra ACT 0200 Australia. **Tel** 011 61 6 267 4268, FAX 011 61 6 267 4263. **ED** Graeme Cohen. **Bk Rev. Circ:** 920.
**Desc:** Carries news items and mathematical articles on tertiary mathematical teaching.
**Ind/Abst** Math. Rev.; Zentralbl. Math. Ihre Grenzgeb.

AT/1032-2302
**GEMS WODEN.** (GEMS.). [GEMSWoden]. **Added/Corp** Australia. Curriculum Development Centre. **VFOAT** Gender Equity in Maths & Science. (1988)-. Periodical. English. qt. **ED** Sue Willis & Margo Hayson. **DD** 507.088042.
**Ind/Abst** Aust. Educ. Index.

●US/1065-7371
**GEOMBINATORICS : [A MINI-JOURNAL OF OPEN PROBLEMS OF COMBINATORIAL AND DISCRETE GEOMETRY AND RELATED AREAS] / UNIVERSITY OF COLORADO AT COLORADO SPRINGS AND CENTER FOR EXCELLENCE IN MATHEMATICAL EDUCATION.** [Geombinatorics]. **Added/Corp** University of Colorado at Colorado Springs. Center for Excellence in Mathematical Education. (1992)-.

Periodical. English. qt. $15.00. Center for Excellence in Mathematical Education, 885 Red Mesa Drive, Colorado Springs CO 80906. **DD** 507.

NE/0046-5755
**GEOMETRIAE DEDICATA.** [Geom. dedic.]. Vol. 1, No. 1 (Nov. 1972)-. Periodical. Multiple languages (English and German). Fifteen times a year. $1,820.00. Kluwer Academic Publishers, Postbus 322, 3300 AH Dordrecht, The Netherlands. **Tel** 011 (31) 78 524400, FAX 011 31 78 183273, telex 20083. **ED** K Strambach and F D Veldkamp. **LC** QA440; .G46. **DD** 516/.005. **CODEN** GEMDAT. **[CCC]. Ad Acc. Pr Rev. Acid Free. Circ:** 600. available on microfilm and microfiche from University Microfilms International (UMI). Documents available from The Genuine Article.
**Desc:** Journal for the publication of research articles on geometry in a wide sense as well as those parts of mathematics which are, at least in part, geometrical in spirit or methods.
**Ind/Abst** Compumath Citation Index [Full Cov.]; Math. Rev.; Ref. Z.; Res. Alert [Full Cov.]; SCISEARCH; Zentralbl. Math. Ihre Grenzgeb.

SZ/1016-443X
**GEOMETRIC AND FUNCTIONAL ANALYSIS : GAFA. VFOAT** GAFA. Vol. 1, No. 1 (1991)-. Periodical. English (French and German). bm. 463.10F Switzerland; 475.00F other. Birkhaeuser Verlag Ag, Klosterberg 23, PO Box 133, CH-4010 Basel Switzerland. **Tel** 011 41 61 2717400, FAX 011 41 0 61 2717666, telex 963475 birk ch. **(Subscription address:** Birkhauser Verlag AG, PO Box 151, CH 4106 Therwil Switzerland; Phone: 011 41 61 7217740**) ED** J. Cheeger, M. Gromov, D. Kazhdan, V. Milman, P. Sarnak, R. Schoen. **LC** QA299.6; .G46. **DD** 515/.05. Index available. cum. index. **Bk Rev. Ad Acc. Circ:** 400 (ctrl).
**Desc:** Publishes major results covering key topics in geometry and analysis, and their interactions: elliptic operators on manifolds; global variational calculus, especially as related to sympletic geometry; concentration phenomenon and geometric inequalities; asymptotic geometry where the dimension goes to infinity; geometric aspects of operator and approximation theories; and geometric problems arising in statistical mechanics.
**Ind/Abst** Math. Rev.; Zentralbl. Math. Ihre Grenzgeb.

RU/0134-8817
**GEOMETRICHESKII SBORNIK. Added/Corp** Tomskii Gosudarstvennyi Universitet Imeni V. Kuibysheva. (1962)-. Russian. Izdatelstvo Tomskogo Universiteta / Tomsk State University, Prospekt Lenina 36, 634050 Tomsk Russia. **Tel** 23-44-65, FAX 22-24-66, telex 128258. **LC** QA440; .G4614.
**Ind/Abst** Zentralbl. Math. Ihre Grenzgeb.

GW/0720-2598
**GEOMETRY.** [Geometry]. **Added/Corp** Heidelberger Akademie der Wissenschaften Fachsingformationszentrum Erergie, Physik, Mathematik. (1981)-. Periodical. English (French and German). Twelve times a year. $135.00. Scientific Information Service Inc., 7 Woodland Avenue, Larchmont NY 10538. **Tel** (914)834-8864. **(Subscription address:** North America/ Journal Fulfillment Services, 44 Hartz Way, Secaucus, NJ 07094**)**

●US/1072-947X
**GEORGIAN MATHEMATICAL JOURNAL.** [Georgian math. j.]. Vol. 1, No. 1 (Jan. 1994)-. Periodical. English. Six times a year. $175.00 US; $205.00 other. Plenum Press, 233 Spring Street, New York NY 10013-1578. **Tel** (212)620-8000, (800)221-9369, FAX (212)463-0742, (212)807-1047, telex 23/421139. **DD** 510. **CODEN** GMJOE5.

●NE
**GEWINA. See** Science and Technology.

UK/0017-0895
**GLASGOW MATHEMATICAL JOURNAL.** [Glasg. math. j.]. Vol. 8, Pt. 1 (Jan. 1967)-. Periodical. English. Three times a year. £68.00 UK and Europe; $125.00 other. Oxford University Press, Walton Street, Oxford OX2 6DP England. **Tel** 011 44 865 56767, FAX 011 44 865 267773, telex 837330 OXPRES G. **(Subscription address:** Oxford University Press / USA, Journals Marketing Department, Oxford University Press, 2001 Evans Road, Cary NC 27513.**) LC** QA1; .G52. **CODEN** GLMJAS. **[CCC]. Pr Rev.** available in microform from University Microfilms International (UMI). ***Continues*** *Proceedings of the Glasgow Mathematical Association.*
**Ind/Abst** Math. Rev.

CI/0017-095X
**GLASNIK MATEMATICKI. SERIJA III.** [Glas. mat.]. **Added/Corp** Drustvo Matematicara i Fizicara SRH. Sveucilliste u Zagrebu. Institut za Matematiku. Sveucilliste u Zagrebu. Matematicki Odjel. (1966)-. Periodical. English (French and German; summaries and/or abstracts in Serbo-Croatian (Roman)). sa (2 issues). $30.00. University of Zagreb / Sveuciliste u Zagrebu, PO Box 815, TRG Marsala Tita 14, 41000 Zagreb Croatia. **Tel** (041)272-411. **LC** QA1; .G53. **CODEN** GLMAB2. Documents available from Ask*IEEE. ***Supersedes*** *Glasnik Matematicko-Fizicki i Astronomski. Serija II.*
**Ind/Abst** INSPEC (1981-); Math. Rev.; Zentralbl. Math. Ihre Grenzgeb.

GW/0932-7991
**GLOTTOMETRIKA. See** Linguistics.

●US/1065-7339
**GRADUATE STUDIES IN MATHEMATICS.** [Grad. stud. math.]. **Added/Corp** American Mathematical Society. **VFOAT** GSM. Vol. 1 (1993)-. Monographic series. English. ir. Price varies per volume. American Mathematical Society, PO Box 6248, Providence RI 02940-6248. **Tel** (800)321-4267, (401)455-4000, FAX (401)331-3842, telex 797192. **(Subscription address:** American Mathematical Society, PO Box 5904, Boston MA 02206-5904.**) DD** 510. **[CCC].**

US/0072-5285
**GRADUATE TEXTS IN MATHEMATICS.** [Grad. texts math.]. (1971)-. Monographic series. English. ir. Price varies per volume. Springer Verlag New York Inc., PO Box 19386 Books, Newark NJ 07195. **Tel** (201)348-4033. **(Subscription address:** North America/ Journal Fulfillment Services, 44 Hartz Way, Secaucus, NJ 07094**) LC** UNC.
**Desc:** Contains articles on all types and courses of mathematics.
**Ind/Abst** Math. Rev.; Zentralbl. Math. Ihre Grenzgeb.

US/0161-3324
**GRAPH THEORY NEWSLETTER.** ***Ceased.*** [Graph theor. newsl.]. **Added/Corp** Western Michigan University. Dept. of Mathematics. Vol. 1 (1971)-(19??). Newsletter. English. qt. Western Michigan University / Mathematics, Mathematics Department GTN, Kalamazoo MI 49009. **Tel** (616)383-6165. **ED** Garry L Johns. **DD** 511. **CODEN** GTNED9. **Circ:** 180 (ctrl).
**Desc:** Abstracts of recent papers in graph theory; announcements relating to graph theory, conferences, changes of addresses, and announcements of recent books in graph theory.
**Ind/Abst** Zentralbl. Math. Ihre Grenzgeb.

JA/0911-0119
**GRAPHS AND COMBINATORICS.** [Graphs comb.]. **VFOAT** Graphs & Combinatorics. Vol. 1, No. 1 (1985)-. Periodical. English. Four times a year. DM490.00. Springer-Verlag Tokyo, 37-3 Hongo 3-Chrome, Bunkyo-ku, Tokyo 113 Japan. **Tel** 011 81 3 38120331, FAX 011 81 3 38120719, telex 26536 SREBS J. **(Subscription address:** Springer Verlag New York Inc. / for North America, 44 Hartz Way, Secaucus NJ 07096.**) ED** Hoon Heng Ten. **CODEN** GRCOE5. **[CCC]. Pr Rev.** available on microfilm and microfiche from University Microfilms International (UMI). Documents available from The Genuine Article, Ask*IEEE.
**Desc:** Features original papers, survey articles, short communications and announcements; covers all aspects of combinatorial mathematics.
**Ind/Abst** Compumath Citation Index [Full Cov.]; INSPEC (1986-); Math. Rev. (1985-); Res. Alert [Full Cov.]; SCISEARCH; Zentralbl. Math. Ihre Grenzgeb.

FR
**GROUPE D'ETUDE D'ALGEBRE. EXPOSES. Main/Corp** Groupe d'Etude d'Algebre. Vol. 1 (1975/76)-. French. Institut Henri Poincare, 11 rue Pierre et Marie Curie, 75231 Paris Cedex 05 France. **ED** Marie-Paule Malliavin. ***Supersedes in part*** *Seminaire P. Dubreil, F. Aribaud et M. P. Malliavin. Algebre.*

FR
**GROUPE D'ETUDE D'ANALYSE ULTRAMETRIQUE. EXPOSES.** ***Ceased.*** **Main/Corp** Groupe d'Etude d'Analyse Ultrametrique (Paris, France). **Added/Corp** Institut Henri Poincare. (1975)-(19??). French. an. Institut Henri Poincare, 11 rue Pierre et Marie Curie, 75231 Paris Cedex 05 France. **LC** QA300; .G76a. **DD** 515/.1. ***Continues*** *Groupe de Travail d'Analyse Ultrametrique.*

FR
**GROUPE D'ETUDE DE THEORIES STABLES. [EXPOSES]. Main/Corp** Groupe d'Etude de Theories Stables. **Added/Corp** Universite Pierre et Marie Curie. Institut Henri Poincare. (1977/1978)-. Periodical. French.
**Ind/Abst** Zentralbl. Math. Ihre Grenzgeb.

GW
**GRUNDLEHREN DER MATHEMATISCHEN WISSENSCHAFTEN. VFOAT** Comprehensive Texts in Mathematics; Series of Comprehensive Texts in Mathematics. (1976)-. Monographic series. English. ir. Price varies per volume. Springer Verlag New York Inc., PO Box 19386 Books, Newark NJ 07195. **Tel** (201)348-4033. **(Subscription address:** Springer Verlag New York Inc. / for North America, 44 Hartz Way, Secaucus NJ 07096.**) LC** UNC. ***Continues*** *Grundlehren der Mathematischen Wissenschaften in Einzeldarstellungenmit Besonderer Berucksichtigung der Anwendungsgebiete.*
**Ind/Abst** Math. Rev.

GW
**GRUNDWISSEN MATHEMATIK.** Vol. 1, (1983)-. Monographic series. German. Springer-Verlag GmbH & Company KG, Heidelberger Platz 3, D 14197 Berlin Germany. **Tel** 011 49 30 8207223, FAX 011 49 30 8214091, telex 183 319 SPBLN D. **(Subscription address:** Springer Verlag New York Inc. / for North America, 44 Hartz Way, Secaucus NJ 07096.**)**
**Ind/Abst** Math. Rev.; Zentralbl. Math. Ihre Grenzgeb.

II/0379-3419
**GUJARAT STATISTICAL REVIEW. See** Mathematics-Abstracting, Bibliographies and Statistics.

US/0362-8191
**HANDBOOK OF TABLES FOR MATHEMATICS. Added/Corp** Chemical Rubber Company. **VFOAT** CRC Handbook of Tables for Mathematics. 3rd Ed. (1967)-. English. ir. $7.95 per issue. CRC Press Inc., 2000 Corporate Boulevard Northwest, Boca Raton FL 33431. **Tel** (407)994-0555, (800)272-7737, FAX (407)998-9784, telex 568689. **LC** QA47; .H32. **DD** 510/.21/2. ***Continues*** *Handbook of Mathematical Tables.*

JA/0018-2079
**HIROSHIMA MATHEMATICAL JOURNAL.** [Hiroshima math. j.]. **Added/Corp** Hiroshima Daigaku. Sugaku Kyoshitsu. Vol. 1, No. 1 (July 1971)-. Periodical. English. ir. Hiroshima University / Department of Mathematics, Faculty of Science, Hiroshima Japan. **LC** QA1; .H572. **DD** 510/5. **CODEN** HMTJAD. ***Continues*** *Hiroshima Daigaku. Journal of Science of the Hiroshima University. Series A-I, Mathematics, 0386-3026.*
**Ind/Abst** Math. Rev.; Zentralbl. Math. Ihre Grenzgeb.

US/0315-0860
**HISTORIA MATHEMATICA.** [Hist. math.]. **Added/Corp** International Commission on the History of Mathematics. Canadian Society for the History and Philosophy of Mathematics. Vol. 1 (Feb. 1974)-. Academic Scholarly Publication. English (Multiple languages). qt (4 issues). $127.00 US and Canada; $156.00 other. Academic Press, Inc., 6277 Sea Harbor Drive, Orlando FL 32887. **Tel** (800)543-9534, (407)345-4100, FAX (407)363-9661. **ED** Eberhard Knobloch and David E. Rowe. **LC** QA21; .H54. **DD** 510/.9. **CODEN** HIMADS. **[CCC]. Pr Rev.** Documents available from The Genuine Article.
**Desc:** Concerned with the history of all aspects of the mathematical sciences in all parts of the world and from all historical periods. Also includes occasional biographies of mathematicians and historians, articles on organizations and institutions, essays on historiography, and the interactions among all facets of mathematical activity and other aspects of culture and society.
**Ind/Abst** Am. Hist. Life (1983-); Compumath Citation Index [Full Cov.]; Math. Rev.; Res. Alert [Full Cov.]; SCISEARCH; Soc. Sci. Cit. Index [Select. Cov.]; Zentralbl. Math. Ihre Grenzgeb.

US/0899-2428
**HISTORY OF MATHEMATICS.** [Hist. math.]. **Added/Corp** American Mathematical Society. Vol. 1 (1988)-. Monographic series. English. ir. Price varies per volume. American Mathematical Society, PO Box 6248, Providence RI 02940-6248. **Tel** (800)321-4267, (401)455-4000, FAX (401)331-3842, telex 797192. **(Subscription address:** American Mathematical Society, PO Box 5904, Boston MA 02206-5904.**) DD** 510. **[CCC].**

GW/0073-2842
**HOCHSCHULBUCHER FUER MATHEMATIK.** [Hochsch.b. Math.]. (1953)-. Monographic series. German. ir. **UDC** 51.
**Ind/Abst** Zentralbl. Math. Ihre Grenzgeb.

JA/0385-4035
**HOKKAIDO MATHEMATICAL JOURNAL.** [Hokkaido math. j.]. **Added/Corp** Hokkaido Daigaku, Sapporo, Japan. Rigakubu. Sugakuka. Vol. 1 (Oct. 1972)-. Periodical. English. Three times a year. $363.00. **(Subscription address:** Kinokuniya Company Ltd., 38-1 Sakuragaoka 5, chome Setagaya-ku, Tokyo 156 Japan.**) LC** QA1; .H632. **DD** 510/.5. **CODEN** HMAJDN. ***Supersedes*** *Hokkaido Daigaku, Sapporo, Japan. Rigakubu. Journal of the Faculty of Science, Hokkaido University. Series I. Mathematics.*
**Ind/Abst** Math. Rev.; Zentralbl. Math. Ihre Grenzgeb.

US/0362-1588
**HOUSTON JOURNAL OF MATHEMATICS.** [Houst. j. math.]. **Added/Corp** University of Houston. Dept. of Mathematics. Vol. 1 (1975)-. Periodical. English. Four times a year (Mar., june, Sept., Dec.). $90.00. University of Houston / Mathematics, C/O G. Auchmuty, 3800 Cullen, Department of Mathematics, Houston TX 77204-5883. **Tel** (713)743-3500. **ED** G. Auchmuty. **LC** QA1; .H68. **DD** 510/.5. **CODEN** HJMADZ. Index available (Bound in December issue, price included). **Pr Rev. Circ:** 450. Documents available from The Genuine Article, Ask*IEEE.
**Desc:** An original research from all areas of mathematics.

**Ind/Abst** Compumath Citation Index [Full Cov.]; INSPEC (1976-); Math. Rev.; Res. Alert [Full Cov.]; SCISEARCH; Zentralbl. Math. Ihre Grenzgeb.

CC/1000-0577
**HSI TUNG KO HSUEH YU SHU HSUEH.** **Added/Corp** Chung-kuo ko Hsueh Yuan. Hsi Tung ko Hsueh yen Chiu so. **VFOAT** Journal of Systems Science and Mathematical Sciences. Vol. 1, No. 1 (1981)-. Periodical. Chinese (summaries and/or abstracts in English). qt. $51.20. Science Press, 16 Donghuangchenggen North Street, Beijing 100707, People's Republic of China. **Tel** 011 86 1 4019821, 011 86 1 4010642, FAX 011 86 1 4012180, 011 86 1 4019810, telex 210147. **LC** Q295; .H725. **DD** 003. **CODEN** XKSHEW. **Ad Acc. Circ:** 6,000.
**Ind/Abst** Math. Rev.; Zentralbl. Math. Ihre Grenzgeb.

●US/1065-8297
**HUMANISTIC MATHEMATICS NETWORK JOURNAL.** [Humanist. Math. Netw. j.]. **Added/Corp** Humanistic Mathemataics Network. **VFOAT** HMN Journal. No. 7 (Apr. 1992)-. English. Humanistic Mathematics Network, Alvin M White, Harvey Mudd College, Claremont CA 91711. **DD** 510. ***Continues*** *Newsletter (Humanistic Mathematics Network), 1047-627X.*

US
**HYPOTENUSE.** **Main/Corp** Research Triangle Institute. English. bm. Research Triangle Institute, PO Box 12194, Research Triangle Park NC 27709.
**Ind/Abst** Ind. Hyg. Dig.

US
**ILLINOIS INVENTORY OF EDUCATIONAL PROGRESS. MATHEMATICS ITEM RESULTS.**
**Added/Corp** Illinois Office of Education. Dept. of Planning, Research, and Evaluation. **VFOAT** I.I.E.P. Mathematics Item Results; IIEP Mathematics Item Results. (19??)-. English. Illinois State Board of Education, 100 North First Street, Springfield IL 62777. **LC** QA13.5.I3; I4. **DD** 510/.7/10773.

US/0019-2082
**ILLINOIS JOURNAL OF MATHEMATICS.** [Ill. j. math.]. **Added/Corp** University of Illinois (Urbana-Champaign Campus) University of Illinois at Urbana-Champaign. Vol. 1 (Mar. 1957)-. Periodical. English (French). Four times a year. $108.00. University of Illinois Press, 1325 South Oak Street, Champaign IL 61820. **Tel** (217)333-0950, FAX (217)244-8082. **ED** Stephanie Alexander, Earl R. Berkson, E. Graham Evans Jr., Adolf Hildebrand, Maung Min-oo, Philippe Toudeur and Lou van der Dries. **LC** QA1; .I45. **DD** 510.5. **CODEN** IJMTAW. **[CCC].** Index available (bound in Dec. issue). **Pr Rev. Circ:** 1,000. available on microfilm and microfiche from University Microfilms International (UMI). Documents available from The Genuine Article.
**Desc:** Research in pure and applied mathematics.
**Ind/Abst** Compumath Citation Index [Full Cov.]; Curr. Contents Phys. Chem. Earth Sci.; Int. Aerosp. Abstr.; Math. Rev.; Res. Alert [Full Cov.]; Stat. Theory Method Abstr. (1961-1963, 1967, 1971, 1974-1975, 1977, 1979); Zentralbl. Math. Ihre Grenzgeb.

US
**ILLINOIS MATHEMATICS TEACHER, THE.** **Added/Corp** Illinois Council of Teachers of Mathematics. (19??)-. Periodical. English. Four times a year. $10.00 (individuals), $15.00 (institutions); $50.00 Comes with Illinois Council for Teachers membership. Illinois Council for Teachers of Mathematics / ICTM, 2343 Douglas Road, Oswego IL 60543.

UK/0272-4960
**IMA JOURNAL OF APPLIED MATHEMATICS.** [IMA j. appl. math.]. **Added/Corp** Institute of Mathematics and Its Applications. **VFOAT** Journal of Applied Mathematics; I.M.A. Journal of Applied Mathematics. **VAT** Institute of Mathematics and Its Applications Journal of Applied Mathematics. Vol. 27, No. 1 (Jan. 1981)-. Periodical. English. bm. £225.00 UK and Europe; $410.00 other. Oxford University Press, Walton Street, Oxford OX2 6DP England. **Tel** 011 44 865 56767, FAX 011 44 865 267773, telex 837330 OXPRES G. **(Subscription address:** Oxford University Press / USA, Journals Marketing Department, Oxford University Press, 2001 Evans Road, Cary NC 27513.**)** **ED** J. R. Ockendon and D. A. Spence. **LC** QA1; .I47. **DD** 505. **CODEN** IJAMDM. **[CCC].** Index available. **Ad Acc. Pr Rev.** available on microfilm and microfiche from University Microfilms International (UMI). Documents available from Article Express International, The Genuine Article, Ask*IEEE. ***Continues in part*** *Journal of the Institute of Mathematics and its Applications, 0020-2932.*
**Desc:** Papers in all areas of the application of maths, including analytic and numerical treatments of both physical and non-physical applied mathematical problems and those arising in industry.
**Ind/Abst** Compumath Citation Index [Full Cov.]; Curr. Contents Phys. Chem. Earth Sci.; Curr. Technol. Index; Ei Page One; Eng. Index Annu.; Fluid Abstr., Civil Eng.; Fluid Abstr. Proc. Eng.; FLUIDEX (1981-); INSPEC (Jan. 1981-); Int. Aerosp. Abstr.; Math. Rev.; Pollut. Abstr. Indexes; Res. Alert [Full Cov.]; Sci. Cit. Index; SCISEARCH; Zentralbl. Math. Ihre Grenzgeb.

UK/0265-0754
**IMA JOURNAL OF MATHEMATICAL CONTROL AND INFORMATION.** [IMA j. math. control inf.]. **Added/Corp** Institute of Mathematics and Its Applications. **VFOAT** Journal of Mathematical Control and Information. **VAT** Institute of Mathematics and Its Applications Journal of Mathematical Control and Information. Vol. 1, No. 1 (1984)-. Periodical. English. qt. £120.00 UK and Europe; $210.00 other. Oxford University Press, Walton Street, Oxford OX2 6DP England. **Tel** 011 44 865 56767, FAX 011 44 865 267773, telex 837330 OXPRES G. **(Subscription address:** Oxford University Press / USA, Journals Marketing Department, Oxford University Press, 2001 Evans Road, Cary NC 27513.**)** **ED** C. J. Harris and J. E. Marshall. **LC** QA402.3; .I4575. **DD** 629.8/312. **[CCC].** Index available. **Ad Acc. Pr Rev.** available on microfilm and microfiche from University Microfilms International (UMI). Documents available from Article Express International, The Genuine Article, Ask*IEEE.
**Desc:** Original papers in mathematical control theory, systems theory, and allied information sciences.
**Ind/Abst** Compumath Citation Index [Full Cov.]; Ei Page One; Eng. Index Annu.; INSPEC (1985-); Math. Rev. (1987-); Res. Alert [Full Cov.]; Zentralbl. Math. Ihre Grenzgeb.

UK/0953-0061
**IMA JOURNAL OF MATHEMATICS APPLIED IN BUSINESS AND INDUSTRY.**
**Added/Corp** Institute of Mathematics and Its Applications. **VFOAT** Journal of Mathematics Applied in Business and Industry. **VAT** Institute of Mathematics and Its Applications Journal of Mathematics in Business and Industry. Vol. 2, No. 1 (1989)-. Periodical. English. qt. £120.00 UK and Europe; $210.00 other. Oxford University Press, Walton Street, Oxford OX2 6DP England. **Tel** 011 44 865 56767, FAX 011 44 865 267773, telex 837330 OXPRES G. **(Subscription address:** Oxford University Press / USA, Journals Marketing Department, Oxford University Press, 2001 Evans Road, Cary NC 27513.**)** **LC** HD30.25; .I43. **DD** 650/.01/513. **CODEN** IMJIE9. **[CCC].** available on microfilm and microfiche from University Microfilms International (UMI). ***Continues*** *IMA Journal of Mathematics in Management, 0268-1129.*
**Ind/Abst** Ei Page One; Math. Rev.; Zentralbl. Math. Ihre Grenzgeb.

UK/0265-0746
**IMA JOURNAL OF MATHEMATICS APPLIED IN MEDICINE AND BIOLOGY.** [IMA j. math. appl. med. biol.]. **Added/Corp** Institute of Mathematics and Its Applications. **VFOAT** Journal of Mathematics Applied in Medicine and Biology. **VAT** Institute of Mathematics and Its Applications Journal of Mathematics Applied in Medicine and Biology. Vol. 1, No. 1 (1984)-. Periodical. English. qt. £120.00 UK and Europe; $210.00 other. Oxford University Press, Walton Street, Oxford OX2 6DP England. **Tel** 011 44 865 56767, FAX 011 44 865 267773, telex 837330 OXPRES G. **(Subscription address:** Oxford University Press / USA, Journals Marketing Department, Oxford University Press, 2001 Evans Road, Cary NC 27513.**)** **ED** R. W. Hiorns. **NLM** W1; IM4572. **CODEN** IJMBEG. **[CCC].** Index available. **Ad Acc. Pr Rev.** available on microfilm and microfiche from University Microfilms International (UMI). Documents available from The Genuine Article, BIOSIS Document Express.
**Desc:** Uses of maths in medical and biological research with emphasis upon the special insights and enhanced understanding which arise from these uses.
**Ind/Abst** Anim. Breed. Abstr.; Biol. Abstr. (1986-); Compumath Citation Index [Full Cov.]; Curr. Aware. Biol. Sci., CABS; Curr. Contents Life Sci.; Helminthol. Abstr.; Index Med. (Vol. 1, No. 1, 1984-); Index Vet.; Math. Rev. (1984-); Protozoolog. Abstr.; Res. Alert [Full Cov.]; Rev. Med. Vet. Entomol.; Sci. Cit. Index; SCISEARCH; Vet. Bull.; Zentralbl. Math. Ihre Grenzgeb.

UK/0272-4979
**IMA JOURNAL OF NUMERICAL ANALYSIS.** [IMA j. numer. anal.]. **Added/Corp** Institute of Mathematics and Its Applications. **VAT** Institute of Mathematics and Its Applications Journal of Numerical Analysis. (Jan. 1981)-. Periodical. English. qt. £150.00 UK and Europe; $275.00 other. Oxford University Press, Walton Street, Oxford OX2 6DP England. **Tel** 011 44 865 56767, FAX 011 44 865 267773, telex 837330 OXPRES G. **(Subscription address:** Oxford University Press / USA, Journals Marketing Department, Oxford University Press, 2001 Evans Road, Cary NC 27513.**)** **ED** I. S. Duff and G. A. Watson. **LC** QA297; .I44. **DD** 519.4/05. **CODEN** IJNADH. **[CCC].** Index available. **Ad Acc. Pr Rev.** available on microfilm and microfiche from University Microfilms International (UMI). Documents available from The Genuine Article, Ask*IEEE. ***Continues in part*** *Journal of the Institute of Mathematics and Its Applications, 0020-2932.*
**Desc:** A balanced coverage of both the theoretical and practical aspects of numerical analysis. Papers providing a rigorous analysis of established methods appear alongside articles on new methods which promise wide applicability.
**Ind/Abst** Compumath Citation Index [Full Cov.]; Curr. Contents Phys. Chem. Earth Sci.; Curr. Technol. Index; Fluid Abstr., Civil Eng.; Fluid Abstr. Proc. Eng.; FLUIDEX (1981-); INSPEC (Jan. 1981-); Int. Aerosp. Abstr.; Math. Rev.; Pollut. Abstr. Indexes; Res. Alert [Full Cov.]; Sci. Cit. Index; SCISEARCH; Zentralbl. Math. Ihre Grenzgeb.

UK
**IMA MONOGRAPH SERIES.** **Added/Corp** Institute of Mathematics and Its Applications. Vol. 1 (1985)-. Monographic series. English. ir. Price varies per volume. Oxford University Press, Walton Street, Oxford OX2 6DP England. **Tel** 011 44 865 56767, FAX 011 44 865 267773, telex 837330 OXPRES G. **(Subscription address:** Oxford University Press / USA, Journals Marketing Department, Oxford University Press, 2001 Evans Road, Cary NC 27513.**)**
**Ind/Abst** Math. Rev.; Zentralbl. Math. Ihre Grenzgeb.

US
**IMA VOLUMES IN MATHEMATICS AND ITS APPLICATIONS, THE.** **Added/Corp** University of Minnesota. Institute for Mathematics and Its Applications. Vol. 1 (1986)-. Monographic series. English. ir. £39.00. Springer Verlag New York Inc., PO Box 19386 Books, Newark NJ 07195. **Tel** (201)348-4033.
**Ind/Abst** Math. Rev.; Zentralbl. Math. Ihre Grenzgeb.

US/0899-8248
**IMPACT OF COMPUTING IN SCIENCE AND ENGINEERING.** ***Ceased.*** [Impact comput. sci. eng.]. Vol. 1, No. 1 (Mar. 1989)-Vol. 5, No. 4, (Dec. 1993). Academic Scholarly Publication. English. qt. Academic Press, Inc., 6277 Sea Harbor Drive, Orlando FL 32887. **Tel** (800)543-9534, (407)345-4100, FAX (407)363-9661. **ED** Peter Deuflhard, Ivo Babuska, Franco Brezzi, Jack Dongarra, Iain S Duff, Feng Kang, James Glimm, Wolfgang Hackbusch, Anthony C Hearn, Egon Krause, Oliver McBryan, James Murray, Olivier Pironneau, Werner Rheinboldt, Ulrich Trottenberg, Jurgen Warnatz. **LC** Q183.9; .I49. **DD** 500/.28/5. **CODEN** ICOEEK. **[CCC].** Documents available from Ask*IEEE.
**Desc:** An international, interdisciplinary journal focusing on articles from mathematical and scientific modeling, scientific computing, computer science, and scientific and engineering applications. Articles typically describe real-life problems attacked by a new kind of specifically-adapted algorithm or by any other new computing technique.
**Ind/Abst** ACM Guide Comput. Lit.; Comput. Rev.; INSPEC (1989-); Math. Rev.; Zentralbl. Math. Ihre Grenzgeb.

NE/0019-3577
**INDAGATIONES MATHEMATICAE.** (INDAGATIONES MATHEMATICAE / KONINKLIJKE NEDERLANDSCHE AKADEMIE VAN WETENSCHAPPEN.). [Indag. math.]. **Added/Corp** Koninklijke Nederlandse Akademie van Wetenschappen. Afdeling Natuurkunde. Vol. 1, Fasc. 1-Vol. 51, Fasc. 4; New Ser., Vol. 1. No. 1 (Mar. 1990)-. Dutch (English, French and German). qt (1 volume). Fl410.00. Elsevier Science Publishers BV, PO Box 211, 1000 AE Amsterdam Netherlands. **Tel** 011 31 20 5803642, FAX 011 31 20 5862696, telex 15682. **LC** QA1; .I48. **DD** 510.58. **CODEN** IMTHBJ. **[CCC].** available on microfilm and microfiche from University Microfilms International (UMI). Documents available from The Genuine Article. ***Absorbed*** *Proceedings of the Koninklijke Nederlandse Akademie van Wetenschappen. Series A, Mathematiks, 0023-3358.*
**Ind/Abst** Compumath Citation Index [Full Cov.]; Math. Rev.; Res. Alert [Full Cov.]; Sci. Cit. Index (19??-19??); SCISEARCH; Stat. Theory Method Abstr. (1959, 1971, 1973-1975, 1979-1981, 1984); Zentralbl. Math. Ihre Grenzgeb.

II/0019-5324
**INDIAN JOURNAL OF MATHEMATICS.** [Indian j. math.]. **Added/Corp** Allahabad Mathematical Society. University of Allahabad. Vol. 1, No. 1 (Dec. 1958)-. Periodical. English (French and German). Three times a year. $200.00. Allahabad Mathematical Society, 10 C S P Singh Marg, Allahabad 211 001 India. **Tel** 011 91 11 52208. **(Subscription address:** Prints India, 11 Darya Ganj, New Delhi 110002 India.**)** **LC** QA1; .I495. **CODEN** IJOMAL. Index available. cum. index. **Ad Acc. Circ:** 600.
**Desc:** Publishes original research papers in all branches of mathematics including mathematical statistics.
**Ind/Abst** Int. Aerosp. Abstr.; Math. Rev.; Zentralbl. Math. Ihre Grenzgeb.

II/0537-2038
**INDIAN JOURNAL OF MECHANICS AND MATHEMATICS.** [Indian j. mech. math.]. **Added/Corp** Mathematical Association, Jadavpur. Vol. I (1963)-. Periodical. English. ir. $15.00 (Vols. 8, 9, 10). Indian Books and Periodicals, 2429 Tilak Street, Pahar Ganj, New Delhi 110005 India. **LC** QA801; .I37. **DD** 510/.05. **CODEN** IJMMAB. **Bk Rev.**
**Ind/Abst** Math. Rev.; Zentralbl. Math. Ihre Grenzgeb.

II/0019-5588
**INDIAN JOURNAL OF PURE AND APPLIED MATHEMATICS.** [Indian j. pure appl. math.]. **Added/Corp** National Institute of Sciences of India. Indian National Science Academy. Vol. 1, No. 1

(Jan. 1970)-. Periodical. English. mo. $200.00. Indian National Science Academy, 1 Bahadur Shah Zafar Marg, New Delhi 110 002 India. **(Subscription address:** Prints India, 11 Darya Ganj, New Delhi 110002 India.**) LC** QA1; .I496. **DD** 510/.5. **CODEN** IJMHAU. **Pr Rev.** Documents available from The Genuine Article, Ask*IEEE.
**Ind/Abst** Compumath Citation Index [Full Cov.]; Curr. Contents Phys. Chem. Earth Sci.; INSPEC (Jan. 1970-); Math. Rev.; Res. Alert [Full Cov.]; SCISEARCH; SEA Abstr.; Soc. Sci. Cit. Index [Select. Cov.]; Stat. Theory Method Abstr. (1987); Zentralbl. Math. Ihre Grenzgeb.

II/0019-5693
**INDIAN JOURNAL OF THEORETICAL PHYSICS.** See Physics.

US/0889-6941
**INDIANA MATHEMATICS TEACHER.** (INDIANA MATHEMATICS TEACHER : OFFICIAL JOURNAL OF THE INDIANA COUNCIL OF TEACHERS OF MATHEMATICS.). [Indiana math. teach.]. Vol. 1, No. 1 (Autumn/Winter 1986)-. Periodical. English. sa. $8.00 (regular membership); $2.00 (student membership). Ball State University / Department of Mathematical Sciences, Muncie IN 47306. **DD** 510. **Circ:** 900 (ctrl). ***Continues*** *ICTM Journal.*
**Desc:** Official journal of the Indiana Council of Teachers of Mathematics.

US/0022-2518
**INDIANA UNIVERSITY MATHEMATICS JOURNAL.** [Indiana Univ. math. j.]. **VFOAT** Mathematics Journal. Vol. 20, No. 1 (July 1970)-. English (German, Italian and French). Four times a year. $115.00. Indiana University Mathematics Journal, Swain Hall East 222, Bloomington IN 47405. **Tel** (812)855-2252. **ED** John Brothers. **LC** QA1. **DD** 510/.5. **CODEN** IUMJAB. **[CCC].** Index available. **Pr Rev. Circ:** 1,200. Documents available from The Genuine Article. ***Continues*** *Journal of Mathematics and Mechanics, 0095-9057.*
**Desc:** Significant research articles in both pure and applied mathematics.
**Ind/Abst** Compumath Citation Index [Full Cov.]; Curr. Contents Phys. Chem. Earth Sci.; Int. Aerosp. Abstr.; Math. Rev.; Res. Alert [Full Cov.]; Sci. Cit. Index; SCISEARCH; Zentralbl. Math. Ihre Grenzgeb.

US/0019-8528
**INDUSTRIAL MATHEMATICS.** [Ind. math.]. Vol. 1, (1950)-. Periodical. English. sa. $17.10. Industrial Mathematics Society 48066. **Tel** (313)927-1367. **ED** Robert Schmidt. **LC** TA350; .I5. **DD** 651.26. **CODEN** IMTHAI. cum. index. **Bk Rev. Ad Acc. Circ:** 300. available on microfilm and microfiche from University Microfilms International (UMI). Documents available from Article Express International, Ask*IEEE.
**Desc:** Publishes original papers in applied mathematics; preliminary notes containing novel items of mathematical, scientific, and technical interest, etc.
**Ind/Abst** Bioeng. Abstr.; Ei Page One; Eng. Index Annu. [Select. Cov.]; INSPEC (1971-); Math. Rev.; Qual. Control Appl. Stat.; Zentralbl. Math. Ihre Grenzgeb.

CN/0710-0027
**INFO-MATHS.** [Info-maths]. Vol. 1, No. 1 (1st Sept. 1978)-. Periodical. French. ir. Free. Commission Scolaire Regionale Orleans, CP 5160, Quebec Quebec G1E 6B6 Canada. **DD** 510/.7/1271447. ctrl circ.

CN/0226-2061
**INSTANTANES MATHEMATIQUES.** [Instant. math.]. First issue in Oct. 1964. Periodical. French. ir. $10.00. Instantanes mathematiques, APame, CP 433, Succursale Westmount, Montreal Quebec H3Z 2T5. **DD** 372.7/3044.

US/1058-0573
**INSTITUTE FOR MATH MANIA PRESENTS WONDERFUL IDEAS, THE.** (WONDERFUL IDEAS.). [Inst. Math Mania presents wonderful ideas]. **Added/Corp** Institute for Math Mania. **VFOAT** Wonderful Ideas. (Oct. 1989)-. Periodical. English. Eight times a year (during the school year). $26.00 US; $32.00 Canada and Mexico; $54.00 other. Wonderful Ideas, PO Box 64691, Burlington VT 05406. **Tel** (617)239-1496, FAX (617)239-1496. **ED** Nancy Segal Janes (editor's phone: (800)92-IDEAS). **DD** 510. Index available in last issue of volume--attached. cum. index. **Bk Rev**, (Qty: 2-3). **Circ:** 1,500.
**Desc:** Ideas for teaching, learning and enjoying elementary and middle school mathematics. All activities promote creative thinking, hands-on learning and problem solving.

GW/0722-7906
**INTEGER PROGRAMMING AND RELATED AREAS.** (INTEGER PROGRAMMING AND RELATED AREAS; A CLASSIFIED BIBLIOGRAPHY.). **Added/Corp** Universitat Bonn. Institut fur Okonometrie und Operations Research. (1976)-. Bibliography. English (Multiple languages). ir. Springer-Verlag GmbH & Company KG, Heidelberger Platz 3, D 14197 Berlin Germany. **Tel** 011 49 30 8207223, FAX 011 49 30 8214091, telex 183 319 SPBLN D. **(Subscription address:** Springer Verlag New York Inc. / for North America, 44 Hartz Way, Secaucus NJ 07096.**) LC** Z6654.P75; I57; T57.7. **DD** 016.5197/7.
**Desc:** Vol. for 1976 covers literature through 1975.

SZ/0378-620X
**INTEGRAL EQUATIONS AND OPERATOR THEORY.** [Integr. equ. oper. theory]. Vol. 1 (1978)-. Periodical. English. mo. 848.40F Switzerland; 873.30F other. Birkhaeuser Verlag Ag, Klosterberg 23, PO Box 133, CH-4010 Basel Switzerland. **Tel** 011 41 61 2717400, FAX 011 41 0 61 2717666, telex 963475 birk ch. **(Subscription address:** Birkhauser Verlag AG, PO Box 151, CH 4106 Therwil Switzerland; Phone: 011 41 61 7217740**) ED** I. Gohberg. **LC** QA431; .I48. **DD** 515.4/5/05. **[CCC]. Pr Rev.** available on microfilm and microfiche from University Microfilms International (UMI). Documents available from The Genuine Article.
**Desc:** Devoted to the publication of current research in integral equations, operator theory and related topics, with emphasis on the linear aspects of the theory.
**Ind/Abst** Compumath Citation Index [Full Cov.]; Math. Rev.; Res. Alert [Full Cov.]; SCISEARCH; Zentralbl. Math. Ihre Grenzgeb.

US
**INTERDISCIPLINARY APPLIED MATHEMATICS.** (1991)-. English. Three times a year.
**Desc:** Books in the IAM series will indicate newer ways that existing mathematics may be applied in traditional areas, as well as point towards other innovative areas of application.

US
**INTERDISCIPLINARY MATHEMATICS.** Vol. 1/2-. Monographic series. English. an. Price varies per volume. Math Science Press, 53 Jordan Road, Brookline MA 02146. **Tel** (617)738-0307. **ED** R Hermann.
**Ind/Abst** Math. Rev.; Zentralbl. Math. Ihre Grenzgeb.

UK/0029-5981
**INTERNATIONAL JOURNAL FOR NUMERICAL METHODS IN ENGINEERING.** See Engineering.

SI/0218-1967
**INTERNATIONAL JOURNAL OF ALGEBRA AND COMPUTATION.** [Int. j. algebra comput.]. **VFOAT** Algebra and Computation. Vol. 1, No. 1 (Mar. 1991)-. Periodical. English. Six times a year. $155.00 individuals, $330.00 institutions. World Scientific Publishing Company, PO Box 128, Farrer Road, Singapore 9128 Singapore. **Tel** 011 65 3825663, FAX 011 65 3825919, telex RS 28561 WSPC. **(Subscription address:** US: World Scientific Publishing Co., Inc., 1060 Main Street, River Edge, NJ 07661 Telephone: (201)487-9655, Fax: (201)487-9656; Europe: World Scientific Publishing Co Ltd, 73 Lynton Mead, Totteridge, London N20 8DH United Kingdom Telephone: 011 44 81 4462461, Fax: 011 44 81 4463356; India: World Scientific Publishing Co Pte Ltd, 4911 9th Floor, High Point IV, 45 Palace Road, Bangalore 560 001 India Telephone: (80) 2205972, Fax: (80) 3344593, Telex: 0845-2900 PCO IN; Hong Kong: World Scientific Publishing (HK) Co, PO Box 72482, Kowloon Central Post Office, Hong Kong Telephone: 852-7718791, Fax: 852-7718155**) LC** QA150; .I574. **DD** 512. **CODEN** IACOEA. Documents available from Ask*IEEE.
**Ind/Abst** INSPEC (1991-); Math. Rev.; Zentralbl. Math. Ihre Grenzgeb.

SI/0218-1959
**INTERNATIONAL JOURNAL OF COMPUTATIONAL GEOMETRY & APPLICATIONS.** [Int. j. comput. geom. appl.]. **VFOAT** International Journal of Computational Geometry and Applications; Journal of Computational Geometry & Applications; Journal of Computational Geometry and Applications; Computational Geometry & Applications; Computational Geometry and Applications. Vol. 1, No. 1 (Mar. 1991)-. Periodical. English. qt. $130.00 individuals, $260.00 institutions. World Scientific Publishing Company, PO Box 128, Farrer Road, Singapore 9128 Singapore. **Tel** 011 65 3825663, FAX 011 65 3825919, telex RS 28561 WSPC. **(Subscription address:** US: World Scientific Publishing Co., Inc., 1060 Main Street, River Edge, NJ 07661 Telephone: (201)487-9655, Fax: (201)487-9656; Europe: World Scientific Publishing Co Ltd, 73 Lynton Mead, Totteridge, London N20 8DH United Kingdom Telephone: 011 44 81 4462461, Fax: 011 44 81 4463356; India: World Scientific Publishing Co Pte Ltd, 4911 9th Floor, High Point IV, 45 Palace Road, Bangalore 560 001 India Telephone: (80) 2205972, Fax: (80) 3344593, Telex: 0845-2900 PCO IN; Hong Kong: World Scientific Publishing (HK) Co, PO Box 72482, Kowloon Central Post Office, Hong Kong Telephone: 852-7718791, Fax: 852-7718155**) LC** QA448.D38; I57. **DD** 516/.00285. **CODEN** IJCAEV. Documents available from Ask*IEEE.
**Ind/Abst** INSPEC (1991-); Math. Rev.; Zentralbl. Math. Ihre Grenzgeb.

UK/0020-7160
**INTERNATIONAL JOURNAL OF COMPUTER MATHEMATICS.** [Int. j. comput. math.]. Vol. 1, No. 1 (May 1964)-. Periodical. English. Six times a year. $847.00 (academic institutions), $1321.00 (corporate institutions). Gordon & Breach Science Publishers, PO Box 90, Reading RG1 8JL England. **Tel** 011 44 734 560080, FAX 011 44 734 568211. **(Subscription address:** International Publishers Distributor at one of the following addresses: 820 Town Center Drive, Langhorne, PA 19047; or PO Box 90, Reading Berkshire RG1 8JL UK; or Kent Ridge PO Box 1180, Singapore 9111, Republic of Singapore**) LC** QA76; .I59. **CODEN** IJCMAT. **[CCC].** Index available. cum. index. **Ad Acc, Adv Mgr:** Kathy Langdale. **Pr Rev.** Documents available from Article Express International, The Genuine Article, Ask*IEEE.
**Desc:** Contains work concerning research and development in computer systems and the theory of programming languages and work concerning mathematical techniques of interest to computer users.
**Ind/Abst** Bioeng. Abstr.; Compumath Citation Index [Full Cov.]; Comput. Rev.; Curr. Contents Eng. Tech. Appl. Sci.; Ei Page One; Eng. Index Annu.; INIS Atomindex [Micro.]; INSPEC (Jan. 1968-); Math. Rev.; Pollut. Abstr. Indexes; Res. Alert [Full Cov.]; SCISEARCH; Stat. Theory Method Abstr. (1970, 1972); Zentralbl. Math. Ihre Grenzgeb.

GW/0020-7276
**INTERNATIONAL JOURNAL OF GAME THEORY.** [Int. j. game theory]. **Added/Corp** Institut fuer Hohere Studien und Wissenschaftliche Forschung (Vienna, Austria). Vol. 1 (1971)-. Periodical. English. Four times a year. DM460.00. Physica-Verlag GmbH & Company, Postfach 105280, D-69042 Heidelberg Germany. **Tel** 06221 487-492, FAX 06221 487177 und 487366, telex 461723 sphdb-d. **(Subscription address:** Springer Verlag New York Inc. / for North America, 44 Hartz Way, Secaucus NJ 07096.**) ED** J. Rosenmueller. **LC** QA269; .I55. **DD** 519.3/05. **CODEN** IJGTA2. **[CCC]. Pr Rev.** Documents available from The Genuine Article, Ask*IEEE.
**Desc:** Contains original articles on the theory of games and its applications. A collection of theoretical methods and mathematical models for the study of conflict and cooperation.
**Ind/Abst** ACM Guide Comput. Lit.; Compumath Citation Index [Full Cov.]; Comput. Rev.; Curr. Contents Soc. Behav. Sci.; Econ. Lit. Index; INSPEC (1971-); Int. Abstr. Oper. Res. [Select. Cov.]; J. Econ. Lit. (1986-); Math. Rev.; Res. Alert [Full Cov.]; Soc. Sci. Cit. Index [Full Cov.]; Stat. Theory Method Abstr. (1972, 1974-1975, 1977-1978, 1980-1981); Zentralbl. Math. Ihre Grenzgeb.

●US/1055-7490
**INTERNATIONAL JOURNAL OF MATHEMATICAL AND STATISTICAL SCIENCES.** See Science and Technology.

UK/0020-739X
**INTERNATIONAL JOURNAL OF MATHEMATICAL EDUCATION IN SCIENCE AND TECHNOLOGY.** See Education.

SI/0129-167X
**INTERNATIONAL JOURNAL OF MATHEMATICS.** Vol. 1, No. 1 (Mar. 1990)-. Periodical. English. Six times a year. $210.00 individuals, $420.00 institutions. World Scientific Publishing Company, PO Box 128, Farrer Road, Singapore 9128 Singapore. **Tel** 011 65 3825663, FAX 011 65 3825919, telex RS 28561 WSPC. **(Subscription address:** US: World Scientific Publishing Co., Inc., 1060 Main Street, River Edge, NJ 07661 Telephone: (201)487-9655, Fax: (201)487-9656; Europe: World Scientific Publishing Co Ltd, 73 Lynton Mead, Totteridge, London N20 8DH United Kingdom Telephone: 011 44 81 4462461, Fax: 011 44 81 4463356; India: World Scientific Publishing Co Pte Ltd, 4911 9th Floor, High Point IV, 45 Palace Road, Bangalore 560 001 India Telephone: (80) 2205972, Fax: (80) 3344593, Telex: 0845-2900 PCO IN; Hong Kong: World Scientific Publishing (HK) Co, PO Box 72482, Kowloon Central Post Office, Hong Kong Telephone: 852-7718791, Fax: 852-7718155**) ED** A. Casson and S. Kobayashi. **LC** QA1; .I8325. **DD** 510/.5. **[CCC].** cum. index. **Pr Rev. Circ:** 150.
**Ind/Abst** Math. Rev.; Zentralbl. Math. Ihre Grenzgeb.

US/0161-1712
**INTERNATIONAL JOURNAL OF MATHEMATICS AND MATHEMATICAL SCIENCES.** [Int. j. math. math. sci.]. **Added/Corp** University of Central Florida. Calcutta Mathematical Society. East Carolina University. (March 1978)-. Periodical. English. qt (Mar., June, Sep., Dec.). $100.00. University of Central Florida Department of Mathematics, PO Box 161364, Orlando FL 32816-1364. **Tel** (407)823-2754, (407)823-2478, FAX (407)823-3299. **ED** Dr. Lokenath Debnath. **LC** QA1; .I833. **DD** 510/.8. Index available in last issue of volume--attached. **Pr Rev. Circ:** 325 (ctrl).
**Desc:** A journal devoted to publication of original research papers, research notes, research expository and survey articles with emphasis on unsolved problems and open questions in mathematics and mathematical sciences.
**Ind/Abst** Math. Rev.; Zentralbl. Math. Ihre Grenzgeb.

US/0228-6203
**INTERNATIONAL JOURNAL OF MODELLING & SIMULATION.** See Computers-Simulation.

US
**INTERNATIONAL MATHEMATICS RESEARCH NOTICES.** **Added/Corp** Duke University. Mathematics Dept. No. 1 (1991)-. Periodical. English. ir (12-18 issues per year). $600.00 (institutions), $300.00 (individuals) US; $636.00 (institutions), $336.00 (individuals) other. Duke University Press, PO Box 90660, Durham NC 27708-0660. **Tel** (919)687-3600, (919)688-5134 (orders), FAX (919)688-4574, telex 802829. **ED** Morris Weisfeld.
**Ind/Abst** Math. Rev.; Zentralbl. Math. Ihre Grenzgeb.

UK/0733-1932
**INTERNATIONAL SERIES IN MODERN APPLIED MATHEMATICS AND COMPUTER SCIENCE.** [Int. ser. mod. appl. math. comput. sci.]. Vol. 1 (1981)-. Monographic series. English. ir. Price varies per volume. Oxford University Press, Walton Street, Oxford OX2 6DP England. **Tel** 011 44 865 56767, FAX 011 44 865 267773, telex 837330 OXPRES G.
**Ind/Abst** Math. Rev.

AU
**INTERNATIONALE MATHEMATISCHE NACHRICHTEN.** **VFOAT** International Mathematical News; Nouvelles Mathematique Internationales. (1947)-. Periodical. German (English, German and French). Three times a year (Apr., Aug., Dec.). S300.00. Oesterreichische Math Geslshft Technische University, Wiedner Hauptstrasse 8 10, A-1040 Vienna Austria. **Tel** 0222-58801-5381. **ED** P. Flor. **Bk Rev. Ad Acc. Circ:** 1,500 (ctrl).
**Desc:** News in the mathematical world, book reviews of new mathematical books, and personalities.
**Ind/Abst** Math. Rev.; Zentralbl. Math. Ihre Grenzgeb.

UK/0275-259X
**INTRODUCTORY MATHEMATICS FOR SCIENTISTS AND ENGINEERS.** [Introd. math. sci. eng.]. (19??)-. Monographic series. English. ir. Price varies per volume. John Wiley & Sons Ltd., Baffins Lane, Chichester West Sussex PO19 1UD England. **Tel** 0243 779777, FAX 0243 776128 BTG:JWP001, telex 86290 WIBOOKG. **(Subscription address:** John Wiley & Sons Inc / New Jersey, PO Box 2575, Secaucus NJ 07096-2575.**)**

GW/0020-9910
**INVENTIONES MATHEMATICAE.** [Invent. math.]. Vol. 1 (Feb. 1966)-. Periodical. English (French and German). Twelve times a year. DM3496.00. Springer-Verlag GmbH & Company KG, Heidelberger Platz 3, D 14197 Berlin Germany. **Tel** 011 49 30 8207223, FAX 011 49 30 8214091, telex 183 319 SPBLN D. **(Subscription address:** Springer Verlag New York Inc. / for North America, 44 Hartz Way, Secaucus NJ 07096.**) ED** M Berger, J M Bismut, A Borel, J Coates, A Connes, A A Kirillov, B Mazur, Y Meyer, J W Morgan, R Remmert, and J Sjoestrand. **LC** QA1; .I884. **CODEN** INVMBH. **[CCC].** Index available in last issue of volume--attached. **Pr Rev.** available on microfilm and microfiche from University Microfilms International (UMI). Documents available from The Genuine Article.
**Desc:** A forum for leading fundamental and authoritative papers on mathematics.
**Ind/Abst** Compumath Citation Index [Full Cov.]; Curr. Contents Phys. Chem. Earth Sci.; Int. Aerosp. Abstr.; Math. Rev.; Res. Alert [Full Cov.]; Sci. Cit. Index; SCISEARCH; Zentralbl. Math. Ihre Grenzgeb.

UK/0266-5611
**INVERSE PROBLEMS.** **Added/Corp** Institute of Physics (Great Britain). Vol. 1, No. 1 (Feb. 1985)-. Periodical. English. bm. $616.00. Institute of Physics, Techno House, Redcliffe Way, Bristol BS1 6NX England. **Tel** 011 44 272 297481, FAX 011 44 272 294318, telex 449149 INSTP G. **(Subscription address:** American Institute of Physics, Publishing Sales, 500 Sunnyside Blvd., Woodbury NY 11797.**) ED** M Bertero. **LC** QA1; .I84. **CODEN** INPEEY. **[CCC].** Index available (bound in last issue). **Pr Rev.** available on microfiche. Documents available from The Genuine Article, Ask*IEEE.
**Desc:** An international journal of inverse problems, inverse methods and computerized inversion of data. Aims to combine theoretical, experimental and mathematical papers on inverse problems with numerical and practical approaches to their solution. All inverse problems, inverse methods and data inversion methods are within the scope of the journal.
**Ind/Abst** Compumath Citation Index [Full Cov.]; Curr. Contents Phys. Chem. Earth Sci.; Ei Page One; INSPEC (Feb. 1985-); Math. Rev.; Res. Alert [Full Cov.]; Sci. Cit. Index; SCISEARCH; Zentralbl. Math. Ihre Grenzgeb.

IS/0021-2172
**ISRAEL JOURNAL OF MATHEMATICS.** [Isr. j. math.]. Vol. 1 (Mar. 1963)-. Periodical. English. Twelve times a year. $260.00. Magnes Press, Hebrew University of Jerusalem, PO Box 7695, Jerusalem 91076 Israel. **Tel** 011 972 2 660341, 011 972 2 635291, FAX 011 972 2 633370, telex 25391. **ED** Professor A. Lubotzky. **LC** QA1; .I92. **CODEN** ISJMAP. cum. index (Vols. 1-50). **Pr Rev.** Documents available from The Genuine Article, Ask*IEEE. ***Continues in part*** *Bulletin of the Research Council of Israel. Section F, Mathematics and Physics.*
**Desc:** High quality research papers in many areas of mathematics including, but not limited to logic and set theory, algebra, number theory, analysis, geometry and combinatorics.
**Ind/Abst** Compumath Citation Index [Full Cov.]; Comput. Rev.; Curr. Contents Phys. Chem. Earth Sci.; Energy Res. Abstr.; INSPEC (1981-); Int. Aerosp. Abstr.; Math. Rev.; Res. Alert [Full Cov.]; Sci. Cit. Index; SCISEARCH; Zentralbl. Math. Ihre Grenzgeb.

IS
**ISRAEL MATHEMATICAL CONFERENCE PROCEEDINGS.** **Added/Corp** Universitat Bar-Ilan. Research Institute of Mathematical Sciences. **VFOAT** IMCP. Vol. 1 (1989)-. Monographic series. English. ir. Price varies per volume. American Mathematical Society, PO Box 6248, Providence RI 02940-6248. **Tel** (800)321-4267, (401)455-4000, FAX (401)331-3842, telex 797192. **(Subscription address:** American Mathematical Society, PO Box 5904, Boston MA 02206-5904.**) LC** QA1; .I87.
**Ind/Abst** Zentralbl. Math. Ihre Grenzgeb.

RU/0202-7488
**ITOGI NAUKI I TEHNIKI - VSESOJUZNYI INSTITUT NAUCNOJ I TEHNICESKOJ INFORMACII. SERIJA TEORIJA VEROJATNOSTEJI, MATEMATICESKAJA STATISTIKA, TEORETICESKAJA KIBERNETIKA.** (ITOGI NAUKI I TEKHNIKI: TEORIIA VEROIATNOSTEI, MATEMATICHESKAIA STATISTIKA, TEORETICHESKAIA KIBERNETIKA.). [Itogi nauki i teh. - Vses. inst. naucn. teh. inf., Ser. Teor. verojatn., Mat. stat., Teor. kibern.]. **Added/Corp** Vsesoiuznyi Institut Nauchnoi I Tekhnicheskoi Informatsii (Soviet Union). **VFOAT** Itogi: Nauki I Tekhniki: Seriia Teoriia Veroiatnostei, Matematicheskaia Statistika, Teoreticheskaia Kibernetika; Teoriia Veroiatnostei, Matematicheskaia Statistika, Teoreticheskaia Kibernetika. (1972)-. Russian. VINITI - Vsesoyuznyi Institut Nauchno-Tekhnicheskoi Informatsii, All-Union Scientific and Technical Information Institute, Baltiiskaia Ulitsa 14, 125219 Moscow Russia. **Tel** 238-46-00, FAX 9430060, telex 411160. **LC** QA273; .I83. ***Continues*** *Itogi Nauki: Teoriia Veroiatnostei. Matematicheskai a Statistika.*

RU/0202-7445
**ITOGI NAUKI I TEHNIKI - VSESOJUZNYJ INSTITUT NAUCHOJ I TEHNICESKO J INFORMACII. SERIJA ALGEBRA, TOPOLOGIJA, GEOMETRIJA.** (ITOGI NAUKI I TEKHNIKI : ALGEBRA, TOPOLOGIIA, GEOMETRIIA.). [Itogi nauki teh. - Vses. inst. naucn. teh. inf., Ser. Algebra, Topol., Geom.]. **Added/Corp** Vsesoiuznyu Institut Nauchnoi i Tekhnicheskoi Informatsii (Soviet Union). **VFOAT** Itogi Nauki I Tekhinki: Seriia Algebra, Topologiia, Geometriia. Vol. 10, (1972)-. Russian. 1.78rub. VINITI - Vsesoyuznyi Institut Nauchno-Tekhnicheskoi Informatsii, All-Union Scientific and Technical Information Institute, Baltiiskaia Ulitsa 14, 125219 Moscow Russia. **Tel** 238-46-00, FAX 9430060, telex 411160. **(Subscription address:** V/O Mezhdunarodnaya Kniga, 113095 Dimitrova Ul 39, Moscow, Russia**) LC** QA1; .I954. ***Continues*** *Itogi Nauki: Algebra. Topologiia. Geometriia.*
**Ind/Abst** Zentralbl. Math. Ihre Grenzgeb.

RU/0202-7461
**ITOGI NAUKI I TEHNIKI - VSESOJUZNYJ INSTITUT NAUCNOJ I TEHNICESKOJ INFORMACII. SERIJA PROBLEMY GEOMETRII.** (ITOGI NAUKI I TEKHNIKI. SERIIA PROBLEMY GEOMETRII.). [Itogi nauki teh. - Vses. inst. naucn. teh. inf., Ser. Probl. geom.]. **Added/Corp** Vsesoiuznyi Institut Nauchnoi i Tekhnicheskoi Informatsii (Soviet Union). **VFOAT** Problemy Geometrii Seriia Problemy Geometrii. Vol. 11 (1980)-. Periodical. Russian. ir. VINITI - Vsesoyuznyi Institut Nauchno-Tekhnicheskoi Informatsii, All-Union Scientific and Technical Information Institute, Baltiiskaia Ulitsa 14, 125219 Moscow Russia. **Tel** 238-46-00, FAX 9430060, telex 411160. **LC** QA443; .G45. ***Continues*** *Itogi Nauki i Tekhniki: Problemy Geometrii.*

RU/0202-7453
**ITOGI NAUKI I TEKHNIKI. SERIIA MATEMATICHESKII ANALIZ / GOSUDARSTVENNYI KOMITET SSSR PO NAUKE I TEKHNIKE, AKADEMIIA NAUK SSSR, VSESOIUZNYI INSTITUT NAUCHNOI I TEKHNICHESKOI INFORMATSII.** **Added/Corp** Vsesoiuznyi Institut Nauchnoi i Tekhnicheskoi Informatsii (Soviet Union). **VFOAT** Seriia Matematicheskii Analiz; Matematicheskii Analiz. (1979)-. Russian. ir. VINITI - Vsesoyuznyi Institut Nauchno-Tekhnicheskoi Informatsii, All-Union Scientific and Technical Information Institute, Baltiiskaia Ulitsa 14, 125219 Moscow Russia. **Tel** 238-46-00, FAX 9430060, telex 411160. **(Subscription address:** Victor Kamkin, 4956 Boiling Brook Parkway, Rockville MD 20852.**)** ***Continues*** *Itogi Nauki i Tekhniki. Matematicheskii Analiz.*

RU/0233-6723
**ITOGI NAUKI I TEKHNIKI. SERIIA SOVREMENNYE PROBLEMY MATEMATIKI FUNDAMENTALNYE NAPRAVLENIIA.** **Added/Corp** Vsesoiuznyi Institut Nauchnoi i Tekhnicheskoi Informatsii (Soviet Union). **VFOAT** Seriia Sovremennye Problemy Matematiki; Sovremennye Problemy Matematiki. Fundamentalnye Napravleniia; Itogi Nauki i Tekhniki. Sovremennye Problemy Matematiki; Fundamentalnye Napravleniia. Vol. 1 (1985)-. Russian. ir. VINITI - Vsesoyuznyi Institut Nauchno-Tekhnicheskoi Informatsii, All-Union Scientific and Technical Information Institute, Baltiiskaia Ulitsa 14, 125219 Moscow Russia. **Tel** 238-46-00, FAX 9430060, telex 411160. **LC** QA1; .I956. ***Continues in part*** *Itogi Nauki i Tekhniki. Seriia Sovremennye Problemy Matematiki. Noveishie Dostizheniia.*
**Ind/Abst** Zentralbl. Math. Ihre Grenzgeb.

RU
**ITOGI NAUKI I TEKHNIKI. SERIIA SOVREMENNYE PROBLEMY MATEMATIKI NOVEISHIE DOSTIZHENIIA.** **Added/Corp** Vsesoiuznyi Institut Nauchnoi i Tekhnicheskoi Informatsii (Soviet Union). **VFOAT** Seriia Sovremennye Problemy Matematiki; Sovremennye Problemy Matematiki. Noveishie Dostizheniia; Veishie Dostizheniia; Sovremennye Problemy Matematiki. Vol. 24 (1984)-. Periodical. Russian. sa. 2.30rub (single issue). VINITI - Vsesoyuznyi Institut Nauchno-Tekhnicheskoi Informatsii, All-Union Scientific and Technical Information Institute, Baltiiskaia Ulitsa 14, 125219 Moscow Russia. **Tel** 238-46-00, FAX 9430060, telex 411160. **LC** QA1; .I957. ***Continues in part*** *Itogi Nauki i Tekhniki. Seriia Sovremennye Problemy Matematiki.*

AI
**IZVESTIIA AKADEMII NAUK ARMENII. MATEMATIKA HAYASTANI GITUTYUNNERI AKADEMIAYI TEGHEKAGIR. MATEMATIKA.** **Added/Corp** Hayastani Gitutyunneri Akademia. **VFOAT** Matematika; Matematika; Hayastani Gitutyunneri Akademiayi Teghekagir. Matematika. No. 1 (1991)-. Periodical. Russian (summaries and/or abstracts in Armenian and English; table of contents in Armenian and English). bm. ***Continues*** *Izvestiia Akademii Nauk Armianskoi SSR. Matematika, 0002-3043.*

BW
**IZVESTIIA AKADEMII NAUK BELARUSI. SERIIA FIZIKO-MATEMATISCHEKIKH NAUK.** **Main/Corp** Akademiia Navuk Belaruskai SSR. **Added/Corp** Akademiia Navuk Belaruskai SSR. Izvestiia. Seriia Fiziko-Matematicheskikh Nauk. (1991)-. Byelorussian. **(Subscription address:** Victor Kamkin, 4956 Boiling Brook Parkway, Rockville MD 20852.**)**
**Ind/Abst** Alum. Ind. Abstr.; Chem. Abstr.; Math. Rev.; Met. Abstr.; Rev. Med. Vet. Entomol.

KG
**IZVESTIIA AKADEMII NAUK RESPUBLIKI KYRGYZSTAN. FIZIKO-TEKHNICHESKIE, MATEMATICHESKIE I GORNO-GEOLOGICHESKIE NAUKI.** **See** Physics.

RU
**IZVESTIIA AKADEMII NAUK. SERIIA MATEMATICHESKAIA / ROSSIISKAIA AKADEMIIA NAUK.** ***Title Change.*** **Added/Corp** Rossiiskaia Akademiia Nauk. **VFOAT** Seriia Matematicheskaia; Izvestiia Rossiiskoi Akademii Nauk. Seriia Matematicheskaia. (Mar/Apr 1992)-(199?). Academic Scholarly Publication. Russian (table of contents in English). bm. Izdatelstvo Nauka / Akademiia Nauk, Publishing House of the Russian Academy of Sciences, Leninskii Porspekt 14, 117901 Moscow Russia. **Tel** 011 95 954-21-53, FAX 011 95 938-21-44, telex 411964. **LC** QA1; .I942. ***Continues*** *Izvestiia Akademii Nauk SSSR. Seriia Matematicheskaia, 0373-2436.* ***Continued by*** *Izvestiia Rossiiskoi Akademii Nauk. Seriîia matematicheskaîia.*

UZ/0131-8012
**IZVESTIIA AKADEMII NAUK UZSSR. SERIIA FIZIKO-MATEMATICHESKIKH NAUK.** **See** Physics.

AJ/0002-3108
**IZVESTIJA AKADEMII NAUK AZERBAJDZANSKOJ SSR. SERIJA FIZIKO-TEHNICESKIH I MATEMATICESKIH NAUK.** ***Title Change.*** **See** Physics.

RU/0021-3446
**IZVESTIJA VYSSIH UCEBNYH ZAVEDENIJ. MATEMATIKA.** (IZVESTIIA VYSSHIKH UCHEBNYKH ZAVEDENII. MATEMATIKA / MINISTERSTVO VYSSHEGO OBRAZOVANIIA SSSR.). [Izv. vyss. ucebn. zaved., Mat.]. **Added/Corp** Soviet Union. Ministerstvo Vysshego i Srednego Spetsialnogo Obrazovaniia. Soviet Union. Ministerstvo Vysshego Obrazovaniia. Soviet Union. Gosudarstvennyi Komitet po Narodnomu Obrazovaniiu. **VFOAT** Matematika. (1957)-. Periodical. Russian. mo. $99.95. Kazanskii Universitet / Kazan State University, Ulitsa Lenina 18, 420008 Tatarstan Kazan. **Tel** 32-15-49, FAX 38-73-21, telex 224881. **(Subscription address:** East View Publications Inc., 3020 Harbor Lane North, Suite 110, Minneapolis MN 55447.**)** **LC** QA1; .R78. **CODEN** IVUMBY. **[CCC]**. **Pr Rev.** Documents available from The Genuine Article, Ask*IEEE. ***Absorbed in part*** *Nauchnye Doklady Vysshei Shkoly. Fiziko-Matematicheskie Nauki Fiziko-Matematicheskie Nauki.*
**Ind/Abst** Compumath Citation Index [Full Cov.]; INSPEC (Jan. 1973-); Math. Rev.; Res. Alert [Full Cov.]; SCISEARCH.

●US/1064-5632
**IZVESTIYA. MATHEMATICS.** (IZVESTIYA. MATHEMATICS / RUSSIAN ACADEMY OF SCIENCES.). [Izv., Math.]. **Added/Corp** American Mathematical Society. Rossiiskaia Akademiia Nauk. Vol. 40, No. 1 (1993)-. Periodical. English (translations available in Russian). bm. $808.00 (print or microfiche). American Mathematical Society, PO Box 6248, Providence RI 02940-6248. **Tel** (800)321-4267, (401)455-4000, FAX (401)331-3842, telex 797192. **(Subscription address:** American Mathematical Society, PO Box 5904, Boston MA 02206-5904.**)** **LC** QA1; .M8328. **DD** 510. Index available (bound in sixth issue). ***Continues*** *Mathematics of the USSR. Izvestija, 0025-5726.*
**Desc:** Translation of Russian journal, Izvestiia Rossiiskoi Akademii Nauk Seriia Matematicheskaya, published by the Russian Academy of Sciences. Devoted to current areas of pure mathematics research.
**Ind/Abst** Math. Rev.

GW/0172-8512
**JAHRBUCH UBERBLICKE MATHEMATIK.** [Jahrb. Uberbl. Math.]. **VFOAT** Mathematical Surveys. (1975)-. Periodical. Multiple languages. an. ***Continues*** *Uberblicke Mathematik, 0177-9834.*

GW/0012-0456
**JAHRESBERICHT DER DEUTSCHEN MATHEMATIKER-VEREINIGUNG.** [Jahresber. Dtsch. Math.-Ver.]. **Main/Corp** Deutsche Mathematiker-Vereinigung. Vol. 1 (1890/91)-. Periodical. German (English). qt. DM94.00. BG Teubner GmbH, Postfach 80 10 69, D 75010 Stuttgart Germany. **Tel** 011 49 711 789010, FAX 011 49 711 7890110. **ED** W D Geyer. **LC** QA1; .D4. **CODEN** JDMVA7. **[CCC]**. cum. index. **Bk Rev. Ad Acc. Circ:** 2,400.
**Desc:** Contains main lectures of the annual conferences and special contributions.
**Ind/Abst** Energy Res. Abstr. (March 1982-); Math. Rev.; Stat. Theory Method Abstr. (1969-1970, 1973, 1979, 1982, 1986); Zentralbl. Math. Ihre Grenzgeb.

JA/0916-7005
**JAPAN JOURNAL OF INDUSTRIAL AND APPLIED MATHEMATICS.** **VFOAT** JJIAM. Vol. 8, No. 1, Feb. (1991)-. Periodical. English. Three times a year. $436.00. **(Subscription address:** Kinokuniya Company Ltd., 38-1 Sakuragaoka 5, chome Setagaya-ku, Tokyo 156 Japan.**)** **LC** QA1; .J44. ***Continues*** *Japan Journal of Applied Mathematics, 0910-2043.*
**Ind/Abst** Math. Rev.

US/1058-7349
**JAPANESE JOURNAL OF FUZZY THEORY AND SYSTEMS.** [Jpn. j. fuzzy theory syst.]. **Added/Corp** Japan Society for Fuzzy Theory and Systems. Vol. 1, No. 1 (199?)-. Periodical. English (translations available in Japanese). bm. $695.00. Allerton Press, Inc., 150 Fifth Avenue, New York NY 10011. **Tel** (212)924-3950, FAX (212)463-9684, telex 427441 ALPRES. **LC** QA402; .J37. **DD** 003/.7. **[CCC]**.
**Ind/Abst** Math. Rev.; Zentralbl. Math. Ihre Grenzgeb.

JA/0075-3432
**JAPANESE JOURNAL OF MATHEMATICS.** [Jpn. j. math.]. **Added/Corp** Nihon Sugakkai. Nihon Gakujutsu Kaigi. Gakujutsu Kenkyu Kaigi (Japan). Vol. 1, Nos. 1/2 (1924)-. English (German and French). sa. $303.00. **(Subscription address:** Kinokuniya Company Ltd., 38-1 Sakuragaoka 5, chome Setagaya-ku, Tokyo 156 Japan.**)** **LC** QA1; .J45. **CODEN** JJMAAK.
**Ind/Abst** Math. Rev.; Pollut. Abstr. Indexes; Zentralbl. Math. Ihre Grenzgeb.

CN/0835-3026
**JCMCC : THE JOURNAL OF COMBINATORIAL MATHEMATICS AND COMBINATORIAL COMPUTING.** [JCMCC, J. comb. math. comb. comput.]. **Added/Corp** Charles Babbage Research Centre. **VFOAT** Journal of Combinatorial Mathematics and Combinatorial Computing. Vol. 1 (Apr. 1987)-. Periodical. English. sa. $66.00 (one year=two volumes). Charles Babbage Research Centre, PO Box 272 St Norbert Postal Station, Winnipeg Manitoba R3V 1L6 Canada. **Tel** (204)474-8313, (204)772-2612. **LC** QA164; .J38. **DD** 511/.6/05. **CODEN** JJCCEE. Documents available from Ask*IEEE.
**Ind/Abst** INSPEC (Oct. 1970-); Math. Rev. (1987-); Zentralbl. Math. Ihre Grenzgeb.

US/0885-0062
**JOHNS HOPKINS SERIES IN THE MATHEMATICAL SCIENCES.** [Johns Hopkins ser. math. sci.]. No. 1 (1978)-. Monographic series. English. **LC** UNC. **DD** 510.
**Ind/Abst** Math. Rev.; Zentralbl. Math. Ihre Grenzgeb.

UK/0142-5951
**JOURNAL CONTENTS IN QUANTITATIVE METHODS.** (19??)-. Abstracting/Indexing Service. English. mo. $210.00. University of Manchester / School of Management, PO Box 88, Manchester M60 1QD England. **Tel** 011 44 61 200 3429.

IS/0021-7670
**JOURNAL D' ANALYSE MATHEMATIQUE (JERUSALEM).** (JOURNAL D'ANALYSE MATHEMATIQUE.). [J. anal. math.]. Vol. 1 (1951)-. Periodical. English (French). Three times a year. $190.00. Magnes Press, Hebrew University of Jerusalem, PO Box 7695, Jerusalem 91076 Israel. **Tel** 011 972 2 660341, 011 972 2 635291, FAX 011 972 2 633370, telex 25391. **ED** Lawrence Zalcman. **LC** QA1; .J85. **CODEN** JOAMAV. **Ad Acc. Pr Rev. Circ:** 750. Documents available from The Genuine Article.
**Desc:** Publishes research papers in classical analysis and cognate areas submitted by authors from all over the world.
**Ind/Abst** Compumath Citation Index [Full Cov.]; Curr. Contents Phys. Chem. Earth Sci.; Int. Aerosp. Abstr.; Math. Rev.; Res. Alert [Full Cov.]; SCISEARCH; Zentralbl. Math. Ihre Grenzgeb.

FR/0021-7824
**JOURNAL DE MATHEMATIQUES PURES ET APPLIQUEES.** [J. math. pures appl.]. (1836)-. Periodical. French. Six times a year. 1400.00F France; 1840.00F other. Gauthier-Villars, 15 rue Gossin, 92543 Montrouge Cedex France. **Tel** 33 1 40 92 65 00, FAX 33 1 40 92 65 97. **(Subscription address:** Centrale des Revues, 11 rue Gossin, 92543 Montrouge Cedex France.**)** **ED** Jacques Louis Lions. **LC** QA1; .J9. **DD** 510.5. **CODEN** JMPAAM. **[CCC]. Ad Acc. Pr Rev. Circ:** 1,000. Documents available from The Genuine Article. ***Supersedes*** *Annales de Mathematiques Pures et Appliquees.*
**Desc:** Journal covering mathematics.
**Ind/Abst** Curr. Contents Phys. Chem. Earth Sci.; Energy Res. Abstr.; Int. Aerosp. Abstr.; Math. Rev.; NEXIS; Res. Alert; Sci. Cit. Index; SCISEARCH; Stat. Theory Method Abstr. (1959-1963, 1976, 1978-1979); Zentralbl. Math. Ihre Grenzgeb.

US/0021-8251
**JOURNAL FOR RESEARCH IN MATHEMATICS EDUCATION.** [J. res. math. educ.]. **Added/Corp** National Council of Teachers of Mathematics. ERIC Clearinghouse for Science, Mathematics, and Environmental Education. National Institute of Education (U.S.). Vol. 1, (Jan. 1970)-. Periodical. English. Five times a year. $30.00. National Council of Teachers of Mathematics, 1906 Association Drive, Reston VA 22091. **Tel** (703)620-9840, FAX (703)476-2970. **LC** QA11.A1; J68. **DD** 510/.071. **CODEN** JRMEDN. Index available. cum. index. **Bk Rev. Ad Acc. Pr Rev. Circ:** 6,500 (ctrl). available on microfilm and microfiche from University Microfilms International (UMI). Documents available from The Genuine Article.
**Desc:** Devoted to the interest of teachers of mathematics and mathematics education at all levels. Concerned with research into significant problems in mathematics education. Includes comprehensive reports of empirical studies, summaries of major research studies and articles on current research in the field.
**Ind/Abst** Acad. Search (July 1993-); Contents Pages Educ.; Curr. Contents Soc. Behav. Sci.; Curr. Index J. Educ.; Educ. Index; INFO-SOUTH Abstr.; Mag. Search; PsycINFO; PsycLit; Res. Alert [Full Cov.]; Soc. Sci. Cit. Index [Full Cov.].

GW/0075-4102
**JOURNAL FUER DIE REINE UND ANGEWANDTE MATHEMATIK.** [J. reine angew. Math.]. Vol. 1 (1826)-. Periodical. German. Twelve times a year. $2089.00. Walter de Gruyter Inc., PO Box 303421, D 10728 Berlin Germany. **Tel** 011 49 30 260050, FAX 011 49 30 26005251. **LC** QA1; .J95. **CODEN** JRMAA8. **[CCC]**. cum. index. **Ad Acc. Pr Rev. Circ:** 900. available on microfilm and microfiche from University Microfilms International (UMI). Documents available from The Genuine Article.
**Desc:** Contains original investigations in all branches of pure and applied mathematics.
**Ind/Abst** Compumath Citation Index [Full Cov.]; Curr. Contents Phys. Chem. Earth Sci.; Math. Rev.; Res. Alert [Full Cov.]; Sci. Cit. Index; SCISEARCH; Stat. Theory Method Abstr. (1967-1970, 1983-1984); Zentralbl. Math. Ihre Grenzgeb.

US/0021-8693
**JOURNAL OF ALGEBRA.** [J. algebra]. Vol. 1, No. 1 (April 1964)-. Academic Scholarly Publication. English. Twenty-four times a year. $2100.00 US and Canada; $2437.00 other. Academic Press, Inc., 6277 Sea Harbor Drive, Orlando FL 32887. **Tel** (800)543-9534, (407)345-4100, FAX (407)363-9661. **ED** Walter Feit. **DD** 512. **CODEN** JALGA4. **[CCC]. Pr Rev.** Documents available from The Genuine Article.
**Desc:** Presents carefully selected articles concerning original research in the field of algebra. Articles from related research areas that have a significant bearing on algebra are also included.
**Ind/Abst** Compumath Citation Index [Full Cov.]; Curr. Contents Phys. Chem. Earth Sci.; Int. Aerosp. Abstr.; Math. Rev.; Pollut. Abstr. Indexes; Res. Alert [Full Cov.]; Sci. Cit. Index; SCISEARCH; Zentralbl. Math. Ihre Grenzgeb.

US/0925-9899
**JOURNAL OF ALGEBRAIC COMBINATORICS.** English. qt. $421.00. Kluwer Academic Publishers / Massachusetts, PO Box 358, Accord Station, Hingham MA 02018. **Tel** (617)871-6600. **ED** C.D. Godsil, I. Goulden, and D. Jackson. **Pr Rev. Acid Free.** available on microfilm and microfiche from University Microfilms International (UMI).
**Desc:** The journal publishes papers in which combinatorics and algebra interact in a significant and interesting fashion. This interaction might occur through the study of combinatorial structures using algebraic methods, or the application of combinatorial methods to algebraic problems. The combinatorics might be enumerative, or involve matroids, posets, polytopes, codes, designs, or finite geometries. The algebra could be group theory, representation theory, lattice theory or commutative algebra, to mention just a few possibilities.
**Ind/Abst** Ei Page One; Math. Rev.

●US/1056-3911
**JOURNAL OF ALGEBRAIC GEOMETRY.** [J. algeb. geom.]. **Added/Corp** American Mathematical Society. **VFOAT** Algebraic Geometry. Vol. 1 (1992)-. Periodical. English (French). qt. $208.00. American Mathematical Society, PO Box 6248, Providence RI 02940-6248. **Tel** (800)321-4267, (401)455-4000, FAX (401)331-3842, telex 797192. **(Subscription address:** American Mathematical Society, PO Box 5904, Boston MA 02206-5904.**)** **LC** QA564; .J68. **DD** 510.
**Desc:** Provides a forum for the best work in algebraic geometry.
**Ind/Abst** Math. Rev.

US/0196-6774
**JOURNAL OF ALGORITHMS.** [J. algorithms]. Vol. 1 (March 1980)-. Academic Scholarly Publication. English. bm (6 issues). $271.00 US and Canada; $322.00 other. Academic Press, Inc., 6277 Sea Harbor Drive, Orlando FL 32887. **Tel** (800)543-9534, (407)345-4100, FAX (407)363-9661. **ED** Zvi Galil, David S. Johnson, and Donald E. Knuth. **LC** QA76.6; .J69. **DD** 511/.8. **CODEN** JOALDV. **[CCC]. Pr Rev.** Documents available from The Genuine Article, Ask*IEEE.
**Desc:** Presents papers on algorithms that are inherently discrete and finite and that have some definite mathematical content in a natural way, either in their objective or in their analysis. Features new algorithms and data structures, new analyses or comparisons of known algorithms, complexity studies, and sharply focused review articles of subject areas that are currently active.
**Ind/Abst** ACM Guide Comput. Lit.; Compumath Citation Index [Full Cov.]; Comput. Rev.; INSPEC (March 1981-); Int. Abstr. Oper. Res. [Select. Cov.]; Math. Rev.; Res. Alert [Full Cov.]; SCISEARCH; Zentralbl. Math. Ihre Grenzgeb.

US/1048-9533
**JOURNAL OF APPLIED MATHEMATICS AND STOCHASTIC ANALYSIS.** **See** Computers-Simulation.

FR/1166-3081
**JOURNAL OF APPLIED NON-CLASSICAL LOGICS.** **VFOAT** Journal of Applied Nonclassical Logics. (199?)-. Periodical. English. sa. 530.00F (France); 630.00F (other). Editions Hermes, 14 rue Lantiez, 75017 Paris France. **Tel** 11 33 1 42294466. ***Continues*** *Journal of Non-Classical Logic, 0102-3411.*

UK/0021-9002
**JOURNAL OF APPLIED PROBABILITY.** [J. appl. probab.]. **Added/Corp** Applied Probability Trust. London Mathematical Society. Vol. 1 (June 1964)-. Periodical. English (French). qt. £99.24. Applied Probability, School of Mathematics and Statistics, Sheffield S3 7RH England. **Tel** 011 44 742 824269, FAX 011 44 742 729782. **ED** C. C. Heyde. **LC** QA276; .J65. **CODEN** JPRBAM. **[CCC]**. Index available. cum. index. **Ad Acc. Pr Rev. Circ:** 1,500. Documents available from Article Express International, The Genuine Article, UMI Article Clearinghouse, Ask*IEEE.

**Desc:** Research papers and notes on applications of probability theory to the biological, physical, social, and technological sciences.
**Ind/Abst** ABI/INFORM Glob. Ed.; Anim. Breed. Abstr.; Bioeng. Abstr.; Biostatistica; Compumath Citation Index [Full Cov.]; Curr. Contents Phys. Chem. Earth Sci.; Curr. Index Stat.; Ei Page One; Energy Res. Abstr.; Eng. Index Annu.; INSPEC (Aug. 1969-); Int. Abstr. Oper. Res. [Select. Cov.]; Int. Aerosp. Abstr.; Math. Rev.; Life Sci. Collect.; Plant Breed. Abstr.; Pollut. Abstr. Indexes; Qual. Control Appl. Stat.; Res. Alert [Full Cov.]; Rev. Med. Vet. Entomol.; Sci. Cit. Index; SCISEARCH; Soc. Sci. Cit. Index [Select. Cov.]; Stat. Theory Method Abstr. (1967-1984, 1986); Zentralbl. Math. Ihre Grenzgeb.

●US/1067-5817
**JOURNAL OF APPLIED STATISTICAL SCIENCE.** **See** Statistics.

US/0021-9045
**JOURNAL OF APPROXIMATION THEORY.** [J. approx. theory]. Vol. 1 (June 1968)-. Academic Scholarly Publication. English (German). mo. $773.00 US and Canada; $892.00 other. Academic Press, Inc., 6277 Sea Harbor Drive, Orlando FL 32887. **Tel** (800)543-9534, (407)345-4100, FAX (407)363-9661. **ED** Paul Nevai and Allan Pinkus. **LC** QA221; .J63. **DD** 511/.4/05. **CODEN** JAXTAZ. **[CCC]. Pr Rev.** Documents available from The Genuine Article, Ask*IEEE.
**Desc:** Devoted to new advances in pure and applied approximation theory and related areas.
**Ind/Abst** ACM Guide Comput. Lit.; Compumath Citation Index [Full Cov.]; Comput. Rev.; Curr. Contents Phys. Chem. Earth Sci.; INSPEC (Sept. 1970-); Math. Rev.; Res. Alert [Full Cov.]; Sci. Cit. Index; SCISEARCH; Zentralbl. Math. Ihre Grenzgeb.

US/0176-4268
**JOURNAL OF CLASSIFICATION.** [J. classif.]. **Added/Corp** Classification Society of North America. Vol. 1, No. 1 (1984)-. Periodical. English. Twice a year. $104.00. Springer-Verlag New York Inc., 175 5th Avenue, New York NY 10010. **Tel** (212)460-1500, telex 232 235 SPB UR. **(Subscription address:** Springer Verlag New York Inc. / for North America, 44 Hartz Way, Secaucus NJ 07096.**) ED** P Arabie, A D Gordon, and L Bilger. **[CCC]. Ad Acc. Pr Rev. Circ:** 101. Documents available from The Genuine Article.
**Desc:** Publishes original papers in fields including classification, numerical taxonomy, multidimensional scaling and other ordination techniques, clustering, tree structures and other network models, principal components analysis as well as associated models and algorithms for fitting them.
**Ind/Abst** Biostatistica; Compumath Citation Index [Full Cov.]; Curr. Contents Soc. Behav. Sci.; Curr. Index Stat.; Libr. Inf. Sci. Abstr.; Math. Rev. (1984-); Psychol. Abstr. (1984-); PsycINFO; PsycLit; Res. Alert [Full Cov.]; Soc. Sci. Cit. Index [Full Cov.]; Soc. Res. Methodol. Abstr. (1991-); Zentralbl. Math. Ihre Grenzgeb.

●US/1063-8539
**JOURNAL OF COMBINATORIAL DESIGNS.** [J. comb. des.]. (1993)-. Periodical. English. bm. $240.00 US and Canada; $300.00 Mexico; $322.50 other. John Wiley & Sons, Inc., 605 Third Avenue, New York NY 10158-0012. **Tel** (212)850-6000, (212)850-6645, FAX (212)850-6088, telex 12-7063. **(Subscription address:** John Wiley & Sons / England, Baffins Lane, Chichester, West Sussex PO19 1UD England.**) ED** Charles J. Colbourn, Alexander Rosa and Douglas R. Stinson. **LC** QA166.25; .J68. **DD** 511/.6. **CODEN** JDESEU.
**Desc:** Devoted to the timely publication of the most influential papers in the area of combinatorial design theory.

US/0097-3165
**JOURNAL OF COMBINATORIAL THEORY. SERIES A.** [J. comb. theory. Ser. A]. Vol. 10, No. 1 (Jan. 1971)-. Academic Scholarly Publication. English. Eight times a year. $718.00 US and Canada; $867.00 other. Academic Press, Inc., 6277 Sea Harbor Drive, Orlando FL 32887. **Tel** (800)543-9534, (407)345-4100, FAX (407)363-9661. **ED** Basil Gordon and Bruce Rothschild. **LC** QA164; .J617. **DD** 511/.6. **CODEN** JCBTA7. **[CCC]. Pr Rev.** Documents available from The Genuine Article, Ask*IEEE. ***Continues in part*** *Journal of Combinatorial Theory, 0021-9800.*
**Desc:** Original mathematical research concerned with theoretical and physical aspects of the study of finite and discrete structures in all branches of science. The journal is primarily concerned with structures, designs, and applications of combinatorics.
**Ind/Abst** ACM Guide Comput. Lit.; Compumath Citation Index [Full Cov.]; Comput. Rev.; Curr. Contents Phys. Chem. Earth Sci.; INSPEC (Jan. 1971-); Int. Abstr. Oper. Res. (Jan. 1971-) [Select. Cov.]; Math. Rev.; Res. Alert [Full Cov.]; Sci. Cit. Index; SCISEARCH; Stat. Theory Method Abstr. (1977-1979, 1986); Zentralbl. Math. Ihre Grenzgeb. (Jan. 1971-).

US/0095-8956
**JOURNAL OF COMBINATORIAL THEORY. SERIES B.** [J. comb. theory, Ser. B]. (Feb. 1971)-. Academic Scholarly Publication. English. bm (6 issues). $490.00 US and Canada; $583.00 other. Academic Press, Inc., 6277 Sea Harbor Drive, Orlando FL 32887. **Tel** (800)543-9534, (407)345-4100, FAX (407)363-9661. **ED** Adrian Bondy, U. S. R. Murty and W. R. Pulleyblank. **LC** QA166; .J66. **DD** 511/.5. **CODEN** JCBTB8. **[CCC]. Pr Rev.** Documents available from The Genuine Article, Ask*IEEE. ***Continues in part*** *Journal of Combinatorial Theory, 0021-9800.*
**Desc:** Publishes original mathematical research dealing with theoretical and physical aspects of the study of finite and discrete structures in all branches of science. The journal is primarily concerned with graph theory and matroid theory.
**Ind/Abst** ACM Guide Comput. Lit.; Compumath Citation Index [Full Cov.]; Comput. Rev.; Curr. Contents Clin. Med.; INSPEC (April 1971-); Int. Abstr. Oper. Res. (April 1971-) [Select. Cov.]; Math. Rev.; Res. Alert [Full Cov.]; Sci. Cit. Index; SCISEARCH; Zentralbl. Math. Ihre Grenzgeb. (April 1971-).

II/0250-9628
**JOURNAL OF COMBINATORICS, INFORMATION & SYSTEM SCIENCES.** [J. comb. inf. syst. sci.]. **Added/Corp** Forum for Interdisciplinary Mathematics. **VAT** Journal of Combinatorics, Information and System Sciences. Vol. 1, No. 1, (1976)-. Periodical. English. qt. $95.00. Forum for Interdisciplinary Mathematics, Delhi, India. **(Subscription address:** Prints India, 11 Darya Ganj, New Delhi 110002 India.**) LC** QA164; .J62.
**Ind/Abst** Math. Rev.; Zentralbl. Math. Ihre Grenzgeb.

US/0885-064X
**JOURNAL OF COMPLEXITY.** Vol. 1, No. 1 (Oct. 1985)-. Academic Scholarly Publication. English. qt (4 issues). $175.00 US and Canada; $207.00 other. Academic Press, Inc., 6277 Sea Harbor Drive, Orlando FL 32887. **Tel** (800)543-9534, (407)345-4100, FAX (407)363-9661. **ED** Joseph F. Traub. **LC** QA267; .J68. **DD** 511. **CODEN** JOCOEH. **[CCC].** Documents available from Ask*IEEE.
**Desc:** Original research papers that contain substantial mathematical results on complexity as broadly conceived. Publishes papers that provide major new algorithms or make important progress on upper bounds. Also addresses such complexity topics as physical limits of computation; chaotic behavior and strange attractors; and complexity in biological, physical, or artificial systems.
**Ind/Abst** ACM Guide Comput. Lit.; Comput. Rev.; INSPEC (1985-); Math. Rev. (1985-); Zentralbl. Math. Ihre Grenzgeb.

NE/0377-0427
**JOURNAL OF COMPUTATIONAL AND APPLIED MATHEMATICS.** [J. comput. appl. math.]. **Added/Corp** Koninklijke Vlaamse Ingenieursvereniging. Vol. 1 (March 1975)-. Academic Scholarly Publication. English. Twenty-seven times a year (9 vols.). FI3195.00. Elsevier Science Publishers BV, PO Box 211, 1000 AE Amsterdam Netherlands. **Tel** 011 31 20 5803642, FAX 011 31 20 5862696, telex 15682. **ED** M J Goovaerts, W B Gragg, and L Wuytack. **LC** QA1; .J955. **DD** 519.4/05. **CODEN** JCAMDI. **[CCC]. Pr Rev.** available on microfilm and microfiche from University Microfilms International (UMI). Documents available from Article Express International, The Genuine Article, Ask*IEEE.
**Desc:** Publishes original papers of high scientific standard in all areas of applied mathematics.
**Ind/Abst** ACM Guide Comput. Lit.; Bioeng. Abstr.; Compumath Citation Index [Full Cov.]; Comput. Rev.; Ei Page One; Eng. Index Annu. [Select. Cov.]; GeoRef; INSPEC (March 1983-); Int. Abstr. Oper. Res. [Select. Cov.]; Int. Aerosp. Abstr. (1984-); Math. Rev.; Pollut. Abstr. Indexes; Res. Alert [Full Cov.]; SCISEARCH; Zentralbl. Math. Ihre Grenzgeb.

CC/0254-9409
**JOURNAL OF COMPUTATIONAL MATHEMATICS.** (JOURNAL OF COMPUTATIONAL MATHEMATICS : AN INTERNATIONAL JOURNAL ON NUMERICAL METHODS, ANALYSIS AND APPLICATIONS / EDITED BY EDITORIAL COMMITTEE OF JOURNAL OF COMPUTATIONAL MATHEMATICS.). [J. comput. math.]. Vol. 1, No. 1 (Jan. 1983)-. Periodical. English. qt. DM370.00. VSP International Science Publishers, Godfried van Seystlaan 47, 3703 BR Zeist Netherlands. **Tel** 011 31 3404 25790, FAX 011 31 3404 32081, telex 40217 USP NL. **(Subscription address:** VSP International Science Publishers, PO Box 346, 3700 AH Zeist Netherlands.**) ED** Feng Kang. **CODEN** JCMMEB. **Pr Rev.** Documents available from The Genuine Article, Ask*IEEE.
**Desc:** Covers numerical methods, analysis and applications.
**Ind/Abst** Compumath Citation Index [Full Cov.]; Comput. Rev.; INSPEC (April 1987-); Math. Rev.; Res. Alert [Full Cov.]; SCISEARCH; Zentralbl. Math. Ihre Grenzgeb.

US/0021-9991
**JOURNAL OF COMPUTATIONAL PHYSICS.** **See** Physics.

US/0022-0000
**JOURNAL OF COMPUTER AND SYSTEM SCIENCES.** **See** Computers-Computer Systems.

US/1068-3623
**JOURNAL OF CONTEMPORARY MATHEMATICAL ANALYSIS.** [J. contemp. math. anal.]. **Added/Corp** Haykakan SSH Gitutyunneri Akademia. Vol. 26, No. 1 (1991)-. Periodical. English (translations available in Russian). Six times a year. $800.00. Allerton Press, Inc., 150 Fifth Avenue, New York NY 10011. **Tel** (212)924-3950, FAX (212)463-9684, telex 427441 ALPRES. **LC** QA297; .I9. **DD** 515.3/5/05. **[CCC]. *Continues*** *Izvestiia Akademii Nauk Armianskoi SSR. Matematika. English. Soviet Journal of Contemporary Mathematical Analysis, 0735-2719.*
**Ind/Abst** Math. Rev.

US/0933-2790
**JOURNAL OF CRYPTOLOGY.** (JOURNAL OF CRYPTOLOGY : THE JOURNAL OF THE INTERNATIONAL ASSOCIATION FOR CRYPTOLOGIC RESEARCH.). [J. cryptol.]. **Added/Corp** International Association for Cryptologic Research. Vol. 1, No. 1 (1988)-. Periodical. English. Four times a year. $121.00. Springer-Verlag New York Inc., 175 5th Avenue, New York NY 10010. **Tel** (212)460-1500, telex 232 235 SPB UR. **(Subscription address:** Springer Verlag New York Inc. / for North America, 44 Hartz Way, Secaucus NJ 07096.**) ED** Ernest F Brickell. **LC** Z102.5; .J68. **DD** 652/.805. **CODEN** JOCREQ. **[CCC]. Ad Acc.** available on microfilm and microfiche from University Microfilms International (UMI). Documents available from Article Express International, Ask*IEEE.
**Desc:** Provides a forum for original results in all areas of modern information security - both in cryptography and cryptanalysis.
**Ind/Abst** ACM Guide Comput. Lit.; Comput. Rev.; Ei Page One; Eng. Index Annu.; INSPEC (1988-); Math. Rev. (1988-); Zentralbl. Math. Ihre Grenzgeb.

US/0022-0396
**JOURNAL OF DIFFERENTIAL EQUATIONS.** [J. differ. equ.]. Vol. 1 (Jan. 1965)-. Academic Scholarly Publication. English. Eighteen times a year. $1461.00 US and Canada; $1691.00 other. Academic Press, Inc., 6277 Sea Harbor Drive, Orlando FL 32887. **Tel** (800)543-9534, (407)345-4100, FAX (407)363-9661. **ED** Jack K. Hale. **LC** QA371; .J73. **DD** 515. **CODEN** JDEQAK. **[CCC]. Pr Rev.** Documents available from The Genuine Article, Ask*IEEE. ***Supersedes*** *Contributions to Differential Equations, 0589-5839.*
**Desc:** Concerned with both the theory and the applications of differential equations. The articles published are addressed not only to mathematicians, but also to those engineers, physicists, and other scientists for whom differential equations are valuable research tools.
**Ind/Abst** Compumath Citation Index [Full Cov.]; Comput. Rev.; Curr. Contents Phys. Chem. Earth Sci.; INSPEC (1968-); Int. Aerosp. Abstr.; Math. Rev.; Res. Alert [Full Cov.]; Sci. Cit. Index; SCISEARCH; Zentralbl. Math. Ihre Grenzgeb.

US/0022-040X
**JOURNAL OF DIFFERENTIAL GEOMETRY.** [J. differ. geom.]. **Added/Corp** Lehigh University. Vol. 1 (Mar. 1967)-. Periodical. English. bm. $295.00. International Press, PO Box 2872, Cambridge MA 02238. **Tel** (617)491-0329. **LC** QA641; .J67. **DD** 516/.36/005. **CODEN** JDGEAS. **Pr Rev.** Documents available from The Genuine Article.
**Desc:** The only journal devoted exclusively to differential geometry in the large and to related subjects. It is a central source of information about important developments in modern differential geometry and its relationship to other braches of mathematics.
**Ind/Abst** Compumath Citation Index [Full Cov.]; Math. Rev.; Res. Alert [Full Cov.]; SCISEARCH; Zentralbl. Math. Ihre Grenzgeb.

US/1040-7294
**JOURNAL OF DYNAMICS AND DIFFERENTIAL EQUATIONS.** [J. dyn. differ. equ.]. Vol. 1, No. 1 (Jan. 1989)-. Periodical. English. Four times a year. $195.00 institutions, $60.00 individuals US; $230.00 institutions, $70.00 individuals other. Plenum Press, 233 Spring Street, New York NY 10013-1578. **Tel** (212)620-8000, (800)221-9369, FAX (212)463-0742, (212)807-1047, telex 23/421139. **ED** George R. Sell. **LC** QA370; .J68. **DD** 515/.35/05. **CODEN** JDDEEH. available on microfilm and microfiche from University Microfilms International (UMI). Documents available from Ask*IEEE.
**Desc:** Original papers covering all the classical topics including attractors, bifurcation theory, dichotomies, ergodic theory, finite and infinite dimensional systems and more.
**Ind/Abst** INSPEC (1991-); Math. Rev.; Zentralbl. Math. Ihre Grenzgeb.

US/0022-0531
**JOURNAL OF ECONOMIC THEORY.** **See** Economics-Economic Theory.

NE/0022-0833
**JOURNAL OF ENGINEERING MATHEMATICS.** **See** Engineering.

●US/1069-5869
**JOURNAL OF FOURIER ANALYSIS AND APPLICATIONS, THE.** (1994)-. Periodical. English. qt. $195.00 institution. CRC Press Inc., 2000 Corporate Boulevard Northwest, Boca Raton FL 33431. **Tel** (407)994-0555, (800)272-7737, FAX (407)998-9784, telex 568689. **(Subscription address:** CRC Press Inc., PO Box 750, Pearl River NY 10965.**) ED** John J. Benedetto.
**Desc:** A new mathematical sciences publication devoted to aspects of Fourier analysis and its applications in science and engineering.

US/0022-1236
**JOURNAL OF FUNCTIONAL ANALYSIS.** [J. funct. anal.]. Vol. 1 (May 1967)-. Academic Scholarly Publication. English. Sixteen times a year. $1325.00 US and Canada; $1540.00 other. Academic Press, Inc., 6277 Sea Harbor Drive, Orlando FL 32887. **Tel** (800)543-9534, (407)345-4100, FAX (407)363-9661. **ED** Paul Malliavin, Ralph S. Phillips and Irving Segal. **LC** QA320; .J65. **DD** 517/.5/05. **CODEN** JFUAAW. **[CCC]. Pr Rev.** Documents available from The Genuine Article, Ask*IEEE.
**Desc:** Presents original research papers in all scientific disciplines in which functional analysis plays an important role.
**Ind/Abst** Compumath Citation Index [Full Cov.]; Curr. Contents Phys. Chem. Earth Sci.; INSPEC (April 1972-); Math. Rev.; Pollut. Abstr. Indexes; Res. Alert [Full Cov.]; Sci. Cit. Index; SCISEARCH; Stat. Theory Method Abstr. (1982-1983, 1987); Zentralbl. Math. Ihre Grenzgeb.

US/1050-6926
**JOURNAL OF GEOMETRIC ANALYSIS, THE.** [J. geom. anal.]. Vol. 1, No. 1 (1991)-. Periodical. English. bm. $255.00 (institution); $105.00 (individual). American Mathematical Society, PO Box 6248, Providence RI 02940-6248. **Tel** (800)321-4267, (401)455-4000, FAX (401)331-3842, telex 797192. **ED** Steven G. Krantz. **LC** QA299.6; .J68. **DD** 515/.05. **CODEN** JGANEG.
**Desc:** Serves as a forum for work on the interface of analysis, geometry, and partial differential equations.
**Ind/Abst** Ei Page One; Math. Rev.; Zentralbl. Math. Ihre Grenzgeb.

SZ/0047-2468
**JOURNAL OF GEOMETRY.** [J. geom.]. Vol. 1 (1971)-. Periodical. English (German; summaries and/or abstracts in German). Six times a year. 404.40F Switzerland; 418.50F other. Birkhaeuser Verlag Ag, Klosterberg 23, PO Box 133, CH-4010 Basel Switzerland. **Tel** 011 41 61 2717400, FAX 011 41 0 61 2717666, telex 963475 birk ch. **(Subscription address:** Birkhauser Verlag AG, PO Box 151, CH 4106 Therwil Switzerland; Phone: 011 41 61 7217740**) ED** J. AczÇl, R. Artzy, A. Barlotti, M. Barner, W. Benz, W. Heise, J. W. P. Hirschfield, H. Karzel, H. J. Kroll, W. Leissner, T. G. Ostrom, N. K. Stephanidis, P. V. Ceccherini and G. Tallini. **LC** QA443; .J68. **DD** 516/.2/005. **CODEN** JGMAY9. **[CCC].** available on microfilm and microfiche from University Microfilms International (UMI).
**Desc:** Devoted to the publication of current research developments in the field of geometry, with emphasis on recent results in the foundations of geometry, geometric algebra, finite geometries, combinatorial geometry, and special geometries.
**Ind/Abst** Math. Rev.; Zentralbl. Math. Ihre Grenzgeb.

NE/0393-0440
**JOURNAL OF GEOMETRY AND PHYSICS.** **See** Physics.

NE/0925-5001
**JOURNAL OF GLOBAL OPTIMIZATION : AN INTERNATIONAL JOURNAL DEALING WITH THEORETICAL AND COMPUTATIONAL ASPECTS OF SEEKING GLOBAL OPTIMA AND THEIR APPLICATIONS IN SCIENCE, MANAGEMENT AND ENGINEERING.** Vol. 1, No. 1 (1991)-. Periodical. English. Eight times a year. $800.00. Kluwer Academic Publishers, Postbus 322, 3300 AH Dordrecht, The Netherlands. **Tel** 011 (31) 78 524400, FAX 011 31 78 183273, telex 20083. **ED** R. Horst, V. Bulatov, J. Evtushenko, C. Fleury, and C. Floudas. **LC** QA402.5; .J59; QA402.5; .J68. **DD** 519.3. **CODEN** JGOPEO. **[CCC]. Pr Rev. Acid Free.** available on microfilm and microfiche from University Microfilms International (UMI).
**Desc:** Optimizations is understood in the widest sense including, for example, nonlinear, stochastic and combinatorial programming, multiobjective programming, control, games, geometry and approximations as well as nonlinear systems, algorithms for parallel architectures, etc. Besides research articles and expository papers on theory and algorithms of global optimization, papers on numerical experiments and on applications in engineering, management and the sciences are welcome.
**Ind/Abst** Zentralbl. Math. Ihre Grenzgeb.

US/0364-9024
**JOURNAL OF GRAPH THEORY.** [J. graph theory]. Vol. 1 (Spring 1977)-. Periodical. English. Eight times a year. $584.00 US; $664.00 Canada and Mexico; $694.00 other. John Wiley & Sons, Inc., 605 Third Avenue, New York NY 10158-0012. **Tel** (212)850-6000, (212)850-6645, FAX (212)850-6088, telex 12-7063. **(Subscription address:** John Wiley & Sons / England, Baffins Lane, Chichester, West Sussex PO19 1UD England.**) ED** Fan Chung and Carsten Thomassen. **LC** QA166; .J68. **DD** 510/.5/05. **CODEN** JGTHDO. **[CCC]. Ad Acc. Pr Rev. Circ:** 800. available on microfilm and microfiche from University Microfilms International (UMI). Documents available from The Genuine Article, Ask*IEEE.
**Desc:** Devoted exclusively to the expanding field of graph theory, with emphasis on theorems. Also includes related areas in combinatorics and the interaction of graph theory to other mathematical sciences.
**Ind/Abst** ACM Guide Comput. Lit.; AGRICOLA; Compumath Citation Index [Full Cov.]; Comput. Rev.; INSPEC (Summer 1978-); Int. Abstr. Oper. Res. [Select. Cov.]; Math. Rev.; Res. Alert [Full Cov.]; Sci. Cit. Index; SCISEARCH; Zentralbl. Math. Ihre Grenzgeb.

II/0252-2667
**JOURNAL OF INFORMATION & OPTIMIZATION SCIENCES.** (JOURNAL OF INFORMATION & OPTIMIZATION SCIENCES : A JOURNAL DEVOTED TO ADVANCES IN INFORMATION SCIENCES, OPTIMIZATION SCIENCES AND RELATED ASPECTS.). [J. inf. optim. sci.]. **VFOAT** Journal of Information and Optimization Sciences. Vol. 1, No. 1 (Jan. 1980)-. Periodical. English. Three times a year. $72.00. **(Subscription address:** Prints India, 11 Darya Ganj, New Delhi 110002 India.**) LC** QA75.5; .J63. **DD** 001.5. **CODEN** JIOSDC. **[CCC].** Documents available from Ask*IEEE.
**Ind/Abst** Biostatistica; INSPEC (Jan. 1980-); Int. Abstr. Oper. Res. [Select. Cov.]; Math. Rev.; Oper. Res./Manag. Sci.; Pollut. Abstr. Indexes; Qual. Control Appl. Stat.; Zentralbl. Math. Ihre Grenzgeb.

US/0897-3962
**JOURNAL OF INTEGRAL EQUATIONS AND APPLICATIONS, THE.** [J. integral equ. appl.]. **Added/Corp** Rocky Mountain Mathematics Consortium. Vol. 1, No. 1 (Winter 1988)-. Periodical. English. Four times a year. $165.00. Arizona State University / Rocky Mountain Mathematics Consortium, Department of Mathematics, Box 871904, Tempe AZ 85287-1904. **Tel** (602)965-3788. **LC** QA431; .J66. **DD** 515/.45/05. Documents available from Article Express International. ***Continues** Journal of Integral Equations, 0163-5549.*
**Ind/Abst** Bioeng. Abstr.; Ei Page One; Eng. Index Annu.; Int. Aerosp. Abstr.; Math. Rev. (1988-); Zentralbl. Math. Ihre Grenzgeb.

NE/0928-0219
**JOURNAL OF INVERSE AND ILL-POSED PROBLEMS.** (1992)-. English. bm. DM720.00. VSP International Science Publishers, Godfried van Seystlaan 47, 3703 BR Zeist Netherlands. **Tel** 011 31 3404 25790, FAX 011 31 3404 32081, telex 40217 USP NL. **(Subscription address:** VSP International Science Publishers, PO Box 346, 3700 AH Zeist Netherlands.**) ED** M.M. Lavrent'ev.
**Desc:** Inverse and ill-posed problems appear in mathematical physics and mathematical analysis, geophysics, acoustics, electrodynamics, tomography, medicine and ecology.

●SI/0218-2165
**JOURNAL OF KNOT THEORY AND ITS RAMIFICATIONS.** Vol. 1, No. 1 (Mar. 1992)-. Periodical. English. qt. $130.00 individuals, $260.00 institutions. World Scientific Publishing Company, PO Box 128, Farrer Road, Singapore 9128 Singapore. **Tel** 011 65 3825663, FAX 011 65 3825919, telex RS 28561 WSPC. **(Subscription address:** US: World Scientific Publishing Co., Inc., 1060 Main Street, River Edge, NJ 07661 Telephone: (201)487-9655, Fax: (201)487-9656; Europe: World Scientific Publishing Co Ltd, 73 Lynton Mead, Totteridge, London N20 8DH United Kingdom Telephone: 011 44 81 4462461, Fax: 011 44 81 4463356; India: World Scientific Publishing Co Pte Ltd, 4911 9th Floor, High Point IV, 45 Palace Road, Bangalore 560 001 India Telephone: (80) 2205972, Fax: (80) 3344593, Telex: 0845-2900 PCO IN; Hong Kong: World Scientific Publishing (HK) Co, PO Box 72482, Kowloon Central Post Office, Hong Kong Telephone: 852-7718791, Fax: 852-7718155**) ED** L.H. Kauffman, W.B.R. Lickorish, M. Wadati. **LC** QA612.2; .J68. **DD** 514/.224. **Bk Rev.**
**Desc:** A forum for new developments in knot theory, particularly developments that create connections between knot theory and other aspects of mathematics and natural science.
**Ind/Abst** Math. Rev.

●GW
**JOURNAL OF LIE THEORY.** (Jan. 1995)-. Periodical. English. Twice a year. DM152.00. Heldermann Verlag Berlin, Nassauische Str 26, D 10717 Berlin Germany. **Tel** 011 49 30 870446.

US/0022-247X
**JOURNAL OF MATHEMATICAL ANALYSIS AND APPLICATIONS.** [J. math. anal. appl.]. Vol. 1 (June 1960)-. Academic Scholarly Publication. English. Twenty-four times a year. $2229.00 US and Canada; $2591.00 other. Academic Press, Inc., 6277 Sea Harbor Drive, Orlando FL 32887. **Tel** (800)543-9534, (407)345-4100, FAX (407)363-9661. **ED** Ralph P. Boas and George Leitmann. **LC** QA1; .J958. **DD** 515. **CODEN** JMANAK. **[CCC]. Pr Rev.** Documents available from Article Express International, The Genuine Article, Ask*IEEE.
**Desc:** Presents mathematical papers that treat classical analysis and its numerous applications. The journal emphasizes articles devoted to the mathematical treatment of questions arising in physics, chemistry, biology, and engineering, particularly those that stress analytical aspects and novel problems and their solutions.
**Ind/Abst** Bioeng. Abstr.; Compumath Citation Index [Full Cov.]; Curr. Contents Phys. Chem. Earth Sci.; Ei Page One; Energy Res. Abstr.; Eng. Index Annu.; INIS Atomindex [Micro.]; INSPEC (1968-); Int. Abstr. Oper. Res. [Select. Cov.]; Int. Aerosp. Abstr.; Math. Rev.; Pollut. Abstr. Indexes; Res. Alert [Full Cov.]; Sci. Cit. Index; SCISEARCH; Soc. Sci. Cit. Index [Select. Cov.]; Stat. Theory Method Abstr. (1969, 1971-1972); Zentralbl. Math. Ihre Grenzgeb.

II/0047-2557
**JOURNAL OF MATHEMATICAL AND PHYSICAL SCIENCES.** [J. math. & phys. sci.]. **Added/Corp** Indian Institute of Technology (Madras, India). Vol. 1, (June 1967)-. Periodical. English. Six times a year (Feb., Apr., June, Aug., Oct., Dec.). $50.00 (individuals); $90.00 (institutions). Journal of Mathematical and Physical Science, Room #HSB 249, Indian Institute of Technology, Madras 600036 India. **Tel** 011 91 44 2351338. **ED** P. Achuthan. **LC** QC20; .J646. **DD** 530.15/005. **CODEN** JMPSB9. Index available. cum. index. **Bk Rev. Circ:** 300. Documents available from Ask*IEEE.
**Desc:** Mathematical sciences-continuum mechanics, analysis, probability, combinatorial mathematics, theoretical physics, astrophysics, differential educations and numerical analysis.
**Ind/Abst** INSPEC (June 1969-); Int. Aerosp. Abstr.; Math. Rev.; Zentralbl. Math. Ihre Grenzgeb.

US/0732-3123
**JOURNAL OF MATHEMATICAL BEHAVIOR, THE.** (THE JOURNAL OF MATHEMATICAL BEHAVIOR / THE MADISON PROJECT.). [J. math. behav.]. **Added/Corp** Study Group for Mathematical Behavior. Madison Project (U.S.). Vol. 3, No. 1 (Autumn 1980)-. Periodical. English. qt. $140.00. Ablex Publishing Corporation, 355 Chestnut Street, Norwood NJ 07648. **Tel** (201)767-8450, (201)767-8455 (Customer Service), FAX (201)767-6717. **ED** Robert B. Davis. **LC** QA11.A1; J685. **DD** 370.15/651. **[CCC].** Index available. **Bk Rev. Ad Acc. Circ:** 500. ***Continues** Journal of Children's Mathematical Behavior, 0160-0133.*
**Desc:** Articles addressed toward improving mathematics education either from a theoretical or practical viewpoint.
**Ind/Abst** Curr. Index J. Educ.; Psychol. Abstr. (1980-); PsycINFO; PsycLit.

AU/0303-6812
**JOURNAL OF MATHEMATICAL BIOLOGY.** **See** Biology.

NE/0304-4068
**JOURNAL OF MATHEMATICAL ECONOMICS.** **See** Economics.

US/0924-9907
**JOURNAL OF MATHEMATICAL IMAGING AND VISION.** (1992)-. English. qt. $486.00. Kluwer Academic Publishers / Massachusetts, PO Box 358, Accord Station, Hingham MA 02018. **Tel** (617)871-6600. **ED** Gerhard Ritter. **Pr Rev. Acid Free.** available on microfilm and microfiche from University Microfilms International (UMI).
**Desc:** A technical journal publishing important developments in mathematical imaging. The journal publishes research articles, invited papers, and expository articles. The aim of the jounal is to emphasize the role of mathematics as a rigorous basis for imaging science. This journal provides a sound alternative to present presents journals in this area. The scope of the journal includes: computational models of vision; imaging algebra and mathematical morphology, mathematical methods in reconstruction, compactification, and coding, filter theory, probabilistic, statistical, geometric, topological, and fractal techniques and models in imaging science, inverse optics, and wave theory.
**Ind/Abst** Math. Rev.

US/0022-2488
**JOURNAL OF MATHEMATICAL PHYSICS.** **See** Physics.

US/0022-2496
**JOURNAL OF MATHEMATICAL PSYCHOLOGY.** **See** Psychology.

CC/1000-9191
**JOURNAL OF MATHEMATICAL RESEARCH AND EXPOSITION.** [J. Math. Res. Expo.]. (1981)-. Periodical. English. qt. **DD** 510.
**Ind/Abst** Zentralbl. Math. Ihre Grenzgeb.

●US/1072-3374
**JOURNAL OF MATHEMATICAL SCIENCES.** [J. math. sci.]. **Added/Corp** Consultants Bureau. Vol. 68, No. 1 (Jan. 10, 1994)-. Periodical. English (translations available in Russian). ir (30 issues). $3175.00 US; $3715.00 other. Consultants Bureau, A Division of Plenum Publishing Corporation, 233 Spring Street, New York NY 10013. **Tel** (212)620-8000, (212)620-8466, FAX (212)463-0742, telex 23/421139. **LC** QA1; .J976. **DD** 510. **CODEN** JMTSEW. ***Continues*** *Journal of Soviet Mathematics, 0090-4104.*

II/0449-2757
**JOURNAL OF MATHEMATICAL SCIENCES.** [J. math. sci.]. **Added/Corp** Society of Mathematical Sciences, Delhi (India). Vol. 1 (1966)-. English. an. Society of Mathematical Sciences, Delhi, India. **(Subscription address:** Prints India, 11 Darya Ganj, New Delhi 110002 India.**)** **LC** QA1; .J959. **DD** 510/.5. **CODEN** JOMSB8.
**Ind/Abst** Comput. Rev.; Math. Rev.; Zentralbl. Math. Ihre Grenzgeb.

US/0022-250X
**JOURNAL OF MATHEMATICAL SOCIOLOGY, THE.** **See** Sociology.

US/1052-0600
**JOURNAL OF MATHEMATICAL SYSTEMS, ESTIMATION, AND CONTROL.** **VFOAT** Mathematical Systems, Estimation, and Control. (1991)-. Periodical. English. Four times a year. 504.00F Switzerland; 513.00F other. Birkhauser Boston, Inc., c/o Springer Publishers New York Inc., Customer Service Department, 333 Meadowlands Parkway, Secaucus NJ 07096-2491. **Tel** (201)348-4033, (800)777-4643. **ED** C. F. Martin. **LC** QA402.3; .J68. **DD** 003. **CODEN** JMCOE3. cum. index.
**Desc:** Publishes papers in the areas of systems, estimation and control theory. Papers that make novel applications of good mathematics to problems in estimation and control or the broad area of mathematical systems theory are solicited. Papers are welcomed from throughout the world. Primarily devoted to research papers, but also publishes survey, expository and tutorial papers.
**Ind/Abst** Math. Rev.; Zentralbl. Math. Ihre Grenzgeb.

JA/0023-608X
**JOURNAL OF MATHEMATICS OF KYOTO UNIVERSITY.** **Main/Corp** Kyoto Daigaku. Vol. 1 (Sept. 1961)-. Periodical. Multiple languages (English and French). qt. $448.00. Kyoto Daigaku Rigakubu Sugaku Kyoshitsu, (Department of Mathematics, Faculty of Science, Kyoto University), Oiwakecho, Kitashirakawa, Sakyoku, Kyotoshi, Kyotofu 606 Japan. **(Subscription address:** Kinokuniya Company Ltd., 38-1 Sakuragaoka 5, chome Setagaya-ku, Tokyo 156 Japan.**)** **LC** QA1; .K9. **CODEN** JMKYAZ. **Pr Rev.** Documents available from The Genuine Article. ***Supersedes*** *Kyoto Daigaku. Rigakubu. Memoirs of the College of Science, University of Kyoto. Series A. Mathematics.*
**Ind/Abst** Compumath Citation Index [Full Cov.]; Math. Rev.; Res. Alert [Full Cov.]; SCISEARCH; Zentralbl. Math. Ihre Grenzgeb.

JA/0075-4293
**JOURNAL OF MATHEMATICS, TOKUSHIMA UNIVERSITY.** **Main/Corp** Tokushima Daigaku. Vol. 1 (1967)-. Periodical. English. an. Tokushima University Faculty of Integrated Arts and Sciences, 1-1 Minami-Josanjima-cho, Tokushima-shi, Tokushima-ken Japan 770 Japan. **ED** T. Ishihara and Y. Kametaka. **LC** QA1; .T664a. **DD** 510/.5. **CODEN** JMTUBZ. ***Continues*** *Journal of Gakugei, Tokushima University Mathematics, 0563-6957.*
**Ind/Abst** Math. Rev.; Zentralbl. Math. Ihre Grenzgeb.

PK
**JOURNAL OF MATHEMATICS / UNIVERSITY OF THE PUNJAB.** **Added/Corp** University of the Punjab. Dept. of Mathematics. (19??)-. Periodical. English. an. **LC** QA1; .J9598. **DD** 510/.5.
**Ind/Abst** Math. Rev.; Zentralbl. Math. Ihre Grenzgeb.

US/0047-259X
**JOURNAL OF MULTIVARIATE ANALYSIS.** [J. multivar. anal.]. **VFOAT** Multivariate Analysis. Vol. 1 (Apr. 1971)-. Academic Scholarly Publication. English. Eight times a year. $6254.00 US and Canada; $748.00 other. Academic Press, Inc., 6277 Sea Harbor Drive, Orlando FL 32887. **Tel** (800)543-9534, (407)345-4100, FAX (407)363-9661. **LC** QA278; .J68. **DD** 519.5/3. **CODEN** JMVAAI. **[CCC].** **Pr Rev.** Documents available from Article Express International, The Genuine Article, Ask*IEEE.
**Desc:** Publishes research in the general area of multivariate analysis and presents articles on fundamental theoretical aspects of the field as well as on other aspects concerned with significant applications of new theoretical methods.
**Ind/Abst** ACM Guide Comput. Lit.; Compumath Citation Index [Full Cov.]; Comput. Rev.; Curr. Contents Phys. Chem. Earth Sci.; Curr. Index Stat.; Ei Page One; Eng. Index Annu.; INSPEC (Sept. 1971-); Math. Rev.; Pollut. Abstr. Indexes; Res. Alert [Full Cov.]; Sci. Cit. Index; SCISEARCH; Stat. Theory Method Abstr. (1971-1984, 1986-1987); Zentralbl. Math. Ihre Grenzgeb.

II
**JOURNAL OF NATIONAL ACADEMY OF MATHEMATICS, INDIA.** **Added/Corp** National Academy of Mathematics, India. (19??)-. English. an. $20.00 (members), $50.00 (non-members and libraries). National Academy of Mathematics, India, % Department of Mathematics, University of Gorakhpur, Gorakhpur, India 273001. **LC** PAR.
**Ind/Abst** Zentralbl. Math. Ihre Grenzgeb.

UK/0963-2654
**JOURNAL OF NATURAL GEOMETRY.** [J. nat. geom.]. (1992)-. Periodical. English. qt. **DD** 516.
**Ind/Abst** Zentralbl. Math. Ihre Grenzgeb.

US/0022-314X
**JOURNAL OF NUMBER THEORY.** [J. number theory]. Vol. 1 (Jan. 1969)-. Academic Scholarly Publication. English. mo. $820.00 US and Canada; $976.00 other. Academic Press, Inc., 6277 Sea Harbor Drive, Orlando FL 32887. **Tel** (800)543-9534, (407)345-4100, FAX (407)363-9661. **ED** Hans Zassenhaus. **LC** QA241; .J67. **DD** 512/.81/05. **CODEN** JNUTA9. **[CCC].** **Pr Rev.** Documents available from The Genuine Article, Ask*IEEE.
**Desc:** Features selected research articles that represent the broad spectrum of interest in contemporary number theory and allied areas.
**Ind/Abst** Compumath Citation Index [Full Cov.]; INSPEC (Feb. 1982-); Math. Rev.; Pollut. Abstr. Indexes; Res. Alert [Full Cov.]; SCISEARCH; Zentralbl. Math. Ihre Grenzgeb.

SI/0129-3281
**JOURNAL OF NUMERICAL LINEAR ALGEBRA WITH APPLICATIONS.** ***Ceased.*** Vol. 1, No. 1 (Mar. 1992)-Vol. 1 No. 3 (19??). Periodical. English. qt. World Scientific Publishing Company, PO Box 128, Farrer Road, Singapore 9128 Singapore. **Tel** 011 65 3825663, FAX 011 65 3825919, telex RS 28561 WSPC. **LC** QA184; .J68S. **DD** 512/.5.
**Ind/Abst** Math. Rev.

RM/0379-4024
**JOURNAL OF OPERATOR THEORY.** [J. oper. theory]. **Added/Corp** Institutul National Pentru Creatie StiintificĒa si Tehnica (Romania). Sectia de Matematica. Vol. 1, No. 1 (Winter 1979)-. Periodical. English. qt. $130.00 (institution); $80.00 (individual). American Mathematical Society, PO Box 6248, Providence RI 02940-6248. **Tel** (800)321-4267, (401)455-4000, FAX (401)331-3842, telex 797192. **(Subscription address:** American Mathematical Society, PO Box 5904, Boston MA 02206-5904.**)** Index available (bound in last issue). **Pr Rev.** Documents available from The Genuine Article.
**Desc:** Contains significant research articles in all areas of operator theory. Published by the Institute of Mathematics of the Romanian Academy in Bucharest, Romania.
**Ind/Abst** Math. Rev.; Res. Alert [Full Cov.]; Sci. Cit. Index (19??-19??); SCISEARCH; Zentralbl. Math. Ihre Grenzgeb.

US/0022-3239
**JOURNAL OF OPTIMIZATION THEORY AND APPLICATIONS.** [J. optim. theory appl.]. Vol. 1 (July 1967)-. Periodical. English. Twelve times a year. $925.00 US; $1,080.00 other. Plenum Press, 233 Spring Street, New York NY 10013-1578. **Tel** (212)620-8000, (800)221-9369, FAX (212)463-0742, (212)807-1047, telex 23/421139. **ED** Angelo Miele. **LC** QA402.5; .J6. **CODEN** JOTABN. **[CCC].** Index available. **Pr Rev.** available on microfilm and microfiche from University Microfilms International (UMI). Documents available from Article Express International, The Genuine Article, Ask*IEEE.
**Desc:** Publishes selected papers covering mathematical optimization techniques and their application to science and engineering.
**Ind/Abst** ACM Guide Comput. Lit.; Acoust. Abstr.; Appl. Mech. Rev.; Bioeng. Abstr.; Compumath Citation Index [Full Cov.]; Comput. Rev.; Curr. Contents Eng. Tech. Appl. Sci.; Ei Page One; Energy Res. Abstr.; Eng. Index Annu.; Inf. Sci. Abstr.; INIS Atomindex [Micro.]; INSPEC (Nov. 1967-); Int. Abstr. Oper. Res. (?-?); Int. Aerosp. Abstr.; Math. Rev.; Pollut. Abstr. Indexes; Res. Alert [Full Cov.]; Sci. Cit. Index; SCISEARCH; Soc. Sci. Cit. Index [Select. Cov.]; Zentralbl. Math. Ihre Grenzgeb.

II
**JOURNAL OF ORISSA MATHEMATICAL SOCIETY.** **Added/Corp** Orissa Mathematical Society (India). Vol. 1, No. 1 (Mar. 1982)-. Periodical. English. sa. $40.00. Orissa Mathematical Society, Bhubaneswar, India. **(Subscription address:** Prints India, 11 Darya Ganj, New Delhi 110002 India.**)** **LC** QA1; .J9757. **DD** 510/.5.
**Ind/Abst** Zentralbl. Math. Ihre Grenzgeb.

CC/1000-940X
**JOURNAL OF PARTIAL DIFFERENTIAL EQUATIONS.** **VFOAT** Pien Wei Fen Fang Cheng. (198?)-. Periodical. English (English). qt (4 issues). $160.00. International Academic Publishers, 137 Chaonei Dajie Exhibit Center, Beijing 100010, People's Republic of China. **Tel** 011 86 8316677 530. **LC** QA370; .J7. **DD** 515/.353. **[CCC].** available on microfilm and microfiche from University Microfilms International (UMI).
**Ind/Abst** Math. Rev.; Zentralbl. Math. Ihre Grenzgeb.

NE/0022-4049
**JOURNAL OF PURE AND APPLIED ALGEBRA.** [J. pure appl. algebra]. **VFOAT** Pure and Applied Algebra. Vol. 1 (Jan. 1971)-. Academic Scholarly Publication. English. Twenty-four times a year (8 vols.). Fl2840.00. Elsevier Science Publishers BV, PO Box 211, 1000 AE Amsterdam Netherlands. **Tel** 011 31 20 5803642, FAX 011 31 20 5862696, telex 15682. **ED** P J Freyd and A Heller. **LC** QA150; .J68. **DD** 512/.005. **CODEN** JPAAA2. **[CCC].** **Ad Acc.** **Pr Rev.** available on microfilm and microfiche from University Microfilms International (UMI). Documents available from The Genuine Article.
**Desc:** Concentrates on that part of algebra likely to be of general mathematical interest: algebraic results with immediate applications, and the development of algebraic theories of sufficiently general relevance to allow for future applications.
**Ind/Abst** Compumath Citation Index [Full Cov.]; Curr. Contents Phys. Chem. Earth Sci.; Math. Rev.; Res. Alert [Full Cov.]; Sci. Cit. Index; SCISEARCH; Zentralbl. Math. Ihre Grenzgeb.

US/0022-412X
**JOURNAL OF RECREATIONAL MATHEMATICS.** [J. recreat. math.]. Vol. 1 (Jan. 1968)-. Periodical. English. qt. $82.00. Baywood Publishing Company Inc., 26 Austin Avenue, PO Box 337, Amityville NY 11701. **Tel** (516)691-1270, (800)638-7819, FAX (516)691-1770. **ED** Joseph S Madachy. **LC** QA95; .J85. **CODEN** JRMAB9. **Bk Rev.** Documents available from UMI Article Clearinghouse.
**Desc:** Puzzles, problems and challenges to the solver's ingenuity. Alphabetics, games, polyhedra, topology, map coloring and more, for the math enthusiast.
**Ind/Abst** Acad. Search (July 1993-); Expand. Acad. Index (1989-); Gen. Sci. Index; Gen. Sci. Source (Jul. 1993-); INFO-SOUTH Abstr.; Mag. Search; Math. Rev.; Newsp. Period. Abstr. (1991-); Zentralbl. Math. Ihre Grenzgeb.

US/0090-4104
**JOURNAL OF SOVIET MATHEMATICS.** ***Title Change.*** [J. Sov. math.]. **Added/Corp** Consultants Bureau. Vol. 1 (Jan./Feb. 1973)-Vol. 67 (Dec. 1993). Periodical. English (translations available in Russian). Thirty times a year. Consultants Bureau, A Division of Plenum Publishing Corporation, 233 Spring Street, New York NY 10013. **Tel** (212)620-8000, (212)620-8466, FAX (212)463-0742, telex 23/421139. **ED** R. V. Gamkrelidze, N. N. Ural'tseva, L. D. Faddeev, and O. A. Oleinik. **LC** QA1; .J976. **DD** 510/.5. **CODEN** JSOMARJOSMAR. **[CCC].** available on microfilm and microfiche from University Microfilms International (UMI). ***Formed by the union of*** *Progress in Mathematics, 0079-6433; Problems in Mathematical Analysis* ***and*** *Seminars in Mathematics, 0080-8873.* ***Continued by*** *Journal of Mathematical Sciences (New York, N.Y.), 1072-3374.*
**Ind/Abst** Comput. Inf. Syst. Abstr. J.; INIS Atomindex [Micro.]; Math. Rev.; Pollut. Abstr. Indexes; Zentralbl. Math. Ihre Grenzgeb.

NE/0378-3758
**JOURNAL OF STATISTICAL PLANNING AND INFERENCE.** [J. stat. plann. inference]. Vol. 1 (Feb. 1977)-. Statistical Publication. English. Eighteen times a year (6 volumes). Fl2352.00. Elsevier Science Publishers BV, PO Box 211, 1000 AE Amsterdam Netherlands. **Tel** 011 31 20 5803642, FAX 011 31 20 5862696, telex 15682. **ED** M L Puri. **LC** QA276.A1; J59. **DD** 001.4/22. **CODEN** JSPIDN. **[CCC].** **Pr Rev.** available on microfilm and microfiche from University Microfilms International (UMI). Documents available from The Genuine Article, Ask*IEEE.
**Desc:** Provides a common medium for the dissemination of significant information in all branches of statistics with particular emphasis on statistical planning, and the related areas of combinatorial mathematics and probability theory.
**Ind/Abst** Biostatistica; Compumath Citation Index [Full Cov.]; Curr. Index Stat.; INSPEC (April 1979-); Math. Rev.; Qual. Control Appl. Stat.; Res. Alert [Full Cov.]; SCISEARCH; Soc. Sci. Cit. Index [Select. Cov.]; Stat. Theory Method Abstr. (1978-1984, 1986-1987); Zentralbl. Math. Ihre Grenzgeb.

BG/0256-422X
**JOURNAL OF STATISTICAL RESEARCH - UNIVERSITY OF DACCA. INSTITUTE OF STATISTICAL RESEARCH AND TRAINING.** **See** Statistics.

UK/0747-7171
**JOURNAL OF SYMBOLIC COMPUTATION.** [J. symb. comput.]. Vol. 1, No. 1 (March 1985)-. Academic Scholarly Publication. English. mo. $460.00. Academic Press Ltd., A Division of Harcourt Brace & Company Ltd., 24-28 Oval Road, London NW1 7DX England. **Tel** 071 267 4466, FAX 071 482 2293, 071

485 4752, telex 25775 ACPRES G. **(Subscription address:** Harcourt Brace & Company, Ltd., Foots Cray, High Street, Sidcup Kent DA14 5HP England.**)** **ED** B. Buchberger. **LC** QA76.95; .J68. **DD** 510/.285. **CODEN** JSYCEH. **[CCC].** **Pr Rev.** Documents available from The Genuine Article, Ask*IEEE.
**Desc:** Directed to mathematicians and computer scientists who have a particular interest in symbolic computation. Provides a forum for research in the algorithmic treatment of all types of symbolic objects: objects in formal languages (terms, formulas, programs); algebraic objects (elements in basic number domains, polynomials, residue classes, etc.); and geometrical objects. It is the explicit goal of the journal to promote the integration of symbolic computation by establishing one common avenue of communication for researchers working in the different subareas. It is also important that the algorithmic achievements of these areas should be made available to human problem-solvers in integrated software systems for symbolic computation. To help this integration, the journal publishes invited tutorial surveys as well as applications letters and system descriptions.
**Ind/Abst** ACM Guide Comput. Lit.; Compumath Citation Index [Full Cov.]; Comput. Rev.; Curr. Contents Eng. Tech. Appl. Sci.; Ei Page One; INSPEC (1986); Math. Rev.; Res. Alert [Full Cov.]; Zentralbl. Math. Ihre Grenzgeb.

US/0022-4812
**JOURNAL OF SYMBOLIC LOGIC, THE.** [J. symb. log.]. **Added/Corp** Association for Symbolic Logic. Vol. 1 (Mar. 1936)-. Periodical. English. qt. $230.00. Association for Symbolic Logic, Department of Math, University of Illinois, 1409 West Green Street, Urbana IL 61801. **Tel** (217)333-3350. **(Subscription address:** Association for Symbolic Logic, University of Illinois Press, 54 East Gregory Drive, Champaign IL 61820.**)** **LC** BC1; .J6. **CODEN** JSYLA6. **[CCC].** Index available. cum. index. **Bk Rev**. **Pr Rev. Circ:** 2,600. available on microfilm and microfiche from University Microfilms International (UMI). Documents available from The Genuine Article, Ask*IEEE.
**Desc:** Symbolic and mathematical logic.
**Ind/Abst** Compumath Citation Index [Full Cov.]; Comput. Rev.; Curr. Contents Phys. Chem. Earth Sci.; Humanit. Index; INSPEC (March 1977-); Math. Rev.; Philos. Index; Res. Alert [Full Cov.]; Sci. Cit. Index; SCISEARCH; Soc. Sci. Cit. Index [Select. Cov.]; Zentralbl. Math. Ihre Grenzgeb.

US/1055-789X
**JOURNAL OF TECHNOLOGY IN MATHEMATICS.** ***Ceased.*** (1993)-(199?). Academic Scholarly Publication. English. qt. Academic Press, Inc., 6277 Sea Harbor Drive, Orlando FL 32887. **Tel** (800)543-9534, (407)345-4100, FAX (407)363-9661. **ED** John G Harvey.
**Desc:** Focuses on research related to the use of existing and future technologies in mathematics research, instruction, and learning. Enables those concerned with technology in mathematics to keep abreast of vital research and information.

US/0894-0347
**JOURNAL OF THE AMERICAN MATHEMATICAL SOCIETY.** [J. Am. Math. Soc.]. **Added/Corp** American Mathematical Society. Vol. 1, No. 1 (Jan. 1988)-. Periodical. English. qt. $158.00. American Mathematical Society, PO Box 6248, Providence RI 02940-6248. **Tel** (800)321-4267, (401)455-4000, FAX (401)331-3842, telex 797192. **(Subscription address:** American Mathematical Society, PO Box 5904, Boston MA 02206-5904.**)** **ED** H. Blaine Lawson, Jr., Robert D. MacPherson, Richard Melrose, Andrew Odlyzko and Wilfried Schmid. **LC** QA1; .J9763. **DD** 510/.5. **[CCC].**
**Desc:** Contains research articles of the highest quality in all areas of pure and applied mathematics.
**Ind/Abst** Math. Rev.; Zentralbl. Math. Ihre Grenzgeb.

AT/0263-6115
**JOURNAL OF THE AUSTRALIAN MATHEMATICAL SOCIETY. SERIES A : PURE MATHEMATICS AND STATISTICS.** [J. Aust. Math. Soc., A]. **Added/Corp** Australian Mathematical Society. **VFOAT** Pure Mathematics and Statistics. Vol. 29, Pt. 1 (Feb. 1980)-. Periodical. English. Six times a year (Feb., Apr., June, Aug., Oct., Dec.). 273.00Aus$ Australia; $210.00 US. Australian Mathematical Publishing Association, Department of Mathematics, Australian National University, Canberra ACT 0200 Australia. **Tel** 011 61 6 267 4268, FAX 011 61 6 267 4263. **ED** T. E. Hall. **LC** QA1; .J97643. **DD** 510/.5. **CODEN** JAMADS. **[CCC].** Index available in last issue of volume--attached. **Bk Rev**. **Pr Rev. Circ:** 900. Documents available from The Genuine Article. ***Continues*** *Journal of the Australian Mathematical Society. Series A, Pure Mathematics, 0334-3316.*
**Desc:** Publishes papers on pure mathematics and statistics.
**Ind/Abst** Compumath Citation Index [Full Cov.]; Curr. Contents Phys. Chem. Earth Sci.; Math. Rev.; Res. Alert [Full Cov.]; Sci. Cit. Index; SCISEARCH.

AT/0334-2700
**JOURNAL OF THE AUSTRALIAN MATHEMATICAL SOCIETY. SERIES B : APPLIED MATHEMATICS, THE.** [J. Aust. Math. Soc. Series B, Appl. math.]. **Added/Corp** Australian Mathematical Society. **VFOAT** Applied Mathematics. Vol. 19, Pt. 1 (June 1975)-. Periodical. English. Four times a year (Jan., Apr., July, Oct.). 174.00Aus$ Australia; $134.00 US. Australian Mathematical Publishing Association, Department of Mathematics, Australian National University, Canberra ACT 0200 Australia. **Tel** 011 61 6 267 4268, FAX 011 61 6 267 4263. **ED** E. O. Tuck. **LC** QA1; .J97645. **DD** 510/.5. **CODEN** JAMMDU. **[CCC].** **Bk Rev**. **Pr Rev. Circ:** 830. Documents available from The Genuine Article, Ask*IEEE. ***Continues in part*** *Australian Mathematical Society. Journal of the Australian Mathematical Society, 0004-9735.*
**Desc:** Publishes papers in any field of applied mathematics and related mathematical sciences, excluding statistics.
**Ind/Abst** Compumath Citation Index [Full Cov.]; Curr. Contents Phys. Chem. Earth Sci.; INSPEC (June 1975-); Int. Aerosp. Abstr. (1991-); Math. Rev.; Res. Alert [Full Cov.]; Sci. Cit. Index; SCISEARCH; Stat. Theory Method Abstr. (1980-1981); Zentralbl. Math. Ihre Grenzgeb.

II/0970-5120
**JOURNAL OF THE INDIAN ACADEMY OF MATHEMATICS, THE.** [J. Indian Acad. Math.]. **Main/Corp** Indian Academy of Mathematics. Vol. 1 (March 1979)-. Periodical. English. sa. $24.00. Indian Academy of Mathematics, 46 Shankarbag, Indore 452006 India. **Tel** 31354. **(Subscription address:** Prints India, 11 Darya Ganj, New Delhi 110002 India.**)** **ED** R N Jain. **LC** QA1; .I49a. **DD** 510/.5. Index available. cum. index. **Bk Rev**. **Ad Acc**. **Pr Rev. Circ:** 250 (ctrl).
**Desc:** Publishes research articles from members of the academy on mathematics and its applications.
**Ind/Abst** Math. Rev.; Zentralbl. Math. Ihre Grenzgeb.

II/0019-5839
**JOURNAL OF THE INDIAN MATHEMATICAL SOCIETY, THE.** [J. Indian Math. Soc.]. **Added/Corp** Indian Mathematical Society. Vol. 3 (1911)- Vol. 20, (1933); New Series, Vol. 1 (1934)-?. Periodical. English. qt. $70.00. **(Subscription address:** Prints India, 11 Darya Ganj, New Delhi 110002 India.**)** **CODEN** JIMTA2. cum. index. ***Continues*** *Journal of the Indian Mathematical Club.* ***Continued in part by*** *Mathematics Student (Madras, India), 0025-5742.*
**Ind/Abst** Math. Rev.; Zentralbl. Math. Ihre Grenzgeb.

JA/0915-2350
**JOURNAL OF THE JAPANESE SOCIETY OF COMPUTATIONAL STATISTICS.** **Added/Corp** Japanese Society of Computational Statistics. Vol. 1 (Dec. 1988)-. English. an.
**Ind/Abst** Zentralbl. Math. Ihre Grenzgeb.

KO/0304-9914
**JOURNAL OF THE KOREAN MATHEMATICAL SOCIETY.** [J. Korean Math. Soc.]. **Added/Corp** Taehan Suhakhoe. **VFOAT** Taehan Suhakhoe Chi. (1964)-. English (summaries and/or abstracts in Korean). sa (Feb. and Aug.). Comes with membership. Korean Mathematical Society, 538 Dowha dong 706 Sung Ji, Seoul 121 Korea. **Tel** 011 82 2 7178604. **LC** QA1; .J9765. **DD** 510/.5. **CODEN** JKMSDG.
**Ind/Abst** Math. Rev.; Zentralbl. Math. Ihre Grenzgeb.

UK/0024-6107
**JOURNAL OF THE LONDON MATHEMATICAL SOCIETY.** [J. Lond. Math. Soc.]. **Main/Corp** London Mathematical Society. Vol. 1-44, (1926-1969); Series 2, Vol. 1 (1969)-. Academic Scholarly Publication. English. bm (6 issues). $578.00 US, Canada and Mexico; £298.00 other. Cambridge University Press, The Edinburgh Building, Shaftesbury Road, Cambridge CB2 2RU United Kingdom. **Tel** 011 44 223 312393, FAX 011 44 223 325959. **(Subscription address:** Cambridge University Press / North America, 110 Midland Avenue, Port Chester NY 10573.**)** **ED** I. N. Baker and G. D. James. **LC** QA1; .L53. **DD** 510.5. **CODEN** JLMSAK. Index available in last issue of volume--attached. cum. index. **Bk Rev**. **Pr Rev.** available on microfilm from University Microfilms International (UMI). Documents available from The Genuine Article.
**Desc:** Publishes longer papers, normally in the range of 7 to 17 pages each, from a broad spectrum within mathematics, but with the main emphasis on pure mathematics. These range from number theory to functional analysis, from finite simple groups to the mathematical foundations of quantum theory, from logic and topos theory to the topology of Lie groups.
**Ind/Abst** Compumath Citation Index [Full Cov.]; Curr. Contents Phys. Chem. Earth Sci.; Int. Aerosp. Abstr.; Math. Rev.; Res. Alert [Full Cov.]; Sci. Cit. Index; SCISEARCH; Stat. Theory Method Abstr. (1968-1975, 1979); Zentralbl. Math. Ihre Grenzgeb.

JA/0025-5645
**JOURNAL OF THE MATHEMATICAL SOCIETY OF JAPAN.** [J. Math. Soc. Jpn.]. **Main/Corp** Nihon Sugakkai. Vol. 1 (Sept. 1948)-. Periodical. English. qt. $274.00. Nihon Sugakkai, (Mathematical Soc. of Japan), 25-9-203, Hongo 4 Chome, Bunkyoku, Tokyoto 113 Japan. **(Subscription address:** Maruzen Company Ltd., PO Box 5050, Import & Export Department, Tokyo 100 31 Japan.**)** **LC** QA1; .S85. **DD** 510.6252. **CODEN** NISUBC. cum. index. **Pr Rev.** Documents available from The Genuine Article. ***Supersedes in part*** *Nihon Sugaku Butsuri Gakkai. Proceedings of the Physico-Mathematical Society of Japan.*
**Ind/Abst** Compumath Citation Index [Full Cov.]; Curr. Contents Phys. Chem. Earth Sci.; Math. Rev.; Res. Alert [Full Cov.]; SCISEARCH; Stat. Theory Method Abstr. (1959-1963, 1986); Zentralbl. Math. Ihre Grenzgeb.

NR/0189-8965
**JOURNAL OF THE NIGERIAN MATHEMATICAL SOCIETY.** **Added/Corp** Nigerian Mathematical Society. Vol. 1 (1982)-. English. an. Nigerian Mathematical Society, University Ibadan, Mathematics Department, Ibadan, Nigeria. **LC** QA1; .J9766. **DD** 510/.5.
**Ind/Abst** Math. Rev.; Zentralbl. Math. Ihre Grenzgeb.

UK/0160-5682
**JOURNAL OF THE OPERATIONAL RESEARCH SOCIETY, THE.** (OR; THE JOURNAL OF THE OPERATIONAL RESEARCH SOCIETY.). [J. Oper. Res. Soc.]. **Added/Corp** Operational Research Society (Great Britain). Vol. 29 (Jan. 1978)-. Academic Scholarly Publication. English. mo. £410.00 UK and EEC; £410.00 (surface mail), £492.00 (airmail) other. Macmillan Magazines Ltd., Houndmills, Basingstoke, Hampshire RG21 2XS England. **Tel** 011 44 256 29242, FAX 011 44 256 812358, telex 858493. **ED** John Hough. **LC** Q175; .O59. **DD** 001.4/24/05. **NLM** W1 JO944F. **CODEN** OPRQAK. **[CCC].** Index available (bound in last issue). **Bk Rev**. **Ad Acc**. **Pr Rev.** available on microfilm and microfiche from University Microfilms International (UMI). Documents available from Article Express International, The Genuine Article, Ask*IEEE, UMI Article Clearinghouse. ***Continues*** *Operational Research Quarterly, 0030-3623.*
**Desc:** Papers cover not only the effective application of operational research to real problems, but also the development of new ideas and methodologies, as well as the history of operational research.
**Ind/Abst** ABI/INFORM Glob. Ed.; ABI Inform Ondisc (Jan. 1978-); Acad. Search (July 1993-); Bioeng. Abstr.; Biostatistica; Bus. Index (Jan. 1985-Dec. 1985); Bus. Period. Index; Bus. Source (Jul. 1993-); Coal Abstr.; Compumath Citation Index [Full Cov.]; Contents Pages Manage.; Curr. Contents Eng. Tech. Appl. Sci.; Curr. Contents Soc. Behav. Sci.; Curr. Technol. Index; Ei Page One; EMBASE; Eng. Index Annu.; Gen. BusinessFile (Jan. 1985-Dec. 1985); Gen. Period. Index (Jan. 1985-Dec. 1985); GeoRef; Health Serv. Abstr.; Highw. Res. Abstr.; Hospit. Health Admin. Index; INFO-SOUTH Abstr.; INSPEC (Jan. 1978-); Int. Abstr. Oper. Res. (?-?); Leis. Recreat. Tour. Abstr.; Mag. Search; Manage. Market. Abstr.; Math. Rev.; Oper. Res./Manag. Sci.; Life Sci. Collect.; Qual. Control Appl. Stat.; Res. Alert [Full Cov.]; Risk Abstr.; Rural Dev. Abstr.; Sci. Cit. Index; Selec. Coop. Index Manage. Period; SCISEARCH; Soc. Sci. Cit. Index [Full Cov.]; Stat. Theory Method Abstr. (1982-1984, 1986-1987); Wilson Bus. Abstr.; World Agric. Econ.; Zentralbl. Math. Ihre Grenzgeb.

●US/1061-6292
**JOURNAL OF THE OUGHTRED SOCIETY, THE.** **Added/Corp** Oughtred Society. Vol. 1, No. 1 (Feb. 1992)-. Periodical. English. sa. $10.00. Oughtred Society, 2160 Middlefield Road, Palo Alto CA 94301. **DD** 510.

II/0970-1249
**JOURNAL OF THE RAMANUJAN MATHEMATICAL SOCIETY.** **Added/Corp** Ramanujan Mathematical Society. Vol. 1, No. 1 & 2 (Dec. 1986)-. Periodical. English. sa. $85.00. Ramanujan Mathematical Society, Mysore University, Dr Sampath Kumar, Mysore 570 006 India. **(Subscription address:** Prints India, 11 Darya Ganj, New Delhi 110002 India.**)** **LC** QA1; .J9767. **DD** 510/.5.
**Ind/Abst** Math. Rev. (1988-); Zentralbl. Math. Ihre Grenzgeb.

II/0368-4644
**JOURNAL OF THE UNIVERSITY OF BOMBAY, SCIENCE: PHYSICAL SCIENCES, MATHEMATICS, BIOLOGICAL SCIENCES AND MEDICINE.** [J. Univ. Bombay, Sci.: Phys. Sci., Math., Biol. Sci., Med.]. (1932)-. English. an. **CODEN** JUBSAS.
**Ind/Abst** Zentralbl. Math. Ihre Grenzgeb.

US/0894-9840
**JOURNAL OF THEORETICAL PROBABILITY.** [J. theor. probab.]. Vol. 1, No. 1 (Jan. 1988)-. Periodical. English. Four times a year. $250.00 institutions, $69.00 individuals US; $295.00 institutions, $81.00 individuals other. Plenum Press, 233 Spring Street, New York NY 10013-1578. **Tel** (212)620-8000, (800)221-9369, FAX (212)463-0742, (212)807-1047, telex 23/421139. **ED** A. Mukherjea. **LC** QA273.A1; J68. **DD** 519.2. **CODEN** JTPREO. **[CCC].**

available on microfilm and microfiche from University Microfilms International (UMI).
**Desc:** An international forum for research in all aspects of theoretical probability. Topics include probability theory on semigroups, groups, vector spaces, and other abstract structures as well as random matrices/random operators and applications of these to statistics, computer science, pattern theory, and other disciplines.
**Ind/Abst** Acad. Search (July 1993-); Mag. Search; Math. Rev.; Zentralbl. Math. Ihre Grenzgeb.

UK/0143-9782
**JOURNAL OF TIME SERIES ANALYSIS.** (JOURNAL OF TIME SERIES ANALYSIS / A JOURNAL SPONSORED BY THE BERNOULLI SOCIETY FOR MATHEMATICAL STATISTICS AND PROBABILITY.). [J. time ser. anal.]. **Added/Corp** Bernoulli Society for Mathematical Statistics and Probability. Vol. 1 No. 1 (1980)-. Academic Scholarly Publication. English. Six times a year. £208.00 UK and Europe; $355.00 North America; £229.00 other. Basil Blackwell Publishers Ltd, 108 Cowley Road, Oxford 0X4 1JF England. **Tel** 011 44 865 791100, FAX 011 44 865 791347, telex 837022 OXBOOK G. **(Subscription address:** Blackwell Publishers / UK, Marston Book Services, PO Box 87, Oxford OX2 0DT England.**) ED** M B Priestley. **LC** QA280; .J68. **DD** 519.5/5/05. **CODEN** JTSADL. **[CCC].** Index available. **Ad Acc. Circ:** 1,000. available on microfilm and microfiche from University Microfilms International (UMI). Documents available from Ask*IEEE.
**Desc:** Covers both the basic theory and methodology of time series analysis, and applications to many diverse fields.
**Ind/Abst** Biostatistica (19??-); Curr. Index Stat.; INSPEC (1980-); Math. Rev.; Qual. Control Appl. Stat.; Stat. Theory Method Abstr. (1982-1984, 1986-1987); Zentralbl. Math. Ihre Grenzgeb.

US/0022-5339
**JOURNAL OF UNDERGRADUATE MATHEMATICS. Added/Corp** Guilford College, N.C. College. Dept. of Mathematics. Vol. 1 (Mar. 1969)-. Periodical. English. Twice a year (Mar. & Sept.). $5.00 (individuals); $9.00 (institutions). Guilford College / Department of Mathematics, 5800 West Friendly Avenue, Greensboro NC 27410. **Tel** (919)292-5511, (910)316-2230. **ED** J. R. Boyd. **LC** QA1; .J977. Index available.

CN/0714-7082
**JOURNAL / SASKATCHEWAN MATHEMATICS TEACHERS' SOCIETY.** [J. - Sask. Math. Teach. Soc.]. **VFOAT** S.M.T.S. News/Journal; News/Journal. **VAT** S.M.T.S. News/Journal (Spring, Summer 1980); Saskatchewan Mathematics Teachers' Society; News/Journal (Spring, Summer 1980); News/Journal - Saskatchewan Mathematics Teachers' Society (1980). Vol. 17, No. 4 (Spring/Summer 1980)-. Periodical. English. Three times a year. $8.00. Saskatchewan Mathematics Teachers Society, 2317 Arlington Avenue, PO Box 1108, Saskatoon Saskatchewan S7J 2H8 Canada. **DD** 510/.7. ***Continues** Saskatchewan Mathematics Teachers' Society. News/Journal, 0316-5779.*

FR
**JOURNEES EQUATIONS AUX DERIVEES PARTIELLES. Added/Corp** Universite de Rennes. Laboratoire d'Analyse Fonctionnelle. Societe Mathematique de France. (1975)-. French (English). an.
**Ind/Abst** Zentralbl. Math. Ihre Grenzgeb.

NE/0920-3036
**K-THEORY.** [K-theory]. **VFOAT** K Theory. Vol. 1, No. 1 (1987)-. Periodical. English. bm. $594.00. Kluwer Academic Publishers, Postbus 322, 3300 AH Dordrecht, The Netherlands. **Tel** 011 (31) 78 524400, FAX 011 31 78 183273, telex 20083. **ED** A Bak. **LC** QA612.33; .K27. **DD** 514/.23. **CODEN** KTHEEO. **[CCC]. Ad Acc. Pr Rev. Acid Free. Circ:** 300. available on microfilm and microfiche from University Microfilms International (UMI).
**Desc:** An interdisciplinary journal for the development, application and influence of "K-Theory" in the mathematical sciences.
**Ind/Abst** Math. Rev. (1987-); Zentralbl. Math. Ihre Grenzgeb. (1987-).

JA
**KEIRYO KOKUGOGAKU. VFOAT** Mathematical Linguistics. (May 1957)-. Periodical. Japanese (summaries and/or abstracts in English). qt. $77.00. **(Subscription address:** Japan Publications Trading Company, Ltd., PO Box 5030, Tokyo International, Tokyo 100-31 Japan.**) LC** P9; .K365.
**Ind/Abst** MLA Int. Bibl. Books Artic. Mod. Lang. Lit.; Soc. Plann. Policy Dev. Abstr.

JA/0289-9051
**KOBE JOURNAL OF MATHEMATICS. Added/Corp** Kobe Daigaku. Vol. 1, No. 1 (June 1984)-. Periodical. English. sa. Kobe Daigaku Kyoyobu Sugaku Kyoshitsu, (Dept. of Mathematics, College of Liberal Arts, Kobe University), 2-1, Tsurukabuto 1 Chome, Nadaku, Kobeshi, Hyogoken 657, Japan. **LC** QA1; .K64. ***Continues** Mathematics Seminar Notes, 0385-633X.*
**Ind/Abst** Math. Rev. (1984-); Zentralbl. Math. Ihre Grenzgeb.

JA/0386-5991
**KODAI MATHEMATICAL JOURNAL.** [Kodai math. j.]. **Added/Corp** Tokyo Kogyo Daigaku. Sugaku Kyoshitsu. Vol. 1 (Mar 1978)-. Periodical. English. sa. $303.00. **(Subscription address:** Kinokuniya Company Ltd., 38-1 Sakuragaoka 5, chome Setagaya-ku, Tokyo 156 Japan.**) *Supersedes** Kodai Mathematical Seminar Reports.*
**Ind/Abst** Math. Rev.; Stat. Theory Method Abstr. (1987); Zentralbl. Math. Ihre Grenzgeb.

RU/0321-4729
**KOMBINATORNYI ANALIZ.** [Komb. anal.]. **Added/Corp** Moskovskii Gosudarstvennyi Universitet im. M.V. Lomonosova. Mekhaniko-Matematicheskii Fakultet. (1971)-. Periodical. Russian. **LC** QA164; .K65.
**Ind/Abst** Math. Rev.; Zentralbl. Math. Ihre Grenzgeb.

DK/0023-3323
**KONGELIGE DANSKE VIDENSKABERNES SELSKAB. MATEMATISK-FYSISKE MEDDELELSER.** (MATHEMATISK-FYSISKE MEDDELELSER / DET KGL. DANSKE VIDENSKABERNES SELSKAB.). [K. Dan. vidensk. selsk., Mat.-fys. medd.]. **Added/Corp** Kongelige Danske Videnskabernes Selskab. **VFOAT** Matematisk-Fysiske Meddelelser. Vol. 1 (1917)-. Monographic series. English (Danish). ir (5-6 issues every two years). kr400.00 (latest volume). Munksgaard International Publishers Ltd, PO Box 2148, DK-1016 Copenhagen K Denmark. **Tel** 011 45 33 12 70 30, FAX 011 45 33 12 93 87, telex 19431 MUNKS DK. **LC** AS28; .D215. **CODEN** KDVSAK. **[CCC].** Index Available, published separately, free-automatically sent. Documents available from Ask*IEEE, CASDDS. ***Continues in part** Kongelige Danske Videnskabernes Selskab. Oversigt Over Selskabets Virksomhed.*
**Ind/Abst** Chem. Abstr. (1917-1979); Energy Res. Abstr.; INSPEC (1975-); Math. Rev.; Zentralbl. Math. Ihre Grenzgeb.

DK
**KONGELIGE DANSKE VIDENSKABERNES SELSKAB MATHEMATISK FYSISKE MEDDELESER.** ir. kr400.00 Vol. 42. Munksgaard International Publishers Ltd, PO Box 2148, DK-1016 Copenhagen K Denmark. **Tel** 011 45 33 12 70 30, FAX 011 45 33 12 93 87, telex 19431 MUNKS DK.

RU/0206-6548
**KONSTRUKTIVNAIA TEROIIA FUNKTSII I FUNKTSIONALNYI ANALIZ.** (1977)-. Russian. 1.10rub. Izd-V/O Kazanskogo Universiteta, Ulitsa Lenina 4/5, 42011 G Kazan Russia. **LC** QA331; .K7385.
**Ind/Abst** Zentralbl. Math. Ihre Grenzgeb.

JA/0914-675X
**KUMAMOTO JOURNAL OF MATHEMATICS.** [Kumamoto j. math.]. Periodical. English. ir. Kumamoto Journal of Mathematics, Department of Mathematics, Faculty of Science, Kumamoto University, Kumamoto 860 Japan. **LC** QA1; .K8. **DD** 510. **CODEN** KJMAEZ. Documents available from Ask*IEEE. ***Continues** Kumamoto Journal of Science. (Mathematics), 0385-6763.*
**Ind/Abst** INSPEC (March 1988-); Math. Rev. (1988-); Zentralbl. Math. Ihre Grenzgeb.

KO/0454-8124
**KYUNGPOOK MATHEMATICAL JOURNAL.** [Kyungpook math. j.]. **Added/Corp** Kyongbuk Taehakkyo. Vol. 1 (Jan. 1958)-. Periodical. English. Twice a year (June & Dec.). $20.00. Kyungpook University / Mathematics, Department of Mathematics, Taegu 702 701 South Korea. **Tel** 011 82 53 950-5311. **LC** QA1; .K95. **CODEN** KPMJAW.
**Ind/Abst** Math. Rev.; Zentralbl. Math. Ihre Grenzgeb.

●JA
**KYUSHU JOURNAL OF MATHEMATICS. Added/Corp** Kyushu Daigaku. Graduate School of Mathematics. Vol. 48, No. 1 (Mar. 1994)-. Periodical. English (French and German). sa. Kyushu University / Faculty of Science, 10-1 Hakozaki 6 Chome Higasiku, Fukuokaken 812 Japan. **LC** QA1; .F76. **DD** 510/.5. **Circ:** 700. ***Continues** Memoirs of the Faculty of Science, Kyushu University. Series A, Mathematics.*

LV/0321-2270
**LATVIJSKIJ MATEMATICESKIJ EZEGODNIK.** (LATVIISKII MATEMATICHESKII EZHEGODNIK.). [Latv. mat. ezeg.]. **Added/Corp** Petera Stuckas Latvijas Valsts Universitate. Latvijas PSR Zinatnu Akademija. (1965)-. Periodical. Russian (summaries and/or abstracts in English). an. Zinatne / Science Publishing House, Turgeneva Iela 19, Riga Latvia 1530. **Tel** 3712 212 797. **(Subscription address:** Victor Kamkin, 4956 Boiling Brook Parkway, Rockville MD 20852.**) LC** QA1; .L34. ***Supersedes** Petera Stuckas Latvijas Valsts Universitate. Vychislitelnyi Tsentr. Trudy.*
**Ind/Abst** Int. Aerosp. Abstr.; Math. Rev.; Zentralbl. Math. Ihre Grenzgeb.

CK/0120-1980
**LECTURAS MATEMATICAS.** [Lect. Mat.]. (1980)-. Periodical. Spanish. qt. **DD** 510.
**Ind/Abst** Zentralbl. Math. Ihre Grenzgeb.

GW/0341-633X
**LECTURE NOTES IN BIOMATHEMATICS. See** Biology.

GW/0075-8442
**LECTURE NOTES IN ECONOMICS AND MATHEMATICAL SYSTEMS. See** Economics.

GW/0075-8434
**LECTURE NOTES IN MATHEMATICS (SPRINGER-VERLAG).** (LECTURE NOTES IN MATHEMATICS.). [Lect. notes math.]. (1964)-. Monographic series. English (German and French). ir. Price varies per volume. Springer-Verlag GmbH & Company KG, Heidelberger Platz 3, D 14197 Berlin Germany. **Tel** 011 49 30 8207223, FAX 011 49 30 8214091, telex 183 319 SPBLN D. **(Subscription address:** Springer Verlag New York Inc. / for North America, 44 Hartz Way, Secaucus NJ 07096.**) ED** A. Dold. **LC** QA3; .L28. **CODEN** LNMAA2. **[CCC].** cum. index. Documents available from The Genuine Article, Ask*IEEE.
**Ind/Abst** Compumath Citation Index [Full Cov.]; Ei Page One; INSPEC; Math. Rev.; Res. Alert [Full Cov.]; SCISEARCH; Soc. Sci. Cit. Index [Select. Cov.]; Stat. Theory Method Abstr. (1987); Zentralbl. Math. Ihre Grenzgeb.

US
**LECTURE NOTES IN PURE AND APPLIED MATHEMATICS.** (1971)-. Monographic series. English. ir. Price varies per volume. Marcel Dekker Inc., 270 Madison Avenue, New York NY 10016. **Tel** (212)696-9000, (800)228-1160, FAX (212)685-4540, telex 421419. **(Subscription address:** Marcel Dekker Inc, PO Box 5017, Monticello NY 12701.**)**
**Desc:** Covers topics in pure and applied mathematics such as lie algebras, control theory, topology and more.
**Ind/Abst** Math. Rev.; Zentralbl. Math. Ihre Grenzgeb.

US
**LECTURE NOTES IN STATISTICS.** Vol. 1 (1980)-. Monographic series. English. ir. Price varies per volume. Marcel Dekker Inc., 270 Madison Avenue, New York NY 10016. **Tel** (212)696-9000, (800)228-1160, FAX (212)685-4540, telex 421419. **(Subscription address:** Marcel Dekker Inc, PO Box 5017, Monticello NY 12701.**)**
**Desc:** Topics covered have included incomplete block designs, reliability in the acquisitions process, and randomness.

DK/0065-017X
**LECTURE NOTES SERIES - AARHUS, DENMARK. UNIVERSITET. MATEMATISK INSTITUT. Main/Corp** Aarhus, Denmark. Universitet. Matematisk Institut. (1963)-. English. ir. kr55.00. Matematisk Institut, Aarhus Universitet, Bygning 530, Ny Munkegade, DK-8000 Aarhus C Denmark. **Tel** 011 45 86 127188. **Circ:** 120.
**Desc:** Advanced math courses.
**Ind/Abst** Math. Rev.; Zentralbl. Math. Ihre Grenzgeb.

US/0075-8485
**LECTURES IN APPLIED MATHEMATICS.** [Lect. appl. math.]. **Added/Corp** American Mathematical Society. (1960)-. Monographic series. English. ir. Price varies per volume. American Mathematical Society, PO Box 6248, Providence RI 02940-6248. **Tel** (800)321-4267, (401)455-4000, FAX (401)331-3842, telex 797192. **(Subscription address:** American Mathematical Society, PO Box 5904, Boston MA 02206-5904.**) LC** UNC. **[CCC].**
**Ind/Abst** Math. Rev.; Zentralbl. Math. Ihre Grenzgeb.

II/0970-6313
**LECTURES ON MATHEMATICS AND PHYSICS.** (1953)-. Periodical. English. ir.
**Ind/Abst** Zentralbl. Math. Ihre Grenzgeb.

US/0075-8523
**LECTURES ON MATHEMATICS IN THE LIFE SCIENCES.** [Lect. math. life sci.]. **Added/Corp** American Mathematical Society. (1968)-. Monographic series. English. ir. Price varies per volume. American Mathematical Society, PO Box 6248, Providence RI 02940-6248. **Tel** (800)321-4267, (401)455-4000, FAX (401)331-3842, telex 797192. **(Subscription address:** American Mathematical Society, PO Box 5904, Boston MA 02206-5904.**) LC** UNC. **NLM** W3 LE33. **CODEN** LMLSAA. **[CCC].** Documents available from BIOSIS Document Express, CASDDS.
**Ind/Abst** Biol. Abstr.; Chem. Abstr.; Math. Rev.; Zentralbl. Math. Ihre Grenzgeb.

GW
**LEHRBUCHER UND MONOGRAPHIEN ZUR DIDAKTIK DER MATHEMATIK. Added/Corp** Bibliographisches Institut (Mannheim, Germany). (19??)-. Monographic series. German.
**Ind/Abst** Math. Rev. (1987-); Zentralbl. Math. Ihre Grenzgeb.

GW/0459-021X
**LEITFADEN DER ANGEWANDTEN MATHEMATIK UND MECHANIK.** [Leitf. angew. Math. Mech.]. (1960)-. Monographic series. German.
**Ind/Abst** Math. Rev.; Zentralbl. Math. Ihre Grenzgeb.

NE/0377-9017
**LETTERS IN MATHEMATICAL PHYSICS.** **See** Physics.

US/0278-5307
**LIBERTAS MATHEMATICA.** (LIBERTAS MATHEMATICA / ACADEMIA ROMANO-AMERICANA DE STIINTE SI ARTE.). **Added/Corp** American Romanian Academy of Arts and Sciences. (1981)-. English (French). an (Sept., Or Oct.). $60.00. American Romanian Academy, Math Department, University of Texas Arlington, Arlington TX 76019. **Tel** (817)261-1179, (817)273-3261, FAX (817)794-5802. **ED** Professor C. Corduneanu, (editor's address: PO Box 19408, University of Texas Arlington, Arlington TX 76019, phone: (817)794-5765). **LC** QA1; .L43. **DD** 510/.5. **Bk Rev**, (Qty: 10). **Pr Rev. Circ:** 200. available on CD-ROM from the publisher.
**Desc:** Research journal of ARA (American Romanian Academy of Arts and Science). Besides math research papers, each volume inserts some information concerning ARA, its members, the Romanian mathematical community in the west.
**Ind/Abst** Math. Rev.; Zentralbl. Math. Ihre Grenzgeb.

US/0024-3795
**LINEAR ALGEBRA AND ITS APPLICATIONS.** [Linear algebra appl.]. Vol. 1 (Jan. 1968)-. Academic Scholarly Publication. English. Fifty-four issues per year (18 volumes). $1998.00 US; $2126.00 other. Elsevier Science Publishing Company Inc, Madison Square Station, PO Box 882, New York NY 10159-0882. **Tel** (212)633-3950, FAX (212)633-3990. **ED** Richard A Brualdi and Hans Schneider. **LC** QA251; .L52. **DD** 512/.897. **CODEN** LAAPAW. **[CCC]. Ad Acc. Pr Rev.** available on microfilm and microfiche from University Microfilms International (UMI). Documents available from The Genuine Article, Ask*IEEE.
**Desc:** An internationally renowned source of information on the analytic, algebraic, combinatorial and numerical aspects of linear algebra and matrix theory.
**Ind/Abst** Compumath Citation Index [Full Cov.]; Curr. Contents Phys. Chem. Earth Sci.; INSPEC (1968-); Int. Aerosp. Abstr.; Math. Rev.; Pollut. Abstr. Indexes; Res. Alert [Full Cov.]; Sci. Cit. Index; SCISEARCH; Soc. Sci. Cit. Index [Select. Cov.]; Zentralbl. Math. Ihre Grenzgeb.

US/0308-1087
**LINEAR AND MULTILINEAR ALGEBRA.** [Linear multilinear algebra]. **VFOAT** Linear & Multilinear Algebra. Vol. 1 (1973)-. Periodical. English. qt (3 volumes per year). $806.00 (academic institutions), $1258.00 (corporate institutions). Gordon & Breach Science Publishers, Inc., PO Box 786, Cooper Station, New York NY 10276. **Tel** (212)206-8900, FAX (212)645-2459. **(Subscription address:** International Publishers Distributor at one of the following addresses: 820 Town Center Drive, Langhorne, PA 19047; or PO Box 90, Reading Berkshire RG1 8JL UK; or Kent Ridge PO Box 1180, Singapore 9111, Republic of Singapore) **ED** M. Marcus. **LC** QA184; .L55. **DD** 512/.5/05. **CODEN** LNMLAZ. **[CCC]. Bk Rev. Ad Acc.**
**Ind/Abst** Int. Abstr. Oper. Res. [Select. Cov.]; Math. Rev.; Zentralbl. Math. Ihre Grenzgeb.

RU/0130-9277
**LINGVISTICHESKIE PROBLEMY FUNKTSIONALNOGO MODELIROVANIIA RECHEVOI DEIATELNOSTI.** **See** Linguistics.

US/0363-1672
**LITHUANIAN MATHEMATICAL JOURNAL.** [Lith. math. j.]. **Added/Corp** Consultants Bureau. Vol. 15 (Jan./Mar. 1975)-. Periodical. English (Russian; translations available in Russian). qt (4 issues). $810.00 US; $950.00 other. Consultants Bureau, A Division of Plenum Publishing Corporation, 233 Spring Street, New York NY 10013. **Tel** (212)620-8000, (212)620-8466, FAX (212)463-0742, telex 23/421139. **ED** J. KuGilius. **LC** QA1; .L482. **DD** 510/.5. **CODEN** LMJTD6. **[CCC].** Index available. available on microfilm and microfiche from University Microfilms International (UMI). **Continues** *Lithuanian Mathematical Transactions, 0148-8279.*
**Desc:** This journal focuses on a number of fundamental problems on a wide variety of topics in theoretical mathematics.
**Ind/Abst** Math. Rev.; Pollut. Abstr. Indexes; Zentralbl. Math. Ihre Grenzgeb.

LI/0132-2818
**LITOVSKIJ MATEMATICESKIJ SBORNIK.** (LITOVSKII MATEMATICHESKII SBORNIK.). **Added/Corp** Lietuvos TSR Mokslu Akademija. **VFOAT** Lietuvos Matematikos Rinkinys. (1961)-. Periodical. Russian (summaries and/or abstracts in Lithuanian, English, French and German). Four times a year. $99.95. Mintis / Idea, Z Sierakausko 15, Vilnius 2600 Lithuania. **Tel** 3702 632 943. **(Subscription address:** East View Publications Inc., 3020 Harbor Lane North, Suite 110, Minneapolis MN 55447.) **LC** QA1; .L48.
**Ind/Abst** Eng. Mater. Abstr.; Int. Aerosp. Abstr.; Math. Rev.; Stat. Theory Method Abstr. (1986-1987); Zentralbl. Math. Ihre Grenzgeb.

GW
**LOGIK UND GRUNDLAGEN DER MATHEMATIK.** [Log. Grundl. Math.]. Monographic series. German. Price varies per volume. **LC** QA9; .L65.
**Ind/Abst** Math. Rev.; Zentralbl. Math. Ihre Grenzgeb.

BE/0024-5836
**LOGIQUE ET ANALYSE.** [Log. anal.]. **Added/Corp** Centre National de Recherches de Logique. No. 1 (Jan. 1958)-. Periodical. French. qt. 1200.00F. Universiteit van Ghent, Rozier 44, 9000 Ghent Belgium. **Tel** 011 32 91 643785. **LC** BC1; .L6. **CODEN** LOANAM. ***Continues*** *Bulletin Interieur.*
**Ind/Abst** Math. Rev.; Philos. Index; Soc. Plann. Policy Dev. Abstr.; Zentralbl. Math. Ihre Grenzgeb.

UK/0076-0552
**LONDON MATHEMATICAL SOCIETY LECTURE NOTE SERIES.** [Lect. note ser. - Lond. Math. Soc.]. **Added/Corp** London Mathematical Society. **VFOAT** Lecture Note Series. (1971)-. Monographic series. English. ir. Price varies per volume. Cambridge University Press, The Edinburgh Building, Shaftesbury Road, Cambridge CB2 2RU United Kingdom. **Tel** 011 44 223 312393, FAX 011 44 223 325959. **(Subscription address:** Cambridge University Press / North America, 110 Midland Avenue, Port Chester NY 10573.)
**Desc:** Series on mathematics. Volumes have covered topics such as symplectic geometry, arithmetical functions, and finite geometries and combinatorics.
**Ind/Abst** Math. Rev.; Zentralbl. Math. Ihre Grenzgeb.

UK
**LONDON MATHEMATICAL SOCIETY NEWSLETTER, THE.** **Main/Corp** London Mathematical Society. (19??)-. Newsletter. English. Eleven times a year. Free to members. London Mathematical Society, Burlington House, Piccadilly, London WIV 0NL United Kingdom. **Tel** 071 437 5377, FAX 071 439 4629. **ED** S.M. Oakes. **Ad Acc. Circ:** 2,200.

UK
**LONDON MATHEMATICAL SOCIETY STUDENT TEXTS.** **Added/Corp** London Mathematical Society. (1986)-. Monographic series. English. ir. Price varies per volume. Cambridge University Press, The Edinburgh Building, Shaftesbury Road, Cambridge CB2 2RU United Kingdom. **Tel** 011 44 223 312393, FAX 011 44 223 325959. **(Subscription address:** North America/ Cambridge University Press, 40 West 20th Street, New York, NY 10011-4211; telephone: (212)924-3900)
**Ind/Abst** Math. Rev.; Zentralbl. Math. Ihre Grenzgeb.

RM
**LUCRARILE SEMINARULUI DE MATEMATICA SI FIZICA AL INSTITUTULUI POLITEHNIC "TRAIAN VUIA" TIMISOARA.** **Added/Corp** Institutul Politehnic "Traian Vuia." Seminarul de Matematica si Fizica. **VFOAT** Lucrarile Seminarului de Matematica si Fizica. (1982)-. Periodical. English (French, German, Romanian and Russian). sa. **(Subscription address:** Ilexim Press Department, PO Box 1, 136-1-137, Bucharest, Romania.) **LC** T4; .B84. **DD** 510/.5. Documents available from CASDDS. ***Continues*** *Buletinul Stiintific si Tehnic al Institutului Politehnic "Traian Vuia" Timisoara. Seria Matematica-Fizica.*
**Ind/Abst** Chem. Abstr.

US
**MAA NOTES.** **Added/Corp** Mathematical Association of America. Committee on the Teaching of Undergraduate Mathematics. No. 1 (1983)-. Monographic series. English. Price varies per volume. Mathematical Association of America, 1529 18th Street Northwest, Washington DC 20036. **Tel** (202)387-5200, (800)331-1622, FAX (202)265-2384.
**Ind/Abst** Zentralbl. Math. Ihre Grenzgeb.

GW/0025-2611
**MANUSCRIPTA MATHEMATICA.** [Manuscr. math.]. Vol. 1 (Feb. 14, 1969)-. Periodical. English (French and German; summaries and/or abstracts in French and English). Twelve times a year. DM1548.00. Springer-Verlag GmbH & Company KG, Heidelberger Platz 3, D 14197 Berlin Germany. **Tel** 011 49 30 8207223, FAX 011 49 30 8214091, telex 183 319 SPBLN D. **(Subscription address:** Springer Verlag New York Inc. / for North America, 44 Hartz Way, Secaucus NJ 07096.) **ED** M Barnes, H Brezis, P M Cohn, A Dold, S Hildebrandt, E Hlawka, T Kato, H Kraft, A Prestel, P Roquette and A J Sommese. **LC** QA1; .M267. **DD** 510/.05. **CODEN** MSMHB2. **[CCC]. Pr Rev.** available on microfilm and microfiche from University Microfilms International (UMI). Documents available from The Genuine Article.
**Desc:** Publishes articles on theoretical geodesy, processing techniques of geodetic data and numerical results with special emphasis on physical and mathematical geodesy.
**Ind/Abst** Compumath Citation Index [Full Cov.]; Curr. Contents Phys. Chem. Earth Sci.; Math. Rev.; Res. Alert [Full Cov.]; Sci. Cit. Index; SCISEARCH; Stat. Theory Method Abstr. (1971, 1973-1975, 1977-1984, 1987); Zentralbl. Math. Ihre Grenzgeb.

TZ
**MAT SPECIAL ISSUE.** **Main/Corp** Mathematical Association of Tanzania. **VAT** Mathematical Association of Tanzania Special Issue. English. Tanzania Institute of Education, University of Dar es Salaam, PO Box 35094, Dar es Salaam Tanzania. **LC** QA1; .M42397. **DD** 510/.7/10678.

GW/0340-6253
**MATCH (MULHEIM).** **See** Chemistry.

US/0025-1127
**MATEKON.** **See** Economics.

FI/0025-5149
**MATEMAATTISTEN AINEIDEN AIKAKAUSKIRJA.** **Added/Corp** Matemaattisten Aineiden Opettajien Liitto. Suomen Matematiikan ja Fysiikan Opettajien Liitto. (1937)-. Periodical. Finnish (summaries and/or abstracts in English). Six times a year. Fmk58.00 Finland; Fmk63.00 other. Maolry, Akavatalo Rautatielaisenk 6, 00520 Helsinki 52 Finland. **Tel** 90-1502646. **ED** Kaisa Liisa Peltonen. **LC** QA1; .M27. **DD** 510/.5. **Bk Rev. Ad Acc.**

US/0101-8205
**MATEMATICA APLICADA E COMPUTACIONAL.** (MATEMATICA APLICADA E COMPUTACIONAL / SOCIEDADE BRASILEIRA DE MATEMATICA APPLICADA E COMPUTACIONAL.). [Mat. apl. comput.]. **Added/Corp** Sociedade Brasileira de Matematica Aplicada e Computacional. **VFOAT** Computational and Applied Mathematics. Vol. 1, No. 1 (1982)-. Periodical. English (French and Portuguese; summaries and/or abstracts in Portuguese). Three times a year. 240.00F Switzerland; 248.00F other. Birkhauser Boston, Inc., c/o Springer Publishers New York Inc., Customer Service Department, 333 Meadowlands Parkway, Secaucus NJ 07096-2491. **Tel** (201)348-4033, (800)777-4643. **ED** Carlos A. de Moura, Carlos S. Kubrusly, and Jim Douglas. **LC** QA297; .M355. **DD** 519.4/05. **Pr Rev.** Documents available from The Genuine Article, Ask*IEEE.
**Desc:** Publishes original works in any area of applied mathematics. Features special issues on scientific computing, devoted to those numerical, non-numerical and statistical techniques designed to solve scientific and technological problems with the aid of computers.
**Ind/Abst** Compumath Citation Index [Full Cov.]; Comput. Rev.; INSPEC (1984-); Math. Rev.; Res. Alert [Full Cov.]; Risk Abstr.; SCISEARCH; Zentralbl. Math. Ihre Grenzgeb.

IT/1120-9968
**MATEMATICA E LA SUA DIDATTICA, LA.** [Mat. didatt.]. (1987)-. Periodical. Italian. Three times a year. L40000.00 Italy; L70000.00 other. Pitagora Editrice SRL, Via del Legatore 3, 40127 Bologna Italy. **Tel** 011 39 51 530003, FAX 011 39 51 535301. **UDC** 37.51.

RU/0368-8666
**MATEMATICESKIJ SBORNIK (MOSKVA).** (MATEMATICHESKII SBORNIK / IZDAVAEMYI MOSKOVSKIM MATEMATICHESKIM OBSHCHESTVOM.). [Mat. sb.]. **Added/Corp** Moskovskoe Matematicheskoe Obshchestvo. Akademiia Nauk SSSR. Rossiiskaia Akademiia Nauk. **VFOAT** Recueil Mathematique de la Societe Mathematique de Moscou. (1866)-. Academic Scholarly Publication. Russian (English, French and German; summaries and/or abstracts in English, French and German). mo. $288.00. Izdatelstvo Nauka / Akademiia Nauk, Publishing House of the Russian Academy of Sciences, Leninskii Porspekt 14, 117901 Moscow Russia. **Tel** 011 95 954-21-53, FAX 011 95 938-21-44, telex 411964. **(Subscription address:** East View Publications Inc., 3020 Harbor Lane North, Suite 110, Minneapolis MN 55447.) **LC** QA1; .M4. **CODEN** MATSAB. Index available. cum. index. **Circ:** 2,285. Documents available from CASDDS.
**Ind/Abst** Chem. Abstr. (-1984); Int. Aerosp. Abstr.; Math. Rev. (-1984); Zentralbl. Math. Ihre Grenzgeb.

RU/0025-567X
**MATEMATICHESKIE ZAMETKI.** [Mat. zametki]. **Added/Corp** Akademiia Nauk SSSR. Otdelenie Matematiki. Rossiiskaia Akademiia Nauk. (1967)-. Academic Scholarly Publication. Russian. mo. $176.00. Izdatelstvo Nauka / Akademiia Nauk, Publishing House of the Russian Academy of Sciences, Leninskii Porspekt 14, 117901 Moscow Russia. **Tel** 011 95 954-21-53, FAX 011 95 938-21-44, telex 411964. **(Subscription address:** East View Publications Inc., 3020 Harbor Lane North, Suite 110, Minneapolis MN 55447.) cum. index.
**Ind/Abst** Math. Rev.; Stat. Theory Method Abstr. (1986); Zentralbl. Math. Ihre Grenzgeb.

RU/0234-0879
**MATEMATICHESKOE MODELIROVANIE.** **Added/Corp** Akademiia Nauk SSSR. **VFOAT** MM. (1989)-. Academic Scholarly Publication. Russian. mo. $230.00. Izdatelstvo Nauka / Akademiia Nauk, Publishing House of the Russian

Academy of Sciences, Leninskii Porspekt 14, 117901 Moscow Russia. **Tel** 011 95 954-21-53, FAX 011 95 938-21-44, telex 411964. **(Subscription address:** East View Publications Inc., 3020 Harbor Lane North, Suite 110, Minneapolis MN 55447.**) CODEN** MMODET.

YU/0025-5165
**MATEMATICKI VESNIK.** [Mat. vesn.]. New Series Vol. 1- 1964-. Periodical. Serbo-Croatian (Cyrillic) (English, French and German). Three times a year. **(Subscription address:** Jugoslovenska Knjiga, PO Box 36, YU 11001 Belgrade Yugoslovia.**) LC** QA1; .M4125. **CODEN** MVNSAQ. ***Continues** Drustvo Matematicara I Fizicara Nr Srbije. Vesnik.*
**Ind/Abst** Int. Aerosp. Abstr.; Math. Rev.; Zentralbl. Math. Ihre Grenzgeb.

UN
**MATEMATIKA. Main/Corp** Kharkivskyi Derzhavnyi Universytet Imeni O.M. Horkoho. Russian. 1.80rub each issue. **LC** AS262; .K417; subser.

HU/0025-519X
**MATEMATIKAI LAPOK.** [Mat. l.]. **Added/Corp** Bolyai Janos Matematikai Tarsulat. Vol. 1, (1949)-. Academic Scholarly Publication. Hungarian (summaries and/or abstracts in English and Russian; table of contents in English). Four times a year. Akademiai Kiado, Publishing House of the Hungarian Academy of Sciences, Prielle Kornelia u. 19-35, H-1117 Budapest Hungary. **Tel** 011 36 1 1811991, FAX 011 36 1 1811991, telex 22-6228 AKNYO H. **(Subscription address:** Kultura, Hungarian Foreign Trading Company, PO Box 149, H-1389 Budapest Hungary**) ED** A. Csaszar. **LC** QA1; .M416. **CODEN** MTLPAR. **Bk Rev. Circ:** 1,400 (ctrl). Documents available from Ask*IEEE. ***Supersedes** Matematikai es Fizikai Lapok, 0302-7317.*
**Desc:** Covers algebra, analysis, combinatorics, geometry, number theory, probability and mathematical statistics, topology, mathematical logic and foundations of mathematics.
**Ind/Abst** INSPEC (1976-1979); Math. Rev.; Stat. Theory Method Abstr. (1959-1963, 1968, 1972, 1977, 1979, 1982-1983, 1986); Zentralbl. Math. Ihre Grenzgeb.

PL
**MATEMATYKA. Added/Corp** Wyzsza Szkoa Pedagogiczna w Opolu. Wyzsza Szkoa Pedagogiczna im. Powstancow Slaskich w Opolu. (1956)-. Monographic series. Polish (summaries and/or abstracts in English). bm (5 issues). $35.00. **(Subscription address:** ARS Polona, PO Box 1001, 00068 Warsaw Poland.**) LC** QA1; .M4174.

RU
**MATERIALY PO MATEMATICHESKOMU OBESPECHENIIU EVM. SERIIA FORTRAN. Added/Corp** Akademiia Nauk SSSR. Nauchno-Issledovatelskii Vychislitelnyi Tsentr (Pushchino, Moscow, R.S.F.S.R.). **VFOAT** Seriia Fortran; Fortran; Fortran, Materialy Po Matematicheskomu Obespecheniiu EVM. (19??)-. Monographic series. Russian. Price varies per volume.

●US/1072-4117
**MATH HORIZONS.** [Math horiz.]. **Added/Corp** Mathematical Association of America. **VFOAT** MathHorizons. (Winter 1993)-. Periodical. English. Four times a year. $35.00 nonmembers; $20.00 members. Mathematical Association of America, 1529 18th Street Northwest, Washington DC 20036. **Tel** (202)387-5200, (800)331-1622, FAX (202)265-2384. **DD** 510.

CN/1184-8952
**MATH JOURNAL, THE.** [Math j.]. **Added/Corp** Manitoba Association of Mathematics Teachers. Vol. 16, No. 2 (Feb. 1991)-. Periodical. English. Five times a year. 15.00Can$. Manitoba Teachers Society, 191 Harcourt Street, Winnipeg Manitoba R3J 3H2 Canada. **Tel** (204)888-7961 ext.254, FAX (204)831-0877. **DD** 510. ***Continues** The Manitoba Mathematics Teacher., 0315-9167.*

US/0272-8885
**MATH NOTEBOOK. See** Education-Special Education and Rehabilitation.

YU/0350-2007
**MATHEMATICA BALKANICA. *Ceased.*** [Math. balk.]. Vol. 1 (1971)-Vol 4 (1990). Periodical. English (French, German and Russian). an. IOS Press, Van Diemenstraat 94, 1013 CN Amsterdam Netherlands. **Tel** 011 31 20 6382189, FAX 011 31 20 620 3419. **LC** QA1; .M275. **CODEN** MTMBBP. Documents available from Ask*IEEE.
**Ind/Abst** INSPEC (1972-); Math. Rev.; Zentralbl. Math. Ihre Grenzgeb.

XR/0862-7959
**MATHEMATICA BOHEMICA / CZECHOSLOVAK ACADEMY OF SCIENCES. Added/Corp** Ceskoslovenska Kademie Ed. Matematicky Ustav. (1991)-. Periodical. English. qt. DM252.00 Germany; DM287.00 other. **(Subscription address:** Kubon & Sagner, ABT Zeitschriftenimport, D 80328 Munich Germany.**) LC** QA1; .C39. **CODEN** MABOEF. ***Continues** Casopis pro Pestovani Matematiky, 0528-2195.*
**Ind/Abst** Zentralbl. Math. Ihre Grenzgeb.

US/1065-2965
**MATHEMATICA IN EDUCATION. See** Education.

JA/0025-5513
**MATHEMATICA JAPONICA.** [Math. Jpn.]. **Added/Corp** Osaka Furitsu Daigaku. Sugaku Kyoshitsu. Osaka Kyoiku Daigaku. Sugaku Kyoshitsu. **VFOAT** Mathematica Japonica. Vol. 1, No. 1 (May 1948)-. Periodical. Multiple languages (English, French and German). Six times a year (Jan., Mar., May, July, Sept., Nov.). $404.00. Japenese Association Mathematica Science, Shin Sakaihigashi Building 2 1 18, Sakai Osaka 590 Japan. **Tel** 011 81 722 221850, FAX 011 81 722 227987. **(Subscription address:** Kinokuniya Company Ltd., 38-1 Sakuragaoka 5, chome Setagaya-ku, Tokyo 156 Japan.**) ED** T. Ishihara. **LC** QA1; .M4222. **DD** 510.5. **CODEN** MAJAA9. Index available (Bound in 6th iss. (Nov).). cum. index. **Circ:** 1,000.
**Desc:** These are carefully selected original papers in mathematical sciences submitted from all over the world.
**Ind/Abst** Math. Rev.; Zentralbl. Math. Ihre Grenzgeb.

US/1047-5974
**MATHEMATICA JOURNAL, THE.** [Math. j.]. Vol. 1, Issue 1 (Summer 1990)-. Periodical. English. qt. $55.00 US; $65.00 Canada & Mexico; $87.00 other. Miller Freeman Inc., 600 Harrison Street, San Francisco CA 94107. **Tel** (415)905-2337, FAX (415)905-2240, telex 278273. **(Subscription address:** Palm Coast Data, PO Box 420235, Agency Department, Palm Coast FL 32142.**) LC** QA76.95; .M387. **DD** 510/.285/5369. **[CCC].**
**Desc:** Features scholarly articles, contributed pieces, mathematica news, calendars, new product reviews, and much more. An electronic supplement with tutorials, programs, packages and notebooks is also available.
**Ind/Abst** ACM Guide Comput. Lit. (19??-); Comput. Rev. (19??-).

CC
**MATHEMATICA NUMERICA SINICA.**
**VFOAT** Chi Suan Shu Hsueh. English. qt. RMBY64.40 (airmail), RMBY48.40 (surface mail). Science Press, 16 Donghuangchenggen North Street, Beijing 100707, People's Republic of China. **Tel** 011 86 1 4019821, 011 86 1 4010642, FAX 011 86 1 4012180, 011 86 1 4019810, telex 210147. **CODEN** JSUXDP. Documents available from Ask*IEEE.
**Ind/Abst** INSPEC (1981-); Int. Abstr. Oper. Res. [Select. Cov.]; Math. Rev.; Zentralbl. Math. Ihre Grenzgeb.

AU/0865-2090
**MATHEMATICA PANNONICA.** (199?)-. Periodical. English. sa. Prof I Gy Maurer, Mathematics Institute of Hungarian Science, PO Box 127, 1364 Budapest Hungary. **Tel** 011 36 46 365111 1795.
**Ind/Abst** Math. Rev.; Zentralbl. Math. Ihre Grenzgeb.

DK/0025-5521
**MATHEMATICA SCANDINAVICA.** [Math. scand.]. **Added/Corp** Dansk Matematisk Forening. Vol. 1 (1953)-. Periodical. English (French and German). qt. kr890.00. Aarhus Universitet Matematisk Universitet, Building 530, DK-8000 Aarhus C Denmark. **Tel** 011 45 86 127188. **ED** Jorgen Vesterstrom. **LC** QA1; .M4223. **CODEN** MTSCAN. Index available. **Pr Rev. Circ:** 1,100. Documents available from The Genuine Article. ***Continues** Matematisk Tidsskrift.; **Continues in part** Norsk Matematisk Tidsskrift.*
**Ind/Abst** Compumath Citation Index [Full Cov.]; Comput. Rev.; Math. Rev.; Res. Alert [Full Cov.]; SCISEARCH; Stat. Theory Method Abstr. (1961-1963, 1967, 1971-1972); Zentralbl. Math. Ihre Grenzgeb.

XO/0139-9918
**MATHEMATICA SLOVACA.** [Math. Slovaca]. V. 26- 1976-. Periodical. Multiple languages (Czech, English, French, German, Russian and Slovak). qt. DM146.00 (add DM12.20 for surface mail postage). **(Subscription address:** Slovart GTG Ltd., Krupinska 4, 852 99 Bratislava Slovakia.**) LC** QA1; .M4132. **DD** 510/.5. **CODEN** MASLDM. Documents available from Ask*IEEE. ***Continues** Matematicky Casopis.*
**Ind/Abst** INSPEC (1976-); Math. Rev.; Zentralbl. Math. Ihre Grenzgeb.

RM
**MATHEMATICA / SOCIETATEA DE STIINTE MATEMATICE SI FIZICE.**
**Added/Corp** Societatea de Stiinte Matematice si Fizice din R.P.R. Filiala Cluj. Academia Republicii Socialiste Romania. Filiala Cluj-Napoca. Vol. 1 (1959)-. Periodical. French (English, French, German and Russian). Editura Academia Republicii Socialiste Romania, Calea Victoriei Nr 125, R-79717 Bucuresti Romania. **Tel** telex 10376 PRSFI R. **(Subscription address:** Rompresfilatelia, PO Box 12 201, Bucharest Romania.**) ED** E. Popoviciu. **LC** QA1; .M42. available with charts; available with illustrations. ***Continues** Mathematica (Cluj, Romania : 1929).*

AG/0025-553X
**MATHEMATICAE NOTAE.** [Math. notae]. No. 1 (1941)-. Spanish. be. Unoversidad Nacional Rosario, Avenida Pellegrini 250, 2000 Rosario Argentina. **LC** QA1; .M4225. **DD** 510.5. **CODEN** MANOA3.
**Ind/Abst** Math. Rev.; Zentralbl. Math. Ihre Grenzgeb.

UK/0895-7177
**MATHEMATICAL AND COMPUTER MODELLING.** [Math. comput. model.]. **Added/Corp** International Association for Mathematical and Computer Modelling. Vol. 10, No. 1 (1988)-. Academic Scholarly Publication. English. Twenty-four times a year. $1490.00 The Americas; £1000.00 other. Pergamon Press, An Imprint of Elsevier Science Ltd., The Boulevard, Langford Lane, Kidlington, Oxford OX5 1GB United Kingdom. **Tel** 011 44 865 843000, 011 44 865 843699, FAX 011 44 865 843010. **(Subscription address:** Elsevier Science Ltd. Oxford Fulfillment Centre, PO Box 800, Kidlington, Oxford OX5 1DX United Kingdom.**) ED** E. Y. Rodin. **LC** QA401; .M393. **DD** 001.4/34. **CODEN** MCMOEG. **[CCC]. Pr Rev.** available on microfilm and microfiche from University Microfilms International (UMI). Documents available from The Genuine Article, Ask*IEEE. ***Continues** Mathematical Modelling, 0270-0255.*
**Desc:** Covers disciplines utilizing mathematical modeling as either a theoretical or working tool.
**Ind/Abst** Abstr. Bull. Inst. Pap. Sci. Tech.; Biostatistica; Compumath Citation Index [Full Cov.]; Curr. Aware. Biol. Sci., CABS; Curr. Contents Eng. Tech. Appl. Sci.; Curr. Lit. Sci. Sci.; Ei Page One; EMBASE (1988-); Fluid Abstr., Civil Eng.; Fluid Abstr. Proc. Eng.; FLUIDEX (1988-); INSPEC (1988-); Math. Rev. (1988-); Oper. Res./Manag. Sci.; Res. Alert [Full Cov.]; Risk Abstr.; SCISEARCH; Soc. Sci. Cit. Index [Select. Cov.]; Zentralbl. Math. Ihre Grenzgeb.

US/0025-5564
**MATHEMATICAL BIOSCIENCES. See** Biology.

US/1049-2801
**MATHEMATICAL CHEMISTRY. See** Chemistry.

●UK/1354-6791
**MATHEMATICAL COGNITION.** (1995)-. English. qt. £50.00 EC; $90.00 US; £55.00 other. Lawrence Erlbaum Associates Ltd., 27 Palmeira Mansions, Church Road, Hove East Sussex BN3 2FA England. **Tel** 011 44 273 207411. **(Subscription address:** Turpin Distribution Services Limited, Blackhorse Road, Letchworth, Hertfordshire SG6 1HN, United Kingdom.**) ED** Brian Butterworth and Lisa Cipolotti.
**Desc:** Concerned with advances in the study of mental representation and use of mathematical concepts, and their development in the field. Strives to further understanding of the cognitive processes of mathematics from students of animal behaviour, ethnographers, mathematicians and philosophers.

US/0885-9418
**MATHEMATICAL CONCEPTS AND METHODS IN SCIENCE AND ENGINEERING.** [Math. concepts methods sci. eng.]. (1976)-. Monographic series. English. ir. Price varies per volume. Plenum Press, 233 Spring Street, New York NY 10013-1578. **Tel** (212)620-8000, (800)221-9369, FAX (212)463-0742, (212)807-1047, telex 23/421139. **LC** UNC. **DD** 510.
**Ind/Abst** Math. Rev.; Zentralbl. Math. Ihre Grenzgeb.

US/0076-5325
**MATHEMATICAL ECONOMICS TEXTS. See** Economics.

UK
**MATHEMATICAL EDUCATION FOR TEACHING.** (19??)-. English. ir. £4.00. Jomerton College, H B Shubard, Cambridge CB2 2PH England.

NE/0169-121X
**MATHEMATICAL ENGINEERING IN INDUSTRY.** Vol. 1 No. 1 (1987)-. Periodical. English. qt. DM270.00. VSP International Science Publishers, Godfried van Seystlaan 47, 3703 BR Zeist Netherlands. **Tel** 011 31 3404 25790, FAX 011 31 3404 32081, telex 40217 USP NL. **(Subscription address:** VSP International Science Publishers, PO Box 346, 3700 AH Zeist Netherlands.**) ED** F. A. Goldsworthy. Documents available from Article Express International.
**Desc:** Aimed at bringing to the fore the new mathematical applications in industry. Papers originate from both the academic and industrial sources, the common viewpoint being the industrial context of the work.
**Ind/Abst** Ei Page One; Eng. Index Annu.; Fluid Abstr., Civil Eng.; Fluid Abstr. Proc. Eng.; FLUIDEX; Math. Rev.

UK/0960-1627
**MATHEMATICAL FINANCE : AN INTERNATIONAL JOURNAL OF MATHEMATICS, STATISTICS AND FINANCIAL THEORY.** Vol. 1 (Jan. 1991)-. Periodical. English. Four times a year. $156.00 North America; $178.00 other. Blackwell Publishers, 238 Main Street, Cambridge MA 02142. **Tel** (617)547-7110, (800)835-6770, FAX (617)547-0789. **LC** HF5691; .M27.

[CCC]. available on microfilm and microfiche from University Microfilms International (UMI).
**Ind/Abst** Math. Rev.

UK/0025-5572
**MATHEMATICAL GAZETTE.** (THE MATHEMATICAL GAZETTE.). [Math. gaz.]. **Added/Corp** Mathematical Association. Vol. 1 (April 1894)-. Periodical. English. tq (3 issues). £34.50. Mathematical Association, 259 London Road, Leicester LE2 3BE England. **Tel** 011 44 533 703877. **ED** V. Bryant. **LC** QA1; .M426. **CODEN** MAGAAS. Index Available, published separately, free-automatically sent. cum. index. **Bk Rev. Ad Acc. Circ:** 6,000 (ctrl). available on microfilm and microfiche from University Microfilms International (UMI). ***Supersedes*** *Association for the Improvement of Geometrical Teaching (Great Britain). Report.*
**Desc:** Offers articles on mathematical topics of wide appeal and mathematics teaching at the level of secondary school, college, and university.
**Ind/Abst** Math. Rev. (?-199?); Stat. Theory Method Abstr. (1959-1963, 1967); Zentralbl. Math. Ihre Grenzgeb.

US/0343-6993
**MATHEMATICAL INTELLIGENCER, THE.** [Math. intell.]. Vol. 1 No. 1 (1978)-. Periodical. English. Four times a year. $29.10. Springer-Verlag New York Inc., 175 5th Avenue, New York NY 10010. **Tel** (212)460-1500, telex 232 235 SPB UR. **(Subscription address:** Springer Verlag New York Inc. / for North America, 44 Hartz Way, Secaucus NJ 07096.**) ED** S Axler. **LC** QA1; .M427. **DD** 510/.5. **CODEN** MAINDC. **[CCC]. Pr Rev.** available on microfilm and microfiche from University Microfilms International (UMI). Documents available from The Genuine Article, UMI Article Clearinghouse. ***Continues*** *Mathematical Intelligencer (Berlin, Germany : 1972), 0343-6993.*
**Desc:** Covers a wide range of topics such as people, theorems, philosophy, and history relevant to mathematics, designed for researchers, students, teachers, and others concerned with mathematics.
**Ind/Abst** Acad. Abstr. (July 1993-); Acad. Search (July 1993-); Arts Humanit. Citation Index [Select. Cov.]; Compumath Citation Index [Full Cov.]; Curr. Contents Phys. Chem. Earth Sci.; Energy Res. Abstr. (March 1982-); Expand. Acad. Index (1989-); Gen. Sci. Index; INFO-SOUTH Abstr.; Mag. Search; Math. Rev.; Newsp. Period. Abstr. (1991-); Phys. Briefs; Res. Alert [Full Cov.]; Sci. Cit. Index; SCISEARCH; Soc. Sci. Cit. Index [Select. Cov.]; Zentralbl. Math. Ihre Grenzgeb.

JA/0030-1566
**MATHEMATICAL JOURNAL OF OKAYAMA UNIVERSITY.** [Math. j. Okayama Univ.]. **Added/Corp** Okayama Daigaku. Rigakubu. Sugaku Kyoshitsu. Vol. 1 (Mar. 1952)-. Periodical. English (German and French). sa. Okayama University / Faculty of Science, Tsushima Okayama Japan. **LC** QA1; .M428. **CODEN** MJOKAP.
**Ind/Abst** Math. Rev.; Zentralbl. Math. Ihre Grenzgeb.

JA
**MATHEMATICAL LINGUISTICS. KEIYRKO KOKUGOGAKU. See** Linguistics.

US/0025-5580
**MATHEMATICAL LOG, THE.** [Math. log]. **Added/Corp** Mu Alpha Theta. National High School and Junior College Mathematics Club (U.S.) Mathematical Association of America. National Council of Teachers of Mathematics. (19??)-. Periodical. English. qt. $2.00 US; $5.50 other. Mu Alpha Theta, 601 Elm Avenue/Room 423, Norman OK 73019. **Tel** (405)325-4489. **ED** Dr. Thomas Butts. **Circ:** 30,000. available on microfiche.
**Desc:** Mathematical articles, problems and recreationals appropriate for secondary and junior college students.

●GW/0942-5616
**MATHEMATICAL LOGIC QUARTERLY. VFOAT** MLQ. Vol. 39, No. 1 (1993)-. Periodical. English (French and German). qt. DM366.00. Johann Ambrosius Barth, Prager Strasse 16 B, D 04103 Leipzig Germany. **Tel** 011 49 341 7137570. **(Subscription address:** Huethig Publishing Inc., 29 Macintosh Drive, Oxford CT 06478.**) LC** QA1; .Z38. ***Continues*** *Zeitschrift fuer Mathematische Logik und Grundlagen der Mathematik, 0044-3050.*

SI/0217-2976
**MATHEMATICAL MEDLEY.** [Math. medley]. **Added/Corp** Singapore Mathematical Society. Vol. 1 (1973)-. Periodical. English. tq. Singapore Mathematical Society, Department of Mathematics, University of Singapore, Singapore 10 Singapore.
**Ind/Abst** Math. Rev.; Zentralbl. Math. Ihre Grenzgeb.

GW/0170-4214
**MATHEMATICAL METHODS IN THE APPLIED SCIENCES.** [Math. methods appl. sci.]. Vol. 1, No. 1 (1979)-. Periodical. English (German and French). Fifteen times a year. $995.00. John Wiley & Sons Ltd., Baffins Lane, Chichester West Sussex PO19 1UD England. **Tel** 0243 779777, FAX 0243 776128 BTG:JWP001, telex 86290 WIBOOKG. **(Subscription address:** John Wiley / Philadelphia, PO Box 7247, Philadelphia PA 19170.**) ED** B. Brosowski and G. F. Roach. **LC** QA1; .M46. **DD** 510/.5. **CODEN** MMSCDB. **[CCC].** Index available. **Ad Acc. Pr Rev.** available on microfilm and microfiche from University Microfilms International (UMI). Documents available from Article Express International, The Genuine Article, Ask*IEEE.
**Desc:** The journal is concerned with those mathematical methods which are evidently necessary for the further understanding and thorough analysis of actual problems in the applied sciences.
**Ind/Abst** Appl. Mech. Rev.; Bioeng. Abstr.; Compumath Citation Index [Full Cov.]; Curr. Contents Phys. Chem. Earth Sci.; Ei Page One; Eng. Index Annu. [Select. Cov.]; INSPEC (May 1988-); Int. Aerosp. Abstr.; Math. Rev.; Res. Alert [Full Cov.]; SCISEARCH; Zentralbl. Math. Ihre Grenzgeb.

HU/0209-6137
**MATHEMATICAL METHODS OF OPERATIONS RESEARCH.** [Math. methods oper. res.]. **Added/Corp** Akademiai Kiado. Vol. 1 (1980)-. Academic Scholarly Publication. English. ir. Price varies per volume. Akademiai Kiado, Publishing House of the Hungarian Academy of Sciences, Prielle Kornelia u. 19-35, H-1117 Budapest Hungary. **Tel** 011 36 1 1811991, FAX 011 36 1 1811991, telex 22-6228 AKNYO H.
**Ind/Abst** Math. Rev.; Zentralbl. Math. Ihre Grenzgeb.

●US/1066-5307
**MATHEMATICAL METHODS OF STATISTICS.** [Math. methods stat.]. Vol. 1 (1992)-. Periodical. English. qt (Mar., June, Sept., Dec.). $260.00. Allerton Press, Inc., 150 Fifth Avenue, New York NY 10011. **Tel** (212)924-3950, FAX (212)463-9684, telex 427441 ALPRES. **DD** 519. **[CCC].**

US/1054-6634
**MATHEMATICAL MODELING. VFOAT** Mathematical Modeling, Soviet; Mathematicheskoe Modelirovanie. (1991)-. Periodical. English (Russian). mo. $130.00 (individuals), $330.00 (institutions) US; $160.00 (individuals), $350.00 (institutions) other. Soviet Journals, c/o Allen Press Inc, 1041 New Hampshire Street, Lawrence KS 55044. **Tel** (913)843-1235, FAX (913)843-1274.
**Desc:** This highly technical journal is a leading source of information in the field of mathematical modeling and related fields.

●US/1061-7590
**MATHEMATICAL MODELING AND COMPUTATIONAL EXPERIMENT.** [Math. model. comput. exper.]. **VFOAT** MMCE. (1992)-. Periodical. English. qt. $340.00 (US); $380.00 (Canada & Mexico); $395.00 (other). John Wiley & Sons, Inc., 605 Third Avenue, New York NY 10158-0012. **Tel** (212)850-6000, (212)850-6645, FAX (212)850-6088, telex 12-7063. **(Subscription address:** John Wiley & Sons / England, Baffins Lane, Chichester, West Sussex PO19 1UD England.**) ED** Academician A. A. Samarskii. **DD** 511. **CODEN** MMCEE6.
**Desc:** Describes fast and reliable programs, with particular emphasis on programs for multiprocessor and transputer systems, computational experiments, and detailed computer analysis of important problems, starting with their formulation to finding the optimal conditions and designs.

●US/1067-0688
**MATHEMATICAL MODELLING AND SCIENTIFIC COMPUTING.** (MATHEMATICAL MODELLING AND SCIENTIFIC COMPUTING : AFFILIATED WITH THE INTERNATIONAL ASSOCIATION FOR MATHEMATICAL AND COMPUTER MODELLING.). [Math. model. sci. comput.]. **Added/Corp** International Association for Mathematical and Computer Modelling. (1993)-. Periodical. English. $150.00 (institutions). Principia Scientia, PO Box 31670, St. Louis MO 63131. **DD** 511.

NE/1381-2424
**MATHEMATICAL MODELLING OF SYSTEMS.** (199?)-. Periodical. English. Four times a year. Fl320.00 (institution). Swets & Zeitlinger BV, Heereweg 347B PO Box 825, 2160 SZ Lisse Holland. **Tel** 011 31 2521 35111, FAX 02521-15888, telex 41325. **(Subscription address:** Swets Publishing Service, PO Box 825, 2160 SZ Lisse The Netherlands**)**

SI/0218-2025
**MATHEMATICAL MODELS & METHODS IN APPLIED SCIENCES : MP3SAS.** [Math. models methods appl. sci.]. **VFOAT** Mathematical Models and Methods in Applied Sciences; Mp3sAS. Vol. 1, No. 1 Mar. (1991)-. Periodical. English. Eight times a year. $180.00 individuals, $370.00 institutions. World Scientific Publishing Company, PO Box 128, Farrer Road, Singapore 9128 Singapore. **Tel** 011 65 3825663, FAX 011 65 3825919, telex RS 28561 WSPC. **(Subscription address:** US: World Scientific Publishing Co., Inc., 1060 Main Street, River Edge, NJ 07661 Telephone: (201)487-9655, Fax: (201)487-9656; Europe: World Scientific Publishing Co Ltd, 73 Lynton Mead, Totteridge, London N20 8DH United Kingdom Telephone: 011 44 81 4462461, Fax: 011 44 81 4463356; India: World Scientific Publishing Co Pte Ltd, 4911 9th Floor, High Point IV, 45 Palace Road, Bangalore 560 001 India Telephone: (80) 2205972, Fax: (80) 3344593, Telex: 0845-2900 PCO IN; Hong Kong: World Scientific Publishing (HK) Co, PO Box 72482, Kowloon Central Post Office, Hong Kong Telephone: 852-7718791, Fax: 852-7718155**) LC** QA401; .M396. **DD** 510/.5. **CODEN** MMMSEU. Documents available from Ask*IEEE.
**Ind/Abst** INSPEC (1991-); Math. Rev.; Zentralbl. Math. Ihre Grenzgeb.

US
**MATHEMATICAL NOTES. Added/Corp** Consultants Bureau. Akademiia Nauk SSSR. (Jan./Feb. 1967)-. Periodical. English. Twelve times a year. $1295.00 US; $1515.00 other. Consultants Bureau, A Division of Plenum Publishing Corporation, 233 Spring Street, New York NY 10013. **Tel** (212)620-8000, (212)620-8466, FAX (212)463-0742, telex 23/421139. **LC** QA1; .M753. Documents available from The Genuine Article.
**Ind/Abst** Compumath Citation Index [Full Cov.]; Curr. Contents Phys. Chem. Earth Sci.; Res. Alert [Full Cov.]; Sci. Cit. Index; SCISEARCH.

US
**MATHEMATICAL NOTES. Added/Corp** Princeton University Press. (1967)-. Monographic series. English. ir. Price varies per volume. Princeton University Press, 41 William Street, Princeton NJ 08540. **Tel** (609)258-4900. **(Subscription address:** California Princeton Fulfillment Service, 1445 Lower Ferry Road, Ewing NJ 08618.**)** ***Continues*** *Princeton Mathematical Notes.*
**Ind/Abst** Math. Rev.; Zentralbl. Math. Ihre Grenzgeb.

●US/1067-9073
**MATHEMATICAL NOTES (ROSSIISKAIA AKADEMIIA NAUK).** (MATHEMATICAL NOTES.). [Math. notes]. **Added/Corp** Rossiiskaia Akademiia Nauk. Consultants Bureau. **VFOAT** Matematicheskie Zametki. Vol. 51, No. 1-2 (Jan./Feb. 1992)-. Periodical. English (translations available in Russian). Twelve times a year. $1295.00 US; $1515.00 other. Consultants Bureau, A Division of Plenum Publishing Corporation, 233 Spring Street, New York NY 10013. **Tel** (212)620-8000, (212)620-8466, FAX (212)463-0742, telex 23/421139. **LC** QA1; .M753. **DD** 510. ***Continues*** *Mathematical Notes of the Academy of Sciences of the USSR, 0001-4346.*

NE/0165-2419
**MATHEMATICAL PHYSICS AND APPLIED MATHEMATICS.** [Math. phys. appl. math.]. Vol. 1 (1976)-. Academic Scholarly Publication. English. Price varies per volume. D. Reidel Publishing Company, PO Box 17, 3300 AA Dordrecht The Netherlands. **Tel** 011 31 78 334210, FAX (31) 78 183273, telex 29245 KAPGNL. **CODEN** MPAMD6. Documents available from CASDDS.
**Ind/Abst** Chem. Abstr. (1976-1981); Math. Rev.; Zentralbl. Math. Ihre Grenzgeb.

NE/0921-3767
**MATHEMATICAL PHYSICS STUDIES. See** Physics.

UK/0305-0041
**MATHEMATICAL PROCEEDINGS OF THE CAMBRIDGE PHILOSOPHICAL SOCIETY.** [Math. proc. Camb. Philos. Soc.]. **Main/Corp** Cambridge Philosophical Society. Vol. 77 (Jan. 1975)-. Academic Scholarly Publication. English. bm (6 issues). $372.00 US, Canada & Mexico; £192.00 other. Cambridge University Press, The Edinburgh Building, Shaftesbury Road, Cambridge CB2 2RU United Kingdom. **Tel** 011 44 223 312393, FAX 011 44 223 325959. **(Subscription address:** Cambridge University Press / North America, 110 Midland Avenue, Port Chester NY 10573.**) ED** J. S. Wilson. **LC** Q41; .C17. **DD** 510/.5. **CODEN** MPCPCO. **[CCC]. Pr Rev.** available on microfilm from University Microfilms International (UMI). Documents available from Article Express International, The Genuine Article, Ask*IEEE. ***Continues*** *Cambridge Philosophical Society. Proceedings of the Cambridge Philosophical Society, 0008-1981.*
**Desc:** Publishes original research papers that cover the whole range of pure and applied mathematics, theoretical physics and statistics. All branches of pure mathematics are covered, in particular logic and foundations, number theory, algebra, geometry, algebraic and geometric topology, classical and functional analysis, differential equations, and probability and statistics. On the applied side, mechanics, mathematical physics, relativity and cosmology are included.
**Ind/Abst** Bioeng. Abstr.; Compumath Citation Index [Full Cov.]; Curr. Contents Phys. Chem. Earth Sci.; Ei Page One; Eng. Index Annu.; GeoRef; INSPEC (Jan. 1975-); Int. Aerosp. Abstr.; Math. Rev.; Res. Alert [Full Cov.]; Sci. Cit. Index; SCISEARCH; Stat. Theory Method Abstr. (1979, 1982); Zentralbl. Math. Ihre Grenzgeb.

NE
**MATHEMATICAL PROGRAMMING MASTER INDEX.** (1976)- . Academic Scholarly Publication. English. bm. Elsevier Science Publishers BV, PO Box 211, 1000 AE Amsterdam Netherlands. **Tel** 011 31 20 5803642, FAX 011 31 20 5862696, telex 15682.

NE
**MATHEMATICAL PROGRAMMING. SERIES A : A PUBLICATION OF THE MATHEMATICAL PROGRAMMING SOCIETY.** **Added/Corp** Mathematical Programming Society (U.S.). Vol. 40, No. 1 (Jan. 1988)-. Academic Scholarly Publication. English. Twelve times a year (4 volumes). Fl1336.00. Elsevier Science Publishers BV, PO Box 211, 1000 AE Amsterdam Netherlands. **Tel** 011 31 20 5803642, FAX 011 31 20 5862696, telex 15682. **CODEN** MHPGA4. Documents available from Article Express International, Ask*IEEE. ***Continues in part*** *Mathematical Programming, 0025-5610.*
**Ind/Abst** Bioeng. Abstr.; Ei Page One; Eng. Index Annu.; INSPEC (Sept. 1988-Oct. 1991); Math. Rev.; Pollut. Abstr. Indexes.

SZ/0275-7214
**MATHEMATICAL REPORTS (CHUR, SWITZERLAND).** ***Ceased.*** (MATHEMATICAL REPORTS.). [Math. rep.]. Vol. 1, Pt. 1 (July 1983)-(19??). Monographic series. English. ir. Harwood Academic Publishers, PO Box 90, Reading RG1 8JL England. **Tel** 011 44 734 560080. **(Subscription address:** Harwood Academic Publishers, PO Box 786, Cooper Station, New York NY 10276.**) ED** J. Dieudonne. **LC** UNC. **DD** 510. **[CCC].** Index available. **Bk Rev. Ad Acc.**
**Desc:** State-of-the-art reviews of important current developments.
**Ind/Abst** Math. Rev.; Zentralbl. Math. Ihre Grenzgeb.

JA/0287-9980
**MATHEMATICAL REPORTS OF COLLEGE OF GENERAL EDUCATION, KYUSHU UNIVERSITY.** [Math. rep. Coll. Gen. Educ. Kyushu Univ.]. **VFOAT** Kyushu Daigaku Kyoyobu Sugaku Zasshi. (1964)-. Periodical. English. an. **DD** 510.
**Ind/Abst** Math. Rev.; Zentralbl. Math. Ihre Grenzgeb.

GW/0138-3019
**MATHEMATICAL RESEARCH.** (MATHEMATICAL RESEARCH / MATHEMATISCHE FORSCHUNG : WISSENSCHAFTLICHE BEITRAEGE HERAUSGEGEBEN VON DER AKADEMIE DER WISSENSCHAFTEN DER DDR, ZENTRALINSTITUT FUER MATHEMATIK UND MECHANIK.). [Math. Res.]. **Added/Corp** Akademie der Wissenschaften der DDR. Zentralinstitut fuer Mathematik und Mechanik. **VFOAT** Mathematische Forschung. (1979)-. Monographic series. English. ir. Price varies per volume. Akademie-Verlag GmbH, Muehlenstrasse 33 34, D 13162 Berlin Germany. **Tel** 011 49 30 47889300, FAX 011 49 30 47889357. **(Subscription address:** VCH Publishers Inc., 303 Northwest 12th Avenue, Journals Department, Deerfield FL 33442.**) LC** UNC. Documents available from Ask*IEEE. ***Continues*** *Schriftenreihe des Zentralinstituts fuer Mathematik und Mechanik, 0138-306X.*
**Desc:** Original contributions on all fields of mathematical research, e.g. research monographs, collections of papers to a single topic, reports on congresses to promote quick information and communication.
**Ind/Abst** INSPEC (1986-); Math. Rev.; Zentralbl. Math. Ihre Grenzgeb.

●US/1073-2780
**MATHEMATICAL RESEARCH LETTERS.** (MATHEMATICAL RESEARCH LETTERS : MRL.). [Math. res. lett.]. **VFOAT** MRL. Vol. 1, No. 1 (Jan. 1994)-. Periodical. English. bm. $130.00. International Press, PO Box 2872, Cambridge MA 02238. **Tel** (617)491-0329. **DD** 510.

CC/0255-7789
**MATHEMATICAL RESEARCH REPORT.** [Math. res. rep.]. **VFOAT** Shuxue Yanjiu Baogao. (1979)-. Periodical. Multiple languages. **UDC** 51.
**Ind/Abst** Zentralbl. Math. Ihre Grenzgeb.

US/0025-5629
**MATHEMATICAL REVIEWS. See** Mathematics-Abstracting, Bibliographies and Statistics.

US/0737-4356
**MATHEMATICAL SCIENCES PROFESSIONAL DIRECTORY.** [Math. sci. prof. dir.]. **Added/Corp** American Mathematical Society. (1983)-. English. an (Mar.). $36.00 (institutions & institutions associates); $40.50 (corporate members); $45.00 (non-members). American Mathematical Society, PO Box 6248, Providence RI 02940-6248. **Tel** (800)321-4267, (401)455-4000, FAX (401)331-3842, telex 797192. **(Subscription address:** American Mathematical Society, PO Box 5904, Boston MA 02206-5904.**) ED** Marcia Almeida. **LC** QA1; .M765. **DD** 510/.25/73. ***Continues*** *Mathematical Sciences Administrative Directory, 0543-0895.*
**Desc:** Lists key personnel of over 30 professional mathematical organizations and selected government agencies plus editors of over 100 journals and mathematical sciences departments in universities and in non-academic organizations.

AT/0312-3685
**MATHEMATICAL SCIENTIST.** (THE MATHEMATICAL SCIENTIST.). [Math. sci.]. **Added/Corp** Commonwealth Scientific and Industrial Research Organization (Australia). Division of Mathematics and Statistics. Vol. 1 (Jan. 1976)-. Periodical. English. Twice a year. $15.00 US; £9.75. Applied Probability, School of Mathematics and Statistics, Sheffield S3 7RH England. **Tel** 011 44 742 824269, FAX 011 44 742 729782. **ED** Linda J. Nash. **LC** QA1; .M7654. **DD** 510/.5. **Bk Rev. Circ:** 650.
**Desc:** Publishes papers of general interest in all areas of mathematics.
**Ind/Abst** Energy Res. Abstr. (Sept. 1982-); Math. Rev.; Stat. Theory Method Abstr. (1976-1977, 1979-1984, 1986-1987); Zentralbl. Math. Ihre Grenzgeb.

NE/0165-4896
**MATHEMATICAL SOCIAL SCIENCES. See** Social Sciences.

UK/0025-5653
**MATHEMATICAL SPECTRUM.** [Math. spectr.]. Vol. 1 (1968/1969)-. Periodical. English. Three times a year (September, January and May). $12.35 (one year), $23.10 (two year), $33.90 (three year) North, South and Central America; 17.20Aus$ (one year), 32.26Aus$ (two year), 47.30Aus$ (three year) Australia; £8.00 (one year), £15.00 (two year), £22.00 (three year) other. Applied Probability, School of Mathematics and Statistics, Sheffield S3 7RH England. **Tel** 011 44 742 824269, FAX 011 44 742 729782. **ED** David W. Sharpe. **LC** QA1; .S766. **DD** 510/.05. **CODEN** MSPEB8. Index available. **Bk Rev. Ad Acc. Circ:** 1,800. Documents available from Ask*IEEE.
**Desc:** Articles on all branches of mathematics, book reviews, computer column, problems and solutions. Suitable for students and general readers.
**Ind/Abst** Biostatistica; Fluid Abstr., Civil Eng.; Fluid Abstr. Proc. Eng.; FLUIDEX (1973-1990); INSPEC (1971-); Math. Rev.; Oper. Res./Manag. Sci.; Qual. Control Appl. Stat.

US/0885-4653
**MATHEMATICAL SURVEYS AND MONOGRAPHS.** [Math. surv. monogr.]. **Added/Corp** American Mathematical Society. No. 19 (1984)-. Monographic series. English. ir. Price varies per volume. American Mathematical Society, PO Box 6248, Providence RI 02940-6248. **Tel** (800)321-4267, (401)455-4000, FAX (401)331-3842, telex 797192. **(Subscription address:** American Mathematical Society, PO Box 5904, Boston MA 02206-5904.**) LC** UNC. **DD** 510. ***Continues*** *Mathematical Surveys, 0076-5376.*
**Ind/Abst** Math. Rev.; Zentralbl. Math. Ihre Grenzgeb.

GW/0344-3302
**MATHEMATICAL SYSTEMS IN ECONOMICS.** [Math. syst. econ.]. Monographic series. Multiple languages (English, French and German). ir. Price varies per volume. Athenaum Verlag GmbH, Adelheidstrabe 2, 6240 Tonigstein TS Germany. **Tel** 06174/3021. **ED** R Henn, W Eichhorn, S N Afriat, G Bamberg. **Bk Rev. Ad Acc.**
**Desc:** A survey of one particular subject within the context of mathematical economics, operations research and computer science.
**Ind/Abst** Math. Rev.; Zentralbl. Math. Ihre Grenzgeb.

US/0025-5661
**MATHEMATICAL SYSTEMS THEORY.** [Math. syst. theory]. Vol. 1 (Jan./Feb. 1967)-. Periodical. English. Six times a year. $184.00. Springer-Verlag New York Inc., 175 5th Avenue, New York NY 10010. **Tel** (212)460-1500, telex 232 235 SPB UR. **(Subscription address:** Springer Verlag New York Inc. / for North America, 44 Hartz Way, Secaucus NJ 07096.**) ED** A L Rosenberg. **LC** QA1; .M767. **CODEN** MASTBA. **[CCC].** cum. index. **Pr Rev.** available on microfilm and microfiche from University Microfilms International (UMI). Documents available from The Genuine Article, Ask*IEEE.
**Desc:** Examines the various mathematical aspects of everyday problems in engineering, computer science, and other areas, such as economics and biology, which rely on direct applications of systems ideas.
**Ind/Abst** Compumath Citation Index [Full Cov.]; Comput. Rev.; Curr. Contents Phys. Chem. Earth Sci.; INSPEC (March 1968-); Math. Rev.; Pollut. Abstr. Indexes; Res. Alert [Full Cov.]; Sci. Cit. Index; SCISEARCH; Zentralbl. Math. Ihre Grenzgeb.

US/1055-9426
**MATHEMATICAL WORLD.** [Math. world]. **Added/Corp** American Mathematical Society. Mathematical Association of America. Vol. 1 (1991)-. Monographic series. English. ir. Price varies per volume. American Mathematical Society, PO Box 6248, Providence RI 02940-6248. **Tel** (800)321-4267, (401)455-4000, FAX (401)331-3842, telex 797192. **(Subscription address:** American Mathematical Society, PO Box 5904, Boston MA 02206-5904.**) DD** 510. **[CCC].**
**Ind/Abst** Math. Rev.

US
**MATHEMATICIANS OF OUR TIME.** ***Ceased.*** (1971)-(19??). Monographic series. English. ir. Massachusetts Institute of Technology (MIT) Press, 55 Hayward Street, Cambridge MA 02142-1399. **Tel** (617)253-2889, (617)625-8481, FAX (617)258-6779.
**Ind/Abst** Zentralbl. Math. Ihre Grenzgeb.

US/0730-8639
**MATHEMATICS AND COMPUTER EDUCATION.** [Math. comput. educ.]. Vol. 16, No. 1 (Winter 1982)-. Periodical. English. Three times a year. $62.00 US; $72.00 Canada & Mexico; $75.00 others. Mathematics and Computer Education, PO Box 158, Old Bethpage NY 11804. **Tel** (516)822-5475. **ED** George Miller. **LC** QA13; .M16. **DD** 510/.711. **CODEN** MCEDDA. Index available. cum. index. **Bk Rev. Ad Acc. Pr Rev. Circ:** 1500. available on microfilm and microfiche from University Microfilms International (UMI). Documents available from Ask*IEEE. ***Continues*** *MATYC Journal, 0092-1424.*
**Desc:** Focuses on undergraduate college and university education. From classroom notes to advanced mathematical and computer concepts, to extensive independent reviews of the latest books and software in the fields.
**Ind/Abst** ACM Guide Comput. Lit.; Comput. Lit. Index; Comput. Rev.; Contents Pages Educ.; Curr. Index J. Educ.; Educ. Technol. Abstr.; INSPEC (Winter 1982-); Math. Rev.; Tech. Educ. Train. Abstr.

NE/0378-4754
**MATHEMATICS AND COMPUTERS IN SIMULATION. See** Computers-Simulation.

US/0543-0941
**MATHEMATICS AND ITS APPLICATIONS.** [Math. appl.]. Monographic series. English. ir. Price varies per volume. Gordon & Breach Science Publishers, Inc., PO Box 786, Cooper Station, New York NY 10276. **Tel** (212)206-8900, FAX (212)645-2459. **(Subscription address:** International Publishers Distributor at one of the following addresses: 820 Town Center Drive, Langhorne, PA 19047; or PO Box 90, Reading Berkshire RG1 8JL UK; or Kent Ridge PO Box 1180, Singapore 9111, Republic of Singapore**)** Documents available from Ask*IEEE.
**Ind/Abst** INSPEC; Math. Rev.; Zentralbl. Math. Ihre Grenzgeb.

CN/0848-7499
**MATHEMATICS AND SCIENCES BULLETIN.** [Math. sci. bull.]. **Added/Corp** Alberta. Student Evaluation and Records. (1989/1990)-. Bulletin. English. **DD** 500.71/27123. ***Continues*** *Mathematics & Sciences., 0848-7480.*

US
**MATHEMATICS AND STATISTICS RESEARCH DEPARTMENT PROGRESS REPORT. See** Mathematics-Abstracting, Bibliographies and Statistics.

CN/0823-1117
**MATHEMATICS COUNCIL NEWSLETTER (1983).** (MATHEMATICS COUNCIL NEWSLETTER.). [Math. Counc. newsl.]. **VFOAT** MCATA Newsletter. **VAT** Mathematics Council Alberta Teachers' Association Newsletter. Vol. 1, No. 1 (Jan. 1983)-. Newsletter. English. ir (10 times a year). 25.00Can$ with Delta-K subscription. Alberta Teachers Association, 11010-142 Street, Barnett House, Edmonton Alberta T5N 2R1 Canada. **Tel** (403)453-2411. **DD** 510/.6/07123. **Circ:** 630 (ctrl). ***Absorbed*** *Delta, 0319-8367.*

II/0047-6269
**MATHEMATICS EDUCATION, THE.** [Math. educ.]. (19??)-. Periodical. English. qt (Mar., June, Sept., Dec.). $25.00. J B Prasad Editor, Nirala Nagar PO, Siwan 841226 Saran Bihar India. **(Subscription address:** Prints India, 11 Darya Ganj, New Delhi 110002 India.**) LC** QA1; .M41113. **DD** 510/.5.
**Ind/Abst** Math. Rev.; Zentralbl. Math. Ihre Grenzgeb.

AT/1033-2170
**MATHEMATICS EDUCATION RESEARCH JOURNAL.** [Math. educ. res. j.]. (1989)-. Periodical. English. Three times a year. 75.00Aus$ (institutions), 40.00Aus$ (individuals) Australia; 85.00Aus$ (institutions), 50.00Aus$ (individuals) other. Macquarie University / School of EducationMERGA, MERGA Dr. M. Mitchelmore, NSW 2109 Australia. **Tel** 011 61 2 8058655. **DD** 510.7094. ***Continues*** *Research in Mathematics Education in Australia, 0812-7859.*
**Ind/Abst** Aust. Educ. Index.

UK/0305-7259
**MATHEMATICS IN SCHOOL.** [Math. sch.]. **Added/Corp** Mathematical Association. Vol. 1 (Nov. 1971)-. Periodical. English. Five times a year. £36.00 Europe; £39.00 Other (Institutions). Longman Group Ltd., Fourth Avenue, Longman House, Harlow Essex CM19 5SR England. **Tel** 011 44 279 429655, FAX 011 44 279 431059, telex 81259. **ED** David Neal, Ken Brown, John Bradshaw, Lesley Jones, Michael Cornelius. **[CCC].** Index available. **Bk Rev. Ad Acc. Circ:** 7,800. available on microfilm and microfiche from University Microfilms International (UMI).
**Desc:** Provides a specialist service to mathematics teachers of the 7-16 age group, with practical advice on teaching methods and ideas for class work.

**Ind/Abst** Br. Educ. Index; Curr. Index J. Educ.; Educ. Index; School Organ. Manage. Abstr.; Tech. Educ. Train. Abstr.

US/0076-5392
**MATHEMATICS IN SCIENCE AND ENGINEERING.** [Math. sci. eng.]. Vol. 1 (1961)-. Monographic series. English. ir. Price varies per volume. Academic Press, Inc., 6277 Sea Harbor Drive, Orlando FL 32887. **Tel** (800)543-9534, (407)345-4100, FAX (407)363-9661. **ED** Yoshikazu Sawaragi, Hirotaka Namayama and Tetsuyo Tanino.
**Ind/Abst** Math. Rev.; Zentralbl. Math. Ihre Grenzgeb.

US/0091-7214
**MATHEMATICS INTERNATIONAL.** (MATHEMATICS INTERNATIONAL MICROFORM.). Vol. 2 (1981)-. Monographic series. English (Russian). ir. Price varies per volume. Gordon & Breach Science Publishers, Inc., PO Box 786, Cooper Station, New York NY 10276. **Tel** (212)206-8900, FAX (212)645-2459. **(Subscription address:** Gordon & Breach Science Publishers / England, PO Box 90, Reading RG1 8JL England.) ***Continues*** *Mathematics International.*

JA/0916-6009
**MATHEMATICS JOURNAL OF TOYAMA UNIVERSITY.** [Math. j. Toyama Univ.]. **Added/Corp** Toyama Daigaku. Sugakuka. Vol. 13 (1990)-. English. an. Department of Mathematics / Toyama University, Faculty of Science, Gofuku Toyama 930 Japan. **Tel** 0764 41-1271, FAX 0764 41-2972. **ED** N Kazamaki, M Suzuki, Y Watanabe and N Yoshida. **LC** QA1; .M833. **CODEN** MJTUEG. Documents available from Ask*IEEE. ***Continues*** *Mathematics Reports, Toyama University, 0386-832X.*
**Ind/Abst** INSPEC (1990-); Math. Rev.; Zentralbl. Math. Ihre Grenzgeb.

US
**MATHEMATICS LECTURE SERIES.** (1973)-. Monographic series. English. ir. Price varies per volume. Publish or Perish Inc., PO Box 27703, Houston TX 77027.
**Ind/Abst** Math. Rev. (1987-); Zentralbl. Math. Ihre Grenzgeb.

US/0025-570X
**MATHEMATICS MAGAZINE.** [Math. mag.]. **Added/Corp** Mathematical Association of America. Vol. 21 (Sept./Oct. 1947)-. Periodical. English. Five times a year. $85.00. Mathematical Association of America, 1529 18th Street Northwest, Washington DC 20036. **Tel** (202)387-5200, (800)331-1622, FAX (202)265-2384. **ED** Gerald Alexanderson. **CODEN** MAMGA8. **[CCC].** cum. index. **Bk Rev. Ad Acc. Circ:** 12,000. available on microfilm and microfiche from University Microfilms International (UMI). Documents available from UMI Article Clearinghouse. ***Continues*** *National Mathematics Magazine.*
**Desc:** Covers expository articles, problems and solutions. Provides insight into the history and application of mathematics and points out the challenge and enjoyment in doing mathematics.
**Ind/Abst** Acad. Abstr. Full Text Elite (July 1990-); Acad. Abstr. (July 1990-); Acad. Ind. [Computer File] (1992-); Acad. Search (July 1990-); Curr. Index J. Educ.; Expand. Acad. Index (1989-); Gen. Sci. Index; Gen. Sci. Source (Jul. 1990-); INFO-SOUTH Abstr.; Int. Aerosp. Abstr.; Mag. Search; Math. Rev.; Newsp. Period. Abstr. (1989-); Zentralbl. Math. Ihre Grenzgeb.

US/0025-5718
**MATHEMATICS OF COMPUTATION.** [Math. comput.]. **Added/Corp** National Research Council (U.S.). Division of Mathematics. American Mathematical Society. Vol. 14, No. 69 (Jan. 1960)-. Periodical. English. qt (4 issues). $274.00 (print or microfiche). American Mathematical Society, PO Box 6248, Providence RI 02940-6248. **Tel** (800)321-4267, (401)455-4000, FAX (401)331-3842, telex 797192. **(Subscription address:** American Mathematical Society, PO Box 5904, Boston MA 02206-5904.) **LC** QA47; .M29. **DD** 510. **NLM** W1 MA95. **CODEN** MCMPAF. **[CCC].** Index available (bound in Oct. issue). cum. index. **Bk Rev. Ad Acc. Pr Rev. Circ:** 1,800. available on microfilm and microfiche from University Microfilms International (UMI). Documents available from The Genuine Article, Ask*IEEE. ***Continues*** *Mathematical Tables and Other Aids to Computation, 0891-6837.*
**Desc:** Devoted to papers on advances in numerical analysis, application of computational methods, mathematical tables and other aids to computation.
**Ind/Abst** Abstr. Bull. Inst. Pap. Sci. Tech.; Compumath Citation Index [Full Cov.]; Comput. Rev. (1968-); Curr. Contents Phys. Chem. Earth Sci.; Energy Res. Abstr.; INSPEC (1968-); Int. Aerosp. Abstr.; Math. Rev.; Res. Alert [Full Cov.]; Sci. Cit. Index; SCISEARCH; SPIN (1977-); Stat. Theory Method Abstr. (1961-1963, 1969); Zentralbl. Math. Ihre Grenzgeb.

US/0932-4194
**MATHEMATICS OF CONTROL, SIGNALS, AND SYSTEMS : MCSS.** **See** Engineering.

US/0271-1982
**MATHEMATICS OF FINITE ELEMENTS AND APPLICATIONS, THE.** (THE MATHEMATICS OF FINITE ELEMENTS AND APPLICATIONS : PROCEEDINGS OF THE BRUNEL UNIVERSITY CONFERENCE OF THE INSTITUTE OF MATHEMATICS AND ITS APPLICATIONS HELD IN ...). [Math. finite elem. appl.]. **Added/Corp** Institute of Mathematics and its Applications. Brunel University. Institute of Computational Mathematics. **VFOAT** MAFELAP. (Apr. 1972)-. Academic Scholarly Publication. English. ir. Academic Press, Inc., 6277 Sea Harbor Drive, Orlando FL 32887. **Tel** (800)543-9534, (407)345-4100, FAX (407)363-9661. **ED** J. R. Whiteman. **LC** TA347.F5; C64a. **DD** 620/.001/51535. **CODEN** MFEADM. Documents available from CASDDS.
**Ind/Abst** Chem. Abstr. (1973-1978).

US/0364-765X
**MATHEMATICS OF OPERATIONS RESEARCH.** [Math. oper. res.]. **Added/Corp** Institute of Management Sciences. Operations Research Society of America. Vol. 1 (Feb. 1976)-. Periodical. English. qt. $111.00 US; $119.00 other. Institute of Management Sciences, 290 Westminster Street, Providence RI 02903. **Tel** (401)274-2525, FAX (401)274-3189. **ED** Jan Karel Lenstra. **LC** T57.6.A1; M38. **DD** 658.4/034. **CODEN** MOREDQ. **[CCC]. Pr Rev. Circ:** 2,550. available on microfilm and microfiche from University Microfilms International (UMI). Documents available from Article Express International, The Genuine Article, Ask*IEEE, UMI Article Clearinghouse.
**Desc:** Publishes significant research and reviews that have substantial mathematical interest and relevance to operations research and management science.
**Ind/Abst** ABI/INFORM Glob. Ed.; ABI Inform Ondisc (May 1976-); Acad. Search (July 1993-); ACM Guide Comput. Lit.; Bioeng. Abstr.; Biostatistica; Bus. Index (1985-); Bus. Source (Jul. 1993-); Compumath Citation Index [Full Cov.]; Comput. Rev.; Contents Pages Manage.; Curr. Contents Phys. Chem. Earth Sci.; Ei Page One (1984); Eng. Index Annu.; Gen. BusinessFile (1985-); Gen. Period. Index (1985-); INFO-SOUTH Abstr.; INSPEC (Aug. 1976-); Int. Abstr. Oper. Res. [Full Cov.]; Mag. Search; Math. Rev.; Oper. Res./Manag. Sci.; Pollut. Abstr. Indexes; Qual. Control Appl. Stat.; Res. Alert [Full Cov.]; Sci. Cit. Index; SCISEARCH; Soc. Plann. Policy Dev. Abstr.; Soc. Sci. Cit. Index [Select. Cov.]; Zentralbl. Math. Ihre Grenzgeb.

US/0025-5726
**MATHEMATICS OF THE USSR : IZVESTIJA.** ***Title Change.*** [Math. USSR, Izv.]. **Added/Corp** American Mathematical Society. **VAT** Mathematics of the Union of Soviet Socialist Republics. Izvestija. Vol. 1-39 (Jan./Feb. 1967)-(1992). Periodical. English (Russian). bm (6 issues). American Mathematical Society, PO Box 6248, Providence RI 02940-6248. **Tel** (800)321-4267, (401)455-4000, FAX (401)331-3842, telex 797192. **LC** QA1; .M8328. **CODEN** MUSIAE. **[CCC].** Index available. **Pr Rev.** available on microfilm from University Microfilms International (UMI). Documents available from The Genuine Article. ***Continued by*** *Izvestiia RossiĖiskoĖi Akademii nauk. Seriia Matematicheskaia. English. Izvestiya. Mathematics, 1064-5632.*
**Desc:** Devoted to current areas of pure mathematics research.
**Ind/Abst** Compumath Citation Index [Full Cov.]; Int. Abstr. Oper. Res. [Select. Cov.]; Math. Rev.; Res. Alert [Full Cov.]; Sci. Cit. Index (19??-19??); SCISEARCH; Zentralbl. Math. Ihre Grenzgeb.

US/0025-5734
**MATHEMATICS OF THE USSR : SBORNIK.** ***Title Change.*** **Added/Corp** American Mathematical Society. Akademiia Nauk SSSR. **VAT** Mathematics of the Union of Soviet Socialist Republics. Sbornik. (Jan. 1967)-(1993). Periodical. English (translations available in Russian). bm (6 issues). American Mathematical Society, PO Box 6248, Providence RI 02940-6248. **Tel** (800)321-4267, (401)455-4000, FAX (401)331-3842, telex 797192. **LC** QA1; .M4112. **CODEN** MUSBBS. **[CCC].** Index available. **Pr Rev.** available on microfilm and microfiche from University Microfilms International (UMI). Documents available from The Genuine Article. ***Continued by*** *Matematicheskii Sbornik. English. Sbornik. Mathematics, 1064-5616.*
**Desc:** Cover-to-cover translation of Matematicheskii Sbornik.
**Ind/Abst** Compumath Citation Index [Full Cov.]; Curr. Contents Phys. Chem. Earth Sci.; Math. Rev.; Res. Alert [Full Cov.]; Sci. Cit. Index (19??-19??); SCISEARCH; Zentralbl. Math. Ihre Grenzgeb.

UK/0957-1280
**MATHEMATICS REVIEW.** ***Ceased.*** [Math. rev.]. (1990)-(199?). English. Four times a year (Feb., April, Sept., Nov.). Philip Allan Publishers Ltd, Market Place, Deddington Oxford, OX15 0SE England. **Tel** 011 44 869 38652, FAX 011 44 869 38803. **DD** 510.

II/0025-5742
**MATHEMATICS STUDENT (AHMEDABAD), THE.** (THE MATHEMATICS STUDENT.). [Math. stud.]. **Added/Corp** Indian Mathematical Society. Vol. 1 (March 1933)-. Periodical. English. qt. $70.00. **(Subscription address:** Prints India, 11 Darya Ganj, New Delhi 110002 India.) **ED** A M Vaidya. **LC** QA1; .I53. **DD** 510.5. **CODEN** MTHSBH. **Bk Rev. Ad Acc. Circ:** 1,000 (ctrl). ***Continues in part*** *Journal of the Indian Mathematical Society, 0019-5839.*
**Ind/Abst** Math. Rev.; Zentralbl. Math. Ihre Grenzgeb.

US/0025-5769
**MATHEMATICS TEACHER, THE.** [Math. teach.]. **Added/Corp** National Council of Teachers of Mathematics. Association of Teachers of Mathematics in the Middle States and Maryland. Association of Mathematical Teachers in New England. Vol. 1 (Sept. 1908)-. Periodical. English. Nine times a year. $50.00 (institutions), $45.00 (individuals). National Council of Teachers of Mathematics, 1906 Association Drive, Reston VA 22091. **Tel** (703)620-9840, FAX (703)476-2970. **ED** Harry B. Tunis. **LC** QA1; .N28. **DD** 510/.7. Index available. cum. index. **Bk Rev. Ad Acc. Pr Rev. Circ:** 50,000 (ctrl). available on microfilm and microfiche from University Microfilms International (UMI); available on CD-ROM. Documents available from UMI Article Clearinghouse.
**Desc:** Devoted to the improvement of mathematics instruction in junior high schools, senior high schools, junior colleges and teacher education colleges. Articles cover mathematics content and methods of instruction. Reproducible worksheets, courseware reviews and reviews of new products are also included.
**Ind/Abst** Acad. Ind. [Computer File] (1992-); Comput. Rev.; Contents Pages Educ.; Curr. Index J. Educ.; Educ. Index; Educ. Adm. Abstr.; Except. Child Educ. Resour. (19??-19??); Expand. Acad. Index (1992-); Hum. Resour. Abstr. (?-?); Math. Rev.; Med. Rev. Dig.; Newsp. Period. Abstr. (1989-).

UK/0025-5785
**MATHEMATICS TEACHING.** [Math. teach.]. **Added/Corp** Association of Teachers of Mathematics. **VFOAT** MT. No. 1 (1955)-. Periodical. English. Four times a year. £55.00 (institutions), £21.00 (individuals) surface mail; £58.00 (institutions), £41.00 (individuals) airmail. Association of Teachers of Math, 7 Shaftesbury Street, Derby DE3 8YB England. **Tel** 011 44 0332 346599. **ED** Tony Brown and Laurinda Brown. **Bk Rev. Ad Acc. Circ:** 4,000 (ctrl). available on microfilm and microfiche from University Microfilms International (UMI).
**Desc:** Issues relating to the teaching and learning of mathematics.
**Ind/Abst** Acad. Search (July 1993-); Br. Educ. Index; Curr. Index J. Educ.; Educ. Index; INFO-SOUTH Abstr.; Mag. Search; Res. High. Educ. Abstr.; Tech. Educ. Train. Abstr.

●US/1072-0839
**MATHEMATICS TEACHING IN THE MIDDLE SCHOOL.** **Added/Corp** National Council of Teachers of Mathematics. (1994)-. Periodical. English. qt. $50.00. National Council of Teachers of Mathematics, 1906 Association Drive, Reston VA 22091. **Tel** (703)620-9840, FAX (703)476-2970.

II
**MATHEMATICS TODAY.** **Added/Corp** Professor P.C. Vaidya Sanman Nidhi Trust. (198?)-. English. Twelve times a year. Rs30.00. Mathematics Today, Green Park Extension, New Delhi 110 016 India. **LC** QA1; .M835. **DD** 510/.5.
**Ind/Abst** Math. Rev. (1983-); Zentralbl. Math. Ihre Grenzgeb.

UK/0025-5793
**MATHEMATIKA.** [Mathematika]. **Added/Corp** University College, London. Dept. of Mathematics. Vol. 1, No. 1 (June 1954)-. Periodical. English. sa. £51.00. J W Arrowsmith Ltd, 71 Winterstoke Road, Bristol BS3 2NT England. **Tel** 011 44 272 667545, FAX 011 44 272 637829, telex 851 44246. **LC** QA1; .M84. **DD** 510.5. **CODEN** MTKAAB. Index available. cum. index. **Pr Rev. Circ:** 700 (ctrl). Documents available from The Genuine Article.
**Desc:** Research articles on pure and applied mathematics, short reviews of advanced books on mathematics.
**Ind/Abst** Compumath Citation Index [Full Cov.]; Curr. Contents Phys. Chem. Earth Sci.; Math. Rev.; Res. Alert [Full Cov.]; Sci. Cit. Index; SCISEARCH; Stat. Theory Method Abstr. (1969, 1973); Zentralbl. Math. Ihre Grenzgeb.

GW/0025-5807
**MATHEMATIKUNTERRICHT.** [Mathematikunterricht]. (1???)-. Periodical. German. bm. DM124.80 Germany; DM132.00 other. Erhard Friedrich Verlag, Postfach 100150, D 30917 Seelze Germany. **Tel** 011 49 511 4000452. **UDC** 372.851. **[CCC].**

CN/1187-4821
**MATHEMATIQUE 3031, DEFINITION DU DOMAINE, EXAMENS DE FIN D'ETUDES SECONDAIRES, DE JANVIER ... ET JUIN**. [Math. 3031 def. domaine exam. fin etud. second. janv. juin]. **Added/Corp** Nouveau-Brunswick. Direction des Programmes d'Etudes. **VAT** Mathematique Trois Mille Trente et un, Definition du Domaine, Eexamens de fin d'Etudes Secondaires, de Janvier et Juin. (1991)-. French. **DD** 510.

CN/1187-483X
**MATHEMATIQUE 3032, DEFINITION DU DOMAINE, EXAMENS DE FIN D'ETUDES SECONDAIRES, DE JANVIER ... ET JUIN**. [Math. 3032 defin. domaine exam. fin etud. second. janv. juin]. **Added/Corp** Nouveau-Brunswick. Direction des Programmes d'Etudes. **VAT** Mathematique Trois Mille Trente Deux, Definition du Domaine, Examens de Fin d'Etudes Secondaires, de Janvier et Juin. (1991)-. French. Ministere de l'Education, PO Box 804, Federicton New Brunswick Canada. **DD** 510.

BE
**MATHEMATIQUE ET PEDAGOGIE.** (1975). French. bm. 950.00FB. Societe Belge des Professeurs de Mathematique, 15 rue de la Halle, D-7000 Mons Belgium. **ED** J Bair. ***Continues*** *Mathematica & Paedagogia.*

FR
**MATHEMATIQUES, INFORMATIQUE ET SCIENCES HUMAINES / CENTRE D'ANALYSE ET DE MATHEMATIQUE SOCIALES, LABORATOIRE MIXTE DE L'ECOLE DES HAUTES ETUDES EN SCIENCES SOCIALES ET DU CENTRE NATIONAL DE LA RECHERCHE SCIENTIFIQUE.** **Added/Corp** Ecole des Hautes Etudes en Sciences Sociales. Centre d'Analyse et de Mathematique Sociales. No. 101 (1988)-. Periodical. French. Four times a year. Price varies. Editions du CNRS, 22 rue Saint Armand, F 75015 Paris France. **Tel** 011 33 1 45075050. **(Subscription address:** Regisseur de Revue Mish CAMS, 54 BD Raspail, 75270 Paris Cedex 06 France.**)** **LC** QA1; .M846. **DD** 519.2/05. **CODEN** MSHUEJ. ***Continues*** *Mathematiques et Sciences Humaines, 0025-5815.*

GW/0025-5831
**MATHEMATISCHE ANNALEN.** [Math. ann.]. Vol. 1 (1869)-. Periodical. English (German, French and Italian). Twelve times a year. DM3300.00. Springer-Verlag GmbH & Company KG, Heidelberger Platz 3, D 14197 Berlin Germany. **Tel** 011 49 30 8207223, FAX 011 49 30 8214091, telex 183 319 SPBLN D. **(Subscription address:** Springer Verlag New York Inc. / for North America, 44 Hartz Way, Secaucus NJ 07096.**)** **ED** H Amann, H Bauer Erlangen, J P Bourguignon, H Foellmer, H Grauert, G Harder, F Hirzebruch, N J Hitchin, M Kreck, R Remmert, and W Scharlau. **LC** QA1; .M86. **CODEN** MAANA3. **[CCC].** cum. index. **Pr Rev.** available on microfilm and microfiche from University Microfilms International (UMI). Documents available from The Genuine Article.
**Desc:** Serves specialists in a broad range of fields. Although basically unspecialized, the journal has in recent years earned a high regard for its contributions in the field of analysis.
**Ind/Abst** Compumath Citation Index [Full Cov.]; Curr. Contents Phys. Chem. Earth Sci.; Int. Aerosp. Abstr.; Math. Rev.; Res. Alert [Full Cov.]; Sci. Cit. Index; SCISEARCH; Stat. Theory Method Abstr. (1959-1963, 1967, 1970-1971, 1973, 1977-1980, 1982, 1986); Zentralbl. Math. Ihre Grenzgeb.

GW/0076-5430
**MATHEMATISCHE LEHRBUECHER UND MONOGRAPHIEN. ABTEILUNG 1. MATHEMATISCHE LEHRBUECHER.** (MATHEMATISCHE LEHRBUECHER UND MONOGRAPHIEN. 1. ABTEILUNG, MATHEMATISCHE LEHRBUECHER / HERAUSGEGEBEN VON DER DEUTSCHEN AKADEMIE DER WISSENSCHAFTEN ZU BERLIN, FORSCHUNGSINSTITUT FUER MATHEMATIK.). [Math. LehrbEuch. Monogr., Abt. 1]. **Added/Corp** Deutsche Akademie der Wissenschaften zu Berlin. Forschungsinstitut fuer Mathematik. Deutsche Akademie der Wissenschaften zu Berlin. Institute fuer Mathematik. Deutsche Akademie der Wissenschaften zu Berlin. Zentralinstitut fuer Mathematik und Mechanik. **VFOAT** Mathematische Lehrbuecher. (1952)-. Monographic series. German. ir. Price varies per volume. Akademie-Verlag GmbH, Muehlenstrasse 33 34, D 13162 Berlin Germany. **Tel** 011 49 30 47889300, FAX 011 49 30 47889357. **(Subscription address:** VCH Publishers Inc., 303 Northwest 12th Avenue, Journals Department, Deerfield FL 33442.**)**
**Ind/Abst** Math. Rev.; Zentralbl. Math. Ihre Grenzgeb.

GW/0076-5430
**MATHEMATISCHE LEHRBUECHER UND MONOGRAPHIEN. ABTEILUNG 2. MATHEMATISCHE MONOGRAPHIEN.** (MATHEMATISCHE LEHRBUECHER UND MONOGRAPHIEN. II. ABTEILUNG, MATHEMATISCHE MONOGRAPHIEN.). [Math. Lehrbuech. Monogr. Abt. 2]. **VFOAT** Mathematische Monographien. (1952)-. Monographic series. German. ir. Price varies per volume. Akademie-Verlag GmbH, Muehlenstrasse 33 34, D 13162 Berlin Germany. **Tel** 011 49 30 47889300, FAX 011 49 30 47889357. **(Subscription address:** VCH Publishers Inc., 303 Northwest 12th Avenue, Journals Department, Deerfield FL 33442.**)**
**Ind/Abst** Math. Rev.; Zentralbl. Math. Ihre Grenzgeb.

GW/0025-584X
**MATHEMATISCHE NACHRICHTEN.** [Math. Nachr.]. **Added/Corp** Deutsche Akademie der Wissenschaften zu Berlin. Forschungsinstitut fuer Mathematik. Berlin. Universitat. Mathematisches Institut. Deutsche Akademie der Wissenschaften zu Berlin. Deutsche Akademie der Wissenschaften zu Berlin. Zentralinstitut fuer Mathematik und Mechanik. Vol. 1 (May 1948)-. Periodical. German. bm. $1200.00. Akademie-Verlag GmbH, Muehlenstrasse 33 34, D 13162 Berlin Germany. **Tel** 011 49 30 47889300, FAX 011 49 30 47889357. **(Subscription address:** VCH Publishers Inc., 303 Northwest 12th Avenue, Journals Department, Deerfield FL 33442.**)** **LC** QA1; .B15. **DD** 510.5. **CODEN** MTMNAQ. cum. index. **Pr Rev.** Documents available from The Genuine Article.
**Ind/Abst** Compumath Citation Index [Full Cov.]; Curr. Contents Phys. Chem. Earth Sci.; Math. Rev.; Res. Alert [Full Cov.]; SCISEARCH; Stat. Theory Method Abstr. (1969-1970, 1972-1984, 1987); Zentralbl. Math. Ihre Grenzgeb.

GW/0076-5449
**MATHEMATISCHE SCHULERBUCHEREI.** [Math. Schulerbuch.]. (1954)-. Monographic series. German. ir. Price varies per volume. Deutscher Verlag der Wissenschaften, Taubenstrasste 10, D 10117 Berlin Germany. **Tel** 011 49 30 2291146.
**Ind/Abst** Math. Rev.; Zentralbl. Math. Ihre Grenzgeb.

GW/0720-728X
**MATHEMATISCHE SEMESTERBERICHTE.** [Math. Semesterber.]. Vol. 28, No. 1 (1981)-. Periodical. German. sa. DM84.00. Springer-Verlag GmbH & Company KG, Heidelberger Platz 3, D 14197 Berlin Germany. **Tel** 011 49 30 8207223, FAX 011 49 30 8214091, telex 183 319 SPBLN D. **(Subscription address:** Springer Verlag New York Inc. / for North America, 44 Hartz Way, Secaucus NJ 07096.**)** **ED** N Knoche. **[CCC].** ***Continues*** *Mathematisch-Physikalische Semesterberichte zur Pflege des Zusammenhangs von Schule und Universitat, 0340-4897.*
**Desc:** Contains articles from the research and applications of mathematics that are of importance to mathematicians covering the latest developments in this interdisciplinary field.
**Ind/Abst** Energy Res. Abstr. (March 1982-); Math. Rev.; Zentralbl. Math. Ihre Grenzgeb.

GW/0025-5874
**MATHEMATISCHE ZEITSCHRIFT.** [Math. z.]. (Jan. 1918)-. Periodical. German. Twelve times a year. DM2916.00. Springer-Verlag GmbH & Company KG, Heidelberger Platz 3, D 14197 Berlin Germany. **Tel** 011 49 30 8207223, FAX 011 49 30 8214091, telex 183 319 SPBLN D. **(Subscription address:** Springer Verlag New York Inc. / for North America, 44 Hartz Way, Secaucus NJ 07096.**)** **ED** E Becker, G Carlsson, K Diederich, G Faltings, H Heyer, J Jost, H Knoerrer, and E Zehnder. **LC** QA1; .M88. **CODEN** MAZEAX. **[CCC].** cum. index. **Pr Rev.** available on microfilm and microfiche from University Microfilms International (UMI). Documents available from The Genuine Article.
**Desc:** Contributions range from topics such as algebra to analysis, including applied disciplines.
**Ind/Abst** Compumath Citation Index [Full Cov.]; Curr. Contents Phys. Chem. Earth Sci.; Int. Aerosp. Abstr.; Math. Rev.; Res. Alert [Full Cov.]; Sci. Cit. Index; SCISEARCH; Stat. Theory Method Abstr. (1959-1963, 1966, 1970, 1972-1973, 1976-1977, 1979-1982, 1984, 1986-1987); Zentralbl. Math. Ihre Grenzgeb.

CN/0705-0410
**MATHNEWS.** (MATHNEWS : A NEW WEEKLY PUBLISHED AT THE UNIVERSITY OF WATERLOO.). [MathNEWS]. Jan. 25, 1973-. Periodical. English. wk. Free. MathNews M&C 3038, University of Waterloo, Waterloo Ontario N2L 3G1 Canada. **DD** 378.713/44.

UK/0959-3950
**MATHS & STATS.** [Maths stats]. **VFOAT** Maths and Stats. (1990)-. Periodical. English. qt. Free. CTI, c/o Faculty of Education, University of Birmingham, Birmingham B15 2TT England. **Tel** 011 44 21 414 4800, FAX 021 414 4865. **DD** 510. Index available. cum. index. **Ad Acc. Circ:** 1,500 (ctrl).
**Desc:** Articles and reviews describing the use of computer software in the teaching of mathematics and statistics in higher education.

US
**MATHSCI DISC [COMPUTER FILE].** **Added/Corp** SilverPlatter Information, Inc. American Mathematical Society. **VFOAT** Math Sci Disc. (1940)-. English. sa. $6,750.00 (single user), $10,125.00 (multi-user). Silverplatter Information Inc., 100 River Ridge Drive, Norwood MA 02062. **Tel** (800)343-0064, (617)769-2599, FAX (617)235-1715.
**Desc:** Consists of citations to the world's research literature in mathematics and related areas. Compiled from: Mathematical Reviews and Current Mathematical Publications (1940-1979) of Reviews and Citations compiled from the MathSci online database subfiles, Mathematical Reviews, and current Mathematical Publications, all produced by the American Mathematical Society.

●US/1062-7030
**MATHUSER.** [Mathuser]. **Added/Corp** Wolfram Research, Inc. **VFOAT** Math User. (Spring/Summer 1992)-. Periodical. English. qt. $40.00. Wolfram Research, 100 Trade Center Drive, Champaign IL 61820. **DD** 005.

UK/0025-5998
**MATRIX AND TENSOR QUARTERLY, THE.** ***Ceased.*** [Matrix tensor q.]. (1950)-?. Periodical. English. qt. Power System Studies, PO Box 27, Stafford ST17 4LN England. **LC** QA401; .M44. **DD** 512.896. **CODEN** MATQA5. Documents available from Article Express International, Ask*IEEE.
**Ind/Abst** Bioeng. Abstr.; Ei Page One; Eng. Index Annu.; INSPEC (1968-Vol. 34, No. 4); Math. Rev.; Stat. Theory Method Abstr. (1969).

FR/0249-633X
**MEMOIRE DE LA SOCIETE MATHEMATIQUE DE FRANCE.** [Mem. Soc. math. Fr.]. **Added/Corp** Societe Mathematique de France. Centre National de la Recherche Scientifique (France). No. 1 (1980)-. Periodical. French (English). Four times a year. comes only with Bulletin de la Societe Mathematique de France. Societe Mathematique de France EC Norm Sup Tour L, 1 rue Maurice Arnoux, 92120 Montrouge France. **Tel** 011 33 1 40848054, or 91267464, FAX 011 33 1 40848052, or 91411751. ***Continues*** *Memoire (Societe Mathematique de France).*
**Ind/Abst** Math. Rev.; Zentralbl. Math. Ihre Grenzgeb.

US/0065-9266
**MEMOIRS OF THE AMERICAN MATHEMATICAL SOCIETY.** [Mem. Am. Math. Soc.]. **Main/Corp** American Mathematical Society. No. 1 (1950)-. Periodical. English. bm. $369.00. American Mathematical Society, PO Box 6248, Providence RI 02940-6248. **Tel** (800)321-4267, (401)455-4000, FAX (401)331-3842, telex 797192. **(Subscription address:** American Mathematical Society, PO Box 5904, Boston MA 02206-5904.**)** **LC** QA3; .A57. **DD** 510.82. **CODEN** MAMCAU. **[CCC].** **Pr Rev.** Documents available from The Genuine Article.
**Desc:** Devoted to research in pure and applied mathematics.
**Ind/Abst** Compumath Citation Index [Full Cov.]; Curr. Contents Phys. Chem. Earth Sci.; Int. Aerosp. Abstr.; Math. Rev. (1984-); Res. Alert [Full Cov.]; Sci. Cit. Index; SCISEARCH; Zentralbl. Math. Ihre Grenzgeb.

JA/0389-0252
**MEMOIRS OF THE FACULTY OF SCIENCE, KOCHI UNIVERSITY. SERIES A, MATHEMATICS.** [Mem. Fac. Sci., Kochi Univ., Ser. A, Math.]. **Added/Corp** Kochi Daigaku. Rigakubu. **VFOAT** Kochi Daigaku Rigakuby Kiyo. Sugaku. Vol. 1 (Mar. 1980)-. Periodical. English. Kochi Daigaku Rigakubu, (Faculty of Science, Kochi University), 5-1, Akebonocho 2 Chome, Kochishi, Kochiken 780, Japan. **LC** QA1; .M927.
**Ind/Abst** Math. Rev.; Zentralbl. Math. Ihre Grenzgeb.

JA/0373-6385
**MEMOIRS OF THE FACULTY OF SCIENCE, KYUSHU UNIVERSITY. SERIES A, MATHEMATICS.** ***Title Change.*** [Mem. Fac. Sci., Kyushu Univ., Ser. A]. **Added/Corp** Kyushu Daigaku. Rigakubu. **VFOAT** Kyushu Daigaku Rigakubu Kiyo; Mathematics. Vol. 4, No. 1 (July 1949)-(1993). Periodical. English (French and German). sa. Kyushu University / Faculty of Science, 10-1 Hakozaki 6 Chome Higasiku, Fukuokasi Fukuokaken 812 Japan. **LC** QA1; .F76. **DD** 510/.5. **CODEN** MFKAAF. **Circ:** 700. ***Continues*** *Memoirs of the Faculty of Science, Kyushu Imperial University. Series A, Mathematics.* ***Continued by*** *Kyushu Journal of Mathematics.*
**Ind/Abst** Abstr. J. Earthq. Eng. (?-?); Math. Rev. (?-?); Stat. Theory Method Abstr. (1959-1966); Zentralbl. Math. Ihre Grenzgeb. (?-?).

JA/0388-4112
**MEMOIRS OF THE NATIONAL DEFENSE ACADEMY. MATHEMATICS, PHYSICS, CHEMISTRY, AND ENGINEERING.** [Mem. Natl. Def. Acad., Math., phys., chem., eng.]. **Added/Corp** Boei Daigakko (Japan). **VFOAT** Boei Daigakko Kiyo. Rikogaku Hen; Mathematics, Physics, Chemistry, and Engineering. (1980)-. Periodical. English. qt. National Defense Academy, Hashirimizu 1-10-20, Yokosuka 239 Japan. **LC** Q1; .B63a. **DD** 505. **CODEN** MNDEDHMDPCAW. Documents available from CASDDS. ***Continues*** *Boei Daigakko (Japan). Memoirs of the Defense Academy: Mathematics, Physics, Chemistry, and Engineering.*
**Ind/Abst** Chem. Abstr.; Math. Rev.; Zentralbl. Math. Ihre Grenzgeb.

IT
**MEMORIE LINCEE. MATEMATICA E APPLICAZIONI / CLASSE DI SCIENZE FISICHE, MATEMATICHE E NATURALI.** **Added/Corp** Accademia Nazionale dei Lincei. Classe di Scienze Fisiche, Matematiche e Naturali. **VFOAT** Matematica e Applicazioni; Mem. Mat. Acc. Lincei. Ser. 9, Vol. 1, (1990)-. Monographic series. Italian (English).

Price varies per volume. **LC** QA1; .M84. ***Continues in part*** *Memorie (Accademia Nazionale dei Lincei. Classe di Scienze Fisiche, Matematiche e Naturali).*

GW/0170-9321
**METHODEN UND VERFAHREN DER MATHEMATISCHEN PHYSIK.** [Methoden Verfahren math. Phys.]. (1969)-. Periodical. Multiple languages. ir. DM59.00. Verlag Peter Lang GmbH, Eschborner Landstrasse 42-50, D 60489 Frankfurt Germany. **Tel** 011 49 69 7807050. **ED** Bruno Brosowski and Erich Martensen. **UDC** 53:51-7.
**Desc:** Original papers on Navier-Stokes approximations, spline functions, finite element methods in chemical industry, characterization of optimal points etc.
**Ind/Abst** Zentralbl. Math. Ihre Grenzgeb.

RU/0136-1228
**METODY DISKRETNOGO ANALIZA V ...; SBORNIK TRUDOV.** **Added/Corp** Institut Matematiki (Akademiia Nauk SSSR. Sibirskoe Otdelenie). **VAT** Metody Diskretnogo Analiza ... . (1976)-. Periodical. Russian. **LC** QA1; .D53. ***Continues*** *Diskretnyi Analiz.*
**Ind/Abst** Math. Rev.; Zentralbl. Math. Ihre Grenzgeb.

GW/0026-1335
**METRIKA.** [Metrika]. (1958)-. Periodical. English (German). Six times a year. DM430.00. Physica-Verlag GmbH & Company, Postfach 105280, D-69042 Heidelberg Germany. **Tel** 06221 487-492, FAX 06221 487177 und 487366, telex 461723 sphdb-d. **(Subscription address:** Springer Verlag New York Inc. / for North America, 44 Hartz Way, Secaucus NJ 07096.**)** **ED** W. Uhlmann and O. Krafft. **LC** QA276.A1; M4. **DD** 519.5/05. **CODEN** MTRKA8. **[CCC]. Bk Rev. Ad Acc. Circ:** 700 (ctrl). Documents available from Ask*IEEE. ***Formed by the union of*** *Mitteilungsblatt fuer Mathematische Statistik* ***and*** *Statistische Vierteljahrsschrift, 0255-7479.*
**Desc:** A journal specialized in the field of statistical method and mathematical statistics, in particular in statistical quality control, sampling theory, design of experiments and foundations of statistics. Fields of interest are statistics, stochastics, mathematics, and economics.
**Ind/Abst** Biostatistica; Curr. Index Stat.; Energy Res. Abstr.; INSPEC (1968-); Int. Abstr. Oper. Res. [Select. Cov.]; Math. Rev.; Qual. Control Appl. Stat.; Soc. Res. Methodol. Abstr. (1988-); Stat. Theory Method Abstr. (1959-1963, 1966-1984, 1987); Zentralbl. Math. Ihre Grenzgeb.

US/0026-2285
**MICHIGAN MATHEMATICAL JOURNAL, THE.** [Mich. math. j.]. Vol. 1 (1952)-. Periodical. English. Three times a year. $50.00 (individuals); $90.00 (institutions). University of Michigan / Department of Mathematics, 3220 Angell Hall, Ann Arbor MI 48109-1003. **Tel** (313)747-4462, FAX (313)763-0937. **ED** Douglas G. Dickson. **LC** QA1; .M96. **DD** 510.5. Index available. **Pr Rev. Circ:** 900. Documents available from The Genuine Article.
**Desc:** Research articles on mathematics.
**Ind/Abst** Compumath Citation Index [Full Cov.]; Int. Aerosp. Abstr.; Math. Rev.; Res. Alert [Full Cov.]; Sci. Cit. Index (19??-19??); SCISEARCH; Zentralbl. Math. Ihre Grenzgeb.

UK/0267-5501
**MICROMATH : A JOURNAL OF THE ASSOCIATION OF TEACHERS OF MATHEMATICS.** Vol. 1, No. 1 (1985)-. Academic Scholarly Publication. English. Three times a year. £38.00 (individual), £55.00 (institution). Basil Blackwell Publishers Ltd, 108 Cowley Road, Oxford 0X4 1JF England. **Tel** 011 44 865 791100, FAX 011 44 865 791347, telex 837022 OXBOOK G. **(Subscription address:** Marston Book Services Ltd., PO Box 87, Oxford OX2 0DT England.**)** **ED** Laurinda Brown and Tony Brown. **Bk Rev. Ad Acc. Circ:** 5,000. available on microfilm and microfiche from University Microfilms International (UMI).
**Ind/Abst** Br. Educ. Index.

US/0899-6180
**MISSOURI JOURNAL OF MATHEMATICAL SCIENCES.** [Mo. j. math. sci.]. **Added/Corp** Central Missouri State University. Department of Mathematics and Computer Science. **VFOAT** MJMS. Vol. 0, No. 1 (Fall 1988)-. Periodical. English. Three times a year (Feb., May, Oct.). $11.00 (one year), $17.00 (two year), $23.00 (three year) institutions; $6.00 (one year), $10.00 (two year), $14.00 (three year) individuals. Central Missouri State University / Mathematics & Science, Department of Mathematics and Sciences, Warrensburg MO 64093. **Tel** (816)429-4930. **ED** Terry Goodman. **DD** 510. **Ad Acc. Pr Rev. Circ:** 150.

GW/0340-4358
**MITTEILUNGEN DER MATHEMATISCHEN GESELLSCHAFT IN HAMBURG.** [Mitt. Math. Ges. Hamb.]. **Added/Corp** Mathematische Gesellschaft in Hamburg. (May 1881)-. German (English). ir. Mathematische Gesellschaft in Hamburg, Bundesstrasse 55, D 20146 Hamburg Germany. **Tel** 011 49 40 41235144. **ED** R. Carlsson. **CODEN** MNGBAK. Index available. cum. index. **Ad Acc. Circ:** 800 (ctrl).
**Desc:** Contains mathematical research, biographies of mathematicians, teaching of mathematics.
**Ind/Abst** Math. Rev.; Zentralbl. Math. Ihre Grenzgeb.

SZ/0042-3815
**MITTEILUNGEN DES VEREINIGUNG SCHWEIZERISCHER VERSICHERUNGSMATHEMATIKER.** **See** Insurance.

GW
**MITTEILUNGEN / GESELLSCHAFT FUER ANGEWANDTE MATHEMATIK UND MECHANIK.** **Added/Corp** Gesellschaft fuer Angewandte Mathematik und Mechanik. No. 1 (Mar. 1989)-. Periodical. German.
**Ind/Abst** Math. Rev.; Zentralbl. Math. Ihre Grenzgeb.

GW/0025-5866
**MMU, DER MATHEMATISCHE UND NATURWISSENSCHAFTLICHE UNTERRICHT.** (MATHEMATISCHE UND NATURWISSENSCHAFTLICHE UNTERRICHT.). [MNU, Math. naturwiss. Unterr.]. Vol. 1 (Sept. 1948)-. Academic Scholarly Publication. German. Eight times a year. DM82.00. Ferdinand Dummler Verlag, Postfach 1480, D 53004 Bonn Germany. **Tel** 011 49 228 223031. **CODEN** MNWUAL. **[CCC].** Documents available from CASDDS.
**Ind/Abst** Chem. Abstr.; Energy Res. Abstr. (March 1982-); Zentralbl. Math. Ihre Grenzgeb.

CC
**MO HU SHU HSUEH.** **Added/Corp** Hua Chung Kung Hsueh Yuan (Wu-Chang, Hupeh Province, China). **VFOAT** Fuzzy Mathematics. (Sept. 1981)-. Periodical. Chinese (summaries and/or abstracts in English). qt. Post Office / China, People's Republic of China. **LC** QA248; .M512. **DD** 511.3/22.
**Ind/Abst** Math. Rev.; Zentralbl. Math. Ihre Grenzgeb.

NO/0332-7353
**MODELING, IDENTIFICATION AND CONTROL.** [Model. identif. control]. **Added/Corp** Norges Teknisk-Naturvitenskapelige Forskningsrjad. **VFOAT** MIC. Vol. 1, No. 1 (Jan. 1980)-. Periodical. English. Four times a year (Jan., Apr., July, Oct.). $60.00 (institutions); $25.00 (individuals). Modeling Identification and Control, Div Engineering Cybernetics, N-7034 Trondheim Nth Norway. **Tel** 11 47 7 594376, FAX 011 47 7 594399, telex 55186. **ED** Jens Balchen. **LC** QA401; .M537. **DD** 510/.8. **CODEN** MIDCDA. Index available (Bound in every issue). cum. index. **Pr Rev.** Documents available from Article Express International, The Genuine Article, BIOSIS Document Express, Ask*IEEE.
**Desc:** This bulletin is distributed world-wide. It presents a review of Norwegian research within the fields, and is recognized by specialists has their reviewers.
**Ind/Abst** Abstr. Bull. Inst. Pap. Sci. Tech.; Bioeng. Abstr.; Biol. Abstr.; Curr. Contents Eng. Tech. Appl. Sci.; Ei Page One; Energy Res. Abstr. (July 1981-); Eng. Index Annu.; INSPEC (1980-); Math. Rev.; Life Sci. Collect.; Res. Alert [Full Cov.]; Sci. Cit. Index.

US/1047-5982
**MODERN LOGIC.** [Mod. log.]. Vol. 1, No. 1 (June 1990)-. Periodical. English (French, German, Russian and Spanish). Four times a year (Jan., Apr., July, Oct.). $100.00 (institutions), $36.00 (individuals). Modern Logic Publishing, 2408 1/2 Lincoln Way/Second Floor, Ames IA 50014-1036. **Tel** (515)292-1819. **ED** Irving H. Anellis. **DD** 511. Index available. **Bk Rev**, (Qty: 20-25). **Ad Acc. Circ:** 110 (ctrl).
**Desc:** A vehicle for the rapid publication of historical studies and expository surveys of nineteenth and twentieth century mathematical logic and set theory.
**Ind/Abst** Zentralbl. Math. Ihre Grenzgeb.

GW
**MODERNE MATHEMATIK IN ELEMENTARER DARSTELLUNG.** German. ir. DM29.80. Vandenhoeck & Ruprecht, Robert Bosch Breite 6, D-37079 Goettingen Germany. **Tel** 011 49 551 695911, FAX 011 49 551 695917, telex 965226 VAN d. **ED** Arnold Virsch and Hans G Steiner. **Bk Rev. Ad Acc. Circ:** 3,500.
**Ind/Abst** Math. Rev.; Zentralbl. Math. Ihre Grenzgeb.

AU/0026-9255
**MONATSHEFTE FUER MATHEMATIK.** [Monatsh. Math.]. **Added/Corp** Osterreichische Mathematische Gesellschaft. (1948)-. Periodical. German (English and French; summaries and/or abstracts in English). Eight times a year. $569.00. Springer-Verlag Wien, Sachsenplatz 4 6, PO Box 89, A-1201 Vienna Austria. **Tel** 011 43 1 3302415. **(Subscription address:** Springer Verlag New York Inc. / for North America, 44 Hartz Way, Secaucus NJ 07096.**)** **ED** S Grober, J Hejtmanek, E Hlawka, V Losert, H Reiter, L Schmetterer, W M Schmidt, and K Sigmund. **CODEN** MNMTA2. **[CCC].** cum. index. **Pr Rev.** Documents available from The Genuine Article. ***Continues*** *Monatshefte fur Mathematik und Physik.*
**Desc:** Contains reviews of recent books in the fields of pure and applied mathematics and mathematical physics. Of interest to mathematical libraries and research institutes.
**Ind/Abst** Compumath Citation Index [Full Cov.]; Curr. Contents Phys. Chem. Earth Sci.; Int. Aerosp. Abstr.; Math. Rev.; Res. Alert [Full Cov.]; SCISEARCH; Stat. Theory Method Abstr. (1959-1963, 1966, 1968-1969, 1971, 1973, 1977, 1979, 1982, 1986-1987); Zentralbl. Math. Ihre Grenzgeb.

BL/0100-0934
**MONOGRAFIAS DE MATEMATICA.** [Monogr. mat.]. Monographic series. Portuguese. Price varies per volume.
**Ind/Abst** Math. Rev.; Zentralbl. Math. Ihre Grenzgeb.

MX/0187-4780
**MONOGRAFIAS DEL INSTITUTO DE MATEMATICAS. UNIVERSIDAD NACIONAL AUTONOMA DE MEXICO.** (MONOGRAFIAS DEL INSTITUTO DE MATEMATICAS.). **Added/Corp** Universidad Nacional Autonoma de Mexico. Instituto de Matematicas. (1975)-. Monographic series. Spanish. Price varies per volume.
**Ind/Abst** Math. Rev.; Zentralbl. Math. Ihre Grenzgeb.

PL/0077-0507
**MONOGRAFIE MATEMATYCZNE.** [Monogr. mat.]. Vol. 1 (1932)-. Monographic series. English (French, German and Polish). ir. Price varies per volume. **(Subscription address:** ARS Polona, PO Box 1001, 00068 Warsaw Poland.**)** **LC** UNC.
**Ind/Abst** Math. Rev.; Zentralbl. Math. Ihre Grenzgeb.

SZ/0425-0818
**MONOGRAPHIE ... DE L'ENSEIGNEMENT MATHEMATIQUE.** [Monogr. enseign. math.]. **VFOAT** Monographies de l'Enseignement Mathematique. (1956)-. Monographic series. English (French, German and Italian). ir. Price varies per volume. L'Enseignement Mathematique, 2 4 rue du Lievre, CP 240, CH-1211 Geneva 24 Switzerland. **Tel** 011 41 22 3435060. **LC** UNC. **Circ:** 800.
**Desc:** Monographs on various subjects in mathematics.
**Ind/Abst** Math. Rev.; Zentralbl. Math. Ihre Grenzgeb.

SZ
**MONOGRAPHS IN MATHEMATICS.** Vol. 78 (1983)-. Monographic series. English. Price varies per volume. Birkhaeuser Verlag Ag, Klosterberg 23, PO Box 133, CH-4010 Basel Switzerland. **Tel** 011 41 61 2717400, FAX 011 41 0 61 2717666, telex 963475 birk ch. **LC** UNC. ***Continues*** *Lehrbucher und Monographien aus dem Gebiete der Exakten Wissenschaften. Mathematische Reihe, 1010-724X.*
**Ind/Abst** Math. Rev.; Zentralbl. Math. Ihre Grenzgeb.

US/0027-1322
**MOSCOW UNIVERSITY MATHEMATICS BULLETIN.** [Mosc. Univ. math. bull.]. **Main/Corp** Moskovskii Gosudarstvennyi Universitet IM. M. V. Lomonosova. **VFOAT** Mathematics Bulletin. (19??)-. Bulletin. English (Russian). bm. $800.00. Allerton Press, Inc., 150 Fifth Avenue, New York NY 10011. **Tel** (212)924-3950, FAX (212)463-9684, telex 427441 ALPRES. **CODEN** MUMBA. **[CCC].**
**Ind/Abst** Math. Rev.; Zentralbl. Math. Ihre Grenzgeb.

US/0195-7171
**MULTIPLE LINEAR REGRESSION VIEWPOINTS.** **Added/Corp** Special Interest Group on Multiple Linear Regression. (1970)-. English. Twice a year. $20.00 (institutions), $10.00 (individuals). University of Missouri Department of Behavioral Studies, St. Louis MO 63121. **Tel** (314)553-5785. **ED** Ralph O. Mueller. **LC** QA278.2; .M84. **DD** 519.5/36. cum. index. **Pr Rev. Circ:** 150. available on microfilm and microfiche from University Microfilms International (UMI).
**Desc:** Published to facilitate communication, authorship, creativity and exchange of ideas relating to the teaching, theory and application of MLR.

GW/0065-5295
**NACHRICHTEN DER AKADEMIE DER WISSENSCHAFTEN IN GOTTINGEN. II, MATHEMATISCH-PHYSIKALISCHE KLASSE.** **See** Science and Technology.

JA/0027-7630
**NAGOYA MATHEMATICAL JOURNAL.** [Nagoya math. j.]. **Added/Corp** Nagoya Daigaku. Sugaku Kyoshitsu. Vol. 1 (June 1950)-. Periodical. English (French and German). qt. $339.00. **(Subscription address:** Kinokuniya Company Ltd., 38-1 Sakuragaoka 5, chome Setagaya-ku, Tokyo 156 Japan.**)** **LC** QA1; .N2423. **DD** 510/.5. **CODEN** NGMJA2. cum. index. **Pr Rev.** Documents available from The Genuine Article.
**Ind/Abst** Compumath Citation Index [Full Cov.]; Curr. Contents Phys. Chem. Earth Sci.; Math. Rev.; Res. Alert [Full Cov.]; Sci. Cit. Index; SCISEARCH; Zentralbl. Math. Ihre Grenzgeb.

IR/1015-2857
**NASHR-I RIYAZI.** **VFOAT** Nashr-i Ryazy. (1988)-. Academic Scholarly Publication. Persian. tq. £24.00 Middle East; £25.00 Europe & Asia; £30.00 America & Far East. Iran University Press, 85 Park Avenue, PO Box 15875/4748, Tehran Iran. **Tel** 623232, FAX (008921)4661749, telex 213636-8-D5300. **ED** S. Shahshahani. **Circ:** 3,000.

**Desc:** Strives to cover new advances in mathematics, philosophical and historical aspects of mathematics as well as its applications.

NE/0258-2023
**NATO ASI SERIES. SERIES C, MATHEMATICAL AND PHYSICAL SCIENCES.** [NATO ASI ser., Ser. C : Math. phys. sci.]. **Added/Corp** North Atlantic Treaty Organization. Scientific Affairs Division. **VFOAT** Mathematical and Physical Sciences. (19??)-. Academic Scholarly Publication. English. ir. Price varies per volume. Kluwer Academic Publishers, Postbus 322, 3300 AH Dordrecht, The Netherlands. **Tel** 011 (31) 78 524400, FAX 011 31 78 183273, telex 20083. **(Subscription address:** Kluwer Academic Publishers / US Subscriptions, PO Box 253, Accord Station, Hingham MA 02018.**)** **LC** UNC. **CODEN** NSCSDW. **[CCC].** Documents available from BIOSIS Document Express, CASDDS. ***Continues*** *NATO Advanced Study Institutes Series. Series C, Mathematical and Physical Sciences, 0377-2071.*
**Ind/Abst** Biol. Abstr. (1988-); Chem. Abstr. (1983-); Zentralbl. Math. Ihre Grenzgeb.

US/0548-5932
**NEW MATHEMATICAL LIBRARY.** [New math. libr.]. **Added/Corp** Mathematical Association of America. (1961)-. Monographic series. English. ir. price varies per volume. Mathematical Association of America, 1529 18th Street Northwest, Washington DC 20036. **Tel** (202)387-5200, (800)331-1622, FAX (202)265-2384. **LC** UNC. **DD** 510.
**Ind/Abst** Math. Rev.; Zentralbl. Math. Ihre Grenzgeb.

US/0077-8893
**NEW TRENDS IN MATHEMATICS TEACHING.** **Added/Corp** International Commission on Mathematical Instruction. Unesco. **VFOAT** Tendances Nouvelles de l'Enseignement des Mathematiques. (1966)-. Periodical. English (French). ir. Price varies per volume. UNIPUB, 4611-F Assembly Drive, Lanham MD 20706-4391. **Tel** (800)274-4888, FAX (301)459-0056, telex 28787 GATT CH. **LC** QA11.A1; N38. **DD** 510/.7/1.

●NZ
**NEW ZEALAND JOURNAL OF MATHEMATICS.** **Added/Corp** New Zealand Mathematical Society. University of Auckland. Dept. of Mathematics & Statistics. Vol. 21 (Apr. 1992)-. Periodical. English. ir. $30.00. University of Auckland Math Department, Private Bag 92019, Auckland New Zealand. **Tel** 011 64 9 737999. **LC** QA1; .M411125. ***Continues*** *Mathematical Chronicle, 0581-1155.*

NZ/0549-0510
**NEW ZEALAND MATHEMATICS MAGAZINE, THE.** [N.Z. math. mag.]. **Added/Corp** Auckland Mathematical Association. Auckland, N.Z. University. Dept. of Mathematics. Vol. 1 (Nov. 1963)-. English. Three times a year (May, Aug., Dec.). 40.00NZ$ New Zealand; $18.00 US. Auckland Math Association Inc, PO Box 26-226, Auckland 3 New Zealand. **Tel** 011 64 9 687009. **ED** P. Hughes and S. Martin. **LC** QA11.A1; N4. **Bk Rev. Ad Acc. Circ:** 750 (ctrl).
**Desc:** Mathematics education and items of mathematical interest related to primary and secondary school mathematics prescriptions. Articles and materials for the classroom related to these.
**Ind/Abst** Math. Rev. (?-199?); Zentralbl. Math. Ihre Grenzgeb.

US/0277-1365
**NEWS BULLETIN / NATIONAL COUNCIL OF TEACHERS OF MATHEMATICS.** [News bull. - Natl. Counc. Teach. Math.]. **Added/Corp** National Council of Teachers of Mathematics. **VFOAT** NCTM News Bulletin. **VAT** National Council of Teachers of Mathematics News Bulletin. Vol. 18, No. 1 (Sept. 1981)-. Bulletin. English. Five times a year. Comes with National Council of Teachers of Mathematics membership. National Council of Teachers of Mathematics, 1906 Association Drive, Reston VA 22091. **Tel** (703)620-9840, FAX (703)476-2970. **ED** Cynthia Rosso. **DD** 510. **Circ:** 77,000 (ctrl). ***Continues*** *Newsletter (National Council of Teachers of Mathematics), 0733-8287.*

UK/0465-3696
**NEWS LETTER / MATHEMATICAL ASSOCIATION.** **Main/Corp** Mathematical Association. **VFOAT** Newsletter. (19??)-. Newsletter. English. ir. Free to members. Mathematical Association, 259 London Road, Leicester LE2 3BE England. **Tel** 011 44 533 703877. **ED** D. Peden (editor's address: 23 Patterdale Gardens, High Heaton, Newcastle, NE7 7QX United Kingdom). **Ad Acc. Circ:** 7,000 (ctrl).
**Desc:** House Magazine of the Mathematical Association.

US
**NEWSLETTER - ASSOCIATION FOR WOMEN IN MATHEMATICS.** **Main/Corp** Association for Women in Mathematics. Newsletter. English. bm. $20.00 (individuals), $35.00 (institutions). Wellesley College, Box 178, Wellesley MA 02181. **Tel** (617)237-7517. **ED** Anne Leggett. **Bk Rev. Ad Acc. Circ:** 2,000 (ctrl).
**Desc:** Our letter encourages women to enter and be active in careers in mathematics and related areas, and to promote equal opportunity and equal treatment of women in the mathematical community.

UK
**NEWSLETTER (MATHEMATICAL ASSOCIATION).** (NEWSLETTER.). Newsletter. English. Three times a year (Feb., June, and October). £37.50 (one journal), £50.00 (two journals) comes with membership. Mathematical Association, 259 London Road, Leicester LE2 3BE England. **Tel** 011 44 533 703877. **Ad Acc. Circ:** 6,000 (ctrl).
**Desc:** This is a small booklet sent to members only of the Mathematical Association.

NE
**NIEUWE WISKRANT.** Dutch. Four times a year. $25.00. Freudenthal Institute, Tiberdreef 4 GG Utrecht, Netherlands. **Tel** FAX (0)30 660430. **ED** S Kemme and H B Verhage. Index available. cum. index. **Pr Rev. Circ:** 2,000.
**Desc:** Innovative articles about mathematics education. Many classroom experiences, relevant for teachers.

US/0942-5608
**NON-LINEAR WORLD.** Vol. 1 (1994)-. English. Four times a year. $206.00. Walter de Gruyter Inc. / Hawthorne, 200 Saw Mill River Road, Hawthorne NY 10532. **Tel** (914)747-0110, GERMANY: 011/49/30/260050, FAX (914)747-1326, telex 646677.

UK/0362-546X
**NONLINEAR ANALYSIS.** [Nonlinear anal.]. **VFOAT** Nonlinear Analysis, Theory, Methods & Applications; Nonlinear Analysis, Theory, Methods and Applications. (Sept. 1976)-. Periodical. English. Twenty-four times a year. $1602.00 The Americas; £1075.00 other. Pergamon Press, An Imprint of Elsevier Science Ltd., The Boulevard, Langford Lane, Kidlington, Oxford OX5 1GB United Kingdom. **Tel** 011 44 865 843000, 011 44 865 843699, FAX 011 44 865 843010. **(Subscription address:** Elsevier Science Ltd. Oxford Fulfillment Centre, PO Box 800, Kidlington, Oxford OX5 1DX United Kingdom.**)** **ED** V. Lakshmikantham. **LC** QA299.6; .N66. **DD** 515/.05. **CODEN** NOANDD. **[CCC]. Pr Rev.** available on microfilm and microfiche from University Microfilms International (UMI). Documents available from Article Express International, The Genuine Article, Ask*IEEE.
**Ind/Abst** ACM Guide Comput. Lit.; Appl. Mech. Rev.; Compumath Citation Index [Full Cov.]; Comput. Rev.; Curr. Contents Phys. Chem. Earth Sci.; Ei Page One; Eng. Index Annu. [Select. Cov.]; INSPEC (1977-); Int. Aerosp. Abstr.; Math. Rev.; Pollut. Abstr. Indexes; Res. Alert [Full Cov.]; Sci. Cit. Index; SCISEARCH; Zentralbl. Math. Ihre Grenzgeb.

US/1021-9722
**NONLINEAR DIFFERENTIAL EQUATIONS AND APPLICATIONS.** Vol. 1, No. 1 (Jan. 1994)-. English. Four times a year. 216.20F Switzerland; 226.80F other. Birkhaeuser Verlag Ag, Klosterberg 23, PO Box 133, CH-4010 Basel Switzerland. **Tel** 011 41 61 2717400, FAX 011 41 0 61 2717666, telex 963475 birk ch. **(Subscription address:** Birkhauser Verlag AG, PO Box 151, CH 4106 Therwil Switzerland; Phone: 011 41 61 7217740**)** **ED** L. Salvadori (Chairman - Editorial Committee).
**Desc:** Strives to encourage the interaction between pure mathematics and applied sciences. It strives to provide a forum for research papers on nonlinear differential equations and applications to natural sciences. General theory will include ordinary and partial differential equations (both deterministic and stochastic), variational and topological methods, control theory, qualitative analysis including stability and bifurcation. Applications to natural sciences includes the treatment of problems in classical, statistical and quantum mechanics, electromagnetism, population dynamics, chemical kinetics, combustion theory.

GW/0942-5594
**NONLINEAR DIGEST.** ***Ceased.*** (1993)-Vol. 1. English. sa ((2 issues per volume)). Walter de Gruyter Inc., PO Box 303421, D 10728 Berlin Germany. **Tel** 011 49 30 260050, FAX 011 49 30 26005251. **ED** V Lakshmikantham and M P Singh.
**Desc:** Publishes communications of a more informal, less technical nature, designed for a broader readership. Research papers from any discipline which describe an important problem, present a conjecture of expected outcome and suggest possible approaches to its solution are also welcome in this journal.

NE/0925-6660
**NONLINEAR TOPICS IN THE MATHEMATICAL SCIENCES.** [Nonlinear top. math. sci.]. (1990)-. Monographic series. English. ir.
**Ind/Abst** Math. Rev.; Zentralbl. Math. Ihre Grenzgeb.

UK/0951-7715
**NONLINEARITY (BRISTOL).** (NONLINEARITY.). [Nonlinearity]. **Added/Corp** Institute of Physics (Great Britain) London Mathematical Society. American Institute of Physics. Vol. 1, No. 1 (Feb. 1988)-. Periodical. English (French and German). bm. $538.00. Institute of Physics, Techno House, Redcliffe Way, Bristol BS1 6NX England. **Tel** 011 44 272 297481, FAX 011 44 272 294318, telex 449149 INSTP G. **(Subscription address:** American Institute of Physics, Publishing Sales, 500 Sunnyside Blvd., Woodbury NY 11797.**)** **ED** R. Mackay. **LC** QA427; .N68. **DD** 515. **CODEN** NONLE5. **[CCC].** Index available in last issue of volume--attached. **Circ:** 1,100. available on microfiche. Documents available from The Genuine Article, Ask*IEEE.
**Desc:** Provides results of latest research in nonlinear systems. Covers a wide spectrum ranging from proofs of important theorems to papers presenting ideas, conjectures and numerical or physical experiments of significant physical and mathematical interest.
**Ind/Abst** Abstr. Hum. Comput. Interact.; Compumath Citation Index [Full Cov.]; Curr. Contents, Agric. Biol. Environ. Sci.; INSPEC (Feb. 1988-); Math. Rev.; Res. Alert [Full Cov.]; Sci. Cit. Index; SCISEARCH; Zentralbl. Math. Ihre Grenzgeb.

NO/0801-3500
**NORMAT.** (NORMAT : NORDISK MATEMATISK TIDSKRIFT.). [Normat]. **Added/Corp** Dansk Matematisk Forening. **VFOAT** Nordisk Matematisk Tidskrift. Vol. 1 (1952)-. Periodical. Danish (Scandinavian; summaries and/or abstracts in English). qt. Kr355.00, $64.00. Scandinavian University Press, PO Box 2959 Toeyen, N 0608 Oslo 6 Norway. **Tel** 011 47 2 2575400, FAX 011 47 2 2575353, telex 71896 UROR N. **(Subscription address:** Scandinavian University Press, 200 Meacham Ave., Elmont NY 11003.**)** **ED** Jon Reed. **LC** QA1; .N83. **Bk Rev. Ad Acc. Circ:** 1,500. ***Continues*** *Nordisk Matematisk Tidskrift, 0029-1412.*
**Desc:** Popular scientific journal of mathematics also covering educational aspects.
**Ind/Abst** Math. Rev.; Zentralbl. Math. Ihre Grenzgeb.

NE/0924-6509
**NORTH-HOLLAND MATHEMATICAL LIBRARY.** **See** Library and Information Sciences.

NE/0304-0208
**NORTH-HOLLAND MATHEMATICS STUDIES.** [North-Holl. math. stud.]. (1970)-. Monographic series. English. ir. Price varies per volume. Elsevier Science Publishers BV, PO Box 211, 1000 AE Amsterdam Netherlands. **Tel** 011 31 20 5803642, FAX 011 31 20 5862696, telex 15682. **LC** UNC. **CODEN** NMSTD5. Documents available from Ask*IEEE.
**Ind/Abst** INSPEC; Zentralbl. Math. Ihre Grenzgeb.

NE/0168-1974
**NORTH-HOLLAND SERIES IN STATISTICS AND PROBABILITY.** [North-Holland ser. stat. probab.]. **VAT** North Holland Series in Statistics and Probability. Vol. 1-. Monographic series. English. ir. Price varies per volume. Elsevier Science Publishers BV, PO Box 211, 1000 AE Amsterdam Netherlands. **Tel** 011 31 20 5803642, FAX 011 31 20 5862696, telex 15682. **DD** 519.5. **CODEN** NHSPDQ. Documents available from Ask*IEEE.
**Ind/Abst** INSPEC; Math. Rev.; Zentralbl. Math. Ihre Grenzgeb.

AG/0078-2009
**NOTAS DE ALGEBRA Y ANALISIS.** [Notas Algebra Anal.]. **Added/Corp** Universidad Nacional del Sur. Instituto de Matematica. (1966)-. Monographic series. Spanish. **LC** UNC. **DD** 510.
**Ind/Abst** Math. Rev.; Zentralbl. Math. Ihre Grenzgeb.

AG/0325-8963
**NOTAS DE GEOMETRIA Y TOPOLOGIA / INMABB - CONICET.** ***Suspended.*** Vol. 1 (1980)-Suspended with Issue 1, 1980. Monographic series. Spanish. Price varies per volume. Instituto de Matematica, Universidad Nacional del Sur, Bahia Balanca Argentina.

CL
**NOTAS DE LA SOCIEDAD MATEMATICA DE CHILE.** **Added/Corp** Sociedad Matematica de Chile. Vol. 1, No. 1 (1979)-. Spanish (English).
**Ind/Abst** Math. Rev.; Zentralbl. Math. Ihre Grenzgeb.

AG/0326-1336
**NOTAS DE MATEMATICA DISCRETA.** (NOTAS DE MATEMATICA DISCRETA / INMABB, CONICET.). [Notas mat. discreta]. **Added/Corp** Universidad Nacional de Sur. Instituto de Matematica. Consejo Nacional de Investigaciones Cientificas y Tecnicas (Argentina). No. 1 (1982)-. Monographic series. Spanish. ir. Price varies per volume. Instituto de Matematica / INMABB - UNS - CONICET, Universidad Nacional del Sur, Av. Alem 1253, 8000 Bahia Blanca Argentina. **Tel** 54 091 29557, FAX 54 091 551447. **Circ:** 700 (ctrl).
**Desc:** Collection intended to gather research papers, notes from courses, lectures, seminars, etc. held at the Universidad Nacional del Sur in the fields of combinatory mathematics, graph theory, etc.
**Ind/Abst** Math. Rev.; Zentralbl. Math. Ihre Grenzgeb.

IT
**NOTE DI MATEMATICA.** **Added/Corp** Universita degli Studi di Lecce. Vol. 1, No. 1 (1981)-. Periodical. English. sa. Free on request. Note di Matematica, Univ Degli Studi Dipart Matematica, 73100 Lecce Italy. **Tel** 0832 627443. Index available. cum.

index. **Circ:** 250 (ctrl).
**Desc:** Publishes research articles.
**Ind/Abst** Math. Rev.; Zentralbl. Math. Ihre Grenzgeb.

US
**NOTE PAD.** English. State Bar Association of North Dakota, University of North Dakota, School of Law, Grand Forks ND 58201. **Tel** (701)777-2941, FAX (701)777-2217.

US/0888-6113
**NOTES ON MATHEMATICS AND ITS APPLICATIONS.** [Notes math. its appl.]. Monographic series. English. ir. Price varies per volume. Gordon & Breach Science Publishers, Inc., PO Box 786, Cooper Station, New York NY 10276. **Tel** (212)206-8900, FAX (212)645-2459. **(Subscription address:** International Publishers Distributor at one of the following addresses: 820 Town Center Drive, Langhorne, PA 19047; or PO Box 90, Reading Berkshire RG1 8JL UK; or Kent Ridge PO Box 1180, Singapore 9111, Republic of Singapore**)** **DD** 510.

AT/0818-304X
**NOTES ON PURE MATHEMATICS.** [Notes pure math.]. **Added/Corp** Australian National University. Dept. of Pure Mathematics. Australian National University. Dept. of Mathematics. No. 1 (1968)-. Monographic series. English. Price varies per volume. Australian National University / Department of Mathematics, Department of Pure Mathematics, Canberra ACT 0200 Australia. **LC** UNC.
**Ind/Abst** Math. Rev.

US/0002-9920
**NOTICES OF THE AMERICAN MATHEMATICAL SOCIETY.** [Not. Am. Math. Soc.]. **Main/Corp** American Mathematical Society. Vol. 1 (Feb. 1954)-. English. mo. $255.00. American Mathematical Society, PO Box 6248, Providence RI 02940-6248. **Tel** (800)321-4267, (401)455-4000, FAX (401)331-3842, telex 797192. **(Subscription address:** American Mathematical Society, PO Box 5904, Boston MA 02206-5904.**)** **ED** James Voytuk. **LC** UNC. **DD** 510. **CODEN** AMNOAN. **[CCC].** Index available. **Ad Acc. Circ:** 20,900. available on microfilm and microfiche from University Microfilms International (UMI).
**Desc:** Journal of record of the Society. Meeting/conference announcements, reports on current trends in scientific development, federal funding, news and information of interest to mathematical community.
**Ind/Abst** Comput. Rev.; Math. Rev.; Zentralbl. Math. Ihre Grenzgeb.

US/0885-5862
**NOTRE DAME MATHEMATICAL LECTURES.** [Notre Dame math. lect.]. **Added/Corp** University of Notre Dame. (1942)-. Monographic series. English. ir. Price varies per volume. University of Notre Dame Press, PO Box 635, South Bend IN 46624. **Tel** (219)239-6349, (800)677-3232, FAX (219)239-8148. **(Subscription address:** University of Chicago Press, Book Division, 11030 South Langley Avenue, Chicago IL 60628.**)** **LC** QA1; .N87. **DD** 511.
**Ind/Abst** Math. Rev.

●US/1060-9881
**NOVA JOURNAL OF ALGEBRA AND GEOMETRY.** [Nova j. algebra geom.]. (1992)-. Periodical. English. Four times a year. $165.00. Nova Science Publishers Inc., 6080 Jericho Turnpike, Suite 207, Commack NY 11725-2808. **Tel** (516)499-3103, (516)499-3106, FAX (516)499-3146. **LC** QA150; .N68. **DD** 512/.005.

US
**NTIS ALERT. MATHEMATICAL SCIENCES.** (19??)-. Periodical. English. Twenty-four times a year. $140.00 US; $195.00 other. National Technical Information Service - NTIS, Room 2027S, 5285 Port Royal Road, Springfield VA 22161. **Tel** (703)487-4630, (703)487-4660, (703)487-4650, FAX (703)321-8547, telex 89-9405.

GW/0720-2563
**NUMBER THEORY.** (NUMBER THEORY, INCLUDING ALGEBRAIC GEOMETRY.). **Added/Corp** Heidelberger Akademie der Wissenschaften Fachinformationszentrum Energie, Physik, Mathematik (Eggenstein-Leopoldshafen, Germany). (1981)-. Periodical. English (French and German). Twenty-four times a year. DM155.00 North America; DM210.00 Europe; DM250.00 others. Fachinformationszentrum Karlsruhe, Physics & Math, D 76344 Eggenstein Germany. **Tel** 011 49 7247 808149. **LC** QA241; .N868. **DD** 512/.7/05.

NE/1017-1398
**NUMERICAL ALGORITHMS.** [Numer. algorithms]. Vol. 1 No. 1 (Apr. 1991)-. Periodical. English. Eight times a year. 667.00F (includes distribution costs). Baltzer Science Publishers BV, Asterweg 1A, 1031 HL Amsterdam Netherlands. **Tel** 011 31 20 6370061, FAX 011 31 20 6323651. **LC** QA297; .N952. **CODEN** NUALEG. Documents available from Ask*IEEE.
**Desc:** Covers all aspects of numerical algorithms, theoretical results, implementation, numerical stability, complexity, subroutines and applications.
**Ind/Abst** INSPEC (1991-); Math. Rev.

UK/0720-258X
**NUMERICAL ANALYSIS.** (NUMERICAL ANALYSIS : PROCEEDINGS OF THE DUNDEE CONFERENCE ON NUMERICAL ANALYSIS.). **Main/Conf** Dundee Conference on Numerical Analysis. (1975)-. English. Twelve times a year. Scientific Information Service Inc., 7 Woodland Avenue, Larchmont NY 10538. **Tel** (914)834-8864. **ED** B. Wegner. **LC** QA297; .D85a; QA3; .L28 subser. **DD** 510 S; 519.4. Index available. cum. index. ***Continues*** *Conference on the Numerical Solution of Differential Equations. Conference on the Numerical Solution of Differential Equations : [Proceedings].*
**Desc:** Draws on a worldwide pool of several thousand reviewers.

US/0163-0563
**NUMERICAL FUNCTIONAL ANALYSIS AND OPTIMIZATION.** [Numer. funct. anal. optim.]. Vol. 1 (1979)-. Periodical. English. Ten times a year. $625.00 US; $660.00 other. Marcel Dekker Inc., 270 Madison Avenue, New York NY 10016. **Tel** (212)696-9000, (800)228-1160, FAX (212)685-4540, telex 421419. **(Subscription address:** Marcel Dekker Inc, PO Box 5017, Monticello NY 12701.**)** **ED** M. Z. Nashed. **LC** QA320; .N84. **DD** 515/.7. **CODEN** NFAODL. **[CCC]. Bk Rev. Ad Acc. Pr Rev.** available on microfiche. Documents available from Article Express International, The Genuine Article, Ask*IEEE.
**Desc:** In original research papers, this journal examines the development and applications of functional analysis and operator-theoretic methods in numerical analysis, approximation theory, optimization, control, and systems theory. Emphasis is placed on interaction and unification of these fields, and the use of abstract methods to provide insight and fundamental contributions to problems and models in the natural, physical, engineering, and decision sciences. 'Numerical Functional Analysis and Optimization' features comprehensive survey and expository articles, annotated bibliographies, book reviews, and occasionally an entire issue is devoted to one topic.
**Ind/Abst** Bioeng. Abstr.; Compumath Citation Index [Full Cov.]; Ei Page One; Eng. Index Annu.; INSPEC (1979-); Math. Rev.; Res. Alert [Full Cov.]; SCISEARCH; Soc. Sci. Cit. Index [Select. Cov.]; Zentralbl. Math. Ihre Grenzgeb.

●UK/1070-5325
**NUMERICAL LINEAR ALGEBRA WITH APPLICATIONS.** [Numer. linear algebr. appl.]. **VFOAT** Numerical Linear Algebra. (1993)-. Periodical. English. bm. $275.00. John Wiley & Sons Ltd., Baffins Lane, Chichester West Sussex PO19 1UD England. **Tel** 0243 779777, FAX 0243 776128 BTG:JWP001, telex 86290 WIBOOKG. **(Subscription address:** John Wiley / Philadelphia, PO Box 7247, Philadelphia PA 19170.**)** **ED** O. Axelsson. **DD** 512. **CODEN** NLAAEM.
**Desc:** Emphasizes mathematical rigour in presenting new methods in numerical linear algebra, including their analysis and applications. Also emphasizes analysis of the computational and communication complexity of algorithms in numerical linear algebra when implemented in different computer architectures.

US/0749-159X
**NUMERICAL METHODS FOR PARTIAL DIFFERENTIAL EQUATIONS.** [Numer. methods partial differ. equ.]. Vol. 1, No. 1 (Spring 1985)-. Periodical. English. Six times a year. $578.00 US; $638.00 Canada and Mexico; $660.50 other. John Wiley & Sons, Inc., 605 Third Avenue, New York NY 10158-0012. **Tel** (212)850-6000, (212)850-6645, FAX (212)850-6088, telex 12-7063. **(Subscription address:** John Wiley & Sons / England, Baffins Lane, Chichester, West Sussex PO19 1UD England.**)** **ED** George F. Pinder. **LC** QA377; .N86. **DD** 515.3/53/05. **CODEN** NMPDEB. **[CCC]. Ad Acc.** available on microfilm and microfiche from University Microfilms International (UMI). Documents available from Article Express International.
**Desc:** Presents developments on topics including computational methods, applied numerical analysis and partial differential equations.
**Ind/Abst** Abstr. Bull. Inst. Pap. Sci. Tech.; Ei Page One; Eng. Index Annu.; Math. Rev. (1985-); Mech. Eng. Abstr.; Zentralbl. Math. Ihre Grenzgeb.

UK
**NUMERICAL METHODS IN FRACTURE MECHANICS : PROCEEDINGS OF THE ... INTERNATIONAL CONFERENCE.** **VFOAT** Proceedings of the ... International Conference on Numerical Methods in Fracture Mechanics. (1978)-. English. be. $143.00. Pineridge Press Ltd, Journals Division, 54 Newton Road, Mumbles Swansea SA3 4BQ Wales. **Tel** 011 44 792 361557, FAX 011 44 792 295532.

US/0362-3017
**NUMERICAL SOLUTION OF PARTIAL DIFFERENTIAL EQUATIONS.** (NUMERICAL SOLUTION OF PARTIAL DIFFERENTIAL EQUATIONS: PROCEEDINGS.). **Main/Conf** Symposium on the Numerical Solution of Partial Differential Equation. **Added/Corp** University of Maryland. Institute for Fluid Dynamics and Applied Mathematics. University of Maryland. Computer Science Center. (1965)-. Academic Scholarly Publication. English. ir. Academic Press, Inc., 6277 Sea Harbor Drive, Orlando FL 32887. **Tel** (800)543-9534, (407)345-4100, FAX (407)363-9661. **ED** Bert Hubbard. **LC** QA374; .S94. **DD** 515/.62.

GW/0029-599X
**NUMERISCHE MATHEMATIK.** [Numer. Math.]. Vol. 1 (1959)-. Periodical. English (German). Twelve times a year. DM1746.00. Springer-Verlag GmbH & Company KG, Heidelberger Platz 3, D 14197 Berlin Germany. **Tel** 011 49 30 8207223, FAX 011 49 30 8214091, telex 183 319 SPBLN D. **(Subscription address:** Springer Verlag New York Inc. / for North America, 44 Hartz Way, Secaucus NJ 07096.**)** **ED** R S Varga, I Babuska, F L Bauer, R Bulirsch, P G Ciarlet, G H Golub, A S Householder, H B Keller, B N Parlett, G W Stewart, J Stoer, J Todd, R S Varga, and C Zenger. **LC** QA76.5; .N8. **CODEN** NUMMA7. **[CCC]. Pr Rev.** available on microfilm and microfiche from University Microfilms International (UMI). Documents available from The Genuine Article, Ask*IEEE.
**Desc:** Provides for the international dissemination of contributions dealing with general problems of digital computation.
**Ind/Abst** ACM Guide Comput. Lit.; Appl. Mech. Rev.; Compumath Citation Index [Full Cov.]; Comput. Abstr.; Comput. Rev.; Curr. Contents Phys. Chem. Earth Sci.; INSPEC (1970-); Int. Aerosp. Abstr.; Math. Rev.; Res. Alert [Full Cov.]; Sci. Cit. Index; SCISEARCH; Stat. Theory Method Abstr. (1961-1963, 1966-1969, 1971-1973, 1982); Zentralbl. Math. Ihre Grenzgeb.

XV/0473-7466
**OBZORNIK ZA MATEMATIKO IN FIZIKO.** [Obz. mat. fiz.]. Vol. 1- Mar. 1951-. Academic Scholarly Publication. Slovenian (table of contents in English). bm. $25.00. Komisija za Tisk MFA Srs, Jadranska 19, 61111 Ljubljana Slovenia. **Tel** (061)265-061/53. **ED** Milan Hladnik. **LC** Q4; .O2. **CODEN** OBMFAY. Index available. cum. index. **Bk Rev. Ad Acc. Circ:** 1,500 (ctrl). Documents available from CASDDS.
**Desc:** Professional journal of the Society of Mathematicians, Physicists and Astronomer of the federal state of Slovenia containing, review articles, pedagogical articles, news, book reviews, etc.
**Ind/Abst** Chem. Abstr.; Int. Aerosp. Abstr.; Math. Rev.; Zentralbl. Math. Ihre Grenzgeb.

FR
**OEUVRES DE DESCARTES.** ***Ceased.*** (19??)-Number 12. French. ir. Editions du CNRS, 22 rue Saint Armand, F 75015 Paris France. **Tel** 011 33 1 45075050.

FR
**OFFICIEL DES MATHEMATIQUES CIRCULAIRE D'INFORMATION.** French. mo (except July, Aug. & Sept.). 165.00F. Societe Mathematique de France EC Norm Sup Tour L, 1 rue Maurice Arnoux, 92120 Montrouge France. **Tel** 011 33 1 40848054, or 91267464, FAX 011 33 1 40848052, or 91411751.

CN/0030-3011
**ONTARIO MATHEMATICS GAZETTE.** [Ont. math. gaz.]. **Added/Corp** Ontario Association for Mathematics Education. Ontario Mathematics Commission. Ontario Association of Teachers of Mathematics and Physics. (1962)-. Periodical. English. Three times a year (Apr., Sept., Dec.). 40.00Can$ Canada; 50.00Can$ others. Ontario Association of Mathematics Education, 1 Southdale Drive Attridge, Markham, Ontario, L3P 1J6 Canada. **Tel** (905)294-3511. **ED** Robert Smith and Ron Ripley. **Bk Rev. Circ:** 1,700 (ctrl).
**Desc:** An updating of the Education Acts of the Province of Ontario, lesson strategies for teachers grade K P-University. Summaries of changes in mathematical education in the world over.

US/0030-364X
**OPERATIONS RESEARCH.** [Oper. res.]. **Added/Corp** Operations Research Society of America. Vol. 4 (Feb. 1956)-. Academic Scholarly Publication. English. Six times a year. $135.00 (institutions), $90.00 (individuals) surface mail; $127.00 (individuals), $168.00 (institutions) airmail. Operations Research Society of America, 1314 Guilford Avenue, Baltimore MD 21202. **Tel** (410)850-0300, (800)850-0300. **ED** Donald Ratliff. **NLM** W1 OP148. **CODEN** OPREA1. **[CCC].** Index available. cum. index. **Ad Acc. Pr Rev. Circ:** 11,000. available on microfilm and microfiche from University Microfilms International (UMI). Documents available from Article Express International, The Genuine Article, UMI Article Clearinghouse, Ask*IEEE, CASDDS. ***Continues*** *Journal of the Operations Research Society of America, 0096-3984.*
**Desc:** Devoted principally to theoretical and practical research contributions of archival value.
**Ind/Abst** ABI/INFORM Glob. Ed.; ABI Inform Ondisc (Oct. 1971-); Acad. Search (July 1993-); ACM Guide Comput. Lit.; AGRICOLA; Bioeng. Abstr.; Biostatistica; Bus. Index (1985-); Bus. Period. Index; Bus. Source (Jul. 1993-); Chem. Abstr.; Coal Abstr.; Compumath Citation Index [Full Cov.]; Comput. Rev.; Contents Pages Manage.; Curr. Contents Eng. Tech. Appl. Sci.; Curr. Contents Soc. Behav. Sci.; Ei Page One; Eng. Index

Annu. [Select. Cov.]; Gen. BusinessFile (1985-); Gen. Period. Index (1985-); GeoRef; Hospit. Health Admin. Index; INFO-SOUTH Abstr.; INSPEC (July/Aug. 1968-); Int. Abstr. Oper. Res. [Full Cov.]; Int. Aerosp. Abstr.; Int. Nurs. Index; J. Plan. Lit.; Mag. Search; Manage. Contents; Math. Rev. (1988-); Oper. Res./Manag. Sci.; Peace Res. Abstr. J. (1963-1965); Qual. Control Appl. Stat.; Res. Alert [Full Cov.]; Sci. Cit. Index; Selec. Coop. Index Manage. Period; SCISEARCH; Soc. Sci. Cit. Index [Full Cov.]; Stat. Theory Method Abstr. (1967-1983); UMI ABI/Inform--Bus. Period. Ondisc (Jul. 1987-) [Full Txt.]; Wilson Bus. Abstr.

SZ
**OPERATOR THEORY, ADVANCES AND APPLICATIONS.** Vol. 1 (1979)-. Monographic series. English. ir. Price varies per volume. Birkhaeuser Verlag Ag, Klosterberg 23, PO Box 133, CH-4010 Basel Switzerland. **Tel** 011 41 61 2717400, FAX 011 41 0 61 2717666, telex 963475 birk ch. **ED** I. Gohberg. **LC** UNC.
**Desc:** Devoted to the publication of current research in operator theory, with particular emphasis on applications to classical analysis and the theory of integral equations, as well as to numerical analysis, mathematical physics and mathematical methods in electrical engineering.
**Ind/Abst** Math. Rev.; Zentralbl. Math. Ihre Grenzgeb.

II/0030-3887
**OPSEARCH.** **See** Business-General Management.

RU/0134-3998
**OPTIMIZACIJA.** (OPTIMIZATSIIA.). [Optimizacija]. **Added/Corp** Institut Matematiki (Akademiia Nauk SSSR. Sibirskoe Otdelenie). Vol. 1 (1971)-. Monographic series. Russian. ir. Price varies per volume. Izdatelstvo Nauka / Akademiia Nauk, Publishing House of the Russian Academy of Sciences, Leninskii Porspekt 14, 117901 Moscow Russia. **Tel** 011 95 954-21-53, FAX 011 95 938-21-44, telex 411964. **LC** UNC. ***Continues*** *Optimalnoe Planirovanie.*
**Ind/Abst** Math. Rev.

US
**OPTIMIZATION.** [Optimization]. **Added/Corp** Technische Hochschule Ilmenau. Sektion Mathematik, Rechentechnik und Okonomische Kybernetik. Vol. 8 (1977)-. Periodical. English (German; summaries and/or abstracts in French and Russian). qt. $330.00 (academic institutions), $515.00 (corporate institutions). Gordon & Breach Science Publishers, PO Box 90, Reading RG1 8JL England. **Tel** 011 44 734 560080, FAX 011 44 734 568211. **(Subscription address:** International Publishers Distributor at one of the following addresses: 820 Town Center Drive, Langhorne, PA 19047; or PO Box 90, Reading Berkshire RG1 8JL UK; or Kent Ridge PO Box 1180, Singapore 9111, Republic of Singapore**) LC** QA402.5; .O642. **DD** 519.7/05. **CODEN** OPTZDQ. Documents available from Ask*IEEE. ***Continues in part*** *Mathematische Operationsforschung und Statistik, 0047-6277.*
**Ind/Abst** INSPEC (1985-); Int. Abstr. Oper. Res. [Full Cov.]; Math. Rev.

GW
**OPTIMIZATION TECHNIQUES; PROCEEDINGS OF THE IFIP CONFERENCE ON OPTIMIZATION TECHNIQUES.** **Main/Conf** IFIP Conference on Optimization Techniques. Proceedings. English. Springer-Verlag GmbH & Company KG, Heidelberger Platz 3, D 14197 Berlin Germany. **Tel** 011 49 30 8207223, FAX 011 49 30 8214091, telex 183 319 SPBLN D. **(Subscription address:** Springer Verlag New York Inc. / for North America, 44 Hartz Way, Secaucus NJ 07096.**)**

NE/0167-8094
**ORDER (DORDRECHT).** (ORDER.). [Order]. Vol. 1, No. 1 (1984)-. Periodical. English. qt. $416.00. Kluwer Academic Publishers, Postbus 322, 3300 AH Dordrecht, The Netherlands. **Tel** 011 (31) 78 524400, FAX 011 31 78 183273, telex 20083. **ED** Ivan Rival. **LC** QA171.48; .Q73. **DD** 511.3/2. **[CCC].** Index available. **Bk Rev. Ad Acc. Pr Rev. Acid Free. Circ:** 500. available on microfilm and microfiche from University Microfilms International (UMI). Documents available from The Genuine Article.
**Desc:** Devoted to the theory of ordered sets and its applications. Aims to be an authoritative forum on new and important developments in the subject.
**Ind/Abst** Compumath Citation Index [Full Cov.]; Math. Rev. (1984-); Res. Alert [Full Cov.]; SCISEARCH; Zentralbl. Math. Ihre Grenzgeb.

US/0891-9089
**OREGON MATHEMATICS TEACHER, THE.** [Or. math. teach.]. **Added/Corp** Oregon Council of Teachers of Mathematics. **VFOAT** TOMT. (197?)-. Periodical. English. Six times a year (Jan., Mar., May, Sep., Oct., Nov.). $15.00 (1 year), $28.00 (2 year) US; $20.00 (1 year), $38.00 (2 year) other. Oregon Council of Teachers of Math, 1805 Leo Lane, c/o Jacie Nissen, Newberg OR 97132. **Tel** (503)538-8407. **ED** Anne McEnery-Ogle. **DD** 373. ctrl circ.

JA/0030-6126
**OSAKA JOURNAL OF MATHEMATICS.** [Osaka j. math.]. **Added/Corp** Osaka Daigaku. Sugakuka. Osaka Shiritsu Daigaku. Sugakuka. Vol. 1 (Aug. 1964)-. Periodical. English (French). qt. $399.00. Osaka Daigaku Rigakubu, (Faculty of Science, Okaka University), 1-1 Machikaneyamacho, Toyonakashi, Osakafu, 560 Japan. **(Subscription address:** Kinokuniya Company Ltd., 38-1 Sakuragaoka 5, chome Setagaya-ku, Tokyo 156 Japan.**) LC** QA1; .O72. **DD** 510/.05. **CODEN** OJMAA7. **Pr Rev.** Documents available from The Genuine Article. ***Supersedes*** *Osaka Mathematical Journal; Journal of Mathematics, Osaka City University.*
**Ind/Abst** Compumath Citation Index [Full Cov.]; Curr. Contents Phys. Chem. Earth Sci.; Math. Rev.; Res. Alert [Full Cov.]; SCISEARCH; Stat. Theory Method Abstr. (1969, 1986); Zentralbl. Math. Ihre Grenzgeb.

US/1063-9136
**P-A-M BULLETIN.** [P-A-M bull.]. **Added/Corp** Special Libraries Association. Physics-Astronomy-Mathematics Division. **VFOAT** PAM Bulletin; P A M Bulletin. **VAT** Physics Astronomy Mathematics Bulletin. (19??)-. Bulletin. English. qt (Feb., May, July, Nov.). $9.00. P.A.M. (Physics-Astronomy-Mathematics)Division of the Special Library Association, 1700 18th Street NW, Washington DC 20009. **Tel** (612)624-9395. **ED** Janice Griggs. **DD** 027. **Circ:** 230.

US/0030-8730
**PACIFIC JOURNAL OF MATHEMATICS.** [Pac. j. math.]. **Added/Corp** American Mathematical Society. Institute for Numerical Analysis (U.S.). **VFOAT** Journal of Mathematics. (March 1951)-. Periodical. English. mo (except July and August). $215.00. Pacific Journal of Mathematics, University of California at Berkeley, Department of Mathematics, Berkeley CA 94720. **Tel** (510)642-0116. **(Subscription address:** Pacific Journal of Mathematics, PO Box 4163, Berkeley CA 94704-0163.**) ED** V.S. Varadarajan. **LC** QA1; .P122. **DD** 510.5. **CODEN** PJMAAI. Index available. **Pr Rev. Circ:** 1,500 (ctrl). Documents available from The Genuine Article.
**Desc:** Mathematics research. Back issues available from 1951 onward.
**Ind/Abst** Compumath Citation Index [Full Cov.]; Curr. Contents Phys. Chem. Earth Sci.; Int. Aerosp. Abstr.; Math. Rev.; Pollut. Abstr. Indexes; Res. Alert [Full Cov.]; Sci. Cit. Index; SCISEARCH; Stat. Theory Method Abstr. (1959-1963, 1968, 1972); Zentralbl. Math. Ihre Grenzgeb.

US/1064-9735
**PANAMERICAN MATHEMATICAL JOURNAL.** [Panam. math. j.]. **Added/Corp** University of Central Florida. Dept. of Mathematics. Vol. 1 (1991)-. Periodical. English. qt. $100.00 North America; $105.00 South America; $110.00 other. Dr. Ram U. Verma, 12046 Coed Drive, Orlando FL 32826. **Tel** (407)282-5476. **ED** Dr. Ram U. Verma (telephone 407-282-5476). **LC** QA1; .P16. **DD** 510/.5. Index available (Published separately). cum. index. **Bk Rev. Ad Acc. Circ:** 50.
**Ind/Abst** Math. Rev.; Zentralbl. Math. Ihre Grenzgeb.

US
**PAPERS PRINTED FOR MID-YEAR EXAMINATIONS. SECTION 2. MATHEMATICS, SCIENCES.** **Main/Corp** Harvard University. Faculty of Arts and Sciences. **VFOAT** Mid-Year Examinations; Examinations. Jan. 1967-. English. an. Harvard University Printing Office, Lucy Robinson, Registrar's Office, Holyoke 827, Cambridge MA 02138.

AT
**PARABOLA.** (19??)-. English. Three times a year. 5.00Aus$. University of New South Wales / School of Mathematics, PO Box 1, Kensington 2033 Australia. **Tel** 011 61 2 697 2964, FAX 011 61 2 662 6445. **ED** D. Tacon. **Bk Rev. Ad Acc, Adv Mgr:** D. Tait. **Circ:** 500.

GW/0720-261X
**PARTIAL DIFFERENTIAL EQUATIONS.** **Added/Corp** Heidelberger Akademie der Wissenschaften Fachinformationszentrum Energie, Physik, Mathematik (Eggenstein-Leopoldshafen, Germany). (1981)-. Periodical. English (French and German). mo. $135.00. Scientific Information Service Inc., 7 Woodland Avenue, Larchmont NY 10538. **Tel** (914)834-8864.

US/1054-6618
**PATTERN RECOGNITION AND IMAGE ANALYSIS.** (PATTERN RECOGNITION AND IMAGE ANALYSIS : ADVANCES IN MATHEMATICAL THEORY AND APPLICATIONS IN THE USSR.). [Pattern recognit. image anal.]. **Added/Corp** Nauchnyi Sovet Po Kompleksnoi Probleme "Kibernetika" (Akademiia Nauk SSSR). **VFOAT** Pattern Recognition and Image Analysis, Soviet. Vol. 1, No. 1 (Apr. 1991)-. Periodical. English (translations available in Russian). qt (4 issues). $325.00 US and Canada; $365.00 other. MAIK Nauka / Interperiodica, Ulitsa Profsoyuznaya 90, Moscow 117864 Russia. **(Subscription address:** Interperiodica Publishing, Subscription Office, PO Box 1831, Birmingham AL 35201-1831.**) ED** Yuri Zhuravlev. **LC** TA1650; .R382. **DD** 006.4/2. **Pr Rev.**
**Desc:** Emphasis will be on rapid-publishing of concise articles covering theory, methodology, and practical application. Aims also include publishing papers from proceedings and conferences and state-of-the-art papers.

US/0031-4870
**PENTAGON.** (1941)-. Periodical. English. sa (May, Dec.). $5.00 (one year), $10.00 (two year) US; $7.00 other. Kappa Mu Epsilon, Department of Mathematics, Long Island University, Brookville NY 11548. **Tel** (309)298-1383. **ED** Kent Harris. **Bk Rev. Circ:** 3,000. available on microfilm and microfiche from University Microfilms International (UMI).
**Desc:** Articles of interest for undergraduate students of mathematics.

HU/0031-5303
**PERIODICA MATHEMATICA HUNGARICA.** [Period. math. hung.]. **Added/Corp** Bolyai Janos Matematikai Tarsulat. Vol. 1 (1971)-. Periodical. English (French and German). bm. $622.00. Kluwer Academic Publishers, Postbus 322, 3300 AH Dordrecht, The Netherlands. **Tel** 011 (31) 78 524400, FAX 011 31 78 183273, telex 20083. **ED** Pal Erdos, I. Ratko, and H. Hajnal. **LC** QA1; .P38. **CODEN** PMHGAW. **[CCC]. Bk Rev. Ad Acc. Pr Rev. Acid Free. Circ:** 400. available in microform from University Microfilms International (UMI). Documents available from Ask*IEEE.
**Desc:** The fundamental aim of the journal is to publish original research articles in any area of pure and applied mathematics (algebra, geometry, analysis, etc.).
**Ind/Abst** INSPEC (1975-); Math. Rev.; Stat. Theory Method Abstr. (1972-1977, 1979-1982, 1984, 1986); Zentralbl. Math. Ihre Grenzgeb.

GW/0344-4325
**PERSPECTIVES IN MATHEMATICAL LOGIC.** [Perspect. math. log.]. (1975)-. Monographic series. English. ir. Price varies per volume. Springer-Verlag New York Inc., 175 5th Avenue, New York NY 10010. **Tel** (212)460-1500, telex 232 235 SPB UR. **(Subscription address:** Springer Verlag New York Inc. / for North America, 44 Hartz Way, Secaucus NJ 07096.**) [CCC]. Pr Rev.**
**Desc:** Contains topics on: admissible sets and structures, constructability, general recursion theory, recursion - theoretic, hierarchies, degrees of insolvability, and basic set theory.
**Ind/Abst** Math. Rev.

UK/1062-7901
**PHASE TRANSITIONS AND CRITICAL PHENOMENA.** **See** Physics.

US/0031-8019
**PHILOSOPHIA MATHEMATICA.** [Philos. math.]. **Added/Corp** Association for Philosophy of Mathematics. Canadian Society for the History and Philosophy of Mathematics. Vol. 1, No. 1 (June 1964)-. Academic Scholarly Publication. English (German and French; summaries and/or abstracts in French and German). sa. $60.00. University of Toronto Press, 5201 Dufferin Street, Downsview Ontario M3H 5T8 Canada. **Tel** (416)667-7781, (416)667-7782, FAX (416)667-7803. **ED** Robert Thomas. **LC** QA9; .P45. **DD** 510/.01. **CODEN** PHMAB5. **Bk Rev. Ad Acc. Circ:** 600 (ctrl).
**Desc:** The aim of the journal is scholarly interchange. Contains new work in the philosophy of mathematics, including what can be learned from the study of mathematics. Each issue has articles of interest to both mathematicians and philosophers and those concerned with the teaching of mathematics at every level.
**Ind/Abst** Math. Rev.; Philos. Index; Zentralbl. Math. Ihre Grenzgeb.

US/0031-952X
**PI MU EPSILON JOURNAL.** [Pi Mu Epsilon j.]. **Main/Corp** Pi Mu Epsilon. (Nov. 1949)-. Periodical. English. Twice a year (April & Nov.). $12.00 US; $15.00 other. Pi Mu Epsilon Journal, Professor Dudley, De Pauw University, Greencastle IN 46135. **Tel** (317)658-4728. **ED** Underwood Dudley. **LC** QA1; .P47. **DD** 371.85451. **CODEN** PMEJBR. Index available. **Circ:** 3,500. available on microfilm and microfiche from University Microfilms International (UMI).
**Desc:** Mathematics for the undergraduate and beginning graduate student. Official publication of the Pi Mu Epsilon Honorary Mathematics Society. Mathematics articles and problems, directed at the undergraduate level.
**Ind/Abst** Math. Rev.; Zentralbl. Math. Ihre Grenzgeb.

UK/0269-3666
**PITMAN MONOGRAPHS AND SURVEYS IN PURE AND APPLIED MATHEMATICS.** [Pitman monogr. surv. pure appl. math.]. **VFOAT** Monographs and Surveys in Pure and Applied Mathematics. (1986)-. Monographic series. English. ir. Price varies per volume. Longman Group UK Ltd, Westgate House, The High, 6th Floor, Harlow Essex CM20 1YR England. **Tel** 011 44 0279-442601, FAX 011 44 0279-444501. **LC** UNC. ***Continues*** *Monographs, Advanced Texts, and Surveys in Pure and Applied Mathematics, 8756-7415.*
**Ind/Abst** Math. Rev. (1987-); Zentralbl. Math. Ihre Grenzgeb.

UK/0269-3674
**PITMAN RESEARCH NOTES IN MATHEMATICS SERIES.** [Pitman res. notes math. ser.]. **VFOAT** Research Notes in Mathematics. (198?)-. Monographic series. English. ir. Price varies per volume. John Wiley & Sons Ltd., Baffins Lane, Chichester West Sussex PO19 1UD England. **Tel** 0243 779777, FAX

0243 776128 BTG:JWP001, telex 86290 WIBOOKG. **LC** UNC. ***Continues*** *Research Notes in Mathematics, 0743-0337.*

FR/0397-7471
**PLOT POITIERS.** VFOAT
Poitiers-Limoges-Orleans-Tours. (1976)-. Periodical. French. qt. 80.00F (members), 100.00F (nonmembers) France; 120.00F other. Assn Prof Mathematics Enseign Pub, BP 6759, 45067 Orleans Cedex 2 France. **UDC** 37. ***Continues*** *BROT. Bulletin de la Regionale d'Orleans Tours, 0986-2595.*

UK
**PLUS: A MATHEMATICAL MAGAZINE.**
English. Three times a year. £3.00 (nonmembers), £2.60 (members) UK; £4.10 (nonmembers), £3.70 (members) other. Mathematical Association, 259 London Road, Leicester LE2 3BE England. **Tel** 011 44 533 703877.

GW/0032-7042
**PM. PRAXIS DER MATHEMATIK.** (PRAXIS DER MATHEMATIK.). [PM, Prax. Math.]. Vol. 1 (April 1959)-. Periodical. German. Six times a year. DM91.20 Germany; DM99.00 other. Aulis Verlag Deubner & Company, Antwerpenerstrasse 6 12, 50672 Koln Germany. **Tel** 011 49 221 518051, FAX 011 49 221 518443. **ED** Dietrich Pohlman. **LC** QA1; .P77. **[CCC].** Index Available in last issue of each volume--loose separately paged. **Bk Rev**. **Ad Acc**. **Circ:** 3,000 (ctrl).
**Desc:** Journal for teaching practices in secondary school grades 11 and 12.
**Ind/Abst** Energy Res. Abstr. (March 1982-); Math. Rev.; Zentralbl. Math. Ihre Grenzgeb.

US/1041-3782
**POPULAR STATISTICS.** [Pop. stat.]. (1983)-. Monographic series. English. ir. Price varies per volume. Marcel Dekker Inc., 270 Madison Avenue, New York NY 10016. **Tel** (212)696-9000, (800)228-1160, FAX (212)685-4540, telex 421419. **(Subscription address:** Marcel Dekker Inc, PO Box 5017, Monticello NY 12701.) **DD** 519.
**Desc:** Covers various topics in the statistics field.

PO/0032-5155
**PORTUGALIAE MATHEMATICA.** [Port. math.]. **Added/Corp** Faculdade de Ciencias de Lisboa. Vol. 1 (1937)-. Periodical. English (French, German, Italian and Portuguese). Four times a year. $120.00 Europe; $128.00 others. Portugaliae Mathematica, Avenue da Republica 37 #4, 1000 Lisbon Portugal. **Tel** 011 351 1 7939785. **ED** A. Monteiro. **LC** QA1; .P67. **DD** 510/.5. **CODEN** POMAAJ. cum. index.
**Ind/Abst** Math. Rev.; Stat. Theory Method Abstr. (1959-1966); Zentralbl. Math. Ihre Grenzgeb.

XN/0352-3853
**POSEBNI IZDANIJA - MATEMATICKI FAKULTET NA UNIVERZITETOT "KIRIL I METODIJ", SKOPJE.** (POSEBNI IZDANIJA.). [Poseb. izd. - Mat. fak. Univ. 'Kiril i Metodij' Skopje]. **VFOAT** Editions Speciales - Faculte des Mathematiques de L'Universite 'Kiril i Metodij', Skopje. (1984)-. Monographic series. English. **UDC** 51.
**Ind/Abst** Zentralbl. Math. Ihre Grenzgeb.

●US/0926-2601
**POTENTIAL ANALYSIS : AN INTERNATIONAL JOURNAL DEVOTED TO THE INTERACTIONS BETWEEN POTENTIAL THEORY, PROBABILITY THEORY, GEOMETRY AND FUNCTIONAL ANALYSIS.** Vol. 1, No. 1 (Mar. 1992)-. Periodical. English. bm. $600.00. Kluwer Academic Publishers, Postbus 322, 3300 AH Dordrecht, The Netherlands. **Tel** 011 (31) 78 524400, FAX 011 31 78 183273, telex 20083. **LC** QA404.7; .P65. **DD** 515.9. **CODEN** POANE2. **Pr Rev**. **Acid Free**. available on microfilm and microfiche from University Microfilms International (UMI).
**Desc:** This journal publishes original papers dealing with the applications of potential theory in the following main areas: applications of the classical theory, partial differential equations, elliptic and parabolic operators, boundary problems, nonlinear problems, numerical analysis; harmonic measure, Hausdorff measures, capacities; dirichlet spaces, functional analysis, semi-groups of operators; probabilistic interpretations, Brownian motion, Markov processes, martingales; calculus on the Wiener space, stochastic differential equations, quantum theories; and connections with other theories, such as harmonic analysis, ergodic theory, differential theory, and dynamical systems.

PL
**PRACE IPI PAN / ICS PAS REPORTS.** See Computers.

PL/0239-7978
**PRACE MATEMATYCZNE.** [Rocz. nauk.-dydakt. - Wyz. Szk. Pedagog. im. Komis. Eduk. Nar. Krak., Pr. mat.]. **Main/Corp** Krakow. Wyzsza Szkota Pedagogiczna. Began with No. 4; published in 1966. Monographic series. Polish (summaries and/or abstracts in English, French and Russian). Price varies per volume. **LC** AS142.K66; .A2. ***Continues*** *Matematyka.*

PL
**PRACE NAUKOWE INSTYTUTU MATEMATYKI POLITECHNIKI WROCAWSKIEJ.** **Main/Corp** Politechnika Wrocawska. Instytut Matematyki. **VFOAT** Scientific Papers of the Institute of Mathematics of Wrocaw Technical University. Monographic series. Polish (English and Russian; summaries and/or abstracts in English, Polish and Russian). Price varies per volume. **(Subscription address:** ARS Polona, PO Box 1001, 00068 Warsaw Poland.) **LC** TJ260.A1; B78. ***Continues*** *Politechnika Wrocawska. Instytut Matematyki I Fizyki Teoretycznej. Prace Naukowe.*
**Ind/Abst** Zentralbl. Math. Ihre Grenzgeb.

US/0079-4856
**PRAGUE STUDIES IN MATHEMATICAL LINGUISTICS.** [Prague stud. math. linguist.]. 1966-. English (Russian). ir. John Benjamins BV, Amsteldijk 44, PO Box 75577, 1070 AN Amsterdam Netherlands. **Tel** 011 31 20 6738156, FAX 011 31 20 739773. **(Subscription address:** John Benjamins North America, PO Box 27519, Philadelphia PA 19118-0519.) **NLM** W1 PR224L.
**Desc:** Brings original studies in quantitative and algebraic linguistics from various institutes or mathematicians and experts in machine linguistics from various institutes of the Czechoslovak and Slovak Academies of Sciences and university departments.
**Ind/Abst** Math. Rev.; Zentralbl. Math. Ihre Grenzgeb.

XV
**PREPRINT SERIES OF THE DEPARTMENT OF MATHEMATICS / UNIVERZA V LJUBLJANI, INSTITUT ZA MATEMATIKO, FIZIKO IN MEHANIKO, OFFELEK ZA MATEMATIKO.** No. 14 (1976)-. Periodical. English. an. Institute of Mathematics Physics and Mechanics, PO Box 64, 61111 Ljubljana Slovenia. **Tel** (016)265-061. **ED** Ciril Velkovrh. **Circ:** 200. ***Continues*** *Publications of the Department of Mathematics.*

RU/0134-6350
**PRIKLADNAA MATEMATIKA.** [Prikl. mat.]. (1975)-. Russian. ir. **UDC** 51.
**Ind/Abst** Zentralbl. Math. Ihre Grenzgeb.

RU
**PRIKLADNAIA MATEMATIKA I MEKHANIKA.** **Main/Corp** Kharkivskyi Derzhavnyi Universytet Imeni O.M. Horkoho. Vol. 42 (1977)-. Russian. Six times a year. $211.00. **(Subscription address:** East View Publications Inc., 3020 Harbor Lane North, Suite 110, Minneapolis MN 55447.) **LC** AS262; .K417 subser; QA1. ***Continues*** *Matematika i Mekhanika.*

RU/0032-8235
**PRIKLADNAJA MATEMATIKA I MEHANIKA.** See Engineering-Mechanical Engineering and Machinery.

UK/0032-8294
**PRIMARY MATHEMATICS.** [Prim. math.]. V. 6-Spring 1968-. Periodical. English. Three times a year. $5.00. Pergamon Press, An Imprint of Elsevier Science Ltd., The Boulevard, Langford Lane, Kidlington, Oxford OX5 1GB United Kingdom. **Tel** 011 44 865 843000, 011 44 865 843699, FAX 011 44 865 843010. **(Subscription address:** US/ 395 Saw Mill River Road, Elmsford, NY 10523; Can/ 150 Consumers Road/Suite 104, Willowdale Ontario M2J 1P9; Aus-NZ/ POB 544, Potts Point NSW 2011) **LC** QA135; .T34. **DD** 372.7/05. ***Continues*** *Teaching Arithmetic.*

AT/0816-9349
**PRIME NUMBER.** [Prime number]. (1986)-. Periodical. English. qt. (Comes with Mathematical Assn of Victoria membership). Mathematical Association of Victoria, 61 Blyth Street, Brunswick VIC 3056 Australia. **Tel** 011 61 3 3802399, FAX 011 61 3 3808323. **DD** 372.709945. **Bk Rev**. **Ad Acc**. **Circ:** 2,000 (ctrl). ***Continues*** *Set Two, 0312-5424.*
**Ind/Abst** Aust. Educ. Index.

US/1051-1970
**PRIMUS (TERRE HAUTE, IND.).** (PRIMUS : PROBLEMS, RESOURCES, AND ISSUES IN MATHEMATICS UNDERGRADUATE STUDIES.). [PRIMUS]. **Added/Corp** Rose-Hulman Institute of Technology. **VFOAT** Problems, Resources, and Issues in Mathematics Undergraduate Studies. Vol. 1, No. 1 (March 1991)-. Periodical. English. qt (Mar., Jun., Sep., Dec.). $34.00 US; $40.00 other, postage included. Rose Hulman Institute of Technology, 5500 Wabash Avenue, Terre Haute IN 47803. **Tel** (812)877-8412, FAX (812)877-3198. **ED** Brian J Winkel. **LC** QA11.A1; P74. **DD** 510/.71/1. **[CCC].** available on microfilm and microfiche from University Microfilms International (UMI).
**Desc:** Forum for the exchange of ideas in mathematics education at the college level. Devoted to the dialogue among those interested in undergraduate mathematics.
**Ind/Abst** Curr. Index J. Educ.

US/0079-5194
**PRINCETON MATHEMATICAL SERIES.** (1939)-. Monographic series. English. ir. Price varies per volume. Princeton University Press, 41 William Street, Princeton NJ 08540. **Tel** (609)258-4900. **(Subscription address:** California Princeton Fulfillment Service, 1445 Lower Ferry Road, Ewing NJ 08618.)
**Ind/Abst** Math. Rev.; Zentralbl. Math. Ihre Grenzgeb.

PL/0208-4147
**PROBABILITY AND MATHEMATICAL STATISTICS.** See Mathematics-Abstracting, Bibliographies and Statistics.

US/0079-5607
**PROBABILITY AND MATHEMATICAL STATISTICS (NEW YORK, N.Y.).** (PROBABILITY AND MATHEMATICAL STATISTICS.). [Probab. math. stat.]. (1967)-. Monographic series. English. ir. Price varies per volume. Academic Press, Inc., 6277 Sea Harbor Drive, Orlando FL 32887. **Tel** (800)543-9534, (407)345-4100, FAX (407)363-9661. **ED** M. M. Rao.
**Ind/Abst** Math. Rev.

GW/0720-2628
**PROBABILITY AND STOCHASTIC PROCESSES.** **Added/Corp** Heidelberger Akademie der Wissenschaften Fachsinformationszentrum Energie, Physik, Mathematik. (1981)-. Periodical. English (French and German). mo. $135.00. Scientific Information Service Inc., 7 Woodland Avenue, Larchmont NY 10538. **Tel** (914)834-8864.

US
**PROBABILITY, PURE AND APPLIED.** (1984)-. Monographic series. English. Price varies per volume. Marcel Dekker Inc., 270 Madison Avenue, New York NY 10016. **Tel** (212)696-9000, (800)228-1160, FAX (212)685-4540, telex 421419. **(Subscription address:** Marcel Dekker Inc, PO Box 5017, Monticello NY 12701.)
**Desc:** Each title gives information on probability, including theory and stochastic matrices.
**Ind/Abst** Math. Rev.; Zentralbl. Math. Ihre Grenzgeb.

GW/0178-8051
**PROBABILITY THEORY AND RELATED FIELDS.** [Probab. theory relat. fields]. **VFOAT** Probability Theory. Vol. 71, No. 1 (Jan. 1986)-. English. Twelve times a year. DM2682.00. Springer-Verlag GmbH & Company KG, Heidelberger Platz 3, D 14197 Berlin Germany. **Tel** 011 49 30 8207223, FAX 011 49 30 8214091, telex 183 319 SPBLN D. **(Subscription address:** Springer Verlag New York Inc. / for North America, 44 Hartz Way, Secaucus NJ 07096.) **ED** H Rost. **LC** QA273; .Z4. **DD** 519.2/05. **CODEN** PTRFEU. **[CCC].** **Pr Rev.** available on microfilm and microfiche from University Microfilms International (UMI). Documents available from The Genuine Article. ***Continues*** *Zeitschrift fur Wahrscheinlichkeitstheorie und Verwandte Gebiete, 0044-3719.*
**Desc:** Devoted to research in probability theory on an advanced level; it also publishes papers from other fields such as optimization theory, statistical mechanics, ergodic theory, and measure theory or analytic number theory when they are closely connected with basic problems in probability theory.
**Ind/Abst** Compumath Citation Index [Full Cov.]; Curr. Contents Phys. Chem. Earth Sci.; Curr. Index Stat.; Math. Rev. (1986-); Res. Alert [Full Cov.]; Sci. Cit. Index; SCISEARCH; Stat. Theory Method Abstr. (1986-1987); Zentralbl. Math. Ihre Grenzgeb.

RU
**PROBLEMY MATEMATICHESKOGO ANALIZA.** **Added/Corp** Leningradskii Gosudarstvennyi Universitet Imeni A.A. Zhdanova. Leningradskii Gosudarstvennyi Universitet Imeni A.A. Zhdanova. Kafedra Matematicheskoi Fiziki. (1966)-. Periodical. Russian. bm. St Petersburg State University / Izdatelstvo Leningradskogo Universiteta, Universitetskaia Nab 7/9, 199034 St Petersburg Russia. **Tel** 011 95 218-97-88, FAX 011 95 218-51-52, telex 121481. **LC** QA300; .P962.
**Ind/Abst** Math. Rev.; Zentralbl. Math. Ihre Grenzgeb.

GW
**PROCEEDINGS / CONFERENCE ON COMPACT TRANSFORMATION GROUPS.** **Main/Conf** Conference on Compact Transformation Groups. (1967)-. Proceedings. English. DM32.00. Springer-Verlag New York Inc., 175 5th Avenue, New York NY 10010. **Tel** (212)460-1500, telex 232 235 SPB UR. **(Subscription address:** Springer Verlag New York Inc. / for North America, 44 Hartz Way, Secaucus NJ 07096.) **LC** QA3; .L28 subser; QA387. **DD** 510/.8 S; 512/.55.

UK/0962-8444
**PROCEEDINGS. MATHEMATICAL AND PHYSICAL SCIENCES / THE ROYAL SOCIETY.** **Added/Corp** Royal Society (Great Britain). **VFOAT** Mathematical and Physical Sciences; Proceedings of the Royal Society of London. Series A; Proceedings of the Royal Society. Series A. Vol. 430, No. 1878 (July 1990)-. Academic Scholarly Publication. English. mo. £375.00 UK; $682.00 US; £413.00 other. Royal Society, 6 Carlton House Terrace, London SW1Y 5AG England. **Tel** 011 44 71 839 5561, FAX 071-976 1837, telex 917876 ROYAL G. Documents available from

CASDDS. **Continues** *Royal Society (Great Britain). Proceedings of the Royal Society of London. Series A, Mathematical and Physical Sciences.*
**Ind/Abst** Chem. Abstr.

KO
## PROCEEDINGS OF KIT MATHEMATICS WORKSHOP / KOREA INSTITUTE OF TECHNOLOGY, MATHEMATICS RESEARCH CENTER.
**Added/Corp** Korea Institute of Technology. Mathematics Research Center. **VFOAT** Proceedings of Korea Institute of Technology Mathematics Workshop; Algebra and Topology; Analysis and Geometry. (1986)-. Proceedings. English. **LC** QA8.7; .K57.
**Ind/Abst** Zentralbl. Math. Ihre Grenzgeb.

US/0082-0717
## PROCEEDINGS OF SYMPOSIA IN PURE MATHEMATICS.
[Proc. symp. pure math.]. **Added/Corp** American Mathematical Society. Vol. 1 (1959)-. Monographic series. English. ir. Price varies per volume. American Mathematical Society, PO Box 6248, Providence RI 02940-6248. **Tel** (800)321-4267, (401)455-4000, FAX (401)331-3842, telex 797192. **(Subscription address:** American Mathematical Society, PO Box 5904, Boston MA 02206-5904.**)** **LC** UNC. **[CCC].**
**Ind/Abst** Math. Rev.; Zentralbl. Math. Ihre Grenzgeb.

US/0002-9939
## PROCEEDINGS OF THE AMERICAN MATHEMATICAL SOCIETY.
[Proc. Am. Math. Soc.]. **Main/Corp** American Mathematical Society. Vol. 1 (Feb. 1950)-. Proceedings. English. mo. $605.00. American Mathematical Society, PO Box 6248, Providence RI 02940-6248. **Tel** (800)321-4267, (401)455-4000, FAX (401)331-3842, telex 797192. **(Subscription address:** American Mathematical Society, PO Box 5904, Boston MA 02206-5904.**)** **LC** QA1; .A5215. **DD** 510.6273. **CODEN** PAMYAR. **[CCC].** cum. index. **Pr Rev.** available on microfilm and microfiche from University Microfilms International (UMI). Documents available from The Genuine Article.
**Desc:** Devoted entirely to research in pure and applied mathematics, principally original papers of moderate length. Shorter notes section for very short, yet elegant and polished, papers in mathematics.
**Ind/Abst** Compumath Citation Index [Full Cov.]; Curr. Contents Phys. Chem. Earth Sci.; Math. Rev.; Res. Alert [Full Cov.]; SCISEARCH; Stat. Theory Method Abstr. (1959-1963, 1967, 1972); Zentralbl. Math. Ihre Grenzgeb.

US/0736-587X
## PROCEEDINGS OF THE CONFERENCE - ASSOCIATION FOR COMPUTATIONAL LINGUISTICS. MEETING.
**See** Linguistics.

RM
## PROCEEDINGS OF THE CONFERENCE ON PROBABILITY THEORY.
**Main/Conf** Conference on Probability Theory. **Added/Corp** Academia Republicii Socialiste Romania. Centre of Mathematical Statistics. 4th (1971)-. Proceedings. English. te. Editura Academia Republicii Socialiste Romania, Calea Victoriei Nr 125, R-79717 Bucuresti Romania. **Tel** telex 10376 PRSFI R. **LC** QA273.A1; C65a. **DD** 519.2/05.
**Ind/Abst** Stat. Theory Method Abstr. (1984, 1986).

UK/0013-0915
## PROCEEDINGS OF THE EDINBURGH MATHEMATICAL SOCIETY.
[Proc. Edinb. Math. Soc.]. **Main/Corp** Edinburgh Mathematical Society. (1883)-. Periodical. English. tq. £84.00 UK and Europe; $170.00 other. Oxford University Press, Walton Street, Oxford OX2 6DP England. **Tel** 011 44 865 56767, FAX 011 44 865 267773, telex 837330 OXPRES G. **(Subscription address:** Oxford University Press / USA, Journals Marketing Department, Oxford University Press, 2001 Evans Road, Cary NC 27513.**)** **ED** T. A. Gillespie. **CODEN** PEMSA3. **[CCC].** cum. index. **Pr Rev.** Documents available from The Genuine Article.
**Ind/Abst** Compumath Citation Index [Full Cov.]; Math. Rev.; Res. Alert [Full Cov.]; SCISEARCH; Stat. Theory Method Abstr. (1967-); Zentralbl. Math. Ihre Grenzgeb.

II/0253-4142
## PROCEEDINGS OF THE INDIAN ACADEMY OF SCIENCES. MATHEMATICAL SCIENCES.
(PROCEEDINGS. MATHEMATICAL SCIENCES / INDIAN ACADEMY OF SCIENCES.). [Proc. Indian Acad. Sci., Math. sci.]. **Added/Corp** Indian Academy of Sciences. **VFOAT** Mathematical Sciences; Proceedings of the Indian Academy of Sciences. Mathematical Sciences. Vol. 89, No. 1 (Jan. 1980)-. Academic Scholarly Publication. English. Three times a year. Indian Academy of Sciences Circulation, PO Box 8005, Department of Sadashivanagar, Bangalore 560 080 India. **Tel** 011 91 812 342546, 342310, telex 0845-2178 ACAD IN. **(Subscription address:** Prints India, 11 Darya Ganj, New Delhi 110002 India.**)** **ED** S. G. Dani. **LC** QA11.A1; P76. **DD** 510/.5. **CODEN** PIAMDO. Index available. **Circ:** 750. available on microfilm and microfiche from University Microfilms International (UMI). Documents available from The Genuine Article, Ask*IEEE, CASDDS. **Continues** *Proceedings. A, Mathematical Sciences.*
**Desc:** A leading journal of mathematics, publishing papers on pure and applied mathematics.
**Ind/Abst** Chem. Abstr. (1980-1981); Compumath Citation Index [Full Cov.]; Energy Res. Abstr. (Feb. 1981-); INSPEC (Jan. 1980-); Int. Aerosp. Abstr.; Math. Rev.; Ref. Z.; Res. Alert [Full Cov.]; Zentralbl. Math. Ihre Grenzgeb.

JA/0386-2194
## PROCEEDINGS OF THE JAPAN ACADEMY. SERIES A: MATHEMATICAL SCIENCES.
[Proc. Jpn. Acad. Ser. A]. **Main/Corp** Nihon Gakushiin. Vol. 53 (April 1977)-. Academic Scholarly Publication. English. mo. Nihon Gakushiin, (Japan Academy), 7-32, Ueno Koen, Taitoku, Tokyoto 110 Japan. **(Subscription address:** Maruzen Company Ltd., PO Box 5050, Import & Export Department, Tokyo 100 31 Japan.**)** **LC** QA1; .N525A. **DD** 510/.5. **NLM** W1 PR5853. **CODEN** PJAADT. cum. index. Documents available from The Genuine Article, Ask*IEEE, CASDDS. **Continues in part** *Proceedings of the Japan Academy, 0021-4280.*
**Ind/Abst** Chem. Abstr.; Compumath Citation Index [Full Cov.]; INSPEC (April 1977-); Math. Rev.; Res. Alert [Full Cov.]; SCISEARCH; Zentralbl. Math. Ihre Grenzgeb.

UK/0024-6115
## PROCEEDINGS OF THE LONDON MATHEMATICAL SOCIETY.
[Proc. Lond. Math. Soc.]. **Main/Corp** London Mathematical Society. **Added/Corp** London Mathematical Society. Papers Presented to J. E. Littlewood on His 80th Birthday. London Mathematical Society. Abstracts of Papers Accepted for Publication. Vol. 1, No. 1 (Jan. 1865)-. Periodical. English. bm. £330.00 UK and Europe; $650.00 other. Oxford University Press, Walton Street, Oxford OX2 6DP England. **Tel** 011 44 865 56767, FAX 011 44 865 267773, telex 837330 OXPRES G. **(Subscription address:** Oxford University Press / USA, Journals Marketing Department, Oxford University Press, 2001 Evans Road, Cary NC 27513.**)** **ED** W. D. Evans and J. Wiegold. **LC** QA1; .L5. **DD** 510.08. **CODEN** PLMTAL. **[CCC].** Index available. cum. index. **Ad Acc. Pr Rev. Circ:** 1,400. available on microfilm and microfiche from University Microfilms International (UMI). Documents available from The Genuine Article.
**Desc:** Research papers of a substantial character in the fields of real and complex analysis, differential equations and related areas, topology, geometry, logic, probability and statistics, algebra, number theory, and combinational theory.
**Ind/Abst** Compumath Citation Index [Full Cov.]; Curr. Contents Phys. Chem. Earth Sci.; Math. Rev.; Res. Alert [Full Cov.]; Sci. Cit. Index; SCISEARCH; Stat. Theory Method Abstr. (1959-1963, 1967, 1969-1975); Zentralbl. Math. Ihre Grenzgeb.

UA
## PROCEEDINGS OF THE MATHEMATICAL AND PHYSICAL SOCIETY OF EGYPT.
**Main/Corp** Jam'iyah al-Misriyah lil-'Ulum al-Riyadiyah wa-al-Tabi'iyah. No. 1 (1937)-. Academic Scholarly Publication. English (summaries and/or abstracts in Arabic). an. Documents available from CASDDS.
**Ind/Abst** Chem. Abstr.; Math. Rev.

IE/0035-8975
## PROCEEDINGS OF THE ROYAL IRISH ACADEMY. SECTION A. MATHEMATICAL AND PHYSICAL SCIENCES.
[Proc. R. Ir. Acad., A Math. phys. sci.]. **Main/Corp** Royal Irish Academy. Vol. 69 (1970)-. Proceedings. English. an. 40.00p. Royal Irish Academy, 19 Dawson Street, Dublin 2 Ireland. **Tel** 011 353 1 762570. Documents available from The Genuine Article, Ask*IEEE. **Continues** *T.Proceedings of the Royal Irish Academy. Section A: Mathematical, Astronomical,and Physical Science.*
**Ind/Abst** Curr. Contents Phys. Chem. Earth Sci.; GeoRef (1970-); INSPEC (1970-); Math. Rev.; Res. Alert [Select. Cov.].

UK/0308-2105
## PROCEEDINGS OF THE ROYAL SOCIETY OF EDINBURGH. SECTION A. MATHEMATICA.
(PROCEEDINGS. SECTION A, MATHEMATICS / THE ROYAL SOCIETY OF EDINBURGH.). [Proc. R. Soc. Edinb., Sect. A, Math.]. **Added/Corp** Royal Society of Edinburgh. **VFOAT** Proceedings of the Royal Society of Edinburgh. Section A. Vol. 72, Pt. 1 (1974)-. Periodical. English. bm. £198.00 UK. Royal Society of Edinburgh, 22 24 George Street, Edinburgh EH2 2PQ Scotland. **Tel** 011 44 031-225-6057, FAX 011 44 031-220-6889. **ED** J M Ball. **LC** Q41; .E212. **DD** 510/.5. Index available. cum. index. **Pr Rev. Circ:** 900. Documents available from The Genuine Article, Ask*IEEE, Petroleum Abstracts Document Delivery Service. **Continues in part** *Proceedings. Section A, Mathematical and Physical Sciences, 0080-4541.*
**Desc:** A general mathematics journal publishing papers of international standard across the whole spectrum of mathematics.
**Ind/Abst** Biodeter. Abstr.; Compumath Citation Index [Full Cov.]; Curr. Contents Phys. Chem. Earth Sci.; INSPEC (1983-); Int. Aerosp. Abstr.; Math. Rev.; Pet. Abstr.; Res. Alert [Full Cov.]; Sci. Cit. Index; SCISEARCH; Zentralbl. Math. Ihre Grenzgeb.

US/0149-9963
## PROCEEDINGS OF THE STATISTICAL COMPUTING SECTION.
[Proc. Stat. Comput. Sect.]. **Main/Corp** American Statistical Association. Statistical Computing Section. (1975)-. Statistical Publication. English. an. $48.50. American Statistical Association, 1429 Duke Street, Alexandria VA 22314. **Tel** (703)684-1221, (202)393-3253, FAX (703)684-2037 (orders). **LC** QA276.4; .A43a. **DD** 519.5/01/83. **Circ:** 1,000.
**Ind/Abst** Curr. Index Stat. (199?-).

US/0196-3880
## PROCEEDINGS OF THE TOPOLOGY CONFERENCE, THE.
**Main/Conf** Topology Conference. Proceedings. English. an. Auburn University / Department of Mathematics, Parker Hall, Auburn AL 36849-5310. **Tel** (205)844-4290, FAX (205)844-6555. **ED** Zenor Gruenhage. **LC** QA611.A1; T68 subser. **DD** 514 S; 514. **Pr Rev. Circ:** 350.
**Desc:** Refereed papers presented at the annual topology conference with questions and answers sections at the end.

US/1063-6889
## PROCEEDINGS / SYMPOSIUM ON COMPUTER ARITHMETIC.
[Proc. - Symp. Comput. Arith.]. **Added/Corp** IEEE Computer Society. IEEE Computer Society. Technical Committee on Computer Architecture. **VFOAT** IEEE ... Computer Arithmetic; Computer Arithmetic. 4th (1978)-. English. ir. $74.00 (latest edition). IEEE Computer Society, 10662 Los Vaqueros Circle, PO Box 3014, Los Alamitos CA 90720-1264. **Tel** (714)821-8380, (800)272-6657, FAX (714)821-4641. **LC** QA76.9.C62; S95a. **DD** 004/.01/51. **Continues** *Symposium on Computer Arithmetic. Symposium on Computer Arithmetic : [Papers].*
**Ind/Abst** Index IEEE Publ.

US
## PROCEEDINGS - SYMPOSIUM ON NONLINEAR ESTIMATION THEORY AND ITS APPLICATIONS.
**Main/Conf** Symposium on Nonlinear Estimation Theory and its Applications. 1st- 1970-. Proceedings. English. Western Periodicals Company, 424 East Main Street, Ventura CA 93001. **Tel** (805)641-2665, FAX (805)643-4854. **LC** QA402.3; .S96. **DD** 519.5/4.

US/0743-1643
## PROGRESS IN MATHEMATICS (BOSTON, MASS.).
(PROGRESS IN MATHEMATICS.). [Prog. math.]. Vol. 1 (1979)-. Monographic series. English (French). ir. Price varies per volume. Birkhauser Boston, Inc., c/o Springer Publishers New York Inc., Customer Service Department, 333 Meadowlands Parkway, Secaucus NJ 07096-2491. **Tel** (201)348-4033, (800)777-4643. **(Subscription address:** Birkhauser Boston Books, c/o Springer Verlag, PO Box 19386, Newark, NJ 07195; Phone: (201)348-4033**)** **LC** UNC. **DD** 510.
**Ind/Abst** Math. Rev.; Zentralbl. Math. Ihre Grenzgeb.

SZ
## PROGRESS IN NONLINEAR DIFFERENTIAL EQUATIONS AND THEIR APPLICATIONS.
**VFOAT** PNLDE; Progress in Non-Linear Differential Equations and Their Applications. (1989)-. Monographic series. English. ir. Price varies per volume. Birkhaeuser Verlag Ag, Klosterberg 23, PO Box 133, CH-4010 Basel Switzerland. **Tel** 011 41 61 2717400, FAX 011 41 0 61 2717666, telex 963475 birk ch.
**Ind/Abst** Math. Rev.; Zentralbl. Math. Ihre Grenzgeb.

II/0555-4330
## PROGRESS OF MATHEMATICS.
[Progr. math.]. **Added/Corp** Academy for Progress of Mathematics. Vol. 1 (Mar. 1967)-. Periodical. English. sa. $37.50. Banaras Hindu University Academy of Progress of Mathematics, Varanasi India. **Tel** (0542)54291. **(Subscription address:** Prints India, 11 Darya Ganj, New Delhi 110002 India.**)** **ED** R S Mishra, M W Dhahir, M Hashiguchi, R Miron, H Rund, D A Sprott and B Sinha. **LC** QA1; .P786. **DD** 510/.05. **CODEN** PMTHBS. **Circ:** 250.
**Desc:** Publishes the original research of the members of the Academy in pure and applied mathematics, theoretical physics, astronomy, astrophysics, and statistics, with the cooperation of local and foreign members of the editorial board.
**Ind/Abst** Math. Rev.; Zentralbl. Math. Ihre Grenzgeb.

SP
## PUBLICACIONES DEL DEPARTAMENTO DE MATEMATICAS UNIVERSIDAD DE EXTREMADURA.
**Added/Corp** Universidad de Extremadura (Badajoz, Spain). Departamento de Matematicas. (1983)-. Monographic series. Spanish (English). Price varies per volume.
**Ind/Abst** Zentralbl. Math. Ihre Grenzgeb.

SP
**PUBLICACIONES DEL SEMINARIO MATEMATICO GARCIA DE GALDEANO.** Monographic series. Spanish. Price varies per volume. **LC** QA1; .S3. ***Continues*** *Publicaciones del Seminario Matematico.*
**Ind/Abst** Zentralbl. Math. Ihre Grenzgeb.

SP/0214-1493
**PUBLICACIONS MATEMATIQUES / DEPARTAMENT DE MATEMATIQUES, UNIVERSITAT AUTONOMA DE BARCELONA.** **Added/Corp** Universidad Autonoma de Barcelona. Departament de Matematiques. Vol. 32, No. 1 (Aug. 1988)-. Periodical. English (Catalan, Spanish and French). Twice a year. $70.00 institutions; $33.00 individuals. Departamento de Matematicas, Apartado 53, Universitat Autonoma de Barcelona, 08193 Bellaterra Barcelona Spain. **Tel** 011 34 3 5811304. **LC** QA1; .P82. ***Continues*** *Publications, Seccio de Matematiques.*
**Ind/Abst** Math. Rev. (1988-).

HU/0033-3883
**PUBLICATIONES MATHEMATICAL (DEBRECEN).** (PUBLICATIONES MATHEMATICAE.). [Publ. math.]. **Main/Corp** Kossuth Lajos Tudomanyegyetem. Matematikai Intezet. Vol. 1 (1949)-. Periodical. Hungarian (English, French, German and Russian). Twice a year (Jan. & Aug.). $80.00. Debrecen, Institute Mathematique de Universite, 4010 Debrecen Hungary. **Tel** 36-52-16-857, FAX 36-52-10-936, telex 61-72-200. **(Subscription address:** Kultura, PO Box 149, H 1389 Budapest 62 Hungary.**)** **ED** L. Tamassy. **LC** QA1; .D3. **CODEN** PUMAAR. Index available. **Bk Rev. Ad Acc. Pr Rev. Circ:** 800.
**Desc:** Covers mathematics.
**Ind/Abst** Compumath Citation Index [Full Cov.]; Math. Rev.; Stat. Theory Method Abstr. (1959-1963, 1966, 1968, 1972-1973, 1982-1983, 1986); Zentralbl. Math. Ihre Grenzgeb.

FR/0992-647X
**PUBLICATIONS DE L'INSTITUT DE MATHEMATIQUE DE L'UNIVERSITE DE STRASBOURG.** (1937)-. Monographic series. French. Price varies per volume. Hermann Editeurs Science Arts, 293 rue Lecourbe, 75015 Paris France. **Tel** 011 33 1 45574540. **UDC** 5.
**Ind/Abst** Zentralbl. Math. Ihre Grenzgeb.

FR/0997-5489
**PUBLICATIONS DE L'INSTITUT DE RECHERCHE MATHEMATIQUES DE RENNES.** (1985)-. Monographic series. French. Price varies per volume. **UDC** 51. ***Continues*** *Publications des Seminaires de Mathematiques et Informatique de Rennes, 0997-5349.*
**Ind/Abst** Zentralbl. Math. Ihre Grenzgeb.

YU/0350-1302
**PUBLICATIONS DE L'INSTITUT MATHEMATIQUE (BELGRADE).** (PUBLICATIONS DE L'INSTITUT MATHEMATIQUE.). [Publ. Inst. math.]. Vol. 1 (1947)-V. 14 (1960); New Ser., V. 1 (1961)-. English (French, German and Russian). an (two volumes). $50.00. Matematicki Institut, Knez Mihailova 35, Postfach 367, 11001 Belgrad Yugoslavia. **Tel** (011)630-170. **(Subscription address:** Jugoslovenska Knjiga, PO Box 36, YU 11001 Belgrade Yugoslovia.**)** **ED** Slobodan Aljancic. **Circ:** 600. ***Continues*** *Publications Mathematiques de l'Universite de Belgrade.*
**Desc:** Original research papers in mathematics.
**Ind/Abst** Math. Rev.; Zentralbl. Math. Ihre Grenzgeb.

FR
**PUBLICATIONS DE L'U.E.R. MATHEMATIQUES PURES ET APPLIQUEES / IRMA, UNIVERSITE DES SCIENCES ET TECHNIQUES.** **Added/Corp** Universite des Sciences et Techniques de Lille. U.E.R. Mathematiques Pures et Appliquees. Institut de Recherche de Mathematiques Avancees (Lille, France). Vol. 1, (1979)-. French.
**Ind/Abst** Math. Rev.; Zentralbl. Math. Ihre Grenzgeb.

FR/0259-4897
**PUBLICATIONS DU CENTRE DE RECHERCHES EN MATHEMATIQUES PURES. SERIE I.** [Publ. Cent. rech. math. pures. Ser. I]. Began in 1975. French. an. Centre de Recherches en Mathematiques Pures, PR Gare 2, CH-2002 Neuchatel Switzerland. **LC** QA1; .P83. **DD** 510/.5. ***Continues*** *Publications du Seminaire de Geometrie de l'Universite de Neuchatel. Serie I.*
**Ind/Abst** Math. Rev.; Zentralbl. Math. Ihre Grenzgeb.

FI/0076-1656
**PUBLICATIONS DU DEPARTEMENT DE MATHEMATIQUES.** [Publ. Dep. math.]. Vol. 1 (1964)-Vol. 17, No. 2, (1980); New Series 1 (1982)-. Periodical. French. ir. Price varies. Universite of Claude Bernard / Department of Mathematics, 43 Boulevard dull Novembre 1918, 69622 Villeurbanne Cedex France. **Tel** 011 38 78 898124. ***Continues*** *Annales de l'Universite de Lyon. Troisieme Serie. Sciences. Section A. Sciences Mathematiques et Astronomie.*
**Ind/Abst** Math. Rev.; Zentralbl. Math. Ihre Grenzgeb.

FR/0339-7041
**PUBLICATIONS ECONOMETRIQUES.** (196?)-. Periodical. French. sa. 70.00F France; 148.15F other. Univ Lyon, Dept Mathematique, 43 Blvd du 11 Novembre 1918, 69622 Villeurbanne Cedex France.

FR/0995-4325
**PUBLICATIONS MATHEMATIQUES DE LA FACULTE DES SCIENCES DE BESANCON ANALYSE NON LINEAIRE.** [Publ. math. Fac. sci. Besancon, Anal. non lineaire]. (1974)-. Periodical. French. an. Laboratoire de Mathematiques, UFR Science Tech, 16 Rt de Gray, 25030 Besancon Cedex France. **Tel** 011 33 81 666666. **UDC** 51.
**Ind/Abst** Zentralbl. Math. Ihre Grenzgeb.

FR/0768-9284
**PUBLICATIONS MATHEMATIQUES DE LA FACULTE DES SCIENCES DE BESANCON. THEORIE DES NOMBRES.** [Publ. math. Fac. sci. Besancon, Theor. nr]. (197?)-. Periodical. French. an. Laboratoire de Mathematiques, UFR Science Tech, 16 Rt de Gray, 25030 Besancon Cedex France. **Tel** 011 33 81 666666. **UDC** 51.
**Ind/Abst** Zentralbl. Math. Ihre Grenzgeb.

FR
**PUBLICATIONS MATHEMATIQUES DE L'UNIVERSITE PARIS VII.** **Added/Corp** Universite de Paris VII. U.E.R. de Mathematiques. L.A. 212 du C.N.R.S. (1979)-. Monographic series. French. Price varies per volume. Madame Ehresmann, UER Mathematique, 33 rue Saint-Leu, 80039 Amiens Cedex France. **Tel** 011 33 22 914722. **LC** UNC.
**Ind/Abst** Math. Rev.; Zentralbl. Math. Ihre Grenzgeb.

FR
**PUBLICATIONS MATHEMATIQUES DE L'UNIVERSITE PIERRE ET MARIE CURIE.** **Main/Corp** Universite Pierre et Marie Curie. (19??)-. French. Universite Pierre et Marie Curie, 4 Place Jussieu, Tours 45-62 5E Etage, Paris Cedex France.
**Ind/Abst** Math. Rev.; Zentralbl. Math. Ihre Grenzgeb.

FR/0073-8301
**PUBLICATIONS MATHEMATIQUES. INSTITUT DES HAUTES ETUDES SCIENTIFIQUES.** (PUBLICATIONS MATHEMATIQUES.). [Publ. math., Inst. hautes etud. sci.]. **Main/Corp** Institut des Hautes Etudes Scientifiques (Paris, France). No. 1 (1959)-. French (English and German). Twice a year. 1550.00F. Presses Universitaires de France, Department des Revues, 14 Avenue du Bois de l'Epine, BP 90, 91003 Evry Cedex France. **Tel** (1)60 77 82 05, FAX (1) 60 79 20 45, telex PUF 600 474 F. **(Subscription address:** Publications Mathematiques, IHES 35 Route de Chartes, F 91440 Bures S Yvette France.**)** **ED** Jacques Tits, P. Deligne, M. Gromov, J. Bourgain, D. Sullivan, and R. Thom. **LC** QA1; .P22. **CODEN** PMIHA6. **[CCC].** Index available. **Pr Rev.** Documents available from The Genuine Article.
**Desc:** Appearing in two hardcover volumes each year, this journal presents papers in pure mathematics.
**Ind/Abst** Compumath Citation Index [Full Cov.]; Curr. Contents Phys. Chem. Earth Sci.; Math. Rev.; Res. Alert [Full Cov.]; Sci. Cit. Index; SCISEARCH.

US/0549-4540
**PUBLICATIONS OF THE MATHEMATICAL SOCIETY OF JAPAN.** **Main/Corp** Nihon Sugakkai. (1955)-. Monographic series. English. ir. Price varies per volume. Princeton University Press, 41 William Street, Princeton NJ 08540. **Tel** (609)258-4900.
**Ind/Abst** Zentralbl. Math. Ihre Grenzgeb.

II
**PUBLICATIONS OF THE RAMANUJAN INSTITUTE.** Began in 1969. English. University of Madras Registrar, University Building Chepauk, Madras 600 005 India. **DD** 510/.5.

JA/0034-5318
**PUBLICATIONS OF THE RESEARCH INSTITUTE FOR MATHEMATICAL SCIENCES. SERIES A.** (PUBLICATIONS OF THE RESEARCH INSTITUTE FOR MATHEMATICAL SCIENCES.). [Publ. Res. Inst. Math. Sci., Ser. A]. **Added/Corp** Kyoto Daigaku. Suri Kaiseki Kenkyujo. Vol. 5, No. 1 (July 1969)-. Periodical. English. bm (6 issues). $436.00. **(Subscription address:** Kinokuniya Company Ltd., 38-1 Sakuragaoka 5, chome Setagaya-ku, Tokyo 156 Japan.**)** **CODEN** KRMPBV. **Pr Rev. Circ:** 160. Documents available from The Genuine Article. ***Continues*** *Publications of the Research Institute for Mathematical Sciences. Series A, 0034-5318.*
**Ind/Abst** ACM Guide Comput. Lit.; Compumath Citation Index [Full Cov.]; Comput. Rev.; Math. Rev.; Res. Alert [Full Cov.]; Zentralbl. Math. Ihre Grenzgeb.

YU/0353-8893
**PUBLIKACIJE ELEKTROTEHNICKOG FAKULTETA. SERIJA MATEMATIKA.** **Added/Corp** Univerzitet U Beogradu. Elektrotehnicki Fakultet. **VFOAT** Matematika; Serija Matematika; Publikacije Elektrotehnickog Faculteta Univerziteta U Beogradu. Serija Matematika; Publications of the Faculty of Electrical Engineering, University of Belgrade. Series Mathematics. (1990)-. Serbo-Croatian (Roman). ***Continues*** *Univerzitet U Beogradu. Elektrotehnicki Fakultet.; Publikacije. Serija: Matematika I Fizika.*

YU/0352-5759
**PUNIME MATEMATIKE.** [Pun. mat.]. (1986)-. Periodical. Multiple languages. an. **UDC** 51.
**Ind/Abst** Math. Rev.; Zentralbl. Math. Ihre Grenzgeb.

US/0079-8177
**PURE AND APPLIED MATHEMATICS.** (1970)-. Monographic series. English. ir. Price varies per volume. Marcel Dekker Inc., 270 Madison Avenue, New York NY 10016. **Tel** (212)696-9000, (800)228-1160, FAX (212)685-4540, telex 421419. **(Subscription address:** Marcel Dekker Inc, PO Box 5017, Monticello NY 12701.**)** **ED** Earl J. Taft and Edwin Hweitt.
**Desc:** Strives to cover the various aspects of mathematics, both pure and applied. Topics include Riemannian geometry, stochastic processes, and linear algebra.
**Ind/Abst** Zentralbl. Math. Ihre Grenzgeb.

US/0079-8169
**PURE AND APPLIED MATHEMATICS (NEW YORK. 1949).** (PURE AND APPLIED MATHEMATICS : A SERIES OF MONOGRAPHS AND TEXTBOOKS.). [Pure appl. math.]. (1949)-. Monographic series. English. ir. Price varies per volume. Academic Press, Inc., 6277 Sea Harbor Drive, Orlando FL 32887. **Tel** (800)543-9534, (407)345-4100, FAX (407)363-9661. **ED** Charalambos D. Aliprantis and Owen Burkinshaw. **LC** QA3; .P8. **DD** 510.82.
**Ind/Abst** Math. Rev.; Zentralbl. Math. Ihre Grenzgeb.

II
**PURE AND APPLIED MATHEMATIKA SCIENCES.** **Added/Corp** Mathematika Sciences Society (India). (197?)-. Periodical. English. sa. $200.00. Impex India, 2118 Ansari Road, New Delhi 110002 India. **Tel** 278034. **(Subscription address:** Prints India, 11 Darya Ganj, New Delhi 110002 India.**)** **ED** P L Maggu. **CODEN** PASIDC. **Bk Rev. Ad Acc. Circ:** 500. ***Continues*** *Mathematika Sciences.*
**Desc:** Covers research in operations research, management sciences, computer science, and industrial engineering.
**Ind/Abst** Math. Rev.; Zentralbl. Math. Ihre Grenzgeb.

IT
**QUADERNI DELL'UNIONE MATEMATICA ITALIANA.** **Added/Corp** Unione Matematica Italiana. Vol. 1, (1978)-. Monographic series. Italian. ir. Price varies per volume. Pitagora Editrice SRL, Via del Legatore 3, 40127 Bologna Italy. **Tel** 011 39 51 530003, FAX 011 39 51 535301.
**Ind/Abst** Math. Rev.; Zentralbl. Math. Ihre Grenzgeb.

SA/0379-9468
**QUAESTIONES MATHEMATICAE : JOURNAL OF THE SOUTH AFRICAN MATHEMATICAL SOCIETY : TYDSKRIF VAN DIE SUID-AFRIKAANSE WISKUNDEVERENIGING.** **Added/Corp** South African Mathematical Society. **VFOAT** Journal of the South African Mathematical Society; Tydskrif van die Suid-Afrikaanse Wiskundevereniging; QM; Quaestiones Mathematicae. 1 (1976)-. Periodical. English (German, French and Russian). ir. R25.00 South Africa; $8.75 others. South African Mathematical Society, Potchefstroom University for CHE, Private Bag X6001, Potchefstroom 2520 South Africa. **(Subscription address:** Potchefstroom University for CHE, Department of Mathematics, Potchefstroom 2520 South Africa**)** **ED** HSP Grasser, J W Brewer, GFR Ellis, Roger Entringer, W N Everitt, L Fuchs, K A Hardie, Horst Herrlich, WAJ Luxemburg, D H Martin, A R Mitchell, Paul S Mosterd, Hanno Rund, N Sauer and S Zlobec. **LC** QA1; .Q15. **DD** 510/.5. Index available. cum. index. **Pr Rev. Circ:** 550.
**Desc:** This journal publishes research papers as well as survey and expository articles in the mathematical sciences.
**Ind/Abst** Math. Rev.; Zentralbl. Math. Ihre Grenzgeb.

NE/0033-5177
**QUALITY & QUANTITY.** [Qual. quant.]. **VFOAT** Quality and Quantity. Vol. 1 (Jan. 1967)-. Periodical. English (French). qt. $439.00. Kluwer Academic Publishers, Postbus 322, 3300 AH Dordrecht, The Netherlands. **Tel** 011 (31) 78 524400, FAX 011 31 78 183273, telex 20083. **ED** Vittorio Capecchi, Raymond Boudon, and Charles Kadushin. **LC** H61; .Q18. **NLM** W1 QU158K. **CODEN** QQEJAV. **[CCC]. Pr Rev. Acid Free.** available on microfilm and microfiche from University Microfilms International (UMI). Documents available from The Genuine Article.
**Desc:** An interdisciplinary journal which systematically correlates disciplines such as mathematics and statistics with those of the social sciences, particularly sociology,

economics, and social psychology. The ultimate aim of the journal is to widen the discussion of the most interesting contributions to methodology to scholars of different nations, the objective being the scientific development of social research.
**Ind/Abst** Appl. Soc. Sci. Index Abstr.; Commun. Abstr. (?-?); Compumath Citation Index [Full Cov.]; Curr. Contents Soc. Behav. Sci.; Res. Alert [Full Cov.]; Soc. Plann. Policy Dev. Abstr.; Soc. Sci. Cit. Index [Full Cov.]; Sociol. Abstr. [Full Cov.]; Soc. Res. Methodol. Abstr. (1975-).

GW/0179-3616
**QUANTITATIVE LINGUISTICS. See** Linguistics.

US/1048-8820
**QUANTUM (WASHINGTON, D.C.).** (QUANTUM.). [Quantum]. **Added/Corp** Akademiia Nauk SSSR. Quantum Bureau. American Association of Physics Teachers. National Council of Teachers of Mathematics. National Science Teachers Association. (Jan. 1990)-. Periodical. English (translations available in Russian). Six times a year. $31.10. Springer-Verlag New York Inc., 175 5th Avenue, New York NY 10010. **Tel** (212)460-1500, telex 232 235 SPB UR. **(Subscription address:** Springer Verlag New York Inc. / for North America, 44 Hartz Way, Secaucus NJ 07096.) **ED** Y. Ossipyan, S. L. Glashow, W. P. Thurston. **LC** IN PROCESS; Q1; .Q36. **DD** 500. **[CCC].**
**Desc:** Publishes feature articles that inspire thinking in math and physics. From the "geometry of population genetics" to the "superfluidity of helium II," the journal demonstrates and teaches the thinking paths to a problem, its solutions, and its alternatives. Regular sections such as 'At The Black Board' and 'Brainteasers' are intendended for those who like Olympiads and other problem-solving competitions.
**Ind/Abst** Curr. Index J. Educ.

UK/0033-5606
**QUARTERLY JOURNAL OF MATHEMATICS.** (THE QUARTERLY JOURNAL OF MATHEMATICS. OXFORD SERIES.). [Q. j. math.]. Vol. 1 (Apr. 1930)-. Periodical. English. qt. £95.00 UK and Europe; $165.00 other. Oxford University Press, Walton Street, Oxford OX2 6DP England. **Tel** 011 44 865 56767, FAX 011 44 865 267773, telex 837330 OXPRES G. **(Subscription address:** Oxford University Press / USA, Journals Marketing Department, Oxford University Press, 2001 Evans Road, Cary NC 27513.) **ED** W. Stewart and R. Haydon. **LC** QA1; .Q22. **DD** 510.5. **CODEN** QJMAAT. **[CCC].** Index available. cum. index. **Ad Acc. Pr Rev. Circ:** 1,000. available on microfilm and microfiche from University Microfilms International (UMI). Documents available from The Genuine Article. ***Formed by the union of*** *Messenger of Mathematics* ***and*** *Quarterly Journal of Pure and Applied Mathematics.*
**Desc:** Publishes original contributions to pure mathematics and all the main branches of algebra, analysis, combinatorics and topology.
**Ind/Abst** Compumath Citation Index [Full Cov.]; Curr. Contents Phys. Chem. Earth Sci.; Math. Rev.; Res. Alert [Full Cov.]; Stat. Theory Method Abstr. (1959-1963, 1972, 1974-1975); Zentralbl. Math. Ihre Grenzgeb.

UK/0033-5614
**QUARTERLY JOURNAL OF MECHANICS AND APPLIED MATHEMATICS, THE. See** Engineering-Mechanical Engineering and Machinery.

US/0033-569X
**QUARTERLY OF APPLIED MATHEMATICS.** [Q. appl. math.]. **Added/Corp** Brown University. Vol. 1 (April 1943)-. Periodical. English. qt. $90.00. American Mathematical Society, PO Box 6248, Providence RI 02940-6248. **Tel** (800)321-4267, (401)455-4000, FAX (401)331-3842, telex 797192. **(Subscription address:** American Mathematical Society, PO Box 5904, Boston MA 02206-5904.) **LC** QA1; .Q25. **DD** 510.5. **NLM** W1 QU421. **CODEN** QAMAAY. **[CCC].** Index available (author index in last issue of each volume). **Pr Rev.** available on microfilm and microfiche from University Microfilms International (UMI). Documents available from Article Express International, The Genuine Article, BIOSIS Document Express, Ask*IEEE, CASDDS.
**Desc:** Contains original papers in applied mathematics which have a close connection with applications in industrial or practical science.
**Ind/Abst** Bioeng. Abstr.; Biol. Abstr.; Chem. Abstr.; Compumath Citation Index [Full Cov.]; Comput. Rev.; Curr. Contents Eng. Tech. Appl. Sci.; Curr. Contents Phys. Chem. Earth Sci.; Ei Page One; Energy Res. Abstr.; Eng. Index Annu. [Select. Cov.]; INSPEC (1968-); Int. Aerosp. Abstr.; Math. Rev.; Res. Alert [Full Cov.]; Sci. Cit. Index; SCISEARCH; Stat. Theory Method Abstr. (1970, 1972-1977, 1980-1981); Zentralbl. Math. Ihre Grenzgeb.

CN/0079-8797
**QUEEN'S PAPERS IN PURE AND APPLIED MATHEMATICS.** [Queen's pap. pure appl. math.]. **Main/Corp** Queen's University (Kingston, Ont.). No. 1 (1966)-. Monographic series. English. ir. Price varies per volume. Queens University Campus Bookstore, Kingston Ontario K7L 3N6 Canada. **Tel** (613)545-2955.
**Ind/Abst** Math. Rev.; Zentralbl. Math. Ihre Grenzgeb.

BN/0352-6100
**RADOVI MATEMATICKI / AKADEMIJA NAUKA I UMJETNOSTI BOSNE I HERCEGOVINE. Added/Corp** Akademija Nauka i Umjetnosti Bosne i Hercegovine. Vol. 1, No. 1 (1985)-. Periodical. English (French, German and Russian). sa. Radovi Matematicki, ANU BIH, PP 01-54, 71000 Sarajevo, Bosnia and Hercegovina. **LC** QA1; .R32. ***Continues in part*** *Radovi Odjeljanja Prirodnih i Matematickih Nauka.*
**Ind/Abst** Math. Rev.; Zentralbl. Math. Ihre Grenzgeb.

FR/0764-583X
**RAIRO. MATHEMATICAL MODELLING AND NUMERICAL ANALYSIS.** [Model. math. anal. numer.]. **Added/Corp** Association Francaise Pour la Cybernetique Economique et Technique. Centre National de la Recherche Scientifique (France). **VFOAT** Mathematical Modelling and Numerical Analysis; M=2AN; Modelisation mathematique et Analyse Numerique. (1985)-. Periodical. English (French; summaries and/or abstracts in English and French). Seven times a year. 2090.00F France; 2840.00F other. Dunod Gauthier Villars, 15 rue Gossin, 92543 Montrouge cedex France. **Tel** 011 33 1 46 56 52 66, FAX 011 33 1 46 57 40 69. **(Subscription address:** Centrale des Revues, 11 rue Gossin, 92543 Montrouge Cedex France.) **LC** QA1; .R457. **DD** 519.4. **CODEN** RMMAEV. **[CCC].** Documents available from The Genuine Article, Ask*IEEE. ***Continues*** *RAIRO: Analyse Numerique, 0399-0516.*
**Desc:** Publishes original research and survey papers of high scientific level in numerical analyses and mathematical modelling.
**Ind/Abst** Compumath Citation Index; Curr. Contents Phys. Chem. Earth Sci.; INSPEC (1985-); Math. Rev. (1985-); Res. Alert; Sci. Cit. Index; SCISEARCH; Zentralbl. Math. Ihre Grenzgeb.

II/0079-9602
**RANCHI UNIVERSITY MATHEMATICAL JOURNAL.** [Ranchi Univ. math. j.]. **Added/Corp** Ranchi University. Dept. of Mathematics. Vol. 1 (Mar. 1970)-. Periodical. English. an. $20.00. Ranchi University / Mathematics, Department of Mathematics, Ranchi, India. **(Subscription address:** Prints India, 11 Darya Ganj, New Delhi 110002 India.) **LC** QA1; .R28.
**Ind/Abst** Math. Rev.; Zentralbl. Math. Ihre Grenzgeb.

US/1042-9832
**RANDOM STRUCTURES AND ALGORITHMS.** [Random struct. algorithms]. **VFOAT** Random Structures and Algorithms. (1990)-. Periodical. English. Eight times a year. $346.00 US; $426.00 Canada and Mexico; $456.00 other. John Wiley & Sons, Inc., 605 Third Avenue, New York NY 10158-0012. **Tel** (212)850-6000, (212)850-6645, FAX (212)850-6088, telex 12-7063. **(Subscription address:** John Wiley & Sons / England, Baffins Lane, Chichester, West Sussex PO19 1UD England.) **ED** Michal Karonski and Joel Spencer. **LC** QA166; .R36; QA166.17; .R36. **DD** 519. available on microfilm and microfiche from University Microfilms International (UMI). Documents available from The Genuine Article.
**Desc:** Addresses the rapidly growing interest in the applications of probalistic techniques to problem solving in various areas of mathematics, computer science and operations research. Covers research on discrete random structures, presents the applications of such research to problems in combinatorics and computer science.
**Ind/Abst** Compumath Citation Index [Full Cov.]; Curr. Contents Phys. Chem. Earth Sci.; Math. Rev.; Res. Alert [Full Cov.]; SCISEARCH; Zentralbl. Math. Ihre Grenzgeb.

FR
**RAPPORT NATIONAL DE CONJONCTURE SCIENTIFIQUE : MATHEMATIQUES PURES ET METHODOLOGIE MATHEMATIQUE. Main/Corp** France. Centre National de la Recherche Scientifique. Comite National de la Recherche Scientifique. French. CNRS / Institut d'Information Scientifique et Technique, (Centre National de la Recherche Scientifique), 15 Quai Anatole France, Paris 75700 France. **Tel** 011 33 1 47531515, telex 299 356 F. **LC** QA11.A1; F74A. **DD** 510/.7/2044.

GW/0720-2601
**REAL ANALYSIS. Added/Corp** Heidelberger Akademie der Wissenschaften Fachinformationszentrum Energie, Physik, Mathematik (Eggenstein-Leopoldshafen, Germany). (1981)-. English (French and German). Twelve times a year. $135.00 North American; $168.00 others. Scientific Information Service Inc., 7 Woodland Avenue, Larchmont NY 10538. **Tel** (914)834-8864. **LC** QA299.6; .R4. **DD** 515/.05.

US/0147-1937
**REAL ANALYSIS EXCHANGE.** [Real anal. exch.]. Vol. 1 (1976)-. Periodical. English (French and German). sa. $45.00. Real Analysis Exchange, Mathematics Department, Michigan State University, East Lansing MI 48824. **Tel** (517)353-8489. **ED** Clifford E. Weil. **LC** QA331.5; .R43. **DD** 515/.8/05. **Pr Rev. Circ:** 400 (ctrl).
**Desc:** Research in-roads and survey articles in real variables, real set theory, and real measure theory.
**Ind/Abst** Math. Rev.; Ref. Z.; Zentralbl. Math. Ihre Grenzgeb.

US/0899-014X
**REC NEWSLETTER, THE.** [REC newsl.]. **VFOAT** Recreational & Educational Computing Newsletter. (1986)-. Periodical. English. Eight times a year. $29.00 US; $30.00 Canada & Mexico; $38.00 other. Dr. Michael Ecker, 909 Violet Terrace, Clarks Summit PA 18411. **Tel** (717)586-2784. **ED** Dr. Michael W. Ecker. **DD** 519. **Bk Rev**, (Qty: very few). **Ad Acc.**
**Desc:** This new publication is devoted to the playful connection of computers and educational recreation. It has lot of features such as, programming, fun and challenges. We also have reviews, humor, word games, computer recreation, mathemagic, and our exclusive "Mathemagical Black Holes".

FR/0246-9367
**RECHERCHES EN DIDACTIQUE DES MATHEMATIQUES REVUE.** (1980)-. Periodical. French (English and Spanish). Three times a year. 420.00F France; 510.00F other. Editions La Pensee Sauvage, BP 141, 38002 Grenoble Cedex France. **Tel** 011 33 76871303. **UDC** 51.

FR
**RECHERCHES EN MATHEMATIQUES APPLIQUEES.** (19??)-. French. bm. Masson Editeur, Box Postale 22, 41353 Vineuil 16 France. **Tel** 011 33 54 438994. **(Subscription address:** Masson SA, 7A Boulevard de Perolles,, CH-1701 Fribourg Switzerland.)
**Ind/Abst** Zentralbl. Math. Ihre Grenzgeb.

RU
**REFERATIVNYI ZHURNAL. 13, MATEMATIKA. Added/Corp** Vsesoiuznyi Institut Nauchnoi i Tekhnicheskoi Informatsii (Soviet Union). **VFOAT** Matematika. (1982)-. Abstracting/Indexing Service. Russian. mo. $599 95. VINITI - Vsesoyuznyi Institut Nauchno-Tekhnicheskoi Informatsii, All-Union Scientific and Technical Information Institute, Baltiiskaia Ulitsa 14, 125219 Moscow Russia. **Tel** 238-46-00, FAX 9430060, telex 411160. **(Subscription address:** East View Publications Inc., 3020 Harbor Lane North, Suite 110, Minneapolis MN 55447.) **LC** QA1; .A373. ***Continues*** *Referativnyi Zhurnal. Matematika, 0034-2467.*

AT/0156-7799
**REFLECTIONS.** [Reflections]. (1976)-. Periodical. English. qt. 53.00Aus$ individual; 60.00Aus$ institutional. Mathematical Association of New South Wales, Box 536, Darlinghurst NSW, 2010 Australia. **Tel** 011 61 2 361-5195, FAX 011 61 2 332-2510. **ED** Judy Anderson. **DD** 510.7. **Bk Rev. Circ:** 1,450.
**Ind/Abst** Aust. Educ. Index.

GW/0179-9746
**REGENSBURGER MATHEMATISCHE SCHRIFTEN.** [Regensbg. math. Schr.]. (1977)-. Monographic series. Multiple languages. ir. Price varies per volume. **UDC** 51.
**Ind/Abst** Zentralbl. Math. Ihre Grenzgeb.

GW/0930-4967
**REGENSBURGER TRICHTER, DER.** [Regensbg. Tricht.]. (1973)-. Monographic series. German. ir. Price varies per volume. **UDC** 51.
**Ind/Abst** Zentralbl. Math. Ihre Grenzgeb.

US/0160-7642
**REGIONAL CONFERENCE SERIES IN MATHEMATICS.** [Reg. conf. ser. math.]. **Added/Corp** Conference Board of the Mathematical Sciences. American Mathematical Society. No. 1 (1970)-. Monographic series. English. ir. Price varies per volume. American Mathematical Society, PO Box 6248, Providence RI 02940-6248. **Tel** (800)321-4267, (401)455-4000, FAX (401)331-3842, telex 797192. **(Subscription address:** American Mathematical Society, PO Box 5904, Boston MA 02206-5904.) **LC** QA1; .R33. **DD** 510.8. **[CCC].**
**Ind/Abst** Math. Rev.; Zentralbl. Math. Ihre Grenzgeb.

NE/0921-9315
**REIDEL TEXTS IN THE MATHEMATICAL SCIENCES.** ***Title Change.*** [Reidel texts math. sci.]. (1986)-(199?). Monographic series. English. Kluwer Academic Publishers / Massachusetts, PO Box 358, Accord Station, Hingham MA 02018. **Tel** (617)871-6600. **CODEN** RTMSEW. ***Continued by*** *Kluwer Texts in the Mathematical Sciences.*
**Ind/Abst** Zentralbl. Math. Ihre Grenzgeb.

IT/0392-9523
**RENDICONTI. A, SCIENZE MATEMATICHE E APPLICAZIONI / ISTITUTO LOMBARDO, ACCADEMIA DI SCIENZE E LETTERE. Added/Corp** Istituto Lombardo Accademia di Scienze e Lettere. **VFOAT**

Scienze Matematiche e Applicazioni. Vol. 114 (1980)-. Monographic series. Italian (English). ir. Price varies per volume. Istituto Lombardo, Accademia di Scienze e Lettere, Via Borgonuovo 25, 20121 Milan Italy. **Tel** 011 39 2 86461388. ***Continues in part*** *Rendiconti. A, Scienze Matematiche, Fisiche, Chimiche e Geologiche.*

IT/0009-725X
**RENDICONTI DEL CIRCOLO MATEMATICO DI PALERMO.** [Rend. Circ. Mat. Palermo]. **Added/Corp** Circolo matematico di Palermo. (1887)-. Periodical. Italian (English, French and German). Three times a year. L120000.00. Libreria S F Flaccovio, Via Ruggiero Settimo 37, 90139 Palermo Italy. **Tel** 011 39 91 334323, or 334249, FAX 011 39 91 6112750. **LC** QA1; .C6. **CODEN** RCMMAR. Index available. cum. index. **Bk Rev. Circ:** 600 (ctrl).
**Ind/Abst** Math. Rev.; Stat. Theory Method Abstr. (1959-1963); Zentralbl. Math. Ihre Grenzgeb.

IT
**RENDICONTI DEL SEMINARIO MATEMATICO.** **Main/Conf** Seminario Matematico, Turin. Began in 1930. Italian (English and French). Three times a year. L105000 Italy; L140000 Europe; L200000 other. Rosenberg & Sellier, Via Andrea Doria 14, 10123 Turin Italy. **Tel** 011 39 11 8127808, telex 224202 ROSSELI. **ED** Fulvio Ricci. **LC** QA1; .S43. **DD** 510.82. cum. index. **Bk Rev. Ad Acc. Circ:** 500.
**Desc:** Original articles containing relevant results in mathematics.
**Ind/Abst** Zentralbl. Math. Ihre Grenzgeb.

IT/0370-7377
**RENDICONTI DEL SEMINARIO MATEMATICO E FISICO DI MILANO.** [Rend. Semin. mat. fis. Milano]. **Main/Corp** Seminario Matematico e Fisico di Milano. Vol. 1 (1927)-. Italian (English, French and German). an. Free on request. Seminario Matematico Fisico, Piazza Leonardo da Vinici 132, 20133 Milan Italy. **Tel** 011 39 2 230424. **LC** QA1; .M97. **DD** 510.62452. **CODEN** RSMFAG. cum. index. **Circ:** 300.
**Ind/Abst** Int. Aerosp. Abstr.; Math. Rev.; Zentralbl. Math. Ihre Grenzgeb.

IT/1120-7183
**RENDICONTI DI MATEMATICA E DELLE SUE APPLICAZIONI (1981).** (RENDICONTI DI MATEMATICA E DELLE SUE APPLICAZIONI : RIVISTA TRIMESTRALE PUBBLICATA DA UNIVERSITA DEGLI STUDI DI ROMA (ISTITUTO MATEMATICO GUIDO CASTELNUOVO, ISTITUTO DI MATEMATICA APPLICATA) E ISTITUTO NAZIONALE DI ALTA MATEMATICA.). [Rend. mat. appl.]. **Added/Corp** Universita di Roma. Istituto di Matematica Applicata. Istituto Matematico Guido Castelnuovo. Istituto Nazionale di Alta Matematica (Italy). Series 7, Vol. 1, No. 1 (Jan./March 1981)-. Periodical. Italian (English and French). qt. DM260.00. ESIA Books and Journals, Via Palestro 30, 00185 Rome Italy. **Tel** 011 39 6 4441220, 011 39 6 4441221, FAX 011 39 6 4747743. ***Continues*** *Rendiconti di Matematica, 0034-4427.*
**Ind/Abst** Math. Rev.; Zentralbl. Math. Ihre Grenzgeb.

IT/0041-8994
**RENDICONTI - SEMINARIO MATEMATICO DELLA UNIVERSITA DI PADOVA.** (RENDICONTI DEL SEMINARIO MATEMATICO DELLA UNIVERSITA DI PADOVA.). [Rend. - Semin. mat. Univ. Padova]. **Main/Corp** Padua. Universita. Seminario Matematico. **Added/Corp** Universita di Padova. Seminario Matematico. Vol. 14 (1943)-. Periodical. English (Italian, French and German). sa. L180000 Italy; L230000 other. Cedam Spa, Via Jappelli 5 6, 35121 Padua Italy. **Tel** 011 39 49 65667. **LC** QA1; .P125. **DD** 510/.5. ***Continues*** *Rendiconti del Seminario Matematico della R. Universita di Padova.*
**Ind/Abst** Appl. Mech. Rev.; Math. Rev.; Zentralbl. Math. Ihre Grenzgeb.

NE
**REPORT AM.** 1984-. Monographic series. English. Price varies per volume. Centrum voor Wiskunde en Informatica, PO Box 94079, 1009 GB Amsterdam Netherlands. **Tel** 011 31 20 5929333, FAX 011 31 20 5924199, telex 12571. **Circ:** 250. ***Continues*** *Report TW.*
**Ind/Abst** Math. Rev.

CN/0824-4944
**REPORT FROM THE DEPARTMENT OF MATHEMATICS AND STATISTICS.** [Rep. Dep. Math. Stat.] **VFOAT** Rapport du Department of Mathematics and Statistics. Monographic series. English. Price varies per volume. McGill University / Department of Mathematics and Statistics, Burnside Hall, 805 Sherbrooke Street West, Montreal Quebec H3A 2K6 Canada. **DD** 510.

UK
**REPORT OF COUNCIL.** **Main/Corp** Mathematical Association. English. an. Mathematical Association, 259 London Road, Leicester LE2 3BE England. **Tel** 011 44 533 703877.

JA/0387-8538
**REPORTS OF THE FACULTY OF SCIENCE AND ENGINEERING, SAGA UNIVERSITY MATHEMATICS.** [Rep. Fac. Sci. Eng., Saga Univ., Math.]. English (Japanese). 1 Honjomachi, Saga 830 Japan. **Tel** (0952)24-5191.
**Ind/Abst** Math. Rev.; Zentralbl. Math. Ihre Grenzgeb.

PL/0137-2904
**REPORTS ON MATHEMATICAL LOGIC.** [Rep. math. logic]. V. 1-. Multiple languages (English, French, German and Russian). sa. **(Subscription address:** ARS Polona, PO Box 1001, 00068 Warsaw Poland.**)** **LC** QA9.A1; R45. **CODEN** RMLODX. ***Supersedes*** *Prace Z Logiki.*
**Ind/Abst** Math. Rev.; Philos. Index; Zentralbl. Math. Ihre Grenzgeb.

PL/0034-4877
**REPORTS ON MATHEMATICAL PHYSICS.** **See** Physics.

GW
**RESEARCH AND EXPOSITION IN MATHEMATICS.** **VAT** R and E, Research and Exposition in Mathematics. (1984)-. Monographic series. English. Price varies per volume. **LC** UNC. ***Continues*** *R & E, Research and Education in Mathematics.*
**Ind/Abst** Zentralbl. Math. Ihre Grenzgeb.

US/0735-794X
**RESEARCH FRONTS IN ISI. COMPUMATH.** [Res. fronts ISI/CompuMath]. **VFOAT** Research Fronts in I.S.I. / Compumath. **VAT** Research Fronts in Institute for Scientific Information Compumath. 1981-. Academic Scholarly Publication. English. Institute for Scientific Information, 3501 Market Street, Philadelphia PA 19104. **Tel** (215)386-0100, (800)523-1850, FAX (215)386-6362, telex 84-5305. **(Subscription address:** Institute for Scientific Information, PO Box 71416, Chicago, IL 60694**)**

SZ/0378-6218
**RESULTATE DER MATHEMATIK.** [Result. Math.]. **VFOAT** Mathematical Results; Results in Mathematics. (1978)-. Periodical. German (English and German). Eight times a year. 642.80F Switzerland; 663.00F other. Birkhaeuser Verlag Ag, Klosterberg 23, PO Box 133, CH-4010 Basel Switzerland. **Tel** 011 41 61 2717400, FAX 011 41 0 61 2717666, telex 963475 birk ch. **(Subscription address:** Birkhauser Verlag AG, PO Box 151, CH 4106 Therwil Switzerland; Phone: 011 41 61 7217740**)** **ED** H. J. Arnold. **LC** QA1; .R3645. **DD** 510/.5. **[CCC].** available on microfilm and microfiche from University Microfilms International (UMI).
**Desc:** Publishes mainly research papers in all fields of pure and applied mathematics. A limited number of reviews and field surveys are published provided these serve to further new developments in mathematical research.
**Ind/Abst** Math. Rev.; Zentralbl. Math. Ihre Grenzgeb.

SI/0129-055X
**REVIEWS IN MATHEMATICAL PHYSICS.** **See** Physics.

CK/0034-7426
**REVISTA COLOMBIANA DE MATEMATICAS.** [Rev. colomb. mat.]. **Added/Corp** Sociedad Colombiana de Matematicas. Colombia. Universidad, Bogota. Departamento de Matematicas. Vol. 1 (Mar. 1967)-. Periodical. Spanish (English, French and Portuguese). qt (4 issues). $22.00. Societe Colombiana de Matematicas, Apartado Aereo 2521, Bogota Colombia. **Tel** 011 57 1 2216829. **ED** Xavier Caicedo Ferrer. **LC** QA1; .R369. **CODEN** RCMABQ. Index available (bound in 4th issue). cum. index. **Pr Rev. Circ:** 1,000 (ctrl). ***Supersedes*** *Revista de Matematicas Elementales.*
**Desc:** Research articles in all areas of mathematics.
**Ind/Abst** Math. Rev.; Stat. Theory Method Abstr. (1979); Zentralbl. Math. Ihre Grenzgeb.

MZ/1010-5980
**REVISTA DE CIENCIAS MATEMATICAS.** [Rev. cienc. mat.]. Vol. 5 (1974/75)-. Periodical. Portuguese (English). Ediciones Cubanas, Obispo 527, Altos ESQ Bernaza, CP 10100 Havana Cuba. **Tel** 011 632980, 631942, FAX 011 631011, telex 512337, 6540. ***Formed by the union of*** *Revista de Ciencias Matematicas. Serie A, 0080-2204* ***and*** *Revista de Ciencias Matematicas. Serie B.*
**Ind/Abst** Math. Rev.; Zentralbl. Math. Ihre Grenzgeb.

AG/0041-6932
**REVISTA DE LA UNION MATEMATICA ARGENTINA (1968).** (REVISTA DE LA UNION MATEMATICA ARGENTINA.). [Rev. Union Mat. Argent.]. **Main/Corp** Union Matematica Argentina. **Added/Corp** Union Matematica Argentina. Vol. 24, No. 1, (1968)-. Periodical. Spanish (English). Twice a year. $40.00. Union Matematica Argentina, Guemes 3450, 3000 Santa Fe Argentina. **Tel** 011 54 42 20023 20024. **LC** QA1; .A86. **DD** 510.5. **CODEN** RMAFAG. **Bk Rev. Circ:** 500. ***Continues*** *Revista de la Union Matematica Argentina y de la Asociacion Fisica Argentina, 0327-2583.*
**Desc:** Research papers in all areas of theoretical and applied mathematics. All papers are submitted to referees before being accepted.
**Ind/Abst** Math. Rev.; Zentralbl. Math. Ihre Grenzgeb.

BL/0102-0811
**REVISTA DE MATEMATICA E ESTATISTICA / UNIVERSIDADE ESTADUAL PAULISTA.** **Added/Corp** Universidade Estadual Paulista. Vol. 1 (1983)-. Periodical. Portuguese (table of contents in English). Centro de Publicacoes Culturais e Cientificas, Universidade Estadual Paulista, Caixa Postal 30919, Sao Paulo Brazil.
**Ind/Abst** Math. Rev. (1983-); Zentralbl. Math. Ihre Grenzgeb.

CL/0716-5803
**REVISTA DE MATEMATICAS APLICADAS.** [Rev. mat. apl.]. (1987)-. Periodical. Multiple languages. Twice a year (Jan. and July). $25.00. Univ Chile Facultad Ciencia, Fisica y Matematicas, Casilla 170, Santiago 3 Chile. **Tel** 011 56 2 6711530. **ED** Servet Martinez. **UDC** 51. ***Continues*** *Sigma (Santiago), 0716-3096.*
**Ind/Abst** Zentralbl. Math. Ihre Grenzgeb.

CU
**REVISTA INVESTIGACION OPERACIONAL.** **See** Engineering-Industrial Engineering and Design.

SP/0214-3577
**REVISTA MATEMATICA DE LA UNIVERSIDAD COMPLUTENSE DE MADRID / FACULTAD DE CIENCIAS MATEMATICAS, UNIVERSIDAD COMPLUTENSE DE MADRID.** **Added/Corp** Universidad Complutense de Madrid. Facultad de Ciencias Matematicas. **VFOAT** Revista Matematica. Vol. 1, No. 1-2 (1988)-. Periodical. English (French and Spanish). Three times a year. $52.00. Editorial Complutense, Donoso Cortes 65 1RA Planta, 28003 Madrid Spain. **Tel** 011 34 1 3946372. **LC** QA1; .R394. **DD** 510/.5.
**Desc:** Accepts research and survey papers which meet the following criteria: research papers and unpublished research texts must contain sufficient information and allow the reader to repeat the work carried out by the author. Furthermore, the reader should be able to both evaluate results and conclusions relating to the existing bibliography; and to arrange the paper in the appropriate area of interest in comtemporary mathematics.
**Ind/Abst** Zentralbl. Math. Ihre Grenzgeb.

SP/0213-2230
**REVISTA MATEMATICA IBEROAMERICANA.** **Added/Corp** Instituto de Cooperacion Iberoamericana (Madrid, Spain) Consejo Superior de Investigaciones Cientificas (Spain) Real Sociedad Matematica Espanola. Universidad de Valencia. Comision Asesora de Investigacion Cientifica y Tecnica. Spain. Comision Interministerial de Ciencia y Tecnolog,ia. Vol. 1, No. 1 (1985)-. Periodical. English (French and Spanish). Three times a year. $180.00 institutions; $45.00 individuals. Universidad Autonoma de Madrid / Departamento de Mathematicas, 28049 Madrid Spain. **Tel** 011 34 1 3974930, FAX 011 34 1 3974889. **ED** A. Cordoba. **LC** QA1; .R42. Index available. ***Continues*** *Revista Matematica Hispano-Americana, 0373-0999.*
**Ind/Abst** Math. Rev. (1985-).

FR/0035-1504
**REVUE DE MATHEMATIQUES SPECIALES.** (1890)-. Periodical. French. mo (except July and Aug.). 580.00F. Librairie Vuibert, 63 Boulevard Saint Germain, 75005 Paris France. **Tel** 011 33 1 43256100, FAX 011 33 1 43257586, telex 201005. **LC** QA1; .R45. **DD** 510.5. **Bk Rev. Ad Acc. Circ:** 2,000.

●FR
**REVUE D'HISTOIRE DES MATHEMATIQUES.** (19??)-. Periodical. French. Twice a year. 360.00F France; 400.00F other. Societe Mathematique de France EC Norm Sup Tour L, 1 rue Maurice Arnoux, 92120 Montrouge France. **Tel** 011 33 1 40848054, or 91267464, FAX 011 33 1 40848052, or 91411751. **(Subscription address:** Centrale des Revues, 11 rue Gossin, 92543 Montrouge Cedex France.**)**

BE
**REVUE INFORMATIQUE ET STATISTIQUE DANS LES SCIENCES HUMAINES.** **Added/Corp** Universite de Liege. Laboratoire d'Analyse Statistique des Langues Anciennes. No. 1 (1983)-. Periodical. English (French and Spanish). an (Nov.). 1000F. Centre Informatique de Philosophie et Lettres, Place du 20 Aout 32, B 4000 Liege Belgium. **Tel** 11 32 41 665211, FAX 11 32 41 665702. **ED** J. Denooz. **LC** P98; .I57a. **DD** 410/.28/5. ***Continues*** *International Organization for Ancient Languages Analysis by Computer. Revue - Organisation Internationale pour l'etude des Lagues Anciennes par Ordinateur, 0030-4972.*

RM/0035-3965
**REVUE ROUMAINE DE MATHEMATIQUES PURES ET APPLIQUEES.** (REVUE ROUMAINE DE MATHEMATIQUES PURES ET APPLIQUEES / ACADEMIE DE LA REPUBLIQUE POPULAIRE ROUMAINE.). [Rev. roum. math. pures appl.]. **Added/Corp** Academia Republicii Socialiste Romania. Academia Republicii Populare Romine. Vol. 9, No. 1 (1964)-. Periodical. English (French). Ten times a year. DM645.00. **(Subscription address:** Kubon & Sagner, ABT Zeitschriftenimport, D 80328 Munich Germany.) **LC** QA1; .R445. **CODEN** RRMPB6. Index available. cum. index. **Bk Rev. Ad Acc. Circ:** 1,000 (ctrl). ***Continues*** *Revue de Mathematiques Pures et Appliquees.*
**Desc:** Publishes studies on mathematics, research papers.
**Ind/Abst** Appl. Mech. Rev.; Biostatistica; Comput. Rev.; Int. Aerosp. Abstr.; Math. Rev.; Qual. Control Appl. Stat.; Ref. Z.; Stat. Theory Method Abstr. (1968-1969, 1971, 1973-1975, 1977, 1979, 1982-1984, 1986-1987); Zentralbl. Math. Ihre Grenzgeb.

AT/0310-7205
**RHOMBUS.** [Rhombus]. (1973)-. Periodical. English. qt. (Comes with Mathematical Assn of Western Australia membership). Mathematical Association of Western Australia, PO Box 492, Subiaco 6008 Australia. **Tel** 61 09 349-1380. **DD** 372.73044.
**Ind/Abst** Aust. Educ. Index.

PK/0255-7568
**RIAZI.** (RIAZI : THE SOUVENIR OF KARACHI MATHEMATICAL ASSOCIATION.). [Riazi]. **Added/Corp** Karachi Mathematical Association. **VFOAT** Souvenir of Karachi Mathematical Association. (1978)-. Periodical. English. **LC** QA1; .R46. **DD** 510/.5.
**Ind/Abst** Math. Rev.; Zentralbl. Math. Ihre Grenzgeb.

IT/0048-8283
**RICERCA; MATEMATICHE PURE ED APPLICATE.** **Added/Corp** Istituto Editoriale del Mezzogiorno. Vol. 1 (March 1950)-. Periodical. Italian. tq. Mezzogiorno d'Europa, Via S. Giacomo 19, 80133 Naples Italy. **Tel** 011 39 81 7853640.
**Ind/Abst** Math. Rev.; Zentralbl. Math. Ihre Grenzgeb.

IT/0035-5038
**RICERCHE DI MATEMATICA.** [Ric. mat.]. **Added/Corp** Universita di Napoli. Istituto di Matematica. Vol. 1 (1952)-. Periodical. Italian (English). sa. L47000 Italy; L75000 other. Liguori Libreria Comm, Via Mezzocannone 21 23, 80134 Naples Italy. **Tel** 011 39 81 5527702. **CODEN** RCMTAE. Index available. cum. index. **Circ:** 400.
**Ind/Abst** Math. Rev.; Zentralbl. Math. Ihre Grenzgeb.

IT/0035-6298
**RIVISTA DI MATEMATICA DELLA UNIVERSITA DI PARMA.** [Riv. mat. Univ. Parma]. **Added/Corp** Universita di Parma. Istituto di Matematica. Vol. 1 (1950)-Vol. 10, (1959); Ser. 2, Vol. 1 1960)-Vol. 12, (1971); Ser. 3, Vol. 1 (1972)-Vol. 3 (1974); Ser. 4, Vol. 1 (1975)-. Periodical. Italian. Index available in last issue of volume--attached.
**Ind/Abst** Math. Rev.; Zentralbl. Math. Ihre Grenzgeb.

IT
**RIVISTA DI MATEMATICA PER LE SCIENZE ECONOMICHE E SOCIALI / ASSOCIAZIONE PER LA MATEMATICA APPLICATA ALLE SCIENZE ECONOMICHE E SOCIALI.** **Added/Corp** Associazione per la Matematica Applicata Alle Scienze Economiche e Sociali. Vol. 1, No. 1 (1978)-. Periodical. Italian (English and French). Twice a year (Jan., July). L100000 Italy; L120000 others. AMASES, Un Bocconi V Sarfatti 25, 20136 Milan Italy. **Tel** 011 39 2 58365116. **LC** H61.25; .R58. **DD** 300/.724. **Bk Rev. Ad Acc. Circ:** 2,000.
**Desc:** Applied mathematics to social and economical sciences.
**Ind/Abst** Math. Rev.; Zentralbl. Math. Ihre Grenzgeb.

IT
**RIVISTA DI MATEMATICA PURA ED APPLICATA.** (July 1987)-. Periodical. English (French, German and Italian). Twice a year (May, Nov.). L150000. Aviani Editore, Via Diaz 27, 33019 Tricesimo Italy. **Tel** 011 39 432 46478. **LC** QA1; .R554. **DD** 510. **Ad Acc. Pr Rev.** ctrl circ.
**Ind/Abst** Math. Rev. (1987-).

IT
**RIVISTA DI MATHEMATICA DELLA UNIVERSITA DI PARMA. SERIE 4.** (1975)-. Italian (French, English, German and Spanish). an. Insti di Mathematica, Universita di Parma, Via Universita 12, 43100 Parma Italy.
**Ind/Abst** Math. Rev.

US/0035-7596
**ROCKY MOUNTAIN JOURNAL OF MATHEMATICS, THE.** [Rocky Mt. j. math.]. **Added/Corp** Rocky Mountain Mathematics Consortium. Vol. 1 (Winter 1971)-. Periodical. English. Four times a year. $350.00. Arizona State University / Rocky Mountain Mathematics Consortium, Department of Mathematics, Box 871904, Tempe AZ 85287-1904. **Tel** (602)965-3788. **ED** John McDonald. **LC** QA1; .R597. **DD** 510/.5. **CODEN** RMJMAE. Index available. **Pr Rev. Circ:** 650 (ctrl). Documents available from The Genuine Article, Ask*IEEE.
**Ind/Abst** Compumath Citation Index [Full Cov.]; Energy Res. Abstr. (Oct. 1974-); INSPEC (Winter 1984-); Math. Rev.; Res. Alert [Full Cov.]; SPIN (1977-); Zentralbl. Math. Ihre Grenzgeb.

PL/0373-8302
**ROCZNIKI POLSKOGO TOWARZYSTWA MATEMATYCZNEGO, SERIA 2. WIADOMOSCI MATEMATYCZNE.** (ROCZNIKI. SERIA 2 : WIADOMOSCI MATEMATYCZNE.). [Rocz. Pol. Tow. Mat., Ser. 2]. **Main/Corp** Polskie Towarzystwo Matematyczne. **VFOAT** Wiadomosci Matematiczne; Annales Societatis Mathematicae Polonae. (1955)-. Polish. Twice a year. **(Subscription address:** ARS Polona, PO Box 1001, 00068 Warsaw Poland.) **LC** QA1; .P626. **CODEN** RPTWAD. ***Continues*** *Wiadomosci Matematyczne.*
**Ind/Abst** Math. Rev.

PL/0137-2890
**ROCZNIKI POLSKOGO TOWARZYSTWA MATEMATYCZNEGO, SERIA 3: MATEMATYKA STOSOWANA.** (ROCZNIKI. SERIA III : MATEMATYKA STOSOWANA.). [Rocz. Polsk. Tow. Mat., Ser. 3]. **Main/Corp** Polskie Towarzystwo Matematyczne. **VFOAT** Matematyka Stosowana. 1- 1973-. Polish. Z22.00. Osrodek Rozpowszechniania Wydawnictw Naukowych Pan, Paac Kultury i Nauki, Warszawa Poland. **LC** QA1; .P626A.
**Ind/Abst** Math. Rev.

GW
**ROSTOCKER MATHEMATISCHES KOLLOQUIUM.** Periodical. German (English and Russian). ir (two or three issues per year). DM10.00. Universitaet Rostock, Sektion Mattematik, Universitaetsplatz 1, Rostock O-2500 Germany. **Tel** 0081-369-334, telex 31140. **(Subscription address:** Fa Buchexport, Volkseigener Aussenhandelsbetrieb der DDR, Leninstr 16, Leipzig DDR-7010 East Germany) **ED** G Maess. **LC** QA1; .R67. cum. index. **Circ:** 500 (ctrl).
**Desc:** Publication of original papers (research results). Main topics: mathematical analysis, discrete mathematics, numerical mathematics, and mathematical statistics.
**Ind/Abst** Math. Rev.; Stat. Theory Method Abstr. (1987); Zentralbl. Math. Ihre Grenzgeb.

XR
**ROZPRAVY CESKOSLOVENSKE AKADEMIE VED. RADA MATEMATICKYCH A PRIRODNICH VED.** **Added/Corp** Ceskoslovenska Akademie ved. **VFOAT** Rada Matematickych a Prirodnich ved. (198?)-. Periodical. Czech. ***Continues*** *Rozpravy (Ceskoslovenska Akademie ved). Rada Matematickych a Prirodnich ved, 0069-228X.*
**Ind/Abst** Zentralbl. Math. Ihre Grenzgeb.

PL/0860-2581
**ROZPRAWY MATEMATYCZNE.** [Rozpr. mat.]. **VFOAT** Dissertationes Mathematicae. (1952)-. Monographic series. English (French, German, Polish and Russian). ir. Price varies per volume. Panstwowe Wydawn Naukowe, Miodowa 10, PO Box 391, 00251 Warsaw Poland. **LC** QA1; .D54. **DD** 510. **CODEN** DSMAAH.
**Ind/Abst** Math. Rev.; Stat. Theory Method Abstr. (1969, 1976, 1979, 1982); Zentralbl. Math. Ihre Grenzgeb.

●RU/1061-7566
**RUSSIAN JOURNAL OF COMPUTATIONAL MECHANICS.** See Engineering-Mechanical Engineering and Machinery.

●RU/1061-9208
**RUSSIAN JOURNAL OF MATHEMATICAL PHYSICS.** See Physics.

●NE/0927-6467
**RUSSIAN JOURNAL OF NUMERICAL ANALYSIS AND MATHEMATICAL ANALYSIS.** **VFOAT** Numerical Analysis and Mathematical Modelling. Vol. 7, No. 1 (1992)-. Periodical. English (translations available in Russian). bm. DM940.00. VSP International Science Publishers, Godfried van Seystlaan 47, 3703 BR Zeist Netherlands. **Tel** 011 31 3404 25790, FAX 011 31 3404 32081, telex 40217 USP NL. **(Subscription address:** VSP International Science Publishers, PO Box 346, 3700 AH Zeist Netherlands.) **ED** G. I. Marchuk. **LC** QA297; .S6. **CODEN** RJNMEH. **Pr Rev.** ***Continues*** *Soviet Journal of Nmerical Analysis and Mathematical Modelling, 0169-2895.*
**Desc:** Provides English translations of selected new original Russian papers on the theoretical aspects of numerical analysis and the application of mathematical methods to simulation and modelling.

UK/0036-0279
**RUSSIAN MATHEMATICAL SURVEYS.** [Russ. math. surv.]. **Added/Corp** London Mathematical Society. **VFOAT** Uspekhi Matematicheskikh Nauk. Vol. 15, No. 1 (Jan./Feb. 1960)-. Periodical. English. bm. £326.00. British Library Translated Journals, Boston Spa, Wetherby West Yorkshire LS23 7BQ England. **Tel** 011 44 937 546078. **(Subscription address:** Turpin Transactions Ltd., Blackhorse Road, Letchworth, Herfordshire SG6 1HN United Kingdom; Telephone: (0462) 672555, FAX: (0462) 480947) **ED** J L B Cooper. **LC** QA1; .R82. **Pr Rev.** Documents available from The Genuine Article.
**Ind/Abst** Compumath Citation Index [Full Cov.]; Int. Aerosp. Abstr.; Math. Rev.; Res. Alert [Full Cov.]; Soc. Sci. Cit. Index [Select. Cov.]; Zentralbl. Math. Ihre Grenzgeb.

●US/1066-369X
**RUSSIAN MATHEMATICS.** [Russ. math.]. **VFOAT** Iz. VUZ; Izvestiya Vysshikh Uchebnykh Zavedenii. Matematika. Vol. 36, No. 1 (1992)-. Periodical. English (translations available in Russian). mo. $940.00. Allerton Press, Inc., 150 Fifth Avenue, New York NY 10011. **Tel** (212)924-3950, FAX (212)463-9684, telex 427441 ALPRES. **LC** QA1; .R7813. **DD** 510. **[CCC].** Documents available from Ask*IEEE. ***Continues*** *Soviet Union. Ministerstvo Vysshego i Srednego Spetsialnogo Obrazovaniia. Izvestiia Vysshikh Uchebnykh Zavedenii. Matematika. English. Soviet Mathematics, 0197-7156.*
**Ind/Abst** INSPEC; Math. Rev.

GW/0170-0944
**SACHUNTERRICHT UND MATHEMATIK IN DER PRIMARSTUFE.** [Sachunterr. Math. Prim.stufe]. **VFOAT** SMP. Sachunterricht und Mathematik in der Primarstufe. (1978)-. Periodical. German. mo. DM91.20 Germany; DM103.20 other. Aulis Verlag Deubner & Company, Antwerpenerstrasse 6 12, 50672 Koln Germany. **Tel** 011 49 221 518051, FAX 011 49 221 518443. **UDC** 372.85 :373.3 ***Continues*** *Sachunterricht und Mathematik in der Gundschule, 0342-7404.*

JA/0385-6186
**SAGA DAIGAKU RIKOGAKUBU SHUHO.** See Engineering.

JA/0289-0739
**SAITAMA MATHEMATICAL JOURNAL.** [Saitama math. j.]. Vol. 1 (1983)-. Periodical. English (French and German). an. Free. Saitama University, Department of Mathematics, Faculty of Science, Urawa 338 Japan. **Tel** 011 81 0488 52-2111 ext2423, FAX 48 857 4560. **ED** T Kako, F Sakai, K Takeuchi, and T Mizutani. **LC** QA1; .S28. **DD** 510/.5. cum. index. **Circ:** 500. ***Continues in part*** *Science Reports of Saitama University. Series A, Mathematics, Physics, Chemistry and Biochemistry.*
**Desc:** The aim of this journal is to publish original papers in pure and applied mathematics.
**Ind/Abst** Math. Rev.; Zentralbl. Math. Ihre Grenzgeb.

●US/1064-5616
**SBORNIK. MATHEMATICS.** (SBORNIK. MATHEMATICS / RUSSIAN ACADEMY OF SCIENCES.). **Added/Corp** American Mathematical Society. Rossiiskaia Akademiia Nauk. **VFOAT** Mathematics. Vol. 75, No. 1 (1993)-. Periodical. English (translations available in Russian). mo. $1030.00 (print or microfiche). American Mathematical Society, PO Box 6248, Providence RI 02940-6248. **Tel** (800)321-4267, (401)455-4000, FAX (401)331-3842, telex 797192. **(Subscription address:** American Mathematical Society, PO Box 5904, Boston MA 02206-5904.) **LC** QA1; .M4112. **DD** 510. Index available (bound in fourth issue). ***Continues*** *Mathematics of the USSR. Sbornik, 0025-5734.*
**Desc:** Translation of Russian journal, Matematicheskii Sbornik, published by the Russian Academy of Sciences and the Moscow Mathematical Society.
**Ind/Abst** Math. Rev.; Sci. Cit. Index.

RU
**SBORNIK RABOT PO TEORII OPTIMALNYKH PROTSESSOV.** **Added/Corp** Kaliningradskii Gosudarstvennyi Universitet. Vol. 1 (1973)-. Russian. Kaliningradskii Gosudarstvennyi Universitet / Kaliningrad State University, Ulitsa A Nevskogo 14, 236041 Kaliningrad Russia. **Tel** 46-59-17, FAX 46-58-13, telex 262116. **LC** QA402.5; .S29.

US/0732-7773
**SCHOLASTIC DYNAMATH.** **VFOAT** Dynamath. Vol. 1, No. 1 (Sept. 1982)-. Periodical. English. Eight times a year. $25.00. Scholastic Inc., 2931 East McCarty Street, PO Box 3710, Jefferson City MO 65102-9957. **Tel** (314)636-5271, (800)631-1586. **ED** Jackie Glasthal. **Circ:** 210,000. available on microfilm from University Microfilms International (UMI).
**Desc:** A classroom magazine for children in grades 5 and 6. Includes articles, games, and puzzles which give children a chance to practice math skills.

US/0198-8379
**SCHOLASTIC MATH MAGAZINE.** **VFOAT** Math; Scholastic Math. Vol. 1 (Sept. 19, 1980)-. Periodical. English. Eight times a year. $25.00. Scholastic Inc., 2931 East McCarty Street, PO Box 3710, Jefferson City MO 65102-9957. **Tel** (314)636-5271, (800)631-1586. **ED** Sue Macy. available on microfilm and microfiche from University Microfilms International (UMI).
**Desc:** Math magazine for general math students ages 12-16 and their teachers. Articles and activities focus on problem solving, math on the job, consumer math, and computation practice.

US/1055-1212
**SCHOLASTIC MATH POWER.** [Scholast. math power]. Vol. 1, No. 1 (Sept. 1991)-. Periodical. English. bm. $25.00. Scholastic Inc., 2931 East McCarty Street, PO Box 3710, Jefferson City MO 65102-9957. **Tel** (314)636-5271, (800)631-1586. **DD** 372.

GW/0178-8116
**SCHRIFTENREIHE ANGEWANDTE VERSICHERUNGSMATHEMATIK.** [Schr.reihe angew. Versicher.math.]. Monographic series. German. ir. Price varies per volume. **UDC** 368.
**Ind/Abst** Zentralbl. Math. Ihre Grenzgeb.

GW/0077-1961
**SCHRIFTENREIHE DES MATHEMATISCHEN INSTITUTS DER UNIVERSITAT MUNSTER.** [Schriftenr. Math. Inst. Univ. Munst.]. **Main/Corp** Universitat Munster. Mathematisches Institut. Monographic series. German. Price varies per volume.
**Ind/Abst** Math. Rev.; Zentralbl. Math. Ihre Grenzgeb.

GW
**SCHRIFTENREIHE ZUR MATHEMATIK.** ***Ceased.*** (1955)-(19??). Monographic series. German. ***Continues*** *Schriftenreihe zur Gestaltung des Matematischen Unterrichts.*
**Ind/Abst** Zentralbl. Math. Ihre Grenzgeb.

NE/0926-7220
**SCIENCE & EDUCATION.** **See** Education-Teaching and Curriculum.

CC/1001-6511
**SCIENCE IN CHINA. SERIES A, MATHEMATICS, PHYSICS, ASTRONOMY & TECHNOLOGICAL SCIENCES.** **See** Science and Technology.

FR/0294-0264
**SCIENCES ET TECHNIQUES EN PERSPECTIVE.** **See** Science and Technology.

CL/0716-8446
**SCIENTIA. SERIES A. MATHEMATICAL SCIENCES.** [Scientia, Ser. A, Math. Sci.]. (1988)-. Periodical. English. an. **UDC** 51.
**Ind/Abst** Zentralbl. Math. Ihre Grenzgeb.

US/0276-9670
**SCRIPTA SERIES IN MATHEMATICS.** [Scripta ser. math.]. Monographic series. English. ir. Price varies per volume. John Wiley & Sons, Inc., 605 Third Avenue, New York NY 10158-0012. **Tel** (212)850-6000, (212)850-6645, FAX (212)850-6088, telex 12-7063. **(Subscription address:** John Wiley & Sons / England, Baffins Lane, Chichester, West Sussex PO19 1UD England.**)**

SZ/0272-9903
**SELECTA MATHEMATICA.** ***Title Change.*** (199?)-(199?). English. Four times a year. Birkhaeuser Verlag Ag, Klosterberg 23, PO Box 133, CH-4010 Basel Switzerland. **Tel** 011 41 61 2717400, FAX 011 41 0 61 2717666, telex 963475 birk ch. **ED** R. P. Boas. **[CCC].** ***Continues*** *Selecta Mathematica Sovietica.* ***Continued by*** *Selecta Mathematica. New Series.*
**Desc:** Covers all areas of mathematics, including mathematical physics. Accepts papers by mathematicians from the former Soviet Union, and papers from Russian language journals and collections that are not regularly translated into English.
**Ind/Abst** Math. Rev.; Zentralbl. Math. Ihre Grenzgeb.

SZ
**SELECTA MATHEMATICA. NEW SERIES.** (199?)-. English. Four times a year. 516.20F Switzerland; 526.20F other. Birkhaeuser Verlag Ag, Klosterberg 23, PO Box 151, CH 4106 Therwil Switzerland. **Tel** 011 41 61 2717400, FAX 011 41 0 61 2717666, telex 963475 birk ch. **(Subscription address:** Birkhauser Verlag AG, PO Box 151, CH 4106 Therwil Switzerland; Phone: 011 41 61 7217740**)** **ED** R. P. Boas. ***Continues*** *Selecta Mathematica.*
**Ind/Abst** Math. Rev.; Zentralbl. Math. Ihre Grenzgeb.

US/0272-9903
**SELECTA MATHEMATICA SOVIETICA.** ***Title Change.*** [Sel. math. Sov.]. Vol. 1, No. 1 (1981)-(199?). Periodical. English (Russian). qt. Birkhaeuser Verlag Ag, Klosterberg 23, PO Box 133, CH-4010 Basel Switzerland. **Tel** 011 41 61 2717400, FAX 011 41 0 61 2717666, telex 963475 birk ch. **ED** R P Boas, S Zdravkovska, and M A Brouwers. **LC** QA1; .S414. **DD** 510/.5. **CODEN** SMSODB. **[CCC].** available on microfilm and microfiche from University Microfilms International (UMI). Documents available from Ask*IEEE. ***Continued by*** *Selecta Mathematica.*
**Desc:** Covers all areas of mathematics, including mathematical physics. Papers are selected from Soviet journals and collections that are not regularly translated into English. Also includes previously unpublished papers.
**Ind/Abst** INSPEC (1981-); Math. Rev.; Zentralbl. Math. Ihre Grenzgeb.

US/0094-8837
**SELECTED TABLES IN MATHEMATICAL STATISTICS.** **See** Mathematics-Abstracting, Bibliographies and Statistics.

UK
**SELECTED TOPICS IN GRAPH THEORY.** Vol. 1 (1978)-. Monographic series. English. ir. Price varies per volume. Academic Press, Inc., 6277 Sea Harbor Drive, Orlando FL 32887. **Tel** (800)543-9534, (407)345-4100, FAX (407)363-9661. **LC** QA166; .S46. **DD** 511/.5/05.

US/0065-9274
**SELECTED TRANSLATIONS IN MATHEMATICAL STATISTICS AND PROBABILITY.** [Sel. transl. math. stat. probab.]. **Added/Corp** Institute of Mathematical Statistics. American Mathematical Society. Vol. 1 (1961)-. Monographic series. English. ir. Price varies per volume. American Mathematical Society, PO Box 6248, Providence RI 02940-6248. **Tel** (800)321-4267, (401)455-4000, FAX (401)331-3842, telex 797192. **(Subscription address:** American Mathematical Society, PO Box 5904, Boston MA 02206-5904.**)** **LC** QA273; .S45. **DD** 519.082. **CODEN** SMSRB. **[CCC].**
**Desc:** Mathematical statistics and probabilities.
**Ind/Abst** Zentralbl. Math. Ihre Grenzgeb.

US/0037-1912
**SEMIGROUP FORUM.** [Semigroup forum]. Vol. 1 (Mar. 1970)-. Periodical. English (German, Russian and French). Six times a year. $261.00. Springer-Verlag New York Inc., 175 5th Avenue, New York NY 10010. **Tel** (212)460-1500, telex 232 235 SPB UR. **(Subscription address:** Springer Verlag New York Inc. / for North America, 44 Hartz Way, Secaucus NJ 07096.**)** **ED** J A Goldstein, K H Hofmann, G J Lallement, N R Reilly, and B M Schein. **LC** QA171; .S52. **DD** 512. **CODEN** SMGFAN. **[CCC].** **Pr Rev.** available on microfilm and microfiche from University Microfilms International (UMI). Documents available from The Genuine Article.
**Desc:** Contains survey and research articles, announcements of new results, research problems, short notes, and abstracts and bibliographic items of complete work.
**Ind/Abst** Compumath Citation Index [Full Cov.]; Math. Rev.; Res. Alert [Full Cov.]; Sci. Cit. Index (19??-19??); SCISEARCH; Zentralbl. Math. Ihre Grenzgeb.

FR
**SEMINAIRE CHOQUET. EXPOSES.** 1.-Year; 1962-. Multiple languages (English and French). Institut Henri Poincare, 11 rue Pierre et Marie Curie, 75231 Paris Cedex 05 France. **LC** QA300; .S394B. **DD** 515/.05.

FR/0772-2257
**SEMINAIRE DE MATHEMATIQUE.** **VFOAT** Seminaire de Mathematique. No. 1 (Feb. 1982)-. French (English). Three times a year. Universite Catholique de Louvain / Academie Erasme, Grand rue 25 115, B-1348 Louvain La Neuve Belgium. **Tel** 011 32 10 452395. **LC** WMLC L 83/9710. ***Formed by the union of*** *Seminaire de Mathematique Pure* ***and*** *Seminaire de Mathematiqueappliquee et Mecanique.*

US/1046-5952
**SEMINAIRE DE THEORIE DES NOMBRES / SEMINAIRE DELANGE-PISOT-POITOU.** [Semin. theor. nr.]. **Main/Conf** Seminaire Delange-Pisot-Poitou. 1979-80-. English (French). an. **LC** QA241; .S37A. **DD** 512/.7/05. ***Continues*** *Seminaire Delange-Pisot-Poitou : Exposes.*

GW
**SEMINAIRE DE THEORIE DU POTENTIEL, PARIS : EXPOSES.** No. 1 (1972-1974)-. French. an. Springer-Verlag GmbH & Company KG, Heidelberger Platz 3, D 14197 Berlin Germany. **Tel** 011 49 30 8207223, FAX 011 49 30 8214091, telex 183 319 SPBLN D. **(Subscription address:** Springer Verlag New York Inc. / for North America, 44 Hartz Way, Secaucus NJ 07096.**)** **ED** F Hirsch and G Mokobodzki. **LC** QA3; .L28 subser; QA404.7. **DD** 510 S; 515.7. ***Continues*** *Seminaire de Theorie du Potentiel.*

FR
**SEMINAIRE EQUATIONS AUX DERIVEES PARTIELLES / ECOLE POLYTECHNIQUE, CENTRE DE MATHEMATIQUES.** **Added/Corp** Ecole Polytechnique (France). Centre de Mathematiques. **VFOAT** Seminaire sur les Equations aux Derivees Partielles. (1985/1986)-. French (English). **LC** QA374; .E6942. ***Continues*** *Equations aux Derivees Partielles.*
**Ind/Abst** Zentralbl. Math. Ihre Grenzgeb.

FR
**SEMINAIRE PAUL KREE. EXPOSES.** **Main/Corp** Seminaire Paul Kree. Vol. 1 (1974/75)-. French. Institut Henri Poincare, 11 rue Pierre et Marie Curie, 75231 Paris Cedex 05 France. **LC** QA377; .S44. **DD** 515/.353/08.

FR/0553-2264
**SEMINAIRE SUR LES EQUATIONS AUX DERIVEES PARTIELLES.** **Added/Corp** College de France France. Centre National de la Recherche Scientifique. (1962/1963)-. Periodical. French. an. OFFILIB / Office International de Documentation et Librairie, 48 rue Gay-Lussac, 75240 Paris Cedex 05 France. **Tel** 1 43 29 21 32, FAX 1 43 29 91 67, telex 206 905F. **LC** QA374; .S38.

JA
**SEMINAR ON MATHEMATICAL SCIENCES.** **Added/Corp** Keio Gijuku Daigaku. Suri Kogakuka. (19??)-. Monographic series. English. Price varies per volume. Keio Gijuku Daigaku Riko Gakubu Suri Kagakka, (Dept. of Mathematics, Faculty of Science & Technology, Keio University), 14-1, Hiyoshi 3 Chome, Kohokuku, Yokohamashi, Kanagawaken 223 Japan.
**Ind/Abst** Math. Rev.; Zentralbl. Math. Ihre Grenzgeb.

GW/0940-2268
**SEMINAR SOPHUS LIE : DARMSTADT, ERLANGEN, GREIFSWALD, LEIPZIG.** ***Title Change.*** **Added/Corp** Technische Hochschule Darmstadt. Universitat Erlangen. Ernst-Moritz-Arndt-Universitat Greifswald. Universitat Leipzig. **VFOAT** Seminar Reports (Seminar Sophus Lie). Vol. 1, No. 1 (1991)-(Dec. 1994). Periodical. English. sa. Heldermann Verlag Berlin, Nassauische Str 26, D 10717 Berlin Germany. **Tel** 011 49 30 870446. ***Continued by*** *Journal of Lie Theory.*
**Ind/Abst** Zentralbl. Math. Ihre Grenzgeb.

RM
**SEMINARUL DE OPERATORI LINIARI SI ANALIZA ARMONICA.** **Added/Corp** Universitatea din Timisoara. Sectia de Matematica. (197?)-. Monographic series. English (French). Price varies per volume. Universitetea Timisoara, Bul. V. Parvan, Nr. 4, 1900 Timisoara, Romania. **LC** QA319; .S44.
**Ind/Abst** Zentralbl. Math. Ihre Grenzgeb.

RM
**SEMINARUL DE TEORIA STRUCTURILOR / UNIVERSITATEA DIN TIMISOARA, FACULTATEA DE STIINTE ALE NATURII, SECTIA MATEMATICA.** **Added/Corp** Universitatea din Timisoara. Sectia de Matematica. (19??)-. Monographic series. English. Price varies per volume. Universitetea Timisoara, Bul. V. Parvan, Nr. 4, 1900 Timisoara, Romania. **LC** QA319; .S46. **DD** 515.7/05.
**Ind/Abst** Zentralbl. Math. Ihre Grenzgeb.

RU
**SEMIOTIKA I INFORMATIKA.** **Added/Corp** Vsesoiuznyi Institut Nauchnoi i Tekhnicheskoi Informatsii (Soviet Union). **VFOAT** Semiotics and Informatics. (1975)-. Russian (summaries and/or abstracts in English; table of contents in English). VINITI - Vsesoyuznyi Institut Nauchno-Tekhnicheskoi Informatsii, All-Union Scientific and Technical Information Institute, Baltiiskaia Ulitsa 14, 125219 Moscow Russia. **Tel** 238-46-00, FAX 9430060, telex 411160. **LC** P98; .I52. ***Continues*** *Informatsionnye Voprosy Semiotiki, Lingvistiki i Avtomaticheskogo Perevoda.*
**Ind/Abst** Zentralbl. Math. Ihre Grenzgeb.

US/0747-4946
**SEQUENTIAL ANALYSIS.** [Seq. anal.]. Vol. 3, No. 1 (1984)-. Periodical. English. qt. $385.00 US; $399.00 other. Marcel Dekker Inc., 270 Madison Avenue, New York NY 10016. **Tel** (212)696-9000, (800)228-1160, FAX (212)685-4540, telex 421419. **(Subscription address:** Marcel Dekker Inc, PO Box 5017, Monticello NY 12701.**)** **ED** B. K. Ghosh and P. K. Sen. **LC** QA279.7; .C65. **DD** 519.5/4. **CODEN** SEANEX. **[CCC].** **Bk Rev.** **Ad Acc.** available on microfiche. ***Continues*** *Communications in Statistics. Sequential Analysis, 0731-177X.*
**Desc:** In each issue active and innovative researchers contribute articles covering theoretical, practical, and methodological topics including hypothesis testing, analysis of variance, sample surveys, regression and correlation, experimental design, point and interval estimation, times series analysis, and Bayesian analysis. Readers can expect to encounter a broad spectrum of mathematical tools and concepts, including contributions to pure probability theory that have a clear bearing on sequential analysis.
**Ind/Abst** Biostatistica; Curr. Index Stat.; Math. Rev.; Qual. Control Appl. Stat.; Stat. Theory Method Abstr. (1986-1987); Zentralbl. Math. Ihre Grenzgeb.

BU/0204-4110
**SERDIKA.** (SERDICA; BULGARICAE MATEMATICAE PUBLICATIONES. SERDIKA; BULGARSKO MATEMATICHESKO SPISANIE. SERDIKA; BULGARSKO MATEMATICHESKO SPISANIE.). [Serdika]. **Added/Corp** Edinen Tsentur za Nauka i Podgotovka na Kadri po Matematika i Mekhanika (Bulgarska Akademiia na Naukite). **VFOAT** Serdika; Bulgarsko Matematichesko Spisanie. (1975)-. Periodical. Multiple languages (English, German and Russian). Four times a year. DM117.00. **(Subscription address:** Kubon & Sagner, ABT Zeitschriftenimport, D 80328 Munich Germany.**)** **LC** QA1; .S433. **CODEN** SERDDJ. ***Supersedes*** *Matematicheski Institut (Bulgarska Akademiia na Naukite). Izvestiia.*
**Ind/Abst** Int. Aerosp. Abstr.; Math. Rev.; Zentralbl. Math. Ihre Grenzgeb.

PL
**SERIA CHEMIA.** **Added/Corp** Uniwersytet Im. Adama Mickiewicza W Poznaniu. Wydzia Matematyki, Fizyki I Chemii. No. 11 (1971)-. Academic Scholarly Publication. Polish (summaries and/or abstracts in English). 21.00. Ul Krakowski Azedmiescie 7, 00-068 Warszawa Poland. **LC** QA1; .P682. **CODEN** SCUCDH. Documents available from CASDDS. ***Continues*** *Uniwersytet Im. Adama Mickiewicza W Poznaniu. Wydzia Matematyki, Fizyki I Chemii. Prace Wydziau Matematyki, Fizyki I Chemii. Seria Chemia.*
**Ind/Abst** Chem. Abstr.

PL
**SERIA MATEMATYKA / UNIWERSYTET IM. ADAMA MICKIEWICZA W POZNANIU.** **Added/Corp** Uniwersytet im. Adama Mickiewicza w Poznaniu. Nr. 2 (1975)-. Monographic series. Polish (summaries and/or abstracts in German). Price varies per volume. ***Continues*** *Prace Wydziau Matematyki, Fizyki i Chemii. Seria Matematyka.*

PL/0324-9603
**SERIA MONOGRAFIE - POLITECHNIKA WROCAWSKA, INSTYTUT MATEMATYKI.** [Pr. nauk. Inst. Mat. Politech. Wroc., Monogr.]. **Main/Corp** Politechnika Wrocawska. Instytut Matematyki. **VFOAT** Monografie - Politechnika Wrocawska, Instytut Matematyki. Began in 1974. Monographic series. Polish (summaries and/or abstracts in English and Russian). Price varies per volume. **(Subscription address:** ARS Polona, PO Box 1001, 00068 Warsaw Poland.**)** **LC** TJ260.A1; B78 subser.
**Ind/Abst** Math. Rev.

PL/0324-9611
**SERIA STUDIA I MATERIAY - POLITECHNIKA WROCAWSKA, INSTYTUT MATEMATYKI.** [Pr. nauk. Inst. Mat. Politech. Wroc., Stud. mater.]. **Main/Corp** Politechnika Wrocawska. Instytut Matematyki. **VFOAT** Studies and Research - Wrocaw Technical University, Institute of Mathematics; Studia I Materiay - Politechnika Wrocawska, Instytut Matematyki. No. 10-. Monographic series. Polish (English and Russian; summaries and/or abstracts in English, Polish and Russian). Price varies per volume. **(Subscription address:** ARS Polona, PO Box 1001, 00068 Warsaw Poland.**)** **LC** TJ260.A1; B78 subser. ***Continues*** *Politechnika Wrocawska. Instytut Matematyki I Fizyki Teoretycznej. Studia I Materiay.*
**Ind/Abst** Math. Rev.

SZ/0373-3149
**SERIE INTERNATIONALE D'ANALYSE NUMERIQUE.** (INTERNATIONAL SERIES OF NUMERICAL MATHEMATICS.). [Ser. int. anal. numer.]. **VFOAT** Internationale Schriftenreihe zur Numerischen Mathematik; Serie Internationale d'Analyse Numerique. Vol. 3, (1961)-. Monographic series. English (French and German). ir. Price varies per volume. Birkhaeuser Verlag Ag, Klosterberg 23, PO Box 133, CH-4010 Basel Switzerland. **Tel** 011 41 61 2717400, FAX 011 41 0 61 2717666, telex 963475 birk ch.
**Ind/Abst** Math. Rev.; Zentralbl. Math. Ihre Grenzgeb.

SI/0217-8281
**SERIES IN MODERN APPLIED MATHEMATICS.** [Ser. mod. appl. math.]. (1983)-. Monographic series. English. Price varies per volume. World Scientific Publishing Company, PO Box 128, Farrer Road, Singapore 9128 Singapore. **Tel** 011 65 3825663, FAX 011 65 3825919, telex RS 28561 WSPC. **LC** UNC.
**Ind/Abst** Math. Rev.; Zentralbl. Math. Ihre Grenzgeb.

SI
**SERIES IN PURE MATHEMATICS.** Vol. 1 (1984)-. Monographic series. English. ir. Price varies per volume. World Scientific Publishing Company, PO Box 128, Farrer Road, Singapore 9128 Singapore. **Tel** 011 65 3825663, FAX 011 65 3825919, telex RS 28561 WSPC. **ED** C.C. Hsiung.
**Ind/Abst** Zentralbl. Math. Ihre Grenzgeb.

SI
**SERIES IN REAL ANALYSIS.** Vol. 1 (1988)-. Monographic series. English. Price varies per volume. World Scientific Publishing Company, PO Box 128, Farrer Road, Singapore 9128 Singapore. **Tel** 011 65 3825663, FAX 011 65 3825919, telex RS 28561 WSPC.
**Ind/Abst** Zentralbl. Math. Ihre Grenzgeb.

RU
**SERIIA MATEMATICHESKIKH NAUK.** **VFOAT** Mathematical Sciences Series. (19??)-. Monographic series. Russian. Price varies per volume. St Petersburg State University / Izdatelstvo Leningradskogo Universiteta, Universitetskaia Nab 7/9, 199034 St Petersburg Russia. **Tel** 011 95 218-97-88, FAX 011 95 218-51-52, telex 121481. **LC** AS262; .L422 subser.

NE/0927-6947
**SET-VALUED ANALYSIS.** English. qt. $394.00. Kluwer Academic Publishers, Postbus 322, 3300 AH Dordrecht, The Netherlands. **Tel** 011 (31) 78 524400, FAX 011 31 78 183273, telex 20083. **ED** Biagio Ricceri. **Pr Rev. Acid Free.**
**Desc:** An international journal devoted to all aspects of mathematical analysis involving multifunctions (otherwise called set-valued maps) and topics related to them.

CH/1001-9626
**SHENGWU SHUXUE XUEBAO.** **VFOAT** Journal of Biomathematics. (1986)-. Periodical. Chinese. sa. **DD** 510.
**Ind/Abst** Rev. Plant Pathol.

UK
**SHIVA MATHEMATICS SERIES.** Monographic series. English. Price varies per volume.
**Ind/Abst** Zentralbl. Math. Ihre Grenzgeb.

CC/0583-1431
**SHU HSUEH HSUEH PAO.** **Added/Corp** Chung-Kuo Shu Hsueh Hui. **VFOAT** Acta Mathematica Sinica. (1951)-. Periodical. Chinese (table of contents in English). bm. $117.60. Science Press, 16 Donghuangchenggen North Street, Beijing 100707, People's Republic of China. **Tel** 011 86 1 4019821, 011 86 1 4010642, FAX 011 86 1 4012180, 011 86 1 4019810, telex 210147. **(Subscription address:** China International Book Trading Corporation, PO Box 399, Library Service Department, Beijing 100044 People's Republic of China.**)** Documents available from Ask*IEEE.
**Ind/Abst** INSPEC (Vol. 28, No. 2, March 1985-); Math. Rev.

CC
**SHU HSUEH WU LI HSUEH PAO.** **See** Physics.

CC
**SHU HSUEH YEN CHIU YU PING LUN.** **VFOAT** Journal of Mathematical Research and Exposition; Journal of Mathematical Research & Exposition. Began in 1981. Periodical. Chinese (English). qt. $16.00. China National Publishing Import & Export Corporation, 16 Gongti E Rd., Chaoyang Dist., Beijing 100704, People's Republic of China. **Tel** 011 8601 50630169, 5066688, FAX 011 8601 5063101, 5063010, telex 22313. **LC** QA1; .S4477. **DD** 510/.5.
**Ind/Abst** Math. Rev.

CC/0252-9602
**SHUXUE WULI XUEBAO.** [Shuxue Wuli Xuebao]. **VFOAT** Acta Mathematica Scientia. (1981)-. Periodical. Chinese. qt. 477.50F (includes distribution costs). Baltzer Science Publishers BV, Asterweg 1A, 1031 HL Amsterdam Netherlands. **Tel** 011 31 20 6370061, FAX 011 31 20 6323651. **UDC** 51. **Pr Rev.**

US/0080-5084
**SIAM-AMS PROCEEDINGS.** [SIAM-AMS proc.]. **Added/Corp** American Mathematical Society. Society for Industrial and Applied Mathematics. **VFOAT** S.I.A.M.-A.M.S. Proceedings. Vol. 1 (1969)-. Monographic series. English. ir. Price varies per volume. American Mathematical Society, PO Box 6248, Providence RI 02940-6248. **Tel** (800)321-4267, (401)455-4000, FAX (401)331-3842, telex 797192. **(Subscription address:** American Mathematical Society, PO Box 5904, Boston MA 02206-5904.**)** **CODEN** SAMPBY. **[CCC].** Documents available from CASDDS.
**Ind/Abst** Chem. Abstr.; Math. Rev.; Zentralbl. Math. Ihre Grenzgeb.

US/0036-1399
**SIAM JOURNAL ON APPLIED MATHEMATICS.** [SIAM j. appl. math.]. **Main/Corp** Society for Industrial and Applied Mathematics. **Added/Corp** Society for Industrial and Applied Mathematics. **VFOAT** Applied Mathematics. **VAT** Society for Industrial and Applied Mathematics Journal on Applied Mathematics. Vol. 14 (Jan. 1966)-. Academic Scholarly Publication. English (French, Russian, Spanish and Italian). bm (Feb., Apr., June, Aug., Oct., Dec.). $262.00 US, Canada, and Mexico; $308.00 other. Society for Industrial and Applied Mathematics, 3600 University City Science Center, Philadelphia PA 19104-2688. **Tel** (215)382-9800, (800)447-7426, FAX (215)386-7999, telex 446715. **ED** James P. Keener. **LC** QA1; .S73. **DD** 510/.5. **CODEN** SMJMAP. **[CCC].** Index available. **Ad Acc. Pr Rev. Circ:** 3,000. available in microform. Documents available from Article Express International, The Genuine Article, Ask*IEEE, CASDDS. ***Continues*** *Journal of the Society for Industrial and Applied Mathematics, 0368-4245.*
**Desc:** Contains research articles on the applied mathematics (analytical, stochastic, statistical, numerical) of the physical engineering, biological, medical and social sciences.
**Ind/Abst** Abstr. Bull. Inst. Pap. Sci. Tech.; ACM Guide Comput. Lit.; Acoust. Abstr.; Appl. Sci. Technol. Index; Bioeng. Abstr.; Biostatistica; Chem. Abstr.; Coal Abstr.; Compumath Citation Index [Full Cov.]; Comput. Rev.; Curr. Contents Phys. Chem. Earth Sci.; Ei Page One; EMBASE; Eng. Index Annu.; INSPEC (June 1970-); Int. Abstr. Oper. Res. [Select. Cov.]; Int. Aerosp. Abstr.; Math. Rev.; Oper. Res./Manag. Sci.; Pollut. Abstr. Indexes; Qual. Control Appl. Stat.; Res. Alert [Full Cov.]; Sci. Cit. Index; SCISEARCH; Shock Vibr. Dig.; Stat. Theory Method Abstr. (1969-1975, 1977-1981); Zentralbl. Math. Ihre Grenzgeb.

US/0097-5397
**SIAM JOURNAL ON COMPUTING.** **See** Computers-Data Processing.

US/0363-0129
**SIAM JOURNAL ON CONTROL AND OPTIMIZATION.** [SIAM j. control optim.]. **Main/Corp** Society for Industrial and Applied Mathematics. **VFOAT** Journal on Control and Optimization; Control and Optimization. **VAT** Society for Industrial and Applied Mathematics Journal on Control and Optimization. Vol. 14 (Jan. 1976)-. Periodical. English. bm. $315.00 US, Canada, and Mexico; $360.00 other. Society for Industrial and Applied Mathematics, 3600 University City Science Center, Philadelphia PA 19104-2688. **Tel** (215)382-9800, (800)447-7426, FAX (215)386-7999, telex 446715. **ED** J.C. Willems. **LC** QA402.3; .S22. **DD** 629.8/312/05. **CODEN** SJCODC. **[CCC]. Ad Acc. Circ:** 2,000. Documents available from Article Express International, The Genuine Article, Ask*IEEE. ***Continues*** *SIAM Journal on Control, 0036-1402.*
**Desc:** Contains research articles on the mathematical theory of control and its applications and the associated areas of systems theory and optimization.
**Ind/Abst** ACM Guide Comput. Lit.; Acoust. Abstr.; Appl. Sci. Technol. Index; Bioeng. Abstr.; Compumath Citation Index [Full Cov.]; Comput. Rev.; Curr. Contents Eng. Tech. Appl. Sci.; Curr. Contents Phys. Chem. Earth Sci.; Ei Page One; Eng. Index Annu.; INSPEC (1976-); Int. Aerosp. Abstr.; Math. Rev.; Pollut. Abstr. Indexes; Res. Alert [Full Cov.]; Sci. Cit. Index; SCISEARCH; Soc. Sci. Cit. Index [Select. Cov.]; Zentralbl. Math. Ihre Grenzgeb.

US/0895-4801
**SIAM JOURNAL ON DISCRETE MATHEMATICS.** [SIAM j. discrete math.]. **Added/Corp** Society for Industrial and Applied Mathematics. **VFOAT** Journal on Discrete Mathematics; Discrete Mathematics. **VAT** Society for Industrial and Applied Mathematics Journal on Discrete Mathematics. Vol. 1, No. 1 (Feb. 1988)-. Periodical. English. qt (Feb., May, Aug., Nov.). $238.00 US, Canada, and Mexico; $272.00 other. Society for Industrial and Applied Mathematics, 3600 University City Science Center, Philadelphia PA 19104-2688. **Tel** (215)382-9800, (800)447-7426, FAX (215)386-7999, telex 446715. **ED** Clyde L. Monma. **LC** QA76.9.M35; S56. **DD** 004/.01/51. **[CCC].** Documents available from The Genuine Article. ***Continues in part*** *SIAM Journal on Algebraic and Discrete Methods, 0196-5212.*
**Desc:** Contains research articles on a broad range of topics from pure and applied mathematics including combinatorics and graph theory, discrete optimization and operations research, theoretical computer science, coding and communication theory, and game theory and mathematical modeling.
**Ind/Abst** ACM Guide Comput. Lit.; Biostatistica; Compumath Citation Index [Full Cov.]; Comput. Rev.; Curr. Contents Phys. Chem. Earth Sci.; Int. Abstr. Oper. Res. [Select. Cov.]; Math. Rev. (1988-); Oper. Res./Manag. Sci.; Qual. Control Appl. Stat.; Res. Alert [Full Cov.]; Sci. Cit. Index; SCISEARCH; Zentralbl. Math. Ihre Grenzgeb.

US/0036-1410
**SIAM JOURNAL ON MATHEMATICAL ANALYSIS.** [SIAM j. math. anal.]. **Main/Corp** Society for Industrial and Applied Mathematics. **VFOAT** Journal on Mathematical Analysis. **VAT** Society for Industrial and Applied Mathematics Journal on Mathematical Analysis. Vol. 1 (Feb. 1970)-. Periodical. English. bm (Jan., Mar., May, July, Sept., Nov.). $374.00 US, Canada, and Mexico; $422.00 other. Society for Industrial and Applied Mathematics, 3600 University City Science Center, Philadelphia PA 19104-2688. **Tel** (215)382-9800, (800)447-7426, FAX (215)386-7999, telex 446715. **ED** E. DiBenedetto. **LC** QA300; .S825. **DD** 517/.05. **CODEN** SJMAAH. **[CCC].** Index available. **Ad Acc. Pr Rev. Circ:** 1,355. Documents available from The Genuine Article, Ask*IEEE.
**Desc:** Focuses on those parts of classical and modern analysis that have direct or potential application to the natural sciences and engineering.
**Ind/Abst** ACM Guide Comput. Lit.; Compumath Citation Index [Full Cov.]; Comput. Rev.; Curr. Contents Phys. Chem. Earth Sci.; INSPEC (May 1972-); Int. Aerosp. Abstr.; Math. Rev.; Pollut. Abstr. Indexes; Res. Alert [Full Cov.]; Sci. Cit. Index; SCISEARCH; Zentralbl. Math. Ihre Grenzgeb.

US/0895-4798
**SIAM JOURNAL ON MATRIX ANALYSIS AND APPLICATIONS.** [SIAM j. matrix anal. appl.]. **Added/Corp** Society for Industrial and Applied Mathematics. **VFOAT** Journal on Matrix Analysis and Applications; Matrix Analysis and Applications. **VAT** Society for Industrial and Applied Mathematics Journal on Matrix Analysis and Applications. Vol. 9, No. 1 (Jan. 1988)-. Periodical. English. qt (Jan., Apr., July, Oct.). $254.00 US, Canada, and Mexico; $288.00 other. Society for Industrial and Applied Mathematics, 3600 University City Science Center, Philadelphia PA 19104-2688. **Tel** (215)382-9800, (800)447-7426, FAX (215)386-7999, telex 446715. **ED** G.H. Golub. **LC** QA188; .S53. **DD** 512.9/434/05. **CODEN** SJMAEL. **[CCC].** **Pr Rev.** Documents available from The Genuine Article, Ask*IEEE. ***Continues in part*** *SIAM Journal on Algebraic and Discrete Methods, 0196-5212.*
**Desc:** Contains research articles on the application of matrix analysis to areas such as signal processing, economic and bilogical modelling, and statistics and operations research. Papers that advance both numerical methods and the general theory are welcomed.
**Ind/Abst** ACM Guide Comput. Lit.; Compumath Citation Index [Full Cov.]; Comput. Rev.; Curr. Contents Phys. Chem. Earth Sci.; INSPEC (March 1981-); Math. Rev. (1988-); Pollut. Abstr. Indexes (1988-); Res. Alert [Full Cov.]; Sci. Cit. Index; SCISEARCH; Zentralbl. Math. Ihre Grenzgeb.

US/0036-1429
**SIAM JOURNAL ON NUMERICAL ANALYSIS.** (SIAM JOURNAL ON NUMERICAL ANALYSIS.). [SIAM j. numer. anal.]. **Main/Corp** Society for Industrial and Applied Mathematics. **Added/Corp** Society for Industrial and Applied Mathematics. **VAT** Society for Industrial and Applied Mathematics Journal on Numerical Analysis. Vol. 3 (1966)-. Periodical. English. bm (Feb., Apr., June, Aug., Oct., Dec.). $272.00 US, Canada, and Mexico; $318.00 other. Society for Industrial and Applied Mathematics, 3600 University City Science Center, Philadelphia PA 19104-2688. **Tel** (215)382-9800, (800)447-7426, FAX (215)386-7999, telex 446715. **ED** M. Luskin. **DD** 519. **CODEN** SJNAAM. **[CCC].** **Ad Acc.** **Pr Rev.** **Circ:** 3,000. Documents available from Article Express International, The Genuine Article, Ask*IEEE. ***Continues*** *Journal of the Society for Industrial and Applied Mathematics. Series B, Numerical Analysis, 0887-459X.*
**Desc:** Contains research articles on the development and analysis of numerical methods, including their convergence, stability and error analysis, along with related results in functional analysis and approximation theory. Computational experiments and new types of numerical applications are also included.
**Ind/Abst** ACM Guide Comput. Lit.; Appl. Sci. Technol. Index; Compumath Citation Index [Full Cov.]; Comput. Abstr.; Comput. Rev.; Curr. Contents Phys. Chem. Earth Sci.; Ei Page One; Eng. Index Annu.; INSPEC (July 1968-); Int. Aerosp. Abstr.; Math. Rev.; Pollut. Abstr. Indexes; Res. Alert [Full Cov.]; Sci. Cit. Index; SCISEARCH; Zentralbl. Math. Ihre Grenzgeb.

US/1052-6234
**SIAM JOURNAL ON OPTIMIZATION.** (SIAM JOURNAL ON OPTIMIZATION : A PUBLICATION OF THE SOCIETY FOR INDUSTRIAL AND APPLIED MATHEMATICS.). [SIAM j. optim.]. **Added/Corp** Society for Industrial and Applied Mathematics. **VFOAT** Optimization. **VAT** Society for Industrial and Applied Mathematics Journal on Optimization. Vol. 1, No. 1 (Feb. 1991)-. Periodical. English. qt (Feb., May, Aug., Nov.). $216.00 US, Canada, and Mexico; $246.00 other. Society for Industrial and Applied Mathematics, 3600 University City Science Center, Philadelphia PA 19104-2688. **Tel** (215)382-9800, (800)447-7426, FAX (215)386-7999, telex 446715. **ED** J.E.Dennis, Jr. **LC** QA402.5; .S5442. **DD** 519.3. **CODEN** SJOPE8. **[CCC].**
**Desc:** Contains research and expository articles on the theory and practice of optimization, and papers that link optimization theory with computational practice and applications.
**Ind/Abst** Int. Aerosp. Abstr.

US/0196-5204
**SIAM JOURNAL ON SCIENTIFIC AND STATISTICAL COMPUTING.** ***Title Change.*** [SIAM j. sci. statist. comput.]. **Main/Corp** Society for Industrial and Applied Mathematics. **VAT** Society for Industrial and Applied Mathematics Journal on Scientific and Statistical Computing. Vol. 1-13 (Mar. 1980)-(Nov. 1992). Statistical Publication. English. bm. Society for Industrial and Applied Mathematics, 3600 University City Science Center, Philadelphia PA 19104-2688. **Tel** (215)382-9800, (800)447-7426, FAX (215)386-7999, telex 446715. **ED** Charles William Gear. **LC** QA297; .S587a. **DD** 519.4/05. **CODEN** SIJCD4. **[CCC].** Index available. **Pr Rev.** **Circ:** 1,700. available in microform. Documents available from The Genuine Article, Ask*IEEE. ***Continued by*** *SIAM Journal on Scientific Computing, 1064-8275.*
**Desc:** Contains articles on numerical statistical and nonnumerical techniques, for solving scientific and statistical problems on computers. Emphasis is on the implementation of such techniques with computer languages.
**Ind/Abst** ACM Guide Comput. Lit.; Biostatistica; Comput. Rev.; Curr. Contents Phys. Chem. Earth Sci.; INSPEC (June 1981-); Int. Aerosp. Abstr.; Math. Rev.; Oper. Res./Manag. Sci.; Pollut. Abstr. Indexes; Qual. Control Appl. Stat.; Res. Alert [Full Cov.]; Sci. Cit. Index; SCISEARCH; Zentralbl. Math. Ihre Grenzgeb.

●US/1064-8275
**SIAM JOURNAL ON SCIENTIFIC COMPUTING.** [SIAM j. sci. comput.]. **Added/Corp** Society for Industrial and Applied Mathematics. **VFOAT** Society for Industrial and Applied Mathematics Journal on Scientific Computing. **VAT** Society for Industrial and Applied Mathematics Journal on Scientific Computing. (1993)-. Periodical. English. bm. $286.00 US, Canada, and Mexico; $338.00 other. Society for Industrial and Applied Mathematics, 3600 University City Science Center, Philadelphia PA 19104-2688. **Tel** (215)382-9800, (800)447-7426, FAX (215)386-7999, telex 446715. **ED** J.M. Hyman. **LC** QA297; .S587a. **DD** 519.4/05. **CODEN** SJOCE3. ***Continues*** *SIAM Journal on Scientific and Statistical Computing, 0196-5204.*
**Desc:** Contains research articles on numerical methods and techniques for scientific computation. Papers should address computational issues relevant to the solution of scientific or engineering problems, and should generally include computational results demonstrating the effectiveness of the proposed techniques.
**Ind/Abst** Compumath Citation Index [Full Cov.]; Int. Aerosp. Abstr.; Math. Rev.; Soc. Sci. Cit. Index [Select. Cov.].

US
**SIAM NEWS : A PUBLICATION OF SOCIETY FOR INDUSTRIAL AND APPLIED MATHEMATICS.** **Added/Corp** Society for Industrial and Applied Mathematics. **VFOAT** Society for Industrial and Applied Mathematics News. **VAT** Society for Industrial and Applied Mathematics News. Vol. 6 (Feb. 1973)-. Periodical. English. mo (10 issues). $18.00 US, Canada, and Mexico; $24.00 other. Society for Industrial and Applied Mathematics, 3600 University City Science Center, Philadelphia PA 19104-2688. **Tel** (215)382-9800, (800)447-7426, FAX (215)386-7999, telex 446715. **ED** Lloyd W. Black. **LC** QA1; .S145. **Bk Rev.** **Ad Acc.** **Circ:** 7,500 (ctrl). ***Continues*** *SIAM Newsletter (1968).*
**Desc:** News-journal for the applied mathematics community, with reports on academic and industrial research, federal activities and SIAM activities; includes lists of conferences, meetings, positions, etc.

US/0036-1445
**SIAM REVIEW.** [SIAM rev.]. **Main/Corp** Society for Industrial and Applied Mathematics. **Added/Corp** Society for Industrial and Applied Mathematics. Review. **VAT** Society for Industrial and Applied Mathematics Review. Vol. 1 (Jan. 1959)-. Periodical. English. qt (Mar., June, Sept., Dec.). $158.00 North America; $186.00 other. Society for Industrial and Applied Mathematics, 3600 University City Science Center, Philadelphia PA 19104-2688. **Tel** (215)382-9800, (800)447-7426, FAX (215)386-7999, telex 446715. **ED** Paul Davis. **LC** QA1; .S2. **DD** 519. **CODEN** SIREAD. **[CCC].** Index available. **Bk Rev.** **Ad Acc.** **Pr Rev.** **Circ:** 8,360. Documents available from Article Express International, The Genuine Article, Ask*IEEE, UMI Article Clearinghouse.
**Desc:** Contains primarily expository and survey papers as well as occasional essays on topics of interest to applied mathematicians. Other features are classroom notes, problems and solutions, book reviews.
**Ind/Abst** ACM Guide Comput. Lit.; Appl. Sci. Technol. Index; Biostatistica; Compumath Citation Index [Full Cov.]; Comput. Rev.; Curr. Contents Phys. Chem. Earth Sci.; EMBASE; Eng. Index Annu.; Expand. Acad. Index (1992-); INSPEC (1968-); Int. Abstr. Oper. Res. [Select. Cov.]; Int. Aerosp. Abstr.; Math. Rev.; Newsp. Period. Abstr. (1989-); Oper. Res./Manag. Sci.; Qual. Control Appl. Stat.; Res. Alert [Full Cov.]; Sci. Cit. Index; SCISEARCH; Soc. Sci. Cit. Index [Select. Cov.]; Stat. Theory Method Abstr. (1970-1971, 1973-1981); Zentralbl. Math. Ihre Grenzgeb.

US/1055-1344
**SIBERIAN ADVANCES IN MATHEMATICS.** [Sib. adv. math.]. (1991)-. Periodical. English. Four times a year (Mar., June, Sept., Dec.,). $420.00. Allerton Press, Inc., 150 Fifth Avenue, New York NY 10011. **Tel** (212)924-3950, FAX (212)463-9684, telex 427441 ALPRES. **DD** 510. **[CCC].**
**Ind/Abst** Zentralbl. Math. Ihre Grenzgeb.

●US/1062-8053
**SIBERIAN JOURNAL OF COMPUTER MATHEMATICS.** [Sib. j. comput. math.]. (1992)-. Periodical. English. Four times a year. $395.00. Nova Science Publishers Inc., 6080 Jericho Turnpike, Suite 207, Commack NY 11725-2808. **Tel** (516)499-3103, (516)499-3106, FAX (516)499-3146. **DD** 004.

US
**SIBERIAN JOURNAL OF DIFFERENTIAL EQUATIONS.** (19??)-. English. Four times a year. $395.00. Nova Science Publishers Inc., 6080 Jericho Turnpike, Suite 207, Commack NY 11725-2808. **Tel** (516)499-3103, (516)499-3106, FAX (516)499-3146.

US/0037-4466
**SIBERIAN MATHEMATICAL JOURNAL.** [Sib. math. j.]. **Added/Corp** Consultants Bureau. Vol. 7 (Jan/Feb 1966)-. Periodical. English (Russian). Six times a year. $1430.00 US; $1675.00 other. Consultants Bureau, A Division of Plenum Publishing Corporation, 233 Spring Street, New York NY 10013. **Tel** (212)620-8000, (212)620-8466, FAX (212)463-0742, telex 23/421139. **ED** M. M. Lavrent'ev. **LC** QA1; .S452. **CODEN** SMTJAW. **[CCC].** Index available. **Pr Rev.** available on microfilm and microfiche from University Microfilms International (UMI). Documents available from The Genuine Article.
**Desc:** Provides the English-speaking scientific community with an authoritative translation of math work being done in the education and research center near Novo Sibirisk in Siberia.
**Ind/Abst** Compumath Citation Index [Full Cov.]; Curr. Contents Phys. Chem. Earth Sci.; Int. Aerosp. Abstr.; Math. Rev.; Pollut. Abstr. Indexes; Res. Alert [Full Cov.]; Sci. Cit. Index; SCISEARCH; Zentralbl. Math. Ihre Grenzgeb.

RU/0037-4474
**SIBIRSKIJ MATEMATICESKIH ZURNAL.** (SIBIRSKII MATEMATICHESKII ZHURNAL.). [Sib. mat. z.]. **Added/Corp** Akademiia Nauk SSSR. Sibirskoe Otdelenie. Vol. 1, (May/June 1960)-. Academic Scholarly Publication. Russian. bm. $209.95. Izdatelstvo Nauka / Akademiia Nauk, Publishing House of the Russian Academy of Sciences, Leninskii Porspekt 14, 117901 Moscow Russia. **Tel** 011 95 954-21-53, FAX 011 95 938-21-44, telex 411964. **(Subscription address:** East View Publications Inc., 3020 Harbor Lane North, Suite 110, Minneapolis MN 55447.**)** Index available.
**Ind/Abst** Int. Aerosp. Abstr.; Math. Rev.; Zentralbl. Math. Ihre Grenzgeb.

AT/0314-7606
**SIGMA.** ***Title Change.*** [Sigma]. **VFOAT** Journal of the Mathematical Association of W.A. (1965)-(?). Periodical. English. qt. Mathematical Association of Western Australia, PO Box 492, Subiaco 6008 Australia. **Tel** 61 09 349-1380. **ED** Dr S Willis. **DD** 510.05. ***Continued by*** *Cross Section, 1033-1530.*
**Ind/Abst** Aust. Educ. Index (1974-1986).

GW
**SIGMA SERIES IN APPLIED MATHEMATICS.** Vol. 1 (1985)-. Monographic series. English. Price varies per volume.
**Ind/Abst** Zentralbl. Math. Ihre Grenzgeb.

GW
**SIGMA SERIES IN PURE MATHEMATICS.** (1979)-. Monographic series. English. Price varies per volume. **LC** UNC.
**Ind/Abst** Math. Rev.; Zentralbl. Math. Ihre Grenzgeb.

US/0163-5778
**SIGNUM NEWSLETTER.** **See** Computers.

US/0163-5824
**SIGSAM BULLETIN.** **See** Computers.

BE/0037-5454
**SIMON STEVIN.** ***Title Change.*** [Simon Stevin]. **Added/Corp** Natuur- en Geneeskundige Vennootschap (Netherlands). Vol. 25 (1947)-(19??). Periodical. Multiple languages (Dutch and English). qt. Simon Stevin Wis-Natuurkundig, Tijdschrift Krijgslaan 281, B-9000 Gent Belgium. **Tel** 32 91 225715 ext. 2219. **ED** J. Van Geel (editor's address: Krygslaan 281, B-9000 Gent Belgium). **LC** QA1; .S48. **CODEN** SSWNAX. Index available. **Bk Rev.** ctrl circ. Documents available from Ask*IEEE. ***Formed by the union of*** *Christiaan Huygens; Wis- en Natuurkundig Tijdschrift* ***and*** *Mathematica B.* ***Merged into*** *Bulletin of the Belgian Mathematical Society Simon Stevin.*
**Desc:** Pure and applied mathematics.
**Ind/Abst** INSPEC (1968-1985); Math. Rev.; Zentralbl. Math. Ihre Grenzgeb.

FR/1143-7723
**SINGULARITE LYON.** (SINGULARITE.). (1990)-. Periodical. French. **UDC** 51.
**Ind/Abst** Zentralbl. Math. Ihre Grenzgeb.

GW/0371-0165
**SITZUNGSBERICHTE DER HEIDELBERGER AKADEMIE DER WISSENSCHAFTEN, MATHEMATISCH-NATURWISSENSCHAFTLICHE KLASSE.** **See** Science and Technology.

GW/0371-327X
**SITZUNGSBERICHTE DER SACHSISCHEN AKADEMIE DER WISSENSCHAFTEN ZU LEIPZIG. MATHEMATISCH-NATURWISSENSCHA FTLICHE KLASSE.** [Sitzungsber. Saechs. Akad. Wiss. Leipz., Math.-Nat.wiss. Kl.]. **Added/Corp** Sachsische Akademie der Wissenschaften zu Leipzig. Mathematisch-Naturwissenschaftliche Klasse. Vol. 105, No. 1 (1961)-. Academic Scholarly Publication. German. ir. Price varies per volume. Akademie-Verlag GmbH, Muehlenstrasse 33 34, D 13162 Berlin Germany. **Tel** 011 49 30 47889300, FAX 011 49 30 47889357.

**(Subscription address:** VCH Publishers Inc., 303 Northwest 12th Avenue, Journals Department, Deerfield FL 33442.**)** **LC** AS182; .S214. **CODEN** SSWMAU. Index available in last issue of volume--attached. Documents available from CASDDS. ***Continues*** *Berichte Uber die Verhandlungen der Sachsischen Akademie der Wissenschaften zu Leipzig, 0366-001X.*
**Ind/Abst** Chem. Abstr. (1961-1983); Coal Abstr.; Math. Rev.; Zentralbl. Math. Ihre Grenzgeb.

US/1053-4792
**SMARANDACHE FUNCTION JOURNAL.** [Smarandache funct. j.]. **VFOAT** Smarandache Function. Vol. 1, No. 1 (Dec. 1990)-. English. an (Dec.). $200.00 (library), $100.00. Number Theory Publishing Company, PO Box 10163, Glendale AZ 85318-0163. **ED** Dr. R. Muller. **LC** QA246; .S63. **DD** 512/.72. **Bk Rev**, (Qty: (if they refer to Smarandache function)). **Ad Acc**, **Adv Mgr:** L. Jones. **Pr Rev. Circ:** 5000.
**Desc:** Any article, note, problem, application, etc. which deals with the Smarandache function are published.
**Ind/Abst** Zentralbl. Math. Ihre Grenzgeb.

US/1059-5325
**SOLSTICE (ANN ARBOR, MICH.). See** Geography.

CH/0250-3255
**SOOCHOW JOURNAL OF MATHEMATICS.** [Dongwu shulixue bao]. **VFOAT** Tung Wu Shi Li Hsueh Pao. Vol. 4; Dec. 1978-. Periodical. English (Chinese). sa. NT$600.00 China; $30.00 US. Soochow University Press, Wai Shuang Hsi Shih Lin, Taipei Taiwan. **Tel** 886-2-8819471. **ED** Bang-Yen Chen, L Gross, T Hida, Deng-Yuan Huang, Chii-Ruey Hwang, H Jurgensen, G Kallianpur, H H Kuo, Hang-Chin Lai, Ta-Feng Lin, Tai-Ping Liu, L C Miao, H W Pu, H J Shyr, G G Thierrin, H M Srivastava,. **LC** QA1; .S755. **DD** 510/.5. ctrl circ. ***Continues*** *Soochow Journal of Mathematical & Natural Sciences, 0250-3255.*
**Desc:** Publishes papers with correct, new, nontrivial and interesting results.
**Ind/Abst** Math. Rev.; Zentralbl. Math. Ihre Grenzgeb.

US/1060-0973
**SOURCEBOOK FOR SCIENCE, MATHEMATICS, AND TECHNOLOGY EDUCATION. See** Science and Technology.

GW/0172-6315
**SOURCES IN THE HISTORY OF MATHEMATICS AND PHYSICAL SCIENCES.** [Sources hist. math. phys. sci.]. (1976)-. Monographic series. English. ir. Price varies per volume. Springer-Verlag GmbH & Company KG, Heidelberger Platz 3, D 14197 Berlin Germany. **Tel** 011 49 30 8207223, FAX 011 49 30 8214091, telex 183 319 SPBLN D. **(Subscription address:** Springer Verlag New York Inc. / for North America, 44 Hartz Way, Secaucus NJ 07096.**)**
**Desc:** Contains articles on the history and study of mathematics and physical sciences.
**Ind/Abst** Math. Rev.; Zentralbl. Math. Ihre Grenzgeb.

SA/0038-271X
**SOUTH AFRICAN STATISTICAL JOURNAL. See** Mathematics-Abstracting, Bibliographies and Statistics.

HK/0129-2021
**SOUTHEAST ASIAN BULLETIN OF MATHEMATICS.** [Southeast Asian bull. math.]. **Added/Corp** Southeast Asian Mathematical Society. Vol. 1 (1977)-. Bulletin. English. tq. $62.00. CE Science Press Ltd, 109 115 Queens Road E, Block B 9 F, Hong Kong Hong Kong. **Tel** 11 852 277689. **ED** R F Turner-Smith. **Bk Rev. Ad Acc. Circ:** 450.
**Desc:** Research and expository articles in mathematics.
**Ind/Abst** Math. Rev.; Zentralbl. Math. Ihre Grenzgeb.

US/0197-6788
**SOVIET MATHEMATICS - DOKLADY.** ***Title Change.*** [Sov. math., Dokl.]. **Added/Corp** American Mathematical Society. (Jan./Feb. 1979)-(July/Aug. 1992). Periodical. English (Russian). Three times a year. American Mathematical Society, PO Box 6248, Providence RI 02940-6248. **Tel** (800)321-4267, (401)455-4000, FAX (401)331-3842, telex 797192. **LC** QA1; .A3493. **DD** 510/.5. **[CCC].** Index available. available on microfilm and microfiche from University Microfilms International (UMI). ***Continues*** *Soviet Mathematics, 0038-5573.* ***Continued by*** *Doklady Akademii Nauk. English. Doklady. Mathematics, 1064-5624.*
**Desc:** Presents short articles, averaging three to five pages, covering current research in all fields of pure mathematics.
**Ind/Abst** Int. Abstr. Oper. Res. [Select. Cov.]; Math. Rev.; Zentralbl. Math. Ihre Grenzgeb.

NE/0169-1015
**SPATIAL VISION.** [Spat. vis.]. Vol. 1, No. 1 (1985)-. Periodical. English. qt. DM220.00. VSP International Science Publishers, Godfried van Seystlaan 47, 3703 BR Zeist Netherlands. **Tel** 011 31 3404 25790, FAX 011 31 3404 32081, telex 40217 USP NL. **(Subscription address:** VSP International Science Publishers, PO Box 346, 3700 AH Zeist Netherlands.**)** **ED** David H. Foster and Adam Reeves. **LC** BF469; .S62. **NLM** W1; SP26R. **CODEN** SPVIEU. Documents available from BIOSIS Document Express, Ask*IEEE.
**Ind/Abst** Abstr. Hum. Comput. Interact.; Biol. Abstr. (1985-); INSPEC (1988-); Psychol. Abstr. (1987-); PsycINFO (1990-); PsycLit; Soc. Sci. Cit. Index [Select. Cov.].

AT/0725-1092
**SQUARE ONE SYDNEY.** [Square oneSyd.]. (1980)-. Periodical. English. sa. Mathematical Association of New South Wales, Box 536, Darlinghurst NSW, 2010 Australia. **Tel** 011 61 2 361-5195, FAX 011 61 2 332-2510. **DD** 372.73044.
**Ind/Abst** Aust. Educ. Index.

●US/1061-0022
**ST. PETERSBURG MATHEMATICAL JOURNAL.** [St. Petersbg. math. j.]. **Added/Corp** American Mathematical Society. **VFOAT** Saint Petersburg Mathematical Journal. Vol. 3, No. 1 (1992)-. Periodical. English (translations available in Russian). bm. $977.00. American Mathematical Society, PO Box 6248, Providence RI 02940-6248. **Tel** (800)321-4267, (401)455-4000, FAX (401)331-3842, telex 797192. **(Subscription address:** American Mathematical Society, PO Box 5904, Boston MA 02206-5904.**)** **LC** QA150; .A42. **DD** 512. ***Continues*** *Algebra i Analiz. English. Leningrad Mathematical Journal, 1048-9924.*
**Desc:** Cover-to-cover translation into English of Algebra i Analiz, published by the mathematics section of the Russian Academy of Sciences via the St. Petersburg branch of "Nauka." Contains contributions by some of the most prominent mathematical scientists from the former Soviet Union.
**Ind/Abst** Math. Rev.

IT/1120-4222
**STABILITY & APPLIED ANALYSIS OF CONTINUOUS MEDIA. VFOAT** Stability and Applied Analysis of Continuous Media. (1990)-. Periodical. English. qt. $180.00. Pitagora Editrice SRL, Via del Legatore 3, 40127 Bologna Italy. **Tel** 011 39 51 530003, FAX 011 39 51 535301. **ED** Giovanni Galdi, Brian Straughan and K R Rajagopal. **UDC** 51. Index available. **Pr Rev.** ctrl circ.
**Desc:** Provides a forum for research workers in the field of stability theory; also covers the applied analysis of continuous media with emphasis on nonlinear problems, and new theories.

US
**STATE, DISTRICT, AND REGIONAL REPORT OF STATEWIDE ASSESSMENT RESULTS.** English. an. Florida Department of Education, Tallahassee FL 32301. **LC** LB1050; .F55A. **DD** 371.2/6/09759. ***Continues*** *State & District Report of Results.*

CN/1017-0405
**STATISTICA SINICA. Added/Corp** International Chinese Statistical Association. Chung Yang Yen Chiu Yuan. Institute of Statistical Science. Vol. 1, No. 1 (Jan. 1991)-. Periodical. English. Twice a year (Jan. and July). $60.00 (institutions), $20.00 (individuals). University of Manitoba Department of Statistics, Winnipeg Manitoba R3T 2N2 Canada. **Tel** (204)474-6274, FAX (204)275-5011. **ED** Professor George C. Tiao. **LC** QA276.A1; S83. Index available (Every (2) yrs. and includes 2nd iss. of the even volume.). cum. index. **Circ:** 2,500 (ctrl). Documents available from The Genuine Article.
**Desc:** It publishes original work in both theoretical and applied area of statistics.
**Ind/Abst** Compumath Citation Index [Full Cov.]; Curr. Index Stat.; Res. Alert [Full Cov.]; Soc. Sci. Cit. Index [Select. Cov.].

GW/0173-5896
**STATISTICAL SOFTWARE NEWSLETTER.** [Stat. softw. newsl.]. **Added/Corp** Institut fur Medizinische Informatik und Systemforschung (Gesellschaft fur Strahlen- und Umweltforschung) Gesellschaft fur Strahlen- und Umweltforschung. Institut fur Medizinische Datenverarbeitung. (19??)-. Statistical Publication. English (German). tq. GSF SSN Redaction Medis Inst, Ingolstadterland Strasse 1, W-8042 Neuherberg Germany. **Tel** (089)3787 5365. **LC** QA276.4; .S66. **DD** 519.5/05. **CODEN** SSNEEX. Documents available from Ask*IEEE.
**Ind/Abst** INSPEC (Apr. 1988-1990).

NE/0167-7152
**STATISTICS & PROBABILITY LETTERS.** [Stat. probab. lett.]. **VFOAT** Statistics and Probability Letters. Vol. 1, No. 1 (July 1982)-. Academic Scholarly Publication. English. Sixteen times a year (4 volumes). Fl1340.00. Elsevier Science Publishers BV, PO Box 211, 1000 AE Amsterdam Netherlands. **Tel** 011 31 20 5803642, FAX 011 31 20 5862696, telex 15682. **ED** R A Johnson. **LC** QA276.A1; S742. **DD** 519.5/05. **CODEN** SPLTDC. **[CCC]. Pr Rev.** available on microfilm and microfiche from University Microfilms International (UMI). Documents available from The Genuine Article.
**Desc:** Takes a novel and highly innovative approach to the publication of research findings in statistics and probability.
**Ind/Abst** Compumath Citation Index [Full Cov.]; Curr. Index Stat.; Pollut. Abstr. Indexes; Res. Alert [Full Cov.]; Soc. Sci. Cit. Index [Select. Cov.]; Stat. Theory Method Abstr. (1983-1984, 1986-1987); Zentralbl. Math. Ihre Grenzgeb.

RU
**STATISTIKA RECHI I AVTOMATICHESKII ANALIZ TEKSTA. See** Linguistics.

US/0736-2994
**STOCHASTIC ANALYSIS AND APPLICATIONS.** [Stoch. anal. appl.]. Vol. 1, No. 1 (1983)-. Periodical. English. Five times a year. $595.00 US; $612.50 other. Marcel Dekker Inc., 270 Madison Avenue, New York NY 10016. **Tel** (212)696-9000, (800)228-1160, FAX (212)685-4540, telex 421419. **(Subscription address:** Marcel Dekker Inc, PO Box 5017, Monticello NY 12701.**)** **ED** V. Lakshmikantham and G. S. Ladde. **LC** QA274.2; .S77. **DD** 519.2. **CODEN** SAAPDA. **[CCC]. Pr Rev.** available on microfiche. Documents available from The Genuine Article.
**Desc:** Presents the latest innovations in the field of stochastic theory and its practical applications, as well as the full range of related approaches to analyzing systems under random excitation. In addition, it is the only publication that offers the broad, detailed coverage necessary for the inter-field fertilization of new concepts and ideas, providing the scientific community with a unique and highly useful service.
**Ind/Abst** Compumath Citation Index [Full Cov.]; Curr. Index Stat.; Int. Bibliogr. Rezen. Wissen. Lit. (1984); Int. Bibliogr. Zeitschriftenliteratur Allen Gebieten Wissens; Math. Rev.; Res. Alert [Full Cov.]; Soc. Sci. Cit. Index [Select. Cov.]; Stat. Theory Method Abstr. (1983-1984, 1986-1987); Zentralbl. Math. Ihre Grenzgeb.

NE/0304-4149
**STOCHASTIC PROCESSES AND THEIR APPLICATIONS.** [Stochastic processes their appl.]. **Added/Corp** Bernoulli Society for Mathematical Statistics and Probability. Vol. 1 (Jan. 1973)-. Academic Scholarly Publication. English. Twelve times a year (6 volumes). Fl2340.00. Elsevier Science Publishers BV, PO Box 211, 1000 AE Amsterdam Netherlands. **Tel** 011 31 20 5803642, FAX 011 31 20 5862696, telex 15682. **ED** C C Heyde. **LC** QA274.A1; S77. **DD** 519.2/05. **CODEN** STOPB7. **[CCC]. Pr Rev.** available on microfilm and microfiche from University Microfilms International (UMI). Documents available from The Genuine Article, Ask*IEEE.
**Desc:** Publishes papers in the theory of stochastic processes and their applications.
**Ind/Abst** Biostatistica (Jan. 1973-); Compumath Citation Index [Full Cov.]; Comput. Rev.; Curr. Contents Phys. Chem. Earth Sci.; Curr. Index Stat.; INSPEC (Jan. 1973-); Int. Abstr. Oper. Res. [Select. Cov.]; Math. Rev.; Oper. Res./Manag. Sci. (Jan. 1973-); Qual. Control Appl. Stat. (Jan. 1973-); Res. Alert [Full Cov.]; Sci. Cit. Index; SCISEARCH; Stat. Theory Method Abstr. (1973-1984, 1986-1987); Zentralbl. Math. Ihre Grenzgeb.

SP/0210-7821
**STOCHASTICA.** ***Ceased.*** Catalan (Spanish). Dismar Libros, RDA San Pablo 4, 08001 Barcelona Spain. **Tel** 329 89 52. **LC** QA1; .S787. **DD** 510/.5.
**Ind/Abst** Math. Rev.; Stat. Theory Method Abstr. (1983-1984, 1986-1987).

US/1045-1129
**STOCHASTICS AND STOCHASTICS REPORT.** [Stoch. stoch. rep.]. Vol. 26, No. 1 (1989)-. Periodical. English. ir (4 issues per volume). Price varies. Gordon & Breach Science Publishers, Inc., PO Box 786, Cooper Station, New York NY 10276. **Tel** (212)206-8900, FAX (212)645-2459. **(Subscription address:** International Publishers Distributor at one of the following addresses: 820 Town Center Drive, Langhorne, PA 19047; or PO Box 90, Reading Berkshire RG1 8JL UK; or Kent Ridge PO Box 1180, Singapore 9111, Republic of Singapore**)** **LC** QA274.A1; S78. **DD** 519.2/05. **CODEN** SSTREY. **[CCC].** Documents available from Article Express International, BIOSIS Document Express, Ask*IEEE. ***Continues*** *Stochastics, 0090-9491.*
**Ind/Abst** Bioeng. Abstr.; Biol. Abstr. (1973); Curr. Index Stat.; Ei Page One (1973-); Eng. Index Annu.; INSPEC (1973-); Math. Rev. (-1984).

●US/1070-5511
**STRUCTURAL EQUATION MODELING.** (STRUCTURAL EQUATION MODELING : A MULTIDISCIPLINARY JOURNAL.). **VFOAT** SEM. (1994)-. English. qt. $120.00 US & Canada; $145.00 other. Lawrence Erlbaum Associates, 365 Broadway, Suite 102, Hillsdale NJ 07642. **Tel** (201)666-4110, (800)926-6579, FAX (201)666-2394.

UK
**STRUGGLE : MATHEMATICS FOR LOW ATTAINERS. See** Education-Special Education and Rehabilitation.

PL/0039-3223
**STUDIA MATHEMATICA.** [Stud. math.]. **Added/Corp** Poland. Ministerstwo Wyznan Religijnych i Oswiecenia Publicznego. Vol. 1 (1929)-. Periodical. Polish. ir. $84.00. **(Subscription address:** ARS Polona,

PO Box 1001, 00068 Warsaw Poland.) **LC** QA1; .S8. **CODEN** SMATAZ. cum. index. **Pr Rev. Circ:** 2,000 (ctrl). Documents available from The Genuine Article.
**Desc:** Original papers on functional analysis, abstract methods of mathematical analysis and on the theory of probabilities.
**Ind/Abst** Compumath Citation Index [Full Cov.]; Curr. Contents Phys. Chem. Earth Sci.; Math. Rev.; Res. Alert [Full Cov.]; Stat. Theory Method Abstr. (1959-1963, 1982, 1987); Zentralbl. Math. Ihre Grenzgeb.

HU/0081-6906
**STUDIA SCIENTIARUM MATHEMATICARUM HUNGARICA.** [Stud. sci. math. Hung.]. **Added/Corp** Magyar Tudomanyos Akademia. Vol. 1, No. 1/2 (1966)-. Academic Scholarly Publication. Multiple languages (English, French, German and Russian). Four times a year. $98.00. Akademiai Kiado, Publishing House of the Hungarian Academy of Sciences, Prielle Kornelia u. 19-35, H-1117 Budapest Hungary. **Tel** 011 36 1 1811991, FAX 011 36 1 1811991, telex 22-6228 AKNYO H. **CODEN** SSMHAX. **[CCC].** Documents available from Ask*IEEE. ***Continues*** *Magyar Tudomanyos Akademia Matematikai Kutato Intezetenek Kozlemenyei.*
**Ind/Abst** INSPEC (1988-); Int. Aerosp. Abstr.; Math. Rev.; Zentralbl. Math. Ihre Grenzgeb.

RM/0373-1227
**STUDIA UNIVERSITATIS BABES-BOLYAI : MATHEMATICA.** [Stud. Univ. Babes-Bolyai. Math.]. **Main/Corp** Universitatea "Babes-Bolyai.". Vol. 20, (1975)-. Academic Scholarly Publication. Romanian (English, French and Romanian). Four times a year. DM471.00. **(Subscription address:** Kubon & Sagner, ABT Zeitschriftenimport, D 80328 Munich Germany.**) LC** QA1; .C642a. **DD** 510. **CODEN** SUBMDA. Documents available from CASDDS. ***Continues*** *Studia Universitatis Babes-Bolyai. Series Mathematica-Mechanica, 0370-8659.*
**Ind/Abst** Chem. Abstr.; Int. Aerosp. Abstr.; Math. Rev.; Zentralbl. Math. Ihre Grenzgeb.

GW
**STUDIEN ZUR WISSENSCHAFTS-, SOZIAL- UND BILDUNGSGESCHICHTE DER MATHEMATIK.** (1985)-. Monographic series. German.
**Ind/Abst** Math. Rev.; Zentralbl. Math. Ihre Grenzgeb.

US/0022-2526
**STUDIES IN APPLIED MATHEMATICS (CAMBRIDGE).** (STUDIES IN APPLIED MATHEMATICS.). [Stud. appl. math.]. **Added/Corp** Massachusetts Institute of Technology. Vol. 48 (March 1969)-. Periodical. English. Eight times a year (3 volumes). $370.00 US; $415.00 other. Blackwell Publishers, 238 Main Street, Cambridge MA 02142. **Tel** (617)547-7110, (800)835-6770, FAX (617)547-0789. **ED** D J Benney. **LC** QA1; .J96. **DD** 500.2/05. **CODEN** SAPMB6. **[CCC]. Ad Acc. Pr Rev.** available on microfilm and microfiche from University Microfilms International (UMI). Documents available from Article Express International, The Genuine Article, Ask*IEEE. ***Continues*** *Journal of Mathematics and Physics, 0097-1421.*
**Desc:** Reports research results involving the core concepts of applied mathematics research, including propagation, equilibrium, stability, optimization, and discrete and random processes.
**Ind/Abst** Biceng. Abstr.; Compumath Citation Index [Full Cov.]; Comput. Rev.; Curr. Contents Phys. Chem. Earth Sci.; Ei Page One; EMBASE; Eng. Index Annu.; INSPEC (March 1969-); Int. Aerosp. Abstr.; Math. Rev.; Res. Alert [Full Cov.]; Sci. Cit. Index; SCISEARCH; Zentralbl. Math. Ihre Grenzgeb.

NE
**STUDIES IN COMPUTATIONAL MATHEMATICS.** (1987)-. Monographic series. English. Elsevier Science Publishing Company Inc, Madison Square Station, PO Box 882, New York NY 10159-0882. **Tel** (212)633-3950, FAX (212)633-3990.
**Ind/Abst** Math. Rev. (1987-); Zentralbl. Math. Ihre Grenzgeb.

NE/0049-237X
**STUDIES IN LOGIC AND THE FOUNDATIONS OF MATHEMATICS.** (19??)-. Monographic series. English. ir. Price varies per volume. Elsevier Science Publishing Company Inc, Madison Square Station, PO Box 882, New York NY 10159-0882. **Tel** (212)633-3950, FAX (212)633-3990. **CODEN** SLFMDZ. Documents available from Ask*IEEE.
**Ind/Abst** INSPEC; Zentralbl. Math. Ihre Grenzgeb.

NE/0081-8194
**STUDIES IN MATHEMATICAL AND MANAGERIAL ECONOMICS.** **See** Economics.

NE/0168-2024
**STUDIES IN MATHEMATICS AND ITS APPLICATIONS.** [Stud. math. appl.]. 1-. Monographic series. English. ir. Price varies per volume. Elsevier Science Publishers BV, PO Box 211, 1000 AE Amsterdam Netherlands. **Tel** 011 31 20 5803642, FAX 011 31 20 5862696, telex 15682. **CODEN** SMIADL. Documents available from Ask*IEEE.
**Ind/Abst** INSPEC (1986-); Math. Rev.; Zentralbl. Math. Ihre Grenzgeb.

US/0585-6892
**STUDIES IN MATHEMATICS (NEW HAVEN).** (STUDIES IN MATHEMATICS.). **Added/Corp** School Mathematics Study Group. (1959)-. Monographic series. English. **LC** QA3; .S8527. **DD** 510.82.

IT
**STUDIES IN PROOF THEORY.** Vol. 1 (1984)-. Monographic series. English. ir. Price varies per volume. Bibliopolis, Via Arangio Ruiz 83, 80122 Naples Italy. **Tel** 011 39 81 664606.
**Desc:** Monographs on proof theory and mathematical logic.
**Ind/Abst** Math. Rev. (1987-); Zentralbl. Math. Ihre Grenzgeb.

NE/0081-8542
**STUDIES IN STATISTICAL MECHANICS.** **See** Physics-Analytic and Experimental Mechanics.

US/1040-6441
**STUDIES IN THE DEVELOPMENT OF MODERN MATHEMATICS.** [Stud. dev. mod. math.]. Vol. 1 (1989)-. English. Gordon & Breach Science Publishers, Inc., PO Box 786, Cooper Station, New York NY 10276. **Tel** (212)206-8900, FAX (212)645-2459. **(Subscription address:** International Publishers Distributor at one of the following addresses: 820 Town Center Drive, Langhorne, PA 19047; or PO Box 90, Reading Berkshire RG1 8JL UK; or Kent Ridge PO Box 1180, Singapore 9111, Republic of Singapore**) DD** 500.
**Ind/Abst** Zentralbl. Math. Ihre Grenzgeb.

US/0172-570X
**STUDIES IN THE HISTORY OF MATHEMATICS AND PHYSICAL SCIENCES.** [Stud. hist. math. phys. sci.]. 1-. Monographic series. English. ir. Price varies per volume. Springer-Verlag New York Inc., 175 5th Avenue, New York NY 10010. **Tel** (212)460-1500, telex 232 235 SPB UR. **(Subscription address:** Springer Verlag New York Inc. / for North America, 44 Hartz Way, Secaucus NJ 07096.**) CODEN** SHMSDQ. Documents available from BIOSIS Document Express.
**Desc:** Numbered series.
**Ind/Abst** Biol. Abstr.; Math. Rev.; Zentralbl. Math. Ihre Grenzgeb.

RM/0039-4068
**STUDII SI CERCETARI MATEMATICE.** [Stud. cercet. mat.]. **Added/Corp** Institutul de Matematica (Academia Republicii Populare Romine) Academia Republicii Socialiste Romania. Vol. 1 (1950)-. Periodical. Romanian (English, French, German and Russian). bm (6 issues). DM364.00. **(Subscription address:** Kubon & Sagner, ABT Zeitschriftenimport, D 80328 Munich Germany.**) LC** QA1; .A15. **CODEN** APTMAD. ***Continues*** *Disquisitiones Mathematicae et Physicae* ***and*** *Bulletin Mathematique, 0007-4691.*
**Desc:** Contains articles on mathematics, mathematical logics, numerical analysis, functional analysis and algebra.
**Ind/Abst** Int. Aerosp. Abstr.; Math. Rev.; Stat. Theory Method Abstr. (1966, 1968-1969, 1971, 1973-1975, 1977, 1979, 1986-1987); Zentralbl. Math. Ihre Grenzgeb.

US/0898-9583
**SUGAKU EXPOSITIONS.** [Sugaku expo.]. **Added/Corp** American Mathematical Society. Nihon Sugakkai. Vol. 1, No. 1 (Oct. 1988)-. Periodical. English (translations available in Japanese). sa. $110.00. American Mathematical Society, PO Box 6248, Providence RI 02940-6248. **Tel** (800)321-4267, (401)455-4000, FAX (401)331-3842, telex 797192. **(Subscription address:** American Mathematical Society, PO Box 5904, Boston MA 02206-5904.**) LC** QA1; .S855. **DD** 510/.5. Index available.
**Desc:** Contains translations into English of expository articles from the journal Sugaku, published by Iwanami Shoten, publishers for the Mathematical Society of Japan. Also contains several articles that provide highly informative accounts of a variety of current areas of research.
**Ind/Abst** Zentralbl. Math. Ihre Grenzgeb.

JA/0039-470X
**SUGAKU (TOKYO. 1947).** (SUGAKU.). [Sugaku]. **Added/Corp** Nihon Sugakkai. Iwanami Shoten. Vol. 1 (Apr. 1947)-. Periodical. Japanese. qt. $44.00. Nihon Sugakkai, (Mathematical Soc. of Japan), 25-9-203, Hongo 4 Chome, Bunkyoku, Tokyoto 113 Japan. **(Subscription address:** Kyowa Book Company Inc. 1 38 Kanda Jinbocho Chiyoda Ku, Tokyo 101 Japan (telephone: 11 81 3 3293 0727)**) CODEN** SUGKAQ.
**Ind/Abst** Math. Rev.; Zentralbl. Math. Ihre Grenzgeb.

JA/0386-9555
**SUGAKUSHI KENKYU.** [Sugakushi kenkyu]. **VFOAT** Journal of History of Mathematics, Japan. Periodical. Japanese (Japanese). Nihon Sugakushi Gakkai, c/o Fuji Tanki Daigaku Kagaku-shi Kyoshitsu 7-7, Shimoochiai 1 Shinjuku-ku, Tokyo-to 161 Japan. **LC** QA27.J3; S76.
**Ind/Abst** Math. Rev.; Zentralbl. Math. Ihre Grenzgeb.

UK/0958-6709
**SUMMIT OXFORD.** ***Ceased.*** (SUMMIT.). [Summit Oxf.]. (1990)-(1992). Periodical. English. Four times a year. Philip Allan Publishers Ltd, Market Place, Deddington Oxford, OX15 0SE England. **Tel** 011 44 869 38652, FAX 011 44 869 38803. **DD** 510.505.

FI/0355-1962
**SUOMEN GEODEETTISEN LAITOKSEN TIEDONANTOJA.** **See** Earth Sciences.

JA/0386-2240
**SURI KAGAKU.** **VFOAT** Mathematical Sciences. (1963)-. Academic Scholarly Publication. English. mo. ¥9600. Nyu Saiensusha, Nishiki-cho 3-21, Kanda Chiyoda-ku, Tokyo-to 101 Japan. **LC** Q172; .S9. **CODEN** SUKADJ. Documents available from CASDDS.
**Ind/Abst** Chem. Abstr.

US/0743-0345
**SURVEYS AND REFERENCE WORKS IN MATHEMATICS.** [Surv. ref. works math.]. (1977)-. Monographic series. English. ir. Price varies per volume. John Wiley & Sons Inc / New Jersey, 1 Wiley Drive, Somerset NJ 08875. **Tel** (800)225-5945, (908)469-4400.
**Ind/Abst** Math. Rev.; Zentralbl. Math. Ihre Grenzgeb.

US/1052-9233
**SURVEYS IN DIFFERENTIAL GEOMETRY.** (SURVEYS IN DIFFERENTIAL GEOMETRY : SUPPLEMENT TO THE JOURNAL OF DIFFERENTIAL GEOMETRY.). [Surv. differ. geom.]. **Added/Corp** Lehigh University. No. 1 (1990)-. English. an. $60.00 (institution), $25.00 (individual). American Mathematical Society, PO Box 6248, Providence RI 02940-6248. **Tel** (800)321-4267, (401)455-4000, FAX (401)331-3842, telex 797192. **(Subscription address:** American Mathematical Society, PO Box 5904, Boston MA 02206-5904.**) LC** QA641; .S84. **DD** 516.3/6/005.
**Ind/Abst** Zentralbl. Math. Ihre Grenzgeb.

AU/0938-1953
**SURVEYS ON MATHEMATICS FOR INDUSTRY.** **See** Engineering.

JA/0496-6597
**SUT JOURNAL OF MATHEMATICS.** **Added/Corp** Tokyo Rika Daigaku. **VAT** Science University of Tokyo Journal of Mathematics. Vol. 25, No. 1-. Periodical. English. sa. **LC** QA1; .T17. **DD** 510/.5. ***Continues*** *TRU Mathematics, 0496-6597.*
**Ind/Abst** Zentralbl. Math. Ihre Grenzgeb.

UK/0082-0725
**SYMPOSIA MATHEMATICA.** (SYMPOSIA MATHEMATICA / ISTITUTO NAZIONALE DI ALTA MATEMATICA.). [Symp. Math.]. **Added/Corp** Istituto Nazionale di Alta Mmatematica (Italy). Vol. 1 (1969)-. Periodical. English (French, German and Italian). **DD** 510.
**Ind/Abst** Zentralbl. Math. Ihre Grenzgeb.

US/0883-7066
**SYSTEM DYNAMICS REVIEW.** [Syst. dyn. rev.]. **Added/Corp** System Dynamics Society. Vol. 1, No. 1 (Summer 1985)-. Periodical. English. Four times a year. $195.00. John Wiley & Sons, Inc., 605 Third Avenue, New York NY 10158-0012. **Tel** (212)850-6000, (212)850-6645, FAX (212)850-6088, telex 12-7063. **(Subscription address:** John Wiley & Sons / England, Baffins Lane, Chichester, West Sussex PO19 1UD England.**) ED** George Richardson, Andrew Ford and Erik Mosekilde. **LC** WMLC 93/3892. **DD** 003. **CODEN** SDREEG. **[CCC].** available on microfilm and microfiche from University Microfilms International (UMI). Documents available from The Genuine Article, Ask*IEEE.
**Desc:** Publishes advances in mathematical modeling and computer simulation of dynamic feedback systems; advances in methods of policy analysis based on information feedback and circular causality; generic structures; system dynamics contributions to theory building in the social and natural sciences; policy studies and debate emphasizing the role of feedback and circular causality in problem behavior and developments in strategies for implementation of model-based policy conclusions.
**Ind/Abst** Curr. Contents Soc. Behav. Sci.; INSPEC (1985-); PsycINFO (1990-); PsycLit; Res. Alert [Full Cov.]; Soc. Sci. Cit. Index [Full Cov.].

GW/0232-9298
**SYSTEMS ANALYSIS, MODELLING, SIMULATION.** [Syst. anal. model. simul.]. Vol. 1, No. 1 (1984)-. Periodical. English. qt. $330.00 (academic institutions), $515.00 (corporate institutions). Gordon & Breach Science Publishers, PO Box 90, Reading RG1 8JL England. **Tel** 011 44 734 560080, FAX 011 44 734 568211. **(Subscription address:** International Publishers Distributor at one of the following addresses: 820 Town Center Drive, Langhorne, PA 19047; or PO Box 90,

Reading Berkshire RG1 8JL UK; or Kent Ridge PO Box 1180, Singapore 9111, Republic of Singapore) **LC** QA402; .S969. **DD** 003. **CODEN** SAMSEC. **[CCC]. Pr Rev.** Documents available from The Genuine Article, Ask*IEEE.
**Ind/Abst** ACM Guide Comput. Lit.; Comput. Rev. (1985-); INSPEC (1985-); Math. Rev. (1985-); Res. Alert [Full Cov.].

PL/0137-1223
**SYSTEMS SCIENCE. See** Computers-Computer Systems.

CC/1000-9590
**SYSTEMS SCIENCE AND MATHEMATICAL SCIENCES / EDITED BY INSTITUTE OF SYSTEMS SCIENCE, CHINESE ACADEMY OF SCIENCES.**
**Added/Corp** Chung-Kuo Ko Hsueh Yuan. Hsi Tung Ko Hsueh Yen Chiu So. Vol. 1, No. 1 (Aug. 1988)-. Periodical. English. Four times a year. $370.00. Allerton Press, Inc., 150 Fifth Avenue, New York NY 10011. **Tel** (212)924-3950, FAX (212)463-9684, telex 427441 ALPRES. **LC** Q295; .S962. **DD** 003. **[CCC].**
**Ind/Abst** Zentralbl. Math. Ihre Grenzgeb.

CH/0376-4079
**TAMKANG JOURNAL OF MATHEMATICS.** [Tamkang j. math.]. **Added/Corp** Tan-Chiang Wen Li Hsueh Yuan. Shu Hsueh Yen Chiu So. Vol. 1 (Mar. 1970)-. Periodical. English. Four times a year (Mar., June, Sept., Dec.). $50.00. Tamkang University, 151 Ying-Chuan Road, Math Department, Tamsui Taipei 251 Taiwan. **Tel** 011 886 2 6215656 ext.501-2, FAX 011 886 2 6202613. **ED** Prof. Bit-Shun Tam. **LC** QA1; .T29. **DD** 510/.5. **Pr Rev. Circ:** 350 (ctrl). ***Supersedes*** *Tan-Chiang Shu Hsueh.*
**Desc:** Original research papers on pure and applied mathematics, including statistics.
**Ind/Abst** Math. Rev.; Stat. Theory Method Abstr. (1983-1984, 1986); Zentralbl. Math. Ihre Grenzgeb.

TZ
**TANZANIAN MATHEMATICAL BULLETIN / THE MATHEMATICAL ASSOCIATION OF TANZANIA, THE.**
**Added/Corp** Chama cha Hisabati Tanzania. **VFOAT** Mathematical Bulletin. Vol. 1 (1966)-. Periodical. English (Swahili). Twice a year. $14.00. Mathematical Association of Tanzania, PO Box 35062, Dar es Salaam Tanzania. **Tel** 49192. **ED** F. S. S. Swai and C. B. Alphonce. **LC** WMLC L 83/520. cum. index. **Bk Rev. Ad Acc.**

VM
**TAP CHI TOAN HOC.** Vol. 4- 1976-. Periodical. Vietnamese. qt. **LC** QA1; .T324. ***Continues*** *Tap San Toan Hoc.*
**Ind/Abst** Math. Rev.; Zentralbl. Math. Ihre Grenzgeb.

●US/1073-5836
**TEACHING CHILDREN MATHEMATICS.** (1994)-. Periodical. English. Nine times a year (September-May). $50.00. National Council of Teachers of Mathematics, 1906 Association Drive, Reston VA 22091. **Tel** (703)620-9840, FAX (703)476-2970. Index available in last issue of volume--attached. ***Continues*** *Arithmetic Teacher.*
**Ind/Abst** Mag. Artic. Summar. Elite (June 1994-).

AT/0313-7767
**TEACHING MATHEMATICS.** [Teach. math.]. (1976)-. Academic Scholarly Publication. English. qt. 45.00Aus$ full membership; 35.00Aus$ associate membership. Queensland Association of Mathematics Teachers Inc., PO Box 328, Everton Park QLD 4053 Australia. **Tel** 011 61 7 8552466, FAX 011 61 7 8552466. **ED** John McKinlay. **DD** 510.710943. **Bk Rev.** (Qty: 15-20 per year). **Ad Acc.** Full Page (B&W) 100.00Aus$. Half Page (B&W) 50.00Aus$. **Circ:** 700.
**Ind/Abst** Aust. Educ. Index.

UK/0268-3679
**TEACHING MATHEMATICS AND ITS APPLICATIONS.** (TEACHING MATHEMATICS AND ITS APPLICATIONS / THE INSTITUTE OF MATHEMATICS AND ITS APPLICATIONS.). [Teach. math. appl.]. **Added/Corp** Institute of Mathematics and Its Applications. Vol. 1, No. 1 (1982)-. Periodical. English. qt. £42.00 UK and Europe; $76.00 other. Oxford University Press, Walton Street, Oxford OX2 6DP England. **Tel** 011 44 865 56767, FAX 011 44 865 267773, telex 837330 OXPRES G. **(Subscription address:** Oxford University Press / USA, Journals Marketing Department, Oxford University Press, 2001 Evans Road, Cary NC 27513.**) ED** David Burghes. **[CCC]. Bk Rev. Ad Acc.** available on microfilm and microfiche from University Microfilms International (UMI). ***Continues*** *Journal of Mathematical Modelling for Teachers.*
**Desc:** Provides mathematics teachers in secondary and tertiary education with interesting and stimulating material which can be used in the teaching of mathematics.
**Ind/Abst** Br. Educ. Index.

CN/0823-1664
**TECHNICAL REPORT SERIES OF THE LABORATORY FOR RESEARCH IN STATISTICS AND PROBABILITY.** [Tech. rep. ser. Lab. Res. Stat. Probab.]. **VFOAT** Serie de Monographies du Laboratoire de Recherche en Statistique et Probabilites. Monographic series. English (French). ir (18-20 issues per year). Price varies per volume. Mrs Gill Murray Technical Editor and Coordinator for the Laboratory for Research in Statistics and Probability, Room 611/Arts Tower, Carleton University, Colonel by Drive, Ottawa Ontario K1S 5B6 Canada. **Tel** (613)564-6752, telex 0534232. **ED** D A Dawson, M Csorgo, J N K Rao. **DD** 519/.05. Index available. **Ad Acc. Circ:** 75.
**Desc:** The laboratory has published more than 130 research monographs, lecture notes, and research preprints submitted by members or visiting scientists at the laboratory.

JA/0040-3504
**TENSOR.** (TENSOR.). [Tensor]. **Added/Corp** Tensor Society, Sapporo, Japan. No. 1-9, (1938)-(1949; New Ser., Vol. 1 (June 1950)-. Periodical. English. Three times a year. $386.00. Tenzoru Gakkai, (Tensor Society), Kawaguchi Sukenkyujo, 7-15, Matsugaoka 2 Chome, Chigasakishi, Kanagawaken 253, Japan. **(Subscription address:** Kyowa Book Company Inc., 1 38 Kanda Jinbocho Chiyoda-ku, Tokyo 101 Japan.**) LC** QA1; .T4. **DD** 517.2. **CODEN** TNSRAZ. ctrl circ.
**Ind/Abst** Math. Rev.; Zentralbl. Math. Ihre Grenzgeb.

RU
**TEORIIA FUNKTSII KOMPLEKSNOGO PEREMENNOGO I KRAEVYE ZADACHI.**
**Added/Corp** Chuvashskii Gosudarstvennyi Universitet Im. I.N. Ulianova. (1972)-. Russian. 0.80rub. Chuvashskii Universitet / Chuvash I.N. Ulyanov State University, Moskovskii Prospekt 15, Cheboksary, Chuvash Autonomous Republic. **Tel** 24-03-79, FAX 42-80-90, telex 658127. **LC** QA331; .T37.
**Ind/Abst** Zentralbl. Math. Ihre Grenzgeb.

RU/0207-9941
**TEORIIA OPERATOROV I TEORIIA FUNKTSII. Added/Corp** Leningradskii Gosudarstvennyi Universitet Imeni A.A. Zhdanova. Vol. 1 (1983)-. Periodical. Russian. St Petersburg State University / Izdatelstvo Leningradskogo Universiteta, Universitetskaia Nab 7/9, 199034 St Petersburg Russia. **Tel** 011 95 218-97-88, FAX 011 95 218-51-52, telex 121481.
**Ind/Abst** Zentralbl. Math. Ihre Grenzgeb.

RU/0040-361X
**TEORIIA VEROIATNOSTEI I EE PRIMENENIIA.** [Teor. verojatn. primen.]. **Added/Corp** Akademiia Nauk SSSR. Vol. 1 (1956)-. Academic Scholarly Publication. Russian (French and German; summaries and/or abstracts in English, French and German; table of contents in English, French and German). qt. $142.00. Izdatelstvo Nauka / Akademiia Nauk, Publishing House of the Russian Academy of Sciences, Leninskii Porspekt 14, 117901 Moscow Russia. **Tel** 011 95 954-21-53, FAX 011 95 938-21-44, telex 411964. **(Subscription address:** Victor Kamkin, 4956 Boiling Brook Parkway, Rockville, MD 20852**) LC** QA273; .T4. **CODEN** TVPRA8. cum. index. Documents available from Ask*IEEE, CASDDS.
**Desc:** Emphasis on probabilities.
**Ind/Abst** Chem. Abstr. (?-1973); INSPEC (1968-); Math. Rev.; Zentralbl. Math. Ihre Grenzgeb.

UN/0321-4427
**TEORIJA FUNKCIJ, FUNKCIONALNYJ ANALIZ I IH PRILOZENIJA (HARKOV).** (TEORIIA FUNKTSII, FUNKTSIONALNYI ANALIZ I IKH PRILOZHENIIA.). [Teor. funkc., funkc. anal. ih priloz.]. Periodical. Russian. **LC** QA331.
**Ind/Abst** Int. Aerosp. Abstr.; Math. Rev.; Zentralbl. Math. Ihre Grenzgeb.

UN/0321-3900
**TEORIJA SLUCAINYH PROCESSOV.** (TEORIIA SLUCHAINYKH PROTSESSOV.). [Teor. sluc. processov]. **Added/Corp** Akademiia Nauk Ukrainskoi RSR. Institut Prykladnoi Matematyky i Mekhaniky (Akademiia Nauk Ukrainskoi RSR). Vol. 1 (1973)-. Russian. ir. $4.00. **(Subscription address:** Victor Kamkin, 4956 Boiling Brook Parkway, Rockville MD 20852.**) LC** QA274.A1; T46.
**Desc:** Information on stochastic processes.
**Ind/Abst** Int. Aerosp. Abstr.; Zentralbl. Math. Ihre Grenzgeb.

GW
**TEUBNER-TEXTE ZUR MATHEMATIK.** (19??)-. Monographic series. German (English). ir. Price varies per volume. BSB BG Teubner Verlagsgesellsc, PO Box 930, D 70510 Leipzig Germany. **Tel** 011 49 341 293158.

US/0277-030X
**TEXAS MATHEMATICS TEACHER.**
**Added/Corp** Texas Council of Teachers of Mathematics. Vol. 1 (1954)-. Periodical. English. Four times a year. $8.00. J W Brown, 100 South Glasgow Drive, Dallas TX 75214. **Tel** (214)824-3267. **ED** J. William Brown. **Ad Acc. Circ:** 1,200 (ctrl).
**Desc:** Articles concerning elementary, secondary and college level mathematics - Texas mathematics teacher journal.

BL/0103-491X
**TEXTOS DE METODOS MATEMATICOS.** [Textos metodos mat.]. (1973)-. Monographic series. Portuguese. ir. Price varies per volume. Instituto de Matematica, Rio de Janeiro UFRJ, Brazil. **UDC** 51.
**Ind/Abst** Zentralbl. Math. Ihre Grenzgeb.

NO/0801-3128
**THEORETIC PAPERS / INSTITUTE OF MATHEMATICS, UNIVERSITY OF OSLO.** Monographic series. English. Price varies per volume. Blindern Theoretic Research Team, P.B. 1029, Blindern Oslo 3 Norway. **LC** QA8; .T46. **DD** 510/.1.
**Ind/Abst** Math. Rev.

US/0040-5779
**THEORETICAL AND MATHEMATICAL PHYSICS. See** Physics.

UK/0040-585X
**THEORY OF PROBABILITY AND ITS APPLICATIONS.** [Theory probab. appl.]. **Added/Corp** Society for Industrial and Applied Mathematics. Vol. 1 (Mar. 1956)-. Periodical. English (Russian). qt (Mar., June, Sept., Dec.). $374.00 US, Canada, and Mexico; $420.00 other. Society for Industrial and Applied Mathematics, 3600 University City Science Center, Philadelphia PA 19104-2688. **Tel** (215)382-9800, (800)447-7426, FAX (215)386-7999, telex 446715. **ED** Natascha Artin Brunswick and Bernard Seckler. **LC** QA273; .T413. **DD** 519.1. **CODEN** TPRBAU. **[CCC].** Index available. **Pr Rev. Circ:** 1,050. Documents available from The Genuine Article, Ask*IEEE.
**Desc:** A translation of the Russian journal Teoriya Veroyatnostei i ee Primeneniya, which contains papers on the theory and application of probability, statistics, and stochastic processes.
**Ind/Abst** Compumath Citation Index [Full Cov.]; Curr. Index Stat.; INSPEC (1970-); Int. Abstr. Oper. Res. [Select. Cov.]; Int. Aerosp. Abstr.; Math. Rev.; Pollut. Abstr. Indexes; Res. Alert [Full Cov.]; Sci. Cit. Index; SCISEARCH; Stat. Theory Method Abstr. (1969-1975, 1978-1981, 1986-1987); Zentralbl. Math. Ihre Grenzgeb.

US/0094-9000
**THEORY OF PROBABILITY AND MATHEMATICAL STATISTICS.** [Theory probab. math. stat.]. **Added/Corp** American Mathematical Society. No. 1 (1974)-. Periodical. English. sa (2 issues). $375.00. American Mathematical Society, PO Box 6248, Providence RI 02940-6248. **Tel** (800)321-4267, (401)455-4000, FAX (401)331-3842, telex 797192. **(Subscription address:** American Mathematical Society, PO Box 5904, Boston MA 02206-5904.**) LC** QA273.A1; T453. **DD** 519.2/05. **CODEN** TPMSCO. **[CCC].**
**Desc:** Cover-to-cover translation into English of the Teoriya Veroyatnostei i Matematicheskaya Statistika, published by Kiev University.
**Ind/Abst** Curr. Index Stat.; Math. Rev.; Zentralbl. Math. Ihre Grenzgeb.

US/0095-7380
**THEORY OF STOCHASTIC PROCESSES.** No. 1- 1974-. English. John Wiley & Sons, Inc., 605 Third Avenue, New York NY 10158-0012. **Tel** (212)850-6000, (212)850-6645, FAX (212)850-6088, telex 12-7063. **(Subscription address:** John Wiley & Sons / England, Baffins Lane, Chichester, West Sussex PO19 1UD England.**) LC** QA274.A1; T47. **DD** 519.2/05. **UDC** 519.24.

JA/0040-8735
**TOHOKU MATHEMATICAL JOURNAL.** [Tohoku math. j.]. **Added/Corp** Tohoku Daigaku. Ser. 1, Vol. 1 (July 1911)-. Periodical. English (French, German, Italian and Japanese). qt. $238.00. Tohoku Daigaku, (Tohoku University), 1-1, Katahira 2 Chome, Sendaishi, Miyagiken 980, Japan. **(Subscription address:** Maruzen Company Ltd., PO Box 5050, Import & Export Department, Tokyo 100 31 Japan.**) ED** T. Hayashi. **LC** QA1; .T6. **CODEN** TOMJAM. cum. index. **Pr Rev.** ctrl circ. Documents available from The Genuine Article.
**Ind/Abst** Compumath Citation Index [Full Cov.]; Curr. Contents Phys. Chem. Earth Sci.; Math. Rev.; Res. Alert [Full Cov.]; Sci. Cit. Index; SCISEARCH; Soc. Sci. Cit. Index [Select. Cov.]; Zentralbl. Math. Ihre Grenzgeb.

JA/0912-6112
**TOKEI SURI.** [Tokei suri]. **Added/Corp** Tokei Suri Kenkyujo (Japan). **VFOAT** Proceedings of the Institute of Statistical Mathematics. (1985)-. Periodical. Japanese (Japanese; summaries and/or abstracts in English). sa. $75.00. Monbusho Tokei Suri Kenkyujo, (Inst. of Statistical Mathematics, Ministry of Education), 6-7, Minamiazabu 4 Chome, Minatoku, Tokyoto 106, Japan. **(Subscription address:** Maruzen Company Ltd., PO Box 5050, Import & Export Department, Tokyo 100 31 Japan.**)** ***Continues*** *Tokei Suri Kenkyujo (Japan). Tokei Suri Kenkyujo Iho, 0563-685X.*
**Ind/Abst** Curr. Index Stat.; Math. Rev.

JA
**TOKEI SURI KENKYUJO NENPO.**
**Main/Corp** Tokei Suri Kenkyujo, Tokyo. (19??)-. Japanese. Tokei Suri Kenkyujo, 6-7 Minami Azabu 4-chome Minato-ku, Tokyo 106 Japan. **LC** QA276.A1; T64a.

JA/0387-3870
**TOKYO JOURNAL OF MATHEMATICS.** [Tokyo j. math.]. **Added/Corp** Gakushuin Daigaku. Dept. of Mathematics. **VFOAT** Journal of Mathematics. Vol. 1, No. 1 (July 1978)-. Periodical. English. sa. $266.00. Jochi Daigaku Rikogakubu, (Faculty of Science & Technology, Sophia University), 17-7, Shinjuku 3 Chome, Shinjukuku, Tokyoto 160, Japan. **(Subscription address:** Kinokuniya Company Ltd., 38-1 Sakuragaoka 5, chome Setagaya-ku, Tokyo 156 Japan.**)**
**Ind/Abst** Math. Rev.; Zentralbl. Math. Ihre Grenzgeb.

UK
**TOPICS AND TEXTS IN MATHEMATICS.** Vol. 1 (1984)-. Monographic series. English. AB Academic Publishers, PO Box 42 Bicester, OXON OX6 7NW England. **Tel** 011 44 869 320949.
**Ind/Abst** Zentralbl. Math. Ihre Grenzgeb.

•PO/1230-3429
**TOPOLOGICAL METHODS IN NONLINEAR ANALYSIS. Added/Corp** Centrum im. Juliusza Schaudera (Torun, Poland). **VFOAT** TMNA. Vol. 1, No. 1 (Mar. 1993)-. Periodical. English. qt. $230.00 institution, $115.00 individual. American Mathematical Society, PO Box 6248, Providence RI 02940-6248. **Tel** (800)321-4267, (401)455-4000, FAX (401)331-3842, telex 797192. **(Subscription address:** American Mathematical Society, PO Box 5904, Boston MA 02206-5904.**)**
**Desc:** Contains research and survey papers on a wide range of topics in nonlinear analysis, with a focus on those using topological methods. Published by the Juliusz Schauder Center, with the assistance of Nicolas Copernicus University for Nonlinear Studies in Torun, Poland.

CN/0226-9171
**TOPOLOGIE STRUCTURALE / STRUCTURAL TOPOLOGY.** [Topol. struct.]. **Added/Corp** Universite de Montreal. Structural Topology Research Group. **VFOAT** Structural Topology. (1979)-. Periodical. English (French). Twice a year. 60.00Can$ (institution); 35.00Can$ (individual);. Revue Topologie Structurale, University of Quebec, PO Box 8888 Succ A, Montreal Quebec H3C 3P8 Canada. **Tel** (514)987-7710. **DD** 624.1/05. **Pr Rev. Circ:** 200.
**Desc:** An interdisciplinary journal on the applications of classical and contemporary mathematics, especially geometry to the solution of morphological and structural problems.
**Ind/Abst** Math. Rev.; Zentralbl. Math. Ihre Grenzgeb.

NE/0166-8641
**TOPOLOGY AND ITS APPLICATIONS.** [Topol. appl.] Vol. 11 (Jan. 1980)-. Academic Scholarly Publication. English. Twenty-one times a year (7 volumes). Fl2555.00. Elsevier Science Publishers BV, PO Box 211, 1000 AE Amsterdam Netherlands. **Tel** 011 31 20 5803642, FAX 011 31 20 5862696, telex 15682. **ED** Richard B Sher and Jerry E Vaughan. **LC** QA611.A1; G45. **DD** 514. **CODEN** TIAPD9. **[CCC]. Pr Rev.** available on microfilm and microfiche from University Microfilms International (UMI). Documents available from The Genuine Article. ***Continues*** *General Topology and its Applications.*
**Desc:** Offers broad coverage of the various areas of topological research: the axiomatic, set-theoretic, general, geometric, and algebraic facets of topology as well as areas of interactions between topology and other mathematical disciplines, e.g. topological algebra, topological dynamics, functional analysis, category theory, etc.
**Ind/Abst** Compumath Citation Index [Full Cov.]; Math. Rev.; Pollut. Abstr. Indexes; Res. Alert [Full Cov.]; Zentralbl. Math. Ihre Grenzgeb.

GW/0720-2571
**TOPOLOGY (BERLIN, WEST).** (TOPOLOGY.). [Topology]. **Added/Corp** Heidelberger Akademie der Wissenschaften Fachsinformationszentrum Energie, Physik, Mathematik. (1981)-. English (French and German). Twelve times a year. $140.00. Fachinformationszentrum Karlsruhe, Physics & Math, D 76344 Eggenstein Germany. **Tel** 011 49 7247 808149. **LC** QA611.A1; T668. **DD** 514/.05.
**Ind/Abst** Zentralbl. Math. Ihre Grenzgeb.

UK/0040-9383
**TOPOLOGY (OXFORD).** (TOPOLOGY.). [Topology]. Vol. 1 (Jan./March 1962)-. Periodical. English (French, German and Italian). qt. $701.00 The Americas; £470.00 other. Pergamon Press, An Imprint of Elsevier Science Ltd., The Boulevard, Langford Lane, Kidlington, Oxford OX5 1GB United Kingdom. **Tel** 011 44 865 843000, 011 44 865 843699, FAX 011 44 865 843010. **(Subscription address:** Elsevier Science Ltd. Oxford Fulfillment Centre, PO Box 800, Kidlington, Oxford OX5 1DX United Kingdom.**) ED** B. Birch, S. Donaldson, I. James, F. Kirwan, D. Quillen, R. Cohen, F. Hirzebruch, and L. Siebenmann. **LC** QA611; .T657. **DD** 514/.05. **CODEN** TPLGAF. **[CCC]. Pr Rev.** available on microfilm and microfiche from University Microfilms International (UMI). Documents available from The Genuine Article.
**Ind/Abst** Am. Humanit. Index; Compumath Citation Index [Full Cov.]; Curr. Contents Phys. Chem. Earth Sci.; Math. Rev.; Res. Alert [Full Cov.]; Sci. Cit. Index; SCISEARCH.

US/0146-4124
**TOPOLOGY PROCEEDINGS.** [Topol. proc.]. **Added/Corp** Auburn University. Mathematics Dept. Ohio University. Institute for Medicine and Mathematics. Vol. 1 (1976)-. Monographic series. English. ir. $85.00. Auburn University / Department of Mathematics, Parker Hall, Auburn AL 36849-5310. **Tel** (205)844-4290, FAX (205)844-6555. **ED** Gary Gruenhage (phone: (205)844-6585). **LC** QA611.A1; T68. **DD** 514. Index available. **Pr Rev. Circ:** 300.
**Desc:** Papers presented at the annual Spring Topology Conference.
**Ind/Abst** Math. Rev.; Zentralbl. Math. Ihre Grenzgeb.

SP/0213-8204
**TRABAJOS DE INVESTIGACION OPERATIVA.** Vol. 1, No. 1 (1986)-. Periodical. Spanish (English and French; summaries and/or abstracts in English and Spanish). Three times a year. $20.00. Sociedad de Estadistica e Investigacion Operativa, Hortaleza 104-2 IZDA, 28004 Madrid Spain. **Tel** 011 34 1 3082474. **LC** QA329. **Pr Rev. *Continues in part*** *Trabajos de Estadistica y de Investigacion Operativa, 0041-0241.*
**Desc:** Statistical papers.

US/0002-9947
**TRANSACTIONS OF THE AMERICAN MATHEMATICAL SOCIETY.** [Trans. Am. Math. Soc.]. **Main/Corp** American Mathematical Society. Vol. 1 (Jan. 1900)-. Periodical. English. mo. $980.00. American Mathematical Society, PO Box 6248, Providence RI 02940-6248. **Tel** (800)321-4267, (401)455-4000, FAX (401)331-3842, telex 797192. **(Subscription address:** American Mathematical Society, PO Box 5904, Boston MA 02206-5904.**) LC** QA1; .A522. **DD** 510/.5. **CODEN** TAMTAM. **[CCC].** Index available (bound in Dec. issue). cum. index. **Pr Rev.** available on microfilm and microfiche from University Microfilms International (UMI). Documents available from The Genuine Article.
**Desc:** Devoted entirely to research in pure and applied mathematics and includes longer papers than those published in Proceedings of AMS.
**Ind/Abst** Compumath Citation Index [Full Cov.]; Curr. Contents Phys. Chem. Earth Sci.; Int. Aerosp. Abstr.; Math. Rev.; Pollut. Abstr. Indexes; Res. Alert [Full Cov.]; Sci. Cit. Index; SCISEARCH; Stat. Theory Method Abstr. (1961-1963, 1972-1973); Zentralbl. Math. Ihre Grenzgeb.

US/0077-1554
**TRANSACTIONS OF THE MOSCOW MATHEMATICAL SOCIETY.** [Trans. Mosc. Math. Soc.]. **Main/Corp** Moskovskoe Matematicheskoe Obshchestvo. **Added/Corp** Moskovskoe Matematicheskoe Obshchestvo. American Mathematical Society. London Mathematical Society. **VFOAT** Transactions of the Moscow Mathematical Society. (19??)-. English (Russian). an. $264.00. American Mathematical Society, PO Box 6248, Providence RI 02940-6248. **Tel** (800)321-4267, (401)455-4000, FAX (401)331-3842, telex 797192. **(Subscription address:** American Mathematical Society, PO Box 5904, Boston MA 02206-5904.**) LC** QA1; .M9883. **DD** 510/.5. **CODEN** TMMSD4. **[CCC].**
**Desc:** A translation of the Russian journal, Trudy Moskovskogo Matematicheskogo Obshchestva. Contains the results of original research in pure mathematics.
**Ind/Abst** Math. Rev.; Zentralbl. Math. Ihre Grenzgeb.

XR/0231-9969
**TRANSACTIONS OF THE ... PRAGUE CONFERENCE ON INFORMATION THEORY, STATISTICAL DECISION FUNCTIONS, RANDOM PROCESSES. Main/Conf** Conference on Information Theory, Statistical Decision Functions, Random Processes. **Added/Corp** Ceskoslovenska Akademie Ved. Sekce Technicka. **VFOAT** Information Theory, Statistical Decision Functions, Random Processes. 1st (Nov. 28-30, 1956)-. Statistical Publication. English (French, German and Russian). ir. Kluwer Academic Publishers / Massachusetts, PO Box 358, Accord Station, Hingham MA 02018. **Tel** (617)871-6600. **(Subscription address:** Kluwer Academic Publishers / Netherlands, PO Box 322, 3300 AH Dordrecht Netherlands.**) LC** QA273; .C743. **DD** 519; 311.
**Ind/Abst** Stat. Theory Method Abstr. (1969-1970, 1986-1987).

US/0065-9290
**TRANSLATIONS - AMERICAN MATHEMATICAL SOCIETY.** [Transl. - Am. Math. Soc.]. **Main/Corp** American Mathematical Society. **Added/Corp** United States. Office of Naval Research. (1949)-. Monographic series. English. ir. Price varies per volume. American Mathematical Society, PO Box 6248, Providence RI 02940-6248. **Tel** (800)321-4267, (401)455-4000, FAX (401)331-3842, telex 797192. **(Subscription address:** American Mathematical Society, PO Box 5904, Boston MA 02206-5904.**) LC** QA3; .A572. **[CCC].**
**Ind/Abst** Math. Rev.; Zentralbl. Math. Ihre Grenzgeb.

US/0065-9282
**TRANSLATIONS OF MATHEMATICAL MONOGRAPHS.** [Transl. math. monogr.]. **Added/Corp** American Mathematical Society. (1962)-. Monographic series. English. ir. Price varies per volume. American Mathematical Society, PO Box 6248, Providence RI 02940-6248. **Tel** (800)321-4267, (401)455-4000, FAX (401)331-3842, telex 797192. **(Subscription address:** American Mathematical Society, PO Box 5904, Boston MA 02206-5904.**) LC** UNC. **DD** 510. **[CCC].**
**Ind/Abst** Math. Rev.; Zentralbl. Math. Ihre Grenzgeb.

US/0041-1450
**TRANSPORT THEORY AND STATISTICAL PHYSICS.** **See** Physics-Analytic and Experimental Mechanics.

FR/0766-9968
**TRAVAUX EN COURS.** French. ir. Hermann Editeurs Science Arts, 293 rue Lecourbe, 75015 Paris France. **Tel** 011 33 1 45574540.

RU
**TRUDY. Main/Corp** Akademiia Nauk SSSR. Matematicheskii Institut Im. V. A. Steklova. (1932)-. Academic Scholarly Publication. English (French, German and Russian). ir. Izdatelstvo Nauka / Akademiia Nauk, Publishing House of the Russian Academy of Sciences, Leninskii Porspekt 14, 117901 Moscow Russia. **Tel** 011 95 954-21-53, FAX 011 95 938-21-44, telex 411964. **(Subscription address:** Victor Kamkin, 4956 Boiling Brook Parkway, Rockville MD 20852.**)**

RU/0256-341X
**TRUDY GEOMETRICHESKOGO SEMINARA.** [Tr. Geom. semin.]. **Added/Corp** Kazanskii Gosudarstvennyi Universitet Im. V.I. Ulianova-Lenina. Geometricheskii Seminar. (1975)-. Russian. an. **LC** QA443; .K35. ***Continues*** *Trudy Seminara Kafedry Geometrii, 0130-4836.*
**Ind/Abst** Math. Rev.; Zentralbl. Math. Ihre Grenzgeb.

RU/0371-9685
**TRUDY ORDENA LENINA MATEMATICESKOGO INSTITUTA IM. V.A. STEKLOVA.** (TRUDY MATEMATICHESKOGO INSTITUTA IMENI V.A. STEKLOVA.). [Tr. ordena Lenina Mat. inst. im. V. A. Steklova]. **Added/Corp** Matematicheskii Institut Im. V.A. Steklova. **VFOAT** Trudy Ordena Lenina Matematicheskogo Instituta Imeni V.A. Steklova; Trudy Ordena Lenina i Ordena Oktiabrskoi Revoliutsii Matematicheskogo Instituta Imeni V.A. Steklova; Travaux de l'Institut Mathematique Stekloff. (1935)-. Monographic series. Russian (English, French and German). Price varies per volume. Izdatelstvo Nauka / Akademiia Nauk, Publishing House of the Russian Academy of Sciences, Leninskii Porspekt 14, 117901 Moscow Russia. **Tel** 011 95 954-21-53, FAX 011 95 938-21-44, telex 411964. **LC** QA1; .A4. ***Continues*** *Trudy Fiziko-Matematicheskogo Instituta Imeni V.A. Steklova. Otdel Matematicheskii.*
**Ind/Abst** Int. Aerosp. Abstr.; Math. Rev.

US/0081-5438
**TRUDY ORDENA LENINA MATEMATICHESKOGO INSTITUTA IMENI V. A. STEKLOVA.** (PROCEEDINGS OF THE STEKLOV INSTITUTE OF MATHEMATICS.). [Proc. Steklov Inst. Math.]. **Added/Corp** Matematicheskii Institut im. V.A. Steklova. American Mathematical Society. (19??)-. Proceedings. English (translations available in Russian). qt. $654.00. American Mathematical Society, PO Box 6248, Providence RI 02940-6248. **Tel** (800)321-4267, (401)455-4000, FAX (401)331-3842, telex 797192. **(Subscription address:** American Mathematical Society, PO Box 5904, Boston MA 02206-5904.**) LC** QA1; .A413. **DD** 510. **[CCC].**
**Desc:** This journal is a cover-to-cover translation into English of the Trudy Matematicheskogo Instituta imeni V. A. Steklova of the Russian Academy of Sciences.
**Ind/Abst** Int. Abstr. Oper. Res. [Select. Cov.]; Math. Rev.; Zentralbl. Math. Ihre Grenzgeb.

RU/0321-2971
**TRUDY SEMINARA IMENI I. G. PETROVSKOGO.** [Tr. semin. im. I. G. Petrovskogo]. **Main/Corp** Seminar Imeni I. G. Petrovskogo. Vol. 1 (1975)-. Academic Scholarly Publication. Russian. an. 3.60rub. Izdatelstvo Moskovskogo Universiteta, K-9 Ulitsa Gertsena 5/7, Moscow Russia. **Tel** (301)881-5973. **LC** QA370; .S46a. **CODEN** TSIPDH. Documents available from CASDDS.
**Ind/Abst** Chem. Abstr. (1975-1982); Int. Aerosp. Abstr.; Math. Rev.; Zentralbl. Math. Ihre Grenzgeb.

RU
**TRUDY SEMINARA PO KRAEVYM ZADACHAM / KAZANSKII ORDENA TRUDOVOGO KRASNOGO ZNAMENI GOSUDARSTVENNYI UNIVERSITET IM. V.I. ULIANOVA-LENINA.** [Tr. semin. kraev. zadacam]. **Added/Corp** Kazanskii Gosudarstvennyi Universitet Im. V.I. Ulianova-Lenina. (1966)-. Academic Scholarly Publication. Russian. **CODEN** TSZDAT.

Documents available from CASDDS.
**Ind/Abst** Chem. Abstr.; Int. Aerosp. Abstr.; Math. Rev.; Zentralbl. Math. Ihre Grenzgeb.

RU/0373-4870
**TRUDY SEMINARA PO VEKTORNOMU I TENZORNOMU ANALIZU.** (TRUDY SEMINARA PO VEKTORNOMU I TENZORNOMU ANALIZU S IKH PRILOZHENIIAMI K GEOMETRII, MEKHANIKE I FIZIKE / NAUCHNO-ISSLEDOVATELSKII INSTITUT MATEMATIKI I MEKHANIKI PRI MOSKOVSKOM GOSUDARSTVENNOM UNIVERSITETE.). [Tr. Semin. vektorn. tenzorn. anal.]. **Added/Corp** Moskovskii Gosudarstvennyi Universitet im. M.V. Lomonosova. Nauchno-Issledovatelskii Institut Matematiki. Moskovskii Gosudarstvenny Universitet. Nauchno-Issledovatelskii Institut Matematiki i Mekhaniki. **VFOAT** Abhandlungen aus dem Seminar fur Vektor- und Tensoranalysis Samt Anwendungen auf Geometrie, Mechanik und Physik; Memoires du Seminaire pour l'Analyse Vectorielle et Tensorielle et pour ses Applications a la Geometrie, a la Mecanique et a la Physique. (1933)-. Monographic series. German (French, German, Italian and Russian). Price varies per volume. **LC** QA261; .M6.
**Ind/Abst** Math. Rev.; Zentralbl. Math. Ihre Grenzgeb.

●RU
**TRUDY VYCHISLITELNOGO TSENTRA SO RAN. SERIIA SISTEMNOE MODELIROVANIE / ROSSIISKAIA AKADEMIIA NAUK, SIBIRSKOE OTDELENIE, VYCHISLITELNYI TSENTR.** **Added/Corp** Rossiiskaia Akademiia Nauk. Sibirskoe Otdelenie. Vychislitelnyi Tsentr. **VFOAT** Seriia Sistemnoe Modelirovanie; Sistemnoe Modelirovanie; Trudy VTS SO RAN. Sistemnoe Modelirovanie. (1993)-. Russian. ***Continues*** *Sistemnoe Modelirovanie, 0134-630X.*

JA/0387-4982
**TSUKUBA JOURNAL OF MATHEMATICS.** [Tsukuba j. math.]. **Added/Corp** Tsukuba Daigaku. Sugakukei. Vol. 1 (Dec. 1977)-. Periodical. English. sa. $339.00. **(Subscription address:** Japan Publications Trading Company, Ltd., PO Box 5030, Tokyo International, Tokyo 100-31 Japan.**)** **LC** QA1; .T83. **DD** 510/.5. ***Supersedes*** *Science Reports of the Tokyo Kyoiku Daigaku.*
**Ind/Abst** Math. Rev.; Stat. Theory Method Abstr. (1983-1984, 1986); Zentralbl. Math. Ihre Grenzgeb.

CC
**TZU HSUEH (PEKING, CHINA).** (TZU HSUEH.). **VFOAT** Zi Xue. Periodical. Chinese. RMBY0.36. Science Press, 16 Donghuangchenggen North Street, Beijing 100707, People's Republic of China. **Tel** 011 86 1 4019821, 011 86 1 4010642, FAX 011 86 1 4012180, 011 86 1 4019810, telex 210147. **LC** LC25; .T98. **DD** 374/.1.

US/0041-5995
**UKRAINIAN MATHEMATICAL JOURNAL.** [Ukr. math. j.]. **Added/Corp** Consultants Bureau. Vol. 19 (Jan./Feb. 1967)-. Periodical. English (Russian). mo. $1335.00 US; $1560.00 other. Consultants Bureau, A Division of Plenum Publishing Corporation, 233 Spring Street, New York NY 10013. **Tel** (212)620-8000, (212)620-8466, FAX (212)463-0742, telex 23/421139. **ED** Yu A. Mitropol'skii. **LC** QA1; .U4318. **DD** 510. **CODEN** UKMJB6. **[CCC].** available on microfilm and microfiche from University Microfilms International (UMI).
**Desc:** Publishes articles and brief communications in various areas of pure and applied mathematics. Contains sections devoted to science information, criticism, bibliographies, reviews of problems of current interest.
**Ind/Abst** Math. Rev.; Pollut. Abstr. Indexes; Zentralbl. Math. Ihre Grenzgeb.

●US/1069-5346
**UKRAINIAN MATHEMATICS JOURNAL.** (1993)-. Periodical. English (translations available in Russian). Six times a year. $315.00. Allerton Press, Inc., 150 Fifth Avenue, New York NY 10011. **Tel** (212)924-3950, FAX (212)463-9684, telex 427441 ALPRES.

●UN
**UKRAINSKYI MATEMATYCHNYI ZHURNAL.** **Added/Corp** Instytut Matematyky (Akademiia nauk Ukrainy). T. 44, No 1 (1992)-. Periodical. Ukrainian. mo. **LC** QA1; .U3. ***Continues*** *Ukrainskii Matematicheskii Zhurnal.*

US/0197-3622
**UMAP JOURNAL, THE.** [UMAP j.]. **Added/Corp** Consortium for Mathematics and Its Applications (U.S.) Society for Industrial and Applied Mathematics. Mathematical Association of America. **VFOAT** U.M.A.P. Journal. **VAT** Undergraduate Mathematics Applications Project Journal. Vol. 1, No. 1 (Spring 1980)-. Periodical. English. qt. comes with membership. COMAP Inc, 57 Bedford Street, Suite 210, Lexington MA 02173. **Tel** (617)862-7878, FAX (617)863-1202. **ED** Phillip Straffin and Paul Campbell. **LC** QA11.A1; U48. **DD** 510/.7/1. **Bk Rev**. **Ad Acc**. **Circ:** 2,000.
**Desc:** Math modules, articles and reviews on math applications and the contemporary use and application of math.
**Ind/Abst** Acad. Search (July 1993-); Educ. Index; INFO-SOUTH Abstr.; Mag. Search.

US
**UMAP MODULES.** **See** Mathematics-Abstracting, Bibliographies and Statistics.

US
**UME TRENDS.** (19??)-. Periodical. English. Six times a year. $16.00 US; $24.00 other. Mathematical Association of America, 1529 18th Street Northwest, Washington DC 20036. **Tel** (202)387-5200, (800)331-1622, FAX (202)265-2384. **Bk Rev**.

US/0172-6056
**UNDERGRADUATE TEXTS IN MATHEMATICS.** (1974)-. Monographic series. English. ir. Price varies per volume. Springer-Verlag New York Inc., 175 5th Avenue, New York NY 10010. **Tel** (212)460-1500, telex 232 235 SPB UR. **(Subscription address:** Springer Verlag New York Inc. / for North America, 44 Hartz Way, Secaucus NJ 07096.**)**
**Desc:** Contains articles on analytic number theory, linear algebra, general topology, mathematical logic, applied abstract algebra and calculus.

TU
**UNIVERSITY OF ISTANBUL, FACULTY OF SCIENCE, THE JOURNAL OF MATHEMATICS.** **Added/Corp** Istanbul Universitesi. Fen Fakultesi. **VFOAT** Istanbul Universitesi Fen Fakultesi Matematik Dergisi; Journal of Mathematics; Matematik Dergisi. Vol. 48 (1991)-. Periodical. English (French, German and Italian; summaries and/or abstracts in Turkish). **LC** QA1; .I87. ***Continues*** *Istanbul Universitesi Fen Fakultesi Mecmuas. A Serisi, Srfi ve Tatbiki Matematik (1976).*
**Ind/Abst** Math. Rev.

RU
**UPORIADOCHENNYE MNOZHESTVA I RESHETKI.** (1971)-. Russian. 0.70rub (single issue). Saratov N.G. Chernyshevskii State University, Astrakhanskaya Ulitsa 83, 410071 Saratov Russia. **Tel** 24-16-96, FAX 24-04-46, telex 241125. **LC** QA248; .U56.
**Ind/Abst** Zentralbl. Math. Ihre Grenzgeb.

RU/0042-1316
**USPEHI MATEMATICESKIH NAUK.** (USPEKHI MATEMATICHESKIKH NAUK / VSEOIUZNAIA MATEMATICHESKAIA ASSITSUATSIIA.). [Uspehi mat. nauk]. **Added/Corp** Vsesoiuznaia Matematicheskaia Assotsiatsiia (Soviet Union) Akademiia Nauk SSSR. Moskovskoe Matematicheskoe Obshchestvo. Vol. 1 (1936)-. Academic Scholarly Publication. Russian. bm. $174.00. Izdatelstvo Nauka / Akademiia Nauk, Publishing House of the Russian Academy of Sciences, Leninskii Porspekt 14, 117901 Moscow Russia. **Tel** 011 95 954-21-53, FAX 011 95 938-21-44, telex 411964. **(Subscription address:** Victor Kamkin, 4956 Boiling Brook Parkway, Rockville, MD 20852**)** **LC** QA1; .V63. **CODEN** UMANA5. **[CCC].** Documents available from CASDDS.
**Ind/Abst** Chem. Abstr. (?-1973); Math. Rev.; Zentralbl. Math. Ihre Grenzgeb.

CN/0315-3681
**UTILITAS MATHEMATICA.** [Util. math.]. (May 1972)-. Periodical. English. sa (May, Nov.). $80.00. Utilitas Mathematica Publishing Inc., University of Manitoba, Box 7, University Center, Winnipeg Manitoba R3T 2N2 Canada. **Tel** (204)474-8313, (204)474-8675. **ED** Ralph G. Stanton. **CODEN** UTMADA. **[CCC]. Pr Rev. Circ:** 300. Documents available from The Genuine Article.
**Desc:** A Canadian journal of applied mathematics, computer science, and statistics.
**Ind/Abst** Compumath Citation Index (19??-) [Full Cov.]; Comput. Rev. (19??-); Int. Aerosp. Abstr. (19??-); Math. Rev. (19??-); Res. Alert (19??-) [Full Cov.]; Stat. Theory Method Abstr. (1973-1977, 1980-1984, 1986-1987); Zentralbl. Math. Ihre Grenzgeb. (19??-).

DK/0065-0188
**VARIOUS PUBLICATIONS SERIES - AARHUS UNIVERSITET. MATEMATISK INSTITUT.** (VARIOUS PUBLICATIONS SERIES.). [Var. publ. ser. - Aarhus Univ., Mat. inst.]. **Main/Corp** Aarhus Universitet. Matematisk Institut. No. 1 (1962)-. Monographic series. English. ir. Price varies per volume. Matematisk Institut, Aarhus Universitet, Bygning 530, Ny Munkegade, DK-8000 Aarhus C Denmark. **Tel** 011 45 86 127188. **Circ:** 120.
**Ind/Abst** Math. Rev.

CN/0382-0718
**VECTOR (VANCOUVER).** (VECTOR.). [Vector]. **Added/Corp** British Columbia Association of Mathematics Teachers. Vol. 10, No. 3 (Dec. 1968)-. Periodical. English. ir. 45.00Can$. British Columbia Teachers Federation, 100-550 West 6th Avenue, Vancouver British Columbia V5Z 4P2 Canada. **Tel** (604)871-2283, (800)663-9163, FAX (604)871-2294, (604)871-2290. available on microfilm and microfiche from Micromedia Limited. ***Continues*** *British Columbia Association of Mathematics Teachers. Newsletter, 0382-0726.* ***Continued in part by*** *Newsletter (British Columbia Association of Mathematics Teachers : 1985), 0833-9775.*

GW
**VEROFFENTLICHUNGEN DES LEIBNIZ-ARCHIVS.** **Main/Corp** Hanover. Niedersachsische Landesbibliothek. Leibniz-Archiv. 1-1967-. Monographic series. German. ir. Price varies per volume. Vittorio Klostermann, Frauenlobstrasse 22, D 60487 Frankfurt Germany. **Tel** 011 49 69 9708160. **UDC** 510.
**Ind/Abst** Math. Rev.

RU/0579-9368
**VESTNIK MOSKOVSKOGO UNIVERSITETA SERIIA I, MATEMATIKA, MEKHANIKA.** [Vestn. Mosk. univ., Ser. 1, Mat. mek.]. **Added/Corp** Moskovskii Gosudarstvennyi Universitet Im. M.V. Lomonosova. **VFOAT** Matematika, Mekhanika. (1960)-. Periodical. Russian (summaries and/or abstracts in English). Six times a year. $103.95. Izdatelstvo Moskovskogo Universiteta, K-9 Ulitsa Gertsena 5/7, Moscow Russia. **Tel** (301)881-5973. **(Subscription address:** East View Publications Inc., 3020 Harbor Lane North, Suite 110, Minneapolis MN 55447.**)** **LC** QA1; .M9885. **CODEN** VMMMA5. **[CCC].** Documents available from Article Express International, The Genuine Article, Ask*IEEE. ***Continues in part*** *Vestnik Moskovskogo Universiteta. Seriia Matematiki, Mekhaniki, Astronomii, Fiziki, Khimii.*
**Ind/Abst** Compumath Citation Index [Full Cov.]; Ei Page One; Energy Res. Abstr.; Eng. Index Annu.; INSPEC (July/Aug. 1979-); Int. Aerosp. Abstr.; Math. Rev.; Res. Alert [Full Cov.]; Stat. Theory Method Abstr. (1986-1987); Zentralbl. Math. Ihre Grenzgeb.

US/0278-6419
**VESTNIK MOSKOVSKOGO UNIVERSITETA. SERIIA XV, VYCHISLITELNAIA MATEMATIKA I KIBERNETIKA. ENGLISH.** **See** Computers-Cybernetics.

●RU
**VESTNIK SANKT-PETERBURGSKOGO UNIVERSITETA. SERIIA 1, MATEMATIKA, MEKHANIKA, ASTRONOMIIA.** **Added/Corp** Sankt-Peterburgskii Universitet. **VFOAT** Matematika, Mekhanika, Astronomiia. (1992)-. Periodical. Russian. qt. $70.00. St Petersburg State University / Izdatelstvo Leningradskogo Universiteta, Universitetskaia Nab 7/9, 199034 St Petersburg Russia. **Tel** 011 95 218-97-88, FAX 011 95 218-51-52, telex 121481. **(Subscription address:** Victor Kamkin, 4956 Boiling Brook Parkway, Rockville MD 20852.**)** ***Continues*** *Vestnik Leningradskogo Universiteta. Seriia 1, Matematika, Mekhanika, Astronomiia.*

●US/1063-4541
**VESTNIK ST. PETERSBURG UNIVERSITY: MATHEMATICS.** [Vestn. St. Petersbg. Univ., Math.]. **Added/Corp** Sankt-Peterburgskii Universitet (1992). **VFOAT** Mathematics; Matematika; Vestnik Sankt-Peterburgskogo Universiteta. Matematika. Vol. 25 (1992)-. Periodical. English (translations available in Russian). Four times a year (Jan., Apr., July, Oct.). $655.00. Allerton Press, Inc., 150 Fifth Avenue, New York NY 10011. **Tel** (212)924-3950, FAX (212)463-9684, telex 427441 ALPRES. **LC** QA1; .L42a. **DD** 510. **[CCC].** ***Continues*** *Vestnik Leningrad University: Mathematics, 0146-924X.*
**Ind/Abst** Math. Rev.

II
**VIJNANA PARISHAD ANUSANDHAN PATRIKA.** **Added/Corp** Vijnana Parishad (Allahabad, India). **VFOAT** Research Journal of the Hindi Science Academy. (19??)-. Academic Scholarly Publication. Hindi (summaries and/or abstracts in English). qt. $40.00. Hindi Science Academy Vijnana Parishad, Allahabad India. **(Subscription address:** Prints India, 11 Darya Ganj, New Delhi, 110002 India, (Phone: 011 91 11 3268645)**)** **CODEN** VPAPA9. Documents available from BIOSIS Document Express, CASDDS.
**Ind/Abst** Biol. Abstr.; Chem. Abstr.

AT/0157-759X
**VINCULUM.** (1964)-. Periodical. English. qt. (Comes with Mathematical Assn of Victoria membership). Mathematical Association of Victoria, 61 Blyth Street, Brunswick VIC 3056 Australia. **Tel** 011 61 3 3802399, FAX 011 61 3 3808323. **ED** Roy James. **Bk Rev**. **Ad Acc**. **Circ:** 2,000 (ctrl).
**Ind/Abst** Aust. Educ. Index.

UN/0320-6572
**VISNIK LVIVSKOGO ORDENA LENINA DERZARNOGO UNIVERSITETU IM. IV. FRANKA. SERIJA MEHANIKO-MATEMATICNA.** (VISNIK LVIVSKOGO ORDENA LENINA DERZHARNOGO

UNIVERSITETU. SERIIA MEKHANIKO-MATEMATICHNA.). [Visnik Lviv. Ordena Lenina Derz. Univ. im. Iv. Franka. Ser. meh.-mat.]. **Main/Corp** Lvov. Universitet. Vol. 1-. Periodical. Ukrainian (summaries and/or abstracts in Russian). **LC** QA1; .L83. **UDC** 51; 531; 51-72:53.
**Ind/Abst** Math. Rev.

GW
**VITA MATHEMATICA.** (1987)-. Monographic series. German. Price varies per volume. Birkhaeuser Verlag Ag, Klosterberg 23, PO Box 133, CH-4010 Basel Switzerland. **Tel** 011 41 61 2717400, FAX 011 41 0 61 2717666, telex 963475 birk ch.
**Ind/Abst** Math. Rev. (1987-); Zentralbl. Math. Ihre Grenzgeb.

US
**VNR NEW MATHEMATICS LIBRARY.** (19??)-. Monographic series. English.
**Ind/Abst** Zentralbl. Math. Ihre Grenzgeb.

BW/0234-4823
**VOPROSY ALGEBRY / GOMELSKIFI GOSUDARSTVENNYI UNIVERSITET.** **Added/Corp** Homelski Dziarzhauny Universitet. (1985)-. Russian.
**Ind/Abst** Zentralbl. Math. Ihre Grenzgeb.

KZ
**VOPROSY PRIKLADNOI MATEMATIKI I MEKHANIKI.** **Added/Corp** Qazaqtyng S.M. Kirov Atyndaghy Memlekettik Universiteti. (1974)-. Russian. **LC** QA1; .V57.

RU/0130-0415
**VOPROSY TEORII SISTEM AVTOMATICESKOGO UPRAVLENIJA.** **See** Engineering-Mechanical Engineering and Machinery.

GW
**VORLESUNGEN AUS DEM FACHBEREICH MATHMATIK DER UNIVERSITAT ESSEN.** **Main/Corp** Universitat Essen-Gesamthochschule. Fachbereich Mathematik. (1978)-. Monographic series. German. Price varies per volume.
**Ind/Abst** Math. Rev.; Zentralbl. Math. Ihre Grenzgeb.

CN/1184-1842
**VOTRE GUIDE QUOTIDIEN.** (VOTRE GUIDE QUOTIDIEN / CORD MACINTIRE.). [Votre guide quotid.]. (1991)-. French. 16.00Can$ per volume. Les Editions "Un Monde Different", Local 8, 3400 Boulevard Losch, St-Hubert Quebec J3Y 5T6. **DD** 133.3/35/05.

RU/0321-4117
**VYCHISLITELNAIA I PRIKLADNAIA MATEMATIKA.** Vol. 1 (1965)-. Monographic series. Russian. Price varies per volume. **(Subscription address:** Victor Kamkin, 4956 Boiling Brook Parkway, Rockville MD 20852.)
**Ind/Abst** Int. Aerosp. Abstr.; Zentralbl. Math. Ihre Grenzgeb.

NE/0165-2125
**WAVE MOTION.** [Wave motion]. Vol. 1, No. 1 (Jan. 1979)-. Academic Scholarly Publication. English. Eight times a year (2 vols.). Fl932.00. Elsevier Science Publishers BV, PO Box 211, 1000 AE Amsterdam Netherlands. **Tel** 011 31 20 5803642, FAX 011 31 20 5862696, telex 15682. **ED** J D Achenbach. **LC** QA927; .W37. **DD** 531/.1133. **CODEN** WAMOD9. **[CCC]. Pr Rev.** available on microfilm from University Microfilms International (UMI). Documents available from Article Express International, The Genuine Article, Ask*IEEE.
**Desc:** Devoted to cross fertilization of ideas, and to stimulating interaction between workers in various particular research areas in which wave propagation phenomena play a dominant role.
**Ind/Abst** Acoust. Abstr.; Bioeng. Abstr.; Curr. Contents Eng. Tech. Appl. Sci.; Curr. Contents Phys. Chem. Earth Sci.; Ei Page One; Energy Res. Abstr. (July 1980-); Eng. Index Annu. [Select. Cov.]; GeoRef; INSPEC (Jan. 1979-); Int. Aerosp. Abstr.; Math. Rev.; Ocean. Abstr.; Life Sci. Collect.; Res. Alert [Full Cov.]; Sci. Cit. Index; SCISEARCH; Zentralbl. Math. Ihre Grenzgeb.

UK/0959-7174
**WAVES IN RANDOM MEDIA.** **See** Physics.

AT/1033-3738
**WHAT RESEARCH SAYS TO THE SCIENCE AND MATHEMATICS TEACHER.** **See** Education-Teaching and Curriculum.

●US/1065-9358
**WHAT'S HAPPENING IN THE MATHEMATICAL SCIENCES.** [What's happen. math. sci.]. **Added/Corp** American Mathematical Society. Vol. 1 (1993)-. English. an. $8.00. American Mathematical Society, PO Box 6248, Providence RI 02940-6248. **Tel** (800)321-4267, (401)455-4000, FAX (401)331-3842, telex 797192. **(Subscription address:** American Mathematical Society, PO Box 5904, Boston MA 02206-5904.) **LC** QA1; .W53. **DD** 510. **[CCC].**
**Desc:** Surveys important recent developments in the mathematical sciences. Highlights the excitement and wonder of mathematics.

GW/0934-0505
**WISSENSCHAFTLICHE BEITRAEGE AUS EUROPAISCHEN HOCHSCHULEN REIHE 11 MATHEMATIK.** [Wiss. Beitr. eur. Hochsch., 11 Math.]. (1989)-. Monographic series. Multiple languages. ir.
**Ind/Abst** Zentralbl. Math. Ihre Grenzgeb.

CN/0315-1700
**WORLD DIRECTORY OF HISTORIANS OF MATHEMATICS.** 1st- Ed.; 1972-. Directory. English. ir. $7.00. Historia Mathematica, University of Toronto, Toronto Ontario M5S 1K7 Canada. **Tel** (416)978-5047. **ED** C E Scriba. **LC** QA30; .W59. **DD** 510/.9. **UDC** 51(09)(058.7)(100).
**Desc:** A list of historians of mathematics and their addresses.

II/0512-2740
**WORLD DIRECTORY OF MATHEMATICIANS / PUBLISHED UNDER THE AUSPICES OF THE INTERNATIONAL MATHEMATICAL UNION.** **Added/Corp** International Mathematical Union. Tata Institute of Fundamental Research. Tata Institute of Fundamental Research. School of Mathematics. (1958)-. Directory. English. ir (Published every 4 years). $40.00 (latest volume). American Mathematical Society, PO Box 6248, Providence RI 02940-6248. **Tel** (800)321-4267, (401)455-4000, FAX (401)331-3842, telex 797192. **(Subscription address:** American Mathematical Society, PO Box 5904, Boston MA 02206-5904.) **LC** QA30; .W6. **DD** 510/.25.

TU
**X BILINMEYEN.** (19??)-. Turkish. Twelve times a year. $12.00 Turkey; $13.00 Europe; $14.00 other. X Bilinmeyen, PK 40 Kiziltoprak, Istanbul Turkey.

US/0077-4103
**YEARBOOK - NATIONAL COUNCIL OF TEACHERS OF MATHEMATICS.** (YEARBOOK.). [Yearb. - Natl. Counc. Teach. Math.]. **Added/Corp** National Council of Teachers of Mathematics. (1926)-. Monographic series. English. an. Price varies per volume. National Council of Teachers of Mathematics, 1906 Association Drive, Reston VA 22091. **Tel** (703)620-9840, FAX (703)476-2970. **LC** QA1; .N3. **DD** 510. available on microfilm and microfiche from University Microfilms International (UMI).
**Desc:** An integrated collection of essays focusing on, and treating in depth, a current issue in mathematics education.
**Ind/Abst** Educ. Index.

CC/1000-0887
**YING YUNG SHU HSUEH HO LI HSUEH.** **Added/Corp** Chung-Ching Chiao Tung Hsueh Yuan. **VFOAT** Applied Mathematics and Mechanics. Vol. 1, No. 1 (May 1980)-. Periodical. Chinese (summaries and/or abstracts in English). mo. $54.12. **(Subscription address:** China International Book Trading Corporation, PO Box 399, Library Service Department, Beijing 100044 People's Republic of China.) **LC** TA349; .Y56. **DD** 620.1/01/51.

CC
**YINGYONG SHUXUE XUEBAO.** (YING YUNG SHU HSUEH HSUEN PAO / CHUNG-KUO SHU HSUEH HUI, YING YUNG SHU HSUEH HSUEH PAO PIEN CHI WEI YUAN HUI PIEN CHI.). [Yingyong shuxue xuebao]. **Added/Corp** Chung-kuo Shu Hsueh Hui. **VFOAT** Acta Mathematicae Applicatae Sinica. (Feb. 1978)-. Periodical. Chinese (summaries and/or abstracts in English). qt. $365.00. Chinese Mathematics Society, Science Press, 16 Donghuangchenggen North Street, Beijing 100707, People's Republic of China. **Tel** 011 86 1 4019821, FAX 011 86 4012180, telex 210147. **ED** Hua Luogeng. **LC** QA1; .Y515. **DD** 510/.5. **CODEN** YYSPDS. **Ad Acc. Circ:** 11,000. Documents available from Ask*IEEE.
**Desc:** Provides a forum for Chinese researchers and practitioners and intends to reflect the achievement of Chinese research, advance the development of applied mathematics and promote international academic exchanges.
**Ind/Abst** INSPEC (1978-); Int. Abstr. Oper. Res. [Select. Cov.]; Math. Rev.; Zentralbl. Math. Ihre Grenzgeb.

JA/0044-0523
**YOKOHAMA MATHEMATICAL JOURNAL, THE.** [Yokohama math. j.]. **Added/Corp** Yokohama Shiritsu Daigaku. Bunrigakubu. Sugakuka. Vol. 1 (May 1953)-. Periodical. English. sa. $106.00. Yokohama Shiritsu Daigaku Bunrigakubu Sugaku Katei, (Dept. of Mathematic, Faculty of Liberal Arts & Science, Yokohama City University), 22-2, Seto, Kanazawaku, Yokohamashi, Kanagawaken 236, Japan. **(Subscription address:** Kyowa Book Company Inc., 1 38 Kanda Jinbocho Chiyoda-ku, Tokyo 101 Japan.) **LC** QA1; .Y6.
**Ind/Abst** Math. Rev.; Stat. Theory Method Abstr. (1969, 1984); Zentralbl. Math. Ihre Grenzgeb.

CC
**YUN CHOU HSUEH TSA CHIH.** **VFOAT** Chinese Journal of Operations Research : OR; Chinese Journal of Operations Research. Vol. 1- (Oct. 1982)-. Periodical. Chinese. sa. RMBY0.53. Hsin Hua Shu Tien / Shang-Hai Fa Hsing So, Shanghai, People's Republic of China. **LC** T57.6.A1; Y85. **DD** 001.4/24/05. **UDC** 519.8.
**Ind/Abst** Int. Abstr. Oper. Res. [Full Cov.]; Math. Rev.; Zentralbl. Math. Ihre Grenzgeb.

PL/0044-1899
**ZASTOSOWANIA MATEMATYKI.** [Zastos. mat.]. Vol. 1 (1954)-. Polish (English and Russian). qt. **(Subscription address:** ARS Polona, PO Box 1001, 00068 Warsaw Poland.) **LC** QA1; .Z33. **UDC** 51. **CODEN** ZAMTAK.
**Ind/Abst** Int. Aerosp. Abstr.; Math. Rev.; Stat. Theory Method Abstr. (1959-1963, 1966-1969, 1972, 1976, 1978, 1979-1984, 1987); Zentralbl. Math. Ihre Grenzgeb.

YU
**ZBORNIK RADOVA.** **VFOAT** Recueil des Travaux. Periodical. English (French, German, Russian and Serbo-Croatian (Roman)). Matematicki Institut, Knez Mihailova 35, Postfach 367, 11001 Belgrad Yugoslavia. **Tel** (011)630-170. **LC** Q60; .S7228. ***Continues*** *Matematicki Institut.*
**Ind/Abst** Math. Rev.

GW
**ZDM. ZENTRALBLATT FUER DIDAKTIK DER MATHEMATIK.** **Added/Corp** Universitat Karlsruhe. Zentrum fuer Didaktik der Mathematik. **VFOAT** Zentralblatt fuer Didaktik der Mathematik. Vol. 1 (June 1969)-. German. Six times a year. DM314.00. Fachinformationszentrum Karlsruhe, Physics & Math, D 76344 Eggenstein Germany. **Tel** 011 49 7247 808149. **LC** QA11; .Z18.

GW/0232-2064
**ZEITSCHRIFT FUER ANALYSIS UND IHRE ANWENDUNGEN.** [Z. Anal. ihre Anwend.]. Vol. 1, No. 1 (1982)-. Periodical. German (English and Russian). Four times a year. DM360.00. Heldermann Verlag Berlin, Nassauische Str 26, D 10717 Berlin Germany. **Tel** 011 49 30 870446. **LC** QA300; .B42. **DD** 515/.05. **UDC** 517. Index available. **Bk Rev. Ad Acc. Circ:** 200. ***Continues*** *Beitrage zur Analysis, 0138-4872.*
**Ind/Abst** Math. Rev.; Zentralbl. Math. Ihre Grenzgeb.

GW/0044-2267
**ZEITSCHRIFT FUER ANGEWANDTE MATHEMATIK UND MECHANIK.** [Z. angew. Math. Mech.]. **Added/Corp** Gesellschaft fuer Angewandte Mathematik und Mechanik. Vortrage der Wissenschaftlichen Jahrestagung. **VFOAT** ZAMM; ZAMM, Applied Mathematics and Mechanics. Vol. 1 (Feb. 1921)-. Periodical. German. mo. $1095.00. Akademie-Verlag GmbH, Muehlenstrasse 33 34, D 13162 Berlin Germany. **Tel** 011 49 30 47889300, FAX 011 49 30 47889357. **(Subscription address:** VCH Publishers Inc., 303 Northwest 12th Avenue, Journals Department, Deerfield FL 33442.) **ED** G. Schmidt. **LC** TA3; .Z4. **DD** 510.5. **CODEN** ZAMMAX. **[CCC].** cum. index. **Pr Rev.** available on microfilm from University Microfilms International (UMI). Documents available from Article Express International, The Genuine Article, Ask*IEEE.
**Desc:** Publishes new results and review articles, the proceedings of the annual GAMM conferences, book reviews and information on applied mathematics.
**Ind/Abst** Bioeng. Abstr.; Compumath Citation Index [Full Cov.]; Curr. Contents Eng. Tech. Appl. Sci.; Ei Page One; Eng. Index Annu.; GeoRef; INSPEC (Oct. 1970-); Int. Aerosp. Abstr.; Math. Rev.; Res. Alert [Full Cov.]; Stat. Theory Method Abstr. (1959-1963, 1966-1977, 1979, 1982, 1984, 1986); Zentralbl. Math. Ihre Grenzgeb.

SZ/0044-2275
**ZEITSCHRIFT FUER ANGEWANDTE MATHEMATIK UND PHYSIK : ZAMP.** [Z. angew. Math. Phys.]. **VFOAT** ZAMP. Vol. 1, No. 1 (1950)-. Periodical. English (French and German). bm. 865.60F Switzerland; 881.40F other. Birkhaeuser Verlag Ag, Klosterberg 23, PO Box 133, CH-4010 Basel Switzerland. **Tel** 011 41 61 2717400, FAX 011 41 0 61 2717666, telex 963475 birk ch. **(Subscription address:** Birkhauser Verlag AG, PO Box 151, CH 4106 Therwil Switzerland; Phone: 011 41 61 7217740) **ED** U. Kirchgraber, M. Renardy, I. L. Ryhming, M. Sayir. **LC** QA1; .Z37. **DD** 510/.5. **CODEN** ZAMPDB. **[CCC].** Index Available, published separately, free-automatically sent. **Pr Rev.** available on microfilm from University Microfilms International (UMI). Documents available from The Genuine Article, Ask*IEEE, CASDDS.
**Desc:** Publishes papers in fluid mechanics, mechanics of solids and differential equations/applied mathematics. Also publishes original work in neighbouring domains. Includes a book review section and information on activities, such as upcoming symposia, meetings, and special courses, which are of interest to readers.
**Ind/Abst** ACM Guide Comput. Lit.; Appl. Mech. Rev.; Chem. Abstr.; Compumath Citation Index [Full Cov.]; Comput. Rev.; Curr. Contents Phys. Chem. Earth Sci.; Ei Page One; Energy Res. Abstr.; INSPEC (1968-); Int. Aerosp. Abstr.; Math. Rev.; Met. Abstr.; Pollut. Abstr. Indexes; Res. Alert [Full Cov.]; Sci. Cit. Index; SCISEARCH; Stat. Theory Method Abstr. (1959-1963); Zentralbl. Math. Ihre Grenzgeb.

GW/0044-3050
**ZEITSCHRIFT FUER MATHEMATISCHE LOGIK UND GRUNDLAGEN DER MATHEMATIK.** ***Title Change.*** [Z. math. Logik Grundl. Math.]. **VFOAT** ZML. (1955)-(1992). Periodical. German (French and Russian). bm. Verlag CF Mueller, Verlags GS, D-69018 Heidelberg Germany. **Tel** 011 49 6221 4890. **ED** G Asser and K Schroter. **LC** QA1; .Z38. **DD** 510/.5. **CODEN** ZMLGAQ. cum. index. Documents available from The Genuine Article, Ask*IEEE. ***Continued by*** *Mathematical Logic Quarterly, 0942-5616.*
**Ind/Abst** Compumath Citation Index [Full Cov.]; Comput. Rev.; INSPEC (1968-); Math. Rev.; Philos. Index; Res. Alert [Full Cov.]; Stat. Theory Method Abstr. (1967, 1969, 1971, 1973, 1978, 1984).

AU/0084-537X
**ZEITSCHRIFT FUER NATIONALOKONOMIE. SUPPLEMENTUM.** **VFOAT** Journal of Economics. Supplementum. (1971)-. Monographic series. German. ir. Price varies per volume. Springer-Verlag Wien, Sachsenplatz 4 6, PO Box 89, A-1201 Vienna Austria. **Tel** 011 43 1 3302415. **(Subscription address:** Springer Verlag New York Inc. / for North America, 44 Hartz Way, Secaucus NJ 07096.**)** **ED** D Bos. available on microfilm from University Microfilms International (UMI).
**Desc:** Specializes in mathematical economic theory. It also centers on microeconomic theory but also publishes papers on macroeconomic topics.

GW/0044-4235
**ZENTRALBLATT FUER MATHEMATIK UND IHRE GRENZGEBIETE. See** Mathematics-Abstracting, Bibliographies and Statistics.

PL/0072-470X
**ZESZYTY NAUKOWE - POLITECHNIKA SLASKA. MATEMATYKA. FIZYKA.** (ZESZYTY NAUKOWE POLITECHNIKI SLASKIEJ. MATEMATYKA-FIZYKA.). [Zesz. nauk. - Politech. Sl., Mat. Fiz.]. **Added/Corp** Politechnika Slaska im. W. Pstrowskiego. **VFOAT** Matematyka Fizyuka. (1961)-. Academic Scholarly Publication. Polish (summaries and/or abstracts in English, French, German and Russian). ir. **LC** QA1; .G562. **CODEN** PSMFBT. Documents available from CASDDS.
**Ind/Abst** Chem. Abstr.; Int. Aerosp. Abstr.; Math. Rev.

PL
**ZESZYTY NAUKOWE POLITECHNIKI SLASKIEJ. MATEMATYKA-FIZYKA GEOCHRONOMETRIA. VFOAT** Matematyka-Fizyka. Geochronometria; Matematyka Fizyka. Geochronometria. (1986)-. Periodical. Polish. ir. **LC** QA1; .G562 subser.
**Ind/Abst** Art Archaeol. Tech. Abstr.

GW/0340-9422
**ZOR, ZEITSCHRIFT FUER OPERATIONS RESEARCH : METHODS AND MODELS OF OPERATIONS RESEARCH. VFOAT** Zeitschrift fuer Operations Research; Methods and Models of Operations Research. Vol. 32, Issue 1 (1988)-. Periodical. English. Six times a year. DM290.00 Germany; DM580.00 others. Physica-Verlag GmbH & Company, Postfach 105280, D-69042 Heidelberg Germany. **Tel** 06221 487-492, FAX 06221 487177 und 487366, telex 461723 sphdb-d. **(Subscription address:** Springer Verlag New York Inc. / for North America, 44 Hartz Way, Secaucus NJ 07096.**)** **ED** U. Rieder, ULM. **CODEN** ZMRREP. **[CCC].** Documents available from Ask*IEEE. ***Formed by the union of*** *Zeitschrift fuer Operations Research. Serie A: Theorie* ***and*** *Zeitschrift fuer Operations Research. Serie B: Praxis.*
**Desc:** Areas of mathematical methods and applications in economics, business administration, finance, and engineering are covered.
**Ind/Abst** INSPEC; Int. Abstr. Oper. Res.; Math. Rev.

RU/0044-4669
**ZURNAL VYCISLITELNOJ MATEMATIKI I MATEMATICESKOJ FIZIKI. See** Physics.

## ABSTRACTING, BIBLIOGRAPHIES AND STATISTICS

II
**ALIGARH JOURNAL OF STATISTICS, THE.** **Added/Corp** Aligarh Muslim University. Dept. of Statistics. **VFOAT** AJS; A.J.S. (198?)-. English. an. $20.00. Aligarh Muslim University Department of Statistics, AMU Aligarh 202001 India. **(Subscription address:** Prints India, 11 Darya Ganj, New Delhi, 110002 India, (Phone: 011 91 11 3268645)**)** **LC** QA276.A1; A42. **DD** 519.5.
**Ind/Abst** Biostatistica (19??-); Curr. Index Stat.; Zentralbl. Math. Ihre Grenzgeb.

JA/0020-3157
**ANNALS OF THE INSTITUTE OF STATISTICAL MATHEMATICS.** [Ann. Inst. Stat. Math.]. **Main/Corp** Tokei Suri Kenkyujo (Tokyo, Japan). **VFOAT** AISM. Vol. 1, No. 1 (Aug. 1949)-. Statistical Publication. English. qt. $668.00. Kluwer Academic Publishers, Postbus 322, 3300 AH Dordrecht, The Netherlands. **Tel** 011 (31) 78 524400, FAX 011 31 78 183273, telex 20083. **ED** H. Akaike, S. Konishi, and G. Kitagawa. **LC** QA276; .T6. **DD** 519.905. **CODEN** AISXAD. **[CCC].** cum. index. **Pr Rev. Acid Free.** Documents available from The Genuine Article.
**Desc:** Provides an international forum for the communication of ideas between research statisticians with the goal of advancing human knowledge through the development of the science and technology of statistics. One of the prime objectives is the handling of information that is subject to uncertainty.
**Ind/Abst** Compumath Citation Index [Full Cov.]; Curr. Index Stat.; Int. Aerosp. Abstr.; Math. Rev.; Res. Alert [Full Cov.]; SCISEARCH; SEA Abstr.; Stat. Theory Method Abstr. (1959-1963, 1966-1984, 1986-1987); Zentralbl. Math. Ihre Grenzgeb.

FR
**BULLETIN SIGNALETIQUE. 110.** **Added/Corp** Centre National de la Recherche Scientifique (France) Centre de Documentation Scientifique et Technique. (198?)-. Bulletin. French. mo. 420.00F. Centre National de la Recherche Scientifique, Informascience, 26 rue Boyer, 75971 Paris France. **Tel** 61.41.11.05, telex CNRSDOC 220880 F. **LC** Z6653; .B82; QA1. **DD** 016.51. ***Continues*** *Bulletin Signaletique. 110: Informatique, Automatique, Recherche Operationnelle, Gestion.* ***Continued in part by*** *Pascal Explore. E33, Informatique, 0761-2052; Pascal Explore. E34, Robotique et Automatisatoin des Procesus Industriels, 0761-2060.*

US/0730-6199
**COMPUMATH CITATION INDEX : CMCI.** [CompuMath cit. index]. **Added/Corp** Institute for Scientific Information. **VFOAT** CMCI; C.M.C.I. (1981)-. Abstracting/Indexing Service. English. sa. $2135.00. Institute for Scientific Information, 3501 Market Street, Philadelphia PA 19104. **Tel** (215)386-0100, (800)523-1850, FAX (215)386-6362, telex 84-5305. **(Subscription address:** Institute for Scientific Information, PO Box 71416, Chicago IL 60694.**)** **LC** Z6653; .C84; QA36. **DD** 016.51. cum. index. available on an online database (as Computer & Mathematics Search).
**Desc:** Presents complete bibliographic data and cited references on items contained in over 460 computer science and mathematics journals. Items from over 6,500 of science, social sciences and arts and humanities journals.
**Ind/Abst** Math. Rev.

US/0364-1228
**CURRENT INDEX TO STATISTICS.** (CURRENT INDEX TO STATISTICS, APPLICATIONS, METHODS, AND THEORY.). [Curr. index stat.]. **Added/Corp** American Statistical Association. Institute of Mathematical Statistics. Vol. 1 (1975)-. Abstracting/Indexing Service. English. an. $75.00. Institute of Mathematical Statistics, 3401 Investment Boulevard, Suite 7, Hayward CA 94545-3819. **Tel** (510)783-8141, FAX (510)783-4131. **ED** Richard Burdick. **LC** QA276.A1; C87. **DD** 016.5195/05. **[CCC]. Circ:** 2,000 (ctrl). available on diskette; available on an online database from MATHSCI; and AMS Press, Inc.
**Desc:** Index to the statistical literature of the world. Coverage of 105 core journals in statistics, probability and related fields. Selected articles indexed from other journals. Subject index lists articles alphabetically according to each important word in their titles, and according to carefully selected key words not appearing in titles. Author index lists each article under the name of the author.
**Ind/Abst** Math. Rev.

US/0361-4794
**CURRENT MATHEMATICAL PUBLICATIONS.** [Curr. math. publ.]. **Added/Corp** American Mathematical Society. Vol. 7 (Jan. 10, 1975)-. Abstracting/Indexing Service. English. ir (every three weeks). $394.00. American Mathematical Society, PO Box 6248, Providence RI 02940-6248. **Tel** (800)321-4267, (401)455-4000, FAX (401)331-3842, telex 797192. **(Subscription address:** American Mathematical Society, PO Box 5904, Boston MA 02206-5904.**)** **ED** Robert G. Bartle. **LC** Z6653; .C85; QA36. **DD** 016.51. **CODEN** CUMPBW. **[CCC].** Index available. cum. index. **Circ:** 1,600. available on CD-ROM (MathDisc) from SilverPlatter (US). ***Continues*** *Contents of Contemporary Mathematical Journals and New Publications.*
**Desc:** Subject index of recent and forthcoming mathematical publications that have been classified by the editors of Mathematical Reviews.

II/0379-3419
**GUJARAT STATISTICAL REVIEW.** [Gujarat stat. rev.]. **Added/Corp** Gujarat Statistical Association. (1974)-. Statistical Publication. English. sa. $10.00. I D Patel, Department of Statistics, Gujarat University, Ahmedabad 380009 India. **Tel** 404308. **(Subscription address:** Prints India, 11 Darya Ganj, New Delhi, 110002 India, (Phone: 011 91 11 3268645)**)** **ED** M Sreehari. **LC** QA276.A1; G85. **DD** 519.5/05. **CODEN** GSTRD3. Index available. **Bk Rev. Circ:** 400.
**Ind/Abst** Math. Rev.; Stat. Theory Method Abstr. (1984, 1987); Zentralbl. Math. Ihre Grenzgeb.

US/0025-5629
**MATHEMATICAL REVIEWS.** [Math. rev.]. **Added/Corp** American Mathematical Society. Mathematical Association of America. Vol. 1, No. 1 (Jan. 1940)-. Abstracting/Indexing Service. English. Twelve times a year. $329.00 (print), $4696.00 (annual data access fee). American Mathematical Society, PO Box 6248, Providence RI 02940-6248. **Tel** (800)321-4267, (401)455-4000, FAX (401)331-3842, telex 797192. **(Subscription address:** American Mathematical Society, PO Box 5904, Boston MA 02206-5904.**)** **ED** J. E. Kister. **LC** QA1; .M76. **DD** 510/.5. **NLM** Z 6653 M426. **CODEN** MAREAR. **[CCC].** Index available (author and subject). cum. index. **Bk Rev. Ad Acc. Circ:** 1,900. available on microfilm and microfiche from University Microfilms International (UMI); available on CD-ROM; available on an online database.
**Desc:** Provides reviews of the world's current mathematical literature, classified according to the Mathematics Subject Classification.

US
**MATHEMATICS AND STATISTICS RESEARCH DEPARTMENT PROGRESS REPORT.** **Main/Corp** Oak Ridge National Laboratory. Mathematics and Statistics Research Dept. **VFOAT** Progress Report - Mathematics and Statistics Research Department. English. US Department of Energy Office of Energy Technology, 1000 Independence Avenue SW, Washington DC 20585.

PL/0208-4147
**PROBABILITY AND MATHEMATICAL STATISTICS.** (PROBABILITY AND MATHEMATICAL STATISTICS / INSTITUTE OF MATHEMATICS, POLISH ACADEMY OF SCIENCES.). [Probab. math. stat.]. **Added/Corp** Instytut Matematyczny (Polska Akademia Nauk). Vol. 1, No. 1 (1980)-. Periodical. English (French, German and Russian). ir. Price varies. Institute of Mathematics / Poland, Ul Kopernika 18, 51-617 Wroclaw Poland. **Tel** 21-15-00. **(Subscription address:** ARS Polona, PO Box 1001, 00068 Warsaw Poland.**)** **ED** Kazimeierz Urbanik. **LC** QA273.A1; P76. **DD** 519.2/05. **Ad Acc. Circ:** 1,000.
**Desc:** Publishes original contributions to the theory of probability and mathematical statistics (e.g. random measures, testing of hypotheses, decision theory).
**Ind/Abst** Math. Rev.; Stat. Theory Method Abstr. (1982, 1986-1987); Zentralbl. Math. Ihre Grenzgeb.

US/0733-5830
**PROCEEDINGS OF THE SECTION ON SURVEY RESEARCH METHODS.** [Proc. Sect. Surv. Res. Methods]. **Main/Corp** American Statistical Association. Survey Research Methods Section. (19??)-. Proceedings. English. $81.50. American Statistical Association, 1429 Duke Street, Alexandria VA 22314. **Tel** (703)684-1221, (202)393-3253, FAX (703)684-2037 (orders). **LC** QA276.A1; A47a. **DD** 001.4/22.
**Ind/Abst** Curr. Index Stat. (199?-).

US/1050-6977
**PROGRESS IN PROBABILITY.** [Prog. probab.]. (19??)-. Monographic series. English. ir. Price varies per volume. Birkhauser Boston, Inc., c/o Springer Publishers New York Inc., Customer Service Department, 333 Meadowlands Parkway, Secaucus NJ 07096-2491. **Tel** (201)348-4033, (800)777-4643. **DD** 519. ***Continues*** *Progress in Probability and Statistics, 0749-9175.*
**Ind/Abst** Math. Rev.; Zentralbl. Math. Ihre Grenzgeb.

US/0094-8837
**SELECTED TABLES IN MATHEMATICAL STATISTICS.** **Added/Corp** Institute of Mathematical Statistics. American Mathematical Society. Vol. 1 (1973)-. Monographic series. English. ir. Price varies per volume. American Mathematical Society, PO Box 6248, Providence RI 02940-6248. **Tel** (800)321-4267, (401)455-4000, FAX (401)331-3842, telex 797192. **(Subscription address:** American Mathematical Society, PO Box 5904, Boston MA 02206-5904.**)** **LC** QA276.25; .S43. **DD** 519.5/021/2. **[CCC].**
**Ind/Abst** Stat. Theory Method Abstr. (1982); Zentralbl. Math. Ihre Grenzgeb.

SA/0038-271X
**SOUTH AFRICAN STATISTICAL JOURNAL.** (SOUTH AFRICAN STATISTICAL JOURNAL. SUID-AFRIKAANSE STATISTIESE TYDSKRIF.). [S. Afr. stat. j.]. **Added/Corp** South African Statistical Association. **VFOAT** Suid-Afrikaanse Statistiese Tydskrif. Vol. 1 (1967)-. Statistical Publication. English (Afrikaans). Twice a year (June & Dec.). R50.00. South African Statistical Association, PO Box 27321, Sunnyside 0132 South Africa. **Tel** 021 9380332. **ED** Dr. J. S. Maritz (editor's address: Department of Statistics, University of Sklbunbosch, Sklbunbosch 7600 South Africa, phone: 021 8083244). **LC** QA276.A1; S65. **NLM** HA 1 S719. **CODEN** SASSB5. Each issue contains an index to its own contents (no volume index)--loose. **Pr**

**Rev. Circ:** 700 (ctrl). Documents available from The Genuine Article.
**Desc:** Research and applications of statistics and the usage of data.
**Ind/Abst** Biostatistica; Compumath Citation Index [Full Cov.]; Curr. Index Stat.; Math. Rev.; Oper. Res./Manag. Sci.; Qual. Control Appl. Stat.; Res. Alert [Full Cov.]; Soc. Sci. Cit. Index [Select. Cov.]; Stat. Theory Method Abstr. (1967-1984, 1986-1987); Zentralbl. Math. Ihre Grenzgeb.

CN/1017-0405
**STATISTICA SINICA.** **See** Mathematics.

GW/0233-1888
**STATISTICS (BERLIN, DDR).** (STATISTICS.). [Statistics (Berl. DDR)]. **Added/Corp** Akademie der Wissenschaften der DDR. Zentralinstitut fuer Mathematik und Mechanik. Institut fuer Mathematik (Akademie der Wissenschaften der DDR). Vol. 8 (1977)-. Periodical. English (summaries and/or abstracts in German and Russian). qt. $330.00 (academic institutions), $515.00 (corporate institutions). Gordon & Breach Science Publishers, PO Box 90, Reading RG1 8JL England. **Tel** 011 44 734 560080, FAX 011 44 734 568211. **(Subscription address:** International Publishers Distributor at one of the following addresses: 820 Town Center Drive, Langhorne, PA 19047; or PO Box 90, Reading Berkshire RG1 8JL UK; or Kent Ridge PO Box 1180, Singapore 9111, Republic of Singapore**) ED** Olaf Bunke. **LC** QA276.A1; S74. **DD** 519.5/05. **CODEN** MOSSD5. **[CCC].** Index available. cum. index. **Bk Rev. Ad Acc. Circ:** 900. Documents available from Ask*IEEE. ***Continues in part*** *Mathematische Operationsforschung und Statistik, 0047-6277.*
**Ind/Abst** Curr. Index Stat.; Energy Res. Abstr. (March 1982-); INSPEC (1977-); Math. Rev.; Stat. Theory Method Abstr. (1987).

US
**UMAP MODULES.** **Added/Corp** Consortium for Mathematics and Its Applications (U.S.) Undergraduate Mathematics and Its Applications Project (U.S.). **VFOAT** UMAP Modules / Tools for Teaching / Annual Collection. (1979)-. English. an. $120.00 US; $145.00 others Comes with Consortium for Mathematics and its Applications membership. COMAP Inc, 57 Bedford Street, Suite 210, Lexington MA 02173. **Tel** (617)862-7878, FAX (617)863-1202. **LC** QA11.A1; U5. **DD** 510/.7.

GW/0044-4235
**ZENTRALBLATT FUER MATHEMATIK UND IHRE GRENZGEBIETE.** [Zentralbl. Math. ihre Grenzgeb.]. **Added/Corp** Akademie der Wissenschaften der DDR. Heidelberger Akademie der Wissenschaften. Deutsche Akademie der Wissenschaften zu Berlin. **VFOAT** Mathematics Abstracts. Vol. 1 (April 14, 1931)-. Abstracting/Indexing Service. German. Thirty-two times a year. DM7900.00. Springer-Verlag GmbH & Company KG Heidelberger Platz 3, D 14197 Berlin Germany. **Tel** 011 49 30 8207223, FAX 011 49 30 8214091, telex 183 319 SPBLN D. **(Subscription address:** Springer Verlag New York Inc. / for North America, 44 Hartz Way, Secaucus NJ 07096.**) ED** B Wegner. **LC** QA1; .Z4. **DD** 016.51. **[CCC].** cum. index. available on CD-ROM (CompactMATH); available in microform from University Microfilms International (UMI); available on an online database from STN International (Math) Database. ***Superseded in part by*** *Zentralblatt fuer Mechanik.*
**Desc:** Draws on a worldwide pool of more than 6,000 distinguished reviewers.
**Ind/Abst** Energy Res. Abstr. (Mar. 1982-); Math. Rev.

# MEDICAL SCIENCE AND TECHNOLOGY

CN/1183-6024
**2ND TIER, THE.** [2nd tier]. **Added/Corp** Federation of Medical Specialists of Quebec. **VFOAT** Second Tier. Vol. 11, No. 2 (Apr. 1991)-. Periodical. English. Free to members. FMSQ, Porte 3000 2 Complexe Desjardins, CP 216 Succursale Desjardins, Montreal Quebec H5B 1G8 Canada. **DD** 610/.6/0714. ***Continues*** *FMSQ Information. English., 0849-1054.*

US
**483 VALIDATION MONITOR FOR STERILE, NON-STERILE AND MEDICAL DEVICES.** Began with Vol. 2nd-1 (Jan. 15, 1981). Periodical. English. bw. Bureau of Pharmaceutical Research Inc, 904 Stoneham Drive, Williston Heights, West Chester PA 19382-6670. ***Formed by the union of*** *483 Validation Monitor for Sterile Products; 483 Validation Monitor for Non-Sterile Products* ***and*** *483 Validation Monitor for Medical Devices.*

US/1057-9575
**A & W BASICS IN MEDICINE SERIES.** [A W basics med. ser.]. **VFOAT** A and W Basics in Medicine Series; Basics in Medicine Series. (1991)-. Monographic series. English. sa. $29.95 (single issue). Libra & Gemini Publications, 10703 Paulwood, Houston TX 77071. **DD** 610.

FR/0241-5089
**A. H. AUMONERIES DES HOPITAUX.** **VFOAT** Aumonerie Hopitaux. (1979)-. Periodical. French. Four times a year. 101.18F France; 135.00F France. Aumonerie Nationale Hopitaux, 106 rue du Bac, 75341 Paris Cedex 07 France. **Tel** 011 33 1 43201414. **UDC** 282. ***Continues*** *Aumoniers d'Hopitaux, 0241-5097.*

CN/1183-2096
**A PROPOS (MONTREAL).** (A PROPOS : BULLETIN DE L'ASSOCIATION MEDICALE DU QUEBEC). [A propos]. **Added/Corp** Quebec Medical Association. (1991)-. Bulletin. English (French). qt. Free to members. Quebec Medical Association, 610-1010 Sherbrooke Street West, Montreal Quebec H3A 2R7 Canada. **DD** 610/.9714/05.

US/0092-0371
**AAMC CURRICULUM DIRECTORY.** **See** Education-Higher Education.

US/0360-7437
**AAMC DIRECTORY OF AMERICAN MEDICAL EDUCATION.** **See** Education-Higher Education.

US
**AAMC REPORTER.** **Added/Corp** Association of American Medical Colleges. **VFOAT** Reporter. Vol. 1, No. 1 (Sept. 1991)-. Periodical. English. mo. ***Continues*** *AAMC Weekly Report.*

US/0883-4172
**AAMI MEMBERSHIP DIRECTORY.** [AAMI membsh. dir.]. **Main/Corp** Association for the Advancement of Medical Instrumentation. **VAT** Association for the Advancement of Medical Instrumentation Membership Directory. (198?)-. English. an. $100.00 (two years); $135.00 (individuals), $615.00 (institutions) Comes with Society Biomedical Equipment Technicians & Association for Advancement of Medical Instrumentation membership. Association for the Advancement of Medical Instrumentation, 3330 Washington Boulevard, Suite 400, Arlington VA 22209. **Tel** (703)525-4890, (800)332-2264, FAX (703)276-0793. **ED** Nancy Johnson. **LC** R856.A4; A86a. **DD** 610/.28. **Circ:** 5,000. ***Continues*** *Association for the Advancement of Medical Instrumentation. Membership Directory, 0364-5150.*

US/0739-0270
**AAMI NEWS.** (AAMI NEWS : THE OFFICIAL NEWSLETTER OF THE ASSOCIATION FOR THE ADVANCEMENT OF MEDICAL INSTRUMENTATION.). [AAMI news]. **Added/Corp** Association for the Advancement of Medical Instrumentation. **VAT** Association for the Advancement of Medical Instrumentation News. (19??)-. Periodical. English. Twelve times a year. $80.00. Association for the Advancement of Medical Instrumentation, 3330 Washington Boulevard, Suite 400, Arlington VA 22209. **Tel** (703)525-4890, (800)332-2264, FAX (703)276-0793. **ED** Michael Miller. **Ad Acc. Circ:** 5,000 (ctrl).
**Desc:** To keep AAMI members informed about association policies, programs and meetings; regulatory and legislative actions; and proposed and final publications of the standards program.
**Ind/Abst** Health Devices Alerts.

GW/0002-2993
**ABHANDLUNGEN DER MATHEMATISCH-NATURWISSENSCHAFTLICHEN KLASSE - AKADEMIE DER WISSENSCHAFTEN UND DER LITERATUR.** **See** Science and Technology.

US/0883-2986
**ABMS DIRECTORY OF CERTIFIED PHYSICAL MEDICINE AND REHABILITATION PHYSICIANS.** [ABMS dir. certif. phys. med. rehabil. physiatr.]. **Added/Corp** American Board of Medical Specialties. American Board of Physical Medicine & Rehabilitation. **VFOAT** Directory of Certified Physical Medicine and Rehabilitation Physiatrists. **VAT** American Board of Medical Specialties Directory of Certified Physical Medicine and Rehabilitation Physiatrists. (1985)-. English. be. $24.95. American Board of Medical Specialties, 1 Rotary Center, Suite 805, Evanston IL 60201. **Tel** (708)491-9091. **LC** RM697.U5; A25. **DD** 615.8/2/02573. **NLM** WB 22.1; A1523.

US/0883-2978
**ABMS DIRECTORY OF CERTIFIED PREVENTIVE MEDICINE PHYSICIANS.** [ABMS dir. certif. prev. med. physicians]. **Added/Corp** American Board of Medical Specialties. American Board of Preventive Medicine. **VFOAT** Directory of Certified Preventive Medicine Physicians. **VAT** American Board of Medical Specialties Directory of Certified Preventive Medicine Physicians. (1985)-. English. be. $24.95. American Board of Medical Specialties, 1 Rotary Center, Suite 805, Evanston IL 60201. **Tel** (708)491-9091. **LC** RA423.5; .A25. **DD** 610/.25/73. **NLM** WA 22.1; A1523.

●US
**ABMS RECORD.** **Added/Corp** American Board of Medical Specialties. **VAT** American Board of Medical Specialties Record. Vol. 1, No. 1 (Mar. 1992)-. Periodical. English. bm. American Board of Medical Specialties, 1 Rotary Center, Suite 805, Evanston IL 60201. **Tel** (708)491-9091. ***Continues*** *ABMS Record.*

US/0001-3331
**ABRIDGED INDEX MEDICUS.** **See** Medical Science and Technology-Abstracting, Bibliographies and Statistics.

BU/0001-3536
**ABSTRACTS OF BULGARIAN SCIENTIFIC MEDICAL LITERATURE.** **Added/Corp** Tsentur za Nauchna Informatsiia po Meditsina i Zdaveopazvane (Bulgaria). Vol. 11, No. 1 (Jan.-Mar. 1968)-. Periodical. English (Russian). qt (4 issues). DM122.00. Medical and Public Health Scientific Information Centre, 1 Sveti Georgi Sofojski Street, 1431 Sofia Bulgaria. **(Subscription address:** Kubon & Sagner, ABT Zeitschriftenimport, D 80328 Munich Germany.**) ED** Sv Todorov. **NLM** ZW 1 A165. **Circ:** 515 (ctrl). ***Continues*** *Abstracts of Bulgarian Scientific Literature. Medicine.*
**Desc:** Abstract bulletin on Bulgarian scientific and medical literature. Covers biochemistry, microbiology, physiology, internal medicine, gynecology, obstetrics, dentistry, dermatology, neurology, ophthalmology, otorhinolaryngology, pediatrics, psychiatry, public health, radiology, surgery and toxicology.
**Ind/Abst** Protozoolog. Abstr.

HK/1010-0091
**ABSTRACTS OF CHINESE MEDICINES : ACME.** [Abstr. Chin. med.]. **Added/Corp** Chinese University of Hong Kong. Chinese Medicinal Material Research Centre. **VFOAT** ACME. Vol. 1, No. 1 (Oct. 1986)-. Periodical. English (Portuguese; translations available in Chinese). qt. HK$180.00. Chinese Medicinal Material Research Centre, The Chinese University of Hong Kong, Shatin, N.T., Hong Kong. **Tel** (852)6096140, FAX (852)6035248. **ED** Hson-Mou CHANG, PhD. **NLM** ZWB 50.1; A164.
**Desc:** Key to medical and scientific journals published in China, including Taiwan, related with Chinese herbal medicines for the information of worldwide researchers in medicine and pharmacology. Translates current significant Chinese papers into English abstracts and titles from more than 150 Chinese medical and scientific journals, which are not readily available outside China; information stored in database, retrievable using English keywords, and photocopy of original articles in Chinese, are also available to ACME subscribers on a charge basis.
**Ind/Abst** NAPRALERT.

US/1042-4423
**ABSTRACTS OF CLINICAL CARE GUIDELINES.** **See** Medical Science and Technology-Abstracting, Bibliographies and Statistics.

US/0363-3837
**ABSTRACTS OF CONTRIBUTED PAPERS - MEDICAL CARE SECTION.** (ABSTRACTS OF CONTRIBUTED PAPERS - MEDICAL CARE SECTION, AMERICAN PUBLIC HEALTH ASSOCIATION.). 97th- 1969-. Periodical. English. an. US Department of Health and Human Services National Institutes of Health, 9000 Rockville Pike, Bethesda MD 20892. **Tel** (301)496-9291, FAX (301)496-2443. **NLM** W1 AB879T.
**Desc:** Consists of abstracts of papers from the 97th annual meeting of the Medical Care Section, American Public Health Association.

US/0044-7609
**ACA JOURNAL OF CHIROPRACTIC, THE.** ***Title Change.*** **Main/Corp** American Chiropractic Association. **VAT** American Chiropractic Association Journal of Chiropractic. (19??)-(1992). Periodical. English. mo. Foundation for Chiropractic Education and Research, 1701 Clarendon Boulevard, Arlington VA 22209. **Tel** (703)276-7445, (800)637-6244. **NLM** W1 A113K. available on microfilm and microfiche from University Microfilms International (UMI). ***Continued by*** *Journal of Chiropractic, 0744-9984.*

US/1040-2446
**ACADEMIC MEDICINE.** **See** Education-Higher Education.

●US
**ACCREDITATION MANUAL FOR AMBULATORY HEALTH CARE : AMAHC.** **Added/Corp** Joint Commission on Accreditation of Healthcare Organizations. **VFOAT** AMAHC. (1992)-. English. Joint Commission on Accreditation of Hospitals, 1 Renaissance Boulevard, Headquarters Center, Oakbrook Terrace IL 60181. **Tel** (708)916-5800. ***Continues*** *Ambulatory Health Care Standards Manual, 0898-7351.*

US/1043-6251
**ACP HEALTH LIBRARY.** ***Ceased.*** [ACP health libr.]. **Added/Corp** American College of Physicians. **VAT** American College of Physicians Health Library.

(1990)-(199?). Periodical. English. bm. American College of Physicians, 6th Street and Race Street, Independence Mall West, Philadelphia PA 19106-1572. **Tel** (215)351-2600, (800)523-1546. **DD** 362.

US/1044-4211
**ACPM NEWS.** (ACPM NEWS : THE NEWSLETTER OF THE AMERICAN COLLEGE OF PREVENTIVE MEDICINE.). [ACPM news]. **Added/Corp** American College of Preventive Medicine. **VAT** American College of Preventive Medicine News. (19??)-. Periodical. English. an. $25.00. American College of Preventive Medicine, 1015 15th Street Northwest, Suite 403, Washington DC 20005. **Tel** (202)789-0003. **DD** 610. ***Continues*** *Preventive Medicine Newsletter, 0199-2481.*
**Desc:** Features reports from Officers and the Board of Regents, updates on College committee and task force activities, news of important legislative matters affecting preventive medicine, details of College actions before Congress and other forums, continuing education news, and special project reports.

FR/0075-4463
**ACQUISITIONS MEDICALES RECENTES.** (1916)-. French. an.
**Ind/Abst** Health Plan. Adminis.

BE
**ACTA BELGICA HISTORIAE MEDICINAE : OFFICIAL JOURNAL OF THE BELGIAN ASSOCIATION FOR THE HISTORY OF MEDICINE.** **VFOAT** ABHM. Vol. 1, No. 1 (April 1988)-. Periodical. French (English and Dutch). Four times a year (4 issues). 2000F. Erasmus Hospital - Rheumatology, 808 Lennik Street, 1070 Brussels Belgium. **Tel** 011 32 02 5553431. **ED** Thierry Appelboom. **NLM** W1; AC754N. **Bk Rev**, (Qty: 100). **Ad Acc. Pr Rev. Circ:** 1,000.
**Desc:** History of medicine.

IT/0392-4203
**ACTA BIO-MEDICA DE L'ATENEO PARMENSE.** (ACTA BIO-MEDICA DE L'ATENEO PARMENSE : ORGANO DELLA SOCIETA DI MEDICINA E SCIENZE NATURALI DI PARMA.). [Acta bio-med. Ateneo Parm.]. **Added/Corp** Societ·a di Medicina e Scienze Naturali di Parma. (1981)-. Academic Scholarly Publication. Italian (English; summaries and/or abstracts in English). bm. L5000. Soc Medicina Scienze Naturale, Via Gramsci 14, 43100 Parma Italy. **Tel** 011 39 521 290370. **ED** Paolo Bobbio and Fulvio Allegra. **NLM** W1 AC7631P. **CODEN** ABPADJ. cum. index. **Bk Rev. Circ:** 500 (ctrl). Documents available from BIOSIS Document Express, CASDDS. ***Continues*** *Ateneo Parmense. Acta Bio-Medica, 0004-6351.*
**Ind/Abst** Biol. Abstr.; Chem. Abstr.; EMBASE; Health Plan. Adminis.; Index Med.

YU/0350-5901
**ACTA BIOLOGIAE ET MEDICINAE EXPERIMENTALIS.** **See** Biology.

DK/0105-6255
**ACTA CAMPANOLOGICA.** [Acta campanol.]. (1966)-. Periodical. Multiple languages. Four times a year (Feb., May, Sept., Nov.). kr195.00. Scriptor Publisher APS, Valbygardsvej 64, 2500 Valby Copenhagen Denmark. **Tel** 011 45 1 31174113, FAX 011 45 1 31171947. **DD** 789.5.
**Ind/Abst** RILM Abstr.

BE/0001-5512
**ACTA CLINICA BELGICA.** [Acta clin. belg.]. **Added/Corp** Societe Belge de Medecine Interne. Societe Belge de Biologie Clinique. Vol. 1 (Jan./Feb. 1946)-. Academic Scholarly Publication. Dutch (French and Flemish). Six times a year. 1700F Belgium, 2300F (surface mail) other; 2600F others (airmail). Academisch Ziekenhuis, Jardin Martin V 69, BP 41 4375, 1200 Brussels Belgium. **Tel** 011 32 2 7641869. **NLM** W1 AC7835. **CODEN** ACCBAT. **Pr Rev.** Documents available from The Genuine Article, BIOSIS Document Express, CASDDS. ***Supersedes*** *Bulletins et Comptes Rendus de la Societe Clinique dans Hopitaux de Bruxelles.*
**Ind/Abst** Biol. Abstr.; Chem. Abstr.; Curr. Contents Clin. Med.; EMBASE [Select. Cov.]; Index Med.; Microbiol. Abstr. Sect. B (19??-19??); Nutr. Abstr. Rev., Ser. A, Hum. Exp.; Life Sci. Collect.; PESTDOC; Protozoolog. Abstr.; Res. Alert [Select. Cov.]; SCISEARCH; SportSearch; Virol. AIDS Abstr.

BE/0567-7386
**ACTA CLINICA BELGICA. SUPPLEMENTUM.** [Acta clin. Belg. Suppl.]. (1965)-. Monographic series. English (French and Dutch). ir. Price varies per volume. Academisch Ziekenhuis, Jardin Martin V 69, BP 41 4375, 1200 Brussels Belgium. **Tel** 011 32 2 7641869. **NLM** W1 AC7835A. **CODEN** ACBSB8. Documents available from BIOSIS Document Express, CASDDS.
**Ind/Abst** Biol. Abstr. (-1986); Chem. Abstr.; Health Plan. Adminis.; Index Med.; Life Sci. Collect.

SP/0214-6568
**ACTA ESTOMATOLOGICA VALENCIANA.** [Acta estomatol. valencia.]. (1986)-. Periodical. Multiple languages. tq. Escuela de Estomatologia, Facultad de Medicina, Blasco Ibanez 17, 46010 Valencia Spain. **UDC** 616-31.
**Ind/Abst** Indice Med. Esp.

IT/0587-2421
**ACTA EUROPAEA FERTILITATIS.** [Acta eur. fertil.]. Vol. 1 (March 1969)-. Academic Scholarly Publication. Italian (English, German, French and Spanish). bm. L80000.00. Contraccezione Fertilita Sess, Piazzale Ungheria 73, 90141 Palermo Italy. **Tel** 011 39 91 321922. **NLM** W1 AC802K. **CODEN** AEFTAA. Documents available from BIOSIS Document Express, CASDDS.
**Ind/Abst** Biol. Abstr.; Chem. Abstr.; Dairy Sci. Abstr.; EMBASE; Index Med.; Protozoolog. Abstr.

CI/0065-1206
**ACTA FACULTATIS MEDICAE FLUMENENSIS.** [Acta fac. med. flumenensis]. (1966)-. Periodical. Serbo-Croatian (Cyrillic). Four times a year. Prosveta Export Import Agency, PO Box 180, Terazije 16, 1101 Belgrade Yugoslavia. **Tel** 862-687-441, telex 862-11609. **NLM** W1 AC802N. **CODEN** AFMFBB. Documents available from BIOSIS Document Express, CASDDS.
**Ind/Abst** Biol. Abstr. (1988-); Chem. Abstr.; EMBASE [Select. Cov.].

SZ/0001-5938
**ACTA LEPROLOGICA.** [Acta leprol.]. (1960)-. Academic Scholarly Publication. English (French and Spanish). sa. Free. Ordre de Malte Ciomal, 3 Place Claparede, CH 1205 Geneve Switzerland. **Tel** 011-41-22-468687, FAX (022)347-08-61. **CODEN** ALEPA8. Documents available from CASDDS.
**Ind/Abst** Chem. Abstr.; EMBASE; Health Plan. Adminis.; Index Med. (1978-).

IT/0001-6004
**ACTA MEDICA AUXOLOGICA.** [Acta med. auxol.]. **Added/Corp** Italy. Centro Auxologico Italiano di Piancavallo. Vol. 1 (1969)-. Periodical. English (English, French, German and Italian). Three times a year. $86.00. Vita e Pensiero, Pubblic University, Largo Gemelli 1, 20123 Milan Italy. **Tel** 011 39 2 72342310, 011 39 2 72342370. **NLM** W1 AC86. **CODEN** AMAXBK. Index available. **Bk Rev. Circ:** 1,200 (ctrl). Documents available from BIOSIS Document Express.
**Ind/Abst** Biol. Abstr.; EMBASE; Nutr. Abstr. Rev., Ser. B, Live Feeds and Feed.; Nutr. Abstr. Rev., Ser. A, Hum. Exp.; Life Sci. Collect.; Psychol. Abstr. (1969-).

CR/0001-6012
**ACTA MEDICA COSTARRICENSE.** [Acta med. costarric.]. **Added/Corp** Colegio de Medicos y Cirujanos. (1957)-. Academic Scholarly Publication. Spanish. Three times a year (Apr., Aug., Dec.). Free (postage will varies). Colegio Medicos Y Cirujanos, Apartado 548, 1000 San Jose Costa Rica. **Tel** 011 506 323433. **NLM** W1 AC8333. **CODEN** ATCTAW. Documents available from BIOSIS Document Express, CASDDS.
**Ind/Abst** Biol. Abstr.; Chem. Abstr.; EMBASE; Life Sci. Collect.

CI/1330-0164
**ACTA MEDICA CROATICA : CASOPIS HRVATSKE AKADEMIJE MEDICINSKIH ZNANOSTI.** **Added/Corp** Hrvatska Akademija Medicinskih Znanosti. Vol. 45, 4/5 (1991)-. Academic Scholarly Publication. English (Serbo-Croatian (Roman); summaries and/or abstracts in Serbo-Croatian (Roman)). Five times a year. $150.00. Hravatska Akademija Medicinskih Znanosti / Croatian Academy of Medical Sciences, Subiceva 29, 41000 Zagreb Croatia. **Tel** 011 385 41 419446. **(Subscription address:** Mladost Export Import, PO Box 1028, Ilica 30, 41000 Zagreb Croatia.**)** **NLM** W1; AC8333G. **CODEN** AMCREF. Documents available from BIOSIS Document Express. ***Continues*** *Acta Medica Iugoslavica, 0375-8338.*
**Ind/Abst** Biol. Abstr.; EMBASE; INIS Atomindex [Micro.]; Nucl. Sci. Abstr.; Life Sci. Collect.

DR/0379-4857
**ACTA MEDICA DOMINICANA : REVISTA CIENTIFICA PARA MEDICOS.** (1979)-. Periodical. Spanish. Six times a year. $20.00. Dr. Julio M. Rodriguez / Acta Medica Dominicana, PO Box 20102, Jose Contreras 8, Santa Domingo, Dominican Republic. **Tel** (809)688-4010. **NLM** W1; AC834P. **CODEN** AMDOEB.
**Ind/Abst** EMBASE [Select. Cov.].

JA/0567-7734
**ACTA MEDICA ET BIOLOGICA.** [Acta med. biol.]. **Added/Corp** Niigata Daigaku. Igakubu. Niigata Igakkai. Niigata Daigaku. Igakubu. Niigata Medical Society. Vol. 1 (Mar. 1953)-. Academic Scholarly Publication. Multiple languages (English and German). Four times a year. Niigata Daigaku Igakubu, 757 Ichibancho, Asahimachidori, Niigatashi Niigataken 951 Japan. **(Subscription address:** Japan Publications Trading Company, Ltd., PO Box 5030, Tokyo International, Tokyo 100-31 Japan.**)** **NLM** W1 AC835. **CODEN** AMBNAS. Documents available from BIOSIS Document Express, CASDDS.
**Ind/Abst** Biol. Abstr.; Chem. Abstr.; EMBASE; Nutr. Abstr. Rev., Ser. B, Live Feeds and Feed.; Nutr. Abstr. Rev., Ser. A, Hum. Exp.; Life Sci. Collect.

HU/0236-5286
**ACTA MEDICA HUNGARICA.** [Acta med. Hung.]. **Added/Corp** Magyar Tudomanyos Akademia. **VFOAT** Acta Medica. Vol. 40, No. 1 (1983)-. Academic Scholarly Publication. English. qt. $92.00. Akademiai Kiado, Publishing House of the Hungarian Academy of Sciences, Prielle Kornelia u. 19-35, H-1117 Budapest Hungary. **Tel** 011 36 1 1811991, FAX 011 36 1 1811991, telex 22-6228 AKNYO H. **ED** Ervin Stark. **NLM** W1 AC839J. **CODEN** AMEHDS. Documents available from The Genuine Article, CASDDS. ***Continues*** *Acta Medica Academiae Scientiarum Hungaricae, 0001-5989.*
**Desc:** Publishes original research papers in the field of clinical experimental medicine covering primarily fundamental and applied pathophysiology.
**Ind/Abst** Chem. Abstr. (1983-); Curr. Contents Clin. Med.; Dairy Sci. Abstr.; EMBASE; Health Plan. Adminis.; Index Med.; Life Sci. Collect.; Res. Alert [Full Cov.]; SCISEARCH; SEA Abstr.; SportSearch.

IR/0044-6025
**ACTA MEDICA IRANICA.** [Acta med. Iran.]. **Added/Corp** University of Tehran. Faculty of Medicine. (1956)-. Periodical. English (French and German). Four times a year. 440.00IR $22.00 other. Medical Sciences University of Tehran, Faculty of Medicine, Teheran 14 Iran. **Tel** 6112743. **ED** Parviz Jabal Ameli. **NLM** W1 AC84D. **CODEN** AMEIAS. **Circ:** 2,000. Documents available from BIOSIS Document Express, CASDDS.
**Desc:** Covers health and medical sciences.
**Ind/Abst** Biol. Abstr.; Chem. Abstr.; Health Plan. Adminis.; Nutr. Abstr. Rev., Ser. B, Live Feeds and Feed.; Nutr. Abstr. Rev., Ser. A, Hum. Exp.; Trop. Dis. Bull.

IT
**ACTA MEDICA ITALICA DI MEDICINA TROPICALE E SUBTROPICALE E DI GASTROENTEROLOGIA.** V. 16- 1961-. Periodical. Italian. Clinica Della Mallattie Tropic Via S Lucia, 15 Naples Italy. ***Continues*** *Acta Medica Italica di Malattie Infettive e Parassitarie.*

JA/0386-6092
**ACTA MEDICA KINKI UNIVERSITY.** **Added/Corp** Kinki Daigaku. Kinki University Medical Association. Vol. 1 (Dec. 1976)-. Periodical. English. Kinki Daigaku Igakkai, (Kinki University Medical Assocation), c/o Kinki Daigaku Igakubu Dai, 1 Kaibogaku Kyoshitsu, 380, Nishiyama, Sayamamachi, Minamikawachigun, Osaka 589 Japan. **NLM** W1 AC843. **CODEN** AMKUDT. Documents available from CASDDS.
**Ind/Abst** Chem. Abstr.

MX/0001-5997
**ACTA MEDICA (MEXICO).** (ACTA MEDICA.). [Acta med.]. Began with: Vol. 1 (Jan.-Mar. 1965). Periodical. Spanish. qt. $10,000 Mexico, $20.00 other. Direct Consejo Editoral, Apartado Postal 42-200, Mexico 4 DF Mexico. **LC** PAR. **DD** 610/.5. **NLM** W1 AC824J. **CODEN** ACMDBI. Index available. cum. index. **Bk Rev. Circ:** 1,200 (ctrl). Documents available from BIOSIS Document Express, CASDDS.
**Ind/Abst** Biol. Abstr.; Chem. Abstr.

JA/0001-6055
**ACTA MEDICA NAGASAKIENSIA.** [Acta med. nagasaki.]. **Added/Corp** Nagasaki Daiaku. Igabuku. Vol. 1 (1939)-. Academic Scholarly Publication. English (French and German; summaries and/or abstracts in French and German). ir. Nagasaki Daigaku Igakubu, (School of Medicine, Nagasaki University), 12-4 Sakamotomachi,, Nagasakishi, Nagasakiken 852 Japan. **NLM** W1 AC847.
**Ind/Abst** EMBASE; Nutr. Abstr. Rev., Ser. A, Hum. Exp.; Trop. Dis. Bull.

JA/0386-300X
**ACTA MEDICA OKAYAMA.** [Acta med. Okayama]. **Added/Corp** Okayama Daigaku. Igakubu. Vol. 27 (1973)-. Academic Scholarly Publication. English. Six times a year. Free on request. Okayama University / Japan, School of Medicine, 2 5 1 Shikata Cho, Okayama 700 Japan. **NLM** W1 AC847E. **CODEN** AMOKAG. **Pr Rev.** Documents available from The Genuine Article, BIOSIS Document Express, CASDDS. ***Continues*** *Acta Medicinae Okayama, 0001-6152.*
**Ind/Abst** Biol. Abstr.; Chem. Abstr.; CSA Neuro. Abstr. (?-?); Curr. Aware. Biol. Sci., CABS; Curr. Contents Life Sci.; EMBASE; Health Plan. Adminis.; Immunol. Abstr.; Index Med.; Nutr. Abstr. Rev., Ser. A, Hum. Exp.; Life Sci. Collect.; Res. Alert [Full Cov.]; Rev. Agric. Entomol.; Rev. Med. Vet. Entomol.; Sci. Cit. Index; SCISEARCH; SEA Abstr.; Soc. Sci. Cit. Index [Select. Cov.].

PH/0001-6071
**ACTA MEDICA PHILIPPINA.** [Acta med. Philipp.]. **Added/Corp** University of the Philippines. College of Medicine. University of the Philippines. Institute of Public Health. University of the Philippines. Institute of Hygiene. Vol. 1, No. 1 (July/Sept. 1939)-Vol. 19, 1963; Ser. 2, Vol. 1 (1964)-. Periodical. English. qt. $50.00. Acta Medicina Philippina, College of Medicine, PO Box 593, Manila Philippines. **Tel** 500011-15. **ED** Romeo R. Gulieneg. **NLM** W1 AC8493. **Bk Rev. Ad Acc.** ctrl circ. ***Absorbed*** *Proceedings of the College of*

*Medicine, University of the Philippines.*
**Ind/Abst** EMBASE; Philip. Sci. Technol. Abstr.; Trop. Dis. Bull

PL/0001-608X
**ACTA MEDICA POLONA.** [Acta Med. Pol.]. **Added/Corp** Polska Akademia Nauk. Wydzia VI--Nauk Medycznych. Vol. 1 (1960)-. Periodical. English (French). Four times a year. $60.00 (latest edition). **(Subscription address:** ARS Polona, PO Box 1001, 00068 Warsaw Poland.**) NLM** W1 AC851. **CODEN** AMDPAA. Documents available from BIOSIS Document Express, CASDDS. ***Continues*** *Annals of the Medical Section of the Polish Academy of Sciences.*
**Desc:** Includes reviews of Polish scientific publications.
**Ind/Abst** Biol. Abstr.; Chem. Abstr.; EMBASE; Health Plan. Adminis.; Index Med.; Life Sci. Collect.

PO/0253-0562
**ACTA MEDICA PORTUGUESA.** [Acta med. port.]. Vol. 1, No. 1 (Jan./Feb. 1979)-. Academic Scholarly Publication. English (Portuguese and Spanish). Six times a year. $125.00. Acta Medica Portuguesa, Avenue Almirante Gago, Coutinho 151, Lisbon 1700 Portugal. **Tel** 011 351 8470467. **NLM** W1 AC851D. **CODEN** AMPOD2. Documents available from BIOSIS Document Express, CASDDS.
**Ind/Abst** Biol. Abstr. (1986-); Chem. Abstr.; EMBASE; Index Med.

IT/0001-6098
**ACTA MEDICA ROMANA.** (ACTA MEDICA ROMANA : ANNALI DELLA FACOLTA DI MEDICINA E CHIRURGIA.). [Acta med. rom.]. Vol. 1, No. 1 (July-Dec. 1963)-. Academic Scholarly Publication. Italian. Four times a year. L16000.00 Italy; $185.00 other. Vita e Pensiero, Pubblic University, Largo Gemelli 1, 20123 Milan Italy. **Tel** 011 39 2 72342310, 011 39 2 72342370. **NLM** W1 AC853. **CODEN** AMROBA. Documents available from BIOSIS Document Express, CASDDS.
**Ind/Abst** Biol. Abstr.; Chem. Abstr.; EMBASE.

IT/0065-1389
**ACTA MEDICAE HISTORIAE PATAVINA.** ***Ceased.*** Vol. 1 (1954/55)-(199?). Italian. an. Inst Storia Medicina Universit, Via G Falloppia 50, 35100 Padova Italy. **Tel** 0049/24012. cum. index. **Circ:** 250.
**Ind/Abst** Am. Hist. Life (1989-?).

GW/0172-6099
**ACTA MEDICOTECHNICA (1979).** (ACTA MEDICOTECHNICA.). [Acta med.tech.]. **VFOAT** AM. Acta Medicotechnica. Vol. 27 No. 5 (Oct. 1979)-. Academic Scholarly Publication. Multiple languages (English and German). Twenty-four times a year. DM84.00 Germany; DM94.00 others. Fischer & Pflaum Verlag GmbH, Postfach 190737, D 80607 Heidelberg Germany. **NLM** W1 AC8624. **CODEN** AAMETAR. Documents available from Ask*IEEE. ***Formed by the union of*** *Technik in der Medizin* ***and*** *Medizinal-Markt, 0025-8423.*
**Ind/Abst** EMBASE; Energy Res. Abstr.; INSPEC (Dec. 1980-Dec. 1983).

HU/0236-5391
**ACTA MORPHOLOGICA HUNGARICA.** [Acta morphol. Hung.]. **Added/Corp** Magyar Tudomanyos Akademia. **VFOAT** Acta Morphologica. Vol. 31, No. 1-3 (1983)-. Academic Scholarly Publication. English. qt. $100.00. Akademiai Kiado, Publishing House of the Hungarian Academy of Sciences, Prielle Kornelia u. 19-35, H-1117 Budapest Hungary. **Tel** 011 36 1 1811991, FAX 011 36 1 1811991, telex 22-6228 AKNYO H. **ED** Karoly Lapis (editor's address: Acta Morphologica Hungarica, First Department of Pathology, Semmelweis University Medical School, Ulloi ut 26, H-1085 Budapest Hungary). **LC** QP1; .M3329. **DD** 599/.01/05. **NLM** W1 AC8643. **CODEN** AMHUDE. **[CCC].** cum. index. **Bk Rev. Ad Acc.** Documents available from CASDDS. ***Continues*** *Acta Morphologica Academiae Scientiarum Hungaricae, 0001-6217.*
**Desc:** Aims to promote an integrated approach to experimental medical subjects. It covers the fields from medical morphology to normal and pathological anatomy, forensic medicine and oncology, with emphasis on high resolution papers dealing with electron microscopical findings.
**Ind/Abst** Chem. Abstr. (1983-); CSA Neuro. Abstr. (?-?); Curr. Ref. Fish Res.; EMBASE; Health Plan. Adminis.; Index Med.; Life Sci. Collect.

SW/1101-8429
**ACTA REGIAE SOCIETATIS SCIENTIARUM ET LITTERARUM GOTHOBURGENESIS. BIOMEDICA.** **Added/Corp** Kungl. Vetenskaps- och Vitterhets-Samhallet i Goteborg. **VFOAT** Biomedica. (1991)-. Monographic series. English. ir. Royal Society of Arts and Science in Gothenburg, c/o Goeteborgs Universitetsbibliotek, PO Box 5096, S-402 22 Goetborg, Sweden. **NLM** W1; AC943J.

CI/0001-7019
**ACTA STOMATOLOGICA CROATICA.** [Acta stomatol. croat.]. Vol. 1 (1966)-. Periodical. Serbo-Croatian (Roman). Four times a year. $42.80. Hrvatski Lijecnicki Zbor, Vinogradska 97, 4100 Zagreb Croatia. **(Subscription address:** Mladost Export Import, PO Box 1028, Ilica 30, 41000 Zagreb Croatia.**) NLM** W1 AC949N.
**Ind/Abst** Health Plan. Adminis.; Index Dent. Lit.

IT/1121-2098
**ACTA TECHNOLOGIAE ET LEGIS MEDICAMENTI.** [Acta thechnol. legis medicam.]. (1990)-. Periodical. Multiple languages. Four times a year. L50000.00 Italy; L100000.00 other. Casa Editrice Maccari, Via Trento 53, 43100 Parma Italy. **Tel** 011 39 521 771268, FAX 011 39 521 771268. **UDC** 615. **Circ:** 1,000.

XR/0001-7116
**ACTA UNIVERSITATIS CAROLINAE. MEDICA.** [Acta Univ. Carol., Med.]. **Added/Corp** Universita Karlova. **VFOAT** Medica. (1958)-. Academic Scholarly Publication. Czech (summaries and/or abstracts in English, German and Russian). ir. Price varies. Carolinum Press, Ovochny TRH 5, 11636 Prague 1 Czech Republic. **Tel** 011 42 2 228441. **NLM** W1 AC954K. **CODEN** AUNCA9. Index Available, published separately, free-automatically sent. Documents available from BIOSIS Document Express, CASDDS. ***Continues in part*** *Acta Universitatis Carolinae.*
**Ind/Abst** Biol. Abstr.; Chem. Abstr.; EMBASE; Health Plan. Adminis.; Index Med.; Saf. Health Work; SportSearch.

XR/0567-8250
**ACTA UNIVERSITATIS CAROLINAE. MEDICA. MONOGRAPHIA.** [Acta Univ. Carol., Med., Monogr.]. 10- 1961-. Monographic series. Czech (English and German; summaries and/or abstracts in English, Czech and Russian). Price varies per volume. Carolinum Press, Ovochny TRH 5, 11636 Prague 1 Czech Republic. **Tel** 011 42 2 228441. **NLM** W1 AC954M. **CODEN** AUCMBJ. Documents available from BIOSIS Document Express.
**Ind/Abst** Biol. Abstr.; Health Plan. Adminis.; Index Med.

FI/0355-3221
**ACTA UNIVERSITATIS OULUENSIS. SER. D, MEDICA.** [Acta Univ. Ouluensis. Ser. D, Med.]. No. 1- 1972-. Monographic series. Finnish (English). ir. Price varies per volume. University of Oulu, c/o Leo Hirvonen, 90100 Oulu 10 Finland. **Tel** 358-81-3332133. **NLM** W1 AC954NM. **CODEN** AUODDK. Documents available from BIOSIS Document Express.
**Ind/Abst** Biol. Abstr.; Psychol. Abstr. (1977-); PsycINFO; PsycLit.

XR/0301-2514
**ACTA UNIVERSITATIS PALACKIANAE OLOMUCENSIS FACULTATIS MEDICAE.** [Acta Univ. Palacki. Olomuc. Fac. Med.]. **Added/Corp** Univerzita Palackeho v Olumouci. Lekarska Fakulta. Vol. 22 (1960)-. Academic Scholarly Publication. Czech (German and English; summaries and/or abstracts in English, German and Russian; table of contents in English, German and Russian). Price varies per volume. **(Subscription address:** Artia Pegas Press Ltd., Palac Metro Narodni Trida 25, 11210 Prague 1 Czech Republic.**) NLM** W1 AC954P. **CODEN** AUPMAF. Documents available from BIOSIS Document Express, CASDDS. ***Continues*** *Acta Universitatis Palackianae Olomucensis.*
**Ind/Abst** Biol. Abstr.; Chem. Abstr.; EMBASE; Index Med. (1981-); Saf. Health Work.

XR/0472-8998
**ACTA UNIVERSITATIS PALACKIANAE OLOMUCENSIS FACULTATIS MEDICAE SUPPLEMENTUM.** [Acta Univ. Palacki. Olomuc. Fac. Med., Suppl.]. **Main/Corp** Univerzita Palackeho v Olomouci. Lekarska Fakulta. Monographic series. Multiple languages (Czech, German and Russian). Price varies per volume. **(Subscription address:** Artia Pegas Press Ltd., Palac Metro Narodni Trida 25, 11210 Prague 1 Czech Republic.**) NLM** W1 AC954Q. **CODEN** AOMSAA. Documents available from CASDDS. ***Continues*** *Acta Universitatis Palackianae Olomucensis. Supplementum, 0301-2522.*
**Ind/Abst** Chem. Abstr. (1964-1976).

SW/0282-7476
**ACTA UNIVERSITATIS UPSALIENSIS. COMPREHENSIVE SUMMARIES OF UPPSALA DISSERTATIONS FROM THE FACULTY OF MEDICINE. Added/Corp** Uppsala Universitet. Medicinska Fakulteten. **VFOAT** Comprehensive Summaries of Uppsala Dissertations from the Faculty of Medicine. (198?)-. Monographic series. English. Price varies per volume. **(Subscription address:** Almqvist & Wiksell International, PO Box 4627, S 11691 Stockholm, Sweden**) LC** R5; .A28. **DD** 610/.5. **NLM** W4; U68a. ***Continues*** *Acta Universitatis Upsaliensis. Abstracts of Uppsala Dissertations from the Faculty of Medicine, 0345-004X.*

XR/0001-723X
**ACTA VIROLOGICA (ANGLICKA VERZE).** (ACTA VIROLOGICA.). [Acta virol.]. **Added/Corp** Ceskoslovenska Akademie Ved. Vol. 1 (Jan./March 1957)-. Periodical. English. bm (6 issues). $178.00. Czech Academy of Sciences, Branisovska 31, 37005 Ceske Budejovice, Czech Republic. **Tel** 011 42 38 817 ext. 213, 214. **(Subscription address:** Publications Expediting Inc., 200 Meacham Avenue, Elmont NY 11003.**) ED** L. Borecky and O. G. Andzhaparidze. **NLM** W1 AC9562. **CODEN** AVIRA2. **[CCC].** Index Available, published separately, free-automatically sent. **Pr Rev.** Documents available from The Genuine Article, BIOSIS Document Express, CASDDS.
**Desc:** Articles are presented in basic and applied human, animal, and plant virology. Articles are published from all parts of the world and achieves particularly extensive coverage of the socialist countries.
**Ind/Abst** AgBiotech News Inf.; AGRICOLA [Select. Cov.]; Biol. Abstr.; Chem. Abstr.; CSA Neuro. Abstr. (?-?); Curr. Aware. Biol. Sci., CABS; Curr. Contents Life Sci.; Dairy Sci. Abstr.; EMBASE; Fish Rev. (Jan. 1989-July 1992); Health Plan. Adminis.; Immunol. Abstr.; Index Med.; Index Vet.; Microbiol. Abstr. Sect. B (19??-19??); Microbiol. Abstr. Sect. A; NAPRALERT; Life Sci. Collect.; PESTDOC; Pig News Inf.; Poult. Abstr.; Ref. Upd. Deluxe Ed.; Res. Alert [Full Cov.]; Rev. Med. Vet. Entomol.; Rev. Plant Pathol.; Sci. Cit. Index; SCISEARCH; Vet. Bull.; Trop. Dis. Bull.; Virol. AIDS Abstr.; Wildl. Rev. (Jan. 1989-July 1992).

SP/0212-8608
**ACTAS CLINICAS DELFOS.** [Actas Clin. Delfos]. (1984)-. Periodical. Multiple languages. sa. Centro Medico Delfos, Avd. Hospital Militar 151, 08023 Barcelona Spain. **UDC** 616.

MX/0185-2167
**ACTAS DE LA FACULTAD DE MEDICINA, UNIVERSIDAD AUTONOMA DE GUADALAJARA.** (ACTAS DE LA FACULTAD DE MEDICINA.). [Actas Fac. med., Univ. auton. Guadalajara]. **Added/Corp** Universidad Autonoma de Guadalajara. Facultad de Medicina. Federacion de Colegios de Medicos Cirujanos de Jalisco. **VFOAT** Actas de la Facultad de Medicina de la Universidad Autonoma de Guadalajara. Series 5, Vol. 1, No. 1, (Jan./Apr./80)-. Periodical. Spanish. Three times a year (Apr., Aug., Dec.). $6.00 Mexico; $21.00 others. Federacion del Colegio de Medicad Autonoma de Guadalajar, Guadlajara Mexico. **Tel** 33 15 15 ext. 121. **NLM** W1 AC959E.

SP/0214-3925
**ACTEME. ACTUALIZACION DE TEMAS MEDICOS.** [Acteme, Actual. temas med.]. **VFOAT** Actualizacion de Temas Medicos. (1984)-. Periodical. Spanish. ir. Ediciones Nacionales Especializadas, Modesto Lafuente 41, 28003 Madrid Spain. **UDC** 61.

CN/1180-1050
**ACTION-SANTE (TORONTO).** (ACTION-SANTE / UNIVERSITY OF TORONTO, FACULTE DE MEDECINE.). [Action-sante]. **Added/Corp** University of Toronto. Faculty of Medicine. Vol. 8, No. 1 (Feb. 1990)-. Periodical. French. Six times a year. 36.95Can$. Health News and Medical Sciences Building, University of Toronto Faculty of Medicine, Toronto, Ontario M5S 1A8 Canada. **Tel** (416)978-5411, FAX (416)978-7552. **(Subscription address:** Health News Action Sante, 205 109 Vanderhoof Avenue, Toronto Ontario M4G 2H7 Canada.**) DD** 610/.5.

UK/1351-5268
**ACTIVIN & INHIBIN.** (19??)-. English. £85.00. SUBIS, Mansion House, 19 Kingfield Road, Sheffield S11 9AS England. **Tel** 011 44 114 255 4433, FAX 011 44 114 255 4626.

SP/0365-7965
**ACTUALIDAD MEDICA.** [Actual. Med.]. (1925)-. Periodical. Spanish. bm. Graficas del Sur SA, Boqueron 6, 18001 Granada Spain. **UDC** 61. **CODEN** AUMDA7.
**Ind/Abst** Indice Med. Esp.

BE
**ACTUALITE MEDICAL BELGE.** French (Dutch). 22.50F. Information Medicale Express, Vossegatlaan 16, Bus 40, 1180 Brussel Belgium.

FR
**ACTUALITES MEDICALES INTERNATIONALES EN ANGIOLOGIE.** French. ir. 220.00F France; 330.00F other. Medica Press Intl, 14 rue de Silly, 92000 Boulogne France. **Tel** 011 33 1 48251110.

UK/0360-1293
**ACUPUNCTURE & ELECTRO-THERAPEUTICS RESEARCH.** [Acupunct. electro-therap. res.]. **VAT** Acupuncture and Electro-Therapeutics Research. Vol. 1 (1976)-. Academic Scholarly Publication. English. qt. $150.00. Cognizant Communication Corporation, 3 Hartsdale Road, Elmsford NY 10523. **Tel** (914)592-7720. **ED** Yoshiaki Omura. **LC** RM184; .A285. **DD** 615.8/92. **NLM** W1 AC999K. **CODEN** AEREDS. **[CCC]. Bk Rev. Ad Acc. Pr Rev.** available on microfilm and microfiche from University Microfilms International (UMI). Documents available from Article Express International, The Genuine Article, BIOSIS Document Express, CASDDS.
**Desc:** This journal provides an international forum for the exchange of ideas and promotion of basic and clinical research in acupuncture, electro-therapeutics, and related fields. It aims at providing a better understanding of both the beneficial and adverse effects of these treatments.
**Ind/Abst** Biol. Abstr.; Chem. Abstr.; Cumul. Index Nurs. Allied Health Lit.; Dent. Abstr. (-1991); Ei Page One; EMBASE; Eng. Index Annu.; Health Plan. Adminis.; Index Med. (1981-); Index Dent. Lit.; Index Vet.; Life Sci. Collect.; Psychol. Abstr. (1982-); PsycINFO; PsycLit; Res. Alert [Select. Cov.]; SCISEARCH.

US/0163-1314
**ACUPUNCTURE LETTER, THE.** V. 1- Jan. 1974-. Periodical. English. mo. $20.00 residents, interns & students, $30.00 others. Acupuncture Letter, 250 West 82nd Street/Suite 73, New York NY 10024. **NLM** W1 AC999M.

US/0092-5047
**ACUPUNCTURE (LOS ANGELES).** (ACUPUNCTURE.). V. 1- 1800/1972-. English. National Acupuncture Association, 1033 Gayley Avenue/Suite 200, Los Angeles CA 90024. **LC** Z6665.A45; A27. **DD** 016.615/892. **NLM** ZWB 369 A189.

CN/0706-9812
**ACUPUNCTURE TODAY.** V. 1- Aug. 1977-. Periodical. English. bm. Free to members, $12.00 others. Acupuncture Foundation of Canada, Suite 503, 10 Mary Street, Toronto Ontario M4Y 1P9. **DD** 615/.892/05.

US/0742-1567
**ACUTE CARE MEDICINE.** ***Ceased.*** [Acute care med.]. Began with: Vol. 1, No. 1 (Jan. 1984)-Ceased Vol. 2, No. 7 July 1985. Periodical. English. mo. Acute Care Medicine Publishing NY 10010. **DD** 616. **NLM** W1; AC999Y.

US/0898-2783
**ACUTE CARE THERAPEUTICS.** (ACUTE CARE THERAPEUTICS : ACT.). [Acute care ther.]. **Added/Corp** Pracon Incorporated. **VFOAT** ACT. Vol. 1, No. 1 (1986)-. Periodical. English. Three times a year. Acute Care Therapeutics ACT, 1800 Robert Fulton Drive, Reston VA 22091. **Tel** (703)691-0762. **DD** 616. **NLM** W1; AC999Z. ctrl circ.
**Desc:** Expert reviews of diagnosis and therapy of major conditions faced in critical care medicine.

SA
**ADLER MUSEUM BULLETIN. See** Museums and Galleries.

US/1041-3499
**ADOLESCENT MEDICINE (PHILADELPHIA, PA.).** (ADOLESCENT MEDICINE.). [Adolesc. med.]. Vol. 1, No. 1 (Feb. 1990)-. Periodical. English. Three times a year. $75.00 US and possessions; $85.00 other. Hanley & Belfus Inc., 210 South 13th Street, Philadelphia PA 19107. **Tel** (215)546-7293, FAX (215)790-9330. **LC** RJ550; .A358. **DD** 616/.00835. **NLM** W1; AD37G. **CODEN** AMSRER. **[CCC].** Documents available from BIOSIS Document Express.
**Ind/Abst** Biol. Abstr. (1990-); Comb. Cumul. Index Pediatr. (199?-).

US/0704-4917
**ADRENAL MEDULLA, THE.** [Adrenal medulla]. Vol. 1 (1979)-. Monographic series. English. ir. Price varies per volume. Eden Press, 31A West Minster Avenue, Montreal Quebec H4X 148 Canada. **Tel** (514)488-2066. **LC** QP188.A33; A37. **DD** 612/.45. **NLM** W1 AD388. **CODEN** ADMEEV. Documents available from BIOSIS Document Express.
**Ind/Abst** Biol. Abstr. (1986-).

US
**ADVANCE. Added/Corp** University of Michigan. Medical School. University of Michigan. Hospitals. University of Michigan. School of Nursing. (19??)-. Periodical. English. qt. University of Michigan Medical Center, Office of Planning and Marketing, Department of Public Relations, 300 N Ingalls St. NI4D10, Ann Arbor MI 48109-0475. **Tel** (313)764-2220, FAX (313)747-2104. **ED** Michael Harrison.
**Desc:** Various articles related to medical issues and developments.

US/0741-9783
**ADVANCES.** ***Title Change.*** (ADVANCES : JOURNAL OF THE INSTITUTE FOR THE ADVANCEMENT OF HEALTH.). [Advances]. **Added/Corp** Institute for the Advancement of Health. Fetzer Institute. Vol. 1, No. 1 (Winter 1984)-(19??). Periodical. English. qt. Fetzer Institute, 9292 West KL Avenue, Kalamazoo MI 49009. **Tel** (616)375-2000, FAX (616)372-2163. **ED** Sheldon Lewis. **LC** RC49; .A298. **DD** 616/.001/9. **NLM** W1; AD891. Index available. **Bk Rev. Circ:** 5,000 (ctrl). ***Continued by*** *Advances : The Journal of Mind Body Health.*
**Desc:** Reports on developments in the scientific study of mind-body interactions and health. It is written for professionals and the interested public.
**Ind/Abst** Psychol. Abstr. (1984-); PsycINFO.

US
**ADVANCES FOR MEDICINE.** Vol.1 (1979)-. Periodical. English. qt. Free on request. Hewlett Packard / Massachusetts, 175 Wyman Street, Waltham MA 02154.

AT
**ADVANCES IN BEHAVIOURAL MEDICINE. Added/Corp** Cumberland College of Health Sciences. Vol. 1 (1981)-. English. an. 10.00Aus$. Cumberland College Health Science, PO Box 170, Lidcombe NSW 2141 Australia. **Tel** 011 61 2 6466444. **ED** John L. Sheppard. **NLM** W1 AD436IF.

UK/0272-3840
**ADVANCES IN BIOMATERIALS.** [Adv. biomater.]. Vol. 1 (1980)-. Academic Scholarly Publication. English. ir. Price varies per volume. John Wiley & Sons Ltd., Baffins Lane, Chichester West Sussex PO19 1UD England. **Tel** 0243 779777, FAX 0243 776128 BTG:JWP001, telex 86290 WIBOOKG. **ED** George D. Winter and Jenny Upton. **LC** UNC. **NLM** W3 AD23. **CODEN** ABIODQ. Documents available from Article Express International, BIOSIS Document Express, CASDDS.
**Ind/Abst** Biol. Abstr.; Chem. Abstr.; Eng. Index Annu.

US/1043-3252
**ADVANCES IN BIOMATERIALS (LANCASTER, PA.).** (ADVANCES IN BIOMATERIALS.). [Adv. biomater.]. Vol. 1 (1987)-. English. ir. Technomic Publishing Company, Inc., 851 New Holland Avenue, Box 3535, Lancaster PA 17604. **Tel** (717)291-5609, (800)233-9936, FAX (717)295-4538. **LC** R857.M3; A38. **DD** 610/.28. **NLM** W1; AD448L.

US/0277-0687
**ADVANCES IN DISEASE PREVENTION.** ***Ceased.*** [Adv. dis. prev.]. Vol. 1 (1981)-Completed Series (19??). Periodical. English. an. Springer-Verlag New York Inc., 175 5th Avenue, New York NY 10010. **Tel** (212)460-1500, telex 232 235 SPB UR. **(Subscription address:** Springer Verlag New York Inc. / for North America, 44 Hartz Way, Secaucus NJ 07096.**) ED** Charles B Arnold. **LC** Discard. **NLM** W1 AD548H.

US/0065-2598
**ADVANCES IN EXPERIMENTAL MEDICINE AND BIOLOGY.** [Advan. exp. med. biol.]. **VFOAT** Experimental Medicine and Biology. Vol. 1 (1967)-. Academic Scholarly Publication. English. ir. Price varies per volume. Plenum Press, 233 Spring Street, New York NY 10013-1578. **Tel** (212)620-8000, (800)221-9369, FAX (212)463-0742, (212)807-1047, telex 23/421139. **LC** UNC. **NLM** W1 AD559. **CODEN** AEMBAP. **[CCC].** Documents available from BIOSIS Document Express, CASDDS, ADONIS.
**Ind/Abst** ADONIS; Biol. Abstr.; Chem. Abstr.; Dairy Sci. Abstr.; EMBASE; Energy Res. Abstr. (Aug. 1972-); Health Plan. Adminis.; Index Med.; Index Vet.; INIS Atomindex [Micro.]; Nutr. Abstr. Rev., Ser. A, Hum. Exp.; Life Sci. Collect.; Pig News Inf.; Ref. Upd. Basic Ed.; Ref. Upd. Deluxe Ed.; SportSearch; Vet. Bull.

US/1054-1888
**ADVANCES IN HEALTH ECONOMICS AND HEALTH SERVICES RESEARCH. SUPPLEMENT.** [Adv. health econ. health serv. res., Suppl.]. (1990)-. Monographic series. English. ir. JAI Press Inc., 55 Old Post Road, Suite 2, PO Box 1678, Greenwich CT 06836-1678. **Tel** (203)661-7602, FAX (203)661-0792. **LC** RA410.A1; A38. **DD** 338.4/73621. **NLM** W1; AD621TA.
**Ind/Abst** Health Plan. Adminis.; Hospit. Health Admin. Index (1990-).

US/0197-8322
**ADVANCES IN INFLAMMATION RESEARCH.** [Adv. inflamm. res.]. Vol. 1, (1979)-. Academic Scholarly Publication. English. ir. Price varies per volume. Raven Press, 1185 Avenue of the Americas, 37th Floor, New York NY 10036. **Tel** (212)930-9500, (212)930-9604, FAX (212)869-3495, (212)302-8507, telex 640073. **ED** G. Weissmann. **LC** Discard. **NLM** W1 AD648. **CODEN** ADIRDF. **[CCC].** Documents available from BIOSIS Document Express, CASDDS.
**Ind/Abst** Biol. Abstr.; Chem. Abstr.; Life Sci. Collect.; PESTDOC.

US
**ADVANCES IN LABORATORY AUTOMATION ROBOTICS.** (1984)-. English. **LC** Q183.A1; A38. **DD** 629.8/92. **CODEN** ALOREY. Documents available from CASDDS.
**Ind/Abst** Chem. Abstr.

US/0275-5742
**ADVANCES IN MEDICAL SOCIAL SCIENCE. See** Sociology.

US/1057-6290
**ADVANCES IN MEDICAL SOCIOLOGY. See** Sociology.

US
**ADVANCES IN METALS IN MEDICINE.** Periodical. English. $90.25. JAI Press Inc., 55 Old Post Road, Suite 2, PO Box 1678, Greenwich CT 06836-1678. **Tel** (203)661-7602, FAX (203)661-0792. **ED** M.J. Abrams and B.A. Murrer.

CN/1197-8554
**ADVANCES IN PERITONEAL DIALYSIS.** [Adv. perit. dial.]. **VFOAT** Selected Papers from the Annual Conference on Peritoneal Dialysis; Peritoneal Dialysis Bulletin. 9th Ed. (1989)-. English. Toronto Western Hospital, 399 Bathurst Street, Toronto Ontario, M5T 2S8 Canada. **DD** 617.4/61059. **NLM** W1; CO478.
**Desc:** Information on continuous ambulatory peritoneal dialysis.

US
**ADVANCES IN SPACE BIOLOGY AND MEDICINE. See** Biology.

US/0741-238X
**ADVANCES IN THERAPY.** [Adv. ther.]. Vol. 1, No. 1 (Jan. 1984)-. Periodical. English. bm (Feb., Apr., June, Aug., Oct., Dec.). $60.00. Health Communications Inc., 20 Highland Avenue, Metuchen NJ 08840. **Tel** (908)548-9130, FAX (908)548-8555. **ED** Bruce A. Shapiro. **NLM** W1; AD88K. **[CCC].** Index available. cum. index. **Circ:** 5,000 (ctrl). Documents available from The Genuine Article.
**Desc:** The journal is published bimonthly and is dedicated to the timely publication of studies in clinical medicine and scientific research, case reports, review articles, and other original contributions in the areas of drug therapy, diagnosis, instrumentation, and other related fields, as well as proceedings of symposia and special topics.
**Ind/Abst** Curr. Contents Clin. Med.; EMBASE; Int. Pharm. Abstr.; Res. Alert [Select. Cov.]; SCISEARCH; Soc. Sci. Cit. Index [Select. Cov.].

US
**ADVANCES IN TRAUMA AND CRITICAL CARE.** Vol. 6 (1991)-. English. $69.95. Mosby Year Book Inc., 11830 Westline Industrial Drive, St Louis MO 63146. **Tel** (800)325-4177, (314)872-8370, FAX (314)432-1380, telex 44-2402. ***Continues*** *Advances in Trauma, 0886-7755.*

●US/1076-2191
**ADVANCES IN WOUND CARE.** (ADVANCES IN WOUND CARE : THE JOURNAL FOR PREVENTION AND HEALING.). [Adv. wound care]. Vol. 7, No. 1 (Jan. 1994)-. Periodical. English. bm (6 issues). $50.00 US. Springhouse Corporation, 1111 Bethlehem Pike, Springhouse PA 19477. **Tel** (215)646-8700. **(Subscription address:** S & S Computer, 434 West Downer, Aurora IL 60506.**) DD** 616. ***Continues*** *Decubitus, 0898-1655.*
**Ind/Abst** Cumul. Index Nurs. Allied Health Lit.; Int. Nurs. Index.

US
**ADVANCES. THE JOURNAL OF MIND BODY HEALTH.** English. Four times a year (Jan., Mar., June, Sept.). $39.00 (individuals), $79.00 (institutions) US; $44.00 (individuals), $84.00 (institutions) Canada & Mexico; $46.00 (individuals), $86.00 (institutions) others. Fetzer Institute, 9292 West KL Avenue, Kalamazoo MI 49009. **Tel** (616)375-2000, FAX (616)372-2163. **(Subscription address:** Fulco, Subscription Department, PO Box 3000, Denville, NJ 07834; telephone: (201)627-2427**) ED** Mr. Harris Dienstfrey. Index available (free). cum. index. **Bk Rev**, (Qty: varies). **Pr Rev. Acid Free. Circ:** 3,500.
**Desc:** It examines developments in the study and understanding of mind-body health and encourages discussions and exchanges among researchers, educators and health care professionals.

TU/0304-4939
**AEGEAN MEDICAL JOURNAL.** [Aegean med. j.]. V. 1- 1972-. Periodical. English (summaries and/or abstracts in Turkish). bm. Ege Universitesi / Medicine, School of Medicine, Bornova Izmir Turkey. **NLM** W1 AE14.
**Ind/Abst** EMBASE.

US/0065-3683
**AEROMEDICAL REVIEW.** **See** Aeronautics, Astronautics.

US/0001-9410
**AEROSPACE MEDICINE AND BIOLOGY.** **Added/Corp** United States. National Aeronautics and Space Administration. Scientific and Technical Information Branch. United States. National Aeronautics and Space Administration. Scientific and Technical Information Office. United States. National Aeronautics and Space Administration. Scientific and Technical Information Division. United States. National Aeronautics and Space Administration. Scientific and Technical Information Program. NASA Scientific and Technical Information Facility. (Jan./Mar. 1964)-. English. mo. $215.00. National Aeronautics and Space Administration, 600 Independence Avenue SW, Washington DC 20546. **Tel** (202)453-1000. **(Subscription address:** National Technical Information Service, 5285 Port Royal Road, Springfield, VA 22161**)** **LC** Z6664.3; .A36. **NLM** ZWD 700 A957. cum. index. available on microfilm from University Microfilms International (UMI). ***Continues*** *Aerospace Medicine and Biology.*
**Desc:** A selection of annotated references to unclassified reports and journal articles that were introduced into the NASA scientific and technical information system.

GW/0863-5412
**AERZTEBLATT THUERINGEN.** (1992)-. German. mo. DM50.00 Germany; DM68.00 other. Gustav Fischer Verlag Jena, Postfach 100537, D 07705 Jena Germany. **Tel** 011 49 3641 27332, FAX 011 49 3641 626500. **(Subscription address:** VCH Publishers Inc., 303 Northwest 12th Avenue, Journals Department, Deerfield FL 33442.**)**

●US/1067-8646
**AESCLEPIUS (MARTINEZ, CALIF.).** **See** Architecture.

UK/0141-9536
**AFRICA HEALTH.** [Afr. health]. Vol. 1 (Oct. 1978)-. Periodical. English. Six times a year. $95.00. FSG Communications Ltd., Vine House, Fair Green Reach, Cambridge CB5 0JD England. **Tel** 011 44 638 743633, FAX 011 44 638 743998, telex 9312102384 AH G. **ED** Bryan Pearson. **NLM** W1 AF513. **Bk Rev. Ad Acc. Circ:** 5,000 (ctrl).
**Desc:** An update on health and medicine for doctors in Africa. Covers a broad range of tropical medicine as well as health education and medico/political issues.
**Ind/Abst** Appl. Soc. Sci. Index Abstr.

KE/0378-4851
**AFYA (NAIROBI).** (AFYA.). **Added/Corp** African Medical and Research Foundation. (1967)-. Periodical. English. bm. **NLM** W1 AF75.
**Ind/Abst** Trop. Dis. Bull.

IT
**AGENDA, L'.** Italian. qt (4 issues). L25000.00. L'Agenda Uildm, Via Lissoni 14, 20052 Monza Italy. **Tel** 011 39 39 2496702, 011 39 39 2496703, FAX 011 39 39 2496743. **Bk Rev**, (Qty: 8-10). **Ad Acc, Adv Mgr:** Carla Misto. **Circ:** 8,000 (ctrl).

IT/0392-3002
**AGGIORNAMENTO DEL MEDICO.** [Aggiorn. med.]. (1981)-. Periodical. Italian. mo (10 issues per yer). L40000. Editrice Kurtis Srl, Via Luigi Zoja 30, 20153 Milan Italy. **Tel** 011 39 2 48202740, FAX 011 39 2 48201219. **UDC** 61.

JA/0301-0902
**AICHI IKA DAIGAKU IGAKKAI ZASSHI.** [Aichi Ika Daigaku Igakkai zasshi]. **Main/Corp** Aichi Ika Daigaku Igakkai. **Added/Corp** Aichi Ika Daigaku Igakkai. Journal of the Aichi Medical University Association. **VFOAT** Journal of the Aichi Medical University Association. (1973)-. Periodical. Japanese (table of contents in English). bm. $132.50. Aichi Medical University Association, 21 Karimata, Yazako, Nagakuto-cho Aichi-gun, 480-11, Aichi Japan. **(Subscription address:** Japan Publications Trading Company, Ltd., PO Box 5030, Tokyo International, Tokyo 100-31 Japan.**)** **NLM** W1 AI52E. **CODEN** AIDZAC. Documents available from CASDDS.
**Ind/Abst** Chem. Abstr.; EMBASE [Select. Cov.].

●US/1074-2883
**AIDS & TB WEEKLY ARTICLE SUMMARIES.** [AIDS TB wkly. artic. summ.]. **VFOAT** AIDS and TB Weekly Article Summaries. (1994)-. Periodical. English. wk. $995.00 North America; $1,195.00 other. CW Henderson, PO Box 5528, Atlanta GA 30307-0528. **Tel** (404)377-8895, FAX (404)378-5411. **(Subscription address:** CW Henderson, Subscription Office, PO Box 830409, Birmingham AL 35283-0409.**)** **DD** 616. ***Continues*** *AIDS Article Summaries, 1068-6282.*

FR
**AIMER ET SERVIR.** ***Ceased.*** (19??)-(19??). French. Four times a year. Melle Jeanine Dufrane, 23 rue de Strambruges, B-7991 Neufmaison Belgium. **Bk Rev.** ctrl circ.
**Desc:** How to deal with medicine as a christian.

●US/1067-991X
**AIR MEDICAL JOURNAL.** [Air med. j.]. Vol. 1, Nos. 1-2 (Jan./Feb. 1993)-. Periodical. English. mo (11 issues). $30.00. Mosby Year Book Inc., 11830 Westline Industrial Drive, St Louis MO 63146. **Tel** (800)325-4177, (314)872-8370, FAX (314)432-1380, telex 44-2402. **(Subscription address:** JEMS Communications, PO Box 2789, Carlsbad CA 92018.**)** **DD** 362. **NLM** W1; AI705M. ***Continues*** *Journal of Air Medical Transport, 1046-9095.*

AU/1012-9421
**AK JOURNAL.** ***Title Change.*** (JOURNAL : MITTEILUNGEN DER ARZTEKAMMER FUER STEIERMARK.). [AK J.]. **Added/Corp** Arztekammer fur Steiermark. **VFOAT** AK Journal; AK-Journal. **VAT** Arztekammer Journal. Vol. 34, No. 1 (Jan. 1983)-(198?). Periodical. German. mo. **NLM** W1; JO22L. ***Continues*** *Arztekammer fur Steiermark. Mitteilungen.* ***Continued by*** *Steirisches ArzteJournal.*

JA/0386-6106
**AKITA IGAKU.** [Akita igaku]. **Added/Corp** Akita Igakkai. Akita Daigaku. Igakubu. **VFOAT** Akita Journal of Medicine. Vol. 1, No. 1 (Apr. 1974)-. Periodical. English (Japanese). qt. Akita Daigaku Igakubu, (School of Medicine, Akita University), 1-1 Hondo, 1 Chome, Akitashi, Akitaken 010 Japan. **NLM** W1 AK79. Documents available from CASDDS.
**Ind/Abst** Chem. Abstr.

RU
**AKTUALNYE PROBLEMY REVMATOLOGII.** Vol. 4 (1972)-. Russian. **NLM** W1 AK989DD. ***Continues*** *Problemy Revmatologii.*

GW/0323-651X
**AKTUELLE PROBLEME DER INTENSIVMEDIZIN (LEIPZIG).** (AKTUELLE PROBLEME DER INTENSIVMEDIZIN.). [Aktuelle Probl. Intensivmed.]. Vol. 1 (1982)-. German. an. Price varies per volume. Dr Dietrich Steinkopff Verlag, PO Box 111442, D 64229 Darmstadt Germany. **Tel** 011 49 6151 17450. **ED** L Engelmann, D Schneider, and H Wegner. **NLM** W1; AK9952.

GW/0044-6173
**AKTUELLE TRAUMATOLOGIE.** [Aktuel. Traumatol.]. Vol. 4, (Feb. 1974)-. Academic Scholarly Publication. German (summaries and/or abstracts in English and German). Eight times a year. $222.00. Georg Thieme Verlag Stuttgart, Postfach 301120, D 70451 Stuttgart Germany. **Tel** 011 49 711 89310, FAX 011 49 711 8931298, telex 7 252 275 GTVD. **(Subscription address:** Thieme Medical Publishers Inc., 381 Park Avenue South, New York NY 10016.**)** **NLM** W1 AK996J. **[CCC].** available on microfilm from University Microfilms International (UMI). ***Continues*** *Actuelle Traumatologie.*
**Ind/Abst** EMBASE; Health Plan. Adminis.; Index Med. (1979-); Life Sci. Collect.; SportSearch.

GW/0340-3130
**AKUPUNKTUR / DEUTSCHE ARZTEGESELLSCHAFT FUER AKUPUNKTUR E.V. ... [ET AL.].** **Added/Corp** Deutsche Arztegesellschaft feur Akupunktur. (197?)-. Periodical. German (summaries and/or abstracts in English). Four times a year. DM70.00 Germany; DM77.00 other. Medizinisch Literarische Verlag, Postfach 1151 + 1152, W 3110 Uelzen 1 F R Germany. **Tel** 011 49 581 808151, FAX 011 49 581 808158, telex 841 91326. **NLM** W1; AK996T. **[CCC].**
**Ind/Abst** EMBASE.

GW/0172-9322
**AKUPUNKTURARZT, AURIKULOTHERAPEUT, DER.** **Added/Corp** Deutsche Akademie fuer Akupunktur und Aurikulomedizin. (198?)-. Periodical. German (summaries and/or abstracts in English; table of contents in English). Four times a year. DM92.00. Vieweg Publishing, PO Box 5829, D 65048 Wiesbaden Germany. **Tel** 011 49 611 160230, FAX 011 49 611 160229. **NLM** W1; AK9962. **[CCC].** ***Separated from*** *Deutsche Zeitschrift fuer Akupunktur (Heidelberg, Germany : 1977).*

SU
**AL-FAYSAL AL-TIBBIYAH.** **VFOAT** Alfaisal Medical Journal; Faisal Medical Journal. Periodical. Arabic (English). bm. 50. Majallat Al-Faysal Al-Tibbiyah, Saudi Arabia. **LC** R97.7.A7; F39.

SJ/0253-9691
**AL HAKEEM.** [Hakeem]. Vol. 6 (Nov. 1965)-. Periodical. English (Arabic). ir. University of Khartoum, PO Box 321, Khartoum Sudan. **NLM** W1 HA266. cum. index. ***Continues*** *Hakeim, 0438-413X.*

UA
**AL-JAMIYAH AL-ILMIYAH AL-TULLABIYAH-TIBB AL-AZHAR.** **Added/Corp** Tibb Al-Azhar. Jamiyah Al-Ilmiyah Al-Tullabiyah. Vol. 1, No. 1, (September 1979)-. Periodical. Arabic (English). Three times a year. Mustashfa Al-Husayn Al-Jamii Al-Markaz Al-Dawli Lil-Dirasat Al-Islamiyah, S B 1894, Al-Qahirah Egypt. **LC** R97.7.A7; J35. **DD** 610/.5.

JO/0446-9283
**AL-MAGALLA AL-TIBBIYYA AL-URDUNIYYA.** [al-Magalla al-tibbiyya al-Urduniyya]. **Added/Corp** Jordan Medical Association. Jordan. Khadamat Al-Tibbiyah Al-Malakiyah. **VFOAT** Jordan Medical Journal. (1965)-. Academic Scholarly Publication. Multiple languages. Twice a year (May & Nov.). $20.00. Jordan Medical Journal, PO Box 915, Amman Jordan. **Tel** 962 06 665620. **ED** Fouad Kilani. **CODEN** JOMJAE. Index available. **Ad Acc.** ctrl circ. Documents available from CASDDS.
**Desc:** Original medical papers, reviews, case reports, and brief communications in Arabic and English which have not been published elsewhere.
**Ind/Abst** Chem. Abstr.; EMBASE [Select. Cov.]; Trop. Dis. Bull.

SA
**AL-MAJALLAH AL-TIBBIYAH AL-SAUDIYAH.** Periodical. Arabic. bm. 3 single issue. Wizarat Al-Sihhah Al-Alaqat Al-Ammah, PO Box 10062, Al-Riyad Saudi Arabia. **LC** R97.7.A7; M32.

SJ/1013-1930
**AL-NASRAT AL-TIBIYYA AL-ARABIYYAT.** (ARAB MEDICAL BULLETIN.). [Al-nasrat al-tibiyya al-arabiyyat]. Vol. 4, No 5/7 (May/July 1982)-. Bulletin. English (summaries and/or abstracts in Arabic). mo. **NLM** W1; AR1013C. ***Continues*** *Sudan Medical Bulletin, 0254-9484.*
**Ind/Abst** Trop. Dis. Bull.

US
**ALABAMA MEDICAID.** ***Title Change.*** **See** Insurance.

US/0738-4947
**ALABAMA MEDICINE.** (ALABAMA MEDICINE : JOURNAL OF THE MEDICAL ASSOCIATION OF THE STATE OF ALABAMA.). [Ala. med.]. **Added/Corp** Medical Association of the State of Alabama. Vol. 53, No. 1 (July 1983)-. Academic Scholarly Publication. English. Twelve times a year. $30.00. Medical Association of the State of Alabama, 19 South Jackson Street, Montgomery AL 36104. **Tel** (205)263-6441. **ED** William L. Smith and William H. McDonald. **NLM** W1 AL55T. Index available. **Bk Rev. Ad Acc. Circ:** 5,100. ***Continues*** *Journal of the Medical Association of the State of Alabama, 0025-7044.*
**Ind/Abst** Cumul. Index Nurs. Allied Health Lit.; EMBASE; Health Plan. Adminis.; Hospit. Health Admin. Index; Index Med.; INIS Atomindex [Micro.].

US/0002-4538
**ALASKA MEDICINE.** [Alsk. med.]. **Added/Corp** Alaska State Medical Association. Alaska Dental Society. Vol. 1 (Mar. 1959)-. Periodical. English. Four times a year (Mar., June, Sept., Dec.). $30.00 US; $38.00 Canada; $50.00 others. Alaska Medicine, 4107 Laurel Street, Anchorage AK 99508. **Tel** (907)562-2662, FAX (907)561-2063. **ED** Dr. Donald R. Rogers M. D. **NLM** W1 AL193. Index available. **Bk Rev. Ad Acc. Pr Rev. Circ:** 1,300 (ctrl). available on microfilm and microfiche from University Microfilms International (UMI).
**Desc:** News and information of medical and case reports.
**Ind/Abst** ASTIS Curr. Aware. Bull. (1978-); ASTIS Bibliogr. (1978-); Energy Res. Abstr. (Aug. 1982-); Health Plan. Adminis.; Index Med.; Life Sci. Collect.

CN/0833-8477
**ALBERTA DOCTORS' DIGEST, THE.** [Alta. dr. dig.]. **VFOAT** Doctors' Digest. (Sept. 1976)-. Periodical. English. bm. Alberta Medical Association, 304 CMA Alberta House, 9901-108 Street NW, Edmonton Alberta T5K 1G8 Canada. **Tel** (403)423-2295, FAX (403)425-8037. **ED** Gerald L Higgins and Noel H Hershifield. **DD** 610/.5. **Ad Acc. Circ:** 4,400 (ctrl). ***Continues*** *Doc Tok.*
**Desc:** Provides physicians with information on the political, ethical, economic and societal events shaping the practice of medicine in Alberta.

CN/0706-5493
**ALERT : MEDICAL DEVICES.** **VFOAT** Alerte: Instruments Medicaux. No. 1, (March 29, 1977)-. Periodical. English (French). Health & Welfare Canada / Ottawa, Health Protection Branch, Ottawa Ontario K1A 0L2 Canada. **Tel** (613)954-8842, (613)957-1896.
**Ind/Abst** Health Devices Alerts.

DK/0105-3639
**ALFRED BENZON SYMPOSIUM.** [Alfred Benzon symp.]. **Added/Corp** Alfred Benzon Foundation. (1969)-. Academic Scholarly Publication. English. ir. Price varies per volume. Munksgaard International Publishers Ltd, PO Box 2148, DK-1016 Copenhagen K Denmark. **Tel** 011 45 33 12 70 30, FAX 011 45 33 12 93 87, telex 19431 MUNKS DK. **NLM** W3 AL36. **CODEN** ABSYB2. Documents available from BIOSIS Document Express, CASDDS.
**Desc:** Scientific research within medicine and pharmacology. Each volume is dealing with a specific subject.
**Ind/Abst** Biol. Abstr.; Chem. Abstr.

CN/0228-586X
**ALIVE (VANCOUVER).** **See** Nutrition and Dietetics.

US/0735-2883
**ALL ABOUT MEDICAID.** ***Ceased.*** **See** Insurance.

US/0735-2891
**ALL ABOUT MEDICARE.** ***Ceased.*** **See** Insurance.

US/0194-3766
**ALLIED HEALTH EDUCATION DIRECTORY.** **See** Encyclopedias and General Reference Books.

US
**ALLIED HEALTH EDUCATION NEWSLETTER.** ***Ceased.*** **Added/Corp** American Medical Association. Division of Allied Health Education and Accreditation. (1977)- Ceased (Dec. 1992). Newsletter. English. bm. American Medical Association, 515 North State Street, Chicago IL 60610. **Tel** (312)464-5000, (800)262-2350, FAX (312)464-5831. **ED** William R Burrows. **NLM** W1; AL8269G. Index available. **Bk Rev. Circ:** 1,500 (ctrl).
**Desc:** A multidisciplinary national resource for studies, projects, conferences, and publications, as well as a summation of information and activities relating to allied health education and accreditation.

●US/1076-2809
**ALTERNATIVE AND COMPLEMENTARY THERAPIES.** (1994)-. Periodical. English. bm. $79.00. Mary Ann Liebert Inc., 1651 Third Avenue, New York NY 10128. **Tel** (212)289-2300, (800)M-LIEBERT, FAX (212)289-4697.

NE/0168-8448
**ALTERNATIVE MEDICINE.** ***Ceased.*** [Altern. med.]. Vol. 1, No. 1 (1985)-(1990). Periodical. English. qt. VSP International Science Publishers, Godfried van Seystlaan 47, 3703 BR Zeist Netherlands. **Tel** 011 31 3404 25790, FAX 011 31 3404 32081, telex 40217 USP NL. **(Subscription address:** Aus./NZ: DA Book Pty Ltd, PO Box 163, Mitcham Victoria 3132 Australia; Thailand: Book Promotion & Service Ltd, 59/6 Soi Lung Suan, Ploenchit Road, Pathumwan Bangkok 10500 Thailand; other: European Book Service PBD, Strijkviertel 63, 3454 PK De Meern Netherlands**)** **CODEN** ALTMEA. Documents available from BIOSIS Document Express.
**Desc:** Devoted to fundamental and clinical aspects of traditional, indigenous, unorthodox, and alternative systems of medicine.
**Ind/Abst** Biol. Abstr. (1985-).

US/0743-5533
**ALUMNI DIRECTORY - BOSTON UNIVERSITY. SCHOOL OF MEDICINE. ALUMNI ASSOCIATION.** **See** College and School Publications-Alumni.

US/0739-6899
**ALUMNI DIRECTORY / UNIVERSITY OF MINNESOTA MEDICAL SCHOOL.** **See** College and School Publications-Alumni.

US/0736-6671
**ALUMNI DIRECTORY - UNIVERSITY OF ROCHESTER. SCHOOL OF MEDICINE AND DENTISTRY.** **See** College and School Publications-Alumni.

US/1049-5282
**AMA FREIDA.** (AMA FREIDA [COMPUTER FILE] : FELLOWSHIP AND RESIDENCY ELECTRONIC INTERACTIVE DATABASE ACCESS SYSTEM.). [AMA FREIDA]. **Added/Corp** American Medical Association. Accreditation Council for Graduate Medical Education (U.S.) Information Science Associates. **VFOAT** FREIDA. **VAT** AMA Fellowship and Residency Electronic Interactive Database Access System; Fellowship and Residency Electronic Interactive Database Access System. (1990)-. English. ir. $550.00 medical schools, medical teaching institutions and graduate medical education programs; $1100.00 other. American Medical Association, 515 North State Street, Chicago IL 60610. **Tel** (312)464-5000, (800)262-2350, FAX (312)464-5831. **(Subscription address:** American Medical Association, PO Box 109050, Chicago IL 60610.**)** **DD** 610.
**Desc:** Listing of programs accredited by the Accreditation Council for Graduate Medical Education.

GW/0944-5943
**AMBULANT OPERIEREN.** (19??)-. Four times a year. $102.00. Georg Thieme Verlag Stuttgart, Postfach 301120, D 70451 Stuttgart Germany. **Tel** 011 49 711 89310, FAX 011 49 711 8931298, telex 7 252 275 GTVD. **(Subscription address:** Thieme Medical Publishers Inc., 381 Park Avenue South, New York NY 10016.**)**

US/0897-554X
**AMBULATORY MEDICINE LETTER, THE.** ***Title Change.*** [Ambul. med. lett.]. **VFOAT** Ambulatory Medicine Letter. (1988)-(June 1994). Periodical. English. Twenty-four times a year. J.B. Lippincott Company, 227 East Washington Square, Philadelphia PA 19106-3780. **Tel** (215)238-4200 or 4454, FAX (215)238-4227. **(Subscription address:** J.B. Lippincott, PO Box 350, Hagerstown MD 21740.**)** **DD** 616. **[CCC].** available on microfilm from University Microfilms International (UMI). ***Continued by*** *Primary Care Letter, 1074-2387.*
**Desc:** Summarizing and interpreting advances in outpatient medicine.

US/1066-4076
**AMERICAN ART THERAPY ASSOCIATION NEWSLETTER.** **See** Psychology.

US/1041-3235
**AMERICAN CLINICAL LABORATORY.** [Am. clin. lab.]. Vol. 7, No. 4A (June 1988)-. Academic Scholarly Publication. English. Twelve times a year. $207.00 US; $252.00 other. International Scientific Communications Inc, PO Box 870, 30 Controls Drive, Shelton CT 06484-0870. **Tel** (203)926-9300, FAX (203)926-9310, telex 964292. **ED** Brian Howard and Kara Komornik. **DD** 610. **NLM** W1; AM315C. **CODEN** ACLAE7. **Bk Rev. Ad Acc. Circ:** 72,000 (ctrl). Documents available from CASDDS. ***Continues*** *American Clinical Products Review, 8750-9490.*
**Desc:** Aim is to provide scientists employed in the healthcare professions with news and information about clinical laboratory instruments and related products used for diagnosis and testing. Themes cover instrumentation advances in hospital and private laboratories.
**Ind/Abst** Chem. Abstr.

US/0094-8969
**AMERICAN HOSPITAL ASSOCIATION GUIDE TO THE HEALTH CARE FIELD.** [Am. Hosp. Assoc. guide health care field]. **Added/Corp** American Hospital Association. **VFOAT** Guide to the Health Care Field; A.H.A. Guide to the Health Care Field; AHA Guide to the Health Care Field. (1974)-. Periodical. English. an (July). $75.00 (members); $195.00 (nonmembers). American Hospital Association, 840 North Lake Shore Drive, Chicago IL 60611. **Tel** (312)280-6000, (800)242-2626. **(Subscription address:** American Hospital Association, PO Box 92683, Chicago IL 60675**)** **LC** RA977.A1; A46. **DD** 362.1/1/02573. **NLM** WX 22 AA1 A53. ***Continues*** *AHA Guide to the Health Care Field.*
**Desc:** Published annually, this book lists AHA-registered hospitals with selected profile data, including number of beds, admissions, births, figures on payroll, and personnel. It also provides a series of maps depicting the number of hospitals by city in the U.S.; also includes 80 different classifications identifying services provided by each hospital; health care systems; AHA institutional members; international, national, and regional organizations; state organizations and agencies; and health care providers such as freestanding ambulatory surgery centers, HMOs, freestanding substance abuse, and psychiatric facilities.
**Ind/Abst** Stat. Ref. Index.

US/0091-3960
**AMERICAN JOURNAL OF ACUPUNCTURE.** [Amer. j. acupunct.]. Vol. 1 (Jan./March 1973)-. Academic Scholarly Publication. English. qt. $90.00. American Journal of Acupuncture, 1840 41st Avenue/Suite 102, PO Box 610, Capitola CA 95010. **Tel** (408)475-1700, FAX (408)475-1439. **NLM** W1 AM447. **CODEN** AJAPB9. **[CCC].** Index available. cum. index. **Bk Rev. Ad Acc. Pr Rev. Acid Free. Circ:** 5,000. Documents available from The Genuine Article, BIOSIS Document Express.
**Desc:** As the world's leading English-language acupuncture reference, this journal publishes papers spanning the full spectrum of acupuncture and related modalities from traditional to modern variations plus correlations and combinations with Western medicine. Indispensable for the practitioner who recognizes the value of potentiating healing with complementary therapies, East and West. Includes detailed techniques and applications, methods, and principles, case studies, research, clinical investigation, hypotheses, commentary and historical notes. In addition, each 100-page issue includes abstracts selected from papers and conferences published or presented worldwide.
**Ind/Abst** Biol. Abstr.; Curr. Contents Clin. Med.; Dent. Abstr. (-1991); EMBASE; Index Vet.; Life Sci. Collect.; Res. Alert [Select. Cov.]; Rev. Med. Vet. Mycology; SCISEARCH; Small Anim. Abstr. Bibliogr.

US/0192-415X
**AMERICAN JOURNAL OF CHINESE MEDICINE, THE.** [Am. j. Chin. med.]. **VFOAT** Mei-Chou Chung-Kuo I Hsueh Tsa Chih. Vol. 7, No. 2 (Spring 1979)-. Academic Scholarly Publication. English. Three times a year (four issues in three books). $75.00. The American Journal of Chinese Medicine, IARASM, PO Box 555, Garden City NY 11530. **Tel** (516)292-2767, FAX (516)248-0930. **ED** Frederick F Kao. **LC** R601. **DD** 615/.0951. **NLM** W1 AM449MB. **CODEN** AJCMBA. Index available. **Bk Rev. Ad Acc. Pr Rev. Acid Free.** ctrl circ. available on microfilm and microfiche from University Microfilms International (UMI). Documents available from The Genuine Article, BIOSIS Document Express, CASDDS. ***Continues*** *Comparative Medicine East and West, 0147-2917.*
**Desc:** Publishes original articles and essays related to traditional or ethnomedicine of all cultures. Areas of particular interest include: basic scientific and clinical research in indigenous medical techniques, therapeutic procedures, medicinal plants, and traditional medical theories and concepts.
**Ind/Abst** Anim. Breed. Abstr.; Biol. Abstr.; Chem. Abstr. (1979-1982); Curr. Contents Clin. Med.; EMBASE; Energy Res. Abstr. (July 1982-); Hortic. Abstr.; Index Med.; Index Vet.; NAPRALERT; Life Sci. Collect.; Pig News Inf.; Protozoolog. Abstr.; Psychol. Abstr. (1979-); PsycINFO (?-?); PsycLit; Res. Alert [Select. Cov.]; SCISEARCH; Seed Abstr.; SportSearch; Vet. Bull.

US/0271-3586
**AMERICAN JOURNAL OF INDUSTRIAL MEDICINE.** [Am. j. ind. med.]. Vol. 1, No. 1 (1980)-. Academic Scholarly Publication. English. mo. $1,372.00 US; $1,492.00 Canada and Mexico; $1,537.00 other. John Wiley & Sons, Inc., 605 Third Avenue, New York NY 10158-0012. **Tel** (212)850-6000, (212)850-6645, FAX (212)850-6088, telex 12-7063. **(Subscription address:** John Wiley & Sons / England, Baffins Lane, Chichester, West Sussex PO19 1UD England.**)** **ED** Philip J. Landrigan. **LC** Discard. **NLM** W1 AM468H. **CODEN** AJIMD8. **[CCC]. Pr Rev.** Documents available from The Genuine Article, BIOSIS Document Express, CASDDS.
**Desc:** Publishes original contributions in the fundamental or applied study of occupational disease. Presents both clinical and laboratory findings, as well as general academic and scientific aspects of areas of relevant interest.
**Ind/Abst** Acoust. Abstr.; Agric. Eng. Abstr. (1991-); BioBusiness; Biol. Abstr.; Chem. Abstr. (1980-1985); Chem. Hazards Ind.; Coal Abstr.; CSA Neuro. Abstr. (?-?); Curr. Contents Clin. Med.; Dairy Sci. Abstr.; EMBASE; Health Saf. Sci. Abstr.; Health Plan. Adminis.; Index Med.; Index Vet.; INIS Atomindex [Micro.]; Lab. Hazards Bull.; Leadscan; Life Sci. Collect.; Pig News Inf.; Pollut. Abstr. Indexes; Postharvest News Inf.; Poult. Abstr.; Res. Alert [Full Cov.]; Rev. Agric. Entomol.; Rev. Med. Vet. Entomol.; Rev. Med. Vet. Mycology; Risk Abstr.; Sci. Cit. Index; SCISEARCH; Soc. Sci. Cit. Index [Select. Cov.]; Soils Fert.; Sug. Indus. Abstr.; Toxicol. Abstr.; Weed Abstr.; World Ceram. Abstr.

US/0002-9343
**AMERICAN JOURNAL OF MEDICINE, THE.** [Am. j. med.]. Vol. 1 (July 1946)-. Academic Scholarly Publication. English. mo. $115.00 (institutions), $66.00 (individuals). Excerpta Medica / US, PO Box 3085, Princeton NJ 08543-3085. **Tel** (908)874-8550, FAX (908)874-5611. **(Subscription address:** American Journal of Medicine, PO Box 7723, Riverton NJ 08077-7723.**)** **ED** J. Claude Bennett. **LC** RC60; .A5. **DD** 610.5. **NLM** W1 AM493. **CODEN** AJMEAZ. cum. index. **Pr Rev.** available on microfilm and microfiche from University Microfilms International (UMI). Documents available from The Genuine Article, BIOSIS Document Express, UMI Article Clearinghouse, CASDDS.
**Desc:** Contains the original output of clinical investigators from the USA and many foreign countries. In addition, exciting case reports are published with an eye to anything new and described for the first time. Other features include a clinical-pathologic conference, symposia and essays/editorials on medicine, science and society.
**Ind/Abst** Abr. Index Med.; Acad. Abstr. Full Text Elite (Aug. 1990-); Acad. Abstr. (Aug. 1990-); Acad. Search (Aug. 1990-); AGRICOLA; Annals Behav. Med.; Biol. Abstr.; Biol. Dig.; Biostatistica (19??-19??); Calcium Calcif. Tissue Abstr.; Chem. Abstr.; Cumul. Index Nurs. Allied Health Lit.; Curr. Aware. Biol. Sci., CABS; Curr. Contents Clin. Med.; Curr. Contents Life Sci.; Dairy Sci. Abstr.; EMBASE; Energy Res. Abstr.; Gen. Sci. Source (Jul. 1990-); Health Index (1989-); Health Period. Database [Full Txt.]; Health Plan. Adminis.; Health Ref. Cent. (Jan. 1989-) [Full Cov.]; Health Serv. Abstr.; Helminthol. Abstr. (19??-19??); Immunol. Abstr.; Index Med.; Index Vet.; INFO-SOUTH Abstr.; INIS Atomindex [Micro.]; Int. Pharm. Abstr.; Iowa Drug Inf. Serv. (1967-); J. Watch; Leadscan; Mag. Artic. Summar. Elite (Aug. 1990-); Mag. Artic. Summar. Select (July 1990-); Mag. Artic. Summar. CD-ROM (Aug. 1990-); Mag. Search; Med. Abstr. Newsl.; Microbiol. Abstr. Sect. B; Microbiol. Abstr. Sect. C; Mod. Med.; Newsp. Period. Abstr. (1992-); Nutr. Abstr. Rev., Ser. B, Live Feeds and Feed.; Nutr. Abstr. Rev., Ser. A, Hum. Exp.; Nutr. Res. Newsl.; Oncog. Growth Factors Abstr.; Life Sci. Collect.; PESTDOC; Physic. Medline Plus; Protozoolog. Abstr.; Ref. Upd. Basic Ed.; Ref. Upd. Clinical Ed.; Ref. Upd. Deluxe Ed.; Res. Alert [Full Cov.]; Rev. Med. Vet. Mycology; Rev. Plant Pathol.; Saf. Health Work; Sci. Cit. Index; SCISEARCH; Small Anim. Abstr. Bibliogr.; Soc. Sci. Cit. Index [Select. Cov.]; SportSearch; Stat. Theory Method Abstr. (1959-1963); Sug. Indus. Abstr.; Trop. Dis. Bull.; Virol. AIDS Abstr.; Vocat. Search (Aug. 1990-).

SP/0210-5713
**AMERICAN JOURNAL OF MEDICINE. EDICION ESPANOLA.** [Am. j. med., Ed. esp.]. (1975)-. Periodical. Spanish. mo. Ediciones Doyma SA, Travesera de Gracia 17 21, 08021 Barcelona Spain. **Tel** 011 34 3 2000711, 011 34 3 4145706, FAX 011 34 3 2091136, telex 51964 INK E. **UDC** 61.

US/1059-1494
**AMERICAN JOURNAL OF PAIN MANAGEMENT.** [Am. j. pain manage.]. **Added/Corp** American Academy of Pain Management. **VFOAT** AJPM. Vol. 1, No. 1 (Oct. 1991)-. Periodical. English. Four times a year (Jan., apr., July, Oct.). Free to

(members); $65.00 (non-members); $75.00 others. American Journal of Pain Management, 3600 Sisk Road, Suite 2-D, Modesto CA 95356. **Tel** (209)545-0754. **ED** Robert Supernaw, (editor's address: University of the Pacific, Stockton, CA 95211, phone: (209)946-2300). **LC** RB127; .A43. **DD** 616. **NLM** W1; AM4973. **Bk Rev. Ad Acc, Adv Mgr:** D. McCoy, **Tel** (209)946-3145. **Pr Rev. Circ:** 6,300.

US/0749-3797
**AMERICAN JOURNAL OF PREVENTIVE MEDICINE.** [Am. j. prev. med.]. **Added/Corp** American College of Preventive Medicine. Association of Teachers of Preventive Medicine. Vol. 1, No. 1 (Jan./Feb. 1985)-. Academic Scholarly Publication. English. Six times a year. $165.00 institutions, $82.00 Individuals US; $194.00 institutions, $111.00 individuals other. Oxford University Press / New York, 200 Madison Avenue, New York NY 10016. **Tel** (212)679-7300, (919)677-0977, (800)451-7556, (800)445-9714, FAX (919)677-1303. **(Subscription address:** Oxford University Press / USA, Journals Marketing Department, Oxford University Press, 2001 Evans Road, Cary NC 27513.**) LC** RA421; .A39. **DD** 610/.5. **NLM** W1; AM51D. **CODEN** AJPMEA. **[CCC]. Bk Rev. Ad Acc. Pr Rev. Circ:** 3,000. available on microfilm and microfiche from University Microfilms International (UMI). Documents available from The Genuine Article, BIOSIS Document Express, CASDDS.
**Desc:** Encompasses all the basic and applied sciences that contribute to the promotion of health and the prevention of disease, disability, and premature death.
**Ind/Abst** Biol. Abstr. (1985-); Chem. Abstr. (1985-); Chicano Index; Curr. Contents Clin. Med.; Dev. Med. Child Neurol. (1985-1990); EMBASE; Health Plan. Adminis.; Index Med. (Vol. 1, No. 1, 1985-); Int. Nurs. Index; Linguist. Lang. Behav. Abstr. (1992-); Nutr. Res. Newsl.; Psychol. Abstr. (1989-); PsycINFO; Res. Alert [Select. Cov.]; SCISEARCH; Soc. Plann. Policy Dev. Abstr. (1992-); Soc. Sci. Cit. Index [Select. Cov.]; Sociol. Abstr. (1992-); Trop. Dis. Bull.

US/0002-9629
**AMERICAN JOURNAL OF THE MEDICAL SCIENCES, THE.** [Am. j. med. sci.]. **Added/Corp** Southern Society for Clinical Investigation (U.S.). **VFOAT** Medical Sciences. Vol. 1-26, No. 1-52 (Nov. 1827-Aug. 1840)-. Academic Scholarly Publication. English (summaries and/or abstracts in Interlingua). mo. $130.00 (individuals), $250.00 (institutions) US; $185.00 (individuals), $290.00 (institutions) other. J.B. Lippincott Company, 227 East Washington Square, Philadelphia PA 19106-3780. **Tel** (215)238-4200 or 4454, FAX (215)238-4227. **(Subscription address:** J.B. Lippincott, PO Box 350, Hagerstown MD 21740.**) LC** R11; .A5. **DD** 610/.5. **NLM** W1 AM524. **CODEN** AJMSA9. **[CCC]. Pr Rev.** available on microfilm and microfiche from University Microfilms International (UMI). Documents available from The Genuine Article, BIOSIS Document Express, CASDDS. ***Continues*** *Philadelphia Journal of the Medical and Physical Sciences, 1050-0944;* ***Absorbed*** *Philadelphia Monthly Journal of Medicine and Surgery; American Medical Recorder.*
**Desc:** Scientific medical research.
**Ind/Abst** Abr. Index Med.; Biol. Abstr. (-1981); Chem. Abstr. (1827-1984); Curr. Aware. Biol. Sci., CABS; Curr. Contents Clin. Med.; Curr. Contents Life Sci.; Dairy Sci. Abstr.; EMBASE; Energy Res. Abstr.; Health Plan. Adminis.; Index Med.; Index Vet.; INIS Atomindex [Micro.]; Int. Aerosp. Abstr.; Iowa Drug Inf. Serv. (1966-); Nutr. Res. Newsl.; Life Sci. Collect.; PESTDOC; Physic. Medline Plus; Protozoolog. Abstr.; Ref. Upd. Clinical Ed.; Ref. Upd. Deluxe Ed.; Res. Alert [Full Cov.]; Rev. Med. Vet. Entomol.; Rev. Med. Vet. Mycology; Saf. Health Work; Sci. Cit. Index; SCISEARCH; Soc. Sci. Cit. Index [Select. Cov.]; SportSearch; Trop. Dis. Bull.

●UK/1075-2765
**AMERICAN JOURNAL OF THERAPEUTICS.** (1994)-. Periodical. English. mo. $150.00 US and Canada; £125.00 Europe; £140.00 Other. Chapman & Hall, 2-6 Boundary Row, London SE1 8HN England. **Tel** 011 44 71 865 0066, FAX 011 44 71 522 9623, telex 290164 Chapmag. **(Subscription address:** Chapman & Hall, Cheriton House, North Way, Andover, Hampshire, SP10 5BE England.**)**

US/0001-1843
**AMERICAN MEDICAL NEWS.** [Am. med. news]. **Added/Corp** American Medical Association. Vol. 12, No. 26 (July 1969)-. Periodical. English. wk (48 issues). $139.00 (institution), $99.00 (individual) US. American Medical Association, 515 North State Street, Chicago IL 60610. **Tel** (312)464-5000, (800)262-2350, FAX (312)464-5831. **ED** Dick Walt. **DD** 610. **NLM** W1 AM629G. **[CCC].** Index available ($60.00). **Ad Acc. Circ:** 326,000. available on microfilm and microfiche from University Microfilms International (UMI). ***Continues*** *AMA News, 0275-1003.*
**Desc:** Publishes news and opinions on key issues of political, social and economic significance concerning the practice and delivery of medical care.
**Ind/Abst** Acad. Search (July 1993-); Bus. Index (1985-); Cumul. Index Nurs. Allied Health Lit.; Gen. BusinessFile (1985-); Gen. Period. Index (1985-); Gen. Sci. Source (Jul. 1993-); Health Devices Alerts; Health Index (1989-); Health Period. Database [Full Txt.]; Health Plan. Adminis.; Health Ref. Cent. (Jan. 1989-) [Full Cov.]; Health Source (Jul. 1993-); Hospit. Health Admin. Index; Hospit. Manage. Rev.; INFO-SOUTH Abstr.; Trade Ind. ASAP [Full Txt.]; Trade Ind. Index (1981-) [Full Txt.].

US
**AMERICAN MEDICAL WRITERS ASSOCIATION AMWA JOURNAL.** **VFOAT** AMWA Journal. **VAT** American Medical Writers Association American Medical Writers Association Journal. Vol. 1, No. 1 (Fall 1986)-. Periodical. English. Four times a year. $35.00. American Medical Writers Association, 9650 Rockville Pike, Bethesda MD 20814-3928. **Tel** (301)986-9119. **ED** Ronald J Sanchez. **LC** R119; .M44. **DD** 808/.06661/021. **Bk Rev. Ad Acc. Circ:** 3,500. ***Continues*** *Medical Communications, 0090-046X.*
**Desc:** Dedicated to the improvement of medical communications between medical writers and editors and the general public.
**Ind/Abst** Health Devices Alerts.

UK
**AMRO.** ***Title Change.*** **Added/Corp** Association of Health Care Information and Medical Records Officers (Great Britain). Vol. 29, No. 2 (Aug. 1988)-(19??). Periodical. English. qt (Feb., May, Aug., Nov.). Leefdaal, Pentre Bychan Near Wrexham, Clwyd North Wales UK. **Tel** 011-44-9-78840972. **ED** Mrs. C. Thomson FMR, (editor's address: Warrington District General Hospital, Warrington WA5 1QG England). **NLM** W1; AM924. **Ad Acc, Adv Mgr:** (Editor). **Circ:** 1,000 (ctrl). ***Continues*** *Medical Record and Health Care Information Journal, 0950-5539.* ***Continued by*** *Journal of the Institute of Health Record Information & Management.*
**Ind/Abst** Hospit. Health Admin. Index (Nov. 1988-).

UK/1350-6129
**AMYLOID: THE INTERNATIONAL JOURNAL OF EXPERIMENTAL AND CLINICAL INVESTIGATION.** (19??)-. English. qt. £130.00 (institutional); £88.00 (individual). Parthenon Publishing, Casterton Hall Carnforth, Lancashire LA6 2LA England. **Tel** 011 44 5242 72084, FAX 44-5242-71587.

BL/0301-4487
**ANAIS DA ACADEMIA MINEIRA DE MEDICINA.** **Added/Corp** Academia Mineira de Medicina. Vols. 1/2 (1970/1971)-. Periodical. Portuguese. ir. Price varies. Imprensa Oficial Minas Gerais, Av Aug Lima 270, Bibl e Frieiro, 30190 Belo Horizonte MG Brazil. **NLM** W1 AN108D.

PO/0303-7762
**ANAIS DO INSTITUTO DE HIGIENE E MEDICINA TROPICAL.** [An. Inst. Hig. Med. Trop.]. Vol. 1 (Jan./Dec. 1973)-. Periodical. Portuguese (English). an. 500$00 Portugal; $10.00 US. Instituto de Medicina Tropical, rua da Junqueira 96, 1300 Lisbon Portugal. **Tel** 632141, telex 65086. **NLM** W1 AN111E. **CODEN** AIHTDH. **Bk Rev. Ad Acc. Circ:** 1,000 (ctrl). Documents available from BIOSIS Document Express. ***Supersedes*** *Anais da Escola Nacional de Saude Publica e de Medicina Tropical, 0075-9767.*
**Desc:** Publishes original papers in the domains of medicine, parasitology, public health and microbiology; review articles, research, notes and papers on methods will be considered for publication.
**Ind/Abst** Biol. Abstr.; EMBASE; Index Vet.; Protozoolog. Abstr.; Rev. Med. Vet. Entomol.; Vet. Bull.; Trop. Dis. Bull.

SP/0213-361X
**ANALES DE CUIDADOS INTENSIVOS.** ***Ceased.*** (1985)-(1992). Periodical. Spanish (summaries and/or abstracts in English). bm. C Y S Ediciones SA, Nunez de Balboa 120, 28006 Madrid Spain. **NLM** W1; AN143N.

SP/0034-0634
**ANALES DE LA REAL ACADEMIA NACIONAL DE MEDICINA, MADRID.** (ANALES DE LA REAL ACADEMIA NACIONAL DE MEDICINA.). [An. R. Acad. Nac. Med., Madr.]. **Added/Corp** Real Academia Nacional de Medicina (Spain). Vol. 1 (1879)-. Periodical. Spanish. qt. $60.00. Anales de la Real Academia, Arrieta 12, 28013 Madrid Spain. **Tel** 011 34 1 2470318. **ED** D. Valentin Matilla Gomez. **NLM** W1 AN149J. **Circ:** 2,200 (ctrl).
**Desc:** Specializes in medicine and related sciences.
**Ind/Abst** EMBASE; Health Plan. Adminis.; Index Med.; Indice Med. Esp.; Life Sci. Collect.; SportSearch.

PE
**ANALES DE MEDICINA.** V. 54- Jan./Mar. 1971-. Spanish. qt. Dr Raul Jeri, Apt 5281, Lima 100 Peru. **NLM** W1 AN151A.

SP/0210-5403
**ANALES - INSTITUTO MEDICO BENEFICENCIA.** [An. - Inst. Med. Benefic.]. **VFOAT** Anales - Instituto Medico de la Beneficencia de Navarra; Anales del Instituto Medico de la Beneficencia de Navarra. (1959)-. Periodical. Spanish. Three times a year. Diputacion Foral de Navarra, Ansoleaga 10, Pamplona Spain. **UDC** 61.

●US/1057-2260
**ANALGESIAFILE (SAN ANTONIO, TEXAS).** (ANALGESIAFILE.). [AnalgesiaFile]. **Added/Corp** Dannemiller Memorial Educational Foundation. **VFOAT** Analgesia File; Analgesia File Notebook; AnalgesiaFile Notebook. (Aug 1991)-. English. Twelve times a year. $225.00 (individual), $245.00 (institution) US; $290.00 (individual), $310.00 (institution) other. W.B. Saunders Company, A Subsidiary of Harcourt Brace Jovanovich, Inc., The Curtis Center/Suite 300, Independence Square West, Philadelphia PA 19106-3399. **Tel** (215)238-7800 or, 5587, FAX (215)238-7883, telex 173146. **(Subscription address:** W. B. Saunders Company / North America Subscriptions, c/o Periodicals, 6277 Sea Harbour Drive, 4th Floor, Orlando FL 32887.**) DD** 612.

SP/0212-4572
**ANALISIS CLINICOS.** [Anal. clin.]. **Added/Corp** Ociacion Espa*f*nola de Farmaceuticos Analistas. Sevilla. (1975)-. Periodical. Multiple languages. bm. $62.68 Spain; $106.00 other Europe; $113.00 other. Editorial Garsi SA, Juan Bravo 46, 28006 Madrid, Spain. **Tel** 011 34 1 4021212, telex 98358 GARSI E. **UDC** 616-074.
**Ind/Abst** Indice Med. Esp.

NE/0166-7688
**ANALYSE.** (19??)-. Newsletter. Dutch. Twelve times a year. Fl150.00 Netherlands; Fl162.50 other. Ver van Medische Analisten, Wilhelminapark 52, 3581 NM Utrecht Netherlands. **Tel** 011 31 030523792. Index available. cum. index. **Bk Rev. Ad Acc. Pr Rev. Circ:** 4,000 (ctrl).
**Desc:** Articles on new medical and laboratory technical developments. Contains social news about labor conditions of medical laboratory technologists, including their rights and duties.

US/0743-5797
**ANALYTICAL INSTRUMENTATION.** ***Title Change.*** [Anal. instrum.]. Vol. 13, No. 1 (1984)-(1993). Academic Scholarly Publication. English. qt. Marcel Dekker Inc., 270 Madison Avenue, New York NY 10016. **Tel** (212)696-9000, (800)228-1160, FAX (212)685-4540, telex 421419. **(Subscription address:** Marcel Dekker Inc, PO Box 5017, Monticello NY 12701.**) ED** Galen W. Ewing. **LC** QD53; .C47. **DD** 542/.05. **NLM** W1; AN1917D. **CODEN** ANINE6. **[CCC]. Pr Rev.** available on microfiche. Documents available from Article Express International, The Genuine Article, Ask*IEEE, CASDDS. ***Continues*** *Chemical, Biomedical, and Environmental Instrumentation, 0190-4094.* ***Continued by*** *Instrumentation Science & Technology, 1073-9149.*
**Desc:** Among the many areas covered in this journal are high resolution, high performance techniques in separation science, analysis of trace materials in the environment, the use of computer and microprocessor technology, and creative use of commercial instruments. Also examines state-of-the-art instrumentation technology, ensuring scientists in all fields that they have the top available equipment for their work.
**Ind/Abst** Abstr. Bull. Inst. Pap. Sci. Tech.; Air Pollut. Titles; Anal. Abstr.; Bioeng. Abstr.; Chem. Abstr. (1984-); Curr. Contents Eng. Tech. Appl. Sci.; Curr. Contents Phys. Chem. Earth Sci.; Ei Page One; EMBASE; Energy Res. Abstr.; Eng. Index Annu.; INSPEC (1984-); Mass Spect. Bull.; Phys. Briefs; Res. Alert [Full Cov.]; Sci. Cit. Index; SCISEARCH.

GW/0303-4569
**ANDROLOGIA (BERLIN, WEST).** (ANDROLOGIA : OFFICIAL JOURNAL OF COMITE INTERNATIONAL DE ANDROLOGIA (CIDA).). [Andrologia]. **Added/Corp** Comite International de Andrologia. Deutsche Gesellschaft fuer Andrologie. Vol. 6, No. 1 (1974)-. Academic Scholarly Publication. English (German; summaries and/or abstracts in Spanish and French). Six times a year. DM390.00 Germany; DM396.00 Europe; DM430.00 other. Blackwell Wissenschafts-Verlag, Kurfuerstendamm 57, D 10707 Berlin Germany. **Tel** 011 49 30 32790623, 011 49 30 32790624, FAX 011 49 30 327 90610. **ED** A.F. Holstein. **DD** 616. **NLM** W1 AN215P. **CODEN** ANDRDQ. **[CCC].** Index available. **Bk Rev. Ad Acc. Pr Rev. Circ:** 1,800. available on microfilm from University Microfilms International (UMI). Documents available from The Genuine Article, BIOSIS Document Express, CASDDS, ADONIS. ***Continues*** *Andrologie, 0303-4569.*
**Desc:** Provides an international forum for original papers on the current clinical, morphological, biochemical, and experimental status of organic male infertility and sexual disorder in men.
**Ind/Abst** ADONIS; Anim. Breed. Abstr.; Biol. Abstr.; Chem. Abstr.; CSA Neuro. Abstr. (?-?); Curr. Contents Life Sci.; EMBASE; Index Med.; NAPRALERT; Nutr. Abstr. Rev., Ser. A, Hum. Exp.; Life Sci. Collect.; PESTDOC; Pig News Inf.; Poult. Abstr.; Res. Alert [Full Cov.]; Sci. Cit. Index; SCISEARCH.

FR/0003-3049
**ANGEIOLOGIE.** ***Ceased.*** (ANGEIOLOGIE : REVUE INTERNATIONALE DE DOCUMENTATION SCIENTIFIQUE.). [Angeiologie]. Vol. 11, No. 5 (Nov. 1959)-(1993). Academic Scholarly Publication. English (French). ir (8 no. a year). France Regions Publications, 38 rue Pascal, 75013 Paris France. **Tel** 11 33 1 43315727. **NLM** W1 AN221. **[CCC].** ***Continues*** *Angeiologie et Annales.*
**Ind/Abst** EMBASE.

PL/0303-4135
**ANNALES ACADEMIAE MEDICAE GEDANENSIS.** [Ann. Acad. Med. Gedanensis]. **Main/Corp** Gdansk. Akademia Medyczna. (1971)-. Academic Scholarly Publication. Polish. Medical Academy / Gdansk, Debinki 1, 80-211 Gdansk Poland. **Tel** (58)321914. **CODEN** AAMGBD. Documents available from CASDDS.
**Ind/Abst** Chem. Abstr.; EMBASE [Select. Cov.].

PL/0208-5607
**ANNALES ACADEMIAE MEDICAE SILESIENSIS.** (ANNALES ACADEMIAE MEDICAE SILESIENSIS / SLASKA AKADEMIA MEDYCZNA IM. LUDWIKA WARYNSKIEGO W KATOWICACH.). [Ann. Acad. Med. Siles.]. **Added/Corp** Slaska Akademia Medyczna im. L. Warynskiego. (1978)-. Academic Scholarly Publication. Polish. an. **CODEN** ANSID6. Documents available from CASDDS.
**Ind/Abst** Chem. Abstr.

FI/0066-1996
**ANNALES ACADEMIAE SCIENTIARUM FENNICAE. SER. A5: MEDICA.** [Ann. Acad. Sci. Fenn., Ser. A5]. **VFOAT** Suomalaisen Tiedeakatemian Toimituksia. Ser. A.5, Medica. Vol. 86; 1961-. Monographic series. Multiple languages (French, German and English). Price varies per volume. Akakeeminen-Kirjakuppa, PO Box 128, 00101 Helsinki Finland. **Tel** 011/358/0/90/12141, FAX +358 0 121 4441, telex 125080 AKAHE SF. **NLM** W1 AN307N. available on microfilm and microfiche from University Microfilms International (UMI). ***Continues*** *Annales Academiae Scientiarum Fennicae. Series A. 5. Medica-Anthropologica, 0374-5198.*
**Ind/Abst** EMBASE; Energy Res. Abstr. (March 1972-); Health Plan. Adminis.; Index Med.

MG/0253-6390
**ANNALES DE L'UNIVERSITE DE MADAGASCAR. BIOLOGIE, CLINIQUE, SANTE PUBLIQUE.** **See** Biology.

SP
**ANNALES DE MEDICINA.** Vol. 62 (1976)-. Periodical. Catalan. mo. Ediciones Doyma SA, Travesera de Gracia 17 21, 08021 Barcelona Spain. **Tel** 011 34 3 2000711, 011 34 3 4145706, FAX 011 34 3 2091136, telex 51964 INK E. **NLM** W1 AN559K. ***Continues*** *Anales de Medicina.*
**Ind/Abst** Trop. Dis. Bull.

FR/0221-3796
**ANNALES MEDICALES DE NANCY ET DE L'EST.** [Ann. med. Nancy Est.]. **Added/Corp** Centre Hospitalier et Universitaire de Nancy. Facultes A et B de Medecine. Societe de Medecine de Nancy. (Aug./Sept. 1978)-. Periodical. French (English; summaries and/or abstracts in English). Six times a year. 356.61F France; 350.00F other. Centre Hospitalier Regional de Nancy, Service de Reanimation, Medicale-Centre Hospitalier, Regional, F-54037 Nancy Cedex France. **Tel** 33 83 576161. **ED** Professor Larcan. **NLM** W1 AN449T. **CODEN** AMNADI. **Bk Rev. Ad Acc. Circ:** 3,000 (ctrl). Documents available from BIOSIS Document Express, CASDDS. ***Continues*** *Annales Medicales de Nancy.*
**Ind/Abst** Biol. Abstr. (-1989); Chem. Abstr. (1978-1985); EMBASE [Select. Cov.]; Life Sci. Collect.

FR/0224-5264
**ANNALES SCIENTIFIQUES DE L'UNIVERSITE DE FRANCHE-COMTE-BESANCON. MEDECINE ET PHARMACIE.** **See** Pharmacy and Pharmacology.

PL
**ANNALES SOCIETATIS DOCTRINAE STUDENTIUM ACADEMIAE MEDICAE SILESIENSIS.** Academic Scholarly Publication. Multiple languages (English and Russian). **NLM** W1 AN47KS.

PL/0066-2240
**ANNALES UNIVERSITATIS MARIAE CURIE-SKODOWSKA. SECTIO D, MEDICINA.** [Ann. Univ. Mariae Curie-Skodowska, Sect. D]. **Main/Corp** Uniwersytet Marii Curie-Skodowskiej. **VFOAT** Medicina; Nauki Lekarskie; Roczniki Uniwersytetu Marii Curie-Skodowskiej w Lublinie Dzia D, Nauki Lekarskie. Vol. 1 (1946)-. Polish (English). an. Uniwersytet Marii Curie-Sklodowskiej, Pl Marii Curie-Sklodowskiej 5, 20-031 Lublin Poland. **Tel** 37-53-04, telex 0643223. **NLM** W1 AN47M. **CODEN** AUMKAS. Documents available from BIOSIS Document Express, CASDDS. ***Continued in part by*** *Annales Universitatis Mariae Curie-Skodowska. Sectio DD, Medicina Veterinaria (Lublin, Poland : 1949), 0301-7737.*
**Ind/Abst** Biol. Abstr.; Chem. Abstr. (-1983); Index Med.

GW/0931-9913
**ANNALES UNIVERSITATIS SARAVIENSIS. MEDICINAE. SUPPLEMENT.** [Ann. Univ. Sarav. med., Suppl.]. 1-. Academic Scholarly Publication. German. Price varies per volume. **NLM** W1 AN47R. **CODEN** AUSSEI. Documents available from CASDDS.
**Ind/Abst** Chem. Abstr.

IT/0390-5454
**ANNALI DELL'OSPEDALE MARIA VITTORIA DI TORINO.** [Ann. Osp. Maria Vittoria Torino]. Vol. 17 (1974)-. Periodical. Italian. sa. L15000 Italy; L21000 other. Ospedale Maria Vittoria, Via Cibrario 72, 10144 Turin Italy. **NLM** W1 AN486M. ***Formed by the union of*** *Giornale di Batteriologia, Virologia ed Immunologia ed Annali dell'Ospedale Maria Vittoria di Torino. Parte 1: Sezione Microbiologia, 0301-1453* ***and*** *Giornale di Batteriologia, Virologia ed Immunologia ed Annali dell'Ospedale Maria Vittoria di Torino. Parte 2: Sezione Clinica, 0301-1445.*
**Ind/Abst** Index Med.; Life Sci. Collect.; Trop. Dis. Bull.

IT
**ANNALI DI IGIENE : MEDICINA PREVENTIVA E DI COMUNITA. VFOAT** Annali di Igiene, Medicina Preventiva e di Comunita. Vol. 1, No. 1-2 (Jan./April 1989)-. Periodical. Italian (English). bm. $50.66. Societa Editrice Universo, Via GB Morgagni 1, 00161 Rome Italy. **Tel** 011 39 6 44231171. **NLM** W1; AN491SK. ***Continues*** *Nuovi Annali d'Igiene e Microbiologia.*
**Ind/Abst** Index Med. (1989-); Trop. Dis. Bull.

IT/0003-4630
**ANNALI DI MEDICINA NAVALE.** (1985)-. Periodical. Italian.
**Ind/Abst** Trop. Dis. Bull.

IT
**ANNALI SOTIC.** Aulo Gaggi Editore, Via Andrea Costa 131-5, 40134 Bologna Italy. **Tel** 011 39 51 6142067, telex 43 61 19.

US/0883-6612
**ANNALS OF BEHAVIORAL MEDICINE.** **See** Medical Science and Technology-Abstracting, Bibliographies and Statistics.

FI/0785-3890
**ANNALS OF MEDICINE (HELSINKI).** (ANNALS OF MEDICINE.). [Ann. med.]. **Added/Corp** Suomalainen Laakariseura Duodecim. Vol. 21, No. 1 (Feb. 1989)-. Academic Scholarly Publication. English. bm (6 issues). $274.00 US & Canada; £177.00 other. Blackwell Scientific Publications Ltd, Marston Book Services, PO Box 87, Oxford OX2 ODT UK. **Tel** 011 44 865 791155, FAX 011 44 865 791927, telex 837 515 MARDIS G. **ED** Leena Peltonen. **NLM** W1; AN611D. **CODEN** ANMDEU. Index available. **Ad Acc. Pr Rev. Circ:** 2,000. available on microfilm and microfiche from University Microfilms International (UMI). Documents available from The Genuine Article, BIOSIS Document Express, CASDDS. ***Formed by the union of*** *Annals of Clinical Research, 0003-4762* ***and*** *Medical Biology, 0302-2137.*
**Desc:** Publishes original articles, editorials, reviews and rapidly edited special issues on recent international symposiums.
**Ind/Abst** Biol. Abstr.; Chem. Abstr.; Curr. Aware. Biol. Sci., CABS; Curr. Contents Clin. Med.; Curr. Contents Life Sci.; EMBASE; Health Plan. Adminis.; Index Med. (Feb. 1989-); Indice Med. Esp.; Nutr. Abstr. Rev., Ser. A, Hum. Exp.; PESTDOC; Psychol. Abstr. (1989-); PsycLit; Ref. Upd. Basic Ed.; Ref. Upd. Clinical Ed.; Ref. Upd. Deluxe Ed.; Res. Alert [Full Cov.]; Sci. Cit. Index; SCISEARCH; Soc. Sci. Cit. Index [Select. Cov.]; Trop. Dis. Bull.

SU/0256-4947
**ANNALS OF SAUDI MEDICINE.** [Ann. Saudi med.]. Vol. 5, No. 3 (July 1985)-. Periodical. English (Arabic). bm. Free. King Faisal Specialist Hospital, Publications Office, PO Box 3354, Riyadh 11211 Saudi Arabia. **Tel** 464-7272, telex 401050 ROSPEC SJ. **ED** Peter B Herdson and Saadi Taher. **NLM** W1; AN624T. **CODEN** ANSMEJ. Index available. cum. index. **Bk Rev. Ad Acc. Pr Rev. Circ:** 14,000 (ctrl). Documents available from The Genuine Article, BIOSIS Document Express. ***Continues*** *King Faisal Specialist Hospital Medical Journal, 0253-4770.*
**Desc:** Original articles with clinical focus, case reports, reviews special communications, editorials, letters to the editor, symposia abstracts.
**Ind/Abst** Biol. Abstr.; Curr. Contents Clin. Med.; EMBASE; Helminthol. Abstr. (19??-19??); Index Dent. Lit. (Vol. 5, No. 3, July 1985-); Index Vet.; Protozoolog. Abstr.; Res. Alert [Select. Cov.]; Rev. Med. Vet. Entomol.; Rev. Med. Vet. Mycology; SCISEARCH; Soc. Sci. Cit. Index [Select. Cov.].

SI/0304-4602
**ANNALS OF THE ACADEMY OF MEDICINE, SINGAPORE.** [Ann. Acad. Med. Singap.]. **Added/Corp** Academy of Medicine (Singapore). Vol. 1, (Jan. 1972)-. Periodical. English. Six times a year (Jan., Mar., May, July, Sept., Nov.). $45.00 local housemen and trainees; $90.00 other. Academy of Medicine Singapore, 16 College Road/#01-01, College of Medicine Building, 0316 Singapore. **Tel** 011 65 2245166, FAX 011 65 2255155, telex RS 40173 ACAMED. **(Subscription address:** P.O. Box 694, Tiong Bahru Post Office, 9116 Singapore**)** **ED** S. T. Lee. **NLM** W1 AN626JS. **CODEN** AAMSCG. Index available. cum. index. **Bk Rev. Ad Acc. Circ:** 1,500 (ctrl). Documents available from BIOSIS Document Express. ***Continues*** *Annals of the Academy of Medicine, Singapore.*
**Desc:** Original and review articles on topical medical subjects.
**Ind/Abst** Biol. Abstr. (1986-); EMBASE; Health Plan. Adminis.; Index Med. Jan. 1979-; SportSearch; Trop. Dis. Bull.

II/0379-038X
**ANNALS OF THE NATIONAL ACADEMY OF MEDICAL SCIENCES (INDIA).** [Ann. Natl. Acad. Med. Sci. (India)]. **Main/Corp** National Academy of Medical Sciences (India). Vol. 13 (Jan./March 1977)-. Academic Scholarly Publication. English. qt. $25.00. National Academy of Medical Sciences, New Delhi, India. **(Subscription address:** Prints India, 11 Darya Ganj, New Delhi 110002 India.**)** **NLM** W1 AN626YG. **CODEN** ANAIDI. Documents available from CASDDS. ***Continues*** *Annals of Indian Academy of Medical Sciences, 0019-4263.*
**Ind/Abst** Chem. Abstr.; EMBASE.

US/0077-8923
**ANNALS OF THE NEW YORK ACADEMY OF SCIENCES.** **See** Science and Technology.

FR/0399-3914
**ANNEE DU MEDECIN, L'.** 1976-. Periodical. French. Flammarion Medecine-Sciences, 20 rue de Vaurigard, 75006 Paris France. **ED** P Milliez. **NLM** W1 AN646H.

US
**ANNUAL PROGRESS REPORT / WALTER REED ARMY INSTITUTE OF RESEARCH.** **Added/Corp** Walter Reed Army Institute of Research. (19??)-. English. an. Walter Reed Army Institute of Research, Walter Reed Army Medical Center, Washington DC 20307. available on microfiche (Vols. for (1974-) distributed to depository libraries). ***Continues*** *Research in Biological and Medical Sciences, 0161-3685.*

US/0197-0909
**ANNUAL REPORT - AMERICAN BUREAU FOR MEDICAL ADVANCEMENT IN CHINA, INC.** [Annu. rep. - Am. Bur. Med. Adv. China, inc.]. **Main/Corp** American Bureau for Medical Advancement in China. 1978-. English. an. American Bureau For Medical Advancement In China, 1790 Broadway, New York NY 10010. **NLM** W1 AM292D. ***Continues*** *Annual Report - American Bureau for Medical Aid to China, Inc., 0197-0917.*

II/0255-8726
**ANNUAL REPORT / CENTRAL COUNCIL FOR RESEARCH IN UNANI MEDICINE.** [Annu. rep. - Cent. Counc. Res. Unani Med.]. **Main/Corp** Central Council for Research in Unani Medicine (India). 1978-79 & 1979-80-. English. ir. Government of India / Ministry of Education & Social Welfare, New Delhi 110054 India. **NLM** W2 JI4 C39. ***Continues in part*** *Central Council for Research in Indian Medicine and homeopathy. Annual Report.*

US
**ANNUAL REPORT - CLINICAL APPLICATIONS AND PREVENTION ADVISORY COMMITTEE, NATIONAL INSTITUTES OF HEALTH.** **Main/Corp** National Heart, Lung, and Blood Institute. Clinical Applications and Prevention Advisory Committee. English. an. National Heart Lung and Blood Institute, Division of Heart and Vascular Diseases, Devices and Technology Branch, 9000 Rockville Pike, Bethesda MD 20014.

US/0145-2037
**ANNUAL REPORT - EDUCATIONAL COMMISSION FOR FOREIGN MEDICAL GRADUATES.** **Main/Corp** Educational Commission for Foreign Medical Graduates. (1974)-. English. an. Free. Educa Comm Foreign Medical Graduate, 3624 Market Street, Philadelphia PA 19104. **LC** RA396.A3; E38a. **DD** 610.69/52. **NLM** W1 ED857. ***Continues*** *Annual Report - Educational Council for Foreign Medical Graduates, 0160-7189.*

US
**ANNUAL REPORT FOR THE YEAR ENDED ... / MEXIA STATE SCHOOL.** **Main/Corp** Mexia State School. English. an. Mexia State School, Box 1132, Mexia TX 76667. **LC** HV3006.T42; M495A. **DD** 353.97640072/32.

US/0278-5137
**ANNUAL REPORT / HOWARD UNIVERSITY COLLEGE OF MEDICINE.** **See** Education-Higher Education.

US/0844-9430
**ANNUAL REPORT - MANITOBA HEALTH RESEARCH COUNCIL.** [Annu. rep. - Manit. Health Res. Counc.]. **Main/Corp** Manitoba Health

Research Council. 1982-1983-. English. an. Manitoba Health Research Council, Room S107/759 Bannatyne Avenue, Winnipeg Manitoba R3E 0W3 Canada. **LC** RA185.M3; M36A. **DD** 610/.79.

US/0730-1286
**ANNUAL REPORT / MARCH OF DIMES BIRTH DEFECTS FOUNDATION. Main/Corp** March of Dimes Birth Defects Foundation. (1980)-. English (Spanish and Chinese). an. Free. March of Dimes Birth Defects Foundation, PO Box 1657, Wilkes Barre PA 18703. **Tel** 800 367-6630. **LC** RG626; .M25a. **DD** 618.92/0043/06073. **NLM** W1 MA643. Index available. ***Continues*** *National Foundation. Annual Report, 0735-0163.*

US
**ANNUAL REPORT - MEDICAL DEVICES APPLICATIONS COMMITTEE, NATIONAL INSTITUTES OF HEALTH.** **Main/Corp** National Heart and Lung Institute. Medical Devices Applications Committee. English. an. National Heart Lung and Blood Institute, Division of Heart and Vascular Diseases, Devices and Technology Branch, 9000 Rockville Pike, Bethesda MD 20014.

US/0735-1992
**ANNUAL REPORT - NATIONAL INSTITUTE OF HEALTH (U.S.). DIVISION OF RESEARCH SERVICES.** ***Title Change.*** (ANNUAL REPORT / DIVISION OF RESEARCH SERVICES.). [Annu. rep. - Natl. Inst. Health (U.S.), D v. Res. Serv.]. **Main/Corp** National Institutes of Health (U.S.). Division of Research Services. Fiscal Year 1977-. English. an. National Institutes of Health / Division of Research Sciences, 9000 Rockville Pike, Bethesda MD 20014. **LC** RA11; .D158. **NLM** W2 A N212A. available on microfiche (Vols. distributed to depository libraries). ***Continued by*** *National Institute of Health (U.S.). Division of Research Services. FY ... Annual Report.*

US/0361-9052
**ANNUAL REPORT - NATIONAL PROFESSIONAL STANDARDS REVIEW COUNCIL.** ***Ceased.*** **Main/Corp** United States. National Professional Standards Review Council. (19??)-?. English. an. Professional Standard Review, Professional Standard Review, Washington DC 20202. **LC** RA399.A3; N3a. **DD** 353.008/243. **NLM** W1 NA567.

US
**ANNUAL REPORT / THE ALABAMA MEDICAID AGENCY. Main/Corp** Alabama Medicaid Agency. (19??)-. English. **LC** HD7102.U5; A25. **DD** 362.1/04252/09761. ***Continues*** *Alabama Medicaid.*

UK
**ANNUAL REPORT / THE MEDICAL AND DENTAL DEFENCE UNION OF SCOTLAND LIMITED. Main/Corp** Medical and Dental Defence Union of Scotland. English. **NLM** W1; ME179D. ***Continues*** *Annual Report and Financial Statement - Medical and Dental Defence Union of Scotland Limited, 0144-8730.*

US/0190-5031
**ANNUAL REPORTS ON THE EXCHANGE OF MEDICAL INFORMATION AND SHARING MEDICAL RESOURCES. VFOAT** Exchange of Medical Information and Sharing Medical Resources. Began with 1976/77. English. an. **LC** RA11; .F29. **DD** 353.0084/1. **NLM** W2 A V49AI. ***Formed by the union of*** *Annual Report on Exchange of Medical Information, 0363-5635* ***and*** *Annual Report on Sharing Medical Resources, 0362-0123.*

GW
**ANNUAL REVIEW OF HYDROCEPHALUS.** (19??)-. Monographic series. English. ir. Price varies per volume. Springer-Verlag GmbH & Company KG, Heidelberger Platz 3, D 14197 Berlin Germany. **Tel** 011 49 30 8207223, FAX 011 49 30 8214091, telex 183 319 SPBLN D. **(Subscription address:** Springer Verlag New York Inc. / for North America, 44 Hartz Way, Secaucus NJ 07096.**)**

US/0066-4219
**ANNUAL REVIEW OF MEDICINE.** [Annu. rev. med.]. Vol. 1 (1950)-. Academic Scholarly Publication. English. an (April). $47.00 US; $52.00 other. Annual Reviews Inc., 4139 El Camino Way, PO Box 10139, Palo Alto CA 94303-0139. **Tel** (415)493-4400, (800)523-8635, FAX (415)855-9815. **ED** William P. Creger. **DD** 610.58. **NLM** W1 AN773. **CODEN** ARMCAH. **[CCC].** Index available. cum. index. **Pr Rev.** ctrl circ. available on microfilm and microfiche from University Microfilms International (UMI). Documents available from The Genuine Article, BIOSIS Document Express, CASDDS.
**Desc:** Comprehensive, thorough coverage of latest advances in medicine, written by acknowledged experts in the field. Extensive literature citations included.
**Ind/Abst** Biol. Abstr.; Chem. Abstr.; Curr. Aware. Biol. Sci., CABS; Curr. Contents Clin. Med.; Curr. Contents Life Sci.; EMBASE; Energy Res. Abstr.; Health Plan. Adminis.; Index Med.; Index Sci. Rev. [Full Cov.]; Index Vet.; Nutr. Abstr. Rev., Ser. B, Live Feeds and Feed.; Nutr. Abstr. Rev., Ser. A, Hum. Exp.; Life Sci. Collect.; Protozoolog. Abstr.; Psychol. Abstr. (1969-); PsycINFO; PsycLit; Ref. Upd. Basic Ed.; Ref. Upd. Clinical Ed.; Ref. Upd. Deluxe Ed.; Res. Alert [Full Cov.]; Sci. Cit. Index; SCISEARCH; Soc. Sci. Cit. Index [Select. Cov.]; SportSearch; Vet. Bull.

US/0738-6230
**ANNUAL STATISTICAL REPORT / AMERICAN ASSOCIATION OF COLLEGES OF OSTEOPATHIC MEDICINE. See** Medical Science and Technology-Abstracting, Bibliographies and Statistics.

CN/1182-9648
**ANTIBACTERIAL REVIEW.** [Antibact. rev.]. **Added/Corp** STA Communications. **VFOAT** Anti-Bacterial Review. Vol. 1, No. 1 (Mar. 1990)-. Periodical. English. qt. Limited free distribution. STA Communications Inc., 955 St. John Boulevard, Suite 306, Pt Claire, Quebec H9R 5K3 Canada. **Tel** (514)695-7623. **DD** 615/.329/05.

CN/1182-963X
**ANTIBIOTHERAPIE AUJOURD'HUI.** [Antibiother. aujourd'hui]. **Added/Corp** STA Communications. **VFOAT** Anti Biotherapie Aujourd'Hui. Vol. 1, No 1 (Mar 1990)-. Periodical. French. qt. Limited free distribution. STA Communications Inc., 955 St. John Boulevard, Suite 306, Pt Claire, Quebec H9R 5K3 Canada. **Tel** (514)695-7623. **DD** 615/.329/05.

AT/0729-218X
**ANTIBIOTIC GUIDELINES.** (1978)-. English. an. 15.00Aus$ (two years). Victoria Medical Postgraduate Foundation, PO Box 27, Parkville 3052, Australia. **Tel** 11 61 03 3479633, FAX 11 61 03 3474547. **[CCC].**
**Desc:** The latest information on the drugs guidelines in helping you to select the most appropriate drug treatments for your patients.

●GW
**ANTIINFECTIVE DRUGS AND CHEMOTHERAPY.** (1994)-. Periodical. German. ir (4 to 6 per year). DM150.00. Futuramed GmbH, Postfach 830358, D 830358 Munich Germany. **Tel** 011 49 89 674047. ***Continues*** *Zeitschrift fuer Antimikrobielle Antineoplastische Chemotherapie.*

UK
**ANTIINFLAMMATORY ANTIALLERGIC AND GI PATENT FAST-ALERT.** ***Ceased.*** (19??)-(Apr. 1992). English. Fifty times a year. Current Science / England, Middlesex House, 34-42 Cleveland Street, London W1P 5FB England. **Tel** 011 44 71 580 8393, 011 44 71 323 0323, FAX 011 44 81 580 1938. **(Subscription address:** Current Science, 20 North 3rd Street, Philadelphia PA 19106.**)**

UK/0742-3195
**ANTIMICROBIAL CHEMOTHERAPY SERIES.** [Antimicrob. chemother. ser.]. (1982)-. Monographic series. English. Price varies per volume. John Wiley & Sons Ltd., Baffins Lane, Chichester West Sussex PO19 1UD England. **Tel** 0243 779777, FAX 0243 776128 BTG:JWP001, telex 86290 WIBOOKG. **(Subscription address:** North, South and Central America/ John Wiley & Sons, Inc., Subscription Department, 605 Third Avenue, New York, NY 10158-0012, USA; telephone: (212)850-6645; FAX: (212)850-6021**) ED** R.N. Gruneberg. **NLM** W1 AN875C. ***Continues*** *Antimicrobial Chemotherapy Research Studies Series, 0278-8284.*

US/0738-1751
**ANTIMICROBIC NEWSLETTER, THE.** ***Title Change.*** **See** Biology-Microbiology.

●US/1069-417X
**ANTIMICROBICS AND INFECTIOUS DISEASES NEWSLETTER. See** Biology-Microbiology.

II/0003-5998
**ANTISEPTIC, THE.** [Antiseptic]. (1904)-. Periodical. English. mo. $24.00. Professional Publications Pvt Ltd, PO Box 2, II Main Road, Satya Sai Nagar, Madurai 625003, Tamil Nadu India. **Tel** 35000. **(Subscription address:** Prints India, 11 Darya Ganj, New Delhi 110002 India.**) LC** R97. **DD** 610.5. **NLM** W1 AN888. Index available. **Bk Rev. Ad Acc.** ctrl circ.
**Ind/Abst** EMBASE.

US/0897-9871
**ANTIVIRAL AGENTS BULLETIN.** [Antivir. agents bull.]. Vol. 1, No. 1 (April 1988)-. Periodical. English. Twelve times a year. $350.00 US and North America; $410.00 other. Biotechnology Information Institute, 1700 Rockville Pike, Suite 400, Rockville MD 20852. **Tel** (301)424-0255, FAX (301)424-0257. **ED** Ronald A. Rader. **DD** 615. **NLM** W1; AN869PM. Index available. **Ad Acc.** available on an online database (files 16,636,648/Full-Text) from DIALOG.
**Desc:** A source of information about AIDS and antiviral drug and vaccine development and related activities worldwide. These articles describe and assess commerical and scientific developments, federal and regulatory activities, information resources, treatment advances and trends, patents, announcements of international patent disclosures and abstracts of recent journal articles
**Ind/Abst** Abstr. BioCommer.; F&S Index Plus Text, Int. [Select. Cov.]; PROMT [Full Txt.]; PTS Newsl. Database [Full Txt.].

US/0166-3542
**ANTIVIRAL RESEARCH.** [Antiviral res.]. Vol. 1, No. 1 (March 1981)-. Academic Scholarly Publication. English. mo (3 volumes). Fl1536.00. Elsevier Science Publishers BV, PO Box 211, 1000 AE Amsterdam Netherlands. **Tel** 011 31 20 5803642, FAX 011 31 20 5862696, telex 15682. **ED** A Billiau, E De Clercq, R Whitley, R Dolin, G Galasso and H Schellekens. **NLM** W1 AN869Q. **CODEN** ARSRDR. **[CCC]. Pr Rev.** available on microfilm and microfiche from University Microfilms International (UMI). Documents available from The Genuine Article, BIOSIS Document Express, CASDDS, ADONIS.
**Desc:** Publishes full-length original articles, short definitive papers and review articles, pertaining to the effective control of virus infections in animals and man as well as in plants or lower organisms.
**Ind/Abst** ADONIS; AgBiotech News Inf.; AGRICOLA; Biol. Abstr.; Chem. Abstr.; Curr. Aware. Biol. Sci., CABS; Curr. Contents Life Sci.; EMBASE; For. Prod. Abstr. (19??-19??); For. Abstr.; Health Plan. Adminis.; Hortic. Abstr.; Immunol. Abstr.; Index Med.; Index Vet.; Microbiol. Abstr. Sect. A; NAPRALERT; Life Sci. Collect.; PESTDOC; Pig News Inf.; Potato Abstr.; Ref. Upd. Deluxe Ed.; Res. Alert [Full Cov.]; Rev. Med. Vet. Entomol.; Rev. Med. Vet. Mycology; Rev. Plant Pathol.; Sci. Cit. Index; SCISEARCH; Small Anim. Abstr. Bibliogr.; Vet. Bull.; Trop. Dis. Bull.; Virol. AIDS Abstr.

SP
**ANUARIO ESPANOL Y PORTUGUES DE ANALITICA. VFOAT** Spanish and Portuguese Annual of Analysis. Spanish (Portuguese). 4.500ptas Spain; 9.00ptas North America; 6,500ptas other. Puntex SA, c/ Mare de Deu del Coll 14, 08023 Barcelona Spain. **Tel** (93)237 71 24, FAX (93)217 55 73, telex 97131 GPMM E. **Bk Rev. Ad Acc. Circ:** 10,000.
**Desc:** Medical companies and laboratories. Distributors, trademarks and products listed by specialties.

US
**AOE NEWWORK.** English. qt. $28.00. American Health Information Management Association, Order Unit, PO Box 97349, Chicago IL 60690-7349. **Tel** (312) 787-2672, FAX (312) 787-5926, (312) 787-9793.

US/1058-6385
**AOHA : A PUBLICATION OF THE AMERICAN OSTEOPATHIC HOSPITAL ASSOCIATION.** ***Title Change.*** [AOHA]. **Added/Corp** American Osteopathic Hospital Association. **VAT** American Osteopathic Hospital Association. (1991-1992). Periodical. English. mo. American Osteopathic Hospital Association, 5301 Wisconsin Avenue Northwest, Suite 630, Washington DC 20015. **Tel** (202)686-1700. **DD** 615. **NLM** W1; AO61. ***Continues*** *AOHA Today, 1044-1980.* ***Continued by*** *AOHA Progress.*
**Ind/Abst** Health Plan. Adminis.; Hospit. Health Admin. Index (1991-).

UK/0268-7038
**APHASIOLOGY.** [Aphasiology]. Vol. 1, No. 1 (Jan./Feb. 1987)-. Periodical. English. bm. $336.00 North America; £204.00 UK. Taylor & Francis Ltd., Rankine Road, Basingstoke Hampshire, RG24 8PR United Kingdom. **Tel** 011 44 256 840366, FAX 011 44 256 479438, telex 858540. **(Subscription address:** Taylor & Francis Inc., 1900 Frost Road, Suite 101, Bristol PA 19007-1598.**) ED** Chris Code, Dave Muller and Robert Marshall. **NLM** W1; AP17R. **[CCC]. Pr Rev.** available on microfilm and microfiche from University Microfilms International (UMI). Documents available from The Genuine Article.
**Desc:** Concerned with all aspects of language impairment and related disorders resulting from brain damage. It provides a forum for the exchange of knowledge and the dissemination of current research and expertise in all aspects of aphasia and related topics, from all disciplinary perspectives. Includes papers on clinical, psychological, linguistic and neurological perspectives of aphasia.
**Ind/Abst** Curr. Contents Clin. Med.; EMBASE; Linguist. Lang. Behav. Abstr. (1987-) [Full Cov.]; Res. Alert [Full Cov.]; SCISEARCH; Soc. Plann. Policy Dev. Abstr.; Soc. Sci. Cit. Index [Select. Cov.]; Sociol. Abstr.

UK/1350-4541
**APOPTOSIS.** (19??)-. English. £85.00. SUBIS, Mansion House, 19 Kingfield Road, Sheffield S11 9AS England. **Tel** 011 44 114 255 4433, FAX 011 44 114 255 4626.

US/0003-6609
**APPALACHIA MEDICINE.** **Added/Corp** Appalachian Regional Hospitals, Inc. Vol. 1 (1969)-. Periodical. English. qt. **NLM** W1 AP49. available on microfilm from University Microfilms International (UMI).

US/0362-5443
**APPLICATION OF OPTICAL INSTRUMENTATION IN MEDICINE.** **Added/Corp** United States. Bureau of Radiological Health. (1972)-. Monographic series. English. ir. Price varies per volume. Society of Photo-Optical Instrumentation Engineers, PO Box 10, Bellingham WA 98227. **Tel** (206)676-3290, telex 46-7053. **LC** R857.O6; A65. **DD** 616.07/5/028. **NLM** W1 AP49P.

US
**APPLICATIONS TO THE PROFESSIONAL SCHOOLS AND COLLEGES FOR THE FALL TERM 1948: MEDICINE, DENTISTRY, VETERINARY MEDICINE, PHARMACY, OPTOMETRY, OSTEOPATHY, LAW.** (1949)-. English. Ohio State University / College of Arts and Sciences, Columbus OH 43210. **LC** R745; .G88. **DD** 610.71173.

●GW/0943-0938
**APPLIED PARASITOLOGY.** Vol. 34, No. 1 (1993)-. Periodical. English (German). qt. DM236.00 Germany; DM244.00 other. Gustav Fischer Verlag Jena, Postfach 100537, D 07705 Jena Germany. **Tel** 011 49 3641 27332, FAX 011 49 3641 626500. **(Subscription address:** VCH Publishers Inc., 303 Northwest 12th Avenue, Journals Department, Deerfield FL 33442.**) NLM** W1; AP528KM. **CODEN** APPAEG. ***Continues*** *Angewandte Parasitologie.*
**Ind/Abst** Index Med. (1993-).

US/1057-1590
**APS BULLETIN / AMERICAN PAIN SOCIETY.** **See** Biology-Physiology.

●US/1058-9139
**APS JOURNAL.** (APS JOURNAL: OFFICIAL JOURNAL OF THE AMERICAN PAIN SOCIETY.). [APS j.]. **Added/Corp** American Pain Society. **VAT** American Pain Society Journal. Vol. 1, No. 1 (Spring 1992)-. Periodical. English. qt (4 issues). $105.00 (individuals), $145.00 (institutions). Churchill Livingstone Inc., 650 Avenue of the Americas, New York NY 10011. **Tel** (212)206-5062, FAX (212)727-7808. **(Subscription address:** Churchill Livingstone Inc., 5 South 250 Frontenac Road, Naperville, IL 60563; (telephone: (800)553-5426 or (708)416-3939)**) ED** Kenneth L. Casey. **LC** RB127; .A67. **DD** 616/.0472. **NLM** W1; AP549. **CODEN** APSJEO. **[CCC].** Documents available from The Genuine Article.
**Desc:** Publishes papers on issues and controversies on important advances in the field of pain research, as well as the latest news from the American Pain Society. Readership: neurologists, anesthesiologists, physical therapists, and nurses.
**Ind/Abst** Res. Alert [Full Cov.]; Soc. Sci. Cit. Index [Select. Cov.].

SP
**APUNTS.** Spanish. Centre de Estudis de l'Alt Rendiment Esportiu, Avda. Paissos Catalans S/N, 08950 Esplugues de Llobegrat Barcelona Spain.
**Ind/Abst** Indice Med. Esp.; SPORT Discus.

FR
**ARAB JOURNAL OF MEDICINE: MONTHLY INTERNATIONAL MEDICAL JOURNAL OF THE ARAB DOCTORS.** English. ir. Arab Journal of Medicine, 72 Ave des Champs Elysees, F 75008 Paris France. **Tel** 1 47200777.

GW/0723-5100
**ARAB MEDICO.** (19??)-. Arabic. bm. $39.00. Beta Verlag Marketinggesellschaft, Celsiusstrasse 43, D 53125 Bonn Germany. **Tel** 011 49 228 252061.
**Desc:** Journal for disaster and military medicine forum for the exchange of information.

CN/0345-0988
**ARBETSTERAPEUTEN.** [Arbetsterapeuten]. (1949)-. Periodical. English. Ten times a year. $50.00Can$ Canada; 60.00Can$ other. York Lanes Press, York University, 4700 Keele Street, North York ONT M3J 1P3 Canada. **Tel** (416)736-5843, FAX (416)736-5837. **UDC** 331.881.
**Desc:** Provides for medical services.

RM/0041-6940
**ARCHIVES.** **Main/Corp** Union Medicale Balkanique. Vol. 1 (1963)-. French. bm (6 issues). DM307.00. **(Subscription address:** Kubon & Sagner, ABT Zeitschriftenimport, D 80328 Munich Germany.**)**

BE/0003-9578
**ARCHIVES BELGES DE MEDECINE SOCIALE HYGIENE, MEDECINE DU TRAVAIL ET MEDECINE LEGALE.** [Arch. belg. med. soc. hyg., med. trav. med. leg.]. **VFOAT** Belgisch Archief van Sociale Geneeskunde, Hygieene, Arbeidsgeneeskunde en Gerechtelijke. No. 4 (1946)-. Periodical. French (Dutch and English). bm. 1415F Belgium; 1750F other. Archives Medicine Sociale et d'Hygiene, rue Montagne de l'Oratoire 20, 1010 Brussels Belgium. **NLM** W1 AR305. **CODEN** ABMHAM. **Circ:** 1,000 (ctrl). Documents available from CASDDS. ***Continues*** *Archives de Medecine Sociale et d'Hygiene et Revue de Pathologie et de Physiologie du Travail.*
**Desc:** Original papers on subjects such as hygiene, forensic, social or labour medicine.
**Ind/Abst** Chem. Abstr. (1946-1981); EMBASE; Health Plan. Adminis.; Saf. Health Work.

AE/0020-2460
**ARCHIVES DE L'INSTITUT PASTEUR D'ALGERIE.** [Arch. Inst. Pasteur Algerie]. **Main/Corp** Institut Pasteur d'Algerie. Vol. 1 (1923)-. French (summaries and/or abstracts in English). an. Price varies. Institut Pasteur d'Algeria, rue du Dr. Laveran, Alger Algeria. **NLM** W1 IN509P. available on microfilm from University Microfilms International (UMI). ***Continues in part*** *Archives des Instituts Pasteur de l'Afrique du Nord.*
**Ind/Abst** EMBASE; Health Plan. Adminis.; Index Med.; Index Vet.; Protozoolog. Abstr.; Vet. Bull.; Trop. Dis. Bull.

TI/0020-2509
**ARCHIVES DE L'INSTITUT PASTEUR DE TUNIS.** [Arch. inst. Pasteur Tunis]. **Added/Corp** Institut Pasteur de Tunis. Vol. 1 (1906)-. Periodical. French. Four times a year (Mar., June, Sept., Dec.). $25.00. Institut Pasteur de Tunis, 13 Place Pasteur, BP 74, 1002 Tunis Belvedere Tunisia. **Tel** 011 216 1 283022. **NLM** W1 AR337D. **CODEN** APTUAO. Documents available from BIOSIS Document Express, CASDDS.
**Ind/Abst** Biol. Abstr.; Chem. Abstr.; EMBASE; Health Plan. Adminis.; Index Med. (1978-); Index Vet.; Rev. Med. Vet. Entomol.; Trop. Dis. Bull.

FR/0003-9691
**ARCHIVES DES MALADIES PROFESSIONNELLES DE MEDECINE DU TRAVAIL ET SECURITE SOCIALE.** [Arch. mal. prof. med. trav. secur. soc.]. **Added/Corp** Societes de Medecine du Travail de France. Vol. 7 (1946)-. Academic Scholarly Publication. French. Eight times a year. $241.00. Masson Editeur, Box Postale 22, 41353 Vineuil 16 France. **Tel** 011 33 54 438994. **(Subscription address:** 7A Boulevard de Perolles, CH-1701 Fribourg Switzerland**) NLM** W1 AR3755. **CODEN** AMPMAR. **[CCC].** available on microfilm and microfiche from University Microfilms International (UMI). Documents available from CASDDS. ***Continues*** *Archives des Maladies Professionnelles.*
**Ind/Abst** Chem. Abstr.; Chem. Hazards Ind.; Coal Abstr.; EMBASE; Energy Res. Abstr.; Ergon. Abstr.; Lab. Hazards Bull.; Nutr. Abstr. Rev., Ser. B, Live Feeds and Feed.; Nutr. Abstr. Rev., Ser. A, Hum. Exp.; Life Sci. Collect.; Protozoolog. Abstr.; Rev. Med. Vet. Mycology; Rev. Plant Pathol.; Saf. Health Work; Trop. Dis. Bull.

●MX/0188-0128
**ARCHIVES OF MEDICAL RESEARCH.** **Added/Corp** Instituto Mexicano del Seguro Social. Vol. 23, No. 1 (Spring 1992)-. Periodical. English. qt. $55.00 (institutions), $45.00 (individuals) Mexico; $70.00 (institutions), $60.00 (individuals) other. Inst Mexicano Seguro Social, PO Box 73 032, 06720 Mexico Df Mexico. **Tel** 011 52 5 7610892. **LC** R21; .A735. **NLM** W1; AR455CHJ. ***Continues*** *Archivos de Investigacion Medica, 0066-6769.*

US/8756-0585
**ARCHIVES OF RESEARCH ON INDUSTRIAL CARCINOGENESIS.** [Arch. res. ind. carcinog.]. Vol. 2 (1984)-. Monographic series. English. ir. Price varies per volume. Princeton Scientific Publishing Company Inc., PO Box 2155, Princeton NJ 08543. **Tel** (609)683-4750, FAX (609)683-0838. **ED** Cesare Maltoni and M. A. Mehlman. **LC** UNC. **DD** 616. **NLM** W1; AR487H.
**Desc:** A series of specialized books giving extensive reviews and experimental data for chemicals of industrial significance.

JA
**ARCHIVES OF THE KOHNO CLINICAL MEDICINE RESEARCH INSTITUTE.** **Added/Corp** Kono Rinsho Igaku Kenkyujo. **VFOAT** Kono Rinsho Igaku Kenkyujo Hokan. (1963)-. English. Kono Rinsho Igaku Kenkyujo, (Kohno Clinical Medicine Research Inst.), 28-15, Kitashinagawa, 1 Chome, Shinagawaku, Tokyoto 140 Japan. **NLM** W1; AR489CK.
**Ind/Abst** Trop. Dis. Bull.

IT/0004-0282
**ARCHIVIO ITALIANO DI SCIENZE MEDICHE TROPICALI E DI PARASSITOLOGIA.** (1920)-. Italian. bm. Clin Trop Policlinica Umberto, Rome Italy. Documents available from CASDDS.
**Ind/Abst** Chem. Abstr.

CL/0004-0533
**ARCHIVOS DE BIOLOGIA Y MEDICINA EXPERIMENTALES.** ***Title Change.*** **See** Biology.

SP/0210-5527
**ARCHIVOS DE LA FACULTAD DE MEDICINA DE OVIEDO.** **Added/Corp** Facultad de Medicina de Oviedo. (19??)-. Periodical. Spanish. an. Universidad de Oviedo, Arguelles 19, 33003 Oviedo Spain. **Tel** 011 34 8 5210160. **NLM** W1; AR675Q.

SP/0558-6291
**ARCHIVOS DE LA FACULTAD DE MEDICINA DE ZARAGOZA.** [Arch. Fac. Med. Zaragoza]. Vol. 1 (Jan./Feb. 1932)-. Periodical. Spanish (summaries and/or abstracts in English, German and French). bm. Facultad Medicina Universidad de Zaragoza, Dept Ciencias Morfologicas, E 50009 Zaragoza Spain. **Tel** 011 34 76 359593. **NLM** W1 AR675I.
**Ind/Abst** EMBASE; Indice Med. Esp.

PL/0860-1844
**ARCHIWUM HISTORII I FILOZOFII MEDYCYNY.** (ARCHIWUM HISTORII I FILOZOFII MEDYCYNY / POLSKIE TOWARZYSTWO HISTORII MEDYCYNY I FARMACJI.). [Arch. hist. filoz. med.]. **Added/Corp** Polskie Towarzystwo Historii Medycyny i Farmacji. Vol. 48, Part 3 (1985)-. Periodical. Polish (summaries and/or abstracts in English and Russian). qt. Price on Request. **(Subscription address:** ARS Polona, PO Box 1001, 00068 Warsaw Poland.**) LC** R131; .A65. **DD** 610/.9438. **NLM** W1; AR7552. ***Continues*** *Archiwum Historii Medycyny, 0004-0762.*
**Ind/Abst** Am. Hist. Life (1985-); Index Med. (1985-).

PL/0324-8267
**ARCHIWUM MEDYCYNY SADOWEJ I KRJMINOLOGII.** [Arch. med. sad. kryminol.]. (1968)-. Academic Scholarly Publication. Polish (summaries and/or abstracts in English and Russian). qt. Price on Request. **(Subscription address:** ARS Polona, PO Box 1001, 00068 Warsaw Poland.**) CODEN** AMSKA2. Documents available from CASDDS. ***Continues*** *Archiwum Medycyny Sadowej. Psychiatrii Sadowej i Kryminolog.*
**Ind/Abst** Chem. Abstr.; EMBASE.

FI/0782-226X
**ARCTIC MEDICAL RESEARCH.** [Arch. med. res.]. **Added/Corp** Nordic Council for Arctic Medical Research. (1984)-. Periodical. English. Four times a year. $25.00. Nordic Council for Arctic Medical Research, Matti Nuutinen Aapistie 3, SF-90220 Oulu 22 Finland. **Tel** 011 358 81 334202, FAX 358-81-334765. **ED** J P Hart Hansen, Bert Harvald, Mikael Knip. **LC** RC955; .A76. **DD** 616.9/881. **NLM** W1; AR7558D. **CODEN** AMRSEP. Index available. **Bk Rev. Ad Acc. Pr Rev. Circ:** 2,200 (ctrl). ***Continues*** *Nordic Council for Arctic Medical Research Report, 0355-9823.*
**Ind/Abst** ASTIS Curr. Aware. Bull. (1984-); ASTIS Bibliogr. (1984-); Health Plan. Adminis.; Index Med. (Vol. 19, 1985)-.

UK
**ARMY MEDICAL SERVICES MAGAZINE.** (1948)-. Periodical. English. Three times a year (Feb., June, Oct.). £4.80 UK; £6.30 other. RAMC RHQ / Journal of the RAMC, Keogh Barrack/Ash Vale, Aldershot, Hants GU12 5RQ England. **Tel** 011 44 252 340250. Index available. **Ad Acc.**

II/0253-682X
**AROGYA.** [Arogya]. **Added/Corp** Academy of General Education (Manipala, India) Kasturba Medical College. (1975)-. Periodical. English. sa. $6.00. **NLM** W1 AR852. **CODEN** AROGD8. Documents available from CASDDS.
**Ind/Abst** Chem. Abstr.

BL/0365-0723
**ARQUIVOS BRASILEIROS DE MEDICINA.** [Arq. bras. med.]. **Added/Corp** Universidade do Brasil. Faculdade Nacional de Medicina. Universidade Federal Fluminense. Faculdade de Medicina. Vol. 42 (Jan./Feb. 1952)-. Academic Scholarly Publication. Portuguese (summaries and/or abstracts in English). bm. $80.00. Societe Brasileria de Dermatologia, Av Rio Branco 39 180 Andra, 20090 002 Rio De Jan Rj Brazil. **Tel** 011 55 21 2622825, 011 55 21 2213235. **NLM** W1 AR871. ***Formed by the union of*** *Archivos Brasileiros de Medicina* ***and*** *Arquivos de Clinica.*
**Ind/Abst** EMBASE [Select. Cov.].

BR/0004-2773
**ARQUIVOS CATARINENSES DE MEDICINA.** (ACM. ARQUIVOS CATARINENSES DE MEDICINA.). [Arq. catarinenses med.]. V. 3- Dec. 1974-. Periodical. Portuguese. ir. **NLM** W1 A1136D. ***Continues*** *Arquivos Catarinense de Medicina, 0004-2773.*
**Ind/Abst** Index Med.

PO/0871-3413
**ARQUIVOS DE MEDICINA : REVISTA DE CIENCIA E ARTE MEDICAS.** **Added/Corp** Hospital de S. Joa (Porto, Portugal) Faculdade de Medicina do Porto. (198?)-. Periodical. Portuguese (English). Six times a year. 3000$00 Portugal; 7500$.00 others. Associacao de Estudantes de Faculdade de Medicina do Porto Alamedad, Monteiro Piso 01, Hospital de San Joao, 4200 Porto Portugal. **Tel** 011 351 2 524901. **NLM** W1; AR686.
**Ind/Abst** EMBASE [Select. Cov.].

SZ/0004-2897
**ARS MEDICI, MONATSSCHRIFT FUER ALLGEMEINMEDIZIN.** Vol. 1 (1911)-. Academic Scholarly Publication. German (French). mo. 66.00F. S A E M Verlag AG, Schoenbuehlstrasse 1, CH-8200 Schaffhausen, Switzerland. **Tel** 053-258826, FAX 053-258930. **ED** Dr. Richard Altofer. **NLM** ZW 1 A782. Index available. cum. index. **Bk Rev. Ad Acc. Circ:** 4,500 (ctrl).
**Ind/Abst** EMBASE.

US/0742-1656
**ART THERAPY : JOURNAL OF THE AMERICAN ART THERAPY ASSOCIATION.** See Psychology.

●US/1073-1199
**ARTIFICIAL CELLS, BLOOD SUBSTITUTES, AND IMMOBILIZATION BIOTECHNOLOGY.** (1994)-. Periodical. English. Six times a year. $775.00 US; $796.00 other. Marcel Dekker Inc., 270 Madison Avenue, New York NY 10016. **Tel** (212)696-9000, (800)228-1160, FAX (212)685-4540, telex 421419. **(Subscription address:** Marcel Dekker Inc, PO Box 5017, Monticello NY 12701.**) NLM** W1; AR955G. ***Continues*** *Biomaterials, Artificial Cells, and Immobilization Biotechnology, 1055-7172.*

NE/0924-3054
**ARTIFICIAL ORGANS TODAY : THE OFFICIAL INTERNATIONAL JOURNAL OF THE JAPANESE SOCIETY FOR ARTIFICIAL ORGANS. Added/Corp** Nihon Jinko Zoki Gakkai. Vol. 1, No. (1991)-. Periodical. English. qt. DM330.00. VSP International Science Publishers, Godfried van Seystlaan 47, 3703 BR Zeist Netherlands. **Tel** 011 31 3404 25790, FAX 011 31 3404 32081, telex 40217 USP NL. **(Subscription address:** VSP International Science Publishers, PO Box 346, 3700 AH Zeist Netherlands.**) ED** T. Agishi. **NLM** W1; AR956H. **Pr Rev.** Documents available from The Genuine Article.
**Desc:** Covers a wide spectrum of new and exciting achievements from Japanese researchers in the field of artificial organs, ranging from fundamental research to clinical applications. Topics include blood purification, cardiology, biomaterials and artificial metabolic organs.
**Ind/Abst** Res. Alert [Full Cov.].

NE/0165-5299
**ARTS & WERELD. VAT** Arts en Wereld. Periodical. Dutch. mo. $23.36. Arts en Wereld BV, Traay 186A, 3971 GV Driebergen Netherlands. **NLM** W1 AR959.

GW
**ARZNEIMITTELBRIEF.** German. mo. DM69.00 Germany; DM145.00 other. Westkreuz Druckerei und Verlag, Toepchiner Weg 198-200, D-12309 Berlin Germany. **Tel** 011 49 30 7452047, FAX 011 49 30 7453066. **ED** D. von Gerrath and W. Thimme. Index available. **Circ:** 2,500 (ctrl).
**Desc:** Summary of articles which contain the collected know-how for medicines and therapies used in the doctors daily practice.

AU
**ARZNEIMITTELPRAXIS.** German. ir (4-6 issues per year). $18.00. Medizinische Akademie, Alser Strasse 4, A-1090 Vienna Austria. **Tel** 011 43 222 404005475.

GW/0175-7814
**ARZT IM KRANKENHAUS UND IM GESUNDHEITSWESEN (1981), DER.** (DER ARZT IM KRANKENHAUS UND IM GESUNDHEITSWESEN : MONATSSCHRIFT DES MARBURGER BUNDES.). **Added/Corp** Marburger Bund. **VFOAT** Arzt im Krankenhaus. (1981)-. Periodical. German. mo. **NLM** W1 AR973DC. ***Continues*** *Arzt Im Krankenhaus, 0175-7822.*

GW/0173-5764
**ARZT UND PATIENT (BADEN-BADEN).** (ARZT UND PATIENT.). [Arzt Patient]. 1/80-. Periodical. German. qt. Sun Publishing Ltd., 524 King Street, Fredericton NB E3B 1E6. **NLM** W1 AR982.

SZ/0253-0341
**ARZTE.** (ARZTE. MEDECINS. MEDICI.). [Arzte]. **Added/Corp** Verbindung der Schweizer Arzte. **VFOAT** Medecins; Medici; Schweizerische Arztezeitung; Bulletin des Medecins Suisses. (June 6, 1979)-. Periodical. French (German and Italian). wk. 227.00F. Verlag Hans Huber Ag Bern, Laenggass Strasse 76, CH 3000 Bern 9 Switzerland. **Tel** 011 41 31 3004500. **NLM** W1 AE153M. **Circ:** 26,000. ***Continues*** *Schweizerische Aerztezeitung.*
**Ind/Abst** Saf. Health Work.

GW/0175-5811
**ARZTE-ZEITUNG.** (1982)-. Periodical. German. da. DM149.80 Germany; DM470.00 other. Aerzte Zeitung Verlag GmbH, Postfach 101047, D 63303 Dreieich Germany. **Tel** 11 49 6102 5061488, FAX 11 49 6102 506123. **UDC** 61.

GW/0001-947X
**ARZTEBLATT BADEN-WURTTEMBERG. Added/Corp** Landesarztekammer Baden-Wurttemberg. (1967)-. Periodical. German. mo. $68.60. AW Gentner Verlag, Postfach 101742, D-70015 Stuttgart Germany. **Tel** 011 49 711 636720, FAX 011 49 711 6367247, telex 841 722244. **NLM** W1 AE153S. Index available. **Ad Acc. Circ:** 29,500. ***Continues*** *Arzteblatt Baden-Wurttemberg, 0001-947X.*

GW/0720-6003
**ARZTEZEITSCHRIFT FUER NATURHEILVERFAHREN : ORGAN DES ZENTRALVERBANDES DER ARZTE FUER NATURHEILVERFAHREN E. V. Added/Corp** Zentralverband der Arzte fuer Naturheilverfahren (Germany). Vol. 30, No. 10 (Oct. 1989)-. Periodical. German (summaries and/or abstracts in English and French). Twelve times a year. DM114.00 Germany; DM128.00 others. Medizinisch Literarische Verlag, Postfach 1151 + 1152, W 3110 Uelzen 1 F R Germany. **Tel** 011 49 581 808151, FAX 011 49 581 808158, telex 841 91326. **NLM** W1; AR987G. **[CCC].** ***Continues*** *Arztezeitschrift fÉur Naturheilverfahren und Regulationstherapie.*

GW/0001-9518
**ARZTLICHE JUGENDKUNDE. *Ceased.*** [Arztl. Jugendkd.]. Vol. 52 (July 1959)-(Dec. 1991). Academic Scholarly Publication. German. qt. Johann Ambrosius Barth, Prager Strasse 16 B, D 04103 Leipzig Germany. **Tel** 011 49 341 7137570. **NLM** W1 AE226. ***Continues*** *Gesundheit und Erziehung (Leipzig), 0323-8334.*
**Ind/Abst** EMBASE (?-?); Health Plan. Adminis.; Index Med. (1965-1966); SportSearch (?-?).

GW/0930-1178
**ARZTLICHE MONATSHEFTE.** [Arztl. Mon.hefte]. Vol. 36, No. 1 (Jan. 3, 1986)-. Periodical. German. mo. Deutscher Aerzte Verlag GmbH, Postfach 404265, D-50832 Cologne Germany. **Tel** 011 49 2234 7011219. **NLM** W1; AR96M. **CODEN** AEMOEY. Documents available from BIOSIS Document Express. ***Continues*** *Monatskurse fur die Arztliche Fortbildung, 0026-928X.*
**Ind/Abst** Biol. Abstr. (1986-).

GW/0001-9534
**ARZTLICHE PRAXIS.** [Arztl. prax.]. (1949)-. Periodical. German. ir. DM103.00. Werk Verlag, Dr. E. Banaschewski, Hans Cornelius STR 4, D 81266 Graefelfing Germany. **Tel** 011 49 89 89817122. **ED** Edmund Banaschewski. **NLM** W1 AE412. **[CCC].** Index available. cum. index. **Bk Rev. Ad Acc. Circ:** 54,000. available on microfilm from University Microfilms International (UMI).
**Desc:** The newspaper for the physician in clinics or practice.
**Ind/Abst** Saf. Health Work.

SP/0210-4466
**ASCLEPIO : ARCHIVO IBEROAMERICANO DE HISTORIA DE LA MEDICINA Y ANTROPOLOGIA MEDICA. Added/Corp** Instituto "Arnaldo de Vilanova" de Historia de la Medicina. **VFOAT** Archivo Iberoamericano de Historia de la Medicina y Antropologia Medica. Vol. 16 (1964)-. Periodical. Spanish. sa. 4000ptas Spain; 6000ptas other. Consejo Superior Investigacion Cientificas (CSIC), Vitruvio 8, 28006 Madrid Spain. **Tel** 011 34 1 5612833, FAX 011 34 1 4113077, telex 42182. **LC** R131.A1; A72. **NLM** W1 AS124. ***Continues*** *Archivo Iberoamericano de Historia de la Medicina y Antropologia Medica.*
**Desc:** Publishes research and original articles on the history of medicine and medical anthropology, and on the history of science in general. Contributors are based in Spain and Latin America.
**Ind/Abst** Am. Hist. Life (1983-); Anthropol. Index; Indice Med. Esp.

SI/0129-4881
**ASEAN JOURNAL OF CLINICAL SCIENCES.** [ASEAN j. clin. sci.]. **Added/Corp** ASEAN. (1980)-. Academic Scholarly Publication. English. qt. 124.00Sing$ Singapore; 129.00Sing$ other. Melirwin Enterprises, 126 Joo Seng Road/#06-17, Gold Pine Building, Singapore 1336 Singapore. **Tel** 2808323, FAX 284 6056, telex RS 55674. **NLM** W1; AS129. **CODEN** AJCSDU. **Ad Acc.** Documents available from CASDDS.
**Ind/Abst** Chem. Abstr.; Helminthol. Abstr. (1991-); Trop. Dis. Bull.

US/1062-0281
**ASEPSIS (ARLINGTON, TEX.).** (ASEPSIS.). [Asepsis]. **VFOAT** Asepsis Forum. (197?)-. Periodical. English. qt. Free. Ad/Com Inc. Publishing, 2003 East Lamar Boulevard, Arlington TX 76006-7395. **Tel** (817)795-8247. **DD** 616. **NLM** W1; AS129D.
**Ind/Abst** Cumul. Index Nurs. Allied Health Lit.; Int. Nurs. Index (1990-).

JA/0004-461X
**ASIAN MEDICAL JOURNAL.** [Asian med. j.]. **Added/Corp** Nihon Ishikai. Vol. 1 (Oct. 1958)-. Academic Scholarly Publication. English. mo. $72.00. **(Subscription address:** Japan Publications Trading Company, Ltd., PO Box 5030, Tokyo International, Tokyo 100-31 Japan.**) NLM** W1 AS14. **CODEN** ASMJAB. available on microfilm from University Microfilms International (UMI). Documents available from CASDDS.
**Ind/Abst** Biodeter. Abstr.; Chem. Abstr.; EMBASE; Helminthol. Abstr.; Index Vet.; Microbiol. Abstr. Sect. B (19??-19??); Nutr. Res. Newsl.; Life Sci. Collect.; Protozoolog. Abstr.; Rev. Med. Vet. Entomol.; Rev. Med. Vet. Mycology; Rev. Plant Pathol.; SEA Abstr.; Trop. Dis. Bull.; Virol. AIDS Abstr.

US/1053-7813
**ASIAN MEDICINE.** (ASIAN MEDICINE : THE JOURNAL OF THE AMERICAN COLLEGE OF TRADITIONAL CHINESE MEDICINE / MEI CHOU CHUNG I HSUEH YUAN.). [Asian med.]. **Added/Corp** American College of Traditional Chinese Medicine. **VFOAT** Journal of the American College of Traditional Chinese Medicine. Vol. 8, No. 1, (1990)-. Periodical. English. qt. $25.00. American College of Traditional Chinese Medicine, 2400 Geary Boulevard, San Francisco CA 94115. **Tel** (415)346-7600. **DD** 615. ***Continues*** *Journal of the American College of Traditional Chinese Medicine, 0739-571X.*

●US/1065-2566
**ASPIRE INTERNATIONAL NEWSLETTER.** [Aspire int. newsl.]. **VFOAT** Aspire. Vol. 1, No. 1 (Summer 1992)-. Newsletter. English. qt. $135.00 (institutions). Aspire International Newsletter, Box 1127, One Gustave L Levy Place, New York NY 10029-6574. **DD** 610.

US/1064-4962
**ASSERTIVE UTILIZATION MANAGEMENT REPORT, THE.** [Assert. util. manag. rep.]. (1991)-. Periodical. English. Twelve times a year. $30.00. Mage Corp, 204 East 2nd Avenue, Suite 334, San Mateo CA 94401. **Tel** (415)348-3647. **DD** 610. **Bk Rev**, (Qty: 1-2). ctrl circ.

IS/0334-3871
**ASSIA, JEWISH MEDICAL ETHICS. Added/Corp** Makhon a. sh. Dr. Falk Shlezinger zal le-Heker ha-Refuah a. pi ha-Torah. **VFOAT** Assia; Jewish Medical Ethics. Vol. 1, No. 1 (May 1988)-. Periodical. English (Hebrew). sa. $25.00. Falk Schlesinger Institute MH RE, Sha Are Zedek Hospital, Jeruslem 91031 Isreal. **Tel** 011 972 2 555266. **ED** Dr. Mordechai Halperin. **LC** R724; .A87. **NLM** W1; AS349G. **Ad Acc. Circ:** 500 English, 800 Hebrew.

CN/0820-7399
**ASSOCIATION MONDIALE DES MEDECINS FRANCOPHONES (1982).** (ASSOCIATION MONDIALE DES MEDECINS FRANCOPHONES : [BULLETIN].). [Assoc. mond. med. francoph.]. **Added/Corp** Association Mondiale des Medecins Francophones. No. 8 (July 1982)-. French. sa. Free to members. Association Mondiale des Medecins Francophones, 9 Beckenham Lane, Ottawa Ontario K1J 7J5 Canada. **DD** 610.69/52/0601. **Circ:** 800. ***Continues*** *AMMF, 0820-7380.*

MX/0185-6235
**ATENCION MEDICA.** [Aten. med.]. **VFOAT** Patient Care en Mexico. (1980). Spanish. mo. $80.00. Intersistemas SA de CV, Fernando Alencastre #110, Mexico City DF Mexico. **Tel** 011 52 5 5202073, 011 52 5 5405600. **ED** Martha Castilleja. **NLM** W1 AT212H. **Bk Rev. Ad Acc. Circ:** 16,500 (ctrl).
**Desc:** Continuous medical education articles for general practitioners on day to day practice. Editorial features round table and flow charts.

SP/0212-7601
**ATENCION MEDICA MADRID.** [Aten. med.Madr.]. (1974)-. Periodical. Spanish. bm. Graficas Enar SA, Pedro Muguruza 3/1, 28016 Madrid Spain. **UDC** 61.

UK/0261-4553
**ATPASES.** (19??)-. English. £85.00. SUBIS, Mansion House, 19 Kingfield Road, Sheffield S11 9AS England. **Tel** 011 44 114 255 4433, FAX 011 44 114 255 4626.

IT/0001-4427
**ATTI DELLA ACCADEMIA MEDICA LOMBARDA. Added/Corp** Accademia Medica Lombarda, Milan (1960-). Vol. 15, No. 1 (Apr. 1960)-. Academic Scholarly Publication. Italian. sa. L50000 Italy; L100000 other. Accademia Medica Lombarda, 3 Clinica Chirurgica, Via F Sforza 35, 20122 Milan Italy. **Tel** 02 5408941, FAX 02 5457328. **ED** Emilio Trabucchi. **NLM** W1 AT775. **CODEN** AAMLAR. Documents available from CASDDS.
**Ind/Abst** Chem. Abstr. (-1979); EMBASE; Health Plan. Adminis.; Saf. Health Work.

IT
**ATTI DELLA ACCADEMIA PELORITANA DEI PERICOLANTI. CLASSE DI SCIENZE MEDICO-BIOLOGICHE.** Periodical. Italian (summaries and/or abstracts in English). **LC** R106; .A785. **DD** 610/.5. **NLM** W1 AC645. ***Continues in part*** *Atti Della. Accademia Peloritana.*

BL/0001-1800
**ATUALIDADES MEDICAS.** [Atual. med.]. **VFOAT** AM. Vol. 5 (April 1969)-. Periodical. Portuguese. mo. **NLM** W1 AT875B. ***Continues*** *AM. Revista de Atualidades Medicas.*

# Medical Science and Technology

●UK/1350-9667
**AUDIO JOURNAL OF ONCOLOGY.**
(1994)-. English. qt. $225.00 US and Canada; £130.00 Europe; £145.00 Other. Chapman & Hall, 2-6 Boundary Row, London SE1 8HN England. **Tel** 011 44 71 865 0066, FAX 011 44 71 522 9623, telex 290164 Chapmag. **(Subscription address:** Chapman & Hall, Cheriton House, North Way, Andover, Hampshire, SP10 5BE England.**)**

US/0363-5473
**AUDIT ACTION LETTER, THE.** V. 1- Nov. 1, 1975-. Periodical. English. sm. Patient Care, 690 Kinderkamack Road, Oradell NJ 07649-1506. **NLM** W1 AU202.

US/0363-7387
**AUDIT ACTION LETTER INFORMATION BONUS, THE.** See Business-Accounting.

US/0148-3439
**AUDIT REPORT. BOARD OF MEDICAL EXAMINERS.** (AUDIT REPORT, BOARD OF MEDICAL EXAMINERS (TENNESSEE).). **Main/Corp** Tennessee. Division of State Audit. English. an. Tennessee Comptroller of the Treasury, Nashville TN 37219. **LC** RA396.A4; T37. **DD** 353.9/768/00841.

US/0149-1903
**AUDIT REPORT, BOARD OF PODIATRY.** (AUDIT REPORT, BOARD OF PODIATRY (TENNESSEE).). [Audit rep., Board Podiatry]. **Main/Corp** Tennessee. Division of State Audit. English. Division of State Audit, 1533 Andrew Jackson State Office Building, Nashville TN 37219. **LC** RD563; .T46A. **DD** 353.9/768/0084197585.

AT/0726-3139
**AUSTRALIAN CLINICAL REVIEW. Title Change.** [Aust. clin. rev.]. **Added/Corp** Australian Medical Association. Australian Council on Hospital Standards. AMA/ACHS Peer Review Resource Centre. No. 1 (May 1981)-(199?). Academic Scholarly Publication. English. qt. Blackwell Scientific Publications Australia, 54 University Street, PO Box 378, Carlton Victoria 3053 Australia. **Tel** 011 61 3 3470300, FAX 011 61 3 3475001, telex 10716421. **(Subscription address:** UK/ Marston Book Services, PO Box 87, Oxford UK; US/ 3 Cambridge Center, Suite 208, Cambridge MA 02142; Germany/ Meinekestrasse 4, D-1000 Berlin 15 Germany; France/ Arnette, 2 rue Casimir Delavigne, 75006 Paris France; Austria/ Blackwell MZV, Medizinische Zeitschriftenverlags Gesellschaft, Feldgasse 13, A-1238 Vienna Austria) **ED** John Best. **NLM** W1 AU5185M. Index available. **Bk Rev**. **Circ:** 850. available on microfilm and microfiche from University Microfilms International (UMI). **Continued by** Journal of Quality in Clinical Practice, 1320-5455.
**Desc:** Keeps medical and allied health professions updated on current events in peer review, quality assurance, criteria auditing, utilization review and continuing medical education throughout Australia and the world.
**Ind/Abst** Cumul. Index Nurs. Allied Health Lit.; Health Plan. Adminis.; Hospit. Health Admin. Index; Hum. Resour. Abstr. (?-?); Index Med. (May 1981-).

AT/1031-170X
**AUSTRALIAN COLLEGE OF MIDWIVES INCORPORATED JOURNAL.** [Aust. Coll. Midwives Inc. j.]. **Added/Corp** Australian College of Midwives. **VFOAT** ACMI Journal. Vol. 1, No. 1 (June 1988)-. Periodical. English. Four times a year (Mar., June, Sept., Dec.). 40.00Aus$ Australia; 60.00Aus$ other. Australian College of Midwives, 23-431 St. Kilda Road, Suite 23, Melbourne Victoria 3004 Australia. **Tel** 011 61 3 8045071, FAX 011 61 3 8661370. **ED** Lorraine Wilson. **NLM** W1; AU521S. **Bk Rev**. **Ad Acc**. **Pr Rev. Circ:** 3,500.
**Desc:** Professional journal for midwives and associated health professional.
**Ind/Abst** Health Plan. Adminis.; Int. Nurs. Index (June 1988-).

●AT/1038-1643
**AUSTRALIAN JOURNAL OF MEDICAL SCIENCE.** **Added/Corp** Australian Institute of Medical Scientists. Vol. 13, No. 1 (Feb. 1992)-. Academic Scholarly Publication. English. Four times a year (Feb., May, Aug., Nov.). 50.00Aus$ Australia; 65.00Aus$ other. Australian Journal Medical of Lab Science, PO Box 450, National Secretary, Toowong, Queensland, 4066 Australia. **Tel** 011 61 07 371-3370, FAX 011 61 07 870-4857. **ED** Dr. G. R. Cannell. **CODEN** AUJMEN. Index available (Included in Nov. issue). **Bk Rev**, (Qty: 30). **Ad Acc, Adv Mgr:** B. Walker, **Tel** (07)371-3370. Full Page (B&W) 450.00Aus$. Half Page (B&W) 360.00Aus$. **Pr Rev. Circ:** 2,500 (ctrl). Documents available from CASDDS. **Continues** Australian Journal of Medical Laboratory Science, 0158-4960.
**Desc:** Targeted to members in pathology laboratories, medical and veterinary laboratories of public health departments and universities throughout Australia and many pathology laboratories, research institutes and international libraries.
**Ind/Abst** Chem. Abstr.; Curr. Aware. Biol. Sci., CABS.

AT/1036-9457
**AUSTRALIAN JOURNAL OF MUSIC THERAPY, THE.** [Aust. j. music ther.]. **Added/Corp** Australian Music Therapy Association. (1990)-. English. an. 40.00Aus$. Australian Music Therapy Association, 18 Collins Street, Box Hill, Victoria 3128 Australia. **Tel** 011 61 3 8173129. **ED** Helen Efron and Wendy Taylor. **DD** 615.851540994. **Bk Rev**. **Circ:** 1400 (ctrl).
**Ind/Abst** Aust. Educ. Index (19??-).

●AT/1038-5282
**AUSTRALIAN JOURNAL OF RURAL HEALTH, THE.** **Added/Corp** Association for Australian Rural Nurses. Vol. 1, No. 1 (Nov. 1992)-. Academic Scholarly Publication. English. Four times a year. 140.00Aus$ Australia; 200.00Aus$ other. Blackwell Scientific Publications Australia, 54 University Street, PO Box 378, Carlton Victoria 3053 Australia. **Tel** 011 61 3 3470300, FAX 011 61 3 3475001, telex 10716421. **NLM** W1; AU619.

AT
**AUSTRALIAN MEDICINE : NEWSMAGAZINE OF THE AUSTRALIAN MEDICAL ASSOCIATION.** **Added/Corp** Australian Medical Association. (198?)-. Periodical. English. Twenty-two times a year. 150.00Aus$ Australia; 270.00Aus$ others. Australian Medical Association, PO Box E115, Queen Victoria Terrace, Parkes Australian Capital Territories, 2600 Australia. **Tel** 011 61 6 2705400, FAX 011 61 6 2705499. **ED** Penny Cummins. **NLM** W1; AU633. **Ad Acc, Adv Mgr:** Julie Taylor. **Circ:** 22,000.
**Desc:** News and information of the Australia Medical Association.

AT/0312-8008
**AUSTRALIAN PRESCRIBER.** **Added/Corp** Australia. Dept. of Health. Vol. 1 No. 1 (Oct./Dec. 1975)-. Periodical. English. Four times a year (Feb., May, Aug., Nov.). Free. Australian Prescriber, PO Box 100, Woden Australian Capital Territory 2606 Australia. **Tel** 011 61 6 2897038, FAX 011 61 6 2897694. **ED** Dr. J. S. Dowden. **NLM** W1 AU644E. Index available. cum. index. **Bk Rev**, (Qty: 1). **Pr Rev. Circ:** 60,000 (ctrl).
**Desc:** Review of therapeutics.
**Ind/Abst** Iowa Drug Inf. Serv. (1975-).

AT
**AUSTRALIAN PRIVATE DOCTOR : THE JOURNAL OF PRIVATE DOCTORS OF AUSTRALIA.** **Added/Corp** Private Doctors of Australia. (1985)-. Periodical. English. Six times a year. 70.00Aus$. Private Doctors of Australia, PO Box 390, Wentworthville, NSW 2145 Australia. **Tel** 011 61 02 6365805, FAX 011 61 02 8961651. **ED** Dr. John Mackellar. **NLM** W1; AU644EC. **Bk Rev**, (Qty: 4). **Ad Acc, Adv Mgr:** Ron Hill, **Tel** (08)212 3551. **Circ:** 2,000 (ctrl). **Continues** GP. The Australian & New Zealand General Practitioner, 0158-0787.
**Desc:** Medical policies in Australia.

AT/1030-1933
**AUSTRALIAN THERAPEUTIC DEVICE BULLETIN / DEPARTMENT COMMUNITY SERVICES AND HEALTH.** **Added/Corp** Australia. Dept. of Community Services and Health. Therapeutic Goods Administration (Australia). No. 2 (Nov. 1987)-. Bulletin. English. Three times a year. Free. Australia Department of Health, PO Box 100, Woden ACT 2606 Australia. **Tel** 011 61 6 2398711. **NLM** W1; AU6973. **Continues** Therapeutic Device Bulletin.

US/0893-8474
**AUTISM RESEARCH REVIEW INTERNATIONAL, THE.** See Psychology.

US
**AUTOMATED MEDICAL PAYMENTS NEWS.** (19??)-. Periodical. English. sm. $345.00. Faulkner & Gray Inc., 11 Penn Plaza, 17th Floor, New York NY 10001. **Tel** (212)967-7000, (800)535-8403. **(Subscription address:** Faulkner & Gray, Inc., 118 South Clinton St., Suite 700, Chicago IL 60661.**)**

SP/0214-4077
**AVANCES EN TRAUMATOLOGIA, CIRUGIA, REHABILITACION, MEDICINA PREVENTIVA Y DEL DEPORTE.** [Av. traumatol. cir. rehabil. med. prev. deport.]. **VFOAT** Avances en Traumatologia, Cirugia, Rehabilitacion, Medicina Preventiva y Deportiva. (1985)-. Periodical. Spanish. qt. Puntex SA, Via Laietana 30 4 F, 08003 Barcelona Spain. **Tel** 011 34 3 2680444. **UDC** 61. **Continues** Avances de Traumatologia, Cirugia y Rehabilitacion, Laboral y Deportiva, 0214-4085.
**Ind/Abst** Indice Med. Esp.

●RU/0233-528X
**AVIAKOSMICHESKAIA I EKOLOGICHESKAIA MEDITSINA.** **Added/Corp** Institut Mediko-Biologicheskikh Problem (Russia). **VFOAT** Aerospace and Environmental Medicine. (1992)-. Periodical. Russian (summaries and/or abstracts in English; table of contents in English). Six times a year. $126.00 US; $129.00 other. Izdatelstvo Meditsina / Russian Academy of Medical Sciences, Ulitsa Solyanka 14, 109801 Moscow Russia. **Tel** 011 95 297-05-04. **(Subscription address:** East View Publications Inc., 3020 Harbor Lane North, Suite 110, Minneapolis MN 55447.**) LC** RC1050; .K64. **NLM** W1; AV36. **Continues** Kosmicheskaia Biologiia i Aviakosmicheskaia Meditsina.
**Ind/Abst** Index Med. (1992-).

II/0250-5045
**AVIATION MEDICINE (BANGALORE).** (AVIATION MEDICINE.). [Aviat. med.]. **Added/Corp** Aero Medical Society of India. (1975-). Periodical. English. Twice a year (June, Dec.). $5.20 India; $10.30 US & Canada; $16.05 Europe. Aero Medical Soceity of India, Headquarters West Air Command, IAF PMO, New Delhi, 110010 India. **Tel** 60 661-1228. **ED** Ari Cude Pe Chatterji. **NLM** W1 AV453M. Index available. cum. index. **Bk Rev**. **Ad Acc**. **Circ:** 700. **Continues** Journal of Aero Medical Society of India, 0515-5207.
**Desc:** This field contains original works and applied studies of aerospace medicines.
**Ind/Abst** Int. Aerosp. Abstr.

US/0095-6562
**AVIATION SPACE AND ENVIRONMENTAL MEDICINE.** [Aviat. space environ. med.]. **Added/Corp** Aerospace Medical Association. **VFOAT** Aviation space & environmental medicine. Vol. 46 (Jan. 1975)-. Academic Scholarly Publication. English. mo. $100.00 US; $110.00 other; (airmail postage add $38.00). Aerospace Medical Association, 320 South Henry Street, Alexandria VA 22314. **Tel** (703)739-2240, FAX (703)739-9652. **ED** David R Jones. **LC** RC1050; .A36. **DD** 616.9/8. **NLM** W1 AV47. **CODEN** ASEMCG. **[CCC].** Index available. cum. index. **Bk Rev**. **Ad Acc**. **Pr Rev. Circ:** 5,500. available on microfilm and microfiche from University Microfilms International (UMI). Documents available from The Genuine Article, BIOSIS Document Express, CASDDS. **Continues** Aerospace Medicine, 0001-9402.
**Desc:** Edited for those involved in protecting the health of man in hostile environments. It contains original articles on clinical, investigative and applied medicine.
**Ind/Abst** Aviat. Tradescan [Full Cov.]; Biol. Abstr.; Chem. Abstr.; CIS Abstr.; Cumul. Index Nurs. Allied Health Lit.; Curr. Contents Clin. Med.; Curr. Contents Life Sci.; EMBASE; Energy Res. Abstr. (Oct. 1975-); Ergon. Abstr.; Health Saf. Sci. Abstr.; Index Med.; INIS Atomindex [Micro.]; Int. Aerosp. Abstr.; Nutr. Abstr. Rev., Ser. B, Live Feeds and Feed.; Nutr. Abstr. Rev., Ser. A, Hum. Exp.; Life Sci. Collect.; Psychol. Abstr. (1975-); PsycINFO; PsycLit; PsycScan: Appl. Psych.; Ref. Sources; Res. Alert [Full Cov.]; Risk Abstr.; Saf. Health Work; Sci. Cit. Index; SCISEARCH; Soc. Sci. Cit. Index [Select. Cov.]; SportSearch.

II/0005-2469
**AYU.** [Ayu]. Multiple languages (English and Hindi). 6.00. Gujarata Ayurveda Yunivarsiti, Registrar Dhanvantari Mandir, Jamanagara India. **LC** R606. **NLM** W1 AY966. **Continues** Ayurvedaloka.

AJ/0005-2523
**AZERBAIDZANSKIJ MEDICINSKIJ ZURNAL.** (AZERBAIDZHANSKII MEDITSINSKII ZHURNAL.). [Azerb. med. z.]. **Added/Corp** Azerbaidzhanskii Meditsinskii Institut, Baku. (1928)-. Periodical. Azerbaijani (Russian). **NLM** W1 AZ971. **CODEN** AZMZA6. Documents available from BIOSIS Document Express, CASDDS. **Continues** Bakinskii Meditsinskii Zhurnal.
**Ind/Abst** Biol. Abstr.; Chem. Abstr.

US/0074-8919
**BABOON IN MEDICAL RESEARCH, THE.** (THE BABOON IN MEDICAL RESEARCH : PROCEEDINGS OF THE FIRST INTERNATIONAL SYMPOSIUM ON THE BABOON AND ITS USE AS AN EXPERIMENTAL ANIMAL.). **Main/Conf** International Symposium on the Baboon and its Use as an Experimental Animal. **Added/Corp** Southwest Foundation for Research and Education (San Antonio, Tex.). 1st (1963)-. English. ir. University of Texas Press, PO Box 7819, Austin TX 78713. **Tel** (512)471-4531, FAX (512)320-0668, telex 776453 UTEXPRES AUS. **DD** 619/.98.

US/0746-9500
**BACK PAIN MONITOR. Ceased.** [Back pain monit.]. Vol. 1, No. 1 (Oct. 1983)-Vol. 11, No. 6 (June 1993). Periodical. English. mo. American Health Consultants, 3525 Piedmont Road, Suite 400, Atlanta GA 30305. **Tel** (800)688-2421, (404)262-7436. **NLM** W1; BA187. **[CCC].**

US/0894-7376
**BACKLETTER, THE.** [Backletter]. **VFOAT** Back Letter. (198?)-. Newsletter. English. mo. $89.00 US, Canada & Mexico; $99.00 other. Quest Publishing Company, 1351 Titan Way, Brea CA 92621. **Tel** (714)738-6400, FAX (714)525-6258. **DD** 616.
**Ind/Abst** Health Period. Database [Full Txt.]; Health Ref. Cent. (Jan. 1990-) [Full Txt.] [Full Cov.].

RM
**BACTERIOLOGIA, VIRUSOLOGIA, PARAZITOLOGIA, EPIDEMIOLOGIA / UNIUNEA SOCIETATILOR DE STIINTE MEDICALE DIN ROMANIA.** See Biology-Microbiology.

GW/0724-5297
**BAD INTERN.** (BAD-INTERN : DER BERUFSGENOSSENSCHAFTLICHE ARBEITSMEDIZINISCHE DIENST.). [BAD intern]. **Added/Corp** Berufsgenossenschaftlicher Arbeitsmedizinischer Dienst (Germany). **VFOAT** BAD Intern. **VAT** Berufsgenossenschaftlicher Arbeitsmedizinischer Dienst Intern. (1983)-. Periodical. German. ir. **NLM** W1; BA289C.

CC/0253-3707
**BAIQUIEN YIKE DAXUE XUEBAO.** (PAI CH'IU-EN I K'O TA HSUEH HSUEH PAO. BAIQIUENYIKEDAXUE XUEBAO.). [Baiquien yike daxue xuebao]. **Added/Corp** Pai Ch'iu-en I K'o Ta Hsueh. **VFOAT** Baiqiuenyikedaxue Xuebao; Journal of Bethune Medical College; Baiqiuenyikedaxue Xuebao. (1978)-. Academic Scholarly Publication. Chinese (table of contents in English). bm. $24.00. Baiqiuen Yike Daxue, Xuebao Bianjibu/Norman Bethune, 6, Xinmin Dajie, Changchun, Jilin 130021, Peoples Republic of China. **Tel** 86 431 645911, FAX 86 431 644739. **ED** Li Guangsheng. **NLM** W1 PA273Y. **CODEN** PEIPDB. **Circ:** 2.500 (paid), 1,000 other (ctrl). Documents available from CASDDS.
**Desc:** Information on new developments and research in medical science and technology.
**Ind/Abst** Chem. Abstr.; NAPRALERT.

UK/0005-4216
**BALANCE LONDON.** (BALANCE). [BalanceLond.]. (1961)-. Periodical. English. Six times a year. £10.00 UK & Eire; £20.00 other. British Diabetic Association, 10 Queen Anne Street, London W1M 0BD England. **Tel** 011 44 71 323 1531, FAX 011 44 71 637 3644. **ED** Lesley Hallett and Ed Barrett. **DD** 616.462. Index available. **Bk Rev. Ad Acc. Pr Rev. Circ:** 137,500 (ctrl). ***Continues** Diabetic Journal (London).*
**Desc:** Caters specifically to people with diabetes. Source for diabetic care, new products, medical breakthroughs and advice on how others cope with the disease.

GW
**BALINT-GRUPPE IN KLINIK UND PRAXIS, DIE.** Vol. 1 (1988)-. Monographic series. German. Price varies per volume. Springer-Verlag GmbH & Company KG, Heidelberger Platz 3, D 14197 Berlin Germany. **Tel** 011 49 30 8207223, FAX 011 49 30 8214091, telex 183 319 SPBLN D. **(Subscription address:** Springer Verlag New York Inc. / for North America, 44 Hartz Way, Secaucus NJ 07096.**) LC** WMLC 93/2285. **NLM** W1; BA489.

BG/0301-035X
**BANGLADESH MEDICAL JOURNAL.** [Bangladesh med. j.]. **Added/Corp** Bangladesh Medical Association. New Series Vol. 1, No. 1 (July 1972)-. Academic Scholarly Publication. English. qt. $20.00. Bangladesh Medical Association, B.M.A. House, 15-2 Topkhana Road, Dhaka 2, Bangladesh. **ED** Nazrul Islam. **NLM** W1 BA644. **Bk Rev. Ad Acc. Circ:** 6,000. available with charts; available with illustrations. ***Continues** East Pakistan Medical Journal, 0301-1364.*
**Ind/Abst** EMBASE; Rev. Med. Vet. Entomol.; Trop. Dis. Bull.

BG/0377-9238
**BANGLADESH MEDICAL RESEARCH COUNCIL BULLETIN.** [Bangladesh Med. Res. Counc. bull.]. **Added/Corp** Bangladesh Medical Research Council. Vol. 1 (1975)-. Periodical. English. sa. TK200.00 Bangladesh; $20.00 other. Bangladesh Medical Research Council, Health Institute 2nd Floor, Mohakhali, Dhaka-12 Bangladesh. **Tel** 600992. **ED** S. M. Keramat Ali, N. Islam. **NLM** W1 BA644F. **CODEN** BMRBDI. Index available. **Ad Acc. Circ:** 1,000 (ctrl). Documents available from BIOSIS Document Express.
**Ind/Abst** Biocont. News Inf. (1991-); Biol. Abstr.; EMBASE; Health Plan. Adminis.; Index Med.; Rev. Med. Vet. Entomol.; Rev. Med. Vet. Mycology; Trop. Dis. Bull.

SZ/0067-4524
**BASLER VEROFFENTLICHUNGEN ZUR GESCHICHTE DER MEDIZIN UND DER BIOLOGIE.** No. 1 (1953)-. Monographic series. German (French). ir. Price varies. Schwabe & Company Ltd., Farnsburgerstrasse 8 PF 254, CH-4132 Muttenz 1 Switzerland. **Tel** 011 41 61 4613001, FAX 01 41 61 4612500. **LC** R131.A1; B3. **NLM** W1 BA829. **[CCC].** Index available. **Circ:** 500.
**Desc:** Covers the history of medicine and biology of local interest (Basler Switzerland).

US/1049-4316
**BBI NEWSLETTER, THE.** See Business.

US/0197-7717
**BEHAVIORAL MEDICINE ABSTRACTS.** ***Title Change.*** **See** Medical Science and Technology-Abstracting, Bibliographies and Statistics.

US/0896-4289
**BEHAVIORAL MEDICINE (WASHINGTON, D.C.).** (BEHAVIORAL MEDICINE.). [Behav. med.]. Vol. 14, No. 1 (Spring 1988)-. Periodical. English. qt. $48.00 (individual), $90.00 (institution). Heldref Publications, 1319 Eighteenth Street Northwest, Washington DC 20036-1802. **Tel** (202)296-6267, (800)365-9753, FAX (202)296-5149. **ED** Herbert Benson, Richard Friedman, and Stanislav V. Kasl. **LC** RB152; .J67. **DD** 616.07/1/05. **NLM** W1; BE13GK. **CODEN** BEMEEF. **[CCC].** Index available. cum. index. **Ad Acc. Pr Rev. Acid Free. Circ:** 900. available on microfilm from University Microfilms International (UMI). Documents available from The Genuine Article, BIOSIS Document Express. ***Continues** Journal of Human Stress, 0097-840X.*
**Desc:** An interdisciplinary journal of interest to physicians, psychiatrists, psychologists, nurses, educators, and all who deal with the interaction of behavior and physical health.
**Ind/Abst** Annals Behav. Med.; Appl. Soc. Sci. Index Abstr.; Biol. Abstr. (Spring 1988-); Curr. Contents Clin. Med.; Curr. Contents Soc. Behav. Sci. (Spring 1988-); EMBASE; Geogr. Abstr. Human Geogr.; Health Plan. Adminis.; Index Med. (Spring 1988-); Int. Aerosp. Abstr.; Life Sci. Collect. (Spring 1988-); Psychol. Abstr. (Spring 1988-); PsycINFO (1990-); PsycLit; PsycScan: Appl. Psych.; Res. Alert [Full Cov.]; SCISEARCH; Soc. Sci. Cit. Index (Spring 1988-) [Full Cov.].

CC/1000-1530
**BEIJING YIKE DAXUE XUEBAO.** (PEI-CHING I KO TA HSUEH HSUEH PAO.). [Beijing yike daxue xuebao]. **Added/Corp** Pei-Ching i ko ta Hsueh. **VFOAT** Journal of Beijing Medical University. Vol. 17, No. 4 (1985)-. Academic Scholarly Publication. Chinese. bm. Beijing Yike Daxue / Beijing Medical University, Xueyuan Lu, Beijing 100083, People's Republic of China. **Tel** 861 2091551, FAX 861 2015681. **ED** Feng Chuanhan. **CODEN** BYDXEV. **Pr Rev.** Documents available from CASDDS. ***Continues** Pei-Ching i Hsueh Yuan Hsueh pao.*
**Ind/Abst** Chem. Abstr.; Protozoolog. Abstr.

CC/0253-9713
**BEIJING YIXUE.** (PEI-CHING I HSUEH.). [Beijing yixue]. **Added/Corp** Chung-hua i hsueh hui. Pei-Ching fen hui. **VFOAT** Beijing Medical Journal. (1979)-. Periodical. Chinese (English). bm (6 issues). $42.50. **(Subscription address:** China Books & Periodicals Inc., 2929 24th Street, San Francisco CA 94110.**) CODEN** PCIHD7.
**Ind/Abst** NAPRALERT.

CC/0258-8811
**BEIJING ZHONGYI XUEYUAN XUEBAO.** (PEI-CHING CHUNG I HSUEH YUAN HSUEH PAO.). [Beijing zhongyi xueyuan xuebao]. **Added/Corp** Pei-Ching Chung I Hsueh Yuan. **VFOAT** Journal of Beijing College of Traditional Chinese Medicine. (1959)-. Periodical. Chinese (English). bm (6 issues). $36.75. Beijing Zhongyi Xueyuan, Beijing Institute of Traditional Chinese Medicine, Hepingjie Beikou, Beijing 100029, People's Republic of China. **Tel** 4212731. **(Subscription address:** China Books & Periodicals Inc., 2929 24th Street, San Francisco CA 94110.**) ED** Liu Duzhou. Documents available from BLDSC.
**Desc:** Contains information on Chinese traditional medicine.
**Ind/Abst** Trop. Dis. Bull.

US/1064-1424
**BEING WELL.** (BEING WELL : THE BULLETIN OF THE SOCIETY FOR PROFESSIONAL WEL-BEING.). [Being well]. **Added/Corp** Society for Professional Well-Being. (Oct. 1991)-. Periodical. English. Four times a year (Seasonally). $55.00 (one year); $100.00 (two years). Society Professional Well-Being, 21 West Colony Place, Suite 150, Durham NC 27705. **Tel** (919)419-0011, FAX (919)490-5587. **ED** Marjorie Harrison, Ph.D. **DD** 362. **Bk Rev**, (Qty: 4-6). **Circ:** 500.

SZ/1011-6974
**BEITRAEGE ZUR INFUSIONSTHERAPIE.** [Beitr. Infus.ther.]. **VFOAT** Contributions to Infusion Therapy. Vol. 21 (1988)-. Monographic series. German (English). an. Price varies per volume. S. Karger AG, Allschwilerstrasse 10, PO Box - Postfach - Case Postale, CH-4009 Basel Switzerland. **Tel** 011 41 61 306-1111, FAX 011 41 61 306-1234, telex CH 962 652. **ED** J Eckart, V Kretschmer, K Messmer, H Reissigl, W Stangel, KH Usadel. **NLM** W1; BE342. **CODEN** BEINEM. Documents available from BIOSIS Document Express. ***Continues** Beitrage zu Infusionstherapie und Klinische Ernahrung, 0378-8679.*
**Desc:** Comprises mostly symposium reports and general reviews from the entire field of infusion therapy, transfusion and clinical nutrition, including all related topics.
**Ind/Abst** Biol. Abstr. (1988-); Index Med. (1988-); Ref. Upd. Deluxe Ed.

SZ/0254-8275
**BEITRAEGE ZUR INTENSIV- UND NOTFALLMEDIZIN.** [Beitr. Intensiv- Notf.med.]. Vol. 1 (1983)-. German. an. 90.00F (approx. per volume). S. Karger AG, Allschwilerstrasse 10, PO Box - Postfach - Case Postale, CH-4009 Basel Switzerland. **Tel** 011 41 61 306-1111, FAX 011 41 61 306-1234, telex CH 962 652. **ED** G. Kalff. **NLM** W1; BE344. **[CCC].** Documents available from BIOSIS Document Express.
**Desc:** Represents an overview of current problems in intensive care.
**Ind/Abst** Biol. Abstr.

GW/0005-8149
**BEITRAEGE ZUR ORTHOPADIE UND TRAUMATOLOGIE.** ***Ceased.*** [Beitr. Ortho. Traumatol.]. Vol. 7 (1960)-(Dec. 1990). Academic Scholarly Publication. German. mo. Deutscher Judo Verband, Redaktion Ippon Segewaldweg 40, D 12557 Berlin Germany. **Tel** 011 49 711 210770, telex 051 678. **NLM** W1 BE163. **CODEN** BOTRAJ. **[CCC].** Documents available from BIOSIS Document Express. ***Continues** Beitrage aus dem Gesamten Arbeitsbereich der Orthopadie und Chirurgisch-Medizinischen Technik.*
**Ind/Abst** Biol. Abstr.; EMBASE; Health Plan. Adminis.; Index Med.; Saf. Health Work; SportSearch.

AU
**BEITRAGE ZUR ANAESTHESIOLOGIE, INTENSIV- UND NOTFALLMEDIZIN.** (1990)-. Monographic series. German. ir. Springer-Verlag Wien, Sachsenplatz 4 6, PO Box 89, A-1201 Vienna Austria. **Tel** 011 43 1 3302415. **(Subscription address:** Springer Verlag New York Inc. / for North America, 44 Hartz Way, Secaucus NJ 07096.**) NLM** W1; BE1765. ***Continues** Beitrage zur Anaesthesiologie und Intensivmedizin, 1012-8972.*

BE/0771-5676
**BELGIAN MEDICAL YEAR-BOOK.** [Belg. med. year-b.]. **VFOAT** Belgian Medical Year Book. (1978)-. Dutch (French). an. **NLM** W1 BE462M.

BE/0774-6180
**BEP.** (BULLETIN D'EDUCATION DU PATIENT A SA MALADIE : BEP.). [BEP]. **Added/Corp** Centre d'Education du Patient (Belgium). **VFOAT** BEP. (198?)-. Periodical. French. Four times a year (Mar., June, Sept., Dec.). 650F (individuals), 950F (institutions) Benelux; 700F (individuals), 1050F (institutions) EEC countries; 800F (individuals), 1150F (institutions) others. Centre d'Education du Patient, 1 Ave Therasse, 5530 Yvoir Belgium. **Tel** 011 32 81 422208. **NLM** W1; BU496C.

DK/0107-9786
**BERETNING FOR ... / DEN CENTRALE VIDENSKABSETISKE KOMITE.** **Main/Corp** Centrale Videnskabsetiske Komite (Denmark). **VFOAT** Report for ... / Central Scientific-Ethical Committee of Denmark. 1980-81-. Danish. an. Forskningssekretariatet, Holmens Kanal 7, DK-1060 Kbenhavn K Denmark. **Tel** (01)114300. **LC** R724; .C42A. **DD** 174/.2/09489.

US/0736-7333
**BERKS COUNTY MEDICAL RECORD, THE.** [Berks Cty. med. rec.]. Began with: Vol. 72, No. 7 (Sept. 1981). Periodical. English. mo. Berks County Law Journal, 544 Court Street, PO Box 1058, Reading PA 19603-1058. **Tel** (610)375-4593, FAX (610)373-0256. **NLM** W1 BE671U. ***Continues** Medical Record (Reading, PA.).*

GW/0172-8490
**BERLINER ARZTEBLATT.** [Berl. Arztebl.]. (1956)-. Periodical. German. sm. DM120.00. CB-Verlag Carl Boldt, Baseler Strasse 80, D 12172 Berlin Germany. **Tel** 030 833 60 66, FAX 030 833 91 25. **NLM** W1 BE804. Index available. **Bk Rev. Ad Acc, Adv Mgr:** Peter Geschlius. Full Page (B&W) DM1900.00. Half Page (B&W) DM1000.00. **Acid Free. Circ:** 18,500 (ctrl). ***Absorbed** Zeitschrift fur Arztliche Fortbildung (Berlin);* ***Formed by the union of** Gross-Berliner Arzteblatt, Arztliches Mitteilungsblatt fur Berlin **and** Berliner Arzt.*
**Desc:** Independent magazine for health-politics.

US/0896-6591
**BIBLIOGRAPHIES AND INDEXES IN MEDICAL STUDIES.** [Bibliogr. indexes med. stud.]. (1988)-. Monographic series. English. ir. Price varies per volume. Greenwood Press Inc., PO Box 5007, Westport CT 06881-5007. **Tel** (203)226-3571, FAX (203)222-1502. **DD** 610.

US/0363-0161
**BIBLIOGRAPHY OF BIOETHICS.** **Added/Corp** Kennedy Institute. Center for Bioethics. Kennedy Institute. Vol. 1 (1975)-. Bibliography. English. an. $60.00 US & Canada & Mexico; $70.00 other. Kennedy Institute of Ethics, Georgetown University, Washington DC 20057. **Tel** (800)663-3849, (202)687-3885, FAX (202)687-6770. **ED** Tamar Joy Kahn, LeRoy Walters. **LC** Z6675.E8; B53; R724. **DD** 016.174/2. **NLM** ZW 50 B579. **Circ:** 2,000 (ctrl).
**Desc:** Contains articles with abstracts to literature on ethical, legal, and public policy aspects of health care and biomedical research.

US/0067-7280
**BIBLIOGRAPHY OF THE HISTORY OF MEDICINE.** See Medical Science and Technology-Abstracting, Bibliographies and Statistics.

DK/0006-1786
**BIBLIOTEK FOR LAGER.** [Bibl. lager]. Periodical. Danish. qt. kr250.00. Munksgaard International Publishers Ltd, PO Box 2148, DK-1016 Copenhagen K Denmark. **Tel** 011 45 33 12 70 30, FAX 011 45 33 12 93 87, telex 19431 MUNKS DK. **NLM** W1 BI345. ***Supersedes*** *NYT Bibliotek for Lager.*
**Ind/Abst** EMBASE.

CN/0707-3674
**BIBLIOTHECA MEDICA CANADIANA.**
**See** Library and Information Sciences.

US
**BIENNIAL REPORT OF EXAMINING AND LICENSING BOARDS / MINNESOTA BOARD OF PODIATRY.**
**Main/Corp** Minnesota Board of Podiatry. English. be. 717 Delaware Street SE, Minneapolis MN 55440. **Tel** (612)623-5491. **LC** RD563; .M56A. **DD** 353.97760084/1.

NE/0168-9428
**BIJBLIJVEN.** Vol. 1 (1985)-. Periodical. Dutch. Ten times a year. F270.00. Bohn Stafleu Van Loghum BV, Postbus 246, 3990 GA Houten Netherlands. **Tel** 011 31 3403 95782. **(Subscription address:** Intermedia BV, Postbus 4, 2400 MA Alphen Rijn Netherlands.**) NLM** W1; BI548.

YU/0351-9430
**BILTEN ZA HEMLJ, SIRAK I LEKOVITO BILJE. See** Biology-Botany.

US/0095-0971
**BIO-MEDICAL SCOREBOARD. *Ceased.*** Vol. 1 (Sept. 1974)-Ceased Vol. 12, No. 7 (July 1985). Periodical. English. mo. International Bio-Medical Information Service, PO Box 756, Miami FL 33156. **Tel** (305)271-7272.

●US
**BIOCHEMICAL AND MOLECULAR MEDICINE.** (1994)-. Academic Scholarly Publication. English. bm (6 issues). $414.00 US and Canada; $478.00 other. Academic Press, Inc., 6277 Sea Harbor Drive, Orlando FL 32887. **Tel** (800)543-9534, (407)345-4100, FAX (407)363-9661. ***Continues*** *Biochemical Medicine Metabolic Biology, 0885-4505.*

US/0885-4505
**BIOCHEMICAL MEDICINE AND METABOLIC BIOLOGY. *Title Change.*** [Biochem. med. metabol. biol.]. Vol. 35, No. 1 (Feb. 1986)-(1994). Academic Scholarly Publication. English. bm (including an annual subject index). Academic Press, Inc., 6277 Sea Harbor Drive, Orlando FL 32887. **Tel** (800)543-9534, (407)345-4100, FAX (407)363-9661. **ED** Edward R. B. McCabe, Chandra Mohan and S. P. Bessman. **LC** QP501; .B474. **DD** 612/.015. **NLM** W1; BI621R. **CODEN** BMMBES. **[CCC].** Documents available from The Genuine Article, BIOSIS Document Express, CASDDS. ***Continues*** *Biochemical Medicine, 0006-2944.* ***Continued by*** *Biochemical and Molecular Medicine.*
**Desc:** Papers are published describing original research in biochemistry, physiologic chemistry, and metabolic biology. The primary emphasis is on the determination of the interrelations among reactions, sequences, and formed elements of the cell.
**Ind/Abst** AGRICOLA [Select. Cov.]; Anal. Abstr.; Biol. Abstr. (1986-); Chem. Abstr.; Chem. Titles; Curr. Aware. Biol. Sci., CABS; Curr. Contents Life Sci.; EMBASE; Energy Res. Abstr. (1986-); Health Plan. Adminis.; Index Med. (1986-); Index Vet.; INIS Atomindex [Micro.]; Maize Abstr.; Mass Spect. Bull.; Nutr. Abstr. Rev., Ser. A, Hum. Exp.; Life Sci. Collect. (1986-); PESTDOC (1986-); Potato Abstr.; Protozoolog. Abstr.; Res. Alert [Full Cov.]; Sci. Cit. Index; SCISEARCH; Soc. Sci. Cit. Index [Select. Cov.].

US/0197-8462
**BIOELECTROMAGNETICS.**
[Bioelectromagnetics]. **Added/Corp** Bioelectromagnetics Society (Gaithersburg, Md.). Vol. 1 (1980)-. Academic Scholarly Publication. English. bm. $462.00 US; $522.00 Canada and Mexico; $544.50 other. John Wiley & Sons, Inc., 605 Third Avenue, New York NY 10158-0012. **Tel** (212)850-6000, (212)850-6645, FAX (212)850-6088, telex 12-7063. **(Subscription address:** John Wiley & Sons / England, Baffins Lane, Chichester, West Sussex PO19 1UD England.**) ED** Ben Greenebaum, C. K. Chou, Kjell Hansson-Mild, Donald I. McRee. **LC** QP82.2.E43; B53. **DD** 591.19/17. **NLM** W1 BI663N. **CODEN** BLCTDO. **[CCC]. Pr Rev.** Documents available from The Genuine Article, BIOSIS Document Express, Ask*IEEE, CASDDS.
**Desc:** Devoted to research on biological systems influenced by natural or manufactured electric and/or magnetic fields at frequencies from DC to visible light. Devoted primarily to the publication of data from intensive experimental or clinical studies, but also includes theoretical papers, literature reviews, and brief experimental reports.
**Ind/Abst** Biol. Abstr.; Chem. Abstr.; Curr. Contents Life Sci.; EMBASE; Health Plan. Adminis.; Index Med. (1980-); INIS Atomindex [Micro.]; INSPEC (1982-); Life Sci. Collect.; Ref. Upd. Deluxe Ed.; Res. Alert [Full Cov.]; Sci. Cit. Index; SCISEARCH; Soc. Sci. Cit. Index [Select. Cov.].

UK/0269-9702
**BIOETHICS.** [Bioethics]. Vol. 1, No. 1 (Jan. 1987)-. Academic Scholarly Publication. English. Five times a year. £92.00 UK & Europe; $186.00 North America; £120.00 others. Basil Blackwell Publishers Ltd, 108 Cowley Road, Oxford 0X4 1JF England. **Tel** 011 44 865 791100, FAX 011 44 865 791347, telex 837022 OXBOOK G. **(Subscription address:** Blackwell Publishers / UK, Marston Book Services, PO Box 87, Oxford OX2 0DT England.**) LC** QH332; .B517. **DD** 174/.2/05. **NLM** W1; BI663PE. **[CCC].** available on microfilm and microfiche from University Microfilms International (UMI). Documents available.
**Ind/Abst** Curr. Lit. Fam. Plan. (19??-199?); Int. Bibliogr. Sociol.; Linguist. Lang. Behav. Abstr.; Philos. Index; Soc. Plann. Policy Dev. Abstr.; Soc. Sci. Cit. Index [Full Cov.]; Sociol. Abstr.

●US/1065-7274
**BIOETHICS FORUM. See** Ethics.

US/0886-8913
**BIOETHICS LITERATURE REVIEW. See** Ethics.

UK/0168-8561
**BIOGENIC AMINES. See** Biology-Biochemistry.

US/1055-3150
**BIOGERON (BLOOMINGTON, IND.).** (BIOGERON : THE JOURNAL OF LIFE-EXTENSION SCIENCE.). (1991)-. Periodical. English. qt. $95.00. Biogeron Laboratories Inc, 1821 West Third Street, Suite 202, PO Box 5277, Bloomington IN 47403. **Tel** (812)336-2002, FAX (812)332-5580.

US/1055-5129
**BIOGERON ... LIFE EXTENSION MANUAL.** [Biogeron life ext. man.]. **Added/Corp** Biogeron Laboratories. **VFOAT** Life Extension Manual. 1st Ed. (1991)-. English. $29.95. Biogeron Laboratories Inc, 1821 West Third Street, Suite 202, PO Box 5277, Bloomington IN 47403. **Tel** (812)336-2002, FAX (812)332-5580. **LC** QP85; .B55. **DD** 612.6/8. **NLM** W1; BI665TL.

US/0896-596X
**BIOGERON RESEARCH INDEX. AGING, LONGEVITY, & LIFE EXTENSION. VFOAT** Aging, Longevity, & Life Extension; Aging, Longevity, and Life Extension. Vol. 1, No. 1; Jan. 14, 1988-. Periodical. English. bw. $44.00. Biogeron Laboratories Inc, 1821 West Third Street, Suite 202, PO Box 5277, Bloomington IN 47403. **Tel** (812)336-2002, FAX (812)332-5580. **DD** 618.

SP
**BIOINGENIERIA Y CLINICA.** (19??)-. Spanish. qt. Puntex SA, Via Laietana 30 4 F, 08003 Barcelona Spain. **Tel** 011 34 3 2680444.

RU
**BIOKHIMICHESKAIA EKOLOGIIA I MEDITSINA. Added/Corp** Institut Ekologii Rastenii i Zhivotnykh (Akademiia Nauk SSSR). (1978)-. Russian. ir. 1.20rub (single issue). **LC** R91; .B55.

US
**BIOLAW.** (1986)-. English. an. University Publications of America, 4520 East West Highway 800, Bethesda MD 20814. **Tel** (800)638-8380, (301)654-1550. **ED** James F Childress. ***Continues*** *Bioethics Reporter.*

BU/0204-8817
**BIOLOGIA ET IMMUNOLOGIA REPRODUCTIONIS.** [Biol. immunol. reprod.]. **Added/Corp** Institut po Biologiia i Imunologiia na Razmnozhavaneto i Razviti na Organizmite (Bulgarska Akademiia na Naukite). Vol. 1 (1979)-. Academic Scholarly Publication. English (Bulgarian, English and Russian). Izdatelstvo na Bulgarskata Akademiia Na Naukite, 6 Rouski Boulevard, Sofia Bulgaria. **Tel** FAX 80 13 41, telex 22267 HEMKIK. **NLM** W1 BI671NU. **CODEN** BIMRDD. Documents available from CASDDS.
**Ind/Abst** Chem. Abstr.

●US/1077-1034
**BIOLOGICAL ANALYSIS AND IMAGING METHODS.** (1995)-. Periodical. English. qt. $365.00. Marcel Dekker Inc., 270 Madison Avenue, New York NY 10016. **Tel** (212)696-9000, (800)228-1160, FAX (212)685-4540, telex 421419. ***Continues*** *Journal of Trace and Microprobe Techniques, 0733-4680.*

UK/0142-9612
**BIOMATERIALS.** [Biomaterials]. Vol. 1, No. 1 (Jan. 1980)-. Academic Scholarly Publication. English. Eighteen times a year. $917.00 The Americas; £615.00 other. Butterworth Heinemann Publishers, Linacre House, Jordan Hill, Oxford OX2 8DP England. **Tel** 011 44 865 310366. **(Subscription address:** Elsevier Science Ltd. Oxford Fulfillment Centre, PO Box 800, Kidlington, Oxford OX5 1DX United Kingdom.**) ED** G. W. Hastings, N. A. Peppas, and R. S. Langer. **LC** R857.M3; B568. **DD** 610/.28/05. **NLM** W1 BI852RJ. **CODEN** BIMADU. **[CCC].** Index available. **Ad Acc. Pr Rev.** available on microfilm and microfiche from University Microfilms International (UMI). Documents available from Article Express International, The Genuine Article, BIOSIS Document Express, Ask*IEEE, CASDDS.
**Desc:** Includes papers that study both synthetic and naturally occurring materials. It was established to bring together the work of specialists in many different disciplines and fully reflects on the diversity and rapid growth of this challenging subject. Covers the structure, properties, interactions and functions of biomaterials as well as their clinical applications.
**Ind/Abst** BioBusiness; Biol. Abstr.; Ceram. Abstr.; Chem. Abstr.; Curr. Aware. Biol. Sci., CABS; Curr. Biotechnol.; Curr. Contents Life Sci.; Curr. Technol. Index; Curr. Titl. Dent.; EMBASE; Eng. Index Annu.; Health Plan. Adminis.; Index Med. (-1980); INSPEC (Jan. 1980-); Polymer Contents; Ref. Upd. Deluxe Ed.; Res. Alert [Full Cov.]; Sci. Cit. Index; SCISEARCH.

CK/0120-4157
**BIOMEDICA.** (BIOMEDICA : REVISTA DEL INSTITUTO NACIONAL DE SALUD.). [Biom,edica]. **Added/Corp** Instituto Nacional de Salud (Colombia). Vol. 1, No. 1 (1981)-. Periodical. Spanish (summaries and/or abstracts in English). qt. **NLM** W1 BI853M.
**Ind/Abst** Trop. Dis. Bull.

GW/0232-766X
**BIOMEDICA BIOCHIMICA ACTA. *Ceased.*** **See** Biology.

US/0895-3988
**BIOMEDICAL AND ENVIRONMENTAL SCIENCES. See** Biology.

BE
**BIOMEDICAL & HEALTH RESEARCH : NEWSLETTER / EUROPEAN COMMUNITY. Added/Corp** Commission of the European Communities. DG XII-F-6--Medical Research Division. **VFOAT** Biomedical and Health Research. No. 1 (1990)-. Newsletter. English. tq. Free. A & MJ, Graphic Production S.A., B-1150 Brussels Belgium. **ED** Dr. A. Dickens. **NLM** W1; BI853UG.

US/0742-1796
**BIOMEDICAL ETHICS REVIEWS.** [Biomed. ethics rev.]. (1983)-. English. an. Price varies per volume. Humana Press Inc., 999 Riverview Drive, Suite 208, Totawa NJ 07512. **Tel** (201)256-1699, FAX (201)256-8341. **ED** James Humber and Robert F. Almeder. **LC** R724; .B493. **DD** 174/.2/05. **NLM** W1 B615 (P). Index available. **Bk Rev.**
**Desc:** Reviews on topics of current interest and controversy throughout medicine, including ethical and social policy issues.

US
**BIOMEDICAL INDEX TO PHS-SUPPORTED RESEARCH.**
**Added/Corp** National Institutes of Health (U.S.). Division of Research Grants. **VFOAT** Biomedical Index to PHS Supported Research. **VAT** Biomedical Index to Public Health Service Supported Research. (1988)-. Government Publication. English. ir. Superintendent of Documents, US Government Printing Office, Washington DC 20402. **Tel** (202)275-3328, FAX (202)786-2377. **LC** RA440.6; .U47. **DD** 610/.72073. **NLM** ZW 20.5; B615. ***Continues*** *Research Awards Index, 0147-5320.*

US
**BIOMEDICAL INFORMATICS TODAY.**
**Added/Corp** University of California, Los Angeles. School of Medicine. **VFOAT** UCLA Biomedical Informatics Today. (Sept. 1991)-. Periodical. English.

US/0730-8027
**BIOMEDICAL LABORATORY TECHNICAL REPORT.** [Biomed. Lab. tech. rep.]. Academic Scholarly Publication. English. Price varies per volume. US Army Medical Research and Development Command, Biomedical Laboratory, Aberdeen Proving Ground MD 21010. **CODEN** BLTRDZ. Documents available from CASDDS.
**Ind/Abst** Chem. Abstr.

UK/0961-088X
**BIOMEDICAL LETTERS.** Vol. 46, No. 181 (1991)-. Academic Scholarly Publication. English (French and German). Eight times a year. £200.00. Faculty Press, 88 Regent Street, Cambridge CB2 1DP England. **Tel** FAX 44 553 840695. **LC** QR1; .M624. **DD** 576/.05. **NLM** W1; BI854R. **CODEN** BILEE4. Index available. cum. index. **Bk Rev. Ad Acc.** ctrl circ. Documents available from BIOSIS Document Express, CASDDS. ***Continues*** *Microbios Letters, 0307-5494.*
**Desc:** An international journal for short communications in biomedical research.
**Ind/Abst** Biodeter. Abstr. (1991-); Biol. Abstr.; Chem. Abstr.; Curr. Aware. Biol. Sci., CABS; Microbiol. Abstr. Sect. B; Ref. Upd. Deluxe Ed.

UK/0955-7717
**BIOMEDICAL MATERIALS.** (198?)-. Periodical. English. Twelve times a year. $406.00 The Americas; £272.00 other. Elsevier Advanced Technology, An Imprint of Elsevier Science Ltd., The Boulevard, Langford Lane, Kidlington, Oxford OX5 1GB United Kingdom. **Tel** 011 44 865 843000, 011 44 865 843699,

FAX 011 44 865 843010. **(Subscription address:** Elsevier Science Ltd. Oxford Fulfillment Centre, PO Box 800, Kidlington, Oxford OX5 1DX United Kingdom.**) ED** R. Juniper, P. Read. **NLM** W1; BI854V. **CODEN** BMATEM. **[CCC].** available on microfilm from University Microfilms International (UMI); available on an online database (file 636/Full-Text) from DIALOG. ***Continues*** *Biomedical Polymers.*
**Desc:** International newsletter covering all significant aspects and applications of biomedical polymer technology.
**Ind/Abst** PTS Newsl. Database [Full Txt.].

US/1057-7424
**BIOMEDICAL NEWS SOURCE MIDWEST.** [Biomed. news source midwest]. **VFOAT** Biomedical News Source. (1991)-. Periodical. English. mo. $190.00 (U.S.). The Saber Group, Incorporated, P.O.Box 886, Hudson WI 54016. **Tel** (715)386-5520, FAX (715)386-5520. **ED** G. Thomas. **DD** 362. **NLM** W1; BI854XL. Index available. cum. index. ctrl circ. ***Continues*** *Minnesota Biomed Alert, 1046-5189.*

GW/0934-0734
**BIOMEDICAL PROGRESS.** [Biomed. prog.]. (1988)-. Periodical. English. qt. DM10.00. Medizinish Verlagsgesellschaft, PO Box 1732, W 3550 Marburg F.R.Germany. **Tel** 011 49 6421 22230. **UDC** 61.

JA/0388-6107
**BIOMEDICAL RESEARCH (TOKYO).** (BIOMEDICAL RESEARCH.). [Biomed. res.]. **Added/Corp** Biomedical Research Foundation (Japan). Vol. 1, No. 1 (Feb. 1980)-. Academic Scholarly Publication. English. bm. $234.00. Baiomedikaru Risachi Fandeshon, (Biomedical Research Foundation), 4-1, Nishishinjuku 2 Chome, Shinjukuku, Tokyoto 163 Japan. **(Subscription address:** Maruzen Company Ltd., PO Box 5050, Import & Export Department, Tokyo 100 31 Japan.**) NLM** W1 BI856C. **CODEN** BRESD5. **Pr Rev.** Documents available from The Genuine Article, BIOSIS Document Express, CASDDS.
**Desc:** Publishes original research articles and reviews of high quality in the fields of experimental and medical biology, encouraging interdisciplinary discussion of topics in these fields.
**Ind/Abst** Biol. Abstr.; Chem. Abstr.; Chem. Titles; CSA Neuro. Abstr. (?-?); Curr. Aware. Biol. Sci., CABS; Curr. Contents Life Sci.; Dairy Sci. Abstr.; EMBASE; Life Sci. Collect.; Protozoolog. Abstr.; Res. Alert [Full Cov.]; Sci. Cit. Index; SCISEARCH.

US
**BIOMEDICAL SAFETY & STANDARDS.** **VAT** Biomedical Safety and Standards. Vol. 15, No. 1 (Jan. 1985)-. Periodical. English. sm (published once during January and August). $239.00 US, Canada and Mexico; $269.00 other. Quest Publishing Company, 1351 Titan Way, Brea CA 92621. **Tel** (714)738-6400, FAX (714)525-6258. **ED** Mickey C. Schach and William C. Bayless. **NLM** W1; BI856GH. Index available. **Bk Rev. Ad Acc.** Documents available from UMI Article Clearinghouse. ***Continues*** *Newsletter of Biomedical Safety & Standards, 0048-0282.*
**Desc:** Written for persons involved in medical equipment safety and standards. Covers hazards, product recalls, standards, legal actions, legislation and safety.
**Ind/Abst** Health Devices Alerts; Pharm. News Index (Dec. 1987-).

FR/0753-3322
**BIOMEDICINE & PHARMACOTHERAPY.** [Biomed. pharmacother.]. **VFOAT** Biomedecine & Pharmacotherapie; Biomedicine and Pharmacotherapy; Biomedicine et Pharmacotherapie. Vol. 36, No. 1 (Jan. 1982)-. Academic Scholarly Publication. English (French). Ten times a year (1 volume). 1765.00F France; 2125.00F other. Editions Scientifique Elsevier, 141 rue de Javel, 75747 Paris Cedex 15 France. **Tel** 011 33 1 47 07 11 22, FAX 011 33 1 43 36 80 93. **(Subscription address:** Editions Scientifiques Elsevier / for North America, PO Box 7247-7576, Philadelphia PA 19170-7576.**) NLM** W1 BI857J. **CODEN** BIPHEX. **[CCC]. Pr Rev.** available on microfilm and microfiche from University Microfilms International (UMI). Documents available from The Genuine Article, BIOSIS Document Express, CASDDS, ADONIS. ***Formed by the union of*** *Biomedicine, 0300-0893* ***and*** *Biomedicine Express, 0300-0855.*
**Ind/Abst** ADONIS; Biol. Abstr.; Chem. Abstr.; Curr. Aware. Biol. Sci., CABS; Curr. Contents Life Sci.; EMBASE; Energy Res. Abstr. (Dec. 1982-); Index Med.; Nutr. Abstr. Rev., Ser. B, Live Feeds and Feed.; Nutr. Abstr. Rev., Ser. A, Hum. Exp.; Life Sci. Collect.; PESTDOC; Protozoolog. Abstr.; Ref. Upd. Deluxe Ed.; Res. Alert [Full Cov.]; Sci. Cit. Index; SCISEARCH.

GW/0934-9235
**BIOMETRIE UND INFORMATIK IN MEDIZIN UND BIOLOGIE.** ***Title Change.*** **See** Biology.

US/0149-1008
**BIORESEARCH TODAY. ADDICTION.** ***Ceased.*** **VFOAT** Addiction. **VAT** BioResearch Today. Addiction. Ceased 1990. English. mo. BioSciences Information Service, Biological Abstracts / BIOSIS, 2100 Arch Street, Philadelphia PA 19103-1399. **Tel** (800)523-4806 US, (215)587-4800 Pennsylvania and worldwide, FAX (215)587-2016, telex 831739.
**Desc:** Current awareness journal including abstracts and content summaries involving studies of drug addiction.

US/0149-0982
**BIORESEARCH TODAY. BIRTH DEFECTS.** ***Ceased.*** **VFOAT** Birth Defects. **VAT** BioResearch Today. Birth Defects. Ceased (Dec. 1991). English. mo. BioSciences Information Service, Biological Abstracts / BIOSIS, 2100 Arch Street, Philadelphia PA 19103-1399. **Tel** (800)523-4806 US, (215)587-4800 Pennsylvania and worldwide, FAX (215)587-2016, telex 831739.
**Desc:** Current awareness journal including abstracts and content summaries of studies involving birth defects.

US/0736-6205
**BIOTECHNIQUES.** [BioTechniques]. **VFOAT** Bio Techniques. Vol. 1, No. 1 (March/April 1983)-. Periodical. English. Twelve times a year. $95.00 US & Canada; $125.00 others. Eaton Publishing Company, 154 East Central Street, Natick MA 01760. **Tel** (508)655-8282. **ED** James Ellingbol. **NLM** W1 BI918L. **CODEN** BTNQDO. **[CCC].** cum. index. **Ad Acc. Pr Rev. Circ:** 50,000 (ctrl). Documents available from The Genuine Article, CASDDS. ***Continues*** *Biochromatography, 0888-4404.*
**Desc:** Contains research reports and review articles concerning new laboratory techniques, methods and products of interest to scientists engaged in genetic engineering and general laboratory.
**Ind/Abst** Abstr. BioCommer.; AgBiotech News Inf.; AGRICOLA [Select. Cov.]; Anim. Breed. Abstr.; Biotechnol. Res. Abstr.; Chem. Abstr. (1983-); Curr. Aware. Biol. Sci., CABS; Curr. Biotechnol.; Curr. Contents Life Sci.; EMBASE; Field Crop Abstr.; Food Sci. Technol. Abstr.; Genet. Abstr.; Health Plan. Adminis.; Index Med.; Nucl. Acids Abstr.; Life Sci. Collect.; PESTDOC; Plant Breed. Abstr.; Ref. Upd. Basic Ed.; Ref. Upd. Deluxe Ed.; Res. Alert [Full Cov.]; Rev. Plant Pathol.; Sci. Cit. Index; SCISEARCH; Wheat Barley Trit. Abstr.

UK
**BIOTRANSFORMATIONS : A SURVEY OF THE BIOTRANSFORMATIONS OF DRUGS AND CHEMICALS IN ANIMALS.** **Added/Corp** Royal Society of Chemistry (Great Britain). Vol. 1 (1988)-. English. an. £130.00. Royal Society of Chemistry, Thomas Graham House, Science Park, Cambridge CB4 4WF England. **Tel** 011 44 223 420066, FAX 011 44 223 423429, telex 818293 ROYAL. **(Subscription address:** Royal Society of Chemistry, Distribution Center, Blackhorse Road, Letchworth, SG6 1HN England.**) ED** David R. Hawkins. **NLM** W1; BI919MR. **CODEN** BTRNE2. Documents available from BIOSIS Document Express.
**Desc:** Provides a complete survey of the biotransformation, in vertebrates, of the following: pharmaceuticals, agrochemicals, food additives, environmental chemicals, and industrial chemicals.
**Ind/Abst** Biol. Abstr.

JA
**BITAMIN (VITAMIN).** **See** Chemistry.

RU/0365-9615
**BJULLETEN EKSPERIMENTALNOJ BIOLOGII I MEDICINY.** **See** Biology.

US/0196-1594
**BLACK BAG (WASHINGTON), THE.** ***Title Change.*** (BLACK BAG.). Vol. 1 (1972)-?. Periodical. English. qt. Student Natl Medical Assn, 1012 10th Street NW, Washington DC 20001. **Tel** (202)371-1616. **NLM** W1 BL21. ***Continued by*** *Journal of the Student National Medical Association, 1044-1654.*

UK
**BLACK'S MEDICAL DICTIONARY (LONDON, ENGLAND).** (BLACK'S MEDICAL DICTIONARY.). Began in 1906. English. ir. A & C Black Publishers Ltd, Howard Road, Eaton Socon, Huntingdon CBS PE193EZ England. **Tel** (0480)212666, FAX (0480)405014, telex 32524. **LC** R121; .B598. **DD** 610.3.

GW/0178-8957
**BLICKPUNKT SCHMERZ.** 1985-. Periodical. German. Three times a year. **NLM** W1; BL525.

UK/0306-5472
**BMA NEWS REVIEW.** [BMA news rev.]. **VFOAT** British Medical Association News Review. (1975)-. Periodical. English. mo. £45.00. Professional & Scientific Publishers, Tavistock House, East Tavistock Square, London WC1H 9JR England. **Tel** 011 44 71 387-4499, telex 005311. **(Subscription address:** Professional & Scientific Publishers, PO Box 294, London WC1H 9TB England.**)** ***Continues*** *BMA News, 0306-2368.*
**Desc:** Contains news and information on a wide range of topics of interest and concern to members of the BMA, such as medical politics, as well as finance and the business side of being a doctor. Includes features on other social and health-related subjects.

UK/0269-3879
**BMC. BIOMEDICAL CHROMATOGRAPHY.** **See** Biology.

UK/0959-8138
**BMJ. BRITISH MEDICAL JOURNAL (CLINICAL RESEARCH ED.).** (BMJ : BRITISH MEDICAL JOURNAL / BRITISH MEDICAL ASSOCIATION.). [BMJ, Br. med. j.]. **Added/Corp** British Medical Association. **VFOAT** British Medical Journal. Vol. 297, No. 6640 (July 2, 1988)-. Periodical. English. wk. £158.00 UK & Eire; £262.00 other. BMJ / British Medical Journal Publishing Group, British Medical Association House, Tavistock Square, London WC1H 9JR England. **Tel** 011 44 71 3874499, FAX 011 44 71 383 6402, telex 290034 HBJ MN. **NLM** W1; BM98. **CODEN** BMJOAE. **[CCC]. Pr Rev.** Documents available from ADONIS. ***Continues*** *British Medical Journal (Clinical Research Edition), 0267-0623.*
**Desc:** General journal, with something for everyone regardless of discipline or seniority. Provides an important link between members of the profession at a time of increasing super-specialisation. It covers all branches of medicine and is presented in ways that are accessible to readers from many disciplines. All articles are subjected to extensive peer review and statistical checking before acceptance, and the BMJ publishes fewer than a fifth of the articles it receives. Contains influential editorials on medical, political, and social topics.
**Ind/Abst** ADONIS; Curr. Lit. Fam. Plan.; Genet. Abstr.; Helminthol. Abstr. (1991-); Hum. Genome Abstr.; Index Med. (1988-); Ind. Hyg. Dig. (19??-19??); Nutr. Res. Newsl.; Poult. Abstr.; Soyabean Abstr.; SPORT Discus.

UK
**BMJ. BRITISH MEDICAL JOURNAL (GENERAL PRACTICE ED.).** (BMJ : BRITISH MEDICAL JOURNAL / BRITISH MEDICAL ASSOCIATION.). (19??)-. English. wk. £158.00 UK & Eire. BMJ / British Medical Journal Publishing Group, British Medical Association House, Tavistock Square, London WC1H 9JR England. **Tel** 011 44 71 3874499, FAX 011 44 71 383 6402, telex 290034 HBJ MN.

UK/0959-8146
**BMJ. BRITISH MEDICAL JOURNAL (INTERNATIONAL ED.).** (BMJ : BRITISH MEDICAL JOURNAL / BRITISH MEDICAL ASSOCIATION.). [BMJ, Br. med. j.]. **Added/Corp** British Medical Association. **VFOAT** British Medical Journal; BMJ. Vol. 297, No. 6640 (July 2, 1988)-. Periodical. English. Fifty-two times a year. £194.00. BMJ / British Medical Journal Publishing Group, British Medical Association House, Tavistock Square, London WC1H 9JR England. **Tel** 011 44 71 3874499, FAX 011 44 71 383 6402, telex 290034 HBJ MN. **CODEN** BMJOAE. **[CCC].** available on CD-ROM from Maxwell Electronic Publishing.
**Ind/Abst** AGRICOLA [Select. Cov.]; Annals Behav. Med.; Curr. Aware. Biol. Sci., CABS; EMBASE; Health Index (1989-); Health Period. Database [Full Txt.]; Health Ref. Cent. (Jan. 1989-) [Full Txt.] [Full Cov.]; Highw. Res. Abstr.; Leadscan; Med. Abstr. Newsl.; Oncog. Growth Factors Abstr.; Ref. Upd. Basic Ed.; Ref. Upd. Clinical Ed.; Ref. Upd. Deluxe Ed.; Soc. Sci. Cit. Index [Select. Cov.].

●SA/1019-8350
**BMJ. BRITISH MEDICAL JOURNAL (SOUTH AFRICAN ED.).** [BMJ, Br. med. j. S. Afr. ed.]. **VFOAT** British Medical Journal (South African Ed.). (1992)-. Academic Scholarly Publication. English. mo. R93.48 Spain; R120.00 other. George Warman Publications Pty, PO Box 704, Cape Town 8000 South Africa. **Tel** 011 27 21 245320, FAX 011 27 21 261332, telex 5-21849. **UDC** 61.

IT
**BMJ:BRITISH MEDICAL JOURNAL. ITALIAN EDITION.** ***Suspended.*** (1992)-(July 1993). Italian. Ten times a year. L40.000 Italy; L80.000 other. Editiemme, Via Lanino 5, 20144 Milan Italy. **Tel** 011 39 2 4227946, 011 39 2 4224666, FAX 011 39 2 4120287. ***Continues*** *British Medical Journal. Italian Edition.*

US/1068-3798
**BNA'S HEALTH CARE ELECTRONIC DATA REPORT.** ***Ceased.*** [BNA's health care electron. data rep.]. **Added/Corp** Bureau of National Affairs (Washington, D.C.). **VFOAT** Health Care Electronic Data Report. **VAT** Bureau of National Affairs Health Care Electronic Data Report. Vol. 1, No. 1 (May 12, 1993)-(Dec. 1993). Periodical. English. bw. Bureau of National Affairs Inc., 9435 Key West Avenue, Rockville MD 20850. **Tel** (800)372-1033, (301)258-1033, FAX (301)948-5823. **DD** 362. **[CCC].**

●US/1068-1213
**BNA'S HEALTH CARE POLICY REPORT.** [BNA's health care policy rep.]. **Added/Corp** Bureau of National Affairs (Washington, D.C.). **VFOAT** Health Care Policy Report. **VAT** Bureau of National Affairs' Health Care Policy Report. Vol. 1, No. 1 (Mar. 8, 1993)-. Periodical. English. wk. $682.00. Bureau of National Affairs Inc., 9435 Key West Avenue, Rockville MD 20850. **Tel** (800)372-1033, (301)258-1033, FAX (301)948-5823. **DD** 362. **[CCC].**

SP
**BOEHRINGER MANNHEIM INFORMA DE ACTUALIDADES EN ANALITICA CLINICA Y BIOQUIMICA.** Spanish. ir. Boehringer Mannheim SA, Copernico 61-63, 08006 Barcelona Spain.

JA/0385-1796
**BOEI IKA DAIGAKKO ZASSHI.** [Boei Ika Daigakko zasshi]. **Added/Corp** Boei Ika Daigakko (Japan). **VFOAT** Boei Ika Daigakko Zasshi; Journal of the National Defense Medical College. (1976)-. Periodical. Japanese (English). qt. Boei Ika Daigakko, (National Defense Medical College), 3-2, Namiki, Tokorozawashi, Saitamaken 359 Japan. **NLM** W1; BO114M. **CODEN** BIDZDQ. Documents available from BIOSIS Document Express, CASDDS.
**Ind/Abst** Biol. Abstr.; Chem. Abstr.

PO/0374-6070
**BOLETIM CLINICO DES HOSPITAIS CIVIS DE LISBOA.** Vol. 7 (March/June 1946)-. Bulletin. Portuguese. ir. Livraria Sa da Costa Editora, rua Garrett 100-102, Lisbon 2 Portugal. **LC** RC31.L5; A3. **NLM** W1 BO149. ***Continues*** *Portugal. Direccao Geral dos Hospitais Civis de Lisboa. Boletim Clinico e de Estatistica dos Hospitais Civis de Lisboa.*

BL/0001-3838
**BOLETIM DA ACADEMIA NACIONAL DE MEDICINA.** **Added/Corp** Academia Nacional de Medicina (Brazil). Vol. 1 (April/June 1971)-. Bulletin. Portuguese. ir. Academy National Medicina Biblioteca, Avenue Genl Justo, 365 90 Andar, 20 021 Rio de Janeiro Brazil. **NLM** W1 BO15F. ***Supersedes*** *Boletim da Academia Nacional de Medicina, 0001-3838.*

SP/0210-0940
**BOLETIN DE LA ASOCIACION ESPANOLA DE COLO-PROTOLOGIA.** [Bol. Asoc. Esp. Coloproctol.]. (1978)-. Periodical. Spanish. bm. Editorial Garsi SA, Juan Bravo 46, 28006 Madrid, Spain. **Tel** 011 34 1 4021212, telex 98358 GARSI E. **UDC** 616.3. ***Continues*** *Boletin de la Asociacion Espafnola de Proctologia, 0210-0932.*

PR/0004-4849
**BOLETIN DE LA ASOCIACION MEDICA DE PUERTO RICO.** (BOLETIN - ASOCIACION MEDICA DE PUERTO RICO.). [Bol. Asoc. Med. P. R.]. **Main/Corp** Asociacion Medica de Puerto Rico. (1903)-. Periodical. English. mo. $40.00. Puerto Rican Medical Association, Box 9378, Santurce, Puerto Rico 00908. **Tel** (809)721-6969. **NLM** W1 BO197H.
**Ind/Abst** Cumul. Index Nurs. Allied Health Lit.; Health Plan. Adminis.; Helminthol. Abstr. (1991-); Index Med.; Life Sci. Collect.; Protozoolog. Abstr.; Rev. Med. Vet. Mycology; SportSearch; Trop. Dis. Bull.

SP/0214-2813
**BOLETIN DE LA SOCIEDAD ESPANOLA DE HIDROLOGIA MEDICA.** [Bol. Soc. Esp. Hidrol. Med.]. (1962)-. Periodical. Spanish. tq. Catedra de Hidrologia Medica, Facultad de Medicina, Ciudad Universitaria 28040 Madrid Spain. **UDC** 615.838. ***Continues*** *Boletin Espanol de Hidrologia Medica y Climatologia, 0214-2805.*
**Ind/Abst** Indice Med. Esp.

SP/0301-1143
**BOLETIN DE LA SOCIEDAD VALENCIANA DE PATOLOGIA DIGESTIVA.** [Bol. Soc. Valencia. Patol. Dig.]. Periodical. Spanish. Three times a year. Reycosa Reuniones y Congresos SA, Parque de la Colina 6, 28027 Madrid Spain.
**Ind/Abst** Indice Med. Esp.

BL/0009-0131
**BOLETIN DEL CENTRO PANAMERICANO DE FIEBRE AFTOSA.** **Main/Corp** Pan American Foot and Mouth Disease Center. No. 1 (Jan./Mar. 1971)-. Periodical. Spanish (English). an. $10.00. Centro Pan Am Fiebre, Aftosa Caixa Postal 589, Rio de Janeiro Brasil. **Tel** 011 55 21 7713128, telex 2130253. **NLM** W1 BO281.
**Ind/Abst** Index Vet.; Vet. Bull.

SP/0210-1653
**BOLETIN EPIDEMIOLOGICO SEMANAL - MINISTERIO DE SANIDAD Y CONSUMO. PUBLICACIONES. DOCUMENTACION Y BIBLIOTECA.** (1932)-. Periodical. Spanish. wk. Free upon request. Informacion Sanitaria and Epidemiologica, Paseo del Prado 18-20, 28014 Madrid Spain. **Tel** 011 34 1 420-2176. **UDC** 362.193.
**Ind/Abst** Trop. Dis. Bull.

CL
**BOLETIN HOSPITAL DE VINA DEL MAR.** [Bol. Hosp. V. del Mar. Chile]. **VFOAT** Boletin del Hospital de Vina del Mar; Boletin Trimestrial Hospital de Vina del Mar. V. 1- Jan. 1945-. Periodical. Spanish (summaries and/or abstracts in English). Fundacion Lucas Sierra, Casillo 810, Vina El Mar Chile. **Tel** 011 56 32 68 5944. **NLM** W1 BO44N.

AG/0325-8645
**BOLETIN INFORMATION - CEBIDE.** (BOLETIN / CEBIDE.). [Bol. inf. - CEBIDE]. **Added/Corp** CEBIDE (Center) Argentina. Secretaria de Estado de Ciencia y Tecnologia. Argentina. Secretaria d Estado de Salud Publica. Programa Nacional de Investigaciones en Enfermedades Endemicas (Argentina). **VFOAT** Boletin Informativo, CEBIDE. **VAT** Boletin Information - Centro Bibliografico de Enfermedades Endemicas. (19??)-. Periodical. English (Spanish). Programa Nacional de Investigaciones Enfermedades Endemicas, Buenos Aires Argentina. **NLM** ZWC 705 B688b.

IT/1120-8678
**BOLLETTINO DI FARMACOSORVEGLIANZA.** [Boll. farmacosorvegl.]. (1990)-. Periodical. Italian. ir. Free. Masson S.P.A, Via Statuto 2/4, 20121 Milan Italy. **Tel** 011 39 2 63671, FAX 011 39 2 6367211. **UDC** 615.3.

UK/0268-3369
**BONE MARROW TRANSPLANTATION (BASINGSTOKE).** (BONE MARROW TRANSPLANTATION.). [Bone marrow transplant.]. Vol. 1, No. 1 (May 1986)-. Periodical. English. mo. £290.00 UK; £300.00 (surface mail), £360.00 (airmail) other. Macmillan Magazines Ltd., Houndmills, Basingstoke, Hampshire RG21 2XS England. **Tel** 011 44 256 29242, FAX 011 44 256 812358, telex 858493. **ED** John Goldman, Robert Peter Gale. **NLM** W1; BO707E. **CODEN** BMTRE9. **[CCC].** Index available. **Bk Rev. Ad Acc. Pr Rev. Circ:** 1,000. Documents available from The Genuine Article, BIOSIS Document Express.
**Desc:** Features clinical results in man and experimental results with animals, allografting and autografting, HLA and other methods of selecting donors, graft versus host disease and ways of preventing and treating it and many other topics associated with bone marrow transplantation.
**Ind/Abst** Biol. Abstr. (1986-); Curr. Aware. Biol. Sci., CABS; Curr. Contents Life Sci.; EMBASE; Health Plan. Adminis.; Index Med.; Ref. Upd. Deluxe Ed.; Res. Alert [Full Cov.]; Rev. Med. Vet. Mycology; Sci. Cit. Index; SCISEARCH; Soc. Sci. Cit. Index [Select. Cov.].

GW/0721-9245
**BPT-BERICHT.** (BPT-BERICHT / GSF PROJECTTRAGER.). [BPT-Ber.]. **VFOAT** BPT Bericht. **VAT** Bereich- Projekttragerschaften-Bericht. Began with: 1/77, issued May 1977. Academic Scholarly Publication. German. ir. Gesellschaft fur Strahlen- und Unweltforschung, Ingolstadter Landstr 1, 8042 Neuherberg Germany. **Tel** 089-3187-0, FAX 089-3187-3322, telex 898947-STRAL. **NLM** W1; BP103. **CODEN** BPTBDF. Documents available from CASDDS.
**Ind/Abst** Chem. Abstr. (1977-1985).

XO/0006-9248
**BRATISLAVSKE LEKARSKE LISTY.** [Bratisl. lek. listy]. **Added/Corp** Slovenska Akademia Vied. Vol. 1 (1921)-. Periodical. Multiple languages (Czech and English; summaries and/or abstracts in English, French, German and Russian; table of contents in German, Russian and French). Twelve times a year. DM244.00. **(Subscription address:** Slovart GTG Ltd., Krupinska 4, 852 99 Bratislava Slovakia.**) NLM** W1 BR129. **CODEN** BLLIAX. Documents available from BIOSIS Document Express, CASDDS.
**Ind/Abst** Biol. Abstr.; Chem. Abstr.; Coal Abstr.; EMBASE; Health Plan. Adminis.; Helminthol. Abstr.; Index Med.; Index Vet.; Nutr. Abstr. Rev., Ser. A, Hum. Exp.; Life Sci. Collect.; Protozoolog. Abstr.; Saf. Health Work; SportSearch; Vet. Bull.

BL/0100-879X
**BRAZILIAN JOURNAL OF MEDICAL AND BIOLOGICAL RESEARCH.** [Braz. j. med. biol. res.]. **Added/Corp** Sociedade Brasileira de Biofisica. Associacao Brasileira de Divulgacao Cientifica. **VFOAT** Revista Brasileira de Pesquisas Medicas e Biologicas. Vol. 14, No. 1 (Apr, 1981)-. Academic Scholarly Publication. English. Twelve times a year. $80.00. Associacao Brasileira de Divulgacao Cientifica, Av Bandeirantes 3900 Casa 10, 14049 Ribeirao Preto SP, Brazil. **Tel** 011 55 16 6333825, FAX 011 55 16 6332119, telex 0166354. **ED** Eduardo Moacyr Krieger, Lewis Joel Greene and Sergio Henrique Ferreira. **NLM** W1 BR189N. **CODEN** BJMRDK. **[CCC].** Index available (Dec. iss.). **Ad Acc, Adv Mgr:** L. J. Greene, **Tel** (016)633-3825. **Pr Rev. Circ:** 2,100 (ctrl). available on microfilm from University Microfilms International (UMI). Documents available from The Genuine Article, BIOSIS Document Express, CASDDS. ***Continues*** *Revista Brasileira de Pesquisas Medicas e Biologicas.*
**Ind/Abst** AGRICOLA [Select. Cov.]; Biol. Abstr.; Chem. Abstr.; Chemorecept. Abstr.; CSA Neuro. Abstr.; Curr. Aware. Biol. Sci., CABS; Curr. Contents Life Sci.; Dairy Sci. Abstr.; EMBASE; Health Plan. Adminis.; Helminthol. Abstr. (1991-); Immunol. Abstr.; Index Med.; Index Vet.; Microbiol. Abstr. Sect. B (19??-19??); Microbiol. Abstr. Sect. C; Nutr. Abstr. Rev., Ser. A, Hum. Exp.; Life Sci. Collect.; Pig News Inf.; Protozoolog. Abstr.; Res. Alert [Full Cov.]; Rev. Agric. Entomol.; Rev. Med. Vet. Entomol.; Sci. Cit. Index; SCISEARCH; Soc. Sci. Cit. Index [Select. Cov.]; Soyabean Abstr.; SportSearch; Vet. Bull.; Trop. Dis. Bull.

US/0888-6008
**BREAST DISEASE.** [Breast dis.]. **Added/Corp** Society for the Study of Breast Disease. **VFOAT** Breast Dis. Vol. 1, No. 1 (1987)-. Academic Scholarly Publication. English. qt (1 volume). $215.00 US; $245.00 other. Elsevier Science Publishing Company Inc, Madison Square Station, PO Box 882, New York NY 10159-0882. **Tel** (212)633-3950, FAX (212)633-3990. **ED** Douglas J Marchant. **LC** RC280.B8; B7136. **DD** 616.99/449. **NLM** W1; BR191V. **[CCC].** available on microfilm and microfiche from University Microfilms International (UMI).
**Desc:** Publishes original articles dealing with clinical aspects of human breast disease. The focus of the journal is interdisciplinary and includes, but is not limited to, the disciplines of oncology, surgery, radiology and pathology.
**Ind/Abst** EMBASE; Nutr. Res. Newsl.

●US/1061-4575
**BREAST DISEASES UPDATES.** [Breast dis. updates]. Vol. 1, No. 1 (1992)-. Periodical. English. qt. $60.00 (institutions), $50.00 (individuals). J.B. Lippincott Company, 227 East Washington Square, Philadelphia PA 19106-3780. **Tel** (215)238-4200 or 4454, FAX (215)238-4227. **DD** 616.

●US/1075-122X
**BREAST JOURNAL.** (1995)-. Academic Scholarly Publication. English. bm. $125.00 (institution), $75.00 (individual) US; $150.00 (institution), $100.00 (individual) other. Blackwell Scientific Publishers, 238 Main Street, Cambridge MA 02142. **Tel** (617)547-7110, (800)835-6770, FAX (617)547-0789.

UK/0262-8732
**BRISTOL ADVANCES IN THERAPEUTICS.** (BRISTOL ADVANCES IN THERAPEUTICS / BRISTOL.). [Bristol adv. ther.]. **Added/Corp** Bristol Laboratories. **VFOAT** Advances in Therapeutics. (1979)-. Monographic series. English. ir. Price varies per volume. Bristol Laboratories Inc, Box 657, Syracuse NY 13201. **NLM** W1 BR256.

CN/0007-0556
**BRITISH COLUMBIA MEDICAL JOURNAL.** [B.C. med. j.]. **Added/Corp** British Columbia Medical Association. Vancouver Medical Association. **VFOAT** MJ; MJ. British Columbia Medical Journal. **VAT** MJ. British Columbia Medical Journal. Vol. 1 (1959)-. Periodical. English. Twelve times a year. 50.00Can$ Canada; 65.00Can$ other. British Columbia Medical Association, 115-1665 West Broadway, Vancouver British Columbia V6J 5A4 Canada. **Tel** (604)736-5551, FAX (604)736-4566, (604)733-7317. **ED** Dr. James A. Wilson. **NLM** W1 BR362. **[CCC].** Index available. cum. index. **Bk Rev**, (Qty: 88). **Ad Acc. Pr Rev. Circ:** 7,400 (ctrl). ***Supersedes*** *Vancouver Medical Association. Bulletin of the Vancouver Medical Association., 0366-4821.*
**Desc:** A vehicle for continuing medical education and a forum for association news and member's opinions.

UK/0007-0785
**BRITISH HOMEOPATHIC JOURNAL, THE.** [Br. homoeopath. j.]. **VFOAT** British Homeopathic Journal. Vol. 1 (1911)-. Periodical. English. qt. £36.00. Headley Brothers Ltd., The Invicta Press, Queens Road, Ashford Kent TN24 8HH England. **Tel** 011 44 233 623131. **ED** Peter Fisher. **NLM** W1 BR456. available on microfilm from University Microfilms International (UMI). ***Formed by the union of*** *Journal of the British Homoeopathic Society* ***and*** *British Homoeopathic Review.*
**Ind/Abst** EMBASE.

UK/0143-4977
**BRITISH JOURNAL OF ACUPUNCTURE.** ***Title Change.*** (BRITISH JOURNAL OF ACUPUNCTURE / BRITISH ACUPUNCTURE ASSOCIATION.). [Br. j. acupunct.]. **Added/Corp** British Acupuncture Association. (197?)-(19??). Periodical. English. Twice a year. British Journal of Acupuncture, 108 Cheriton Road, Folkestone Kent CT19 5HF England. **ED** Roger Newman-Turner. **NLM** W1; BR479C. **Bk Rev. Ad Acc. Circ:** 500 (ctrl). ***Continues*** *British Acupuncture Association Journal.* ***Continued by*** *European Journal of Oriental Medicine.*
**Desc:** Covers acupuncture and allied subjects.

UK/0007-0947
**BRITISH JOURNAL OF CLINICAL PRACTICE, THE.** [Br. j. clin. pract.]. Vol. 10, No. 10 (Oct. 1956)-. Academic Scholarly Publication. English. bm. £54.00 UK; $110.00 US; £60.00 other. Medicom UK Ltd, The Quadrant, 118 London Road, Kingston Upon Thames, KT2 6QJ England. **Tel** 011 44 81 541 5666, FAX 011 44 81 541 4746. **ED** Graham Jackson. **LC** R11; .M884. **DD** 610.5. **NLM** W1 BR519RP. **CODEN** BJCPAT. Index available (index published separately). **Bk Rev. Ad Acc. Pr Rev. Circ:** 4,000. Documents available from The Genuine Article, BIOSIS Document Express. ***Continues*** *Medicine Illustrated.*
**Desc:** Publishes original papers, reviews, features, case reports and meeting reports. All papers selected for publication have not been published or accepted for publication elsewhere.
**Ind/Abst** Biol. Abstr. (?-1985); Curr. Contents Clin. Med.; EMBASE; Health Plan. Adminis.; Helminthol. Abstr.; Hospit. Health Admin. Index; Index Med.; Int. Pharm.

Abstr.; Iowa Drug Inf. Serv. (1969-); Nutr. Abstr. Rev., Ser. B, Live Feeds and Feed.; Nutr. Abstr. Rev., Ser. A, Hum. Exp.; Nutr. Res. Newsl.; Life Sci. Collect.; PESTDOC; Protozoolog. Abstr.; Res. Alert [Full Cov.]; Rev. Med. Vet. Mycology; Sci. Cit. Index; SCISEARCH; Spec. Educ. Needs Abstr.

UK/0262-8767
**BRITISH JOURNAL OF CLINICAL PRACTICE. SYMPOSIUM SUPPLEMENT.** [Br. j. clin. pract., Symp. suppl.]. **VFOAT** B.J.C.P. Supplement; BJCP Supplement. (197?)-. Monographic series. English. ir. £18.00 UK; $36.00 other. Medicom UK Ltd, The Quadrant, 118 London Road, Kingston Upon Thames, KT2 6QJ England. **Tel** 011 44 81 541 5666, FAX 011 44 81 541 4746. **NLM** W1 BR519S.
**Ind/Abst** Health Plan. Adminis.; Index Med.

UK/0007-1064
**BRITISH JOURNAL OF HOSPITAL MEDICINE.** [Br. j. hosp. med.]. Vol. 1 (Oct. 1968)-. Academic Scholarly Publication. English. Twenty times a year. £120.00 (institution), £76.00 (individual) UK; £135.00 (institution), £120.00 (individual) other. Mark Allen Publishing Limited, Robjohns Farm, Vicarage Road, Finchingfield CM7 4LJ England. **Tel** 11 44 371 810433. **DD** 610. **NLM** W1 BR537N. **CODEN** BJHMAB. Index Available in first issue of next volume--loose--separately paged. **Pr Rev.** available on microfilm and microfiche from University Microfilms International (UMI). Documents available from The Genuine Article, BIOSIS Document Express, Ask*IEEE, CASDDS. ***Continues** Hospital Medicine.*
**Ind/Abst** Biol. Abstr.; Chem. Abstr. (1968-1983); Cumul. Index Nurs. Allied Health Lit.; Curr. Contents Clin. Med.; EMBASE; Health Devices Alerts; Index Med.; Index Vet.; INSPEC (Jan. 1981-); Int. Nurs. Index; Nutr. Abstr. Rev., Ser. B, Live Feeds and Feed.; Nutr. Abstr. Rev., Ser. A, Hum. Exp.; Life Sci. Collect.; Protozoolog. Abstr.; Res. Alert [Full Cov.]; Rev. Med. Vet. Entomol.; Sci. Cit. Index; SCISEARCH; Soc. Sci. Cit. Index [Select. Cov.]; Vet. Bull.

UK/0961-7930
**BRITISH JOURNAL OF INTENSIVE CARE.** (1991)-. Periodical. English. mo. £84.00 (UK), £114.00 (Europe except UK), £132.00 (other) institutions; £60.00 (UK), £90.00 (Europe except UK), £108.00 (other) individuals. Greycoat Publishing, 1 Harley Street, London W1N 1DA England. **Tel** 11 44 71 6371828, FAX 11 44 71 6313020. **ED** Prof. Michael Rennie (editors telephone: 0382 307572). **NLM** W1; BR544R. Index available. **Bk Rev. Ad Acc, Adv Mgr:** Ashley Walus. **Circ:** 16,000 (ctrl).
**Desc:** Provides a forum for different specialized working in intensive care. Its editorial embraces both academic studies and practical applications providing readers with access to the latest research findings and to tried and tested solution to common problems in the intensive care unit.
**Ind/Abst** EMBASE [Select. Cov.].

UK/0962-1423
**BRITISH JOURNAL OF MEDICAL ECONOMICS, THE.** **See** Economics.

UK/0301-5572
**BRITISH JOURNAL OF SEXUAL MEDICINE.** ***Ceased.*** [Br. j. sex. med.]. Vol. 1 (Sept./Oct. 1973)-Ceased (Dec. 1991). Academic Scholarly Publication. English. bm. Medical News Tribune, Tower House, Southampton Street, London WC2E 7LS England. **Tel** (01)379-6005, FAX 01379 6737, telex 266854. **ED** Alan Riley. **NLM** W1 BR628. **CODEN** BJMEDF. **Bk Rev. Ad Acc. Circ:** 20,000. Documents available from BIOSIS Document Express.
**Desc:** Clinical papers, news and comment on sexual medicine. Principally papers on urology, gynecology, endocrinology, sexually transmitted diseases, reproductive medicine, psychosexual medicine.
**Ind/Abst** Biol. Abstr.; EMBASE; Health Plan. Adminis.

UK/0007-1420
**BRITISH MEDICAL BULLETIN.** [Br. med. bull.]. **Added/Corp** British Council. Medical Dept. Vol. 1 (March 1943)-. Academic Scholarly Publication. English. qt (January, April, July and October). £134.00 Europe; £137.00 Other (Institutions). Churchill Livingstone, 1-3 Baxter's Place, Leith Walk, Edinburgh EH1 3AF Scotland. **Tel** 011 44 31 556 2424, FAX 011 44 31 558 1278, telex 727511. **(Subscription address:** Maruzen Company Ltd., PO Box 5050, Import & Export Department, Tokyo 100 31 Japan.**)** **ED** C A Mims. **LC** R31; .B925. **DD** 610.5. **NLM** W1 BR687. **CODEN** BMBUAQ. **[CCC]. Bk Rev. Ad Acc. Pr Rev.** available on microfilm and microfiche from University Microfilms International (UMI). Documents available from The Genuine Article, BIOSIS Document Express, CASDDS, ADONIS.
**Desc:** Worldwide experts review current knowledge and the latest research in a particular field. Each issue covers a different medical topic.
**Ind/Abst** ADONIS; Anim. Breed. Abstr.; Biol. Abstr.; Chem. Abstr.; CSA Neuro. Abstr. (?-?); Curr. Biotechnol.; Curr. Contents Clin. Med.; Curr. Contents Life Sci.; Dairy Sci. Abstr.; Dev. Med. Child Neurol.; EMBASE; Immunol. Abstr.; Index Med.; Index Vet.; Int. Pharm. Abstr.; Microbiol. Abstr. Sect. B (19??-19??); Nutr. Abstr. Rev., Ser. B, Live Feeds and Feed.; Nutr. Abstr. Rev., Ser. A, Hum. Exp.; Life Sci. Collect.; PESTDOC; Protozoolog. Abstr.; Ref. Upd. Basic Ed.; Ref. Upd. Clinical Ed.; Ref. Upd. Deluxe Ed.; Res. Alert [Full Cov.]; Rev. Med. Vet. Mycology; Rev. Plant Pathol.; Saf. Health Work; Sci. Cit. Index; SCISEARCH; Soc. Sci. Cit. Index [Select. Cov.]; Stat. Theory Method Abstr. (1970); Vet. Bull.; Trop. Dis. Bull.; Virol. AIDS Abstr.

UK/0267-0631
**BRITISH MEDICAL JOURNAL (PRACTICE OBSERVED ED.).** ***Title Change.*** (BRITISH MEDICAL JOURNAL.). [Br. med. j.]. **Added/Corp** British Medical Association. **VFOAT** BMJ. (1981)-(19??). Academic Scholarly Publication. English. wk. BMJ / British Medical Journal Publishing Group, British Medical Association House, Tavistock Square, London WC1H 9JR England. **Tel** 011 44 71 3874499, FAX 011 44 71 383 6402, telex 290034 HBJ MN. **NLM** W1 BR69E. **CODEN** BMJOAE. ***Continues in part** British Medical Journal, 0007-1447.* ***Continued by** British Medical Journal.*
**Ind/Abst** Calcium Calcif. Tissue Abstr.; Coal Abstr.; Cumul. Index Nurs. Allied Health Lit.; Dev. Med. Child Neurol.; EMBASE; Health Serv. Abstr.; Immunol. Abstr.; Int. Pharm. Abstr.; J. Watch; SportSearch; Toxicol. Abstr.

UK/0140-2722
**BRITISH MEDICINE (LONDON : 1972).** ***Ceased.*** (BRITISH MEDICINE; A MONTHLY GUIDE TO CURRENT LITERATURE.). [Brit. med.]. Vol. 1 (Jan. 1972)-Ceased Vol. 19 (1990). Periodical. English. mo. Pergamon Press, An Imprint of Elsevier Science Ltd., The Boulevard, Langford Lane, Kidlington, Oxford OX5 1GB United Kingdom. **Tel** 011 44 865 843000, 011 44 865 843699, FAX 011 44 865 843010. **(Subscription address:** US/ 395 Saw Mill River Road, Elmsford, NY 10523; Can/ 150 Consumers Road/Suite 104, Willowdale Ontario M2J 1P9; Aus-NZ/ POB 544, Potts Point NSW 2011**)** **NLM** ZW 1 B863. **[CCC].** available on microfilm and microfiche from University Microfilms International (UMI). ***Formed by the union of** British Medical Book List and British Medical Index.*
**Ind/Abst** Protozoolog. Abstr.

UK/0950-3005
**BRITISH REVIEW OF BULIMIA + ANOREXIA NERVOSA.** ***Title Change.*** [Br. rev. bulimia anorex. nerv.]. **Added/Corp** Anorexic Family Aid (Charitable Trust). National Information Centre Norwich. **VFOAT** British Review of Bulimia and Anorexia Nervosa. Vol. 1, No. 1 (Nov. 1986)-(199?). Periodical. English. sa. Eating Disorders Association, Sackville Place, 44 Magdalen Street, Norwich NR3 1JE England. **Tel** 011 44 603 621414. **NLM** W1; BR75J. ***Continued by** Eating Disorders Review (Chichester, England), 1067-1633.*
**Ind/Abst** EMBASE; Psychol. Abstr. (1986-); PsycINFO; PsycLit.

US/0898-3070
**BUCKEYE OSTEOPATHIC PHYSICIAN.**
**See** Pharmacy and Pharmacology.

CN/1187-2233
**BULLETIN AMI.** [Bull. AMI]. **Added/Corp** Assistance Medicale Internationale (Societe). **VFOAT** Bulletin de l'AMI. **VAT** Bulletin Assistance Medicale Internationale, Societe. Vol. 1 No 1 (Spring 1991)-. Bulletin. French. Three times a year. Assistance Medicale Internationale, 3540 Ave de Lorimier, Montreal Quebec H2K 3X6 Canada. **Tel** 521-2311. **DD** 362.1/0425. ***Continues** Bulletin de l'Assistance Medicale Internationale., 0382-4462.*

CN/0702-7656
**BULLETIN - ASSOCIATION DES MEDECINS DE LANGUE FRANCAISE DU CANADA (1977).** (BULLETIN - ASSOCIATION DES MEDECINS DE LANGUE FRANCAISE DU CANADA.). **Main/Corp** Association des Medecins de Langue Francaise du Canada. V. 11, No. 1-Jan./Feb. 1977-. Bulletin. French. mo. 145.00Can$ physicians, 45.00Can$ residents/interns, 30.00Can$ students. Association des Medecins de Langue Francaise du Canada, 8355 Boulevard Saint Laurent, Montreal Quebec H2P 2Z6 Canada. **Tel** (514)388-2228. **ED** Andre de Seve. **DD** 610.6/271. **Bk Rev. Ad Acc. Circ:** 15,000 (ctrl).

AT/0156-5184
**BULLETIN / AUSTRALIAN MUSIC THERAPY ASSOCIATION.** **See** Music.

UK/0953-7511
**BULLETIN / BRITISH SOCIETY FOR MUSIC THERAPY.** **See** Music.

CN/1186-0006
**BULLETIN - CANADIAN MEDICAL ASSOCIATION.** ***Ceased.*** (BULLETIN.). [Bull. - Can. Med. Assoc.]. **Main/Corp** Canadian Medical Association. **VAT** Bulletin - Association Medicale Canadienne. (Oct. 1990)-(199?). English (French). Canadian Medical Association, 1867 Alta Vista Drive, Ottawa Ontario K1G 3Y6 Canada. **Tel** (613)731-9331 ext. 2028, FAX (613)731-4797. **DD** 610.

CN/0823-2105
**BULLETIN CANADIEN D'HISTOIRE DE LA MEDECINE.** (CANADIAN BULLETIN OF MEDICAL HISTORY.). [Bull. can. hist. med.]. **Added/Corp** Canadian Society for the History of Medicine. **VFOAT** Bulletin Canadien d'Histoire de la Medecine; MH; CBMH/BCHM. Vol. 4 No. 1 (Summer 1987)-. Bulletin. English (summaries and/or abstracts in French). sa. Canadian Bulletin of Medical History, Charles G Roland MD, 3N10-HSC McMaster University, Hamilton Ontario L8N 3Z5 Canada. **Tel** (416)525-9140. **DD** 610/.971. ***Continues** Bulletin Canadien d'Histoire de la Medecine., 0823-2105.*
**Ind/Abst** Am. Hist. Life (1990-); Can. Period. Index.

CN/0315-2979
**BULLETIN - CORPORATION PROFESSIONNELLE DES MEDECINS DU QUEBEC.** [Bull. - Corp. prof. med. Que.]. **Main/Corp** Corporation Professionnelle des Medecins du Quebec. Vol. 14 (Fevr. 1974)-. Bulletin. French (English). qt. Free on request. Professional Corporation of Physicians of Quebec, 1440 Ouest rue St Catherine, Montreal Quebec H3G 1S5 Canada. **Tel** (514)878-4441, FAX (514)878-4379. **Circ:** 20,000 (ctrl). ***Continues** College des Medecins et Chirurgiens de la Province de Quebec. Bulletin., 0069-5599.*
**Desc:** Pertains to medicine and legislation.

FR/0764-8103
**BULLETIN D'AUDIOPHONOLOGIE, ANNALES SCIENTIFIQUES DE L'UNIVERSITE DE FRANCHE-COMTE. MEDECINE & PHARMACIE.** [Bull. audiophonol. Ann. sci. Univ. Franche-Comte Med. pharm.]. **VFOAT** Bulletin d'Audiophonologie, Annales Scientifiques de l'Universite de Franche-Comte. Medecine et Pharmacie. (1985)-. Bulletin. Multiple languages. Four times a year. 390.00F France; 430.00F other. Association Franc Comtoise d'Audiophonologie, Faculte de Medecine & de Pharmacie, 25030 Besancon France. **Tel** 011 33 1 81665566, FAX 011 33 1 81665573. **UDC** 616.28. ***Continues in part** Bulletin d'Audiophonologie (Besancon), 0338-9405.*

FR/0475-042X
**BULLETIN DE LA SOCIETE DE PATHOLOGIE EXOTIQUE.** Bulletin. French. ir (11 times per year). 131.00F France; $36.00 US; £32.00 UK. Masson SA, Avenue Beauregard 12, CH-1701 Fribourg Switzerland. **Tel** 011 41 37 249585, FAX 011 41 37 247559, telex 942658 SEMI CH.

LU/0037-9247
**BULLETIN DE LA SOCIETE DES SCIENCES MEDICALES DU GRAND-DUCHE DE LUXEMBOURG.** [Bull. Soc. sci. med. Grand-Duche Luxemb.]. **Added/Corp** Societe des Sciences Medicales du Grand-Duche de Luxembourg. (1864)-. Periodical. Multiple languages (English, French and German). ir. Free on request. Societe des Sciences Medicales du Grand-Duche de Luxembourg, M Dicato Luxembourg Medical Center, L 1210 Luxembourg. **Tel** 011 352 44112084. **NLM** W1 BU515. **CODEN** BMGLAO. Documents available from BIOSIS Document Express, CASDDS.
**Ind/Abst** Biol. Abstr.; Chem. Abstr. (1864-1982); EMBASE; Health Plan. Adminis.; Index Med.

SG/0049-1101
**BULLETIN DE LA SOCIETE MEDICALE D'AFRIQUE NOIRE DE LANGUE FRANCAISE.** (DAKAR MEDICAL.). [Bull. Soc. med. Afr. noire lang. fr.]. **Added/Corp** Societe Medicale d'Afrique Noire de Langue Francaise. Vol. 24 (1979)-. Academic Scholarly Publication. French (summaries and/or abstracts in English and French). sa. 500.00F French speaking Africa; 600.00F other. Society Medical d'Afrique Noire Langue Francaise, Boite Postale 450, Dakar Senegal. **NLM** W1 DA243M. **CODEN** DAMDD5. Index available. **Bk Rev.** Documents available from BIOSIS Document Express. ***Continues** Bulletin de la Societe Medicale d'Afrique Noire de Langue Francaise, 0049-1101.*
**Desc:** Publications on tropical diseases.
**Ind/Abst** Biol. Abstr.; EMBASE; Helminthol. Abstr. (19??-19??); Index Med. (1979-); Protozoolog. Abstr.; Rev. Med. Vet. Mycology; SportSearch; Trop. Dis. Bull.

FR/0001-4079
**BULLETIN DE L'ACADEMIE NATIONALE DE MEDICINE.** [Bull. Acad. natl. med.]. **Added/Corp** Academie Nationale de Medecine (France). (1947)-. Bulletin. French. Nine times a year. 620.00F France; 650.00F other. L'Academie Nationale Medicine, 16 rue Bonaparte, 75272 Paris Cedex 06 France. **Tel** 011 33 1 43269680. **NLM** W1 BU525. **CODEN** BANMAC. **[CCC]. Pr Rev.** Documents available from The Genuine Article, CASDDS. ***Continues** Bulletin de l'Academie de Medecine.*
**Ind/Abst** Chem. Abstr.; Curr. Contents Clin. Med.; EMBASE; GeoRef; Health Plan. Adminis.; Helminthol. Abstr. (1991-); Index Med. (1979-); Index Vet.; Nutr. Abstr. Rev., Ser. A, Hum. Exp.; Life Sci. Collect.;

Protozoolog. Abstr.; Res. Alert [Select. Cov.]; Saf. Health Work; Soc. Sci. Cit. Index [Select. Cov.]; SportSearch; Trop. Dis. Bull.

FR
**BULLETIN DE L'AGMF.** Bulletin. French. Ten times a year. Assn Gen Des Medecins France, 30 Blvd Pasteur, 75740 Paris Cedex 15 France. **Tel** 011 33 1 45675506.

FR/0030-4565
**BULLETIN DE L'ORDRE DES MEDECINS.** [Bull. Ordre med.]. (1941)-. Periodical. French. ir (11 issues). $40.00. Masson Editeur, Box Postale 22, 41353 Vineuil 16 France. **Tel** 011 33 54 438994. **UDC** 61.

BE/0377-8231
**BULLETIN ET MEMOIRES DE L'ACADEMIE ROYALE DE MEDECINE DE BELGIQUE.** [Bull. mem. Acad. r. med. Belg.]. Vol. 130 (Jan. 1975)-. Academic Scholarly Publication. French (English). mo (11y). 3000F. Academie Royale de Medecine de Belgique, Palais Academies, rue Decale 1, 1000 Bruxelles Belgium. **Tel** 11 32 2 5112471, FAX (02)502-0712. **LC** R41; .B82. **NLM** W1 BU652P. **CODEN** BMABDZ. **Bk Rev**. Documents available from BIOSIS Document Express, CASDDS. ***Formed by the union of*** *Bulletin de l'Academie Royale de Medecine de Belgique, 0001-4168* ***and*** *Memoires de l'Academie Royale de Medecine de Belgique, 0065-0595.*
**Ind/Abst** Biol. Abstr.; Chem. Abstr.; EMBASE; Health Plan. Adminis.; Index Med.

CN/0705-3029
**BULLETIN - INTERNATIONAL ASSOCIATION FOR MOBILIZATION OF CREATIVITY.** **Main/Corp** International Association for Mobilization of Creativity. **VFOAT** I. A. M. C. Bulletin. **VAT** International Association for Mobilization of Creativity Bulletin; Bulletin. Association Internationale pour la Mobilisation de la Creativite. V. 1- Jan. 1978-. Bulletin. English (French). bm. Price varies per volume. International Association for Mobilization of Creativity, Box 123, Montreal Quebec H3X 3T3 Canada. **DD** 615/.8515.

JA/0495-7792
**BULLETIN - JOURNAL OF THE TOKYO WOMEN'S MEDICAL COLLEGE.** **Added/Corp** Tokyo Joshi Ika Daigaku. Heart Institute Japan. Vol. 1, No. 1 (July 1957)-. Bulletin. Japanese (English). mo. ¥6000. Society of Tokyo Women's Medical College, 8-1 Kawadacho, Shinjuku-ku, Tokyo 162 Japan. **Tel** telex 2322317-TWMILIB-J. **DD** 616.1. **NLM** W1 BU847I. **CODEN** BHIJAR. cum. index. **Ad Acc. Circ:** 1,700 (ctrl). Documents available from CASDDS.
**Ind/Abst** Chem. Abstr. (1979-1980).

US/0098-5880
**BULLETIN - LUZERNE COUNTY MEDICAL SOCIETY, THE.** **Added/Corp** Luzerne County Medical Society. Vol. 3 (Oct. 1931)-. Bulletin. English. qt (March, June, Sep., Dec.). $20.00. Luzerne County Medical Society, 130 South Franklin Street, Wilks Barre PA 18701. **Tel** (717)823-0917. **ED** Edward Lottick. **NLM** W1 BU674. **Ad Acc. Circ:** 675.
**Desc:** Brief, socio-economic, up-to-date information on medicine and health care on a national, state, and local basis. Includes editorial, new members roster and committees listed.

US/0098-5872
**BULLETIN - MARION COUNTY MEDICAL SOCIETY.** ***Title Change.*** (THE MARION COUNTY MEDICAL SOCIETY BULLETIN.). [Bull. - Marion Cty. Med. Soc.]. **Added/Corp** Marion County Medical Society. Vol. 50 (Jan. 1959)-(19??). Periodical. English. ir. Indianapolis Medical Society, 631 East New York Street, Indianapolis IN 46202. **Tel** (317)639-3406. **NLM** W1 MA654C. ***Continues*** *Bulletin of the Indianapolis Medical Society.* ***Continued by*** *Indianapolis Medical Society Bulletin.*

US/0007-4888
**BULLETIN OF EXPERIMENTAL BIOLOGY AND MEDICINE.** [Bull. exp. biol. med.]. **VFOAT** Biulleten Eksperimentalnoi Biologii i Meditsiny. Vol. 41 (Jan. 1956)-. Academic Scholarly Publication. English (Russian). mo. $1430.00 US; $1675.00 other. Consultants Bureau, A Division of Plenum Publishing Corporation, 233 Spring Street, New York NY 10013. **Tel** (212)620-8000, (212)620-8466, FAX (212)463-0742, telex 23/421139. **ED** A. D. Ado. **LC** R850. **DD** 619.05. **NLM** W1 BU772. **CODEN** BEXBAN. **[CCC].** Index available. available on microfilm and microfiche from University Microfilms International (UMI). Documents available from The Genuine Article, BIOSIS Document Express, CASDDS.
**Desc:** This important Soviet journal publishes accounts of experimental research on urgent problems of modern biology and medicine. Conducted by members of the Academy of Medical Science of the USSR.
**Ind/Abst** Biol. Abstr. (?-1984); Calcium Calcif. Tissue Abstr.; Chem. Abstr.; CSA Neuro. Abstr. (?-?); Curr. Contents Life Sci.; Dairy Sci. Abstr.; EMBASE; Helminthol. Abstr. (1991-); Immunol. Abstr.; Index Med.; Index Vet.; INIS Atomindex [Micro.]; Microbiol. Abstr. Sect. B (19??-19??); NAPRALERT; Life Sci. Collect.; Pollut. Abstr. Indexes; Protozoolog. Abstr.; Res. Alert [Full Cov.]; Sci. Cit. Index; SCISEARCH; Soc. Sci. Cit. Index [Select. Cov.]; Toxicol. Abstr.

UK
**BULLETIN OF MEDICAL ETHICS.** **See** Ethics.

II/0302-2404
**BULLETIN OF POSTGRADUATE INSTITUTE OF MEDICAL EDUCATION AND RESEARCH, CHANDIGARH.** [Bull. Postgrad. Inst. Med. Educ. Res., ChandÂigarh]. **Main/Corp** Postgraduate Institute of Medical Education and Research, Chandigarh. **VFOAT** Bulletin P.G.I.; Bulletin, Postgraduate Institute of Medical Education and Research, Chandigarh. (196?)-. Bulletin. English. Four times a year. **(Subscription address:** Prints India, 11 Darya Ganj, New Delhi 110002 India, telephone: 011 91 11 3268645) **NLM** W1 BU835M. **CODEN** BPIRD8. Documents available from BIOSIS Document Express, CASDDS.
**Ind/Abst** Biol. Abstr.; Chem. Abstr.; EMBASE; Trop. Dis. Bull.

CN/0001-4311
**BULLETIN OF THE ACADEMY OF MEDICINE, TORONTO.** **Main/Corp** Academy of Medicine, Toronto, Ont. Vol. 1 (1927)-. Bulletin. English. ir. Academy of Medicine / Canada, 288 Bloor Street West, Toronto Ontario M5S 1V8 Canada. **NLM** W1 BU84L.

US/0014-0937
**BULLETIN OF THE ESSEX COUNTY MEDICAL SOCIETY, THE.** **Added/Corp** Essex County Medical Society (N. J.). (193?)-. Bulletin. English. mo (9 issues). Comes with membership to Essex County Medical Society. Essex County Medical Society, 80 Pompton Ave., Verona NJ 07044. **Tel** (201)239-9392. **ED** Enio Callouri, M.D. **NLM** W1 BU846M. **Ad Acc.** available with illustrations.

US/0007-5140
**BULLETIN OF THE HISTORY OF MEDICINE.** [Bull. hist. med.]. **Added/Corp** American Association for the History of Medicine. Johns Hopkins University. Institute of the History of Medicine. American Association of the History of Medicine. Transactions. Vol. 7, No. 1 (Jan. 1939)-. Periodical. English. Four times a year (March, June, Sept. and Dec.). $61.50 US; $65.50 Canada and Mexico; $72.20 other. Johns Hopkins University Press, 2715 North Charles Street, Baltimore MD 21218-4319. **Tel** (410)516-6987, FAX (410)516-6968. **ED** Gert Brieger and Jerome Bylebyl. **LC** R11; .B93. **DD** 610. **NLM** W1 BU85X. **[CCC].** Index Available Received separately--bound from publisher. cum. index. **Bk Rev. Ad Acc. Pr Rev. Circ:** 2,250. available on microfilm and microfiche from University Microfilms International (UMI). Documents available from The Genuine Article, BIOSIS Document Express, CASDDS. ***Continues*** *Bulletin of the Institute of the History of Medicine.*
**Desc:** Articles analyze advances in medical science, examine changes in clinical practices, and explore how the responses of societies to health care needs have varied over time and across cultures. Updates readers on national and international activities in the field.
**Ind/Abst** Am. Hist. Life (1963-); Am. Bibliogr. Slavic East Europ. Stud.; Annu. Bibliogr. Engl. Lang. Lit.; Biol. Abstr.; Chem. Abstr.; Curr. Contents Clin. Med.; Curr. Contents Life Sci.; EMBASE; Health Plan. Adminis.; Index Med.; Index Vet.; Life Sci. Collect.; Res. Alert [Full Cov.]; Sci. Cit. Index; SCISEARCH; Soc. Sci. Cit. Index [Select. Cov.].

II/0304-9558
**BULLETIN OF THE INDIAN INSTITUTE OF HISTORY OF MEDICINE.** **Added/Corp** Central Council for Research in Indian Medicine and Homoeopathy. Vol. 4 (Jan. 1974)-. Bulletin. English (summaries and/or abstracts in Hindi). sa. $30.00. **(Subscription address:** Prints India, 11 Darya Ganj, New Delhi 110002 India.) **LC** R605; .O82. **DD** 610/.954. **NLM** W1 BU852EM. ***Continues*** *Institute of History of Medicine. Bulletin, 0304-9566.*

II/0575-1772
**BULLETIN OF THE INSTITUTE OF POST GRADUATE MEDICAL EDUCATION AND RESEARCH.** **Main/Corp** Calcutta. Institute of Post Graduate Medical Education and Research. Vol. 1 (Jan. 1959)-. Bulletin. English. qt. $25.00. Institute of Post Graduate Medical Education & Research / Calcutta, Calcutta, India. **(Subscription address:** Prints India, 11 Darya Ganj, New Delhi 110002 India.)

JA
**BULLETIN OF THE KOHNO CLINICAL MEDICINE RESEARCH INSTITUTE.** **Added/Corp** Kohno Clinical Medicine Research Institute. (19??)-. Bulletin. English. Kono Rinsho Igaku Kenkyujo, (Kohno Clinical Medicine Research Inst.), 28-15, Kitashinagawa, 1 Chome, Shinagawaku, Tokyoto 140 Japan.
**Ind/Abst** Trop. Dis. Bull.

US/0028-7091
**BULLETIN OF THE NEW YORK ACADEMY OF MEDICINE (1925).** (BULLETIN OF THE NEW YORK ACADEMY OF MEDICINE.). [Bull. N. Y. Acad. Med.]. **Added/Corp** New York Academy of Medicine. 2nd Ser., Vol. 1 (March 1925)-. Academic Scholarly Publication. English. Twice a year. $35.00 US and Canada; $40.00 other. New York Academy of Medicine, 2 East 103rd Street, New York NY 10029. **Tel** (212)876-8200. **ED** Dr. Robert J. Haggerty. **LC** R15; .N62. **DD** 610.62747. **NLM** W1 BU874. **CODEN** BNYMAM. **Bk Rev. Pr Rev. Circ:** 4,000 (ctrl). available on microfilm and microfiche from University Microfilms International (UMI). Documents available from The Genuine Article, BIOSIS Document Express, CASDDS. ***Continues*** *New York Academy of Medicine. Transactions of the New York Academy of Medicine, 0892-4503.*
**Desc:** The bulletin is a scholarly and scientific journal. It publishes papers presented at meetings, abstracts of original investigation, essays on medical history, book reviews, case reports, etc.
**Ind/Abst** Biol. Abstr.; Chem. Abstr. (1925-1983); Crim. Justice Abstr.; Cumul. Index Nurs. Allied Health Lit.; Curr. Contents Clin. Med.; Dairy Sci. Abstr.; EMBASE; Energy Res. Abstr.; Health Plan. Adminis.; Immunol. Abstr.; Index Med.; Int. Nurs. Index; Med. Abstr. Newsl.; Mod. Med.; Numis. Lit.; Nutr. Abstr. Rev., Ser. A, Hum. Exp.; Nutr. Res. Newsl.; Life Sci. Collect.; PESTDOC; Protozoolog. Abstr.; Res. Alert [Select. Cov.]; SCISEARCH; Soc. Sci. Cit. Index [Select. Cov.]; SportSearch; Trop. Dis. Bull.

US/0199-7378
**BULLETIN OF THE OCMA, THE.** [Bull. OCMA]. **Main/Corp** Orange County Medical Association. **VFOAT** Bulletin of the Orange County Medical Association. (19??)-. Periodical. English. Twelve times a year. $24.00. Orange County Medical Association, 300 South Flower Street, Orange CA 92668. **Tel** (714)978-1770, FAX (714)978-6039. **ED** Arthur D. Silk and Jacquiline E. Falgren. **NLM** W1 BU88. **Ad Acc. Circ:** 2,850. ***Continues*** *Bulletin of the Orange County Medical Association, 0272-9059.*
**Desc:** News and information on the state and county legislation and medicine issues from the Orange County medical community.

JA
**BULLETIN OF THE OSAKA MEDICAL COLLEGE.** **Added/Corp** Osaka Ika Daigaku. Vol. 34, No. 1, 2 (Nov. 1988)-. Bulletin. English. sa. Osaka Medical College, 2-7 Daigakumachi Takatsuki, Osaka Japan. **Tel** 0276-83-1221. **NLM** W1; BU883G. **CODEN** BOMCEB. Documents available from BIOSIS Document Express. ***Continues*** *Bulletin of the Osaka Medical School, 0030-6142.*
**Ind/Abst** Biol. Abstr. (1990-); Health Plan. Adminis.; Index Med. (1988-).

SZ/0042-9686
**BULLETIN OF THE WORLD HEALTH ORGANIZATION.** [Bull. W.H.O.]. **Main/Corp** World Health Organization. **Added/Corp** World Health Organization. Bulletin de l'Organisation Mondiale de la Sante. **VFOAT** Bulletin de l'Organisation Mondiale de la Sante. (1948)-. Academic Scholarly Publication. English (French). bm. $152.00 Surface Mail; $165.00 (airmail) Europe; $183.00 (airmail) other. World Health Organization, Distribution and Sales, 20 Avenue Appia, CH-1211 Geneva 27 Switzerland. **Tel** 011 41 22 7912111, FAX 011 41 22 7880401. **LC** R5; .W62. **DD** 610.82. **NLM** W1 BU896N. **CODEN** BWHOA6. **Pr Rev.** available on microfilm and microfiche from University Microfilms International (UMI); available on an online database (file 149/Full-Text) from DIALOG. Documents available from The Genuine Article, BIOSIS Document Express, CASDDS. ***Continues*** *Interim Commission of the World Health Organization. Bulletin.*
**Desc:** Presents original research findings selected on the basis of their immediate or potential relevance to problems of human health. Records work from leading authorities the world over, offering access to new laboratory, clinical and epidemiological data drawn from a broad range of fields. Whether based on molecular biology or in chemoprophylaxis, all papers share the capacity of advanced health efforts.
**Ind/Abst** Appl. Soc. Sci. Index Abstr.; Biol. Abstr.; Chem. Abstr. (1947-1983); Curr. Contents Clin. Med.; Curr. Contents Life Sci.; Dairy Sci. Abstr.; Dent. Abstr. (-1991); EMBASE; Environ. Period. Bibliogr. (?-?); Fish Rev.; Health Saf. Sci. Abstr.; Health Period. Database [Full Txt.]; Helminthol. Abstr. (1991-); Immunol. Abstr.; Index Med.; Index Vet.; Int. Pharm. Abstr.; Microbiol. Abstr. Sect. B (19??-19??); Microbiol. Abstr. Sect. C; NAPRALERT; Nematol. Abstr.; Nutr. Abstr. Rev., Ser. B, Live Feeds and Feed.; Nutr. Abstr. Rev., Ser. A, Hum. Exp.; Nutr. Res. Newsl.; Life Sci. Collect.; PESTDOC; Pollut. Abstr. Indexes; Poult. Abstr.; Protozoolog. Abstr.; Ref. Upd. Deluxe Ed.; Res. Alert [Full Cov.]; Rev. Med. Vet. Entomol.; Rev. Med. Vet. Mycology; Rev. Plant Pathol.; Rural Dev. Abstr.; Saf. Health Work; Sci. Cit. Index; SCISEARCH; Small Anim. Abstr. Bibliogr.; Soc. Sci. Cit. Index [Select. Cov.]; Soc. Work Abstr. (?-?); Vet. Bull.; Trop. Dis. Bull.; Virol. AIDS Abstr.; Wildl. Rev.

JA/0513-1812
**BULLETIN OF THE YAMAGUCHI MEDICAL SCHOOL.** [Bull. Yamaguchi Med. Sch.]. **Added/Corp** Yamaguchi Kenritsu Ika Daigaku.

**VFOAT** Yamaguchi Ika Daigaku Kiyo. (Feb. 1953)-. Academic Scholarly Publication. English (French and German). ir. Yamaguchi Medical School, Yamaguchi Prefecture. **NLM** W1 BU897F. **CODEN** BYMSAN. Documents available from BIOSIS Document Express, CASDDS.
**Ind/Abst** Biol. Abstr. (-1989); Chem. Abstr.; EMBASE; Trop. Dis. Bull.

JA/0040-8921
**BULLETIN OF TOKYO MEDICAL AND DENTAL UNIVERSITY, THE.** [Bull. Tokyo Med. Dent. Univ.]. **Main/Corp** Tokyo Ika Shika Daigaku. **Added/Corp** Tokyo Medical and Dental University. No. 1 (March 1954)-. Bulletin. English. qt. Free on request. Tokyo Medical and Dental University / Tokyoto, 5 45 Yushima 1 Chome, Bunkyo Ku Tokyoto 113 Japan. **NLM** W1 BU898M. **CODEN** BTMDAB. Index available. cum. index. **Ad Acc. Circ:** 1,500. Documents available from BIOSIS Document Express, CASDDS.
**Ind/Abst** Biol. Abstr.; Chem. Abstr. (1954-1982); Curr. Titl. Dent.; EMBASE; Health Plan. Adminis.; Index Med.; Index Dent. Lit.; Nutr. Res. Newsl.; SEA Abstr.; Trop. Dis. Bull.

CN/0315-2979
**BULLETIN - PROFESSIONAL CORPORATION OF PHYSICIANS OF QUEBEC.** [Bull. - Corp. prof. med. Que.]. **Main/Corp** Professional Corporation of Physicians of Quebec. Vol. 14 (Feb. 1974)-. Bulletin. French (English). Four times a year (Feb., Apr., June, Sept., (two issues in Nov. & Dec.)). Free. Professional Corporation of Physicians of Quebec, 1440 Ouest rue St Catherine, Montreal Quebec H3G 1S5 Canada. **Tel** (514)878-4441, FAX (514)878-4379. Index available. cum. index. **Bk Rev**, (Qty: 28). **Circ:** 20,500. ***Continues** College des Medecins et Chirurgiens de la Province de Quebec. Bulletin, 0069-5599.*
**Ind/Abst** Point Repere (1984-Vol. 30, No. 4 Nov./Dec. 1990).

II/0255-7207
**BULLETIN / RAJENDRA MEMORIAL RESEARCH INSTITUTE OF MEDICAL SCIENCES.** [Bull. - Rajendra Meml. Res. Inst. Med. Sci.]. **Added/Corp** Rajendra Memorial Research Institute of Medical Sciences. Rajendra Memorial Research Society for Medical Sciences. (197?)-. Bulletin. English. sa. **NLM** W1 BU478HD.

CN/0838-1380
**BULLETIN, UNIVERSITY-INDUSTRY PROGRAMS.** (BULLETIN, PROGRAMMES UNIVERSITE-INDUSTRIE / CONSEIL DE RECHERCHES MEDICALES DU CANADA.). [Bull. univ.-ind. programs]. **Added/Corp** Conseil de Recherches Medicales (Canada). **VFOAT** Bulletin, University-Industry Programs. Vol. 3, No 2 (Apr. 1991)-. Bulletin. French (English). **DD** 610/.72071/05. ***Separated from** Newsletter - Medical Research Council., 0047-6560.*

CN/0838-1380
**BULLETIN, UNIVERSITY-INDUSTRY PROGRAMS / MEDICAL RESEARCH COUNCIL OF CANADA.** [Bull. univ.-ind. programs]. **Added/Corp** Medical Research Council (Canada). **VFOAT** Bulletin, Pyrogrammes Universite-Industrie. Vol. 3, No. 2 (Apr. 1991)-. Bulletin. English (French). Medical Research Council of Canada, Jeanne Mance Building/20th Floor, Ottawa Ontario K1A 0W9 Canada. **Tel** (613)996-8182. **DD** 610/.72071/05. ***Separated from** Newsletter - Medical Research Council., 0047-6560.*

AQ
**BULLETIN / UNIVERSITY OF HEALTH SCIENCES, ANTIGUA, SCHOOL OF MEDICINE.** **Main/Corp** University of Health Sciences Antigua. School of Medicine. (19??)-. English. University of Health Sciences Antigua / School of Medicine, St. John's Antigua & Barbuda.

UK/0305-4179
**BURNS : JOURNAL OF THE INTERNATIONAL SOCIETY FOR BURN INJURIES.** **Added/Corp** International Society for Burn Injuries. **VFOAT** Journal of the International Society for Burn Injuries. Vol. 15 No. 1 (Feb. 1989)-. Periodical. English. Eight times a year. $276.00 The Americas; £185.00 other. Butterworth Heinemann Publishers, Linacre House, Jordan Hill, Oxford OX2 8DP England. **Tel** 011 44 865 310366. **(Subscription address:** Elsevier Science Ltd. Oxford Fulfillment Centre, PO Box 800, Kidlington, Oxford OX5 1DX United Kingdom.**) NLM** W1; BU9732F. **[CCC]. Pr Rev.** Documents available from The Genuine Article. ***Continues** Burns, Including Thermal Injury.*
**Ind/Abst** Cumul. Index Nurs. Allied Health Lit.; Curr. Contents Clin. Med.; EMBASE; Health Plan. Adminis.; Index Med. (Feb. 1989-); Physic. Medline Plus; Protozoolog. Abstr.; Res. Alert [Select. Cov.]; Rev. Med. Vet. Mycology; SCISEARCH; Soc. Sci. Cit. Index [Select. Cov.].

SP/0212-6176
**BUTLLETI EPIDEMIEOLOGIC GENERALITAT VALENCIANA.** [Butll. epidemiol. Gen. Valencia.]. **VFOAT** Boletin Epidemiologico Generalidad Valenciana; Butlleti Epidemieologic Generalitat Valenciana. (1983)-. Periodical. Spanish. mo. Generalidad Valenciana, Colon 48, 46004 Valencia Spain. **UDC** 362.193.

SP/0211-6340
**BUTLLETI EPIDEMIOLOGIC DE CATALUNYA.** [Butll. epidemiol. Catalunya]. **VFOAT** BEC. Butlleti Epidemiologic de Catalunya. (1980)-. Periodical. Catalan. mo. Generalidad de Cataluna, Travesia de Les Corts 131-159, 08028 Barcelona Spain. **UDC** 362.193.
**Ind/Abst** Trop. Dis. Bull.

JA/0286-2190
**BYOTAI SEIRI (OSAKA. 1982).** **See** Philosophy.

CN/0068-8258
**C.A.R. SCOPE.** **Main/Corp** Canadian Arthritis and Rheumatism Society. **VFOAT** Carscope. V. 1- Jan. 1960-. Periodical. English. mo. Club Culturel Les Philanthropes, Suite 3235, 1, Place Ville-Marie, Montreal Quebec H3B 3M7.

US/0148-2394
**CA SELECTS: ANTI-INFLAMMATORY AGENTS & ARTHRITIS.** **See** Chemistry-Abstracting, Bibliographies and Statistics.

US/0882-6447
**CADUCEUS (SPRINGFIELD, ILL.).** (CADUCEUS : A MUSEUM QUARTERLY FOR THE HEALTH SCIENCES.). [Caduceus]. **Added/Corp** Southern Illinois University School of Medicine. Dept. of Medical Humanities. Southern Illinois University School of Medicine. Division of Biomedical Communications. Medical Illustration. Vol. 1, No. 1 (Spring 1985)-. Periodical. English. Three times a year. $45.00 (individuals); $60.00 (institutions). Department of Medical Humanities, Southern Illinois University, School of Medicins, PO Box 19230, Springfield IL 62794-9230. **Tel** (217)782-4261. **ED** Glen W. Davidson. **DD** 610. **NLM** W1; CA1297. **Bk Rev. Ad Acc. Circ:** 150.
**Desc:** Focus on medical artifacts, medical practice and institutions for health care delivery to inform readers on contexts from which contemporary health care issues have emerged.
**Ind/Abst** Except. Hum. Exp.; Health Plan. Adminis.; Index Med. (1985-).

BE/0376-7639
**CAHIERS DE MEDECINE DU TRAVAIL.** [Cah. med. trav.]. **Added/Corp** Association Professionnelle Belge des Medecins du Travail. Institut des Hautes Etudes de Belgique. **VFOAT** Cahiers voor Bedrijfsbeneesheren; Cahiers voor Arbeidsgeneeskunde. (19??)-. Monographic series. French (Dutch). Four times a year. 2100.00F Belgium; 2600.00f other. Assn Prof Belge Medec Travail, 128 Avenue Henri Jaspar, 1060 Brussels Belgium. **Tel** 011 32 2 5382820, FAX 011 32 2 5387932, telex 27036. **NLM** W1 CA1382M. **CODEN** CMTVAS. Index available. **Bk Rev. Ad Acc.** ctrl circ. Documents available from CASDDS.
**Ind/Abst** Chem. Abstr.; EMBASE; Saf. Health Work.

FR/0007-9936
**CAHIERS DE MEDECINE INTERPROFESSIONNELLE.** [Cah. med. interprof.]. (1961)-. Periodical. French. qt. 411.36F France; 420.00F other. Docis, 31 rue Mederic, 75832 Paris Cedex 17 France. **Tel** 011 33 1 47660230. **UDC** 614.25.

FR/0338-3849
**CAHIERS D'ENSEIGNEMENT DE LA SOFCOT.** **Added/Corp** Societe Francaise de Chirurgie Orthopedique et Traumatologique. **VAT** Cahiers d'Enseignement de la Societe Francaise de Chirurgie Orthopedique et Traumatologique. (1975)-. Monographic series. French. Price varies per volume. Expansion Scientifique Francaise, 31 Boulevard de la Tour-Maubourg, 75007 Paris France. **Tel** 011 33 1 40 62 64 00, 011 33 1 40626439. **NLM** W1 CA141. **CODEN** CENSE5.

BE/0771-0313
**CAHIERS DU G.E.R.M, LES.** [Cah. G.E.R.M.]. **VFOAT** Cahiers du Groupe d'Etude pour Une Reforme de la Medecine. (1981)-. Periodical. French. Four times a year. 1000.00F (individuals), 1600.00F (institutions) Belgium; 1450.00F (individuals), 2100.00F (institutions) other. Groupe d'Etude pour une Reforme de la Medecine, Chee Waterloo 255 BTE 12, 1060 Brussels Belgium. **Tel** 011 32 2 5344254, FAX 011 32 2 5342097. **UDC** 61. ***Continues** G.E.R.M. Lettre d'Information, 0771-0267.*

FR
**CAHIERS INTEGRES DE MEDECINE.** No. 1, (Oct. 10, 1970)-. Periodical. French. S P P I F, Zi de Vineuil, BP 22, F-41350 Vineuil France.

FR/0338-1439
**CAHIERS MEDICAUX.** [Cah. med.]. Vol. 1- 5 Sept. 1975-. Academic Scholarly Publication. French. wk. SIMEP Editions, 38-46 rue de Bruxelles, BP 1214, 69611 Villeubranne CDX France. **NLM** W1 CA146E. **CODEN** CAMEDV. Documents available from CASDDS.
***Supersedes** Cahiers Medicaux Lyonnais.*
**Ind/Abst** Chem. Abstr. (1975-1984).

NE/0921-3457
**CAHIERS VAN DE STICHTING BIO-WETENSCHAPPEN EN MAATSCHAPPIJ.** [Cah. Bio-Wet. Maatsch.]. **Added/Corp** Stichting Bio-Wetenschappen en Maatschappij. **VFOAT** Cahiers Bio-Wetenschappen en Maatschappij. (197?)-. Periodical. Dutch. qt. Fl30.00. Stichting Biowetenschappen & Maatschapij, Postbus 19301, 3501 DH Utrecht Netherlands. **Tel** 011 31 30 315915. **NLM** W1; CA152.

GW/0724-7141
**CALCIUM ANTAGONISMUS AKTUELL.** [Calcium-Antagon. aktuell]. **VFOAT** Calcium-Antagonismus Aktuell. Vol. 1-. Periodical. German. Three times a year. **NLM** W1; CA163R.

II/0008-0667
**CALCUTTA MEDICAL JOURNAL.** [Calcutta med. j.]. **Added/Corp** Calcutta Medical Club. Vol. 1 (July 1906)-. Academic Scholarly Publication. English. mo. $35.00. Calcutta Medical Club, C.M.C. House, 91B Chittaranjan Avenue, 700073, Calcutta India. **Tel** (33)270171. **(Subscription address:** Prints India, 11 Darya Ganj, New Delhi 110002 India.**) LC** R97. **DD** 610/.5. **NLM** W1 CA19. **CODEN** CMJRAY. Documents available from BIOSIS Document Express, CASDDS.
**Ind/Abst** Biol. Abstr. (?-1980); Chem. Abstr. (1906-1982); EMBASE [Select. Cov.]; Protozoolog. Abstr.

US
**CALIFORNIA HEALTH LAW REPORT.** ***Ceased.*** **See** Law.

US
**CALIFORNIA MEDICAL ASSISTANT, THE.** (19??)-. Periodical. English. Six times a year. $15.00. California Medical Assistant Association, 50 1st Street / #300, San Francisco CA 94105. **Tel** (415)764-4828.

US/8750-1813
**CALIFORNIA PHYSICIAN.** **Added/Corp** California Medical Association. Vol. 1, No. 1 (Sept. 1984)-. Periodical. English. mo. $3.00 members; $35.00 non-members. California Medical Association, PO Box 7690, San Franciso CA 94120-5179. **Tel** (415)541-0900, FAX (415)882-5116. **ED** Kelly Guncheon. **[CCC].** Index available. **Ad Acc, Adv Mgr:** Robert Shapiro. Full Page (B&W) $1570.00. Half Page (B&W) $1025.00. **Circ:** 33,000. ***Continues** CMA News, 0273-8244.*
**Desc:** Conveys to its members information of professional and personal interest to physicians, including issues concerning medical practice management, socioeconomics, opinion surveys, legislative and government developments, vital legal decisions and opinions, and financial and personal development.

●US/0963-1801
**CAMBRIDGE QUARTERLY OF HEALTHCARE ETHICS : CQ : THE INTERNATIONAL JOURNAL FOR HEALTHCARE ETHICS COMMITTEES.** **VFOAT** CQ; Cambridge Quarterly of Health Care Ethics. Vol. 1, No. 1 (Winter 1992)-. Academic Scholarly Publication. English. qt. $94.00 US, Canada & Mexico; £55.00 other. Cambridge University Press / New York, 40 West 20th Street, New York NY 10011-4211. **Tel** (212)924-3900, (800)221-4512. **(Subscription address:** Cambridge University Press / Outside of North America, Journal Fulfillment Department, The Edinburgh Building, Cambridge CB2 2RU United Kingdom.**) ED** David Thomasma, Thomasine Kushner, and Steve Heilig. **LC** R724; .C327. **NLM** W1; CA4538G.
**Desc:** Specifically designed to meet the needs of professionals serving on healthcare ethics committee in hospitals, nursing homes, hospices and rehabilitation centers. The aim of the journal is to analyze the facts, the applicable principles and the precedents in terms of the Ethics Committee experience.

CN/0843-994X
**CANADIAN JOURNAL OF CME.** (THE CANADIAN JOURNAL OF CME : CONTINUING MEDICAL EDUCATION.). [Can. j. CME]. **VFOAT** Continuing Medical Education. **VAT** Canadian Journal of Continuing Medical Education. Vol. 1, No. 1 (Apr. 1989)-. Periodical. English. mo. 68.00Can$ Canada; 86.00Can$ other. STA Communications Inc., 955 St. John Boulevard, Suite 306, Pt Claire, Quebec H9R 5K3 Canada. **Tel** (514)695-7623. **DD** 610/.5.

CN/0839-1866
**CANADIAN JOURNAL OF DIAGNOSIS.** (THE CANADIAN JOURNAL OF DIAGNOSIS.). [Can. j. diagn.]. **VFOAT** Diagnosis. Vol. 4, No. 6 (June 1987)-. Periodical. English. mo. Free to general practitioners, family physicians and selected specialists; 102.00Can$

Canada; 129.00Can$ other. STA Communications Inc., 955 St. John Boulevard, Suite 306, Pt Claire, Quebec H9R 5K3 Canada. **Tel** (514)695-7623. **DD** 616.07/5/05/. **NLM** W1; CA586J. ***Continues** Diagnosis (Canadian Ed.), 0825-4656.*

CN/0008-4158
**CANADIAN JOURNAL OF MEDICAL TECHNOLOGY.** [Can. j. med. technol.]. **Added/Corp** Canadian Society of Laboratory Technologists. Vol. 1, (Oct. 1938)-. Periodical. English (French; summaries and/or abstracts in French). qt. 19.26Can$ Canada; 20.00Can$ other. Canadian Society of Laboratory Technologists, Box 2830 LCD 1, Hamilton Ontario L8N 3N8 Canada. **Tel** (905)528-8642, FAX (905)528-4968. **ED** Leslie D. Mellor and Kurt H. Davis. **NLM** W1 CA594L. **CODEN** CJMTAY. Index available. cum. index. **Bk Rev. Ad Acc. Circ:** 22,500 (ctrl). Documents available from BIOSIS Document Express, CASDDS. ***Absorbed in part** Canadian Society of Laboratory Technologists. News Bulletin, 0045-5377.* ***Superseded in part by** Canadian Society of Laboratory Technologists. News Bulletin, 0381-5846.*
**Desc:** Medical laboratory technology subjects, human interest, membership information including clinical chemistry, hematology, microbiology, histopathology, and immunohematology.
**Ind/Abst** Biol. Abstr.; Chem. Abstr. (1938-1983); Cumul. Index Nurs. Allied Health Lit.; Health Plan. Adminis.; Hospit. Health Admin. Index; Index Med.; Nutr. Abstr. Rev., Ser. B, Live Feeds and Feed.; Nutr. Abstr. Rev., Ser. A, Hum. Exp.; Life Sci. Collect.; Protozoolog. Abstr.

CN/0828-7643
**CANADIAN JOURNAL OF MEDICAL TECHNOLOGY (ED. FRANCAISE).** (CANADIAN JOURNAL OF MEDICAL TECHNOLOGY : PUBLICATION OFFICIELLE, ASSOCIATION CANADIENNE DES TECHNOLOGISTES DE LABORATOIRE.). [Can. j. med. technol.]. **Added/Corp** Association Canadienne des Technologistes de Laboratoire. **VFOAT** Medical Technology. Vol. 47, No. 1 (Mars 1985)-. Periodical. French (summaries and/or abstracts in English). qt. 18.00Can$ Canada; 20.00Can$ other. Canadian Society of Laboratory Technologists, Box 2830 LCD 1, Hamilton Ontario L8N 3N8 Canada. **Tel** (905)528-8642, FAX (905)528-4968. **DD** 610.69/53/0971.

CN/1185-7196
**CANADIAN LIPIDOLOGY REVIEW.** [Can. lipidol. rev.]. **Added/Corp** STA Communications. Vol. 1, No. 1 (Jan. 1991)-. Periodical. English. qt. Limited free distribution. STA Communications Inc., 955 St. John Boulevard, Suite 306, Pt Claire, Quebec H9R 5K3 Canada. **Tel** (514)695-7623. **DD** 616.3/997/005.

CN/0838-9845
**CANADIAN MEDICAL DEVICE DIRECTORY, THE.** [Can. med. device dir.]. **VFOAT** Canadian Medical Device Directory. 1985-. Directory. English. ir. **DD** 681/.761/02571.

CN/0225-9451
**CANADIAN MEDICAL EDUCATION STATISTICS.** **See** Medical Science and Technology-Abstracting, Bibliographies and Statistics.

CN
**CANADIAN MEDICAL LIVES.** **Added/Corp** Hannah Institute for the History of Medicine. **VFOAT** Canadian Medical Lives Series. No. 1 (1989)-. Monographic series. English. ir. Price varies per volume. Fitzhenry & Whiteside, 195 Allstate Parkway, Markham Ont L3R 4T8 Canada. **Tel** 800-387-9776, (905)477-9700. **NLM** WZ 140; DC2 C212.

CN/0319-6283
**CANADIAN MUSIC THERAPY JOURNAL.** **See** Music.

SP
**CANTABRIA MEDICA.** Spanish. ir. Sindicato Medico Libre, General Mola 27, 39004 Santander Spain.

●US/1076-1047
**CAPITATION & MEDICAL PRACTICE.** **VFOAT** Capitation and Medical Practice. (1994)-. English. mo. $189.00 US and Canada. Aspen Publishers Inc., 7201 McKinney Circle, Frederick MD 21701. **Tel** (800)234-1660, (301)698-7100, FAX (301)251-5784, telex 5106014543. **(Subscription address:** Aspen Publishers Inc., PO Box 990, Frederick MD 21701.**)**

UK/0266-0970
**CARE OF THE CRITICALLY ILL.** (19??)-. Periodical. English. Six times a year. £30.00 (individuals) UK; £35.00 (individuals), £40.00 (institutions) Europe; £45.00 others. Macmillan Magazines Ltd., Houndmills, Basingstoke, Hampshire RG21 2XS England. **Tel** 011 44 256 29242, FAX 011 44 256 812358, telex 858493. **(Subscription address:** MacMillian Magazines Publishing Ltd, Hainault Road Little Health, Romford Essex RM6 5NP England.**)** **NLM** W1; CA777T. **CODEN** CCILED.
**Ind/Abst** EMBASE.

TR/0374-7042
**CARIBBEAN MEDICAL JOURNAL.** [Caribb. med. j.]. **Added/Corp** Caribbean Commonwealth Medical Associations. Trinidad and Tobago Medical Associations. (1938)-. Periodical. English. qt. **NLM** W1 CA788. **CODEN** CMJUA9. Documents available from BIOSIS Document Express.
**Ind/Abst** Biol. Abstr.; Trop. Dis. Bull.

US/0098-0153
**CARLE SELECTED PAPERS.** [Carle sel. pap.]. **Added/Corp** Carle Clinic Association, Urbana, Ill. Carle Foundation Hospital, Urbana, Ill. Vol. 27 (Fall 1974)-. Periodical. English. Twice a year (Spring & Fall). Free. Carle Clinic Association, 6111 West Park Street, Urbana IL 61801. **Tel** (217)337-3327. **NLM** W1 CA793. **CODEN** CCCFAT. Documents available from BIOSIS Document Express, CASDDS. ***Continues** Selected Papers of the Carle Clinic and Carle Foundation, 0093-5565.*
**Ind/Abst** Biol. Abstr. (1984-); Chem. Abstr.

US/1061-9259
**CASE MANAGER.** **See** Insurance.

XR/0008-7335
**CASOPIS LEKARU CESKYCH.** [Cas. lek. cesk.]. Vol. 1 1862-. Periodical. Czech (summaries and/or abstracts in English, French, German and Russian; table of contents in English, French, German and Russian). wk. $155.90. **(Subscription address:** Artia Pegas Press Ltd., Palac Metro Narodni Trida 25, 11210 Prague 1 Czech Republic.**)** **NLM** W1 CA919. **CODEN** CLCEAL. **[CCC].** Documents available from CASDDS.
**Ind/Abst** Chem. Abstr.; Dairy Sci. Abstr.; EMBASE; Helminthol. Abstr. (1991-); Index Med.; Index Vet.; Nutr. Abstr. Rev., Ser. B, Live Feeds and Feed.; Nutr. Abstr. Rev., Ser. A, Hum. Exp.; Life Sci. Collect.; Rev. Med. Vet. Mycology; Saf. Health Work; SportSearch; Trop. Dis. Bull.

US
**CATALOG OF PUBLICATIONS, AUDIOVISUALS, & SOFTWARE.** **Main/Corp** National Library of Medicine (U.S.). **Added/Corp** National Institutes of Health (U.S.). **VFOAT** Catalog of Publications, Audiovisuals, and Software. (May 1991)-. Catalog. English. Office of Inquiries and Publications Management, National Library of Medicine, 8600 Rockville Pike, Bethesda MD 20209. **Tel** (202)783-3238. ***Continues** Publications (National Library of Medicine (U.S.)).*

UK/0008-8226
**CATHOLIC MEDICAL QUARTERLY : JOURNAL OF THE GUILD OF CATHOLIC DOCTORS.** **Added/Corp** Guild of Catholic Doctors (Great Britain). (Oct. 1947)-. Periodical. English. Four times a year (Feb., May, Aug., Nov.). £15.00. Guild of Catholic Doctors, 60 Grove End Road, London NW8 9NH England. **Tel** 011 44 71 266 4246, FAX 011 44 71 266 2316. **NLM** W1 CA972. ***Continues** Catholic Medical Guardian.*

BL/0101-1782
**CEARA MEDICO.** (CEARA MEDICO : ORGAO DO CENTRL MEDICO CEARENSE.). [Ceara med]. Began with: Yearly V. 5, March 1917. Academic Scholarly Publication. Portuguese. qt. **NLM** W1 CE113. ***Continues** Norte Medico.*
**Ind/Abst** EMBASE.

UK/0142-8020
**CELL CALCIUM.** **Added/Corp** University of Sheffield. Biomedical Information Service. **VFOAT** Monthly Bibliography on Cell Calcium. Vol. 1, No. 1 (Jan. 1976)-. Periodical. English. mo. £120.00. SUBIS, Mansion House, 19 Kingfield Road, Sheffield S11 9AS England. **Tel** 011 44 114 255 4433, FAX 011 44 114 255 4626.

UK/0969-0239
**CELLULOSE.** (19??)-. Periodical. English. qt. $250.00 US and Canada; £145.00 Europe; £160.00 Other. Chapman & Hall, 2-6 Boundary Row, London SE1 8HN England. **Tel** 011 44 71 865 0066, FAX 011 44 71 522 9623, telex 290164 Chapmag. **(Subscription address:** Chapman & Hall, Cheriton House, North Way, Andover, Hampshire, SP10 5BE England.**)**

●US
**CENTERWATCH.** (June 1994)-. Periodical. English. Four times a year. $295.00. CenterWatch, 19 Rockingham Street, Cambridge MA 02139. **Tel** (617)784-0039, FAX (617)784-1795. **ED** Robert Whitaker.
**Desc:** Covers trends and information on clinical medical research. Includes strategic issues for people trying to raise funds for research - serves to link clinical centers with research sponsors.

RH/0008-9176
**CENTRAL AFRICAN JOURNAL OF MEDICINE.** [Cent. Afr. j. med.]. Vol. 1 (Jan. 1955). Periodical. English. mo. $105.00 surface mail; $210.00 airmail. Central African Journal of Medicine, PO Box A195, Avondale Harare Zimbabwe. **Tel** 791631. **ED** H M Chinyanga and F K Nkrumah. **NLM** W1 CE301. **CODEN** CAJMA3. Index available. **Bk Rev. Ad Acc. Pr Rev. Circ:** 1,300. Documents available from The Genuine Article, BIOSIS Document Express, CASDDS.
**Desc:** General medicine pertaining to Africa and Zimbabwe in particular.
**Ind/Abst** Abstr. Anthropol.; Biol. Abstr.; Chem. Abstr.; Curr. Contents Clin. Med.; Dairy Sci. Abstr.; EMBASE; Health Plan. Adminis.; Helminthol. Abstr. (19??-19??); Index Med.; Maize Abstr.; Nutr. Abstr. Rev., Ser. B, Live Feeds and Feed.; Nutr. Abstr. Rev., Ser. A, Hum. Exp.; Nutr. Res. Newsl.; Protozoolog. Abstr.; Res. Alert [Select. Cov.]; Rev. Agric. Entomol.; Rev. Med. Vet. Entomol.; Rev. Med. Vet. Mycology; Rev. Plant Pathol.; SCISEARCH; Trop. Dis. Bull.

FR/0008-9826
**CENTRE MEDICAL (MOULINS).** (CENTRE MEDICAL.). **Added/Corp** Societe de Medecine du Centre. Ecole de Medecine de Clermont-Ferrand. Institut d'Hydrologie. **VFOAT** Centre Medical Scientifique; Centre Medical Scientifique et Professionnel. (1931)-. Periodical. French. mo. **NLM** W1 CE485. cum. index. ***Continues** Centre Medical et Pharmaceutique, 0008-9826.*

SP/0210-6361
**CENTRO MEDICO.** [Cent. med.]. (1979)-. Periodical. Spanish. bm. Publicidad Belen y Medina, Balmes 114 2/2, 08008 Barcelona Spain. **UDC** 61.

US/1040-8827
**CEREBROVASCULAR AND BRAIN METABOLISM REVIEWS.** [Cerebrovasc. brain metab. rev.]. Vol. 1, No. 1 (Spring 1989)-. Periodical. English. qt. $140.00 (individuals), $185.00 (institutions) US; $170.00 (individuals), $225.00 (institutions) other. Raven Press, 1185 Avenue of the Americas, 37th Floor, New York NY 10036. **Tel** (212)930-9500, (212)930-9604, FAX (212)869-3495, (212)302-8507, telex 640073. **LC** RC386; .C46. **DD** 616.8/1/005. **NLM** W1; CE582F. **CODEN** CEMREV. **[CCC].** available on microfilm and microfiche from University Microfilms International (UMI). Documents available from The Genuine Article, BIOSIS Document Express.
**Ind/Abst** Biol. Abstr. (1989-); Curr. Aware. Biol. Sci., CABS; Curr. Contents Clin. Med.; Curr. Contents Life Sci.; Health Plan. Adminis.; Index Med. (1989-); Ref. Upd. Deluxe Ed.; Res. Alert [Full Cov.]; Sci. Cit. Index; SCISEARCH.

TU/0254-4113
**CERRAHPASA MEDICAL REVIEW.** [Cerrahpasa med. rev.]. Vol. 1-. Academic Scholarly Publication. English. an. Free. **NLM** W1 CE856.
**Ind/Abst** EMBASE.

TU/0376-7833
**CERRAHPASA TIP FAKULTESI DERGISI.** [Cerrahpasa Tp Fak. derg.]. **Added/Corp** Istanbul Universitesi. Cerrahpasa Tip Fakultesi. **VFOAT** Journal of the Cerrahpasa Medical Faculty. (1970)-. Academic Scholarly Publication. Turkish (summaries and/or abstracts in English). qt. Istanbul Universitesi, Dergi Kurulu Cerrahpasa Tip FA, 34303 Istanbul Turkey. **Tel** 011 90 1 5884800. **ED** Vural Solok. **NLM** W1 CE587. **CODEN** CTFDDO. Documents available from BIOSIS Document Express.
**Ind/Abst** Biol. Abstr.; EMBASE [Select. Cov.].

CE/0011-2232
**CEYLON JOURNAL OF MEDICAL SCIENCE.** **Added/Corp** University of Sri Lanka. Vol. 6 (1949)-. Periodical. English. Twice a year. $10.00. University of Colombo, The Librarian, 94 Munidasa Cumaratunga, Mawatha Colombo 3 Sri Lanka. ***Continues** Ceylon Journal of Science. Section D: Medical Science.*
**Ind/Abst** Agrofor. Abstr. (1991-); Dairy Sci. Abstr.; Nutr. Abstr. Rev., Ser. B, Live Feeds and Feed.; Nutr. Abstr. Rev., Ser. A, Hum. Exp.; Trop. Dis. Bull.

CE/0009-0875
**CEYLON MEDICAL JOURNAL.** [Ceylon med. j.]. New Series, V. 1- May 1952-. Periodical. English. qt. $80.00. Sri Lanka Medical Association, 6 Wijerama Mawatha, Colombo 7 Sri Lanka. **Tel** 693324. **ED** C G Uragoda and Colvin Goonaratna. **NLM** W1 CE945. Index available. cum. index. **Bk Rev. Ad Acc. Circ:** 1,000 (ctrl). ***Supersedes** Journal. British Medical Association. Ceylon Branch.*
**Ind/Abst** EMBASE; Health Plan. Adminis.; Index Med.; Nutr. Abstr. Rev., Ser. B, Live Feeds and Feed.; Nutr. Abstr. Rev., Ser. A, Hum. Exp.; Protozoolog. Abstr.; SportSearch; Trop. Dis. Bull.

CH
**CHANG-KENG I HSUEH TSA CHIH / CHANG-KENG CHI NIEN I YUAN / CHANG GUNG MEDICAL JOURNAL / CHANG GUNG MEMORIAL HOSPITAL.** **Added/Corp** Chang-Keng Chi Nien i Yuan. **VFOAT** Chang Gung Medical Journal; Chang-Keng i Hsueh. (19??)-. Periodical. Chinese (English). qt. Chang-Keng chi Nien i Yuan, Taipei Taiwan. **CODEN** CIHCEN. ***Continues** Chang-Keng i Hsueh, 0255-8270.*

CH/0255-8270
**CHANGGENG YIXUE.** ***Title Change.*** (CHANG KENG I HSUEH.). **VFOAT** Chang Gung Medical Journal; Chang-Keng i Hsueh tsa Chih. Vol. 1, (1976)-(19??).

Periodical. Chinese (English). qt. Chang Keng Medical Evalu Assn, Taipei Taiwan. **NLM** W1 CH1233R. ***Continued by*** *Chang-Keng i Hsueh tsa Chih.*
**Ind/Abst** Health Plan. Adminis.; Index Med. (v9n1,1986-).

US/1070-6771
**CHANGING MEDICAL MARKETS. See** Business-Marketing.

GW/0232-7090
**CHARITE-ANNALEN. Added/Corp** Humboldt-UniversitËat zu Berlin. Bereich Medizin. **VFOAT** Charite Annalen. (19??)-. Bulletin. German. Akademie-Verlag GmbH, Muehlenstrasse 33 34, D 13162 Berlin Germany. **Tel** 011 49 30 47889300, FAX 011 49 30 47889357. **(Subscription address:** VCH Publishers Inc., 303 Northwest 12th Avenue, Journals Department, Deerfield FL 33442.**) ED** H. Mau.

CC
**CHE-CHIANG CHUNG I HSUEH YUAN HSUEH PAO. Added/Corp** Che-Chiang Chung i Hsueh Yuan. **VFOAT** Journal of Zhejiang Traditional Chinese Medical College. (1977)-. Periodical. Chinese. bm. Science Press, 16 Donghuangchenggen North Street, Beijing 100707, People's Republic of China. **Tel** 011 86 1 4019821, 011 86 1 4010642, FAX 011 86 1 4012180, 011 86 1 4019810, telex 210147. **LC** R97.7.C5; C39. **DD** 610/.951.

US/0749-906X
**CHE VUOI?. VFOAT** Che Vuoi. 1 (Fall 1984)-. Periodical. English (English). qt. $20.00. Che Vuoi, 63 Duke Ellington Blvd., No. 5, New York NY 10025. **DD** 616.

AT/0812-9630
**CHECK. VFOAT** Continuous Home Evaluation of Clincial Knowledge. (1980)-. English. Eleven times a year (June/July issues combined). 75.00Aus$ (medical graduates with 6 units & medical students with 12 units); 140.00Aus$ (college members with 12 units); 150.00Aus$ (medical graduates with 12 units). RACGP / Check Programme, 70 Jolimont Street, Jolimont Victoria 3002 Australia. **Tel** 011 61 3 654 3000, FAX 011 61 3 65 5723, telex 33532.
**Desc:** News and information on clinical knowledge for home care.

IT
**CHECK UP INCONTRI.** Nuova Scerpa Ed SRL, Via Le Molise 56, 20137 Milan Italy.

US
**CHEM PACKAGE.** (19??)-. English. ir. $795.00 (includes Healthcare Hazardous Materials Management and Healthcare Environmental Management System). ECRI Emergency Care Research Institute, 5200 Butler Pike, Plymouth Meeting PA 19462. **Tel** (215)825-6000, FAX (215)834-1275, telex 510-660-8023.

CH
**CHENG-KUNG TA HSUEH HSUEH PAO. JEN WEN, SHE HUI, KO CHI, I HSUEH PIEN. See** Humanities.

PH/0300-0974
**CHEST DISEASES.** (CHEST DISEASES : OFFICIAL PUBLICATION OF THE QUEZON INSTITUTE.). [Chest dis.]. **Added/Corp** Quezon Institute. Vol. 8, No. 2 (June 1972)-. Periodical. English. sa. The Quezon Institute, PO Box 3256, Manila Philippines. **NLM** W1 CH419. ***Continues*** *Bulletin of the Quezon Institute, 0300-094X.*
**Ind/Abst** Philip. Sci. Technol. Abstr.

JA/0303-5476
**CHIBA IGAKU ZASSHI.** [Chiba igaku zasshi]. **Added/Corp** Chiba Igakkai (Founded 1922). **VFOAT** Chiba Medical Journal. (1974)-. Periodical. Japanese. bm. $125.50. Chiba Igakkai, (Chiba Medical Society), Chiba Daigaku Igakubu, 8-1 Inohana 1 Chome, Chibashi, Chibaken 280 Japan. **(Subscription address:** Japan Publications Trading Company, Ltd., PO Box 5030, Tokyo International, Tokyo 100-31 Japan.**) NLM** W1 CH428I. **CODEN** CIZAAZ. Documents available from BIOSIS Document Express, CASDDS. ***Continues*** *Chiba Igakkai Zasshi, 0009-3459.*
**Ind/Abst** Biol. Abstr.; Chem. Abstr.

US/0009-3637
**CHICAGO MEDICINE. Added/Corp** Chicago Medical Society. Vol. 63 No. 28 (1961)-. Periodical. English. Twenty-four times a year. $30.00. Chicago Medical Society, 515 North Dearborn, Chicago IL 60610. **Tel** (412)670-2550. **ED** Gary Baldwin. **NLM** W1 CH5992. Index available. **Bk Rev**, (Qty: 72). **Ad Acc, Adv Mgr:** Kristi Zernia, **Tel** (312)670-2550 ext. 228. Full Page (B&W) $360.00 (24 times). Half Page (B&W) $195.00 (24 times). **Circ:** 11,000. ***Continues*** *Chicago Medical Society. Bulletin.*

CC
**CHIH CHIAO I SHENG TSA CHIH. VFOAT** Chijiao-Yisheng Zazhi. (1973)-. Periodical. Chinese. bm. **LC** R97.7.C5; C458.
**Ind/Abst** NAPRALERT.

CC
**CHINA MEDICAL ABSTRACTS. VFOAT** Chung-Kuo I Hsueh Wen Chai. Vol. 1, No. 1 (June 1981)-. English. bm. $22.00. **(Subscription address:** China International Book Trading Corporation, PO Box 399, Library Service Department, Beijing 100044 People's Republic of China.**) NLM** ZW 1 C542.
**Ind/Abst** NAPRALERT.

US/0090-5003
**CHINA MEDICAL REPORTER.** V. 1- Feb. 1973-. Periodical. English. mo. PO Box 2342, Palo Alto CA 94305. **NLM** W1 CH755.

CC/0366-6999
**CHINESE MEDICAL JOURNAL.** [Chin. med. j.]. **Added/Corp** Chung-Hua i Hsueh Hui, Peiping. **VFOAT** Chung-Hua Hsueh Tsa Chih. Ying-Wen Pan. New Series Vol. 1-4, (Jan. 1975)-(Dec. 1978); Vol. 92 (Jan. 1979)-. Academic Scholarly Publication. English (Chinese; translations available in Chinese). mo. $181.00. TWL Publishing Pte Ltd., 25 Genting Road, 07 01 Soon Seng, Singapore 1334 Singapore. **Tel** 011 65 7438606. **NLM** W1 CH775B. **CODEN** CMJODS. Documents available from The Genuine Article, BIOSIS Document Express, CASDDS. ***Continues*** *China's Medicine.*
**Ind/Abst** Biol. Abstr.; Chem. Abstr.; Coal Abstr.; Curr. Contents Clin. Med.; Curr. Contents Phys. Chem. Earth Sci.; Dairy Sci. Abstr.; Dent. Abstr. (-1991); EMBASE [Select. Cov.]; Health Plan. Adminis.; Helminthol. Abstr. (19??-19??); Index Med.; Int. Pharm. Abstr.; Med. Abstr. Newsl.; NAPRALERT; Nutr. Abstr. Rev., Ser. B, Live Feeds and Feed.; Nutr. Abstr. Rev., Ser. A, Hum. Exp.; Nutr. Res. Newsl.; PESTDOC; Protozoolog. Abstr.; Res. Alert [Full Cov.]; Rev. Med. Vet. Entomol.; Rev. Med. Vet. Mycology; Rev. Plant Pathol.; Sci. Cit. Index; SCISEARCH; Soc. Sci. Cit. Index [Select. Cov.]; SportSearch; Trop. Dis. Bull.

UK/1001-9294
**CHINESE MEDICAL SCIENCES JOURNAL.** [Chin. med. sci. j.]. **Added/Corp** Chung-kuo I Hsueh ko Hsueh Yuan. **VFOAT** Chung-kuo I Hsueh ko Hsueh Tsa Chih. Vol. 6, No. 1 (Mar. 1991)-. Periodical. English. qt. £85.00 UK; $132.00 other. Taylor & Francis Ltd., Rankine Road, Basingstoke Hampshire, RG24 8PR United Kingdom. **Tel** 011 44 256 840366, FAX 011 44 256 479438, telex 858540. **(Subscription address:** Taylor & Francis Inc., 1900 Frost Road, Suite 101, Bristol PA 19007-1598.**) ED** Gu Fangzhou, Chairman. **NLM** W1; CH775H. **CODEN** CMSJEP. available on microfilm and microfiche from University Microfilms International (UMI). Documents available from BIOSIS Document Express. ***Continues*** *Proceedings of the Chinese Academy of Medical Sciences and the Peking Union Medical College, 0258-8757.*
**Desc:** Publishes original research papers, review papers and short communications on almost every branch of basic and clinical medicine, pharmacology and traditional Chinese medicine, submitted form medical colleges throughout the PRC. Also features occasional supplements focusing on special professional fields.
**Ind/Abst** Biol. Abstr. (1991-); EMBASE [Select. Cov.]; Index Med. (1991-); Trop. Dis. Bull.

●US/1054-4704
**CHINESE MEDICINE AND HEALTH. Added/Corp** Institute for Advanced Research in Asian Science and Medicine. (1992)-. Periodical. English. qt. $25.00. Institute for Advanced Research in Asian Science and Meicine, PO Box 555, Garden City NY 11530.

●US
**CHIROPRACTIC COLLEGE DIRECTORY, THE. Added/Corp** American Chiropractic Association. 3rd Ed. (1992-93)-. Directory. English. ir. KM Enterprises, PO Box 25978, Los Angeles CA 90025. **Tel** (310)398-9135. **NLM** WB 22.1; C51. ***Continues*** *Chiropractic College Admissions and Curriculum Directory, 0899-3807.*

US
**CHIROPRACTIC LEGAL UPDATE. See** Law.

US/1041-2360
**CHIROPRACTIC PRODUCTS.** [Chiropr. prod.]. (198?)-. Periodical. English. Seven times a year. Novicom Inc, 3510 Torrance Boulevard, Suite 315, Torrance CA 90503. **Tel** (310)316-8112. **ED** Marvin Rosenfeld. **DD** 615. **Bk Rev. Ad Acc. Circ:** 35,000 (ctrl).
**Desc:** Latest products and service news along with a featured subject for every issue.

CN/0824-9709
**CHIROPRACTIC RESEARCH ARCHIVES COLLECTION.** [Chiropr. res. arch. coll.]. **VFOAT** CRAC. **VAT** CRAC. Chiropractic Research Archives Collection. Vol. 1 (1984)-. English. an. $60.00. Clemmer Health Sciences Library, Canadian Memorial Chiropractic College, 1900 Bayview Avenue, Toronto Ontario M4G 3E6 Canada. **Tel** 482-2340. **ED** R Gitelman and J C Callaghan. **DD** 615.5/34. **Circ:** 2,000. ***Continues*** *Archives (Canadian Memorial Chiropractic College).*
**Desc:** A specialized recurring bibliography. Offers subject, author and abstract access to over 4,000 relevant chiropractic, osteopathic and medical references.

JA/0386-8109
**CHIRYOGAKU.** [Chiryogaku]. **VFOAT** Biomedicine & Therapeutics. Vol. 1, No. 1 (1978)-. Periodical. Japanese. mo. Raifu Saiensu Shuppan K K, Masuda Bldg, Kyobashi 2-5-10, Chuo-ku, Tokyo-to 104 Japan. **NLM** W1; CH872. **CODEN** CHRYDT. Documents available from CASDDS.
**Ind/Abst** Chem. Abstr.

UK/0264-9640
**CHLOROPLASTS.** (19??)-. Periodical. English. £85.00. SUBIS, Mansion House, 19 Kingfield Road, Sheffield S11 9AS England. **Tel** 011 44 114 255 4433, FAX 011 44 114 255 4626.

KO
**CHOESIN UIHAK. THE NEW MEDICAL JOURNAL. VFOAT** New Medical Journal. (1958)-. Academic Scholarly Publication. Korean (summaries and/or abstracts in English). mo. W12,000. **LC** R97.7.K6; C47. **DD** 610/.5. **NLM** W1 CH881. **CODEN** CHOUAX. Documents available from CASDDS.
**Ind/Abst** Chem. Abstr. (?-1974).

KO
**CHOKSIPCHA PYONGWON CHI. Main/Corp** Soul Choksipcha Pyongwon. **VFOAT** Medical Journal of the Red Cross Hospital. Periodical. Korean (summaries and/or abstracts in English). Taehan Choksipcha S A, 523-1 Majang-dong Songdong-ku, Seoul Korea. **LC** R97.7.K6; S66A. **DD** 610/.5.

KO/1013-3968
**CHONNAM JOURNAL OF MEDICAL SCIENCES.** [Chonnam j. med. sci.]. **Added/Corp** Chonnam Taehakkyo. Research Institute of Medical Sciences. Vol. 1, No. 1 (1988)-. English. sa. $30.00. Research Institute of Medical Sciences, 5 Hakdong Chonnam University Medical, Kwangju 501 190 Korea. **Tel** 011 82 62 232-1244. **NLM** W1; CH904W. **CODEN** CJMSEZ. Documents available from BIOSIS Document Express.
**Ind/Abst** Biol. Abstr. (1991-); Trop. Dis. Bull.

JA
**CHOONPA IGAKU. JAPANESE JOURNAL OF MEDICAL ULTRASONICS. Added/Corp** Nippon ChÂoonpa Igakkai. **VFOAT** Japanese Journal of Medical Ultrasonics. (1976)-. Periodical. Japanese. sa. $270.00. Nihon Choonpa Igakkai, (Japan Society of Ultrasonics in Medicine), 26-9, Hongo 2 Chome, Bunkyoku, Tokyoto 113 Japan. **(Subscription address:** Kyowa Book Company Inc., 1-38 Kanda Jinbo-Cho, Chiyoda-Ku, Tokyo 101, Japan (Phone: 03-3293-0727)**) NLM** W1 CH908. ***Continues*** *Nippon Choonpa Igakkai Kenkyu Happyokai Koen Ronbun Shu.*
**Ind/Abst** EMBASE.

KO
**CHOSON TAEHAKKYO UIDAE NONMUNJIP. Added/Corp** Choson Taehakkyo. Uihak Yonguso. **VFOAT** Medical Journal of Chosun University; Choson Taehakkyo Uihak Nonmunjip; Choson Uidae Nonmunjip. Periodical. Korean (English). qt. Choson Taehakkyo Uihak Yonguso, 17 Pullo-dong, Tong-ku Kwangju-si Korea. **LC** R97.7.K6; U39. **NLM** W1; CH913T. ***Continues*** *Uihak Yongu.*

US
**CHRISTIAN MEDICAL & DENTAL SOCIETY JOURNAL. Added/Corp** Christian Medical Dental Society. **VFOAT** CMDS Journal. Vol. 19, No. 3 (Fall 1988)-. Periodical. English. qt. $25.00 (one year), $45.00 (two year), $55.00 (three year). Christian Medical & Dental Society, 1616 Gateway Boulevard, Box 830689, Richardson TX 75083. **Tel** (214)783-8384, FAX (214)783-0921. **ED** David B. Biebel. **NLM** W1; CH9317. **Bk Rev**, (Qty: 4). **Ad Acc. Pr Rev. Circ:** 11,000. available on microfilm. ***Continues*** *Christian Medical Society Journal, 0009-546X.*
**Desc:** Vehicle designed to express views and concerns on issues of faith and practice for medical/dental professionals and students, as well as others interested in Christian whole person medicine.
**Ind/Abst** Christ. Period. Index (19??-).

II
**CHRISTIAN MEDICAL JOURNAL OF INDIA : QUARTERLY JOURNAL OF THE CHRISTIAN MEDICAL ASSOCIATION OF INDIA. Added/Corp** Christian Medical Association of India. (1986)-. Periodical. English. qt. $25.00. Christian Medical Association of India, Plot No 2, A-3 Local Shopping Centre, Janakpuri New Delhi 110 058 India. **(Subscription address:** Prints India, 11 Darya Ganj, New Delhi 110002 India.**) LC** RA529; .C54. **DD** 610/.5. **NLM** W1; CH932. ***Continues*** *Journal of the Christian Medical Association of India.*

UK/0967-3849
**CHROMOSOME RESEARCH.** (19??)-. English. Eight times a year. $460.00 US; £270.00 other. Rapid Communications of Oxford Ltd, The Old Malthouse, Paradise Street, Oxford OX1 1LD England. **Tel** 011 44 0865 790447, FAX 011 44 0865 244012, telex 9403712. **[CCC].**

CN/0228-8699
**CHRONIC DISEASES IN CANADA.** [Chronic dis. Can.]. Vol. 1, No. 1 (June 1980)-. Periodical. English (French). bm. Free. Chronic Diseases in Canada, 145D LCDC Building/Health Welfare, Ottawa Ontario K1A 0L2 Canada. **Tel** (613)957-1767, (613)957-1788, FAX (613)952-7009. **ED** Walter Litven. **LC** RA644.8.C2; C48. **DD** 614/.4/0971. Index available. cum. index. **Bk Rev. Circ:** 4,000 (ctrl).
**Ind/Abst** PAIS Int. Print (1991-).

US
**CHRONIC PAIN LETTER.** (1984)-. Periodical. English. Six times a year. $35.00 (physicians, health professionals, and institutions); $20.00 (individuals and students). Dolak Inc., PO Box 1303, Old Chelsea Station, New York NY 10011. **Tel** (212)473-7187. **UDC** 61. **Bk Rev.**
**Desc:** Brings current information on the management of chronic pain to the sufferer, the family, the helper, and the professional.

KO
**CHUCHE UIHAK. VFOAT** Juche Uihak. V. 1, No. 1(1982)-. Periodical. Korean (summaries and/or abstracts in English). Kwahak, Paekkwa Sajon Chulpansa, Changgyong 2-dong Sosong-kuyok, Pyongyang-si North Korea. **LC** R97.7.K6; C49.

CC/0254-1785
**CHUNG-HUA CH'I KUAN I CHIH TSA CHIH.** [Zhonghua qiguan yizhi zazhi]. **VFOAT** Zhonghua Qiguan Yizhi Zazhi; Chinese Journal of Organ Transplantation. Vol. 1. Periodical. Chinese. qt. $5.04. Science Press, 16 Donghuangchenggen North Street, Beijing 100707, People's Republic of China. **Tel** 011 86 1 4019821, 011 86 1 4010642, FAX 011 86 1 4012180, 011 86 1 4019810, telex 210147. **ED** Qiu Fa-zu. **NLM** W1 CH977M. **Bk Rev. Ad Acc. Circ:** 3,500.
**Desc:** Organ transplantations including kidney, liver, pancreas, spleen, bone marrow, endocrine, glands, heart, lung, intestine, etc. Studying on dialysis, preservation of donor organ, immunology, immunosuppressive treatment.

CH/0578-1337
**CHUNG-HUA I HSUEH TSA CHIH (TAIPEI TAIWAN).** (CHUNG-HUA I HSUEH TSA CHIH.). **Added/Corp** Chung-Hua i Hsueh Hui (China : Republic : 1949- ). **VFOAT** Chinese Medical Journal (Taipei); Chinese Medical Journal. (Jan. 1954)-. Academic Scholarly Publication. Chinese (English). mo. Chinese Medical Association, Taipei Taiwan. **LC** R97.7.C5; C4594. **DD** 610/.5. **NLM** W1 CH982E. **CODEN** CIHCDM. Documents available from CASDDS.
**Ind/Abst** Chem. Abstr.; EMBASE [Select. Cov.]; Health Plan. Adminis.; Index Med.

CC/0578-1426
**CHUNG-HUA NEI KO TSA CHIH.** [Chung-hua nei ko tsa chih]. **Added/Corp** Chung-hua Ii Hsueh hui. Nei ko Hsueh hui. **VFOAT** Chinese Journal of Internal Medicine; Zhonghua Neike Zazhi. (1953)-. Academic Scholarly Publication. Chinese. mo. $68.04. **(Subscription address:** China International Book Trading Corporation, PO Box 399, Library Service Department, Beijing 100044 People's Republic of China.**)** **DD** 616. **NLM** W1 CH983. **CODEN** CHHNAB. Documents available from CASDDS.
**Ind/Abst** Chem. Abstr.; Index Med. (1979-); NAPRALERT.

CC/0529-5858
**CHUNG I TSA CHIH. Added/Corp** Chung-hua Chuan kuo Chung i Hsueh Hui. Chung i Yen Chiu Yuan (Peking, China). **VFOAT** Journal of Traditional Chinese Medicine; Zhongyi Zazhi. (1955)-. Periodical. Chinese. mo. $17.80. **(Subscription address:** China International Book Trading Corporation, PO Box 399, Library Service Department, Beijing 100044 People's Republic of China.**)** **LC** R97.7.C5; J68. **DD** 610. **NLM** W1 CH985R. ***Continues*** *Pei-Ching Chung I.*
**Desc:** Contains information on Chinese medicine.

CC
**CHUNG I YAO HSUEH PAO. VFOAT** Zhongyiyaoxuebao. Periodical. Chinese. qt. RMBY0.30. Hei-Lung-Chiang Chung I Hsueh Yuan, Ha-Erh-Pin Shih yu Chu, Harbin Heilungkiang, People's Republic of China. **LC** R97.7.C5; C46. **DD** 610/.951.

●CC/1003-5370
**CHUNG-KUO CHUNG HSI I CHIEH HO TSA CHIH. Added/Corp** Chung-kuo Chung Hsi i Chieh Ho Hsueh Hui. Chung-kuo Chung i Yen Chiu Yuan. **VFOAT** Zhongguo Zhongxiyi Jiehe Zazhe; Chinese Journal of Integrated Traditional and Western Medicine. (1992)-. Periodical. Chinese (summaries and/or abstracts in English). mo. $38.77. Chung-kuo Kuo Chi Tu Shu Mao i Tsung Kung Ssu, PO Box 399, Peking, China. **(Subscription address:** China International Book Trading Corporation, PO Box 399, Library Service Department, Beijing 100044 People's Republic of China.**)** **LC** R97.7.C5; C459. **DD** 610/.5. ***Continues*** *Chung Hsi i Chieh Ho Tsa Chih.*

CH/0258-8021
**CHUNG-KUO SHENG WU I HSUEH KUNG CHENG HSUEH PAO.** [Zhongguo shengwu yixue, gongcheng xuebao]. **VFOAT** Chinese Journal of Biomedical Engineering. Vol. 1, (Nov. 1982)-. Academic Scholarly Publication. Chinese (summaries and/or abstracts in English). qt. $18.00 (add $6.70 surface mail), (add $10.00 airmail). Chung-Kuo Tu Shu Shin Chu Kou Tsung Kung SSU, 137 Chao Nei Ta Chieh, Beijing, People's Republic of China. **Tel** 440731 203, FAX 401 5664, telex 22313 CPC CN. **LC** R856.A1. **DD** 610/.28. **NLM** W1; CH991AR. **CODEN** ZSYXEI. **Ad Acc.** Documents available from Article Express International, BIOSIS Document Express, Ask*IEEE, CASDDS.
**Ind/Abst** Biol. Abstr. (1987-); Chem. Abstr.; Ei Page One; EMBASE; Eng. Index Annu.; INSPEC (1985-).

KO
**CHUNGNAM UIDAE CHAPCHI.**
**Added/Corp** Chungnam Taehakkyo. Chiyok Sahoe Uihak Yonguso. **VFOAT** Chungnam Medical Journal. (197?)-. Periodical. Korean (summaries and/or abstracts in English). **LC** R97.7.K6; C52. Documents available from CASDDS.
**Ind/Abst** Chem. Abstr.

SP/0212-6052
**CIENCIA MEDICA.** [Cienc. med.]. **VFOAT** Ciencia Medica para la Practica Diaria. (1983)-. Periodical. Spanish. Eleven times a year. $80.00 Europe; $120.00 other. Alpe Editores SA, C Pedro Rico 27 Oficinas 11 & 12, 28029 Madrid Spain. **Tel** 011 34 7338811. **UDC** 61.
**Ind/Abst** EMBASE [Select. Cov.].

DR
**CIENCIAS DE LA SALUD : ORGANO DE DIFUSION CIENTIFICA DE LA FACULTAD DE CIENCIAS DE LA SALUD, UNIVERSIDAD AUTONOMA DE SANTO DOMINGO. Added/Corp** Universidad Autonoma de Santo Domingo. Facultad de Ciencias de la Salud. (198?)-. Periodical. Spanish (summaries and/or abstracts in English). sa. **NLM** W1; CI259C.
**Ind/Abst** Trop. Dis. Bull.

BL
**CIENCIAS MEDICAS.** [Cienc. med.]. (1968)-. Periodical. Portuguese. **NLM** W1 CI263.
**Ind/Abst** EMBASE.

BL/0101-4501
**CIENCIAS MEDICAS (NITEROI).** (CIENCIAS MEDICAS / UNIVERSIDADE FEDERAL FLUMINENSE.). [Cienc. med.]. **Added/Corp** Universidade Federal Fluminense. Universidade Federal Fluminense. Centro de Ciencias Medicas. Vol. 1, No. 1 (July/Dec. 1981)-. Periodical. Portuguese (summaries and/or abstracts in English). sa. Free on request. Centro Ciencias Medicas, UFF Hosp, Univ A Pedro, Predio An 4, 24030 Niteroi RJ Brazil. **Tel** 719 5064. **NLM** W1 CI262V.

US/0163-0075
**CINCINNATI MEDICINE. Added/Corp** Academy of Medicine of Cincinnati. Vol. 1 (Fall 1978)-. Periodical. English. Four times a year (Jan., Apr., July, Oct.). $10.00 US; $15.00 other. Academy Journal Publishing Company, 320 Broadway, Cincinnati OH 45202. **Tel** (513)421-7010, FAX (513)721-4378. **ED** Rhonda Tepe. **NLM** W1 CI334V. **Ad Acc.** ***Supersedes*** *Cincinnati Journal of Medicine, 0009-6873.*
**Desc:** A view on the health care reform. Takes a look at various health care reform packages, either proposed or enacted.

SZ/0379-8100
**CIOMS CALENDAR. Added/Corp** Council for International Organizations of Medical Sciences. **VFOAT** Calendar of Congresses of Medical Sciences; Calendrier des Congres des Sciences Medicales. **VAT** Council for International Organizations of Medical Sciences Calendar of International and Regional Congresses of Medical Sciences. (1977)-. English (French). an. $9.00. C I O M S Publications, Avenue Appia, 1211 Geneva 27 Switzerland. **Tel** 011 41 22 913406, telex 845 27821. **NLM** W 3.5 C143. Index available. **Ad Acc. Circ:** 2,000. ***Continues*** *CIOMS Calendar of International and Regional Congresses of Medical Sciences, 0379-8100.*
**Desc:** Calendar of congresses of medical sciences.

US
**CIR NEWS / THE COMMITTEE OF INTERNS AND RESIDENTS. Added/Corp** Committee of Interns and Residents (New York, N.Y.). **VAT** Committee of Interns and Residents News. Vol. 9, No. 2 (August/Sept. 1980)-. Periodical. English. Seven times a year. Committee of Interns & Residents, 386 Park Avenue South, New York NY 10016. **Tel** (212)725-5500. ***Continues*** *CIR Bulletin.*

FR/0264-6900
**CIRCULATION ET METABOLISME DU CERVEAU.** (CIRCULATION ET METABOLISME DU CERVEAU : ORGANE OFFICIEL DE LA SOCIETE DE CIRCULATION ET METABOLISME DU CERVEAU.). [Circ. metab. cerveau]. **Added/Corp** Societe de Circulation et Metabolisme du Cerveau. **VFOAT** Cerebral Circulation and Metabolism; Cerebral Circulation & Metabolism. Vol. 1 No. 1 (April 1983)-. Periodical. French (English). Four times a year. 553.38F (institutions), 401.57F (individuals) France; 650.00F (institutions), 520.00F (individuals) other. John Libbey Eurotext Ltd, 6 rue Blanche, Isabelle Trope, 92120 Montrouge France. **Tel** 011 33 1 47358552. **(Subscription address:** ATEI John Libbey Eurotext, 23 25 rue Fernand Combette, 93100 Montreuil France.**)** **NLM** W1; CI743P. **CODEN** CMCEEW. Documents available from BIOSIS Document Express, CASDDS.
**Ind/Abst** Biol. Abstr. (1985-); Chem. Abstr.; EMBASE.

JM/1018-9041
**CLAN. CARIBBEAN LABORATORY ACTION NEWS.** [CLAN, Caribb. lab. action news]. (1991)-. Periodical. English. tq. Free. CAREC (Caribbean Epidemiology Centre), 16-18 Jamaica Boulevard, PO Box 164, Federation Park, Port-of-Spain Trinidad. **(Subscription address:** The Press - University of the West Indies, 1A Aqueduct Flats, Mona Campus, Kingston 7, Jamaica**)** **UDC** 61. **CODEN** NU054.
**Desc:** Provides information on laboratory medicine and is a vehicle for communication among laboratory scientists and technologists in the Caribbean.

US/1055-6656
**CLEFT PALATE-CRANIOFACIAL JOURNAL.** [Cleft palate-craniofac. j.]. **Added/Corp** American Cleft Palate-Craniofacial Association. **VFOAT** Cleft Palate Craniofacial Journal. Vol. 28, No. 1 (Jan. 1991)-. Academic Scholarly Publication. English. Six times a year. $147.00 (institutions), $106.00 (individuals) US & Canada; $178.00 (institutions), $137.00 (individuals) other. Decker Periodicals Publishing Inc, PO Box 620, Station A, Hamilton Ontario L8N 3K7 Canada. **Tel** (416)522-7017, (800) 568-7281, FAX (416)522-7839. **ED** Stewart Rood. **LC** RD525; .C55. **DD** 617/225043. **NLM** W1; CL146. **CODEN** CPJOEG. Documents available from The Genuine Article. ***Continues*** *Cleft Palate Journal, 0009-8701.*
**Desc:** International, interdisciplinary publication covering growth, development, diagnosis, and treatment of individuals with craniofacial anomalies. Each issue summarizes clinical and research activities in cleft palate and other craniofacial disabilities, together with research in related laboratory sciences.
**Ind/Abst** Curr. Contents Clin. Med.; Curr. Contents Life Sci.; EMBASE; Health Plan. Adminis.; Index Med. (1991-); Linguist. Lang. Behav. Abstr.; Life Sci. Collect.; Res. Alert [Full Cov.]; Sci. Cit. Index; SCISEARCH; Soc. Plann. Policy Dev. Abstr.; Soc. Sci. Cit. Index [Select. Cov.]; Sociol. Abstr.

US/0891-1150
**CLEVELAND CLINIC JOURNAL OF MEDICINE.** [Clevel. Clin. j. med.]. **Added/Corp** Cleveland Clinic Educational Foundation. Vol. 54, No. 1 (Jan./Feb. 1987)-. Academic Scholarly Publication. English. bm. $30.00 (individuals), $40.00 (institutions). Cleveland Clinic, 9500 Euclid Avenue, Cleveland OH 44195. **Tel** (216)444-2662, FAX (216)444-9385. **ED** Herbert P. Wiedemann, M.D. **LC** R11; .C57. **DD** 610. **NLM** W1; CL162M. **CODEN** CCJMEL. **[CCC].** Index available. **Ad Acc. Pr Rev. Circ:** 90,000. available on microfilm and microfiche from University Microfilms International (UMI). Documents available from The Genuine Article, BIOSIS Document Express. ***Continues*** *Cleveland Clinic Quarterly, 0009-8787.*
**Desc:** Briefs readers on new developments that affect the practice of medicine. Primary audience is internists and cardiologists. Contents include Highlights from Medical Grand Rounds, Highlights from CME, Current Drug Therapy, Clinical Applications of Research.
**Ind/Abst** Biol. Abstr. (1987-); Curr. Contents Clin. Med.; EMBASE (1987-); Energy Res. Abstr. (1987-); Health Plan. Adminis.; Index Med. (1987-); INIS Atomindex [Micro.]; Mod. Med.; Life Sci. Collect. (1987-); Res. Alert [Select. Cov.]; Rev. Med. Vet. Entomol.; Rev. Med. Vet. Mycology; SCISEARCH; Soc. Sci. Cit. Index [Select. Cov.].

US
**CLEVELAND PHYSICIAN.** (1964)-. Periodical. English. Twelve times a year. $24.00. Academy of Medicine of Cleveland, 11001 Cedar Avenue, Cleveland OH 44106. **Tel** (216)229-2200. **ED** Richard J. Nowak. **Ad Acc. Circ:** 4,300. ***Supersedes*** *Academy of Medicine of Cleveland. Bulletin.*
**Desc:** A publication of the Academy of Medicine of Cleveland and Cleveland Medical Library containing socio-economic issues of interest to the medical community.

US/0069-4770
**CLIN-ALERT.** [Clin-alert]. **VFOAT** Clin Alert. (1962)-. Abstracting/Indexing Service. English. Twenty-four times a year. $99.95 (one year), $185.00 (two year), $273.00 (three year) US; $109.95 (one year), $202.00 (two year), $300.00 (three year) other. Learned Information Inc., 143 Old Marlton Pike, Medford NJ 08055-8750. **Tel** (609)654-6266, FAX (609)654-4309. **ED** Ramona M. Scheible (editor's telephone: (812)738-7115). **DD** 615. **NLM** ZQZ 42 C641. **[CCC].** Index available. cum. index. ctrl circ.
**Desc:** For physicians, pharmacologists, and attorneys who research adverse drug reactions, drug interactions, and related therapeutic hazards.

UK/0144-7777
**CLINICA.** [Clinica]. (1980)-. Periodical. English. wk. $750.00 US/Canada; ¥128,000 Japan; £420.00 UK, Europe, N.Africa/Mid East, other. PJB Publications, 18-20 Hill Rise, Richmond Surrey TW10 6UA England. **Tel** 011 44 81 948 3262. **ED** Peter Charlish. **CODEN** CLNCD5.

[CCC]. **Ad Acc. Circ:** 10,000. Documents available from UMI Article Clearinghouse.
**Desc:** Offers information on medical/surgical equipment, specialties, disposables, reagents and instrumentation. Covers all aspects of the medical device market place as a weekly international publication.
**Ind/Abst** Pharm. News Index (Dec. 1982-); Trade Ind. Index.

SP/0210-4660
**CLINICA ANESTESIOLOGICA.** ***Ceased.*** [Clin. anestesiol.]. (1977)-Vol. 13 (19??). Monographic series. Spanish. qt. Salvat Editores SA, Calle Mallorca 45-49, Barcelona 08029 Spain. **Tel** 011 34 3 2010911, FAX 011 34 3 321-0565, telex SAEDI E 53132. **(Subscription address:** Salvat Publicaciones Cientificas SA, Avda Burgos 19 50 D, Madrid 28036 Spain**) UDC** 616.

IT/0391-2035
**CLINICA E LABORATORIO (ROMA).** (CLINICA E LABORATORIO.). [Clin. lab.]. (1977)-. Academic Scholarly Publication. Italian (English; summaries and/or abstracts in English). Four times a year. L80000 individuals; L140000 institutions. Il Pensiero Scientifico Editore s.r.l., Via Bradano 3C, 00199 Rome Italy. **Tel** 011 39 6 86207158, 86207159, 86207168, 86207169, FAX 011 39 6 86207160. **ED** G. Sprovieri, M. Rossi. **NLM** W1 CL366V. **CODEN** CLLADN. Index available. **Bk Rev. Ad Acc, Adv Mgr:** Dott Dalla, **Tel** 06-86207165. Full Page (B&W) L1.650.000. **Circ:** 1,300. Documents available from CASDDS.
**Ind/Abst** Anal. Abstr.; Chem. Abstr.; EMBASE; Index Med.

IT/0009-9007
**CLINICA EUROPEA.** ***Ceased.*** [Clin. eur.]. (1962)-(1992). Academic Scholarly Publication. Italian (English and French). qt. Clinica Europea, Via Concordia 20, Rome Italy. **Tel** 06/7943327-7576475. **ED** Lino Busnco and Fausto Federici. **NLM** W1 CL372. **CODEN** CLEUAB. Index available. **Bk Rev. Ad Acc. Circ:** 3,000. Documents available from BIOSIS Document Express, CASDDS.
**Ind/Abst** Biol. Abstr. (1985-); Chem. Abstr.; EMBASE.

SP/0210-7945
**CLINICA RURAL.** [Clin. rural]. (1965)-. Periodical. Spanish. mo. Jose Boada Sallares, Ronda de San Pedro 22, 08010 Barcelona Spain. **UDC** 61.

IT/0009-9074
**CLINICA TERAPEUTICA, LA.** ***Ceased.*** [Clin. Ter.]. (May 1951)-(19??). Periodical. Italian. mo. Societa Editrice Universo, Via GB Morgagni 1, 00161 Rome Italy. **Tel** 011 39 6 44231171. **DD** 616. **NLM** W1 CL582. **CODEN** CLTEA4. Documents available from BIOSIS Document Express, CASDDS.
**Ind/Abst** Biol. Abstr.; Chem. Abstr.; EMBASE; Health Plan. Adminis.; Index Med.; PESTDOC.

US/0891-2238
**CLINICAL ANATOMY (NORWALK, CONN.).** (CLINICAL ANATOMY.). (1989)-. English. be. $265.00 US; $340.00 other. Appleton Century Crofts, Prentice Hall, 200 Old Tappan Road, Old Tappan NJ 07675. **Tel** (201)767-5188, (800)922-0579. **DD** 611.

IT/0392-856X
**CLINICAL AND EXPERIMENTAL RHEUMATOLOGY.** [Clin. exp. rheumatol.]. **VFOAT** Rheumatology. Vol. 1, No. 1 (Jan./Mar. 1983)-. Academic Scholarly Publication. English. bm. L125000 (Italy); $170.00 (airmail), $140.00 (surface mail) other. Clinical and Experimental Rheumatology, Via S Maria 31, 56126 Pisa Italy. **Tel** 050/40124, FAX 050/553444. **ED** Stefano Bombardieri, Graham Hughes, Haralampos M Moutsopoulos, and Paul E Phillips. **NLM** W1 CL664F. **CODEN** CERHDP. Index available. cum. index. **Bk Rev. Ad Acc. Pr Rev. Circ:** 1,300. Documents available from The Genuine Article, CASDDS.
**Desc:** An international journal of rheumatic and connective tissue diseases. Includes original articles, review articles, case reports, letters to the editor and book reviews.
**Ind/Abst** Chem. Abstr. (1983-); Curr. Aware. Biol. Sci., CABS; Curr. Contents Clin. Med.; Curr. Contents Life Sci.; EMBASE; Health Plan. Adminis.; Index Med. (Vol. 1, No. 1, 1983-); Nutr. Abstr. Rev., Ser. A, Hum. Exp.; Res. Alert [Full Cov.]; Sci. Cit. Index; SCISEARCH; Soc. Sci. Cit. Index [Select. Cov.].

UK/0147-958X
**CLINICAL AND INVESTIGATIVE MEDICINE.** (CLINICAL AND INVESTIGATIVE MEDICINE. MEDICINE CLINIQUE ET EXPERIMENTALE.). [Clin. invest. med.]. **VFOAT** Medicine Clinique et Experimentale. Vol. 1 (1978)-. Academic Scholarly Publication. English (summaries and/or abstracts in French). Six times a year. $150.00. University of Toronto Press, 5201 Dufferin Street, Downsview Ontario M3H 5T8 Canada. **Tel** (416)667-7781, (416)667-7782, FAX (416)667-7803. **ED** Carl A. Goresky. **NLM** W1 CL664G. **CODEN** CNVMDL. **[CCC]. Bk Rev. Ad Acc. Pr Rev. Circ:** 1,300. available on microfilm from University Microfilms International (UMI). Documents available from The Genuine Article, BIOSIS Document Express, CASDDS.
**Desc:** Represents the majority of Canadian biomedical scientists through the publication of high-quality research and review articles and addresses itself to members of the international research community of clinical investigation.
**Ind/Abst** Biol. Abstr.; Chem. Abstr.; Curr. Aware. Biol. Sci., CABS; Curr. Contents Clin. Med.; Curr. Contents Life Sci.; Dairy Sci. Abstr.; EMBASE; Health Plan. Adminis.; Index Med. (1978-); Nutr. Abstr. Rev., Ser. B, Live Feeds and Feed.; Nutr. Abstr. Rev., Ser. A, Hum. Exp.; Life Sci. Collect.; Protozoolog. Abstr.; Ref. Upd. Deluxe Ed.; Res. Alert [Full Cov.]; Sci. Cit. Index; SCISEARCH; Soc. Sci. Cit. Index [Select. Cov.].

NE
**CLINICAL ASPECTS OF BIOMEDICINE.** (1991)-. Monographic series. English. Price varies per volume. Elsevier Science Publishers Ltd, Crown House, Linton Road, Barking Essex IG11 8JU England. **Tel** 011 44 81 5947272, FAX 081-594-5942, telex 896950. **NLM** W1; CL668JK. **CODEN** CABMEZ. Documents available from BIOSIS Document Express.
**Ind/Abst** Biol. Abstr. (1991-).

UK/0959-9851
**CLINICAL AUTONOMIC RESEARCH : OFFICIAL JOURNAL OF THE CLINICAL AUTONOMIC RESEARCH SOCIETY.** **Added/Corp** Clinical Autonomic Research Society. Vol. 1, No. 1 (March 1991)-. Periodical. English. bm. $355.00 US; £210.00 other. Rapid Communications of Oxford Ltd, The Old Malthouse, Paradise Street, Oxford OX1 1LD England. **Tel** 011 44 0865 790447, FAX 011 44 0865 244012, telex 9403712. **ED** Prof C J Mathias. **NLM** W1; CL668KH. **CODEN** CAURE9. **[CCC].** Index available. cum. index. **Bk Rev. Ad Acc. Pr Rev. Acid Free.** Documents available from The Genuine Article.
**Desc:** Interdisciplinary journal drawing together research on the autonomic nervous system. Scope includes neurology, cardiology, physiology, pharmacology and biochemistry.
**Ind/Abst** Curr. Aware. Biol. Sci., CABS; Index Med. (Mar. 1991-); Res. Alert [Full Cov.]; Soc. Sci. Cit. Index [Select. Cov.].

UK/0268-0033
**CLINICAL BIOMECHANICS (BRISTOL).** (CLINICAL BIOMECHANICS.). [Clin. biomech.]. **Added/Corp** Osteopathic Association of Great Britain. Vol. 1, No. 1 (Feb. 1986)-. Periodical. English. Eight times a year. $291.00 The Americas; £195.00 other. Butterworth Heinemann Publishers, Linacre House, Jordan Hill, Oxford OX2 8DP England. **Tel** 011 44 865 310366. **(Subscription address:** Elsevier Science Ltd. Oxford Fulfillment Centre, PO Box 800, Kidlington, Oxford OX5 1DX United Kingdom.**) ED** A. Kim Burton and Jon H. Thompson. **NLM** W1; CL668TH. **CODEN** CLBIEW. **[CCC].** Index available. **Ad Acc. Pr Rev.** available on microfilm and microfiche from University Microfilms International (UMI). Documents available from Article Express International, The Genuine Article, BIOSIS Document Express.
**Desc:** An international multidisciplinary journal publishing original research papers, letters, reviews and abstracts on clinical aspects of biomechanics related to dysfunction of the musculo-skeletal system.
**Ind/Abst** Biol. Abstr. (1986-); Curr. Contents Clin. Med.; EMBASE; Eng. Index Annu.; Res. Alert [Full Cov.]; Soc. Sci. Cit. Index [Select. Cov.].

FI/0358-4879
**CLINICAL CHEMICA (OULU).** (CLINICA CHEMICA.). No. 1-. Monographic series. English (Finnish). ir. Price varies per volume. Professor Sakari Piha, University of Oulu, 90100 Oulu 10 Finland. **Tel** 358-81-332133. **ED** Leo Hirvonen. **NLM** W1 AC954NM no.33 etc. **Ad Acc. Circ:** 500 (ctrl).
**Desc:** Monographs, reviews and dissertations in the field of clinical chemistry.

US
**CLINICAL DIAGNOSIS BY LABORATORY METHODS; A WORKING MANUAL OF CLINICAL PATHOLOGY.** (19??)-. English. ir. price varies per volume. W.B. Saunders Company, A Subsidiary of Harcourt Brace Jovanovich, Inc., The Curtis Center/Suite 300, Independence Square West, Philadelphia PA 19106-3399. **Tel** (215)238-7800 or, 5587, FAX (215)238-7883, telex 173146. **(Subscription address:** W. B. Saunders Company / North America Subscriptions, c/o Periodicals, 6277 Sea Harbour Drive, 4th Floor, Orlando FL 32887.**)**

US/0735-9306
**CLINICAL ECOLOGY.** ***Title Change.*** (CLINICAL ECOLOGY : ARCHIVES OF THE SOCIETY FOR CLINICAL ECOLOGY.). [Clin. ecol.]. **Added/Corp** Society for Clinical Ecology (U.S.). Vol. 1, No. 1 (Spring 1982)-(19??). Periodical. English. qt. Clinical Ecology Publishing Inc., 3069 South Detroit Way, Denver CO 80210. **Tel** (303)831-7335. **ED** John W. Gerrard and Del Stigler. **LC** RC585; .C55. **DD** 616.97/005. **NLM** W1; CL694W. **CODEN** CLIEEL. **Bk Rev. Ad Acc. Circ:** 1,200 (ctrl). Documents available from BIOSIS Document Express. ***Continues*** *Archives for Clinical Ecology.* ***Continued by*** *Environmental Medicine.*
**Desc:** Publishes original research and review literature on environmental medicine and clinical ecology, describing the intersection of allergy, immunology, toxicology, nutrition and individual adaptation.
**Ind/Abst** Art Archaeol. Tech. Abstr.; Biol. Abstr. (1987-); For. Prod. Abstr.; Index Vet.; Maize Abstr.; Nutr. Abstr. Rev., Ser. A, Hum. Exp.; Nutr. Res. Newsl.; Potato Abstr.; Rev. Med. Vet. Mycology.

US/0894-1025
**CLINICAL HEMOSTASIS REVIEW.** (CLINICAL HEMOSTASIS REVIEW : CHR.). [Clin. hemost. rev.]. **VFOAT** CHR. Vol. 1, No. 1 (Jan. 1987)-Vol. 8 (Jan. 1993)-. Periodical. English. Twelve times a year. $45.00 one year; $85.00 two year. Hemostasis Resources Inc, 800 Clermont Street, Denver CO 80220. **Tel** (303)399-3336. **ED** Rebecca Jensen. **DD** 616. **NLM** W1; CL71H. **Ad Acc, Adv Mgr:** G. Ens, **Tel** (803)399-3336. **Circ:** 5,000 (ctrl).
**Desc:** Covers concepts in coagulation. Each issue contains an in-depth articles on a selected topic in hemostasis and presents a related case. The newsletter also includes a self assessment by which AMA-approved CMD and CEU credits can be earned.

GW/0941-0198
**CLINICAL INVESTIGATOR, THE.** ***Title Change.*** **Added/Corp** Gesellschaft Deutscher Naturforscher und Arzte. Vol. 70, No. 1 (Jan. 1992)-(Jan. 1, 1995). Periodical. English. mo. Springer-Verlag GmbH & Company KG, Heidelberger Platz 3, D 14197 Berlin Germany. **Tel** 011 49 30 8207223, FAX 011 49 30 8214091, telex 183 319 SPBLN D. **(Subscription address:** Springer Verlag New York Inc. / for North America, 44 Hartz Way, Secaucus NJ 07096.**) NLM** W1; CL717. **CODEN** CINVE8. **[CCC].** Documents available from The Genuine Article, ADONIS. ***Continues*** *Klinische Wochenschrift, 0023-2173.* ***Continued by*** *Journal of Molecular Medicine, 0946-2716.*
**Ind/Abst** ADONIS; Curr. Contents Clin. Med.; Curr. Contents Life Sci.; Index Med. (1992-); Ref. Upd. Basic Ed.; Ref. Upd. Clinical Ed.; Ref. Upd. Deluxe Ed.; Res. Alert [Full Cov.]; Sci. Cit. Index (19??-19??); SCISEARCH; Soc. Sci. Cit. Index [Select. Cov.].

●US/1068-1191
**CLINICAL INVESTIGATOR NEWS.** [Clin. investig. news]. (Mar. 1993)-. Periodical. English. mo. $548.00 US & Canada; $578.00 other. CTB International Publishing Inc., PO Box 218, Maplewood NJ 07040. **Tel** (201)379-7749, FAX (201)379-1158. **DD** 615.

US/0366-6743
**CLINICAL JOURNAL (MANHASSET).** (CLINICAL JOURNAL.). **Added/Corp** North Shore University Hospital. Medical Staff. Vol. 1, Spring (1978)-. Periodical. English. sa (2 issues). $11.00. North Shore University Hospital, 300 Community Drive, Manhasset NY 11030. **Tel** (516)562-0100. **NLM** W1 CL72B.

US/0749-8047
**CLINICAL JOURNAL OF PAIN, THE.** [Clin. j. pain]. **Added/Corp** American Academy of Pain Medicine. Vol. 1, No. 1 (1985)-. Periodical. English. qt. $96.00 (individuals), $155.00 (institutions) US; $125.00 (individuals), $185.00 (institutions) other. Raven Press, 1185 Avenue of the Americas, 37th Floor, New York NY 10036. **Tel** (212)930-9500, (212)930-9604, FAX (212)869-3495, (212)302-8507, telex 640073. **ED** Gerald M. Aronoff. **DD** 616. **NLM** W1; CL724. **[CCC]. Pr Rev.** available on microfilm and microfiche from University Microfilms International (UMI). Documents available from The Genuine Article.
**Desc:** A multidisciplinary journal for all clinicians involved in pain management. Explores all aspects of pain and its effective treatment.
**Ind/Abst** Annals Behav. Med.; Curr. Contents Clin. Med.; EMBASE; Index Med. (1989-); Res. Alert [Full Cov.]; SCISEARCH; Soc. Sci. Cit. Index [Select. Cov.].

JA
**CLINICAL JOURNAL OF TRADITIONAL CHINESE MEDICINE. CHUI RINSHO.** Japanese. qt. ¥6400.00 Japan; ¥8120.00 other. Toyo Gakujutsu Shuppansha, 1-5-3 ch Miyakubo Ichikawashi, Chibaken 272 Japan. **Tel** 011 81 473 718337.

US/0192-1282
**CLINICAL LAB PRODUCTS.** (1972)-. Periodical. English. mo. $60.00 US; $125.00 (surface mail), $250.00 (airmail) other. Clinical Lab Products Inc, PO Box 69, Amherst NH 03031. **Tel** (603)673-7555, FAX (603)672-5625. **ED** Jane Pluke. **Ad Acc. Circ:** 53,000 (ctrl).
**Desc:** New products in the clinical diagnostic field.

BE
**CLINICAL LABORATORY INTERNATIONAL.** English. ir. $70.00. Pan European Publishing Company, rue Verte 216, 1210 Brussels 21 Belgium. **Tel** 011 32 2 2420611. **UDC** 61.
**Ind/Abst** Abstr. BioCommer.

US
**CLINICAL LABORATORY PRODUCT COMPARISON SYSTEM.** **Added/Corp** ECRI (Organization). **VFOAT** Product Comparison System. Vol. 1 (1985)-. English. mo. $595.00. ECRI Emergency Care

Research Institute, 5200 Butler Pike, Plymouth Meeting PA 19462. **Tel** (215)825-6000, FAX (215)834-1275, telex 510-660-8023. available on CD-ROM from DIALOG.

US/0093-8076
## CLINICAL LABORATORY REFERENCE.
**VFOAT** CLR. 1st Ed. (1974)-. Periodical. English. an. $29.00 US; $35.00 other. Medical Economics Publishing, Five Paragon Drive, Second Floor, Montvale NJ 07645. **Tel** (800)432-4570, (201)358-2210. **ED** Robert J. Fitzgibbon. **LC** RB36.2; .C553. **DD** 338.4/7/616075. **NLM** QY 26 C641. **Ad Acc. Circ:** 50,000.
**Desc:** The clinical laboratorian's reference for diagnostic reagents, tests, systems and instrumentation.

US/0894-959X
## CLINICAL LABORATORY SCIENCE.
(CLINICAL LABORATORY SCIENCE : JOURNAL OF THE AMERICAN SOCIETY FOR MEDICAL TECHNOLOGY.). [Clin. lab. sci.]. **Added/Corp** American Society for Medical Technology. Vol. 1, No. 1 (Jan./Feb. 1988)-. Academic Scholarly Publication. English. bm (6 issues). $60.00 (institutions), $40.00 (individuals) US; $65.00 Canada; $80.00 other. American Society of Clinical Laboratory Science, 7910 Woodmont Avenue, Suite 1301, Bethesda MD 20814. **Tel** (301)657-2768, (301)654-1622, FAX (301)654-1622. **ED** Greg D. Goss. **DD** 610. **NLM** W1; CL726DK. Index available. **Bk Rev. Ad Acc. Pr Rev. Acid Free. Circ:** 20,000 (ctrl). available on microfilm and microfiche from University Microfilms International (UMI). Documents available from CASDDS. ***Continues*** *Journal of Medical Technology, 0741-5397.*
**Desc:** Contains articles covering all subspecialties of medical technology with peer-reviewed reports published in the journal's academic section and feature articles and departments covering current events within the field.
**Ind/Abst** Chem. Abstr.; Cumul. Index Nurs. Allied Health Lit.; EMBASE; Hospit. Health Admin. Index; Index Vet.; Life Sci. Collect.; Rev. Med. Vet. Mycology.

US/0746-469X
## CLINICAL LASER MONTHLY. *Ceased.*
[Clin. laser mon.]. (1983)-(Dec. 1994). Periodical. English. mo. American Health Consultants, 3525 Piedmont Road, Suite 400, Atlanta GA 30305. **Tel** (800)688-2421, (404)262-7436. **NLM** W1; CL726DR. **[CCC].**
**Ind/Abst** Cumul. Index Nurs. Allied Health Lit.

UK/0267-6605
## CLINICAL MATERIALS.
[Clin. mater.]. Vol. 1, No. 1 (Feb. 1986)-. Academic Scholarly Publication. English. Twelve times a year. $678.00 The Americas; £455.00 other. Elsevier Applied Science, An Imprint of Elsevier Science Ltd., The Boulevard, Langford Lane, Kidlington, Oxford OX5 1GB United Kingdom. **Tel** 011 44 865 843000, 011 44 865 843699, FAX 011 44 865 843010. **(Subscription address:** Elsevier Science Ltd. Oxford Fulfillment Centre, PO Box 800, Kidlington, Oxford OX5 1DX United Kingdom.**) ED** C. Doyle. **NLM** W1; CL727. **CODEN** CLNME2. **[CCC].** available on microfilm and microfiche from University Microfilms International (UMI). Documents available from Article Express International, The Genuine Article, BIOSIS Document Express, CASDDS. ***Absorbed*** *Critical Reviews in Biocompatibility, 0748-5204.*
**Desc:** Satisfies a demand for rapid publication and cross-fertilization of ideas in the development and clinical application of materials in surgical, medical and dental practice. Will provide a common reference for practising clinicians, bioengineers, biochemists and materials scientists, who are involved in the design, development and applications of new materials and devices for use in patient care.
**Ind/Abst** Biol. Abstr. (1991-); Chem. Abstr.; EMBASE; Eng. Index Annu.; Met. Abstr.; Res. Alert [Full Cov.].

US/0412-7994
## CLINICAL MEDICINE (WINNETKA. 1940). *Ceased.*
(CLINICAL MEDICINE.). Vol. 47, No. 9 (1940)-?. Periodical. English. mo. NURSECOM Inc., 1211 Locust Street, Philadelphia PA 19107. **Tel** (215)545-7222, (800)242-6757, FAX (215)545-8107. **NLM** W1 CL73TC. ***Continues*** *Clinical Medicine and Surgery, 0092-6477;* ***Absorbed*** *Southern General Practitioner; Mississippi Valley Medical Journal, 0096-5480; Antibiotics & Chemotherapy, 0570-3123.*

●US/1063-0279
## CLINICAL PERFORMANCE AND QUALITY HEALTH CARE.
(1993)-. Periodical. English. qt. $106.00 institution; $96.00 individual (US). Slack Inc., 6900 Grove Road, Thorofare NJ 08086. **Tel** (609)848-1000, (800)257-8290, FAX (609)853-5991, telex 517108 SLACK INC VD. **NLM** W1; CL762M.

●US
## CLINICAL PRACTICE GUIDELINE.
**Added/Corp** United States. Agency for Health Care Policy and Research. No. 1 (1992)-. Monographic series. English. Price varies per volume. **NLM** W1; CL767JE.
**Ind/Abst** Abstr. Clin. Care Guidel.; Index Med. (1992-).

●US/1066-677X
## CLINICAL PRACTICE GUIDELINES.
[Clin. pract. guidel.]. **Added/Corp** American College of Physicians. (1992)-. English. an. $71.00 (non-members), $60.00 (members). American College of Physicians, 6th Street and Race Street, Independence Mall West, Philadelphia PA 19106-1572. **Tel** (215)351-2600, (800)523-1546. **(Subscription address:** American College of Physicians, PO Box 7777 R 0320, Philadelphia PA 19175.**) DD** 616.

US/0009-9279
## CLINICAL RESEARCH. *Title Change.*
[Clin. res.]. **Added/Corp** American Federation for Clinical Research. American Society for Clinical Investigation. Vol. 6 (Jan. 1958)-(Dec. 1994). Periodical. English. bm. Slack Inc., 6900 Grove Road, Thorofare NJ 08086. **Tel** (609)848-1000, (800)257-8290, FAX (609)853-5991, telex 517108 SLACK INC VD. **DD** 610. **NLM** W1 CL778. **CODEN** CLREAS. **[CCC].** available on microfilm and microfiche from University Microfilms International (UMI). Documents available from The Genuine Article, BIOSIS Document Express. ***Continues*** *Clinical Research Proceedings, 0096-0004;* ***Continues in part*** *Journal of Clinical Investigation, 0021-9738.* ***Continued by*** *Journal of Investigative Medicine.*
**Desc:** Includes abstracts submitted to the annual meeting of the American Society for Clinical Investigation.
**Ind/Abst** Biol. Abstr.; Curr. Contents Life Sci.; EMBASE; Health Plan. Adminis.; Hospit. Health Admin. Index; Index Med. (1984-); Nutr. Res. Newsl.; Life Sci. Collect.; PESTDOC; Protozoolog. Abstr.; Ref. Upd. Basic Ed.; Ref. Upd. Deluxe Ed.; Res. Alert [Full Cov.]; Risk Abstr.; Sci. Cit. Index; SCISEARCH; Soc. Sci. Cit. Index [Select. Cov.]; SportSearch.

US
## CLINICAL RESEARCH ASSOCIATES NEWSLETTER.
**Added/Corp** Clinical Research Associates. (197?)-. Newsletter. English. mo. $44.00 (1 year), $82.00 (2 year), $114.00 (3 year). Clinical Research Associates, 3707 North Canyon Road/Suite 6, Provo UT 84604. **Tel** (801)226-2121, FAX (801)226-4726. Index available. **Circ:** 20,000.

US
## CLINICAL STUDIES.
1- 1971-. Academic Scholarly Publication. English. ir. Elsevier Science Publishing Company Inc, Madison Square Station, PO Box 882, New York NY 10159-0882. **Tel** (212)633-3950, FAX (212)633-3990.

US/0009-9295
## CLINICAL SYMPOSIA (1957).
(CLINICAL SYMPOSIA.). [Clin. symp.]. **Added/Corp** Ciba Pharmaceutical Products, Inc. Ciba Pharmaceutical Company. CIBA-GEIGY Corporation. Pharmaceuticals Division. Vol. 9 (Jan./Feb. 1957)-. Periodical. English. qt (4 issues). $27.97 (one year), $55.94 (two year), $83.91 (three year). Ciba Pharmaceutical Company, 420 Madison Avenue, Suite 400, New York NY 10017. **Tel** (212)832-8888. **ED** Maria E. Brown. **LC** R11; .C583. **DD** 616.05. **NLM** W1 CL796. Index available. cum. index. ***Continues*** *Ciba Clinical Symposia, 0362-5060.*
**Ind/Abst** Cumul. Index Nurs. Allied Health Lit.; Energy Res. Abstr. (April 1982-); Health Plan. Adminis.; Index Med.; Physic. Medline Plus.

US
## CLINICAL SYMPOSIA ... ANNUAL.
***Ceased.*** **Added/Corp** Ciba Pharmaceutical Company. (1975)-Vol. 44. Periodical. English. an. Ciba Geigy, PO Box 18060, Newark NJ 07101. **Tel** (800)631-1181. **LC** R11; .C584. **DD** 616/.005.

US
## CLINICAL THERMOLOGY.
(1991)-. Monographic series. English. ir. Price varies per volume. Springer-Verlag New York Inc., 175 5th Avenue, New York NY 10010. **Tel** (212)460-1500, telex 232 235 SPB UR. **(Subscription address:** Springer Verlag New York Inc. / for North America, 44 Hartz Way, Secaucus NJ 07096.**) ED** M. Gauthrie.
**Desc:** Deals with diagnosis and therapy.

DK/0902-0063
## CLINICAL TRANSPLANTATION.
[Clin. transplant.]. Vol. 1 (1987)-. Periodical. English. bm. kr1270.00 US, Canada and Japan; kr1250.00 other. Munksgaard International Publishers Ltd, PO Box 2148, DK-1016 Copenhagen K Denmark. **Tel** 011 45 33 12 70 30, FAX 011 45 33 12 93 87, telex 19431 MUNKS DK. **ED** John S Najarian and Richard L Simmons. **NLM** W1; CL797KF. **CODEN** CLTRED. **[CCC].** Index available. **Ad Acc. Pr Rev. Circ:** 1,000 (ctrl). Documents available from The Genuine Article.
**Desc:** Channel of communication for all those involved in the care of people who require or have had organ or tissue transplants. Provides complete spectrum of present and possible future transplant operations.
**Ind/Abst** Curr. Contents Clin. Med.; EMBASE; Protozoolog. Abstr.; Res. Alert [Select. Cov.]; Rev. Med. Vet. Mycology; SCISEARCH; Soc. Sci. Cit. Index [Select. Cov.].

US/0882-6617
## CLINICAL UPDATE.
[Clin. update]. **Added/Corp** Mayo Clinic. **VFOAT** Mayo Clinical Update; Update. Vol. 1, No. 1 (Winter 1985)-. Periodical. English. qt. Free to medical professionals. Mayo Clinic, 200 First Street Southwest, Rochester MN 55905. **Tel** (800)633-4567. **DD** 616. **NLM** W1; CL799RE.

US/0887-6169
## CLINICAL VISION SCIENCES. *Title Change.*
[Clin. vis. sci.]. Vol. 1, No. 1 (1986)-(19??). Periodical. English. Six times a year. Pergamon Press Inc., 660 White Plains Road, Tarrytown NY 10591-5153. **Tel** (914)524-9200, FAX (914)333-2444, telex 13-7328. **(Subscription address:** UK/ Headington Hill Hall, Oxford OX3 0BW; Can/ 150 Consumers Road/ Suite 104, Willowdale Ontario M2J 1P9; Aus-NZ/ PO Box 544, Potts Point NSW 2011**) ED** E Zrenner, I Bodis-Wollner, and R F Hess. **DD** 617. **NLM** W1; CL799RH. **[CCC]. Pr Rev.** available on microfilm and microfiche from University Microfilms International (UMI). Documents available from The Genuine Article, Ask*IEEE. ***Merged into*** *Vision Research.*
**Desc:** Encourages the publication of detailed studies that use clinical material to address important issues in basic science and the use of basic scientific methods to address questions of clinical relevance. Studies include psychophysics, electrophysiology, visual development, neuropharmacology and physiological optics.
**Ind/Abst** Curr. Aware. Biol. Sci., CABS; Curr. Contents Life Sci.; EMBASE; INSPEC (1987-); Res. Alert [Full Cov.]; Sci. Cit. Index; SCISEARCH; Soc. Sci. Cit. Index [Select. Cov.].

SP
## CLINICAS DE MEDICINA DEPORTIVA.
Spanish. McGraw Hill, Interamericana de Espana SA, Manuel Ferrero 13, 28036 Madrid Spain.

US/1052-0627
## CLINICIAN REVIEWS.
[Clin. rev.]. Vol. 1, No. 1 (Feb. 1991)-. Periodical. English. Ten times a year. $55.00 US; $85.00 other. Williams & Wilkins Company, 428 East Preston Street, Baltimore MD 21202-3993. **Tel** (410)528-4000, (800)638-6423, FAX (410)528-8596, telex 87669. **(Subscription address:** Williams & Wilkins, PO Box 64380, Baltimore MD 21264.**) DD** 616. **NLM** W1; CL805H. **[CCC].** Documents available from Quick Copies.
**Desc:** A "reader friendly" journal for physician assistants and nurse practitioners with easy-to-digest articles on new therapeutic drugs and procedures.

CN/0832-9184
## CLINICIEN.
(LE CLINICIEN.). [Clinicien]. Vol. 1, No. 1 (Oct. 1986)-. Periodical. French. ir. 102.00Can$ Canada; 129.00Can$ other. STA Communications Inc., 955 St. John Boulevard, Suite 306, Pt Claire, Quebec H9R 5K3 Canada. **Tel** (514)695-7623. **DD** 616.07/05.

US/0272-5231
## CLINICS IN CHEST MEDICINE.
[Clin. chest med.]. Vol. 1, No. 1 (Jan. 1980)-. Periodical. English. qt. $99.00 (individual), $119.00 (institution) US; $129.00 (individual), $136.00 (institution) other. W.B. Saunders Company, A Subsidiary of Harcourt Brace Jovanovich, Inc., The Curtis Center/Suite 300, Independence Square West, Philadelphia PA 19106-3399. **Tel** (215)238-7800 or, 5587, FAX (215)238-7883, telex 173146. **(Subscription address:** W. B. Saunders Company / North America Subscriptions, c/o Periodicals, 6277 Sea Harbour Drive, 4th Floor, Orlando FL 32887.**) ED** R.A. Mathay, G.R. Olsen, A.M. Fein and T.E. King, Jr. **LC** RC941. **DD** 617/.54/005. **UDC** 616.24. **NLM** W1 CL831AG. **[CCC].** Index available. **Pr Rev. Circ:** 3,500. available on microfilm and microfiche from University Microfilms International (UMI). Documents available from The Genuine Article.
**Desc:** Practical updates for the clinician on the latest advances. Each issue addresses a single topic in patient care.
**Ind/Abst** Cumul. Index Nurs. Allied Health Lit.; Curr. Contents Clin. Med.; EMBASE; Health Plan. Adminis.; Index Med. (Jan. 1980-); Microbiol. Abstr. Sect. B; Nutr. Abstr. Rev., Ser. A, Hum. Exp.; Life Sci. Collect.; Physic. Medline Plus; Protozoolog. Abstr.; Res. Alert [Full Cov.]; Sci. Cit. Index; SCISEARCH; Soc. Sci. Cit. Index [Select. Cov.].

US/0193-743X
## CLINICS IN DIAGNOSTIC ULTRASOUND.
[Clin. diagn. ultrasound]. Vol. 1 (1979)-. Monographic series. English. Three times a year. Price varies per volume. Churchill Livingstone, 1-3 Baxter's Place, Leith Walk, Edinburgh EH1 3AF Scotland. **Tel** 011 44 31 556 2424, FAX 011 44 31 558 1278, telex 727511. **(Subscription address:** US and Canada/ Churchill Livingstone Inc., 5 South 250 Frontenac Road, Naperville, IL 60563; (telephone: (800)553-5426 or (708)416-3939)**) ED** Kenneth J. Taylor. **LC** UNC. **NLM** W1 CL831BC. **CODEN** CDULDB. Documents available from BIOSIS Document Express.
**Desc:** Book series presenting practical, up-to-the-minute material on the latest ultrasonographic techniques, indications for their use and their value in diagnosis. Each volume provides in-depth coverage of a specific topic of contemporary significance.
**Ind/Abst** Biol. Abstr. (?-1980); Health Plan. Adminis.; Index Med. (1988-).

US/0272-2712
## CLINICS IN LABORATORY MEDICINE.
[Clin. lab. med.]. **VFOAT** Laboratory Medicine. Vol. 1, No. 1 (March 1981)-. Periodical. English. qt. $82.00 (individual), $100.00 (institution) US; $113.00 (individual), $119.00 (institution) other. W.B. Saunders Company, A Subsidiary of Harcourt Brace Jovanovich, Inc., The Curtis

Center/Suite 300, Independence Square West, Philadelphia PA 19106-3399. **Tel** (215)238-7800 or, 5587, FAX (215)238-7883, telex 173146. **(Subscription address:** W. B. Saunders Company / North America Subscriptions, c/o Periodicals, 6277 Sea Harbour Drive, 4th Floor, Orlando FL 32887.**) ED** Edward Yeager. **LC** RB37.A1. **DD** 616.07/05. **NLM** W1 CL831CC. **CODEN** CLMED6. **[CCC]. Pr Rev. Circ:** 2,000. available on microfilm and microfiche from University Microfilms International (UMI). Documents available from The Genuine Article, BIOSIS Document Express.
**Desc:** Practical updates for the clinician on the latest advances. Each issue addresses a single topic in patient care.
**Ind/Abst** Biol. Abstr.; Curr. Contents Clin. Med.; EMBASE; Health Plan. Adminis.; Index Med. (1981-); Nutr. Abstr. Rev., Ser. A, Hum. Exp.; Res. Alert [Select. Cov.]; SCISEARCH; Soc. Sci. Cit. Index [Select. Cov.].

CN/0825-3005
**CLINIMED.** (CLINIMED [ENREGISTREMENT SONORE] / DE MEDIFACTS LTEE.). [Clinimed]. Vol. 1, No. 1 (Jan. 27, 1976)-. Periodical. French. mo. 48.00Can$ Canada; 65.00Can$ other. Medifacts Group Ltd, 20 Camelot Drive, Suite 600, Ottawa Ontario K2A 0G3 Canada. **Tel** (613)728-4655. **DD** 610.

US
**CLINMED-CD.** (19??)-. English. bm. $850.00. Silverplatter Information Inc., 100 River Ridge Drive, Norwood MA 02062. **Tel** (800)343-0064, (617)769-2599, FAX (617)235-1715.
**Desc:** A subset of MEDLINE database.

NE/0366-676X
**CLIO MEDICA.** [Clio med.]. **Added/Corp** International Academy of the History of Medicine. **VFOAT** Acta Academiae Internationalis Historiae Medicinae. Vol. 1 (Nov. 1965)-. Periodical. English (French and German). ir. Fl160.00. Editions Rodopi BV, Keizersgracht 302-304, 1016 Ex Amsterdam Netherlands. **Tel** 011 31 20 6227507, FAX 011 31 20 380948. **LC** R131.A1; C48. **NLM** W1 CL933. Index available. **Bk Rev. Ad Acc. Circ:** 350.
**Ind/Abst** Am. Hist. Life (1965-); Health Plan. Adminis.; Index Med.

RM
**CLUJUL MEDICAL. Added/Corp** Institutul Medico-Farmaceutic, Cluj. Univnea Societatilor de Stiinte Medical Fialiala Cluj. Societatea Stiintelor Medicale Filiala Cluj. Vol.1, (Feb. 1920)-. Academic Scholarly Publication. Romanian. Four times a year. DM193.00. **(Subscription address:** Kubon & Sagner, ABT Zeitschriftenimport, D 80328 Munich Germany.**) NLM** W1 CL934. **CODEN** CLUMBY. Documents available from BIOSIS Document Express, CASDDS.
**Desc:** Review of medicine with articles on original orientation and experimental, clinical and laboratory medicine.
**Ind/Abst** Biol. Abstr.; Chem. Abstr.

CN/0820-3946
**CMAJ. CANADIAN MEDICAL ASSOCIATION JOURNAL.** (CMAJ : CANADIAN MEDICAL ASSOCIATION JOURNAL : JOURNAL DE L'ASSOCIATION MEDICALE CANADIENNE.). [CMAJ, Can. Med. Assoc. j.]. **Added/Corp** Canadian Medical Association. **VFOAT** Canadian Medical Association Journal; Journal de l'Association Medicale Canadienne. **VAT** Canadian Medical Association Journal (1985). Vol. 133, No. 5 (Sept. 1, 1985)-. Periodical. English (French). Twenty-four times a year. 90.00Can$ Canada; $115.00 other. Canadian Medical Association, 1867 Alta Vista Drive, Ottawa Ontario K1G 3Y6 Canada. **Tel** (613)731-9331 ext. 2028, FAX (613)731-4797. **(Subscription address:** Canadian Medical Association, CMA House, PO Box 8650, Ottawa Ontario K1G 0G8 Canada.**) DD** 610/.971. **[CCC]. Bk Rev. Ad Acc. Pr Rev. Acid Free.** available on microfiche. Documents available from BIOSIS Document Express, CASDDS. ***Continues** Canadian Medical Association. Canadin Medical Association Journal, 0008-4409.*
**Desc:** A general scientific medical journal that includes notices of upcoming conferences, book reviews, summaries of CMA policies and news. Also includes features of interest to members of the Association and others in the health care professions.
**Ind/Abst** Biol. Abstr.; Biol. Dig.; Can. Index; Can. Period. Index (19??-); Chem. Abstr.; Curr. Aware. Biol. Sci., CABS; Curr. Contents Clin. Med.; EMBASE; Index Med.; Int. Nurs. Index; Int. Pharm. Abstr.; Med. Abstr. Newsl.; Sci. Cit. Index; SPORT Discus; Virol. AIDS Abstr.

●US/1066-3703
**CODE OF FEDERAL REGULATIONS UPDATE. 21 CFR, DRUGS AND MEDICAL DEVICES. See** Pharmacy and Pharmacology.

FR/0335-5306
**COEUR ET SANTE PARIS.** [Coeur et sante Paris]. (1974)-. Periodical. French. qt. 97.94F France; 130.00F other. Edicardio, 9 rue Laborde, F 75008 Paris France. **Tel** 011 33 1 45220663. **UDC** 61.

US/0275-8091
**COLLECTIONS (PHILADELPHIA, PA.).** (COLLECTIONS : THE NEWSLETTER OF THE ARCHIVES AND SPECIAL COLLECTIONS ON WOMEN IN MEDICINE, THE MEDICAL COLLEGE OF PENNSYLVANIA.). **Added/Corp** Medical College of Pennsylvania. Archives and Special Collections on Women in Medicine. (19??)-. Newsletter. English. Twice a year. Free. Medical College of Pennsylvania, Arch Spec College of Women Medicine, Philadelphia PA 19129. **Tel** (215)842-7124. **Circ:** 8,500 (ctrl).
**Desc:** Articles by archives collections, activities, and researchers, lists of acquisitions, news items about archives activities, list of donors and information on exhibits.

US/0742-8057
**COLLEGE REVIEW (DENVER, COLO.), THE.** (THE COLLEGE REVIEW : A PUBLICATION OF THE AMERICAN COLLEGE OF MEDICAL GROUP ADMINISTRATORS.). [Coll. rev.]. **Added/Corp** American College of Medical Group Administrators. Vol. 1, No. 1 (Spring 1984)-. Periodical. English. qt. $30.00. Medical Group Management Association, 104 Inverness Terrace East, Englewood CO 80112. **Tel** (303)397-7879, FAX (303)799-1683. **ED** Keith Jones. **DD** 362. **NLM** W1; CO1985. **Circ:** 765 (ctrl).
**Desc:** Contains in-depth informed researched looks at the vast array of issues that face medical group administrators today.
**Ind/Abst** Health Plan. Adminis.; Hospit. Health Admin. Index.

CK/0120-8322
**COLOMBIA MEDICA : CM. Added/Corp** Universidad del Valle. Corporacion Editora Medica del Valle. **VFOAT** CM. (19??)-. Periodical. Spanish. Four times a year. 15.00Col$. Colombia Medica, Corp ED Medic de Valle, AA 8025 Cali Colombia. **Tel** 011 57 23 581939. **ED** Dr. Francisco Falabella. **NLM** W1; CO219P. **Ad Acc. Pr Rev. Circ:** 1,500. ***Continues** Acta Medica del Valle.*

US/0199-7343
**COLORADO MEDICINE (1980).** (COLORADO MEDICINE.). [Colo. med.]. **Added/Corp** Colorado Medical Society. Rocky Mountain Medical Conference. Vol. 77, (Jan. 1980)-. Academic Scholarly Publication. English. Twelve times a year. $35.00. Colorado Medical Society, PO Box 17550, Denver CO 80217. **Tel** (303)779-5455. **ED** William Pierson. **LC** R11; .R67. **DD** 610/.5. **NLM** W1 CO25LD. Index available (Bound in December issue, publish in December). **Bk Rev**, (Qty: 1-3). **Ad Acc. Circ:** 5,000. available on microfilm and microfiche from University Microfilms International (UMI). ***Continues** Rocky Mountain Medical Journal, 0035-760X.*
**Desc:** On the Colorado medicine.
**Ind/Abst** EMBASE; Health Plan. Adminis.; Index Med.; SportSearch.

●US
**COMMUNICATION AND LANGUAGE INTERVENTION SERIES. See** Physically Impaired.

UK/0267-3320
**COMMUNICATIONS IN LABORATORY MEDICINE.** ***Ceased.*** (1985)-(Jan. 1994). Periodical. English. bm. Interlaboratory Communications, 1 Hithercroft Court, Wallingford, Oxon OX10 9BT England. **Tel** 011 44 0491 26333, FAX 011 44 0491 26939. **ED** Dr. P.J. Wood. **NLM** W1; CO4278. Index available. **Bk Rev. Ad Acc. Pr Rev. Circ:** 1,000.
**Desc:** Clinical biochemistry and associated sciences.

US
**COMMUNITY INTEGRATION : THE NEWSLETTER OF THE REHABILITATION RESEARCH AND TRAINING CENTER ON COMMUNITY INTEGRATION OF PERSONS WITH TRAUMATIC BRAIN INJURY, AT THE STATE UNIVERSITY OF NEW YORK AT BUFFALO. Added/Corp** State University of New York at Buffalo. Rehabilitation Research and Training Center on Community Integration of Persons with Traumatic Brain Injury. Vol. 1, No. 1, (Aug./Sept. 1990)-. Newsletter. English.

US
**COMPACT CAMBRIDGE MEDLINE [COMPUTER FILE]. Added/Corp** Cambridge Scientific Abstracts, Inc. National Library of Medicine (U.S.). **VFOAT** Cambridge MEDLINE; MEDLINE. (Jan./June 1986)-. Periodical. English. mo. Cambridge Scientific Abstracts, 7200 Wisconsin Avenue, #601, Bethesda MD 20814-4823. **Tel** (301)961-6750, (800)843-7751, FAX (301)961-6720. Index available. **Bk Rev. Ad Acc.** available via Internet (to the current year's abstracts and five-year backfiles) from Cambridge Scientific Abstracts.
**Desc:** Source for biomedical literature, including research, clinical practice, administration, policy issues, and health care services.

SZ/0379-7996
**COMPENDIA RHEUMATOLOGICA.** (1976)-. Monographic series. German (French and English). ir. Price varies per volume. Eular Verlag, Missionsstrasse 36, CH-4012 Basel Switzerland. **Tel** 011 41 61 2611317, FAX 011 41 61 256213, telex 963 755 REIN CH. **ED** H. Mathies and F. J. Wagenhauser. **NLM** W1 CO439R.

MX/0185-1934
**COMPENDIUM DE INVESTIGACIONES CLINICAS LATINOAMERICANAS.** [Compend. invest. clin. latinoam.]. (198?)-. Academic Scholarly Publication. Spanish (summaries and/or abstracts in English). bm (6 issues). $38.00 US, Canada, Mexico & Pan America; $48.00 Europe; $56.00 other. Intersistemas SA de CV, Fernando Alencastre #110, Mexico City DF Mexico. **Tel** 011 52 5 5202073, 011 52 5 5405600. **ED** Juan del Rio H. **NLM** W1 CO448. **CODEN** CLATDP. **Circ:** 5,500 (ctrl). Documents available from BIOSIS Document Express.
**Desc:** Clinical and pharmacological research studies and clinical therapeutic trials.
**Ind/Abst** Biol. Abstr.; EMBASE.

UK/0950-6667
**COMPLEMENTARY MEDICINE INDEX : CURRENT AWARENESS TOPICS SERVICES. Added/Corp** British Library. Medical Information Service. Research Council for Complementary Medicine (England). **VFOAT** Current Awareness Topics Services. Vol. 1, (1986)-. Periodical. English (German and French). Twelve times a year. £50.00 UK & ECC; £65.00 other. British Library / Publications Sale Unit, Boston Spa, Wetherby, West Yorkshire LS23 7BQ England. **Tel** 011 44 937 546546 546543, FAX 011 44 937 546333, telex 557381. **ED** Stephen Andrews. **NLM** ZWB 300; C761. Index available. cum. index. **Bk Rev. Ad Acc. Pr Rev. Circ:** 300.
**Desc:** Bibliography to the literature of alternative and complementary medicine.

UK/0965-2299
**COMPLEMENTARY THERAPIES IN MEDICINE.** (1993)-. Periodical. English. Four times a year. £104.00 Europe; £105.00 Other (Institutions). Churchill Livingstone, 1-3 Baxter's Place, Leith Walk, Edinburgh EH1 3AF Scotland. **Tel** 011 44 31 556 2424, FAX 011 44 31 558 1278, telex 727511. **(Subscription address:** Maruzen Company Ltd., PO Box 5050, Import & Export Department, Tokyo 100 31 Japan.**) NLM** W1; CO4512. ***Continues** Complementary Medical Research.*

●UK/1353-6117
**COMPLEMENTARY THERAPIES IN NURSING AND MIDWIFERY.** (1994)-. Periodical. English. bm. £67 Europe; £68 Other (Institutions). Churchill Livingstone, 1-3 Baxter's Place, Leith Walk, Edinburgh EH1 3AF Scotland. **Tel** 011 44 31 556 2424, FAX 011 44 31 558 1278, telex 727511. **(Subscription address:** Maruzen Company Ltd., PO Box 5050, Import & Export Department, Tokyo 100 31 Japan.**)**

US
**COMPREHENSIVE DISSERTATION INDEX. Added/Corp** University Microfilms International. (1973/77)-. English. an. $660.00. University Microfilms International, 300 North Zeeb Road, Ann Arbor MI 48106-1346. **Tel** (313)761-4700, (800)521-0600 Exts. 2490, 2491, FAX (313)973-1540. Index available. **Bk Rev. Ad Acc. Circ:** 3,000 (ctrl).
**Desc:** Comprehensive index to 850,000 doctoral dissertations available on demand from University Microfilm. Base volumes with supplements printed annually.

US/1040-4074
**COMPREHENSIVE MEDLINE/EBSCO CD-ROM.** (COMPREHENSIVE MEDLINE/EBSCO CD-ROM. [COMPUTER FILE].). [Compr. MEDLINE/Ebsco CD-ROM]. **Added/Corp** National Library of Medicine (U.S.) EBSCO Electronic Information. **VFOAT** Comprehensive MEDLINE EBSCO CD-ROM; MEDLINE EBSCO CD-ROM. (1986)-. Periodical. English. mo. $1095.00 US and Canada; $1145.00 other (for current plus two year backfile); $1495.00 US and Canada; $1595.00 other (for current plus five year backfile); $2195.00 US and Canada; $2345.00 other (for current plus nine year backfile); $2795.00 US and Canada; $2995.00 other (for current plus backfile to 1966). National Library of Medicine, 8600 Rockville Pike, Bethesda MD 20894. **Tel** (301)496-6308. **(Subscription address:** EBSCO Publishing-Peabody, 83 Pine Street, Peabody MA 01960; telephone: North America/ (800)653-2726; other (508)535-8500; FAX: (508)535-8545**) DD** 610.
**Desc:** Includes MeSH search capabilities, interface for ordering full text of referenced documents, SDI, bibliography production, and compilation of system-use statistics. Menu choices include options for the library patron as well as the professional searcher.

US/0098-8243
**COMPREHENSIVE THERAPY.** [Compr. ther.]. **Added/Corp** American Society of Contemporary Medicine and Surgery. Vol. 1 (May 1975)-. Periodical. English. Twelve times a year. $159.00 US; $189.00 other.

# Medical Science and Technology

American Society Contemporary Medicine and Surgery, 233 East Erie Street, Suite 710, Chicago IL 60611. **Tel** (800)621-4002, (312)951-1400, FAX (312)951-1400. **ED** David Bellows M. D. and Randall T. Bellows M. D. **LC** [R11; .C59]. **DD** 610/.5. **NLM** W1 CO453K. **Bk Rev**. **Circ:** 1,300.
 **Desc:** News and information covering different areas of medicine.
 **Ind/Abst** Cumul. Index Nurs. Allied Health Lit.; Curr. Index J. Educ.; EMBASE; Energy Res. Abstr. (March 1982-); Index Med.; INIS Atomindex [Micro.]; Nutr. Res. Newsl.

US/0163-0547
**COMPUTERS & MEDICINE. See** Computers.

US/0573-2107
**COMPUTERS IN BIOMEDICAL RESEARCH.** [Comput. biomed. res.]. Vol. 1 (1965)-. English. Mount Melleray Abbey, Cappoquin Ireland. **Tel** 058 54404. **NLM** W1 CO457U. **CODEN** CPBRAF. Documents available from BIOSIS Document Express.
 **Ind/Abst** Biol. Abstr. (?-1974); Biostatistica (?-?); Curr. Aware. Biol. Sci., CABS.

US/0737-8556
**COMPUTING PHYSICIAN.** [Comput. phys.]. Vol. 1, No. 1 (April 1983)-. Periodical. English. mo. $80.00. PW Communications, Inc., 515 Madison Avenue, New York NY 10022. **NLM** W1; CO4575.

SP/0213-5884
**COMUNIDAD Y DROGAS.** [Comunidad drog.]. (1986)-. Periodical. Spanish. qt. Free upon request. Ministerio de Sanidad y Consumo, Paseo del Prado 18 20, 28071 Madrid Spain. **Tel** 011 34 1 420-2227, 420-2051. **UDC** 613.8.
 **Ind/Abst** Indice Med. Esp.

FR/0010-5309
**CONCOURS MEDICAL.** [Coucours med.]. Vol. 1 (1879)-. Periodical. French. Forty times a year (Includes supplements). 626.84F Doctors France & EEC Countries; 640.00F Doctors French Overseas Dept. & Terr. EEC Countries; 930.46F France; 950.00F French Overseas Dept. & Terr. EEC Countries (others); 1,020.00F Doctors (others); 1,220.00F French Overseas Dept. & Terr. EEC Countries (others). Concours Medical, 37 rue de Bellefond, 75441 Paris Cedex 09 France. **Tel** 011 33 1 45963200. **ED** Jacque Pouletty. **NLM** W1 CO462. **CODEN** COMEAO. **[CCC].** Bk Rev. Ad Acc. Pr Rev. Circ: 55,000 (ctrl). Documents available from BIOSIS Document Express, CASDDS.
 **Desc:** Medical review regarding continuous information on therapeutic medicine and ethics.
 **Ind/Abst** Biol. Abstr.; Chem. Abstr.; Coal Abstr.; EMBASE; Energy Res. Abstr.; Health Plan. Adminis.; Saf. Health Work; SportSearch.

IT/1122-0279
**CONFINIA CEPHALALGICA.** (19??)-. Periodical. Italian. tq. $103.00. Masson S.P.A, Via Statuto 2/4, 20121 Milan Italy. **Tel** 011 39 2 63671, FAX 011 39 2 6367211. **ED** Gian Camillo Manzoni.

US/0010-6178
**CONNECTICUT MEDICINE.** [Conn. med.]. **Added/Corp** Connecticut State Medical Society. Vol. 22, No. 8 (Aug. 1958)-. Periodical. English. Twelve times a year. $25.00. Connecticut Medicine, 160 St Ronan Street, New Haven CT 06511. **Tel** (203)865-0587. **ED** Robert V. Massey M.D. **NLM** W1 CO711N. Index available (Dec. iss.). **Bk Rev**. **Ad Acc**. **Pr Rev**. **Circ:** 6,500 (ctrl).
**Continues** Connecticut State Medical Journal, 0096-0179.
 **Ind/Abst** CIS Abstr.; Cumul. Index Nurs. Allied Health Lit.; EMBASE; Energy Res. Abstr.; Health Plan. Adminis.; Index Med.; INIS Atomindex [Micro.]; Life Sci. Collect.; Saf. Health Work; SportSearch.

US/8756-9086
**CONNECTIVE ISSUES.** [Connect. issues]. Periodical. English. qt. $25.00. The National Marfan Foundation, Washington NY 11050. **Tel** (516)883-8712. **ED** Priscilla Ciccariello and Joe Kolman. **DD** 616. **Ad Acc**. **Circ:** 8,000.
 **Desc:** Articles by, about, and for people, and their families, with the Marfan Syndrome. Information for the layman and the professional. Human interest stories and information regarding research.

JA/0916-572X
**CONNECTIVE TISSUE TOKYO. 1989.** [Connect. tissue Tokyo, 1989]. (1989)-. Periodical. Multiple languages. qt. Japanese Society for Connective Tissue Research, 1-1 Shinjuku 6-chome, Shinjuku-ku 160 Tokyo, Japan. **Tel** (3)3352-6335. **DD** 616.77. **Continues** Ketsugo Soshiki, 0389-7079.
 **Ind/Abst** EMBASE.

US
**CONOMIKES MEDICARE HOTLINE.**
English. mo (with July-Aug. combined). $117.00. Conomikes Reports, 6033 West Century Boulevard, Suite 990, Los Angeles CA 90045. **Tel** (213)645-5100. **ED** George S. Conomikes.
 **Desc:** Deals with Medicare coding and reimbursement.

US/0890-4383
**CONOMIKES REPORTS ON MEDICAL PRACTICE MANAGEMENT : AN INFORMATION SERVICE OF CONOMIKES ASSOCIATES, INC.** [Conomikes rep. med. pract. manage.]. **Added/Corp** Conomikes Associates, Inc. (Marina del Rey, Calif.). **VFOAT** ConomikesReports on Medical Practice Management; ConomikesReports; Conomikes Reports. (198?)-. Periodical. English. mo (except combined July/Aug. and Dec./Jan.). $98.00 (1 year), $196.00 (2 year). Conomikes Reports, 6033 West Century Boulevard, Suite 990, Los Angeles CA 90045. **Tel** (213)645-5100. **ED** George S. Conomikes. **DD** 610. **Circ:** 3,500.

US/0737-4674
**CONSENSUS DEVELOPMENT CONFERENCE SUMMARIES.** (CONSENSUS DEVELOPMENT CONFERENCE SUMMARIES / NATIONAL INSTITUTES OF HEALTH.). [Consens. dev. conf. summ.]. **Added/Corp** National Institutes of Health (U.S.). Vol. 3 (1980)-. English. an. Free on request. US Department of Health and Human Services National Institutes of Health, 9000 Rockville Pike, Bethesda MD 20892. **Tel** (301)496-9291, FAX (301)496-2443. **NLM** W3 CO978NM. **Continues** National Institutes of Health Consensus Development Conference Summaries, 0195-6213.
 **Ind/Abst** Abstr. Clin. Care Guidel.; Health Plan. Adminis.; Index Med.

SP/1131-4184
**CONSULTA MADRID. 1983.** [ConsultaMadr., 1983]. (1983)-. Periodical. Spanish. wk. Edilerner SA, Paseo de la Castellana 53/2, 28046 Madrid Spain. **UDC** 61. **Continues** Consulta Semanal, 1131-4176.

US/0010-7069
**CONSULTANT (HACKENSACK).** (CONSULTANT.). [Consult.]. **Added/Corp** Smith, Kline & French Laboratories. Vol. 1 (April 1961)-. Periodical. English. mo. $70.00 US; $90.00 other. Cliggott Publishing Company, 55 Holly Hill Lane, Box 4010, Greenwich CT 06830. **Tel** (203)661-0600, (212)993-0440. **ED** Bernice Shaw Ullrich. **LC** [R11; .C629]. **DD** 616/.005. **NLM** W1 CO752. **[CCC].** Pr Rev. Circ: 124,386. available on microfilm and microfiche from University Microfilms International (UMI); available on an online database (files 149,648/Full-Text) from DIALOG.
 **Desc:** A primary care journal which emphasizes the "how to" aspect of medicine. Helps readers resolve common questions in everyday practice and provides peer references so doctors can measure their techniques, etc.
 **Ind/Abst** Acad. Abstr. Full Text Elite (Jan. 1992-); Acad. Abstr. (Jan. 1992-); Acad. Search (Jan. 1992-); Bus. ASAP (1990-) [Full Txt.]; Bus. Index (1985-); Cumul. Index Nurs. Allied Health Lit.; Foods Adlibra; Gen. BusinessFile (1985-); Health Index (1989-); Health Period. Database [Full Txt.]; Health Plan. Adminis.; Health Ref. Cent. (Jan. 1989-) [Full Cov.]; Hospit. Health Admin. Index (Vol. 28, No. 1, 1988-Dec. 1991); INFO-SOUTH Abstr.; Int. Nurs. Index; Mag. Search.

SZ
**CONTACT : A BI-MONTHLY PUBLICATION OF THE CHRISTIAN MEDICAL COMMISSION, WORLD COUNCIL OF CHURCHES. Added/Corp** World Council of Churches. Christian Medical Commission. (1970)-. Periodical. English (French, Spanish and Portuguese). bm (6 issues). Free to developing countries; 15.00F industrialized countries. World Council of Churches, PO Box 2100, CH 1211 Geneva 2 Switzerland. **Tel** 011 41 22 7906076, FAX 011 41 22 7910361, telex 23 423 OIK CH. **ED** Sandra Freeman. **NLM** W1; CO755VE. cum. index. **Bk Rev**. **Circ:** 26,000.
 **Desc:** Bulletin of the Christian Medical Commission reporting topical, innovative approaches to the promotion of health.
 **Ind/Abst** Trop. Dis. Bull.

US/1040-2217
**CONTEMPORARY PERSPECTIVES IN REHABILITATION.** (CONTEMPORARY PERSPECTIVES IN REHABILITATION : CPR.). [Contemp. perspect. rehabil.]. **VFOAT** CPR. Vol. 1 (1986)-. Monographic series. English. Price varies per volume. FA Davis Company, 1915 Arch Street, Philadelphia PA 19103. **Tel** (800)523-4049, (215)568-2270, FAX (215)568-5065, telex 83-4837. **DD** 615. **NLM** W1; CO769NS. **CODEN** CPRHEZ.

●US
**CONTINUING CARE CONNECTION : LINKING LONG-TERM, HOME AND COMMUNITY CARE SYSTEMS. See** Sociology-Social Services and Welfare.

US/0160-6980
**CONTINUING EDUCATION FOR HEALTH CARE PROVIDERS. See** Education-Adult and Continuing Education.

US/0193-2349
**CONTINUING EDUCATION IN ORTHOPAEDIC SURGERY. SOUND RECORDING.** [Contin. educ. orthop. surg.]. **Added/Corp** Orthopaedic Audio-Synopsis Foundation. **VFOAT** Orthopaedic Audio-Synopsis Continuing Education in Orthopaedic. Vol. 8, No. 1 (April 1976)-. Periodical. English. Twelve times a year. $150.00 US & Canada & Mexico; $160.00 Central America & Caribbean; $165.00 Europe & South America; 170.00 other. Orthopaedic Audio Synopsis Foundation, 1510 Oxley Street, Suite B Box H, South Pasadena CA 91031. **Tel** (310)682-1760. **ED** Alice Harri. **DD** 617. **NLM** W1 CO775S. available on audiocassette. **Continues** Orthopaedic Audio-Synopsis.
 **Desc:** Sixty minute audio cassette tape on topics of interest to the Orthopaedic Surgeon.

US/0148-1010
**CONTINUING EDUCATION LECTURES.** [Contin. educ. lect.]. **Main/Corp** Society of Nuclear Medicine. Southeastern Chapter. Academic Scholarly Publication. English. an. $25.00. Society of Nuclear Medicine Southeastern Chapter, 5987 Turpin Hill Drive, Cincinnati OH 45244. **Tel** (513)231-6955. **ED** Vincent J Sodd. **CODEN** CELEDK. Index available. **Ad Acc**. Documents available from CASDDS.
 **Ind/Abst** Chem. Abstr.

●US
**CONTINUING MEDICAL EDUCATION DIRECTORY / AMERICAN MEDICAL ASSOCIATION. See** Encyclopedias and General Reference Books.

US/0891-5059
**CONTRACT HEALTHCARE. Ceased.** [Contract healthc.]. **Added/Corp** Medill School of Journalism. Magazine Publishing Program. **VFOAT** Contract Health Care. (Feb. 1988)-(19??). Periodical. English. Ten times a year. Contract Healthcare, % Fern R Potvin, 1290 Wall Street West, Lyndhurst NJ 07071. **DD** 338.
 **Ind/Abst** Health Plan. Adminis.; Hospit. Health Admin. Index (May,1989-Nov/Dec,1989 L).

US/0886-8220
**CONTRIBUTIONS IN MEDICAL STUDIES.** [Contrib. med. stud.]. No. 16 (1986)-. Monographic series. English. ir. Price varies per volume. Greenwood Press Inc., PO Box 5007, Westport CT 06881-5007. **Tel** (203)226-3571, FAX (203)222-1502. **DD** 610. **NLM** W1; CO778NHE. **Continues** Contributions in Medical History, 0147-1058.

SP/0213-8328
**CONTROL DE CALIDAD ASISTENCIAL. Ceased.** [Control calid. asist.]. **VFOAT** CCA. (1986)-(19??). Periodical. Spanish. qt. Editorial Garsi SA, Juan Bravo 46, 28006 Madrid, Spain. **Tel** 011 34 1 4021212, telex 98358 GARSI E. **UDC** 614.
 **Ind/Abst** Indice Med. Esp.

US/0197-2456
**CONTROLLED CLINICAL TRIALS.** [Control. clin. trials]. **Added/Corp** Society for Clinical Trials (U.S.). Vol. 1 (May 1980)-. Academic Scholarly Publication. English. Six times a year (1 volume). $285.00 US; $325.00 other. Elsevier Science Publishing Company Inc, Madison Square Station, PO Box 882, New York NY 10159-0882. **Tel** (212)633-3950, FAX (212)633-3990. **ED** Curtis L Meinert. **LC** R850.A1; C673. **DD** 616/.0072. **NLM** W1 CO779F. **CODEN** CCLTDH. **[CCC].** **Bk Rev**. **Ad Acc**. **Pr Rev**. **Circ:** 1,750. available on microfilm and microfiche from University Microfilms International (UMI). Documents available from The Genuine Article, ADONIS.
 **Desc:** Provides authoritative coverage of the design, methods and operational aspects of prospective follow-up studies with an emphasis on controlled clinical trials.
 **Ind/Abst** ADONIS; Annals Behav. Med.; Biostatistica; Curr. Aware. Biol. Sci., CABS; Curr. Contents Life Sci.; EMBASE; Health Plan. Adminis.; Index Med. (1980-); Int. Pharm. Abstr.; Oper. Res./Manag. Sci.; Life Sci. Collect.; PESTDOC; Qual. Control Appl. Stat.; Ref. Upd. Deluxe Ed.; Res. Alert [Full Cov.]; Sci. Cit. Index; SCISEARCH; Trop. Dis. Bull.

US/0882-5319
**CONVENTION REPORTER.** [Conv. report.]. English. ir. Physicians World Comm Group, 400 Plaza Drive, Secaucus NJ 07096. **Tel** (201)865-7500. **DD** 610.

US/0749-8055
**CONVULSIVE THERAPY.** [Convuls. ther.]. **VFOAT** Convulsive Ther. Vol. 1, No. 1 (1985)-. Periodical. English. qt. $118.00 (individuals), $210.00 (institutions) US; $155.00 (individuals), $245.00 (institutions) other. Raven Press, 1185 Avenue of the Americas, 37th Floor, New York NY 10036. **Tel** (212)930-9500, (212)930-9604, FAX (212)869-3495, (212)302-8507, telex 640073. **ED** Charles Horn Kellner. **DD** 616. **NLM** W1; CO785. **CODEN** COTHE4. **[CCC].** **Pr Rev**. available on microfilm and microfiche from University Microfilms International (UMI). Documents available from The Genuine Article, BIOSIS Document Express.
 **Desc:** Covers all aspects of contemporary ECT, reporting on major clinical and research developments

worldwide.
**Ind/Abst** Biol. Abstr. (1986-); Curr. Contents Clin. Med.; EMBASE; Psychol. Abstr. (1988-); PsycINFO; PsycLit; Res. Alert [Select. Cov.]; SCISEARCH; Soc. Sci. Cit. Index [Select. Cov.].

US/0192-4842
**COOPERATION (JEFFERSON CITY).** (COOPERATION.). **Added/Corp** Missouri Association of Osteopathic Physicians and Surgeons. Periodical. English. Four times a year. $30.00. Missouri Osteopathic Association, PO Box 748, Jefferson City MO 65102. **Tel** (314)634-3415. **ED** E. H. Borman. **NLM** W1 CO816. **Ad Acc. Circ:** 1,800 (ctrl).
**Desc:** Policy update in health care covering government bills, rules and regulations, new medical trends, scientific and management articles and association news.

NE/0167-8965
**CORE JOURNALS IN CLINICAL PHARMACOLOGY.** **VFOAT** Clinical Pharmacology. Vol. 1, No. 1 (Jan. 1983)-. Academic Scholarly Publication. English. mo. $100.00. Elsevier Science Publishers BV, PO Box 211, 1000 AE Amsterdam Netherlands. **Tel** 011 31 20 5803642, FAX 011 31 20 5862696, telex 15682. **NLM** ZQV 38; C797. **CODEN** CJCPD9.

US/1040-4066
**CORE MEDLINE/EBSCO CD-ROM.** (CORE MEDLINE/EBSCO CD-ROM [COMPUTER FILE].). [Core MEDLINE/Ebsco CD-ROM]. **Added/Corp** National Library of Medicine (U.S.) EBSCO Electronic Information. **VFOAT** Core MEDLINE EBSCO CD ROM; MEDLINE EBSCO CD ROM. (Jan. 1986/Mar. 1988)-. Abstracting/Indexing Service. English. qt. $715.50 US & Canada; $740.15 Far East & Australia; $750.50 other. EBSCO Publishing / Boston, 83 Pine Street, Peabody MA 01960. **Tel** (800)653-2726 North America, (508)535-8500, FAX (508)535-8545. **DD** 610.
**Desc:** Includes over 560 journals which are indexed on one disc. Features include unlimited searching of the MEDLINE data subset; Access of information by author, title, subject, CAS Registry Number, ISSN, keyword, year of publication and journal title; Offers user security with library maintained user files; Will store queries for future search (SDI); Will save search strategies and resultus for future recall, etc.

GW/0070-0347
**CORPUS MEDICORUM GRAECORUM.** **Added/Corp** Deutsche Akademie der Wissenschaften zu Berlin. Akademie der Wissenschaften der DDR. Akademie der Wissenschaften in Berlin (1991-). Vol. 1 (1908)-. Monographic series. Arabic (English, French, German, Greek and Modern, Latin; translations available in Greek, Modern and German, French). Price varies per volume. Akademie-Verlag GmbH, Muehlenstrasse 33 34, D 13162 Berlin Germany. **Tel** 011 49 30 47889300, FAX 011 49 30 47889357. **(Subscription address:** VCH Publishers Inc., 303 Northwest 12th Avenue, Journals Department, Deerfield FL 33442.**)** **LC** R126.A1; C6. **NLM** WZ 292 C816.

SP
**CORREO BACTERIOLOGICO.** Spanish. mo. Lilly Indiana de Espana SA, Paseo de la Industria S/N, 28100 Alcobendas (Madrid) Spain.

IT/0390-8798
**CORRIERE DEL MEDICO.** [Corr. medico]. (1954)-. Periodical. Italian. bw. L90000.00. Techniware, Via A Rizzoli 2, 20132 Milan Italy. **Tel** 011 39 2 58084410. **UDC** 61.

US/0735-6188
**COST EFFECTIVENESS RESOURCE PERSONNEL DIRECTORY.** (COST EFFECTIVENESS RESOURCE PERSONNEL DIRECTORY / AMERICAN MEDICAL ASSOCIATION, DIVISION OF HEALTH SERVICE, DEPARTMENT OF HEALTH CARE FINANCING AND ORGANIZATION.). [Cost eff. resour. pers. dir.]. **Added/Corp** American Medical Association. Dept. of Health Care Financing and Organization. **VFOAT** A.M.A. Cost Effectiveness Resource Personnel Directory; AMA Cost Effectiveness Resource Personnel Directory. (19??)-. Directory. English. $3.00. AMA Department of Health Care and Financing Organization, 535 North Dearborn Street, Chicago IL 60610. **LC** R712.A1; C67. **DD** 610/.68/1.

US/0146-1117
**COUNCIL NOTES - INDIANA FAMILY HEALTH COUNCIL, INC.** (COUNCIL NOTES.). **Main/Corp** Indiana Family Health Council. No. 1- Winter 1977-. Periodical. English. qt. Indiana Family Health Council, 21 Beachway Drive/Suite B, Indianapolis IN 46224. **Tel** (317)247-9151.

FR/0290-5736
**COURRIER DE LA SCLEROSE EN PLAQUES, LE.** (1963)-. Periodical. French. Twice a year (Jan. & Dec.). 70.00F. LFSEP - Secretariat, 17 Bould Auguste Blanqui, 75013 Paris France. **Tel** 011 33 1 40786900, FAX 011 33 1 45894057. **ED** M. Jacques Bonneau. **UDC** 616.8. Index available. cum. index. **Ad Acc. Pr Rev. Circ:** 6,000.
**Desc:** News and information relating to or affecting sclerosis.

US/0590-0301
**COURTROOM MEDICINE.** **See** Law.

US/0886-9634
**CRANIO.** (CRANIO : THE JOURNAL OF CRANIOMANDIBULAR PRACTICE.). [Cranio]. **VFOAT** Journal of Craniomandibular Practice. Vol. 3, No. 1 (Feb. 1985)-. Periodical. English. Four times a year. $55.00 (individual), $97.00 (institutions) US; $75.00 (individual), $117.00 (institutions) other. Chroma Inc., PO Box 8887, Chattanooga TN 37414. **Tel** (800)624-4141. **DD** 616. **NLM** W1; CR115D. **CODEN** CRANEG. **Ad Acc. Pr Rev.** Documents available from The Genuine Article, BIOSIS Document Express. ***Continues** Journal of Cranio-Mandibular Practice, 0734-5410.*
**Desc:** Presents complete coverage of temporomandibular joint study outlining all of the most significant advances in clinical methods, technology, and therapeutics.
**Ind/Abst** Biol. Abstr. (1987-); Curr. Contents Clin. Med.; Curr. Titl. Dent.; Dent. Abstr. (-1991); Health Plan. Adminis.; Index Dent. Lit. (1985-); Res. Alert [Select. Cov.]; SCISEARCH.

US/1050-009X
**CRANIO CLINICS INTERNATIONAL.** [Cranio clin. int.]. Vol. 1, No. 1 (1991)-. Periodical. English. Three times a year. $125.00 (3 volume set). Williams & Wilkins Company, 428 East Preston Street, Baltimore MD 21202-3993. **Tel** (410)528-4000, (800)638-6423, FAX (410)528-8596, telex 87669. **(Subscription address:** Williams & Wilkins, PO Box 64380, Baltimore, MD 21264**)** **DD** 612. **NLM** W1; CR117. Documents available from Quick Copies.

US/0162-7279
**CRANIOFACIAL GROWTH SERIES.** **Added/Corp** University of Michigan. Center for Human Growth and Development. No. 1 (1972)-. Monographic series. English. ir. Price varies per volume. Center of Human Growth and Development, 300 North Ingalls Building, Ann Arbor MI 48106. **Tel** (313)764-2443. **ED** David S. Carlson, James A. McNamara. **LC** UNC. **NLM** W1 CR118. **Circ:** 1,000.
**Desc:** Internationally renowned researchers and clinicians in medicine, anatomy, dentistry, orthodontics and other fields examine important topics in craniofacial biology in this series of monographs.

US/0270-7462
**CRITICAL CARE.** [Crit. care]. **Main/Corp** Society of Critical Care Medicine. (1980)-. English. an. $53.00 US and Canada; $55.00 other. Society of Critical Care Medicine, 8101 East Kaiser Boulevard, Anaheim CA 92808. **Tel** (714)282-6000. **LC** RC86; .S617. **DD** 616/.028. **NLM** W1 CR216D.

●US/1067-9502
**CRITICAL CARE ALERT.** [Crit. care alert]. **Added/Corp** American Health Consultants. Vol. 1, No. 1 (Apr. 1993)-. Periodical. English. mo. $158.00. American Health Consultants, 3525 Piedmont Road, Suite 400, Atlanta GA 30305. **Tel** (800)688-2421, (404)262-7436. **(Subscription address:** American Health Consultants, PO Box 95278, Chicago IL 60694.**)** **DD** 362.

●US/1070-4523
**CRITICAL CARE MANAGEMENT.** (1993)-. Periodical. English. mo. $158.00. American Health Consultants, 3525 Piedmont Road, Suite 400, Atlanta GA 30305. **Tel** (800)688-2421, (404)262-7436. **(Subscription address:** American Health Consultants, PO Box 95278, Chicago IL 60694.**)**

US/0892-3930
**CRITICAL CARE OUTLOOK.** ***Ceased.*** [Crit. care outlook]. Vol. 1, No. 1 (June 1988)-?. Periodical. English. mo (ten issues per year). Quality Medical Publishing, 11970 Borman Drive, Suite 222, St. Louis MO 63146. **Tel** (314)878-7808, (800)423-6865, FAX (314)878-9937. **DD** 610.
**Desc:** Each issues contains valuable information in the areas of ethics, medicine, drug therapy and nursing.

UK/0956-2257
**CRITICAL ISCHAEMIA.** [Crit. ischaem.]. (1989)-. Periodical. English. qt (Mar, June, Sept, Dec). $125.00 US; $115.00 Europe. Cambridge Medical Publications Ltd, Wicker House High Street, Worthing West Sussex, BN11 1DJ England. **Tel** 011 44 903 205884, FAX 011 44 903 34862, telex 878372 PPSLTI. **DD** 616.13. **Ad Acc. Acid Free.**
**Desc:** An international journal covering reviews and comment on all aspects of critical limb ischaemia and peripheral arterial occlusive disease, including pathophysiology, biochemistry, surgery and clinical aspects.

US/0892-0915
**CRITICAL REVIEWS IN NEUROBIOLOGY.** [Crit. rev. neurobiol.]. **VFOAT** CRC Critical Reviews in Neurobiology. **VAT** Chemical Rubber Company Critical Reviews in Neurobiology. Vol. 3 Issue 1 (1987)-. Academic Scholarly Publication. English. qt. $84.00 (individual), $265.00 (institution). Begell House Inc., PO Box 1109, Pearl River NY 10965. **Tel** (212)725-1999. **ED** Charles B. Nemeroff. **LC** RC321; .C73. **DD** 599. **NLM** W1; CR216ZD. **CODEN** CCNBE8. **[CCC].** Documents available from The Genuine Article, BIOSIS Document Express, CASDDS. ***Continues** CRC Critical Reviews in Clinical Neurobiology, 0742-941X.*
**Desc:** Provides up-to-date information from pertinent neurobiological disciplines with particular relevance to clinical neurobiological or psychiatric problems.
**Ind/Abst** Biol. Abstr. (1987-); Chem. Abstr. (1987-); Curr. Aware. Biol. Sci., CABS; Curr. Contents Clin. Med.; EMBASE; Index Med. (1987-); Life Sci. Collect.; Res. Alert [Full Cov.]; Sci. Cit. Index; SCISEARCH; Soc. Sci. Cit. Index [Select. Cov.].

US/0896-2960
**CRITICAL REVIEWS IN PHYSICAL AND REHABILITATION MEDICINE.** **See** Biology-Botany.

CI/0353-9504
**CROATIAN MEDICAL JOURNAL.** [Croat. med. j.]. **VFOAT** CMJ. (1992)-. Periodical. English. qt. **(Subscription address:** Mladost Export Import, PO Box 1028, Ilica 30, 41000 Zagreb Croatia.**)** **UDC** 61. ***Continues** Radovi Medicinskog Fakulteta u Zagrebu, 0033-8575.*
**Ind/Abst** EMBASE [Select. Cov.].

US/1054-4305
**CRYONICS (RIVERSIDE, CALIF.).** (CRYONICS.). [Cryonics]. **Added/Corp** Alcor Life Extension Foundation. (198?)-. Periodical. English. mo. $15.00 US; $20.00 Canada and Mexico; and $25.00 other. Alcor Life Extension Foundation, 7895 East Acoma Drive, Suite 110, Scottsdale AZ 85260. **Tel** (602)922-9013. **DD** 614.

●CN/1193-7343
**CSRO. CANADIAN SPINAL RESEARCH ORGANIZATION.** (CANADIAN SPINAL RESEARCH ORGANIZATION QUARTERLY : CSRO.). [CSRO, Can. Spinal Res. Organ.]. **Added/Corp** Canadian Spinal Research Organization. **VFOAT** CSRO; OCRME; Organisme Canadien de Recherche sur la Moelle Epiniere. **VAT** Canadian Spinal Research Organization. Volume 3, Issue 2 (Summer 1992)-. Periodical. English (French). qt. Free to members. Spinal Cord Society of Canada, 120 Newkirk Road, Unit 32, Richmond Hill, Ontario L4C 9S7 Canada. **Tel** (905)508-4000, 800 361-4004. **DD** 616.8. ***Continues** Spinal Cord Society Canada (Bulletin)., 1184-8472.*

●US/1062-6743
**CTDNEWS (PHILADELPHIA, PA.).** (CTD NEWS.). [CTDnews]. **VFOAT** CTD News. **VAT** Cumulative Trauma Disorder News. (Jan. 1992)-. Periodical. English. Twelve times a year. $110.00 US; $125.00 other. CTDnews Inc., 10 Railroad Street, PO Box 239, Haverford PA 19041. **Tel** (215)896-2770, FAX (215)289-2654. **DD** 616. Index available (published in June and December). cum. index. **Bk Rev. Ad Acc. Circ:** 1,500 (ctrl). available on an online database from NEWSNET.

SP
**CUADERNOS DE BIOESTADISTICA Y SUS APLICACIONES INFORMATICAS.** Spanish. Facultad Medicina Universidad de Zaragoza, Dept Ciencias Morfologicas, E 50009 Zaragoza Spain. **Tel** 011 34 76 359593.

SP
**CUADERNOS FORMACION CONTINUADA. AEFA.** Spanish. ir. Editorial Garsi SA, Juan Bravo 46, 28006 Madrid, Spain. **Tel** 011 34 1 4021212, telex 98358 GARSI E.

SP
**CUADERNOS VALENCIANOS DE HISTORIA DE LA MEDICINA Y DE LA CIENCIA.** **Added/Corp** Instituto de Historia de la Medicina, Valencia. Facultad de Medicina de Valencia. Catedra de Historia de la Medicina. 16 (1975)-. Monographic series. Spanish. ir. Price varies per volume. Instituto Historia de la Medecina, Paseo al Mar, Valencia Spain. **Tel** 96 3690400. **NLM** W1 CU142MA. ***Continues** Cuadernos Hispanicos de Historia de la Medicina Y de la Ciencia.*

US/0090-1377
**CUMULATED ABRIDGED INDEX MEDICUS.** **See** Medical Science and Technology-Abstracting, Bibliographies and Statistics.

US/0090-1423
**CUMULATED INDEX MEDICUS.** **See** Medical Science and Technology-Abstracting, Bibliographies and Statistics.

US/0893-0198
**CURA ANIMARUM.** (CURA ANIMARUM : A JOURNAL FOR THE ADVANCEMENT OF RELIGIOUS CARE OF TROUBLED PERSONS.). **Added/Corp** Association of Mental Health Clergy (U.S.). Vol. 36, No. 1 (May 1984)-. Periodical. English. ir. Association of Mental Health Clergy, 11701 Van Brady Road, Upper Marlboro

# Medical Science and Technology

MD 20772. **Tel** (202)373-7035. **DD** 253. *Continues AMHC Forum, 0883-0401.*
**Ind/Abst** Abstr. Res. Pastor. Care Couns.; Hospit. Health Admin. Index (1984-); Index Book Rev. Relig.; Relig. Index One Period.

NE/0168-6917
**CURRENT CLINICAL PRACTICE SERIES.** [Curr. clin. pract. ser.]. **VFOAT** CCP. (1982)-. Academic Scholarly Publication. English. ir. Price varies per volume. Excerpta Medica Publishing Group, PO Box 548, 1000 AM Amsterdam Netherlands. **Tel** 011 31 20 5803243. **(Subscription address:** Elsevier Science Inc. / New York Books, 655 Avenue of the Americas, New York NY 10010.) **NLM** W1 CU786M. **CODEN** CCPSEZ. **[CCC].** Documents available from CASDDS.
**Ind/Abst** Chem. Abstr.

SP
**CURRENT CONCEPTS IN ONCOLOGY.**
Spanish. ir. Cyanamid, Cristobal Bordiu 35, 28003 Madrid Spain.

US/0891-3358
**CURRENT CONTENTS. CLINICAL MEDICINE.** See Medical Science and Technology-Abstracting, Bibliographies and Statistics.

●US/1073-1237
**CURRENT CONTENTS. CLINICAL MEDICINE (CD-ROM VERSION).** See Medical Science and Technology-Abstracting, Bibliographies and Statistics.

US/1062-3159
**CURRENT CONTENTS ON DISKETTE. CLINICAL MEDICINE.** See Medical Science and Technology-Abstracting, Bibliographies and Statistics.

US/1062-3116
**CURRENT CONTENTS ON DISKETTE WITH ABSTRACTS. CLINICAL MEDICINE.** See Medical Science and Technology-Abstracting, Bibliographies and Statistics.

UK/0968-6053
**CURRENT DIAGNOSTIC PATHOLOGY.**
(19??)-. Periodical. English. Four times a year. £160.00 Europe; £161.00 Other (Institutions). Churchill Livingstone, 1-3 Baxter's Place, Leith Walk, Edinburgh EH1 3AF Scotland. **Tel** 011 44 31 556 2424, FAX 011 44 31 558 1278, telex 727511. **(Subscription address:** Maruzen Company Ltd., PO Box 5050, Import & Export Department, Tokyo 100 31 Japan.)

US/0092-8682
**CURRENT MEDICAL DIAGNOSIS & TREATMENT.** [Curr. med. diagn. treat.]. **VAT** Current Medical Diagnosis and Treatment. (1974)-. English. an. $41.95. Appleton Century Crofts, Prentice Hall, 200 Old Tappan Road, Old Tappan NJ 07675. **Tel** (201)767-5188, (800)922-0579. **ED** Marcus A. Krupp, Milton J. Chatton and Lawrence M. Tierney, Jr. **LC** RC71; .A14. **DD** 616.07/5/05. **NLM** W1 CU788M. *Continues Current Diagnosis & Treatment.*
**Desc:** Provides useful and comprehensive information on currently accepted methods of diagnosis and treatment of medical diseases and disorders.

UK/0269-185X
**CURRENT MEDICAL LITERATURE. GROWTH AND GROWTH FACTORS.**
[Curr. med. lit., Growth growth factors]. (1986)-. Periodical. English. qt. £20.00 UK; $40.00 other. Current Medical Literature Ltd., 40-42 Osnaburgh Street, London NW1 3ND England. **Tel** 011 44 71 4658377, FAX 011 44 71 4658380. **(Subscription address:** Royal Society Medicine Services, 1 Wimpole Street, London W1M 8AE England.) **DD** 016.6126.

UK/0300-7995
**CURRENT MEDICAL RESEARCH AND OPINION.** [Curr. med. res. opin.]. Vol. 1 (1972)-. Academic Scholarly Publication. English. Ten times a year. £100.00. Clayton-Wray Publishers Ltd., 1A High Street, Alton Hants GU34 1BA England. **Tel** 011 44 420 87293. **NLM** W1 CU794. **CODEN** CMROCX. **Pr Rev.** available on microfilm and microfiche from University Microfilms International (UMI). Documents available from The Genuine Article, CASDDS.
**Ind/Abst** Chem. Abstr.; Curr. Contents Clin. Med.; EMBASE; Health Plan. Adminis.; Index Med.; Int. Pharm. Abstr.; Nutr. Res. Newsl.; Life Sci. Collect.; PESTDOC; Res. Alert [Full Cov.]; Rev. Med. Vet. Mycology; Sci. Cit. Index; SCISEARCH; Trop. Dis. Bull.

UK/0141-9951
**CURRENT MEDICAL RESEARCH AND OPINION SUPPLEMENT.** [Curr. med. res. opin. Suppl.]. (1975)-. Monographic series. English. ir. Price varies per volume. Clayton-Wray Publishers Ltd., 1A High Street, Alton Hants GU34 1BA England. **Tel** 011 44 420 87293.
**Ind/Abst** EMBASE.

US/0734-9939
**CURRENT MEDICINE.** [Curr. med.]. Vol. 1 (1983)-. Periodical. English. ir. John Wiley & Sons, Inc., 605 Third Avenue, New York NY 10158-0012. **Tel** (212)850-6000, (212)850-6645, FAX (212)850-6088, telex 12-7063. **(Subscription address:** John Wiley & Sons / England, Baffins Lane, Chichester, West Sussex PO19 1UD England.) **ED** Gary L Gitnick. **LC** R11; .C873. **DD** 616/.005. **NLM** W1 CU796F.

●UK/1070-5295
**CURRENT OPINION IN CRITICAL CARE.**
(1994)-. Periodical. English. bm (6 issues). $259.95 (institutions); $129.95 (individuals). Current Science / England, Middlesex House, 34-42 Cleveland Street, London W1P 5FB England. **Tel** 011 44 71 580 8393, 011 44 71 323 0323, FAX 011 44 81 580 1938. **(Subscription address:** Current Science, 20 North 3rd Street, Philadelphia PA 19106.)

●US/1070-5287
**CURRENT OPINION IN PULMONARY MEDICINE.** (1994)-. Periodical. English. Six times a year. $129.95 (individuals); $259.95 (institutions). Current Science / England, Middlesex House, 34-42 Cleveland Street, London W1P 5FB England. **Tel** 011 44 71 580 8393, 011 44 71 323 0323, FAX 011 44 81 580 1938. **(Subscription address:** Current Science, 20 North 3rd Street, Philadelphia PA 19106.)

US
**CURRENT OPINION IN THERAPEUTIC PATENTS.** English. mo. £2675.00 UK; $5000.00 other. Current Patents Ltd, 34-42 Cleveland Street, London W1P 5FB England. **Tel** 011 44 71 323 0323.

UK
**CURRENT PROBLEMS / COMMITTEE ON SAFETY OF MEDICINES.** **Added/Corp** Great Britain. Committee on Safety of Medicines. No. 1 (Sept. 1975)-. Periodical. English. Three times a year. Free on request to qualified subscribers. Committee on Safety of Medicine, Market Towers, 1 Nine Elms Lane, London SW8 5NQ United Kingdom. **Tel** 011 44 71 2730451. **NLM** W1; CU8033L.
**Ind/Abst** Trop. Dis. Bull.

●US/1068-2252
**CURRENT REVIEW OF CEREBROVASCULAR DISEASE.** [Curr. rev. cerebrovasc. dis.]. 1st Edition (1993)-. English. an (Dec.). $99.95. Current Science, 20 North 3rd Street, Philadelphia PA 19106. **Tel** (215)574-2266, (800)552-5866, FAX (215)574-2270. **DD** 616.

●US/1072-8392
**CURRENT REVIEW OF MAGNETIC RESONANCE IMAGING.** (1994)-. English. Current Science, 20 North 3rd Street, Philadelphia PA 19106. **Tel** (215)574-2266, (800)552-5866, FAX (215)574-2270.

●US/1069-5850
**CURRENT REVIEW OF PAIN.** (1994)-. Periodical. English. an. $103.45 US & Canada; $114.95 Mexico, South & Central America. Current Science, 20 North 3rd Street, Philadelphia PA 19106. **Tel** (215)574-2266, (800)552-5866, FAX (215)574-2270.

US/0167-7209
**CURRENT REVIEWS IN BIOMEDICINE.**
[Curr. rev. biomed.]. 1-. Academic Scholarly Publication. English. Price varies per volume. Elsevier Science Publishing Company Inc, Madison Square Station, PO Box 882, New York NY 10159-0882. **Tel** (212)633-3950, FAX (212)633-3990. **NLM** W1 CU8093L. **CODEN** CRBID5. Documents available from CASDDS.
**Ind/Abst** Chem. Abstr.

US/0011-393X
**CURRENT THERAPEUTIC RESEARCH.**
See Pharmacy and Pharmacology.

US/0893-763X
**CURRENT THERAPY NEWSLETTER.**
[Curr. ther. newsl.]. Vol. 1, No. 1 (1987)-. Periodical. English. Six times a year. $150.00. Current Therapy, 4873 Dogwood Avenue, Seal Beach CA 90740. **Tel** (310)594-8737. **ED** Ellyn Siegal Edelman. **DD** 616. **NLM** W1; CU819TH. ctrl circ.

US/0732-4448
**CURRENT TOPICS IN CHINESE SCIENCE. SECTION G, MEDICAL SCIENCE.** [Curr. top. Chin. sci., Sect. G, Med. sci.]. **VFOAT** Medical Science. Vol. 1 (1982)-. English. an. Gordon & Breach Science Publishers, Inc., PO Box 786, Cooper Station, New York NY 10276. **Tel** (212)206-8900, FAX (212)645-2459. **(Subscription address:** International Publishers Distributor at one of the following addresses: 820 Town Center Drive, Langhorne, PA 19047; or PO Box 90, Reading Berkshire RG1 8JL UK; or Kent Ridge PO Box 1180, Singapore 9111, Republic of Singapore) **LC** R97. **DD** 610/.5. **NLM** W1; CU82DR.

**CODEN** CGMSDD. Documents available from BIOSIS Document Express.
**Ind/Abst** Biol. Abstr. (-1982).

UK/0011-3999
**CURRENT WORK IN THE HISTORY OF MEDICINE.** **Added/Corp** Wellcome Institute for the History of Medicine. Wellcome Historical Medical Library. No. 1 (Jan./Mar. 1954)-. Periodical. English. qt. £33.00. Professional & Scientific Publishers, Tavistock House, East Tavistock Square, London WC1H 9JR England. **Tel** 011 44 71 387-4499, telex 005311. **(Subscription address:** Professional & Scientific Publishers, PO Box 294, London WC1H 9TB England.) **LC** R131.A1; C8. **DD** 610; 016.
**Desc:** A bibliographic register of articles and books in all languages, and their authors, this is an indispensable companion for those concerned with any aspect of the subject.

US/8750-8699
**CURRENTS IN AFFECTIVE ILLNESS.** See Psychology.

US
**CUTTING EDGE - AMERICAN MEDICAL RECORDS ASSOCIATION.** English. qt. $100.00. American Health Information Management Association, Order Unit, PO Box 67349, Chicago IL 60690-7349. **Tel** (312) 787-2672, FAX (312) 787-5926, (312) 787-9793.

US/0070-2455
**CYSTIC FIBROSIS CLUB ABSTRACTS.**
[Cyst. Fibros. Club abstr.]. **Main/Corp** Cystic Fibrosis Club. Meeting. **Added/Corp** Cystic Fibrosis Foundation. National Cystic Fibrosis Research Foundation (U.S.). No. 3 (1962)-. Academic Scholarly Publication. English. an. Cystic Fibrosis Foundation, 6000 Executive Blvd., Suite 309, Rockville MD 20852. **Tel** (301)881-9130. **DD** 616.3. **NLM** W1 CY751.
**Ind/Abst** EMBASE.

US
**CYSTIC FIBROSIS (NATIONAL INSTITUTE OF ARTHRITIS, DIABETES, AND DIGESTIVE AND KIDNEY DISEASES (U.S.)).** (CYSTIC FIBROSIS.). **VFOAT** NIADDK Research Advances. English. an. National Institutes of Health, 9000 Rockville Pike, Bethesda MD 20014. **Tel** (301)496-6975. **NLM** W1; CY749. *Continues National Institute of Arthritis, Metabolism, and Digestive Diseases (U.S.).*

UK/0268-1625
**CYTOSKELETON SHEFFIELD.**
(CYTOSKELETON.). [Cytoskeleton Sheff.]. (1986)-. English. mo. £105.00. SUBIS, Mansion House, 19 Kingfield Road, Sheffield S11 9AS England. **Tel** 011 44 114 255 4433, FAX 011 44 114 255 4626. **DD** 016.5748734. **[CCC].**

US/0731-4027
**D-J-M ENZYME REPORT.** *Title Change.* See Biology.

US/0011-586X
**DALLAS MEDICAL JOURNAL.** [Dallas med. j.]. **Added/Corp** Dallas County Medical Society (Tex.). (1901)-. Periodical. English. mo. $36.00 US, Canada, and Mexico; $50.00 other. Dallas County Medical Society, PO Box 4680 Station A, Dallas TX 75208-0680. **Tel** (214)948-3622. **ED** Linda C. Chandler. **DD** 610. **NLM** W1 DA353. **Ad Acc. Pr Rev. Circ:** 4,400 (ctrl).
**Desc:** News, announcements, and articles of socioeconomic and clinical interest.

CH/0258-3291
**DANGDAI YIXUE.** (TANG TAI I HSUEN.). [Dangdai yixue]. **VFOAT** Medicine Today. No. 1- 1973-. Periodical. Chinese. mo. **ED** Y F Liao and C H Chou. **LC** R97.7.C5; T36. **NLM** W1 TA5398I.

DK/0011-6092
**DANISH MEDICAL BULLETIN.** *Ceased.*
[Dan. med. bull.]. **Added/Corp** Almindelige Danske Lgeforening. Denmark. Sundhedsstyrelsen. Kbenhavns Universitet. Medicinske Fakultet. Kbenhavns Universitet. Lgevidenskabelige Fakultet. Aarhus Universitet. Lgevidenskabelige Fakultet. Odense Universitet. Lgevidenskabelige Fakultet. **VFOAT** DMB. Vol. 1, No. 1 (Mar. 1954)-Series complete. English (summaries and/or abstracts in Interlingua). ir. Den Almindelige Danske, Laegeforening Esplanaden 8A, 1263 Copenhagen K Denmark. **Tel** 011 45 31 385500. **ED** Erik Juhl and John Christiansen. **DD** 610. **NLM** W1 DA545. **CODEN** DMBUAE. Index available. **Ad Acc. Pr Rev. Circ:** 5,200. available on microfilm and microfiche from University Microfilms International (UMI). Documents available from The Genuine Article, BIOSIS Document Express, CASDDS.
**Desc:** Scientific publication.
**Ind/Abst** Biol. Abstr. (1988-); Chem. Abstr.; Curr. Aware. Biol. Sci.; CABS; Curr. Contents Clin. Med.; Curr. Contents Life Sci.; Curr. Titl. Abstr.; Dairy Sci. Abstr.; EMBASE; Health Plan. Adminis.; Hum. Rights Intern. Rep.; Immunol. Abstr.; Index Med.; Nutr. Abstr. Rev., Ser. B, Live Feeds and Feed.; Nutr. Abstr. Rev., Ser. A, Hum.

Exp.; Nutr. Res. Newsl.; Life Sci. Collect.; Pollut. Abstr. Indexes; Ref. Upd. Deluxe Ed.; Res. Alert [Full Cov.]; Rural Dev. Abstr.; Sci. Cit. Index; SCISEARCH; Soc. Sci. Cit. Index [Select. Cov.]; Trop. Dis. Bull.

US/0735-3863
**DATA PROCESSING AUDITING REPORT.** ***Ceased.*** (DATA PROCESSING AUDITING REPORT : DPAR.). [Data process. audit. rep.]. **VFOAT** DPAR; D.P.A.R. (1983)-(Nov. 1986). Periodical. English. mo. John Wiley & Sons, Inc., 605 Third Avenue, New York NY 10158-0012. **Tel** (212)850-6000, (212)850-6645, FAX (212)850-6088, telex 12-7063. **(Subscription address:** John Wiley & Sons / England, Baffins Lane, Chichester, West Sussex PO19 1UD England.) **ED** Michael Strober. **[CCC]. Bk Rev.**
**Desc:** Investigation of a broad range of eating disorders. Articles from biomedical and the behavioral sciences.

CN/1180-5358
**DECISIONS - MEDICAL RESEARCH COUNCIL (CANADA).** (DECISIONS.). [Decis. - Med. Res. Counc.]. **Main/Corp** Medical Research Council (Canada). **VFOAT** Decisions. **VAT** Decisions - Conseil de Recherches Medicales (Canada). Vol. 1, No. 1 (June 1990)-. Periodical. English (French). **DD** 354.710084/1/05.

US/0898-1655
**DECUBITUS (CHICAGO, ILL.).** ***Title Change.*** (DECUBITUS.). [Decubitus]. Vol. 1, No. 1 (Feb. 1988)-Vol. 6, No. 6 (Nov. 1993). Periodical. English. bm. SPRINGHOUSE, 103 North Second Street/Suite 200, Dundee IL 60118. **Tel** (708)426-6100, (800)621-4432. **DD** 616. **NLM** W1; DE111C. **[CCC]. Pr Rev.** ***Continued by*** *Advances in Wound Care.*
**Desc:** The resource for all healthcare professionals interested in prevention and treatment of pressure ulcers, containing the latest information in the pressure ulcer field.
**Ind/Abst** Cumul. Index Nurs. Allied Health Lit.; Health Plan. Adminis.; Int. Nurs. Index (Vol. 1 No. 1, 1988-?).

US/0011-7781
**DELAWARE MEDICAL JOURNAL.** [Del. med. j.]. **Added/Corp** Medical Society of Delaware. Vol. 32, No. 2 (Feb. 1960)-. Periodical. English. Twelve times a year. $20.00. Medical Society of Delaware, 1925 Lovering Avenue, Wilmington DE 19806. **Tel** (302)658-3957. **ED** E. Wayne Martz M.D. **NLM** W1 DE1234. Index available (Bound in 12th issue). cum. index. **Bk Rev**, (Qty: 4). **Ad Acc. Pr Rev. Circ:** 1,600. available on microfilm and microfiche from University Microfilms International (UMI). ***Continues*** *Delaware State Medical Journal, 0092-7295.*
**Desc:** Exists to reflect and promote the public perception of the medical profession, and to provide educational material related to scientific medicine. Its practice and to keep members of the profession informed of the trends, changes, and directions in medicine practice.
**Ind/Abst** Energy Res. Abstr.; Health Plan. Adminis.; Index Med.; INIS Atomindex [Micro.]; Life Sci. Collect.; SportSearch.

JA
**DENSHI IGAKU / MEDICAL ELECTRONICS.** [Denshi igaku]. **Added/Corp** Denpa Jikkensha. **VFOAT** Medical Electronics. (1966)-. Academic Scholarly Publication. Japanese. Denpa Jikkensha, 15-4 Shimouma 6-chome, Setagaya-ku Tokyo 154 Japan. **CODEN** DEIGDM. Documents available from CASDDS.
**Ind/Abst** Chem. Abstr.

FR
**DEPENSES OBLIGATOIRES DE SANTE, STATISTIQUES DEPARTEMENTALES / MINISTERE DE LA SANTE ET DE LA SECURITE SOCIALE, DIRECTION GENERALE DE LA SANTE, BUREAU DES AFFAIRES GENERALES, LES.** **Added/Corp** France. Direction Generale de la Sante. Bureau des Affaires Generales. (19??)-. French. **LC** RA410.55.F8; D46. **DD** 338.4/33621/0944021.

NE
**DERMATO SELECTIEF. See** Science and Technology.

US/0098-471X
**DETROIT MEDICAL NEWS. Added/Corp** Wayne County Medical Society, Detroit. Vol. 25 (Sept. 5, 1933)-. Periodical. English. wk. $40.00. Wayne County Medical Society, 1010 Antietam, Detroit MI 48207. **Tel** (313)567-1640, FAX (313)567-2065. **ED** Susan Adelman, MD. **NLM** W1 DE533. **Ad Acc. Circ:** 4,000. ***Continues*** *Wayne County Medical Society. Bulletin.*
**Desc:** Contains reports of the activities of the Wayne County Medical Society as well as state and AMA news.

●US/1058-2797
**DETWILER DIRECTORY OF MEDICAL MARKET SOURCES, THE.** [Detwiler dir. med. mark. sources]. (1992)-. Directory. English. an. $195.00. SM Detwiler & Associates, Inc., PO Box 15308, Fort Wayne IN 46885. **Tel** (219)749-6534. **DD** 610.

GW/0178-3351
**DEUTSCHE MEDIZIN.** Four times a year. DM98.00. Springer-Verlag GmbH & Company KG, Heidelberger Platz 3, D 14197 Berlin Germany. **Tel** 011 49 30 8207223, FAX 011 49 30 8214091, telex 183 319 SPBLN D. **(Subscription address:** Springer Verlag New York Inc. / for North America, 44 Hartz Way, Secaucus NJ 07096.) **[CCC].**

GW/0012-0472
**DEUTSCHE MEDIZINISCHE WOCHENSCHRIFT.** [Dtsch. med. Wochenschr.]. **VFOAT** German Medical Monthly; DMW, Deutsche Medizinische Wochenschrift. **VAT** DMW. Vol. 1, (Sept 25, 1875)-. Academic Scholarly Publication. German (summaries and/or abstracts in English and Spanish). wk. $266.00. Georg Thieme Verlag Stuttgart, Postfach 301120, D 70451 Stuttgart Germany. **Tel** 011 49 711 89310, FAX 011 49 711 8931298, telex 7 252 275 GTVD. **(Subscription address:** Thieme Medical Publishers Inc., 381 Park Avenue South, New York NY 10016.) **NLM** W1 DE758. **CODEN** DMWOAXDDMWDF. **[CCC].** Index Available, published separately, free-automatically sent. **Pr Rev.** available on microfilm and microfiche from University Microfilms International (UMI). Documents available from The Genuine Article, BIOSIS Document Express, CASDDS, ADONIS.
**Ind/Abst** ADONIS; Biol. Abstr. (1980-); Chem. Abstr.; Curr. Contents Clin. Med.; Curr. Contents Life Sci.; Dairy Sci. Abstr.; EMBASE; Health Plan. Adminis.; Helminthol. Abstr. (19??-19??); Index Med.; Index Vet.; NAPRALERT; Nutr. Abstr. Rev., Ser. B, Live Feeds and Feed.; Nutr. Abstr. Rev., Ser. A, Hum. Exp.; Life Sci. Collect.; PESTDOC; Pig News Inf.; Protozoolog. Abstr.; Res. Alert [Full Cov.]; Rev. Med. Vet. Entomol.; Rev. Med. Vet. Mycology; Saf. Health Work; Sci. Cit. Index; SCISEARCH; Soc. Sci. Cit. Index [Select. Cov.]; SportSearch; Trop. Dis. Bull.

GW
**DEUTSCHE ZEITSCHRIFT FUER AKUPUNKTUR : DZA. Added/Corp** Osterreichische Gesellschaft fuer Akupunktur und Auriculotherapie. Forschungsgemeinschaft fuer Akupunktur (Germany) Gesellschaft der Arzte fuer Erfahrungsheilkunde (Germany). **VFOAT** DZA. (1977)-. Periodical. German (summaries and/or abstracts in English). bm. Karl F Haug Verlag GmbH and Company, Postfach 102840, D 69018 Heidelberg Germany. **Tel** 011 49 6221 40620. **NLM** W1; DE894. ***Continued in part by*** *Akupunturarzt, Aurikulotherapeut.*
**Ind/Abst** EMBASE.

GW/0012-1207
**DEUTSCHES ARZTEBLATT.** (1872)-. Periodical. German. wk (Thurs.). DM502.99 Germany; DM642.20 other. Deutscher Aerzte Verlag GmbH, Postfach 404265, D-50832 Cologne Germany. **Tel** 011 49 2234 7011219. **Bk Rev. Ad Acc. Circ:** 210,000 (ctrl).
**Desc:** Contains updates on current research in the medical field, continuing education opportunities, health, career policies and commentaries.

GW/0176-3695
**DEUTSCHES ARZTEBLATT AUSG. C.** (19??)-. Periodical. German. wk. DM483.00 Germany; DM561.00 other. Deutscher Aerzte Verlag GmbH, Postfach 404265, D-50832 Cologne Germany. **Tel** 011 49 2234 7011219. **UDC** 61.

US/8756-5641
**DEVELOPMENTAL NEUROPSYCHOLOGY.** [Dev. neuropsychol.]. Vol. 1, No. 1 (1985)-. Periodical. English. qt. $195.00 US & Canada; $220.00 other. Lawrence Erlbaum Associates, 365 Broadway, Suite 102, Hillsdale NJ 07642. **Tel** (201)666-4110, (800)926-6579, FAX (201)666-2394. **ED** Francis J Pirozzolo. **LC** WMLC 93/1384. **DD** 618. **NLM** W1; DE997UE. **CODEN** DENEE8. **Ad Acc. Pr Rev.** available on microfilm and microfiche from University Microfilms International (UMI). Documents available from The Genuine Article, BIOSIS Document Express.
**Ind/Abst** Biol. Abstr. (1986-); Curr. Contents Soc. Behav. Sci.; Dev. Med. Child Neurol.; Psychol. Abstr. (1985-); PsycINFO; PsycLit; Res. Alert [Full Cov.]; Soc. Sci. Cit. Index [Full Cov.].

SZ
**DEVENIR.** French. qt. 118.00F institution; 86.00 individual. Medecine et Hygiene, Case Postale 456, CH-1211 Geneve 4 Switzerland. **Tel** 011 41 22 3469355, 011 41 22 3469356. Index available. **Bk Rev. Ad Acc.**
**Desc:** European review on child development.

US/0273-3137
**DEVICE TECHNIQUES.** [Device tech.]. 1980. Periodical. English. bm. DEVTEQ, PO Box 3175, Walnut Creek CA 94598. **Tel** (510)945-0137. **ED** Marvin Shepherd. **Circ:** 300.
**Desc:** Practical guidelines in the safe and proper use of medical devices for nurses and engineers.

US/0098-7573
**DEVICES & DIAGNOSTICS LETTER. VAT** Devices and Diagnostics Letter. Vol. 1 (Nov. 15, 1974)-. Periodical. English. Fifty-one times per year (published weekly except last week of Dec.). $717.00 US, Canada and Mexico; $792.00 other. Washington Business Information Inc., 1117 North 19th Street, Suite 200, Arlington VA 22209. **Tel** (703)247-3433, (800)426-0416, FAX (703)247-3421. **ED** Joe Wilcox. **NLM** W1 DE9992. **[CCC].** available on an online database (file 158/Full-Text) from DIALOG.
**Desc:** For executives concerned with government regulation of medical devices and in vitro diagnostic products.

AG/0012-1762
**DIA MEDICO, EL. VFOAT** Dia Medico. Aniversario. Vol. 1 (Aug. 6, 1928)-. Periodical. Spanish. Eleven times a year. Marcelo Cristian Repetto, Calle Tucman 2012 40, Piso 1050 Capital Federal Argentina. **NLM** W1 DI132.

NE
**DIABC.** Dutch. mo. Diabetes Ver Nederland, Postbus 933, 3800 AX Amersfoort Netherlands. **Tel** 011 31 033 630566.

UK/0263-7294
**DIABETES MELLITUS.** [Diabetes mellitus]. (1983)-. English. mo. £105.00. SUBIS, Mansion House, 19 Kingfield Road, Sheffield S11 9AS England. **Tel** 011 44 114 255 4433, FAX 011 44 114 255 4626. **DD** 016.616462.

GW/0178-8345
**DIAGNOSE & LABOR.** [Diagn. & Labor]. **VFOAT** Diagnose und Labor. (Mar. 1985)-. Periodical. German. Four times a year. DM28.00 Germany; DM36.00 others. Medizinish Verlagsgesellschaft, PO Box 1732, W 3550 Marburg F.R.Germany. **Tel** 011 49 6421 22230. **NLM** W1; DI23. **CODEN** DILAEE. Documents available from BIOSIS Document Express, CASDDS. ***Continues*** *Laboratoriumsblaetter, 0023-673X.*
**Ind/Abst** Biol. Abstr.; Chem. Abstr.

IT/1120-7108
**DIAGNOSIS MILANO.** ***Ceased.*** [Diagnosis Milano]. (19??)-(Dec. 1993). Periodical. Italian. qt. Masson S.P.A, Via Statuto 2/4, 20121 Milan Italy. **Tel** 011 39 2 63671, FAX 011 39 2 6367211. **UDC** 616.

US/0163-3228
**DIAGNOSIS (ORADELL, N.J.).** ***Ceased.*** (DIAGNOSIS.). [Diagnosis]. (March/April 1979)-(Jan. 1989). Periodical. English. mo. Medical Economics Data, Five Paragon Drive, PO Box 27, Montvale NJ 07645. **Tel** (800)442-6657, (201)358-7200. **ED** Harry Atkins. **LC** RC71; .A142. **DD** 616.07/05. **NLM** W1 DI258B. **[CCC]. Ad Acc. Circ:** 100,000 (ctrl).
**Desc:** Serves primary care physicians; focus is on the diagnostic process - history taking, physical examination, therapeutic trials, laboratory tests, x-ray, ECG and other modalities that led to swift and accurate diagnosis on detection of disease.

●SZ/1070-3608
**DIAGNOSTIC AND THERAPEUTIC ENDOSCOPY.** (1994)-. Periodical. English. ir. Gordon & Breach Science Publishers, PO Box 90, Reading RG1 8JL England. **Tel** 011 44 734 560080, FAX 011 44 734 568211. **(Subscription address:** International Publishers Distributor at one of the following addresses: 820 Town Center Drive, Langhorne, PA 19047; or PO Box 90, Reading Berkshire RG1 8JL UK; or Kent Ridge PO Box 1180, Singapore 9111, Republic of Singapore)

US/0198-6627
**DIAGNOSTIC DIALOG. See** Chemistry.

US/1054-9609
**DIAGNOSTICS INTELLIGENCE.** (DIAGNOSTICS INTELLIGENCE : MONTHLY INTELLIGENCE FOR THE MEDICAL DIAGNOSTIC INDUSTRY.). [Diagn. intell.]. (1989)-. Periodical. English. mo. $414.00 US & Canada; $434.00 other. CTB International Publishing Inc., PO Box 218, Maplewood NJ 07040. **Tel** (201)379-7749, FAX (201)379-1158. **DD** 338. **[CCC].**

GW/0340-5680
**DIAGNOSTIK.** [Diagnostik]. Academic Scholarly Publication. German. Georg Thieme Verlag Stuttgart, Postfach 301120, D 70451 Stuttgart Germany. **Tel** 011 49 711 89310, FAX 011 49 711 8931298, telex 7 252 275 GTVD. **(Subscription address:** Thieme Medical Publishers Inc., 381 Park Avenue South, New York NY 10016.) **NLM** W1 DI259AF. **CODEN** DGNKA2. Documents available from CASDDS.
**Ind/Abst** Chem. Abstr.; EMBASE; SportSearch.

PL/0012-1932
**DIAGNOSTYKJA LABORATORYJNA.** (DIAGNOSTYKA LABORATORYJNA / POLSKIE TOWARZYSTWO DIAGNOSTYKI LABORATORYJNEJ.). [Diagn. lab.]. **Added/Corp** Polskie Towarzystwo Diagnostyki Laboratoryjnej. (19??)-. Periodical. Polish (summaries and/or abstracts in English and Russian). Four times a year. Price on Request. **(Subscription address:** ARS Polona, PO Box 1001, 00068 Warsaw Poland.) **CODEN** DLJNAQ. Documents available from CASDDS.
**Ind/Abst** Chem. Abstr.

# Medical Science and Technology

**US/0090-2934**
**DIALYSIS & TRANSPLANTATION.** [Dial. transplant.]. **VAT** Dialysis and Transplantation. Vol. 1 (Apr./May 1972)-. Academic Scholarly Publication. English. mo. $60.00 (one year), $115.00 (two year), $165.00 (three year) surface mail; $105.00 (one year), $205.00 (two year), $300.00 (three year) airmail. Creative Age Publications, 7628 Densmore Avenue, Van Nuys CA 91406. **Tel** (800)624-4196. **ED** Dan Gordon and Barbara Feiner. **NLM** W1 DI261N. **CODEN** DITRD2. Index available. cum. index. **Bk Rev. Ad Acc. Pr Rev. Circ:** 18,000 (ctrl). Documents available from The Genuine Article, BIOSIS Document Express, CASDDS.
 **Desc:** Technical articles report on development and technical aspects of new procedures, techniques, equipment, materials, processes and systems.
 **Ind/Abst** Biol. Abstr.; Chem. Abstr. (1972-1983); Curr. Contents Clin. Med.; EMBASE; Health Devices Alerts; Nutr. Abstr. Rev., Ser. B, Live Feeds and Feed.; Nutr. Abstr. Rev., Ser. A, Hum. Exp.; Life Sci. Collect.; Res. Alert [Select. Cov.]; SCISEARCH.

SP
**DIARIO DE CONGRESOS MEDICOS.**
Spanish. Ediciones Doyma SA, Travesera de Gracia 17 21, 08021 Barcelona Spain. **Tel** 011 34 3 2000711, 011 34 3 4145706, FAX 011 34 3 2091136, telex 51964 INK E.

**US/0415-8407**
**DIGEST OF CHIROPRACTIC ECONOMICS, THE. VFOAT** Chiropractic Economics. (19??)-. Periodical. English. bm. $27.00 US and Mexico; $29.00 Canada; $40.00 other. Chiropractic News Publishing Corporation, 29229 West 6 Mile Road, Livonia MI 48152. **Tel** (313)427-5720, FAX (313)427-2760. **ED** Keith Tosolt. **NLM** W1 DI539. **Bk Rev. Ad Acc. Circ:** 41,200 (ctrl).
 **Desc:** Topics of interest to chiropractors including techniques, finances, business management, books, nutrition, and sports injuries.

**US/0732-7498**
**DIRECTIONS (KANSAS CITY, MO.).**
(DIRECTIONS / MID-WEST HEALTH CONGRESS.). Vol. 1, No. 1 (Jan./Feb./Mar. 1982)-. Periodical. English. qt. $12.00. Mid-West Health Congress, 729 E 70, Kansas City MO 64131.

**US/0543-2774**
**DIRECTORY. See** Library and Information Sciences.

**US/0732-3468**
**DIRECTORY / AAMC GROUP ON MEDICAL EDUCATION.** [Dir. - AAMC Group Med. Educ.]. **Main/Corp** AAMC Group on Medical Education. **VAT** Directory - Association of American Medical Colleges Group on Medical Education. 1981-1982-. Directory. English. AAMC Group on Medical Education, One Dupont Circle NW/Suite 200, Washington DC 20036. **LC** R735.A4; A23A. **DD** 610/.7/1173. **Continues** AAMC Group on Medical Education. Membership Roster.

US
**DIRECTORY, AVIATION MEDICAL EXAMINERS. VFOAT** Aviation Medical Examiners. Government Publication. English. US Department of Transportation / Federal Aviation Administration, 800 Independence Avenue Southwest, Washington DC 20591. **Tel** (202)367-3484, FAX (202)367-3505. **NLM** W 22 AA1 D4.

**US/0883-5330**
**DIRECTORY OF BIOMEDICAL AND HEALTH CARE GRANTS.** [Dir. biomed. heal. care grants]. (1985)-. Directory. English. an. $84.50 North America; $101.40 other. Oryx Press, 4041 North Central Avenue, #700, Phoenix AZ 85012-3397. **Tel** (800)279-ORYX, (602)265-2651, FAX (602)265-6250, (800)279-4663, (800)279-6799. **(Subscription address:** Eurospan Ltd., Journals and Serials Division, 3 Henrietta Street, Covent Garden, London WC2E 8LU England.**) LC** R850.A1; D57. **DD** 610/.79. **NLM** W 22; AA1 D55.
 **Desc:** Provides up-to-date information on nearly 3,000 funding sources. Listings span the spectrum of financial support from corporate, foundation, and professional associations to federal and local governments.

US
**DIRECTORY OF BIOMEDICAL ETHICS ORGANIZATIONS / AHA. Added/Corp** American Hospital Association. (1989)-. English. an. American Hospital Association, 840 North Lake Shore Drive, Chicago IL 60611. **Tel** (312)280-6000, (800)242-2626.

**US/0161-5793**
**DIRECTORY OF CLINICAL FELLOWSHIPS IN MEDICINE : UNITED STATES AND CANADA.** Directory. English. $12.00. Graduate Publications, PO Box 6610, Ventura CA 93003. **LC** R840; .D57. **DD** 610/.7/9.

**US/0149-3760**
**DIRECTORY OF DOCTORS OF OSTEOPATHY LICENSED AND REGISTERED IN TENNESSEE.** 1976-. Directory. English. State Licensing Board for the Healing Arts, TDPH State Office Building, Ben Allen Road, Nashville TN 37216. **LC** RZ333; .D55. **DD** 615/.533/025768. **NLM** WB 22 AT2 D53. **Continues** Directory of Doctors of Osteopathy Licensed in Tennessee.
 **Desc:** Contains State Licensing Board for the Healing Arts act, and Osteopathic Practice Act.

**US/0744-0804**
**DIRECTORY OF FEDERAL HEALTH/MEDICINE GRANTS AND CONTRACTS PROGRAMS.** [Dir. Fed. health/med. grants contracts programs]. **VAT** Directory of Federal Health Medicine Grants and Contracts Programs. 1st- Ed.; 1979-. Directory. English. Science & Health Publications Inc, 10000 Falls Road/Suite 306, Potomac MD 20850. **LC** RA440; .D57. **DD** 610/.79. **NLM** W 22 AA1 D58.

**US/0892-0109**
**DIRECTORY OF GRADUATE MEDICAL EDUCATION PROGRAMS. Title Change.** [Dir. grad. med. educ. programs]. **Added/Corp** American Medical Association. Accreditation Council for Graduate Medical Education (U.S.) (1987/1988)-(1992/1993). Directory. English. an. 535 North Dearborn Street, Chicago IL 60610. **Tel** (312)280-7168. **ED** Anne Crowley. **LC** R840; .D56. **DD** 610/.7/1173. **NLM** WX 22; AA1 D595. **[CCC]. Continues** Directory of Residency Training Programs. **Continued by** Graduate Medical Education Directory.

**US/0095-7925**
**DIRECTORY OF HEALTH SCIENCES LIBRARIES IN THE UNITED STATES. See** Library and Information Sciences.

US
**DIRECTORY OF JAPANESE HEALTHCARE INDUSTRY.** Directory. English. an. $450.00. Japan Publications Inc, 150 Post Street, Suite 500, San Francisco CA 94108. **Tel** (415)772-5555.
 **Desc:** A comprehensive directory for individuals and companies seeking information on manufacturers and distributors participating in all segments of the Japanese healthcare market.

UK
**DIRECTORY OF MEDICAL AND HEALTH CARE LIBRARIES IN THE UNITED KINGDOM AND REPUBLIC OF IRELAND. See** Library and Information Sciences.

US
**DIRECTORY OF MEDICAL COMPUTER SYSTEMS. See** Computers.

US
**DIRECTORY OF MEDICAL INSTITUTIONS CONDUCTING RESEARCH AND SERVICES FOR PERSONS WITH THE MARFAN SYNDROME AND RELATED CONNECTIVE TISSUE DISORDERS.** Directory. an. National Marfan Foundation, 382 Main Street, Port Washington MD 11050. **Tel** (516)883-8712. **ED** Priscilla Ciccariello. ctrl circ. available on videocassette.
 **Desc:** Listing of institutions that treat people with the Marfan Syndrome.

US
**DIRECTORY OF MEDICAL PRACTICE POSITIONS.** Fall (1991)-. Directory. English. **NLM** WX 22; AA1 D5994.

**US/1063-1712**
**DIRECTORY OF MEDICAL REHABILITATION PROGRAMS.** [Dir. med. rehabil. programs]. **Added/Corp** Health Care Investment Analysts, Inc. NovaCare (Firm). (1990)-. Directory. English. an. $202.95. HCIA, 300 East Lombard Street, Baltimore MD 21202. **Tel** (410)576-9600, (800)568-3282. **DD** 362.

**US/0160-6468**
**DIRECTORY OF MEDICAL SCHOOLS WORLDWIDE. See** Education-Higher Education.

US
**DIRECTORY OF MEDICAL VIDEO PROGRAMS, THE. VFOAT** Medical Video Programs. (1990)-. Directory. English. an. Med AV Publishing Company, 521 Lafayette Avenue, Hawthorne NJ 07506. **Tel** (201)423-3330. **Continues** Directory of Medical Audio/Visual Programs for the Health Sciences and Related Fields, 0891-947x.

**US/0892-2756**
**DIRECTORY OF ONLINE HEALTHCARE DATABASES, THE. Ceased.** [Dir. online healthc. databases]. Vol. 1 (1986)-Ceased Vol. 5. Directory. English. an. Medical Data Exchange Inc, 445 South San Antonio Road/Suite 102, Los Altos CA 94022. **Tel** (415)941-3600, FAX (415)941-3683. **ED** Karen Peterkin and Donald Black. **DD** 610. **NLM** W 22.1; D5985.
 **Desc:** An easy-to-use guide to 202 online databases in the healthcare field. Each reference includes: database title, producer, vendors, cost, file size and summary of contents.

**II/0253-7656**
**DIRECTORY OF PARA-MEDICAL INSTITUTIONS OF INDIA.** [Dir. para med. inst. India]. Directory. English. Central Bureau of Health Intelligence, Directorate General of Health Services, Nirman Bhavan, New Delhi 110011 India. **Tel** 3019544. **NLM** W 22 JI4 D56.

US
**DIRECTORY OF PREVENTIVE MEDICINE RESIDENCY PROGRAMS IN THE UNITED STATES AND CANADA.**
**Main/Corp** American College of Preventive Medicine. 1st Edition (1979)-. English. an. $15.00. American College of Preventive Medicine, 1015 15th Street Northwest, Suite 403, Washington DC 20005. **Tel** (202)789-0003.
 **Desc:** Provides comprehensive information on all aspects of residency training programs in the field. Included for each program are program director, address, telephone, training capacity, funded slots, numbers of residents, data on average stipends and other benefits, degrees awarded, area of emphasis, as well as a narrative description presenting on overview and special features.

**US/1060-1759**
**DIRECTORY OF PUBLISHED PROCEEDINGS. SERIES MLS, MEDICAL/LIFE SCIENCES.** [Dir. publ. proc., Ser. MLS Med./life sci.]. **VFOAT** InterDok Directory of Published Proceedings. Series MLS, Medical/Life Sciences. Vol. 1 (1991)-. Directory. English. an. $125.00. InterDok Corporation, PO Box 326, Harrison NY 10528. **Tel** (914)835-3506, FAX (914)835-6757. **DD** 610. **NLM** ZW 3; D598. **Continues in part** Directory of Published Proceedings. Series SEMT: Science/Engineering/Medicine/Technology, 0012-3293.

**US/0419-3350**
**DIRECTORY OF PUBLISHED PROCEEDINGS. SERIES SEMT, SCIENCE/ENGINEERING/MEDICINE/ TECHNOLOGY. ANNUAL CUMULATIVE VOLUME / INTERDOK. See** Science and Technology.

US
**DIRECTORY OF PUBLISHED PROCEEDINGS. SERIES SEMT SCIENCE/ENGINEERING/MEDICINE/ TECHNOLOGY. CUMULATED INDEX SUPPLEMENT. See** Science and Technology.

**US/0192-8104**
**DIRECTORY OF SUBSPECIALTY FELLOWSHIP TRAINING PROGRAMS.**
Directory. English. Association of Professors of Medicine, One Dupont Circle, Washington DC 20036. **LC** R840; .D59. **DD** 616/.026/079.

**US/0196-6340**
**DIRECTORY - TEXAS OSTEOPATHIC MEDICAL ASSOCIATION. Main/Corp** Texas Osteopathic Medical Association. 1978/79-. Directory. English. an. Texas Osteopathic Medical Association, 226 Bailey Avenue, Fort Worth TX 76107. **Tel** (817)336-0549. **NLM** WB 22 AT4 T4D. **Ad Acc. Circ:** 3,500 (ctrl). **Continues** Membership Directory - Texas Osteopathic Medical Association, 0190-7026.

**US/0011-5029**
**DISEASE-A-MONTH.** (DISEASE-A-MONTH : DM.). [Dis.-mon.]. **VFOAT** DM; Disease A Month; Disease-A-Month Series. (Oct. 1954)-. Academic Scholarly Publication. English. mo. $110.00 (institutions), $72.00 (individuals) US; $122.00 (institutions), $84.00 (individuals) other. Mosby Year Book Inc., 11830 Westline Industrial Drive, St Louis MO 63146. **Tel** (800)325-4177, (314)872-8370, FAX (314)432-1380, telex 44-2402. **ED** Roger C. Bone. **LC** R11; .D2. **DD** 610/.5. **NLM** W1 D116. **[CCC]. Pr Rev.** available on microfilm and microfiche from University Microfilms International (UMI). Documents available from The Genuine Article.
 **Desc:** Addressed to the general internist. Contains single topic discussions that focus on the integrated management of a particular disease. Emphasis is on the practical information needed by practicing physicians.
 **Ind/Abst** Abr. Index Med.; EMBASE; Health Plan. Adminis.; Index Med.; Nutr. Abstr. Rev., Ser. A, Hum.

Exp.; Nutr. Res. Newsl.; Life Sci. Collect.; Physic. Medline Plus; Res. Alert [Full Cov.]; Sci. Cit. Index; SCISEARCH; Soc. Sci. Cit. Index [Select. Cov.].

US/8756-5447
**DM & S ADP PLAN.** (DM & S ADP PLAN / VETERANS ADMINISTRATION.). **Main/Corp** United States. Veterans Administration. Dept. of Medicine and Surgery. Medical Information Resources Management Office. **VFOAT** DM and S ADP Plan. **VAT** Department of Medicine and Surgery Automated Data Processing Plan. English. an. US Veterans Administration / Washington DC, 810 Vermont Avenue Southwest, Washington DC 20420. **Tel** (202)393-2124. **LC** UB369; .U57C. **DD** 353.0081/2. available on microfiche (Vols. for (1985-) distributed to depository libraries).

UK/0142-8640
**DNA SHEFFIELD.** (DNA.). [DNA Sheff.]. **VFOAT** Deoxyribonucleic Acid. (1975)-. English. mo. £80.00. SUBIS, Mansion House, 19 Kingfield Road, Sheffield S11 9AS England. **Tel** 011 44 114 255 4433, FAX 011 44 114 255 4626. **DD** 016.574873282.

US/0011-5088
**DO, THE.** **Main/Corp** American Osteopathic Association. **VAT** The Doctor of Osteopathy. (19??)-. Periodical. English. Twelve times a year. $50.00 US; $90.00 others. American Osteopathic Association, 142 East Ontario Street, Chicago IL 60611-2864. **Tel** (312)280-5800. **NLM** W1 D127.
**Ind/Abst** Int. Pharm. Abstr.

IT
**DOCTOR NUTRIZIONE.** ***Ceased.*** (1988)-(1992). Italian. bm. Arte Edizioni Srl, Via Ambrogio Figino 16, 20156 Milan Italy. **Tel** 011 39 2 330241.

TU/1010-7584
**DOGA. TURK TIP VE ECZACILIK DERGISI.** **VFOAT** Turk Tip ve Eczacilik Dergisi; Doga. Turkish Journal of Medicine and Pharmacy; Turkish Journal of Medicine and Pharmacy. (1986)-. Multiple languages. Scientific and Technical Research Council of Turkey, Ataturk Bulvari 221, Kavaklidere Ankara Turkey. **Tel** 3420845, FAX 1175902, telex BTAK TR 43186. ***Continues*** *Doga. Bilim Dergisi. Seri C, Tip, 0254-2331.*
**Ind/Abst** EMBASE [Select. Cov.].

JA/0385-5023
**DOKKYO JOURNAL OF MEDICAL SCIENCES.** [Dokkyo j. med. sci.]. **Added/Corp** Dokkyo Igakkai. Dokkyo Ika Daigaku. Vol. 1 (Oct. 1974)-. Academic Scholarly Publication. Multiple languages (English and German). sa. Dokkyo Journal of Medical Sciences, 880 Kitakobayashi Mibumachish, Tochigiken 321 02 Japan. **NLM** W1 DO634. **CODEN** DJMSDB. Documents available from CASDDS.
**Ind/Abst** Chem. Abstr.; EMBASE [Select. Cov.].

GW/0342-0795
**DOKUMENTATION : MEDIZIN IM UMWELTSCHUTZ.** [Dok. Med. Umweltschutz]. **VFOAT** Medizin im Umweltschutz. V. 1- Jan. 1977-. English (German). qt. Idis Oeffentl Gesundheitswesen, Postfach 201012, D33548 Bielefeld F R Germany. **Tel** 011 49 521 86033. **NLM** ZW 1 D658. ***Supersedes*** *Dokumentation: Reinhaltung der Luft + Medizin.*

SP/0214-0659
**DOLOR.** [Dolor]. (1986)-. Periodical. Spanish (summaries and/or abstracts in English). Four times a year. 3500ptas Spain; 4000ptas other. Publicidad Permanayer SA, Mallorca 310, 08037 Barcelona Spain. **Tel** 011 34 3 207-5920, FAX 011 34 3 257-6642. **UDC** 61. **Bk Rev. Ad Acc. Pr Rev. Circ:** 10,000.
**Desc:** Topics on pain.

US
**DORLAND'S ILLUSTRATED MEDICAL DICTIONARY.** (1957)-. English. ir. $39.95. W.B. Saunders Company, A Subsidiary of Harcourt Brace Jovanovich, Inc., The Curtis Center/Suite 300, Independence Square West, Philadelphia PA 19106-3399. **Tel** (215)238-7800 or, 5587, FAX (215)238-7883, telex 173146. **(Subscription address:** W. B. Saunders Company / North America Subscriptions, c/o Periodicals, 6277 Sea Harbour Drive, 4th Floor, Orlando FL 32887.**)** **LC** R121; .D73. **DD** 610/.3/21. ***Continues*** *American Illustrated Medical Dictionary.*

US
**DORLAND'S POCKET MEDICAL DICTIONARY.** (194?)-. Periodical. English. ir. Holt Rinehart and Winston, 6277 Sea Harbor Drive, Orlando FL 32887. **Tel** (407)345-2000, 800 545-2522. **LC** R121; .A5. **DD** 610/.3. ***Continues*** *American Pocket Medical Dictionary.*

SZ/1011-288X
**DOULEUR ET ANALGESIE.** (1988)-. French. qt. Medecine et Hygiene, Case Postale 456, CH-1211 Geneve 4 Switzerland. **Tel** 011 41 22 3469355, 011 41 22 3469356.
**Ind/Abst** EMBASE [Select. Cov.].

●US/1073-8169
**DR. ATKINS' HEALTH REVELATIONS.** [Dr. Atkins' health revel.]. **VFOAT** Health Revelations. (Mar. 1993)-. Newsletter. English. Twelve times a year. $39.95. Wellness Communications, PO Box 25948, Alexandria PA 22313. **Tel** (703)548-2400, (800)336-4893, FAX (703)549-0182. **ED** Joe Wargo. **DD** 613. Index available. cum. index. **Ad Acc. Circ:** 65,000.
**Desc:** Information on nutrients and herbs used in complementary medicine to help the body enhance and heal itself.

US/1068-2953
**DR. WILLIAM CAMPBELL DOUGLASS' SECOND OPINION.** [Dr. William Campbell Douglass' second opin.]. **VFOAT** Second Opinion. Vol. 1, No. 1 (Mar. 1991)-. Periodical. English. mo. $49.00 one year, $89.00 two year. Soundview Communications Inc., 7000 Peachtree, Dunwoody Road #5, Atlanta GA 30328. **Tel** (404)399-1877, (800)728-2288, FAX (404)399-0815. **(Subscription address:** Second Opinion, PO Box 467939, Atlanta GA 30346.**)** **ED** Dr. William Campbell Douglass. **DD** 610. Index available (published in Jan. issue). cum. index. **Circ:** 55,000. ***Continues*** *Doctor's People.*
**Desc:** Contains consumer-oriented alternative health information.
**Ind/Abst** Acad. Abstr. (Jan. 1992-); Acad. Search (Jan. 1992-); Health Source (Jan. 1992-).

US
**DRAFT, FULL DESIGNATION RENEWAL APPLICATION.** (DRAFT OF FULL DESIGNATION RENEWAL APPLICATION HEALTH PLANNING AND DEVELOPMENT SOUTH CAROLINA AREA II.). **Main/Corp** Three Rivers Health Systems Agency, Inc. **VFOAT** Full Designation Renewal Application. 197 -). English. Three Rivers Health, PO Box 5472, Cayce W Cola SC 29171-5472.

US/0741-6512
**DRG MONITOR.** ***Ceased.*** [DRG monit.]. **VFOAT** D.R.G. Monitor. **VAT** Diagnosis Related Group Monitor. Vol. 1, No. 1 (Sept. 1983)-Ceased (Dec. 1990). Periodical. English. mo. Hanley & Belfus Inc., 210 South 13th Street, Philadelphia PA 19107. **Tel** (215)546-7293, FAX (215)790-9330. **NLM** W1; DR3588. **[CCC].**
**Ind/Abst** Health Plan. Adminis.; Hospit. Health Admin. Index (Vol. 6, No. 1, 1988-?).

US/1058-241X
**DRUG TARGETING AND DELIVERY.** ***Title Change.*** [Drug target. deliv.]. (1992)-(1993). Monographic series. English. qt. Academic Press, Inc., 6277 Sea Harbor Drive, Orlando FL 32887. **Tel** (800)543-9534, (407)345-4100, FAX (407)363-9661. **ED** Alfred Stracher. **DD** 615. **[CCC].** ***Continued by*** *Drug Delivery.*
**Desc:** Focuses on drug delivery technology at the theoretical as well as practical level. Provides a single literature source for both the academic and industrial communities in this advancing area of study. Includes basic research, development, and application principles on the molecular, cellular, and higher levels of target sites, as well as physical, chemical and immunokinetic modes of delivery.

US/0001-7094
**DRUG THERAPY (NEW YORK, N.Y.).** ***Ceased.*** (DRUG THERAPY.). [Drug ther.]. **VFOAT** Physicians Prescribing Update, Drug Therapy; Drug Therapy, Physicians Prescribing Update. Vol. 1, No. 1 (Jan. 1971)-(Aug. 1994). Academic Scholarly Publication. English. mo. Excerpta Medica / US, PO Box 3085, Princeton NJ 08543-3085. **Tel** (908)874-8550, FAX (908)874-5611. **DD** 615. **NLM** W1 DR61. **CODEN** ORTHDZ. **[CCC].** Index available. **Ad Acc. Pr Rev. Circ:** 110,000 (ctrl). available on microfilm and microfiche from University Microfilms International (UMI). Documents available from CASDDS.
**Desc:** A journal for primary care physicians that provides timely information concerning new drug developments and the medical treatment of diseases.
**Ind/Abst** Bibliogr. Mission.; Chem. Abstr.; EMBASE; Int. Pharm. Abstr.; Life Sci. Collect.; PESTDOC.

BE
**D'SANTE.** (19??)-. French. mo. 499.00F Belgium; 800.00F other. D'Sante, 51 rue Auguste Danse, 1180 Brussels Belgium. **Tel** 011 32 2 3430700.
**Ind/Abst** Point Repere (19??-19??).

FI/0012-7183
**DUODECIM.** [Duodecim]. **Added/Corp** Societas Medicorum Fennica "Duodecim", Helsingfors. No. 1 (1885)-. Academic Scholarly Publication. Finnish (summaries and/or abstracts in English). Twenty-three times a year. Finnish Medical Society, Kalevankatu 11 A, 00100 Helsinki Finland. **Tel** 011 358 0 611050, FAX 011 358 0 611004. **NLM** W1 DU705Z. **CODEN** DUODAG. **Ad Acc. Circ:** 17,500 (ctrl). Documents available from CASDDS.
**Ind/Abst** Chem. Abstr.; Curr. Biotechnol.; EMBASE; Health Plan. Adminis.; Index Med.; SportSearch.

SP/0211-9536
**DYNAMIS (GRANADA).** (DYNAMIS.). [Dynamis]. **Added/Corp** Universidad de Granada. Departamento de Historia de la Medicina. Vol. 1 (1981)-. Periodical. Spanish (English). an. 3090ptas. Universidad de Granada / Campus de Cartuja, 18071 Granada Spain. **Tel** 011 34 58 243930, 243931. **LC** R131.A1; D96. **DD** 610/.9. **NLM** W1; DY988N.
**Ind/Abst** Am. Hist. Life (1981-); Indice Med. Esp.

UK/0308-6275
**DYSLEXIA REVIEW.** [Dyslexia rev.]. English. ir. Dyslexia Inst, 133 Gresham Road, Staines TW18 2AJ England. **NLM** W1 DY99.

KE/0012-835X
**EAST AFRICAN MEDICAL JOURNAL, THE.** [East Afr. med. j.]. **Added/Corp** Medical Association of East Africa. British Medical Association. Vol.9 (April 1932)-. Periodical. English. mo. $375.00 US. East African Medical Journal, Box 41632, Nairobi Kenya East Africa. **Tel** 11 254 2 724711. **ED** E. G. Kasili. **LC** R98; .E3. **DD** 610.5. **NLM** W1 EA824. **CODEN** EAMJAV. Index available. cum. index. **Bk Rev. Ad Acc. Pr Rev. Circ:** 4,500. Documents available from The Genuine Article, CASDDS. ***Continues*** *Kenya and East African Medical Journal.*
**Desc:** Medical subjects based on clinical findings.
**Ind/Abst** AGRICOLA; Chem. Abstr.; Curr. Contents Clin. Med.; Curr. Titl. Dent.; Dairy Sci. Abstr.; EMBASE; Food Sci. Technol. Abstr.; Geogr. Abstr. Human Geogr.; Health Plan. Adminis.; Helminthol. Abstr. (19??-19??); Highw. Res. Abstr.; Index Med.; Index Dent. Lit.; Index Vet.; Int. Dev. Abstr.; Microbiol. Abstr. Sect. B; Nutr. Abstr. Rev., Ser. A, Hum. Exp.; Nutr. Res. Newsl.; Life Sci. Collect.; Protozoolog. Abstr.; Res. Alert [Full Cov.]; Rev. Agric. Entomol.; Rev. Med. Vet. Entomol.; Rev. Med. Vet. Mycology; Rev. Plant Pathol.; Risk Abstr. (19??-19??); Sci. Cit. Index; SCISEARCH; Soc. Sci. Cit. Index [Select. Cov.]; Spec. Educ. Needs Abstr.; Vet. Bull.; Trop. Dis. Bull.

US/1050-6675
**EAST TEXAS MEDICINE.** [East Tex. med.]. (Oct. 1989)-. Periodical. English. bm. $25.00 US; $100.00 other. East Texas Medicine, 777 South Broadway/Suite 207, Tyler TX 75701. **Tel** (214)592-8533. **ED** Gary Boyd. **DD** 610. **NLM** W1; EA835. Index available. cum. index. **Ad Acc. Circ:** 2,500 (ctrl).
**Desc:** Contains current medical topics.

UK/1351-5276
**EATING DISORDERS.** (19??)-. English. £75.00. SUBIS, Mansion House, 19 Kingfield Road, Sheffield S11 9AS England. **Tel** 011 44 114 255 4433, FAX 011 44 114 255 4626.

●US/1076-2825
**ECOSYSTEM HEALTH AND MEDICINE.** (1995)-. Academic Scholarly Publication. English. qt. $120.00 (institution), $80.00 (individual); $140.00 (institution), $95.00 (individual) other. Blackwell Scientific Publishers, 238 Main Street, Cambridge MA 02142. **Tel** (617)547-7110, (800)835-6770, FAX (617)547-0789.

US/0896-6613
**EDELL HEALTH LETTER, THE.** ***Ceased.*** [Edell health lett.]. (198?)-(Dec. 1993). Periodical. English. Ten times a year. Edell Health Letter, 301 Howard Street/ 18th Floor, San Francisco CA 94105. **Tel** (415)512-9100, FAX (415)512-9600. **(Subscription address:** PO Box 57812, Boulder, CO 80322-7812**)** **ED** Claire Ellis. **DD** 616. **Circ:** 50,000. available on an online database (file 149/Full-Text) from DIALOG. ***Continues*** *People's Medical Journal, 0741-2886.*
**Desc:** Consists of short, informative abstracts of articles published in the professional literature on a wide variety of topics such as contraception, Alzheimer's disease, blood pressure, nutrition, asthma, smoking, and cancer detection.
**Ind/Abst** Acad. Abstr. Full Text Elite (Jan. 1992-); Acad. Abstr. (Jan. 1992-); Acad. Search (Jan. 1992-); Consum. Health Nutr. Index; Health Index (1989-); Health Period. Database [Full Txt.]; Health Ref. Cent. (Jan. 1989-) [Full Txt.] [Full Cov.]; Health Source (Jan. 1992-); INFO-SOUTH Abstr.; Mag. Search.

US/0013-1091
**EDUCACION MEDICA Y SALUD.** [Educ. med. salud]. **Added/Corp** Pan American Federation of Associations of Medical Schools. Pan American Health Organization. Vol. 1 (Oct./Dec. 1966)-. Periodical. Spanish (Portuguese and English). Four times a year (Jan., Apr., July, Oct.). $20.00. Pan American Health Organization, 525 23rd Street Northwest, Office District Sales, Washington DC 20037. **Tel** (202)293-8130, FAX (202)338-0869. **ED** Jorge Haddad (telephone: (202)861-3295). **NLM** W1 ED69. Index available. cum. index. **Bk Rev. Circ:** 5,800 (ctrl). available on an online database from MEDLINE.
**Desc:** Published to support manpower development activities in the countries of the region and to disseminate modern techniques for the teaching-learning process in the health sciences in general.
**Ind/Abst** Health Plan. Adminis.; Index Med.; Trop. Dis. Bull.

US/0888-7640
**EDUCATIONAL SERIES ON CHINESE MEDICINE.** [Educ. ser. Chin. med.]. No. 1-. Monographic series. English (translations available in Chinese). Price varies per volume. Oriental Healing Arts

Institute, 1945 Palo Verde Avenue, Suite 208, Long Beach CA 90815. **Tel** (213)431-3544, FAX (213)594-6513. **DD** 615. **NLM** W1; ED878D.

GW
**EEG-EMG.** [EEG-EMG]. **VAT** Eletroenzephalographie - Elektromyographie. Vol. 1, (1970)-. German. qt. $177.00. Georg Thieme Verlag Stuttgart, Postfach 301120, D 70451 Stuttgart Germany. **Tel** 011 49 711 89310, FAX 011 49 711 8931298, telex 7 252 275 GTVD. **(Subscription address:** Thieme Medical Publishers Inc., 381 Park Avenue South, New York NY 10016.**) NLM** W1 E22. **CODEN** EEGEAE. **Pr Rev.** available on microfilm from University Microfilms International (UMI). Documents available from The Genuine Article, BIOSIS Document Express.
**Ind/Abst** Biol. Abstr. (1986-); Curr. Contents Clin. Med.; EMBASE; Energy Res. Abstr. (Sept. 1980-); Health Plan. Adminis.; Index Med. (Mar. 1976-Dec. 1992); Res. Alert [Full Cov.]; SCISEARCH; Soc. Sci. Cit. Index [Select. Cov.].

TU/1016-9113
**EGE TIP DERGISI.** [Ege tip derg.]. (1962)-. Periodical. Turkish. qt. 100.00TL. Ege Universitesi Tip Fakultesi, Yayin Alt-Komitesi Yayin Burosu, Bornova Izmir Turkey. **Tel** 9051 18 18 20 3103, FAX 9051 18 28 52. **ED** Emel Tumbay. **UDC** 61.

NE/0166-008X
**EHBO VOORPOST VAN DE DOKTER.** **VAT** Eerste Hulp bij Ongelukken Voorpost van de Dokter. (Jan./Feb. 1977)-. Periodical. Dutch. mo. Stichting Voorpost, Kapelweg 34, 3951 AD Maarn Hol Netherlands. **NLM** W1 E27. ***Supersedes*** *Voorpost van de Dokter, 0166-9109.*

US/0724-6706
**EINSTEIN QUARTERLY, THE.** (THE EINSTEIN QUARTERLY JOURNAL OF BIOLOGY AND MEDICINE.). [Einstein q.]. **Added/Corp** Albert Einstein College of Medicine. **VFOAT** Einstein Quarterly. Vol. 1, No. 1 (April 1982)-. Academic Scholarly Publication. English. Four times a year. $94.00. Springer-Verlag New York Inc., 175 5th Avenue, New York NY 10010. **Tel** (212)460-1500, telex 232 235 SPB UR. **(Subscription address:** Springer Verlag New York Inc. / for North America, 44 Hartz Way, Secaucus NJ 07096.**) ED** L Rosenthal and S Douros. **NLM** W1; EI507. **[CCC].** available in microform from University Microfilms International (UMI). Documents available from CASDDS.
**Desc:** Presents investigations into disciplines at the interface of medicine and the social sciences - medico-legal and technical studies, epidemiology and public policy, and the history of medicine - in addition to basic scientific research and clinical investigations.
**Ind/Abst** Chem. Abstr.

JA
**EIZO JOHO MEDIKARU. IMAGE TECHNOLOGY & INFORMATION DISPLAY. MEDICINE.** Japanese. mo. $200.00. Sangyo Kaihatsu Kiko K.K., Nishikawa Pakingu Biru, 1-1, Kanda Izumichi, Chiyodaku, Tokyoto 101 Japan. **(Subscription address:** Maruzen Company Ltd., PO Box 5050, Import & Export Department, Tokyo 100 31 Japan.**)**

AI/0514-7484
**EKSPERIMENTAL EV KLINIKAKAN BZHSHKUTYAN.** (EKSPERIMENTALNAIA I KLINICHESKAIA MEDITSINA / PORJARARAKAN EV KLINIKAKAN BZHSHKUTYUN / AKADEMIIA NAUK ARMIANSKOI SSR.). [Eksp. klinik. bzhshk.]. **Added/Corp** Haykakan SSH Gitutyunneri Akademia. **VFOAT** Porjararakan ev Klinikakan Bzhshkutyun. (1989)-. Academic Scholarly Publication. Russian (summaries and/or abstracts in Armenian and English; table of contents in Armenian and English). bm. $109.95. Akademiia Nauk Armianskoi / Armenian Academy of Sciences, Prospekt Marshala Bagramyana 24, 375019 Yerevan Armenia. **Tel** 52 45 80, telex 243344. **(Subscription address:** East View Publications Inc., 3020 Harbor Lane North, Suite 110, Minneapolis MN 55447.**) CODEN** EKMEEM. Documents available from BIOSIS Document Express, CASDDS. ***Continues*** *Zhurnal Eksperimentalnoi i Klinicheskoi Meditsiny, 0514-7484.*
**Ind/Abst** Biol. Abstr.; Chem. Abstr.

BU/0367-0643
**EKSPERIMENTALNA MEDITSINA I MORFOLOGIIA.** [Eksp. med. morfol.]. **Added/Corp** Bulgaria. Ministerstvo na Narodnoto Zdrave. Vol. 1, (1962)-. Academic Scholarly Publication. Bulgarian (summaries and/or abstracts in Russian and English). Four times a year. DM66.00. Ministerstvo Nordnoto Zdrave, 11 PL Slaveikov, Sofia Bulgaria. **(Subscription address:** Kubon & Sagner, ABT Zeitschriftenimport, D 80328 Munich Germany.**) NLM** W1 EK283. **CODEN** EKMMA8. Documents available from CASDDS.
**Ind/Abst** Chem. Abstr.; EMBASE [Select. Cov.]; Index Med.

LV
**EKSPERIMENTALNAIA MEDITSINA.** **Added/Corp** Latvian S. S. R. Veselibas Aizsardzibas Ministrija. Latvijas Padomju Socialistiskas Republikas Zinatnu Akademija. Otdelenie Khimicheskikh i Biologicheskikh Nauk. **VFOAT** Seriia "Eksperimentalnaia Meditsina". (1978)-. Monographic series. Russian. Zinatne / Science Publishing House, Turgeneva lela 19, Riga Latvia 1530. **Tel** 3712 212 797. **NLM** W1 EK482E. **CODEN** EKMEDL. Documents available from CASDDS.
**Ind/Abst** Chem. Abstr.

BE/0424-8120
**ELECTRODIAGNOSTIC-THERAPIE.** [Electrodiagn.-ther.]. (1964)-. French. qt.
**Ind/Abst** Health Plan. Adminis.

US/0923-0475
**ELECTRON MICROSCOPY IN BIOLOGY AND MEDICINE.** **See** Biology.

US/0271-1877
**ELECTRON MICROSCOPY IN HUMAN MEDICINE.** V. 1- 1978-. Academic Scholarly Publication. English. an. **CODEN** EMHMDY. Each issue contains an index to its own contents (no volume index)--loose. Documents available from CASDDS.
**Ind/Abst** Chem. Abstr.

●NE
**EMBASE LIST OF JOURNALS INDEXED.** **See** Medical Science and Technology-Abstracting, Bibliographies and Statistics.

NE
**EMBASE [ONLINE DATABASE].** **See** Medical Science and Technology-Abstracting, Bibliographies and Statistics.

US/1042-2978
**EMERGENCY DEPARTMENT LAW.** **See** Law.

US/0748-8947
**EMERGENCY MEDICINE (GLENDALE, CALIF.).** (EMERGENCY MEDICINE SOUND RECORDING.). [Emerg. med.]. **Added/Corp** Audio-Digest Foundation. **VFOAT** Audio-Digest Emergency Medicine. Vol. 1, No. 1 (Oct. 1, 1984)-. Periodical. English. sm. $179.76 US; $202.80 Canada; $247.44 other (audiocassette). Audio-Digest Foundation, 1577 Chevy Chase Drive, Glendale CA 91206. **Tel** (213)245-8505, (800)423-2308, FAX (818)240-7379. **ED** Claron L. Oakley. **DD** 617. Index available. ctrl circ.
**Desc:** Interactive system of audio cassette postgraduate medical education, with each one-hour program eligible for two Category I credit hours.

US/1040-7901
**EMERGENCY PHYSICIAN REPORT.** (1990)-. Periodical. English. Three times a year. $52.50. Mosby Year Book Inc., 11830 Westline Industrial Drive, St Louis MO 63146. **Tel** (800)325-4177, (314)872-8370, FAX (314)432-1380, telex 44-2402.

●US/1062-3175
**EMERGING ISSUES IN BIOMEDICAL POLICY.** [Emerg. issues biomed. policy]. Vol. 1 (1992)-. Periodical. English. Columbia University Press, 136 South Broadway, Irvington NY 10533. **Tel** (914)591-9111. **LC** R724; .E52. **DD** 174/.2/05. **NLM** W1; EM664M.

TS/0250-6882
**EMIRATES MEDICAL JOURNAL.** [Emir. med. j.]. **Added/Corp** United Arab Emirates. Ministry of Health. Vol. 1 (April 1980)-. Academic Scholarly Publication. English. ir. Emirates Medical Association, PO Box 6600, Dubai United Arab Emirates. **Tel** 011 971 4 377377. **NLM** W1 EM661VN.
**Ind/Abst** EMBASE; Trop. Dis. Bull.

US/0740-9087
**EMPLOYERS' HEALTH COSTS SAVINGS LETTER.** Vol. 1, No. 1 (Aug. 1983). Periodical. English. mo. $157.00. Health Resources Publishing, 3100 Highway 138, Wall Township NJ 07719-1442. **Tel** (908)681-1133, FAX (908)681-0490. **ED** Robert K. Jenkins. **[CCC].** Index available. cum. index.
**Desc:** The latest news on what other employers are doing to appropriately save on health care spending.

US
**EMS MEDICAL ADVISOR.** (19??)-. English. Four times a year. $47.00. Scott Bourn Associates, 557 Burbank Street, Unit B, Broomfield CO 80020. **Tel** (303)460-0900, (800)669-9448, FAX (303)460-0985. **Circ:** 1,000.

US/0743-4510
**ENCYCLOPEDIA OF MEDICAL ORGANIZATIONS AND AGENCIES.** [Encycl. med. organ. agencies]. 1st Ed. (1983)-. English. an. $220.00. Gale Research Inc., 835 Penobscot Building, Detroit MI 48226. **Tel** (800)877-GALE, (313)961-2242, FAX (313)961-6083, telex TWX 810-221-7086. **ED** Karen Boyden. **LC** R712.A1; E53. **DD** 362.1/025/73.
**Desc:** Furnishes current information on more than 12,000 major public and private agencies in medicine and related fields. Entries are arranged into 69 chapters covering specific areas of modern health care and medicine.

JA
**ENDAI NAIYO SHOROKU, NIHON KETSUGO SOSHIKI GAKKAI SOKAI.** **VFOAT** Nihon Ketsugo Soshiki Gakkai Sokai Endai Naiyo Shoroku. Academic Scholarly Publication. Japanese. **NLM** W1 EN274S. **CODEN** NSSHDB. Documents available from CASDDS.
**Ind/Abst** Chem. Abstr.

GW/0933-811X
**ENDOSKOPIE HEUTE.** **Added/Corp** Deutsche Gesellschaft fuer Endoskopie und Bildgebende Verfahren. **VFOAT** German journal of Endoscopy and Other Imaging Methods. (198?)-. Periodical. German (summaries and/or abstracts in English; table of contents in English). qt. Karl Demeter Verlag, Wuermstrasse 13, Postfach 1660, W 8032 Graefelfing Germany. **Tel** 011 49 89 852033, FAX 011 49 89 9543347, telex 524068 Delta D. **NLM** W1; EN424.
**Ind/Abst** EMBASE.

SP/0423-121X
**ENFERMEDADES DEL TORAX.** [Enferm. torax]. (1952)-. Academic Scholarly Publication. Spanish. qt. Ministerio de Sanidad y Consumo Publicaciones Documentacion y Biblioteca, Pasco del Prado 18-20, 28014 Madrid Spain. **NLM** W1 EN589. Index Available Received separately--bound from publisher.
**Ind/Abst** EMBASE; Indice Med. Esp.

CL/0716-2774
**ENFOQUES EN ATENCION PRIMARIA.** **Added/Corp** Sociedad de Profesionales para el Apoyo de la Salud Materno Infantil. Vol. 1, No. 1 (Mar. 1986)-. Periodical. Spanish. Four times a year. $27.00 Latin America; $37.00 other. Ediciones Paesmiltda, Casilla 121-A Correo 29, Santiago Chile. **Tel** 011 56 2 336916, FAX 011 56 2 6321571. **ED** Juanita Rojas. **NLM** W1; EN639L. **Bk Rev. Ad Acc, Adv Mgr:** Suzamme Aurelius, **Tel** 6394560. **Circ:** 200 (ctrl).

JA/0389-4290
**ENSHO.** (ENSHO : NIHON ENSHO GAKKAI ZASSHI.). [Ensho]. **Added/Corp** Nihon Ensho Gakkai. **VFOAT** Japanese Journal of Inflammation. (1981)-. Periodical. Japanese (summaries and/or abstracts in English; table of contents in English). qt. Nihon Ensho Gakkai, (Japanese Society of Inflammation), 9-6-505, Otsuka 3 Chome, Bunkyoku, Tokyoto 112 Japan. **NLM** W1; EN910. **CODEN** ENSHEE. Documents available from CASDDS.
**Ind/Abst** Chem. Abstr.

US/0734-3531
**ENTEROVIRUS SURVEILLANCE.** (CENTERS FOR DISEASE CONTROL ENTEROVIRUS SURVEILLANCE.). 1970-1979-. English. Centers for Disease Control, 1600 Clifton Road NE, Atlanta GA 30333. **Tel** (404)639-3311, FAX (404)639-3296. **LC** RA644.E54; C47. **DD** 614.5/7.

CN/0833-9880
**ENTRE LE POUCE ET L'INDEX.** (ENTRE LE POUCE ET L'INDEX / L'ASSOCIATION DES PROFESSIONNELS POUR LA PREVENTION DES INFECTIONS.). [Entre pouce index]. Vol. 1, No. 1 (Fall 1985)-. Periodical. French. Three times a year. Association des Professionnels pour la Prevention des Infections, 264 Boulevard Dorchester Est, 7 Etage, Montreal Quebec H2X 3L4 Canada. **DD** 616.9/045.

US
**ENVIRONMENTAL MEDICINE.** (19??)-. English. Four times a year (Mar., June, Sept., Dec.). $32.00 Canada, $38.00 England & South America, $42.00 Australia (individuals); $78.00 Canada, $84.00 England & South America, $88.00 Australia (institutions). Environmental Medicine Publishing Company, Inc., PO Box 101059, Denver CO 80210. **Tel** (303)831-7335. ***Continues*** *Clinical Ecology.*

JA/0287-0517
**ENVIRONMENTAL MEDICINE : ANNUAL REPORT OF THE RESEARCH INSTITUTE OF ENVIRONMENTAL MEDICINE, NAGOYA UNIVERSITY.** **Added/Corp** Nagoya Daigaku. Kankyo Igaku Kenkyujo. (1982)-. Academic Scholarly Publication. English. ir. Free on request. The Research Institute of Environmental Medicine, Nagoya University, Nagoya Japan. **Tel** 011 81 52 781 5111, FAX 011 81 52 781 9117. **ED** Hideki Yamamura. **LC** RA565.A1; E587. **DD** 616.9/8/005. **NLM** W1; EN984UK. **Circ:** 400 (ctrl). Documents available from CASDDS. ***Continues*** *Annual Report of the Research Institute of Environmental Medicine, Nagoya University, 0469-4759.*
**Desc:** Covers environmental health and environmentally induced diseases.
**Ind/Abst** Chem. Abstr.; EMBASE.

US/1062-3736
**ENVIRONMENTAL PHYSICIAN, THE.** (THE ENVIRONMENTAL PHYSICIAN : NEWSLETTER OF THE AMERICAN ACADEMY OF ENVIRONMENTAL MEDICINE.). [Environ. physician]. **Added/Corp** American Academy of Environmental Medicine. Vol. 25, No. 3 (Fall 1991). Newsletter. English. qt. $30.00 US; $32.00

Canada. American Academy of Environmental Medicine, AAEM, PO Box 16106, Denver CO 80216. **DD** 616. ***Continues*** *A.A.E.M. Newsletter.*

FR
**EPILEPSIES.** English. Five times a year. 280.00F (individuals), 460.00F (institutions) EEC; 313.42F (individuals), 489.72F (institutions) France; 460.00F (individuals), 530.00F (institutions) other. John Libbey Eurotext Ltd, 6 rue Blanche, Isabelle Trope, 92120 Montrouge France. **Tel** 011 33 1 47358552.
**Ind/Abst** EMBASE.

NE/0922-9833
**EPILEPSY RESEARCH. SUPPLEMENT.** [Epilepsy res., Suppl.]. (1988)-. Monographic series. English. Price varies per volume. Elsevier Science Publishers BV, PO Box 211, 1000 AE Amsterdam Netherlands. **Tel** 011 31 20 5803642, FAX 011 31 20 5862696, telex 15682. **NLM** W1; EP455KEA.
**Ind/Abst** Health Plan. Adminis.; Index Med. (1988-).

●UK
**EPSTEIN-BARR VIRUS REPORT.** (1994)-. English. bm. $140.00 (institution), $100.00 (individual) US; £68.00 (institution), £49.00 (individual) UK & Europe; £84.00 (institution), £62.00 (individual) other. Royal Society of Medicine Press, 1 Wimpole Street, London W1M 8AE England. **Tel** 011 44 71 2902928.

GW/0014-0082
**ERFAHRUNGSHEILKUNDE.** [Erfahr.-Heilkd.]. Academic Scholarly Publication. German. mo. DM192.00. Karl F Haug Verlag GmbH and Company, Postfach 102840, D 69018 Heidelberg Germany. **Tel** 011 49 6221 40620. **ED** Gyorgy Irmey. **NLM** W1 ER221. **CODEN** ERFAAK. Index available. cum. index. **Bk Rev. Ad Acc. Circ:** 8,400. Documents available from CASDDS.
**Desc:** Contains research articles on clinical reports about the latest advances in biological medicine, diet therapy, cellular therapy, neural therapy, oxygen therapy, biological cancer control and therapy, phytotherapy, acupuncture, etc.
**Ind/Abst** Chem. Abstr.; Energy Res. Abstr. (Feb. 1975-).

SP
**ERGA NOTICIAS.** Spanish. bm. Free. Inst Nac Seguridad Higiene Trabajo, Calle Dulcet 2 10, 08034 Barcelona Spain. **Tel** 011 34 3 2800102. **UDC** 61.

GW/0170-2327
**ERGO-MED.** [Ergo-Med]. (Sept. 1977)-. German. bm (Feb., Apr., June, Aug., Oct., Dec.). DM76.20 Germany; DM90.60 other. Dr. Curt Haefner Verlag GmbH, Bachstrasse 14, Postfach 106060, D 69050 Heidelberg Germany. **Tel** 011 49 6221 49063. **ED** Curt Haefner. **NLM** W1 ER31. **[CCC].** Index available. cum. index. **Bk Rev. Ad Acc. Circ:** 2,000 (ctrl).
**Ind/Abst** Ergon. Abstr.

UK/0952-3391
**ESAO PROCEEDINGS / EUROPEAN SOCIETY FOR ARTIFICIAL ORGANS.** [ESAO proc.]. **Main/Corp** European Society for Artificial Organs. Meeting. (Sept. 1-3, 1982)-. Proceedings. English. an. Holt Saunders Ltd, High Street, Foots Cray Sidcup, Kent DA14 5HP England. **Tel** 011 44 81 300 3322. **NLM** W1; EU731T; W1; LI4071 v.1 suppl.1 etc. ***Continues*** *Proceedings European Society for Artificial Organs (ESAO).*

FR/0248-9643
**EST MEDECINE.** [Est med.]. Vol. 1, No 1 (Jan. 1, 1981)-. Periodical. French. Twenty times a year (No issues in July/Aug.). 313.42F. Region Sante, 305 B Centre D'Affaries Object, 92661 Asnieres Cedex France. **Tel** 011 33 1 47931804, FAX 011 33 1 47910540. **ED** Dr. Geraud Gay. **NLM** W1 ES74. **Bk Rev. Ad Acc, Adv Mgr:** A. Trebucq. **Pr Rev. Circ:** 7,200. ***Continues in part*** *Medecine, Revue Medicale Inter-Regionale du Nord & de L'est, 0153-8748.*

CN
**ESTIMATES. PART III, MEDICAL RESEARCH COUNCIL. Main/Corp** Canada. **VFOAT** Budget des Depenses. Partie III, Conseil de Recherches Medicales. (19??)-. English (French). $3.00 Canada; $3.60 other. Canada Communication Group Publishers, Order Processing, Ottawa Ontario K1A 0S9 Canada. **Tel** (819)956-4800, (819)956-4802. **LC** RA184; .C3a. **DD** 354.710084/1.

US
**ETHICAL CURRENTS. See** Ethics.

US
**ETHICAL ISSUES IN MEDICINE.** ***Ceased.*** **See** Ethics.

UK/0266-688X
**ETHICS & MEDICINE : A CHRISTIAN PERSPECTIVE ON ISSUES IN BIOETHICS. VFOAT** Ethics and Medicine. (1985)-. Periodical. English. Three times a year (March, June and October). £11.85 UK; £12.70 other. Paternoster Press, A division of Send the Light Ltd., PO Box 300, Kingstown Broadway, Cumbria CA3 0QS England. **Tel** 011 44 228 512512, FAX 011 44 228 514949. **NLM** W1; ET436L.
**Desc:** Review of medical ethics from Christian perspectives.
**Ind/Abst** Relig. Theol. Abstr. (199?-).

US/1071-3778
**ETHICS AND MEDICS.** [Ethics medics]. **Added/Corp** Pope John XXIII Medical-Moral Research and Education Center. **VFOAT** Ethics & Medics. Vol. 1 (Jan./Feb. 1976)-. Periodical. English. mo (12 issues). $15.00 US; $18.00 other. Pope John XXIII Center, 186 Forbes Road, Braintree MA 02184. **Tel** (617)848-6965. **ED** David Beauregard. **DD** 241. Index available. cum. index. **Circ:** 25,000. available on videocassette.
**Desc:** News and information on medical ethics issues.

GW/0935-7335
**ETHIK IN DER MEDIZIN. See** Ethics.

ET
**ETHIOPIAN JOURNAL OF HEALTH DEVELOPMENT, THE. See** Public Health and Safety.

ET/0014-1755
**ETHIOPIAN MEDICAL JOURNAL.** [Ethiop. med. j.]. (1962)-. Academic Scholarly Publication. English. Four times a year (Jan., Apr., July, Oct.). $40.00. Ethiopian Medical Association, Box 3472, Addis Ababa Ethiopia. **Tel** ADDIS ABABA 15 81 74. **ED** Dr. F. T. Lester and Dr. Hagos Beyene (phone: 158174). **NLM** W1 ET439. **CODEN** EMDJA2. Index available. cum. index. **Bk Rev. Ad Acc. Pr Rev. Circ:** 800. Documents available from The Genuine Article, BIOSIS Document Express.
**Desc:** Devoted to the advancement and dissemination of knowledge pertaining to medicine in Ethiopia and other developing countries.
**Ind/Abst** Biol. Abstr.; Curr. Contents Clin. Med.; EMBASE; Health Plan. Adminis.; Helminthol. Abstr. (19??-19??); Index Med.; Nutr. Abstr. Rev., Ser. A, Hum. Exp.; Life Sci. Collect.; Protozoolog. Abstr.; Res. Alert [Select. Cov.]; Rev. Med. Vet. Entomol.; SCISEARCH; Soc. Sci. Cit. Index [Select. Cov.]; Virol. AIDS Abstr.

FR/0766-4214
**ETUDES ET TRAVAUX SUR CENDRARS. Added/Corp** Universite de Paris X: Nanterre. Centre de Semiotique Textuelle. (1987)-. Monographic series. French. qt. Price varies per volume. Publidix Universite de Paris, X 200 Ave de la Republique, 92001 Nanterre Cedex France. **ED** Edmond M. Lipiansky. **LC** UNC.

RW
**ETUDES RWANDAISES. SERIE LETTRES ET SCIENCES HUMAINES / UNIVERSITE NATIONALE DU RWANDA. Added/Corp** Universite Nationale du Rwanda. **VFOAT** Serie Lettres et Sciences Humaines; Lettres et Sciences Humaines. Vol. 1, No 2 (1987)-. Periodical. French. sa. **LC** DT450; .E88. **DD** 967.571/005. ***Continues in part*** *Etudes Rwandaises.*

IT/0014-2573
**EUROPA MEDICOPHYSICA.** [Eur. Medicophys.]. (1965)-. Periodical. Multiple languages. qt. $90.00 (individuals), $140.00 (institutions). Edizioni Minerva Medica, Corso Bramante 83-85, 10126 Turin Italy. **Tel** 011 39 11 678282, FAX 011 39 11 674502. **UDC** 615. **CODEN** EUMP-A.
**Desc:** Official journal of the Italian Society of Physical Medicine and Rehabilitation and of the European Federation of Physical Medicine and Rehabilitation.

US/1047-5354
**EUROPEAN CLINICAL LABORATORY.** [Eur. clin. lab.]. (1988)-. Periodical. English. bm. $108.00. International Scientific Communications Inc, PO Box 870, 30 Controls Drive, Shelton CT 06484-0870. **Tel** (203)926-9300, FAX (203)926-9310, telex 964292. **DD** 610. **NLM** W1; EU613P. ***Continues*** *International Clinical Products Review, 0888-7128.*
**Ind/Abst** Abstr. BioCommer.; Anal. Abstr.; Curr. Biotechnol.

SZ/0071-2655
**EUROPEAN CONFERENCE ON MICROCIRCULATION.** ***Ceased.*** [Eur. Conf. Microcirc.]. **Main/Corp** European Conference on Microcirculation. 1st (1960)-?. English (French and German). be. S. Karger AG, Allschwilerstrasse 10, PO Box - Postfach - Case Postale, CH-4009 Basel Switzerland. **Tel** 011 41 61 306-1111, FAX 011 41 61 306-1234, telex CH 962 652. **NLM** W3 EU78. **CODEN** EKMZAD. Documents available from BIOSIS Document Express.
**Ind/Abst** Biol. Abstr. (-1981).

UK/0263-9114
**EUROPEAN JOURNAL OF CHIROPRACTIC.** [Eur. j. chiropr.]. **Added/Corp** European Chiropractors' Union. Vol. 30, No. 2 (June 1982)-. Academic Scholarly Publication. English. tq (3 issues). $118.00 (institutions), $55.00 (individuals) US & Canada; £69.00 (institutions), £37.50 (individuals) Europe; £76.00 (institutions), £37.50 (individuals) other. Blackwell Scientific Publications Ltd, Marston Book Services, PO Box 87, Oxford OX2 ODT UK. **Tel** 011 44 865 791155, FAX 011 44 865 791927, telex 837 515 MARDIS G. **ED** S. Leyson. **NLM** W1 EU72BN. **[CCC]. Bk Rev. Ad Acc. Circ:** 1,000. available on microfilm and microfiche from University Microfilms International (UMI). ***Continues*** *Bulletin of the European Chiropractors' Union, 0423-6793.*
**Desc:** Scholarly articles fully backed up by sound research are accepted. Journal also encourages postgraduate work in chiropractic and education.

GW/0014-2972
**EUROPEAN JOURNAL OF CLINICAL INVESTIGATION.** [Eur. j. clin. invest.]. Vol. 1 (Mar 1970)-. Academic Scholarly Publication. English. mo (12 issues). $431.00 US & Canada; £251.50 Europe; £278.00 other. Blackwell Scientific Publications Ltd, Marston Book Services, PO Box 87, Oxford OX2 ODT UK. **Tel** 011 44 865 791155, FAX 011 44 865 791927, telex 837 515 MARDIS G. **ED** R. Arnold. **LC** R850.A1; E9. **DD** 616/.005. **NLM** W1 EU72C. **CODEN** EJCIB8. **[CCC]. Ad Acc. Pr Rev. Circ:** 1,600. available on microfilm and microfiche from University Microfilms International (UMI). Documents available from The Genuine Article, BIOSIS Document Express, CASDDS, ADONIS. ***Supersedes*** *Archiv fur Klinische Medizin, 0365-3773.*
**Desc:** Cultivation of clinical research by methods of natural science.
**Ind/Abst** ADONIS; Biol. Abstr.; Chem. Abstr.; Curr. Contents Life Sci.; Dairy Sci. Abstr.; EMBASE; Energy Res. Abstr. (Jan. 1971-); Health Plan. Adminis.; Index Med.; Nutr. Res. Newsl.; Life Sci. Collect.; PESTDOC; Protozoolog. Abstr.; Ref. Upd. Basic Ed.; Ref. Upd. Clinical Ed.; Ref. Upd. Deluxe Ed.; Res. Alert [Full Cov.]; Sci. Cit. Index; SCISEARCH; Soc. Sci. Cit. Index [Select. Cov.]; SportSearch.

UK/0960-135X
**EUROPEAN JOURNAL OF CLINICAL INVESTIGATION SUPPLEMENT.** [Eur. j. clin. investig., Suppl.]. **Added/Corp** European Society for Clinical Investigation. (1990)-. Academic Scholarly Publication. English. an. Blackwell Scientific Publications Ltd, Marston Book Services, PO Box 87, Oxford OX2 ODT UK. **Tel** 011 44 865 791155, FAX 011 44 865 791927, telex 837 515 MARDIS G.
**Ind/Abst** EMBASE.

UK/1969-9546
**EUROPEAN JOURNAL OF EMERGENCY MEDICINE.** (19??)-. Periodical. English. Four times a year. $225.00 US and Canada; £130.00 Europe; £145.00 Other. Chapman & Hall, 2-6 Boundary Row, London SE1 8HN England. **Tel** 011 44 71 865 0066, FAX 011 44 71 522 9623, telex 290164 Chapmag. **(Subscription address:** Chapman & Hall, Cheriton House, North Way, Andover, Hampshire, SP10 5BE England.**)**

NE/0929-0273
**EUROPEAN JOURNAL OF HEALTH LAW. See** Law.

FR/0223-5234
**EUROPEAN JOURNAL OF MEDICINAL CHEMISTRY.** [Eur. j. med. chem.]. **VFOAT** Chimica Therapeutica. Vol. 9 (Jan./Feb. 1974)-. Academic Scholarly Publication. English (French and German). Twelve times a year (1 volume). 2150.00F France; 2570.00F other. Editions Scientifique Elsevier, 141 rue de Javel, 75747 Paris Cedex 15 France. **Tel** 011 33 1 47 07 11 22, FAX 011 33 1 43 36 80 93. **(Subscription address:** Editions Scientifiques Elsevier / for North America, PO Box 7247-7576, Philadelphia PA 19170-7576.**) ED** C. Combet Farnoux and O. Lafont. **NLM** W1 EU72DI. **CODEN** EJMCA5. **[CCC].** Index available. **Bk Rev. Ad Acc. Pr Rev. Circ:** 1,500 (ctrl). Documents available from The Genuine Article, BIOSIS Document Express, CASDDS, ADONIS. ***Continues*** *Chimica Therapeutica, 0009-4374.*
**Desc:** Publishes studies on all aspects of medicinal chemistry.
**Ind/Abst** ADONIS; Biol. Abstr.; Chem. Abstr.; Curr. Chem. React.; Curr. Contents Life Sci.; EMBASE; Energy Res. Abstr.; For. Prod. Abstr. (1991-); For. Abstr.; Helminthol. Abstr.; Index Chem.; NAPRALERT; Nematol. Abstr.; Life Sci. Collect.; PESTDOC; Protozoolog. Abstr.; Ref. Upd. Deluxe Ed.; Res. Alert [Full Cov.]; Rev. Med. Vet. Mycology; Sci. Cit. Index; SCISEARCH.

●FR/1165-0478
**EUROPEAN JOURNAL OF MEDICINE.** French. mo. 490.00F France; $175.00 (institution), $106.00 (individual). La Presse Medicale, 120 Boulevard Street Germain, 75006 Paris France. **Tel** 011 33 1 46342160, FAX 011 33 1 44072032. **ED** Prof Leon Perlemuter. **NLM** W1; EU72DIC. **Bk Rev**, (Qty: 12). **Ad Acc, Adv Mgr:** Mme Laska, **Tel** 33 1 45 502308. **Circ:** 11,000.
**Ind/Abst** Curr. Aware. Biol. Sci., CABS.

●UK
**EUROPEAN JOURNAL OF ORIENTAL MEDICINE.** (1993)-. Academic Scholarly Publication. English. sa. £13.00 Europe; £18.00 other. Council for Acupuncture, 179 Gloucester Place, London NW1 6DX England. **Tel** 081 883 8431, FAX 071 724 5330. **ED** Carol Daglish. **Bk Rev**, (Qty: 12). **Ad Acc, Adv Mgr:** Carol Daglish, **Tel** 081 883 8431. **Pr Rev. Acid Free. Circ:** 5,000 (ctrl). ***Continues*** *British Journal of Acupuncture.*

# Medical Science and Technology

GW/0939-6365
**EUROPEAN JOURNAL OF PAIN, THE.** [Eur. j. pain]. VFOAT Journal of Pain. (1990)-. Periodical. Multiple languages. Four times a year. DM112.00 Germany; DM116.00 others. Verlag fuer Medizin VFM, Postfach 105767, W-6900 Heidelberg 1 Germany. **Tel** 011 49 6221 406248, FAX 011 49 6221 400727, telex 461683HVVFM D. **UDC** 61. *Continues Schmerz (Heidelberg), 0174-4895.*
**Ind/Abst** EMBASE.

US/0163-2787
**EVALUATION & THE HEALTH PROFESSIONS.** [Eval. health prof.]. VFOAT EHP. VAT Evaluation and the Health Professions. Vol. 1 (Spring 1978)-. English. qt (Mar., June, Sept., Dec.). $160.00. SAGE Periodical Press, 2455 Teller Road, Thousand Oaks CA 91320. **Tel** (805)499-0721, FAX (805)499-0871, telex 100799. **ED** R. Barker Bausell (Universty of Maryland). **LC** RA399.A1; E9. **DD** 362.1. **NLM** W1 EV13F. **[CCC].** **Pr Rev.** **Acid Free.** available on microfilm and microfiche from University Microfilms International (UMI). Documents available from The Genuine Article.
**Desc:** Provides a forum for all health professionals interested or engaged in the development, implementation and evaluation of health programs.
**Ind/Abst** AGRICOLA; Biostatistica (19??-19??); Cumul. Index Nurs. Allied Health Lit.; Curr. Contents Soc. Behav. Sci.; Curr. Index J. Educ.; EMBASE; Hospit. Health Admin. Index; Hum. Resour. Abstr.; Middle East Abstr. Index; Psychol. Abstr. (1984-); PsycINFO; PsycLit; Res. Alert [Full Cov.]; Sage Fam. Stud. Abstr. (?-?); Soc. Plann. Policy Dev. Abstr.; Soc. Sci. Cit. Index [Full Cov.]; Trop. Dis. Bull.; Work Relat. Abstr.

NE/0014-4053
**EXCERPTA MEDICA. SECTION 1. ANATOMY, ANTHROPOLOGY, EMBRYOLOGY AND HISTOLOGY.** See Medical Science and Technology-Abstracting, Bibliographies and Statistics.

●NE
**EXCERPTA MEDICA. SECTION 30. CLINICAL AND EXPERIMENTAL PHARMACOLOGY.** See Medical Science and Technology-Abstracting, Bibliographies and Statistics.

US/0149-9742
**EXTRAMURAL RESEARCH PROGRAMS SUPPORTED BY THE FOOD AND DRUG ADMINISTRATION.** Main/Corp United States. Food and Drug Administration. Office of Science. Extramural Research Staff. VFOAT FDA Extramural Research Programs. English. US Food and Drug Administration / FDA, 5600 Fishers Lane, Room 14-71, Rockville MD 20857. **Tel** (301)443-2410, FAX (301)443-0755. **LC** R854.U5; U538A. **DD** 610/.7/2073.

US
**FAA OFFICE OF AVIATION MEDICINE REPORTS.** English. Aviation Medicine, 800 Independence Avenue SW, Washington DC 20591.
**Ind/Abst** Psychol. Abstr.

GW/0937-8898
**FACHMEDIEN GESUNDHEIT 1989.** [Fachmed. Gesundh. 1989]. VFOAT GSK-Fachmedien Gesundheit (1989). (19??)-. German. qt (4 issues). DM380.00. GSK, Ges F Strukturanalysen, Wilh Schiedermaier Strasse 14, 84347 Pfarrkirchen Germany. **Tel** 011 49 85611796. **UDC** 61 :659.4. *Continues GSK-Fachmedien Gesundheit, 0935-8358.*

US/0161-5580
**FALK SYMPOSIUM.** [Falk Symp.]. (19??)-. English. ir. Falk Foundation EV, PO Box 6529, D 79041 Freiburg Germany. **Tel** 011 49 761 130340, telex 772458 FALK D. **NLM** W3 FA17. **CODEN** FASYDI. Documents available from CASDDS.
**Ind/Abst** Chem. Abstr.

US/0014-7257
**FAMILY HEALTH BULLETIN.** Vol. 1 (1958)-. Bulletin. English. qt. Free. Maternal and Child Health Branch of the California State Department of Health Services, Room 350 OB 8, Sacramento CA 95814. **NLM** W1 FA432BR.

US/1041-2271
**FAMILY PRACTICE NEWSLETTER, THE.** (THE FAMILY PRACTICE NEWSLETTER / EAST CAROLINA UNIVERSITY, SCHOOL OF MEDICINE, DEPARTMENT OF FAMILY MEDICINE.). [Fam. pract. newsl.]. **Added/Corp** East Carolina University. Dept. of Family Medicine. (1986)-. Newsletter. English. Twenty-four times a year. $65.00 (one year), $110.00 (two years), $150.00 (three years). Informed, PO Box 669, Mount Gretna PA 17064. **Tel** (717)531-8186. **ED** Dr. Colin P. Kerr M.D. **DD** 616. Index available. cum. index. **Circ:** 1,000.

US
**FAMILY SYSTEMS MEDICINE NEWSLETTER.** See Health and Personal Fitness.

US/1047-8892
**FAULKNER & GRAY'S MEDICINE & HEALTH.** [Faulkner Gray's med. health]. VFOAT Faulkner and Gray's Medicine and Health; Medicine and Health; Medicine & Health. Vol. 43, No. 45 (Nov. 13, 1989)-. Periodical. English. Fifty times a year. $495.00. Faulkner & Gray Inc., 11 Penn Plaza, 17th Floor, New York NY 10001. **Tel** (212)967-7000, (800)535-8403. **ED** Janet Firshein. **LC** RA395.A3; W37. **DD** 362.1/0973/05. **NLM** W1; FA964. ctrl circ. *Continues Medicine & Health, 1047-8884.*
**Desc:** Health policy newsletter reporting on and interpreting weekly developments in Congress, the White House, and the executive departments.
**Ind/Abst** Hospit. Health Admin. Index (Nov. 13, 1989-).

US
**FDA DRUG AND DEVICE PRODUCT APPROVALS LIST / (U.S.) FOOD AND DRUG ADMINISTRATION.** See Pharmacy and Pharmacology.

US
**FEDERAL PERSONNEL MANUAL SYSTEM. FPM SUPPLEMENT 792-1. OCCUPATIONAL HEALTH SERVICES FOR FEDERAL CIVILIAN EMPLOYEES.** See Public Administration-Civil Service.

US/0430-2869
**FEELINGS & THEIR MEDICAL SIGNIFICANCE.** [Feel. their med. signif.]. V. 1 (Dec. 1958)-. Periodical. English. bm. Free to health professionals. Ross Laboratories, 625 Cleveland Avenue, Columbus OH 43216. **Tel** (614)227-3333. **DD** 616. **NLM** W1 FE399.

NE/0167-7004
**FERNSTROM FOUNDATION SERIES.** [Fernstrom found. ser.]. **Added/Corp** Eric K. Fernstrom Foundation. Vol. 1 (1982)-. Monographic series. English. Price varies per volume. Elsevier Science Publishers BV, PO Box 211, 1000 AE Amsterdam Netherlands. **Tel** 011 31 20 5803642, FAX 011 31 20 5862696, telex 15682. **NLM** W1 FE746S. **CODEN** FFOSDF. Documents available from CASDDS.
**Ind/Abst** Chem. Abstr.; EMBASE.

US/0015-0282
**FERTILITY AND STERILITY.** [Fertil. steril.]. **Added/Corp** American Fertility Society. American Society for the Study of Sterility. Vol. 1 (Jan. 1950)-. Academic Scholarly Publication. English. mo. $125.00 (individual), $175.00 (institution). The American Fertility Society, 1209 Montgomery Highway, Birmingham AL 35216-2809. **Tel** (205)978-5000, FAX (205)978-5005. **ED** Roger D. Kempers. **LC** RC889; .A532. **DD** 616.69. **NLM** W1 FE839. **CODEN** FESTAS. Index available (bound in last issue). cum. index. **Bk Rev.** **Ad Acc.** **Pr Rev. Circ:** 14,000. available on microfilm. Documents available from The Genuine Article, BIOSIS Document Express, CASDDS.
**Desc:** Keeps physicians abreast of the latest developments in the field.
**Ind/Abst** AGRICOLA; Anim. Breed. Abstr.; Biol. Abstr.; Chem. Abstr.; Comb. Cumul. Index Ob./Gyn.; Curr. Aware. Biol. Sci., CABS; Curr. Biotechnol.; Curr. Contents Clin. Med.; Curr. Contents Life Sci.; Curr. Lit. Fam. Plan.; Dairy Sci. Abstr.; EMBASE; Energy Res. Abstr.; Health Plan. Adminis.; Index Med.; Index Vet.; INIS Atomindex [Micro.]; Int. Aerosp. Abstr.; Int. Pharm. Abstr.; Iowa Drug Inf. Serv. (1970-); Med. Abstr. Newsl.; Mod. Med.; NAPRALERT; Nutr. Abstr. Rev., Ser. B, Live Feeds and Feed.; Nutr. Abstr. Rev., Ser. A, Hum. Exp.; Life Sci. Collect.; PESTDOC; Physic. Medline Plus; Protozoolog. Abstr.; Ref. Upd. Basic Ed.; Ref. Upd. Deluxe Ed.; Res. Alert [Full Cov.]; Sci. Cit. Index; SCISEARCH; Soc. Sci. Cit. Index [Select. Cov.]; SportSearch; Vet. Bull.

US/0740-3178
**FERTILITY ASSISTANCE.** (FERTILITY ASSISTANCE / INSTITUTE FOR FERTILITY ASSISTANCE.). [Fertil. assist.]. Periodical. English. mo. $72.00. Institute of Fertility Assistance, 120 North 4th Avenue, Ann Arbor MI 48104-1402. **DD** 304. *Continues Surrogate Parenting News, 0736-7325.*

IT
**FIDIA RESEARCH SERIES.** **Added/Corp** FIDIA. (1985)-. Academic Scholarly Publication. English. ir. Price varies per volume. Springer-Verlag GmbH & Company KG, Heidelberger Platz 3, D 14197 Berlin Germany. **Tel** 011 49 30 8207223, FAX 011 49 30 8214091, telex 183 319 SPBLN D. **(Subscription address:** Springer Verlag New York Inc. / Order Dept. North America, 44 Hartz Way, Secaucus NJ 07096.) **NLM** W1; FI322. **CODEN** FRSEEA. Documents available from CASDDS.
**Ind/Abst** Chem. Abstr. (1985-).

US/0739-8131
**FILIPINO PHYSICIANS IN AMERICA.** [Filip. phys. Am.]. V. 1-. English. Phillipine Hertitage Publications, PO Box 1606, Indianapolis IN 46206. **LC** R697.F6; F55. **DD** 610/.92/2; B.

US/0071-4909
**FILM REFERENCE GUIDE FOR MEDICINE AND ALLIED SCIENCES.** **Added/Corp** United States. Federal Advisory Council on Medical Training Aids. Library of Congress. United States. Interdepartmental Committee on Medical Training Aids. (June 1956)-. Government Publication. English. an. Superintendent of Documents, US Government Printing Office, Washington DC 20402. **Tel** (202)275-3328, FAX (202)786-2377. **LC** R835; .F5. **DD** 610.84. **NLM** ZW 18 F487.

FI/0015-2501
**FINSKA LAKARESALLSKAPETS HANDLINGAR.** [Fin. Lakaresallsk. handl.]. **Main/Corp** Finska Lakaresallskapet. Vol. 1 (1841)-. Periodical. Finnish. an. Fmk160.00. Finska Lalaresallskapet, PB 316, 00171 Helsingfors Finland. **Tel** 011 358 90 665576. **(Subscription address:** Centre Exchange Publishing Scientifque, Rauhankatu 15 B, 00170 Helsinki Finland.) **NLM** W1 FI605C.
**Ind/Abst** EMBASE.

IT/0367-326X
**FITOTERAPIA.** See Biology-Botany.

FR/0985-2662
**FLASH ETAT-UNIS.** See Biology.

FR/0985-2654
**FLASH JAPON.** See Biology.

FR/0769-1432
**FLASH ... SUR LA RECHERCHE SCIENTIFIQUE ET MEDICALE A L'UNIVERSITE PIERRE ET MARIE CURIE.** (1981)-. French. an. **NLM** W1; FL595.

US/1051-578X
**FLEX AND SPEX INFORMATION BULLETIN.** [FLEX SPEX inf. bull.]. **Added/Corp** Federation of State Medical Boards of the United States. (1990)-. Bulletin. English. Federation of State Medical Boards of the United States Inc, 2630 West Freeway/Suite 138, Fort Worth TX 76102-7199. **DD** 610. *Continues FLEX Information Bulletin.*

US
**FLORIDA MEDICAL DIRECTORY.** **Main/Corp** Florida Medical Association. (1938)-. Directory. English. an (published in April or May). $75.00. Florida Medical Association Inc, PO Box 2411, ATTN: Directory, Jacksonville FL 32203. **Tel** (904)356-1571, FAX (904)353-1247. **ED** R. G. Lacsamana. **LC** R712.A2; F63. **DD** 614.2409759. **Ad Acc. Circ:** 15,500.
**Desc:** Scientific material targeted towards the medical profession in Florida.

US/0733-1223
**FLORIDA RELATIVE VALUE STUDIES.** [Fla. relat. value stud.]. Began in 1962. English. ir. $17.50. Florida Medical Association Inc, PO Box 2411, ATTN: Directory, Jacksonville FL 32203. **Tel** (904)356-1571, FAX (904)353-1247. **LC** R728.5. **DD** 338.4/361/09759. **NLM** W1; FL52JK.

US/0744-589X
**FMG, THE.** (THE FMG : THE NEWSLETTER FOR THE FOREIGN MEDICAL GRADUATE / SPECIAL COMMITTEE ON FOREIGN MEDICAL GRADUATES OF THE NEW YORK COUNTY MEDICAL SOCIETY.). VFOAT F.M.G. VAT Foreign Medical Graduate. Vol. 1, No. 1 (Apr. 1982)-. Newsletter. English. qt. Special Committee on Foreign Medical Graduates, New York County Medical Society, 40 West 57th Street, New York NY 10019.

US/0885-7032
**FMG NEWSLETTER / CIVIC RESEARCH CENTER.** [FMG newsl.]. **Added/Corp** Civic Research Center (Memphis, Tenn.). VAT Foreign Medical Graduates Newsletter. (19??)-. Newsletter. English. mo (10 issues). $55.00 (institutions), $40.00 (individuals) US; $65.00 other. FMG Newsletter, PO Box 41831, Memphis TN 38174. **Tel** (901)522-6112. **DD** 610.

US
**FOCUS (BOSTON, MASS.).** (FOCUS.). Began in Sept. 1971. Periodical. English. wk. Harvard University / Boston, News Office for the Medical Area, 25 Shattuck Street, Boston MA 02115. *Continues Harvard Medical Area Newsletter and Focus on Medical Area Meetings.*

GW/0940-9998
**FOCUS MUL : ZEITSCHRIFT FUER WISSENSCHAFT, FORSCHUNG UND LEHRE AN DER MEDIZINISCHEN UNIVERSITAT ZU LUBECK.** (1991)-. Periodical. German. qt. Hansisches Verlagskontor Herr Scheffler, Herr Scheffler Mengstr, Postfach 2051,

D-23552 Luebeck 1 Germany. **Tel** 011 49 451 16050. ***Continues*** *Focus MHL, 0176-3857.*
**Ind/Abst** Chem. Abstr.

US/0887-1566
**FOCUS ON AUTISTIC BEHAVIOR.** [Focus autistic behav.]. (1986)-. Periodical. English. bm (6 issues). $24.00 (individuals), $45.00 (institutions) US and Canada; $65.00 other. Pro-Ed Inc., 8700 Shoal Creek Boulevard, Austin TX 78757-6897. **Tel** (512)451-3246, FAX (512)451-8542. **LC** RJ506.A9; F63. **DD** 616. **CODEN** FAUBES.
**Ind/Abst** Acad. Search (July 1993-); Except. Child Educ. Resour.; INFO-SOUTH Abstr.; Mag. Search; Psychol. Abstr. (1986-); PsycINFO; PsycLit.

US
**FOCUS ON RURAL HEALTH.** English. Four times a year. Free on request. University of North Dakota School of Medicine, The Center for Rural Health, 501 Columbia Road North, Grand Forks ND 58203. **Tel** (701)777-3848. **ED** Ross Collins.

HU/0015-5314
**FOGORVOSI SZEMLE.** [Fogorv. sz.]. Vol. 1, (1908)-. Periodical. Hungarian. ir. $36.00. **(Subscription address:** Kultura, PO Box 149, H 1389 Budapest 62 Hungary**)** **NLM** W1 FO122. ***Supersedes*** *Magyar Fogorvosk Lapja.*
**Ind/Abst** Index Med.; Index Dent. Lit.

BL/0015-5454
**FOLHA MEDICA.** (A FOLHA MEDICA.). [Folha med.]. (1920)-. Periodical. Portuguese. mo. Cidade-Editora Cientifica Ltda., PO Box 4847, Rua Mexico 90 - 2 andar, 20031 Rio de Janeiro Brazil. **NLM** W1 FO125H. Index Available in first issue of next volume--loose--separately paged.
**Ind/Abst** EMBASE [Select. Cov.].

XO/0430-8611
**FOLIA FACULTATIS MEDICAE UNIVERSITATIS COMENIANAE BRATISLAVIENSIS.** [Folia Fac. Med. Univ. Comen. Bratisl.]. **Main/Corp** Bratislava. Univerzita. Lekarska Fakulta. Czech (summaries and/or abstracts in Russian and English). Ustredna Kniznica a SIS Lekarskej Fakulty UK, Odborarske nam 14 813 72, Bratislava Slovakia. **NLM** W1 FO176. **CODEN** FFMDAP. Documents available from BIOSIS Document Express.
**Ind/Abst** Biol. Abstr.; EMBASE [Select. Cov.].

PL/0015-5616
**FOLIA MEDICA CRACOVIENSIA.** [Folia med. crac.]. **Added/Corp** Polska Akademia Nauk. Oddzial w Krakowie. Komisja Nauk Medycznych. Vol. 1 (1959)-. Academic Scholarly Publication. Polish (summaries and/or abstracts in English). Sixteen times a year (Publishes four issues per volume). **(Subscription address:** ARS Polona, PO Box 1001, 00068 Warsaw Poland.**)** **NLM** W1 FO225. **CODEN** FMCRAW. Documents available from BIOSIS Document Express, CASDDS.
**Ind/Abst** Biol. Abstr.; Chem. Abstr.; EMBASE [Select. Cov.]; Index Med.

BN/0350-0705
**FOLIA MEDICA FACULTATIS MEDICINAE UNIVERSITATIS SARAEVIENSIS.** [Folia med. Fac. med. Univ. Saraev.]. **Added/Corp** Univerzitet v Sarajevo. **VFOAT** Folia Medica Saraeviensis. Vol.1 (Oct. 1966)-. Academic Scholarly Publication. English (summaries and/or abstracts in Serbian). **NLM** W1 FO225F. **CODEN** FOMDBL. Documents available from CASDDS.
**Ind/Abst** Chem. Abstr. (-1985); EMBASE; Trop. Dis. Bull.

BU/0204-8043
**FOLIA MEDICA (PLOVDIV).** (FOLIA MEDICA.). [Folia med.]. **Added/Corp** Vissh Meditsinski Institut "I.P. Pavlov," Plovdiv. Vol. 1 (1959)-. Academic Scholarly Publication. Multiple languages (English, French, German and Russian). sa. Available on exchange basis only. Academia Medica IP Pavlov, 8 Tsanko Djustabanov St, Plovdiv Bulgaria. **NLM** W1 FO22. **CODEN** FOLMA8. Documents available from BIOSIS Document Express, CASDDS.
**Ind/Abst** Biol. Abstr. (-1984); Chem. Abstr.; EMBASE; Health Plan. Adminis.; Saf. Health Work.

SZ
**FORSCHENDE KOMPLEMENTARMEDIZIN.** (19??)-. German. Six times a year. $92.00. S. Karger AG, Allschwilerstrasse 10, PO Box - Postfach - Case Postale, CH-4009 Basel Switzerland. **Tel** 011 41 61 306-1111, FAX 011 41 61 306-1234, telex CH 962 652. **ED** D. Melchart, A. Stacher, D.G.S. Thilo-Korner, M. Ullmann.

GW/0440-1298
**FORSCHUNG UND ERGEBNISSE DES BEREICHES MEDIZIN.** Periodical. German. Martin-Luther-Universitat Halle-Wittenberg, August-Bebel-Strasse 13, DDR-4010 Halle Germany. **Tel** 895 271, telex 04 353 UNI HAL DD. **LC** AS182; .H125 subser [RS1]. **DD** 610/.5.

GW/0170-3331
**FORTSCHRITT UND FORTBILDUNG IN DER MEDIZIN.** (FORTSCHRITT UND FORTBILDUNG IN DER MEDIZIN : JAHRBUCH / .... INTERDISZIPLINARES FORUM DER BUNDESARZTEKAMMER.). [Fortschr. Fortbild. Med.]. **Main/Conf** Interdisziplinares Forum der Bundesarztekammer. **Main/Corp** Interdisziplinares Forum der Bundesarztekammer. **Added/Corp** Bundesaerztekammer. **VFOAT** Jahrbuch. (1976/1977)-. German. an. DM45.00. Bundesaerztekammer, PO Box 41 02 20, Herbert-Lewin-Str. 1, D 50931 Cologne Germany. **Tel** 011 49 221 4004240. **NLM** W3; IN11888L.
**Ind/Abst** EMBASE [Select. Cov.].

GW/0938-9407
**FORTSCHRITTE DER DIAGNOSTIK.** (Apr. 15, 1990)-. Periodical. German. qt. Urban & Vogel, Postfach 152209, D-80052 Munich Germany. **Tel** 011 49 89 53292140, FAX 089/536052, telex 521701. **NLM** W1; FO853D.

GW/0015-8178
**FORTSCHRITTE DER MEDIZIN.** [Fortschr. Med.]. Vol. 1 (Jan. 1883)-. Academic Scholarly Publication. German (summaries and/or abstracts in English and French). Thirty-six times a year. DM202.00 Germany; DM284.00 other. Urban & Vogel, Postfach 152209, D-80052 Munich Germany. **Tel** 011 49 89 53292140, FAX 089/536052, telex 521701. **ED** T V Keil. **NLM** W1 FO86. **CODEN** FMDZAR. **[CCC]**. Index available. **Bk Rev. Ad Acc. Circ:** 40,000 (ctrl). Documents available from CASDDS. ***Absorbed*** *Medizinische Praxis, 0175-6125.*
**Desc:** Medical magazine for the whole field of practical medicine.
**Ind/Abst** Chem. Abstr.; EMBASE; Health Plan. Adminis.; Index Med.; Nutr. Abstr. Rev., Ser. B, Live Feeds and Feed.; Nutr. Abstr. Rev., Ser. A, Hum. Exp.; Life Sci. Collect.; Protozoolog. Abstr.; SportSearch.

GW/0932-5611
**FORTSCHRITTE DER MEDIZIN. SUPPLEMENT : DIE KONGRESSINFORMATION FUER DIE PRAXIS.** (1985)-. Monographic series. German. ir. Price varies per volume. Urban & Vogel, Postfach 152209, D-80052 Munich Germany. **Tel** 011 49 89 53292140, FAX 089/536052, telex 521701. **NLM** W1; FO86BA.
**Ind/Abst** EMBASE.

CN/0836-3463
**FORUM / ASSOCIATION OF CANADIAN MEDICAL COLLEGES.** [Forum - Assoc. Can. Med. Coll.]. **Added/Corp** Association of Canadian Medical Colleges. Vol. 20, No. 1 (Dec./Jan. 1987)-. Periodical. English (summaries and/or abstracts in French). Six times a year (Jan., Mar., May, July, Sept., Nov.). 30.00Can$ Canada; 35.00Can$ US; 40.00Can$ others. Association of Canadian Medical Colleges, 774 Echo Drive, Ottawa, Ontario K1S 5P2 Canada. **Tel** (613)730-0687. **DD** 610/.7/1171. **NLM** W1; FO943Q. ***Continues*** *Association of Canadian Medical Colleges. ACMC Forum., 0317-5006.*

SP/0212-9965
**FORUM BARCELONA.** [ForumBarc.]. (1984)-. Periodical. Spanish. Eleven times a year. Mayo SA, Muntaner 374-376, 08006 Barcelona Spain. **Tel** 209 02 55, FAX 202 06 43. **ED** Jose Mayoral and Josep Ferrando. **UDC** 61. **Ad Acc.** ***Continues*** *Forum Medico, 0212-7369.*
**Desc:** Information about the more relevant national and international meetings of medicine.

US/0148-4710
**FORUM ON INFECTION.** V. 1- June 1974-. Monographic series. English. bm. Price varies per volume. Biomedical Information Corporation, 800 Second Avenue, New York NY 10017. **Tel** (212)262-9662. **NLM** W1 FO958G.

IT/0015-9271
**FRACASTORO, IL.** [Fracastoro]. Vol. 1- June 1905-. Academic Scholarly Publication. Italian (summaries and/or abstracts in French, English and German). qt. $13.00. Istituti Ospitalieri Verona, Piazza a Stefani 1, Verona Italy. **Tel** (045)932370. **NLM** W1 FR138. **CODEN** FRACAC. **Bk Rev. Ad Acc. Circ:** 2,000 (ctrl). Documents available from BIOSIS Document Express.
**Desc:** Covers general medicine, clinical problems, laboratory epidemiology, and psychiatry.
**Ind/Abst** Biol. Abstr.; EMBASE.

US
**FREELANCE DIRECTORY.** **See** Journalism.

US/1066-8322
**FRONTIERS IN HEADACHE RESEARCH.** [Front. headache res.]. Vol. 1 (1991)-. Academic Scholarly Publication. English. ir. Price varies per volume. Raven Press, 1185 Avenue of the Americas, 37th Floor, New York NY 10036. **Tel** (212)930-9500, (212)930-9604, FAX (212)869-3495, (212)302-8507, telex 640073. **ED** Jes Olesen. **DD** 616. **NLM** W1; FR945YD. **CODEN** FHREE3. Documents available from CASDDS.
**Ind/Abst** Chem. Abstr.

US/1062-5380
**FSMBNEWSLINE (FORT WORTH, TEX.).** (FSMBNEWSLINE.). [FSMBNewsline]. **Added/Corp** Federation of State Medical Boards of the United States. **VFOAT** FSMB Newsline. **VAT** Federation of State Medical Boards Newsline. Dec. (1991)-. Periodical. English. Six times a year. $25.00. Federation of State Medical Boards of the United States, 6000 West Place, Suite 707, Ft Worth TX 76107. **Tel** (817)735-8445, FAX (817)738-6629. **DD** 610. ***Continues*** *FSMB Newsletter, 0888-5664.*

GW/0863-2693
**FUER DIE MEDIZINISCHE PRAXIS.** [Fuer med. Prax.]. (1988)-. Monographic series. English. ir. Price varies per volume. Gustav Fischer Verlag Jena, Postfach 100537, D 07705 Jena Germany. **Tel** 011 49 3641 27332, FAX 011 49 3641 626500. **CODEN** FMPREX. Documents available from BIOSIS Document Express.
**Ind/Abst** Biol. Abstr.

JA
**FUJITA GAKUEN IGAKKAISHI.** [Fujita Gakuen Igakkaishi]. **Added/Corp** Fujita Gakuen Igakkai. Nagoya Hoken Eisei Daigaku. **VFOAT** Bulletin of the Fujita-Gakuen Medical Society. (1977)-. Periodical. Japanese. an. Nagoya Hoken Eisei Daigaku, Do Igakkai, Fujita Gakkuen Igakkai, 1-98 Dengakuga, Kubo, Kutsuaki-cho, Toyoake, Aichi-ken 470-11 Japan. **CODEN** FGIGDO. Documents available from CASDDS.
**Ind/Abst** Chem. Abstr.

JA
**FUKUOKA ACTA MEDICA.** **VFOAT** Fukuoka Igaku Zasshi. V. 20- 1927-. Periodical. Japanese (summaries and/or abstracts in English). mo. Fukuoka Igakkai, (Fukuoka Medical Soceity), Kyushu Daigaku Igakubu, 1-1, Maidashi 3 Chome, Higashiku, Fukuokashi, Fukuokaken 812 Japan. **(Subscription address:** Japan Publications Trading Company, Ltd., PO Box 5030, Tokyo International, Tokyo 100-31 Japan.**)** ***Continues*** *Fukuoka-Ikwadaigaku-Zasshi.*
**Ind/Abst** Index Med.

JA/0016-254X
**FUKUOKA IGAKU ZASSHI.** ([FUKUOKA IGAKU ZASSHI] [FUKUOKA MEDICAL JOURNAL] FUKUOKA ACTA MEDICA.). [Fukuoka igaku zasshi]. **Added/Corp** Fukuoka Igakkai. Kyusku Teikoku Daigaku. Igakubu. **VFOAT** Fukuoka Medical Journal; Fukuoka Acta Medica. Vol. 33 (1940)-. Academic Scholarly Publication. Japanese. Kyushu University / Kyushu Association of Neuro-Psychiatry, Fukuoka 812, 3-1-1 Maidashi Higashiku Japan. **NLM** W1; FU503. **CODEN** FKIZA4. Documents available from BIOSIS Document Express, CASDDS. ***Continues*** *Fukuoka Ika Daigaku Zasshi.*
**Ind/Abst** Biol. Abstr.; Chem. Abstr.; EMBASE; Health Plan. Adminis.; Index Med.

JA/0016-2582
**FUKUSHIMA IGAKU ZASSHI.** (FUKUSHIMA IGAKU ZASSHI. FUKUSHIMA MEDICAL JOURNAL.). [Fukushima igaku zasshi]. **VFOAT** Fukushima Medical Journal. (1951)-. Periodical. Japanese. qt. $162.00. Fukushima Society of Medical Science, 1 Hikarigaoka, 960-12 Fukushima Japan. **(Subscription address:** Japan Publications Trading Company, Ltd., PO Box 5030, Tokyo International, Tokyo 100-31 Japan.**)** **NLM** W1 FU512. **CODEN** FSIZAQ. Documents available from CASDDS.
**Ind/Abst** Chem. Abstr.; EMBASE [Select. Cov.].

JA/0016-2590
**FUKUSHIMA JOURNAL OF MEDICAL SCIENCE.** [Fukushima J. Med. Sci.]. **Added/Corp** Fukushima Kenritsu Ika Daigaku. Vol. 1 (Mar 1954)-. Periodical. English. qt. Fukushima Medical College Library, 5 75 Sugitsumacho, Fukushimashi 960 Japan. **Tel** 0245 211211. **NLM** W1 FU515. **CODEN** FJMSAU. Documents available from CASDDS.
**Ind/Abst** Chem. Abstr. (-1987); EMBASE; Health Plan. Adminis.; Index Med.; Trop. Dis. Bull.

GW/0722-3684
**FUNKTIONELLE BIOLOGIE & MEDIZIN.** **See** Biology.

CN/0225-395X
**FUTURE HEALTH.** (FUTURE HEALTH. PERSPECTIVES SANTE.). [Future health]. **Added/Corp** Canadians for Health Research. **VFOAT** Perspectives Sante; Sante a l'Avenir. Vol. 1 (Dec. 1979)-. Periodical. English (French). qt. 15.00Can$. Canadians for Health Research, PO Box 126, Westmount Quebec H3Z 2T1 Canada. **Tel** (514)398-7478, FAX (514)398-8361. **ED** Heather Pengelley. **DD** 610/.7/2071. **NLM** W1 FU612. **Bk Rev**, (Qty: approx. 2/yr). **Circ:** 2,000 (ctrl). ***Formed by the union of*** *Canadians for Health Research. Newsletter, 0226-1340* ***and*** *Nouvelles des C R M, 0226-1332.*
**Desc:** Health science research in Canada, articles by scientists, voluntary health associations, health workers, the public government departments. News, people, items and book reviews and announcements of meetings.

XR/0072-0038
**FYSIATRICKY A REUMATOLOGICKY VESTNIK.** [Fysiatr. reumatol. vestn.]. **Added/Corp** Ceskoslovenska Fysiatricka Spolecnost. Ceskoslovenska Lekarska Spolecnost J.E. Purkyne. Reumatologicka Sekce. Vol. 44 (June 1966)-. Periodical. Czech (summaries and/or abstracts in English and Russian). Four times a year. $54.80. Avicenum Medical Press, Malostranske Nam 28, 11802 Prague Czech Republic. **Tel** 011 42 2 530643. **(Subscription address:** Artia Pegas Press Ltd., Palac Metro Narodni Trida 25, 11210 Prague 1 Czech Republic.) **NLM** W1 FY634. **CODEN** FYRVAX. **[CCC].** ***Continues*** *Fysiatricky Vestnik.*
**Ind/Abst** EMBASE.

●IT/1120-8392
**G & B : GIORNALE DI CLINIA MEDICA & BASI RAZIONALI DELLA TERAPIA.** **VFOAT** Giornale di Clinia Medica & Basi Razionali Della Terapia; Giornale di Clinia Medica e Basi Razionali Della Terapia; G e B. (1993)-. Periodical. Italian. Twenty times a year. $130.00. Piccin Editore, Via Altinate 107, 35121 Padua Italy. **Tel** 011 39 49 655566, FAX 011 39 49 8750693. **CODEN** GCMTEX. ***Formed by the union of*** *Giornale di Clinica Medica* ***and*** *Basi Razionali Della Terapia.*

SP/0304-4858
**GACETA MEDICA DE BILBAO.** [Gac. med. Bilbao]. (1971)-. Periodical. Spanish (table of contents in English). **NLM** W1 GA23N. **CODEN** GCMBA9. Documents available from CASDDS. ***Continues*** *Gaceta Medica del Norte.*
**Ind/Abst** Chem. Abstr.; Indice Med. Esp.

VE/0367-4762
**GACETA MEDICA DE CARACAS.** [Gac. med. Caracas]. Vol. 1- Apr. 1893-. Academic Scholarly Publication. Spanish (English). qt. Free. Academia Nacional de Medicina, Apartado de Correo 804, Caracas 1010-A Venezuela. **Tel** 483/36/91. **NLM** W1 GA231.
**Ind/Abst** EMBASE; Trop. Dis. Bull.

MX/0016-3813
**GACETA MEDICA DE MEXICO.** [Gac. med. Mex.]. 1864-1900. Periodical. Spanish. mo. $50.00. Unidad de Conjunto Centro Med Nac, Bloque B Av Cuauhtemoc 330, Mexico 7 DF Mexico. **Tel** 52/5/564/5019. **LC** R21; .G2. **DD** 610.6272. **NLM** W1 GA258. **CODEN** GMMEAK. **Circ:** 5,000. available on microfilm from University Microfilms International (UMI). Documents available from CASDDS.
**Ind/Abst** Chem. Abstr.; Index Med.; Life Sci. Collect.

●UK/0966-6362
**GAIT & POSTURE.** **VFOAT** Gait and Posture. Vol. 1, No. 1 (Mar. 1993)-. Periodical. English. Four times a year. $187.00 The Americas; £125.00 other. Butterworth Heinemann Publishers, Linacre House, Jordan Hill, Oxford OX2 8DP England. **Tel** 011 44 865 310366. **(Subscription address:** Elsevier Science Ltd. Oxford Fulfillment Centre, PO Box 800, Kidlington, Oxford OX5 1DX United Kingdom.) **LC** QP310.W3; G34. **DD** 612.7/6/05. **NLM** W1; GA363G.
**Desc:** Provides a vehicle for the publication of up-to-date basic and clinical research on all aspects of locomotion and balance.
**Ind/Abst** Soc. Sci. Cit. Index [Select. Cov.].

SP/0304-4866
**GALICIA CLINICA.** [Galicia clin.]. (1929)-. Periodical. Spanish. mo. Asociacion de Prensa Medica ES, Juana de Vega 13 2, E 15004 La Corun Spain. **Tel** 011 34 81 222596. **UDC** 61.
**Ind/Abst** EMBASE [Select. Cov.]; Indice Med. Esp.

US/0740-7025
**GAP CONFERENCE REPORT / RESEARCH PROGRAM, CYSTIC FIBROSIS FOUNDATION.** [GAP conf. rep.]. **Main/Corp** Cystic Fibrosis Foundation. Research Program. **VFOAT** G.A.P. Conference Report. Vol. 4, No. 1-. English. ir. Cystic Fibrosis Foundation, 6000 Executive Blvd., Suite 309, Rockville MD 20852. **Tel** (301)881-9130. ***Continues*** *Cystic Fibrosis "GAP" Conference Report, 0196-2418.*

KO/0377-9483
**GATORRIG DAIHAG UIHAG-BU RONMUN-JIB.** (KATOLLIK TAEHAK UIHAKPU NONMUNJIP.). [Gatorrig Daihag Uihag-bu Ronmun-jib]. **Added/Corp** Katollik Taehak (Seoul, Korea). Taehagwon. Katollik Taehak (Seoul, Korea). Uihakpu. **VFOAT** Theses of Catholic Medical College; Journal of Catholic Medical College. (1957)-. Periodical. Korean (English). qt. **LC** R97.7.K6; K37. **NLM** W1 KA89K. **CODEN** KTUNAA. Documents available from BIOSIS Document Express, CASDDS.
**Ind/Abst** Biol. Abstr.; Chem. Abstr.

FR/0760-758X
**GAZETTE MEDICALE.** [Gaz. med.]. V. 91 No. 1 (with No. 6 12/01/84)-. Periodical. French. wk. Gazette Medicale de France, 123 rue de Tocqueville, 75017 Paris France. **Tel** 1 47 66 52 36. **NLM** W1; GA756D. **[CCC].** ***Continues*** *Gazette Medicale de France (Paris, France : 1969), 0016-5557.*
**Ind/Abst** Biodeter. Abstr.; Dairy Sci. Abstr.; Helminthol. Abstr. (1991-); Index Vet.; Nutr. Abstr. Rev., Ser. A, Hum. Exp.; Protozoolog. Abstr.; Rev. Agric. Entomol.; Rev. Med. Vet. Entomol.; Rev. Med. Vet. Mycology; SCISEARCH; SportSearch.

IT/0393-3660
**GAZZETTA MEDICA ITALIANA, ARCHIVIO PER LE SCIENZE MEDICHE.** Vol. 143 (Jan./Feb. 1984)-. Periodical. Italian. Six times a year. $95.00 (individuals), $145.00 (institutions). Edizioni Minerva Medica, Corso Bramante 83-85, 10126 Turin Italy. **Tel** 011 39 11 678282, FAX 011 39 11 674502. ***Formed by the union of*** *Archivio per le Scienze Mediche, 0004-0312* ***and*** *Gazzetta Medica Italiana, 0016-5670.*
**Desc:** Covers clinical and experimental medicine and surgery.
**Ind/Abst** EMBASE.

NE/0921-5360
**GEDRAG & GEZONDHEID.** See Psychology.

GW/0016-6006
**GELBEN HEFTE, DIE.** Vol. 1 (1961)-. Periodical. German. qt. DM36.00. Medizinish Verlagsgesellschaft, PO Box 1732, W 3550 Marburg F.R.Germany. **Tel** 011 49 6421 22230.

JA/0388-6719
**GENDAI TOYO IGAKU.** [Gendai Toyo igaku]. **VFOAT** Journal of Traditional Sino-Japanese Medicine. Vol. 1, No. 1 (July 1980)-. Academic Scholarly Publication. Japanese. qt. $108.00. Igaku Shuppan Senta, (Medical Publications Center Inc.), Toshimaya Biru, 5-1, Sarugakucho 1 Chome, Chiyodaku, Tokyoto 101 Japan. **(Subscription address:** Kyowa Book Company, Inc., 1-38 Kanda Jinbo-Cho, Chiyoda-Ku Tokyo 101, Japan) **NLM** W1 GE184G. **CODEN** GTIGDO. Documents available from CASDDS.
**Ind/Abst** Chem. Abstr.

UK/1356-1308
**GENE THERAPY.** (19??)-. English. £110.00. SUBIS, Mansion House, 19 Kingfield Road, Sheffield S11 9AS England. **Tel** 011 44 114 255 4433, FAX 011 44 114 255 4626.

NE/0168-437X
**GENEES- EN VERBANDMIDDELENINDUSTRIE / CENTRAAL BUREAU VOOR DE STATISTIEK, HOOFDAFDELING STATISTIEKEN VAN INDUSTRIE EN BOUWNIJVERHEID.** **VFOAT** Manufacture of Drugs, Medicines, and Dressings. Dutch (summaries and/or abstracts in English). an. Fl9.50. Centraal Bureau voor de Statistiek, AFD ALG Zaken, Postbus 959, 2270 AZ Voorburg Netherlands. **Tel** 011 31 70 3373800, FAX 011 31 038 7429, telex 32692 CBS NL. **LC** HD9671.N4; G45. ***Continues*** *Genees- en Verbandmiddelenindustrie Produktiestatistieken.*

NE/0016-6464
**GENEESKUNDIGE GIDS (1969- ).** (1969)-. Periodical. German. bw.

NE/0304-4629
**GENEESMIDDELENBULLETIN.** See Pharmacy and Pharmacology.

FR/0183-4568
**GENERALISTE PARIS, LE.** (GENERALISTE.). (1975)-. Periodical. French. wk (Twice a week except for the month of Aug.). 156.71F France; 1050.00F others. Editions Medecin Generaliste, 11 Blvd Sebastopol, 75001 Paris France. **Tel** 011 33 1 42336174. **UDC** 61. **[CCC].**

US/1061-2289
**GENESIS REPORT/DX, THE.** (THE GENESIS REPORT / DX : BUSINESS IMPLICATIONS OF TECHNOLOGY INNOVATION IN DIAGNOSTIC MEDICINE.). [Genes. rep./Dx]. **VFOAT** Genesis Report Dx. (1991)-. Periodical. English. bm. $795.00 US; $850.00 other. Genesis Group, 29 Park Street, Montclair NJ 07042. **Tel** (201)509-7735 or, 509-7740. **DD** 338. **NLM** W1; GE276K.

US
**GEORGIA MANAGED CARE.** English. Eight times a year (4 newsletters and 4 directories, alternating months). $150.00. Harkey and Associates Inc., PO Box 159025, 2000 Richard Jones Road, Suite 170, Nashville TN 37215. **Tel** (615)385-4131, FAX (615)385-4979.

SZ/0016-9161
**GESNERUS.** [Gesnerus]. **Added/Corp** Schweizerische Gesellschaft fur Geschichte der Medizin und der Naturwissenschaften. Vol. 1, (1943)-. Periodical. German. Three times a year. 95.00F Europe; 104.00F other. Sauerlaender AG, Laurenzenvorstadt 89, CH 5001 Aarau Switzerland. **Tel** 011 41 64 268626. **NLM** W1; GE823. **[CCC].**
**Ind/Abst** Am. Hist. Life (1988-); Health Plan. Adminis.; Index Med.; Math. Rev.

GW/0016-9307
**GESUNDHEITSPOLITISCHE UMSCHAU.** See Pharmacy and Pharmacology.

GW
**GESUNDHEITSREPORT INTERN.** (19??)-. German. mo. DM96.00. Extec Marketing GmbH, Rosenaeckerstr 30, W 7046 Gaeufelden FR Germany. **Tel** 011 49 7032 78030.

●US/1066-2367
**GETTING THE MOST FOR YOUR MEDICAL DOLLAR.** See Consumer Interests.

●NE
**GEWINA.** See Science and Technology.

GH/0016-9560
**GHANA MEDICAL JOURNAL.** [Ghana med. j.]. V. 1- 1962-. Periodical. English. ir. Ghana Medical Journal, Box 297, Accra Ghana Africa. **NLM** W1 GH377. **CODEN** GHMJAY. Documents available from BIOSIS Document Express.
**Ind/Abst** Biol. Abstr.; EMBASE; Nutr. Abstr. Rev., Ser. B, Live Feeds and Feed.; Nutr. Abstr. Rev., Ser. A, Hum. Exp.

JA/0072-4521
**GIFU DAIGAKU IGAKUBU KIYO.** (GIFU DAIGAKU IGAKUBU KIYO. ACTA SCHOLAE MEDICINALIS UNIVERSITATIS IN GIFU.). [Gifu Daigaku Igakubu kiyÂo]. **Added/Corp** Gifu Daigaku. Igakubu. **VFOAT** Acta Scholae Medicinales Universitatis in Gifu; Kiyo-Igakubu, Gifu Daigaku. (1967)-. Periodical. Japanese (summaries and/or abstracts in English; table of contents in English). Six times a year. Free. Gifu Daigaku Igakubu Kiyo, 40 Tsukasacho, Gifushi Gifu Ken 500 Japan. **NLM** W1 GI113N. **CODEN** GDIKAN. Index available in last issue of volume--attached. Documents available from BIOSIS Document Express, CASDDS. ***Continues*** *Gifu Ika Daigaku Kiyo. Acta Scholae Medicinalis in Gifu.*
**Ind/Abst** Biol. Abstr.; Chem. Abstr.

IT/0391-8866
**GIORNALE DEI CONGRESSI MEDICI : GCM : L'AGGIORNAMENTO IN DIRETTA DAI CONGRESSI, IL.** (19??)-. Periodical. Italian. bm. L50000, $35.53. CIC Edizioni Internazionali, Via L Spallanzani 11, 00161 Rome Italy. **Tel** 011 39 6 841-2673, FAX 011 39 6 844-3365, telex 622099 CIC I. **ED** Andrea Salvati. **NLM** W1; GI313.

IT/0393-8492
**GIORNALE DEL MEDICO, IL.** (1985)-. Periodical. Italian. sw. L17000 Italy. Masson S.P.A, Via Statuto 2/4, 20121 Milan Italy. **Tel** 011 39 2 63671, FAX 011 39 2 6367211. **UDC** 61.

IT/0017-0364
**GIORNALE DI MEDICINA MILITARE.** [G. med. milit.]. (1908)-. Periodical. Italian. Six times a year. $75.00. M D Uff AMM Spec G Medicina MI, via Marsala 104, 00185 Rome Italy. **Tel** 011 39 6 47357939. **ED** Stato Maggiore Esercito. **NLM** W1 GI617H. **CODEN** GMMIAW. Index available. cum. index. **Bk Rev. Ad Acc. Pr Rev.** ctrl circ. Documents available from CASDDS. ***Continues*** *Giornale Medico del Regio Esercito.*
**Desc:** Medicine and related science papers and general culture topics.
**Ind/Abst** Chem. Abstr.; EMBASE; Saf. Health Work.

IT/0017-0445
**GIORNALE ITALIANO DI CHEMIOTERAPIA.** ***Ceased.*** [G. ital. chemioter.]. (1954)-(1989). Academic Scholarly Publication. Italian (summaries and/or abstracts in English). an. Edizioni Minerva Medica, Corso Bramante 83-85, 10126 Turin Italy. **Tel** 011 39 11 678282, FAX 011 39 11 674502. **ED** C Grassi. **NLM** W1 GI769. **CODEN** GICTAL. **Ad Acc.** Documents available from CASDDS.
**Desc:** Journal addressed to practitioners and specialists in chemotherapy in Italy and abroad. It deals with topics in chemotherapy, scientific practice and research.
**Ind/Abst** Chem. Abstr.; EMBASE; Health Plan. Adminis.; Index Med.; Index Dent. Lit.

IT/0391-9889
**GIORNALE ITALIANO DI MEDICINA DEL LAVORO.** [G. ital. med. lav.]. **Added/Corp** Fondazione Clinica del Lavoro. Vol. 1 (July 1979)-. Academic Scholarly Publication. Italian. bm. L160000 Italy; L320000 other. Giardini Editori Stampatori, Via Santa Bibbiana 28, 56127 Pisa Italy. **Tel** 011 39 50 934242. **NLM** W1 GI779. **CODEN** GIMLDG. Documents available from BIOSIS Document Express, CASDDS.
**Ind/Abst** Biol. Abstr.; Chem. Abstr.; EMBASE; Health Plan. Adminis.; Index Med.; Ind. Hyg. Dig.

IT/0393-5957
**GIORNALE ITALIANO DI RICERCHE CLINICHE E TERAPEUTICHE.** [G. ital. ric. clin. ter.]. (1979)-. Periodical. Italian. sm. Esi Stampa Medica Srl, Casella Postale 42, 20097 San Donato Mil Italy. **Tel** 11 39 2 5274241, FAX 11 39 2 55600670, telex 324894. **UDC** 615.4.
**Ind/Abst** EMBASE.

# Medical Science and Technology

CN/0700-8139
**GLAS K O H T-A.** **Main/Corp** Koordinacijski Odbor Hrvata Toronto. Began publication in 1972. Periodical. Serbo-Croatian (Roman). mo. GLAS K O H T-A, PO Box 235 Station T, Toronto Ontario M6B 4A1 Canada. **Tel** (416)781-0359. **DD** 971/.004/91823. **Circ:** 1,000.
**Desc:** We list past and coming events i.e. mainly lectures, write-ups on lectures, and health, tidbits about members, write-ups about our health fair outlines and outings.

YU/0081-3966
**GLAS. ODELJENJE MEDICINSKIH NAUKA.** [Glas - Srp. akad. nauka umet., Od. med. nauka]. **VFOAT** Glas. (1949)-. Academic Scholarly Publication. Serbo-Croatian (Roman) (summaries and/or abstracts in English and French). Glas Srpske Akademie Nauka, Knez Milhailova 35, Belgrad Yugoslavia. **CODEN** SUGMAW. Documents available from BIOSIS Document Express.
**Ind/Abst** Biol. Abstr.; EMBASE; Index Med.

BG
**GLIMPSE : INTERNATIONAL CENTRE FOR DIARRHOEAL DISEASE RESEARCH, BANGLADESH NEWSLETTER.** **Added/Corp** International Centre for Diarrhoeal Disease Research, Bangladesh. **VFOAT** International Centre for Diarrhoeal Disease Research, Bangladesh Newsletter. Vol. 1, No. 1 (Jan. 1979)-. Newsletter. English. bm.
**Ind/Abst** Trop. Dis. Bull.

UK/1356-1316
**GLYCOBIOLOGY RESEARCH.** (19??)-. English. £115.00. SUBIS, Mansion House, 19 Kingfield Road, Sheffield S11 9AS England. **Tel** 011 44 114 255 4433, FAX 011 44 114 255 4626.

UK/0969-3653
**GLYCOSYLATION AND DISEASE.** (19??)-. English. bm. $295.00 US; £175.00 other. Rapid Communications of Oxford Ltd, The Old Malthouse, Paradise Street, Oxford OX1 1LD England. **Tel** 011 44 0865 790447, FAX 011 44 0865 244012, telex 9403712.

IT
**GO-GIOVANE ODONTOIATRIA.** (19??)-. Periodical. Italian. qt. 37000L. Masson S.P.A, Via Statuto 2/4, 20121 Milan Italy. **Tel** 011 39 2 63671, FAX 011 39 2 6367211.

XN/0065-1214
**GODISEN ZBORNIK NA MEDICINSKIOT FAKULTET VO SKOPJE.** (GODISEN ZBORNIK NA MEDICINSKIOT FAKULTET VO SKOPJE / UNIVERZITET NA NARODNA REPUBLIKA MAKEDONIJA.). [God. zb. Med. fak. Skopje]. **Added/Corp** Medicinski Fakultet vo Skopje. **VFOAT** Acta Facultatis Medicinae Skopiensis. (1954)-. Macedonian (French, German and Serbo-Croatian (Roman); summaries and/or abstracts in English). ir. Price varies. **(Subscription address:** Jugoslovenska Knjiga, PO Box 36, YU 11001 Belgrade Yugoslavia.**) NLM** W1 GO414. **CODEN** GZMSAH. **[CCC].** Documents available from CASDDS.
**Ind/Abst** Chem. Abstr.; Health Plan. Adminis.

CI/0352-664X
**GODISNJAK VOJNOMEDICINSKE AKADEMIJE.** (GODISNJAK VOJNOMEDICINSKE AKADEMIJE / ANNUAL OF THE MILITARY MEDICAL ACADEMY.). [God. Vojnomed. akad.]. **Added/Corp** Vojnomedicinska Akademija (Yugoslavia). **VFOAT** Annual of the Military Medical Academy; Godisnjak Vma. Vol. 26 (1984)-. Periodical. Serbo-Croatian (Roman) (summaries and/or abstracts in English, French and Russian; table of contents in English, French and Russian). an. Prosveta Export Import Agency, PO Box 180, Terazije 16, 1101 Belgrade Yugoslavia. **Tel** 862-687-441, telex 862-11609. **LC** UH295.Y8; B4. **DD** 616.9/8023. **NLM** W1; GO414J. **Continues** Zbornik Vojnomedicinske Akademije.
**Ind/Abst** Index Dent. Lit. (1984-1987).

US
**GOVERNMENT RELATIONS NOTE.** V. 1- Jan. 16, 1975-. Periodical. English. National Health Council Inc, 350 Fifth Avenue/Room 1118, New York NY 10018. **Tel** (212)268-8900. **NLM** W1 GO879N.

US
**GRADUATE EDUCATION BULLETIN.** **Main/Corp** Uniformed Services University of the Health Sciences. **VFOAT** Graduate Education in the Basic Medical Sciences. Bulletin. English. an. Uniformed Services University of the Health Sciences, 4301 Bridge Road, Bethesda MD 20814-4799.

●US
**GRADUATE MEDICAL EDUCATION DIRECTORY.** See Encyclopedias and General Reference Books.

DK/0254-2609
**GRADUATE MEDICAL EDUCATION IN THE EUROPEAN REGION. SUPPLEMENTARY REPORT.** [Grad. med. educ. Eur. reg., Suppl. rep.]. 1st-. English. ir. World Health Organization / Denmark, Scherfigsvej 8, 2100 Copenhagen 0 Denmark. **Tel** 011 45 39171717. **NLM** W 20 P246GA.

US/1053-6620
**GRAND ROUNDS PRESS, THE.** [Grand rounds press]. (1991)-. Monographic series. English. qt. $21.95 (single issue). The Grand Rounds Press, Whittle Direct Books, 505 Market Street, Knoxville TN 37902. **DD** 610.

CN/0703-2595
**GRANTS AND AWARDS GUIDE - MEDICAL RESEARCH COUNCIL.** (GRANTS AND AWARDS GUIDE.). **Main/Corp** Medical Research Council (Canada). **VFOAT** Guide de Subventions et Bourses. 1970-. Periodical. English (French). an. Medical Research Council / Canada, Jeanne Mance Building, 20th Floor, Ottawa Ontario K1A 0W9 Canada. **Tel** (613)954-1382. **DD** 610./7/2071. **NLM** W 20.5; G764.

CN/0823-9266
**GREAT EXPECTATIONS.** [Great Expect.]. **VFOAT** Guide for Expectant Parents. Periodical. English. qt (Jan., Apr., July, Oct.). Free. Great Expectations, 269 Richmond Street W/Circulation, Toronto, Ontario M5V 1X1 Canada. **Tel** (416)596-8680, FAX (416)596-1991. **ED** Fran Fearmley. **DD** 618.24.

US/1041-2352
**GREAT IDEAS FOR LONG TERM CARE.** [Gt. ideas long term care]. (198?)-. Periodical. English. mo. $39.00. Eymann Publications, PO Box 3577, Reno NV 89505. **Tel** (702)333-6651. **DD** 618.

GW/0341-7344
**GRUPPENPRAXIS, DIE.** V. 1- ; Nov. 1974-. Periodical. German. Arzte Infound Verlag, Postfach 222, Stuttgart 70 Germany. **NLM** W1 GR937.

CC/1001-9448
**GUANGDONG YIXUE.** (KUANG-TUNG I HSUEH.). [Guangdong yixue]. **Added/Corp** Chung-Hua I Hsueh Hui (China : 1949- ). Kuang-Tung Fen Hui. **VFOAT** Guangdong Medical Journal. (19??)-. Periodical. Chinese. bm. RMBY1.60. Guangdong Yixue Qingbao Yanjiusuo, Guangdong Medical Information Institute, N0. 2, Jinbuli, Huifu Xilu, Guangzhou, Guangdong 510180, People's Republic of China. **Tel** 884610. **ED** Z. Fumin. **CODEN** GUYIEG. Documents available from BLDSC, CASDDS.
**Desc:** Medical periodical reflecting all the latest developments in the medical sciences.
**Ind/Abst** Chem. Abstr.

UY
**GUIA DE MEDICAMENTOS.** Spanish. Editorial Publifarma, Juan B Blanco 861, AP 201, Montevideo Uruguay.

CN/1183-0689
**GUIDE BOUNTY DE LA GROSSESSE, LE.** [Guide Bounty grossesse]. **VFOAT** Grossesse. No 1 (1991)-. Periodical. French. sa. Limited free distribution. Bounty Family Publications, Unite 2, 746 Ave Warden, Scarborough, Ontario M1L 4A2. **DD** 618.2.

US/0085-1353
**GUIDE TO BIOMEDICAL STANDARDS, THE.** **VFOAT** Biomedical Standards. 1st Ed. (1971)-. English. an. $40.00. Quest Publishing Company, 1351 Titan Way, Brea CA 92621. **Tel** (714)738-6400, FAX (714)525-6258. **ED** Allan F. Pacela. **LC** R856.6; .G84. **DD** 610/.28. **NLM** ZW 26; G946. Index available.
**Desc:** Directory of United States, international and other national standards that control or regulate medical equipment and medical-care facilities.

US
**GUIDE TO MEDICAL AND SCIENCE NEWS MEDIA.** See Journalism.

UK/0265-2730
**GUIDE TO POSTGRADUATE DEGREES, DIPLOMAS AND COURSES IN MEDICINE.** (GUIDE TO POSTGRADUATE DEGREES, DIPLOMAS AND COURSES IN MEDICINE / COUNCILS FOR POSTGRADUATE MEDICAL EDUCATION, NATIONAL ADVICE CENTRE.). [Guide postgrad. degrees diplomas courses med.]. **Added/Corp** National Advice Centre (Great Britain). (1983)-. Periodical. English. an. £13.50. National Advice Centre, Intelligene Woodlands Ford, Midlothian EH37 5RE England. **Tel** 011 44 875 320063. **NLM** W 22; FA1 B93s. **Continues** Summary of Postgraduate Diplomas and Courses in Medicine.

US/1045-0548
**... GUIDE TO THE NATION'S HOSPICES, THE.** [Guide nation's hosp.]. **Added/Corp** National Hospice Organization (U.S.). (1984)-. English. an (July). $85.00. National Hospice Organization, 1901 North Moore Street, Suite 901, Arlington VA 22209-1706. **Tel** (703)243-5900, FAX (703)525-5762. **ED** Margaret Duncan, (phone: (703)243-5900). **LC** R726.8; .G85. **DD** 362.1/75. **NLM** WX 22; AA1 G9. **Circ:** 2,000. **Continues** Hospices Coast to Coast, 0743-5029.
**Desc:** A nationwide directory of hospice programs by state, city, and services.

●CN/1188-1380
**GUIDE UNIVERSITAIRE DE LA MEDECINE.** (GUIDE UNIVERSITAIRE DE LA MEDECINE, UNIVERSITY GUIDE FOR MEDICINE.). [Guide univ. med.]. **VFOAT** Guide de la Medecine; University Guide for Medicine. (1992)-. French (summaries and/or abstracts in English). 2.95Can$. Publications Universitaires, CP 32048, Montreal (Quebec) H2L 4Y5. **DD** 610.

US/0270-0646
**GUIDELINES IN MEDICINE.** [Guidel. med.]. Vol. 1 (1979)-. Monographic series. English. Price varies per volume. University Park Press, PO Box 4034, New York NY 10163. **LC** UNC. **NLM** W1 GU78Y. **CODEN** GUMEDB. Documents available from BIOSIS Document Express.
**Ind/Abst** Biol. Abstr. (?-1979).

US
**GUIDES TO EVALUATION OF PERMANENT IMPAIRMENT.** (19??)-. English. ir. $69.95 (nonmember). American Medical Association, 515 North State Street, Chicago IL 60610. **Tel** (312)464-5000, (800)262-2350, FAX (312)464-5831. **(Subscription address:** American Medical Association, PO Box 109050, Chicago IL 60610.**)**
**Desc:** Resource for use by physicians, attorneys and health care professionals to make evaluations.

UK/0952-0643
**GULLET.** **Title Change.** Vol. 1, No. 1 (Sept. 1990)-(19??). Periodical. English. qt. Longman Group Ltd., Fourth Avenue, Longman House, Harlow Essex CM19 5SR England. **Tel** 011 44 279 429655, FAX 011 44 279 431059, telex 81259. **ED** J.R. Bennet and G.G. Jamieson. **NLM** W1; GU809. **[CCC].** Index available. cum. index. **Bk Rev**. **Ad Acc**. **Pr Rev**. available on microfilm and microfiche from University Microfilms International (UMI). **Merged into** Diseases of the Esophagus.
**Desc:** Research and commissioned reviews on all aspects of disorders of the gullet.
**Ind/Abst** EMBASE.

US
**GUNDERSEN MEDICAL JOURNAL, THE.** **Added/Corp** Gundersen Medical Foundation. Vol. 1, No. 1 (Dec. 1991)-. Periodical. English. **NLM** W1; GU809L.

CH/0028-0275
**GUOLI TAIWAN DAXUE YIXUEYUAN YANJIU BAOGAO.** [Guoli Taiwan Daxue Yixueyuan Yanjiu Baogao]. **VFOAT** Memoirs of the College of Medicine of the National Taiwan University; Memoirs of the Faculty of Medicine, National Taiwan University. (1947)-. Multiple languages. ir. **CODEN** KTHYAC.
**Ind/Abst** Crop Physiol. Abstr.; Rev. Plant Pathol.; Sorghum Mill. Abstr.

CH/0253-3197
**GUOLI ZHONGGUO YIYAO YANJIUSUO YANJIU BAOGAO.** (KUO LI CHUNG-KUO I YAO YEN CHIU SO YEN CHIU PAO KAO.). [Guoli zhongguo yiyao yanjiusuo yanjiu baogao]. **Added/Corp** Kuo li Chung-kuo i yao yen Chiu so (China (Republic : 1949- )). **VFOAT** Annual Reports of the National Research Institute of Chinese Medicine. (19??)-. Chinese (English). National Research Institute of Chinese Medicine. **CODEN** KCIKDT.
**Ind/Abst** NAPRALERT.

US/0882-696X
**GUTHRIE JOURNAL OF THE DONALD GUTHRIE FOUNDATION FOR MEDICAL RESEARCH, THE.** [Guthrie j. Donald Guthrie Found. Med. Res.]. **Added/Corp** Donald Guthrie Foundation for Medical Research. **VFOAT** Guthrie Journal. Vol. 55, No. 1 (Summer 1985)-. Academic Scholarly Publication. English. qt. Free on request. Guthrie Foundation, Sayre PA 18840. **Tel** (717)888-6666 ext. 4620. **DD** 616. **NLM** W1; GU829F. **Continues** Guthrie Bulletin of the Donald Guthrie Foundation for Medical Research, 0735-4592.
**Ind/Abst** EMBASE; Health Devices Alerts; Life Sci. Collect.; Saf. Health Work.

UK
**GUY'S GAZETTE.** **Added/Corp** Guy's Hospital. Vol. 104, No. 2399 (Feb. 1990)-. Periodical. English. mo. Gazette Office, 238 St. Thomas Street, London SE1 9RT England. **NLM** W1; GU837. **Continues** Guy's Hospital Gazette.

SI/0300-4090
**H.K.I.M.S. HONG KONG INDEX OF MEDICAL SPECIALTIES.** (HONG KONG INDEX OF MEDICAL SPECIALTIES.). [HKIMS Hong Kong index med. spec.]. **VFOAT** HKIMS; H.K.I.M.S. Vol. 1, No. 1 (November 1972)-. Chinese. Three times a year. 110.00Sing$ (airmail), 60.00Sing$ (surface mail). MIMS Asia, 135 Cecil Street, 13-00 LKN Building, Singapore 0106 Singapore. **Tel** 011 65 2233788, FAX 011 65 2214788.

UK/0952-2433
**H.M. QUEEN ELIZABETH THE QUEEN MOTHER FELLOWSHIP.** [H.M. Queen Elizabeth the Queen Mother fellowsh.]. **VFOAT** HM Queen Elizabeth the Queen Mother Fellowship. Monographic series. English. an. Price varies per volume. **NLM** W1; HM676.

TU/0259-2282
**HACETTEPE MEDICAL JOURNAL.** [Hacet. med. j.]. **Added/Corp** Hacettepe Universitesi. Tp Fakultesi. **VFOAT** Hacettepe tp Dergisi. Vol. 16, No. 1 (Jan. 1983)-. Periodical. English. Four times a year. Hacettepe University Press / Turkey, Faculty of Medicine, Hacettepe 06100 Ankara Turkey. **NLM** W1; HA152M. **CODEN** HMJOEG. Documents available from BIOSIS Document Express. ***Continues*** *Hacettepe Bulletin of Medicine/Surgery, 0017-6451.*
**Ind/Abst** Biol. Abstr. (1983-); EMBASE [Select. Cov.].

●UK/1351-8216
**HAEMOPHILIA.** (1995)-. Academic Scholarly Publication. English. Four times a year. $160.00 (institutions), $76.00 (individuals) US & Canada; £100.00 (institutions), £47.50 (individuals) Europe; £110.00 (institutions), £52.50 (individuals) other. Blackwell Scientific Publications Ltd, Marston Book Services, PO Box 87, Oxford OX2 ODT UK. **Tel** 011 44 865 791155, FAX 011 44 865 791927, telex 837 515 MARDIS G.

GW/0720-9355
**HAEMOSTASEOLOGIE.** [Hamostaseologie]. Vol. 1, No. 1, (March 1981)-. Academic Scholarly Publication. German (table of contents in English). qt. DM178.00 Europe; $110.60 other. F K Schattauer Verlagsgesellschaft mbH, Postfach 10 45 45, D 70040 Stuttgart Germany. **Tel** 011 49 711 2298726. **ED** E. Deutsch, D. L. Heene, H. G. Lasch, K. Lechner, R. Marx and P. Matis. **NLM** W1 HA155W. **CODEN** HAEMD2. **[CCC]**. Index available. **Bk Rev**. **Ad Acc**. Documents available from CASDDS.
**Ind/Abst** Chem. Abstr.; EMBASE.

SZ/0301-0147
**HAEMOSTASIS.** [Haemostasis]. Vol. 1 (1972)-. Academic Scholarly Publication. English. bm. $296.00. S. Karger AG, Allschwilerstrasse 10, PO Box - Postfach - Case Postale, CH-4009 Basel Switzerland. **Tel** 011 41 61 306-1111, FAX 011 41 61 306-1234, telex CH 962 652. **ED** H. C. Hemker, T. Lindhout, J. Rosing. **NLM** W1 HA1653. **CODEN** HMTSB7. **[CCC]**. Index available. **Ad Acc**. **Pr Rev**. available on microfilm from University Microfilms International (UMI). Documents available from The Genuine Article, BIOSIS Document Express, CASDDS. ***Supersedes*** *Coagulation, 0009-9902.*
**Desc:** Thorough coverage of the complex processes which underlie the hemostatic mechanism is given in this journal. Original papers report the latest findings on the pathology, physiology and biochemistry of hemorrhagic disease and thrombosis. In addition to in-depth studies of such topics as blood coagulation factors and fibrinolysis, readers will find extensive data on heparin and oral anticoagulation. Also provides practical information on the diagnosis and treatment of bleeding disorders and on fibrinolytic treatment. These experimental and clinical investigations are supported by occasional authoritative reviews to make the journal a full record of current research and its clinical implications.
**Ind/Abst** Biol. Abstr.; Chem. Abstr.; Curr. Contents Life Sci.; Dairy Sci. Abstr.; EMBASE; Health Plan. Adminis.; Index Med.; Life Sci. Collect.; Protozoolog. Abstr.; Ref. Upd. Deluxe Ed.; Res. Alert [Full Cov.]; Sci. Cit. Index; SCISEARCH; SportSearch.

US
**HAEOE HANIN UIRYO CHONGNAM.** **VFOAT** Medical Directory of Overseas Koreans. Korean (English). $16.00. **LC** RT25.A2; H33. ***Continues*** *Haeoe Hanin Kanhowon Chongnam.*

AT/0312-6137
**HANDBOOK - FACULTY OF MEDICINE, UNIVERSITY OF NEW SOUTH WALES.** [Handb. - Fac. Med., Univ. N.S.W.]. **Main/Corp** New South Wales. University, Kensington. Faculty of Medicine. Began in 1961. Academic Scholarly Publication. English. an. 4.00Aus$. University of New South Wales / Faculty of Medicine, PO Box 1, Kensington New South Wales 2133 Australia. **Tel** (02)385-2450, FAX (02)662-2573. **LC** R831.N46; A27A. **DD** 610/.7/11944. **Circ:** 2,800 (ctrl).
**Desc:** General information relating to course content, rules and procedures for undergraduate and postgraduate studies in medicine. Also student services and staff listing.

NE
**HANDBOOK OF ELECTROENCEPHALOGRAPHY AND CLINICAL NEUROPHYSIOLOGY.** (1971)-. Monographic series. English. ir. price varies per volume. Elsevier Science Publishers BV, PO Box 211, 1000 AE Amsterdam Netherlands. **Tel** 011 31 20 5803642, FAX 011 31 20 5862696, telex 15682. **(Subscription address:** Elsevier Science Inc. / New York Books, 655 Avenue of the Americas, New York NY 10010.**)** **NLM** WL 150 H236.
**Ind/Abst** EMBASE.

NE/0167-5567
**HANDBOOK OF INFLAMMATION.** [Handb. inflamm.]. Vol. 1 (1979)-. Monographic series. English. ir. Price varies per volume. Elsevier Science Publishers BV, PO Box 211, 1000 AE Amsterdam Netherlands. **Tel** 011 31 20 5803642, FAX 011 31 20 5862696, telex 15682. **LC** RB131; .H27. **NLM** W1 HA51PS.

II/0253-7621
**HANDBOOK OF MEDICAL EDUCATION.** [Handb. med. educ.]. English. an. 8.00. Association of Indian Universities, AIU House, 16 Kotla Marg, New Delhi 110002 India. **Tel** 11-3310059, FAX 11-3315105, telex 31-66180 AIU-IN. **LC** R814.A6. **DD** 610/.7/1154. **NLM** W 22 J14 H2.

US/0072-9841
**HANDBOOK OF MEDICAL TREATMENT.** (1949)-. Monographic series. English. ir. Price varies per volume. Mosby Year Book Inc., 11830 Westline Industrial Drive, St Louis MO 63146. **Tel** (800)325-4177, (314)872-8370, FAX (314)432-1380, telex 44-2402.

US
**HANDBOOK ON THE LATE EFFECTS OF POLIOMYELITIS FOR PHYSICIANS AND SURVIVORS.** (1988)-. Periodical. English. $6.75 US; $8.00 Canada/Mexico and Overseas. Gazette International Networking Institute, 5100 Oakland Avenue, Number 206, St Louis MO 63110. **Tel** (314)534-0475, FAX (314)534-5070. **ED** Gini Laurie, Frederick M Maynard, Armin Fischer, and Judy Raymond.
**Desc:** A 48-page booklet in dictionary format, this publication contains information about clinical problems associated with the late effects of polio based on the experiences of physicians and polio survivors.

US
**HANDBUCH DER HAUT- UND GESCHLECHTSKRANKHEITEN. ERGANZUNGSWERK.** Monographic series. English. bm. Price varies per volume. Springer-Verlag New York Inc., 175 5th Avenue, New York NY 10010. **Tel** (212)460-1500, telex 232 235 SPB UR. **(Subscription address:** Springer Verlag New York Inc. / for North America, 44 Hartz Way, Secaucus NJ 07096.**)** **ED** J Jadassohn.

CC/1002-0837
**HANGTIAN YIXUE YU YIXUE GONGCHENG.** **VFOAT** Space Medicine & Medical Engineering. (1988)-. Periodical. Chinese (summaries and/or abstracts in English). qt. Space Medicine & Medical Engineering, PO Box 5104, Beijing 100094, People's Republic of China. **ED** Professor Wei Jinhe. **DD** 616.98021.
**Desc:** Articles including space life sciences, aerospace medicine, physiology, psychology, biology, medical engineering investigations on environmental control, life support systems, safety and rescue under emergencies in aircrafts and spacecrafts, theory and application of manmachine-environment system engineering, ergonomics, measuring and processing of biomedical signals, and technology for ground simulation of aerospace environmental factors.

KO/0250-9083
**HANGUG NUIHAG DOSEGWAN.** **See** Library and Information Sciences.

KO/0379-1521
**HANGUK UIKWAHAK : THE OFFICIAL JOURNAL OF RESEARCH INSTITUTE OF MEDICAL SCIENCE OF KOREA.** Began with Jan. 1969 issue. Academic Scholarly Publication. English (Korean). qt. Union of Concerned Scientists, 26 Church Street, Cambridge MA 02238. **Tel** (617)546-5552, FAX (617)864-9405. **LC** R97.7.K6. **NLM** W1 HA524K. **CODEN** HAUID2. Documents available from CASDDS.
**Ind/Abst** Chem. Abstr.; Energy Res. Abstr. (Sept. 1980-).

KO/0254-5942
**HANNYAN NUI-DAI HAGSUR JI.** (HANYANG UIDAE HAKSULCHI.). [Hannyan nui-dai hagsur ji]. **Added/Corp** Hanyang Taehakkyo. Uikwa Taehak. **VFOAT** Journal of Hanyang Medical College. Vol. 1, No. 1 (1981)-. Periodical. Korean (summaries and/or abstracts in English). Hanyang Taehakkyo Uikwa Taehak, Seoul Korea. **LC** R97.7.K6; H38. **NLM** W1 HA539. **CODEN** HIHAD3. Documents available from CASDDS.
**Ind/Abst** Chem. Abstr.

BL/0100-3283
**HANSENOLOGIA INTERNATIONALIS.** [Hansenol. int.]. **Added/Corp** Sao Paulo (Brazil : State). Divisao de Hansenologia e Dermatologia Sanitaria. (1976)-. Periodical. English (Portuguese, Italian, Spanish and French; summaries and/or abstracts in English). sa. Instituto de Saude, Div Hanse, Nologia Dermatologia Sanitaria, PST8027 01000 Sao Paulo Brazil. **NLM** W1 HA538. **CODEN** HAINDP. Documents available from BIOSIS Document Express. ***Continues*** *Revista Brasileira de Leprologia.*
**Ind/Abst** Biol. Abstr.; EMBASE; Index Med.; Trop. Dis. Bull.

IS/0017-7768
**HAREFUAH.** [Harefuah]. **Added/Corp** Histadrut ha-Refuit be-Yisrael. (1924)-. Academic Scholarly Publication. Hebrew (summaries and/or abstracts in English). ir. $300.00. Israel Medical Association, 39 Shaul Hamelech Boulevard, Tel Aviv 64928 Israel. **Tel** 3 266968. **NLM** W1 HA579. **CODEN** HAREA6HAREH6. Documents available from BIOSIS Document Express, CASDDS.
**Ind/Abst** Biol. Abstr.; Chem. Abstr.; EMBASE; Index Med.; Nutr. Abstr. Rev., Ser. B, Live Feeds and Feed.; Nutr. Abstr. Rev., Ser. A, Hum. Exp.; Life Sci. Collect.; Protozoolog. Abstr.; Rev. Med. Vet. Entomol.; Rev. Med. Vet. Mycology; Rev. Plant Pathol.

US/1052-1577
**HARVARD HEALTH LETTER.** (HARVARD HEALTH LETTER / FROM HARVARD MEDICAL SCHOOL.). [Harv. health lett.]. **Added/Corp** Harvard Medical School. Vol. 15, No. 11 (Oct. 1990)-. Periodical. English. mo (12 issues). $24.00 US; $30.00 Canada. Harvard Medical School, 164 Longwood Avenue, 1st Floor, Boston MA 02115. **Tel** (617)432-1485, FAX (617)432-1506. **(Subscription address:** Palm Coast Data, PO Box 420285, Agency Department, Palm Coast, FL 32142; Telephone: (800)829-9171**)** **ED** William I. Bennett. **LC** RC81.A1; H35. **DD** 610/.5. **CODEN** HHLEET. Index available. cum. index. **Circ:** 315,000. available on microfiche; available on CD-ROM; available on an online database (files 149,647/Full-Text) from DIALOG. Documents available from UMI Article Clearinghouse, Magazine Collection. ***Continues*** *Harvard Medical School Health Letter, 0161-7486.*
**Desc:** Newsletter of general health information written by doctors of Harvard Medical School. Treats serious medical topics with in-depth analysis.
**Ind/Abst** Acad. Abstr. Full Text Elite (Oct. 1990-) [Full Txt.]; Acad. Abstr. (Oct. 1990-); Acad. Search (Oct. 1990-); Cumul. Index Nurs. Allied Health Lit.; Gen. Period. Index (1990-); Health Index (1990-); Health Period. Database [Full Txt.]; Health Ref. Cent. (Jan. 1989-) [Full Txt.] [Full Cov.]; Health Source (Oct. 1990-) [Full Txt.]; INFO-SOUTH Abstr.; Mag. Artic. Summar. Elite (Oct. 1990-) [Full Txt.]; Mag. Artic. Summar. Select (Oct. 1990-) [Full Txt.]; Mag. Artic. Summar. CD-ROM (Oct. 1990-); Mag. Index Plus (1990-); Mag. Index. Sel. (1990-); Mag. Search; Newsp. Period. Abstr. (1992-); Mag. Index; Vocat. Search (Oct. 1990-) [Full Txt.].

US/0191-7757
**HARVARD MEDICAL ALUMNI BULLETIN.** **See** College and School Publications-Alumni.

US/0073-0874
**HARVEY LECTURES, THE.** [Harvey lect.]. **Added/Corp** Harvey Society of New York. New York Academy of Medicine. Series 1 (1906)-. English. ir. Price varies per volume. Wiley Liss, 605 3rd Avenue, New York NY 10158. **Tel** (212)850-8800, (212)850-6645. **ED** Ruth Sager and J. Michael. **LC** R111.H33. **DD** 610/.5. **NLM** W1 HA707. **CODEN** HALEAA. cum. index. **Pr Rev.** Documents available from The Genuine Article, BIOSIS Document Express, CASDDS.
**Desc:** Includes a list of members of the Harvey Society.
**Ind/Abst** Biol. Abstr.; Chem. Abstr.; Energy Res. Abstr. (Aug. 1982-); Health Plan. Adminis.; Index Med.; Index Sci. Rev. [Full Cov.]; Res. Alert [Full Cov.]; Sci. Cit. Index; SCISEARCH.

US/0093-0334
**HASTINGS CENTER REPORT, THE.** [Hastings Cent. rep.]. **Main/Corp** Hastings Center. **Added/Corp** Institute of Society, Ethics, and the Life Sciences. Hastings Center. Report. Vol. 1 (June 1971)-. Periodical. English. bm. $75.00 (institutions), $55.00 (individuals) US; $80.00 (institutions), $65.00 (individuals) other. The Hastings Center, 255 Elm Road, Briarcliff Manor NY 10510-9974. **Tel** (914)762-8500, FAX (914)762-2124. **ED** Courtney S. Campbell and Bette-Jane Crigger. **LC** R724; .H27b. **DD** 174/.2/05. **NLM** W1 HA75. **CODEN** HSCRAS. Index available. **Bk Rev**. **Circ:** 11,500. available on microfilm and microfiche from University Microfilms International (UMI); available on an online database (file 149/Full-Text) from DIALOG. Documents available from The Genuine Article, BIOSIS Document Express, UMI Article Clearinghouse. ***Absorbed in part*** *Studies - Hastings Center, 0093-3252.*
**Desc:** Focuses on ethical issues in medicine, biology, law, social sciences, and the professions.
**Ind/Abst** Acad. Abstr. Full Text Elite (July 1990-); Acad. Abstr. (July 1990-); Acad. Ind. [Computer File] (1988-); Acad. Search (July 1990-); Biogr. Index; Biol. Abstr.; Cumul. Index Nurs. Allied Health Lit.; Curr. Contents Soc. Behav. Sci.; Curr. Lit. Fam. Plan.; Energy Res. Abstr.

(April 1982-); Expand. Acad. Index (1988-); Gen. Sci. Index; Gen. Sci. Source (Jul. 1990-); Health Index (1989-); Health Period. Database [Full Txt.]; Health Plan. Adminis.; Health Ref. Cent. (Jan. 1989-) [Full Txt.] [Full Cov.]; Hospit. Manage. Rev. (19??-19??); Index Med.; Index Book Rev. Relig.; Index Period. Artic. Relat. Law; INFO-SOUTH Abstr.; Mag. Search; Middle East Abstr. Index; Newsp. Period. Abstr. (1988-); PAIS Int. Print (1991-); Philos. Index; Physic. Medline Plus; Relig. Index One Period. (1973-); Res. Alert [Full Cov.]; Soc. Plann. Policy Dev. Abstr.; Soc. Sci. Source (Jul. 1990-); Soc. Sci. Cit. Index [Full Cov.]; Soc. Sci. Index; Soc. Sci. Index Fulltext (Aug. 1988-) [Full Txt.]; Soc. Work Abstr. [Select. Cov.]; Sociol. Abstr.; SportSearch.

US/0017-8594
**HAWAII MEDICAL JOURNAL (1962).** (HAWAII MEDICAL JOURNAL.). [Hawaii med. j.]. **Added/Corp** Hawaii Medical Association. Hawaii Society of Medical Technologists. Vol. 21, No. 4 (Mar/Apr. 1962)-. Academic Scholarly Publication. English. mo. $25.00. Hawaii Medical Association, 1360 South Beretania Street, Honolulu HI 96814-1514. **Tel** (808)536-7702, FAX (808)528-2376. **ED** Dr. Norm Goldstein. **NLM** W1 HA968. **CODEN** HWMJAE. Index available (Bound in Mar. iss.). **Bk Rev**, (Qty: 2-3). **Ad Acc. Pr Rev. Circ:** 1,700 (ctrl). available on microfilm and microfiche from University Microfilms International (UMI). Documents available from BIOSIS Document Express, CASDDS. ***Continues*** *Hawaii Medical Journal and Inter-Island Nurses Bulletin.* ***Continued in part by*** *Directory of Hawaii Physicians, 1046-5510.*
**Desc:** Contains health related scientific articles relative to Hawaii and the Pacific. Information on the news of local physicians, editorials, continuing medical education events.
**Ind/Abst** Biol. Abstr.; Chem. Abstr.; EMBASE; Energy Res. Abstr. (Aug. 1982-); Health Plan. Adminis.; Index Med.; Nutr. Abstr. Rev., Ser. B, Live Feeds and Feed.; Nutr. Abstr. Rev., Ser. A, Hum. Exp.; Life Sci. Collect.; Protozoolog. Abstr.; Soc. Work Abstr. [Select. Cov.]; SportSearch.

US
**HAWKEYE OSTEOPATHIC JOURNAL.** **Added/Corp** Iowa Osteopathic Medical Association. Vol. 1, No. 1 (May 1, 1983)-. Periodical. English. bm (6 issues). $30.00. Iowa Osteopathic Medical Association, 1113 Locust, Suite 2B, Des Moines IA 50309. **Tel** (515)283-0005. **ED** Dana Shaffer. **NLM** W1; HA958. **Ad Acc.**
**Desc:** Publication of the Iowa Osteopathic Medical Association. Presents news of the Association and information on osteopathic medicine.

UK
**HEALING HAND, THE.** **See** Religion and Theology.

US/1055-0054
**HEALING HEALTHCARE NETWORK NEWSLETTER.** [Heal. healthc. netw. newsl.]. **VFOAT** Healing Healthcare. Vol. 1, No. 1 Fall (1990)-. Periodical. English. qt (Jan., Apr., July, Oct.). $35.00 (one year), $65.00 (two year). Healing Healthcare Network News, PO Box 339, Brighton CO 80601. **Tel** (303)659-2446, FAX (303)659-7995. **ED** Leanne Raiser Carlson. **DD** 362. **Circ:** 500.
**Desc:** Describes/features innovative healing programs in hospitals.

US/0897-3598
**HEALTH ADVOCATE (MADISON, WIS.).** (HEALTH ADVOCATE : NEWSLETTER OF THE NATIONAL HEALTH LAW PROGRAM.). [Health advocate]. **Added/Corp** National Health Law Program. **VFOAT** Newsletter of the National Health Law Program. No. 133 (Summer 1982)-. Newsletter. English. qt. $20.00. National Health Law Program Incorporated, 2639 South La Cienega Boulevard, Los Angeles CA 90034. **Tel** (301)204-6010, FAX (301)204-0891. **DD** 344. **NLM** W1; HE204. ***Continues*** *National Health Law Program. NHeLP Health Advocate, 0272-7102.*

●US/1075-024X
**HEALTH ALLIANCE ALERT.** **See** Insurance.

UK/0267-2170
**HEALTH & LIBERATION : ANTI-APARTHEID MOVEMENT HEALTH COMMITTEE NEWSLETTER.** **VFOAT** Anti-Apartheid Movement Health Committee Newsletter; Health and Liberation. (1982)-. Newsletter. English. AAM Health Committee, 13 Mandela Street, London NW1 England.

●US/1066-1786
**HEALTH & MEDICAL YEAR BOOK.** [Health med. year book]. **Added/Corp** P.F. Collier, Inc. **VFOAT** Health and Medical Year Book. (1992)-. English. **LC** RA773; .H26. **DD** 610/.5. ***Continues*** *Health & Medical Horizons, 0734-5003.*

US
**HEALTH & WEALTH GUARDIAN.** 462 South Gilbert Road, Mesa AZ 85204.

CN/0849-830X
**... HEALTH & WELL-BEING RESOURCES DIRECTORY, THE.** [Health well-being resour. dir.]. **Added/Corp** Circle Institute. **VFOAT** Health and Well-Being Resources Directory. (1990/1991)-. Directory. English. be. $4.00 per volume. Circle Institute, PO Box 3113, Halifax Nova Scotia B3J 3G6 Canada. **DD** 613.

US/1062-6107
**HEALTH BUSINESS.** ***Title Change.*** **See** Business-Marketing.

US
**HEALTH CARE.** English. $8.95. First Publishing Inc., 2100 Riverchase Center, Suite 110, Birmingham AL 35244. **Tel** (205)733-1970, FAX (205)733-1974.

●UK/1065-3058
**HEALTH CARE ANALYSIS.** (HEALTH CARE ANALYSIS. : THE EUROPEAN JOURNAL OF HEALTH CARE PHILOSOPHY, POLICY AND VALUES.). [Health care anal.]. (1993)-. Periodical. English. Four times a year. $185.00. John Wiley & Sons Ltd., Baffins Lane, Chichester West Sussex PO19 1UD England. **Tel** 0243 779777, FAX 0243 776128 BTG:JWP001, telex 86290 WIBOOKG. **(Subscription address:** John Wiley / Philadelphia, PO Box 7247, Philadelphia PA 19170.**) ED** David Seedhouse. **DD** 362. **NLM** W1; HE298J. **CODEN** HCAVEO.
**Desc:** International journal which seeks to analyze health care from multiple perspectives. Publishes original empirical or conceptual research, but especially encourages the reflective combination of both.

CN/0316-2141
**HEALTH CARE DIGEST.** V. 1- Mar. 1974-. Periodical. English. bm. $6.00 Canada; $8.00 US; $5.00 other. Health Care Digest, 1450 Don Mills Road, Don Mills Ontario M3B 2X7 Canada. **DD** 338.4/7/61028.
**Ind/Abst** Health Plan. Adminis.

US
**HEALTH CARE ETHICS USA.** English. qt. $20.00 US; $25.00 other. Center for Health Care Ethics, 1402 South Grand Boulevard, St. Louis MO 63104. **Tel** (314)577-8000. **ED** Mary E. Hogan. **NLM** W1; HE299GP. cum. index. **Pr Rev. Circ:** 1,000.

US/0197-4246
**HEALTH CARE FINANCING ADMINISTRATION RULINGS ON MEDICARE, MEDICAID, PROFESSIONAL STANDARDS REVIEW, AND RELATED MATTERS.** **See** Insurance.

US
**HEALTH CARE MARKETER.** English. United Communications Group, 11300 Rockville Pike, Suite 1100, Rockville MD 20852. **Tel** (301)816-8950 ext. 223, FAX (301)816-8945.

UK
**HEALTH CARE PARLIAMENTARY MONITOR.** English. Twenty times a year. £249.00 UK; £300.00 other. Cadmus Newsletter Ltd, Southbank House, Black Ponce Road, London SE1 7SJ England. **Tel** (071)587-1441, (071)735-8171, FAX (071)735-1555. **ED** Pauline Chudley and Rodney Deitch. Index available. cum. index. **Bk Rev. Circ:** 1,000 (ctrl). available on diskette.
**Desc:** Covers all UK parliamentary, civil service and political developments which are relevant to the subject area of health care and community developments.

CN/1186-8201
**HEALTH CARE PRODUCTS AND CAPABILITIES IN ALBERTA.** [Health care prod. capabil. Alta.]. **Added/Corp** Alberta. Alberta Technology, Research and Telecommunications. Canada. Industry, Science and Technology Canada. **VFOAT** Directory. (1991)-. English. be. **DD** 381/.45613/0257123.

●US/1067-2214
**HEALTH CARE REFORM WEEK.** Vol. 21, No. 42 (Nov. 9, 1992)-. Periodical. English. Forty-eight times a year. $447.00. United Communications Group, 11300 Rockville Pike, Suite 1100, Rockville MD 20852. **Tel** (301)816-8950 ext. 223, FAX (301)816-8945. **NLM** W1; HE299R. ***Continues*** *Health Policy Week, 0732-7439.*
**Ind/Abst** Hospit. Health Admin. Index (1992-).

US/0883-900X
**HEALTH CARE RESOURCES IN PENNSYLVANIA, LONG TERM CARE FACILITIES.** 1981-. English. an. State Health Data Center, Pennsylvania Department of Health, PO Box 90, Harrisburg PA 17108. **LC** RA997.5.P4; L66. **DD** 362.1/6/09748021. ***Continues*** *Long Term Care Facilities, 0883-7414.*

US/0745-1717
**HEALTH CARE SYSTEMS (NEW YORK, N.Y.).** (HEALTH CARE SYSTEMS.). [Health care syst.]. Vol. 19, No. 10 (Oct. 1982)-. Periodical. English. mo. $30.00. Miller Freeman Inc., 600 Harrison Street, San Francisco CA 94107. **Tel** (415)905-2337, FAX (415)905-2240, telex 278273. **NLM** W1 HE302T. **[CCC].** ***Continues*** *Health Care Product News, 0018-5566.*

UK/0267-3223
**HEALTH CARE UK.** **Added/Corp** Chartered Institute of Public Finance and Accountancy. (1984)-. Periodical. English. an. £22.00. **(Subscription address:** BEBC Distribution, PO Box 1496 Poole, Dorser BH12 3YD United Kingdom.**) NLM** W1; HE303C.

US/0362-8337
**HEALTH CAREERS.** 1975/76-. English. United Hospital Fund of New York, 3 East 54th Street, New York NY 10022. **Tel** (212)645-2500. **LC** R690; .H4. **DD** 362.1/023.

CN/0701-1210
**HEALTH CAREERS NEWS.** **See** Occupations and Careers.

US/0740-2406
**HEALTH COST MANAGEMENT.** ***Ceased.*** [Health cost manage.]. **VFOAT** HCM. Vol. 1, No. 1 (Oct. 1983)-Ceased with Vol. 5, No. 4. Periodical. English. bm. Health Cost Management Association, PO Box 641, Bryn Mawr PA 19010. **Tel** (215)546-4995. **NLM** W1; HE315R.
**Ind/Abst** Health Plan. Adminis.; Hospit. Health Admin. Index (1984-).

US/0046-7022
**HEALTH DEVICES.** [Health devices]. **Added/Corp** Emergency Care Research Institute. Vol. 1 (Jan. 1971)-. Periodical. English. mo. Free to members of Health Devices Systems. ECRI Emergency Care Research Institute, 5200 Butler Pike, Plymouth Meeting PA 19462. **Tel** (215)825-6000, FAX (215)834-1275, telex 510-660-8023. **ED** R. Mosenkis. **LC** R856.A1; H4. **DD** 610/.28. **NLM** W1 HE317K. **[CCC]. Bk Rev**. available on microfiche. Documents available from UMI Article Clearinghouse.
**Desc:** A journal reporting comparative medical device evaluations with brand-name ratings, and reporting hazards and problems with hospital devices.
**Ind/Abst** Health Plan. Adminis.; Pharm. News Index (Sept. 1984-).

US/0163-0458
**HEALTH DEVICES ALERTS.** **See** Medical Science and Technology-Abstracting, Bibliographies and Statistics.

US/0278-3452
**HEALTH DEVICES SOURCEBOOK.** [Health devices sourceb.]. **Added/Corp** ECRI (Organization) Emergency Care Research Institute. (1979)-. English. an. $285.00. ECRI Emergency Care Research Institute, 5200 Butler Pike, Plymouth Meeting PA 19462. **Tel** (215)825-6000, FAX (215)834-1275, telex 510-660-8023. **ED** Robert Mosenkis. **LC** R856.48; .H4. **DD** 681/.761/029473. **NLM** W 26 H433. **[CCC].**
**Desc:** A single-volume reference source where you can locate quickly, information about products, manufacturers, service companies, leasing companies, and equipment rebuilders.

UK/0141-1403
**HEALTH EQUIPMENT NOTE.** **Added/Corp** Gt. Brit. Dept. of Health and Social Security. Great Britain. Welsh Office. Scotland. Home and Health Dept. (1975)-. Monographic series. English. ir. Price varies per volume. Her Majesty's Stationery Office, 51 Nine Elms Lane, London SW8 5DR England. **Tel** 011 44 71 873 8459, 011 44 71 873 8499, FAX 011 44 71 873 8499, 011 44 71 873 8456, telex 297138. **(Subscription address:** Her Majesty's Stationery Office, PO Box 276, Publications Centre, London SW8 5DT England.**) NLM** W1 HE329. ***Continues*** *Hospital Equipment Note, 0072-6028 .*

US/0193-7928
**HEALTH FUNDS DEVELOPMENT LETTER.** (1978)-. Periodical. English. Twelve times a year. $177.00 (one year), $319.00 (two years), $451.00 (three years); $137.00 (introductory subscription). Health Resources Publishing, 3100 Highway 138, Wall Township NJ 07719-1442. **Tel** (908)681-1133, FAX (908)681-0490. **ED** Robert K Jenkins. **[CCC]. Bk Rev. Ad Acc.** ctrl circ.
**Desc:** Monthly report sharing news of critical federal and foundation funding opportunities and trends, read by development directors and grants officers.

US/0892-7731
**HEALTH INDUSTRY BUYERS GUIDE : HIBG.** [Health ind. buy. guide]. **VFOAT** HIBG. 44th Ed. (1983/1984)-. Consumer Publication. English. an (Dec.). $130.00 US; $135.00 Canada, $155.00 other. Springhouse Corporation, 1111 Bethlehem Pike, Springhouse PA 19477. **Tel** (215)646-8700. **DD** 610. **NLM** W 26; S966. Index available (free). **Ad Acc.** available on microfilm from University Microfilms International (UMI). ***Continues*** *Surgical Trade Buyer's Guide, 0081-9654.*
**Desc:** The most comprehensive directory of healthcare products and services published for the healthcare distribution industry.

US/0745-4678
**HEALTH INDUSTRY TODAY.** [Health ind. today]. **VFOAT** HIT. (1983)-. Periodical. English. mo (11 issues). $277.00 US; $283.00 Canada; $295.00 other. Business Word Inc., 5350 South Roslyn Street, Suite 400, Englewood CA 80111-2125. **Tel** (303)290-8500, FAX (303)290-9025. **DD** 338. **NLM** W1 HE351B. **CODEN** HITOD3. **Ad Acc.** ctrl circ. available on microfilm and microfiche from University Microfilms International (UMI); available on an online database (files 15,648/Full-Text) from DIALOG. ***Continues** Surgical Business, 0039-6095.*
**Desc:** The magazine for healthcare distribution executives. Provides unique in-depth coverage of the most current industry news, trends, developments and new products and services.
**Ind/Abst** BioBusiness (1989-); Hospit. Health Admin. Index (Vol. 50, No. 1, 1987-Vol.52, No. 12, 1989); Hospit. Manage. Rev. (19??-19??); Predicasts; Trade Ind. ASAP [Full Txt.]; Trade Ind. Index [Full Txt.].

●UK
**HEALTH INFORMATICS.** (1994)-. Periodical. English. Four times a year. £78.00 Europe; £79.00 Other (Institutions). Churchill Livingstone, 1-3 Baxter's Place, Leith Walk, Edinburgh EH1 3AF Scotland. **Tel** 011 44 31 556 2424, FAX 011 44 31 558 1278, telex 727511. **(Subscription address:** Maruzen Company Ltd., PO Box 5050, Import & Export Department, Tokyo 100 31 Japan.**)**

UK/0969-0719
**HEALTH INFORMATICS EUROPE.** English. qt. £40.00. British Journal Healthcare Computing, 45 Woodland Grove, Weybridge Surrey KT13 9EQ England. **Tel** 011 44 932 852776, FAX 01-247-0671. **(Subscription address:** Pillar Publications, 45 Woodland Grove, Waybridge, Surrey KT13 9EQ England.**)**

US
**HEALTH LAW DIGEST / NATIONAL HEALTH LAWYERS ASSOCIATION. See** Law.

CN/0226-8841
**HEALTH LAW IN CANADA. See** Law.

US/0163-3996
**HEALTH LAW PROJECT LIBRARY BULLETIN. See** Law.

US/0736-3443
**HEALTH LAWYER, THE. See** Law.

US/0882-598X
**HEALTH LETTER (WASHINGTON, D.C.).** (HEALTH LETTER / THE PUBLIC CITIZEN HEALTH RESEARCH GROUP.). [Health lett. (Wash. D.C.)]. **Added/Corp** Public Citizen Health Research Group. Vol. 1, No. 1 (March/April 1985)-. Periodical. English. mo. $18.00 (1 year), $30.00 (2 year), $42.00 (3 year). Health Letter, 2000 P Street NW, Washington DC 20036. **Tel** (202)833-3000, FAX (202)296-1727. **ED** Sidney M Wolfe. **DD** 361. Index available. cum. index. **Circ:** 90,000.
**Desc:** The medical field from a consumer advocacy standpoint.
**Ind/Abst** Consum. Health Nutr. Index; Mag. Artic. Summar. Select (July 1990-Sept. 1990).

UK/0265-6647
**HEALTH LIBRARIES REVIEW. See** Library and Information Sciences.

●US/1074-4770
**HEALTH MANAGEMENT TECHNOLOGY.** [Health manag. technol.]. Vol. 15, No. 1 (Jan. 1994)-. Periodical. English. Twelve times a year. $29.00 US, $39.00 Canada & Mexico, $49.00 others (surface mail); $89.00 (one year), $169.00 (two years) others (airmail). Argus Business, 6151 Powers Ferry Road, Atlanta GA 30339. **Tel** (404)995-2500, (800)233-3359. **(Subscription address:** Sunbelt Fulfillment Services, P. O. Box 41530, Nashville, TN 37204, telephone: (615)377-3322 or (800)888-5139**) DD** 616. **NLM** W1; HE413QD. **Circ:** 16,000. available on microfilm and microfiche from University Microfilms International (UMI); available on an online database (Files 15,675/Full Text) from DIALOG. ***Continues** Computers in Healthcare, 0745-1075.*

UK/0955-2065
**HEALTH MANPOWER MANAGEMENT.** [Health manpow. manag.]. Vol. 14, No. 2 (Sept. 1988)-. Periodical. English. Five times a year. $689.00. MCB University Press, 60 62 Toller Lane, Bradford West Yorkshire BD8 9BX England. **Tel** 011 44 274 499821, FAX 011 44 274 547143, telex 51317 MCBUNI G. **(Subscription address:** MCB University Press / US and Canada Subscriptions, PO Box 10812, Birmingham AL 35201-0812.**) ED** Alison Hyde. **NLM** W1; HE413QP. Documents available from UMI Article Clearinghouse. ***Continues** Health Services Manpower Review, 0306-0233.*
**Desc:** Coverage of human resource issues within the health care industry. Each issue carries a wide range of articles, together with shorter news items, and a regular NAHSPO news section. Directed at human resource professionals and general managers in the health care industry, as well as to managers from professional backgrounds, and those in the trade union movement.
**Ind/Abst** ABI/INFORM Glob. Ed.; Hospit. Health Admin. Index (1988-); Trop. Dis. Bull.

US/0735-9683
**HEALTH MARKETING QUARTERLY.** [Health market q.]. Vol. 1, No. 1 (Fall 1983)-. Periodical. English. qt (Published during the academic year). $265.00 US; $371.00 other. The Haworth Press Inc, 10 Alice Street, Binghamton NY 13904-1580. **Tel** (607)722-5857, (800)3-HAWORTH, FAX (607)722-1424. **ED** William J. Winston (editor's address: Managing and Marketing Consultant, PO Box 8566, Berkeley, CA 94707). **NLM** W1; HE414D. **Bk Rev. Ad Acc. Pr Rev. Acid Free. Circ:** 272. available on microfilm and microfiche from University Microfilms International (UMI). Documents available from UMI Article Clearinghouse, Haworth Document Delivery Service. ***Continues** Health & Medical Care Services Review.*
**Desc:** An applied journal for marketing health and human services. Supplies "how-to" marketing tools for specific delivery systems. Each issue of the journal is devoted to a select health service-group practice marketing, mental health marketing, long-term care marketing and serves as a basic resource for marketing the selected service.
**Ind/Abst** ABI/INFORM Glob. Ed.; ABI Inform Ondisc (Winter 1984-); ABI/INFORM Ondisc: Expr. Ed.; Commun. Abstr.; Gen. BusinessFile (1992-); Health Plan. Adminis.; Hospit. Health Admin. Index; Hospit. Manage. Rev.; PsycINFO; Soc. Plann. Policy Dev. Abstr.

CN/0821-3925
**HEALTH NEWS (TORONTO).** (HEALTH NEWS / UNIVERSITY OF TORONTO, FACULTY OF MEDICINE.). [Health news]. **Added/Corp** University of Toronto. Faculty of Medicine. Vol. 1, No. 1 (Feb. 1983)-. Periodical. English. bm. 18.95Can$ (one year), 34.95Can$ (two year), 46.95Can$ (three year) Canada; 24.95Can$ (one year), 45.95Can$ (two year), 61.95Can$ (three year) other. Health News and Medical Sciences Building, University of Toronto Faculty of Medicine, Toronto, Ontario M5S 1A8 Canada. **Tel** (416)978-5411, FAX (416)978-7552. **(Subscription address:** Health News, 109 Vanderhoof Avenue, Suite 205, Toronto, Ontario M4G 2H7 Canada**) ED** June V Engel. **DD** 610/.5.
**Desc:** Contains health information for the lay public from the University of Toronto's Faculty of Medicine.
**Ind/Abst** Can. Index; Can. Period. Index (19??-); Consum. Health Nutr. Index; Cumul. Index Nurs. Allied Health Lit.; Health Period. Database [Full Txt.]; Health Ref. Cent. (Jan. 1989-) [Full Txt.] [Full Cov.]; SPORT Discus.

US/1060-605X
**HEALTH ONE MEDICAL JOURNAL.** ***Title Change.*** [Health One med. j.]. **Added/Corp** Health One Corporation. Office of Medical Education and Research. Vol. 1, No. 1 (Jan. 1992)-(1992). Periodical. English. qt. Office of Medical Education and Research, Medical Affairs Division, Health 1 Corp., 2810 57th Avenue N., Minneapolis MN 55430. **DD** 616. ***Continued by** Medical Journal of HealthSpan, 1069-0174.*

NE/0168-8510
**HEALTH POLICY (AMSTERDAM).** (HEALTH POLICY.). [Health policy]. **Added/Corp** National Commission for Health Certifying Agencies (U.S.). Vol. 4, No. 1 (1984)-. Academic Scholarly Publication. English. Twelve times a year (4 vols.). $751.00. Elsevier Science Ireland Ltd., Bay 15, Shannon Industrial Estate, Co Clare Ireland. **Tel** 011 353 61 471944. **ED** Jan Blanpain, Karen Davis, and Akira Koizumi. **NLM** W1; HE473P. **[CCC].** available on microfilm and microfiche from University Microfilms International (UMI). ***Continues** Health Policy and Education, 0165-2281.*
**Desc:** A vehicle for the exploration and discussion of health policy issues and aimed in particular at enhancing communications between health policy researchers, legislators, decision-makers, and other professionals concerned with implementing policy particularly in the industrialized nations.
**Ind/Abst** EMBASE; Health Plan. Adminis.; Hospit. Health Admin. Index; PAIS Int. Print (1991-); Trop. Dis. Bull.

US/0888-9465
**HEALTH PROFESSIONS REPORT.** [Health prof. rep.]. Vol. 13, No. 7 (April 4, 1984)-. Periodical. English. bw. $270.00 (one year), $525.00 (two year). Whitaker Newsletter, PO Box 340, 313 South Avenue, Suite 202, Fanwood NJ 07023-0340. **Tel** (201)889-6336, FAX (201)889-6339. **(Subscription address:** Whitaker Newsletters, PO Box 192, Fanwood NJ 07923.**) ED** Anne Bittner. **DD** 610. **[CCC]. *Continues** Health Planning & Manpower Report, 0362-3165.*
**Desc:** Reports on the education and training of doctors, nurses, and allied health professionals. Includes pending legislation, information on public and private funding sources, cost-cutting measures, curriculum ideas, recruiting efforts and admissions policies, new medical breakthroughs, scientific research and advanced programs from America's leading medical training facilities.

US
**HEALTH PROFESSIONS SCHOOLS. SELECTED ENROLLMENT DATA.** English. an. US Department of Health & Human Services National Center for Health Statistics, 6525 Belcrest Road, Room 1140, Hyattsville MD 20782. **Tel** (301)436-7016, FAX (301)436-4258. **NLM** W 19 H434.

AT/1036-1073
**HEALTH PROMOTION JOURNAL OF AUSTRALIA.** English. Three times a year (Apr., July, Dec.). 30.00Aus$ (members of the Australian Association of Health); 40.00Aus$ (non-members); 50.00Aus$ (institutions). HPJA, PO Box 14, West Perth WA 6872 Australia. **Tel** 011 61 9 3512365. **ED** Dr. Ray James. **Bk Rev.** ctrl circ.

US/0278-6133
**HEALTH PSYCHOLOGY. See** Psychology.

US
**HEALTH REFERENCE CENTER [COMPUTER FILE]. See** Medical Science and Technology-Abstracting, Bibliographies and Statistics.

US/0731-5694
**HEALTH SCIENCE REVIEW (NEW YORK, N.Y.).** (HEALTH SCIENCE REVIEW.). [Health sci. rev.]. Vol. 1, No. 1 (Apr. 1982)-. Periodical. English. ir. KPR Infor/Media Corporation, 605 Third Avenue, New York NY 10158. **Tel** (212)878-3700. **ED** Linda Stanley. **NLM** W1 HE534M. ctrl circ.
**Desc:** Various topics of interest to physicians and the medical community.

CN/0708-9465
**HEALTH SCIENCES INFORMATION IN CANADA. LIBRARIES.** ***Ceased.*** **See** Library and Information Sciences.

US/0162-0843
**HEALTH SCIENCES SERIALS. See** Library and Information Sciences.

UK/0268-0459
**HEALTH SERVICE ABSTRACTS. See** Medical Science and Technology-Abstracting, Bibliographies and Statistics.

US/0017-9124
**HEALTH SERVICES RESEARCH.** (HEALTH SERVICES RESEARCH ; HSR.). [Health serv. res.]. **Added/Corp** Association for Health Services Research. Hospital Research and Educational Trust. Association of University Programs in Health Administration. **VFOAT** HSR. Vol. 1 (Summer 1966)-. Academic Scholarly Publication. English. Six times a year (Feb., Apr., June, Aug., Oct., Dec.). $60.00. American College of Healthcare Executives, 840 North Lake Shore Drive, c/o J. Flory, Chicago IL 60611. **Tel** (312)943-0544 ext. 3000, FAX (312)943-3791. **(Subscription address:** FDN American College of Healthcare Executives, Order Processing Center, 1951 Cornell Avenue, Melrose Park IL 60160.**) ED** Gordon DeFriese. **LC** RA960; .H5815. **DD** 362.1/05. **NLM** W1 HE576E. **CODEN** HESRA. **Pr Rev. Circ:** 2,600. available on microfilm and microfiche from University Microfilms International (UMI). Documents available from The Genuine Article, UMI Article Clearinghouse.
**Desc:** Provides advance information on new trends and techniques. It focuses on empirical studies addressing major policy issues and organizational settings, emphasizing scholarly research and its applications to improved health care delivery.
**Ind/Abst** ABI/INFORM Glob. Ed.; ABI Inform Ondisc (Spring 1983-); Acad. Search (July 1993-); Biostatistica (1974-); Bus. Index (1985-); Bus. Source (Jul. 1993-); Cumul. Index Nurs. Allied Health Lit.; Curr. Contents Soc. Behav. Sci.; EMBASE; Energy Res. Abstr. (Aug. 1982-); Gen. BusinessFile (1985-); Gen. Period. Index (1985-); Health Plan. Adminis.; Health Source (Jul. 1993-); Hospit. Health Admin. Index; Hospit. Manage. Rev. (Spring 1983-); Index Med.; INFO-SOUTH Abstr.; Int. Pharm. Abstr.; Mag. Search; Res. Alert [Full Cov.]; Soc. Sci. Cit. Index [Full Cov.]; Trade Ind. ASAP [Full Txt.]; Trade Ind. Index [Full Txt.]; Trop. Dis. Bull.

US/0194-3049
**HEALTH SYSTEMS REPORT ALMANAC ON FEDERAL HEALTH ISSUES, PROPOSALS, ADMINISTRATIVE ACTIONS, LEGISLATION, PUBLIC LAWS. See** Law.

US/0892-0036
**HEALTH TECHNOLOGY CASE STUDY.** [Health technol. case study]. **VFOAT** Case Study Series; OTA Case Studies; O.T.A. Case Studies. 22 (March 1983)-. Monographic series. English. Price varies per volume. Iowa Department of Corrections, 523 East 12th Street, Capitol Annex, Des Moines IA 50319. **Tel** (515)281-4811, FAX (515)281-7345. **DD** 338. **NLM** W1; HE589K.

US
**HEALTH TECHNOLOGY MANAGEMENT.** (19??)-. English. ir. $360.00. ECRI Emergency Care Research Institute, 5200 Butler Pike, Plymouth Meeting PA 19462. **Tel** (215)825-6000, FAX (215)834-1275, telex 510-660-8023.

US/1041-6072
**HEALTH TECHNOLOGY TRENDS.** [Health technol. trends]. **Added/Corp** ECRI (Organization). Vol. 1, No. 1 (March 1989)-. Periodical. English. mo. $275.00. ECRI Emergency Care Research Institute, 5200 Butler Pike, Plymouth Meeting PA 19462. **Tel** (215)825-6000, FAX (215)834-1275, telex 510-660-8023. **DD** 362. **NLM** W1; HE589M. **[CCC].**
**Desc:** Gives you the critical information you need in just minutes. No extraneous material. Just practical recommendations to support your day-to-day decisions and to give you clear insight into tomorrow's health care delivery systems. You'll get help in developing key strategies, outpacing your competition and creating strong profit centers.
**Ind/Abst** Hospit. Manage. Rev. (19??-).

●US
**HEALTHCARE CD-ROM/CD-I DIRECTORY.** **VFOAT** CD-ROM/CD-I Directory; Interactive Healthcare Directory. CD-ROM. (1994)-. Directory. English. an. $72.00. Stewart Publishing Inc., 6471 Merritt Court, Alexandria VA 22312. **Tel** (703)354-8155. ***Continues*** *Healthcare CD-ROM Directory, 1074-6064.*

US/1074-6064
**HEALTHCARE CD-ROM DIRECTORY.** ***Title Change.*** [Healthc. CD-ROM dir.]. **VFOAT** CD-ROM Directory; CD-ROM; Interactive Healthcare Directory. CD-ROM. (1991)-(1993). Directory. English. Stewart Publishing Inc., 6471 Merritt Court, Alexandria VA 22312. **Tel** (703)354-8155. **LC** R119.9; .H43. **DD** 610. **NLM** ZW 18; H4343. ***Continues in part*** *Interactive Healthcare Directory.* ***Continued by*** *Healthcare CD-ROM/CD-I Directory.*

US/0894-9980
**HEALTHCARE COMMUNITY RELATIONS & MARKETING LETTER.** [Healthc. community relat. mark. lett.]. **VFOAT** Health Care Community Relations & Marketing Letter. Vol. 1, No. 1 (July 1987)-. Periodical. English. Twelve times a year. $197.00 (one year), $354.00 (two years), $500.00 (three years); $137.00 (introductory subscription). Health Resources Publishing, 3100 Highway 138, Wall Township NJ 07719-1442. **Tel** (908)681-1133, FAX (908)681-0490. **DD** 362. **[CCC].** Index available. **Bk Rev. Ad Acc.**
**Desc:** Written for the professional manager, the letter with help you stay atop of the latest innovations and keep pace with the changes in the healthcare field.

US/0899-9287
**HEALTHCARE FORUM JOURNAL, THE.** [Healthc. forum j.]. **Added/Corp** Healthcare Forum (Organization). **VFOAT** Health Care Forum Journal. Vol. 30, No. 4 (July/August 1987)-. Periodical. English. bm. $45.00 US; $60.00 Canada & Mexico; $90.00 other. Healthcare Forum Journal, 830 Market Street/8th Floor, San Francisco CA 92102. **Tel** (415)421-8810, FAX (415)421-8837. **ED** Susan Anthony. **DD** 362. **NLM** W1; HE298PJ. Index available (published in Nov. issue). cum. index. **Ad Acc, Adv Mgr:** Gayle Samuelson. **Circ:** 26,000 (ctrl). available on microfilm and microfiche from University Microfilms International (UMI); available on an online database. Documents available from UMI Article Clearinghouse. ***Continues*** *Healthcare Forum.*
**Desc:** Analyzes, interprets, and advises industry leaders of emerging trends in the everchanging healthcare industry. In-depth articles focus on innovative strategies and solutions to management challenges.
**Ind/Abst** ABI/INFORM Glob. Ed.; ABI Inform Ondisc (1987-); Cumul. Index Nurs. Allied Health Lit. (1987-); Hospit. Health Admin. Index (July/Aug. 1987-); Hospit. Manage. Rev.

US/0891-9267
**HEALTHCARE MANAGEMENT TEAM LETTER.** **VFOAT** Health Care Management Team Letter. (May 1985)?-. Periodical. English. mo. $137.00. Health Resources Publishing, 3100 Highway 138, Wall Township NJ 07719-1442. **Tel** (908)681-1133, FAX (908)681-0490. **ED** Robert K. Jenkins. **DD** 362. Index available. cum. index.
**Desc:** Contains information which is useful to management teams.

US/1068-0802
**HEALTHCARE PACKAGING.** ***Ceased.*** **See** Packaging.

US
**HEALTHCARE PRODUCT COMPARISON SYSTEM - IMAGING AND RADIOLOGY.** (19??)-. English. mo. $595.00. ECRI Emergency Care Research Institute, 5200 Butler Pike, Plymouth Meeting PA 19462. **Tel** (215)825-6000, FAX (215)834-1275, telex 510-660-8023.

US
**HEALTHCARE PRODUCT COMPARISON SYSTEM - SURGICAL.** (19??)-. English. qt. $320.00. ECRI Emergency Care Research Institute, 5200 Butler Pike, Plymouth Meeting PA 19462. **Tel** (215)825-6000, FAX (215)834-1275, telex 510-660-8023.

US/1046-4603
**HEALTHCARE RECRUITMENT RESOURCE GUIDE.** ***Title Change.*** [Healthc. recruit. resour. guide]. **Added/Corp** Recruitment Resources, Inc. **VFOAT** Health Care Recruitment Resource Guide. (1989)-(199?). English. an. Florida Reference Press, 720 East Fletcher Avenue/Suite 110, Tampa FL 33612. **LC** R697.A4; H42. **DD** 610/.25/73. ***Continued by*** *Healthcare Recruitment Resource Guide (Baltimore, Md.), 1046-4603.*

●US/1046-4603
**HEALTHCARE RECRUITMENT RESOURCE GUIDE.** [Healthc. recruit. resour. guide]. Vol. 1 (1992)-. English. $155.00. National Health Publishing, 428 East Preston Street, Baltimore MD 21202-3923. **Tel** (301)363-6400. **DD** 610. **NLM** W 22; AA1 H55. ***Continues*** *Healthcare Recruitment Resource Guide (Clearwater, Fla.), 1046-4603.*

US/1049-4499
**HEALTHCARE TECHNOLOGY BUSINESS OPPORTUNITIES.** (19??)-. English. Twelve times a year. $295.00. American Health Consultants, 3525 Piedmont Road, Suite 400, Atlanta GA 30305. **Tel** (800)688-2421, (404)262-7436. **(Subscription address:** American Health Consultants, PO Box 95278, Chicago IL 60694.**) [CCC].** available on an online database (file 636/Full-Text) from DIALOG.

US/1047-7276
**HEALTHCARE TRENDS & TRANSITION.** [Healthc. trends transit.]. **VFOAT** Healthcare Trends and Transition. Vol. 1, No. 1 (Dec. 1989)-. Periodical. English. mo. $12.00. NEX Inc., 606 South Schumaker Drive, Salisbury MD 21801. **DD** 610.
**Ind/Abst** Cumul. Index Nurs. Allied Health Lit.; Health Plan. Adminis.; Hospit. Health Admin. Index (Dec. 1989-May 1991).

US
**HEALTHCARE VIDEODISC DIRECTORY.** **See** Photography and Video.

US
**HEALTHPLAN / NATIONAL LIBRARY OF MEDICINE / [COMPUTER FILE].** (19??)-. Periodical. English. qt. $950.00. Silverplatter Information Inc., 100 River Ridge Drive, Norwood MA 02062. **Tel** (800)343-0064, (617)769-2599, FAX (617)235-1715.
**Desc:** Bibliographic file with abstracts covering the non-clinical aspects of health care delivery, including all aspects of administration and planning of health care facilities, health insurance and financial management, licensure and related topics.

US
**HEALTHTRAC.** English. Twenty-four times a year (Published weekly during the regular legislative session, semi-monthly during the pre-session, and monthly for the balance of the year.). $185.00 state & local government; $385.00 individuals. Healthtrac Inc, PO Box 13552, Tallahassee FL 32317. **Tel** (904)222-8180, (800)533-5259, FAX (904)222-4893. **ED** Christine Jordan Sexton. **Circ:** 145 (ctrl).
**Desc:** Covers healthcare news and current issues.

CN/0849-3111
**HEARTBEAT (VANCOUVER).** (HEARTBEAT / HEART AND STROKE FOUNDATION OF B.C. & YUKON.). [Heartbeat]. **Added/Corp** Heart and Stroke Foundation of B.C. & Yukon. (Summer 1990)-. Periodical. English. qt. Heart and Stroke Foundation of British Columbia and Yukon, 1212 West Broadway, Vancouver, British Columbia V6H 3V2 Canada. **DD** 362.1/9612/0060711. ***Continues*** *Heart to Heart (Vancouver, B.C.), 0834-4779.*

CC/1000-1581
**HEBEI YIXUEYUAN XUEBAO.** (HO-PEI I HSUEH YUAN HSUEH PAO.). [Hebei yixueyuan xuebao]. **Added/Corp** Ho-Pei i Hsueh Yuan. **VFOAT** Acta Academiae Medicinae Hebei. (19??)-. Periodical. Chinese (summaries and/or abstracts in English; table of contents in English). qt. $18.84. Shihjiazhuan Ho Pei I Hseuh Yuan Hubei Yixuetuan, Beijing, China. **(Subscription address:** China National Publishers / Industry & Trade, PO Box 782, Beijing, China.**) CODEN** HYXUEI. Documents available from CASDDS.
**Ind/Abst** Chem. Abstr.

GW/0017-9604
**HEILBERUFE, DIE.** 1.- Yearly volume; 1949-. Periodical. German. mo. $28.00, $4.00 (single issue). VCH Publishers Inc, 220 East 23rd Street, New York NY 10010. **Tel** (212)683-8333, , FAX (212)481-0897. **(Subscription address:** VCH Publishers Inc., 303 Northwest 12th Avenue, Journals Department, Deerfield FL 33442.**) NLM** W1 HE733. **[CCC].**

UK/1351-5284
**HELICOBACTER.** (19??)-. English. £85.00. SUBIS, Mansion House, 19 Kingfield Road, Sheffield S11 9AS England. **Tel** 011 44 114 255 4433, FAX 011 44 114 255 4626.

CN/0226-6644
**HEMOPHILIE DE NOS JOURS, L'.** V. 14, No. 2- 2nd Quarterly, 1977-. Periodical. French. qt. Societe Canadienne de l'Hemophilie, 460 Jarvis, Toronto Ontario M4Y 2H5 Canada. **DD** 616.1/572/00971.

US/0194-1100
**HENRY E. SIGERIST SUPPLEMENTS TO THE BULLETIN OF THE HISTORY OF MEDICINE, THE.** [Henry E. Sigerist suppl. Bull. hist. med.]. No. 1 (1978)-. Monographic series. English. ir. Price varies per volume. Johns Hopkins University Press, 2715 North Charles Street, Baltimore MD 21218-4319. **Tel** (410)516-6987, FAX (410)516-6968. **LC** UNC. **NLM** W1 HE896. ***Supersedes*** *Bulletin of the History of Medicine. Supplements.*
**Ind/Abst** Health Plan. Adminis.; Index Med. (1978-1985).

US/0018-0416
**HENRY FORD HOSPITAL MEDICAL JOURNAL.** ***Ceased.*** [Henry Ford Hosp. med. j.]. **Main/Corp** Henry Ford Hospital. **Added/Corp** Edsel B. Ford Institute for Medical Research. Vol. 15, No. 2 (Summer 1967)-Vol. 40, No. 4, (Oct. 1992). English. qt. Henry Ford Hospital, 2921 W Grand Boulevard 411, Detroit MI 48202. **Tel** (313)876-2028. **ED** Raymond C Mellinger and Sarah Whitehouse. **LC** R11; .H48. **NLM** W1 HE901H. **CODEN** HFHJA6. Index available. cum. index. **Bk Rev. Pr Rev. Circ:** 10,000. available on microfilm and microfiche from University Microfilms International (UMI). Documents available from BIOSIS Document Express, CASDDS. ***Continues*** *Henry Ford Hospital. Henry Ford Hospital Medical Bulletin, 0096-1868.*
**Desc:** Work of current Henry Ford Hospital staff, alumni, participants in sponsored symposia. Broad scientific forum for all areas: clinical, research, technical, administrative, and patient care delivery.
**Ind/Abst** Biol. Abstr.; Chem. Abstr.; EMBASE; Health Plan. Adminis.; Index Med.; Life Sci. Collect.; Saf. Health Work.

US
**HEPATOLOGY.** English. mo. $215.00 (individual), $338.00 (institution) US; $256.00 (individual), $378.00 (institution) other. W.B. Saunders Company, A Subsidiary of Harcourt Brace Jovanovich, Inc., The Curtis Center/Suite 300, Independence Square West, Philadelphia PA 19106-3399. **Tel** (215)238-7800 or, 5587, FAX (215)238-7883, telex 173146. **(Subscription address:** W. B. Saunders Company / North America Subscriptions, c/o Periodicals, 6277 Sea Harbour Drive, 4th Floor, Orlando FL 32887.**)**

NE
**HEPATOLOGY LETTERS.** Academic Scholarly Publication. English. Six times a year (1 volume). Fl443.00 (includes postage). Elsevier Science Publishers BV, PO Box 211, 1000 AE Amsterdam Netherlands. **Tel** 011 31 20 5803642, FAX 011 31 20 5862696, telex 15682.

PL/0018-0599
**HERBA POLONICA.** **See** Biology-Botany.

GW/0720-0730
**HERZ + GEFASSE.** [Herz Gefasse]. **VFOAT** Herz und Gefassse. (Jan. 1981)-. Periodical. German. mo. Perimed Spitta Med Verlagsges, Marienbergstrasse 78, D 90411 Nuernberg Germany. **Tel** 011 49 911 952800. **NLM** W1 HE986UF.

BU/0018-8247
**HIGIENA I ZDRAVEOPAZVANE.** (KHIGIENA I ZDRAVEOPAZVANE.). [Hig. zdraveopaz.]. **VFOAT** Higiena i Zdraveopazvane. (1966)-. Periodical. Bulgarian (summaries and/or abstracts in English and Russian; table of contents in English and Russian). Six times a year. 62.00F. Hemus Foreign Trade Organization, 14 Benkovsky St., 1000 Sofia Bulgaria. **Tel** 011 359 2 882544. **NLM** W1 KH387. **CODEN** KHZDAN. Documents available from BIOSIS Document Express, CASDDS. ***Continues*** *Khigiena.*
**Ind/Abst** Biol. Abstr. (-1989); Chem. Abstr.; EMBASE [Select. Cov.]; Saf. Health Work.

BL/0101-9597
**HILEIA MEDICA.** [Hilela med.]. Vol. 1, No. 1 (Oct. 1979)-. Periodical. Portuguese (summaries and/or abstracts in English and French). sa. Universidade Federal Do Para, Campus University, Guama Biblio Ctrl, 66000 Belem Para Brazil. **Tel** 011 55 91 2292088. **NLM** W1 HI406G.

BL/0101-9600
**HILEIA MEDICA. SUPLEMENTO.** [Hileia med., Supl.]. **Added/Corp** Universidade Federal do Para. Centro de Ciencias da Saude. No. 1 (Aug. 1980)-. Periodical. Portuguese. sa. Centro de Ciencias da Saude, Praca Camelo Salgarda 1, 66-00 Belem-Para Brasil. **NLM** W1 HI406H.

JA/0018-2044
**HIROSAKI IGAKU.** (HIROSAKI IGAKU. HIROSAKI MEDICAL HOURNAL.). [Hirosaki igaku]. **Added/Corp** Hirosaki Daigaku. Igakubu. **VFOAT** Hirosaki Medical Journal. (1950)-. Academic Scholarly Publication. Japanese (summaries and/or abstracts in English and German). qt. Hiroshaki Daigaku Igakubu, (School of Medicine, Hirosaki Universty), 5, Zaifucho, Hirosakishi, Aomoriken 036 Japan. **NLM** W1; HI559. **CODEN** HIRIA6. Documents available from BIOSIS Document Express, CASDDS.
**Ind/Abst** Biol. Abstr. (-1983); Chem. Abstr.; EMBASE [Select. Cov.]; Saf. Health Work.

JA/0018-2087
**HIROSHIMA DAIGAKU IGAKU ZASSHI.** [Hiroshima Daigaku igaku zasshi]. **Added/Corp** Hiroshima Daigaku. Igakubu. **VFOAT** Medical Journal of Hiroshima University. (1962)-. Periodical. Japanese (table of contents in English). Hiroshima Daigaku Igaku Shuppankai, (Hiroshima University Medical Press), 2-3, Kasumi 1 Chome, Minamiku, Hiroshimashi, Hiroshimaken 734 Japan. **NLM** W1 GE169. **CODEN** HDIZAB. Documents available from BIOSIS Document Express, CASDDS. ***Continues** Gencho Hiroshima Igaku.*
**Ind/Abst** Biol. Abstr.; Chem. Abstr.

JA/0018-2052
**HIROSHIMA JOURNAL OF MEDICAL SCIENCES.** [Hiroshima j. med. sci.]. **Added/Corp** Hiroshima Ika Daigaku. Hiroshima Daigaku. Igakubu. Vol. 1 (Dec. 1951)-. Academic Scholarly Publication. English. qt. Hiroshima University School of Medicine, Kasumi-Cho, Hiroshima Japan. **NLM** W1 HI591. **CODEN** HIJMAC. available on microfilm and microfiche from University Microfilms International (UMI). Documents available from BIOSIS Document Express, CASDDS.
**Ind/Abst** Biol. Abstr.; Chem. Abstr.; EMBASE; Health Plan. Adminis.; Index Med.; Life Sci. Collect.

SP/0018-2125
**HISPALIS MEDICA.** (1943)-. Periodical. Spanish. mo. 30ptas. Hispalis Medica, Gravina 29, Seville Spain. **Tel** 954-221751. **ED** M Rios Mozo. **Bk Rev. Ad Acc. Circ:** 1,000.
**Ind/Abst** Indice Med. Esp.; Nutr. Abstr. Rev., Ser. B, Live Feeds and Feed.; Nutr. Abstr. Rev., Ser. A, Hum. Exp.

FR/0440-8888
**HISTOIRE DES SCIENCES MEDICALES.** **Added/Corp** Societe Fracaise d'Histoire de la Medecine. Vol. 1 (Jan./Mar. 1967)-. Periodical. French. qt. 600.00F EEC Countries; 660.00F other. Soc Fran D Histoire Medecine, 38 Bis rue de Courlancy, 51100 Reims France. **Tel** 011 33 26 483260, FAX 011 33 26 483271. **ED** J. Samion-Contet. **[CCC].** cum. index. **Bk Rev.**
**Ind/Abst** Am. Hist. Life (1989-).

CN/0826-0125
**HLABC FORUM. See** Library and Information Sciences.

US
**HMO PPO DIRECTORY.** Directory. English. an. $206.50. Medical Economics Data, Five Paragon Drive, PO Box 27, Montvale NJ 07645. **Tel** (800)442-6657, (201)358-7200.

UK
**HMSO MEDICAL SERIES.** (19??)-. English. ir. Price varies per volume. Her Majesty's Stationery Office, 51 Nine Elms Lane, London SW8 5DR England. **Tel** 011 44 71 873 8459, 011 44 71 873 8499, FAX 011 44 71 873 8499, 011 44 71 873 8456, telex 297138. **(Subscription address:** Her Majesty's Stationery Office, PO Box 276, Publications Centre, London SW8 5DT England.**)**

JA/0367-6110
**HOKEN BUTSURI.** (HOKEN BUTSURI : JOURNAL OF THE JAPAN HEALTH PHYSICS SOCIETY.). [Hoken butsuri]. **Added/Corp** Nihon Hoken Butsuri Gakkai. (1966)-. Academic Scholarly Publication. Japanese (summaries and/or abstracts in English; table of contents in English). qt. $148.00. **(Subscription address:** Kyowa Book Company Inc., 1-38 Kanda Jinbo-Cho, Chiyoda-Ku Tokyo 101, Japan**) CODEN** HOKBAQ. Documents available from CASDDS.
**Ind/Abst** Chem. Abstr.

JA/0367-6102
**HOKKAIDO IGAKU ZASSHI.** [Hokkaido igaku zasshi]. **Added/Corp** Hokkaido Igakkai. **VFOAT** Hokkaido Journal of Medical Science. (1923)-. Academic Scholarly Publication. Japanese. bm. $114.00. **(Subscription address:** Kyowa Book Company Inc., 1-38 Kanda Jinbo-Cho, Chiyoda-Ku Tokyo 101, Japan**) NLM** W1 HO4891. **CODEN** HOIZAK. Documents available from BIOSIS Document Express, CASDDS.
**Ind/Abst** Biol. Abstr.; Chem. Abstr.; Index Dent. Lit.

US/0898-6029
**HOLISTIC MEDICINE (SEATTLE, WASH.).** (HOLISTIC MEDICINE : NEWSLETTER OF THE AMERICAN HOLISTIC MEDICAL ASSOCIATION AND THE AMERICAN HOLISTIC MEDICAL FOUNDATION / AMERICAN HOLISTIC MEDICAL ASSOCIATION.). [Holist. med.]. **Added/Corp** American Holistic Medical Association. American Holistic Medical Foundation. (197?)-. Periodical. English. Four times a year (Jan., Apr., July., Oct.). $30.00 US; $50.00 other. American Holistic Medical Association, 4101 Lake Boone Trail, Suite 201, Raleigh NC 27607. **Tel** (919)787-5181, FAX (919)787-4916. **ED** Rueben Dowtin, (phone: (919-787-5181 Ext. 8247). **DD** 613. **NLM** W1; HO491QAC. **Bk Rev. Ad Acc, Adv Mgr:** R. Dowtin. **Circ:** 1,300 (ctrl).
**Desc:** Contains holistic medical care and nutrition information for health professionals and the general public. Including scientific articles and personal insights of biographical and inspirational nature.
**Ind/Abst** Health Period. Database.

US/1072-3617
**HOME CARE REPORT.** English. Twelve times a year. $100.00. W.D. Cabin & Associates, PO Box 438, Totowa NJ 07511. **Tel** (201)263-2017, FAX (201)263-1832. **ED** William D. Cabin. **Ad Acc. Circ:** 500.
**Desc:** Provides information on the home health care field; for those who give or receive medical attention in the home rather than the hospital.

US/0734-7588
**HOME HEALTH JOURNAL.** ***Ceased.*** [Home health j.]. Vol. 1, No. 1 (Nov. 1980)-(1987). Periodical. English. mo. Home Health Journal, 1539 Parental Home Road, Jacksonville FL 32216-3098. **Tel** (904)725-5133. **ED** Jocelyn W Griffo. **DD** 362. **NLM** W1; HO502U. **Bk Rev. Ad Acc. Circ:** 10,000 (ctrl).
**Desc:** Provides independent reporting of substantive, comprehensive, in-depth news and features from the US health care system's most recent spin-off, home health care; for business providers of home health care nationwide, including agency administrators, owners, clinical and management staffs.
**Ind/Abst** Hospit. Health Admin. Index (Vol. 4, 1983-Vol. 8, No. 12, 1987).

●US/1069-4560
**HOMECARE DIRECTION.** [Homecare dir.]. **Added/Corp** Beacon Health Corporation. **VFOAT** Home Care Direction. Vol. 1, No. 1 (June 1993)-. Periodical. English. Twelve times a year. $187.00 (one year); $337.00 (two years); $449.00 (three years). Beacon Health Corporation, 1001 West Glen Oaks Lane, Suite 104, Mequon WI 53092. **Tel** (800)553-2041, (414)241-3765, FAX (414)241-4488. **NLM** W1; HO505G. Index available. cum. index. ctrl circ.
**Desc:** News and information about homecare.

US/0882-9152
**... HOMECARE MARKET REPORT, THE.** English. $40.00 US; $60.00 other. Homecare, 2048 Cotner Avenue, Los Angeles CA 90025. **Tel** (310)477-1033. **ED** Andria Segedy. **LC** HD9995.H563; U544. **DD** 381/.45681761. **Ad Acc. Circ:** 11,400 (ctrl).
**Desc:** A business magazine devoted to the home health care market.

NE/0534-9303
**HORMONAL STEROIDS : PROCEEDINGS. Main/Conf** International Congress on Hormonal Steroids. (1962)-. Proceedings. English. ir. $166.75. Elsevier Science Publishers BV, PO Box 211, 1000 AE Amsterdam Netherlands. **Tel** 011 31 20 5803642, FAX 011 31 20 5862696, telex 15682.

JA
**HOSHASEN IGAKU SOGO KENKYUJO NENPO. Main/Corp** Hoshasen Igaku Sogo Kenkyujo (Japan). (19??)-. Japanese. an. Free. Hoshasen Igaku Sogo Kenkyujo, 9-1 Anakawa 4-chome, Chiba 280 Japan. **Tel** 0472-51-2111. **ED** Mikio Shikita. **LC** R895.A1; H67a. **NLM** W1 HO69FE. ctrl circ.

US/0742-969X
**HOSPICE JOURNAL, THE. See** Sociology-Social Services and Welfare.

US/0898-7270
**HOSPIMEDICA.** ***Ceased.*** Vol. 1, No. 3 (Jan./Feb. 1984)-(July 1992). Periodical. English. Nine times a year. Techcom Inc, PO Box 5017, Westport CT 06881. **DD** 616. **NLM** W1; HO69HH. **[CCC]. Circ:** 27,000. ***Continues** Hospitals & Healthcare International, 0898-7262.*
**Desc:** A hospital journal read by senior decision-makers, such as chief medical officers and department heads. Provides a platform for the discussion of topical issues, and a conduit for the world-wide dissemination of information related to the newest technologies, systems, trends and methods. Publishes exclusive articles from leading specialists in disciplines such as radiology, anaesthesiology, cardiology, and critical care. Contains a broad range of information on new products and literature, significant events and meetings, and industry news.
**Ind/Abst** Health Devices Alerts.

SP/0211-4437
**HOSPITAL COMARCAL.** [Hosp. comarc.]. (1980)-. Periodical. Spanish. Three times a year. Hospital Comarcal de Estella, 31200 Estella (Navarra) Spain. **UDC** 61.

UK/0262-3145
**HOSPITAL DOCTOR.** [Hosp. dr.]. (1978)-. Periodical. English. wk (46 issues per year). £70.00 UK; £94.00 other Europe; £114.00 other. Reed Business Publishing Group / England, Quadrant House, Quadrant Sutton Surrey, SM2 5AS England. **Tel** 011 44 81 652-3500. **(Subscription address:** Reed Healthcare Subscriptions, 120 126 Lavender Avenue, Mitcham Surrey CR4 3HP United Kingdom.**) DD** 610. **Ad Acc. Circ:** 36,000 (ctrl). ***Continues** On Call.*
**Desc:** Newspaper for doctors working in hospitals.

US/8756-8519
**HOSPITAL ETHICS. See** Ethics.

US/0884-8998
**HOSPITAL HOME HEALTH.** ***Ceased.*** [Hosp. home health]. **Added/Corp** American Health Consultants. (19??)-(Dec. 1994). Periodical. English. mo. American Health Consultants, 3525 Piedmont Road, Suite 400, Atlanta GA 30305. **Tel** (800)688-2421, (404)262-7436. **DD** 362.
**Desc:** Devoted exclusively to the success of hospital-based home care.

US/0098-180X
**HOSPITAL INFECTION CONTROL.** Vol. 1 (Nov. 1974)-. Periodical. English. mo. $269.00. American Health Consultants, 3525 Piedmont Road, Suite 400, Atlanta GA 30305. **Tel** (800)688-2421, (404)262-7436. **(Subscription address:** American Health Consultants, PO Box 95278, Chicago IL 60694.**) NLM** W1 HO799. **[CCC].** available on microfilm and microfiche from University Microfilms International (UMI).
**Ind/Abst** Cumul. Index Nurs. Allied Health Lit.; Health Devices Alerts; Health Plan. Adminis.; Hospit. Health Admin. Index.

US/0441-2745
**HOSPITAL MEDICINE (NEW YORK, N.Y.).** (HOSPITAL MEDICINE.). [Hosp. med.]. **Added/Corp** Wallace Laboratories. Vol. 1 (Sept. 1964)-. Periodical. English. mo. $80.00 (institutions), $45.00 (individuals). Excerpta Medica / US, PO Box 3085, Princeton NJ 08543-3085. **Tel** (908)874-8550, FAX (908)874-5611. **(Subscription address:** Hospital Medicine, PO Box 3095, Denville NJ 07834.**) ED** Marian Berger. **LC** R11; .H6. **DD** 610. **NLM** W1 HO817J. **[CCC]. Ad Acc.** ctrl circ. available on microfilm and microfiche from University Microfilms International (UMI).
**Desc:** The journal for the primary care physician in both office and hospital-based practice. Areas covered in this highly illustrated journal cover the entire range of clinical medicine in an up-to-date and precise manner.
**Ind/Abst** Cumul. Index Nurs. Allied Health Lit.

US/0888-2428
**HOSPITAL PHYSICIAN (SURGERY/EMERGENCY/SPECIALTIES ED.).** (HOSPITAL PHYSICIAN.). [Hosp. physician]. (June 1985)-. Periodical. English. mo. $65.00 US; $85.00 Canada; $130.00 other. Turner White Communications, 125 Strafford Avenue, Suite 220, Wayne PA 19087. **Tel** (215)975-4541. **ED** Joseph Hoffman. **DD** 617. **Ad Acc. Pr Rev. Circ:** 89,000 (ctrl). available on microfilm from University Microfilms International (UMI). ***Formed by the union of** Hospital Physician (Surgical Edition) **and** Hospital Physician (ER Staff Edition).*
**Ind/Abst** Abstr. Clin. Care Guidel.; Int. Pharm. Abstr.

SP/0213-4845
**HOSPITAL PRACTICE (ED. EN ESPANOL).** ***Ceased.*** [Hosp. pract. (Ed. esp.)]. (1986)-(Dec. 1994). Periodical. Spanish. Ten times a year. Ediciones Doyma SA, Travesera de Gracia 17 21, 08021 Barcelona Spain. **Tel** 011 34 3 2000711, 011 34 3 4145706, FAX 011 34 3 2091136, telex 51964 INK E. **UDC** 61.

US/8750-2836
**HOSPITAL PRACTICE (OFFICE EDITION).** (HOSPITAL PRACTICE.). [Hosp. pract.]. Vol. 16, No. 1 (Jan. 1981)-. Periodical. English. mo. $54.00 (one year), $95.00 (two year) US; $68.00 (one year), $115.00 (two year) other. HP Publishing Company, 55 Fifth Avenue, 14th Floor, New York NY 10003-4301. **Tel** (212)989-2100, FAX (212)989-2100. **LC** R11; .H828. **DD** 616. **NLM** W1; HO87GB. Index available. **Ad Acc. Pr Rev. Circ:** 10,000 (ctrl). available on microfilm and microfiche from University Microfilms International (UMI). Documents available from The Genuine Article. ***Continues in part** Hospital Practice, 0018-5809.*
**Desc:** Publishes reviews, revisions and articles. Oriented to expose concepts in the areas of the physiopathology, of the diagnostic sides and of the therapeutic sides.
**Ind/Abst** Abr. Index Med.; Cumul. Index Nurs. Allied Health Lit.; Curr. Contents Clin. Med.; EMBASE; Helminthol. Abstr. (1991-); Hospit. Health Admin. Index; Index Med.; Index Vet.; INIS Atomindex [Micro.]; Microbiol. Abstr. Sect. B (19??-19??); Physic. Medline Plus; Protozoolog. Abstr.; Res. Alert [Select. Cov.]; Rev. Med. Vet. Mycology; SCISEARCH; Soc. Sci. Cit. Index [Select. Cov.]; SportSearch.

CN/0823-6798
**HOSPITAL PRODUCTS AND TECHNOLOGY.** ***Ceased.*** [Hosp. prod. technol.]. Vol. 1, No. 1 (May 1983)-(19??). Periodical. English. bm. Maclean Hunter Canada / Montreal, 1001 bvd. de Maisonneuve W., Montreal, Quebec H3A 3E1 Canada. **Tel** 514-845-5141, FAX 514-845-4302, telex 055-60604. **ED** Earl Damude, Tom Gale, and Leo Cuarbonneau. **DD** 381/.45681761/05. **Ad Acc. Circ:** 20,000 (ctrl).

**Desc:** News and new products tabloid for health care professionals in Canada exploring the interfaces among medical device technology, patient care quality and health care economics.

US
**HOSPITAL REHAB.** (19??)-. English. $219.00. American Health Consultants, 3525 Piedmont Road, Suite 400, Atlanta GA 30305. **Tel** (800)688-2421, (404)262-7436. **(Subscription address:** American Health Consultants, PO Box 95278, Chicago IL 60694.)
**Ind/Abst** Hospit. Manage. Rev. (19??-).

US
**HOSPITAL RISK CONTROL SYSTEM.** (19??)-. English. mo. $695.00. ECRI Emergency Care Research Institute, 5200 Butler Pike, Plymouth Meeting PA 19462. **Tel** (215)825-6000, FAX (215)834-1275, telex 510-660-8023.

UK/0305-4136
**HOSPITAL UPDATE.** [Hosp. update]. (1975)-. Periodical. English. mo. £47.00 UK; £60.00 Europe; £66.00 other. Reed Business Publishing Group / England, Quadrant House, Quadrant Sutton Surrey, SM2 5AS England. **Tel** 011 44 81 652-3500. **(Subscription address:** Reed Healthcare Subscriptions, 120 126 Lavender Avenue, Mitcham Surrey CR4 3HP United Kingdom.) **NLM** W1 HO894K.
**Ind/Abst** Life Sci. Collect. (19??-).

US/0747-6116
**HOST/PATHOGEN NEWS.** [Host/pathog. news]. **VFOAT** Host Pathogen News. Periodical. English. qt. $16.00 US; $20.00 other. South Peace Regional Planning Commission, 200 Windsor Court, 9835-101 Aveneu, Brande Prairie, Alta T8V 5V4 Canada. **DD** 616.

CH
**HSUEH PAO (SHAN-TUNG CHUNG I HSUEH YUAN).** (HSUEH PAO / JOURNAL OF SHANDONG COLLEGE OF TRADITIONAL CHINESE MEDICINE / SHAN-TUNG CHUNG I HSUEH YUAN.). **Added/Corp** Shan-Tung Chung i Hsueh Yuan. **VFOAT** Journal of Shandong College of Traditional Chinese Medicine; Shan-Tung Chung I Hsueh Yuan Hsueh Pao. (19??)-. Periodical. Chinese (Chinese). qt. $17.70. Science Press, 16 Donghuangchenggen North Street, Beijing 100707, People's Republic of China. **Tel** 011 86 1 4019821, 011 86 1 4010642, FAX 011 86 1 4012180, 011 86 1 4019810, telex 210147. **(Subscription address:** China International Book Trading Corporation, PO Box 399, Library Service Department, Beijing 100044 People's Republic of China.) **LC** R97.7.C5; H83. **DD** 610/.5. **Ad Acc. Circ:** 7,000.
**Desc:** Introduces traditional chinese medicine.

CC/0257-7712
**HUA-HSI I KO TA HSUEH HSUEH PAO.** [J. West China Univ. Med. Sci.]. **VFOAT** Journal of West China University of Medical Sciences; Huaxi Yike Daxue Xuebao. (March 1986)-. Academic Scholarly Publication. Chinese. qt. $15.04. **(Subscription address:** China International Book Trading Corporation, PO Box 399, Library Service Department, Beijing 100044 People's Republic of China.) **NLM** W1; HU429C. **CODEN** HYDXET. Documents available from BIOSIS Document Express, CASDDS. ***Continues*** *Ssu-Chuan I Hsueh Yuan Hsueh Pao.*
**Ind/Abst** Biol. Abstr. (1986-); Chem. Abstr. (1986-); EMBASE [Select. Cov.]; Food Sci. Technol. Abstr.; Index Med. (1986-); Index Vet.; Protozoolog. Abstr.

CC/1000-243X
**HUBEI YIXUEYUAN XUEBAO. VFOAT** Acta Academiae Medicinae Hubei. (1980)-. Periodical. Chinese. qt. Editorial Board of the Journal of Hubei Medical College, 20 East Lake Road, Wuhan, Hubei, People's Republic of China. **DD** 610.
**Ind/Abst** EMBASE [Select. Cov.].

NE/0018-7070
**HUISARTS EN WETENSCHAP.** [Huisarts wet.]. (1957)-. Periodical. Dutch. Thirteen times a year. Fl137.03. Bohn Stafleu Van Loghum BV, Postbus 246, 3990 GA Houten Netherlands. **Tel** 011 31 3403 95782. **(Subscription address:** Intermedia BV, Postbus 4, 2400 MA Alphen Rijn Netherlands.)
**Ind/Abst** EMBASE [Select. Cov.].

US/0885-0615
**HUMAN RESEARCH REPORT.** [Hum. res. rep.]. Vol. 1, No. 1 (Jan. 1986)-. Periodical. English. mo. $167.00 US; $172.00 Canada and Mexico; $197.00 other. The Deem Corporation, PO Box 44069, Omaha NE 68144. **Tel** (402)895-5748, FAX (402)895-2306. **ED** Dennis Maloney. **LC** R853.H8; H83. **DD** 346. **NLM** W1; HU4626.
**Desc:** Provides advance tips on federal research regulations, federal laws, and lawsuits against researchers in human experimentation. Helps readers limit their liability in biomedical and behavioral research projects.

UK/0142-811X
**HUMAN SEXUALITY.** [Hum. sex.]. (1977)-. English. mo. £85.00. SUBIS, Mansion House, 19 Kingfield Road, Sheffield S11 9AS England. **Tel** 011 44 114 255 4433, FAX 011 44 114 255 4626. **DD** 016.6126.

CN/0828-7090
**HUMANE MEDICINE.** [Hum. med.]. **VFOAT** Humane Medicine Journal. Vol. 1, No. 1 (March 1985)-. Periodical. English. qt (Jan., Apr., July, Oct.). 52.00Can$ Canada; $62.00 other. Canadian Medical Association, 1867 Alta Vista Drive, Ottawa Ontario K1G 3Y6 Canada. **Tel** (613)731-9331 ext. 2028, FAX (613)731-4797. **(Subscription address:** Canadian Medical Association, CMA House, PO Box 8650, Ottawa Ontario K1G 0G8 Canada.) **DD** 610.69/6. **NLM** W1; HU479T. **[CCC]. Ad Acc. Pr Rev. Acid Free.** available on CD-ROM; available on microfilm and microfiche from University Microfilms International (UMI). Documents available from The Genuine Article.
**Desc:** Provides an international forum for the discussion of critical ethical and philosophical issues that concern those dedicated to promoting compassionate health care.
**Ind/Abst** Can. Index (?-?); Can. Period. Index (19??-)(1990-); Curr. Contents Clin. Med.; Res. Alert [Select. Cov.]; SCISEARCH; Soc. Sci. Cit. Index [Select. Cov.].

CC/1000-5625
**HUNAN YIKE DAXUE XUEBAO.** (HU-NAN I KOTA HSUEH HSUEH PAO.). [Hunan yike daxue xuebao]. **Added/Corp** Hu-nan I Ko Ta Hsueh. **VFOAT** Hunan Yike Daxue Xuebao; Bulletin of Hunan Medical University. (1989)-. Periodical. Chinese. qt. **(Subscription address:** China National Publishers / Industry & Trade, PO Box 782, Beijing, China.) **CODEN** HYXBET. Documents available from BIOSIS Document Express, CASDDS. ***Continues*** *Hu-nan I Hsueh Yuan Hsueh Pao, 0253-3170.*
**Ind/Abst** Biol. Abstr. (1989-); Chem. Abstr.

GW/0172-3790
**HYGIENE + MEDIZIN.** [Hyg. + Med.]. **VFOAT** Hygiene und Medizin. (197?)-. Periodical. German (summaries and/or abstracts in English and German). Twelve times a year. DM133.00. MHP Verlag GmbH, Ostring 13, D 65205 Wiesbaden Germany. **Tel** 011 49 6122 770931, FAX 011 49 6122 76331. **ED** H. P. Werner. **NLM** W1 HY474. **CODEN** HYMEDG. Index available. **Bk Rev. Ad Acc. Pr Rev. Circ:** 5,000 (ctrl). Documents available from BIOSIS Document Express.
**Desc:** International journal for applied hygiene and preventive medicine in hospitals and practice. Official information bulletin of the German Society for Hospital Hygiene.
**Ind/Abst** Biol. Abstr. (-1989); EMBASE.

UK/0143-117X
**HYPERTENSION SHEFFIELD.** (HYPERTENSION.). [Hypertension Sheff.]. (1979)-. English. mo. £75.00. SUBIS, Mansion House, 19 Kingfield Road, Sheffield S11 9AS England. **Tel** 011 44 114 255 4433, FAX 011 44 114 255 4626. **DD** 016.574.

IT/0394-817X
**I CARE.** [I Care]. (1976)-. Periodical. Italian. qt. L35000 Italy; L45000 other. Centro Rieuducazione Ortofonica, P le Porta Al Prato 34-35, 50123 Florence Italy. **Tel** 011 39 55 215113, FAX 011 39 55 216014. **UDC** 376.3. **Bk Rev.** ctrl circ.

US
**IACFA NEWSLETTER.** Newsletter. English. Four times a year (Mar., June, Sept., Dec.). $15.00. International Association of Cystic Fibrosis, 2656 Euclid Heights Boulevard, Apartment 102, Cleveland OH 44106. **Tel** (216)321-3774, FAX (508)456-8387. **ED** Barbara Palys, Jan Sperry and Chris Miller (European Editor). **Circ:** 3,400.

CK/0121-0793
**IATREIA MEDELLIN.** [Iatreia Medellin]. (1988)-. Periodical. Spanish. tq. $40.00. Universidad de Antioquia / Medicina, Facultad de Medicina, 1226 Medellin Colombia. **Tel** 011 57 4 263-7954, 011 57 4 263-6446. **ED** Federico Diaz M.D. **DD** 610. Index available (in Nov. issue). **Pr Rev. Circ:** 1,000.
**Ind/Abst** EMBASE [Select. Cov.].

DK/0905-717X
**IATROGENICS : THE OFFICIAL JOURNAL OF THE INTERNATIONAL SOCIETY FOR THE PREVENTION OF IATROGENIC COMPLICATIONS (ISPIC).** **Added/Corp** International Society for the Prevention of Iatrogenic Complications. Vol. 1, Issue 1 (Jan./Mar. 1991)-. Periodical. English. qt. Kr500.00. Munksgaard International Publishers Ltd, PO Box 2148, DK-1016 Copenhagen K Denmark. **Tel** 011 45 33 12 70 30, FAX 011 45 33 12 93 87, telex 19431 MUNKS DK. **NLM** W1; IA225. **CODEN** ITRNEB.
**Ind/Abst** EMBASE.

JA
**ICMR ANNALS : ANNUAL REPORTS OF THE INTERNATIONAL CENTER FOR MEDICAL RESEARCH.** [ICMR annals]. **Added/Corp** International Center for Medical Research. **VAT** International Center for Medical Research Annals. Vol. 1 (1981)-. Periodical. English. Kobe Daigaku Igakubu Fuzoku Igaku Kenkyu Kokusai Koryu Senta, (International Center for Medical Research, School of Medicine, Kobe University), 5-1, Kusunokicho 7 Chome, Chuoku,, Kobeshi, Hyogoken 650 Japan. **NLM** W1 IC409. **CODEN** ICMRDE. Documents available from BIOSIS Document Express, CASDDS.
**Ind/Abst** Biol. Abstr.; Chem. Abstr.; Trop. Dis. Bull.

US/8756-7857
**ICU FORUM.** [ICU forum]. **VAT** Intensive Care Unit Forum. Periodical. English. bm. Free. ICU Forum, PO Box 8025 Wainwright Station, San Antonio TX 78208. **DD** 616.

NE/0303-870X
**IFIP MEDICAL INFORMATICS MONOGRAPH SERIES.** V. 1- 1974-. Academic Scholarly Publication. English. ir. Elsevier Science Publishing Company Inc, Madison Square Station, PO Box 882, New York NY 10159-0882. **Tel** (212)633-3950, FAX (212)633-3990. **NLM** W1 I227M.

JA/0915-8669
**IGAKU KENSA. VFOAT** Japanese Journal of Medical Technology (Tokyo. 1991); Nihon Rinsho Eisei Kensa Gishikaishi (Tokyo. 1991). (1991)-. Periodical. Japanese. mo. **DD** 610. Documents available from CASDDS. ***Continues*** *Eisei Kensa, 0367-052X.*
**Ind/Abst** Chem. Abstr.

JA/0039-2359
**IGAKU NO AYUMI.** [Igaku no ayumi]. (Mar. 1946)-. Periodical. Japanese. wk. $786.00. Ishiyaku Publishers Inc., 7-10 Honkomagome 1 Chome, Bunkyo-ku, Tokyo Japan. **(Subscription address:** Kyowa Book Co., Inc., 1- 38 Kanda Jinbo-Cho Chiyoda-Ku, Tokyo 101, Japan) **CODEN** IGAYAY. Documents available from CASDDS.
**Ind/Abst** Chem. Abstr.

JA/0019-1604
**IGAKU TO SEIBUTSUGAKU.** [Igaku to seibutsugaku]. **VFOAT** Medicine and Biology. (1942)-. Periodical. Japanese. mo. Tokyo Ogata Igaku Kagaku Kenkyujo, Tokyo Japan. **DD** 610. Documents available from CASDDS.
**Ind/Abst** Chem. Abstr.

JA/0389-3898
**IGAKU TO YAKUGAKU.** [Igaku to yakugaku]. **VFOAT** Journal of Medicine (Tokyo. 1979). (1979)-. Periodical. Japanese. mo. Shizen Kagakusha, (Shizen Kagakusha Co., Ltd.), Kudan Sentoraru Biru,, 1-4, Iidabashi 2 Chome, Chiyodaku, Tokyoto 102 Japan. **DD** 610. Documents available from CASDDS.
**Ind/Abst** Chem. Abstr.

JA/0385-440X
**IKA KIKAIGAKU.** (IKA-KIKAIGAKU. JAPANESE JOURNAL OF MEDICAL INSTRUMENTATION.). [Ika kikaigaku]. **Added/Corp** Nippon Ika Kikai Gakkai. **VFOAT** Japanese Journal of Medical Instrumentation. (1976)-. Academic Scholarly Publication. Japanese (table of contents in English). Twelve times a year. $144.00. Nihon Ika Kikai Gakkai, (Medical Instruments Soc. of Japan), 39-15, Hongo 3 Chome, Bunkyoku, Tokyoto 113 Japan. **(Subscription address:** Kyowa Book Company Inc., 1 38 Kanda Jinbocho Chiyoda-ku, Tokyo 101 Japan.) **NLM** W1 IK257. ***Continues*** *Ika Kikaigaku Zasshi, 0019-440X.*
**Ind/Abst** EMBASE.

US/0018-9960
**ILAR NEWS.** [ILAR news]. **Main/Corp** Institute of Laboratory Animal Resources (U.S.). **VAT** Institute of Laboratory Animal Resources News. Vol. 10 (Oct. 1966)-. Periodical. English. Four times a year. Free on request. National Academy Press, 2101 Constitution Avenue NW, Lockbox 285, Washington DC 20055. **Tel** (800)624-6242, (202)334-3313, FAX (202)334-2451. **(Subscription address:** Institute of Laboratory Animal Resources, National Research Council, Box 285, Washington DC 20055.) **ED** Dorothy D. Greenhouse. **LC** QL55; .I45. **DD** 591/.07/24. **NLM** W1 I245. **Circ:** 2,100 (ctrl). ***Continues*** *Information on Laboratory Animals for Research.*
**Desc:** Provides information and discussion on the use of animals in biomedical research, including state-of-the-art techniques, unusual animal models and genetic stocks, perspectives and commentary, guidelines and legislation affecting animal use, and news items.
**Ind/Abst** AgBiotech News Inf.; AGRICOLA [Full Cov.]; Anim. Breed. Abstr.; Fish Rev. (19??-199?); Index Vet.; Pig News Inf.; Vet. Bull.; Wildl. Rev. (19??-199?).

US/0147-0191
**ILLINOIS CONFERENCE ON MEDICAL INFORMATION SYSTEMS.** 1st- 1974-. Periodical. English. an. **NLM** W3 IL37.

US/1044-6400
**ILLINOIS MEDICINE.** (ILLINOIS MEDICINE / ILLINOIS STATE MEDICAL SOCIETY.). [Ill. med.]. **Added/Corp** Illinois State Medical Society. Vol. 1, No. 2 (Jan. 6, 1989)-. Academic Scholarly Publication. English. Twenty-four times a year. $12.00 US, Cuba, Puerto Rico, Philippines & Mexico; $12.50 Canada; $19.00 other. Illinois Medicine, 20 North Michigan Avenue, Suite 700, Chicago IL 60602. **Tel** (312)782-1654, (800)782-4767, FAX (312)782-2023. **ED** Lynn Koslowsky. **DD** 610. **NLM** W1; IL417L. **Ad Acc, Adv Mgr:** Carla Nolen. **Circ:** 20,000. available on microfilm from University Microfilms International (UMI). Documents available from BIOSIS Document Express, CASDDS. ***Continues*** *IMJ. Illinois Medical Journal, 0019-2120.*

**Desc:** Brings Illinois physicians balanced, accurate news and comments on health care issues and professional concerns.
**Ind/Abst** Biol. Abstr.; Chem. Abstr.; Energy Res. Abstr.; Highw. Res. Abstr.; Hospit. Manage. Rev. (19??-); Index Med.; INIS Atomindex [Micro.]; Life Sci. Collect.; Soc. Welf. Soc. Plan./Policy Soc. Dev.

SP
**IM; INFORMATICA EN MEDICINA Y BIOLOGIA.** (19??)-. Academic Scholarly Publication. Spanish (summaries and/or abstracts in English). Four times a year. 4800ptas. ICR SA, Calle Gayarre 13-1-3, 08014 Barcelona, Spain. **Tel** 011 39 3 4313561.

UK/0265-0746
**IMA JOURNAL OF MATHEMATICS APPLIED IN MEDICINE AND BIOLOGY.** **See** Mathematics.

CN/0383-9710
**IMAGE (VANCOUVER).** (IMAGE.). **Added/Corp** Kinsmen Rehabilitation Foundation of British Columbia. (1971)-. Periodical. English. qt (Mar., June, Sept., Dec.). free. Kinsmen Rehabilitation Foundation of British Columbia, 2256 West 12th Avenue, Vancouver BC V6K 4L2 Canada. **Tel** (604)736-8841 (VOICE), (604)738-0603 (TDD), FAX (604)738-0015. **ED** Bruce Crump. **DD** 362.4/06/2711. **Bk Rev. Ad Acc. Circ:** 20,000 (ctrl). ***Continues*** *Image 5, 0315-324X; Information Bulletin (Disabled Living Resource Centre).*
**Desc:** Articles on medical, social service and technological advances and issues of interest to physically disabled people, health care, and social service professionals, and the general public. Includes D.L.R.C. Bulletin which is a selective bibliography of publications, equipment and services dealing with independent living for physically disabled. Issues are topic-oriented, i.e. gardening, sexuality, etc.

SZ
**IMAGING AND SURGICAL ANATOMY.** ***Title Change.*** (1992)-(199?). English. an. S. Karger AG, Allschwilerstrasse 10, PO Box - Postfach - Case Postale, CH-4009 Basel Switzerland. **Tel** 011 41 61 306-1111, FAX 011 41 61 306-1234, telex CH 962 652. **ED** W Lierse. ***Continues*** *Bibliotheca Anatomica.* ***Continued by*** *Imaging and Clinical Anatomy.*
**Desc:** A large number of the volumes in this series focus on problems in microcirculation. This preferential coverage is a service to general medicine in that the small and lymphatic vessels rarely receive such exclusive and thorough attention.
**Ind/Abst** Ref. Upd. Deluxe Ed.

UK/0267-2928
**IMLS GAZETTE.** [IMLS gaz.]. Vol. 29, No. 1 (Jan. 1985)-. Periodical. English. mo. £42.00. Institute of Medical Laboratory Sciences, 12 Queen Anne Street, London W1M 0AU England. **Tel** 01-636 8192, FAX 01-436 4946. **ED** R Owen. **NLM** W1; IM4573. Index available. cum. index. ***Continues*** *Gazette of the Institute of Medical Laboratory Sciences, 0307-5656.*
**Ind/Abst** Health Serv. Abstr.

US
**IMMI : THE INDEX OF MEDIEVAL MEDICAL IMAGES IN NORTH AMERICA.** **VFOAT** Index of Medieval Medical Images in North America; IMMI Newsletter. Vol. 1, No. 1 (Jan. 1989)-. Periodical. English. UCLA School of Medicine, Medical History Division, Department of Anatomy and Cell Biology, Los Angeles CA 90024.

NE/0926-2067
**IMMUNOASSAY KIT DIRECTORY. SERIES A, CLINICAL CHEMISTRY, THE.** **VFOAT** Clinical Chemistry; IKAD. Series A, Clinical Chemistry. Vol. 1, Pt. 1 (May 1991)-. Directory. English. Five times a year (5 issues per year). $980.00. Kluwer Academic Publishers, Postbus 322, 3300 AH Dordrecht, The Netherlands. **Tel** 011 (31) 78 524400, FAX 011 31 78 183273, telex 20083. **ED** John Seth. **NLM** QY 26; I33. **Pr Rev. Acid Free.** available on microfilm and microfiche from University Microfilms International (UMI).
**Desc:** Provides clinical chemists with comparative aspects of over 1500 commercially available kits on peptide, steroid and thyroid hormones, proteins, tumor markers, therapeutic drugs.

FR
**IMPACT INTERNAT.** French. Impact Medecin, 20 Boulevard Du Parc, 92521 Neuilly, Seine Cedex France. **Tel** 011 33 1 46413333, FAX 011 33 1 46410200.

FR
**IMPACT MEDECIN (NOUV. FORMULE).** (IMPACT MEDECIN.). No. 1 (Jan. 21, 1989)-. Periodical. French. wk. Impact Medecin, 20 Boulevard Du Parc, 92521 Neuilly, Seine Cedex France. **Tel** 011 33 1 46413333, FAX 011 33 1 46410200. **NLM** W1; IM591C. ***Continues*** *Impact Medecin, Le Praticien; P.P.P., 0755-382X.*

FR
**IMPACT MEDECIN QUOTIDIEN.** French. ir. 280.00F. Impact Medecine, 20 Bld du Parc, 92521 Neuilly Seine Cedex France. **Tel** 011 33 1 46413300.

US/1059-3489
**IMPLANT SOCIETY, THE.** (THE IMPLANT SOCIETY : [PERIODICAL].). [Implant Soc.]. Vol. 1, No. 1 (Mar./Apr. 1990)-. Periodical. English. bm. $188.00 (one year), $288.00 (two years), $368.00 (three years) US; $135.00 (one year), $245.00 (two years), $330.00 (three years) other. Implant Society, One Kendall Square, Suite 2200, Cambridge MA 02139. **Tel** (617)621-7170. **ED** M Thompson. **DD** 617. **NLM** W1; IM595G. Index available (bound in every issue). cum. index. **Circ:** 15,000.
**Ind/Abst** Index Dent. Lit. (1990-).

●US/1063-8520
**IMPULSE (CHAMPAIGN, ILL.).** **See** Dance.

US
**IN CONFIDENCE.** English. bm. $67.50 (members); $75.00 (non-members). American Health Information Management Association, Order Unit, PO Box 97349, Chicago IL 60690-7349. **Tel** (312) 787-2672, FAX (312) 787-5926, (312) 787-9793.

US/1047-0549
**IN HEALTH.** ***Title Change.*** [In health]. Vol. 4, No. 1 (Jan./Feb. 1990)-Vol. 5, No. 7 (Dec./Jan. 1992). Periodical. English. bm. PO Box 56863, Boulder CO 80322-6863. **LC** R773; .I5. **DD** 610/.5. **NLM** W1; IN102K. **CODEN** IHEAER. ***Continues*** *Hippocrates (Sausalito, CA), 0892-2977.* ***Merged with*** *Health (Family Media, Inc.), 0279-3547* ***to form*** *Health (San Francisco, Calif.), 1059-938X.*
**Ind/Abst** Gen. Sci. Source (Jan. 1992-); Health Ref. Cent. (Jan. 1989-) [Full Txt.] [Full Cov.]; Mag. Artic. Summar. Select (Jan. 1992-); Mag. Index Plus (1990-1992); Read. Guide Abstr. Select Ed.; Mag. Index (?-?).

US/1042-7430
**IN-SERVICE REVIEWS IN CLINICAL LABORATORY SCIENCE.** (IN-SERVICE REVIEWS IN CLINICAL LABORATORY SCIENCE [SOUND RECORDING].). [In-serv. rev. clin. lab. sci.]. **Added/Corp** American Society for Medical Technology. **VFOAT** In Service Reviews in Clinical Laboratory Science. (198?)-. Periodical. English. mo. $175.00. Educational Reviews Inc., 6801 Cahaba Valley Road, Birmingham AL 35242. **Tel** (205)991-5188, (800)633-4743, FAX (205)995-1926. **DD** 610. ***Continues*** *In Service Reviews in Medical Laboratory Technology, 1041-0074.*

US/1041-0104
**IN SERVICE REVIEWS IN DIAGNOSTIC MEDICAL SONOGRAPHY.** (IN SERVICE REVIEWS IN DIAGNOSTIC MEDICAL SONOGRAPHY [SOUND RECORDING].). **VFOAT** In-Service Reviews in Diagnostic Medical Sonography. (19??)-. Periodical. English. mo. $175.00. Educational Reviews Inc., 6801 Cahaba Valley Road, Birmingham AL 35242. **Tel** (205)991-5188, (800)633-4743, FAX (205)995-1926. **DD** 616.

US/0363-521X
**IN VITRO. MONOGRAPH.** **See** Biology.

US/0733-1398
**IN VIVO (NEW YORK, N.Y.).** **See** Business.

US/0019-3879
**INDEX MEDICUS (1960).** **See** Medical Science and Technology-Abstracting, Bibliographies and Statistics.

II/1013-5499
**INDEX MEDICUS FOR WHO SOUTH-EAST ASIA REGION.** **Added/Corp** World Health Organization. Regional Office for South-East Asia. **VFOAT** Index Medicus for WHO South East Asia Region; WHO Index Medicus for WHO South-East Asia Region. Vol. 1 (June 1980)-. English. an. Oxford University Press, Walton Street, Oxford OX2 6DP England. **Tel** 011 44 865 56767, FAX 011 44 865 267773, telex 837330 OXPRES G. **(Subscription address:** Oxford University Press / USA, Journals Marketing Department, Oxford University Press, 2001 Evans Road, Cary NC 27513.) **NLM** ZW 1 I38.

BL/0100-4743
**INDEX MEDICUS LATINO-AMERICANO.** ***Suspended.*** (INDEX MEDICUS LATINO-AMERICANO / BIBLIOTECA REGIONAL DE MEDICINA, ORGANIZACION PANAMERICANA DE LA SALUD.). [Index med. lat.-am.]. **Added/Corp** Biblioteca Regional de Medicina e Ciencias da Saude (Sao Paulo, Brazil) Centro Latino-Americano de Informacao em Ciencias da Saude. **VFOAT** Index Medicus Latino Americano. Vol. 1, No. 1 (Jan./June 1979)-Vol. 13 No. 1/2. Portuguese (Spanish). qt. $25.00 Brazil; $40.00 Latin American countries; $100.00 other. Organizacao Pan American da Saude, rua Botucatu 862, 04023 Sao Paulo SP Brazil. **Tel** (011)549-2611, telex 11 22143. **LC** Z6661.L29; I53; R21. **DD** 016.61. **NLM** ZW 1 I38522. **Circ:** 500. available on CD-ROM from BIREME; available on an online database.
**Desc:** Approximately 450 Latin American biomedical journals analyzed. Published with abstracts of most articles. Subject headings in English, Spanish, and Portuguese.
**Ind/Abst** Trop. Dis. Bull.

US
**INDEX MEDICUS / NATIONAL LIBRARY OF MEDICINE. [MICROFICHE].** **See** Medical Science and Technology-Abstracting, Bibliographies and Statistics.

II/0019-5677
**INDIAN JOURNAL OF HISTORY OF MEDICINE.** V. 1- June 1956-. Periodical. English. ir. Hindustan Book Agency, 17 UB Jawahar Nagar, Delhi 7 India. **LC** R131.A1; I48.

II/0019-5332
**INDIAN JOURNAL OF MEDICAL EDUCATION.** **Added/Corp** Indian Association for the Advancement of Medical Education. (Oct. 1961)-. Periodical. English. Three times a year. $48.00. Association for the Advencement of Medical Education, Vellore, Madras State, India. **(Subscription address:** Prints India, 11 Darya Ganj, New Delhi, 110002 India, (Phone: 011 91 11 3268645)) **LC** R735.A1; I5. **NLM** W1 IN2125.

II/0970-955X
**INDIAN JOURNAL OF MEDICAL RESEARCH. SECTION A, INFECTIOUS DISEASES.** [Indian j. med. res., Sect. A, Infect. dis.]. **Added/Corp** Indian Council of Medical Research. **VFOAT** Infectious Diseases. Vol. 89 (Jan. 1989)-. Periodical. English. mo. $90.00. Indian Council of Medical Research, PO Box 4508 Ansari Nagar, New Delhi 110029 India. **Tel** 011 91 11 653980. **(Subscription address:** Prints India, 11 Darya Ganj, New Delhi 110002 India.) **ED** G V Satvavati and N Medappa. **DD** 610. **CODEN** IMADEH. Index available. cum. index. **Bk Rev. Ad Acc. Pr Rev. Circ:** 1,000 (ctrl). Documents available from The Genuine Article, BIOSIS Document Express. ***Continues in part*** *Indian Journal of Medical Research, 0019-5340.*
**Desc:** Journal publishing all aspects of medical research that contribute significantly to the advancement of knowledge in medical sciences.
**Ind/Abst** Biol. Abstr. (1989-); Curr. Contents Life Sci.; EMBASE; Helminthol. Abstr. (1991-); Life Sci. Collect.; Protozoolog. Abstr.; Res. Alert [Full Cov.]; Rev. Med. Vet. Entomol.; Rev. Med. Vet. Mycology; Saf. Health Work; Sci. Cit. Index; SCISEARCH; Soc. Sci. Cit. Index [Select. Cov.].

II/0970-9568
**INDIAN JOURNAL OF MEDICAL RESEARCH. SECTION B, BIOMEDICAL RESEARCH OTHER THAN INFECTIOUS DISEASES.** [Indian j. med. res., Sect. B, Biomed. res. other than infect. dis.]. **Added/Corp** Indian Council of Medical Research. **VFOAT** Biomedical Research Other Than Infectious Diseases. Vol. 90 (Feb. 1989)-. Periodical. English. mo. $90.00. Indian Council of Medical Research, PO Box 4508 Ansari Nagar, New Delhi 110029 India. **Tel** 011 91 11 653980. **(Subscription address:** Prints India, 11 Darya Ganj, New Delhi 110002 India.) **ED** G V Satvavati and N Medappa. **DD** 610. **CODEN** IMBDEM. Index available. cum. index. **Bk Rev. Ad Acc. Pr Rev. Circ:** 1,000 (ctrl). Documents available from The Genuine Article, BIOSIS Document Express. ***Continues in part*** *Indian Journal of Medical Research, 0019-5340.*
**Desc:** Journal publishing all aspects of medical research that contribute significantly to the advancement of knowledge in medical sciences.
**Ind/Abst** Biol. Abstr. (1989-); Curr. Contents Life Sci.; EMBASE [Select. Cov.]; Nucl. Sci. Abstr.; Life Sci. Collect.; Protozoolog. Abstr.; Res. Alert [Full Cov.]; Rev. Agric. Entomol.; Rev. Med. Vet. Entomol.; Rev. Med. Vet. Mycology; Saf. Health Work; Sci. Cit. Index; SCISEARCH; Sel. Water Resour. Abstr.; Soc. Sci. Cit. Index [Select. Cov.].

II/0019-5359
**INDIAN JOURNAL OF MEDICAL SCIENCES.** [Indian j. med. sci.]. Vol. 1 (July 1947)-. Academic Scholarly Publication. English. mo. $45.00. Indian Journal Medical Science Road, Back Bay VW, 3 A Charni Rd Grd, Bombay 400 004, India. **(Subscription address:** Prints India, 11 Darya Ganj, New Delhi 110002 India.) **ED** J C Patel. **NLM** W1 IN215. **CODEN** INJMAO. Index available. cum. index. **Bk Rev. Ad Acc. Circ:** 3,500 (ctrl). Documents available from BIOSIS Document Express, CASDDS. ***Continues*** *Medical Bulletin.*
**Desc:** Covers information on medical sciences.
**Ind/Abst** Biol. Abstr.; Chem. Abstr.; EMBASE [Select. Cov.]; Index Med.; Life Sci. Collect.; Rev. Med. Vet. Mycology; Rev. Plant Pathol.; SEA Abstr.; Trop. Dis. Bull.

II/0301-1216
**INDIAN JOURNAL OF PREVENTIVE AND SOCIAL MEDICINE.** [Indian j. prev. soc. med.]. **Added/Corp** Indian Public Health Association. (19??)-. Periodical. English. qt. $30.00. **(Subscription address:** Prints India, 11 Darya Ganj, New Delhi 110002 India.)

●II
**INDIAN JOURNAL OF UNANI MEDICINE : DEVOTED TO INTERDISCIPLINARY RESEARCH IN UNANI MEDICINE AND ALLIED SCIENCES.** **Added/Corp** Central Council for Research in Unani Medicine (India). **VFOAT**

Devoted to Interdisciplinary Research in Unani Medicine and Allied Sciences; Unani Medicine; Indian J. Unani Medicine. Vol. 1, No. 1 (Jan./June 1991)-. Periodical. English. sa. $10.00. Central Council for Research in Unani Medicine, 5 Panchsheel Shopping Center, New Delhi 110017 India. **(Subscription address:** Prints India, 11 Darya Ganj, New Delhi 110002 India.) **LC** R97; .I56. **DD** 615.5/3.

II/0019-5863
**INDIAN MEDICAL GAZETTE.** [Indian med. gaz.]. Vol. 1 (May 1961)-. Periodical. English. mo. $30.00. Savory Chambers, Wallace Street, 40001 Bombay India. **(Subscription address:** Prints India, 11 Darya Ganj, New Delhi, 110002 India, (Phone: 011 91 11 3268645)) **NLM** W1 IN25. **CODEN** IMGAAY. Documents available from CASDDS.
**Ind/Abst** Chem. Abstr. (1866-1982); EMBASE.

II/0019-5871
**INDIAN MEDICAL JOURNAL.** [Indian med. j.]. (1910)-. Academic Scholarly Publication. English. mo. $20.00. Indian Books and Periodicals, 2429 Tilak Street, Pahar Ganj, New Delhi 110005 India. **(Subscription address:** Prints India, 11 Darya Ganj, New Delhi, 110002 India, (Phone: 011 91 11 3268645)) **NLM** W1 IN252. **CODEN** IMJUA7. Documents available from CASDDS. ***Continues*** *All-India Hospital Assistant's Journal.*
**Ind/Abst** Chem. Abstr.; EMBASE.

II/0019-6169
**INDIAN PRACTITIONER.** (1947)-. Periodical. English. mo. $40.00. The Indian Practitioner, David Sassoon Building/3rd Floor, 143 Mahatma Gandhi Road, Bombay 400 023 India. **Tel** 27 38 09. **(Subscription address:** Prints India, 11 Darya Ganj, New Delhi, 110002 India, (Phone: 011 91 11 3268645)) **ED** S A Nanivadekar. Index available. cum. index. **Bk Rev. Ad Acc. Circ:** 17,000 (ctrl).
**Desc:** Journal devoted to medicine, public health and surgery.

US
**INDIANA HAND CENTER NEWSLETTER.** English. qt (seasonally). $100.00. Foundation for Hand Research and Education, PO Box 80434, Indianapolis IN 46280. **Tel** (317)471-4313. **ED** Kathy Meier. **Circ:** 500.
**Desc:** Current techniques and issues in hand surgery and rehabilitation.

US/0746-8288
**INDIANA MEDICINE.** (INDIANA MEDICINE : THE JOURNAL OF THE INDIANA STATE MEDICAL ASSOCIATION.). [Indiana med.]. **Added/Corp** Indiana State Medical Association. Vol. 77, No. 1 (Jan. 1984)-. Academic Scholarly Publication. English. Six times a year (Jan., March, May, July, Sep., Nov.). $14.00 (libraries), $15.00 (others) US; $15.00 (libraries), $17.00 (others) Canada; $16.00 (libraries), $18.00 (others) other. Indiana Medicine, 322 Canal Walk, Indianapolis IN 46202. **Tel** (317)261-2060, FAX (317)261-2076. **ED** Tina Sims. **LC** R15; .I43. **DD** 610. **NLM** W1; IN304R. Index available. **Ad Acc, Adv Mgr:** same as editor. **Pr Rev. Circ:** 7,000 (ctrl). available on microfilm from University Microfilms International (UMI). ***Continues*** *Journal of the Indiana State Medical Association, 0019-6770.*
**Desc:** Focus on socioeconomic, practice management, legal, legislative, ethical and financial issues affecting medicine. Contents include association activities and peer-reviewed scientific articles.
**Ind/Abst** Cumul. Index Nurs. Allied Health Lit.; EMBASE; Energy Res. Abstr.; Hospit. Health Admin. Index; Index Med.; INIS Atomindex [Micro.]; Int. Nurs. Index; Life Sci. Collect.; SportSearch.

SP
**INDICE MEDICO ESPANOL.** **See** Medical Science and Technology-Abstracting, Bibliographies and Statistics.

US/0275-0236
**INFECTION CONTROL DIGEST.** ***Ceased.*** [Infect control dig.]. Vol. 1, No. 1 (Jan. 1980)-Ceased Vol. 7, No. 12. Periodical. English. mo. American Hospital Association, 840 North Lake Shore Drive, Chicago IL 60611. **Tel** (312)280-6000, (800)242-2626. **NLM** W1 IN406B. available in microform.

US
**INFECTION REPORTER, THE.** Vol. 1, No. 1 (Jan. 1984)-. English. mo. The Infection Reporter, PO Box 54209, Philadelphia PA 19105. **Tel** (215)592-9342.

US/0162-6493
**INFECTIOUS DISEASE PRACTICE.** (19??)-. Periodical. English. mo. $89.00 US; $111.00 other. MBC Publications Inc., Winthrop University Hospital, Mineola, Long Island NY 11501. **Tel** (516)663-2505. **ED** Dean Laux. **Bk Rev. Circ:** 1,500.
**Desc:** Medical information for physicians in infectious diseases.

GW/0178-9090
**INFEKTIONEN UND KLINIKHYGIENE.** ***Ceased.*** (1985)-(19??). Periodical. German. qt. Vieweg Publishing, PO Box 5829, D 65048 Wiesbaden Germany. **Tel** 011 49 611 160230, FAX 011 49 611 160229. **UDC** 616.9-022.1.

US/0360-3997
**INFLAMMATION.** [Inflammation]. **Added/Corp** International Inflammation Research Society. Vol. 1 (Mar. 1975)-. Periodical. English. Six times a year. $320.00 institutions, $77.00 individuals US; $375.00 institutions, $90.00 individuals other. Plenum Press, 233 Spring Street, New York NY 10013-1578. **Tel** (212)620-8000, (800)221-9369, FAX (212)463-0742, (212)807-1047, telex 23/421139. **ED** Gerald Weissmann. **LC** RB131; .I518. **DD** 616/.047. **NLM** W1 IN41KR. **CODEN** INFLD4. **[CCC].** Index available. **Pr Rev.** available on microfilm and microfiche from University Microfilms International (UMI). Documents available from The Genuine Article, BIOSIS Document Express, CASDDS, ADONIS.
**Desc:** An international journal devoted to experimental and clinical studies of the physiology, biochemistry, cell biology and pharmacology of inflammation.
**Ind/Abst** ADONIS; Biol. Abstr.; Chem. Abstr.; Curr. Contents Life Sci.; Dairy Sci. Abstr.; EMBASE; Energy Res. Abstr. (Oct. 1981-); Immunol. Abstr.; Index Med.; Index Vet.; INIS Atomindex [Micro.]; Life Sci. Collect.; PESTDOC; Ref. Upd. Deluxe Ed.; Res. Alert [Full Cov.]; Sci. Cit. Index; SCISEARCH; Vet. Bull.

SZ/1023-3830
**INFLAMMATION RESEARCH.** (19??)-. English. Twelve times a year (plus two supplements). 1280.60F Switzerland; 1303.40F other. Birkhaeuser Verlag Ag, Klosterberg 23, PO Box 133, CH-4010 Basel Switzerland. **Tel** 011 41 61 2717400, FAX 011 41 0 61 2717666, telex 963475 birk ch. **(Subscription address:** Birkhauser Verlag AG, PO Box 151, CH 4106 Therwil Switzerland; Phone: 011 41 61 7217740) ***Continues*** *Agents and Actions.*
**Desc:** Official journal of the European Histamine Research Society, the European Inflammation Society, and the British Inflammation Research Association.

US/1047-5028
**INFLAMMATORY DISEASE AND THERAPY.** [Inflamm. dis. ther.]. (1989)-. Monographic series. English. Price varies per volume. Marcel Dekker Inc., 270 Madison Avenue, New York NY 10016. **Tel** (212)696-9000, (800)228-1160, FAX (212)685-4540, telex 421419. **(Subscription address:** Marcel Dekker Inc, PO Box 5017, Monticello NY 12701.) **DD** 616. **NLM** W1; IN41LA. **CODEN** IDITE8. Documents available from BIOSIS Document Express, CASDDS.
**Ind/Abst** Biol. Abstr.; Chem. Abstr.

NE/0925-4692
**INFLAMMOPHARMACOLOGY. VFOAT** Inflammo Pharmacology. Vol. 1, No. 1 (1991)-. Academic Scholarly Publication. English. qt. $378.00. Kluwer Academic Publishers, Postbus 322, 3300 AH Dordrecht, The Netherlands. **Tel** 011 (31) 78 524400, FAX 011 31 78 183273, telex 20083. **ED** K.D. Rainsford. **NLM** W1; IN41LF. **CODEN** IAOAES. **[CCC]. Pr Rev. Acid Free.** available on microfilm and microfiche from University Microfilms International (UMI). Documents available from CASDDS.
**Desc:** Publishes papers on inflammation and its pharmacological control emphasizing comparisons of different inflammatory states, and the actions, therapeutic efficacy and safety of drugs employed in the treatment of inflammatory.
**Ind/Abst** Chem. Abstr.; Curr. Aware. Biol. Sci., CABS; EMBASE.

US/0362-3351
**INFLUENZA SURVEILLANCE (1973).** (INFLUENZA SURVEILLANCE.). [Influ. surveill.]. **VFOAT** Influenza Surveillance Report; Influenza Report. No. 90 (1973-1974-1975)-. English. ir. US Department of Health and Human Services, 200 Independence Avenue Southwest, Washington DC 20201. **LC** RA644.I6. **DD** 614.5/18/0973021. **NLM** W2 A C7CI. available on microfiche (Vols. for (July 1979- June 1981-) distributed to depository libraries). ***Continues*** *Influenza-Respiratory Disease Surveillance, 0362-3343.*

GW
**INFORMATIK, BIOMETRIE UND EPIDEMIOLOGIE IN MEDIZIN UND BIOLOGIE.** German. Four times a year. DM288.00 Germany; DM296.00 other. Gustav Fischer Verlag Stuttgart, Postfach 720143, Wollgrasweg 49, D 70577 Stuttgart Germany. **Tel** 011 49 711 458030, FAX 0711-4580334, telex 2627-7111488. **(Subscription address:** VCH Publishers Inc., 303 Northwest 12th Avenue, Journals Department, Deerfield FL 33442.)

●UK/1353-8861
**INFORMATION MANAGEMENT IN HEALTH CARE / IM & T SERVICE.** (1994)-. Periodical. English. Three times a year. £95.00 (Institutions). Churchill Livingstone, 1-3 Baxter's Place, Leith Walk, Edinburgh EH1 3AF Scotland. **Tel** 011 44 31 556 2424, FAX 011 44 31 558 1278, telex 727511. **(Subscription address:** Maruzen Company Ltd., PO Box 5050, Import & Export Department, Tokyo 100 31 Japan.)

●UK/1353-887X
**INFORMATION MANAGEMENT IN HEALTH CARE / PRIMARY CARE SERVICE.** (1994)-. Periodical. English. Three times a year. £85.00 (Institutions). Churchill Livingstone, 1-3 Baxter's Place, Leith Walk, Edinburgh EH1 3AF Scotland. **Tel** 011 44 31 556 2424, FAX 011 44 31 558 1278, telex 727511. **(Subscription address:** Maruzen Company Ltd., PO Box 5050, Import & Export Department, Tokyo 100 31 Japan.)

●US/1065-8009
**INFORMATION SYSTEMS IN GROUP PRACTICE SURVEY. Added/Corp** Center for Research in Ambulatory Health Care Administration (U.S.). (1992)-. English. be. $35.00. Center for Research in Ambulatory Health Care Administration, 104 Inverness Terrace East, Englewood CO 80112.

US/0160-757X
**INFUSION (ANDOVER).** ***Suspended.*** (INFUSION.). Vol. 1, Sept. 1977-Suspended with Vol. 13. Periodical. English. bm. $12.00. Artemis Publishing, 12 High Street, Andover MA 01810. **NLM** W1; IN445. **[CCC].**
**Ind/Abst** EMBASE; Int. Pharm. Abstr.

KO
**IN'GAN KWAHAK. VFOAT** Human Science. Academic Scholarly Publication. English (Korean). Songsim Chungang Yuji Chaedan, 94-195 Yongdungpo-dong Yongdungpo-ku, Seoul South Korea. **LC** R97.7.K6; I53. **NLM** W1 IN447E. **CODEN** INKWDS. Documents available from CASDDS.
**Ind/Abst** Chem. Abstr.

CN/0705-369X
**INJURED ATHLETE, THE.** V. 1- 1977-. Periodical. English. qt. Free. Ontario Athletic Therapist Association, 559 Jarvis Street, Toronto Ontario M4Y 2J1 Canada. **DD** 617/.1027/062713. ctrl circ.

US/1056-473X
**INJURIES, WOUNDS, AND MULTIPLE BODY DAMAGES.** (1991)-. Periodical. English. mo. $240.00. Abbe Publishers Association, Virginia Division, 4111 Gallows Road, Annandale VA 22003.

UK/0020-1383
**INJURY.** (INJURY. THE BRITISH JOURNAL OF ACCIDENT SURGERY.). [Injury]. Vol. 1 (July 1969)-. Academic Scholarly Publication. English. Ten times a year. $321.00 The Americas; £215.00 other. Butterworth Heinemann Publishers, Linacre House, Jordan Hill, Oxford OX2 8DP England. **Tel** 011 44 865 310366. **(Subscription address:** Elsevier Science Ltd. Oxford Fulfillment Centre, PO Box 800, Kidlington, Oxford OX5 1DX United Kingdom.) **ED** O. N. Tubbs (editor's address: The General Hospital, Birmingham United Kingdom). **[CCC].** Index available. **Bk Rev. Ad Acc. Pr Rev. Circ:** 1,150. available on microfilm and microfiche from University Microfilms International (UMI). Documents available from The Genuine Article, BIOSIS Document Express.
**Desc:** Offers wide-ranging coverage of all aspects of trauma, including injuries of the head, chest and abdomen, as well as fractures and soft tissue injuries.
**Ind/Abst** Biol. Abstr.; Curr. Contents Clin. Med.; EMBASE; Hospit. Health Admin. Index; Index Med.; Res. Alert [Select. Cov.]; SCISEARCH; SPORT Discus; SportSearch.

NE/0378-3790
**INORGANIC PERSPECTIVES IN BIOLOGY AND MEDICINE.** **See** Biology.

US/0046-9580
**INQUIRY (CHICAGO).** (INQUIRY.). [Inq.]. **Added/Corp** Blue Cross Association. Division of Research. Vol. 1 (Aug. 1963)-. Academic Scholarly Publication. English. Four times a year (Mar., June, Sept., Dec.). $70.00 US Possessions & Canada; $125.00 others. Blue Cross Association, PO Box 527, Glenview IL 60025. **Tel** (708)724-9280, FAX (708)729-2199. **ED** Phillip Puchalski. **LC** RA410.A1; I58. **NLM** W1 IN456K. **CODEN** INQYA. **[CCC].** cum. index. **Pr Rev. Circ:** 2,500 (ctrl). available on microfilm and microfiche from University Microfilms International (UMI). Documents available from The Genuine Article, UMI Article Clearinghouse.
**Desc:** Seeks to contribute to the continued improvement in the nation's health care system by providing a thoughtful forum for the communication and discussion of relevant public policy issues, innovative concepts, and original research and demonstrations in the areas of health care organization, provision, and financing.
**Ind/Abst** ABI/INFORM Glob. Ed.; ABI Inform Ondisc (Spring 1988-); Acad. Abstr. Full Text Elite (July 1990-); Acad. Abstr. (July 1990-); Acad. Search (July 1990-); Bus. Index (1985-); Bus. Period. Index; Chicano Index; Cumul. Index Nurs. Allied Health Lit.; Econ. Lit. Index (199?-); EMBASE; Energy Res. Abstr. (1982-); Gen. BusinessFile (1985-); Gen. Period. Index (1985-); Health Plan. Adminis.; Health Source (Jul. 1990-); Hospit. Health Admin. Index; Hospit. Manage. Rev.; Humanit. Source (Jul. 1990-); Index Med.; INFO-SOUTH Abstr.; Int. Pharm. Abstr.; J. Econ. Lit.; Mag. Search; PAIS Int. Print (1991-); Res. Alert [Full Cov.]; Soc. Sci. Cit. Index [Full Cov.]; Trade Ind. Index; Trop. Dis. Bull.; Wilson Bus. Abstr.

PL
**INSEMINATOR.** **Added/Corp** Panstwowe Wydawnictwo Rolnicze i Lesne. Vol. 12, No. 1 (1976)-. Periodical. Polish. qt. **(Subscription address:** ARS Polona, PO Box 1001, 00068 Warsaw Poland.**)**

NE/0378-0546
**INSERM SYMPOSIUM.** **Main/Corp** Institut National de la Sante et de la Recherche Medicale (France). **VAT** Institut Nacional de la Sante et de la Recherche Medicale Symposium. No. 1 (1975)-. Academic Scholarly Publication. English. ir. Price varies per volume. Elsevier Science Publishers BV, PO Box 211, 1000 AE Amsterdam Netherlands. **Tel** 011 31 20 5803642, FAX 011 31 20 5862696, telex 15682. **NLM** W3 I328E. **CODEN** INSSDM. Documents available from CASDDS.
**Ind/Abst** Chem. Abstr.

US/1043-8467
**INSIGHT INTO COURTS.** **See** Law.

GW/0932-4682
**INSTAND SCHRIFTENREIHE / INSTITUT FUR STANDARDISIERUNG UND DOKUMENTATION IM MEDIZINISCHEN LABORATORIUM E.V. (INSTAND).** [INSTAND Schr.reihe]. Vol. 1-. Periodical. German. Springer-Verlag New York Inc., 175 5th Avenue, New York NY 10010. **Tel** (212)460-1500, telex 232 235 SPB UR. **(Subscription address:** Springer Verlag New York Inc. / for North America, 44 Hartz Way, Secaucus NJ 07096.**)** **NLM** W1; IN485.

FR/0020-2142
**INSTANTANES MEDICAUX, LES.** [Instant. med.]. No. 1, (Dec. 1949)-. Periodical. French. mo. Editions Techniques, 141 rue de Javel, 75747 Paris Cedex 15 France. **Tel** 011 33 1 45589100. **[CCC].**
**Ind/Abst** Saf. Health Work.

●US/1073-9149
**INSTRUMENTATION SCIENCE AND TECHNOLOGY.** [Instrum. sci. technolog.]. **VFOAT** Instrumentation Science and Technology. (1994)-. Academic Scholarly Publication. English. qt. $350.00 US; $364.00 other. Marcel Dekker Inc., 270 Madison Avenue, New York NY 10016. **Tel** (212)696-9000, (800)228-1160, FAX (212)685-4540, telex 421419. **(Subscription address:** Marcel Dekker Inc, PO Box 5017, Monticello NY 12701.**)** **LC** QD53; .C47. **DD** 542. **CODEN** ISCTEF. ***Continues*** *Analytical Instrumentation, 0743-5797.*
**Ind/Abst** Abstr. Bull. Inst. Paper Chem.; Air Pollut. Titles; Bioeng. Abstr.; Chem. Abstr.; Curr. Contents Phys. Chem. Sci.; EMBASE; Energy Res. Abstr.; Eng. Index Annu.; Sci. Cit. Index.

GW
**INTENSIV.** (19??)-. Four times a year. $71.00. Georg Thieme Verlag Stuttgart, Postfach 301120, D 70451 Stuttgart Germany. **Tel** 011 49 711 89310, FAX 011 49 711 8931298, telex 7 252 275 GTVD. **(Subscription address:** Thieme Medical Publishers Inc., 381 Park Avenue South, New York NY 10016.**)**

GW
**INTENSIV UND NOTFALLBEHANDLUNG.** (19??)-. German. Four times a year. DM96.00. Dustri-Verlag, Dr Karl Feistle, Postfach 49, D 82032 Deisenhofen Germany. **Tel** 011 49 89 6138610, FAX 011 49 89 6135412. ***Continues*** *Intensivbehandlung.*

GW/0341-3063
**INTENSIVBEHANDLUNG.** ***Title Change.*** [Intensivbehandlung]. Vol. 1 (1 Quarter 1976)-(Jan. 1992). Periodical. German (summaries and/or abstracts in English). qt. Dustri-Verlag, Dr Karl Feistle, Postfach 49, D 82032 Deisenhofen Germany. **Tel** 011 49 89 6138610, FAX 011 49 89 6135412. **ED** Gepler, Pilgrim, Landauer, Ludriug. **NLM** W1 IN652ZU. **CODEN** NTNSDQ. **[CCC]. Bk Rev. Ad Acc.** ctrl circ. Documents available from BIOSIS Document Express. ***Continued by*** *Intensiv und Notfallbehandlung.*
**Ind/Abst** Biol. Abstr. (1976-1990); EMBASE; Energy Res. Abstr. (Sept. 1982-); Life Sci. Collect.

UK/0265-5241
**INTENSIVE & CRITICAL CARE DIGEST.** [Intensive crit. care dig.]. **VFOAT** Intensive and Critical Care Digest. Periodical. English. sa. King & Wirth Publishing Company Ltd., 85 Campden Street Kensington, London W8 7EN England. **Tel** 011 44 81 455 0760, FAX 011 44 81 2018955, telex 13139. **NLM** W1; IN6522.
**Ind/Abst** Health Devices Alerts.

GW/0342-4642
**INTENSIVE CARE MEDICINE.** [Intensive care med.]. Vol. 3 (1977)-. Academic Scholarly Publication. English. Twelve times a year. DM698.00. Springer-Verlag GmbH & Company KG, Heidelberger Platz 3, D 14197 Berlin Germany. **Tel** 011 49 30 8207223, FAX 011 49 30 8214091, telex 183 319 SPBLN D. **(Subscription address:** Springer Verlag New York Inc. / for North America, 44 Hartz Way, Secaucus NJ 07096.**)** **ED** F. Lemaire. **NLM** W1 IN6523. **CODEN** ICMED9. **[CCC]. Pr Rev.** available on microfilm and microfiche from University Microfilms International (UMI). Documents available from The Genuine Article, BIOSIS Document Express, CASDDS. ***Continues*** *European Journal of Intensive Care Medicine, 0340-0964.*
**Desc:** Provides a medium for the communication and exchange of current work and ideas in this field. Intended for all involved in intensive medical care, physicians, anaesthetists, surgeons, pediatricians, and all concerned with the pre-clinical subjects and medical sciences basic to these disciplines.
**Ind/Abst** Biol. Abstr. (1989-); Chem. Abstr. (1977-1983); Curr. Contents Clin. Med.; EMBASE; Energy Res. Abstr. (May 1979-); Health Devices Alerts; Index Med.; Int. Nurs. Index; Nutr. Abstr. Rev., Ser. A, Hum. Exp.; Res. Alert [Full Cov.]; Sci. Cit. Index; SCISEARCH; Soc. Sci. Cit. Index [Select. Cov.].

GW/0935-1701
**INTENSIVE CARE MEDICINE SUPPLEMENT.** [Intensive care med., Suppl.]. (19??)-. Monographic series. English. ir. Price varies per volume. Springer-Verlag GmbH & Company KG, Heidelberger Platz 3, D 14197 Berlin Germany. **Tel** 011 49 30 8207223, FAX 011 49 30 8214091, telex 183 319 SPBLN D. **(Subscription address:** Springer Verlag New York Inc. / for North America, 44 Hartz Way, Secaucus NJ 07096.**)** **UDC** 616-08.
**Ind/Abst** EMBASE.

NE
**INTENSIVE CARE REVIEW.** (19??)-. Periodical. English. mo (10 issues). Fl80.19 Belgium and Netherlands; Fl109.43 other Europe; Fl119.81 other. Medical Transfer BV, Postbus 12627, 1100 AP Amsterdam Netherlands. **Tel** 011 31 20 6951056.

UK/0266-7037
**INTENSIVE CARE WORLD (BALDOCK).** (INTENSIVE CARE WORLD.). [Intensive care world]. **Added/Corp** World Federation of Societies of Intensive & Critical Care Medicine. **VFOAT** ICW. Vol. 1, No. 1 (May/June 1984)-. Periodical. English. qt (Mar., Jun., Sep., Dec.). £45.00. King & Wirth Publishing Company Ltd., 85 Campden Street Kensington, London W8 7EN England. **Tel** 011 44 81 455 0760, FAX 011 44 81 2018955, telex 13139. **ED** G. Dobb. **NLM** W1; IN6525. **Bk Rev. Ad Acc. Circ:** 20,000 (ctrl). ***Continues*** *Critical Care International.*
**Desc:** Review articles on critical/intensive care medicine.
**Ind/Abst** Health Devices Alerts.

UK
**INTENSIVE THERAPY AND CLINICAL MONITORING.** ***Ceased.*** Vol. 8, No. 1 (Jan./Feb. 1987)-(19??). Periodical. English. mo. Medical News Tribune, Tower House, Southampton Street, London WC2E 7LS England. **Tel** (01)379-6005, FAX 01379 6737, telex 266854. **ED** Michael Rennie. **NLM** W1; IN6528. **Bk Rev. Ad Acc. Circ:** 11,500. ***Continues*** *British Journal of Parenteral Therapy.*
**Ind/Abst** Int. Pharm. Abstr.; Nutr. Abstr. Rev., Ser. A, Hum. Exp.

GW/0175-3851
**INTENSIVMEDIZIN + NOTFALLMEDIZIN.** (INTENSIVMEDIZIN + NOTFALLMEDIZIN : ORGAN DER DEUTSCHEN UND DER OSTERREICHISCHEN GESELLSCHAFT FUER INTERNISTISCHE INTENSIVMEDIZIN, DER SEKTION NEUROLOGIE DER DGIM UND DER SEKTION INTENSIVMEDIZIN IM BERUFSVERBAND DEUTSCHER INTERNISTEN E.V.). [Intensivmed. Notf.med.]. **Added/Corp** Deutsche Gesellschaft fuer Internistische Intensivmedizin. Osterreichische Gesellschaft fuer Internistische Intensivmedizin. Deutsche Gesellschaft fuer Internistische Intensivmedizin. Sektion Neurologie. Berufsverband Deutscher Internisten. Sektion Intensivmedizin. **VFOAT** Intensivmedizin und Notfallmedizin; Intensivmedizin. Vol. 20, No. 4 (1983)-. Periodical. German (English). Eight times a year. DM428.00. Dr Dietrich Steinkopff Verlag, PO Box 111442, D 64229 Darmstadt Germany. **Tel** 011 49 6151 17450. **(Subscription address:** Springer Verlag New York Inc. / for North America, 44 Hartz Way, Secaucus NJ 07096.**)** **NLM** W1; IN653H. **CODEN** INNOEK. **[CCC].** Documents available from BIOSIS Document Express. ***Continues*** *Intensivmedizin, 0303-6251.*
**Ind/Abst** Biol. Abstr. (1989-); EMBASE [Select. Cov.].

UK/0142-2367
**INTERNATIONAL CONGRESS AND SYMPOSIUM SERIES / ROYAL SOCIETY OF MEDICINE.** [Int. congr. symp. ser., R. Soc. Med.]. **Added/Corp** Royal Society of Medicine (Great Britain). No. 1 (1978)-. Academic Scholarly Publication. English. Price varies per volume. Academic Press Ltd., A Division of Harcourt Brace & Company Ltd., 24-28 Oval Road, London NW1 7DX England. **Tel** 071 267 4466, FAX 071 482 2293, 071 485 4752, telex 25775 ACPRES G. **(Subscription address:** Harcourt Brace Jovanovich Limited, Footscray High Street, Sidcup, Kent DA14 5HP UK, (Phone: 081-300-3322)**)** **LC** UNC. **NLM** W3 IN207. **CODEN** RMISDU. **[CCC].** Documents available from BIOSIS Document Express, CASDDS.
**Ind/Abst** Biol. Abstr.; Chem. Abstr.

NE/0531-5131
**INTERNATIONAL CONGRESS SERIES.** [Int. Congr. ser.]. **Added/Corp** Excerpta Medica Foundation. No. 1 (1952)-. Monographic series. English (French and German). ir. Price varies per volume. Elsevier Science Publishers BV, PO Box 211, 1000 AE Amsterdam Netherlands. **Tel** 011 31 20 5803642, FAX 011 31 20 5862696, telex 15682. **(Subscription address:** Elsevier Science Inc. / New York Books, 655 Avenue of the Americas, New York NY 10010.**)** **LC** UNC. **NLM** W 3 EX89. **CODEN** EXMDA4. **[CCC].** available on CD-ROM. Documents available from CASDDS.
**Ind/Abst** Chem. Abstr.; EMBASE; Index Vet.; Int. Aerosp. Abstr.; Life Sci. Collect.; Vet. Bull.

BE
**INTERNATIONAL HOSPITAL EQUIPMENT : IHE.** **VFOAT** IHE; I.H.E. (19??)-. Periodical. English. Nine times a year. $95.00. Pan European Publishing Company, rue Verte 216, 1210 Brussels 21 Belgium. **Tel** 011 32 2 2420611. **(Subscription address:** Elsevier Librico NV, Div Pepco Groenstraat 216, 1210 Brussels 21 Belgium.**)** **DD** 681/.761/0294.

●UK/1353-4505
**INTERNATIONAL JOURNAL FOR QUALITY IN HEALTH CARE : JOURNAL OF THE INTERNATIONAL SOCIETY FOR QUALITY IN HEALTH CARE.** **Added/Corp** International Society for Quality in Health Care. Vol. 6, No. 1 (Mar. 1994)-. Periodical. English. qt. $224.00 The Americas; £150.00 other. Pergamon Press, An Imprint of Elsevier Science Ltd., The Boulevard, Langford Lane, Kidlington, Oxford OX5 1GB United Kingdom. **Tel** 011 44 865 843000, 011 44 865 843699, FAX 011 44 865 843010. **(Subscription address:** Elsevier Science Ltd. Oxford Fulfillment Centre, PO Box 800, Kidlington, Oxford OX5 1DX United Kingdom.**)** **NLM** W1; IN7652I. ***Continues*** *Quality Assurance in Health Care, 1040-6166.*

UK/0334-0139
**INTERNATIONAL JOURNAL OF ADOLESCENT MEDICINE AND HEALTH.** [Int. j. adolesc. med. health]. Vol. 1, No. 1-2 (Jan./June 1985)-. Periodical. English. qt. $200.00. Freund Publishing House Ltd, PO Box 35010, 61 Nachmani Street, Tel Aviv 61350 Israel. **Tel** 011 972 3 5662925, FAX 011 972 3 5605335. **(Subscription address:** Freund Publishing House Ltd., Suite 500 Chesham House, 150 Regent Street, London W1R 5FA England.**)** **ED** E. Chigier. **NLM** W1; IN7652T. **CODEN** IJAHE8. Documents available from BIOSIS Document Express.
**Ind/Abst** Biol. Abstr. (1985-1988); EMBASE; Psychol. Abstr. (1985-); PsycINFO; PsycLit.

UK/0105-6263
**INTERNATIONAL JOURNAL OF ANDROLOGY.** [Int. j. androl.]. **Added/Corp** Comite Internacional de Andrologia. Vol. 1, No. 1 (Feb. 1978)-. Academic Scholarly Publication. English. bm (6 issues). $217.00 US & Canada; £140.00 other. Blackwell Scientific Publications Ltd, Marston Book Services, PO Box 87, Oxford OX2 ODT UK. **Tel** 011 44 865 791155, FAX 011 44 865 791927, telex 837 515 MARDIS G. **NLM** W1 IN7653V. **CODEN** IJANDP. **[CCC]. Bk Rev. Ad Acc. Pr Rev.** ctrl circ. available on microfilm and microfiche from University Microfilms International (UMI). Documents available from The Genuine Article, BIOSIS Document Express, CASDDS.
**Ind/Abst** AGRICOLA; Anim. Breed. Abstr.; Biol. Abstr.; Chem. Abstr.; CSA Neuro. Abstr. (?-?); Curr. Aware. Biol. Sci., CABS; Curr. Contents Life Sci.; EMBASE; Index Med.; Index Vet.; NAPRALERT; Life Sci. Collect.; Pig News Inf.; Ref. Upd. Deluxe Ed.; Res. Alert [Full Cov.]; Sci. Cit. Index; SCISEARCH; Vet. Bull.

DK/0106-1607
**INTERNATIONAL JOURNAL OF ANDROLOGY. SUPPLEMENT.** [Int. j. androl., Suppl.]. No. 1 (1978)-. Monographic series. English. ir. Comes with International Journal of Andrology. Blackwell Scientific Publications Ltd, Marston Book Services, PO Box 87, Oxford OX2 ODT UK. **Tel** 011 44 865 791155, FAX 011 44 865 791927, telex 837 515 MARDIS G. **NLM** W1 IN7653VD. **CODEN** IJSPDJ. Documents available from BIOSIS Document Express, CASDDS.
**Ind/Abst** Biol. Abstr.; Chem. Abstr.

NE/0924-8579
**INTERNATIONAL JOURNAL OF ANTIMICROBIAL AGENTS.** Vol. 1 (1991)-. Academic Scholarly Publication. English. Eight times a year (2 volumes). Fl992.00. Elsevier Science Publishers BV, PO Box 211, 1000 AE Amsterdam Netherlands. **Tel** 011 31 20 5803642, FAX 011 31 20 5862696, telex 15682. **NLM** W1; IN7654P. **CODEN** IAAGEA. **[CCC].** available on microfilm and microfiche from University Microfilms International (UMI). Documents available from CASDDS. ***Continues*** *Antimicrobial Agents Annual (Amsterdam, Netherlands).*
**Desc:** Provides up-to-date and comprehensive reference information on the physical, chemical, pharmacological, in vitro and clinical properties of individual antimicrobial agents, and immunotherapy.
**Ind/Abst** Chem. Abstr.; EMBASE.

US/1057-4263
**INTERNATIONAL JOURNAL OF ARTS MEDICINE.** (INTERNATIONAL JOURNAL OF ARTS MEDICINE : IJAM.). [Int. j. arts med.]. **Added/Corp** International Arts Medicine Association. International Society for Music in Medicine. **VFOAT** IJAM. Vol. 1, No. 1 (Fall 1991)-. Periodical. English. sa. $20.00. MMB Music, Inc., 10370 Page Industrial Boulevard, St. Louis MO 63132. **Tel** (314)427-5660, 800 543-3771. **ED** Rosalie Rebollo Pratt, EdD. **LC** R702.5; .I58. **DD** 616. **NLM** W1; IN7655HI. **Pr Rev.**
**Desc:** The International Journal of Arts Medicine contains peer-reviewed theoretical, clinical and philosophical articles by prominent physicians, arts therapists and arts educators pertaining to Arts Medicine. IJAM presents current research and clinical information, covers international conferences, and features reviews of media resources and interviews with Arts Medicine professionals.
**Ind/Abst** Music Index (Vol. 1, No. 1, 1991-).

●US/1070-5503
**INTERNATIONAL JOURNAL OF BEHAVIORAL MEDICINE.** **See** Psychology.

UK/0020-7101
**INTERNATIONAL JOURNAL OF BIOMEDICAL COMPUTING.** [Int. j. bio-med. comput.]. Vol. 1 (Jan. 1970)-. Academic Scholarly Publication. English. Twelve times a year (4 vols.). $862.00. Elsevier Science Ireland Ltd., Bay 15, Shannon Industrial Estate, Co Clare Ireland. **Tel** 011 353 61 471944. **ED** J.G. Llaurado, J.H. Mitchell, and A. Hasman. **NLM** W1 IN76558. **CODEN** IJBCBT. **[CCC].** Index available. **Pr Rev.** available on microfilm and microfiche from University Microfilms International (UMI). Documents available from Article Express International, The Genuine Article, BIOSIS Document Express, Ask*IEEE, CASDDS.
**Desc:** An international forum for the presentation of original work, interpretative reviews, commentaries and discussion of fundamental research and new developments in the application of the various types of computers (digital, analogue and hybrid) to medicine in particular and the biosciences in general.
**Ind/Abst** Biol. Abstr.; Biostatistica (19??-); Chem. Abstr.; Compumath Citation Index [Full Cov.]; Comput. Rev.; Curr. Aware. Biol. Sci., CABS; Curr. Contents Eng. Tech. Appl. Sci.; Curr. Contents Life Sci.; Ei Page One; EMBASE; Eng. Index Annu.; Immunol. Abstr.; Index Med.; INSPEC (Jan. 1974-); Math. Rev.; Life Sci. Collect.; Phys. Med. Biol. (19??-19??); Ref. Upd. Deluxe Ed.; Res. Alert [Full Cov.]; Sci. Cit. Index; SCISEARCH; Soc. Sci. Cit. Index [Select. Cov.].

US/1047-1979
**INTERNATIONAL JOURNAL OF CLINICAL ACUPUNCTURE.** [Int. j. clin. acupunct.]. Vol. 1, No. 1 (1990)-. Periodical. English. qt. $100.00 individuals, $210.00 institutions US; $135.00 individuals, $240.00 institutions other. Allerton Press, Inc., 150 Fifth Avenue, New York NY 10011. **Tel** (212)924-3950, FAX (212)463-9684, telex 427441 ALPRES. **LC** RM184; .I56. **DD** 615.8/92/05. **NLM** W1; IN766DH. **[CCC].**

GW/0940-5437
**INTERNATIONAL JOURNAL OF CLINICAL AND LABORATORY RESEARCH.** **See** Biology.

GW/0179-1958
**INTERNATIONAL JOURNAL OF COLORECTAL DISEASE.** [Int. j. colorectal dis.]. **VFOAT** Colorectal Disease. Vol. 1, No. 1 (Jan. 1986)-. Periodical. English. qt. DM348.00. Springer-Verlag GmbH & Company KG, Heidelberger Platz 3, D 14197 Berlin Germany. **Tel** 011 49 30 8207223, FAX 011 49 30 8214091, telex 183 319 SPBLN D. **(Subscription address:** Springer Verlag New York Inc. / for North America, 44 Hartz Way, Secaucus NJ 07096.**)** **ED** R John Nicholls. **NLM** W1; IN766DP. **CODEN** IJCDE6. **[CCC]. Pr Rev.** available on microfilm and microfiche from University Microfilms International (UMI). Documents available from The Genuine Article, BIOSIS Document Express.
**Desc:** Reports the progress and practice of all specialties studying and treating colorectal disease. Contains original articles of high scientific quality and includes symposia and reviews of subjects of topical interest.
**Ind/Abst** Biol. Abstr.; Curr. Contents Clin. Med.; EMBASE; Index Med. (1986-); Nutr. Abstr. Rev., Ser. A, Hum. Exp.; Res. Alert [Select. Cov.]; SCISEARCH.

UK/0265-6736
**INTERNATIONAL JOURNAL OF HYPERTHERMIA.** (INTERNATIONAL JOURNAL OF HYPERTHERMIA : THE OFFICIAL JOURNAL OF EUROPEAN SOCIETY FOR HYPERTHERMIC ONCOLOGY, NORTH AMERICAN HYPERTHERMIA GROUP.). [Int. j. hypertherm.]. **Added/Corp** European Society for Hyperthermic Oncology. North American Hyperthermia Group. Japanese Society of Hyperthermic Oncology. Vol. 1, No. 1 (Jan.-Mar. 1985)-. Academic Scholarly Publication. English. bm. £284.00 UK; $469.00 other. Taylor & Francis Ltd., Rankine Road, Basingstoke Hampshire, RG24 8PR United Kingdom. **Tel** 011 44 256 840366, FAX 011 44 256 479438, telex 858540. **(Subscription address:** Taylor & Francis Inc., 1900 Frost Road, Suite 101, Bristol PA 19007-1598.**)** **ED** Stan B. Field, George M. Hahn, Jens Overgaard, and T. Sugahara. **NLM** W1; IN768I. **CODEN** IJHYEQ. **[CCC]. Pr Rev.** available on microfilm and microfiche from University Microfilms International (UMI). Documents available from The Genuine Article, BIOSIS Document Express, Ask*IEEE, CASDDS.
**Desc:** Provides a forum for the publication of research and clinical papers on hyperthermia, which fall largely into the following categories: clinical studies, biological studies and techniques of heat delivery and temperature measurement.
**Ind/Abst** Biol. Abstr. (1985-); Chem. Abstr. (1985-); Curr. Aware. Biol. Sci., CABS; Curr. Contents Life Sci.; EMBASE; Index Med. (Vol. 1, No. 1, 1985-); INSPEC (1986-); Res. Alert [Full Cov.]; Sci. Cit. Index; SCISEARCH; Vet. Bull.

UK/0955-9930
**INTERNATIONAL JOURNAL OF IMPOTENCE RESEARCH.** Vol. 1, No. 1 (Aug. 1989)-. Periodical. English. qt. $123.00 (institution), $73.00 (individual) US; £74.00 (institution), £44.00 (individual) other. Royal Society of Medicine Press, 1 Wimpole Street, London W1M 8AE England. **Tel** 011 44 71 2902928. **ED** Dr William L Furlow and Dr Gorm Wagner. **NLM** W1; IN768T.
**Desc:** Brings together the multidisciplinary approaches which lead to a better understanding of sexual function and dysfunction.

US
**INTERNATIONAL JOURNAL OF MEDICAL AND BIOLOGICAL FRONTIERS.** (19??)-. Periodical. English. Four times a year. $385.00. Nova Science Publishers Inc., 6080 Jericho Turnpike, Suite 207, Commack NY 11725-2808. **Tel** (516)499-3103, (516)499-3106, FAX (516)499-3146.

●UK
**INTERNATIONAL JOURNAL OF OBESITY AND RELATED METABOLIC DISORDERS : JOURNAL OF THE INTERNATIONAL ASSOCIATION FOR THE STUDY OF OBESITY.** **Added/Corp** International Association for the Study of Obesity. **VFOAT** International Journal of Obesity. Vol. 16, No. 1 (Jan. 1992)-. Periodical. English. mo (12 issues). £235.00 UK and EEC countries; £255.00 (surface mail), £306.00 (airmail) other. Macmillan Magazines Ltd., Houndmills, Basingstoke, Hampshire RG21 2XS England. **Tel** 011 44 256 29242, FAX 011 44 256 812358, telex 858493. **NLM** W1; IN77PG. ***Continues*** *International Journal of Obesity, 0307-0565.*

US/0884-8297
**INTERNATIONAL JOURNAL OF PSYCHOSOMATICS.** [Int. j. psychosom.]. Vol. 31, No. 1-. Periodical. English. qt. $50.00 (direct to IPI) US, Canada, and Mexico; $60.00 (direct to IPI) other. International Journal of Psychosomatics, PO Box 1296, Philadelphia PA 19105. **Tel** (215)525-5511. **ED** Donald R Morse. **DD** 616. **NLM** W1; IN777P. **CODEN** IJOPEY. Index available. **Bk Rev. Ad Acc. Pr Rev. Circ:** 1,000 (ctrl). available on microfilm and microfiche from University Microfilms International (UMI). Documents available from BIOSIS Document Express. ***Continues*** *Journal of the American Society of Psychosomatic Dentistry and Medicine, 0003-1194.*
**Desc:** Psychosomatic (mind/body) aspects of health and disease.
**Ind/Abst** Annals Behav. Med.; Biol. Abstr. (1984-); Curr. Titl. Dent.; EMBASE; Energy Res. Abstr. (1984-); Index Med.; Index Dent. Lit.; Psychol. Abstr. (1984-); PsycINFO; PsycLit.

●US
**INTERNATIONAL JOURNAL OF REHABILITATION AND HEALTH.** (1994)-. Periodical. English. Four times a year. $115.00 institutions, $40.00 individuals US; $135.00 institutions, $47.00 individuals other. Plenum Press, 233 Spring Street, New York NY 10013-1578. **Tel** (212)620-8000, (800)221-9369, FAX (212)463-0742, (212)807-1047, telex 23/421139. ***Continues*** *Journal of Rehabilitation and Health.*

NE/0924-6479
**INTERNATIONAL JOURNAL OF RISK & SAFETY IN MEDICINE, THE.** **VFOAT** Risk & Safety in Medicine; International Journal of Risk and Safety in Medicine; Risk and Safety in Medicine. Vol. 1, No. 1 (June 1990)-. Academic Scholarly Publication. English. Six times a year (2 volumes). Fl980.00. Elsevier Science Publishers BV, PO Box 211, 1000 AE Amsterdam Netherlands. **Tel** 011 31 20 5803642, FAX 011 31 20 5862696, telex 15682. **NLM** W1; IN786. **CODEN** IJMDEM. **[CCC].** ***Absorbed*** *Iatrogenics: Safety in Health Care.*
**Ind/Abst** EMBASE; Int. Pharm. Abstr.

UK/0266-4623
**INTERNATIONAL JOURNAL OF TECHNOLOGY ASSESSMENT IN HEALTH CARE.** [Int. j. technol. assess. health care]. Vol. 1, No. 1 (Jan. 1985)-. Academic Scholarly Publication. English. qt (4 issues). $134.00 US, Canada & Mexico; £86.00 other. Cambridge University Press, The Edinburgh Building, Shaftesbury Road, Cambridge CB2 2RU United Kingdom. **Tel** 011 44 223 312393, FAX 011 44 223 325959. **(Subscription address:** Cambridge University Press / North America, 110 Midland Avenue, Port Chester NY 10573.**)** **ED** Stanley J. Reiser and Egon Jonsson. **LC** R855; .I57. **DD** 610/.28. **NLM** W1; IN791MC. **[CCC].** available on microfilm from University Microfilms International (UMI).
**Desc:** Serves as a forum for the wide range of professionals interested in the assessment of medical technology, its consequences for patients and its impact on society. Covers the generation, evaluation, diffusion and use of health care technology. In addition to general essays, regular columns on technology assessment reports, reviews and announcements, thematic sections are published.
**Ind/Abst** EMBASE; Health Devices Alerts; Health Plan. Adminis.; Hum. Resour. Abstr. (?-?).

UK/0196-1365
**INTERNATIONAL JOURNAL OF THERAPEUTIC COMMUNITIES.** ***Title Change.*** [Int. j. ther. communities]. **Added/Corp** Association of Therapeutic Communities. Vol. 1 (Spring 1980)-. Periodical. English. qt. Association of Therapeutic Communities, The Retreat, York YO1 5BN England. **Tel** 011 44 904 412551. **(Subscription address:** PO Box 109, Dorking Surrey England**)** **ED** David Millard and Keith Beach. **LC** RC489.T67; I57. **DD** 616.89/14. **NLM** W1; IN791NJ. **CODEN** IJTCDJ. **Bk Rev. Ad Acc. Circ:** 500. available on microfilm from University Microfilms International (UMI). ***Continued by*** *Therapeutic Communities, 0964-1866.*
**Desc:** Original articles, community studies and shorter pieces on therapeutic institutions and other social systems.
**Ind/Abst** Appl. Soc. Sci. Index Abstr.; EMBASE; Int. Bibliogr. Sociol.; Psychol. Abstr. (1988-); PsycINFO; PsycLit.

CH/0377-0168
**INTERNATIONAL JOURNAL OF ZOONOSES.** ***Ceased.*** [Int. j. zoonoses]. Vol. 1 (June 1974)-Ceased (Jan. 1987). Periodical. English. sa. International Laboratory for Zoonoses, Number 2 Lane 7 Tsingtien Street, Taipei Taiwan. **NLM** W1 IN792. **CODEN** IJZODH. Documents available from BIOSIS Document Express, CASDDS.
**Ind/Abst** AGRICOLA; Biol. Abstr.; Chem. Abstr.; EMBASE; Index Med.; Index Vet.; Life Sci. Collect.; Protozoolog. Abstr.; SEA Abstr.; Vet. Bull.

US
**INTERNATIONAL MED-TECH DIRECTORY : THE INTERNATIONAL GUIDE TO PUBLIC HEALTH CARE COMPANIES.** (1991)-. Directory. English. Med-Tech Group, Division of D. H. Blair & Co., 44 Wall Street, New York NY 10005. **NLM** W 22.1; I612. ***Continues*** *Med Tech Directory, 1045-3121.*

US
**INTERNATIONAL MEDICAL DEVICE REGULATORY MONITOR.** (19??)-. English. mo. $495.00. Newsletter Services Inc, 9700 Philadelphia Court, Lanham MD 20706. **Tel** (800)345-2611. ***Separated from*** *International Drug & Device Regulatory Monitor.*

●US
**INTERNATIONAL MEDICAL IMAGE REGISTRY.** Vol. 1 (1995)-. Periodical. English. bm (6 issues). $75.00 (individuals), $100.00 (institutions), $85.00 (individuals), $125.00 (institutions) other. Raven Press, 1185 Avenue of the Americas, 37th Floor, New York NY 10036. **Tel** (212)930-9500, (212)930-9604, FAX (212)869-3495, (212)302-8507, telex 640073.

US/1040-7588
**INTERNATIONAL MEDICAL TRIBUNE SYNDICATE.** [Int. med. trib. synd.]. **VFOAT** IMTS. Periodical. English. wk. $120.00 (individuals). Ira Weinstein MD, 257 Park Avenue South, New York NY 10010. **Tel** (212)674-8500, FAX (212)529-8490, telex 147103 IMTS. **ED** Jeanne Kassler and Anne Landry. **DD** 610. available on an online database from Dialcom Inc.

UK/0143-4853
**INTERNATIONAL MEDICINE (LONDON).** ***Suspended.*** (INTERNATIONAL MEDICINE.). [Int. med.]. Vol. 1, July 1979-?. Periodical. English. qt. $56.00. Franklin Scientific Publications, 371 Kennington Lane, London SE11 5RA England. **Tel** 582-5344. **ED** D Geoffrey Brandon. **NLM** W1 IN823U. **Circ:** 5,000.
**Desc:** Review articles of general medical interest to doctors working in all fields of medicine.

UK/0143-4853
**INTERNATIONAL MEDICINE. SUPPLEMENT.** [Int. med. Suppl.]. No. 1-. Monographic series. English. ir. Price varies per volume. Franklin Scientific Publications, 371 Kennington Lane, London SE11 5RA England. **Tel** 582-5344. **ED** D Geoffrey Brandon. **NLM** W1; IN823W. **Circ:** 5,000.
**Desc:** Topics in all branches of medicine written with the non-specialist in mind.

US/1065-1586
**INTERNATIONAL TRAVEL IMMUNIZATIONS.** ***Title Change.*** [Int. travel immun.]. (1992)-(1992). English. Shoreland Medical Marketing, 2620 Lefeber Avenue, Milwaukee WI 53213-1224. **DD** 314. ***Continued by*** *Travel and Routine Immunizations.*

US/0020-9546
**INTERNIST (SAN FRANCISCO, CALIF.), THE.** (THE INTERNIST.). [Internist]. **Added/Corp** American Society of Internal Medicine. (19??)-. Periodical. English. mo. $12.00 (members), $24.00 (non-members) US & Canada; $30.00 (other). American Society of Internal Medicine, 1101 Vermont Avenue NW/Suite 500, Washington DC 20005. **Tel** (202)289-1700. **DD** 362. available on microfilm and microfiche from University Microfilms International (UMI).
**Ind/Abst** Health Plan. Adminis.; Hospit. Health Admin. Index; PESTDOC.

GW/0020-9570
**INTERNISTISCHE PRAXIS.** [Internist. Prax.]. Vol. 1 (1961)-. Academic Scholarly Publication. German. Four times a year. Hans Marseille Verlag GmbH, Buerkleinstrasse 12, D 80538 Munich Germany. **Tel** 011 49 89 227988, FAX 011 49 89 2904643. **ED** H. Feiereis. **NLM** W1 IN968. **CODEN** INPXAJ. **[CCC].** Index available. cum. index. **Bk Rev.** available on microfilm from University Microfilms International (UMI).
**Ind/Abst** EMBASE.

US/0896-5021
**INTERNIST'S CLINICAL UPDATE.** ***Ceased.*** (INTERNIST'S CLINICAL UPDATE : A TWICE-MONTHLY DIGEST OF NEW DEVELOPMENTS IN INTERNAL MEDICINE SPONSORED BY ALBERT EINSTEIN COLLEGE OF MEDICINE/MONTEFIORE MEDICAL CENTER.). [Internist's clin. update]. **Added/Corp** Albert Einstein College of Medicine. Montefiore Medical Center. Vol. 1, No. 1 (Jan. 5, 1988)-(199?). Periodical. English. sm. Educational Reviews Inc., 6801 Cahaba Valley Road, Birmingham AL 35242. **Tel** (205)991-5188, (800)633-4743, FAX (205)995-1926. **DD** 616.

US/1056-9618
**INTERSTUDY QUALITY EDGE, THE.** ***Title Change.*** (THE INTERSTUDY QUALITY EDGE : MEASUREMENT AND MANAGEMENT OF CLINICAL OUTCOMES.). [Interstudy qual. edge]. **Added/Corp** InterStudy (Center). **VFOAT** Quality Edge. Vol. 1, No. 1 (1991)-(19??). Periodical. English. sa. Interstudy, PO Box 4366, St. Paul MN 55104. **Tel** (612)858-9291. **LC** RA399.A3; I57. **DD** 362.1/068/5. **NLM** W1; IN982RN. ***Split into*** *Interstudy Competitive Edge* ***and*** *Interstudy Quality Edge.*

IT
**INTERVISTA MEDICA.** Esam Editrice SRL, Via Reno 21, 00198 Rome Italy.

US/0190-3500
**INVENTORY OF HEALTH CARE FACILITY SURVEYORS, UNITED STATES.** **Added/Corp** United States. Division of Medical Care Standards. United States. Health Services Administration. Division of Provider Standards and Certification. (1972)-. Periodical. English. be. **NLM** W1 IN993V.

UK/0261-4952
**INVERTEBRATE NEUROBIOLOGY.** [Invertebr. neurobiol.]. (1982)-. English. mo. £105.00. SUBIS, Mansion House, 19 Kingfield Road, Sheffield S11 9AS England. **Tel** 011 44 114 255 4433, FAX 011 44 114 255 4626. **DD** 016.59204805. **[CCC].**

VE/0535-5133
**INVESTIGACION CLINICA.** [Invest. clin.]. No. 1 (July 1960)-. Academic Scholarly Publication. Spanish (English). qt. Bs80.00 Venezuela; $20.00 other. Investigacion Clinica, Apartado 1151, Maracaibo Venezuela. **Tel** (061)525291. **ED** Slavia Ryder. **NLM** W1 IN993W. **CODEN** ICLIAD. ctrl circ. Documents available from The Genuine Article, BIOSIS Document Express, CASDDS.
**Ind/Abst** Biol. Abstr.; Chem. Abstr.; EMBASE [Select. Cov.]; Health Plan. Adminis.; Nutr. Abstr. Rev., Ser. B, Live Feeds and Feed.; Nutr. Abstr. Rev., Ser. A, Hum. Exp.; Protozoolog. Abstr.; Res. Alert [Select. Cov.]; SCISEARCH.

MX/0377-0206
**INVESTIGACION MEDICA INTERNACIONAL.** [Invest. med. int.]. (1974)-. Academic Scholarly Publication. Spanish (summaries and/or abstracts in English). Four times a year. $110.00. Mundo Medico SA, Ejecricto Nacional 381, 11520 Mexico DF Mexico. **Tel** 011 52 5 2038111. **ED** Harry Swartz and Marco Antonio Tovar Sosa. **NLM** W1 IN993X. **CODEN** IMEIDH. **Ad Acc, Adv Mgr:** Oscar Bagnarelli. **Circ:** 7,000 (ctrl). Documents available from BIOSIS Document Express, CASDDS.
**Desc:** Scholarly articles and research studies from South American doctors and scientists covering all aspects of medical and pharmacological research, including cytology, pathology and clinical aspects.
**Ind/Abst** Biol. Abstr. (1986-); Chem. Abstr.; EMBASE [Select. Cov.]; Nutr. Abstr. Rev., Ser. B, Live Feeds and Feed.; Nutr. Abstr. Rev., Ser. A, Hum. Exp.; Life Sci. Collect.; Protozoolog. Abstr.

SP/0212-6605
**INVESTIGACION Y CLINICA LASER : ORGANO DEL GRUPO DE EXPERIMENTACION E INVESTIGACION CLINICA LASER (GRUPO LASER-ESPANA).** **Added/Corp** Grupo de Investigacion y Experimentacion Clinica Laser (Grupo Laser-Espana). Vol. 1, No. 1 (Enero/Marzo 1984)-. Periodical. Spanish (summaries and/or abstracts in English). qt. Etecnes, Travesera de Gracia 15, Barcelona 08021 Spain. **Tel** FAX 011 34 3 2096918. **NLM** W1; IN994E.

US/0746-8709
**IOWA MEDICINE.** (IOWA MEDICINE : JOURNAL OF THE IOWA MEDICAL SOCIETY.). [Iowa med.]. **Added/Corp** Iowa Medical Society. Vol. 74, No. 1 (Jan. 1984)-. Periodical. English. Twelve times a year. $25.00. Iowa Medical Society, 1001 Grand Avenue, West Des Moines IA 50265. **Tel** (515)223-1401, FAX (515)223-8420. **ED** Marion Alberts. **LC** R15; .I62. **DD** 610/.5. **NLM** W1; IO295FF. Index available. cum. index. **Bk Rev. Ad Acc, Adv Mgr:** Jane Nieland. **Circ:** 4,870. ***Continues*** *Journal of the Iowa Medical Society, 0021-0587.*
**Desc:** Contains articles on the scientific and social economic side of medicine plus public health material.
**Ind/Abst** Cumul. Index Nurs. Allied Health Lit.; Energy Res. Abstr.; Hospit. Health Admin. Index; Index Med.; INIS Atomindex [Micro.]; SportSearch.

IR/0253-0716
**IRANIAN JOURNAL OF MEDICAL SCIENCES.** [Iran. j. med. sci.]. **Added/Corp** Danishgah-i Shiraz. Medical School. Vol. 10, No. 1-4 (1979)-. Periodical. English. qt. $80.00. Shiraz University of Medical Sciences, Nemazee Hospital, Shiraz, Iran. **Tel** (71)61089. **ED** K. Vessal. **NLM** W1 IR328. **CODEN** IJMSDW. Documents available from BIOSIS Document Express, CASDDS. ***Continues*** *Pahlavi Medical Journal.*
**Ind/Abst** Biol. Abstr. (19??-1983); Chem. Abstr. (1979-1980); EMBASE [Select. Cov.]; Life Sci. Collect.

US/0193-7758
**IRB.** **See** Ethics.

IE/0021-1265
**IRISH JOURNAL OF MEDICAL SCIENCE.** [Ir. j. med. sci.]. **Added/Corp** Royal Academy of Medicine in Ireland. (1922)-. Academic Scholarly Publication. English. mo. 48p EEC countries; 60p others. Royal Academy of Medicine Ireland, 6 Kildare Street, Dublin 2 Ireland. **Tel** 011-353-1-767650, FAX 011-353-1-611684. **ED** Thomas F Gorey. **NLM** W1 IR429. **CODEN** IJMSAT. Index available (published separately). cum. index. **Bk Rev. Ad Acc, Adv Mgr:** D. Korcel. **Pr Rev. Circ:** 1,500 (ctrl). available on microfilm and microfiche from University Microfilms International (UMI). Documents available from The Genuine Article, BIOSIS Document Express, CASDDS. ***Continues*** *Dublin Journal of Medical Science.*
**Desc:** Medical and allied sciences research.
**Ind/Abst** Biol. Abstr.; Chem. Abstr.; Curr. Contents; Curr. Contents Clin. Med.; EMBASE [Select. Cov.]; Index Med.; Microbiol. Abstr. Sect. B (19??-19??); Mod. Med.; Nucl. Sci. Abstr.; Nutr. Abstr. Rev., Ser. B, Live Feeds and Feed.; Nutr. Abstr. Rev., Ser. A, Hum. Exp.; Nutr. Res. Newsl.; Life Sci. Collect.; PESTDOC; Protozoolog. Abstr.; Res. Alert [Select. Cov.]; Rev. Med. Vet. Mycology; SCISEARCH; SportSearch.

IE/0332-3102
**IRISH MEDICAL JOURNAL.** [Ir. med. j.]. **Added/Corp** Irish Medical Association. **VFOAT** Journal of the Irish Medical Association. Vol. 67, No. 13 (July 13, 1974)-. Periodical. English. Six times a year (Jan., Mar., May, Jul., Sep., Nov.). £75.00 Europe; £90.00 other. Irish Medical Journal, 10 Fitzwilliam Place, Dublin 2 Ireland. **Tel** 353 1 6767273, FAX 353 1 6612758. **ED** Dr. J;ohn Murphy. **NLM** W1 IR449E. **CODEN** IMDJBD. **Bk Rev.** (Qty: 6). **Ad Acc. Circ:** 6,200. Documents available from The Genuine Article, CASDDS. ***Continues*** *Journal of the Irish Medical Association of Eire, 0021-129X.*
**Ind/Abst** Chem. Abstr.; Curr. Contents Clin. Med.; EMBASE; Index Med.; Life Sci. Collect.; Res. Alert [Select. Cov.]; Rev. Med. Vet. Mycology; SCISEARCH; Soc. Sci. Cit. Index [Select. Cov.]; SportSearch.

UK/0142-8152
**IRON METABOLISM.** [Iron metab.]. (1979)-. English. mo. £85.00. SUBIS, Mansion House, 19 Kingfield Road, Sheffield S11 9AS England. **Tel** 011 44 114 255 4433, FAX 011 44 114 255 4626. **DD** 016.6123924.

JA/0021-1699
**IRYO.** [Iryo]. **Added/Corp** Iryo Dokokai. **VFOAT** Medical Journal of National Hospitals and Sanitoriums of Japan; Japanese Journal of the National Medical Services. Vol. 1 (1946)-. Academic Scholarly Publication. Japanese (summaries and/or abstracts in English; table of contents in English). mo. $211.50. Kokuritsu Iryo Gakkai, (Japanese Soc. of National Medical Services), Koseisho Hoken Iryokyoku, 2-2, Kasumigaseki 1 Chome, Chiyodaku, Tokyoto 100 Japan. **(Subscription address:** Japan Publications Trading Company, Ltd., PO Box 5030, Tokyo International, Tokyo 100-31 Japan.**)** **NLM** W1 IR629. **CODEN** IRYOAV. Documents available from BIOSIS Document Express, CASDDS.
**Ind/Abst** Biol. Abstr.; Chem. Abstr.; EMBASE [Select. Cov.]; Life Sci. Collect.

JA/0289-8055
**IRYO JOHOGAKU.** [Iryo Johogaku]. **VFOAT** Japan Journal of Medical Informatics; Journal of Japan Association for Medical Informatics. (1982)-. Periodical. Japanese (English). Four times a year. $184.00. Japanese Journal of Medical Informatics, 4-16 Yayoi 2-Chome, Bunkyo-ku 113 Tokyo Japan. **(Subscription address:** Kyowa Book Company Inc., 1 38 Kanda Jinbocho Chiyoda-ku, Tokyo 101 Japan.**)** **DD** 610. ***Continues*** *MEDINFO Kenkyukai Shiryo, 0289-8047.*
**Ind/Abst** EMBASE.

US/0021-1753
**ISIS.** **See** Science and Technology.

IT
**ISIS NEWS.** (Jan. 1985)-. Periodical. English. mo. Isis Informazione Stampa, Largo Arenula 26, 00186 Rome Italy.

US/0160-3787
**ISOZYMES.** ***Ceased.*** **See** Biology-Biochemistry.

IS/0021-2180
**ISRAEL JOURNAL OF MEDICAL SCIENCES.** [Isr. j. med. sci.]. Vol. 1, (Jan. 1965)-. Academic Scholarly Publication. English. Twelve times a year. $75.00 (institutions & individuals) Israel; $115.00 (individuals), $165.00 (institutions) other. Israel Journal of Medical Sciences, National Council for Research and Development, 2 Etzel Street, French Hill, 97853 Jerusalem Israel. **Tel** 02-817727, FAX 972-2-815722. **ED** Professor Moshe Prywes M.D. **LC** R97. **NLM** W1 IS63TU. **CODEN** IJMDAI. Index available. cum. index. **Bk Rev. Ad Acc, Adv Mgr:** S. Noy, **Tel** (2) 972-817727. **Pr Rev. Circ:** 5,000. available on microfilm from University Microfilms International (UMI). Documents available from The Genuine Article, BIOSIS Document Express, CASDDS. ***Formed by the union of*** *Israel Medical Journal* ***and*** *Israel Journal of Experimental Medicine.*
**Desc:** These are articles on experimental and chemical medicine, epidemiology and public health. A periodic special issues on specific subjects and international proceedings.
**Ind/Abst** Biol. Abstr.; Chem. Abstr.; Curr. Aware. Biol. Sci., CABS; Curr. Contents Life Sci.; Dairy Sci. Abstr.; EMBASE; Helminthol. Abstr. (19??-19??); Index Med.; Nutr. Abstr. Rev., Ser. B, Live Feeds and Feed.; Nutr. Abstr. Rev., Ser. A, Hum. Exp.; Nutr. Res. Newsl.; Life Sci. Collect.; PESTDOC; Protozoolog. Abstr.; Ref. Upd. Basic Ed.; Ref. Upd. Deluxe Ed.; Res. Alert [Full Cov.]; Rev. Med. Vet. Entomol.; Rev. Med. Vet. Mycology; Rev. Plant Pathol.; Sci. Cit. Index; SCISEARCH; Small Anim. Abstr. Bibliogr.; Soc. Sci. Cit. Index [Select. Cov.]; SportSearch; Trop. Dis. Bull.

SZ/1010-8408
**ISSUES IN BIOMEDICINE.** **See** Biology.

US/8756-8160
**ISSUES IN LAW & MEDICINE.** **See** Law.

CN/1182-8757
**ISSUES (PENTICTON).** **See** Parapsychology and Occultism.

TU/0379-1173
**ISTANBUL TIP FAKULTESI MECMUASI. MONOGRAFI SERISINDEN.** **Added/Corp** Istanbul Ueniversitesi. Tip Fakultesi. No. 28 (1961)-. Monographic series. Turkish (English; summaries and/or abstracts in German). Price varies per volume. Istanbul Tip Fakultesi, Dekanligi Capa, 34390, Istanbul, Turkey. **NLM** W1 IS782M. ***Continues*** *Istanbul Ueniversitesi Tip Fakultesi Mecmuasi. Monografi Serisi, 0379-1181.*
**Ind/Abst** EMBASE.

TU/0301-7362
**ISTANBUL TP FAKULTESI MECMUASI.** [Istanbul Tp Fak. Mecm.]. **Added/Corp** Istanbul Universitesi. Tp Fakultesi. (1970)-. Periodical. Turkish. Six times a year. Free on request. Istanbul Universitesi Tip Fak, Dekanligi Yayin Komisyonu, Capa Istanbul Turkey. **Tel** 011 90 212 5342562. **NLM** W1 IS782. **CODEN** TFMEAC. ***Continues*** *Tp Fakultesi Mecmuasi, 0047-1623.*

II
**ISTERSCOPIA NELLA PRATICA CLINICA-S, L'.** (19??)-. Italian. $20.00. S O G S R L, Galleria Storione 2A, 35128 Padua Italy. **Tel** 011 39 49 8756900.

IT/0393-5620
**ISTISAN-CONGRESSI.** **VFOAT** Istisan Congressi. (1985)-. Monographic series. English (Italian). Price varies per volume. **NLM** W1; IS812.

HU/0865-0497
**ITD. IZOTOPTECHNIKA, DIAGNOSZTIKA.** [itd, Izottech. diagn.]. **VFOAT** Izotoptechnika, Diagnosztika. (1989)-. Periodical. Multiple languages. qt. **UDC** 621.039. Documents available from CASDDS. ***Continues*** *Izotoptechnika, 0004-7201.*
**Ind/Abst** Chem. Abstr.

RU
**ITOGI NAUKI I TEKHNIKI: MEDITSINSKAIA GEOGRAFIIA.** **See** Geography.

JA/0287-0894
**IYAKUHIN KENKYU.** [Iyakuhin kenkyu]. **Added/Corp** Nihon Koteisho Kyokai. **VFOAT** Iyakuhin Kenkyu. (1970)-. Periodical. Japanese. Six times a year. Y60000.00 (enterprises); Y12000 (individuals) Comes with Society of Japanese Pharmacopoeia membership. Society of Japanese Pharmacopoeia, Shibuya 2 12 15 Shibuya Ku, Tokyo 150 Japan. **Tel** 81 3 3400 5634, or 5635. **CODEN** IYKEDH. Documents available from CASDDS.
**Ind/Abst** Chem. Abstr.

RU
**IZOBRETENIIA I RATSIONALIZATORSKIE PREDLOZHENIIA V OBLASTI MEDITSINY.** **Added/Corp** Vsesoiuznyi Nauchno-Issledovatelskii Institut Meditsinskoi i Mediko-Tekhnicheskoi Informatsii (Soviet Union). Vol. 1 (1973)-. Russian. 0.20rub (single issue). Vses Nauchno-issl, ZH-240 Moskvoretskaia Naberezhnaia 2A, Moscow Russia. **LC** R856.A1; I94. **NLM** W1 IZ65G.

BU/0323-9438
**IZVESTIJA - DRZAVEN INSTITUT ZA KONTROL NA LEKARSTVENITE SREDSTVA.** (IZVESTIIA / MINISTERSTVO NA NARODNOTO ZDRAVE, MEDITSINSKA AKADEMIIA, DURZHAVEN INSTITUT ZA KONTROL NA LEKARSTVENITE SREDSTVA.). [Izv. - Drz. inst. kontrol lek. sreds.]. **Added/Corp** Durzhaven Institut za Kontrol na Lekarstvenite Sredstva. (1967)-. Periodical. Bulgarian. Izdatelstvo Meditsina i Fizkultura, 11 Pl. Slaveikov, Sofiia Bulgaria. **CODEN** IDISD4. Documents available from CASDDS.
**Ind/Abst** Chem. Abstr.

AU/0379-2595
**JAHRBUCH - STEIERMARKISCHE GEBIETSKRANKENKASSE FUR ARBEITER UND ANGESTELLTE.** **Main/Corp** Steiermarkische Gebietskrankenkasse fur Arbeiter und Angestellte. (1974)-. German. an. Josef-Pongratz-Platz 1, 8011 Graz Austria. **LC** HD7102.A9; S84B. **NLM** W1 ST436. ***Continues*** *Steierarkische Gebietskrankenkasse fur Arbeiter und Angstellte. Jahresbericht.*

SZ/1016-1562
**JAHRESBERICHT - SCHWEIZERISCHE AKADEMIE DER MEDIZINISCHEN WISSENSCHAFTEN (1988).** (JAHRESBERICHT / SCHWEIZERISCHE AKADEMIE DER MEDIZINISCHEN WISSENSCHAFTEN.). [Jahresber. - Schweiz. Akad. Med. Wiss.]. **Added/Corp** Schweizerische Akademie der Medizinischen Wissenschaften. (1988)-. Periodical. German (French and English). an. Schweizerische Akademie Medizinischen Wissenschaften, Wissenschaften Petersplatz 18, CH 4051 Basel Switzerland. **NLM** W1; JA204L. ***Continues*** *Bulletin der Schweizerischen Akademie der Medizinischen Wissenschaften, 0036-7494.*
**Ind/Abst** Health Plan. Adminis.

SP/0211-4445
**JAMA EN ESPANOL.** [JAMA Esp.]. **VFOAT** Journal of the American Medical Association en Espanol. V. 1- Jan. 1975-. Periodical. Spanish. mo. Editorial Eco SA, De la Cruz 44, Barcelona 34 Spain. **NLM** W1 J221D.

FR/1140-5031
**JAMA H (ED. FRANCAISE).** (JAMA H.). [JAMA H Ed. fr.]. **VFOAT** JAMA Journal of the American Medical Association (Ed. Hospitaliere); Journal of the American Medical Association H (Ed. Francaise). (1989)-. Periodical. French. mo. 295.00F (1 year), 395.00F (2 year) France; 530.00F (1 year), 750.00F (2 year) other. Publs Medic Internationales, 24 Bis Bv Verd de St. Julien, 92190 Meudon France. **Tel** 011 33 1 45078300. **UDC** 61.

FR/0221-7678
**JAMA JOURNAL OF THE AMERICAN MEDICAL ASSOCIATION. EDITION FRANCAISE.** (JAMA : JOURNAL OF THE AMERICAN MEDICAL ASSOCIATION.). [J.A.M.A., J. Am. Med. Assoc., Ed. fr.]. **Added/Corp** American Medical Association. **VFOAT** J.A.M.A.; Journal of the American Medical Association. Vol. 1 (Jan. 1980)-. Periodical. French. Thirty-three times a year. 295.00F (1 year), 395.00F (2 year) France; 530.00F (1 year), 750.00 (2 year) other. JAMA, 24 Bis Rd Verd de St. Julien, F-92190 Meudon France. **Tel** 011 33 1 45078300, FAX 011 33 1 46230021. **[CCC].**
**Ind/Abst** AgBiotech News Inf.; Biol. Dig.; Curr. Aware. Biol. Sci., CABS; Ref. Upd. Basic Ed.; Ref. Upd. Clinical Ed.; Ref. Upd. Deluxe Ed.

US/0098-7484
**JAMA : THE JOURNAL OF THE AMERICAN MEDICAL ASSOCIATION.** [JAMA j. Am. Med. Assoc.]. **Added/Corp** American Medical Association. **VFOAT** Journal of the American Medical Association; J.A.M.A. Vol. 173, No. 9 (July 2, 1960)-. Academic Scholarly Publication. English (French and Spanish). wk (48 issues). $140.00 (institution), $120.00 (individual) US. American Medical Association, 515 North State Street, Chicago IL 60610. **Tel** (312)464-5000, (800)262-2350, FAX (312)464-5831. **ED** George D. Lundberg. **LC** R15; .A48. **DD** 610/.5. **NLM** W1 J221. **CODEN** JAMAAP. **[CCC].** Index available (bound in last issue). **Bk Rev. Ad Acc. Pr Rev. Acid Free. Circ:** 279,600. available on microfilm and microfiche from University Microfilms International (UMI); available on an online database (files 149,442,647,648/Full-Text) from DIALOG; and MEDIS. Documents available from The Genuine Article, BIOSIS Document Express, UMI Article Clearinghouse, CASDDS, Documents on Demand. ***Continues*** *Journal of the American Medical Association, 0002-9955.*
**Desc:** The official communication of organized medicine. It is a general medical journal with a mission to educate.
**Ind/Abst** Abr. Index Med.; Abstr. Clin. Care Guidel.; Acad. Abstr. Full Text Elite (Jan. 1989-); Acad. Abstr. (Jan. 1989-); Acad. Ind. [Computer File] (1988-); Acad. Search (Jan. 1989-); AGRICOLA [Select. Cov.]; Annals Behav. Med.; Biol. Abstr.; Biostatistica; Chem. Abstr.; Chem. Hazards Ind.; Crim. Justice Abstr.; CSA Neuro. Abstr. (?-?); Cumul. Index Nurs. Allied Health Lit.; Curr. Biotechnol.; Curr. Contents Clin. Med.; Curr. Contents Life Sci.; Curr. Lit. Fam. Plan.; Dairy Sci. Abstr.; Dent. Abstr.; Dev. Med. Child Neurol.; EMBASE; Energy Res. Abstr.; Environ. Abstr.; Expand. Acad. Index (1987-); Foods Adlibra; Gen. Period. Index (1987-); Gen. Sci. Index; Gen. Sci. Source (Jan. 1989-); Health Saf. Sci. Abstr.; Health Devices Alerts; Health Index (1989-); Health Period. Database [Full Txt.]; Health Ref. Cent. (Jan. 1989-) [Full Txt.] [Full Cov.]; Health Source (Jan. 1989-); Helminthol. Abstr. (19??-19??); High. Educ. Abstr. (1968-19??); Hospit. Health Admin. Index; Hospit. Manage. Rev.; Hum. Genome Abstr.; Immunol. Abstr.; Index Med.; Index Period. Artic. Relat. Law; Index Vet.; Ind. Hyg. Dig. (19??-19??); INFO-SOUTH Abstr.; INIS Atomindex [Micro.]; Int. Nurs. Index; Int. Pharm. Abstr.; Iowa Drug Inf. Serv. (1966-); J. Watch; Lab. Hazards Bull.; Mag. Artic. Summar. Elite (Jan. 1989-); Mag. Artic. Summar. Select (Jan. 1989-); Mag. Artic. Summar. CD-ROM (Jan. 1989-); Mag. ASAP Plus [Full Txt.]; Mag. ASAP Sel. [Full Txt.]; Mag. Index Plus (1989-); Mag. Index. Sel. (1987-); Mag. Search; Med. Abstr. Newsl.; Microbiol. Abstr. Sect. B; Microbiol. Abstr. Sect. A; Microbiol. Abstr. Sect. C; Mod. Med.; NAPRALERT; Newsp. Period. Abstr. (1986-); Nutr. Abstr. Rev., Ser. B, Live Feeds and Feed.; Nutr. Abstr. Rev., Ser. A, Hum. Exp.; Nutr. Res. Newsl.; Life Sci. Collect.; PESTDOC; Physic. Medline Plus; Pig News Inf.; Pollut. Abstr. Indexes; Poult. Abstr.; Protozoolog. Abstr.; Psychol. Abstr.; Res. Alert [Full Cov.]; Resource/One Ondisc (1986-); Rev. Agric. Entomol.; Rev. Med. Vet. Entomol.; Rev. Med. Vet. Mycology; Rev. Plant Pathol.; Risk Abstr.; Sci. Cit. Index; SCISEARCH; Soc. Sci. Cit. Index [Select. Cov.]; SPORT Discus; SportSearch; Mag. Index (1988-); Vet. Bull.; Trade Ind. ASAP [Full Txt.]; Trade Ind. Index [Full Txt.]; Trop. Dis. Bull.; Virol. AIDS Abstr.; Vocat. Search (Jan. 1989-); Weed Abstr.

SP
**JANO. GUIA DE CONGRESOS MEDICOS.** Spanish. Ediciones Doyma SA, Travesera de Gracia 17 21, 08021 Barcelona Spain. **Tel** 011 34 3 2000711, 011 34 3 4145706, FAX 011 34 3 2091136, telex 51964 INK E.

SP/0210-220X
**JANO. MEDICINA Y HUMANIDADES.** [Jano, Med. humanid.]. (1971)-. Periodical. Spanish. Forty-Four times a year. $101.00. Ediciones Doyma SA, Travesera de Gracia 17 21, 08021 Barcelona Spain. **Tel** 011 34 3 2000711, 011 34 3 4145706, FAX 011 34 3 2091136, telex 51964 INK E. **UDC** 61. **[CCC].**

NE/0021-4264
**JANUS (AMSTERDAM).** ***Ceased.*** (JANUS.). [Janus]. Vol. 1; July/Aug. 1896-Ceased ?. Periodical. French (German and English). qt. E M Bruins, Joh Verhulststraat 185, Amsterdam The Netherlands. **LC** R131.A1. **NLM** W1 JA864. **CODEN** JNUSA6. cum. index.
**Desc:** Includes section "Review Bibliography."

**Ind/Abst** Am. Hist. Life (1957-1965, 1971-); Chem. Bus. Bull.; Chem. Bus. NewsBase (1989-); Chem. Bus. Update; Math. Rev.; Zentralbl. Math. Ihre Grenzgeb.

JA
**JAPAN INTRACTABLE DISEASES RESEARCH FOUNDATION PUBLICATION.** Monographic series. English. Price varies per volume. University of Tokyo Press, 7 3 1 Hongo Bunkyo-ku, Tokyo 113 Japan. **Tel** 011 81 3 3811 0964. **NLM** W1; JA876J. ***Continues*** *Japan Medical Research Foundation Publication.*

JA
**JAPAN MEDICAL JOURNAL. NIHON IJI SHIMPO.** Japanese. wk. $396.00. Shukan Nippon Iji Shinposha, 2-9, Kanda Surugadai, Chiyodaku, Tokyoto 101-91 Japan. **(Subscription address:** Kyowa Book Company Inc., 1-38 Kanda Jinbo-Cho, Chiyoda-Ku, Tokyo 101, Japan (Phone: 03-3293-0727)**)**

SP
**JAPAN REPORT SERIES MEDICAL TECHNOLOGY.** English. mo. $430.00. Newmedia International Japan, AV Infanta Carlota 123 5 A, 08029 Barcelona Spain. **Tel** 011 34 3 4195690, FAX 414 42 13. **(Subscription address:** Newmedia International Japan, Midland Bank 196 Oxford Street AC 41217380, London W1A 1 EZ England**)**
**Ind/Abst** PROMT [Full Txt.]; PTS Newsl. Database [Full Txt.].

JA/0021-5112
**JAPANESE JOURNAL OF MEDICAL SCIENCE & BIOLOGY.** [Jpn. j. med. sci. biol.]. **Added/Corp** Kokuritsu Yobo Eisei Kenkyujo (Japan). **VAT** Japanese Journal of Medical Science and Biology. Vol. 5 (1952)-. Academic Scholarly Publication. English. bm. $100.00. Koseisho Kokuritsu Yobo Eisei Kenkyujo, (National Inst. of Health, Ministry of Health & Welfare), 10-35, Kamiosaki 2 Chome, Shinagawaku, Tokyoto 141 Japan. **(Subscription address:** Maruzen Company Ltd., PO Box 5050, Import & Export Department, Tokyo 100 31 Japan.**) NLM** W1 JA975. **CODEN** JJMCAQ. **Pr Rev.** ctrl circ. Documents available from The Genuine Article, BIOSIS Document Express, CASDDS. ***Continues*** *Japanese Medical Journal, 0368-3095.*
**Desc:** Publishes full communications, reviews, and epidemiological reports dealing with all aspects of medical science and biology.
**Ind/Abst** AGRICOLA; Biodeter. Abstr. (1991-); Biol. Abstr.; Chem. Abstr.; Curr. Contents Life Sci.; Dairy Sci. Abstr.; EMBASE; Helminthol. Abstr. (19??-19??); Index Med.; Index Vet.; NAPRALERT; Nutr. Res. Newsl.; Life Sci. Collect.; Pig News Inf.; Protozoolog. Abstr.; Res. Alert [Full Cov.]; Rev. Med. Vet. Entomol.; Sci. Cit. Index; SCISEARCH; SEA Abstr.; Small Anim. Abstr. Bibliogr.; Soc. Sci. Cit. Index [Select. Cov.]; Vet. Bull.; Trop. Dis. Bull.

SP
**JAPANESE REPORT SERIES : MEDICAL TECHNOLOGY.** English. mo. $430.00 US; £265.00 UK. Newmedia International Japan, AV Infanta Carlota 123 5 A, 08029 Barcelona Spain. **Tel** 011 34 3 4195690, FAX 414 42 13. **UDC** 63.

US/0091-2751
**JCU : JOURNAL OF CLINICAL ULTRASOUND.** [J. clin. ultrasound]. **Added/Corp** American Institute of Ultrasound in Medicine. **VFOAT** Journal of Clinical Ultrasound. Vol. 1 (March 1973)-. Academic Scholarly Publication. English. Nine times a year. $333.00 US; $423.00 Canada and Mexico; $456.75 other. John Wiley & Sons, Inc., 605 Third Avenue, New York NY 10158-0012. **Tel** (212)850-6000, (212)850-6645, FAX (212)850-6088, telex 12-7063. **(Subscription address:** John Wiley & Sons / England, Baffins Lane, Chichester, West Sussex PO19 1UD England.**) ED** Russell L. Deter. **LC** RM862.7; .J18. **DD** 616.07/5. **NLM** W1 J223Y. **CODEN** JCULDD. **[CCC]. Ad Acc. Pr Rev. Circ:** 6,500. available on microfilm and microfiche from University Microfilms International (UMI). Documents available from The Genuine Article, BIOSIS Document Express, Ask*IEEE.
**Desc:** Devoted exclusively to the clinical applications of ultrasound in medicine. Coverage is provided on ultra-sound's current use in evaluating disorders affecting the central nervous system, fetus and placenta, gastrointestinal system, reproductive system and urinary system.
**Ind/Abst** Biol. Abstr.; Curr. Contents Clin. Med.; EMBASE; Energy Res. Abstr. (April 1977-); Health Devices Alerts; Helminthol. Abstr. (1991-); Index Med.; INIS Atomindex [Micro.]; INSPEC (Sept. 1981-); Life Sci. Collect.; Physic. Medline Plus; Protozoolog. Abstr.; Ref. Upd. Deluxe Ed.; Res. Alert [Full Cov.]; Sci. Cit. Index; SCISEARCH.

US/0190-1818
**JHP, JOURNAL OF HOMEOPATHIC PRACTICE.** **VFOAT** Journal of Homeopathic Practice. Vol. 1 (Spring 1978)-. Periodical. English. qt. $10.00 (North America), $20.00 (other). Journal of Homeopathic Practice, 5916 Charbot West, Oakland CA 94618-1932. **LC** RX1; .J16. **DD** 615/.532/05. **NLM** W1 J39.

CC/0253-3685
**JIANGSU YIYAO.** (CHIANG-SU I YAO.). [Jiangsu yiyao]. **VFOAT** Jiangsuyiyao; Jiangsu Medical Journal. (1974)-. Periodical. Chinese (table of contents in English). mo. Chiang-su Jen Min Chu Pan She, Post Office Nan-Ching Shin, Nan-Ching Shin, People's Republic of China. **NLM** W1 CH423C. **CODEN** CIYADX. Documents available from CASDDS.
**Ind/Abst** Chem. Abstr.; NAPRALERT.

CC/0253-9799
**JIANGSU ZHONGYI ZAZHI.** (CHIANG-SU CHUNG I TSA CHIH.). [Jiangsu zhongyi zazhi]. **VFOAT** Jiangsu Journal of Traditional Chinese Medicine. Began with: V. 1, No. 1 in 1980. Academic Scholarly Publication. Chinese. bm. **NLM** W1 CH423BD. **CODEN** CIYCD5. Documents available from CASDDS.
**Ind/Abst** Chem. Abstr. (1980-1984).

JA/0387-0308
**JICHI IKA DAIGAKU KIYO.** [Jichi Ika Daigaku kiyo]. **VFOAT** Jichi Medical School Journal. (1978)-. Periodical. Multiple languages. an. Jichi Ika Daigaku, (Jichi Medical School), 3311-1, Yakushiji, Minamikawachimachi, Kawachigun, Tochigiken 329-04, Japan. **DD** 060. Documents available from CASDDS.
**Ind/Abst** Chem. Abstr.

JA/0021-6968
**JIKEIKAI MEDICAL JOURNAL.** [Jikeikai med. j.]. **Added/Corp** Jikei Daigaku. Igakubu. Tokyo Jikeikai Ika Daigaku. Vol. 1 (1954)-. Academic Scholarly Publication. English (Japanese). ir. Jikeikai University School of Medicine, 25 8 3 Chome Nishi Shinbashi, Tokyo 105 Japan. **ED** Kenji Sakurai, Satoshi Kurihara, Shin-Ichi Hayashi, Akio Kobayashi, Haruo Kameda, Kihei Maekawa, Sachio Mochizuki, Ken-Ichi Kobayashi, Shin-Ichiro Ushigome, Kazuo Urata. **NLM** W1 JI612. **CODEN** JMEJASOJMEJAS. **[CCC].** cum. index. ctrl circ. Documents available from BIOSIS Document Express, CASDDS.
**Ind/Abst** Anal. Abstr.; Biol. Abstr.; Chem. Abstr.; EMBASE [Select. Cov.]; SEA Abstr.; Trop. Dis. Bull.

JA/0007-5124
**JIKKEN DOBUTSU.** [Jikken dobutsu]. **Added/Corp** Nihon Jikken Dobutsu Kenkyukai. **VFOAT** Experimental Animals. Vol. 17 (1968)-. Academic Scholarly Publication. Japanese (English). qt. $140.00. University of Tokyo Institute of Medical Science, Shirokanedai, Minatoku Tokyo Japan. **(Subscription address:** Kyowa Book Company, Inc., 1 38 Kanda Jinbocho Chiyoda Ku Tokyo 101 Japan**) NLM** W1 JI625. **CODEN** JIDOAA. **[CCC].** Index available. cum. index. **Bk Rev. Ad Acc. Pr Rev. Circ:** 2,200. Documents available from The Genuine Article, BIOSIS Document Express, CASDDS. ***Continues** Jikken Dobutsu Iho.*
**Ind/Abst** Biol. Abstr.; Chem. Abstr.; EMBASE; Index Med.; Index Vet.; Nutr. Abstr. Rev., Ser. B, Live Feeds and Feed.; Poult. Abstr.; Protozoolog. Abstr.; Res. Alert [Select. Cov.]; Small Anim. Abstr. Bibliogr.; Vet. Bull.

CC/0253-2719
**JILINYIKE DAXUE XUEBAO.** (CHI-LIN I KO TA HSUEH HSUEH PAO.). [Jilin yike daxue xuebao]. **VFOAT** Jilinyikedaxue Xuebao. Vol. 1- ; 1978-. Academic Scholarly Publication. Chinese. qt. **LC** R97.7.C5; C42A. **CODEN** CIKPD8. Documents available from CASDDS.
**Ind/Abst** Chem. Abstr.

CC/1000-9965
**JINAN DAXUE XUEBAO ZIRAN KEXUE YU YIXUE BAN.** (JINAN DAXUE XUEBAO.). **VFOAT** Journal of Jinan University (Natural Science and Medicine Ed.). (1989)-. Periodical. Chinese. qt. Jinan University / Journal Editorial Department, (Jinan Daxue / Xuebao Bianjibu), Building 75, 2nd Floor, Room 217, Shipai, Guangzhou, Guangdong, 510632 People's Republic of China. **Tel** 5516511. **ED** W. Weiliang. **DD** 506. Documents available from CASDDS, BLDSC, CASDDS. ***Continues** Jinan Li-Yi Xuebao, 1000-5064.*
**Ind/Abst** Chem. Abstr.

JA/0300-0818
**JINKO ZOKI.** [Jinko zoki]. **Added/Corp** Nihon Jinko Zoki Gakkai. **VFOAT** Artificial Organs. (1972)-. Periodical. Japanese. qt. Japanese Society for Artificial Organs, 4-16 Yayoi 2-chome, Bunkyo-ku 103 Tokyo Japan. **CODEN** JNZKA7. Documents available from BIOSIS Document Express, CASDDS. ***Continues** Journal of the Japanese Society for Artificial Organs and Tissues, 0300-0826.*
**Ind/Abst** Biol. Abstr. (1988-); Chem. Abstr. (1985-1989); EMBASE.

●US
**JOB CHOICES ... IN HEALTHCARE.** **See** Occupations and Careers.

US/1058-112X
**JOHNS HOPKINS CENTER FOR ALTERNATIVES TO ANIMAL TESTING : NEWSLETTER, THE.** [Johns Hopkins Cent. Altern. Anim. Test.]. **Added/Corp** Johns Hopkins Center for Alternatives to Animal Testing. Vol. 1, No. 1 (Fall 1982)-. Newsletter. English. Three times a year. Free, US; $30.00 other. Johns Hopkins University Press, 2715 North Charles Street, Baltimore MD 21218-4319. **Tel** (410)516-6987, FAX (410)516-6968. **DD** 179. **NLM** W1; JO14R.
**Ind/Abst** AGRICOLA [Select. Cov.].

US/1042-1882
**JOHNS HOPKINS MEDICAL LETTER HEALTH AFTER 50, THE.** [Johns Hopkins med. lett. health 50]. **Added/Corp** Johns Hopkins Medical Institutions. **VFOAT** Health After 50; Johns Hopkins Medical Letter Health After Fifty. Vol. 1, Issue 1 (Mar. 1989)-. Periodical. English. mo. $20.00 US; $29.00 Canada; $30.00 other. Medletter Associates Inc., 632 Broadway, 11th Floor, New York NY 10012. **Tel** (212)505-2255 ext. 100. **ED** Simeon Margolis, M.D. and Hamilton Moses III, M.D. **DD** 362. cum. index. **Circ:** 100 (ctrl).
**Desc:** Consumers guide to health care.
**Ind/Abst** Consum. Health Nutr. Index (Jan. 1990); Cumul. Index Nurs. Allied Health Lit.; INIS Atomindex [Micro.]; Med. Abstr. Newsl.

US
**JOINT MEMBERSHIP DIRECTORY / THE ASSOCIATION OF BIOMEDICAL COMMUNICATIONS DIRECTORS, THE ASSOCIATION OF MEDICAL ILLUSTRATORS, THE HEALTH SCIENCES COMMUNICATIONS ASSOCIATION.** **See** Communication.

NE/0166-2430
**JONXIS LECTURES, THE.** [Jonxis lect.]. **Added/Corp** Rijksuniversiteit te Groningen. Faculteit der Geneeskunde. Foundation for Higher Medical Education Netherlands Antilles. Vol. 1 (1978)-. Academic Scholarly Publication. English. ir. Price varies per volume. Elsevier Science Publishers BV, PO Box 211, 1000 AE Amsterdam Netherlands. **Tel** 011 31 20 5803642, FAX 011 31 20 5862696, telex 15682. **NLM** W3 JO44. **CODEN** JOLEDV. **[CCC].** Documents available from BIOSIS Document Express, CASDDS.
**Ind/Abst** Biol. Abstr.; Chem. Abstr.

BG/1012-8697
**JOPSOM. JOURNAL OF PREVENTIVE AND SOCIAL MEDICINE.** (JOURNAL OF PREVENTIVE AND SOCIAL MEDICINE : JOPSOM : A BI-ANNUAL JOURNAL OF THE NATIONAL INSTITUTE OF PREVENTIVE AND SOCIAL MEDICINE.). [JOPSOM, J. prevent. soc. med.]. **Added/Corp** National Institute of Preventive and Social Medicine (Bangladesh). **VFOAT** JOPSOM; J.O.P.S.O.M. Vol. 1, No. 1, May (1982)-. Periodical. English. sa. **NLM** W1; JO843F.

US/0745-2624
**JOURNAL - AMERICAN ASSOCIATION FOR MEDICAL TRANSCRIPTION.** (JOURNAL : JOURNAL OF THE AMERICAN ASSOCIATION FOR MEDICAL TRANSCRIPTION.). [J.-Am. Assoc. Med. Transcr.]. **Added/Corp** American Association for Medical Transcription. **VFOAT** Journal of the American Association for Medical Transcription. Vol. 1, No. 1 (Summer 1982)-. Periodical. English. qt. American Association for Medical Transcription, PO Box 576187, Modesto CA 95357-6187. **Tel** (800)982-2182. **ED** Claudia Tessier. **DD** 651. **NLM** W1 JO22C.
**Desc:** JAAMT is the official journal of the American Association for Medical Transcription, distributed to over 10,000 medical transcriptionists, supervisors, educators, medical record directors, physicians, and allied health professionals. Topics include medical language, medicine, pharmaceutical updates, medical references, stylistic preferences, editing practices, technological updates, education, supervision, and training.
**Ind/Abst** Health Plan. Adminis.

US/0148-4869
**JOURNAL - ASSOCIATION FOR HOSPITAL MEDICAL EDUCATION.** **Added/Corp** Association for Hospital Medical Education. (Summer/Fall 1976)-. Periodical. English. qt. **NLM** W1 JO2224. ***Supersedes** AHME Journal, 0090-7782.*

US/0030-1132
**JOURNAL - COLLEGE OF MEDICINE, THE OHIO STATE UNIVERSITY.** (COLLEGE OF MEDICINE JOURNAL.). **Added/Corp** Ohio State University. College of Medicine. Vol. 14 (Autumn 1963)-. Periodical. English. Three times a year. Free. Medical Administration Center, Ohio State University, 370 West 9th Avenue, Columbus OH 43210. **Tel** (614)422-5672. **ED** Ernest W. Johnson. **NLM** W1; CO186. **Bk Rev. Circ:** 13,200 (ctrl). ***Continues** Health Center Journal.*

FR/0021-7883
**JOURNAL DE MEDECINE DE LYON.** [J. med. Lyon]. No. 1 (1920)-. Academic Scholarly Publication. French (summaries and/or abstracts in English and Esperanto). Eleven times a year. 200.00F France; 400.00F other. Sedip Communications, 75 Cours Albert Thomas, 69447 Lyon Cedex 3 France. **Tel** 011 33 72352372, FAX 011 33 72352345. **ED** Michel Evreux. **NLM** W1 JO319C. **CODEN** JMLYA6. **Bk Rev. Ad Acc, Adv Mgr:** F. Balula. **Circ:** 3,000. Documents available from BIOSIS Document Express, CASDDS.
**Ind/Abst** Biol. Abstr. (-1987); Chem. Abstr.; EMBASE [Select. Cov.].

FR/0021-7905
**JOURNAL DE MEDECINE DE STRASBOURG.** [J. med. Strasb.]. **Added/Corp** Universite de Strasbourg. Faculte de Medecine. (1970)-. Academic Scholarly Publication. French (French; summaries and/or abstracts in English). mo. 420.00F France; 590.00F other. Expansion Scientifique Francaise, 31 Boulevard de la Tour-Maubourg, 75007 Paris France. **Tel** 011 33 1 40 62 64 00, 011 33 1 40626439. **NLM** W1 JO319T. **CODEN** JMSTBR. **[CCC].** Documents available from CASDDS. ***Supersedes** Strasbourg Medical.*
**Ind/Abst** Chem. Abstr.; EMBASE [Select. Cov.]; Life Sci. Collect.; Saf. Health Work.

FR/0987-2825
**JOURNAL DE MEDECINE PRATIQUE.** ***Ceased.*** **VFOAT** JMP. Vol. 1, No. 1 (1987)-(1991). Periodical. French. wk. Expansion Scientifique Francaise, 31 Boulevard de la Tour-Maubourg, 75007 Paris France. **Tel** 011 33 1 40 62 64 00, 011 33 1 40626439. **NLM** W1; JO323R.

FR
**JOURNAL DE READAPTATION MEDICALE.** French. qt. 510.00F France; $136.00 US; £109.00 other. Masson SA, Avenue Beauregard 12, CH-1701 Fribourg Switzerland. **Tel** 011 41 37 249585, FAX 011 41 37 247559, telex 942658 SEMI CH. available on microfilm and microfiche from University Microfilms International (UMI).

FR/0245-5811
**JOURNAL DE TRAUMATOLOGIE.** [J. traumatol.]. Vol. 1, No.1 (1980)-. Academic Scholarly Publication. English (French). qt. 152.00F Switzerland; $82.00 other. Masson SA, Avenue Beauregard 12, CH-1701 Fribourg Switzerland. **Tel** 011 41 37 249585, FAX 011 41 37 247559, telex 942658 SEMI CH. **(Subscription address:** 7A Boulevard de Perolles, CH-1701 Fribourg Switzerland**) NLM** W1 JO366C.
**Ind/Abst** EMBASE.

FR/0245-5552
**JOURNAL D'ECHOGRAPHIE ET DE MEDECINE ULTRASONORE : JEMU.** [J.E.M.U. J. echogr. med. ultrason.]. **VFOAT** JEMU; J.E.M.U. Vol. 1 (1980)-. Periodical. French (summaries and/or abstracts in English). bm. $160.00. Masson Editeur, Box Postale 22, 41353 Vineuil 16 France. **Tel** 011 33 54 438994. **(Subscription address:** 7A Boulevard de Perolles, CH-1701 Fribourg Switzerland**) NLM** W1 JO237B. **[CCC].** available on microfilm and microfiche from University Microfilms International (UMI).
**Ind/Abst** EMBASE.

FR/0294-0736
**JOURNAL D'ECONOMIE MEDICALE.** [J. econ. med.]. Vol. 1, No. 1 (Jan./Mars 1983)-. Periodical. French (summaries and/or abstracts in French and English; table of contents in French and English). Eight times a year. 742.41F (individuals), 843.29F (institutions) France; 913.00F (individuals), 1020.00F (institutions) others. Editions Alexandre Lacassagne, 162 Avenue Lacassagne, 69424 Lyon Cedex 03 France. **Tel** 011 33 72 334040. **(Subscription address:** Diffusion Eska, 27 rue Dunois, 75013 Paris France.**) NLM** W1; JO237D. **[CCC].** ***Continues** Bulletin d'Economie Medicale, 0769-9654.*
**Ind/Abst** EMBASE.

FR/1153-0863
**JOURNAL DU SIDA PARIS, LE.** (LE JOURNAL DU SIDA.). **Added/Corp** Association pour la Recherche Clinique Contre l'AIDS-SIDA et sa Therapeutique (France). (1990)-. Periodical. French. mo (11 issues). 489.72F France; 650.00F other. Arcat Sida, 57 rue St Louis en l Ile, 75004 Paris France. **Tel** 011 33 1 43546715. **UDC** 616.97. ***Continues** SIDA. Savoir, Informer, Debattre, Analyser, 0996-6625.*
**Ind/Abst** Trop. Dis. Bull.

UK/0951-2578
**JOURNAL / INSTITUTE OF STERILE SERVICES MANAGEMENT.** **Added/Corp** Institute of Sterile Services Management. **VFOAT** Journal of Sterile Services Management. (1988)-. Periodical. English. bm. Angwin Associates, Sills 7 Kendal Drive, Beeston Nottingham NG9 3AW England. **Tel** 011 44 602 704464. **NLM** W1; JO478M. ***Continues** Journal of Sterile Services Management.*
**Ind/Abst** Hospit. Health Admin. Index (1988-1989).

FR/0241-0109
**JOURNAL INTERNATIONAL DE MEDECINE, LE.** (LE JOURNAL INTERNATIONAL DE MEDECINE : JIM.). [J. int. med.]. **VFOAT** JIM; J.I.M. Vol. 1, No. 1 (Oct. 1979)-. Periodical. French. ir. 181.00F France; 385.00F other. Abstract, 25 Bis Av Pierre Grenier, 92100 Boulogne Billanct France. **Tel** 011 33 1 49100606. **NLM** W1 JO479D.

II/0971-071X
**JOURNAL INTERNATIONAL MEDICAL SCIENCES ACADEMY.** [J. Int. Med. Sci. Acad.]. **VFOAT** JIMSA. (1987)-. Periodical. English. qt. International Medical Sciences Academy, National Medical Library Building, Ansari Nagar, Ring Road, 110029 New Delhi India. **Tel** (11)654660. **UDC** 61.
**Ind/Abst** EMBASE [Select. Cov.].

US/1055-0887
**JOURNAL OF ADDICTIVE DISEASES.**
**See** Drug Abuse and Alcoholism.

US/1054-139X
**JOURNAL OF ADOLESCENT HEALTH.** (JOURNAL OF ADOLESCENT HEALTH : OFFICIAL PUBLICATION OF THE SOCIETY FOR ADOLESCENT MEDICINE.). [J. adolens. health]. **Added/Corp** Society for Adolescent Medicine (U.S.). Vol. 12, No. 1 (Jan. 1991)-. Academic Scholarly Publication. English. Twelve times a year (2 volumes). $335.00 US; $397.00 other. Elsevier Science Publishing Company Inc, Madison Square Station, PO Box 882, New York NY 10159-0882. **Tel** (212)633-3950, FAX (212)633-3990. **LC** RJ550; .J67. **DD** 616/.005. **NLM** W1; JO533RS. **CODEN** JADHE5. **[CCC]. Pr Rev.** available on microfilm and microfiche from University Microfilms International (UMI). Documents available from The Genuine Article, BIOSIS Document Express. ***Continues*** *Journal of Adolescent Health Care, 0197-0070.*
**Ind/Abst** Annals Behav. Med.; Biol. Abstr.; Cumul. Index Nurs. Allied Health Lit.; Curr. Contents Clin. Med.; Curr. Contents Soc. Behav. Sci.; EMBASE; Health Plan. Adminis.; Index Med. (Jan. 1991-); Res. Alert [Full Cov.]; Risk Abstr.; SCISEARCH; Soc. Plann. Policy Dev. Abstr.; Soc. Sci. Cit. Index [Full Cov.]; SPORT Discus.

US/0894-5888
**JOURNAL OF ADVANCEMENT IN MEDICINE.** (JOURNAL OF ADVANCEMENT IN MEDICINE / SPONSORED BY THE AMERICAN COLLEGE OF ADVANCEMENT IN MEDICINE.). [J. adv. med.]. **Added/Corp** American College of Advancement in Medicine. Vol. 1, No. 1 (Spring 1988)-. Periodical. English. qt. $215.00 US; $250.00 other. Human Sciences Press, PO Box 735, 233 Spring Street, New York NY 10013. **Tel** (212)620-8000, FAX (212)807-1047, telex 23421139. **(Subscription address:** Eurospan Ltd., Journals and Serials Division, 3 Henrietta Street, Covent Garden, London WC2E 8LU England.**) ED** Derrick Lonsdale. **DD** 610. **NLM** W1; JO533UG. **CODEN** JAMEE7. **[CCC].** available on microfilm and microfiche from University Microfilms International (UMI).
**Desc:** Dedicated to research on emerging and innovative advances in medical science, with a particular focus on nutritional/preventative medicine. Special emphasis is given to nonsurgical, less invasive, and nontoxic methods of diagnosis and treatment.

NE/0165-0327
**JOURNAL OF AFFECTIVE DISORDERS.** [J. affective disord.]. Vol. 1 (March 1979)-. Academic Scholarly Publication. English. Sixteen times a year (4 vols.). Fl1828.00. Elsevier Science Publishers BV, PO Box 211, 1000 AE Amsterdam Netherlands. **Tel** 011 31 20 5803642, FAX 011 31 20 5862696, telex 15682. **ED** E S Paykel and G Winokur. **NLM** W1 JO534B. **CODEN** JADID7. **[CCC]. Pr Rev.** available on microfilm and microfiche from University Microfilms International (UMI). Documents available from The Genuine Article, BIOSIS Document Express, CASDDS, ADONIS.
**Desc:** Publishes papers concerned with affective disorders in the widest sense: depression, mania and anxiety.
**Ind/Abst** ADONIS; Biol. Abstr.; Chem. Abstr.; Curr. Aware. Biol. Sci., CABS; Curr. Contents Life Sci.; EMBASE; Index Med.; Life Sci. Collect.; Psychol. Abstr. (1979-); PsycINFO; PsycLit; Ref. Upd. Deluxe Ed.; Res. Alert [Full Cov.]; Sci. Cit. Index; SCISEARCH; Soc. Sci. Cit. Index [Select. Cov.].

●US/1059-924X
**JOURNAL OF AGROMEDICINE.** Vol. 1 (Spring 1992)-. English. qt (4 issues). $75.00 US; $105.00 other. The Haworth Press Inc, 10 Alice Street, Binghamton NY 13904-1580. **Tel** (607)722-5857, (800)3-HAWORTH, FAX (607)722-1424. **ED** Stanley H. Schuman, MD, DrPH, Medical University of South Carolina. **NLM** W1; JO534JD. **Acid Free.** Documents available from Haworth Document Delivery Service, Documents on Demand.
**Ind/Abst** Abstr. Anthropol.; AGRICOLA; Biostatistica; Environ. Abstr.; Environ. Period. Bibliogr.; Food Sci. Technol. Abstr.; Geogr. Abstr. Human Geogr.; Health Saf. Sci. Abstr.; Helminthol. Abstr.; Int. Dev. Abstr.

US/0090-7421
**JOURNAL OF ALLIED HEALTH.** [allied health]. **Added/Corp** Association of Schools of Allied Health Professions. American Society of Allied Health Professions. (Nov. 1972)-. Academic Scholarly Publication. English. Four times a year. $75.00 US & US Posessions, Canada & Mexico; $90.00 others. American Society of Allied Health Professionals, 1730 M Street Northwest, Suite 500, Washington DC 20036. **Tel** (202)293-4848, FAX (202)293-4852. **ED** Thomas Elwood. **LC** R690; .J65. **DD** 610.69/53/05. **NLM** W1 JO534V. ctrl circ. available on microfilm and microfiche from University Microfilms International (UMI).
**Desc:** The official publication of the Association of Schools of Allied Health Professions. The journal is the only interdisciplinary allied health publication, publishing scholarly works related to research and development, feature articles, research abstracts, and book reviews. Readers of the journal comprise allied health leaders, educators, and faculty.
**Ind/Abst** Cumul. Index Nurs. Allied Health Lit.; Curr. Index J. Educ.; Health Plan. Adminis.; Hospit. Health Admin. Index; Hospit. Manage. Rev.; Index Med.

UK/0959-9886
**JOURNAL OF ALTERNATIVE AND COMPLEMENTARY MEDICINE.** [J. altern. complement. med.]. **VFOAT** Journal of Alternative and Complementary Medicine. (1987)-. Periodical. English. Twelve times a year. £27.50 UK; £32.00 Europe & Eire; £40.00 other. Journal of Alternative and Complementary Medicine, Homewood NHS Trust, Guildford Road, Chertsey Surrey KT16 OQA. **Tel** 011 44 0276 51522, FAX 011 44 0276 51557. **ED** Leon Chaitow. **DD** 615.5. Index available. cum. index. **Bk Rev**, (Qty: 36). **Ad Acc**, **Adv Mgr:** Elaine Curtis, **Tel** 0932 874333. **Circ:** 5,000 (ctrl). ***Continues*** *Journal of Alternative Medicine, 0950-5466.*
**Desc:** A journal for healthcare professionals in all the natural therapies.

●US/1075-5535
**JOURNAL OF ALTERNATIVE AND COMPLEMENTARY MEDICINE (NEW YORK, N.Y.), THE.** (THE JOURNAL OF ALTERNATIVE AND COMPLEMENTARY MEDICINE : RESEARCH ON PARADIGM, PRACTICE, AND POLICY.). **VFOAT** Alternative and Complementary Medicine. (1994)-. Periodical. English. qt. $110.00. Mary Ann Liebert Inc., 1651 Third Avenue, New York NY 10128. **Tel** (212)289-2300, (800)M-LIEBERT, FAX (212)289-4697. **ED** Marc S. Micozzi. **Pr Rev.**
**Desc:** For physicians and individuals seeking information on nontraditional medical practices.

UK/0951-1830
**JOURNAL OF AMBULATORY MONITORING.** [J. ambul. monit.]. Vol. 1, No. 1 (Jan./March 1988)-. Periodical. English. qt. £115.00 UK; $190.00 other. Taylor & Francis Ltd., Rankine Road, Basingstoke Hampshire, RG24 8PR United Kingdom. **Tel** 011 44 256 840366, FAX 011 44 256 479438, telex 858540. **(Subscription address:** Taylor & Francis Inc., 1900 Frost Road, Suite 101, Bristol PA 19007-1598.**) ED** Shlomo Stern and Stuart Meldrum (associate editor). **NLM** W1; JO535CV. **[CCC].** available on microfilm from University Microfilms International (UMI).
**Desc:** Covers all aspects of ambulatory, or personal, monitoring, including ECG, EEG, pH, blood-pressure, respiration and activity monitoring. Publishes clinical and technical research papers, reviews and equipment validations. The official journal of The International Society for Holter Monitoring.
**Ind/Abst** Ergon. Abstr.

US/0744-8481
**JOURNAL OF AMERICAN COLLEGE HEALTH.** (JOURNAL OF AMERICAN COLLEGE HEALTH : J OF ACH.). [J. Am. coll. health]. **Added/Corp** Helen Dwight Reid Educational Foundation. American College Health Association. **VFOAT** J of ACH; J. of A.C.H.; J.A.C.H.; JACH; College Health. Vol. 30, No. 5 (April 1982)-. Periodical. English. bm. $49.00 (individual), $85.00 (institution). Heldref Publications, 1319 Eighteenth Street Northwest, Washington DC 20036-1802. **Tel** (202)296-6267, (800)365-9753, FAX (202)296-5149. **ED** John M Dorman, Clifford B Reifler, Allan J Schwartz, and Paula L Swinford. **LC** RA564.5; .J65. **DD** 613/.088375. **NLM** W1 JO535D. **[CCC]. Bk Rev. Ad Acc. Circ:** 1,800. available on microfilm and microfiche from University Microfilms International (UMI). ***Continues*** *Journal of the American College Health Association, 0164-4300.*
**Desc:** Provides a forum on college health care. Covers developments and research in this broad field, including clinical and preventive medicine, health promotion and education, administration, mental health, nursing, and medicine. The journal features major research articles and, in clinical and program notes, describes how individual colleges and universities have dealt with on-campus health issues.
**Ind/Abst** Acad. Search (Jan. 1994-); Appl. Soc. Sci. Index Abstr.; Cumul. Index Nurs. Allied Health Lit.; Curr. Index J. Educ.; Curr. Lit. Fam. Plan.; Educ. Index; Educ. Adm. Abstr.; EMBASE; Health Source (Jul. 1993-); High. Educ. Abstr.; Index Med.; INFO-SOUTH Abstr.; Mag. Search; Phys. Educ. Index; Psychol. Abstr. (1982-); PsycINFO; PsycLit; SportSearch.

TU
**JOURNAL OF ANKARA MEDICAL SCHOOL. Added/Corp** Ankara Universitesi Tp Fakultesi. **VFOAT** Ankara tp Bulteni. Vol. 11, No. 1 (1989)-. Academic Scholarly Publication. Turkish (English, French and German). qt. Ankara Universitesi Tip, Fakultesi Yayn Komisyonu Baskanlg, Ankara Turkey. ***Continues*** *Ankara tp Bulteni, 0252-970X.*
**Ind/Abst** EMBASE.

US/1067-4640
**JOURNAL OF ANTHROPOSOPHIC MEDICINE.** [J. anthropos. med.]. **Added/Corp** Physician's Association for Anthroposophic Medicine. (19??)-. Periodical. English. Four times a year. $50.00 US; $60.00 other. Physician's Association for Anthroposophic Medicine, 7953 California Avenue, Fair Oaks CA 95628. **Tel** (916)969-8250, FAX (916)966-5314. **ED** Edwin H. Funk, M. D. and Christa van Tellingen-van Heek, M. D. **DD** 616. **Bk Rev. Ad Acc. Circ:** 500.
**Desc:** Publish quality original articles on anthroposophic medicine and other related topics.

II/0377-0400
**JOURNAL OF APPLIED MEDICINE.** Vol. 1 (Jan. 1975)-. Academic Scholarly Publication. English. mo. $30.00. Living Media India Ltd., PO Box 706, Faridabad 121007 India. **(Subscription address:** Prints India, 11 Darya Ganj, New Delhi, 110002 India, (Phone: 011 91 11 3268645)**) ED** G S Sainani. **NLM** W1 JO541H. **CODEN** JAMED6. **Bk Rev. Ad Acc. Circ:** 10,000 (ctrl). Documents available from CASDDS.
**Desc:** A medical review journal to keep Indian doctors abreast with international developments in the field of medicine.
**Ind/Abst** Chem. Abstr.

UK/0140-511X
**JOURNAL OF AUDIOVISUAL MEDIA IN MEDICINE, THE.** [J. audiov. media med.]. **Added/Corp** Institute of Medical and Biological Illustration. Vol. 1 (Feb. 1978)-. Periodical. English. qt. $157.00 The Americas; £105.00 other. Butterworth Heinemann Publishers, Linacre House, Jordan Hill, Oxford OX2 8DP England. **Tel** 011 44 865 310366. **(Subscription address:** Elsevier Science Ltd. Oxford Fulfillment Centre, PO Box 800, Kidlington, Oxford OX5 1DX United Kingdom.**) ED** K. P. Duguid (editor's address: Department of Medical Illustration, University of Aberdeen, Scotland United Kingdom). **NLM** W1 JO546T. **CODEN** JAUMD2. **[CCC].** Index available. **Bk Rev. Ad Acc. Circ:** 1,030. available on microfilm and microfiche from University Microfilms International (UMI). Documents available from BIOSIS Document Express. ***Supersedes*** *Medical and Biological Illustration, 0025-6978.*
**Desc:** Provides a vehicle for the inter-change of information and ideas on the development, implementation and use of audiovisual media for education, record and research purposes in all areas of the health sciences.
**Ind/Abst** Biol. Abstr. (1986-); Educ. Technol. Abstr.; Index Med.; Index Vet.; Life Sci. Collect.; Res. High. Educ. Abstr.; Vet. Bull.

II
**JOURNAL OF AYURVEDA (JAIPUR, INDIA).** (JOURNAL OF AYURVEDA.). **Added/Corp** National Institute of Ayurveda (India). **VFOAT** Ayurveda Thraimasiki. Vol. 1 No. 1 (Jan. 1981)-. Periodical. English (Hindi and Sanskrit). qt. $10.00. **NLM** W1; JO547S.

BG/1015-0870
**JOURNAL OF BANGLADESH COLLEGE OF PHYSICIANS & SURGEONS.** [J. Bangladesh Coll. Phys. Surg.]. **Added/Corp** Bamaladesa Kalaja aba Phijisiyanasa anda Sarjanasa. **VFOAT** Journal of Bangladesh College of Physicians and Surgeons; Journal of BCPS. Vol. 1, No. 1 (Aug. 1983)-. Periodical. English. sa. Journal Committee, Mohakhali 1212, Dacca, Bangladesh. **NLM** W1; JO552.
**Ind/Abst** EMBASE [Select. Cov.].

US/0160-7715
**JOURNAL OF BEHAVIORAL MEDICINE.**
**See** Psychology.

US/0094-2499
**JOURNAL OF BIOCOMMUNICATION, THE.** [J. biocommun.]. **Added/Corp** Association of Medical Illustrators. Health Sciences Communications Association. Vol. 1 (June 1974)-. Periodical. English. qt. $40.00 (one year), $77.00 (two year), $114.00 (three year) US and Canada; $43.00 (one year), $83.00 (two year), $123.00 (three year) all other (surface delivery); $54.00 (one year), $105.00 (two year), $156.00 (three year) Europe and North America (air mail); $58.00 (one year), $113.00 (two year), $168.00 (three year) other (air mail). Journal of Biocommunication, 1 wedgewood Drive, Suite 28, c/o Easter Bisiness Service, Jewet City CT 06351. **Tel** (203)376-8150, FAX (203)376-6621. **LC** R118; .J68. **DD** 610/.7/8. **NLM** W1 JO563I. **Acid Free.** available on microfilm and microfiche from University Microfilms International (UMI).
**Desc:** Dedicated to serving as a showcase of biocommunication techniques; describing proven and experimental procedures in medical art and illustration, instructional design, information retrieval, and other communication modalities applied in the health sciences; encouraging the sharing of biocommunication materials; promoting acceptance so that articles and information may influence the course of the profession and contributions may receive appropriate recognition.
**Ind/Abst** Cumul. Index Nurs. Allied Health Lit.; Curr. Index J. Educ.; Energy Res. Abstr. (Aug. 1982-); Index Med.; Middle East Abstr. Index.

US/0021-9304
**JOURNAL OF BIOMEDICAL MATERIALS RESEARCH.** [J. biomed. materi. res.]. **Added/Corp** Society for Biomaterials. European Society for Biomaterials. Nihon Baiomateriaru Gakkai. Vol. 1, Mar. (1967)-. Periodical. English. mo. $1,236.00 (US); $1,356.00 (Canada & Mexico); $1,401.00 (other);. John Wiley & Sons, Inc., 605 Third Avenue, New York NY 10158-0012. **Tel** (212)850-6000, (212)850-6645, FAX (212)850-6088, telex 12-7063. **(Subscription address:** John Wiley & Sons / England, Baffins Lane, Chichester, West Sussex PO19 1UD England.) **ED** A. Norman Cranin. **LC** R856; .J6. **DD** 610/.28. **NLM** W1 JO564P. **CODEN** JBMRBG. **[CCC]. Ad Acc. Circ:** 1,600. available on microfilm and microfiche from University Microfilms International (UMI). Documents available from Article Express International, The Genuine Article, BIOSIS Document Express, CASDDS.
**Desc:** Published in two sections, the journal offers a monthly research publication. Part A, the monthly, features topics ranging from alloys, polymers and ceramics to surgery, dentistry and implanted devices. The new Applied Biomaterials section covers product and engineering, pioneering surgical techniques and details on government regulations.
**Ind/Abst** BioBusiness; Bioeng. Abstr.; Biol. Abstr.; Calcium Calcif. Tissue Abstr.; Ceram. Abstr.; Chem. Abstr.; Curr. Biotechnol.; Curr. Contents Life Sci.; Curr. Titl. Dent.; Ei Page One; EMBASE; Energy Res. Abstr.; Eng. Index Annu.; Health Devices Alerts; Index Med.; INIS Atomindex [Micro.]; Int. Aerosp. Abstr.; Life Sci. Collect.; Ref. Upd. Deluxe Ed.; Res. Alert [Full Cov.]; Sci. Cit. Index; SCISEARCH.

●SZ/1021-7770
**JOURNAL OF BIOMEDICAL SCIENCE.** **Added/Corp** Kuo Chia ko Hsueh Wei Yuan Hui. (1994)-. Periodical. English. Four times a year. $247.00. S. Karger AG, Allschwilerstrasse 10, PO Box - Postfach - Case Postale, CH-4009 Basel Switzerland. **Tel** 011 41 61 306-1111, FAX 011 41 61 306-1234, telex CH 962 652. **ED** C.C. Chang. **NLM** W1; JO564TK.
**Desc:** Devoted to the promotion of basic medical science and its significance for human welfare. Encourages interdisciplinary dialogue between basic and clinical sciences, as well as advances in the fundamental and molecular aspects of medicine. Emphasis is also given to basic studies on the pathogenesis and treatment of diseases.

●US
**JOURNAL OF BRAIN IMAGING AND BEHAVIOR.** (1994)-. Periodical. English. Four times a year. $150.00 institutions, $50.00 individuals US; $175.00 institutions, $59.00 individuals other. Plenum Press, 233 Spring Street, New York NY 10013-1578. **Tel** (212)620-8000, (800)221-9369, FAX (212)463-0742, (212)807-1047, telex 23/421139.

UK/0951-5038
**JOURNAL OF BRITISH MUSIC THERAPY.** **See** Music.

US/0273-8481
**JOURNAL OF BURN CARE & REHABILITATION, THE.** [J. burn care rehabil.]. **Added/Corp** American Burn Association. American Association of Tissue Banks. Skin Council. **VFOAT** Journal of Burn Care and Rehabilitation. Vol. 1, No. 1 (Sept./Oct. 1980)-. Academic Scholarly Publication. English. bm (6 issues). $92.00 (institutions), $57.00 (individuals) US; $104.00 (institutions), $69.00 (individuals) other. Mosby Year Book Inc., 11830 Westline Industrial Drive, St Louis MO 63146. **Tel** (800)325-4177, (314)872-8370, FAX (314)432-1380, telex 44-2402. **ED** Charles R. Baxter and William W. Monafo. **DD** 617. **NLM** W1 JO57R. **CODEN** JBCRD2. **[CCC].** Index available. **Bk Rev. Ad Acc. Pr Rev. Circ:** 6,000 (ctrl). available on microfilm and microfiche from University Microfilms International (UMI). Documents available from BIOSIS Document Express, CASDDS.
**Desc:** Provides information about care of burn patients from emergency treatment through rehabilitation. Articles of report findings of researchers, clinicians and other burn specialists.
**Ind/Abst** Biol. Abstr.; Chem. Abstr.; Cumul. Index Nurs. Allied Health Lit.; EMBASE; Index Med. (1987-); Int. Nurs. Index (1986-).

IT/1120-009X
**JOURNAL OF CHEMOTHERAPY (FLORENCE).** (JOURNAL OF CHEMOTHERAPY.). [J. chemother.]. **Added/Corp** Mediterranean Society of Chemotherapy. Mediterranean Society of Therapy. Vol. 1, No. 1 (Feb. 1989)-. Periodical. English (Italian). Six times a year. L100000 Italy; $100.00 other. Scrit Srl, Via Galliano 135, 50144 Florence Italy. **Tel** 011 39 55 331766, FAX 011 39 55 331641. **ED** Mary Forrest. **NLM** W1; JO5826. **CODEN** JCHEEU. **[CCC].** Index available. **Pr Rev. Circ:** 500. Documents available from The Genuine Article, BIOSIS Document Express, CASDDS. ***Continues*** *Chemioterapia, 0392-906X.*
**Desc:** Publishes articles on oncological, immunomodulating and antimicrobial chemotherapy.
**Ind/Abst** Biol. Abstr.; Chem. Abstr.; Curr. Contents Clin. Med.; EMBASE; Helminthol. Abstr. (1991-); Index Med. (1989-); Res. Alert [Select. Cov.]; Rev. Med. Vet. Entomol.; Rev. Med. Vet. Mycology; SCISEARCH.

UK/0143-8042
**JOURNAL OF CHINESE MEDICINE, THE.** [J. Chin. med.]. No. 1 (Summer 1979)-. Periodical. English. Three times a year. £18.00 UK; £20.00 (airmail) Europe; £22.00 (airmail) other; £19.00 (surface mail) all countries. Journal of Chinese Medicine, 22 Cromwell Road, Hove Sussex BN3 3EB England. **Tel** FAX 0273 748588. **ED** Peter Deadman. **NLM** W1 JO583J. Index available. cum. index. **Bk Rev. Ad Acc. Circ:** 2,000.
**Desc:** Covers the theory and practice of traditional Chinese medicine with emphasis on acupuncture.

US/0744-9984
**JOURNAL OF CHIROPRACTIC.** [J. chiropr.]. **Added/Corp** American Chiropractic Association. Vol. 19, No. 1 (Jan. 1982)-. Periodical. English. Twelve times a year. $80.00. American Chiropractic Association, 1701 Clarendon Boulevard, Arlington VA 22209. **Tel** (703)276-8800. **ED** Harry Weiner. **NLM** W1 JO5842. Index available. **Bk Rev. Ad Acc. Circ:** 23,000 (ctrl). available on microfilm and microfiche from University Microfilms International (UMI). ***Continues*** *ACA Journal of Chiropractic, 0044-7609.*
**Desc:** Journal carrying professional papers, association activities, letters, editorials, book reviews, and various news items of interest to the chiropractic profession.
**Ind/Abst** Health Period. Database.

UK/0141-3317
**JOURNAL OF CHRONIC DISEASES AND THERAPEUTICS RESEARCH.** [J. chronic dis. ther. res.]. V. 1- 1977-. Periodical. English. qt. International Society for the Prevention of Stress, 9 Suffold Drive, Laidon Essex SS15 6PL England. **NLM** W1 JO585T.

US/1046-7890
**JOURNAL OF CLINICAL ETHICS, THE.** **See** Ethics.

US/0021-9738
**JOURNAL OF CLINICAL INVESTIGATION, THE.** [J. clin. invest.]. **Added/Corp** American Society for Clinical Investigation. Vol. 1 (Oct. 1924)-. Academic Scholarly Publication. English. Twelve times a year. $380.00 Europe; $285.00 other. Rockefeller University Press, 222 East 70th Street, New York NY 10021. **Tel** (212)327-8572, FAX (212)327-7944. **(Subscription address:** Rockefeller University Press, Box 5108 GPO, New York NY 10087-5108.) **ED** Bruce E. Scharshmidt. **LC** R11; .J67. **DD** 616/.005. **NLM** W1 JO588H. **CODEN** JCINAO. **[CCC].** Index available. cum. index. **Ad Acc. Circ:** 6,420. available on an online database from BRS; available on microfilm and microfiche from University Microfilms International (UMI). Documents available from The Genuine Article, BIOSIS Document Express, CASDDS. ***Continued in part by*** *Clinical Research, 0009-9279.*
**Desc:** Official journal of the Society for Clinical Investigation. Represents a forum for research which links basic science to clinical practice.
**Ind/Abst** Abr. Index Med.; AgBiotech News Inf.; AGRICOLA; Biol. Abstr.; Calcium Calcif. Tissue Abstr.; Chem. Abstr.; Chem. Titles; Chemorecept. Abstr.; CSA Neuro. Abstr.; Curr. Aware. Biol. Sci., CABS; Curr. Contents Life Sci.; Dairy Sci. Abstr.; EMBASE; Energy Res. Abstr.; Food Sci. Technol. Abstr.; Genet. Abstr.; Health Period. Database; Helminthol. Abstr. (19??-19??); Hum. Genome Abstr.; Immunol. Abstr.; Index Med.; Index Vet.; INIS Atomindex [Micro.]; Int. Aerosp. Abstr.; Iowa Drug Inf. Serv. (1966-); Microbiol. Abstr. Sect. B; Microbiol. Abstr. Sect. C; Nutr. Abstr. Rev., Ser. B, Live Feeds and Feed.; Nutr. Abstr. Rev., Ser. A, Hum. Exp.; Nutr. Res. Newsl.; Oncog. Growth Factors Abstr.; Life Sci. Collect.; PESTDOC; Physic. Medline Plus; Protozoolog. Abstr.; Ref. Upd. Basic Ed.; Ref. Upd. Clinical Ed.; Ref. Upd. Deluxe Ed.; Res. Alert [Full Cov.]; Rev. Med. Vet. Mycology; Rev. Plant Pathol.; Saf. Health Work; Sci. Cit. Index; SCISEARCH; SportSearch; Stat. Theory Method Abstr. (1959-1963); Vet. Bull.; Trop. Dis. Bull.; Virol. AIDS Abstr.

US
**JOURNAL OF CLINICAL INVESTIGATION. [MICROFICHE], THE.** (19??)-. English. ir. University Microfilms International, 300 North Zeeb Road, Ann Arbor MI 48106-1346. **Tel** (313)761-4700, (800)521-0600 Exts. 2490, 2491, FAX (313)973-1540.

US/0887-8013
**JOURNAL OF CLINICAL LABORATORY ANALYSIS, THE.** [J. clin. lab. anal.]. Vol. 1, No. 1 (1987)-. Periodical. English. Six times a year. $462.00 US; $522.00 Canada and Mexico; $544.50 other. John Wiley & Sons, Inc., 605 Third Avenue, New York NY 10158-0012. **Tel** (212)850-6000, (212)850-6645, FAX (212)850-6088, telex 12-7063. **(Subscription address:** John Wiley & Sons / England, Baffins Lane, Chichester, West Sussex PO19 1UD England.) **ED** Robert M. Nakamura and Ralph A. Reisfeld. **DD** 616. **NLM** W1; JO588J. **CODEN** JCANEM. **[CCC]. Pr Rev.** Documents available from The Genuine Article, BIOSIS Document Express, CASDDS. ***Absorbed*** *Diagnostic and Clinical Immunology, 0895-0458.*
**Desc:** Publishes original articles on newly developing assays, with emphasis on their application in clinical laboratory testing.
**Ind/Abst** Biol. Abstr. (1987-); Chem. Abstr.; CSA Neuro. Abstr. (?-?); Curr. Contents Life Sci.; EMBASE; Food Sci. Technol. Abstr.; Helminthol. Abstr. (1991-); Immunol. Abstr.; Index Med.; Oncog. Growth Factors Abstr.; Protozoolog. Abstr.; Ref. Upd. Deluxe Ed.; Res. Alert [Full Cov.]; Rev. Med. Vet. Mycology; Sci. Cit. Index; SCISEARCH; Virol. AIDS Abstr.

US
**JOURNAL OF CLINICAL LABORATORY ASSAY.** (19??)-. Periodical. English. Four times a year. $65.00. Field & Wood Inc., 4156 Manayunk Avenue, Philadelphia PA 19128. **Tel** (215)828-4010. **(Subscription address:** Field & Wood, PO Box 975, Blue Bell PA 19422.) **UDC** 61.

US/0748-1977
**JOURNAL OF CLINICAL MONITORING.** [J. clin. monit.]. Vol. 1, No. 1 (Jan. 1985)-. Periodical. English. bm. $253.00 (institutions), $150.00 (individuals) US; $274.00 (institutions), $174.00 (individuals) Canada; $323.00 (institutions), $213.00 (individuals) other. Little Brown & Company, 34 Beacon Street, Boston MA 02108. **Tel** (617)227-0730, (800)759-0190. **(Subscription address:** Little Brown and Company, PO Box 7671, Riverton NJ 08077-7671.) **DD** 616. **NLM** W1; JO5893ME. **CODEN** JCMOEH. **[CCC]. Pr Rev.** available on microfilm from University Microfilms International (UMI). Documents available from Article Express International, The Genuine Article.
**Ind/Abst** Curr. Contents Clin. Med.; Ei Page One; EMBASE; Eng. Index Annu.; Health Devices Alerts; Index Med. (1985-); Res. Alert [Full Cov.]; SCISEARCH.

AT/0967-5868
**JOURNAL OF CLINICAL NEUROSCIENCE.** (19??)-. Periodical. English. Four times a year. £135.00 (Institutions); £85.00 (Individual). Churchill Livingstone, 1-3 Baxter's Place, Leith Walk, Edinburgh EH1 3AF Scotland. **Tel** 011 44 31 556 2424, FAX 011 44 31 558 1278, telex 727511. **(Subscription address:** Maruzen Company Ltd., PO Box 5050, Import & Export Department, Tokyo 100 31 Japan.)

●US/1068-9583
**JOURNAL OF CLINICAL PSYCHOLOGY IN MEDICAL SETTINGS.** **See** Psychology.

●US/1076-1608
**JOURNAL OF CLINICAL RHEUMATOLOGY.** English. bm. $74.00 (individual), $114.00 (institution), US; $99.00 (individual), $139.00 (institution). Williams & Wilkins Company, 428 East Preston Street, Baltimore MD 21202-3993. **Tel** (410)528-4000, (800)638-6423, FAX (410)528-8596, telex 87669. **(Subscription address:** Williams & Wilkins, PO Box 64380, Baltimore MD 21264.) Documents available from Quick Copies.

CN/0894-1912
**JOURNAL OF CONTINUING EDUCATION IN THE HEALTH PROFESSIONS, THE.** [J. contin. educ. health prof.]. **Added/Corp** Alliance for Continuing Medical Education. Society of Medical College Directors of Continuing Medical Education. **VFOAT** JCEHP. Vol. 8, No. 1 (1988)-. Periodical. English. qt. $38.00 (individuals), $68.00 (institutions) US & Canada; $58.00 (individuals), $88.00 (institutions) other. Decker Periodicals Publishing Inc, PO Box 620, Station A, Hamilton Ontario L8N 3K7 Canada. **Tel** (416)522-7017, (800) 568-7281, FAX (416)522-7839. **ED** James Mullins. **LC** R845; .M6. **DD** 610/.7/15. **NLM** W1; JO595YW. **CODEN** JCHPET. **[CCC].** Index available. **Bk Rev**, (Qty: 12). **Pr Rev. Circ:** 2,500. available on microfilm and microfiche from University Microfilms International (UMI). ***Continues*** *Mobius, 0272-3425.*
**Desc:** Devoted to the theory and practice of continuing education in all health professions. Covers a wide range of subjects that affect the lifelong professional commitment, competence, and performance of the health professionals.
**Ind/Abst** Cumul. Index Nurs. Allied Health Lit.; Curr. Index J. Educ.

CN/0712-9912
**JOURNAL OF CONTINUING MEDICAL EDUCATION.** (JOURNAL OF CONTINUING MEDICAL EDUCATION / UNIVERSITY OF WESTERN ONTARIO.). [J. contin. med. educ.]. Vol. 1, No. 1 (Sept. 1981)-. Periodical. English. sa. Free. University of Western Ontario Department of Continuing Medical Education, London Ontario N6A 5C1 Canada. **DD** 610/.5.

US/0883-9441
**JOURNAL OF CRITICAL CARE.** [J. crit. care]. Vol. 1, No. 1 (Mar. 1986)-. Periodical. English. qt. $99.00 (individual), $151.00 (institution) US $167.00 (individual), $183.00 (institution) other. W.B. Saunders Company, A Subsidiary of Harcourt Brace Jovanovich, Inc., The Curtis Center/Suite 300, Independence Square West, Philadelphia PA 19106-3399. **Tel** (215)238-7800 or, 5587, FAX (215)238-7883, telex 173146.

**(Subscription address:** W. B. Saunders Company / North America Subscriptions, c/o Periodicals, 6277 Sea Harbour Drive, 4th Floor, Orlando FL 32887.**)** **ED** David R. Dantzker. **DD** 616. **NLM** W1; JO612BG. **CODEN** JCCAER. **[CCC].** **Pr Rev.** Documents available from The Genuine Article, BIOSIS Document Express, CASDDS.
**Desc:** Presents basic and clinical research, pertinent reviews, ethical and legal controversies, and important abstracts in the area of critical care. Contains articles encompassing all specialties and subspecialties of critical care.
**Ind/Abst** Biol. Abstr.; Chem. Abstr.; Curr. Contents Clin. Med.; EMBASE; Health Devices Alerts; Mod. Med.; Res. Alert [Select. Cov.]; SCISEARCH.

US/1040-0257
**JOURNAL OF CRITICAL ILLNESS, THE.** [J. crit. illn.]. Vol. 1, No. 1 (Jan. 1986)-. Periodical. English. mo. $70.00 US; $90.00 other. Cliggott Publishing Company, 55 Holly Hill Lane, Box 4010, Greenwich CT 06830. **Tel** (203)661-0600, (212)993-0440. **ED** Ellen M Rosen. **DD** 616. **NLM** W1; 612BJ. **[CCC].** Index available. **Bk Rev.** **Ad Acc.** ctrl circ. available on microfilm.
**Desc:** Presents practical and authoritative information on the diagnosis and management of clinical problems in critically ill patients. It includes original review articles, instructions on specific procedures, etc.

US/8756-4793
**JOURNAL OF DIAGNOSTIC MEDICAL SONOGRAPHY.** **Added/Corp** Society of Diagnostic Medical Sonographers (U.S.). **VFOAT** JDMS. Vol. 1, No. 1 (Jan./Feb. 1985)-. Periodical. English. bm. $75.00 (individuals), $110.00 (institutions) US; $99.00 (individuals), $130.00 (institutions) other. J.B. Lippincott Company, 227 East Washington Square, Philadelphia PA 19106-3780. **Tel** (215)238-4200 or 4454, FAX (215)238-4227. **(Subscription address:** J.B. Lippincott, PO Box 350, Hagerstown MD 21740.**)** **DD** 616. **NLM** W1; JO621F. **[CCC].** **Pr Rev.** available on microfilm and microfiche from University Microfilms International (UMI). Documents available from The Genuine Article.
**Ind/Abst** Acoust. Abstr.; EMBASE; Res. Alert [Select. Cov.]; SCISEARCH.

UK/0307-5095
**JOURNAL OF ELECTROPHYSIOLOGICAL TECHNOLOGY.** [J. electrophysiol. technol.]. **Added/Corp** Electrophysiological Technologists' Association. Association Pour la Promotion des Techniques Eelectrophysiologiques. Fachvereinigung der Elektrophysiologischen Assistenten. Vol. 1 (March 1975)-. Academic Scholarly Publication. English (English, French and German). Four times a year (Mar., June, Sept., Dec.). £25.00 surface mail. EPTA, C/O Mrs. L. O'Neill, EEG Department, Leicester Royal, 1NF Leicester LE1 SWW England. **ED** C. Green and R. Pottinger. **NLM** W1 JO633H. cum. index. **Bk Rev.** **Ad Acc, Adv Mgr:** B. Bragg. **Circ:** 700.
**Desc:** Articles of interest to clinical electrophysiologists and technicians.
**Ind/Abst** EMBASE.

UK/0968-0519
**JOURNAL OF ENDOTOXIN RESEARCH.** (19??)-. Periodical. English. £299.00 Europe; £302.00 Other (Institutions). Churchill Livingstone, 1-3 Baxter's Place, Leith Walk, Edinburgh EH1 3AF Scotland. **Tel** 011 44 31 556 2424, FAX 011 44 31 558 1278, telex 727511. **(Subscription address:** Maruzen Company Ltd., PO Box 5050, Import & Export Department, Tokyo 100 31 Japan.**)**

US/0094-730X
**JOURNAL OF FLUENCY DISORDERS.** [J. fluen. disord.]. **Added/Corp** Research Foundation for Communication Disorders. Vol. 1 (July 1974)-. Academic Scholarly Publication. English. Four times a year (1 volume). $254.00 US; $284.00 other. Elsevier Science Publishing Company Inc, Madison Square Station, PO Box 882, New York NY 10159-0882. **Tel** (212)633-3950, FAX (212)633-3990. **ED** Anthony A Zenner and P Helbert Damste. **LC** RC423.A1; J66. **DD** 616.8/55/005. **NLM** WI J065M. **CODEN** JFDID8. **[CCC].** **Ad Acc.** **Pr Rev.** available on microfilm and microfiche from University Microfilms International (UMI). Documents available from The Genuine Article, BIOSIS Document Express.
**Desc:** Provides coverage of clinical and theoretical aspects of stuttering, including the latest remediation techniques.
**Ind/Abst** Biol. Abstr.; Curr. Contents Soc. Behav. Sci.; EMBASE; Linguist. Lang. Behav. Abstr. (1978-) [Full Cov.]; Psychol. Abstr. (1981-); PsycINFO (1990-); PsycLit; Res. Alert [Full Cov.]; Soc. Plann. Policy Dev. Abstr.; Soc. Sci. Cit. Index [Full Cov.]; Sociol. Abstr.; Spec. Educ. Needs Abstr.

BE/0770-9471
**JOURNAL OF HEAD & NECK PATHOLOGY.** ***Ceased.*** [J. head neck pathol.]. **VFOAT** Journal of Head and Neck Pathology. (1982)-Vol. 11 No. 5 (June 1993). Periodical. Dutch (English and French). bm. Centre Tete et Cou Hoofd en Hals Centrum, Av du Duc Jean 71-73, 1080 Bruxelles Belgium. **Tel** (02)424 12 12, FAX (02)425 70 76. **ED** De Lathouwer. **NLM** W1; JO669RR. **Bk Rev.** **Ad Acc.** **Circ:** 10,000 (ctrl). ***Continues*** *Postgraduate Journal for Mouth, Head and Neck Pathology.*
**Desc:** Aim is to elucidate all aspects of current knowledge concerning head and neck pathology; plans to stimulate the mutual interest of all disciplines involved, directly or indirectly.
**Ind/Abst** Curr. Titl. Dent.

US/0890-6874
**JOURNAL OF HEALTH OCCUPATIONS EDUCATION.** [J. health occup. educ.]. **Added/Corp** American Vocational Association. Health Occupations Education Division. Vol. 1, No. 1 (Spring 1986)-. Periodical. English. Twice a year (May, Nov.). $20.00 division members, $25.00 others. Journal of Health Occupations Education, NC State University, Box 7801, Raleigh NC 27695. **Tel** (919)515-2234, FAX (919)515-7634. **ED** Norma Walters (editor's address: 235 George C Wallace, Auburn University, Auburn, AL 36849), Beverly Richards (editor's address: Penn State University, 105 Rackley Building, University Park, PA 16802). **LC** R847.A1; J68. **DD** 610/.7/1. **NLM** W1; JO67BIK. Index available. **Bk Rev.** **Pr Rev.**
**Desc:** Developed to facilitate communication among members of the profession on current methods of research and findings in the field, on current program trends and issues in health care, and on media resources which have an impact on health occupations education.

US/0361-6878
**JOURNAL OF HEALTH POLITICS, POLICY AND LAW.** **See** Law.

US/0898-2740
**JOURNAL OF HEALTHCARE EDUCATION AND TRAINING.** [J. healthc. educ. train.]. **Added/Corp** American Society for Healthcare Education and Training. American Hospital Association. Vol. 1, No. 1 (Summer 1986)-. Periodical. English. tq. Comes with American Society of Healthcare Education & Training membership. American Hospital Association, 840 North Lake Shore Drive, Chicago IL 60611. **Tel** (312)280-6000, (800)242-2626. **DD** 610. **NLM** W1; JO67BN.
**Desc:** American Society for Healthcare Education and Training. This journal publishes reports of new developments, innovations, research and trends in the field of health care, education and training.
**Ind/Abst** Hospit. Health Admin. Index (1986-).

US/0884-1225
**JOURNAL OF HYPERBARIC MEDICINE.** ***Title Change.*** (JOURNAL OF HYPERBARIC MEDICINE : JOURNAL OF THE UNDERSEA MEDICAL SOCIETY, INC.). [J. hyperb. med.]. **Added/Corp** Undersea Medical Society. Undersea and Hyperbaric Medical Society. Vol. 1, No. 1 (Winter 1986)-(19??). Periodical. English. qt. Undersea and Hyperbaric Medical Society, 10531 Metropolitan Avenue, Kensington MD 20895. **Tel** (301)942-2980. **ED** Enrico Camporesi. **DD** 615. **NLM** W1; JO674P. **Bk Rev.** **Ad Acc.** **Pr Rev.** **Circ:** 1,800 (ctrl). ***Continues*** *Hyperbaric Oxygen Review, 0195-9263.* ***Merged with*** *Undersea Biomedical Research, 0093-5387;* ***Absorbed by*** *Undersea & Hyperbaric Medicine, 1066-2936.*
**Desc:** Original research and clinical applications in the field of hyperbaric medicine.

US/0899-8299
**JOURNAL OF IMA, THE.** (THE JOURNAL OF IMA / ISLAMIC MEDICAL ASSOCIATION OF NORTH AMERICA.). [J. IMA]. **Added/Corp** Islamic Medical Association of North America. **VFOAT** JIMA. (19??)-. Periodical. English. Four times a year (Jan., April, July, Oct.). $50.00 US; $60.00 other. Islamic Medical Association, 4121 South Fairview Avenue, Suite 203, Downers Grove IL 60515. **Tel** (708)852-2122, FAX (708)969-9237. **ED** H. E. Fadel (editor's address: 818 St. Sebastian Way, Suite 200, Augusta, GA 30901). **DD** 616. **NLM** W1; JO676B. **Ad Acc.** **Circ:** 2,000.

●US/1068-7777
**JOURNAL OF INFECTIOUS DISEASE PHARMACOTHERAPY.** **See** Pharmacy and Pharmacology.

US/0885-0666
**JOURNAL OF INTENSIVE CARE MEDICINE.** [J. intensive care med.]. Vol. 1, No. 1 (Jan./Feb. 1986)-. Academic Scholarly Publication. English. bm. $135.00 (institution), $110.00 (individual) US; $165.00°(institution), $120.00 (individual) other. Blackwell Scientific Publishers, 238 Main Street, Cambridge MA 02142. **Tel** (617)547-7110, (800)835-6770, FAX (617)547-0789. **DD** 616. **NLM** W1; JO716D. **[CCC].** available on microfilm and microfiche from University Microfilms International (UMI).
**Ind/Abst** EMBASE.

US/0363-2768
**JOURNAL OF INTER-AMERICAN MEDICINE, THE.** V. 1- Mar. 1976-. Periodical. English (Spanish; summaries and/or abstracts in Spanish and English). qt. American Hospital of Miami, 11750 Bird Road, Miami FL 33175. **NLM** W1 JO716E.

UK/0300-0605
**JOURNAL OF INTERNATIONAL MEDICAL RESEARCH, THE.** [J. int. med. res.]. Vol. 1 (1972)-. Academic Scholarly Publication. English (summaries and/or abstracts in French, German and Spanish). bm. $110.00. Cambridge Medical Publications Ltd, Wicker House High Street, Worthing West Sussex, BN11 1DJ England. **Tel** 011 44 903 205884, FAX 011 44 903 34862, telex 878372 PPSLTI. **ED** Malcolm Lauer, Robert J. Kasprowicz. **NLM** W1 JO718K. **CODEN** JIMRBV. **[CCC].** **Ad Acc.** **Pr Rev.** **Circ:** 4,000. available on microfilm from University Microfilms International (UMI). Documents available from The Genuine Article, BIOSIS Document Express, CASDDS.
**Desc:** Medical research predominantly in comparative drug evaluation.
**Ind/Abst** Biol. Abstr.; Chem. Abstr.; CSA Neuro. Abstr. (?-?); Curr. Contents Clin. Med.; Curr. Contents Life Sci.; EMBASE; Health Saf. Sci. Abstr.; Highw. Res. Abstr.; Index Med.; Nutr. Abstr. Rev., Ser. B, Live Feeds and Feed.; Nutr. Abstr. Rev., Ser. A, Hum. Exp.; Nutr. Res. Newsl.; Life Sci. Collect.; PESTDOC; Pollut. Abstr. Indexes; Protozoolog. Abstr.; Res. Alert [Full Cov.]; Rev. Med. Vet. Mycology; Rev. Plant Pathol.; Sci. Cit. Index; SportSearch; Trop. Dis. Bull.

US/0161-7702
**JOURNAL OF INTERNATIONAL PHYSICIANS.** V. 1- 1976-. Periodical. English. bm. $30.00. Pacifica Ventures, 1030 North Kings Highway, Cherry Hill NJ 08034. **NLM** W1 JO719.

US/0194-1658
**JOURNAL OF INTRAVENOUS THERAPY (LOS ANGELES).** (JOURNAL OF INTRAVENOUS THERAPY.). **Added/Corp** I.V. Therapy Association of the U.S.A. **VFOAT** Journal of I.V. Therapy. (Jan./Feb. 1977)-. Periodical. English. bm. $24.00 US; $28.00 Canada; $38.00 other. Journal of Intravenous Therapy, Box 67159, Century City, Los Angeles CA 90067. **Tel** (310)475-5141. **ED** William J Kurdi. **NLM** W1; JO721. **Bk Rev.** **Ad Acc.** **Circ:** 3,000 (ctrl). ***Absorbed*** *Western States IV Therapy Journal, 0363-4302.*
**Desc:** Covers all aspects of intravenous therapy.

●US
**JOURNAL OF INVESTIGATIVE MEDICINE.** (Dec. 1994)-. Periodical. English. bm. $90.00 (members); $95.00 (nom-members). Slack Inc., 6900 Grove Road, Thorofare NJ 08086. **Tel** (609)848-1000, (800)257-8290, FAX (609)853-5991, telex 517108 SLACK INC VD. ***Continues*** *Clinical Research, 0009-9279.*

KO/1011-8934
**JOURNAL OF KOREAN MEDICAL SCIENCE.** [J. Korean med. sci.]. **Added/Corp** Taehan Uihak Hyophoe. Punkwa Hakhoe Hyobuihoe. Vol. 1, No. 1 (1986)-. Periodical. English. Four times a year. Korean Medical Association, 302 75 Dong du Ichon Dong, Yongsan ku 140 031 Seoul, Korea. **Tel** 011 2 822 7983807. **NLM** W1; JO733I. **CODEN** JKMSEH. Documents available from BIOSIS Document Express, CASDDS.
**Ind/Abst** Biol. Abstr.; Chem. Abstr.; Health Plan. Adminis.

US/0022-2143
**JOURNAL OF LABORATORY AND CLINICAL MEDICINE, THE.** [J. lab. clin. med.]. **Added/Corp** Central Society for Clinical Research (U.S.). Vol. 1 (Oct. 1915)-. Academic Scholarly Publication. English. mo. $215.00 (institutions), $107.00 (individuals) US; $236.00 (institutions), $128.00 (individuals) other. Mosby Year Book Inc., 11830 Westline Industrial Drive, St Louis MO 63146. **Tel** (800)325-4177, (314)872-8370, FAX (314)432-1380, telex 44-2402. **ED** Thomas M. Daniel. **LC** R11; .J695. **NLM** W1 JO734. **CODEN** JLCMAK. **[CCC].** Index available. **Ad Acc.** **Pr Rev.** **Circ:** 4,262. available on microfilm and microfiche from University Microfilms International (UMI). Documents available from The Genuine Article, BIOSIS Document Express, CASDDS, ADONIS.
**Desc:** Presents articles of interest to physicians, academic clinical scientists, and laboratory consultants with an interest in clinical investigation and research.
**Ind/Abst** Abr. Index Med.; ADONIS; Biol. Abstr.; Calcium Calcif. Tissue Abstr.; Chem. Abstr.; CSA Neuro. Abstr. (?-?); Curr. Aware. Biol. Sci., CABS; Curr. Contents Life Sci.; Dairy Sci. Abstr.; EMBASE; Energy Res. Abstr.; Health Period. Database; Helminthol. Abstr.; Immunol. Abstr.; Index Med.; INIS Atomindex [Micro.]; Iowa Drug Inf. Serv. (1966-); Nutr. Abstr. Rev., Ser. B, Live Feeds and Feed.; Nutr. Abstr. Rev., Ser. A, Hum. Exp.; Life Sci. Collect.; PESTDOC; Physic. Medline Plus; Protozoolog. Abstr.; Ref. Upd. Basic Ed.; Ref. Upd. Deluxe Ed.; Res. Alert [Full Cov.]; Rev. Med. Vet. Mycology; Rev. Plant Pathol.; Saf. Health Work; Sci. Cit. Index; SCISEARCH; Soc. Sci. Cit. Index [Select. Cov.]; SportSearch; Trop. Dis. Bull.

●US/1073-1105
**JOURNAL OF LAW, MEDICINE & ETHICS, THE.** **See** Law.

US/1050-6934
**JOURNAL OF LONG-TERM EFFECTS OF MEDICAL IMPLANTS.** (LONG-TERM EFFECTS OF MEDICAL IMPLANTS.). [J. long-term eff. med. implants]. **VFOAT** Long Term Effects of Medical Implants. Vol. 1, Issue 1 (1991)-. Academic Scholarly Publication. English. Four times a year. $84.00 (individual), $210.00 (institution). Begell House Inc., PO Box 1109, Pearl River NY 10965. **Tel** (212)725-1999. **ED** Stephen D Bruck. **DD** 617. **CODEN** JLEIEM. **[CCC]. Pr Rev.** Documents available from The Genuine Article, CASDDS.
**Desc:** This journal aims towards better understanding of the mechanisms of failure of pre-clinically tested medical implants during long-term in vivo service life both in appropriate animal models and in humans, and establishing an effective linkage between pre-clinical and clinical studies.
**Ind/Abst** Chem. Abstr.; Curr. Contents Clin. Med.; Curr. Contents Life Sci.; Res. Alert [Full Cov.]; Sci. Cit. Index.

UK/0268-9235
**JOURNAL OF MANAGEMENT IN MEDICINE.** [J. manage. med.]. Vol. 1, No. 1 (1987)-. Periodical. English. bm. $589.00. MCB University Press, 60 62 Toller Lane, Bradford West Yorkshire BD8 9BX England. **Tel** 011 44 274 499821, FAX 011 44 274 547143, telex 51317 MCBUNI G. **(Subscription address:** MCB University Press / US and Canada Subscriptions, PO Box 10812, Birmingham AL 35201-0812.**) ED** Frada Eskin. **NLM** W1; JO748DK. **Bk Rev.** Documents available from UMI Article Clearinghouse.
**Desc:** A leading journal devoted to the publication of original papers addressing issues of health care management. Under the guidance of its eminent International Editorial Board, the journal provides a valuable forum for the management issues related to medical care, offering contributions from both academic and professional fields.
**Ind/Abst** ABI/INFORM Glob. Ed.

GW/0935-6339
**JOURNAL OF MANUAL MEDICINE.** ***Ceased.*** Vol. 4, No. 1 (1989)-Vol. 6, No. 6 (1992). Periodical. English. Six times a year. Springer-Verlag GmbH & Company KG, Heidelberger Platz 3, D 14197 Berlin Germany. **Tel** 011 49 30 8207223, FAX 011 49 30 8214091, telex 183 319 SPBLN D. **(Subscription address:** Springer Verlag New York Inc. / for North America, 44 Hartz Way, Secaucus NJ 07096.**) ED** J Dvorak, H Baumgartner, and W Gilliar. **NLM** W1; JO748FG. **[CCC].** ***Continues*** *Manual Medicine, 0254-9522.*
**Desc:** Fulfills the long-standing need for an exchange of information among practitoners of manual medicine all over the world. Reflecting the growing importance in the field of manual medicine, articles exclusively in English (under the auspices of Federation Internationale de Medicine Manuelle) are published.
**Ind/Abst** EMBASE.

MY/0126-7752
**JOURNAL OF MEDICAL AND HEALTH LABORATORY TECHNOLOGY, MALAYSIA.** **Added/Corp** Institute of Medical & Health Laboratory Technology, Malaysia. (1974)-. English. an. $3.00. Institute of Medical and Health, Laboratory of Technology, Institute of Medical Research, Jalan Pahang Kuala Lumpur Malaysia. **NLM** W1 JO749NV.

CC/1000-9094
**JOURNAL OF MEDICAL COLLEGES OF PLA.** [J. Med. Coll. PLA]. **Added/Corp** China. Chung-Kuo Jen Min Chieh Fang Chun. **VAT** Journal of Medical Colleges of People's Liberation Army. Vol. 1, No. 1 (March 1986)-. Academic Scholarly Publication. English. qt. $70.50. China National Publishing Import & Export Corporation, 16 Gongti E Rd., Chaoyang Dist., Beijing 100704, People's Republic of China. **Tel** 011 8601 50630169, 5066688, FAX 011 8601 5063101, 5063010, telex 22313. **(Subscription address:** PO Box 88, Beijing 100704 China**) ED** Wu Zhongli. **NLM** W1; JO749T. **CODEN** JMCPE6. **Ad Acc.** Documents available from CASDDS.
**Ind/Abst** Chem. Abstr. (1986-); CSA Neuro. Abstr. (?-?); Trop. Dis. Bull.

US/1056-2478
**JOURNAL OF MEDICAL EDUCATION TECHNOLOGIES.** [J. med. educ. technol.]. Vol. 1, No. 1 (Summer 1990)-. Periodical. English. qt. $40.00 (North America), $55.00 (includes postage) other (members of Society for Applied Learning Technology); $60.00 (North America), $75.00 (includes postage) other (non-members). Society for Applied Learning Technology Institute, 50 Culpeper Street, Warrenton VA 22186. **Tel** (703)347-0055, FAX (703)349-3169. **DD** 610. **[CCC].**

UK/0306-6800
**JOURNAL OF MEDICAL ETHICS.** [J. med. ethics]. **Added/Corp** Society for the Study of Medical Ethics (Great Britain). Vol. 1, April (1975)-. Academic Scholarly Publication. English. qt. £100.00 other. BMJ / British Medical Journal Publishing Group, British Medical Association House, Tavistock Square, London WC1H 9JR England. **Tel** 011 44 71 3874499, FAX 011 44 71 383 6402, telex 290034 HBJ MN. **ED** Raanan Gillon. **NLM** W1 JO75I. **CODEN** JMETDR. **Pr Rev.** available on microfilm and microfiche from University Microfilms International (UMI). Documents available from The Genuine Article, BIOSIS Document Express, UMI Article Clearinghouse.
**Desc:** A leading international journal in the field of medical ethics. It publishes interdisciplinary articles on the ethical aspects of health care.
**Ind/Abst** Acad. Search (July 1993-); Biol. Abstr.; Cumul. Index Nurs. Allied Health Lit.; Curr. Contents Clin. Med.; Curr. Contents Soc. Behav. Sci.; EMBASE; Expand. Acad. Index (1989-); Gen. Sci. Source (Jul. 1993-); Index Med.; INFO-SOUTH Abstr.; Mag. Search; Newsp. Period. Abstr. (1991-); Life Sci. Collect.; Res. Alert [Full Cov.]; Sci. Cit. Index; SCISEARCH; Soc. Sci. Source (Jul. 1993-); Soc. Sci. Cit. Index [Full Cov.]; Soc. Sci. Index Fulltext (Sept. 1988-) [Full Txt.].

US/1041-3545
**JOURNAL OF MEDICAL HUMANITIES, THE.** [J. med. humanit.]. Vol. 10, No. 1 (Spring/Summer 1989)-. Periodical. English. qt. $170.00 US; $200.00 other. Human Sciences Press, PO Box 735, 233 Spring Street, New York NY 10013. **Tel** (212)620-8000, FAX (212)807-1047, telex 23421139. **(Subscription address:** Eurospan Ltd., Journals and Serials Division, 3 Henrietta Street, Covent Garden, London WC2E 8LU England.**) ED** Charles Perakis. **LC** R724; .B483. **DD** 174/.2/05. **NLM** W1; JO75NJ. **[CCC].** available on microfilm and microfiche from University Microfilms International (UMI). Documents available from BIOSIS Document Express. ***Continues*** *Journal of Medical Humanities and Bioethics, 0882-6498.*
**Desc:** Continues to feature original papers that explore the relationships between medicine and the humanities. Highlighting the connections between medicine and art, ethics, history, literature, music, philosophy, religion, psychiatry/behavioral sciences, and jurisprudence. The journal aims to further the understanding of the art of medicine from a humanistic perspective. Prominent specialists in their respective fields contribute articles that are responsive to the concerns of both the scholar and clinician.
**Ind/Abst** Biol. Abstr. (1989-); Health Plan. Adminis.; Hospit. Health Admin. Index (1989-); Philos. Index (1989-); Soc. Plann. Policy Dev. Abstr.

UK
**JOURNAL OF MEDICAL SCREENING.** (19??)-. English. £92.00. BMJ / British Medical Journal Publishing Group, British Medical Association House, Tavistock Square, London WC1H 9JR England. **Tel** 011 44 71 3874499, FAX 011 44 71 383 6402, telex 290034 HBJ MN.

NE/0360-5310
**JOURNAL OF MEDICINE AND PHILOSOPHY, THE.** [J. med. philos.]. **Added/Corp** Society for Health and Human Values. Vol. 1 (March 1976)-. Periodical. English. bm. $394.00. Kluwer Academic Publishers, Postbus 322, 3300 AH Dordrecht, The Netherlands. **Tel** 011 (31) 78 524400, FAX 011 31 78 183273, telex 20083. **ED** H Tristram Engelhardt Jr. **LC** R723; .J66. **DD** 610/.1. **NLM** W1 JO758G. **CODEN** JMPHDCJOMPDZ. **[CCC]. Bk Rev. Ad Acc. Pr Rev. Circ:** 2,000. available on microfilm and microfiche from University Microfilms International (UMI). Documents available from The Genuine Article, UMI Article Clearinghouse.
**Desc:** Explores the shared themes and concerns of philosophy and the medical sciences.
**Ind/Abst** Acad. Search (July 1993-); Crim. Penol. Police Sci. Abstr.; Curr. Contents Soc. Behav. Sci.; Energy Res. Abstr. (Aug. 1982-); Expand. Acad. Index (1989-); Gen. Sci. Source (Jul. 1993-); Guide Soc. Sci. Relig.; Health Plan. Adminis.; Hospit. Health Admin. Index; Humanit. Index; Humanit. Source (Jul. 1993-); Index Med.; Index Period. Artic. Relat. Law; INFO-SOUTH Abstr.; Int. Bibliogr. Sociol.; Int. Nurs. Index; Mag. Search; Newsp. Period. Abstr. (1991-); Philos. Index; Res. Alert [Full Cov.]; Soc. Plann. Policy Dev. Abstr.; Soc. Sci. Cit. Index [Full Cov.]; Sociol. Abstr.

US/0025-7850
**JOURNAL OF MEDICINE (WESTBURY).** (JOURNAL OF MEDICINE; CLINICAL, EXPERIMENTAL AND THEORETICAL.). [J. med.]. Vol. 1 (1970)-. Academic Scholarly Publication. English. Six times a year. $140.00 US; $175.00 other. PJD Publications Ltd., PO Box 966, Westbury NY 11590. **Tel** (516)626-0650, FAX (516)626-5546. **ED** J.L. Ambrus and Siva Sankar. **LC** R11; .J73. **NLM** W1 JO757WC. **CODEN** JNMDBO. **[CCC]. Bk Rev. Ad Acc. Pr Rev.** available on microfilm from University Microfilms International (UMI). Documents available from The Genuine Article, BIOSIS Document Express, CASDDS. ***Continues*** *Medicina Experimentalis.*
**Desc:** Covering all areas of medicine, for universities and medical libraries.
**Ind/Abst** Biol. Abstr.; Chem. Abstr.; Cumul. Index Nurs. Allied Health Lit.; EMBASE; Energy Res. Abstr. (1971-); Index Med.; Leg. Resour. Index (1980-?); PESTDOC; Res. Alert [Select. Cov.]; Saf. Health Work; SCISEARCH; SportSearch.

UK/0265-2048
**JOURNAL OF MICROENCAPSULATION.** See Pharmacy and Pharmacology.

GW/0946-2716
**JOURNAL OF MOLECULAR MEDICINE.** (19??)-. English. Twelve times a year. DM498.00. Springer-Verlag GmbH & Company KG, Heidelberger Platz 3, D 14197 Berlin Germany. **Tel** 011 49 30 8207223, FAX 011 49 30 8214091, telex 183 319 SPBLN D. **(Subscription address:** Springer Verlag New York Inc. / for North America, 44 Hartz Way, Secaucus NJ 07096.**)** ***Continues*** *The Clinical Investigator.*

US/0022-2917
**JOURNAL OF MUSIC THERAPY.** See Music.

US/1047-7837
**JOURNAL OF NATUROPATHIC MEDICINE, THE.** [J. naturopath. med.]. Vol. 1, No. 1 (July 1990)-. Periodical. English. an. $95.00 (institutions), $65.00 (individuals) US; $100.00 (institutions), $75.00 (individuals) other. The Journal Management Group Inc, 10 Morgan Avenue, Norwalk CT 06851. **Tel** (203)866-7664. **DD** 613. **NLM** W1; JO777TD. **Ad Acc. Pr Rev. Acid Free.**
**Desc:** Publishes peer reviewed research in traditional medicine pertinent to the naturopathic physician and other primary caregivers.

●US/1076-2752
**JOURNAL OF OCCUPATIONAL AND ENVIRONMENTAL MEDICINE.** (JOURNAL OF OCCUPATIONAL AND ENVIRONMENTAL MEDICINE. OFFICIAL PUBLICATION OF THE AMERICAN COLLEGE OF OCCUPATIONAL AND ENVIRONMENTAL MEDICINE.). **Added/Corp** American College of Occupational and Environmental Medicine. (1995)-. Periodical. English. mo. $114.00 (individual), $149.00 (institution), US; $195.00 (individual), $194.00 (nstitution). Williams & Wilkins Company, 428 East Preston Street, Baltimore MD 21202-3993. **Tel** (410)528-4000, (800)638-6423, FAX (410)528-8596, telex 87669. **(Subscription address:** Williams & Wilkins, PO Box 64380, Baltimore MD 21264.**)** Documents available from Quick Copies.
**Desc:** Original articles on occupational medical practice, including; epidemiology, toxicology, health screening, ergonomics, assessment, rehabilitation, health education, and administration.

US/0022-3298
**JOURNAL OF ORGONOMY, THE.** Vol. 1 (Nov. 1967)-. Periodical. English. Twice a year (May & Nov.). $40.00 (one year), $70.00 (two years), $95.00 (three years). Orgonomic Publishers, PO Box 1169, Iverness CA 94937. **Tel** (415)669-1551. **ED** Barbara G. Koopman. **LC** RZ460; .J66. **NLM** W1 JO804MK. Index available. cum. index. **Bk Rev. Circ:** 1,000 (ctrl). available on microfilm and microfiche from University Microfilms International (UMI).
**Desc:** Continues the work of Wilhelm Reich with translations, clinical and research papers on psychiatry, medicine, physics, childrearing, and education.

US/0885-3924
**JOURNAL OF PAIN AND SYMPTOM MANAGEMENT.** **Added/Corp** University of Wisconsin--Madison. Dept. of Anesthesiology. Vol. 1, No. 1 (Winter 1986)-. Academic Scholarly Publication. English. Eight times a year (1 volume). $230.00 US; $275.00 other. Elsevier Science Publishing Company Inc, Madison Square Station, PO Box 882, New York NY 10159-0882. **Tel** (212)633-3950, FAX (212)633-3990. **ED** George Heidrich and Russell Portenoy. **LC** RB127; .P76. **DD** 615. **NLM** W1; JO826F. **[CCC]. Bk Rev. Ad Acc. Pr Rev. Circ:** 4,000. available on microfilm and microfiche from University Microfilms International (UMI). Documents available from The Genuine Article. ***Continues*** *PRN Forum, 0743-345X.*
**Desc:** A peer reviewed medical journal publishing clinically relevant research in pain and symptom control.
**Ind/Abst** Abstr. Res. Pastor. Care Couns. (19??-); Annals Behav. Med.; Child Dev. Abstr. Bibliogr.; Cumul. Index Nurs. Allied Health Lit.; Curr. Aware. Biol. Sci., CABS; Curr. Contents Clin. Med.; EMBASE; Index Med. (1994-); Int. Nurs. Index (1986-); Nurs. Abstr.; PESTDOC; Psychol. Abstr. (1986-); PsycINFO; PsycLit; Res. Alert [Select. Cov.]; SCISEARCH; Soc. Plann. Policy Dev. Abstr.; Soc. Sci. Cit. Index [Select. Cov.].

US/0896-6966
**JOURNAL OF PHARMACOEPIDEMIOLOGY.** [J. pharmacoepidemiol.]. Vol. 1, No. 1 (1990)-. Periodical. English. Twice a year. $75.00 US; $105.00 other. The Haworth Press Inc, 10 Alice Street, Binghamton NY 13904-1580. **Tel** (607)722-5857, (800)3-HAWORTH, FAX (607)722-1424. **ED** Jack E. Fincham (editor's address: Samford University, School of Pharmacy, Birmingham, AL 35229). **DD** 615. **NLM** W1; JO829ML. **CODEN** JPHAE7. **Bk Rev. Ad Acc. Pr Rev. Acid Free. Circ:** 204. available on microfilm and microfiche from University Microfilms International (UMI). Documents available from BIOSIS Document Express,

Haworth Document Delivery Service.
**Desc:** The fast-growing field related to the assessment of drug therapy after the distribution and "Post-Marketing" phase utilizing epidemiological research methods. Provides new insights in post-marketing assessment and drug surveillance; benefit-to-risk profiles of existing and newly developed pharmaceutical products; beneficial and adverse reactions to drugs; methodologies to study the outcomes of drug therapy.
**Ind/Abst** Biol. Abstr. (1991-); Biostatistica (199?-199?); Int. Pharm. Abstr.; Soc. Plann. Policy Dev. Abstr.

II/0022-3859
**JOURNAL OF POSTGRADUATE MEDICINE (BOMBAY).** (JOURNAL OF POST GRADUATE MEDICINE.). [J. postgrad. med.]. **Added/Corp** Seth Gordhandas Sunderdas Medical College. K[ing] E[dward] M[emorial] Hospital, Bombay. Vol. 1, (April 1955)-. Periodical. English. Four times a year (Jan., Apr., July, Oct.). $50.00. Journal of Post-Graduate Medicine, Bombay, India. **(Subscription address:** Prints India, 11 Darya Ganj, New Delhi 110002 India.**)** **ED** S. D. Bhandarkar. **NLM** W1 JO838. **CODEN** JPMDA3. Index available. **Bk Rev. Ad Acc. Circ:** 1,000 (ctrl). Documents available from BIOSIS Document Express, CASDDS.
**Desc:** Original articles describing clinical and experimental work and case reports on various subspecialties of modern medicine.
**Ind/Abst** Biol. Abstr.; Chem. Abstr. (1955-1982); Index Med.

US/0731-8332
**JOURNAL OF PRISON & JAIL HEALTH.** ***Ceased.*** **See** Law-Law Enforcement and Criminology.

US/1040-8800
**JOURNAL OF PROSTHETICS AND ORTHOTICS.** (JOURNAL OF PROSTHETICS AND ORTHOTICS : JPO.). [J. prosthet. orthot.]. **Added/Corp** American Academy of Orthotists and Prosthetists. American Orthotic and Prosthetic Association. **VFOAT** JPO. Vol. 1, No. 1 (Oct. 1988)-. Periodical. English. Four times a year (Jan., Apr., July, Oct.). $60.00 US; $80.00 others. American Academy of Prosthetics and Orthotics, 1650 King Street, Suite 500, Alexandria VA 22314. **Tel** (703)836-7116, FAX (708)836-0838. **ED** C. Micheal Schuch, (phone: (703)836-7118). **LC** RD130; .J68. **DD** 617.9/5. **NLM** W1; JO851E. Index available. **Bk Rev,** (Qty: 10-20). **Ad Acc, Adv Mgr:** Amy Coniglio, **Tel** (703)836-7118. **Pr Rev. Circ:** 4,500 (ctrl). available on microfilm and microfiche from University Microfilms International (UMI). Documents available from The Genuine Article. ***Formed by the union of*** *Clinical Prosthetics and Orthotics, 0735-0090* ***and*** *Orthotics and Prosthetics, 0030-5928.*
**Desc:** Provides the latest research and clinical thinking in orthotics and prosthetics, including information on new devices, fitting techniques and patient management experiences.
**Ind/Abst** Res. Alert [Full Cov.]; SCISEARCH; Soc. Sci. Cit. Index [Select. Cov.].

UK/0022-3999
**JOURNAL OF PSYCHOSOMATIC RESEARCH.** [J. psychosom. res.]. Vol. 1 (Feb. 1956)-. Academic Scholarly Publication. English. Eight times a year. $641.00 The Americas; £430.00 other. Pergamon Press, An Imprint of Elsevier Science Ltd., The Boulevard, Langford Lane, Kidlington, Oxford OX5 1GB United Kingdom. **Tel** 011 44 865 843000, 011 44 865 843699, FAX 011 44 865 843010. **(Subscription address:** Elsevier Science Ltd. Oxford Fulfillment Centre, PO Box 800, Kidlington, Oxford OX5 1DX United Kingdom.**)** **ED** Geoffrey Lloyd. **LC** RC52; .J6. **DD** 616.8; 616.08*. **NLM** W1 JO859. **CODEN** JPCRAT. **[CCC]. Pr Rev.** available on microfilm and microfiche from University Microfilms International (UMI). Documents available from The Genuine Article, BIOSIS Document Express, CASDDS.
**Desc:** Papers published in the journal reflect current research in the psychosomatic approach from both an experimental and a clinical viewpoint, and subject its theories to scientific examination.
**Ind/Abst** Annals Behav. Med.; Appl. Soc. Sci. Index Abstr.; Biol. Abstr.; Chem. Abstr.; Curr. Aware. Biol. Sci., CABS; Curr. Contents Clin. Med.; Curr. Contents Soc. Behav. Sci.; Dev. Med. Child Neurol.; EMBASE; High. Educ. Abstr. (1978-); Index Med.; Middle East Abstr. Index; Nutr. Abstr. Rev., Ser. A, Hum. Exp.; Life Sci. Collect.; Psychol. Abstr. (1956-); PsycINFO; PsycLit; Res. Alert [Full Cov.]; Sci. Cit. Index; SCISEARCH; Soc. Plann. Policy Dev. Abstr.; Soc. Sci. Cit. Index [Full Cov.]; Sociol. Abstr.; Women Stud. Abstr.

UK/0957-4832
**JOURNAL OF PUBLIC HEALTH MEDICINE.** [J. public health med.]. **Added/Corp** Royal Colleges of Physicians of the United Kingdom. Faculty of Public Health Medicine. Vol. 12, No. 1 (Feb. 1990)-. Periodical. English. qt. £90.00 UK and Europe; $165.00 other. Oxford University Press, Walton Street, Oxford OX2 6DP England. **Tel** 011 44 865 56767, FAX 011 44 865 267773, telex 837330 OXPRES G. **(Subscription address:** Oxford University Press / USA, Journals Marketing Department, Oxford University Press, 2001 Evans Road, Cary NC 27513.**)** **NLM** W1; JO859QH. **CODEN** JPHME9. **[CCC].** available on microfilm and microfiche from University Microfilms International (UMI). Documents available from The Genuine Article.
***Continues*** *Community Medicine, 0142-2456.*
**Ind/Abst** Appl. Soc. Sci. Index Abstr.; Curr. Contents Clin. Med.; Curr. Contents Soc. Behav. Sci.; EMBASE; Health Plan. Adminis.; Index Med. (1990-); Res. Alert [Full Cov.]; SCISEARCH; Soc. Sci. Cit. Index [Full Cov.]; Trop. Dis. Bull.

●AT
**JOURNAL OF QUALITY IN CLINICAL PRACTICE.** (1994)-. Academic Scholarly Publication. English. qt. 199.00Aus$ Australia; ¥12000 Japan; $120.00 other. Blackwell Scientific Publications Australia, 54 University Street, PO Box 378, Carlton Victoria 3053 Australia. **Tel** 011 61 3 3470300, FAX 011 61 3 3475001, telex 10716421. ***Continues*** *Australian Clinical Review.*

●US/0883-0444
**JOURNAL OF REFRACTIVE AND CORNEAL SURGERY. Added/Corp** International Society of Refractive Keratoplasty. Vol. 10, No. 1 (Jan./Feb. 1994)-. Periodical. English. bm. $120.00 (individual), $136.00 (institution). Slack Inc., 6900 Grove Road, Thorofare NJ 08086. **Tel** (609)848-1000, (800)257-8290, FAX (609)853-5991, telex 517108 SLACK INC VD. **NLM** W1; JO866JM. **CODEN** JRCSEG. ***Continues*** *Refractive & Corneal Surgery, 1042-962X.*
**Ind/Abst** Index Med. (1994-).

US/1068-9591
**JOURNAL OF REHABILITATION AND HEALTH.** ***Title Change.*** (1994)-(1994). Periodical. English. qt. Plenum Press, 233 Spring Street, New York NY 10013-1578. **Tel** (212)620-8000, (800)221-9369, FAX (212)463-0742, (212)807-1047, telex 23/421139. ***Continued by*** *International Journal of Rehabilitation and Health.*

UK/0022-4251
**JOURNAL OF REPRODUCTION & FERTILITY.** (JOURNAL OF REPRODUCTION AND FERTILITY.). [J. reprod. fertil.]. **Added/Corp** Society for the Study of Fertility. International Planned Parenthood Federation. Indian Society for the Study of Reproduction. Society for the Study of Fertility. Proceedings. **VFOAT** Journal of Reproduction & Fertility. Vol. 1 (Feb. 1960)-(19??). Academic Scholarly Publication. English. Six times a year. $420.00 US; £220.00 UK. The Journal of Reproduction & Fertility Ltd., 22 Newmarket Rd., Cambridge CB5 8DT England. **Tel** 011 44 0223 351809, FAX 011 44 0223 359754. **(Subscription address:** Portland Press Ltd., Commerce Way, Whitehall Industrial Estate, Colchester CO2 8HP England.**)** **ED** Barbara Weir. **LC** QP251; .J75. **NLM** W1 JO868K. **CODEN** JRPFA4. **[CCC].** Index available. cum. index. **Bk Rev. Ad Acc. Pr Rev. Circ:** 2,200 (ctrl). available with charts; available with illustrations. Documents available from The Genuine Article, BIOSIS Document Express, CASDDS. ***Supersedes*** *Studies on Fertility, 0562-4142.* ***Continued in part by*** *Journal of Reproduction & Fertility. Abstract Series, 0954-0725.*
**Desc:** Covers reproductive morphology, physiology, biochemistry and pathology in man and other animals. Also veterinary problems of fertility and lactation.
**Ind/Abst** Abstr. Anthropol.; AgBiotech News Inf.; AGRICOLA [Select. Cov.]; Anim. Breed. Abstr.; Biol. Agric. Index; Biol. Abstr.; Chem. Abstr.; Curr. Aware. Biol. Sci., CABS; Curr. Biotechnol.; Dairy Sci. Abstr.; EMBASE; Fish Rev.; Index Med.; Key Word Index Wildl. Res.; NAPRALERT; Nutr. Abstr. Rev., Ser. B, Live Feeds and Feed.; Life Sci. Collect.; PESTDOC; Pig News Inf.; Poult. Abstr.; Ref. Upd. Basic Ed.; Ref. Upd. Deluxe Ed.; Res. Alert [Full Cov.]; Sci. Cit. Index; SCISEARCH; Stat. Theory Method Abstr. (1986); Wildl. Rev.

UK/0449-3087
**JOURNAL OF REPRODUCTION AND FERTILITY. SUPPLEMENT.** [J. reprod. fert. Suppl.]. **Added/Corp** Society for the Study of Fertility. (1966)-. Academic Scholarly Publication. English. bm. The Journal of Reproduction & Fertility Ltd., 22 Newmarket Rd., Cambridge CB5 8DT England. **Tel** 011 44 0223 351809, FAX 011 44 0223 359754. **(Subscription address:** Portland Press Ltd., Commerce Way, Whitehall Industrial Estate, Colchester CO2 8HP England.**)** **NLM** W1 JO868KA. **CODEN** JRFSAR. **[CCC].** Documents available from BIOSIS Document Express, CASDDS.
**Ind/Abst** AGRICOLA [Select. Cov.]; Biol. Abstr.; Chem. Abstr.; Index Med.

II
**JOURNAL OF RESEARCH AND EDUCATION IN INDIAN MEDICINE, THE.** Vol. 1 (Jan./Mar. 1982)-. Periodical. English. qt. $75.00. Journal of Research & Education in Indian Medicine, Varanasi, India. **(Subscription address:** Prints India, 11 Darya Ganj, New Delhi 110002 India.**)** **NLM** W1; JO868T.

●UK
**JOURNAL OF SEROTONIN RESEARCH.** (1994)-. English. qt. $170.00 (institution), $120.00 (individual) US; £95.00 (institution), £65.00 (individual) other. Royal Society of Medicine Press, 1 Wimpole Street, London W1M 8AE England. **Tel** 011 44 71 2902928.

●UK/0962-1105
**JOURNAL OF SLEEP RESEARCH. Added/Corp** European Sleep Research Society. **VFOAT** JSR. Vol. 1, No. 1 (Mar. 1992)-. Academic Scholarly Publication. English. Four times a year. $163.00 US & Canada; £96.00 Europe; £105.50 other. Blackwell Scientific Publications Ltd, Marston Book Services, PO Box 87, Oxford OX2 ODT UK. **Tel** 011 44 865 791155, FAX 011 44 865 791927, telex 837 515 MARDIS G. **LC** QP425; .J62. **DD** 612.8/21. **NLM** W1; JO877FR. **CODEN** JSRSEU.
**Ind/Abst** Curr. Aware. Biol. Sci., CABS; Soc. Sci. Cit. Index [Select. Cov.].

US/1058-1588
**JOURNAL OF SPINE RESEARCH.** ***Ceased.*** (1993)-(Nov. 1993). Periodical. English. qt. Allen Press Inc., 810 East 10th Street, PO Box 1897, Lawrence KS 66044-8897. **Tel** (913)843-1221, (800)627-0629, FAX (913)843-1274. **Ad Acc. Acid Free.**
**Desc:** Aims to advance all research related to understanding the anatomy, physiology, biomechanics, and function of the back and spine in health and disease. The purpose of the journal is to provide a forum for the presentation of systematic, well-designed, scientific research in the fields of orthopedics, rheumatology, and neurosurgery related to back and spine.

US/0711-7075
**JOURNAL OF SYSTEMIC THERAPIES.** (1993)-. English. Four times a year. $55.00 (institutions); $70.00 others. Guilford Publications Inc., 72 Spring Street, New York NY 10012. **Tel** (212)431-9800, (800)365-7006, FAX (212)966-6708. **ED** Donald Efron. ***Continues*** *Journal of Strategic Therapies.*

●UK
**JOURNAL OF TELEMEDICINE AND TELECARE.** Vol.1 (1995)-. English. qt. $172.00 (institution), $128.00 (individual) US; £98.00 (institution), £72.00 (individual) other. Royal Society of Medicine Press, 1 Wimpole Street, London W1M 8AE England. **Tel** 011 44 71 2902928.

US/0893-7400
**JOURNAL OF THE AMERICAN ACADEMY OF PHYSICIAN ASSISTANTS.** [J. Am. Acad. Physician Assist.]. **Added/Corp** American Academy of Physician Assistants. Vol. 1, No. 1 (Jan./Feb. 1988)-. Periodical. English. Ten times a year. $42.00 (individuals), $62.00 (institutions). Medical Economics Publishing, Five Paragon Drive, Second Floor, Montvale NJ 07645. **Tel** (800)432-4570, (201)358-2210. **ED** Leslie A. Kole and Nancy J. Johnson. **DD** 610. **NLM** W1; JO907XD. **[CCC].** Index available. **Bk Rev. Ad Acc. Pr Rev.** available on microfilm and microfiche from University Microfilms International (UMI).
**Desc:** Provides clinical information and news to the practicing physician assistant and surgical assistant. Features original contributions, clinical review articles, and legislative, academic, ethical, and health policy reports. Original articles focus on the causes, diagnosis, and treatment of medical and and surgical conditions seen by physician assistants.
**Ind/Abst** Cumul. Index Nurs. Allied Health Lit.

US/0002-7243
**JOURNAL OF THE AMERICAN ANALGESIA SOCIETY.** ***Title Change.*** [J. Am. Analg. Soc.]. **Main/Corp** American Analgesia Society. **VFOAT** Journal - American Analgesia Society. (1963)-(199?). Academic Scholarly Publication. English. sa. Arthur A Weiner DMD, 1110 North Main Street, Randolph MA 02368. **Tel** (617)963-0250. **ED** Arthur A Weiner. **DD** 615. **NLM** W1 JO222TK. **CODEN** JAASBK. cum. index. **Bk Rev. Ad Acc. Circ:** 750 (ctrl). Documents available from CASDDS. ***Merged into*** *Anesthesia Progress, 0003-3006.*
**Desc:** Articles, abstracts and books that deal with Nitrous Oxide-Oxygen Relative analgesia in dentistry and with behavior modification and management of the apprehensive patient.
**Ind/Abst** Chem. Abstr.

AG/0325-9226
**JOURNAL OF THE AMERICAN MEDICAL ASSOCIATION EN ARGENTINA.** [J. Am. Med. Assoc. Argent.]. **Added/Corp** American Medical Association. **VFOAT** Revista de la Asociacion Medica Americana en Argentina. Vol. 1 (March 1979)-. Periodical. Spanish. mo.

●US/1067-5027
**JOURNAL OF THE AMERICAN MEDICAL INFORMATICS ASSOCIATION.** [J. Am. Med. Inform. Assoc.]. **Added/Corp** American Medical Informatics Association. **VFOAT** A.JAMIA. (1994)-. Periodical. English. bm. $98.00 (individual), $175.00 (institution) US; $108.00 (individual), $185.00 (institution) Other. Hanley & Belfus Inc., 210 South 13th Street, Philadelphia PA 19107. **Tel** (215)546-7293, FAX (215)790-9330. **DD** 610. **NLM** W1; JO909NI. **[CCC].**

US/0098-8421
**JOURNAL OF THE AMERICAN MEDICAL WOMEN'S ASSOCIATION (1972).** (JOURNAL OF THE AMERICAN MEDICAL WOMEN'S ASSOCIATION.). [J. Am. Med. Women's Assoc.]. **Main/Corp** American Medical Women's Association. **VFOAT** JAMWA. Vol. 27, No. 3 (March 1972)-. Academic Scholarly Publication. English. Six times a year (Jan., Mar., May, July, Sept., Nov.). $50.00. American Medical Women's Association, 801 North Fairfax Street, Suite 400, Alexandria VA 22314. **Tel** (703)838-0500, FAX (703)549-3864. **ED** Wendy Chavkin MD. MPH (phone: (212)387-3864). **LC** R15; .A7413. **DD** 610/.5. **NLM** W1 JO909S. **[CCC].** Index available (Bound in Nov. iss.). **Bk Rev. Ad Acc. Pr Rev. Circ:** 13,000. available on microfilm and microfiche from University Microfilms International (UMI). ***Continues*** *Woman Physician, 0002-7103.*
**Desc:** Reports on sex bias in medical education, maternity rights and benefits. The status of women physicians, and dual-doctor families. Includes scholarly articles on such women's health issues as fetal alcohol syndrome, the pain of dysmenorrhea, and conservative treatment for breast cancer. Commentary on the political scene, news of women in medicine, discussion of student issues, and much more.
**Ind/Abst** Energy Res. Abstr. (Aug. 1982-); Index Med.; Multicult. Educ. Abstr.; Life Sci. Collect.; Stud. Women Abstr.; Women Stud. Abstr.

US/0098-6151
**JOURNAL OF THE AMERICAN OSTEOPATHIC ASSOCIATION, THE.** [J. Am. Osteopath. Assoc.]. **VFOAT** JAOA; Journal AOA. Vol. 1, No. 1 (Sept. 1901)-. Academic Scholarly Publication. English. mo. $50.00 US; $90.00 other. American Osteopathic Association, 142 East Ontario Street, Chicago IL 60611-2864. **Tel** (312)280-5800. **ED** George W. Northup. **LC** RZ301. **DD** 615. **NLM** W1 J222F. **CODEN** JAOAAZ. **Bk Rev. Ad Acc. Circ:** 30,500 (ctrl). available on microfilm and microfiche from University Microfilms International (UMI). Documents available from BIOSIS Document Express, CASDDS. ***Continues*** *Journal of the American Osteopathic Association, 0003-0287.*
**Desc:** The official scientific publication of the American Osteopathic Association. It documents osteopathic contributions in all scientific and clinical medical fields.
**Ind/Abst** Biol. Abstr.; Chem. Abstr.; Cumul. Index Nurs. Allied Health Lit.; EMBASE; Energy Res. Abstr.; Health Period. Database; Index Med.; INIS Atomindex [Micro.]; Nutr. Abstr. Rev., Ser. B, Live Feeds and Feed.; Nutr. Abstr. Rev., Ser. A, Hum. Exp.; Life Sci. Collect.; Protozoolog. Abstr.; Rev. Med. Vet. Mycology; Risk Abstr.; Saf. Health Work; SCISEARCH; SportSearch.

US/0195-2307
**JOURNAL OF THE AMERICAN PARAPLEGIA SOCIETY.** [J. Am. Parapleg. Soc.]. **Added/Corp** American Paraplegia Society. Vol. 1, No. 1 (April 1978)-. Periodical. English. qt. Free to members. American Paraplegia Society, 75 20 Astoria Boulevard, Jackson Heights NY 11370. **Tel** (718)803-3782. **NLM** W1 JO91D.
**Ind/Abst** Index Med.

US/0004-1858
**JOURNAL OF THE ARKANSAS MEDICAL SOCIETY, THE.** [J. Ark. Med. Soc.]. Vol. 3- June 1906-. Periodical. English. mo. $22.00. Arkansas Medical Society, PO Box 5776, Little Rock AR 72215. **Tel** (501)224-8967, FAX (501)224-6489. **ED** Stephanie Percefull. **NLM** W1 JO911W. **CODEN** JAMSAB. Index available. cum. index. **Ad Acc, Adv Mgr:** Editor. **Pr Rev. Circ:** 3,400 (ctrl). Documents available from CASDDS. ***Continues*** *Monthly Bulletin of the Arkansas Medical Society.*
**Desc:** Scientific articles and socio-economic news items pertaining to the medical profession.
**Ind/Abst** Chem. Abstr.; Energy Res. Abstr.; Index Med.; INIS Atomindex [Micro.]; Nutr. Abstr. Rev., Ser. B, Live Feeds and Feed.; Nutr. Abstr. Rev., Ser. A, Hum. Exp.; Life Sci. Collect.; SportSearch.

BA/1015-6321
**JOURNAL OF THE BAHRAIN MEDICAL SOCIETY.** **VFOAT** Magallet Gamiyyat al-Atibb al-Bahrayniyyat. (1989)-. English. Bahrain Medical Society, PO Box 26136, Manama, Bahrain. **Tel** (973)742666.
**Ind/Abst** EMBASE [Select. Cov.].

II
**JOURNAL OF THE CHRISTIAN MEDICAL ASSOCIATION OF INDIA.** **Main/Corp** Christian Medical Association of India. V. 1- 1926-. Periodical. English. qt. $8.00. Hindustan Book Agency, 17 UB Jawahar Nagar, Delhi 7 India. ***Continues*** *Medical Missions in India.*

●US/1057-3321
**JOURNAL OF THE CHRONIC FATIGUE SYNDROMES.** **VFOAT** Journal of Chronic Fatigue Syndromes. (Apr. 1995)-. Periodical. English. qt. $75.00 US; $105.00 other. The Haworth Press Inc, 10 Alice Street, Binghamton NY 13904-1580. **Tel** (607)722-5857, (800)3-HAWORTH, FAX (607)722-1424. **Acid Free.** Documents available from Haworth Document Delivery Service.
**Desc:** Presents cutting-edge research, debate, discussion and clinical data relating to CFIDS.

UA/0013-2411
**JOURNAL OF THE EGYPTIAN MEDICAL ASSOCIATION.** (THE JOURNAL OF THE EGYPTIAN MEDICAL ASSOCIATION.). [J. Egypt. Med. Assoc.]. **Added/Corp** Jamiyah Al-Tibbiyah Al-Misriyah. Vol. 36, No. 5/6 (1953)-. Periodical. English (Arabic and French; summaries and/or abstracts in Arabic). mo. **NLM** W1 JO92E. Documents available from CASDDS. ***Continues*** *Journal of the Royal Egyptian Medical Association.*
**Ind/Abst** Chem. Abstr.; Life Sci. Collect.; Trop. Dis. Bull.

IQ/0041-9419
**JOURNAL OF THE FACULTY OF MEDICINE, BAGHDAD.** (JOURNAL.). **Main/Corp** Bagdad. Jami'at Baghdad. Faculty of Medicine. Vol. 13 (Jan. 1949)-Vol. 21 (1957); New Ser., Vol. 1 (Jan. 1959)-. Periodical. Arabic (English). qt. **DD** 610. **CODEN** JFAQAE. Documents available from CASDDS. ***Continues*** *Bagdad. Royal College of Medicine of Iraq. Journal.*
**Ind/Abst** Chem. Abstr.; Trop. Dis. Bull.

US/0015-4148
**JOURNAL OF THE FLORIDA MEDICAL ASSOCIATION (1974).** (THE JOURNAL OF THE FLORIDA MEDICAL ASSOCIATION.). [J. Fla. Med. Assoc.]. **Added/Corp** Florida Medical Association. Vol. 61 (Jan. 1974)-. Academic Scholarly Publication. English. mo. $31.80 (one year), $63.60 (two years), $95.40 (three years) Florida; $30.00 (one year), $60.00 (two years), $90.00 (three years) other. Florida Medical Association Inc, PO Box 2411, ATTN: Directory, Jacksonville FL 32203. **Tel** (904)356-1571, FAX (904)353-1247. **ED** Jacques R. Caldwell M.D. **NLM** W1 JO922M. **CODEN** JFMAAQ. Index available (published in Dec. issue). cum. index (published in Dec. issue). **Bk Rev**, (Qty: 6-10 per year). **Ad Acc, Adv Mgr:** Joy Freiha. **Pr Rev. Circ:** 17,000. available on microfilm and microfiche from University Microfilms International (UMI). Documents available from CASDDS. ***Continues*** *J.F.M.C., Journal of the Florida Medical Association, 0091-6757.*
**Desc:** Peer reviewed medical journal with scientific articles as well as medical-legal, medical economics, editorials and other nonscientific features.
**Ind/Abst** Chem. Abstr.; Cumul. Index Nurs. Allied Health Lit.; EMBASE [Select. Cov.]; Energy Res. Abstr. (Jan. 1974-); Index Med.; INIS Atomindex [Micro.]; Nutr. Abstr. Rev., Ser. B, Live Feeds and Feed.; Nutr. Abstr. Rev., Ser. A, Hum. Exp.; Life Sci. Collect.; Protozoolog. Abstr.

HK/0929-6646
**JOURNAL OF THE FORMOSAN MEDICAL ASSOCIATION / TAI-WAN I CHIH.** **Added/Corp** Tai-Wan I Hsueh Hui. **VFOAT** Tai-Wan I Chih. Vol. 90, No. 1 (Jan. 1991)-. Periodical. English. Twelve times a year. $60.00 China; $70.00 others. Formosan Medical Association, 1 Chang Te Street, Taipei 10016 Taiwan. **Tel** 886 2 3810367. **NLM** W1; JO922QH. **CODEN** JFASEO. ***Continues*** *Tai-Wan I Hsueh Hui Tsa Chih, 0371-7682.*
**Ind/Abst** EMBASE [Select. Cov.]; Helminthol. Abstr. (1991-); Index Med. (1991-); NAPRALERT; Rev. Med. Vet. Mycology; Trop. Dis. Bull.

US/0022-5045
**JOURNAL OF THE HISTORY OF MEDICINE AND ALLIED SCIENCES.** [J. hist. med. allied sci.]. **Added/Corp** Yale University. Dept. of the History of Science and Medicine. Yale University. Dept. of the History of Medicine. Vol. 1 (Jan. 1946)-. Periodical. English. Four times a year. $45.00 (individuals), $65.00 (institutions) US; $55.00 (individuals), $75.00 (institutions) others. Journal History of Medicine Allied Sciences, PO Box 487, Canton MA 02021. **Tel** (617)828-8450. **ED** Robert J. T. Joy. **LC** R131.A1; J6. **DD** 610.9. **NLM** W1 JO928Q. **CODEN** JHMAA6. Index available. cum. index. **Bk Rev. Ad Acc. Pr Rev. Circ:** 1,500 (ctrl). available on microfilm and microfiche from University Microfilms International (UMI). Documents available from The Genuine Article, BIOSIS Document Express, CASDDS.
**Desc:** Broad coverage of medicine and allied sciences from an historical perspective throughout the ages and the world.
**Ind/Abst** Am. Hist. Life (1954-); Annu. Bibliogr. Engl. Lang. Lit.; Arts Humanit. Citation Index [Select. Cov.]; Biol. Abstr.; Chem. Abstr.; Curr. Contents Clin. Med.; Energy Res. Abstr. (Aug. 1982-); Index Med.; Middle East Abstr. Index; Life Sci. Collect.; Res. Alert [Full Cov.]; Sci. Cit. Index; SCISEARCH; Soc. Sci. Cit. Index [Select. Cov.].

HK/1010-8424
**JOURNAL OF THE HONG KONG MEDICAL ASSOCIATION.** [J. Hong Kong Med. Assoc.]. **Added/Corp** Hong Kong Medical Association. **VFOAT** Hsiang-Kang i Hsueh Hui i Kan. Vol. 37, No. 1 (March 1985)-. Periodical. English. qt. $20.00. Hong Kong Medical Association, GPO Box 1957, 15 Hennesy Road, Hong Kong. **Tel** 5-278891. **NLM** W1; JO928Z. **CODEN** JHKAEY. Documents available from BIOSIS Document Express. ***Continues*** *Bulletin-Journal of the Hong Kong Medical Association.*
**Ind/Abst** Biol. Abstr. (1986-); EMBASE [Select. Cov.].

II/0019-5847
**JOURNAL OF THE INDIAN MEDICAL ASSOCIATION.** [J. Indian Med. Assoc.]. Vol. 1 (Sept. 1931)-. Academic Scholarly Publication. English. mo. $60.00. Journal of the Indian Medical Association, 53 Creek Row, Calcutta 700 014 India. **(Subscription address:** Prints India, 11 Darya Ganj, New Delhi 110002 India.**)** **NLM** W1 JO931. **CODEN** JIMAAD. available on microfilm from University Microfilms International (UMI). Documents available from BIOSIS Document Express, CASDDS. ***Supersedes*** *Indian Medical World.*
**Ind/Abst** Biol. Abstr.; Chem. Abstr. (1931-1980); EMBASE [Select. Cov.]; Helminthol. Abstr.; Index Med.; NAPRALERT; Life Sci. Collect.; Protozoolog. Abstr.; Rev. Med. Vet. Entomol.; Rev. Med. Vet. Mycology; Rev. Plant Pathol.; SportSearch; Trop. Dis. Bull.

II/0022-507X
**JOURNAL OF THE INDIAN MEDICAL PROFESSION.** **VFOAT** JIMP Annual. V. 1- 1954-. Periodical. English. mo. United Asia Publishers, 12 Rampart Row, Bombay 1 India.

UK
**JOURNAL OF THE INSTITUTE OF HEALTH RECORD INFORMATION & MANAGEMENT.** (19??)-. English. Four times a year. £24.00. IHRIM Publications, 93 Moss Bank, Winsford Cheshire CW7 2EW England. **Tel** 011 44 94874573. ***Continues*** *AMRO.*

NP
**JOURNAL OF THE INSTITUTE OF MEDICINE.** **Added/Corp** Institute of Medicine (Kathmandu, Nepal). Vol. 1, No. 1 (Feb. 1979)-. Periodical. English (Nepali). Twice a year. $10.00. Institute of Medicine, PO Box 2533, Maharajgunj, Kathmandu, Nepal. **NLM** W1 JO931MM.
**Ind/Abst** EMBASE [Select. Cov.].

●US/1060-3085
**JOURNAL OF THE INTERAMERICAN MEDICAL AND HEALTH ASSOCIATION.** **Added/Corp** Interamerican Medical and Health Association. **VFOAT** JIMHA. (1992)-. Academic Scholarly Publication. English. Three times a year. $60.00 (institution) North America, Europe and Japan. Interamerican Medical and Health Association, 3025 St. James Drive, Boca Raton FL 33434. **Tel** (407)483-6573. **NLM** W1; JO931UE.

IE/0374-8405
**JOURNAL OF THE IRISH COLLEGES OF PHYSICIANS AND SURGEONS.** [J. Ir. Coll. Physicians Surg.]. **Main/Corp** Irish Colleges of Physicians and Surgeons. Vol. 1 (July 1971)-. Academic Scholarly Publication. English. qt. 57.00p Ireland/UK; 63.00p other EEC; 69.00p (surface), 75.00p (air) other. Mercer Library, Lower Mercer Street, Dublin 2 Ireland. **Tel** 011 351 1 4780674, FAX 011 353 4780934. **ED** Austin Leahy. **NLM** W1 JO932E. **CODEN** IPSJB7. **[CCC].** Index available. **Bk Rev. Ad Acc. Pr Rev. Circ:** 4,000. Documents available from BIOSIS Document Express. ***Supersedes*** *Journal of the Royal College of Surgeons in Ireland, 0035-8827.*
**Desc:** Reviews and original research papers on the practice, ethics, and science of medicine and all of its specialities. Regular editorial contributions featuring topical and controversial issues in medicine. Articles on medical history and philosophy, especially if they have an Irish perspective and letters from readers.
**Ind/Abst** Biol. Abstr.; EMBASE [Select. Cov.].

US/0023-0294
**JOURNAL OF THE KENTUCKY MEDICAL ASSOCIATION, THE.** [J. Ky. Med. Assoc.]. **Main/Corp** Kentucky Medical Association. Vol. 62, No. 11 (Nov. 1964)-. Academic Scholarly Publication. English. Twelve times a year. $25.00. Kentucky Medical Association, 301 North Hurstbourne Parkway, Suite 200, Louisville KY 10222. **Tel** (502)456-6200, FAX (502)426-6877. **ED** A. Evan Overstreet M. D. **DD** 616. **NLM** W1 JO934KN. **CODEN** JKMAB5. Index available (Bound in next issue, in December for $3.00). cum. index. **Bk Rev. Ad Acc, Adv Mgr:** Sue Tharp, **Tel** (502)426-6200. **Circ:** 5,500 (ctrl). available on microfilm from University Microfilms International (UMI). Documents available from BIOSIS Document Express, CASDDS. ***Continues*** *Journal of the Kentucky State Medical Association.*
**Desc:** Scientific articles, membership news, socioeconomic articles, and CME courses.
**Ind/Abst** Biol. Abstr.; Chem. Abstr.; Cumul. Index Nurs. Allied Health Lit.; EMBASE [Select. Cov.]; Energy Res. Abstr. (April 1978-); Index Med.; Protozoolog. Abstr.; Rev. Med. Vet. Mycology; Rev. Plant Pathol.; SportSearch.

KU/0023-5776
**JOURNAL OF THE KUWAIT MEDICAL ASSOCIATION, THE.** [Magalla al-Gamiyya at-tibiyya al-Kuwaitiyya]. **VFOAT** Magalla Al-Gamiyya At-Tibiyya Al-Kuwaitiyya. Vol. 1 (March 1967)-. Periodical. English. qt. 2.00KD. Kuwait Medical

Association, PO Box 1202, Editorial Section, Safat Kuwait. **Tel** 011 965 5333278, FAX 011 965 5333276. **ED** Abdulla A Al-Rashred, Mohammed Aref, Majeed Alwan, Nicholas Miller, Ahmed Teebi, David Wright. **NLM** W1 JO934T. **CODEN** KMAJAJ. **Ad Acc. Pr Rev. Circ:** 4,000. Documents available from CASDDS.
**Ind/Abst** Chem. Abstr.; EMBASE; Protozoolog. Abstr.; Rev. Med. Vet. Mycology; Rev. Plant Pathol.; Trop. Dis. Bull.

US/0024-6921
**JOURNAL OF THE LOUISIANA STATE MEDICAL SOCIETY, THE.** [J. La. State Med. Soc.]. **Added/Corp** Louisiana State Medical Society. Vol. 105, No. 1 (Jan. 1953)-. Academic Scholarly Publication. English. mo. $18.00 US; $21.00 other. Louisiana State Medical Society, 3501 North Causeway Boulevard, Suite 800, Metairie LA 70002. **Tel** (504)832-9815, FAX (504)833-7685. **ED** Conway Magee. **DD** 610. **NLM** W1; JO22P. **CODEN** JLSMAW. Index available in last issue of volume--attached. **Bk Rev**, (Qty: 1-2/yr). **Ad Acc, Adv Mgr:** Ann Goocer. **Pr Rev. Circ:** 6400 (ctrl). available on microfilm and microfiche from University Microfilms International (UMI). Documents available from BIOSIS Document Express, CASDDS. ***Continues*** *New Orleans Medical and Surgical Journal New Orleans, La. : 1873), 0097-1790.*
**Desc:** Includes scientific manuscripts, editorial column, book reviews, medical student section, calendar, new members, auxiliary report, and EKG of the month.
**Ind/Abst** Biol. Abstr.; Chem. Abstr.; Energy Res. Abstr.; Hospit. Health Admin. Index; Index Med.; Life Sci. Collect.; Saf. Health Work; SportSearch.

US/0025-7028
**JOURNAL OF THE MEDICAL ASSOCIATION OF GEORGIA.** [J. Med. Assoc. Georgia]. **Main/Corp** Medical Association of Georgia. Vol. 1 (1911)-. Periodical. English. mo. $40.00 North America; $100.00 other. Medical Assn of Georgia, 938 Peachtree St. NE, Atlanta GA 30309. **Tel** (404)876-7535, FAX (404)874-5641. **ED** Charles R Underwood. **LC** R15; .G53. **DD** 610.62758. **NLM** W1 JO939H. Index available (bound in Dec. issue). cum. index. **Bk Rev. Ad Acc. Pr Rev. Circ:** 7,000 (ctrl). available on microfilm from University Microfilms International (UMI).
**Desc:** Contains political and social economic articles related to medicine.
**Ind/Abst** Cumul. Index Nurs. Allied Health Lit.; Energy Res. Abstr. (Sept. 1975-); Hospit. Health Admin. Index; Index Med.; Life Sci. Collect.; SportSearch.

TH/0025-7036
**JOURNAL OF THE MEDICAL ASSOCIATION OF THAILAND.** [J. Med. Assoc. Thail.]. **Added/Corp** Phaetaya Samakorn haeng Prathet Thai. (1941)-. Academic Scholarly Publication. English (summaries and/or abstracts in Thai). mo. $40.00 (surface mail), $50.00 (airmail). Medical Association Thailand, 67 9 Soi Soonvichai New Pech, Buri Road Bangkok 10 Thailand. **Tel** 4113111, 4110263. **NLM** W1 JO939P. **CODEN** JMTHBU. Documents available from BIOSIS Document Express, CASDDS. ***Continues*** *Medical Journal of the Medical Association of Thailand.*
**Ind/Abst** Biol. Abstr.; Chem. Abstr.; EMBASE [Select. Cov.]; Helminthol. Abstr.; Index Med.; Nutr. Abstr. Rev., Ser. A, Hum. Exp.; Protozoolog. Abstr.; Rev. Med. Vet. Mycology; Rev. Plant Pathol.; SEA Abstr.; Trop. Dis. Bull.

US/0026-6396
**JOURNAL OF THE MISSISSIPPI STATE MEDICAL ASSOCIATION.** [J. Miss. State Med. Assoc.]. **Main/Corp** Mississippi State Medical Association. **Added/Corp** Mississippi State Medical Association. Vol. 1 (Jan. 1960)-. Periodical. English. mo. $35.00 US; $45.00 other. Mississippi State Medical Association Journal, PO Box 5229, Jackson MS 39296. **Tel** (601)354-5433, FAX (601)352-4834. **ED** M.W. Lockey. **DD** 610. **NLM** W1 JO94N. **CODEN** MSMJB8MIMIA. Index available. cum. index. **Ad Acc. Circ:** 2,800 (ctrl). available on microfilm and microfiche from University Microfilms International (UMI). ***Supersedes*** *Mississippi Doctor.*
**Desc:** Contains scientific articles, socioeconomic issues and association news.
**Ind/Abst** Energy Res. Abstr.; Hospit. Health Admin. Index; Index Med.; Mod. Med.; SportSearch.

US/0892-0249
**JOURNAL OF THE N.J. ASSOCIATION OF OSTEOPATHIC PHYSICIANS AND SURGEONS, THE.** [J. N.J. Assoc. Osteopath. Physicians Surg.]. **Added/Corp** New Jersey Association of Osteopathic Physicians and Surgeons. **VFOAT** Journal of the New Jersey Association of Osteopathic Physicians and Surgeons. Vol. 83, No. 1 (Jan. 1984)-. Periodical. English. Twelve times a year. $15.00 (members); $25.00 (non-members). New Jersey Association of Osteopathic Physicians & Surgeons, 1212 Stuyvesant Avenue, Trenton NJ 08618. **Tel** (609)393-8114. **ED** Eleanore A. Farley. **DD** 615. Index available. **Bk Rev. Ad Acc. Circ:** 1,800 (ctrl). ***Continues*** *NJAOPS Journal (Trenton, N.J. : 1981), 8756-7024.*

II/0377-0621
**JOURNAL OF THE NATIONAL INTEGRATED MEDICAL ASSOCIATION.** **Added/Corp** National Integrated Medical Association. Vol. 14, No. 4 (Apr. 1972)-. Periodical. English. mo. $28.00. National Integrated Medical Association, G/2 Mohan Kunj Jyotiba Phule Marg, Dadar Bombay-400 014 India. **Tel** 453-608. **(Subscription address:** Prints India, 11 Darya Ganj, New Delhi 110002 India.**) NLM** W1 JO941K. ***Continues*** *National Medical Journal Amalgamating with Journal of the National Integrated Medical Association, 0377-0621.*

US/0027-9684
**JOURNAL OF THE NATIONAL MEDICAL ASSOCIATION.** [J. Natl. Med. Assoc.]. (Jan./Mar 1909)-. Periodical. English. mo. $100 institution, $85.00 individual (US). Slack Inc., 6900 Grove Road, Thorofare NJ 08086. **Tel** (609)848-1000, (800)257-8290, FAX (609)853-5991, telex 517108 SLACK INC VD. **ED** Calvin Sampson. **LC** R15. **DD** 610/.5. **NLM** W1 JO941N. **CODEN** JNMAAE. **Bk Rev. Ad Acc. Pr Rev. Circ:** 25,407 (ctrl). available on microfilm and microfiche from University Microfilms International (UMI). Documents available from The Genuine Article, BIOSIS Document Express, CASDDS.
**Desc:** Provides the most intense and thorough focus on urban medicine available for physicians who serve the health care needs of American urban populations.
**Ind/Abst** Biol. Abstr.; Chem. Abstr.; Cumul. Index Nurs. Allied Health Lit.; Curr. Contents Clin. Med.; EMBASE; Energy Res. Abstr.; Index Med.; Int. Pharm. Abstr.; Nutr. Abstr. Rev., Ser. B, Live Feeds and Feed.; Nutr. Abstr. Rev., Ser. A, Hum. Exp.; Life Sci. Collect.; Protozoolog. Abstr.; Psychol. Abstr. (1977-); PsycINFO; PsycLit; Res. Alert [Select. Cov.]; Rev. Med. Vet. Mycology; SCISEARCH; Soc. Sci. Cit. Index [Select. Cov.].

US/0276-2293
**JOURNAL OF THE NATIONAL REYE'S SYNDROME FOUNDATION.** ***Suspended.*** [J. Natl. Reye's Syndr. Found.]. Vol. 1, No. 1-?. Periodical. English. National Reye's Syndrome Foundation, PO Box 829, Bryan OH 43506. **NLM** W1 JO941PI.

PK/0030-9982
**JOURNAL OF THE PAKISTAN MEDICAL ASSOCIATION.** ***Suspended.*** (JPMA. THE JOURNAL OF THE PAKISTAN MEDICAL ASSOCIATION.). [J. Pak. Med. Assoc.]. **Added/Corp** Pakistan Medical Association. **VFOAT** Journal of the Pakistan Medical Association. Vol. 24, No. 3 (1974)-(19??). Academic Scholarly Publication. English. mo. Pakistan Medical Association, PMA House Garden Road, Karachi 3 Pakistan. **Tel** (021)714632. **ED** S. J. Zuberi. **NLM** W1 J514K. **CODEN** JJPAD4JPKMAK. Index available. **Bk Rev. Ad Acc.** ctrl circ. available on microfilm and microfiche from University Microfilms International (UMI). Documents available from CASDDS. ***Continues*** *Journal of the Pakistan Medical Association, 0030-9982.*
**Desc:** Research on medical and public health problems.
**Ind/Abst** Chem. Abstr. (1974-1983); EMBASE [Select. Cov.]; Helminthol. Abstr. (1991-); Index Med.; Life Sci. Collect.; Rev. Agric. Entomol.; Rev. Med. Vet. Entomol.; Trop. Dis. Bull.

US/0479-9534
**JOURNAL OF THE PENNSYLVANIA OSTEOPATHIC MEDICAL ASSOCIATION, THE.** [J. Pa. Osteopath. Med. Assoc.]. **Added/Corp** Pennsylvania Osteopathic Medical Association. **VFOAT** POMA Journal. (1957)-. Periodical. English. Five times a year. Free to libraries on request; $20.00 other. Pennsylvania Osteopathic Association, 1330 Eisenhower Boulevard, Harrisburg PA 17111. **Tel** (717)939-9318, FAX (717)929-7255. **ED** Leonard H. Finkelstein; Susan M. Folmer and Mario E.J. Lanni, managing editors. **DD** 610. **Ad Acc. Circ:** 3,200 (ctrl).
**Desc:** Professional articles of interest to osteopathic physicians on medicine, and surgery; news from osteopathic colleges, hospitals, current legislation.

UK/0035-8665
**JOURNAL OF THE ROYAL ARMY MEDICAL CORPS.** [J. R. Army Med. Corps]. **Main/Corp** Great Britain. Army. Royal Army Medical Corps. Vol. 1 (July 1903)-. Periodical. English. Three times a year (Feb., June, Oct.). £13.50 UK; £15.00 other. RAMC RHQ / Journal of the RAMC, Keogh Barrack/Ash Vale, Aldershot, Hants GU12 5RQ England. **Tel** 011 44 252 340250. **LC** UH201; .G6. **NLM** W1 JO95Q. Index available. **Bk Rev. Ad Acc. Circ:** 1,500.
**Desc:** Medical articles and case reports on various diseases, medical book reviews; reports on medical lectures, publications, abstracts and summaries by Royal Army Medical Corps Officers.
**Ind/Abst** EMBASE; Ergon. Abstr.; Helminthol. Abstr. (1991-); Index Med.; Rev. Med. Vet. Entomol.; SportSearch.

UK/0035-8819
**JOURNAL OF THE ROYAL COLLEGE OF PHYSICIANS OF LONDON.** [J. R. Coll. Physicans Lond.]. **Main/Corp** Royal College of Physicians of London. Vol. 1, (Oct. 1966)-. Academic Scholarly Publication. English. Six times a year (Jan., Mar., May, July, Sept., Nov.). £40.00 UK and Republic of Ireland; £55.00 other. Royal College of Physicians, 11 St Andrews Place, Regents Park, London NW1 4LE England. **Tel** 011 44 71 935 1174, FAX 011 44 71 487 5218. **ED** Dr. R. Mahler. **LC** R31; .R69. **NLM** W1 JO95U. **CODEN** RCPJAX. Index available. cum. index. **Bk Rev**, (Qty: (25-30)). **Ad Acc, Adv Mgr:** PRC Assoc., **Tel** 081-786-7376. **Pr Rev. Circ:** 12,500. Documents available from The Genuine Article, BIOSIS Document Express.
**Desc:** Medicine and the medical specialties.
**Ind/Abst** Biodeter. Abstr.; Biol. Abstr.; CIS Abstr.; Cumul. Index Nurs. Allied Health Lit.; Curr. Contents Clin. Med.; EMBASE [Select. Cov.]; Index Med.; Nutr. Abstr. Rev., Ser. A, Hum. Exp.; Nutr. Res. Newsl.; Life Sci. Collect.; Res. Alert [Full Cov.]; Saf. Health Work; Sci. Cit. Index; SCISEARCH; Soc. Sci. Cit. Index [Select. Cov.]; SportSearch; Trop. Dis. Bull.

UK/0035-9033
**JOURNAL OF THE ROYAL NAVAL MEDICAL SERVICE.** [J. R. Nav. Med. Serv.]. **Added/Corp** Great Britain. Royal Naval Medical Service. Royal Naval Medical School (Great Britain). Vol. 1, No. 1 (Jan. 1915)-. Academic Scholarly Publication. English. Three times a year. £15.00. Journal of Royal Naval Medical Service, Monckton House, Institute of Naval Medicine, Gosport Hants P012 2DL England. **Tel** 011 44 705 822351 Ext. 41346, FAX 011 44 705 504823. **ED** F R Wilkes. **NLM** W1 JO951E. **CODEN** JRNMAF. Index available in last issue of volume--attached. **Bk Rev. Ad Acc. Circ:** 1,000 (ctrl). available on microfilm and microfiche from University Microfilms International (UMI). Documents available from BIOSIS Document Express, CASDDS.
**Desc:** Articles on clinical and occupational medicine of relevance to The Royal Navy.
**Ind/Abst** Biol. Abstr. (-1975); Chem. Abstr.; EMBASE [Select. Cov.]; Index Med.; Saf. Health Work; Trop. Dis. Bull.

UK/0141-0768
**JOURNAL OF THE ROYAL SOCIETY OF MEDICINE.** [J.R. Soc. Med.]. **Main/Corp** Royal Society of Medicine (Great Britain). Vol. 71 (Jan. 1978)-. Academic Scholarly Publication. English. mo. $195.00 US; £98.00 UK & Europe; £106.00 other. Royal Society of Medicine Press, 1 Wimpole Street, London W1M 8AE England. **Tel** 011 44 71 2902928. **ED** A Harding Rains. **LC** R35; .R7. **DD** 610/.8. **NLM** W1 JO951H. **CODEN** JRSMD9. **[CCC]**. Index available. **Bk Rev. Ad Acc. Pr Rev. Circ:** 19,000. available on microfilm and microfiche from University Microfilms International (UMI). Documents available from The Genuine Article, CASDDS, ADONIS. ***Continues*** *Proceedings of the Royal Society of Medicine, 0035-9157.*
**Desc:** General medical journal publishing clinical research and reviews across the range of specialties.
**Ind/Abst** ADONIS; Arts Humanit. Citation Index [Select. Cov.]; Chem. Abstr.; CSA Neuro. Abstr. (?-?); Cumul. Index Nurs. Allied Health Lit.; Curr. Aware. Biol. Sci., CABS; Curr. Contents Clin. Med.; Curr. Contents Life Sci.; Curr. Titl. Dent.; Dairy Sci. Abstr.; Dev. Med. Child Neurol.; EMBASE; Helminthol. Abstr. (1991-); Index Med.; Index Vet.; Int. Pharm. Abstr.; Med. Abstr. Newsl.; Nutr. Abstr. Rev., Ser. A, Hum. Exp.; Nutr. Res. Newsl.; Life Sci. Collect.; PESTDOC; Protozoolog. Abstr.; Ref. Upd. Clinical Ed.; Ref. Upd. Deluxe Ed.; Res. Alert [Full Cov.]; Res. High. Educ. Abstr.; Rev. Med. Vet. Entomol.; Sci. Cit. Index; SCISEARCH; Soc. Sci. Cit. Index [Select. Cov.]; Trop. Dis. Bull.

UK
**JOURNAL OF THE ROYAL SOCIETY OF MEDICINE. SUPPLEMENT.** (1982)-. Monographic series. English. Price varies per volume. Royal Society of Medicine Press, 1 Wimpole Street, London W1M 8AE England. **Tel** 011 44 71 2902928. **Pr Rev.**
**Ind/Abst** Curr. Aware. Biol. Sci., CABS; EMBASE.

HK/0379-3176
**JOURNAL OF THE SOCIETY OF COMMUNITY MEDICINE HONG KONG.**
**See** Public Health and Safety.

US/0038-3139
**JOURNAL OF THE SOUTH CAROLINA MEDICAL ASSOCIATION (1975).** (THE JOURNAL OF THE SOUTH CAROLINA MEDICAL ASSOCIATION.). [J. S. C. Med. Assoc.]. **Added/Corp** South Carolina Medical Association. Vol. 71, No. 10 (Oct. 1975)-. Periodical. English. mo. $25.00. South Carolina Medical Association, PO Box 11888, Capitol Station, Columbia SC 29211. **Tel** (803)798-6207, FAX (803)772-6783. **ED** Joy Drennen. **DD** 610. Index available (Dec. issue). **Ad Acc. Pr Rev. Circ:** 4,500 (ctrl). available on microfilm and microfiche from University Microfilms International (UMI); available on photocopies from University Microfilms International (UMI). ***Continues*** *Journal (South Carolina Medical Association), 0038-3139.*
**Desc:** A scientific publication for practicing physicians, containing scientific articles and association news with some socioeconomic information.
**Ind/Abst** Energy Res. Abstr.; Index Med.

US/1044-1654
**JOURNAL OF THE STUDENT NATIONAL MEDICAL ASSOCIATION.** ***Title Change.*** [J. Stud. Natl. Med. Assoc.]. **Added/Corp** Student National Medical Association. **VFOAT** Journal of the SNMA; SNMA Journal. Vol. 1, No. 1 (Spring 1989)-(1993). Periodical. English. qt. $10.00. Spectrum Unlimited, 4000 Davey Street/Suite 602, New Orleans LA 70122. **DD** 610. ***Continues*** *Black Bag, 0196-1594.* ***Continued by*** *Journal for Minority Medical Students, 1074-5807.*

US/0040-3318
**JOURNAL OF THE TENNESSEE MEDICAL ASSOCIATION.** [J. Tenn. Med. Assoc.]. Vol. 56, No. 5 (May 1963)-. Academic Scholarly Publication. English. mo. $20.00 US; $26.00 other. Tennessee Medical Association, PO Box 120909, Nashville TN 37212. **Tel** (615)385-2100, FAX (615)383-5918. **ED** John B Thomison. **NLM** W1 JO957M. Index available. **Ad Acc. Circ:** 6,650 (ctrl). ***Continues*** *Journal of the Tennessee State Medical Association, 0735-7338.*
**Desc:** Scientific information and news about legislative, socioeconomic, educational, and medical activities in the state.
**Ind/Abst** EMBASE [Select. Cov.]; Energy Res. Abstr.; Hospit. Health Admin. Index; Index Med.; Life Sci. Collect.; SportSearch.

US
**JOURNAL OF THE US ARMY MEDICAL DEPARTMENT, THE.** **VAT** Journal of the United States Army Medical Department. (Nov./Dec. 1989)-. Periodical. English. mo. Commander in Chief, 7th Medical Command, Attn Editor, APO New York NY 09102-3304. **LC** RC970; .U53. **DD** 616.9/8023/05. ***Continues*** *Medical Bulletin (United States. Army. Medical Command, 7th).*

II/0970-4396
**JOURNAL OF THE VIVEKANANDA INSTITUTE OF MEDICAL SCIENCES.** [J. Vivekananda Inst. Med. Sci.]. **Added/Corp** Vivekananda Institute of Medical Sciences (Calcutta, India) Ramakrishna Mission Seva Pratishthan (Calcutta, India). (197?)-. Periodical. English. sa. $12.00. Ramakrishna Mission, Institute of Culture, Calcutta, India. **(Subscription address:** Prints India, 11 Darya Ganj, New Delhi 110002 India.**)** **NLM** W1; JO961J.

US/0883-5993
**JOURNAL OF THORACIC IMAGING.** [J. thorac. imaging]. **Added/Corp** Aspen Systems Corporation. Society of Thoracic Radiology. **VFOAT** Thoracic Imaging; JTI. Vol. 1, No. 1 (Dec. 1985)-. Periodical. English. qt. $145.00 (individuals), $164.00 (institutions) US; $178.00 (individuals), $196.00 (institutions) other. Raven Press, 1185 Avenue of the Americas, 37th Floor, New York NY 10036. **Tel** (212)930-9500, (212)930-9604, FAX (212)869-3495, (212)302-8507, telex 640073. **ED** Eric N. C. Milue. **DD** 617. **NLM** W1; JO996ID. **CODEN** JTIME8. **[CCC]. Ad Acc. Pr Rev. Circ:** 900. available on microfilm from University Microfilms International (UMI). Documents available from The Genuine Article, BIOSIS Document Express.
**Desc:** Provides a forum for the discussion of all aspects of the diagnosis of chest disease using imaging techniques, including conventional chest radiography, tomography, computed tomography, digitized radiography, ultrasound, nuclear medicine, magnetic resonance imaging, and all other promising techniques.
**Ind/Abst** Biol. Abstr. (1986-), (1986-1990-); Curr. Contents Clin. Med.; EMBASE; Index Med. (1985-); INIS Atomindex [Micro.]; Res. Alert [Select. Cov.]; Rev. Med. Vet. Mycology; SCISEARCH.

NE/0929-5305
**JOURNAL OF THROMBOSIS AND THROMBOLYSIS.** (19??)-. English. qt. $406.00. Kluwer Academic Publishers, PO Box 322, 3300 AH Dordrecht, The Netherlands. **Tel** 011 (31) 78 524400, FAX 011 31 78 183273, telex 20083.

CC/0257-716X
**JOURNAL OF TONGJI MEDICAL UNIVERSITY.** [J. Tongji Med. Univ.]. **Added/Corp** Tung Chi i Ko ta Hsueh (Wu-han Shih, China). **VFOAT** Tung Chi I Ko Ta Hsueh Hsueh Pao. Vol. 6, No. 1 (1986)-. Periodical. English. qt. $48.10. China National Publishing Import & Export Corporation, 16 Gongti E Rd., Chaoyang Dist., Beijing 100704, People's Republic of China. **Tel** 011 8601 50630169, 5066688, FAX 011 8601 5063101, 5063010, telex 22313. **NLM** W1; JO966JF. Documents available from CASDDS. ***Continues*** *Acta Academiae Medicinae Wuhan, 0253-3316.*
**Ind/Abst** Chem. Abstr.; EMBASE [Select. Cov.]; Index Med. (1986-).

GW/0931-2838
**JOURNAL OF TRACE ELEMENTS AND ELECTROLYTES IN HEALTH AND DISEASE.** Vol. 1, No. 1 (Sept. 1987)-. Periodical. English. qt. $265.00, $229.00 (membership) North America; DM450.00, DM320.00 (membership) other. Walter de Gruyter Inc., PO Box 303421, D 10728 Berlin Germany. **Tel** 011 49 30 260050, FAX 011 49 30 26005251. **(Subscription address:** US and Canada/ 200 Saw Mill River Road, Hawthorne, NY 10532**)** **ED** P Bratter, K D Kruse-Jarres, I Lombeck, and W Paterno. **NLM** W1; JO966KDR. **CODEN** JTEDET. **[CCC]. Bk Rev. Ad Acc. Pr Rev. Circ:** 800. Documents available from The Genuine Article, CASDDS.
**Desc:** Covers theoretical and applied aspects of trace elements and electrolytes in medicine. It covers the following topics: analytical methods, metabolism (biochemistry and pathobiochemistry), nutrition, toxicology, epidemiology, and clinical applications (diagnosis and therapy).
**Ind/Abst** Chem. Abstr.; Chem. Hazards Ind.; Curr. Contents Life Sci.; Dairy Sci. Abstr.; EMBASE; Index Med. (1987-); Lab. Hazards Bull.; Nutr. Abstr. Rev., Ser. B, Live Feeds and Feed.; Nutr. Abstr. Rev., Ser. A, Hum. Exp.; Pig News Inf.; Res. Alert [Full Cov.]; Sci. Cit. Index; SCISEARCH.

US/0896-548X
**JOURNAL OF TRACE ELEMENTS IN EXPERIMENTAL MEDICINE, THE.** [J. trace elem. exp. med.]. **Added/Corp** International Society for Trace Element Research in Humans. (1988)-. Periodical. English. Four times a year. $298.00 (US); $338.00 (Canada and Mexico); $353.00 (other). John Wiley & Sons, Inc., 605 Third Avenue, New York NY 10158-0012. **Tel** (212)850-6000, (212)850-6645, FAX (212)850-6088, telex 12-7063. **(Subscription address:** John Wiley & Sons / England, Baffins Lane, Chichester, West Sussex PO19 1UD England.**)** **ED** Ananda S. Prasad. **DD** 612. **NLM** W1; JO966KDW. **CODEN** JTEMEM. Documents available from BIOSIS Document Express, CASDDS.
**Desc:** An international periodical focusing on the role of trace elements in human health and disease. Comprehensive coverage of health problems caused by trace element excess or deficiency in human diets is presented, with special attention given to the clinical, nutritional, biochemical, immunological, and toxicological aspects of trace elements.
**Ind/Abst** Biol. Abstr. (1988-); Chem. Abstr.; CSA Neuro. Abstr. (?-?); EMBASE; Health Saf. Sci. Abstr.; Ref. Upd. Deluxe Ed.

US/0270-661X
**JOURNAL OF TRADITIONAL ACUPUNCTURE, THE.** [J. tradit. acupunct.]. **Added/Corp** Centre for Traditional Acupuncture Foundation. Traditional Acupuncture Foundation. Vol. 1, No. 1 (Summer 1977)-. Academic Scholarly Publication. English. ir. $35.00 membership. Traditional Acupuncture Institute, American City Building / Suite 108, Columbia MD 21044. **Tel** (301)997-4888. **LC** RM184; .J68. **DD** 615.8/92/05. **NLM** W1 JO966KE. **Bk Rev.** ctrl circ.
**Desc:** A scholarly journal published to further the knowledge and practice of traditional acupuncture.

CC/0254-6272
**JOURNAL OF TRADITIONAL CHINESE MEDICINE.** [J. tradit. Chin. med.]. **Added/Corp** Chung i Yen Chiu Yuan (Peking, China) Chung-hua Chuan kuo Chung i Hsueh Hui. **VFOAT** Chung I Ysa Chih Ying Wen Pan. Vol. 1, No. 1 (Sept. 1981)-. English. qt. $82.60. China National Publishing Import & Export Corporation, 16 Gongti E Rd., Chaoyang Dist., Beijing 100704, People's Republic of China. **Tel** 011 8601 50630169, 5066688, FAX 011 8601 5063101, 5063010, telex 22313. **ED** Hu Ximing. **NLM** W1 JO966KF. **CODEN** JTCMEC. **Bk Rev. Ad Acc.** Documents available from BIOSIS Document Express.
**Desc:** Provides information of clinical and basic investigation on traditional Chinese medicine and acupuncture, together with Chinese medical history and lectures on acupuncture.
**Ind/Abst** Biol. Abstr.; Helminthol. Abstr.; Index Med.; NAPRALERT.

SW/0345-5564
**JOURNAL OF TRAFFIC MEDICINE.** (JOURNAL OF TRAFFIC MEDICINE : OFFICIAL ORGAN OF THE INTERNATIONAL ASSOCIATION FOR ACCIDENT AND TRAFFIC MEDICINE.). [J. traffic med.]. **Added/Corp** International Association for Accident and Traffic Medicine. Vol. 9, No. 1 (March 1981)-. Periodical. English. qt. 75.00F. International Association of Traffic Medicine, Kytosuontie 11, SF 00300 Helsinki Finland. **Tel** 011 45 1 4735500, FAX 011 45 1 4775450. **NLM** W1; JO966KG. ***Continues*** *Journal of Traffic Medicine/IAATM Newsletter, 0345-5564.*
**Desc:** An international journal of traffic safety, with its main focus on the broad area of traffic safety with an emphasis on the medical aspects.
**Ind/Abst** EMBASE; Highw. Res. Abstr.

CN/1195-1982
**JOURNAL OF TRAVEL MEDICINE.** (19??)-. English. Four times a year. $70.00 (institutions), $53.00 (individuals) US & Canada; $85.00 (institutions), $68.00 (individuals) other. Decker Periodicals Publishing Inc, PO Box 620, Station A, Hamilton Ontario L8N 3K7 Canada. **Tel** (416)522-7017, (800) 568-7281, FAX (416)522-7839.

●UK/1353-8012
**JOURNAL OF VASCULAR INVESTIGATION.** (1994)-. Periodical. English. Four times a year. £179.00 Europe; £180.00 Other (Institutions). Churchill Livingstone, 1-3 Baxter's Place, Leith Walk, Edinburgh EH1 3AF Scotland. **Tel** 011 44 31 556 2424, FAX 011 44 31 558 1278, telex 727511. **(Subscription address:** Maruzen Company Ltd., PO Box 5050, Import & Export Department, Tokyo 100 31 Japan.**)**

US/1042-5268
**JOURNAL OF VASCULAR MEDICINE AND BIOLOGY.** ***Ceased.*** [J. vasc. med. biol.]. Vol. 1, No. 1 (Feb. 1989)-(19??). Academic Scholarly Publication. English. bm (6 issues). Blackwell Scientific Publishers, 238 Main Street, Cambridge MA 02142. **Tel** (617)547-7110, (800)835-6770, FAX (617)547-0789. **DD** 616. **NLM** W1; JO97BK. **CODEN** JVBIE9. **[CCC].** available on microfilm and microfiche from University Microfilms International (UMI). Documents available from ADONIS.
**Ind/Abst** ADONIS (19??-19??); EMBASE (19??-19??).

●UK/1352-0504
**JOURNAL OF VIRAL HEPATITIS.** (199?)-. Academic Scholarly Publication. English. Six times a year. $230.00 (institutions), $99.00 (individuals) US & Canada; £135.00 (institutions), £59.50 (individuals) Europe; £148.50 (institutions), £65.00 (individuals) other. Blackwell Scientific Publications Ltd, Marston Book Services, PO Box 87, Oxford OX2 ODT UK. **Tel** 011 44 865 791155, FAX 011 44 865 791927, telex 837 515 MARDIS G.

US/0892-1997
**JOURNAL OF VOICE.** (JOURNAL OF VOICE : OFFICIAL JOURNAL OF THE VOICE FOUNDATION.). [J. voice]. **Added/Corp** Voice Foundation. Vol. 1, No. 1 (March 1987)-. Periodical. English. qt. $99.00 (individuals), $172.00 (institutions) US; $126.00 (individuals), $194.00 (institutions) other. Raven Press, 1185 Avenue of the Americas, 37th Floor, New York NY 10036. **Tel** (212)930-9500, (212)930-9604, FAX (212)869-3495, (212)302-8507, telex 640073. **ED** Robert Thayer Sataloff. **LC** QP306; .J68. **DD** 612/.78/05. **NLM** W1; JO972. **CODEN** JOVOEA. **[CCC].** available on microfilm and microfiche from University Microfilms International (UMI). Documents available from The Genuine Article, BIOSIS Document Express.
**Desc:** Publishes pertinent clinical and research articles on the care of the human voice. Includes topics on basic voice science, acoustics, anatomy, synthesis, medical and surgical treatment of voice problems, voice therapy, and voice pedagogy.
**Ind/Abst** Biol. Abstr.; EMBASE; Music Index (1989-); Res. Alert [Select. Cov.]; SCISEARCH; Soc. Sci. Cit. Index [Select. Cov.].

UK/0953-9859
**JOURNAL OF WILDERNESS MEDICINE.** **Added/Corp** Wilderness Medical Society. Vol. 1, No. 1 (1990)-. Periodical. English. qt. $175.00 US and Canada; £140.00 Europe; £140.00 other. Chapman & Hall, 2-6 Boundary Row, London SE1 8HN England. **Tel** 011 44 71 865 0066, FAX 011 44 71 522 9623, telex 290164 Chapmag. **(Subscription address:** Chapman & Hall, Cheriton House, North Way, Andover, Hampshire, SP10 5BE England.**)** **ED** Paul S. Auerbach, Oswald Oelz. **LC** RC1220.M6; J68. **DD** 616.02/5. **NLM** W1; JO972CP. **CODEN** JWMEEP. Documents available from The Genuine Article, ADONIS.
**Desc:** Publishes original research on all aspects of medicine in hostile natural environments including: high altitude and climbing medicine, cold and heat-related phenomena, natural environmental disasters, immersion and near-drowning, diving and barotrauma, hazardous plants, reptiles, insects and marine animals, animal attacks, search and rescue, ethical and legal issues, medicine in remote environments, travel medicine, survival physiology, aeromedical transport and wilderness trauma management.
**Ind/Abst** ADONIS; Curr. Contents Clin. Med.; EMBASE; Environ. Period. Bibliogr.; Res. Alert [Select. Cov.]; SCISEARCH.

●US/1059-7115
**JOURNAL OF WOMEN'S HEALTH.** (JOURNAL OF WOMEN'S HEALTH : THE OFFICIAL PUBLICATION OF THE SOCIETY FOR THE ADVANCEMENT OF WOMEN'S HEALTH RESEARCH.). [J. women's health]. **Added/Corp** Society for the Advancement of Women's Health Research. Vol. 1, No. 1 (Spring 1992)-. Periodical. English. bm. $130.00. Mary Ann Liebert Inc., 1651 Third Avenue, New York NY 10128. **Tel** (212)289-2300, (800)M-LIEBERT, FAX (212)289-4697. **ED** Anne Colston Wentz and Florence Haseltine. **LC** RA564.85; .J68. **DD** 616/.0082. **NLM** W1; JO972R. **CODEN** JWOHEA. **Bk Rev. Ad Acc. Pr Rev.**
**Desc:** Publishes papers on diseases or conditions that hold greater risk for or are more prevalent among women. Contains original articles and review articles, and includes point - counterpoint discussions, reviews of important meetings, abstracts of selected seminars, news from women's health networks, and other material relevant to the professional advancement of women's health specialization.

●UK/0969-0700
**JOURNAL OF WOUND CARE.** [J. wound care]. (1992)-. Periodical. English. Ten times a year. £59.50 UK; $128.00 US and Canada; £66.00 Europe; £80.00 (airspeed) other. Macmillan Magazines Ltd., Houndmills, Basingstoke, Hampshire RG21 2XS England. **Tel** 011 44 256 29242, FAX 011 44 256 812358, telex 858493.

CC/0258-0659
**JOURNAL OF XIAN MEDICAL UNIVERSITY.** (HSI-AN I KO TA HSUEH HSUEH PAO / XIAN YIKEDAXUE XUEBAO / JOURNAL OF XIAN MEDICAL UNIVERSITY.). [J. Xian Med. Univ.]. **Added/Corp** Hsi-An i ko ta Hsueh. **VFOAT** Xian Yikedaxue Xuebao; Journal of Xian Medical University. Vol. 7, No. 1 (1986)-. Academic Scholarly Publication. Chinese (English). Four times a year. Xian Medical University, 16 Scarlet-Bird Avenue, South Suburb, 710061 Xian, People's Republic of China. **ED** Han Weidong. **NLM** W1; HS799G. **CODEN** XYDXEZ. Index available. cum. index. **Photos. Ad Acc, Adv Mgr:** Yue Mangsheng, **Tel** 029 5261609-2266. Full Page (B&W) $200.00. Half Page (B&W) $100.00. Full Page (Color) $400.00. Half Page (Color) $200.00. **Pr Rev. Circ:** 3,000. Documents available from BIOSIS Document Express, Magazine Collection, UMI Article Clearinghouse, The Genuine Article, BLDSC, CASDDS. ***Continues*** *Hsi-An i Hsueh Yuan Hsueh Pao, 0257-313X.*
**Desc:** Represents the latest achievement, technics and experience in scientific research, teaching and medical care of the University, reports recent developments in medicine at home and abroad; improves academic exchange for the purpose of giving service to flourishing science, training qualified personnel and building China in to a powerful modern country. The main content is basic medicine, clinical medicine, preventive medicine, traditional Chinese medicine, combination of traditional Chinese and Western medicine, introduction to latest technic and methods.
**Ind/Abst** Biol. Abstr. (1986-); Chem. Abstr. (1988); EMBASE [Select. Cov.].

US/0030-1876
**JOURNAL - OKLAHOMA STATE MEDICAL ASSOCIATION.** (THE JOURNAL / OKLAHOMA STATE MEDICAL ASSOCIATION.). [J. - Okla. State Med. Assoc.]. **Added/Corp** Oklahoma State Medical Association. **VFOAT** Journal of the Oklahoma State Medical Association. Vol. 60, No. 8 (Aug. 1967)-. Periodical. English. mo. $30.00. Oklahoma State Medical Association, 601 NW Expressway, Oklahoma City OK 73118. **Tel** (405)843-9571. **ED** Susan Records. **DD** 610. Index available (In Dec. issue). **Bk Rev. Ad Acc. Circ:** 3,900 (ctrl). available on microfilm and microfiche from University Microfilms International (UMI). ***Continues*** *Journal of the Oklahoma State Medical Association, 0030-1876.*
**Desc:** A scientific publication written by and for the physicians of Oklahoma.
**Ind/Abst** Energy Res. Abstr.; Hospit. Health Admin. Index; Index Med.; Nutr. Abstr. Rev., Ser. B, Live Feeds and Feed.; Nutr. Abstr. Rev., Ser. A, Hum. Exp.; Rev. Med. Vet. Entomol.; SportSearch.

US/0896-7210
**JOURNAL WATCH.** See Medical Science and Technology-Abstracting, Bibliographies and Statistics.

PH
**JPMA : JOURNAL OF THE PHILIPPINE MEDICAL ASSOCIATION.** Vol. 58, No. 3 (June-July 1982 1982)-. Periodical. English. qt. $30.00. Philippine Medical Association, North Avenue Dilaman, Quezon City Philippines. ***Continues*** *Journal of the Philippine Medical Association, 0031-7748.*
**Ind/Abst** Philip. Sci. Technol. Abstr.

US
**JPRS REPORT. SCIENCE & TECHNOLOGY. USSR: SPACE BIOLOGY & SPACE MEDICINE.** ***Ceased.***
**VFOAT** J.P.R.S. Report. Science & Technology; USSR: Space Biology & Aerospace Medicine. **VAT** Joint Publications Research Service Report. Science & Technology. USSR: Space Biology & Aerospace Medicine. (1987)-(1988). Periodical. English. ir. Joint Publications Research Services, PO Box 12507, Arlington VA 22209. ***Continues*** *USSR Report. Space Biology and Aerospace Medicine, 0196-9269.*

JA/0389-1844
**JUNKAN SEIGYO.** [Junkan seigyo]. **VFOAT** Circulation Control. (1980)-. Periodical. Multiple languages. sa. Kodama K.K., (Kodama Ltd.), 3-2, Kanda Sakumacho, Chiyodaku, Tokyoto 101 Japan. **DD** 616.1. Documents available from CASDDS.
**Ind/Abst** Chem. Abstr.

KO/0253-6250
**JUNNAN NUIDAIJI.** (CHUNGANG UIDAE CHI.). [Junnan nuidaiji]. **Added/Corp** Chungang Taehakkyo. Uikwa Taehak. **VFOAT** Chung-Ang Journal of Medicine. (1981)-. Periodical. Korean (summaries and/or abstracts in English). qt. **NLM** W1 CH9912J. **CODEN** CJMEDQ. Documents available from BIOSIS Document Express, CASDDS. ***Continues*** *Chungang Uidae Chapji.*
**Ind/Abst** Biol. Abstr.; Chem. Abstr.; Energy Res. Abstr. (1981-); Helminthol. Abstr. (1991-); Trop. Dis. Bull.; Weed Abstr.

JA/0022-6769
**JUNTENDO IGAKU.** [Juntendo igaku]. **Added/Corp** Juntendo Igakkai. **VFOAT** Juntendo Medical Journal. (1955)-. Periodical. Japanese. qt. Juntendo Igakkai, (Juntendo Medical Society), 1-1, Hongo 2 Chome, Bunkyoku, Tokyoto 113 Japan. **CODEN** JUIZAG. Documents available from CASDDS. ***Continues*** *Juntendo Igaku Zasshi.*
**Ind/Abst** Chem. Abstr.

FR/0768-6625
**JUSQU'A LA MORT ACCOMPAGNER LA VIE.** **VFOAT** JALMALV. (1985)-. Periodical. French. qt. 110.00F France; 130.00F (surface mail), 150.00F (air mail) other. JALMALV, 4 rue Hector Berlioz, 38000 Grenoble France. **Tel** 011 33 76 510851. **UDC** 362.1(449.91).

JA/0022-7226
**JUZEN IGAKKAI ZASSHI.** (KANAZAWA DAIGAKU JUZEN IGAKKAI ZASSHI.). [JÂuzen Igakkai zasshi]. **Added/Corp** Kanazawa Daigaku. Juzen Igakkai. **VFOAT** Journal of the Juzen Medical Society; Juzen Igakkai Zasshi. (1896)-. Periodical. Japanese (summaries and/or abstracts in English). bm. Kanazawa Daigaku Juzen Igakkai, (Juzen Medical Soc. of Kanazawa University), 13-1, Takaramachi, Kanazawashi, Ishikawaken 920 Japan. **CODEN** JUZIAG. Documents available from CASDDS.
**Ind/Abst** Chem. Abstr.

JA/0913-2384
**KAGAKU RYOHO NO RYOIKI (1987).** (KAGAKU RYOHO NO RYOIKI.). [Kagaku ryoho no ryoiki]. **Added/Corp** Kagaku Ryoho Kenkyukai. **VFOAT** Antibiotics and Chemotherapy; Antibiotics & Chemotherapy. (1987)-. Periodical. Japanese. mo. Iyaku Janarusha, Medicine & Drug Journal Co., Ltd., 3-28, Hiranocho, Higashiku, Osakashi, Osakafu 541 Japan. **NLM** W1; KO618K. **CODEN** KRRYEI. Documents available from CASDDS. ***Continues*** *Kosei Busshitsu Kara Kagaku Ryoho no Ryoiki, 0911-3045.*
**Ind/Abst** Chem. Abstr.

JA/0385-5759
**KANAZAWA IKA DAIGAKU ZASSHI.** (KANAZAWA IKA DAIGAKU ZASSHI. JOURNAL OF KANAZAWA MEDICAL UNIVERSITY.). [Kanazawa Ika Daigaku zasshi]. **Added/Corp** Kanazawa Ika Daigaku. Kanazawa Ika Daigaku Igakkai. **VFOAT** Journal of Kanazawa Medical University. Vol. 1 (Mar. 1976)-. Periodical. English (Japanese). qt. Kanazawa Ika Daigaku Iggakai, (Medical Soc. of Kanazawa Medical University), 1-1, Daigaku, Uchinadamachi, Kahokugun, Ishikawaken 920-02, Japan. **NLM** W1 KA4379. **CODEN** KIDZDN. Documents available from CASDDS.
**Ind/Abst** Chem. Abstr.

JA/0369-3570
**KANKYO IGAKU KENKYUJO NENPO.** [Kankyo Igaku Kenkyujo nenpo]. **Added/Corp** Nagoya Daigaku. Kankyo Igaku Kenkyujo. **VFOAT** Annals of the Research Institute of Environmental Medicine, Nagoya University. (1949)-. Japanese. an. Nagoya Daigaku Kankyo Igaku Kenkyujo, (Research Inst. of Environmental Medicine, Nagoya University), Furocho, Chikusaku, Nagoyashi, Aichiken 464 Japan. **CODEN** NDKIA2. Documents available from CASDDS.
**Ind/Abst** Chem. Abstr.

JA/0022-8400
**KANSAI IKA DAIGAKU ZASSHI.** (KANSAI IKA DAIGAKU ZASSHI. JOURNAL OF THE KANSAI MEDICAL SCHOOL.). [Kansai Ika Daigaku zasshi]. **Main/Corp** Kansai Ika Daigaku. **VFOAT** Journal of the Kansai Medical School. (1948)-. Periodical. Japanese (English). qt. Society of Kansai Medical University, 1 Fumizonocho, Moriguchi-shi, 570 Osaka Japan. **NLM** W1 KA502V. **CODEN** KIDZAK. Documents available from BIOSIS Document Express, CASDDS.
**Ind/Abst** Biol. Abstr. (-1988); Chem. Abstr.; EMBASE [Select. Cov.].

FI/0355-4813
**KANSANELAKELAITOKSEN JULKAISUJA. AL.** **VFOAT** Publications of the Social Insurance Institution, Finland. No. 1 (1974)-. Monographic series. Finnish (summaries and/or abstracts in English). Price varies per volume. **NLM** W1; KA505.

FI/0355-4821
**KANSANELAKELAITOKSEN JULKAISUJA. M.** See Insurance.

US/8755-0059
**KANSAS MEDICINE.** (KANSAS MEDICINE : THE JOURNAL OF THE KANSAS MEDICAL SOCIETY.). [Kans. med.]. **Added/Corp** Kansas Medical Society. Vol. 86, No. 1 (Jan. 1985)-. Academic Scholarly Publication. English. Twelve times a year. $45.00 (US), $50.00 (other) with directory; $25.00 (US), $30.00 (other) without directory. Kansas Medical Society, 623 West 10th Avenue, Topeka KS 66612. **Tel** (913)235-2383, (800)332-0156. **LC** R15; .K27. **DD** 610/.6/0781. **NLM** W1; KA575. **CODEN** KAMEEI. Index available in last issue of volume--attached. **Ad Acc, Adv Mgr:** Susan Ward. **Pr Rev. Circ:** 3,700. available on microfilm and microfiche from University Microfilms International (UMI). Documents available from BIOSIS Document Express, CASDDS. ***Continues*** *Kansas Medical Society. Journal of the Kansas Medical Society, 0022-8699.*
**Desc:** Scientific / medical material and articles on practice management and socio-economic issues for Kansas physicians.
**Ind/Abst** Biol. Abstr.; Chem. Abstr. (1985-); Energy Res. Abstr. (1985-); Hospit. Health Admin. Index (1985-); Index Med. (1985-); Nucl. Sci. Abstr. (1985-); SportSearch (1985-).

JA/0451-4203
**KANZO (TOKYO, JAPAN : 1960).** (KANZO.). [Kanzo]. **Added/Corp** Nihon Kanzo Gakkai. **VFOAT** Acta Hepatologica Japonica. (1960)-. Academic Scholarly Publication. Japanese (English). mo. $308.00. Nihon Kanzo Gakkai, (Japan Soc. of Hepatology), 1-1, Hongo 4 Chome, Bunkyoku, Tokyoto 113 Japan. **(Subscription address:** Kyowa Book Company Inc., 1-38 Kanda Jinbo-Cho, Chiyoda-Ku Tokyo 101, Japan) **CODEN** KNZOAU. Documents available from CASDDS.
**Ind/Abst** Chem. Abstr.; EMBASE.

CH/0257-5655
**KAO-HSIUNG I HSUEH KO HSUEH TSA CHIH.** [Gaoxiong yixue Kexue zazhi]. **VFOAT** Kaohsiung Journal of Medical Sciences; Kaohsiung I Chih. (1985)-. Academic Scholarly Publication. Chinese (English). mo. Kaohsiung Medical Institute, Kaohsiung Taiwan. **UDC** 61. **NLM** W1; KA754C. **CODEN** KHHCE2. Documents available from BIOSIS Document Express, CASDDS.
**Ind/Abst** Biocont. News Inf.; Biol. Abstr. (1986-); Chem. Abstr. (1986-); EMBASE [Select. Cov.]; Helminthol. Abstr. (1991-); Maize Abstr.; Nutr. Abstr. Rev., Ser. B, Live Feeds and Feed.; Rice Abstr.

JA
**KARADA NO KAGAKU.** [Karada no kagaku]. **VFOAT** Popular Medicine. (1956)-. Academic Scholarly Publication. Japanese. bm. RMBY4.80. Science Press, 16 Donghuangchenggen North Street, Beijing 100707, People's Republic of China. **Tel** 011 86 1 4019821, 011 86 1 4010642, FAX 011 86 1 4012180, 011 86 1 4019810, telex 210147. **ED** Bao Guohua. **CODEN** KARKAN. **Ad Acc. Circ:** 600,000. Documents available from CASDDS.
**Desc:** Publishes short articles by experts in their particular lines, including traditional, Chinese medicine, and reports on the latest achievements in medicine and pharmacy.
**Ind/Abst** Chem. Abstr. (1965-1985).

GW/0022-9113
**KARTEI DER PRAKTISCHEN MEDIZIN.** [Kartei prakt. Med.]. (19??)-. Periodical. German. Twenty-four times a year. $164.00. Hippokrates Verlag, Postfach 102263, W 70018 Stuttgart Germany. **Tel** 011 49 711 89310. **(Subscription address:** Thieme Medical Publishers Inc., 381 Park Avenue South, New York NY 10016.) **UDC** 61(01).

VE/0075-5222
**KASMERA.** [Kasmera]. (1962)-. Periodical. Spanish. an. **DD** 616.07.
**Ind/Abst** Trop. Dis. Bull.

JA/0386-5924
**KAWASAKI IGAKKAISHI.** (KAWASAKI IGAKKAI SHI.). **Added/Corp** Kawasaki Igakkai. **VFOAT** Kawasaki Medical Journal. (1975)-. Academic Scholarly Publication. Japanese (summaries and/or abstracts in English). sa. Kawasaki Igakkai, (Kawasaki Medical School), 577, Matsushima, Kurashikishi, Okayamaken 701-01 Japan. **NLM** W1 KA93KI. Documents available from CASDDS.
**Ind/Abst** Chem. Abstr.

JA/0385-0234
**KAWASAKI MEDICAL JOURNAL.** [Kawasaki med. j.]. **Added/Corp** Kawasaki Ika Daigaku. Kawasaki Igakkai. Vol. 1 (1975)-. Academic Scholarly Publication. English (French and German). qt. Kawasaki Medical Society, 577 Matsushima Kurashikishi, Okayamaken 701-01 Japan. **ED** Tetsuo Kimoto and Yoshihito Yawata. **NLM** W1 KA93L. **CODEN** KAMJDW. Index available. cum. index. **Bk Rev. Ad Acc. Circ:** 800 (ctrl). Documents available from BIOSIS Document Express, CASDDS.
**Ind/Abst** Biol. Abstr.; Chem. Abstr.; EMBASE [Select. Cov.]; Nutr. Res. Newsl.; SEA Abstr.; Trop. Dis. Bull.

RU/0368-4814
**KAZANSKIJ MEDICINSKIJ ZURNAL.** (KAZANSKII MEDITSINSKII ZHURNAL.). [Kaz. med. z.]. (1901)-. Academic Scholarly Publication. Russian. Six times a year. $99.95. **(Subscription address:** East View Publications Inc., 3020 Harbor Lane North, Suite 110, Minneapolis MN 55447.) **NLM** W1 KA98. **CODEN** KAMZA9. Documents available from BIOSIS Document Express, CASDDS.
**Ind/Abst** Biol. Abstr.; Chem. Abstr.; Int. Aerosp. Abstr.

JA/0368-5179
**KEIO IGAKU.** [Keio igaku]. **Added/Corp** Keio Igakkai. **VFOAT** Journal of the Keio Medical Society. (1921)-. Periodical. Japanese. bm. Keio University School of Medicine, Shinanomachi Shinjuku-ku, Tokyo Japan 160. **Tel** 81-3-353-1211. **CODEN** KEIGAS. Documents available from CASDDS.
**Ind/Abst** Chem. Abstr.

JA/0022-9717
**KEIO JOURNAL OF MEDICINE.** [Keio j. med.]. **Added/Corp** Keio Gijuku Daigaku. Igakubu. Vol. 1 (Jan. 1952)-. Academic Scholarly Publication. English. qt.

$98.00. Keio University School of Medicine, Shinanomachi Shinjuku-ku, Tokyo Japan 160. **Tel** 81-3-353-1211. **(Subscription address:** Kyowa Book Company Inc., 1 38 Kanda Jinbocho Chiyoda-ku, Tokyo 101 Japan.**)** **ED** Toyomi Fujino. **NLM** W1 KE381. **CODEN** KJMEA9. Index available. cum. index. **Circ:** 1,200 (ctrl). Documents available from BIOSIS Document Express, CASDDS.
**Desc:** Covers general medicine and basic surgery.
**Ind/Abst** Biol. Abstr.; Chem. Abstr.; EMBASE [Select. Cov.]; Index Med.; SEA Abstr.; Trop. Dis. Bull.

US/0162-9840
**KEITHWOOD DIRECTORY OF HOSPITAL & SURGICAL SUPPLY DEALERS.** **VFOAT** Directory of Hospital & Surgical Supply Dealers. **VAT** Keithwood Directory of Hospital and Surgical Supply Dealers. Directory. English. $45.00. Keithwood Company, 18th and Courtland Sts, Philadelphia PA 19140. **LC** HD9994.U5; K44.

JA/0301-2611
**KENSA TO GIJUTSU.** **VFOAT** Modern Medical Laboratory. (1973)-. Periodical. Japanese. Thirteen times a year. ¥16100. Igaku Shoin Ltd., 5-24-3 Hongo Bunkyo-ku, Tokyo 113 Japan. **Tel** 011 81 3 817 5670. **NLM** W1 KE651. **CODEN** KTGIDU. Documents available from CASDDS.
**Ind/Abst** Chem. Abstr.

CN/0823-9827
**KEYS TO HEALTH.** (KEYS TO HEALTH / SASKATCHEWAN COUNCIL FOR ALTERNATE THERAPY.). [Keys health]. **Added/Corp** Saskatchewan Council for Alternate Therapy. (1982)-. Periodical. English. qt. Free to Members. Saskatchewan Council for Alternate Therapy, PO Box 2437, Prince Albert Saskatchewan. **DD** 610/.5.

US
**KILLERS AND CRIPPLERS, THE.**
**Added/Corp** National Health Education Committee. (19??)-. English. an. David McKay Company Inc, 2 Park Avenue, New York NY 10016. ***Continues*** *Facts on the Major Killing and Crippling Diseases in the United States Today.*
**Desc:** Facts on major diseases in the United States today.

GW/0340-5877
**KINDERARZT, DER.** [Kinderarzt]. **VFOAT** Der Kinderarzt (Lubeck). (1970)-. Periodical. German. mo. DM175.00 Germany; DM185.00 other. Hansisches Verlagskontor Herr Scheffler, Herr Scheffler Mengstr, Postfach 2051, D-23552 Luebeck 1 Germany. **Tel** 011 49 451 16050. **UDC** 616-053.2. ***Continues*** *Mitteilungen fuer Kinderarzte, 0462-9345.*

SU/0254-413X
**KING ABDULAZIZ MEDICAL JOURNAL.** [King Abdulaziz med. j.]. **VFOAT** Majallat Al-Malik Abd Al-Aziz Al-Tibbiyah. Vol. 1, No. 1 (Mar. 1981)-. Academic Scholarly Publication. Arabic (English). qt. **NLM** W1 KI65. **CODEN** KAMJEX. Documents available from CASDDS.
**Ind/Abst** Chem. Abstr. (1981-1984).

UK/0085-2546
**KING'S GAZETTE.** Periodical. English. Three times a year. **NLM** W1 KI714S. ***Continues*** *King's College Hospital Gazette, 0309-7366.*

JA/0385-8367
**KINKI DAIGAKU IGAKU ZASSHI.** (KINKI DAIGAKU IGAKU ZASSHI. MEDICAL JOURNAL OF KINKI UNIVERSITY.). [Kinki Daigaku igaku zasshi]. **Added/Corp** Kinki Daigaku Igakkai. **VFOAT** Medical Journal of Kinki University. (1976)-. Periodical. Japanese (summaries and/or abstracts in English). Kinki Daigaku Igaku Kai, 377-2 Ohno-higashi, Osaka Sayama-shi, 589, Osaka, Japan. **NLM** W1 KI718S. **CODEN** KDIZDD. Documents available from BIOSIS Document Express, CASDDS.
**Ind/Abst** Biol. Abstr. (1985-); Chem. Abstr.; EMBASE [Select. Cov.]; Energy Res. Abstr. (Oct. 1980-).

HU/0023-1878
**KISERLETES ORVOSTUDOMANY.** [Kis,erl. orvostud.]. **Added/Corp** Orvos-Egeszsegugyi Szakszervezet. (1949)-. Periodical. Hungarian. bm. **LC** R850; .K47. **NLM** W1 KI845. **CODEN** KIORAH. Documents available from CASDDS.
**Ind/Abst** Chem. Abstr.

JA/0023-1908
**KITA KANTO IGAKU.** (KITA KANTO IGAKU / THE KITAKANTO MEDICAL JOURNAL.). [Kita Kanto igaku]. **Added/Corp** Kita Kanto Igakkai. **VFOAT** Kitakanto Medical Journal. (1951)-. Academic Scholarly Publication. Japanese (summaries and/or abstracts in English). bm (6 issues). $104.00. Gumma Daigaku Igakubu, 3-39-22 Showa-machi, Maebashi-shi Gumma Japan. **Tel** 0272 (31)7221. **(Subscription address:** Japan Publications Trading Company, Ltd., PO Box 5030, Tokyo International, Tokyo 100-31 Japan.**)** **ED** M. Miura, H. Yamanaka, S. Hirai, H. Ishikawa, K. Kasahara, and Y. Nakazato. **CODEN** KKAIA2. **Circ:** 1,000. Documents available from BIOSIS Document Express, CASDDS.
**Desc:** Contributions from members of the Kitakanto Medical Society including original articles, reviews and case reports.
**Ind/Abst** Biol. Abstr.; Chem. Abstr.; EMBASE [Select. Cov.]; Saf. Health Work.

JA/0023-1924
**KITASATO ARCHIVES OF EXPERIMENTAL MEDICINE, THE.** ***Ceased.*** [Kitasato arch. exp. med.]. **Added/Corp** Kitasato Kenkyujo. (1917)-(May 1994). Academic Scholarly Publication. English (French and German). qt. Kitasato Kenkyujo, (Kitasato Institute), 9-1, Shirokane 5 Chome, Minatoku, Tokyoto 108, Japan. **(Subscription address:** Japan Publications Trading Company, Ltd., PO Box 5030, Tokyo International, Tokyo 100-31 Japan.**)** **LC** R850.A1; K57. **NLM** W1 KI855. **CODEN** KAEMAW. Documents available from BIOSIS Document Express, CASDDS.
**Ind/Abst** Anim. Breed. Abstr.; Biol. Abstr.; Chem. Abstr.; EMBASE; Index Med.; Index Vet.; Pig News Inf.; Rev. Agric. Entomol.; Rev. Med. Vet. Entomol.; Vet. Bull.

JA/0385-5449
**KITASATO IGAKU.** [Kitasato igaku]. **Added/Corp** Kitasato Igakkai. **VFOAT** Kitasato Medicine. (1971)-. Periodical. Japanese. bm. Kitasato Igakkai, (Kitasato Medical Soc.), 15-1, Kitasato 1 Chome, Sagamiharashi, kanagawaken 228, Japan. **CODEN** KIIGDP. Documents available from CASDDS.
**Ind/Abst** Chem. Abstr.

NE
**KLIK.** (19??)-. Periodical. Dutch. mo (11 issues). Fl62.26 Netherlands; Fl72.64 Europe; Fl88.68 other. St. Maandblad Klik, Postbus 297, 3500 AG Utrecht Netherlands. **Tel** 011 31 30 316343.

RU/0023-2149
**KLINICESKAJA MEDICINA.** (KLINICHESKAIA MEDITSINA.). [Klin. med.]. **Added/Corp** Russian S.F.S.R. Narodnyi Komissariat Zdravookhraneniia. Russian S.F.S.R. Glavnoe Upravlenie Nauchnymi Uchrezhdeniiami. Soviet Union. Ministerstvo Zdravookhranenniia. (1923)-. Academic Scholarly Publication. Russian (summaries and/or abstracts in English; table of contents in English and German). Six times a year. $89.95. Izdatelstvo Meditsina / Russian Academy of Medical Sciences, Ulitsa Solyanka 14, 109801 Moscow Russia. **Tel** 011 95 297-05-04. **(Subscription address:** East View Publications Inc., 3020 Harbor Lane North, Suite 110, Minneapolis MN 55447.**)** **LC** R91; .K376. **NLM** W1 KL187. **CODEN** KLMIAZ. **[CCC]**. Index available. cum. index. **Bk Rev. Pr Rev.** Documents available from The Genuine Article, BIOSIS Document Express, CASDDS.
**Ind/Abst** Biol. Abstr.; Chem. Abstr.; Dairy Sci. Abstr.; EMBASE [Select. Cov.]; Helminthol. Abstr. (19??-19??); Index Med.; Microbiol. Abstr. Sect. B (19??-19??); PESTDOC; Protozoolog. Abstr.; Res. Alert [Full Cov.]; Rev. Med. Vet. Entomol.; Rev. Med. Vet. Mycology; Sci. Cit. Index; SCISEARCH; Soc. Sci. Cit. Index [Select. Cov.]; Virol. AIDS Abstr.

GW/0341-2350
**KLINIKARZT, DER.** Yearly V. 1- June 28, 1972-. Periodical. German. **NLM** W1 KL313. ***Supersedes*** *Med. Ass, 0341-2466.*

DK/0902-2767
**KLINISK SYGEPLEJE.** [Klin. sygepl.]. (1987)-. Periodical. Danish. bm. kr260.00. Munksgaard International Publishers Ltd, PO Box 2148, DK-1016 Copenhagen K Denmark. **Tel** 011 45 33 12 70 30, FAX 011 45 33 12 93 87, telex 19431 MUNKS DK. **DD** 610 610.73. **CODEN** 61.7.

JA/0075-6431
**KOBE DAIGAKU IGAKUBU KIYO.** [Kobe Daigaku Igakubu Kiyo]. **Added/Corp** Kobe Daigaku. Igakubu. **VFOAT** Medical Journal of Kobe University. (1968)-. Periodical. Japanese (summaries and/or abstracts in English). qt. Kobe University School of Medicine, 7 Kusunoki Cho, Kobe Japan. **CODEN** KDIKAX. Documents available from BIOSIS Document Express, CASDDS. ***Continues*** *Kobe Ika Daigaku Kiyo.*
**Ind/Abst** Biol. Abstr. (-1987); Chem. Abstr.; EMBASE [Select. Cov.].

JA/0023-2513
**KOBE JOURNAL OF MEDICAL SCIENCES.** [Kobe j. med. sci.]. (1954)-. Academic Scholarly Publication. English. bm. ¥1000. Kobe University School of Medicine, 7 Kusunoki Cho, Kobe Japan. **NLM** W1 KO2817. **CODEN** KJMDA6. Index Available, published separately, free-automatically sent. Documents available from BIOSIS Document Express, CASDDS. ***Continues*** *Hyogo Journal of the Medical Sciences.*
**Ind/Abst** Biol. Abstr.; Chem. Abstr.; EMBASE [Select. Cov.]; Index Med.; NAPRALERT; Life Sci. Collect.; Trop. Dis. Bull.

JA/0300-9149
**KOKUBYO GAKKAI ZASSHI.** [Kokubyo Gakkai Zasshi]. **Main/Corp** Kokubyo Gakkai. **Added/Corp** Kokubyo Gakkai. Journal of the Japan Stomatological Society. **VFOAT** Journal of the Japan Stomatological Society; Vierteljahrschrift - Japanische Gesellschaft fur Stomatologie. Vol. 1 (June 1927)-. Periodical. Japanese (summaries and/or abstracts in English and German). qt. $128.50. Kokubyo Gakkai, (Japan Stomatological Soc.), 44-2, Komagome 1 Chome, Toshimaku, Tokyoto 170, Japan. **(Subscription address:** Japan Publications Trading Company, Ltd., PO Box 5030, Tokyo International, Tokyo 100-31 Japan.**)** **NLM** W1 KO296. **CODEN** KOGZA9. Documents available from CASDDS.
**Ind/Abst** Chem. Abstr.; Index Med.; Index Dent. Lit.

JA
**KOKURITSU TAMA KENKYUJO NEMPO.** **Main/Corp** Kokuritsu Tama Kenkyujo. Began with the report for 1955. Japanese (English). an. Kokuritsu Tama Kenkyujo, 2-1 Aobacho 4-chome, Higashimurayama Japan. **Tel** (0423)91-8211. **ED** Tatsuo Mori. **LC** RC154.A1; K640. Index available. ctrl circ.

GW/0723-5364
**KOPFSCHMERZ.** Monographic series. English. Price varies per volume. G Braun Verlag, Postfach 1709, D 76006 Karlsruhe Germany. **Tel** 011 49 721 165392.

SI
**KOREAN INDEX OF MEDICAL SPECIALITIES.** Three times a year. $36.00. Medidata Pte. Ltd., 15 McCallum Street, 04-01 Natwest, Singapore 0106 Singapore. **Tel** 011 65 2233788.

HU/0139-4509
**KORHAZ- ES ORVOSTECHNIKA.** (KORHAZ- ES ORVOSTECHNIKA : AZ ORSZAGOS KORHAZ- ES ORVOSTECHNIKAI INTEZET TUDOMANYOS FOLYOIRATA.). [Korh.- orvtech.]. **Added/Corp** Orszagos Korhaz- es Orvostechnikai Intezet (Hungary). Vol. 18, No. 1 (Jan. 1980)-. Academic Scholarly Publication. Hungarian (summaries and/or abstracts in English and Russian). bm. $14.00 Austria, Croatia, Yugoslavia, Slovenia, Ukraine, Czech Republic, Slovakia, & Romania; $18.00 other. Akademiai Kiado, Publishing House of the Hungarian Academy of Sciences, Prielle Kornelia u. 19-35, H-1117 Budapest Hungary. **Tel** 011 36 1 1811991, FAX 011 36 1 1811991, telex 22-6228 AKNYO H. **(Subscription address:** Kultura, Hungarian Foreign Trading Company, PO Box 149, H-1389 Budapest 62 Hungary (011 36 1 359370)**)** **NLM** W1 KO611V. ***Continues*** *Orvos es Technika, 0473-4424.*
**Ind/Abst** Energy Res. Abstr. (Oct. 1981-).

IS/0023-4109
**KOROT.** (19??)-. Periodical. English (Hebrew). an. $25.50. Magnes Press, Hebrew University of Jerusalem, PO Box 7695, Jerusalem 91076 Israel. **Tel** 011 972 2 660341, 011 972 2 635291, FAX 011 972 2 633370, telex 25391. **ED** Professor S. Kottek. Index available. cum. index. **Circ:** 500. ***Continues*** *Koroth.*
**Desc:** This journal includes social, philosophical and ethical aspects and with special emphasis on the Jewish contribution to the medicine and life science fields.

IS
**KOROTH (JERUSALEM : 1951).** ***Title Change.*** (KOROTH.). **Added/Corp** Hevrah Le-toldot Ha-refuah U-madae Ha-teva Be-Yisrael. Akademyah Li-refuah Bi-Yerushalayim. **VFOAT** Koroth. (1952)-(19??). Periodical. English (Hebrew). an. Magnes Press, Hebrew University of Jerusalem, PO Box 7695, Jerusalem 91076 Israel. **Tel** 011 972 2 660341, 011 972 2 635291, FAX 011 972 2 633370, telex 25391. **ED** Professor S. Kottek. **NLM** W1 KO615. cum. index. **Circ:** 500. ***Continued by*** *Korot.*
**Desc:** This journal includes social, philosophical and ethical aspects and with special emphasis on the Jewish contribution to the medicine and life science fields.
**Ind/Abst** Am. Hist. Life (1963-1975).

KO
**KORYO TAEHAKKYO UIKWA TAEHAK NONMUNJIP. KOREA UNIVERSITY MEDICAL JOURNAL.** **Main/Corp** Koryo Taehakkyo. Uikwa Taehak. **Added/Corp** Koryo Taehakkyo. Uikwa Taehak. Korea University Medical Journal. **VFOAT** Korea University Medical Journal. (19??)-. Academic Scholarly Publication. English (Korean). **LC** R97.7.K6; K67a. **NLM** W1; KO616HD. **CODEN** KTUNDD. Documents available from BIOSIS Document Express, CASDDS.
**Ind/Abst** Biol. Abstr.; Chem. Abstr.; EMBASE; Trop. Dis. Bull.

JA/0910-6073
**KOSANKINBYO KENKYUSHO ZASSHI.** [Kosankinbyo Kenkyusho zasshi]. **VFOAT** Kokenshi. (1984)-. Periodical. Japanese (summaries and/or abstracts in English). Four times a year. Tohoku Daigaku Kosankinbyo Ken, 4 1 Seiryocho Sendaishi, Miyagiken 980 Japan. **DD** 616.9. ***Continues*** *Kosankinbyo Kenkyu Zasshi, 0368-6078.*
**Ind/Abst** EMBASE [Select. Cov.].

JA/0022-5274
**KOTSU IGAKU.** [Kotsu igaku]. **Added/Corp** Nihon Kotsu Igakkai. **VFOAT** Journal of Transportation Medicine. (1947)-. Periodical. Japanese (summaries and/or abstracts in English). bm. Japanese Association of Transportation Medicine, 2-1 Yoyogi, Shibuya-ku 151 Tokyo Japan. **CODEN** KOIGAU. Documents available from CASDDS.
**Ind/Abst** Chem. Abstr. (1947-1986); EMBASE.

GW/0023-4486
**KRANKENDIENST.** (19??)-. Periodical. German. mo. DM54.00. Lambertus-Verlag GmbH, Postfach 1026, 79010 Freiburg, Germany. **Tel** 011 49 761 3 68 25 0, FAX 011 49 761 3 70 64. **UDC** 362.1. Index available. cum. index. **Bk Rev.** **Ad Acc.** **Circ:** 4,000.

CH
**KUO CHIA I HSUEH TSA CHIH.** **VFOAT** Kuo Chia I Hsueh. First published in 1983. Periodical. Chinese. qt. $200.00. Kuo Chia I Hsueh Tsa Chih She, PO Box 44-45, Taipei Shih Taiwan. **LC** R97.7.C5; K84. **DD** 610/.951.

JA/0023-5679
**KURUME MEDICAL JOURNAL.** [Kurume Med. J.]. **Added/Corp** Kurume Daigaku. Igakubu. Vol. 1 (Jan./Mar. 1954)-. Academic Scholarly Publication. English. qt. $95.00. Kurume University, School of Medicine, Kurume Shi Japan. **Tel** 942 35 3311 ext. 3030, FAX 942 32 0900. **(Subscription address:** Japan Publications Trading Company, Ltd., PO Box 5030, Tokyo International, Tokyo 100-31 Japan.**)** **ED** Takashi Akasu. **NLM** W1 KU722. **CODEN** KRMJAC. Index available. **Circ:** 550 (institutions) (ctrl). Documents available from BIOSIS Document Express, CASDDS.
**Ind/Abst** Biol. Abstr.; Chem. Abstr.; EMBASE [Select. Cov.]; Index Med.; Nutr. Abstr. Rev., Ser. A, Hum. Exp.; SEA Abstr.; Trop. Dis. Bull.

JA/0368-5829
**KYORIN IGAKKAI ZASSHI.** [Kyorin Igakukai zasshi]. **Added/Corp** Kyorin Igakkai. **VFOAT** Journal of the Kyorin Medical Society. (1970)-. Periodical. Japanese (summaries and/or abstracts in English). qt. Kyorin Medical Society, 6-20-2 Shinkawa, Mitaka City, Tokyo 181 Japan. **CODEN** KIZSB8. Documents available from CASDDS.
**Ind/Abst** Chem. Abstr.

JA
**KYOTO FURITSU IKA DAIGAKU ZASSHI.** [Kyoto Furitsu Ika Daigaku zasshi]. **Added/Corp** Kyoto Furitsu Ika Daigaku. **VFOAT** Journal of Kyoto Prefectural Medical University; Journal of Kyoto Prefectural Universty of Medicine. (1927)-. Periodical. Japanese (summaries and/or abstracts in English). mo. Kyoto Furitsu Ika Daigaku Igakkai, (Medical Soc. of Kyoto Prefectural University of Medicine), 465, Kajiicho, Hirokoji Agaru,, Kawaramachi Doori, Kamigyoku, Kyotoshi, Kyotofu 602, Japan. **CODEN** KFIZAO. Documents available from BIOSIS Document Express, CASDDS.
**Ind/Abst** Biol. Abstr.; Chem. Abstr.

NE/0368-7368
**LAB-INSTRUMENTEN AMSTERDAM.** (LAB-INSTRUMENTEN). (1965)-. Periodical. Dutch. mo. Fl90.00 Netherlands; Fl107.50 other. ADEX CV, PO Box 328, 3760 AH Soest Netherlands. **Tel** 011 31 2155 10034, FAX 011 31 2155 25576. **UDC** 53.

US/1045-7313
**LAB REPORT.** [Lab rep.]. Vol. 11, No. 9 (Sept. 1989)-. Periodical. English. Eleven times a year (July/Aug., iss. combined). $99.00 (one year), $170.00 (two year), $240.00 (three year). G & R Publications Inc, 185 Devonshire Street, 9th Floor, Boston MA 02110. **Tel** (617)338-8860, FAX (617)338-9895. **ED** Dr. Raymond Gambino M. D. **DD** 616. **NLM** W1; LA131DE. **[CCC].** Index available. cum. index. **Pr Rev.** ***Continues*** *Lab Report for Physicians, 0278-5161.*
**Desc:** Updates on the laboratory diagnosis for the physicians.

US/0192-7698
**LAB (RIDGEWOOD).** (LAB.). **VFOAT** Laboratory Medicine for Practicing Physicians. V. 1- May/June 1978-. Periodical. English. bm. $15.00. Peer Communications Group, Box 691, 615 Franklin Turnpike, Ridgewood NJ 07451. **NLM** W1 LA123.

US/1054-0970
**LABMEDICA (WILTON, CONN.).** ***Title Change.*** (LABMEDICA.). [Labmedica]. (1984)-(199?). Periodical. English (summaries and/or abstracts in Arabic, French, German and Spanish). bm. Techcom Inc, PO Box 5017, Westport CT 06881. **DD** 616. **NLM** W1; LA131P. ***Continued by*** *LabMedica International, 1068-1760.*
**Ind/Abst** Chem. Hazards Ind.; Curr. Biotechnol.; Lab. Hazards Bull.

GW/0170-205X
**LABOR-MEDIZIN (GIT-VERLAG GIEBELER).** (LABOR-MEDIZIN.). [Lab.-Med.]. **VFOAT** Labor Medizin. Vol. 7, No.1 (Jan. 1984)-. Academic Scholarly Publication. German (summaries and/or abstracts in English). Ten times a year. DM120.00. GIT Verlag GmbH, Roblerstrabe 90, Postfach 110564, D 64220 Darmstadt Germany. **Tel** 011 49 6151 8090-0, FAX 011 49 6151 8090-45. **NLM** W1; LA18R. **CODEN** LAMEET. Documents available from CASDDS. ***Continues*** *Git Labor-Medizin, 0170-205X.*
**Ind/Abst** Anal. Abstr.; Chem. Abstr. (1984-); Chem. Hazards Ind.; Lab. Hazards Bull.

GW/0342-3026
**LABORATORIUMSMEDIZIN.** **Added/Corp** Deutsche Gesellschaft fur Laboratoriumsmedizin. Arbeitsgemeinschaft der Facharzte fur Laboratoriumsmedizin. Osterreichische Gesellschaft fur Medizinische und Chemische Labordiagnostik. Osterreichische Gesellschaft fur Laboratoriumsmedizin. **VFOAT** Laboratoriums Medizin. Vol. 1, (May 1977)-. Academic Scholarly Publication. German (summaries and/or abstracts in English). ir. DM198.00. Blackwell Wissenschafts-Verlag, Kurfuerstendamm 57, D 10707 Berlin Germany. **Tel** 011 49 30 32790623, 011 49 30 32790624, FAX 011 49 30 327 90610. **ED** L. Thomas. **NLM** W1 LA2055D. **CODEN** LABOD3. **[CCC].** Index available. **Bk Rev.** **Ad Acc.** **Circ:** 7,800 (ctrl). Documents available from CASDDS. ***Absorbed*** *Medizinische Laboratorium.*
**Desc:** Clinical chemistry, haematology, microscopy, laboratory automation, immunology, bacteriology, haemostaseology, serology, chromatography, RIA (radioimmunoassay), and epidemiology.
**Ind/Abst** Chem. Abstr.; EMBASE.

US/0160-8584
**LABORATORY AND RESEARCH METHODS IN BIOLOGY AND MEDICINE.** ***Ceased.*** **See** Biology.

UK/0458-5933
**LABORATORY ANIMAL HANDBOOKS.** Began publication with No. 2 in 1969. Monographic series. English. ir. Price varies per volume. Royal Society of Medicine Press, 1 Wimpole Street, London W1M 8AE England. **Tel** 011 44 71 2902928. **Circ:** 1,700. ***Continues*** *Laboratory Animal Symposia.*
**Desc:** All aspects of laboratory animal science including microbiology, nutrition, pathology, toxicology, etc.
**Ind/Abst** Index Vet.; Vet. Bull.

US/0007-5027
**LABORATORY MEDICINE.** [Lab. med.]. **Added/Corp** American Society of Clinical Pathologists. Vol. 1 (Jan. 1970)-. Academic Scholarly Publication. English. mo. $55.00 (institutions), $50.00 (individuals) US; $70.00 (institutions), $65.00 (individuals) other. American Society of Clinical Pathologists, 2100 West Harrison Street, c/o L. Fields, Chicago IL 60612. **Tel** (312)738-1336, (800)621-4142, FAX (312)738-1619. **(Subscription address:** Japan/ Woodbell Scope Inc., Mansui Building, 9-18, Kanda-Surugadai 2-Chome, Chiyoda-Ku, Tokyo 101 Japan**)** **ED** Paul Sher and Deborah Mercer. **LC** RB37.A1; L33. **NLM** W1 LA219R. **CODEN** LBMEBX. Index available. **Bk Rev.** **Ad Acc.** **Pr Rev.** **Circ:** 155,000. available on microfilm and microfiche from University Microfilms International (UMI). Documents available from The Genuine Article, CASDDS. ***Formed by the union of*** *Bulletin of Pathology* ***and*** *Technical Bulletin of the Registry of Medical Technologists, 0097-0654.*
**Ind/Abst** Chem. Abstr.; Curr. Aware. Biol. Sci., CABS; Curr. Contents Clin. Med.; EMBASE; Protozoolog. Abstr.; Res. Alert [Select. Cov.]; Rev. Med. Vet. Entomol.; Rev. Med. Vet. Mycology; Risk Abstr.; SCISEARCH; Soc. Sci. Cit. Index [Select. Cov.].

US/1050-9658
**LABORATORY MEDICINE ABSTRACT AND COMMENT.** ***Ceased.*** [Lab. med. abstr. comment]. Vol. 1 (1991)-Ceased with Vol. 3, No. 6 (1993). Periodical. English. Ten times a year. Churchill Livingstone Inc., 650 Avenue of the Americas, New York NY 10011. **Tel** (212)206-5062, FAX (212)727-7808. **(Subscription address:** Churchill Livingstone Inc., 5 South 250 Frontenac Road, Naperville, IL 60563 (telephone: (800)553-5426 or (708)416-3939)**)** **ED** Calvin L. Strand. **DD** 615.
**Desc:** Contains summaries of the most important articles in laboratory medicine published in a wide range of journals. Each summary is followed by an editorial comment on the significance and relevancy to daily practice of the finding reported in the article. Readership: pathologists and medical technicians.

GW/0344-1733
**LABORPRAXIS.** [Laborprax.]. (1977)-. Academic Scholarly Publication. German. Twelve times a year. DM170.00 Germany; DM190.00 other. Vogel Verlag, Postfach 6740, D-97064 Wuerzburg Germany. **Tel** 011 49 931 4182145, 011 49 931 4182483, FAX 011 49 931 4182670, telex 841 680131. **NLM** W1; LA236G. **CODEN** LAPRDE. **[CCC].** **Ad Acc.** **Circ:** 14,050 (ctrl). Documents available from CASDDS.
**Ind/Abst** Chem. Abstr.; EMBASE.

GW/0171-4279
**LABORPRAXIS IN DER MEDIZIN.** [Lab.-Prax. Med.]. **VAT** Labor Praxis in der Medizin. Began with: Feb. 20, 1978. Periodical. German. sa. $8.11. Vogel Verlag, Postfach 6740, D-97064 Wuerzburg Germany. **Tel** 011 49 931 4182145, 011 49 931 4182483, FAX 011 49 931 4182670, telex 841 680131. **NLM** W1 LA236L.
**Ind/Abst** Energy Res. Abstr. (Feb. 1983-).

SW/0023-7205
**LAKARTIDNINGEN.** [Lakartidningen]. V. 62- 1965-. Academic Scholarly Publication. Swedish. wk. Kr572.00. Swedish Medical Association, PO Box 5603, S-11486 Stockholm Sweden. **Tel** (08)7903300, FAX (08)207435. **ED** Bosse Tolander. **UDC** 667.6. **NLM** W1 LA256L. Index available. **Bk Rev.** **Ad Acc.** **Pr Rev.** **Circ:** 32,000. ***Continues*** *Svenska Lakartidningen.*
**Desc:** General medicine journal.
**Ind/Abst** EMBASE; Energy Res. Abstr.; Index Med.; Int. Pharm. Abstr.; Rev. Med. Vet. Entomol.; Saf. Health Work; SportSearch.

UK/0140-6736
**LANCET (BRITISH EDITION).** (THE LANCET.). [Lancet]. Vol. 1, No. 1 (Oct. 1823)-. Academic Scholarly Publication. English. Fifty-two times a year. £145.00 (institution), £90.00 (individual) UK & Europe; £155.00 (institution), £110.00 (individual) other. Lancet Ltd, 46 Bedford Square, London WC1B 3SL England. **Tel** 011 44 1 436 4981, FAX (617)868-7738. **(Subscription address:** The Lancet, PO Box 64342, Baltimore MD 21264.**)** **LC** R31; .L3. **NLM** W1 LA453. **CODEN** LANCAO. **[CCC].** **Pr Rev.** **Circ:** 20,000. available on microfilm and diskette from University Microfilms International (UMI); available on CD-ROM. Documents available from BIOSIS Document Express, UMI Article Clearinghouse, CASDDS, Documents on Demand.
**Desc:** Original articles providing basic information on diagnostic methodology.
**Ind/Abst** AGRICOLA; Biodeter. Abstr.; Biol. Abstr.; Biol. Dig.; Calcium Calcif. Tissue Abstr.; Chem. Abstr.; Chem. Hazards Ind.; Crim. Penol. Police Sci. Abstr.; Curr. Contents Clin. Med.; Curr. Contents Life Sci.; Dev. Med. Child Neurol.; EMBASE; Environ. Abstr.; Food Sci. Technol. Abstr.; Gen. Period. Index (1988-); Genet. Abstr.; Health Saf. Sci. Abstr.; Health Devices Alerts; Health Serv. Abstr.; Helminthol. Abstr. (1991-); Hospit. Manage. Rev.; Hum. Genome Abstr.; Immunol. Abstr.; Index Med.; Index Vet.; Int. Pharm. Abstr.; Lab. Hazards Bull.; Leadscan; Microbiol. Abstr. Sect. A; Newsp. Period. Abstr. (1989-); Nutr. Abstr. Rev., Ser. A, Hum. Exp.; PESTDOC; Physic. Medline Plus; Pig News Inf.; Poult. Abstr.; Protozoolog. Abstr.; Rev. Med. Vet. Mycology; Rice Abstr.; Risk Abstr.; Saf. Health Work; Small Anim. Abstr. Bibliogr.; Soc. Sci. Cit. Index [Select. Cov.]; Soils Fert.; Soyabean Abstr.; SPORT Discus; SportSearch; Vet. Bull.; Trop. Dis. Bull.; Virol. AIDS Abstr.; Weed Abstr.

NE/0923-7577
**LANCET ED. FRANCAISE.** ***Ceased.*** (THE LANCET.). [Lancet Ed. fr.]. (1989)-(1993). Academic Scholarly Publication. French. mo. Editions Scientifique Elsevier, 141 rue de Javel, 75747 Paris Cedex 15 France. **Tel** 011 33 1 47 07 11 22, FAX 011 33 1 43 36 80 93. **UDC** 61. **[CCC].** available on microfilm and microfiche from University Microfilms International (UMI).
**Ind/Abst** Int. Pharm. Abstr.

IT/0393-0637
**LANCET EDIZIONE ITALIANA, THE.** [Lancet Ed. ital.]. (1984)-. Periodical. Italian. Ten times a year. L88000 Italy. Masson S.P.A, Via Statuto 2/4, 20121 Milan Italy. **Tel** 011 39 2 63671, FAX 011 39 2 6367211. **UDC** 61.
**Desc:** Coverage includes original articles, news and comments, editorials and letters to the editors. A selection of relevant and interesting articles are carefully chosen by the editorial panel members.

JA/0916-6386
**LANCET NIHONGO-BAN, THE.** (THE LANCET.). [Lancet Nihongo-ban]. **VFOAT** Ransetto. Nihongo-ban. (1991)-. Academic Scholarly Publication. Japanese. mo. ¥26460.00. Elsevier Science Publishers, 20-12, Yushima 3-chome, Bunkyo-ku, Tokyo 113 Japan. **DD** 610.
**Desc:** Special features of this edition are: wide coverage including original articles, news and comments, editorials and letters to the editors. A selection of articles are chosen by the editorial panel members and translated into the Japanese language.

US/0099-5355
**LANCET (NORTH AMERICAN EDITION), THE.** (THE LANCET.). [Lancet]. No. 7453 (July 2, 1966)-. Periodical. English. wk. $207.00 US; $229.00 Canada. The Lancet, 655 Avenue of the Americas, 5th Floor, New York NY 10010. **Tel** (212)633-3800, FAX (212)633-3850. **(Subscription address:** Lancet, PO Box 64342, Baltimore MD 21264.**)** **LC** R31; .L3. **DD** 610/.5. **NLM** W1 LA453B. **CODEN** LANAA1. **[CCC].** Index available (bound in last issue). **Bk Rev.** **Ad Acc.** **Pr Rev.** **Circ:** 15,000. available on CD-ROM. Documents available from The Genuine Article, BIOSIS Document Express, ADONIS.
**Desc:** Covers developments worldwide in general medicine and clinical research.
**Ind/Abst** Acad. Abstr. Full Text Elite (Jan. 1989-); Acad. Abstr. (Jan. 1989-); Acad. Ind. [Computer File] (1988-); Acad. Search (Jan. 1989-); ADONIS; AGRICOLA [Select. Cov.]; Arts Humanit. Citation Index [Select. Cov.]; Biol. Abstr.; Cumul. Index Nurs. Allied Health Lit.; Expand. Acad. Index (1988-); Foods Adlibra; Gen. Sci. Index (1992-); Gen. Sci. Source (Jan. 1989-); Health Index (1989-); Health Period. Database [Full Txt.]; Health Ref. Cent. (Jan. 1989-) [Full Txt.] [Full Cov.]; Health Source (Jan. 1989-); Hospit. Manage. Rev.; Ind. Hyg. Dig. (19??-19??); INFO-SOUTH Abstr.; J. Watch (199?-); Mag. Artic. Summar. Elite (Jan. 1989-); Mag. Artic. Summar. Select (Jan. 1989-); Mag. Artic. Summar. CD-ROM (Jan. 1989-); Mag. ASAP Plus [Full Txt.]; Mag. Index Plus (1992-); Mag. Search; Med. Abstr. Newsl.; Microbiol. Abstr. Sect. B; Oncog. Growth Factors Abstr.; Life Sci. Collect.; Popul. Index; Ref. Upd. Basic Ed.; Ref. Upd. Clinical Ed.; Ref. Upd. Deluxe Ed.; Res. Alert [Full

Cov.]; Sci. Cit. Index; SCISEARCH; Sel. Water Resour. Abstr.; Toxicol. Abstr.; Trade Ind. ASAP [Full Txt.]; Trade Ind. Index [Full Txt.]; Vocat. Search (Jan. 1989-).

SP
**LANCET (SPANISH EDITION), THE.**
Spanish. Ediciones Doyma SA, Travesera de Gracia 17 21, 08021 Barcelona Spain. **Tel** 011 34 3 2000711, 011 34 3 4145706, FAX 011 34 3 2091136, telex 51964 INK E.

●US/1067-2036
**LAPAROSCOPIC SURGERY UPDATE.**
[Laparosc. surg. update]. Vol. 1, No. 1 (Mar. 1993)-. Periodical. English. mo. $245.00 (one year), $390.00 (two year), $490.00 (three year). Global Success Corporation, 2400 Ninth Street North, Suite 450, Naples FL 33940. **Tel** (813)261-4335, FAX (813)261-6713. **ED** Greg Freeman. **DD** 617. Index available. cum. index. ctrl circ.

UK/0268-8921
**LASERS IN MEDICAL SCIENCE.** [Lasers med. sci.]. **Added/Corp** European Laser Association. Vol. 1, No. 1 (Jan. 1986)-. Periodical. English. qt (4 issues). £99.00 (institution), £70.00 (individual) UK/Europe;'$178.00 (institution), $128.00 (individual) other. Harcourt Brace & Company Ltd., Foots Cray, High Street, Sidcup Kent DA14 5HP England. **Tel** 011 44 81 300 3322, FAX 011 44 81 309 0807. **(Subscription address:** W. B. Saunders Company / North America Subscriptions, c/o Periodicals, 6277 Sea Harbour Drive, 4th Floor, Orlando FL 32887.**) ED** S. G. Bown, J. A. S. Carruth, G. Jori and L. O. Svaasand. **NLM** W1; LA783F. **CODEN** LMSCEZ. **[CCC].** Documents available from The Genuine Article, BIOSIS Document Express.
**Desc:** A journal that is establishing itself as a leading international publication to bring together the work of clinicians and basic scientists in the rapidly expanding field of the medical applications of lasers. In addition to original and review articles, the journal includes comment on important laser literature published elsewhere and a diary of forthcoming laser meetings.
**Ind/Abst** Biol. Abstr. (1986-); Curr. Contents Clin. Med.; Curr. Contents Life Sci.; EMBASE; Res. Alert [Full Cov.]; Sci. Cit. Index.

NE/0925-8434
**LASERS IN MEDICINE.** ***Ceased.*** Vol. 1, Issue 1, Jan. (1991)-Vol. 3. Periodical. English. Eleven times a year (1 volume). Excerpta Medica Publishing Group, PO Box 548, 1000 AM Amsterdam Netherlands. **Tel** 011 31 20 5803243. **(Subscription address:** Elsevier Scientific Publishers, Ltd, Customer Relations Manager, PO Box 85, Limerick, Ireland**) NLM** ZWB 117; L343. **CODEN** LMEDE2. **[CCC].**

●US/1067-716X
**LATEST WORD (PHILADELPHIA, PA.), THE.** (THE LATEST WORD.). [Latest word]. **VAT** Latest Word. (1993)-. Periodical. English. bm. $29.00 (individual), $39.00 (institution) US; $54.00 other. W.B. Saunders Company, A Subsidiary of Harcourt Brace Jovanovich, Inc., The Curtis Center/Suite 300, Independence Square West, Philadelphia PA 19106-3399. **Tel** (215)238-7800 or, 5587, FAX (215)238-7883, telex 173146. **(Subscription address:** W. B. Saunders Company / North America Subscriptions, c/o Periodicals, 6277 Sea Harbour Drive, 4th Floor, Orlando FL 32887.**) DD** 610.

IT/0391-3147
**LAVORO E MEDICINA.** [Lav. med.]. (1947)-. Periodical. Italian. Three times a year. L200000 Italy. Ediz Culturali Internazionali ECIG, Via Caffaro 19 Int 10, 16124 Genoa, Italy. **Tel** 011 39 10 208800. **(Subscription address:** Italia Srl, C SO Brescia 75, 10152 Turin, Italy.**) UDC** 61. **CODEN** LAVM-A.

US/0277-8459
**LAW, MEDICINE & HEALTH CARE.** ***Title Change.*** **See** Law.

US
**LAWYERS' GUIDE TO MEDICAL PROOF.** **See** Law.

US/8755-5891
**LAWYER'S MEDICAL DIGEST.** **See** Law.

IT
**LEADERSHIP MEDICA.** Italian. mo. Free on request. Cesil, Via Olmetto 5, 20123 Milan Italy. **Tel** 011 39 2 878397. **ED** Genina Iacoboni.

LE/0023-9852
**LEBANESE MEDICAL JOURNAL.** (LE JOURNAL MEDICAL LIBANAIS.). [Leban. med. j.]. V. 3-Jan. 1950-. Periodical. French (Arabic and English). bm. Inter Commerce Center, PO Box 11-9450, Beirut Lebanon. **NLM** W1 JO517. **CODEN** LMJJA7. Index available in last issue of volume--attached. ***Continues*** *Revue Medicale Libanaise.*
**Ind/Abst** Index Med.

GW/0172-7788
**LECTURE NOTES IN MEDICAL INFORMATICS.** (1978)-. Monographic series. English. ir. Price varies per volume. Springer-Verlag GmbH & Company KG, Heidelberger Platz 3, D 14197 Berlin Germany. **Tel** 011 49 30 8207223, FAX 011 49 30 8214091, telex 183 319 SPBLN D. **(Subscription address:** Springer Verlag New York Inc. / for North America, 44 Hartz Way, Secaucus NJ 07096.**) ED** D. A. B. Lindberg and P. L. Reichertz. **LC** UNC. **NLM** W1 LE334N.
**Desc:** Contains articles on therapeutic studies, decision-making systems approach in acute diseases, and topics in image science.
**Ind/Abst** Ei Page One; Math. Rev.; Zentralbl. Math. Ihre Grenzgeb.

US/0190-2350
**LEGAL ASPECTS OF MEDICAL PRACTICE.** **See** Law.

XO/0457-4214
**LEKARSKY OBZOR.** [Lek. obz.]. (1952)-. Academic Scholarly Publication. Slovak (summaries and/or abstracts in English, German and Russian; table of contents in English, German and Russian). mo. DM91.82. Slovart GTG LTD, Krupinska 4, 852 99 Bratislava, Slovakia. **Tel** 011 42 7 839471 2. **(Subscription address:** Artia Pegas Press Ltd., Palac Metro Narodni Trida 25, 11210 Prague 1 Czech Republic.**) NLM** W1 LE685. **CODEN** LEOBAK. Documents available from CASDDS.
**Ind/Abst** Chem. Abstr.; Curr. Biotechnol.; EMBASE [Select. Cov.]; Helminthol. Abstr.; Saf. Health Work.

PL/0024-0745
**LEKARZ WOJSKOWY.** [Lek. wojs.]. **Added/Corp** Polish Army Medical Corps. Journal. (1920)-. Periodical. Polish. **NLM** W1 LE7671. **CODEN** LEKWAT. Documents available from CASDDS.
**Ind/Abst** Chem. Abstr.

US/1042-6922
**LENS AND EYE TOXICITY RESEARCH.** ***Title Change.*** [Lens eye toxic. res.]. **Added/Corp** International Society of Ocular Toxicology. Congress. International Society of Ocular Toxicology. Vol. 6, No. 1 & 2 (1989)-(19??). Academic Scholarly Publication. English. qt. Marcel Dekker Inc., 270 Madison Avenue, New York NY 10016. **Tel** (212)696-9000, (800)228-1160, FAX (212)685-4540, telex 421419. **(Subscription address:** Marcel Dekker Inc, PO Box 5017, Monticello NY 12701.**) ED** Sidney Lerman, Otto Hockwin, Kazuyuki Susaki. **LC** RE401; .L46. **DD** 617.7/1. **NLM** W1; LE829. **CODEN** LETRET. **[CCC].** Documents available from CASDDS. ***Continues*** *Lens Research, 0738-1441.* ***Merged into*** *Journal of Toxicology / Cutaneous and Ocular Toxicology.*
**Desc:** As the official journal of the International Society of Ocular Toxicology, 'Lens and Eye Toxicity Research' provides a forum for the latest developments in drug-induced ocular side effects and methods (both in vivo and in vitro) to monitor such effects. The proceedings of the ISOT Congress, which is held every two years, are also published as special issues. In addition, articles presented examine such topics as biochemistry and metabolism of the normal, aging, and cataractous lens; the development of medical therapy to inhibit and prevent cataract progression; biophysical basis of lens transparency; recombinant DNA research; the correlation between structure and function; lens protein structure and function including x-ray crystallographic, biophysical, and metabolic studies; and the ocular lens as a model for geriatric research.
**Ind/Abst** Chem. Abstr.; Curr. Aware. Biol. Sci., CABS; EMBASE; Ref. Upd. Deluxe Ed.

UK
**LEPRA REPORT.** **Main/Corp** British Leprosy Relief Association. (1957)-. English. an. British Leprosy Relief Association, Manfield House 376 Strand Ste 54, London WC2R OLR England. **NLM** W1 BR662. ***Continues*** *Report of the British Empire Leprosy Relief Association.*

UK/0305-7518
**LEPROSY REVIEW.** [Lepr. rev.]. **Added/Corp** British Leprosy Relief Association. British Empire Leprosy Relief Association. Vol. 1 (Jan. 1930)-. Academic Scholarly Publication. English. Four times a year. £30.00 UK. Lepra, Fairfax House, Causton Road, Colchester C01 1PU England. **Tel** 011 44 206562286, FAX 011 44 206762151. **ED** J.L. Turk, Royal college of Surgeons, 35/43 Lincoln's Inn, Fields, London WC2A 3PN England UK; Telephone: 11 44 071 4053474. **NLM** W1 LE872. **CODEN** LEREAA. **[CCC].** Index available in last issue of volume--attached. **Bk Rev**, (Qty: 3/yr). **Ad Acc, Adv Mgr:** Jennet Batten, **Tel** 11 44 0865 873899. **Pr Rev. Circ:** 1,700. Documents available from The Genuine Article, BIOSIS Document Express, CASDDS. ***Supersedes*** *Leprosy Notes.*
**Desc:** Research and control of leprosy.
**Ind/Abst** Biol. Abstr.; Chem. Abstr. (1930-1983); Curr. Aware. Biol. Sci., CABS; Curr. Contents Clin. Med.; EMBASE; Helminthol. Abstr.; Index Med.; Microbiol. Abstr. Sect. B; Life Sci. Collect.; Res. Alert [Full Cov.]; Sci. Cit. Index; SCISEARCH; Soc. Sci. Cit. Index [Select. Cov.]; Trop. Dis. Bull.; Virol. AIDS Abstr.

US/0024-1288
**LET'S LIVE.** **See** Nutrition and Dietetics.

FR/0296-9009
**LETTRE DE L'INFECTIOLOGUE, LA.**
(1985)-. Periodical. French. Twenty times a year. 381.98F France; 480.00F other. Edimark, 207 rue Gallieni, 92100 Boulogne France. **Tel** 011 33 1 48251159. **UDC** 616.9.

FR
**LETTRE DES SYSTEMES D'INFORMATIONS MEDICALISEES.**
French. qt. 240.00F. Direction Hopitaux, 8 rue de Segur, 75007 Paris France. **Tel** 011 33 1 4056 4374, FAX 011 33 1 40564963.

FR
**LETTRE DU MEDECIN.** French. ESPACE, 4888 St. Denis, Montreal Quebec H2J 2L6 Canada. **Tel** (514)844-9858.

FR/0153-4742
**LETTRE MEDICALE, LA.** ***Suspended.*** [Lett. med.]. (1977)-(Oct. 1993). Periodical. French. mo. La Lettre Medicale, BP 179, 75523 Paris Cedex 11 France. **Tel** 011 33 1 47004917. **UDC** 61. ***Continues*** *Lettre Medicale d'Information, 0336-1853.*

US/1059-6593
**LIFE-LINE (NATIONAL HYDROCEPHALUS FOUNDATION).**
(LIFE-LINE : NEWSLETTER OF THE NATIONAL HYDROCEPHALUS FOUNDATION.). **Added/Corp** National Hydrocephalus Foundation. **VFOAT** Life Line. Vol. 8, No. 3 (Autumn 1991)-. Newsletter. English. qt. $10.00 (includes membership). Life-Line, 400 North Michigan Avenue, Suite 1102, Chicago IL 60611-4102. **DD** 616. ***Continues*** *Newsletter of the National Hydrocephalus Foundation.*

CN/0383-8099
**LIFE SUPPORT.** V. 1- Mar. 1976-. Periodical. English. bm. $5.00. Association of Casualty Care Personnel, PO Box 901, Oshawa Ontario L1H 7N1 Canada. **DD** 362.1/04/25.

UK/0261-989X
**LIFE SUPPORT SYSTEMS.** ***Ceased.*** (LIFE SUPPORT SYSTEMS : THE JOURNAL OF THE EUROPEAN SOCIETY FOR ARTIFICIAL ORGANS.). [Life support syst.]. Vol. 1, No. 1 (Jan./March 1983)-Ceased Vol. 6, No. 2. Academic Scholarly Publication. English. qt. W.B. Saunders Company, A Subsidiary of Harcourt Brace Jovanovich, Inc., The Curtis Center/Suite 300, Independence Square West, Philadelphia PA 19106-3399. **Tel** (215)238-7800 or, 5587, FAX (215)238-7883, telex 173146. **(Subscription address:** W. B. Saunders Company / North America Subscriptions, c/o Periodicals, 6277 Sea Harbour Drive, 4th Floor, Orlando FL 32887.**) ED** M Black. **LC** RC86. **DD** 616/.028. **NLM** W1; I407I. **CODEN** LSSYD6. **[CCC]. Bk Rev. Ad Acc. Circ:** 350. Documents available from BIOSIS Document Express, CASDDS.
**Desc:** Artificial organs, orthopedics, transplants, bioengineering, biomaterials, bioprostheses, intensive care, fluid delivery systems, dialysis, instrumentation, organ preservation, and regeneration.
**Ind/Abst** Biol. Abstr.; Chem. Abstr. (1983-); EMBASE; Index Med.

IT
**LIGAND QUARTERLY NOTIZIE TECHNICHE.** (19??)-. Italian (English). Four times a year. L70000 Italy; L105000 other. Clas International, Via Pace 8, 25122 Brescia Italy. **Tel** 011 39 30 3772712. **ED** G. M. Lanesi. Index available. **Bk Rev**, (Qty: 5/yr). **Ad Acc, Adv Mgr:** Dott Roseua Rebuglio. **Pr Rev. Circ:** 6,000.
**Desc:** Diagnostic Laboratory - Immunoassay

CI/0024-3477
**LIJECNICKI VJESNIK.** [Lijec. vjesn.]. **VFOAT** Liecnicki Viestnik. (1879)-. Academic Scholarly Publication. Serbo-Croatian (Roman) (summaries and/or abstracts in English). mo. $120.00. Lijecnicki Vjesnik, PO Box 1028 Ilica 30, 41000 Zagreb Croatia. **Tel** 011 385 41 422425. **ED** Ivan Bakran. **NLM** W1 LI511K. **CODEN** LIVJA5. Index available. cum. index. **Ad Acc. Pr Rev. Circ:** 7,400 (ctrl). Documents available from CASDDS.
**Desc:** Official journal of the Medical Association of Croatia. Publishes articles from clinical and experimental medicine.
**Ind/Abst** Chem. Abstr.; EMBASE [Select. Cov.]; Index Med.; Saf. Health Work.

●UN/1019-5297
**LIKARSKA SPRAVA.** (LIKARSKA SPRAVA / MINISTERSTVO OKHORONY ZDOROVIA UKRAINY.). [Likar. sprava]. **Added/Corp** Ukraine. Ministerstvo Okhorony Zdorovia. (1992)-. Periodical. Ukrainian (Russian; summaries and/or abstracts in English; table of contents in English). mo. $129.95. **(Subscription address:** East View Publications Inc., 3020 Harbor Lane North, Suite 110, Minneapolis MN 55447.**) CODEN** LISPEC. Documents available from BIOSIS Document Express.
**Ind/Abst** Biol. Abstr.; Index Med. (1992-).

FR/0981-1095
**LILLE MEDICAL (1987).** (LILLE MEDICAL.). [Lille med.]. Vol. 27, No. 1 (Jan. 1987)-. Periodical.

French. Ten times a year. 375.00F. Association Medi-Press, 1 Place de Verdun, 59045 Lille Cedex France. **NLM** W1; LI5238. **CODEN** LIMEEH. **Ad Acc.** available with charts; available with illustrations. Documents available from BIOSIS Document Express. ***Continues*** *LARC Medical, 0242-9462.*
**Ind/Abst** Biol. Abstr. (1988-); Coal Abstr.

US
**LIMITED MOBILITY & IMMOBILIZED PATIENT PRODUCTS.** English. qt. Free (North America). Card-Zine Communications Inc, 7537 North Ridge, Suite A, Chicago IL 60645. **Tel** (312)338-9333, FAX (312)338-9302. **Ad Acc. Circ:** 75,000 (ctrl).

CH/0258-4697
**LIN CHUANG I HSUEH.** [Linchuang yixue]. **VFOAT** Clinical Medicine. Began Jan. 1978-. Periodical. Chinese. mo. **NLM** W1 LI623L.

US/0024-3639
**LINACRE QUARTERLY, THE. See** Ethics.

●US/1065-5832
**LINK (DURHAM, N.C.), THE. See** Sociology-Social Services and Welfare.

CN/1184-6828
**LINK TO THE ONTARIO SOCIETY OF OCCUPATIONAL THERAPISTS, THE.** [Link Ont. Soc. Occup. Ther.]. **Added/Corp** Ontario Society of Occupational Therapists. **VFOAT** Link. No. 1 (Apr. 1990)-. Periodical. English. bm. 25.00Can$. Ontario Society of Occupational Therapists, 55 Eglinton Avenue East, Suite 210, Toronto ONT M4P 1G8. **Tel** (416)322-3011, FAX (416)322-6705. **DD** 615.8/515/060713. ***Continues*** *Ontario Society of Occupational Therapists Newsletter., 0831-9723.*

CN/0824-7536
**LIST OF CERTIFIED HEALTH CARE PRODUCTS AND SERVICES.** ***Title Change.*** (LIST OF CERTIFIED HEALTH CARE PRODUCTS AND SERVICES / CANADIAN STANDARDS ASSOCIATION.). [List certif. health care prod. serv.]. **Main/Corp** Canadian Standards Association. **Added/Corp** Canadian Standards Association. Health Care Technology Program. (1980)-(199?). English. an. Canadian Standards Association, 178 Rexdale Boulevard, Rexdale Ontario M9W 1R3 Canada. **Tel** (416)747-4000, (416)747-4044, telex 06-989344. **DD** 381/.45610/28. ***Continued by*** *Canadian Standards Association. List of CSA Certified Health Care Products and Services, 1200-1678.*

CN/1200-1678
**LIST OF CSA CERTIFIED HEALTH CARE PRODUCTS AND SERVICES.** [List CSA certif. health care prod. serv.]. **Main/Corp** Canadian Standards Association. **VFOAT** List of Canadian Standards Association Certified Health Care Products and Services. (199?)-. English. 45.00Can$. Canadian Standards Association, 178 Rexdale Boulevard, Rexdale Ontario M9W 1R3 Canada. **Tel** (416)747-4000, (416)747-4044, telex 06-989344. **DD** 338.4/7681761. ***Continues*** *Canadian Standards Association. List of Certified Health Care Products and Services., 0824-7536.*

NE/0923-5582
**LIST OF JOURNALS ABSTRACTED.** ***Title Change.*** **See** Medical Science and Technology-Abstracting, Bibliographies and Statistics.

CN/1184-6038
**LISTE DES NOUVELLES ACQUISITIONS - HOPITAL SAINT-VINCENT, OTTAWA, ONT. BIBLIOTHEQUE.** (LISTE DES NOUVELLES ACQUISITIONS). [Liste nouv. acquis. - H„op. St.-Vincent Ott. Ont., Bibl.]. **Main/Corp** Saint Vincent Hospital (Ottawa, Ont.). Library. **VFOAT** List of Recent Acquisitions. Vol. 11, No. 2 (May 1990)-. Periodical. English (French). bm. Limited free distribution. Saint Vincent Hospital, Library, 60 Cambridge Street, Ottawa, Ontario K1R 7A5 Canada. **DD** 016.61. ***Continues*** *Saint Vincent Hospital (Ottawa, Ont.). Library. Nouvelles Acquisitions., 0848-5453.*

US/0278-9671
**LITERATURE AND MEDICINE.** [Lit. med.]. Vol. 1 (1982)-. Periodical. English. Twice a year. $38.00 US; $41.50 Canada and Mexico; $41.90 other. Johns Hopkins University Press, 2715 North Charles Street, Baltimore MD 21218-4319. **Tel** (410)516-6987, FAX (410)516-6968. **ED** Anne Hudson Jones. **LC** PN56.M38; L57. **DD** 809/.93356. **[CCC]. Bk Rev. Ad Acc. Circ:** 600. available on microfilm from University Microfilms International (UMI). Documents available from The Genuine Article.
**Desc:** Focusing on an emerging specialty of the medical humanities. Devoted to examining the connections between the two disciplines.
**Ind/Abst** Arts Humanit. Citation Index [Full Cov.]; Curr. Contents Arts Humanit.; Index Med.; Lit. Crit. Regist.; MLA Int. Bibl. Books Artic. Mod. Lang. Lit.; Res. Alert [Full Cov.].

SZ/1011-2928
**LITHIUM THERAPY MONOGRAPHS.** ***Ceased.*** [Lithium ther. monogr.]. (1987)-?. Monographic series. English. S. Karger AG, Allschwilerstrasse 10, PO Box - Postfach - Case Postale, CH-4009 Basel Switzerland. **Tel** 011 41 61 306-1111, FAX 011 41 61 306-1234, telex CH 962 652. **ED** F N Johnson. **NLM** W1; LI822. **CODEN** LTMOEM. **[CCC].** Index available. ctrl circ. Documents available from BIOSIS Document Express.
**Desc:** Reflects the recent explosion of research into the biological effects of lithium.
**Ind/Abst** Biol. Abstr.; Ref. Upd. Deluxe Ed.

FR/0248-3521
**LITTERATURE, MEDECINE, SOCIETE.** [Litt. med. soc.]. **VFOAT** LMS; L.M.S. No. 1 (1979)-. Monographic series. French. an. Price varies per volume. Universite de Nantes, 2 Chemin de la Houssiniere, 44072 Nantes France. **Tel** 011 33 40 373037, 373004. **NLM** W1; LI858.

US
**LOGIN BROTHERS HEALTH SCIENCES LIBRARY NEWSLETTER.** (19??)-. Newsletter. English. Twelve times a year. Free on request. Login Brothers Book Company, 1436 West Randolph Street, Chicago IL 60607. **Tel** (312)733-6424, (800)621-4249, FAX (312)666-2680, (800)339-1077.
**Desc:** Supplies information on the latest publications in the various fields of medicine.

IT
**LOGOPEDIA CONTEMPORANEA.** (19??)-. Italian. Three times a year. L30000.00 Italy; L45000.00 other. Anna Rosa Noci Franceschini, Direttore V Baldesi 6, 50131 Florence Italy. **Tel** 011 39 55 587749.

US/1062-2616
**LONG-TERM CARE EXECUTIVE NETWORK.** ***Ceased.*** **VFOAT** Long Term Care Executive Network; Executive Network. (1992)-(199?). Periodical. English. mo. Aspen Publishers Inc., 7201 McKinney Circle, Frederick MD 21701. **Tel** (800)234-1660, (301)698-7100, FAX (301)251-5784, telex 5106014543. **NLM** W1; LO7899KD.

US/0743-1422
**LONG TERM CARE MANAGEMENT.** ***Title Change.*** Vol. 13, No. 8 (Mar. 1, 1984)-(19??). Periodical. English. sm. Faulkner & Gray Inc., 11 Penn Plaza, 17th Floor, New York NY 10001. **Tel** (212)967-7000, (800)535-8403. **ED** Spencer Vibbert. **NLM** W1; LO7899M. **Bk Rev.** ctrl circ. available on an online database (file 636/Full-Text) from DIALOG. ***Continues*** *Long Term Care, 0192-7701.* ***Continued by*** *Report on Long Term Care.*
**Desc:** Reports on breaking developments in nursing home marketing, gerontology, Medicare and Medicaid reimbursement, ethics, legal issues and congressional activity.

CN/1180-2189
**LONG TERM CARE MONITOR.** [Long term care monit.]. **Added/Corp** Carswell Legal Publications. **VFOAT** Long Term Care. Vol. 1, No. 1 (Mar. 1990)-. Periodical. English. Ten times a year. 83.00Can$. MPL Communications, 133 Richard Street West, Suite 700, Toronto Ontario M5H 3M8 Canada. **Tel** (416)869-1177, FAX (416)869-0456. **DD** 362.1/6/097105.
**Desc:** Newsletter for administrators of long-term care facilities. Provides practical advice and news about ongoing issues in the long-term care sector.

US
**LONG-TERM CARE NEWS / HOSPITAL ASSOCIATION OF NEW YORK STATE.** ***Title Change.*** **See** Sociology-Social Services and Welfare.

BE/0024-6956
**LOUVAIN MEDICAL.** [Louv. med.]. **Added/Corp** Universite Catholique de Louvain. Association des Medecins Anciens Etudiants. Cercle Medical Saint-Luc. Universite Catholique de Louvain. Faculte de Medecine. Vol. 86 (Jan. 1967)-. Academic Scholarly Publication. French. Ten times a year. 1500F Belgium; 2000F others. UCL-5265, 52 Avenue E Mounier, 1200 Bruxelles Belgium. **Tel** 011 32 2 7641111. **NLM** W1 LO956. **CODEN** LOMEAL. available on microfilm from University Microfilms International (UMI). Documents available from CASDDS. ***Formed by the union of*** *Revue Mediale de Louvain* ***and*** *Recipe.*
**Ind/Abst** Chem. Abstr.; EMBASE [Select. Cov.]; Life Sci. Collect.

FR/0766-5466
**LYON MEDITERRANEE MEDICAL. MEDECINE DU SUD-EST.** [Lyon Mediterr. med., med. Sud-Est]. (1973)-. Periodical. French. mo (10 issues per year). 274.24F France; 250.00F other. Galliena Promotion, 58 A rue du Dessous des Berges, 75013 Paris France. **Tel** 011 33 1 45849766. **UDC** 61(449). ***Continues*** *Lyon Mediterranee Medical, 0399-032X.*

UK/1351-5322
**LYSOSOMES & ENDOCYTOSIS.** (19??)-. English. £85.00. SUBIS, Mansion House, 19 Kingfield Road, Sheffield S11 9AS England. **Tel** 011 44 114 255 4433, FAX 011 44 114 255 4626. ***Continues*** *Lysosomes.*

US/0724-6811
**M.D. COMPUTING.** (M.D. COMPUTING : COMPUTERS IN MEDICAL PRACTICE.). [M.D. comput.]. **Added/Corp** American Association for Medical Systems and Informatics. **VFOAT** Computers in Medical Practice; Medcomp; MD Computing. Vol. 1, No. 1 (1984)-. Periodical. English. Six times a year. $99.40. Springer-Verlag New York Inc., 175 5th Avenue, New York NY 10010. **Tel** (212)460-1500, telex 232 235 SPB UR. **(Subscription address:** Springer Verlag New York Inc. / for North America, 44 Hartz Way, Secaucus NJ 07096.**) ED** W V Slack and E S Boro. **LC** R858.A1; M18. **DD** 610/.28/5. **NLM** W1; MD9994. **[CCC]. Ad Acc. Pr Rev. Circ:** 10,000. Documents available from The Genuine Article, Ask*IEEE. ***Absorbed*** *Medical Computer Journal, 0888-3416.*
**Desc:** Covers the use of computers in medical practice with office management, clinical data collection, literature reference, hardware and software reviews.
**Ind/Abst** Compumath Citation Index [Full Cov.]; Comput. Database; Comput. Lit. Index; EMBASE; Index Med.; Inf. Sci. Abstr. [Full Cov.]; INSPEC (Jan./Feb. 1985-); Int. Pharm. Abstr.; Microcomput. Index (May 1984-)(1984-); Res. Alert [Full Cov.]; SCISEARCH; Soc. Sci. Cit. Index [Select. Cov.]; Zentralbl. Math. Ihre Grenzgeb.

IE/0300-8223
**M.I.M.S. IRELAND.** (MIMS IRELAND.). [MIMS Ireland]. **VFOAT** M.I.M.S. Ireland. **VAT** Monthly Index of Medical Specialties. Ireland. (19??)-. English. mo. Free to doctors in the Republic of Ireland; £75.00 Ireland, England, Scotland, Wales, and Northen Ireland; £101.40 other. Irish Medical Times, 15 Harcourt Street, Dublin 2 Ireland. **Tel** 011 353 1 757461.

UK/0142-8195
**MACROPHAGES SHEFFIELD.** (MACROPHAGES.). [Macrophages Sheff.]. (1976)-. English. mo. £110.00. SUBIS, Mansion House, 19 Kingfield Road, Sheffield S11 9AS England. **Tel** 011 44 114 255 4433, FAX 011 44 114 255 4626. **DD** 016.61242. **[CCC].**

SP/0213-9510
**MADRID, UNE.** [UNE Madr.]. **Added/Corp** Associacion Espanola de Normalizacion y Certificacion. (1981)-. Periodical. Spanish. mo. 9000.00ptas. AENOR Asociacion Espanola de Normalizacion y Certificacion, Fernandez de la Hoz 52, 28010 Madrid Spain. **Tel** 011 34 1 4104851, 011 34 1 4104855, FAX 410 49 76, telex 46545. **UDC** 006. ***Continues*** *Boletin de la Normalizacion Espanola, 0210-2315.*

CN/0847-9380
**MAGAZINE PAIN DE VIE.** [Mag. Pain vie]. Vol. 12, No. 2 (Spring 1989)-. Periodical. French. qt. Distribution gratuite restreinte. Pain de Vie, CP 723, St-Hyacinthe Quebec J2S 7P5 Canada. **DD** 220/.05. ***Continues*** *Pain de Vie (Saint-Hyacinthe, Quebec)., 0228-7072.*

US
**MAGNES LECTURE SERIES.** Vol. 1 (1984)-. Monographic series. English. Price varies per volume. **LC** UNC. **NLM** W1; MA333. **CODEN** MLSEEB. Documents available from BIOSIS Document Express.
**Ind/Abst** Biol. Abstr. (?-1987).

UK/0953-1424
**MAGNESIUM RESEARCH : OFFICIAL ORGAN OF THE INTERNATIONAL SOCIETY FOR THE DEVELOPMENT OF RESEARCH ON MAGNESIUM.** Vol. 1, No. 1/2 (July 1988)-. Periodical. English. an. £65.00 (surface mail), £75.00 (airmail) UK; $120.00 (surface mail), $140.00 (airmail) other. John Libbey & Company Ltd, 13 Smiths Yard, Summerley Street, London SW18 4HR England. **Tel** 01-947 2777, FAX 01-947 2664, telex 94013503 JOHN G. **ED** Jean Durlach. **NLM** W1; MA335E. **Bk Rev. Ad Acc. Circ:** 75 (ctrl). Documents available from CASDDS.
**Desc:** The official journal of the Society for the Development of Research on Magnesium-SDRM. The aim of the journal is to publish original articles on magnesium from all fields of research and from every country. It is the only journal in its field that is truly international and interdisciplinary.
**Ind/Abst** Chem. Abstr.; Ref. Upd. Deluxe Ed.

HU/0025-0066
**MAGYAR BELORVOSI ARCHIVUM (1955).** (MAGYAR BELORVOSI ARCHIVUM.). [Magy. belorv. arch.]. **Added/Corp** Magyar Belgyogyasz Tarsasag. Orvos-Egeszsegugyi Szakszervezet. Belgyogyasz Szakcsoport. Orvos-Egeszsegugyi Szakszervezet. Ideg-, Elme Szakcsoport. Vol. 8 (1955)-. Academic Scholarly Publication. Hungarian (Hungarian; summaries and/or abstracts in Russian, English, French and German). bm. $34.00 Austria, Croatia, Czech Republic, Slovakia, Romania, Yugoslavia, Slovenia and Ukraine; $38.00 other. Akademiai Kiado, Publishing House of the Hungarian Academy of Sciences, Prielle Kornelia u. 19-35, H-1117 Budapest Hungary. **Tel** 011 36 1 1811991, FAX 011 36 1 1811991, telex 22-6228 AKNYO H. **(Subscription address:** Kultura, PO Box 149, H 1389 Budapest 62 Hungary.**) NLM** W1 MA394. **CODEN** MBARAM. Documents available from CASDDS.

*Continues in part* *Magyar Belorvosi Archivum Es Ideggyogyaszati Szemle, 0301-7850.*
**Ind/Abst** Chem. Abstr.; Energy Res. Abstr. (Dec. 1979-).

HU/0139-4495
**MAGYAR REUMATOLOGIA.** (MAGYAR REUMATOLOGIA / MAGYAR REUMATOLOGUSOK EGYESULETENEK ES A MAGYAR BALNEOKLIMATOLOGIAI EGYESULETENEK A FOLYOIRATA.). [M. rheumatol.]. Vol. 21, (Jan. 1980)-. Periodical. Hungarian. qt. Ifsusagi Lap es Konyvkiado Vallalat, Revay U, 16, 1374, Budapest, Hungary. **Tel** 361-113-7038. **NLM** W1 MA408D. ***Continues*** *Rheumatologia, Balneologia, Allergologia.*
**Ind/Abst** EMBASE [Select. Cov.]; Energy Res. Abstr. (Sept. 1980-).

IO/0377-1121
**MAJALAH KEDOKTERAN INDONESIA.** **VFOAT** Journal of the Indonesian Medical Association. Periodical. Indonesian (English). **NLM** W1 MA492K. ***Continues*** *Madjalah Kedokteran Indonesia, 0464-3186.*

IR/0254-4571
**MAJALLAH-I NIZAM-I PIZISHKI-I IRAN.** (MAJALLAH-I NIZAM-I PIZISHKI-I IRAN / THE JOURNAL OF THE IRANIAN MEDICAL COUNCIL.). [Majallah-i Nizam-i pizishki-i Iran]. **Added/Corp** Nizam-i Pizishki-i Iran. **VFOAT** Journal of the Iranian Medical Council. (197?)-. Periodical. Persian. ir. Iranian Medical Council, 40 Shirin Avenue, PO Box 3474, Ehran Iran. **Tel** 821111-821113. **NLM** W1 JO9315.

UA
**MAJALLAT AL-KHADAMAT AL-SIHHIYAH LI-IQLIM SHARQ AL-BAHR AL-MUTAWASSIT.** **Added/Corp** World Health Organization. Regional Office for the Eastern Mediterranean. **VFOAT** Eastern Mediterranean Region Health Services Journal. (198?)-. Periodical. Arabic (English and French). sa. **NLM** W1; MA492KW.
**Ind/Abst** Trop. Dis. Bull.

US/0090-6506
**MAJOR MEDICAL PLANS : SELECTED COLLECTIVE BARGAINING AGREEMENTS, CALIFORNIA.** **See** Insurance.

CN/0228-8702
**MALADIES CHRONIQUES AU CANADA.** [Mal. chron. Can.]. **Added/Corp** Canada. Health and Welfare Canada. Vol. 1, No. 1 (June 1980)-. French. qt (Feb., May., Aug., Nov.). Free. Chronic Diseases in Canada, 145D LCDC Building/Health Welfare, Ottawa Ontario K1A 0L2 Canada. **Tel** (613)957-1767, (613)957-1788, FAX (613)952-7009. **ED** Walter Litven. **DD** 614/.4/0971. Index available. cum. index. **Bk Rev.** **Pr Rev.** **Circ:** 3,500 (ctrl).

FR
**MALADIES METABOLIQUES. E81.** French. 832.12F France; 860.00F other. Institut de l'Information Scientique et Technique (INIST), 2 Allee du Parc de Brabois, 54514 Vandoeuvre Nancy Cedex France. **Tel** 011 33 83 504600, FAX 011 33 83 504650. ***Continues*** *Pascal Explore. E81: Maladies Metaboliques.*

US/0738-1956
**MALPRACTICE REPORTER. HOSPITALS, THE.** **See** Law.

US/0749-3495
**MALPRACTICE REPORTER. PODIATRY, THE.** **See** Law.

US/0145-9783
**MAN AND MEDICINE.** **See** Ethics.

US/1049-457X
**MANAGED CARE INSIGHTS.** [Manag. care insights]. **VFOAT** Insights. Vol. 1, No. 1 (Spring 1990)-. Periodical. English. qt. Free on request. Scott-Levin Associates, 60 Blacksmith Road, Newtown PA 18940. **Tel** (215)860-0440, FAX (215)860-5477. **DD** 362. **NLM** W1; MA57JF.

US/0744-4966
**MANHATTAN MEDICINE.** ***Title Change.*** (MANHATTAN MEDICINE : [OFFICIAL PUBLICATION OF THE NEW YORK COUNTY MEDICAL SOCIETY] / NEW YORK COUNTY MEDICAL SOCIETY.). **Added/Corp** Medical Society of the County of New York. **VFOAT** MM. Vol. 1, No. 1 (Jan. 1982)-(19??). Periodical. English. ir. New York County Medical Society, 15 East 26th Street, 11th Floor, New York NY 10010. **Tel** (212)684-4670. **ED** Nancy L. Adams. **Bk Rev.** **Ad Acc.** **Circ:** 6,000 (ctrl). ***Continued by*** *MM News.*
**Desc:** Contains articles about political issues confronting doctors in Manhattan (malpractice insurance costs, etc.), not technical material. About goings-on at the Medical Society, the AMA, the State Medical Society, etc.

CN/0025-2255
**MANITOBA MEDICAL REVIEW (MICROFICHE).** (MANITOBA MEDICAL REVIEW.). V. 13- Jan. 1933-. Periodical. English. mo. **DD** 610/.5. available on microfilm from University Microfilms International (UMI).

CN/0832-6096
**MANITOBA MEDICINE.** [Manit. med.]. **Added/Corp** University of Manitoba. Faculty of Medicine. Vol. 57, No. 1 (Spring 1987)- Vol. 63 (1993)-. Periodical. English. Four times a year (During the seasons). $20.00 one year. University of Manitoba Faculty of Medicine, 750 Bannatyne Avenue, Winnipeg Manitoba R3E 0W3 Canada. **Tel** (204)788-6557. **ED** Dr. I. Carr, S105-750 Bannatyne Avenue, Winnipeg MANI R3E OW3, (204)789-3660. **DD** 610/.97127. **Bk Rev.** ctrl circ. ***Continues*** *University of Manitoba Medical Journal, 0076-4108.*

US
**MANUAL OF MEDICAL THERAPEUTICS / DEPARTMENT OF MEDICINE, WASHINGTON UNIVERSITY SCHOOL OF MEDICINE.** **Added/Corp** Washington University. Department of Medicine. (19??)-. English. ir. $23.50. Little Brown & Company, 34 Beacon Street, Boston MA 02108. **Tel** (617)227-0730, (800)759-0190.

GW/0025-2514
**MANUELLE MEDIZIN.** [Man. Med.]. **Added/Corp** Deutsche Gesellschaft fuer Manuelle Medizin. (19??)-. Periodical. German. Six times a year. DM222.00. Springer-Verlag GmbH & Company KG, Heidelberger Platz 3, D 14197 Berlin Germany. **Tel** 011 49 30 8207223, FAX 011 49 30 8214091, telex 183 319 SPBLN D. **(Subscription address:** Springer Verlag New York Inc. / for North America, 44 Hartz Way, Secaucus NJ 07096.**)** **ED** H Baumgartner, E Frolich, and H D Wolff. **NLM** W1 MA635. **[CCC].** available on microfilm from University Microfilms International (UMI).
**Desc:** Reports on research and practical developments as well as news in the fields of orthopedics, traumatology, internal medicine, and rheumatology.
**Ind/Abst** EMBASE.

US/0882-3634
**MARKER (NEW YORK, N.Y.), THE.** (THE MARKER / HUNTINGTON'S DISEASE FOUNDATION OF AMERICA.). [Marker]. Periodical. English. Three times a year. Huntington's Disease Foundation of America, 250 West 57th Street, New York NY 10107. **DD** 616. **NLM** W1; MA657. ***Continues*** *Newsletter (Committee to Combat Huntington's Disease), 0882-3642.*

UK/0951-3175
**MARKET LETTER.** **See** Pharmacy and Pharmacology.

MR/0025-388X
**MAROC MEDICAL.** (AL-MAGHRIB AL-TIBBI.). [Maroc med.]. V. 1- Oct. 1978-. Academic Scholarly Publication. French. Maroc Medical Hopital, Avicenne, Rabat Morocco. **NLM** W1 MA66B. ***Supersedes*** *Maroc Medical, 0025-388X.*
**Ind/Abst** EMBASE; Index Med.

US/0886-0572
**MARYLAND MEDICAL JOURNAL (1985).** (MARYLAND MEDICAL JOURNAL : MMJ.). [Md. med. j.]. **Added/Corp** Medical and Chirurgical Faculty of the State of Maryland. **VFOAT** MMJ. Vol. 34, No. 1 (Jan. 1985)-. Periodical. English. mo. $45.00 US; $57.00 other. Maryland Medical Journal, 1211 Cathedral Street, Baltimore MD 21201. **Tel** (410)539-0872, FAX (410)547-0915. **ED** Victor R. Hrehorovich and Henry P. Laughlin. **LC** R11; .M36. **DD** 610/.5. **NLM** W1; MA76M. **CODEN** MMJRA8. Index available. **Bk Rev,** (Qty: 10-12). **Ad Acc.** **Pr Rev.** **Circ:** 7,200 (ctrl). available on microfilm and microfiche from University Microfilms International (UMI). Documents available from BIOSIS Document Express. ***Continues*** *Maryland State Medical Journal, 0025-4363.*
**Desc:** Focuses on original research, case studies and review articles, as well as material on health-related legislation, medical history, practice management and member-related information.
**Ind/Abst** Biol. Abstr. (1985-1989); Crim. Justice Abstr. (-199?); Cumul. Index Nurs. Allied Health Lit.; EMBASE [Select. Cov.]; Energy Res. Abstr.; Index Med. (1985-); INIS Atomindex [Micro.]; Int. Nurs. Index; Life Sci. Collect.; SportSearch.

US/0273-8929
**MASSACHUSETTS MEDICAL NEWS.** [Mass. med. news]. **VFOAT** MMN. Vol. 1 (Nov. 21/28, 1980)-. Periodical. English. Nine times a year. Free on request. Massachusetts General Hospital / Massachusetts Medical News, Fruit Street, Boston MA 02114.

PL/0025-5246
**MATERIA MEDICA POLONA (ENGLISH EDITION).** **See** Pharmacy and Pharmacology.

RU
**MATERIALY PROBLEMNOI KOMISSII AKADEMII MEDITSINSKIKH NAUK SSSR "KOR', VIRUSNYE ENTSEFALITY, POLIOMIELIT" / AKADEMIA MEDITSINSKIKH NAUK SSSR, INSTITUT POLIOMIELITA I VIRUSNYKH ENTSEFALITEV.** **Added/Corp** Akademiia Meditsinskikh Nauk SSSR. Problemnaia Komissia "Kor', Virusnye Entsefality, Poliomielit". Akademiia Meditsinskikh Nauk SSSR. Institut Poliomielita i Virusnykh Entsefalitov. Vol. 3 (1968)-. Monographic series. Russian. Price varies per volume. **NLM** W1 MA944C. ***Continues*** *Materialy Problemnoi Komissii Akademii Meditsinskikh Nauk SSSR Poliomielit I Virusnye Entsefality.*

GW/0934-8832
**MATRIX (STUTTGART).** ***Title Change.*** (MATRIX : COLLAGEN AND RELATED RESEARCH.). [Matrix]. **VFOAT** Collagen and Related Research. Vol. 9, Nr. 1 (Jan. 1989)-Vol. 13, No. 6 (Nov. 1993). Academic Scholarly Publication. English. Nine times a year. Gustav Fischer Verlag Stuttgart, Postfach 720143, Wollgrasweg 49, D 70577 Stuttgart Germany. **Tel** 011 49 711 458030, FAX 0711-4580334, telex 2627-7111488. **ED** S. Gay and E.J. Miller. **LC** QP552.C6; M38. **DD** 591.1/85. **NLM** W1; MA974. **CODEN** MTRXEH. **[CCC].** **Pr Rev.** Documents available from The Genuine Article, BIOSIS Document Express, CASDDS. ***Continues*** *Collagen and Related Research, 0174-173X.* ***Continued by*** *Matrix Biology, 0945-053X.*
**Desc:** Provides an international and interdisciplinary forum for the publications of original articles on collagen. The scope of the journal covers the biochemistry, embryology, histology, immunology, pathology and physiology of collagen and related macromolecules as well as the pathology of the various connective tissues.
**Ind/Abst** Biol. Abstr. (1989-); Chem. Abstr. (1989-); Curr. Aware. Biol. Sci., CABS; EMBASE; Index Med. (Jan. 1989-); Res. Alert [Full Cov.]; Sci. Cit. Index; SCISEARCH.

CH/0254-1319
**MAZUIXEE ZAZHII.** ***Title Change.*** (MA TSUI HSUEH TSA CHIH / ANAESTHESIOLOGICA SINICA.). [Mazuixue zazhi]. **Added/Corp** Chung-hua Min Kuo ma Tsui i Hsueh Hui. **VFOAT** Anaesthesiologica Sinica; Acta Anaesthesiologica Sinica. (1960)-Vol. 31, No. 4 (Dec. 1993). Periodical. Chinese (English). Four times a year. Chung-hau Min Kuo Ma Tsui Hui, Taipei Taiwan. **NLM** W1; MA102. ***Continued by*** *Acta Anaesthesiologica Sinica.*
**Ind/Abst** Index Med. (Vol. 23, No. 1, 1985-).

BU/0324-119X
**MBI. MEDICO-BIOLOGIC INFORMATION.** [MBI, Med. biol. inf.]. **VFOAT** Medico-Biologic Information; MBI; Medico Biologic Information. (1970)-. Periodical. English (Bulgarian). bm (6 issues). Free on request. Pharmachim, 16 Iliensko Chaussee, 1220 Sofia Bulgaria. **ED** A. Damyanov. **LC** RM1; .M16. **NLM** W1 M22. **Ad Acc.** **Circ:** 2,000. available with illustrations.
**Ind/Abst** EMBASE [Select. Cov.].

CN/0024-905X
**MCGILL MEDICAL JOURNAL.** ***Ceased.*** [McGill med. j.]. Ceased (1981). Academic Scholarly Publication. English (French). ir. McGill Medical Science Center, 3655 Drummond Street, McIntyre Medical Sci, Montreal Quebec H3A 1W8 Canada. **NLM** W1 MA158E. ***Continues*** *McGill Medical Undergraduate Journal, 0381-0720.*
**Ind/Abst** EMBASE.

US/0734-1970
**MCGRAW-HILL'S MEDICAL UTILIZATION REVIEW.** [McGraw-Hill's med. util. rev.]. **VFOAT** Medical Utilization Review; Utilization Review Letter. Vol. 10, No. 15 (Aug. 1, 1982)-. Periodical. English. sm. $385.00. Faulkner & Gray Inc., 11 Penn Plaza, 17th Floor, New York NY 10001. **Tel** (212)967-7000, (800)535-8403. **NLM** W1; MC998H. ***Continues*** *PSRO Letter, 0149-5844.*

●US/1061-4370
**MDA REPORTS.** [MDA rep.]. **Added/Corp** Muscular Dystrophy Association. **VAT** Muscular Dystrophy Association Reports. Vol. 1, No. 1 (Spring 1992)-. Periodical. English. qt. Free. Muscular Dystrophy Association / Arizona, 3561 East Sunrise Drive, Tucson AZ 85718. **Tel** (602)529-2000. **DD** 616. **NLM** W1; MD9996. ***Continues*** *MDA Newsmagazine, 8750-2321.*

US/0890-7587
**MDR WATCH.** [MDR watch]. **Added/Corp** Washington Business Information, Inc. **VAT** Medical Device Reporting Watch. No. 1 (Nov. 1986)-. Periodical. English. Twelve times a year. $647.00 North America; $702.00 other. Washington Business Information Inc., 1117 North 19th Street, Suite 200, Arlington VA 22209. **Tel** (703)247-3433, (800)426-0416, FAX (703)247-3421. **ED** Denise Elliiott. **DD** 346. **NLM** W1; M295E. **[CCC].**

UK/0264-1410
**MEAD JOHNSON ADVANCES IN THERAPEUTICS.** [Mead Johnson adv. ther.]. **Added/Corp** Bristol-Myers Co. Ltd. Mead Johnson Division. **VFOAT** Advances in Therapeutics. Vol. 1, (1979)-. Monographic series. English. ir. Price varies per volume. **NLM** W1 ME103M.

US/0190-0749
**MEAD JOHNSON SYMPOSIUM ON PERINATAL AND DEVELOPMENTAL MEDICINE.** ***Ceased.*** [Mead Johnson sympos. perinat. dev. med.]. **Added/Corp** Mead Johnson &

Company. No. 1 (June 1972)-(19??). Monographic series. English. be. Mead Johnson, Evansville IN 47721. **Tel** (812)429-6321. **NLM** W3 ME375. **CODEN** MJSMDK. Documents available from CASDDS.
**Ind/Abst** Chem. Abstr. (?-?).

US/0883-1750
**MED DEV.** [Med dev]. **VFOAT** Medical Devices. Periodical. English. qt. $60.00. Biellambe, PO Box 21451, Sarasota FL 33583. **Tel** (813)922-6353. **ED** John J Lamb. **DD** 681. **Circ:** 50.
**Desc:** Basis of information is Food and Drug Administration publications on medical devices. Other interests are materials used in implants and testing of medical devices.

GW/0934-3148
**MED-REPORT.** (19??)-. Periodical. German. Twenty-four times a year. DM148.00. Blackwell Wissenschafts-Verlag, Kurfuerstendamm 57, D 10707 Berlin Germany. **Tel** 011 49 30 32790623, 011 49 30 32790624, FAX 011 49 30 327 90610. **UDC** 616.

NZ
**MED TEC INTERNATIONAL. Added/Corp** IAMLT (Association). No. 24, (1976)-. Periodical. English (French and German). Twice a year (Mar., Nov.). 25.00NZ$ one year; 40.00NZ$ two years. International Association of Medical Laboratory Technicians, 19 Taihiki Road Clarks Beach RD4, Pukekohe 1850 New Zealand. **Tel** 011 64 92321441, FAX 011 46 8 109061. **ED** Desmond Philip. **NLM** W1; ME108F. **Ad Acc. Circ:** 16,000 (ctrl). ***Continues** IAMLT Newsletter.*
**Desc:** Journal of International Association of Medical Laboratory Technology, containing articles on subjects of general interest to all branches of Medical Laboratory Technology as well as Association and Society news.

FR/0999-6338
**MEDECIN BIOPATHOLOGISTE PARIS, LE.** (LE MEDECIN BIOPATHOLOGISTE.). (1989)-. Periodical. French (English). bm. 330.00F. Medecin Biopathologiste, 133 Bd du Montparnasse, 75014 Paris France. **Tel** 33 1 43203838, FAX 33 1 43229103. **UDC** 616-074/-078. **Bk Rev. Ad Acc, Adv Mgr:** Dr. Laget, **Tel** 33 1 40476060. **Circ:** 4,000.

CN/0025-6692
**MEDECIN DU QUEBEC.** (LE MEDICIN DU QUEBEC.). [Med. Que.]. **Added/Corp** Federation des Medecins Omnipraticiens du Quebec. Vol. 1 (June 1965)-. Periodical. French (summaries and/or abstracts in English). mo. Free, general or public hospitals; 75.00Can$ other. Federation of General Practitioners of Quebec, 1440 St Catherine Street West/Suite 1100, Montreal Quebec H3G 1R8 Canada. **Tel** (514)878-1911, FAX (514)878-4455. **ED** Georges Boileau. **NLM** W1 ME118C. Index available (bound in Jan. issue). cum. index. **Bk Rev**, (Qty: 50). **Ad Acc. Pr Rev. Circ:** 19,200 (ctrl).
**Desc:** Socio-economic content addressed to the Quebec medical profession.
**Ind/Abst** Health Devices Alerts; Point Repere (1983-).

FR/0294-0817
**MEDECINE AERONAUTIQUE ET SPATIALE.** [Med. aeronaut. spat.]. **Added/Corp** Societe Francaise de Physiologie et de Medecine Aeronautiques et Cosmonautiques. Vol. 21, No. 81 (1st Quarterly 1982)-. Academic Scholarly Publication. French (table of contents in English). qt. 420.00F France; 470.00F other. Air France / Societe France de Medicine Aerospatiale, 1 Square Max Hymans, 75757 Paris Cedex 15 France. **Tel** 011 33 1 43239422. **LC** RC1050; .R5. **DD** 616.9/8021/05. **NLM** W1; ME127KA. Documents available from CASDDS. ***Continues in part** Medecine Aeronautique et Spatiale, Medecine Subaquatique et Hyperbare, 0399-6417.*
**Ind/Abst** Chem. Abstr.; Int. Aerosp. Abstr.; Saf. Health Work.

SG/0465-4668
**MEDECINE D'AFRIQUE NOIRE.** [Med. Afr. Noire]. (1954)-. French. Eleven times a year. 330.00F France and French-speaking Africa; 460.00F other. Medecine d'Afrique Noire, 9, rue Truguet, 83000 TOULON France. **Tel** 011 33 94 62 7575, FAX 011 33 94 93 5169, telex 400 287 FC 300. **CODEN** MAFNA.
**Ind/Abst** EMBASE [Select. Cov.]; Nutr. Abstr. Rev., Ser. A, Hum. Exp.; Protozoolog. Abstr.; Rev. Med. Vet. Mycology; Trop. Dis. Bull.

FR/0543-2243
**MEDECINE DE L'HOMME PARIS.** (1968)-. Periodical. French. Six times a year. 330F France; 350F others. Centre Catholique Medecins France, 5 Avenue de l'Observatoire, 75006 Paris France. **Tel** 011 33 1 46345975, FAX 011 33 1 43547007. **UDC** 61.

FR
**MEDECINE DOUCE.** French. 198.00F France; 250.00F other. Medecine Douce, 49 Ave Franklin D Roosevelt, 75008 Paris France. **Tel** 011 33 1 42891083, FAX 011 33 1 42250838.

FR/0300-4937
**MEDECINE ET ARMEES. See** Military and Defense.

FR/1246-7391
**MEDECINE ET DROIT.** (19??)-. Academic Scholarly Publication. French. Six times a year. 575.00F France; 640.00F other. Editions Scientifique Elsevier, 141 rue de Javel, 75747 Paris Cedex 15 France. **Tel** 011 33 1 47 07 11 22, FAX 011 33 1 43 36 80 93. **(Subscription address:** Editions Scientifiques Elsevier / for North America, PO Box 7247-7576, Philadelphia PA 19170-7576.**)**

SZ/0025-6749
**MEDECINE ET HYGIENE.** [Med. hyg.]. Vol. 1, No. 1 (May 1, 1943)-. Academic Scholarly Publication. French. ir. 88.00F Switzerland; 168.00F other. Medecine et Hygiene, Case Postale 456, CH-1211 Geneva 4 Switzerland. **Tel** 011 41 22 3469355, 3469356, FAX (022)47 56 10, telex 421 859 MEDHY. **NLM** W1 ME1393. **CODEN** MEHGAB. **[CCC].** available on microfilm from University Microfilms International (UMI). Documents available from CASDDS.
**Ind/Abst** Chem. Abstr.; EMBASE [Select. Cov.]; Index Dent. Lit.

FR/0399-077X
**MEDECINE ET MALADIES INFECTIEUSES.** [Med. mal. infect.]. (1971)-. Periodical. Multiple languages. mo. Soc Francaise d Editions Med, 22 rue du Chateau des Rentiers, 75013 Paris France. **Tel** 011 33 1 45835054. **UDC** 616.9. **Pr Rev.** Documents available from The Genuine Article.
**Ind/Abst** Curr. Contents Clin. Med.; EMBASE; Helminthol. Abstr. (1991-); Index Vet.; Pig News Inf.; Protozoolog. Abstr.; Res. Alert [Select. Cov.]; Rev. Med. Vet. Mycology; SCISEARCH; Soils Fert.; Trop. Dis. Bull.

FR/0398-7604
**MEDECINE ET NUTRITON.** [Med. Nutr.]. Vol. 12 (Jan. 1976)-. Academic Scholarly Publication. French. bm. 330.00F (France); 380.00F (other). Editions la Simarre, ZI 2 rue Joseph Cugnot, 37300 Joue-les-Tours France. **Tel** 11 33 47 535366, or 535134. **NLM** W1 ME1396. **CODEN** MENUDI. **[CCC].** Documents available from CASDDS. ***Continues** Annales d'Hygiene de Langue Francaise. Medecine et Nutrition, 0398-7582.*
**Ind/Abst** AGRICOLA; Chem. Abstr.; EMBASE [Select. Cov.]; Nutr. Abstr. Rev., Ser. A, Hum. Exp.; Life Sci. Collect.; Potato Abstr.; Rural Dev. Abstr.; Saf. Health Work.

FR/1150-5966
**MEDECINE FOETALE ET ECHOGRAPHIE EN GYNECOLOGIE.** (1990)-. Periodical. French. qt. 350.00F France; 500.00F other. **UDC** 618. Index Available published separately, bound from publisher, free-automatically sent. cum. index. **Ad Acc, Adv Mgr:** Dr. Niddam.

FR
**MEDECINE HOSPITALIERE, LA.** ***Ceased.*** (19??)-(19??). French. Masson Editeur, Box Postale 22, 41353 Vineuil 16 France. **Tel** 011 33 54 438994. available on microfilm and microfiche from University Microfilms International (UMI).

CN/1182-1507
**MEDECINE MODERNE, RAPPORT SPECIAL.** [Med. mod., rapp. spec.]. Jan. (1990)-. Periodical. French. mo. 30.00Can$. Southam Information and Technology Group Inc., 1450 Don Mills Road, Don Mills Ontario M3B 2X7 Canada. **Tel** (416)445-6641, (800)668-2374, FAX (416)442-2261. **DD** 610/.5. ***Continues** Medecine Moderne du Canada., 0025-6803.*

FR/0767-0974
**MEDECINE SCIENCES : M/S. See** Biology.

CN/0228-409X
**MEDECINE TRADITIONNELLE CHINOISE ET ACUPUNCTURE.** (MEDECINE TRADITIONNELLE CHINOISE ET ACUPUNCTURE : ORGANE OFFICIEL DE L'ASSOCIATION INTERNATIONALE DE MEDECINE TRADITIONNELLE CHINOISE ET DE L'ASSOCIATION D'ACUPUNCTURE DU QUEBEC.). [med. tradit. chin. acupunct.]. Vol. 4, No. 1-. Periodical. English (French). qt. $6.00 inside Quebec, $10.00 outside Quebec. Acupuncture Association of Quebec, 4251 Hochelaga Street East, Montreal Quebec H1V 1C1. **DD** 610/.951. ***Continues** Acupuncture (Montreal, Quebec), 0228-4081.*

UK/0144-4271
**MEDECONOMICS.** [Medeconomics]. (1980)-. Periodical. English. mo (12 issues). £62.00 UK; £91.00 Eire & Europe; £138.00 America, Middle East, Africa & India; £140.00 Australia, New Zealand & Japan; £91.00 other. Haymarket Publishing Ltd., 12 14 Ansdell Street, London W8 5TR England. **Tel** 011 44 483 733800, FAX 011 44 483 776573. **(Subscription address:** Haymarket Publishing Ltd, PO Box 219, Subscriptions Department, Woking Surrey GU21 1ZW, United Kingdom.**) [CCC].**

AU/0253-7419
**MEDEQUIP.** ***Ceased.*** [Medequip]. (1982)-(19??). Periodical. English (German). ir (7-10 issues yearly). Blackwell MZV Medizinische Zeitschriftenverlags Gesellschaft, Feldgasse 13, A-1238 Vienna Austria. **Tel** 011 43 1 8893646, FAX 011 43 1 889364724. **(Subscription address:** UK/ Marston Book Services, PO Box 87, Oxford UK; US/ 3 Cambridge Center, Suite 208, Cambridge MA 02142; Aus/ 54 University Street, Carlton Victoria 3053 Australia; Germany/ Meinekestrasse 4, D-1000 Berlin 15 Germany; France/ Arnette, 2 rue Casimir Delavigne, 75006 Paris France**) NLM** W 26 M488. available on microfilm and microfiche from University Microfilms International (UMI).

BE
**MEDEX.** (19??)-. French. Four times a year. 1750F. ICS Belgium, Waterloosesteenweg 935 937, B-1180 Brussels Belgium. **Tel** 011 32 2 3754439, FAX 374 25 56. **ED** J. P. Dehaspe. **Ad Acc. Circ:** 10,000 (ctrl).
**Desc:** Medications index.

US
**MEDI PAGES.** (19??)-. English. an. $39.95. Medi Pages, PO Box 1548, Lewiston NY 14092. **Tel** (716)284-4277. ***Continues** Health and Medical Care Directory.*

CN/0382-8808
**MEDI-US.** V. 1- Fall 1975-. Periodical. French. ir. Association des Etudiants en Medecine, Universite de Montreal, CP 6128, Montreal Quebec H3C 3J7 Canada. **DD** 610.7/11/714281. ***Supersedes** Mum.*

FR
**MEDIAS.** French. Les Temps Medias, 55 rue Amsterdam, 75008 Paris France.

FR
**MEDIAS HEBDO.** French. Medias Service Abonnements, 55 rue d Amsterdam, 75008 Paris France.

●UK/0962-9351
**MEDIATORS OF INFLAMMATION.** (1992)-. Periodical. English. bm. $445.00 US; £260.00 other. Rapid Communications of Oxford Ltd, The Old Malthouse, Paradise Street, Oxford OX1 1LD England. **Tel** 011 44 0865 790447, FAX 011 44 0865 244012, telex 9403712. **NLM** W1; ME156DK. **CODEN** MNFLEF. **[CCC]. Ad Acc. Acid Free.** Documents available from ADONIS.
**Desc:** Promotes the rapid publication of original and fundamental research articles on all aspects of cellular mediators.
**Ind/Abst** ADONIS; Sci. Cit. Index.

US
**MEDIC. METODOLOGIA E DIDATTICA CLINICA.** (19??)-. Periodical. English. Four times a year. L80000 institutions; L60000 individuals. Il Pensiero Scientifico Editore s.r.l., Via Bradano 3C, 00199 Rome Italy. **Tel** 011 39 6 86207158, 86207159, 86207168, 86207169, FAX 011 39 6 86207160. **Ad Acc.** Full Page (B&W) L2.000.000. **Circ:** 3,000.

CI/0351-0093
**MEDICA JADERTINA.** [Med. jadert.]. (1969)-. Periodical. Serbo-Croatian (Roman). Four times a year. Scientific Unit of the Medical Center Zadar, I. G. Kovacica 5, 57000 Zadar Croatia. **Tel** (57)24-677. **(Subscription address:** Mladost Export Import, PO Box 1028, Ilica 30, 41000 Zagreb Croatia.**) UDC** 61. **CODEN** MEJAD6.
**Ind/Abst** EMBASE [Select. Cov.].

GW/0172-9160
**MEDICA (STUTTGART).** (MEDICA.). [Medica]. V. 1, No. 1 (15. Jan. 1980)-. Periodical. German. sm. Georg Thieme Verlag Stuttgart, Postfach 301120, D 70451 Stuttgart Germany. **Tel** 011 49 711 89310, FAX 011 49 711 8931298, telex 7 252 275 GTVD. **(Subscription address:** Thieme Medical Publishers Inc., 381 Park Avenue South, New York NY 10016.**) NLM** W1 ME156T.

US
**MEDICAL ABBREVIATIONS - 8600 CONVENIENCES AT THE EXPENSE OF COMMUNICATIONS AND SAFETY.** English. be. $11.95. Neil M Davis Associates, 1143 Wright Drive, Huntington Valley PA 19006. **Tel** (215)947-1752, FAX (215)938-1937. **ED** Neil M. Davis. Each issue contains an index to its own contents (no volume index)--loose. cum. index. **Bk Rev. Ad Acc.**

US/0730-7810
**MEDICAL ABSTRACTS NEWSLETTER. See** Medical Science and Technology-Abstracting, Bibliographies and Statistics.

US/0745-0907
**MEDICAL ADVERTISING NEWS.** ***Title Change.* See** Business-Advertising and Public Relations.

US/0543-2480
**MEDICAL ALMANAC.** (1961/62)-. Periodical. English. ir. W.B. Saunders Company, A Subsidiary of Harcourt Brace Jovanovich, Inc., The Curtis Center/Suite 300, Independence Square West, Philadelphia PA 19106-3399. **Tel** (215)238-7800 or, 5587, FAX (215)238-7883, telex 173146. **(Subscription address:** W. B. Saunders Company / North America Subscriptions, c/o Periodicals, 6277 Sea Harbour Drive, 4th Floor, Orlando FL 32887.**) ED** P S Nagan. **LC** R104; .M4. **DD** 610.82.

US/0363-0366
**MEDICAL AND HEALTH ANNUAL.** See Encyclopedias and General Reference Books.

US/0749-9973
**MEDICAL AND HEALTH INFORMATION DIRECTORY.** [Med. health inf. dir.]. 1st Ed. (1977)-. Directory. English. ir. $485.00. Gale Research Inc., 835 Penobscot Building, Detroit MI 48226. **Tel** (800)877-GALE, (313)961-2242, FAX (313)961-6083, telex TWX 810-221-7086. **ED** Karen Boyden. **LC** R118.4.U6; M43. **DD** 610/.72073. **NLM** W 22; AA1 K9M.
**Desc:** Provides descriptive information on some 16,400 national, international, and state professional and voluntary associations, federal and state agencies, foundations and grant-awarding organizations, research centers, medical and allied health schools, and more. Contains essential contact data and descriptive details on more than 9,700 libraries, audiovisual producers and services, publications, publishers, and databases. Also contains current data on over 23,000 clinics, treatment centers, care programs, counseling/diagnostic services, and other health services.

US/0145-9740
**MEDICAL ANTHROPOLOGY.** See Anthropology.

US/0745-5194
**MEDICAL ANTHROPOLOGY QUARTERLY.** See Anthropology.

US/0091-7877
**MEDICAL BOOK GUIDE.** 1974-. Periodical. English. an. GK Hall & Co, 100 Front Street, Riverside NJ 08075. **Tel** (800)257-5755 ext. 2223. **LC** Z6660; .M39; R129. **DD** 016.61.

US/0889-5538
**MEDICAL BUSINESS JOURNAL, THE.** ***Title Change.*** [Med. bus. j.]. Vol. 1, No. 1 (Jan. 1985)-?. Periodical. English. sm. Faulkner & Gray Inc., 11 Penn Plaza, 17th Floor, New York NY 10001. **Tel** (212)967-7000, (800)535-8403. **LC** RA410.A1; M38. **DD** 338.4/73621/0973. **NLM** W1; ME25B. ***Absorbed by*** *Health Business, 1062-6107.*
**Ind/Abst** Abstr. BioCommer. (-19??).

US/0025-7079
**MEDICAL CARE.** [Med. care]. **Added/Corp** American Public Health Association. Medical Care Section. Vol. 1, No. 1 (Jan./Mar. 1963)-. Periodical. English. mo. $143.00 (individuals), $244.00 (institutions) US; $183.00 (individuals), $283.00 (institutions) other. J.B. Lippincott Company, 227 East Washington Square, Philadelphia PA 19106-3780. **Tel** (215)238-4200 or 4454, FAX (215)238-4227. **(Subscription address:** J.B. Lippincott, PO Box 350, Hagerstown MD 21740.**) ED** Duncan Neuhauser. **LC** RA1; .M43. **DD** 362.1/0973. **NLM** W1 ME25L. **CODEN** MDLCBDMELAA. **[CCC]. Ad Acc. Pr Rev. Circ:** 2,926. available on microfilm and microfiche from University Microfilms International (UMI). Documents available from The Genuine Article, BIOSIS Document Express.
**Desc:** International journal for original articles describing significant current developments in medical care.
**Ind/Abst** Biol. Abstr. (1988-); Chicano Index; Cumul. Index Nurs. Allied Health Lit.; Curr. Contents Clin. Med.; Curr. Contents Soc. Behav. Sci.; EMBASE; Energy Res. Abstr. (Aug. 1982-); Health Plan. Adminis.; Health Serv. Abstr.; Hospit. Health Admin. Index; Hospit. Manage. Rev.; Index Med.; Int. Nurs. Index; Int. Pharm. Abstr.; Life Sci. Collect.; Psychol. Abstr. (1986-); PsycINFO; PsycLit; Res. Alert [Full Cov.]; Sci. Cit. Index; SCISEARCH; Soc. Plann. Policy Dev. Abstr.; Soc. Sci. Cit. Index [Full Cov.]; Sociol. Abstr.; Trop. Dis. Bull.

US/0025-7087
**MEDICAL CARE REVIEW.** [Med. care rev.]. **Added/Corp** Michigan. University. Bureau of Public Health Economics. **VFOAT** MCR. Vol. 24, No. 1 (Jan. 1967)-. Academic Scholarly Publication. English. qt. $95.00. SAGE Periodical Press, 2455 Teller Road, Thousand Oaks CA 91320. **Tel** (805)499-0721, FAX (805)499-0871, telex 100799. **ED** Thomas G. Rundall A. Malone. **LC** RA410; .P8. **DD** 362.1/0973. **NLM** ZWA 100 P973. **CODEN** MDCRB. **[CCC]. Bk Rev. Pr Rev. Circ:** 1,300. available on microfilm and microfiche from University Microfilms International (UMI). ***Continues*** *Public Health Economics and Medical Care Abstracts.*
**Desc:** Features carefully peer-reviewed scholarly papers, along with commentaries, that analyze, critique, and synthesize the literature and research in these and other important areas: the financing of health services; organizational structure and behavior; physician-hospital relationships; patient behavior; and political issues.
**Ind/Abst** Health Plan. Adminis.; Hospit. Health Admin. Index; Hum. Resour. Abstr. (?-?); Int. Pharm. Abstr.; PAIS Int. Print (1991-); Soc. Work Abstr. (?-?).

HK
**MEDICAL CHINA. NEWSFILE / CHUNG-KUO I HSUEH. NEWSFILE.** ***Suspended.*** **VFOAT** Newsfile; Chung-kuo i Hsueh. Newsfile. (19??)-(Oct. 1991). Periodical. English. Twenty-five times a year. $475.00. Medical China Publishing Ltd, 4306 China Resources Building, 26 Harbour Road, Wanchai Hong Kong. **Tel** 011 852 5 5736211, FAX 011 852 5 8913831, telex 68444. **NLM** W1; ME25V. Index available. cum. index.

US/0025-7125
**MEDICAL CLINICS OF NORTH AMERICA, THE.** [Med. clin. North Am.]. Vol. 1 (July 1917)-. Academic Scholarly Publication. English. bm. $77.00 (individual), $100.00 (institution) US; $113.00 (individual), $120.00 (institution) other. W.B. Saunders Company, A Subsidiary of Harcourt Brace Jovanovich, Inc., The Curtis Center/Suite 300, Independence Square West, Philadelphia PA 19106-3399. **Tel** (215)238-7800 or, 5587, FAX (215)238-7883, telex 173146. **(Subscription address:** W. B. Saunders Company / North America Subscriptions, c/o Periodicals, 6277 Sea Harbour Drive, 4th Floor, Orlando FL 32887.**) ED** Barbara Cohen-Kligerman. **LC** RC60. **NLM** W1 ME252R. **CODEN** MCNAA9. **[CCC].** Index available. cum. index. **Pr Rev. Circ:** 35,500. available on microfilm and microfiche from University Microfilms International (UMI). Documents available from The Genuine Article, BIOSIS Document Express, CASDDS. ***Continues*** *Medical Clinics of Chicago, 0096-7041.*
**Desc:** Clinical updates on management and techniques written by experts in the field. Topics are those of current concerns to internists. Each issue is different topic.
**Ind/Abst** Abr. Index Med.; Biol. Abstr.; Chem. Abstr.; Cumul. Index Nurs. Allied Health Lit.; Curr. Contents Clin. Med.; Curr. Contents Life Sci.; EMBASE; Energy Res. Abstr.; Helminthol. Abstr.; Index Med.; INIS Atomindex [Micro.]; Int. Pharm. Abstr.; Life Sci. Collect.; PESTDOC; Physic. Medline Plus; Protozoolog. Abstr.; Ref. Upd. Basic Ed.; Ref. Upd. Deluxe Ed.; Res. Alert [Full Cov.]; Sci. Cit. Index; SCISEARCH; Soc. Sci. Cit. Index [Select. Cov.]; SportSearch.

US/0162-2382
**MEDICAL COMPUTING SERIES.** V. 1-. Monographic series. English. Price varies per volume. John Wiley & Sons, Inc., 605 Third Avenue, New York NY 10158-0012. **Tel** (212)850-6000, (212)850-6645, FAX (212)850-6088, telex 12-7063. **(Subscription address:** John Wiley & Sons / England, Baffins Lane, Chichester, West Sussex PO19 1UD England.**) ED** D W Hill. **NLM** W1 ME265.

GW/0179-1826
**MEDICAL CORPS INTERNATIONAL.** ***Ceased.*** (198?)-(1993). Periodical. English. Beta Verlag Marketing Gesellschaft, POB 130121, Celsiusstrasse 43, W-4300 Bonn 1 Germany. **NLM** W1; ME271H.
**Ind/Abst** Trop. Dis. Bull.

US/0272-989X
**MEDICAL DECISION MAKING.** See Computers-Artificial Intelligence.

US/0194-844X
**MEDICAL DEVICE & DIAGNOSTIC INDUSTRY.** [Med. device diagn. ind.]. **VAT** Medical Device and Diagnostic Industry. (June 1979)-. Academic Scholarly Publication. English. Twelve times a year. Cannon Communications, Inc., 3340 Ocean Park Boulevard / #1000, Santa Monica CA 90405. **Tel** (310)392-5509, 762-2193. **ED** Cheryl Doriot. **DD** 610. **NLM** W1 ME2966I. **CODEN** MDIIDI. **Circ:** 31,932. Documents available from Article Express International, The Genuine Article, CASDDS.
**Ind/Abst** BioBusiness; Bioeng. Abstr.; Ceram. Abstr.; Chem. Abstr.; Ei Page One; Eng. Index Annu.; Health Devices Alerts; Res. Alert [Full Cov.]; Soc. Sci. Cit. Index [Select. Cov.].

●US/1060-8338
**MEDICAL DEVICE APPROVAL LETTER.** [Med. device approv. lett.]. **Added/Corp** Washington Information Source. (1992)-. Periodical. English. mo. $495.00. Washington Information Source Company, 6506 Old Stage Road, Suite 700, Rockville MD 20852. **ED** Kenneth Reid. **DD** 362. **[CCC]. Bk Rev,** (Qty: 2-3). Documents available.
**Desc:** Lists 510(k)s approved by the FDA monthly for new devices and diagnostics. Provides news/analysis about FDA approval requirements; documents, including 510k(s); and PMAs through RECORD-RETRIEVE service.

US/1068-9311
**MEDICAL DEVICE REGISTER : SUPPLEMENT.** [Med. device regist., Suppl.]. (1989)-. English. an. $106.50. Medical Economics Data, Five Paragon Drive, PO Box 27, Montvale NJ 07645. **Tel** (800)442-6657, (201)358-7200. **DD** 681.

US/1048-6690
**MEDICAL DEVICE TECHNOLOGY.** [Med. device technol.]. (Jan./Feb. 1990)-. Periodical. English. Ten times a year. £32.00 Europe; £80.00 other. Advanstar Communications Inc., 131 West First Street, Duluth MN 55802. **Tel** (218)723-9477, (800)346-0085. **(Subscription address:** Advanstar Communications / UK Subscriptions, Park West, Sealand Road, Circulation Department, Chester CH1 4RN England.**) ED** Stefan Schuber. **DD** 616. **NLM** W1; ME2966M. ctrl circ. Documents available from The Genuine Article.
**Desc:** Editorial is written for professionals in the European medical device and diagnostics market and includes information on regulatory and legal affairs.
**Ind/Abst** Int. Pharm. Abstr.; Res. Alert [Full Cov.].

US
**MEDICAL DEVICE TRACKING.** (19??)-. English. ir. $295.00. ECRI Emergency Care Research Institute, 5200 Butler Pike, Plymouth Meeting PA 19462. **Tel** (215)825-6000, FAX (215)834-1275, telex 510-660-8023.

US
**MEDICAL DEVICES. Main/Corp** United States. Food and Drug Administration. **VFOAT** Pocket Supplement to Preamble Compilation. Apr. 1978-Mar. 1980-. English. an. US Department of Health and Human Services, 200 Independence Avenue Southwest, Washington DC 20201.

US/0888-7136
**MEDICAL DEVICES BULLETIN.** (MEDICAL DEVICES BULLETIN / NATIONAL CENTER FOR DEVICES AND RADIOLOGICAL HEALTH.). [Med. devices bull.]. **Added/Corp** National Center for Devices and Radiological Health (U.S.) Center for Devices and Radiological Health (U.S.). **VFOAT** DRH Medical Devices Bulletin. Vol. 1, No. 1 (Aug. 1983)-. Periodical. English. mo. Free. National Center for Devices & Radiological Health, HFZ-30, 12720 Twinburg Parkway, Rockville MD 20857. **Tel** (301)443-5807. **DD** 615. **NLM** W1; ME2966N.
**Ind/Abst** Health Devices Alerts.

US/0163-2426
**MEDICAL DEVICES, DIAGNOSTICS & INSTRUMENTATION REPORTS.** [Med. devices diagn. instrum. rep.]. **VFOAT** Gray Sheet; MDDI Reports. **VAT** Medical Devices, Diagnostics and Instrumentation Reports. (19??)-. Government Publication. English. wk. $690.00. FDC Reports Inc., 5550 Friendship Boulevard/Suite 1, Chevy Chase MD 20815. **Tel** (301)657-9830. **ED** Meg Bryant and Cole Palmer Werber. **CODEN** MDDIDR. **[CCC]. Ad Acc.** ctrl circ. Documents available from UMI Article Clearinghouse.
**Desc:** Provides in-depth, specialized coverage of the medical devices, diagnostics and instrumentation industries. Spectrum of coverage includes regulatory agency and congressional activities, industry developments and investor/financial news.
**Ind/Abst** Health Devices Alerts (19??-); Pharm. News Index (Dec. 1977-); PROMT (19??-); Trade Ind. Index (19??-).

US/0748-4852
**MEDICAL DEVICES REPORT.** (19??)-. Periodical. English. wk (50 issues per year). $435.00 US; $480.00 other. Medical Devices Report, PO Box 1062, Manassas VA 22110. **Tel** (703)361-6472. **ED** Steve Butchock. **NLM** W1; ME2966S. ***Absorbed*** *Washington Radiology Report., 0748-8033.*
**Desc:** Information on medical equipment, supplies, patents, and equipment failure.
**Ind/Abst** Health Devices Alerts.

SA
**MEDICAL DIGEST, THE.** Periodical. English. mo ((Feb.-Nov.)). R30.00 South Africa; R63.00 North America; R54.00 other. MIMS Pty Ltd., PO Box 2059, Pretoria 0001 South Africa. **Tel** 011 27 12 348-5010, FAX 011 27 12 477716. **Ad Acc. Circ:** 5,266 (ctrl).
**Desc:** Contains scientific articles and abstracts.

US/1052-0325
**MEDICAL DIRECTIONS (MERCER ISLAND, WASH.).** (MEDICAL DIRECTIONS.). [Med. dir.]. Vol. 1, No. 1 (June 1990)-. Periodical. English. Twelve times a year. $46.00. Medical Directions Publishing, PO Box 513, Woodlands Hills CA 91365. **Tel** (818)703-4031. **ED** John M. Harris, Jr. **DD** 610. **NLM** W1; ME2996. Index available. cum. index. **Circ:** 300 (ctrl).
**Desc:** Abstracts of current medical literature dealing with cost-effective medicine.

US/0273-0561
**MEDICAL DIRECTORY OF NEW YORK STATE. Added/Corp** Medical Society of the State of New York (1807-). (1950)-. English. an (Sept.). $113.66 New York; $105.00 others. Medical Society of New York, 420 Lakeville Road, Lake Success NY 11040. **Tel** (516)488-6100. **ED** Michael Martino. **NLM** W 22 AN6 M4. **Ad Acc. Circ:** 30,000 (ctrl). ***Continues*** *Medical Directory of New York, New Jersey and Connecticut.*
**Desc:** Directory listing New York State doctors and staff lists of New York State hospitals.

US/0025-7206
**MEDICAL ECONOMICS.** [Med. econ.]. Vol. 1 (Oct. 1923)-. Periodical. English. sm. $99.00 US; $159.00 other. Medical Economics Publishing, Five Paragon Drive, Second Floor, Montvale NJ 07645. **Tel** (800)432-4570, (201)358-2210. **(Subscription address:** Fulco Medical Economics, PO Box 3000, Denville NJ 07834.**) ED** H.S. Baketel. **LC** R723.5; .M4. **DD** 610. **NLM** W1 ME309H. available on an online database (file 648/Full-Text) from DIALOG.
**Desc:** Designed to advise the office-based doctor in the non-clinical areas of practice management, professional relations, malpractice concerns, and personal finance.
**Ind/Abst** Bus. Index (1985-); Cumul. Index Nurs. Allied

Health Lit.; Gen. BusinessFile (1985-); Gen. Period. Index (1985-); Health Plan. Adminis.; Health Ref. Cent. (1987-) [Select. Cov.]; Hospit. Health Admin. Index; Hospit. Manage. Rev.; Index Med.; Mag. Search; PAIS Int. Print (1991-); Trade Ind. ASAP [Full Txt.]; Trade Ind. Index (1981-) [Full Txt.].

UK/0308-0110
**MEDICAL EDUCATION.** [Med. educ.]. **Added/Corp** Association for the Study of Medical Education. Vol. 10 (Jan. 1976)-. Academic Scholarly Publication. English. bm (6 issues). $231.00 US & Canada; £135.50 Europe; £149.00 other. Blackwell Scientific Publications Ltd, Marston Book Services, PO Box 87, Oxford OX2 ODT UK. **Tel** 011 44 865 791155, FAX 011 44 865 791927, telex 837 515 MARDIS G. **ED** J. H. Walton. **LC** R735.A1; B7. **DD** 610/.7/11. **NLM** W1 ME309KE. **[CCC].** Index available (bound in last issue). **Bk Rev. Ad Acc. Pr Rev. Circ:** 1,540. available on microfilm and microfiche from University Microfilms International (UMI). Documents available from The Genuine Article, ADONIS. ***Continues*** *British Journal of Medical Education, 0007-1110.*
**Desc:** Covers all topical issues of undergraduate, postgraduate and continuing education.
**Ind/Abst** ADONIS; Cumul. Index Nurs. Allied Health Lit.; Curr. Contents Clin. Med.; Educ. Technol. Abstr.; EMBASE; Index Med.; Middle East Abstr. Index; Multicult. Educ. Abstr.; Nutr. Abstr. Rev., Ser. A, Hum. Exp.; Life Sci. Collect.; Psychol. Abstr. (1986-); PsycINFO; PsycLit; Res. Alert [Full Cov.]; Res. High. Educ. Abstr.; Sci. Cit. Index; SCISEARCH; Soc. Sci. Cit. Index [Select. Cov.]; SportSearch; Stud. Women Abstr.; Tech. Educ. Train. Abstr.; Trop. Dis. Bull.

US/0194-147X
**MEDICAL ELECTRONIC PRODUCTS.** [Med. electron. prod.]. **Added/Corp** Medical Electronics Society. Vol. 8, No. 5 (Oct. 1977)-. Periodical. English. Six times a year. Measurement & Data Corporation, 2994 West Liberty Avenue, Pittsburgh PA 15216. **Tel** (412)343-9666, FAX (412)343-9685. **DD** 629. **NLM** W1 ME309LR. ***Continues*** *Med News.*

US/0361-4174
**MEDICAL ELECTRONICS & EQUIPMENT NEWS. VAT** Medical Electronics and Equipment News. Periodical. English. bm. $40.00 US; $60.00 other. Reilly Publishing Company, 523 Busse Highway, Park Ridge IL 60068. **Tel** (312)693-3773. **DD** 610. **CODEN** MEEQA. available on microfilm from University Microfilms International (UMI). ***Continues*** *Medical Electronics News, 0025-7230.*

US/0149-9734
**MEDICAL ELECTRONICS (PITTSBURGH, PA.).** (MEDICAL ELECTRONICS.). [Med. electron.]. **Added/Corp** Medical Electronics Society. **VFOAT** MED. Medical Electronics. Vol.8, No. 5 (Oct. 1977)-. Periodical. English. bm. $22.00 (one year), $35.00 (two year) US; $35.00 other. Measurement & Data Corporation, 2994 West Liberty Avenue, Pittsburgh PA 15216. **Tel** (412)343-9666, FAX (412)343-9685. **ED** Milton H Aronson and Harish Saluja. **LC** R856.A1; M385. **DD** 629. **NLM** W1 ME309LR. **Bk Rev. Ad Acc. Circ:** 101,000 (ctrl). available on microfilm and microfiche from University Microfilms International (UMI). ***Continues*** *Medical Electronics & Data, 0098-3446.*
**Ind/Abst** Comput. Lit. Index; Health Devices Alerts; Hospit. Health Admin. Index.

US/0162-816X
**MEDICAL EQUIPMENT CLASSIFIED, THE.** (1978)-. Periodical. English. mo. $18.00. GOVESCO Publications, Box 29268, Minneapolis MN 55429.

JA/0025-8830
**MEDICAL EQUIPMENT JOURNAL OF JAPAN.** (19??)-. Periodical. English. mo. $138.00. Genyosha, 18-2, Shibuya 3 Chome, Shibuyaku, Tokyoto 150, Japan. **(Subscription address:** Kyowa Book Company Inc., 1 38 Kanda Jinbocho Chiyoda-ku, Tokyo 101 Japan.**)**

US/0886-0653
**MEDICAL ETHICS ADVISOR. See** Ethics.

GW/0724-8172
**MEDICAL FOCUS (WURZBURG, GERMANY).** (MEDICAL FOCUS.). Vol. 1 (May 1983)-. Periodical. English (Chinese). bm. $46.00. Beta Verlag Marketinggesellsch., Celsiusstrasse 43, PO Box 140121, W 5300 Bonn 1 Germany. **Tel** 011 49 228 252061, FAX (0220) 25 20 67, (0228)25 82 96, telex 8 869 536 beta d. **ED** Werner Skolaut. **NLM** W1; ME321R. **[CCC]. Ad Acc. Pr Rev. Circ:** 25,000 (ctrl). ***Continues*** *Export Markt. Physicians' and Hospital Supply.*
**Desc:** Covering medical, laboratory and hospital supplies with feature articles and new product reviews.
**Ind/Abst** Nonwovens Abstr.

UK/0261-3646
**MEDICAL FORUM (OXFORD, OXFORDSHIRE).** ***Ceased.*** (MEDICAL FORUM.). No. 1 (1981)-(19??). Periodical. English. qt. SK&F Labs, Mundells, Welwyn Garden City, Hert England. **Tel** 0865-724631. **NLM** W1 ME322E.

AT
**MEDICAL FRAUD AND OVERSERVICING / THE PARLIAMENT OF THE COMMONWEALTH OF AUSTRALIA, JOINT COMMITTEE OF PUBLIC ACCOUNTS. See** Law.

US/0899-8949
**MEDICAL GROUP MANAGEMENT JOURNAL.** [Med. group manage. j.]. **Added/Corp** Medical Group Management Association. **VFOAT** MGM Journal; MGMA Journal. (Nov./Dec. 1987)-. Periodical. English. bm. $43.00. Medical Group Management Association, 104 Inverness Terrace East, Englewood CO 80112. **Tel** (303)397-7879, FAX (303)799-1683. **ED** Fred E Graham and Derrol D Moorhead. **LC** R729.5.G6; M44. **DD** 610/.65/05. **NLM** W1; JO334GE. **CODEN** MGMJET. Index available. **Bk Rev. Ad Acc. Circ:** 14,000 (ctrl). available on microfilm and microfiche from University Microfilms International (UMI). ***Continues*** *Medical Group Management, 0025-7257.*
**Desc:** Ideas and techniques for group practice management including building, personnel management, finance, marketing and general management.
**Ind/Abst** Hospit. Health Admin. Index (Nov./Dec. 1987-); Hospit. Manage. Rev.

US/0025-7265
**MEDICAL GROUP NEWS.** ***Ceased.*** Vol. 1 (1968)-Vol 21. Periodical. English. bm. Global Medical Press, PO Box 36, Glencoe IL 60022. **Tel** (312)441-6474. **ED** Carol Brierly. **LC** R11; .M653. **NLM** W1 ME334K. **Ad Acc. Circ:** 54,000 (ctrl).
**Desc:** News and features specifically for physicians and administrators in group practice.

UK/0025-7273
**MEDICAL HISTORY.** [Med. hist.]. **Added/Corp** Wellcome Institute for the History of Medicine. Wellcome Historical Medical Library. Wellcome Institute of the History of Medicine. Cambridge University History of Medicine Society. British Society for the History of Medicine. Vol. 1 (Jan. 1957)-. Academic Scholarly Publication. English. qt. £94.00. Professional & Scientific Publishers, Tavistock House, East Tavistock Square, London WC1H 9JR England. **Tel** 011 44 71 387-4499, telex 005311. **(Subscription address:** Professional & Scientific Publishers, PO Box 294, London WC1H 9TB England.**) ED** W.F. Bynum, V. Nutton. **LC** R131.A1; M4. **DD** 610.9. **NLM** W1 ME338. **CODEN** MDHIAA. Index available. **Bk Rev. Ad Acc. Pr Rev. Circ:** 800. available on microfilm from University Microfilms International (UMI). Documents available from The Genuine Article, BIOSIS Document Express.
**Desc:** The official organ of the Wellcome Institute for the History of Medicine, this journal is devoted to all aspects of the history of medicine and the many disciplines that impinge upon it. Its concern is to deepen the understanding of medicine in the widest sense, which also embraces literary and legal history, medical sociology, ethnology, theology, and the history of art and technology.
**Ind/Abst** Am. Hist. Life (1967-); Biol. Abstr.; Br. Archaeol. Bibliogr.; Curr. Contents Clin. Med.; EMBASE; Helminthol. Abstr.; Index Med.; Middle East Abstr. Index; Life Sci. Collect.; Protozoolog. Abstr.; Res. Alert [Full Cov.]; Rev. Med. Vet. Entomol.; Sci. Cit. Index; SCISEARCH; Trop. Dis. Bull.

UK/0950-5571
**MEDICAL HISTORY. SUPPLEMENT.** [Med. his., Suppl.]. **Added/Corp** Wellcome Institute for the History of Medicine. No. 1 (1981)-. Monographic series. English. an. Price varies per volume; comes with Medical History. Professional & Scientific Publishers, Tavistock House, East Tavistock Square, London WC1H 9JR England. **Tel** 011 44 71 387-4499, telex 005311. **NLM** W1; ME338A. Index available. **Pr Rev. Circ:** 700.
**Ind/Abst** Index Med.

US/0274-614X
**MEDICAL HOTLINE.** ***Suspended.*** [Med. hotline]. -Suspended with Jan. 1985 issue cd's. Periodical. English. mo. Ovation Magazine, 33 West 60th St, New York NY 10023. **Tel** (212)765-5110.

US/0892-2772
**MEDICAL HUMANITIES REVIEW.** [Med. humanit. rev.]. **Added/Corp** University of Texas Medical Branch at Galveston. Institute for the Medical Humanities. **VFOAT** MHR. Vol. 1, No. 1 (Jan. 1987)-. Periodical. English. sa. $40.00 (institutions), $20.00 (individuals) US; $45.00 (institutions), $25.00 (individuals) other. Institute for the Medical Humanities, The University of Texas Medical Branch, Galveston TX 77555. **Tel** (409)772-2376, FAX (409)772-5640. **ED** Ronald A. Carson and Thomas H. Murray. **LC** WMLC 93/1867. **DD** 610. **NLM** ZW 50; M4893. **Bk Rev**, (Qty: 40). **Ad Acc, Adv Mgr:** Diane Pfeil. **Circ:** 1,000.
**Desc:** Provides timely and substantial reviews of significant new works in the medical humanities. Includes review essays, thematic reviews, and comparative reviews.
**Ind/Abst** Book Rev. Index; Philos. Index.

UK/0306-9877
**MEDICAL HYPOTHESES.** [Med. hypotheses]. Vol. 1 (Jan./Feb. 1975)-. Academic Scholarly Publication. English. mo. £421.00 Europe; £423.00 Other (Institutions). Churchill Livingstone, 1-3 Baxter's Place, Leith Walk, Edinburgh EH1 3AF Scotland. **Tel** 011 44 31 556 2424, FAX 011 44 31 558 1278, telex 727511. **(Subscription address:** Maruzen Company Ltd., PO Box 5050, Import & Export Department, Tokyo 100 31 Japan.**) ED** David F Horrobin. **LC** R5; .M39. **DD** 610/.5. **NLM** W1 ME341D. **CODEN** MEHYDY. **[CCC]. Pr Rev.** available on microfilm from University Microfilms International (UMI). Documents available from The Genuine Article, BIOSIS Document Express, CASDDS, ADONIS.
**Desc:** Devoted entirely to the publication of ideas in medicine and the related biomedical sciences. Every issue offers the opportunity to share the knowledge, opinions and criticisms of experts from around the world who are exchanging views and compounding theories which may lead to important discoveries.
**Ind/Abst** ADONIS; Anim. Breed. Abstr.; Biol. Abstr.; Chem. Abstr.; CSA Neuro. Abstr. (?-?); Curr. Aware. Biol. Sci., CABS; Curr. Contents Clin. Med.; Curr. Contents Life Sci.; Dairy Sci. Abstr.; EMBASE; Index Med.; Index Vet.; Nematol. Abstr.; Nutr. Abstr. Rev., Ser. A, Hum. Exp.; Life Sci. Collect.; Protozoolog. Abstr.; Ref. Upd. Basic Ed.; Ref. Upd. Deluxe Ed.; Res. Alert [Full Cov.]; Sci. Cit. Index; SCISEARCH; Soc. Sci. Cit. Index [Select. Cov.]; Vet. Bull.; Virol. AIDS Abstr.

AT
**MEDICAL IMAGING AND MONITORING.** English. qt. 60.00Aus$. Reed Business Publishing Pty Ltd. / Australia, 1 5 Railway Street, Level 12 North Tower, Chatswood W 2067 NSW Australia. **Tel** 011 61 2 3725222, FAX 011 61 2 4197533. **ED** Jane Kahler. **Bk Rev. Ad Acc, Adv Mgr:** David Strong. **Circ:** 3000 (ctrl).
**Desc:** To provide users of medical diagnostic and patient monitoring equipment with news and product information.

●US/1073-1202
**MEDICAL IMAGING (PORTSMOUTH, R.I.).** (MEDICAL IMAGING : THE BUSINESS MAGAZINE FOR TECHNOLOGY MANAGEMENT.). [Med. imaging]. Vol. 9, No. 1 (Jan. 1994)-. Periodical. English. Twelve times a year. $50.00. Second Source Publications Inc., PO Box 930, Portsmouth RI 02871. **Tel** (401)683-7470. **DD** 338. **NLM** W1; ME341EJ. ***Continues*** *Second Source Imaging, 1053-6876.*

SI
**MEDICAL INDEXES.** MIMS Asia, 135 Cecil Street, 13-00 LKN Building, Singapore 0106 Singapore. **Tel** 011 65 2233788, FAX 011 65 2214788.

US/0275-1461
**MEDICAL INDUSTRY ANALYSIS SERVICE.** [Med. ind. anal. serv.]. (April 1980)-. Monographic series. English. mo. Price varies per volume. Creative Strategies International, 4340 Stevens Creek Blvd., Suite 275, San Jose CA 95129. **NLM** W1 ME341U. ***Continues*** *Medical Industry Analysis.*

●US/1060-5193
**MEDICAL INDUSTRY EXECUTIVE.** [Med. ind. exec.]. Feb. (1992)-. Periodical. English. bm. $45.00 US; $95.00 other. Medical Industry Publications, Inc., 1190 Hightower Trail, Atlanta GA 30350. **Tel** (404)988-9797, FAX (404)594-6998. **ED** Elizabeth R. Porter. **DD** 681. **Ad Acc, Adv Mgr:** Larry Jacobs, **Tel** (603)772-0730. **Circ:** 40,000 (ctrl).
**Desc:** Targets CEO's and upper management of medical device, equipment and supply manufacturers. Editorial focuses on health care, legislation, new medical products and developments, equipment, diagnostic products and home medical equipment.

UK/0307-7640
**MEDICAL INFORMATICS. See** Computers-Data Processing.

US
**MEDICAL INNOVATION AT THE CROSSROADS. Added/Corp** Institute of Medicine (U.S.). Committee on Technological Innovation in Medicine. Vol. 1 (1990)-. Monographic series. English. ir. Price varies per volume. National Academy Press, 2101 Constitution Avenue NW, Lockbox 285, Washington DC 20055. **Tel** (800)624-6242, (202)334-3313, FAX (202)334-2451. **NLM** W1; ME342F.

US/0896-4831
**MEDICAL INTERFACE.** [Med. interface]. Vol. 1, No. 1 (Jan. 1988)-. Periodical. English. mo. $68.00 (individual); $90.00 (institutions) US; $90.00 (individual); $110.00 (institutions) other. Medicom International Inc, 66 Palmer Avenue, Suite 49, Bronxville NY 10708. **Tel** (914)337-7878, FAX (914)337-5023. **ED** Stanton Mehr. **LC** WMLC 93/1425. **DD** 362. **NLM** W1; ME342P. **Ad Acc, Adv Mgr:** Jane Armstrong. **Pr Rev. Circ:** 28,000 (ctrl).
**Desc:** An interface of managed healthcare topics.
**Ind/Abst** Int. Pharm. Abstr.

CN
**MEDICAL JOURNAL. Main/Corp** University of Toronto. Vol. 54, (Dec. 1976)-. Periodical. English. Three times a year. 25.00Can$. University of Toronto Medical Journal, Medical Society of University Toronto, Toronto ONT Canada. **Tel** (416)978-8730. ***Continues*** *University of Toronto Medical Journal.*

II/0377-1237
**MEDICAL JOURNAL, ARMED FORCES INDIA.** [Med. j. Armed Forces India]. Vol. 30, No. 4 (Oct. 1974)-. Periodical. English. qt. $34.00. **(Subscription address:** Prints India, 11 Darya Ganj, New Delhi 110002 India.) **NLM** W1 ME344M. ***Continues*** *Armed Forces Medical Journal, India, 0004-2218.*
**Ind/Abst** Energy Res. Abstr. (March 1981-); Nutr. Abstr. Rev., Ser. A, Hum. Exp.; Trop. Dis. Bull.

AT/0025-729X
**MEDICAL JOURNAL OF AUSTRALIA.** [Med. j. Aust.]. **Added/Corp** Australian Medical Association. British Medical Association. Vol. 1 (July 1914)-. Academic Scholarly Publication. English. sm. 225.00Aus$ Australia; 295.00Aus$ New Zealand, Papua New Guinea, New Caledonia, Solomon Islands, & Vanuatu; 325.00Aus$ other. Australasian Medical Publishing Company, 76 Berry Street Level 1, North Sydney 2059 Australia. **Tel** 011 61 2 9548666, FAX 11 61 02 5023626. **(Subscription address:** Australasian Medical Publishing Co., Private Bag 901, North Sydney 2059 Australia) **ED** Laurel Thomas. **NLM** W1 ME345. **CODEN** MJAUAJ. Index Available Published separately--free--upon request. **Bk Rev. Ad Acc. Pr Rev. Circ:** 22,000 (ctrl). available on microfilm and microfiche from University Microfilms International (UMI). Documents available from The Genuine Article, BIOSIS Document Express, CASDDS. ***Formed by the union of*** *Australasian Medical Gazette, 0314-5158* ***and*** *Australian Medical Journal, 0314-514X.*
**Desc:** Provides practitioners with original reports. Also provides the latest clinical infomation from Australia and surrounding countries.
**Ind/Abst** Aust. Leg. Mon. Dig.; Biodeter. Abstr. (1991-); Biol. Abstr.; Chem. Abstr.; Chem. Hazards Ind.; CSA Neuro. Abstr. (?-?); Cumul. Index Nurs. Allied Health Lit.; Curr. Aware. Biol. Sci., CABS; Curr. Biotechnol.; Curr. Contents Clin. Med.; Dairy Sci. Abstr.; Dev. Med. Child Neurol.; EMBASE; Helminthol. Abstr. (19??-19??); Highw. Res. Abstr.; Hortic. Abstr.; Index Med.; Index Vet.; Int. Pharm. Abstr.; Iowa Drug Inf. Serv. (1969-); Lab. Hazards Bull.; Mod. Med.; NAPRALERT; Nutr. Abstr. Rev., Ser. A, Hum. Exp.; Nutr. Res. Newsl. (-1987); Life Sci. Collect.; PESTDOC; Protozoolog. Abstr.; Ref. Upd. Basic Ed.; Ref. Upd. Deluxe Ed.; Res. Alert [Full Cov.]; Rev. Agric. Entomol.; Rev. Med. Vet. Entomol.; Rev. Med. Vet. Mycology; Rice Abstr.; Risk Abstr.; Saf. Health Work; Sci. Cit. Index; SCISEARCH; Soc. Sci. Cit. Index [Select. Cov.]; SportSearch; Vet. Bull.; Trop. Dis. Bull.; Virol. AIDS Abstr.; Wheat Barley Trit. Abstr.

IQ/0253-0759
**MEDICAL JOURNAL OF BASRAH UNIVERSITY, THE.** [Med. j. Basrah Univ.]. **Added/Corp** Jamiat Al-Basrah. College of Medicine. **VFOAT** Majallah Al-Tibbiyah Li-Jamiat Al-Basrah. Vol. 1, No. 1 (June 1977)-. Periodical. English (summaries and/or abstracts in Arabic). **NLM** W1 ME345CJ.
**Ind/Abst** Trop. Dis. Bull.

TU/1017-7698
**MEDICAL JOURNAL OF EGE UNIVERSITY.** [Med. j. Ege Univ.]. (1991)-. Periodical. English. qt. 100.00TL. Ege Universitesi Tip Fakultesi, Yayin Alt-Komitesi Yayin Burosu, Bornova Izmir Turkey. **Tel** 9051 18 18 20 3103, FAX 9051 18 28 52. **UDC** 61.
**Desc:** Publishes research papers, case reports, and news on any field of medicine.

MY/0300-5283
**MEDICAL JOURNAL OF MALAYSIA.** (THE MEDICAL JOURNAL OF MALAYSIA.). [Med. j. Malaysia]. **Added/Corp** Malaysian Medical Association. Vol. 27 (1972)-. Academic Scholarly Publication. English. Four times a year. 240.00Mal$. Medical Association of Malaysia, 4th Floor Mma House, 124 Jalan Pahang, 53000 Kuala Lumpur Malaysia. **Tel** 011 60 3 4420617. **NLM** W1 ME35. **CODEN** MJMLAI. Documents available from BIOSIS Document Express, CASDDS. ***Continues*** *Medical Journal of Malaya.*
**Ind/Abst** Biol. Abstr.; Chem. Abstr.; Cumul. Index Nurs. Allied Health Lit.; EMBASE [Select. Cov.]; Index Med.; Trop. Dis. Bull.

ZA/0047-651X
**MEDICAL JOURNAL OF ZAMBIA.** [Med. j. Zambia]. (1967)-. Academic Scholarly Publication. English. Six times a year. Zambia Medical Association, PO Box 717, Ndola Zambia. **CODEN** MJZAAG. Documents available from BIOSIS Document Express.
**Ind/Abst** Biol. Abstr.; EMBASE.

CN/0833-2207
**MEDICAL JOURNAL - UNIVERSITY OF TORONTO.** (UNIVERSITY OF TORONTO MEDICAL JOURNAL.). [Med. j. - Univ. Tor.]. **VFOAT** University of Toronto Medical Journal (1976). (1976)-. Periodical. English. Three times a year. 25.00Can$ one year; 50.00Can$ patron. University of Toronto Medical Sciences Building, Room 2141, Toronto Ontario M5S 1A8 Canada. **Tel** (800)633-6088. **ED** Cindy Grief and Matthew Stanbrock, (phone: 978-8730). **DD** 610. **Bk Rev. Ad Acc, Adv Mgr:** Kenmars Inc., **Tel** (416)864-9132. **Circ:** 1,200. ***Continues*** *University of Toronto Medical Journal (1965), 0833-2193.*

UK/0308-3616
**MEDICAL LABORATORY SCIENCES.** ***Title Change.*** [Med. lab. sci.]. **Added/Corp** Institute of Medical Laboratory Sciences (Great Britain). Vol. 33-49 No. 4 (Jan. 1976)-(Dec. 1992). Academic Scholarly Publication. English. qt. Blackwell Scientific Publications Ltd, Marston Book Services, PO Box 87, Oxford OX2 ODT UK. **Tel** 011 44 865 791155, FAX 011 44 865 791927, telex 837 515 MARDIS G. **(Subscription address:** UK/ Marston Book Services, PO Box 87, Oxford UK; US/ 3 Cambridge Center, Suite 208, Cambridge MA 02142; Aus/ 54 University Street, Carlton Victoria 3053 Australia; Germany/ Meinekestrasse 4, D-1000 Berlin 15 Germany; France/ Arnette, 2 rue Casimir Delavigne, 75006 Paris France; Austria/ Blackwell MZV, Medizinische Zeitschriftenverlags Gesellschaft, Feldgasse 13, A-1238 Vienna Austria) **ED** A D Farr. **NLM** W1 ME361E. **CODEN** MLASDU. **[CCC]. Bk Rev. Ad Acc. Pr Rev. Circ:** 18,300. available on microfilm and microfiche from University Microfilms International (UMI). Documents available from The Genuine Article, BIOSIS Document Express, CASDDS. ***Continues*** *Medical Laboratory Technology, 0022-2607.* ***Continued by*** *British Journal of Biomedical Science, 0967-4845.*
**Desc:** Worldwide papers are published on all aspects of medical laboratory sciences with particular emphasis on the major disciplines of blood transfusion, cellular pathology, clinical chemistry, haematology, immunology and microbiology.
**Ind/Abst** Anal. Abstr.; Biol. Abstr.; Chem. Abstr.; Cumul. Index Nurs. Allied Health Lit.; Curr. Biotechnol.; Curr. Contents Life Sci.; Dairy Sci. Abstr.; EMBASE; Food Sci. Technol. Abstr.; Index Med.; Index Vet.; Microbiol. Abstr. Sect. B; Microbiol. Abstr. Sect. A; Nutr. Abstr. Rev., Ser. A, Hum. Exp.; Life Sci. Collect.; Protozoolog. Abstr.; Res. Alert [Full Cov.]; Sci. Cit. Index; SCISEARCH; Soc. Sci. Cit. Index [Select. Cov.]; SportSearch; Trop. Dis. Bull.

UK/0950-0294
**MEDICAL LABORATORY SCIENCES. SUPPLEMENT.** [Med. lab. sci., Suppl.]. (1986)-. Academic Scholarly Publication. English. ir. Blackwell Scientific Publications Ltd, Marston Book Services, PO Box 87, Oxford OX2 ODT UK. **Tel** 011 44 865 791155, FAX 011 44 865 791927, telex 837 515 MARDIS G.
**Ind/Abst** EMBASE.

UK/0263-8568
**MEDICAL LABORATORY SCIENTIFIC OFFICERS REGISTER, THE.** **Added/Corp** Medical Laboratory Technicians Board. (1979)-. Periodical. English. an. £15.00. Council for the Professions Supplementary to Medicine, 184 Kennington Park Road, London SE11 4BU England. **Tel** 011 44 71 582-0866. **NLM** QZ 22 FA1 M489L. ***Continues*** *Medical Laboratory Technicians Register.*

UK/0140-3028
**MEDICAL LABORATORY WORLD.** [Med. lab. world.]. Vol. 1 (Sept. 1977)-. Academic Scholarly Publication. English. Eleven times a year. $178.00 US & Canada; £48.00 UK. Wilmington Publishing Ltd., PO Box 200, Field End Road, Ruislip Middx HA4 OSY England. **Tel** 011 44 81 841 3970, FAX 011 44 81 841 9676. **ED** Susan Pearson. **NLM** W1 ME361KR. **CODEN** MLWODQ. **Ad Acc. Circ:** 10,000 (ctrl). Documents available from CASDDS.
**Desc:** Covers all equipment and techniques associated with all aspects of medical laboratory sciences. News, comments, and articles of general interest are also covered.
**Ind/Abst** Abstr. BioCommer. (19??-); Chem. Abstr. (19??-); Curr. Biotechnol. (19??-).

US/0896-0275
**MEDICAL LASER BUYERS' GUIDE. See** Economics-Industry and Production.

US/0892-3108
**MEDICAL LASER INDUSTRY REPORT.** ***Title Change.*** **See** Economics-Industry and Production.

US
**MEDICAL LASER REPORT. See** Economics-Industry and Production.

US/0098-4833
**MEDICAL LAW LETTER FOR PHYSICIANS, SURGEONS & HEALTH PROFESSIONALS, THE. See** Law.

UK/0957-9346
**MEDICAL LAW REPORTS. See** Law.

●UK/0967-0742
**MEDICAL LAW REVIEW. See** Law.

SP/0025-732X
**MEDICAL LETTER.** (19??)-. Spanish. bw. $84.00. Prous Science Publishers, Apartado de Correos 540, 08080 Barcelona Spain. **Tel** 011 34 3 4592220, FAX 011 34 3 4581535. **UDC** 61.

●US/1067-1269
**MEDICAL LITIGATION ALERT. See** Law.

US
**MEDICAL MALPRACTICE. See** Insurance.

US/0893-8229
**MEDICAL MALPRACTICE DEFENSE REPORTER, THE.** ***Ceased.*** **See** Law.

US/0885-744X
**MEDICAL MALPRACTICE PREVENTION.** ***Suspended.*** **See** Law.

US/0025-7354
**MEDICAL MARKETING & MEDIA. See** Business-Marketing.

US/0093-1314
**MEDICAL MEETINGS.** [Med. meet.]. Vol. 1, (1973)-. Periodical. English. Eight times a year. $48.00 US; $64.00 other. Laux Company Inc, 63 Great Road, Maynard MA 01754. **Tel** (508)897-5552, FAX (508)897-6824. **ED** Betsy Bair Cassidy. **DD** 610. **NLM** W1 ME384K. **[CCC]. Ad Acc, Adv Mgr:** B Ventre. **Circ:** 14,000 (ctrl).
**Desc:** Reports on the healthcare meetings industry, with news, departments, informative features and updates on destinations where medical meetings are held.

US
**MEDICAL MEETINGS ANNUAL DIRECTORY.** (1975)-. Directory. English. an (November). $25.00 US; $30.00 others. Laux Company Inc, 63 Great Road, Maynard MA 01754. **Tel** (508)897-5552, FAX (508)897-6824. **ED** Betsy Bair. **Ad Acc, Adv Mgr:** B. Ventre. **Circ:** 14,000 (ctrl).

US/1055-5951
**MEDICAL MONITOR.** [Med. monit.]. **Added/Corp** Gardiner-Caldwell SynerMed. University of Texas Health Science Center at Houston. Vol. 1, No. 1 (Apr. 1991)-. Periodical. English. Free. Gardiner-Caldwell Synermed, Route 513 and Trimmer Road, PO Box 458, Califon NJ 07830. **DD** 616. **NLM** W1; ME3936.

US/0025-7397
**MEDICAL-MORAL NEWSLETTER, THE.** Vol. 2, No. 5 (Jan. 1966)-. Periodical. English. Ten times a year (except July and Aug.). $25.00 US, $33.00 Canada & Mexico, $37.00 others (surface mail); $41.00 (airmail). Ayd Medical Communications, 1130 East Cold Spring Lane, Baltimore MD 21239. **Tel** (301)433-9220, FAX (301)532-5419. **ED** Frank J. Ayd Jr. Index available. cum. index. **Bk Rev. Circ:** 800. ***Continues*** *Medical Newsletter for Religious.*
**Desc:** In-depth analysis of medical/ethical topics with special emphasis on the background, present status, and possible ramifications of current thinking.

CN/0846-1309
**MEDICAL NETWORKS.** (MEDICAL NETWORKS / CONTINUING MEDICAL EDUCATION, FACULTY OF MEDICINE, MEMORIAL UNIVERSITY OF NEWFOUNDLAND.). [Med. netw.]. **Added/Corp** Memorial University of Newfoundland. Continuing Medical Education. Vol. 1, No. 1 (Aug. 1990)-. Periodical. English. bm. Free. Continuing Medical Education, Faculty of Medicine, Memorial Univeristy of Newfoundland, Room 2901, Health Science Centre, Prince Philip Drive, St. John's, Newfoundland A1B 3V6 Canada. **DD** 610/.71/5.

US/1054-3066
**MEDICAL NEWS REPORT.** [Med. news rep.]. Vol. 1, No. 1 (Oct. 1991)-. Periodical. English. mo. $150.00. Rundown/Standish Publishing, POB 335, Ardmore PA 19003. **Tel** (215)664-3322, FAX (215)664-3322. **ED** Kim Standish. **DD** 362.

US/0895-4313
**MEDICAL OFFICE REPORT.** [Med. off. rep.]. (1988)-. Periodical. English. mo. $158.00. Washington G 2 Reports, 1111 14th Street NW, Suite 711, Washington DC 20005. **Tel** (202)789-1034, FAX (202)289-4062. **ED** Dennis W. Weissman and D. J. Curren. **DD** 362.

US/0090-1474
**MEDICAL OPINION (NEW YORK, N.Y.).** (MEDICAL OPINION.). [Med. opin.]. V. 1 (May 1972)-. Periodical. English. mo. $14.00 US; $18.00 other. Weston Communications, Inc., 575 Madison Avenue, New York NY 10022. **LC** R11; .M7252. **DD** 610/.5. **NLM** W1 ME409C. ***Supersedes*** *Medical Opinion, 0090-1474.*

●US/1067-4195
**MEDICAL OUTCOMES & GUIDELINES ALERT.** [Med. outcomes guidel. alert]. **Added/Corp** Faulkner & Gray's Healthcare Information Center. **VFOAT** Medical Outcomes and Guidelines Alert. (1993)-. Periodical. English. Twenty-four times a year. $395.00. Faulkner & Gray Inc., 11 Penn Plaza, 17th Floor, New York NY 10001. **Tel** (212)967-7000, (800)535-8403. **DD** 362.

US
**MEDICAL OUTCOMES & GUIDELINES SOURCEBOOK.** (19??)-. Directory. English. an. $235.00. Faulkner & Gray Inc., 11 Penn Plaza, 17th Floor, New York NY 10001. **Tel** (212)967-7000, (800)535-8403.

UK/0143-0203
**MEDICAL PHYSICS HANDBOOKS. See** Physics.

US/0094-2405
**MEDICAL PHYSICS (LANCASTER).** See Physics.

US/0163-1802
**MEDICAL PHYSICS MONOGRAPH.** See Physics.

CN/0025-7435
**MEDICAL POST, THE.** Vol. 1 (Sept. 14, 1965)-. Periodical. English. Forty-Four times a year. 59.00Can$ Canada; 120.00Can$ other. MacLean Hunter Ltd. Business Publishers / Canada, Box 9100, Station A, Toronto ONT M5W 1A5 Canada. **Tel** (416)946-8420, (800)567-0444. **(Subscription address:** Indas, 35 Riviera Drive, Building 17, Markham Ontario L3R 8N4 Canada.) **NLM** W1 ME412M. **[CCC].** available on microfilm from University Microfilms International (UMI).
**Ind/Abst** Can. Index.

SZ/1011-7571
**MEDICAL PRINCIPLES AND PRACTICE.** (MEDICAL PRINCIPLES AND PRACTICE : INTERNATIONAL JOURNAL OF THE KUWAIT UNIVERSITY, HEALTH SCIENCE CENTRE.). [Med. princ. pract.]. **Added/Corp** Jamiat al-Kuwayt. Health Science Centre. (Sept. 1988)-. Periodical. English. Four times a year (one volume per year). $178.00. S. Karger AG, Allschwilerstrasse 10, PO Box - Postfach - Case Postale, CH-4009 Basel Switzerland. **Tel** 011 41 61 306-1111, FAX 011 41 61 306-1234, telex CH 962 652. **ED** B. Al-Nakib. **NLM** W1; ME416RS. **[CCC].** Index available. cum. index. **Ad Acc. Circ:** 1,800 (ctrl). available on microfiche; available on microfilm; available in microform. Documents available from BIOSIS Document Express.
**Desc:** General medical journal that focuses on recent advances made in basic medical sciences and clinical practice. It reflects the broad spectrum of work conducted by scientists and physicians from around the world at the Kuwait University faculty of medicine since its foundation in 1976. The international character of their contributions has resulted in the journal attracting original papers, reviews, reports and short communications not only from Kuwait and the Middle East, but also from the international scientific and medical communities as a whole.
**Ind/Abst** Biol. Abstr.; EMBASE; Ref. Upd. Deluxe Ed.

US/0885-1158
**MEDICAL PROBLEMS OF PERFORMING ARTISTS.** [Med. probl. perform. artists]. **VFOAT** MPPA. Vol. 1, No. 1 (March 1986)-. Periodical. English. qt. $48.00 (US & possessions), $58.00 (other) individual; $58.00 (US & possessions), $68.00 (other) institution. Hanley & Belfus Inc., 210 South 13th Street, Philadelphia PA 19107. **Tel** (215)546-7293, FAX (215)790-9330. **ED** Alice Bronfonbrener. **LC** WMLC 93/433. **DD** 616. **CODEN** MPPAEC. **[CCC]. Bk Rev. Ad Acc. Pr Rev. Circ:** 2,500. Documents available from The Genuine Article, BIOSIS Document Express.
**Desc:** Covers medical and psychological problems of vocalist, instrumentalists, dancers and other performing artists, including original research and reviews.
**Ind/Abst** Arts Humanit. Citation Index [Full Cov.]; Biol. Abstr. (1986-); Curr. Contents Clin. Med.; Music Index; Res. Alert [Select. Cov.]; Risk Abstr.; SCISEARCH; Soc. Sci. Cit. Index [Select. Cov.].

US/0893-6250
**MEDICAL PRODUCT MANUFACTURING NEWS.** (MEDICAL PRODUCT MANUFACTURING NEWS.). [Med. prod. manuf. news]. **Added/Corp** Canon Communications, Inc. (198?)-. Periodical. English. Ten times a year. Free on request to qualified subscribers; $95.00 other. Canon Communications Inc, 3340 Ocean Park Boulevard, Suite 1000, Santa Monica CA 90405. **Tel** (310)392-5509, (312)762-2193, FAX (310)453-2584. **ED** Ingrid Birze. **Ad Acc. Circ:** 20,000 (ctrl).
**Desc:** Product tabloid featuring the latest equipment, materials, components, and services for medical device and medical electronics manufacturers.

US/0279-4802
**MEDICAL PRODUCTS SALES.** [Med. prod. sales]. **Added/Corp** American Surgical Trade Association. Health Industry Distributors Association (U.S.). **VFOAT** MPS; M.P.S. Vol. 12, No. 5 (May 1981)-. Periodical. English. mo. $49.95. McKnight Medical Communications Inc, 1419 Lake Cook Road, Suite 110, Deerfield IL 60015. **Tel** (708)647-0259, (800)451-7838. **(Subscription address:** Hallmark Data Systems, PO Box 1165, Skokie IL 60076.) **ED** William C. Briggs and Heather Schroeder. **NLM** W1 ME4173. **[CCC]. Ad Acc. Circ:** 24,000 (ctrl). available on microfilm from University Microfilms International (UMI). ***Continues** MPS. Medical Products Salesman, 0192-432X.*
**Desc:** The dealer/distributor news magazine of health care product sales and marketing.
**Ind/Abst** Hospit. Health Admin. Index (1981-1986).

CN/0835-3069
**MEDICAL PSYCHOTHERAPY.** ***Ceased.*** [Med. psychother.]. Vol. 1 (1988)-Vol. 5 (March 1993). English. an. Hogrefe and Huber Publishers, PO Box 2487, Kirkland WA 98083. **Tel** (800)228-3749, (206)820-1500, FAX (206)823-8324. **(Subscription address:** US/ PO Box 51, Lewiston, NY 14092; Germany/ Daimlerstrasse 40, W-7000 Stuttgart 50; Switzerland/ Laenggass Strasse 76, CH-3000 Bern 9) **LC** RC321; .M39. **DD** 616.89/14/05. **NLM** W1; ME421T. available on microfilm and microfiche from University Microfilms International (UMI).

US/0276-3869
**MEDICAL REFERENCE SERVICES QUARTERLY.** See Library and Information Sciences.

UK/0141-2256
**MEDICAL RESEARCH COUNCIL ANNUAL REPORT.** [Annu. rep. - Med. Res. Counc.]. **Main/Corp** Medical Research Council (Great Britain). (April 1965-March 1966)-. English. an. £10.00. Medical Research Council, 20 Park Cresent, London W1N 4AL England. **Tel** 011 44 71 636 5422. **NLM** W2; FA1 M37r. ***Continues** Medical Research Council (Great Britain). Report of the Medical Research Council.*

UK/0309-0132
**MEDICAL RESEARCH COUNCIL HANDBOOK.** (HANDBOOK / MEDICAL RESEARCH COUNCIL (GREAT BRITAIN).). **Main/Corp** Medical Research Council (Great Britain). (1970/71)-. English. an. £10.00. Medical Research Council, 20 Park Cresent, London W1N 4AL England. **Tel** 011 44 71 636 5422. **LC** R854.G7; M44. **DD** 610/.72/042. **NLM** W 22 FA1; M495H.

US
**MEDICAL RESEARCH FUNDING BULLETIN.** **Added/Corp** Science Support Center. (1972)-. Bulletin. English. tm. $68.00 US; $72.00 Canada; $92.00 other. Science Support Center, PO Box 7507 FDR Station, New York NY 10150. **Tel** (212)371-3398. **ED** Carroll Jordon. **Bk Rev. Ad Acc. Circ:** 3,000 (ctrl).
**Desc:** Information on government and private agency grants and contracts available to support health science programs at universities and medical centers.

US/1052-9152
**MEDICAL RESEARCH FUNDING NEWS.** ***Ceased.*** [Med. res. funding news]. Vol. 1, No. 1 (Jan 31, 1991)-(1992). Periodical. English. sm. Faulkner & Gray Inc., 11 Penn Plaza, 17th Floor, New York NY 10001. **Tel** (212)967-7000, (800)535-8403. **DD** 610. available on an online database (file 636/Full-Text) from DIALOG.

US/0083-3541
**MEDICAL RESEARCH IN THE VETERANS' ADMINISTRATION.** **Main/Corp** United States. Veterans Administration. 1962/63-. English. US Veterans Administration / Washington DC, 810 Vermont Avenue Southwest, Washington DC 20420. **Tel** (202)393-2124. **LC** RA11; .F32. **DD** 610/.7/2073. **NLM** W2 A V54MO. ***Continues** Medical Research in the Veteran's Administration, 0083-3541.*

UK
**MEDICAL RESEARCH INDEX.** ***Title Change.*** 4th Ed. (1971)-?. English. Longman Group Ltd., Fourth Avenue, Longman House, Harlow Essex CM19 5SR England. **Tel** 011 44 279 429655, FAX 011 44 279 431059, telex 81259. **(Subscription address:** Fourth Avenue, Harlow Essex CM19 5AA England) ***Continued by** Medical Research Centres.*

CN/1186-2858
**MEDICAL REVIEW OF MEETINGS & LISTINGS, THE.** [Med. rev. meet. listings]. **VAT** Medical Review of Meetings and Listings. Vol. 1, No. 1 (Mar. 1991)-. Periodical. English. ir. Parkhurst Publishing, 400 McGill 3rd Floor, Montreal Quebec H2Y 2G1 Canada. **Tel** (514)397-8833, (514)397-9393. **DD** 610/.5.

US/0892-3736
**MEDICAL ROUNDS.** ***Ceased.*** [Med. rounds]. Vol. 1, No. 1 (1988)-(1990). Periodical. English. bm. Little Brown & Company, 34 Beacon Street, Boston MA 02108. **Tel** (617)227-0730, (800)759-0190. **DD** 610. **NLM** W1; ME4594.

US/0738-6060
**MEDICAL SCHOOL ADMISSION REQUIREMENTS, UNITED STATES AND CANADA.** See Education-Higher Education.

UK/0269-8951
**MEDICAL SCIENCE RESEARCH.** [Med. sci. res.]. Vol. 15, No. 1 (Jan. 1987)-. Academic Scholarly Publication. English. Twelve times a year. $998.00 US; £421.00 Europe; £525.00 other. Chapman & Hall, 2-6 Boundary Row, London SE1 8HN England. **Tel** 011 44 71 865 0066, FAX 011 44 71 522 9623, telex 290164 Chapmag. **(Subscription address:** International Thomson Publishing Svcs. Ltd., Subscription Department North Way Andover, Hampshire SP10 5BE England.) **ED** S. Johnson. **NLM** W1; ME46R. **CODEN** MSCREJ. **[CCC]. Bk Rev.** available on an online database; available on microfiche. Documents available from BIOSIS Document Express, CASDDS. ***Continues** IRCS Medical Science, 0268-8220.*
**Desc:** Journal for rapid publication and effective dissemination of original articles over the entire field of medical and biomedical science. Its scope embraces both clinical studies and basic research.
**Ind/Abst** Anim. Breed. Abstr.; Biol. Abstr. (1987-); Calcium Calcif. Tissue Abstr.; Chem. Abstr. (1987-); CSA Neuro. Abstr.; Curr. Aware. Biol. Sci., CABS; Curr. Contents Life Sci.; Dairy Sci. Abstr.; EMBASE; Helminthol. Abstr. (19??-19??); Hortic. Abstr.; Immunol. Abstr.; Index Med.; Index Vet.; Microbiol. Abstr. Sect. B; Microbiol. Abstr. Sect. A; Microbiol. Abstr. Sect. C; Nutr. Abstr. Rev., Ser. B, Live Feeds and Feed.; Nutr. Abstr. Rev., Ser. A, Hum. Exp.; PESTDOC; Poult. Abstr.; Protozoolog. Abstr.; Psychol. Abstr. (1983-); PsycINFO (1990-); PsycLit; Ref. Upd. Deluxe Ed.; Rev. Agric. Entomol.; Rev. Med. Vet. Entomol.; Rev. Med. Vet. Mycology; Sci. Cit. Index; Small Anim. Abstr. Bibliogr.; Soc. Sci. Cit. Index [Select. Cov.]; Vet. Bull.; Virol. AIDS Abstr.; Weed Abstr.

US/0199-4905
**MEDICAL SCIENCES BULLETIN.** See Pharmacy and Pharmacology.

US/0073-7518
**MEDICAL SERIES, BULLETIN.** **Main/Corp** Industrial Hygiene Foundation of America. Began publication on Apr. 15, 1937. Bulletin. English. ir. Industrial Health Foundation, 34 Penn Circle West, Pittsburgh PA 15206. **Tel** (412)363-6600, FAX (412)363-6605. **LC** HD7260; .I374. **Circ:** 2,000 (ctrl).

●US/1059-907X
**MEDICAL SOFTWARE REVIEWS.** [Med. softw. rev.]. Vol. 1, No. 1 (Jan. 1992)-. Periodical. English. Twelve times a year. $75.00 (individuals); $90.00 (institutions) North America; $94.00 (individuals), $109.00 (institutions) others. Healthcare Computing Publications, Inc., 462-2nd Street, Brooklyn NY 11215-2503. **Tel** (718)499-5910. **DD** 610. **NLM** W1; ME4972.
**Desc:** Devoted to helping physicians with independent and objective reviews of medical software.

US/1041-6501
**MEDICAL STAFF LEADER.** [Med. staff lead.]. **Added/Corp** American Hospital Association. Vol. 18, No. 1 (Jan. 1989)-. Periodical. English. mo. $22.00 US; $35.00 other. American Hospital Publishing Inc., (A Subsidiary of the American Hospital Association), PO Box 92683, Chicago IL 60675. **Tel** (312)440-6836, (800)621-6902, FAX (312)951-8491. **DD** 658. **NLM** W1; ME498KL. available on microfilm and microfiche from University Microfilms International (UMI). ***Continues** Medical Staff News, 8756-680X.*

US/0360-7623
**MEDICAL STUDENT (DARIEN).** (MEDICAL STUDENT.). **Added/Corp** Pfizer Pharmaceuticals. Roerig Division. Pfizer Inc. Pfizer Laboratories Division. Vol. 1, (1974)-. Periodical. English. Four times a year. Free. Mark Powley Associates Inc, 88 Main Street, New Canaan CT 06840. **Tel** (203)972-1902. **NLM** W1 ME4985D.

US/0147-5711
**MEDICAL SUBJECT HEADINGS. ANNOTATED ALPHABETIC LIST.** See Library and Information Sciences.

US/0891-3994
**MEDICAL SUBJECT HEADINGS. SUPPLEMENTARY CHEMICAL RECORDS.** See Library and Information Sciences.

US/0161-3278
**MEDICAL SUBJECT HEADINGS. TREE ANNOTATIONS.** Began with 1977. English. an. $18.00. National Technical Information Service - NTIS, Room 2027S, 5285 Port Royal Road, Springfield VA 22161. **Tel** (703)487-4630, (703)487-4660, (703)487-4650, FAX (703)321-8547, telex 89-9405. **NLM** Z 695.9 M489. available on microfiche (Vols. for (1983-1984) distributed to depository libraries).

US/0147-099X
**MEDICAL SUBJECT HEADINGS. TREE STRUCTURES.** See Library and Information Sciences.

●US
**MEDICAL SUPPLY CATALOG / U.S. PUBLIC HEALTH SERVICE.** **Main/Corp** PHS Supply Service Center (U.S.). **VFOAT** PHS Medical Supply Catalog. (1992)-. Catalog. English. PHS Supply Service Center, Director, Perry Point MD 21902. ***Continues** Health Resources and Services Administration Medical Supply Catalog.*

UK/0142-159X
**MEDICAL TEACHER.** [Med. teach.]. Vol. 1 (Jan./Feb. 1979)-. Academic Scholarly Publication. English. qt (Mar., June, Sept., Dec.). £154.00. Carfax Publishing Company, PO Box 25 Abingdon, Oxfordshire OX14 3UE England. **Tel** 011 44 235 555335, FAX (0279)31067, telex 817484. **(Subscription address:** US and Canada/ PO Box 2025, Dunnellon, FL 34430-2025; telephone:(904)489-6996) **ED** R. M. Harden. **NLM** W1 ME517M. **[CCC]. Bk Rev. Ad Acc. Pr Rev.** available on microfiche. Documents available from The Genuine Article.
**Desc:** Addresses the needs of teachers and

administrators for the practical training of students for the health care professions.
**Ind/Abst** Cumul. Index Nurs. Allied Health Lit.; Curr. Contents Clin. Med.; Curr. Index J. Educ.; Educ. Technol. Abstr.; EMBASE; Index Med. (Vol. 7, No. 1, 1983-); Int. Nurs. Index; Res. Alert [Select. Cov.]; Res. High. Educ. Abstr.; SCISEARCH; Soc. Sci. Cit. Index [Select. Cov.]; Tech. Educ. Train. Abstr.

UK/0309-2666
**MEDICAL TECHNOLOGIST AND SCIENTIST, THE.** ***Ceased.*** Vol. 5, No. 11 (Nov. 1975)-(19??). Periodical. English. mo. A E Morgan Publications Ltd, Stanley House, 9 West Street, Epsom Surrey KT18 7RL England. **Tel** 011 44 3727 41411, FAX 0372 744493, telex 291561 VIA SOS G. **ED** Karen Broadribb. **NLM** W1 ME518T. **Bk Rev. Ad Acc. Circ:** 8,000 (ctrl). available on microfilm and microfiche from University Microfilms International (UMI). ***Continues*** *Medical Technologist, 0300-5879.*
**Desc:** Laboratory instrumentation, (medical) analytical and diagnostic equipment and processes.
**Ind/Abst** Abstr. BioCommer.

US/0899-3092
**MEDICAL TECHNOLOGY.** [Asp. med. technol.]. 1989-. Monographic series. English. Price varies per volume. Gordon & Breach Science Publishers, Inc., PO Box 786, Cooper Station, New York NY 10276. **Tel** (212)206-8900, FAX (212)645-2459. **(Subscription address:** International Publishers Distributor at one of the following addresses: 820 Town Center Drive, Langhorne, PA 19047; or PO Box 90, Reading Berkshire RG1 8JL UK; or Kent Ridge PO Box 1180, Singapore 9111, Republic of Singapore**)** **DD** 616.

SA
**MEDICAL TECHNOLOGY SA. Added/Corp** Society of Medical Laboratory Technologists of South Africa. **VFOAT** Geneeskundige Tegnologie SA. Vol. 1, No. 1 (Mar. 1987)-. Periodical. English (Afrikaans). Six times a year (Feb., Apr., June, Aug., Oct., Dec.). R50.00 South Africa; R80.00 others. Medical Technology News Investments, PO Box 843, 7655 Wellington South Africa. **Tel** 011 27 2211 25247, FAX 011 27 2211 25229. **ED** Mr. C Blow. **NLM** W1; ME521G. **Ad Acc. Pr Rev. Circ:** 6,000 (ctrl). ***Continues*** *South African Journal of Medical Laboratory Technology.*
**Desc:** Information and news with the medical technology in South Africa.

JA/0389-1887
**MEDICAL TECHNOLOGY (TOKYO. 1973).** (RINSHO KENSAGAKU ZASSHI.). [Med. technol.]. **VFOAT** Medical Technology. (1973)-. Periodical. Japanese. mo. Ishiyaku Shuppan K.K., (Ishiyaku Publishers, Inc.), 7-10, Honkomagome 1 Chome, Bunkyoku Tokyoto 113 Japan. **NLM** W1 RI2165H. **CODEN** METCDS. Documents available from CASDDS.
**Ind/Abst** Chem. Abstr.

NE/0266-2078
**MEDICAL TEXTILES.** [Med. text.]. **Added/Corp** Shirley Institute. Vol. 1, No. 1 (May 1984)-. Periodical. English. Twelve times a year. $404.00 The Americas; £271.00 other. Elsevier Advanced Technology, An Imprint of Elsevier Science Ltd., The Boulevard, Langford Lane, Kidlington, Oxford OX5 1GB United Kingdom. **Tel** 011 44 865 843000, 011 44 865 843699, FAX 011 44 865 843010. **(Subscription address:** Elsevier Science Ltd. Oxford Fulfillment Centre, PO Box 800, Kidlington, Oxford OX5 1DX United Kingdom.**)** **ED** Edward Love and Peter Lennox-Kerr. **NLM** W1; ME521T. **[CCC].** available on microfilm from University Microfilms International (UMI); available on an online database (file 636/Full-Text) from DIALOG.
**Desc:** Covers all major aspects and applications of medical textile technology.
**Ind/Abst** Nonwovens Abstr.; PTS Newsl. Database [Full Txt.]; Text. Technol. Dig.

US/0279-9340
**MEDICAL TRIBUNE (1980).** ***Title Change.*** (MEDICAL TRIBUNE.). [Med. trib.]. Vol. 21, No. 17 (May 7, 1980)-(19??). Periodical. English. Twenty-six times a year. Medical Tribune Inc, 257 Park Avenue South, New York NY 10010. **Tel** (212)674-8500, FAX (212)529-8490, telex 14-7103. **ED** William Ingram. **LC** R5; .M4. **DD** 610/.5. **NLM** W1 ME5268. **[CCC]. Bk Rev. Ad Acc. Circ:** 150,000 (ctrl). available on microfilm and microfiche from University Microfilms International (UMI). ***Continues*** *Medical Tribune and Medical News, 0098-6240;* ***Absorbed*** *Therapaeia, 0888-2592; Sexual Medicine Today, 0149-2926; Hospital Tribune, 0018-5876; Medical News & International Report.* ***Split into*** *Medical Tribune for the Family Physician* ***and*** *Medical Tribune for the Internist & Cardiologist.*
**Desc:** Written by professionals for professionals. 25 years serving the medical community. Coverage on medical news, medicolegal drug hearings, meetings, infection control, and more.

●US
**MEDICAL TRIBUNE FOR THE FAMILY PHYSICIAN.** **VFOAT** Medical Tribune. Vol. 34, No. 17 (Thursday, Sept. 9, 1993)-. Periodical. English. Twenty-four times a year. $75.00. Medical Tribune Inc, 257 Park Avenue South, New York NY 10010. **Tel** (212)674-8500, FAX (212)529-8490, telex 14-7103. **NLM** W1; ME5295. ***Continues in part*** *Medical Tribune (New York, N.Y. : 1980), 0279-9340.*

US/0279-9340
**MEDICAL TRIBUNE FOR THE INTERNIST & CARDIOLOGIST.** (19??)-. English. Twenty-four times a year. $75.00. Medical Tribune Inc, 257 Park Avenue South, New York NY 10010. **Tel** (212)674-8500, FAX (212)529-8490, telex 14-7103. **[CCC].** ***Continues in part*** *Medical Tribune New York.*

GW
**MEDICAL TRIBUNE. GERMAN EDITION.** (19??)-. German. wk. DM111.00 Germany; DM179.00. Medical Tribune Verlagsges GmbH, Rheinstrasse 19, D 65185 Wiesbaden Germany. **Tel** 011 49 611 17050.

US/0279-9340
**MEDICAL TRIBUNE. MICROFORM.** (1980)-. English. Medical Tribune, Rheinstrasse 19, W-62 Wiesbaden 1 Germany. **LC** Microfilm (o) 84/2020. **[CCC].** ***Continues*** *Medical Tribune and Medical News.*

US
**MEDICAL UPDATE.** (1976)-. Periodical. English. mo. $12.00. Benjamin Franklin Literary and Medical Society, 1100 Waterway Boulevard, Indianapolis IN 46206. **Tel** (317)636-8881, FAX (317)637-0126. **ED** Cory Servaas.
**Desc:** For consumers interested in the latest in health care advise, preventive medicine, nutrition and better health habits.
**Ind/Abst** Consum. Health Nutr. Index; Health Index (1989-); Health Period. Database [Full Txt.]; Health Ref. Cent. (Jan. 1989-) [Full Txt.] [Full Cov.].

US/0732-0183
**MEDICAL UPDATE (CHICAGO, ILL.).** (MEDICAL UPDATE : THE WORLD BOOK FAMILY HEALTH ANNUAL.). [Med. update]. **Added/Corp** World Book, Inc. (1982)-. English. an. World Book - Childcraft International, 510 Merchandise Mart Plaza, Chicago IL 60654. **Tel** (800)621-8202. **LC** RC81.A1; M43. **DD** 610/.5.

US
**MEDICAL USES OF STATISTICS.** **See** Medical Science and Technology-Abstracting, Bibliographies and Statistics.

●US
**MEDICAL UTILIZATION MANAGEMENT.** **Added/Corp** Faulkner & Gray's Healthcare Information Center. Vol. 22, No. 2 (Jan. 20, 1994)-. Periodical. English. Twenty-four times a year. $395.00. Faulkner & Gray Inc., 11 Penn Plaza, 17th Floor, New York NY 10001. **Tel** (212)967-7000, (800)535-8403. **NLM** W1; ME53G. ***Continues*** *Medical Utilization Review.*

US/1050-9984
**MEDICAL UTILIZATION REVIEW DIRECTORY.** [Med. util. rev. dir.]. **VFOAT** Medical Utilization Review. (1991)-. Directory. English. an. $365.00. Faulkner & Gray Inc., 11 Penn Plaza, 17th Floor, New York NY 10001. **Tel** (212)967-7000, (800)535-8403. **LC** RA972; .M4. **DD** 362.1/068. **NLM** WX 22; AA1 M4.
**Desc:** Main listing describes free standing medical utilization review companies, insurance-based review programs, major users of utilization review and industry consultants.

●US/1072-6039
**MEDICAL WASTE ANALYST.** [Med. waste anal.]. Vol. 2, No. 2 (Nov. 1993)-. Periodical. English. mo. $245.00. Technomic Publishing Company, Inc., 851 New Holland Avenue, Box 3535, Lancaster PA 17604. **Tel** (717)291-5609, (800)233-9936, FAX (717)295-4538. **LC** WMLC 93/3495. **DD** 363. **NLM** W1; ME538BE. ***Continues*** *Regulatory Analyst. Medical Waste, 1065-1063.*

US/1058-2711
**MEDICAL WASTE MONITOR.** [Med. waste monit.]. Vol. 1, No. 1 (May 1991)-. Periodical. English. bm. Free on request. MedX, Inc., PO Box 025499, Miami FL 33102-5499. **Tel** (800)527-0666, (305)885-4004, FAX ((305)888-9637. **ED** Julie Gonzalez. **DD** 363. Index available. cum. index. **Circ:** 150,000 (ctrl). available on CD-ROM; available on microfilm.

US/1048-4493
**MEDICAL WASTE NEWS.** [Med. waste news]. **Added/Corp** Business Publishers. (1989)-. Periodical. English. bw (26 issues). $390.00. Business Publishers Inc., 951 Pershing Drive, Silver Spring MD 20910-4464. **Tel** (301)587-6300, (800)274-0122, FAX (301)585-9075. **DD** 363. **NLM** W1; ME538BL. **[CCC].** available on an online database (file 636/Full-Text) from DIALOG.
**Desc:** Covers the treatment, management, and disposal of medical and infectious waste.
**Ind/Abst** PTS Newsl. Database [Full Txt.].

UK
**MEDICAL WORLD AND NEWSLETTER.** (19??)-. English. ir. ASTMS / England, 79 Camden Road, London NW1 9ES England. **Tel** 011 44 71 2674422.

US
**MEDICAL WORLD ANNUAL.** Began in 1963. English. an. McGraw Hill Publishing Company, Inc., 1221 Avenue of the Americas, New York NY 10020. **Tel** (212)512-6410, (800)525-5003, FAX (212)512-6111. **LC** R101; .M438. **DD** 610/.5.

UK
**MEDICAL WORLD (LONDON, ENGLAND : 1969).** (MEDICAL WORLD.). Vol. 107, No. 1 (Jan. 1969)-. Periodical. English. mo. $4.82. ASTMS / England, 79 Camden Road, London NW1 9ES England. **Tel** 011 44 71 2674422. ***Continues*** *Medical World and Newsletter, 0260-3101.*

CN/0828-3575
**MEDICAL WORLD MAGAZINE.** [Med. world mag.]. **VFOAT** Medical World. 1st Issue (1985)-. Periodical. English. bm. Free, 15.00Can$ other. Medical World Magazine, 2 Bloor Street West/Suite 700, Toronto Ontario M4W 3R1 Canada. **DD** 610/.5.

US/0025-763X
**MEDICAL WORLD NEWS.** ***Suspended.*** [Med. world news]. (April 22, 1960)-Suspended (Feb. 1994). Periodical. English. Twelve times a year. $38.00 US; $52.75 Canada; $68.00 other. Miller Freeman Inc., 600 Harrison Street, San Francisco CA 94107. **Tel** (415)905-2337, FAX (415)905-2240, telex 278273. **ED** Annette Ostreicher. **LC** R11; .M864. **DD** 610/.5. **NLM** W1 ME5472. **CODEN** MDWNA. **[CCC]. Bk Rev. Ad Acc. Circ:** 125,000 (ctrl). available on microfilm and microfiche from University Microfilms International (UMI); available on an online database (file 149/Full-Text) from DIALOG. Documents available from UMI Article Clearinghouse.
**Desc:** Analysis of contemporary medical practice designed to help the physician keep up-to-date on legislative, clinical and socio-economic aspects of American medicine.
**Ind/Abst** ABI/INFORM Glob. Ed.; ABI Inform Ondisc (March 1974-March 1977); Acad. Ind. [Computer File] (1982-); Acad. Search (July 1993-); AGRICOLA; Biol. Dig.; Cumul. Index Nurs. Allied Health Lit.; Curr. Lit. Fam. Plan.; Expand. Acad. Index (1992-); F&S Index Plus Text, Int. [Select. Cov.]; Gen. Period. Index (1992-); Health Devices Alerts; Health Index (1989-); Health Period. Database [Full Txt.]; Health Ref. Cent. (Jan. 1989-) [Full Txt.] [Full Cov.]; Hospit. Health Admin. Index; Hospit. Manage. Rev.; INFO-SOUTH Abstr.; Int. Pharm. Abstr.; Mag. ASAP Plus [Full Txt.]; Mag. Index Plus (1992-); Mag. Search; Newsp. Period. Abstr. (1988-); PROMT; Trade Ind. ASAP [Full Txt.]; Women Stud. Abstr.

US/0094-5811
**MEDICAL WORLD NEWS REVIEW.** V. 1-May 1974-. Periodical. English. qt. $10.00. McGraw Hill Publishing Company, Inc., 1221 Avenue of the Americas, New York NY 10020. **Tel** (212)512-6410, (800)525-5003, FAX (212)512-6111. **LC** R11. **DD** 610/5. **NLM** W1 ME5473.

US/0025-7664
**MEDICAMUNDI.** ***Ceased.*** [Medicamundi]. Vol. 1 (1955)-(19??). Academic Scholarly Publication. English. bm. North America Phillips Company, Hearing Aid Division, 100 East 42nd Street, New York NY 10017. **NLM** W1 ME5505. **CODEN** MEMUAA. Documents available from Ask*IEEE.
**Ind/Abst** EMBASE; Energy Res. Abstr.; INSPEC (Vol. 14 No. 2-).

US
**MEDICARE REIBURSEMENT MANUAL FOR CLINICAL LABORATORIES.** English. an (published each spring). 225.00 subscribers of National Intelligence Report; $275.00 other. Washington G 2 Reports, 1111 14th Street NW, Suite 711, Washington DC 20005. **Tel** (202)789-1034, FAX (202)289-4062.

JA/0025-7699
**MEDICINA.** [Medicina]. (1964)-. Periodical. Japanese. mo. Igaku Shoin, (Igaku Shoin Ltd.), 24-3, Hongo 5 Chome, Bunkyoku, Tokyoto 113-9, Japan. **CODEN** MDCHBH. Documents available from CASDDS. ***Formed by the union of*** *Rinsho Naika Shonika* ***and*** *SogÂo Igaku.*
**Ind/Abst** Chem. Abstr.

SP/0300-8169
**MEDICINA & HISTORIA.** (19??)-. Periodical. Spanish. Five times a year. free. J Uriach y CIA SA, Decano Bahi 59-67, 08026 Barcelona Spain. **Tel** 34-3-347 1511, FAX 34-3-456 0639, telex 52963 URIAC.

**ED** J. Uriach and Dega Bahi. cum. index. **Bk Rev. Circ:** 70,000.
**Desc:** Publication on the history of medicine.

AG/0025-7680
**MEDICINA (BUENOS AIRES).** (MEDICINA : ORGANO DE LA SOCIEDAD ARGENTINA DE INVESTIGACION CLINICA.). [Medicina, B. Aires]. **Added/Corp** Sociedad Argentina de Investigacion Clinica. (1940)-. Academic Scholarly Publication. Spanish (summaries and/or abstracts in English, French and German). Six times a year. $70.00 Latin America; $90.00 other. Instituto de Investigaciones Medicas, Donato Alvarez 3150, 1427 Buenos Aires Argentina. **Tel** 11 54 522 0061, 522064, FAX 11 54 5732619. **ED** Amaedo P Barousse, Aquiles J Roncoroni, Christiane D Pasqualini, Juan Antonio Barcat, Jorge Firmat, Samuel Finkielnan. **LC** R21; .M37. **NLM** W1 ME551K. **CODEN** MEDCAD. Index available. cum. index. **Bk Rev**, (Qty: 26). **Ad Acc, Adv Mgr:** Delisio Horacio J. **Pr Rev. Circ:** 4,500 (ctrl). available on microfilm from University Microfilms International (UMI). Documents available from The Genuine Article, BIOSIS Document Express, CASDDS.
**Desc:** Contains articles on clinical and experimental medicine, reviews, case reports, clinical-pathological conferences, editorials and book reviews.
**Ind/Abst** Biol. Abstr.; Chem. Abstr.; CSA Neuro. Abstr. (?-?); EMBASE [Select. Cov.]; Index Med.; Microbiol. Abstr. Sect. C; Nutr. Abstr. Rev., Ser. A, Hum. Exp.; Life Sci. Collect.; Protozoolog. Abstr.; Res. Alert [Full Cov.]; Sci. Cit. Index; SCISEARCH; Soc. Sci. Cit. Index [Select. Cov.]; SportSearch; Trop. Dis. Bull.

SP/0025-7753
**MEDICINA CLINICA.** [Med. clin.]. (1943)-. Academic Scholarly Publication. Spanish. wk. $99.00. Ediciones Doyma SA, Travesera de Gracia 17 21, 08021 Barcelona Spain. **Tel** 011 34 3 2000711, 011 34 3 4145706, FAX 011 34 3 2091136, telex 51964 INK E. **ED** D Ciril Rozman. **NLM** W1 ME569. **CODEN** MCLBA2. **[CCC].** Index available. cum. index. **Bk Rev. Ad Acc. Pr Rev. Circ:** 12,000 (ctrl). Documents available from The Genuine Article, BIOSIS Document Express, CASDDS.
**Desc:** Contents include clinical research studies selected on their medical interest, scientific quality and practical value. Publishes studies oriented to continuation of the medical formation.
**Ind/Abst** Biol. Abstr.; Chem. Abstr.; Curr. Contents Clin. Med.; EMBASE [Select. Cov.]; Helminthol. Abstr. (19??-19??); Index Med.; Indice Med. Esp.; Microbiol. Abstr. Sect. B; Microbiol. Abstr. Sect. C; Nutr. Abstr. Rev., Ser. A, Hum. Exp.; Life Sci. Collect.; Protozoolog. Abstr.; Res. Alert [Full Cov.]; Rev. Med. Vet. Entomol.; Rev. Med. Vet. Mycology; Sci. Cit. Index; SCISEARCH; Soc. Sci. Cit. Index [Select. Cov.]; Virol. AIDS Abstr.

SP
**MEDICINA DE EMPRESA.** Spanish. Sociedad Catalana de Seguridad y Medicina del Trabajo, Tapineria 10/2, 08002 Barcelona Spain.

MX/0300-3833
**MEDICINA DE POSTGRADO.** ***Ceased.*** Periodical. Spanish. mo. Novaro Internacionale sa Calle 5 No 12, Naucalpan Mexico.

IT/0025-7818
**MEDICINA DEL LAVORO.** (LA MEDICINA DEL LAVORO.). [Med. lav.]. Vol. 16 (1925)-. Academic Scholarly Publication. Italian (English, French and German; summaries and/or abstracts in English and German). bm. L90000 (Italy); L125000 (Europe); L135000 (other). Casa Editrice Mattioli, Via Codura 1B, 43036 Fidenza PR Italy. **Tel** 39 524 84547. **LC** RC963; .A437. **NLM** W1 ME578T. **CODEN** MELAAD. Index available (bound in Jan. issue). **Ad Acc. Circ:** 2,000. Documents available from BIOSIS Document Express, CASDDS. ***Continues*** *Lavoro (Clinica delle Malattie Professionali di Milano).*
**Ind/Abst** Anal. Abstr.; Biol. Abstr.; Chem. Abstr.; Chem. Hazards Ind.; EMBASE; Ergon. Abstr.; Index Med.; Ind. Hyg. Dig.; Lab. Hazards Bull.; Saf. Health Work; Trop. Dis. Bull.

IT
**MEDICINA DEMOCRATICA.** Medicina Democratica, Via Carracci 2, 20149 Milan Italy.

IT
**MEDICINA DI LABORATORIO, LA.** (19??)-. Italian. Four times a year. $180.00. Piccin Editore, Via Altinate 107, 35121 Padua Italy. **Tel** 011 39 49 655566, FAX 011 39 49 8750693.

IT/1120-3773
**MEDICINA E INFORMATICA.** [Med. inform.]. (1984)-. Periodical. Multiple languages (English). Four times a year. L80000 (individuals), L135000 (institutions). Il Pensiero Scientifico Editore s.r.l., Via Bradano 3C, 00199 Rome Italy. **Tel** 011 39 6 86207158, 86207159, 86207168, 86207169, FAX 011 39 6 86207160. **ED** Sergio L. Magalini, Fabrizio Ricci and Riccardo Maceratini. **UDC** 610. **Bk Rev. Ad Acc, Adv Mgr:** Dott Dalla, **Tel** 06-86207165. Full Page (B&W) L1.650.000. **Circ:** 1,050.

IT/0025-7834
**MEDICINA E MORALE.** [Med. morale]. **Added/Corp** Universita Cattolica del Sacro Cuore. Facolta di Medicina e Chirurgia. (1939)-. Periodical. Italian (French and Spanish; summaries and/or abstracts in French, Spanish and English). Six times a year. L50000 (Italy); L80000 (other). Medicina Morale Universita Cattolica, Sacro Cuore L Go F Vito 1, 00168 Rome Italy. **Tel** 11 39 6 30154842.

SP
**MEDICINA INTEGRAL.** Spanish. IDEPSA International Ediciones Publs SA, Principe de Vergara 112 1F, 28002 Madrid Spain. **Tel** 011 34 1 5637306.
**Ind/Abst** Indice Med. Esp.

SP/0210-5691
**MEDICINA INTENSIVA / SOCIEDAD ESPANOLA DE MEDICINA INTENSIVA Y UNIDADES CORONARIAS. Added/Corp** Sociedad Espanola de Medicina Intensiva y Unidades Coronarias. (197?)-. Periodical. Spanish (summaries and/or abstracts in English; table of contents in English). Nine times a year. $75.00. IDEPSA International Ediciones Publs SA, Principe de Vergara 112 1F, 28002 Madrid Spain. **Tel** 011 34 1 5637306. **NLM** W1; ME597M.
**Ind/Abst** EMBASE; Indice Med. Esp.

SP
**MEDICINA MILITAR.** Spanish. Puntex SA, Via Laietana 30 4 F, 08003 Barcelona Spain. **Tel** 011 34 3 2680444.
**Ind/Abst** Indice Med. Esp.

IT
**MEDICINA MODERNA.** Italian. mo. L10000. Tecniche Nuove SPA, Via Ciro Menotti 14, 20129 Milan Italy. **Tel** 011 39 2 75701, FAX 011 39 2 7610351, telex 334647 TECHS I.

IT/0392-4548
**MEDICINA OGGI.** [Med. oggi]. (1981)-. Periodical. Italian (summaries and/or abstracts in English). qt. $95.00. Casa Editrice Libraria Idelson Gnocchi, via Alcide De Gasperi 55, 80133 Naples Italy. **Tel** 011 39 81 5524733. **UDC** 61.
**Ind/Abst** EMBASE [Select. Cov.].

IT/0391-7231
**MEDICINA OSPEDALIERA ROMANA.** (MEDICINA OSPEDALIERA ROMANA : ORGANO UFFICIALE DELLA SOCIETA DI MEDICINA OSPEDALIERA.). [Med. osp. rom.]. Vol. 1, N. 1 (Mar. 1980)-. Periodical. English (Italian). qt. **NLM** W1 ME5926F.

IT/0025-7893
**MEDICINA PSICOSOMATICA.** [Med. psicosom.]. **Added/Corp** Societa Italiana di Medicina Psicosomatica. (1956)-. Periodical. Italian. qt. L60000 Italy; L120000 other. Societa Editrice Universo, Via GB Morgagni 1, 00161 Rome Italy. **Tel** 011 39 6 44231171. **NLM** W1 ME614. **CODEN** MDPSAC. Documents available from BIOSIS Document Express.
**Ind/Abst** Biol. Abstr.; EMBASE; Psychol. Abstr. (1972-); PsycINFO; PsycLit.

BL/0076-6046
**MEDICINA RIBEIRAO PRETO.** (MEDICINA.). [Medicina Ribeirao Preto]. (1961)-. Periodical. Portuguese. qt. Biblioteca Central do Campus de Ribeirao Preto, Campus Universidade - USP, CEP 14049, Ribeirao Preto, Sao Paulo, Brazil. **UDC** 61.
**Ind/Abst** EMBASE [Select. Cov.].

IT/0025-7915
**MEDICINA SOCIALE.** [Med. soc.]. (1950)-. Periodical. Italian. Six times a year. L40000.00 Italy; L80000.00 other. Casa Editrice Maccari, Via Trento 53, 43100 Parma Italy. **Tel** 011 39 521 771268, FAX 011 39 521 771268. **UDC** 61. **CODEN** MESOA.

IT/0580-9320
**MEDICINA TERMALE E CLIMATOLOGIA.** ***Ceased.*** [Med. term. climatol.]. (1969)-(19??). Periodical. English (Italian and German). qt. Libreria Dello Studente, Viale Romagna 37, 20133 Milan Italy. **NLM** W1 ME629E. **CODEN** MTCLD7. Documents available from CASDDS.
**Ind/Abst** Chem. Abstr. (1969-1982).

UK
**MEDICINE AND GLOBAL SOCIETY.** (199?)-. English. qt. £80.00. BMJ / British Medical Journal Publishing Group, British Medical Association House, Tavistock Square, London WC1H 9JR England. **Tel** 011 44 71 3874499, FAX 011 44 71 383 6402, telex 290034 HBJ MN. ***Continues*** *PSR Quarterly : A Journal of Medicine and Global Survival., 1051-2438.*

UK
**MEDICINE AND GLOBAL SURVIVAL. See** Public Health and Safety.

UK/0748-8009
**MEDICINE AND WAR.** [Med. war]. **Added/Corp** Medical Association for the Prevention of War. Medical Association for Prevention of War (Australia). Vol. 1, No. 1 (Jan./April 1985)-. Periodical. English. qt. $110.00. Frank Cass & Company Ltd, Newbury House, 890-900 Eastern Avenue, Newbury Park, Ilford, Essex IG2 7HH United Kingdom. **Tel** 011 44 81 599 8866, FAX 011 44 81 599 0984, telex 897719. **ED** Douglas Holdstock, FRCP, UK. **LC** RC970; .M43. **DD** 327.1/7. **NLM** W1; ME649W. **CODEN** MEWAE4. **[CCC]. Ad Acc, Adv Mgr:** Anne Kidson. available on microfilm and microfiche from University Microfilms International (UMI). ***Continues*** *Journal of the Medical Association for Prevention of War.*
**Desc:** A journal of international medical concern on the biosocial, psychological and medical aspects of war and other social violence.
**Ind/Abst** Curr. Mil. Pol. Lit.; Index Med. (Vol. 1, No. 1, 1985-); PAIS Int. Print (1991-); Peace Res. Abstr. J. (1985-).

US/0025-7974
**MEDICINE (BALTIMORE).** (MEDICINE.). [Medicine]. Vol. 1 (May 1922)-. Academic Scholarly Publication. English. bm. $75.00 (individual), $140.00 (institution) US; $102.00 (individual), $167.00 (institution). Williams & Wilkins Company, 428 East Preston Street, Baltimore MD 21202-3993. **Tel** (410)528-4000, (800)638-6423, FAX (410)528-8596, telex 87669. **(Subscription address:** Williams & Wilkins, PO Box 64380, Baltimore MD 21264.**) ED** J. H. Talbott. **LC** R11; .M87. **DD** 610.5. **NLM** W1 ME648. **CODEN** MEDIAV. **[CCC].** cum. index. **Ad Acc. Pr Rev. Circ:** 7,900. available on microfilm. Documents available from , The Genuine Article, BIOSIS Document Express, CASDDS, Documents on Demand, Quick Copies.
**Desc:** General medicine review journal to cover areas of interest to the internists, including literature review and follow-up studies.
**Ind/Abst** Abr. Index Med.; Biol. Abstr.; Chem. Abstr.; Curr. Aware. Biol. Sci., CABS; EMBASE; Energy Inf. Abstr.; Energy Res. Abstr.; Environ. Abstr.; Health Period. Database [Full Txt.]; Index Med.; Iowa Drug Inf. Serv. (1971-); Nucl. Sci. Abstr.; Nutr. Abstr. Rev., Ser. A, Hum. Exp.; Nutr. Res. Newsl.; Life Sci. Collect.; Physic. Medline Plus; Protozoolog. Abstr.; Ref. Upd. Basic Ed.; Ref. Upd. Deluxe Ed.; Res. Alert [Full Cov.]; Rev. Med. Vet. Mycology; Sci. Cit. Index; SCISEARCH.

BE
**MEDICINE BIOLOGIE ENVIRONMENT.** 1000.00F. Inst Natl Ecology Cancerology, Rue des Frifiers 24 Bis, 1000 Brussels Belgium. **Tel** 011 32 2 2190830.

FR
**MEDICINE D'AFRIQUE NOIRE.** Yearly V. 1- March 11, 1954-. Periodical. French. ir. $26.61. Medecine d'Afrique Noire, 9, rue Truguet, 83000 TOULON France. **Tel** 011 33 94 62 7575, FAX 011 33 94 93 5169, telex 400 287 FC 300.
**Ind/Abst** Helminthol. Abstr. (19??-19??); Rev. Med. Vet. Entomol.

UK
**MEDICINE DIGEST.** Vol. 1 (1974)-. Periodical. English. Twelve times a year. $78.00. Medicine Digest, 15 McCallum Street, 04 01 Natwest, Singapore 0106 Singapore. **Tel** 011 65 2238788. **ED** H. de Glanville. **Bk Rev. Ad Acc. Circ:** 23,000 (ctrl).
**Desc:** General medicine information for the tropical countries.
**Ind/Abst** Trop. Dis. Bull.

HK
**MEDICINE DIGEST. ASIA.** (1983)-. English (Multiple languages). Twelve times a year. $64.00 (one year). Medicine Digest Asia, 200 Lockhart Road, Room 1501, Wanchai Hong Kong Hong Kong. **Tel** 011 852 5 5199303, FAX 011 852 5 5073817. **ED** Dr. Hugh de Glanville (editor's address: 45 Woodland Grove, Weybridge, Surrey KT13 9EQ, U.K. phone: 932-858035). **Ad Acc, Adv Mgr:** Mary, **Tel** 519 9303. **Circ:** 29,600 (SE Asia), 8,200 (Pakistan), 10,000 (China) (ctrl).

●US/1057-9354
**MEDICINE, EXERCISE, NUTRITION, AND HEALTH.** [Med. exerc. nutr. health]. Vol. 1, No. 1 (Jan./Feb. 1992)-. Academic Scholarly Publication. English. bm. $130.00 (institution), $70.00 (individual) US; $160.00 (institution), $100.00 (individual) other. Blackwell Scientific Publishers, 238 Main Street, Cambridge MA 02142. **Tel** (617)547-7110, (800)835-6770, FAX (617)547-0789. **DD** 613. **NLM** W1; ME651G. **[CCC].**

UK/0144-0403
**MEDICINE INTERNATIONAL. THE MONTHLY ADD-ON JOURNAL. UK EDITION.** (MEDICINE INTERNATIONAL.). [Med. int. Mon. add-on j. UK ed.]. Vol. 1, No. 1 (Jan. 1981)-. Periodical. English. Twelve times a year. £68.40 UK; £72.00 other. Medicine Group (Journals) Ltd., Publishing House / United Kingdom, 62 Stert Street, Abingdon Oxon OX14 3UQ England. **Tel** 011 44 235 555770, FAX 011 44 235 554691, telex 85183147. **NLM** W1 ME6533K. Index available. cum. index. **Bk Rev. Ad Acc.** ctrl circ. ***Continues*** *Medicine.*
**Ind/Abst** Energy Res. Abstr. (Jan. 1982-); Protozoolog. Abstr.; Trop. Dis. Bull.

UK/0144-0411
**MEDICINE INTERNATIONAL. THE QUARTERLY ADD-ON JOURNAL.** [Med. int. Q. add-on j.]. (1981)-. Periodical. English. Four times a year (Mar., June, Sept., Dec.). £72.00. Medicine Group

# Medical Science and Technology

(Journals) Ltd., Publishing House / United Kingdom, 62 Stert Street, Abingdon Oxon OX14 3UQ England. **Tel** 011 44 235 555770, FAX 011 44 235 554691, telex 85183147. **Continues** Medicine. The Quarterly Add-on Journal, 0142-1182.

●US/1066-4149
**MEDICINE (NEW YORK, N.Y. 1993).** (MEDICINE : THE YEAR IN REVIEW / MEDICAL TRIBUNE.). (1993)-. English. $49.95. Medical Tribune Inc, 257 Park Avenue South, New York NY 10010. **Tel** (212)674-8500, FAX (212)529-8490, telex 14-7103.

CN/0225-3895
**MEDICINE NORTH AMERICA.** No. 1 (March 1980)-. Periodical. English. mo (10 issues). $70.00 US; 65.00Can$ Canada; $98.00 other. C M E Publishing, 400 McGill 3rd Floor, Montreal Quebec H2Y 2G1, Canada. **Tel** (514)397-9393, FAX (514)397-0228. **ED** Ian R. Hart (editor's address: Division of Endocrinology, A6, Ottawa Civic Hospital, 1053 Carling Avenue, Ottawa, Ontario Canada K1Y 4E9). **DD** 610/.5. **NLM** W1 ME6533T. Index available. cum. index. **Ad Acc**, **Adv Mgr:** C.Bourke. **Circ:** 30,000 (ctrl).
**Desc:** Textbook of general medicine in journal format published a chapter at a time over a 3 year publishing cycle.
**Ind/Abst** Cumul. Index Nurs. Allied Health Lit.

SP
**MEDICINE (SPANISH EDITION).** (MEDICINE.). (19??)-. Spanish. ir (25 issues). $85.00. IDEPSA International Ediciones Publs SA, Principe de Vergara 112 1F, 28002 Madrid Spain. **Tel** 011 34 1 5637306.

SW/0346-542X
**MEDICINSK TEKNIK.** (1973)-. Periodical. Swedish. bm. Kr209.00 Scandinavia; Kr275.00 other. Medicinsk Teknik, Jovisgatan 4, S-151 64 Sodertalj Sweden. **Tel** 011 46 755 60554. **UDC** 615.4.

YU/0301-083X
**MEDICINSKA ISTRAZIVANJA. SUPPLEMENTUM.** VFOAT Medical Investigations. Vol. 1 (1971)-. Serbo-Croatian (Roman) (table of contents in English). **NLM** W1 ME739B.

RU/0025-8075
**MEDICINSKAJA TEHNIKA.** (MEDITSINSKAIA TEKHNIKA.). [Med. teh.]. **Added/Corp** Soviet Union. Ministerstvo Zdravookhraneniia. Vol. 1 (Jan./Feb. 1967)-. Academic Scholarly Publication. Russian (summaries and/or abstracts in English; table of contents in English). Six times a year. $89.95. **(Subscription address:** East View Publications Inc., 3020 Harbor Lane North, Suite 110, Minneapolis MN 55447.**) NLM** W1 ME804. **CODEN** MEDTBV. Documents available from Article Express International, Ask*IEEE, CASDDS.
**Ind/Abst** Chem. Abstr.; Ei Page One; Eng. Index Annu.; Index Med.; INSPEC (Jan./Feb. 1972-); Int. Aerosp. Abstr.

CI/0352-602X
**MEDICINSKI ANALI.** (MEDICINSKI ANALI / OPCA BOLNICA SPLIT, JEDINICA ZA ZNANSTVENI RAD.). [Med. an.]. **Added/Corp** Opca Bolnica Split. Jedinica za Znanstveni Rad. (1985)-. Periodical. Serbo-Croatian (Roman). sa. **CODEN** MEDAEB. Documents available from CASDDS. **Continues** Anali Opce Bolnice Split, 0350-1132.
**Ind/Abst** Chem. Abstr.

YU/0350-1221
**MEDICINSKI CASOPIS.** VFOAT Medical Journal; Revue Medicale. (1961)-. Periodical. Serbo-Croatian (Roman) (summaries and/or abstracts in English, French, German and Russian). Srpsko Lekarsko Drustvo, Stomatoloski Glasnik, Rankeova 4, Stomatoloski Glasnik, Narodnog Fronta 1/II, 11000 Belgrad Yugoslavia. **Tel** 11/686864. **NLM** W1 ME745N.

YU/0025-8105
**MEDICINSKI PREGLED.** [Med. pregl.]. (1948)-. Academic Scholarly Publication. Serbo-Croatian (Cyrillic). bm (6 issues). $60.00. Serbian Medical Society, Dzordza Vasingtona 19, 11000 Belgrade Yugoslavia. **Tel** 011 346 090. **ED** Vojislav Nikolic. **NLM** W1 ME74655. **CODEN** MEPEAB. cum. index. **Bk Rev**. **Ad Acc**. **Circ:** 1,300 (ctrl). Documents available from BIOSIS Document Express, CASDDS.
**Desc:** Original articles and case reports from all medical fields; reviews of interesting articles published in other journals.
**Ind/Abst** Biol. Abstr.; Chem. Abstr.; Index Med.

XV/0025-8121
**MEDICINSKI RAZGLEDI.** [Med. razgledi]. (1961)-. Academic Scholarly Publication. Slovenian (summaries and/or abstracts in English; table of contents in English). qt. 50.000 Din Yugoslavia; $24.00 US. Medicinski Razgledi, Korytkova 2, 61105 Ljubljana Slovenia. **Tel** (061)442-356. **ED** Zlatko Fras. **NLM** W1 ME7466J. **CODEN** MRAZAM. Index available. cum. index. **Bk Rev** **Ad Acc**. **Circ:** 3,200 (ctrl). Documents available from BIOSIS Document Express, CASDDS.
**Desc:** Medical practice, research and review articles.
**Ind/Abst** Biol. Abstr.; Chem. Abstr.

IT
**MEDICO D'ITALIA.** Free. Fed Nazionale Ordini Medici, Cola di Rienzo 80/A, 00192 Rome Italy.

IT/0390-0347
**MEDICO E PAZIENTE.** [Med. paziente]. (1975)-. Periodical. Italian. Eighteen times a year. L52000.00 Italy. Edifarm, Viale Sabotino 19 2, 20135 Milan Italy. **Tel** 011 39 2 58318401. **UDC** 61.

US/0278-9779
**MEDICO INTERAMERICANO.** [Med. interam.]. **Added/Corp** Interamerican College of Physicians & Surgeons. Vol. 1 No. 1, (January 1982)-. Periodical. Spanish. Twelve times a year. $45.00. Medico Interamericano, 299 Madison Avenue, New York NY 10017. **Tel** (212)697-3175. **NLM** W1; ME7678.

SP/0214-6363
**MEDICO MADRID, EL.** (MEDICO; PROFESION Y HUMANIDADES.). [Medico Madr.]. (1980)-. Periodical. Spanish. wk. 5500.00ptas Spain; 6000.00ptas other. SANED SA, Paseo de la Habana 202 Bis, 28036 Madrid Spain. **Tel** 011 34 1 5553508. **UDC** 61.

NR/0253-0961
**MEDICOM.** [Medicom]. Vol. 1, No. 1 (July-Sept. 1979)-. Periodical. English. an. N15.00 Nigeria; $5.00 US. Les Amis, Alexander Brown Hall, University College Hospital, Ibadan Nigeria. **NLM** W1 ME776. **Ad Acc**. **Circ:** 2,000.

IT
**MEDICUS.** Ceased. (19??)-(June 1993). Italian. Medicine Communication, Via E Ponti 49, 20143 Milan Italy. **Tel** 011 39 2 89125353.

IT/1121-2810
**MEDIFAX ROMA.** (MEDIFAX.). [Medifax Roma]. (1991)-. Periodical. Italian. Three times a year. Free on request. Il Pensiero Scientifico Editore s.r.l., Via Bradano 3C, 00199 Rome Italy. **Tel** 011 39 6 86207158, 86207159, 86207168, 86207169, FAX 011 39 6 86207160. **UDC** 61. **Ad Acc**. Full Page (B&W) L3.500.000. **Circ:** 27,500.

NE
**MEDIFO.** Ceased. (19??)-(Jan. 1992). English. Intermedia BV, Postbus 4, 2400 M Alphen Rijn Netherlands. **Tel** 011 31 1720 66855.

US/8750-9741
**MEDIGRAM (EAST LANSING, MICH. : 1985).** (MEDIGRAM.). [Medigram]. **Added/Corp** Michigan State Medical Society. Vol. 1, No. 1 (Jan. 1985)-. Periodical. English. Forty-six times a year (Weekly except July, Aug. and last week of Dec.). $50.00. Michigan State Medical Society, 120 West Saginaw Street, East Lansing MI 48823. **Tel** (517)337-1351, FAX (517)337-2490. **Separated from** Michigan Medicine, 0026-2293.

●US/1065-0725
**MEDIGUIDE TO DEPRESSION IN PRIMARY CARE.** (1992)-. Periodical. English. qt. Free. Dellacorte Publications, 919 3rd Avenue, New York NY 10022-3904. **Tel** (212)751-2806. **NLM** W1; CL84.

US/0738-2995
**MEDIGUIDE TO PAIN.** (MEDIGUIDE TO PAIN / PROVIDED AS A PROFESSIONAL SERVICE BY KNOLL PHARMACEUTICAL COMPANY.). [Mediguide pain]. **Added/Corp** Knoll Pharmaceutical Company. Endo Laboratories. Vol. 1, Issue 1 (1980)-. Periodical. English. qt. $24.00. Dellacorte Publications, 919 3rd Avenue, New York NY 10022-3904. **Tel** (212)751-2806. **NLM** W1 ME787GH.

IO/0126-0901
**MEDIKA.** See Pharmacy and Pharmacology.

BU/0204-6725
**MEDIKO-BIOLOGICESKAJA INFORMACIJA.** (MEDIKO-BIOLOGICHESKAIA INFORMATSIIA : MBI.). [Med.-biol. inf.]. VFOAT Mediko Biologicheskaia Informatsiia; MBI. (1967)-. Periodical. Bulgarian. bm. Pharmachim, 16 Iliensko Chaussee, 1220 Sofia Bulgaria. **CODEN** MBIID4. Documents available from CASDDS.
**Ind/Abst** Chem. Abstr.

BU/0323-9802
**MEDIKO-BIOLOGICNI PROBLEMI.** See Biology.

BE/0304-4823
**MEDIKON.** [Medikon]. VFOAT Medikon National; Medikon Nationaal. 1st- 1972-. Periodical. Multiple languages (Dutch, English and French; summaries and/or abstracts in Dutch, English and French). mo. Medikon Scientific Publishing, Citadellaan 36, B-9000 Ghent Belgium. **NLM** W1 ME7884M.
**Ind/Abst** Life Sci. Collect.

NR
**MEDILAG.** (1967)-. Periodical. English. sa. Students Union / University of Lagos, College of Medicine, PMB 12003, Lagos Nigeria.

US/0363-3926
**MEDIQUIZ ANNUAL.** (1975)-. English. an. $50.00. Romaine Pierson Publishing Inc., 80 Shore Road, Port Washington NY 11050. **Tel** (516)883-6350. **ED** C. A. Ragan Jr. and F. Coulston. **NLM** W1 ME7887.

NE
**MEDISCH CONTACT.** Dutch. wk. Fl144.50 Netherlands; Fl254.50 other. Uitgeverij Misset, Postbus 4, 7000 AH Doetinchem Netherlands. **Tel** 011 31 3465 58222. **ED** C Spreeuwenberg. Index available. cum. index. **Bk Rev** **Ad Acc**. **Pr Rev**. **Circ:** 28,000 (ctrl).
**Desc:** Journal for the members of the Dutch medical association.

NE/0167-6601
**MEDISCH JAAR, HET.** (1975)-. Dutch. an. F99.50. Libresso BV, Postbus 878, 7400 GA Deventer Netherlands. **Tel** 011 31 5700 47421. **ED** Bohn Schelrema and Molhena. **NLM** W1 ME7895. **Circ:** 3,000.
**Desc:** Medical news of the previous year.

NE/0924-2554
**MEDISCHE INSTRUMENTEN- EN ORTHOPEDISCHE ARTIKELENINDUSTRIE, TANDTECHNISCHE WERKPLAATSEN / CENTRAAL BUREAU VOOR DE STATISTIEK, HOOFDAFDELING STATISTIEDEN VAN INDUSTRIE EN BOUWNIJVERHEID.** VFOAT Medical Instruments and Orthopedical Articles Industry, Dental Technical Workshops. 1980-1981-. Dutch (summaries and/or abstracts in English). an. Fl7.00. Centraal Bureau voor de Statistiek, AFD ALG Zaken, Postbus 959, 2270 AZ Voorburg Netherlands. **Tel** 011 31 70 3373800, FAX 011 31 038 7429, telex 32692 CBS NL. **LC** HD9994.N4; M43.

UK
**MEDISTAT / WORLD MEDICAL MARKET ANALYSIS.** English. mo. £195.00. MDIS Ltd, MDIS House, 8 Eastgate Square Are, Chichester PO19 1JN England. **Tel** 0243 533322, FAX 0243 533418. **ED** Karen Simpkins. Index available. **Bk Rev**. **Ad Acc**. **Pr Rev**. **Circ:** 600.
**Desc:** Analysis of medical devices and equipment markets worldwide.

FR/0302-9263
**MEDITERRANEE MEDICALE.** [Mediterr. med.]. No. 1 (1973)-. Academic Scholarly Publication. French. Twenty times a year (No issues in July/Aug.). 313.42F. Region Sante, 305 B Centre D'Affaries Object, 92661 Asnieres Cedex France. **Tel** 011 33 1 47931804, FAX 011 33 1 47910540. **ED** Professor R. Raoult. **NLM** W1 ME794M. **CODEN** MDTMBF. **[CCC]**. **Bk Rev** **Ad Acc**, **Adv Mgr:** A. Trebucq. Documents available from BIOSIS Document Express. **Formed by the union of** Corse Medicale; Sud Medical; Marseille Chirurgical, 0025-4045; Marseille Medical **and** Archives de Medecine.
**Ind/Abst** Biol. Abstr. (-1983); EMBASE; Saf. Health Work; Trop. Dis. Bull.

BU/0324-1440
**MEDITSINSKA TEKHNIKA / MA-TSENTR ZA NAUCHNA INFORMATSIIA PO MEDITSINA I ZDRAVEOPAZVANE S TSENTRALNA MEDITSINSKA BIBLIOTEKA.** **Added/Corp** Tsentralna Meditsinska Biblioteka. MA - Tsent'r za Nauchna Informatsiia po Meditsina i Zdraveopazvane. (1968)-. Academic Scholarly Publication. Bulgarian. qt. $20.40. **(Subscription address:** Hemus Foreign Trade Organization, 6 Tzar Osvoboditel Boulevard, 1000 Sofia Bulgaria.**) CODEN** MDTEDR. Documents available from CASDDS.
**Ind/Abst** Acoust. Abstr.; Chem. Abstr.

●RU/0869-7760
**MEDITSINSKAIA POMOSHCH / MEDICAL CARE / MINISTERSTVO ZDRAVOOKHRANENIA RF.** **Added/Corp** Russia (Federation). Ministerstvo Zdravookhraneniia. (1993)-. Periodical. Russian (summaries and/or abstracts in English; table of contents in English). bm. Izdatelstvo Meditsina / Russian Academy of Medical Sciences, Ulitsa Solyanka 14, 109801 Moscow Russia. **Tel** 011 95 297-05-04. **(Subscription address:** Victor Kamkin, 4956 Boiling Brook Parkway, Rockville MD 20852.) Index available in last issue of volume--attached. **Bk Rev**. Documents available from CASDDS. **Formed by the union of** Feldsher i Akusherka, 0014-9772 **and** Meditsinskaia Sestra, 0025-8342.
**Ind/Abst** Chem. Abstr.; Int. Nurs. Index; SportSearch.

UZ/0025-830X
**MEDITSINSKII ZHURNAL UZBEKISTANA.** [Med. z. Uzb.]. (1957)-. Academic Scholarly Publication. Russian. Six times a year. $129.95. **(Subscription address:** East View Publications Inc., 3020 Harbor Lane North, Suite 110, Minneapolis MN

55447.) **NLM** W1 ME8085. **CODEN** MZUZA8. Documents available from BIOSIS Document Express, CASDDS.
**Ind/Abst** Biol. Abstr.; Chem. Abstr.

GW/0323-5386
**MEDIZIN AKTUELL.** Vol. 1 (Jan. 1975)-. Periodical. German (Russian). mo. DM90.00. Selecta Verlagsgesellschaft mbH, Postfach 4240, c/o Mrs. Riemer, D-65032 Wiesbaden Germany. **Tel** 011 49 611 1705261. **ED** Petra Beuse, Gertraud Mietzelfeld, & Wiebke Seydel. **NLM** W1 ME81N. **Ad Acc.**

GW/0939-351X
**MEDIZIN, GESELLSCHAFT, UND GESCHICHTE : JAHRBUCH DES INSTITUTS FUER GESCHICHTE DER MEDIZIN DER ROBERT BOSCH STIFTUNG.** **Added/Corp** Robert Bosch Stiftung. Institut fuer Geschichte der Medizin. **VFOAT** MedGG. Bd. 8 (1989)-. German (English; summaries and/or abstracts in English). an. DM48.00. Franz Steiner Verlag GmbH, Postfach 101061, D 70009 Stuttgart Germany. **Tel** 011 49 0711 2582372, FAX 011 49 0711 2582290, telex 723636 daz d. **ED** Robert Jutte. **NLM** W1; ME81W. **Bk Rev**, (Qty: 4-6/yr). **Ad Acc**, **Adv Mgr:** MS. Szoradi. **Circ:** 200. ***Continues*** *Jahrbuch des Instituts fuer Geschichte der Medizin der Robert Bosch Stiftung, 0175-6788.*
**Desc:** The objective of this yearbook is to serve researchers in the history of medicine and pharmaceutics in an interdisciplinary way which also takes into account social history, folklore, language and literature as well as art. It is dedicated to all aspects of illness and health.

GW/0323-6153
**MEDIZIN UND GESELLSCHAFT.** [Med. Ges.]. Academic Scholarly Publication. German. ir. Price varies per volume. Campus Verlag, Heelstrasse 149, D-60488 Frankfurt Germany. **Tel** 011 49 69 96751606, FAX 011 49 69 7682046. **ED** H U Deppe, H Fredrich, R Muller. **NLM** W1 ME814GH. **Bk Rev**. **Ad Acc. Circ:** 1,000. ***Continues*** *Zeitschrift fur Arztliche Fortbildung. Beiheft, 0323-8970.*
**Ind/Abst** EMBASE.

GW/0025-8431
**MEDIZINHISTORISCHES JOURNAL.** [Medizinhist. J.]. **VAT** Medizin Historisches Journal. Vol. 1, (1966)-. Periodical. German (English). qt. DM136.00 Germany; DM144.00 other. Gustav Fischer Verlag Stuttgart, Postfach 720143, Wollgrasweg 49, D 70577 Stuttgart Germany. **Tel** 011 49 711 458030, FAX 0711-4580334, telex 2627-7111488. **(Subscription address:** VCH Publishers Inc., 303 Northwest 12th Avenue, Journals Department, Deerfield FL 33442.) **LC** R131.A1; M43. **DD** 610/.9. **NLM** W1 ME818M. **[CCC].** cum. index.
**Ind/Abst** Am. Hist. Life (1988-).

GW/0723-5003
**MEDIZINISCHE KLINIK (MUNCHEN. 1983).** (MEDIZINISCHE KLINIK.). [Med. Klin.]. Vol. 78, No. 1 (Jan. 21, 1983)-. Periodical. German (summaries and/or abstracts in English). Twelve times a year. DM196.80 Germany; DM231.00 other. Urban & Vogel, Postfach 152209, D-80052 Munich Germany. **Tel** 011 49 89 53292140, FAX 089/536052, telex 521701. **(Subscription address:** Verlegerdienst Muenchen, Postfach 1280, D 82197 Gilching Germany.) **NLM** W1 ME8236TC. **[CCC]. Pr Rev.** ***Continues*** *Medizinische Klinik (Klinik-Ausg.), 0722-9321.*
**Ind/Abst** CSA Neuro. Abstr. (?-?); EMBASE [Select. Cov.]; Energy Res. Abstr.; Index Med. Vol. 81, No. 1, 1986-; Life Sci. Collect.; PESTDOC; Saf. Health Work; Soc. Sci. Cit. Index [Select. Cov.].

GW
**MEDIZINISCHE KLINIK. SUPPLEMENT.** Vol. 1 (1985/1986)-. Periodical. German. Fifty-two times a year. Urban & Vogel, Postfach 152209, D-80052 Munich Germany. **Tel** 011 49 89 53292140, FAX 089/536052, telex 521701. **NLM** W1; ME8236TCG.
**Ind/Abst** Index Med. (1985-1986).

GW/0076-6151
**MEDIZINISCHE LANDERKUNDE.** (MEDIZINISCHE LANDERKUNDE. GEOMEDICAL MONOGRAPH SERIES.). **Added/Corp** Heidelberger Akademie der Wissenschaften. Mathematisch-Naturwissenschaftliche Klasse. **VFOAT** Geomedical Monograph Series. (1967)-. Monographic series. English (German). ir. Price varies per volume. Springer Verlag New York Inc., PO Box 19386 Books, Newark NJ 07195. **Tel** (201)348-4033. **ED** Helmut J. Jusatz. **NLM** W1 ME825N.
**Desc:** A series on regional studies in geographical medicine.

GW/0025-8474
**MEDIZINISCHE MONATSSCHRIFT (STUTTGART).** (MEDIZINISCHE MONATSSCHRIFT, ZEITSCHRIFT FUR ALLGEMEINE MEDIZIN UND THERAPIE.). Vol. 1-. Periodical. German. mo. DM99.00. Wissenschaftliche Verlagsgesellschaft mbH, Postfach 101061, D 70009 Stuttgart Germany. **Tel** 011 49 711 258200, FAX 011 49 711 2582290, telex 723636 DAZ D. Index available in last issue of volume--attached. **Bk Rev. Ad Acc. Circ:** 12,000 (ctrl).

GW/0025-8512
**MEDIZINISCHE WELT.** [Med. Welt]. **VFOAT** Med Welt. (1960)-. Academic Scholarly Publication. German. Twelve times a year (plus supplements). DM275.00 Europe; $161.90 other. F K Schattauer Verlagsgesellschaft mbH, Postfach 10 45 45, D 70040 Stuttgart Germany. **Tel** 011 49 711 2298726. **ED** H. G. Lasch, P. Matis, and G. Oehler. **NLM** W1 ME842S. **CODEN** MEWEAC. **[CCC]. Pr Rev.** Documents available from The Genuine Article, BIOSIS Document Express, CASDDS. ***Continues*** *Die Medizinische, 0342-1147;* ***Absorbed*** *Medwelt Compact.*
**Ind/Abst** Biol. Abstr.; Chem. Abstr.; Curr. Contents Clin. Med.; EMBASE [Select. Cov.]; Energy Res. Abstr.; Helminthol. Abstr. (1991-); Index Med.; Nutr. Abstr. Rev., Ser. A, Hum. Exp.; Life Sci. Collect.; PESTDOC; Protozoolog. Abstr.; Res. Alert [Select. Cov.]; Rev. Med. Vet. Entomol.; Rev. Med. Vet. Mycology; Saf. Health Work; SCISEARCH; Soc. Sci. Cit. Index [Select. Cov.].

GW/0944-6885
**MEDIZINPRODUKTE JOURNAL.** (19??)-. German. qt. DM39.00. Wissenschaftliche Verlagsgesellschaft mbH, Postfach 101061, D 70009 Stuttgart Germany. **Tel** 011 49 711 258200, FAX 011 49 711 2582290, telex 723636 DAZ D. **ED** G. Schorn.

GW/0344-9416
**MEDIZINTECHNIK (STUTTGART).** (MEDIZINTECHNIK.). [Medizintechnik]. **VFOAT** Engineering in Medicine. (April 1978)-. Academic Scholarly Publication. German (English; summaries and/or abstracts in English). bm (6 issues). DM120.90 Germany; DM134.70 other. AW Gentner Verlag, Postfach 101742, D-70015 Stuttgart Germany. **Tel** 011 49 711 636720, FAX 011 49 711 6367247, telex 841 722244. **ED** R. D. Bockman. **NLM** W1 ME858A. **CODEN** MDZNDG. **Bk Rev. Ad Acc. Circ:** 6,500. Documents available from CASDDS. ***Continues*** *Medizinische Technik, 0025-8504.*
**Desc:** Covers the general field of medical technology, diagnosis, and therapeutic rehabilitation.
**Ind/Abst** Chem. Abstr.; EMBASE.

US
**MEDLARS.** Sheldon Kotzin, Bibliographic Services Division, Building 38A/Room 4N419, National Library of Medicine, 8600 Rockville Pike, Bethesda MD 20894. **Tel** (301)496-6193.
**Desc:** Worldwide coverage of the biomedical journal literature.

US
**MEDLINE KNOWLEDGE FINDER. / MODEL UM-11.** English. qt. $2220.00 (institutions), $1420.00 (individuals) US; $2270.00 (institutions), $1470.00 (individuals) Canada; $2280.00 (institutions), $1480.00 (individuals) Europe; $2345.00 (institutions), $1545.00 (individuals) other. Aries Systems Corporation, 200 Sutton Street, North Andover MA 01845. **Tel** (508)975-7570, FAX (508)975-3811.
**Desc:** Contains citations from MEDLINE database for current year and ten prior years.

US
**MEDLINE KNOWLEDGE FINDER. UM-5.** English. qt. $1620.00 (institutions), $1020.00 (individuals) US; $1670.00 (institutions), $1070.00 (individuals) Canada; $1680.00 (institutions), $1080.00 (individuals) Europe; $1745.00 (institutions), $1145.00 (individuals) other. Aries Systems Corporation, 200 Sutton Street, North Andover MA 01845. **Tel** (508)975-7570, FAX (508)975-3811.
**Desc:** Unabridged MEDLINE database for current year and four prior years.

US
**MEDLINE [COMPUTER FILE].** **Added/Corp** National Library of Medicine (U.S.) SilverPlatter Information, Inc. (1983-1984)-. Abstracting/Indexing Service. English. qt. $1045.00 The Americas; $1150.00 other (1988- present). Silverplatter Information Inc., 100 River Ridge Drive, Norwood MA 02062. **Tel** (800)343-0064, (617)769-2599, FAX (617)235-1715.
**Desc:** Contains the MEDLINE database of the National Library of Medicine from 1983 to the present. Includes bibliographic citations and abstracts for biomedical literature in English and all foreign languages and is fully indexed. System requirements: IBM PC, XT, AT or compatible; 512K RAM (640K recommended); MS-DOS or PC-DOS 2.1; floppy disk drive or hard disk drive; CD-ROM drive; printer (optional).

US/0097-9732
**MEDOC.** ***Ceased.*** **See** Medical Science and Technology-Abstracting, Bibliographies and Statistics.

FR/0294-1007
**MEDSUBHYP.** [MEDSUBHYP]. **VFOAT** Medecine Subaquatique et Hyperbare. (1982)-. Periodical. French. qt. **UDC** 61:623.74. ***Continues in part*** *Medecine Aeronautique et Spatiale, Medecine subaquatique et Hyperbare, 0399-6417.*
**Ind/Abst** Aquat. Sci. Fish. Abstr. (Computer File).

GW/0941-682X
**MEDWELT COMPACT.** ***Title Change.*** No. 12 (July 1991)-No. 11 (June 1992). Periodical. German. sm. F K Schattauer Verlagsgesellschaft mbH, Postfach 10 45 45, D 70040 Stuttgart Germany. **Tel** 011 49 711 2298726. ***Continues*** *Med Welt, 0937-3004.* ***Absorbed by*** *Medizinische Welt, 0025-8512.*

PL/0025-8601
**MEDYCYNA DOSWIADCZALNA I MIKROBIOLOGIA.** [Med. dosw. mikrobiol.]. **Added/Corp** Panstwowy Zakad Higieny. Polskie Towarzystwo Mikrobiologow. Vol. 1 (1949)-. Academic Scholarly Publication. Polish (summaries and/or abstracts in English, French and Russian). Four times a year. Price varies. Panstwowe Wydawn Naukowe, Miodowa 10, PO Box 391, 00251 Warsaw Poland. **(Subscription address:** ARS Polona, PO Box 1001, 00068 Warsaw Poland.) **LC** R91; .M428. **NLM** W1 ME866. **CODEN** MDMIAZ. Documents available from BIOSIS Document Express, CASDDS. ***Supersedes*** *Medycyna Doswiadczalna i Spoteczna.*
**Ind/Abst** Biol. Abstr.; Chem. Abstr.; EMBASE [Select. Cov.]; Index Med.; Life Sci. Collect.; Trop. Dis. Bull.

PL/0465-5893
**MEDYCYNA PRACY.** [Med. pr.]. Vol. 1-2, (1948)-(1949); New Series, Vol. 1 (1950)-. Academic Scholarly Publication. Polish (summaries and/or abstracts in Russian and English). bm. Price on Request. **(Subscription address:** ARS Polona, PO Box 1001, 00068 Warsaw Poland.) **NLM** W1 ME8697. **CODEN** MEPAAX. Documents available from CASDDS.
**Ind/Abst** Ceram. Abstr.; Chem. Abstr.; Coal Abstr.; Index Med.; Saf. Health Work; SportSearch; Trop. Dis. Bull.

PL/0867-3055
**MEDYK WARSZAWA.** (MEDYK.). (1990)-. Periodical. Polish. mo. $24.00. **(Subscription address:** ARS Polona, PO Box 1001, 00068 Warsaw Poland.) **UDC** 614(438).

US/1046-6983
**MEETINGS INMED.** [Meet. inmed]. **VFOAT** Meetings in Med. Vol. 1, No. 1 (Jan. 1988)-. Periodical. English. Four times a year (Feb., May, Aug., Nov.). $45.00. Scientific Meetings Publishing, PO Box 81662, San Diego CA 92138. **Tel** (619)270-2910, FAX (619)270-2910. **DD** 610.
**Desc:** A leading source of information on forthcoming events of all important medical, dental and health sciences meeting held throughout the world.

US/0747-8372
**MEMBERSHIP DIRECTORY / AMERICAN CHIROPRACTIC ASSOCIATION.** **Main/Corp** American Chiropractic Association. (1983)-. Directory. English. an. $100.00 (nonmembers), $20.00 (members). American Chiropractic Association, 1701 Clarendon Boulevard, Arlington VA 22209. **Tel** (703)276-8800. **LC** RZ233; .A47. **DD** 615.5/34/02573. **NLM** WB 22; AA1 A33o. **Circ:** 16,000. ***Continues*** *Official Membership Directory - American Chiropractic Association, 0569-3837.*
**Desc:** List of names, addresses, and phone numbers.

●US
**MEMBERSHIP DIRECTORY / AMERICAN COLLEGE OF OCCUPATIONAL AND ENVIRONMENTAL MEDICINE.** **Main/Corp** American College of Occupational and Environmental Medicine. (1993)-. Directory. English. American College of Occupational and Environmental Medicine, 55 West Seegers Road, Arlington Heights IL 60005. **Tel** (708)228-6850. **NLM** WA 22; AA1 A53m. ***Continues*** *American College of Occupational Medicine. Membership Directory.*

US
**MEMBERSHIP DIRECTORY / AMERICAN COLLEGE OF OCCUPATIONAL MEDICINE.** ***Title Change.*** **Main/Corp** American College of Occupational Medicine. Began with (1988/1989)-(1991/1992). Directory. English. **NLM** WA 22; AA1 A53m. ***Continues*** *American Occupational Medical Association. Membership Directory - American Occupational Medical Association, 0190-1664.* ***Continued by*** *American College of Occupational and Environmental Medicine. Membership Directory.*

US/1053-0967
**MEMBERSHIP DIRECTORY / AMERICAN COLLEGE OF PHYSICIANS.** **See** Encyclopedias and General Reference Books.

US
**MEMBERSHIP DIRECTORY / AMERICAN MEDICAL WRITERS ASSOCIATION.** **See** Societies and Clubs.

US
**MEMBERSHIP DIRECTORY / MEDICAL SOCIETY OF NEW JERSEY.** Directory. English. be. $79.50 (NJ residents includes 6% sales tax); $75.00 (others). Medical Society of New Jersey, 2 Princess Road, Lawrenceville NJ 08648. **Tel** (609)896-1766, FAX (609) 896-1368.

US/8755-2892
**MEMBERSHIP DIRECTORY / NATIONAL ASSOCIATION FOR MUSIC THERAPY.** See Music.

JA
**MEMOIRS OF NATIONAL INSTITUTE OF POLAR RESEARCH. SERIES E : BIOLOGY AND MEDICAL SCIENCE.** See Biology.

CH
**MEMOIRS OF THE COLLEGE OF MEDICINE OF THE NATIONAL TAIWAN UNIVERSITY.** **Main/Corp** Tai-Wan Ta Hsueeh, Tai-pei. College of Medicine. (19??)-. English (Chinese). **Ind/Abst** Trop. Dis. Bull.

CN/0824-3093
**MENNONITE MEDICAL MESSENGER (WINNIPEG, MAN.).** (MENNONITE MEDICAL MESSENGER.). [Mennon. med. mssenger]. Periodical. English. qt. $8.00. Mennonite Medical Association, 3003 Benham Avenue, Elkhart IN 46517-1999. **Tel** (219)295-3726. **ED** John Bender. **DD** 289.7. **Circ:** 2,000 (ctrl).
**Desc:** Information, promotion and theological treatment of a holistic approach to health care. The magazine addresses health care professionals, especially doctors, nurses and administrators.

●US/1072-3714
**MENOPAUSE (NEW YORK, N.Y.).** (MENOPAUSE : JOURNAL OF THE NORTH AMERICAN MENOPAUSE SOCIETY.). (1994)-. Periodical. English. qt. $89.00 (individuals), $105.00 (institutions) US; $100.00 (individuals), $116.00 (institutions) other. Raven Press, 1185 Avenue of the Americas, 37th Floor, New York NY 10036. **Tel** (212)930-9500, (212)930-9604, FAX (212)869-3495, (212)302-8507, telex 640073.

US/0747-8461
**MEN'S HEALTH (EMMAUS, PA. 1985).** ***Title Change.*** (MEN'S HEALTH.). [Men's health]. Vol. 1, No. 1 (Feb. 1983)-(1992). Periodical. English. qt. Rodale Press Inc., 400 South 10th Street, Emmaus PA 18098. **Tel** (215)967-5171, (800)666-2503. **DD** 613. available on microfilm and microfiche from University Microfilms International (UMI). ***Continued by*** *Men's Confidential.*
**Desc:** A newsletter that pays particular attention to topics such as vasectomy, hernia, drugs, sexual dysfunction, male stress syndrome, and prostate cancer.
**Ind/Abst** Acad. Abstr. Full Text Elite (Jan. 1992-) [Full Txt.]; Acad. Abstr. (Jan. 1992-); Consum. Health Nutr. Index (Jan. 1990); Foods Adlibra (19??-1992); Gen. Period. Index (1989-); Health Source (Jan. 1992-) [Full Txt.]; INFO-SOUTH Abstr.; Mag. Artic. Summar. Select (Jan. 1992-) [Full Txt.]; Mag. Artic. Summar. CD-ROM (Jan. 1992-); Mag. Search; Mag. Index (1989-?); Vocat. Search (Jan. 1992-) [Full Txt.].

US/1064-685X
**MENTAL HEALTH-HUMAN RESOURCES CONFERENCE GUIDE.** [Ment. health-hum. resour. conf. guide]. **VFOAT** Conference Guide; Mental Health Human Resources Conference Guide. Vol. 6, No. 1 (Jan. 1988)-. Periodical. English. mo (except Aug. & Dec.). $30.00. Mental Health Conference Guide, 826 9th Street, Greeley CO 80631. **Tel** (303)351-6688. **ED** Byron Norton. **DD** 362. **NLM** W 3.5; M5485. **Ad Acc, Adv Mgr:** Jody Bowland. ctrl circ. ***Continues*** *Conference Connection.*

US/0883-3443
**MENTAL HEALTH SYSTEMS SOFTWARE DIRECTORY.** ***Ceased.*** (MENTAL HEALTH SYSTEMS SOFTWARE DIRECTORY / AMERICAN ASSOCIATION FOR MEDICAL SYSTEMS AND INFORMATICS.). [Ment. health syst. softw. dir.]. (1985)-(19??). Directory. English. AMIA, 4915 St Elmo Avenue, Suite 302, Bethesda MD 20814. **DD** 362. **NLM** WM 22; AA1 M549.
**Desc:** Original manuscripts of each symposium.

US/0076-6526
**MERCK MANUAL OF DIAGNOSIS AND THERAPY, THE.** [Merck man. diagn. ther.]. **Added/Corp** Merck & Co. Merck Sharp & Dohme. **VFOAT** Merck Manual. 8th Ed. (1950)-. Monographic series. English. ir (every 5 years). Price varies per volume. Merck & Company, PO Box 2000, Rahway NJ 07065. **Tel** (908)594-4600. **LC** RC55; .M4. **DD** 615.5/8/05. **NLM** WB 100 M555M. ***Continues*** *Merck Manual of Therapeutics and Materia Medica.*

US/0093-0997
**MERIDIAN (LOS ANGELES).** (MERIDIAN.). [Meridian]. V. 1- Nov. 1973-. Periodical. English. ir. Acupuncture Research Institute CA 90031. **NLM** W1 ME951E.

●US/1065-2760
**METHODS & TECHNIQUES FOR THE CLINICAL LABORATORY.** **VFOAT** Methods and Techniques for the Clinical Laboratory. (1993)-. Monographic series. English. qt. $145.00 (institutions). Field & Wood, Inc., 4156 Manayunk Avenue, Philadelphia PA 19128. **Tel** (215)828-4010.

GW/0026-1270
**METHODS OF INFORMATION IN MEDICINE.** [Methods inf. med.]. **VFOAT** Methodik der Information in der Medizin. Vol. 1 (Jan. 1962)-. Academic Scholarly Publication. English (German; summaries and/or abstracts in German and English). qt. DM366.00 (institutions), DM271.00 (individuals) Europe; $227.00 (institutions), $165.00 (individuals) other. F K Schattauer Verlagsgesellschaft mbH, Postfach 10 45 45, D 70040 Stuttgart Germany. **Tel** 011 49 711 2298726. **ED** G. Wagner, P. L. Reichertz and D. A. B. Lindberg. **LC** R51; .M55. **DD** 025/.0661/05. **NLM** W1 ME9617M. **CODEN** MIMCAI. **[CCC].** Index available. cum. index. **Bk Rev. Ad Acc. Pr Rev.** ctrl circ. Documents available from The Genuine Article, BIOSIS Document Express, Ask*IEEE. ***Supersedes*** *Medizinische Dokumentation.*
**Desc:** International journal in the field of methodology of medical research, documentation, information science and medical information science and medical informatics. Its chief aim is the promotion of this field of science by the dissemination of new knowledge and the publication of new developments on the sector of medical information processing.
**Ind/Abst** Biol. Abstr.; Curr. Contents Clin. Med.; EMBASE; Energy Res. Abstr.; Index Med.; INSPEC (April 1970-); Int. Pharm. Abstr.; Libr. Inf. Sci. Abstr.; Life Sci. Collect.; Res. Alert [Full Cov.]; Sci. Cit. Index; SCISEARCH; Soc. Sci. Cit. Index [Select. Cov.].

US/0738-856X
**METHOTREXATE UPDATE.** [Methotrexate update]. Summer 1983-. Periodical. English. qt. $3.00 single issue. American Society of Swedish Engineers, One Dag Hammerskjold Plaza, Suite 3800, New York NY 10017.

FR/1258-780X
**METIERS DE LA PETITE ENFANCE.** (19??)-. Periodical. French. Ten times a year. 180.00F France; 250.00F other. Expansion Scientifique Francaise, 31 Boulevard de la Tour-Maubourg, 75007 Paris France. **Tel** 011 33 1 40 62 64 00, 011 33 1 40626439.

NE/0167-5885
**MEYLER AND PECK'S DRUG-INDUCED DISEASES.** [Meyler Peck's drug-induced dis.]. **VFOAT** Meyler and Peck's Drug Induced Diseases. Vol. 5 (1980)-. Academic Scholarly Publication. English. ir. Price varies per volume. Elsevier Science Publishers BV, PO Box 211, 1000 AE Amsterdam Netherlands. **Tel** 011 31 20 5803642, FAX 011 31 20 5862696, telex 15682. **LC** RC90; .D7. **NLM** W1 ME996J. **CODEN** MPDID9. Documents available from CASDDS. ***Continues*** *Drug-Induced Diseases.*
**Ind/Abst** Chem. Abstr.

SP
**MG. MEDICINA GENERAL.** Spanish. Laboratorios Lederle, Apartado 471, 28080 Madrid Spain.

CN/0831-2249
**MHLA BULLETIN.** See Library and Information Sciences.

CN/0848-9009
**MHLA NEWS.** See Library and Information Sciences.

US/1047-2509
**MIAMI MEDICAL LETTER.** (MIAMI MEDICAL LETTER : UPDATED MEDICAL INFORMATION FOR YOUR FAMILY.). [Miami med. lett.]. **Added/Corp** Cedars Medical Center. (1987)-. Periodical. English (Spanish). Twelve times a year. $36.00 North America; $48.00 other. Miami Medical Letter Inc., 9700 Southwest 67th Avenue, Miami FL 33156. **Tel** (305)284-8466, FAX (305)284-1019. **(Subscription address:** Box 3708, Miami FL 33265**) ED** Rosario A. Levine. **DD** 616. Index available. cum. index. **Ad Acc.**
**Desc:** Health information for the general public.

US/1047-2495
**MIAMI MEDICAL LETTER EN ESPANOL.** (MIAMI MEDICAL LETTER EN ESPANOL : NUEVOS INFORMES PARA SU FAMILIA.). [Miami med. lett. esp.]. (1987)-. Periodical. Spanish (English). mo. $36.00 North America; $48.00 other. Miami Medical Letter Inc., 9700 Southwest 67th Avenue, Miami FL 33156. **Tel** (305)284-8466, FAX (305)284-1019. **(Subscription address:** Box 3708, Miami FL 33265**) ED** Rasario A Levine. **DD** 616. Index available. cum. index. **Ad Acc.**
**Desc:** Health information for the lay public.

US
**MIAMI MEDICINE.** ***Ceased.*** **Added/Corp** Dade County Medical Association. Vol. 43, No. 10 (Oct. 1973)-(19??). Periodical. English. mo. Dade County Medical Association, 444 Brickell Avenue, Miami FL 33131. **Tel** (305)324-8717. **NLM** W1; MI155. ***Continues*** *Bulletin of the Dade County Medical Association.*

US/0026-2293
**MICHIGAN MEDICINE.** [Mich. med.]. **Added/Corp** Michigan State Medical Society. **VFOAT** Michigan Medicine/Medigram. Vol. 63, No. 7 (1964)-. Periodical. English. mo. $100.00 (1 year), $185.00 (2 year) including subscription to Medigram. Michigan State Medical Society, 120 West Saginaw Street, East Lansing MI 48823. **Tel** (517)337-1351, FAX (517)337-2490. **ED** Betty J McNerney. **LC** R15; .M613. **DD** 610.62774. **NLM** W1 MI22J. Index available. **Ad Acc. Circ:** 11,000. available on microfilm and microfiche from University Microfilms International (UMI). ***Continues*** *Journal of the Michigan State Medical Society, 0098-7522.* ***Continued in part by*** *Medigram (East Lansing, Mich. : 1985), 8750-9741.*
**Desc:** Socioeconomic medical news.
**Ind/Abst** Cumul. Index Nurs. Allied Health Lit.; Energy Res. Abstr. (1972-); Index Med.; Int. Nurs. Index; Saf. Health Work; SportSearch.

UK/0891-060X
**MICROBIAL ECOLOGY IN HEALTH AND DISEASE.** [Microb. ecol. health dis.]. **Added/Corp** Society for Intestinal Microbial Ecology and Disease. Society for Microbial Ecology and Disease. Vol. 1 (1988)-. Periodical. English. Six times a year. $425.00. John Wiley & Sons Ltd., Baffins Lane, Chichester West Sussex PO19 1UD England. **Tel** 0243 779777, FAX 0243 776128 BTG:JWP001, telex 86290 WIBOOKG. **(Subscription address:** John Wiley / Philadelphia, PO Box 7247, Philadelphia PA 19170.**) ED** S. P. Borriello. **LC** QR171.A1; M53. **DD** 616/.01/05. **NLM** W1; MI263G. **CODEN** MEHDE6. **[CCC].** Index available. **Bk Rev. Ad Acc.** available on microfilm and microfiche from University Microfilms International (UMI). Documents available from BIOSIS Document Express.
**Desc:** Presents research on different human microbial ecosystems and their role in health and disease. Topics include: investigative methods, animal and in vitro models, the effect of antibiotics or diet on the commensal flora or its development, alterations in the host environment, the role of immunological and other mechanisms that help maintain a stable flora, and the clinical application of the commensal flora in treatment and prevention of disease.
**Ind/Abst** Biol. Abstr. (1990-); Curr. Aware. Biol. Sci., CABS; Dairy Sci. Abstr.; Environ. Period. Bibliogr. (?-?); Food Sci. Technol. Abstr.; Microbiol. Abstr. Sect. B; Nutr. Abstr. Rev., Ser. A, Hum. Exp.; Rev. Med. Vet. Mycology; Sci. Cit. Index.

IT/1120-3811
**MICROCIRCOLAZIONE OGGI.** [Microcircolaz. oggi]. (1984)-. Periodical. Italian. Three times a year. Il Pensiero Scientifico Editore s.r.l., Via Bradano 3C, 00199 Rome Italy. **Tel** 011 39 6 86207158, 86207159, 86207168, 86207169, FAX 011 39 6 86207160. **ED** C. Allegra. **UDC** 616.6.

UK/1350-4916
**MICROCIRCULATION.** (19??)-. Periodical. English. Four times a year. $205.00 US and Canada; £130.00 Europe; £145.00 Other. Chapman & Hall, 2-6 Boundary Row, London SE1 8HN England. **Tel** 011 44 71 865 0066, FAX 011 44 71 522 9623, telex 290164 Chapmag. **(Subscription address:** Chapman & Hall, Cheriton House, North Way, Andover, Hampshire, SP10 5BE England.**)**

US/0740-9451
**MICROCIRCULATION, ENDOTHELIUM, AND LYMPHATICS.** Vol. 1, No. 1 (Feb. 1984)-. Academic Scholarly Publication. English. bm (February, April, June, August, October and December). $230.00 North America; $288.00 other. Butterworth Heinemann / Woburn, MA, 225 Wildwood Avenue, Unit B, Woburn MA 01801. **Tel** (800)366-2665, FAX (617)928-2620, telex 880052. **ED** Burton M Altura (editor's address: State University of New York - Downstate Medical Center, Brooklyn NY). **LC** QP106.6; .M534. **DD** 612.1/35. **NLM** W1; MI298F. **CODEN** MELYEL. **[CCC].** Index available. **Ad Acc. Pr Rev.** available on microfilm and microfiche from University Microfilms International (UMI). Documents available from BIOSIS Document Express, CASDDS.
**Desc:** An international rapid communication journal that publishes papers on any topic related to microscopic blood vessels in health and disease, including basement membranes, vascular smooth muscle cells, formed elements, endothelium, lymphatic blood vessels, lymph, geometry and rheology. This includes the physiology, pharmacology, morphology, pathology, biophysics, and biochemistry of these important blood vessels.
**Ind/Abst** Biol. Abstr. (1985-); Chem. Abstr. (1984-); EMBASE; Index Med. (1984); Ref. Upd. Deluxe Ed.; Sci. Cit. Index (19??-19??); SCISEARCH.

UK/0263-1016
**MIDDLE EAST HEALTH (1981).** (MIDDLE EAST HEALTH.). [Middle East health]. Vol. 5, No. 8 (Sept. 1981)-. Periodical. English. Nine times a year. $125.00. Print Design Services Ltd., 254 Upper Richmond Road West, London SW14 8AG England. **Tel** 011 44 81 8789130. **NLM** W1 MI32K. ***Continues*** *MEH. Middle East Health Supply & Service, 0309-2003.*
**Ind/Abst** Curr. Titl. Dent.

JA/0026-3532
**MIE MEDICAL JOURNAL.** [Mie med. j.]. **Added/Corp** Mie Daigaku. Igakubu. Vol. 3 (June 1952)-. Academic Scholarly Publication. English. tq. Mie University School of Medicine, 2 174 Endobashi Tsu, Mie Ken Japan. **NLM** W1 MI34. **CODEN** MMJJAI. Documents

available from BIOSIS Document Express, CASDDS. ***Continues*** *Journal of the Mie Medical College, 0368-3133.*
**Ind/Abst** Biol. Abstr.; Chem. Abstr.; EMBASE [Select. Cov.]; Index Vet.; Nutr. Abstr. Rev., Ser. A, Hum. Exp.; Small Anim. Abstr. Bibliogr.; Trop. Dis. Bull.

GW/0720-0536
**MIKROOEKOLOGIE UND THERAPIE.** (MIKROOEKOLOGIE UND THERAPIE. MICROECOLOGY AND THERAPY.). [Mikroolog. Ther.]. **Added/Corp** Institut fuer Mikrooekologie. **VFOAT** Microecology and Therapy. Vol. 7 (1977)-. Academic Scholarly Publication. German (English and German; summaries and/or abstracts in English and German). ir. DM79.00 Europe. Institut fuer Mikrooekologie, Postfach 1765, D 35727 Herborn Germany. **Tel** 011 49 27722404. **NLM** W1 MI424. **CODEN** MITHE4. Documents available from CASDDS. ***Continues*** *Uber die Behandlungen mit Physiologischen Bakterien, 0720-1648.*
**Ind/Abst** Chem. Abstr. (1984-); Protozoolog. Abstr.

US/0026-4075
**MILITARY MEDICINE.** [Mil. med.]. **Added/Corp** Association of Military Surgeons of the United States. Vol. 116, No. 1 (Jan. 1955)-. Academic Scholarly Publication. English. Twelve times a year. $45.00 (one year), $80.00 (two years), $115.00 (three years) US and US possessions, $50.00 (one year), $90.00 (two years), $130.00 (three years) other surface mail; $115.00 (one year), $155.00 (two years), $195.00 (three years) airmail. Association of Military Surgeons of the United States, 9320 Old Georgetown Road, Bethesda MD 20814. **Tel** (301)897-8800. **ED** John C. Duffy. **LC** RD1; .A7. **NLM** W1 MI488. **CODEN** MMEDA9. **[CCC].** Index available. cum. index. **Bk Rev. Ad Acc. Pr Rev. Circ:** 16,500 (ctrl). available on microfilm and microfiche from University Microfilms International (UMI). Documents available from The Genuine Article, BIOSIS Document Express, CASDDS. ***Continues*** *Military Surgeon (Washington, D.C. : 1907), 0096-6827.*
**Desc:** Concerning medical activities of the Federal Medical Services; means of communication among members. An exchange of scientific and technological developments of medicine.
**Ind/Abst** Biol. Abstr.; Chem. Abstr. (1955-1983); Cumul. Index Nurs. Allied Health Lit.; Curr. Contents Clin. Med.; Curr. Mil. Pol. Lit.; EMBASE; Energy Res. Abstr.; Helminthol. Abstr. (19??-19??); Index Med.; Index Vet.; Iowa Drug Inf. Serv. (1969-); Nutr. Abstr. Rev., Ser. A, Hum. Exp.; Life Sci. Collect.; Protozoolog. Abstr.; Psychol. Abstr. (1955-); PsycINFO; PsycLit; Res. Alert [Select. Cov.]; Rev. Med. Vet. Entomol.; Rev. Med. Vet. Mycology; Risk Abstr.; Saf. Health Work; SCISEARCH; Small Anim. Abstr. Bibliogr.; Soc. Sci. Cit. Index [Select. Cov.]; SportSearch; Virol. AIDS Abstr.

IT
**MILLECONGRESSI.** Italian. sa. L180000.00. Mediamed Srl, Via Gradoli 18, 00189 Rome Italy. **Tel** 011 39 6 33266530.

SA/0076-8847
**MIMS DESK REFERENCE.** **See** Pharmacy and Pharmacology.

II/0970-1036
**MIMS INDIA.** **See** Pharmacy and Pharmacology.

UK/0302-4172
**MIMS MIDDLE EAST.** [MIMS Middle East]. **VFOAT** M.I.M.S. Middle East. **VAT** Monthly Index of Medical Specialties. Middle East. (197?)-. Trade Publication. English. bm. £25.30. A E Morgan Publications Ltd, Stanley House, 9 West Street, Epsom Surrey KT18 7RL England. **Tel** 011 44 3727 41411, FAX 0372 744493, telex 291561 VIA SOS G. **ED** Frances Wilson. **Ad Acc. Circ:** 19,000.
**Desc:** Lists prescribable drugs for medical practitioners.

JA/0540-1259
**MINAMI OSAKA BYOIN IGAKU ZASSHI.** [Minami Osaka Byoin Igaku Zasshi]. **VFOAT** Journal of Minami Osaka Hospital; Medical Journal of Minami Osaka Hospital. (1953)-. Japanese. Three times a year. Minami Osaka Hospital, 18-18 Higashi-Kagaya 1-chome, Suminoe-ku, 559, Osaka, Japan. **CODEN** MOBZA6. ctrl circ.
**Ind/Abst** EMBASE [Select. Cov.].

●CN/1195-1990
**MIND / BODY MEDICINE.** (February 1995)-. English. qt. $120.00 (institutions), $80.00 (individuals) US & Canada; $138.00 (institutions), $108.00 (individuals) other. Decker Periodicals Publishing Inc, PO Box 620, Station A, Hamilton Ontario L8N 3K7 Canada. **Tel** (416)522-7017, (800) 568-7281, FAX (416)522-7839.

US/0026-556X
**MINNESOTA MEDICINE.** [Minn. med.]. **Added/Corp** Minnesota Medical Association. Minnesota State Medical Association. Vol. 1 (Jan. 1918)-. Academic Scholarly Publication. English. mo. $36.00 US; $60.00 other. Minnesota Medical Association, 3433 Broadway Street Northeast, Suite 300, Minneapolis MN 55413-1761. **Tel** (612)378-1875, (800)999-1875, FAX (612)378-3875. **ED** Richard L. Reece and Meredith McNab. **LC** R15; .M64. **DD** 610.5. **NLM** W1 MI699. **CODEN** MIMDAL. **[CCC]. Bk Rev. Ad Acc. Pr Rev. Circ:** 8,000. available on microfilm and microfiche from University Microfilms International (UMI). Documents available from The Genuine Article, BIOSIS Document Express, CASDDS.
**Ind/Abst** Biol. Abstr.; Chem. Abstr.; Cumul. Index Nurs. Allied Health Lit.; EMBASE; Energy Res. Abstr.; Index Med.; Mod. Med.; Life Sci. Collect.; Res. Alert [Select. Cov.]; SCISEARCH; SportSearch.

US
**MINORITY BIOMEDICAL SUPPORT PROGRAM : A DIRECTORY OF THE RESEARCH PROJECTS.** **Main/Corp** Research Resources Information Center. Directory. English. US Department of Health and Human Services National Institutes of Health, 9000 Rockville Pike, Bethesda MD 20892. **Tel** (301)496-9291, FAX (301)496-2443. Each issue contains an index to its own contents (no volume index)--loose.

US/0085-3488
**MINORITY STUDENT OPPORTUNITIES IN UNITED STATES MEDICAL SCHOOLS.** **See** Education-Higher Education.

US
**MISCELLANEOUS PAPERS / HISTORY OF MEDICINE SOCIETY OF APPALACHIA.** **Added/Corp** History of Medicine Society of Appalachia. No. 1 (1990)-. Monographic series. English. Price varies per volume. **NLM** W1; MI791D.

US
**MISSISSIPPI STATE MEDICAL ASSOCIATION DIRECTORY.** Directory. English. an. $50.00. Mississippi State Medical Association Journal, PO Box 5229, Jackson MS 39296. **Tel** (601)354-5433, FAX (601)352-4834. **Ad Acc.**

US/0026-6620
**MISSOURI MEDICINE.** [Mo. med.]. Vol.50 (Jan. 1953)-. Academic Scholarly Publication. English. mo. $20.00. Missouri State Medical Association, 113 Madison Box 1028, Jefferson City MO 65101. **Tel** (314)636-5151, FAX (314)636-8552. **ED** Angie Allen. **NLM** W1 MI878. Index available. cum. index (Dec. issue). **Ad Acc. Pr Rev. Circ:** 7,200. available on microfilm and microfiche from University Microfilms International (UMI). ***Continues*** *Missouri State Medical Association. Journal.*
**Desc:** Published for Missouri physicians. Scientific articles are previously unpublished clinical, review, and investigative articles. News articles cover organizational, economic, political, legislative, social and personal medical activities.
**Ind/Abst** EMBASE [Select. Cov.]; Energy Res. Abstr.; Index Med.; Life Sci. Collect.; SportSearch.

GW
**MITGLIEDER DER DEUTSCHEN GESELLSCHAFT FUR INNERE MEDIZIN.** **Main/Corp** Deutsche Gesellschaft fur Innere Medizin. (19??)-. German. **LC** R713.45; .D48a. **DD** 610.69/52/02543.

GW
**MITGLIEDER-VERZEICHNIS MIT UBERSICHT DER ARBEITS-, LANDES-, REGIONAL- UND STADTGRUPPEN / DEUTSCHE GESELLSCHAFT FUER HERPETOLOGIE UND TERRARIENKUNDE E.V.** **Main/Corp** Deutsche Gesellschaft fur Herpetologie und Terrarienkunde. **VFOAT** Mitgliederverzeichnis mit Ubersicht der Arbeits-, Landes-, Regional- und Stadtgruppen.; Mitglieder-Verzeichnis.; Mitgliederverzeichnis. (19??)-. German. **LC** QL35; .D48a. **DD** 597.6/06/043. ***Continues*** *Deutsche Gesellschaft fur Herpetologie und Terrarienkunde. Stadtgruppen- und Mitgliederverzeichnis.*
**Desc:** Information concerning herpetologists.

UK/0142-8217
**MITOCHONDRIA / ISSUED MONTHLY BY UNIVERSITY OF SHEFFIELD BIOMEDICAL INFORMATION SERVICE.** **Added/Corp** University of Sheffield. Biomedical Information Service. (197?)-. Periodical. English. sm. £105.00. SUBIS, Mansion House, 19 Kingfield Road, Sheffield S11 9AS England. **Tel** 011 44 114 255 4433, FAX 011 44 114 255 4626. **LC** Z5322.C3; M57. **[CCC].**

GW
**MITTEILUNGEN ARBEITSGEMEINSCHAFT FUER KLINISCHE NEPHROLOGIE.** German. an. DM32.00. Vandenhoeck & Ruprecht, Robert Bosch Breite 6, D-37079 Goettingen Germany. **Tel** 011 49 551 695911, FAX 011 49 551 695917, telex 965226 VAN d.

GW
**MITTEILUNGEN DER ARBEITSSTELLE FUR ETHNOMEDIZIN.** **Main/Corp** Arbeitsstelle fur Ethnomedizin. No.1-. Periodical. German. Arbeitsstelle fur Ethnomedizin, Germany.

US/0541-5489
**MLA NEWS.** **See** Library and Information Sciences.

US/0580-7247
**MLO, MEDICAL LABORATORY OBSERVER.** [MLO: Med. lab. obs.]. **VFOAT** Medical Laboratory Observer. Vol. 1 (July 1969)-. Periodical. English. mo. $65.00 US; $75.00 other. Medical Economics Publishing, Five Paragon Drive, Second Floor, Montvale NJ 07645. **Tel** (800)432-4570, (201)358-2210. **(Subscription address:** Fulco Medical Economics, PO Box 3000, Denville NJ 07834.**) ED** Robert J. Fitzgibbon. **LC** RB36; .M17. **DD** 610/.28. **NLM** W1 M386R. **CODEN** MLOBAC. **[CCC]. Ad Acc. Circ:** 60,000 (ctrl). available on an online database (file 648/Full-Text) from DIALOG. Documents available from BIOSIS Document Express.
**Desc:** Purpose is to improve the management skills of clinical laboratory supervisors.
**Ind/Abst** Biol. Abstr. (-1985); Cumul. Index Nurs. Allied Health Lit.; Health Plan. Adminis.; Hospit. Health Admin. Index; Trade Ind. ASAP [Full Txt.]; Trade Ind. Index (1981-) [Full Txt.].

US
**MM NEWS.** (19??)-. Periodical. English. Six times a year. $15.00. New York County Medical Society, 15 East 26th Street, 11th Floor, New York NY 10010. **Tel** (212)684-4670. ***Continues*** *Manhattan Medicine, 0744-4966.*
**Desc:** Contains articles about political issues confronting doctors in Manhattan (malpractice insurance costs, etc.), not technical material. About goings-on at the Medical Society, the AMA, the State Medical Society, etc.

GW/0340-8183
**MMG, MEDIZIN, MENSCH, GESELLSCHAFT.** ***Ceased.*** [MMG, Med. Mensch, Ges.]. **VFOAT** Medizin, Mensch, Gesellschaft. (1976)-(199?). Periodical. German (summaries and/or abstracts in English). qt. Ferdinand Enke Verlag, Ruedigerstrasse 14, D-70469 Stuttgart Germany. **Tel** 011 49 711 8931124, 011 49 711 893123. **NLM** W1 M386W.
**Ind/Abst** EMBASE; Int. Bibliogr. Sociol.; Soc. Plann. Policy Dev. Abstr.

GW/0341-3098
**MMW. MUNCHENER MEDIZINISCHE WOCHENSCHRIFT.** [MMW; Munch. med. Wochenschr.]. **VFOAT** Munchener Medizinische Wochenschrift. Vol. 116 (Jan. 4, 1974)-. Academic Scholarly Publication. German (summaries and/or abstracts in English). wk. DM192.00 Germany; DM210.00 other. MMV Medizin Verlag, Postfach 801246, Neumarkter Street 18, W-8000 Muenchen 80 F R Germany. **Tel** 011/49/89/9269070, FAX 089/48189-633, telex 522053. **ED** Dr. Aumiller, (phone: 011 49 89 43189 640). **NLM** W1 M386Z. **CODEN** MMMWD7. **[CCC].** Index available. cum. index (published two times a year). **Ad Acc, Adv Mgr:** W. Beuse, **Tel** 089-43189-642-676. **Pr Rev. Circ:** 55,000 (ctrl). Documents available from CASDDS. ***Continues*** *Munchener Medizinische Wochenschrift, 0027-2973.*
**Desc:** Medical journal.
**Ind/Abst** Chem. Abstr.; Curr. Biotechnol.; EMBASE [Select. Cov.]; Energy Res. Abstr. (March 1982-); Microbiol. Abstr. Sect. B (19??-19??); Life Sci. Collect.; PESTDOC; Protozoolog. Abstr.; Rev. Med. Vet. Entomol.; Rev. Med. Vet. Mycology; Saf. Health Work; SportSearch.

AT/0312-875X
**MODERN MEDICINE.** [Mod. med.]. **VFOAT** Modern Medicine of Australia. Vol. 15 (Jan. 1972)-. Periodical. English. Twelve times a year. 105.00Aus$ Australia; 140.00Aus$ (surface mail), 175.00Aus$ (airmail) New Zealand, Fiji, & Papua New Guinea; 165.00Aus$ (surface mail), 265.00Aus$ (airmail) Britain, Europe, & US; 140.00Aus$ (surface mail), 225.00Aus$ (airmail) Asia. Modern Medicine of Australia Pty., 15 Grosvenor Street, Suite 3, Neutral Bay New South Wales, 2089 Australia. **Tel** 011 61 2 9082 155, FAX 011 61 2 9081 961. **ED** Dr. John Ellald, (editor's address: PO Box 114, Neutal Bay New South Wales 2089 Australia). **NLM** W1 MO14. **Bk Rev**, (Qty: 25). **Ad Acc, Adv Mgr:** T. Scott, **Tel** (02)908-2155. **Pr Rev. Circ:** 20,999 (ctrl). ***Continues*** *Modern Medicine of Australia, 0026-8089.* ***Continued in part by*** *Malaria in Australia.*

UK/0262-4273
**MODERN MEDICINE (BECKENHAM).** (MODERN MEDICINE.). [Mod. med.]. V. 16- Jan. 1971-. Periodical. English. mo. **NLM** W1 MO139M. available on microfilm from University Microfilms International (UMI). ***Continues*** *Modern Medicine of Great Britain Ltd.*

US/0026-8070
**MODERN MEDICINE (MINNEAPOLIS).** **See** Medical Science and Technology-Abstracting, Bibliographies and Statistics.

NE/0929-0141
**MODERN MEDICINE (NEDERLANDSE ED.).** (MODERN MEDICINE.). (1976)-. Academic Scholarly Publication. Dutch. mo. Fl181.13 Netherlands; Fl252.83 other. Bugamor International, De Haak 58, 1353 AE Almere Netherlands. **Tel** 011 31 36 5382297. **ED** G. Geerling. Index available. **Bk Rev. Ad Acc. Pr Rev.** ctrl

circ.
**Desc:** Medical, practical, and scientific information for general practitioners and internists.

UK/0306-6657
**MODERN MEDICINE OF IRELAND.** [Mod. med. Irel.]. (1971)-. Periodical. English. Twelve times a year. £60.00 UK; £75.00 others. Findlay Publications Ltd, Franks Hall, Horton Kirby, Kent DA4 9LL England. **Tel** 011 44 (0322)222222, FAX 011 44 (0322)289577. **NLM** W1 MO165I. available on microfilm from University Microfilms International (UMI).

CN/0825-0464
**MODULE D'AUTOFORMATION.** [Module autoform.]. **Added/Corp** Federation des Medecins Omnipraticiens du Quebec. No. 1 (1984)-. Monographic series. French. ir. Price varies per volume. Federation des Medecins Omnipracticiens du Quebec, Bureau 1100/1440 Ouest rue Ste-Catherine, Montreal Quebec H3G 1R8 Canada. **Tel** (514)878-1911. **DD** 610/.715. **Circ:** 1,000.

UK/0098-2997
**MOLECULAR ASPECTS OF MEDICINE.** [Mol. aspects med.]. Vol. 1 (1976)-. Academic Scholarly Publication. English. bm. $477.00 The Americas; £320.00 other. Pergamon Press, An Imprint of Elsevier Science Ltd., The Boulevard, Langford Lane, Kidlington, Oxford OX5 1GB United Kingdom. **Tel** 011 44 865 843000, 011 44 865 843699, FAX 011 44 865 843010. **(Subscription address:** Elsevier Science Ltd. Oxford Fulfillment Centre, PO Box 800, Kidlington, Oxford OX5 1DX United Kingdom.**)** **ED** H. Baum. **LC** RB112; .M64. **DD** 616.07. **NLM** W1 MO195H. **CODEN** MAMED5MAMED. **[CCC].** available on microfilm and microfiche from University Microfilms International (UMI). Documents available from The Genuine Article, BIOSIS Document Express, CASDDS.
**Ind/Abst** Biol. Abstr.; Chem. Abstr.; Curr. Aware. Biol. Sci., CABS; EMBASE; Index Med.; Index Sci. Rev. [Full Cov.]; Life Sci. Collect.; Res. Alert [Full Cov.]; Sci. Cit. Index; SCISEARCH.

UK/1356-1324
**MOLECULAR BIOLOGY TECHNIQUES.** (19??)-. English. £105.00. SUBIS, Mansion House, 19 Kingfield Road, Sheffield S11 9AS England. **Tel** 011 44 114 255 4433, FAX 011 44 114 255 4626.

US/1057-2805
**MOLECULAR GENETIC MEDICINE. See** Biology-Genetics.

●US/1076-1551
**MOLECULAR MEDICINE (CAMBRIDGE, MASS.).** (MOLECULAR MEDICINE.). (1994)-. Academic Scholarly Publication. English. Seven times a year. $150.00 (institution), $95.00 (individual)US; $180.00 (institution), $120.00 (individual). Blackwell Scientific Publishers, 238 Main Street, Cambridge MA 02142. **Tel** (617)547-7110, (800)835-6770, FAX (617)547-0789.

US/0149-6735
**MONTEFIORE MEDICINE.** V. 1- Summer 1976-. Periodical. English. qt. Montefiore Hospital and Medical Center, 111 East 210 Street, Bronx NY 10467. **NLM** W1 MO583P.

US/0883-0266
**MONTHLY PRESCRIBING REFERENCE.** **VFOAT** MPR. (June 1985)-. Periodical. English. mo. $95.00 (institutions); $78.00 physicians; $39.00 (individuals) other. Prescribing Reference Inc, PO Box 844, Pearl River NY 10965. **Tel** (800)436-9269, FAX (212)732-2360. **ED** Hany Eskalis. **DD** 615. **NLM** QV 772; M789. Index available. cum. index. **Ad Acc. Pr Rev. Circ:** 115,000 (ctrl). available on microfilm from University Microfilms International (UMI).
**Desc:** Prescribing reference for office based physicians, including information on the top 2,000 prescribed drugs.

PK/0379-2617
**MOTHER & CHILD (LAHORE). See** Family and Marriage.

SW/0347-0989
**MOTPOL.** V. 54, No. 5- 1976-. Periodical. Swedish. ir. Progek / Sweden, Progr Ekonomitjaenst, Box 31003, S 400 32 Goeteborg Sweden. **Tel** 011 46 31 243425. **NLM** W1 MO949F. ***Continues*** *MFT. Medicinska Foreningarnas Tidskrift.*

US/0027-2507
**MOUNT SINAI JOURNAL OF MEDICINE, NEW YORK, THE.** [Mt. Sinai j. med.]. **Added/Corp** Mount Sinai Hospital (New York, N.Y.). Committee on Medical Education and Publications. Mount Sinai Medical Center (New York, N.Y.). **VFOAT** Mount Sinai Journal of Medicine. Vol. 37 (Jan./Feb. 1970)-. Academic Scholarly Publication. English. Six times a year. $75.00 US and Canada; $80.00 other. Mount Sinai Journal of Medicine, Box 1094 50 East 98th Street, New York NY 10029. **Tel** (212)241-6108, . **LC** R11; .N724. **DD** 610/.5. **NLM** W1 MO95KG. **CODEN** MSJMAZ. **Pr Rev.** available on microfilm and microfiche from University Microfilms International (UMI). Documents available from The Genuine Article, BIOSIS Document Express, CASDDS. ***Continues*** *Journal of the Mount Sinai Hospital, New York, 0099-9695.*
**Ind/Abst** Biol. Abstr.; Chem. Abstr.; Curr. Contents Clin. Med.; EMBASE [Select. Cov.]; Energy Res. Abstr. (Dec. 1974-); Index Med.; Nutr. Res. Newsl.; Life Sci. Collect.; Protozoolog. Abstr.; Res. Alert [Full Cov.]; Rev. Med. Vet. Entomol.; Sci. Cit. Index; SCISEARCH; Soc. Sci. Cit. Index [Select. Cov.]; SportSearch.

FR
**MOUTON, LE.** French. ir. 321.60F. Editions Maloine, 27 rue de l'Ecole de Medecine, F-75006 Paris France. **Tel** 011 33 1 43256045, FAX 011 33 1 46340589, telex 203215 F.

US/1046-137X
**MOVING AHEAD (CHICAGO, ILL.).** (MOVING AHEAD : A PUBLICATION OF THE AMERICAN CONGRESS OF REHABILITATION MEDICINE, HEAD INJURY INTERDISCIPLINARY SPECIAL INTEREST GROUP.). [Mov. ahead]. **Added/Corp** American Congress of Rehabilitation Medicine. Head Injury Interdisciplinary Special Interest Group. Vol. 1, Issue 1 (Jan. 1986)-. Periodical. English. tq. $30.00. ACRM Head Injury Interdisciplinary Special Interest Group, PO Box 271475, Concord CA 94527. **DD** 615.

UK/0143-0130
**MRC NEWS.** **VFOAT** Medical Research Council News. (1978)-.
**Ind/Abst** Trop. Dis. Bull.

US/1051-9661
**MRO ALERT. See** Law.

RU
**MRZ. MEDITSINSKII REFERATIVNYI ZHURNAL.** **Added/Corp** Vsesoiuznyi Nauchno-Issledovatelskii Institut Meditsinskoi i Mediko-Tekhnicheskoi Informatsii. **VFOAT** Meditsinskii Referativnyi Zhurnal. Vol. 19 (1975)-. Russian (table of contents in English). **NLM** ZW 1 M4915. ***Continues*** *Meditsinskii Referativnyi Zhurnal.*

IT
**MT : MEDICAL TOP.** ***Suspended.*** (19??)-Suspended (Dec. 1990). Periodical. Italian. Twelve times a year. Masson S.P.A, Via Statuto 2/4, 20121 Milan Italy. **Tel** 011 39 2 63671, FAX 011 39 2 6367211.

US/1060-7609
**MT TODAY.** (MT TODAY : A WEEKLY NEWSMAGAZINE FOR MEDICAL LABORATORY PROFESSIONALS.). [MT today]. (1991)-. Periodical. English. wk. $13.00. Valley Forge Press, 1288 Valley Forge Road, Box 1135, Valley Forge PA 19482. **Tel** (800)220-4979, (215)935-3301. **DD** 610.

US/0734-6875
**MUSIC THERAPY PERSPECTIVES. See** Music.

GW/0933-6885
**MUSIK-, TANZ- UND KUNSTTHERAPIE. See** Music.

UK/1351-5292
**MYCOBACTERIA.** (19??)-. English. £85.00. SUBIS, Mansion House, 19 Kingfield Road, Sheffield S11 9AS England. **Tel** 011 44 114 255 4433, FAX 011 44 114 255 4626.

FR/0248-9635
**N.P.N. MEDECINE.** (NORD PICARDIE NORMANDIE MEDECINE.). [N.P.N. med.]. **VFOAT** Nord Picardie Normandie Medecine. Vol. 1, No. 1 (Jan. 1, 1981)-. Academic Scholarly Publication. French. Ten times a year (Except July/Aug.). 313.42F. Region Sante, 305 B Centre D'Affaries Object, 92661 Asnieres Cedex France. **Tel** 011 33 1 47931804, FAX 011 33 1 47910540. **ED** Dr. Beuard Devulder. **NLM** W1 NP404. **Bk Rev.** ***Continues in part*** *Medecine, Revue Medicale Inter-Regionale du Nord & de l'Est, 0153-8748.*
**Ind/Abst** EMBASE.

JA/0027-7622
**NAGOYA JOURNAL OF MEDICAL SCIENCE.** [Nagoya j. med. sci.]. **Added/Corp** Aichi Ika Daigaku. Nagoya Ika Daigaku. Nagoya Daigaku. Igakubu. Nagoya Teikoku Daigaku. Igakuba. Vol. 2 (1927)-. Academic Scholarly Publication. English (French and German). sa. Nagoya University School of Medicine, Tsurumai Cho Showa Ku, Nagoya Japan. **LC** R97; .N3. **DD** 610.5. **NLM** W1 NA113. **CODEN** NJMSAG. Documents available from BIOSIS Document Express, CASDDS. ***Continues*** *AICHI Journal of Experimental Medicine.*
**Ind/Abst** Biol. Abstr.; Chem. Abstr.; EMBASE; Index Med.; SEA Abstr.; Trop. Dis. Bull.

JA/0027-7649
**NAGOYA MEDICAL JOURNAL.** [Nagoya med. j.]. **Added/Corp** Nagoya Shiritsu Daigaku. Igakubu. Vol. 1 (Jan. 1953)-. Academic Scholarly Publication. English. qt. Free. Nagoya City University Medical School, Kawasumi Mizuho-cho, Mizuho-ku Nagoya 467 Japan. **Tel** 052-851-4166. **ED** Makoto Sasaki, Akira Masaoka, Tomohiro Matsuda, Ryo Tanaka, Yoshiro Wada, Nobuo Matsui. **NLM** W1 NA115. **CODEN** NMJOAA. **Bk Rev. Circ:** 750. Documents available from BIOSIS Document Express, CASDDS.
**Desc:** Official publication of the Nagoya City University Medical School for original articles (and occasional reviews) in all branches of medical sciences.
**Ind/Abst** Biol. Abstr.; Chem. Abstr.; Dairy Sci. Abstr.; SEA Abstr.; Trop. Dis. Bull.

JA/0027-7606
**NAGOYA SHIRITSU DAIGAKU IGAKKAI ZASSHI. JOURNAL OF THE NAGOYA CITY UNIVERSITY MEDICAL ASSOCIATION.** [Nagoya Shiritsu Daigaku Igakkai Zasshi]. **Added/Corp** Nagoya Shiritsu Daigaku. Igakkai. **VFOAT** Journal of the Nagoya City University Medical School; Journal of the Nagoya City University Medical Association. (1950)-. Academic Scholarly Publication. Japanese (table of contents in English). qt. $81.00. Nagoya City University Medical Association, 1 Kawasumi Mizuhocho, Mizuho-ku Nagoya-shi, 467 Aichi Japan. **(Subscription address:** Japan Publications Trading Company, Ltd., PO Box 5030, Tokyo International, Tokyo 100-31 Japan.**)** **NLM** W1 NA1154. **CODEN** NASDA6. Documents available from CASDDS.
**Ind/Abst** Chem. Abstr.; EMBASE [Select. Cov.].

CC/1000-5331
**NANJING YIXUEYUAN XUEBAO.** (NAN-CHING I HSUEH YUAN HSUEH PAO.). [Nanjing yixueyuan xuebao]. **Added/Corp** Nan-Ching i Hsueh Yuan. **VFOAT** Nanjing Yixueyuan Xuebao; Acta Academiae Medicinae Nanjing. (19??)-. Academic Scholarly Publication. Chinese. qt. Nanjing Yixueyuan / Nanjing Institute of Medical Sciences, 140 Hanzhong lu, Nanjing, Jiangsu 210029, People's Republic of China. **Tel** 649141. **ED** W. Jingjiang. **CODEN** NAYXEW. Documents available from CASDDS, BLDSC, CASDDS.
**Ind/Abst** Chem. Abstr.

UK/0957-4484
**NANOTECHNOLOGY (BRISTOL). See** Engineering.

JA/0469-5550
**NARA IGAKU ZASSHI.** [Nara igaku zasshi]. **VFOAT** Journal of Nara Medical Association. (1949)-. Academic Scholarly Publication. Japanese (summaries and/or abstracts in English). bm. $88.50. Nara Igakkai, (Nara Medical Assoc.), Nara Kenritsu Ika Daigaku, Shijomachi, Kashiharashi, Naraken 634 Japan. **(Subscription address:** Japan Publications Trading Company, Ltd., PO Box 5030, Tokyo International, Tokyo 100-31 Japan.**)** **NLM** W1 NA171. **CODEN** NAIZAM. Index available in last issue of volume--attached. Documents available from BIOSIS Document Express, CASDDS.
**Ind/Abst** Biol. Abstr.; Chem. Abstr.; EMBASE [Select. Cov.]; Helminthol. Abstr.; Protozoolog. Abstr.; Rev. Med. Vet. Mycology.

YU/0351-7462
**NARODNA ZDRAVSTVENA KULTURA U SR SRBIJI.** [Nar. zdrav. kult. SR Srb.]. **VFOAT** Folk Health Culture in the Socialist Republic of Serbia. Vol. 1- 1976-. Monographic series. Serbo-Croatian (Roman) (summaries and/or abstracts in English). Price varies per volume. **ED** J Tucakov. **NLM** W1 PO863 knijiga 10, etc.
**Ind/Abst** Annu. Bibliogr. Engl. Lang. Lit.

US/0027-8785
**NATIONAL BOARD EXAMINER, THE.** [Natl. Board exam.]. **Added/Corp** National Board of Medical Examiners. (1954)-. English. qt. free on request. National Board of Medical Examiners, 3930 Chestnut Street, Philadelphia PA 19104. **Tel** (215)349-6400. **LC** R745; .N23. **NLM** W1 NA328. ***Continues*** *Diplomate, 0096-0209.*

US/1055-6044
**NATIONAL DIGEST OF HEALTH AND MEDICINE.** (1991)-. Periodical. English. mo. $39.00. United States Medical Information Center, 1133 Fifteenth Street NW, Wahington DC 20005.

US/0892-6972
**NATIONAL DIRECTORY OF HEAD INJURY REHABILITATION SERVICES.** (NATIONAL DIRECTORY OF HEAD INJURY REHABILITATION SERVICES : A REFERENCE GUIDE TO PROGRAMS AND FACILITIES IN THE UNITED STATES OFFERING SPECIALIZED TREATMENT FOR HEAD INJURED PERSONS.). [Natl. dir. head inj. rehabil. serv.]. **Added/Corp** National Head Injury Foundation (U.S.). **VFOAT** NHIF National Directory of Head Injury Rehabilitation Services. (1984)-. Directory. English. Twelve times a year. $60.00 members; $70.00 non-members. National Head Injury Foundation, 1776 Massachusetts Avenue Northwest, Washington DC 20036. **Tel** (800)444-6443, (202)296-6443. **ED** Mary S. Rutter. **NLM** WL 22; AA1 N175. **Ad Acc, Adv Mgr:** Kim Arline, **Tel** (202)296-6443. **Circ:** 10,000.
**Desc:** Information on over 400 specialized head injury rehabilitation programs nationwide.

US/0739-6724
**NATIONAL DIRECTORY OF HOLISTIC HEALTH PROFESSIONALS, THE.** [Natl. dir. holistic health prof.]. **Main/Corp** Association for Holistic Health (U.S.). **VFOAT** Association for Holistic Health Directory. 1st Vol. -. Directory. English. Association For Holistic Health, PO Box 9532, San Diego CA 92109. **LC** R723. **DD** 613. **NLM** W 22; AA1 A7.

AT/0155-9567
**NATIONAL DIRECTORY OF INTERNSHIPS, RESIDENCIES & REGISTRARSHIPS, AUSTRALIA.** ***Suspended.*** [Natl. dir. internsh. resid. regist., Aust.]. (1978)-?. Directory. English. Vic Medical Postgraduate Foundation, 22 Lascelles Avenue, Trawalla/Toorak 3142 Australia. **NLM** W 22; KA8 N2. **[CCC].**

US/0145-689X
**NATIONAL DISEASE AND THERAPEUTIC INDEX.** English. IMS America Ltd, Butler Pike & Maple Avenue, Ambler PA 19002. **LC** RM263; .N36. **DD** 615/.58/0973. **NLM** QV 772 N2762.

US
**NATIONAL DISEASE AND THERAPEUTIC INDEX (NDTI). DIAGNOSIS / IMS AMERICA.** **VFOAT** Diagnosis; N.D.T.I. Diagnosis Reference File; NDTI. Diagnosis. Began with: 1960. Periodical. English. qt. IMS America Ltd, Butler Pike & Maple Avenue, Ambler PA 19002. **NLM** QV 772; N27621.

US
**NATIONAL DISEASE AND THERAPEUTIC INDEX (NDTI). DRUG NATIONAL ESTIMATES / IMS AMERICA.** **Added/Corp** IMS America Ltd. **VFOAT** Drug National Estimates; NDTI. Drug National Estimates. (1972)-. English. an. IMS America Ltd, Butler Pike & Maple Avenue, Ambler PA 19002. **NLM** QV 772; N276214. ***Continues in part*** *National Disease and Therapeutic Index (NDTI). National Estimates.*

US/1071-1201
**NATIONAL GUIDE TO FUNDING IN HEALTH.** [Natl. guide funding health]. **Added/Corp** Foundation Center. 2nd Ed. (1990)-. Periodical. English. ir. Foundation Center, 79 Fifth Avenue, Department EN, New York NY 10003. **Tel** (212)620-4230, (800)424-9836, FAX (212)807-3677. **LC** RA410.A1; N37. **DD** 362.

US
**NATIONAL HEAD INJURY FOUNDATION CATALOGUE OF EDUCATIONAL MATERIALS.** English. an. National Head Injury Foundation, 1776 Massachusetts Avenue Northwest, Washington DC 20036. **Tel** (800)444-6443, (202)296-6443. **ED** Sharon Gloger Friedman.

●US/1071-6262
**NATIONAL HEAD INJURY FOUNDATION'S TBI CHALLENGE!, THE.** [National Head Injury Foundation's TBI challenge!]. **Added/Corp** National Head Injury Foundation (U.S.). **VFOAT** TBI Challenge!. (Feb. 1993)-. Periodical. English. qt. comes with membership. National Head Injury Foundation, 1776 Massachusetts Avenue Northwest, Washington DC 20036. **Tel** (800)444-6443, (202)296-6443. **DD** 362. ***Continues*** *Newsletter - National Head Injury Foundation.*

US/0146-6690
**NATIONAL INSTITUTES OF HEALTH ANNUAL REPORT OF INTERNATIONAL ACTIVITIES.** (NATIONAL INSTITUTES OF HEALTH ANNUAL REPORT OF INTERNATIONAL ACTIVITIES / PREPARED BY JOHN E. FOGARTY INTERNATIONAL CENTER FOR ADVANCED STUDY IN THE HEALTH SCIENCES.). **Main/Corp** John E. Fogarty International Center for Advanced Study in the Health Sciences. **Added/Corp** National Institutes of Health (U.S.). Began with (1968/69)-. English. an. John E Fogarty International Center for Advanced Study in the Health Sciences, 9000 Rockville Pike, Bethesda MD 20205. **LC** RA11; .D13. **DD** 610/.72. **NLM** W2 A N206N. available on microfiche (Vols. for (1985-) distributed to depository libraries).

US/0270-6768
**NATIONAL INTELLIGENCE REPORT. CLINICAL LABS/BLOOD BANKS.** [Natl. intell. rep., Clin. labs/blood banks]. **VFOAT** Clinical Labs/Blood Banks; National Intelligence Report on Clinical Labs/Blood Banks. **VAT** National Intelligence Report. Clinical Labs Blood Bank. (1979)-. Periodical. English. Twenty-two times a year (published monthly except once in Aug. and Dec.). $198.00 subscribers to other Washington G-2 reports; $220.00 other. Washington G 2 Reports, 1111 14th Street NW, Suite 711, Washington DC 20005. **Tel** (202)789-1034, FAX (202)289-4062. **ED** Dennis W. Weissman and D. J. Curren. ctrl circ.

US/0733-9844
**NATIONAL JOURNAL OF MEDICINE & MEDICAL RESEARCH.** **VFOAT** National Journal of Medicine and Medical Research; Journal of Medicine; Journal of Medicine & Medical Research; Journal of Medicine and Medical Research. Vol. 1-. Periodical. English. mo. $156.00. ASA-Association Staffing, PO Box 1643, Casselberry FL 32707-1643. **NLM** W1 NA486SM.

US/0149-9939
**NATIONAL LIBRARY OF MEDICINE AUDIOVISUALS CATALOG.** ***Ceased.*** **See** Library and Information Sciences.

US
**NATIONAL LIBRARY OF MEDICINE CURRENT CATALOG.** ***Ceased.*** **Main/Corp** National Library of Medicine (U.S.). **VFOAT** NLM Current Catalog. (1988)-(Dec. 1993). Catalog. English. qt. National Library of Medicine, 8600 Rockville Pike, Bethesda MD 20894. **Tel** (301)496-6308. ***Continues*** *National Library of Medicine (U.S.) National Library of Medicine Current Catalog Annual National Library of Medicine Current Catalog. Annual Cumulation;* ***Absorbed*** *National Library of Medicine (U.S.) National Library of Medicine Current Catalog Cumulative.*

US/0163-4569
**NATIONAL LIBRARY OF MEDICINE PROGRAMS AND SERVICES.** **See** Library and Information Sciences.

II/0970-258X
**NATIONAL MEDICAL JOURNAL OF INDIA, THE.** [Natl. med. j. India]. **Added/Corp** All-India Institute of Medical Sciences. **VFOAT** NMJI. Vol. 1, No. 1 (Jan./Feb. 1988)-. Periodical. English. bm. £45.00 UK and Europe; $75.00 other. Oxford University Press, Walton Street, Oxford OX2 6DP England. **Tel** 011 44 865 56767, FAX 011 44 865 267773, telex 837330 OXPRES G. **(Subscription address:** Oxford University Press / USA, Journals Marketing Department, Oxford University Press, 2001 Evans Road, Cary NC 27513.**)** **LC** R97; .N37. **NLM** W1; NA526. **CODEN** NMJIEU. **[CCC].** available on microfilm and microfiche from University Microfilms International (UMI). Documents available from BIOSIS Document Express.
**Ind/Abst** Biol. Abstr. (1989-); EMBASE [Select. Cov.]; Helminthol. Abstr. (1991-); Protozoolog. Abstr.

US/1052-309X
**NATIONAL MEDICAL-LEGAL JOURNAL.** **See** Law.

US/1075-3753
**NATIONAL NETWORK (DALLAS, TEX.).** (NATIONAL NETWORK : THE NEWSLETTER OF THE HOSPITAL LIBRARIES SECTION OF THE MEDICAL LIBRARY ASSOCIATION.). [Natl. netw.]. **Main/Corp** Medical Library Association. Hospital Library Section. (197?)-. Periodical. English. qt. $20.00. Medical Library Association, Suite 300, Six North Michigan Avenue, Chicago IL 60602-4805. **Tel** (312)419-9094, FAX (312)419-8950. **DD** 027.

US/0363-7174
**NATIONAL PHYSICIAN ASSISTANT PROGRAM PROFILE, THE.** **Main/Corp** Association of Physician Assistant Programs. 1st- Ed.; 1975/76-. English. Association of Physician Assistant Programs, 1117 North 19th Street, Arlington VA 22209. **LC** R847.5; .A88A. **DD** 610.73/7/071.

US/0273-4974
**NATIONAL REPORT COMPUTERS AND HEALTH.** **See** Computers.

IT/1121-1350
**NATOM. FARMACIA NATURALE.** [NATOM, Farm. nat.]. **VFOAT** Farmacia Naturale. (1991)-. Periodical. Italian. Nine times a year. L70000.00 Italy; L140000.00 Europe; L190000.00 other. Tecniche Nuove SPA, Via Ciro Menotti 14, 20129 Milan Italy. **Tel** 011 39 2 75701, FAX 011 39 2 7610351, telex 334647 TECHS I. **UDC** 615.32. ***Continues*** *NATOM (Milano), 0394-8196.*

GW/0934-7909
**NATUR-UND GANZHEITSMEDIZIN : NGM.** **VFOAT** Natur- und GanzheitsMedizin; NGM. (198?)-. Periodical. German (summaries and/or abstracts in English). Comes with Die Medizinische Welt. F K Schattauer Verlagsgesellschaft mbH, Postfach 10 45 45, D 70040 Stuttgart Germany. **Tel** 011 49 711 2298726. **ED** Marcela Ullmann. **NLM** W1; NA922. **[CCC].** Index available. cum. index. **Bk Rev. Ad Acc. Circ:** 15,000.
**Desc:** Magazine dealing with natural and holistic medicine from a strictly scientific angle. Based on classical medical education.

AT
**NATURAL THERAPIST.** ***Ceased.*** (19??)-(199?). Research Publications Pty Ltd., 27A Boronia Road, Vermont 3133 Victoria Australia. **Tel** 03 8731450.

●US
**NATURE MEDICINE.** (Jan. 1995)-. Periodical. English. Twelve times a year. $295.00 US; £350.00 other. Nature Publishing Company, 65 Bleecker Street, 12th Floor, New York NY 10012. **Tel** (212)477-9600, (800)524-0328, FAX (212)477-8020. **(Subscription address:** Nature Order Department, Macmillan Magazines, Ltd., Brunel Road, Basingstoke, Hants RG21 2XS England.**)**

GW/0177-6754
**NATURHEILPRAXIS MIT NATURMEDIZIN.** [N. Nat.heilprax. Nat.med.]. **VFOAT** N. Naturheilpraxis Mit Naturmedizin. Vol. 37 (May 1984)-. Periodical. German. mo. DM56.10 Germany; DM60.30 other. Richard Pflaum Verlag Gmbh, Postfach 190737, D 80607 Munich Germany. **Tel** 011 49 89 126070, FAX 011 49 89 12607200, telex 5216075. **NLM** W1; NA843R. ***Continues*** *Naturheilpraxis.*

US
**NATUROPATHIC PHYSICIAN / THE AMERICAN ASSOCIATION OF NATUROPATHIC PHYSICIANS, THE.** **Added/Corp** American Association of Naturopathic Physicians. **VFOAT** AANP Newsletter. Vol. 6, No. 3 (Summer 1991)-. Periodical. English. Four times a year (Mar., June, Sept., Dec.). $36.00 US; $55.00 others. American Association of Naturopathic Physicians, PO Box 20386, Seattle WA 98102. **Tel** (206)323-7610. **ED** Paul Bergner, (editor's address: 725 Southeast 28th, Portland, OR 97214, phone: (503)231-8257). **NLM** W1; NA899G. **Bk Rev,** (Qty: 8-12). **Ad Acc. Circ:** 1,500. ***Continues*** *AANP Quarterly.*

US/0895-8211
**NAVY MEDICINE.** [Navy med.]. **Added/Corp** United States. Naval Medical Command. United States. Navy. Medical Dept. United States. Navy Dept. Bureau of Medicine and Surgery. Vol. 78, No. 2 (March/April 1987)-. Government Publication. English. bm. $11.00 domestic; $13.75 other. Superintendent of Documents, US Government Printing Office, Washington DC 20402. **Tel** (202)275-3328, FAX (202)786-2377. **DD** 359. **NLM** W2; A5 B9me. available on microfilm and microfiche from University Microfilms International (UMI). ***Continues*** *U.S. Navy Medicine, 0364-6807.*
**Desc:** The official publication of the Navy Medical Department. It is intended for Medical Department personnel and contains professional information relative to medicine, dentistry, and the allied health sciences.
**Ind/Abst** Index Dent. Lit. (1987-); Life Sci. Collect. (1987-).

US/0896-6443
**NCCLS DOCUMENT.** **See** Biology.

●US
**NCRR REPORTER / NATIONAL CENTER FOR RESEARCH RESOURCES.** **Added/Corp** National Center for Research Resources (U.S.) Research Resources Information Center. **VFOAT** National Center for Research Resources Reporter. Vol. 17, No. 3 (May/June 1993)-. Government Publication. English. bm. $9.50 US; $11.90 other. Superintendent of Documents, US Government Printing Office, Washington DC 20402. **Tel** (202)275-3328, FAX (202)786-2377. **NLM** W1; NC998M. ***Continues*** *Reporter (National Center for Research Resources (U.S.)), 1057-9400.*
**Desc:** Provides information on current research in the medical field. contains articles, research highlights, research focus reports, and announcements of meetings.

UK/0306-5464
**NDC PAPER.** [NDC paper]. **Added/Corp** Scottish Sub-Aqua Club. Vol. 1, (1974)-. Periodical. English. **NLM** W1 N123P.

US/0091-6730
**NEBRASKA MEDICAL JOURNAL, THE.** [Nebr. med. j.]. **Added/Corp** Nebraska Medical Association. Nebraska State Medical Association. Vol. 56, No. 12 (Dec. 1971)-. Periodical. English. Twelve times a year. $23.00. Nebraska Medical Association Inc, 233 South 13th Street, Suite 1512, Lincoln NE 68508. **Tel** (402)474-4472, FAX (402)474-2198. **ED** Benjamin Gelber. **NLM** W1 NE1145. **CODEN** NBMJAZ. cum. index. **Ad Acc. Pr Rev. Circ:** 2,200. available on microfilm and microfiche from University Microfilms International (UMI). Documents available from CASDDS. ***Continues*** *Nebraska State Medical Journal, 0028-1956.*
**Ind/Abst** Chem. Abstr.; Cumul. Index Nurs. Allied Health Lit.; Energy Res. Abstr. (1982-); Index Med.; Life Sci. Collect.; SportSearch.

NE
**NEDERLANDS MILITAIR GENEESKUNDIG TIJDSCHRIFT.** **Added/Corp** Netherlands (Kingdom, 1815- ). Leger. Inspectie van de Geneeskundige Dienst. Dec. (1947)-. Periodical. Dutch. mo. Free on request for Netherlands military; F23.50 Netherlands; F34.00 other. Mindefensie, Postbus 20701, 2500 ES Den Haag Netherlands. **LC** RC971; .N4. **NLM** W1 NE138.

NE
**NEDERLANDS TIJDSCHRIFT VOOR DIETISTEN.** (19??)-. Dutch. Taak Van Poortvliestraat 3, OSS Netherlands.

NE/0028-2162
**NEDERLANDS TIJDSCHRIFT VOOR GENEESKUNDE.** [Ned. tijdschr. geneeskd.]. (1957)-. Academic Scholarly Publication. Dutch. wk. Fl234.25. Libresso BV, Postbus 878, 7400 GA Deventer Netherlands. **Tel** 011 31 5700 47421. **NLM** W1 NE147. **CODEN** NETJAN. Documents available from CASDDS. ***Supersedes*** *Nederlandsch Tijdschrift voor Geneeskunde.*
**Ind/Abst** Chem. Abstr.; Dairy Sci. Abstr.; EMBASE; Helminthol. Abstr. (19??-19??); Hortic. Abstr.; Index Med.; Index Dent. Lit.; Index Vet.; Nutr. Abstr. Rev., Ser. A, Hum. Exp.; Ornamental Hort. (1991-); Life Sci. Collect.; PESTDOC; Potato Abstr.; Protozoolog. Abstr.; Rev. Med. Vet. Mycology; Saf. Health Work; Small Anim. Abstr. Bibliogr.; Soyabean Abstr.; SportSearch; Trop. Dis. Bull.

US
**NEEDLE, THE. Added/Corp** American Academy of Acupuncture Medicine. Vol. 2, No. 1 (4th quarter, 1982)-. Periodical. English. qt. Brown University / Box 1951, Providence RI 02912. **NLM** W1; NE193KM. ***Continues*** *American Academy of Acupuncture Medicine : Journal, 0278-8918.*

GW/0300-8371
**NEUE MUNCHNER BEITRAGE ZUR GESCHICHTE DER MEDIZIN UND NATURWISSENSCHAFTEN. MEDIZINHISTORISCHE REIHE.** (1970)-. Monographic series. German. ir. Price varies per volume. Werner Fritish Verlag, Promenadeplatz 11, D 80333 Munich Germany. **ED** H. Goerke. **NLM** W1 NE264E.

GW/0172-9225
**NEURALTHERAPIE NACH HUNEKE. VFOAT** Freudenstadter Vortrage. Vol. 1- 1974-. German. Karl F Haug Verlag GmbH and Company, Postfach 102840, D 69018 Heidelberg Germany. **Tel** 011 49 6221 40620. **NLM** W1 NE323D.
**Desc:** Consists of the proceedings of the 13th/14th working meeting of the Internationale Medizinische Gesellschaft fur Neuralthearpie nach Huneke.

•UK/0969-9961
**NEUROBIOLOGY OF DISEASE.** (199?)-. Academic Scholarly Publication. English. Six times a year. $169.00 (institutions), $68.00 (individuals) US & Canada; £99.00 (institutions), £40.00 (individuals) Europe; £109.00 (institutions), £44.00 (individuals) other. Blackwell Scientific Publications Ltd, Marston Book Services, PO Box 87, Oxford OX2 ODT UK. **Tel** 011 44 865 791155, FAX 011 44 865 791927, telex 837 515 MARDIS G.

US
**NEW DEFINITION / THE CENTER FOR CASE MANAGEMENT, INC, THE. Added/Corp** Center for Case Management (South Natick, Natick, Mass.). Vol. 6, No. 2 (Spring/Summer 1991)-. Periodical. English. Four times a year. $25.95. Center for Case Management Inc., 6 Pleasant Street, South Natick MA 01760. **Tel** (508)651-2600, FAX (508)655-0858. **ED** Karen Zander. **NLM** W1; NE372I. ***Continues*** *Definition.*

US
**NEW DIRECTORY OF MEDICAL SCHOOLS, THE.** 1962-. Directory. English. Aurea Publications, Allenhurst NJ 07711. **ED** A S White and E Pokress. **NLM** W 22 N525.

US
**NEW DRUG BUYER, THE.** (19??)-. Periodical. English. Twenty-four times a year. $345.00. Faulkner & Gray Inc., 11 Penn Plaza, 17th Floor, New York NY 10001. **Tel** (212)967-7000, (800)535-8403.

UK/0958-9422
**NEW DRUGS AND NOVEL COMPOUNDS IN MEDICINE AND PHARMACOLOGY.** **See** Pharmacy and Pharmacology.

US/0360-2613
**NEW DYNAMICS OF PREVENTIVE MEDICINE. Added/Corp** International Academy of Preventive Medicine. Vol. 1 (1974)-. Monographic series. English. ir. Symposia Foundation, 863 Heather Way, Carlsbad CA 92009. **NLM** W1 NE374J.
**Desc:** Consists of selected papers from the 5th meeting of the International Academy of Preventive Medicine.

US/0028-4793
**NEW ENGLAND JOURNAL MEDICINE, THE.** (THE NEW ENGLAND JOURNAL MEDICINE. MICROFORM.). **Added/Corp** Massachusetts Medical Society. Vol. 198 (Feb. 23, 1928)-. Periodical. English. wk. New England Journal of Medicine, 1440 Main Street, Waltham MA 02154-1649. **Tel** (617)893-3800, (800)843-6356, FAX (617)647-5785, telex 5106015660 NEJM BOS UQ. **[CCC].** cum. index. ***Continues*** *Boston Medical and Surgical Journal, 0096-6762.*
**Ind/Abst** INFO-SOUTH Abstr.; Psychol. Abstr. (1928-).

US/0277-996X
**NEW ENGLAND JOURNAL OF HUMAN SERVICES.** **See** Sociology-Social Services and Welfare.

US/0028-4793
**NEW ENGLAND JOURNAL OF MEDICINE, THE.** [N. Engl. j. med.]. **Added/Corp** Massachusetts Medical Society. Vol. 198 (Feb. 23, 1928)-. Academic Scholarly Publication. English. Fifty-two times a year. $145.00. New England Journal of Medicine, 1440 Main Street, Waltham MA 02154-1649. **Tel** (617)893-3800, (800)843-6356, FAX (617)647-5785, telex 5106015660 NEJM BOS UQ. **(Subscription address:** New England Journal of Medicine, PO Box 9135, Waltham MA 02154.**) ED** Arnold S. Relman. **LC** R11; .B7. **DD** 610/.5. **NLM** W1 NE388. **CODEN** NEJMAG. **[CCC].** cum. index. **Bk Rev. Ad Acc, Adv Mgr Tel** (617)893-6742. **Pr Rev. Circ:** 225,000. available on CD-ROM (x) from Maxwell Electronic Publishing; available on microfilm and microfiche from University Microfilms International (UMI); available on an online database (file 444/Full-Text) from DIALOG. Documents available from The Genuine Article, BIOSIS Document Express, UMI Article Clearinghouse, CASDDS, Documents on Demand. ***Continues*** *Boston Medical and Surgical Journal, 0096-6762.*
**Desc:** A general medical journal with current updates in the latest news and breakthroughs of the medical field.
**Ind/Abst** Abr. Index Med.; Abstr. Anthropol. (19??-); Abstr. Soc. Gerontol. (?-?); Abstr. Clin. Care Guidel.; Acad. Abstr. Full Text Elite (Sept. 1984-) [Full Txt.]; Acad. Abstr. (Sept. 1984-); Acad. Ind. [Computer File] (1988-); Acad. Search (Sept. 1984-); AGRICOLA [Select. Cov.]; Annals Behav. Med.; Biodeter. Abstr.; Biol. Abstr.; Biol. Dig.; Calcium Calcif. Tissue Abstr.; Chem. Abstr.; Consum. Health Nutr. Index; Crim. Justice Abstr.; CSA Neuro. Abstr. (?-?); Cumul. Index Nurs. Allied Health Lit.; Curr. Aware. Biol. Sci., CABS; Curr. Contents Clin. Med.; Curr. Contents Life Sci.; Curr. Lit. Fam. Plan.; Dairy Sci. Abstr.; Dent. Abstr. (-199?); Dev. Med. Child Neurol.; EMBASE; Energy Inf. Abstr.; Energy Res. Abstr.; Environ. Abstr.; Expand. Acad. Index (1988-); Food Sci. Technol. Abstr.; Foods Adlibra; Gen. Period. Index (1987-); Gen. Sci. Index; Gen. Sci. Source (Jan. 1988-) [Full Txt.]; Genet. Abstr.; Health Saf. Sci. Abstr.; Health Devices Alerts; Health Index (1989-); Health Period. Database; Health Ref. Cent. (Jan. 1989-) [Full Cov.]; Health Serv. Abstr.; Health Source (Sep. 1984-) [Full Txt.]; Helminthol. Abstr. (1991-); Hospit. Manage. Rev.; Hum. Genome Abstr.; Immunol. Abstr.; Index Med.; Index Period. Artic. Relat. Law; Index Vet.; Ind. Hyg. Dig. (19??-19??); INFO-SOUTH Abstr.; Int. Aerosp. Abstr.; Int. Pharm. Abstr.; Iowa Drug Inf. Serv. (1966-); J. Watch; Leadscan; Mag. Artic. Summar. Elite (Jan. 1984-) [Full Txt.]; Mag. Artic. Summar. Select (Jan. 1984-); Mag. Artic. Summar. CD-ROM (Sept. 1984-); Mag. Index Plus (1989-); Mag. Index. Sel. (1987-); Mag. Search; Maize Abstr.; Med. Abstr. Newsl.; Microbiol. Abstr. Sect. B; Microbiol. Abstr. Sect. C; NAPRALERT; Newsp. Period. Abstr. (1987-); Nutr. Abstr. Rev., Ser. A, Hum. Exp.; Nutr. Res. Newsl.; Oncog. Growth Factors Abstr.; PESTDOC; Physic. Medline Plus; Pollut. Abstr. Indexes; Popul. Index; Poult. Abstr.; Protozoolog. Abstr.; Psychol. Abstr. (1928-); PsycINFO; PsycLit; Ref. Upd. Basic Ed.; Ref. Upd. Clinical Ed.; Ref. Upd. Deluxe Ed.; Res. Alert [Full Cov.]; Resource/One Ondisc (1987-); Rev. Med. Vet. Entomol.; Rev. Med. Vet. Mycology; Risk Abstr.; Saf. Health Work; Sci. Cit. Index; SCISEARCH; Soc. Plann. Policy Dev. Abstr.; Soc. Sci. Cit. Index [Select. Cov.]; Soc. Work Abstr. (1987-) [Select. Cov.]; Sociol. Abstr.; SPORT Discus; SportSearch; Mag. Index (1988-); Vet. Bull.; Toxicol. Abstr.; Trade Ind. Index; Trop. Dis. Bull.; Virol. AIDS Abstr.; Vocat. Search (Sept. 1984-) [Full Txt.]; Women Stud. Abstr.

US/0028-4793
**NEW ENGLAND JOURNAL OF MEDICINE (OVERSEAS ED.).** (THE NEW ENGLAND JOURNAL OF MEDICINE.). **Added/Corp** Massachusetts Medical Society. (198?)-. Periodical. English. Fifty-two times a year. $188.00 institutions; $157.00 physicians; $102.00 individuals. New England Journal of Medicine, 1440 Main Street, Waltham MA 02154-1649. **Tel** (617)893-3800, (800)843-6356, FAX (617)647-5785, telex 5106015660 NEJM BOS UQ. **(Subscription address:** New England Journal of Medicine, PO Box 9135, Waltham MA 02154.**) NLM** W1; NE388B. **[CCC]. Pr Rev.**

•US/1063-7389
**NEW HORIZONS (BALTIMORE, MD.).** (NEW HORIZONS : AN OFFICIAL PUBLICATION OF THE SOCIETY OF CRITICAL CARE MEDICINE.). [New horiz.]. **Added/Corp** Society of Critical Care Medicine. Vol. 1, No. 1 (Feb. 1993)-. Periodical. English. qt. $95.00 (individual), $126.00 (institution) US; $120.00 (individual), $151.00 (institution) other. Williams & Wilkins Company, 428 East Preston Street, Baltimore MD 21202-3993. **Tel** (410)528-4000, (800)638-6423, FAX (410)528-8596, telex 87669. **(Subscription address:** Williams & Wilkins, PO Box 64380, Baltimore MD 21264.**) DD** 617. **NLM** W1; NE4242. **[CCC].** Documents available from Quick Copies.
**Desc:** Each issue focuses on one topic, bringing coverage to ICU and CCU specialists.

US/0270-7748
**NEW IMAGE OF MAN IN MEDICINE, A.** [New image man med.]. Vol. 1-. Academic Scholarly Publication. English. ir. Futura Publishing Company Inc., 135 Bedford Road, PO Box 418, Armonk NY 10504-0418. **Tel** (914)273-1014, (800)877-8761, FAX (914)273-1015, (914)273-1016. **LC** R723; .N443. **DD** 306. **CODEN** NIMED4. Documents available from CASDDS.
**Ind/Abst** Chem. Abstr.

US/0885-842X
**NEW JERSEY MEDICINE.** (NEW JERSEY MEDICINE : THE JOURNAL OF THE MEDICAL SOCIETY OF NEW JERSEY.). [N.J. med.]. **Added/Corp** Medical Society of New Jersey. Vol. 82, No. 10 (Oct. 1985)-. Periodical. English. mo. $35.00 North America; $50.00 other. Medical Society of New Jersey, 2 Princess Road, Lawrenceville NJ 08648. **Tel** (609)896-1766, FAX (609) 896-1368. **ED** Howard D Slobodien. **LC** R15; .N515. **DD** 610/.5. **NLM** W1; NE446P. Index available. cum. index. **Bk Rev. Ad Acc. Pr Rev. Circ:** 11,000. available on microfilm and microfiche from University Microfilms International (UMI). ***Continues*** *Journal of the Medical Society of New Jersey, 0025-7524.*
**Desc:** Scientific and socio-economic journal.
**Ind/Abst** CSA Neuro. Abstr. (?-?); Hospit. Health Admin. Index; Index Med. Oct. 1985-; Soc. Plann. Policy Dev. Abstr.; Sociol. Abstr.; SportSearch.

US/0748-8777
**NEW MEDICAL SCIENCE.** [New med. sci.]. Vol. 1, No. 1 (July 1984)-. Periodical. English. bm. Moorhead Publications Inc, Conway Court, 810 South Waukegan Road, Suite 200, Lake Forest IL 60045. **Tel** (708)615-8333, FAX (708)615-8345. **ED** Marc Kusinitz. **DD** 610. **Circ:** 90,000.
**Desc:** Explores the new frontiers in medical technology today.

US/0196-4852
**NEW MEXICO STATE MEDICAL FACILITIES PLAN. Main/Corp** New Mexico. State Health Planning and Development Bureau. 1978/79-. English. an. New Mexico Department of Health, 1190 St. Francis Drive, Santa Fe NM 87502. **Tel** (505)827-2613. **NLM** W2 AN5 H5NA. ***Continues*** *New Mexico State Plan for Hospitals and Health Facilities Survey, Construction and Modernization, 0192-1053.*

US/0028-6451
**NEW PHYSICIAN.** [New physician]. **Added/Corp** Student American Medical Association. American Medical Student Association. (1957)-. Periodical. English. Nine times a year. $22.00. American Medical Student Association, 1890 Preston White Drive, Reston VA 22091. **Tel** (703)620-6600. **ED** Richard Camer. **NLM** W1 NE484I. Index available. **Bk Rev. Ad Acc. Circ:** 40,000 (ctrl). available on microfilm and microfiche from University Microfilms International (UMI). ***Continues*** *Student American Medical Association. Journal.*
**Desc:** News and feature coverage on social, political, and ethical issues in medical education and health care delivery, primary care clinical columns, etc.
**Ind/Abst** Hospit. Health Admin. Index (1966-1989).

US/0361-6347
**NEW TITLES IN BIOETHICS. Added/Corp** National Reference Center for Bioethics Literature. Vol. 1, (May 1975)-. Periodical. English. Four times a year. $20.00 US; $30.00 other; Annual Cumulation: $15.00 US, Canada & Mexico; $20.00 other. Kennedy Institute of Ethics, Georgetown University, Washington DC 20057. **Tel** (800)663-3849, (202)687-3885, FAX (202)687-6770. **ED** Lucinda Fitch Huttlinger. **LC** Z6675.E8; N48; R724. **DD** 016.174/2. **NLM** ZW 50 N532. **Circ:** 1,200 (ctrl).

US/0160-7162
**NEW VISTAS IN COUNSELING SERIES.** Vol. 1 (1977)-. Monographic series. English. ir. Price varies per volume. Human Sciences Press, PO Box 735, 233 Spring Street, New York NY 10013. **Tel** (212)620-8000, FAX (212)807-1047, telex 23421139. **LC** UNC. **NLM** W1 NE513K.

US
**NEW YORK AND NEW JERSEY REGIONAL MEDICAL LIBRARY NEWS.** **See** Library and Information Sciences.

US/0898-6401
**NEW YORK DOCTOR, THE.** [N. Y. dr.]. Vol. 1, No. 1 (April 1988)-. Periodical. English. Twenty-six times a year. $65.00 (one year); $110.00 (two years); $150.00 (three years). Chase Communications Group, 2535 Beechwood Avenue, PO Box 9001, Mt Vernon NY 10552. **Tel** (914)699-2020. **ED** Gerald L. Taylor. **DD** 610. ctrl circ.
**Desc:** Offers nonclinical, local, hard news to New York City physicians, and covers hospital politics, malpractice cases, medical ethics, insurance, legislation, regulation and commercial real estate.

US/0196-6871
**NEW YORK MEDICAL QUARTERLY, THE.** [N. Y. med. q.]. Vol. 1 (Summer 1979)-. Academic Scholarly Publication. English. qt. New York Medical Publ Corp, 370 7th Avenue/Room 322, New York NY 10001. **Tel** (212)371-1000. **LC** R11. **DD** 610/.5. **NLM** W1

NE697AL. **CODEN** NYMQDG. Documents available from BIOSIS Document Express, CASDDS.
**Ind/Abst** Biol. Abstr. (1988-); Chem. Abstr.

US/0028-7628
**NEW YORK STATE JOURNAL OF MEDICINE.** ***Ceased.*** [N. Y. State j. med.]. **Added/Corp** New York State Medical Association. Medical Society of the State of New York (1807- ). Vol. 1, Jan. 1901-Ceased with Issue for March 1993. Academic Scholarly Publication. English. mo. Medical Society of the State of New York, 420 Lakeville Road, Lake Success NY 11042. **Tel** (516)488-6100, FAX (516)488-1267. **ED** Pascal James Imperato. **LC** R11; .N74. **DD** 610.5. **NLM** W1 NE885. **CODEN** NYSJAM. **Bk Rev. Ad Acc. Pr Rev. Circ:** 28,000 (ctrl). Documents available from The Genuine Article, BIOSIS Document Express, CASDDS. ***Continues*** *Transactions. New York State Medical Association for the Year, 1044-6443;* ***Absorbed*** *Medical Society of the State of New York. Transactions.*
**Desc:** Peer reviewed general medical journal; independent editorial content emphasis on commentary, research, and news.
**Ind/Abst** Biol. Abstr.; Chem. Abstr.; Crim. Penol. Police Sci. Abstr.; Cumul. Index Nurs. Allied Health Lit.; Curr. Contents Clin. Med.; EMBASE; Energy Res. Abstr.; Index Med.; Index Vet.; Int. Aerosp. Abstr.; Iowa Drug Inf. Serv. (1969-); Mod. Med.; Nutr. Res. Newsl.; Life Sci. Collect.; PESTDOC; Protozoolog. Abstr.; Psychol. Abstr. (1927-); PsycINFO; PsycLit; Res. Alert [Full Cov.]; Rev. Med. Vet. Mycology; Risk Abstr.; Saf. Health Work; Sci. Cit. Index; SCISEARCH; Soc. Sci. Cit. Index [Select. Cov.]; SportSearch.

NZ/1171-0195
**NEW ZEALAND JOURNAL OF MEDICAL LABORATORY SCIENCE.** (NEW ZEALAND JOURNAL OF MEDICAL LABORATORY SCIENCE : OFFICIAL PUBLICATION OF THE NEW ZEALAND INSTITUTE OF MEDICAL LABORATORY SCIENCE INCORPORATED.). [N.Z. j. med. lab. sci.]. **Added/Corp** New Zealand Institute of Medical Laboratory Science. **VFOAT** Medical Laboratory Science. Vol. 45, No. 1 (Mar. 1991)-. Periodical. English. qt (Mar., May, Aug., Nov.). 33.00NZ$ New Zealand; 39.60NZ$ other. New Zealand Journal of Medical Laboratory, PO Box 9095 Newmarket, Auckland New Zealand. **Tel** 011 64 093797440. **NLM** W1; NE973L. **CODEN** NZJMEV. **Bk Rev. Ad Acc. Pr Rev. Circ:** 1,500 (ctrl). Documents available from BIOSIS Document Express. ***Continues*** *New Zealand Journal of Medical Laboratory Technology, 0028-8349.*
**Ind/Abst** Biol. Abstr. (1991-); Cumul. Index Nurs. Allied Health Lit.

NZ/0028-8446
**NEW ZEALAND MEDICAL JOURNAL.** [N. Z. med. j.]. **Added/Corp** Medical Association of New Zealand. (1887)-. Academic Scholarly Publication. English. Twenty-two times a year. 236.25NZ$ New Zealand; $135.00 other. New Zealand Medical Journal, PO Box 156, Wellington New Zealand. **Tel** 011 64 4 472-4741, FAX 011 64 4 471-0838. **ED** R.G. Robinson. **NLM** W1 NE977. **CODEN** NZMJAX. **[CCC]. Bk Rev. Ad Acc. Pr Rev. Circ:** 5,500. Documents available from The Genuine Article, BIOSIS Document Express, CASDDS.
**Desc:** Journal of the New Zealand Medical Association. Original clinical articles, related to medical practice and health care. Includes correspondence and news.
**Ind/Abst** Biodeter. Abstr. (1991-); Biol. Abstr.; Chem. Abstr.; Cumul. Index Nurs. Allied Health Lit.; Curr. Contents Clin. Med.; Dairy Sci. Abstr.; Dev. Med. Child Neurol.; EMBASE [Select. Cov.]; Helminthol. Abstr. (19??-19??); Highw. Res. Abstr.; Index Med.; Iowa Drug Inf. Serv. (1969-); Nutr. Abstr. Rev., Ser. A, Hum. Exp.; Nutr. Res. Newsl.; Life Sci. Collect.; PESTDOC; Protozoolog. Abstr. (-1989); Res. Alert [Full Cov.]; Rev. Med. Vet. Entomol.; Rev. Med. Vet. Mycology; Risk Abstr.; Saf. Health Work; Sci. Cit. Index; SCISEARCH; Soc. Sci. Cit. Index [Select. Cov.]; SportSearch.

CN/0715-5379
**NEWS / BRITISH COLUMBIA MEDICAL ASSOCIATION.** [News - B.C. Med. Assoc.]. **Added/Corp** British Columbia Medical Association. (1981)-. Periodical. English. British Columbia Medical Association, 115-1665 West Broadway, Vancouver British Columbia V6J 5A4 Canada. **Tel** (604)736-5551, FAX (604)736-4566, (604)733-7317. **ED** Bob Young. **DD** 362.1/09711. **Ad Acc. Circ:** 6,200 (ctrl).
**Desc:** Articles on news, politics and more pertaining to the practice of medicine in British Columbia and/or membership in the British Columbia Medical Association.

US/0196-3856
**NEWS FROM ABMAC.** **Main/Corp** American Bureau for Medical Advancement in China. **VAT** News from American Bureau for Medical Advancement in China. V. 40- Sept. 1979-. English. bm. American Bureau For Medical Advancement In China, 1790 Broadway, New York NY 10010. **LC** HV688.C4; A55. **DD** 362.1/0425/0951. ***Continues*** *ABMAC Bulletin, 0001-0529.*

US/0027-965X
**NEWS (NATIONAL LIBRARY OF MEDICINE (US)).** **See** Library and Information Sciences.

US/0028-9264
**NEWS OF NEW YORK.** **Added/Corp** Medical Society of the State of New York. (19??)-. Periodical. English. mo (12 issues). $36.00. Medical Society of the State of New York, 420 Lakeville Road, Lake Success NY 11042. **Tel** (516)488-6100, FAX (516)488-1267. **ED** Charlotte K. Petersen. **NLM** W1 ME493A. **Ad Acc, Adv Mgr:** Colleen Caplan. **Circ:** 30,000 (ctrl).
**Desc:** Social, political and economic news of the Medical Society of New York State, with emphasis on the people of the society.

US
**NEWSEARCH.** Vol. 1, No. 1 (August 1984)-. Periodical. English. qt. Stuart Pharmaceuticals, Hanby Building, Concourt Plaza, Wilmington DE 19806. **NLM** W1; NE997RD.

CN/0715-2396
**NEWSLETTER / ALBERTA HERITAGE FOUNDATION FOR MEDICAL RESEARCH.** [Newsl. - Alta. Herit. Found. Med. Res.]. **Main/Corp** Alberta Heritage Foundation for Medical Research. (1981)-. Periodical. English. Four times a year. Free. Alberta Heritage Foundation for Medical Research, 10180-101st Street, Suite 3125, Edmonton Alberta T5J 3S4 Canada. **Tel** (403)423-5727, FAX (403)429-3509. **ED** Lois Hammond. **DD** 610/.7/207123. **Circ:** 3,500 (ctrl).

US/0270-2673
**NEWSLETTER - AMERICAN ASSOCIATION OF TISSUE BANKS.** [Newsl. - Am. Assoc. Tissue Banks]. **Main/Corp** American Association of Tissue Banks. Newsletter. English. qt. $100.00 includes annual membership. American Association of Tissue Banks, 1350 Beverly Road/#220A, McLean VA 22101-3917. **Tel** (703)827-9582. **ED** Jeanne Mowe and Pamela Valeiras. **Bk Rev. Circ:** 700 (ctrl).
**Desc:** Informs members about the current affairs in tissue banking, including regulatory and legislative activities affecting the various specialities within the tissue banking community; advises organizations and individuals wishing to establish or expand banking activities; provides updates on actions taken by AATB's BOG; publishes proceedings of meetings, workshops, and special events.

US/1052-7982
**NEWSLETTER / AMERICAN FEDERATION FOR CLINICAL RESEARCH.** **Added/Corp** American Federation for Clinical Research. **VFOAT** American Federation for Clinical Research Newsletter. Vol. 1, No. 1 (Dec. 1988)-. Academic Scholarly Publication. English. Four times a year. $48.00 nonmembers. Slack Inc., 6900 Grove Road, Thorofare NJ 08086. **Tel** (609)848-1000, (800)257-8290, FAX (609)853-5991, telex 517108 SLACK INC VD. **DD** 610. **Ad Acc.** Documents available from BIOSIS Document Express, CASDDS.
**Desc:** Represents a forum for research which links basic science to clinical practice. Each issue includes summaries of emerging avenues of investigation.
**Ind/Abst** Biol. Abstr.; Biotechnol. Res. Abstr.; Chem. Abstr.; Dairy Sci. Abstr.; EMBASE; Helminthol. Abstr.; Index Med.; Index Sci. Rev.; Index Vet.; Rev. Plant Pathol.; Saf. Health Work; Vet. Bull.; Trop. Dis. Bull. (-19??).

US/0250-4294
**NEWSLETTER - IFLA. SECTION OF BIOLOGICAL AND MEDICAL SCIENCES LIBRARIES.** **See** Library and Information Sciences.

US/0363-4671
**NEWSLETTER - INSTITUTE OF MEDICINE.** [Newsl. - Inst. Med.]. **Main/Corp** Institute of Medicine (U.S.). (Dec. 1972)-. Newsletter. English. Six times a year. Free on request. National Academy Press, 2101 Constitution Avenue NW, Lockbox 285, Washington DC 20055. **Tel** (800)624-6242, (202)334-3313, FAX (202)334-2451. **(Subscription address:** Institute of Medicine, Box 285, Washington DC 20055.**)** **NLM** W1 NE998JH.
**Desc:** Information on program and general activities of the Institute of Medicine.

CN/0047-6560
**NEWSLETTER - MEDICAL RESEARCH COUNCIL (OTTAWA).** (NEWSLETTER - MEDICAL RESEARCH COUNCIL.). [Newsl. - Med. Res. Counc.]. **Main/Corp** Medical Research Council (Canada). **VFOAT** Actualites - Conseil de Recherches Medicales. Vol. 1 (Oct. 15, 1970)-. Newsletter. Multiple languages (English and French). qt. Free on request. Medical Research Council / Canada, Jeanne Mance Building, 20th Floor, Ottawa Ontario K1A 0W9 Canada. **Tel** (613)954-1382. ***Absorbed*** *University-Industry Bulletin, 1187-3701.* ***Continued in part by*** *Bulletin, University-Industry Programs, 0838-1380.*

US
**NEWSLETTER (NATIONAL HEAD INJURY FOUNDATION (U.S.)).** ***Title Change.*** (NEWSLETTER / NATIONAL HEAD INJURY FOUNDATION, INC.). **Added/Corp** National Head Injury Foundation (U.S.). (19??)-(19??). Newsletter. English. qt. National Head Injury Foundation, 1776 Massachusetts Avenue Northwest, Washington DC 20036. **Tel** (800)444-6443, (202)296-6443. ***Continued by*** *TBI Challenge.*

US/1047-2517
**NEWSLETTER OF THE AMERICAN INSTITUTE OF STRESS, THE.** [Newsl. Am. Inst. stress]. **Added/Corp** American Institute of Stress. (1988)-. Newsletter. English. mo. $35.00 US; (add $10.00 postage) other. American Institute of Stress, 124 Park Avenue, Yonkers NY 10703. **Tel** (914)963-1200, FAX (914)965-6267. **ED** Paul J Rosch (editor's address: 924 Park Avenue, Yonkers NY 10703; editor's telephone: (914)963-1200). **DD** 616. **Bk Rev**, (Qty: 12 per year). **Circ:** 2,000. ***Continues*** *Practical Stress Management.*
**Desc:** Contains articles on health, medicine, and stress.

US/0378-6781
**NEWSLETTER ON DENGUE, YELLOW FEVER, AND AEDES AEGYPTI IN THE AMERICAS.** **Added/Corp** Pan American Health Organization. Vol. 5, No. 2 (Aug. 1976)-. Periodical. English. qt. Pan American Health Organization, 525 23rd Street Northwest, Office District Sales, Washington DC 20037. **Tel** (202)293-8130, FAX (202)338-0869. **LC** RA644.D4; D45. **DD** 614.5/71/097. **NLM** W1 NE998WM. ***Continues*** *Dengue Newsletter for the Americas, 0376-818X.*

US/0736-4873
**NEWSLETTER - PEOPLE'S MEDICAL SOCIETY (U.S.).** (NEWSLETTER / PEOPLE'S MEDICAL SOCIETY.). [Newsl. - People's Med. Soc. (U.S.)]. **Added/Corp** People's Medical Society (U.S.). **VFOAT** People's Medical Society Newsletter. (Winter 1983)-. Newsletter. English. bm. Free with People's Medical Society membership. People's Medical Society, 462 Walnut Street, Allentown PA 18102. **Tel** (610)770-1670. **ED** Paula Brisco. Index available. **Circ:** 25,000. available on an online database (file 149/Full-Text) from DIALOG.
**Desc:** Focuses on patient's rights, malpractice, second opinions, quality and access to medical care, health insurance, sources of health information, hospital mortality rates and related topics.
**Ind/Abst** Acad. Abstr. Full Text Elite (Jan. 1992-) [Full Txt.]; Acad. Abstr. (Jan. 1992-); Acad. Search (Jan. 1992-); Consum. Health Nutr. Index (Jan. 1990); Health Index (1989-); Health Period. Database [Full Txt.]; Health Ref. Cent. (Jan. 1989-) [Full Txt.] [Full Cov.]; Health Source (Jan. 1992-); INFO-SOUTH Abstr.; Mag. Artic. Summar. Elite (Jan. 1992-) [Full Txt.]; Mag. Artic. Summar. CD-ROM (Jan. 1992-); Mag. Search.

AT/0816-8059
**NEWSLETTER - SCHOOL OF MEDICAL EDUCATION, UNIVERSITY OF NEW SOUTH WALES.** (NEWLETTER.). [Newsl. - Sch. Med. Educ. Univ. N. S. W.]. **Added/Corp** University of New South Wales. School of Medical Education. Regional Teacher Training Centre for Health Personnel. (Dec.-Jan. 1984)-. Periodical. English. bm. **NLM** W1; NE997TN. ***Continues*** *Newsletter (University of New South Wales. Centre for Medical Education Research and Development), 0158-9121.*

US/1057-6371
**NEWSLINE / AMERICAN MEDICAL ASSOCIATION AUXILIARY, INC.** [Newsline - Am. Med. Assoc., Aux.]. **Added/Corp** American Medical Association. Auxiliary. Vol. 1, No. 1 (Aug. 1991)-. Periodical. English. bm. $5.00. Newsline, American Medical Association Auxilary, 515 North State Street, Chicago IL 60610. **DD** 610. **NLM** W1; NE996YL. ***Formed by the union of*** *AMA-ERF News; County Connection; Health Projects News; Legislation News; Membership News* ***and*** *National News.*

NE/0922-744X
**NG. NIEUWSBLAD GEZONDHEIDSZORG.** ***Ceased.*** (NG). [NG, Nieuwsbl. gezondheidsz.]. **VFOAT** Nieuwsblad Gezondheidszorg. (1989)-(1993). Periodical. Dutch. mo. Mediselect BV, Postbus 28091, 3838 ZH Hoogland Netherlands. **Tel** 011 31 33 808020, FAX 00 31 33 805881. **UDC** 613/614. **Ad Acc. Circ:** 13,000 (ctrl).
**Desc:** General information on medical, economical, and political issues for medical target groups.

US
**NHIC NEWSLETTER.** Newsletter. English. sa. Free. National Health Information Council, Room 1514 Jeannie Mance Building, Ottawa ONT K1A 0K9 Canada. **Tel** (613)957-0690, FAX (613)941-4539.

US/0161-1607
**NHRC REPORT.** [NHRC rep.]. **Main/Corp** Naval Health Research Center. **Added/Corp** Naval Health Research Center. Report. **VAT** Naval Health Research Center Report. (197?)-. English. an. Department of the Navy Navy Health Research Center, Commanding Officer, PO Box 85122, San Diego CA 92138-9174. **Tel** (619)553-8428. **ED** Brenda M Crooks. **LC** RC981; .N29a. **DD** 613/.088359. **NLM** W2 A5 N19N. **Circ:** 500 (ctrl).

*Continues Abstracts of Completed Research - Naval Health Research Center, 0164-0518.*
**Desc:** Command historical summary.
**Ind/Abst** Psychol. Abstr. (1975-).

JA/0029-0424
**NICHIDAI IGAKU ZASSHI.** [Nichidai igaku zasshi]. **Added/Corp** Nihon Daigaku Igakkai. **VFOAT** Nihon University Medical Journal; Journal of Nihon University Medical Association. (1937)-. Academic Scholarly Publication. Japanese (summaries and/or abstracts in English). mo. Nihon Daigaku Igakkai, (Nihon University Medical Assoc.), 30-1, Oyaguchi Kamicho, Itabashiku, Tokyoto 173, Japan. **NLM** W1 NI348. **CODEN** NICHAS. Documents available from BIOSIS Document Express, CASDDS.
**Ind/Abst** Biol. Abstr.; Chem. Abstr.; EMBASE.

GW/0028-9795
**NIEDERSACHSISCHES ARZTEBLATT.** Vol. 1 (1947)-. Periodical. German. sm. Schluetersche Verlag Druckerei, Postfach 5440, D-30054 Hannover Germany. **Tel** 011 49 511 85500, FAX 011 49 511 1236400, telex 923978. **NLM** W1 NI376.

GW/0300-5224
**NIEREN- UND HOCKDRUCKKRANKHEITEN.** [Nieren-Hochdruckkr.]. (1972)-. Academic Scholarly Publication. German. mo. DM228.00. Dustri-Verlag, Dr Karl Feistle, Postfach 49, D 82032 Deisenhofen Germany. **Tel** 011 49 89 6138610, FAX 011 49 89 6135412. **NLM** W1 NI376V. **CODEN** NIHOD9. **[CCC]. Bk Rev. Ad Acc. Pr Rev.** ctrl circ. Documents available from The Genuine Article, CASDDS.
**Ind/Abst** Chem. Abstr.; EMBASE; Life Sci. Collect.; Res. Alert [Select. Cov.]; SCISEARCH.

NR/0331-4316
**NIGERIAN JOURNAL OF MEDICAL SCIENCES.** [Niger. j. med. sci.]. V. 1- Jan./Mar. 1979-. Academic Scholarly Publication. English. qt. **NLM** W1 NI392E. **CODEN** NJMSDJ. Documents available from CASDDS.
**Ind/Abst** Chem. Abstr.

NR/0300-1652
**NIGERIAN MEDICAL JOURNAL.** [Niger. med. j.]. **Added/Corp** Nigeria Medical Association. Vol. 1 (Jan. 1971)-. Periodical. English. bm. $136.00 US; $168.00 other. Nigerian Medical Association, PO Box 60382, Ikoyi Lagos Nigeria. **NLM** W1 NI41. **CODEN** NGMDAI. Documents available from BIOSIS Document Express. ***Continues** Journal of the Nigeria Medical Association, 0300-1652.*
**Ind/Abst** Biol. Abstr.; Index Med.

CN/0849-2646
**NIGHTINGALE (OTTAWA).** (THE NIGHTINGALE.). [Nightingale]. **Added/Corp** Nightingale Research Foundation. Vol. 1, No. 3 (Spring 1990)-. Periodical. English. qt. Free to members. Nightingale Research Foundation, c/o Dr. Byron Hyde, 383 Danforth Avenue, Ottowa, Ontario K2A 0E1 Canada. **DD** 616.7/4/005. ***Continues** Nightingale Research Foundation (Bulletin)., 0849-2638.*

US/8755-4674
**NIH DATA BOOK.** (NIH DATA BOOK : BASIC DATA RELATING TO THE NATIONAL INSTITUTES OF HEALTH.). [NIH data book]. **Added/Corp** National Institutes of Health (U.S.). Office of the Associate Director, Program Planning and Evaluation. National Institutes of Health (U.S.). Division of Research Grants. **VFOAT** N.I.H. Data Book. **VAT** National Institutes of Health Data Book. (1982)-. Periodical. English. an. Free on request. US Department of Health and Human Services National Institutes of Health, 9000 Rockville Pike, Bethesda MD 20892. **Tel** (301)496-9291, FAX (301)496-2443. **ED** Patricia McKinley. **LC** RA11; .D159. **DD** 610/.79. **NLM** W2; A N208b. Index available. **Circ:** 10,000. ***Continues** Basic Data Relating to the National Institutes of Health.*
**Desc:** 46 tables of data on funding of health-related research, primarily by the National Institute of Health.

US
**NIH NEWS & FEATURES / NATIONAL INSTITUTES OF HEALTH. Added/Corp** National Institutes of Health (U.S.). **VFOAT** NIH News and Features. (199?)-. Periodical. English. Twelve times a year. Free. National Institute of Health, 9000 Rockville Pike, Building 31/Room 2B-03, Bethesda MD 20892. **Tel** (301)496-9291. ***Continues** News and Features from NIH.*

US/0164-162X
**NIH RESEARCH ADVANCES. VAT** National Institutes of Health Research Advances. 1976-. Periodical. English. an. US Department of Health and Human Services National Institutes of Health, 9000 Rockville Pike, Bethesda MD 20892. **Tel** (301)496-9291, FAX (301)496-2443. **NLM** W1 N317C. ***Continues** Research Advances, 0098-6593.*

JA/0047-1887
**NIHON HOIGAKU ZASSHI.** [Nippon hoigaku zasshi]. **Added/Corp** Nihon Hoi Gakkai. **VFOAT** Japanese Journal of Legal Medicine. (1944)-. Academic Scholarly Publication. Japanese. bm. $188.00. Nihon Hoigakkai, (Medico-Legal Soc. of Japan), Tokyo Daigaku Igakubu, Hoigaku Kyoshitsu, 3-1, Hongo 7 Chome, Bunkyoku, Tokyoto 113, Japan. **(Subscription address:** Japan Publications Trading Company, Ltd., PO Box 5030, Tokyo International, Tokyo 100-31 Japan.**) CODEN** NHOZAX. Documents available from CASDDS.
**Ind/Abst** Chem. Abstr.; EMBASE; Index Med.

JA/0916-085X
**NIHON IYO MASU SUPEKUTORU GAKKAI KOENSHU. VFOAT** Proceedings of the Japanese Society for Biomedical Mass Spectrometry2. (1988)-. Academic Scholarly Publication. Multiple languages. an. **DD** 545.33. Documents available from CASDDS. ***Continues** Iyo Masu Kenkyukai Koenshu, 0910-870X.*
**Ind/Abst** Chem. Abstr.

JA
**NIHON KAGAKU RYOHO GAKKAI SOKAI SHOROKUSHU. Main/Corp** Nihon Kagaku Ryoho Gakkai. Japanese. mo. ¥10,000 Japan; $140.00 other. Nihon Kagaku Ryoho Gakkai, (Japan Soc. of Chemotherapy), 20-8, Kamiosaki 2 Chome, Shinagawaku, Tokyoto 141, Japan. **LC** RM260; .N53A. **Ad Acc. Circ:** 4,500 (ctrl).

JA/0386-3980
**NIHON RAIGAKKAI ZASSHI.** (NIPPON RAI GAKKAI ZASSHI.). [Nihon Raigakkai zasshi]. **Added/Corp** Nihon Rai Gakkai. **VFOAT** Japanese Journal of Leprosy. Vol. 46 (Jan./Mar. 1977)-. Academic Scholarly Publication. Japanese (summaries and/or abstracts in English; table of contents in English). Four times a year. ¥6000. Japanese Leprosy Association, 2 1 4 Chome Aobacho Higashi, Murayama Shi Tokyo Japan. **Tel** 011 81 3 342391821. **NLM** W1 NI927V. **CODEN** NRGZDW. Documents available from BIOSIS Document Express, CASDDS. ***Continues** Repura, 0024-1008.*
**Ind/Abst** Biol. Abstr.; Chem. Abstr.; EMBASE; Index Med.; Trop. Dis. Bull.

JA/0047-1852
**NIHON RINSHO.** [Nihon rinsho]. **VFOAT** Japanese Journal of Clinical Medicine; Nippon Rinsho. (1943)-. Periodical. Japanese. mo. $464.50. Nippon Rinshosha, (Nippon Rinshosha Co., Ltd.), 3-1, Doshomachi, Higashiku, Osakashi, Osakafu 541, Japan. **(Subscription address:** Japan Publications Trading Company, Ltd., PO Box 5030, Tokyo International, Tokyo 100-31 Japan.**) NLM** W1 NI928M. ***Formed by the union of** Chuo Igaku; Gendai No Igaku; Jikken Chiryo; Osaka Iji Shinshi; Rinko; Rinsho to Yakubutsu **and** Yuseigaku.*
**Ind/Abst** Index Med.

JA
**NIHON TEITAION KENKYUKAI KAISHI. Added/Corp** Nihon Teitaion Kenkyukai. **VFOAT** Journal of the Japanese Society for Hypothermia. (1981)-. Academic Scholarly Publication. Japanese (summaries and/or abstracts in English). sa. Nihon Teitaion Kenkyukai Jimukyoku, (Japanese Soc. for Hypothermia), Kokuritsu Shoni Byoin Shinzo, Kekkan Geka, 35-31, Taishido, 3 Chome, Setagayaku, Tokyoto 154, Japan. **NLM** W1; NI429R. Documents available from CASDDS.
**Ind/Abst** Chem. Abstr.

JA/0546-0352
**NIHON UNIVERSITY JOURNAL OF MEDICINE, THE.** [Nihon Univ. j. med.]. **Main/Corp** Nihon Daigaku. Igakubu. **VFOAT** Journal of Medicine. Vol. 1 (1959)-. Academic Scholarly Publication. English. bm (Feb., Apr., June, Aug., Oct., Dec.). Nihon University School of Medicine, Maruzen Company Ltd, PO Box 5050, 100-31 Tokyo Japan. **Tel** 011/81/3/2789223, FAX 011/81/3/274/2270, telex 781/26517. **ED** Yukiyasu Sezai. **NLM** W1 NI431. **CODEN** NUMDAE. Documents available from BIOSIS Document Express, CASDDS.
**Desc:** Provides a channel for the publication of original contributions on the medical science.
**Ind/Abst** Biol. Abstr. (19??-); Chem. Abstr. (19??-); EMBASE (19??-) [Select. Cov.]; SEA Abstr. (19??-).

JA/0029-0440
**NIIGATA IGAKKAI ZASSHI.** [Niigata Igakkai zasshi]. **Added/Corp** Niigata Igakkai. **VFOAT** Niigata Medical Journal. (1946)-. Academic Scholarly Publication. Japanese. mo. Niigata Igakkai, (Niigata Medical Society), Niigata Daigaku Fuzoku Toshokan, Asahimachi Bunkan, 757, Ichibancho, Asahimachi Doori, Niigatashi, Niigataken 950 Japan. **CODEN** NIGZAY. Documents available from CASDDS. ***Continues** Hokuetsu Igakkai Zasshi.*
**Ind/Abst** Chem. Abstr.

JA/0047-1801
**NIPPON DAICHO KOMONBYO GAKKAI ZASSHI.** (NIPPON DAICHO KOMONBYO GAKKAI ZASSHI JOURNAL OF THE JAPAN SOCIETY OF COLO-PROCTOLOGY.). [Nippon Daicho KomonbyÅo Gakkai zasshi]. **Added/Corp** Nippon Daicho Komonbyo Gakkai. **VFOAT** Journal of the Japan Society of Colo-Proctology. (1967)-. Academic Scholarly Publication. Japanese (summaries and/or abstracts in English). Eight times a year. $160.00. Japan Society of Colo-Proctology, 11-1 Omori-Nishi 6-chome, Ota-ku 143 Tokyo Japan. **(Subscription address:** Kyowa Book Company Inc., 1 38 Kanda Jinbocho Chiyoda-ku, Tokyo 101 Japan.**) NLM** W1 NI888C. **CODEN** NDKGAU. Documents available from BIOSIS Document Express. ***Continues** Nippon Chokucho Komonbyo Gakki Zasshi.*
**Ind/Abst** Biol. Abstr.; EMBASE.

JA/0048-0444
**NIPPON IKA DAIGAKU ZASSHI.** [Nippon Ika Daigaku zasshi]. **Added/Corp** Nippon Ika Daigaku. **VFOAT** Journal of Nippon Medical School. (1923)-. Academic Scholarly Publication. Japanese (Japanese; summaries and/or abstracts in English). qt. Medical Association / Nippon Medical School, 1 5 Sendagi, 1 Chome, Bunkyoku Tokyo Japan. **NLM** W1 NI91. **CODEN** NIDZAJ. Documents available from BIOSIS Document Express, CASDDS.
**Ind/Abst** Biol. Abstr.; Chem. Abstr.; EMBASE [Select. Cov.]; Index Med.

JA/0021-4493
**NIPPON ISHIKAI ZASSHI. JOURNAL OF THE JAPAN MEDICAL ASSOCIATION. Main/Corp** Nihon Ishikai. **Added/Corp** Nippon Ishikai. Sokai Keika. **VFOAT** Journal of the Japan Medical Association; Journal of the Japanese Medical Association. (1937)-. Academic Scholarly Publication. Japanese. mo. **NLM** W1 NI912S. Documents available from CASDDS. ***Continues** Isei.*
**Ind/Abst** Chem. Abstr.; Life Sci. Collect.

JA/0029-0343
**NIPPON ONSEN KIKO BUTSURI IGAKKAI ZASSHI.** [Nippon Onsen Kiko Butsuri Igakkai Zasshi]. **VFOAT** Journal of Japanese Association of Physical Medicine, Balneology and Climatology. (1962)-. Periodical. Japanese. qt. $184.00. Japanese Association of Physical Medicine Balneology and Climatology, Ishizuka Yaesu Building, 5-20 Yaesu 1-chome, Chuo-ku 103 Tokyo Japan. **(Subscription address:** Kyowa Book Company Inc., 1 38 Kanda Jinbocho Chiyoda-ku, Tokyo 101 Japan.**) CODEN** NOKBAO. ***Continues** Nihon Onsen Kiko Gakkai Zasshi, 0369-4240.*
**Ind/Abst** EMBASE.

JA/0301-2581
**NISSEI BYOIN IGAKU ZASSHI. Main/Corp** Nisssei Byoin. **VFOAT** Journal of the Nissei Hospital. (1973)-. Academic Scholarly Publication. Japanese (summaries and/or abstracts in English; table of contents in English). Nissei Byoin, (Nissei Hospital), 3-8, Itachibori 6 Chome, Nishiku, Osakashi, Osakafu 550 Japan. **NLM** W1 NI983Q. Documents available from CASDDS.
**Ind/Abst** Chem. Abstr.

UK/1351-525X
**NITRIC OXIDE.** (19??)-. English. £105.00. SUBIS, Mansion House, 19 Kingfield Road, Sheffield S11 9AS England. **Tel** 011 44 114 255 4433, FAX 011 44 114 255 4626.

US/0146-3055
**NLM TECHNICAL BULLETIN, THE.** **See** Library and Information Sciences.

UK/0952-3480
**NMR IN BIOMEDICINE.** [NMR biomed.]. **VFOAT** NIB. Vol. 1, No. 1 (Feb. 1988)-. Periodical. English. Eight times a year. $595.00. John Wiley & Sons Ltd., Baffins Lane, Chichester West Sussex PO19 1UD England. **Tel** 0243 779777, FAX 0243 776128 BTG:JWP001, telex 86290 WIBOOKG. **(Subscription address:** John Wiley / Philadelphia, PO Box 7247, Philadelphia PA 19170.**) ED** John R. Griffiths and Truman R. Brown. **DD** 574. **NLM** W1; N168G. **CODEN** NMRBEF. **[CCC].** Index available. **Bk Rev. Ad Acc.** available on microfilm and microfiche from University Microfilms International (UMI). Documents available from The Genuine Article, Ask*IEEE.
**Desc:** Publishes original papers in which nuclear magnetic resonance spectroscopy is used for investigating basic biochemical and clinical problems. Papers describe advances in the understanding of the biochemistry and physiology of normal and diseased organs, tissues and cells and the application of these advances to the treatment of disease.
**Ind/Abst** Curr. Aware. Biol. Sci., CABS; Curr. Contents Life Sci.; Index Med. (1988-); INSPEC (Feb. 1990-); Life Sci. Collect.; Res. Alert [Full Cov.]; Sci. Cit. Index; SCISEARCH.

NE
**NOBEL LECTURES OF PHYSIOLOGY OR MEDICINE.** ***Ceased.*** (19??)-Series complete. Academic Scholarly Publication. English. ir. Elsevier Science Publishers BV, PO Box 211, 1000 AE Amsterdam Netherlands. **Tel** 011 31 20 5803642, FAX 011 31 20 5862696, telex 15682.

SW/0029-1420
**NORDISK MEDICIN.** [Nord. med.]. **VFOAT** NM. (1939)-. Periodical. Swedish (summaries and/or abstracts in English; table of contents in English). mo (except July and Aug.). Kr215.00 Sweden; Kr255.00 other. Nordisk Medicin, Box 5603, S-114 86 Stockholm Sweden. **Tel** 011 46 8 7903495, 011 46 8 7903496. **NLM** W1 NO211. Index available in last issue of volume--attached. ***Formed by the union of** Hospitalstidende Finskafa Laekaresaellskapets Handlingar; Duodecim; Norsk Magasin for Laegevidenskapen; Medicinsk Revue;*

*Hygiea* **and** *Svenska Laekaresaellskapets Foerhandlingar.*
**Ind/Abst** Index Med.; Nutr. Abstr. Rev., Ser. A, Hum. Exp.; Saf. Health Work; Trop. Dis. Bull.

SW/0303-6480
**NORDISK MEDICINHISTORISK AARSBOK.** [Nord. medicinhist. aarsb.]. **Added/Corp** Medicinhistoriska Museet (Stockholm, Sweden). (1968)-. Periodical. English (Danish, English, French, German, Norwegian and Swedish). an. Museum of Medical History, (Medicinhistoriska Museet), Aasoegatan 146, 116 32 Stockholm Sweden. **Tel** 011 08 6 642 41 66, FAX 011 08 644 02 86. **LC** R538.5; .M42. **DD** 610/.5. **NLM** W1 NO211M. ***Continues*** *Medicinhistorisk Aarsbok, 0078-1061.*
**Ind/Abst** Am. Hist. Life (19??-).

US
**NORTHERN CALIFORNIA MEDICINE.** English. mo. $48.00 (one year), $89.00 (two year). Northern California Medicine, 1611 Telegraph Road, Suite 1201, Oakland CA 94611. **Tel** (510)832-3364, FAX (510)832-3368. **Bk Rev. Ad Acc, Adv Mgr:** Kate Lynn, **Tel** (510)832-3364. **Circ:** 25,000 (ctrl).
**Desc:** Independent medical business newsletter gives up-to-date information in all aspects of the medical and business fields.

GR/0369-5700
**NOSOKOMEIAKA HRONIKA.** (NOSOKOMEIAKA CHRONIKA : DIMENIAIA EKDOSE TES HENOSEOS EPISTEMONIKOU PROSOPIKOU THERAPEUTÂERIOU "HO EUANGELISMOS".). [Nosokom. Hron.]. **Added/Corp** Henosis Epistemonikou Prosopikou TherapÂeuteriou "Ho Euangelismos.". **VFOAT** Nosokomiaka Chronika : Bi-Monthly Publication of the "Evangelismos Hospital" Scientific Society. (19??)-. Academic Scholarly Publication. Greek, Modern. bm. Henoseos Epistemonikou Prosopikou Therapeuteriou ho Euangelismos, Athens 140, Greece. **CODEN** NSKCAL. Documents available from CASDDS.
**Ind/Abst** Chem. Abstr.; EMBASE.

SP
**NOTICIAS MEDICAS.** Spanish. Editores Medicos SA, Calle Gabriela Mistral 2, 28035 Madrid Spain. **Tel** 011 34 1 3860033, 34 1 3860366, FAX 34 1 3739907.

UY
**NOTICIAS : ORGANO OFICIAL DEL SINDICATO MEDICO DEL URUGUAY.** **Added/Corp** Sindicato Medico del Uruguay. (198?)-. Periodical. Spanish (translations available in English). **NLM** W1; NO769.
**Ind/Abst** Trop. Dis. Bull.

IT
**NOTIZIARIO : AITN, IL.** (19??)-. Italian. Four times a year. Free on request. Assoc It Tecnici Neurofisiopat, Corso San Maurizio 12 Bis, 10124 Turin Italy. **Tel** 011 39 11 2399.

ER
**NOUKOGUDE EESTI TERVISHOID. ZDRAVOOKHRNENIE SOVETSKOI ESTONII.** **Added/Corp** Estonia. Tervishoiu Ministeerium. **VFOAT** Zdravookhranenie Sovetskoi Estonii. (1958)-. Periodical. Estonian (summaries and/or abstracts in Russian). bm. $18.00. **(Subscription address:** Victor Kamkin, 4956 Boiling Brook Parkway, Rockville MD 20852.) **LC** R96.E8; N6. **NLM** W1 NO825.

FR/0293-9495
**NOUVELLE GAZETTE DE LA TRANSFUSION : BULLETIN D'INFORMATION DE L'ADTS, LA.** ***Title Change.*** **Added/Corp** ADTS (Association). Vol. 4, No. 25 (Nov./Dec. 1981)-(1992). Bulletin. French. Adts Gazette de la Transfusion, 125 RTE De Stanlingrad Hop Avic, F 93000 Bobigny France. **Tel** 011 33 1 48955671. **NLM** W1; NO834CK. ***Continues*** *Gazette de la Transfusion.* ***Continued by*** *Gazette de la Transfusion (Miribel, France : 1992).*

FR/0246-0122
**NOUVELLE REVUE DE MEDECINE DE TOULOUSE.** ***Ceased.*** [Nouv. rev. med. Toulouse]. Vol. 1, No. 1 (Jan. 1983)-Ceased ?. Academic Scholarly Publication. French. mo. Revue de Medecine de Toulouse, 37 Allees Jules Guesde, Toulouse 31 France. **NLM** W1; NO834FT. Documents available from CASDDS. ***Absorbed*** *Revue de Medecine de Toulouse, 0556-753X.*
**Ind/Abst** Chem. Abstr. (1983-); EMBASE (1983-); Life Sci. Collect. (1983-).

CN/0318-0549
**NOUVELLES DE LA F M O Q (ENGLISH EDITION).** (NOUVELLES DE LA F M O Q.). **Main/Corp** Federation des Medecins Omnipraticiens du Quebec. Vol. 4, April 1975-. Periodical. French. Federation of General Practitioners of Quebec, 1440 St Catherine Street West/Suite 1100, Montreal Quebec H3G 1R8 Canada. **Tel** (514)878-1911, FAX (514)878-4455. **DD** 362.1/09714. ctrl circ. ***Supersedes*** *Federation of General Practitioners of Quebec. F M O Q News, 0318-0557.*

CN/0838-2638
**NOVA SCOTIA MEDICAL JOURNAL, THE.** [N.S. med. j.]. **Added/Corp** Medical Society of Nova Scotia. Vol. 67, No. 1; (Feb. 1988)-. Periodical. English. bm. 25.00Can$ Canada; 30.00Can$ US; 35.00Can$ other. Medical Society of Nova Scotia, 5 Spectacle Lake Drive Business Park, Darmouth, Nova Scotia B3B 1X7 Canada. **Tel** (902)453-0205, FAX (902)454-7488. **ED** J. F. O'Conner. **DD** 610/.9716. **NLM** W1; NO921J. Index available. **Bk Rev. Ad Acc. Circ:** 2,500 (ctrl). ***Continues*** *Nova Scotia Medical Bulletin, 0029-5094.*
**Desc:** Articles on all aspects of medicine.
**Ind/Abst** EMBASE [Select. Cov.]; Nutr. Res. Newsl.

●US
**NTIS ALERT. MEDICINE & BIOLOGY.** **Added/Corp** United States. National Technical Information Service. **VFOAT** Medicine & Biology; NTIS Alert. Medicine and Biology; Medicine and Biology. Vol. 92, No. 01 (Jan. 7, 1992)-. Periodical. English. Twenty-four times a year. $105.00 North America; $145.00 other. National Technical Information Service - NTIS, Room 2027S, 5285 Port Royal Road, Springfield VA 22161. **Tel** (703)487-4630, (703)487-4660, (703)487-4650, FAX (703)321-8547, telex 89-9405. **NLM** ZW1; M48935. ***Continues*** *Medicine & Biology, 0364-6432.*

US/0896-0607
**NUCLEAR MEDICINE (NEW YORK, N.Y.).** (NUCLEAR MEDICINE.). [Nucl. med.]. (1990)-. Monographic series. English. an. Price varies per volume. Gordon & Breach Science Publishers, Inc., PO Box 786, Cooper Station, New York NY 10276. **Tel** (212)206-8900, FAX (212)645-2459. **(Subscription address:** International Publishers Distributor at one of the following addresses: 820 Town Center Drive, Langhorne, PA 19047; or PO Box 90, Reading Berkshire RG1 8JL UK; or Kent Ridge PO Box 1180, Singapore 9111, Republic of Singapore) **NLM** W1; NU124K. ***Continues*** *Monographs in Nuclear Medicine, 0882-6455.*

SP
**NUEVA BIOMETRICA.** Spanish. Biolecta SA, Paseo de la Castellana 268, 28046 Madrid Spain.

US/0892-6204
**NUTRITION UPDATE (SAN CLEMENTE, CALIF.).** (NUTRITION UPDATE. RESEARCH IN HOLISTIC HEALTH AND NUTRITION). [Nutr. update]. (198?)-. Periodical. English. Twelve times a year. $72.00. Nutrition Update, PO Box 216, San Clemente CA 92672. **Tel** (714)498-7359. **ED** Lyn Darnell. **DD** 613. **Circ:** 200 (ctrl).
**Desc:** Abstracts of research from medical journals on nutritions and preventive medicine.

KO/0254-5985
**NYEIBAN NUIHAG HOI JI.** (YEBANG UIHAKHOE CHI.). [Nyeiban nuihag hoi ji]. **Main/Corp** Taehan Yebank Uihakhoe. **VFOAT** The Korean Journal of Preventive Medicine. Began in 1968. Academic Scholarly Publication. English (Korean). **LC** RA421. **NLM** W1; YE463M. **CODEN** YUHCA5. Documents available from CASDDS.
**Ind/Abst** Chem. Abstr.

CN
**OAHA NEWS BULETIN.** English. bm (pubilshed Jan., Mar., May, July, Sep., Nov.). $7.50. Ontario Association Non Profit Homes, 7050 Weston Road, Suite 605, Woodbridge, Ontario, L4L 8G7 Canada. **Tel** (416)851-8821, FAX (416)851-5597. **ED** Donna Cote. **Ad Acc, Adv Mgr:** B. Sherrer, **Tel** (416)884-3710.
**Desc:** Association house organ for non-profit long-term care providers.

●US/1060-3220
**O&P BUSINESS NEWS.** **See** Business.

●US/1071-7323
**OBESITY RESEARCH.** [Obes. res.]. **Added/Corp** North American Association for the Study of Obesity. (1993)-. Periodical. English. bm. $180.00 (Institutions), $105.00 (Individuals) US; $200.00 (Institutions), $130.00 (Individuals) Other. North American Study Obesity, 6400 Perkins Road, Baton Rouge LA 70808. **Tel** (504)765-0934, FAX (504)765-0935. **ED** George A. Bray. **DD** 616. **NLM** W1; OB402KC. Index available (Published in November). **Bk Rev. Ad Acc. Pr Rev. Circ:** 450 (ctrl).

US/0279-9529
**OBSERVER (PHILADELPHIA, PA.).** (AMERICAN COLLEGE OF PHYSICIANS OBSERVER.). [Observer]. **Added/Corp** American College of Physicians. **VFOAT** Observer. Vol. 1, No. 1/2 (Jan./Feb. 1981)-. Periodical. English. mo. $12.00. American College of Physicians, 6th Street and Race Street, Independence Mall West, Philadelphia PA 19106-1572. **Tel** (215)351-2600, (800)523-1546. **(Subscription address:** American College of Physicians, PO Box 7777 R 0320, Philadelphia PA 19175.) **NLM** W1 AM326R. **[CCC].** ***Continues*** *Forum on Medicine.*
**Ind/Abst** Hospit. Health Admin. Index (1981-1987).

UK
**OCCASIONAL PAPER.** **Added/Corp** Royal College of General Practitioners. (1991)-. Monographic series. English. ir. Price varies per volume. World Wide Subscription Services, Unit 4, Gibbs Reed Farm, East Sussex TN5 7HE England. **Tel** (0580)200657, FAX (0580)200616. **NLM** W1; OC544ZB. ***Continues*** *Journal of the Royal College of General Practitioners. Occasional Paper.*

UK
**OCCASIONAL PAPERS / NUFFIELD PROVINCIAL HOSPITALS TRUST.** No. 1 (1984)-. Monographic series. English. Price varies per volume. **NLM** W1; OC544ZD.

●UK/1351-0711
**OCCUPATIONAL AND ENVIRONMENTAL MEDICINE.** **See** Industrial Health and Safety.

US
**OCCUPATIONAL MEDICAL DIGEST, THE.** Vol. 1, No. 1 (Jan. 1988)-. Periodical. English. Twelve times a year. $225.00. Seak Inc., PO Box 729, East Falmouth MA 02541. **Tel** (508)548-7023, FAX (508)540-8304. **ED** Steven Bahitsky. ctrl circ. available in Loose-leaf.

●UK/0962-7480
**OCCUPATIONAL MEDICINE.** **Added/Corp** Society of Occupational Medicine. Vol. 42, No. 1 (Feb. 1992)-. Periodical. English. Six times a year. $187.00 The Americas; £125.00 other. Butterworth Heinemann Publishers, Linacre House, Jordan Hill, Oxford OX2 8DP England. **Tel** 011 44 865 310366. **(Subscription address:** Elsevier Science Ltd. Oxford Fulfillment Centre, PO Box 800, Kidlington, Oxford OX5 1DX United Kingdom.) **NLM** W1; OC583W. **CODEN** OCMEE8. Documents available from The Genuine Article, BIOSIS Document Express. ***Continues*** *Journal of the Society of Occupational Medicine, 0301-0023.*
**Ind/Abst** Biol. Abstr.; Coal Abstr.; EMBASE; Index Med.; Ind. Hyg. Dig. (1992-); Life Sci. Collect.; Pollut. Abstr. Indexes; Res. Alert [Select. Cov.]; Saf. Health Work; Soc. Sci. Cit. Index [Select. Cov.].

JA/0472-4674
**OCHANOMIZU IGAKU ZASSHI.** [Ochanomizu igaku zasshi]. **VFOAT** The Ochanomizu Medical Journal; Ochanomizu Medical Journal. Began in 1952. Academic Scholarly Publication. Japanese. qt. Tokyo Ikashika Daigaku, 3 Yushima, Bunkyo-ku Tokyo Japan. **ED** Hinoyuki Oshima, Shin-ich Shina and Takehito Takano. **CODEN** OCIZAD. ctrl circ. Documents available from CASDDS. ***Supersedes*** *Ochanomizu Gakkai Shi.*
**Ind/Abst** Chem. Abstr.

US/1050-0650
**OCULAR THERAPEUTICS AND MANAGEMENT.** [Ocul. ther. manage.]. Vol. 1, No. 1 (Mar./Apr. 1990)-. Periodical. English. bm. $69.00. Ocular Therapeutics and Management, 4765 Woodvale Drive, Atlanta GA 30327. **Tel** (404)252-0639, FAX (404)252-0326. **DD** 617.

●US/0000-1406
**OFFICIAL AMERICAN BOARD OF MEDICAL SPECIALTIES (ABMS) DIRECTORY OF BOARD CERTIFIED MEDICAL SPECIALISTS, THE.** (THE OFFICIAL ABMS DIRECTORY OF BOARD CERTIFIED MEDICAL SPECIALISTS.). [Off. Am. Board Med. Spec. (ABMS) dir. board certif. med. spec.]. **Added/Corp** American Board of Medical Specialties. **VFOAT** Directory of Board Certified Medical Specialists; Official American Board of Medical Specialties Directory of Board Certified Medical Specialists. **VAT** Official American Board of Medical Specialists Directory of Board Certified Specialists. 26th Ed. (1994)-. English. an. $425.00. Marquis Who's Who, A Reed Reference Publishing Company, Part of Reed International PLC, 121 Chanlon Road, New Providence NJ 07974. **Tel** (908)464-6800, (800)521-8110, FAX (908)665-6688, telex 138 755. **LC** R712.A1; O335. **DD** 610.69/52/02573. **NLM** W 22; AA1 O32. **[CCC].** ***Formed by the union of*** *Directory of Medical Specialists, 0070-5829* ***and*** *Official American Board of Medical Specialties (ABMS) Directory of Board Certified Medical Specialists, 0000-1406.*
**Desc:** Gives current information on practicing physicians - name, address, telephone number, medical school and year of degree to current academic appointments, academic titles, fellowships, etc

US/0000-1406
**OFFICIAL AMERICAN BOARD OF MEDICAL SPECIALTIES (ABMS) DIRECTORY OF BOARD CERTIFIED MEDICAL SPECIALISTS, THE.** ***Title Change.*** [Off. Am. Board Med. Spec. (ABMS) dir. board certif. med. spec.]. **Added/Corp** American Board of Medical Specialties. ABMS Research and Education Foundation.

VFOAT Directory of Board Certified Medical Specialists; Official ABMS Directory of Board Certified Medical Specialists. **VAT** Official American Board of Medical Specialties Directory of Board Certified Medical Specialists. (1993)-(1993). English. be (main volume published in even years, supplement in odd years). Marquis Who's Who, A Reed Reference Publishing Company, Part of Reed International PLC, 121 Chanlon Road, New Providence NJ 07974. **Tel** (908)464-6800, (800)521-8110, FAX (908)665-6688, telex 138 755. **LC** R729.5.S6; A25. **DD** 610. **NLM** W 22; AA1 O32. **[CCC].** available on magnetic tape and CD-ROM. ***Continues*** *ABMS Compendium of Certified Medical Specialists, 0884-1543.* ***Merged with*** *Directory of Medical Specialists, 0070-5829* ***to form*** *Official ABMS Directory of Board Certified Medical Specialists, 0000-1406.*

DK/0108-5344
**OFTALMOLOG.** [Oftalmolog]. (1981)-. Periodical. Multiple languages. Four times a year (Feb., May, Sept., Nov.). kr195.00. Scriptor Publisher APS, Valbygardsvej 64, 2500 Valby Copenhagen Denmark. **Tel** 011 45 1 31174113, FAX 011 45 1 31171947. **DD** 617.7. **CODEN** 61.67.

US/0892-2454
**OHIO MEDICINE.** (OHIO MEDICINE : JOURNAL OF THE OHIO STATE MEDICAL ASSOCIATION.). [Ohio med.]. **Added/Corp** Ohio State Medical Association. **VFOAT** Ohio State Medical Journal. Vol. 83, No. 1 (Jan. 1987)-. Periodical. English. mo. $35.00 US; $82.00 others. Ohio State Medical Association, 1500 Lake Shore Drive, Columbus OH 43204. **Tel** (614)486-2401. **ED** Karen S. Edwards. **DD** 610. **NLM** W1; OH37H. **Ad Acc, Adv Mgr:** G. Auigley, **Tel** (513)779-7177. **Circ:** 14,000-15,000 (ctrl). ***Continues*** *Ohio State Medical Journal, 0030-1124.*
**Desc:** For member physicians of the Ohio State Medical Association. Features healthcare reform, legislation and legal news related to the OSMA.
**Ind/Abst** EMBASE [Select. Cov.]; Energy Res. Abstr. (1987-); Index Med. (1987-); Life Sci. Collect. (1987-).

CN/0831-6465
**OMNI.** (L'OMNI : BULLETIN DE L'ASSOCIATION DES MEDECINS OMNIPRATICIENS DE MONTREAL.). [Omni]. **VFOAT** Omni. Vol. 1, No. 1 (Jan. Feb. 1978)-. Bulletin. French. Free. Association des Medecins Omnipracticiens de Montreal, Bureau 1100, 1440 Ouest rue Ste-Catherine, Montreal Quebec H3G 1R8 Canada. **DD** 610.69/52/06071427.

IT/0390-6825
**OMNIA MEDICA ET THERAPEUTICA. ARCHIVIO.** [Omnia med. ther. Arch.]. Academic Scholarly Publication. Italian. qt. Price varies per volume. Edizione Omnia Medica, Via S Michele Degli Scalzi 63, Pisa Italy. **NLM** W1 OM884D. **CODEN** OMTAAT. Documents available from BIOSIS Document Express, CASDDS.
**Ind/Abst** Biol. Abstr. (-1976); Chem. Abstr. (1972-1980).

CN/1195-0242
**OMNIPRATICIEN (SCARBOROUGH).** (L'OMNIPRATICIEN.). [Omnipraticien]. **Added/Corp** Thomson Healthcare Communications. April 22, (1993)-. Periodical. French. sm. 45.32Can$ (one year); 65.00Can$ (two years). Thomson Healthcare, 1120 Birchmount Road, Suite 200, Scarborough Ontario M1K 5G4 Canada. **Tel** (905)750-8900. **DD** 362.1.

●US/1059-2725
**ONLINE JOURNAL OF CURRENT CLINICAL TRIALS, THE.** (THE ONLINE JOURNAL OF CURRENT CLINICAL TRIALS [COMPUTER FILE].). [Online j. curr. clin. trials]. **Added/Corp** American Association for the Advancement of Science. OCLC. **VFOAT** Current Clinical Trials. (1992)-. Periodical. English. ir. $110.00. American Association for the Advancement of Science, 1333 H Street Northwest, Washington DC 20005. **Tel** (202)326-6400, (203)326-6417, (202)326-6430, FAX (202)842-1065. **(Subscription address:** Subscription Department OJC, PO Box 3000, Denville NJ 07834.**) ED** Maria Lebron. **DD** 616. **CODEN** OJCTEI. cum. index. available on microfiche from American Association Advancement Science; available on an online database from American Association Advancement Science. Documents available.
**Desc:** Publishes original research reports, reviews, meta-analyses and editorials on trials of therapies, procedures and other interventions relevant to care in all fields.

CN/0030-302X
**ONTARIO MEDICAL REVIEW. Added/Corp** Ontario Medical Association. Vol. 10, No. 3 (June 1943)-. Periodical. English. mo. 47.00Can$ Canada; 54.00Can$ US; 70.00Can$ other. Ontario Medical Association, 525 University Avenue, Suite 300, Toronto Ontario M5G 2K7, Canada. **Tel** (416)599-2580. **ED** R. David Fletcher. **NLM** W1 ON672. Index available. **Bk Rev. Ad Acc. Circ:** 17,500 (ctrl). ***Continues*** *Ontario Medical Association. Bulletin.*
**Desc:** Contains articles on health care delivery, medical economics, politics, education, physicians' lifestyles, and medico-legal matters.

CN/0228-877X
**ONTARIO MEDICAL TECHNOLOGIST / ONTARIO SOCIETY OF MEDICAL TECHNOLOGISTS.** [Ont. Med. Technol.]. **VFOAT** Technologist. Vol. 1, No. 1 (March 1980)-. Periodical. English. qt. $50.00 U.S. Ontario Medical Technologist, Suite 600/234 Eglinton Avenue East, Toronto Ontario M4P 1K5 Canada. **Tel** (416)485-6768. **ED** Peter Drury. **DD** 610.73/7/05. **Bk Rev. Ad Acc. Circ:** 5,000 (ctrl). ***Continues*** *Newsletter (Ontario Society of Medical Technologists), 0380-1888.*
**Desc:** Scientific articles dealing with medical laboratory technology.

GW/0178-1715
**OP-JOURNAL.** [OP-J.]. **VFOAT** Operationssaal-Journal. (1985)-. Periodical. German. tq. $59.00. Georg Thieme Verlag Stuttgart, Postfach 301120, D 70451 Stuttgart Germany. **Tel** 011 49 711 89310, FAX 011 49 711 8931298, telex 7 252 275 GTVD. **(Subscription address:** Thieme Medical Publishers Inc., 381 Park Avenue South, New York NY 10016.**) UDC** 61.

US
**OPERATING ROOM PRODUCT DIRECTORY : ORPD / ASSOCIATION OF OPERATING ROOM NURSES, INC.** ***Title Change.*** **Added/Corp** Association of Operating Room Nurses. **VFOAT** ORPD; AORN's OR Product Directory; O.R. Product Directory; OR Product Directory. 3rd Ed. (1990)-(1993). English. Association of Operating Room Nurses, Inc., 2170 South Parker Road, Suite 300, Denver CO 80231-5711. **Tel** (303)755-6300, (303)755-6304. **NLM** WO 22; AA1 O61. ***Continues*** *O.R. Product Directory.* ***Continued by*** *O.R. Product Directory (Denver, Colo. : 1993).*

US
**OPERATING ROOM RISK MANAGEMENT.** (19??)-. English. mo. $365.00. ECRI Emergency Care Research Institute, 5200 Butler Pike, Plymouth Meeting PA 19462. **Tel** (215)825-6000, FAX (215)834-1275, telex 510-660-8023.

IT/0392-5153
**OPERATORE SANITARIO, L'.** [Oper. sanit.]. **Added/Corp** ACOS (Association). (19??)-. Periodical. Italian. Three times a year (Apr., Aug., Dec.). L30000 Europe; L35000 other. Association Catt Operatori Sanitari, Via Gregorio VII 111, 00165 Rome Italy. **Tel** 011 39 631953, FAX 011 39 6 631953. **NLM** W1 OP151. **Bk Rev**, (Qty: 12-15). **Ad Acc. Pr Rev. Circ:** 10,000 (ctrl).
**Desc:** Includes information concerning regional chapters of ACOS.

UK
**OPM NEWS (LONDON, ENGLAND).** (OPM NEWS : OFFSHORE PARA-MEDICINE NEWSLETTER.). **VFOAT** Offshore Para-Medicine Newsletter. Newsletter. English. mo. **NLM** W1; OP42.

SW/0030-414X
**OPUSCULA MEDICA.** ***Ceased.*** [Opusc. med.]. **Added/Corp** Stockholm. Sodersjukhuset. (Jan. 1956)-(Dec. 1992). Academic Scholarly Publication. Swedish (summaries and/or abstracts in English). Four times a year. Opuscula Medica Supplementum, Sodersjukhuset, S 100 64 Stockholm Sweden. **NLM** W1 OP94. **CODEN** OPMEAR.
**Ind/Abst** EMBASE [Select. Cov.]; Saf. Health Work; Trop. Dis. Bull.

●UK
**ORAL DISEASES.** (1994)-. Periodical. English. qt. £125.00 UK and EEC countries; £135.00 (surface mail), £162.00 (air mail) other. Macmillan Magazines Ltd., Houndmills, Basingstoke, Hampshire RG21 2XS England. **Tel** 011 44 256 29242, FAX 011 44 256 812358, telex 858493.
**Desc:** Covers all research related to oral diseases, including the basic sciences, clinical research, and analytical epidemiology.

HU/0030-6002
**ORVOSI HETILAP.** [Orv. hetil.]. **Added/Corp** Magyar Orvosok Szabad Szakszervezete. Orvos-Egeszsegugyi Szakszerve-Zet. **VFOAT** OH. Vol. 1 (June 4, 1857)-. Academic Scholarly Publication. Hungarian (summaries and/or abstracts in German, Russian and English). wk. $128.00. Akademiai Kiado, Publishing House of the Hungarian Academy of Sciences, Prielle Kornelia u. 19-35, H-1117 Budapest Hungary. **Tel** 011 36 1 1811991, FAX 011 36 1 1811991, telex 22-6228 AKNYO H. **(Subscription address:** Kultura, Hungarian Foreign Trading Company, PO Box 149, H-1389 Budapest 12 Hungary (011 36 1 359370)**) LC** R96.H8; O7. **NLM** W1 OR877.
**Ind/Abst** EMBASE; Helminthol. Abstr. (1991-); Index Med.; Protozoolog. Abstr.; SportSearch.

HU/0030-6037
**ORVOSKEPZES (BUDAPEST).** (ORVOSKEPZES.). [Orvoskepzes]. **Added/Corp** Orvosi Tovabbkepzes Koezponti Bizottsag. (1911)-. Periodical. Hungarian. bm. $23.00. **(Subscription address:** Kultura, PO Box 149, H 1389 Budapest 62 Hungary.**) LC** R91; .O7. **NLM** W1 OR881. **CODEN** ORVOAE. Documents available from BIOSIS Document Express.
**Ind/Abst** Biol. Abstr.; EMBASE [Select. Cov.]; Energy Res. Abstr. (Dec. 1979-).

HU/0010-3551
**ORVOSTORTENETI KOZLEMENYEK.** **See** History(General).

JA/0030-6096
**OSAKA CITY MEDICAL JOURNAL.** [Osaka City Med. J.]. (1954)-. Academic Scholarly Publication. English (French and German; summaries and/or abstracts in French and German). sa. Osaka City Medical Center, 4-54 Asahimachi, 1-chome Abeno-ku, 545 Osaka Japan. **NLM** W1 OS104. **CODEN** OCMJAJ. Documents available from BIOSIS Document Express, CASDDS.
**Ind/Abst** Biol. Abstr.; Chem. Abstr.; EMBASE; Energy Res. Abstr.; Index Med.; Nutr. Abstr. Rev., Ser. A, Hum. Exp.

JA/0030-6169
**OSAKA DAIGAKU IGAKU ZASSHI.** (MEDICAL JOURNAL OF OSAKA UNIVERSITY.). [Med. j. Osaka Univ.]. **Added/Corp** Osaka Daigaku. Igakubu. Vol. 1, No. 1 (1949)-. Academic Scholarly Publication. English. ir. University of Tokyo, Faculty of Medicine, 7-3-1 Hongo, Bunkyo-ku, Tokyo 113 Japan. **NLM** W1 ME352H. **CODEN** MJOUAL. Documents available from BIOSIS Document Express, CASDDS.
**Ind/Abst** Biol. Abstr.; Chem. Abstr. (-1985); EMBASE; Index Med.; Saf. Health Work; SEA Abstr.; Trop. Dis. Bull.

JA/0030-6118
**OSAKA IKA DAIGAKU ZASSHI.** [Osaka Ika Daigaku zasshi]. **Added/Corp** Osaka Ika Daigaku Igakkai. Osaka Ika Daigaku. **VFOAT** Journal of Osaka Medical College. (1950)-. Academic Scholarly Publication. Japanese (summaries and/or abstracts in English). qt. $74.00. Osaka Ika Daigaku Igakkai, (Medical Soc. of Osaka Medical College), 2-7, Daigakumachi, Takatsukishi, Osakafu 569 Japan. **(Subscription address:** Japan Publications Trading Company, Ltd., PO Box 5030, Tokyo International, Tokyo 100-31 Japan.**) CODEN** OIDZAU. Documents available from CASDDS. ***Continues*** *Osaka Koto Igaku Senmon Gakko Zasshi.*
**Ind/Abst** Chem. Abstr.

CN/0085-4557
**OSLER LIBRARY NEWSLETTER.** [Osler Lib. newsl.]. **Added/Corp** McGill University. Medical Library. No. 1 (June 1969)-. Newsletter. English. Three times a year. Free on request. McGill University / Osler Library, 3655 Drummond Street, Montreal Quebec H3G 1Y6 Canada. **Tel** (514)398-4720, FAX (514)398-5747. **Circ:** 1,500 (ctrl).
**Desc:** News and articles about the Osler Library and William Osler.

SW/0345-8865
**OSSA.** ***Ceased.*** [Ossa]. Vol. 1 (1974)-(Sept. 1994). Monographic series. English (German; summaries and/or abstracts in Russian). an. University of Stockholm-Ossa, Professor Gejvall, Osteological Research Lab, S 171 71 Solna Sweden. **NLM** W1 OS548. **CODEN** OIJRD5. Documents available from BIOSIS Document Express.
**Ind/Abst** Anthropol. Lit.; Biol. Abstr.; Br. Archaeol. Bibliogr.; GeoRef.

US/0092-9336
**OSTEOPATHIC ANNALS.** ***Ceased.*** [Osteopath. ann.]. Vol. 1 (Oct. 1973)-?. Periodical. English. mo. Haymarket Doyma Inc, 53 Park Place/8th Floor, Suite 1010, New York NY 10007. **Tel** (212)766-7200. **LC** RZ301; .O55. **DD** 615. **NLM** W1 OS801.
**Ind/Abst** EMBASE.

US/0894-3311
**OSTEOPOROSIS UPDATE.** 1987-. English. ir. $79.00. Radiology Research and Education Foundation, 3rd & Parnassus Avenue/Suite C324, San Francisco CA 94143-0628. **DD** 616.

AU/0029-8786
**OSTERREICHISCHE ARZTEZEITUNG.** [Osterr. Arzteztg.]. (1945)-. Periodical. German. Osterreische Arztekammer, Weihburggasse 10-12, A-1010, Wien, Austria. **Tel** (1)5124486. **UDC** 61. **CODEN** OEAEB.
**Ind/Abst** EMBASE [Select. Cov.].

US/0889-5899
**OSTOMY/WOUND MANAGEMENT.** [Ostomy/wound manage.]. **VFOAT** Ostomy Wound Management. (198?)-. Periodical. English. qt. $16.00 (US), $20.00 (other). Health Management Publishing Inc., 550 American Avenue, Circulation Department, King of Prussia PA 19406. **Tel** (215)337-4466, (800)237-7285, FAX (215)337-0890. **DD** 616. **NLM** W1; OS963. ***Continues*** *Ostomy Management, 0274-7944.*
**Ind/Abst** Cumul. Index Nurs. Allied Health Lit.; Health Plan. Adminis.

US/0893-1712
**OT WEEK.** **See** Education-Special Education and Rehabilitation.

●US/1077-1123
**OTOLOGY-NEUROTOLOGY (NEW YORK, N.Y.).** (OTOLOGY-NEUROTOLOGY : OFFICIAL JOURNAL OF THE PROSPER MENIERE SOCIETY.). **Added/Corp** Prosper Meniere Society. (1995)-. Periodical. English. qt. $109.00 (institutions), $85.00 (individuals) US; $134.00 (institutions), $110.00 (individuals) other. Thieme Medical Publishers Inc., 381 Park Avenue South, Suite 1201, New York NY 10016. **Tel** (212)683-5088, (212)683-5089, FAX (212)779-9020, telex 220 862 TSINC UR.

FR
**OTORHINOLARYNGOLOGIE, STOMATOLOGIE, PATHOLOGIE, CERVICOFACIALE, E72.** French. 959.74F France; 1000.00F other. Institut de l'Information Scientifique et Technique Technologie Medecine, 2 Allee du Parc de Brabois, 54514 Vandoeuvre Nancy France. **Tel** 011 33 83 504664. ***Continues*** *Pascal Explore E72 : Otorhinolaryngologie, Stomatologie, Pathologie, Cervicofaciale.*

FR/0048-2366
**OUEST MEDICAL PARIS.** [Ouest Med. Paris]. (1948)-. Periodical. French. Ten times a year. 259.55F France; 520.00F other. Medialogues, 58 Avenue de la Marne, 96200 Asnieres France. **Tel** 011 33 1 47931804. **UDC** 61. **Pr Rev.**
**Ind/Abst** Virol. AIDS Abstr.

US
**OUTCOMES MEASUREMENT AND MANAGEMENT.** (19??)-. English. bm (6 issues). $150.00. Zitter Group & Center, 90 New Montgomery Street, San Francisco CA 94105. **Tel** (415)495-2450. **ED** Susan Keller. **Circ:** 4,000.
**Desc:** Provides outcomes information for medical and pharmaceutical executives.

US/0737-4429
**OUTLOOK / EDUCATIONAL COMMISSION FOR FOREIGN MEDICAL GRADUATES.** [Outlook]. **VFOAT** E.C.F.M.G. Outlook; ECFMG Outlook. Winter 1983-. Periodical. English. qt. Free. Educational Commission for Foreign Medical Graduates, 2000 Pennsylvania Avenue NW/Suite 3600, Washington DC 20006. **Tel** (202)293-9320, FAX (202)457-0751. **ED** Wendy Waddell Steele. **Circ:** 9,000.
**Desc:** International medical education.

US/1056-3172
**OVATION REPORT ON COST EFFECTIVE PRODUCTS, THE.** **Added/Corp** Ovation Healthcare Research, Inc. Vol. 1, No. 1 (1991)-. Periodical. English. qt. Ovation Healthcare Research, 600 Central Avenue, #333, Highland Park IL 60035. **DD** 616.

UK/0030-7661
**OXFORD MEDICAL SCHOOL GAZETTE.** **Added/Corp** Oxford University. Medical School. Vol. 1 (1949)-. Periodical. English. Three times a year. £4.50. Oxford University Press, Walton Street, Oxford OX2 6DP England. **Tel** 011 44 865 56767, FAX 011 44 865 267773, telex 837330 OXPRES G. **(Subscription address:** Oxford University Press / USA, Journals Marketing Department, Oxford University Press, 2001 Evans Road, Cary NC 27513.**)** **NLM** W1 OX621. cum. index.

UK
**OXFORD MONOGRAPHS ON MEDICAL GENETICS.** (1966)-. Monographic series. English. ir. Price varies per volume. Oxford University Press, Walton Street, Oxford OX2 6DP England. **Tel** 011 44 865 56767, FAX 011 44 865 267773, telex 837330 OXPRES G. **(Subscription address:** Oxford University Press / USA, Journals Marketing Department, Oxford University Press, 2001 Evans Road, Cary NC 27513.**)** **ED** Martin Bobrow, Peter S. Harper, Arno G. Motulsky and Charles Scriver.

US/0743-507X
**P & S / THE COLLEGE OF PHYSICIANS AND SURGEONS OF COLUMBIA UNIVERSITY.** **VFOAT** P and S. Began with: Vol. 1, No. 1, issued 1981. Periodical. English. Free. P & S Editor, Office of the Dean, College of Physicians and Surgeons, 630 West 168th Street, New York NY 10032. **Tel** (212)305-3900, (212)305-4521. **ED** Donald F Tapley. **NLM** W1 P129C. **Bk Rev. Circ:** 20,000 (ctrl). ***Continues*** *P & S Alumni Journal, 0742-8421; P&S Alumni Journal.*
**Desc:** A non-technical news and features publication reporting on contemporary issues in medicine, as well as research, teaching, and clinical care activities of faculty and students.

US
**P S R MONITOR.** ir (four to six issues per year). $50.00. Physicians for Social Responsibility, 1000 16th Street NW, Suite 810, Washington DC 20036. **Tel** (202)785-8777. **ED** Sally James. **Circ:** 8,000 (ctrl).
**Desc:** Legislative alert newsletter for PSR members working to prevent nuclear war and other enviornmental catastrophes.

US/8756-0321
**PACIFIC JOURNAL OF ORIENTAL MEDICINE, THE.** (THE PACIFIC JOURNAL OF ORIENTAL MEDICINE : A PUBLICATION OF THE SAN FRANCISCO COLLEGE OF ACUPUNCTURE & ORIENTAL MEDICINE.). **VAT** Pac. J. Orient. Med. Vol. 1, No. 1 (Fall 1984)-. Periodical. English. qt. $10.00 students, $20.00 others. San Francisco College of Acupuncture and Oriental Medicine, 2051 Market Street, San Francisco CA 94114-1363. **LC** R581; .P33. **DD** 610/.95.

US
**PACKAGING OF HEALTHCARE DEVICES AND PRODUCTS.** (1990)-. Proceedings. English. an. $125.00. Technomic Publishing Company, Inc., 851 New Holland Avenue, Box 3535, Lancaster PA 17604. **Tel** (717)291-5609, (800)233-9936, FAX (717)295-4538.
**Desc:** A forum for the presentation of new developments in the area of specialized packaging. Details advances in packaging materials, design, processing, sterilization, function and performance, solid waste management and environmental considerations, legislation and regulation, end-use aspects, and applications and markets.

US/8756-2650
**PAFAMS UPDATE.** (PAFAMS UPDATE / PANAMERICAN FEDERATION OF ASSOCIATIONS OF MEDICAL SCHOOLS.). [PAFAMS update]. **VAT** Panamerican Federation of Associations of Medical Schools Update. Vol. 1, No. 1 (April 1984)-. Periodical. English. Free. Educational Commission for Foreign Medical Graduates, 2000 Pennsylvania Avenue NW/Suite 3600, Washington DC 20006. **Tel** (202)293-9320, FAX (202)457-0751. **DD** 610. **NLM** W1; PA267E. **Circ:** 2,000.
**Desc:** Medical education throughout the Americas.

IT
**PAGINE DI PSICOMOTRICITA.** (19??)-. Italian. Four times a year. L25000. Soc Italiana Psicomotricita, Via Pace 9, 20121 Milan Italy.

NE/0169-1112
**PAIN CLINIC, THE.** [Pain clin.]. Vol. 1, No. 1 (1986)-. Periodical. English. qt. DM210.00. VSP International Science Publishers, Godfried van Seystlaan 47, 3703 BR Zeist Netherlands. **Tel** 011 31 3404 25790, FAX 011 31 3404 32081, telex 40217 USP NL. **(Subscription address:** VSP International Science Publishers, PO Box 346, 3700 AH Zeist Netherlands.**)** **ED** G. M. Wyant and T. P. Nash. **NLM** W1; PA293F. **CODEN** PACLEA. Documents available from The Genuine Article, BIOSIS Document Express.
**Desc:** Focuses on the clinical methods used and the problems involved in the diagnosis and treatment of persistent and recurrent types of pain.
**Ind/Abst** Biol. Abstr. (1986-); EMBASE; Psychol. Abstr. (1986-); PsycINFO; PsycLit; Res. Alert [Full Cov.]; Soc. Sci. Cit. Index [Select. Cov.].

US/0938-9016
**PAIN DIGEST.** [Pain dig.]. Vol. 1, No. 1 (1991)-. Periodical. English. Six times a year. $147.00. Springer-Verlag New York Inc., 175 5th Avenue, New York NY 10010. **Tel** (212)460-1500, telex 232 235 SPB UR. **(Subscription address:** Springer Verlag New York Inc. / for North America, 44 Hartz Way, Secaucus NJ 07096.**)** **ED** P. P. Raj. **LC** RB127; .P33223. **DD** 616/.0472/05. **NLM** W1; PA293K. **CODEN** PADIE6. **[CCC].** available on microfilm and microfiche from University Microfilms International (UMI).
**Desc:** An international multidisciplinary journal. Provides a comprehensive means of surveying developments in anesthesiology, neurology, oncology, physical medicine, psychiatry, orthopaedics and nursing. Gives physicians a compact, reliable source for news of advances in the specialty of pain medicine. Features special pathbreaking articles, information on government policies affecting pain management, insurance issues, and breakthroughs in the industry.

US/1056-294X
**PAIN MANAGEMENT UPDATE.** [Pain manage. update]. **VFOAT** Pain Management. Vol. 1, No. 1 (1991)-. Periodical. English. qt. Free. Neuromed, Inc., 5000-A Oakes Road, Ft. Lauderdale FL 33314. **DD** 616.

●US
**PAIN MEDICINE JOURNAL CLUB JOURNAL.** (1995)-. Periodical. English. bm (6 issues). $75.00 (individuals), $110.00 (institutions) US; $85.00 (individuals), $120.00 (institutions) other. Raven Press, 1185 Avenue of the Americas, 37th Floor, New York NY 10036. **Tel** (212)930-9500, (212)930-9604, FAX (212)869-3495, (212)302-8507, telex 640073.

NE/0921-3287
**PAIN RESEARCH AND CLINICAL MANAGEMENT.** Vol. 1 (1987)-. Monographic series. English. ir. Price varies per volume. Elsevier Science Publishers BV, PO Box 211, 1000 AE Amsterdam Netherlands. **Tel** 011 31 20 5803642, FAX 011 31 20 5862696, telex 15682. **(Subscription address:** Elsevier Science Inc. / New York Books, 655 Avenue of the Americas, New York NY 10010.**)** **NLM** W1; PA296L. **Pr Rev.**

●UK/0968-1302
**PAIN REVIEWS.** (1994/95)-. English. qt. $125.00 (institution), $90.00 (individual) North America; £65.00 (institution), £40.00 (individual) Europe; £75.00 (institution), £50.00 (individual) other. Edward Arnold, 338 Euston Road, London NW1 3BH England. **Tel** 011 44 71 873 6000, FAX 011 44 071 873 6325. **(Subscription address:** Turpin Distribution Services Limited, Blackhorse Road, Letchworth, Hertfordshire SG6 1HN, United Kingdom.**)** **ED** Keith Budd and Wolfgang Hamann.
**Desc:** The primary aim of the journal is not only to present the latest clinical information, but also to bridge the gap between basic science and clinical medicine in complementary paired articles, thus enabling basic scientists and clinicians to keep abreast of new ideas and developments beyond the confines of their particular specialism. The journal encompasses the whole spectrum of pain, its basis and management.
**Ind/Abst** CSA Neuro. Abstr. (19??-).

NE/0167-6482
**PAIN. SUPPLEMENT (AMSTERDAM).** (PAIN. SUPPLEMENT.). [Pain. Suppl.]. **Added/Corp** International Association for the Study of Pain. Vol. 1 (1981)-. English. ir (every 3 years). $97.00. IASP Publications, 909 43rd Street, Suite 306, Seattle WA 98105. **Tel** (206)547-6409. **NLM** W1 PA29A.
**Ind/Abst** Index Med.

UK/0961-4591
**PALLIATIVE CARE INDEX.** [Palliative care index]. **VFOAT** Current Awareness Topics Services. Palliative Care Index. (1991)-. Periodical. English. Twelve times a year. £50.00 UK & ECC; $65.00 others. British Library / Publications Sale Unit, Boston Spa, Wetherby, West Yorkshire LS23 7BQ England. **Tel** 011 44 937 546546 546543, FAX 011 44 937 546333, telex 557381. Index available. **Bk Rev. Ad Acc.** ctrl circ. ***Continues*** *Current Awareness Topics Services. Terminal Care Index, 0953-6779.*
**Desc:** Information and news and on the care of the terminally ill patients.

UK/0269-2163
**PALLIATIVE MEDICINE.** [Palliat. med.]. Vol. 1, No. 1 (1987)-. Periodical. English. qt. $230.00 North America; £148.00 Europe; £159.00 Other. Edward Arnold, 338 Euston Road, London NW1 3BH England. **Tel** 011 44 71 873 6000, FAX 011 44 071 873 6325. **(Subscription address:** Edward Arnold, PO Box 386, Avenel NJ 07001-0386.**)** **ED** D. Doyle. **NLM** W1; PA367H. **CODEN** PAMDE2. Documents available from BIOSIS Document Express.
**Desc:** Dedicated to improving clinical practice in the palliative care of patients with far-advanced disease, this journal is intended for medical, nursing and other related disciplines concerned with patient care. It provides a focus for doctors, nurses, physiotherapists, psychologists, social workers, clergy, administrators, occupational therapists and volunteer organizers. Such a multidisciplinary approach is the hallmark of effective patient care, and the journal is a professional window on that care. The journal publishes original papers, review articles, and case reports. It provides up-to-date information: drug and device assessments, calendars of meetings and employment opportunities.
**Ind/Abst** Biol. Abstr. (1991-); Index Med.

US/1052-1372
**P&T (LAWRENCEVILLE, N.J.).** (P&T : A PEER-REVIEWED JOURNAL FOR FORMULARY MANAGEMENT.). [P&T]. **VFOAT** P and T. **VAT** Pharmacy & Therapeutics; Pharmacy and Therapeutics. Vol. 15, No. 7 (July 1990)-. Periodical. English. mo. $75.00 (institutions), $55.00 (individuals). Excerpta Medica / US, PO Box 3085, Princeton NJ 08543-3085. **Tel** (908)874-8550, FAX (908)874-5611. **(Subscription address:** P & T, PO Box 3000, Denville NJ 07834.**)** **DD** 615. **NLM** W1; P134. **CODEN** PPTTEK. **[CCC].** ***Continues*** *Hospital Therapy, 8750-6831.*
**Desc:** Designed to assist members of pharmacy and therapeutics committees in carrying out their functions. These include formulary management, establishment of medication-related policies and more.

IT/0031-0808
**PANMINERVA MEDICA.** [Panminerva med.]. **Added/Corp** Associazione Medica Italiana. Vol. 1 (May 1959)-. Periodical. English. qt. $90.00 (individuals), $140.00 (institutions). Edizioni Minerva Medica, Corso Bramante 83-85, 10126 Turin Italy. **Tel** 011 39 11 678282, FAX 011 39 11 674502. **ED** Tomaso Oliaro. **NLM** W1 PA494. **CODEN** PMMDAE. **Pr Rev.** available on microfilm from University Microfilms International (UMI). Documents available from The Genuine Article, BIOSIS Document Express, CASDDS.
**Desc:** A review journal survey which summarizes the entire original articles and abstracts of articles published in European journals.
**Ind/Abst** Biol. Abstr.; Chem. Abstr.; Curr. Contents Clin. Med.; Index Med.; Nucl. Sci. Abstr.; Life Sci. Collect.; Res. Alert [Select. Cov.]; SCISEARCH; Soc. Plann. Policy Dev. Abstr.

SP
**PANORAMA ACTUAL DEL MEDICAMENTO.** Spanish. Consejo General de Colegios Oficiales Farmaceuticos, Villanueva 11, 28001 Madrid Spain.

FR
**PANORAMA DU MEDECIN.** French. da. 250.00F. Panorama du Medecin, 37 Avenue des Champs Elysees, F-75008 Paris France. **Tel** 011 33 1 49536800.

UK/0957-4190
**PAPILLOMAVIRUS REPORT.** Vol. 1, No. 1 (Jan. 1990)-. Periodical. English. bm. $140.00 (institution), $100.00 (individual) US; £68.00 (institution), £49.00 (individual) UK & Europe; £84.00 (institution), £62.00 (individual) other. Royal Society of Medicine Press, 1 Wimpole Street, London W1M 8AE England. **Tel** 011 44 71 2902928. **NLM** ZQW 165.5.P2; P213.

PP/0031-1480
**PAPUA NEW GUINEA MEDICAL JOURNAL.** [P. N. G. med. j.]. **Added/Corp** Medical Society of Papua New Guinea. Papua New Guinea. Dept. of Public Health. Vol. 14, No. 3 (Sept. 1971)-. Academic Scholarly Publication. English. qt. k.60.00 institutions; k.50.00 individuals. Medical Society-Papua New Guinea, Box 60, Goroka EHP Papua New Guinea. **Tel** 011 675 712200, FAX 011 675 721998, telex NE 72654. **ED** Michael Alpers. **CODEN** PGMJBP. Index available. **Bk Rev. Ad Acc. Pr Rev. Circ:** 300 (ctrl). available on microfilm from University Microfilms International (UMI). Documents available from The Genuine Article, BIOSIS Document Express. ***Continues** Papua and New Guinea Medical Journal.*
**Desc:** Articles on health, medicine and human biology in Papua, New Guinea and elsewhere.
**Ind/Abst** Biol. Abstr.; Curr. Contents Clin. Med.; EMBASE; Helminthol. Abstr. (1991-); Index Med.; Res. Alert [Select. Cov.]; Rev. Med. Vet. Entomol.; SCISEARCH; Soc. Sci. Cit. Index [Select. Cov.]; Trop. Dis. Bull.

CL/0716-0720
**PARASITOLOGIA AL DIA : REVISTA DE LA SOCIEDAD CHILENA DE PARASITOLOGIA.** **Added/Corp** Sociedad Chilena de Parasitologia. (19??)-. Periodical. Spanish. sa (June & Dec.). $40.00. University of Chile Facultad Medicina, Casilla 9183, Santiago Chile. **Tel** 011 56 2 7370081 ext. 5340, FAX 56 2 5510174. **LC** RC119; .P349. **DD** 616.9/6/005. **NLM** W1; PA636D.
**Ind/Abst** Trop. Dis. Bull.

UK/0964-7570
**PARASITOLOGY.** (19??)-. English. £115.00. SUBIS, Mansion House, 19 Kingfield Road, Sheffield S11 9AS England. **Tel** 011 44 114 255 4433, FAX 011 44 114 255 4626.

CN/0824-7315
**PARKINSON NETWORK.** [Parkinson netw.]. Bulletin # 27 (March 1984)-. Periodical. English. qt. $10.00 U.S. Parkinson Foundation of Canada 222, PO Box 110, Toronto Ontario M5G 2C2 Canada. **Tel** (416)964-1155. **ED** Sandie Burke. **DD** 616.8/33/006071. **Ad Acc. Circ:** 5,500 (ctrl). ***Continues** Bulletin (Parkinson Foundation of Canada), 0711-236X.*
**Desc:** Facts, theories, and hopes for future cure research. Reports of activities pleas for help either financially or as volunteers.

UK/1353-8020
**PARKINSONISM AND RELATED DISORDERS.** (19??)-. English. Four times a year. $187.00 The Americas; £125.00 other. Butterworth Heinemann Publishers, Linacre House, Jordan Hill, Oxford OX2 8DP England. **Tel** 011 44 865 310366. **(Subscription address:** Elsevier Science Ltd. Oxford Fulfillment Centre, PO Box 800, Kidlington, Oxford OX5 1DX United Kingdom.**)**

CN/0707-8617
**PATH FINDER (VANCOUVER).** (PATH FINDER.). Feb. 1978-. Periodical. English. bm. Free. R A Rockerbie, Editor, Intersociety Council of Laboratory Medicine of Canada, 7755 Jensen Place, Burnaby British Columbia V5A 2A7 Canada. **DD** 616.07/5/0971.

BE/0770-4224
**PATIENT CARE NEDERLAND.** (PATIENT CARE.). [Patient care Ned.]. **VFOAT** Het Tijdschrift Voor de Huisarts. (1974)-. Periodical. Dutch. mo. F125.00. ICS Belgium, Waterloosesteenweg 935 937, B-1180 Brussels Belgium. **Tel** 011 32 2 3754439, FAX 374 25 56. **UDC** 61.

US/0738-3991
**PATIENT EDUCATION AND COUNSELING.** [Patient educ. couns.]. **Added/Corp** Excerpta Medica (Firm). Vol. 5, No. 1 (1983)-. Academic Scholarly Publication. English. Six times a year (2 vols.). $311.00. Elsevier Science Ireland Ltd., Bay 15, Shannon Industrial Estate, Co Clare Ireland. **Tel** 011 353 61 471944. **ED** Edward E. Bartlett and Ruud Jonkers. **LC** R727.3; .P374. **DD** 362.1/7. **NLM** W1; PA9632E. **[CCC].** Index available. **Bk Rev. Ad Acc. Pr Rev. Circ:** 1,000. available on microfilm and microfiche from University Microfilms International (UMI). Documents available from The Genuine Article. ***Continues** Patient Counselling and Health Education, 0190-2040.*
**Desc:** Applied research in patient education and counseling, managers, and others involved in patient education and counseling.
**Ind/Abst** AGRICOLA; Annals Behav. Med.; Cumul. Index Nurs. Allied Health Lit.; Curr. Contents Soc. Behav. Sci.; EMBASE; Hospit. Health Admin. Index; Nutr. Res. Newsl.; Psychol. Abstr. (1985-); PsycINFO; PsycLit; Res. Alert [Full Cov.]; Soc. Sci. Cit. Index [Full Cov.]; Stud. Women Abstr.; Tech. Educ. Train. Abstr.

NZ/0110-4578
**PATIENT MANAGEMENT.** Vol. 1, (June 1972)-. Periodical. English. Twelve times a year. 105.00NZ$ New Zealand; 135.00NZ$ Pacific Region; 180.00NZ$ US, Canada and Asia; 193.00NZ$ UK, Europe & other. ADIS International Ltd, 41 Centorian Drive, Private Bag 65901, Mairangi Bay, Auckland 10 New Zealand. **Tel** 011 64 9 4798100, FAX 011 64 9 4791418. **NLM** W1 PA9634. ***Supersedes** Medical Equipment.*

NZ/0314-660X
**PATIENT MANAGEMENT (SEAFORTH).** ***Title Change.*** (PATIENT MANAGEMENT.). [Patient manage.]. Vol. 1, No. 1 (June 1977)-(19??). Periodical. English. mo. ADIS International Ltd, 41 Centorian Drive, Private Bag 65901, Mairangi Bay, Auckland 10 New Zealand. **Tel** 011 64 9 4798100, FAX 011 64 9 4791418. **(Subscription address:** US/ 582 Middletown Boulevard B-30, Langhorne, PA 19047-1822; HK/ 18/F Tung Sun Commercial Centre, 194-200 Lockhard Road, Wanchai Hong Kong**) ED** Graeme S. Avery and Sandra Wilson. **NLM** W1 PA9632G. cum. index. **Ad Acc. Circ:** 5,000 (ctrl). ***Continued by** GP General Practitioner, 1039-7469.*
**Desc:** Discusses the place and interrelationship of diagnostic, therapeutic and supportive measures in the overall treatment of disease states. Aimed at the general and hospital practitioner.

CN/1188-0236
**PATIENT OF THE MONTH PROGRAM.** English. Eight times a year. $200.00 (nonmembers), $145.00 (members). Decker Periodicals Publishing Inc, PO Box 620, Station A, Hamilton Ontario L8N 3K7 Canada. **Tel** (416)522-7017, (800) 568-7281, FAX (416)522-7839.

GW/0177-8161
**PATIENTORIENTIERTE ALLGEMEINMEDIZIN.** [Patientorient. Allg.med.]. V. 1-. German. Springer-Verlag New York Inc., 175 5th Avenue, New York NY 10010. **Tel** (212)460-1500, telex 232 235 SPB UR. **(Subscription address:** Springer Verlag New York Inc. / for North America, 44 Hartz Way, Secaucus NJ 07096.**) NLM** W1 PA965H.

IT/1120-8627
**PEDAGOGIA MEDICA.** ***Ceased.*** [Pedagog. med.]. (1987)-(1992). Periodical. Italian. qt. Masson S.P.A, Via Statuto 2/4, 20121 Milan Italy. **Tel** 011 39 2 63671, FAX 011 39 2 6367211. **ED** Ottavio Albano. **UDC** 37.04 :61. **Bk Rev. Ad Acc. Circ:** 5,000 (ctrl).

SA/1017-1711
**PEDMED.** [Pedmed]. **VFOAT** S.A. Paediatric Medicine; South African Paediatric Medicine. (1987)-. Periodical. English. Six times a year. R38.76 South Africa; R60.00 other. George Warman Publications Pty, PO Box 704, Cape Town 8000 South Africa. **Tel** 011 27 21 245320, FAX 011 27 21 261332, telex 5-21849. **UDC** 616-053.2. **Bk Rev. Ad Acc. Circ:** 2,900 (ctrl).

JA/0388-4171
**PEIN KURINIKKU.** [Pein kurinikku]. **VFOAT** Journal of Pain Clinic. (1980)-. Periodical. Japanese. bm. $210.00. Shinko Koeki K.K. Isho Shuppanbu, (Publication of Medical Books, Shinko Trading Co., Ltd.), 8-18, Minamiazabu 2 Chome, Minatoku, Tokyoto 106, Japan. **(Subscription address:** Maruzen Company Ltd., PO Box 5050, Import & Export Department, Tokyo 100 31 Japan.**) DD** 616.072.

US/0031-4595
**PENNSYLVANIA MEDICINE.** (PENNSYLVANIA MEDICINE : OFFICIAL PUBLICATION OF THE PENNSYLVANIA MEDICAL SOCIETY.). [Pa. med.]. **Added/Corp** Pennsylvania Medical Society. Vol. 69, No. 3 (Mar. 1966)-. Academic Scholarly Publication. English. mo (12 issues). $20.00 US and Canada; $30.00 other. Pennsylvania Medical Society, 77 East Park Drive, Harrisburg PA 17105. **Tel** (717)558-7750. **ED** Mary L. Uehlein. **LC** R11; .P43. **NLM** W1 PE385K. **CODEN** PNMDAL. **Ad Acc. Circ:** 17,000. Documents available from BIOSIS Document Express, CASDDS. ***Continues** Pennsylvania Medical Journal (1928), 0096-0667.*
**Desc:** Socioeconomic and political news affecting the practice of medicine in Pennsylvania.
**Ind/Abst** Biol. Abstr.; Chem. Abstr.; Cumul. Index Nurs. Allied Health Lit.; EMBASE; Health Devices Alerts; Index Med.; Life Sci. Collect.; Saf. Health Work.

UK/0301-0066
**PERCEPTION (LONDON).** **See** Psychology.

GW/0935-0020
**PERFUSION : DURCHBLUTUNGSSTORUNGEN UND ARTERIOSKLEROSE IN KLINIK UND PRAXIS.** (198?)-. Periodical. German (English; summaries and/or abstracts in English). Six times a year. **NLM** W1; PE786E. Index available. **Bk Rev. Circ:** 8,000.

US/1054-3392
**PERINATAL NEONATAL PRACTICE.** (1991)-. Periodical. English. bm. $32.00. Knolls Publishing Group, 201 Littleton Road, Morris Plains NJ 07950. **Tel** (201)285-0855.

●US/1070-8979
**PERIOPERATIVE OPTIONS AND OPPORTUNITIES.** [Perioper. options oppor.]. (1992)-. Periodical. English. bm. $40.00 (one year), $75.00 (two year). Nursing Renaissance Inc, 260 Mohawk Drive, Boulder CO 80303. **Tel** (303)499-6029. **DD** 610.

US/1045-2338
**PERMUTED MEDICAL SUBJECT HEADINGS.** **See** Library and Information Sciences.

UK
**PERSISTENT PAIN: MODERN METHODS OF TREATMENT.** **VFOAT** Modern Methods of Treatment. V. 1- 1977-. Monographic series. English. ir. Price varies per volume. Grune & Stratton Inc., 6277 Sea Harbor Drive, Orlando FL 32887. **Tel** (800)782-4479, (407)345-2567. **ED** S Lipton.

●US/1065-0687
**PERSONAL MEDICAL ADVISOR.** (PERSONAL MEDICAL ADVISOR [COMPUTER FILE].). **Added/Corp** Medical Data Exchange, Inc. EBSCO Publishing (firm). **VFOAT** EBSCO CD-ROM. (1992)-. Periodical. English. (one time CD-ROM). $299.00. EBSCO Publishing / Boston, 83 Pine Street, Peabody MA 01960. **Tel** (800)653-2726 North America, (508)535-8500, FAX (508)535-8545. Index available. **Pr Rev.**
**Desc:** Provides current medical reference information from seven health treatment publications.

SW
**PERSONALSITUATIONEN.** **Main/Corp** Svenska Landstingsforbundet. Swedish. Landstingsforbundet, PO Box 6606, 11384 Stockholm Sweden. **Tel** 08 2365 60. **LC** RA410.9.S8; S89A. **DD** 331.12/5161/09485.

US/0886-2125
**PERSONNEL POSTSCRIPT.** **Added/Corp** Medical Group Management Association. Vol. 1 No. 1 (1986)-. Periodical. English. qt. $65.00 MGMA members, $95.00 non-members. Medical Group Management Association, 104 Inverness Terrace East, Englewood CO 80112. **Tel** (303)397-7879, FAX (303)799-1683. **DD** 658.

US/0730-7950
**PERSONS ENROLLED FOR MEDICARE.** **See** Insurance.

US/0031-5982
**PERSPECTIVES IN BIOLOGY AND MEDICINE.** **See** Biology.

SZ/0272-6327
**PERSPECTIVES IN BIOMECHANICS.** [Perspect. biomech.]. Vol. 1, Pt. A (1980)-. Periodical. English. ir. Price varies. Harwood Academic Publishers, PO Box 90, Reading RG1 8JL England. **Tel** 011 44 734 560080. **(Subscription address:** Harwood Academic Publishers, PO Box 786, Cooper Station, New York NY 10276.**) ED** D. N. Ghista. **DD** 574. **NLM** W3 PE871AG.

US/1049-3247
**PERSPECTIVES IN CLINICAL MEDICINE.** (1991)-. Periodical. English. Free. Radius Scientific, Inc., 1 Harmon Meadow Boulevard, 4th Floor, Secaucus NJ 07094.

US/0898-6770
**PERSPECTIVES IN HYPERTENSION SERIES.** [Perspect. hypertens. ser.]. **VFOAT** Perspectives in Hypertension. Vol. 1 (1987)-. Monographic series. English. ir. Price varies per volume. **(Subscription address:** Raven Press Book Department, 1185 Avenue of the Americas, New York NY 10036.**) DD** 616. **NLM** W1; PE871APH.
**Ind/Abst** Biol. Abstr. (1987-).

US/0018-4195
**PERSPECTIVES IN LONG-TERM CARE.** V. 1- Jan./Feb. 1970-. Periodical. English. bm. **NLM** W1 PE871AT. ***Formed by the union of** Homemaker-Home Health Aide Bulletin, 0441-1153 **and** Chronic Illness News Letter, 0578-0349.*

US/0889-8413
**PERSPECTIVES ON PREVENTION.** ***Ceased.*** [Perspect. prev.]. Vol. 1, Issue 1 (Fall 1986)-Vol. 2, Issue 3 (?). Periodical. English. qt. Association of Teachers of Preventive Medicine, 1030 15th Street NW/Suite 410, Washington DC 20005. **DD** 362. **NLM** W1; PE872JE.
**Ind/Abst** Nutr. Res. Newsl.

US/1066-3533
**PERSPECTIVES ON THE MEDICAL TRANSCRIPTION PROFESSION.** [Perspect. med. transcr. prof.]. **Added/Corp** Health

Professions Institute. **VFOAT** Perspectives. (1990)-. Periodical. English. qt. $50.00 US; $60.00 Canada; $70.00 other. Health Professions Institute, PO Box 801, Modesto CA 95353. **Tel** (209)551-2112, FAX (209)551-0404. **ED** Sally C. Pitman. **DD** 610. Index available. cum. index. **Bk Rev**, (Qty: 4-6). **Ad Acc. Circ:** 2,000. available on audiocassette.
**Desc:** Of interest to medical transcriptionists (MTs), MT service owners, MT educators, and hospital MT departments.

HU/0139-4215
**PEST MEGYEI ORVOS-GYOGYSZERESZ NAPOK TUDOMANYOS KOZLEMENYEI.** [Pest M. Orv.-Gyogyszeresz Napok tud. kozl.]. 1978-. Hungarian. an. **NLM** W3 PE66. ***Continues*** *Pest Megyei Orvosi Napok Tudomanyos Kozlemenyei 0200-1225.*

GW/0937-0277
**PFLEGEN AMBULANT.** [Pfleg. ambul.]. (1990)-. Periodical. German. bm. DM39.60 Germany; DM48.30 other Europe; DM75.60 other. Bibliomed Medizinische Verlag, Postfach 150 Nuernberger St 10, W 34201 Melsungen F R Germany. **Tel** 011 49 5661 6001, FAX 011 49 5661 8360. **UDC** 616-083 :614.88.

GW/0233-237X
**PHARMACOKINETICS.** ***Ceased.*** **See** Pharmacy and Pharmacology.

US/0031-7179
**PHAROS OF ALPHA OMEGA ALPHA-HONOR MEDICAL SOCIETY, THE.** [Pharos Alpha Omega Alpha Honor Med. Soc.]. **Main/Corp** Alpha Omega Alpha. **VFOAT** Pharos. Vol.1 (1938)-. Periodical. English. qt. $10.00. Alpha Omega Alpha Honor Medical Society, 525 Middlefield Road/Suite 130, Menlo Park CA 94025. **Tel** (415)329-0291, FAX (415)329-1618. **ED** Robert J Glaser. **LC** LJ105.A6. **DD** 378/.1985461. **NLM** W1 PH328. Index available. **Bk Rev. Circ:** 60,000 (ctrl).
**Desc:** Non-technical articles relating to medicine.
**Ind/Abst** Cumul. Index Nurs. Allied Health Lit.; Energy Res. Abstr. (Aug. 1982-); Index Med.

US/0031-7306
**PHILADELPHIA MEDICINE.** **Added/Corp** Philadelphia County Medical Society. Vol.37, No.43 (June 13, 1942)-. Periodical. English. mo (12 issues). $15.00 US; $40.00 other. Philadelphia County Medical Society, 2100 Spring Garden Street, Philadelphia PA 19130. **Tel** (215)564-3059, FAX (215)563-3627. **ED** William Weiss, M.D. **NLM** W1 PH414. Index available. **Ad Acc. Circ:** 4,500 (ctrl). ***Continues*** *Weekly Roster and Medical Digest and Medical Digest.*
**Desc:** Medical oriented article news and classified ads.

NE/0376-7418
**PHILOSOPHY AND MEDICINE.** **See** Philosophy.

US
**PHILSOM/S : PERIODICAL HOLDINGS IN THE LIBRARY OF THE SCHOOL OF MEDICINE BY SUBJECT.** **See** Library and Information Sciences.

IT/1120-1797
**PHYSICA MEDICA.** (1987)-. Italian. qt. GESA, Piazza Monte Ceneri 13, CH 6901 Lugano Italy. ***Continues*** *Fisica in Medicina, 1120-1916.*
**Ind/Abst** EMBASE.

US/8750-7544
**PHYSICIAN ASSISTANT (1983).** (PHYSICIAN ASSISTANT : THE OFFICIAL JOURNAL OF THE AMERICAN ACADEMY OF PHYSICIAN ASSISTANTS.). [Phys. assist.]. **Added/Corp** American Academy of Physician Assistants. **VFOAT** Physician Assistant & Health Practitioner; Physician Assistant and Health Practitioner. Vol. 7, No. 1 (Jan. 1983)-. Periodical. English. mo. $65.00 (institutions), $55.00 (individuals). Excerpta Medica / US, PO Box 3085, Princeton NJ 08543-3085. **Tel** (908)874-8550, FAX (908)874-5611. **(Subscription address:** Physician Assistant, PO Box 3000, Denville NJ 07834.**)** **ED** Bob Dedonato DeDonato, Lucy Kavaler, and Robert Spencer. **LC** R697.P45; H43. **DD** 610.73/7. **NLM** W1; PH774Q. **[CCC].** cum. index. **Bk Rev. Ad Acc. Circ:** 20,935 (ctrl). available on microfilm and microfiche from University Microfilms International (UMI). ***Continues*** *Physician Assistant, Health Practitioner, 0197-713X.*
**Desc:** Clinical and practice related information geared to the physician assistant profession.
**Ind/Abst** Cumul. Index Nurs. Allied Health Lit.; Hospit. Health Admin. Index; Int. Nurs. Index.

US
**PHYSICIAN ASSISTANT NEWSLETTER OF ETHICS.** **See** Ethics.

●US/1064-4563
**PHYSICIAN COMPENSATION AND PRODUCTION SURVEY.** (PHYSICIAN COMPENSATION AND PRODUCTION SURVEY : ... REPORT BASED ON ... DATA / MEDICAL GROUP MANAGEMENT ASSOCIATION.). **Added/Corp** Medical Group Management Association. Center for Research in Ambulatory Health Care Administration (U.S.). (1992)-. English. $130.00. Center for Research in Ambulatory Health Care Administration, 104 Inverness Terrace East, Englewood CO 80112. **NLM** W1; PH775G.

US/0192-2963
**PHYSICIAN EAST.** [Phys. east]. (Jan. 1979)-. Periodical. English. Twelve times a year. Physician East, 60 State Street/Suite 3330, Boston MA 02109. **NLM** W1 PH776. ***Supersedes*** *Massachusetts Physician, 0025-4851.*

US/1051-2632
**PHYSICIAN MARKETPLACE UPDATE.** ***Ceased.*** [Physician marketpl. update]. **Added/Corp** Center for Health Policy Research (American Medical Association) American Medical Association. Vol. 1, No. 1 (Jan. 1990)-(Nov. 1992). English. Six times a year. American Medical Association, 515 North State Street, Chicago IL 60610. **Tel** (312)464-5000, (800)262-2350, FAX (312)464-5831. **DD** 362. ***Continues*** *SMS Report (Chicago, Ill. : 1987).*

US
**PHYSICIAN REFERRAL UPDATE.** (19??)-. English. mo. $195.00. Admissions Marketing Report, 3050 Presidential Drive, Suite 111, Atlanta GA 30340. **Tel** (404)457-6105. **ED** Richard Cohen (Editor's Phone: (415)454-8887). **Ad Acc. Circ:** 350.

US/0276-8283
**PHYSICIANS' CURRENT PROCEDURAL TERMINOLOGY.** **See** Encyclopedias and General Reference Books.

US/8750-9407
**PHYSICIANS FINANCIAL NEWS.** **See** Business-Banking and Finance.

●US/1053-9727
**PHYSICIANS' GUIDE TO RARE DISEASES.** [Physicians' guide rare dis.]. **Added/Corp** National Organization for Rare Disorders. (1991)-. English. $67.00. Dowden Publishing Company, 110 Summit Avenue, Montvale NJ 07645. **Tel** (201)391-9100, FAX (201)391-2778. **DD** 616. **NLM** WB 39; P578.

US/0079-192X
**PHYSICIAN'S HANDBOOK.** [Physician's handb.]. (1941)-. English. ir (every three years). $16.50. Appleton & Lange, (A Subsidiary of Simon & Schuster), 25 Van Zant Street, East Norwalk CT 06855. **Tel** (203)838-4400, (800)423-1359, FAX (203)854-9486. **ED** Marcus A. Krupp, Lawrence M. Tierney Jr., Robert L. Roe and Carlos A. Camargo. **LC** RC55; .P4. **DD** 616.075.
**Desc:** Describes the most serviceable diagnostic tests and emphasizes anatomic, physiologic, and pharmacologic bases for understanding diagnostic data and therapeutic interventions.

US/0031-9066
**PHYSICIAN'S MANAGEMENT.** [Physician's manage.]. (1961)-. Periodical. English. mo. $50.00 US and possessions; $75.00 Canada; $110.00 other. Advanstar Communications Inc., 131 West First Street, Duluth MN 55802. **Tel** (218)723-9477, (800)346-0085. **ED** Robert A Feigenbaum. **LC** R728; .P5. **DD** 362. **NLM** W1 PH828. **[CCC]. Ad Acc. Circ:** 110,885 (ctrl). available on microfilm and microfiche from University Microfilms International (UMI). ***Absorbed*** *Surgeon's Management.*
**Desc:** Serves medical and osteopathic physicians; the doctor's business journal.
**Ind/Abst** Account. Tax Datab. (1987-); Hospit. Health Admin. Index.

US/1042-2625
**PHYSICIAN'S MARKETING & MANAGEMENT.** [Phys. mark. manage.]. **VFOAT** Physician's Marketing and Management. (1988)-. Periodical. English. mo. $189.00 physicians, $239.00 institution. American Health Consultants, 3525 Piedmont Road, Suite 400, Atlanta GA 30305. **Tel** (800)688-2421, (404)262-7436. **(Subscription address:** American Health Consultants, PO Box 95278, Chicago IL 60694.**)** **DD** 610. ***Continues*** *Physician's Marketing, 0883-1459.*
**Ind/Abst** Hospit. Manage. Rev.

US
**PHYSICIANS MEDICARE AUTHORITY.** English. Sixteen times a year (Updates in Jan., Apr., July, Oct. & Special Alert publishes monthly). $245.00. Berman & Associates Inc., PO Box 292918, Dayton OH 45429. **Tel** (800)442-1554, (513)438-1100, FAX (513)438-1164. **ED** Patricia Johnson, (editor's address: 5600 Kentshire Drive, Suite 3, Dayton, OH 45440 (phone: (513)438-1100).
**Desc:** Medicare Part B reference manual.

●US/1065-6545
**PHYSICIAN'S MEDLINE PLUS.** **See** Medical Science and Technology-Abstracting, Bibliographies and Statistics.

CN/1187-5062
**PHYSICIAN'S NEWSLETTER - SASKATCHEWAN. SASKATCHEWAN HEALTH.** (PHYSICIAN'S NEWSLETTER.). [Physician's newsl. - Sask., Sask. Health]. **Added/Corp** Saskatchewan. Saskatchewan Health. Saskatchewan. Medical Care Insurance Branch. No. 1 (Nov. 25, 1991)-. Newsletter. English. mo. Saskatchewan Health, T C Douglas Building, 3475 Albert Street, Regina Saskatchewan S4S 6X6 Canada. **DD** 610.69.

US/1055-629X
**PHYSICIAN'S PAYMENT UPDATE.** [Physician's paym. update]. **Added/Corp** American Health Consultants. (198?)-. Periodical. English. mo. $259.00. American Health Consultants, 3525 Piedmont Road, Suite 400, Atlanta GA 30305. **Tel** (800)688-2421, (404)262-7436. **(Subscription address:** American Health Consultants, PO Box 95278, Chicago IL 60694.**)** **DD** 362. ***Continues*** *Physician's Payment Advisory, 1050-8791.*
**Desc:** Devoted entirely to all the payment and reimbursement issues affecting physicians in solo and group practices.

US
**PHYSICIAN'S RELATIONS ADVISOR.** ***Title Change.*** (19??)-(199?). English. American Health Consultants, 3525 Piedmont Road, Suite 400, Atlanta GA 30305. **Tel** (800)688-2421, (404)262-7436. ***Continued by*** *Physician's Relations Update.*
**Desc:** Specifically written to help physician relations professionals lead their hospitals into the future. You'll discover how to promote loyalty and goodwill with physicians, gain a competitive edge in the market place, recruit and retain top-notch doctors, steer clear of medical staff conflicts and related liability, and comply with a host of murky regulations governing hospital-physician ties.
**Ind/Abst** Hospit. Manage. Rev. (19??-199?).

US/1047-3793
**PHYSICIAN'S WEEKLY.** (PHYSICIAN'S WEEKLY [POSTER].). [Physician's wkly.]. (198?)-. Periodical. English. wk. Free on request. Whittle Communications, 333 Main Avenue, Knoxville TN 37902. **Tel** (615)595-5000, FAX (615)595-5877. **DD** 610.

US
**PHYSIFAX.** **Main/Corp** Meducation International. English. Meducation International Ltd, Multimedia Communications in Medical Education, Montclair NJ 07042. **LC** RC55; .M397A. **DD** 616/.002/02.

GW/0940-6689
**PHYSIKALISCHE MEDIZIN, REHABILITATIONSMEDIZIN, KURORTMEDIZIN.** [Phys. Med. Rehabil.med. Kurortmed.]. (1991)-. Periodical. Multiple languages. bm (Feb., Apr., June, Aug., Oct., Dec.). $103.00. Georg Thieme Verlag Stuttgart, Postfach 301120, D 70451 Stuttgart Germany. **Tel** 011 49 711 89310, FAX 011 49 711 8931298, telex 7 252 275 GTVD. **(Subscription address:** Thieme Medical Publishers Inc., 381 Park Avenue South, New York NY 10016.**)** **UDC** 615.8. ***Continues*** *Zeitschrift fuer Physiotherapie, 0003-9357.*

CN/0300-0508
**PHYSIOTHERAPY CANADA.** [Physiother. Can.]. **VFOAT** Physiotherapie Canada. V. 24, No. 3 (July 1972)-. Periodical. English (French). Four times a year. 40.00Can$. Canadian Physiotherapy Association, 890 Yonge Street/9th Floor, Toronto Ontario M4W 3P4 Canada. **Tel** (416)924-5312, FAX (416)924-7335. **ED** Diane Charter. **DD** 615/.8/05. **NLM** W1 PH968. **CODEN** PTHCAZ. **[CCC].** Index available. **Bk Rev. Ad Acc. Circ:** 7,625 (ctrl). available on microfilm and microfiche from University Microfilms International (UMI). Documents available from BIOSIS Document Express. ***Continues*** *Journal of the Canadian Physiotherapy Association, 0008-4751.*
**Desc:** Articles on research, clinical practice, education and administration relevant to physical rehabilitation. Also book reviews, abstracts, coming events and news reports.
**Ind/Abst** Biol. Abstr.; Cumul. Index Nurs. Allied Health Lit.; EMBASE; Health Plan. Adminis.; Hospit. Health Admin. Index.

GW/0944-7113
**PHYTOMEDICINE.** (19??)-. English. Four times a year. DM356.00 Germany; DM364.00 other. Gustav Fischer Verlag Stuttgart, Postfach 720143, Wollgrasweg 49, D 70577 Stuttgart Germany. **Tel** 011 49 711 458030, FAX 0711-4580334, telex 2627-7111488. **(Subscription address:** VCH Publishers Inc., 303 Northwest 12th Avenue, Journals Department, Deerfield FL 33442.**)**

SP
**PICM PROFESION. INVESTIGACION Y CLINICA MEDICA.** Spanish. Editorial Garsi SA, Juan Bravo 46, 28006 Madrid, Spain. **Tel** 011 34 1 4021212, telex 98358 GARSI E.

HK
**PIMS.** Chinese. Three times a year. 60.00Sing$ (surface mail), 110.00Sing$ (airmail). MIMS Asia, 135 Cecil Street, 13-00 LKN Building, Singapore 0106 Singapore. **Tel** 011 65 2233788, FAX 011 65 2214788.

US/0894-6779
**PLASMAPHERESIS.** ***Title Change.*** [Plasmapheresis]. **Added/Corp** American Blood Resources Association. (1987-1992). Periodical. English. mo. American Blood Resources Association, PO Box 669, Annapolis MD 21403. **Tel** (410)263-8296. **ED** Robert W Reilly. **DD** 362. **NLM** W1; PL112. Index available. cum. index. **Ad Acc.** ctrl circ. ***Formed by the union of*** *ABRA newsletter; Plasma quarterly, 0739-8751.* ***Continued by*** *Journal (American Blood Resources Association).*

XR/0551-1038
**PLZENSKY LEKARSKY SBORNIK.** [Plzen. lek. sb.]. **Added/Corp** Universita Karlova Fakulta Lekarska. Pobocka v Plzni. **VFOAT** Pilezenskii Meditsinskii Sbornik; Plzen Medical Report. (1956)-. Periodical. Czech (summaries and/or abstracts in English and Russian). ir. Charles University / Univerzita Karlova, Ovocnytrh 5, 116 36 Prague 1 Czech Republic. **Tel** 228441. **NLM** W1 PL274.

US/0093-2248
**PMBR, PHYSICIANS'S MEDICAL BOOK REFERENCE.** **VFOAT** Physician's Medical Book Reference. (1974)-. English. an. $25.95. Medi-Facts Publishing Company, 2337 Lemoine Avenue, Fort Lee NJ 07024. **LC** Z6658; .P12. **DD** 016.61. **NLM** ZWB 100 P114.

US/1055-0178
**POCKET PDR [COMPUTER FILE].** **VAT** Pocket Physician's Desk Reference. (1991)-. English. an. $119.00 (diskette). Medical Economics Data, Five Paragon Drive, PO Box 27, Montvale NJ 07645. **Tel** (800)442-6657, (201)358-7200. available in print (Physicians' Desk Reference); available on CD-ROM (Physicians' Desk Reference (Compact Disc Ed.)).
**Desc:** System requirement: pocket computer by Selectronics.

US
**POL ADVISOR.** (19??)-. Periodical. English. qt. $59.00 US; $75.00 other. Medical Economics Publishing, Five Paragon Drive, Second Floor, Montvale NJ 07645. **Tel** (800)432-4570, (201)358-2210.

IT
**POLICLINICO; SEZIONE CHIRURGICA.** (1893)-. Periodical. Italian (summaries and/or abstracts in French and English). bm. L80000 (Italy); $120.00 (other). Edizioni Luigi Pozzi Srl, Via Panama 68, 00198 Rome Italy. **Tel** (06)8553548, FAX (06)8554105.

IT/0048-4717
**POLICLINICO, SEZIONE MEDICA.** [Policlin., Sez. Med.]. (1893)-. Periodical. Italian. bm. Edizione Luigi Pozzi S.r.l., Via Panama 68, 00198, Roma, Italy. **Tel** (6)8553548. **CODEN** PSMDAMPSMDAM.
**Ind/Abst** EMBASE [Select. Cov.].

PL/0370-0747
**POLIMERY W MEDYCYNIE.** [Polim. med.]. **Added/Corp** Akademia Medyczna we Wrocawiu. Zakad Chirurgii Doswiadczalnej i Badania Tworzyw Sztucznych. **VFOAT** Polimery V Meditsine; Polymere in der Medizin; Polymers in Medicine. Vol. 1 (1970)-. Multiple languages (English, German, Polish and Russian). qt. $40.00. **(Subscription address:** ARS Polona, PO Box 1001, 00068 Warsaw Poland.**) NLM** W1 PO213M. **CODEN** PMYMAX. Documents available from CASDDS.
**Ind/Abst** Chem. Abstr.; Index Med.

US
**POLIO NETWORK NEWS.** **Added/Corp** Gazette International Networking Institute. International Polio Network. (198?)-. Periodical. English. qt (Feb., May, Aug., Nov.). $20.00 US; $24.00 other. Gazette International Networking Institute, 5100 Oakland Avenue, Number 206, St Louis MO 63110. **Tel** (314)534-0475, FAX (314)534-5070. **ED** Joan Headley. **NLM** W1; PO2155L. **Ad Acc. Circ:** 4,000.
**Desc:** The quarterly newsletter of International Polio Network, it contains current information about the late effects of polio and topics related to disability.

PL/0867-8383
**POLISH JOURNAL OF OCCUPATIONAL MEDICINE AND ENVIRONMENTAL HEALTH.** ***Title Change.*** **Added/Corp** Instytut Medycyny Pracy Im. Prof. Dr. Med. Jerzego Nofera. Polskie Towarzystwo Medycyny Pracy. Vol. 4, No. 1 (1991)-(19??). Periodical. English. Four times a year. Nofer Inst of Occupational Medicine, PO Box 199, 8 Southwest Tersey Street, 90-950 Lodz Poland. **Tel** 011 48 42 314745, 011 48 42 314625, 011 48 42 314911, e mail:GeoNet Mull:imp-dyrekcja, FAX 011 48 42 348331, 011 48 42 556102, telex 885360 IMP PL, 885130 CITOZ PL, 885130 IMP PL. **ED** Janusz Indulski. **NLM** W1; PO23LG. Index available (annual authors index). **Bk Rev**, (Qty: 4). **Ad Acc. Pr Rev.** ctrl circ. ***Continues*** *Polish Journal of Occupational Medicine.* ***Continued by*** *International Journal of Occupational Medicine and Environmental Health.*
**Ind/Abst** EMBASE; Index Med. (1991-?); Ref. Z.

PL/0032-3756
**POLSKI TYGODNIK LEKARSKI (1960).** (POLSKI TYGODNIK LEKARSKI.). [Pol. tyg. lek.]. **Added/Corp** Polskie Towarzystwo Lekarskie. Vol. 15 (Jan. 1960)-. Periodical. Polish. wk. Price on Request. **(Subscription address:** ARS Polona, PO Box 1001, 00068 Warsaw Poland.**) NLM** W1 PO29. ***Continues in part*** *Polski Tygodnik Lekarski I Wiadomosci Lekarskie, 0860-8849.*
**Ind/Abst** EMBASE [Select. Cov.]; Index Med.; Protozoolog. Abstr.; Rev. Med. Vet. Entomol.; Saf. Health Work; SportSearch.

IT/0392-9264
**POLSO, IL.** [... Polso]. (1976)-. Periodical. Italian. ir (18 issues). L38000 Italy. Masson S.P.A, Via Statuto 2/4, 20121 Milan Italy. **Tel** 011 39 2 63671, FAX 011 39 2 6367211. **UDC** 61.

US/0272-6335
**POLYMERS IN BIOLOGY AND MEDICINE.** **See** Biology.

UK/0143-4225
**POLYPEPTIDES SHEFFIELD.** (POLYPEPTIDES.). [Polypeptides Sheff.]. (1980)-. English. mo. £75.00. SUBIS, Mansion House, 19 Kingfield Road, Sheffield S11 9AS England. **Tel** 011 44 114 255 4433, FAX 011 44 114 255 4626. **DD** 016.612405. **[CCC].**

XR/0301-2549
**POLYTHEMATICAL COLLECTED REPORTS OF THE MEDICAL FACULTY OF THE PALACKY UNIVERSITY.** **Main/Corp** Univerzita Palackeho v Olomouci. Lekarska Fakulta. Vol. 10 (1964)-. Periodical. Multiple languages (Czech, English, German and Russian). Statni Pedagogicke Nakladatelstvi, Ostrovni 30, 113 01 Prague 1 Czech Republic. **Tel** (2)203787, FAX (2)293883. **ED** F Santavy. ***Continues*** *Polythematicky Sbornik Praci Lekarske Fakulty Palackeho University v Olomouci.*

US/8756-646X
**PORTLAND PHYSICIAN SCRIBE, THE.** ***Title Change.*** (PORTLAND PHYSICIAN SCRIBE.). [Portland phys. scribe]. **Added/Corp** Multnomah County Medical Society. **VFOAT** Scribe. Vol. 1, No. 1 (Jan. 1983)-Vol. 10, No. 4 (Feb. 21, 1992). Periodical. English. bw. Multnomah County Medical Society, 4540 SW Kelly, Portland OR 97201. **Tel** (503)222-9977, FAX (503)222-3164. **DD** 362. ***Continues*** *Portland Scribe, 0032-4930.* ***Continued by*** *Scribe (Portland, Or. : 1992).*

US/1051-6492
**POST-POLIO DIRECTORY.** [Post-polio dir.]. **VAT** Post Polio Directory. (1989)-. Directory. English. an (Mar.). $3.00 US; $4.00 others. Gazette International Networking Institute, 5100 Oakland Avenue, Number 206, St Louis MO 63110. **Tel** (314)534-0475, FAX (314)534-5070. **ED** Joan Headley. **LC** RC180.A1; P67. **DD** 362. **NLM** WC 22.1; P857. ***Continues*** *Polio Network News.*
**Desc:** Lists clinics, health professionals, and support groups that is knowledgeable about the effects of polio. Contains over 500 entries including an international section.

US
**POSTDOCTORAL RESEARCH FELLOWSHIP OPPORTUNITIES / NATIONAL INSTITUTES OF HEALTH.** **Main/Corp** National Institutes of Health (U.S.). (199?)-. Catalog. English. National Institutes of Health Medical Staff Fellowship Program, Building 31 Room 4804, Bethesda MD 20205. **Tel** (301)496-2427. ***Continues*** *National Institutes of Health (U.S.). Postdoctoral Research Fellowship Opportunities Catalog.*

UK/0142-7946
**POSTGRADUATE DOCTOR. AFRICA.** [Postgrad. doc., Afr.]. (1979)-. Periodical. English. mo. £18.00 UK and Europe; 25.00 other. Barker Publications Limited, Barker House, 539 London Road, Isleworth, Middlesex TW7 4DA United Kingdom. **Tel** 011 44 81 847 1774, FAX 011 44 81 568 2766, telex 896691 TLXIRG. **ED** D Harvey. **NLM** W1 PO955H. **[CCC].** Index available. cum. index. **Bk Rev. Ad Acc. Circ:** 9,000 (ctrl). available on microfilm.
**Desc:** Review articles on clinical medicine in primary care.
**Ind/Abst** Protozoolog. Abstr.; Trop. Dis. Bull.

UK/0267-0275
**POSTGRADUATE DOCTOR. CARIBBEAN.** (POSTGRADUATE DOCTOR.). [Postgrad. dr., Caribb.]. **VFOAT** Postgraduate Doctor--Caribbean. (198?)-. Periodical. English. bm. Barker Publications Limited, Barker House, 539 London Road, Isleworth, Middlesex TW7 4DA United Kingdom. **Tel** 011 44 81 847 1774, FAX 011 44 81 568 2766, telex 896691 TLXIRG. **NLM** W1; PO955HCH. **[CCC].**

UK/0140-7724
**POSTGRADUATE DOCTOR. MIDDLE EAST EDITION.** (POSTGRADUATE DOCTOR. MIDDLE EAST.). [Postgrad. doct., Middle East ed.]. (1978)-. Periodical. English. Twelve times a year. £59.00 UK and Europe; £77.00 other. Barker Publications Limited, Barker House, 539 London Road, Isleworth, Middlesex TW7 4DA United Kingdom. **Tel** 011 44 81 847 1774, FAX 011 44 81 568 2766, telex 896691 TLXIRG. **ED** D. Harvey. **NLM** W1 PO955HD. **[CCC].** Index available. cum. index. **Bk Rev. Ad Acc. Circ:** 20,000 (ctrl).
**Desc:** Review articles on clinical medicine in primary care.
**Ind/Abst** Protozoolog. Abstr.; Trop. Dis. Bull.

UK/0032-5473
**POSTGRADUATE MEDICAL JOURNAL.** [Postgrad. med. j.]. **Added/Corp** Fellowship of Postgraduate Medicine. Vol. 1, No. 1 (1925)-. Academic Scholarly Publication. English. mo (12 issues). £130.00 UK and EEC; £140.00. Professional & Scientific Publishers, Tavistock House, East Tavistock Square, London WC1H 9JR England. **Tel** 011 44 71 387-4499, telex 005311. **(Subscription address:** Professional & Scientific Publishers, PO Box 294, London WC1H 9TB England.**) ED** B.I. Hoffbrand. **NLM** W1 PO957H. **CODEN** PGMJAO. **[CCC]. Bk Rev. Ad Acc. Pr Rev. Circ:** 2,000. available on microfilm and microfiche from University Microfilms International (UMI). Documents available from The Genuine Article, BIOSIS Document Express, CASDDS. ***Supersedes*** *Fellowship of Medicine and Postgraduate Medical Association. Bulletin.*
**Desc:** Focuses attention on current methods of diagnosis, treatment and other important clinical topics. Its interdisciplinary approach reflects everyday clinical practice. Each issue publishes: review articles, single subject symposia, correspondence, conference proceedings and diary of forthcoming events, regular series on community medicine, diagnostic images, emergencey medicine, etc.
**Ind/Abst** Biol. Abstr.; Chem. Abstr.; Curr. Contents Clin. Med.; Dairy Sci. Abstr.; EMBASE; Food Sci. Technol. Abstr.; Helminthol. Abstr. (19??-19??); Index Med.; Int. Pharm. Abstr.; Nutr. Abstr. Rev., Ser. A, Hum. Exp.; Nutr. Res. Newsl.; Life Sci. Collect.; PESTDOC; Protozoolog. Abstr.; Ref. Upd. Basic Ed.; Ref. Upd. Deluxe Ed.; Res. Alert [Full Cov.]; Rev. Med. Vet. Entomol.; Rev. Med. Vet. Mycology; Sci. Cit. Index; SCISEARCH; Soc. Sci. Cit. Index [Select. Cov.]; Trop. Dis. Bull.

UK/0370-0593
**POSTGRADUATE MEDICAL JOURNAL. SUPPLEMENT.** **Added/Corp** Fellowship of Postgraduate Medicine. (19??)-. Academic Scholarly Publication. English. ir. Price varies per volume. Professional & Scientific Publishers, Tavistock House, East Tavistock Square, London WC1H 9JR England. **Tel** 011 44 71 387-4499, telex 005311. **CODEN** PMESAJ. Documents available from CASDDS.
**Ind/Abst** Chem. Abstr.

US/0032-5481
**POSTGRADUATE MEDICINE.** [Postgrad. med.]. **Added/Corp** Interstate Post Graduate Medical Association of North America. Vol. 1 (Jan. 1947)-. Academic Scholarly Publication. English. Sixteen times a year. $54.00 US; $58.88 Canada; $130.00 other. McGraw Hill Publishing Company, Inc., 1221 Avenue of the Americas, New York NY 10020. **Tel** (212)512-6410, (800)525-5003, FAX (212)512-6111. **(Subscription address:** McGraw Hill / Minnesota, 4530 West 77th Street, Suite 350, Minneapolis MN 55435.**) ED** Glen C. Griffin. **LC** R11; .P74. **DD** 616.05. **NLM** W1 PO958. **CODEN** POMDAS. **[CCC].** Index available. cum. index. **Bk Rev. Ad Acc. Pr Rev. Circ:** 125,600 (ctrl). available on microfilm and microfiche from University Microfilms International (UMI); available on an online database (file 149,624/Full-Text) from DIALOG. Documents available from The Genuine Article, BIOSIS Document Express, CASDDS.
**Desc:** For physicians in family practice, internal medicine, and other primary care specialties. Clinical articles by physicians focus on information about diagnosis and treatment of common conditions. Includes a symposium of articles on a specific disease topic and a quiz that physicians can submit for continuing education credit.
**Ind/Abst** Abr. Index Med.; Abstr. Clin. Care Guidel.; Biol. Abstr.; Chem. Abstr.; Consum. Health Nutr. Index; Cumul. Index Nurs. Allied Health Lit.; Curr. Contents Clin. Med.; EMBASE; Energy Res. Abstr.; Health Devices Alerts; Health Index (1991-); Health Period. Database [Full Txt.]; Health Ref. Cent. (Jan. 1989-) [Full Txt.] [Full Cov.]; Helminthol. Abstr.; Index Med.; Iowa Drug Inf. Serv. (1969-); Med. Abstr. Newsl.; Mod. Med.; Nutr. Abstr. Rev., Ser. A, Hum. Exp.; Nutr. Res. Newsl.; Life Sci. Collect.; Physic. Medline Plus; Protozoolog. Abstr.; Res. Alert [Full Cov.]; Rev. Med. Vet. Entomol.; Rev. Med. Vet. Mycology; Risk Abstr.; Saf. Health Work; Sci. Cit. Index; SCISEARCH; Soc. Sci. Cit. Index [Select. Cov.]; SPORT Discus; SportSearch.

XR/0032-6291
**PRACOVNI LEKARSTVI.** [Prac. lek.]. Vol. 1 (Sept. 1949)-. Academic Scholarly Publication. Czech. ir. $81.90. **(Subscription address:** Artia Pegas Press Ltd., Palac Metro Narodni Trida 25, 11210 Prague 1 Czech Republic.**) NLM** W1 PR135. **CODEN** PRLFAG. **[CCC].** Documents available from CASDDS.
**Ind/Abst** Acoust. Abstr.; Chem. Abstr.; Coal Abstr.; EMBASE; Ergon. Abstr.; Saf. Health Work; Trop. Dis. Bull.

US
**PRACTICAL CLINICAL GUIDES.** Vol. 1 (1990)-. Monographic series. English. ir. Price varies per volume. Marcel Dekker Inc., 270 Madison Avenue, New

York NY 10016. **Tel** (212)696-9000, (800)228-1160, FAX (212)685-4540, telex 421419. **(Subscription address:** Marcel Dekker Inc, PO Box 5017, Monticello NY 12701.**)** **NLM** W1; PR1385.

US/0742-1435
**PRACTICE LIFE.** ***Ceased.*** (PRACTICE LIFE : A PRACTICE PRODUCTIVITY.). [Pract. life]. Ceased (Oct. 1989). Periodical. English. mo. Medaphis Corporations, 210 Interstate North/Suite 600, Atlanta GA 30339.

US/0888-9066
**PRACTICE PERSONNEL BULLETIN.** ***Ceased.*** **See** Business-Personnel Management.

FR/0182-1377
**PRACTICIENS ET 3 EME AGE.** [Med. 3 Eme Age]. **VFOAT** Medecine et Troisieme Age. (1977)-. Periodical. French. mo (8 issues). 333.01F France; 500.00F other. Soc Francaise d Editions Med, 22 rue du Chateau des Rentiers, 75013 Paris France. **Tel** 011 33 1 45835054. **UDC** 61.

IT/0391-7282
**PRACTITIONER EDIZIONE ITALIANA.** ***Suspended.*** [Practitioner Ed. ital.]. (1978)-(July 1993). Periodical. Italian. Eighteen times a year. L44000.00 Italy; L88000.00 other. Editiemme, Via Lanino 5, 20144 Milan Italy. **Tel** 011 39 2 4227946, 011 39 2 4224666, FAX 011 39 2 4120287. **UDC** 61.

GW/0937-552X
**PRAEVENTION UND REHABILITATION.** [Pravent. Rehabil.]. (1989)-. Periodical. Multiple languages. qt. DM96.00. Dustri-Verlag, Dr Karl Feistle, Postfach 49, D 82032 Deisenhofen Germany. **Tel** 011 49 89 6138610, FAX 011 49 89 6135412. **UDC** 61.

IT
**PRATICA PSICOMOTORIA.** (19??)-. Italian. Three times a year. L40000. Centro Pubblicazione Veneto, Cas Postale 3, 31033 Castelfranco Veneto Italy. **Tel** 011 39 49 8751291.

FR/0750-6155
**PRATIQUE MEDICALE, LA.** ***Ceased.*** [Prat. med.]. 1 (Jan. 8 1982)-Ceased Vol. 41 (1988). Periodical. French. Forty-two times a year. Masson SA, Avenue Beauregard 12, CH-1701 Fribourg Switzerland. **Tel** 011 41 37 249585, FAX 011 41 37 247559, telex 942658 SEMI CH. **(Subscription address:** 7A Boulevard de Perolles, CH-1701 Fribourg Switzerland**)** **NLM** W1 PR299D. **[CCC].** available on microfilm and microfiche from University Microfilms International (UMI). ***Formed by the union of*** *Psychiatrie du Praticien, 0248-1758; Gynecologie Obstetrique du Praticien* ***and*** *Dermatologie du Praticien, 0248-9686.*

GW/0176-4616
**PRAXIS KURIER, KONGRESS-SYNOPSE AKTUELL : PK.** [Kongr.-Synop. aktuell]. **VFOAT** Praxis Kurier, Kongress Synopse Aktuell; Kongress-Synopse Aktuell; PK Kongress-Synopse Aktuell; Praxis Kurier; PK; P.K.; P.K. Kongress-Synopse Aktuell. No. 1 (June 22, 1983)-. Periodical. German. wk. $30.44. Selecta Verlagsgesellschaft mbH, Postfach 4240, c/o Mrs. Riemer, D-65032 Wiesbaden Germany. **Tel** 011 49 611 1705261. **NLM** W1 PR328D.

GW/0722-477X
**PRAXIS MEDIZINISCHER DOKUMENTATION / DEUTSCHER VERBAND MEDIZINISCHER DOKUMENTARE E.V.** [Prax. med. Dok.]. **Added/Corp** Deutscher Verband Medizinischer Dokumentare. **VFOAT** PMD. No. 1 (1981)-. Periodical. German. qt. DM40.00 US; DM46.40 other. PWD Verlagsgesellschaft, Goethestr 21, W-8000 Munich 2 F R Germany. **Tel** 011 49 89 591964, 011 49 89 591965, FAX 011 49 89 553079, telex 5216808. **ED** Ulli Hoffmann. **NLM** W1; PR329H. **Ad Acc, Adv Mgr:** Doris Tegethoff, **Tel** (0891)5919 64 ext. 165. ***Separated from*** *Krankenhaus-Technik.*

GW/0941-1046
**PRAXISMAGAZIN.** (1992)-. Twelve times a year. DM184.00. Springer-Verlag GmbH & Company KG, Heidelberger Platz 3, D 14197 Berlin Germany. **Tel** 011 49 30 8207223, FAX 011 49 30 8214091, telex 183 319 SPBLN D. **(Subscription address:** Springer Verlag New York Inc. / for North America, 44 Hartz Way, Secaucus NJ 07096.**)** **[CCC].**

FR/0983-5075
**PRECEPTA MEDICA.** No. 1 (April 87)-. Periodical. French. Edimedica, 146 Boulevard Voltaire, 92600 Asnieres France. **Tel** 011 33 1 47935603. **NLM** W1; PR33Q.

US/1049-023X
**PREHOSPITAL AND DISASTER MEDICINE.** (PREHOSPITAL AND DISASTER MEDICINE : THE OFFICIAL JOURNAL OF THE NATIONAL ASSOCIATION OF EMS PHYSICIANS AND THE WORLD ASSOCIATION FOR EMERGENCY AND DISASTER MEDICINE IN ASSOCIATION WITH THE ACUTE CARE FOUNDATION.). [Prehosp. disaster med.]. **Added/Corp** National Association of EMS Physicians (U.S.) World Association for Emergency and Disaster Medicine. Acute Care Foundation. Vol. 4 No. 1 (July/Sept. 1989)-. Periodical. English. qt. $89.00 (one year), $159.00 (two year). Mosby Year Book Inc., 11830 Westline Industrial Drive, St Louis MO 63146. **Tel** (800)325-4177, (314)872-8370, FAX (314)432-1380, telex 44-2402. **(Subscription address:** JEMS Communications, PO Box 2789, Carlsbad CA 92018.**)** **DD** 617. **NLM** W1; PR37K. ***Formed by the union of*** *Journal of the World Association for Emergency and Disaster Medicine, 0882-7397* ***and*** *Journal of Prehospital Medicine.*
**Ind/Abst** Cumul. Index Nurs. Allied Health Lit.; Health Devices Alerts.

AG/0032-745X
**PRENSA MEDICA ARGENTINA.** [Prensa med. argent.]. Vol. 1, (June 1914)-. Academic Scholarly Publication. Spanish (summaries and/or abstracts in English). Ten times a year (monthly except Jan. & Feb.). $120.00. Prensa Medica Argentina, Junin 845, Buenos Aires Argentina. **Tel** 011 54 1 9619793 or 9619782, , FAX 011 54 1 9619494. **ED** Pablo A. Lopez. **NLM** W1 PR405. **CODEN** PMARAUPMARA4. Index available. **Bk Rev. Ad Acc. Circ:** 5,000. available on microfilm and microfiche from University Microfilms International (UMI). Documents available from The Genuine Article, BIOSIS Document Express, CASDDS.
**Desc:** General medicine, clinical practice and surgery.
**Ind/Abst** Biol. Abstr.; Chem. Abstr. (1914-1983); Dairy Sci. Abstr.; EMBASE [Select. Cov.]; Helminthol. Abstr. (19??-19??); Life Sci. Collect.; Protozoolog. Abstr.; Res. Alert [Select. Cov.]; Rev. Med. Vet. Entomol.; SCISEARCH; Small Anim. Abstr. Bibliogr.; Virol. AIDS Abstr.

UK/0959-6682
**PRESCRIBER.** (19??)-. English. Twenty-four times a year. £36.00 hospitals, £72.00 UK; £95.00 others. A and M Publishing Ltd, 180 Upper Richmond Road Cambridge, Putney London SW15 2SH England. **Tel** 011 44 81 780 2741. **ED** Tim Dean. Index available. cum. index. **Ad Acc, Adv Mgr:** Peter Saver. **Pr Rev. Circ:** 19,000 (ctrl).
**Desc:** Forum for rational prescribing and formula development.

US/1040-1342
**PRESS REPORT, THE.** ***Ceased.*** [Press rep.]. Periodical. English. mo. American Health Consultants, 3525 Piedmont Road, Suite 400, Atlanta GA 30305. **Tel** (800)688-2421, (404)262-7436. **DD** 610.

FR/0755-4982
**PRESSE MEDICALE (1983), LA.** (LA PRESSE MEDICALE.). [Presse med.]. Vol. 12, No. 1 (8 Jan. 1983)-. Academic Scholarly Publication. French (summaries and/or abstracts in English). wk (44 issues per year). $310.00. Masson Editeur, Box Postale 22, 41353 Vineuil 16 France. **Tel** 011 33 54 438994. **ED** Claudio Ortolani. **NLM** W1 PR455. **CODEN** PRMEEM. **[CCC]. Bk Rev. Ad Acc. Pr Rev. Circ:** 40,000. available on microfilm and microfiche from University Microfilms International (UMI). Documents available from The Genuine Article, BIOSIS Document Express, CASDDS. ***Continues*** *Nouvelle Presse Medicale, 0301-1518.*
**Desc:** A reference publication for all hospital doctors.
**Ind/Abst** Biol. Abstr.; Calcium Calcif. Tissue Abstr.; Chem. Abstr.; CSA Neuro. Abstr. (?-?); Curr. Contents Clin. Med.; Curr. Contents Life Sci.; EMBASE; Energy Res. Abstr. (Jan. 1983-); Helminthol. Abstr. (1991-); Immunol. Abstr.; Index Med.; Microbiol. Abstr. Sect. B (19??-19??); Microbiol. Abstr. Sect. C; Nutr. Abstr. Rev., Ser. A, Hum. Exp.; Life Sci. Collect.; PESTDOC; Protozoolog. Abstr.; Ref. Upd. Basic Ed.; Ref. Upd. Deluxe Ed.; Res. Alert [Full Cov.]; Rev. Med. Vet. Entomol.; Saf. Health Work; Sci. Cit. Index; SCISEARCH; Soc. Sci. Cit. Index [Select. Cov.]; Trop. Dis. Bull.; Virol. AIDS Abstr.

US/0889-0242
**PRESSURE (BETHESDA, MD.).** (PRESSURE / UNDERSEA MEDICAL SOCIETY.). [Pressure]. **Added/Corp** Undersea Medical Society. (19??)-. Periodical. English. Six times a year (Feb., Apr., June, Aug., Oct., Dec.). $25.00. Undersea and Hyperbaric Medical Society, 10531 Metropolitan Avenue, Kensington MD 20895. **Tel** (301)942-2980. **ED** Gail S. Makulowich. **DD** 616. **Bk Rev. Ad Acc. Circ:** 3,000 (ctrl).

UK/0300-2659
**PREVENT.** [Prevent]. Vol. 1 (1972/73)-. Periodical. English. bm (6 issues). $28.00. Experts Publishers, 124 Uptown Lane, London E7 England. **LC** RA421; .P677. **DD** 614.4/4. **NLM** W1 PR493.

US/0091-7435
**PREVENTIVE MEDICINE (1972).** (PREVENTIVE MEDICINE.). [Prev. med. (1972)]. **Added/Corp** American Health Foundation. Vol. 1 (Mar. 1972)-. Academic Scholarly Publication. English. bm (6 issues). $264.00 US and Canada. Academic Press, Inc., 6277 Sea Harbor Drive, Orlando FL 32887. **Tel** (800)543-9534, (407)345-4100, FAX (407)363-9661. **ED** Ernst L. Wynder and Jerome D. Cohen. **LC** RA421; .P684. **DD** 613. **NLM** W1 PR507K. **CODEN** PVTMA3. **[CCC]. Pr Rev.** Documents available from The Genuine Article, BIOSIS Document Express, CASDDS.
**Desc:** Dedicated to the entire field of preventive medicine and public health. Emphasizes practical implications, includes both research and clinical practice reports as well as articles on important current or historical events in preventive medicine.
**Ind/Abst** AGRICOLA [Select. Cov.]; Biol. Abstr.; Chem. Abstr.; Coal Abstr.; Curr. Contents Clin. Med.; Dev. Med. Child Neurol.; EMBASE; Energy Res. Abstr. (1975-); Foods Adlibra; Index Med.; Nutr. Abstr. Rev., Ser. A, Hum. Exp.; Nutr. Res. Newsl.; Life Sci. Collect.; Res. Alert [Full Cov.]; Sci. Cit. Index; SCISEARCH; Soc. Sci. Cit. Index [Select. Cov.]; Trop. Dis. Bull.

IT/1120-2971
**PREVENZIONE OGGI.** [Prev. oggi]. (1989)-. Periodical. Italian. qt. L55000.00 Italy; L107000.00 other. Istituto Poligrafico Zecca Stato, Piazza Verdi 10, 00198 Rome Italy. **Tel** 011 39 6 85082307, 011 39 6 85082221. **UDC** 614.8.

●US
**PRIMARY CARE LETTER.** (1994)-. Periodical. English. bw. $92.00 US; $116.00 other. J.B. Lippincott Company, 227 East Washington Square, Philadelphia PA 19106-3780. **Tel** (215)238-4200 or 4454, FAX (215)238-4227. **(Subscription address:** J.B. Lippincott, PO Box 350, Hagerstown MD 21740.**)** ***Continues*** *Ambulatory Medicine Letter.*
**Desc:** Review of developments in outpatient diagnosis, therapeutics, and screening.

●US/1071-2496
**PRIMARY CARE NEWSLETTER. See** Sociology-Social Services and Welfare.

US/1040-2497
**PRIMARY CARE REPORTS.** ***Ceased.*** [Prim. care rep.]. Vol. 4, No. 7 (July 1988)-(December 1992). Periodical. English. mo. American Health Consultants, 3525 Piedmont Road, Suite 400, Atlanta GA 30305. **Tel** (800)688-2421, (404)262-7436. **DD** 616. **NLM** W1; PR522AK. ***Continues*** *Advanced Clinical Updates, 0893-9837.*
**Desc:** Provides the latest information in primary care. Each monthly issue is devoted to a single topic of vital importance to the primary care physician.

US/0032-891X
**PRIVATE PRACTICE.** ***Ceased.*** **Added/Corp** Congress of County Medical Societies. Vol. 1 (Feb. 1969)-(May 1994). Periodical. English. mo. Private Practice, PO Box 890547, Oklahoma City OK 73189. **Tel** (405)692-4466, FAX (405)692-4446. **ED** Brian Sherman. **LC** R11; .P75. **DD** 610/.5. **NLM** W1 PR532. Index available. **Bk Rev. Ad Acc, Adv Mgr:** Debra Griffith. **Circ:** 140,000 (ctrl). available on microfilm and microfiche from University Microfilms International (UMI).
**Desc:** Social-economic journal.

UK
**PROBLEMS AND PROGRESS IN MEDICAL CARE; ESSAYS ON CURRENT RESEARCH. Added/Corp** Nuffield Provincial Hospitals Trust. **VFOAT** Portfolio for Health. (1964)-. Monographic series. English. ir. Price varies per volume. Oxford University Press, Walton Street, Oxford OX2 6DP England. **Tel** 011 44 865 56767, FAX 011 44 865 267773, telex 837330 OXPRES G. **(Subscription address:** Oxford University Press / USA, Journals Marketing Department, Oxford University Press, 2001 Evans Road, Cary NC 27513.**)**

US/0889-4701
**PROBLEMS IN CRITICAL CARE.** ***Ceased.*** [Probl. crit. care]. Vol. 1, No. 1 (Jan./March 1987)-(Dec. 1992). Periodical. English. qt. J.B. Lippincott Company, 227 East Washington Square, Philadelphia PA 19106-3780. **Tel** (215)238-4200 or 4454, FAX (215)238-4227. **LC** RC86; .P76. **DD** 616/.028/05. **NLM** W1; PR573L. **[CCC].** cum. index. available on microfilm from University Microfilms International (UMI).
**Ind/Abst** EMBASE.

PL/0303-2264
**PROBLEMY MEDYCYNY WIEKU ROZWOJOWEGO.** [Probl. med. wieku rozw.]. Vol. 1 (1972)-. Periodical. Polish (summaries and/or abstracts in English). Twice a year. **(Subscription address:** ARS Polona, PO Box 1001, 00068 Warsaw Poland.**)** **NLM** W1 PR5806. **CODEN** PMWRA4. Documents available from CASDDS.
**Ind/Abst** Chem. Abstr. (1972-1977); Index Med.

PL/0137-4982
**PROBLEMY SZKOLNICTWA I NAUK MEDYCZNYCH.** [Probl. szk. nauk med.]. Vol. 1 (1976)-. Periodical. Polish. qt. Price on Request. **(Subscription address:** ARS Polona, PO Box 1001, 00068 Warsaw Poland.**)** **NLM** W1 PR5815F.

PL/0370-2219
**PROBLEMY TECHNIKI W MEDYCYNIE.** (PROBLEMY TECHNIKI W MEDYCYNIE: ORGAN CENTRALNOGO OSRODKA TECHNIKI MEDYCZNEJ.). [Probl. tech. med.]. **Added/Corp** Centralny Osrodek Techniki Medycznej (Poland). (1970)-. Academic Scholarly Publication. Polish (summaries and/or abstracts in English, German and Russian). sa. Price on Request. **(Subscription address:** ARS Polona, PO Box 1001,

00068 Warsaw Poland.) **CODEN** PTMDBU. Documents available from CASDDS.
**Ind/Abst** Chem. Abstr.

US/0191-1856
**PROCEEDINGS OF THE ANNUAL COCCIDIOIDOMYCOSIS STUDY GROUP MEETING.** **Added/Corp** Coccidioidomycosis Study Group. (1976)-. Proceedings. English. **NLM** W1 PR584LTG. ***Continues*** *Progress Report of the Veterans Administration-Armed Forces Coccidioidomycosis Study Group, 0191-3255.*
**Desc:** Consists of proceedings of the 21st?- annual meetings.

US/0276-1483
**PROCEEDINGS OF THE ... ANNUAL MEETING OF THE SOCIETY OF PROSPECTIVE MEDICINE.** [Proc. annu. meet. Soc. Prospect. Med.]. **Main/Corp** Society of Prospective Medicine. Meeting. 16th (Oct./Nov. 1, 1980)-. Proceedings. English. an (Fall). $35.00 (nonmembers), free (members). Society of Prospective Medicine, PO Box 55110, Indianapolis IN 46205. **Tel** (317)549-3600, FAX (317)549-3670. **LC** RA422; .S5a. **DD** 362.1/0973. ***Continues*** *Proceedings of the Annual Meeting on Prospective Medicine and Health Hazard Appraisal.*

UK/0258-6185
**PROCEEDINGS OF THE EUROPEAN PROSTHODONTIC ASSOCIATION, THE.** (19??)-. Periodical. English. an. £10.00. European Prosthodontic Association, c/o Dr. P.R. Likeman, Floor 20 Guys Hospital, London SE1 9RT Egland. **Tel** 011 71 955 4026, FAX 011 71 407 6736. **ED** Dr. P.R. Likeman. **UDC** 616.314. **Circ:** 450.

JA/0914-4404
**PROCEEDINGS OF THE ICMR SEMINAR.** **Added/Corp** International Center for Medical Research. (198?)-. Academic Scholarly Publication. English. Kobe Daigaku Igakubu Fuzoku Igaku Kenkyu Kokusai Koryu Senta, (International Center for Medical Research, School of Medicine, Kobe University), 5-1, Kusunokicho 7 Chome, Chuoku,, Kobeshi, Hyogoken 650 Japan. **NLM** W1; IC409L. Documents available from CASDDS.
**Ind/Abst** Chem. Abstr.

UK/0534-9354
**PROCEEDINGS OF THE INTERNATIONAL CONGRESS ON MEDICAL RECORDS.** (1952)-. Proceedings. English. ir. **LC** RA976; .I5.
**Desc:** Information on clinical medicine.

CH/0255-6596
**PROCEEDINGS OF THE NATIONAL SCIENCE COUNCIL, REPUBLIC OF CHINA. PART B, LIFE SCIENCES.** [Proc. Natl. Sci. Counc. Repub. China, Part B, Life sci.]. **Added/Corp** Kuo Chia Ko Hsueh Wei Yuan Hui. **VFOAT** Life Sciences; Yen Chiu Hui Kan. Sheng Ming Ko Hsueh; Sheng Ming Ko Hsueh. Vol. 8, No. 1 (Jan. 1984)-. Academic Scholarly Publication. English (summaries and/or abstracts in Chinese). qt. $16.00 surface mail; $18.00 (air mail) Hong Kong, Macao, Asia, & Pacific Area; $19.00 (air mail) America, Europe, & Africa. National Science Council, Republic of China, Math Res Promotion Center NTU, Taipei Taiwan. **Tel** 011 886 2 3633860. **ED** Jung-Yaw Lin. **LC** Q72.5; .P76. **DD** 574/.05. **NLM** W1; PR586CC. **CODEN** PNBSEF. Index available. **Circ:** 2,400. available on microfiche. Documents available from BIOSIS Document Express, CASDDS. ***Continues*** *Proceedings of the National Science Council, Republic of China. Part B, Basic Science, 0253-6870.*
**Ind/Abst** AgBiotech News Inf.; Anim. Breed. Abstr.; Biol. Abstr. (1984-); Chem. Abstr. (1984-); Crop Physiol. Abstr.; Food Sci. Technol. Abstr.; Index Med. (Vol. 8, No. 1, 1984-); Index Vet.; Int. Aerosp. Abstr. (1984-); Plant Breed. Abstr.; Poult. Abstr.; Rice Abstr.; SEA Abstr.; Soils Fert.; Vet. Bull.; Wildl. Rev.

US/0037-9727
**PROCEEDINGS OF THE SOCIETY FOR EXPERIMENTAL BIOLOGY AND MEDICINE.** [Proc. Soc. Exp. Biol. Med.]. **Main/Corp** Society for Experimental Biology and Medicine (New York, N.Y.). Vol. 1 (1903/04)-. Academic Scholarly Publication. English. Eleven times a year (except August). $240.00 (institution), $130.00 (individual) US; $265.00 (institution), $160.00 (individual) other. Blackwell Scientific Publishers, 238 Main Street, Cambridge MA 02142. **Tel** (617)547-7110, (800)835-6770, FAX (617)547-0789. **LC** QP1; .S8. **DD** 616.07/05. **NLM** W1 PR5865. **CODEN** PSEBAA. **[CCC]**. **Pr Rev.** Documents available from The Genuine Article, BIOSIS Document Express, CASDDS.
**Desc:** Interdisciplinary journal which publishes the results of investigative research in biomedicine.
**Ind/Abst** AgBiotech News Inf.; AGRICOLA [Select. Cov.]; Anim. Breed. Abstr.; Biol. Abstr.; Calcium Calcif. Tissue Abstr.; Chem. Abstr.; Chem. Titles; CSA Neuro. Abstr.; Curr. Aware. Biol. Sci., CABS; Curr. Contents Life Sci.; Dairy Sci. Abstr.; EMBASE; Energy Res. Abstr.; Fish Rev.; Food Sci. Technol. Abstr.; Immunol. Abstr.; Index Med.; Int. Aerosp. Abstr.; Iowa Drug Inf. Serv. (1968-); Maize Abstr.; NAPRALERT; Nucl. Sci. Abstr.; Nutr. Abstr. Rev., Ser. B, Live Feeds and Feed.; Nutr. Abstr. Rev., Ser. A, Hum. Exp.; Life Sci. Collect.; PESTDOC; Pig News Inf.; Poult. Abstr.; Ref. Upd. Basic Ed.; Ref. Upd. Deluxe Ed.; Res. Alert [Full Cov.]; Rev. Med. Vet. Entomol.; Sci. Cit. Index; SCISEARCH; Soyabean Abstr.; Trop. Dis. Bull.; Virol. AIDS Abstr.; Wildl. Rev.

●US/1065-9889
**PROCEEDINGS OF THE SOCIETY OF MAGNETIC RESONANCE IN MEDICINE.**
**See** Physics-Magnetism.

NZ/0301-6331
**PROCEEDINGS OF THE UNIVERSITY OF OTAGO MEDICAL SCHOOL.** [Proc. Univ. Otago Med. Sch.]. **Main/Corp** University of Otago. Medical School. **Added/Corp** Otago Medical School Research Society. Vol. 1 (1922)-. Academic Scholarly Publication. English. Three times a year. $24.00. Otago Medical School Research Faculty, PO Box 913, Dunedin 9000 New Zealand. **Tel** 011 64 24 791200. **NLM** W1 PR587EN.
**Ind/Abst** EMBASE [Select. Cov.]; Life Sci. Collect.

NE/0084-1641
**PROCEEDINGS OF THE WORLD CONGRESS.** **Main/Conf** World Congress on Fertility and Sterility. 1st- 1953-. Proceedings. English (Spanish, French and German). Excerpta Medica Publishing Group, PO Box 548, 1000 AM Amsterdam Netherlands. **Tel** 011 31 20 5803243. **LC** RC889; .W62. **DD** 612.6. **NLM** W3 WO541.

US
**PROCEEDINGS / THE ANNUAL SYMPOSIUM ON COMPUTER APPLICATIONS IN MEDICAL CARE.** **Added/Corp** Institute of Electrical and Electronics Engineers. IEEE Computer Society. 4th (1980)-. Proceedings. English. AMIA, 4915 St Elmo Avenue, Suite 302, Bethesda MD 20814. **Pr Rev.** ***Continues*** *Symposium on Computer Application in Medical Care. Proceedings - Symposium on Computer Application in Medical Care, 0195-4210.*
**Ind/Abst** Index Med. (1991-).

FR/0762-4476
**PROCOF MEDICAL.** (PROCOF MEDICAL : ANNUAIRE MEDICAL ET PHARMACEUTIQUE DE FRANCE.). [PROCOF med.]. **VFOAT** Annuaire Medical et Pharmaceutique de France. Ed. 1981/82-. French. an. **NLM** W 22; GF7 P9.

US/1064-8526
**PRODUCT DEVELOPMENT DIRECTORY.** (PRODUCT DEVELOPMENT DIRECTORY : AN HISTORICAL INDEX TO FDA 510(K) FILINGS BY PRODUCT CATEGORY / FROM MEDICAL DEVICE REGISTER.). [Product dev. dir.]. **Added/Corp** United States. Food and Drug Administration. Medical Device Register, Inc. Medical Economics Data (Firm). (1987)-. Directory. English. an. $206.50. Medical Economics Data, Five Paragon Drive, PO Box 27, Montvale NJ 07645. **Tel** (800)442-6657, (201)358-7200. **LC** R855; .P76. **DD** 681/.761/029473. **NLM** W 26; M489201.

US/1064-850X
**PRODUCT SOS.** [Product SOS]. **Added/Corp** Directory Systems, Inc. Situation Occurrence Service. Medical Economics Data (Firm). **VFOAT** Product SOS Historical. (1985)-. English. an. $325.00. Medical Economics Data, Five Paragon Drive, PO Box 27, Montvale NJ 07645. **Tel** (800)442-6657, (201)358-7200. **LC** R856.48; .P76. **DD** 363.1/8.
**Desc:** A complete, unedited listing of every medical device problem report filed with the U.S. Food and Drug Administration for the previous year. Each listing is based upon a specific device problem which resulted in an injury or death, and includes the product and company involved, the date, the complete text of the report, and the FDA's review of the situation.

SP
**PROFESION MEDICA.** Spanish. SANED SA, Paseo de la Habana 202 Bis, 28036 Madrid Spain. **Tel** 011 34 1 5553508.

US/0555-3385
**PROFESSIONAL LIABILITY NEWSLETTER.** **See** Insurance.

US/0033-0140
**PROFESSIONAL MEDICAL ASSISTANT, THE.** [Prof. med. assist.]. **Added/Corp** American Association of Medical Assistants. **VFOAT** PMA. Vol. 1 (July/Aug. 1968)-. Periodical. English. Six times a year. $30.00. American Association Medical Assistant, 20 North Wacker Drive, Suite 1575, Chicago IL 60606-2903. **Tel** (312)899-1500. **ED** Karen S. Rodd. **LC** R728.8; .P7. **DD** 610.69/53/05. **NLM** W1 PR59. Index available. cum. index. **Bk Rev.** **Ad Acc.** **Circ:** 13,000. available on microfilm and microfiche from University Microfilms International (UMI). ***Continues*** *American Association of Medical Assistants. AAMA Bulletin.*
**Desc:** Articles by and for medical assistants (medical secretaries, clinical assistants technicians) stressing their importance in helping doctors respond successfully to the demands for medical services.
**Ind/Abst** Cumul. Index Nurs. Allied Health Lit.

UK/0969-434X
**PROFESSIONAL UPDATE.** (19??)-. Newsletter. English. Ten times a year. £72.00 Europe; £73.00 Other (Institutions). Churchill Livingstone, 1-3 Baxter's Place, Leith Walk, Edinburgh EH1 3AF Scotland. **Tel** 011 44 31 556 2424, FAX 011 44 31 558 1278, telex 727511. **(Subscription address:** Maruzen Company Ltd., PO Box 5050, Import & Export Department, Tokyo 100 31 Japan.)

US/0278-5374
**PROGRAM HIGHLIGHTS.** (PROGRAM HIGHLIGHTS / DIVISION OF RESEARCH RESOURCES.). [Program highlights]. **Main/Corp** National Institutes of Health (U.S.). Division of Research Resources. 1979-. English. an. Free. Office of Science and Health Reports, Division of Research Resources, National Institute of Health, Bethesda MD 20205. **Tel** (301)496-5545. **ED** Edward Post. **LC** R854.U5. **DD** 610/.72073. **NLM** W2 A N167P. **Circ:** 12,000 (ctrl).
**Desc:** Review of biomedical research performed in research centers supported by the NIH Division of Research Resources.

FR
**PROGRES EN ANDROLOGIE.** (1987)-. Periodical. French. Doin Editeurs, 8 Place de l'Odeon, F 75006 Paris France. **Tel** 011 33 1 46332237. **NLM** W1; PR64G.

SZ/1017-8686
**PROGRESS IN APPLIED MICROCIRCULATION (ENGLISH ED.).** (PROGRESS IN APPLIED MICROCIRCULATION.). [Prog. appl. microcirc.]. **VFOAT** Mikrozirkulation in Forschung und Klinik. Vol. 1 (1983)-. Academic Scholarly Publication. English. an. 130.00F (approx. per volume). S. Karger AG, Allschwilerstrasse 10, PO Box - Postfach - Case Postale, CH-4009 Basel Switzerland. **Tel** 011 41 61 306-1111, FAX 011 41 61 306-1234, telex CH 962 652. **ED** K. Messmer. **LC** UNC. **NLM** W1; PR666FI. **CODEN** PAMIEH. Documents available from BIOSIS Document Express, CASDDS.
**Desc:** Knowledge of the physiology and pathology of microcirculation has grown rapidly in recent years, making the collaboration between specialists from basic research (morphology, physiology, rheology, biophysics) and clinicians crucial. This series provides just such a forum for the exchange of ideas and information. Each volume in the series covers a topical aspect of microcirculation and deals with it on an interdisciplinary basis. Besides offering an overview of developments in the field, contributions also present the latest results of original research by recognized authorities.
**Ind/Abst** Biol. Abstr.; Chem. Abstr. (1983-); Ref. Upd. Deluxe Ed.

GW/0177-8757
**PROGRESS IN CLINICAL BIOCHEMISTRY AND MEDICINE.** **See** Biology-Biochemistry.

UK
**PROGRESS IN CLINICAL MEDICINE.** Vol. 1-. English. Churchill Livingstone, 1-3 Baxter's Place, Leith Walk, Edinburgh EH1 3AF Scotland. **Tel** 011 44 31 556 2424, FAX 011 44 31 558 1278, telex 727511. **LC** R31; .P78. **DD** 616/.005. **NLM** W1; PR668GBF.

JA
**PROGRESS OF DIGESTIVE ENDOSCOPY.** **Added/Corp** Nippon Shokaki Naishikyo Gakkai. Kanto Chihokai. Vol. 1 (1972)-. Proceedings. Japanese. ¥10300. Kyowa Kikaku Tsushin, (Kyowa Kikaku Tsushin Co., Ltd.), Shinbashi Ekimae Biru, 1 Gokan, 2-20, Shinbashi, Minatoku, Tokyoto 105 Japan. **NLM** W1 PR687R.
**Desc:** Proceedings of the Nippon Shokaki Naishikyo Gakkai Kanto Chihokai.

IT
**PROGRESSI CLINICI. MEDICINA.** Vol. 1, No. 1 (1984)-. Periodical. Italian. Six times a year (Feb., Apr., June. Aug., Oct., Dec.). $180.00. Piccin Editore, Via Altinate 107, 35121 Padua Italy. **Tel** 011 39 49 655566, FAX 011 39 49 8750693. **NLM** W1; PR697G.

AU
**PROMED.** (19??)-. Twelve times a year. $139.00. Springer-Verlag Wien, Sachsenplatz 4 6, PO Box 89, A-1201 Vienna Austria. **Tel** 011 43 1 3302415. **(Subscription address:** Springer Verlag New York Inc. / for North America, 44 Hartz Way, Secaucus NJ 07096.)

US/0161-6471
**PROMOTING COMMUNITY HEALTH.** English. an. $1.20. Health Services Administration Services, Rockville MD 20857. **LC** RA445; .P69. **DD** 362.1.

FR/0152-2108
**PROSPECTIVE ET SANTE.** [Prospect. sante]. No. 1 (1977)-. Periodical. French. qt. $15.96. P S P, 9 rue Alfred de Vigny, 75008 Paris France. **Tel** 01 763 41 33. **ED** Michel Salomon. **NLM** W1 PR767. Index available. cum. index. **Bk Rev. Ad Acc. Circ:** 10,000.
**Desc:** Interdisciplinary journal for the science of life and health.

UK/0267-1336
**PROSTAGLANDIN PERSPECTIVES.** [Prostaglandin perspect.]. **Added/Corp** May & Baker. Vol. 1, No. 1 (1984)-. English. qt. Rhone Poulenc Ltd, Rainham Road South, Dagenhm Essex RM10 7EX England. **Tel** 01 592 3060. **NLM** W1; PR769Y.

US/0162-9352
**PROSTAGLANDINS & THERAPEUTICS.** **VAT** Prostaglandins and Therapeutics. V. 1- Spring 1975-. Periodical. English. qt. Upjohn Co, 7000 Portage Road, Kalamazoo MI 48008. **Tel** (616)323-4000. **NLM** W1 PR77T.

UK/0952-3278
**PROSTAGLANDINS, LEUKOTRIENES, AND ESSENTIAL FATTY ACIDS.** [Prostaglandins, leukot. essent. fat. acids]. Vol. 31, No. 1 (Jan. 1988)-. Academic Scholarly Publication. English. mo. £1001.00 Europe; £1005.00 Other (Institutions). Churchill Livingstone, 1-3 Baxter's Place, Leith Walk, Edinburgh EH1 3AF Scotland. **Tel** 011 44 31 556 2424, FAX 011 44 31 558 1278, telex 727511. **(Subscription address:** Maruzen Company Ltd., PO Box 5050, Import & Export Department, Tokyo 100 31 Japan.**) ED** D F Horrobin. **NLM** W1; PR77TJ. **CODEN** PLEAEU. **[CCC]. Pr Rev.** available on microfilm and microfiche from University Microfilms International (UMI). Documents available from The Genuine Article, BIOSIS Document Express, CASDDS, ADONIS. ***Continues*** *Prostaglandins, Leukotrienes, and Medicine, 0262-1746.*
**Desc:** Publishes high-quality papers in this fast-developing field of prostaglandins, leukotrienes and essential fatty acids research, particularly relating to their role in clinical medicine.
**Ind/Abst** ADONIS; Anim. Breed. Abstr.; Biol. Abstr. (1988-); Chem. Abstr.; Curr. Aware. Biol. Sci., CABS; Curr. Biotechnol.; Curr. Contents Life Sci.; EMBASE; Helminthol. Abstr.; Index Med. (1988-); PESTDOC; Ref. Upd. Basic Ed.; Ref. Upd. Deluxe Ed.; Res. Alert [Full Cov.]; Sci. Cit. Index; SCISEARCH; Soc. Sci. Cit. Index [Select. Cov.]; Weed Abstr.

FR
**PROVENCE MEDICALE.** French. ir. 120.00F France; 170.00F other. Nouvelles Edit Medicales France, BP 451, 95005 Cergy Pontoise France. **Tel** 011 33 1 44644400.

PL/0033-2240
**PRZEGLAD LEKARSKI.** (PRZEGLAD LEKARSKI : ORGAN TOWARZYSTWA LEKARSKIEGO KRAKOWSKIEGO, ODDZIAU, PTL.). [Prz. lek.]. **Added/Corp** Polskie Towarzystwo Lekarskie. Krakowski Oddzia. (1945)-. Academic Scholarly Publication. Polish (summaries and/or abstracts in English and Russian; table of contents in English and Russian). mo. Price on Request. **(Subscription address:** ARS Polona, PO Box 1001, 00068 Warsaw Poland.**) NLM** W1 PR932. **CODEN** PRLKAV. Documents available from CASDDS.
**Ind/Abst** Chem. Abstr.; EMBASE [Select. Cov.]; Index Med.; Saf. Health Work; Trop. Dis. Bull.

PE
**PSICOACTIVA : REVISTA CIENTIFICA DEL CENTRO DE INFORMACION Y EDUCACION PARA LA PREVENCION DEL ABUSO DE DROGAS.** **See** Drug Abuse and Alcoholism.

US/1051-2438
**PSR QUARTERLY (BALTIMORE, MD.), THE.** ***Title Change.*** (THE PSR QUARTERLY : A JOURNAL OF MEDICINE & GLOBAL SURVIVAL.). [PSR q.]. **Added/Corp** Physicians for Social Responsibility (U.S.). **VAT** Physicians for Social Responsibility quarterly. (1991)-(1992). Periodical. English. qt. Williams & Wilkins Company, 428 East Preston Street, Baltimore MD 21202-3993. **Tel** (410)528-4000, (800)638-6423, FAX (410)528-8596, telex 87669. **(Subscription address:** US/ PO Box 64380, Baltimore, MD 21264-4380; Japan/ Igaku-Shoin MYW Ltd, 1-28-36 Hongo, Bunkyo-ku Tokyo 113 Japan; European/ The Broadway House, 2-6 Fulham Broadway, London SW6 1AA England; telephone: (800)638-6423**) LC** RA441; .P78. **DD** 363.3/47/05. **NLM** W1; P95. **[CCC].** Documents available from Quick Copies. ***Continued by*** *Medicine and Global Society.*
**Desc:** First journal to promote investigation of medical, scientific, public health, and bioethical problems that have evolved in the wake of the nuclear age.
**Ind/Abst** Environ. Period. Bibliogr.

UK/0264-1801
**PSYCHOLOGICAL MEDICINE. MONOGRAPH SUPPLEMENT.** **See** Psychology.

US/0033-3174
**PSYCHOSOMATIC MEDICINE.** [Psychosom. med.]. **Added/Corp** American Psychosomatic Society. National Research Council (U.S.). Committee on Problems of Neurotic Behavior. American Society for Research in Psychosomatic Problems. Vol. 1 (Jan. 1939)-. Academic Scholarly Publication. English. bm. $152.00 (indiviual), $313.00 (institution) US; $182.00 (individual), $343.00 (institution) other. Williams & Wilkins Company, 428 East Preston Street, Baltimore MD 21202-3993. **Tel** (410)528-4000, (800)638-6423, FAX (410)528-8596, telex 87669. **(Subscription address:** Williams & Wilkins, PO Box 64380, Baltimore MD 21264.**) ED** Donald Oken. **LC** RC49; .P8. **DD** 616. **NLM** W1 PS82. **CODEN** PSMEAP. **[CCC]. Pr Rev.** available on microfilm and microfiche from University Microfilms International (UMI). Documents available from The Genuine Article, BIOSIS Document Express, CASDDS, Quick Copies.
**Desc:** Interdisciplinary journal devoted to behavioral biology. Delivers up-to-date, authoritative reports for psychiatrists, clinical psychologists, behavioral scientists and general practitioners.
**Ind/Abst** Annals Behav. Med.; Biol. Abstr.; Chem. Abstr.; Crim. Justice Abstr.; Curr. Contents Clin. Med.; Curr. Contents Life Sci.; Curr. Contents Soc. Behav. Sci.; EMBASE; Energy Res. Abstr. (Aug. 1976-); High. Educ. Abstr. (1976-); Index Med.; Med. Abstr. Newsl.; Life Sci. Collect.; Psychol. Abstr. (1939-); PsycINFO; PsycLit; Ref. Sources; Ref. Upd. Deluxe Ed.; Res. Alert [Full Cov.]; Risk Abstr.; Sci. Cit. Index; SCISEARCH; Soc. Plann. Policy Dev. Abstr.; Soc. Sci. Cit. Index [Full Cov.]; Soc. Welf. Soc. Plan./Policy Soc. Dev.; Sociol. Abstr.

NE
**PSYCHOSOMATIC MEDICINE : PROCEEDINGS OF THE ... INTERNATIONAL CONGRESS OF THE ACADEMY OF PSYCHOSOMATIC MEDICINE.** **Added/Corp** Excerpta Medica Foundation. (1966)-. English. ir. Price varies per volume. S. Karger AG, Allschwilerstrasse 10, PO Box - Postfach - Case Postale, CH-4009 Basel Switzerland. **Tel** 011 41 61 306-1111, FAX 011 41 61 306-1234, telex CH 962 652.

US/0033-3182
**PSYCHOSOMATICS (WASHINGTON, D.C.).** (PSYCHOSOMATICS.). [Psychosomatics]. **Added/Corp** Academy of Psychosomatic Medicine. Vol. 1 (Jan./Feb. 1960)-. Academic Scholarly Publication. English. bm. $149.00 US; $164.00 other (institution). American Psychiatric Press Inc., 1400 K Street Northwest, Suite 1101, Washington DC 20005. **Tel** (202)682-6222, FAX (202)789-2648. **ED** Leo Cristofar. **LC** RC49; .P83. **DD** 616.08/05. **NLM** W1 PS822. **CODEN** PSYCBC. **Ad Acc. Pr Rev. Circ:** 43,106. available on microfilm and microfiche from University Microfilms International (UMI). Documents available from The Genuine Article, BIOSIS Document Express, CASDDS.
**Desc:** Publishes original research on clinical topics in medical psychiatry.
**Ind/Abst** Biol. Abstr.; Chem. Abstr.; Cumul. Index Nurs. Allied Health Lit.; Curr. Contents Clin. Med.; Curr. Contents Soc. Behav. Sci.; EMBASE; Energy Res. Abstr. (Aug. 1982-); Index Med.; Med. Abstr. Newsl.; Mod. Med.; Life Sci. Collect.; Psychol. Abstr. (1966-); PsycINFO; PsycLit; Res. Alert [Full Cov.]; Sci. Cit. Index; SCISEARCH; Soc. Sci. Cit. Index [Full Cov.]; Soc. Work Abstr. [Select. Cov.].

US/0732-7986
**PSYCHOTHERAPY RESEARCH REVIEW SERIES.** [Psychother. res. rev. ser.]. (19??)-. Monographic series. English. ir. Price varies per volume. Guilford Publications Inc., 72 Spring Street, New York NY 10012. **Tel** (212)431-9800, (800)365-7006, FAX (212)966-6708.

US/1050-1835
**PTSD RESEARCH QUARTERLY.** [PTSD res. q.]. **VAT** Post-Traumatic Stress Disorder Research Quarterly; Post Traumatic Stress Disorder Research Quarterly. (1990)-. Periodical. English. qt. Free. National Center for Post-Traumatic Stress Disorder (116D), VA Medical Center, White River Junction VT 05001. **DD** 616.

AG
**PUBLICACION.** **Main/Corp** Buenos Aires. Universidad Nacional. Instituto de Enfermedades Infecciosas. Spanish.

CN/0704-0148
**PUBLICATION OF THE HANNAH INSTITUTE FOR THE HISTORY OF MEDICINE.** **Main/Corp** Hannah Institute for the History of Medicine. V. 1- 1977-. Periodical. English. Free. The Hannah Institute for the History of Medicine, Suite 105/50 Prince Arthur Avenue, Toronto Ontario M5R 1B5 Canada. **DD** 610/.5. **NLM** W1 PU69.

US/0743-6017
**PUBLICATIONS IN INDIANA MEDICAL HISTORY.** [Pub. Ind. med. hist.]. No. 1-. Monographic series. English. ir. Price varies per volume. Indiana Historical Society, 315 West Ohio Street, Indianapolis IN 46202. **Tel** (317)232-1882. **NLM** W1; PU732F.

IO/0165-7259
**PUBLIKATIES VAN DE GEZONDHEIDSORGANISATIE T. N. O. SERIE A : ALGEMENE ONDERWERPEN.** **VFOAT** Proceedings of the Organization for Health Research T. N. O. General Subjects. No. 1- 1958-. Monographic series. Dutch (English). Price varies per volume. **NLM** W1 PU7393.

DK/0105-4139
**PUBLIKATION - INSTITUT FOR SOCIAL MEDICIN, KBENHAVNS UNIVERSITET.** (PUBLICATION - INSTITUTE OF SOCIAL MEDICINE, UNIVERSITY OF COPENHAGEN.). 5- 1974-. Monographic series. Danish. Price varies per volume. University of Copenhagen Institute of Social Medicine, Copenhagen Denmark. **NLM** W1 PU676. ***Continues*** *Publikation - Institut for Social Medicin, Kbenhavns Universitet, 0105-4139.*

US
**PUBLISHED SEARCH BIBLIOGRAPHIES FROM THE NTIS BIBLIOGRAPHIC DATA BASE. HEALTH AND MEDICINE / U.S. DEPARTMENT OF COMMERCE, NATIONAL TECHNICAL INFORMATION SERVICE.** **See** Medical Science and Technology-Abstracting, Bibliographies and Statistics.

PR/0738-0658
**PUERTO RICO HEALTH SCIENCES JOURNAL.** **Added/Corp** University of Puerto Rico Medical Sciences Campus. Vol. 1, No. 1 (Mar. 1982)-. Academic Scholarly Publication. English (summaries and/or abstracts in Spanish). Three times a year. $30.00 (institutions), $20.00 (individuals). Puerto Rico Health Sciences, University of Puerto Rico, Department of Medical Sciences, GPO Box 5067, San Juan, Puerto Rico 00936. **Tel** (809)758-2525 ext. 1719. **ED** Rafael Villavicencio. **NLM** W1 PU787JR. **CODEN** PRHJDB. Index available. cum. index. **Bk Rev. Ad Acc. Pr Rev. Circ:** 600. Documents available from CASDDS.
**Desc:** Strives to publish research findings by local investigators and by Puerto Ricans abroad. It also promotes the publication of research done by students on campus.
**Ind/Abst** Chem. Abstr.; Index Med. (Vol. 4, No. 1, 1985-).

UK
**PULSE.** (19??)-. English. wk. £93.00 UK & Ireland; $196.00 other. Morgan Grampian, 40 Beresford Street Woolwich, London SE18 6BQ England. **Tel** 011 44 81 855 7777, FAX 011 44 81 855 5548, telex 896238.

UK/0048-6000
**PULSE LONDON. 1959.** [Pulse Lond. 1959]. English. wk. £90.50 UK and Northern Ireland; $190.00 other. Morgan Grampian, 40 Beresford Street Woolwich, London SE18 6BQ England. **Tel** 011 44 81 855 7777, FAX 011 44 81 855 5548, telex 896238.

II/0033-4340
**PUNJAB MEDICAL JOURNAL.** 1- 1951-. Periodical. English. ir. Hindustan Book Agency, 17 UB Jawahar Nagar, Delhi 7 India.

US/1044-5854
**PXE AWARENESS.** (PXE AWARENESS / NATIONAL ASSOCIATION FOR PSEUDOXANTHOMA ELASTICUM.). [PXE aware.]. **Added/Corp** National Association for Pseudoxanthoma Elasticum. **VAT** Pseudozanthoma Elasticum Awareness. Vol. 1, No. 1 (Jan. 1989)-. Periodical. English. qt. Free to members. National Association for Pseudoxanthoma Elasticum, PO Box 6925, Albany NY 12203-1938. **DD** 616.

US
**QI/TQM.** (19??)-. English. $289.00. American Health Consultants, 3525 Piedmont Road, Suite 400, Atlanta GA 30305. **Tel** (800)688-2421, (404)262-7436. **(Subscription address:** American Health Consultants, PO Box 95278, Chicago IL 60694.**)**
**Ind/Abst** Hospit. Manage. Rev. (19??-).

●UK
**QJM : MONTHLY JOURNAL OF THE ASSOCIATION OF PHYSICIANS.** **Added/Corp** Association of Physicians of Great Britain and Ireland. **VFOAT** Monthly Journal of the Association of Physicians. Vol. 87, 7 (July 1994)-. Periodical. English. mo. $255.00. Oxford University Press, Walton Street, Oxford OX2 6DP England. **Tel** 011 44 865 56767, FAX 011 44 865 267773, telex 837330 OXPRES G. **(Subscription address:** Oxford University Press / USA, Journals Marketing Department, Oxford University Press, 2001 Evans Road, Cary NC 27513.**) LC** R31; .Q2. **NLM** W1; QJ102K. Index available. cum. index. **Ad Acc. Circ:** 2,500. ***Continues*** *Quarterly Journal of Medicine, 0033-5622.*
**Desc:** Covers the whole field of medicine with emphasis on internal medicine. Reports advances of importance and significance in both diagnosis and treatment. Many papers are concerned with the development of growing points of current interest.
**Ind/Abst** ADONIS; Biol. Abstr.; Curr. Aware. Biol. Sci., CABS; Curr. Contents Clin. Med.; Curr. Contents Life Sci.;

Dairy Sci. Abstr.; EMBASE; Health Serv. Abstr.; Helminthol. Abstr.; Int. Pharm. Abstr.; Nutr. Abstr. Rev., Ser. A, Hum. Exp.; Nutr. Res. Newsl.; Life Sci. Collect.; Protozoolog. Abstr.; Ref. Upd. Basic Ed.; Ref. Upd. Deluxe Ed.; Res. Alert [Full Cov.]; Rev. Med. Vet. Entomol.; Index Med. (1994-); Sci. Cit. Index; SCISEARCH; Trop. Dis. Bull.

SP/0213-4462
**QUADERN CAPS.** [Quad. CAPS]. **VFOAT** Quadern Centre d'Analisis i Programes Sanitaris; Quaderns CAPS. (1984)-. Monographic series. Spanish. Four times a year. 4000ptas. Centro de Analisis y Programas Sanitarios, 150 1 2, 08036 Barcelona Spain. **Tel** 011 34 3 3226554, FAX 3 410 97 42. **(Subscription address:** Suport Services, Paris 150, 08036 Barcelona Spain.**)** **UDC** 614. **Circ:** 3,000.
**Desc:** An open publication to the cultural reflexion about health policies, ways of life and work, mixed with various opinions and analyses about medicine.

IT
**QUADERNI DI CURE PALLIATIVE.** (19??)-. Periodical. Italian. qt. 75000L. Masson S.P.A, Via Statuto 2/4, 20121 Milan Italy. **Tel** 011 39 2 63671, FAX 011 39 2 6367211. **ED** Marcello Tamburini.

IT/0392-9620
**QUADERNI MARCHIGIANI DI MEDICINA.** ***Suspended.*** (1983)-Suspended with Issue 2(1993). Periodical. Italian (English; summaries and/or abstracts in English). bm. L50000. Il Lavoro Editoriale, Via Piave 32, 60123 Ancona Italy. **Tel** 011 39 71 52735, FAX 011 39 71 36202. **NLM** W1; QU152L. Index available. **Bk Rev. Ad Acc. Circ:** 1,000 (ctrl).
**Ind/Abst** EMBASE [Select. Cov.].

FR/0997-9638
**QUALITE SANTE PARIS.** ***Suspended.*** (QUALITE SANTE.). (1989)-Suspended (1993). Periodical. French. Six times a year. Heral, 44 rue Jules Ferry, 94400 Vitry-sur-Seine France. **Tel** 011 33 1 46825300. **UDC** 61. ***Continues*** *Revue des Professions de Sante.*

US/0885-713X
**QUALITY ASSURANCE AND UTILIZATION REVIEW : OFFICIAL JOURNAL OF THE AMERICAN COLLEGE OF UTILIZATION REVIEW PHYSICIANS.** ***Title Change.*** [Qual. assur. util. rev.]. **Added/Corp** American College of Utilization Review Physicians. (1986-1992). Periodical. English. qt. Williams & Wilkins Company, 428 East Preston Street, Baltimore MD 21202-3993. **Tel** (410)528-4000, (800)638-6423, FAX (410)528-8596, telex 87669. **(Subscription address:** US/ PO Box 64380, Baltimore, MD 21264-4380; Japan/ Igaku-Shoin MYW Ltd, 1-28-36 Hongo, Bunkyo-ku Tokyo 113 Japan; European/ The Broadway House, 2-6 Fulham Broadway, London SW6 1AA England; telephone: (800)638-6423**)** **DD** 610. **NLM** W1; QU153KF. **[CCC]. Pr Rev.** Documents available from Quick Copies. ***Continued by*** *American Journal of Medical Quality, 1062-8606.*
**Desc:** Articles on utilization review, quality assurance, cost containment, diagnosis related groups, risk management, and peer review.
**Ind/Abst** Health Plan. Adminis.; Hospit. Health Admin. Index (1986-).

US/1058-6415
**QUALITY HEALTHCARE & OUTCOMES.** [Qual. healthc. outcomes]. **Added/Corp** Excerpta Medica (Firm). CR Group. **VFOAT** Quality Healthcare and Outcomes; Quality. No. 1 (Oct. 1991)-. Periodical. English. Three times a year. Excerpta Medica Publishing Group, PO Box 548, 1000 AM Amsterdam Netherlands. **Tel** 011 31 20 5803243. **DD** 362.

●UK/0963-8172
**QUALITY IN HEALTH CARE : QHC.** **VFOAT** QHC. Vol. 1, No. 1 (Mar. 1992)-. Periodical. English. qt. £97.00. BMJ / British Medical Journal Publishing Group, British Medical Association House, Tavistock Square, London WC1H 9JR England. **Tel** 011 44 71 3874499, FAX 011 44 71 383 6402, telex 290034 HBJ MN. **ED** Fiona Moss. **NLM** W1; QU158LAH. **Bk Rev. Pr Rev.**
**Desc:** The journal aims to monitor the relationship between clinical and medical audit and quality assurance programs, the development of clinical and medical audit as local activities and as large national initiatives, the integration of medical audit into medical practice, the impact of medical and clinical audit on postgraduate and undergraduate training and education, and the relationship between management and quality initiatives.

US
**QUALITY IN HEALTHCARE MANAGEMENT.** English. Twice a year. $26.00 US; $30.36 other. Macmillan Professional Journal, 30 Vreeland Road, Florham Park NJ 07932. **Tel** (201)822-1622, FAX (201)822-2498.

US
**QUALITY MANAGEMENT UPDATE.** (19??)-. Periodical. English. Twenty-four times a year. $275.00. Faulkner & Gray Inc., 11 Penn Plaza, 17th Floor, New York NY 10001. **Tel** (212)967-7000, (800)535-8403.

US/1040-0079
**QUALITY RESOURCE MONITOR.** ***Ceased.*** [Qual. resour. monit.]. **Added/Corp** Medical Management Analysis International. (19??)-(19??). Periodical. English. bm. Quality Resource Monitor, PO Box 2106, Rockville MD 20852. **DD** 362.

US
**QUANTUM MEDICINE.** Vol. 1, No. 1 and 2 (Jan., April 1988)-. Periodical. English. qt. Quantum Medicine, 910 East Victory Drive, Savannah GA 31405. ***Absorbed*** *Basal Facts, 0147-9679.*

US/0196-5530
**QUARTERLY INDEX TO CURRENT CONTENTS. LIFE SCIENCES.** [Q. index curr. contents, Life sci.]. **VFOAT** Q.U.I.C.C./L.S.; QUICC/LS. Began with 1980, Issues 1-13. Academic Scholarly Publication. English. qt. $150.00 US and Canada. Institute for Scientific Information, 3501 Market Street, Philadelphia PA 19104. **Tel** (215)386-0100, (800)523-1850, FAX (215)386-6362, telex 84-5305. **(Subscription address:** Institute for Scientific Information, PO Box 71416, Chicago, IL 60694**)** **LC** Z5321; .Q37; QH301. **DD** 016.574. **NLM** ZW 1 C959B.

UK/0033-5622
**QUARTERLY JOURNAL OF MEDICINE, THE.** ***Title Change.*** [Q. j. med.]. **Added/Corp** Association of Physicians of Great Britain and Ireland. **VFOAT** QJM. Vol. 1 (Oct. 1907)-Vol. 24, (July 1931); New Ser., Vol. 1 (Jan. 1932)-Vol. 87, No. 6 (June 1994). Academic Scholarly Publication. English. mo. Oxford University Press, Walton Street, Oxford OX2 6DP England. **Tel** 011 44 865 56767, FAX 011 44 865 267773, telex 837330 OXPRES G. **(Subscription address:** Oxford University Press / USA, Journals Marketing Department, Oxford University Press, 2001 Evans Road, Cary NC 27513.**)** **ED** J. S. Cameron. **LC** R31; .Q2. **NLM** W1; QU278. **CODEN** QJMEA7. **[CCC].** Index available. cum. index. **Ad Acc. Pr Rev. Circ:** 2,500. available on microfilm and microfiche from University Microfilms International (UMI). Documents available from The Genuine Article, BIOSIS Document Express, CASDDS, ADONIS. ***Continued by*** *QJM.*
**Desc:** Covers the whole field of medicine with emphasis on internal medicine. Reports advances of importance and significance in both diagnosis and treatment, and many of its papers are concerned with the development of growing points of current interest.
**Ind/Abst** ADONIS; Biol. Abstr.; Chem. Abstr. (1907-1983); Curr. Aware. Biol. Sci., CABS; Curr. Contents Clin. Med.; Curr. Contents Life Sci.; Dairy Sci. Abstr.; EMBASE; Health Serv. Abstr.; Helminthol. Abstr.; Index Med.; Int. Pharm. Abstr.; Iowa Drug Inf. Serv. (1968-19??); Nutr. Abstr. Rev., Ser. A, Hum. Exp.; Nutr. Res. Newsl.; Life Sci. Collect.; Protozoolog. Abstr.; Ref. Upd. Basic Ed.; Ref. Upd. Deluxe Ed.; Res. Alert [Full Cov.]; Rev. Med. Vet. Entomol.; Rev. Med. Vet. Mycology; Sci. Cit. Index; SCISEARCH; Stat. Theory Method Abstr. (1959-1963); Trop. Dis. Bull.

GW/0176-912X
**QUINOLONES BULLETIN : REPORTS ON GYRASE INHIBITORS.** 1984-. Bulletin. English. **NLM** W1; QU94.

YU/0351-4331
**RAD DISPANZERA ZA PLUCNE BOLESTI I TUBERKULOZU.** [Rad dispanz. plucne boles. tuberk.]. 1973-. Periodical. Serbo-Croatian (Roman). **NLM** W2 GS4.1 V8I4R. ***Continues*** *Rad Antituberkuloznih Dispanzera, 0485-8506.*

AT/0033-8273
**RADIOGRAPHER.** (THE RADIOGRAPHER : THE OFFICIAL JOURNAL OF THE AUSTRALASIAN INSTITUTE OF RADIOGRAPHY.). [Radiographer]. **Added/Corp** Australian Institute of Radiography. Australian Institute of Radiography. (1949)-. Academic Scholarly Publication. English. Four times a year (Mar., June, Sept., Dec.). 45.00Aus$. Australian Institute of Radiography, 32 Bedford Street, 1st Floor, PO Box 1169, Collingwood Victoria 3066 Australia. **Tel** 011 61 03 419 3336, FAX 011 61 03 416 0783. **ED** J. Lane. **CODEN** RDGRAJ. Index available. **Bk Rev. Ad Acc. Pr Rev. Circ:** 3,300 (ctrl). Documents available from Ask*IEEE, CASDDS.
**Desc:** News and information radiography, radiation therapy, ultrasound, and others articles.
**Ind/Abst** Chem. Abstr. (1948/1949-1984); Energy Res. Abstr.; INSPEC (1982-).

II/0485-9561
**RAJASTHAN MEDICAL JOURNAL, THE.** [Rajasthan med. j.]. **Added/Corp** Rajasthan (India). Directorate of Medical and Health Services. Rajasthan (India). Directorate of Medical, Health, and Family Planning. Rajasthan (India). Directorate of Medical, Health & Family Welfare Services. (19??)-. Periodical. English. qt. $14.50. Directorate of Medical & Health Services, Rajasthan, Jaipur, India. **(Subscription address:** Prints India, 11 Darya Ganj, New Delhi 110002 India.**)** **NLM** W1 RA463.

IT/0391-1675
**RAPPORTI ISTISAN.** **Added/Corp** Istituto Superiore di Sanita (Italy). **VFOAT** ISTISAN. (1977)-. Academic Scholarly Publication. English (Italian). **NLM** W1; RA489J. **CODEN** RAISEF. Documents available from CASDDS.
**Ind/Abst** Chem. Abstr. (1985-).

IT
**RASSEGNA DI MEDICINA DEI LAVORATORI.** (19??)-. Italian. Four times a year. L80000 Italy; L160000 other. Ediesse / Rome, Via Dei Frentani 4A, 00185 Rome Italy. **Tel** 011 39 6 44870286, 44870288, FAX 011 39 6 4481260. Index available (bound in last issue).

IT/0033-9695
**RASSEGNA INTERNAZIONALE DI CLINICA E TERAPIA.** [Rass. Int. Clin. Ter.]. Vol. 1 (1920)-. Academic Scholarly Publication. Italian. Six times a year. $50.00. Bruno Buonomo La Rossa, Pallonetto S Chiara 8, 80134 Naples Italy. **Tel** 011 39 81 5520424. **NLM** W1 RA789. available on microfilm and microfiche from University Microfilms International (UMI).
**Ind/Abst** CSA Neuro. Abstr. (?-?); EMBASE [Select. Cov.]; Life Sci. Collect. (1985-).

IT/0033-9776
**RASSEGNA MEDICA SARDA.** [Rass. med. Sarda]. Vol. 38 (1936)-. Academic Scholarly Publication. Italian. **NLM** W1 RA885V. **CODEN** RMSAAN. Documents available from CASDDS. ***Continues*** *Societa fra i Cultori Delle Scienze Mediche e Naturali di Cagliari. Atti.*
**Ind/Abst** Chem. Abstr.; EMBASE; Life Sci. Collect.; Saf. Health Work.

US/0190-5139
**RATE REVIEW TOPICS.** V. 1- June 1, 1977-. Periodical. English. sm. $85.00. Miller and Byrne, 1370 Piscard Drive, Rockville MD 20850. **NLM** W1 RA9477.

CN/0712-5364
**REACH (VANCOUVER).** ***Ceased.*** (REACH.). [Reach]. (1977)-(1993). Periodical. English. qt. Canadian Diabetic Association, British Columbia Division, 4480 Main Street, Vancouver British Columbia V5V 3R3 Canada. **DD** 616.4/62/005.

AT/0157-7271
**REACTIONS.** ***Title Change.*** [Reactions]. No. 1 (Jan. 25, 1980)-(19??). Periodical. English. wk. ADIS Press International, 582 Middletown Boulevard B-30, Langhorne PA 19047-1822. **Tel** (215)752-4500, 011 64 9 4798100, 8525 892 0633, FAX (215)752-4541, 8525 834 5554. **(Subscription address:** NZ/ Centorian Drive, Mairangi Bay, Private Bag, Auckland 10 New Zealand; HK/ 18/F Tung Sun Commercial Centre, 194-200 Lockhard Road, Wanchai Hong Kong**)** **ED** Rennie C Heel. **NLM** W1 RE1H. **[CCC].** Index Available, published separately, free-automatically sent. cum. index. **Bk Rev. Ad Acc. Circ:** 800 (ctrl). ***Continued by*** *Reactions Weekly, 0114-9954.*
**Desc:** Current international reports on adverse drug reactions, interactions, overdose, poisoning, abuse and drug addiction.

US/0737-0822
**READINGS AND PERSPECTIVES IN MEDICINE.** ***Ceased.*** [Read. perspect. med.]. **Added/Corp** Duke University. Medical Center. Booklet No. 1- ?. Monographic series. English. ir. Duke University Medical Center, Medical History Program and the Trent Collection, Durham NC 27710. **NLM** W1 RE103F.

●US/1060-5673
**READMORE REPORTER, THE.** (THE READMORE REPORTER: FOR THE MEDICAL LIBRARY COMMUNITY.). **VFOAT** Readmore Reporter for the Medical Library Community. (1992)-. Periodical. English. qt. Readmore, Inc., 22 Courtlanot Street, New York NY 10007.

FR/0765-5290
**REANIMATION, SOINS INTENSIFS, MEDECINE D'URGENCE.** [Reanim., soins intensifs, med. urgence]. (1985)-. Periodical. French. bm. 1100.00F France; 1420.00F other. Expansion Scientifique Francaise, 31 Boulevard de la Tour-Maubourg, 75007 Paris France. **Tel** 011 33 1 40 62 64 00, 011 33 1 40626439. **ED** C. Chopin. **UDC** 616. **Circ:** 3,000.
**Ind/Abst** EMBASE.

US/0730-8019
**RECENT ADVANCES IN CLINICAL THERAPEUTICS.** [Recent adv. clin. ther.]. Vol. 1 (1981)-. Academic Scholarly Publication. English. ir. Academic Press, Inc., 6277 Sea Harbor Drive, Orlando FL 32887. **Tel** (800)543-9534, (407)345-4100, FAX (407)363-9661. **ED** Jack Z. Yetiv and Joseph R. Bianchine. **NLM** W3 RE341. **CODEN** RETHDU. Documents available from CASDDS.
**Ind/Abst** Chem. Abstr. (1981-1983).

UK/0143-6775
**RECENT ADVANCES IN CLINICAL VIROLOGY.** ***Ceased.*** [Recent adv. clin. virol.]. Began with: No. 1, published 1977-?. English. ir. Churchill Livingstone, 1-3 Baxter's Place, Leith Walk, Edinburgh EH1 3AF Scotland. **Tel** 011 44 31 556 2424, FAX 011 44 31 558 1278, telex 727511. **(Subscription address:** US/ Churchill Livingstone, Fulfillment Office, PO Box 11318, Birmingham, AL 35202) **ED** A P Waterson. **NLM** W1 RE105UC.

UK/0143-6791
**RECENT ADVANCES IN MEDICINE (EDINBURGH).** (RECENT ADVANCES IN MEDICINE.). [Recent adv. med.]. (1924)-. English. ir (every five years). Price varies per volume. Longman Group Ltd., Fourth Avenue, Longman House, Harlow Essex CM19 5SR England. **Tel** 011 44 279 429655, FAX 011 44 279 431059, telex 81259. **(Subscription address:** Churchill Livingstone / US, 5 S 250 Frontenac Road, Naperville IL 60563.) **LC** Discard.

UK/0261-1449
**RECENT ADVANCES IN OCCUPATIONAL HEALTH.** ***Ceased.*** [Recent adv. occup. health]. No. 1-Ceased with Vol. 3. Periodical. English. ir. Churchill Livingstone, 1-3 Baxter's Place, Leith Walk, Edinburgh EH1 3AF Scotland. **Tel** 011 44 31 556 2424, FAX 011 44 31 558 1278, telex 727511. **(Subscription address:** US/ Churchill Livingstone, Fulfillment Office, PO Box 11318, Birmingham, AL 35202) **ED** J C McDonald. **LC** RC967; .R42. **DD** 613.6/2/05. **NLM** W1 RE105VNM.

US/0148-2319
**RECENT ADVANCES IN ULTRASOUND IN BIOMEDICINE.** V. 1-. English. Research Studies Press / Forest Grove, PO Box 92, Forest Grove OR 91776. **LC** R857.U48; R4. **DD** 616.07/54.

CN/0228-0655
**RECENT AND RECOMMENDED MEDICAL BOOKS.** (RECENT AND RECOMMENDED MEDICAL BOOKS - BRITISH COLUMBIA MEDICAL LIBRARY SERVICES.). [Recent recomm. med. books]. **Main/Corp** British Columbia Medical Library Service. **VAT** Selective List for Hospital Libraries. 1979-. English. an. 5.00Can$. British Columbia Medical Library Service, 1807 West 10th Avenue, Vancouver British Columbia V6J 2A9 Canada. **Tel** (604)733-6671, FAX (604)737-8582. **ED** C William Fraser and Lenore Mason. **DD** 016.61. **Circ:** 275. ***Continues*** *British Columbia Medical Library Service. Recent and Recommended Texts, 0228-0647.*
**Desc:** Both a core list of medical books and a selected list for hospital libraries.

US/0899-0778
**RECENT TITLES IN LAW FOR THE SUBJECT SPECIALIST. MEDICINE AND HEALTH LAW.** **See** Law.

US/1043-3163
**RECOVERY NOW.** [Recovery now]. (1988)-. Periodical. English. Eleven times a year (Dec./Jan. issues combined). $36.00. Recovery Now, PO Box 280, Throggs Neck Station, Bronx NY 10465-9998. **Tel** (212)653-0321. **DD** 616.

●UK/1351-0002
**REDOX REPORT.** (1994)-. English. Four times a year. £200.00 Europe; £202.00 Other (Institutions). Churchill Livingstone, 1-3 Baxter's Place, Leith Walk, Edinburgh EH1 3AF Scotland. **Tel** 011 44 31 556 2424, FAX 011 44 31 558 1278, telex 727511. **(Subscription address:** Maruzen Company Ltd., PO Box 5050, Import & Export Department, Tokyo 100 31 Japan.)

CN/0704-3899
**REFERENCE LIST OF HEALTH SCIENCE RESEARCH IN CANADA.** **VFOAT** Repertoire de Recherches en Sante au Canada. 1969/70-. English (French). an. Medical Research Council / Canada, Jeanne Mance Building, 20th Floor, Ottawa Ontario K1A 0W9 Canada. **Tel** (613)954-1382. **DD** 610'.7'2071. **NLM** W 22 DC2 R3. ***Continues*** *Reference List of Medical Research Projects in Canada, 0527-6535.*

US
**REFERENCE UPDATE BASIC EDITION [COMPUTER FILE].** **See** Medical Science and Technology-Abstracting, Bibliographies and Statistics.

US
**REFERENCE UPDATE DELUXE EDITION [COMPUTER FILE].** **See** Medical Science and Technology-Abstracting, Bibliographies and Statistics.

US/0034-3188
**REGAN REPORT ON MEDICAL LAW.** **See** Law.

UK/0960-7889
**REGULATORY AFFAIRS JOURNAL.** [Regul. aff. j.]. Vol. 1 (Nov./Dec. 1990)-. Periodical. English. mo (Published on the first day of each month). £720.00 Europe; £780.00 other. Regulatory Affairs Journal, PO Box 635, Maidenhead Berkshire, SL6 6TW England. **Tel** 011 44 1276 476432, FAX 011 44 1276 75603. **ED** Robin Harmon. **DD** 363.1946. Index available. cum. index. **Bk Rev**. **Ad Acc**. **Pr Rev**. ctrl circ.
**Desc:** Full coverage of regulatory matters in all of the following markets: ethical pharmaceuticals, OTC medicines, biotechnology, medical devices, veterinary products, cosmetics and toiletries, agrochemicals, food and labelling.

●UK
**REGULATORY AFFAIRS JOURNAL (DEVICES), THE.** Vol. 1 (1993)-. English. qt. £395.00 Europe; £430.00 other. Regulatory Affairs Journal, PO Box 635, Maidenhead Berkshire, SL6 6TW England. **Tel** 011 44 1276 476432, FAX 011 44 1276 75603.

US/1065-1063
**REGULATORY ANALYST. MEDICAL WASTE.** ***Title Change.*** [Regul. anal., Med. waste]. **Added/Corp** Warren, Gorham & Lamont, Inc. **VFOAT** Medical Waste. (1992)-(1993). Periodical. English. mo. Technomic Publishing Company, Inc., 851 New Holland Avenue, Box 3535, Lancaster PA 17604. **Tel** (717)291-5609, (800)233-9936, FAX (717)295-4538. **DD** 363. **NLM** W1; RE173JF. **[CCC]**. ***Continued by*** *Medical Waste Analyst, 1072-6039.*

●CN/1192-2508
**REHAB & COMMUNITY CARE MANAGEMENT.** [Rehab communtiy care manag.]. **VFOAT** Rehab and Community Care Management. Vol. 1, No. 1 (June 1992)-. Periodical. English. Four times a year (Feb., May, Sept., Nov.). 25.58Can$. BCS Communications Ltd., 101 Thorncliffe Park Drive, Toronto Ontario M4H 1M2 Canada. **Tel** (416)421-7944, FAX (416)421-0966. **ED** H. Dostal. **DD** 362.1. **Bk Rev**, (Qty: 8-12). **Ad Acc**. **Circ:** 20,000 (ctrl).
**Desc:** News and information of interest to those involved with rehabilitation and community care management.

SA/0034-3501
**REHABILITASIE IN SUID-AFRIKA.** [Rehabil. S.-Afr.]. **Added/Corp** South Africa. Dept. of Labour. South African Rehabilitation Council. **VFOAT** Rehabilitation in South Africa; Rehabilitasie in S. A. Vol. 1 (Mar. 1957)-. Academic Scholarly Publication. Multiple languages (Afrikaans and English). qt. Department of Man Power, PO Box X117, 0001 Pretoria South Africa. **Tel** (12)3106358. **NLM** W1 RE173M.
**Ind/Abst** Cumul. Index Nurs. Allied Health Lit.; EMBASE.

US/0885-1123
**REHABILITATION REPORT.** ***Ceased.*** [Rehabil. rep.]. Began with: Vol. 1, No. 1 (Sept. 1985)-(1988). Periodical. English. mo. Hanley & Belfus Inc., 210 South 13th Street, Philadelphia PA 19107. **Tel** (215)546-7293, FAX (215)790-9330. **DD** 615. **NLM** W1; RE175CH.

GW/0034-3536
**REHABILITATION (STUTTGART).** (REHABILITATION.). [Rehabilitation]. **Added/Corp** Deutsche Vereinigung fuer die Rehabilitation Behinderter. Vol. 15 (1962)-. Academic Scholarly Publication. English (French and German; summaries and/or abstracts in French and German; table of contents in German). qt. $109.00. Georg Thieme Verlag Stuttgart, Postfach 301120, D 70451 Stuttgart Germany. **Tel** 011 49 711 89310, FAX 011 49 711 8931298, telex 7 252 275 GTVD. **(Subscription address:** Thieme Medical Publishers Inc., 381 Park Avenue South, New York NY 10016.) **NLM** W1 RE173U. **[CCC]**. available on microfilm from University Microfilms International (UMI). ***Continues*** *Internationale Zeitschrift fur Physikalische Medizin und Rehabilitation.*
**Ind/Abst** EMBASE; Index Med.; SportSearch.

US/1058-4811
**RELAX (BANNOCKBURN, ILL.).** **See** Travel and Tourism.

UK/0142-8357
**RENAL TRANSPLANTATION AND DIALYSIS.** [Renal transplant. dial.]. (1971)-. English. mo. £75.00. SUBIS, Mansion House, 19 Kingfield Road, Sheffield S11 9AS England. **Tel** 011 44 114 255 4433, FAX 011 44 114 255 4626. **DD** 016.574. **[CCC]**. **Ad Acc**.
**Desc:** Current awareness service for researchers.

US
**RENALIFE : THE QUARTERLY JOURNAL OF THE NATIONAL ASSOCIATION OF PATIENTS ON HEMODIALYSIS AND TRANSPLANTATION.** **VFOAT** Renal Life. Vol. 2, No. 5 (Dec. 1985)-. Periodical. English. qt. $50.00. American Association of Kidney Patients, 1 Davis Boulevard/Suite LL1, Tampa FL 33606. **Tel** (813)251-0725. **NLM** W1; RE198J. ***Continues*** *NAPHT News, 0363-4701.*

CN
**REPORT - MEDICAL RESEARCH COUNCIL.** **Main/Corp** Medical Research Council (Canada). **VFOAT** Rapport - Conseil de Recherches Medicales. No. 1 (1966)-. Monographic series. English (French). ir. Price varies per volume. Medical Research Council / Canada, Jeanne Mance Building, 20th Floor, Ottawa Ontario K1A 0W9 Canada. **Tel** (613)954-1382. **LC** R854.C3; M4. ***Absorbed*** *Rapport, No. 4, 1970.*

US/0278-6354
**REPORT / NATIONAL COUNCIL ON HEALTH CARE TECHNOLOGY.** [Rep. - Natl. Counc. Health Care Technol. (U.S.)]. **Main/Corp** National Council on Health Care Technology (U.S.). English. an. National Center for Health Care Technology, 5600 Fishers Lane, Rockville MD 20857. **LC** R854.U5; N27A. **DD** 353.00841.

PL
**REPORT OF SCIENTIFIC ACTIVITIES.** **Main/Corp** Polska Akademia Nauk. Centrum Medycyny Doswiadczalnej I Klinicznej. 1967/71-. Polish (English). Orpan Palace of Culture and Science, Warsaw Poland. **LC** R854.P6; P64A.

AT/0727-3738
**REPORT OF THE AUSTRALIA AND NEW ZEALAND COMBINED DIALYSIS AND TRANSPLANT REGISTRY.** [Rep. Aust. N. Z. comb. dial. transplant regist.]. (1978)-. English. an. 30.00Aus$. Queen Elizabeth Hospital, Renal Unit, 28 Woodville Road, Woodville South, 5011 Australia. **Tel** 011 61 8 450222, FAX 011 61 8 459699. **ED** Dr. A. P. S. Disney. **DD** 312.361. ctrl circ.

CN
**REPORT OF THE PRESIDENT - MEDICAL RESEARCH COUNCIL OF CANADA.** **Main/Corp** Medical Research Council of Canada. **VFOAT** Rapport du President. 1969/70-. English (French). an. Information Canada, 171 Slater Street, Ottawa Ontario K1A 0S9 Canada. **Tel** (819)997-1095.

CN/0384-2029
**REPORT OF THE PRESIDENT - MEDICAL RESEARCH COUNCIL (OTTAWA).** (REPORT OF THE PRESIDENT - MEDICAL RESEARCH COUNCIL.). **Main/Corp** Medical Research Council (Canada). **VFOAT** Rapport du President - Conseil de Recherches Medicales. **VAT** Rapport du President - Conseil de Recherches Medicales (Ottawa); MRC Report of the President; Medical Research Council Report of the President; Rapport du President du CRM; Rapport du President du Conseil de Recherches Medicales. 1969/70-. Periodical. English (French). an. Medical Research Council of Canada, Jeanne Mance Building/20th Floor, Ottawa Ontario K1A 0W9 Canada. **Tel** (613)996-8182. **NLM** W2; DC2 M5r. ***Continues*** *Medical Research Council (Canada). Annual Report, 0384-2215; Annual Review on Support of University Research;* ***Absorbed*** *Compte Rendu Annuel sur l'Aide Apportee a la Recherche Scientifique dans les Universites, 1970/71, 0384-2010.*

UK/0072-6109
**REPORT ON CONFIDENTIAL ENQUIRIES INTO MATERNAL DEATHS IN ENGLAND AND WALES.** **Added/Corp** Great Britain. Ministry of Health. Great Britain. Dept. of Health and Social Security. (1954)-. English. ir. Her Majesty's Stationery Office, 51 Nine Elms Lane, London SW8 5DR England. **Tel** 011 44 71 873 8459, 011 44 71 873 8499, FAX 011 44 71 873 8499, 011 44 71 873 8456, telex 297138. **(Subscription address:** PO Box 276, Public Centre, London SW8 5DT England) **LC** RG530.3.G72; E547. **NLM** W1 RE212VM no.1 etc.

US
**REPORT ON LONG TERM CARE.** ***Ceased.*** (19??)-(19??). Periodical. English. sm. Faulkner & Gray Inc., 11 Penn Plaza, 17th Floor, New York NY 10001. **Tel** (212)967-7000, (800)535-8403. ***Continues*** *Long Term Care Management, 0743-1422.*

US/1064-4148
**REPORT ON MEDICAL GUIDELINES & OUTCOMES RESEARCH. ANNOTATED DIRECTORY OF MEDICAL PRACTICE GUIDELINES.** [Rep. med. guidel. outcomes res., Annot. dir. med. pract. guidel.]. **Added/Corp** Health & Sciences Communications. **VFOAT** Annotated Directory of Medical Practice Guidelines; Report on Medical Guidelines and Outcomes Research. Annotated Directory of Medical Practice Guidelines. (Mar. 1, 1991)-. Directory. English. sm. $495.00. Capitol Publications, 1101 King Street, Suite 444, Alexandria VA 22314. **Tel** (703)683-4100, (800)655-5597. **(Subscription address:** Capitol Publications, PO Box 1453, Alexandria, VA 22313) **DD** 362. **NLM** W 22; AA1 R34.

US
**REPORT ON MEDICAL SCHOOL FACULTY SALARIES.** **See** Education-Higher Education.

US/0095-0831
**REPORT TO THE CONGRESS - LISTER HILL NATIONAL CENTER FOR BIOMEDICAL COMMUNICATIONS.** (REPORT TO THE CONGRESS.). **Main/Corp** Lister Hill National Center for Biomedical Communications. English. 8600 Rockville Pike, Bethesda MD 20014. **LC** R118; .L55A. **DD** 610/.7.

US/1057-9400
**REPORTER - NATIONAL CENTER FOR RESEARCH RESOURCES (U.S.).** ***Title Change.*** (REPORTER / NATIONAL CENTER FOR RESEARCH RESOURCES.). [Report. - Natl. Cent. Res. Resour. (U. S.)]. **Added/Corp** National Center for Research Resources (U.S.) Research Resources Information Center. **VFOAT** Research Resources Reporter. Vol. 15, No. 1 (Jan. 1991)-Vol. 17, No. 2 (Mar./Apr. 1993). Government Publication. English. mo. Superintendent of Documents, US Government Printing Office, Washington DC 20402. **Tel** (202)275-3328, FAX (202)786-2377. **DD** 619. **NLM** W1; RE212RL. ***Continues*** *Research Resources Reporter, 0160-807X.* ***Continued by*** *NCRR Reporter.*

US/1045-0246
**RESCUE (SOLANA BEACH, CALIF.).** (RESCUE.). [Rescue]. **VFOAT** Rescue Magazine. Vol. 2, Issue 3 (May/June 1989)-. Periodical. English. bm. $14.95 (one year), $27.95 (two year). Mosby Year Book Inc., 11830 Westline Industrial Drive, St Louis MO 63146. **Tel** (800)325-4177, (314)872-8370, FAX (314)432-1380, telex 44-2402. **(Subscription address:** JEMS Communications, PO Box 2789, Carlsbad CA 92018.**) DD** 363. **NLM** W1; RE2145R. ***Continues*** *Rescue Magazine, 1041-0651.*

UK/0143-3083
**RESEARCH AND CLINICAL FORUMS.** [Res. clin. forums]. Vol. 1 (1979)-. Academic Scholarly Publication. English. ir. Price varies per volume. Wells Medical, 14B Chapel Place, Royal Turbridge, Wells Kent TN1 1BP England. **Tel** 011 44 892-511600. **NLM** W3 RE457. **CODEN** RCLFD4. **[CCC].** ctrl circ. Documents available from CASDDS.
**Desc:** Proceedings of medico-scientific meetings.
**Ind/Abst** Chem. Abstr.

AT/0157-745X
**RESEARCH AND DEVELOPMENT MONOGRAPH - UNIVERSITY OF NEW SOUTH WALES, CENTRE FOR MEDICAL EDUCATION, RESEARCH AND DEVELOPMENT.** (RESEARCH AND DEVELOPMENT MONOGRAPH / THE UNIVERSITY OF NEW SOUTH WALES, CENTRE FOR MEDICAL EDUCATION RESEARCH AND DEVELOPMENT [AND] WORLD HEALTH ORGANIZATION, REGIONAL TEACHER TRAINING CENTRE FOR HEALTH PERSONNEL.). [Res. dev. monogr. - Univ. New South Wales Cent. Med. Educ. Res. Dev.]. **Added/Corp** University of New South Wales. Centre for Medical Education Research and Development. Regional Teacher Training Centre for Health Personnel. (19??)-. Monographic series. English. ir. Price varies per volume. University of New South Wales / Centre for Medical Education Research and Development, Kensington New South Wales Australia. **NLM** W1 RE215BM.

US/0080-1518
**RESEARCH CENTERS DIRECTORY.** [Res. cent. dir.]. **Added/Corp** Gale Research Company. Gale Research Inc. 2nd Ed. (1965)-. Directory. English. an (July). $455.00. Gale Research Inc., 835 Penobscot Building, Detroit MI 48226. **Tel** (800)877-GALE, (313)961-2242, FAX (313)961-6083, telex TWX 810-221-7086. **ED** Thomas Cichonski. **LC** AS25; .D5. **DD** 001. **NLM** Q 180.U5 D598A. ***Continues*** *Directory of University Research Bureaus and Institutes.*
**Desc:** Covers 13,000 research units in all fields and reflects current trends in university-related research in the United States and Canada. An expanded section focuses on university research parks and technology transfer centers that represent joint ventures between business, industry, and universities.

US
**RESEARCH GRANTS / [PREPARED BY NATIONAL INSTITUTES OF HEALTH, DIVISION OF RESEARCH GRANTS, STATISTICS AND ANALYSIS BRANCH].** **Added/Corp** National Institutes of Health (U.S.) National Institutes of Health (U.S.). Division of Research Grants. Statistics and Analysis Branch. National Institutes of Health (U.S.). Division of Research Grants. Information Systems Branch. Statistical Analysis Unit. **VFOAT** N.I.H. Research Grants; NIH Research Grants. (1968)-. English. an. Free on request. National Institute of Health, 9000 Rockville Pike, Building 31/Room 2B-03, Bethesda MD 20892. **Tel** (301)496-9291. **LC** R850.A1; U48. **DD** 610/.72/073. **NLM** WA 22 AA1 R46.

GW/0300-9130
**RESEARCH IN EXPERIMENTAL MEDICINE.** [Res. exp. med.]. **VFOAT** Zeitschrift fuer die Gesamte Experimentelle Medizin Einschliesslich Experimenteller Chirurgie. Vol. 157 (1972)-. Academic Scholarly Publication. English (German). Six times a year. DM980.00. Springer-Verlag GmbH & Company KG, Heidelberger Platz 3, D 14197 Berlin Germany. **Tel** 011 49 30 8207223, FAX 011 49 30 8214091, telex 183 319 SPBLN D. **(Subscription address:** Springer Verlag New York Inc. / for North America, 44 Hartz Way, Secaucus NJ 07096.**) ED** F -D Goebel. **LC** R850.A1; Z43. **DD** 619/.05. **NLM** W1 RE227FK. **CODEN** REXMAS. **[CCC]. Pr Rev.** available on microfilm from University Microfilms International (UMI). Documents available from The Genuine Article, BIOSIS Document Express, CASDDS, ADONIS. ***Continues*** *Zeitschrift fuer die Gesamte Experimentelle Medizin Einschliesslich Experimenteller Chirurgie, 0044-2534.*
**Desc:** Publishes original papers pertinent to the development or application of new methods or devices in experimental medicine and surgery.
**Ind/Abst** ADONIS; Biol. Abstr.; Chem. Abstr.; Curr. Contents Life Sci.; Dairy Sci. Abstr.; EMBASE; Energy Res. Abstr. (Feb. 1974-); Index Med.; Nutr. Abstr. Rev., Ser. A, Hum. Exp.; Life Sci. Collect.; PESTDOC; Res. Alert [Full Cov.]; Sci. Cit. Index; SCISEARCH.

US
**RESEARCH IN MEDICAL EDUCATION : PROCEEDINGS OF THE ... ANNUAL CONFERENCE.** **See** Education-Higher Education.

US/0275-4959
**RESEARCH IN THE SOCIOLOGY OF HEALTH CARE.** **See** Sociology.

US
**RESEARCH PAPERS / HISTORY OF MEDICINE ASSOCIATES.** **Added/Corp** University of Arkansas for Medical Sciences. History of Medicine Associates. No. 1 (1990)-. Monographic series. English. Price varies per volume. **NLM** W1; RE2324.

UK/0143-7984
**RESEARCH PUBLICATIONS OF THE WELLCOME UNIT FOR THE HISTORY OF MEDICINE.** [Res. publ. - Wellcome Unit Hist. Med.]. **VFOAT** Research Publications. No. 2-. Monographic series. English. ir. Price varies per volume. **NLM** W1 RE233Q. ***Continues*** *Research Publications (Wellcome Unit for the History of Medicine).*

US/0193-2209
**RESEARCH REPORT - OKLAHOMA MEDICAL RESEARCH FOUNDATION.** v. 1- 1977-. Periodical. English. **NLM** W1 RE234G. ***Continues*** *Research Reporter (Oklahoma City).*

AT/1031-4717
**RESEARCH REPORT - ROYAL PRINCE ALFRED HOSPITAL.** (RESEARCH REPORT / ROYAL PRINCE ALFRED HOSPITAL.). [Res. rep. - R. Prince Alfred Hosp.]. **Added/Corp** Royal Prince Alfred Hospital (Sidney, N.S.W.) Royal Prince Alfred Hospital (Sydney, N.S.W.). Annual Report. (19??)-. English. ir. **NLM** W 20.5; R4345.

US/0034-5555
**RESIDENT AND STAFF PHYSICIAN.** [Resid. staff physician]. **VFOAT** Resident and Staff Physician. Vol. 15, No. 7 (July 1969)-. Periodical. English. mo. $55.00 US; $92.00 other. Romaine Pierson Publishing Inc., 80 Shore Road, Port Washington NY 11050. **Tel** (516)883-6350. **ED** Alfred Jay Bollet. **DD** 610. **NLM** W1 RE245. **Bk Rev. Ad Acc. Circ:** 100,000 (ctrl). available on microfilm and microfiche from University Microfilms International (UMI). ***Continues*** *Resident Physician, 0482-3834.*
**Desc:** Clinical journal directed toward residents and full-time hospital staff.
**Ind/Abst** Hospit. Health Admin. Index (1969-1990); Int. Pharm. Abstr. (199?-).

●US/1061-6632
**RESIDENTS' PRESCRIBING REFERENCE.** [Resid. prescr. ref.]. **VFOAT** Prescribing Reference. Vol. 1, No.1 Spring/Summer (1992)-. Periodical. English. sa. $30.00 (institutions). Prescribing Reference Inc, PO Box 844, Pearl River NY 10965. **Tel** (800)436-9269, FAX (212)732-2360. **DD** 615.

US/0738-0496
**RESMEDICA.** [ResMedica]. **Added/Corp** St. John's Mercy Medical Center (Saint Louis, Mo.). **VFOAT** Res Medica. Vol. 1, No. 2 (Aug. 1983)-. Periodical. English. Four times a year. Res Medica, St John's Mercy Medical Center, 615 South New Ballas Road, Suite 114, St Louis MO 63141. **Tel** (314)569-6990. **ED** Thomas F. Frawley and Jane Wilson. **NLM** W1; RE246H. **Circ:** 16,000 (ctrl). ***Continues*** *ResMedicus.*

US/1040-3957
**RESPONSE (LEBANON, PA.).** (RESPONSE.). [Response]. (1988)-. Periodical. English. mo. $16.00 (general), $10.00 (student). D J Russell, PO Box 719, Lebanon PA 17042. **DD** 610.

GW/0178-2525
**RETTUNGSDIENST.** (198?)-. Periodical. German (summaries and/or abstracts in English). Twelve times a year. DM72.50. Stumpf & Kossendey GmbH, Postfach 1153, W-2905 Edewecht Germany. **Tel** 011 49 04405-7073, FAX 011 49 04405-7744. **NLM** W1; RE2509F. Index available. **Bk Rev.** ctrl circ. ***Continues*** *Rettungssanitater.*

PL/0034-6233
**REUMATOLOGIA.** [Reumatologia]. **Added/Corp** Instytut Reumatologiczny. Polskie Towarzystwo Reumatologiczne. Vol. 1, No. 1, (1963)-. Academic Scholarly Publication. Polish (summaries and/or abstracts in English and Russian). qt. Price on Request. **(Subscription address:** ARS Polona, PO Box 1001, 00068 Warsaw Poland.**) NLM** W1 RE251H. **CODEN** RMTOA2. Index Available in first issue of next volume--loose--separately paged. Documents available from BIOSIS Document Express, CASDDS.
**Ind/Abst** Biol. Abstr.; Chem. Abstr.; EMBASE [Select. Cov.].

AT/0157-9347
**REVIEW PAPER - UNIVERSITY OF NEW SOUTH WALES, CENTRE FOR MEDICAL EDUCATION RESEARCH AND DEVELOPMENT.** (REVIEW PAPER / THE UNIVERSITY OF NEW SOUTH WALES, CENTRE FOR MEDICAL EDUCATION RESEARCH AND DEVELOPMENT [AND] WORLD HEALTH ORGANIZATION, REGIONAL TEACHER TRAINING CENTRE FOR HEALTH PERSONNEL.). [Rev. pap. - Univ. New South Wales, Cent. Med. Educ. Res. Dev.]. **Added/Corp** University of New South Wales. Centre for Medical Education Research and Development. Regional Teacher Training Centre for Health Personnel. (1979)-. Monographic series. English. ir. Price varies per volume. University of New South Wales / Centre for Medical Education Research and Development, Kensington New South Wales Australia. **NLM** W1 RE257CC.

UK/0954-139X
**REVIEWS IN MEDICAL MICROBIOLOGY : A JOURNAL OF THE PATHOLOGICAL SOCIETY OF GREAT BRITAIN AND IRELAND.** **Added/Corp** Pathological Society of Great Britain and Ireland. (1990)-. Periodical. English. qt. $255.00 US and Canada; £150.00 Europe; £165.00 Other. Chapman & Hall, 2-6 Boundary Row, London SE1 8HN England. **Tel** 011 44 71 865 0066, FAX 011 44 71 522 9623, telex 290164 Chapmag. **(Subscription address:** Chapman & Hall, Cheriton House, North Way, Andover, Hampshire, SP10 5BE England.**) NLM** W1; RE257CFL. **CODEN** RMEMER. **[CCC].** available on microfilm and microfiche from University Microfilms International (UMI).
**Desc:** Up-to-the-minute reviews covering the very latest research and techniques. Internationally acknowledged experts worldwide will provide reviews of topics in medical microbiology, virology, mycology, parasitology, clinical microbiology and hospital infection.
**Ind/Abst** Biodeter. Abstr. (1991-); Curr. Aware. Biol. Sci., CABS; EMBASE; Helminthol. Abstr. (1991-); Index Vet.; Leis. Recreat. Tour. Abstr.; Protozoolog. Abstr.; Rev. Med. Vet. Mycology; Small Anim. Abstr. Bibliogr.; Vet. Bull.; Trop. Dis. Bull.

BL/0102-2105
**REVISTA AMRIGS.** [Rev. AMRIGS]. (197?)-. Periodical. Portuguese (summaries and/or abstracts in English). ir. $50.00. Associacao Medica Do Rio Grande Do Sul, Av Ipiranga 5311, 90620 Porto Alegre RS Brasil. **Tel** 011 55 512 368111. **ED** Angelo Alves de Mattos and M. T. Barros. **NLM** W1 RE264. Index available. cum. index. **Ad Acc. Circ:** 7,000 (ctrl). ***Continues*** *Revista da AMRIGS, 0102-2105.*
**Ind/Abst** Index Med. (1979-).

BL/0100-3232
**REVISTA BRASILEIRA DE CLINICA E TERAPEUTICA.** (REVISTA BRASILEIRA DE CLINICA E TERAPEUTICA : CT.). [Rev. bras. cl,in. ter.]. **VFOAT** Clinica e Terapeutica; CT. Vol. 41, No. 1 (Jan. 1984)-. Periodical. Portuguese (summaries and/or abstracts in English). mo. $80.00. **NLM** W1; RE311EB. Documents available from BIOSIS Document Express. ***Continues*** *Clinica e Terapeutica, 0100-3232.*
**Ind/Abst** Biol. Abstr.; EMBASE [Select. Cov.]; Trop. Dis. Bull.

BL/0034-7256
**REVISTA BRASILEIRA DE MALARIOLOGIA E DOENCAS TROPICAIS.** ***Ceased.*** Vol. 1 (Jan. 1949)-Ceased Vol. 38 (1986). Periodical. Portuguese (summaries and/or abstracts in English). an. SUCAM Esplan Ministerios, Bloco G, 2000 Rio de Janeiro Brazil. **Tel** 225 9428, FAX 061 225 8645, telex 611603. **Circ:** 3,000 (ctrl).
**Ind/Abst** Index Med.; Trop. Dis. Bull.

BL/0034-7264
**REVISTA BRASILEIRA DE MEDICINA.** [Rev. Bras. med.]. Vol. 1 (Jan. 1944)-. Academic Scholarly Publication. Portuguese (summaries and/or abstracts in English). mo (except combined Jan./Feb.). $250.00. Moreira Jr Editora Medica Ltda, Rue Henrique Martins 493, 04504 Sao Paulo SP Brazil. **Tel** 011 55 11 8849911, FAX 011 55 11 2800491. **NLM** W1 RE3429. **CODEN** RBMEAU. **Ad Acc. Circ:** 25,000. Documents

# Medical Science and Technology

available from CASDDS.
**Desc:** Scientific articles.
**Ind/Abst** Chem. Abstr. (1944-1983); EMBASE [Select. Cov.]; Helminthol. Abstr.; Life Sci. Collect.; Protozoolog. Abstr.; Trop. Dis. Bull.

BL/0303-7657
**REVISTA BRASILEIRA DE SAUDE OCUPACIONAL.** See Industrial Health and Safety.

SP
**REVISTA CLINICA ESPANOLA. NUEVOS ARCHIVOS DE LA FACULTAD DE MEDICINA.** Spanish. IDEPSA International Ediciones Publs SA, Principe de Vergara 112 1F, 28002 Madrid Spain. **Tel** 011 34 1 5637306.

CR/0253-2948
**REVISTA COSTARRICENSE DE CIENCIAS MEDICAS.** [Rev. costarric. cienc. med.]. **Added/Corp** Caja Costarricense de Seguro Social. Centro de Docencia e Investigacion. Subdireccion de Ciencias Medicas. Vol. 1, No. 1 (June 1980)-. Academic Scholarly Publication. Spanish (summaries and/or abstracts in English). Twice a year. $10.00 Central & Pan America; $15.00 others. Caja Costarricense de Seguro Social, Apartado 10105, San Jose Costa Rica. **Tel** 011 506 234033. **ED** Jessie Orlich. **NLM** W1 RE359BL. **CODEN** RCCMEF. **Bk Rev. Ad Acc. Circ:** 2,500. Documents available from BIOSIS Document Express.
**Desc:** Covers all medical subjects, especially clinical applications and laboratory practice and research. General essays may be accepted if applicable to clinical practice.
**Ind/Abst** Biol. Abstr.; EMBASE.

CU/1012-3172
**REVISTA CUBANA DE HEMATOLOGIA INMUNOLOGIA Y HEMOTERAPIA.** [Rev. cuba. hematol. inmunol. hemoter.]. (1985)-. Periodical. Spanish. Three times a year. $28.00 North America; $30.00 South America; $38.00 other. Ediciones Cubanas, Obispo 527, Altos ESQ Bernaza, CP 10100 Havana Cuba. **Tel** 011 632980, 631942, FAX 011 631011, telex 512337, 6540. **NLM** W1; RE3594E. **CODEN** RCHHEP. Documents available from BIOSIS Document Express.
**Desc:** Exposition of articles with the purpose of offering up to date information to the increasing number of doctors and other professionals interested in the three specialties. The journal serves as a scientific information exchange between specialists of other countries, fundamentally Latin American ones.
**Ind/Abst** Biol. Abstr. (1988-); Soc. Plann. Policy Dev. Abstr.

CU/0864-0300
**REVISTA CUBANA DE INVESTIGACIONES BIOMEDICAS.**
**Added/Corp** Centro Nacional de Informacion de Ciencias Medicas. **VFOAT** RCIB; IB. Vol. 1, No. 1 (1982)-. Periodical. Spanish (summaries and/or abstracts in English, French and Russian). Three times a year. $21.00 North America; $23.00 South America; $28.00 other. Ediciones Cubanas, Obispo 527, Altos ESQ Bernaza, CP 10100 Havana Cuba. **Tel** 011 632980, 631942, FAX 011 631011, telex 512337, 6540. **NLM** W1; RE3597.
**Desc:** Magazine with a scientific and technical character. Publishes previously unpublished studies of Cuban author, with a wide experience in biomedical researches.
**Ind/Abst** EMBASE [Select. Cov.].

CU/0034-7523
**REVISTA CUBANA DE MEDICINA.**
**Suspended.** [Rev. Cuba. med.]. **Added/Corp** Cuba. Ministerio de Salud Publica. Consejo Cientifico. Centro Nacional de Informacion de Ciencias Medicas. Vol. 1 (1962)-Suspended (1992). Academic Scholarly Publication. Spanish. Three times a year. Ediciones Cubanas, Obispo 527, Altos ESQ Bernaza, CP 10100 Havana Cuba. **Tel** 011 632980, 631942, FAX 011 631011, telex 512337, 6540. **NLM** W1 RE362. **CODEN** RCBMA6. **Circ:** 50,000 (ctrl). Documents available from CASDDS.
**Desc:** Containing articles of general interest and on medical specialities, mainly by Cuban authors.
**Ind/Abst** Chem. Abstr.; EMBASE [Select. Cov.]; Life Sci. Collect.; Trop. Dis. Bull.

●BL
**REVISTA DA ASSOCIACAO MEDICA BRASILEIRA. Added/Corp** Associacao Medica Brasileira. **VFOAT** Journal of the Brazilian Medical Association. Vol. 38 (1992)-. Periodical. Portuguese (summaries and/or abstracts in English; table of contents in English). Six times a year. AMB Associacao Medica Brasileira, Rua Sao Carlos do Pinhal 324, 0133 Sao Paulo SP Brazil. **Tel** 011 55 11 2893511. **NLM** W1; RE366RM. **Continues** Associacao Medica Brasileira. AMB, 0102-843X.
**Ind/Abst** Index Med.

RM/0377-7871
**REVISTA DE CHIRURGIE, ONCOLOGIE, RADIOLOGIE, O.R.L. OFTALMOLOGIE, STOMATOLOGIE. SERIA : STOMATOLOGIE.** [Rev. chir. oncol. radiol. o.r.l. oftalmol. stomatol., Ser. stomatol.]. **Added/Corp** Societatea de Stomatologie. **VFOAT** Stomatologie. Vol. 21, No. 4 (July/Sept. 1974)-. Periodical. Romanian (summaries and/or abstracts in English, French, German and Russian). Four times a year. $20.00. Uniunea Societatilor de Stiinte Medicale din Romania, Str. Progresului Nr. 10, Bucurest Romania. (**Subscription address:** Orion Press SRL, SPL Independentei 202-A, Bucharest 6 Romania.) **NLM** W1 RE378G. **CODEN** RCOSDO. Index available. **Bk Rev. Ad Acc.** available with charts; available with illustrations. Documents available from BIOSIS Document Express, CASDDS. **Continues** Stomatologie, 0039-1719.
**Desc:** Contains articles on theoretical and practical matters in the speciality.
**Ind/Abst** Biol. Abstr.; Chem. Abstr.; Index Dent. Lit. (Vol. 31, No. 1, 1984-).

SP
**REVISTA DE LA ASOCIACION CASTELLANA DE APARATO DIGESTIVO.** Spanish. Jarpyo Editores SA, Antonio Lopez Aguados 4, 28029 Madrid, Spain. **Tel** 011 34 1 3144338, 011 34 1 3144458.

AG/0014-6722
**REVISTA DE LA FACULTAD DE CIENCIAS MEDICAS DE CORDOBA.**
**Added/Corp** Facultad de Ciencias Medicas de Cordoba. Universidad Nacional de Cordoba. Vol. 12 (1954)-. Periodical. Spanish. ir. Facultad de Ciencias Medicas, Ciudad Universitia, Cordoba 32 Argentina. **NLM** W1 RE408. **Continues** Revista de la Facultad de Ciencias Medicas de la Universidad Nacional de Cordoba.
**Ind/Abst** Index Med.; SportSearch.

SP/1130-4405
**REVISTA DE LA MEDICINA TRADICIONAL CHINA.** [Rev. med. tradic. china]. **VFOAT** Zhongyi Zazhi (Ed. Espa/nola). (1990)-. Periodical. Spanish. qt. $90.00. Sinomed S.L., Londres n017 3rd D, 28028 Madrid Spain. **Tel** (91)361-1266, FAX (91)361-1266. **ED** Angela Re Catalina. **UDC** 615.804.1. **Ad Acc. Circ:** 3,000 (ctrl).
**Desc:** Medical sciences such as homeopathy and acupuncture.
**Ind/Abst** NAPRALERT.

SP
**REVISTA DE LA REAL ACADEMIA DE MEDICINA DE BARCELONA.** Spanish. Real Academia de Medicina de Barcelona, Carmen 47, 08001 Barcelona Spain.

PE/0254-3435
**REVISTA DE LA SANIDAD DE LAS FUERZAS POLICIALES.** [Rev. Sanid. fuerzas polic.]. **Added/Corp** Peru. Sanidad de las Fuerzas Policiales. Vol. 41, No. 1 (Jan./June 1980)-. Periodical. Spanish. sa (2 issues). $30.00 Peru; $40.00 Pan America; $45.00 other. F Raul Jeri, Apartment 5281, Lima 100 Peru. **Tel** 224395. **ED** F. Raul Jeri. **NLM** W1 RE41S. Index available. **Bk Rev. Ad Acc. Circ:** 8,000 (ctrl). **Continues** Revista de la Sanidad del Ministerio del Interior, 0379-3907.
**Desc:** Original articles in areas of health and military medicine, pharmacy, dentistry, nursing, and review articles.
**Ind/Abst** Energy Res. Abstr. (April 1983-).

SP/0212-0771
**REVISTA DE LA SOCIEDAD ANDALUZA DE TRAUMATOLOGIA Y ORTOPEDIA.** (1981)-. Periodical. Spanish (Spanish). qt. Editorial Garsi SA, Juan Bravo 46, 28006 Madrid, Spain. **Tel** 011 34 1 4021212, telex 98358 GARSI E. **NLM** W1; RE412JK.
**Ind/Abst** Indice Med. Esp.

CU/0037-847X
**REVISTA DE LA SOCIEDAD CUBANA DE HISTORIA DE LA MEDICINA.** (REVISTA.). [Rev. Soc. cuba. hist. med.]. **Main/Corp** Sociedad Cubana de Historia de la Medicina. Vol. 1 (1958)-. Periodical. Spanish. qt. **NLM** W1 RE412S.
**Ind/Abst** Am. Hist. Life (1958-1962).

SP/0210-3451
**REVISTA DE LA SOCIEDAD ESPANOLA DE DIALISIS Y TRANSPLANTE.**
**Suspended. Added/Corp** Sociedad Espanola de Dialisis y Trasplante. **VFOAT** Revista S. E. D. Y. T.; SEDYT. Vol. 1 (Jan. 1979)-(19??). Periodical. English (Spanish). qt. Hospital Clinico Universitario, Madre Vedruna 18 IZQ, 50008 Zaragoza Spain. **Tel** 011 34 976 356400. **NLM** W1 RE414G.
**Ind/Abst** EMBASE; Indice Med. Esp.

RM/0377-4988
**REVISTA DE MEDICINA INTERNA, NEUROLOGIE, PSIHIATRIE, NEUROCHIRURGIE, DERMATO-VENEROLOGIE. DERMATO-VENEROLOGIE.** (REVISTA DE MEDICINA-INTERNA, NEUROLOGIE, PSIHIATRIE, NEUROCHIRURGIE, DERMATO-VENEROLOGIE; 10 DERMATO-VENEROLOGIE.). [Rev. med. interna neurol. psihiatr. neurochir. derm.-venerol., Derm.-venerol.]. **Added/Corp** Societatea de Dermato-Venerologie. Uniunea Societatilor de Stiinte Medicale din Republica Socialista Romania. **VFOAT** Dermato-Venerologie. Vol. 19 (Jan. 1974)-. Academic Scholarly Publication. Romanian (summaries and/or abstracts in English, French, German and Russian). qt. Uniunea Societ Stiinte Medical, Str Progresului 8, Bucharest Romania. **NLM** W1 RE427G. **CODEN** RMIDDJ. Documents available from BIOSIS Document Express, CASDDS. **Continues** Dermato-Venerologie, 0011-9024.
**Desc:** Review for information and orientation on relevant matters.
**Ind/Abst** Biol. Abstr.; Chem. Abstr. (1974-1982); EMBASE.

AG/0326-3428
**REVISTA DE NEFROLOGIA, DIALISIS Y TRANSPLANTE : PUBLICACION CONJUNTA DE LA ASOCIACION REGIONAL DE DIALISIS Y TRASPLANTES RENALES DE CAPITAL FEDERAL Y PROVINCIA DE BUENOS AIRES Y LA SOCIEDAD ARGENTINA DE NEFROLOGIA. Added/Corp** Asociacion Regional de Dialisis y Transplantes Renales de Capital Federal y Provincia de Buenos Aires. Sociedad Argentina de Nefrologia. (198?)-. Periodical. Spanish. Four times a year (Mar., June, Sept., Dec.). $40.00. Association Regional Dialsis y Transplantes Renales, Avenue Pueyrredon 1132, Piso 3 # 19, 118 Buenos Aires Argentina. **Tel** 011 54 1 9614010. **NLM** W1; RE446C. **Ad Acc, Adv Mgr:** Nelida Pecoraro, **Tel** 01 825 0023. **Circ:** 1,500 (ctrl).

SP
**REVISTA DE SANIDAD MILITAR.** Spanish. Escuela de Aplicacion de Sanidad Military, Camino de los Ingenieros 6, 19 Madrid Spain. **LC** RC970; .M4. **NLM** W1 RE496D. **Continues** Medicina y Cirugia de Guerra.

BL/0101-5575
**REVISTA DO HCPA & FACULDADE DE MEDICINA DA UNIVERSIDADE FEDERAL DO RIO GRANDE DO SUL.** [Rev. HCPA Fac. Med. Univ. Fed. Rio Gd. Sul]. **VFOAT** Revista do Hospital de Clinicas de Porto Alegre e Faculdade de Medicina da Universidade Federal do Rio Grande do Sul. (1981)-. Periodical. Multiple languages. sa. Revista HCPA, Rua Ramiro Barcelos 2350, 90210 Porto Alegre, Brazil. **Tel** (512)316699. **UDC** 61.
**Ind/Abst** EMBASE [Select. Cov.].

BL/0041-8781
**REVISTA DO HOSPITAL DAS CLINICAS.** [Rev. Hosp. Clin.]. **Added/Corp** Universidade de Sao Paulo. Faculdade de Medicina. Universidade de Sao Paulo. Hospital das Clinicas. **VFOAT** HC. Vol. 1 (Jan. 1946)-. Academic Scholarly Publication. Portuguese (English and Spanish). Six times a year (Feb., Apr., June, Aug., Oct., Dec.). $110.00. Revista Hospital das Clinicas, Caixa Postal 8091, Sao Paulo Brazil. **ED** Prof. Dr. Mitja Polak. **NLM** W1 RE52. **CODEN** RHCFAP. Index available. cum. index. **Bk Rev. Ad Acc, Adv Mgr Tel** 282-2511 R.4235. **Circ:** 6,000 (ctrl). Documents available from BIOSIS Document Express, CASDDS.
**Desc:** General news and information in medicine.
**Ind/Abst** Biol. Abstr.; Chem. Abstr.; Dairy Sci. Abstr.; EMBASE; Helminthol. Abstr.; Index Med.; Life Sci. Collect.; Protozoolog. Abstr.; Trop. Dis. Bull.

PO
**REVISTA DO HOSPITAL DE EGAS MONIZ.** Vol. 4 (1987)-. Periodical. Portuguese (Portuguese). qt. **NLM** W1; RE52F. **Continues** Boletim do Hospital de Egas Moniz.

EC/0034-9313
**REVISTA ECUATORIANA DE MEDICINA Y CIENCIAS BIOLOGICAS. Suspended.** [Rev. ecuat. med. cienc. biol.]. **VFOAT** Medicina Y Ciencias Biologicas. Vol. 1, No. 1 (Jan./Mar. 1963)-(1992). Periodical. Spanish (summaries and/or abstracts in English). qt. Ctr Nac Documentos Cientificos Ecatoriana, Quito Ecuador. **NLM** W1 RE524M. **CODEN** REMBA8. Documents available from BIOSIS Document Express.
**Ind/Abst** Biol. Abstr.; Saf. Health Work.

SP/0048-7791
**REVISTA ESPANOLA DE REUMATISMO Y ENFERMEDADES OSTEOARTICULARES.** [Rev. esp. reum. enferm. osteoartic.]. (June 1945)-. Academic Scholarly

Publication. Spanish. Four times a year. $17.00. Editorial ECO, S A Calle de la Cruz 44, Barcelona 34 Spain.
**Ind/Abst** EMBASE; Life Sci. Collect.; Saf. Health Work.

BL/0034-9585
**REVISTA GOIANA DE MEDICINA.** [Rev. Goiana med.]. Vol. 1 (July/Sept. 1955)-. Academic Scholarly Publication. Portuguese (Portuguese). qt. **NLM** W1 RE581G. available on microfilm from University Microfilms International (UMI).
**Ind/Abst** EMBASE; Rev. Med. Vet. Entomol.; Trop. Dis. Bull.

SP
**REVISTA IBEROAMERICANA DE FERTILIDAD Y REPRODUCCION HUMANA.** Spanish (English). mo. 5OOOptas Spain; $60.00 other. Nuevas Creaciones Medicas, C Santillana del Mar, 3 Chalet 44, 28660 Boadilla del Monte Madrid Spain. **Tel** 011 34 1 6321544, 011 34 1 6321608, FAX 011 34 1 6321544. Index available. **Ad Acc. Circ:** 10,000 (ctrl).
**Desc:** Publishes different medical reviews on topics such as sexually transmitted diseases and psychosomatic disorders.
**Ind/Abst** Indice Med. Esp.

SP
**REVISTA IBEROAMERICANA DE TROMBOSIS Y HEMOSTASIA.** Spanish. Editorial Garsi SA, Juan Bravo 46, 28006 Madrid, Spain. **Tel** 011 34 1 4021212, telex 98358 GARSI E.
**Ind/Abst** Indice Med. Esp.

BL
**REVISTA MEDICA DA BAHIA. Added/Corp** Associacao Bahiana de Medicina. Vol. 1 (June 1933)-. Periodical. Portuguese. tq.
**Ind/Abst** Trop. Dis. Bull.

CR/0034-9909
**REVISTA MEDICA DE COSTA RICA.** [Rev. med. Costa Rica]. **Added/Corp** Asociacion de Medicos Especialistas de la Salud Publica de Costa Rica. Colegio de Medicos y Cirujanos (San Jose, Costa Rica) Centro de Estudios Medicos "Moreno Canas.". (194?)-. Periodical. Spanish (summaries and/or abstracts in English). Three times a year. Revista Medica de Costa Rica, Apartado Postal 978-1000, San Jose Costa Rica. **Tel** 2552969, FAX 2552969. **ED** Manuel Zeledon, M.D. **NLM** W1 RE617G. Index available. **Ad Acc. Circ:** 5,000 (ctrl). ***Continues** Revista Medica (San Jose, Costa Rica).*
**Ind/Abst** EMBASE [Select. Cov.].

MZ
**REVISTA MEDICA DE MOCAMBIQUE. Added/Corp** Instituto Nacional da Saude (Mozambique) Universidade Eduardo Mondlane. Faculdade de Medicina. (198?)-. Periodical. Portuguese (summaries and/or abstracts in English).
**Ind/Abst** Helminthol. Abstr. (1991-); Protozoolog. Abstr.; Trop. Dis. Bull.

PN/0379-1629
**REVISTA MEDICA DE PANAMA.** [Rev. med. Panama]. **Added/Corp** Academia Panamena de Medicina y Cirugia. Vol. 1 (Jan./April 1976)-. Periodical. Spanish (English). Three times a year. $35.00 (1 year), $65.00 (2 year), $90.00 (3 year). Academia Panamena Medicina y Cirugia, Apartado 6225, Panama 5 Republic of Panama. **Tel** 011 507 615321, FAX 011 507 619250. **ED** Carlos Calero. **NLM** W1 RE612M. Index available. **Bk Rev. Ad Acc. Pr Rev. Circ:** 1,200 (ctrl). ***Supersedes** Revista Medica de Panama.*
**Desc:** Medical themes of clinical research and experiments.
**Ind/Abst** Index Med.

CL
**REVISTA MEDICA DE VALPARAISO. Added/Corp** Sociedad Medica de Valparaiso. **VAT** RMV. (Feb. 1948)-. Periodical. Spanish. Four times a year. $30.00. Sociedad Medica de Valparaiso, Calle Honpaneda, 2653 Valparaiso Chile. **NLM** W1 RE6284.

MX/0018-5604
**REVISTA MEDICA DEL HOSPITAL COLONIA.** [Rev. med. Hosp. Colonia]. **Added/Corp** Ferrocarriles Nacionales de Mexico. Asociacion Medica. Hospital Colonia, Mexico. (1953)-. Periodical. Spanish. bm. Avenida Ejercito Nacional, No 884-201, Mexico 5 DF Mexico. **NLM** W1 RE631D.

BL/0100-0195
**REVISTA MEDICA DO ESTADO DO RIO DE JANEIRO.** [Rev. med. Estado Rio de Jan.]. V. 1-Jan./April 1977-. Academic Scholarly Publication. Portuguese. bm. Free. Secretaria do Estado de Saude, rua Moncorvo Filho 100, 2 Andar, 20 211 Rio de Janeiro Brazil. **Tel** 232 6811. **NLM** W1 RE635U. ***Continues** RM. Revista Medica do Estado do Rio de Janeiro, 0100-0195.*
**Ind/Abst** EMBASE.

BO/0482-6760
**REVISTA MEDICA (LA PAZ).** (REVISTA MEDICA.). V. 1- Jan./April 1977-. Periodical. Spanish. **NLM** W1 RE606GD.
**Ind/Abst** Rev. Med. Vet. Entomol.

MX/0484-7849
**REVISTA MEDICA (MEXICO).** (REVISTA MEDICA DEL INSTITUTO MEXICANO DEL SEGURO SOCIAL.). [Rev. med.]. **Added/Corp** Instituto Mexicano del Seguro Social. **VFOAT** Revista Medica. Vol. 21, No. 3 (May/Jun. 1983)-. Periodical. Spanish (table of contents in English and Spanish). bm. **ED** J. S. Palencia. **CODEN** RMEDAU. Documents available from BIOSIS Document Express. ***Continues** Revista Medica (Instituto Mexicano del Seguro Social).*
**Ind/Abst** Biol. Abstr.; EMBASE [Select. Cov.].

RM
**REVISTA MEDICALA ROMANA. Added/Corp** Societatea Nationala de Medicina Generala. Uniunea Societatilor de Stiinte Medicale. Vol. 39, (1991)-. Periodical. Romanian (table of contents in English and French). mo. DM168.00. Uniunea Societatilor de Stiinte Medicale din Romania, Str. Progresului Nr. 10, Bucurest Romania. **(Subscription address:** Kubon & Sagner, ABT Zeitschriftenimport, D 80328 Munich Germany.) ***Continues** Revista Viata Medicala.*

RM
**REVISTA MEDICO-CHIRURGICALA.** (1887)-. Periodical. Romanian. Four times a year. DM189.00. **(Subscription address:** Kubon & Sagner, ABT Zeitschriftenimport, D 80328 Munich Germany.) Documents available from CASDDS.
**Ind/Abst** Chem. Abstr.

BL/0101-5907
**REVISTA PARAENSE DE MEDICINA.** [Rev. Para. med.]. Yearly V. 1, No. 1 (Jan./July 1979)-. Periodical. Portuguese. sa. **NLM** W1 RE712B.

BL/0048-7864
**REVISTA PAULISTA DE HOSPITAIS.** [Rev. paul. hosp.]. Vol. 1 (Jan. 1953)-. Academic Scholarly Publication. Portuguese. mo. $70.00. **NLM** W1 RE7125. **Ad Acc. Circ:** 20,000 (ctrl).
**Desc:** Covers general medicine.
**Ind/Abst** EMBASE.

BL/0035-0362
**REVISTA PAULISTA DE MEDICINA.** [Rev. paul. med.]. **Added/Corp** Associacao Paulista de Medicina. (1941)-. Academic Scholarly Publication. Portuguese. bm. $116.70. Associacao Paulista de Medicina, CX Postal 2103, Sao Paulo SP Brazil. **Tel** 232 3141, FAX 55 11 607 7979. **ED** Professor Dra Linamara and R. Batlistella. **NLM** W1 RE7126. **Bk Rev**, (Qty: 4). **Circ:** 5,000 (ctrl). ***Continues** Revista (Associacao Paulista de Medicina).*
**Ind/Abst** EMBASE [Select. Cov.]; Index Med.

RU/0256-5528
**REVMATOLOGIJA.** (REVMATOLOGIIA.). [Revmatologija]. **Added/Corp** Vsesoiuznoe Nauchnoe Revmatologicheskoe Obshchestvo (Soviet Union). (1983)-. Russian (summaries and/or abstracts in English). Four times a year. $36.00. Izdatelstvo Meditsina / Russian Academy of Medical Sciences, Ulitsa Solyanka 14, 109801 Moscow Russia. **Tel** 011 95 297-05-04. **(Subscription address:** Victor Kamkin, 4956 Boiling Brook Parkway, Rockville MD 20852.) **NLM** W1 RE74K. ***Continues** Voprosy Revmatizma.*
**Desc:** Information on rheumatology.
**Ind/Abst** Index Med.

BE/0250-488X
**REVUE BELGE D'ACUPUNCTURE.** [Rev. belg d'acupunct.]. **VFOAT** Belgisch Tijdschrift der Akupunktuur. No 1- March 1978-. Periodical. French (Dutch). qt. $22.00. Association Belge Medecins Acupunctue, 49 A Square Ambiorix, 1040 Brussels Belgium. **NLM** W1 RE741L.

CN/1185-720X
**REVUE CANADIENNE DE LIPIDOLOGIE.** [Rev. can. lipidol.]. **Added/Corp** STA Communications. Vol. 1, No 1 (Jan. 1991)-. Periodical. French. qt. Limited free distribution. STA Communications Inc., 955 St. John Boulevard, Suite 306, Pt Claire, Quebec H9R 5K3 Canada. **Tel** (514)695-7623. **DD** 616.3/997/005.

FR/0557-7721
**REVUE DE MEDECINE DE TOURS.** [Rev. med. Tours]. Vol. 1, No. 1 (Jan./Febr. 1967)-. Periodical. French. Eight times a year. 260.00F (France); 270.00F (other). Editions la Simarre, ZI 2 rue Joseph Cugnot, 37300 Joue-les-Tours France. **Tel** 11 33 47 535366, or 535134. **NLM** W1 RE794R.
**Ind/Abst** EMBASE [Select. Cov.].

FR/0300-0559
**REVUE DE MEDECINE DU TRAVAIL.** (REVUE DE MEDECINE DU TRAVAIL : BULLETIN DU GROUPEMENT NATIONAL D'ETUDE DES MEDECINS DU BATIMENT ET DES TRAVAUX PUBLICS.). [Rev. med. trav.]. **Added/Corp** Groupement National d'Etude des Medecins du Batiment et des Travaux Publics. (1972)-. Periodical. French. Five times a year. 300.00F France; 450.00F other. Groupement Nationale d'Etude Recherches, 6 rue Paul Valery, 75116 Paris France. **(Subscription address:** Revue de Medecine du Travail, 7 rue La Perouse, F 75116 Paris France.) **NLM** W1 RE794V. ***Continues** Bulletin du Groupement National d'Etude des Medecins du Batiment et des Travaux Publics.*
**Ind/Abst** Coal Abstr.; Saf. Health Work.

FR
**REVUE DE PRATICIEN. MEDECINE GENERALE, LA. VFOAT** Medecine Generale. No. 1 (Sept. 17, 1987)-. Periodical. French. Forty times a year. 832.52 (institutions), 587.66F (individual doctors) France; 1050.00F other. JB Bailliere, 37 Avenue des Champs Elysees, 75008 Paris France. **Tel** 011 33 1 49536900. **NLM** W1; RE8393L. ***Separated from** Revue de Praticien, 0035-2640.*
**Ind/Abst** EMBASE [Select. Cov.].

FR/0242-9454
**REVUE D'EDUCATION MEDICALE.** [Rev. educ. med.]. Vol. 5, No. 1 (Jan. 1982)-. Periodical. French (summaries and/or abstracts in English and French). mo. 101 Avenue de Clichy, 75017 Paris France. **Tel** 1 47 75 30 62. **NLM** W1; RE748G. ***Continues** Revue Francaise d'Education Medicale.*

FR/0035-2330
**REVUE D'HISTOIRE DE LA MEDECINE HEBRAIQUE. Added/Corp** Societe d'Histoire de la Medecine Hebraique. **VFOAT** Ketav-at Lahakirat Toledot Ha-Refuah Ha-Ivrit. (1948)-. Periodical. French (summaries and/or abstracts in Hebrew). qt. $11.31. Revue D'Histoire de La Medecine Hebraique, 177 Bd Malesherbes, 75017 Paris 17E France. **Tel** 227 97 11. **ED** Simon Isidore. cum. index. **Bk Rev.**
**Desc:** History of Hebrew medicine, medical ethic.

FR/0035-2640
**REVUE DU PRACTICIEN, LA.** [Rev. prat.]. Vol. 1 (Oct. 1951)-. Academic Scholarly Publication. French (English). wk (60 no. a year). $1665.03F (institutions), 837.41F (individual doctors) France; 2100.00F other. JB Bailliere, 37 Avenue des Champs Elysees, 75008 Paris France. **Tel** 011 33 1 49536900. **NLM** W1 RE8391. **[CCC].** Index available. cum. index. **Bk Rev. Ad Acc. Circ:** 50,000 (ctrl). ***Formed by the union of** Paris Medical, 0369-8300 **and** Revue Generale de Clinique et de Therapeutique, 0368-3397. **Continued in part by** Revue du Praticien. Medecine Generale.*
**Ind/Abst** EMBASE [Select. Cov.]; Energy Res. Abstr. (July 1973-); Saf. Health Work; SportSearch.

BE/0259-8582
**REVUE INTERNATIONALE DES SERVICES DE SANTE DES FORCES ARMEES : ORGANE DU COMITE INTERNATIONAL DE MEDECINE ETUDE PHARMACIE MILITAIRES.** [Rev. int. serv. sante forces armees]. **VFOAT** International Review of the Armed Forces Medical Services. Vol. 59, Nos. 1,2,3, (March 1986)-. Periodical. French (English). Four times a year (Mar., June, Sept., Dec.). 1800F. Comite International de Medecine et de Pharmacie Militaires, rue Saint Laurent 79, B-4000 Liege Belgium. **Tel** (41) 22 21 83, FAX 32 41/22 21 50. **ED** M Cools. **NLM** W1; RE895K. Index available (Bound in 4th iss. (Dec.).). **Bk Rev. Ad Acc. Circ:** 3,000 (ctrl). Documents available from BIOSIS Document Express. ***Continues** Revue Internationale des Services de Sante des Armees de Terre, de mer et de l'Air, 0035-3469.*
**Desc:** All matters interesting the armed forces medical service.
**Ind/Abst** Biol. Abstr.; Protozoolog. Abstr.

FR/0035-3493
**REVUE INTERNATIONALE D'OCEANOGRAPHIE MEDICALE.** [Rev. int. oceanogr. med.]. **Added/Corp** Centre d'Etudes et de Recherches de Biologie et d'Oceanographie Medicale. **VFOAT** R.I.O.M. (1966)-. Academic Scholarly Publication. French (English). Four times a year (Mar., June, Sept., Dec.). 441.00F. Centre Etudes Recherch Biologi, 1 Ave Jean Lorrain, 06300 Nice France. **Tel** 011 33 93 897249. **LC** RA600; .R47. **NLM** W1 RE898T. **CODEN** RVOMAY. Documents available from BIOSIS Document Express, CASDDS. ***Supersedes** Centre d'Etudes et de Recherches de Biologie et d'Oceanographie Medicale. Cahiers du C.E.R.B.O.M.*
**Ind/Abst** Aquat. Sci. Fish. Abstr. (Computer File); Biol. Abstr.; Chem. Abstr.; EMBASE; Energy Res. Abstr.; Mar. Sci. Contents Tables; Ocean. Abstr.; Life Sci. Collect.

FR/0246-0831
**REVUE INTERNATIONALE DU TRACHOME ET DE PATHOLOGIE OCULAIRE TROPICALE ET SUBTROPICALE ET DE SANTE PUBLIQUE. See** Medical Science and Technology-Ophthalmology.

MR/0251-0758
**REVUE MAROCAINE DE MEDECINE ET SANTE.** [Rev. maroc. med. sante]. **VFOAT** Tibb Wa-Al-Sihhah. 1- 1979-. Academic Scholarly Publication. French. qt. **NLM** W1 RE902L. **CODEN** RMMSDG. Documents available from CASDDS.
**Ind/Abst** Chem. Abstr. (1978-1981); EMBASE; Life Sci. Collect.

BE/0035-3639
**REVUE MEDICALE DE BRUXELLES.** [Rev. med. Brux.]. Began in 1944?. Periodical. French. mo. 1200F Belgium; 2000F other. ULB-FAC Medecine Bureau Info Medicale, 2 rue Evers, 1000 Bruxelles Belgium. **Tel** 02/539.23.12. **NLM** W1 RE907Z. **CODEN** RMBRDQ. **Bk Rev. Ad Acc.** Documents available from BIOSIS Document Express. ***Absorbed*** *Bruxelles Medical.*
**Desc:** Covers original or review articles for postgraduate and general practitioners.
**Ind/Abst** Biol. Abstr.; EMBASE [Select. Cov.]; Index Med.

SZ/0035-3655
**REVUE MEDICALE DE LA SUISSE ROMANDE.** [Rev. med. suisse romande]. Vol.1 (Jan. 1881). Academic Scholarly Publication. French. mo. 110.00F. Revue Medicale de la Suisse Romande, AV. Bellefontaine 2, Case Postale 3093, 1002 Lausanne. **Tel** 021 23 98 66. **ED** E C Bonard and J P Berger. **NLM** W1 RE907S. **CODEN** RMSRA6. Index available. **Ad Acc. Circ:** 4,800. Documents available from BIOSIS Document Express. ***Absorbed*** *Bulletin de la Societe Medicale Romande.*
**Desc:** Medical journal of the Medical Society of Switzerland.
**Ind/Abst** Biol. Abstr.; EMBASE [Select. Cov.]; Index Med.; Nutr. Abstr. Rev., Ser. A, Hum. Exp.; Life Sci. Collect.; Rev. Med. Vet. Entomol.; Saf. Health Work; SportSearch.

FR/0767-2004
**REVUE MEDICALE DE L'ASSURANCE MALADIE.** [Rev. med. assur. mal.]. (1970)-. Academic Scholarly Publication. French. Four times a year. 123.22F. UCANSS, 33 Avenue du Maine, BP 45 & 46, 75755 Paris Cedex 15 France. **Tel** 011 33 1 45388149, 011 33 1 45388148. **UDC** 368.4.

BE/0370-629X
**REVUE MEDICALE DE LIEGE.** [Rev. med. Liege]. Vol. 1 (July 1946)-. Academic Scholarly Publication. French. Twelve times a year. 2000F Belgium; 2800F other. University de Liege, Institut de Medicine, rue Alex Bouvy 13, B-4020 Liege Belgium. **Tel** 041 437572. **ED** H. Kulbertus. **NLM** W1 RE9087. **CODEN** RMLIAC. Index available. **Circ:** 3,000. available on microfilm from University Microfilms International (UMI). Documents available from BIOSIS Document Express, CASDDS.
**Desc:** An technical journal of interest to physicians covering all aspects of the medical profession.
**Ind/Abst** Biol. Abstr.; Chem. Abstr.; EMBASE [Select. Cov.]; Index Med.; Life Sci. Collect.; Rev. Med. Vet. Entomol.; Saf. Health Work; SportSearch.

FR/0247-7750
**REVUE PRESCRIRE, LA.** [Rev. Prescr.]. (1980)-. Periodical. French. mo (11 issues). 734.57 (non-profit institutions and individuals), 1469.14F (other institutions), France; 809.57 (non-profit institutions and individuals), 1544.14F (other institutions) other. La Revue Prescrire, BP 459/83 Blvd. Voltaire, 75011 Paris Cedex 11 France. **Tel** 011 33 1 47009445, FAX 48-07-87-32. **ED** Gilles Bardelay. **UDC** 61. Index available. cum. index. **Bk Rev. Pr Rev. Circ:** 25,000 (ctrl).
**Desc:** Independent comparative information on drugs and therapeutics for general practitioners and pharmacists.
**Ind/Abst** Int. Pharm. Abstr.

SP/0211-7274
**RHEUMA (MADRID).** [Rheuma Madr.]. (1981)-. Periodical. Spanish. bm. 51580ptas Spain; 6000ptas other. Jarpyo Editores SA, Antonio Lopez Aguados 4, 28029 Madrid, Spain. **Tel** 011 34 1 3144338, 011 34 1 3144458. **UDC** 616-002.77. **Ad Acc. Circ:** 2,000.

GW/0721-8222
**RHEUMA, SCHMERZ & ENTZUNDUNG.** **VFOAT** Rheuma, Schmerz und Entzundung. Vol. 1, No. 1 (1981)-. Periodical. German. Twelve times a year. $195.00. PMI Verlag GmbH, August-Schanz Strasse 21, D 60433 Frankfurt Germany. **Tel** 011 49 69 5480000, FAX 069/548000-77, telex 412952 PMI D. **NLM** W1 RH267.

●US/1061-222X
**RHODE ISLAND MEDICINE.** [R. I. med.]. **Added/Corp** Rhode Island Medical Society. Vol. 75, No. 1 (Jan. 1992)-. Periodical. English. mo. $40.00 US; $45.00 other. Rhode Island Medical Journal, 106 Francis Street, Providence RI 02903. **Tel** (401)331-3207. **ED** Stanley M. Aronson. **DD** 616. **NLM** W1; RH523. **CODEN** RIMEEF. Index available. **Bk Rev**, (Qty: 4-6). **Ad Acc, Adv Mgr:** James P.Wilson. **Circ:** 2,000. ***Continues*** *Rhode Island Medical Journal, 0363-7913.*
**Ind/Abst** Cumul. Index Nurs. Allied Health Lit.; Energy Res. Abstr.; Index Med. (1992-); Life Sci. Collect.

IT
**RIABILITAZIONE, LA.** (19??)-. Periodical. Italian. qt. $117.00. Masson S.P.A, Via Statuto 2/4, 20121 Milan Italy. **Tel** 011 39 2 63671, FAX 011 39 2 6367211. **ED** Ivano Colombo.

IT/1120-379X
**RICERCA & PRATICA.** (RICERCA & PRACTICA ISTITUTO MARIO NEGRI.). **VFOAT** Ricerca e Pratica. (1985)-. Italian. Six times a year. L80000 individuals; L120000 institutions. Il Pensiero Scientifico Editore s.r.l., Via Bradano 3C, 00199 Rome Italy. **Tel** 011 39 6 86207158, 86207159, 86207168, 86207169, FAX 011 39 6 86207160. **ED** Daniele Coen. **Circ:** 1,700.
**Ind/Abst** EMBASE.

IT/0035-5259
**RIFORMA MEDICA.** (RIFORMA MEDICA; GIORNALE INTERNAZIONALE SETTIMANALE DE MEDICINA, CHIRURGIA E SCIENZE AFFINI.). [Riforma med.]. Vol. 1 (Jan. 1885)-. Academic Scholarly Publication. Italian (summaries and/or abstracts in French, English and German). Three times a year. $90.00 (individuals), $140.00 (institutions). Edizioni Minerva Medica, Corso Bramante 83-85, 10126 Turin Italy. **Tel** 011 39 11 678282, FAX 011 39 11 674502. **ED** T Oliaro. **NLM** W1 RI168L. **CODEN** RIMEAB. **Bk Rev. Ad Acc.** Documents available from CASDDS.
**Desc:** Journal addressed to practitioners in Italy and abroad. It deals with topics in medicine and pharmacology, scientific practice and research.
**Ind/Abst** Chem. Abstr.; CIS Abstr.; EMBASE [Select. Cov.]; Saf. Health Work.

JA/0485-1420
**RINSHO KENSA.** [Rinsho kensa]. **VFOAT** Journal of Medical Technology. Began in 1957. Academic Scholarly Publication. Japanese. mo (with one special issue). $121.80. Igaku Shoin Ltd., 5-24-3 Hongo Bunkyo-ku, Tokyo 113 Japan. **Tel** 011 81 3 817 5670. **ED** Tadashi Kawai. **UDC** 615.4. **CODEN** RNKNAT. Index available. cum. index. **Ad Acc. Circ:** 12,000. Documents available from CASDDS.
**Ind/Abst** Chem. Abstr.; Curr. Biotechnol.

US/0273-3617
**RISK MANAGEMENT REPORT, MEDICAL RECORDS, THE.** ***Title Change.*** [Risk manage. rep., med. rec.]. **VFOAT** Medical Records. Vol. 1, No. 1 (April 1983)-?. Periodical. English. bm. Cox Publications, PO Box 20316, Billings MT 59104-0316. **Tel** (406)256-8822. **ED** Meridith B Cox. ***Continued by*** *Health Insurance/Medical Records Risk Management Reporter, 0883-6671.*
**Desc:** Legal liability involving medical records and ways to reduce liability risks.

US/0893-8245
**RISK MANAGEMENT REPORTER FOR THE HEALTH CARE PROFESSIONAL, THE.** **See** Law.

IT/0035-5836
**RIVISTA DEGLI INFORTUNI E DELLE MALATTIE PROFESSIONALI.** (RIVISTA DEGLI INFORTUNI E DELLE MALATTIE PROFESSIONALI : PUBBLICAZIONE BIMESTRALE DELL'I.N.A.I.L.). [Riv. infort. mal. prof.]. **Added/Corp** Istituto Nazionale Fascista per l'Assicurazione Contro gli Infortuni Sul Lavoro (Italy) I.N.A.I.L. (1941)-. Academic Scholarly Publication. Italian. Six times a year. L80000 Italy; L90000 others. Interantional Rivista Infortuni, Via IV Novembre 144, 00187 Rome Italy. **Tel** 011 39 6 672041. **LC** HD7816.I8; R3. **NLM** W1 RI349. **CODEN** RIMPAA. Documents available from CASDDS. ***Continues*** *Infortuni e Malattie Professionali.*
**Ind/Abst** Chem. Abstr.; Saf. Health Work.

IT
**RIVISTA DEL MEDICO PRATICO, LA.** (19??)-. Periodical. Italian. wk. $100.00. Masson S.P.A, Via Statuto 2/4, 20121 Milan Italy. **Tel** 011 39 2 63671, FAX 011 39 2 6367211. **ED** Carlo Grassi.

IT/0391-2825
**RIVISTA DI MEDICINA DEL LAVORO ED IGIENE INDUSTRIALE.** **See** Industrial Health and Safety.

IT/0394-9982
**RIZA PSICOSOMATICA.** (1980)-. Academic Scholarly Publication. Italian. mo. L78000 Italy. Edizioni Riza, Via Luigi Anelli 1, 20122 Milan, Italy. **Tel** 011 39 2 58301022. **UDC** 615.8.

●US/1355-8382
**RNA. THE OFFICIAL PUBLICATION OF THE RNA SOCIETY.** (March 1995)-. Academic Scholarly Publication. English. Ten times a year. $299.00. Cambridge University Press / New York, 40 West 20th Street, New York NY 10011-4211. **Tel** (212)924-3900, (800)221-4512.
**Desc:** Covers research in all areas of RNA structure and function in eukaryotic, prokaryotic and viral systems. Also covers areas such as mRNA structure, function and biogenesis, and alternative processing.

UK
**ROCK CARLING FELLOWSHIP.** 1964?-. Monographic series. English. an. Price varies per volume.

PL/0523-1507
**ROCZNIKI AKADEMII MEDYCZNEJ IM. JULIANA MARCHLEWSKIEGO W BIAYMSTOKU. SUPLEMENT.** [Rocz. Akad. Med. Juliana Marchlewskiego Biayst., Supl.]. **VFOAT** Annales Academiae Medicae Bialostocensis. Supplementum. Vol. 1 (1958)-. Monographic series. Polish (summaries and/or abstracts in English and Russian). Price varies per volume. Medical Academy, Kilinskiego 1 Bialystok, 15 230 Poland. **Tel** 225-70, FAX 24907 48-85, telex 85 2200 AM PL. **NLM** W1 RO221AN. **CODEN** RMJSAW. Documents available from BIOSIS Document Express.
**Ind/Abst** Biol. Abstr.; Index Med.

PL/0067-6489
**ROCZNIKI AKADEMII MEDYCZNEJ W BIAYMSTOKU.** [Rocz. Akad. Med. Biaymst.]. **Added/Corp** Akademii Medycznej W Biaymstoku. **VFOAT** Annales Academiae Medicae Bialostocensis. (1989)-. Polish (English; summaries and/or abstracts in Russian). Medical Academy, Kilinskiego 1 Bialystok, 15 230 Poland. **Tel** 225-70, FAX 24907 48-85, telex 85 2200 AM PL. **NLM** W1; RO221AR. ***Continues*** *Roczniki Akademii Medycznej Im. Juliana Marchlewskiego W Biaymstoku, 0067-6489.*
**Ind/Abst** Index Med. (1988-1989).

RM/0048-8585
**ROMANIAN MEDICAL REVIEW.** [Rom. med. rev.]. **Added/Corp** Centrul de Documentare Medicala (Bucharest, Romana). Vol. 9, No. 2 (1966)-. Periodical. English (Romanian). qt. Medical Publishing House, 7 Aristide Briand Street, Bucharest Romania. **NLM** W1; RO329. **CODEN** RMDRAX. ***Continues*** *Rumanian Medical Review.*
**Ind/Abst** Life Sci. Collect.

●RU/0869-2106
**ROSSISKII MEDITSINSKII ZHURNAL : ORGAN MINISTERSTVA ZDRAVOOKHRANENIIA RSFSR.** **Added/Corp** Russian S.F.S.R. Ministerstvo Zdravookhraneniia. Russia (Federation). Ministerstvo Zdravookhraneniia. **VFOAT** Russian Medical Journal; Rossiysky Meditsinsky Zhurnal. (1992)-. Periodical. Russian (summaries and/or abstracts in English; table of contents in English). mo. $105.00. Izdatelstvo Meditsina / Russian Academy of Medical Sciences, Ulitsa Solyanka 14, 109801 Moscow Russia. **Tel** 011 95 297-05-04. **(Subscription address:** Victor Kamkin, 4956 Boiling Brook Parkway, Rockville MD 20852.**) LC** R91; .S68. **NLM** W1; RO452J. **CODEN** RMZHEF. ***Continues*** *Sovetskaia Meditsina, 0038-5077.*

CN/0823-4639
**ROSTER DE L'ACTL.** [Roster ACTL]. **Main/Corp** Canadian Society of Laboratory Technologists. **VFOAT** CSLT Roster. **VAT** Roster de l'Association Canadienne des Technologistes de Laboratoire of Laboratory Technologists. 1 Mar. 1983-. English (French). an. Canadian Society of Laboratory Technologists, Box 2830 LCD 1, Hamilton Ontario L8N 3N8 Canada. **Tel** (905)528-8642, FAX (905)528-4968. **ED** Kurt H Davis. **DD** 610.69/53/06071. **Circ:** 3,000 (ctrl). ***Continues*** *Canadian Society of Laboratory Technologists. Roster, 0318-1561.*
**Desc:** Listing of certified members in good standing with the national certifying body.

US
**ROSTER ISSUE OF THE NORTH CAROLINA MEDICAL JOURNAL.** (19??)-. English. an (March). $55.00. North Carolina Medical Society, PO Box 27167, Raleigh NC 27611. **Tel** (919)833-3836, FAX (919)833-2023. **Ad Acc, Adv Mgr:** Don French, **Tel** (919)467-8515. **Circ:** 8,500 (ctrl).
**Desc:** Membership listing- Names and addresses of society members.

US/0160-9440
**ROSTER OF MEMBERS - ASSOCIATION FOR HOSPITAL MEDICAL EDUCATION.** **Main/Corp** Association for Hospital Medical Education. English. an. SYS Systems Association, 2011 Crystal Drive/#200, Arlington VA 22202-3702. **LC** R735.A1. **DD** 610/.71/073. **NLM** WX 22.1 A849R.

UK/0268-3091
**ROUND TABLE SERIES / ROYAL SOCIETY OF MEDICINE SERVICES.** [Round table ser. - R. Soc. Med. Serv.]. **Added/Corp** Royal Society of Medicine Services (Great Britain). No. 1 (1985)-. Monographic series. English. Price varies per volume. Royal Society of Medicine Press, 1 Wimpole Street, London W1M 8AE England. **Tel** 011 44 71 2902928. **NLM** W1; RO489J. ***Continues*** *Forum Series (Royal Society of Medicine (Great Britain)), 0144-5618.*
**Ind/Abst** EMBASE.

GW/0933-0089
**RWI-MITTEILUNGEN.** [RWI-Mitt.]. **VFOAT** Rheinisch-Westfalisches Institut-Mitteilungen; Rheinisch-Westfalisches Institut feur Wirtschaftsforschung-Mitteilungen. (1987)-. Periodical. German. Duncker und Humblot Verlag, Postfach 410329, D-12113 Berlin Germany. **Tel** 011 49 30 79000612, 011

49 30 79000613. **UDC** 330. ***Continues*** *Mitteilungen - Rheinisch-Westfalisches Institut feur Wirtschaftsforschung Essen, 0035-4465.*

JA/0289-1530
**RYUKYU DAIGAKU IGAKKAI ZASSHI.** [Ryukyu Daigaku Igakkai zasshi]. **VFOAT** Ryukyu Medical Journal; Ryukyu Daigaku Igakubu Kiyo. (1983)-. Periodical. Multiple languages. qt. Ryukyu Daigaku Igakubu, (Faculty of Medicine, University of the Ryukyus), 3-1, Yogi 1 Chome, Nahashi, Okinawaken 902, Japan. **DD** 610. Documents available from CASDDS. ***Continues*** *Ryukyu Daigaku Hokengaku Igaku Zasshi, 0285-9270.*
**Ind/Abst** Chem. Abstr.

GW/0340-644X
**SAARLANDISCHES ARZTEBLATT.** [Saarl. Arztebl.]. **Added/Corp** Arztekammer des Saarlandes. Vol. 1 (1948)-. Academic Scholarly Publication. German. Twelve times a year. DM84.11 Germany; DM105.00 others. Deutscher Aerzte Verlag GmbH, Postfach 404265, D-50832 Cologne Germany. **Tel** 011 49 2234 7011219. **NLM** W1 SA104.
**Ind/Abst** EMBASE.

US/0886-2826
**SACRAMENTO MEDICINE.** [Sacram. med.]. **Added/Corp** Sacramento-El Dorado Medical Society. (19??)-. Periodical. English. Eleven times a year (July/Aug. iss. combined). $24.00. Sacramento El-Dorado Medical Society, 5380 Elvas Avenue, Sacramento CA 95819. **Tel** (916)452-2671. **ED** Dr. Richard Johnson M.D. **DD** 610. **Bk Rev**. **Ad Acc**, **Adv Mgr:** Chris Albeson, **Tel** (916)452-2671. **Pr Rev. Circ:** 1,700. ***Continues*** *Bulletin - Sacramento County Medical Society, 0098-4515.*

IT
**SAGGI.** (19??)-. Periodical. Italian. sa. 45000L. Masson S.P.A, Via Statuto 2/4, 20121 Milan Italy. **Tel** 011 39 2 63671, FAX 011 39 2 6367211. **ED** Giorgio Moretti.

UK/0036-2778
**SAINT BARTHOLOMEW'S HOSPITAL JOURNAL.** **Added/Corp** Saint Bartholomew's Hospital (London, England). **VFOAT** Journal; St. Bartholomew's Hospital Journal. (1893)-. Periodical. English. qt. £10.00 England; £8.00 other. Saint Bartholomews Hospital, Medical College West Smithfield, London EC1 7BE England. **Tel** 011 44 71 606-7404. **ED** Kate Feary (editor's phone: 071-601-8871). **NLM** W1 SA164. **Bk Rev**, (Qty: 16). **Ad Acc**. **Circ:** 1,200.

JA/0370-8241
**SAISHIN IGAKU.** [Saishin Igaku]. **VFOAT** Modern Medicine (Osaka); Recent Medicine (Osaka). (1946)-. Japanese. Twelve times a year. $288.00. Saishin Igaku Sha, Century Building, 5-8 Hiranocho 2-chome, Chuo-ku, 541, Osaka Japan. **(Subscription address:** Kyowa Book Company Inc., 1 38 Kanda Jinbocho Chiyoda-ku, Tokyo 101 Japan.**)** **CODEN** SAIGAK. Documents available from CASDDS.
**Ind/Abst** Chem. Abstr.; EMBASE [Select. Cov.].

JA/0385-5074
**SAITAMA IKA DAIGAKU ZASSHI.** (SAITAMA IKA DAIGAKU ZASSHI. JOURNAL OF SAITAMA MEDICAL SCHOOL.). [Saitama Ika Daigaku zasshi]. **Added/Corp** Saitama Ika Daigaku. Saitama Ika Daigaku Igakkai. **VFOAT** Journal of Saitama Medical School. (1974)-. Periodical. Japanese (summaries and/or abstracts in English). Medical Society of Saitama Medical School, 38 Morohongo, Moroyama, Iruma-gun, 350-04, Saitama, Japan. **NLM** W1 SA274. **CODEN** SIDZD9. Documents available from BIOSIS Document Express, CASDDS.
**Ind/Abst** Biol. Abstr. (1986-); Chem. Abstr. (-1988); EMBASE [Select. Cov.].

GW/0178-7969
**SALIX.** (1985)-. Periodical. German (English). sa. MW-Verlag, Postfach 338, D-8700, Wurzburg 11. **NLM** W1; SA330.

SP
**SALUD RURAL. T.S.R.** Spanish. Twenty times a year. 5.000ptas Spain; 8.000ptas other. Jarpyo Editores SA, Antonio Lopez Aguados 4, 28029 Madrid, Spain. **Tel** 011 34 1 3144338, 011 34 1 3144458. **(Subscription address:** Antonio Lopez Aguado 1-4, 28029 Madrid Spain**)** **Ad Acc**. **Circ:** 19,000 (ctrl).

IT/0392-4505
**SALUTE E TERRITORIO.** **Added/Corp** Giunta Regionale Toscana. (197?)-. Periodical. Italian. bm. L55000 Italy; L65000 other. Mozzon Giuntina SPA, Via Mannelli 29R, 50136 Florence, Italy. **Tel** 011 39 55 2476781, FAX 055/2478568. **NLM** W1; SA405.

US
**SAM-CD : SCIENTIFIC AMERICAN MEDICINE ON CD-ROM.** English. qt. $651.00. Scientific American Medicine, 415 Madison Avenue, New York NY 10017. **Tel** (212)754-0550, (800)333-1199.
**Desc:** Includes the 2,300-page text of Scientific American Medicine with full-color photographs, x-rays, line drawings and tables. Also included is the complete library of DISCOTEST interactive patient management problems available for CME credits.

SA/0256-9574
**SAMJ. SOUTH AFRICAN MEDICAL JOURNAL.** [SAMJ, S. Afr. med. j.]. **VFOAT** South African Medical Journal; SAMT. Suid-Afrikaanse Mediese Tydskrif. (1985)-. Periodical. English. wk. Medical Association of South Africa, Private Bag X1, 7430 Pinelands South Africa. **Tel** 011 27 21 5313081, FAX 534126, telex 5-20378 CT. **UDC** 61. Documents available from CASDDS.
**Ind/Abst** Chem. Abstr.

US
**SAN DIEGO PHYSICIAN.** **Added/Corp** San Diego County Medical Society. Vol. 55, (Jan. 1969)-. Periodical. English. Twelve times a year. $25.00. San Diego County Medical Society, PO Box 23581, San Diego CA 92123. **Tel** (619)565-8888, FAX (619)569-1334. **ED** Dr. James L. Rice M. D. Index available (Bound in next iss.). **Bk Rev**, (Qty: 2). **Ad Acc**, **Adv Mgr:** E. Persian. **Circ:** 3,500 (ctrl). ***Continues*** *Bulletin- San Diego County Medical Society.*
**Desc:** This is distributed to all major San Diego County health agencies, hospital administrators and public relations directors, state and national legislators, medical schools, libraries and medical societies.

US/0361-705X
**SAN FRANCISCO MEDICINE.** **Added/Corp** San Francisco Medical Society. (Jan. 1976)-. Periodical. English. mo. $33.00. San Francisco Medical Society, 1409 Sutter Street, San Francisco CA 94109. **Tel** (415)561-0850, FAX (415)561-0833. **ED** Toni Brayer. **NLM** W1 SA5768. Index available. **Bk Rev**. **Ad Acc**. **Circ:** 3,300. ***Continues*** *Bulletin - San Francisco Medical Society, 0036-4142.*

IT
**SANARE INFIRMOS.** (19??)-. Italian. Three times a year. L20000.00 Italy; L30000.00 Europe; L45000.00 other. Europa Scienze Umane Editrice, Via Olgettina 60, 20132 Milan Italy. **Tel** 011 39 2 26410150.

KO/0257-2389
**SANNEB MISAINMURHAG HOIJI.** (SANOP MISAENGMUL HAKHOE CHI.). [Sanneb misainmurhag hoiji]. **Added/Corp** Hanguk Sanop Misaengmul Hakhoe. **VFOAT** Korean Journal of Applied Microbiology and Bioengineering; Hanguk Sanop Misaengmul Hakhoe Chi. (197?)-. Academic Scholarly Publication. English (Korean). Six times a year. $40.00. Korean Society of Applied Microbiology, 93 1 Mojin Dong Sungdond Ku, Seoul Korea. **Tel** 011 82 1 447-1487. **LC** QR53; .S35. **NLM** W1; SA783. **CODEN** SMHAEH. Documents available from BIOSIS Document Express, CASDDS.
**Ind/Abst** BioBusiness; Biol. Abstr. (1985-); Chem. Abstr.

SP/0211-0873
**SANT PAU.** Periodical. Catalan. **NLM** W1; SA783S. ***Continues*** *Anales del Hospital de la Santa Cruz y San Pablo, 0301-3626.*
**Ind/Abst** Indice Med. Esp.

FR/0293-5945
**SANTE 2000 MEDECINE.** [Sante 2000 med.]. **VFOAT** Sante Deux Mille Medecine; Afrique Sante Deux Mille Medecine; Afrique Sante 2000 Medecine. Began with: V. 1, No. 1 (March/April 1982). Periodical. French. qt. **NLM** W1 SA834.

PH/0371-3520
**SANTO TOMAS JOURNAL OF MEDICINE.** [St. Tomas j. med.]. Vol. 2, No. 2 (March 1947)-. Academic Scholarly Publication. English. qt. University of Santo Tomas Faculty of Medicine and Surgery, Manila Philippines. **NLM** W1; SA869. ***Continues*** *U.S.T. Journal of Medicine.*
**Ind/Abst** EMBASE; Philip. Sci. Technol. Abstr.

JA/0036-472X
**SAPPORO IGAKU ZASSHI.** (SAPPORO IGAKU ZASSHI. THE SAPPORO MEDICAL JOURNAL.). [Sapporo igaku zasshi]. **Added/Corp** Sapporo Ika Daigaku. **VFOAT** Sapporo Medical Journal. (1952)-. Periodical. Japanese (English; summaries and/or abstracts in English; table of contents in English). bm. Sapporo Medical College, South 1, West 17, Sapporo, Japan 060. **NLM** W1 SA9417. **CODEN** SIZSAR. Documents available from BIOSIS Document Express, CASDDS. ***Continues*** *Sapporo Ika Daigaku. Kiyo.*
**Ind/Abst** Biol. Abstr.; Chem. Abstr.; EMBASE [Select. Cov.]; Saf. Health Work.

JA/0389-3944
**SAPPORO IKA DAIGAKU JINBUN SHIZEN KAGAKU KIYO.** [Sapporo Ika Daigaku jinbun shizen kagaku kiyo]. **Added/Corp** Sapporo Igaku Daigaku. **VFOAT** Journal of Liberal Arts and Sciences, Sapporo Medical College. (1979)-. Periodical. Japanese. Sapporo Ika Daigaku, (Sapporo Medical College), Nishi 17 Chome, Minami 1 JO, Chuoku, Sapporoshi, Hokkaido 060 Japan. **CODEN** SIDKDW. Documents available from BIOSIS Document Express, CASDDS. ***Continues*** *Sapporo Ika Daigaku. Sapporo Igaku Daigaku Shingaku Katei Kiyo.*
**Ind/Abst** Biol. Abstr.; Chem. Abstr.

IT/0393-1447
**SARCOIDOSIS.** [Sarcoidosis]. **Added/Corp** International Committee on Sarcoidosis. Vol. 1, No. 1 (Sept. 1984)-. Periodical. English. sa (Mar., and Sept.). $67.00. PCA Publishing Commun Advert, Via Clerici 12, 20032 Brusuglio Cormano, Italy. **Tel** 011 39 2 663000802. **ED** Geraint D James. **NLM** W1; SA9428T. **Bk Rev**. **Ad Acc**. **Circ:** 1,000.
**Ind/Abst** EMBASE [Select. Cov.]; Index Med. (1984-); Sci. Cit. Index; Soc. Sci. Cit. Index [Select. Cov.].

JA
**SASEBO SHIRITSU SOGO BYOIN IGAKU GYOSEKI SHU.** Periodical. Japanese. Sasebo Shiritsu Sogo Byoin Ikyoku, (Sasebo City General Hospital), 10-3, Shimanjicho, Saseboshi, Nagasakiken 857 Japan. **NLM** W1 SA943C. ***Supersedes*** *Sasebo Shiritsu Shimin Byoin Igaku Gyoseki Shu.*

CN/1182-0063
**SASKATCHEWAN MEDICAL JOURNAL.** [Sask. med. j.]. **Added/Corp** Saskatchewan Medical Association. University of Saskatchewan. Continuing Medical Education. Vol. 1, No. 1 Feb. (1990)-. Periodical. English. qt. $20.00 per year. University of Saskatchewan Department of Continuing Medical Education, 408 Ellis Hall, Saskatoon Saskatchewan S7N 0W0 Canada. **Tel** (306)966-7790. **DD** 610/.97124/05. ***Continues*** *C M E News, 0701-4880.*

SU/0379-5284
**SAUDI MEDICAL JOURNAL.** [Saudi med. j.]. Vol. 1, July (1979)-. Periodical. English (Arabic; table of contents in Arabic). mo. £30.00. Fisher Duncan, 10 Barley MOW Passage, Chiswick, London W4 4PH England. **Tel** 011 44 81 9446477, FAX 011 44 81 74263024. **ED** Saleh Al-Deeb MD. **NLM** W1 SA966. **CODEN** SAMJDI. **[CCC]**. Index available. **Bk Rev**. **Ad Acc**, **Adv Mgr:** Peter Carpenter. **Pr Rev. Circ:** 24,000 (ctrl). available on microfilm and microfiche from University Microfilms International (UMI). Documents available from The Genuine Article, BIOSIS Document Express.
**Desc:** General medical journal.
**Ind/Abst** Biol. Abstr.; Curr. Contents Clin. Med.; EMBASE [Select. Cov.]; Helminthol. Abstr. (19??-19??); Index Vet.; Nutr. Abstr. Rev., Ser. A, Hum. Exp.; Life Sci. Collect. (1990-); Protozoolog. Abstr.; Res. Alert [Select. Cov.]; Rev. Med. Vet. Entomol.; Soc. Sci. Cit. Index [Select. Cov.]; Sug. Indus. Abstr.; Trop. Dis. Bull.

XR/0036-5327
**SBORNIK LEKARSKY.** [Sb. lek.]. **Added/Corp** Universita Karlova. Fakulta Vseobecneho Lekarstvi. Universita Karlova. Fakulta Lekarska. **VFOAT** Archives Bohemes de Medecine. (1887)-. Academic Scholarly Publication. Slovak (summaries and/or abstracts in English and Russian). Twelve times a year. $66.80. **(Subscription address:** Artia Pegas Press Ltd., Palac Metro Narodni Trida 25, 11210 Prague 1 Czech Republic.**)** **NLM** W1 SB471. **CODEN** SBLEA2. Documents available from CASDDS.
**Ind/Abst** Chem. Abstr.; EMBASE [Select. Cov.]; Index Med.; Nutr. Abstr. Rev., Ser. A, Hum. Exp.; Life Sci. Collect.; Saf. Health Work; SportSearch.

RU
**SBORNIK NAUCHNO-PRAKTICHESKIKH RABOT - MINISTERSTVO ZDRAVOOKHRANENIIA RSFSR, CHETVERTOE GLAVNOE UPRAVLENIE.** **Added/Corp** Russia (R.S.F.S.R.) Ministerstvo Zdravookhraneniia. Chetvertoe Glavnoe Upravlenie. Vol. 1 (1970)-. Russian. **NLM** W1 SB471X.

RU/0300-0168
**SBORNIK NAUCNYH TRUDOV - KLINIKA NERVNYH BOLEZNEJ IRKUTSKOGO MEDICINSKOGO INSTITUTA.** (NAUCHNYE TRUDY.). [Sb. naucn. tr. - Klin. nervn. bolezn. Irkutsk. med. inst.]. **Main/Corp** Irkutskii Meditsinskii Institut. Klinika Nervnykh Boleznei. (19??)-. Monographic series. Russian. Price varies per volume.

XR/0049-5514
**SBORNIK VEDECKYCH PRACI LEKARSKE FAKULTY KARLOVY UNIVERSITY V HRADCI KRALOVE.** [Sb. ved. pr. lek. fak. Univ. Karlovy Hradci Kralove]. **Main/Corp** Prague. Universita Karlova Lekarska Fakulta v Hdadci Kralove. **Added/Corp** Karlova Universita. Lekarska Fakulta v Hradci Kralove. **VFOAT** Collection of Scientific Works of the Faculty of Medicine of Charles University; Sbornik Nauchnykh Rabot Meditsinskogo Fakulteta Karlova Universiteta v Gradtse Kralove. (1958)-. Academic Scholarly Publication. Czech. ir. **(Subscription address:** Artia Pegas Press Ltd., Palac Metro Narodni Trida 25, 11210 Prague 1 Czech Republic.**)** **LC** R95.P7; A28. **NLM** W1 SB702P. **CODEN** SVLKAO. Documents available from BIOSIS Document Express, CASDDS.
**Ind/Abst** Biol. Abstr.; Chem. Abstr.; EMBASE [Select. Cov.]; Index Med.; Postharvest News Inf.

US
**SCALPEL (BRONXVILLE, N.Y.).** (THE SCALPEL / ALPHA EPSILON DELTA, THE PREMEDICAL HONOR SOCIETY.). **Added/Corp** Alpha Epsilon Delta. **VFOAT** Scalpel of Alpha Epsilon Delta. Vol. 1, No. 1 (Jan. 1931)-. Periodical. English. sa. $3.50. Scalpel, 7 Brookside Circle, c/o Dr. M. Moore, Bronxville NY 10708. **NLM** W1 SC141.

NO/1103-8128
**SCANDINAVIAN JOURNAL OF OCCUPATIONAL THERAPY.** (19??)-. English. qt (4 issues). Kr560.00, $90.00. Scandinavian University Press, PO Box 2959 Toeyen, N 0608 Oslo 6 Norway. **Tel** 011 47 2 2575400, FAX 011 47 2 2575353, telex 71896 UROR N. **(Subscription address:** Scandinavian University Press, 200 Meacham Ave., Elmont NY 11003.**)**

SW/0036-5505
**SCANDINAVIAN JOURNAL OF REHABILITATION MEDICINE.** [Scand. j. rehabil. med.]. Vol. 1 (1969)-. Academic Scholarly Publication. English. qt. Kr720.00, $118.00. Scandinavian University Press, PO Box 2959 Toeyen, N 0608 Oslo 6 Norway. **Tel** 011 47 2 2575400, FAX 011 47 2 2575353, telex 71896 UROR N. **(Subscription address:** Scandinavian University Press, 200 Meacham Ave., Elmont NY 11003.**) ED** Olle Hook. **NLM** W1 SC153N. **CODEN** SJRMAA. **Pr Rev.** Documents available from The Genuine Article, BIOSIS Document Express.
**Desc:** A forum for research into rehabilitation medicine. The journal deals with the medical, psychological, social, economic and technological aspects of rehabilitation. Focuses on work physiology, neurophysiology, physiotherapy, psychology, work tests and development of technical aids.
**Ind/Abst** Biol. Abstr.; Cumul. Index Nurs. Allied Health Lit.; Curr. Contents Clin. Med.; Dev. Med. Child Neurol.; EMBASE; Ergon. Abstr.; Except. Child Educ. Resour. (19??-19??); Index Med.; Life Sci. Collect.; PsycINFO (?-?); PsycLit; Res. Alert [Select. Cov.]; Soc. Sci. Cit. Index [Select. Cov.]; SportSearch.

SW/0346-8720
**SCANDINAVIAN JOURNAL OF REHABILITATION MEDICINE. SUPPLEMENT.** [Scand. j. rehabil. med., Suppl.]. (1970)-. Academic Scholarly Publication. English. ir. Price varies per volume. Scandinavian University Press, PO Box 2959 Toeyen, N 0608 Oslo 6 Norway. **Tel** 011 47 2 2575400, FAX 011 47 2 2575353, telex 71896 UROR N. **(Subscription address:** Scandinavian University Press, 200 Meacham Ave., Elmont NY 11003.**) NLM** W1 SC153P. **CODEN** SJRSDV. Documents available from BIOSIS Document Express.
**Ind/Abst** Biol. Abstr.; EMBASE; Index Med.

SW/0300-8037
**SCANDINAVIAN JOURNAL OF SOCIAL MEDICINE.** [Scand. j. soc. med.]. **Added/Corp** Scandinavian Association for Social Medicine. Vol. 1, No. 1 (1973)-. Academic Scholarly Publication. English. qt. Kr840.00, $135.00. Scandinavian University Press, PO Box 2959 Toeyen, N 0608 Oslo 6 Norway. **Tel** 011 47 2 2575400, FAX 011 47 2 2575353, telex 71896 UROR N. **(Subscription address:** Scandinavian University Press, 200 Meacham Ave., Elmont NY 11003.**) ED** Lars Olov Bygren. **NLM** W1; SC154BJ. **CODEN** SJSMAF. **Pr Rev.** Documents available from The Genuine Article, BIOSIS Document Express. ***Continues** Acta Socio-Medica Scandinavica.*
**Desc:** Presents research papers on the functioning of the Scandinavian welfare states and sociomedical problems encountered. Most of the journal's articles are based upon original research accepted after peer review, but the journal also publishes articles concerning research on policy matters.
**Ind/Abst** Biol. Abstr.; Cumul. Index Nurs. Allied Health Lit.; Curr. Contents Clin. Med.; Curr. Contents Soc. Behav. Sci.; Curr. Titl. Dent.; Dent. Abstr. (-199?); EMBASE; Index Med.; Life Sci. Collect.; Res. Alert [Full Cov.]; Risk Abstr.; Saf. Health Work; Soc. Sci. Cit. Index [Full Cov.]; SportSearch; Trop. Dis. Bull.

SW/0301-7311
**SCANDINAVIAN JOURNAL OF SOCIAL MEDICINE. SUPPLEMENTUM.** [Scand. j. soc. med., Suppl.]. **VFOAT** Scandinavian Journal of Social Medicine. Supplement. (1973)-. Academic Scholarly Publication. English. ir. Comes with Scandinavian Journal of Social Medicine. Scandinavian University Press, PO Box 2959 Toeyen, N 0608 Oslo 6 Norway. **Tel** 011 47 2 2575400, FAX 011 47 2 2575353, telex 71896 UROR N. **(Subscription address:** Scandinavian University Press, 200 Meacham Ave., Elmont NY 11003.**) NLM** W1; SC154BK. **CODEN** SJSSD2. Documents available from BIOSIS Document Express. ***Continues** Acta Socio-Medica Scandinavica. Supplement.*
**Ind/Abst** Biol. Abstr.; Cumul. Index Nurs. Allied Health Lit.; EMBASE; Index Med.; Life Sci. Collect.

US/0733-4397
**SCHEDULE OF NIH CONFERENCES.** **Main/Corp** National Institutes of Health (U.S.). Division of Research Grants. **VFOAT** Schedule of N.I.H. Conferences. **VAT** Schedule of National Institutes of Health Conferences. Began with Oct. 1969. Periodical. English. qt. Division of Research Grants, National Institutes of Health, Bethesda MD 20205. **NLM** W 3.5 S414.

US/0197-7210
**SCHISTO UPDATE.** **See** Medical Science and Technology-Abstracting, Bibliographies and Statistics.

GW/0932-433X
**SCHMERZ, DER.** **Added/Corp** Serturner Gesellschaft. Gesellschaft zum Studium des Schmerzes fuer Deutschland, Osterreich and die Schweiz. Vol. 1, No. 1 (July 1987)-. Periodical. German (summaries and/or abstracts in English). Six times a year. DM218.00. Springer-Verlag GmbH & Company KG, Heidelberger Platz 3, D 14197 Berlin Germany. **Tel** 011 49 30 8207223, FAX 011 49 30 8214091, telex 183 319 SPBLN D. **(Subscription address:** Springer Verlag New York Inc. / for North America, 44 Hartz Way, Secaucus NJ 07096.**) ED** H Bergmann and M Zimmermann. **NLM** W1; DE478. **[CCC].** available on microfilm and microfiche from University Microfilms International (UMI).

GW/0178-692X
**SCHMERZDIAGNOSTIK UND THERAPIE.** [Schmerzdiagn. Ther.]. Vol. 1-. Periodical. German (English). ir. **NLM** W1; SC18J.

GW/0170-0596
**SCHMERZSTUDIEN.** V. 1-. Academic Scholarly Publication. German. ir. Price varies per volume. VCH Publishers Inc, 220 East 23rd Street, New York NY 10010. **Tel** (212)683-8333, , FAX (212)481-0897. **(Subscription address:** VCH Publishers Inc., 303 Northwest 12th Avenue, Journals Department, Deerfield FL 33442.**) NLM** W1 SC18M. **CODEN** SCHMDG. Documents available from CASDDS.
**Ind/Abst** Chem. Abstr. (1978-1981).

GW/0174-4771
**SCHRIFTENREIHE DER DEUTSCHEN GESELLSCHAFT FUER MEDIZINISCHE DOKUMENTATION, INFORMATIK UND STATISTIK E. V.** **Added/Corp** Deutsche Gesellschaft fuer Medizinische Dokumentation, Informatik und Statistik. No. 1 (1978)-. Monographic series. German. Price varies per volume. F K Schattauer Verlagsgesellschaft mbH, Postfach 10 45 45, D 70040 Stuttgart Germany. **Tel** 011 49 711 2298726. **NLM** W1 SC329F.

US/0731-5406
**SCHUMPERT MEDICAL QUARTERLY.** ***Ceased.*** [Schumpert med. q.]. **Added/Corp** Schumpert Medical Center. Vol. 1, No. 1 (June 1982)-Vol. 9, No. 3 (June 1992). Periodical. English. Four times a year. Schumpert Medical Center, PO Box 21976, Department of Medical Publishers, Shreveport LA 71120. **Tel** (318)227-6602. **ED** Merrilee S. Leatherman. **NLM** W1 SC373. Index available. cum. index. **Ad Acc. Circ:** 7,000 (ctrl).
**Desc:** Each issue devoted to one specialty. Provides forum for exchange of ideas and gives practical clinical information from various specialties for primary care physicians treating various patients.

SZ/0036-7672
**SCHWEIZERISCHE MEDIZINISCHE WOCHENSCHRIFT.** [Schweiz. med. Wochenschr.]. **VFOAT** Journal Suisse de Medecine. Vol. 50 (Jan. 1920)-. Academic Scholarly Publication. German (French; summaries and/or abstracts in German). Fifty-two times a year. 166.00F Switzerland; 179.00F Europe; 198.00F other. Schwabe & Company Ltd., Farnsburgerstrasse 8 PF 254, CH-4132 Muttenz 1 Switzerland. **Tel** 011 41 61 4613001, FAX 01 41 61 4612500. **ED** G. Riva, P. W. Straub, B. Truniger and A. Uehlinger. **NLM** W1 SC485. **CODEN** SMWOAS. **[CCC].** Index available in last issue of volume--attached. **Bk Rev. Ad Acc. Pr Rev. Circ:** 5,300 (ctrl). Documents available from The Genuine Article, BIOSIS Document Express, CASDDS. ***Continues** Correspondenz-Blatt fuer Schweizer Artze.*
**Desc:** Information about all fields of medicine.
**Ind/Abst** AgBiotech News Inf.; Biol. Abstr.; Chem. Abstr.; Curr. Contents Clin. Med.; EMBASE; Helminthol. Abstr.; Index Med.; Index Dent. Lit.; Nutr. Abstr. Rev., Ser. A, Hum. Exp.; Life Sci. Collect.; PESTDOC; Protozoolog. Abstr.; Ref. Upd. Basic Ed.; Ref. Upd. Deluxe Ed.; Res. Alert [Full Cov.]; Rev. Med. Vet. Entomol.; Rev. Med. Vet. Mycology; Saf. Health Work; Sci. Cit. Index; SCISEARCH; Small Anim. Abstr. Bibliogr.; Soc. Sci. Cit. Index [Select. Cov.]; SportSearch.

SZ/0250-5525
**SCHWEIZERISCHE MEDIZINISCHE WOCHENSCHRIFT. SUPPLEMENTUM.** [Schweiz. med. Wochenschr., Suppl.]. Vol. 1 (April 1975)-. Academic Scholarly Publication. German (French and German). ir. Comes with journal: 166.00F Switzerland; 179.00F Europe; 198.00F other. Schwabe & Company Ltd., Farnsburgerstrasse 8 PF 254, CH-4132 Muttenz 1 Switzerland. **Tel** 011 41 61 4613001, FAX 01 41 61 4612500. **NLM** W1 SC485C. **CODEN** SMWSD9. Documents available from CASDDS.
**Ind/Abst** Chem. Abstr. (1976-1982); Index Med.

GW/0722-3625
**SCHWERPUNKT MEDIZIN.** (SCHWERPUNKT MEDIZIN : S.M.). **VFOAT** S.M.; SM. Began with 1978. Periodical. German (summaries and/or abstracts in English and German). ir. Selecta Verlagsgesellschaft mbH, Postfach 4240, c/o Mrs. Riemer, D-65032 Wiesbaden Germany. **Tel** 011 49 611 1705261. **NLM** W1 SC643H.

GW/0340-5303
**SCHWESTER. DER PFLEGER, DIE.** (1975)-. Periodical. German. Twelve times a year. DM54.00 Germany; DM 60.60 others. Bibliomed Medizinische Verlag, Postfach 150 Nuernberger St 10, W 34201 Melsungen F R Germany. **Tel** 011 49 5661 6001, FAX 011 49 5661 8360. **UDC** 362.14. **CODEN** 616-083.

●US/1068-6738
**SCIENTIFIC AMERICAN FRONTIERS (MAGAZINE).** (SCIENTIFIC AMERICAN FRONTIERS.). [Sci. Am. front.]. **VFOAT** Scientific American Frontiers Magazine. (1994)-. Periodical. English. mo. $36.00. Scientific American Medicine, 415 Madison Avenue, New York NY 10017. **Tel** (212)754-0550, (800)333-1199. **(Subscription address:** CDS Agency Hard Copy, PO Box 4966, Des Moines IA 50340.**) DD** 505.

US/0194-9063
**SCIENTIFIC AMERICAN MEDICINE.** (1978)-. Periodical. English. mo. $373.00 (institution), $313.00 (individual) US; $395.50 (institution), $335.50 (individual) Canada; $428.50 (institution), $336.50 (individual) other (surface mail). Scientific American Medicine, 415 Madison Avenue, New York NY 10017. **Tel** (212)754-0550, (800)333-1199. **ED** Edward Rubenstein. **Ad Acc. Pr Rev. Circ:** 30,000. available on CD-ROM; available on an online database from BRS.
**Desc:** Contains current patient-care information in the 15 subspecialties of medicine.

●US/1068-6746
**SCIENTIFIC AMERICAN SCIENCE & MEDICINE.** [Sci. Am. sci. med.]. **VFOAT** Scientific American Science and Medicine. (1994)-. Periodical. English. bm (6 issues). $59.00 (one year), $89.00 (two year). Scientific American Medicine, 415 Madison Avenue, New York NY 10017. **Tel** (212)754-0550, (800)333-1199. **(Subscription address:** CDS Agency Hard Copy, PO Box 4966, Des Moines IA 50340.**) DD** 505. **NLM** W1; SC833P.
**Desc:** Describes the process and the results of research that is relevant to the practice of medicine. Designed to make biomedical science accessible to practicing physicians.

UK/0884-8319
**SCIENTIFIC SERIALS REVIEW. BIOMEDICINE.** ***Ceased.*** **See** Biology.

US
**SCOPE NOTE / JOSEPH AND ROSE KENNEDY INSTITUTE OF ETHICS, GEORGETOWN UNIVERSITY.** **Added/Corp** Kennedy Institute of Ethics. National Reference Center for Bioethics Literature. **VFOAT** Scope Note Series. (1982)-. Monographic series. English. ir. Price varies per volume. Kennedy Institute of Ethics, Georgetown University, Washington DC 20057. **Tel** (800)663-3849, (202)687-3885, FAX (202)687-6770. **ED** Doris Goldstein. **LC** R724; .S395. **NLM** ZW 50; S422.

UK/0036-9330
**SCOTTISH MEDICAL JOURNAL.** [Scott. med. j.]. **Added/Corp** Royal Medico-Chirurgical Society of Glasgow. Edinburgh Medico-Chirurgical Society. Scottish Society for Experimental Medicine. Vol. 1 (Jan. 1956)-. Academic Scholarly Publication. English. Six times a year. $99.00. Durrant Periodicals, Winton LEA Pencaitland, East Lothian EH34 5AY Scotland. **Tel** 011 44 875 340354. **NLM** W1 SC902. **CODEN** SMDJAK. **[CCC]. Pr Rev.** Documents available from The Genuine Article, BIOSIS Document Express, CASDDS. ***Formed by the union of** Glasgow Medical Journal **and** Edinburgh Medical Journal.*
**Ind/Abst** Appl. Soc. Sci. Index Abstr.; Biol. Abstr.; Chem. Abstr.; Curr. Contents Clin. Med.; Curr. Contents Life Sci.; EMBASE; Health Serv. Abstr.; Index Med.; Nutr. Res. Newsl.; Life Sci. Collect.; PESTDOC; Potato Abstr.; Protozoolog. Abstr.; Res. Alert [Full Cov.]; Sci. Cit. Index; SCISEARCH; Soc. Sci. Cit. Index [Select. Cov.]; SportSearch; Trop. Dis. Bull.

US
**SCRIBE.** (1991). English. $36.00 (1 year), $60.00 (2 year). Multnomah County Medical Society, 4540 SW Kelly, Portland OR 97201. **Tel** (503)222-9977, FAX (503)222-3164. ***Continues** Portland Physician Scribe, 8756-646X.*

US
**SCRIPPS CLINIC UPDATE.** (19??)-. Periodical. English. Six times a year. Free on request. Scripps Research Institute, 10666 North Torrey Pines Road, La Jolla CA 92037. **Tel** (619)554-8040. ***Absorbed** Scientific Report, 0361-3054.*

BU/0582-3250
**SCRIPTA SCIENTIFICA MEDICA.** [Scr. sci. med.]. **Added/Corp** Vissh Meditsinski Institut - Varna. Vol. 4, No. 2 (1965)-. Academic Scholarly Publication. Bulgarian (English; summaries and/or abstracts in English and Russian; table of contents in English and Russian). an. Free on request. Higher Institute of Medicine, 55 Marin Drinov Street, Varna 9002 Bulgaria. **Tel** 052 225421. **NLM** W1 SC938. **CODEN** SSCMBX. Documents available from CASDDS. ***Continues*** *Nauchni Trudove of the Vissh Meditsinski Institut, Varna.*
**Ind/Abst** Chem. Abstr.; Saf. Health Work; Trop. Dis. Bull.

JA/1010-5441
**SEAMIC INFORMATION RETRIEVAL ON CURRENT LITERATURE. SERIES M, MALARIA.** **See** Public Health and Safety.

JA/0387-737X
**SEAMIC NEWS LETTER.B.** **Added/Corp** Nihon Kokusai Iryodan. Tonan Ajia Iryo Joho Senta. Nihon Kohusoi Iryodan. Vol. 1 (Feb. 1979)-. Periodical. English. sa. Tonan Ajia Iryo Joho Senta, (Southeast Asian Medical Information Center), 7-2, Shinbashi 4 Chome, Minatoku, Tokyoto 105, Japan.
**Ind/Abst** Trop. Dis. Bull.

US/1054-9358
**SEARCH (NEW YORK, N.Y. 1991).** (SEARCH : THE ROCKEFELLER UNIVERSITY MAGAZINE.). [Search]. **Added/Corp** Rockefeller University. **VFOAT** Rockefeller University Magazine. Premier Issue (Spring 1991)-. Periodical. English. Twice a year. Free on request. Rockefeller University Press, 222 East 70th Street, New York NY 10021. **Tel** (212)327-8572, FAX (212)327-7944. **ED** Doron Weber. **DD** 001. **Circ:** 10,000.

US/0890-1570
**SECOND OPINION (PARK RIDGE, ILL.).** (SECOND OPINION.). [Second opin.]. **Added/Corp** Park Ridge Center (Ill.). Vol. 1 (1986)-. Periodical. English. Four times a year (Jan, Apr, July, Oct). $45.00 (one year), $80.00 (two years), $115.00 (three years). Park Ridge Center, 211 East Ontario, Suite 800, Chicago IL 60611. **Tel** (312)266-2222, FAX (312)266-6086. **ED** Martin E. Marty and Barbara Hofmaier. **LC** R724; .S398. **DD** 174/.2/05. **NLM** W1; SE217W. Index available. cum. index. **Bk Rev. Pr Rev. Circ:** 2,000. available on an online database (file 149/Full-Text) from DIALOG.
**Desc:** Non-denominational interdisciplinary book-like journal focuses on medical ethics and health-faith issues. Includes case studies, interviews, articles and extensive illustrations.
**Ind/Abst** Abstr. Res. Pastor. Care Couns. (19??-); Acad. Abstr. Full Text Elite (Jan. 1992-); Acad. Abstr. (Jan. 1992-); Acad. Search (Jan. 1992-); Christ. Period. Index (19??-); Cumul. Index Nurs. Allied Health Lit.; Health Index (1989-); Health Period. Database [Full Txt.]; Health Plan. Adminis.; Health Ref. Cent. (Jan. 1989-) [Full Txt.] [Full Cov.]; Health Source (Mar. 1992-); Hospit. Health Admin. Index (1986-); Index Book Rev. Relig.; INFO-SOUTH Abstr.; Int. Nurs. Index; Mag. Search; Relig. Index One Period.

US/0738-8802
**SECOND OPINIONS ON HEALTH CARE ISSUES.** ***Ceased.*** [Second opin. health care issues]. **Added/Corp** Thompson, Mohr & Associates. **VFOAT** Second Opinions; 2nd Opinions on Health Care Issues. (198?)-(19??). Periodical. English. qt. SENSS Inc, 1079 Wigtown Court, Weaton IL 60187. **Tel** (312)653-7939. **ED** David R Thompson and Richard E Thompson. Index available. cum. index. **Circ:** 300.

US/1053-6876
**SECOND SOURCE IMAGING.** ***Title Change.*** [Second source imaging]. **VFOAT** Imaging. Vol. 5, No. 4 (May 1990)-(199?). Periodical. English. mo. Second Source Publications Inc., PO Box 930, Portsmouth RI 02871. **Tel** (401)683-7470. **DD** 338. ***Continues in part*** *Second Source, 0892-3426.* ***Continued by*** *Medical Imaging (Portsmouth, R.I.), 1073-1202.*

NE/0167-8523
**SECRETORY PROCESS, THE.** [Secret. process]. Vol. 1 (1982)-. Academic Scholarly Publication. English. ir. Price varies per volume. Elsevier Science Publishers BV, PO Box 211, 1000 AE Amsterdam Netherlands. **Tel** 011 31 20 5803642, FAX 011 31 20 5862696, telex 15682. **ED** A. M. Poisner and J. M. Trifaro. **LC** UNC. **NLM** W1 SE2205. **CODEN** SEPREI. **Pr Rev.** Documents available from CASDDS.
**Ind/Abst** Chem. Abstr.

JA/0387-2289
**SEI MARIANNA IKA DAIGAKU ZASSHI.** **Added/Corp** Sei Marianna Ika Daigaku. **VFOAT** St. Marianna Medical Journal. (19??)-. Periodical. Japanese (summaries and/or abstracts in English). qt. Sei Marianna Ika Daigaku Igakkai, (St. Marianna Medical Society), 16-1, Sugao 2 Chome, Miyamaeku, Kawasakishi, Kanagawaken 213, Japan. **NLM** W1 SE249J. **CODEN** SMIZDS. Documents available from CASDDS.
**Ind/Abst** Chem. Abstr.

FR/1163-1961
**SEIN PARIS, LE.** (LE SEIN.). (1991)-. Periodical. French. qt. $145.00. Masson SA, Avenue Beauregard 12, CH-1701 Fribourg Switzerland. **Tel** 011 41 37 249585, FAX 011 41 37 247559, telex 942658 SEMI CH. **UDC** 61.

JA
**SEITAI JOHO KAGAKU KENKYU.** **VFOAT** Biomedical Information Science. 1- 1976-. Japanese (Japanese). Kobe Daigaku Igakubu, Dai-2 Seirigabu Kyoshitsu Kusunokicho 6-chome Ikuta-ku 650, Koba Japan. **LC** RA409.5; .S33.

GW/0852-4877
**SELECTA / DAS WOCHENMAGAZIN DES ARZTES.** Dr Ildar Idris, Pasinger Str 8, W-8033 Planegg Germany.

IT
**SELECTA MEDICA. GASTROENTEROLOGIA.** (19??)-. Periodical. Italian. bm. Masson S.P.A, Via Statuto 2/4, 20121 Milan Italy. **Tel** 011 39 2 63671, FAX 011 39 2 6367211. **ED** Gabriele Bianchi Porro.

GW/0582-4877
**SELECTA PLANEGG.** [Selecta Planegg]. (1959)-. Periodical. German. Fifty-two times a year. DM103.00. Selecta Verlagsgesellschaft mbH, Postfach 4240, c/o Mrs. Riemer, D-65032 Wiesbaden Germany. **Tel** 011 49 611 1705261. **UDC** 615/618. **[CCC].**

GW/0721-8184
**SELECTA (PLANEGG, GERMANY).** (SELECTA. SUPPLEMENT.). [Sel., Suppl.]. No. 1 (Sept. 7, 1981)-. Periodical. German. qt. Selecta Verlagsgesellschaft mbH, Postfach 4240, c/o Mrs. Riemer, D-65032 Wiesbaden Germany. **Tel** 011 49 611 1705261. **NLM** W1; SE32KM.

US/0361-3046
**SELECTED STUDIES IN MEDICAL CARE AND MEDICAL ECONOMICS.** English. an. Blue Cross Association, PO Box 527, Glenview IL 60025. **Tel** (708)724-9280, FAX (708)729-2199. **LC** RA410.53; .S43. **DD** 362.1/05. **NLM** W 22 AA1 S4.

AG
**SEMANA MEDICA (BUENOS AIRES, ARGENTINA : 1894).** (LA SEMANA MEDICA.). (1894)-. Periodical. Spanish (summaries and/or abstracts in English). Forty-Four times a year. $150.00. La Semana Medica, Arenales 3574, Buenos Aires 1425 Argentina. **ED** Eduardo F. Mele. **NLM** W1 SE44. Index available. cum. index. **Bk Rev. Ad Acc. Circ:** 7,000.

MX/0037-1823
**SEMANA MEDICA DE MEXICO.** (19??)-. Periodical. English. sm. Semana Medica SA, Queretaro 183 Col Roma, 06700 Mexico City DF Mexico. **Tel** 574-50-33.

SP
**SEMER.** Spanish. SANED SA, Paseo de la Habana 202 Bis, 28036 Madrid Spain. **Tel** 011 34 1 5553508.
**Ind/Abst** Indice Med. Esp.

SP
**SEMINARIOS DE ROENTGENELOGIA.** Spanish. Editorial Cientifico Medica / Barcelona, Via Layetana 53, 08003 Barcelona Spain.

US/1047-1227
**SEMINARS IN CHIROPRACTIC.** ***Ceased.*** [Semin. chiropr.]. **VFOAT** SIC. Vol. 1, No. 1 (Winter 1990)-(19??). Monographic series. English. qt. **DD** 615. **NLM** W1; SE487EH.

US/0894-0959
**SEMINARS IN DIALYSIS.** [Sem. dial.]. Vol. 1, No. 1 (Jan. 1988)-. Academic Scholarly Publication. English. qt. $130.00 (institution), $85.00 (individual) US; $165.00 (institutions), $115.00 (individuals) other. Blackwell Scientific Publishers, 238 Main Street, Cambridge MA 02142. **Tel** (617)547-7110, (800)835-6770, FAX (617)547-0789. **DD** 616. **NLM** W1; SE487NH. **[CCC]. Pr Rev.** Documents available from The Genuine Article.
**Desc:** Practical, peer-reviewed, clinical review articles and features covering peritoneal and hemodialysis for nephrologists and dialysis professionals.
**Ind/Abst** Curr. Contents Clin. Med.; Res. Alert [Select. Cov.]; Soc. Sci. Cit. Index [Select. Cov.].

●CN/1198-7340
**SEMINARS IN HEADACHE MANAGEMENT.** (March 1995)-. English. qt. $78.00 (institutions), $52.00 (individuals) US & Canada; $105.00 (institutions), $79.00 (individuals) other. Decker Periodicals Publishing Inc, PO Box 620, Station A, Hamilton Ontario L8N 3K7 Canada. **Tel** (416)522-7017, (800) 568-7281, FAX (416)522-7839.

●US
**SEMINARS IN ORTHODONTICS.** (1995)-. English. qt. $105.00 (institution), $94.00 (individual). W.B. Saunders Company, A Subsidiary of Harcourt Brace Jovanovich, Inc., The Curtis Center/Suite 300, Independence Square West, Philadelphia PA 19106-3399. **Tel** (215)238-7800 or, 5587, FAX (215)238-7883, telex 173146. **(Subscription address:** W. B. Saunders Company / North America Subscriptions, c/o Periodicals, 6277 Sea Harbour Drive, 4th Floor, Orlando FL 32887.**)**

KO
**SEOUL JOURNAL OF MEDICINE, THE.** **Added/Corp** Soul Taehakkyo. Uikwa Taehak. Vol. 26, No. 1 (Mar. 1985)-. Periodical. English (summaries and/or abstracts in Korean). qt. **NLM** W1; SE633. Documents available from CASDDS. ***Continues*** *Soul Uidae Haksulchi, 0253-2972.*
**Ind/Abst** Chem. Abstr.; EMBASE [Select. Cov.]; Trop. Dis. Bull.

JA/0289-8020
**SERAPYUTIKKU RISACHI.** **VFOAT** Therapeutic Research. Vol. 1, No. 1 (1984)-. Periodical. Japanese (summaries and/or abstracts in English). Twelve times a year. $342.00. Life Science Publishing Co. Ltd., Mihashi Building, 11-7 Nihombashi, Kobuna-cho Chuo-ku, 103 Tokyo, Japan. **(Subscription address:** Kyowa Book Company Inc., 1 38 Kanda Jinbocho Chiyoda-ku, Tokyo 101 Japan.**) NLM** W1; SE707. **CODEN** THREEL. Documents available from CASDDS.
**Ind/Abst** Chem. Abstr. (1984-); EMBASE [Select. Cov.].

US
**SERIAL PUBLICATIONS CURRENTLY RECEIVED AND ON ORDER - EASTERN VIRGINIA MEDICAL SCHOOL, NORFOLK, VA. MOORMAN MEMORIAL LIBRARY.** **See** Library and Information Sciences.

GW/0944-7105
**SEXUOLOGIE.** **See** Sexual Life.

CC/1000-7377
**SHAANXI YIXUE ZAZHI.** **VFOAT** Shaanxi Medical Journal. (1987)-. Periodical. Chinese. mo. **DD** 610. Documents available from CASDDS.
**Ind/Abst** Chem. Abstr.

CH
**SHAN-HSI CHUNG I.** **VFOAT** Shanxi Zhongyi. Periodical. Chinese. bm. NT$0.25. Hsi-An Shih Yu Cheng Chu, China. **LC** R97.7.C5; S47.

CC/1000-0496
**SHANDONG YIKE DAXUE XUEBAO.** (SHAN-TUNG I KO TA HSUEH HSUEH PAO.). [Shandong yike daxue xuebao]. **Added/Corp** Shan-Tung I Ko Ta Hsueh. **VFOAT** Acta Academiae Medicinae Shandong. (1986)-. Academic Scholarly Publication. Chinese (summaries and/or abstracts in English and Chinese). qt. Shandong Yike Daxue, Xuebao Bianjibu, No. 44, Wenhua Xilu, Jinan, Shandong 250012, People's Republic of China. **Tel** 0531 252424, FAX 0531 613813. **(Subscription address:** China International Book Trading Corporation, PO Box 399, Library Service Department, Beijing 100044 People's Republic of China.**) ED** Xi Yaosheng. **CODEN** SYXBEE. **Circ:** 8,000. Documents available from BLDSC, CASDDS. ***Continues*** *Shan-Tung I Hsueh Yuan Hsueh Pao, 0254-6159.*
**Ind/Abst** Chem. Abstr.

CC
**SHANG-HAI CHEN CHIU TSA CHIH.** **VFOAT** Shanghai Journal of Acupuncture. First published in Feb. 1982-. Periodical. Chinese (summaries and/or abstracts in English). qt. RMBY0.30. Guozi Shudian, PO Box 399, Chegongzhuang Xilu 35, Beijing, People's Republic of China. **Tel** 1 8414284, FAX 1 8412023, telex 22496. **ED** Chao Tsen-Wu. **LC** RM184; .S45 . **DD** 615.8/92/05. **Bk Rev. Ad Acc. Circ:** 20,000.
**Desc:** Covers clinical studies on neurophysiological and biochemical basis of acupuncture analgesia, and clinical study on acupuncture treatment for gastric and duodenal ulcers.

CC/0257-8131
**SHANGHAI YIKE DAXUE XUEBAO.** (SHANG-HAI I KO TA HSUEH HSUEH PAO.). [Shanghai yike daxue xuebao]. **Added/Corp** Shang-hai i Ko Ta Hsueh. **VFOAT** Acta Academiae Medicinae Shanghai. (1986)-. Academic Scholarly Publication. Chinese (summaries and/or abstracts in English; table of contents in English). Six times a year. Science Press, 16 Donghuangchenggen North Street, Beijing 100707, People's Republic of China. **Tel** 011 86 1 4019821, 011 86 1 4010642, FAX 011 86 1 4012180, 011 86 1 4019810, telex 210147. **(Subscription address:** China International Book Trading Corporation, PO Box 399, Library Service Department, Beijing 100044 People's Republic of China.**) NLM** W1; SH125H. **CODEN** SYDXEE. Documents available from BIOSIS Document Express, CASDDS. ***Continues*** *Shang-hai Ti 1 i Hsueh Yuan Hsueh Pao (1964), 0253-3650.*
**Ind/Abst** Biol. Abstr. (1991-); Chem. Abstr. (1986-).

CC/0253-9934
**SHANGHAI YIXUE.** (SHANG-HAI I HSUEH. SHANGHAI YIXUE.). [Shanghai yixue]. **VFOAT** Shanghai yixue. (19??)-. Academic Scholarly Publication. Chinese. Twelve times a year. $27.36. **(Subscription address:** China International Book Trading Corporation, PO Box

399, Library Service Department, Beijing 100044 People's Republic of China.) **LC** R97.7.C5; S514. **NLM** W1 SH127K. **CODEN** SIHSD8. Documents available from CASDDS.
**Ind/Abst** Chem. Abstr.; NAPRALERT.

CH/0253-9853
**SHANXI XIN YIYAO.** (SHAN-HSI HSIN I YAO.). [Shanxi xin yiyao]. Began in 1972. Academic Scholarly Publication. Chinese. mo. NT$0.25. Hsi-An Shih Yu Chu China Mainland, China. **LC** R97.7.C5; S48. **DD** 610/.5. **CODEN** SHIYDO. Documents available from CASDDS.
**Ind/Abst** Chem. Abstr.; NAPRALERT.

CH/1001-9626
**SHENGWU SHUXUE XUEBAO. See** Mathematics.

US/1048-0846
**SHEPARD'S MEDICAL MALPRACTICE CITATIONS. See** Law.

US
**SHEPHERD SYSTEM, THE.** (19??)-. English. Four times a year. $210.00 US, Canada and Mexico; $245.00 other. Quest Publishing Company, 1351 Titan Way, Brea CA 92621. **Tel** (714)738-6400, FAX (714)525-6258.

JA/0912-3016
**SHIGA IKA DAIGAKU ZASSHI.** [Shiga Ika Daigaku zasshi]. **VFOAT** Journal of Shiga University of Medical Science. (1986)-. Academic Scholarly Publication. Multiple languages. an. Shiga Ika Daigaku, (Shiga University of Medical Science), Seta Tsukinowacho, Otsushi, Shigaken 520-21 Japan. **DD** 610. Documents available from CASDDS.
**Ind/Abst** Chem. Abstr.

JA
**SHIKOKU ACTA MEDICA.** (19??)-. Academic Scholarly Publication. English. bm. Tokushima Igakkai, (Tokushima Medical Assoc.), Tokushima Daigaku Igakubu, 18-15, Kuramotocho 3 Chome, Tokushimashi, Tokushimaken 770, Japan. **(Subscription address:** Japan Publications Trading Company, Ltd., PO Box 5030, Tokyo International, Tokyo 100-31 Japan.**)**
**Ind/Abst** EMBASE [Select. Cov.]; Trop. Dis. Bull.

JA/0037-3699
**SHIKOKU IGAKU ZASSHI.** (SHIKOKU IGAKU ZASSHI SHIKOKU ACTA MEDICA. SHIKOKU MEDICAL JOURNAL.). [Shikoku Igaku Zasshi]. **VFOAT** Shikoku Acta Medica; Shikoku Medical Journal. (1950)-. Academic Scholarly Publication. Japanese (summaries and/or abstracts in English). Six times a year. $84.50. Tokushima Igakkai, (Tokushima Medical Assoc.), Tokushima Daigaku Igakubu, 18-15, Kuramotocho 3 Chome, Tokushimashi, Tokushimaken 770, Japan. **(Subscription address:** Japan Publications Trading Company, Ltd., PO Box 5030, Tokyo International, Tokyo 100-31 Japan.**)** **NLM** W1 SH329. **CODEN** SKIZAB. Documents available from BIOSIS Document Express, CASDDS.
**Ind/Abst** Biol. Abstr. (1961-1980); Chem. Abstr.; EMBASE.

JA/0370-999X
**SHINDAN TO CHIRYO.** [Shindan To Chiryo]. **VFOAT** Diagnosis and Treatment. (1926)-. Academic Scholarly Publication. Japanese. Twelve times a year. Shindan to Chiryo Co. Ltd., 406 Marunouchi Building Marunouchi, Tokyo Japan. **Tel** 011 81 3 32144950. **CODEN** SHCHA8. Documents available from CASDDS. ***Continues** Kinsei Igaku.*
**Ind/Abst** Chem. Abstr.

JA/0001-8724
**SHINKEI KENKYU NO SHIMPO.** [Shinkei Kenkyu no shimpo]. **VFOAT** Recent Advance in Research of the Nervous System; Advances in Neurological Sciences. (1956)-. Academic Scholarly Publication. Japanese (summaries and/or abstracts in English). bm. ¥32340.00. Igaku Shoin Ltd., 5-24-3 Hongo Bunkyo-ku, Tokyo 113 Japan. **Tel** 011 81 3 817 5670. **NLM** W1 SH3305. **CODEN** SKNSAF. Documents available from BIOSIS Document Express, CASDDS.
**Ind/Abst** Biol. Abstr.; Chem. Abstr.; EMBASE.

JA/0385-0307
**SHINSHIN IGAKU.** (SHINSHIN IGAKU. JAPANESE JOURNAL OF PSYCHOSOMATIC MEDICINE.). [Shinshin igaku]. **Added/Corp** Nippon Shika Ishikai. **VFOAT** Japanese Journal of Psychosomatic Medicine. (1976)-. Periodical. Japanese (summaries and/or abstracts in English). Eight times a year. ¥14,160. Igaku Shoin Ltd., 5-24-3 Hongo Bunkyo-ku, Tokyo 113 Japan. **Tel** 011 81 3 817 5670. **NLM** W1 SH3329. **CODEN** SHIGD4. Documents available from BIOSIS Document Express, CASDDS. ***Continues** Seishin Shintai Igaku.*
**Ind/Abst** Biol. Abstr.; Chem. Abstr.; EMBASE.

JA/0037-3826
**SHINSHU IGAKU ZASSHI.** (SHINSHU IGAKU ZASSHI. SHINSHU MEDICAL JOURNAL.). [Shinshu igaku zasshi]. **VFOAT** Shinshu Medical Journal. (1952)-. Academic Scholarly Publication. Japanese. ir. $122.50. Shinshu Igakkai, (Shinshu Medical Society), c/o Shinshu Daigaku Igakubu, 1-1, Asahi 3 Chome, Matsumotoshi, Naganoken 390, Japan. **(Subscription address:** Japan Publications Trading Company, Ltd., PO Box 5030, Tokyo International, Tokyo 100-31 Japan.**)** **CODEN** SIZAA7. Documents available from BIOSIS Document Express, CASDDS.
**Ind/Abst** Biol. Abstr. (1986-1989); Chem. Abstr.; EMBASE.

JA/0037-3826
**SHINSHU MEDICAL JOURNAL. VFOAT** Shinshu Medical Journal. (1952)-. Academic Scholarly Publication. English. Six times a year. $122.50. **(Subscription address:** Japan Publications Trading Company, Ltd., PO Box 5030, Tokyo International, Tokyo 100-31 Japan.**)**
**Ind/Abst** EMBASE [Select. Cov.].

JA/0559-8672
**SHINYAKU TO RINSHO.** [Shinyaku to rinsho]. **VFOAT** Journal of New Remedies & Clinics; Journal of New Remedies and Clinics. (1952)-. Periodical. Japanese. mo. $277.00. **(Subscription address:** Japan Publications Trading Company, Ltd., PO Box 5030, Tokyo International, Tokyo 100-31 Japan.**)** **CODEN** SHRIAI.

JA
**SHITSUGI OTO. Added/Corp** Nihon Iji Shimpo. No. 1 (1973)-. Periodical. Japanese. ¥4800. Nihon Iji Shimposha, 2-9 Kanda Surugadai Chiyoda-ku, Tokyo 101 Japan. **Tel** FAX 03 3292 1550. **LC** R97.7.J3; S58.

JA/0388-9734
**SHOJINKAI IGAKUSHI.** [Shojinkai igakushi]. **VFOAT** Matsushita Medical Journal; Matsushita Bulletin for Medical Science. (1980)-. Academic Scholarly Publication. Japanese. an. Shojinkai, 2-35, Sotojimacho, Moriguchishi, Osakafu 570, Japan. **DD** 610. Documents available from CASDDS. ***Continues** Shojinkaishi, 0388-9726.*
**Ind/Abst** Chem. Abstr.

CH/0254-0142
**SHOU I KO CHI TSA CHIH.** [Shouyi keji zazhi]. **VFOAT** Shouyi Keji Zazhi. Academic Scholarly Publication. Chinese. bm. NT$0.35. Chung-kuo Nung Yeh Ko Hsueh Yuan, Lan-Chou Shou I Yen Chiu So, Lan-chou Shih, People's Republic of China. **LC** SF604; .S45. **CODEN** SKZADO. Documents available from CASDDS.
**Ind/Abst** Chem. Abstr. (1982).

CC/1001-2389
**SHOUDU YIXUEYUAN XUEBAO. VFOAT** Journal of Capital Institute of Medicine. (1987)-. Periodical. Chinese. qt. **DD** 610. ***Continues** Beijing di er Yixueyuan Xuebao, 1000-0291.*
**Ind/Abst** Protozoolog. Abstr.

JA/0037-4342
**SHOWA IGAKKAI ZASSHI.** (ZASSHI.). [Showa Igakkai Zasshi]. **Main/Corp** Showa Igakkai. **Added/Corp** Showa Medical Association. Showa Igakkai Zasshi. (1939)-. Academic Scholarly Publication. English. Showa Medical Association, 508 Hatanodai 1-chome, Shinagawa-ku, 142, Tokyo, Japan. **NLM** W1 SH56. **CODEN** SIGZAL. Documents available from CASDDS.
**Ind/Abst** Chem. Abstr.; EMBASE [Select. Cov.].

JA/0915-6380
**SHOWA UNIVERSITY JOURNAL OF MEDICAL SCIENCES, THE. Added/Corp** Showa Igakkai. Showa Daigaku. Vol. 1, No. 1/2 (Dec. 1989)-. Periodical. English. Showa Medical Association, 508 Hatanodai 1-chome, Shinagawa-ku, 142, Tokyo, Japan. **NLM** W1; SH562S.

US/1041-2832
**SICKNESS & WELLNESS PUBLICATIONS.** [Sick. wellness publ.]. **VFOAT** Sickness and Wellness Publications; Publications Sickness & Wellness. Vol. 1 (1989)-. English. $39.50 (print), $89.50 (electronic edition). John Gordon Burke Publisher Inc., PO Box 1492, Evanston IL 60204. **Tel** (708)866-8625, FAX (708)866-8625. **ED** Gerald Shields. **LC** Z6664.A1; S53; RA773. **DD** 016.616. **NLM** ZW 1; S566. Index available. available on an online database (as an electronic information service).
**Desc:** An index and description of newsletters and other similar publications devoted to sickness and wellness and written for the lay person.

SP
**SIDAPRESS.** Spanish. sa. 700.00ptas Spain; 1700.00ptas other. Comision Ciudadana Anti Sida Bizcaya, Dos de Mayo 6-1 DCHA, 48003 Bilbao Spain. **Tel** 011 34 4 416005.

US/0163-5697
**SIGBIO NEWSLETTER. See** Computers.

CH/0254-0088
**SILI ZHONGGUO YIYAO XUEYUAN YANJIU NIANBAO.** (SSU LI CHUNG-KUO I YAO HSUEH YUAN YEN CHIU NIEN PAO.). [Sili zhongguo yiyao xueyuan yanjiu nianbao]. **VFOAT** China Medical College Annual Bulletin. Chinese (English; summaries and/or abstracts in English). an. China Medical College, 2 Ying-Tsai Road, Taichung Taiwan. **NLM** W1 SS19.

IT/1120-673X
**SIMG : MEDICINA GENERALE.** Italian. mo. L35.000. Utet Periodici Scient, Viale Tunisia 37, 20124 Milan Italy. **Tel** 011 39 2 29003555. **ED** Romolo Saccomani. Index available. cum. index. **Ad Acc. Circ:** 70,000 (ctrl).

SI/0037-5675
**SINGAPORE MEDICAL JOURNAL.** [Singapore med. j.]. **Added/Corp** Singapore Medical Association. (1960)-. Academic Scholarly Publication. English. bm (6 issues). 120.00Sing$ Singapore; 150.00Sing$ ASEAN countries; 240.00Sing$ other. Singapore Medical Association, 2 College Road Level 2, Alumni Medicine, Singapore 0316 Singapore. **Tel** 011 65 2231264, 011 65 2238767. **NLM** W1 SI523. **CODEN** SIMJA3. Documents available from BIOSIS Document Express. ***Supersedes** Alumni Association, Malaya. Proceedings.*
**Ind/Abst** Biol. Abstr.; Cumul. Index Nurs. Allied Health Lit.; EMBASE [Select. Cov.]; Index Med.; Index Dent. Lit.; Life Sci. Collect.; SportSearch; Trop. Dis. Bull.

US/0161-8105
**SLEEP (NEW YORK, N.Y.).** (SLEEP.). [Sleep]. **Added/Corp** American Sleep Disorders Association. Sleep Research Society. Association for the Psychophysiological Study of Sleep. European Sleep Research Society. Association of Sleep Disorders Centers. Vol. 1 (Sept. 1978)-. Academic Scholarly Publication. English. ir (10 issues). $185.00 (institutions), $129.00 (individuals) US; $220.00 (institutions), $159.00 (individuals) other. Association of Professional Sleep Society, 1610 14th Street Northwest 300, Rochester MN 55901. **Tel** (507)287-6006. **(Subscription address:** Sleep, PO Box 1897, Lawrence KS 66044-8897.**)** **LC** QP425; .S65. **DD** 612/.821/05. **NLM** W1; SL569. **CODEN** SLEED6. **[CCC]. Ad Acc. Pr Rev. Acid Free.** Documents available from The Genuine Article, BIOSIS Document Express, CASDDS.
**Desc:** Publishes articles which range from clinical investigations of sleep/wake disorders and medical problems during sleep to investigations of the basic physiological and biochemical events and anatomichological and psycho-physiological research as well as research in circadian and biological rhythms.
**Ind/Abst** Biol. Abstr.; Chem. Abstr.; CSA Neuro. Abstr. (?-?); Curr. Aware. Biol. Sci., CABS; Curr. Contents Life Sci.; Dev. Med. Child Neurol.; EMBASE; Index Med.; Med. Abstr. Newsl.; Life Sci. Collect.; Psychol. Abstr. (1979-); PsycINFO; PsycLit; Ref. Upd. Deluxe Ed.; Res. Alert [Full Cov.]; Sci. Cit. Index; SCISEARCH; Soc. Sci. Cit. Index [Select. Cov.]; SportSearch.

US/0748-5352
**SLEEP WATCHERS.** [Sleep watch.]. Periodical. English. qt. $25.00. Cameron Harris Editor, Sleep Disorders Center, Mayo Clinic, Rochester MN 55905. **Tel** (507)285-4150. **ED** Cameron Harris. **DD** 616. **Bk Rev. Ad Acc.** ctrl circ.
**Desc:** Sleepwatchers is the journal of polygomnography technology. It carries articles and discussion on the technical aspects of the clinical and research study of sleep.

●US/1060-8427
**SMART DRUG NEWS.** (SMART DRUG NEWS : THE NEWSLETTER OF THE COGNITIVE ENHANCEMENT RESEARCH INSTITUTE.). [Smart drug news]. **Added/Corp** Cognitive Enhancement Research Institute. Vol. 1, No. 1 (Jan. 1992)-. Periodical. English. Ten times a year. $44.00. Cognitive Enhancement Research Institute, PO Box 4029, Menlo Park CA 94026. **Tel** (415)321-2374. **DD** 615. **NLM** W1; SM27.

US
**SOAP NEWSLETTER.** Newsletter. English. ir. $80.00 active and associate members, 40.00 other. Baylor College of Medicine, Department of Anesthesiology, 6550 Fannin, #1003 Smith Tower, Houston TX 77030. **Tel** (713)793-2900, FAX (713)795-0117. **ED** Stephen Longmire, M.D. & B. Wycke Baker M.D. ctrl circ.
**Desc:** Newsletter for physicians interested in the problems and practice of the perinatal period.

UK/0951-631X
**SOCIAL HISTORY OF MEDICINE : THE JOURNAL OF THE SOCIETY FOR THE SOCIAL HISTORY OF MEDICINE. Added/Corp** Society for the Social History of Medicine. Vol. 1, No. 1 (April 1988)-. Periodical. English. tq. £50.00 UK and Europe; $93.00 other. Oxford University Press, Walton Street, Oxford OX2 6DP England. **Tel** 011 44 865 56767, FAX 011 44 865 267773, telex 837330 OXPRES G. **(Subscription address:** Oxford University Press / USA, Journals Marketing Department, Oxford University Press, 2001 Evans Road, Cary NC 27513.**)** **ED** Ann Digby, Richard Smith and Roger Cooter. **LC** R131.A1; S58. **DD** 610/.9. **NLM** W1; SO105P. **[CCC].** Index available. cum. index. **Bk Rev. Ad Acc. Circ:** 600. available on microfilm and microfiche from University Microfilms International (UMI). Documents available from The Genuine Article. ***Continues** Society for the Social History of Medicine Bulletin, 0307-6792.*
**Desc:** All aspects of health, illness and medical treatment, as well as the biological aspects of normal life,

with patients within their economic, social and political environments and with systems of health and welfare provision.
**Ind/Abst** Am. Hist. Life (1989-); Arts Humanit. Citation Index [Select. Cov.]; Curr. Contents Soc. Behav. Sci.; Res. Alert [Full Cov.]; Soc. Plann. Policy Dev. Abstr.; Soc. Sci. Cit. Index [Full Cov.].

US/0277-9536
**SOCIAL SCIENCE & MEDICINE (1982).** **See** Social Sciences.

US/0575-5964
**SOCIOECONOMIC REPORT. Main/Corp** California Medical Association. Bureau of Research and Planning. Periodical. English. bm. California Medical Association, PO Box 7690, San Franciso CA 94120-5179. **Tel** (415)541-0900, FAX (415)882-5116.

FR
**SOMATOTHERAPIES ET SOMATOLOGIE.** French (English). Four times a year. 350.00F France; 380.00F other. Innovation Psychiatrique, Docteur Meyer, 20 Place des Halles, 67000 Strasbourg France. **Tel** 011 33 88224692, FAX 011 33 88325124. **ED** Docteur Meyer. Index available. **Bk Rev**, (Qty: 3). **Ad Acc. Pr Rev.**
**Desc:** International journal of the body in psychotherapy and body psychotherapy. Includes autism, sexology, psychosis, and training.

GW/0931-2447
**SONDERBANDE ZUR STRAHLENTHERAPIE UND ONKOLOGIE.** ***Ceased.*** [Sonderbd. Strahlenther. Onkol.]. (1987)-?. Monographic series. German (English). Urban & Schwarzenberg, Landwehrstr 61, W-8 Munchen 2 Germany. **NLM** W1; SO8877D. ***Continues*** *Sonderbande zur Strahlentherapie, 0371-3822.*
**Ind/Abst** Energy Res. Abstr.; Index Med. (1987-).

SA/0379-6175
**SOUTH AFRICAN JOURNAL OF PHYSIOTHERAPY.** [S. Afr. j. physiother.]. **VFOAT** Suid-Afrikaanse Tydskrif Fisioterapie. (1955)- Vol. 49 (Feb. 1993)-. Periodical. Multiple languages (English). Four times a year (Feb., May, Aug., Nov.). R90.00 South Africa; R150.00 other. Mara Communications, PO Box 695, Edenvale 1610 South Africa. **Tel** 011 27 11 453-2746, FAX 011 27 11 453-1689. **ED** Dr. J. Beenhakker. **UDC** 615.8. Index available (Bound in Feburary issue). **Bk Rev. Ad Acc. Circ:** 2,300 (ctrl). ***Continues*** *Physiotherapy.*
**Ind/Abst** EMBASE.

SA/0038-2469
**SOUTH AFRICAN MEDICAL JOURNAL.** [S. Afr. med. j.]. **Added/Corp** Medical Association of South Africa. **VFOAT** Suid-Afrikaanse Mediese Tydskrif; SAMJ; SAMT; Suid-Afrikaanse Tydskrif vir Geneeskunde; Suid-Afrikaanse Mediese Joernal; SAMJSAMT. Vol. 6, No. 1 (Jan. 9, 1932)-. Academic Scholarly Publication. English (Afrikaans). mo. R180.00 South Africa; R275.00 other. Medical Association of South Africa, Private Bag X1, 7430 Pinelands South Africa. **Tel** 011 27 21 5313081, FAX 534126, telex 5-20378 CT. **ED** N C Lee. **LC** R98; .S63. **DD** 610/.5. **NLM** W1 SO906H. **CODEN** SAMJAF. Index available. **Bk Rev. Ad Acc. Pr Rev. Circ:** 13,400. available on microfilm and microfiche from University Microfilms International (UMI). Documents available from The Genuine Article, BIOSIS Document Express, CASDDS. ***Continues*** *Journal (Medical Association of South Africa).*
**Desc:** Original research, news, medical information and opinions.
**Ind/Abst** Biol. Abstr.; Calcium Calcif. Tissue Abstr.; Chem. Abstr. (1932-1985); Cumul. Index Nurs. Allied Health Lit.; Curr. Contents Clin. Med.; Dairy Sci. Abstr.; Dev. Med. Child Neurol.; EMBASE; Helminthol. Abstr. (19??-19??); Index Med.; Index Vet.; Iowa Drug Inf. Serv.; Maize Abstr.; Microbiol. Abstr. Sect. B; Microbiol. Abstr. Sect. C; Mod. Med.; Nutr. Abstr. Rev., Ser. A, Hum. Exp.; Nutr. Res. Newsl.; Life Sci. Collect.; PESTDOC; Protozoolog. Abstr.; Ref. Upd. Basic Ed.; Ref. Upd. Deluxe Ed.; Res. Alert [Full Cov.]; Rev. Agric. Entomol.; Rev. Med. Vet. Entomol.; Rev. Med. Vet. Mycology; Saf. Health Work; Sci. Cit. Index; SCISEARCH; Soc. Sci. Cit. Index [Select. Cov.]; Soyabean Abstr.; Vet. Bull.; Trop. Dis. Bull.; Virol. AIDS Abstr.

US/0038-3317
**SOUTH DAKOTA JOURNAL OF MEDICINE.** [S. D. j. med.]. **Added/Corp** South Dakota State Medical Association. American Academy of Family Physicians. South Dakota Chapter. American College of Surgeons. South Dakota Chapter. South Dakota Psychiatric Association. Vol. 18 No. 3 (Mar. 1965)-. Periodical. English. Twelve times a year. $15.00 US; $18.00 other. South Dakota State Medical Association, 1323 South Minnesota Avenue, Sioux Falls SD 57105. **Tel** (605)336-1965, FAX (605)336-0270. **ED** J. W. Freeman and J. F. Barlow. **NLM** W1 SO917. **CODEN** SDMEAL. Index available (December issue). **Ad Acc, Adv Mgr:** J. Spars, **Tel** (605)336-1965. **Pr Rev. Circ:** 1,400 (ctrl). Documents available from BIOSIS Document Express, CASDDS. ***Continues*** *South Dakota Journal of Medicine and Pharmacy, 0096-8420.*

**Desc:** Scientific articles related to medicine.
**Ind/Abst** Biol. Abstr.; Chem. Abstr.; Energy Res. Abstr. (1976-); Index Med.

US/0886-2079
**SOUTH FLORIDA MEDICAL REVIEW.** ***Ceased.*** [South Fla. med. rev.]. Began in (1985)-?. Periodical. English. bw. 100 Northeast 7th Street, Miami FL 33132. **Tel** (305)377-3721. **ED** Av Goldstein. **DD** 362. **Circ:** 14,500.

UK/0266-0342
**SOUTHAMPTON MEDICAL JOURNAL.** [Southampt. med. j.]. **Added/Corp** Southampton Postgraduate Medical and Dental Federation. Vol. 1, No. 1 (Spring 1984)-. Periodical. English. Three times a year. £4.50. Southampton Postgraduate Medical and Dental Federation, South Academic Block, General Hospital, Southampton SO9 4XY England. **Tel** 0703 777222. **NLM** W1; SO924M. **Bk Rev. Ad Acc. Pr Rev.** ctrl circ.
**Desc:** Local medical news and other topics of interest relating to our health.

TH/0038-3619
**SOUTHEAST ASIAN JOURNAL OF TROPICAL MEDICINE AND PUBLIC HEALTH, THE.** **See** Public Health and Safety.

US/0097-5419
**SOUTHERN MEDICINE.** [South. med.]. **Added/Corp** Southern Medical Association. Vol. 60, No. 1 (Feb. 1972)-. Periodical. English. Four times a year. comes with Southern Medical Association membership. Southern Medical Association, PO Box 190088, 35 Lakeshore Drive, Birmingham AL 35219-0088. **Tel** (800)423-4992, (205)945-1840, FAX (205)942-0642. **ED** J. Graham Simth Jr. M.D. **LC** R11; .S66. **DD** 610/.5. **NLM** W1 SO956X. **CODEN** SNMDBL. ***Continues*** *Southern Medical Bulletin, 0038-433X.*

PK/1017-4699
**SPECIALIST KARACHI. VFOAT** Quarterly Specialist; Specialist Quarterly. (1984)-. English. qt. Doctor Publications, PO Box 8766, Raja Ghazanfar Ali Road, Saddar, Karachi, Pakistan. **Tel** (21)527556.
**Ind/Abst** EMBASE [Select. Cov.].

US/0738-470X
**SPECTRUM (ROCKVILLE, MD.).** ***Ceased.*** (SPECTRUM / CYSTIC FIBROSIS FOUNDATION.). [Spectrum]. Vol. 1, No. 1 Feb. (1981)- ?. Periodical. English. an. Cystic Fibrosis Foundation, 6000 Executive Blvd., Suite 309, Rockville MD 20852. **Tel** (301)881-9130. **NLM** W1 SP32R.

CN/1184-8472
**SPINAL CORD SOCIETY CANADA.** ***Title Change.*** (SPINAL CORD SOCIETY CANADA : SCSC.). [Spinal Cord Soc. Can.]. **Added/Corp** Spinal Cord Society Canada. **VFOAT** Societe de la Moelle Epiniere du Canada. Volume 1, Issue 1 (Nov./Dec. 1990)-Vol. 3, Issue 1 (Spring 1992). Periodical. English (French). bm. Spinal Cord Society of Canada, 120 Newkirk Road, Unit 32, Richmond Hill, Ontario L4C 9S7 Canada. **Tel** (905)508-4000, 800 361-4004. **DD** 616.8. ***Continued by*** *Canadian Spinal Research Organization Quarterly, 1193-7343.*

US/0362-2436
**SPINE (PHILADELPHIA, PA. 1976).** (SPINE.). [Spine (Phila. Pa. 1976)]. Vol. 1 (March 1976)-. Academic Scholarly Publication. English. Twenty-four times a year. $239.00 (individuals), $439.00 (institutions) US; $429.00 (individuals), $539.00 (institutions) other. J.B. Lippincott Company, 227 East Washington Square, Philadelphia PA 19106-3780. **Tel** (215)238-4200 or 4454, FAX (215)238-4227. **(Subscription address:** J.B. Lippincott, PO Box 350, Hagerstown MD 21740.**) ED** Henry LaRocca. **LC** RD768; .S67. **DD** 617/.375/005. **NLM** W1 SP47. **CODEN** SPINDD. **[CCC]. Ad Acc. Pr Rev. Circ:** 8,223. available on microfilm and microfiche from University Microfilms International (UMI). Documents available from The Genuine Article, BIOSIS Document Express, CASDDS.
**Desc:** Information gathered from disciplines dealing with the human spine. Includes research and case reports. Treatments and practice methods are also included.
**Ind/Abst** Biol. Abstr.; Calcium Calcif. Tissue Abstr.; Chem. Abstr. (1976-1983); CSA Neuro. Abstr. (?-?); Cumul. Index Nurs. Allied Health Lit.; Curr. Contents Clin. Med.; Dev. Med. Child Neurol.; EMBASE; Energy Res. Abstr. (July 1982-); Index Med.; Life Sci. Collect.; Physic. Medline Plus; Res. Alert [Select. Cov.]; Rev. Med. Vet. Mycology; Soc. Sci. Cit. Index [Select. Cov.].

US/1058-1421
**SPINE REHABILITATION.** ***Ceased.*** (1993)-(199?). Periodical. English. qt. Allen Press Inc., 810 East 10th Street, PO Box 1897, Lawrence KS 66044-8897. **Tel** (913)843-1221, (800)627-0629, FAX (913)843-1274. **Ad Acc. Acid Free.**
**Desc:** Committed to an understanding of conservative care as the primary model for treatment of spinal disorders. Articles provide clinical evidence of research on care and treatment of spine and back problems. The range of discussion includes orthopedic, neurologic, physical, occupational, psychological, psychiatric, chiropractic, and multidisciplinary approaches to patient care.

GW
**SPRINGER SERIES IN BRAIN DYNAMICS.** Vol. 1 (1988)-. Monographic series. English. Price varies per volume. Springer-Verlag GmbH & Company KG, Heidelberger Platz 3, D 14197 Berlin Germany. **Tel** 011 49 30 8207223, FAX 011 49 30 8214091, telex 183 319 SPBLN D. **(Subscription address:** Springer Verlag New York Inc. / for North America, 44 Hartz Way, Secaucus NJ 07096.**) NLM** W1; SP685ME.

AT/0813-1988
**SPUMS JOURNAL.** (SPUMS JOURNAL / SOUTH PACIFIC UNDERWATER MEDICINE SOCIETY.). [SPUMS j.]. **Added/Corp** South Pacific Underwater Medicine Society. (19??)-. Periodical. English. qt (Mar., June, Sept., Dec.). $80.00. South Pacific Underwater Medicine Society, Spring Street, Melbourne, Victoria, 3000 Australia. **Tel** 011 61 3 8194898. **(Subscription address:** SPUMS Journal, Australian & New Zealand College of Anaesthetists, Spring Street, Melbourne VIC 3000 Australia.**) ED** D. G. Walker. **NLM** W1; SP82. **Bk Rev. Ad Acc. Circ:** 900 (ctrl).

YU/0049-0210
**SRPSKI ARHIV ZA CELOKUPNO LEKARSTVO. / ARCHIVES SERBES DE MEDECINE GENERAL / SERBIAN ARCHIVES OF GENERAL MEDICINE.** **Added/Corp** Srpsko Lekarsko Drustvo, Belgrad. **VFOAT** Serbisches Archiv fur die Allgemeine Medizin; Archives Serbes de Medecine General; Serbian Archives of General Medicine. (1872)-. Academic Scholarly Publication. Serbo-Croatian (Cyrillic) (table of contents in English, French and German). mo. SRPSKE Sekarske Drustvo, Belgrade Yugoslavia. **(Subscription address:** Mladost Export Import, PO Box 1028, Ilica 30, 41000 Zagreb Croatia.**) LC** R91; .S75. **NLM** W1 SR671. **CODEN** SACLA5. Documents available from BIOSIS Document Express.
**Ind/Abst** Biol. Abstr.; EMBASE; Index Med.; Saf. Health Work.

US/0892-1334
**ST. LOUIS METROPOLITAN MEDICINE.** [St. Louis metrop. med.]. **Added/Corp** St. Louis Metropolitan Medical Society. **VFOAT** Saint Louis Metropolitan Medicine; Metro Medicine. Vol. 1 (1979)-. Periodical. English. Twelve times a year. $8.00 (members); $25.00 (non-members). St Louis Metropolitan Medical Society, 3839 Lindell Boulevard, St Louis MO 63108. **Tel** (314)371-5225. **ED** Linda A. Fisher. **DD** 362. Index available. **Bk Rev. Ad Acc. Circ:** 3,100 (ctrl). ***Formed by the union of*** *St. Louis County Medical Society Bulletin, 0098-583X* ***and*** *St. Louis Medicine.*
**Desc:** Data on business matters relating to the medicine field.

IT/0038-9323
**STAMPA MEDICA.** [Stampa med.]. (1955)-. Periodical. Italian. Nineteen times a year. L20000 Italy; L45000 Europe; L70000 Western Hemisphere and Asia; L65000 Africa; L93000 other. Esi Stampa Medica Srl, Casella Postale 42, 20097 San Donato Mil Italy. **Tel** 11 39 2 5274241, FAX 11 39 2 55600670, telex 324894. **UDC** 614. Index available. cum. index. **Bk Rev. Ad Acc. Circ:** 100,000 (ctrl).

US/0739-0564
**STANDARDS MONITOR.** (STANDARDS MONITOR : AAMI STANDARDS AND RECOMMENDED PRACTICES, A PROGRESS REPORT AND NOTIFICATION OF PROPOSED ACTION.). [Stand. monit.]. **Main/Corp** Association for the Advancement of Medical Instrumentation. Periodical. English. bm. $70.00. Association for the Advancement of Medical Instrumentation, 3330 Washington Boulevard, Suite 400, Arlington VA 22209. **Tel** (703)525-4890, (800)332-2264, FAX (703)276-0793. **ED** Michael Miller, Nancy Johnson. **Ad Acc. Circ:** 5,000.
**Desc:** Reports on status of AAMI standards, recommended practices and other technical documents, as well as committee activity.

●US/1062-7162
**STANDARDS OF MEDICAL CARE.** (1992)-. Periodical. English. qt. $795.00. R&R Publishing, 1000 Potomac Street NW, Suite 401, Washington DC 20007.

IT/1120-527X
**STARBENE MILANO.** [Starbene Milano]. (1978)-. Periodical. Italian. mo. L31200 Italy; L57000 other. Arnoldo Mondadori Editore, UFF Cont Abbonamenti, 20090 Segrate MI Italy. **Tel** 011 39 2 75422015, telex 320457 MONDMI I. **UDC** 613.

IE
**STATISTICAL INFORMATION RELEVANT TO THE HEALTH SERVICES.** **See** Medical Science and Technology-Abstracting, Bibliographies and Statistics.

●UK/0962-2802
**STATISTICAL METHODS IN MEDICAL RESEARCH. VFOAT** SM in MR. Vol. 1, No. 1 (1992)-. Statistical Publication. English. qt. $190.00 North America; £97.50 Europe; £110.00 Other. Edward Arnold,

338 Euston Road, London NW1 3BH England. **Tel** 011 44 71 873 6000, FAX 011 44 071 873 6325. **(Subscription address:** Edward Arnold, PO Box 386, Avenel NJ 07001-0386.**) ED** Brian S. Everitt, Graham Dunn and Theodore R. Holford. **LC** R853.S7; S77. **DD** 610/.72. **NLM** W1; ST317D.
**Desc:** Devoted exclusively to the powerful statistical techniques available to the medical profession. Each issue will focus on a particular theme, and will consist of five of more review papers which indicate the successes and failures of the application of these statistical methods in medical research and give an overall impression of the contributions they have made.
**Ind/Abst** Curr. Aware. Biol. Sci., CABS; Index Med.; Stat. Theory Method Abstr.

UK/0277-6715
**STATISTICS IN MEDICINE.** **See** Medical Science and Technology-Abstracting, Bibliographies and Statistics.

US/0742-8871
**STATUS REPORT - UNITED STATES. HEALTH CARE FINANCING ADMINISTRATION. OFFICE OF RESEARCH AND DEMONSTRATIONS.** (STATUS REPORT.). [Status rep. - U.S., Health Care Financ. Adm., Off. Res. Demonstr.]. **Added/Corp** United States. Health Care Financing Administration. Office of Research and Demonstrations. (April 1983)-. Government Publication. English. an. $17.00. Superintendent of Documents, US Government Printing Office, Washington DC 20402. **Tel** (202)275-3328, FAX (202)786-2377. **ED** Gerri Michael Dyer. **LC** RA410.53; .S73. **DD** 338.4/33621/0973. **NLM** W 20.5; R4206. **Circ:** 3,000. ***Continues*** *Research and Demonstrations in Health Care Financing.*
**Desc:** Provides brief synopses and current status of intramural and extramural research and demonstration projects funded by the Health Care Financing Administration that relate to the Medicare and Medicaid programs.

US
**STEDMAN'S MEDICAL DICTIONARY.** (194?)-. Monographic series. English. ir. Price varies per volume. Williams & Wilkins Company, 428 East Preston Street, Baltimore MD 21202-3993. **Tel** (410)528-4000, (800)638-6423, FAX (410)528-8596, telex 87669. **(Subscription address:** Williams & Wilkins, PO Box 64380, Baltimore MD 21264.**)** Documents available from Quick Copies. ***Continues*** *Stedman, Thomas Lathrop, 1853-1938. A Practical Medical Dictionary.*

AU
**STEIRISCHES ARZTEJOURNAL : MITTEILUNGEN DER ARZTEKAMMER FUER STEIERMARK.** **Added/Corp** Arztekammer fur Steiermark. **VFOAT** Steirische Arzte Journal; Arzte Journal. (1990)-. Periodical. German. mo. **NLM** W1; ST435L. ***Continues*** *Journal (Arztekammer fur Steiermark), 1012-9421.*

●CN
**STITCHES : THE JOURNAL OF MEDICAL HUMOUR.** (1993)-. Periodical. English. Ten times a year (July/Aug. & Nov./Dec. issues combined). 40.00Can$. Stitches, 14845 Yonge Street, Suite 300, Aurora Ontario L4G 6H8 Canada. **Tel** (905)841-5607, FAX (905)841-5688. **ED** Simon Hally. **NLM** W1; ST525. **Bk Rev**, (Qty: 10). **Ad Acc. Circ:** 42,000 (ctrl). ***Continues*** *Punch Digest for Canadian Doctors, 1182-5405.*
**Desc:** A journal of medical wit and humor.

IT/0393-4292
**STORIA E MEDICINA POPOLARE.** **Added/Corp** Centro "Storia e Medicina Popolare". (Nov. 1983)-. Periodical. Italian. Storia Medicina Popolare, Via Ferruccio 26, 00185 Rome Italy. **NLM** W1; ST697C.

UK/0748-8386
**STRESS MEDICINE.** [Stress med.]. Vol. 1, No. 1 (Jan.-March 1985)-. Periodical. English. Four times a year. $495.00. John Wiley & Sons Ltd., Baffins Lane, Chichester West Sussex PO19 1UD England. **Tel** 0243 779777, FAX 0243 776128 BTG:JWP001, telex 86290 WIBOOKG. **(Subscription address:** John Wiley / Philadelphia, PO Box 7247, Philadelphia PA 19170.**) ED** David Wheatley and John M. Ivancevich, North American editor. **DD** 616. **NLM** W1; ST799M. **CODEN** STMEEZ. **[CCC]. Pr Rev. Circ:** 2,000. available on microfilm and microfiche from University Microfilms International (UMI). Documents available from The Genuine Article, BIOSIS Document Express.
**Desc:** Publishes papers on physiological and psychological aspects of stress and their interaction, and the investigation of the mechanisms of stress induced diseases.
**Ind/Abst** Annals Behav. Med.; Arts Humanit. Citation Index [Select. Cov.]; Biol. Abstr. (1989-); Curr. Contents Clin. Med.; Curr. Contents Soc. Behav. Sci.; EMBASE; Health Saf. Sci. Abstr.; Psychol. Abstr. (1987-); PsycINFO (1990-); PsycLit; Res. Alert [Full Cov.]; Soc. Sci. Cit. Index [Full Cov.].

US/1049-7463
**STROKE. CLINICAL UPDATES.** [Stroke clin. updates]. **Added/Corp** National Stroke Association (U.S.). **VFOAT** Stroke. Vol. 1, Issue 1 (April 1990)-. Periodical. English. Six times a year. $35.00 (Comes with National Stroke Association Membership). National Stroke Association, 8480 East Orchard Road, Suite 1000, Englewood CO 80111-5015. **Tel** (303)771-1700, FAX (303)771-1886. **DD** 616. **NLM** W1; ST81R.

US
**STUDENT COURSE EVALUATIONS, CORE CLERKSHIPS / HARVARD MEDICAL SCHOOL, COMMITTEE ON EDUCATIONAL EVALUATION.** **Added/Corp** Harvard Medical School. Committee on Educational Evaluation. **VFOAT** Student Course Evaluation Guide; HMS Student Core Clerkship Evaluations. Vol. 11 (1989/1990)-. Periodical. English. Committee on Educational Evaluation, Harvard Medical School, 10 Shattuck Street, Boston MA 02115. ***Continues*** *Core Clerkships, Student Course Evaluation.*

US/0274-6018
**STUDENT DOCTOR.** [Stud. dr.]. **Added/Corp** Student Osteopathic Medical Association. Vol. 1, (Jan./Feb. 1980)-. Periodical. English. Four times a year (Special iss. in Oct.). $25.00. National Soma, 142 East Ontario Street, Chicago IL 60611. **Tel** (800)237-7662, FAX (312)280-5893.

IT
**STUDI SULLA TOSCANA MEDICEA.** 1-. Monographic series. Italian. ir. Price varies per volume. Casa Editrice Leo S. Olschki, Viuzzo del Pozzetto, Casella Postale 66, 50126 Florence Italy. **Tel** 011 39 55 6530684, FAX 011 39 55 6530214.

XO/0371-2222
**STUDIA PNEUMOLOGICA ET PHTISEOLOGICA CECHOSLOVACA.** [Stud. pneumol. phtiseol. cechosl.]. (1970)-. Academic Scholarly Publication. Czech (summaries and/or abstracts in English and Russian). mo. Vydavatelstivi Osveta / Education, Osloboditelov 21, O36 54 Martin Slovakia. **Tel** (842)341-21, FAX 7 350-36. **NLM** W1 ST885K. **CODEN** SPPCAC. Documents available from CASDDS. ***Continues*** *Rozhledy v Tuberkulose a v Nemocech Plicnich.*
**Ind/Abst** Chem. Abstr.; Coal Abstr.; EMBASE; Saf. Health Work; Trop. Dis. Bull.

PL/0860-9594
**STUDIA SOCIETATIS SCIENTIARUM TORUNENSIS. SECTIO H, MEDICINA.** [Stud. Soc. Sci. Torun., Sect. H, Med.]. (1989)-. Polish (English). ir. varies. Towarzystow Noukowe w Toruniu, U1 Wysoka 16, 87-100 Torun Poland. **Tel** 239-41, telex 552388 FSBH PL. **ED** Lech Bieganowski. **UDC** 61. Index available. **Circ:** 300 (ctrl).
**Desc:** Works of different fields of medicine.

GW/0081-7333
**STUDIEN ZUR MEDIZINGESCHICHTE DES NEUNZEHNTEN JAHRHUNDERTS.** [Stud. Medizingesch. neunzehnten Jahrhunderts]. (1967)-. Academic Scholarly Publication. German. ir. Price varies per volume. Vandenhoeck & Ruprecht, Robert Bosch Breite 6, D-37079 Goettingen Germany. **Tel** 011 49 551 695911, FAX 011 49 551 695917, telex 965226 VAN d. **ED** Walter Heischvel-Artelt and and Edith Maun. **NLM** W1 ST913K. **CODEN** SMNJA2. **Ad Acc.** Documents available from CASDDS.
**Ind/Abst** Chem. Abstr.

GW/0323-4126
**STUDIENMATERIAL ZUR WEITERBILDUNG MEDIZINISCH-TECHNISCHER LABORASSISTENTEN.** [Studienmater. Weiterbild. med.-tech. Laborassistenten]. **VFOAT** Studienmaterial; Studienmaterial zur Weiterbildung Medizinisch-Technischer Assistenten. Periodical. German. ir. Institut fur Weiterbildung Mittlerer Medizinischer, Fachkrafte Rubensstrasse, O-1500 Potsdam Germany. **NLM** W1 ST915B. **CODEN** SWMTAT. Documents available from CASDDS.
**Ind/Abst** Chem. Abstr.

NE/0925-1421
**STUDIES IN ANCIENT MEDICINE.** Vol. 1 (1991)-. Monographic series. English (German). ir. Price varies per volume. E. J. Brill, Postbus 9000, 2300 PA Leiden Netherlands. **Tel** 011 31 71 312624, FAX 011 31 71 317532, telex 39296 BRILL NL. **NLM** W1; ST918K.

II
**STUDIES IN HISTORY OF MEDICINE AND SCIENCE.** Vol. 9, No. 1-2 (March/June 1985)-. Periodical. English. qt. Rs100.00, Rs25.00 (single issues) India; £20.00, £5.00 (single issues) UK; $25.00, $6.00 (single issues) other. Institute of History of Medicine & Medical Research, Hamdard Nagar, New Delhi 110062 India. **NLM** W1; ST92QH. Index available. cum. index. **Bk Rev. Circ:** 600 (ctrl). ***Continues*** *Studies in History of Medicine.*
**Ind/Abst** Am. Hist. Life (1985-).

US/0585-6906
**STUDIES IN MEDICAL GEOGRAPHY.** [Stud. med. geogr.]. Monographic series. English. ir. Price varies per volume. Hafner Press, 866 Third Avenue, NY NY 10022. **Tel** (212)702-4200. **ED** David Loiterstein. **NLM** W1 ST921. **CODEN** SMDGAB. Documents available from BIOSIS Document Express.
**Ind/Abst** Biol. Abstr.

FI/0781-1705
**STUK-A.** [STUK-A]. **VFOAT** Sateilyturvakeskus-A. (1984)-. English. ir. Sateilyturvakeskus, Helsinki Finland. **UDC** 614.8. Documents available from CASDDS. ***Continues*** *STL-A, 0355-7006.*
**Ind/Abst** Chem. Abstr.

GW/0939-5911
**SUCHT.** (1991)-. Periodical. Multiple languages. bm. DM140.00. Neuland Verlagsgesellschaft, Markt 24-26, D 21502 Geesthacht Germany. **Tel** 011 49 4152 81342. **UDC** 61.
**Ind/Abst** EMBASE.

II
**SUDHANIDHI.** Vol. 1 (Jan. 1973)-. Periodical. Hindi (Hindi). mo. 8.00. **LC** R97.7.H5; S9.

GW/0039-4564
**SUDHOFFS ARCHIV.** (SUDHOFFS ARCHIV. BEIHEFTE.). [Sudhoffs Arch.]. (1966)-. Monographic series. German (English and French). sm. DM148.00. Franz Steiner Verlag GmbH, Postfach 101061, D 70009 Stuttgart Germany. **Tel** 011 49 0711 2582372, FAX 011 49 0711 2582290, telex 723636 daz d. **ED** Peter Dilg, Menso Folkerts, Gundolf Keil, Fritz Krafft and Rolf Winau. **NLM** W1 SU189A. **CODEN** SZWBAC. **[CCC]. *Continues*** *Sudhoffs Archiv fuer Geschichte der Medizin und der Naturwissenschaften. Beihefte.*
**Desc:** Covers the history of medical science.
**Ind/Abst** GeoRef; Index Med.

JA/0285-8177
**SUMITOMO BYOIN IGAKU ZASSHI.** [Sumitomo ByÅoin igaku zasshi]. **Added/Corp** Sumitomo Byoin. **VFOAT** Medical Journal of Sumitomo Hospital. (1974)-. Academic Scholarly Publication. Japanese. Sumitomo Byoin, Naka-no-Shima 5-2-2, Kita-ku, Osaka-shi 530 Japan. **CODEN** SBIZDJ. Documents available from CASDDS.
**Ind/Abst** Chem. Abstr.

US
**SUMMARY OF MEDICAL PROGRAMS.** English. mo. US Veterans Administration / Washington DC, 810 Vermont Avenue Southwest, Washington DC 20420. **Tel** (202)393-2124. **NLM** W2; A V49sg. available on microfiche (Vols. for (Jan. 1980- ) distributed to depository libraries). Documents available from Documents on Demand. ***Continues*** *Veterans Administration; Summary of Medical Programs.*
**Ind/Abst** Am. Stat. Index.

JA/0289-5102
**SUNAGAWA SHIRITSU BYOIN IGAKU ZASSHI.** [Sunagawa Shiritsu Byoin igaku zasshi]. **VFOAT** Journal of Sunagawa City Medical Center. (1984)-. Periodical. Multiple languages. an. Sunagawa City Medical Center, 6-1 West 4-jo, North 4-jo Sunagawa-shi, 073-01 Hokkaido, Japan. **DD** 610.
**Ind/Abst** EMBASE [Select. Cov.].

FI/0039-5560
**SUOMEN LAAKARILEHTI. FINLANDS LAKARTIDNING.** **Added/Corp** Suomen Laakariliito. **VFOAT** Finlands Lakartidning. (1946)-. Periodical. Finnish. Thirty-three times a year. Fmk615.00 Scandinavia; Fmk750.00 other. Finnish Medical Association, PO Box 49, Makelankatu 2, 00501 Helskini Finland. **Tel** 011 358 0 90 393 091. **NLM** W1 SU605. Index Available, published separately, free-automatically sent. ***Supersedes*** *Suomen Laakari - Liiton Aikauslehiti.*

FI/0786-2180
**SUOMEN LAAKETILASTO / LAAKEINFORMAATION JA -TILASTOINNIN YHTEISTYOTOIMIKUNTA.** **See** Medical Science and Technology-Abstracting, Bibliographies and Statistics.

GW/0930-4061
**SUPPLEMENT (DARMSTADT).** ***Ceased.*** (SUPPLEMENT / GIT VERLAG.). [Supplement]. **VFOAT** Chromatographie; Mikroskopie, Elektronenmikroskopie; GIT Supplement. (198?)-(19??). German (summaries and/or abstracts in English). ir. GIT Verlag GmbH, Roblerstrabe 90, Postfach 110564, D 64220 Darmstadt Germany. **Tel** 011 49 6151 8090-0, FAX 011 49 6151 8090-45. **NLM** W1; SU692. ***Continues*** *Supplement (G-I-T Verlag Ernst Giebeler), 0930-4061.* ***Continued in part by*** *GIT Spezial. Chromatographie, 0940-032X.*
**Ind/Abst** Anal. Abstr.

CN/0821-1590
**SUPPLEMENT ONE, HEALTH SCIENCES BOOKS & JOURNALS.** See Publishing-Books and Bookmaking.

XR/0049-5522
**SUPPLEMENTUM SBORNIKU VEDECKYCH PRACI LEKARSKE FAKULTY UNIVERZITY KARLOVY V HRADCI KRALOVE.** [Suppl. Sb. ved. pr. Lek. fak. Univ. Karlovy Hradci Kralove]. **Added/Corp** Karlova Universita. Lekarska Fakulta v Hradci Kralove. **VFOAT** Prilozhenie k Sborniku Nauchnykh Rabot Meditsinskogo Fakulteta Karlova Universiteta v Gradtse Kralove. (1958)-. Periodical. Czech (summaries and/or abstracts in Russian and English). ir. Charles University / Univerzita Karlova, Ovocnytrh 5, 116 36 Prague 1 Czech Republic. **Tel** 228441. **(Subscription address:** Artia Pegas Press Ltd., Palac Metro Narodni Trida 25, 11210 Prague 1 Czech Republic.**)** **NLM** W1 SB702PA. **CODEN** SVKSA9. Documents available from BIOSIS Document Express.
**Ind/Abst** Biol. Abstr.; Index Med.

US/0164-4238
**SURGICAL TECHNOLOGIST, THE.** [Surg. technol.]. **Added/Corp** Association of Surgical Technologists. Vol. 11 (Jan./Feb. 1979)-. Periodical. English. Twelve times a year. $36.00 US; $48.00 others. Association of Surgical Technologists, 7108-C South Alton Way, Engelwood CO 80112. **Tel** (303)694-9130, FAX (303)694-9169. **ED** Sharon Prague. **NLM** W1 SU768. Index available (Bound in December issue). **Bk Rev. Ad Acc. Pr Rev. Circ:** 16,000. ***Continues*** *OR Tech, 0275-4622.*
**Desc:** The purpose of this journal is advance the quality of surgical patient care by providing a forum for the exchange of knowledge in the field of surgical technology and by promoting a high standard of surgical technology performance. Emphasis is given to surgical procedures and products, aseptic technique, regulatory and legislative issues, and professional development.
**Ind/Abst** Cumul. Index Nurs. Allied Health Lit.; Health Devices Alerts; Health Plan. Adminis.; Hospit. Health Admin. Index; Index Med.

CN/0833-7926
**SURVEILLANCE.** (SURVEILLANCE : MEDICAL DEVICES.). [Surveill.]. No. 1 (July 9, 1987)-. Periodical. English (French). ir. Health & Welfare Canada / Ottawa, Health Protection Branch, Ottawa Ontario K1A 0L2 Canada. **Tel** (613)954-8842, (613)957-1896. **DD** 610/.28.
**Ind/Abst** Dairy Sci. Abstr.; Health Devices Alerts; Index Vet.; Vet. Bull.

BU/0562-7192
**SUVREMENNA MEDICINA.** (SUVREMENNA MEDITSINA.). [Suvrem. med.]. **Added/Corp** Bulgaria. Ministerstvo na Narodnoto Zdrave i Sotsialnite Grizhi. Bulgaria. Ministerstvo na Narodnoto Zdrave. **VFOAT** Savremenna Meditsina. Vol. 1 (Jan./Feb. 1950)-. Academic Scholarly Publication. Bulgarian (summaries and/or abstracts in English and Russian; table of contents in English and Russian). bm (6 issues). $90.00. Medicina I Fizkultru, Pl Slaveikov 11, Sofiya Bulgaria. **(Subscription address:** Hemus Foreign Trade Organization, 6 Tzar Osvoboditel Boulevard, 1000 Sofia Bulgaria.**)** **NLM** W1 SU926. **CODEN** SUMEA4. Documents available from CASDDS. ***Supersedes*** *Bulgarski Lekarski Suiuz. Suvremenna Meditsina.*
**Ind/Abst** Chem. Abstr.; EMBASE; Saf. Health Work.

SZ/0251-1665
**SWISS MED.** [Swiss med]. (197?)-. Academic Scholarly Publication. German (French, Italian and English). Twelve times a year. 100.00F Switzerland; 120.00F Europe; 200.00F other. Verlag Dr Felix Wuest AG, Seestrasse 5/Postfach, CH-8700 Kuesnacht Switzerland. **Tel** 011 41 1 9110055, FAX (01)9106080, telex 825705. **NLM** W1 SW406M. Index available. ctrl circ.
**Ind/Abst** EMBASE.

GW/0341-6321
**SYMPOSIA MEDICA HOECHST.** [Symp. med. Hoechst]. (1973)-. Academic Scholarly Publication. English (summaries and/or abstracts in German). an. Price varies per volume. F K Schattauer Verlagsgesellschaft mbH, Postfach 10 45 45, D 70040 Stuttgart Germany. **Tel** 011 49 711 2298726. **ED** E. Lindenlaub. **NLM** W3 SY1055. **CODEN** SMHODO. ctrl circ. Documents available from CASDDS.
**Ind/Abst** Chem. Abstr.

NE/0166-1167
**SYMPOSIA OF THE GIOVANNI LORENZINI FOUNDATION.** [Symp. Giovanni Lorenzini Found.]. **Added/Corp** Fondazione Giovanni Lorenzini. Vol. 1 (1978)-. Academic Scholarly Publication. English. Price varies per volume. Elsevier Science Publishers BV, PO Box 211, 1000 AE Amsterdam Netherlands. **Tel** 011 31 20 5803642, FAX 011 31 20 5862696, telex 15682. **NLM** W3 SY1056. **CODEN** SGLFD9. Documents available from CASDDS.
**Ind/Abst** Chem. Abstr.

US/0081-1548
**SYMPOSIA OF THE SOCIETY FOR THE STUDY OF INBORN ERRORS OF METABOLISM.** **Main/Corp** Society for the Study of Inborn Errors of Metabolism. **Added/Corp** Society for the Study of Inborn Errors of Metabolism. Proceedings of the Society for the Study of Inborn Errors of Metabolism. **VFOAT** Proceedings of the Symposia of the Society for the Study of Inborn Errors of Metabolism. (1963)-. English. University Park Press, PO Box 4034, New York NY 10163. **CODEN** PSSMDE. Documents available from BIOSIS Document Express.
**Ind/Abst** Biol. Abstr. (1975-1980); Calcium Calcif. Tissue Abstr. (-1981).

US/1065-1357
**TABER'S CYCLOPEDIC MEDICAL DICTIONARY.** [Taber's cyclop. med. dict.]. **VFOAT** Cyclopedic Medical Dictionary. (1940)-. English. ir (Feb. every four years). $27.50 (with index); $29.95 (without index). FA Davis Company, 1915 Arch Street, Philadelphia PA 19103. **Tel** (800)523-4049, (215)568-2270, FAX (215)568-5065, telex 83-4837. **LC** R121.T18. **DD** 610.

KO/1010-0695
**TAEHAN HANUI HAKHOE CHI.** **VFOAT** The Journal of Korean Oriental Medical Society; Journal of Korean Oriental Medical Society. Academic Scholarly Publication. Korean (Korean). Taehan Hanui Hakhoe, 929-4 Chegi-dong Tongdaemun-ku, Seoul Korea. **LC** R97.7.K6. **NLM** W1; TA392G. Documents available from CASDDS.
**Ind/Abst** Chem. Abstr.

KO/0023-4028
**TAEHAN UIHAK HYOPHOE CHAPCHI.** **Main/Corp** Taehan Uihak Hyophoe, Seoul, Korea. (1958)-. Academic Scholarly Publication. Korean. Korean Medical Association, 302 75 Dong du Ichon Dong, Yongsan ku 140 031 Seoul, Korea. **Tel** 011 2 822 7983807.
**Ind/Abst** EMBASE [Select. Cov.].

KO
**TAEHAN UIHAK HYOPHOE CHI.** **Main/Corp** Taehan Uihak Hyophoe. **VFOAT** Journal of the Korean Medical Association. Academic Scholarly Publication. Korean (Korean). Taehan Uihak Hyophoe, CPO Box 2062, Seoul Korea. **LC** R97.7.K6; T34A. **DD** 610/.5. **NLM** W1 TA396. **CODEN** THUHA7. Documents available from CASDDS.
**Ind/Abst** Chem. Abstr.; EMBASE.

GW/0494-464X
**TAGLICHE PRAXIS.** [Tagl. prax.]. (1960)-. Academic Scholarly Publication. German. Four times a year. Hans Marseille Verlag GmbH, Buerkleinstrasse 12, D 80538 Munich Germany. **Tel** 011 49 89 227988, FAX 011 49 89 2904643. **ED** Lubeck H. Feiereis. **NLM** W1 TA39. **[CCC]**. Index Available, published separately, free-automatically sent. **Ad Acc.**
**Ind/Abst** EMBASE.

JA/0389-9071
**TAIRYOKU KENKYU.** (TAIRYOKU KENKYU : TAIRYOKU IGAKU KENKYUJO HOKOKU.). [Tairyoku kenkyu]. **Added/Corp** Tairyoku Igaku Kenkyujo (Tokyo, Japan) Meiji Seimei Kosei Jigyodan. **VFOAT** Bulletin of the Physical Fitness Research Institute. (1963)-. Academic Scholarly Publication. Japanese (English). Meiji Life Foundation of Health Welfare, 150 Tobukicho, Hachioji City 192 Tokyo Japan. **CODEN** TAKNAS. Documents available from BIOSIS Document Express, CASDDS.
**Ind/Abst** Biol. Abstr.; Chem. Abstr.; EMBASE.

JA/0372-1566
**TAISHA.** [Taisha]. **VFOAT** Metabolism and Disease. Began in 1964. Academic Scholarly Publication. Japanese. Fifteen times a year. $384.00. Nakayama Shoten, 25-14, Hakusan 1 Chome, Bunkyoku, Tokyoto 113, Japan. **(Subscription address:** Kyowa Book Company Inc., 1-38 Kanda Jinbo-Cho, Chiyoda-Ku, Tokyo 101, Japan (Phone: 03-3293-0727)**)** **CODEN** TSHAAW. Documents available from CASDDS.
**Ind/Abst** Chem. Abstr.

US/8756-212X
**TAIWAN REVIEW.** Periodical. English. ABMAC, 2 East 103rd Street, New York NY 10029. **DD** 610. **NLM** W1; TA442T.

US/1046-1906
**TARGETED DIAGNOSIS AND THERAPY.** (1988)-. Monographic series. English. ir. Price varies per volume. Marcel Dekker Inc., 270 Madison Avenue, New York NY 10016. **Tel** (212)696-9000, (800)228-1160, FAX (212)685-4540, telex 421419. **(Subscription address:** Marcel Dekker Inc, PO Box 5017, Monticello NY 12701.**)** **DD** 616. **NLM** W1; TA579. **CODEN** TDTSEB.

US/1040-1334
**TEACHING AND LEARNING IN MEDICINE.** [Teach. learn. med.]. Vol. 1, No. 1 (1989)-. Periodical. English. qt. $195.00 US & Canada; $220.00 other. Lawrence Erlbaum Associates, 365 Broadway, Suite 102, Hillsdale NJ 07642. **Tel** (201)666-4110, (800)926-6579, FAX (201)666-2394. **ED** Terrill A Mast and Howard Barrows. **DD** 610. **NLM** W 18; T2509.
**Desc:** An international forum for scholarly, state of the art research on teaching and learning processes as they relate to the education of medical professionals. This journal addresses practical issues and provides the analysis and empirical research needed to facilitate decision making about medical education at all levels.

US
**TEACHING CASES & PREHOSPITAL CARE.** (19??)-. English. Four times a year. $340.00. Scott Bourn Associates, 557 Burbank Street, Unit B, Broomfield CO 80020. **Tel** (303)460-0900, (800)669-9448, FAX (303)460-0985. **ED** Scott Bourn. cum. index.
**Desc:** Educational material for EMS personnel.

FR/0766-5725
**TECHN. BIOL. - 1985.** (TECHNIQUE & BIOLOGIE.). **VFOAT** Technique et Biologie; TB. Vol. 11 No. 62 (Feb. 1985)-. Academic Scholarly Publication. French. bm. 220.00F, 170.00F (students) France; 320.00 other. Societe Francaise D'Editions Medicales, 22-24 rue du Chateau des Rentiers, 75013 Paris France. **Tel** (1)45-83-50-54, FAX (1)45-83-13-54. **NLM** W1; TE160. **CODEN** TEBIEY. **[CCC]. Ad Acc. Circ:** 6,000. Documents available from CASDDS. ***Continues*** *Technicien Biologiste, 0337-9965.*
**Ind/Abst** Chem. Abstr. (-1988).

US
**TECHNICAL NOTES : MEDLARS INDEXING INSTRUCTIONS : SUPPLEMENT.** **Main/Corp** United States. National Library of Medicine. Bibliographic Service Divison. Index Section. (1975)-. English. ir. $23.50 North America; $25.50 other. Bibliographic Services Division, Building 38A/Room 4N419, National Library of Medicine, 8600 Rockville Pike, Bethesda MD 20894.

US
**TECHNICAL REPORT SAM-TR.** **Main/Corp** United States. School of Aerospace Medicine. **VFOAT** Report SAM-TR; SAM-TR. No. 64-75 (Dec. 1964)-. English. AL/DOKL, Brooks Air Force Base TX 78235-5000. ***Continues*** *United States. School of Aerospace Medicine. Technical Documentary Report, SAM-TDR.*
**Ind/Abst** Psychol. Abstr. (196?-).

NE/0928-7329
**TECHNOLOGY AND HEALTH CARE : OFFICIAL JOURNAL OF THE EUROPEAN SOCIETY FOR ENGINEERING AND MEDICINE.** (19??)-. Academic Scholarly Publication. English. Four times a year (1 volume). Fl489.00. Elsevier Science Publishers BV, PO Box 211, 1000 AE Amsterdam Netherlands. **Tel** 011 31 20 5803642, FAX 011 31 20 5862696, telex 15682. **[CCC].**

●US/1051-5682
**TECHNOLOGY FOR HOME CARE.** (1992)-. Periodical. English. mo. $95.00. ECRI Emergency Care Research Institute, 5200 Butler Pike, Plymouth Meeting PA 19462. **Tel** (215)825-6000, FAX (215)834-1275, telex 510-660-8023.

US/0892-7332
**TECHNOLOGY FOR LABORATORY MEDICINE.** ***Ceased.*** (TECHNOLOGY FOR LABORATORY MEDICINE / ECRI.). [Technol. lab. med.]. **Added/Corp** ECRI (Organization). Vol. 1, No. 1 (May 1987)-Ceased Jan. (1993). Periodical. English. mo. ECRI Emergency Care Research Institute, 5200 Butler Pike, Plymouth Meeting PA 19462. **Tel** (215)825-6000, FAX (215)834-1275, telex 510-660-8023. **DD** 610. **NLM** W1; TE211DL.

US/8756-8608
**TECHNOLOGY FOR MATERIALS MANAGEMENT.** ***Ceased.*** [Technol. mater. manage.]. Vol. 5, No. 7 (Jan. 1985)-Ceased March (1993). Periodical. English. mo. ECRI Emergency Care Research Institute, 5200 Butler Pike, Plymouth Meeting PA 19462. **Tel** (215)825-6000, FAX (215)834-1275, telex 510-660-8023. **ED** J Nobel. **DD** 658. **[CCC]. Bk Rev.** ***Continues*** *Health Devices Update. Materials Management.*
**Desc:** A newsletter for materials managers, purchasing agents, and CSR supervisors summarizing health care technology issues, product recalls, hazards, and problems.

US/1049-4324
**TECHTRANSFER NEWS.** [TechTransfer news]. **VFOAT** Tech Transfer News. Vol. 1, No. 1 (Mar. 1990)-. Periodical. English. ir. $300.00. TechTransfer Services, 69 Midland Avenue, Tarrytown NY 10591. **Tel** (914)631-2699. **ED** Marvin Margothes. **DD** 621.
**Desc:** Provides information on technology for medical diagnostics and laboratory instruments, offered by nonprofit research organizations and government agencies internationally.

SP
**TECNICAS DE LABORATORIO.** Academic Scholarly Publication. Spanish. Publica SA / Barcelona, Travesera de Las Corts 354, 08015 Barcelona Spain. Documents available from CASDDS.
**Ind/Abst** Chem. Abstr.; Food Sci. Technol. Abstr.; Indice Med. Esp.

JA/0387-5547
**TEIKYO IGAKU ZASSHI.** [Teikyo igaku zasshi]. **Added/Corp** Teikyo Daigaku. Igakubu. **VFOAT** Teikyo Medical Journal. (1978)-. Periodical. Japanese (summaries and/or abstracts in English). Four times a year. Teikyo University School of Medicine, c/o Shoma-ka 11-1, Kaga 2-chome, Itabashi-ku, 173, Tokyo, Japan. **CODEN** TIGZDZ. Documents available from CASDDS.
**Ind/Abst** Chem. Abstr.; EMBASE [Select. Cov.]; Energy Res. Abstr. (Dec. 1979-).

US
**TELEMEDICINE.** (19??)-. English. Twelve times a year. $397.00. Miller Freeman Inc., 600 Harrison Street, San Francisco CA 94107. **Tel** (415)905-2337, FAX (415)905-2240, telex 278273.

SP
**TEMAS ACTUALES DE MEDICINA GENERAL.** English. McGraw Hill, Interamericana de Espana SA, Manuel Ferrero 13, 28036 Madrid Spain.

FR/0378-8407
**TEMPO MEDICAL INTERNATIONAL.** [Tempo med. int.rn]. **VFOAT** Tempo Medical. (1977)-. Periodical. French. Thirty-five times a year. 441.00F France; 540.00F other. Tempo Medical, 8 rue Torricelli, 75017 Paris France. **Tel** 011 33 1 44093600, FAX (1)40 68 08 19. **UDC** 611.7. **[CCC].**

IT
**TEMPO MEDICO.** Italian. Thirty-nine times a year. L30000.00 Italy; L75000.00 other. Editiemme, Via Lanino 5, 20144 Milan Italy. **Tel** 011 39 2 4227946, 011 39 2 4224666, FAX 011 39 2 4120287. **Bk Rev. Ad Acc, Adv Mgr:** Cozzi Elisabetta, **Tel** 011 39 2 422 1240. **Circ:** 75,000 (ctrl).

US/1048-3926
**TENNESSEE MANAGED CARE.** [Tenn. manag. care]. (1987)-. Periodical. English. Ten times a year. $157.00 (6 newsletters plus 4 supplements). Harkey and Associates Inc., PO Box 159025, 2000 Richard Jones Road, Suite 170, Nashville TN 37215. **Tel** (615)385-4131, FAX (615)385-4979. **DD** 338.

RU/0040-3660
**TERAPEVTICESKIJ ARHIV.** (TERAPEVTICHESKII ARKHIV.). [Ter. arh.]. Vol. 1 (1923)-. Academic Scholarly Publication. Russian (summaries and/or abstracts in English). mo. $120.00. Izdatelstvo Meditsina / Russian Academy of Medical Sciences, Ulitsa Solyanka 14, 109801 Moscow Russia. **Tel** 011 95 297-05-04. **(Subscription address:** Victor Kamkin, 4956 Boiling Brook Parkway, Rockville, MD 20852) **NLM** W1 TE511. **CODEN** TEARAI. **Pr Rev.** Documents available from The Genuine Article, BIOSIS Document Express, CASDDS.
**Desc:** Information on therapeutics.
**Ind/Abst** Biol. Abstr.; Chem. Abstr.; Curr. Contents Clin. Med.; EMBASE [Select. Cov.]; Helminthol. Abstr.; Index Med.; Life Sci. Collect.; PESTDOC; Protozoolog. Abstr.; Res. Alert [Full Cov.]; Rev. Med. Vet. Entomol.; Rev. Med. Vet. Mycology; Sci. Cit. Index (19??-19??); SCISEARCH; Sug. Indus. Abstr.

IT
**TERAPIA MODERNA.** [Ter. mod.]. (1965)-. Academic Scholarly Publication. Italian. Four times a year. L130000 individuals; L160000 institutions. Il Pensiero Scientifico Editore s.r.l., Via Bradano 3C, 00199 Rome Italy. **Tel** 011 39 6 86207158, 86207159, 86207168, 86207169, FAX 011 39 6 86207160. **CODEN** TPMDAB. Index available. **Circ:** 1,000. Documents available from CASDDS.
**Ind/Abst** Chem. Abstr.; EMBASE [Select. Cov.].

US/0275-1453
**TEXAS DO.** [Tex. DO]. **Added/Corp** Texas Osteopathic Medical Association. **VAT** Texas Doctor of Osteopathy. Vol. 37, No.7 (Aug. 1980)-. Periodical. English. Eleven times a year (Except Apr.). Texas Osteopathic Medical Association, 226 Bailey Avenue, Fort Worth TX 76107. **Tel** (817)336-0549. **NLM** W1 TE694. **Ad Acc. Circ:** 3,500 (ctrl). available on microfilm from University Microfilms International (UMI). ***Continues*** *Texas Osteopathic Physicians Journal, 0275-1445.*

US/0040-4470
**TEXAS MEDICINE.** [Tex. med.]. **Added/Corp** Texas Medical Association. Vol. 62 (May 1966)-. Academic Scholarly Publication. English. Twelve times a year. $40.00. Texas Medical Association, 401 West 15th Street, Austin TX 78701. **Tel** (512)370-1300, FAX (512)370-1630. **ED** Rae Vajgert. **LC** R11; .T43. **NLM** W1 TE787. **CODEN** TXMDAX. Index available. **Ad Acc. Pr Rev. Circ:** 29,000. available on microfilm and microfiche from University Microfilms International (UMI). Documents available from CASDDS. ***Continues*** *Texas State Journal of Medicine, 0096-7165.*
**Desc:** Clinical medical journal and organizational publication for Texas Medical Association.
**Ind/Abst** Chem. Abstr.; Chicano Index; Cumul. Index Nurs. Allied Health Lit.; EMBASE [Select. Cov.]; Energy Res. Abstr.; Index Med.; Med. Abstr. Newsl.; Life Sci. Collect.; Protozoolog. Abstr.; Saf. Health Work; SportSearch.

SZ/1013-2007
**TEXTE ZUR GESCHICHTE DER PRAVENTIVMEDIZIN : TGP / HERAUSGEGEBEN VON ERWIN BRAUN GESELLSCHAFT FUR PRAVENTIVMEDIZIN.** [Texte Gesch. Prav.med.]. **VFOAT** TGP. V. 1-. Monographic series. German (French and Latin). Price varies per volume. **NLM** W1; TE995.

NE/0167-9902
**THEORETICAL MEDICINE.** [Theor. med.]. Vol. 4, No. 1 (Feb. 1983)-. Academic Scholarly Publication. English. qt. $386.00. Kluwer Academic Publishers, Postbus 322, 3300 AH Dordrecht, The Netherlands. **Tel** 011 (31) 78 524400, FAX 011 31 78 183273, telex 20083. **ED** Kazem Sadegh-Zadeh and David Thomasma. **LC** R723; .T42. **DD** 610/.1. **NLM** W1; TH12J. **CODEN** THMEDT. **[CCC].** Index available. **Bk Rev. Ad Acc. Pr Rev. Acid Free. Circ:** 450. available on microfilm and microfiche from University Microfilms International (UMI). Documents available from The Genuine Article. ***Continues*** *Metamedicine, 0166-2031.*
**Desc:** Provides a forum for interdisciplinary studies in the philosophy and methodology of the medical practice and research. Is an important communication medium in the area of the philosophy and methodology of medicine and, as such, offers comprehensive bibliographies, reviews of significant literature, information about current scholarly activities in the field, including partial proceedings of selected meetings, and an opinions section for readers' commentaries.
**Ind/Abst** Curr. Contents Soc. Behav. Sci.; EMBASE; Energy Res. Abstr. (Feb. 1983-); Index Med. (Vol. 5, No. 1, 1984-); Philos. Index (Vol. 5, No. 1, 1984-); Res. Alert [Full Cov.]; Soc. Sci. Cit. Index [Full Cov.].

UK/0964-1866
**THERAPEUTIC COMMUNITIES.** [Ther. communities]. **Added/Corp** Association of Therapeutic Communities. (1992)-. Periodical. English. qt. £48.00 (institutions), £24.00 (individuals) UK; £60.00 (institutions), £32.00 (individuals) other. Association of Therapeutic Communities, The Retreat, York YO1 5BN England. **Tel** 011 44 904 412551. ***Continues*** *International Journal of Therapeutic Communities, 0196-1365.*

US/0163-4356
**THERAPEUTIC DRUG MONITORING.** **See** Pharmacy and Pharmacology.

FR/0989-6171
**THERAPEUTIQUE ACTUELLE : TA.** ***Suspended.*** **VFOAT** TA; Therapeutical Advances. (June 1988)-Suspended (1993). Periodical. French. ir (5-6 per year). C et P Communications Sante, 134 Avenue de Villiers, 75017 Paris France. **Tel** 011 33 1 44404050, FAX 011 33 1 44400180. **NLM** W1; TH179L.

HU/0133-3909
**THERAPIA HUNGARICA (ENGLISH EDITION).** (THERAPIA HUNGARICA.). [Ther. Hung.]. **VFOAT** Hungarian Medical Journal. Vol. 1 (1953)-. Academic Scholarly Publication. English. ir. Free on request. Therapia Hungarica, Vorosmarty Ter 4, Budapest 5 Hungary. **Tel** 36 1 1427989, FAX 36 1 1427959, telex 226571. **ED** Dr. P Braun (editor's address: PO Box 64, 1367 Budapest 5 Hungary). **NLM** W1; TH635. **CODEN** THHUAF. Documents available from CASDDS.
**Ind/Abst** Chem. Abstr. (-1988); EMBASE [Select. Cov.]; Index Med.; Life Sci. Collect.; PESTDOC.

GW/0040-5965
**THERAPIE DER GEGENWART.** ***Ceased.*** (DIE THERAPIE DER GEGENWART : MEDIZINISCH-CHIRURGISCHE RUNDSCHAU FUER PRAKTISCHE ARZTE.). [Ther. Ggw.]. Vol. 36 (Jan. 1895)-(Sept. 1993). Periodical. German. mo. Urban & Vogel, Postfach 152209, D-80052 Munich Germany. **Tel** 011 49 89 53292140, FAX 089/536052, telex 521701. **ED** T U Keil. **NLM** W1 TH643. **CODEN** THGEAU. **[CCC]. Bk Rev. Ad Acc. Circ:** 36,000 (ctrl). Documents available from CASDDS. ***Continues*** *Medizinisch-Chirurgische Rundschau.*
**Desc:** Young journal with compact information, journalist research and a wide readers service for the G.P.
**Ind/Abst** Chem. Abstr.; EMBASE; Energy Res. Abstr.; Life Sci. Collect.; PESTDOC.

GW/0040-5973
**THERAPIEWOCHE.** [Therapiewoche]. **Added/Corp** Deutsche Therapiewoche. Vol. 1 (1950/1951)-. Academic Scholarly Publication. German. Forty-eight times a year. DM118.00 Germany; DM138.00 others. G Braun Verlag, Postfach 1709, D 76006 Karlsruhe Germany. **Tel** 011 49 721 165392. **NLM** W1 TH659. **CODEN** THEWA6. Documents available from CASDDS.
**Ind/Abst** Chem. Abstr.; EMBASE [Select. Cov.]; Energy Res. Abstr. (Feb. 1973-); PESTDOC.

AU/0258-848X
**THERAPIEWOCHE OSTERREICH.** [Ther.woche Osterr.]. (1986)-. Periodical. German. mo. Therapiewoche Verlag Ges.m.b.H, Protschhofstr. 12 A-5082, Grodig/Salzburg, Germany. **Tel** (6246)3408.
**Ind/Abst** EMBASE [Select. Cov.].

SZ/0256-6869
**THERAPIEWOCHE SCHWEIZ.** [Ther.woche Schweiz]. (1985)-. Periodical. German. mo. **UDC** 61.
**Ind/Abst** EMBASE [Select. Cov.].

US/0882-3758
**THERMOLOGY.** (THERMOLOGY : THE JOURNAL OF THE AMERICAN ACADEMY OF THERMOLOGY.). [Thermology]. **Added/Corp** American Academy of Thermology. Vol. 1, No. 1 (April 1985)-. Periodical. English. Four times a year. Thermology, PO Box 1324, Vienna VA 22180. **Tel** (703)938-6140, FAX (703)938-1482. **ED** Sumio Vematsu. **DD** 616. **NLM** W1; TH68R. Index available. **Bk Rev. Ad Acc. Pr Rev. Circ:** 3,000. ***Continues*** *Thermology Quarterly, 0742-7050.*
**Desc:** A medical journal presenting the most recent scientific studies involving liquid crystal and/or infrared imaging (thermography).

FR/0399-0648
**THESINDEX MEDICAL.** [Thesindex med.]. 1976/77-. French. an. **NLM** ZW 4 T413. ***Continues*** *Index Alphabetique Annuel des Sujets Traites dans les Theses de Medecine, 0399-0621.*
**Desc:** Consists of an index of these defended in France and in certain universities of French-speaking countries.

AU/0934-9669
**THROMBOTIC AND HEMORRHAGIC DISORDERS.** English. qt. DM224.00. Springer-Verlag GmbH & Company KG, Heidelberger Platz 3, D 14197 Berlin Germany. **Tel** 011 49 30 8207223, FAX 011 49 30 8214091, telex 183 319 SPBLN D. **(Subscription address:** Springer Verlag New York Inc. / for North America, 44 Hartz Way, Secaucus NJ 07096.) **ED** E Deutsch. **[CCC].**
**Desc:** Provides recent advances, presenting original research papers, short communications, and reviews of the following topics: mechanisms involved in physiological and pathological haemostasis; development of in vivo and in vitro methods; basic and clinical investigations with therapeutic application of drugs; mechanisms underlying the therapeutic actions.

SZ/0896-341X
**THYMUS UPDATE.** (1988)-. Monographic series. English. an. Price varies per volume. Harwood Academic Publishers, PO Box 90, Reading RG1 8JL England. **Tel** 011 44 734 560080. **LC** UNC. **DD** 616. **NLM** W1; TH958T. **CODEN** THUPEZ.

UK/0142-8349
**THYROID HORMONES.** [Thyroid horm.]. (1976)-. English. mo. £110.00. SUBIS, Mansion House, 19 Kingfield Road, Sheffield S11 9AS England. **Tel** 011 44 114 255 4433, FAX 011 44 114 255 4626. **DD** 016.61244.

CC/0253-9896
**TIANJIN YIYAO.** (TIEN-CHIN I YAO.). [Tianjin yiyao]. **Added/Corp** Tien-chin Shih i Yao ko Hsueh Chi Shu Ching Pao Chan. Tsa Chih Tsu. (19??)-. Academic Scholarly Publication. Chinese. mo. Tianjin Yixue Keji Qingbao Yanjiusuo, Tianjin Medical Science and Technology Information Institute, 131 Chengdu Dao, Tianjin 300050 People's Republic of China. **Tel** 311705. **ED** Zhang Ying-fu. **LC** R97.7.C5; T54. **NLM** W1 TI345. **CODEN** TIYADG. **Ad Acc.** Documents available from BIOSIS Document Express, CASDDS.
**Desc:** It's a comprehensive medical magazine that includes the content of basic medicine, clinical medicine and pharmacology.
**Ind/Abst** Biol. Abstr.; Chem. Abstr.; Curr. Biotechnol.

II/0970-1257
**TIBETAN MEDICINE.** (TIBETAN MEDICINE = GSO RIG.). [Tibetan med.]. **Added/Corp** Library of Tibetan Works & Archives. **VFOAT** Gso Rig. (1980)-. Periodical. English. an. $10.00. Library of Tibetan Works & Archives, Dharamsala, India. **(Subscription address:** Prints India, 11 Darya Ganj, New Delhi 110002 India.) **NLM** W1; TI1001.

SW/1100-6323
**TIDSKRIFT FOR MEDICINSK OCH TEKNISK FOTOGRAFI.** **See** Photography and Video.

NO/0029-2281
**TIDSSKRIFT FOR DEN NORSKE LAEGEFORENING; TIDSSKRIFT FOR PRAKTISK MEDISIN. THE JOURNAL OF THE NORWEGIAN MEDICAL ASSOCIATION.** **Main/Corp** Norske Laegeforening. **VFOAT** Journal of the Norwegian Medical Association; Tidsskrift for Praktisk Medicin. Vol. 10 (Jan. 1890)-. Academic Scholarly Publication. Norwegian (summaries and/or abstracts in English). Thirty times a year. Kr650.00 Norway and Scandinavia; Kr850.00 other. Tidsskrift for den Norske, Fjellveien 5, N 1324 Lysaker Norway. **Tel** 011 47 2 124600. **ED** Ole K. Harlem. **NLM** W1 NO266.

**CODEN** TNLAAH. Index available. **Bk Rev**. **Ad Acc**. **Circ:** 15,000. ***Continues*** *Tidsskrift for Praktisk Medicin*.
**Desc:** Membership news and advertisements. Scientific and clinical medicine.
**Ind/Abst** EMBASE [Select. Cov.]; Index Med.; SportSearch.

GW
**TIERLABORATORIUM / HERAUSGEGEBEN VON DEN ZENTRALEN TIERLABORATORIEN UND DEM INSTITUT FUER VERSUCHSTIERKUNDE DER FREIEN UNIVERSITAT BERLIN.** See Veterinary Sciences.

NE/0925-2819
**TIJDSCHRIFT VOOR GENEESKUNDE & ETHIEK.** **VFOAT** TGE. (1991)-. Periodical. Dutch. Four times a year. Fl65.00 (institutions), Fl50.00 (individuals) Netherlands; Fl75.00 (institutions), Fl60.00 (individuals) other. Van Gorcum & Company BV, PO Box 43, NL 9400 AA Assen Netherlands. **Tel** 011 31 5920 46846, FAX 011 31 5920 72064.

HK
**TIMS.** Chinese. Three times a year. 60.00Sing$ (surface mail), 110.00Sing$ (airmail). MIMS Asia, 135 Cecil Street, 13-00 LKN Building, Singapore 0106 Singapore. **Tel** 011 65 2233788, FAX 011 65 2214788.

TU
**TIP DUNYASI.** **VFOAT** Tib Dunyasi. V. 1- Jan. 1928. Periodical. Turkish (Turkish). **NLM** W1 TI1002.

●US/1076-3279
**TISSUE ENGINEERING.** (1994)-. Periodical. English. qt. $170.95. Mary Ann Liebert Inc., 1651 Third Avenue, New York NY 10128. **Tel** (212)289-2300, (800)M-LIEBERT, FAX (212)289-4697.
**Desc:** Focuses on engineering new tissue. Applies principles and methods of engineering and the life sciences toward the fundamental understanding of structure-function relationships in normal and pathologic tissue and the development of biological substitutes.

US
**TJFR HEALTH NEWS REPORTER.** English. mo. $298.00 corporate; $198.00 non-profit. TJFR Publishing Company, 545 North Maple Avenue, 2nd Floor, Ridgewood NJ 07450. **Tel** (201)444-6061, FAX (201)444-5919. **ED** Erilyn B. Riley. **Bk Rev**, (Qty: 12). **Ad Acc**.
**Desc:** Covers health media.

US
**TMA ACTION.** **Main/Corp** Texas Medical Association. **VAT** Texas Medical Association Action. (19??)-. Periodical. English. mo. Texas Medical Association, 401 West 15th Street, Austin TX 78701. **Tel** (512)370-1300, FAX (512)370-1630. **ED** Jon R. Hornaday. **Circ:** 25,000.
**Desc:** Information on non-clinical activities, policies, and news of interest to physicians and medical student members of the Texas Medical Association.

JA/0440-0852
**TO SHIN, HAI.** **VFOAT** Lung & Heart. (1960)-. Periodical. Multiple languages. qt. Kokuseido Shuppan K.K., (Kokuseido Publishing Co., Ltd.), 23-5-202, Hongo 3 Chome, Bunkyoku, Tokyoto 113 Japan. **DD** 616.2. Documents available from CASDDS. ***Continues*** *Hai, 0436-5712*.
**Ind/Abst** Chem. Abstr.

US/0091-2360
**TODAY'S CHIROPRACTIC.** Vol. 1 (Jan./Feb. 1972)-. Periodical. English. bm (6 issues). $24.00 (one year), $40.00 (two year), $56.00 (three year). Life Chiropractic College, 1269 Barclay Circle, Marietta GA 30060. **Tel** (404)424-0554 ext. 225, FAX (404)429-8359. **ED** James B. Panter. **LC** RZ201; .T62. **DD** 615/.534/05. **NLM** W1 TO161. **Bk Rev**, (Qty: 18). **Ad Acc**, **Adv Mgr:** Cheryl DiDuro. **Pr Rev. Circ:** 38,000. available on microfilm from University Microfilms International (UMI).
**Desc:** Covers chiropractic, health, nutrition, exercise and celebrities.

US/0147-4782
**TODAY'S CLINICIAN.** (TODAY'S CLINICIAN AND POSTGRADUATE EDUCATION AT COMMUNITY HOSPITALS.). V. 1- Sept. 1977-. Periodical. English. mo. $20.00. Weston Communications, Inc., 575 Madison Avenue, New York NY 10022. **LC** R11; .T6. **DD** 610/.5. **NLM** W1 TO161K.

CN
**TODAY'S HEALTH REPORT.** ***Ceased.*** English. mo. Thomson Healthcare, 1120 Birchmount Road, Suite 200, Scarborough Ontario M1K 5G4 Canada. **Tel** (905)750-8900. ***Continues*** *Today's Health, 0821-6819*.

US/1059-0242
**TODAY'S TEAM.** [Today's team]. (1990)-. Periodical. English. mo. $220.00 (sold only in bulk). Wentworth Publishing Company, 1866 Colonial Village Lane, Lancaster PA 17605. **Tel** (800)331-5196, (717)393-1000. **(Subscription address:** Wentworth Publishing Co., PO Box 10488, Lancaster PA 17605.**)** **DD** 658.

US/0741-2320
**TODAY'S THERAPEUTIC TRENDS.** (TODAY'S THERAPEUTIC TRENDS : THE JOURNAL OF NEW DEVELOPMENTS IN CLINICAL MEDICINE.). [Today's ther. trends]. **VFOAT** Journal of New Developments in Clinical Medicine. Vol. 1, No. 1 (April 1983)-. Periodical. English. qt. $20.00 (one year), $35.00 (two year). Communications Media Education, PO Box 712, Princeton Junction NJ 08550. **Tel** (609)799-2300, (800)221-3899, FAX (609)275-8745. **NLM** W1 TO172M. **Circ:** 3,500.
**Desc:** Reviews of clinical experience with new or existing drug products or medical instrumentation, applicable to clinicians and medical investigators.
**Ind/Abst** Bibliogr. Mission.; EMBASE [Select. Cov.]; Ind. Hyg. Dig. (19??-).

NE
**TOEGEPASTE WETENSCHAP.** **VFOAT** TNO Magazine; Toegepaste Wetenschap TNO. (Jan. 1985)-. Periodical. Dutch. mo. Friese Pers, Boekerij, Postbus 619, Drachten The Netherlands.

JA/0040-8670
**TOHO IGAKKAI ZASSHI.** [Toho Igakkai zasshi]. **Main/Corp** Toho Igakkai. **VFOAT** Journal of the Medical Society of Toho University. Academic Scholarly Publication. Japanese (summaries and/or abstracts in English; table of contents in French). bm. Toho Daigaku Igakkai, (Medical Soc. of Toho University), 21-16, Omori Nishi 5 Chome, Otaku, Tokyoto 143, Japan. **(Subscription address:** Japan Publications Trading Company, Ltd., PO Box 5030, Tokyo International, Tokyo 100-31 Japan.**)** **NLM** W1 TO182. **CODEN** TOIZAG. Documents available from BIOSIS Document Express, CASDDS.
**Ind/Abst** Biol. Abstr.; Chem. Abstr.; EMBASE [Select. Cov.].

JA/0040-8727
**TOHOKU JOURNAL OF EXPERIMENTAL MEDICINE, THE.** [Tohoku j. exp. med.]. **Added/Corp** Tohoku Daigaku. **VFOAT** Tohoku Jikkenigaku. Vol. 1 (1920)-. Academic Scholarly Publication. English (German). mo. $450.00. Tohoku Janaru Kankokai, (Tohoku University Medical Press), 2-1, Seiryomachi, Sendaishi, Miyagiken 980 Japan. **(Subscription address:** Maruzen Company Ltd., PO Box 5050, Import & Export Department, Tokyo 100 31 Japan.**)** **NLM** W1 TO182U. **CODEN** TJEMAO. cum. index. **Pr Rev.** ctrl circ. available on microfilm and microfiche from University Microfilms International (UMI). Documents available from The Genuine Article, BIOSIS Document Express, CASDDS. ***Absorbed in part*** *Tohoku Daigaku. Anatomische Institut Arbeiten.* ***and*** *Mitteilungen Uber Allgemeine Pathologie und pathologische Natomie*.
**Desc:** Official publication of the Tohoku University for all original works in all branches of medical sciences.
**Ind/Abst** Anim. Breed. Abstr.; Biol. Abstr.; Chem. Abstr.; CSA Neuro. Abstr. (?-?); Curr. Biotechnol.; Curr. Contents Life Sci.; EMBASE [Select. Cov.]; Immunol. Abstr.; Index Med.; NAPRALERT; Nutr. Abstr. Rev., Ser. A, Hum. Exp.; Life Sci. Collect.; Protozoolog. Abstr.; Res. Alert [Full Cov.]; Rev. Med. Vet. Entomol.; Rev. Med. Vet. Mycology; Saf. Health Work; Sci. Cit. Index; SCISEARCH; SEA Abstr.; Trop. Dis. Bull.; Virol. AIDS Abstr.; Weed Abstr.

JA/0385-0005
**TOKAI JOURNAL OF EXPERIMENTAL AND CLINICAL MEDICINE.** (THE TOKAI JOURNAL OF EXPERIMENTAL AND CLINICAL MEDICINE.). [Tokai j. exp. clin. med.]. **Added/Corp** Tokai Daigaku. School of Medicine. Tokai Medical Association. Vol. 1 (Jan. 1976)-. Academic Scholarly Publication. English. Six times a year. $84.50. **(Subscription address:** Japan Publications Trading Company, Ltd., PO Box 5030, Tokyo International, Tokyo 100-31 Japan.**)** **NLM** W1 TO1847CJ. **CODEN** TJEMDR. Documents available from BIOSIS Document Express, CASDDS.
**Ind/Abst** Biol. Abstr.; Chem. Abstr.; EMBASE [Select. Cov.]; Index Med.; SEA Abstr.; Trop. Dis. Bull.

SP
**TOKO-GINECOLOGIA PRACTICA.** Spanish. Editorial Garsi SA, Juan Bravo 46, 28006 Madrid, Spain. **Tel** 011 34 1 4021212, telex 98358 GARSI E.
**Ind/Abst** Indice Med. Esp.

JA/0040-8875
**TOKUSHIMA JOURNAL OF EXPERIMENTAL MEDICINE, THE.** [Tokushima j. exp. med.]. **Added/Corp** Tokushima Daigaku. Igakubu. Vol. 1 (March 1954)-. Academic Scholarly Publication. English (German). qt. Tokushima University, School of Medicine, 18-15 Kuramoto-cho 3-chome, Tokushima-shi, Tokushima-ken 770 Japan. **Tel** 0886-31-3111, FAX 0886-33-0771. **ED** Kenji Shima. **NLM** W1 TO186. **CODEN** TJXMAH. Documents available from BIOSIS Document Express, CASDDS.
**Ind/Abst** Biol. Abstr.; Chem. Abstr. (-1987); EMBASE [Select. Cov.]; Index Med.; Nutr. Abstr. Rev., Ser. A, Hum. Exp.; Trop. Dis. Bull.

JA/0040-8905
**TOKYO IKA DAIGAKU ZASSHI.** (ZASSHI - TOKYO IKA DAIGAKU. THE JOURNAL OF TOKYO MEDICAL COLLEGE.). [Tokyo Ika Daigaku zasshi]. **Main/Corp** Tokyo Ika Daigaku. **Added/Corp** Tokyo Ika Daigaku. Igakkai. **VFOAT** Journal of Tokyo Medical College. (1947)-. Periodical. Japanese (summaries and/or abstracts in English). bm. Medical Society of Tokyo Medical College, 1-1 Shinjuku 6-chome, Shinjuku-ku, 160, Tokyo, Japan. **NLM** W1 TO1962. **CODEN** TIDZAH. Documents available from BIOSIS Document Express, CASDDS. ***Continues*** *Tokyo Igaku Senmongakko. Zasshi*.
**Ind/Abst** Biol. Abstr.; Chem. Abstr.; EMBASE [Select. Cov.]; Saf. Health Work.

JA/0375-9172
**TOKYO JIKEIKAI IKA DAIGAKU ZASSHI.** [Tokyo Jikeikai Ika Daigaku zasshi]. **Added/Corp** Tokyo Jikeikai Ika Daigaku. **VFOAT** Tokyo Jikeikai Medical Journal. (1951)-. Periodical. Japanese (summaries and/or abstracts in English). bm. Jikei University School of Medicine, 25-8 Nishishinbashi, 3-chome Minato-ku, 105, Tokyo, Japan. **NLM** W1 TO1976. **CODEN** TJIDAH. Documents available from BIOSIS Document Express, CASDDS. ***Continues*** *Seiikai Zasshi*.
**Ind/Abst** Biol. Abstr.; Chem. Abstr.; EMBASE [Select. Cov.].

JA/0040-9022
**TOKYO JOSHI IKA DAIGAKU ZASSHI.** [Tokyo Joshi Ika Daigaku zasshi]. **Added/Corp** Tokyo Joshi Ika Daigaku Gakkai. **VFOAT** Journal of Tokyo Women's Medical College; Tokyo Joshi Ikadaigaku Zasshi. (1931)-. Periodical. Japanese (summaries and/or abstracts in English). mo. $160.50. Society of Tokyo Women's Medical College, 8-1 Kawadacho, Shinjuku-ku, Tokyo 162 Japan. **Tel** telex 2322317-TWMILIB-J. **(Subscription address:** Japan Publications Trading Company, Ltd., PO Box 5030, Tokyo International, Tokyo 100-31 Japan.**)** **NLM** W1 TO1989. **CODEN** TJIZAF. Documents available from CASDDS.
**Ind/Abst** Chem. Abstr.; EMBASE [Select. Cov.].

FR
**TONUS MEDICAL.** French. bw. 150.00F (one year), 250.00F (two year), 350.00F (three year). Tonus, 29 rue FG Poissonniere, 75009 Paris France. **Tel** 011 33 1 42471317.

US/0885-971X
**TOPICS IN ACUTE CARE AND TRAUMA REHABILITATION.** ***Ceased.*** [Top. acute care trauma rehabil.]. **VFOAT** TACTR. Vol. 1, No. 1, July (1986)-Ceased with Oct. (1988). Periodical. English. qt. Aspen Publishers Inc., 7201 McKinney Circle, Frederick MD 21701. **Tel** (800)234-1660, (301)698-7100, FAX (301)251-5784, telex 5106014543. **DD** 617. **NLM** W1; TO539B. **[CCC]**. available on microfilm and microfiche from University Microfilms International (UMI).
**Ind/Abst** Cumul. Index Nurs. Allied Health Lit.

US/0882-5645
**TOPICS IN PAIN MANAGEMENT.** [Top. pain manage.]. Vol. 1, No. 1 (June 1985)-. Periodical. English. mo. $95.00 (individuals), $120.00 (institution) US; $115.00 (individuals), $140.00 (institutions) other. Williams & Wilkins Company, 428 East Preston Street, Baltimore MD 21202-3993. **Tel** (410)528-4000, (800)638-6423, FAX (410)528-8596, telex 87669. **(Subscription address:** Williams & Wilkins, PO Box 64380, Baltimore MD 21264.**)** **ED** Joel R. Saper. **DD** 616. **NLM** W1; TO54FD. **[CCC]**. Documents available from Quick Copies.
**Desc:** Reviews of journals and provides in-depth information needed to deal with pain disorders.

CN/0836-7655
**TOURBILLON DE LA SQTRP, LE.** **VAT** Tourbillon de la Societe Quebecoise des Therapeutes en Readaptation Physique. Vol. 7, No. 5 (March/April 1987)-. Periodical. French. bm. Free to members. Societe Quebecoise des Therapeutes en Readaptation Physique, 1150 East Boulevard Saint-Joseph, Montreal Quebec H2J 1L5 Canada. **Tel** (514)522-1310. **DD** 615.8/2/09714. **Ad Acc. Circ:** 700 (ctrl). ***Continues*** *Oui-Dire (Montreal, Quebec), 0710-4367*.

FR
**TOUT PREVOIR.** French. bm. 60.00F. Assn Generare Medecine France, 30 Boulvard Pasteur, 75740 Paris Cedex 15 France.

JA
**TOYO IGAKU.** **VFOAT** Oriental Medicine. Japanese. bm (6 issues). $98.00. **(Subscription address:** Kyowa Book Company Inc., 1-38 Kanda Jinbo-Cho Chiyoda Ku, Tokyo 101 Japan)

JA/0385-4469
**TOYO IGAKU.** [Toyo Igaku]. (1973)-. Periodical. Japanese. bm. $310.00. **(Subscription address:** Maruzen Company Ltd., PO Box 5050, Import & Export Department, Tokyo 100 31 Japan.**)** **DD** 610.

FR/1142-2866
**TPH. THERAPEUTIQUE ET PRATIQUE HOSPITALIERES PARIS.** (TPH.). **VFOAT** Therapeutique et Pratique Hospitalieres (Paris). (1989)-. Periodical. French. Five times a year (plus 2 or 3 special issues). 245.00F France; 250.00F other. C & P, 134 Ave. de Villiers, 75017 Paris France. **Tel** 011 33 1 44404050. **UDC** 615.8.

GW
**TRACE ELEMENTS IN ELECTROLYTES.** (19??)-. English. qt. $98.00 (individuals), $125.00 (institutions). Dustri-Verlag, Dr Karl Feistle, Postfach 49, D 82032 Deisenhofen Germany. **Tel** 011 49 89 6138610, FAX 011 49 89 6135412. ***Continues*** *Trace Elements in Medicine, 0174-7371.*

GW/0174-7371
**TRACE ELEMENTS IN MEDICINE.** ***Title Change.*** [Trace elem. med.]. Vol. 1, No. 1 (1st Quarter, 1984)-(1994). Academic Scholarly Publication. English. qt. Dustri-Verlag, Dr Karl Feistle, Postfach 49, D 82032 Deisenhofen Germany. **Tel** 011 49 89 6138610, FAX 011 49 89 6135412. **NLM** W1; TR108D. **CODEN** TEMDE6. **[CCC]. Pr Rev.** Documents available from The Genuine Article, BIOSIS Document Express, CASDDS. ***Continued by*** *Trace Elements in Electrolytes.*
**Ind/Abst** Biol. Abstr. (1986-); Chem. Abstr. (1984-); Curr. Aware. Biol. Sci., CABS; Curr. Contents Clin. Med.; EMBASE; Nutr. Abstr. Rev., Ser. A, Hum. Exp.; Nutr. Res. Newsl.; Res. Alert [Full Cov.]; Sci. Cit. Index; SCISEARCH.

CC/0258-8803
**TRADITIONAL CHINESE MEDICINE DIGEST.** ***Ceased.*** **VFOAT** Chung I Hui Tsui. Vol. 1, No. 1 (1984)-?. Periodical. English. qt. SHK International Services Ltd, 22P 151 Gloucester Road, Hong Kong Hong Kong. **Tel** 5 8325100. **NLM** ZW 1; T763.

II/0025-7109
**TRADITIONAL MEDICAL SYSTEMS.** Vol. 1, No. 1 (1980)-. Periodical. English. qt. $45.00. K K Roy Private Ltd, PO Box 10210, 55 Gariahat Road, Calcutta 700019 India. **Tel** 91 33-474872, 91 33-475069. **ED** K K Roy. Index available. **Bk Rev**. **Ad Acc. Circ:** 3,000. ***Absorbed*** *Medical Checklist.*
**Desc:** Carries specialized articles on traditional medical systems and herbal medicine.

FR
**TRAITE D'ANATOMIE HUMAINE.** French. ir. Scientific & Med Publ France, 100 East 42nd Street, Suite 1002, New York NY 10017. **Tel** (212)983-6278.

US/0010-1087
**TRANSACTIONS & STUDIES OF THE COLLEGE OF PHYSICIANS OF PHILADELPHIA.** [Trans. stud. Coll. Physicians Philadelphia]. **Main/Corp** College of Physicians of Philadelphia. **VFOAT** Transactions and Studies of the College of Physicians of Philadelphia; Medicine & History; Medicine and History. (June 1938)-. Periodical. English. an (Sept.). $15.00. College of Physicians of Philadelphia, 19 South 22nd Street, Philadelphia PA 19103. **Tel** (215)563-3737, FAX (215)561-6477. **ED** Thomas A. Horrocks. **LC** R15; .P5. **NLM** W1 TR2231. **CODEN** TSCPAI. **Circ:** 2,500. Documents available from BIOSIS Document Express, CASDDS. ***Continues*** *Transactions of the College of Physicians of Philadelphia (1875), 0093-2949.*
**Desc:** Current medical topics, medical ethics and medical history.
**Ind/Abst** Biol. Abstr.; Chem. Abstr.; Cumul. Index Nurs. Allied Health Lit.; Energy Res. Abstr. (Aug. 1982-); Index Med.

US/0361-5537
**TRANSACTIONS - NORTH CAROLINA MEDICAL SOCIETY.** **Main/Corp** North Carolina Medical Society. (19??)-. English. an. 222 North Person Street, Raleigh NC 27611. **LC** R15; .N9. **DD** 610/.6/2756. ***Continues*** *Transactions of the Medical Society of the State of North Carolina.*

●US/1064-4709
**TRANSACTIONS OF THE ACADEMY OF INSURANCE MEDICINE: 1992, VOLUME LXXVI.** **See** Insurance.

US/0065-7778
**TRANSACTIONS OF THE AMERICAN CLINICAL AND CLIMATOLOGICAL ASSOCIATION.** [Trans. Am. Clin. Climatol. Assoc.]. **Main/Corp** American Clinical and Climatological Association. Vol. 49 (1933)-. English. an (Aug.). $35.00. American Clinical & Climatological Association, 200 First Street Southwest, Rochester MN 55905. **NLM** W1 TR224L. **CODEN** TACCAN. **Circ:** 500 (ctrl). Documents available from BIOSIS Document Express, CASDDS. ***Continues*** *Transactions of the American Climatological and Clinical Association, 0732-3255.*
**Ind/Abst** Biol. Abstr. (-1982); Chem. Abstr. (1933-1979); EMBASE; Energy Res. Abstr.; Index Med.

US/0066-9458
**TRANSACTIONS OF THE ASSOCIATION OF AMERICAN PHYSICIANS.** [Trans. Assoc. Am. Physicians]. **Main/Corp** Association of American Physicians. Vol. 1 (1886)-. English. an. $52.50 US; $63.00 other. Association of American Physicians, PO Box 3000, Denville NJ 07834. **(Subscription address:** Fulco, 30 Broad Street, Denville NJ 07834.**) LC** R15; .A95. **NLM** W1 TR225J. **CODEN** TAAPAI. cum. index. Documents available from CASDDS.
**Desc:** Contains manuscripts based on presentations at the annual meeting of the Association of American Physicians.
**Ind/Abst** Chem. Abstr.; EMBASE; Energy Res. Abstr. (March 1979-); Index Med.

US/0066-9598
**TRANSACTIONS OF THE ASSOCIATION OF LIFE INSURANCE MEDICAL DIRECTORS OF AMERICA, ANNUAL MEETING.** ***Title Change.*** **See** Insurance.

UK/0076-6011
**TRANSACTIONS OF THE MEDICAL SOCIETY.** (TRANSACTIONS - MEDICAL SOCIETY OF LONDON.). [Trans. Med. Soc.]. **Main/Corp** Medical Society of London. Vol. 13 (1890)-. English. an (July). £15.00. Medical Society of London, 11 Chandos Street, Cavendish Square, London W1M 0EB England. **Tel** 071 580 1043, FAX 071 580 5743. **ED** Mr. P. S. London. **NLM** W1; TR226J. **Circ:** 600. ***Continues*** *Medical Society of London. Proceedings.*
**Desc:** Papers presented to the Society in each year.
**Ind/Abst** Index Med.

US/0887-7963
**TRANSFUSION MEDICINE REVIEWS.** [Transfus. med. rev.]. Vol. 1, No. 1 (April 1987)-. Periodical. English. qt (Jan., Apr., July, Oct.). $74.00 (individual), $104.00 (institution), US; $124.00 (individual), $132.00 (institutions) other. W.B. Saunders Company, A Subsidiary of Harcourt Brace Jovanovich, Inc., The Curtis Center/Suite 300, Independence Square West, Philadelphia PA 19106-3399. **Tel** (215)238-7800 or, 5587, FAX (215)238-7883, telex 173146. **(Subscription address:** W. B. Saunders Company / North America Subscriptions, c/o Periodicals, 6277 Sea Harbour Drive, 4th Floor, Orlando FL 32887.**) ED** Morris A. Blajchman. **DD** 615. **NLM** W1; TR228WB. **CODEN** TMEREU. **[CCC].** Index available. cum. index. **Bk Rev. Ad Acc. Pr Rev. Circ:** 2,000. available on microfilm. Documents available from BIOSIS Document Express.
**Desc:** Provides an informational forum for the publication of review articles on clinical and research topics in transfusion medicine.
**Ind/Abst** Biol. Abstr. (1991-); Index Med. (1987-); Ref. Upd. Deluxe Ed.

UK/0955-3886
**TRANSFUSION SCIENCE.** [Transfus. sci.]. Vol. 10, No. 1 (1989)-. Periodical. English. qt. $336.00 The Americas; £225.00 other. Pergamon Press, An Imprint of Elsevier Science Ltd., The Boulevard, Langford Lane, Kidlington, Oxford OX5 1GB United Kingdom. **Tel** 011 44 865 843000, 011 44 865 843699, FAX 011 44 865 843010. **(Subscription address:** Elsevier Science Ltd. Oxford Fulfillment Centre, PO Box 800, Kidlington, Oxford OX5 1DX United Kingdom.**) ED** G. Rock. **NLM** W1; TR228WH. **CODEN** TRASEE. **[CCC]. Pr Rev.** available on microfilm and microfiche from University Microfilms International (UMI). Documents available from The Genuine Article, BIOSIS Document Express. ***Continues*** *Plasma Therapy & Transfusion Technology, 0278-6222.*
**Desc:** Presents original articles relating to scientific and clinical studies in the areas of immunohematology, transfusion practice and apheresis. Topics covered include the collection and processing of blood, compatibility testing and guidelines for the use of blood products.
**Ind/Abst** Biol. Abstr. (1991-); Curr. Aware. Biol. Sci., CABS; Curr. Contents Clin. Med.; EMBASE; Immunol. Abstr.; Res. Alert [Select. Cov.].

US/0041-1337
**TRANSPLANTATION.** [Transplantation]. **Added/Corp** Transplantation Society. Vol. 1 (Jan. 1963)-. Academic Scholarly Publication. English. Twenty-four times a year. $260.00 (individual), $415.00 (institution) US; $330.00 (individual), $485.00 (institution). Williams & Wilkins Company, 428 East Preston Street, Baltimore MD 21202-3993. **Tel** (410)528-4000, (800)638-6423, FAX (410)528-8596, telex 87669. **(Subscription address:** Williams & Wilkins, PO Box 64380, Baltimore MD 21264.**) ED** Anthony P. Monaco. **LC** QP89; .T72. **DD** 617/.95. **NLM** W1 TR234S. **CODEN** TRPLAU. **[CCC]. Ad Acc. Pr Rev. Circ:** 2,600. available on microfilm. Documents available from The Genuine Article, BIOSIS Document Express, CASDDS, ADONIS, Quick Copies. ***Supersedes*** *Transplantation Bulletin, 0564-1217.*
**Desc:** Original papers and abstracts from every specialty, including immunology, hematology, endocrinology, and embryology.
**Ind/Abst** ADONIS; AgBiotech News Inf.; Anim. Breed. Abstr.; Arts Humanit. Citation Index [Select. Cov.]; Biol. Abstr.; Chem. Abstr.; CSA Neuro. Abstr. (?-?); Curr. Aware. Biol. Sci., CABS; Curr. Contents Life Sci.; EMBASE; Energy Res. Abstr.; Immunol. Abstr.; Index Med.; Nucl. Sci. Abstr.; Pig News Inf.; Protozoolog. Abstr.; Ref. Upd. Basic Ed.; Ref. Upd. Clinical Ed.; Ref. Upd. Deluxe Ed.; Res. Alert [Full Cov.]; Rev. Med. Vet. Mycology; Sci. Cit. Index; SCISEARCH; Soc. Sci. Cit. Index [Select. Cov.]; Vet. Bull.; Virol. AIDS Abstr.

IT
**TRATTATO ENCICLOPEDICO DI ANESTESIA RIANIMAZIONE E TERAPIA INTENSIVA.** Italian. Piccin Editore, Via Altinate 107, 35121 Padua Italy. **Tel** 011 39 49 655566, FAX 011 39 49 8750693.

US
**TRAVEL MEDICINE ADVISOR.** (19??)-. English. ir. $268.00. American Health Consultants, 3525 Piedmont Road, Suite 400, Atlanta GA 30305. **Tel** (800)688-2421, (404)262-7436. **(Subscription address:** American Health Consultants, PO Box 95278, Chicago IL 60694.**)**

UK/0267-3606
**TRAVEL MEDICINE INTERNATIONAL.** [Travel med. int.]. 2, 2 (Summer 1984)-. Periodical. English. Six times a year. £160.00 (institutions), £120.00 (individuals) UK; £162.00 (institutions), £145.00 (individuals) other. Mark Allen Publishing Limited, Robjohns Farm, Vicarage Road, Finchingfield CM7 4LJ England. **Tel** 11 44 371 810433. **NLM** W1; TR296. ***Continues*** *Travel and Traffic Medicine International, 0263-8657.*
**Ind/Abst** Trop. Dis. Bull.

US/0892-774X
**TREE TRIMMER, THE.** **Added/Corp** National Library of Medicine (U.S.) Medical Subject Headings, Tree Structures, 1987. (1987)-. English. an. $57.00. Clintworth Publications, 2018 Griffith Park Boulevard, Suite 325, Los Angeles CA 90039. **Tel** (213)661-3469. **DD** 582.

US
**TRENDS :AMERICAN SOCIETY OF ALLIED HEALTH PROFESSIONS.** **Added/Corp** American Society of Allied Health Professions. (198?)-. Periodical. English. Ten times a year (monthly with July/Aug. & Dec./Jan. issues combined). $55.00 US, Canada, and Mexico; $72.00 other. American Society of Allied Health Professionals, 1730 M Street Northwest, Suite 500, Washington DC 20036. **Tel** (202)293-4848, FAX (202)293-4852. ***Continues*** *Allied Health Trends.*

US
**TRENDS IN BHPR PROGRAM STATISTICS. GRANTS, AWARDS, LOANS.** **See** Medical Science and Technology-Abstracting, Bibliographies and Statistics.

US/1046-4948
**TRIAD (FARMINGTON, MICH.).** (TRIAD : OFFICIAL JOURNAL OF THE MICHIGAN ASSOCIATION OF OSTEOPATHIC PHYSICIANS AND SURGEONS.). [Triad]. **Added/Corp** Michigan Association of Osteopathic Physicians and Surgeons. (1989)-. Periodical. English. bm. $30.00 US; $70.00 other. Michigan Association of Osteopathic Physicians and Surgeons, 33100 Freedom Road, Farmington MI 48024. **Tel** (313)476-2800, FAX (313)476-1834. **ED** Melvin Linden. **DD** 616. **NLM** W1; TR42. **Ad Acc, Adv Mgr:** Mark Scheible, **Tel** (313)476-2800. **Pr Rev. Circ:** 3,000 (ctrl). ***Continues*** *Michigan Osteopathic Journal, 0026-2374.*
**Desc:** Scientific articles and socio-economic features informative to the Michigan Osteopathic Community.

SZ/0041-2597
**TRIANGLE (ENGLISH EDITION).** (TRIANGLE.). [Triangle]. **Added/Corp** Sandoz AG. **VFOAT** Sandoz Journal of Medical Science. Vol. 1 (1952)-. Academic Scholarly Publication. English. tq. **NLM** W1 TR446. **CODEN** TRGLAJ. Documents available from CASDDS.
**Ind/Abst** Chem. Abstr. (-1982); EMBASE; Trop. Dis. Bull.

SP
**TRIBUNA MEDICA.** Spanish. $85.00. Editorial Garsi SA, Juan Bravo 46, 28006 Madrid, Spain. **Tel** 011 34 1 4021212, telex 98358 GARSI E.

●UK/1351-8488
**TUMOR TARGETING.** (1995)-. Periodical. English. Four times a year. $225.00 US and Canada; £130.00 Europe; £145.00 Other. Chapman & Hall, 2-6 Boundary Row, London SE1 8HN England. **Tel** 011 44 71 865 0066, FAX 011 44 71 522 9623, telex 290164 Chapmag. **(Subscription address:** Chapman & Hall, Cheriton House, North Way, Andover, Hampshire, SP10 5BE England.**)**

TI/0041-4131
**TUNISIE MEDICALE, LA.** [Tunisie Med.]. **Added/Corp** Ordre des Medecins de Tunisie. Societe Tunisienne des Sciences Medicales. (1929)-. Academic Scholarly Publication. French. Six times a year. $32.00. Tunisie Medicale, 18 rue de Russie, Tunis Tunisia. **NLM** W1 TU726. ***Continues*** *Revue Tunisienne des Sciences*

*Medicales.*
**Ind/Abst** EMBASE [Select. Cov.]; Helminthol. Abstr. (1991-); Index Med.; SportSearch; Trop. Dis. Bull.

TU
**TURK HIJIYEN VE DENEYSEL BIYOLOJI DERGISI.** **Added/Corp** Refik Saydam Hfzsshha Enstitusu. **VFOAT** Turkish Bulletin of Hygiene and Experimental Biology. (1982)-. Periodical. Turkish (summaries and/or abstracts in English and Turkish). tq. Documents available from CASDDS. ***Continues*** *Turk Hijiyen ve Tecrubi Biyoloji Dergisi (1977).*
**Ind/Abst** Chem. Abstr.; Protozoolog. Abstr.; Rev. Med. Vet. Mycology; Trop. Dis. Bull.

GW/0935-3216
**TW-PADIATRIE.** **VFOAT** Therapiewoche-Padiatrie. (1988)-. German. bm. G Braun Verlag, Postfach 1709, D 76006 Karlsruhe Germany. **Tel** 011 49 721 165392.
**Ind/Abst** EMBASE [Select. Cov.].

JA/0387-0723
**UCHU KOKU KANKYO IGAKU.** (UCHU KOKU KANKYO IGAKU / NIHON UCHU KOKU KANKYO IGAKKAI.). [Uchu Koku Kankyo Igaku]. **Added/Corp** Nihon Uchu Koku Kankyo Igakkai. **VFOAT** Japanese Journal of Aerospace and Environmental Medicine. (1978)-. Academic Scholarly Publication. Japanese. Four times a year. $116.50. Nihon Uchu Koku Kankyo Igakkai, (Japan Soc. of Aerospace & Environmental Medicine), c/o Tokyo Jikeikai Ika Daigaku, Uchu Igaku Kenkyushitsu, 25-8, Nishishinbashi 3 Chome, Minatoku, Tikyoto 105, Japan. **(Subscription address:** Japan Publications Trading Company, Ltd., PO Box 5030, Tokyo International, Tokyo 100-31 Japan.**) CODEN** UKKIDT. Documents available from CASDDS. ***Continues*** *Koku Uchu Igaku Shirigaku.*
**Ind/Abst** Chem. Abstr. (1978-1983); EMBASE; Int. Aerosp. Abstr.; Psychol. Abstr. (1978-).

DK/0041-5782
**UGESKRIFT FOR LAGER.** [Ugeskr. lager]. **Added/Corp** Almindelige Danske Lgeforening. **VFOAT** Ugeskr. Lger. Vol. 1 (1839)-. Academic Scholarly Publication. Danish. wk. kr1320.00. Den Almindelige Danske, Laegeforening Esplanaden 8A, 1263 Copenhagen K Denmark. **Tel** 011 45 31 385500. **NLM** W1 UG13. **CODEN** UGLAAD. available on microfilm. Documents available from BIOSIS Document Express, CASDDS.
**Ind/Abst** Art Archaeol. Tech. Abstr.; Biol. Abstr.; Chem. Abstr. (1839-1984); EMBASE; Energy Res. Abstr.; Helminthol. Abstr. (19??-19??); Index Med.; Ornamental Hort.; Life Sci. Collect.; Protozoolog. Abstr.; Rev. Med. Vet. Mycology; Rice Abstr.; Saf. Health Work; SportSearch.

JA/0042-6857
**UIRUSU.** (UIRUSU. VIRUS.). [Uirusu]. **Added/Corp** Nihon Uirusu Gakkai. **VFOAT** Virus. Vol. 1 (April 1951)-. Periodical. Japanese (summaries and/or abstracts in English). sa. $90.00. Bureau Gravimetrique Intl, 18 Av Ed Belin, 31055 Toulouse Cedex France. **Tel** 61 33 29 80, FAX 61 25 30 98, telex 530776F. **(Subscription address:** Kyowa Book Company Inc., 1 38 Kanda Jinbocho Chiyoda-ku, Tokyo 101 Japan.**) DD** 576. **NLM** W1 UI332U. **CODEN** UIRUAF. Documents available from BIOSIS Document Express, CASDDS.
**Ind/Abst** Biol. Abstr.; Chem. Abstr.; EMBASE; Index Med.; Life Sci. Collect.

KO
**UIRYO POHOM YONBO.** ***Title Change.*** **See** Insurance.

UK/0041-6193
**ULSTER MEDICAL JOURNAL.** [Ulster med. j.]. **Added/Corp** Ulster Medical Society. Vol. 1 (Jan. 1932)-. Academic Scholarly Publication. English. sa. £30.00. Ulster Medical Society, 97 Lisburn Road, Whitla Medical Building, Belfast, BT9 7AF Northern Ireland. **Tel** 44 232 222043, 44 232 221487. **ED** D R Hadden. **NLM** W1 UL72X. Index available. cum. index. **Bk Rev. Ad Acc. Pr Rev. Circ:** 1,000. available on microfilm and microfiche from University Microfilms International (UMI). Documents available from The Genuine Article. ***Supersedes*** *Transactions of the Ulster Medical Society.*
**Desc:** Accepts original clinical and scientific papers, including case reports and historical commentaries, on general and specialist topics in all fields of medicine.
**Ind/Abst** Curr. Contents Clin. Med.; Curr. Contents Life Sci.; EMBASE [Select. Cov.]; Index Med.; Int. Nurs. Index; Life Sci. Collect.; Poult. Abstr.; Res. Alert [Select. Cov.]; SportSearch; Trop. Dis. Bull.

GW/0172-4614
**ULTRASCHALL IN DER MEDIZIN.** (ULTRASCHALL IN DER MEDIZIN : ORGAN DER DEUTSCHEN GESELLSCHAFT FUER ULTRASCHALL IN DER MEDIZIN, [DER] OSTERREICHISCHEN GESELLSCHAFT FUER ULTRASCHALL IN DER MEDIZIN, [DER] SCHWEIZERISCHEN GESELLSCHAFT FUER ULTRASCHALL IN MEDIZIN UND BIOLOGIE.). [Ultraschall Med.]. **Added/Corp** Osterreichische Gesellschaft fuer Ultraschall in der Medizin. Schweizerische Gesellschaft fuer Ultraschall in Medizin und Biologie. Deutsche Gesellschaft fuer Ultraschall in der Medizin. Vol. 1, No. 1, (May 1980)-. Periodical. German (summaries and/or abstracts in English). bm. $165.00. Georg Thieme Verlag Stuttgart, Postfach 301120, D 70451 Stuttgart Germany. **Tel** 011 49 711 89310, FAX 011 49 711 8931298, telex 7 252 275 GTVD. **(Subscription address:** Thieme Medical Publishers Inc., 381 Park Avenue South, New York NY 10016.**) NLM** W1 UL7301. **[CCC]. Pr Rev.** Documents available from The Genuine Article.
**Ind/Abst** Curr. Contents Clin. Med.; EMBASE; Index Med.; Int. Nurs. Index; Protozoolog. Abstr.; Res. Alert [Full Cov.]; Sci. Cit. Index; SCISEARCH.

GW/0930-8040
**ULTRASCHALL IN KLINIK UND PRAXIS.** Vol. 1, No. 1 (Oct. 1986)-. Periodical. German (summaries and/or abstracts in English). qt. DM234.00. Springer-Verlag GmbH & Company KG, Heidelberger Platz 3, D 14197 Berlin Germany. **Tel** 011 49 30 8207223, FAX 011 49 30 8214091, telex 183 319 SPBLN D. **(Subscription address:** Springer Verlag New York Inc. / for North America, 44 Hartz Way, Secaucus NJ 07096.**) ED** H Bartels, R Erbel, M Hansmann, and R Otto. **NLM** W1; UL733. **[CCC].** available on microfilm and microfiche from University Microfilms International (UMI).

US/0098-0382
**ULTRASOUND IN MEDICINE.** **Main/Corp** American Institute of Ultrasound in Medicine. (1975)-. Monographic series. English. an. Price varies per volume. Plenum Press, 233 Spring Street, New York NY 10013-1578. **Tel** (212)620-8000, (800)221-9369, FAX (212)463-0742, (212)807-1047, telex 23/421139. **LC** RC78.7.U4; A5a. **DD** 616.07/54. **NLM** W3 UL849. ***Supersedes*** *Annual Scientific Conference of the American Institute of Ultrasound in Medicine, 0065-8871.*

US/0301-5629
**ULTRASOUND IN MEDICINE & BIOLOGY.** [Ultrasound med. biol.]. **Added/Corp** World Federation for Ultrasound in Medicine and Biology. **VFOAT** Ultrasound in Medicine and Biology. Vol. 1 (Sept. 1973)-. Periodical. English. Nine times a year. $634.00 The Americas; £425.00 other. Pergamon Press, An Imprint of Elsevier Science Ltd., The Boulevard, Langford Lane, Kidlington, Oxford OX5 1GB United Kingdom. **Tel** 011 44 865 843000, 011 44 865 843699, FAX 011 44 865 843010. **(Subscription address:** Elsevier Science Ltd. Oxford Fulfillment Centre, PO Box 800, Kidlington, Oxford OX5 1DX United Kingdom.**) ED** Denis N. White. **LC** RM862.7; .U47. **DD** 616.07/54. **NLM** W1 UL751. **CODEN** USMBA3. **[CCC]. Ad Acc. Pr Rev.** ctrl circ. available on microfilm and microfiche from University Microfilms International (UMI). Documents available from Article Express International, The Genuine Article, BIOSIS Document Express, Ask*IEEE.
**Desc:** Papers in the journal deal with the physics, instrumentation and biological effects of this form of energy on all living systems, from lower organisms to man. Particular emphasis is placed on the practical application of ultrasonic techniques in clinical medicine.
**Ind/Abst** Acoust. Abstr.; AGRICOLA; Biol. Abstr.; Comput. Inf. Syst. Abstr. J. [Full Cov.]; Cumul. Index Nurs. Allied Health Lit.; Curr. Contents Clin. Med.; Ei Page One; EMBASE; Eng. Index Annu.; Environ. Period. Bibliogr. (?-?); Health Saf. Sci. Abstr.; Helminthol. Abstr. (1991-); Index Med.; INSPEC (Sept. 1973-); Int. Aerosp. Abstr.; Int. Build. Serv. Abstr.; Mech. Eng. Abstr.; Life Sci. Collect.; Phys. Med. Biol. (19??-19??); Pollut. Abstr. Indexes; Res. Alert [Full Cov.]; Sci. Cit. Index; SCISEARCH; Solid State Supercond. Abstr.

US/0894-8771
**ULTRASOUND QUARTERLY.** [Ultrasound q.]. Vol. 6 No. 1 (1988)-. Periodical. English. qt. $110.00 (individuals), $145.00 (institutions) US; $138.00 (individuals), $170.00 (institutions) other. Raven Press, 1185 Avenue of the Americas, 37th Floor, New York NY 10036. **Tel** (212)930-9500, (212)930-9604, FAX (212)869-3495, (212)302-8507, telex 640073. **ED** Roger C. Sanders. **LC** RC78.7.U4; U47. **DD** 616. **NLM** W1; UL751M. **CODEN** ULQUEZ. **[CCC].** available on microfilm and microfiche from University Microfilms International (UMI). Documents available from BIOSIS Document Express. ***Continues*** *Ultrasound Annual, 0888-8264.*
**Desc:** Brings together original articles on diagnostic ultrasound, reviews new diagnostic information obtained by recent technological advances, and clarifies well established and controversial subjects.
**Ind/Abst** Biol. Abstr. (1989-); EMBASE.

US/1055-7997
**ULTRASOUND SOURCEBOOK & REFERENCE GUIDE.** [Ultrasound sourceb. ref. guide]. **Added/Corp** Society of Diagnostic Medical Sonographers (U.S.). **VFOAT** Ultrasound Sourcebook and Reference Guide. 1st Ed. (1991)-. English. J.B. Lippincott Company, 227 East Washington Square, Philadelphia PA 19106-3780. **Tel** (215)238-4200 or 4454, FAX (215)238-4227. **LC** RC78.7.U4; U48. **DD** 616.07/543.

●US/1062-080X
**UN-COMMON SENSE (LONG BEACH, CALIF.).** (UN-COMMON SENSE.). [Uncommon sense]. **VFOAT** Uncommon Sense. (1992)-. Periodical. English. mo. $139.00. Practice Performance Publishing, Inc., 2508 East Willow, Suite 302, Long Beach CA 90806. **Tel** (310)595-1728. **DD** 610.

US
**UNDERWATER AND HYPERBARIC MEDICINE.** **Added/Corp** Undersea and Hyperbaric Medical Society. United States. National Oceanic and Atmospheric Administration. United States. Navy. Vol. 2 No. 3 (May/June 1987)-. Periodical. English. Six times a year. $100.00. Undersea and Hyperbaric Medical Society, 10531 Metropolitan Avenue, Kensington MD 20895. **Tel** (301)942-2980. **ED** Leon J. Greenbaum Jr. **LC** RC1015; .U48. **DD** 616.9/8022/05. **NLM** ZWD 650; U56. Index available. cum. index. **Circ:** 200. ***Continues*** *Underwater Medicine, 0886-3474.*
**Desc:** Abstracts of the current literature relating to underwater and hyperbaric medicine.

US/0191-2534
**UNDERWATER MEDICINE AND RELATED SCIENCES.** (UNDERWATER MEDICINE AND RELATED SCIENCES; A GUIDE TO THE LITERATURE.). [Underw. med. relat. sci.]. Vol. 1, (1968/71)-. Monographic series. English. ir. Price varies per volume. Plenum Press, 233 Spring Street, New York NY 10013-1578. **Tel** (212)620-8000, (800)221-9369, FAX (212)463-0742, (212)807-1047, telex 23/421139. **ED** M.F. Werts and C.W. Shilling. **DD** 616. **NLM** ZWD 650 S556AB. **Bk Rev. Ad Acc. Pr Rev.** ctrl circ.

US
**UNIFORMED SERVICES MEDICAL/DENTAL FACILITIES IN THE U.S.A.** ***Title Change.*** **Added/Corp** United States. American Forces Information Services. **VFOAT** Uniformed Services Medical, Dental Facilities in the U.S.A. (19??)-(198?). English. ir. American Forces Information Service, 601 North Fairfax Street/#310, Alexandria VA 22314-2007. **LC** Discard. ***Continued by*** *Uniformed Services Medical/Dental Facilities Worldwide.*
**Desc:** Available only to Department of Defense personnel.

CK/0120-7504
**UNIMETRO : ORGANO DE INFORMACION E INVESTIGACION.** **Added/Corp** Corporacion Universitaria Metropolitana Ciencias de la Salud (Barranquilla, Colombia). Vol. 1, No. 1 (1985)-. Periodical. Spanish. sa. $15.00. Univ Metropolitana Cienc Salud, CRA-42F 75B-169 Apartado Aereo, 50576 Barranquilla Colombia. **NLM** W1; UN139D. Index available. **Ad Acc. Circ:** 2,000.
**Desc:** Information and research for the different programs of the University of Health Sciences.

CN/0041-6959
**UNION MEDICALE DU CANADA.** [Union med. Can.]. Vol. 1 (Jan. 1872)-. Academic Scholarly Publication. French (English; summaries and/or abstracts in French and English). mo. 90.00Can$ US; 75.00Can$ Canada; 105.00Can$ other. Association des Medecins de Langue Francaise du Canada, 8355 Boulevard Saint Laurent, Montreal Quebec H2P 2Z6 Canada. **Tel** (514)388-2228. **ED** Fernand Taras. **NLM** W1 UN208. **CODEN** UMCAAA. **Bk Rev. Ad Acc. Pr Rev. Circ:** 13,000 (ctrl). Documents available from The Genuine Article, CASDDS. ***Absorbed*** *Association des Medecins de Langue Francaise de l'Amerique du Nord. Bulletin, 0700-592X;* ***Absorbed in part*** *Bulletin d'Information a l'Attention des Pharmaciens des Etablissements, 0845-3063.*
**Desc:** Medical journal containing clinical and research papers, review articles, and continuing medical education. Read by general practitioners, certified specialists, interns and residents.
**Ind/Abst** Chem. Abstr.; Curr. Contents Clin. Med.; EMBASE; Helminthol. Abstr. (1991-); Index Med.; Life Sci. Collect.; Point Repere (1983-); Protozoolog. Abstr.; Res. Alert [Select. Cov.]; SportSearch.

US/1069-6725
**UNIVERSAL HEALTHCARE ALMANAC, THE.** [Univers. healthc. alm.]. **Added/Corp** R-C Publications. **VFOAT** Universal Health Care Almanac. 1st Ed. (1984/1985)-. Periodical. English. Four times a year. $140.00 (new subscription), $110.00 (renewal subscription). Silver & Cherner Ltd., PO Box 35425, Phoenix AZ 85069. **Tel** (602)995-9447, FAX (602)996-9458. **DD** 362. Index available.

US/1059-3438
**UNIVERSAL MEDICAL DEVICE NOMENCLATURE SYSTEM.** (UNIVERSAL MEDICAL DEVICE NOMENCLATURE SYSTEM (ENGLISH/RUSSIAN EDITION)). [Univers. med. device nomencl. syst.]. **Added/Corp** ECRI. **VFOAT** Nomenklaturnaia/Kodiruiushchaia Sistema Meditsinskoi Tekhniki; Universalnaia Nomenklaturnaia Sistema i Sistema Kodirovaniia Meditsinskoi Tekhniki na Russkom i Angliiskom iazykakh; Universal Medical Device Nomenclature System in Russian and English; Universal Nomenclature and Coding System for Medical Devices in Russian and English; Nomenklaturnaia/Kodiruiushchaia [i.e. Nomenklaturnaia/Kodiruiushchaia] Sistema Meditsinskoi Tekhniki. Vol. 1 (1991)-. English. ECRI Emergency Care Research Institute, 5200 Butler Pike, Plymouth Meeting PA 19462. **Tel** (215)825-6000, FAX (215)834-1275, telex 510-660-8023. **DD** 610.

US/0736-7406
**UNIVERSITY OF CHICAGO SICKLE CELL CENTER HEMOGLOBIN SYMPOSIA, THE.** **VFOAT** Symposia. Vol. 1-. Academic Scholarly Publication. English. an. Price varies per volume. Elsevier Science Publishers Ltd, Crown House, Linton Road, Barking Essex IG11 8JU England. **Tel** 011 44 81 5947272, FAX 081-594-5942, telex 896950. **DD** 616.1/527/005. **NLM** W3 UN94. Documents available from CASDDS.
**Ind/Abst** Chem. Abstr.

US/0737-1276
**UNIVERSITY OF MINNESOTA CONTINUING MEDICAL EDUCATION.** [Univ. Minn. contin. med. educ.]. Vol. 1 (1982)-. Academic Scholarly Publication. English. ir. Price varies per volume. University of Minnesota Press, 2037 University Avenue Southeast, Minneapolis MN 55414. **Tel** (612)642-2516, (612)624-0005. **LC** UNC. **DD** 610. **NLM** W1 UN944T. **CODEN** UMCEEQ. Documents available from CASDDS.
**Ind/Abst** Chem. Abstr.

US
**UNIVERSITY OF MINNESOTA MEDICAL BULLETIN.** **Added/Corp** University of Minnesota. Hospitals. Vol. 27 (1955)-. Periodical. English. qt. Minnesota Medical Foundation, Box 193 UMHC, Minneapolis MN 55455. **Tel** (612)625-1440. **ED** Jean Murray. **NLM** W1 MI773. **Circ:** 20,000 (ctrl). ***Continues*** *University of Minnesota. Hospitals. Bulletin of the University of Minnesota Hospitals and the Minnesota Medical Foundation.*
**Desc:** Informs readers about the medical school. Features faculty, students, alumni and medical advances.

IT
**UNIVERSO DIABETE : RIVISTA INFORMAZIONE E ISTRUZIONE SUL DIABETE.** (19??)-. Italian. bm (5 issues). L20000. Universo Diabete, C So Vittorio Emanuele 3, 86100 Campobasso Italy. **Tel** 011 39 874 92806.

SA/0258-929X
**UPDATE CAPE TOWN.** [Update Cape Town]. (1986)-. Periodical. English. Twelve times a year. R102.60 South Africa; R140.00 other. George Warman Publications Pty, PO Box 704, Cape Town 8000 South Africa. **Tel** 011 27 21 245320, FAX 011 27 21 261332, telex 5-21849. **UDC** 61. **Ad Acc. Circ:** 8,400 (ctrl).

GW/0933-6788
**UPDATE IN INTENSIVE CARE AND EMERGENCY MEDICINE.** (1986)-. Monographic series. German. ir. Springer Verlag New York Inc., PO Box 19386 Books, Newark NJ 07195. **Tel** (201)348-4033. **UDC** 616.

SW/0300-9734
**UPSALA JOURNAL OF MEDICAL SCIENCES.** [Ups. j. med. sci.]. Vol. 77, No. 1 (1983)-. Academic Scholarly Publication. English. Three times a year. Kr375.00, $62.00. Scandinavian University Press, PO Box 2959 Toeyen, N 0608 Oslo 6 Norway. **Tel** 011 47 2 2575400, FAX 011 47 2 2575353, telex 71896 UROR N. **(Subscription address:** Scandinavian University Press, 200 Meacham Ave., Elmont NY 11003.**) UDC** 61. **NLM** W1 UP67K. **CODEN** UJMSAP. **Pr Rev.** Documents available from The Genuine Article, BIOSIS Document Express, CASDDS. ***Continues*** *Acta Societas Medicorum Upsaliensis.*
**Desc:** Publishes clinical and experimental original works in the medical field.
**Ind/Abst** Biol. Abstr.; Chem. Abstr.; Curr. Aware. Biol. Sci., CABS; Curr. Contents Clin. Med.; EMBASE; Helminthol. Abstr. (1991-); Index Med.; Nutr. Res. Newsl.; Life Sci. Collect.; Ref. Upd. Deluxe Ed.; Res. Alert [Full Cov.]; Sci. Cit. Index; SCISEARCH.

SW/0300-9726
**UPSALA JOURNAL OF MEDICAL SCIENCES. SUPPLEMENT.** [Ups. j. med. sci., Suppl.]. **Added/Corp** Upsala Medical Society. (1971)-. English. ir. Kr375.00, $62.00 (Comes with Upsala Journal of Medical Sciences). Scandinavian University Press, PO Box 2959 Toeyen, N 0608 Oslo 6 Norway. **Tel** 011 47 2 2575400, FAX 011 47 2 2575353, telex 71896 UROR N. **(Subscription address:** Scandinavian University Press, 200 Meacham Ave., Elmont NY 11003.**) NLM** W1 UP67L. **CODEN** UJMSBQ. Documents available from BIOSIS Document Express, CASDDS. ***Continues*** *Acta Societatis Medicorum Upsaliensis. Supplement.*
**Ind/Abst** Biol. Abstr.; Chem. Abstr. (1972-1982); Curr. Aware. Biol. Sci., CABS; Index Med.

FR/0923-2524
**URGENCES MEDICALES (PARIS).** (URGENCES MEDICALES : REVUE EUROPEENNE D'OXYOLOGIE.). [Urgences med.]. **Added/Corp** Societe Francaise de Medecine de Catastrophe. Vol. 8, No. 1 (1989)-. Academic Scholarly Publication. French (English). bm (1 volume). 975.00F France; 1090.00F other. Editions Scientifique Elsevier, 141 rue de Javel, 75747 Paris Cedex 15 France. **Tel** 011 33 1 47 07 11 22, FAX 011 33 1 43 36 80 93. **(Subscription address:** Editions Scientifiques Elsevier / for North America, PO Box 7247-7576, Philadelphia PA 19170-7576.**) NLM** W1; UR245. **CODEN** URGME3. **[CCC].** available on microfilm and microfiche from University Microfilms International (UMI). Documents available from BIOSIS Document Express. ***Continues*** *Convergences Medicales, 0750-0785.*
**Ind/Abst** Biol. Abstr.; EMBASE.

SP
**URGENCIAS.** Spanish. Urgencias, Meson de Paredes 73, 28012 Madrid Spain.

US
**USAF MEDICAL SERVICE DIGEST / UNITED STATES AIR FORCE.** **Added/Corp** United States. Air Force Medical Service. **VFOAT** Medical Service Digest. **VAT** United States Air Force Medical Service Digest. Vol. 35, No. 2 (Summer 1984)-. Government Publication. English. qt. $5.00; $1.75 (single issues) US; $6.25; $2.19 (single issues) other. Superintendent of Documents, US Government Printing Office, Washington DC 20402. **Tel** (202)275-3328, FAX (202)786-2377. ***Continues*** *Medical Service Digest, 0041-7491.*

IT
**USMED : ULTRASUONI IN MEDICINA.** Novappia Editrice, Via Appia Nuova 206, 00183 Rome Italy.

UK/0264-410X
**VACCINE.** [Vaccine]. Vol. 1, No. 1 (Dec. 1983)-. Academic Scholarly Publication. English. Sixteen times a year. $857.00 The Americas; £575.00 other. Butterworth Heinemann Publishers, Linacre House, Jordan Hill, Oxford OX2 8DP England. **Tel** 011 44 865 310366. **(Subscription address:** Elsevier Science Ltd. Oxford Fulfillment Centre, PO Box 800, Kidlington, Oxford OX5 1DX United Kingdom.**) ED** R. E. Spier. **NLM** W1; VA239. **CODEN** VACCDE. **[CCC].** Index available. **Bk Rev. Ad Acc. Pr Rev.** available on microfilm and microfiche from University Microfilms International (UMI). Documents available from The Genuine Article, CASDDS, ADONIS.
**Desc:** A journal for all those involved with the research and development, production and use of both human and veterinary vaccines. It publishes reviews, original research papers, short communications, editorials, comment pieces, book reviews, patent reports, meeting reports and a calendar of forthcoming meetings.
**Ind/Abst** ADONIS; AgBiotech News Inf.; AGRICOLA; Chem. Abstr.; Curr. Aware. Biol. Sci., CABS; Curr. Biotechnol.; Curr. Contents, Agric. Biol. Environ. Sci.; Curr. Contents Life Sci.; Dairy Sci. Abstr.; EMBASE; Immunol. Abstr.; Index Med. (Vol. 1, No. 1, 1983-); Index Vet.; Microbiol. Abstr. Sect. B; Microbiol. Abstr. Sect. A; Life Sci. Collect.; PESTDOC; Pig News Inf.; Poult. Abstr.; Protozoolog. Abstr.; Ref. Upd. Deluxe Ed.; Res. Alert [Full Cov.]; Sci. Cit. Index; SCISEARCH; Small Anim. Abstr. Bibliogr.; Soc. Sci. Cit. Index [Select. Cov.]; Vet. Bull.; Trop. Dis. Bull.; Virol. AIDS Abstr.

US/0899-4056
**VACCINES (COLD SPRING HARBOR, N.Y.).** (VACCINES.). [Vaccines]. **Added/Corp** Cold Spring Harbor Laboratory. (1985)-. English. an. $100.00. Cold Spring Harbor Laboratory, 10 Skyline Drive, Plainview NY 11803. **Tel** (516)349-1930, (800)843-4388, FAX (516)349-1946. **LC** QR189; .V26. **DD** 615/.372. **CODEN** VMAVEA.

US/0740-901X
**VANDERBILT MEDICAL ALUMNI DIRECTORY.** **See** College and School Publications-Alumni.

US/1067-5051
**VASCULAR FORUM.** ***Ceased.*** [Vasc. forum]. Vol. 1, No. 1 (Mar. 1993)-Vol. 2 No. 6 (19??). Periodical. English. bm (6 issues). Futura Publishing Company Inc., 135 Bedford Road, PO Box 418, Armonk NY 10504-0418. **Tel** (914)273-1014, (800)877-8761, FAX (914)273-1015, (914)273-1016. **DD** 617.

US/8756-3401
**VASCULAR VIEWS.** ***Ceased.*** [Vasc. views]. Periodical. English. mo. Vascular Training Center, PO Box 35598, Tucson AZ 85740. **Tel** (602)293-1156. **ED** Ann C Belanger and Bette G Newton. **DD** 616. Index available. cum. index.
**Desc:** Newsletter designed for those interested in vascular disease and/or noninvasive vascular technology. Topics include anatomy/physiology, pathophysiology, diagnosis, therapy and others.

GW/0930-3677
**VERBANDTECHNIK.** Vol. 1, No. 1 (Sept. 1985)-. Periodical. German (summaries and/or abstracts in English). bm. Verlag Bernd Von Hallern, Dorpstroot 14, D 21709 Burweg Germany. **Tel** 011 49 4144 5655. **NLM** W1; VE216.

BE/0302-6469
**VERHANDELINGEN - KONINKLIJKE ACADEMIE VOOR GENEESKUNDE VAN BELGIE.** [Verh., K. Acad. Geneeskd. Belg.]. **Main/Corp** Koninklijke Academie voor Geneeskunde van Belgie. (1973)-. Academic Scholarly Publication. Dutch (English and French). Six times a year. 2750F. Verhandelingen Koninklijke Academie voor Geneeskunde van Belgie, Hortogelijkestr 1, Brussels 1 Belgium. **Tel** 011 32 2 5117897, 5115210. **NLM** W1 VE475KA. **CODEN** VKGBAU. **Circ:** 400 (ctrl). Documents available from CASDDS. ***Continues*** *Verhandelingen (Koninklijke Vlaamse Academie voor Geneeskunde van Belgie).*
**Ind/Abst** Chem. Abstr.; Index Med.; Trop. Dis. Bull.

GW/0724-6765
**VERHANDLUNGSBERICHT DER DEUTSCHEN GESELLSCHAFT FUR LASERMEDIZIN E.V. / ... TAGUNG.** [Verhandlungsber. Dtsch. Ges. Lasermed. e.V.]. **Main/Conf** Deutsche Gesellschaft fur Lasermedizin. **Main/Corp** Deutsche Gesellschaft fur Lasermedizin. Tagung. 1. (3.-6. Nov. 1982)-. German. **NLM** W1; DE7903V.

SZ
**VEROFFENTLICHUNGEN.** **Main/Corp** Schweizerische Gesellschaft fur Geschichte der Medizin und der Naturwissenschaften. Vol. 1 (1922)-. Monographic series. German. ir. Price varies per volume. Sauerlaender AG, Laurenzenvorstadt 89, CH 5001 Aarau Switzerland. **Tel** 011 41 64 268626.

GW/0933-4548
**VERSICHERUNGSMEDIZIN.** [Versicherungsmedizin]. **Added/Corp** Verband der Lebensversicherungsunternehmen (Germany) Verband der Privaten Krankenversicherung. **VFOAT** Versicherungs Medizin. Vol. 40, No. 1 (Jan. 1988)-. Periodical. German (summaries and/or abstracts in English). bm. DM22.43. Verlag Versicherungswirtschaft, Klosestrasse 20 24, D-76137 Karlsruhe Germany. **Tel** 011 49 721 35090, FAX 011 49 721 31833. **NLM** W1; VE791K. **CODEN** VERSEU. Documents available from BIOSIS Document Express. ***Continues*** *Lebensversicherungs Medizin.*
**Ind/Abst** Biol. Abstr.; EMBASE [Select. Cov.]; Index Med. Jan. 1988-.

●XR
**VESTNIK AKADEMIE VED CESKE REPUBLIKY.** **Added/Corp** Akademie Ved Ceske Republiky. **VFOAT** Vestnik AVCR. (1993)-. Periodical. Czech (table of contents in English). sa. DM184.80 Germany; DM219.80 other. Academia, Publishing House of the Czechoslovak Academy of Sciences, Czech AC SCI, Vodickova 40, PO Box 896, 112 29 Prague 1, Czech Republic. **Tel** 011 42 2 245117. **(Subscription address:** Kubon & Sagner, ABT Zeitschriftenimport, D 80328 Munich Germany.**) LC** AS142; .C41. ***Continues*** *Vestnik Ceskoslovenske Akademie Ved, 0009-0492.*

RU/0002-3027
**VESTNIK AKADEMII MEDITSINSKIKH NAUK SSSR.** ***Title Change.*** [Vestn. Akad. med. nauk SSSR]. **Added/Corp** Akademiia Meditsinskikh nauk SSSR. (1946)-(1992). Academic Scholarly Publication. Russian. **(Subscription address:** Victor Kamkin, 4956 Boiling Brook Parkway, Rockville MD 20852.**) NLM** W1; VE816. **CODEN** VAMNAQ. **[CCC]. Pr Rev.** Documents available from BIOSIS Document Express, CASDDS. ***Continued by*** *Vestnik Rossiiskoi Akademii Meditsinskih nauk.*
**Ind/Abst** Biol. Abstr.; Chem. Abstr. (-1991); Index Med.; Int. Aerosp. Abstr.; Int. Nurs. Index; Nutr. Abstr. Rev., Ser. A, Hum. Exp.; Life Sci. Collect.; Rev. Med. Vet. Entomol.; Sci. Cit. Index (19??-19??); SCISEARCH; SportSearch; Sug. Indus. Abstr.

XR/0009-0492
**VESTNIK CESKOSLOVENSKE AKADEMIE VED.** ***Title Change.*** **Added/Corp** Ceskoslovenska Akademie Ved. **VFOAT** Vestnik CSAV. (1953)-(19??). Academic Scholarly Publication. Czech (summaries and/or abstracts in English and Russian; table of contents in English and Russian). bm. Academia, Publishing House of the Czechoslovak Academy of Sciences, Czech AC SCI, Vodickova 40, PO Box 896, 112 29 Prague 1, Czech Republic. **Tel** 011 42 2 245117. **ED** Josef Riman. **LC** AS142; .C41. **NLM** W1 CE87K. Index available. **Circ:** 1,800. Documents available from BIOSIS Document Express, CASDDS. ***Continues*** *Vestnik Ceske Akademie Ved a Umeni.* ***Continued by*** *Vestnik Akademie Ved Ceske Republiky.*
**Desc:** Reports on all activities of the Czechoslovak Academy of Sciences and also publishes articles on the current state and prospects in the individual sciences.
**Ind/Abst** Biol. Abstr. (?-?); Chem. Abstr. (?-?).

●RU
**VESTNIK ROSSIISKOI AKADEMII MEDITSINSKIH NAUK / ROSSIISKAIA AKADEMIIA MEDITSINSKIKH NAUK.** **Added/Corp** Rossiiskaia Akademiia Meditsinskikh Nauk. (1992)-. Periodical. Russian (summaries and/or abstracts in English; table of contents in English). Six times a year. $189.95. Izdatelstvo Meditsina / Russian Academy of Medical Sciences, Ulitsa Solyanka 14, 109801 Moscow Russia. **Tel** 011 95 297-05-04. **(Subscription address:** East View Publications Inc., 3020 Harbor Lane North, Suite 110, Minneapolis MN 55447.**) NLM** W1; VE844N. **CODEN** VAMEE3. Documents available from The Genuine Article. ***Continues*** *Vestnik Akademii*

*Meditsinskikh Nauk SSSR, 0002-3027.*
**Ind/Abst** Index Med. (1992-); Res. Alert [Full Cov.]; Sci. Cit. Index; Soc. Sci. Cit. Index [Select. Cov.].

RM/0042-5036
**VIATA MEDICALA.** (VIATA MEDICALA / EDITATA DE UNIUNEA SOCIETATILOR DE STIINTE MEDICALE DIN REPUBLICA SOCIALISTA ROMANIA.). [Viata med.]. **Added/Corp** Uniunea Societatilor de Stiinte Medicale. Vol. 22 (Aug. 1974)-. Periodical. Romanian (table of contents in English and Russian). mo. DM210.00. **(Subscription address:** Kubon & Sagner, ABT Zeitschriftenimport, D 80328 Munich Germany.**)** **NLM** W1 VI169C. ***Continues in part** Viata Medicala, 0042-5036.*
**Ind/Abst** Int. Nurs. Index; Saf. Health Work.

AT/0813-6394
**VICTORIAN BRANCH NEWS.** [Vic. Branch news]. **Added/Corp** Australian Medical Association. Victorian Branch. **VFOAT** A.M.A. Victorian Branch News. (1982)-. Periodical. English. mo. 20.00Aus$. Australian Medical Association / Victorian Branch, 293 Royal Parade, Parkville Victoria 3052 Australia. **Tel** FAX 011 61 3 3479871. **DD** 610.5. **Ad Acc.** ***Continues** Monthly Paper - Australian Medical Association, Victorian Branch and the Medical Society of Victoria, 0572-1253.*

FR/0042-5583
**VIE MEDICALE, LA.** ***Ceased.*** [Vie med.]. Vol. 50 (1969)-?. Periodical. French. mo. Les Editions de la Vie Medicale, 133 Bis rue de l'Universite, 75007 Paris France. **Tel** 45.55.95.52. ***Formed by the union of** Vie Medicale. Actualite Professionnelle, 0505-4958; Vie Medicale. Enquete, 0991-9120; Vie Medicale. Specialite, 0506-8983 **and** Vie Medicale. Therapeutique, 0991-9139.*

CN/1182-3143
**VIES A VIH.** (VIES A VIH : BULLETIN FRANCOPHONE DU COMITE SIDA AIDE MONTREAL.). [Vies Vih]. **Added/Corp** Comite SIDA Aide Montreal. Vol. 5, No 1 (Jan. 1990)-. Bulletin. French. mo. Limited free distribution. Comite SIDA Aide Montreal, 3600 Avenue de l'Hotel-de-Ville, Montreal, Quebec H2X 3M2 Canada. **DD** 362.1/969792/00971428. ***Continues** Virulent (Montreal, Quebec)., 1182-3151.*

US/0190-3535
**VIEWPOINT (NEW YORK. 1968). See** Insurance.

US/0279-6023
**VIRGINIA LIFELINE.** (VIRGINIA LIFELINE : OFFICIAL PUBLICATION OF VIRGINIA ASSOCIATION OF VOLUNTEER RESCUE SQUADS.). **Added/Corp** Virginia Association of Volunteer Rescue Squads. (19??)-. Periodical. English. mo. $7.50. Virginia Association of Volunteer Rescue Squads, 2015 Staples Mill Road/Suite 429, Richmond VA 23230. **Tel** (804)355-5757. ***Continues** First Aid Bulletin, 0273-8309.*

US
**VIRGINIA MASON CLINIC BULLETIN.** Vol. 40, No. 4 (Winter 1986/87)-. Academic Scholarly Publication. English. qt. Virginia Mason Clinic, 1100 Ninth Avenue, PO Box 900, Seattle WA 98111. **NLM** W1; VI779G. ***Continues** Bulletin of the Mason Clinic, 0025-4657.*
**Ind/Abst** EMBASE.

US/1052-4231
**VIRGINIA MEDICAL QUARTERLY : VMQ.** [Va. med. q.]. **Added/Corp** Medical Society of Virginia. **VFOAT** VMQ. Vol. 117, No. 7 (Summer 1990)-. Academic Scholarly Publication. English. qt (Jan., Apr., July, Oct.). $24.00 US; $30.00 other. Medical Society of Virginia, 4205 Dover Road, Richmond VA 23221. **Tel** (804)353-2721, FAX (804)355-6189. **ED** Edwin L. Kendig, Jr. MD. **DD** 610. **NLM** W1; VI81I. Index available (with Oct. issue). **Bk Rev**, (Qty: 6-10). **Ad Acc, Adv Mgr:** Anne Hill, **Tel** (804)353-2721. **Pr Rev. Circ:** 7,000. available on magnetic tape, an online database, and CD-ROM; available on microfilm and microfiche from University Microfilms International (UMI). ***Continues** Virginia Medical, 0146-3616.*
**Desc:** Medical journal of the Medical Society of Virginia. Contains medical articles plus features and news of interest to physicians.
**Ind/Abst** EMBASE; Energy Res. Abstr.; Health Plan. Adminis.; Index Med. (1990-).

US
**VITAL SIGNS.** (19??)-. Periodical. English. Four times a year. $25.00. MD Resources Inc., 9360 Sunset Drive #139, Miami FL 33183. **Tel** (305)271-9213. **ED** Wendy Perlman, Carol Maxfield, and Richard Steinkohl.
**Desc:** Newsletter published for clients, physicians and affiliated companies of MD Resources Inc.

RU/0026-9050
**VOENNO-MEDICINSKIJ ZURNAL.** (VOENNO-MEDITSINSKII ZHURNAL.). [Voenno-med. z.]. (1944)-. Periodical. Russian. mo. $99.95. Voenizdat, Bolshoi Kiselnii per., 14 Moscow Russia. **(Subscription address:** East View Publications Inc., 3020 Harbor Lane North, Suite 110, Minneapolis MN 55447.**)** **NLM** W1 VO22. **CODEN** VMEZA4. available on microfilm from University Microfilms International (UMI). Documents available from CASDDS.
**Ind/Abst** Chem. Abstr.; Index Med.; Int. Aerosp. Abstr.; Int. Nurs. Index.

XR/0372-7025
**VOJENSKE ZDRAVOTNICKE LISTY.** [Vojen. zdrav. listy]. (1925)-. Periodical. Multiple languages. Magnet-Press s.p., Vlasislavova 26 116 66, Prague Czech Republic. **Tel** (2)260651-9. **UDC** 61+355.
**Ind/Abst** EMBASE [Select. Cov.].

YU/0042-8450
**VOJNOSANITETSKI PREGLED.** (VOJNOSANITETSKI PREGLED; CASOPIS LEKARA I FARMACEUTA JUGOSLOVENSKE NARODNE ARMYE.). [Vojnosanit. pregl.]. **VFOAT** Military-Medical and Pharmaceutical Review; Revue de Medecine et Pharmacie Militaires; Zhurnal Voennoi Meditsiny i Farmatsii. (1944)-. Academic Scholarly Publication. Serbo-Croatian (Cyrillic) (summaries and/or abstracts in English, French and Russian). bm. $78.00. Saveznog Sekretarijat Narodnu, Odbranu S Uprave Crontravsk 17, 11000 Belgrade Yugoslavia. **(Subscription address:** Jugoslovenska Knjiga, PO Box 36, YU 11001 Belgrade Yugoslovia.**)** **NLM** W1 VO455E.
**Ind/Abst** EMBASE [Select. Cov.]; Index Med.; Int. Pharm. Abstr. (199?-); Saf. Health Work.

US/0193-2179
**VOLUNTARY EFFORT QUARTERLY.** V. 1-Feb. 1979-. Periodical. English. qt. The Voluntary Effort, 840 North Lake Shore Drive, Chicago IL 60611. **NLM** W1 VO594F.

RU/0137-0618
**VOPROSY KLINICESKOJ MEDICINY (DUSANBE).** (VOPROSY KLINICHESKOI MEDITSINY.). **Added/Corp** Respublikanskaia Klinicheskaia Bolnitsa No. 3 (Tajik S.S.R.). Vol. 1 (1970)-. Russian. **NLM** W1 VO634L.

RU/0042-8787
**VOPROSY KURORTOLOGII, FIZIOTERAPII I LECEBNOJ FIZICESKOJ KULTURY.** (VOPROSY KURORTOLOGII, FIZIOTERAPII I LECHEBNOI FIZICHESKOI KULTURY.). [Vopr. kurortol., fizioter. lec. fiz. kult.]. **Added/Corp** Soviet Union. Ministerstvo Zdravookhraneniia. (1955)-. Academic Scholarly Publication. Russian. Six times a year. $69.95. **(Subscription address:** East View Publications Inc., 3020 Harbor Lane North, Suite 110, Minneapolis MN 55447.**)** **NLM** W1 VO636. **CODEN** VKFLAL. Documents available from CASDDS. ***Continues** Voprosy Kurortologii.*
**Ind/Abst** Chem. Abstr.; Index Med.; Int. Aerosp. Abstr.

JA/0289-730X
**WAKAN IYAKU GAKKAISHI.** [Wakan Iyaku Gakkaishi]. **VFOAT** Journal of Medical and Pharmaceutical Society for Wakan-Yaku. (1984)-. Academic Scholarly Publication. English (Japanese). Three times a year. $172.00. Wakan Iyaku Gakkai, (Medical & Pharmaceutical Soc. for Wakan-Yaku), Toyama Ika Yakka Daigaku, Wakan Yaku Kenkyujo, 2630, Sugitani, Toyamashi, Toyamaken 930-01 Japan. **(Subscription address:** Japan Publications Trading Company, Ltd., PO Box 5030, Tokyo International, Tokyo 100-31 Japan.**)** **DD** 615. Documents available from CASDDS. ***Continues** Wakan-Yaku Shinpojumu, 0388-7413.*
**Ind/Abst** Chem. Abstr.

JA/0043-0013
**WAKAYAMA IGAKU.** [Wakayama igaku]. **Added/Corp** Wakayama Igakkai. **VFOAT** Journal of the Wakayama Medical Society. (1950)-. Academic Scholarly Publication. Japanese (summaries and/or abstracts in English). qt. The Wakayama Medical Society, 9 Kyuban-cho, Wakayama-shi 640 Japan. **NLM** W1 WA215. **CODEN** WKMIAO. Documents available from CASDDS.
**Ind/Abst** Chem. Abstr. (19??-); EMBASE (19??-) [Select. Cov.].

JA/0511-084X
**WAKAYAMA MEDICAL REPORTS.** [Wakayama med. rep.]. **Added/Corp** Wakayama Kenritsu Ika Daigaku. Vol. 1 (May 1953)-. Academic Scholarly Publication. English. ir. Free. Wakayama Medical College Library, Wakayama Japan. **NLM** W1 WA231. **CODEN** WKMRAH. Documents available from BIOSIS Document Express, CASDDS.
**Ind/Abst** Biol. Abstr.; Chem. Abstr.; EMBASE; SEA Abstr.; Trop. Dis. Bull.

TH/0125-1643
**WARASAN KROMKANPAET LAE ANAMAI.** (JOURNAL OF THE DEPARTMENT OF MEDICAL AND HEALTH SERVICES.). **Added/Corp** Thailand. Dept. of Medical and Health Services. Vol. 1, No. 3 (May 1973)-. Periodical. Thai (English; summaries and/or abstracts in English and Thai). **NLM** W1 JO918X. ***Continues** Warasan Kromkanpaet Lae Anamai, 0125-1643.*

●US/1069-4218
**WARNING LETTER BULLETIN. See** Pharmacy and Pharmacology.

GW/0043-2156
**WEHRMEDIZINISCHE MONATSSCHRIFT.** [Wehrmed. Monatsschr.]. **Added/Corp** Deutsche Gesellschaft fur Wehrmedizin und Wehrpharmazie (Germany) Germany (West). Bundesministerium der Verteidigung. Germany (West). Sanitats- und Gesundheitswesens der Bundeswehr. (19??)-. Academic Scholarly Publication. Multiple languages. mo. DM96.00, $69.48 Germany; DM104.40, $75.56 other. Umschau Verlag, Postfach 110262, D-60037 Frankfurt Germany. **Tel** 011 49 69 2600692, FAX 011 49 69 2600223, telex 411964. **CODEN** WEMOBZ. **[CCC]**. Index available (Free). **Bk Rev. Ad Acc. Circ:** 5,300. Documents available from CASDDS.
**Ind/Abst** Chem. Abstr. (19??-); Energy Res. Abstr. (Aug. 1976-); SportSearch (19??-).

US
**WESLEY W. SPINK LECTURES ON COMPARATIVE MEDICINE.** English. ir. University of Minnesota Press, 2037 University Avenue Southeast, Minneapolis MN 55414. **Tel** (612)642-2516, (612)624-0005.

NR/0189-160X
**WEST AFRICAN JOURNAL OF MEDICINE.** [West Afr. j. med.]. **Added/Corp** West African College of Physicians. West African College of Surgeons. (1981)-. Periodical. English (French; summaries and/or abstracts in French). qt. West African College of Physicians & Surgeons, PMB 2023, 6 Taylor Drive, Yaba Lagos Nigeria. **Tel** 800140 4. **NLM** W1 WE329D. **Bk Rev. Ad Acc. Pr Rev. Circ:** 1,500.
**Desc:** Devoted to the publication of scientific information derived from research and clinical observations in all fields of health.
**Ind/Abst** Health Plan. Adminis. (19??-).

JM/0043-3144
**WEST INDIAN MEDICAL JOURNAL, THE.** [West Indian med. j.]. **Added/Corp** University of the West Indies (Mona, Jamaica). Vol. 1 (1951)-. Academic Scholarly Publication. English. qt. $60.00. West Indian Medical Journal, Faculty of Medical Sciences, University of West Indies, Mona Kingston 7 Jamaica. **Tel** (809)927-1214, FAX (809)927-2556. **ED** Vasil Persaud. **NLM** W1 WE389. **CODEN** WIMJAD. Index available. **Bk Rev. Ad Acc. Pr Rev. Circ:** 2,000. available on microfilm from University Microfilms International (UMI); available on CD-ROM. Documents available from The Genuine Article, CASDDS. ***Supersedes** Jamaica Medical Review.*
**Desc:** Medical research in clinical and community medicine in the English speaking Caribbean.
**Ind/Abst** Chem. Abstr.; Curr. Contents Clin. Med.; EMBASE [Select. Cov.]; Helminthol. Abstr. (19??-19??); Hospit. Health Admin. Index; Index Med.; Index Vet.; Int. Nurs. Index; Microbiol. Abstr. Sect. B (19??-19??); NAPRALERT; Life Sci. Collect.; Protozoolog. Abstr.; Res. Alert [Select. Cov.]; Rev. Med. Vet. Mycology; Trop. Dis. Bull.; Virol. AIDS Abstr.; Weed Abstr.

UK
**WEST OF ENGLAND MEDICAL JOURNAL.** Vol. 105 (March 1990)-. Periodical. English. qt. £25.00. Clinical Press, Redland Green Farm Redland, Bristol BS6 7HF England. **Tel** 011 44 272 237709, 011 44 272 420256. **ED** M. G. Wilson. **NLM** W1; WE403. **Bk Rev. Ad Acc. Circ:** 9,000. ***Continues** Bristol Medico-Chirurgical Journal (1963).*
**Desc:** Scientific articles on medicine and surgery and comments on local medical affairs (West of England).
**Ind/Abst** Index Med. (1990-).

US/0043-3284
**WEST VIRGINIA MEDICAL JOURNAL.** [West Va. med. j.]. **Added/Corp** West Virginia State Medical Association. Vol.1 (Aug. 1906)-. Academic Scholarly Publication. English. mo. $36.00 US; $60.00 other. West Virginia Medical Journal, 4307 MacCorkle Avenue SE, PO Box 4106, Charleston WV 25364. **Tel** (304)925-0342, FAX (304)925-0345. **ED** Stephen D Ward MD. **NLM** W1 WE456. Index available. **Ad Acc, Adv Mgr:** Michelle Young. **Pr Rev. Circ:** 2,627 (ctrl). available on microfilm and microfiche from University Microfilms International (UMI). ***Supersedes** West Virginia State Medical Association. Transactions.*
**Desc:** Scientific, socio-economic news of medicine in West Virginia. Official journal of West Virginia State Medical Association.
**Ind/Abst** EMBASE; Energy Res. Abstr. (1977-); Index Med.; Int. Nurs. Index; Life Sci. Collect.; SportSearch.

US
**WESTERN BIOETHICS NETWORK. See** Ethics.

US/0093-0415
**WESTERN JOURNAL OF MEDICINE, THE.** [West. j. med.]. **Added/Corp** California Medical Association. Vol. 120 (Jan. 1974)-. Academic Scholarly Publication. English. mo. $40.00 (one year), $70.00 (two year) US & Canada; $70.00 (one year) $120.00 (two

year) other. California Medical Association, PO Box 7690, San Francisco CA 94120-5179. **Tel** (415)541-0900, FAX (415)882-5116. **(Subscription address:** Western Journal of Medicine, PO Box 7602, c/o Nila Nichols, Circulation Department, San Francisco CA 94120-7602.**) ED** Linda Hawes Clever. **LC** R15; .C235. **DD** 610/.5. **NLM** W1 WE632J. **CODEN** WJMDA2. **[CCC].** Index available. **Ad Acc, Adv Mgr:** John Cook, **Tel** (415)882-5178. **Pr Rev. Circ:** 50,000. available on microfilm from University Microfilms International (UMI); available on an online database (file 149/Full-Text) from DIALOG. Documents available from The Genuine Article, CASDDS. ***Continues*** *California Medicine, 0008-1264;* ***Absorbed*** *Arizona Medicine, 0004-1556.*
**Desc:** Contains articles for physicians on medical practice and research. Content is of interest to general physicians, specialists and health-care workers. Includes coverage of medical socioeconomics.
**Ind/Abst** Abstr. Res. Pastor. Care Couns.; AGRICOLA; Chem. Abstr. (-1988); Chicano Index; Coal Abstr.; Cumul. Index Nurs. Allied Health Lit.; Curr. Contents Clin. Med.; Dairy Sci. Abstr.; EMBASE; Energy Res. Abstr. (1975-); Health Devices Alerts; Health Index (1989-); Health Period. Database [Full Txt.]; Health Ref. Cent. (Jan. 1989-) [Full Txt.] [Full Cov.]; Helminthol. Abstr.; Index Med.; Int. Nurs. Index; Iowa Drug Inf. Serv. (1967-); Med. Abstr. Newsl.; Microbiol. Abstr. Sect. B (19??-19??); Microbiol. Abstr. Sect. C; Mod. Med.; Nutr. Res. Newsl.; Life Sci. Collect.; Physic. Medline Plus; Protozoolog. Abstr.; Res. Alert [Full Cov.]; Risk Abstr.; Saf. Health Work; Sci. Cit. Index; SCISEARCH; Soc. Sci. Cit. Index [Select. Cov.]; SportSearch; Virol. AIDS Abstr.

PL/0043-5147
**WIADOMOSCI LEKARSKIE (1960).**
(WIADOMOSCI LEKARSKIE : ORGAN POLSKIEGO TOWARZYSTWA LEKARSKIEGO.). [Wiad. lek.]. **Added/Corp** Polskie Towarzystwo Lekarskie. (1960)-. Academic Scholarly Publication. Polish (Polish; summaries and/or abstracts in English and Russian). sm (24 issues). Price on Request. **(Subscription address:** ARS Polona, PO Box 1001, 00068 Warsaw Poland.**) CODEN** WILEAR. Documents available from BIOSIS Document Express, CASDDS. ***Continues in part*** *Polski Tygodnik Lekarski I Wiadomosci Lekarskie, 0860-8849.*
**Ind/Abst** Biol. Abstr.; Chem. Abstr.; Index Med.; Nutr. Abstr. Rev., Ser. A, Hum. Exp.; Life Sci. Collect.

PL/0510-4262
**WIADOMOSCI MELIORACYJNE I LAKARSKIE.** [Wiad. melior. lakarskie]. **Added/Corp** Stowarzyszenie Naukowo-Techniczne Inzynierow i Technikow Wodno-Melioracyjnych. Vol. 2 (1959)-. Periodical. Polish. mo. Price on Request. **(Subscription address:** ARS Polona, PO Box 1001, 00068 Warsaw Poland.**)**
**Ind/Abst** AGRICOLA.

AU/0043-5325
**WIENER KLINISCHE WOCHENSCHRIFT.**
[Wien. Klin. Wochenschr.]. **Added/Corp** Gesellschaft der Aerzte in Wien. Vol. 1, No. 1 (Apr. 1888)-. Academic Scholarly Publication. German. Twenty-four times a year. $307.00. Springer-Verlag Wien, Sachsenplatz 4 6, PO Box 89, A-1201 Vienna Austria. **Tel** 011 43 1 3302415. **(Subscription address:** Springer Verlag New York Inc. / for North America, 44 Hartz Way, Secaucus NJ 07096.**) ED** O Kraupp and H Sinzinger. **NLM** W1 WI28. **CODEN** WKWOAO. **[CCC]. Pr Rev.** available on microfilm from University Microfilms International (UMI). Documents available from The Genuine Article, BIOSIS Document Express, CASDDS.
**Desc:** Goals are the medical education/development of doctors and the documentation of medical research results in Austria. Original articles and surveys from all medical specialties, clinical and applied.
**Ind/Abst** Biol. Abstr.; Chem. Abstr.; Curr. Contents Clin. Med.; Dairy Sci. Abstr.; EMBASE [Select. Cov.]; Helminthol. Abstr. (19??-19??); Index Med.; Nutr. Abstr. Rev., Ser. A, Hum. Exp.; Life Sci. Collect.; PESTDOC; Res. Alert [Full Cov.]; Rev. Med. Vet. Entomol.; Rev. Med. Vet. Mycology; Saf. Health Work; Sci. Cit. Index; SCISEARCH; Soc. Sci. Cit. Index [Select. Cov.].

AU/0300-5178
**WIENER KLINISCHE WOCHENSCHRIFT. SUPPLEMENTUM.** [Wien. klin. Wochenschr., Suppl.]. No. 1 (1972)-. Academic Scholarly Publication. German. Price varies per volume. Springer-Verlag Wien, Sachsenplatz 4 6, PO Box 89, A-1201 Vienna Austria. **Tel** 011 43 1 3302415. **(Subscription address:** Springer Verlag New York Inc. / for North America, 44 Hartz Way, Secaucus NJ 07096.**) NLM** W1 WI28A. **CODEN** WKWSA2. available on microfilm from University Microfilms International (UMI). Documents available from BIOSIS Document Express, CASDDS.
**Ind/Abst** Biol. Abstr.; Chem. Abstr. (1972-1981); EMBASE [Select. Cov.]; Index Med.

AU/0043-5341
**WIENER MEDIZINISCHE WOCHENSCHRIFT.** [Wien. med. Wschr.]. Vol. 1 (April 5, 1851)-. Academic Scholarly Publication. German (English). Twenty times a year. S1790.00 Austria; S1960.00 other. Blackwell MZV Medizinische Zeitschriftenverlags Gesellschaft, Feldgasse 13, A-1238 Vienna Austria. **Tel** 011 43 1 8893646, FAX 011 43 1 889364724. **ED** G. Hitzenberger, H. Sterz and G.S. Barolin. **NLM** W1; WI336. **CODEN** WMWOA4. Index available. **Bk Rev. Ad Acc. Pr Rev. Circ:** 4,150. available on microfilm and microfiche from University Microfilms International (UMI). Documents available from The Genuine Article, CASDDS, ADONIS.
**Ind/Abst** ADONIS; Chem. Abstr. (1851-1983); EMBASE; Index Med.; Nutr. Abstr. Rev., Ser. A, Hum. Exp.; Life Sci. Collect.; PESTDOC; Res. Alert [Select. Cov.].

US
**WILDERNESS MEDICINE LETTER : THE OFFICIAL NEWSLETTER OF THE WILDERNESS MEDICAL SOCIETY.**
**Added/Corp** Wilderness Medical Society. Vol. 7, No. 1 (Jan. 1990)-. Periodical. English. Four times a year. $30.00. Wilderness Medical Society, PO Box 2463, Indianapolis IN 46206. **Tel** (317)631-1745, FAX (317)634-7817. **ED** Karl Neumann. **NLM** W1; WI48. **Bk Rev. Ad Acc. Circ:** 3,000 (ctrl). ***Continues*** *Wilderness Medicine.*

US
**WILMER RETINA UPDATE, THE.** Vol. 1 (1995)-. Periodical. English. bm (6 issues). $60.00 (individuals), $85.00 (institutions) US; $75.00 (individuals), $100.00 (institutions) other. Raven Press, 1185 Avenue of the Americas, 37th Floor, New York NY 10036. **Tel** (212)930-9500, (212)930-9604, FAX (212)869-3495, (212)302-8507, telex 640073.

US
**WINDHOVER'S HEALTH CARE STRATEGIST. Added/Corp** Windhover Information Inc. **VFOAT** Health Care Strategist. (19??)-. English. an. $695.00. Windhover Information, PO Box 360, South Norwalk CT 06856. **Tel** (203)838-4401. ***Continues*** *Wilkerson's Health Care Strategist.*

US/0043-6542
**WISCONSIN MEDICAL JOURNAL.** [Wisc. med. j.]. Vol. 1 (Jan. 1903)-. Academic Scholarly Publication. English. mo. $35.00 US; $40.00 other. State Medical Society of Wisconsin, PO Box 1109, Madison WI 53701. **Tel** (608)257-6781, FAX (608)283-5401. **ED** Russell King. **LC** R11; .W7. **DD** 610.5. **NLM** W1 WI801G. Index available. cum. index. **Ad Acc, Adv Mgr:** Lynne Bjorgo. **Circ:** 7,400 (ctrl).
**Desc:** Contains scientific articles, socioeconomic organizational, medical meetings, classified advertisements, physical news, and special articles.
**Ind/Abst** Cumul. Index Nurs. Allied Health Lit.; EMBASE [Select. Cov.]; Energy Res. Abstr.; Index Med.; Med. Abstr. Newsl.; Life Sci. Collect.

US/0736-4318
**WISCONSIN PUBLICATIONS IN THE HISTORY OF SCIENCE AND MEDICINE.**
[Wis. publ. hist. sci. med.]. No. 1 (1982)-. Monographic series. English. Three times a year. Price varies per volume. University of Wisconsin Press, Journal Division, 114 North Murray Street, Madison WI 53715. **Tel** (608)262-4952, FAX (608)262-8909. **ED** William Coleman, David C. Lindberg, and Ronald L. Numbers. **NLM** W1 WI805.

GW/0138-1067
**WISSENSCHAFTLICHE ZEITSCHRIFT - ERNST-MORITZ-ARNDT- UNIVERSITAT GRIEFSWALD. MEDIZINISCHE REIHE.**
**Added/Corp** Ernst-Moritz-Arndt-Universitat Greifswald. **VAT** Wissenschaftliche Zeitschrift der Ernst Moritz Arndt Universitat Griefswald. Medizinische Reihe. (1972)-. German. qt. 12.20M Germany; 12.70M other. LKG Leipziger Kommissions & Grossbuchhandel, Leninstrasse 16, Postfach 520, D 04005 Leipzig, Germany. **Tel** 011 49 341 71370. **NLM** W1 WI984. **CODEN** WZERDH. Documents available from CASDDS.
**Ind/Abst** Chem. Abstr.

KO
**WOLGAN HANUIYAK CHONGBO. VFOAT** Hanuiyak Chongbo; Oriental Medicine Information. Periodical. Korean (Korean). W7,400. Sung Mun Book Company, CPO Box 2485, Seoul Korea. **LC** R97.7.K6; W64.

US/0162-6892
**WOMEN IN MEDICAL ACADEMIA.** V. 1- Winter 1977-. Periodical. English. American Medical Women's Association / Arizona, Professional Resources Research Center, PO Box 43011, Tucson AZ 85733. **NLM** W1 WO481.

●US
**WOMEN'S HEALTH JOURNAL.** Vol. 1 (1995)-. English. qt. $95.00 US & Canada; $120.00 other. Lawrence Erlbaum Associates, 365 Broadway, Suite 102, Hillsdale NJ 07642. **Tel** (201)666-4110, (800)926-6579, FAX (201)666-2394.

●US/1062-4163
**WOMEN'S HEALTH LETTER.** [Women's health lett.]. (1992)-. Periodical. English. Twelve times a year. $24.00 US; $25.32 Canada; $25.92 Mexico; $31.92 other. Women's Health Letter, 2245 East Colorado Blvd., Suite 104, Pasadena CA 91107. **Tel** (818)798-0638, FAX (818)798-0639. **ED** Kerri Bodmer. **DD** 362. **Bk Rev**, (Qty: 8/year). **Circ:** 10,000.
**Desc:** Review of women's health news and information.

US/1055-6370
**WORCESTER MEDICINE.** [Worcest. med.]. **Added/Corp** Worcester District Medical Society. **VFOAT** WM. Vol. 55, No. 4 (Winter 1990)-. Periodical. English. qt. Worcester Dis Medical Society, 321 Main Street, Worcester MA 01608. **Tel** (617)753-1579. **DD** 610. **NLM** W1; WO8454. ***Continues*** *Worcester Medical News.*

AT/0813-4472
**WORKING PAPER - UNIVERSITY OF NEWCASTLE, FACULTY OF MEDICINE.**
(WORKING PAPER / THE UNIVERSITY OF NEWCASTLE, FACULTY OF MEDICINE.). [Work. pap. - Univ. Newctle. Fac. Med.]. **Added/Corp** University of Newcastle. Faculty of Medicine. No. 1 (1975)-. Monographic series. English. ir. Price varies per volume. University of Newcastle Faculty of Education, NSW 2308 Australia. **NLM** W1 WO848DS.

NE/0259-7284
**WORKSHOP CONFERENCES HOECHST.** [Workshop Conf. Hoechst]. V. 1- 1973-. Periodical. English. Excerpta Medica Publishing Group, PO Box 548, 1000 AM Amsterdam Netherlands. **Tel** 011 31 20 5803243. **CODEN** WCHODW. Documents available from BIOSIS Document Express.
**Ind/Abst** Biol. Abstr.

US/0890-4480
**WORLD BOOK HEALTH & MEDICAL ANNUAL, THE.** [World Book health med. annu.]. **Added/Corp** World Book, Inc. **VFOAT** World Book Health and Medical Annual; Health & Medical Annual; Health and Medical Annual. (1987)-. English. an. $27.90. World Book Encyclopedia Inc., 2515 East 43rd Street, Chattanooga TN 37422. **Tel** (800)874-0520, (615)867-9081. **LC** RA431; .W65. **DD** 610. Index available.
**Desc:** Subject specialists have composed the 'Special Reports' in each volume, and science, technical, and health writers have contributed to the 'file' or encyclopedia-type articles.

SZ/0512-2759
**WORLD DIRECTORY OF MEDICAL SCHOOLS. Added/Corp** World Health Organization. **VFOAT** Repertoire Mondial des Ecoles de Medecine. (1953)-. Monographic series. English (French). ir. Price varies per volume. World Health Organization, Distribution and Sales, 20 Avenue Appia, CH-1211 Geneva 27 Switzerland. **Tel** 011 41 22 7912111, FAX 011 41 22 7880401. **LC** R711; .W6. **DD** 610.71. **NLM** W 22 W927.
**Desc:** Concise profiles of schools of undergraduate medical education throughout the world.

GW/0049-8122
**WORLD MEDICAL JOURNAL.** [World med. j.]. **Added/Corp** World Medical Association. Vol. 1 (Jan. 1954)-. Periodical. English. bm (6 issues). DM39.25 Germany; DM48.00 other; Free to members of the World Medical Association. Deutscher Aerzte Verlag GmbH, Postfach 404265, D-50832 Cologne Germany. **Tel** 011 49 2234 7011219. **LC** R5; .W66. **DD** 610.621. **NLM** W1 WO895. Index available (bound in Jan. issue). available on microfilm and microfiche from University Microfilms International (UMI). ***Continues*** *World Medical Association. Bulletin, 1047-1928.*
**Ind/Abst** Hospit. Health Admin. Index; Life Sci. Collect.

US/1062-7731
**WORLD MEDICAL REVIEWS IN PARKINSON'S DISEASE.** ***Ceased.*** [World med. rev. Parkinson's dis.]. Vol. 1, No. 1 (1992)-(July 1993). Periodical. English. qt. World Medical Reviews Corporation, PO Box 639, Tenafly NJ 07670. **Tel** (201)567-1629. **DD** 616.

US/0161-2875
**WORLD MEETINGS. MEDICINE.**
**Added/Corp** World Meetings Information Center. Vol. 1 (Jan. 1978)-. Periodical. English. qt. $165.00 US; $180.00 other. Macmillan Publishing Company, 100 Front Street, Box 500, Riverside NJ 08075-7500. **Tel** (800)257-5755, (609)461-6500, FAX (609)461-7070. **ED** Clark Hansen. **NLM** W 3.5 W921. **CODEN** WMMEDT. **Circ:** 400.
**Desc:** Registry of future meetings on the subject of medicine, psychiatry, biology, clinical research, pharmacology, pediatrics and other pertinent topics.

US/0190-0617
**WORLDWIDE BIOMEDICAL MEETINGS, CONFERENCES, AND EXHIBITIONS.** V. 1- Apr. 1977-. Periodical. English. qt. Robert First, Inc., 405 Lexington Avenue, New York NY 10017. **NLM** W 3.5 W929.

US/0146-8014
**WORLDWIDE GUIDE TO MEDICAL ELECTRONICS MARKETING REPRESENTATION, THE.** **See** Library and Information Sciences.

●US/1067-1927
**WOUND REPAIR AND REGENERATION.** [Wound repair regen.]. **Added/Corp** Wound Healing Society. European Tissue Repair Society. Vol. 1, No. 1 (Jan./Mar. 1993)-. Periodical. English. qt. $83.00 (institutions), $55.00 (individuals) US; $100.50 (institutions), $72.50 (individuals) other. Mosby Year Book Inc., 11830 Westline Industrial Drive, St Louis MO 63146. **Tel** (800)325-4177, (314)872-8370, FAX (314)432-1380, telex 44-2402. **DD** 617. **NLM** W1; WO935GK. **[CCC]. Ad Acc. Pr Rev.**
**Desc:** Serves general surgeons, dermatologists, plastic surgeons, and basic scientists. Publishes original papers on new developments, techniques, research findings and other information pertinent to wound management.

US/1044-7946
**WOUNDS (KING OF PRUSSIA, PA.).** (WOUNDS : A COMPENDIUM OF CLINICAL RESEARCH AND PRACTICE.). Vol. 1, No. 1 (Apr. 1989)-. Periodical. English. bm. $60.00. Health Management Publishing Inc., 550 American Avenue, Circulation Department, King of Prussia PA 19406. **Tel** (215)337-4466, (800)237-7285, FAX (215)337-0890. **DD** 617. **NLM** W1; WO935L. Documents available from The Genuine Article.
**Ind/Abst** Curr. Contents Clin. Med.; Res. Alert [Select. Cov.].

US/0741-8523
**WRAP UP (NORWOOD, N.J.).** (WRAP-UP.). Sept. 1983-. English. qt. $12.00 US; $15.00 other. American Overseas Book Company, 550 Walnut Street, Norwood NJ 07648. **Tel** (201)767-7600, (201)784-0263, FAX (201)784-0263, telex 882384. **ED** D J Palus and Cicely Marks. **Bk Rev. Ad Acc. Circ:** 4,500.
**Desc:** Provides subscription update information, new books, audiovisuals, and computer software, brief bibliographies, customer staff changes and awards, and brief articles by customers.

●DK/0908-665X
**XENOTRANSPLANTATION.** (1994)-. Periodical. English. qt. kr1110.00 US & Canada; kr 1140.00 other. Munksgaard International Publishers Ltd, PO Box 2148, DK-1016 Copenhagen K Denmark. **Tel** 011 45 33 12 70 30, FAX 011 45 33 12 93 87, telex 19431 MUNKS DK.
**Desc:** Discusses new findings in the field of organ and tissue transplantation across species barriers.

US/0044-0086
**YALE JOURNAL OF BIOLOGY AND MEDICINE, THE.** [Yale j. biol. med.]. Vol. 1; Oct. 1928-. Academic Scholarly Publication. English. bm. $90.00 (institutions), $60.00 (individuals) US; $98.00 (institutions), $68.00 (individuals) other. Yale Journal of Biology and Medicine, 333 Cedar Street, New Haven CT 06510. **Tel** (203)785-4251. **ED** Philip K Bondy. **LC** R11. **DD** 610.5. **NLM** W1 YA454. **CODEN** YJBMAU. **[CCC].** Index available. **Bk Rev. Ad Acc. Pr Rev. Circ:** 600. available on microfilm and microfiche from University Microfilms International (UMI). Documents available from The Genuine Article, BIOSIS Document Express, CASDDS.
**Desc:** Original contributions, medical reviews, case reports, medical history, symposia related to biomedical matters.
**Ind/Abst** AGRICOLA [Select. Cov.]; Biol. Abstr.; Biol. Dig.; Chem. Abstr.; Curr. Contents Life Sci.; EMBASE; Energy Res. Abstr.; Index Med.; Index Vet.; Nutr. Abstr. Rev., Ser. A, Hum. Exp.; Nutr. Res. Newsl.; Life Sci. Collect.; Ref. Upd. Deluxe Ed.; Res. Alert [Full Cov.]; Rev. Med. Vet. Mycology; Sci. Cit. Index; SCISEARCH; Wildl. Rev.

JA/0513-1731
**YAMAGUCHI IGAKU.** [Yamaguchi igaku]. **Added/Corp** Yamaguchi Daigaku Igakkai. **VFOAT** Yamaguchi Medical Journal. (1953)-. Periodical. Japanese (summaries and/or abstracts in English). bm (6 issues). Yamaguchi Kenritsu Ika Daigaku Igakkai, 1144 Kogushi Ube-shi, Yamaguchi Ken 755 Japan. **NLM** W1 YA669K. **CODEN** YIKUAO. Documents available from CASDDS.
**Ind/Abst** Chem. Abstr.; EMBASE [Select. Cov.].

JA/0912-0025
**YAMANASHI IKA DAIGAKU ZASSHI.** [Yamanashi Ika Daigaku zasshi]. **Added/Corp** Yamanashi Ika Daigaku Igakkai. Yamanashi Ika Daigaku Ishikai. **VFOAT** Yamanashi Medical Journal. (1986)-. Periodical. Japanese. Yamanashi Ika Daigaku igakkai, (Medical Soc. of Yamanashi Medical College), 210, Shimogato, Tamahocho, Nakakomagun, Yamanashiken 409-38, Japan. **NLM** W1; YA677G. **CODEN** YIDZE8. Documents available from CASDDS.
**Ind/Abst** Chem. Abstr.

US/1054-772X
**YEAR BOOK OF CLINICAL MICROBIOLOGY.** **See** Biology-Microbiology.

US/0734-3299
**YEAR BOOK OF CRITICAL CARE MEDICINE, THE.** [Year book crit. care med.]. **VFOAT** Critical Care Medicine. **VAT** Yearbook of Critical Care Medicine. (1983)-. English. an. $54.95 (latest edition). Mosby Year Book Inc., 11830 Westline Industrial Drive, St Louis MO 63146. **Tel** (800)325-4177, (314)872-8370, FAX (314)432-1380, telex 44-2402. available on CD-ROM (as ClinMED-CD) from SilverPlatter (US).

US/0896-4475
**YEAR BOOK OF INFERTILITY, THE.** [Year b. infertil.]. **Added/Corp** Year Book Medical Publishers. **VFOAT** Infertility. (1989)-. English. an. $64.95 (latest edition). Mosby Year Book Inc., 11830 Westline Industrial Drive, St Louis MO 63146. **Tel** (800)325-4177, (314)872-8370, FAX (314)432-1380, telex 44-2402. **LC** IN PROCESS. **DD** 616. **NLM** W1; YE182L. **CODEN** YBINEG.

US/0084-3873
**YEAR BOOK OF MEDICINE, THE.** [Year book med.]. **VFOAT** Yearbook of Medicine. (1949)-. English. an. $59.95. Mosby Year Book Inc., 11830 Westline Industrial Drive, St Louis MO 63146. **Tel** (800)325-4177, (314)872-8370, FAX (314)432-1380, telex 44-2402. **LC** R101; .Y35. **DD** 616. **NLM** W1 YE26. ***Continues*** *Year Book of General Medicine, 0093-3635.*

US/8756-3460
**YEAR BOOK OF REHABILITATION, THE.** ***Ceased.*** [Year b. rehabil.]. **VFOAT** Yearbook of Rehabilitation. (1986)-(1992). English. an. Mosby Year Book Inc., 11830 Westline Industrial Drive, St Louis MO 63146. **Tel** (800)325-4177, (314)872-8370, FAX (314)432-1380, telex 44-2402. **LC** RM930.A1; Y43. **DD** 617. **NLM** ZWB 320; Y39. ***Continues*** *Year Book of Physical Medicine and Rehabilitation.*

US/0084-358X
**YEARBOOK AND DIRECTORY OF OSTEOPATHIC PHYSICIANS.** [Yearb. dir. osteopath. phys.]. **VFOAT** American Osteopathic Association Yearbook and Directory of Osteopathic Physicians; AOA Directory of Osteopathic Physicians. **VAT** Association of Osteopathic Physicians Directory of Osteopathic Physicians. Directory. English. an. $35.00. American Osteopathic Association, 142 East Ontario Street, Chicago IL 60611-2864. **Tel** (312)280-5800. **ED** Thomas W Allen. **DD** 615. **NLM** WB 22 DA2 D5983. **Ad Acc. Circ:** 21,000 (ctrl). ***Continues*** *Directory of Osteopathic Physicians.*
**Desc:** A compendium of osteopathic medical information, it lists all osteopathic physicians, alphabetically and geographically, as well as hospital, school, certification, licensing, and statistical data.

JA/0372-7726
**YOKOHAMA IGAKU.** (YOKOHAMA IGAKU. YOKOHAMA MEDICAL JOURNAL.). [Yokohama igaku]. **VFOAT** Yokohama Medical Journal. (1948)-. Periodical. Japanese. bm. $139.50. Medical Association of Yokohama City University, 2-33 Urafunecho, Minami-ku, Yokohama-shi, 232 Kanagawa, Japan. **(Subscription address:** Japan Publications Trading Company, Ltd., PO Box 5030, Tokyo International, Tokyo 100-31 Japan.**) NLM** W1 YO667. **CODEN** YKIGAK. Documents available from BIOSIS Document Express, CASDDS.
**Ind/Abst** Biol. Abstr. (-1989); Chem. Abstr.; EMBASE [Select. Cov.].

JA/0044-0531
**YOKOHAMA MEDICAL BULLETIN.** [Yokohama med. bull.]. Vol. 1 Oct. (1950)-. Academic Scholarly Publication. English (German and French). Three times a year. Yokohama National University / Education, Faculty of Education, Publishing Committee, 156 Tokiwadai, Hodogaya-ku, Yokohama, 240, Japan. **Tel** 045-787-2556, FAX 045-787-2560. **ED** Tomoo Ohshima. **NLM** W1 YO671. **CODEN** YMBUA7. **Circ:** 1,000 (ctrl). Documents available from BIOSIS Document Express, CASDDS.
**Ind/Abst** Biol. Abstr.; Chem. Abstr.; EMBASE [Select. Cov.]; Nutr. Abstr. Rev., Ser. A, Hum. Exp.; SEA Abstr.

JA/0513-5710
**YONAGO ACTA MEDICA.** [Yonago acta med.]. **Added/Corp** Tottori University. Medical School. Vol. 1 (July 1954)-. Academic Scholarly Publication. Multiple languages (English, French and German). Tottori Daigaku Igakubu, (School of Medicine, Tottori University), 86, Nishimachi, Yonagoshi, Tottoriken 683 Japan. **NLM** W1 YO681. **CODEN** YOAMAQ. Documents available from CASDDS.
**Ind/Abst** Chem. Abstr.; EMBASE [Select. Cov.]; Helminthol. Abstr. (1991-); Rev. Med. Vet. Mycology; Trop. Dis. Bull.

JA/0044-0558
**YONAGO IGAKU ZASSHI.** [Yonago igaku zasshi]. **VFOAT** Journal of the Yonago Medical Association. (1948)-. Periodical. Japanese. bm. Yonago Igakkai, (Yonago Medical Assoc.), Tottori Daigaku Igakubu, 86, Nishimachi, Yonagoshi, Tottoriken 683 Japan. **DD** 610. Documents available from CASDDS.
**Ind/Abst** Chem. Abstr.

KO/0513-5796
**YONSEI MEDICAL JOURNAL.** [Yonsei med. j.]. **Added/Corp** Yonse Tachakkyo, Seoul, Korea. Uikwa Tachak. Vol. 1 (1960)-. Academic Scholarly Publication. English. qt. Free. Yonsei University International, College of Medicine, CPO Box 8044, Seoul Korea. **Tel** 392-0161. **ED** Jung-Koo Youn. **NLM** W1 YO682. **CODEN** YOMJA9. Index available. **Circ:** 2,000 (ctrl). Documents available from CASDDS.
**Ind/Abst** Chem. Abstr.; EMBASE [Select. Cov.]; Index Med.

GW/0724-9004
**ZAC, ZEITSCHRIFT FUER ANTIMIKROBIELLE, ANTINEOPLASTISCHE CHEMOTHERAPIE.** ***Title Change.*** (ZEITSCHRIFT FUER ANTIMIKROBIELLE, ANTINEOPLASTISCHE CHEMOTHERAPIE : ZAC / HERAUSGEGEBEN VON DER PAUL-EHRLICH-GESELLSCHAFT FUER CHEMOTHERAPIE E.V.). [ZAC, Z. antimikrob. antineoplast. Chemother.]. **Added/Corp** Paul-Ehrlich-Gesellschaft. **VFOAT** ZAC; Zeitschrift fur Antimikrobielle und Antineoplastische Chemotherapie. Vol. 1, Nos. 1 & 2 (1983)-(Sept. 1994). Academic Scholarly Publication. German (summaries and/or abstracts in English). qt. Futuramed GmbH, Postfach 830358, D 830358 Munich Germany. **Tel** 011 49 89 674047. **NLM** W1; ZE234. Index available. **Bk Rev. Ad Acc.** Documents available from CASDDS. ***Continued by*** *Antiinfective Drugs and Chemotherapy ADC.*
**Ind/Abst** Chem. Abstr. (?-?); EMBASE (?-?).

IT/0044-1570
**ZACCHIA.** [Zacchia]. (1921)-. Academic Scholarly Publication. Italian. qt. L70000 Italy; L140000 other. Societa Editrice Universo, Via GB Morgagni 1, 00161 Rome Italy. **Tel** 011 39 6 44231171. **NLM** W1 ZA33. **CODEN** ZACCAL. Documents available from CASDDS.
**Ind/Abst** Chem. Abstr.; EMBASE.

YU/0352-1788
**ZBORNIK RADOVA PRIRODNO-MATEMATICKOG FAKULTETA. SERIJA ZA BIOLOGIJU.** **See** Biology.

RU/0044-1945
**ZDOROVE.** [Zdorove]. **Added/Corp** Soviet Union. Ministerstvo Zdravookhraneniia. (1955)-. Periodical. Russian. mo. $89.95. **(Subscription address:** East View Publications Inc., 3020 Harbor Lane North, Suite 110, Minneapolis MN 55447.**) NLM** W1 ZD832.
**Ind/Abst** Int. Aerosp. Abstr.

TA/0514-2415
**ZDRAVOOHRANENIE TADZIKISTANA.** (ZDRAVOOKHRANENIE TADZHIKISTANA / MINISTERSTVO ZDRAVOOKHRANENIIA TADZHIKSKOÊI SSR.). [Zdravoohr. Tadz.]. **Added/Corp** Tajik S.S.R. Vazorati Nigahdorii Tandurusti. Ittifoqi Kasabai Korkunoni Tib (Tajik S.S.R.). Komiteti Respublikavi. **VFOAT** Nigahdorii Tandurustii Tojikiston. (1933)-. Periodical. Russian (summaries and/or abstracts in English and Tajik; table of contents in English and Tajik). bm. Minzdrav Tadzhikskoj SSR, Ulitsa Putovskogo 59, 734026 Dushanbe Tajikstan. **NLM** W1 ZD8545. **CODEN** ZDTAAJ. Documents available from CASDDS.
**Ind/Abst** Chem. Abstr.; EMBASE [Select. Cov.].

BW/0044-1961
**ZDRAVOOKHRANENIE BELORUSSII.** [Zdravoohran. Beloruss.]. **Added/Corp** Byelorussian SSR. Ministerstvo Zdravookhraneniia. (1955)-. Academic Scholarly Publication. Russian (summaries and/or abstracts in English; table of contents in English). mo. $149.95. **(Subscription address:** East View Publications Inc., 3020 Harbor Lane North, Suite 110, Minneapolis MN 55447.**) NLM** W1 ZD8525. **CODEN** ZDBEA9. Documents available from BIOSIS Document Express, CASDDS.
**Ind/Abst** Biol. Abstr.; Chem. Abstr.; EMBASE.

XV/0350-0063
**ZDRAVSTVENI VESTNIK.** [Zdrav. vestn.]. (1946)-. Periodical. Slovenian. mo. Slovensko Zdravnisko Drustvo, PO Box 26, Komenskega 4, 61001 Ljubljana Slovenia. **Tel** (61)317-868. **UDC** 61. **CODEN** ZDVEA7. Documents available from The Genuine Article.
**Ind/Abst** EMBASE [Select. Cov.]; Res. Alert [Select. Cov.].

GW/0720-0587
**ZEITSCHRIFT FUER BADER- UND KLIMAHEILKUNDE.** [Z. Bader- Klimaheilkd.]. 27.- Yearly volume; Jan./Mar. 1980-. Academic Scholarly Publication. German. bm. Futura Publishing Company Inc., 135 Bedford Road, PO Box 418, Armonk NY 10504-0418. **Tel** (914)273-1014, (800)877-8761, FAX (914)273-1015, (914)273-1016. **NLM** W1 ZE237C. ***Continues*** *Zeitschrift fur Agewandte Bader- und Klimaheilkunde, 0084-5280.*
**Ind/Abst** EMBASE.

GW/0044-2542
**ZEITSCHRIFT FUER DIE GESAMTE INNERE MEDIZIN UND IHRE GRENZGEBIETE.** ***Ceased.*** [Z. ges. inn. Med. ihre Grenzgeb.]. Vol. 1, (1946)-(19??). Academic Scholarly Publication. German (summaries and/or abstracts in English, German and Russian; table of contents in English and Russian). mo. Georg Thieme Verlag

Stuttgart, Postfach 301120, D 70451 Stuttgart Germany. **Tel** 011 49 711 89310, FAX 011 49 711 8931298, telex 7 252 275 GTVD. **(Subscription address:** Thieme Medical Publishers Inc., 381 Park Avenue South, New York, NY 10016) **NLM** W1 ZE266. **CODEN** ZGIMAL. **[CCC].** Index Available, published separately, free-automatically sent. Documents available from CASDDS.
**Ind/Abst** Chem. Abstr.; Curr. Biotechnol.; EMBASE [Select. Cov.]; Index Med.; Nutr. Abstr. Rev., Ser. A, Hum. Exp.; Life Sci. Collect.

GW/0343-8554
**ZEITSCHRIFT FUER LYMPHOLOGIE.** [Z. Lymphol.]. **Added/Corp** Deutsche Gesellschaft fuer Lymphologie. **VFOAT** Journal of Lymphology. Vol. 1 (Sept. 1977)-. Academic Scholarly Publication. English (German). sa. DM117.00 Europe; $65.40 other. F K Schattauer Verlagsgesellschaft mbH, Postfach 10 45 45, D 70040 Stuttgart Germany. **Tel** 011 49 711 2298726. **ED** A. Gregl, E. Kuhnke, H. Schoberth. **NLM** W1 ZE445D. **CODEN** ZELYDR. **[CCC].** Index available. **Bk Rev. Ad Acc.** Documents available from BIOSIS Document Express, CASDDS.
**Desc:** The journal of the German Society of Lymphology.
**Ind/Abst** Biol. Abstr.; Chem. Abstr.; EMBASE; Helminthol. Abstr.; Index Med.; Index Vet.; Life Sci. Collect.

SZ/0514-8782
**ZEITSCHRIFT FUER MILITARMEDIZIN.** Academic Scholarly Publication. German. bm. Deutscher Judo Verband, Redaktion Ippon Segewaldweg 40, D 12557 Berlin Germany. **Tel** 011 49 711 210770, telex 051 678. **LC** RC970; .Z45. **NLM** W1 ZE465. **CODEN** ZEMIAF. Documents available from CASDDS.
**Ind/Abst** Chem. Abstr.

GW/0720-9762
**ZEITSCHRIFT FUER PHYSIKALISCHE MEDIZIN, BALNEOLOGIE, MED. KLIMATOLOGIE.** ***Title Change.*** [Z. phys. Med. Balneol. med. Klimatol.]. **Added/Corp** Deutsche Gesellschaft fuer Physikalische Medizin und Rehabilitation. (1981)-(19??). Academic Scholarly Publication. German. bm. Karl Demeter Verlag, Wuermstrasse 13, Postfach 1660, W 8032 Graefelfing Germany. **Tel** 011 49 89 852033, FAX 011 49 89 9543347, telex 524068 Delta D. **NLM** W1; ZE532VK. **CODEN** ZPMKDX. Documents available from CASDDS. ***Continues*** *Zeitschrift fuer Physikalische Medizin, 0044-3344.* ***Merged with*** *Zeitschrift fuer Physiotherapie* ***to form*** *Physikalische Medizin, Rehabilitationsmedizin, Kurortmedizin.*
**Ind/Abst** Chem. Abstr.

GW/0340-5613
**ZEITSCHRIFT FUER PSYCHOSOMATISCHE MEDIZIN UND PSYCHOANALYSE.** [Z. Psychosom. Med. Psychoanal.]. Vol. 13 (1967)-. Academic Scholarly Publication. German. qt. DM136.00. Vandenhoeck & Ruprecht, Robert Bosch Breite 6, D-37079 Goettingen Germany. **Tel** 011 49 551 695911, FAX 011 49 551 695917, telex 965226 VAN d. **NLM** W1 ZE566. **CODEN** ZPPSB2. **[CCC]. Pr Rev.** Documents available from The Genuine Article, BIOSIS Document Express. ***Continues*** *Zeitschrift fuer Psycho-Somatische Medizin, 0375-5355.*
**Ind/Abst** Biol. Abstr.; Curr. Contents Clin. Med.; Curr. Contents Soc. Behav. Sci.; EMBASE; Index Med.; Psychol. Abstr. (1967-); PsycINFO (1956-); PsycLit; Res. Alert [Full Cov.]; Sci. Cit. Index; SCISEARCH; Soc. Sci. Cit. Index [Full Cov.].

GW
**ZEITSCHRIFT FUER TRANSPLANTATIONSMEDIZIN.** German (English). qt. DM64.00 Germany; DM70.00 other. Wolfgang Pabst Verlag, Am Eichengrund 28, D 49525 Lengerich Germany. **Tel** 011 49 5484 308, FAX 011 49 5484 550. **ED** A E Lison. Index available. cum. index. **Bk Rev. Ad Acc. Circ:** 1,600 (ctrl).
**Desc:** Articles about organ transplantation.

SZ/1017-1584
**ZEITSCHRIFT FUER UNFALLCHIRURGIE UND VERSICHERUNGSMEDIZIN.** [Z. Unfallchir. Versicher.med.]. **Added/Corp** Schweizerische Gesellschaft fuer Unfallmedizin und Berufskrankheiten. **VFOAT** Revue de Traumatologie et d'Assicurologie. Vol. 83, No. 1 (1990)-. Periodical. German (French; summaries and/or abstracts in English). qt (4 issues). 116.00F. Verlag Hans Huber Ag Bern, Laenggass Strasse 76, CH 3000 Bern 9 Switzerland. **Tel** 011 41 31 3004500. **ED** E. Frei. **LC** RD92; .Z43. **DD** 617.1/005. **NLM** W1; ZE629K. **CODEN** ZUVEES. Index available. **Bk Rev. Ad Acc. Circ:** 800. ***Continues*** *Zeitschrift fuer Unfallchirurgie, Versicherungsmedizin und Berufskrankheiten, 0254-6310.*
**Desc:** Offical journal of the Swiss Society for Accident Medicine and Occupational Diseases.
**Ind/Abst** Health Plan. Adminis.; Index Med. (1990-).

GW/0233-1608
**ZEITSCRHIFT FUR KLINISCHE MEDIZIN (BERLIN, DDR).** ***Ceased.*** (ZEITSCHRIFT FUER KLINISCHE MEDIZIN : ZKM.). [Z. Klin. Med. (Berl. DDR)]. **Added/Corp** Gesellschaft fur Klinische Medizin der DDR. **VFOAT** ZKM. Vol. 40, No. 1 (Jan. 1985)-(1993). Academic Scholarly Publication. German (summaries and/or abstracts in English). bm. Selecta Verlagsgesellschaft mbH, Postfach 4240, c/o Mrs. Riemer, D-65032 Wiesbaden Germany. **Tel** 011 49 611 1705261. **ED** H David. **NLM** W1; ZE433S. **CODEN** ZKMEEF. Index available. cum. index. **Bk Rev. Ad Acc. Circ:** 6,800 (ctrl). Documents available from The Genuine Article, BIOSIS Document Express, CASDDS. ***Continues*** *Deutsche Gesundheitswesen, 0012-0219.*
**Desc:** Publishes original papers and surveys that deal with the results from clinically relevant basic and current research and clinical practice, as well as with theoretical medical problems.
**Ind/Abst** Biol. Abstr. (1988-); Chem. Abstr. (1985-); Dairy Sci. Abstr.; EMBASE [Select. Cov.]; Helminthol. Abstr. (19??-19??); Nutr. Abstr. Rev., Ser. A, Hum. Exp.; Life Sci. Collect.; Protozoolog. Abstr.; Res. Alert [Select. Cov.]; Rev. Med. Vet. Entomol.; Rev. Med. Vet. Mycology; Saf. Health Work.

GW/0173-3338
**ZENTRALBLATT FUER ARBEITSMEDIZIN, ARBEITSSCHUTZ, PROPHYLAXE UND ERGONOMIE.** [Zentralbl. Arbeitsmed., Arbeitsschutz, Prophyl. Ergon.]. **Added/Corp** Bundesanstalt fuer Arbeitsschutz und Unfallforschung. Vol. 30, No. 4 (April 1980)-. Academic Scholarly Publication. German (summaries and/or abstracts in English). Twelve times a year. DM211.20 Germany; DM240.00 other. Dr. Curt Haefner Verlag GmbH, Bachstrasse 14, Postfach 106060, D 69050 Heidelberg Germany. **Tel** 011 49 6221 49063. **NLM** W1 ZE767M. **CODEN** ZAAEDK. Documents available from CASDDS. ***Continues*** *Zentralblatt fuer Arbeitsmedizin, Arbeitsschutz, und Prophylaxe, 0340-7047.*
**Ind/Abst** Acoust. Abstr.; Chem Inform; Chem. Abstr.; Coal Abstr.; EMBASE; Energy Res. Abstr. (April 1981-); Ergon. Abstr.

CC/1000-1743
**ZHEJIANG YIKE DAXUE XUEBAO.** (CHE-CHIANG I KO TA HSUEH HSUEH PAO.). [Zhejiang yike daxue xuebao]. **Added/Corp** Che-chiang i Ko Ta Hsueh. **VFOAT** Journal of Zhejiang Medical University; Zhejiang Yikedaxue Xuebao. (197?)-. Academic Scholarly Publication. Chinese (summaries and/or abstracts in English). bm. $12.00. Zhejiang Yike Daxue, Xuebao Bianji Shi, 157 Yan'an Road, Hangzhou, Zhejiang 310006 People's Republic of China. **Tel** 0571 7022700, FAX 0571 7071571. **ED** Z. Shu. **NLM** W1; CH153C. **CODEN** ZYDXDM. **Ad Acc, Adv Mgr:** Z. Lianrong. **Circ:** 5,000. Documents available from BIOSIS Document Express, CASDDS.
**Ind/Abst** Biol. Abstr. (1985-); Chem. Abstr.; NAPRALERT.

CC/0411-8421
**ZHEJIANG ZHONGYI ZAZHI.** [Zhejiang zhongyi zazhi]. **VFOAT** Zhejiang Journal of Traditional Medicine. (19??)-. Academic Scholarly Publication. Chinese. mo. $1.90 (per issue). Zhejiang Sheng Zhongyiyao Yanjiusuo, Zhejiang Provincial Institute of Traditional Chinese Medicine, 26 Tianmushan Lu, Hangzhou, Zhejiang 310007, People's Republic of China. **(Subscription address:** China International Book Trading Corporation, PO Box 399, Library Service Department, Beijing 100044 People's Republic of China.)
**Desc:** Contains information about Chinese traditional medicine.
**Ind/Abst** NAPRALERT.

CC/1000-0607
**ZHENCI YANJIU.** (CHEN TZU YEN CHIU.). [Zhenci yanjiu]. **Added/Corp** Chung-Kuo i Hsueh Ko Hsueh Yuan. I Hsueh Ching Pao Yen Chiu So. Chung i Yen Chiu Yuan (Peking, China). Chen Chiu Yen Chiu So. (1980)-. Periodical. Chinese (summaries and/or abstracts in English; table of contents in English). qt. $38.70. Science Press, 16 Donghuangchenggen North Street, Beijing 100707, People's Republic of China. **Tel** 011 86 1 4019821, 011 86 1 4010642, FAX 011 86 1 4012180, 011 86 1 4019810, telex 210147. **(Subscription address:** China International Book Trading Corporation, PO Box 399, Library Service Department, Beijing 100044 People's Republic of China.) **NLM** W1; CH411G. ***Continues*** *Chen Tzu Ma Tsui, 1000-7814.*
**Ind/Abst** Index Med.

CC/0376-2491
**ZHONG HUA YI XUE ZA ZHI.** (CHUNG-HUA I HSUEH TSA CHIH.). [Zhong hua yi xue za zhi]. **Added/Corp** Chung-hua i Hsueh hui (1914?-1949). **VFOAT** Chinese Medical Journal; Zhongua Yixue Zazhi; National Medical Journal of China. (Nov. 1915)-. Periodical. Chinese (English). mo. $68.04. **(Subscription address:** China International Book Trading Corporation, PO Box 399, Library Service Department, Beijing 100044 People's Republic of China.) **LC** PAR. **NLM** W1 CH982H. **CODEN** CHHTAT.
**Ind/Abst** NAPRALERT.

CC/0254-1440
**ZHONG SHAN YIXUEYUAN XUEBAO.** (CHUNG-SHAN I HSUEH YUAN HSUEH PAO.). [Zhong Shan yixueyuan xuebao]. **Added/Corp** Chung-shan I Hsueh Yuan (Canton, China). **VFOAT** Acta Academiae Medicinae Zhong Shan. Vol. 1 (1980)-. Periodical. Chinese (summaries and/or abstracts in English). qt. RMBY2.50. University of Medical Sciences / Zhongshan Yike Daxue, Editorial Board of Academics, 74 Zhongshan Erlu, Guangzhou, Guangdong 510089, People's Republic of China. **ED** P. Wenwei. **LC** R97.7.C5; C53. **DD** 610/.5. **NLM** W1 CH991G. Documents available from BLDSC.

CC/1001-6627
**ZHONGGUO JISHENGCHONGBING FANGZHI ZAZHI.** **VFOAT** Chinese Journal of Parasitic Disease Control. (1988)-. Periodical. Chinese. qt. **DD** 574.23.
**Ind/Abst** Protozoolog. Abstr.

CC/1000-7423
**ZHONGGUO JISHENGCHONGXUE YU JISHENGCHONGPING ZAZHI.** (CHUNG-KUO CHI SHENG CHUNG HSUEH YU CHI SHENG CHUNG PING TSA CHIH.). [Zhongguo jishengchongxue yu jishengchongping zazhi]. **Added/Corp** Chung-kuo yu Fang i Hsueh ko Hsueh Yuan. Chi Sheng Chung Ping yen Chiu so. **VFOAT** Chinese Journal of Parasitology and Parasitic Diseases. (1987)-. Periodical. Chinese (summaries and/or abstracts in English; table of contents in English). qt. $10.60. **(Subscription address:** China International Book Trading Corporation, PO Box 399, Library Service Department, Beijing 100044 People's Republic of China.) **NLM** W1; CH986H. ***Continues*** *Chi Sheng Chung Hsueh Yu Chi Sheng Chung Ping Tsa Chih, 1000-1808.*
**Ind/Abst** Biocont. News Inf.; Helminthol. Abstr.; Index Med. (1987-); Index Vet.; Nematol. Abstr.; Pig News Inf.; Protozoolog. Abstr.; Rev. Agric. Entomol.; Rev. Med. Vet. Entomol.; Rev. Med. Vet. Mycology.

CC/0258-4646
**ZHONGGUO YIKE DAXUE XUEBAO.** (CHUNG-KUO I KO TA HSUEH HSUEH PAO.). [Zhongguo yike daxue xuebao]. **Added/Corp** Chung-Kuo i Ko Ta Hsueh. **VFOAT** Journal of China Medical University. (197?)-. Academic Scholarly Publication. Chinese (summaries and/or abstracts in English; table of contents in English). bm. **NLM** W1; CH9817CEK. **CODEN** ZYDXEN. Documents available from BIOSIS Document Express, CASDDS.
**Ind/Abst** Biol. Abstr. (1986-); Chem. Abstr. (1984-).

CC/0253-3774
**ZHONGGUO YIXUE KEXUEYUAN XUEBAO.** (CHUNG-KUO I HSUEH KO HSUEH YUAN HSUEH PAO.). [Zhongguo yixue kexueyuan xuebao]. **VFOAT** Acta Academiae Medicinae Sinicae. Vol. 1 (1979)-. Academic Scholarly Publication. Chinese (summaries and/or abstracts in English). bm. $29.28. **(Subscription address:** China International Book Trading Corporation, PO Box 399, Library Service Department, Beijing 100044 People's Republic of China.) **NLM** W1 CH988CE. **CODEN** CIHPDR. Documents available from BIOSIS Document Express, CASDDS.
**Ind/Abst** Biol. Abstr. (1986-); Chem. Abstr.; Index Med. (1979-).

CC/0254-9042
**ZHONGGUO YIXUE WENZHAI. ZHONGYI.** (CHUNG-KUO I HSUEH WEN CHAI. CHUNG I.). [Zhongguo yixue wenzhai, Zhongyi]. **VFOAT** China Medical Abstracts. Section, Traditional Medicine. Vol. 6. Periodical. Chinese. bm. $28.00. Science Press, 16 Donghuangchenggen North Street, Beijing 100707, People's Republic of China. **Tel** 011 86 1 4019821, 011 86 1 4010642, FAX 011 86 1 4012180, 011 86 1 4019810, telex 210147. **ED** Gong Shuxian and Xiao Shuchun. **NLM** ZW 1 C555. **Ad Acc. Circ:** 40,000. ***Continues*** *Chung I Wen Chai, 0253-2220.*
**Desc:** Abstracts from 116 Chinese medical journals on traditional Chinese medicine, herbal drugs, acupuncture, and moxibustion, and other therapies, Chinese medicine combines with western medicine, etc.

CC/0255-2930
**ZHONGGUO ZHENJIU.** (CHUNG-KUO CHEN CHIU.). [Zhongguo zhenjiu]. **Added/Corp** Chung-hua Chuan kuo Chung i Chen Chiu Hsueh Hui. Chung i Yen Chiu Yuan (Peking, China). Chen Chiu Yen Chiu So. **VFOAT** Chinese Acupuncture and Moxibustion; Chinese Acupuncture & Moxibustion. (Aug. 1981)-. Periodical. Chinese (summaries and/or abstracts in English; table of contents in English). bm. China Ocean Press, 1 Fuxingmenwai Street, Beijing 100860 China. **Tel** 011 86 1 8532211 ext. 5913. **NLM** W1; CH986.
**Ind/Abst** EMBASE.

CC/1001-5302
**ZHONGGUO ZHONGYAO ZAZHI.** (CHUNG-KUO CHUNG YAO TSA CHIH.). [Zhongguo zhongyao zazhi]. **Added/Corp** Chung-kuo Yao Hsueh Hui. Chung i Yen Chiu Yuan (Peking, Chia). Chung Yao Yen Chiu So. **VFOAT** China Journal of Chinese Materia Medica; Zhongguo Zhongyao Zazhi. Vol. 1 (Jan. 1989)-. Academic Scholarly Publication. Chinese (summaries and/or abstracts in English; table of contents in English). mo. $76.80. **(Subscription address:** China International Book Trading Corporation, PO Box 399, Library Service Department, Beijing 100044 People's Republic of China.) **NLM** W1; CH986L. **CODEN** ZZZAE3. Documents available from BIOSIS Document Express, CASDDS. ***Continues*** *Chung Yao Tung Pao (Peking, China : 1981),*

*0254-0029.*
**Ind/Abst** Biol. Abstr. (1989-); Chem. Abstr.; Index Med. (1989-).

CC/0254-1424
**ZHONGHUA WULIYIXUE ZAZHI.** (CHUNG-HUA WU LI I HSUEH TSA CHIH.). [Zhonghua wuli yixue zazhi]. **Added/Corp** Ho-pei I Hsueh Yuan. **VFOAT** Zhonghua Wuliyixue Zazhi; Chinese Journal of Physical Medicine. Vol. 1 (1979)-. Periodical. Chinese (table of contents in English). qt. Hebei Academy of Medical Sciences / Hebei Yixue Yuan, 5 Chang-an Xilu, Shijiazhuang, Hebei 050017, People's Republic of China. **Tel** 44121. **(Subscription address:** China International Book Trading Corporation, PO Box 399, Library Service Department, Beijing 100044 People's Republic of China.**)** **ED** Bei Chi. **NLM** W1 CH985D. **Bk Rev. Ad Acc. Circ:** 10,000 (ctrl). Documents available from BLDSC.

CC/0255-7053
**ZHONGHUA YISHI ZAZHI.** (CHUNG-HUA I SHIH TSA CHIH.). [Zhonghua yishi zazhi]. **VFOAT** Chinese Journal of Medical History. Aug. 1980-. Periodical. Chinese. qt. RMBY9.20. Science Press, 16 Donghuangchenggen North Street, Beijing 100707, People's Republic of China. **Tel** 011 86 1 4019821, 011 86 1 4010642, FAX 011 86 1 4012180, 011 86 1 4019810, telex 210147. **LC** R601. **DD** 610/.951. **NLM** W1 CH982HM. **Circ:** 8,000. ***Continues in part*** *I Hsueh Shih Yu Pao Chien Tsa Chih.*
**Desc:** History of Chinese (minor nationalities traditional, modern), world medicine, medical literature research; medical relics; theoretical studies; medical history teaching; book reviews, etc.
**Ind/Abst** Am. Hist. Life (1991-).

CC/0253-9624
**ZHONGHUA YUFANG-YIXUE ZAZHI.** (CHUNG-HUA YU FANG I HSUEH TSA CHIH.). [Zhonghua yufang-yixue zazhi]. **Added/Corp** Chung-hua i Hsueh Hui, Peiping. **VFOAT** Zhonghua Yufangyixue Zazhi; Chinese Journal of Preventive Medicine. (1967)-. Academic Scholarly Publication. Chinese (table of contents in English). qt. $3.00. **(Subscription address:** China International Book Trading Corporation, PO Box 399, Library Service Department, Beijing 100044 People's Republic of China.**)** **NLM** W1 CH985H. **CODEN** CHYCDW. Documents available from BIOSIS Document Express, CASDDS.
**Ind/Abst** Biol. Abstr. (1985-); Chem. Abstr.; Index Med. (1979-); Rev. Med. Vet. Mycology.

CH/0529-5769
**ZHONGUA MINGUO MAZUI XUEHUI ZAZHI.** (CHUNG-HUA MIN KUO MA TSUI HSUEH HUI TSA CHIH.). [Zhonghua minguo mazui xuehui zazhi]. **VFOAT** Acta Anaesthesiologica Sinica; Chung-Hua Ma Tsui Tsa Chih. Began with: Vol. 1, 1961. Periodical. English (Chinese). qt. National Anaesthesiologic Scie Soc, Taipei Taiwan. **NLM** W1 CH982R.
**Ind/Abst** Index Med.

CH/1001-4454
**ZHONGYAOCAI.** **VFOAT** Journal of Chinese Medicinal Materials. (1985)-. Periodical. Chinese. mo. **DD** 615.1.
**Ind/Abst** Rev. Plant Pathol.; Seed Abstr.

AG/0514-7972
**ZOONOSES.** [Zoonoses]. V. 1- Mar./June 1978-. Periodical. English. qt. Pan American Zoonoses Center, Casilla de Correo 23, Ramos Mejia Argentina. **LC** RC113.5; .Z67. **DD** 616.9/5/05. **NLM** W1 ZO614R.
**Ind/Abst** Life Sci. Collect.

## ABSTRACTING, BIBLIOGRAPHIES AND STATISTICS

US/0146-5066
**5-YEAR CUMULATED BIBLIOGRAPHY OF ORTHOPAEDIC SURGERY.** **Added/Corp** National Library of Medicine (U.S.). **VAT** Five-Year Cumulated Bibliography of Orthopaedic Surgery. (1966/70)-. English. ir. Price varies per volume. Journal of Bone and Joint Surgery, 20 Pickering Street, Needham MA 02192-3157. **Tel** (617)449-9738, FAX (617)449-9742. **NLM** ZWE 168 A616.

US/0001-3331
**ABRIDGED INDEX MEDICUS.** (ABRIDGED INDEX MEDICUS / NATIONAL LIBRARY OF MEDICINE.). **Added/Corp** National Library of Medicine (U.S.) Medical Library Association. (Jan. 1970)-. Abstracting/Indexing Service. English. Twelve times a year. $55.00. Superintendent of Documents, US Government Printing Office, Washington DC 20402. **Tel** (202)275-3328, FAX (202)786-2377. **DD** 016. **NLM** ZW 1 A158. **CODEN** AIXMA. **Circ:** 4,700. available on CD-ROM (BIBLIOMED) from Digital Diagnostics Inc.; and (CORE MEDLINE) EBSCO Publishing - Peabody. ***Continues*** *American Medical Association. Abridged Index Medicus.*
**Desc:** A bibliography based on articles from 118 English-language journals. Designed for the need of the individual practitioner and libraries of small hospitals and clinics.

UK/0263-6778
**ABSTRACTS IN BIOCOMMERCE.** (ABSTRACTS IN BIOCOMMERCE : ABC.). [Abstr. biocommer.]. **VFOAT** ABC; A.B.C. Vol. 1, No. 1 (Aug. 9, 1982)-. Abstracting/Indexing Service. English. Twenty-four times a year. $439.00 Europe; $836.00 others. Biocommerce Data Ltd, 95 High Street, Slough Berks SL1 1DH United Kingdom. **Tel** 011 44 753-511777, FAX 011 44 753 512239. **ED** A Crafts-Lighty. **NLM** Z 7914.B33; A164. Index available. cum. index. **Ad Acc. Circ:** 500 (ctrl). available on an online database (File CELL) from DATA-STAR; and (File 286) DIALOG; available on diskette (as PC-ABC) from the publisher.
**Desc:** A business news monitoring service summarising important events in the biotechnology industry worldwide. A comprehensive system indexing articles in major newsletters, magazines and newspapers. Some additional US and UK newspapers that are not individually mentioned are monitored.

US/1047-4862
**ABSTRACTS IN SOCIAL GERONTOLOGY.** (ABSTRACTS IN SOCIAL GERONTOLOGY.). [Abstr. soc. gerontol.]. **Added/Corp** National Council on the Aging. Vol. 33, No. 1 (March 1990)-. Abstracting/Indexing Service. English. qt. $164.00. SAGE Periodical Press, 2455 Teller Road, Thousand Oaks CA 91320. **Tel** (805)499-0721, FAX (805)499-0871, telex 100799. **LC** IN PROCESS. **DD** 362. **NLM** ZWT 100; C976. **Acid Free. Circ:** 8,400. available on microfilm and microfiche from University Microfilms International (UMI). ***Continues*** *Current Literature on Aging, 0011-3662.*
**Desc:** Provides abstracts and bibliographies of major articles, books, reports, and other materials on all aspects of social gerontology.

US/1042-4423
**ABSTRACTS OF CLINICAL CARE GUIDELINES.** [Astr. clin. care guidel.]. **Added/Corp** Joint Commission on Accreditation of Healthcare Organizations. Vol. 1, No. 1 (Jan./Feb. 1989)-. Abstracting/Indexing Service. English. Ten times a year. $95.00 US; $105.00 other. Mosby Year Book Inc., 11830 Westline Industrial Drive, St Louis MO 63146. **Tel** (800)325-4177, (314)872-8370, FAX (314)432-1380, telex 44-2402. **DD** 610. **NLM** ZW 84.1; A1645. Index available. cum. index. **Circ:** 2,500.
**Desc:** Assists in the dissemination of clinical care guidelines.

US/0001-4249
**ACADEMY BOOKMAN, THE.** [Acad. bookm.]. V. 1- Spring 1948-. Periodical. English. sa. $20.00. New York Academy of Medicine, 2 East 103rd Street, New York NY 10029. **Tel** (212)876-8200. **ED** B A Kirkpatrick. **LC** Z881; .N6395. **DD** 016.61. **NLM** Z 675.M4 N532F. Index available. cum. index. **Bk Rev. Circ:** 400 (ctrl).

●US/1066-1107
**AIDS ABSTRACTS (ATLANTA, GA.).** (AIDS ABSTRACTS.). (1993)-. Abstracting/Indexing Service. English. mo (one complete directory plus monthly updates). $995.00 US, Canada and Mexico; $1,195.00 other. CW Henderson, PO Box 5528, Atlanta GA 30307-0528. **Tel** (404)377-8895, FAX (404)378-5411. **(Subscription address:** CW Henderson, Subscription Office, PO Box 830409, Birmingham AL 35283-0409.**)**

US/1052-0287
**AIDS BIBLIOGRAPHY.** [AIDS bibliogr.]. **Added/Corp** National Library of Medicine (U.S.). Reference Section. **VAT** Acquired Immunodeficiency Syndrome Bibliography. Vol. 1, No. 1 (Jan./March 1988)-. Government Publication. English. mo. $76.00 US; $95.00 other. Superintendent of Documents, US Government Printing Office, Washington DC 20402. **Tel** (202)275-3328, FAX (202)786-2377. **LC** Z6664.A27; A39; RC607.A26. **DD** 016.61697/92. **NLM** ZWD 308; A2877. ***Continues*** *Acquired Immunodeficiency Syndrome (AIDS).*

US
**AMERICAN HOSPITAL ASSOCIATION HOSPITAL STATISTICS.** **Added/Corp** American Hospital Association. **VFOAT** AHA Hospital Statistics. (1990-91)-. Statistical Publication. English. an. $139.00 (non-members), $59.00 (members). American Hospital Association, 840 North Lake Shore Drive, Chicago IL 60611. **Tel** (312)280-6000, (800)242-2626. **NLM** W1; AM433CM. ***Continues*** *Hospital Statistics, 0090-6662.*

US/0090-1385
**ANESTHESIOLOGY BIBLIOGRAPHY.** ***Ceased.*** **Added/Corp** American Society of Anesthesiologists. Vol. 1, (1968)-Vol. 26, No. 4, (Dec. 1993). English. qt. Wood Library Museum of Anesthesiology, 520 North Northwest, Park Ridge IL 60068. **Tel** (312)825-5586. **NLM** ZWO 200 A582. **Circ:** 400.
**Desc:** This quarterly index contains current anesthesia related references retrieved by medlars.

US/0883-6612
**ANNALS OF BEHAVIORAL MEDICINE.** (ANNALS OF BEHAVIORAL MEDICINE : A PUBLICATION OF THE SOCIETY OF BEHAVIORAL MEDICINE.). [Annals behav. med.]. **Added/Corp** Society of Behavioral Medicine (U.S.). Vol. 7, No. 1 (1985)-. Abstracting/Indexing Service. English. Four times a year (Jan., Apr., July, Oct.). $125.00. Society of Behavioral Medicine, 103 South Adams Street, Rockville MD 20850. **Tel** (301)251-2790, FAX (310)279-6749. **ED** W. Stewart Agras. **LC** R726.5; .B4263. **DD** 616/.001/9. **NLM** W1; AN56T. **CODEN** ABMEEH. **Bk Rev. Ad Acc. Pr Rev. Acid Free. Circ:** 3,000 (ctrl). Documents available from BIOSIS Document Express. ***Continues*** *Behavioral Medicine Update, 0742-5554;* ***Absorbed*** *Behavioral Medicine Abstracts.*
**Desc:** The definitive source for comprehensive reviews of topics involving the interactions of behavior and health. Features peer-reviewed reviews of cutting edge research and invited analyses by authorities in the field.
**Ind/Abst** Abstr. Anthropol. (19??-); Annals Behav. Med.; Biol. Abstr. (1986-); Cumul. Index Nurs. Allied Health Lit.; EMBASE; Linguist. Lang. Behav. Abstr.; Psychol. Abstr. (1979-); PsycINFO (1990-); Soc. Plann. Policy Dev. Abstr.; Soc. Work Abstr. [Select. Cov.]; Sociol. Abstr.

US/0732-4545
**ANNOTATED STUDENT AFFAIRS BIBLIOGRAPHY.** (ANNOTATED STUDENT AFFAIRS BIBLIOGRAPHY / ASSOCIATION OF AMERICAN MEDICAL COLLEGES.). [Annot. stud. aff. bibliogr.]. **Added/Corp** Association of American Medical Colleges. (1979)-. Bibliography. English. be. $2.95. Association of Medical Colleges, One Dupont Circle NW/Suite 200, Washington DC 20036. **Tel** (202)828-0570. **ED** Janet Bickel and Mary Cureton. **LC** Z5818.M43; A56; R745. **DD** 016.61/07/1173. **Circ:** 2,000.
**Desc:** Summarizes major articles on medical school curricula, admission, financial aid and counselling resources and on student's characteristics and career choices. Includes sections on minorities and women in medicine.

US/0738-6230
**ANNUAL STATISTICAL REPORT / AMERICAN ASSOCIATION OF COLLEGES OF OSTEOPATHIC MEDICINE.** [Annu. stat. rep. - Am. Assoc. Coll. Osteopath. Med.]. **Added/Corp** American Association of Colleges of Osteopathic Medicine. American Association of Colleges of Osteopathic Medicine. Office of Information Services. (1981)-. Statistical Publication. English. an. $13.00. American Association of Colleges of Osteopathic Medicine, 6110 Executive Boulevard, Suite 405, Rockville MD 20852. **Tel** (301)468-0990. **NLM** W 18 A615A.

US
**ANNUAL STATISTICAL REPORT / EMILY P. BISSELL HOSPITAL.** **Main/Corp** Emily P. Bissell Hospital. **Added/Corp** Emily P. Bissell Hospital. Annual Report. **VFOAT** Annual Report. (19??)-. Statistical Publication. English. an. Emily P Bissell Hospital, 3000 Newport Gap Pike, Wilmington DE 19808. **LC** RA982.W582; E473a. **DD** 362.1/1.097512.

VE
**ANUARIO DE EPIDEMIOLOGIA Y ESTADISTICA VITAL.** Statistical Publication. Spanish. an. Ministerio de Sanidad y Asistencia Social, Direccion General/G-820, Caracas Venezuela. **LC** RA234; .B32. **DD** 312/.0987. **NLM** W2 DV4 D3A. ***Continues*** *Anuario de Epidemiologia y Estadistica Vital.*

US/0272-586X
**ARKANSAS HEALTH MANPOWER STATISTICS : LICENSED PRACTICAL NURSES.** **VFOAT** Licensed Practical Nurses. 1978-. English. Arkansas Health Services Agency, 4815 West Markham Street, Little Rock AR 72205. **Tel** (501)661-2509, FAX (501)661-2399. **NLM** W2 AA8 D63AL. ***Continues in part*** *Arkansas Health Manpower Statistics, 0197-6478.*

US/0272-5878
**ARKANSAS HEALTH MANPOWER STATISTICS : REGISTERED NURSES.** **VFOAT** Registered Nurses. 1978-. English. Arkansas Health Services Agency, 4815 West Markham Street, Little Rock AR 72205. **Tel** (501)661-2509, FAX (501)661-2399. **NLM** W2 AA8 D63AP. ***Continues in part*** *Arkansas Health Manpower Resources, 0197-6478.*

US/0197-7717
**BEHAVIORAL MEDICINE ABSTRACTS.** ***Title Change.*** [Behav. med. abstr.]. **Added/Corp** Society of Behavioral Medicine (U.S.). Vol. 1, No. 1 (Jan.-Mar. 1980)-Vol. 12 (1991). Abstracting/Indexing Service. English. qt. Society of Behavioral Medicine, 103 South Adams Street, Rockville MD 20850. **Tel** (301)251-2790, FAX (310)279-6749. **ED** Frances J Keefe. **LC** R726.5; .B425. **DD** 616/.0019. **NLM** ZWM 425; B419. **Ad Acc. Circ:** 2,000. ***Absorbed by*** *Annals of Behavioral Medicine.*
**Desc:** Contains 250-300 abstracts per issue from recently published articles on disease prevention and

health promotion. Covers a wide variety of disciplines and supplies complete citations.
**Ind/Abst** Soc. Work Abstr. [Select. Cov.].

UY
**BIBLIOGRAFIA URUGUAYA DE MEDICINA : PUBLICACIONES PERIODICAS.** 1973/74-. Spanish. Universidad de la Republica de Uruguay / Medicina, Facultad de Medicina, General Flores 2125, Montevideo Uruguay.

UK/0006-1565
**BIBLIOGRAPHY OF REPRODUCTION.** ***Title Change.* See** Biology-Abstracting, Bibliographies and Statistics.

US/0067-7280
**BIBLIOGRAPHY OF THE HISTORY OF MEDICINE.** (BIBLIOGRAPHY OF THE HISTORY OF MEDICINE / NATIONAL LIBRARY OF MEDICINE.). **Added/Corp** National Library of Medicine (U.S.) United States. Public Health Service. (1965)-. Abstracting/Indexing Service. English. ir. $19.00 (1991 - latest edition). US Department of Health and Human Services National Institutes of Health, 9000 Rockville Pike, Bethesda MD 20892. **Tel** (301)496-9291, FAX (301)496-2443. **ED** James H Cassedy. **LC** Z6660; .B582. **DD** 016.61/09. **NLM** ZWZ 40 B582. cum. index. **Circ:** 1,500.
**Desc:** Citations of journals to current world-wide historical literature pertaining to the history of medicine and related sciences and specialties.

●US/1068-5693
**BIOENGINEERING ABSTRACTS (1993).** (BIOENGINEERING ABSTRACTS.). [BioEng. abstr.]. **Added/Corp** Cambridge Scientific Abstracts, Inc. Engineering Information Inc. Vol. 20, No. 1 (1993)-. Abstracting/Indexing Service. English. mo. $585.00 US; $695.00 other. Cambridge Scientific Abstracts, 7200 Wisconsin Avenue, #601, Bethesda MD 20814-4823. **Tel** (301)961-6750, (800)843-7751, FAX (301)961-6720. **DD** 610. available via Internet (to the current year's abstracts and five-year backfiles) from Cambridge Scientific Abstracts. ***Continues*** *Engineering Index Bioengineering and Biotechnology Abstracts, 1041-2913.*
**Desc:** International scope of bioengineering and biomedical engineering literature.

US/0275-1712
**BIOGRAPHICAL DIRECTORY OF THE AMERICAN ACADEMY OF PEDIATRICS.** (BIOGRAPHICAL DIRECTORY OF THE AMERICAN ACADEMY OF PEDIATRICS / COMPILED FOR THE ACADEMY BY JAQUES CATTELL PRESS, R.R. BOWKER COMPANY.). **Main/Corp** American Academy of Pediatrics. **Added/Corp** Jaques Cattell Press. 1st Ed. (1980)-. Directory. English. ir. Price varies per volume. R R Bowker, A Reed Reference Publishing Company, Part of Reed International PLC, PO Box 31, 121 Chanlon Drive, New Providence NJ 07974. **Tel** (908)464-6800, (800)521-8110, FAX (908)665-6688, telex 138-755. **LC** RJ43.A1; A45a. **DD** 618.92/00092/2; B. **NLM** WS 22 AA1 A4B.

US/0272-3603
**BIOGRAPHICAL DIRECTORY OF THE AMERICAN PODIATRY ASSOCIATION.** **Main/Corp** American Podiatry Association. (1980)-. Directory. English. ir. Price varies per volume. R R Bowker, A Reed Reference Publishing Company, Part of Reed International PLC, PO Box 31, 121 Chanlon Drive, New Providence NJ 07974. **Tel** (908)464-6800, (800)521-8110, FAX (908)665-6688, telex 138-755. **LC** RD563; .A582b. **DD** 617/.585/00922; B. **NLM** WE 22 AA1 A556.

US
**BIOGRAPHICAL DIRECTORY OF THE FELLOWS & MEMBERS OF THE AMERICAN PSYCHIATRIC ASSOCIATION.** **Main/Corp** American Psychiatric Association. **VFOAT** Biographical Directory of the American Psychiatric Association. (1973)-. Directory. English. ir. Price varies per volume. R R Bowker, A Reed Reference Publishing Company, Part of Reed International PLC, PO Box 31, 121 Chanlon Drive, New Providence NJ 07974. **Tel** (908)464-6800, (800)521-8110, FAX (908)665-6688, telex 138-755.

●UK
**BIOTECHNOLOGY ABSTRACTS.** **VFOAT** Derwent Biotechnology Abstracts. (1993)-. Abstracting/Indexing Service. English. Twenty-six times a year. $1750.00. Derwent Publications Ltd., Derwent House 14, Great Queen Street, London WC2B 5DF England. **Tel** 011 44 71 3442800. **NLM** Z 7914.B33; D484. ***Continues*** *Derwent Biotechnology Abstracts, 0262-5318.*
**Desc:** Covers all aspects of biotechnology from genetic manipulation through biochemical engineering and fermentation to downstream processing. Papers dealing exclusively with the application of the products of biotechnological processes in nonindustrial fields, methods of nonindustrial waste disposal when unrelated to the processing of industrial waste and when no economically valuable product is formed, or brewing and the preparation of established fermented foods and feedstuffs are not included.

US/0733-5709
**BIOTECHNOLOGY RESEARCH ABSTRACTS.** ***Ceased.*** [Biotechnol. res. abstr.]. **Added/Corp** Cambridge Scientific Abstracts, Inc. Vol. 1, No. 1 (Jan. 1984)-(19??). Abstracting/Indexing Service. English. bm (double issue in Dec.). Cambridge Scientific Abstracts, 7200 Wisconsin Avenue, #601, Bethesda MD 20814-4823. **Tel** (301)961-6750, (800)843-7751, FAX (301)961-6720. **ED** Darrell Stover. **LC** TP248.2; .B57. **DD** 660/.6. **NLM** ZQW 25; B616. Index available. cum. index. **Bk Rev**. available on magnetic tape; available on CD-ROM; available on an online database. ***Continued in part by*** *Medical & Pharmaceutical Biotechnology Abstracts, 1063-1178* ***and*** *Agricultural & Environmental Biotechnology Abstracts, 1063-1151.*
**Desc:** Covers genetic engineering, cloning vectors, gene manipulation, transfer, and expression; patents issued in the US, products and applications of biotechnology, and much more. Provides important information for scientists in wide-ranging fields for specialists concerned with pollution and environment and for academic, governmental, and industrial information specialists.

US/0896-4572
**BREASTFEEDING ABSTRACTS.** [Breastfeed. abstr.]. **Added/Corp** La Leche League International. Vol. 1, No. 1 (Summer 1981)-. Periodical. English. Four times a year (Feb., May, Aug., Nov.). $12.50 (non-members); $50.00 (members) Comes in combination with Breastfeeding Resource Centers membership Professional & New Beginnings. La Leche League International, 9616 Minneapolis Avenue, Franklin Park IL 60131. **Tel** (708)455-7730. **(Subscription address:** 3022 Huntington Drive, Arlington Heights, IL 60004, telephone: (708)577-2625**)** **LC** Discard. **DD** 618. **NLM** ZWS 125; B828.

FR/0998-678X
**BULLETIN BIBLIOGRAPHIQUE O.R.S.T.O.M. SANTE.** Vol. 2, No. 1 (1990)-. Bulletin. French. sa. 90.00F France; 100.00F other. Editions de l'ORSTOM, 72 Route d'Aulnay, 93143 Bondy Cedex France. **Tel** 011 33 1 48025500. Index available. **Circ:** 300. available on diskette.
**Desc:** Bibliography on Health Sciences including epidemiology, medical entomology, parasitology, virology, nutrition, medical anthropology.

UK/0008-0586
**CALCIFIED TISSUE ABSTRACTS.** ***Title Change.*** [Calcif. tissue abstr.]. **Added/Corp** Information Retrieval Limited. Cambridge Scientific Abstracts, Inc. Medical Research Council (Great Britain). Mineral Metabolism Unit. (Apr. 1969)-(1993). Abstracting/Indexing Service. English. qt (plus annual index). Cambridge Scientific Abstracts, 7200 Wisconsin Avenue, #601, Bethesda MD 20814-4823. **Tel** (301)961-6750, (800)843-7751, FAX (301)961-6720. **ED** Graciela Duran-Troise. **LC** QP88.2; .C35. **DD** 599/.019214. **NLM** ZWE 200; C144. Index available. cum. index (annual). **Bk Rev**. available on magnetic tape; available on an online database from DIALOG; and BRS; available on CD-ROM from Compact Cambridge. ***Continued by*** *Calcium and Calcified Tissue Abstracts, 1069-5540.*
**Desc:** Assembles pertinent findings drawn from wide-ranging disciplines, eliminating the need for exhaustive investigations. From bone tumors and diseases to cellular studies, the journal covers all aspects of bone mineral metabolism. Each issue cites revealing new research into intestinal absorption of calcium, phosphorus, and magnesium, osteoporosis, and a host of other topics essential to medical research.

●US/1069-5540
**CALCIUM AND CALCIFIED TISSUE ABSTRACTS.** **Added/Corp** Cambridge Scientific Abstracts, Inc. (1994)-. Abstracting/Indexing Service. English. qt (4 issues). $495.00 US; $575.00 other. Cambridge Scientific Abstracts, 7200 Wisconsin Avenue, #601, Bethesda MD 20814-4823. **Tel** (301)961-6750, (800)843-7751, FAX (301)961-6720. **NLM** ZWE 200; C144. available via Internet (to the current year's abstracts and five-year backfiles) from Cambridge Scientific Abstracts. ***Continues*** *Calcified Tissue Abstracts, 0008-0586.*

CN/0225-9451
**CANADIAN MEDICAL EDUCATION STATISTICS.** [Can. med. educ. stat.]. **Added/Corp** Association of Canadian Medical Colleges. **VFOAT** Statistiques Relatives a l'Enseignement Medical au Canada. (1977/78)-. English (French). an. 30.00Can$. Association of Canadian Medical Colleges, 774 Echo Drive, Ottawa, Ontario K1S 5P2 Canada. **Tel** (613)730-0687. **ED** E Ryten. **DD** 610/.7/1171. **NLM** W 18 C213. Index available. **Circ:** 300.
**Desc:** Statistics on enrollment, graduation, admissions, fees, post-MD. residency training, of Canadian Medical Schools.

BL
**CATALOGO COLETIVO DE PUBLICACOES PERIODICAS EM CIENCIAS BIOMEDICAS.** Portuguese. Av General Justo, 171 4 Po S Andar, CEP 20000 Rio de Janeiro Brazil. **LC** Z6660; .C35; R129. **DD** 016.61/05.

US/0009-3939
**CHILD DEVELOPMENT ABSTRACTS AND BIBLIOGRAPHY.** [Child dev. abstr. bibliogr.]. **Added/Corp** Society for Research in Child Development. National Research Council (U.S.). Committee on Child Development. Vol. 2 (Feb. 1928)-. Abstracting/Indexing Service. English. Three times a year. $68.00. University of Chicago Press / Journals Division, PO Box 37005, 5720 South Woodlawn, Chicago IL 60637. **Tel** (312)753-3347, FAX (312)753-0811. **(Subscription telephone:** (312)753-8083**)** **ED** Neil Joseph Salkind. **LC** HQ750.A1; C47. **DD** 305.2/3. **NLM** ZWS 100 C536. **Bk Rev. Acid Free.** available on microfilm and microfiche from University Microfilms International (UMI). ***Continues*** *Selected Child Development Abstracts Currently Published in the Journal of Nervous and Mental Disease, the Wistar Institute Bibliographic Service, American Journal of Diseases of Children, Archives of Neurology and Psychiatry, Psychological Abstracts, Physiological Abstracts, Biological Abstracts, Chemical Abstracts, Endocrinology.*
**Desc:** Source for references to the current literature related to growth and development of children.

●US
**CINAHL (PEABODY, MASS.).** (CINAHL [COMPUTER FILE] / EBSCO CD-ROM.). (1993)-. English. mo. $1095.00. EBSCO Publishing / Boston, 83 Pine Street, Peabody MA 01960. **Tel** (800)653-2726 North America, (508)535-8500, FAX (508)535-8545.
**Desc:** Nursing and allied health professionals who want information applicable to their specialties can find it in this comprehensive database.

US/0884-8092
**COMBINED CUMULATIVE INDEX TO OBSTETRICS AND GYNECOLOGY.** [Comb. cumul. index obstet. gynecol.]. **VFOAT** Obstetrics and Gynecology. Vol. 1 (1985)-. Abstracting/Indexing Service. English. an. $130.00 (Volume 7). Numarc Book Corporation, 60 Alcona Avenue, Buffalo NY 14226. **Tel** (716)834-1390. **ED** Carl W. Hepp. **DD** 618. Index available. ctrl circ.
**Desc:** Original subject and author indexing to seven of the most widely read obstetrical and gynecological specialty journals.

US/0190-4981
**COMBINED CUMULATIVE INDEX TO PEDIATRICS.** [Comb. cumul. index pediatr.]. Vol. 1 (1978)-. Abstracting/Indexing Service. English. an. $127.50. Numarc Book Corporation, 60 Alcona Avenue, Buffalo NY 14226. **Tel** (716)834-1390. **ED** Carl W. Hepp. **LC** Z6671.5; .C65; RJ45. **DD** 016.61892. **NLM** ZWS 100 C731. Index available. cum. index. **Circ:** 2,000 (ctrl).
**Desc:** Original subject and author indexing to sixteen of the most widely read pediatric specialty journals.

UK
**COMMUNICABLE DISEASE STATISTICS / OFFICE OF POPULATION CENSUSES AND SURVEYS [AND] COMMUNICABLE DISEASE SURVEILLANCE CENTRE OF THE PUBLIC HEALTH LABORATORY SERVICE.** **Added/Corp** Great Britain. Office of Population Censuses and Surveys. Communicable Disease Surveillance Centre of the Public Health Laboratory Service (Great Britain). (1979)-. English. an. Her Majesty's Stationery Office, 51 Nine Elms Lane, London SW8 5DR England. **Tel** 011 44 71 873 8459, 011 44 71 873 8499, FAX 011 44 71 873 8499, 011 44 71 873 8456, telex 297138. **(Subscription address:** Her Majesty's Stationery Office, PO Box 276, Publications Centre, London SW8 5DT England.**)** **LC** RA643.7.G7; S73. **DD** 312/.39/0942. ***Continues*** *Statistics of Infectious Diseases.*

US
**CONNECTICUT'S PRIVATE MENTAL HOSPITALS : INPATIENT STATISTICS FOR YEAR ENDING ... / PREPARED BY STATISTICS SECTION, CONNECTICUT STATE DEPARTMENT OF MENTAL HEALTH.** **Added/Corp** Connecticut. Dept. of Mental Health. Statistics Section. **VFOAT** Private Mental Hospitals, Inpatient Statistics. (19??)-. English. an. Statistics Section / Hartford, Connecticut State Department of Mental Health, 90 Washington Street, Hartford CT 06115. **LC** RC445.C78; C69. **DD** 362.2/1/09746.

CN
**CONTACT /REVUE OFFICIELLE DE L ASSOCIATION QUEBECOICE DES ARCHIVISTES MEDICALES.** French. Four times a year (Published March, June, Sept. and Dec.).

25.42Can$. Asociation que Archivistes Medicales, 4257 Place Viger, PO Box 1020, Rock Forest, Quebec, JIN 1Y9 Canada. **Tel** (819)567-6935, FAX (819)823-0799.

US/0141-7711
## CSA NEUROSCIENCES ABSTRACTS.
[CSA neurosci. abstr.]. **VFOAT** C.S.A. Neurosciences Abstracts; Neurosciences Abstracts. **VAT** Cambridge Scientific Abstracts Neurosciences Abstracts. Vol. 1, No. 1 (Jan. 1983)-. Abstracting/Indexing Service. English. mo (includes annual index). $740.00 US; $815.00 other. Cambridge Scientific Abstracts, 7200 Wisconsin Avenue, #601, Bethesda MD 20814-4823. **Tel** (301)961-6750, (800)843-7751, FAX (301)961-6720. **ED** Mary Brazier and Jaun M. Saavedra. **LC** QP351; .C75. **DD** 591.1/88. **NLM** ZWL 100 C958. Index available. cum. index. available on magnetic tape; available on an online database; available on CD-ROM; available via Internet (to the current year's abstracts and five-year backfiles) from Cambridge Scientific Abstracts.
**Desc:** Covers all aspects of vertebrate and invertebrate neuroscience, emphasizing basic research studies. Each issue examines specific topics such as aging, degeneration and repair, neuropharmacology, molecular neurobiology, genetics, sleep, neural correlates of behavior, immunology and much more.

US/0090-1377
## CUMULATED ABRIDGED INDEX MEDICUS.
(CUMULATED ABRIDGED INDEX MEDICUS / NATIONAL LIBRARY OF MEDICINE.). **Added/Corp** National Library of Medicine (U.S.) Medical Library Association. (1970)-. English. an. $104.00. Superintendent of Documents, US Government Printing Office, Washington DC 20402. **Tel** (202)275-3328, FAX (202)786-2377. **LC** Z6660; .C79. **DD** 016.61. **NLM** ZW 1 A158.
**Desc:** A cumulation in one volume of the citations appearing in the monthly Abridged Index Medicus. Contains subject and author sections.

US/0090-1423
## CUMULATED INDEX MEDICUS.
[Cumul. index med.]. **Added/Corp** American Medical Association. National Library of Medicine (U.S.). (1960)-. Abstracting/Indexing Service. English. an. $301.00 (1991) US; $37.00 (1991) other. National Library of Medicine, 8600 Rockville Pike, Bethesda MD 20894. **Tel** (301)496-6308. **LC** Z6660; .I422. **DD** 016.61. **NLM** ZW 1 I384. **Circ:** 5,000. available on microfilm and microfiche from University Microfilms International (UMI); available on microfiche; available in reprints from University Microfilms International (UMI). ***Continues*** *Quarterly Cumulative Index Medicus.*
**Desc:** A cumulation of the citations appearing in Index Medicus for the previous year. Includes author and subject sections-Medical Subject Headings, List of Journals Indexed in Index Medicus, and Bibliography of Medical Reviews.

US/0146-5554
## CUMULATIVE INDEX TO NURSING & ALLIED HEALTH LITERATURE.
[Cumul. index nurs. allied health lit.]. **Added/Corp** Glendale Adventist Medical Center. Seventh-Day Adventist Hospital Association. **VFOAT** Nursing and Allied Health (CINAHL); Nursing and Allied Health Index; CINAHL. **VAT** Cumulative Index to Nursing and Allied Health Literature. Vol. 22 (1977)-. Abstracting/Indexing Service. English. bm. $295.00. CINAHL Information Systems, 1509 Wilson Terrace, Glendale CA 91209. **Tel** (818)409-8005. **(Subscription address:** CINAHL Information Systems, PO Box 871, Glendale, CA 91209**) ED** Delauna Lockwood. **LC** Z6675.N7; C8; RT41. **DD** 016.61/073. **NLM** ZWY 100 C971. Index available. cum. index. **Ad Acc. Circ:** 5,300. available on microfilm and microfiche from University Microfilms International (UMI); available on magnetic tape; available on CD-ROM from SilverPlatter (US); and Compact Cambridge; available on an online database from DIALOG; DATA-STAR; and (label- NAHL) BRS/Colleague. ***Continues*** *Cumulative Index to Nursing Literature, 0011-3018;* ***Absorbed*** *Nursing and Allied Health Index, 0744-8732.* ***Continued in part by*** *Nursing and Allied Health Index, 0744-8732.*
**Desc:** Contains citations from nursing and allied health journals; includes a subject headings list.

US
## CUMULATIVE INDEX TO NURSING & ALLIED HEALTH LITERATURE. [MICROFICHE].
(19??)-. English. ir. University Microfilms International, 300 North Zeeb Road, Ann Arbor MI 48106-1346. **Tel** (313)761-4700, (800)521-0600 Exts. 2490, 2491, FAX (313)973-1540. available in print.

UK/0895-9803
## CURRENT ADVANCES IN CANCER RESEARCH.
[Curr. adv. cancer res.]. Vol. 1, No. 1 (Jan. 1988)-. Abstracting/Indexing Service. English. mo. $857.00 The Americas; £575.00 other. Elsevier Geo Abstracts, An Imprint of Elsevier Science Ltd., The Boulevard, Langford Lane, Kidlington, Oxford OX5 1GB United Kingdom. **Tel** 011 44 865 843000, 011 44 865 843699, FAX 011 44 865 843010. **(Subscription address:** Elsevier Science Ltd. Oxford Fulfillment Centre, PO Box 800, Kidlington, Oxford OX5 1DX United Kingdom.**) LC** Z6664.C2; C87. **DD** 616. **NLM** ZQZ 200; C9758. available on microfilm and microfiche from University Microfilms International (UMI).
**Desc:** Designed to provide biologists working in any area of the subject with a current literature searching service which is fast, comprehensive, economical, and above all, easy to use. More than 2,000 journals covering all aspects of cancer research will be scanned each month. Titles will be presented under 35 major subject headings with full cross referencing.

●UK/0964-8720
## CURRENT ADVANCES IN ENDOCRINOLOGY AND METABOLISM.
**VFOAT** Current Advances in Endocrinology & Metabolism. Vol. 9, No. 1 (Jan. 1992)-. Abstracting/Indexing Service. English. mo. $775.00 The Americas; £520.00 other. Elsevier Geo Abstracts, An Imprint of Elsevier Science Ltd., The Boulevard, Langford Lane, Kidlington, Oxford OX5 1GB United Kingdom. **Tel** 011 44 865 843000, 011 44 865 843699, FAX 011 44 865 843010. **(Subscription address:** Elsevier Science Ltd. Oxford Fulfillment Centre, PO Box 800, Kidlington, Oxford OX5 1DX United Kingdom.**) ED** Harry Smith. **LC** QP1; .C9. **DD** 016.5911. **NLM** ZWK 102; C976. available on microfilm and microfiche from University Microfilms International (UMI). ***Continues*** *Current Advances in Physiology, 0741-1693.*
**Desc:** Provides current awareness service in the fields of endocrinology and metabolism studies.

●UK/0964-8747
## CURRENT ADVANCES IN IMMUNOLOGY & INFECTIOUS DISEASES.
**VFOAT** Current Advances in Immunology and Infectious Diseases. Vol. 9, No. 1 (Jan. 1992)-. Abstracting/Indexing Service. English. mo. $1021.00 The Americas; £685.00 other. Elsevier Geo Abstracts, An Imprint of Elsevier Science Ltd., The Boulevard, Langford Lane, Kidlington, Oxford OX5 1GB United Kingdom. **Tel** 011 44 865 843000, 011 44 865 843699, FAX 011 44 865 843010. **(Subscription address:** Elsevier Science Ltd. Oxford Fulfillment Centre, PO Box 800, Kidlington, Oxford OX5 1DX United Kingdom.**) ED** Harry Smith. **LC** Z6663.I4; C87; QR180. **DD** 016.5912/9. **NLM** ZWQ 504; C9755. available on microfilm and microfiche from University Microfilms International (UMI). ***Continues*** *Current Advances in Immunology, 0741-1650.*
**Desc:** A current literature searching service which enables pure and applied scientists to keep abreast of the ever increasing literature being published in their subject area, by providing a subject categorized listing of titles, authors, bibliographic details and authors' addresses. A few major subject areas covered are: immunoglobulin; medical and veterinary mycology; AIDS and HIV; and network theory.

UK/0741-1677
## CURRENT ADVANCES IN NEUROSCIENCE.
[Curr. adv. neurosci.]. (1984)-. Abstracting/Indexing Service. English. mo. $1029.00 The Americas; £690.00 other. Elsevier Geo Abstracts, An Imprint of Elsevier Science Ltd., The Boulevard, Langford Lane, Kidlington, Oxford OX5 1GB United Kingdom. **Tel** 011 44 865 843000, 011 44 865 843699, FAX 011 44 865 843010. **(Subscription address:** Elsevier Science Ltd. Oxford Fulfillment Centre, PO Box 800, Kidlington, Oxford OX5 1DX United Kingdom.**) ED** Harry Smith (editor's address: Department of Botany, University of Leicester, University Road, Leicester LE1 7QQ UK) and Peter N Campbell (editor's address: Department of Biochemistry, University College, London WC1E 6BT UK). **LC** QP351; .C85. **DD** 599/.0188. **NLM** ZWL 100; C976. **Circ:** 1,200. available on microfilm and microfiche from University Microfilms International (UMI). ***Continues in part*** *Current Awareness in Biological Sciences.*
**Desc:** Gives listings of titles of neuro-scientific papers published throughout the world classified into 134 major areas. Full bibliographical citations and reprint addresses are included.

●UK/0965-0512
## CURRENT ADVANCES IN TOXICOLOGY.
Vol. 9, No. 1 (Jan. 1992)-. Abstracting/Indexing Service. English. mo. $656.00 The Americas; £440.00 other. Elsevier Geo Abstracts, An Imprint of Elsevier Science Ltd., The Boulevard, Langford Lane, Kidlington, Oxford OX5 1GB United Kingdom. **Tel** 011 44 865 843000, 011 44 865 843699, FAX 011 44 865 843010. **(Subscription address:** Elsevier Science Ltd. Oxford Fulfillment Centre, PO Box 800, Kidlington, Oxford OX5 1DX United Kingdom.**) ED** Harry Smith. **LC** Z6665.A1; C87. **DD** 016.6159. **NLM** ZQV 600; C976. **Circ:** 1,000. available on microfilm and microfiche from University Microfilms International (UMI). ***Continues*** *Current Advances in Pharmacology & Toxicology, 0741-1685.*
**Desc:** Provides a current awareness service in the realm of toxicology. Classified by subject.

AT/0727-2545
## CURRENT AUSTRALIAN HEALTH SERIALS.
**Added/Corp** Australia. Dept. of Health. Central Library. (1979)-. English. ir. Australian Government Publishing Service, GPO Box 84, Canberra ACT 2601 Australia. **Tel** 011 61 6 2954411, FAX 011 61 6 2954455. **NLM** ZW 1 C93.

US/1052-9063
## CURRENT BIBLIOGRAPHIES IN MEDICINE.
[Curr. bibliogr. med.]. **Added/Corp** National Library of Medicine (U.S.). **VFOAT** CBM. (1988)-. Monographic series. English. ir (approximately 20 bibliographies issued annually). $60.00 domestic; $75.00 other. Superintendent of Documents, US Government Printing Office, Washington DC 20402. **Tel** (202)275-3328, FAX (202)786-2377. **LC** Z6660; .U66b. **DD** 610. **NLM** ZW 1; N272. ***Continues*** *Literature Search, 0083-2251;* ***Absorbed*** *Specialized Bibliography Series, 0276-234X.*
**Desc:** Publishes approximately 20 bibliographies per year on a variety of biomedical topics similar to those covered previously in the NLM Literature Search series.
**Ind/Abst** Dairy Sci. Abstr.; Missionalia.

UK/0960-5037
## CURRENT BIOTECHNOLOGY.
**Added/Corp** Royal Society of Chemistry (Great Britain). Vol. 9, Issue 1 (Jan. 1991)-. Abstracting/Indexing Service. English. mo (12 issues). £436.00 EC and other; $790.00 US. Royal Society of Chemistry, Thomas Graham House, Science Park, Cambridge CB4 4WF England. **Tel** 011 44 223 420066, FAX 011 44 223 423429, telex 818293 ROYAL. **(Subscription address:** Turpin Distribution Services Limited, Blackhorse Road, Letchworth, Hertfordshire SG6 1HN, United Kingdom.**) LC** TP248.2; .C87. **DD** 660.6/05. **NLM** ZQU 4; C7964. **CODEN** CUBIER. Index available. **Ad Acc.** available on an online database from CAN/OLE; ESA-IRS; DIALOG; and DATA-STAR. ***Continues*** *Current Biotechnology Abstracts, 0264-3391.*
**Desc:** A current awareness periodical which reports on the latest scientific, technical and commercial advances in the field of biotechnology- the development of biological systems to create useful products. It covers the production and use of biological, inorganic, organic chemicals for the agricultural, food, pharmaceutical and other industries and biotechnology in energy production and waste treatment.

US/0891-3358
## CURRENT CONTENTS. CLINICAL MEDICINE.
[Curr. contents, Clin. med.]. **Added/Corp** Institute for Scientific Information. **VFOAT** Clinical Medicine; CM; Current Contents. CM; CC/CM. Vol. 15, No. 1 (Jan. 5, 1987)-. Abstracting/Indexing Service. English. wk. $488.00 print; $779.00 combined with diskette. Institute for Scientific Information, 3501 Market Street, Philadelphia PA 19104. **Tel** (215)386-0100, (800)523-1850, FAX (215)386-6362, telex 84-5305. **(Subscription address:** Institute for Scientific Information, PO Box 71416, Chicago IL 60694.**) DD** 610. **NLM** ZW 1; C95. **CODEN** CCCMEK. available on diskette; available on magnetic tape and an online database (as Current Contents Search); available on CD-ROM. Documents available from The Genuine Article. ***Continues*** *Current Contents. Clinical Practice, 0091-1704.*
**Desc:** Reproduces the table of contents of issues of journals in a range of medical disciplines.
**Ind/Abst** Curr. Contents Clin. Med.; Health Devices Alerts; Res. Alert [Full Cov.]; Sci. Cit. Index; SCISEARCH; Soc. Sci. Cit. Index [Full Cov.].

●US/1073-1237
## CURRENT CONTENTS. CLINICAL MEDICINE (CD-ROM VERSION).
(CURRENT CONTENTS. CLINICAL MEDICINE [COMPUTER FILE].). **Added/Corp** Institute for Scientific Information. **VFOAT** Clinical Medicine. (1994)-. English. wk. $1995.00. Institute for Scientific Information, 3501 Market Street, Philadelphia PA 19104. **Tel** (215)386-0100, (800)523-1850, FAX (215)386-6362, telex 84-5305. **(Subscription address:** Institute for Scientific Information, PO Box 71416, Chicago, IL 60694**)** available in print; available on diskette; available on magnetic tape and an online database.
**Desc:** Covers the latest issues of the world's leading journals in a wide range of medical disciplines.

US/1062-3159
## CURRENT CONTENTS ON DISKETTE. CLINICAL MEDICINE.
(CURRENT CONTENTS ON DISKETTE. CLINICAL MEDICINE [COMPUTER FILE].). [Curr. contents diskette, Clin. med.]. **VFOAT** Clinical Medicine. Vol. 18, Issue 1 (Jan. 1, 1990)-. Periodical. English. wk. $487.00. Institute for Scientific Information, 3501 Market Street, Philadelphia PA 19104. **Tel** (215)386-0100, (800)523-1850, FAX (215)386-6362, telex 84-5305. **(Subscription address:** Institute for Scientific Information, PO Box 71416, Chicago, IL 60694**) DD** 016. available in print (As: Current Contents. Clinical Medicine); available on magnetic tape and an online database; available on CD-ROM.
**Desc:** Covers the latest issues of the world's leading journals in a wide range of medical disciplines.

US/1062-3116
## CURRENT CONTENTS ON DISKETTE WITH ABSTRACTS. CLINICAL MEDICINE.
(CURRENT CONTENTS ON DISKETTE WITH ABSTRACTS. CLINICAL MEDICINE [COMPUTER FILE].). [Curr. contents diskette abstr., Clin. med.]. **VFOAT** Clinical Medicine. Vol. 19, Issue 18 (May 6, 1991)-. Periodical. English. wk. $525.00. Institute for Scientific Information, 3501 Market Street, Philadelphia

PA 19104. **Tel** (215)386-0100, (800)523-1850, FAX (215)386-6362, telex 84-5305. **(Subscription address:** Institute for Scientific Information, PO Box 71416, Chicago IL 60694.**) DD** 016. available in print (As: Current Contents. Clinical Medicine); available on magnetic tape and an online database; available on CD-ROM.
**Desc:** Covers journals in a wide range of medical disciplines.

US/0882-2441
**CURRENT RESEARCH UPDATES. OBSTETRICS & GYNECOLOGY.** [Curr. res. updates, Obstet. gynecol.]. **VFOAT** Obstetrics & Gynecology; Obstetrics and Gynecology; Current Research Updates in Obstetrics & Gynecology. (198?)-. Periodical. English. Twelve times a year. $135.00 (institution), $80.00 (individual). Current Research Updates Publishing, PO Box 2831, Bellingham WA 98227. **Tel** (206)647-1568. **ED** Karen S. Stephan. **DD** 618. Index available. cum. index. **Circ:** 400.
**Desc:** Abstracts of all relevant papers appearing in more than 800 worldwide professional journals. Approximately 200 abstracts per month. Full citation and author address.

UK/0262-5318
**DERWENT BIOTECHNOLOGY ABSTRACTS.** ***Title Change.*** [Derwent biotechnol. abstr.]. Vol. 1, No. 1 (July 15, 1982)-(Mar. 1993). Abstracting/Indexing Service. English. bw. Derwent Publications Ltd., Derwent House 14, Great Queen Street, London WC2B 5DF England. **Tel** 011 44 71 3442800. **LC** TP248.13; .D47. **DD** 660.6/05. **NLM** Z 7914.B33; D484. Index available. ctrl circ. ***Continued by*** *Biotechnology Abstracts.*
**Desc:** Covers all aspects of biotechnology from genetic manipulation through biochemical engineering and fermentation to downstream processing. Papers dealing exclusively with the application of the products of biotechnological processes in nonindustrial fields, methods of nonindustrial waste disposal when unrelated to the processing of industrial waste and when no economically valuable product is formed, or brewing and the preparation of established fermented foods and feedstuffs are not included.

UK/0012-1622
**DEVELOPMENTAL MEDICINE & CHILD NEUROLOGY.** [Dev. med. child neurol.]. **Added/Corp** National Spastics Society (Great Britain). Medical Education and Information Unit. Spastics Society. Medical Education and Information Unit. Spastics International Medical Publications. MacKeith Press. American Academy for Cerebral Palsy. American Academy For Cerebral Palsy & Developmental Medicine. British Paediatric Neurology Association. **VFOAT** Developmental Medicine and Child Neurology. Vol. 4, No. 1 (Feb. 1962)-. Abstracting/Indexing Service. English (summaries and/or abstracts in French, German and Spanish). mo (2 supplements and index). $137.00 US, Canada & Mexico; £92.00 other. Cambridge University Press, The Edinburgh Building, Shaftesbury Road, Cambridge CB2 2RU United Kingdom. **Tel** 011 44 223 312393, FAX 011 44 223 325959. **(Subscription address:** Cambridge University Press / North America, 110 Midland Avenue, Port Chester NY 10573.**) ED** Martin C. O. Bax. **LC** RJ1; .D4. **DD** 616.8. **NLM** W1 DE997T. **CODEN** DMCNAW. **[CCC].** Index available. cum. index. **Bk Rev. Ad Acc. Pr Rev. Circ:** 5,500. available on microfilm and microfiche from University Microfilms International (UMI). Documents available from The Genuine Article, BIOSIS Document Express. ***Continues*** *Cerebral Palsy Bulletin.* ***Continued in part by*** *American Academy For Cerebral Palsy & Developmental Medicine. Meeting. Abstracts.*
**Desc:** The official journal of the American Academy for Cerebral Palsy and Developmental Medicine and the British Paediatric Neurology Association. Covers a wide range of clinical topics involving diseases or disabilities of children. Also of interest to specialists engaged in medical research in pediatrics, genetics, orthopedics, rheumatology, endocrinology, neurology, and other relevant areas. Features original articles, case reports, assessments, letters to the editor, book reviews, current articles listings and notices.
**Ind/Abst** Annals Behav. Med.; Biol. Abstr.; Cumul. Index Nurs. Allied Health Lit.; Curr. Aware. Biol. Sci., CABS; Curr. Contents Clin. Med.; Curr. Contents Life Sci.; Dev. Med. Child Neurol.; EMBASE; Except. Child Educ. Resour.; Health Period. Database; Health Plan. Adminis.; Index Med.; Leadscan; Nutr. Abstr. Rev., Ser. B, Live Feeds and Feed. (1962-); Nutr. Abstr. Rev., Ser. A, Hum. Exp.; Nutr. Res. Newsl.; Life Sci. Collect.; Protozoolog. Abstr.; Psychol. Abstr. (1962-); PsycINFO; PsycLit; Ref. Upd. Deluxe Ed.; Res. Alert [Full Cov.]; Sci. Cit. Index; SCISEARCH; Soc. Sci. Cit. Index [Select. Cov.]; Spec. Educ. Needs Abstr.; Trop. Dis. Bull.; Women Stud. Abstr.

UK
**DIAGNOSTIC TUMOUR BIBLIOGRAPHIES.** 1-. Monographic series. English. Price varies per volume. **NLM** ZQZ 241; D536.

●NE
**EMBASE LIST OF JOURNALS INDEXED.** **Added/Corp** Excerpta Medica (Firm). **VFOAT** List of Journals Indexed. (1993)-. Abstracting/Indexing Service. English. an. Elsevier Science Publishing Company Inc, Madison Square Station, PO Box 882, New York NY 10159-0882. **Tel** (212)633-3950, FAX (212)633-3990. ***Continues*** *List of Journals Abstracted (1983).*
**Desc:** Complete listing of biomedical journals which are screened for items for inclusion in the EMBASE database and other Excerpta Medica services.

NE
**EMBASE [ONLINE DATABASE].** Abstracting/Indexing Service. English. Excerpta Medica / Electronic Publishing Division, Molenwerf 1, 1014 AG Amsterdam, PO Box 2227, 1000 CE Amsterdam, The Netherlands. **Tel** 020 5803201, FAX 020 5803214, telex 18582.
**Desc:** Database consisting of over 7980 biomedical scientific journals. Of these, over 2500 are screened cover-to-cover for all biomedical scientific information. Covers all journals which are included in the Excerpta Medica journal collection.

US/1041-2913
**ENGINEERING INDEX BIOENGINEERING AND BIOTECHNOLOGY ABSTRACTS.** ***Title Change.* See** Engineering-Abstracting, Bibliographies and Statistics.

NE/0014-4053
**EXCERPTA MEDICA. SECTION 1. ANATOMY, ANTHROPOLOGY, EMBRYOLOGY AND HISTOLOGY.** [Excerpta Med., Sect. 1]. **VFOAT** Anatomy, Anthropology, Embryology and Histology. **VAT** Excerpta Medica. Section One. Anatomy, Anthropology, Embryology and Histology. Vol. 1 (Oct. 1947)-. Abstracting/Indexing Service. English. Sixteen times a year (2 volumes). Fl1776.00. Excerpta Medica Publishing Group, PO Box 548, 1000 AM Amsterdam Netherlands. **Tel** 011 31 20 5803243. **(Subscription address:** Excerpta Medica Journals, PO Box 85, Limerick Ireland.**) NLM** ZW 1 E954. **CODEN** AAEHA9. **[CCC].** Index Available, published separately, free-automatically sent. **Ad Acc. Circ:** 300. available on microfilm from University Microfilms International (UMI); available on CD-ROM from SilverPlatter (US). Documents available from CASDDS.
**Desc:** Covers primarily normal anatomy and embryology in distinction to pathological anatomy and teratology, which are to be found in the abstract journals on 'General Pathology and Pathological Anatomy' and 'Developmental Biology and Teratology', respectively.
**Ind/Abst** Anthropol. Index; Chem. Abstr.

NE/0014-407X
**EXCERPTA MEDICA. SECTION 3. ENDOCRINOLOGY.** **Added/Corp** Excerpta Medica Foundation. **VFOAT** Excerpta Medica. Section Three, Endocrinology; Endocrinology. Vol. 26, No. 1 (Jan. 1972)-. Abstracting/Indexing Service. English. Twenty-four times a year (3 vols.). Fl2610.00. Excerpta Medica Publishing Group, PO Box 548, 1000 AM Amsterdam Netherlands. **Tel** 011 31 20 5803243. **(Subscription address:** Excerpta Medica Journals, PO Box 85, Limerick Ireland.**) NLM** ZW 1 E956. **[CCC].** Index Available, published separately, free-automatically sent. available on microfilm from University Microfilms International (UMI); available on CD-ROM. ***Continues*** *Excerpta Medica. Section 3. Endocrinology, Experimental and Clinical.*
**Desc:** Covers both normal and abnormal, clinical and experimental endocrinology.

●NE
**EXCERPTA MEDICA. SECTION 4. MICROBIOLOGY, BACTERIOLOGY, MYCOLOGY, PARASITOLOGY, AND VIROLOGY.** **Added/Corp** Excerpta Medica (Firm). **VFOAT** Microbiology, Bacteriology, Mycology, Parasitology, and Virology. Vol. 70, Issue 1 (1992)-. Abstracting/Indexing Service. English. Thirty-two times a year (4 volumes). Fl3712.00. Excerpta Medica Publishing Group, PO Box 548, 1000 AM Amsterdam Netherlands. **Tel** 011 31 20 5803243. **(Subscription address:** Excerpta Medica Journals, PO Box 85, Limerick Ireland.**) NLM** ZW 1; E9571. **CODEN** MBVMA. available on CD-ROM from SilverPlatter (US). ***Continues*** *Excerpta Medica. Section 4, Microbiology;* ***Absorbed*** *Virology, 0031-6520.*
**Desc:** Contains information on the general aspects of infectious diseases, diagnosis, treatment, epidemiology and prevention of diseases.

NE/0014-4096
**EXCERPTA MEDICA. SECTION 5. GENERAL PATHOLOGY AND PATHOLOGICAL ANATOMY.** [Excerpta Med., Sect. 5]. **Added/Corp** Excerpta Medica (Firm). **VFOAT** Excerpta Medica; General Pathology and Pathological Anatomy. **VAT** Excerpta Medica. Section Five. General Pathology and Pathological Anatomy. Vol. 1, (July 1948)-. Abstracting/Indexing Service. English. Twenty-four times a year (3 vols.). Fl2700.00. Excerpta Medica Publishing Group, PO Box 548, 1000 AM Amsterdam Netherlands. **Tel** 011 31 20 5803243. **(Subscription address:** Excerpta Medica Journals, PO Box 85, Limerick Ireland.**) LC** RB1; .G4. **DD** 616.0758. **NLM** ZW 1 E958. **CODEN** GPPABB. **[CCC].** Index Available, published separately, free-automatically sent. available on microfilm from University Microfilms International (UMI); available on CD-ROM from SilverPlatter (US). Documents available from CASDDS.
**Desc:** Organized into three major divisions: general pathology, organ pathology and a special chapter for techniques and laboratory methods.
**Ind/Abst** Chem. Abstr.

NE/0014-410X
**EXCERPTA MEDICA. SECTION 6. INTERNAL MEDICINE.** [Excerpta med., Sect. 6. Intern. med.]. **VFOAT** Internal Medicine. **VAT** Excerpta Medica. Section Six. Internal Medicine. Vol. 1 (Oct. 1947)-. Abstracting/Indexing Service. English. Twenty-four times a year (3 vols.). Fl2595.00. Excerpta Medica Publishing Group, PO Box 548, 1000 AM Amsterdam Netherlands. **Tel** 011 31 20 5803243. **(Subscription address:** Excerpta Medica Journals, PO Box 85, Limerick Ireland.**) NLM** ZW 1 E959. **CODEN** IMDCBQ. **[CCC].** Index Available, published separately, free-automatically sent. **Ad Acc. Circ:** 350. available on microfilm from University Microfilms International (UMI); available on CD-ROM. Documents available from CASDDS.
**Desc:** Provides abstracts of articles on diseases affecting the various organ system in adults.
**Ind/Abst** Chem. Abstr.

NE/0373-6512
**EXCERPTA MEDICA. SECTION 7. PEDIATRICS AND PEDIATRIC SURGERY.** [Excerpta Med., Sect. 7, Pediatr. pediatr. surg.]. **VFOAT** Pediatrics and Pediatric Surgery. **VAT** Excerpta Medica. Section Seven. Pediatrics and Pediatric Surgery. Vol. 26 (1972)-. Abstracting/Indexing Service. English. Eighteen times a year (3 vols.). Fl2673.00. Excerpta Medica Publishing Group, PO Box 548, 1000 AM Amsterdam Netherlands. **Tel** 011 31 20 5803243. **(Subscription address:** Excerpta Medica Journals, PO Box 85, Limerick Ireland.**) NLM** ZW 1 E96. **CODEN** PPSUDH. **[CCC]. Ad Acc. Circ:** 400. available on microfilm from University Microfilms International (UMI); available on CD-ROM. ***Continues*** *Excerpta Medica. Section 7. Pediatrics.*
**Desc:** Covers all aspects of development and disease in childhood and adolescence, including somatic, mental and emotional development, genetics, the perinatal period, nutrition, preventive and social pediatrics and social pediatrics and the diseases of childhood.

NE/0014-4126
**EXCERPTA MEDICA. SECTION 8. NEUROLOGY AND NEUROSURGERY.** **VFOAT** Neurology and Neurosurgery. Vol. 22 (1969)-. Abstracting/Indexing Service. English. Thirty-two times a year (4 vols.). Fl3524.00. Excerpta Medica Publishing Group, PO Box 548, 1000 AM Amsterdam Netherlands. **Tel** 011 31 20 5803243. **(Subscription address:** Excerpta Medica Journals, PO Box 85, Limerick Ireland.**) NLM** ZW 1 E961. **CODEN** NLNSB2. **[CCC].** Index Available, published separately, free-automatically sent. available on microfilm from University Microfilms International (UMI); available on CD-ROM. ***Continues*** *Excerpta Medica. Section 8A. Neurology and Neurosurgery.*
**Desc:** Devoted primarily to the diagnosis and treatment (both medical and surgical) of diseases of the nervous system.

NE/0014-4134
**EXCERPTA MEDICA. SECTION 9. SURGERY.** ***Title Change.*** [Excerpta Med., Sect. 9, Surg.]. **VFOAT** Surgery. **VAT** Excerpta Medica. Section Nine. Surgery. Vol. 1 (1947)-?. Abstracting/Indexing Service. English. Twenty-four times a year (3 volumes). Excerpta Medica Publishing Group, PO Box 548, 1000 AM Amsterdam Netherlands. **Tel** 011 31 20 5803243. **(Subscription address:** Elsevier Scientific Publishers, Ltd, Customer Relations Manager, PO Box 85, Limerick, Ireland**) NLM** ZW 1 E962. **CODEN** EMSGAY. **[CCC]. Ad Acc. Circ:** 250. available on microfilm from University Microfilms International (UMI); available on CD-ROM. Documents available from CASDDS. ***Continued by*** *Excerpta Medica. Section 28, Urology.*
**Desc:** Provides abstracts of the most important articles on surgery of the various organ systems and anatomical areas in adults. Attention is also given to the problems to the general surgeon and the organization of surgical care in the hospital.
**Ind/Abst** Chem. Abstr.

NE/0014-4142
**EXCERPTA MEDICA. SECTION 10. OBSTETRICS AND GYNECOLOGY.** **VFOAT** Obstetrics and Gynaecology. **VAT** Excerpta Medica. Section Ten. Obstetrics and Gynecology. Vol. 1 (1948)-. Abstracting/Indexing Service. English. Twenty times a year (2 vols.). Fl2530.00. Excerpta Medica Publishing Group, PO Box 548, 1000 AM Amsterdam Netherlands. **Tel** 011 31 20 5803243. **(Subscription address:** Excerpta Medica Journals, PO Box 85, Limerick Ireland.**) NLM** ZW 1 E963. **CODEN** EMOGAE. **[CCC].** available on microfilm from University Microfilms International (UMI); available on CD-ROM. Documents available from CASDDS.
**Desc:** Contains an introductory chapter on general

subjects such as embryology, congenital malformations, chromosomes and heredity.
**Ind/Abst** Chem. Abstr.

NE/0014-4169
**EXCERPTA MEDICA. SECTION 12. OPHTHALMOLOGY.** [Excerpta med., Sect. 12, Ophthalmol.]. **VFOAT** Ophthalmology. **VAT** Excerpta Medica. Section Twelve. Ophthalmology. Vol. 1 (May 1947)-. Abstracting/Indexing Service. English. Sixteen times a year (2 vols.). Fl1692.00. Excerpta Medica Publishing Group, PO Box 548, 1000 AM Amsterdam Netherlands. **Tel** 011 31 20 5803243. **(Subscription address:** Excerpta Medica Journals, PO Box 85, Limerick Ireland.**) NLM** ZW 1 E965. **CODEN** OPHYAS. **[CCC].** Index Available, published separately, free-automatically sent. available on microfilm from University Microfilms International (UMI); available on CD-ROM. Documents available from CASDDS.
**Desc:** The organization of the abstracts in this journal is anatomical and etiological in nature.
**Ind/Abst** Chem. Abstr.

NE/0014-4177
**EXCERPTA MEDICA. SECTION 13. DERMATOLOGY AND VENEREOLOGY.** [Excerpta Med., Sect. 13, Dermatol.]. **VFOAT** Dermatology and Venereology. **VAT** Excerpta Medica. Section Thirteen. Dermatology and Venereology. (1947)-. Abstracting/Indexing Service. English. Sixteen times a year (2 vols.). Fl2056.00. Excerpta Medica Publishing Group, PO Box 548, 1000 AM Amsterdam Netherlands. **Tel** 011 31 20 5803243. **(Subscription address:** Excerpta Medica Journals, PO Box 85, Limerick Ireland.**) NLM** ZW 1 E966. **CODEN** DVENB4. **[CCC]. Ad Acc. Circ:** 350. available on microfilm from University Microfilms International (UMI); available on CD-ROM from SilverPlatter (US). Documents available from CASDDS.
**Desc:** Primarily devoted to the diagnosis and treatment of skin disease and venereal disease.
**Ind/Abst** Chem. Abstr.

NE/0014-4185
**EXCERPTA MEDICA. SECTION 14. RADIOLOGY.** [Excerpta med., Sect. 14, Radiol.]. **VFOAT** Radiology. **VAT** Excerpta Medica. Section Fourteen. Radiology. Vol. 1 (June 1947)-. Abstracting/Indexing Service. English. Twenty times a year (2 vols.). Fl2594.00. Excerpta Medica Publishing Group, PO Box 548, 1000 AM Amsterdam Netherlands. **Tel** 011 31 20 5803243. **(Subscription address:** Excerpta Medica Journals, PO Box 85, Limerick Ireland.**) NLM** ZW 1 E967. **CODEN** RDGYA6. **[CCC].** Index Available, published separately, free-automatically sent. available on microfilm from University Microfilms International (UMI); available on CD-ROM. Documents available from CASDDS.
**Desc:** Covers both radiodiagnosis and radiotherapy.
**Ind/Abst** Chem. Abstr.

NE/0014-4207
**EXCERPTA MEDICA. SECTION 16. CANCER.** [Excerpta Med., Sect. 16, Cancer]. **VFOAT** Cancer. **VAT** Excerpta Medica. Section Sixteen. Cancer. Vol. 20 (Jan. 1972)-. Abstracting/Indexing Service. English. Thirty-two times a year (4 vols.). Fl3524.00. Excerpta Medica Publishing Group, PO Box 548, 1000 AM Amsterdam Netherlands. **Tel** 011 31 20 5803243. **(Subscription address:** Excerpta Medica Journals, PO Box 85, Limerick Ireland.**) NLM** ZW 1 E969. **CODEN** CEXCA3. **[CCC].** available on microfilm from University Microfilms International (UMI); available on CD-ROM from SilverPlatter (US). Documents available from CASDDS. ***Continues*** *Cancer, Experimental and Clinical.*
**Desc:** Begins with a chapter on general aspects of the cancer problem such as different methods of diagnosis and therapy, multiple tumors, metastasis, cancer incidence, mortality, prevention and control followed by chapters on experimental cancer research and on clinical aspects of cancer.
**Ind/Abst** Chem. Abstr.

NE
**EXCERPTA MEDICA. SECTION 17. PUBLIC HEALTH, SOCIAL MEDICINE AND EPIDEMIOLOGY. Added/Corp** Excerpta Medica (Firm). **VFOAT** Public Health, Social Medicine and Epidemiology. Vol. 50, Issue 2 (1988)-. Abstracting/Indexing Service. English. Twenty-four times a year (3 volumes). Fl2487.00. Excerpta Medica Publishing Group, PO Box 548, 1000 AM Amsterdam Netherlands. **Tel** 011 31 20 5803243. **(Subscription address:** Excerpta Medica Journals, PO Box 85, Limerick Ireland.**) NLM** ZW 1; E971. available on CD-ROM from SilverPlatter (US). ***Continues*** *Excerpta Medica. Section 17, Public Health, Social Medicine and Hygiene.*
**Desc:** Contains information on all aspects of public health and social medicine. Also includes health planning and education, epidemiology and prevention of communicable diseases and more.

NE/0014-4223
**EXCERPTA MEDICA. SECTION 18. CARDIOVASCULAR DISEASES AND CARDIOVASCULAR SURGERY. VFOAT** Cardiovascular Diseases and Cardiovascular Surgery. Vol. 10 (1966)-. Abstracting/Indexing Service. English. Twenty-four times a year (3 vols.). Fl2748.00. Excerpta Medica Publishing Group, PO Box 548, 1000 AM Amsterdam Netherlands. **Tel** 011 31 20 5803243. **(Subscription address:** Excerpta Medica Journals, PO Box 85, Limerick Ireland.**) [CCC].** Index Available, published separately, free-automatically sent. **Ad Acc. Circ:** 300. available on microfilm from University Microfilms International (UMI); available on CD-ROM. ***Continues*** *Excerpta Medica. Section 18. Cardiovascular Diseases.*
**Desc:** Covers both the surgical and the nonsurgical aspects of cardiovascular disease.

NE/0014-4231
**EXCERPTA MEDICA. SECTION 19. REHABILITATION AND PHYSICAL MEDICINE. Added/Corp** Excerpta Medica Foundation. **VFOAT** Rehabilitation and Physical Medicine. Vol. 7 (Jan. 1964)-. Abstracting/Indexing Service. English. Eight times a year (1 volume). Fl1103.00. Excerpta Medica Publishing Group, PO Box 548, 1000 AM Amsterdam Netherlands. **Tel** 011 31 20 5803243. **(Subscription address:** Excerpta Medica Journals, PO Box 85, Limerick Ireland.**) NLM** ZW 1 E973. **[CCC]. Ad Acc. Circ:** 350. available on microfilm from University Microfilms International (UMI); available on CD-ROM. ***Continues*** *Excerpta Medica. Section 19. Rehabilitation.*
**Desc:** Reflects the multiplicity of aspects of physical medicine and the care of the disabled which it covers.

NE/0014-424X
**EXCERPTA MEDICA. SECTION 20. GERONTOLOGY AND GERIATRICS. VFOAT** Gerontology and Geriatrics. Vol. 1 (July 1958)-. Abstracting/Indexing Service. English. Eight times a year (1 volume). Fl1282.00. Excerpta Medica Publishing Group, PO Box 548, 1000 AM Amsterdam Netherlands. **Tel** 011 31 20 5803243. **(Subscription address:** Excerpta Medica Journals, PO Box 85, Limerick Ireland.**) [CCC].** Index Available, published separately, free-automatically sent. available on microfilm from University Microfilms International (UMI); available on CD-ROM.
**Desc:** Covers all aspects of aging, biomedical gerontology, the somatic, mental and emotional problems of the aged, and the social and organizational aspects of the care of the long-term elderly patient.

NE/0014-4258
**EXCERPTA MEDICA. SECTION 21. DEVELOPMENTAL BIOLOGY AND TERATOLOGY. Added/Corp** Excerpta Medica Foundation. National Institute of Child Health and Human Development (U.S.). **VFOAT** Developmental Biology and Teratology. Vol. 5 (1965)-. Abstracting/Indexing Service. English. Twelve times a year (2 volumes). Fl2108.00. Excerpta Medica Publishing Group, PO Box 548, 1000 AM Amsterdam Netherlands. **Tel** 011 31 20 5803243. **(Subscription address:** Excerpta Medica Journals, PO Box 85, Limerick Ireland.**) [CCC].** Index Available, published separately, free-automatically sent. available on microfilm from University Microfilms International (UMI); available on CD-ROM. ***Continues*** *Excerpta Medica. Section 21. Human Developmental Biology.*
**Desc:** Covers normal and pathological as well as experimental and clinical aspects of embryology and development, with emphasis on teratology.

NE/0014-4266
**EXCERPTA MEDICA. SECTION 22. HUMAN GENETICS. Added/Corp** Excerpta Medica Foundation. **VFOAT** Human Genetics. Vol. 1, No. 5 (Jan. 1963)-. Abstracting/Indexing Service. English. Twenty times a year (2 vols.). Fl2398.00. Excerpta Medica Publishing Group, PO Box 548, 1000 AM Amsterdam Netherlands. **Tel** 011 31 20 5803243. **(Subscription address:** Excerpta Medica Journals, PO Box 85, Limerick Ireland.**) LC** QH431; .H835. **DD** 573.2/1. **NLM** ZW 1 E976. **[CCC]. Ad Acc. Circ:** 535 (ctrl). available on microfilm from University Microfilms International (UMI); available on CD-ROM. ***Continues*** *Human Genetics Abstracts.*
**Desc:** Contains information on general genetics, and the genetics of lower organisms. Of potential interest to human medicine, molecular and cytogenetics.

NE/0014-4274
**EXCERPTA MEDICA. SECTION 23. NUCLEAR MEDICINE.** [Excerpta Med., Sect. 23, Nucl. med.]. **VFOAT** Nuclear Medicine. **VAT** Excerpta Medica. Section Twenty Three. Nuclear Medicine. Vol. 1 (Jan. 1964)-. Abstracting/Indexing Service. English. Sixteen times a year (2 vols.). Fl1810.00. Excerpta Medica Publishing Group, PO Box 548, 1000 AM Amsterdam Netherlands. **Tel** 011 31 20 5803243. **(Subscription address:** Excerpta Medica Journals, PO Box 85, Limerick Ireland.**) NLM** ZW 1 E977. **CODEN** NUMEAH. **[CCC]. Ad Acc. Circ:** 250. available on microfilm from University Microfilms International (UMI); available on CD-ROM. Documents available from CASDDS.
**Desc:** Covers both the diagnostic and the therapeutic applications of radioisotopes in biomedicine.
**Ind/Abst** Chem. Abstr.

NE/0014-4282
**EXCERPTA MEDICA. SECTION 24. ANESTHESIOLOGY. VFOAT** Anesthesiology. Vol. 1 (Jan. 1966)-. Abstracting/Indexing Service. English. Ten times a year (1 volume). Fl1392.00. Excerpta Medica Publishing Group, PO Box 548, 1000 AM Amsterdam Netherlands. **Tel** 011 31 20 5803243. **(Subscription address:** Excerpta Medica Journals, PO Box 85, Limerick Ireland.**) [CCC]. Ad Acc. Circ:** 450. available on microfilm from University Microfilms International (UMI); available on CD-ROM from SilverPlatter (US).
**Desc:** The main information content in this abstract journal is organized in chapters on general, local and special anesthesia, each of which is further subdivided on the basis of the specific technique being used or the type of surgery being performed.

NE/0014-4290
**EXCERPTA MEDICA. SECTION 25. HEMATOLOGY. VFOAT** Hematology. Vol. 1 (Apr. 1967)-. Abstracting/Indexing Service. English. Twenty-four times a year (3 vols.). Fl2637.00. Excerpta Medica Publishing Group, PO Box 548, 1000 AM Amsterdam Netherlands. **Tel** 011 31 20 5803243. **(Subscription address:** Excerpta Medica Journals, PO Box 85, Limerick Ireland.**) [CCC]. Ad Acc. Circ:** 250. available on microfilm from University Microfilms International (UMI); available on CD-ROM.
**Desc:** Covers all aspects of the blood cells, the hematopoietic and reticuloendothelial conditions, including separate chapters on the blood coagulation, under both normal and pathological conditions, and including separate chapters on the blood groups and blood transfusion.

NE/0014-4304
**EXCERPTA MEDICA. SECTION 26. IMMUNOLOGY, SEROLOGY AND TRANSPLANTATION. VFOAT** Immunology, Serology and Transplantation. Vol. 1 (July 1967)-. Abstracting/Indexing Service. English. Thirty-two times a year (4 vols.). Fl3276.00. Excerpta Medica Publishing Group, PO Box 548, 1000 AM Amsterdam Netherlands. **Tel** 011 31 20 5803243. **(Subscription address:** Excerpta Medica Journals, PO Box 85, Limerick Ireland.**) NLM** ZW 1 E978C. **[CCC].** available on microfilm from University Microfilms International (UMI); available on CD-ROM. ***Supersedes in part*** *Excerpta Medica. Section 4, Medical Microbiology, Immunology and Serology.*
**Desc:** Reflects the many specific concepts dealt with in the immunological literature. General chapters deal with antigens, antibodies, antigen-antibody reactions, complement, specific and non-specific inhibition of the immune response, autoimmunity, etc.

NE/0014-4312
**EXCERPTA MEDICA. SECTION 27. BIOPHYSICS, BIOENGINEERING AND MEDICAL INSTRUMENTATION. VFOAT** Biophysics, Bioengineering and Medical Instrumentation. Vol. 3 (1969)-. Abstracting/Indexing Service. English. Ten times a year (1 volume). Fl1588.00. Excerpta Medica Publishing Group, PO Box 548, 1000 AM Amsterdam Netherlands. **Tel** 011 31 20 5803243. **(Subscription address:** Excerpta Medica Journals, PO Box 85, Limerick Ireland.**) NLM** ZW 1 E978E. **[CCC].** Index Available, published separately, free-automatically sent. cum. index. **Ad Acc. Circ:** 440 (ctrl). available on microfilm from University Microfilms International (UMI); available on CD-ROM from SilverPlatter (US). ***Continues*** *Excerpta Medica. Section 27. Medical Instrumentation.*
**Desc:** This abstract journal starts with chapters on the basic concepts of biophysics and bio-engineering, instrumentation (amplifiers, generators, recorders, cameras, etc.) and computers.
**Ind/Abst** Health Devices Alerts.

NE/0014-4320
**EXCERPTA MEDICA. SECTION 28. UROLOGY AND NEPHROLOGY. VFOAT** Urology and Nephrology. (1969)-. Abstracting/Indexing Service. English. Sixteen times a year (2 vols.). Fl1810.00. Excerpta Medica Publishing Group, PO Box 548, 1000 AM Amsterdam Netherlands. **Tel** 011 31 20 5803243. **(Subscription address:** Excerpta Medica Journals, PO Box 85, Limerick Ireland.**) ED** Z Szendroi. **NLM** ZW 1 E978H. **[CCC].** Index Available, published separately, free-automatically sent. **Ad Acc. Circ:** 350. available on microfilm from University Microfilms International (UMI); available on CD-ROM. ***Continues*** *Excerpta Medica. Section 28, Urology.*
**Desc:** Consists of several chapters each in urology and on diseases of the kidney, both subdivided on an anatomical and etiopathological basis into some 15 subheadings.

●NE
**EXCERPTA MEDICA. SECTION 30. CLINICAL AND EXPERIMENTAL PHARMACOLOGY. Added/Corp** Excerpta Medica (Firm). **VFOAT** Clinical and Experimental Pharmacology. Vol. 78, Issue 1 (1992)-. Abstracting/Indexing Service. English. Thirty-two times a year (4 volumes). Fl4220.00. Excerpta Medica Publishing Group, PO Box 548, 1000 AM Amsterdam Netherlands. **Tel** 011 31 20 5803243. **(Subscription address:**

Excerpta Medica Journals, PO Box 85, Limerick Ireland.) **NLM** ZW 1; E978JC. **CODEN** ESCPER. available on CD-ROM from SilverPlatter (US). ***Formed by the union of*** *Excerpta Medica. Section 30, Pharmacology, 0167-9643* ***and*** *Excerpta Medica. Section 130, Clinical Pharmacology.*
**Desc:** Contains information on all aspects of experimental and clinical pharmacology.

NE/0014-4363
**EXCERPTA MEDICA. SECTION 32. PSYCHIATRY.** **VFOAT** Psychiatry. Vol. 22, No. 1 (Jan. 1969)-. Abstracting/Indexing Service. English. Twenty times a year (2 vols.). Fl2282.00. Excerpta Medica Publishing Group, PO Box 548, 1000 AM Amsterdam Netherlands. **Tel** 011 31 20 5803243. **(Subscription address:** Excerpta Medica Journals, PO Box 85, Limerick Ireland.**)** **NLM** ZW 1 E978L. **[CCC].** available on microfilm from University Microfilms International (UMI); available on CD-ROM. ***Continues*** *Excerpta Medica. Section 8B, Psychiatry.*
**Desc:** Covers all aspects of the work and training of the psychiatrist.

NE
**EXCERPTA MEDICA. SECTION 36. HEALTH POLICY, ECONOMICS, AND MANAGEMENT.** **Added/Corp** Excerpta Medica (Firm). **VFOAT** Health Policy, Economics, and Management. Vol. 24, Issue 1 (1988)-. Abstracting/Indexing Service. English. bm (1 volume). Fl1168.00. Excerpta Medica Publishing Group, PO Box 548, 1000 AM Amsterdam Netherlands. **Tel** 011 31 20 5803243. **(Subscription address:** Excerpta Medica Journals, PO Box 85, Limerick Ireland.**)** **NLM** ZW 1; E978R. **CODEN** HEHMDB. available on CD-ROM; available in microform from University Microfilms International (UMI). ***Continues*** *Health Economics and Hospital Management, 0300-5321.*
**Desc:** Contains information on the economic, social and political aspects of healthcare and its organization.

NE/0167-9171
**EXCERPTA MEDICA. SECTION 37. DRUG LITERATURE INDEX.** ***Ceased.*** [Excerpta med. Sect. 37, Drug lit. index]. **Added/Corp** Excerpta Medica (Firm). **VFOAT** Drug literature index. Vol. 12, Issue 1 (1980)-Vol. 22 (?). Abstracting/Indexing Service. English. Twenty-four times a year. Excerpta Medica Publishing Group, PO Box 548, 1000 AM Amsterdam Netherlands. **Tel** 011 31 20 5803243. **NLM** ZQV 55 D794. available on microfilm from University Microfilms International (UMI); available on CD-ROM. ***Continues*** *Drug Literature Index, 0376-5091.*
**Desc:** Provides a comprehensive and up-to-date bibliographic tool which can be used to find significant information on the effects of all drugs and potential drugs reported in the primary biomedical and chemical literature from all major countries in the world.

NE/0167-9090
**EXCERPTA MEDICA. SECTION 38. ADVERSE REACTIONS TITLES.** [Excerpta Med., 38, Adverse react. titles]. **Added/Corp** Excerpta Medica (Firm). **VFOAT** Adverse Reactions Titles. Vol. 15, Issue 1 (1980)-. Abstracting/Indexing Service. English. Twelve times a year (1 volume). Fl1950.00. Excerpta Medica Publishing Group, PO Box 548, 1000 AM Amsterdam Netherlands. **Tel** 011 31 20 5803243. **(Subscription address:** Excerpta Medica Journals, PO Box 85, Limerick Ireland.**)** **NLM** ZQZ 42 A244. available on microfilm from University Microfilms International (UMI); available on CD-ROM. ***Continues*** *Adverse Reactions Titles.*

NE/0304-4041
**EXCERPTA MEDICA. SECTION 40. DRUG DEPENDENCE, ALCOHOL ABUSE, AND ALCOHOLISM.** **Added/Corp** Excerpta Medica (Firm). **VFOAT** Drug Dependence, Alcohol Abuse, and Alcoholism. Vol. 16, Issue 1 (1988)-. Abstracting/Indexing Service. English. bm (1 volume). Fl1098.00. Excerpta Medica Publishing Group, PO Box 548, 1000 AM Amsterdam Netherlands. **Tel** 011 31 20 5803243. **(Subscription address:** Excerpta Medica Journals, PO Box 85, Limerick Ireland.**)** **LC** HV5801; .D6. **DD** 016.36229. **NLM** ZW 1; E9639. **CODEN** DDAAEQ. **[CCC].** available on microfilm from University Microfilms International (UMI); available on CD-ROM. ***Continues*** *Excerpta Medica. Section 40, Drug Dependence.*
**Desc:** Contains information on all aspects of the abuse of drugs, alcohol and organic solvents.

NE/0300-5194
**EXCERPTA MEDICA. SECTION 46. ENVIRONMENTAL HEALTH AND POLLUTION CONTROL.** [Excerpta Med., Sect. 46]. **Added/Corp** Excerpta Medica (Firm) Netherlands. Ministerie van Volksgezondheid en Milieuhygiene. **VFOAT** Environmental Health and Pollution Control. Vol. 17, Issue 1 Abstracts No. 1-240 (1980)-. Abstracting/Indexing Service. English. Ten times a year (1 volume). Fl1544.00. Excerpta Medica Publishing Group, PO Box 548, 1000 AM Amsterdam Netherlands. **Tel** 011 31 20 5803243. **(Subscription address:** Excerpta Medica Journals, PO Box 85, Limerick Ireland.**)** **NLM** ZW 1; E978T. **CODEN** EHPCA6. **[CCC].** available on microfilm from University Microfilms International (UMI); available on CD-ROM. ***Continues*** *Environmental Health and Pollution Control, 0300-5194.*
**Desc:** Covers all aspects of air, water and soil pollution, noise hindrance and radioactivity as related to the outdoor environment.

NE/0303-8459
**EXCERPTA MEDICA. SECTION 50. EPILEPSY ABSTRACTS.** **Added/Corp** Excerpta Medica (Firm). **VFOAT** Epilepsy Abstracts. Vol. 13, Issue 1 (1980)-. Abstracting/Indexing Service. English. Six times a year (1 volume). Fl937.00. Excerpta Medica Publishing Group, PO Box 548, 1000 AM Amsterdam Netherlands. **Tel** 011 31 20 5803243. **(Subscription address:** Excerpta Medica Journals, PO Box 85, Limerick Ireland.**)** **NLM** ZWL 385; E64. **CODEN** EMEPAP. **[CCC].** available on microfilm from University Microfilms International (UMI); available on CD-ROM. ***Continues*** *Epilepsy Abstracts, 0013-9599.*
**Desc:** Includes material on both the experimental aspects of seizures and convulsions and the diagnosis and treatment of clinical forms of epilepsy and other convulsive syndromes.

NE/0167-8353
**EXCERPTA MEDICA. SECTION 52. TOXICOLOGY.** [Excerpta Med., 52 Toxicol.]. **Added/Corp** Excerpta Medica (Firm). **VFOAT** Excerpta Medica. Section Fifty-Two, Toxicology; Toxicology. Vol. 1, Issue 1 Abstracts No. 1-380 (1983)-. Abstracting/Indexing Service. English. Twenty times a year (2 vols.). Fl2150.00. Excerpta Medica Publishing Group, PO Box 548, 1000 AM Amsterdam Netherlands. **Tel** 011 31 20 5803243. **(Subscription address:** Excerpta Medica Journals, PO Box 85, Limerick Ireland.**)** **ED** J B Bijlsma, A J Dunning, G E Farrar, P J Gaillard, L E Meltzer, P J Vinken. **NLM** ZW 1 E978WD. **CODEN** TXICDD. **[CCC].** available on microfilm from University Microfilms International (UMI); available on CD-ROM. ***Continues in part*** *Excerpta Medica. Section 30, Pharmacology and Toxicology, 0014-4347.*
**Desc:** Covers areas including food additives and contaminants, cosmetics and toiletries, agrochemicals, industrial chemicals, radiation and radioactive materials.

NE/0304-3789
**EXCERPTA MEDICA. SECTION 65. CANCER IMMUNOLOGY. LITERATURE INDEX.** V. 1- 1975-. Abstracting/Indexing Service. English. mo. $40.00. Excerpta Medica Publishing Group, PO Box 548, 1000 AM Amsterdam Netherlands. **Tel** 011 31 20 5803243. **LC** RC268.3; .C34. **DD** 016.6169/94/079. **NLM** ZQZ 200 C2167. available on CD-ROM.

US/0736-4342
**GERONTOLOGICAL ABSTRACTS.** ***Ceased.*** [Gerontol. abstr.]. Vol. 1 (Nov. 1976)-Ceased (1984). Abstracting/Indexing Service. English. ir (11 no. a year). University of Michigan Dental School, Dept. of Cell Biology, Ann Arbor MI 48109. **Tel** (313)764-1555. **NLM** ZWT 100 G372.

US/0163-0458
**HEALTH DEVICES ALERTS.** [Health devices alerts]. **Added/Corp** Emergency Care Research Institute. Vol. 1 (April 15, 1977)-. Abstracting/Indexing Service. English. ir (76 issues). $695.00 US; $710.00 Canada; $725.00 other (includes Health Devices Alerts Abstracts and Health Devices Alerts action items; comes also with Health Devices Systems membership). ECRI Emergency Care Research Institute, 5200 Butler Pike, Plymouth Meeting PA 19462. **Tel** (215)825-6000, FAX (215)834-1275, telex 510-660-8023. **ED** Eileen M. McDaniel. **NLM** ZW 26 H434. **[CCC].** Index available (free). **Circ:** 2,500. available on CD-ROM; available on an online database (ECRINET) from DIALOG.
**Desc:** Abstracts of reported hazards, recalls, and problems with medical devices and equipment, often with recommendation action.

●US/1065-0679
**HEALTH PLANNING AND ADMINISTRATION.** (HEALTH PLANNING AND ADMINISTRATION [COMPUTER FILE] : EBSCO CD-ROM.). **Added/Corp** EBSCO Publishing (Firm) National Library of Medicine (U.S.) United States. Dept. of Health and Human Services. **VFOAT** EBSCO CD-ROM. (1992)-. Abstracting/Indexing Service. English. qt. $795.00. EBSCO Publishing / Boston, 83 Pine Street, Peabody MA 01960. **Tel** (800)653-2726 North America, (508)535-8500, FAX (508)535-8545. Index available. **Pr Rev.**
**Desc:** A database of over 475,000 citations provided by the US National Library of Medicine and the American Hospital Association, Health Planning & Administration covers the nonclinical aspects of the planning and administration of health care delivery. Also included are health care facilities, health insurance, HMOs, staffing, quality, licensure and accreditation.

US
**HEALTH REFERENCE CENTER [COMPUTER FILE].** **VFOAT** InfoTrac Health Reference Center. (19??)-. Abstracting/Indexing Service. English. mo. $6000.00 (with InfoTrac workstation), $5000.00 (without hardware) basic subscription; $5300.00 (with InfoTrac workstation), $4300.00 (without hardware) school year subscription. Information Access Company, 362 Lakeside Drive, Foster City CA 94404. **Tel** (800)227-8431.
**Desc:** Comprehensive integrated system designed to meet a variety of health and medical information needs. Provides information from periodicals, pamphlets and reference books.

UK/0268-0459
**HEALTH SERVICE ABSTRACTS.** [Health serv. abstr.]. **Added/Corp** Great Britain. Dept. of Health and Social Security Library. Vol. 1, No. 1 (May 1985)-. Abstracting/Indexing Service. English. mo. £36.00. Department of Health and Social Security Library, PO Box 21, Stanmore, Middlesex HA7 1AY England. **Tel** 011 44 71 9722000, 9728161. ***Formed by the union of*** *Current Literature on Health Services, 0141-0571; Current Literature on General Medical Practice* ***and*** *Hospital Abstracts, 0018-5507.*

●US/1077-1719
**HOSPITAL AND HEALTH ADMINISTRATION INDEX.** (1995)-. Abstracting/Indexing Service. English. tq. $255.00 US; $300.00 other. American Hospital Association, 840 North Lake Shore Drive, Chicago IL 60611. **Tel** (312)280-6000, (800)242-2626. ***Continues*** *Hospital Literature Index, 0018-5736.*

US
**HOSPITAL AND HEALTH ADMINISTRATION INDEX. ANNUAL CUMULATION.** (19??)-. English. an. $310.00 (nonmember), $240.00 (member). American Hospital Association, 840 North Lake Shore Drive, Chicago IL 60611. **Tel** (312)280-6000, (800)242-2626. **(Subscription address:** American Hospital Publ. Inc., PO Box 92567, Chicago IL 60675.**)**

US/0018-5736
**HOSPITAL LITERATURE INDEX.** ***Title Change.*** [Hosp. lit. index]. **Added/Corp** American Hospital Association. Library of the American Hospital Association, Asa S. Bacon Memorial. Vol. 13, No. 2 (Dec. 1957)-(1994). Abstracting/Indexing Service. English. qt. American Hospital Association, 840 North Lake Shore Drive, Chicago IL 60611. **Tel** (312)280-6000, (800)242-2626. **LC** Z6675.H75; H67; RA963. **DD** 016.3621/1. **NLM** ZWX 100 H828. **Circ:** 2,500. available on CD-ROM (as Health Planning and Administration Database - HEALTH); available on an online database (as Health Planning and Administration Database - HEALTH) from Pan American Health Organization (Brazil); (as Health Planning and Administration Database - HEALTH) FRG MEDLARS Center; (as Health Planning and Administration Database - HEALTH) NLA (National Library of Australia); (as Health Planning and Administration Database - HEALTH) NLM; (as Health Planning and Administration Database - HEALTH) DIALOG; and (as Health Planning and Administration Database - HEALTH) BRS; available on microfilm and microfiche from University Microfilms International (UMI). ***Continues*** *Hospital Periodical Literature Index.* ***Continued by*** *Hospital and Health Administration Index, 1077-1719.*
**Desc:** Provides information on the organization and administration, economics, laws and regulations, and policy and planning of health care delivery. Gives special emphasis to three areas: the theory of health care systems in general, health care in industrialized countries (primarily the United States), and the provision of health care both inside and outside of health care facilities.

US/0737-903X
**HOSPITAL MANAGEMENT REVIEW.** [Hosp. manage. rev.]. **Added/Corp** Health Systems Resources. (Jan. 1982)-. Abstracting/Indexing Service. English. Eleven times a year (monthly except July). $87.00 (one year), $154.00 (two year) $221.00 (three year) US and Canada; $99.00 (one year) other. COR Healthcare Resources, (A Division of COR Research Inc.), PO Box 40959, Santa Barbara CA 93140. **Tel** (805)564-2177, FAX (805)564-2146. **ED** Dean H Anderson. **[CCC].** **Bk Rev.**
**Desc:** Informative summaries of key articles and research reports selected from more than 100 publications in the health care and management fields.

CN/1195-4000
**HOSPITAL MORBIDITY - CANADIAN CENTRE FOR HEALTH INFORMATION.** (HOSPITAL MORBIDITY / STATISTICS CANADA, CANADIAN CENTRE FOR HEALTH INFORMATION / LA MORBIDITE HOSPITALIERE / STATISTIQUE CANADA, CENTRE CANADIEN D'INFORMATION SUR LA SANTE.). [Hosp. morb. - Can. Cent. Health Inf.]. **Added/Corp** Canadian Centre for Health Information. **VFOAT** Morbidite Hospitaliere. (1990/91)-. English (French). an. 35.00Can$ Canada; $37.00. Statistics Canada, Publications Sales & Services, Main Building Room 1710, Ottawa Ontario K1A 0T6 Canada. **Tel** (613)951-5078, (800)267-6677, FAX (613)951-1584, telex 053-3585. **DD** 304.6/4/0971021. Index available. cum. index. **Ad Acc.** **Pr Rev.** **Circ:** 2,000. ***Continues*** *Health Reports. Supplement. Hospital Morbidity, 1190-2464.*
**Desc:** The latest information on health issues, reported in

comprehensive articles covering important topics from the incidence of a given disease, through its risk factors and morbidity rates, to hospitalization costs and stay and discharge data. Information is presented in its demographic context, along with international comparisons and assessments of the socio-economic impact on Canadians.

CN/0383-574X
**HOSPITAL STATISTICS. VOLUME 1. BEDS, SERVICES, PERSONNEL.** (HOSPITAL STATISTICS, V. I; BEDS, SERVICES, PERSONNEL. LA STATISTIQUE HOSPITALIERE, V. I; LITS, SERVICES, PERSONNEL.). **Main/Corp** Canada. Statistics Canada. Hospitals Section. **VFOAT** Statistique Hospitaliere, V. I; Lits, Services, Personnel. (1973)-. English (French). an. $3.50. Information Canada, 171 Slater Street, Ottawa Ontario K1A 0S9 Canada. **Tel** (819)997-1095. ***Formed by the union of*** *Canada. Statistics Canada. Hospitals Section. Hospital Statistics, V. I; Hospital Beds., 0383-5715; Canada. Statistics Canada. Hospital Section. Hospital Statistics, V. II; Hospital Services., 0383-5723* ***and*** *Canada. Statistics Canada. Hospitals Section. Hospital Statistics, V. III; Hospital Personnel., 0383-5731.*

US/0307-112X
**IMMUNOLOGY ABSTRACTS.** [Immunol. abstr.]. **Added/Corp** Information Retrieval Limited. Cambridge Scientific Abstracts, Inc. Vol. 1 (Jan. 1976)-. Abstracting/Indexing Service. English. mo (includes annual index). $945.00 US; $995.00 other. Cambridge Scientific Abstracts, 7200 Wisconsin Avenue, #601, Bethesda MD 20814-4823. **Tel** (301)961-6750, (800)843-7751, FAX (301)961-6720. **ED** David Cheyney. **LC** QR180; .I532. **DD** 599/.02/905. **NLM** ZQW 504 I33. Index Available Published separately--free--upon request. cum. index. **Bk Rev**. available on magnetic tape; available on an online database from DIALOG; and BRS; available on CD-ROM from Compact Cambridge; available via Internet (to the current year's abstracts and five-year backfiles) from Cambridge Scientific Abstracts.
**Desc:** Immune system of man and animals; immune system disorders such as AIDS, response to infections, tumors, transplantation, and genetic characteristics.

US/0019-3879
**INDEX MEDICUS (1960).** (INDEX MEDICUS / NATIONAL LIBRARY OF MEDICINE.). [Index med.]. **Added/Corp** National Library of Medicine (U.S.). New Series, Vol. 1, No. 1, (Jan. 1960)-. Abstracting/Indexing Service. English. mo. $284.00 US; $355.00 other. Superintendent of Documents, US Government Printing Office, Washington DC 20402. **Tel** (202)275-3328, FAX (202)786-2377. **LC** Z6660; .I42. **DD** 016.61. **NLM** ZW 1 I384. cum. index. **Circ:** 6,000. available on CD-ROM (Comprehensive MEDLINE) from EBSCO Publishing - Peabody; available on microfiche from University Microfilms International (UMI). ***Continues*** *Current List of Medical Literature;* ***Absorbed*** *Monthly Bibliography of Medical Reviews, 0027-0202.*
**Desc:** A bibliographic listing of references to current articles from approximately 3,600 of the world's biomedical journals. Consists of a subject and name section, a Bibliography of Medical Reviews, and List of Journals Indexed in Index Medicus.
**Ind/Abst** Dairy Sci. Abstr.; Popul. Index; Rev. Med. Vet. Mycology; Rev. Plant Pathol.

US
**INDEX MEDICUS / NATIONAL LIBRARY OF MEDICINE. [MICROFICHE].** (19??)-. English. qt. University Microfilms International, 300 North Zeeb Road, Ann Arbor MI 48106-1346. **Tel** (313)761-4700, (800)521-0600 Exts. 2490, 2491, FAX (313)973-1540. available in print.

SP
**INDICE MEDICO ESPANOL. Added/Corp** Instituto de Informacion y Documentacion en Biomedicina (Valencia, Spain). Vol. 1 (Jan./March 1965)-. Abstracting/Indexing Service. Spanish. sa (2 issues). 6000ptas (institution) Spain. Centro Documentacion Informati Biomedica, Avd Blasco Ibanez 17, 46010 Valencia Spain. **Tel** 011 34 6 3610373, 3692466, FAX 011 34 6 3613975. **Circ:** 800 (ctrl). available on CD-ROM.
**Desc:** The only national list that compiles and analyzes the investigative works published in Spanish biomedical magazines. An extensive work which covers over 10,000 articles from over 160 magazines.
**Ind/Abst** Nutr. Abstr. Rev., Ser. B, Live Feeds and Feed.; Nutr. Abstr. Rev., Ser. A, Hum. Exp.

US/0098-2393
**INTERNATIONAL BIBLIOGRAPHY OF THE FORENSIC SCIENCES, THE.** ***Suspended.*** (1975)-?. Bibliography. English. an. Inform / Kansas, PO Box 8282, Wichita KS 67208. **Tel** (316)689-3707. **ED** W G Eckert. **NLM** ZW 700 I61.

US/0090-0575
**INTERNATIONAL BIBLIOGRAPHY ON BURNS.** (INTERNATIONAL BIBLIOGRAPHY ON BURNS : FOR BETTER PATIENT CARE, RESEARCH, AND TEACHING.). **Added/Corp** American Burn Research Corporation. Institute for Burn Medicine. National Institute for Burn Medicine. (1969)-. Bibliography. English. an. $40.00. National Institute for Burn Medicine, 909 East Ann Street, Ann Arbor MI 48104. **Tel** (313)769-9000. **ED** Irving Feller. **LC** Z6667.B8; F4; RD96.4. **DD** 016.617/11. **Circ:** 500.
**Desc:** Updates of what has been published world-wide, specific to burn care. Each supplement includes citations for approximately 2,000 articles.

US/0360-1196
**INTERNATIONAL BIBLIOGRAPHY ON BURNS. SUPPLEMENT.** Vol. 1 (1970)-. Bibliography. English. an. $25.00. University of Michigan Burn Center Library, 1500 East Medical Center Drive, 1B401 Box 0033, Ann Arbor MI 48109. **Tel** (313)936-9666. **ED** C A Jones and I Feller. **LC** Z6667.B8; F4 SUPPL; RD96.4. **DD** 016.617/11. **NLM** ZWO 704 F381I. **Circ:** 200.
**Desc:** Listing, by subject with author and subject indexes, of material written on burn care from around the world. Includes 13 major headings, some of which are: epidemiology, treatment, outcome, prevention, medical/legal aspects, rehabilitation, audio visual and prevention materials sections.

US/0020-8124
**INTERNATIONAL NURSING INDEX.** [Int. nurs. index]. **Added/Corp** American Journal of Nursing Company. Institute for Scientific Information. National Library of Medicine (U.S.) American Nurses Association. National League for Nursing. Vol. 1 (1966)-. Abstracting/Indexing Service. English. Four times a year (3 regular issues plus 1 cumulative issue). $280.00 (one year), $499.00 (two year). American Journal of Nursing Company, 555 West 57th Street, New York NY 10019-2961. **Tel** (212)582-8820, FAX (212)586-5462. **(Subscription address:** International Nursing Index, 555 West 57th Street, 13th Floor, New York NY 10019.**) ED** Frederick W. Pattison. **LC** Z6675.N7; I5. **DD** 610.73/016. **NLM** ZWY 100 I61. **Ad Acc. Circ:** 2,000. available on CD-ROM from EBSCO Publishing - Peabody; available on microfilm and microfiche from University Microfilms International (UMI); available on microfilm.
**Desc:** Indexes more than 320 nursing magazines, and nursing articles drawn from 2,600 medical and related health journals.

UK/0959-9886
**JOURNAL OF ALTERNATIVE AND COMPLEMENTARY MEDICINE.** **See** Medical Science and Technology.

US/0896-7210
**JOURNAL WATCH.** [J. watch]. **Added/Corp** Massachusetts Medical Society. (1987)-. Abstracting/Indexing Service. English. Twenty-four times a year. $79.00 US; $95.00 other. New England Journal of Medicine, 1440 Main Street, Waltham MA 02154-1649. **Tel** (617)893-3800, (800)843-6356, FAX (617)647-5785, telex 5106015660 NEJM BOS UQ. **(Subscription address:** New England Journal of Medicine, PO Box 9135, Waltham MA 02154.**) ED** Anthony L. Komaroff. **DD** 610. available on an online database (through BRS/Colleague).
**Desc:** A surveillance newsletter summarizing key articles from 25 major medical journals. Includes information on developments in primary care.

JA/0023-5326
**KUMAMOTO MEDICAL JOURNAL, THE.** [Kumamoto med. j.]. **Added/Corp** Kumamoto Daigaku. Igakubu. Kumamoto Ika Daigaku. Vol. 1, (July 1938)-. Academic Scholarly Publication. English (German). ir. Kumamoto Diaguku Igakubu Library, Kumamoto Japan. **Tel** 096-344-2111. **NLM** W1 KU699. **CODEN** KUMJAX. **Circ:** 450 (ctrl). Documents available from CASDDS.
**Desc:** Covers materials and methods or cases in clinical and autopsy report, results, discussion, acknowledgments, and references.
**Ind/Abst** Chem. Abstr.; EMBASE [Select. Cov.]; Helminthol. Abstr. (1991-); SEA Abstr.

US
**LILACS ON CD-ROM.** English. Three times a year. $500.00. Bireme Latin America & CARI Center, Lilacs CD-ROM, Rua Botucatu 862, 04023 Sao Paulo SP Brazil. **Tel** 011 55 11 5492611.
**Desc:** Contains bibliographic citations provided by regional medical centers throughout Latin America.

NE/0923-5582
**LIST OF JOURNALS ABSTRACTED.** ***Title Change.*** **Added/Corp** Excerpta Medica (Firm). **VFOAT** EMBASE List of Lournals Abstracted. (1983)-(1992). Abstracting/Indexing Service. English. an. Excerpta Medica Publishing Group, PO Box 548, 1000 AM Amsterdam Netherlands. **Tel** 011 31 20 5803243. **NLM** ZW 1; E979E. ***Continues*** *Excerpta Medica. List of Journals Abstracted (1979), 0167-6180.* ***Continued by*** *EMBASE List of Journals Indexed.*

US/0093-3821
**LIST OF JOURNALS INDEXED IN INDEX MEDICUS.** (LIST OF JOURNALS INDEXED IN INDEX MEDICUS / NATIONAL LIBRARY OF MEDICINE.). **Added/Corp** National Library of Medicine (U.S.). (1960)-. English. an. $16.00 US; $20.00 other. National Library of Medicine, 8600 Rockville Pike, Bethesda MD 20894. **Tel** (301)496-6308. **LC** Z6660; .U66a. **DD** 016.61. **NLM** ZW 1 L772.
**Desc:** A listing of the 2,800 journals being indexed for Index Medicus as of January 1989. Listed in four sections: 1) by abbreviated title, followed by full title; 2) full title, followed by abbreviated title; 3) by subject field, and 4) by country of origin.

US/0736-7139
**LIST OF SERIALS INDEXED FOR ONLINE USERS.** (LIST OF SERIALS INDEXED FOR ONLINE USERS / (U.S.) NATIONAL LIBRARY OF MEDICINE.). **Added/Corp** National Library of Medicine (U.S.) United States. National Technical Information Service. National Library of Medicine (U.S.). Library Operations. (1983)-. English. an. $32.00 North America; $57.00 other. National Library of Medicine, 8600 Rockville Pike, Bethesda MD 20894. **Tel** (301)496-6308. **(Subscription address:** National Technical Information Service, 5285 Port Royal Road, Springfield, VA 22161**) LC** Z6660; .L66; R129. **DD** 016.61/05. **NLM** ZW 1 L774. ***Continues*** *List of Serials and Monographs Indexed for Online Users, 0196-755X.*

HU/0025-0252
**MAGYAR ORVOSI BIBLIOGRAFIA. VFOAT** Bibliographia Medica Hungarica. Began publication in 1957. Periodical. Hungarian. ir. **LC** Z6661.H93; M3.

US
**MATERNAL AND CHILD HEALTH STATISTICS : NORTH CAROLINA.** 1972-. English. an. North Carolina Department of Health Resources, Division of Health Services, Raleigh NC 27611. **LC** RG530.3.U52; N674. **DD** 312/.23756. **UDC** 312:613.95(756).

US/0730-7810
**MEDICAL ABSTRACTS NEWSLETTER.** [Med. abstr. newsl.]. (1981)-. Abstracting/Indexing Service. English. mo. $24.95 (one year), $39.95 (two year) US; $28.95 (surface mail) other. Medical Abstracts Newsletter, PO Box 2170, Teaneck NJ 07666. **Tel** (201)836-5030. **ED** Toni L Goldfarb. **LC** Discard. Index available. **Bk Rev**, (Qty: 2-3). **Circ:** 10,000.
**Desc:** Summarizes the research studies doctors read, in plain english the layman can easily understand. Each issue provides brief summaries (abstracts) of the latest breakthroughs and discoveries selected from over 140 authoritative medical journals.
**Ind/Abst** Consum. Health Nutr. Index.

US/0000-085X
**MEDICAL AND HEALTH CARE BOOKS AND SERIALS IN PRINT.** [Med. health care books ser. print]. (1985)-. English. an. $225.00. R R Bowker, A Reed Reference Publishing Company, Part of Reed International PLC, PO Box 31, 121 Chanlon Drive, New Providence NJ 07974. **Tel** (908)464-6800, (800)521-8110, FAX (908)665-6688, telex 138-755. **LC** Z6658; .B65; R129. **DD** 016.61. **NLM** ZW 1; B787. **[CCC]**. ***Continues*** *Medical Books and Serials in Print, 0000-0574.*
**Desc:** Contains listings under 6,000 targeted medical and allied health subject areas for more than 65,000 books and over 15,000 US and international serials that let you cover every aspect of the biomedical and health sciences.

●US/1063-1178
**MEDICAL & PHARMACEUTICAL BIOTECHNOLOGY ABSTRACTS.** [Med. pharm. biotechnol. abstr.]. **Added/Corp** Cambridge Scientific Abstracts, Inc. **VFOAT** Medical and Pharmaceutical Biotechnology Abstracts. Vol. 1, No. 1 (1993)-. Abstracting/Indexing Service. English. bm (6 issues). $275.00 US; $285.00 other. Cambridge Scientific Abstracts, 7200 Wisconsin Avenue, #601, Bethesda MD 20814-4823. **Tel** (301)961-6750, (800)843-7751, FAX (301)961-6720. **DD** 615. available on magnetic tape, an online database, and CD-ROM; available via Internet (to the current year's abstracts and five-year backfiles) from Cambridge Scientific Abstracts. ***Continues in part*** *Biotechnology Research Abstracts, 0733-5709.*
**Desc:** New applications for biotechnology in medicine and phamacology, human health, and the diagnosis and treatment of disease are highlighted in this journal. Topics include: genetic engineering and gene therapy - drug development and drug delivery systems - vaccines, blood factors, and products - antisense technology, and many other key areas.

US
**MEDICAL USES OF STATISTICS.** (19??)-. Monographic series. English. ir. $43.45. New England Journal of Medicine, 1440 Main Street, Waltham MA 02154-1649. **Tel** (617)893-3800, (800)843-6356, FAX (617)647-5785, telex 5106015660 NEJM BOS UQ.

US/0097-9732
**MEDOC.** ***Ceased.*** (MEDOC; A COMPUTERIZED INDEX TO U.S. GOVERNMENT DOCUMENTS IN THE MEDICAL AND HEALTH SCIENCES.). [MEDOC]. **Added/Corp** Spencer S. Eccles Medical Sciences Library. **VFOAT** Computerized Index to U.S. Government Documents in the Medical and Health Sciences; Index to U.S. Government Documents in the Medical and Health Sciences. Vol. 1 (1974)-Vol. 20, No. 4 (Dec. 1993). Abstracting/Indexing Service. English. qt. MEDOC, University of Utah, Spencer Eccles Health Science

Library, Salt Lake City UT 84112. **Tel** (801)581-5268, FAX (801)581-3632. **ED** Michael Thelin. **NLM** ZW 1 M106. **Circ:** 400.
**Desc:** Index to US Government publications in the health and medical sciences.

US
**MEDSTAT REPORT.** ***Ceased.*** (19??)-(19??). English. Twice a year. Medstat Systems Inc., 777 East Eisenhower Boulevard, Ann Arbor MI 48108.

US/0026-8070
**MODERN MEDICINE (MINNEAPOLIS).** (MODERN MEDICINE.). Vol. 1 (Oct. 1932)-. Abstracting/Indexing Service. English. mo. $50.00 US and possessions; $75.00 Canada; $110.00 other. Advanstar Communications Inc., 131 West First Street, Duluth MN 55802. **Tel** (218)723-9477, (800)346-0085. **ED** Martin M Stevenson. **LC** R11; .M95. **DD** 616/.005. **NLM** W1 MO142. **Ad Acc. Circ:** 123,096 (ctrl). available on microfilm and microfiche from University Microfilms International (UMI).
**Desc:** A clinical journal serving family physicians, general practitioners, cardiologists, internists, and osteopaths.

US/0112-8868
**NEW ZEALAND MEDICAL WORKFORCE STATISTICS ... .** 1984/1985-. English. te (summaries in other years). $20.00. Management Services and Research Unit, Department of Health, PO Box 5013, Wellington New Zealand. **Tel** 844-1671, telex NZ 3571. **ED** Alan Morris and Carol Leatham. **LC** PAR. **DD** 331.7/6161/09931021. **Circ:** 400 (ctrl). ***Continues*** *New Zealand Medical Manpower Statistics.*
**Desc:** Numerical data and commentaries on questionnaire survey of registered practising medical practitioners. Full coverage, medical council survey in conjunction with the Department of Health. Full analysis published.

US/0195-3354
**NURSING ABSTRACTS.** [Nurs. abstr.]. Vol. 1 (1979)-. Abstracting/Indexing Service. English. bm. $340.00 US and Canada; $385.00 other; Back volumes available- $160.00 US, $165.00 other. Nursing Abstracts Company Inc, Box 295, Forest Hills NY 11375. **Tel** (718)268-5344. **ED** D Dolgins. **DD** 610. **NLM** ZWY 100 N971. Index available (annual index included).
**Desc:** Reviews articles in over 70 nursing journals in all specialties of nursing. Abstracts are concise and easy to understand. Each issue contains more than 300 items, indexed by subject, and a list of journals; an annual index with more than 10,00 entries, listed by author, subject matter and publication for quick reference and research is included in the price of subscription. Back volumes are available at $160.00 each, plus $20.00 foreign postage. A truly useful, valuable and timesaving tool.

US
**NURSING & ALLIED HEALTH CINAHL CAMBRIDGE. CD-ROM.** English. mo. $1095.00 US and Canada; $1335.00 other except UK, Australia and Asia. Cambridge Scientific Abstracts, 7200 Wisconsin Avenue, #601, Bethesda MD 20814-4823. **Tel** (301)961-6750, (800)843-7751, FAX (301)961-6720. Index available. **Bk Rev. Ad Acc.** available in print.

US
**NURSING & ALLIED HEALTH (CINAHL)-CD [COMPUTER FILE].** **Added/Corp** Glendale Adventist Medical Center. **VFOAT** Nursing and Allied Health (CINAHL)-CD; CINAHL-CD. (19??)-. English. bm. $1250.00. Silverplatter Information Inc., 100 River Ridge Drive, Norwood MA 02062. **Tel** (800)343-0064, (617)769-2599, FAX (617)235-1715. available in print.
**Desc:** Nursing and allied health professionals who want information applicable to their specialties can find it in this comprehensive database.

US/1043-8963
**ONCOGENES AND GROWTH FACTORS ABSTRACTS.** [Oncog. growth factors abstr.]. **Added/Corp** Cambridge Scientific Abstracts, Inc. **VFOAT** Oncogenes Abstracts. Vol. 1, No. 1 (June 1989)-. Abstracting/Indexing Service. English. qt (plus annual index). $275.00 US; $285.00 other. Cambridge Scientific Abstracts, 7200 Wisconsin Avenue, #601, Bethesda MD 20814-4823. **Tel** (301)961-6750, (800)843-7751, FAX (301)961-6720. **ED** Robert H. Bassin and David S. Salomon. **LC** RC268.42; .O5253. **DD** 616.99/4071. **NLM** ZQZ 202; O56. Index available. available on magnetic tape; available on an online database; available on CD-ROM; available via Internet (to the current year's abstracts and five-year backfiles) from Cambridge Scientific Abstracts.
**Desc:** Surveys and summarizes hundreds of conference proceedings, books, and research reports to cover every aspect of oncogene research into the molecular basis of malignant transformations. Suggests new directions for research and in helping scientists avoid dead ends or costly duplication of work.

US/0733-4060
**ONGOING CURRENT BIBLIOGRAPHY OF PLASTIC AND RECONSTRUCTIVE SURGERY (1980).** (ONGOING CURRENT BIBLIOGRAPHY OF PLASTIC AND RECONSTRUCTIVE SURGERY.). **Added/Corp** American Society of Plastic and Reconstructive Surgeons. Educational Foundation. Symposium. Plastic Surgery Educational Foundation (American Society of Plastic and Reconstructive Surgeons). **VFOAT** Plastic Surgery. Vol. 8, No. 3 (May-June 1980)-. Periodical. English. bm. $60.00 North america; $75.00 other. Plastic Surgery Education Foundation, 23 Pinewood Farm Street, Medlars DM, Owings Mills MD 22117. **Tel** (301)252-4022. **NLM** ZWO 600; M11. ***Continues*** *Current Bibliography of Plastic and Reconstructive Surgery, 0149-5348.*

NE/0014-4371
**ORTHOPEDIC SURGERY.** **Added/Corp** Excerpta Medica Foundation. Vol. 11 (Jan. 1966)-. Abstracting/Indexing Service. English. Ten times a year (1 volume). Fl1203.00. Excerpta Medica Publishing Group, PO Box 548, 1000 AM Amsterdam Netherlands. **Tel** 011 31 20 5803243. **(Subscription address:** Excerpta Medica Journals, PO Box 85, Limerick Ireland.**) LC** RD701; .O78. **NLM** ZW 1 E978M. **[CCC]. Ad Acc. Circ:** 350. available on microfilm from University Microfilms International (UMI); available on CD-ROM. ***Continues*** *Orthopedics and Traumatology.*
**Desc:** Covers the entire area of orthopedics. Contains an introductory chapter on general orthopedics, subdivided on an anatomical basis, followed by chapters covering growth and development (including congenital malformations and growth deformities), physical examination and diagnostic procedures, instrumentation, biomechanics, and experimental orthopedics.

●US/1065-6545
**PHYSICIAN'S MEDLINE PLUS.** (PHYSICIAN'S MEDLINE PLUS [COMPUTER FILE] : EBSCO CD-ROM.). **Added/Corp** EBSCO Publishing (Firm). **VFOAT** EBSCO CD-ROM. (1992)-. Abstracting/Indexing Service. English. qt. $399.00. EBSCO Publishing / Boston, 83 Pine Street, Peabody MA 01960. **Tel** (800)653-2726 North America, (508)535-8500, FAX (508)535-8545. Index available. **Pr Rev.**
**Desc:** Unique subset of the National Library of Medicine's (NLM) MEDLINE file. Quarterly updates allow for instant access to data from the 200 journals most subscribed to by physicians. The database includes more than 100 journals from the Brandon and Hill "List of Books and Journals for the Small Medical Library" and over 100 titles in the Abridged Index Medicus. Searchable Full Text coverage of The New England Journal of Medicine is a standard feature of Physician's MEDLINE Plus. Physicians now have all this information at their fingertips, without the costs associated with on-line searching.

DK/0906-9666
**PROGRAM OF PLENARY SESSIONS AND ADVANCE ABSTRACTS OF SHORT COMMUNICATIONS.** [Program plenary sess. adv. abstr. short commun]. **VFOAT** Program of Plenary Sessions and Advance Abstracts of Short Papers. (1984)-. Monographic series. English. ir. Price varies per volume. Scandinavian University Press, PO Box 2959 Toeyen, N 0608 Oslo 6 Norway. **Tel** 011 47 2 2575400, FAX 011 47 2 2575353, telex 71896 UROR N. **DD** 612.4. ***Continues*** *Advance Abstracts of Short Papers - Symposion Deutsche Gesellschaft fur Endokrinologie, 0302-9522.*

US
**PUBLISHED SEARCH BIBLIOGRAPHIES FROM THE NTIS BIBLIOGRAPHIC DATA BASE. HEALTH AND MEDICINE / U.S. DEPARTMENT OF COMMERCE, NATIONAL TECHNICAL INFORMATION SERVICE.** **Added/Corp** United States. National Technical Information Service. **VFOAT** Published Search Bibliographies from the N.T.I.S. Bibliographic Data Base. Physical Sciences; Health and Medicine. (19??)-. English. ir. Free on request. National Technical Information Service - NTIS, Room 2027S, 5285 Port Royal Road, Springfield VA 22161. **Tel** (703)487-4630, (703)487-4660, (703)487-4650, FAX (703)321-8547, telex 89-9405.

●US/1076-2833
**QUINTESSENCE (CHICAGO, ILL.).** (QUINTESSENCE : EXCELLENCE IN ENVIRONMENTAL CONTAMINATION & TOXICOLOGY.). (1994)-. Periodical. English. Six times a year. $200.00 (North America), $210.00 (other) institutions; $99.00 individuals. SCIPRESS, 3200 North Lake Shore Drive, # 1903, Chicago IL 60657. **Tel** (312)975-0648. **ED** Herbert N. Nigg (editor's address: University of Florida, Institute of Food and Agricultural Sciences, 700 Experiment Station Road, Lake Alfred, FL 33850; FAX: (813)956-4631). Index available (subject index).
**Desc:** An interdisciplinary synthesis of the most important scientific studies describing original experimental or theoretical work concerning contaminants in the environment. Studies published worldwide describing significant advances in air, water, and soil contamination and pollution, as well as methodology, and work in the related disciplines.

US
**REFERENCE UPDATE BASIC EDITION [COMPUTER FILE].** Abstracting/Indexing Service. English. wk. $399.00 (diskette), $299.00 (modem). Research Information Systems, 2355 Camino Vida Roble, Carlsbad CA 92009. **Tel** (619)438-5526, (619)438-5547.
**Desc:** Current awareness service for scientists in the fields of biology and medicine. Covers approximately 430 journals.

US
**REFERENCE UPDATE CLINICAL EDITION [COMPUTER FILE].** Abstracting/Indexing Service. English. mo. $75.00. Research Information Systems, 2355 Camino Vida Roble, Carlsbad CA 92009. **Tel** (619)438-5526, (619)438-5547.
**Desc:** Covers internal medicine and related areas. Allows those in the fields of biology and medicine to stay abreast of current literature.

US
**REFERENCE UPDATE DELUXE EDITION [COMPUTER FILE].** Abstracting/Indexing Service. English. wk. $499.00 (diskette), $399.00 (modem). Research Information Systems, 2355 Camino Vida Roble, Carlsbad CA 92009. **Tel** (619)438-5526, (619)438-5547.
**Desc:** Current awareness service for scientists in the fields of biology and medicine. A comprehensive software package that provides the rapid display of citations of newly published articles, based on a variety of user-identified criteria.

NO/0802-1473
**REGIONAL DELIGHET.** **VFOAT** Regional Mortality. English (Norwegian). Central Bureau of Statistics / Norway, PO Box 8131 DEP, N-0033 Oslo 1 Norway. **Tel** 011 47 2 2864964, FAX 011 47 2 864973. **LC** HA1501 subser; HB1445. **DD** 314.81 s; 304.6/4/09481021.

US/0197-7210
**SCHISTO UPDATE.** [Schisto update]. **Added/Corp** Edna McConnell Clark Foundation. National Library of Medicine (U.S.). (July 1977/Dec. 1978)-. Periodical. English. Four times a year. Edna McConnell Clark Foundation, 250 Park Avenue, New York NY 10017. **ED** Linda Lange. **NLM** ZWC 810 S3365.
**Desc:** Lists articles concerned with schistosomiasis that have appeared in approximately 2,300 journals published throughout the world which were indexed in MEDLARS.

UK/0267-0348
**SELECTED BIBLIOGRAPHIES ON AGEING.** [Sel. bibliogr. ageing]. **Added/Corp** Centre for Policy on Ageing (London, England). Vol. 1 (1984)-. Monographic series. English. ir. Price varies per volume. Centre for Policy on Aging, 25-31 Ironmonger Row, London EC1R 3QP England. **Tel** 011 44 712531787. **(Subscription address:** CPA Bailey Distribution Ltd., Learoyd Road, Mountfield Industry ES, Kent TN28 8X4 England.**) ED** Gillian Crosby. **LC** UNC. **NLM** ZWT 100; S464. **Circ:** 500 (ctrl).

US/0884-1152
**SELECTED MEDICAL CARE STATISTICS.** **See** Military and Defense-Abstracting, Bibliographies and Statistics.

CN/0705-8322
**SERVICE DE LA BIBLIOTHEQUE: SUPPLEMENT AU GUIDE DE L'USAGER.** **Main/Corp** Association de Paralysie Cerebrale du Quebec. (1977)-. French. an. Association de Paralysie Cerebrale du Quebec / Charlesbourg, 4765 1st Avenue/Suite 300, Charlesbourg Quebec G1H 2T3 Canada. **DD** 016.6168/36.

IE
**STATISTICAL INFORMATION RELEVANT TO THE HEALTH SERVICES.** **Main/Corp** Ireland (Eire). Dept. of Health. Planning Unit. Statistical Publication. English. 40. Government Publications, 4 5 Harcourt Road, Dublin 2 Ireland. **Tel** 011 353 1 6613111 Ext.4005. **LC** RA407.5.I73; I74A. **DD** 362.1/09417.

US/0098-8057
**STATISTICAL REPORT - LOUISIANA, HEALTH AND SOCIAL AND REHABILITATION SERVICES ADMINISTRATION (ANNUAL).** (STATISTICAL REPORT.). **Main/Corp** Louisiana. Health and Social and Rehabilitation Services Administration. (19??)-. Statistical Publication. English. an. Health & Social & Rehabilitation Services Administration, PO Box 60630, Public Health Station, New Orleans LA 70160. **LC** RA981.L6; A328. **DD** 362.1/1/09763. ***Continues*** *Louisiana. State Dept. of Hospitals. Annual Statistical Report.*

UK/0277-6715
**STATISTICS IN MEDICINE.** [Stat. med.]. Vol. 1 No. 1 (Jan/March 1982)-. Periodical. English. Twenty-four times a year. $895.00. John Wiley & Sons Ltd., Baffins Lane, Chichester West Sussex PO19 1UD England. **Tel**

0243 779777, FAX 0243 776128 BTG:JWP001, telex 86290 WIBOOKG. **(Subscription address:** John Wiley / Philadelphia, PO Box 7247, Philadelphia PA 19170.) **ED** T. Colton, L. Freedman, T. Johnson, and D. Machin. **LC** RA409; .S687. **DD** 610/.72. **NLM** W1 ST319N. **CODEN** SMEDDA. **[CCC]. Pr Rev. Circ:** 1,100. available on microfilm and microfiche from University Microfilms International (UMI). Documents available from The Genuine Article, BIOSIS Document Express.
**Desc:** Publishes papers on practical applications of statistics and other quantitative methods to medicine. Covers all aspects of the collection, analysis, presentation and interpretation of medical data. The journal emphasizes the relevance of numerical techniques and explains statistical and quantitative ideas in a medical context.
**Ind/Abst** Biol. Abstr. (1987-); Biostatistica; Compumath Citation Index [Full Cov.]; Curr. Aware. Biol. Sci., CABS; Curr. Contents Clin. Med.; Curr. Contents Life Sci.; Curr. Contents Phys. Chem. Earth Sci.; Curr. Index Stat.; EMBASE; Index Med.; Protozoolog. Abstr.; Qual. Control Appl. Stat.; Res. Alert [Full Cov.]; Rev. Med. Vet. Entomol.; Risk Abstr.; SCISEARCH; Soc. Sci. Cit. Index [Select. Cov.]; Stat. Theory Method Abstr. (1983); Trop. Dis. Bull.; Virol. AIDS Abstr.

CN/0524-5354
**STATISTICS OF HOSPITAL CASES DISCHARGED. BRITISH COLUMBIA.** (STATISTICS OF HOSPITAL CASES DISCHARGED.). **Main/Corp** British Columbia. Hospital Programs. Research Division. No. 14- 1974-. English. an. Hospital Programs, Parliament Buildings, Victoria British Columbia Canada. **LC** RA983.A4; B683. **DD** 362.1/1/09711. ***Continues** Statistics of Hospital Cases Discharged, 0524-5354.*

CN/0524-5451
**STATISTICS OF HOSPITALIZED ACCIDENTS : BRITISH COLUMBIA.** **Main/Corp** British Columbia. Hospital Programs. Research Division. (1973)-. English. an. Ministry of Health / Victoria, 1515 Blanshard Street, Victoria British Columbia V8W 3C8 Canada. **Tel** 387-2749. **LC** RA407.5.C2; B75. **DD** 312/.4/09711. **NLM** W2 DC2.1 B8H83S. ***Continues** Statistics of Hospitalized Accidents, British Columbia, 0524-5451.*
**Desc:** Province of British Columbia accidents statistics.

CN/0821-1582
**SUGGESTED LIST OF MEDICAL BOOKS & JOURNALS.** Sept. 1982-. English. be. Ontario Medical Association, 525 University Avenue, Suite 300, Toronto Ontario M5G 2K7, Canada. **Tel** (416)599-2580. **DD** 016.61. ***Continues** Suggested List of Basic Books & Journals (Ontario Medical Association), 0821-1558.*

FI/0786-2180
**SUOMEN LAAKETILASTO / LAAKEINFORMAATION JA -TILASTOINNIN YHTEISTYOTOIMIKUNTA.** **VFOAT** Finnish Statistics on Medicines. (1987)-. English (Finnish). an. National Board of Health Pharmaceutical Bureau, PO Box 221, SF-00531 Helsinki Finland. **LC** RM138; .S86.

JA
**TOSHO MOKUROKU - KOKU IGAKU JIKKENTAI.** **Main/Corp** Japan. Koku Igaku Jikkentai. Multiple languages (Japanese, English and German). Koku Igaku Jikkentai, 2-10 Sakaecho 1-chome, Tachikawa Japan. **LC** Z6664.3; .J362A; RC1062. **NLM** Z 675.M4 K79T.

US/0140-5365
**TOXICOLOGY ABSTRACTS.** [Toxicol. abstr.]. **Added/Corp** Cambridge Scientific Abstracts. Information Retrieval Limited. Vol. 1 (Jan. 1978)-. Abstracting/Indexing Service. English. mo (includes annual index). $795.00 US; $965.00 other. Cambridge Scientific Abstracts, 7200 Wisconsin Avenue, #601, Bethesda MD 20814-4823. **Tel** (301)961-6750, (800)843-7751, FAX (301)961-6720. **ED** Roberta Gardner. **LC** RA1190; .T695. **DD** 615.9/005. **NLM** ZQV 600.3 T763. Index available. **Bk Rev.** available on magnetic tape and an online database; available on CD-ROM (POLTOX) from Cambridge Scientific Abstracts; available on an online database from Pollution and Toxicology Database; available on magnetic tape from Pollution and Toxicology Database; available via Internet (to the current year's abstracts and five-year backfiles) from Cambridge Scientific Abstracts.
**Desc:** Covers every aspect of toxicology: industrial chemicals, pharmaceuticals, food, agrochemicals, cosmetics, toiletries, household. Social poisons, and toxicity studies in man and animals.
**Ind/Abst** World Surf. Coat. Abstr.

US
**TRENDS IN BHPR PROGRAM STATISTICS. GRANTS, AWARDS, LOANS.** **VFOAT** Trends in B.H.P.R. Program Statistics. Grants, Awards, Loans. **VAT** Trends in Bureau of Health Professions Program Statistics. Grants, Awards, Loans. FY 1957-79-. English. an. US Department of Health and Human Services, 200 Independence Avenue Southwest, Washington DC 20201. ***Continues** Trends in BHM Program Statistics. Grants, Awards, Loans, 0147-3425.*

UK/0041-3240
**TROPICAL DISEASES BULLETIN.** **Added/Corp** Bureau of Hygiene and Tropical Diseases (London, England) Tropical Diseases Bureau (London, England). Vol. 1 (Nov. 15, 1912)-. Abstracting/Indexing Service. English. mo. $290.00. CAB International Centre, Wallingford, Oxon OX10 8DE United Kingdom. **Tel** 44 491 832111, FAX 44 491 833508, telex 847964 (COMAGG G). **ED** Carolyn A Brown. **LC** RC960; .L78. **DD** 616. cum. index. **Bk Rev. Ad Acc. Circ:** 1,400. ***Supersedes** Bulletin of the Sleeping Sickness Bureau and the Kala Azar Bulletin.*
**Desc:** Contains critical abstracts of selected papers on clinical, field and laboratory studies pertaining to international public health. The material is selected by the Bureau of Hygiene and Tropical Diseases' scientific staff from the joint bibliographic collection with the London School of Hygiene and Tropical Medicine of journals plus books, reports etc. The abstracts, many written by internationally recognized experts, are supplemented regularly with reviews and features such as points of view, essay-type book reviews and bibliographies of Chinese literature.
**Ind/Abst** Helminthol. Abstr. (19??-19??); Index Med.; Protozoolog. Abstr.; Rev. Med. Vet. Entomol.

CN/1195-4086
**TUBERCULOSIS STATISTICS / STATISTICS CANADA, CANADIAN CENTRE FOR HEALTH INFORMATION.** **Added/Corp** Canadian Centre for Health Information. **VFOAT** Statistique de la Tuberculose. (1991)-. English (French). an. 13.00Can$ Canada; $14.00 other. Statistics Canada, Publications Sales & Services, Main Building Room 1710, Ottawa Ontario K1A 0T6 Canada. **Tel** (613)951-5078, (800)267-6677, FAX (613)951-1584, telex 053-3585. **LC** RA644.T7; H36. **DD** 614.5/42/0971021. ***Continues** Health Reports. Supplement. Tuberculosis Statistics, Morbidity and Mortality, 1180-2413.*

US/0741-6326
**U.S. MEDICAL LICENSURE STATISTICS ... AND LICENSURE REQUIREMENTS ... .** [U.S. med. licens. stat. licens. require.]. **Added/Corp** American Medical Association. Survey & Data Resources. **VFOAT** US Medical Licensure Statistics ... and Licensure Requirements ...; Medical Licensure Statistics; Licensure Requirements. (1982)-. English. an (Apr.). $70.00 (members); $100.00 (non-members). American Medical Association, 515 North State Street, Chicago IL 60610. **Tel** (312)464-5000, (800)262-2350, FAX (312)464-5831. **(Subscription address:** American Medical Association, PO Box 109050, Chicago IL 60610.) **ED** Catherine M. Bidese. **LC** RA396.A3; U2. **DD** 362.1/72. **NLM** W1; US830. **Circ:** 2,500 (ctrl).
**Desc:** The only single source reference guide to U.S. medical licensure, with up-to-date statistics and state requirements for medical licensure in the U.S.

US
**UCLA UAF BIBLIOGRAPHY IN MENTAL RETARDATION.** **Main/Corp** University of California, Los Angeles. University Affiliated Facilities. **VFOAT** Bibliography in Mental Retardation. V. 1- Sept. 1971-. Bibliography. English. mo. University of California at Los Angeles / Affiliated Facilities, Los Angeles CA 90024. **LC** Z6677; .C354. **DD** 016.3623/05. **UDC** 616.89-008.454.

US/0896-5919
**VIROLOGY & AIDS ABSTRACTS.** [Virol. AIDS abstr.]. **Added/Corp** Cambridge Scientific Abstracts, Inc. **VFOAT** Virology and AIDS Abstracts; Virology Abstracts. Vol. 21, No. 3 (Mar. 1988)-. Abstracting/Indexing Service. English. mo (includes annual index). $845.00 US; $900.00 other. Cambridge Scientific Abstracts, 7200 Wisconsin Avenue, #601, Bethesda MD 20814-4823. **Tel** (301)961-6750, (800)843-7751, FAX (301)961-6720. **ED** Darrell Stover. **LC** QR360; .V513. **DD** 576/.64/05. **NLM** ZQW 160; V819. Index available. cum. index. **Bk Rev.** available on magnetic tape; available on an online database; available on CD-ROM; available via Internet (to the current year's abstracts and five-year backfiles) from Cambridge Scientific Abstracts. ***Continues** Virology Abstracts, 0042-6830.*
**Desc:** All aspects of research relating to viruses, including effects on humans, animals, and plants. Special emphasis on acquired immune deficiency syndrome (AIDS).

## ALLERGY AND IMMUNOLOGY

US/0883-2994
**ABMS DIRECTORY OF CERTIFIED ALLERGY AND IMMUNOLOGY PHYSICIANS.** [ABMS dir. certif. allergy immunol. physicians]. **Added/Corp** American Board of Medical Specialties. American Board of Allergy and Immunology. **VFOAT** Directory of Certified Allergy and Immunology Physicians; ABMS ... Directory of Certified Allergists and Immunologists. **VAT** American Board of Medical Specialties Directory of Certified Allergy and Immunology Physicians. (1985)-. English. be. $24.95. American Board of Medical Specialties, 1 Rotary Center, Suite 805, Evanston IL 60201. **Tel** (708)491-9091. **LC** RC583; .A17. **DD** 616.97/0025/73. **NLM** QW 522.1; A1523.

US/1041-4487
**ACQUIRED IMMUNE DEFICIENCY SYNDROME NEWSLETTER.** ***Title Change.*** [Acquir. immune defic. syndr. newsl.]. **VFOAT** AIDS Newsletter. Vol. 1, No. 1 (Sept. 1, 1988)-(199?). Newsletter. English. ir (48 issues). AIDS Newsletter, 1680 North Vine Street/Suite 316, Los Angeles CA 90028. **Tel** (310)461-0768. **ED** James Goode. **DD** 616. **Pr Rev. Circ:** 350. ***Merged into** Aids Weekly, 1069-1456.*
**Desc:** All current aids abstracts from all known medical journals.

US/0178-2134
**ADVANCES IN IMMUNITY AND CANCER THERAPY.** [Adv. immun. cancer ther.]. Vol. 1 (1985)-. Monographic series. English. ir. Price varies per volume. Springer-Verlag New York Inc., 175 5th Avenue, New York NY 10010. **Tel** (212)460-1500, telex 232 235 SPB UR. **(Subscription address:** Springer Verlag New York Inc. / for North America, 44 Hartz Way, Secaucus NJ 07096.) **LC** RC271.I45; A35. **DD** 616.99/4061. **NLM** W1; AD646. **CODEN** AICTER. Documents available from BIOSIS Document Express.
**Ind/Abst** Biol. Abstr. (1985-); Health Plan. Adminis.; Index Med. (1985-); INIS Atomindex [Micro.].

US/0065-2776
**ADVANCES IN IMMUNOLOGY.** ***Title Change.*** [Adv. Immunol.]. **Added/Corp** Institute of Water Pollution Control. Vol. 1 (1961)-(19??). Academic Scholarly Publication. English. an. Academic Press, Inc., 6277 Sea Harbor Drive, Orlando FL 32887. **Tel** (800)543-9534, (407)345-4100, FAX (407)363-9661. **ED** W H Taliferro and J H Humphrey. **LC** QR180; .A2. **DD** 615.3705. **NLM** W1 AD647. **CODEN** ADIMAV. **[CCC]. Pr Rev.** available on microfilm. Documents available from The Genuine Article, BIOSIS Document Express, CASDDS. ***Continues** Institute of Sewage Purification. Journal and Proceedings, 0368-0215.* ***Merged with** Institution of Water Engineers and Scientists. Journal of the Institution of Water Engineers and Scientists, 0309-1600* ***and** Public Health Engineer, 0300-5925* ***to form** Water and Environmental Management, 0951-7359.*
**Ind/Abst** AgBiotech News Inf.; Anim. Breed. Abstr.; Biol. Abstr.; Chem. Abstr.; Curr. Aware. Biol. Sci., CABS; Dairy Sci. Abstr.; EMBASE; Energy Res. Abstr. (Oct. 1975-); Index Med.; Index Sci. Rev. [Full Cov.]; Index Vet.; Nutr. Abstr. Rev., Ser. B, Live Feeds and Feed.; Nutr. Abstr. Rev., Ser. A, Hum. Exp.; Life Sci. Collect.; Protozoolog. Abstr.; Ref. Upd. Basic Ed.; Ref. Upd. Clinical Ed.; Ref. Upd. Deluxe Ed.; Res. Alert [Full Cov.]; Sci. Cit. Index; SCISEARCH; Vet. Bull.; Trop. Dis. Bull.

UK
**ADVANCES IN IMMUNOPHARMACOLOGY : PROCEEDINGS OF THE INTERNATIONAL CONFERENCE ON IMMUNOPHARMACOLOGY.** **Main/Conf** International Conference on Immunopharmacology. **VFOAT** Proceedings of the ... International Conference on Immunopharmacology. 1st (July 1980)-. Proceedings. English. ir. Pergamon Press, An Imprint of Elsevier Science Ltd., The Boulevard, Langford Lane, Kidlington, Oxford OX5 1GB United Kingdom. **Tel** 011 44 865 843000, 011 44 865 843699, FAX 011 44 865 843010. **(Subscription address:** US/ 395 Saw Mill River Road, Elmsford, NY 10523; Can/ 150 Consumers Road/Suite 104, Willowdale Ontario M2J 1P9; Aus-NZ/ POB 544, Potts Point NSW 2011) **LC** RM370; .I56A. **DD** 615/.7. **NLM** W3; IN181W.

US
**ADVANCES IN MOLECULAR AND CELLULAR IMMUNOLOGY.** Vol. 1 (1993)-. Periodical. English. $180.50. JAI Press Inc., 55 Old Post Road, Suite 2, PO Box 1678, Greenwich CT 06836-1678. **Tel** (203)661-7602, FAX (203)661-0792. **ED** B. Singh.

UK/0960-5428
**ADVANCES IN NEUROIMMUNOLOGY.**
**See** Medical Science and Technology-Neurology.

US/0892-8762
**AGING, IMMUNOLOGY AND INFECTIOUS DISEASE.** [Aging immunol. infect. dis.]. **VFOAT** Aging; Immunology and Infectious Disease. Vol. 1, No. 1 (1988)-. Periodical. English. qt. $137.00 US and Canada; $167.00 other. Mary Ann Liebert Inc., 1651 Third Avenue, New York NY 10128. **Tel** (212)289-2300, (800)M-LIEBERT, FAX (212)289-4697. **ED** Jeanette Thorbecke. **LC** QR180; .A32. **DD** 616.97/079/005. **NLM** W1; AG344. **CODEN** AIIDE9. **Pr Rev.** Documents available from BIOSIS Document Express.
**Desc:** Publishes papers on immunology and infectious diseases as related to aging. Provides a forum for basic

studies on host defense mechanisms, in vivo in animal models and in man, as well as in vitro and at the molecular level.
**Ind/Abst** Biol. Abstr. (1988-).

GW
**AIDS.** Vol. 1 (1985)-. Periodical. German. **NLM** W1; AI696C.
**Ind/Abst** Curr. Titl. Dent.; Virol. AIDS Abstr.

US/0894-931X
**AIDS.** ***Ceased.*** (AIDS : A QUARTERLY BIBLIOGRAPHY FROM ALL FIELDS OF PERIODICAL LITERATURE.). [AIDS]. **Added/Corp** Lincoln Associates (Madison, Wis.). **VAT** Acquired Immune Deficiency Syndrome; Acquired Immunodeficiency Syndrome. Vol. 1, No. 1 (Spring 1987)-?. Bibliography. English. qt. Lincoln Associates, Box 507, Madison WI 53701. **DD** 616.

●US/1066-1107
**AIDS ABSTRACTS (ATLANTA, GA.).** **See** Medical Science and Technology-Abstracting, Bibliographies and Statistics.

●UK/0968-5480
**AIDS ABSTRACTS : INTERNATIONAL LITERATURE ON ACQUIRED IMMUNODEFICIENCY SYNDROME AND RELATED RETROVIRUSES.** **Added/Corp** University of Leeds. Oncology Information Service. Vol. 9, No. 1 (Jan. 1993)-. Periodical. English. mo. £138.00. Carfax Publishing Company, PO Box 25 Abingdon, Oxfordshire OX14 3UE England. **Tel** 011 44 235 555335, FAX (0279)31067, telex 817484. **(Subscription address:** US and Canada/ PO Box 2025, Dunnellon, FL 34430-2025; telephone:(904)489-6996**)** **ED** Arthur W. Boylston. **NLM** ZWD 308; A28772. available on microfiche. ***Continues*** *AIDS Information.*

UK/0953-0096
**AIDS ACTION.** **Added/Corp** Appropriate Health Resources & Technologies Action Group. **VAT** Acquired Immune Deficiency Syndrome Action. Issue 1 (Nov. 1987)-. Periodical. English (French, Spanish and Portuguese). qt. $40.00 institutions; $20.00 individuals. AHRTAG, 1 London Bridge Street, 3 Castle, London SE1 9SG England. **Tel** 011 44 71 378 1403, FAX 011 44 71 403 6003, telex 912881 TXG. **ED** Hilary Hughes. **NLM** W1; AI696CE. **Bk Rev. Circ:** 80,000.
**Desc:** Newsletter containing practical information for health workers and communities in developing countries about HIV infection and AIDS.
**Ind/Abst** Trop. Dis. Bull.

US/0887-0292
**AIDS ALERT.** ***Ceased.*** [AIDS alert]. **Added/Corp** American Health Consultants. **VFOAT** Acquired Immunodeficiency Syndrome Alert. Vol. 1, No. 1 (Jan. 1986)-(Dec. 1994). Periodical. English. mo. American Health Consultants, 3525 Piedmont Road, Suite 400, Atlanta GA 30305. **Tel** (800)688-2421, (404)262-7436. **ED** Terri Thornton. **DD** 614. **NLM** W1; AI696CH. available on an online database (file4 149/Full-Text) from DIALOG.
**Desc:** Covers up-to-the minute developments and guidance on the entire spectrum of AIDS challenges, including treatment, precautions, screening, diagnosis and policy.
**Ind/Abst** Cumul. Index Nurs. Allied Health Lit.; Health Index (1989-); Health Period. Database [Full Txt.]; Health Ref. Cent. (Jan. 1989-) [Full Cov.]; Trop. Dis. Bull.

SA/1016-4731
**AIDS ANALYSIS AFRICA.** **Added/Corp** Aids Policy Research Group (South Africa). Vol. 1, No. 1 (June/July 1990)-. Periodical. English. bm. £60.00. Africa Analysis Ltd, Suite 71 Ludgate House, 107 111 Fleet Street, London EC41 2AB England. **Tel** 011 44 71 353 1117, FAX 011 44 71 353 1516. **ED** Alan Whiteside and Rex Wisbury. **LC** RA644.A25; A3322. **DD** 362.1/969792/0096805. **Bk Rev. Circ:** 250.
**Desc:** A newsletter reporting developments in AIDS control, management and finance in Africa. Also addresses company and agency reactions.

US/0887-3852
**AIDS & PUBLIC POLICY JOURNAL.** [AIDS public policy j.]. **VFOAT** AIDS and Public Policy Journal; APPJ. **VAT** Acquired Immune Deficiency Syndrome & Public Policy Journal; Acquired Immunodeficiency Syndrome & Public Policy Journal. Vol. 1, No. 1 (July 1986)-. Periodical. English. qt (Jan., Apr., Jul., Nov.). $105.00 US; $115.00 other. University Publishing Group Inc., 107 East Church Street, Frederick MD 21701-5441. **Tel** (301)694-8531, (800)654-8188. **ED** Edward N. Brandt. **LC** RA644.A25; A352. **DD** 362.1/969792/0097305. **NLM** W1; AI696CHD. **Bk Rev. Pr Rev.**
**Desc:** The journal is devoted to providing a forum for the in-depth analysis, discussion, and debate of the humerous and controversial issues surrounding the AIDS epidemic. Serves as a vehicle for the development, review, and criticism of proposals and guidelines for appropriate private, institutional, and public response to AIDS.
**Ind/Abst** EMBASE; Linguist. Lang. Behav. Abstr.; PAIS Int. Print; Soc. Plann. Policy Dev. Abstr.; Sociol. Abstr.

US/1055-0380
**AIDS & SOCIETY.** [AIDS soc.]. **Added/Corp** African-Caribbean Institute (Hanover, N.H.) International Development Research Centre (Canada) United States. Bureau of the Census. **VFOAT** AIDS and Society. **VAT** Acquired Immune Deficiency Syndrome & Society. Vol. 1, No. 1 (Oct. 1989)-. Periodical. English (summaries and/or abstracts in French and Spanish). Four times a year (Jan., Apr., July, Oct.). $18.00 (individuals); $30.00 (institutions). African Carribean Institute, 4 West Wheelock Street, Hanover NH 03755. **Tel** (802)649-5296. **ED** Erika Stecklare, Circulation Manager. **LC** RA644.A25; A287. **DD** 362.1/9697/92 2 20. **NLM** W1; AI696CHDG. **Bk Rev. Ad Acc. Circ:** 2,000 (ctrl).
**Desc:** Information in AIDS for social and behavioral scientists, educators, policy makers, in longer articles as well as news briefs.

US
**AIDS & TB ARTICLE SUMMARIES.** ***Title Change.*** (1993)-(1993). English. wk. CW Henderson, PO Box 5528, Atlanta GA 30307-0528. **Tel** (404)377-8895, FAX (404)378-5411. ***Continues*** *AIDS Article Summaries.* ***Continued by*** *AIDS & TB Weekly Article Summaries.*

US
**AIDS & TB WEEKLY ABSTRACTS FROM CONFERENCE PROCEEDINGS.** (19??)-. Proceedings. English. wk (48 issues). $995.00 US, Canada and Mexico; $1,195.00 other (includes complimentary binder). CW Henderson, PO Box 5528, Atlanta GA 30307-0528. **Tel** (404)377-8895, FAX (404)378-5411. **(Subscription address:** AIDS and TB Weekly Article Summaries, PO Box 830409, Birmingham AL 35283-0409.**)** Index available (3 quarterly). cum. index (end of the year). ***Continues*** *AIDS & TB Abstracts from Conference Proceedings.*

●US
**AIDS & TB WEEKLY ARTICLE SUMMARIES.** (1993)-. English. wk (48 issues). $995.00 US, Canada and Mexico; $1,195.00 other (includes complimentary binder). CW Henderson, PO Box 5528, Atlanta GA 30307-0528. **Tel** (404)377-8895, FAX (404)378-5411. **(Subscription address:** AIDS and TB Weekly Article Summaries, PO Box 830409, Birmingham AL 35283-0409.**)** Index available (3 quarterly). cum. index (end of the year). ***Continues*** *AIDS & TB Article Summaries.*

US/1068-6282
**AIDS ARTICLE SUMMARIES.** ***Title Change.*** (1993)-(1993). Periodical. English. Forty-eight times a year. CW Henderson, PO Box 5528, Atlanta GA 30307-0528. **Tel** (404)377-8895, FAX (404)378-5411. **(Subscription address:** CW Henderson, Subscription Office, PO Box 830409, Birmingham AL 35283-0409.**)** ***Continued by*** *AIDS & TB Article Summaries.*

US/0895-9765
**AIDS CABISCO NEWS.** [AIDS Cabisco news]. **Added/Corp** AIDS Cabisco. Vol. 1, No. 1 (Sept. 1987)-. Periodical. English. bm. Free. AIDS Cabisco News, 2700 York Road, Burlington NC 27215. **DD** 614.

UK/0954-0121
**AIDS CARE.** [AIDS care]. Vol. 1, No. 1 (1989)-. Periodical. English. Four times a year. £160.00. Carfax Publishing Company, PO Box 25 Abingdon, Oxfordshire OX14 3UE England. **Tel** 011 44 235 555335, FAX (0279)31067, telex 817484. **(Subscription address:** US and Canada/ PO Box 2025, Dunnellon, FL 34430-2025; telephone:(904)489-6996**)** **ED** Lorraine Sherr and Robert Bor. **LC** RC607.A26; A3463. **NLM** W1; AI696CHF. **CODEN** AIDCEF. **[CCC].** Index available. cum. index. **Bk Rev. Ad Acc. Pr Rev. Circ:** 650. available on microfiche. Documents available from The Genuine Article, BIOSIS Document Express.
**Desc:** Provides research and reports from the many complimentary disciplines involved in AIDS/HIV, including: psychology, sociology, epidemiology, social work, anthropology, social aspects of medicine, nursing, education, etc.
**Ind/Abst** Appl. Soc. Sci. Index Abstr.; Biol. Abstr. (1989-); Curr. Contents Soc. Behav. Sci.; EMBASE; Health Plan. Adminis.; Index Med. (1989-); Int. Nurs. Index; Linguist. Lang. Behav. Abstr.; Psychol. Abstr. (1989-); PsycINFO; Res. Alert [Full Cov.]; Risk Abstr.; Sci. Cit. Index (19??-19??); Soc. Plann. Policy Dev. Abstr.; Soc. Sci. Cit. Index [Full Cov.]; Sociol. Abstr.; Trop. Dis. Bull.

US
**AIDS CASES, STATE OF NEW JERSEY, AS OF ... .** English. mo. New Jersey Department of Health, John Fitch Plaza, CN-360, Trenton NJ 08625. **Tel** (609)292-7837, FAX (609)984-5474. ctrl circ.

US/1043-1543
**AIDS CLINICAL CARE.** **See** Medical Science and Technology-Communicable Diseases.

US/0899-0263
**AIDS CLINICAL DIGEST.** ***Ceased.*** [AIDS clin. dig.]. **Added/Corp** American Health Consultants. **VAT** Acquired Immune Deficiency Syndrome Clinical Digest. Vol. 1, No. 1 (July 1, 1988)-Ceased (Sept 1991). Periodical. English. sm. American Health Consultants, 3525 Piedmont Road, Suite 400, Atlanta GA 30305. **Tel** (800)688-2421, (404)262-7436. **DD** 616. **NLM** W1; AI696CHH.

US/1045-2877
**AIDS CLINICAL REVIEW.** [AIDS clin. rev.]. **VAT** Acquired Immunodeficiency Syndrome Clinical Review. (1989)-. English. an. $145.00. Marcel Dekker Inc., 270 Madison Avenue, New York NY 10016. **Tel** (212)696-9000, (800)228-1160, FAX (212)685-4540, telex 421419. **(Subscription address:** Marcel Dekker Inc, PO Box 5017, Monticello NY 12701.**)** **ED** Paul Volberding and Mark A Jacobson. **LC** RC607.A26; A345727. **DD** 616.97/92/005. **NLM** W1; AI696CHJ. **CODEN** ACLREO.
**Ind/Abst** Health Plan. Adminis.; Index Med. (1989-).

US/0893-7613
**AIDS CRISIS, THE.** [AIDS crisis]. **VAT** Acquired Immune Deficiency Syndrome Crisis. 1987-. Periodical. English. an. $60.00. Social Issues Resources Crisis Inc, PO Box 2348, Boca Raton FL 33427-2348. **Tel** (407)994-0079, (800)327-0513. **ED** Eleanor Goldstein. **LC** RA644.A25; A355. **DD** 362.1/9697/9. Index available. available on CD-ROM.
**Desc:** Contains 80 articles relating to the AIDS virus.

●US/1065-6162
**AIDS DIRECTORY, THE.** (THE AIDS DIRECTORY : AN ESSENTIAL GUIDE TO THE 1500 LEADERS IN RESEARCH POLICY, ADVOCACY, AND FUNDING.). (1992)-. Directory. English. ir (every 1-2 years). $250.00. Buraff Publications Inc., 714 Church Street, Alexandria VA 22314. **Tel** (800)333-1291, (703)739-8500.
**Desc:** Information on those organizations helping in the fight against AIDS.

US/0895-8882
**AIDS EDUCATION.** ***Title Change.*** [AIDS educ.]. Vol. 1, No. 1 (Sept. 1987)-(19??). Periodical. English. Ten times a year (Sept. through June). National Professional Resources, PO Box 1479, 25 South Regent Street, Port Chester NY 10573. **Tel** (914)937-8879, FAX (914)937-9327. **ED** Janet Simon. **DD** 614. **Bk Rev. Circ:** 2,000. ***Merged with*** *Substance Abuse in Schools.*
**Desc:** Educational programs to combat AIDS.

GW/0179-3098
**AIDS-FORSCHUNG.** (AIDS-FORSCHUNG : AIFO.). [AIDS-Forsch.]. **VFOAT** AIFO; Acquired Immune Deficiency Syndrome Research. Vol. 1, No. 1 (Jan. 1986)-. Academic Scholarly Publication. German (summaries and/or abstracts in English). Twelve times a year. DM180.00. Verlag RS Schulz, Postfach 1780, D 82317 Starnberger Germany. **Tel** 011 49 8151 1490. **NLM** W1; AI696CK. **CODEN** AIFOER. Documents available from BIOSIS Document Express, CASDDS.
**Ind/Abst** Biol. Abstr.; Chem. Abstr. (1986-); EMBASE; PAIS Int. Print; Trop. Dis. Bull.

NE/1013-7785
**AIDS HEALTH PROMOTION, EXCHANGE.** (AIDS HEALTH PROMOTION EXCHANGE / WORLD HEALTH ORGANIZATION, GLOBAL PROGRAMME ON AIDS, HEALTH PROMOTION UNIT.). [AIDS health promot., Exch.]. **Added/Corp** Global Programme on AIDS (World Health Organization). Health Promotion Unit. Koninklijk Instituut voor de Tropen. **VAT** Acquired Immune Deficiency Syndrome Health Promotion Exchange. (1988)-. Periodical. English. Four times a year. Fl35.00. Royal Tropical Institute, Information & Documentation, Mauritskade 63, 1092 AD Amsterdam Netherlands. **Tel** 11 31 20 5688330, FAX 11 31 20 6654423, telex 15080 KIT NL. **ED** Maria de Bruyn and Marianne W. Sermars; Telephone: 11 31 20 5688428. **LC** WMLC 93/1464. **NLM** W1; AI696CM.
**Desc:** Designed to communicate the range of educational approaches and materials being used by different countries in their efforts to inform the general public about the AIDS risk and encourage changes in behaviour. Features editorial material, original reports, brief notes under a "country watch" rubric and black and white illustrations taken from some of the more imaginative educational campaigns.

US/0899-742X
**AIDS/HIV RECORD.** ***Ceased.*** [AIDS/HIV rec.]. **VFOAT** AIDS HIV Record. **VAT** Acquired Immune Deficiency Syndrome/Human Immunodeficiency Virus record. Vol. 2, No. 11 and 12 (June 15, 1988)-?. Periodical. English. sm. The AIDS Record, 1612 18th Street NW, Washington DC 20009. **Tel** (202)393-2437, FAX (202)337-4251. **DD** 362. **NLM** W1; AI696CD. ***Continues*** *AIDS Record, 0891-3765.*

US/1057-5065
**AIDS/HIV TREATMENT DIRECTORY.** (AIDS/HIV TREATMENT DIRECTORY / COMPILED AND PUBLISHED BY AMERICAN FOUNDATION FOR AIDS RESEARCH (AMFAR).). [AIDS/HIV treat. dir.]. **Added/Corp** American Foundation for AIDS Research. Pharmaceutical Manufacturers Association. **VFOAT** AIDS, HIV Treatment Directory. **VAT** Acquired Immune Deficiency Syndrome Human Immunodeficiency Virus Treatment Directory. Vol. 4, No. 1 (June 1990)-. Directory. English. qt (published within the seasons). $55.00 US; $77.00 other. AmFAR Treatment Directory, 733 3rd

Avenue, 12th Floor, New York NY 10017. **Tel** (212)682-7440, FAX (212)682-9812. **ED** Jon Engbretson. **DD** 616. **NLM** QV 22.1; A514. Index available. cum. index. **Pr Rev.** ***Continues*** *AIDS/HIV Experimental Treatment Directory, 0898-5030.*
**Desc:** The most comprehensive source of information on treatments in development for AIDS and HIV infection, related opportunistic infections and neoplasms. The Directory also includes key lists, indices, glossary, and reviews of emerging new topics. All entries are backed by continuous tracking of the medical literature and key research conferences.

UK/0953-1580
**AIDS INFORMATION.** ***Title Change.***
**Added/Corp** University of Leeds. Oncology Information Service. **VAT** Aquired Immune Deficiency Syndrome Information. Began with: Vol. 1, No. 1 (1985)-Vol. 8 (1992). Periodical. English. mo. Carfax Publishing Company, PO Box 25 Abingdon, Oxfordshire OX14 3UE England. **Tel** 011 44 235 555335, FAX (0279)31067, telex 817484. **(Subscription address:** US and Canada/ PO Box 2025, Dunnellon, FL 34430-2025; telephone:(904)489-6996**) LC** RC607.A26; A347427. **DD** 616.97/92. **NLM** ZWD 308; A28772. **[CCC].** ***Continued by*** *AIDS Abstracts (Abingdon, England).*
**Desc:** Current awareness service listing research papers, reviews, letters reporting original research, editorials, case reports and clinical trials concerning all aspects of human and simian retroviruses and the acquired immunodeficiency syndrome.

US/1044-2138
**AIDS INFORMATION SOURCEBOOK.**
***Ceased.*** [AIDS info. sourceb.]. **VAT** Acquired Immune Deficiency Syndrome Information Sourcebook. 1st Ed (1988)-3rd Edition (1992). English. an. Oryx Press, 4041 North Central Avenue, #700, Phoenix AZ 85012-3397. **Tel** (800)279-ORYX, (602)265-2651, FAX (602)265-6250, (800)279-4663, (800)279-6799. **ED** H Robert Malinowsky and Gerald J Perry. **LC** RC607.A26. **DD** 614. **NLM** W 22; AA1 A24.
**Desc:** Covers of 800 organizations in the US and Canada that provide outreach services, educational programs, and AIDS "hotlines".

US
**AIDS LAW AND LITIGATION REPORTER.** English. mo. $495.00. University Publishing Group Inc., 107 East Church Street, Frederick MD 21701-5441. **Tel** (301)694-8531, (800)654-8188.

US/0896-6370
**AIDS LAW REPORTER, THE.** ***Ceased.*** **See** Law.

UK/0952-7427
**AIDS LETTER, THE.** **Added/Corp** Royal Society of Medicine (Great Britain) Royal Society of Medicine Services (Great Britain). **VAT** The Acquired Immune Deficiency Syndrome Letter. Vol. 1, No. 1 (June 1987)-. Periodical. English. bm. $32.00 US; £16.00 other. Royal Society of Medicine Press, 1 Wimpole Street, London W1M 8AE England. **Tel** 011 44 71 2902928. **ED** V G Daniels and M W Adler. **NLM** W1; AD696DEB. **Circ:** 1,800.
**Desc:** Provides information on research and treatment for AIDS, and related political and social issues.

US/0893-1526
**AIDS LITERATURE & NEWS REVIEW.**
[AIDS lit. news rev.]. **VFOAT** AIDS Literature and News Review. **VAT** Acquired Immune Deficiency Syndrome Literature and News Review. (1987)-. Periodical. English. mo. $225.00 US; $235.00 other. University Publishing Group Inc., 107 East Church Street, Frederick MD 21701-5441. **Tel** (301)694-8531, (800)654-8188. **ED** N. Quist. **LC** RC607.A26; A34794. **DD** 616.97/92/005. **NLM** ZWD 308; A28773.
**Desc:** Provides comprehensive and interdisciplinary coverage of AIDS-related literature and current developments in medicine, law, public policy, and the social sciences. Surveying hundreds of journals, newsletters, newspapers, and special reports, ALNR brings you comprehensive summaries - most written by the author's themselves - organized and sorted in 25 areas of study.

US/0899-1464
**AIDS LITIGATION REPORTER.** **See** Medical Science and Technology-Forensic Medicine, Medical Jurisprudence.

UK/0269-9370
**AIDS (LONDON).** (AIDS.). [AIDS]. **VAT** Acquired Immune Deficiency Syndrome. Vol. 1, No. 1 (May 1987)-. Periodical. English. Twelve times a year. $144.95 (individuals); $345.00 (institutions). Current Science / England, Middlesex House, 34-42 Cleveland Street, London W1P 5FB England. **Tel** 011 44 71 580 8393, 011 44 71 323 0323, FAX 011 44 81 580 1938. **(Subscription address:** Current Science, 20 North 3rd Street, Philadelphia PA 19106.**) LC** RC607.A26; A34415. **DD** 616.97/92/005. **NLM** W1; AI696B. **CODEN** AIDSET. **[CCC].** Index available. **Ad Acc.** **Pr Rev.** **Circ:** 3,100. available on diskette. Documents available from The Genuine Article, BIOSIS Document Express, CASDDS.
**Desc:** Directed toward researchers, clinicians and policy makers involved with AIDS. Featuring rapid publication of the foremost data and research, cited in Medline and Current Contents. Each issue features one review, updated CDC/WHO statistics and a bibliography of the current world literature published during the previous month.
**Ind/Abst** Biol. Abstr.; Chem. Abstr.; Chem. Hazards Ind.; Curr. Aware. Biol. Sci., CABS; EMBASE; Health Plan. Adminis.; Index Med. (1987-); Lab. Hazards Bull.; Physic. Medline Plus; Psychol. Abstr. (1988-); PsycINFO; Res. Alert [Full Cov.]; Sci. Cit. Index; SCISEARCH; Soc. Sci. Cit. Index [Select. Cov.]; Trop. Dis. Bull.

US/0899-6733
**AIDS NEWS REPORTER, THE.** **VAT** Acquired Immune Deficiency Syndrome News Reporter. 1988-. Periodical. English. mo. $150.00. Loy & Loy Communications Corporation, PO Box 4310, Sunland CA 91040.

UK/0268-8360
**AIDS NEWSLETTER (LONDON, ENGLAND).** (AIDS NEWSLETTER.). **Added/Corp** Great Britain. Bureau of Hygiene and Tropical Diseases. (1986)-. Periodical. English. $180.00. CAB International Centre, Wallingford, Oxon OX10 8DE United Kingdom. **Tel** 44 491 832111, FAX 44 491 833508, telex 847964 (COMAGG G). **NLM** W1; AI696DB.
**Ind/Abst** Chem. Hazards Ind.; Lab. Hazards Bull.

US/0893-5068
**AIDS PATIENT CARE.** [AIDS patient care]. **VAT** Acquired Immuned Deficiency Syndrome Patient Care. Vol. 1, No. 1 (June 1987)-. Periodical. English. bm. $97.00. Mary Ann Liebert Inc., 1651 Third Avenue, New York NY 10128. **Tel** (212)289-2300, (800)M-LIEBERT, FAX (212)289-4697. **ED** Michael Gottlieb, MD. **LC** RC607.A26; A34858. **DD** 362.1/969792/005. **NLM** W1; AI696DD. **CODEN** APACEF. **Ad Acc.** Documents available from The Genuine Article.
**Desc:** Publishes articles that span the specturm of HIV disease diagnosis, treatment, prevention, and education. Presents material that can be applied to daily clinical practice. For physicians, nurses, administrators, educators and other professionals in AIDS care.
**Ind/Abst** Cumul. Index Nurs. Allied Health Lit.; Curr. Contents Soc. Behav. Sci.; EMBASE; Health Index (1989-); Health Period. Database; Health Ref. Cent. (Jan. 1989-) [Full Cov.]; Res. Alert [Full Cov.]; Soc. Sci. Cit. Index [Full Cov.].

US/0899-9449
**AIDS (PHOENIX, ARIZ.).** ***Ceased.*** (AIDS : ACQUIRED IMMUNE DEFICIENCY SYNDROME.). **VFOAT** Acquired Immune Deficiency Syndrome. **VAT** Acquired Immune Deficiency Syndrome; Acquired Immunodeficiency Syndrome. 1st Ed. (1985)-Ceased (1989). English. sa. Oryx Press, 4041 North Central Avenue, #700, Phoenix AZ 85012-3397. **Tel** (800)279-ORYX, (602)265-2651, FAX (602)265-6250, (800)279-4663, (800)279-6799. **ED** D A Tyckoson. **LC** Z6664.A27; A36; RC607.A26. **DD** 016.3621/969792. **NLM** ZWD 308; A2874.
**Ind/Abst** Microbiol. Abstr. Sect. B; Microbiol. Abstr. Sect. A; Microbiol. Abstr. Sect. C; Protozoolog. Abstr.; Ref. Upd. Clinical Ed.; Ref. Upd. Deluxe Ed.

US/0887-1493
**AIDS POLICY & LAW.** **See** Law.

US/1053-0894
**AIDS READER, THE.** [AIDS read.]. Vol. 1, No. 1 (Jan./Feb. 1991)-. Periodical. English. bm. $100.00 (libraries, double subscription) US. SCP Communications Inc, 134 West 29th Street, New York NY 10001. **Tel** (212)714-1740, FAX (212)629-3760. **LC** RC607.A26; A34887. **DD** 616.97/92/005. **NLM** W1; AI696DGD.

US
**AIDS REFERENCE AND RESEARCH COLLECTION.** English. an. $195.00. University Publishing Group Inc., 107 East Church Street, Frederick MD 21701-5441. **Tel** (301)694-8531, (800)654-8188.

US/0893-5084
**AIDS REPORT (WESTPORT, CONN.).**
(AIDS REPORT.). **VAT** Acquired Immune Deficiency Syndrome Report. (1987)-. Periodical. English. mo (12 issues per volume). $31.00 US, Canada and Mexico; $40.00 other. Food & Nutrition Press Inc, 2 Corporate Drive, PO Box 374, Trumbull CT 06611. **Tel** (203)261-8587, FAX (203)261-9724. **ED** John J. O'Neil. **DD** 616.
**Desc:** Provides developments in the medical, social, economic, regulatory and political aspects of AIDS.

US/0889-2229
**AIDS RESEARCH AND HUMAN RETROVIRUSES.** [AIDS res. hum. retrovir.]. **VAT** Acquired Immune Deficiency Syndrome Research and Human Retrovuses; Acquired Immunodeficiency Syndrome Research and Human Retroviruses. Vol. 3, No. 1 (Spring 1987)-. Periodical. English. mo. $327.00. Mary Ann Liebert Inc., 1651 Third Avenue, New York NY 10128. **Tel** (212)289-2300, (800)M-LIEBERT, FAX (212)289-4697. **ED** Dani Bolognesi, PhD and Jefferey Laurence, MD. **LC** RC607.A26; A35. **DD** 616.97/92/0072. **NLM** W1; A11666. **CODEN** ARHRE7. **Ad Acc.** **Pr Rev.** Documents available from The Genuine Article, BIOSIS Document Express, CASDDS. ***Continues*** *AIDS Research, 0737-6006.*
**Desc:** Provides a forum for publication of original articles in the multidisciplinary study of retrovirus associated diseases with emphasis on the acquired immunodeficiency syndrome. Attentive to the investigations of new viruses pertaining to cancer, degenerative diseases and the immune system in general.
**Ind/Abst** Biol. Abstr. (1987-); Chem. Abstr.; Curr. Aware. Biol. Sci., CABS; Curr. Contents Life Sci.; EMBASE; Genet. Abstr.; Health Plan. Adminis.; Immunol. Abstr.; Index Med. (1987-); Microbiol. Abstr. Sect. A; Ref. Upd. Deluxe Ed.; Res. Alert [Full Cov.]; Rev. Med. Vet. Entomol.; Sci. Cit. Index; SCISEARCH; Soc. Sci. Cit. Index [Select. Cov.]; Trop. Dis. Bull.; Virol. AIDS Abstr.

US/1056-1080
**AIDS RESEARCH REVIEWS.** [AIDS res. rev.]. **VFOAT** Acquired Immunodeficiency Syndrome Research Reviews. Vol. 1 (1991)-. Academic Scholarly Publication. English. $165.00. Marcel Dekker Inc., 270 Madison Avenue, New York NY 10016. **Tel** (212)696-9000, (800)228-1160, FAX (212)685-4540, telex 421419. **(Subscription address:** Marcel Dekker Inc, PO Box 5017, Monticello NY 12701.**) LC** RC607.A26; A3514. **DD** 616.97/92/005. **NLM** W1; AI696FG. **CODEN** ARRVEZ. Documents available from CASDDS.
**Ind/Abst** Chem. Abstr.

US/1040-6778
**AIDS SCAN.** ***Ceased.*** (AIDS SCAN : CURRENT LITERATURE IN PERSPECTIVE.). [AIDS scan]. Vol. 1, No. 1 (1989)-Ceased (Nov. 1990). Periodical. English. qt. Mosby Year Book Inc., 11830 Westline Industrial Drive, St Louis MO 63146. **Tel** (800)325-4177, (314)872-8370, FAX (314)432-1380, telex 44-2402. **LC** PAR. **DD** 616. **NLM** ZWD 308; A2879. **Ad Acc.**
**Desc:** Keeps clinicians, clinical administrators, researchers, and public policy makers abreast of important trends, discoveries, and developments in AIDS. Coverage reflects the full spectrum of AIDS-related topics, including: biology of HIV and its biologic relatives, vaccine research and development, infection control precautions, public education, and management of major clinical manifestations.

●US/1067-0718
**AIDS TARGETED INFORMATION.** [AIDS target. inf.]. **Added/Corp** American Foundation for Aids Research. (1993)-. Periodical. English. mo. $365.00 (institution) US. Williams & Wilkins Company, 428 East Preston Street, Baltimore MD 21202-3993. **Tel** (410)528-4000, (800)638-6423, FAX (410)528-8596, telex 87669. **(Subscription address:** Williams & Wilkins, PO Box 64380, Baltimore, MD 21264**) DD** 362. **NLM** ZWD 308; A288. Documents available from Quick Copies. ***Continues*** *AIDS Targeted Information Newsletter, 0892-0125.*
**Desc:** A compendium of the latest articles chronicling medical knowledge and research about AIDS from over 100 journals.

US/0892-0125
**AIDS TARGETED INFORMATION NEWSLETTER.** ***Title Change.*** (AIDS TARGETED INFORMATION NEWSLETTER : A.T.I.N.). [AIDS targeted inf. newsl.]. **Added/Corp** American Foundation for AIDS Research. **VFOAT** A.T.I.N.; ATIN. Vol. 1, No. 1 (Jan. 1987)-(199?). Newsletter. English. mo. Williams & Wilkins Company, 428 East Preston Street, Baltimore MD 21202-3993. **Tel** (410)528-4000, (800)638-6423, FAX (410)528-8596, telex 87669. **(Subscription address:** US/ PO Box 64380, Baltimore, MD 21264-4380; Japan/ Igaku-Shoin MYW Ltd, 1-28-36 Hongo, Bunkyo-ku Tokyo 113 Japan; European/ The Broadway House, 2-6 Fulham Broadway, London SW6 1AA England; telephone: (800)638-6423**) DD** 616. **NLM** ZWD 308; A288. Documents available from Quick Copies. ***Continued by*** *AIDS Targeted Information, 1067-0718.*
**Desc:** A compendium of the latest articles chronicling medical knowledge and research about AIDS from over 100 journals.

US
**AIDS THERAPIES.** English. ir (one complete directory plus monthly updates). $995.00 US, Canada and Mexico; $1,195.00 other. CW Henderson, PO Box 5528, Atlanta GA 30307-0528. **Tel** (404)377-8895, FAX (404)378-5411. **(Subscription address:** PO Box 830409, Birmingham, AL 35283-0409; telephone: (800)633-4931 or (205)995-1567, FAX: (205)995-1588**)** available on an online database (file 16,636/Full-Text) from DIALOG. ***Continues*** *DAITA.*

US/1052-4207
**AIDS TREATMENT NEWS.** [AIDS treat. news]. **VAT** Acquired Immunodeficiency Syndrome Treatment News. No. 21 (1987)-. Periodical. English. sm. $230.00. AIDS Treatment News Publications, PO Box 411256, San Francisco CA 94141. **Tel** (415)255-0588, (800)873-2812, FAX (415)255-4659. **ED** John S. James. **LC** WMLC 93/1430. **DD** 616. **NLM** W1; AI696G. Index available. cum. index. **Circ:** 5,000 (ctrl). ***Continues*** *On Guard (San Francisco, Calif.).*
**Desc:** Reports on experimental and complementary treatments, especially those available now. Also examines the ethical and public-policy issues around AIDS research and treatment access.

US/1053-9093
**AIDS UPDATE (ALBANY, N.Y.).** ***Ceased.*** (AIDS UPDATE.). [AIDS update]. **Added/Corp** New York (State). Dept. of Social Services. Rockefeller College of Public Affairs and Policy. Social Welfare Continuing Education Program. No. 1 (Fall 1987)-(19??). Periodical. English. qt. Department of Social Services / New York, 135 Western Avenue, Albany NY 12222. **Tel** (518)442-5731. **DD** 362. **NLM** W1; AI696GD.

US/1042-4784
**AIDS UPDATE (RESTON, VA.).** ***Ceased.*** (AIDS UPDATE.). [AIDS update]. **VAT** Acquired Immune Deficiency Syndrome Update. Vol. 1, No. 1 (Jan. 1988)-(199?). Periodical. English. wk (48 issues per year). Cancer Letter Inc, PO Box 15189, Washington DC 20003. **Tel** (202)543-7665, FAX (202)543-6879. **DD** 616. **NLM** W1; AI696GE. **Bk Rev. Circ:** 750.
**Desc:** Covers AIDS/HIV research policy, funding and scientific advances.

US/1040-6247
**AIDS UPDATES.** [AIDS updates]. **VAT** Acquired Immune Deficiency Syndrome Updates; Acquired Immunodeficiency Syndrome Updates. Vol. 1, No. 1 (Sept./Oct. 1988)-. Periodical. English. bm. J.B. Lippincott Company, 227 East Washington Square, Philadelphia PA 19106-3780. **Tel** (215)238-4200 or 4454, FAX (215)238-4227. **LC** RC607.A26; A368. **DD** 616.97/92/005. **NLM** W1; AI696GG. **CODEN** AIUPE3.
**Ind/Abst** EMBASE.

US
**AIDS WATCH. See** Medical Science and Technology-Communicable Diseases.

UK
**AIDS WATCH.** ***Ceased.*** **Added/Corp** International Planned Parenthood Federation. Norges Rde kors. Panos Institute. No. 1 (1988)-Ceased (April 1991). Periodical. English. qt. International Planned Parenthood Federation, Regent's College, Inner Circle, Regent's Park, London NW1 4NS England. **Tel** 011 44 71 486 0741, FAX 011 44 71 487 7950, telex 919573 IPEPEE G. **NLM** W1; AI696H.

US/1069-1456
**AIDS WEEKLY.** [AIDS wkly.]. **VFOAT** CDC AIDS Weekly. (Jan. 7, 1991)-. Periodical. English. wk (48 issues). $995.00 US, Canada and Mexico; $1,195.00 other. CW Henderson, PO Box 5528, Atlanta GA 30307-0528. **Tel** (404)377-8895, FAX (404)378-5411. **(Subscription address:** CW Henderson, Subscription Office, PO Box 830409, Birmingham AL 35283-0409.**) DD** 616. **NLM** W1; AI696HH. available on an online database (file 16,149/Full-Text) from DIALOG. ***Continues*** *CDC AIDS Weekly, 0884-903X;* ***Absorbed*** *AIDSMonthly (Treatment Edition); AIDSMonthly (Journal Edition); AIDSMonthly (Healthcare Edition); AIDSMonthly (Education Edition); AIDSMonthly (Government Edition); AIDSMonthly (Psychosocial Edition); AIDSMonthly (Workplace Edition); AIDSMonthly (Research Edition); AIDSMonthly (International Edition); AIDSMonthly (Service Organization Edition)* ***and*** *AIDSMonthly (Business and Finance Edition).*
**Desc:** Delivers a detailed account of the latest AIDS information by regularly monitoring and abstracting over 8,000 journals to keep you thoroughly informed.
**Ind/Abst** AIDS Abstr.; Health Index (1991-); Health Period. Database [Full Txt.]; Health Ref. Cent. (Jan. 1989-) [Full Txt.] [Full Cov.].

GW/0934-1129
**AIDS WIESBADEN.** ***Ceased.*** [AIDS Wiesb.]. **VFOAT** Acquired Immune Deficiency Syndrome (Wiesbaden). (1988)-(19??). Periodical. German. bm. Vieweg Publishing, PO Box 5829, D 65048 Wiesbaden Germany. **Tel** 011 49 611 160230, FAX 011 49 611 160229. **UDC** 612.017.1 :616.
**Desc:** Supplies information about AIDS for clinical and practical use.

US
**AIDS (WYLIE, TEX.).** (AIDS.). English. be. Information Aids Inc., 2812 Exchange Street, Wylie TX 75098. **Tel** (214)442-0167.

US/1059-8855
**AIDSMONTHLY (GOVERNMENT ED.).** ***Title Change.*** (AIDSMONTHLY.). [AIDSmonthly]. **VFOAT** AIDS Monthly. **VAT** Acquired Immune Deficiency Syndrome Monthly. Government Edition. (Jan. 1992)-(19??). Periodical. English. mo. CW Henderson, PO Box 5528, Atlanta GA 30307-0528. **Tel** (404)377-8895, FAX (404)378-5411. **DD** 362. ***Merged into*** *AIDS Weekly, 1069-1456.*

US/1059-8820
**AIDSMONTHLY (HEALTHCARE ED.).** ***Title Change.*** (AIDSMONTHLY.). [AIDSmonthly]. **VFOAT** AIDS Monthly. **VAT** Acquired Immune Deficiency Syndrome Monthly. Healthcare Edition. Jan. (1992)-(199?). Periodical. English. mo. AIDS Weekly, PO Box 830409, Birmingham AL 35283. **Tel** (205)995-1567. **DD** 362. ***Merged into*** *AIDS Weekly.*

US/1059-8901
**AIDSMONTHLY (INTERNATIONAL ED.).** ***Title Change.*** (AIDSMONTHLY.). [AIDSmonthly]. **VFOAT** AIDS Monthly. **VAT** Acquired Immune Deficiency Syndrome Monthly. International Edition. (Jan. 1992)-(19??). Periodical. English. mo. CW Henderson, PO Box 5528, Atlanta GA 30307-0528. **Tel** (404)377-8895, FAX (404)378-5411. **DD** 362. ***Merged into*** *AIDS Weekly, 1069-1456.*

US/1059-8812
**AIDSMONTHLY (JOURNAL ED.).** ***Title Change.*** (AIDSMONTHLY.). [AIDSmonthly]. **VFOAT** AIDS Monthly. **VAT** Acquired Immune Deficiency Syndrome Monthly. Journal Edition. (Jan. 1992)-(19??). Periodical. English. mo. CW Henderson, PO Box 5528, Atlanta GA 30307-0528. **Tel** (404)377-8895, FAX (404)378-5411. **DD** 362. ***Merged into*** *AIDS Weekly, 1069-1456.*

US/1059-8871
**AIDSMONTHLY (LEGAL ED.).** ***Ceased.*** (AIDSMONTHLY.). [AIDSmonthly]. **VFOAT** AIDS Monthly. **VAT** Acquired Immune Deficiency Syndrome Monthly. Legal Edition. (Jan. 1992)-(19??). Periodical. English. mo. AIDS Monthly, PO Box 830409, Birmingham AL 35283-0409. **DD** 340.

US/1059-8863
**AIDSMONTHLY (PSYCHOSOCIAL ED.).** ***Title Change.*** (AIDSMONTHLY.). [AIDSmonthly]. **VFOAT** AIDS Monthly. **VAT** Acquired Immune Deficiency Syndrome Monthly. Psychosocial Edition. (Jan. 1992)-(19??). Periodical. English. mo. CW Henderson, PO Box 5528, Atlanta GA 30307-0528. **Tel** (404)377-8895, FAX (404)378-5411. **DD** 362. ***Merged with*** *AIDS Weekly, 1069-1456.*

US/1059-8898
**AIDSMONTHLY (RESEARCH ED.).** ***Title Change.*** (AIDSMONTHLY.). [AIDSmonthly]. **VFOAT** AIDS Monthly. **VAT** Acquired Immune Deficiency Syndrome Monthly. Research Edition. (Jan. 1992)-(19??). Periodical. English. mo. CW Henderson, PO Box 5528, Atlanta GA 30307-0528. **Tel** (404)377-8895, FAX (404)378-5411. **DD** 616. ***Merged with*** *AIDS Weekly, 1069-1456.*

US/1059-891X
**AIDSMONTHLY (SERVICE ORGANIZATION ED.).** ***Title Change.*** (AIDSMONTHLY.). [AIDSmonthly]. **VFOAT** AIDS Monthly. **VAT** Acquired Immune Deficiency Syndrome Monthly. Service Organization Edition. (Jan. 1992)-(19??). Periodical. English. mo. CW Henderson, PO Box 5528, Atlanta GA 30307-0528. **Tel** (404)377-8895, FAX (404)378-5411. **DD** 362. ***Merged with*** *AIDS Weekly, 1069-1456.*

US/1059-8804
**AIDSMONTHLY (TREATMENT ED.).** ***Title Change.*** (AIDSMONTHLY.). [AIDSmonthly]. **VFOAT** AIDS Monthly. **VAT** Acquired Immune Deficiency Syndrome Monthly. Treatment ed. (Jan. 1992)-(19??). Periodical. English. mo. CW Henderson, PO Box 5528, Atlanta GA 30307-0528. **Tel** (404)377-8895, FAX (404)378-5411. **DD** 616. ***Merged with*** *AIDS Weekly, 1069-1456.*

US/1059-888X
**AIDSMONTHLY (WORKPLACE ED.).** ***Title Change.*** (AIDSMONTHLY.). [AIDSmonthly]. **VFOAT** AIDS Monthly. **VAT** Acquired Immune Deficiency Syndrome Monthly. Workplace Edition. (Jan. 1992)-(19??). Periodical. English. mo. CW Henderson, PO Box 5528, Atlanta GA 30307-0528. **Tel** (404)377-8895, FAX (404)378-5411. **DD** 362. ***Merged with*** *AIDS Weekly, 1069-1456.*

MX/0002-5151
**ALERGIA (MEXICO).** (ALERGIA; REVISTA IBEROAMERICANA DE ALERGOLOGIA.). [Alergia]. (1953)-. Academic Scholarly Publication. Spanish (English; summaries and/or abstracts in English). Six times a year. $120.00. Alergia, Dr. J. P. Martin, Fuente del Emperador 6, 53950 Naucalpan mexico. **Tel** 011 52 2511849, FAX 011 52 2513975. **ED** Jesus Perez Martin. **NLM** W1 AL316C. **CODEN** ALEGAF. Index available. cum. index. **Bk Rev. Ad Acc. Pr Rev. Circ:** 3,000 (ctrl). Documents available from BIOSIS Document Express.
**Desc:** These are the original articles on allergy and immunology.
**Ind/Abst** Biol. Abstr.; EMBASE [Select. Cov.]; Index Med.

US/1053-1092
**ALLERGIC DISEASE AND THERAPY.** [Allerg. dis. ther.]. Vol. 1 (1990)-. Monographic series. English. ir. Price varies per volume. Marcel Dekker Inc., 270 Madison Avenue, New York NY 10016. **Tel** (212)696-9000, (800)228-1160, FAX (212)685-4540, telex 421419. **(Subscription address:** Marcel Dekker Inc, PO Box 5017, Monticello NY 12701.**) DD** 616. **NLM** W1; AL538. **CODEN** ADITEM.
**Desc:** Series covering such topics as asthma, childhood rhinitis and sinusitis, and the molecular biology of the allergic immune response.

FR/0397-9148
**ALLERGIE ET IMMUNOLOGIE PARIS.** (1969)-. Periodical. English (French). Ten times a year. 479.92F France; 600.00F other. Editions du Porphyre, 4 Place du 18 Juin 1940, 75006 Paris France. **Tel** 011 33 1 42221894. **UDC** 616-056.3.
**Ind/Abst** EMBASE; Health Plan. Adminis.

GW/0323-4398
**ALLERGIE UND IMMUNOLOGIE.** ***Ceased.*** [Allerg. Immunol.]. Vol. 17 (1971)-(Dec. 1991). Periodical. German. qt. Johann Ambrosius Barth, Prager Strasse 16 B, D 04103 Leipzig Germany. **Tel** 011 49 341 7137570. **ED** H Ambrosius Kleine-Natrop, and Lunzenauer. **NLM** W1 AL557E. **CODEN** ALIMCL. **Bk Rev. Ad Acc.** ctrl circ. Documents available from BIOSIS Document Express, CASDDS. ***Continues*** *Allergie und Asthma, 0375-8443.*
**Desc:** Publishes original articles and survey reports of the entire field of immunology and allergology. Experimental immunological investigations are also taken into consideration as clinical immunological and allergological ones.
**Ind/Abst** Biol. Abstr. (?-?); Chem. Abstr. (?-?); EMBASE (?-?); Health Plan. Adminis. (?-?); Index Med. (?-?); Nutr. Abstr. Rev., Ser. B, Live Feeds and Feed. (?-?); Nutr. Abstr. Rev., Ser. A, Hum. Exp. (?-?); Life Sci. Collect. (?-?).

SP/0301-0546
**ALLERGOLOGIA ET IMMUNOPATHOLOGIA.** [Allergol. immunopathol.]. **Added/Corp** International Association of Asthmology. Sociedad Espanola de Alergia. Sociedad Latinoamericana de Alergia e Inmunologia. Vol. 1 (Jan./Feb. 1973)-. Academic Scholarly Publication. Spanish (English). bm. $69.72 Spain; $109.00 other Europe; $133.00 other. Editorial Garsi SA, Juan Bravo 46, 28006 Madrid, Spain. **Tel** 011 34 1 4021212, telex 98358 GARSI E. **NLM** W1; AL563. **CODEN** AGIMBJ. **[CCC]. Bk Rev. Ad Acc. Pr Rev. Circ:** 1,100. Documents available from CASDDS.
**Ind/Abst** Chem. Abstr.; Cumul. Index Nurs. Allied Health Lit.; Dairy Sci. Abstr.; EMBASE; Health Plan. Adminis.; Immunol. Abstr.; Index Med.; Index Vet.; Indice Med. Esp.; Nutr. Abstr. Rev., Ser. B, Live Feeds and Feed.; Nutr. Abstr. Rev., Ser. A, Hum. Exp.; Nutr. Res. Newsl.; Life Sci. Collect.; Protozoolog. Abstr.; Rev. Med. Vet. Entomol.; Rev. Med. Vet. Mycology.

GW/0344-5062
**ALLERGOLOGIE.** [Allergologie]. Vol. 1, No. 1 (1. Quarterly 1978)-. Academic Scholarly Publication. German (summaries and/or abstracts in English). mo. DM228.00. Dustri-Verlag, Dr Karl Feistle, Postfach 49, D 82032 Deisenhofen Germany. **Tel** 011 49 89 6138610, FAX 011 49 89 6135412. **ED** Fudis and Wiesbaden. **NLM** W1; AL563. **CODEN** ALLRDI. **[CCC].** Index available. **Bk Rev. Ad Acc. Pr Rev.** ctrl circ. Documents available from The Genuine Article, CASDDS.
**Ind/Abst** Chem. Abstr.; EMBASE; Entomol. Abstr.; Nutr. Abstr. Rev., Ser. A, Hum. Exp.; Res. Alert [Select. Cov.]; Rev. Agric. Entomol.; Rev. Med. Vet. Entomol.; SCISEARCH.

CN/0824-1333
**ALLERGY ALERT.** (ALLERGY ALERT / ALLERGY FOUNDATION OF CANADA.). [Allergy alert]. **Added/Corp** Allergy Foundation of Canada. No. 19 (Spring 1980)-. Periodical. English. qt (4 issues). Comes with Allergy Foundation of Canada membership. Allergy Foundation of Canada, PO Box 1904, Saskatoon Saskatchewan S7K 3S5 Canada. **Tel** (306)373-7591. **ED** Sandy Woynarski. **DD** 616.97/005. **Bk Rev. Circ:** 650 (ctrl). ***Continues*** *Newsletter (Allergy Foundation of Canada), 0824-1325.*
**Desc:** Allergy information on foods, products, environmental information and doctor information.

CN/0838-1925
**ALLERGY & CLINICAL IMMUNOLOGY NEWS.** (ALLERGY & CLINICAL IMMUNOLOGY NEWS : OFFICIAL ORGAN OF THE INTERNATIONAL ASSOCIATION OF ALLERGY [I.E. ALLERGOLOGY] AND CLINICAL IMMUNOLOGY.). [Allergy clin. immunol. news]. **Added/Corp** International Association of Allergology and Clinical Immunology. **VFOAT** Allergy and Clinical Immunology News; ACI News. Vol. 1, No. 1 (Jan. 1989)-. Periodical. English. bm (6 issues). DM124.00 (institutions), DM107.00 (individuals). Verlag Hans Huber Ag Bern, Laenggass Strasse 76, CH 3000 Bern 9 Switzerland. **Tel** 011 41 31 3004500. **(Subscription address:** Hogrefe & Huber Publishers, Seattle Office, Box 2487, Kirkland WA 98083.**) ED** A.L. de Weck. **DD** 616.97/005. **NLM** W1; AL559L. **Circ:** 7,000.
**Desc:** The goal is to establish a rapid communication channel that will allow clinicians and basic researchers to disseminate information about allergic mechanisms and diseases.

US/1059-4205
**ALLERGY CONNECTIONS.** [Allergy connect.]. (1991)-. Periodical. English. qt. $8.00. Allergy Connections, PO Box 154, Pewaukee WI 53072. **DD** 616.

DK/0105-4538
**ALLERGY (COPENHAGEN).** (ALLERGY.). [Allergy]. **VFOAT** Acta Allergologica. (1978)-. Academic Scholarly Publication. English. mo. kr2260.00 US, Canada and Japan; kr1240.00 other. Munksgaard International Publishers Ltd, PO Box 2148, DK-1016 Copenhagen K Denmark. **Tel** 011 45 33 12 70 30, FAX 011 45 33 12 93 87, telex 19431 MUNKS DK. **ED** Gunnar

Bendixen. **NLM** W1 AL564. **CODEN** LLRGDY. **[CCC].** Index available. **Bk Rev. Ad Acc. Pr Rev. Circ:** 1,000. Documents available from The Genuine Article, BIOSIS Document Express, CASDDS, ADONIS. ***Continues*** *Acta Allergologica, 0001-5148.*
**Desc:** Publishes information on the clinical application of allergology and immunology as well as laboratory and experimental research relevant to clinical practice.
**Ind/Abst** ADONIS; Biol. Abstr.; Chem. Abstr.; Curr. Aware. Biol. Sci., CABS; Dairy Sci. Abstr.; EMBASE; Energy Res. Abstr. (Jan. 1979-); Food Sci. Technol. Abstr.; Health Plan. Adminis.; Immunol. Abstr.; Index Med.; Index Vet.; Microbiol. Abstr. Sect. C; Nutr. Abstr. Rev., Ser. B, Live Feeds and Feed.; Nutr. Abstr. Rev., Ser. A, Hum. Exp.; Nutr. Res. Newsl.; Life Sci. Collect.; PESTDOC; Pig News Inf.; Protozoolog. Abstr.; Res. Alert [Full Cov.]; Rev. Med. Vet. Entomol.; Rev. Med. Vet. Mycology; Saf. Health Work; Sci. Cit. Index; SCISEARCH.

US/1046-9354
**ALLERGY PROCEEDINGS.** (ALLERGY PROCEEDINGS : THE OFFICIAL JOURNAL OF REGIONAL AND STATE ALLERGY SOCIETIES.). [Allergy proc.]. Vol. 9, No. 5 (Sept./Oct. 1988)-. Academic Scholarly Publication. English (Spanish). Six times a year. $65.00 individuals, $95.00 institutions. Oceanside Publications, 95 Pitman Street, Providence RI 02906. **Tel** (401)331-2510, FAX (401)331-5138. **ED** G. Settipane. **DD** 616. **NLM** W1; AL5632L. **CODEN** ALPRE5. Index available. **Ad Acc. Pr Rev. Circ:** 3,000 (ctrl). Documents available from The Genuine Article, CASDDS. ***Continues*** *New England and Regional Allergy Proceedings, 0742-2814.*
**Desc:** Original research reports and review articles in allergy and immunology. Offical journal of regional and state allergy societies.
**Ind/Abst** Chem. Abstr. (1988-); Curr. Contents Clin. Med.; EMBASE; Index Med. (1988-); Nutr. Abstr. Rev., Ser. A, Hum. Exp.; Nutr. Res. Newsl.; Res. Alert [Select. Cov.]; Rev. Med. Vet. Entomol.; Rev. Med. Vet. Mycology; SCISEARCH.

DK/0108-1675
**ALLERGY SUPPLEMENTUM.** (ALLERGY. SUPPLEMENT.). [Allergy suppl.]. No. 4 (1985)-. Monographic series. English. mo. kr2260.00 US, Canada and Japan; kr2240.00 other (comes with subscription to Allergy). Munksgaard International Publishers Ltd, PO Box 2148, DK-1016 Copenhagen K Denmark. **Tel** 011 45 33 12 70 30, FAX 011 45 33 12 93 87, telex 19431 MUNKS DK. Documents available from BIOSIS Document Express, CASDDS. ***Continues*** *Allergy Supplementum, 0108-1675.*
**Ind/Abst** Biol. Abstr. (1989-); Chem. Abstr.; Curr. Aware. Biol. Sci., CABS; EMBASE.

DK/1046-7408
**AMERICAN JOURNAL OF REPRODUCTIVE IMMUNOLOGY : AJRI.** [Am. j. reprod. immunol.]. **VFOAT** AJRI. Vol. 19, No. 1 (Jan. 1989)-. Academic Scholarly Publication. English. mo. kr2500.00 US and Canada; kr2550.00 other. Munksgaard International Publishers Ltd, PO Box 2148, DK-1016 Copenhagen K Denmark. **Tel** 011 45 33 12 70 30, FAX 011 45 33 12 93 87, telex 19431 MUNKS DK. **DD** 616. **NLM** W1; AM521NE. **CODEN** AJRIE8. **[CCC].** Documents available from The Genuine Article, BIOSIS Document Express, CASDDS. ***Continues*** *American Journal of Reproductive Immunology and Microbiology, 8755-8920.*
**Ind/Abst** Anim. Breed. Abstr.; Biol. Abstr. (1989-); Chem. Abstr. (1989-); Curr. Aware. Biol. Sci., CABS; Curr. Contents Life Sci.; EMBASE; Immunol. Abstr.; Index Med. (Jan. 1989-); INIS Atomindex [Micro.]; Life Sci. Collect. (1989-); Res. Alert [Full Cov.]; Sci. Cit. Index; SCISEARCH.

US/1050-6586
**AMERICAN JOURNAL OF RHINOLOGY.** **See** Medical Science and Technology-Otorhinolaryngology.

IT/0365-169X
**ANNALI ITALIANI DI DERMATOLOGIA CLINICA E SPERIMENTALE.** **See** Medical Science and Technology-Dermatology.

IT/0003-472X
**ANNALI SCLAVO. COLLANA MONOGRAFICA.** **Added/Corp** Istituto Sieroterapico e Vaccinogeno Toscano "Sclavo". (1984)-. Monographic series. English (Italian). **NLM** W1; AN549. **CODEN** ASCLAZ.
**Ind/Abst** Health Plan. Adminis.; Index Med. (1984-).

US/0003-4738
**ANNALS OF ALLERGY.** [Ann. allergy]. **Added/Corp** American College of Allergists. American College of Allergy and Immunology. Vol. 1 (July/Aug. 1943)-. Academic Scholarly Publication. English (summaries and/or abstracts in Spanish). mo. $60.00. American College of Allergy and Immunology, 85 West Algonquin Road, Suite 550, Arlington Height IL 60005. **Tel** (708)427-1200. **ED** J. A .Bellanti. **DD** 616. **NLM** W1 AN56. **CODEN** ANAEA3. **Bk Rev. Ad Acc. Pr Rev. Circ:** 6,100. available on microfilm and microfiche from University Microfilms International (UMI). Documents available from The Genuine Article, BIOSIS Document Express, CASDDS.
**Desc:** Diagnosis, prognosis, treatment of allergic disorders, case reports, some papers on immunology, CME articles, abstracts, clinical allergy-immunology rounds, editorials, and news items are included.
**Ind/Abst** Biol. Abstr.; Chem. Abstr.; Curr. Aware. Biol. Sci., CABS; Curr. Contents Clin. Med.; Dairy Sci. Abstr.; EMBASE; Food Sci. Technol. Abstr.; Health Plan. Adminis.; Helminthol. Abstr. (1991-); Immunol. Abstr.; Index Med.; Index Vet.; Iowa Drug Inf. Serv. (1966-); Med. Abstr. Newsl.; Microbiol. Abstr. Sect. C; Mod. Med.; NAPRALERT; Nutr. Abstr. Rev., Ser. B, Live Feeds and Feed.; Nutr. Abstr. Rev., Ser. A, Hum. Exp.; Nutr. Res. Newsl.; Life Sci. Collect.; PESTDOC; Physic. Medline Plus; Postharvest News Inf.; Potato Abstr.; Protozoolog. Abstr.; Ref. Upd. Clinical Ed.; Ref. Upd. Deluxe Ed.; Res. Alert [Full Cov.]; Rev. Med. Vet. Entomol.; Rev. Med. Vet. Mycology; Rev. Plant Pathol.; Saf. Health Work; Sci. Cit. Index; SCISEARCH; Soc. Sci. Cit. Index [Select. Cov.]; Soyabean Abstr.; Sug. Indus. Abstr.; Vet. Bull.; Virol. AIDS Abstr.

US/0882-2239
**ANNUAL REPORT OF INTRAMURAL ACTIVITIES - NATIONAL INSTITUTE OF ALLERGY AND INFECTIOUS DISEASES (U.S.).** **See** Medical Science and Technology-Communicable Diseases.

US/0732-0582
**ANNUAL REVIEW OF IMMUNOLOGY.** [Annu. rev. immunol.]. Vol. 1 (1983)-. Academic Scholarly Publication. English. an (April). $48.00 US; $53.00 other. Annual Reviews Inc., 4139 El Camino Way, PO Box 10139, Palo Alto CA 94303-0139. **Tel** (415)493-4400, (800)523-8635, FAX (415)855-9815. **ED** William E. Paul. **LC** QR180; .A576. **DD** 616.07/9/05. **NLM** W1 AN772H. **CODEN** ARIMDU. **[CCC].** Index available. cum. index. **Pr Rev.** ctrl circ. available on microfilm and microfiche from University Microfilms International (UMI). Documents available from The Genuine Article, BIOSIS Document Express, CASDDS.
**Desc:** Comprehensive, thorough coverage of latest advances in immunology, written by acknowledged experts in the field. Extensive literature citations included.
**Ind/Abst** AgBiotech News Inf.; Anim. Breed. Abstr.; Biol. Agric. Index; Biol. Abstr.; Chem. Abstr. (1983-); Curr. Aware. Biol. Sci., CABS; Curr. Contents Life Sci.; EMBASE; Immunol. Abstr.; Index Med. (Vol. 1, 1983-); Index Sci. Rev. [Full Cov.]; Life Sci. Collect.; Protozoolog. Abstr.; Ref. Upd. Basic Ed.; Ref. Upd. Clinical Ed.; Ref. Upd. Deluxe Ed.; Res. Alert [Full Cov.]; Rev. Med. Vet. Entomol.; Sci. Cit. Index; SCISEARCH; Trop. Dis. Bull.

DK/0903-4641
**APMIS : ACTA PATHOLOGICA, MICROBIOLOGICA ET IMMUNOLOGICA SCANDINAVICA.** **VFOAT** Acta Pathologica, Microbiologica, et Immunologica Scandinavica. Vol. 96, No. 1 (Jan. 1988)-. Periodical. English. mo. kr2450.00 US and Canada; kr2430.00 other. Munksgaard International Publishers Ltd, PO Box 2148, DK-1016 Copenhagen K Denmark. **Tel** 011 45 33 12 70 30, FAX 011 45 33 12 93 87, telex 19431 MUNKS DK. **NLM** W1; AP18. **[CCC]. Pr Rev.** Documents available from The Genuine Article, CASDDS, ADONIS. ***Formed by the union of*** *Acta Pathologica, Microbiologica et Immunologica Scandinavica. Section A, Pathology, 0108-0164; Acta Pathologica, Microbiologica et Immunologica Scandinavica. Section B, Microbiology, 0108-0180* ***and*** *Acta Pathologica, Microbiologica et Immunologica Scandinavica. Section C, Immunology, 0108-0202.*
**Ind/Abst** ADONIS; AGRICOLA [Select. Cov.]; Chem. Abstr.; Curr. Aware. Biol. Sci., CABS; Curr. Contents Life Sci.; Curr. Titl. Dent.; Dairy Sci. Abstr.; EMBASE; Health Plan. Adminis.; Helminthol. Abstr. (19??-19??); Immunol. Abstr.; Index Med. (1988-); Index Vet.; PESTDOC; Pig News Inf.; Poult. Abstr.; Protozoolog. Abstr.; Res. Alert [Full Cov.]; Rev. Med. Vet. Entomol.; Sci. Cit. Index; SCISEARCH; Vet. Bull.; Trop. Dis. Bull.

DK/0903-465X
**APMIS. ACTA PATHOLOGICA, MICROBIOLOGICA ET IMMUNOLOGICA SCANDINAVICA. SUPPLEMENTUM.** (APMIS SUPPLEMENTUM.). [APMIS, Acta pathol. microbiol. immunol. Scand., Suppl.]. **VFOAT** Acta Pathologica Microbiologica et Immunologica Scandinavica. (1988)-. Monographic series. English. mo. kr2450.00 US, Canada & Japan; kr2430.00 other. Munksgaard International Publishers Ltd, PO Box 2148, DK-1016 Copenhagen K Denmark. **Tel** 011 45 33 12 70 30, FAX 011 45 33 12 93 87, telex 19431 MUNKS DK. **LC** R81; .A312. **NLM** W1; AP18a. **CODEN** AISSE2APSUEN. Documents available from BIOSIS Document Express. ***Continues*** *Acta Pathologica, Microbiologica, et Immunologica Scandinavica. Supplement, 0108-0172.*
**Ind/Abst** Biol. Abstr.; Curr. Aware. Biol. Sci., CABS; EMBASE; Health Plan. Adminis.; Index Med. No. 1, 1988-.

GW/0936-8671
**ARBEITEN AUS DEM PAUL-EHRLICH-INSTITUT (BUNDESAMT FUER SERA UND IMPFSTOFFE) ZU FRANKFUERT A.M.** [Arb. Paul-Ehrlich-Inst. Bundesamt Sera Impfst. Frankf. Main.]. **Added/Corp** Paul-Ehrlich-Institut, Bundesamt fuer Sera und Impfstoffe. **VFOAT** Arbeiten aus Dem Paul-Ehrlich-Institut. (1988)-. Monographic series. English (German). ir. Price varies per volume. Gustav Fischer Verlag Stuttgart, Postfach 720143, Wollgrasweg 49, D 70577 Stuttgart Germany. **Tel** 011 49 711 458030, FAX 0711-4580334, telex 2627-7111488. **ED** R. Kurth. **LC** QR180; .F72. ***Continues*** *Arbeiten aus Paul-Ehrlich-Institut (Bundesamt fuer Sera und Impfstoffe), Dem Georg-Speyer-Haus und Dem Ferdinand-Blum-Institut zu Frankfurt A.M., 0066-5665.*
**Ind/Abst** Health Plan. Adminis.

MG/0020-2495
**ARCHIVES DE L'INSTITUT PASTEUR DE MADAGASCAR.** [Arch. Inst. Pasteur Madagascar]. Vol. 22 (1954)-. Periodical. French (English). Twice a year. Free. Institut Pasteur de Madagascar, BP 1274 Antananarive, Tananarive Madagascar. **Tel** 011 261 2 26492. **ED** D. Coulanges. **LC** R108; .T27. **NLM** W1 AR337. **CODEN** AINMAN. Index available. **Bk Rev. Ad Acc. Circ:** 900 (ctrl). Documents available from BIOSIS Document Express. ***Continues*** *Archives de l'Institut Pasteur de Tananarive, 0301-4517.*
**Ind/Abst** Biol. Abstr.; Health Plan. Adminis.; Helminthol. Abstr.; Index Med. (1978-); Index Vet.; Life Sci. Collect.; Protozoolog. Abstr.; Rev. Med. Vet. Entomol.; Vet. Bull.; Trop. Dis. Bull.

●US/1071-0906
**ARCHIVES OF STD/HIV RESEARCH.** [Arch. STD/HIV res.]. **VFOAT** Archives of STD HIV Research. **VAT** Archives of Sexually Transmitted Diseases/Human Immunodeficiency Viruses Research. Vol. 6, Issues 1, 2 (1992)-. Periodical. English. qt. $180.00 (institutions), $160.00 (individuals) US, Canada & Mexico; $190.00 (institutions), $170.00 (individuals) other. Reproductive Health Center, 78 Surfsong Road, Kiawah Island SC 29455. **Tel** (803)768-5556. **DD** 616. **NLM** W1; AR488P. ***Continues*** *Archives of AIDS Research, 0899-4811.*

PL/0004-069X
**ARCHIVUM IMMUNOLOGII ET THERAPIAE EXPERIMENTALIS.** [Arch. immunol. ther. exp.]. **Added/Corp** Instytut Immunologii i Terapii Doswiadczalnej (Polska Akademia Nauk) Instytut Immunologii i Terapii Doswiadczalnej im. Ludwika Hirszfelda. Vol. 10 (1962)-. Academic Scholarly Publication. English (Polish). bm. $108.00. **(Subscription address:** ARS Polona, PO Box 1001, 00068 Warsaw Poland.**) ED** J. Inglot. **CODEN** AITEAT. Documents available from BIOSIS Document Express, CASDDS. ***Continues*** *Archivum Immunologii i Terapii Dowiadczalnej.*
**Ind/Abst** Anal. Abstr.; Biol. Abstr.; Chem. Abstr.; EMBASE; Health Plan. Adminis.; Immunol. Abstr.; Index Med.; Index Vet.; Life Sci. Collect.; SCISEARCH.

JA/0021-4884
**ARERUGI.** (ARERUGI. JAPANESE JOURNAL OF ALLERGOLOGY.). [Arerugi]. **VFOAT** Japanese Journal of Allergology. (1952)-. Academic Scholarly Publication. Japanese (Japanese; summaries and/or abstracts in English). mo. $272.00. Nihon Arerugi Gakkai, (Japanese Society of Allergology), c/o Nihon Ika Daigaku Biseibutsu, Men Ekigaku Kyoshitsu, 1-5, Sendagi, 1 Chome, Bunkyoku, Tokyoto 113 Japan. **(Subscription address:** Japan Publications Trading Company, Ltd., PO Box 5030, Tokyo International, Tokyo 100-31 Japan.**) NLM** W1 AR7563. **CODEN** ARERAM. available on CD-ROM. Documents available from BIOSIS Document Express, CASDDS.
**Ind/Abst** Biol. Abstr.; Chem. Abstr.; EMBASE [Select. Cov.]; Index Med.; Rev. Med. Vet. Entomol.; Rev. Med. Vet. Mycology; Soyabean Abstr.

TH/0125-877X
**ASIAN PACIFIC JOURNAL OF ALLERGY AND IMMUNOLOGY.** (ASIAN PACIFIC JOURNAL OF ALLERGY AND IMMUNOLOGY / LAUNCHED BY THE ALLERGY AND IMMUNOLOGY SOCIETY OF THAILAND ?). [Asian Pac. j. allergy immunol.]. **Added/Corp** Allergy and Immunology Society of Thailand. Vol. 1, No. 1 (June 1983)-. Periodical. English. Twice a year (June & Dec.). $60.00 (institutions), $40.00 (individual) non-members of Asia, Pacific Society of Allergy and Immunology; $30.00 (individual) members of Asia, Pacific Society of Allergy and Immunology. Asian Pacific Journal of Allergy & Immunology, 420 6 Rajvihi, Mahidol University of Micro, Bangkok 10400 Thailand. **Tel** 011 66 2 2483191, FAX 011 66 2 4121371, telex 84770 UNIMAHI TH. **ED** Prasert Thongcharoen. **NLM** W1 AS14F. **CODEN** APJIEA. Index available. cum. index. **Bk Rev. Ad Acc. Pr Rev. Circ:** 1,000 (ctrl). Documents available from The Genuine Article, BIOSIS Document Express.
**Ind/Abst** Biol. Abstr. (1986-); Curr. Contents Clin. Med.;

EMBASE; Health Plan. Adminis.; Helminthol. Abstr. (1991-); Immunol. Abstr.; Index Med. (Vol. 1, No. 1, 1983-); Index Vet.; Nutr. Res. Newsl.; Protozoolog. Abstr.; Res. Alert [Select. Cov.]; Rev. Med. Vet. Entomol.; Rev. Med. Vet. Mycology; SCISEARCH; Virol. AIDS Abstr.

US/0899-7470
**ASTHMA & ALLERGY ADVOCATE.** [Asthma allergy advocate]. **Added/Corp** American Academy of Allergy and Immunology. American College of Allergy & Immunology. Asthma & Allergy Foundation of America. **VFOAT** Asthma and Allergy Advocate. (198?)-. Periodical. English. qt. American Academy of Allergy and Immunology, 611 East Wells Street, Milwaukee WI 53202. **Tel** (414)272-6071. **DD** 616.

UK/0142-8365
**AUTOIMMUNE DISEASES.** [Autoimmune dis.]. (1973)-. English. bm. £115.00. SUBIS, Mansion House, 19 Kingfield Road, Sheffield S11 9AS England. **Tel** 011 44 114 255 4433, FAX 011 44 114 255 4626. **DD** 016.574. **Bk Rev. Ad Acc.**
**Desc:** Current awareness service for researchers and clinicians.

SZ/0891-6934
**AUTOIMMUNITY (CHUR, SWITZERLAND).** (AUTOIMMUNITY.). [Autoimmunity]. Vol. 1, No. 1 (1988)-. Periodical. English. ir (3 issues per volume). $1080.00 (university and hospital libraries); $1686.00 other. Harwood Academic Publishers, PO Box 90, Reading RG1 8JL England. **Tel** 011 44 734 560080. **ED** Terence J. Wilkin. **LC** QR188.3; .A98. **DD** 616.07/9/05. **NLM** W1; AU872. **CODEN** AUIMEI. **[CCC].** Documents available from The Genuine Article.
**Ind/Abst** Curr. Aware. Biol. Sci., CABS; Curr. Contents Life Sci.; EMBASE; Health Plan. Adminis.; Protozoolog. Abstr.; Res. Alert [Select. Cov.]; SCISEARCH.

US/0891-2076
**BASIC & CLINICAL IMMUNOLOGY.** [Basic clin. immunol.]. **VFOAT** Basic and Clinical Immunology. 1st Ed. (1976)-. English. be. $29.00 per issue. Appleton Century Crofts, Prentice Hall, 200 Old Tappan Road, Old Tappan NJ 07675. **Tel** (201)767-5188, (800)922-0579. **LC** RC582; .B39. **DD** 616. **NLM** W1; BA813J. Index available.

US/0195-4261
**BASIC AND CLINICAL IMMUNOLOGY (NEW YORK).** (BASIC AND CLINICAL IMMUNOLOGY.). (197?)-. Monographic series. English. ir. Price varies per volume. John Wiley & Sons, Inc., 605 Third Avenue, New York NY 10158-0012. **Tel** (212)850-6000, (212)850-6645, FAX (212)850-6088, telex 12-7063. **(Subscription address:** John Wiley & Sons / England, Baffins Lane, Chichester, West Sussex PO19 1UD England.**)**

GW/0301-0457
**BEHRING INSTITUTE MITTEILUNGEN.** [Behring Inst. Mitt.]. **VFOAT** Behring Institute Research Communications. (1972)-. Academic Scholarly Publication. German (English). ir (2 or 3 per year). $7.00. Behringwerke, Emil Von Behring STR 76, D 35041 Marburg Germany. **Tel** 011 49 6421 392793. **LC** RM31. **DD** 615/.1/05. **NLM** W1 BE139. **CODEN** BHIMA2. Documents available from CASDDS. ***Continues*** *Behringswerk-Mitteilungen, 0067-4885.*
**Ind/Abst** Chem. Abstr.; EMBASE; Health Plan. Adminis.; Index Med. (1983-).

US/1058-708X
**BETA (SAN FRANCISCO, CALIF.).** (BETA : BULLETIN OF EXPERIMENTAL TREATMENTS FOR AIDS : A PUBLICATION OF THE SAN FRANCISCO AIDS FOUNDATION.). [Beta]. **Added/Corp** San Francisco AIDS Foundation. **VFOAT** Bulletin of Experimental Treatments for AIDS. (Nov. 1989)-. Bulletin. English. qt. $45.00 (individuals); $95.00 (institutions). BETA Publications Aids Foundation, 2115 Fourth Street, Berkeley CA 94710. **Tel** (800)327-9893. **ED** Ron Baker (phone: (510)549-4300). **LC** IN PROCESS. **DD** 616. **NLM** W1; BE9553.

US/0278-9566
**BI-ANNUAL REVIEW OF ALLERGY.** ***Ceased.*** [Bi-annu. rev. allergy]. (1979)-(1983). English. be. Medical Exam Publishing Company, 52 Vanderbilt Avenue Elsevier, New York NY 10017-3808. **Tel** (212)463-1052. **LC** RC583; .A47. **DD** 616.97/005. **NLM** W1 B112. ***Continues*** *Annual Review of Allergy, 0090-1083.*
**Desc:** Review of recent allergy research and literature with commentary by noted specialists.

US/0149-1032
**BIORESEARCH TODAY. CANCER C. IMMUNOLOGY.** ***Ceased.*** **See** Medical Science and Technology-Neoplasma, Neoplastic.

IT/0021-2547
**BOLLETTINO DELL'ISTITUTO SIEROTERAPICO MILANESE.** ***Ceased.*** [Boll. Ist. sieroter. milan.]. **Main/Corp** Milan. Istituto Sieroterapico Milanese. **VFOAT** Bollettino dell'Istituto Sieroterapico Milanese Serafino Belfanti. Vol. 19 (June 1940)-Vol. 70. Periodical. Italian (Italian). bm. Institute Sieroterapico Milanese, Via Darwin, 20143 Milan Italy. **NLM** W1 IS865. **CODEN** BISMAP. Documents available from BIOSIS Document Express, CASDDS. ***Continues*** *Bollettino dell'Istituto Sieroterapico Milanese.*
**Ind/Abst** Biodeter. Abstr.; Biol. Abstr.; Chem. Abstr.; Dairy Sci. Abstr.; EMBASE; Health Plan. Adminis.; Helminthol. Abstr. (1991-); Index Med.; Index Vet.; Nutr. Abstr. Rev., Ser. B, Live Feeds and Feed.; Nutr. Abstr. Rev., Ser. A, Hum. Exp.; Life Sci. Collect.; Protozoolog. Abstr.; Rev. Med. Vet. Entomol.; Vet. Bull.; Trop. Dis. Bull.

US/0889-1591
**BRAIN, BEHAVIOR, AND IMMUNITY.** **See** Medical Science and Technology-Neurology.

FR/0020-2452
**BULLETIN DE L'INSTITUT PASTEUR.** [Bull. Inst. Pasteur]. **Main/Corp** Institut Pasteur (Paris, France). Vol. 1 (1903)-. Academic Scholarly Publication. French (English). qt (1 volume). 895.00F France; 1050.00F other. Editions Scientifique Elsevier, 141 rue de Javel, 75747 Paris Cedex 15 France. **Tel** 011 33 1 47 07 11 22, FAX 011 33 1 43 36 80 93. **(Subscription address:** Editions Scientifiques Elsevier / for North America, PO Box 7247-7576, Philadelphia PA 19170-7576.**) ED** P. Meyer, W. H. Fridman, C. Hannoun, A. Ryter and M. Schwartz. **LC** R108; .I6453. **DD** 610.82. **NLM** W1 BU541D. **CODEN** BIPAA8. **[CCC].** Index available. **Bk Rev. Ad Acc. Pr Rev. Circ:** 1,000 (ctrl). available on microfilm and microfiche from University Microfilms International (UMI). Documents available from The Genuine Article, BIOSIS Document Express, CASDDS, ADONIS.
**Desc:** Publishes reviews on all aspects of microbiology, immunology, virology, and infectious diseases, with a view to providing researchers and teaching staffs in these fields.
**Ind/Abst** ADONIS; AgBiotech News Inf.; Bibliogr. Mission.; Biocont. News Inf.; Biol. Abstr.; Chem. Abstr.; Curr. Contents Life Sci.; Dairy Sci. Abstr.; EMBASE; Energy Res. Abstr. (April 1982-); Index Vet.; Life Sci. Collect.; Protozoolog. Abstr.; Ref. Upd. Deluxe Ed.; Res. Alert [Full Cov.]; Rev. Med. Vet. Entomol.; Rev. Med. Vet. Mycology; Sci. Cit. Index; SCISEARCH; Vet. Bull.; Trop. Dis. Bull.

US/1040-7111
**CA SELECTS: AIDS & RELATED IMMUNODEFICIENCIES.** **See** Chemistry-Abstracting, Bibliographies and Statistics.

US
**CALIFORNIA HIV TESTING AND COUNSELING MONTHLY REPORT.** **Added/Corp** California. Office of AIDS. HIV Testing Unit. (Jan. 1990)-. Periodical. English. mo. ***Continues*** *Alternative Test Site Report.*

US
**CDC HIV : AIDS PREVENTION NEWSLETTER.** **See** Medical Science and Technology-Communicable Diseases.

US/0008-8749
**CELLULAR IMMUNOLOGY.** [Cell. immunol.]. Vol. 1 (May 1970)-. Academic Scholarly Publication. English. Fourteen times a year. $1325.00 US and Canada; $1590.00 other. Academic Press, Inc., 6277 Sea Harbor Drive, Orlando FL 32887. **Tel** (800)543-9534, (407)345-4100, FAX (407)363-9661. **ED** H. Sherwood Lawrence. **LC** QR185.C4; C4. **DD** 574.8/765. **NLM** W1 CE129. **CODEN** CLIMB8. **[CCC]. Pr Rev.** Documents available from The Genuine Article, BIOSIS Document Express, CASDDS.
**Desc:** Devoted to the publication of original investigations concerned with the immunological activities of cells in experimental or clinical situations. The scope of the journal encompasses the broad area of in vitro and in vivo studies of cellular responses.
**Ind/Abst** AgBiotech News Inf.; Anim. Breed. Abstr.; Biol. Abstr.; Chem. Abstr.; Curr. Aware. Biol. Sci., CABS; Curr. Contents Life Sci.; Dairy Sci. Abstr.; EMBASE; Energy Res. Abstr. (Feb. 1972-); Genet. Abstr.; Health Plan. Adminis.; Helminthol. Abstr. (19??-19??); Immunol. Abstr.; Index Med.; Index Vet.; INIS Atomindex [Micro.]; Microbiol. Abstr. Sect. B; Microbiol. Abstr. Sect. C; NAPRALERT; Nutr. Abstr. Rev., Ser. A, Hum. Exp.; Oncog. Growth Factors Abstr.; Life Sci. Collect.; PESTDOC; Pig News Inf.; Protozoolog. Abstr.; Ref. Upd. Basic Ed.; Ref. Upd. Deluxe Ed.; Res. Alert [Full Cov.]; Rev. Med. Vet. Mycology; Rev. Plant Pathol.; Sci. Cit. Index; SCISEARCH; Vet. Bull.; Trop. Dis. Bull.; Virol. AIDS Abstr.

SZ/1015-0145
**CHEMICAL IMMUNOLOGY.** [Chem. immunol.]. Vol. 46 (1989)-. English. Twice a year. 200.00F (approx. per volume). S. Karger AG, Allschwilerstrasse 10, PO Box - Postfach - Case Postale, CH-4009 Basel Switzerland. **Tel** 011 41 61 306-1111, FAX 011 41 61 306-1234, telex CH 962 652. **ED** L. Adorini, K. Arai, F.W. Fitch, K. Ishazaka, B.H. Waksman, H. Waldmann. **LC** IN PROCESS. **NLM** W1; CH25G. **CODEN** CHMIEP. **Pr Rev.** Documents available from The Genuine Article, BIOSIS Document Express, CASDDS. ***Continues*** *Progress in Allergy, 0079-6034.*
**Desc:** Has presented annual collections of review articles on topics of major interest, authored by recognized international authorities. The series earned itself a reputation through the high scientific quality of its contents as well as the appropriateness of selected topics. The series will reflect both the changing scope of the field, and the rapid developments with a larger output of volumes in areas where recent research has been concentrated.
**Ind/Abst** Biol. Abstr.; Chem. Abstr.; EMBASE; Index Med. (1989-); Ref. Upd. Clinical Ed.; Ref. Upd. Deluxe Ed.; Res. Alert [Full Cov.]; Sci. Cit. Index; SCISEARCH.

US/0896-2359
**CIVIC HEALTH OCCASIONAL PAPER.** [Civ. health occas. pap.]. **Added/Corp** Discreet Medical Testing, Inc. **VFOAT** Civic Health. **VAT** Acquired Immune Deficiency Syndrome Testing in a Democratic Society. (1987)-. Monographic series. English. ir. Discreet Medical Testing, Inc., 902 North Grang Avenue, Santa Ana CA 92701. **DD** 614.

US
**CLINICAL ALLERGY AND IMMUNOLOGY SERIES.** (19??)-. Monographic series. English. ir. Price varies per volume. Marcel Dekker Inc., 270 Madison Avenue, New York NY 10016. **Tel** (212)696-9000, (800)228-1160, FAX (212)685-4540, telex 421419. **(Subscription address:** Marcel Dekker Inc, PO Box 5017, Monticello NY 12701.**)**

UK/0263-4848
**CLINICAL ALLERGY. SUPPLEMENT.** [Clin. allergy. Suppl.]. (1980)-. Monographic series. English. ir. Price varies per volume. Blackwell Scientific Publications Ltd, Marston Book Services, PO Box 87, Oxford OX2 ODT UK. **Tel** 011 44 865 791155, FAX 011 44 865 791927, telex 837 515 MARDIS G. **Circ:** 1,750.

●US/1071-4138
**CLINICAL AND DIAGNOSTIC LABORATORY IMMUNOLOGY (CD-ROM).** (CLINICAL AND DIAGNOSTIC LABORATORY IMMUNOLOGY [COMPUTER FILE].). **Added/Corp** American Society for Microbiology. (1994)-. English. Six times a year. $207.00 (print), $240.00 (CD-ROM) US. American Society for Microbiology, 1325 Massachusetts Avenue Northwest, Washington DC 20005-4171. **Tel** (202)737-3600, FAX (202)737-0367. **(Subscription address:** American Society for Microbiology, Journals Subscription Department, PO Box 11127, Birmingham AL 35201-1127.**)** available in print from the publisher.

●US/1071-412X
**CLINICAL AND DIAGNOSTIC LABORATORY IMMUNOLOGY (PRINT).** (CLINICAL AND DIAGNOSTIC AND LABORATORY IMMUNOLOGY.). **Added/Corp** American Society for Microbiology. (1994)-. Periodical. English. Six times a year. $207.00 (print), $240.00 (CD-ROM) US. American Society for Microbiology, 1325 Massachusetts Avenue Northwest, Washington DC 20005-4171. **Tel** (202)737-3600, FAX (202)737-0367. **(Subscription address:** American Society for Microbiology, Journals Subscription Department, PO Box 11127, Birmingham AL 35201-1127.**) NLM** W1; CL654C. available on CD-ROM from the publisher.
**Desc:** Devoted to the advancement and dissemination of new knowledge about all aspects of clinical laboratory immunology.

UK/0954-7894
**CLINICAL AND EXPERIMENTAL ALLERGY.** (CLINICAL AND EXPERIMENTAL ALLERGY : JOURNAL OF THE BRITISH SOCIETY FOR ALLERGY AND CLINICAL IMMUNOLOGY.). [Clin. exp. allergy]. **Added/Corp** British Society for Allergy and Clinical Immunology. Vol. 19, No. 1 (Jan. 1989)-. Academic Scholarly Publication. English. mo (12 issues). $506.00 US & Canada; £297.00 Europe; £326.00 other. Blackwell Scientific Publications Ltd, Marston Book Services, PO Box 87, Oxford OX2 ODT UK. **Tel** 011 44 865 791155, FAX 011 44 865 791927, telex 837 515 MARDIS G. **NLM** W1; CL654L. **CODEN** CLEAEN. **[CCC]. Pr Rev.** available on microfilm and microfiche from University Microfilms International (UMI). Documents available from The Genuine Article, BIOSIS Document Express, ADONIS. ***Continues*** *Clinical Allergy, 0009-9090.*
**Ind/Abst** ADONIS; Biol. Abstr.; Curr. Aware. Biol. Sci., CABS; Curr. Contents Clin. Med.; Curr. Contents Life Sci.; Dairy Sci. Abstr.; EMBASE; Health Plan. Adminis.; Immunol. Abstr.; Index Med. (Jan. 1989-); Nutr. Abstr. Rev., Ser. A, Hum. Exp.; Nutr. Res. Newsl.; PESTDOC; Postharvest News Inf.; Ref. Upd. Clinical Ed.; Ref. Upd. Deluxe Ed.; Res. Alert [Full Cov.]; Rev. Med. Vet. Entomol.; Rev. Med. Vet. Mycology; Sci. Cit. Index; SCISEARCH; Trop. Dis. Bull.

UK/0009-9104
**CLINICAL AND EXPERIMENTAL IMMUNOLOGY.** (CLINICAL AND EXPERIMENTAL IMMUNOLOGY : AN OFFICIAL JOURNAL OF THE BRITISH SOCIETY FOR IMMUNOLOGY.). [Clin. exp. immunol.]. **Added/Corp** British Society for Immunology. Vol. 1 (Jan. 1966)-. Academic Scholarly Publication. English. mo (12 issues). $760.00 US & Canada; £445.50 Europe; £490.00 other. Blackwell Scientific Publications Ltd, Marston Book Services, PO Box 87, Oxford OX2 ODT UK. **Tel** 011 44 865 791155, FAX 011 44 865 791927, telex 837 515 MARDIS G. **ED** J. L. Turk. **LC** RC583; .C55. **DD** 616.0705. **NLM** W1 CL664. **CODEN** CEXIAL. **[CCC].** Index available. **Ad Acc. Pr Rev. Circ:** 1,740 (ctrl). available on microfilm and microfiche from University Microfilms International (UMI). Documents available from The Genuine Article, BIOSIS Document Express, CASDDS, ADONIS.
**Desc:** Publishes material describing original research on the role of immunology in the diagnosis and pathogenesis of disease, including allergy.
**Ind/Abst** ADONIS; AgBiotech News Inf.; Anim. Breed. Abstr.; Biol. Abstr.; Chem. Abstr.; CSA Neuro. Abstr. (?-?); Curr. Aware. Biol. Sci., CABS; Curr. Contents Life Sci.; Dairy Sci. Abstr.; EMBASE; Genet. Abstr.; Health Plan. Adminis.; Helminthol. Abstr. (19??-19??); Immunol. Abstr.; Index Med.; Index Vet.; Microbiol. Abstr. Sect. B; Microbiol. Abstr. Sect. C; Nutr. Abstr. Rev., Ser. A, Hum. Exp.; Oncog. Growth Factors Abstr.; Life Sci. Collect.; PESTDOC; Protozoolog. Abstr.; Ref. Upd. Basic Ed.; Ref. Upd. Deluxe Ed.; Res. Alert [Full Cov.]; Rev. Med. Vet. Mycology; Rice Abstr.; Sci. Cit. Index; SCISEARCH; Soc. Sci. Cit. Index [Select. Cov.]; Soyabean Abstr.; SportSearch; Vet. Bull.; Trop. Dis. Bull.; Virol. AIDS Abstr.

●UK/1072-1630
**CLINICAL AND EXPERIMENTAL METABOLISM.** (1994)-. Periodical. English. Three times a year. $170.00. Harcourt Brace & Company Ltd., Foots Cray, High Street, Sidcup Kent DA14 5HP England. **Tel** 011 44 81 300 3322, FAX 011 44 81 309 0807. **(Subscription address:** W. B. Saunders Company / North America Subscriptions, c/o Periodicals, 6277 Sea Harbour Drive, 4th Floor, Orlando FL 32887.**)**

US/0090-1229
**CLINICAL IMMUNOLOGY AND IMMUNOPATHOLOGY.** [Clin. immunol. immunopathol.]. Vol. 1 (Oct. 1972)-. Academic Scholarly Publication. English. mo. $782.00 US and Canada; $951.00 other. Academic Press, Inc., 6277 Sea Harbor Drive, Orlando FL 32887. **Tel** (800)543-9534, (407)345-4100, FAX (407)363-9661. **ED** Noel R. Rose and Stanley Cohen. **LC** RC583; .C56. **DD** 616.07/9/05. **NLM** W1 CL715. **CODEN** CLIIAT. **[CCC]. Pr Rev.** Documents available from The Genuine Article, BIOSIS Document Express, CASDDS.
**Desc:** Publishes original research on the molecular and cellular bases of immunological disease. The journal also features short analytical reviews of timely topics in basic immunology, case reports, and letters to the editor.
**Ind/Abst** Biol. Abstr.; Chem. Abstr.; Curr. Contents Clin. Med.; Curr. Contents Life Sci.; Dairy Sci. Abstr.; EMBASE; Energy Res. Abstr. (April 1974-); Health Plan. Adminis.; Helminthol. Abstr. (1991-); Immunol. Abstr.; Index Med.; INIS Atomindex [Micro.]; Nutr. Abstr. Rev., Ser. B, Live Feeds and Feed.; Nutr. Abstr. Rev., Ser. A, Hum. Exp.; Oncog. Growth Factors Abstr.; Life Sci. Collect.; Protozoolog. Abstr.; Ref. Upd. Basic Ed.; Ref. Upd. Deluxe Ed.; Res. Alert [Full Cov.]; Sci. Cit. Index; SCISEARCH; Small Anim. Abstr. Bibliogr.; Virol. AIDS Abstr.

●US/1061-6969
**CLINICAL IMMUNOLOGY DIGEST.** (1992)-. Periodical. English. qt. $50.00. F.J. Fontana, 1012 North Peak, #1, Dallas TX 75204. ***Continues*** *Immunological Disorders Update, 1056-4896.*

US/0197-1859
**CLINICAL IMMUNOLOGY NEWSLETTER.** [Clin. immunol. newsl.]. Vol. 1 (Jan. 7, 1980)-. Newsletter. English. Twelve times a year (1 volume). $180.00 US; $234.00 other. Elsevier Science Publishing Company Inc, Madison Square Station, PO Box 882, New York NY 10159-0882. **Tel** (212)633-3950, FAX (212)633-3990. **ED** Herman Friedman, Mario R Escobar, and Noel R Rose. **DD** 616. **NLM** W1 CL715G. **CODEN** CIMNDC. **[CCC]. Circ:** 1,000. Documents available from BIOSIS Document Express.
**Desc:** Brings readers concise and practical reports on topics of immediate importance, such as monoclonal antibodies, acquired immunodeficiency syndrome, interferon, and immunology of tumors. Also includes new ideas for detection, case studies, guest editorials, and announcements of meetings and events of importance.
**Ind/Abst** Biol. Abstr.; Immunol. Abstr.; Index Vet.; Life Sci. Collect.; Trop. Dis. Bull.; Virol. AIDS Abstr.

●NZ/1172-7039
**CLINICAL IMMUNOTHERAPEUTICS. See** Pharmacy and Pharmacology.

US/0731-8235
**CLINICAL REVIEWS IN ALLERGY.** [Clin. rev. allergy]. Vol. 1, No. 1 (Mar. 1983)-. Academic Scholarly Publication. English. qt. $190.00 US; $215.00 other. Humana Press Inc., 999 Riverview Drive, Suite 208, Totawa NJ 07512. **Tel** (201)256-1699, FAX (201)256-8341. **ED** M. Eric Gershwin, M.D. **NLM** W1; CL779LF. **CODEN** CRVADD. **[CCC]. Ad Acc. Pr Rev. Circ:** 500. Documents available from The Genuine Article, BIOSIS Document Express, CASDDS.
**Desc:** Publishes scholarly review papers, with each issue devoted to the same topics, in an attempt to provide comprehensive treatment, by a revolving series to Topic Editors, on a subject of critical importance to allergists.
**Ind/Abst** Biol. Abstr.; Chem. Abstr. (1983-); Curr. Aware. Biol. Sci., CABS; Curr. Contents Clin. Med.; Curr. Contents Life Sci.; Dairy Sci. Abstr.; Health Plan. Adminis.; Index Med. (1983-); Index Sci. Rev. [Full Cov.]; Nutr. Res. Newsl.; Postharvest News Inf.; Ref. Upd. Clinical Ed.; Ref. Upd. Deluxe Ed.; Res. Alert [Full Cov.]; Rev. Med. Vet. Entomol.; Rev. Med. Vet. Mycology; Sci. Cit. Index; SCISEARCH; Soyabean Abstr.

US
**COMMON SENSE ABOUT AIDS.** (19??)-. English. $199.00. American Health Consultants, 3525 Piedmont Road, Suite 400, Atlanta GA 30305. **Tel** (800)688-2421, (404)262-7436. **(Subscription address:** American Health Consultants, PO Box 95278, Chicago IL 60694.**)**

UK/0147-9571
**COMPARATIVE IMMUNOLOGY, MICROBIOLOGY AND INFECTIOUS DISEASES. See** Biology-Microbiology.

SZ
**COMPLEMENT PROFILES.** ***Ceased.*** Vol. 1 (1993)-(1993). Monographic series. English. an. S. Karger AG, Allschwilerstrasse 10, PO Box - Postfach - Case Postale, CH-4009 Basel Switzerland. **Tel** 011 41 61 306-1111, FAX 011 41 61 306-1234, telex CH 962 652. **ED** J. M. Cruse and R. E. Lewis, Jr. **NLM** W1; CO451VM. **Pr Rev.** Documents available from BIOSIS Document Express.
**Desc:** Authored by internationally renowned investigators, volumes in this new series will feature the latest developments in complement research.
**Ind/Abst** Biol. Abstr.; Index Med.; Ref. Upd. Deluxe Ed.

US/0149-1148
**COMPREHENSIVE IMMUNOLOGY.** ***Ceased.*** [Compr. immunol.]. V. 1-Ceased ?. Academic Scholarly Publication. English. ir. Plenum Press, 233 Spring Street, New York NY 10013-1578. **Tel** (212)620-8000, (800)221-9369, FAX (212)463-0742, (212)807-1047, telex 23/421139. **ED** R A Good and S B Day. **NLM** W1 CO4523. **CODEN** COIMDV. Index Available Published separately--free--upon request. Documents available from BIOSIS Document Express, CASDDS.
**Ind/Abst** Biol. Abstr.; Chem. Abstr.; Life Sci. Collect.

SW/0255-7983
**CONCEPTS IN IMMUNOPATHOLOGY.** [Concepts immunopathol.]. Vol. 1 (1985)-. Monographic series. English. an. 200.00F (approx. per volume). S. Karger AG, Allschwilerstrasse 10, PO Box - Postfach - Case Postale, CH-4009 Basel Switzerland. **Tel** 011 41 61 306-1111, FAX 011 41 61 306-1234, telex CH 962 652. **ED** J. M. Cruse and R. E. Lewis Jr. **NLM** W1; CO459RH. **[CCC].** Documents available from BIOSIS Document Express.
**Desc:** Volumes in this series offer a consolidated overview of work from the many disciplines attempting to understand how immune responses are involved in disease. Authored by invited experts, each volume presents review articles that describe and interpret the essential lines of progress on a given topic. Editorial priority is given to those rapidly developing areas that hold the greatest promise of contributing to the understanding of major human diseases. Though authored by specialists, chapters are written to serve the scientific community at large.
**Ind/Abst** Biol. Abstr.; Index Med. (1985-); Ref. Upd. Deluxe Ed.

UK
**CONTEMPORARY ISSUES IN CLINICAL IMMUNOLOGY AND ALLERGY.** 1-. Monographic series. English. Price varies per volume. **NLM** W1 CO769MQD.

US/0093-4054
**CONTEMPORARY TOPICS IN IMMUNOBIOLOGY.** [Contemp. top. immunobiol.]. (1972)-. Academic Scholarly Publication. English. ir. Price varies per volume. Plenum Press, 233 Spring Street, New York NY 10013-1578. **Tel** (212)620-8000, (800)221-9369, FAX (212)463-0742, (212)807-1047, telex 23/421139. **LC** QR180; .C632. **DD** 574.2/9/05. **NLM** W1 CO77. **CODEN** CTIBBV. **[CCC].** Documents available from CASDDS.
**Ind/Abst** AGRICOLA; Chem. Abstr.; Energy Res. Abstr. (Jan. 1981-); Index Med.; INIS Atomindex [Micro.]; Life Sci. Collect.

US/0090-8800
**CONTEMPORARY TOPICS IN MOLECULAR IMMUNOLOGY.** [Contemp. topics mol. immunol.]. Vol. 2 (1973)-. Academic Scholarly Publication. English. ir. Price varies per volume. Plenum Press, 233 Spring Street, New York NY 10013-1578. **Tel** (212)620-8000, (800)221-9369, FAX (212)463-0742, (212)807-1047, telex 23/421139. **LC** QR180; .C635. **DD** 574.2/9/05. **NLM** W1 CO77K. **CODEN** CTMIB4. Documents available from CASDDS. ***Continues*** *Contemporary Topics in Immunochemistry, 0161-4304.*
**Ind/Abst** Chem. Abstr.; Energy Res. Abstr. (Aug. 1982-); Health Plan. Adminis.; Index Med.

SZ/0301-3081
**CONTRIBUTIONS TO MICROBIOLOGY AND IMMUNOLOGY.** [Contrib. microbiol. immunol.]. Vol. 1 (1973)-. Monographic series. English (French and German). an. 250.00F (approx. per volume). S. Karger AG, Allschwilerstrasse 10, PO Box - Postfach - Case Postale, CH-4009 Basel Switzerland. **Tel** 011 41 61 306-1111, FAX 011 41 61 306-1234, telex CH 962 652. **ED** J. M. Cruse and R. E. Lewis Jr. **NLM** W1 CO778UK. **CODEN** CMIMBF. **[CCC].** Documents available from BIOSIS Document Express, CASDDS. ***Continues*** *Bibliotheca Microbiologica, 0067-8058.*
**Desc:** Contemporary studies in this field are now primarily devoted to increasing our understanding of the human immune system. Through publications which emphasize themes related to microorganisms responsible for disease and concentrate on the molecular construction of respective antibodies, this series continues to adapt to concerns which are directing research efforts in microbiology and immunology.
**Ind/Abst** AGRICOLA [Select. Cov.]; Biol. Abstr.; Chem. Abstr.; Index Med.; Index Vet.; Microbiol. Abstr. Sect. B (19??-19??); Life Sci. Collect.; Ref. Upd. Deluxe Ed.; Vet. Bull.

SP/0214-3755
**CORE JOURNALS EN ALERGIA E INMUNOLOGIA.** (1986)-. Periodical. Spanish. mo. Mayo SA, Muntaner 374-376, 08006 Barcelona Spain. **Tel** 209 02 55, FAX 202 06 43. **(Subscription address:** Laboratorios Lesvi, Poligono Industrial can Pelegri, 08740 San Andres de la Barca Barcelona Spain**) ED** Josce Mayoral and Josep M Ferrando. **UDC** 616(048.1). **Circ:** 2,000.
**Desc:** Contains a review of the literature recently published in the most relevant journals of this specialty.

US/1040-8401
**CRITICAL REVIEWS IN IMMUNOLOGY.** [Crit. rev. immunol.]. **VFOAT** CRC Critical Reviews in Immunology. **VAT** Chemical Rubber Company Critical Reviews in Immunology. Vol. 1, Issue 2 (1980)-. Academic Scholarly Publication. English. Four times a year. $84.00 (individual); 4265.00 (other). Begell House Inc., PO Box 1109, Pearl River NY 10965. **Tel** (212)725-1999. **ED** M. Z. Atassi. **LC** QR180; .C18. **DD** 574.2/9/05. **NLM** W1; CR1243. **CODEN** CCRIDE. **[CCC].** Documents available from The Genuine Article, BIOSIS Document Express, CASDDS. ***Continues*** *CRC Critical Reviews in Immunology, 0197-3355.*
**Desc:** Contains critical and timely review articles, in various aspects of contemporary immunology, from a wide variety of disciplines.
**Ind/Abst** AgBiotech News Inf.; Anim. Breed. Abstr.; Biol. Abstr.; Chem. Abstr.; Curr. Aware. Biol. Sci., CABS; Curr. Contents Life Sci.; EMBASE; Immunol. Abstr.; Index Med. (1980-); Life Sci. Collect.; Ref. Upd. Basic Ed.; Ref. Upd. Deluxe Ed.; Res. Alert [Full Cov.]; Sci. Cit. Index.

●UK/0964-8747
**CURRENT ADVANCES IN IMMUNOLOGY & INFECTIOUS DISEASES. See** Medical Science and Technology-Abstracting, Bibliographies and Statistics.

UK/0952-8075
**CURRENT AIDS LITERATURE. Added/Corp** Great Britain. Bureau of Hygiene and Tropical Diseases. Vol. 1, No. 1 (Jan. 1988)-. Periodical. English. mo. $475.00. CAB International Centre, Wallingford, Oxon OX10 8DE United Kingdom. **Tel** 44 491 832111, FAX 44 491 833508, telex 847964 (COMAGG G). **(Subscription address:** CAB International, Subscriptions Department, Wallingford, OX OX108DE England**) ED** Caroline J Akehurst. **NLM** ZWD 308; C976. **Circ:** 1,000. available on CD-ROM; available on an online database from DATA-STAR; BRS; and DIMDI. ***Continues*** *AIDS and Retroviruses Update.*
**Desc:** Provides annotations from world medical and scientific publications, books, reports, ect. on HIV and AIDS worldwide.

US/0736-4350
**CURRENT CONCEPTS IN ALLERGY AND CLINICAL IMMUNOLOGY.** ***Ceased.*** [Curr. concepts allergy clin. immunol.]. **Added/Corp** New York Allergy Society. Lederle Laboratories. Vol. 1 (1971)-?. Periodical. English. Three times a year. New York Allergy Society, 428 West 59th Street, Roosevelt Hospital, New York NY 10019. **Tel** (212)554-7192. **NLM** W1 CU7873. cum. index. **Circ:** 2,500.
**Desc:** Timely reviews of topics in allergy immunology interested for updating physicians in practice regarding clinical disorders.

US/0952-7915
**CURRENT OPINION IN IMMUNOLOGY.** [Curr. opin. immunol.]. Vol. 1, No. 1 (Sept./Oct. 1988)-. Periodical. English. Six times a year. $147.00

(individuals); $440.00 (institutions). Current Science / England, Middlesex House, 34-42 Cleveland Street, London W1P 5FB England. **Tel** 011 44 71 580 8393, 011 44 71 323 0323, FAX 011 44 81 580 1938. **(Subscription address:** Current Science, 20 North 3rd Street, Philadelphia PA 19106.) **ED** F. W. Alt, P. Marrack, and I. M. Roitt. **NLM** W1; CU799GDL. **CODEN** COPIEL. **[CCC]. Ad Acc. Pr Rev. Circ:** 2,500. available on diskette. Documents available from The Genuine Article, BIOSIS Document Express.
**Desc:** Directed toward researchers and practicing immunologists. Presents review articles from an area of concentration covering an entire year's literature with annotated references. Each issue features a bibliography of the current world literature published during the previous year.
**Ind/Abst** Anim. Breed. Abstr.; Biol. Abstr.; Curr. Aware. Biol. Sci., CABS; Curr. Contents Life Sci.; EMBASE; Health Plan. Adminis.; Helminthol. Abstr. (1991-); Immunol. Abstr.; Protozoolog. Abstr.; Ref. Upd. Deluxe Ed.; Res. Alert [Full Cov.]; Rev. Med. Vet. Entomol.; Sci. Cit. Index; SCISEARCH; Trop. Dis. Bull.

UK/0898-5871
**CURRENT TOPICS IN AIDS.** [Curr. topics AIDS]. **VAT** Current Topics in Acquired Immunodeficiency Syndrome. Vol. 1 (1987)-. Monographic series. English. ir. Price varies per volume. John Wiley & Sons Ltd., Baffins Lane, Chichester West Sussex PO19 1UD England. **Tel** 0243 779777, FAX 0243 776128 BTG:JWP001, telex 86290 WIBOOKG. **LC** RC607.A26; C88. **DD** 616.97/92. **NLM** W1; CU819U.

US
**CURRENT TOPICS IN IMMUNOLOGY.** No. 1 (1974)-. Monographic series. English. ir. Price varies per volume. Williams & Wilkins Company, 428 East Preston Street, Baltimore MD 21202-3993. **Tel** (410)528-4000, (800)638-6423, FAX (410)528-8596, telex 87669. Documents available from Quick Copies.

GW/0070-217X
**CURRENT TOPICS IN MICROBIOLOGY AND IMMUNOLOGY.** [Curr. top. microbiol. immunol.]. **VFOAT** Ergebnisse der Mikrobiologie und Immunitatsforschung; CTMI. (1967)-. Academic Scholarly Publication. English (German). ir. Price varies per volume. Springer-Verlag GmbH & Company KG, Heidelberger Platz 3, D 14197 Berlin Germany. **Tel** 011 49 30 8207223, FAX 011 49 30 8214091, telex 183 319 SPBLN D. **(Subscription address:** Springer Verlag New York Inc. / for North America, 44 Hartz Way, Secaucus NJ 07096.) **LC** QR1; .E6. **NLM** W1 CU82K. **CODEN** CTMIA3. **[CCC].** cum. index. Documents available from The Genuine Article, BIOSIS Document Express, CASDDS. ***Continues** Ergebnisse der Mikrobiologie, Immunitatsforschung und Experimentellen Therapie, 0367-1003.*
**Desc:** Articles on molecular biology of adenoviruses.
**Ind/Abst** AgBiotech News Inf.; AGRICOLA; Anim. Breed. Abstr.; Biol. Abstr.; Chem. Abstr.; Curr. Aware. Biol. Sci., CABS; EMBASE; Genet. Abstr.; Health Plan. Adminis.; Helminthol. Abstr.; Immunol. Abstr.; Index Med.; Index Sci. Rev. [Full Cov.]; Index Vet.; Microbiol. Abstr. Sect. B; Microbiol. Abstr. Sect. C; Oncog. Growth Factors Abstr.; Life Sci. Collect.; Poult. Abstr.; Protozoolog. Abstr.; Ref. Upd. Basic Ed.; Ref. Upd. Deluxe Ed.; Res. Alert [Full Cov.]; Sci. Cit. Index; SCISEARCH; Vet. Bull.; Trop. Dis. Bull.; Virol. AIDS Abstr.

US/1051-7685
**DAITA.** ***Title Change.*** (DAITA : CURRENT AIDS THERAPIES : INCLUDING THE DIRECTORY OF ANTIVIRAL AND IMMUNOMODULATORY THERAPIES FOR AIDS AND GUIDE TO OPPORTUNISTIC INFECTIONS.). **VFOAT** Directory of Antiviral and Immunomodulatory Therapies for AIDS. (1990)-(19??). Directory. English. mo (one complete directory plus monthly updates). AIDS Weekly, PO Box 830409, Birmingham AL 35283. **Tel** (205)995-1567. **(Subscription address:** PO Box 830409, Birmingham, AL 35283-0409; telephone: (800)633-4931, FAX: (205)995-1588) ***Separated from** CDC AIDS Weekly, 0884-903X.* ***Continued by** AIDS Therapies.*

US/0273-2254
**DERMATOLOGY & ALLERGY. See** Medical Science and Technology-Dermatology.

US/0145-305X
**DEVELOPMENTAL AND COMPARATIVE IMMUNOLOGY.** [Dev. comp. immunol.]. **Added/Corp** International Society of Developmental and Comparative Immunology. **VFOAT** Journal of Developmental and Comparative Immunology. Vol. 1 (Jan. 1977)-. Academic Scholarly Publication. English. bm. $701.00 The Americas; £470.00 other. Pergamon Press, An Imprint of Elsevier Science Ltd., The Boulevard, Langford Lane, Kidlington, Oxford OX5 1GB United Kingdom. **Tel** 011 44 865 843000, 011 44 865 843699, FAX 011 44 865 843010. **(Subscription address:** Elsevier Science Ltd. Oxford Fulfillment Centre, PO Box 800, Kidlington, Oxford OX5 1DX United Kingdom.) **ED** Edwin L. Cooper. **LC** QR180; .D46. **DD** 591.2/9/05. **NLM** W1 DE997PM. **CODEN** DCIMDQ. **[CCC]. Pr Rev.** available on microfilm and microfiche from University Microfilms International (UMI). Documents available from The Genuine Article, BIOSIS Document Express, CASDDS.
**Desc:** Serves as a world forum for the rapid dissemination of original research that treats the development and maturation of the immune system in the broadest sense, emphasizing ontogenetic (including aging) and phylogenetic aspects. Encompasses (among other subjects) mechanisms of recognition of self and non-self at the cellular, molecular, and organismic levels.
**Ind/Abst** AgBiotech News Inf.; AGRICOLA [Select. Cov.]; Biocont. News Inf.; Biol. Abstr.; Chem. Abstr.; Curr. Contents, Agric. Biol. Environ. Sci.; Curr. Contents Life Sci.; Curr. Ref. Fish Res.; Dairy Sci. Abstr.; EMBASE; Energy Res. Abstr. (April 1982-); Health Plan. Adminis.; Helminthol. Abstr. (19??-19??); Immunol. Abstr.; Index Med.; Index Vet.; INIS Atomindex [Micro.]; Life Sci. Collect.; Protozoolog. Abstr.; Res. Alert [Full Cov.]; Rev. Agric. Entomol.; Rev. Med. Vet. Entomol.; Sci. Cit. Index; SCISEARCH; Vet. Bull.

SZ/1044-6672
**DEVELOPMENTAL IMMUNOLOGY.** [Dev. immunol.]. Vol. 1, No. 1 (1990)-. Periodical. English. qt (2 volumes). $373.00 (academic institutions), $582.00 (corporate institutions). Harwood Academic Publishers, PO Box 90, Reading RG1 8JL England. **Tel** 011 44 734 560080. **(Subscription address:** International Publishers Distributor at one of the following addresses: 820 Town Center Drive, Langhorne, PA 19047; or PO Box 90, Reading Berkshire RG1 8JL UK; or Kent Ridge PO Box 1180, Singapore 9111, Republic of Singapore) **ED** Harold von Boehmer and Tadamitsu Kishimoto. **LC** QR184.5; .D48. **DD** 591.2/9. **NLM** W1; DE9970. **CODEN** DEIME7. **[CCC].**
**Desc:** Covering cellular and molecular areas of developmental immunology, this journal reports on both ontogenetic and phylogenetic elements by way of contributions from experts in the field.
**Ind/Abst** Curr. Aware. Biol. Sci., CABS; Index Med. (1990-).

NE/0167-8418
**DEVELOPMENTS IN HEMATOLOGY AND IMMUNOLOGY. See** Medical Science and Technology-Hematology.

US/0163-5921
**DEVELOPMENTS IN IMMUNOLOGY.** ***Ceased.*** [Dev. immunol.]. Vol. 1 (1978)-Series Complete. Academic Scholarly Publication. English. ir. Elsevier Science Publishing Company Inc, Madison Square Station, PO Box 882, New York NY 10159-0882. **Tel** (212)633-3950, FAX (212)633-3990. **LC** UNC. **NLM** W1 DE997WM. **CODEN** DEIMD6. Documents available from BIOSIS Document Express, CASDDS.
**Ind/Abst** Biol. Abstr.; Chem. Abstr.; Life Sci. Collect.

US
**DIRECTORY OF AIDS RELATED PERIODICALS. VFOAT** NAN Directory of AIDS Related Periodicals; NAN Directory of AIDS-Related Periodicals. (Spring 1988)-. Directory. English. National AIDS Network, Clearinghouse and Resource Development, Washington DC. **NLM** ZWD 308; D599.

IT/0392-6699
**EOS (ROMA).** (EOS : RIVISTA DI IMMUNOLOGIA ED IMMUNOFARMACOLOGIA.). [Eos]. (1981)-. Periodical. Italian (English). qt. Editrice Sigma Tau, Via Sudafrica 20, 00144 Rome Italy. **Tel** 011 39 6 91391. **NLM** W1; EO24Z. **CODEN** EOSSDJ. Documents available from The Genuine Article, BIOSIS Document Express, CASDDS.
**Ind/Abst** Biol. Abstr. (1985-); Chem. Abstr.; Curr. Contents Life Sci.; EMBASE; Immunol. Abstr.; Res. Alert [Full Cov.]; Sci. Cit. Index; SCISEARCH.

UK/0960-7420
**EUROPEAN JOURNAL OF IMMUNOGENETICS : OFFICIAL JOURNAL OF THE BRITISH SOCIETY FOR HISTOCOMPATABILITY AND IMMUNOGENETICS. Added/Corp** British Society for Histocompatibility and Immunogenetics. Vol. 18, Nos. 1/2 (Feb./Apr. 1991)-. Academic Scholarly Publication. English. bm (6 issues). $299.00 US and Canada; £175.00 Europe; £192.50 other. Blackwell Scientific Publications Ltd, Marston Book Services, PO Box 87, Oxford OX2 ODT UK. **Tel** 011 44 865 791155, FAX 011 44 865 791927, telex 837 515 MARDIS G. **LC** QR184; .J68. **DD** 574.2/9. **NLM** W1; EU72DFJ. **CODEN** EJOIE3. **[CCC].** available on microfilm and microfiche from University Microfilms International (UMI). Documents available from The Genuine Article, CASDDS. ***Continues** Journal of Immunogenetics, 0305-1811.*
**Ind/Abst** Chem. Abstr. (1991-); Curr. Aware. Biol. Sci., CABS; Curr. Contents Life Sci.; EMBASE; Genet. Abstr.; Health Plan. Adminis.; Immunol. Abstr.; Index Med.; Ref. Upd. Deluxe Ed.; Res. Alert [Full Cov.]; Sci. Cit. Index; SCISEARCH; Trop. Dis. Bull.

GW/0014-2980
**EUROPEAN JOURNAL OF IMMUNOLOGY.** [Eur. j. immunol.]. Vol. 1 (Jan. 1971)-. Academic Scholarly Publication. English. mo. $798.00. VCH Gesellschaft GmbH, Postfach 101161, D 69451 Weinheim Germany. **Tel** 011 49 6201 606459, FAX 011 49 6201 606184. **(Subscription address:** VCH Publishers Inc., 303 Northwest 12th Avenue, Journals Department, Deerfield FL 33442.) **LC** QR180; .E8. **DD** 616.07/9/05. **NLM** W1 EU72DG. **CODEN** EJIMAF. **[CCC]. Pr Rev.** available on microfilm. Documents available from The Genuine Article, BIOSIS Document Express, CASDDS, Documents on Demand.
**Desc:** Publishes research reports and short communications from all fields relevant to immunochemistry, physical chemistry of immunological processes, cellular immunology, mediators of cell-to-cell interaction, immunopathology, immunogenetics, and clinical immunology.
**Ind/Abst** AgBiotech News Inf.; AGRICOLA; Anim. Breed. Abstr.; Biol. Abstr.; Chem. Abstr.; CSA Neuro. Abstr. (?-?); Curr. Aware. Biol. Sci., CABS; Curr. Contents Life Sci.; Dairy Sci. Abstr.; EMBASE; Energy Inf. Abstr.; Energy Res. Abstr. (Jan. 1974-); Environ. Abstr.; Genet. Abstr.; Health Plan. Adminis.; Helminthol. Abstr. (1991-); Hum. Genome Abstr.; Immunol. Abstr.; Index Med.; Index Vet.; Microbiol. Abstr. Sect. B; Microbiol. Abstr. Sect. C; NAPRALERT; Nucl. Acids Abstr.; Oncog. Growth Factors Abstr.; Life Sci. Collect.; PESTDOC; Pig News Inf.; Poult. Abstr.; Protozoolog. Abstr.; Ref. Upd. Basic Ed.; Ref. Upd. Deluxe Ed.; Res. Alert [Full Cov.]; Rev. Med. Vet. Entomol.; Rev. Med. Vet. Mycology; Sci. Cit. Index; SCISEARCH; Vet. Bull.; Trop. Dis. Bull.; Virol. AIDS Abstr.

NE/0014-4304
**EXCERPTA MEDICA. SECTION 26. IMMUNOLOGY, SEROLOGY AND TRANSPLANTATION. See** Medical Science and Technology-Abstracting, Bibliographies and Statistics.

●US
**EXERCISE IMMUNOLOGY REVIEW.** Vol. 1 (1995)-. English. an (Published in March). $18.00 (individual), $30.00 (institution); $20.00 (individual), $32.00 (institution) other. Human Kinetics Publishers Inc, 1607 North Market Street, PO Box 5076, Champaign IL 61825-5076. **Tel** (217)351-5076, FAX (217)351-2674. **ED** Roy J. Shephard.
**Desc:** Committed to developing and enriching knowledge in all aspects of immunology that relate to sport, exercise, and regular physical activity.

SZ/0254-9670
**EXPERIMENTAL AND CLINICAL IMMUNOGENETICS.** [Exp. clin. immunogenet.]. (April 1984)-. Academic Scholarly Publication. English. qt. $208.00. S. Karger AG, Allschwilerstrasse 10, PO Box - Postfach - Case Postale, CH-4009 Basel Switzerland. **Tel** 011 41 61 306-1111, FAX 011 41 61 306-1234, telex CH 962 652. **ED** K. Bauer. **NLM** W1; EX464H. **CODEN** ECIME4. **[CCC]. Ad Acc. Pr Rev.** available on microfilm; available on microfiche. Documents available from The Genuine Article, BIOSIS Document Express, CASDDS.
**Desc:** Basic findings constitute the main body of this publication. They will continue to remain of importance as the journal charts the explosive growth of immunogenetics as a basic biological science with increasing impact on clinical concerns and other applications. Contributions from international sources offer readers experimental data on proteins of immunological relevance, the MHC of various species, and other cell surface antigens including blood group epitopes. Special attention is also given to reports on recent advances in the evolution and ontogeny of the immunoglobulin superfamily and other molecules of immunological interest and in the genetics of the immune response.
**Ind/Abst** AgBiotech News Inf.; Anim. Breed. Abstr.; Biol. Abstr.; Chem. Abstr. (1984-); Curr. Aware. Biol. Sci., CABS; Curr. Contents Life Sci.; EMBASE; Health Plan. Adminis.; Index Med.; Ref. Upd. Deluxe Ed.; Res. Alert [Full Cov.]; Sci. Cit. Index; SCISEARCH.

●NE/0928-8244
**FEMS IMMUNOLOGY AND MEDICAL MICROBIOLOGY. Added/Corp** Federation of European Microbiological Societies. **VFOAT** Immunology and Medical Microbiology. Vol. 6, No. 1 (Jan. 1993)-. Academic Scholarly Publication. English. mo (3 volumes). Fl1320.00; Fl7467.00 combination subscription to all 4 FEMS' journals. Elsevier Science Publishers BV, PO Box 211, 1000 AE Amsterdam Netherlands. **Tel** 011 31 20 5803642, FAX 011 31 20 5862696, telex 15682. **NLM** W1; FE548S. **CODEN** FIMIEVFMIMEH. **[CCC].** Documents available from ADONIS. ***Separated from** FEMS Microbiology Letters, 0378-1097.*
**Ind/Abst** ADONIS; Sci. Cit. Index.

NE/0920-8534
**FEMS MICROBIOLOGY IMMUNOLOGY.** ***Title Change.* See** Biology-Microbiology.

US/1047-0719
**FOCUS (SAN FRANCISCO, CALIF.).** (FOCUS : A GUIDE TO AIDS RESEARCH.). [Focus]. **Added/Corp** AIDS Health Project. Vol. 1, No. 1 (Dec. 1985)-. Periodical. English. Twelve times a year. $36.00 (individuals), $90.00 (institutions) US; $48.00 (individuals), $110.00 (institutions) other. Regents University California / AIDS Health Project, Box 0884, San Francisco CA 94143. **Tel** (415)476-6430, FAX (415)476-7996. **DD** 614. **NLM** W1; FO1002G. **Bk Rev.**
**Desc:** A guide to AIDS research and counseling.

IT/1120-7892
**GIAIDS. GIORNALE ITALIANO DELL' AIDS.** [GIAIDS, G. ital. AIDS]. **VFOAT** Giornale Italiano dell' Acquired Immunodeficiency Syndrome; Giornale Italiano dell' AIDS. (1990)-. Periodical. Italian. Four times a year. L80000 (individuals), L140000 (institutions). Il Pensiero Scientifico Editore s.r.l., Via Bradano 3C, 00199 Rome Italy. **Tel** 011 39 6 86207158, 86207159, 86207168, 86207169, FAX 011 39 6 86207160. **ED** Ferdinando Dianzani and Elio Guzzanti. **UDC** 616.9. **Bk Rev**. **Ad Acc**. Full Page (B&W) L1.650.000. **Circ:** 5,500.

IT/1120-6373
**GIORNALE ITALIANO DI ALLERGOLOGIA E IMMUNOLOGIA CLINICA.** [G. ital. allergol. immunol. clin.]. (1991)-. Periodical. Italian. bm. L100000 (Italy); $100.00 (other). Editrice Kurtis Srl, Via Luigi Zoja 30, 20153 Milan Italy. **Tel** 011 39 2 48202740, FAX 011 39 2 48201219. **UDC** 616-056.3. ***Continues*** *Folia Allergologica et Immunologica Clinica, 0303-8432.*

US/1063-0627
**HARVARD AIDS INSTITUTE SERIES ON GENE REGULATION OF HUMAN RETROVIRUSES.** [Harv. AIDS Inst. ser. gene regul. hum. retrovir.]. **Added/Corp** Harvard AIDS Institute. Vol. 1 (1991)-. Academic Scholarly Publication. English. ir. Price varies per volume. Raven Press, 1185 Avenue of the Americas, 37th Floor, New York NY 10036. **Tel** (212)930-9500, (212)930-9604, FAX (212)869-3495, (212)302-8507, telex 640073. **ED** William A. Haseltine, Flossie Wong-Staal and Mitsauki Yoshida. **DD** 616. **CODEN** HAIRE4. Documents available from CASDDS.
**Ind/Abst** Chem. Abstr.

US
**HEPATITIS B COALITION NEWS.** (19??)-. Newsletter. English. Free to health care workers and concerned community members; $20.00 requested donation. Hepatitis B Coalition, 1573 Selby Avenue, Suite 229, St. Paul MN 55104-6328. **Tel** (612)647-9009, FAX (612)647-9131. available via Internet.
**Desc:** Promotes hepatitis B vaccination for all infants and adolescents; HBsAg screening for all pregnant women; testing and vaccination for high-risk groups; and education and treatment for hepatitis B carriers.

US/1048-759X
**HIV/AIDS SURVEILLANCE.** [HIV/AIDS surveill.]. **Added/Corp** Centers for Disease Control (U.S.) Center for Infectious Diseases (U.S.). Division of HIV/AIDS. National Center for Infectious Diseases (U.S.). Division of HIV/AIDS. **VFOAT** HIV/AIDS Surveillance Report. **VAT** Human Immunodeficiency Virus, Acquired Immunodeficiency Syndrome Surveillance. (Feb. 1988)-. Periodical. English. mo. Free on request. National AIDS Clearing House, PO Box 6003, Rockville MD 20850. **Tel** (800)221-3908. **DD** 616. **NLM** W2; A A372a. ***Continues*** *AIDS Weekly Surveillance Report, 1041-5319.*

US
**HIV/AIDS UPDATE / PENNSYLVANIA DEPARTMENT OF HEALTH, BUREAU OF HIV/AIDS.** **See** Public Health and Safety.

US/0198-8859
**HUMAN IMMUNOLOGY.** [Hum. immunol.]. **Added/Corp** American Association for Clinical Histocompatibility Testing. Vol. 1 (July 1980)-. Academic Scholarly Publication. English. mo (3 volumes). $655.00 US; $717.00 other. Elsevier Science Publishing Company Inc, Madison Square Station, PO Box 882, New York NY 10159-0882. **Tel** (212)633-3950, FAX (212)633-3990. **ED** D Bernard Amos, Jeffrey R Dawson and Jon J van Rood. **LC** QR180; .H85. **DD** 616.07/9/05. **NLM** W1 HU448H. **CODEN** HUIMDQ. **[CCC]**. **Ad Acc**. **Pr Rev**. **Circ:** 650. available on microfilm and microfiche from University Microfilms International (UMI). Documents available from The Genuine Article, BIOSIS Document Express, CASDDS.
**Desc:** Devoted to an understanding of the ontogeny, mechanisms, regulation and control of immune responsiveness.
**Ind/Abst** Biol. Abstr.; Chem. Abstr.; Curr. Aware. Biol. Sci., CABS; Curr. Contents Life Sci.; EMBASE; Genet. Abstr.; Health Plan. Adminis.; Hum. Genome Abstr.; Immunol. Abstr.; Index Med.; Life Sci. Collect.; Protozoolog. Abstr.; Ref. Upd. Basic Ed.; Ref. Upd. Clinical Ed.; Ref. Upd. Deluxe Ed.; Res. Alert [Full Cov.]; Sci. Cit. Index; SCISEARCH.

US/0272-457X
**HYBRIDOMA.** [Hybridoma]. Vol. 1, No. 1 (1981)-. Academic Scholarly Publication. English. bm. $251.00. Mary Ann Liebert Inc., 1651 Third Avenue, New York NY 10128. **Tel** (212)289-2300, (800)M-LIEBERT, FAX (212)289-4697. **ED** Zenon Steplewski. **LC** QR185.8.H93; H9. **DD** 574.2/9. **NLM** W1 HY26. **CODEN** HYBRDY. **Bk Rev**. **Ad Acc**. **Pr Rev**. Documents available from The Genuine Article, CASDDS, Documents on Demand. ***Absorbed*** *Monoclonal Antibodies.*
**Desc:** Publishes papers in the fields of molecular immunology and experimental and clinical immunotherapy. Includes papers on the application of monoclonal antibodies for diagnostics and therapy and is a primary venue for original publications on the varied aspects of hybridoma research.
**Ind/Abst** AgBiotech News Inf.; AGRICOLA; Anim. Breed. Abstr.; Biotechnol. Res. Abstr.; Chem. Abstr.; CSA Neuro. Abstr. (?-?); Curr. Aware. Biol. Sci., CABS; Curr. Biotechnol.; Curr. Contents Life Sci.; EMBASE; Energy Inf. Abstr.; Environ. Abstr.; Genet. Abstr.; Health Plan. Adminis.; Helminthol. Abstr. (1991-); Immunol. Abstr.; Index Med.; Index Vet.; Nematol. Abstr.; Oncog. Growth Factors Abstr.; Life Sci. Collect.; PESTDOC; Poult. Abstr.; Protozoolog. Abstr.; Ref. Upd. Deluxe Ed.; Res. Alert [Full Cov.]; Sci. Cit. Index; SCISEARCH; Vet. Bull.; Trop. Dis. Bull.

UK/0887-7750
**IMMUNE INTERVENTION.** [Immune interv.]. Vol. 1-. Academic Scholarly Publication. English. Price varies per volume. Academic Press Ltd., A Division of Harcourt Brace & Company Ltd., 24-28 Oval Road, London NW1 7DX England. **Tel** 071 267 4466, FAX 071 482 2293, 071 485 4752, telex 25775 ACPRES G. **(Subscription address:** Harcourt Brace Jovanovich Limited, Footscray High Street, Sidcup, Kent DA14 5HP UK, (Phone: 081-300-3322)) **ED** I M Roitt. **DD** 616. **NLM** W1; IM458P. **CODEN** IMMIEO. Documents available from CASDDS.
**Ind/Abst** Chem. Abstr. (1984-).

GW/0340-1162
**IMMUNITAT UND INFEKTION.** [Immun. Infekt.]. Vol. 1 (Oct. 1973)-. Academic Scholarly Publication. German (summaries and/or abstracts in English). bm. DM99.00 Germany; DM108.00 other. Richard Pflaum Verlag Gmbh, Postfach 190737, D 80607 Munich Germany. **Tel** 011 49 89 126070, FAX 011 49 89 12607200, telex 5216075. **NLM** W1 IM46. **CODEN** IMINDI. **[CCC]**. **Pr Rev**. Documents available from The Genuine Article, BIOSIS Document Express, CASDDS.
**Ind/Abst** Biol. Abstr.; Chem. Abstr.; Curr. Contents Clin. Med.; EMBASE; Immunol. Abstr.; Index Med.; Life Sci. Collect.; Protozoolog. Abstr.; Res. Alert [Full Cov.]; Sci. Cit. Index; SCISEARCH; Soc. Sci. Cit. Index [Select. Cov.]; Trop. Dis. Bull.

●US/1074-7613
**IMMUNITY (CAMBRIDGE, MASS.).** (IMMUNITY.). [Immunity]. Vol. 1, No. 1 (Apr. 1994)-. Periodical. English. mo. $385.00 (institution) US; $445.00 (institution) other. Cell Press, 50 Church Street, Cambridge MA 02138. **Tel** (617)661-7060, FAX (617)661-7061. **DD** 574. **NLM** W1; IM4723.

UK/0262-8740
**IMMUNOASSAY. SUPPLEMENT.** [Immunoass., Suppl.]. **Added/Corp** University of Sheffield. Biomedical Information Service. (1980)-. Academic Scholarly Publication. English. Twenty-four times a year. £160.00 with Immunoassay (Annotations). SUBIS, Mansion House, 19 Kingfield Road, Sheffield S11 9AS England. **Tel** 011 44 114 255 4433, FAX 011 44 114 255 4626. **CODEN** ISUPDO. Documents available from CASDDS.
**Ind/Abst** Chem. Abstr.

GW/0930-9160
**IMMUNOASSAY TECHNOLOGY. *Ceased.*** [Immunoass. technol.]. Vol. 1 (1985)-Vol. 2 (19??). English. Walter de Gruyter Inc., PO Box 303421, D 10728 Berlin Germany. **Tel** 011 49 30 260050, FAX 011 49 30 26005251. **(Subscription address:** US and Canada/ 200 Saw Mill River Road, Hawthorne, NY 10532) **NLM** W1; IM449R. **CODEN** IMTCE7. Documents available from BIOSIS Document Express, CASDDS.
**Ind/Abst** Biol. Abstr. (1985-?); Chem. Abstr. (?-?).

GW/0171-2985
**IMMUNOBIOLOGY (1979).** (IMMUNOBIOLOGY.). [Immunobiology]. **VFOAT** Zeitschrift fur Immunitatsforschung. Vol. 156, (Aug. 1979)-. Academic Scholarly Publication. English. ir. DM896.00 Germany; DM916.00 other. Gustav Fischer Verlag Stuttgart, Postfach 720143, Wollgrasweg 49, D 70577 Stuttgart Germany. **Tel** 011 49 711 458030, FAX 0711-4580334, telex 2627-7111488. **(Subscription address:** VCH Publishers Inc., 303 Northwest 12th Avenue, Journals Department, Deerfield FL 33442.) **ED** D Gemsa. **LC** QR180; .Z44. **DD** 599/.02/9. **NLM** W1 IM483. **CODEN** IMMND4. **[CCC]**. **Bk Rev**. **Ad Acc**. **Pr Rev**. **Circ:** 650. Documents available from The Genuine Article, BIOSIS Document Express, CASDDS. ***Continues*** *Zeitschrift fur Immunitatsforschung. Immunobiology., 0340-904X.*
**Desc:** Publishes research findings that have fundamental importance as a link between researchers and clinicians active at the experimental levels of immunobiology, serology, hematology, allergy, infectious diseases, transplantations, as well as nonspecific resistance.
**Ind/Abst** AgBiotech News Inf.; AGRICOLA [Select. Cov.]; Anim. Breed. Abstr.; Biol. Abstr.; Chem. Abstr.; Curr. Aware. Biol. Sci., CABS; Curr. Contents Life Sci.; Dairy Sci. Abstr.; EMBASE; Energy Res. Abstr. (Nov. 1971-); Immunol. Abstr.; Index Med.; Index Vet.; Life Sci. Collect.; Protozoolog. Abstr.; Ref. Upd. Basic Ed.; Ref. Upd. Deluxe Ed.; Res. Alert [Full Cov.]; Rev. Med. Vet. Mycology; Sci. Cit. Index; SCISEARCH; Vet. Bull.; Trop. Dis. Bull.

UK/1067-795X
**IMMUNODEFICIENCY (CHUR, SWITZERLAND).** (IMMUNODEFICIENCY.). [Immunodefic.]. (Oct. 1993)-. Periodical. English. ir. Harwood Academic Publishers, PO Box 90, Reading RG1 8JL England. **Tel** 011 44 734 560080. **(Subscription address:** International Publishers Distributor at one of the following addresses: 820 Town Center Drive, Langhorne, PA 19047; or PO Box 90, Reading Berkshire RG1 8JL UK; or Kent Ridge PO Box 1180, Singapore 9111, Republic of Singapore) **DD** 616. **CODEN** IUNOEZ. ***Continues*** *Immunodeficiency Reviews, 0893-5300.*

UK/0893-5300
**IMMUNODEFICIENCY REVIEWS. *Title Change.*** [Immunodefic. rev.]. Vol. 1, No. 1 (1988)-(1994). Periodical. English. qt (1 volume). Harwood Academic Publishers, PO Box 90, Reading RG1 8JL England. **Tel** 011 44 734 560080. **(Subscription address:** International Publishers Distributor at one of the following addresses: 820 Town Center Drive, Langhorne, PA 19047; or PO Box 90, Reading Berkshire RG1 8JL UK; or Kent Ridge PO Box 1180, Singapore 9111, Republic of Singapore) **LC** QR188.35; .I45. **DD** 616.97/9/005. **NLM** W1; IM484I. **CODEN** IMMREH. **[CCC]**. Documents available from BIOSIS Document Express. ***Continued by*** *Immunmodeficiency, 1067-795X.*
**Ind/Abst** Biol. Abstr. (1990-); Curr. Aware. Biol. Sci., CABS; EMBASE; Health Plan. Adminis.; Index Med. (1988-).

US/0093-7711
**IMMUNOGENETICS (NEW YORK).** (IMMUNOGENETICS.). [Immunogenetics]. Vol. 1 (Feb. 1974)-. Periodical. English. Twelve times a year. DM1512.00. Springer-Verlag GmbH & Company KG, Heidelberger Platz 3, D 14197 Berlin Germany. **Tel** 011 49 30 8207223, FAX 011 49 30 8214091, telex 183 319 SPBLN D. **(Subscription address:** Springer Verlag New York Inc. / for North America, 44 Hartz Way, Secaucus NJ 07096.) **ED** J Klein and E Moeller. **LC** QR184; .I44. **DD** 574.2/9. **NLM** W1 IM485. **CODEN** IMNGBK. **[CCC]**. **Pr Rev**. available on microfilm and microfiche from University Microfilms International (UMI). Documents available from The Genuine Article, BIOSIS Document Express, CASDDS, Documents on Demand.
**Desc:** Covers such topics as immunogenetics of cell interaction, immunogenetics of tissue differentiation and development, phylogeny of alloantigens and immune response and genetics and biochemistry of alloantigens.
**Ind/Abst** AgBiotech News Inf.; AGRICOLA; Biol. Abstr.; Chem. Abstr.; Curr. Contents Life Sci.; EMBASE; Energy Inf. Abstr.; Environ. Abstr.; Genet. Abstr.; Hum. Genome Abstr.; Immunol. Abstr.; Index Med.; Nucl. Acids Abstr.; Life Sci. Collect.; PESTDOC; Protozoolog. Abstr.; Ref. Upd. Basic Ed.; Ref. Upd. Deluxe Ed.; Res. Alert [Full Cov.]; Sci. Cit. Index; SCISEARCH.

IT
**IMMUNOLOGIA CLINICA. *Ceased.*** Vol. 7, No. 1 (March 1988)-(Dec. 1993). Periodical. English (summaries and/or abstracts in Italian). qt. Masson SA, Avenue Beauregard 12, CH-1701 Fribourg Switzerland. **Tel** 011 41 37 249585, FAX 011 41 37 247559, telex 942658 SEMI CH. **NLM** W1; IM493. **CODEN** IMCLEH. Documents available from BIOSIS Document Express. ***Continues*** *Immunologia Clinica e Sperimentale, 0392-6702.*
**Ind/Abst** Biol. Abstr. (1988-); EMBASE.

PL/0324-8534
**IMMUNOLOGIA POLSKA.** [Immunol. pol.]. **Added/Corp** Polskie Towarzystwo Immunologiczne. (1976)-. Academic Scholarly Publication. Polish (summaries and/or abstracts in English). qt. $45.00. **(Subscription address:** ARS Polona, PO Box 1001, 00068 Warsaw Poland.) **LC** QR180; .I5335. **NLM** W1 IM495. **CODEN** IMPODM. Documents available from BIOSIS Document Express, CASDDS. ***Supersedes*** *Annals of Immunology, 0044-8338.*
**Ind/Abst** Biol. Abstr.; Chem. Abstr.; EMBASE; Energy Res. Abstr. (March 1983-).

SZ/0257-277X
**IMMUNOLOGIC RESEARCH.** [Immunol. res.]. Vol. 1 (1986)-. Academic Scholarly Publication. English. qt. $266.00. S. Karger AG, Allschwilerstrasse 10, PO Box - Postfach - Case Postale, CH-4009 Basel Switzerland. **Tel** 011 41 61 306-1111, FAX 011 41 61 306-1234, telex CH 962 652. **ED** J. M. Cruse and R. E. Lewis. **NLM** W1; IM498. **CODEN** IMRSEB. **[CCC]**. **Pr Rev**. available in microform. Documents available from The Genuine Article, BIOSIS Document Express, CASDDS. ***Continues*** *Survey of Immunologic Research, 0252-9564.*
**Desc:** Represents a unique publishing medium for the presentation, interpretation and clarification of complex scientific data in a novel format different from papers presented in the classical, orthodox style. The scope of the journal encompasses the immunologic subspecialties including cellular, molecular, genetic, and biochemical as well as clinical and pathological aspects of immunologic research. Other topics chosen for emphasis include transplantation, immunophysiology, and immunopharmacology.
**Ind/Abst** Anim. Breed. Abstr.; Biol. Abstr. (1986-); Chem. Abstr. (1986-); Curr. Aware. Biol. Sci., CABS; Curr. Contents Life Sci.; EMBASE; Index Med. (1986-); Ref.

Upd. Basic Ed.; Ref. Upd. Deluxe Ed.; Res. Alert [Full Cov.]; Rev. Med. Vet. Entomol.; Sci. Cit. Index; SCISEARCH.

US/1056-4896
**IMMUNOLOGICAL DISORDERS UPDATE.** ***Title Change.*** [Immunol. disord. update]. **VFOAT** I D Update. (April/June 1991)-(1992). Periodical. English. qt. F.J. Fontana, 1012 North Peak, #1, Dallas TX 75204. **DD** 616. ***Continued by*** *Clinical Immunology Digest, 1061-6969.*

US/0882-0139
**IMMUNOLOGICAL INVESTIGATIONS.** [Immunol. invest.]. Vol. 14, No. 1 (Feb. 1985)-. Academic Scholarly Publication. English. Six times a year. $635.00 US; $656.00 other. Marcel Dekker Inc., 270 Madison Avenue, New York NY 10016. **Tel** (212)696-9000, (800)228-1160, FAX (212)685-4540, telex 421419. **(Subscription address:** Marcel Dekker Inc, PO Box 5017, Monticello NY 12701.**) ED** Carel J. Van Oss. **LC** QR180; .I527. **DD** 616.07/9/05. **NLM** W1; IM5103. **CODEN** IMINEJ. **[CCC]. Pr Rev.** Documents available from The Genuine Article, BIOSIS Document Express, CASDDS. ***Continues*** *Immunological Communications, 0090-0877;* ***Absorbed*** *Clinical Immunology Reviews, 0277-9366.*
**Desc:** Disseminates immunological developments on a worldwide basis and encompasses all facets of fundamental and applied immunology, including immunohematology and the studies of allergies. This journal provides information presented in the form of original research articles and book reviews giving an in-depth examination of the latest advances in molecular and cellular immunology.
**Ind/Abst** AgBiotech News Inf.; Anim. Breed. Abstr.; Biol. Abstr. (1985-); Chem. Abstr. (1985-); Curr. Aware. Biol. Sci., CABS; Curr. Contents Life Sci.; EMBASE; Helminthol. Abstr. (1991-); Immunol. Abstr.; Index Med. (1985-); Index Vet.; Poult. Abstr.; Protozoolog. Abstr.; Ref. Upd. Deluxe Ed.; Res. Alert [Full Cov.]; Sci. Cit. Index; SCISEARCH; Vet. Bull.; Virol. AIDS Abstr.

DK/0105-2896
**IMMUNOLOGICAL REVIEWS.** [Immunol. rev.]. Vol. 33 (1977)-. Academic Scholarly Publication. English. bm. kr2160.00 US, Canada and Japan; kr2140.00 other. Munksgaard International Publishers Ltd, PO Box 2148, DK-1016 Copenhagen K Denmark. **Tel** 011 45 33 12 70 30, FAX 011 45 33 12 93 87, telex 19431 MUNKS DK. **ED** Goran Moller. **LC** UNC. **NLM** W1 IM512. **CODEN** IMRED2. **[CCC].** cum. index. **Ad Acc. Pr Rev. Circ:** 2,000 (ctrl). Documents available from The Genuine Article, BIOSIS Document Express, CASDDS, ADONIS. ***Continues*** *Transplantation Reviews, 0082-5948.*
**Desc:** Publishes invited reviews within the fields of clinical and experimental immunology.
**Ind/Abst** ADONIS; AgBiotech News Inf.; Biol. Abstr.; Chem. Abstr.; CSA Neuro. Abstr. (?-?); Curr. Contents Life Sci.; EMBASE; Genet. Abstr.; Helminthol. Abstr. (1991-); Immunol. Abstr.; Index Med.; Index Sci. Rev. [Full Cov.]; Life Sci. Collect.; Protozoolog. Abstr.; Res. Alert [Full Cov.]; Sci. Cit. Index; SCISEARCH.

FR/0755-0871
**IMMUNOLOGIE MEDICALE.** ***Title Change.*** No. 1 (1983)-(19??). Periodical. French. qt. Editions de l'Interligne, 47 rue de Charonne, 75011 Paris France. **Tel** 011 33 1 48068466. **NLM** W1; IM515. ***Merged into*** *Infectiologie Immunologie.*

UKU/0130-2019
**IMMUNOLOGIJA I ALLERGIJA.** (IMMUNOLOGIIA I ALLERGIIA.). **Added/Corp** Ukraine. Ministerstvo Okhorony Zdorovia. (1975)-. Periodical. Russian. **LC** QR180; .I5337. **NLM** W1 IM52K. Documents available from CASDDS. ***Formed by the union of*** *Immunologija, 0300-0567;* ***Allergija, 0303-5433 and*** *Vakciny i Syvorotki, 0301-1887.*
**Ind/Abst** Chem. Abstr.

RU/0206-4952
**IMMUNOLOGIJA (MOSKVA).** (IMMUNOLOGIIA.). [Immunologija]. **Added/Corp** Akademiia Meditsinskikh Nauk SSSR. (1980)-. Academic Scholarly Publication. Russian (summaries and/or abstracts in English). Six times a year. $129.95. Izdatelstvo Meditsina / Russian Academy of Medical Sciences, Ulitsa Solyanka 14, 109801 Moscow Russia. **Tel** 011 95 297-05-04. **(Subscription address:** East View Publications Inc., 3020 Harbor Lane North, Suite 110, Minneapolis MN 55447.**) NLM** W1 IM52B. **CODEN** IMUNDA. Documents available from BIOSIS Document Express, CASDDS.
**Ind/Abst** Biol. Abstr.; Chem. Abstr.; EMBASE.

●US/1192-5612
**IMMUNOLOGIST (TORONTO).** (THE IMMUNOLOGIST : OFFICIAL ORGAN OF THE INTERNATIONAL UNION OF IMMUNOLOGICAL SOCIETIES.). [Immunologist]. **Added/Corp** International Union of Immunological Societies. Vol. 1, No. 1 (Jan. 1993)-. Periodical. English. Six times a year. DM124.00 (institutions), DM107.00 (individuals). Hogrefe Verlag fuer Psychologie, Rohnsweg 25, D 37085 Goettingen Germany. **Tel** 011 49 551 496090, FAX 011 49 551 4960988. **(Subscription address:** Hogrefe & Huber Publishers, Seattle Office, Box 2487, Kirkland WA 98083.**) ED** J.B. Natvig. **DD** 616.07/9/05. **NLM** W1; IM524. **Circ:** 5,000.
**Desc:** Serves as a forum for all matters immunological. Provides an opportunity to communicate directly with researchers as well as a wide range of medical clinicians working in the fields where applied immunology is already beginning to make a difference.

UK/0019-2805
**IMMUNOLOGY.** [Immunology]. **Added/Corp** British Society for Immunology. Vol. 1 (Jan. 1958)-. Academic Scholarly Publication. English. mo (12 issues). $551.00 US & Canada; £323.00 Europe; £355.50 other. Blackwell Scientific Publications Ltd, Marston Book Services, PO Box 87, Oxford OX2 ODT UK. **Tel** 011 44 865 791155, FAX 011 44 865 791927, telex 837 515 MARDIS G. **ED** M. W. Steward. **LC** QR180; .I53. **DD** 615.3706242. **NLM** W1 IM53. **CODEN** IMMUAM. **[CCC].** Index available (bound in last issue). **Bk Rev. Ad Acc. Pr Rev. Circ:** 2,300. available on microfilm and microfiche from University Microfilms International (UMI). Documents available from The Genuine Article, BIOSIS Document Express, CASDDS, ADONIS.
**Desc:** Publishes work in all areas of immunology.
**Ind/Abst** ADONIS; AgBiotech News Inf.; AGRICOLA; Anim. Breed. Abstr.; Biol. Abstr.; Chem. Abstr.; CSA Neuro. Abstr. (?-?); Curr. Aware. Biol. Sci., CABS; Dairy Sci. Abstr.; EMBASE; Food Sci. Technol. Abstr.; Genet. Abstr.; Health Plan. Adminis.; Helminthol. Abstr. (19??-19??); Immunol. Abstr.; Index Med.; Microbiol. Abstr. Sect. B; Microbiol. Abstr. Sect. C; NAPRALERT; Nutr. Abstr. Rev., Ser. B, Live Feeds and Feed.; Nutr. Abstr. Rev., Ser. A, Hum. Exp.; Nutr. Res. Newsl.; Oncog. Growth Factors Abstr.; Life Sci. Collect.; PESTDOC; Pig News Inf.; Poult. Abstr.; Protozoolog. Abstr.; Ref. Upd. Basic Ed.; Ref. Upd. Deluxe Ed.; Res. Alert [Full Cov.]; Rev. Med. Vet. Entomol.; Rev. Med. Vet. Mycology; Sci. Cit. Index; SCISEARCH; Trop. Dis. Bull.; Virol. AIDS Abstr.

US/0307-112X
**IMMUNOLOGY ABSTRACTS. See** Medical Science and Technology-Abstracting, Bibliographies and Statistics.

US/0889-8561
**IMMUNOLOGY AND ALLERGY CLINICS OF NORTH AMERICA.** [Immunol. allergy clin. North Am.]. Vol. 7, No. 1 (April 1987)-. Academic Scholarly Publication. English. qt. $89.00 (individuals), $111.00 (institutions) US; $124.00 (institutions), $131.00 (individuals) other. W.B. Saunders Company, A Subsidiary of Harcourt Brace Jovanovich, Inc., The Curtis Center/Suite 300, Independence Square West, Philadelphia PA 19106-3399. **Tel** (215)238-7800 or, 5587, FAX (215)238-7883, telex 173146. **(Subscription address:** W. B. Saunders Company / North America Subscriptions, c/o Periodicals, 6277 Sea Harbour Drive, 4th Floor, Orlando FL 32887.**) ED** Barbara Conover. **DD** 616. **NLM** W1; IM533. **[CCC].** Index available. **Pr Rev. Circ:** 600. available on microfilm and microfiche from University Microfilms International (UMI). Documents available from The Genuine Article, CASDDS. ***Continues in part*** *Clinics in Immunology and Allergy, 0260-4639.*
**Desc:** Contains practical updates for the clinician on the latest advances. Each issue addresses a single topic in patient care.
**Ind/Abst** Chem. Abstr. (April 1987-); Curr. Contents Life Sci.; EMBASE; Res. Alert [Full Cov.]; Sci. Cit. Index; SCISEARCH; Soc. Sci. Cit. Index [Select. Cov.].

US/0194-7508
**IMMUNOLOGY & ALLERGY PRACTICE.** ***Ceased.*** [Immunol. allergy pract.]. **Added/Corp** American Association for Clinical Immunology and Allergy. **VAT** Immunology and Allergy Practice. Vol. 1 (Mar./Apr. 1979)-Vol. 16 (1994). Periodical. English. mo. Macor Publishing Company, 116 West 32nd Street/8th Floor, New York NY 10001. **Tel** (212)736-6688, FAX (212)564-1763. **ED** Sidney Friedlaender. **LC** RC581; .I44. **DD** 616.9/7/005. **NLM** W1 IM53B. **[CCC]. Bk Rev. Ad Acc. Circ:** 19,000 (ctrl).
**Desc:** Original, review and state-of-the art articles covering important aspects of clinical immunology and allergy.
**Ind/Abst** EMBASE.

AT/0818-9641
**IMMUNOLOGY AND CELL BIOLOGY.** [Immunol. cell biol.]. **Added/Corp** University of Adelaide. Australian Society for Immunology. Vol. 65, Pt. 1 (Feb. 1987)-. Academic Scholarly Publication. English. Six times a year. 286.00Aus$ Australia; 369.00Aus$ Australia. Blackwell Scientific Publications Australia, 54 University Street, PO Box 378, Carlton Victoria 3053 Australia. **Tel** 011 61 3 3470300, FAX 011 61 3 3475001, telex 10716421. **(Subscription address:** UK/ Marston Book Services, PO Box 87, Oxford UK; US/ 3 Cambridge Center, Suite 208, Cambridge MA 02142; Germany/ Meinekestrasse 4, D-1000 Berlin 15 Germany; France/ Arnette, 2 rue Casimir Delavigne, 75006 Paris France; Austria/ Blackwell MZV, Medizinische Zeitschriftenverlags Gesellschaft, Feldgasse 13, A-1238 Vienna Austria) **ED** I. Kotlarski. **LC** QH301; .A8. **DD** 616.07/9. **NLM** W1; IM53BF. **CODEN** ICBIEZ. **[CCC].** Index available. cum. index. **Pr Rev. Circ:** 1,100. available on microfilm and microfiche from University Microfilms International (UMI). Documents available from The Genuine Article, BIOSIS Document Express, CASDDS, ADONIS. ***Continues*** *Australian Journal of Experimental Biology and Medical Science, 0004-945X.*
**Desc:** Publishes original works on research or concepts of immunology and cell biology.
**Ind/Abst** ADONIS; AGRICOLA [Select. Cov.]; Biol. Abstr. (1987-); Chem. Abstr.; Curr. Aware. Biol. Sci., CABS; Curr. Biotechnol.; Curr. Contents Life Sci.; Dairy Sci. Abstr.; EMBASE; Health Plan. Adminis.; Helminthol. Abstr. (1991-); Index Med. (1987-); Index Vet.; Protozoolog. Abstr.; Ref. Upd. Deluxe Ed.; Res. Alert [Full Cov.]; Rev. Agric. Entomol.; Rev. Med. Vet. Entomol.; Rev. Med. Vet. Mycology; Sci. Cit. Index; SCISEARCH; Vet. Bull.; Trop. Dis. Bull.

UK/0959-4957
**IMMUNOLOGY AND INFECTIOUS DISEASES.** **VFOAT** Immunology and Infectious Diseases. Vol. 1, No. 1 (Dec. 1990)-. Periodical. English. Four times a year. $425.00 US; £250.00 other. Rapid Communications of Oxford Ltd, The Old Malthouse, Paradise Street, Oxford OX1 1LD England. **Tel** 011 44 0865 790447, FAX 011 44 0865 244012, telex 9403712. **(Subscription address:** Rapid Communications of Oxford Ltd, ITPS, Cheriton House, North Way, Andover Mants SP10 5BE UK**) ED** R.K. Chandra. **NLM** W1; IM53BGL. **CODEN** IINDEK. **[CCC].** Index available. cum. index. **Bk Rev. Ad Acc. Pr Rev. Acid Free.**
**Desc:** Scope includes immunoregulation, immunochemistry and virulence factors.
**Ind/Abst** Curr. Aware. Biol. Sci., CABS; Immunol. Abstr.; Index Vet.; Nutr. Abstr. Rev., Ser. A, Hum. Exp.; Pig News Inf.; Vet. Bull.

NE/0165-2478
**IMMUNOLOGY LETTERS.** [Immunol. lett.]. Vol. 1 (July 1979)-. Academic Scholarly Publication. English. Fifteen times a year (5 volumes). Fl2600.00. Elsevier Science Publishers BV, PO Box 211, 1000 AE Amsterdam Netherlands. **Tel** 011 31 20 5803642, FAX 011 31 20 5862696, telex 15682. **ED** P Perlmann, H von Boehmer, L Brent, A Bussard, B Cinader, J Gergely, M W Hess, T Honjo, E Klein, M Kronenberg, I Pecht, K Shortman and C Terhorst. **NLM** W1 IM53D. **CODEN** IMLED6. **[CCC]. Pr Rev.** available on microfilm and microfiche from University Microfilms International (UMI). Documents available from The Genuine Article, BIOSIS Document Express, CASDDS, Documents on Demand, ADONIS.
**Desc:** Provides a vehicle for the rapid publication of short, complete and definitive reports, minireviews and letters to the editor covering all aspects of immunology.
**Ind/Abst** ADONIS; AgBiotech News Inf.; Anim. Breed. Abstr.; Biol. Abstr.; Chem. Abstr.; CSA Neuro. Abstr. (?-?); Curr. Aware. Biol. Sci., CABS; Curr. Biotechnol.; Curr. Contents Life Sci.; EMBASE; Energy Inf. Abstr.; Environ. Abstr.; Genet. Abstr.; Helminthol. Abstr. (1991-); Immunol. Abstr.; Index Med.; Index Vet.; Microbiol. Abstr. Sect. B (19??-19??); Microbiol. Abstr. Sect. C; Life Sci. Collect.; Postharvest News Inf.; Poult. Abstr.; Protozoolog. Abstr.; Ref. Upd. Basic Ed.; Ref. Upd. Deluxe Ed.; Res. Alert [Full Cov.]; Rev. Agric. Entomol.; Rev. Med. Vet. Entomol.; Rev. Med. Vet. Mycology; Sci. Cit. Index; SCISEARCH; Vet. Bull.; Virol. AIDS Abstr.

US/0092-6019
**IMMUNOLOGY SERIES.** [Immunol. ser.]. Vol. 1 (1973)-. Monographic series. English. ir. Price varies per volume. Marcel Dekker Inc., 270 Madison Avenue, New York NY 10016. **Tel** (212)696-9000, (800)228-1160, FAX (212)685-4540, telex 421419. **(Subscription address:** Marcel Dekker Inc, PO Box 5017, Monticello NY 12701.**) ED** N. Rose. **LC** UNC. **NLM** W1 IM53K. **CODEN** IMSED7. **[CCC].** Documents available from CASDDS.
**Desc:** This is an ongoing series. Each title has a different subject.
**Ind/Abst** Chem. Abstr.; Health Plan. Adminis.; Life Sci. Collect.

UK
**IMMUNOLOGY. SUPPLEMENT.** Vol. 1 (1988)-. Monographic series. English. ir. Price varies per volume. Blackwell Scientific Publications Ltd, Marston Book Services, PO Box 87, Oxford OX2 ODT UK. **Tel** 011 44 865 791155, FAX 011 44 865 791927, telex 837 515 MARDIS G.
**Ind/Abst** Index Med. (1988-).

UK/0167-5699
**IMMUNOLOGY TODAY (AMSTERDAM. REGULAR ED.).** (IMMUNOLOGY TODAY.). [Immunol. today]. **VFOAT** IT. Vol. 1 (July 1980)-. Academic Scholarly Publication. English. Twelve times a year (plus compendium and index). $514.00 The Americas; £345.00 other. Elsevier Trends Journals, An Imprint of Elsevier Science Ltd., The Boulevard, Langford Lane, Kidlington, Oxford OX5 1GB United Kingdom. **Tel** 011 44 865 843000, 011 44 865 843699, FAX 011 44 865 843010. **(Subscription address:** Elsevier Science Ltd. Oxford Fulfillment Centre, PO Box 800, Kidlington, Oxford OX5 1DX United Kingdom.**) ED** John R. Inglis. **NLM** W1 IM53P. **CODEN** IMTOD8. **[CCC]. Bk Rev. Ad Acc. Circ:** 6,200. available on microfilm from University Microfilms International (UMI). Documents available from The Genuine Article, BIOSIS Document Express, CASDDS, ADONIS.
**Desc:** Provides critical synthesis of what is new and exciting in all branches of basic and applied immunology.
**Ind/Abst** Abstr. BioCommer.; ADONIS; AgBiotech News Inf.; Anim. Breed. Abstr.; Biol. Abstr.; Chem. Abstr.; CSA Neuro. Abstr. (?-?); Curr. Aware. Biol. Sci., CABS; Curr.

Contents Life Sci.; Dairy Sci. Abstr.; EMBASE; Genet. Abstr.; Health Plan. Adminis.; Immunol. Abstr.; Index Med. (1988-); Index Vet.; Life Sci. Collect.; Plant Breed. Abstr.; Protozoolog. Abstr.; Ref. Upd. Basic Ed.; Ref. Upd. Clinical Ed.; Ref. Upd. Deluxe Ed.; Res. Alert [Full Cov.]; Sci. Cit. Index; SCISEARCH; Soc. Sci. Cit. Index [Select. Cov.]; Vet. Bull.; Trop. Dis. Bull.; Virol. AIDS Abstr.

US/0271-3284
**IMMUNOLOGY TRIBUNE.** ***Ceased.*** [Immunol. trib.]. Vol. 1 (Feb. 1979)-?. Periodical. English. mo. MDT Publications, PO Box 581, Sheffield MA 01257. **Tel** (713)668-6700. **ED** M D Tatkon and J Goodman. **NLM** W1 IM53T. **Bk Rev.**

●US/1058-6687
**IMMUNOMETHODS (SAN DIEGO, CALIF.).** (IMMUNOMETHODS.). [ImmunoMethods]. **VFOAT** Immuno Methods. Vol. 1, No. 1 (Aug. 1992)-. Academic Scholarly Publication. English. bm. $148.00 US and Canada. Academic Press, Inc., 6277 Sea Harbor Drive, Orlando FL 32887. **Tel** (800)543-9534, (407)345-4100, FAX (407)363-9661. **ED** John J. Langone. **DD** 616. **CODEN** IMUME8. **[CCC].** Documents available from CASDDS.
**Desc:** Provides focused, detailed, and authoritative reports on immunological techniques and procedures. Encompasses humoral and cellular immunity and biological mediators that can affect the integrity and function of the immune system. Includes both endogenous substances and environmental agents.
**Ind/Abst** Chem. Abstr.

US
**IMMUNOPATHOLOGY IMMUNOTHERAPY FORUM.** (1988)-. Periodical. English. bm. $40.00. World Medical Communications Organizations, 7 Ridgedale Avenue, Cedar Knolls NJ 07927. **Tel** (201)455-1121. **NLM** W1; IM53V. ***Continues*** *Immunopathology Immunotherapy Letter, 0882-5262.*

US/0162-3109
**IMMUNOPHARMACOLOGY.** [Immunopharmacology]. Vol. 1, (Dec. 1978)-. Academic Scholarly Publication. English. Nine times a year (3 vols.). Fl1506.00. Elsevier Science Publishers BV, PO Box 211, 1000 AE Amsterdam Netherlands. **Tel** 011 31 20 5803642, FAX 011 31 20 5862696, telex 15682. **ED** J R Battisto. **NLM** W1 IM56. **CODEN** IMMUDP. **[CCC]. Bk Rev. Ad Acc. Pr Rev.** ctrl circ. available on microfilm and microfiche from University Microfilms International (UMI). Documents available from The Genuine Article, BIOSIS Document Express, CASDDS, ADONIS.
**Desc:** Provides a medium for the publication of investigations pertaining to immunology, pharmacology and toxicology. Interface between disciplines of immunology and pharmacology.
**Ind/Abst** ADONIS; Biol. Abstr.; Chem. Abstr.; Chem. Titles; Curr. Aware. Biol. Sci., CABS; Curr. Contents Life Sci.; EMBASE; Immunol. Abstr.; Index Med.; Index Vet.; NAPRALERT; Life Sci. Collect.; PESTDOC; Ref. Upd. Deluxe Ed.; Res. Alert [Full Cov.]; Rev. Med. Vet. Mycology; Sci. Cit. Index; SCISEARCH; Vet. Bull.

US/0892-3973
**IMMUNOPHARMACOLOGY AND IMMUNOTOXICOLOGY.** [Immunopharmacol. immunotoxicol.]. Vol. 9, No. 1 (Mar. 1987)-. Periodical. English. qt. $475.00 US; $489.00 other. Marcel Dekker Inc., 270 Madison Avenue, New York NY 10016. **Tel** (212)696-9000, (800)228-1160, FAX (212)685-4540, telex 421419. **(Subscription address:** Marcel Dekker Inc, PO Box 5017, Monticello NY 12701.**) ED** Michael A. Chirigos, Gloria H. Heppner, Ronald B. Herberman and Jacques Descotes. **DD** 615. **NLM** W1; IM566. **CODEN** IITOEF. **[CCC]. Pr Rev.** available in microform. Documents available from The Genuine Article, BIOSIS Document Express, CASDDS, ADONIS. ***Continues*** *Journal of Immunopharmacology, 0163-0571.*
**Desc:** For the numerous researchers who need to know more about the mechanisms by which immune systems carry out their various functions, this journal provides a current, comprehensive resource. Offers readers an interdisciplinary approach to subjects - integrating pharmacology and toxicology with immunology. It presents original scientific papers, brief communications, reviews, and research and clinical studies using immunomodifying agents for cancer, immunodeficiency disorders, chronic infections, allergies, and inflammatory disorders.
**Ind/Abst** ADONIS; Biol. Abstr. (1987-); Chem. Abstr.; Curr. Aware. Biol. Sci., CABS; Curr. Contents Life Sci.; EMBASE; Helminthol. Abstr. (1991-); Index Med. (1987-); PESTDOC; Ref. Upd. Deluxe Ed.; Res. Alert [Full Cov.]; Rev. Med. Vet. Mycology; Sci. Cit. Index; SCISEARCH.

US
**IMMUNOPHARMACOLOGY REVIEWS.** (1990)-. Monographic series. English. ir. Price varies per volume. Plenum Press, 233 Spring Street, New York NY 10013-1578. **Tel** (212)620-8000, (800)221-9369, FAX (212)463-0742, (212)807-1047, telex 23/421139. **ED** John W. Hadden and Andor Szentivanyi. **LC** RM370; .I465. **DD** 615/.37. **CODEN** IMNREM. Documents available from BIOSIS Document Express, CASDDS.
**Ind/Abst** Biol. Abstr.; Chem. Abstr.

NE/1380-2933
**IMMUNOTECHNOLOGY.** (1995)-. Academic Scholarly Publication. English. Four times a year (1 volume). Fl419.00. Elsevier Science Publishers BV, PO Box 211, 1000 AE Amsterdam Netherlands. **Tel** 011 31 20 5803642, FAX 011 31 20 5862696, telex 15682.

US
**IMMUNOTHERAPY AND CLINICAL CANCER IMMUNOLOGY. Main/Corp** International Cancer Research Data Bank. Periodical. English. US Department of Health and Human Services National Institutes of Health, 9000 Rockville Pike, Bethesda MD 20892. **Tel** (301)496-9291, FAX (301)496-2443.

US/0019-9567
**INFECTION AND IMMUNITY. See** Biology-Microbiology.

US/0739-7348
**INFECTIOUS DISEASE ALERT.** (INFECTIOUS DISEASE ALERT / WG&L.). [Infect. dis. alert]. Vol. 1, No. 1 (Oct. 1, 1981)-. Periodical. English. sm. $116.00. American Health Consultants, 3525 Piedmont Road, Suite 400, Atlanta GA 30305. **Tel** (800)688-2421, (404)262-7436. **(Subscription address:** American Health Consultants, PO Box 95278, Chicago IL 60694.**) ED** Jeffrey E Galpin, Lawrence A May. **DD** 616. **NLM** W1 IN406HM. **[CCC].** Index available. **Ad Acc. Circ:** 3,500.
**Desc:** An update of current developments in infections disease and immunology.

US/1078-2850
**INFECTIOUS DISEASE WEEKLY.** (19??)-. English. wk (48 issues). $995.00 US, Canada and Mexico; $1195.00 other. CW Henderson, PO Box 5528, Atlanta GA 30307-0528. **Tel** (404)377-8895, FAX (404)378-5411. **(Subscription address:** CW Henderson, Subscription Office, PO Box 830409, Birmingham AL 35283-0409.**)**
**Desc:** Features worldwide research breakthroughs, original reporting, abstracts from conference proceedings, and highlights from relevant journals. Topics include the latest in prevention, diagnosis and treatment common and uncommon infectious diseases; government action and programs and hospital policies.

SP/0212-3800
**INFECTOLOGIKA.** [Infectologika]. V. 4, No. 1 (Jan./Feb. 1983)-. Periodical. Spanish. bm. Alpe Editores SA, C Pedro Rico 27 Oficinas 11 & 12, 28029 Madrid Spain. **Tel** 011 34 7338811. **NLM** W1; IN406W. **CODEN** INFEEI. Documents available from BIOSIS Document Express. ***Continues*** *Immunologika.*
**Ind/Abst** Biol. Abstr. (1985-).

SP/0213-9626
**INMUNOLOGIA (1987).** (INMUNOLOGIA.). [Inmunologia]. Vol. 6, No. 1 (Jan./Mar. 1987)-. Periodical. Spanish (English). Four times a year. $39.00. Ediciones Doyma SA, Travesera de Gracia 17 21, 08021 Barcelona Spain. **Tel** 011 34 3 2000711, 011 34 3 4145706, FAX 011 34 3 2091136, telex 51964 INK E. **ED** D. Jordi Vives Puiggros. **NLM** W1; IN454F. **CODEN** INMNEC. **Circ:** 3,000. Documents available from CASDDS. ***Continues*** *Revista Doyma de Inmunologia.*
**Desc:** Exclusive spokes-piece of the research and clinical training in immunology.
**Ind/Abst** Chem. Abstr.; Indice Med. Esp.; Sci. Cit. Index (19??-19??); SCISEARCH.

CN/1187-5674
**INTER-VIH.** [Inter-VIH]. **Added/Corp** Centre Hospitalier de Verdun. Departement de Sante Communautaire. **VAT** Inter-Virus de l'Immunodeficience Humaine. Vol. 1, No 1 (July 1991)-. Periodical. French. Limited free distribution. DSC Verdun, 4000 Boulevard Lasalle, Verdun Quebec H4G 2A3 Canada. **DD** 616.97/92/005.

●SZ/1018-2438
**INTERNATIONAL ARCHIVES OF ALLERGY AND IMMUNOLOGY.** (1992)-. Periodical. English. mo. $1383.00. S. Karger AG, Allschwilerstrasse 10, PO Box - Postfach - Case Postale, CH-4009 Basel Switzerland. **Tel** 011 41 61 306-1111, FAX 011 41 61 306-1234, telex CH 962 652. **ED** G. Wick. **NLM** W1; IN7042. **[CCC].** Documents available from The Genuine Article, BIOSIS Document Express. ***Continues*** *International Archives of Allergy and Applied Immunology, 0020-5915.*
**Desc:** Provides an important forum for all areas of modern immunology. The journal bridges the gap between basic and clinical aspects of immunology and publishes work in the fields of clinical immunology, allergy, immunopathology and transplantation, cellular immunology, immunogenetics, molecular biology, immunopharmacology and immunoendocrinology, mucosal immunity, phylogeny, ontogeny and aging, immunology of infectious and connective tissue diseases.
**Ind/Abst** Biol. Abstr.; Curr. Aware. Biol. Sci., CABS; Index Med.; Ref. Upd. Basic Ed.; Ref. Upd. Deluxe Ed.; Res. Alert [Full Cov.]; Sci. Cit. Index; SCISEARCH.

SZ/0074-4220
**INTERNATIONAL CONVOCATION ON IMMUNOLOGY. [PROCEEDINGS].** ***Ceased.*** 1st (1968)-Series complete with 9th Convocation. English. ir. S. Karger AG, Allschwilerstrasse 10, PO Box - Postfach - Case Postale, CH-4009 Basel Switzerland. **Tel** 011 41 61 306-1111, FAX 011 41 61 306-1234, telex CH 962 652. **[CCC].**

UK/0953-8178
**INTERNATIONAL IMMUNOLOGY.** [Int. immunol.]. Vol. 1, No. 1 (1989)-. Periodical. English. mo. £295.00 UK and Europe; $495.00 other. Oxford University Press, Walton Street, Oxford OX2 6DP England. **Tel** 011 44 865 56767, FAX 011 44 865 267773, telex 837330 OXPRES G. **(Subscription address:** Oxford University Press / USA, Journals Marketing Department, Oxford University Press, 2001 Evans Road, Cary NC 27513.**) NLM** W1; IN7652BR. **CODEN** INIMEN. **[CCC].** available on microfilm and microfiche from University Microfilms International (UMI). Documents available from The Genuine Article, BIOSIS Document Express, ADONIS.
**Ind/Abst** ADONIS; AgBiotech News Inf.; Anim. Breed. Abstr.; Biol. Abstr.; Curr. Aware. Biol. Sci., CABS; Curr. Contents Life Sci.; EMBASE; Genet. Abstr.; Health Plan. Adminis.; Immunol. Abstr.; Index Vet.; Oncog. Growth Factors Abstr.; Protozoolog. Abstr.; Res. Alert [Full Cov.]; Rev. Agric. Entomol.; Rev. Med. Vet. Entomol.; Sci. Cit. Index; SCISEARCH; Vet. Bull.; Trop. Dis. Bull.

IT/0394-6320
**INTERNATIONAL JOURNAL OF IMMUNOPATHOLOGY AND PHARMACOLOGY.** [Int. j. immunopathol. pharmacol.]. **VFOAT** IJIPP. (198?)-. Periodical. English. Three times a year. L190000 Italy; $190.00 other. Cattedra Immunologia Conti., Universita Via Vestini, 66100 Chieti Italy. **Tel** 39 871 355293, FAX 39 871 561635. **NLM** W1; IN768JF. **CODEN** IJIPE4. **Ad Acc.** Documents available from The Genuine Article, BIOSIS Document Express.
**Ind/Abst** Biol. Abstr. (1991-); Curr. Aware. Biol. Sci., CABS; Curr. Contents Life Sci.; EMBASE; Res. Alert [Full Cov.]; Sci. Cit. Index; SCISEARCH.

SZ/0255-9625
**INTERNATIONAL JOURNAL OF IMMUNOTHERAPY.** [Int. j. immunother.]. **VFOAT** Immunotherapy. Vol. 1, No. 1 (1985)-. Periodical. English. qt. 260.00F Europe; 265.00F other. Bioscience Ediprint Inc, rue Alexandre Gavard 16, 1227 Carouge Geneva Switzerland. **Tel** 011 41 22 3003383. **NLM** W1; IN768M. **CODEN** IJIMET. **[CCC]. Pr Rev.** available on microfilm from University Microfilms International (UMI). Documents available from The Genuine Article, BIOSIS Document Express, CASDDS.
**Ind/Abst** Biol. Abstr. (1985-); Chem. Abstr. (1985-); Curr. Aware. Biol. Sci., CABS; Curr. Contents Life Sci.; Dairy Sci. Abstr.; EMBASE; Immunol. Abstr.; Int. Pharm. Abstr.; PESTDOC; Res. Alert [Full Cov.]; Sci. Cit. Index; SCISEARCH.

UK/0956-4624
**INTERNATIONAL JOURNAL OF STD & AIDS. Added/Corp** Royal Society of Medicine Services (Great Britain). **VFOAT** International Journal of STD and AIDS. **VAT** International Journal of Sexually Transmitted Diseases & Acquired Immunodificiency Syndrome. Vol. 1, No. 1 (Jan. 1990)-. Periodical. English. bm. $172.00 (institution), $128.00 (individual) US; £98.00 (institution), £72.00 (individual) other. Royal Society of Medicine Press, 1 Wimpole Street, London W1M 8AE England. **Tel** 011 44 71 2902928. **LC** RC201.A1; I7. **DD** 616.95/1/005. **NLM** W1; IN791F. **CODEN** INSAE3. **[CCC]. Pr Rev.** Documents available from The Genuine Article, ADONIS.
**Desc:** Publishes clinically oriented papers on the investigation and treatment of both the "traditional" sexually transmitted diseases (STD) and AIDS/HIV.
**Ind/Abst** ADONIS; Curr. Aware. Biol. Sci., CABS; Curr. Contents Clin. Med.; EMBASE; Health Plan. Adminis.; Res. Alert [Select. Cov.]; Soc. Sci. Cit. Index [Select. Cov.]; Trop. Dis. Bull.

SZ/0883-0185
**INTERNATIONAL REVIEWS OF IMMUNOLOGY.** [Int. rev. immunol.]. Vol. 1, No. 1 (1986)-. Periodical. English. Fifty times a year. Price varies. Harwood Academic Publishers, PO Box 90, Reading RG1 8JL England. **Tel** 011 44 734 560080. **(Subscription address:** Harwood Academic Publishers, PO Box 786, Cooper Station, New York NY 10276.**) ED** Heinz Kohler and Constantin Bona. **DD** 616. **NLM** W1; IN835DL. **CODEN** IRIMEH. **[CCC].** Documents available from BIOSIS Document Express.
**Desc:** Covers the whole of immunology -- research, progress, debate and discovery, and brings recent research and comment from around the world to a single source.
**Ind/Abst** Biol. Abstr.; Curr. Aware. Biol. Sci., CABS; Index Med.

US/0894-3745
**ISI ATLAS OF SCIENCE. IMMUNOLOGY.** [ISI atlas of science, Immunol.]. **Added/Corp** Institute for Scientific Information. **VFOAT** Atlas of Science. Immunology. **VAT** Institute for Scientific Information Atlas

of Science. Immunology. Vol. No. 1, Issue No. 1 (1988)-. Academic Scholarly Publication. English. qt. $95.00 individuals, $295.00 libraries. Institute for Scientific Information, 3501 Market Street, Philadelphia PA 19104. **Tel** (215)386-0100, (800)523-1850, FAX (215)386-6362, telex 84-5305. **(Subscription address:** Institute for Scientific Information, PO Box 71416, Chicago, IL 60694**)** **LC** QR180; .I83. **DD** 574.2/9/05. **NLM** W1; IS405W. **CODEN** IASIE4. **[CCC].** Documents available from BIOSIS Document Express. ***Continues in part*** *ISI Atlas of Science, 0278-2898.*
**Ind/Abst** Biol. Abstr. (1988-).

US
## ISSUES (AIDS PROJECT LOS ANGELES).
(ISSUES.). English. qt. AIDS Project Los Angeles, 6721 Romaine Street, Los Angeles CA 90038-2425. **Tel** (213)962-1600 ext. 534.

US/0894-9255
## JOURNAL OF ACQUIRED IMMUNE DEFICIENCY SYNDROMES. *Title Change.*
[J. acquir. immune defic. syndr.]. Vol. 1, No. 1 (1988)-(199?). Periodical. English. Fifteen times a year (3 vols. of 5 issues each). Raven Press, 1185 Avenue of the Americas, 37th Floor, New York NY 10036. **Tel** (212)930-9500, (212)930-9604, FAX (212)869-3495, (212)302-8507, telex 640073. **ED** William A. Haseltine, Paul A. Volberding, and William A. Blattner. **LC** RC607.A26; J68. **DD** 616.97/92/005. **NLM** W1; JO533PS. **CODEN** JAISET. **[CCC]. Pr Rev.** available on microfilm and microfiche from University Microfilms International (UMI). Documents available from The Genuine Article, BIOSIS Document Express, CASDDS. ***Continued by*** *Journal of Acquired Immune Deficiency Syndromes and Human Retrovirology.*
**Desc:** Provides a synthesis of AIDS-related information from all relevant clinical and basic sciences. Guided by an eminent international editorial board, JAIDS combines peer-reviewed original articles on vital topics in the field. Included are reviews of current research, results of clinical trials, case reports, and discussions of national policy issues.
**Ind/Abst** Biol. Abstr. (1988-); Chem. Abstr.; Curr. Aware. Biol. Sci., CABS; Curr. Contents Life Sci.; EMBASE; Health Period. Database; Health Ref. Cent. (Jan. 1989-) [Full Cov.]; Immunol. Abstr.; Index Med. (1988-); Index Vet.; Protozoolog. Abstr.; Res. Alert [Full Cov.]; Rev. Med. Vet. Mycology; Risk Abstr.; Sci. Cit. Index; SCISEARCH; Small Anim. Abstr. Bibliogr.; Soc. Sci. Cit. Index [Select. Cov.]; Vet. Bull.; Trop. Dis. Bull.

US
## JOURNAL OF ACQUIRED IMMUNE DEFICIENCY SYNDROMES AND RETROVIROLOGY.
(199?)-. Periodical. English. Fifteen times a year (3 vols. of 5 issues each). $401.00 (institutions), $168.00 (individuals) US; $451.00 (institutions), $225.00 (individuals) other. Raven Press, 1185 Avenue of the Americas, 37th Floor, New York NY 10036. **Tel** (212)930-9500, (212)930-9604, FAX (212)869-3495, (212)302-8507, telex 640073. ***Continues*** *Journal of Acquired Immune Deficiency Syndromes, 0894-9255.*
**Desc:** Provides a synthesis of AIDS-related information from all relevant clinical and basic sciences. Included are reviews of current research, results of clinical trials, case reports, and discussions of national policy issues.

US/0091-6749
## JOURNAL OF ALLERGY AND CLINICAL IMMUNOLOGY.
(THE JOURNAL OF ALLERGY AND CLINICAL IMMUNOLOGY : OFFICIAL ORGAN OF AMERICAN ACADEMY OF ALLERGY.). [J. allergy clin. immunol.]. **Added/Corp** American Academy of Allergy. Vol. 48, (July 1971)-. Academic Scholarly Publication. English. mo. $199.00 (institutions), $102.00 (individuals) US; $231.00 (institutions), $134.00 (individuals) other. Mosby Year Book Inc., 11830 Westline Industrial Drive, St Louis MO 63146. **Tel** (800)325-4177, (314)872-8370, FAX (314)432-1380, telex 44-2402. **ED** Burton Zweiman. **NLM** W1 JO534S. **CODEN** JACIBY. **[CCC].** Index available. cum. index. **Ad Acc. Circ:** 7,990. available on microfilm and microfiche from University Microfilms International (UMI). Documents available from The Genuine Article, BIOSIS Document Express, CASDDS, ADONIS. ***Continues*** *Journal of Allergy, 0021-8707.*
**Desc:** Serves the clinical allergist and immunologist, and dermatologists, internists, general practitioners, pediatricians, and otolaryngologists concerned with clinical manifestations of allergies in their practice.
**Ind/Abst** Abr. Index Med.; ADONIS; AGRICOLA [Select. Cov.]; Biol. Abstr.; Biol. Dig.; Chem. Abstr.; Curr. Aware. Biol. Sci., CABS; Curr. Contents Clin. Med.; Curr. Contents Life Sci.; Dairy Sci. Abstr.; EMBASE; Energy Res. Abstr. (Nov. 1971-); Entomol. Abstr.; For. Prod. Abstr.; Helminthol. Abstr. (19??-19??); Immunol. Abstr.; Index Med.; Iowa Drug Inf. Serv.; Maize Abstr.; Med. Abstr. Newsl.; Microbiol. Abstr. Sect. C; Mod. Med.; NAPRALERT; Nutr. Abstr. Rev., Ser. A, Hum. Exp.; Nutr. Res. Newsl.; Life Sci. Collect.; PESTDOC; Physic. Medline Plus; Ref. Upd. Basic Ed.; Ref. Upd. Deluxe Ed.; Res. Alert [Full Cov.]; Rev. Med. Vet. Entomol.; Rev. Med. Vet. Mycology; Saf. Health Work; Sci. Cit. Index; SCISEARCH; Soc. Sci. Cit. Index [Select. Cov.]; Soyabean Abstr.; Virol. AIDS Abstr.

UK/0896-8411
## JOURNAL OF AUTOIMMUNITY.
[J. autoimmun.]. Vol. 1 (1988)-. Academic Scholarly Publication. English. Six times a year. $355.00. Academic Press Ltd., A Division of Harcourt Brace & Company Ltd., 24-28 Oval Road, London NW1 7DX England. **Tel** 071 267 4466, FAX 071 482 2293, 071 485 4752, telex 25775 ACPRES G. **(Subscription address:** Harcourt Brace & Company, Ltd., Foots Cray, High Street, Sidcup Kent DA14 5HP England.**)** **ED** J. F. Bach, I. M. Roitt, N. Talal and L. Chatenoud. **NLM** W1; JO547NJ. **CODEN** JOAUEP. **[CCC]. Pr Rev.** Documents available from The Genuine Article, BIOSIS Document Express.
**Desc:** Publishes papers related to the diverse aspects of autoimmunity: the mechanism of selfrecognition, regulation of autoimmune responses, experimental autoimmune diseases, diagnostic autoantibody tests, and the epidemiology, pathophysiology, and treatment of autoimmune diseases. Special, but not exclusive, attention will be given to papers dealing with genetic, molecular biology and cellular aspects of the discipline.
**Ind/Abst** Anim. Breed. Abstr.; Biol. Abstr.; Curr. Aware. Biol. Sci., CABS; Curr. Contents Life Sci.; EMBASE; Health Plan. Adminis.; Immunol. Abstr.; Index Med.; Res. Alert [Full Cov.]; Sci. Cit. Index; SCISEARCH.

UK/0141-2760
## JOURNAL OF CLINICAL & LABORATORY IMMUNOLOGY.
[J. clin. lab. immunol.]. **VAT** Journal of Clinical and Laboratory Immunology. Vol. 1 (June 1978)-. Academic Scholarly Publication. English. mo. £395.00 ECC countries; £495.00 others; $975.00 US. Teviot Scientific Publications, 82 Great King Street, Edinburgh EH3 6QU Scotland. **Tel** 011 44 31 3328764, FAX 011 44 31 3432633. **ED** W. J. Irvine. **NLM** W1 JO587AE. **CODEN** JLIMDJ. **[CCC]. Bk Rev. Ad Acc. Pr Rev. Circ:** 300. Documents available from The Genuine Article, CASDDS.
**Desc:** An international journal concerning immunology in all areas relevant to the understanding of the role of immunology in health and disease.
**Ind/Abst** Chem. Abstr.; Dairy Sci. Abstr.; EMBASE; Index Med.; Microbiol. Abstr. Sect. B; Life Sci. Collect.; Protozoolog. Abstr.; Ref. Upd. Deluxe Ed.; Res. Alert [Full Cov.]; Rev. Med. Vet. Mycology; SCISEARCH.

US/0736-4393
## JOURNAL OF CLINICAL IMMUNOASSAY.
[J. clin. immunoass.]. Vol. 6, No. 1 (Spring 1983)-. Academic Scholarly Publication. English (Italian and German). qt. $52.00 US; $64.00 other. Clinical Ligand Assay Society, 3139 S Wayne Road, Wayne MI 48184. **Tel** (313)722-6290. **ED** Gerald D Nordblom. **NLM** W1 JO588DC. **CODEN** JCLIES. Index available. cum. index. **Bk Rev. Ad Acc. Pr Rev. Circ:** 1,650 (ctrl). available on microfilm from University Microfilms International (UMI). Documents available from The Genuine Article, CASDDS. ***Continues*** *Ligand Quarterly, 0199-4794.*
**Desc:** Contains articles related to ligand methodology (advances and reviews) and associated problems such as data reduction, equipment, quality control and related clinical information.
**Ind/Abst** Chem. Abstr. (1983-); Curr. Aware. Biol. Sci., CABS; Curr. Contents Life Sci.; EMBASE; Ref. Upd. Deluxe Ed.; Res. Alert [Select. Cov.]; SCISEARCH; Soc. Sci. Cit. Index [Select. Cov.].

US/0271-9142
## JOURNAL OF CLINICAL IMMUNOLOGY.
[J. clin. immunol.]. Vol. 1, No. 1 (Jan. 1981)-. Academic Scholarly Publication. English. Six times a year. $335.00 institutions, $68.00 individuals US; $390.00 institutions, $80.00 individuals other. Plenum Press, 233 Spring Street, New York NY 10013-1578. **Tel** (212)620-8000, (800)221-9369, FAX (212)463-0742, (212)807-1047, telex 23/421139. **ED** Sudhir Gupta. **LC** RC581; .J68. **DD** 616.07/9/05. **NLM** W1 JO588DE. **CODEN** JCIMDO. **[CCC].** Index available. **Pr Rev.** available on microfilm and microfiche from University Microfilms International (UMI). Documents available from The Genuine Article, BIOSIS Document Express, CASDDS, ADONIS.
**Desc:** This journal is devoted exclusively to clinical immunology and its application to the practice of medicine.
**Ind/Abst** ADONIS; Biol. Abstr.; Chem. Abstr.; Curr. Aware. Biol. Sci., CABS; Curr. Contents Life Sci.; EMBASE; Helminthol. Abstr. (1991-); Immunol. Abstr.; Index Med.; INIS Atomindex [Micro.]; Life Sci. Collect.; Protozoolog. Abstr.; Ref. Upd. Basic Ed.; Ref. Upd. Clinical Ed.; Ref. Upd. Deluxe Ed.; Res. Alert [Full Cov.]; Sci. Cit. Index; SCISEARCH; Soc. Sci. Cit. Index [Select. Cov.].

US/0022-1007
## JOURNAL OF EXPERIMENTAL MEDICINE, THE.
[J. exp. med.]. Vol. 1 (Jan. 1896)-. Academic Scholarly Publication. English. Twelve times a year. $325.00 Europe; $240.00 other. Rockefeller University Press, 222 East 70th Street, New York NY 10021. **Tel** (212)327-8572, FAX (212)327-7944. **ED** Zanvil A. Cohn, Anthony Cerami and Maclyn McCarty. **NLM** W1 JO644Q. **CODEN** JEMEAV. **[CCC].** Index available in last issue of volume--attached. cum. index. **Pr Rev. Circ:** 3,853. available on microfilm and microfiche from University Microfilms International (UMI). Documents available from The Genuine Article, BIOSIS Document Express, CASDDS.
**Desc:** Publishes the most significant research in immunology and experimental medicine.
**Ind/Abst** AgBiotech News Inf.; Anim. Breed. Abstr.; Biol. Abstr.; Chem. Abstr.; Curr. Aware. Biol. Sci., CABS; Curr. Contents Life Sci.; Dairy Sci. Abstr.; EMBASE; Energy Res. Abstr.; Genet. Abstr.; Helminthol. Abstr. (19??-19??); Hum. Genome Abstr.; Immunol. Abstr.; Index Med.; Index Vet.; INIS Atomindex [Micro.]; Microbiol. Abstr. Sect. B; Microbiol. Abstr. Sect. C; Nutr. Abstr. Rev., Ser. B, Live Feeds and Feed.; Nutr. Abstr. Rev., Ser. A, Hum. Exp.; Oncog. Growth Factors Abstr.; Life Sci. Collect.; PESTDOC; Protozoolog. Abstr.; Ref. Upd. Basic Ed.; Ref. Upd. Clinical Ed.; Ref. Upd. Deluxe Ed.; Res. Alert [Full Cov.]; Rev. Med. Vet. Mycology; Sci. Cit. Index; SCISEARCH; Stat. Theory Method Abstr. (1959-1963); Vet. Bull.; Trop. Dis. Bull.; Virol. AIDS Abstr.

US/0197-1522
## JOURNAL OF IMMUNOASSAY.
[J. immunoass.]. Vol. 1 (1980)-. Academic Scholarly Publication. English. qt. $395.00 US; $409.00 other. Marcel Dekker Inc., 270 Madison Avenue, New York NY 10016. **Tel** (212)696-9000, (800)228-1160, FAX (212)685-4540, telex 421419. **(Subscription address:** Marcel Dekker Inc, PO Box 5017, Monticello NY 12701.**)** **ED** W. H. C. Walker. **LC** RB46.5; .J67. **DD** 616.07/56. **NLM** W1 JO676D. **CODEN** JOU!DK. **[CCC]. Bk Rev. Ad Acc. Pr Rev.** ctrl circ. available on microfiche. Documents available from The Genuine Article, BIOSIS Document Express, CASDDS.
**Desc:** Presents up-to-the-minute coverage of this rapidly expanding field, providing practical, hands-on information with an emphasis on applications. This publication features advances in radioimmunoassay, receptor assay, cytochemical bioassay, and ligand assay using tracer or biological markers of ligand-receptor interaction; the latest automation techniques to facilitate quicker, more accurate results; ongoing coverage of data reduction and interpretation to help solve theoretical and experimental problems; and much more.
**Ind/Abst** Biol. Abstr.; Chem. Abstr.; Curr. Aware. Biol. Sci., CABS; Curr. Contents Life Sci.; EMBASE; Helminthol. Abstr. (1991-); Immunol. Abstr.; Index Med.; Index Vet.; INIS Atomindex [Micro.]; Life Sci. Collect.; Poult. Abstr.; Protozoolog. Abstr.; Ref. Upd. Deluxe Ed.; Res. Alert [Full Cov.]; Rev. Med. Vet. Mycology; Sci. Cit. Index; SCISEARCH; Vet. Bull.; Trop. Dis. Bull.

NE/0022-1759
## JOURNAL OF IMMUNOLOGICAL METHODS.
[J. immunol. methods]. **VFOAT** Immunological Methods. Vol. 1 (Sept. 1971)-. Academic Scholarly Publication. English. Twenty-two times a year (11 vols.). Fl4609.00; Fl4819.00 combination subscription with Immunotechnology. Elsevier Science Publishers BV, PO Box 211, 1000 AE Amsterdam Netherlands. **Tel** 011 31 20 5803642, FAX 011 31 20 5862696, telex 15682. **ED** V Nussenzweig and M W Turner. **LC** QR183; .J68. **DD** 616.07/9/05. **NLM** W1 JO676K. **CODEN** JIMMBG. **[CCC]. Pr Rev.** available on microfilm and microfiche from University Microfilms International (UMI). Documents available from The Genuine Article, BIOSIS Document Express, CASDDS, Documents on Demand, ADONIS.
**Ind/Abst** ADONIS; AgBiotech News Inf.; Anal. Abstr.; BioBusiness (-1990); Biol. Abstr.; Chem. Abstr.; Curr. Biotechnol.; Curr. Contents Life Sci.; Dairy Sci. Abstr.; EMBASE; Energy Inf. Abstr.; Environ. Abstr.; Helminthol. Abstr. (1991-); Immunol. Abstr.; Index Med.; Int. Aerosp. Abstr.; Microbiol. Abstr. Sect. B; Microbiol. Abstr. Sect. A; Nutr. Abstr. Rev., Ser. B, Live Feeds and Feed.; Nutr. Abstr. Rev., Ser. A, Hum. Exp.; Life Sci. Collect.; Pig News Inf.; Protozoolog. Abstr.; Ref. Upd. Basic Ed.; Ref. Upd. Deluxe Ed.; Res. Alert [Full Cov.]; Rev. Med. Vet. Mycology; Rev. Plant Pathol.; Sci. Cit. Index; SCISEARCH; Small Anim. Abstr. Bibliogr.; Trop. Dis. Bull.; Virol. AIDS Abstr.

IT/1120-3765
## JOURNAL OF IMMUNOLOGICAL RESEARCH : JIR : THE JOURNAL OF THE ITALIAN FEDERATION OF IMMUNOLOGICAL SOCIETIES. *Ceased.*
**Added/Corp** Italian Federation of Immunological Societies. **VFOAT** JIR. (198?)-(Dec. 1992). Periodical. Italian. qt. Il Pensiero Scientifico Editore s.r.l., Via Bradano 3C, 00199 Rome Italy. **Tel** 011 39 6 86207158, 86207159, 86207168, 86207169, FAX 011 39 6 86207160. **NLM** W1; JO676R. Documents available from The Genuine Article.
**Ind/Abst** Res. Alert [Full Cov.]; Sci. Cit. Index; SCISEARCH.

US/0022-1767
## JOURNAL OF IMMUNOLOGY (1950), THE.
(THE JOURNAL OF IMMUNOLOGY : OFFICIAL JOURNAL OF THE AMERICAN ASSOCIATION OF IMMUNOLOGISTS.). [J. immunol.]. **Added/Corp** American Association of Immunologists. Vol. 64, No. 1 (Jan. 1950)-. Academic Scholarly Publication. English. sm (24 issues). $300.00 (institution), $170.00 (institution) US; $390.00 (institution), $260.00 (individual) other, surface mail. American Association of Immunologists, 9650 Rockville Pike, Bethesda MD 20814. **Tel** (301)571-1792. **(Subscription address:** Fulco, 30 Broad Street, Denville NJ 07834.**)** **LC** QR180; .J6. **DD** 615. **NLM** W1 JO677.

**CODEN** JOIMA3. **[CCC].** Index available (bound in last issue). **Pr Rev.** available on microfilm. Documents available from The Genuine Article, BIOSIS Document Express, CASDDS. ***Continues*** *Journal of Immunology, Virus-Research & Experimental Chemotherapy, 1047-7381.*
**Desc:** Original research papers on cellular immunology; immunochemistry and molecular immunology; immunogenetics and immunoregulation; immunopathology and clinical immunology; immunopharmacology; microbial immunology; and tumor and transplantation immunology.
**Ind/Abst** Abr. Index Med.; AgBiotech News Inf.; AGRICOLA; Anim. Breed. Abstr.; Annals Behav. Med.; Biol. Agric. Index; Biol. Abstr.; Calcium Calcif. Tissue Abstr.; Chem. Abstr.; Chemorecept. Abstr.; CSA Neuro. Abstr. (?-?); Curr. Aware. Biol. Sci., CABS; Dairy Sci. Abstr.; EMBASE; Energy Res. Abstr.; Genet. Abstr.; Health Index (1989-1991); Health Period. Database; Helminthol. Abstr.; Hum. Genome Abstr.; Immunol. Abstr.; Index Med.; INIS Atomindex [Micro.]; Int. Aerosp. Abstr.; Microbiol. Abstr. Sect. B; Microbiol. Abstr. Sect. C; NAPRALERT; Nucl. Acids Abstr.; Oncog. Growth Factors Abstr.; Life Sci. Collect.; PESTDOC; Physic. Medline Plus; Pig News Inf.; Poult. Abstr.; Protozoolog. Abstr.; Ref. Upd. Basic Ed.; Ref. Upd. Deluxe Ed.; Res. Alert [Full Cov.]; Rev. Med. Vet. Entomol.; Rev. Med. Vet. Mycology; Sci. Cit. Index; SCISEARCH; Trop. Dis. Bull.; Virol. AIDS Abstr.

US/1053-8550
**JOURNAL OF IMMUNOTHERAPY.** ***Title Change.*** (JOURNAL OF IMMUNOTHERAPY : OFFICIAL JOURNAL OF THE SOCIETY FOR BIOLOGICAL THERAPY.). [J. immunother.]. **Added/Corp** Society for Biological Therapy. Vol. 10, No. 1 (Feb. 1991)-(199?). Academic Scholarly Publication. English. bm. Raven Press, 1185 Avenue of the Americas, 37th Floor, New York NY 10036. **Tel** (212)930-9500, (212)930-9604, FAX (212)869-3495, (212)302-8507, telex 640073. **LC** RM270; .J68. **DD** 615/.37. **NLM** W1; JO679G. **CODEN** JOIME7. **[CCC].** available on microfilm and microfiche from University Microfilms International (UMI). Documents available from The Genuine Article, BIOSIS Document Express, CASDDS. ***Continues*** *Journal of Biological Response Modifiers, 0732-6580.* ***Continued by*** *Journal of Immunotherapy with Emphasis on Tumor Immunology, 1067-5582.*
**Desc:** This journal publishes basic scientific and clinical studies of the immunologic response to tumors and other diseases. It addresses the latest advances in basic cytokine research (interferons, interluekins, and newly described factors); immune regulation; immune response to diseases and associated antigens; growth factors and their receptors; hematopoietic factors; monoclonal antibodies; therapuetic studies in animal models; immunotherapy research, including active immunization and adaptive immunotherapy in animal models and humans; and clinical trials.
**Ind/Abst** Biol. Abstr. (1991-); Chem. Abstr. (1991-); Curr. Aware. Biol. Sci., CABS; Curr. Contents Life Sci.; EMBASE; Health Plan. Adminis.; Index Med. (1991-); INIS Atomindex [Micro.]; Int. Pharm. Abstr.; PESTDOC; Ref. Upd. Deluxe Ed.; Res. Alert [Full Cov.]; Sci. Cit. Index; SCISEARCH.

●US/1067-5582
**JOURNAL OF IMMUNOTHERAPY WITH EMPHASIS ON TUMOR IMMUNOLOGY : OFFICIAL JOURNAL OF THE SOCIETY FOR BIOLOGICAL THERAPY.** [J. immunother. emphas. immunol.]. **Added/Corp** Society for Biological Therapy. **VFOAT** Journal of Immunotherapy. Vol. 13, No. 1 (Jan. 1993)-. Academic Scholarly Publication. English. Eight times a year. $2088.00 (individuals), $385.00 (institutions) US; $274.00 (individuals), $474.00 (institutions) other. Raven Press, 1185 Avenue of the Americas, 37th Floor, New York NY 10036. **Tel** (212)930-9500, (212)930-9604, FAX (212)869-3495, (212)302-8507, telex 640073. **DD** 615. **NLM** W1; JO679G. **CODEN** JIEIEZ. Documents available from BIOSIS Document Express, CASDDS. ***Continues*** *Journal of Immunotherapy, 1053-8550.*
**Ind/Abst** Biol. Abstr.; Chem. Abstr.; Index Med.

SP/1018-9068
**JOURNAL OF INVESTIGATIONAL ALLERGOLOGY & CLINICAL IMMUNOLOGY.** (JOURNAL OF INVESTIGATIONAL ALLERGOLOGY & CLINICAL IMMUNOLOGY : OFFICIAL ORGAN OF THE INTERNATIONAL ASSOCIATION OF ASTHMOLOGY (INTERASMA) AND SOCIEDAD LATINOAMERICANA DE ALERGIA E INMUNOLOGIA.). [J. investig. allergol. clin. immunol.]. **Added/Corp** International Association of Asthmology. Sociedad Latinoamericana de Alergia e Inmunologia. **VFOAT** Journal of Investigational Allergology and Clinical Immunology. Vol. 1, No. 1 (Feb. 1991)-. Periodical. English (summaries and/or abstracts in Spanish). bm. $100.00. Prous Science Publishers, Apartado de Correos 540, 08080 Barcelona Spain. **Tel** 011 34 3 4592220, FAX 011 34 3 4581535. **NLM** W1; JO727I. **CODEN** JIAIEF. Documents available from The Genuine Article.
**Ind/Abst** Curr. Contents Clin. Med.; Res. Alert [Select. Cov.]; SCISEARCH.

●US/1069-7438
**JOURNAL OF NEURO-AIDS.** See Medical Science and Technology-Neurology.

●US/1049-5150
**JOURNAL OF NUTRITIONAL IMMUNOLOGY.** See Nutrition and Dietetics.

●US/1065-1799
**JOURNAL OF PHARMACEUTICAL CARE IN AIDS/HIV TREATMENT.** **VFOAT** Journal of Pharmaceutical Care in AIDS/HIV Treatment. (1995)-. English. qt. $60.00 US; $84.00 other. The Haworth Press Inc, 10 Alice Street, Binghamton NY 13904-1580. **Tel** (607)722-5857, (800)3-HAWORTH, FAX (607)722-1424. **Acid Free.** Documents available from Haworth Document Delivery Service.

NE/0165-0378
**JOURNAL OF REPRODUCTIVE IMMUNOLOGY.** [J. reprod. immunol.]. Vol. 1 (Jan./Feb. 1979)-. Academic Scholarly Publication. English. Nine times a year (3 vols.). $613.00. Elsevier Science Ireland Ltd., Bay 15, Shannon Industrial Estate, Co Clare Ireland. **Tel** 011 353 61 471944. **ED** W.D. Billington and A.E. Beer. **NLM** W1 JO868N. **CODEN** JRIMDR. **[CCC].** **Pr Rev.** available on microfilm and microfiche from University Microfilms International (UMI). Documents available from The Genuine Article, BIOSIS Document Express, CASDDS.
**Desc:** Devoted to the publication of suitable material within the general field of the immunology of reproduction, interpreted in its widest sense.
**Ind/Abst** AgBiotech News Inf.; Anim. Breed. Abstr.; Biol. Abstr.; Chem. Abstr.; Curr. Aware. Biol. Sci., CABS; Curr. Contents Life Sci.; Dairy Sci. Abstr.; EMBASE; Immunol. Abstr.; Index Med.; Index Vet.; NAPRALERT; Life Sci. Collect.; Pig News Inf.; Ref. Upd. Deluxe Ed.; Res. Alert [Full Cov.]; Sci. Cit. Index; SCISEARCH; Vet. Bull.

US/1055-3290
**JOURNAL OF THE ASSOCIATION OF NURSES IN AIDS CARE, THE.** See Medical Science and Technology-Nursing.

●US/1074-2395
**JOURNAL OF THE PHYSICIANS ASSOCIATION FOR AIDS CARE.** [J. Physicians Assoc. AIDS Care]. **Added/Corp** Physicians Association for AIDS Care. **VFOAT** AIDS Care; JPAAC. Vol. 1, No. 1 (Jan. 1994)-. Periodical. English. mo. $60.00 US; $100.00 other. Physicians Association for AIDS Care, 101 West Grand Avenue, Suite 200, Chciago IL 60610. **Tel** (312)222-1326, FAX (312)222-0329. **DD** 362. **NLM** W1; JO946N. ***Continues*** *PAACnotes, 1059-7913.*

JA/0387-1010
**KANSEN, ENSHO, MENEKI.** [Kansen, ensho, meneki]. **VFOAT** Infection, Inflammation & Immunity; Infection, Inflammation and Immunity. (1971)-. Periodical. Japanese. bm. Iyaku no Monsha, Nihonbashi, Honcho 3-3 Chou-ku, Tokyo-to 103 Japan. **CODEN** KEMEDB. Documents available from BIOSIS Document Express, CASDDS.
**Ind/Abst** Biol. Abstr.; Chem. Abstr.

UK/0142-8160
**LEUCOCYTES.** (1976)-. English. Twenty-four times a year. £120.00. SUBIS, Mansion House, 19 Kingfield Road, Sheffield S11 9AS England. **Tel** 011 44 114 255 4433, FAX 011 44 114 255 4626. **[CCC].** **Ad Acc.**
**Desc:** Current awareness service for researchers and clinicians.

US/0197-4041
**LIGAND REVIEW, THE.** [Ligand rev.]. V. 1- Fall 1979-. Academic Scholarly Publication. English. qt. $20.00. Technical & Professional Services Inc, 940 Crossroad Boulevard, Seguin TX 78155. **NLM** W1 LI468B. **CODEN** LRVWD8. Documents available from CASDDS.
**Ind/Abst** Chem. Abstr.

US/0740-7394
**LINSCOTT'S DIRECTORY OF IMMUNOLOGICAL AND BIOLOGICAL REAGENTS.** [Linscott's Dir. ... immunol. biol. reagents]. **VFOAT** Directory of Immunological and Biological Reagents; Linscotts. 2nd Ed. (1982/1983)-. English. be. $75.00. Linscott's Directory, 4877 Grange Road, Santa Rosa CA 95404. **Tel** (707)544-9555. **ED** William D. Linscott. **LC** QR183; .L56. **DD** 574.19/2/0294. **NLM** QW 22.1; L759. Index available. **Bk Rev.** **Ad Acc.** **Circ:** 8,000 (ctrl). ***Continues*** *Linscott's Catalog of Immunological and Biological Reagents.*
**Desc:** Lists sources for 30,000 reagents used in bio-medical and immunological research.

US/1042-4075
**MA REPORT (FAIRFAX, VA.), THE.** (THE MA REPORT / MOTHERS OF ASTHMATICS, INC.). [MA rep.]. **Added/Corp** Mothers of Asthmatics. **VAT** Mothers of Asthmatics Report. (198?)-. Periodical. English. Twelve times a year. $25.00 one year; $50.00 two year. Mothers of Asthmatics Inc., 3554 Chain Bridge Road, Suite 200, Fairfax VA 22030. **Tel** (703)385-4403, FAX (703)352-4354. **ED** Jennifer Miller. **DD** 616. **Circ:** 4,000.
**Desc:** A newsletter with practical and educational information, medical updates and other useful resources regarding allergies and asthma.

RU
**MATERIALY SIMPOZIUMOV PO OBSHCHEI IMMUNOLOGII / AKADEMIIA MEDITSINSKIKH NAUK SSSR, INSTITUT EPIDEMIOLOGII I MIKROBIOLOGII IM. N.F. GAMALEI.** **Added/Corp** Institut Epidemiologii i Mikrobiologii Imeni N.F. Gamalei. **VFOAT** Voprosy Immunologii. (1967)-. Russian (summaries and/or abstracts in English). **LC** WMLC 91/1723. **NLM** W1 MA944L.

US/1061-5458
**MAXWELL COMPACT LIBRARIES. AIDS.** (MAXWELL COMPACT LIBRARIES. AIDS [COMPUTER FILE].). [Maxwell compact libr., AIDS]. **VFOAT** AIDS. (1989)-. English. qt. $695.00 (institution) US. Macmillan New Media, 124 Mt. Auburn Street, Cambridge MA 02138. **Tel** (617)661-2955, (800)342-1338, FAX (617)868-7738. **DD** 616. ***Continues*** *Compact Library, AIDS, 0899-997X.*
**Desc:** A comprehensive collection of databases on the clinical, social, economic and political aspects of AIDS research and treatment. It includes the complete text of 10,000 AIDS-related articles from ten major medical journals.

JA/0910-3740
**MEDICAL IMMUNOLOGY.** [Med. immunol.]. **VFOAT** Men'eki to Shikkan (1985). (1985)-. Periodical. Japanese. mo. Kokusai Isho Shuppan, 26-4, Hongo 3 Chome, Bunkyoku, Tokyoto 113, Japan. **DD** 616. Documents available from CASDDS. ***Continues*** *Men'eki to Shikkan, 0389-7419.*
**Ind/Abst** Chem. Abstr.

GW/0300-8584
**MEDICAL MICROBIOLOGY AND IMMUNOLOGY.** See Biology-Microbiology.

BL/0073-9901
**MEMORIAS DO INSTITUTO BUTANTAN (SAO PAULO).** (MEMORIAS DO INSTITUTO DE BUTANTAN.). [Mem. Inst. Butantan]. **Added/Corp** Instituto Butantan. **VFOAT** Memorias do Instituto Butantan. (1918)-. Periodical. Portuguese (English, French and German). **NLM** W1 ME903H. **CODEN** MIBUAH. Documents available from BIOSIS Document Express, CASDDS. ***Absorbed*** *Colectanea dos Trabalhos do Instituto de Butantan.*
**Ind/Abst** Biol. Abstr.; Chem. Abstr.; Helminthol. Abstr. (1991-); Index Med. (1965-1976-77); Index Vet.; Trop. Dis. Bull.

JA/0289-3371
**MEN'EKI YAKURI SHINPOJUMU.** See Pharmacy and Pharmacology.

US/0026-0495
**METABOLISM, CLINICAL AND EXPERIMENTAL.** [Metab. clin. exp.]. Vol. 1 (Jan. 1952)-. Academic Scholarly Publication. English. mo. $174.00 (individual), $232.00 (institution) US; $278.00 (individual), $306.00 (institution) other. W.B. Saunders Company, A Subsidiary of Harcourt Brace Jovanovich, Inc., The Curtis Center/Suite 300, Independence Square West, Philadelphia PA 19106-3399. **Tel** (215)238-7800 or, 5587, FAX (215)238-7883, telex 173146. **(Subscription address:** W. B. Saunders Company / North America Subscriptions, c/o Periodicals, 6277 Sea Harbour Drive, 4th Floor, Orlando FL 32887.**)** **ED** James B. Field. **LC** RB147; .M48. **DD** 616.3/9. **NLM** W1 ME961P. **CODEN** METAAJ. **[CCC].** **Pr Rev.** Documents available from The Genuine Article, BIOSIS Document Express, CASDDS.
**Desc:** This eminent journal is regarded by clinicians and researchers alike as an authoritative sources of practical information on metabolic processes and diseases in the area of nutrition, endocrines, genetics, dystrophies, diabetes, and gout.
**Ind/Abst** AGRICOLA [Select. Cov.]; Biol. Abstr.; Chem. Abstr.; Chem. Titles; CSA Neuro. Abstr.; Curr. Aware. Biol. Sci., CABS; Curr. Contents Life Sci.; Dairy Sci. Abstr.; EMBASE; Energy Res. Abstr.; Index Med.; Nutr. Abstr. Rev., Ser. A, Hum. Exp.; Nutr. Res. Newsl.; Life Sci. Collect.; PESTDOC; Ref. Upd. Basic Ed.; Ref. Upd. Deluxe Ed.; Res. Alert [Full Cov.]; Sci. Cit. Index; SCISEARCH; Soc. Sci. Cit. Index [Select. Cov.]; SPORT Discus; SportSearch; Sug. Indus. Abstr.

US
**MICHIGAN HIV REPORT / DEPARTMENT OF PUBLIC HEALTH.** See Public Health and Safety.

JA/0385-5600
**MICROBIOLOGY AND IMMUNOLOGY.** [Microbiol. immunol.]. **Added/Corp** Nihon Saikin Gakkai. Nihon Uirusu Gakkai. Nihon Meneki Gakkai. Vol. 21, No. 1 (1977)-. Academic Scholarly Publication. English. mo. $255.00. Gakkaishi Kanko Senta, (Center for Academic Publications, Japan), 4-16, Yayoi 2 Chome, Bunkyoku, Tokyoto 113, Japan. **(Subscription address:** Maruzen

Company Ltd., PO Box 5050, Import & Export Department, Tokyo 100 31 Japan.) **LC** QR1; .J36. **DD** 616/.01. **NLM** W1 MI292K. **CODEN** MIIMDV. **Pr Rev.** Documents available from The Genuine Article, BIOSIS Document Express, CASDDS. ***Continues*** *Japanese Journal of Microbiology, 0021-5139.*
**Ind/Abst** AgBiotech News Inf.; AGRICOLA [Select. Cov.]; Biol. Abstr.; Chem. Abstr.; CSA Neuro. Abstr. (?-?); Curr. Biotechnol.; Curr. Contents Life Sci.; Dairy Sci. Abstr.; EMBASE; Immunol. Abstr.; Index Med.; Index Dent. Lit.; Index Vet.; Microbiol. Abstr. Sect. B; Microbiol. Abstr. Sect. A; NAPRALERT; Life Sci. Collect.; PESTDOC; Pig News Inf.; Ref. Upd. Deluxe Ed.; Res. Alert [Full Cov.]; Rev. Med. Vet. Entomol.; Rev. Med. Vet. Mycology; Sci. Cit. Index; SCISEARCH; Vet. Bull.; Trop. Dis. Bull.; Virol. AIDS Abstr.

US/1056-2915
**MIRA (SAN FRANCISCO, CALIF.).**
***Suspended.*** (MIRA : MULTICULTURAL INQUIRY AND RESEARCH ON AIDS : QUARTERLY NEWSLETTER.). [MIRA]. **Added/Corp** Multicultural Inquiry and Research on AIDS (Project). **VFOAT** MIRA Newsletter; Multicultural Inquiry and Research on AIDS. **VAT** Multicultural Inquiry and Research on AIDS. (198?)-Suspended (July, 1993). Newsletter. English. Four times a year. MIRA, 5815 Third Street, San Francisco CA 94124. **Tel** (415)822-7114 & 822-4115. **DD** 614. **NLM** W1; MI782D.

US/0891-3676
**MODERN CONCEPTS IN IMMUNOLOGY.**
[Mod. concepts immunol.]. Vol. 1-. Monographic series. English. Price varies per volume. John Wiley & Sons, Inc., 605 Third Avenue, New York NY 10158-0012. **Tel** (212)850-6000, (212)850-6645, FAX (212)850-6088, telex 12-7063. **(Subscription address:** John Wiley & Sons / England, Baffins Lane, Chichester, West Sussex PO19 1UD England.) **DD** 616. **NLM** W1; MO125S.

UK/0161-5890
**MOLECULAR IMMUNOLOGY.** [Mol. immunol.]. Vol. 16 (Jan. 1979)-. Academic Scholarly Publication. English. Eighteen times a year. $1349.00 The Americas; £905.00 other. Pergamon Press, An Imprint of Elsevier Science Ltd., The Boulevard, Langford Lane, Kidlington, Oxford OX5 1GB United Kingdom. **Tel** 011 44 865 843000, 011 44 865 843699, FAX 011 44 865 843010. **(Subscription address:** Elsevier Science Ltd. Oxford Fulfillment Centre, PO Box 800, Kidlington, Oxford OX5 1DX United Kingdom.) **ED** Michel Fougereau. **LC** QR180; .I5. **DD** 574.2/9. **NLM** W1 MO196K. **CODEN** MOIMD5. **[CCC]. Pr Rev.** available on microfilm and microfiche from University Microfilms International (UMI). Documents available from The Genuine Article, BIOSIS Document Express, CASDDS, ADONIS. ***Continues*** *Immunochemistry (Oxford, England : 1965), 0019-2791.*
**Desc:** Primarily devoted to the publication and communication of immunological knowledge which can be delineated at the molecular level. Within this framework it publishes contributions concerned with the molecular analysis of the cellular components and processes which underlie the biological behavior of cells involved in immune phenomena.
**Ind/Abst** ADONIS; AgBiotech News Inf.; Anim. Breed. Abstr.; Biol. Abstr.; Chem. Abstr.; Chem. Titles; Curr. Aware. Biol. Sci., CABS; Curr. Contents Life Sci.; EMBASE; Energy Res. Abstr. (Dec. 1979-); Genet. Abstr.; Immunol. Abstr.; Index Med.; Index Vet.; Microbiol. Abstr. Sect. B (19??-19??); Oncog. Growth Factors Abstr.; Life Sci. Collect.; PESTDOC; Pig News Inf.; Poult. Abstr.; Ref. Upd. Basic Ed.; Ref. Upd. Deluxe Ed.; Res. Alert [Full Cov.]; Rev. Med. Vet. Entomol.; Rev. Med. Vet. Mycology; Sci. Cit. Index; SCISEARCH; Vet. Bull.; Trop. Dis. Bull.; Virol. AIDS Abstr.; Weed Abstr.

UK/0261-4960
**MONOCLONAL ANTIBODIES.** [Monoclon. antibod.]. (1982)-. English. Twenty-four times a year. £115.00. SUBIS, Mansion House, 19 Kingfield Road, Sheffield S11 9AS England. **Tel** 011 44 114 255 4433, FAX 011 44 114 255 4626. **DD** 016.5990293. **[CCC]. Bk Rev. Ad Acc.**
**Desc:** Current awareness service for researchers and clinicians.

SW/0077-0760
**MONOGRAPHS IN ALLERGY.** [Monogr. allergy]. Vol. 1 (1966)-. Monographic series. English. an. 220.00F (approx. per volume). S. Karger AG, Allschwilerstrasse 10, PO Box - Postfach - Case Postale, CH-4009 Basel Switzerland. **Tel** 011 41 61 306-1111, FAX 011 41 61 306-1234, telex CH 962 652. **ED** L. A. Hanson, F. Shakib. **DD** 616. **NLM** W1 MO567E. **CODEN** MOALAR. **[CCC]. Pr Rev.** Documents available from The Genuine Article, BIOSIS Document Express, CASDDS.
**Desc:** Volumes in this series focus on areas of allergy and immunology characterized by exceptional importance and growth. Given the complexity of developments in these fields, volumes perform a major service by centralizing and synthesizing vast amounts of data normally scattered throughout the literature. In addition to their value as progress reports, these monographs have proved useful in clarifying both the clinical implications of present knowledge and the directions which further work must take.
**Ind/Abst** Biol. Abstr.; Chem. Abstr. (1966-1983); Index Med.; Life Sci. Collect.; Ref. Upd. Deluxe Ed.; Res. Alert [Full Cov.]; Sci. Cit. Index.

●US/1068-7629
**MUCOSAL IMMUNOLOGY UPDATE : OFFICIAL PUBLICATION OF THE SOCIETY FOR MUCOSAL IMMUNOLOGY.** (1993)-. Periodical. English. Four times a year. $70.00 (institutions), $45.00 (individuals) US; $92.00 (institutions), $60.00 (individuals) other. Raven Press, 1185 Avenue of the Americas, 37th Floor, New York NY 10036. **Tel** (212)930-9500, (212)930-9604, FAX (212)869-3495, (212)302-8507, telex 640073. **NLM** W1; MU346.

US
**NATIONAL AIDS INFORMATION CLEARINGHOUSE CONFERENCE CALENDAR.** **Added/Corp** National AIDS Information Clearinghouse (U.S.). **VFOAT** Conference Calendar. (Jan. 1991)-. Periodical. English. **NLM** W 22.1; N155. ***Continues*** *NAIC Conference Calendar.*

●SZ/1018-8916
**NATURAL IMMUNITY.** (Jan./Feb. 1992)-. Periodical. English. bm. $266.00. S. Karger AG, Allschwilerstrasse 10, PO Box - Postfach - Case Postale, CH-4009 Basel Switzerland. **Tel** 011 41 61 306-1111, FAX 011 41 61 306-1234, telex CH 962 652. **ED** R.B. Herberman. **NLM** W1; NA805C. **CODEN** NAIMEL. **[CCC].** Documents available from The Genuine Article, BIOSIS Document Express. ***Continues*** *Natural Immunity and Cell Growth Regulation, 0254-7600.*
**Desc:** Offers a unique collection of original research on natural immune effector mechanisms against cancer and infectious diseases. Readers will find information on the role of natural killer cells, MHC-nonrestricted T cells, macrophages and granulocytes in antitumor immunity and other biological functions. Also included is research on the molecular aspects of killer cell-target cell interactions, membrane structures involved in signal transduction and activation, and regulation of oncolytic cells by cytokines.
**Ind/Abst** Biol. Abstr.; Curr. Aware. Biol. Sci., CABS; Curr. Contents Life Sci.; Index Med. (1992-); Ref. Upd. Deluxe Ed.; Res. Alert [Select. Cov.].

US
**NEEDLE TIPS.** (19??)-. Newsletter. English. Free to health care workers and concerned community members; $20.00 requested donation. Immunization Action Coalition, 1573 Selby Avenue, Suite 229, St. Paul MN 55104-6328. **Tel** (612)647-9009, FAX (612)647-9131. available via Internet.
**Desc:** Published by the Immunization Action Coalition, a non-profit organization promoting physician, community, and family awareness of and responsibility for appropriate immunization of all people of all ages against all vaccine-preventable diseases.

●US
**NEWSLETTER FOR PEOPLE WITH LACTOSE INTOLERANCE AND MILK ALLERGY.** Newsletter. English. Four times a year (Winter, Spring, Summer, Fall). $15.00 (one year); $28.00 (two years); $42.00 (three years). Commerical Writing Service, PO Box 3074, Iowa City IA 52244. **Circ:** 1,000.

US/0147-7277
**NIAID MANUAL OF TISSUE TYPING TECHNIQUES.** [NIAID man. tissue typing tech.]. **Main/Corp** United States. National Institute of Allergy and Infectious Diseases. Allergic and Immunologic Diseases Program. **VAT** National Institute of Allergy and Infectious Diseases Manual of Tissue Typing Techniques. English. United States National Institute of Allergy and Infectious Diseases, Immunology Allergic and Immunologic Diseases Program, Bethesda MD 20205. **LC** QR184.3; .U55A. **DD** 616.07/9. ***Continues*** *NIAID Manual of Tissue Typing Techniques, 0147-7277.*

UK/0141-9838
**PARASITE IMMUNOLOGY.** [Parasite immunol.]. Vol. 1 (Spring 1979)-. Academic Scholarly Publication. English. mo (12 issues). $563.00 (institutions), $99.00 (individuals) US & Canada; £330.00 (institutions), £59.00 (individuals) Europe; £363.00 (institutions), £65.00 (individuals) other. Blackwell Scientific Publications Ltd, Marston Book Services, PO Box 87, Oxford OX2 ODT UK. **Tel** 011 44 865 791155, FAX 011 44 865 791927, telex 837 515 MARDIS G. **ED** G. A. T. Targett and Bridget M. Ogilvie. **NLM** W1 PA635U. **CODEN** PAIMD8. **[CCC].** Index available (bound in last issue). **Ad Acc. Circ:** 515 (ctrl). available on microfilm and microfiche from University Microfilms International (UMI). Documents available from The Genuine Article, BIOSIS Document Express, CASDDS, ADONIS.
**Desc:** Covers research on parasite immunology in the general sense, emphasis on how hosts control parasites and the immunopathological reactions in parasitic infections.
**Ind/Abst** ADONIS; AgBiotech News Inf.; AGRICOLA [Select. Cov.]; Anim. Breed. Abstr.; Biol. Abstr.; Chem. Abstr.; Curr. Aware. Biol. Sci., CABS; Curr. Contents Life Sci.; EMBASE; Helminthol. Abstr. (19??-19??); Immunol. Abstr.; Index Med.; Index Vet.; Microbiol. Abstr. Sect. C; Life Sci. Collect.; Poult. Abstr.; Protozoolog. Abstr.; Ref. Upd. Deluxe Ed.; Res. Alert [Full Cov.]; Rev. Med. Vet. Entomol.; Sci. Cit. Index; SCISEARCH; Vet. Bull.; Trop. Dis. Bull.

FR/1146-5506
**PASCAL. E 62, IMMUNOLOGIE.** **VFOAT** PASCAL. E 62, Immunology; PASCAL. Soixante-Deux, Immunologie. (1990)-. Periodical. Multiple languages. Ten times a year. 1340.00F France; 1425.00F other. CNRS / Institut d'Information Scientifique et Technique, (Centre National de la Recherche Scientifique), 15 Quai Anatole France, Paris 75700 France. **Tel** 011 33 1 47531515, telex 299 356 F. **(Subscription address:** Institut d'Information Scientifique et Technique Diffusion, 2 Allee du Parc de Brabois, 54514 Vandoeuvre Nancy France.) **UDC** 011. ***Continues*** *Pascal Explore. E62, Immunologie, 0761-2141.*

US/1045-5418
**PEDIATRIC AIDS AND HIV INFECTION.** [Pediatr. AIDS HIV infect.]. **Added/Corp** Mary Ann Liebert, Inc. Vol. 1, No. 1 (1990)-. Periodical. English. bm. $106.00. Mary Ann Liebert Inc., 1651 Third Avenue, New York NY 10128. **Tel** (212)289-2300, (800)M-LIEBERT, FAX (212)289-4697. **ED** Mhairi MacDonald and Harold Ginzburg. **LC** RJ387.A25; P42. **DD** 362.1/98929792/005. **NLM** W1; PE163D. **CODEN** PAHIEQ. Documents available from The Genuine Article.
**Desc:** Publishes critical articles, review papers and original research on the methods of diagnosis and treatment of obstetric, pediatric and adolescent patients with HIV infection. Topics include epidemiology, molecular biology, clinical presentation, diagnosis and treatment, pathology, virology, reproductive aspects and relevant legal, ethical community and psychosocial issues in caring for the family with HIV infection.
**Ind/Abst** Cumul. Index Nurs. Allied Health Lit.; Curr. Contents Clin. Med.; EMBASE; Res. Alert [Select. Cov.]; Risk Abstr.; SCISEARCH; Soc. Sci. Cit. Index [Select. Cov.]; Trop. Dis. Bull.

DK/0905-6157
**PEDIATRIC ALLERGY AND IMMUNOLOGY : OFFICIAL PUBLICATION OF THE EUROPEAN SOCIETY OF PEDIATRIC ALLERGY AND IMMUNOLOGY.** **Added/Corp** European Society of Pediatric Allergy and Immunology. Vol. 1, No. 1 (Oct. 1990)-. Periodical. English. qt. kr880.00 (institution), kr470.00 (individual) US, Canada and Japan; kr850.00 (institution), kr440.00 (individual) other. Munksgaard International Publishers Ltd, PO Box 2148, DK-1016 Copenhagen K Denmark. **Tel** 011 45 33 12 70 30, FAX 011 45 33 12 93 87, telex 19431 MUNKS DK. **ED** Bengt Bjoerksten. **NLM** W1; PE163M. **[CCC]. Ad Acc. Pr Rev. Circ:** 600.
**Desc:** Publishes original contributions and comprehensive reviews related to the understanding and treatment of immune deficiency, allergic inflammatory and infectious diseases in children.
**Ind/Abst** Curr. Aware. Biol. Sci., CABS; EMBASE.

US/0883-1874
**PEDIATRIC ASTHMA, ALLERGY & IMMUNOLOGY.** **See** Medical Science and Technology-Pediatrics.

IT/1120-2556
**PERSPECTIVES IN E.N.T.-IMMUNOLOGY.** (1987)-. English. Edizioni Luigi Pozzi Srl, Via Panama 68, 00198 Rome Italy. **Tel** (06)8553548, FAX (06)8554105.
**Ind/Abst** EMBASE.

DK/0905-4383
**PHOTODERMATOLOGY, PHOTOIMMUNOLOGY & PHOTOMEDICINE.** **See** Medical Science and Technology-Dermatology.

●US
**POSITIVE LIVING.** **See** Public Health and Safety.

CN/0831-0998
**PRACTICAL ALLERGY & IMMUNOLOGY.** [Pract. allergy immunol.]. **Added/Corp** Medicopea (Firm). Vol. 1, (Apr. 1986)-. Periodical. English. Six times a year (Feb., Apr., June, Aug., Oct., Dec.). $60.00 Canada; $72.00 US; $94.00 other. Medicopea International, 3333 Cote Vertu Boulevard, Suite 300, Montreal QUE H4R 2N1 Canada. **Tel** (514)331-4561, FAX (514)336-1129. **DD** 616.97/005. **NLM** W1; PR138J. Index available. **Bk Rev. Ad Acc. Circ:** 8,941.
**Desc:** It provides practical information of the specific problems encountered by the allergist and immunologist. Each issue contains general topics, and regular departments includes clinical presentation, aids, updates, allergy updated, dermatology updates, and pediatrics updates.

UK/0262-8783
**PRACTICAL METHODS IN CLINICAL IMMUNOLOGY SERIES.** [Pract. methods clin. immunol.]. **VFOAT** Practical Methods in Clinical Immunology. 1-. Monographic series. English. ir. Price varies per volume. Churchill Livingstone, 1-3 Baxter's Place, Leith Walk, Edinburgh EH1 3AF Scotland. **Tel** 011 44 31 556 2424, FAX 011 44 31 558 1278, telex 727511.

(Subscription address: US/ Churchill Livingstone, Fulfillment Office, PO Box 11318, Birmingham, AL 35202) ED R C Nairn. DD 616.07/9/05. NLM W1 PR142K.

NE
**PROGRESS IN IMMUNOLOGY.** Main/Conf International Congress of Immunology. 1- 1971-. English. te. North-Holland Publishing Company, PO Box 211, Amsterdam The Netherlands. LC QR180.3; .I56A. DD 574.2/9. NLM W3 PR947F.

SZ
**PROGRESS REPORT / GLOBAL PROGRAMME ON AIDS.** Main/Corp Global Programme on AIDS (World Health Organization). No. 3 (May 1988)-. English. LC RA644.A25; G56. NLM W1; GL362V. *Continues Special Programme on AIDS (World Health Organization). Progress Report.*

CN/0849-3138
**QUARTERLY / THE ALLERGY AND ENVIRONMENTAL HEALTH ASSOCIATION.** [Q. - Allergy Environ. Health Assoc.]. Added/Corp Allergy and Environmental Health Association. VFOAT AEHA Quarterly. (1990)-. Periodical. English. qt. Free to members (membership: $20.00 per year). Allergy and Environmental Health Association, 10 George Street North, Cambridge, Ontario N1S 2M7 Canada. DD 616.9/8. *Continues Quarterly (Human Ecology Foundation of Canada)., 0846-541X.*

GW
**QUINTESSENZ BIBLIOTHEK. ASTHMA UND ALLERGIE.** VFOAT Asthma und Allergie; Bibliothek Asthma und Allergie. Bd. 1-(1991)-. Monographic series. German. Price varies per volume. NLM W1; QU964H.

CN/1189-3087
**RAPPORT D'ACTIVITES / CENTRE QUEBECOIS DE COORDINATION SUR LE SIDA.** See Public Health and Safety.

RU/0202-9030
**REFERATIVNYJ ZURNAL - VSESOJUZNYJ INSTITUT NAUCNOJ I TEHNICESKOJ INFORMACII. 53. IMMUNOLOGIJA. ALLERGOLOGIJA.** (REFERATIVNYI ZHURNAL. IMMUNOLOGIIA. ALLERGOLOGIIA.). Added/Corp Vsesoiuznyi Institut Nauchnoi i Tekhnicheskoi Informatsii. VFOAT Immunologiia; Allergologiia. (1978)-. Abstracting/Indexing Service. Russian. mo. $299.95. VINITI - Vsesoyuznyi Institut Nauchno-Tekhnicheskoi Informatsii, All-Union Scientific and Technical Information Institute, Baltiiskaia Ulitsa 14, 125219 Moscow Russia. Tel 238-46-00, FAX 9430060, telex 411160. NLM ZQW 4 R332. *Continues in part Referativnyi Zhurnal. Obshchie Voprosy Patologii.*

US/0896-0623
**REGIONAL IMMUNOLOGY.** *Ceased.* [Reg. immunol.]. Vol. 1, No. 1 (July/Aug. 1988)-(199?). Periodical. English. bm. John Wiley & Sons, Inc., 605 Third Avenue, New York NY 10158-0012. Tel (212)850-6000, (212)850-6645, FAX (212)850-6088, telex 12-7063. (Subscription address: John Wiley & Sons / England, Baffins Lane, Chichester, West Sussex PO19 1UD England.) ED J Wayne Streilein. DD 616. NLM W1; RE173BJF. CODEN REGIE3. [CCC]. available on microfilm and microfiche from University Microfilms International (UMI). Documents available from BIOSIS Document Express.
Desc: The first journal to focus on immune phenomena that occur in specific regions, organs, and tissues of the body.
Ind/Abst Biol. Abstr. (1989-); Curr. Aware. Biol. Sci., CABS; EMBASE; Index Med. (July/Aug. 1988-).

US/0161-3618
**REPORT FROM THE DIRECTOR, NATIONAL INSTITUTE OF ALLERGY AND INFECTIOUS DISEASES.** See Medical Science and Technology-Communicable Diseases.

FR/0923-2494
**RESEARCH IN IMMUNOLOGY (PARIS).** (RESEARCH IN IMMUNOLOGY.). [Res. immunol.]. Vol. 140, No. 1 (Jan. 1989)-. Academic Scholarly Publication. English (summaries and/or abstracts in French). Nine times a year (1 volume). 1875.00F (regular subscription), 4310.00F (combination subscription with Research in Microbiology and Research in Virology) France; 2215.00F (regular subscription), 5083.00 (combination subscription with Research in Microbiology and Research in Virology) other. Editions Scientifique Elsevier, 141 rue de Javel, 75747 Paris Cedex 15 France. Tel 011 33 1 47 07 11 22, FAX 011 33 1 43 36 80 93. (Subscription address: Editions Scientifiques Elsevier / for North America, PO Box 7247-7576, Philadelphia PA 19170-7576.) NLM W1; RE227FV. CODEN RIMME5. [CCC]. Pr Rev. available on microfilm and microfiche from University Microfilms International (UMI). Documents available from The Genuine Article, BIOSIS Document Express, CASDDS, ADONIS. *Continues Annales de l'Institut Pasteur. Immunology, 0769-2625.*
Ind/Abst ADONIS; Anim. Breed. Abstr.; Biol. Abstr.; Chem. Abstr.; Curr. Aware. Biol. Sci., CABS; Curr. Contents Life Sci.; EMBASE; Immunol. Abstr.; Index Med.; Index Vet.; PESTDOC; Protozoolog. Abstr.; Ref. Upd. Deluxe Ed.; Res. Alert [Full Cov.]; Rev. Med. Vet. Mycology; Sci. Cit. Index; SCISEARCH; Vet. Bull.; Trop. Dis. Bull.

NE/0167-6091
**RESEARCH MONOGRAPHS IN IMMUNOLOGY.** [Res. monogr. immunol.]. Vol. 1 (1980)-. Academic Scholarly Publication. English. ir. Price varies per volume. Elsevier Science Publishers BV, PO Box 211, 1000 AE Amsterdam Netherlands. Tel 011 31 20 5803642, FAX 011 31 20 5862696, telex 15682. LC UNC. DD 616.07/9. NLM W1 RE232GS. CODEN RMIMDC. Documents available from BIOSIS Document Express, CASDDS.
Ind/Abst Biol. Abstr. (-1981); Chem. Abstr.; Life Sci. Collect.

PL
**RESEARCH REPORT (INSTYTUT IMMUNOLOGII I TERAPII DOSWIADCZALNEJ IM. LUDWIKA HIRSZFELDA).** (RESEARCH REPORT / POLISH ACADEMY OF SCIENCES, LUDWIK HIRSZFELD INSTITUTE OF IMMUNOLOGY AND EXPERIMENTAL THERAPY.). (1985/87)-. English. be. (Subscription address: ARS Polona, PO Box 1001, 00068 Warsaw Poland.) NLM W1; RE234AWCM. *Continues Annual Report / Instytut Immunologii i Terapii Doswiadczalnej (Polska Akademia Nauk.*

FR
**RETROVIRUS.** Vol. 1, No. 1 (Sept. 1988)-. Periodical. French (summaries and/or abstracts in English and French). qt. $100.00. Retrovirus Public Press Intl, 62 rue Ivan Tourgueniev, 78380 Bougival France. NLM W1; RE2509D.
Ind/Abst EMBASE.

UK/0952-7168
**REVIEWS ON IMMUNOASSAY TECHNOLOGY.** Vol. 1 (1988)-. Academic Scholarly Publication. English. be. Macmillan Publishing Company, 866 3rd Avenue, New York NY 10022. Tel (212)702-2000, (800)257-5755. NLM W1; RE257M. Documents available from CASDDS.
Ind/Abst Chem. Abstr. (1988-).

SP/0214-1477
**REVISTA ESPANOLA DE ALERGOLOGIA E INMUNOLOGIA CLINICA : ORGANO OFICIAL DE LA SOCIEDAD ESPANOLA DE ALERGOLOGIA E INMUNOLOGIA CLINICA.** Added/Corp Sociedad Espanola de Alergologia e Inmunologia Clinica. Vol. 1, Num. 1 (Feb. 1986)-. Periodical. Spanish (summaries and/or abstracts in English; table of contents in English). bm. 3.300ptas. Editorial Saned SA, Apolonio Morales 6, 28036 Madrid Spain. Tel 011 34 1 359-4092, FAX 011 34 1 457-9918. ED Miguel Angel Renart Pita. NLM W1; RE5266. Bk Rev. Ad Acc. Circ: 2,000 (ctrl).
Desc: Original articles and revisions on allergology and clinical immunology. Reviews books in the field.
Ind/Abst EMBASE; Indice Med. Esp.

FR/0335-7457
**REVUE FRANCAISE D'ALLERGOLOGIE ET D'IMMUNOLOGIE CLINIQUE.** [Rev. fr. allergol. immunol. clin.]. Added/Corp Societe Francaise d'Allergologie. Vol. 14 (Jan./Feb. 1974)-. Academic Scholarly Publication. French (summaries and/or abstracts in English). Four times a year. 700.00F France; 920.00F other. Expansion Scientifique Francaise, 31 Boulevard de la Tour-Maubourg, 75007 Paris France. Tel 011 33 1 40 62 64 00, 011 33 1 40626439. NLM W1 RE844E. Pr Rev. available on microfilm from University Microfilms International (UMI). Documents available from The Genuine Article. *Continues Revue Francaise d'Allergologie, 0035-2845.*
Ind/Abst Curr. Contents Clin. Med.; EMBASE; Nutr. Abstr. Rev., Ser. A, Hum. Exp.; Life Sci. Collect.; Res. Alert [Select. Cov.]; Rev. Med. Vet. Entomol.; Saf. Health Work.

JA/0910-4186
**RINPAGAKU.** [Rinpagaku]. Added/Corp Nihon Rinpakei Kenkyukai. VFOAT Japanese Journal of Lymphology. (1978)-. Periodical. Japanese. sa. Nihon Rinpakei Kenkyukai, (Japanese Soc. of Lymphology), Tokyo Ika Daigaku Dai, 1 Kaibogaku Kyoshitsu, 1-1, Shinjuku 6 Chome, Shinjukuku, Tokyoto 160, Japan. CODEN RINPEJ. Documents available from CASDDS.
Ind/Abst Chem. Abstr.

IT/0035-6204
**RIVISTA DI EMOTERAPIA ED IMMUNOEMATOLOGIA.** [Riv. Emoter. Immunoematol.]. Vol. 1 (1954)-. Periodical. Italian. qt (4 issues). L30.000 Italy; $50.00 other. EMP, Via Riviera 39, 27100 Pavia Italy. Tel 011 39 382 526253. UDC 61. CODEN REIMAL.
Ind/Abst Index Med.

●US
**RMI ... REVIEW OF HIV & AIDS RESEARCH.** Added/Corp Reliance Medical Information, Inc. VFOAT RMI ... Review of HIV and AIDS Research; Review of HIV & AIDS Research; Review of HIV and AIDS Research. (1992)-. English. NLM ZWD 308; R627.

US/1049-8966
**RN-AIDSLINE.** *Ceased.* See Medical Science and Technology-Nursing.

RM/1220-8485
**ROUMANIAN ARCHIVES OF MICROBIOLOGY AND IMMUNOLOGY.** [Rom. arch. microbiol. immunol.]. Added/Corp Institutul Cantacuzino. VFOAT Romanian Archives of Microbiology and Immunology. Vol. 50, No. 1 (Jan./Mar. 1991)-. Periodical. English (summaries and/or abstracts in French). qt. DM294.00. (Subscription address: Kubon & Sagner, ABT Zeitschriftenimport, D 80328 Munich Germany.) NLM W1; RO489H. CODEN RAMIE5. *Continues Archives Roumaines de Pathologie Experimentales et de Micorbiologie, 0004-0037.*
Ind/Abst EMBASE [Select. Cov.]; Index Med. (1991-).

UK/0300-9475
**SCANDINAVIAN JOURNAL OF IMMUNOLOGY.** [Scand. j. immunol.]. Added/Corp Scandinavian Society for Immunology. Vol. 1 (Feb. 1972)-. Academic Scholarly Publication. English. mo (12 issues). $409.00 US & Canada; £264.00 other. Blackwell Scientific Publications Ltd, Marston Book Services, PO Box 87, Oxford OX2 ODT UK. Tel 011 44 865 791155, FAX 011 44 865 791927, telex 837 515 MARDIS G. ED M. Harboe and J. B. Natvig. LC QR180; .S33. DD 574.2/9/05. NLM W1 SC15E. CODEN SJIMAX. [CCC]. Index available (bound in last issue). Ad Acc. Pr Rev. Circ: 1,200. available on microfilm and microfiche from University Microfilms International (UMI). Documents available from The Genuine Article, BIOSIS Document Express, CASDDS, ADONIS.
Desc: International papers within the various fields of cellular and molecular immunology.
Ind/Abst ADONIS; AGRICOLA; Biol. Abstr.; Chem. Abstr.; Curr. Contents Life Sci.; Dairy Sci. Abstr.; EMBASE; Energy Res. Abstr. (July 1975-); Genet. Abstr.; Helminthol. Abstr. (19??-19??); Immunol. Abstr.; Index Med.; Microbiol. Abstr. Sect. B; NAPRALERT; Life Sci. Collect.; Protozoolog. Abstr.; Ref. Upd. Basic Ed.; Ref. Upd. Deluxe Ed.; Res. Alert [Full Cov.]; Sci. Cit. Index; SCISEARCH; Trop. Dis. Bull.; Virol. AIDS Abstr.

NO/0301-6323
**SCANDINAVIAN JOURNAL OF IMMUNOLOGY. SUPPLEMENT.** [Scand. j. immunol., Suppl.]. No. 1 (1973)-. Academic Scholarly Publication. English. ir. Comes with subscription to Scandinavian Journal of Immunology. Blackwell Scientific Publications Ltd, Marston Book Services, PO Box 87, Oxford OX2 ODT UK. Tel 011 44 865 791155, FAX 011 44 865 791927, telex 837 515 MARDIS G. NLM W1 SC15EC. CODEN SJISDK. [CCC]. Documents available from BIOSIS Document Express, CASDDS.
Ind/Abst Biol. Abstr.; Chem. Abstr.; Curr. Aware. Biol. Sci., CABS; Index Med.; Life Sci. Collect.

US/1058-6598
**SCOTT KING'S DIABETES INTERVIEW.** [Scott King's diabetes interview]. VFOAT Diabetes Interview; Interview. (1991)-. Periodical. English. mo. $14.00 US; $16.50 Canada; $19.00 other. Sugar Happy, 3715 Balboa Street, San Francisco CA 94121. Tel (800)347-4848, (415)387-4737, FAX (415)387-3604. ED Scott King. DD 616. Bk Rev, (Qty: 3). Ad Acc. Pr Rev. Circ: 30,000. *Continues Dial News.*
Desc: Only national diabetes newspaper in publication. Mission is to provide information on health and diabetes care.

UK/1044-5323
**SEMINARS IN IMMUNOLOGY.** [Semin. immunol.]. Vol. 1, Issue 1 (Sept. 1989)-. Academic Scholarly Publication. English. bm (6 issues). $185.00. Academic Press Ltd., A Division of Harcourt Brace & Company Ltd., 24-28 Oval Road, London NW1 7DX England. Tel 071 267 4466, FAX 071 482 2293, 071 485 4752, telex 25775 ACPRES G. (Subscription address: Harcourt Brace & Company, Ltd., Foots Cray, High Street, Sidcup Kent DA14 5HP England.) DD 616. NLM W1; SE489BE. CODEN SEIME2. [CCC]. Documents available from CASDDS.
Desc: Features in-depth reviews of a single topic in immunology. Contains reviews that are lively, readable and most importantly substantive enough to cite in your own work.
Ind/Abst Chem. Abstr. (1989-); Immunol. Abstr.; Index Med. (1989-).

CN/1198-7421
**SEMINARS IN OTOLARYNGIC ALLERGY.** (March 1995)-. English. qt. $78.00 (institutions), $52.00 (individuals) US & Canada; $105.00 (institutions), $79.00 (individuals) other. Decker Periodicals Publishing Inc, PO Box 620, Station A, Hamilton Ontario L8N 3K7 Canada. Tel (416)522-7017, (800) 568-7281, FAX (416)522-7839.

CC/1001-2478
**SHANGHAI MIANYIXUE ZAZHI.** **VFOAT** Shanghai Journal of Immunology. (1981)-. Periodical. Chinese. bm. **DD** 574.29.
**Ind/Abst** Protozoolog. Abstr.

SP
**SIDAHORA :UN PROYECTO DEL DEPARTAMENTO DE PUBLICACIONES DEL PWA COALITION, NY.** **Added/Corp** People with AIDS Coalition. **VFOAT** SIDA Ahora. (1989)-. Periodical. English (Spanish). qt. $20.00. PWA Coalition Newsline / New York, 50 West 17th Street, 8th Floor, New York NY 10011. **Tel** (212)647-1415, FAX (212)647-1419. **ED** Luis Lopez. **NLM** W1; SI252. **Circ:** 12,000.
**Desc:** Written for and by Latinos with AIDS.

US
**SIDAMERICA.** Spanish. ir (approximately 2 issues per year). Free. Panos Institute, 1717 Massachusetts Avenue Northwest, Suite 301, Washington DC 20036. **Tel** (202)483-0044, FAX (202)483-3059.
**Desc:** For those working on HIV / AIDS throughout the Americas. Focuses on needs and issues in the region.

US/0037-6337
**SKIN & ALLERGY NEWS.** **See** Medical Science and Technology-Dermatology.

JA/0910-5042
**SOSHIRAN ENGLISH ED.** [Soshiran Engl. ed.]. **VFOAT** Sino-Japanese Journal of Allergology and Immunology (English Ed.). (1983)-. Academic Scholarly Publication. English. an. Nitchu Men'eki Arerugi Kaigi, (Sino-Japanese Meeting on Allergology & Immunology), Nippon Zoki Seiyaku K.K., 2-10, Hiranomachi, Higashiku, Osakashi, Osakafu 541, Japan. **DD** 616.97. Documents available from CASDDS.
**Ind/Abst** Chem. Abstr.

SZ/0887-3488
**SOVIET MEDICAL REVIEWS. SECTION D, IMMUNOLOGY REVIEWS.** ***Ceased.*** [Sov. med. rev., D Immunol. rev.]. **Added/Corp** Soviet Medical Reviews (Firm : Chur, Switzerland). **VFOAT** Immunology Reviews; Immunology; Soviet Medical Reviews. Immunology. Vol. 1 (1987)-(1993). English. an. Harwood Academic Publishers, PO Box 90, Reading RG1 8JL, England. **Tel** 011 44 734 560080. **(Subscription address:** International Publishers Distributor at one of the following addresses: 820 Town Center Drive, Langhorne, PA 19047; or PO Box 90, Reading Berkshire RG1 8JL UK; or Kent Ridge PO Box 1180, Singapore 9111, Republic of Singapore**)** **LC** QR180; .S66. **DD** 616.07/9/05. **NLM** W1; SO996LD. **CODEN** SMDREE. **[CCC].**

SZ/0896-601X
**SOVIET MEDICAL REVIEWS SUPPLEMENT SERIES. SECTION D, IMMUNOLOGY.** [Sov. med. rev., Suppl. ser., Immunol.]. **VFOAT** Immunology. Vol. 1 (1988)-. English. ir. Harwood Academic Publishers, PO Box 90, Reading RG1 8JL England. **Tel** 011 44 734 560080. **(Subscription address:** International Publishers Distributor at one of the following addresses: 820 Town Center Drive, Langhorne, PA 19047; or PO Box 90, Reading Berkshire RG1 8JL UK; or Kent Ridge PO Box 1180, Singapore 9111, Republic of Singapore**)** **NLM** W1; SO996LH.

US/0895-755X
**SPOTLIGHT ON AIDS.** **VAT** Spotlight on Acquired Immune Deficiency Syndrome. Periodical. English. mo. $40.00 US; $45.00 Canada. Associated Physicians Publishing Company, PO Box 181, Harrison NY 10528.

US/0344-4325
**SPRINGER SEMINARS IN IMMUNOPATHOLOGY.** [Springer semin. immunopathol.]. **VFOAT** Seminars in Immunopathology. Vol. 1 (1978)-. Academic Scholarly Publication. English. Four times a year. DM490.00. Springer-Verlag GmbH & Company KG, Heidelberger Platz 3, D 14197 Berlin Germany. **Tel** 011 49 30 8207223, FAX 011 49 30 8214091, telex 183 319 SPBLN D. **(Subscription address:** Springer Verlag New York Inc. / for North America, 44 Hartz Way, Secaucus NJ 07096.**)** **ED** P A Miescher and H L Spiegelberg. **LC** UNC. **NLM** W1 SP685J. **CODEN** SSIMDV. **[CCC].** **Pr Rev.** available on microfilm from University Microfilms International (UMI). Documents available from The Genuine Article, CASDDS, ADONIS.
**Desc:** Aim of this journal is to keep clinicians and pathologists up-to-date on developments in the field of immunopathology.
**Ind/Abst** ADONIS; Chem. Abstr.; Curr. Contents Life Sci.; EMBASE; Index Med.; Life Sci. Collect.; Protozoolog. Abstr.; Ref. Upd. Basic Ed.; Ref. Upd. Deluxe Ed.; Res. Alert [Full Cov.]; Sci. Cit. Index; SCISEARCH; Trop. Dis. Bull.

●UK/0967-0149
**THERAPEUTIC IMMUNOLOGY.** Vol. 1, No. 1 (Jan. 1994)-. Academic Scholarly Publication. English. Six times a year. $231.00 (institutions), $106.00 (individuals) US & Canada; £135.00 (institutions), £62.50 (individuals) Europe; £149.00 (institutions), £68.50 (individuals) other. Blackwell Scientific Publications Ltd, Marston Book Services, PO Box 87, Oxford OX2 ODT UK. **Tel** 011 44 865 791155, FAX 011 44 865 791927, telex 837 515 MARDIS G.

NE/0165-6090
**THYMUS.** [Thymus]. Vol. 1 (Sept. 1979)-. Academic Scholarly Publication. English. ir (Eight issues per year). $311.00. Kluwer Academic Publishers, Postbus 322, 3300 AH Dordrecht, The Netherlands. **Tel** 011 (31) 78 524400, FAX 011 31 78 183273, telex 20083. **ED** Jean-Louis Touraine. **NLM** W1 TH958. **CODEN** THYMDB. **[CCC].** **Bk Rev.** **Ad Acc.** **Pr Rev.** **Acid Free.** **Circ:** 1,000. available on microfilm and microfiche from University Microfilms International (UMI). Documents available from The Genuine Article, BIOSIS Document Express, CASDDS.
**Desc:** Devoted to the rapid publication of papers (original papers, review articles, short communications and letters to the editor), within the fields of thymology, immunobiology and clinical immunology.
**Ind/Abst** Biol. Abstr.; Chem. Abstr.; Curr. Aware. Biol. Sci., CABS; Curr. Contents Life Sci.; EMBASE; Fish Rev. (Jan. 1989-July 1992); Index Med.; Index Vet.; Life Sci. Collect.; Poult. Abstr.; Ref. Upd. Deluxe Ed.; Res. Alert [Full Cov.]; Sci. Cit. Index; SCISEARCH; Vet. Bull.; Wildl. Rev. (Jan. 1989-July 1992).

US
**TOTAL AIDS CASES, UTAH AND UNITED STATES.** **See** Public Health and Safety.

FR/1166-5300
**TRANSCRIPTASE : REVUE CRITIQUE DE L'ACTUALIT,E SCIENTIFIQUE INTERNATIONALE SUR LE SIDA.** (1991)-. Periodical. French. Eleven times a year. 350.00F (institutions), 250.00F (individuals) Europe; 450.00 (institutions), 350.00 (individuals) other. Association Pistes, 192 rue Lecourbe France. **Tel** 011 33 1 53688888. **ED** Giulles Piacoux (editor's address: Hospital de P'institor Pasteur, 211 rue de Vaugirard, 25015 Paris, France; phone 45688196). **NLM** W1; TR228J. Index available. cum. index. **Ad Acc,** **Adv Mgr:** Mayle Didier. **Circ:** 3,000 (ctrl).

●US/0966-3274
**TRANSPLANT IMMUNOLOGY.** Vol. 1, No. 1 (Mar. 1993)-. Academic Scholarly Publication. English. qt. £140.00 (institution), £67.50 (individual) EC; $250.00 (institution), $125.00 (individual) US; £160.00 (institution), £77.50 (individual) other. Edward Arnold, 338 Euston Road, London NW1 3BH England. **Tel** 011 44 71 873 6000, FAX 011 44 071 873 6325. **(Subscription address:** Edward Arnold, PO Box 386, Avenel NJ 07001-0386.**)** **ED** I.V. Hutchinson. **NLM** W1; TR233E. **CODEN** TRIME2. Documents available from CASDDS.
**Desc:** Devoted exclusively to the immunobiology of transportation, the journal includes original articles and reviews on all aspects of immunology as they related to clinical and experimental transplantation. Coverage includes major and minor allogeneic and xenogeneic histocompatibility antigens; the T processing, presentation and recognition of allo and xenoantigens; adhesion molecules, endothelial cells and lymphocyte migration; and infection and other complications.
**Ind/Abst** Chem. Abstr.; Curr. Aware. Biol. Sci., CABS; EMBASE; Immunol. Abstr.

US/0748-1861
**TRANSPLANTATION AND IMMUNOLOGY LETTER.** **See** Medical Science and Technology-Surgery.

US/1050-625X
**TREATMENT ISSUES.** (TREATMENT ISSUES : THE GMHC NEWSLETTER OF EXPERIMENTAL AIDS THERAPIES.). [Treat. issues]. **Added/Corp** Gay Men's Health Crisis, Inc. Vol. 1, No. 1 (Nov. 27, 1987)-. English. Ten times a year. $30.00 individuals, $50.00 institutions. Gay Men Health Crisis - GMHC, Medical Information, 129 West 20th Street, New York NY 10011. **Tel** (212)807-7517. **LC** RC607.A26; T74. **DD** 616.97/9206/05.
**Desc:** Community-based newsletter devoted to AIDS/HIV treatment and medical information. Provides timely, accurate information about treatments so that people affected by HIV disease can make more informed health care decisions.

●US/1056-7909
**VACCINE RESEARCH.** [Vaccine res.]. Vol. 1, No. 1 (Spring 1992)-. Academic Scholarly Publication. English. qt. $172.95. Mary Ann Liebert Inc., 1651 Third Avenue, New York NY 10128. **Tel** (212)289-2300, (800)M-LIEBERT, FAX (212)289-4697. **ED** Michael Hanna, Jr. **DD** 616. **NLM** W1; VA242B. **CODEN** VAREES. Documents available from CASDDS.
**Desc:** A central resource of documentation of basic and applied research in vaccine development and application. Publishes original investigative and theoretical papers describing principles and technologies that can be applied to the development of new vaccines and the improvement of safety and efficacy of existing vaccines as well as important biologic and immunologic principles relevant to host-vaccine interactions.
**Ind/Abst** Chem. Abstr.

●US/1074-2921
**VACCINE WEEKLY.** (1994)-. English. wk. $995.00 US, Canada and Mexico; $1,195.00 other. CW Henderson, PO Box 5528, Atlanta GA 30307-0528. **Tel** (404)377-8895, FAX (404)378-5411. **(Subscription address:** CW Henderson, Subscription Office, PO Box 830409, Birmingham AL 35283-0409.**)**
**Desc:** Concentrates on vaccine-related news and research. Topics include therapeutic vaccines for AIDS, cancer, and other diseases, efficacy and safety trials, and FDA regulations and approvals.

US/0882-8245
**VIRAL IMMUNOLOGY.** [Viral immunol.]. Vol. 1, No. 1 (Spring 1987)-. Academic Scholarly Publication. English. qt. $179.95. Mary Ann Liebert Inc., 1651 Third Avenue, New York NY 10128. **Tel** (212)289-2300, (800)M-LIEBERT, FAX (212)289-4697. **ED** Gordon Dressman, Ronald Kennedy, Robert Lanford, and Tran Chanh. **DD** 616. **NLM** W1; VI763. **CODEN** VIIMET. **Pr Rev.** Documents available from The Genuine Article, BIOSIS Document Express, CASDDS.
**Desc:** Centralizes research in viral immunology. Contains articles and features regular mini-reviews of relevant literature, as well as clinical and veterinary articles, and laboratory research. Topics covered include human and animal viral immunology, research and development of viral vaccines.
**Ind/Abst** Biol. Abstr. (1987-); Chem. Abstr.; Curr. Aware. Biol. Sci., CABS; Curr. Contents Life Sci.; EMBASE; Health Plan. Adminis.; Immunol. Abstr.; Index Med. (1987-);; Index Vet.; Res. Alert [Full Cov.]; Trop. Dis. Bull.; Virol. AIDS Abstr.

US/0896-5919
**VIROLOGY & AIDS ABSTRACTS.** **See** Medical Science and Technology-Abstracting, Bibliographies and Statistics.

SZ/1011-5773
**WHO AIDS SERIES.** [WHO AIDS ser.]. **Added/Corp** World Health Organization. **VAT** World Health Organization Acquired Immune Deficiency Syndrome Series. (1988)-. Monographic series. English. ir. Comes with WHO Global Subscription Package. World Health Organization, Distribution and Sales, 20 Avenue Appia, CH-1211 Geneva 27 Switzerland. **Tel** 011 41 22 7912111, FAX 011 41 22 7880401. **LC** UNC. **NLM** W1; WH45K. **CODEN** WASEEA. Documents available from BIOSIS Document Express.
**Desc:** Features documents and reports issued by WHO Global Programme on AIDS. Responsible for acting as the world's directing and coordinating authority on questions of AIDS research and prevention, issues information meeting the highest standards of validity and objectivity. Recent topics include guidelines for AIDS sterilization and disinfection and nursing management of persons infected with HIV.
**Ind/Abst** Biol. Abstr. (1988-); EMBASE.

UK/0954-6510
**WORLDAIDS.** **Added/Corp** Panos Institute. Great Britain. Bureau of Hygiene and Tropical Diseases. **VFOAT** World AIDS. No. 1 (Jan. 1989)-. Periodical. English. bm. £15.00. Panos Publications Limited, 9 White Lion Street, London N19PD England. **Tel** 011 44 71 2781111, telex 9419293. **LC** RA644.A25; W6. **NLM** W1; WO901L.
**Ind/Abst** Hum. Rights Intern. Rep.

SZ/0256-2308
**YEAR IN IMMUNOLOGY, THE.** ***Ceased.*** [Year immunol.]. (1982)-Series complete with Volume 7 (1993). Periodical. English. an. S. Karger AG, Allschwilerstrasse 10, PO Box - Postfach - Case Postale, CH-4009 Basel Switzerland. **Tel** 011 41 61 306-1111, FAX 011 41 61 306-1234, telex CH 962 652. **ED** J M Cruse and R E Lewis Jr. **LC** QR180; .Y43. **DD** 616.07/9/05. **NLM** W1; SU921H v.2 no.3 etc. **[CCC].** Documents available from BIOSIS Document Express.
**Desc:** Annual presentation of ongoing research in the eclectic science of immunology. It is designed to give the reader an overview of the most significant developments that occured in various aspects of immunology in the year immediately preceding publication. Volumes, which consist of interpretive reviews written by invited scientists, thus undertake the vital task of helping the immunologists to keep in touch with the latest ideas and developments in their field.
**Ind/Abst** Biol. Abstr.; Index Med. (1984-1985)(1984-85-); Ref. Upd. Deluxe Ed.

CC/1000-484X
**ZHONGGUO MIANYIXUE ZAZHI.** **VFOAT** Chinese Journal of Immunology. (1985)-. Academic Scholarly Publication. Chinese. bm. **DD** 616.079. Documents available from CASDDS.
**Ind/Abst** Chem. Abstr.

CC/0254-5101
**ZHONGHUA WEISHENGWUXUE HE MIANYIXUE ZAZHI.** (CHUNG-HUA WEI SHENG WU HSUEH HO MIEN I HSUEH TSA CHIH.). [Zhonghua weishengwuxue he mianyixue zazhi]. **Added/Corp** Chung-Hua i Hsueh Hui (China : 1949- ). Wei Sheng Wu Ho Mien i Hsueh Hui. **VFOAT** Chinese Journal of Microbiology and Immunology; Zhonghua Weishengwuxue He Mianyixue Zazhi. (1981)-. Academic Scholarly Publication. Chinese (summaries and/or

abstracts in English). bm. Society of Microbiology and Immunology, Chinese Medical Association, c/o National Vaccine & Serum Institute, chaoyangqu, Beijing, 100024 China. **NLM** W1 CH985C. **CODEN** ZWMZDP. Documents available from CASDDS.
**Ind/Abst** Chem. Abstr.

RU/0372-9311
**ZHURNAL MIKROBIOLOGII, EPIDEMIOLOGII I IMMUNOBIOLOGII.** [Z. mikrobiol. epidemiol. immunobiol.]. **Added/Corp** Vsesoiuznoe Nauchnoe Obshchestvo Mikrobiologov, Epidemiologov i Parazitologov Im. I.I. Mechnikova. (1935)-. Academic Scholarly Publication. Russian (summaries and/or abstracts in English; table of contents in English). Six times a year. $159.95. Izdatelstvo Meditsina / Russian Academy of Medical Sciences, Ulitsa Solyanka 14, 109801 Moscow Russia. **Tel** 011 95 297-05-04. **(Subscription address:** East View Publications Inc., 3020 Harbor Lane North, Suite 110, Minneapolis MN 55447.) **NLM** W1; ZH421. **CODEN** ZMEIAV. **[CCC]. Pr Rev.** Documents available from The Genuine Article, BIOSIS Document Express, CASDDS. ***Formed by the union of*** *Zhurnal Epidemiologii I Mikrobiologii* ***and*** *Zhurnal Mikrobiologii I Immunolobiologii.*
**Ind/Abst** Biol. Abstr.; Chem. Abstr.; Curr. Biotechnol.; Curr. Contents Life Sci.; EMBASE [Select. Cov.]; Helminthol. Abstr. (19??-19??); Index Med.; Int. Aerosp. Abstr.; Microbiol. Abstr. Sect. B (19??-19??); Microbiol. Abstr. Sect. A; Microbiol. Abstr. Sect. C; Life Sci. Collect.; Protozoolog. Abstr.; Res. Alert [Full Cov.]; Rev. Med. Vet. Entomol.; Rev. Med. Vet. Mycology; Sci. Cit. Index; SCISEARCH; Trop. Dis. Bull.; Virol. AIDS Abstr.

## ANATOMY

SZ/0001-5180
**ACTA ANATOMICA.** [Acta anat.]. Vol. 1 (1945)-. Academic Scholarly Publication. English (French and German; summaries and/or abstracts in French, German and English). mo. $1353.00. S. Karger AG, Allschwilerstrasse 10, PO Box - Postfach - Case Postale, CH-4009 Basel Switzerland. **Tel** 011 41 61 306-1111, FAX 011 41 61 306-1234, telex CH 962 652. **ED** HW Denker, AW English. **LC** QL801; .A2. **DD** 611.05. **NLM** W1 AC752. **CODEN** ACATA5. **[CCC].** Index available in last issue of volume--attached. cum. index. **Ad Acc. Pr Rev.** available on microfilm and microfiche from University Microfilms International (UMI). Documents available from The Genuine Article, BIOSIS Document Express, CASDDS. ***Continues*** *Bio-Morphosis.*
**Desc:** Concise reports from major laboratories throughout the world present original findings on all levels of organization of modern anatomical research, from subcellular to organismal. Studies in traditional areas of anatomical investigation are published along with contributions from non-traditional areas such as cell biology, neuroscience, developmental biology and functional and evolutionary morphology. This unique combination supports the journal's aim of representing all areas of modern research in anatomy.
**Ind/Abst** AGRICOLA [Select. Cov.]; Anim. Breed. Abstr.; Biol. Abstr.; Calcium Calcif. Tissue Abstr.; Chem. Abstr.; CSA Neuro. Abstr.; Curr. Aware. Biol. Sci., CABS; Curr. Contents Life Sci.; Curr. Ref. Fish Res.; Curr. Titl. Dent.; Dairy Sci. Abstr.; EMBASE; Health Plan. Adminis.; Index Med.; Index Vet.; Int. Aerosp. Abstr.; Nutr. Abstr. Rev., Ser. B, Live Feeds and Feed.; Nutr. Abstr. Rev., Ser. A, Hum. Exp.; Life Sci. Collect.; Pig News Inf.; Poult. Abstr.; Ref. Upd. Deluxe Ed.; Res. Alert [Full Cov.]; Sci. Cit. Index; SCISEARCH; Small Anim. Abstr. Bibliogr.; Soc. Sci. Cit. Index [Select. Cov.]; Vet. Bull.; Wildl. Rev.

GW/0301-5556
**ADVANCES IN ANATOMY, EMBRYOLOGY AND CELL BIOLOGY.** [Adv. anat., embryol. cell biol.]. **VFOAT** Revuews d'Anatomie et de Morphologie Experimentale; Ergebnisse der Anatomie und Entwicklungsgeschichte. Vol. 47 (1973)-. Monographic series. German (summaries and/or abstracts in English). ir. Price varies per volume. Springer Verlag New York Inc., PO Box 19386 Books, Newark NJ 07195. **Tel** (201)348-4033. **ED** F. Beck, W. Hild, W. Kritz, J.E. Pauly, Y. Sano, T.H. Schiebler, R. Ortmann. **LC** QL801; .E67. **DD** 574.4/08. **NLM** W1 AD433K. Documents available from The Genuine Article. ***Continues*** *Ergebnisse der Anatomie und Entwicklungsgeschichte, 0071-1098.*
**Ind/Abst** Index Med.; Index Sci. Rev. [Full Cov.]; Life Sci. Collect.; Res. Alert [Full Cov.]; Sci. Cit. Index; SCISEARCH.

UK/0269-0071
**ADVANCES IN PINEAL RESEARCH. See** Biology.

SP/0569-9894
**ANALES DE ANATOMIA.** [An. anat.]. (1952)-. Academic Scholarly Publication. Spanish. sa. Facultad Medicina Universidad de Zaragoza, Dept Ciencias Morfologicas, E 50009 Zaragoza Spain. **Tel** 011 34 76 359593. **NLM** W1 AN129. **CODEN** AANOA7. **[CCC].** Documents available from CASDDS.
**Ind/Abst** Chem. Abstr.; EMBASE [Select. Cov.]; Indice Med. Esp.

SP
**ANATOMIA HUMANA.** Spanish. **NLM** W1 AN192FJ.

FI/0358-4895
**ANATOMICA, PATHOLOGICA, MICROBIOLOGICA.** No. 1-. English (Finnish). ir. Fmk75.00 Finland; $15.00 US. Prof Leo Hirvonen, University of Oulu, 90100 Oulu 10 Finland. **Tel** 358-81-332133. **ED** Leo Hirvonen. **UDC** 611; 616; 579. **NLM** W1 AC954NM. **Ad Acc. Circ:** 450 (ctrl).
**Desc:** Monographs, reviews and dissertations in the fields of normal and pathological anatomy and microbiology.

US/0003-276X
**ANATOMICAL RECORD, THE.** [Anat. rec.]. **Added/Corp** American Association of Anatomists. American Society of Zoologists. Wistar Institute of Anatomy and Biology. Vol. 1 (Nov. 24, 1906)-. Academic Scholarly Publication. English. mo. $2,220.00 US; $2,340.00 Canada and Mexico; $2,385.00 other. John Wiley & Sons, Inc., 605 Third Avenue, New York NY 10158-0012. **Tel** (212)850-6000, (212)850-6645, FAX (212)850-6088, telex 12-7063. **(Subscription address:** John Wiley & Sons / England, Baffins Lane, Chichester, West Sussex PO19 1UD England.) **ED** Aaron J Ladman. **LC** QL801; .A45. **DD** 611.05. **NLM** W1 AN193. **CODEN** ANREAK. **[CCC]. Ad Acc. Pr Rev.** Documents available from The Genuine Article, BIOSIS Document Express, CASDDS.
**Desc:** A forum for research dealing with diverse aspects of the organization of biological structure and its functional significance. Includes regular research reports, review articles, special communications, and commentaries on all areas of the anatomical sciences.
**Ind/Abst** AgBiotech News Inf.; AGRICOLA; Anim. Breed. Abstr.; Biol. Agric. Index; Biol. Abstr.; Calcium Calcif. Tissue Abstr.; Chem. Abstr.; CSA Neuro. Abstr.; Curr. Aware. Biol. Sci., CABS; Curr. Contents Life Sci.; Curr. Ref. Fish Res.; Curr. Titl. Dent.; Dairy Sci. Abstr.; EMBASE; Fish Rev.; Health Plan. Adminis.; Index Med.; Index Vet.; INIS Atomindex [Micro.]; Int. Aerosp. Abstr.; Nutr. Abstr. Rev., Ser. B, Live Feeds and Feed.; Life Sci. Collect.; Pig News Inf.; Poult. Abstr.; Ref. Upd. Basic Ed.; Ref. Upd. Deluxe Ed.; Res. Alert [Full Cov.]; Sci. Cit. Index; SCISEARCH; Vet. Bull.; Wildl. Rev.

US/0749-3002
**ANATOMICAL RECORD. SUPPLEMENT, THE.** [Anat. rec., Suppl.]. (1983)-. Monographic series. English. ir. Price varies per volume. John Wiley & Sons, Inc., 605 Third Avenue, New York NY 10158-0012. **Tel** (212)850-6000, (212)850-6645, FAX (212)850-6088, telex 12-7063. **(Subscription address:** John Wiley & Sons / England, Baffins Lane, Chichester, West Sussex PO19 1UD England.) **LC** W1. **DD** 611. **NLM** W1; AN193A.
**Ind/Abst** Index Med.

GW/0003-2786
**ANATOMISCHER ANZEIGER.** ***Title Change.*** [Anat. Anz.]. Vol. 1 (June 1, 1886)-(1991). Academic Scholarly Publication. English (German and French). ir (6 times per year). Gustav Fischer Verlag Jena, Postfach 100537, D 07705 Jena Germany. **Tel** 011 49 3641 27332, FAX 011 49 3641 626500. **(Subscription address:** 303 NW 12th Avenue, Deerfield Beach FL 33442; telephone: (305)428-5566) **ED** G H Schumacher. **LC** QL801. **NLM** W1 AN207. **CODEN** ANANAU. **[CCC].** Index available. **Bk Rev. Ad Acc. Pr Rev. Circ:** 690. Documents available from BIOSIS Document Express, CASDDS. ***Continued by*** *Annals of Anatomy, 0940-9602.*
**Desc:** Presents papers dealing with the entire field of anatomy, histology, embryology and adjacent fields. To a restricted extent the "Anatomischer Anzeiger" will also be available for texts of personal matters, data of congresses, etc. Intended for all anatomists engaged in research or teaching, specialists engaged in adjacent fields and all who are interested in morphology.
**Ind/Abst** Anim. Breed. Abstr.; Biol. Abstr.; Chem. Abstr.; Curr. Ref. Fish Res.; Dairy Sci. Abstr.; EMBASE; Health Plan. Adminis.; Index Med.; Index Vet.; Nutr. Abstr. Rev., Ser. B, Live Feeds and Feed.; Life Sci. Collect.; Pig News Inf.; Poult. Abstr.; Rev. Agric. Entomol.; Sci. Cit. Index; SCISEARCH; Small Anim. Abstr. Bibliogr.; Vet. Bull.

GW/0340-2061
**ANATOMY AND EMBRYOLOGY.** [Anat. embryol.]. (1974)-. Academic Scholarly Publication. English (French and German). Twelve times a year. DM2680.00. Springer-Verlag GmbH & Company KG, Heidelberger Platz 3, D 14197 Berlin Germany. **Tel** 011 49 30 8207223, FAX 011 49 30 8214091, telex 183 319 SPBLN D. **(Subscription address:** Springer Verlag New York Inc. / for North America, 44 Hartz Way, Secaucus NJ 07096.) **ED** R Bellairs, B Christ, G Gabella, W Kriz, E Mugnaini, F Walberg, and K Zilles. **LC** QL951; .Z4. **DD** 596/.03. **NLM** W1 AN211. **CODEN** ANEMDG. **[CCC]. Ad Acc. Pr Rev.** available on microfilm from University Microfilms International (UMI). Documents available from The Genuine Article, BIOSIS Document Express, CASDDS. ***Continues*** *Zeitschrift fur Anatomie und Entwicklungsgeschichte, 0044-2232.*
**Desc:** Publishes original articles on anatomy, neuroanatomy, histology, morphological endocrinology, and embryology of vertebrates and especially, of man.
**Ind/Abst** AgBiotech News Inf.; Anim. Breed. Abstr.; Biol. Abstr.; Chem. Abstr. (1974-1983); Curr. Aware. Biol. Sci., CABS; Curr. Contents Life Sci.; Dairy Sci. Abstr.; EMBASE; Index Med.; Index Vet.; Life Sci. Collect.; Pig News Inf.; Poult. Abstr.; Ref. Upd. Deluxe Ed.; Res. Alert [Full Cov.]; Sci. Cit. Index; SCISEARCH; Small Anim. Abstr. Bibliogr.; Vet. Bull.

●GW/0940-9602
**ANNALS OF ANATOMY. Added/Corp** Anatomische Gesellschaft. **VFOAT** Anatomischer Anzeiger. Vol. 174, No. 1 (Feb. 1992)-. Periodical. German (English). Six times a year. DM660.00 Germany; DM672.00 other. Gustav Fischer Verlag Jena, Postfach 100537, D 07705 Jena Germany. **Tel** 011 49 3641 27332, FAX 011 49 3641 626500. **(Subscription address:** VCH Publishers Inc., 303 Northwest 12th Avenue, Journals Department, Deerfield FL 33442.) **CODEN** ANANEY. Documents available from The Genuine Article. ***Continues*** *Anatomischer Anzeiger, 0003-2786.*
**Ind/Abst** Curr. Aware. Biol. Sci., CABS; Curr. Contents Life Sci.; Res. Alert [Full Cov.]; Sci. Cit. Index; Soc. Sci. Cit. Index [Select. Cov.].

US
**ANNUAL FINANCIAL STATEMENT / ANATOMICAL BOARD OF THE STATE OF TEXAS. Main/Corp** Anatomical Board of the State of Texas. English. an. University of Texas / Medical Branch, 301 University Boulevard, Galveston TX 77550. **LC** QM33.2.T4; A5A. **DD** 354.97640072/236841.

US
**ANNUAL MEETING OF THE BOARD, ... MINUTES / ANATOMICAL BOARD OF THE STATE OF TEXAS. Main/Corp** Anatomical Board of the State of Texas. English. an. University of Texas / Medical Branch, 301 University Boulevard, Galveston TX 77550. **LC** QM33.2.T4; A5B. **DD** 353.97640084/1.

FR/0395-501X
**ARCHIVES D'ANATOMIE ET DE CYTOLOGIE PATHOLOGIQUES.** [Arch. anat. cytol. pathol.]. Vol. 24, (1976)-. Academic Scholarly Publication. French (summaries and/or abstracts in English). bm. 1290.00F France; 1620.00F other. Semaine de Hopitaux, 31 Boulevard de la Tour-Maubourg, 75007 Paris, France. **Tel** 011 33 1 40 62 64 00. **NLM** W1 AR312E. **CODEN** AACPDQ. **[CCC]. Bk Rev. Ad Acc. Circ:** 1,500. Documents available from BIOSIS Document Express, CASDDS. ***Continues*** *Archives d'Anatomie Pathologique, 0003-9608.*
**Ind/Abst** Biol. Abstr.; Chem. Abstr.; CIS Abstr.; EMBASE; Index Med.; Life Sci. Collect.; Protozoolog. Abstr.; Saf. Health Work.

UK/0148-5016
**ARCHIVES OF ANDROLOGY.** [Arch. androl.]. Vol. 1, No. 1 (1978)-. Academic Scholarly Publication. English. bm. $450.00 North America; £273.00 UK. Taylor & Francis Ltd., Rankine Road, Basingstoke Hampshire, RG24 8PR United Kingdom. **Tel** 011 44 256 840366, FAX 011 44 256 479438, telex 858540. **(Subscription address:** Taylor & Francis Inc., 1900 Frost Road, Suite 101, Bristol PA 19007-1598.) **ED** E. S. E. Hafez (editor's address: Reproductive Health Center, 78 Surfsong Road, Kiawah Island, South Carolina 29455). **LC** QP253; .A7. **DD** 612.6/1. **NLM** W1 AR436. **CODEN** ARANDR. **[CCC].** Index available. **Bk Rev. Ad Acc. Pr Rev. Circ:** 700. available on microfilm and microfiche from University Microfilms International (UMI). Documents available from The Genuine Article, BIOSIS Document Express, CASDDS, ADONIS.
**Desc:** Publishes research papers, review articles, and short communications in areas of reproduction, fertility and regulation, and infertility in the human and animal male. Aspects covered include: anatomical, morphological, ultrastructural, physiological, endocrinological, immunological, neurological, microbiological, pathological, psychiatric, fertility regulation and contraception.
**Ind/Abst** ADONIS; Anim. Breed. Abstr.; Biol. Abstr.; Chem. Abstr.; CSA Neuro. Abstr. (?-?); Curr. Aware. Biol. Sci., CABS; Curr. Contents Life Sci.; EMBASE; Health Plan. Adminis.; Index Med. (1978-); Med. Abstr. Newsl.; NAPRALERT; Life Sci. Collect.; Pig News Inf.; Ref. Upd. Deluxe Ed.; Res. Alert [Full Cov.]; Sci. Cit. Index; SCISEARCH.

IT/0004-0223
**ARCHIVIO ITALIANO DI ANATOMIA E DI EMBRIOLOGIA.** ***Title Change.*** [Arch. ital. anat. embriol.]. **Added/Corp** Societa Italiana di Anatomia. Consiglio Nazionale delle Ricerche (Italy). **VFOAT** Italian Journal of Anatomy and Embryology. Vol. 1 (Feb. 1902)-(19??). Periodical. Italian (English; summaries and/or abstracts in English, German and French). qt. Mozzon Giuntina SPA, Via Mannelli 29R, 50136 Florence, Italy. **Tel** 011 39 55 2476781, FAX 055/2478568. **ED** Giuseppe Carlo Balboni. **NLM** W1; AR58. **CODEN** AIAEA2. **Bk Rev. Ad Acc. Circ:** 500 (ctrl). Documents available from BIOSIS Document Express, CASDDS. ***Continued by*** *Italian Journal of*

*Anatomy & Embriology.*
**Desc:** Publishes scientific papers concerning subjects of anatomy, histology, embryology, histochemistry, etc.
**Ind/Abst** Biol. Abstr.; Chem. Abstr.; EMBASE; Index Med.; Index Vet.; Life Sci. Collect.; Vet. Bull.

SP
**ARCHIVOS DE ANATOMIA Y EMBRIOLOGIA.** Spanish. Editorial Complutense, Donoso Cortes 65 1RA Planta, 28003 Madrid Spain. **Tel** 011 34 1 3946372.
**Ind/Abst** Indice Med. Esp.

RU/0004-1947
**ARKHIV ANATOMII, GISTOLOGII I EMBRIOLOGII.** ***Title Change.*** [Arh. anat., gistol. embriol.]. **Added/Corp** Soviet Union. Ministerstvo Zdravookhraneniia. Soviet Union. Narodnyi Komissariat Zdravookhraneniia. Vsesoiuznoe Nauchnoe Obshchestvo Anatomov, Gistologov i Embriologov (Soviet Union). **VFOAT** Archives Russes d'Anatomie, d'Histologie et d'Embryologie. Vol. 10 (1931)-(1994). Periodical. Russian (summaries and/or abstracts in English). mo. Izdatelstvo Meditsina / Russian Academy of Medical Sciences, Ulitsa Solyanka 14, 109801 Moscow Russia. **Tel** 011 95 297-05-04. **NLM** W1 AR828. **CODEN** AAGEAA. Documents available from BIOSIS Document Express, CASDDS. ***Continues*** *Russkii Arkhiv Anatomii, Gistologii i Embryologii.* ***Continued by*** *Morfologiia.*
**Ind/Abst** Biol. Abstr.; Chem. Abstr.; Index Med.; Int. Aerosp. Abstr.; Life Sci. Collect.; SportSearch.

SZ/0067-7833
**BIBLIOTHECA ANATOMICA.** ***Title Change.*** [Bibl. anat.]. Vol. 1 (1961)- (1992). Periodical. English (French). an. S. Karger AG, Allschwilerstrasse 10, PO Box - Postfach - Case Postale, CH-4009 Basel Switzerland. **Tel** 011 41 61 306-1111, FAX 011 41 61 306-1234, telex CH 962 652. **ED** W Lierse. **UDC** 611. **NLM** W1 BI394. **CODEN** BIANA6. **[CCC].** Documents available from BIOSIS Document Express, CASDDS. ***Continued by*** *Imaging and Surgical Anatomy.*
**Desc:** Largely focuses on problems in microcirculation, a service to general medicine in that the small and lymphatic vessels rarely receive such attention. Material includes clinical aspects, methodology, and symposia reports, bringing theory closer to practice.
**Ind/Abst** Biol. Abstr.; Chem. Abstr.; Health Plan. Adminis.; Index Med.; Life Sci. Collect.

FR/0989-8972
**BIOLOGICAL STRUCTURES AND MORPHOGENESIS.** ***Ceased.*** [Biol. struct. morphog.]. **VFOAT** Archives d'Anatomie Microscopique et de Morphologie Experimentale. Vol. 1, No. 1 (1988)-Vol. 4, No. 4 (June 1993). Periodical. English. qt. Masson SA, Avenue Beauregard 12, CH-1701 Fribourg Switzerland. **Tel** 011 41 37 249585, FAX 011 41 37 247559, telex 942658 SEMI CH. **(Subscription address:** 7A Boulevard de Perolles, CH-1701 Fribourg Switzerland**)** **NLM** W1; BI759LN. **CODEN** BSTME2. available on microfilm and microfiche from University Microfilms International (UMI). Documents available from BIOSIS Document Express. ***Continues*** *Archives d'Anatomie Microscopique et de Morphologie Experimentale, 0003-9594.*
**Ind/Abst** Biol. Abstr.; EMBASE; Index Med. (1988-).

FR/0376-6160
**BULLETIN DE L'ASSOCIATION DES ANATOMISTES.** [Bull. Assoc. anat.]. **Added/Corp** Association des anatomistes. (Feb./Mar. 1973)-. Bulletin. French. qt. 680.00F (Europe); 800.00F (other). Association des Anatomistes, BP 184, 54505 Vandoeuvre Nancy France. **Tel** 11 33 83 592833, FAX 11 33 83 446065. **LC** QL801; .A9. **DD** 599/.04. **NLM** W1 BU529. **CODEN** ANOBAU. Documents available from BIOSIS Document Express. ***Continues*** *Comptes Rendus de l'Association des Anatomistes, 0066-8915.*
**Desc:** Includes the association's compted rendus, 21-1926- issued as numbers of the bulletin.
**Ind/Abst** Biol. Abstr.; EMBASE; Health Plan. Adminis.; Index Med.

CC/0529-1356
**CHIEH P'OU HSUEH PAO.** **Added/Corp** Chung-kuo Chieh p'ou Hsueh hui. **VFOAT** Acta Anatomica Sinica. (1953)-. Periodical. Chinese (summaries and/or abstracts in English, German and Russian).
**Ind/Abst** NAPRALERT.

US/0897-3806
**CLINICAL ANATOMY (NEW YORK, N.Y.).** (CLINICAL ANATOMY.). [Clin. anat.]. **Added/Corp** American Association of Clinical Anatomists. Meeting. American Association of Clinical Anatomists. British Association of Clinical Anatomists. (1988)-. Periodical. English. Six times a year. $498.00 US; $%58.00 Canada and Mexico; $%80.50 other. John Wiley & Sons, Inc., 605 Third Avenue, New York NY 10158-0012. **Tel** (212)850-6000, (212)850-6645, FAX (212)850-6088, telex 12-7063. **(Subscription address:** John Wiley & Sons / England, Baffins Lane, Chichester, West Sussex PO19 1UD England.**)** **ED** Donald R. Cahill. **DD** 611. **NLM** W1; CL653. **CODEN** CLANE8.
**Desc:** Provides a medium for the exchange of current information between anatomists and clinicians. Embraces anatomy in all its aspects-gross, histologic, developmental, and neurologic-as applied to medical practice.
**Ind/Abst** EMBASE; Ref. Upd. Deluxe Ed.

●US/1058-8388
**DEVELOPMENTAL DYNAMICS.** [Dev. dyn.]. **Added/Corp** American Association of Anatomists. Vol. 193, No. 1 (Jan. 1992)-. Academic Scholarly Publication. English. mo. $1,296.00 (US); $1,416.00 other. John Wiley & Sons, Inc., 605 Third Avenue, New York NY 10158-0012. **Tel** (212)850-6000, (212)850-6645, FAX (212)850-6088, telex 12-7063. **(Subscription address:** John Wiley & Sons / England, Baffins Lane, Chichester, West Sussex PO19 1UD England.**)** **ED** Paul Goetinck. **LC** QL801; .A4. **DD** 611. **NLM** W1; DE997NJH. **CODEN** DEDYEI. Documents available from The Genuine Article, BIOSIS Document Express, CASDDS. ***Continues*** *American Journal of Anatomy, 0002-9106.*
**Desc:** Provides a focus for communication among developmental biologists who study the emergence of form during animal development. It is an international forum for information derived from analytical and theoretical investigations on the mechanisms that control morphogenesis.
**Ind/Abst** Biol. Abstr. (1992-); Chem. Abstr. (1992-); Curr. Aware. Biol. Sci., CABS; Curr. Contents Life Sci.; EMBASE; Energy Res. Abstr.; Index Med. (1992-); INIS Atomindex [Micro.]; Ref. Upd. Deluxe Ed.; Res. Alert [Full Cov.]; Sci. Cit. Index; SCISEARCH.

NE/0924-3860
**EUROPEAN JOURNAL OF MORPHOLOGY.** [Eur. j. morphol.]. Vol. 28 (1990)-. Academic Scholarly Publication. English. qt. FI526.00 (Institutions). Swets & Zeitlinger BV, Heereweg 347B PO Box 825, 2160 SZ Lisse Holland. **Tel** 011 31 2521 35111, FAX 02521-15888, telex 41325. **(Subscription address:** Swets Publishing Service, PO Box 825, 2160 SZ Lisse The Netherlands**)** **ED** J Drukker, A Huson, A Kaufman, T Pexieder, D W Scheureman. **LC** QL799; .A25. **DD** 591.4. **NLM** W1; EU72DIE. **CODEN** EJMOEB. **[CCC].** Documents available from The Genuine Article, BIOSIS Document Express, CASDDS. ***Continues*** *Acta Morphologica Neerlando-Scandinavica, 0001-6225.*
**Desc:** The scope can be described as covering the entire field of vertebrate morphology with certain emphasis on human anatomy and clinical anatomy and embryology. In the field of anatomy, main topics are: developmental anatomy, functional anatomy - mainly anatomy and the locomotor apparatus and neuroanatomy.
**Ind/Abst** Biol. Abstr. (1991-); Chem. Abstr. (1956-1983); CSA Neuro. Abstr.; Curr. Aware. Biol. Sci., CABS; Curr. Contents Life Sci.; EMBASE; Index Med. (1990-); Life Sci. Collect.; Res. Alert [Full Cov.]; Sci. Cit. Index; SCISEARCH.

NE/0014-4096
**EXCERPTA MEDICA. SECTION 5. GENERAL PATHOLOGY AND PATHOLOGICAL ANATOMY.** **See** Medical Science and Technology-Abstracting, Bibliographies and Statistics.

SZ
**IMAGING AND CLINICAL ANATOMY.** (19??)-. English. an. 150.00F (approx. per volume). S. Karger AG, Allschwilerstrasse 10, PO Box - Postfach - Case Postale, CH-4009 Basel Switzerland. **Tel** 011 41 61 306-1111, FAX 011 41 61 306-1234, telex CH 962 652. **ED** A. W. English. ***Continues*** *Imaging and Surgical Anatomy.*
**Desc:** A large number of the volumes in this series focus on problems in microcirculation. Material includes clinical aspects, methodology and symposia reports bringing theory closer to practice.

IT
**ITALIAN JOURNAL OF ANATOMY & EMBRIOLOGY.** (19??)-. English. Four times a year. L15000 Italy; L20000 others. Mozzon Giuntina SPA, Via Mannelli 29R, 50136 Florence, Italy. **Tel** 011 39 55 2476781, FAX 055/2478568. ***Continues*** *Archivio Italiano di Anatomia e Embrilogia, 0004-0223.*

UK/0021-8782
**JOURNAL OF ANATOMY.** [J. anat.]. **Added/Corp** Anatomical Society of Great Britain and Ireland. Vol. 51 (Oct. 1916)-. Academic Scholarly Publication. English. bm (6 issues). $662.00 US, Canada & Mexico; £352.00 other. Cambridge University Press, The Edinburgh Building, Shaftesbury Road, Cambridge CB2 2RU United Kingdom. **Tel** 011 44 223 312393, FAX 011 44 223 325959. **(Subscription address:** Cambridge University Press / North America, 110 Midland Avenue, Port Chester NY 10573.**)** **ED** P. K. Thomas. **LC** QL801; .J7. **DD** 596/.04/05. **CODEN** JOANAY. **Bk Rev. Pr Rev.** available on microfilm and microfiche from University Microfilms International (UMI). Documents available from The Genuine Article, BIOSIS Document Express, CASDDS. ***Continues*** *Journal of Anatomy and Physiology.*
**Desc:** Publishes original papers, book reviews and invited review articles from all over the world. Covers all aspects of normal human and comparative anatomy including applied anatomy, physical anthropology, neurology, endocrinology, embryology, stereology, histology, histochemistry, and electron microscopy with special emphasis on experimental morphology.
**Ind/Abst** AGRICOLA; Biol. Abstr.; Chem. Abstr.; CSA Neuro. Abstr. (?-?); Curr. Contents Life Sci.; Curr. Ref. Fish Res.; Curr. Titl. Dent.; Dairy Sci. Abstr.; EMBASE; Fish Rev.; GeoRef; Index Med.; Index Vet.; Key Word Index Wildl. Res.; Nutr. Abstr. Rev., Ser. B, Live Feeds and Feed.; Life Sci. Collect.; Pig News Inf.; Ref. Upd. Basic Ed.; Ref. Upd. Deluxe Ed.; Res. Alert [Full Cov.]; Sci. Cit. Index; SCISEARCH; Small Anim. Abstr. Bibliogr.; Vet. Bull.; Wildl. Rev.

II/0003-2778
**JOURNAL OF THE ANATOMICAL SOCIETY OF INDIA.** **Main/Corp** Anatomical Society of India. Vol. 1 (June 1952)-. Periodical. English. sa. $35.00. Anatomical Society of India, Department of Anatomy, MLB Medical College, Jhansi 284 128 India. **Tel** 2032. **(Subscription address:** Prints India, 11 Darya Ganj, New Delhi, 110002 India, (Phone: 011 91 11 3268645)**)** **ED** G. S. Longia, Vinod Kumar. **LC** QM1; .A7162. **DD** 611.06254. **NLM** W1 JO911Q. **CODEN** JAINAA. Index available. **Bk Rev. Ad Acc. Circ:** 650-700 (ctrl). Documents available from CASDDS.
**Ind/Abst** Chem. Abstr.; Index Vet.; Vet. Bull.

JA/0022-7722
**KAIBOGAKU ZASSHI.** (KAIBOGAKU ZASSHI / ACTA ANATOMICA NIPPONICA.). [Kaibogaku zasshi]. **Added/Corp** Nippon Kaibo Gakkai. **VFOAT** Acta Anatomica Nipponica; Japanese Zeitschrift fur Anatomie. Vol. 1 (Aug. 1928)-. Academic Scholarly Publication. Japanese (summaries and/or abstracts in English and German). Six times a year. $264.50. University of Japan, Japanese Association of Anatomists, Nihon Kaibo Gakkai, 731 Hongo Bunkyo Tokyo Japan. **(Subscription address:** Japan Publications Trading Company, Ltd., PO Box 5030, Tokyo International, Tokyo 100-31 Japan.**)** **NLM** W1 KA4062. **CODEN** KAIZAN. Documents available from BIOSIS Document Express.
**Ind/Abst** Biol. Abstr.; EMBASE; Index Med.

●RU/0004-1947
**MORFOLOGIIA.** (1992)-. Russian (English). mo. $99.95. **(Subscription address:** East View Publications Inc., 3020 Harbor Lane North, Suite 110, Minneapolis MN 55447.**)** ***Continues*** *Archiv Anatomii, Gistologii i Embriologii.*

GW/0172-9187
**MORPHOLOGIA MEDICA.** [Morphol. med.]. Vol. 1, No. 1 (Feb. 1981)-. Academic Scholarly Publication. German (summaries and/or abstracts in English). bm. $118.00. VCH Publishers Inc, 220 East 23rd Street, New York NY 10010. **Tel** (212)683-8333, , FAX (212)481-0897. **(Subscription address:** VCH Publishers Inc., 303 Northwest 12th Avenue, Journals Department, Deerfield FL 33442.**)** **NLM** W1 MO915H. **CODEN** MOMDDW.
**Ind/Abst** EMBASE; Index Med.

GW/0303-2418
**NORMALE UND PATHOLOGISCHE ANATOMIE.** [Norm. pathol. Anat.]. (1970)-. Monographic series. German. ir. Price varies per volume. Georg Thieme Verlag Stuttgart, Postfach 301120, D 70451 Stuttgart Germany. **Tel** 011 49 711 89310, FAX 011 49 711 8931298, telex 7 252 275 GTVD. **(Subscription address:** Thieme Medical Publishers Inc., 381 Park Avenue South, New York NY 10016.**)** **NLM** W1 NO254T. ***Continues*** *Zwanglose Abhandlungen aus Demgebiet der Normalen und Pathologischenanatomie.*
**Ind/Abst** Index Med.

JA/0030-154X
**OKAJIMAS FOLIA ANATOMICA JAPONICA.** Vol. 14, Issue 3 (June 1936)-. Academic Scholarly Publication. English (German). bm. $312.00. Okajima Foria Anatomika Yaponika Henshubu, (Editorial Board of Okajima Folia Anatomica Japonica), c/o Keio Daigaku Igakubu, Kaibogaku Kyoshitsu, 35 Shinanomachi, Shinjukuku, Tokyoto 160, Japan. **(Subscription address:** Japan Publications Trading Company, Ltd., PO Box 5030, Tokyo International, Tokyo 100-31 Japan.**)** **NLM** W1 OK102. **CODEN** OFAJAE. cum. index. Documents available from BIOSIS Document Express. ***Continues*** *Folia Anatomica Japonica.*
**Ind/Abst** AGRICOLA; Biol. Abstr.; EMBASE; Index Med.; Life Sci. Collect.

FR/0761-1900
**PASCAL FOLIO. F53, ANATOMIE ET PHYSIOLOGIE DES VERTEBRES.** **VFOAT** Anatomie et Physiologie des Vertebres; Vertebrates Anatomy and Physiology. No. 1 (1984)-. Periodical. French (English). mo. Centre de Documentation Scientifique et Technique, Centre National de la Recherche Scientifique, 26 rue Boyer, 75971 Paris Cedex 20 France. **Tel** (1) 43 58 35 59, telex CNRSDOC

220880F. **NLM** ZQ 1; P289. ***Continues in part*** *Bulletin Signaletique. 365, Zoologie des Vertebres, Ecologie Animale, Physiologie Appliquee Humaine.*

US/0092-6930
**PROCEEDINGS OF THE CAJAL CLUB.** (PROCEEDINGS.). **Main/Corp** Cajal Club. V. 1 (1973)-. Proceedings. English. University of Texas / Medical Branch, 301 University Boulevard, Galveston TX 77550. **LC** QP351; .C28A. **DD** 612/.8/06273. **NLM** W1 PR5848N.

JA
**RINSHO TO KAIBO SEMINA.** **VFOAT** Readings on Advanced Functional Anatomy Seminar. V. 1 (July/Sept. 1983)-. Japanese. Ishiyaku Shuppan K.K., (Ishiyaku Publishers, Inc.), 7-10, Honkomagome 1 Chome, Bunkyoku Tokyoto 113 Japan. **ED** Hoshino Kazumasa. **NLM** W3 RI195L.

GW/0930-1038
**SURGICAL AND RADIOLOGIC ANATOMY (ENGLISH ED.).** (SURGICAL AND RADIOLOGIC ANATOMY : SRA.). [Surg. radiol. anat.]. **VFOAT** SRA. Vol. 8, No. 1 (1986)-. Periodical. English. Four times a year. 1945.00F. Springer-Verlag France, 26 rue des Carmes, F 75005 Paris France. **Tel** 011 33 1 44411599, FAX 011 33 43250225. **(Subscription address:** Springer Verlag New York Inc. / for North America, 44 Hartz Way, Secaucus NJ 07096.**) ED** J.P. Chevrel. **NLM** W1; SU76D. **Pr Rev.** Documents available from The Genuine Article. ***Continues*** *Anatomia Clinica. English Ed., 0343-6098.*
**Desc:** Designed to provide clinicians, whether general practitioners, or specialists, surgeons or radiologists, with information to keep them up to date in this field and to open up a pathway to applications in their particular specialty.
**Ind/Abst** Curr. Contents Clin. Med.; EMBASE; Index Med. (1986-); Res. Alert [Full Cov.]; Sci. Cit. Index; SCISEARCH.

GW/0066-1562
**VERHANDLUNGEN DER ANATOMISCHEN GESELLSCHAFT.** [Verh. Anat. Ges.]. **Main/Corp** Anatomische Gesellschaft. Vol. 1 (1887)-. Academic Scholarly Publication. German. ir. $97.00. VCH Gesellschaft GmbH, Postfach 101161, D 69451 Weinheim Germany. **Tel** 011 49 6201 606459, FAX 011 49 6201 606184. **(Subscription address:** VCH Publishers Inc., 303 Northwest 12th Avenue, Journals Department, Deerfield FL 33442.**) LC** QL801; .A57. **NLM** W1 VE483K. **CODEN** VHAGAS. Documents available from BIOSIS Document Express, CASDDS.
**Ind/Abst** Biol. Abstr. (19??-); Chem. Abstr. (19??-); Index Med. (19??-); Index Vet. (19??-).

## ANESTHESIOLOGY

US/0094-6354
**AANA JOURNAL.** **See** Medical Science and Technology-Nursing.

US/0199-2554
**AANA NEWSBULLETIN.** **See** Medical Science and Technology-Nursing.

US/0883-122X
**ABMS DIRECTORY OF CERTIFIED ANESTHESIOLOGISTS.** ***Title Change.*** [ABMS dir. certif. anesth.]. **Added/Corp** American Board of Medical Specialties. American Board of Anesthesiology. **VFOAT** Directory of Certified Anesthesiologists. **VAT** American Board of Medical Specialties Directory of Certified Anesthesiologists. (1985)-(199?). Directory. English. be. American Board of Medical Specialties, 1 Rotary Center, Suite 805, Evanston IL 60201. **Tel** (708)491-9091. **LC** RD78.62.U6; A25. **DD** 617/.96/02573. **NLM** WO 222.1; A1523. ***Continued by*** *Official American Board of Medical Specialties (ABMS) Directory of Board Certified Anesthesiologists, 0000-1546.*

BE/0001-5164
**ACTA ANAESTHESIOLOGICA BELGICA.** [Acta anaesthesiol. belg.]. Vol. 1 (March 1950)-. Periodical. French (Dutch and English). Four times a year. 2400F Belgium; 2800F others. Association for the Society of Scientifique Medica Belgique, Avenue Circulaire 138A, B-1180 Brussels Belgium. **Tel** 011 32 2 3745158. **ED** G. Rolly. **NLM** W1 AC749. **CODEN** AABEAJ. **Bk Rev. Ad Acc. Circ:** 800. Documents available from BIOSIS Document Express, CASDDS.
**Desc:** All aspects related to anesthesiology, (anesthesia, pain treatment, intensive care, emergency medicine, etc.), basic research and clinical practice.
**Ind/Abst** Biol. Abstr.; Chem. Abstr.; EMBASE; Index Med.

IT/0374-4965
**ACTA ANAESTHESIOLOGICA ITALICA.** [Acta anaesthesiol. ital.]. Vol. 23 (Jan./Feb. 1972)-. Academic Scholarly Publication. Italian (French, German and Italian; summaries and/or abstracts in English). Four times a year. L80000.00 Italy; L120000.00 other. La Garangola, Via Montona 4, 35137 Padua Italy. **Tel** 011 39 49 8750550, FAX 011 39 49 8751743. **NLM** W1 AC751C. **CODEN** AANIBO. Index available. **Bk Rev. Ad Acc, Adv Mgr:** A. Pagamento. **Pr Rev. Circ:** 1700 (ctrl). Documents available from BIOSIS Document Express, CASDDS. ***Continues*** *Acta Anaesthesiologic.*
**Ind/Abst** Biol. Abstr.; Chem. Abstr.; EMBASE [Select. Cov.].

DK/0001-5172
**ACTA ANAESTHESIOLOGICA SCANDINAVICA.** [Acta anaesthesiol. Scand.]. Vol. 1 (1957)-. Academic Scholarly Publication. English. Eight times a year. kr1180.00 US, Canada and Japan; kr1085.00 other. Munksgaard International Publishers Ltd, PO Box 2148, DK-1016 Copenhagen K Denmark. **Tel** 011 45 33 12 70 30, FAX 011 45 33 12 93 87, telex 19431 MUNKS DK. **ED** Jan Eklund. **UDC** 616-089.5. **NLM** W1 AC7515. **CODEN** AANEAB. **[CCC]. Pr Rev.** Documents available from The Genuine Article, BIOSIS Document Express, UMI Article Clearinghouse, CASDDS, ADONIS.
**Desc:** Publishes papers on original work in anaesthesiology and subjects related to its basic sciences.
**Ind/Abst** ADONIS; Biol. Abstr.; Chem. Abstr.; CSA Neuro. Abstr. (?-?); Cumul. Index Nurs. Allied Health Lit.; Curr. Aware. Biol. Sci., CABS; Curr. Contents Clin. Med.; Curr. Contents Life Sci.; EMBASE; Energy Res. Abstr.; Health Devices Alerts; Index Med.; Index Vet.; INIS Atomindex [Micro.]; Nutr. Abstr. Rev., Ser. A, Hum. Exp.; Life Sci. Collect.; PESTDOC; Protozoolog. Abstr.; Ref. Upd. Deluxe Ed.; Res. Alert [Full Cov.]; Sci. Cit. Index; SCISEARCH; Soc. Sci. Cit. Index [Select. Cov.]; Vet. Bull.

DK/0515-2720
**ACTA ANAESTHESIOLOGICA SCANDINAVICA. SUPPLEMENT.** [Acta anaesthesiol. Scand., Suppl.]. Vol. 1 (1959)-. Academic Scholarly Publication. English. kr1180.00 US, Canada & Japan; kr1085.00 other (included with Acta Anaesthesiologica Scandinavica). Munksgaard International Publishers Ltd, PO Box 2148, DK-1016 Copenhagen K Denmark. **Tel** 011 45 33 12 70 30, FAX 011 45 33 12 93 87, telex 19431 MUNKS DK. **NLM** W1 AC75151. **CODEN** AASXAP. **[CCC].** Documents available from BIOSIS Document Express, CASDDS.
**Ind/Abst** Biol. Abstr.; Chem. Abstr.; Curr. Aware. Biol. Sci., CABS; EMBASE; Energy Res. Abstr. (1976-); Index Med.; Life Sci. Collect.

●CC
**ACTA ANAESTHESIOLOGICA SINICA.** **Added/Corp** Chung-hua Min Kuo Ma Tsui Hsueh Hui. **VFOAT** Ma Tsui Hsueh Tsa Chih. Vol. 32, No. 1 (Mar. 1994)-. Periodical. Chinese (English). Four times a year. Chung-hau Min Kuo Ma Tsui Hui, Taipei Taiwan. **NLM** W1; AC7516. ***Continues*** *Ma Tsui Hsueh Tsa Chih, 0254-1319.*
**Ind/Abst** Index Med. (1994-).

US/0737-6146
**ADVANCES IN ANESTHESIA.** [Adv. anesth.]. Vol. 1 (1984)-. English. ir. Price varies. Mosby Year Book Inc., 11830 Westline Industrial Drive, St Louis MO 63146. **Tel** (800)325-4177, (314)872-8370, FAX (314)432-1380, telex 44-2402. **ED** T. James Gallagher. **LC** RD78.3; .A38. **DD** 617/.96/05. **NLM** W1; AD422. **[CCC].**

●US/1078-4500
**AMERICAN JOURNAL OF ANESTHESIOLOGY, THE.** (1995)-. Periodical. English. bm (6 issues). $85.00 (institutions), $65.00 (individuals) US; $110.00 (institutions), $90.00 (individuals) other. Excerpta Medica / US, PO Box 3085, Princeton NJ 08543-3085. **Tel** (908)874-8550, FAX (908)874-5611. **(Subscription address:** American Journal of Anesthesiology, PO Box 3000, Denville NJ 07834.**)** ***Continues*** *Anesthesiology Review, 0093-4437.*
**Desc:** Presents fresh informative scientific, original, and review articles as well as symposia and news reports on matters of concern to the practicing anesthesiologist.

●US/1066-8977
**AMERICAN SOCIETY OF POST ANESTHESIA NURSES (ASPAN).** **See** Medical Science and Technology-Nursing.

UK/0003-2409
**ANAESTHESIA.** [Anaesthesia]. **Added/Corp** Association of Anaesthetists of Great Britain and Ireland. Vol. 1 (Oct. 1946)-. Academic Scholarly Publication. English. mo. £175.00 (institution), £68.00 (individual) UK & Europe; $315.00 (institution), $122.00 (individual) other. Harcourt Brace & Company Ltd., Foots Cray, High Street, Sidcup Kent DA14 5HP England. **Tel** 011 44 81 300 3322, FAX 011 44 81 309 0807. **(Subscription address:** W. B. Saunders Company / North America Subscriptions, c/o Periodicals, 6277 Sea Harbour Drive, 4th Floor, Orlando FL 32887.**) ED** M. Morgan. **DD** 617. **NLM** W1 AN103R. **CODEN** ANASAB. **[CCC]. Bk Rev. Pr Rev.** available on microfilm and microfiche from University Microfilms International (UMI). Documents available from The Genuine Article, CASDDS.
**Desc:** Publishes original articles of current clinical and scientific interest related to the practice of the modern specialty of anaesthesia and its scientific basis.
**Ind/Abst** Abr. Index Med.; Chem. Abstr.; Curr. Aware. Biol. Sci., CABS; Curr. Contents Clin. Med.; Curr. Contents Life Sci.; EMBASE; Health Devices Alerts; Health Plan. Adminis.; Index Med.; Life Sci. Collect.; PESTDOC; Res. Alert [Full Cov.]; Sci. Cit. Index; SCISEARCH; Soc. Sci. Cit. Index [Select. Cov.].

AT/0310-057X
**ANAESTHESIA AND INTENSIVE CARE.** [Anaesth. intensive care]. Vol. 1 (Aug. 1972)-. Academic Scholarly Publication. English. bm. 144.00Aus$ (institution), 102.00Aus$ (individual) Australia; 244.00Aus$ (institution), 144.00Aus$ (individual) other. Anaesthesia and Intensive Care, PO Box 600, Edgecliff NSW 2027, Australia. **Tel** 011 61 2 3274022, FAX 011 61 2 3277666. **ED** B. F. Horan. **UDC** 616-089.5. **NLM** W1 AN103T. **Bk Rev. Ad Acc. Pr Rev.** available on microfilm from University Microfilms International (UMI). Documents available from The Genuine Article.
**Desc:** Published by the Australian Society of Anaesthetists, this journal presents original articles of scientific and clinical related disciplines. Frequent symposium issues, comprehensive review articles, dissertations on the history of anesthesia and education and training in these specialties are informative and authoritative. This journal is international in readership.
**Ind/Abst** Cumul. Index Nurs. Allied Health Lit.; Curr. Contents Clin. Med.; EMBASE; Health Devices Alerts; Index Med.; Nutr. Abstr. Rev., Ser. B, Live Feeds and Feed.; Nutr. Abstr. Rev., Ser. A, Hum. Exp.; Life Sci. Collect.; Res. Alert [Full Cov.]; Sci. Cit. Index; SCISEARCH; Soc. Sci. Cit. Index [Select. Cov.].

UK/0263-1512
**ANAESTHESIA (EDINBURGH).** (ANAESTHESIA.). [Anaesthesia]. **VFOAT** Anaesthesia Review. (1982)-. Periodical. English. $150.00. Churchill Livingstone, 1-3 Baxter's Place, Leith Walk, Edinburgh EH1 3AF Scotland. **Tel** 011 44 31 556 2424, FAX 011 44 31 558 1278, telex 727511. **(Subscription address:** PO Box 11318, Birmingham, AL 35202**) ED** Ronald D Miller. **LC** RD78.3; .A5. **DD** 617/.96/05. **NLM** W1 AN103G. **CODEN** ANRVE7. Documents available from BIOSIS Document Express.
**Ind/Abst** Biol. Abstr. (1991-); Protozoolog. Abstr.; Ref. Upd. Deluxe Ed.

HU/0133-5405
**ANAESTHESIOLOGIA ES INTENSIV THERAPIA.** [Anaesthesiol. intensiv ther.]. **Added/Corp** Magyar Anaesthesiologiai es Reanimatios Tarsasag. Magyar Anaesthesiologiai es Intenziv Therapias Tarsasag. **VFOAT** Aneszteziologia es Intenziv Terapia. (1972)-. Academic Scholarly Publication. Hungarian (summaries and/or abstracts in English; table of contents in English). bm. Akademiai Kiado, Publishing House of the Hungarian Academy of Sciences, Prielle Kornelia u. 19-35, H-1117 Budapest Hungary. **Tel** 011 36 1 1811991, FAX 011 36 1 1811991, telex 22-6228 AKNYO H. **(Subscription address:** Kultura, PO Box 149, H 1389 Budapest 62 Hungary.**) NLM** W1; AN103XM. **CODEN** AITHD7. Documents available from CASDDS. ***Continues*** *Anaesthesiologia es Reanimatio.*
**Ind/Abst** Chem. Abstr. (1971-1982).

FI/0358-4836
**ANAESTHESIOLOGICA (OULU).** (ANAESTHESIOLOGICA.). [Anaesthesiologica]. No. 1-. Monographic series. English (Finnish). ir. Price varies per volume. Prof Leo Hirvonen, University of Oulu, 90100 Oulu 10 Finland. **Tel** 358-81-332133. **ED** Leo Hirvonen. **UDC** 616-089.5. **NLM** W1 AC954NM no.12 etc. cum. index. **Ad Acc. Circ:** 450 (ctrl).
**Desc:** Monographs, reviews, and dissertation in the field of surgical anesthesiology.

GW/0170-5334
**ANAESTHESIOLOGIE UND INTENSIVMEDIZIN (ERLANGEN).** (ANAESTHESIOLOGIE UND INTENSIVMEDIZIN : INFORMATIONEN DER DEUTSCHEN GESELLSCHAFT FUER ANAESTHESIOLOGIE UND INTENSIVMEDIZIN UND DES BERUFSVERBANDES DEUTSCHER ANAESTHESISTEN.). [Anaesthesiol. Intensivmed.]. **Added/Corp** Deutsche Gesellschaft fuer Anaesthesiologie und Intensivmedizin. Berufsverband Deutscher Anaesthesisten. Vol. 9 (Sept. 1978)-. Academic Scholarly Publication. German. Twelve times a year. DM72.00 Germany; DM85.20 others. Perimed Spitta Med Verlagsges, Marienbergstrasse 78, D 90411 Nuernberg Germany. **Tel** 011 49 911 952800. **NLM** W1; AN1919S. **CODEN** ATIMDA. Documents available from CASDDS. ***Continues*** *Anaesthesiologische Informationen, 0341-2555.*
**Ind/Abst** Chem. Abstr.; EMBASE.

GW/0323-4983
**ANAESTHESIOLOGIE UND REANIMATION.** [Anaesthesiol. Reanim.]. **Added/Corp** Gesellschaft fur Anaesthesiologie und Reanimation der DDR. Vol. 1 , (1976)-. Academic Scholarly Publication. German (summaries and/or abstracts in English). Six times a year. $80.87. Selecta Verlagsgesellschaft mbH, Postfach 4240, c/o Mrs. Riemer, D-65032 Wiesbaden Germany. **Tel** 011 49 611 1705261. **NLM** W1 AN103Z. **CODEN** ANREDN. **[CCC].** Documents available from CASDDS.
**Ind/Abst** Chem. Abstr. (1976-1982); EMBASE [Select. Cov.]; Health Plan. Adminis.; Index Med.

CN/0824-7412
**ANAESTHESIOLOGY.** (ANAESTHESIOLOGY : SOUND RECORDING.). [Anaesthesiology]. No. 1 (1983)-. Periodical. English. Medifacts Group Ltd, 20 Camelot Drive, Suite 600, Ottawa Ontario K2A 0G3 Canada. **Tel** (613)728-4655. **DD** 617/.96/05. **UDC** 616-089.5.
**Ind/Abst** Cumul. Index Nurs. Allied Health Lit.

GW/0003-2417
**ANAESTHESIST, DER.** [Anaesthesist]. **Added/Corp** Osterreiche Gesellschaft fuer Anaesthesiologie und Reanimation. Deutsche Gesellschaft fuer Anaesthesie und Wiederbelebung. Schweizerische Gesellschaft fuer Anaesthesiologie und Wiederbelebung. (1952)-. Academic Scholarly Publication. German. Twelve times a year. DM468.00. Springer-Verlag GmbH & Company KG, Heidelberger Platz 3, D 14197 Berlin Germany. **Tel** 011 49 30 8207223, FAX 011 49 30 8214091, telex 183 319 SPBLN D. **(Subscription address:** Springer Verlag New York Inc. / for North America, 44 Hartz Way, Secaucus NJ 07096.**) ED** A Doenicke, O Mayrhofer, and H Schaer. **NLM** W1 AN1046. **CODEN** ANATAE. **[CCC]. Ad Acc. Pr Rev.** available on microfilm and microfiche from University Microfilms International (UMI). Documents available from The Genuine Article, BIOSIS Document Express, CASDDS, ADONIS.
**Desc:** Offers articles from the whole field of anesthesiology and basic research on the subject. Original research studies, new technological developments, letters to the editor, transactions of conferences, detailed of periodical articles in the overview field of interest to anesthetists, surgeons.
**Ind/Abst** ADONIS; Biol. Abstr.; Chem. Abstr.; Curr. Contents Clin. Med.; EMBASE; Energy Res. Abstr.; Health Plan. Adminis.; Index Med.; Int. Aerosp. Abstr.; Life Sci. Collect.; PESTDOC; Res. Alert [Full Cov.]; Sci. Cit. Index; SCISEARCH.

●UK
**ANAESTHETIC PHARMACOLOGY REVIEW.** Vol. 1, No. 1 (1993)-. Periodical. English. qt (Feb., May, Aug., Nov.). £60.00 (individuals), £85.00 (institutions) Europe; £68.00 (individuals), £94.00 (institutions) other. Castle House Publications Ltd, 28-30 Church Road, Tunbridge Wells Kent, TN1 1JP England. **Tel** 011 44 892 539606, FAX 011 44 892 517005, telex 957565 CBJ AG. **NLM** W1; AN1046E. Index available.

●US/1071-569X
**ANALGESIA (ELMSFORD, N.Y.).** (ANALGESIA.). (1994)-. Periodical. English. Six times a year. $95.00 US; $125.00 other. Cognizant Communication Corporation, 3 Hartsdale Road, Elmsford NY 10523. **Tel** (914)592-7720. **[CCC].** Index available (bound in last issue).

GW/0939-2661
**ANASTHESIOLOGIE, INTENSIVMEDIZIN, NOTFALLMEDIZIN, SCHMERZTHERAPIE : AINS. Added/Corp** Deutsche Gesellschaft Fur Anasthesiologie und Intensivmedizin. **VFOAT** AINS. Vol. 26, No. 1 (Feb. 1991)-. Periodical. German (English; summaries and/or abstracts in English; table of contents in English). Eight times a year. $223.00. Georg Thieme Verlag Stuttgart, Postfach 301120, D 70451 Stuttgart Germany. **Tel** 011 49 711 89310, FAX 011 49 711 8931298, telex 7 252 275 GTVD. **(Subscription address:** Thieme Medical Publishers Inc., 381 Park Avenue South, New York NY 10016.**) NLM** W1; AN1919L. ***Continues*** *Anasthesie, Intensivtherapie, Notfallmedizin, 0174-1837.*
**Ind/Abst** EMBASE; Health Plan. Adminis.; Index Med. (1991-).

GW/0171-1814
**ANASTHESIOLOGIE UND INTENSIVMEDIZIN (BERLIN, WEST).** (ANAESTHESIOLOGIE UND INTENSIVMEDIZIN.). [Anasthesiol. Intensivmed.]. **VFOAT** Anaesthesiology and Intensive Care Medicine. (1978)-. Academic Scholarly Publication. German (English). ir. Price varies per volume. Springer-Verlag GmbH & Company KG, Heidelberger Platz 3, D 14197 Berlin Germany. **Tel** 011 49 30 8207223, FAX 011 49 30 8214091, telex 183 319 SPBLN D. **(Subscription address:** Springer Verlag New York Inc. / for North America, 44 Hartz Way, Secaucus NJ 07096.**) LC** UNC. **NLM** W1 AN103YJ. **CODEN** ANIMD2. **[CCC].** Documents available from The Genuine Article, BIOSIS Document Express, CASDDS. ***Continues*** *Anaesthesiologie und Wiederbelebung.*
**Ind/Abst** Biol. Abstr.; Chem. Abstr.; Curr. Contents Clin. Med.; EMBASE; Res. Alert [Select. Cov.]; Soc. Sci. Cit. Index [Select. Cov.].

IT/0570-0760
**ANESTESIA E RIANIMAZIONE.** [Anest. rianim.]. (Sept. 1960)-. Academic Scholarly Publication. Italian (summaries and/or abstracts in English). Four times a year. L40.000. Systems SRL, Via Olanda 6, 20083 Gaggiano Mi Italy. **Tel** 011 39 2 90841814. Index available. **Bk Rev. Ad Acc. Circ:** 4,000 (ctrl).
**Ind/Abst** EMBASE.

IT
**ANESTESIOLOGIA CLINICA.** (19??)-. Italian. Three times a year. L110000.00 Italy; L220000.00 other. Verduci Editore, Via Gregorio VII 186, 00165 Rome Italy. **Tel** 011 39 6 39375224.

RU/0201-7563
**ANESTEZIOLOGIJA I REANIMATOLOGIJA.** (ANESTEZIOLOGIIA I REANIMATOLOGIIA.). [Anest. i reanim.]. **Added/Corp** Soviet Union. Ministerstvo Zdravookhraneniia. Vsesoiuznoe Nauchnoe Obshchestvo Anesteziologov i Reanimatologov (Soviet Union). (Jan./Feb. 1977)-. Academic Scholarly Publication. Russian (summaries and/or abstracts in English). bm. $79.95. Izdatelstvo Meditsina / Russian Academy of Medical Sciences, Ulitsa Solyanka 14, 109801 Moscow Russia. **Tel** 011 95 297-05-04. **(Subscription address:** East View Publications Inc., 3020 Harbor Lane North, Suite 110, Minneapolis MN 55447.**) NLM** W1 AN217R. **CODEN** AREAD8. Index available. **Bk Rev.** Documents available from BIOSIS Document Express, CASDDS. ***Continues*** *Eksperimentalnaia Khirurgiia i Anesteziologiia.*
**Ind/Abst** Biol. Abstr.; Chem. Abstr.; EMBASE; Index Med.

PL/0324-8216
**ANESTEZJA, REANIMACJA, INTENSYWNA TERAPIA.** [Anest. reanim. intensywna ter.]. **Added/Corp** Towarzystwo Anestezjologow Polskich. Vol. 5- (Jan./March 1973)-. Academic Scholarly Publication. Polish (summaries and/or abstracts in Russian and English; table of contents in English and Russian). qt. $99.00. **(Subscription address:** ARS Polona, PO Box 1001, 00068 Warsaw Poland.**) NLM** W1 AN217Y. **CODEN** ARITCG. Documents available from CASDDS. ***Continues*** *Anestezja I Reanimacja.*
**Ind/Abst** Chem. Abstr.

US/0003-2999
**ANESTHESIA AND ANALGESIA.** [Anesth. analg.]. **Added/Corp** International Anesthesia Research Society. **VFOAT** Anesthesia & Analgesia. Vol. 36 (Jan./Feb. 1957)-. Academic Scholarly Publication. English. mo. $157.00 (individual), $222.00 (institution), US; $202.00 (individual), $267.00 (institution) other. Williams & Wilkins Company, 428 East Preston Street, Baltimore MD 21202-3993. **Tel** (410)528-4000, (800)638-6423, FAX (410)528-8596, telex 87669. **(Subscription address:** Williams & Wilkins, PO Box 64380, Baltimore MD 21264.**) ED** Nicholas M. Greene. **DD** 617. **NLM** W1 AN218. **CODEN** AACRAT. **[CCC]. Bk Rev. Ad Acc. Pr Rev. Circ:** 17,000. available on microfilm and microfiche from University Microfilms International (UMI). Documents available from , The Genuine Article, BIOSIS Document Express, CASDDS, Quick Copies. ***Continues*** *Current Researchs in Anesthesia & Analgesia, 0099-8125.*
**Desc:** The official journal of the International Anesthesia Research Society. This journal publishes original research and clinical articles for practicing physicians and allied medical personnel.
**Ind/Abst** Abr. Index Med.; Biol. Abstr.; Chem. Abstr.; Cumul. Index Nurs. Allied Health Lit.; Curr. Aware. Biol. Sci., CABS; Curr. Contents Clin. Med.; Curr. Contents Life Sci.; EMBASE; Health Devices Alerts; Health Plan. Adminis.; Index Med.; Index Vet.; Int. Nurs. Index; Iowa Drug Inf. Serv. (1968-); Life Sci. Collect.; PESTDOC; Physic. Medline Plus; Pig News Inf.; Ref. Upd. Basic Ed.; Ref. Upd. Deluxe Ed.; Res. Alert [Full Cov.]; Sci. Cit. Index; SCISEARCH; Soc. Sci. Cit. Index [Select. Cov.].

US/1055-7601
**ANESTHESIA & PAIN CONTROL IN DENTISTRY.** ***Title Change.*** **See** Dentistry.

US/1050-8775
**ANESTHESIA MALPRACTICE PROTECTOR.** (ANESTHESIA MALPRACTICE PROTECTOR / AMERICAN HEALTH CONSULTANTS.). [Anesth. malpract. prot.]. **Added/Corp** American Health Consultants. (Aug. 1989)-. Periodical. English. mo. $219.00 (without Continuing Medical Education credits); $269.00 (with Continuing Medical Education credits). American Health Consultants, 3525 Piedmont Road, Suite 400, Atlanta GA 30305. **Tel** (800)688-2421, (404)262-7436. **(Subscription address:** American Health Consultants, PO Box 95278, Chicago IL 60694.**) LC** KF2910.A53; A133. **DD** 346.7303/32; 347.306332. **NLM** W1; AN218L. ***Continues*** *Anesthesiology Alert.*
**Desc:** Addresses legal problems and rapidly changing legal issues that affect the field of anesthesiology. Brings the latest news covering malpractice legislation, regulation and pending cases.

US/0003-3006
**ANESTHESIA PROGRESS. See** Dentistry.

US/0740-1914
**ANESTHESIAFILE.** [Anesthesiafile]. **Added/Corp** Anesthesiology Society (San Antonio, Tex.). **VFOAT** Anesthesia File. (198?)-. English. mo. $225.00 (individual), $245.00 (institution) US; $290.00 (individual) $310.00 (institution) other. W.B. Saunders Company, A Subsidiary of Harcourt Brace Jovanovich, Inc., The Curtis Center/Suite 300, Independence Square West, Philadelphia PA 19106-3399. **Tel** (215)238-7800 or, 5587, FAX (215)238-7883, telex 173146. **(Subscription address:** W. B. Saunders Company / North America Subscriptions, c/o Periodicals, 6277 Sea Harbour Drive, 4th Floor, Orlando FL 32887.**) ED** Vincent Collins, Betty Johnson, Janet Connolly. **DD** 617.

FR/0996-8296
**ANESTHESIE REANIMATION PRATIQUE PARIS.** (ANESTHESIE REANIMATION PRATIQUE.). (1989)-. Periodical. French. mo (10 issues). 342.80F France; 350.00F other. Len Medical, 48 Bis Avenue Kleber, F-75116 Paris France. **Tel** 011 33 1 47550606. **ED** Dr. A. Marsac. **UDC** 616-089.5. **Ad Acc.**

US/1050-6470
**ANESTHESIOLOGIST'S CLINICAL UPDATE.** ***Ceased.*** (ANESTHESIOLOGIST'S CLINICAL UPDATE : A MONTHLY DIGEST OF NEW DEVELOPMENTS IN ANESTHESIOLOGY / SPONSORED BY ALBERT EINSTEIN COLLEGE OF MEDICINE/MONTEFIORE MEDICAL CENTER.). [Anesthesiol. clin. update]. **Added/Corp** Albert Einstein College of Medicine. Montefiore Medical Center. (1989)-Vol. 5. Periodical. English. mo. Educational Reviews Inc., 6801 Cahaba Valley Road, Birmingham AL 35242. **Tel** (205)991-5188, (800)633-4743, FAX (205)995-1926. **DD** 617.

US/0889-8537
**ANESTHESIOLOGY CLINICS OF NORTH AMERICA.** [Anesthesiol. clin. North Am.]. Vol. 5, No. 1 (March 1987)-. Academic Scholarly Publication. English. qt. $93.00 (individual), $110.00 (institution) US; $130.00 (individual), $141.00 (institution) other. W.B. Saunders Company, A Subsidiary of Harcourt Brace Jovanovich, Inc., The Curtis Center/Suite 300, Independence Square West, Philadelphia PA 19106-3399. **Tel** (215)238-7800 or, 5587, FAX (215)238-7883, telex 173146. **(Subscription address:** W. B. Saunders Company / North America Subscriptions, c/o Periodicals, 6277 Sea Harbour Drive, 4th Floor, Orlando FL 32887.**) DD** 616. **NLM** W1; AN22J. **[CCC].** available on microfilm and microfiche from University Microfilms International (UMI). Documents available from CASDDS. ***Continues in part*** *Clinics in Anaesthesiology, 0261-9881.*
**Ind/Abst** Chem. Abstr. (1987-); EMBASE; Nutr. Abstr. Rev., Ser. A, Hum. Exp.

US/0271-1265
**ANESTHESIOLOGY (GLENDALE, CALIF.).** (ANESTHESIOLOGY [SOUND RECORDING].). [Anesthesiolog.]. **Added/Corp** Audio-Digest Foundation. **VFOAT** Audio-Digest Anesthesiology; Audio Digest Anesthesiology. (1959)-. Periodical. English. sm (24 issues). $179.76 US; $202.80 Canada; $247.44 other (audiocassette). Audio-Digest Foundation, 1577 Chevy Chase Drive, Glendale CA 91206. **Tel** (213)245-8505, (800)423-2308, FAX (818)240-7379. **ED** Claron L. Oakley. **DD** 617. **NLM** W1 AU201D. Index available. ctrl circ.
**Desc:** An interactive system of audio cassette postgraduate medical education, with each one-hour program eligible for two Category I credit hours.

US/0003-3022
**ANESTHESIOLOGY (PHILADELPHIA).** (ANESTHESIOLOGY.). [Anesthesiology]. **Added/Corp** American Society of Anesthesiologists. American Society of Anesthesiologists. Vol. 1 (July 1940)-. Academic Scholarly Publication. English. mo. $120.00 (individuals), $200.00 (institutions) US; $190.00 (individuals), $270.00 (institutions) other. J.B. Lippincott Company, 227 East Washington Square, Philadelphia PA 19106-3780. **Tel** (215)238-4200 or 4454, FAX (215)238-4227. **(Subscription address:** J.B. Lippincott, PO Box 350, Hagerstown MD 21740.**) ED** Lawrence J. Saidman. **DD** 617. **NLM** W1 AN22H. **CODEN** ANESAV. **[CCC].** cum. index. **Bk Rev. Ad Acc. Pr Rev. Circ:** 32,768. available on microfilm and microfiche from University Microfilms International (UMI). Documents available from The Genuine Article, BIOSIS Document Express, CASDDS.
**Desc:** Editorials, articles, laboratory reports, clinical and case reports, reports from scientific meetings.
**Ind/Abst** Abr. Index Med.; Biol. Abstr.; Calcium Calcif. Tissue Abstr.; Chem. Abstr.; CSA Neuro. Abstr.; Curr. Contents Clin. Med.; Curr. Contents Life Sci.; EMBASE; Health Devices Alerts; Health Plan. Adminis.; Index Med.; Index Vet.; INIS Atomindex [Micro.]; Int. Aerosp. Abstr.; Nutr. Abstr. Rev., Ser. B, Live Feeds and Feed.; Nutr. Abstr. Rev., Ser. A, Hum. Exp.; Life Sci. Collect.; PESTDOC; Physic. Medline Plus; Pig News Inf.; Ref. Upd. Basic Ed.; Ref. Upd. Deluxe Ed.; Res. Alert [Full Cov.]; Sci. Cit. Index; SCISEARCH; Soc. Sci. Cit. Index [Select. Cov.].

US/1063-8571
**ANESTHESIOLOGY RESIDENT, THE.** ***Ceased.*** [Anesthesiol. resid.]. (1992)-(1994). Periodical. English. bm. Slack Inc., 6900 Grove Road, Thorofare NJ 08086. **Tel** (609)848-1000, (800)257-8290, FAX (609)853-5991, telex 517108 SLACK INC VD. **NLM** W1; AN22JR.

US/0093-4437
**ANESTHESIOLOGY REVIEW.** ***Title Change.*** [Anesthesiol. rev.]. Vol. 1 (Feb. 1974)-(19??). Academic Scholarly Publication. English. bm. Excerpta Medica / US,

PO Box 3085, Princeton NJ 08543-3085. **Tel** (908)874-8550, FAX (908)874-5611. **LC** RD78.3; .A55. **DD** 617/.96/05. **NLM** W1 AN22K. **[CCC].** Index available in last issue of volume--attached. **Bk Rev. Ad Acc. Pr Rev. Circ:** 12,000. ***Continued by*** *American Journal of Anesthesiology.*
**Desc:** Presents fresh informative scientific, original, and review articles as well as symposia and news reports on matters of concern to the practicing anesthesiologist.
**Ind/Abst** EMBASE; Health Devices Alerts.

FR/0750-7658
**ANNALES FRANCAISES D'ANESTHESIE ET DE REANIMATION.** [Ann. fr. anesth. reanim.]. **Added/Corp** Societe Francaise d'Anesthesie et de Reanimation. Vol. 1 (1982)-. Academic Scholarly Publication. French (English and French). bm. $237.00. Masson Editeur, Box Postale 22, 41353 Vineuil 16 France. **Tel** 011 33 54 438994. **(Subscription address:** 7A Boulevard de Perolles, CH-1701 Fribourg Switzerland**) NLM** W1 AN408S. **CODEN** AFAREO. **[CCC].** Documents available from The Genuine Article, CASDDS. ***Formed by the union of*** *Anesthesie, Analgesie, Reanimation, 0003-3014* ***and*** *Annales de l'Anesthesiologie Francaise, 0003-4061.*
**Ind/Abst** Chem. Abstr.; Curr. Contents Clin. Med.; EMBASE; Index Med.; Life Sci. Collect.; PESTDOC; Res. Alert [Select. Cov.]; SCISEARCH.

US/0270-5877
**ASA NEWSLETTER (PARK RIDGE).** (ASA NEWSLETTER.). [ASA newsl.]. **Main/Corp** American Society of Anesthesiologists. **Added/Corp** American Society of Anesthesiologists. Newsletter. **VAT** American Society of Anesthesiologists Newsletter. Vol. 29, No. 11 (Nov. 1965)-. Newsletter. English. mo. $12.00 (nonmembers), Free (members). American Society of Anesthesiologists, 520 North Northwest Highway, Park Ridge IL 60068. **Tel** (708)825-5586. **NLM** W1 A15V. ***Continues*** *Newsletter - American Society of Anesthesiologists.*
**Ind/Abst** Abstr. Clin. Care Guidel.

UK/0950-3501
**BAILLIERE'S CLINICAL ANAESTHESIOLOGY. VFOAT** Anaesthesiology; Clinical Anaesthesiology. Vol. 1, No. 1 (Mar. 1987)-. Periodical. English. qt (4 issues). £86.00 (institution). Harcourt Brace & Company Ltd., Foots Cray, High Street, Sidcup Kent DA14 5HP England. **Tel** 011 44 81 300 3322, FAX 011 44 81 309 0807. **(Subscription address:** W. B. Saunders Company / North America Subscriptions, c/o Periodicals, 6277 Sea Harbour Drive, 4th Floor, Orlando FL 32887.**) NLM** W1; BA46D. **Pr Rev.** ***Continues in part*** *Clinics in Anaesthesiology, 0261-9881.*
**Ind/Abst** Curr. Contents Clin. Med.; EMBASE; SCISEARCH.

UK/0007-0912
**BRITISH JOURNAL OF ANAESTHESIA.** [Br. j. anaesth.]. Vol. 1 (1923)-. Academic Scholarly Publication. English. mo. £149.00. Professional & Scientific Publishers, Tavistock House, East Tavistock Square, London WC1H 9JR England. **Tel** 011 44 71 387-4499, telex 005311. **ED** G. Smith. **NLM** W1 BR503. **CODEN** BJANAD. **[CCC]. Pr Rev.** available on microfilm and microfiche from University Microfilms International (UMI). Documents available from The Genuine Article, BIOSIS Document Express, CASDDS.
**Desc:** Publishes original work in all branches of anaesthesia, including the application of basic sciences, with review articles and new equipment reports. All subscribers also receive the "Handbook of British Anaesthesia", an annual compendium of information of anaesthetic interest at the national level, in a single source reference.
**Ind/Abst** Biol. Abstr.; Chem. Abstr.; CSA Neuro. Abstr. (?-?); Curr. Aware. Biol. Sci., CABS; Curr. Contents Clin. Med.; Curr. Contents Life Sci.; Dairy Sci. Abstr.; EMBASE; Health Devices Alerts; Health Plan. Adminis.; Health Serv. Abstr.; Index Med.; Index Vet.; Iowa Drug Inf. Serv. (1969-); Nutr. Abstr. Rev., Ser. B, Live Feeds and Feed.; Nutr. Abstr. Rev., Ser. A, Hum. Exp.; Life Sci. Collect.; PESTDOC; Physic. Medline Plus; Pig News Inf.; Protozoolog. Abstr.; Ref. Upd. Basic Ed.; Ref. Upd. Deluxe Ed.; Res. Alert [Full Cov.]; Sci. Cit. Index; SCISEARCH; Vet. Bull.

FR/0007-9685
**CAHIERS D'ANESTHESIOLOGIE.** [Cah. Anesthesiol.]. (April 1953)-. Academic Scholarly Publication. French. ir. 600.00F. Blackwell Scientific Publishers / Arnette, 2 rue Casimir-Delavigne, 75006 Paris France. **Tel** 011 33 1 44860770, FAX 011 33 1 46336797. **(Subscription address:** Service Abbonements, 1 rue de Lille, 75007 Paris France.**) DD** 617.96. **NLM** W1 CA134. **CODEN** CAANBU. **[CCC].** available on microfilm and microfiche from University Microfilms International (UMI). Documents available from CASDDS.
**Ind/Abst** Chem. Abstr. (1953-1983); EMBASE; Health Plan. Adminis.; Index Med.

US/1060-8532
**CANA, INC. See** Medical Science and Technology-Nursing.

CN/0832-610X
**CANADIAN JOURNAL OF ANAESTHESIA.** [Can. j. anaesth.]. **Added/Corp** Canadian Anaesthetists' Society. **VFOAT** Journal Canadien d'Anesthesie. Vol. 34, No. 1 (Jan. 1987)-. Academic Scholarly Publication. English (French; summaries and/or abstracts in French). mo. 204.00Can$ (institutions), 156.00Can$ (individuals) US and Canada; 226.00Can$ (institutions), 177.00Can$ (individuals) other; Supplement included. Canadian Anaesthetists Society, 1 Eglinton Avenue East/ Suite 208, Toronto Ontario M4P 3A1 Canada. **Tel** (416)480-0602. **ED** David R. Bevan (editor's telephone number: (514)848-9649). **DD** 617/.96/05. **NLM** W1; CA569E. **CODEN** CJOAEP. **[CCC].** Index available. cum. index. **Bk Rev. Ad Acc. Circ:** 5,040. available on microfilm and microfiche from University Microfilms International (UMI). Documents available from The Genuine Article, BIOSIS Document Express, CASDDS. ***Continues*** *Canadian Anaesthetists' Society. Canadian Anaesthetists' Society Journal, 0008-2856.*
**Desc:** International anaesthesia medical journal publishing reports of current investigation, review articles, editorials, clinical and technical reports, abstracts from the literature, book reviews, continuing medical education articles, and annual meeting abstracts.
**Ind/Abst** Biol. Abstr. (1987-); Chem. Abstr. (1987-); CSA Neuro. Abstr. (?-?); Cumul. Index Nurs. Allied Health Lit.; Curr. Contents Clin. Med.; Curr. Contents Life Sci.; EMBASE; Health Devices Alerts; Health Plan. Adminis.; Hospit. Health Admin. Index; Index Med. (1987-); INIS Atomindex [Micro.]; Iowa Drug Inf. Serv.; Life Sci. Collect.; Ref. Upd. Deluxe Ed.; Res. Alert [Full Cov.]; Sci. Cit. Index; SCISEARCH.

US/1046-1795
**CARDIOTHORACIC AND VASCULAR ANESTHESIA UPDATE.** [Cardiothorac. vasc. anesth. update]. (1990)-. English. an. $111.00 (individual), $144.00 (institution) US; $172.00 other. W.B. Saunders Company, A Subsidiary of Harcourt Brace Jovanovich, Inc., The Curtis Center/Suite 300, Independence Square West, Philadelphia PA 19106-3399. **Tel** (215)238-7800 or, 5587, FAX (215)238-7883, telex 173146. **(Subscription address:** W. B. Saunders Company / North America Subscriptions, c/o Periodicals, 6277 Sea Harbour Drive, 4th Floor, Orlando FL 32887.**) NLM** W1; CA77MDW. **[CCC].**

IT/0390-6310
**COLLANA DI AGGIORNAMENTI IN ANESTESIA E RIANIMAZIONE.** Periodical. Italian. Piccin Editore, Via Altinate 107, 35121 Padua Italy. **Tel** 011 39 49 655566, FAX 011 39 49 8750693. **UDC** 616-089.5. **NLM** W1 CO167CR.

SP/0214-9370
**CORE JOURNALS EN ANESTESIOLOGIA.** [Core j. anestesiol.]. (1990)-. Periodical. Spanish. Four times a year. Mayo SA, Muntaner 374-376, 08006 Barcelona Spain. **Tel** 209 02 55, FAX 202 06 43. **ED** Jose Mayoral and Josep Ferrando. **UDC** 616-089.5(048.3). **Circ:** 1,000.
**Desc:** Abstracts of world literature on anesthesiology.

US/1048-2687
**CRNA.** (CRNA : THE JOURNAL OF NURSE ANESTHETISTS.). [CRNA]. **VAT** Certified Registered Nurse Anesthetists. (1990)-. Periodical. English. qt (Feb., Mau, Aug., Nov.). $59.00 (individual), $84.00 (institution), US; $99.00 (individual), $106.00 (institution), other. W.B. Saunders Company, A Subsidiary of Harcourt Brace Jovanovich, Inc., The Curtis Center/Suite 300, Independence Square West, Philadelphia PA 19106-3399. **Tel** (215)238-7800 or, 5587, FAX (215)238-7883, telex 173146. **(Subscription address:** W. B. Saunders Company / North America Subscriptions, c/o Periodicals, 6277 Sea Harbour Drive, 4th Floor, Orlando FL 32887.**) DD** 617. **NLM** W1; CR217G. **[CCC].**
**Ind/Abst** Cumul. Index Nurs. Allied Health Lit.

UK/0883-4490
**CURRENT EUROPEAN ANAESTHESIOLOGY.** (CURRENT EUROPEAN ANAESTHESIOLOGY : THE YEARBOOK OF THE EUROPEAN ACADEMY OF ANAESTHESIOLOGY.). [Curr. Eur. anaesthesiol.]. **Added/Corp** European Academy of Anaesthesiology. Vol. 1 (1985)-. English. ir. John Wiley & Sons Ltd., Baffins Lane, Chichester West Sussex PO19 1UD England. **Tel** 0243 779777, FAX 0243 776128 BTG:JWP001, telex 86290 WIBOOKG. **DD** 617. **NLM** W1; CU788GK.

UK/0269-6959
**CURRENT MEDICAL LITERATURE. ANAESTHESIOLOGY / THE ROYAL SOCIETY OF MEDICINE. Added/Corp** Royal Society of Medicine (Great Britain). **VFOAT** Anaesthesiology. (198?)-. Periodical. English. qt. £20.00 UK; $40.00 US; £20.00 other. Current Medical Literature Ltd., 40-42 Osnaburgh Street, London NW1 3ND England. **Tel** 011 44 71 4658377, FAX 011 44 71 4658380. **(Subscription address:** Royal Society Medicine Services, 1 Wimpole Street, London W1M 8AE England.**) NLM** ZWO 200; C976.

UK/0952-7907
**CURRENT OPINION IN ANAESTHESIOLOGY.** [Curr. opin. anaesthesiol.]. **Added/Corp** European Academy of Anaesthesiology. Vol. 1 No. 1 (May/June 1988)-. Academic Scholarly Publication. English. Six times a year. $169.95 (individual); $345.50 (institution). Current Science / England, Middlesex House, 34-42 Cleveland Street, London W1P 5FB England. **Tel** 011 44 71 580 8393, 011 44 71 323 0323, FAX 011 44 81 580 1938. **(Subscription address:** Current Science, 20 North 3rd Street, Philadelphia PA 19106.**) ED** Cedric Prys-Roberts. **NLM** W1; CU799GB. **[CCC]. Circ:** 3,200. available on diskette.
**Desc:** Directed toward researchers and practicing anesthesiologists. Presents review articles from an area of concentration covering an entire year's literature with annotated references. Each issue features a bibliography of the current world literature published during the previous year.
**Ind/Abst** Cumul. Index Nurs. Allied Health Lit.; EMBASE.

US/0164-310X
**CURRENT REVIEWS FOR NURSE ANESTHETISTS.** [Curr. rev. nurse anesth.]. **Added/Corp** Mount Sinai Medical Center (Miami Beach, Fla.). Dept. of Anesthesiology. Vol. 1, (1978)-. Monographic series. English. Twenty-six times a year. $175.00. Current Reviews, 7480 Fairway Drive, Suite 106, Miami Lakes FL 33014. **Tel** (305)822-1415, FAX (305)823-9367. **ED** Frank Moya, M.D. (editor's address: Department of Anesthesiology, and Director, The Pain Center, Mount Sinai Medical Center, Miami Beach, Florida). **NLM** W1 CU8093K.
**Desc:** These are lessons consists of current information, written by leading authorities, and the latest techniques, prefaced with specific objectives to be achieved in that lesson.
**Ind/Abst** Cumul. Index Nurs. Allied Health Lit.

US/0891-9917
**CURRENT REVIEWS IN CLINICAL ANESTHESIA.** [Curr. rev. clin. anesth.]. **Added/Corp** Mount Sinai Medical Center (Miami Beach, Fla.). Dept. of Anesthesiology. (1980)-. Periodical. English. Twenty-six times a year. $250.00. Current Reviews, 7480 Fairway Drive, Suite 106, Miami Lakes FL 33014. **Tel** (305)822-1415, FAX (305)823-9367. **ED** Frank Moya, M.D. (editor's address: Department of Anesthesiology, and Director, The Pain Center, Mount Sinai Medical Center, Miami Beach, Florida). **DD** 617. **NLM** W1; CU8093LD.
**Desc:** These are lessons consisting of current information written by leading authorities about the latest anesthesia techniques.

UK/0144-8684
**CURRENT TOPICS IN ANAESTHESIA.** [Curr. top. anaesth.]. **VFOAT** Current Topics in Anaesthesia Series. 1-. Monographic series. English. Price varies per volume. Edward Arnold, 338 Euston Road, London NW1 3BH England. **Tel** 011 44 71 873 6000, FAX 011 44 071 873 6325. **UDC** 616-089.5. **NLM** W1 CU82.

US/1058-1200
**DRIPPS' INTRODUCTION TO ANESTHESIA.** (1991)-. English. ir. W.B. Saunders Company, A Subsidiary of Harcourt Brace Jovanovich, Inc., The Curtis Center/Suite 300, Independence Square West, Philadelphia PA 19106-3399. **Tel** (215)238-7800 or, 5587, FAX (215)238-7883, telex 173146. **(Subscription address:** W. B. Saunders Company / North America Subscriptions, c/o Periodicals, 6277 Sea Harbour Drive, 4th Floor, Orlando FL 32887.**)**

FR
**ENCYCLOPEDIE MEDICO-CHIRURGICALE : MEDECINE GENERALE ET SPECIALITES. ANESTHESIE ET REANIMATION. See** Medical Science and Technology-Surgery.

UK/0265-0215
**EUROPEAN JOURNAL OF ANAESTHESIOLOGY.** [Eur. j. anaesthesiol.]. **Added/Corp** European Academy of Anaesthesiology. Vol. 1, No. 1 (March 1984)-. Academic Scholarly Publication. English. Six times a year. $426.00 US & Canada; £275.00 other. Blackwell Scientific Publications Ltd, Marston Book Services, PO Box 87, Oxford OX2 ODT UK. **Tel** 011 44 865 791155, FAX 011 44 865 791927, telex 837 515 MARDIS G. **NLM** W1; EU638. **CODEN** EJANEG. **[CCC]. Pr Rev.** available on microfilm and microfiche from University Microfilms International (UMI). Documents available from The Genuine Article, BIOSIS Document Express, CASDDS.
**Ind/Abst** Biol. Abstr. (1987-); Chem. Abstr. (1984-); Curr. Contents Clin. Med.; EMBASE; Health Plan. Adminis.; Index Med. (Vol. 1, No. 1, 1984-); Res. Alert [Select. Cov.]; SCISEARCH.

UK/0952-1941
**EUROPEAN JOURNAL OF ANAESTHESIOLOGY. SUPPLEMENT.** (1987)-. Academic Scholarly Publication. English.

Blackwell Scientific Publications Ltd, Marston Book Services, PO Box 87, Oxford OX2 ODT UK. **Tel** 011 44 865 791155, FAX 011 44 865 791927, telex 837 515 MARDIS G. **NLM** W1; EU638B. **CODEN** EJSUEP.
**Ind/Abst** EMBASE; Health Plan. Adminis.; Index Med. (1987-).

NE/0014-4282
**EXCERPTA MEDICA. SECTION 24. ANESTHESIOLOGY.** See Medical Science and Technology-Abstracting, Bibliographies and Statistics.

UK/0260-2873
**HANDBOOK OF BRITISH ANAESTHESIA.** [Handb. Br. anaesth.]. **VFOAT** British Journal of Anaesthesia. 1979/80-. English. an. **UDC** 616-089.5. **NLM** W1 HA51IG.

JA/0367-5947
**HOKURIKU MASUIGAKU ZASSHI.** [Hokuriku masuigaku zasshi]. **VFOAT** Hokuriku Journal of Anesthesiology. V. 1- Nov. 1967-. Periodical. Japanese (Japanese). an. Nihon Masui Gakkai Hokuriku Chihokai, (Hokuriku Branch, Japan Soc. of Anesthesiology), Kanazawa Daigaku Igakubu Masuigaku, Kyoshitsu, 13-1, Takaramachi, Kanazawashi, Ishikawaken 920 Japan. **UDC** 616-089.5. **NLM** W1 HO491K. **CODEN** HKMZAC. Documents available from BIOSIS Document Express.
**Ind/Abst** Biol. Abstr.; EMBASE.

II/0019-5049
**INDIAN JOURNAL OF ANAESTHESIA.** [Indian j. anaesth.]. **Added/Corp** Indian Society of Anaesthetists. **VFOAT** Indian Journal of Ansthesia. (1953)-. Periodical. English. bm. $60.00. Indian Society of Anaethetists, Calcutta, India. **(Subscription address:** Prints India, 11 Darya Ganj, New Delhi, 110002 India, (Phone: 011 91 11 3268645)) **NLM** W1 IN206N.

GW/0173-2315
**INTENSIVMEDIZINISCHE PRAXIS.** [Intensivmed. Prax.]. (1979)-. Academic Scholarly Publication. German. sa. **NLM** W1 IN653P. ***Supersedes*** *Anasthesiologische und Intensivmedizinische Praxis, 0303-6200.*
**Ind/Abst** EMBASE; Index Med.

US/0020-5907
**INTERNATIONAL ANESTHESIOLOGY CLINICS.** [Int. anesthesiol. clin.]. **VFOAT** I.A.C. Vol. 1, No. 1 (Aug. 1962)-. Academic Scholarly Publication. English. qt. $150.00 (institutions), $135.00 (individuals) US; $165.00 (institutions), $150.00 (individuals) Canada; $194.00 (institutions), $155.00 (individuals) other. Little Brown & Company, 34 Beacon Street, Boston MA 02108. **Tel** (617)227-0730, (800)759-0190. **(Subscription address:** Little Brown and Company, PO Box 7671, Riverton NJ 08077-7671.) **ED** Mary B. Donchez. **LC** RD81.A1; I55. **DD** 617/.96/05. **NLM** W1 IN702. **CODEN** IACLAV. **[CCC]. Pr Rev. Circ:** 3,500. available on microfilm and microfiche from University Microfilms International (UMI). Documents available from The Genuine Article, BIOSIS Document Express, CASDDS.
**Desc:** Features guest editors and contributors who focus on one topic per issue that is of clinical importance in anesthesiology.
**Ind/Abst** Biol. Abstr.; Chem. Abstr.; Cumul. Index Nurs. Allied Health Lit.; Curr. Contents Clin. Med.; EMBASE; Energy Res. Abstr. (Mar. 1982-); Health Devices Alerts; Index Med.; Res. Alert [Full Cov.]; Sci. Cit. Index; SCISEARCH; Soc. Sci. Cit. Index [Select. Cov.].

NE/0169-1066
**JAPANESE ANAESTHESIA JOURNALS' REVIEW.** ***Ceased.*** [Jpn. anaesth. j. rev.]. Vol. 1, No. 1-Ceased with Vol. 4. Periodical. English. qt. VSP International Science Publishers, Godfried van Seystlaan 47, 3703 BR Zeist Netherlands. **Tel** 011 31 3404 25790, FAX 011 31 3404 32081, telex 40217 USP NL. **(Subscription address:** Aus./NZ: DA Book Pty Ltd, PO Box 163, Mitcham Victoria 3132 Australia; Thailand: Book Promotion & Service Ltd, 59/6 Soi Lung Suan, Ploenchit Road, Pathumwan Bangkok 10500 Thailand; other: European Book Service PBD, Strijkviertel 63, 3454 PK De Meern Netherlands) **ED** T Oyama. **UDC** 616.089.5. **NLM** W1; JA949. **CODEN** JAJREV. **Ad Acc.** Documents available from BIOSIS Document Express.
**Desc:** A journal enhancing the accessibility of research and clinical data in anaesthesia originating in Japan and containing the most important articles and latest findings.
**Ind/Abst** Biol. Abstr. (1986-).

GW
**JOURNAL OF ANESTHESIA.** English. Four times a year. DM260.00. Springer-Verlag GmbH & Company KG, Heidelberger Platz 3, D 14197 Berlin Germany. **Tel** 011 49 30 8207223, FAX 011 49 30 8214091, telex 183 319 SPBLN D. **(Subscription address:** Springer Verlag New York Inc. / for North America, 44 Hartz Way, Secaucus NJ 07096.)

JA/0913-8668
**JOURNAL OF ANESTHESIA. Added/Corp** Nihon Masui Gakkai. Vol. 1, No. 1 (Mar. 1987)-. Periodical. English. Four times a year. DM260.00. Springer-Verlag Tokyo, 37-3 Hongo 3-Chrome, Bunkyo-ku, Tokyo 113 Japan. **Tel** 011 81 3 38120331, FAX 011 81 3 38120719, telex 26536 SREBS J. **(Subscription address:** Springer Verlag New York Inc. / for North America, 44 Hartz Way, Secaucus NJ 07096.) **NLM** W1; JO536DN.

US/1053-0770
**JOURNAL OF CARDIOTHORACIC AND VASCULAR ANESTHESIA.** [J. cardiothorac. vasc. anesth.]. Vol. 5, No. 1 (Feb. 1991)-. Periodical. English. bm. $128.00 (individual), $162.00 (institution), US; $186.00 (individual), $202.00 (institution) other. W.B. Saunders Company, A Subsidiary of Harcourt Brace Jovanovich, Inc., The Curtis Center/Suite 300, Independence Square West, Philadelphia PA 19106-3399. **Tel** (215)238-7800 or, 5587, FAX (215)238-7883, telex 173146. **(Subscription address:** W. B. Saunders Company / North America Subscriptions, c/o Periodicals, 6277 Sea Harbour Drive, 4th Floor, Orlando FL 32887.) **DD** 617. **NLM** W1; JO574VC. **CODEN** JCVAEK. ***Continues*** *Journal of Cardiothoracic Anesthesia, 0888-6296.*
**Ind/Abst** EMBASE; Health Plan. Adminis.; Index Med. (Feb. 1991-).

US/0952-8180
**JOURNAL OF CLINICAL ANESTHESIA.** [J. clin. anesthes.]. **VFOAT** JCA. Vol. 1, No. 1 (1988)-. Periodical. English. Eight times a year. $200.00 US; $250.00 other. Butterworth Heinemann / Woburn, MA, 225 Wildwood Avenue, Unit B, Woburn MA 01801. **Tel** (800)366-2665, FAX (617)928-2620, telex 880052. **(Subscription address:** Elsevier Science Inc. / New York Books, 655 Avenue of the Americas, New York NY 10010.) **ED** J Kitz (editor's address: Department of Anesthesia, Harvard Medical School, and Massachusetts General Hospital, Boston, MA). **DD** 617. **NLM** W1; JO587AF. **CODEN** JCLBE7. **[CCC].** Index available. **Bk Rev. Ad Acc.** available on microfilm and microfiche from University Microfilms International (UMI). Documents available from The Genuine Article.
**Desc:** Serves as a forum for practical clinical information for the anesthesiologist from resident level onward. The scope of the journal will be of direct relevance to anesthesia practice and includes drugs, techniques, monitoring and equipment, critical care, pharmacokinetics and physiology.
**Ind/Abst** Curr. Contents Clin. Med.; EMBASE; Health Plan. Adminis.; Index Med. (1988-); Int. Nurs. Index; Ref. Upd. Deluxe Ed.; Res. Alert [Select. Cov.].

GW/0341-5023
**KLINISCHE ANASTHESIOLOGIE UND INTENSIVTHERAPIE.** [Klin. Anaesthesiol. Intensivther.]. (1974)-. Monographic series. German. ir. Price varies per volume. Springer-Verlag New York Inc., 175 5th Avenue, New York NY 10010. **Tel** (212)460-1500, telex 232 235 SPB UR. **(Subscription address:** Springer Verlag New York Inc. / for North America, 44 Hartz Way, Secaucus NJ 07096.) **UDC** 616-089.5. **NLM** W1 KL434. **CODEN** KAINDO. Documents available from CASDDS.
**Desc:** Numbered series.
**Ind/Abst** Chem. Abstr.; Index Med.

UK/0267-0003
**LECTURES IN ANAESTHESIOLOGY.** ***Ceased.*** [Lect. anaesthesiol.]. No. 1 (1985)-Ceased (Dec. 1988). Periodical. English. sa. Mosby Year Book Inc., 11830 Westline Industrial Drive, St Louis MO 63146. **Tel** (800)325-4177, (314)872-8370, FAX (314)432-1380, telex 44-2402. **UDC** 616-089.5. **NLM** W1; LE336. ***Continues*** *WFSA Lectures.*

US/0892-2438
**LITERATURE SCAN. ANESTHESIOLOGY.** ***Suspended.*** [Lit. scan, Anesthesiol.]. **VFOAT** Anesthesiology. Vol. 1 No. 1 (June 1987)-(19??). Periodical. English. bm. World Medical Communications Organizations, 7 Ridgedale Avenue, Cedar Knolls NJ 07927. **Tel** (201)455-1121. **ED** Robert K. Stoelting. **DD** 617. **Bk Rev. Ad Acc. Circ:** 26,000 (ctrl).
**Desc:** Journal and book reviews in anesthesiology with personal commentary on each review.

US/0738-1018
**MALPRACTICE REPORTER. ANESTHESIOLOGY, THE.** See Law.

JA/0021-4892
**MASUI.** (MASUI.). [Masui]. **Added/Corp** Nippon Masui Gakki. **VFOAT** Japanese Journal of Anesthesiology. Vol. 1 (1952)-. Academic Scholarly Publication. Japanese (summaries and/or abstracts in English). mo. $478.00. **(Subscription address:** Kyowa Book Company Inc., 1 38 Kanda Jinbocho Chiyoda-ku, Tokyo 101 Japan.) **NLM** W1 MA933. **CODEN** MASUAC. Documents available from BIOSIS Document Express.
**Ind/Abst** Biol. Abstr.; EMBASE; Index Med.

JA/0385-1664
**MASUI TO SOSEI.** [Masui to sosei]. **Added/Corp** Hiroshima Masui Igakkai. **VFOAT** Hiroshima Journal of Anesthesia. (1978)-. Periodical. Japanese (summaries and/or abstracts in English). qt. Hiroshima University School of Medicine, Kasumi-Cho, Hiroshima Japan. **CODEN** MASODV. Documents available from CASDDS. ***Continues*** *Hiroshima Masui Igakkai. Hiroshima Masui Igakkai Zasshi, 0440-8764.*
**Ind/Abst** Chem. Abstr.; EMBASE [Select. Cov.].

LE/0544-0440
**MIDDLE EAST JOURNAL OF ANESTHESIOLOGY.** [Middle East j. anaesthesiol.]. **Added/Corp** Middle East Society of Anaesthesiologists. American University of Beirut Medical Center. Anesthesiology Dept. **VFOAT** Middle East Journal of Anesthesiology. Vol. 7, No. 1 (Feb. 1983)-. Periodical. English. Three times a year (Feb., June, and Oct.). $40.00. Middle East Journal, Box 1136044, American University Beirut, Beirut Lebanon. **Tel** 340460, telex 20801 LE. **ED** Anis Baraka, Maurice Baroody and Musa Muallem. **NLM** W1 MI32R. **CODEN** MEJAA3. Index available. **Bk Rev. Ad Acc. Circ:** 500 (ctrl). ***Continues*** *Middle East Journal of Anaesthesiology.*
**Ind/Abst** Index Med.

US/1055-5137
**MILESTONES IN ANESTHESIA.** [Milest. anesth.]. Vol. 1, No. 1 (Mar. 1991)-. Periodical. English. Three times a year. Medicine Group USA, 301 Oxford Valley Road, Suite 804A, Yardley PA 19067. **DD** 617.

IT/0375-9393
**MINERVA ANESTESIOLOGICA.** [Minerva anestesiol.]. **Added/Corp** Societa Italiana di Anestesia, Analgesia, Rianimazione e Terapia Intensiva. Societa Italiana di Anestesiologia. Societa Italiana di Anestesia e Rianimazione. Vol. 19 (Jan. 1953)-. Academic Scholarly Publication. Italian. mo. $110.00 (individuals), $150.00 (institutions). Edizioni Minerva Medica, Corso Bramante 83-85, 10126 Turin Italy. **Tel** 011 39 11 678282, FAX 011 39 11 674502. **ED** O Zaffiiu. **NLM** W1 MI631. **CODEN** MIANAP. **Bk Rev. Ad Acc.** available on microfilm from University Microfilms International (UMI). Documents available from CASDDS. ***Continues*** *Giornale Italiano di Anestesiologia.*
**Ind/Abst** Chem. Abstr.; EMBASE; Index Med.

NE/0921-8769
**NEDERLANDS TIJDSCHRIFT VOOR ANESTHESIOLOGIE.** [Ned. tijdschr. anesthesiol.]. (1988)-. Periodical. Dutch. qt. Fl100.00 Netherlands; Fl103.77 other. Bugamor International, De Haak 58, 1353 AE Almere Netherlands. **Tel** 011 31 36 5382297. **UDC** 616-089.5.

US/0897-7437
**NURSE ANESTHESIA.** ***Ceased.*** [Nurse anesth.]. **VFOAT** Nurse Anesthesia. Vol. 1, No. 1 (Mar. 1990)-(Jan. 1994). Periodical. English. qt. Appleton & Lange, (A Subsidiary of Simon & Schuster), 25 Van Zant Street, East Norwalk CT 06855. **Tel** (203)838-4400, (800)423-1359, FAX (203)854-9486. **ED** Wynne R. Waugaman. **DD** 617. **NLM** W1; NU551. **[CCC]. Ad Acc. Pr Rev. Acid Free.**
**Desc:** This quarterly, peer-reviewed journal provides the latest insight on research and clinical practice in nurse anesthesia through original articles, detailed clinical reviews, descriptions of new techniques, and actual case analysis, point/counterpoint and ask the expert.
**Ind/Abst** Cumul. Index Nurs. Allied Health Lit.; Health Plan. Adminis.; Int. Nurs. Index (1990-).

US/0275-665X
**OBSTETRIC ANESTHESIA DIGEST.** [Obstet. anesthes. dig.]. Vol. 1, No. 1 (Mar. 1981)-. Periodical. English. qt. $86.00 (individuals), $108.00 (institutions) US; $112.00 (individuals), $135.00 (institutions) other. Raven Press, 1185 Avenue of the Americas, 37th Floor, New York NY 10036. **Tel** (212)930-9500, (212)930-9604, FAX (212)869-3495, (212)302-8507, telex 640073. **ED** G. F. Marx and G. M. Bassell. **DD** 615. **NLM** W1 OB495. **CODEN** OADIDS. **[CCC].** Index available. **Circ:** 800.
**Desc:** Abstracts of obstetrics, obstetrics anesthesia and neonatology with critical commentary.

●US/0000-1546
**OFFICIAL AMERICAN BOARD OF MEDICAL SPECIALTIES (ABMS) DIRECTORY OF BOARD CERTIFIED ANESTHESIOLOGISTS, THE.** (THE OFFICIAL AMERICAN BOARD OF MEDICAL SPECIALTIES (ABMS) DIRECTORY OF BOARD CERTIFIED ANESTHESIOLOGISTS.). [Off. Am. Board Med. Spec. (ABMS) dir. board certif. anesthesiol.]. **Added/Corp** American Board of Medical Specialties. **VFOAT** Directory of Board Certified Anesthesiologists; Official ABMS Directory of Board Certified Anesthesiologists. 5th Ed. (1994)-. English. be. American Board of Medical Specialties, 1 Rotary Center, Suite 805, Evanston IL 60201. **Tel** (708)491-9091. **LC** RD78.62.U6; A25. **DD** 617/.96/02573. ***Continues*** *ABMS Directory of Certified Anesthesiologists, 0883-122X.*

FR/0990-1310
**OXYMAG : JOURNAL D'INFORMATION PROFESSIONNELLE DES INFIRMIERS ANESTHESISTES.** No. 1 (March 1988)-. Periodical. French. qt. 176.79F France; 180.50F other. Oxymag, 9 Bis Passage Dartois Bidot, F 94100 Saint Maur France. **Tel** 011 33 1 976000. **NLM** W1; OX63J.

FR/0761-2303
**PASCAL EXPLORE. E83, ANESTHESIE ET REANIMATION. VFOAT** Anesthesie et Reanimation; Anesthesiology and Resuscitation. No. 1

(1984)-. Periodical. French. mo. Institut de l'Information Scientique et Technique (INIST), 2 Allee du Parc de Brabois, 54514 Vandoeuvre Nancy Cedex France. **Tel** 011 33 83 504600, FAX 011 33 83 504650. **NLM** ZQ 1; B936QH. ***Continues*** *Bulletin Signaletique. 349, Anesthesie, Reanimation.*

FR
**PEDIATRIC ANAESTHESIA.** (19??)-. English. qt. 866.80F (institutions), 636.63F (individuals) France. Librairie Arnette, Serv Abonn, 2 rue Casimir Delavigne, 75006 Paris France. **Tel** 011 33 1 45852705.

US/0896-5315
**PRACTICAL REVIEWS IN ANESTHESIOLOGY.** (PRACTICAL REVIEWS IN ANESTHESIOLOGY [SOUND RECORDING].). [Pract. rev. anesthesiol.]. **Added/Corp** Educational Reviews, Inc. Montefiore Medical Center. **VFOAT** Practical Reviews. Vol. 1, No. 1 (June, 1976)-. Periodical. English. mo. $175.00 Physicians/Dentists; $125.00 Residents. Educational Reviews Inc., 6801 Cahaba Valley Road, Birmingham AL 35242. **Tel** (205)991-5188, (800)633-4743, FAX (205)995-1926. **DD** 617.

US/0889-4698
**PROBLEMS IN ANESTHESIA.** ***Ceased.*** [Probl. anesth.]. Vol. 1, No. 1 (Jan./March 1987)-(Oct./Dec. 1994). Periodical. English. qt. J.B. Lippincott Company, 227 East Washington Square, Philadelphia PA 19106-3780. **Tel** (215)238-4200 or 4454, FAX (215)238-4227. **(Subscription address:** J.B. Lippincott, PO Box 350, Hagerstown MD 21740.**) LC** RD82.5; .P76. **DD** 617. **NLM** W1; PR573KJ. **[CCC].** cum. index. available on microfilm from University Microfilms International (UMI).

US/0164-1700
**PROCEEDINGS - AMERICAN SOCIETY FOR THE ADVANCEMENT ANESTHESIA IN DENTISTRY.** [Proc. - Am. Soc. Adv. Anesth. Dent.]. **Main/Corp** American Society for the Advancement of Anesthesia in Dentistry. **VFOAT** Pain Control in Dentistry; A.A.S.A.A.D. Pain Control in Dentistry. (1973)-. Proceedings. English. Twice a year. $65.00. American Society for the Advancement of Anesthesia in Dentistry, 475 White Plains, Eastchester NY 10707. **Tel** (914)961-8136. **ED** Louis L. Zall (editor's address: 211 Broadway, Bayonne, NJ 07002). **LC** RK1; .A64. **DD** 617. **NLM** W1 PR5822. **Bk Rev. Ad Acc. Circ:** 1,100 (ctrl).

US/0099-1546
**PROGRESS IN ANESTHESIOLOGY.** [Progr. anesthesiol.]. Vol. 1 (1975)-. Monographic series. English. mo. $295.00 (individuals), $325.00 (institutions) US; $360.00 (individuals), $390.00 (individual) other. W.B. Saunders Company, A Subsidiary of Harcourt Brace Jovanovich, Inc., The Curtis Center/Suite 300, Independence Square West, Philadelphia PA 19106-3399. **Tel** (215)238-7800 or, 5587, FAX (215)238-7883, telex 173146. **(Subscription address:** W. B. Saunders Company / North America Subscriptions, c/o Periodicals, 6277 Sea Harbour Drive, 4th Floor, Orlando FL 32887.**) NLM** W1 PR666FG. **CODEN** PRANDM.

US/0891-5784
**PROGRESS IN ANESTHESIOLOGY (SAN ANTONIO, TEX.).** (PROGRESS IN ANESTHESIOLOGY.). [Prog. anesthesiol.]. **Added/Corp** Dannemiller Memorial Educational Foundation (San Antonio, Tex.). Vol. 1, No. 1 (1987)-. Periodical. English. mo. $295.00. Dannemiller Memorial Education Foundation, 12500 Network Boulevard, Suite 101, San Antonio TX 78249. **Tel** (512)641-8311, (800)328-2308, FAX (512)641-8329. **ED** James Eisenkraft. **DD** 617. ***Continues*** *Clinical Anesthesiology, 0883-0282.*
**Desc:** Continuing education program for the anesthesiology specialist. Topics encompass a full range of clinical and research concerns of current interest from diagnosis and etiology to treatment and follow-up therapy. Provides clinically valuable insights from active practitioners who understand the needs and constraints of today's specialist.

UK/0309-2305
**RECENT ADVANCES IN ANAESTHESIA AND ANALGESIA.** [Recent adv. anaesth. analg.]. (1932)-. Academic Scholarly Publication. English. ir. Price varies per volume. Longman Group Ltd., Fourth Avenue, Longman House, Harlow Essex CM19 5SR England. **Tel** 011 44 279 429655, FAX 011 44 279 431059, telex 81259. **(Subscription address:** Churchill Livingstone / US, 5 S 250 Frontenac Road, Naperville IL 60563.**) ED** R. S. Atkinson and A. P. Adams. **NLM** W1 RE105RG. **CODEN** RAAADM. Documents available from CASDDS.
**Ind/Abst** Chem. Abstr.

US/0363-471X
**REFRESHER COURSES IN ANESTHESIOLOGY.** **Added/Corp** American Society of Anesthesiologists. **VFOAT** ASA Refresher Courses in Anesthesiology. Vol. 2 (1974)-. Periodical. English. an. $23.95 (individuals), $26.95 (institutions) US; $29.95 (individuals), $32.95 (institutions) other. J.B. Lippincott Company, 227 East Washington Square, Philadelphia PA 19106-3780. **Tel** (215)238-4200 or 4454, FAX (215)238-4227. **(Subscription address:** J.B. Lippincott, PO Box 350, Hagerstown MD 21740.**) ED** S.G. Hershey. **NLM** W1 RE1717. **[CCC].** available on microfilm from University Microfilms International (UMI). ***Continues*** *Regional Refresher Courses in Anesthesiology, 0093-7401.*
**Desc:** A project of the Continuing Education Program of the American Society of Anesthesiologists.

US/0146-521X
**REGIONAL ANESTHESIA.** [Reg. anesth.]. Vol. 1 (Oct./Dec. 1976)-. Academic Scholarly Publication. English. bm (6 issues). $136.00 (institution), $102.00 (individual) US. Churchill Livingstone Inc., 650 Avenue of the Americas, New York NY 10011. **Tel** (212)206-5062, FAX (212)727-7808. **(Subscription address:** Churchill Livingstone Inc., 5 South 250 Frontenac Road, Naperville, IL 60563; (telephone: (800)553-5426 or (708)416-3939)**) ED** Benjamin Coving. **LC** RD84. **DD** 617/.964/05. **UDC** 616-089.5. **NLM** W1 RE173BI. **CODEN** RGANDZ. **[CCC]. Ad Acc. Pr Rev. Circ:** 4,988. available on microfilm and microfiche from University Microfilms International (UMI). Documents available from The Genuine Article, BIOSIS Document Express, CASDDS.
**Desc:** Original articles, case reports, clinical workshops, and other data for local anesthetics.
**Ind/Abst** Biol. Abstr.; Chem. Abstr.; Curr. Contents Clin. Med.; Health Plan. Adminis.; Res. Alert [Select. Cov.].

BL/0034-7094
**REVISTA BRASILEIRA DE ANESTESIOLOGIA.** [Rev. bras. anestesiol.]. Year 1- April 1951-. Academic Scholarly Publication. Portuguese (English and Spanish). bm. $80.00. Sociedade Brasileira de Anestesiologia, Rua Professor Alfredo Gomes 36, 22251 Rio de Janeiro RJ Brazil. **Tel** (021)2666324. **ED** Antonio Liete Oliva Filho. **UDC** 616-089.8. **NLM** W1; RE304. **CODEN** RBANAV. Index available. cum. index. **Bk Rev. Ad Acc. Circ:** 5,150. available on microfilm and microfiche from University Microfilms International (UMI). Documents available from BIOSIS Document Express, CASDDS.
**Desc:** Experimental and clinical research and information in anesthesiology and related fields.
**Ind/Abst** Biol. Abstr.; Chem. Abstr.; EMBASE; Life Sci. Collect.

SP/0034-9356
**REVISTA ESPANOLA DE ANESTESIOLOGIA Y REANIMACION.** [Rev. esp. anestesiol. reanim.]. **Added/Corp** Sociedad Espanola de Anestesiologia y Reanimacion. (1968)-. Academic Scholarly Publication. Spanish. bm (6 issues). $53.00. Ediciones Doyma SA, Travesera de Gracia 17 21, 08021 Barcelona Spain. **Tel** 011 34 3 2000711, 011 34 3 4145706, FAX 011 34 3 2091136, telex 51964 INK E. **ED** R. Garcia Guasch. **NLM** W1 RE527. **CODEN** REANBJ. **[CCC].** Index available. cum. index. **Bk Rev. Ad Acc. Pr Rev. Circ:** 4,000 (ctrl). Documents available from CASDDS. ***Continues*** *Revista Espanola de Anestesiologia.*
**Desc:** Bulletin of actual medical reports.
**Ind/Abst** Chem. Abstr.; EMBASE [Select. Cov.]; Index Med.; Indice Med. Esp.

MX/0185-1012
**REVISTA MEXICANA DE ANESTESIOLOGIA Y REANIMACION.** (19??)-. Spanish. Four times a year (Feb, May, Aug., Nov.). $70.00. Societe Mexico de Anestesiologia AC, Insurgentes Sur #636 Desp 502, 03100 Mexico DF Mexico. **Tel** 011 52 6691659, 011 52 6691457, FAX 011 52 6691659. **ED** Dr. Jose de Jesus Jaramillo-Magana. Index available (published in Dec.). **Ad Acc, Adv Mgr:** Yolanda Celis. **Pr Rev. Circ:** 2000. available on CD-ROM. Documents available from Correo.

GW/0342-4448
**SCHRIFTENREIHE INTENSIVMEDIZIN, NOTFALLMEDIZIN, ANASTHESIOLOGI.** **VFOAT** Intensivmedizin, Notfallmedizin, Anasthesiologie. INA; INA. Vol. 1 (1976)-. Academic Scholarly Publication. German. ir. Price varies per volume. Georg Thieme Verlag Stuttgart, Postfach 301120, D 70451 Stuttgart Germany. **Tel** 011 49 711 89310, FAX 011 49 711 8931298, telex 7 252 275 GTVD. **(Subscription address:** Thieme Medical Publishers Inc., 381 Park Avenue South, New York NY 10016.**) NLM** W3 SC427Z. **CODEN** SINADI. Documents available from CASDDS.
**Ind/Abst** Chem. Abstr.

US/0277-0326
**SEMINARS IN ANESTHESIA.** [Semin. anesth.]. Vol. 1, No. 1 (Mar. 1982)-. Academic Scholarly Publication. English. qt (Mar., June, Sept., Dec.). $75.00 (individual), $123.00 (institution) US; $132.00 (one year), $146.00 (istitution) other. W.B. Saunders Company, A Subsidiary of Harcourt Brace Jovanovich, Inc., The Curtis Center/Suite 300, Independence Square West, Philadelphia PA 19106-3399. **Tel** (215)238-7800 or, 5587, FAX (215)238-7883, telex 173146. **(Subscription address:** W. B. Saunders Company / North America Subscriptions, c/o Periodicals, 6277 Sea Harbour Drive, 4th Floor, Orlando FL 32887.**) ED** Ronald L. Katz. **UDC** 616-089.5. **NLM** W1 SE486T. **CODEN** SEANDW. **[CCC].** Index available (bound in issue). **Pr Rev.** Documents available from CASDDS.
**Desc:** Provides anesthesiologists with a review of important topics in the field. Devoted to a topic of particular interest in which invited experts discuss a wealth of clinical experience.
**Ind/Abst** Chem. Abstr.; EMBASE; Risk Abstr.; Sci. Cit. Index (19??-19??); SCISEARCH.

US/0279-4829
**SURGICAL PRODUCT NEWS.** ***Title Change.*** [Surg. prod. news]. Vol. 1, No. 1 (Sept. 1981)-(19??). Periodical. English. bm. Gordon Publications Inc, A Subsidiary of Cahners Publishing Company, 301 Gibraltar Drive, Box 650, Morris Plains NJ 07950. **Tel** (201)292-5100. **ED** Paul Gregory. **[CCC]. Ad Acc. Circ:** 75,000 (ctrl). ***Continued by*** *Surgical Products, 1062-4732.*
**Desc:** Providing surgeons, anesthesiologists, and hospital department heads with news on new medical/surgical products, equipment and services, and instruments used in the operating room, post-op and emergency departments.

US/0039-6206
**SURVEY OF ANESTHESIOLOGY.** [Surv. anesthesiol.]. Vol. 1 (Feb. 1957)-. Periodical. English. bm. $87.00 (individual), $112.00 (institution) US; $114.00 (individual), $139.00 (institutions) other. Williams & Wilkins Company, 428 East Preston Street, Baltimore MD 21202-3993. **Tel** (410)528-4000, (800)638-6423, FAX (410)528-8596, telex 87669. **(Subscription address:** Williams & Wilkins Williams & Wilkins, PO Box 64380, PO Box 64380, Baltimore Baltimore MD MD 21264 21264.**) ED** Burnell R. Brown, Jr. **LC** RD81.A1; S8. **DD** 615.78105; 617.9605. **NLM** ZWO 200 S963. **CODEN** SANEA5. **[CCC]. Ad Acc. Circ:** 5,350. available on microfilm. Documents available from Quick Copies.
**Desc:** Condensations with critical comments of important anaesthesiology-related literature from around the world.
**Ind/Abst** Life Sci. Collect.

US/8756-8578
**TECHNOLOGY FOR ANESTHESIA.** [Technol. anesth.]. **Added/Corp** Emergency Care Research Institute. (198?)-. Periodical. English. mo. $95.00 US; $105.00 Canada; $125.00 other. ECRI Emergency Care Research Institute, 5200 Butler Pike, Plymouth Meeting PA 19462. **Tel** (215)825-6000, FAX (215)834-1275, telex 510-660-8023. **ED** J. Nobel. **DD** 617. **[CCC].** ***Continues*** *Health Devices Update. Anesthesia.*
**Desc:** A newsletter for anesthesiologists and anesthetists summarizing health care technology issues and reporting product recalls, hazards, and problems.

GW/0179-8669
**THEORETICAL SURGERY.** ***Ceased.*** **See** Medical Science and Technology-Surgery.

TU/1016-5150
**TURK ANESTEZIYOLOJI VE REANIMASYON CEMIYETI MECMUASI.** **VFOAT** Journal of the Turkish Anaesthesiology and Reanimation Society. (1972)-. Turkish. qt. Logos Yayincilik A.S., Altan Erbulak Sok., Birlik Apt. No. 7/6, Mecidiyekoy 80300, Istanbul Turkey.
**Ind/Abst** EMBASE [Select. Cov.].

US/1073-5437
**YEAR BOOK OF ANESTHESIA AND PAIN MANAGEMENT, THE.** ***Title Change.*** [Year b. anesth. pain manage.]. **VFOAT** Yearbook of Anesthesia and Pain Management. (1992)-(1993). English. an. Mosby Year Book Inc., 11830 Westline Industrial Drive, St Louis MO 63146. **Tel** (800)325-4177, (314)872-8370, FAX (314)432-1380, telex 44-2402. **LC** RD81.A1; Y4. **DD** 617. **NLM** W1; YE108. ***Continues*** *Year Book of Anesthesia, 0084-3652.* ***Continued by*** *Year Book of Anesthesiology and Pain Management.*

US
**YEAR BOOK OF ANESTHESIOLOGY AND PAIN MANAGEMENT, THE.** [Year b. anesth. pain manage.]. (1993)-. English. an. Mosby Year Book Inc., 11830 Westline Industrial Drive, St Louis MO 63146. **Tel** (800)325-4177, (314)872-8370, FAX (314)432-1380, telex 44-2402. **LC** RD81.A1; Y4. **DD** 617. ***Continues*** *Yearbook of Anesthesia and Pain Management.*

CC/0254-1416
**ZHONGHUA MAZUIXUE ZAZHI.** (CHUNG-HUA MA TSUI HSUEH TSA CHIH.). [Zhonghua mazuixue zazhi]. **Added/Corp** Ho-pei Sheng i Hsueh k'o Hsueh Yuan. I Hsueh ch'ing pao yen Chiu so. **VFOAT** Chinese Journal of Anesthesiology. (1981)-. Periodical. Chinese (summaries and/or abstracts in English). qt. **NLM** W1 CH982KM. **CODEN** ZMZADD.
**Ind/Abst** NAPRALERT.

## BIOTECHNOLOGY

US
**AAMI STANDARDS AND RECOMMENDED PRACTICES.** **Added/Corp** Association for the Advancement of Medical Instrumentation. (19??)-. English. ir. $495.00 (non-members), $365.00 (members). Association for the Advancement of Medical Instrumentation, 3330 Washington Boulevard, Suite 400, Arlington VA 22209. **Tel** (703)525-4890, (800)332-2264, FAX (703)276-0793. **LC** R856.6; .A17. **DD** 610.28.

UK/0263-6778
**ABSTRACTS IN BIOCOMMERCE.** **See** Medical Science and Technology-Abstracting, Bibliographies and Statistics.

GW/0138-4988
**ACTA BIOTECHNOLOGICA.** [Acta biotechnol.]. **Added/Corp** Akademie der Wissenschaften der DDR. Institut fuer Technische Chemie. Institut fuer Technische Mikrobiologie (Germany) Institut fuer Enzymologie und Technische Mikrobiologie (Germany). Vol. 1, No. 1 (1981)-. Academic Scholarly Publication. English (German and Russian). qt. $295.00. Akademie-Verlag GmbH, Muehlenstrasse 33 34, D 13162 Berlin Germany. **Tel** 011 49 30 47889300, FAX 011 49 30 47889357. **(Subscription address:** VCH Publishers Inc., 303 Northwest 12th Avenue, Journals Department, Deerfield FL 33442.**)** **ED** M. Ringpfeil and G. Vetterlein. **LC** TA164; .A35. **DD** 574/.05. **NLM** W1 AC764M. **CODEN** ACBTDD. **[CCC]**. Index available. **Bk Rev. Ad Acc. Pr Rev. Circ:** 450 (ctrl). available on an online database. Documents available from The Genuine Article, BIOSIS Document Express, CASDDS.
**Desc:** Publishes original papers, short communications, reports and reviews from the whole field of biotechnology.
**Ind/Abst** AgBiotech News Inf.; BioBusiness; Biocont. News Inf. (1991-); Biol. Abstr.; Biotechnol. Res. Abstr.; Chem. Abstr.; Coal Abstr.; Curr. Aware. Biol. Sci., CABS; Curr. Biotechnol.; Curr. Contents, Agric. Biol. Environ. Sci.; Dairy Sci. Abstr.; EMBASE; Food Sci. Technol. Abstr.; Index Vet.; Microbiol. Abstr. Sect. B; Microbiol. Abstr. Sect. A; Microbiol. Abstr. Sect. C; PESTDOC; Pig News Inf.; Plant Breed. Abstr.; Res. Alert [Full Cov.]; Rev. Plant Pathol.; Sci. Cit. Index; SCISEARCH; Sug. Indus. Abstr.; Vet. Bull.; Virol. AIDS Abstr.; Weed Abstr.; Wheat Barley Trit. Abstr.

NE
**ADONIS CD-ROM.** (19??)-. Abstracting/Indexing Service. English. wk. FI32000.00. ADONIS BV, PO Box 17005, 1001 JA Amsterdam Netherlands. **Tel** 011 31 20 6262629.
**Desc:** A CD-ROM system that enables you to print on-site, high quality copies of scientific articles published in authoritative journals. Journals are primarily from biomedical disciplines.

US/1053-4490
**ADVANCES IN APPLIED BIOTECHNOLOGY SERIES.** [Adv. appl. biotechnol. ser.]. Vol. 1 (1989)-. Monographic series. English. ir. Price varies per volume. Gulf Publishing Company / Texas, PO Box 2608, Houston TX 77252. **Tel** (800)231-6275, (713)529-4301, FAX (713)520-4433. **DD** 660. **NLM** W1; AD433N. **CODEN** AASEE6. Documents available from BIOSIS Document Express, CASDDS.
**Ind/Abst** Biol. Abstr.; Chem. Abstr.

US/0360-9960
**ADVANCES IN BIOENGINEERING.** **See** Engineering.

US/0736-2293
**ADVANCES IN BIOTECHNOLOGICAL PROCESSES.** [Adv. biotechnol. process.]. Vol. 1 (1983)-. Academic Scholarly Publication. English. ir. Price varies per volume. John Wiley & Sons, Inc., 605 Third Avenue, New York NY 10158-0012. **Tel** (212)850-6000, (212)850-6645, FAX (212)850-6088, telex 12-7063. **(Subscription address:** John Wiley & Sons / England, Baffins Lane, Chichester, West Sussex PO19 1UD England.**)** **ED** Avshalom Mizrahi and Antonius L. van Wezel. **LC** TP248.3; .A385. **DD** 660/.6/05. **NLM** W1 AD449M. **CODEN** ABIPDT. **[CCC]**. Documents available from Article Express International, BIOSIS Document Express, CASDDS.
**Ind/Abst** AGRICOLA [Select. Cov.]; BioBusiness; Biol. Abstr.; Chem. Abstr. (1983-); Eng. Index Annu.; Health Plan. Adminis.; Immunol. Abstr.; Index Med. Vol. 3, 1984-; Microbiol. Abstr. Sect. A; Life Sci. Collect.; PESTDOC.

UK
**ADVANCES IN GENE TECHNOLOGY.** (1990)-. Periodical. English. ir. $90.25. JAI Press Inc., 55 Old Post Road, Suite 2, PO Box 1678, Greenwich CT 06836-1678. **Tel** (203)661-7602, FAX (203)661-0792. **LC** IN PROCESS.

UK/0954-9897
**AGBIOTECH NEWS AND INFORMATION.** **See** Agriculture-Abstracting, Bibliographies and Statistics.

US/1066-0569
**AGBIOTECH STOCK LETTER.** [AgBiotech stock lett.]. (198?)-. Periodical. English. mo. $165.00. Agbiotech Investors, PO Box 40460, Berkeley CA 94704. **DD** 630.
**Ind/Abst** Abstr. BioCommer.

US/0899-3998
**AGBIOTECHNOLOGY NEWS.** ***Title Change.*** [AgBiotechnol. news]. **VFOAT** AG Biotechnology News. Vol. 4, No. 3 (May/June 1987)-(199?). Periodical. English. bm. Freiberg Publishing, Box 7, Cedar Falls IA 50613-0007. **Tel** (319)277-3599. **DD** 630. **CODEN** AGBNEO. Documents available from The Genuine Article, BIOSIS Document Express. ***Continues*** *Agricultural Biotechnology News, 0748-822X.* ***Continued by*** *Biotech Reporter, 1069-4773.*
**Desc:** News magazine featuring the latest information and trends available in the field of agricultural biotechnology, both research and business.
**Ind/Abst** Abstr. BioCommer. (-199?); AGRICOLA [Select. Cov.]; BioBusiness (1987-); Biol. Abstr. (1987-); Foods Adlibra; Infomat Int. Bus.; Res. Alert [Full Cov.].

●US/1063-1151
**AGRICULTURAL & ENVIRONMENTAL BIOTECHNOLOGY ABSTRACTS.** **See** Agriculture-Abstracting, Bibliographies and Statistics.

IT/1120-6012
**AGRO-INDUSTRY HI-TECH.** **See** Agriculture.

US/0749-3223
**AMERICAN BIOTECHNOLOGY LABORATORY.** [Am. biotechnol. lab.]. **VFOAT** American Biotechnology Laborarory. News Edition; ABL. (Dec. 1983)-. Academic Scholarly Publication. English. Eight times a year. $144.00 US; $171.00 other. International Science Communications Inc, PO Box 870, 30 Controls Drive, Shelton CT 06430. **Tel** (203)926-9300. **ED** Brian Howard. **DD** 574. **NLM** W1; AM281V. **CODEN** ABLAEY. **Pr Rev. Circ:** 73,000. Documents available from The Genuine Article, CASDDS.
**Ind/Abst** Abstr. BioCommer. (-199?); AGRICOLA [Select. Cov.]; BioBusiness; Biotechnol. Res. Abstr.; Chem. Abstr. (1983-); Curr. Aware. Biol. Sci., CABS; Curr. Biotechnol.; Curr. Contents, Agric. Biol. Environ. Sci.; Life Sci. Collect.; Protozoolog. Abstr.; Res. Alert [Full Cov.]; SCISEARCH.

US/1049-5398
**ANIMAL BIOTECHNOLOGY.** **See** Veterinary Sciences.

US/0090-6964
**ANNALS OF BIOMEDICAL ENGINEERING.** [Ann. biomed. eng.]. **Added/Corp** Biomedical Engineering Society. **VFOAT** Biomedical Engineering. Vol. 1 (Sept. 1972)-. Academic Scholarly Publication. English. bm (6 issues). $450.00 (institution), $150.00 (individual) US; $480.00 (institution), $180.00 (individual) other. Blackwell Scientific Publishers, 238 Main Street, Cambridge MA 02142. **Tel** (617)547-7110, (800)835-6770, FAX (617)547-0789. **ED** Hun H. Sun. **LC** R856.A1; A55. **DD** 610/.28. **NLM** W1 AN564. **CODEN** ABMECF. **[CCC]**. Index available (bound in Dec. issue). **Pr Rev.** available on microfilm and microfiche from University Microfilms International (UMI). Documents available from Article Express International, The Genuine Article, BIOSIS Document Express, Ask*IEEE. ***Absorbed*** *Journal of Bioengineering, 0145-3068.*
**Desc:** Publishes reports of original research on the application of sound engineering theory or practice to significant biomedical questions and problems.
**Ind/Abst** Appl. Mech. Rev.; Biol. Abstr.; Ceram. Abstr.; CSA Neuro. Abstr.; Curr. Aware. Biol. Sci., CABS; Curr. Contents Life Sci.; Ei Page One; EMBASE; Energy Res. Abstr. (April 1974-); Eng. Index Annu.; Health Plan. Adminis.; Index Med.; INIS Atomindex [Micro.]; INSPEC (Dec. 1974-); Int. Aerosp. Abstr.; Life Sci. Collect.; Phys. Med. Biol. (19??-19??); Res. Alert [Full Cov.]; Sci. Cit. Index; SCISEARCH.

US/8756-8144
**ANNUAL REPORT - NATIONAL INSTITUTES OF HEALTH (U.S.). BIOMEDICAL ENGINEERING AND INSTRUMENTATION BRANCH.** (ANNUAL REPORT FY ... / BIOMEDICAL ENGINEERING AND INSTRUMENTATION BRANCH, DIVISION OF RESEARCH SERVICES, NATIONAL INSTITUTES OF HEALTH.). [Annu. rep. - Natl. Inst. Health (U.S.), Biomed. Eng. Instrum. Branch]. **Main/Corp** National Institutes of Health (U.S.). Biomedical Engineering and Instrumentation Branch. English. an. **LC** R856.4. **DD** 610/.28. **NLM** W1; AN759ES. available on microfiche (Vols. for (1984) distributed to depository libraries). ***Continues*** *National Institutes of Health (U.S.). Division of Research Resources. Annual Report, 0730-8892.*

UK/0263-2535
**ANNUAL REPORT OF THE OXFORD ORTHOPAEDIC ENGINEERING CENTRE.** [Annual rep. Oxf. Orthop. Eng. Cent.]. Began with: 1 (1974). English. an. Nuffield Orthopaedic Centre, Headington, Oxford, 0X3 7LD England. **NLM** W1; AN76WF.

US/0147-0876
**ANNUAL REPORTS OF PROGRESS - REHABILITATION ENGINEERING CENTER AT RANCHO LOS AMIGOS HOSPITAL.** **VFOAT** Annual Progress Report - Rehabilitation Engineering Center at Rancho Los Amigos Hospital. No. 1- Dec. 1971/Nov. 1972-. Periodical. English. an. **NLM** W1 AN769GT.

US
**APPLIED BIOCHEMISTRY AND BIOTECHNOLOGY.** ***Title Change.*** **See** Biology-Biochemistry.

GW/0175-7598
**APPLIED MICROBIOLOGY AND BIOTECHNOLOGY.** **See** Biology-Microbiology.

US/0734-5151
**ARIES' BIOTECHNOLOGY CHEMONOMIES REPORT.** [Aries' biotechnol. chemon. rep.]. **VFOAT** Biotechnology Chemonomics Report; Biotechnology Chemonomics. Vol. 1, No. 1 (Sept. 1982)-. Periodical. English. mo. $290.00. Economics of Technologies, PO Box 6558, 49 East 41st Street, New York NY 10163. **Tel** (718)429-3132. **ED** Robert S Aries, Sigm Xi.
**Desc:** Deals with economic comments on the basic trends, marketing, costs and effects of technology and technical transfer with or without patents of the chemical process industries, particularly biotechnology.

US
**ARIS FUNDING REPORT / BIOMEDICAL SCIENCES.** English. ir (published every six weeks). $225.00. Academic Research Information System, 2940 16th Street, Suite 314, San Francisco CA 94103. **Tel** (415)558-8133, FAX (415)558-8135. **ED** Betty L. Traynor. available on diskette.
**Desc:** Provides grant information in the biomedical sciences from both federal and private sources.

US/1054-2027
**ASFA MARINE BIOTECHNOLOGY ABSTRACTS.** **See** Biology-Marine Biology.

US/0887-3127
**ASIAN MEDICAL & BIOTECHNOLOGY NEWS.** [Asian med. biotechnol. news]. **VFOAT** Asian Medical & Biotechnology News. (1985)-. Periodical. English. bm (6 issues). $65.00. Asian Medical & Biotechnology, PO Box 1182, Ames IA 50010. **Tel** (515)296-9919. **DD** 605.

AT/1036-7128
**AUSTRALASIAN BIOTECHNOLOGY.** [Australas. biotechnol.]. **Added/Corp** Australian Biotechnology Association. Vol. 1, No. 1 (Aug. 1991)-. Periodical. English. Six times a year. 72.00Aus$ (Australia); 96.00Aus$ (other). Australian Biotechnology Association Ltd, PO Box 4, Gardenvale 3185 Australia. **Tel** 011 61 3 5968879, FAX 011 61 3 5968874. **ED** M. J. Playne. **NLM** W1; AU237. **CODEN** AUBIE5. **Bk Rev**, (Qty: 10). **Ad Acc, Adv Mgr:** Gary Dolder. **Pr Rev. Circ:** 1,000. ***Formed by the union of*** *ABA Bulletin* ***and*** *Australian Journal of Biotechnology.*
**Desc:** Reports on the activities of biobusiness in Australia and New Zealand; on the commercialization of new products and processes; on political, government and regulatory decisions affecting the performance of biobusinesses and on export opportunities.
**Ind/Abst** Abstr. BioCommer. (199?-); BioBusiness (1992-); Curr. Aware. Biol. Sci., CABS; Food Sci. Technol. Abstr.; Soc. Sci. Cit. Index [Select. Cov.].

AT/0158-9938
**AUSTRALASIAN PHYSICAL & ENGINEERING SCIENCES IN MEDICINE.** (AUSTRALASIAN PHYSICAL & ENGINEERING SCIENCES IN MEDICINE / SUPPORTED BY THE AUSTRALASIAN COLLEGE OF PHYSICAL SCIENTISTS IN MEDICINE AND THE AUSTRALASIAN ASSOCIATION OF PHYSICAL SCIENCES IN MEDICINE.). [Australas. phys. eng. sci. med.]. **Added/Corp** Australasian College of Physical Scientists in Medicine. Australasian Association of Physical Sciences in Medicine. **VFOAT** Australasian Physical and Engineering Sciences in Medicine. New Series, Vol. 3, No. 1, Serial No. 86 (Jan/Feb 1980)-. Academic Scholarly Publication. English. Four times a year (Mar., Jun., Sept., Dec.). 45.00Aus$ (surface mail), 55.00Aus$ (economy airmail) individuals; 80.00Aus$ (surface mail), 90.00Aus$ (economy airmail) library or business. Australasian Physical & Engineering Sciences in Medicine, Department of Medical Physics, Royal Adelaide Hospital, Adelaide, South Australia 5000. **Tel** 011 61 8 224 5651, FAX 011 61 8 223 2071, telex AA 89764. **ED** Associate Professor A.H. Beddoe. **NLM** W1 AU335H. **CODEN** AUPMDI. Index available (volume index bound in last issue). **Bk Rev. Ad Acc. Pr Rev. Circ:** 500. Documents available from Article Express International, BIOSIS Document Express, Ask*IEEE, CASDDS. ***Continues*** *Australasian Physical Sciences in Medicine, 0157-9738.*
**Desc:** Application of the physical sciences and engineering to medical and clinical problems. Back issues available.

**Ind/Abst** Biol. Abstr. (1985-); Chem. Abstr.; Comput. Inf. Syst. Abstr. J. [Full Cov.]; Elect. Comm. Abstr.; Eng. Index Annu.; Health Plan. Adminis.; Index Med. (1983-); INSPEC (Jan.-Feb. 1980-); Mater. Sci. Eng. Abstr.; Phys. Med. Biol. (19??-19??); Pollut. Abstr. Indexes; Solid State Supercond. Abstr.

AT/1032-8068
**AUSTRALIAN AND NEW ZEALAND BIOTECHNOLOGY DIRECTORY. VFOAT** Australian and New Zealand Biotechnology Directory. 1st ed. (1989)-. Directory. English. an. 70.00Aus$. Australian Industrial Publishers Pty Ltd, 2 Wilford Avenue, Linderdale South Australia 5032 Australia. **Tel** (618)234-0022, FAX (618)234-0058. **ED** Michael Deves. **Ad Acc. Circ:** 1,000.
**Desc:** A directory of Australian and New Zealand Biotechnology companies.

US/0095-0963
**AUTOMEDICA (NEW YORK).** (AUTOMEDICA.). [Automedica]. Vol. 1 (Jan. 1974)-. Periodical. English. qt (1 volume). $816.00 (academic institutions), $1,273.00 (corporate institutions). Gordon & Breach Science Publishers, Inc., PO Box 786, Cooper Station, New York NY 10276. **Tel** (212)206-8900, FAX (212)645-2459. **(Subscription address:** Gordon & Breach Science Publishers / England, PO Box 90, Reading RG1 8JL England.**)** **LC** R858.A1; A9. **DD** 610/.28/54. **NLM** W1 AU873P. **CODEN** AUMDC9. **[CCC].** Documents available from Article Express International, BIOSIS Document Express, Ask*IEEE.
**Ind/Abst** Biol. Abstr. (-1984); Comput. Rev.; Ei Page One; Energy Res. Abstr. (May 1974-); Eng. Index Annu.; INSPEC (1974-).

●US
**BBSRC BUSINESS. Main/Corp** Biotechnology and Biological Sciences Research Council. (1994)-. Newsletter. English. qt. Biotechnology and Biological Sciences Research Council, Polaris House, North Star Avenue, Swindon SN2 1UH England. **Tel** 011 44 793 413200, FAX 011 44 793 413201. **ED** Dr. Monica Winstanley. **Circ:** 5,000 (ctrl).

CN
**BC BIOTECHNOLOGY ALLIANCE BIOFAX.** English. sm. Free to members; 200.00Can$ (corporate membership). Biotechnology Alliance, Suite 800, 4710 Kingsway, Burnaby, British Columbia V5H 4M2 Canada.
**Ind/Abst** Abstr. BioCommer.

UK
**BIA NEWSLETTER.** Newsletter. English. mo. Free to members; membership rates available on application. BioIndustry Association, 1 Queen Anne's Gate, London SW1H 9BT United Kingdom.
**Ind/Abst** Abstr. BioCommer.

NZ/0113-1060
**BIO-INPHARMA.** ***Title Change.*** [Bio-inpharma]. **VFOAT** BioInpharma; Biopharma; ADIS Bio-Inpharma. No. 1 (Jan. 17, 1987)-?. Periodical. English. sm. ADIS International Ltd, 41 Centorian Drive, Private Bag 65901, Mairangi Bay, Auckland 10 New Zealand. **Tel** 011 64 9 4798100, FAX 011 64 9 4791418. **(Subscription address:** US/ 582 Middletown Boulevard B-30, Langhorne, PA 19047-1822; HK/ 18/F Tung Sun Commercial Centre, 194-200 Lockhard Road, Wanchai Hong Kong**)** **NLM** W1; BI667J. **[CCC].** ***Continued by*** *Inpharma, 0156-2703.*
**Desc:** Current awareness service covering research projects and marketed products in biotechnology. Unique emphasis on application of biotechnology in diagnostic and clinical use.

US/0959-2989
**BIO-MEDICAL MATERIALS AND ENGINEERING.** [Bio-med. mater. eng.]. **VFOAT** Biomedical Materials and Engineering. Vol. 1, No. 1 (1990)-. Academic Scholarly Publication. English. Four times a year. $425.00 The Americas; £285.00 other. Pergamon Press, An Imprint of Elsevier Science Ltd., The Boulevard, Langford Lane, Kidlington, Oxford OX5 1GB United Kingdom. **Tel** 011 44 865 843000, 011 44 865 843699, FAX 011 44 865 843010. **(Subscription address:** Elsevier Science Ltd. Oxford Fulfillment Centre, PO Box 800, Kidlington, Oxford OX5 1DX United Kingdom.**)** **ED** T. Yokobori. **LC** R857.M3; B48. **DD** 610/.28. **NLM** W1; BI854X. **CODEN** BMENEO. available on microfilm and microfiche from University Microfilms International (UMI). Documents available from The Genuine Article, CASDDS.
**Desc:** Interdisciplinary journal that publishes original research papers, review articles and brief notes on materials and engineering for biological and medical systems.
**Ind/Abst** Alum. Ind. Abstr.; Chem. Abstr.; Eng. Mater. Abstr.; Index Med. (1991-); Met. Abstr.; Res. Alert [Full Cov.].

FR/0292-8418
**BIO-SCIENCES.** [Bio-sciences]. **VFOAT** Biosciences. No. 1 (Jan./Feb. 1982)-. Academic Scholarly Publication. French (summaries and/or abstracts in English). Six times a year. 380.00F (one year), 650.00F (two year) France; 450.00F (one year), 750.00F (two year) other. Biosciences, BP 19, 78117 Chateaufort France. **Tel** 011 33 1 39565210. **NLM** W1; BI91WP. **CODEN** BIOSER. Documents available from CASDDS.
**Ind/Abst** Chem. Abstr.; Curr. Biotechnol.; Energy Res. Abstr. (Feb. 1983-).

US
**BIOCENTURY : THE BERNSTEIN REPORT ON BIOBUSINESS.** (19??)-. English. wk (50 issues). $735.00. BioCentury Publications Inc., PO Box 3415, Redwood City CA 94064. **Tel** (415)347-1043.
**Ind/Abst** Abstr. BioCommer.

PL/0208-5216
**BIOCYBERNETICS AND BIOMEDICAL ENGINEERING / POLISH ACADEMY OF SCIENCES, INSTITUTE OF BIOCYBERNETICS AND BIOMEDICAL ENGINEERING.** Vol. 1, No. 1/2-. Periodical. English. **NLM** W1 BI662M.

●US/1068-5693
**BIOENGINEERING ABSTRACTS (1993).** **See** Medical Science and Technology-Abstracting, Bibliographies and Statistics.

UK/0142-0674
**BIOENGINEERING CURRENT AWARENESS NOTIFICATION : BECAN.** **VFOAT** BECAN. Periodical. English. mo. **LC** R856.A1; B54. **DD** 610/.28.

GW/0178-2029
**BIOENGINEERING (GRAFELFING, GERMANY).** ***Ceased.*** (BIOENGINEERING.). [Bioengineering]. **VFOAT** Bio Engineering. (198?)-Issue 6 (1994). Academic Scholarly Publication. German. Six times a year. Resch Media Mail Verlag GmbH, Postfach 1260, D 82166 Graefelfing Germany. **Tel** 011 49 89 8580710. **LC** TP248.13; .B54. **DD** 660/.6. **NLM** W1; BI663ND. **CODEN** BENGEQ. Documents available from The Genuine Article, CASDDS.
**Ind/Abst** Chem. Abstr. (1986-); Curr. Biotechnol.; Food Sci. Technol. Abstr.; Res. Alert [Full Cov.].

UK/0951-5291
**BIOENGINEERING NOW.** [Bioeng. now]. (1987)-. English. bm. £85.00 Europe; £100.00 other. Sarratt Information Services, 68 St Andrews Road, Henly Thames, Oxon RG9 1JE England. **Tel** 011 44 81 422 4384. **ED** Brandl Graham Kay. **DD** 610.28. Index available (Published separately). **Circ:** 50.
**Desc:** This Publication is a bibliographic listing of world wide articles published on bioengineering and biomaterials

FR/0294-3506
**BIOFUTUR.** [Biofutur]. (1982)-. Academic Scholarly Publication. French (English). mo (11 issues). 795.00F France; 915.00F other. Editions Scientifique Elsevier, 141 rue de Javel, 75747 Paris Cedex 15 France. **Tel** 011 33 1 47 07 11 22, FAX 011 33 1 43 36 80 93. **(Subscription address:** Editions Scientifiques Elsevier / for North America, PO Box 7247-7576, Philadelphia PA 19170-7576.**)** **LC** TP248.13; .B545. **DD** 660/.6/05. **NLM** W1; BI665KE. **CODEN** BIOFEM. **[CCC]. Pr Rev.** available on microfilm and microfiche from University Microfilms International (UMI). Documents available from The Genuine Article. ***Absorbed*** *Biofutur. Technoscope, 0992-4221.*
**Ind/Abst** AgBiotech News Inf.; Biodeter. Abstr. (1991-); Curr. Aware. Biol. Sci., CABS; Curr. Biotechnol.; Curr. Contents, Agric. Biol. Environ. Sci.; Dairy Sci. Abstr.; EMBASE; For. Abstr.; Helminthol. Abstr. (1991-); Hortic. Abstr.; Index Vet.; Infomat Int. Bus.; Maize Abstr.; Methods Organ. Synth.; Nematol. Abstr.; Nutr. Abstr. Rev., Ser. B, Live Feeds and Feed.; PESTDOC; Plant Breed. Abstr.; Plant Genet. Resour. Abstr.; Potato Abstr.; Protozoolog. Abstr.; Res. Alert [Full Cov.]; Rev. Agric. Entomol.; Rev. Plant Pathol.; SCISEARCH; Soc. Sci. Cit. Index [Select. Cov.]; Weed Abstr.; World Agric. Econ.

US/0886-7461
**BIOINVENTION.** [BioInvention]. **VFOAT** Bio Invention. Vol. 5, No. 1 (Jan. 1986)-. Periodical. English. Twelve times a year. $425.00. Biosource, Inc., PO Box 550, Howell NJ 07731. **Tel** (908)905-5728, FAX (908)905-5847. **ED** Thomas J. Puskar. **DD** 660. **NLM** W1; BI667JK. available in bound issues. ***Continues*** *Biotechnology Patent Digest, 0730-1057.*
**Ind/Abst** Abstr. BioCommer. (-199?).

US/1056-9138
**BIOLOGICAL EFFECTS OF NONIONIZING ELECTROMAGNETIC RADIATION DIGEST UPDATE (PHILADELPHIA, PA.).** (BIOLOGICAL EFFECTS OF NONIONIZING ELECTROMAGNETIC RADIATION DIGEST UPDATE.). **Added/Corp** Information Ventures, Inc. **VFOAT** BENER Digest Update. Vol. 1, No. 1 (June 1991)-. Periodical. English. qt. $315.00. Information Ventures Inc., 1500 Locust Street, Suite 3216, Philadelphia PA 19102. **Tel** (215)732-9083, FAX (215)732-3754. **ED** Robert Goldberg. **DD** 574. **CODEN** BENUEY. Index available (bound in all issues). available on CD-ROM from Info Ventures.
**Desc:** Documents and critically reviews current research on the biological and health effects of nonionizing electromagnetic radiation.

US/1055-7172
**BIOMATERIALS, ARTIFICIAL CELLS, AND IMMOBILIZATION BIOTECHNOLOGY.** ***Title Change.*** [Biomater. artif. cells immobil. biotechnol.]. **Added/Corp** International Society for Artificial Cells and Immobilization Biotechnology. Vol. 19, No. 1 (1991)-(19??). Academic Scholarly Publication. English. qt. Marcel Dekker Inc., 270 Madison Avenue, New York NY 10016. **Tel** (212)696-9000, (800)228-1160, FAX (212)685-4540, telex 421419. **(Subscription address:** Marcel Dekker Inc, PO Box 5017, Monticello NY 12701.**)** **ED** T M S Chang, P E Barre and C J Chiu. **LC** R856.A1; B56. **DD** 610/.28. **NLM** W1; BI852RR. **CODEN** BACBEU. **[CCC].** Documents available from Article Express International, The Genuine Article, BIOSIS Document Express, Ask*IEEE, CASDDS. ***Continues*** *Biomaterials, Artificial Cells, and Artificial Organs, 0890-5533.* ***Continued by*** *Artificial Cells, Blood Substitutes, and Immobilization Biotechnology.*
**Desc:** Covers artificial replacement on three structural levels: molecules, cells, and organs. Integrates biotechnology, polymer chemistry, and engineering in the development of biomaterials, artificial cells, and artificial organs.
**Ind/Abst** BioBusiness (1991-); Bioeng. Abstr. (1991-); Biol. Abstr. (1991-); Chem. Abstr. (1991-); Curr. Contents Clin. Med.; Ei Page One (1991-); EMBASE; Energy Res. Abstr. (1991-); Eng. Index Annu.; Eng. Index Energy Abstr. (1991-); Health Plan. Adminis.; Index Med. (1991-); INSPEC (1991-); Mater. Sci. Eng. Abstr.; Met. Abstr. (1991-); Life Sci. Collect. (1991-); Ref. Upd. Deluxe Ed.; Res. Alert [Full Cov.]; Sci. Cit. Index; SCISEARCH.

●US/1076-6286
**BIOMATERIALS SCIENCE AND ENGINEERING.** (1994)-. Periodical. English. qt. $156.00. Mary Ann Liebert Inc., 1651 Third Avenue, New York NY 10128. **Tel** (212)289-2300, (800)M-LIEBERT, FAX (212)289-4697.

BE/0778-4910
**BIOMEDICAL & HEALTH RESEARCH.** [Biomed. health res.]. **VFOAT** Biomedical and Health Research; Newsletter Biomedical & Health Research. (1990)-. Periodical. Multiple languages. qt. Free. Commission of the European Communities, DG XII-E-4, Medical Research Division, Rue de la Loi 200, B-1049 Brussels, Belgium. **Tel** FAX 011 32 2 2955365. **ED** A Dickens. **UDC** 167(4). **CODEN** CE.
**Desc:** Provides news and information on biomedical research. Also announces recent publications and conferences in the field.

US/0006-3398
**BIOMEDICAL ENGINEERING.** [Biomed. eng.]. **Added/Corp** Consultants Bureau. Vol. 1 (Jan. 1967)-. Academic Scholarly Publication. English (Russian). bm. $945.00 US; $1105.00 other. Consultants Bureau, A Division of Plenum Publishing Corporation, 233 Spring Street, New York NY 10013. **Tel** (212)620-8000, (212)620-8466, FAX (212)463-0742, telex 23/421139. **ED** V. A. Viktorov. **LC** R856; .M4513. **DD** 610/.28. **NLM** W1 BI854I. **CODEN** BIOEAF. **[CCC].** available on microfilm and microfiche from University Microfilms International (UMI). Documents available from Article Express International, BIOSIS Document Express, Ask*IEEE, CASDDS.
**Desc:** Covers recent advances in the growing field of biomedical technology, instrumentation, and administration.
**Ind/Abst** Bioeng. Abstr.; Biol. Abstr. (?-1984); Chem. Abstr.; Ei Page One; EMBASE; Energy Res. Abstr. (May 1974-); Eng. Index Annu.; Health Plan. Adminis.; Index Med.; INIS Atomindex [Micro.]; INSPEC (Jan.-Feb. 1972-).

US/0194-2778
**BIOMEDICAL ENGINEERING AND COMPUTATION SERIES.** [Biomed. eng. comput. ser.]. Vol. 1-. Monographic series. English. ir. Price varies per volume. Harwood Academic Publishers / New York, PO Box 786, Cooper Station, New York NY 10276. **Tel** (212)206-8900, (201)643-7500. **(Subscription address:** International Publishers Distributor at one of the following addresses: 820 Town Center Drive, Langhorne, PA 19047; or PO Box 90, Reading Berkshire RG1 8JL UK; or Kent Ridge PO Box 1180, Singapore 9111, Republic of Singapore**)** **ED** Dhanjoo N Ghista. **NLM** W1 BI854IH.

US/0190-0951
**BIOMEDICAL ENGINEERING AND HEALTH SYSTEMS.** (19??)-. Monographic series. English. ir. Price varies per volume. John Wiley & Sons Inc / New Jersey, 1 Wiley Drive, Somerset NJ 08875. **Tel** (800)225-5945, (908)469-4400. **(Subscription address:** John Wiley & Sons / England, Baffins Lane, Chichester, West Sussex PO19 1UD England.**)**
**Ind/Abst** Math. Rev.

●US/1062-5488
**BIOMEDICAL ENGINEERING CITATION INDEX.** (BIOMEDICAL ENGINEERING CITATION INDEX [COMPUTER FILE] : A CD-ROM DATABASE WITH ABSTRACTS.). **Added/Corp** Institute for Scientific Information. **VFOAT** Biomedical Engineering. (1992)-. English. bm. $2,250.00. Institute for Scientific Information, 3501 Market Street, Philadelphia PA 19104. **Tel** (215)386-0100, (800)523-1850, FAX (215)386-6362, telex 84-5305. **(Subscription address:** Institute for Scientific Information, PO Box 71416, Chicago, IL 60694**)**

US/0899-8205
**BIOMEDICAL INSTRUMENTATION & TECHNOLOGY.** (BIOMEDICAL INSTRUMENTATION AND TECHNOLOGY : JOURNAL OF THE ASSOCIATION FOR THE ADVANCEMENT OF MEDICAL INSTRUMENTATION.). [Biomed. instrum. technol.]. **Added/Corp** Association for the Advancement of Medical Instrumentation. **VFOAT** Biomedical Instrumentation and Technology. Vol. 23, No. 1 (Jan./Feb. 1989)-. Periodical. English. bm. $96.00 (institutions), $72.00 (individuals) US and Possessions; $106.00 (institutions), $82.00 (individuals) other. Hanley & Belfus Inc., 210 South 13th Street, Philadelphia PA 19107. **Tel** (215)546-7293, FAX (215)790-9330. **ED** Gail Corbett. **LC** R856.A1; B575. **DD** 610/.28/05. **NLM** W1; BI854MN. **CODEN** BITYE2. **[CCC]. Bk Rev. Ad Acc. Circ:** 5,500. Documents available from Article Express International, The Genuine Article, BIOSIS Document Express, Ask*IEEE. ***Formed by the union of*** *Medical Instrumentation, 0090-6689* ***and*** *Biomedical Technology Today, 0883-9093.*
**Desc:** Leading authorities provide data on biomedical and biotechnical applications of medical instrumentation and articles exploring the tools and techniques used in a host of medical situations. Also includes articles on the management and maintenance of equipment.
**Ind/Abst** Biol. Abstr.; Comput. Inf. Syst. Abstr. J. [Full Cov.]; Elect. Comm. Abstr.; EMBASE; Eng. Index Annu.; Health Devices Alerts; Health Plan. Adminis.; Index Med. Feb. 1989-; INIS Atomindex [Micro.]; INSPEC (Jan./Feb. 1989-); Res. Alert [Full Cov.]; Soc. Sci. Cit. Index [Select. Cov.].

●US/1064-699X
**BIOMEDICAL LIBRARY ACQUISITIONS BULLETIN [COMPUTER FILE].** **See** Library and Information Sciences.

US
**BIOMEDICAL MARKET NEWSLETTER.** [Biomed. mark. newsl.]. Vol. 1, No. 1 (Sept. 1991)-. Newsletter. English. mo. $395.00 (one yar), $655.00 (two year), $915.00 (three year) surface mail; $584.00 air mail. Biomedical Market Newsletter, 3237 Idaho Place, Costa Mesa CA 92626. **Tel** (714)434-9500, (800)875-8181. **DD** 338. available on an online database (files 16,636/Full-Text) from DIALOG.
**Ind/Abst** PROMT [Full Txt.]; PTS Newsl. Database [Full Txt.].

US/0192-1266
**BIOMEDICAL PRODUCTS.** [Biomed. prod.]. (19??)-. Periodical. English. mo. $30.00 US, Canada and Mexico; $42.00 (surface mail), $93.00 (airmail) other. Cahners Publishing Company, 249 West 17th Street, New York NY 10011. **Tel** (212)645-0067, FAX (212)242-6987. **(Subscription address:** Gordon Publications, Inc., Paid Circulation Department, 301 Gibralter Drive, Box 650, Morris Plains NJ 07950-0650.**)** **DD** 610. **[CCC].**
**Desc:** Reaches directors, principle investigators, biochemists, chemists, medical researchers, microbiologists, professors and medical school teachers in the life science/biotech research laboratories of universities, medical institutions, pharmaceutical companies, industry, and biotechnology and research centers.

II/0970-938X
**BIOMEDICAL RESEARCH.** [Biomed. res.]. Vol. 1 (Jan. 1990)-. Periodical. English. sa. $60.00. Scientific Publishers, PO Box 91, Ratanada Road, Jodhpur 342011 India. **(Subscription address:** Prints India, 11 Darya Ganj, New Delhi 110002 India.**)** **NLM** W1; BI8564. **CODEN** BIRSE8. Documents available from BIOSIS Document Express.
**Ind/Abst** Biol. Abstr. (1991-); EMBASE [Select. Cov.].

●BU
**BIOMEDICAL REVIEWS.** Vol. 1 (1992)-. Periodical. English. DM86.00. **(Subscription address:** Kubon & Sagner, ABT Zeitschriftenimport, D 80328 Munich Germany.**)** **NLM** W1; BI856GGG.

US/1051-2020
**BIOMEDICAL SCIENCE AND TECHNOLOGY.** ***Ceased.*** (BIOMEDICAL SCIENCE AND TECHNOLOGY : RESEARCH, ENGINEERING, AND MANUFACTURING.). [Biomed. sci. technol.]. (1991)-(19??). Academic Scholarly Publication. English. qt. Academic Press, Inc., 6277 Sea Harbor Drive, Orlando FL 32887. **Tel** (800)543-9534, (407)345-4100, FAX (407)363-9661. **ED** Robert D Gold. **LC** R856.A1; B577. **DD** 610/.28/05. **NLM** W1; BI856GL. **[CCC]. Pr Rev.** Documents available from The Genuine Article.
**Desc:** Dedicated to covering the development and production of devices and instruments used in medicine and health care. Publishes peer-reviewed technical articles and other information of interest and applicability to a broad range of those working to create, develop, and manufacture the materials and products used by the medical community. Technical articles, whether tutorial or describing specific applications, are written so that their application across many specialty fields is evident. Attention is also given to the transfer of new technologies from the academic or government research lab to the commercial product manufacture.
**Ind/Abst** Res. Alert [Full Cov.].

US/0067-8856
**BIOMEDICAL SCIENCES INSTRUMENTATION.** [Biomed. sci. instrum.]. **Main/Conf** International ISA Biomedical Sciences Instrumentation Symposium. V. 7- 1970-. Academic Scholarly Publication. English. an. $34.50 plus shipping. Instrument Society of America, 67 Alexander Drive, Research Triangle NC 27709. **Tel** (919)549-8411, FAX (919)549-8288, telex 802 540. **LC** R856; .N33. **DD** 610'.28. **NLM** W1 BI856J. **CODEN** BMSIA7. **[CCC].** available on microfilm and microfiche from University Microfilms International (UMI). Documents available from Article Express International, CASDDS. ***Continues*** *National Biomedical Sciences Instrumentation; Proceedings / National Biomedical Sciences Instrumentation Symposium, 0067-8856;* ***Absorbed*** *Rocky Mountain Bioengineering Symposium. Conference Record.*
**Desc:** Proceedings of the jointly-sponsored ISA Biomedical Sciences Division/Rocky Mountain Bioengineering Symposium/Engineering in Medicine and Science Group of IEEE Conference.
**Ind/Abst** Bioeng. Abstr.; Chem. Abstr.; Ei Page One; EMBASE; Energy Res. Abstr. (June 1971-); Eng. Index Annu.; Health Plan. Adminis.; Index Med.

US/0147-2682
**BIOMEDICAL TECHNOLOGY INFORMATION SERVICE.** [Biomed. technol. inf. serv.]. Vol. 4 (Jan. 31, 1977)-. Newsletter. English. sm (published once during January and August). $266.00 US, Canada and Mexico; $304.00 other. Quest Publishing Company, 1351 Titan Way, Brea CA 92621. **Tel** (714)738-6400, FAX (714)525-6258. **ED** Allan F. Pacela. **DD** 610. **NLM** W1 BI856T. **CODEN** BTISE6. **[CCC].** Index available. **Bk Rev.** Documents available from UMI Article Clearinghouse. ***Formed by the union of*** *Advanced Biomedical Technology, 0094-0100; Biomedical Inventions Reporter, 0094-0119; Government Documents Review, 0094-0127* ***and*** *Health Care Statistics Report, 0094-0135.*
**Desc:** Covers advances in medical technology and instrumentation.
**Ind/Abst** Pharm. News Index (Dec. 1987-).

●US/1073-1210
**BIOMEDICAL TECHNOLOGY MANAGEMENT.** [Biomed. technol. manag.]. **VFOAT** Technology. Vol. 5, No. 1 (Jan.-Feb. 1994)-. Periodical. English. Six times a year. Free to qualified subscribers; $35.00 other. Second Source Publications Inc., PO Box 930, Portsmouth RI 02871. **Tel** (401)683-7470. **DD** 610. **NLM** W1; BI856U. ***Continues*** *Second Source Biomedical, 1053-6868.*

GW/0013-5585
**BIOMEDIZINISCHE TECHNIK.** [Biomed. Tech.]. **VFOAT** Biomedical Engineering. Vol. 16 (Feb. 1971)-. Academic Scholarly Publication. German (English; summaries and/or abstracts in English and German). bm. DM418.00 Germany; DM470.00 other. Fachverlag Schiele & Schoen, Markgrafenstrasse 11, W-1000 Berlin 61 Germany. **Tel** 011/49/30/2516029, FAX 011/49/30/2517248, telex 841/181470. **LC** R856.A1. **NLM** W1 BI858. **CODEN** BMZTA7. **[CCC]. Pr Rev.** Documents available from Article Express International, The Genuine Article, Ask*IEEE, CASDDS. ***Continues*** *Elektromedizin.*
**Ind/Abst** Chem. Abstr.; Curr. Contents Clin. Med.; EMBASE; Energy Res. Abstr. (July 1974-); Eng. Index Annu. [Select. Cov.]; Health Plan. Adminis.; Index Med.; INSPEC (Feb. 1971-); Life Sci. Collect.; Protozoolog. Abstr.; Res. Alert [Full Cov.]; Saf. Health Work; Sci. Cit. Index; SCISEARCH; Soc. Sci. Cit. Index [Select. Cov.].

US/0888-7470
**BIOPROCESS TECHNOLOGY.** [Bioprocess technol.]. Vol. 1 (1986)-. Monographic series. English. Price varies per volume. Marcel Dekker Inc., 270 Madison Avenue, New York NY 10016. **Tel** (212)696-9000, (800)228-1160, FAX (212)685-4540, telex 421419. **(Subscription address:** Marcel Dekker Inc, PO Box 5017, Monticello NY 12701.**)** **DD** 660. **NLM** W1; BI88U. **CODEN** BPTEEP. Documents available from CASDDS.
**Desc:** Covers topics in biotechnology such as anaerobic fermentation, yeast strain selections and sensors in bioprocess control.
**Ind/Abst** Chem. Abstr.

UK/0269-7572
**BIORECOVERY (BERKHAMSTED).** (BIORECOVERY.). [Biorecovery]. Vol. 1, No. 1 (1988)-. Periodical. English. ir (four issues per volume). $114.00 (four issues). AB Academic Publishers, PO Box 42 Bicester, OXON OX6 7NW England. **Tel** 011 44 869 320949. **CODEN** BRECEQ. Documents available from The Genuine Article, BIOSIS Document Express, CASDDS, Documents on Demand.
**Ind/Abst** Biodeter. Abstr. (1991-); Biol. Abstr. (1989-); Chem. Abstr.; Curr. Biotechnol.; Energy Inf. Abstr.; Environ. Abstr.; Environ. Period. Bibliogr.; Res. Alert [Full Cov.].

US/0887-6207
**BIOSCAN.** [BioScan]. **VAT** Bio Scan. Vol. 1 (1987)-. English. bm. $950.00 North America; $1120.00 other. Oryx Press, 4041 North Central Avenue, #700, Phoenix AZ 85012-3397. **Tel** (800)279-ORYX, (602)265-2651, FAX (602)265-6250, (800)279-4663, (800)279-6799. **(Subscription address:** Eurospan Ltd., Journals and Serials Division, 3 Henrietta Street, Covent Garden, London WC2E 8LU England.**)** **LC** HD9999.B44; B56. **DD** 338.7/6208/025. **NLM** QT 22.1; B615. available in Loose-leaf; available on diskette; available on an online database.
**Desc:** A comprehensive and up-to-date information service covering 550 US companies and 365 foreign companies actively involved in product research and development. Reports on industry leaders and identifies new and emerging companies. Information includes product development, business strategy, investments, parent company and percentage owned, financial information, research and development activities, history and new facility information.

●JA/0916-8451
**BIOSCIENCE, BIOTECHNOLOGY, AND BIOCHEMISTRY.** **Added/Corp** Nihon Nogei Kagakkai. Vol. 56, No. 1 (Jan. 1992)-. Periodical. English. mo. $350.00. **(Subscription address:** Japan Publications Trading Company, Ltd., PO Box 5030, Tokyo International, Tokyo 100-31 Japan.**)** **LC** IN PROCESS; QH301; .B56. **NLM** W1; BI91H. **CODEN** BBBIEJ. **[CCC].** Documents available from The Genuine Article, Documents on Demand. ***Continues*** *Agricultural and Biological Chemistry, 0002-1369.*
**Ind/Abst** Biol. Agric. Index; Curr. Aware. Biol. Sci., CABS; Curr. Contents, Agric. Biol. Environ. Sci.; Curr. Contents Life Sci.; Environ. Abstr.; Food Sci. Technol. Abstr.; Foods Adlibra; Ref. Upd. Deluxe Ed.; Res. Alert [Full Cov.]; Sci. Cit. Index; Soc. Sci. Cit. Index [Select. Cov.].

UK/0956-5663
**BIOSENSORS & BIOELECTRONICS.** **See** Biology-Biochemistry.

NE/0923-179X
**BIOSEPARATION.** Vol. 1, No. 1 (May 1990)-. Periodical. English. bm. $644.00. Kluwer Academic Publishers, Postbus 322, 3300 AH Dordrecht, The Netherlands. **Tel** 011 (31) 78 524400, FAX 011 31 78 183273, telex 20083. **ED** Tony Atkinson. **NLM** W1; BI915W. **CODEN** BISPE4. **[CCC]. Pr Rev. Acid Free.** available on microfilm and microfiche from University Microfilms International (UMI). Documents available from The Genuine Article, CASDDS.
**Desc:** Publishes papers on all aspects of separation science applicable or potentially applicable to commercial scale biotechnological processes.
**Ind/Abst** Chem. Abstr.; Curr. Aware. Biol. Sci., CABS; Food Sci. Technol. Abstr.; Res. Alert [Full Cov.].

GW/0931-1408
**BIOTEC (STUTTGART).** (BIOTEC.). [Biotec]. Vol. 1 (1987)-. Monographic series. English (English). bm. L70000.00. Clas International, Via Pace 8, 25122 Brescia Italy. **Tel** 011 39 30 3772712. **NLM** W1; BI918KH. **CODEN** BITCE4. **Bk Rev**, (Qty: 15-20/yr). **Ad Acc, Adv Mgr:** Michele Francaviglia. **Pr Rev. Circ:** 4000. Documents available from BIOSIS Document Express, CASDDS.
**Desc:** Biotechnology applicated to different fields of medicine.
**Ind/Abst** AGRICOLA [Select. Cov.]; Biol. Abstr. (1988-); Chem. Abstr.; Ei Page One.

US/0899-5702
**BIOTECH BUSINESS.** [Biotech bus.]. (Jan. 1988)-. Periodical. English. mo. $150.00. Worldwide Videotex, PO Box 3273, Boynton Beach FL 33424-3273. **Tel** (407)738-2276, FAX (407)738-2275. **ED** Mark Wright. **DD** 338. **Bk Rev**, (Qty: 12). available on an online database (file 636/Full-Text) from DIALOG; and NEWSNET.
**Desc:** Provides news and information on biotechnology products and companies.
**Ind/Abst** PTS Newsl. Database [Full Txt.].

US/1067-2818
**BIOTECH BUYERS' GUIDE.** (BIOTECH BUYERS' GUIDE / AMERICAN CHEMICAL SOCIETY.). [Biotech buy. guide]. **Added/Corp** American Chemical Society. Vol. 1 (1990)-. Consumer Publication. English. an. $50.00. American Chemical Society, 1155 Sixteenth Street Northwest, Washington DC 20036. **Tel** (800)333-9511, (800)227-5558, (614)447-3776, FAX (202)833-7736. **ED** Louis Gonzalez. **LC** HD9706.65.B55; B56. **DD** 660. **NLM** QT 22.1; B616. **CODEN** BBGUEC. **Ad Acc. Circ:** 65,000.
**Desc:** Complete directory to biotechnology products and services, from lab bench to pilot plant.

US/1067-1196
**BIOTECH DAILY.** ***Title Change.*** [Biotech dly.]. Vol. 1, No. 1 (Aug. 11, 1992)-(199?). Periodical. English. da. King Publishing Group, 627 National Press Building, Washington DC 20045. **Tel** (202)638-4260, FAX (202)662-9744. **LC** TP248.13; .B5583. **DD** 660/.6/05. **NLM** W1; BI918KRF. ***Continues*** *Genetic Engineering Letter, 0276-1882.* ***Merged with*** *Pharmaceutical Daily, 1071-5096* ***to form*** *Pharmaceutical & Biotech Daily, 1074-8636.*
**Ind/Abst** Abstr. BioCommer.

GW/0938-7501
**BIOTECH FORUM EUROPE.** ***Ceased.*** [Biotech forum Eur.]. **Added/Corp** Arbeitsgesellschaft fuer Gen-Diagnostik. Osterreichische Gesellschaft fuer Bioiprozesstechnik. **VFOAT** BFE. Vol. 7, No. 1 (March 1990)-(19??). Academic Scholarly Publication. English. bm. British Science Fiction Association Ltd, 60 Bournemouth Road, Folkestone Kent CT19 5AZ England. **CODEN** BFOEEW. **[CCC].** Documents available from The Genuine Article, CASDDS. ***Continues*** *Biotec Europe, 0937-0412.*
**Ind/Abst** Abstr. BioCommer.; AgBiotech News Inf.; AGRICOLA [Select. Cov.]; Chem. Abstr.; Ei Page One; Food Sci. Technol. Abstr.; PESTDOC; Plant Breed. Abstr.; Plant Genet. Resour. Abstr.; Res. Alert [Full Cov.]; Rev. Agric. Entomol.; Seed Abstr.; Weed Abstr.

UK/0953-2226
**BIOTECH KNOWLEDGE SOURCES.** (BIOTECH KNOWLEDGE SOURCES : BKS.). [Biotech. knowl. sources]. **Added/Corp** British Library. Biotechnology Information Service. BioCommerce Data Ltd. **VFOAT** BKS. (1987)-. Periodical. English. Twelve times a year. £158.00 Europe; $300.00 other. Biocommerce Data Ltd, 95 High Street, Slough Berks SL1 1DH United Kingdom. **Tel** 011 44 753-511777, FAX 011 44 753 512239. **ED** R. Wakerfort. **NLM** ZQT 34; B61578. Index available. cum. index. **Bk Rev. Ad Acc. Circ:** 200 (ctrl).
**Desc:** A alerting service listing new books, market surveys and other publications on biotechnology and forthcoming conferences and courses worldwide. Includes reviews of new information products and case studies of services.

UK
**BIOTECH NEWS.** (198?)-. Periodical. English. mo. £82.50 UK; £87.50 airmail. Springfield Information Services / Petersborough, PO Box 31, Cross Street Court, Peterborough PE1 1SD England. **Tel** 011 44 733 267272. **NLM** W1; BI918KT. Documents available from CASDDS.
**Ind/Abst** Abstr. BioCommer.; Chem. Abstr.

US/0898-2813
**BIOTECH PATENT NEWS.** [Biotech pat. news]. (1987)-. Periodical. English. Twelve times a year. $95.00 US; $110.00 other. Biotech Patent News, PO Box 4482, Metuchen NJ 08840. **Tel** (908)549-1356, FAX (908)549-1356. **ED** Richard S. Parr. **DD** 610. **Ad Acc, Adv Mgr:** Alicia Parr. **Circ:** 180. available on an online database (files 16,636/Full-Text) from DIALOG; and (dialog-predicasts).
**Desc:** Newsletter exclusively devoted to worldwide patent, licensing and litigation information relating to biotechnology.
**Ind/Abst** Abstr. BioCommer.; PROMT [Full Txt.]; PTS Newsl. Database [Full Txt.].

US/1069-4773
**BIOTECH REPORTER.** [Biotech report.]. Vol. 10, No. 6 (May 1993)-. Periodical. English. mo. $135.00. Freiberg Publishing, Box 7, Cedar Falls IA 50613-0007. **Tel** (319)277-3599. **DD** 630. ***Continues*** *Agbiotechnology News, 0899-3998.*

●UK
**BIOTECHNOLOGY ABSTRACTS. See** Medical Science and Technology-Abstracting, Bibliographies and Statistics.

US
**BIOTECHNOLOGY ABSTRACTS [COMPUTER FILE] / DERWENT PUBLICATIONS, LTD. Added/Corp** SilverPlatter Information, Inc. Derwent Publications, Ltd. Periodical. English. qt. $1750.00 academic institutions; $4900.00 multi-user; $2450.00 all others. Silverplatter Information Inc., 100 River Ridge Drive, Norwood MA 02062. **Tel** (800)343-0064, (617)769-2599, FAX (617)235-1715. **(Subscription address:** Non-North America orders/ Silverplatter Information BV, PC Hoofstrat 116 II, 1071 CD Amsterdam Netherlands**)**
**Desc:** Contains abstracts of major scientific publications, conference proceedings, and patent literature covering all aspects of biotechnology and includes all industrial uses of microorganisms, enzymes and cell culture, as well as plant micropropagation.

UK/0734-9750
**BIOTECHNOLOGY ADVANCES.** [Biotechnol. adv.]. Vol. 1, No. 1 (1983)-. Academic Scholarly Publication. English. qt. $425.00 The Americas; £285.00 other. Pergamon Press, An Imprint of Elsevier Science Ltd., The Boulevard, Langford Lane, Kidlington, Oxford OX5 1GB United Kingdom. **Tel** 011 44 865 843000, 011 44 865 843699, FAX 011 44 865 843010. **(Subscription address:** Elsevier Science Ltd. Oxford Fulfillment Centre, PO Box 800, Kidlington, Oxford OX5 1DX United Kingdom.**) ED** Murray Moo Young. **LC** TP248.2; .B55. **DD** 660/.6/05. **NLM** W1; BI918MF. **CODEN** BIADDD. **[CCC]. Pr Rev.** available on microfilm and microfiche from University Microfilms International (UMI). Documents available from Article Express International, The Genuine Article, CASDDS, ADONIS.
**Desc:** Journal is devoted to all areas of biotechnology including relevant aspects of its disciplinary underpinnings in biology, chemistry and engineering. The primary purpose is to provide regular, rapid but authoritative reviews of important advances in this field for students, researchers, managers and others in industry, government and academia.
**Ind/Abst** ADONIS; AgBiotech News Inf.; AGRICOLA [Select. Cov.]; BioBusiness; Biodeter. Abstr. (19??-19??); Biostatistica; Chem. Abstr. (1983-); Curr. Aware. Biol. Sci., CABS; Curr. Biotechnol.; Curr. Contents, Agric. Biol. Environ. Sci.; Eng. Index Annu.; For. Prod. Abstr.; Index Sci. Rev. [Full Cov.]; Maize Abstr.; Nutr. Abstr. Rev., Ser. B, Live Feeds and Feed.; Oper. Res./Manag. Sci.; Life Sci. Collect. (1985-); PESTDOC; Plant Breed. Abstr.; Plant Genet. Resour. Abstr.; Postharvest News Inf.; Res. Alert [Full Cov.]; Sci. Cit. Index; SCISEARCH; Weed Abstr.

US/0885-4513
**BIOTECHNOLOGY AND APPLIED BIOCHEMISTRY.** [Biotechnol. appl. biochem.]. **Added/Corp** International Union of Biochemistry. Vol. 8, No. 1 (Feb. 1986)-. Academic Scholarly Publication. English. Six times a year (including an annual subject index). $185.00 US; £105.00 UK. Portland Press Ltd., PO Box 32 Commerce Way, Colchester CO2 8HP Essex England. **Tel** 011 44 206 796351, FAX 011 44 206 799331, telex 987275 BIOSOC G. **ED** P. N. Campbell. **LC** QP501; .J66. **DD** 660/.6. **NLM** W1; BI918MJ. **CODEN** BABIEC. **[CCC]. Pr Rev.** Documents available from The Genuine Article, BIOSIS Document Express, CASDDS. ***Continues*** *Journal of Applied Biochemistry, 0161-7354.*
**Desc:** A journal devoted to biochemistry and molecular biology, and the role they play in the development of biotechnology. Results of fundamental studies directly related to the design of new biotechnology, the improvement of existing biochemical processes, and the preparation, utilization, conversion, or application of biological materials are emphasized.
**Ind/Abst** Abstr. Bull. Inst. Pap. Sci. Tech.; AgBiotech News Inf.; AGRICOLA [Select. Cov.]; BioBusiness; Biodeter. Abstr.; Biol. Abstr. (1986-); Chem. Abstr. (1986-); Coal Abstr. (1986-); Curr. Aware. Biol. Sci., CABS; Curr. Biotechnol.; Curr. Contents, Agric. Biol. Environ. Sci.; Curr. Contents Life Sci.; EMBASE (1986-); Energy Res. Abstr. (1986-); Food Sci. Technol. Abstr.; Foods Adlibra; Genet. Abstr.; Health Plan. Adminis.; Immunol. Abstr.; Index Med. (1986-); Microbiol. Abstr. Sect. B (19??-19??); Microbiol. Abstr. Sect. A; Microbiol. Abstr. Sect. C; Life Sci. Collect. (1986-); PESTDOC; Protozoolog. Abstr.; Res. Alert [Full Cov.]; Rev. Agric. Entomol.; Rev. Med. Vet. Entomol.; Rev. Med. Vet. Mycology; Sci. Cit. Index; SCISEARCH.

US/0006-3592
**BIOTECHNOLOGY AND BIOENGINEERING.** [Biotechnol. bioeng.]. **VFOAT** Biotechnology & Bioengineering. Vol. 4 (March 1962)-. Academic Scholarly Publication. English. Twenty-four times a year. $1,680.00 US; $1,920.00 Canada and Mexico; $2,010.00 other. John Wiley & Sons, Inc., 605 Third Avenue, New York NY 10158-0012. **Tel** (212)850-6000, (212)850-6645, FAX (212)850-6088, telex 12-7063. **(Subscription address:** John Wiley & Sons / England, Baffins Lane, Chichester, West Sussex PO19 1UD England.**) ED** Eleftherios T. Papoutsakes. **LC** QH324; .B5. **DD** 574. **NLM** W1 BI918N. **CODEN** BIBIAU. **[CCC]. Pr Rev.** available on microfilm and microfiche from University Microfilms International (UMI). Documents available from Article Express International, The Genuine Article, BIOSIS Document Express, CASDDS, ADONIS. ***Continues*** *Journal of Biochemical and Microbiological Technology and Engineering.*
**Desc:** An international forum for original research on all aspects of biochemical and microbial technology, this journal's purview encompasses a wide range of disciplines. Included among the topics covered are insights into biotechnology in energy production and conservation, computer applications in fermentation technology and single-cell protein from renewable and nonrenewable sources.
**Ind/Abst** Abstr. Bull. Inst. Pap. Sci. Tech.; ADONIS; AgBiotech News Inf.; AGRICOLA [Select. Cov.]; Agric. Eng. Abstr. (1991-); AQUAREF; BioBusiness; Biodeter. Abstr. (19??-19??); Bioeng. Abstr.; Biol. Agric. Index; Biol. Abstr.; Biotechnol. Res. Abstr.; Chem. Abstr.; Chem. Titles; Coal Abstr.; Comput. Inf. Syst. Abstr. J. [Full Cov.]; Crop Physiol. Abstr.; Curr. Aware. Biol. Sci., CABS; Curr. Biotechnol.; Curr. Contents, Agric. Biol. Environ. Sci.; Curr. Contents Life Sci.; Dairy Sci. Abstr.; Ei Page One; Elect. Comm. Abstr.; EMBASE; Energy Res. Abstr.; Eng. Index Annu.; Environ. Eng. Abstr.; Food Sci. Technol. Abstr.; Foods Adlibra; For. Prod. Abstr. (1991-); For. Abstr.; Gas Abstr.; Health Plan. Adminis.; Hortic. Abstr.; INIS Atomindex [Micro.]; Int. Aerosp. Abstr.; Mater. Sci. Eng. Abstr.; Mech. Eng. Abstr.; Microbiol. Abstr. Sect. B; Microbiol. Abstr. Sect. A; Microbiol. Abstr. Sect. C; Nutr. Abstr. Rev., Ser. B, Live Feeds and Feed.; Life Sci. Collect.; PESTDOC; Plant Grow. Reg. Abstr.; Pollut. Abstr. Indexes; Proc. Chem. Eng.; Ref. Upd. Deluxe Ed.; Res. Alert [Full Cov.]; Rev. Agric. Entomol.; Rev. Med. Vet. Mycology; Rice Abstr.; Sci. Cit. Index; SCISEARCH; Solid State Supercond. Abstr.; Soyabean Abstr.; Sug. Indus. Abstr.; Theoret. Chem. Eng.; Weed Abstr.

US/0572-6565
**BIOTECHNOLOGY AND BIOENGINEERING SYMPOSIUM.** [Biotechnol. bioeng. symp.]. No. 1 (1969)-. English. an. Price varies per volume. John Wiley & Sons, Inc., 605 Third Avenue, New York NY 10158-0012. **Tel** (212)850-6000, (212)850-6645, FAX (212)850-6088, telex 12-7063. **(Subscription address:** John Wiley & Sons / England, Baffins Lane, Chichester, West Sussex PO19 1UD England.**) NLM** W3 BI617. **CODEN** BIBSBR. Documents available from Article Express International, BIOSIS Document Express, CASDDS.
**Ind/Abst** BioBusiness; Bioeng. Abstr.; Biol. Abstr.; Chem. Abstr.; Coal Abstr.; Curr. Biotechnol.; Curr. Contents, Agric. Biol. Environ. Sci.; Curr. Contents Life Sci.; Dairy Sci. Abstr.; Ei Page One; EMBASE; Energy Res. Abstr. (Aug. 1977-); Eng. Index Annu.; Food Sci. Technol. Abstr.; INIS Atomindex [Micro.]; Nutr. Abstr. Rev., Ser. B, Live Feeds and Feed.; Nutr. Abstr. Rev., Ser. A, Hum. Exp.; Life Sci. Collect.; Proc. Chem. Eng.; Theoret. Chem. Eng.

BU
**BIOTECHNOLOGY AND BIOTECHNOLOGICAL EQUIPMENT.** English (Bulgarian). qt. $120.00. Diagnosis Press Ltd., 125 Tsarigradsko Boulevard, Bl 2520, Sofia 1113 Bulgaria. **Tel** 011 359 2 705176. Documents available from The Genuine Article.
**Ind/Abst** Res. Alert.

NE
**BIOTECHNOLOGY AND DEVELOPMENT MONITOR. Added/Corp** Netherlands. Directoraat-Generaal Internationale Samenwerking. Universiteit van Amsterdam. **VFOAT** Monitor. No. 1 (Sept. 1989)-. Periodical. English. Documents available from The Genuine Article.
**Ind/Abst** Abstr. BioCommer.; Plant Genet. Resour. Abstr.; Res. Alert [Full Cov.].

UK/0264-8725
**BIOTECHNOLOGY & GENETIC ENGINEERING REVIEWS.** [Biotechnol. genet. eng. rev.]. **VFOAT** Biotechnology and Genetic Engineering Reviews. Vol. 1 (1984)-. Academic Scholarly Publication. English. an. £95.00. Intercept Ltd., PO Box 716, Andover Hampshire SP10 1YG England. **Tel** 011 44 264 334748, FAX 011 44 264 334058, telex 41103 PEPSOS G. **LC** TP248.13; .B56. **DD** 660/.6/05. **NLM** W1; BI918Q. **CODEN** BGERES. **[CCC].** Index available. Documents available from The Genuine Article, CASDDS.
**Desc:** Articles covering developments in industrial, agricultural and medical applications of biotechnology (wide sense) with particular emphasis on the genetic manipulation of the organisms concerned.
**Ind/Abst** AGRICOLA [Select. Cov.]; BioBusiness (Vol. 1, 1984-); Chem. Abstr. (1984-); Curr. Biotechnol.; Health Plan. Adminis.; Index Med. (Vol. 1, 1984-);; Index Sci. Rev. [Full Cov.]; PESTDOC; Potato Abstr.; Res. Alert [Full Cov.]; SCISEARCH.

UK/0261-6904
**BIOTECHNOLOGY BULLETIN.** [Biotechnol. bull.]. (1982)-. Periodical. English. mo. $395.00. Legal Studies and Services Publishing Ltd., 9 13 St. Andrew Street, London EC4A 3AE England. **Tel** 011 44 71 936 2016. **(Subscription address:** IBC Subscription Services, IBC House, Vickers Drive Weybridge, Surrey KT13 0XS England.**)**
**Ind/Abst** Abstr. BioCommer.; AGRICOLA [Select. Cov.]; Chem. Bus. Bull.; Chem. Bus. NewsBase (1989-); Chem. Bus. Update; Curr. Biotechnol.

UK/0965-9595
**BIOTECHNOLOGY BUSINESS NEWS.** [Biotechnol. bus. news]. (1991)-. Periodical. English. bw. £390.00 UK; £414.00 other. Financial Times Business Information Ltd., Tower House, Southampton Street, London WC2E 7HA England. **Tel** 011 44 71 353 1040.
**Ind/Abst** Abstr. BioCommer.

UK
**BIOTECHNOLOGY BUSINESS NEWS / FINANCIAL TIMES.** (199?)-. Periodical. English. bw. £390.00 UK; £414.00 other. Financial Times Business Information Ltd., Tower House, Southampton Street, London WC2E 7HA England. **Tel** 011 44 71 353 1040. available on an online database (files 16,636/Full-Text) from DIALOG.
**Ind/Abst** PROMT [Full Txt.]; PTS Newsl. Database [Full Txt.].

US/0892-7987
**BIOTECHNOLOGY BUSINESS REPORT.** [Biotechnol. bus. rep.]. (1986)-. Periodical. English. mo. $239.00. Quest Ventures, PO Box 146671, Chicago IL 60614-6671. **DD** 338.
**Desc:** Written for business professionals interested in the commercial development of genetic engineering and

technology. News and editorial articles by industry experts address joint ventures, new products, marketing strategies and patent positions in biotech.

US/1057-607X
**BIOTECHNOLOGY CITATION INDEX.** (BIOTECHNOLOGY CITATION INDEX [COMPUTER FILE].). [Biotechnol. cit. index]. **Added/Corp** Institute for Scientific Information. (Jul/Aug 1991)-. English. ir. $1969.00. Institute for Scientific Information, 3501 Market Street, Philadelphia PA 19104. **Tel** (215)386-0100, (800)523-1850, FAX (215)386-6362, telex 84-5305. **(Subscription address:** Institute for Scientific Information, PO Box 71416, Chicago IL 60694.**)** **LC** TP248.13; .B58. **DD** 016.

US/1055-2162
**BIOTECHNOLOGY, CURRENT PROGRESS.** [Biotechnol. curr. prog.]. **VFOAT** Biotechnology. Vol. 1 (1991)-. Periodical. English. ir. $68.00. Technomic Publishing Company, Inc., 851 New Holland Avenue, Box 3535, Lancaster PA 17604. **Tel** (717)291-5609, (800)233-9936, FAX (717)295-4538. **LC** TP248.13; .B5755. **DD** 660/.6/05. **NLM** W1; BI918PH. **CODEN** BCUPE6. Documents available from BIOSIS Document Express.
**Ind/Abst** Biol. Abstr. (1991-).

US/1059-7352
**BIOTECHNOLOGY DIRECTORY (NEW YORK, N.Y.), THE.** (THE BIOTECHNOLOGY DIRECTORY.). [Biotechnol. dir.]. (1985)-. Directory. English. an. $240.00. Stockton Press, 49 West 24th Street, New York NY 10010. **Tel** (800)221-2123, (212)673-4400, FAX (212)673-9842. **ED** J Coombs. **LC** TP248.3; .I56. **DD** 660/.6/025. **NLM** QT 22.1; B616b. **[CCC].** ***Continues*** *International Biotechnology Directory, 0265-3877.*

US/0955-6621
**BIOTECHNOLOGY EDUCATION.** ***Ceased.*** [Biotechnol. educ.]. (1989)-Vol. 3, No. 4. Periodical. English. qt. Helix Publishing, 1 Howard Court, 94-96 Blackheath Hill, Greenwich, London SE10 8AF United Kingdom. **ED** Paul Wymer. **LC** TP248.13; .B576. **NLM** W1; BI918LDK. Documents available from The Genuine Article.
**Desc:** Provides an enabling resource to teachers of biology, biochemistry and allied subjects who wish to introduce aspects of biotechnology into their existing courses. Articles give details of simple, tried and tested class experiments to illustrate practical applications.
**Ind/Abst** AgBiotech News Inf.; Curr. Aware. Biol. Sci., CABS; Curr. Index J. Educ.; Res. Alert [Full Cov.].

GW/0935-1043
**BIOTECHNOLOGY FOCUS.** [Biotechnol. focus]. (1988)-. English (translations available in German). ir. John Wiley & Sons, Inc., 605 Third Avenue, New York NY 10158-0012. **Tel** (212)850-6000, (212)850-6645, FAX (212)850-6088, telex 12-7063. **LC** TP248.13; .J353. **DD** 660/.6. **NLM** W1; JA168.

GW/0938-5584
**BIOTECHNOLOGY (FRANKFURT 1991).** **VFOAT** Biotechnology : Apparatus, Plant, and Equipment. (1991)-. Periodical. English. mo. £121.00 EC; $220.00 US; £121.00 other. Royal Society of Chemistry, Thomas Graham House, Science Park, Cambridge CB4 4WF England. **Tel** 011 44 223 420066, FAX 011 44 223 423429, telex 818293 ROYAL. **(Subscription address:** Turpin Distribution Services Limited, Blackhorse Road, Letchworth, Hertfordshire SG6 1HN, United Kingdom.**)** **UDC** 57.08.
**Desc:** Contains abstracts on the practical methods and hardware used by biotechnologists, with emphasis on environmental and safety aspects, downstream processing, microbiological corrosion and the control, design and construction of biochemical reactors.

US/1052-6153
**BIOTECHNOLOGY HANDBOOKS.** [Biotechnol. handb.]. Vol. 1 (1987)-. Monographic series. English. ir. Price varies per volume. Plenum Press, 233 Spring Street, New York NY 10013-1578. **Tel** (212)620-8000, (800)221-9369, FAX (212)463-0742, (212)807-1047, telex 23/421139. **ED** Tony Atkinson and Roger F. Sherwood. **DD** 660. **NLM** W1; BI918PQ. **CODEN** BHANE3.
**Ind/Abst** AGRICOLA [Select. Cov.].

US/0934-943X
**BIOTECHNOLOGY IN AGRICULTURE AND FORESTRY.** [Biotechnol. agricult. for.]. (1986)-. Monographic series. English. ir. Price varies per volume. Birkhaeuser Boston Books, Springer Verlag, POB 19386, Newark NJ 07195. **Tel** (201)348-4033. **ED** Y.P.S. Bajaj. **LC** UNC.

US/0891-9283
**BIOTECHNOLOGY IN JAPAN NEWSSERVICE.** ***Ceased.*** [Biotechnol. Jpn. newsserv.]. **Added/Corp** Japan Pacific Associates. **VFOAT** Biotechnology in Japan. (198?)-(Dec. 1993). Periodical. English. mo. Japan Pacific Association, 467 Hamilton Avenue/Suite 2, Palo Alto CA 94301. **Tel** (415)322-8441, FAX (415)322-8454. **ED** Yoriko Kishimoto. **DD** 620. ctrl circ.
**Desc:** Covers biotechnology trends and developments in Japan for biotechnology, technical, or business managers.
**Ind/Abst** Abstr. BioCommer.; Curr. Biotechnol.

US
**BIOTECHNOLOGY IN JAPAN YEARBOOK.** **Added/Corp** Nikkei Biotechnology. Japan Pacific Associates. (1990/1991)-. English. Japan Pacific Association, 467 Hamilton Avenue/Suite 2, Palo Alto CA 94301. **Tel** (415)322-8441, FAX (415)322-8454.

UK/0952-147X
**BIOTECHNOLOGY INFORMATION NEWS.** ***Ceased.*** **Added/Corp** British Library. Biotechnology Information Service. No. 16 (Mar. 1988)-No. 25/26. Periodical. English. Four times a year. British Library Science Reference Information Service, 25 Southampton Building, London WC21 1AW England. **Tel** 011 44 1 6361544. **Ad Acc. Circ:** 1,300 (ctrl). ***Continues*** *News (European Biotechnology Information Project).*
**Ind/Abst** Abstr. BioCommer. (-19??).

US/0277-9773
**BIOTECHNOLOGY INVESTMENT OPPORTUNITIES.** [Biotechnol. investm. oppor.]. **VFOAT** Biotechnology. (Sept. 1981)-. Periodical. English. Twelve times a year. $195.00 US; $220.00 other. High Tech Publishing Company, 10 Ridge Road, PO Box 1923, Brattleboro VT 05301. **Tel** (802)254-3539. available on an online database from DATA-STAR; and BRS.
**Ind/Abst** PTS Newsl. Database [Full Txt.].

US/0730-031X
**BIOTECHNOLOGY LAW REPORT.** [Biotechnol. law rep.]. Vol. 1, No. 1 (Jan. 1982)-. Periodical. English. bm. $491.00. Mary Ann Liebert Inc., 1651 Third Avenue, New York NY 10128. **Tel** (212)289-2300, (800)M-LIEBERT, FAX (212)289-4697. **ED** Gerry Elman. **LC** KF3827.G4; A132. **DD** 344.73/095; 347.30495. **NLM** W1; BI918R. **CODEN** BLREEL. **Bk Rev. Ad Acc.** Documents available from The Genuine Article.
**Desc:** A record of the evolving body of law governing biotechnology, particularly in the industries in which new products from these technologies are developing the most rapidly: pharmaceuticals, chemicals, agriculture, food processing, energy, mineral recovery, and waste treatment. All legal aspects are reported, and critical documents are reproduced.
**Ind/Abst** BioBusiness (1987-); Res. Alert [Full Cov.]; Soc. Sci. Cit. Index [Select. Cov.].

UK/0141-5492
**BIOTECHNOLOGY LETTERS.** [Biotechnol. lett.]. Vol. 1 (1979)-. Academic Scholarly Publication. English. mo. £270.00 (institution), £86.00 (individual) UK; $540.00 (institution), $172.00 (individual) US. Chapman & Hall, 2-6 Boundary Row, London SE1 8HN England. **Tel** 011 44 71 865 0066, FAX 011 44 71 522 9623, telex 290164 Chapmag. **(Subscription address:** International Thomson Publishing Svcs. Ltd., Subscription Department North Way Andover, Hampshire SP10 5BE England.**)** **ED** J. D. Bulock. **LC** QR53; .B536. **DD** 660/.6/05. **UDC** 663.15. **NLM** W1 BI918T. **CODEN** BILED3. **[CCC]. Ad Acc. Pr Rev. Circ:** 1,000. Documents available from The Genuine Article, BIOSIS Document Express, CASDDS, Documents on Demand.
**Desc:** Short original communications of new work in any topic relevant to the practical applications of biological reactions including process and reactor design.
**Ind/Abst** AgBiotech News Inf.; AGRICOLA [Select. Cov.]; BioBusiness; Biocont. News Inf. (19??-19??); Biodeter. Abstr. (19??-19??); Biol. Abstr.; Biotechnol. Res. Abstr.; Chem. Abstr.; Chem. Titles; Curr. Aware. Biol. Sci., CABS; Curr. Biotechnol.; Curr. Contents, Agric. Biol. Environ. Sci.; Curr. Contents Life Sci.; Dairy Sci. Abstr.; EMBASE; Energy Inf. Abstr.; Environ. Abstr.; Food Sci. Technol. Abstr.; Foods Adlibra; For. Prod. Abstr. (1991-); For. Abstr.; Genet. Abstr.; Health Saf. Sci. Abstr.; Hortic. Abstr.; Immunol. Abstr.; Maize Abstr.; Microbiol. Abstr. Sect. B; Microbiol. Abstr. Sect. A; Microbiol. Abstr. Sect. C; Nutr. Abstr. Rev., Ser. A, Hum. Exp.; Life Sci. Collect.; PESTDOC; Plant Genet. Resour. Abstr.; Plant Grow. Reg. Abstr.; Pollut. Abstr. Indexes; Ref. Upd. Deluxe Ed.; Res. Alert [Full Cov.]; Rev. Agric. Entomol.; Rev. Med. Vet. Entomol.; Sci. Cit. Index; SCISEARCH; Soyabean Abstr.; Sug. Indus. Abstr.; Weed Abstr.

GW/0930-8938
**BIOTECHNOLOGY MONOGRAPHS.** [Biotechnol. monogr.]. Vol. 1 (1985)-. Academic Scholarly Publication. English. ir. Price varies per volume. Springer-Verlag GmbH & Company KG, Heidelberger Platz 3, D 14197 Berlin Germany. **Tel** 011 49 30 8207223, FAX 011 49 30 8214091, telex 183 319 SPBLN D. **(Subscription address:** Springer Verlag New York Inc. / for North America, 44 Hartz Way, Secaucus NJ 07096.**)** **ED** S. Aiba, L.T. Fan, A. Fiechter, J. Klein, K. Schuegerl. **NLM** W1; BI18LF. **CODEN** BIMOE5. Documents available from BIOSIS Document Express, CASDDS.
**Desc:** Series covering all aspects of biotechnology including biomedical engineering.
**Ind/Abst** Biol. Abstr. (1985-); Chem. Abstr. (1985-).

US/0738-4076
**BIOTECHNOLOGY MONTHLY UPDATE.** [Biotechnol. mon. update]. **VFOAT** Biotechnology. English. mo. $150.00 US; $175.00 other. G V Olsen Associates, 123 Picketts Ridge Road, West Redding CT 06896. **Tel** (203)938-4188, FAX (203)938-4186. **ED** Gustav V Olsen. **Circ:** 75.

US/0275-7559
**BIOTECHNOLOGY (NEW YORK, N.Y. : 1983).** (BIOTECHNOLOGY.). [Biotechnology]. Periodical. English. bm. $78.00. Bio/Technology, Subscription Department, PO Box 316, Martinsville NJ 08836. **Tel** (212)477-9600. **ED** Douglas McCormich. **Bk Rev. Ad Acc. Circ:** 15,000.
**Desc:** Industrial biology, news research products and techniques from start to full scale processes profiles on films and personalities.
**Ind/Abst** Abstr. BioCommer.; BioBusiness; For. Prod. Abstr.; Genet. Abstr.; Maize Abstr.; Ornamental Hort.; Plant Breed. Abstr.; Plant Grow. Reg. Abstr.; Potato Abstr.; Ref. Upd. Deluxe Ed.; Rice Abstr.

US/0273-3226
**BIOTECHNOLOGY NEWS.** [Biotechnol. news]. Vol. 1, No. 1 (Jan. 1, 1981)-. Periodical. English. Thirty times a year. $538.00 US & Canada; $561.00 other. CTB International Publishing Inc., PO Box 218, Maplewood NJ 07040. **Tel** (201)379-7749, FAX (201)379-1158. **ED** Christopher Brogna. **DD** 660. **NLM** W1; BI918TG. **CODEN** BINWEY. **[CCC].** Index available (2/yr). cum. index. **Bk Rev. Ad Acc.**
**Desc:** Covers genetic engineering, enzymes, diagnostics, fermentation, monoclonals, applied molecular biology, tissue culture, plant biotechnology and microbial technology.
**Ind/Abst** Abstr. BioCommer.; AGRICOLA [Select. Cov.]; Chem. Bus. Bull.; Chem. Bus. NewsBase (1989-); Chem. Bus. Update; Chem. Ind. Notes; Curr. Biotechnol.

US
**BIOTECHNOLOGY NEWSWATCH.** Vol. 7, No. 23 Dec. 7, (1987)-. Newsletter. English. sm. $875.00 US and Canada; $915.00 other. McGraw Hill Publishing Company, Inc., 1221 Avenue of the Americas, New York NY 10020. **Tel** (212)512-6410, (800)525-5003, FAX (212)512-6111. **(Subscription address:** McGraw Hill Management Information Center, 1221 Avenue of the Americas, 36th Floor, New York NY 10020.**)** available on an online database (file 624/Full-Text) from DIALOG. ***Continues*** *McGraw-Hill's Biotechnology Newswatch, 0275-3685.*
**Ind/Abst** AGRICOLA [Select. Cov.]; Chem. Bus. Bull.; Chem. Bus. NewsBase (1989-); Chem. Bus. Update; Curr. Biotechnol.; Trade Ind. Index.

US/8756-7938
**BIOTECHNOLOGY PROGRESS.** [Biotechnol. prog.]. **Added/Corp** American Institute of Chemical Engineers. American Institute of Chemical Engineers. Food, Pharmaceutical, and Bioengineering Division. American Chemical Society. **VFOAT** BiotechnologyProgress. Vol. 1, No. 1 (March 1985)-. Academic Scholarly Publication. English. Six times a year. $365.00 (institution) US. American Chemical Society, 1155 Sixteenth Street Northwest, Washington DC 20036. **Tel** (800)333-9511, (800)227-5558, (614)447-3776, FAX (202)833-7736. **(Subscription address:** American Chemical Society / Ohio, Department L 0011, Columbus OH 43268-0011.**)** **ED** Jerome S. Schultz. **LC** TP248.13; .B578. **DD** 660/.6/05. **NLM** W1; BI918V. **CODEN** BIPRET. **[CCC]. Pr Rev. Acid Free.** available on microfilm and microfiche from University Microfilms International (UMI). Documents available from Article Express International, The Genuine Article, BIOSIS Document Express, CASDDS, Documents on Demand.
**Desc:** Focuses on the application of fundamental chemical and engineering principles to biological phenomena and to processor product design.
**Ind/Abst** Abstr. BioCommer.; AGRICOLA [Select. Cov.]; Appl. Sci. Technol. Index (1991-); BioBusiness; Biodeter. Abstr. (19??-19??); Biol. Abstr. (1985-); Biotechnol. Res. Abstr.; Chem. Abstr. (1985-); Coal Abstr.; Curr. Aware. Biol. Sci., CABS; Curr. Contents, Agric. Biol. Environ. Sci.; Eng. Index Annu.; Environ. Abstr.; Food Sci. Technol. Abstr.; Foods Adlibra; Gas Abstr.; Microbiol. Abstr. Sect. B; PESTDOC; Ref. Upd. Deluxe Ed.; Res. Alert [Full Cov.]; Rice Abstr.; SCISEARCH; Sug. Indus. Abstr.

US/0733-5709
**BIOTECHNOLOGY RESEARCH ABSTRACTS.** ***Ceased.*** **See** Medical Science and Technology-Abstracting, Bibliographies and Statistics.

US/0749-0372
**BIOTECHNOLOGY SOFTWARE.** [Biotechnol. softw.]. **VFOAT** Biotechnology Software Report; BSR. Vol. 1, No. 1 (Sept./Oct. 1984)-. Periodical. English. bm. $108.00. Mary Ann Liebert Inc., 1651 Third Avenue, New York NY 10128. **Tel** (212)289-2300, (800)M-LIEBERT, FAX (212)289-4697. **ED** Kevin Ahern and Indira Rajagopal. **DD** 001. **NLM** W1; BI918Y. **CODEN** BSOFEO.
**Desc:** Interface between computers and the researcher who is not a computer scientist. Prevents the duplication of effort that exists when a new computer application is designed that has already been devised in another laboratory.

UK/0951-208X
**BIOTECHNOLOGY TECHNIQUES.**
[Biotechnol. tech.]. Vol. 1, No. 1 (Mar. 1987)-. Periodical. English. Twelve times a year. £216.00 (institution), £70.00 (individual) UK; $432.00 (institution), $140.00 (individual) US. Chapman & Hall, 2-6 Boundary Row, London SE1 8HN England. **Tel** 011 44 71 865 0066, FAX 011 44 71 522 9623, telex 290164 Chapmag. **(Subscription address:** International Thomson Publishing Svcs. Ltd., Subscription Department North Way Andover, Hampshire SP10 5BE England.**) ED** Colin Retledge. **NLM** W1; BI9184. **CODEN** BTECE6. **[CCC].** Index available. **Bk Rev. Ad Acc. Pr Rev. Circ:** 600. available on microfilm from University Microfilms International (UMI). Documents available from The Genuine Article, BIOSIS Document Express, CASDDS, Documents on Demand.
**Desc:** Provides working accounts of innovative and improved procedures that have been demonstrated experimentally.
**Ind/Abst** AgBiotech News Inf.; AGRICOLA [Select. Cov.]; Anal. Abstr.; BioBusiness; Biodeter. Abstr. (19??-19??); Biol. Abstr. (1987-); Chem. Abstr.; Curr. Aware. Biol. Sci., CABS; Curr. Biotechnol.; Curr. Contents, Agric. Biol. Environ. Sci.; Dairy Sci. Abstr.; Environ. Abstr.; Field Crop Abstr.; For. Prod. Abstr. (1991-); Immunol. Abstr.; Microbiol. Abstr. Sect. B; Microbiol. Abstr. Sect. A; Microbiol. Abstr. Sect. C; Nutr. Abstr. Rev., Ser. B, Live Feeds and Feed.; PESTDOC; Res. Alert [Full Cov.]; Rice Abstr.; Weed Abstr.

US/0898-2848
**BIOTECHNOLOGY THERAPEUTICS.**
[Biotechnol. ther.]. Vol. 1, No. 1 (1989)-. Periodical. English. qt. $325.00 US; $339.00 other. Marcel Dekker Inc., 270 Madison Avenue, New York NY 10016. **Tel** (212)696-9000, (800)228-1160, FAX (212)685-4540, telex 421419. **(Subscription address:** Marcel Dekker Inc, PO Box 5017, Monticello NY 12701.**) ED** Steven Gillis, Arthur Ammann and Susanna Cunningham-Rundles. **LC** RM666.R37; B56. **DD** 610/.28. **NLM** W1; BI9185. **CODEN** BITHEJ. **[CCC]. Ad Acc. Pr Rev.** ctrl circ. Documents available from The Genuine Article, ADONIS.
**Desc:** This journal is devoted solely to presenting results of preclinical and clinical trials throughout all phases of biotechnologically produced therapeutic agents. Emphasizes the utility of a broad array of rapidly emerging products from molecular biology for potential and actual medicine practice. This journal features superior, original contributions by both researchers and clinicians comprising basic and applied research articles, review articles, short reports, conference papers, and symposia as topical volumes. It details these agents' success in the treatment of the entire range of diseases, including infections, malignancies, immunological disease, hematologic disorders, and others.
**Ind/Abst** ADONIS; Curr. Aware. Biol. Sci., CABS; EMBASE; Ref. Upd. Deluxe Ed.; Res. Alert [Full Cov.].

●US/1061-3471
**BIOTECHNOLOGY WEEK.** (1992)-. Periodical. English. sm. Cahners Publishing Company, 249 West 17th Street, New York NY 10011. **Tel** (212)645-0067, FAX (212)242-6987. **(Subscription address:** Cahners Publishing Company / Colorado, Paid Subscription Service Center, PO Box 7610, Highlands Ranch CO 80126-7610.**)** Documents available from The Genuine Article.
**Ind/Abst** Res. Alert [Full Cov.].

CU/0864-4551
**BIOTECNOLOGIA APLICADA : REVISTA DE LA SOCIEDAD IBEROLATINOAMERICANA PARA INVESTIGACIONES SOBRE INTERFERON Y BIOTECNOLOGIA EN SALUD.** **Added/Corp** Sociedad Iberolatinoamericana para Investigaciones sobre Interferon y Biotecnologia en Salud. Vol. 7, No. 1 (1990)-. Periodical. English (Spanish). Three times a year (April, Aug., Dec.). DM60.00. Palacio de las Convenciones, PO Box 6072, 6 Habana Cuba. **Tel** (7)21-8008, FAX (53 7)218070, (53 7)336008. **ED** Ileana Filgueiras (21-8854). **NLM** W1; BI918LB. Index available (Published in April). cum. index. **Ad Acc, Adv Mgr:** Alfredo Delgado, **Tel** 21-8854. **Circ:** 3,000 (ctrl). Documents available from CASDDS. ***Continues** Interferon y Biotecnologia, 0258-9222.*
**Desc:** This journal is the vehicle of communication among Latin American specialists in the fields of biotechnology and its applications. This journal publishes original articles and reviews.
**Ind/Abst** Chem. Abstr.; EMBASE [Select. Cov.]; Rev. Med. Vet. Entomol.; Soils Fert.

RU/0234-2758
**BIOTEHNOLOGIA (MOSKVA).**
(BIOTEKHNOLOGIIA.). [Biotehnologia]. (1985)-. Academic Scholarly Publication. Russian (table of contents in English). mo. $162.00. **(Subscription address:** Victor Kamkin, 4956 Boiling Brook Parkway, Rockville MD 20852.**) CODEN** BTKNEZ. Documents available from BIOSIS Document Express, CASDDS.
**Ind/Abst** BioBusiness; Biocont. News Inf.; Biodeter. Abstr.; Biol. Abstr.; Chem. Abstr. (1985-); Curr. Biotechnol.; Hortic. Abstr.; Index Vet.; PESTDOC; Postharvest News Inf.; Potato Abstr.; Rev. Med. Vet. Entomol.

US/0890-734X
**BIOTEKHNOLOGIIA.** ***Title Change.*** (SOVIET BIOTECHNOLOGY.). [Soviet biotechnol.]. **VFOAT** Biotekhnologiya. No. 1 (1986)-(1993). Periodical. English (translations available in Russian). bm. Allerton Press, Inc., 150 Fifth Avenue, New York NY 10011. **Tel** (212)924-3950, FAX (212)463-9684, telex 427441 ALPRES. **LC** TP248.19.S65; B56. **DD** 660/.6/0947. **NLM** W1; SO996C. **CODEN** SOVBE2. **[CCC]. *Continued by*** *Russian Biotechnology.*
**Ind/Abst** AGRICOLA [Select. Cov.]; Biocont. News Inf. (1991-); Biodeter. Abstr. (1991-); Dairy Sci. Abstr.; For. Prod. Abstr. (1991-); Hortic. Abstr.; Microbiol. Abstr. Sect. A; Nutr. Abstr. Rev., Ser. B, Live Feeds and Feed.; Nutr. Abstr. Rev., Ser. A, Hum. Exp.; Rev. Agric. Entomol.; Rev. Med. Vet. Entomol.; Rev. Plant Pathol.; Soils Fert.; Sug. Indus. Abstr.; Wheat Barley Trit. Abstr.

BU
**BIOTEKHNOLOGIIA & BIOTEKHNIKA : IZDANIE NA NATSIONALNIIA SUVET PO BIOTEKHNOLOGIIA KUM DURZHAVNIIA KOMITET ZA IZSLEDVANIIA I TEKHNOLOGII.**
**Added/Corp** Natsionalen Suvet po Biotekhnologiia Kum Durzhavniia Komitet za Izsledvaniia i Tekhnologii (Bulgaria). **VFOAT** Biotekhnologiia i Biotekhnika; Biotechnology and Bioindustry; Biotechnology & Bioindustry; Journal of Biotechnology and Bioindustry. (19??)-. Periodical. Bulgarian (English; summaries and/or abstracts in Russian). Twice a year. DM75.00. **(Subscription address:** Kubon & Sagner, ABT Zeitschriftenimport, D 80328 Munich Germany.**) LC** TP248.13; .B585. Documents available from CASDDS.
**Ind/Abst** Chem. Abstr.

CR/0255-7924
**BOLETIN DE BIOTECNOLOGIA : ORGANO DE DIFUSION DEL COMITE PERMANENTE DE BIOTECNOLOGIA DE LA ASOCIACION INTERCIENCIA.**
**Added/Corp** Consejo Nacional de Investigaciones Cientificas y Tecnologicas (Costa Rica) Asociacion Interciencia. Comite Permanente de Biotecnologia. (198?)-. Periodical. Spanish (English). sa.
**Ind/Abst** Trop. Dis. Bull.

●UK/0967-4845
**BRITISH JOURNAL OF BIOMEDICAL SCIENCE.** **Added/Corp** Institute of Medical Laboratory Sciences (Great Britain) Royal Society of Medicine Services (Great Britain). Vol. 50, No. 1 (Mar. 1993)-. Academic Scholarly Publication. English. qt. **CODEN** BJMSEO. **[CCC].** Documents available from CASDDS. ***Continues** Medical Laboratory Sciences, 0308-3616.*
**Desc:** Includes information on medical sciences and technology.
**Ind/Abst** Chem. Abstr.; Sci. Cit. Index.

US/1040-9416
**BT CATALYST.** (BT CATALYST / NORTH CAROLINA BIOTECHNOLOGY CENTER.). [BT catal.]. **Added/Corp** North Carolina Biotechnology Center. **VAT** Biotechnology Catalyst. Vol. 1 No. 1 (Nov. 1987)-. Periodical. English. mo. Free. North Carolina Biotechnology Center, PO Box 13547, Research Triangle Park NC 27709-3547. **DD** 620. available on an online database (file 636/Full-Text) from DIALOG.
**Ind/Abst** Abstr. BioCommer.; PTS Newsl. Database [Full Txt.].

●CN/1188-455X
**CANADIAN BIOTECH NEWS.** [Can. biotech news]. Vol. 1, No. 1 (Jan. 15, 1992)-. Periodical. English. bw. $450.00 (one year), $720.00 (two year) institutions; $160.00 (one year), $256.00 (two year) individuals. Canadian Biotech News Service, 340 Richmond Road, Ottawa, Ontario K2A 0E8 Canada. **Tel** (613)726-0115, FAX (613)726-7344. **ED** Peter Winter (editor's address: 20 Stone Park Lane, Nepean, Ontario K2H 9P4 Canada). **DD** 620.8. Index available (published separately). cum. index. **Bk Rev**, (Qty: 50). **Ad Acc, Adv Mgr:** Carole Cheetham. **Circ:** 3,000. available on microfilm; available on microfiche. ***Continues** New Biotech Busine$$ Canada., 0838-5777.*
**Desc:** Progress and prospects of the Canadian biotech industry. Details on companies, products, and emerging research and development.
**Ind/Abst** Abstr. BioCommer.

US/0884-7479
**CAS BIOTECH UPDATES. BIOSENSORS.** **Added/Corp** American Chemical Society. Chemical Abstracts Service. **VFOAT** Biosensors. **VAT** Chemical Abstracts Service Biotech Updates. Biosensors. (198?)-. Periodical. English. bw. $215.00. Chemical Abstracts Service, (Subsidiary of The American Chemical Society), 2540 Olentangy River Road, PO Box 3012, Columbus OH 43210-0012. **Tel** (614)447-3731, (800)753-4227, FAX (614)447-3751. **(Subscription address:** Chemical Abstracts Service, Customer Service Department, PO Box 3012, Columbus OH 43210.**) DD** 610. **CODEN** CBUBE2.
**Desc:** Provides information on the use of immobilized enzymes, immunological components, and cell fractions or whole cells for biochemical analysis, body fluid monitoring, and diagnostics. Coverage includes electrodes, thermistors, transistors and light-detection-type biosensors in the detection and determination of sample components.

US/1040-709X
**CAS BIOTECH UPDATES. CELL & TISSUE CULTURE.** [CAS biotech updates, Cell tissue cult.]. **Added/Corp** American Chemical Society. Chemical Abstracts Service. **VFOAT** CAS Biotech Updates. Cell and Tissue Culture; Cell & Tissue Culture; Cell and Tissue Culture. **VAT** Chemical Abstracts Service Biotech Updates. Cell & Tissue Culture. (Jan. 9, 1989)-. English. bw. $215.00. Chemical Abstracts Service, (Subsidiary of The American Chemical Society), 2540 Olentangy River Road, PO Box 3012, Columbus OH 43210-0012. **Tel** (614)447-3731, (800)753-4227, FAX (614)447-3751. **(Subscription address:** Chemical Abstracts Service, Customer Service Department, PO Box 3012, Columbus OH 43210.**) DD** 574. **CODEN** CUCCEE.

US/0884-7452
**CAS BIOTECH UPDATES. ENVIRONMENTAL BIOTECHNOLOGY.**
[CAS biotech updates, Environ. biotechnol.]. **Added/Corp** American Chemical Society. Chemical Abstracts Service. **VFOAT** Environmental Biotechnology. **VAT** Chemical Abstract Service Biotech Updates Environmental Biotechnology. (Jan. 13, 1986)-. Periodical. English. bw. $215.00. Chemical Abstracts Service, (Subsidiary of The American Chemical Society), 2540 Olentangy River Road, PO Box 3012, Columbus OH 43210-0012. **Tel** (614)447-3731, (800)753-4227, FAX (614)447-3751. **(Subscription address:** Chemical Abstracts Service, Customer Service Department, PO Box 3012, Columbus OH 43210.**) DD** 574. **CODEN** CBEBEO.

US/1040-7081
**CAS BIOTECH UPDATES. ENZYMES IN BIOTECHNOLOGY.** [CAS biotech updates, Enzym. biotechnol.]. **Added/Corp** American Chemical Society. Chemical Abstracts Service. **VFOAT** Enzymes in Biotechnology. **VAT** Chemical Abstracts Service Biotech Updates. Enzymes in Biotechnology. (Jan. 9, 1989)-. English. bw. $215.00. Chemical Abstracts Service, (Subsidiary of The American Chemical Society), 2540 Olentangy River Road, PO Box 3012, Columbus OH 43210-0012. **Tel** (614)447-3731, (800)753-4227, FAX (614)447-3751. **(Subscription address:** Chemical Abstracts Service, Customer Service Department, PO Box 3012, Columbus OH 43210.**) DD** 660. **CODEN** CUEBEL.

BE
**CEREVISIA AND BIOTECHNOLOGY.**
English (French and Dutch). qt. 2000F Belgium; 2300F other. S C Cepia, Groene Dreef 11, 9830 Sint Marten Latem Belgium. **Tel** 011 32 91 825695. **ED** Ing L Lenges and E Van Schoonenberghe. ***Continues** Cerevisia; Belgian Journal of Food Chemistry and Biotechnology.*

UK/0277-4038
**CHEMICAL ENGINEERING ASPECTS OF BIOMEDICINE RESEARCH STUDIES SERIES.** [Chem. eng. asp. biomed. res. stud. ser.]. 1-. Monographic series. English. ir. Price varies per volume. John Wiley & Sons Ltd., Baffins Lane, Chichester West Sussex PO19 1UD England. **Tel** 0243 779777, FAX 0243 776128 BTG:JWP001, telex 86290 WIBOOKG. **(Subscription address:** North, South and Central America/ John Wiley & Sons, Inc., Subscription Department, 605 Third Avenue, New York, NY 10158-0012, USA; telephone: (212)850-6645; FAX: (212)850-6021**) ED** Horst Chmiel. **NLM** WI CH248F.

GW/0722-6764
**CHEMIE IN LABOR UND BIOTECHNIK : CLB.** **See** Chemistry.

IT/0392-839X
**CHIMICA OGGI.** [Chim. oggi]. **VFOAT** Chemistry Today; Chimicaoggi. Vol. 1 (March 1983)-. Periodical. English (Italian). ir (10 issues). L185000 Italy; L380000 other. Tekno Scienze, Via Vincenzo Gioberti 1, 20123 Milan Italy. **Tel** 011 39 2 4818118. **CODEN** CHOGDS. Index available. Documents available from CASDDS.
**Ind/Abst** Anal. Abstr.; Chem. Abstr. (1983-); Chem. Bus. Bull.; Chem. Bus. NewsBase (1987-); Chem. Bus. Update; Curr. Biotechnol.; Fluid Abstr., Civil Eng.; Fluid Abstr. Proc. Eng.; FLUIDEX; Int. Pharm. Abstr.; PESTDOC; Proc. Chem. Eng.; Soc. Sci. Cit. Index [Select. Cov.]; Theoret. Chem. Eng.

US/1042-749X
**CHINESE JOURNAL OF BIOTECHNOLOGY.** [Chin. j. biotechnol.]. Vol. 4, No. 1 (1989)-. Periodical. English (translations available in Chinese). Four times a year. $415.00. Allerton Press, Inc., 150 Fifth Avenue, New York NY 10011. **Tel** (212)924-3950, FAX (212)463-9684, telex 427441 ALPRES. **LC** TP248.13; .C48. **DD** 660/.6. **NLM** W1;

CH761. **[CCC].**
**Ind/Abst** AgBiotech News Inf.; Field Crop Abstr.; Health Plan. Adminis.; Index Med. (1988-); Irr. Drain. Abstr.; Plant Breed. Abstr.; Plant Grow. Reg. Abstr.; Potato Abstr.; Rice Abstr.; Soils Fert.; Wheat Barley Trit. Abstr.

CN/0715-4828
**CIRCUIT (FREDERICTON).** (CIRCUIT / PROGRAMME DE GENIE MEDICAL DES HOPITAUX DU N.-B.). [Circuit]. Vol. 1-. Periodical. English (French). bm. Free. Circuit, c/o Institute of Biomedical Engineering, University of New Brunswick, PO Box 4400, Fredericton New Brunswick E3B 5A3 Canada. **Tel** (506)453-4966. **ED** Virginia Patterson. **DD** 610/.28/09715. **Circ:** 175. ***Formed by the union of*** *New Brunswick Hospitals Medical Engineering Program. Newsletter, 0383-0586* ***and*** *New Brunswick Hospitals Medical Engineering Program. Circulaire, 0383-0594.*

US/1046-3305
**CLINICAL BIOTECHNOLOGY.** ***Ceased.*** [Clin. biotechnol.]. Vol. 1, No. 1 (Nov./Dec. 1989)-(19??). Periodical. English. mo. Mary Ann Liebert Inc., 1651 Third Avenue, New York NY 10128. **Tel** (212)289-2300, (800)M-LIEBERT, FAX (212)289-4697. **(Subscription address:** Roland Nardone, Ph.D.**)** **DD** 620. **NLM** W1; CL668W. **Pr Rev.** Documents available from The Genuine Article.
**Desc:** Focuses on those aspects of biotechnology research which have a strong nexus with the clinical sciences, especially for understanding the pathological state and for diagnosis, prognosis, and therapy.
**Ind/Abst** Res. Alert [Full Cov.].

US/0277-0393
**CLINICAL ENGINEERING INFORMATION SERVICE.** [Clin. eng. inf. serv.]. **VFOAT** CEIS. Vol. 1, No. 1 (Jan./Feb. 1977)-. Periodical. English. Six times a year. $110.00 (one year); $210.00 (two years. Scientific Enterprises Inc, 5104 Randolph Road, North Little Rock AR 72116. **Tel** (501)771-1775, FAX (501)771-1775. **ED** David Simmons. **NLM** W1; CL696CJ. Index Available published separately, bound from publisher, free-automatically sent. cum. index.
**Desc:** A unique newsletter serving as a resource to administrators, hospital engineers, clinical / biomedical engineers, and biomedical equipment technicians in management and technology. Topics such as use of computers, safety, helpful suggestions, technical discussions and maintenance management and FDA recalls are covered in each issue. Forms and policy statements that can be used in a subscriber's program are frequently published. Over 30 pages per issue and a binder is furnished with the first issue each year.
**Ind/Abst** Health Devices Alerts; Hospit. Health Admin. Index (1983-1987).

US/0730-7578
**CLINICAL INSTRUMENT SYSTEMS : CIS.** [Clin. instrum. syst.]. **VFOAT** CIS; C.I.S. Vol. 1, No. 1 (Aug. 1980)-. Periodical. English. Ten times a year. $225.00. Clinical Instrument Systems, 447 Glenbrook Road, Stamford CT 06906. **Tel** (203)329-9220, FAX (203)327-3462. **ED** Nelson L. Alpert. **NLM** W1 CL715N. Index available. cum. index. **Pr Rev.**
**Desc:** A technical information resource providing laboratory personnel and pathologists with information on instrumentation in fields of clinical chemistry, RIA, hematology, microbiology and blood banking.

UK/0143-0815
**CLINICAL PHYSICS AND PHYSIOLOGICAL MEASUREMENT.** ***Title Change.*** **See** Physics.

JA
**COMLINE NEWS SERVICE.** mo. ¥90,000 Japan; $700.00 other. COMLINE Business Data Inc., 1-12-5 Hamamatsutho, Minato-ku Tokyo 105 Japan.
**Ind/Abst** Abstr. BioCommer.

UK/0266-7061
**COMPUTER APPLICATIONS IN THE BIOSCIENCES.** **See** Computers.

NE/0169-2607
**COMPUTER METHODS AND PROGRAMS IN BIOMEDICINE.** [Comput. methods programs biomed.]. Vol. 20, No. 1 (May 1985)-. Academic Scholarly Publication. English. Nine times a year (3 volumes). $726.00. Elsevier Science Ireland Ltd., Bay 15, Shannon Industrial Estate, Co Clare Ireland. **Tel** 011 353 61 471944. **ED** W. Schneider, R.E. Smith, S. Kaihara, and T. Groth. **NLM** W1; CO457I. **CODEN** CMPBEK. **[CCC].** available on microfilm and microfiche from University Microfilms International (UMI). Documents available from Article Express International, The Genuine Article, BIOSIS Document Express, Ask*IEEE. ***Continues*** *Computer Programs in Biomedicine, 0010-468X.*
**Desc:** Audience is all life science researchers, clinicians, statisticians, health scientists, computer scientists, programmers and bio-engineers, engaged in applying and teaching biomedical information processing.
**Ind/Abst** Anim. Breed. Abstr.; Biol. Abstr. (1985-); Compumath Citation Index [Full Cov.]; Comput. Rev.; Curr. Aware. Biol. Sci., CABS; Curr. Contents Life Sci.; Ei Page One; EMBASE; Eng. Index Annu.; Health Plan. Adminis.; Helminthol. Abstr.; Index Med. (May 1985-); INSPEC (May 1985-); Ref. Upd. Deluxe Ed.; Res. Alert [Full Cov.]; Sci. Cit. Index; SCISEARCH; Soc. Sci. Cit. Index [Select. Cov.].

US/0010-4809
**COMPUTERS AND BIOMEDICAL RESEARCH.** [Comput. biomed. res.]. **Added/Corp** American Association for Medical Systems and Informatics. Vol. 1 (March 1967)-. Academic Scholarly Publication. English. bm (6 issues). $247.00 US and Canada; $302.00 other. Academic Press, Inc., 6277 Sea Harbor Drive, Orlando FL 32887. **Tel** (800)543-9534, (407)345-4100, FAX (407)363-9661. **ED** Homer R. Warner. **DD** 574. **NLM** W1 CO457R. **CODEN** CBMRB7. **[CCC].** **Pr Rev.** Documents available from The Genuine Article, BIOSIS Document Express, Ask*IEEE, CASDDS.
**Desc:** Provides researchers with up-to-date information concerning the use of computers in biomedicine.
**Ind/Abst** ACM Guide Comput. Lit.; Anim. Breed. Abstr.; Biol. Abstr.; Chem. Abstr.; Compumath Citation Index [Full Cov.]; Comput. Rev.; CSA Neuro. Abstr. (?-?); Cumul. Index Nurs. Allied Health Lit.; Curr. Contents Eng. Tech. Appl. Sci.; Curr. Contents Life Sci.; EMBASE; Energy Res. Abstr.; Health Saf. Sci. Abstr.; Health Plan. Adminis.; Index Med.; Index Vet.; INIS Atomindex [Micro.]; INSPEC (1968-); Int. Aerosp. Abstr.; Life Sci. Collect.; Pollut. Abstr. Indexes; Ref. Upd. Deluxe Ed.; Res. Alert [Full Cov.]; Sci. Cit. Index; SCISEARCH; Soc. Sci. Cit. Index [Select. Cov.]; Trop. Dis. Bull.

US/0010-4825
**COMPUTERS IN BIOLOGY AND MEDICINE.** [Comput. biol. med.]. Vol. 1 (Aug. 1970)-. Academic Scholarly Publication. English. bm. $604.00 The Americas; £405.00 other. Pergamon Press, An Imprint of Elsevier Science Ltd., The Boulevard, Langford Lane, Kidlington, Oxford OX5 1GB United Kingdom. **Tel** 011 44 865 843000, 011 44 865 843699, FAX 011 44 865 843010. **(Subscription address:** Elsevier Science Ltd. Oxford Fulfillment Centre, PO Box 800, Kidlington, Oxford OX5 1DX United Kingdom.**)** **ED** Robert S. Ledley. **LC** R858.A1; C65. **DD** 610/.285/4. **NLM** W1 CO457T. **CODEN** CBMDAW. **[CCC].** **Pr Rev.** available on microfilm and microfiche from University Microfilms International (UMI). Documents available from Article Express International, The Genuine Article, BIOSIS Document Express, Ask*IEEE, CASDDS, ADONIS.
**Desc:** A medium of international communication on the revolutionary advances being made in the application of the computer to the fields of bioscience and medicine. It encourages the exchange of research, instruction, ideas and information on all aspects of the growing use of computers.
**Ind/Abst** ADONIS; Bioeng. Abstr.; Biol. Abstr.; Biostatistica; Chem. Abstr.; Compumath Citation Index [Full Cov.]; Comput. Abstr.; Comput. Rev.; CSA Neuro. Abstr. (?-?); Cumul. Index Nurs. Allied Health Lit.; Curr. Aware. Biol. Sci., CABS; Curr. Contents Eng. Tech. Appl. Sci.; Curr. Contents Life Sci.; Ei Page One; EMBASE; Energy Res. Abstr. (Sept. 1971-); Eng. Index Annu.; Health Saf. Sci. Abstr.; Health Plan. Adminis.; Index Med.; Inf. Sci. Abstr.; INSPEC (Aug. 1970-); Int. Aerosp. Abstr.; Life Sci. Collect.; Pollut. Abstr. Indexes; Protozoolog. Abstr.; Res. Alert [Full Cov.]; Sci. Cit. Index; SCISEARCH.

US/0734-1407
**CRC HANDBOOK OF CLINICAL ENGINEERING.** [CRC handb. clin. eng.]. **VFOAT** Handbook of Clinical Engineering; C.R.C. Handbook of Clinical Engineering. **VAT** Chemical Rubber Company Handbook of Clinical Engineering. Vol. 1 (1980)-. English. ir. Price varies per volume. CRC Press Inc., 2000 Corporate Boulevard Northwest, Boca Raton FL 33431. **Tel** (407)994-0555, (800)272-7737, FAX (407)998-9784, telex 568689. **NLM** W1 C559. Each issue contains an index to its own contents (no volume index)--loose.

US/0278-940X
**CRITICAL REVIEWS IN BIOMEDICAL ENGINEERING.** [Crit. rev. biomed. eng.]. **VFOAT** C.R.C. Critical Reviews in Biomedical Engineering; CRC Critical Reviews in Biomedical Engineering. **VAT** Chemical Rubber Company Critical Reviews in Biomedical Engineering. Vol. 7, Issue 1 (1981)-. Periodical. English. Six times a year. $99.95 (individual), $389.00 (institution). Begell House Inc., PO Box 1109, Pearl River NY 10965. **Tel** (212)725-1999. **ED** Gerald D. Fasman. **LC** R856.A1; C5. **DD** 610/.28/05. **NLM** W1 CR216W. **CODEN** CRBEDR. **[CCC].** Documents available from Article Express International, The Genuine Article, BIOSIS Document Express, Ask*IEEE. ***Continues*** *Critical Reviews in Bioengineering, 0731-6984.*
**Desc:** Provides critical evaluations of current research and development including interpretive of major problems.
**Ind/Abst** Biol. Abstr.; Curr. Aware. Biol. Sci., CABS; Curr. Contents Life Sci.; EMBASE; Energy Res. Abstr. (1981-); Eng. Index Annu.; Health Plan. Adminis.; Index Med.; Index Sci. Rev. [Full Cov.]; INSPEC (1983-); Life Sci. Collect.; Res. Alert [Full Cov.]; Sci. Cit. Index; SCISEARCH; SportSearch.

US/0738-8551
**CRITICAL REVIEWS IN BIOTECHNOLOGY.** [Crit. rev. biotechnol.]. **Added/Corp** Chemical Rubber Company. **VFOAT** C.R.C. Critical Reviews in Biotechnology; CRC Critical Reviews in Biotechnology. **VAT** Chemical Rubber Company Critical Reviews in Biotechnology. Vol. 1, Issue 1 (1983)-. Academic Scholarly Publication. English. qt. $285.00 institution. CRC Press Inc., 2000 Corporate Boulevard Northwest, Boca Raton FL 33431. **Tel** (407)994-0555, (800)272-7737, FAX (407)998-9784, telex 568689. **(Subscription address:** CRC Press Inc., PO Box 750, Pearl River NY 10965.**)** **ED** Graham G. Stewart & Inge Russell. **LC** TP248.13; .C74. **DD** 660/.6. **NLM** W1; CR216ZB. **CODEN** CRBTE5. **[CCC].** **Pr Rev.** Documents available from Article Express International, The Genuine Article, CASDDS.
**Desc:** Provides a forum for critical evaluation of current and recent publications and for state-of-the-art reports from various geographic areas around the world.
**Ind/Abst** AgBiotech News Inf.; AGRICOLA [Select. Cov.]; Biocont. News Inf. (19??-19??); Biodeter. Abstr. (1991-); Biotechnol. Res. Abstr.; Chem. Abstr. (1983-); Crop Physiol. Abstr.; Curr. Aware. Biol. Sci., CABS; Curr. Biotechnol.; Curr. Contents, Agric. Biol. Environ. Sci.; Eng. Index Annu. [Select. Cov.]; Field Crop Abstr.; Food Sci. Technol. Abstr.; Health Plan. Adminis.; Index Med. (Vol. 6, No. 1, 1987-); Index Sci. Rev. [Full Cov.]; Maize Abstr.; Life Sci. Collect.; PESTDOC; Ref. Upd. Deluxe Ed.; Res. Alert [Full Cov.]; Rev. Plant Pathol.; Sci. Cit. Index; SCISEARCH.

●UK/0964-8712
**CURRENT ADVANCES IN APPLIED MICROBIOLOGY & BIOTECHNOLOGY.** **See** Biology-Abstracting, Bibliographies and Statistics.

US/0735-956X
**CURRENT AWARENESS IN BIOTECHNOLOGY.** [Curr. aware. biotech.]. Dec. 1981-. English. ir. Bernard Wolnak and Associates, 360 North Michigan Avenue/Suite 706, Chicago IL 60601. **Tel** (312)782-4926. **ED** Bernard Wolnak. ctrl circ.
**Desc:** Presents a realistic perspective and a critical evaluation of the many and varied developments in biotechnology that can have an impact in the commercial world.

UK/0960-5037
**CURRENT BIOTECHNOLOGY.** **See** Medical Science and Technology-Abstracting, Bibliographies and Statistics.

UK/0958-1669
**CURRENT OPINION IN BIOTECHNOLOGY.** Vol. 1, No. 1 (Oct. 1990)-. Academic Scholarly Publication. English. Six times a year. $265.00 (individual); $630.00 (institution). Current Science / England, Middlesex House, 34-42 Cleveland Street, London W1P 5FB England. **Tel** 011 44 71 580 8393, 011 44 71 323 0323, FAX 011 44 81 580 1938. **(Subscription address:** Current Science, 20 North 3rd Street, Philadelphia PA 19106.**)** **LC** TP248.13; .C87. **DD** 660/.6. **NLM** W1; CU799GBL. **CODEN** CUOBE3. **[CCC].** Documents available from The Genuine Article, BIOSIS Document Express, CASDDS.
**Desc:** Directed toward researchers and educators in biotechnology. Presents review articles from an area of concentration covering an entire year's literature with annotated references. Each issue features evaluations and complete listing of key references and patents.
**Ind/Abst** AgBiotech News Inf.; Biol. Abstr. (1992-); Chem. Abstr. (1990-); Curr. Aware. Biol. Sci., CABS; Plant Breed. Abstr.; Ref. Upd. Deluxe Ed.; Res. Alert [Full Cov.].

NE/0924-1949
**CURRENT PLANT SCIENCE AND BIOTECHNOLOGY IN AGRICULTURE.** **See** Biology-Botany.

NE/0920-9069
**CYTOTECHNOLOGY (DORDRECHT).** **See** Biology-Cytology and Histology.

GW/0934-3792
**DECHEMA BIOTECHNOLOGY CONFERENCES.** **Added/Corp** Dechema. **VFOAT** DECHEMA Biotechnology Conferences Series. Vol. 1 (1987)-. Monographic series. English. an. VCH Gesellschaft GmbH, Postfach 101161, D 69451 Weinheim Germany. **Tel** 011 49 6201 606459, FAX 011 49 6201 606184. **(Subscription address:** VCH Publishers Inc., 303 Northwest 12th Avenue, Journals Department, Deerfield FL 33442.**)** **NLM** W1; DE111AL. Documents available from CASDDS.
**Ind/Abst** Chem. Abstr.

UK/0262-5318
**DERWENT BIOTECHNOLOGY ABSTRACTS.** ***Title Change.*** **See** Medical Science and Technology-Abstracting, Bibliographies and Statistics.

US/0882-6005
**DIRECTORY OF CONSULTANTS IN BIOTECHNOLOGY, THE.** [Dir. consult. biotechnol.]. (1985)-. English. ir. $85.00. **(Subscription address:** Research Publications Inc. / Microfilm, 12 Lunar Drive Drawer AB, Woodbridge CT 06525.**)** **LC** TP248.17; .D57. **DD** 660/.6/02573.

●US/1060-4200
**DIRECTORY OF PLANT BIOTECHNOLOGY COMPANIES IN USA/ BY FORE.** See Biology-Botany.

US/1041-2913
**ENGINEERING INDEX BIOENGINEERING AND BIOTECHNOLOGY ABSTRACTS.** ***Title Change.*** **See** Engineering-Abstracting, Bibliographies and Statistics.

FR/1141-5134
**ENGLISH AUDIO REVIEWS ENGLISH ED.** (1990)-. English. bm. 640.81F individuals; 876.90F institutions. English Audio Reviews, 14 Ave Beausejour BP 36, 95380 Louvres France. **Tel** 011 33 1 34689250. **ED** Richard Edelstein, MD. **UDC** 374.7. **CODEN** 802.0.
**Desc:** English language training audio journal. EAR provides practical language help, vocabulary, exercises and standard letters for professional correspondence for all those in the biomedical professions whose first language is not English.

●US/1065-707X
**ENTREZ (BETHESDA, MD.).** (ENTREZ. SEQUENCES [COMPUTER FILE].). **Added/Corp** National Center for Biotechnology Information (U.S.). **VFOAT** Sequences. (1992)-. Government Publication. English. bm. $76.00 US; $87.74 South America; $97.94 Europe; $106.94 Middle East and Africa; $107.66 Asia the Pacific and Australia; $84.80 Canada; $84.98 Mexico. Superintendent of Documents, US Government Printing Office, Washington DC 20402. **Tel** (202)275-3328, FAX (202)786-2377. **NLM** W1; EN98K.

UK/0141-0229
**ENZYME AND MICROBIAL TECHNOLOGY.** [Enzyme microb. technol.]. Vol. 1 (Jan. 1979)-. Academic Scholarly Publication. English. mo. $825.00 US; $925.00 other. Butterworth Heinemann / Woburn, MA, 225 Wildwood Avenue, Unit B, Woburn MA 01801. **Tel** (800)366-2665, FAX (617)928-2620, telex 880052. **(Subscription address:** Elsevier Science Inc. / New York Books, 655 Avenue of the Americas, New York NY 10010.**) LC** TP248.E5; E565. **DD** 660/.6/05. **NLM** W1 EN986P. **CODEN** EMTED2. **[CCC].** available on microfilm and microfiche from University Microfilms International (UMI). Documents available from Article Express International, The Genuine Article, BIOSIS Document Express, CASDDS, ADONIS.
**Ind/Abst** ADONIS; Biocont. News Inf.; Bioeng. Abstr.; Biol. Abstr.; Chem. Abstr.; Curr. Aware. Biol. Sci., CABS; Curr. Biotechnol.; Curr. Contents, Agric. Biol. Environ. Sci.; Curr. Contents Life Sci.; Ei Page One; EMBASE; Eng. Index Annu.; Food Sci. Technol. Abstr.; Foods Adlibra; For. Prod. Abstr.; Life Sci. Collect.; PESTDOC; Ref. Upd. Deluxe Ed.; Res. Alert; Rev. Plant Pathol.; Sci. Cit. Index; SCISEARCH; Sug. Indus. Abstr.

US/0094-8500
**ENZYME ENGINEERING.** [Enzym. eng.]. **Added/Corp** American Institute of Chemical Engineers. New York Academy of Sciences. Vol. 1 (1972)-. Monographic series. English. ir. Price varies per volume. Plenum Press, 233 Spring Street, New York NY 10013-1578. **Tel** (212)620-8000, (800)221-9369, FAX (212)463-0742, (212)807-1047, telex 23/421139. **LC** TP248.E5; E57. **DD** 660/.63. **NLM** W3 EN696. **CODEN** ENENDT. Documents available from CASDDS.
**Desc:** Consists of papers presented at the Engineering Foundation Conference on Enzyme Engineering.
**Ind/Abst** AGRICOLA; BioBusiness; Chem. Abstr.; Dairy Sci. Abstr.; PESTDOC.

US
**ENZYME ENGINEERING AND BIOTECHNOLOGY.** (19??)-. English. Eighteen times a year. $675.00 US; $765.00 other; combined with Molecular Biotechnology: $755.00 US, $855.00 other. Humana Press Inc., 999 Riverview Drive, Suite 208, Totawa NJ 07512. **Tel** (201)256-1699, FAX (201)256-8341. **ED** Howard H. Weetall. ***Continues in part*** *Applied Biochemistry and Biotechnology, 0273-2289.*

NE
**EUROPEAN BIOTECHNOLOGY INFORMATION SERVICE.** (1991)-. Periodical. English. ASFRA BV, Voorhaven 33, 1135 BL Edam The Netherlands. **Tel** 011 31 02993 72751, FAX 011 31 02993 72877.
**Ind/Abst** Abstr. BioCommer.

FR/0765-2046
**EUROPEAN BIOTECHNOLOGY NEWSLETTER (PARIS).** (EUROPEAN BIOTECHNOLOGY NEWSLETTER.). [Eur. biotechnol. newsl.]. **VFOAT** EBN. No. 1 (April 4, 1986)-. Academic Scholarly Publication. English. Twenty-two times a year. 3350.00F France; 3500.00F other. Editions Scientifique Elsevier, 141 rue de Javel, 75747 Paris Cedex 15 France. **Tel** 011 33 1 47 07 11 22, FAX 011 33 1 43 36 80 93. **(Subscription address:** Editions Scientifiques Elsevier / for North America, PO Box 7247-7576, Philadelphia PA 19170-7576.**) CODEN** EBNWEI. **[CCC].** Documents available from CASDDS. ***Continues*** *Biotechnology Insight.*
**Ind/Abst** Abstr. BioCommer.; AGRICOLA [Select. Cov.]; BioBusiness (1988-); Chem. Abstr.; Chem. Ind. Notes (1986-); Curr. Biotechnol.

HU/0237-0743
**FOLIA BIOTECHNOLOGICA.** [Folia biotechnol.]. (1984)-. Monographic series. English. ir. OMIKK, 1428 Budapest, PF 12, Hungary. **Tel** (361)-118-1994, FAX (361)-138-2414, telex 22-4944 omikk h. **UDC** 57.08. Documents available from CASDDS.
**Ind/Abst** Chem. Abstr.

US/0890-5436
**FOOD BIOTECHNOLOGY.** [Food biotechnol.]. Vol. 1, No. 1 (1987)-. Periodical. English. Three times a year. $440.00 US; $450.50 (other). Marcel Dekker Inc., 270 Madison Avenue, New York NY 10016. **Tel** (212)696-9000, (800)228-1160, FAX (212)685-4540, telex 421419. **(Subscription address:** Marcel Dekker Inc, PO Box 5017, Monticello NY 12701.**) ED** Dietrich Knorr. **LC** TP248.65.F66; F66. **DD** 664. **NLM** W1; FO435C. **CODEN** FBIOEE. **[CCC]. Pr Rev.** available on microfiche. Documents available from Article Express International, The Genuine Article, BIOSIS Document Express, CASDDS, Documents on Demand.
**Desc:** This journal brings together the most current research on biotechnology in the areas of food production and processing. Among the subjects treated in detail are agricultural chemicals, analytical methods, biopolymers, enzymes, fermentation technology, food additives, microbiology, molecular biology, nutrition, safety and toxicology, tissue culture, unit operations and novel food processes. The first periodical devoted to this field, this international, peer-reviewed journal includes articles reporting basic and applied research, review articles, book reviews, and letters to the editor.
**Ind/Abst** AGRICOLA; BioBusiness; Biocont. News Inf.; Biodeter. Abstr.; Biol. Abstr. (1987-); Chem. Abstr.; Curr. Aware. Biol. Sci., CABS; Curr. Biotechnol.; Curr. Contents, Agric. Biol. Environ. Sci.; Ei Page One; Eng. Index Annu.; Environ. Abstr.; Food Sci. Technol. Abstr.; Microbiol. Abstr. Sect. A; Nutr. Abstr. Rev., Ser. B, Live Feeds and Feed.; Nutr. Abstr. Rev., Ser. A, Hum. Exp.; Ref. Upd. Deluxe Ed.; Res. Alert [Full Cov.]; Rev. Med. Vet. Mycology; SCISEARCH; Sug. Indus. Abstr.

UK/0952-357X
**FOOD BIOTECHNOLOGY (LONDON).** (FOOD BIOTECHNOLOGY.). [Food biotechnol.]. (1987)-. Academic Scholarly Publication. English. Elsevier Science Publishers Ltd, Crown House, Linton Road, Barking Essex IG11 8JU England. **Tel** 011 44 81 5947272, FAX 081-594-5942, telex 896950. **LC** TP248.65.F66; F65. **DD** 664. Documents available from CASDDS.
**Ind/Abst** AGRICOLA [Full Cov.]; Chem. Abstr.; PESTDOC.

US/0893-6129
**FRONTIERS IN IMMUNOASSAY AND BIOTECHNOLOGY.** ***Ceased.*** [Front. immunoass. biotechnol.]. Vol. 6, No. 1 (Jan. 1985)-(19??). Periodical. English. Ten times a year. Scientific Newsletter Enterprises Inc., RD 4 Box 7, Middleton NY 10940. **ED** John F. Zack Jr. **LC** RB46.5; .F76. **DD** 616.07/56. **NLM** W1; FR945YK. Index available. **Circ:** 500. ***Continues*** *Frontiers in Immunoassay.*
**Desc:** Contains developments in clinical biotechnology and non-isotopic immunoassay field, products, services, government regulations, books, calendar and bibliography.
**Ind/Abst** Abstr. BioCommer. (-199?).

NE/0921-3775
**FRONTIERS OF MEDICAL AND BIOLOGICAL ENGINEERING.** (FRONTIERS OF MEDICAL AND BIOLOGICAL ENGINEERING : THE INTERNATIONAL JOURNAL OF THE JAPAN SOCIETY OF MEDICAL ELECTRONICS AND BIOLOGICAL ENGINEERING.). [Front. med. biol. eng.]. **Added/Corp** Nihon ME Gakkai. Vol. 1 No. 1 (1988)-. Periodical. English. qt. DM340.00. VSP International Science Publishers, Godfried van Seystlaan 47, 3703 BR Zeist Netherlands. **Tel** 011 31 3404 25790, FAX 011 31 3404 32081, telex 40217 USP NL. **(Subscription address:** VSP International Science Publishers, PO Box 346, 3700 AH Zeist Netherlands.**) ED** T. Togawa. **NLM** W1; FR946GN. **CODEN** FMBEEQ. **Bk Rev. Ad Acc.** Documents available from BIOSIS Document Express.
**Desc:** Aims to introduce research and applications in the field of medical and biological engineering from Japan and other countries to a world-wide readership.
**Ind/Abst** Biol. Abstr. (1991-); Health Plan. Adminis.

CN/1180-5668
**FRONTIERS (POINTE-CLAIRE).** (FRONTIERS.). [Frontiers]. **Added/Corp** STA Communications. Vol. 1, No. 1 (Aug. 1990)-. Periodical. English. qt. Limited free distribution. STA Communications Inc., 955 St. John Boulevard, Suite 306, Pt Claire, Quebec H9R 5K3 Canada. **Tel** (514)695-7623. **DD** 660/.6/05.

GW/0930-4320
**GBF MONOGRAPHS / GESELLSCHAFT FUER BIOTECHNOLOGISCHE FORSCHUNG.** **VFOAT** G.B.F. Monographs; G.B.F. Monographien; GBF Monographien. Vol. 8 (1987)-. Monographic series. English (German). Price varies per volume. VCH Publishers Inc, 220 East 23rd Street, New York NY 10010. **Tel** (212)683-8333, , FAX (212)481-0897. **(Subscription address:** VCH Publishers Inc., 303 Northwest 12th Avenue, Journals Department, Deerfield FL 33442.**) NLM** W1; GB22. Documents available from CASDDS. ***Continues*** *GBF Monograph Series, 0930-4312.*
**Ind/Abst** Biodeter. Abstr.; Chem. Abstr.; Sug. Indus. Abstr.

US/1063-0341
**GEN GUIDE TO BIOTECHNOLOGY COMPANIES.** [GEN guide biotechnol. co.]. **VFOAT** Guide to Biotechnology Companies; Genetic Engineering News Guide to Biotechnology Companies. (1985)-. English. an. $128.95. Mary Ann Liebert Inc., 1651 Third Avenue, New York NY 10128. **Tel** (212)289-2300, (800)M-LIEBERT, FAX (212)289-4697. **LC** TP248.17; .G46. **DD** 338.7/6606/025.

US/1050-3862
**GENETIC ANALYSIS, TECHNIQUES AND APPLICATIONS.** **See** Biology-Genetics.

UK/0959-020X
**GENETIC ENGINEER & BIOTECHNOLOGIST, THE.** [Genet. eng. biotechnol.]. **VFOAT** Genetic Engineer and Biotechnologist. Vol. 10, Issue 1 (March/April 1990)-. Academic Scholarly Publication. English. qt. £146.00. Carfax Publishing Company, PO Box 25 Abingdon, Oxfordshire OX14 3UE England. **Tel** 011 44 235 555335, FAX (0279)31067, telex 817484. **(Subscription address:** US and Canada/ PO Box 2025, Dunnellon, FL 34430-2025; telephone:(904)489-6996**) ED** Roderick N. Greenshields. **NLM** W1; GE2785. **CODEN** GEBIER. **[CCC]. Bk Rev. Ad Acc. Circ:** 500. available on microfiche from University Microfilms International (UMI). Documents available from The Genuine Article, CASDDS. ***Continues*** *International Industrial Biotechnology, 0269-7815.*
**Desc:** Covers business, finance and research and development.
**Ind/Abst** Abstr. BioCommer.; AgBiotech News Inf.; BioBusiness (1990-); Biodeter. Abstr. (1991-); Chem. Abstr.; Chem. Bus. Bull.; Chem. Bus. NewsBase (1990-); Chem. Bus. Update; Curr. Aware. Biol. Sci., CABS; Food Sci. Technol. Abstr.; PESTDOC; Res. Alert [Full Cov.]; Rev. Plant Pathol.; Soc. Sci. Cit. Index [Select. Cov.]; Weed Abstr.

US/0196-3716
**GENETIC ENGINEERING.** **See** Biology-Genetics.

AU
**GENETIC ENGINEERING AND BIOTECHNOLOGY MONITOR / UNITED NATIONS INDUSTRIAL DEVELOPMENT ORGANIZATION.** **See** Biology-Genetics.

US/0890-0906
**GENETIC ENGINEERING AND BIOTECHNOLOGY RELATED FIRMS WORLDWIDE DIRECTORY.** [Genet. eng. biotechnol. relat. firms worldw. dir.]. (1986)-. Directory. English. $299.00 US; $314.00 Canada; $334.00 other. Mega-Type Publications, 186 Route 571 Bldg 3A, PO Box 664, Princeton NJ 08550. **Tel** (800)962-7004, (609)275-6900, FAX (609)275-8011. **DD** 660. **NLM** QH 442; G3285. ***Continues*** *Genetic Engineering and Biotechnology Firms Worldwide Directory, 0892-0710.*
**Desc:** Worldwide directory listing over 5500 firms in the US and sixty foreign countries. Complete address information as well as free form text listings.

NE/0921-2604
**GENETIC ENGINEERING AND BIOTECHNOLOGY YEARBOOK.** [Genet. eng. biotechnol. yearb.]. (19??)-. Academic Scholarly Publication. English. an. Price varies. Elsevier Science Publishers BV, PO Box 211, 1000 AE Amsterdam Netherlands. **Tel** 011 31 20 5803642, FAX 011 31 20 5862696, telex 15682. **(Subscription address:** Elsevier Science Inc. / New York Books, 655 Avenue of the Americas, New York NY 10010.**) LC** TP248.2; .G46. **DD** 660/.6/05. **NLM** TP 248.2; G328.

US/0740-9737
**GENEWATCH.** (GENEWATCH : A NEWSLETTER OF THE COMMITTEE FOR RESPONSIBLE GENETICS.). [Genewatch]. **Added/Corp** Committee for Responsible Genetics. **VFOAT** Gene Watch. (1984)-. Periodical. English. bm. $24.00 (individuals), $30.00 (institutions), $15.00 (students). Council for Responsible Genetics, 5 Upland Road, Suite 3, Cambridge MA 02140. **Tel** (617)868-0870, FAX (617)491-5344. **ED** Judith Glaubman. **DD** 363. **CODEN** GEWAE6. cum. index (brochure). **Bk Rev**, (Qty: varies). **Circ:** 900.
**Desc:** Analyzes politics, ethics and social impacts of

genetic engineering and new biotechnology. Feature articles, news notes, reviews and resources.
**Ind/Abst** AGRICOLA [Select. Cov.]; Altern. Press Index (199?-); BioBusiness (1988-).

JA/0385-6151
**HAKKOKOGAKU KAISHI.** ***Title Change.*** (HAKKO KOGAKKAI SHI / HAKKOKOGAKU KAISHI.). [Hakkokogaku Kaishi]. **Added/Corp** Nihon Hakko Kogakkai. **VFOAT** Hakkokogaku Kaishi; Hakkokogaku. (1977)-(1992). Academic Scholarly Publication. Japanese (summaries and/or abstracts in English; table of contents in English). bm. Nihon Hakko Kogakkai, (Society of Fermentation Technology, Japan), Osaka Daigaku Kogakubu, 2-1, Yamadaoka, Suitashi, Osakafu 565 Japan. **(Subscription address:** Kyowa Book Company Inc., 1 38 Kanda Jinbocho Chiyoda-ku, Tokyo 101 Japan.**) LC** TP500; .H35. **CODEN** HKOKDE. **Pr Rev.** Documents available from The Genuine Article, BIOSIS Document Express, CASDDS. ***Continues in part*** *Hakko Kogaku Zasshi.* ***Continued by*** *Seibutsu Kogakkai shi.*
**Ind/Abst** BioBusiness (19??-19??); Biol. Abstr. (19??-19??); Chem. Abstr. (19??-19??); Curr. Biotechnol. (19??-19??); Curr. Contents, Agric. Biol. Environ. Sci. (19??-19??); EMBASE (19??-19??); Food Sci. Technol. Abstr. (19??-19??); Life Sci. Collect. (19??-19??); PESTDOC (19??-19??); Res. Alert (19??-19??) [Full Cov.]; Rice Abstr. (19??-19??).

US
**IBA REPORTS.** English. bm. Free to members. Industrial Biotechnology Association, 1625 K Street NW, Suite 1100, Washington DC 20006.
**Ind/Abst** Abstr. BioCommer.

US/0739-5175
**IEEE ENGINEERING IN MEDICINE AND BIOLOGY MAGAZINE.** (IEEE ENGINEERING IN MEDICINE AND BIOLOGY MAGAZINE : THE QUARTERLY MAGAZINE OF THE ENGINEERING IN MEDICINE & BIOLOGY SOCIETY.). [IEEE eng. med. biol. mag.]. **Added/Corp** IEEE Engineering in Medicine and Biology Society. **VFOAT** I.E.E.E. Engineering in Medicine and Biology Magazine; E.M.B. Magazine; EMB Magazine. **VAT** Institute of Electrical and Electronics Engineers Engineering in Medicine and Biology Magazine. Vol. 1, No. 2 (June 1982)-. Periodical. English. bm. $115.00. IEEE, Institution of Electrical and Electronics Engineers, Inc., 345 East 47th Street, New York NY 10017-2394. **Tel** (908)981-1393, FAX (908)981-9667. **(Subscription address:** IEEE / Institute of Electrical and Electronics Engineers, 445 Hoes Lane, PO Box 1331, Piscataway NJ 08855-1331.**) LC** R856.A1; E54. **DD** 610/.28. **NLM** W1 IE222H. **CODEN** IEMBDE. **[CCC]. Pr Rev.** Documents available from Article Express International, The Genuine Article, Ask*IEEE. ***Continues*** *Engineering in Medicine & Biology, 0278-0054.*
**Desc:** Covers general and technical articles on current technologies and methods used in biomedical and clinical engineering; societal implications of medical technologies, current news items; patent descriptions, and correspondence. Special interest departments, students, law, clinical engineering, ethics, new products, society news, historical features, government.
**Ind/Abst** Bioeng. Abstr.; Curr. Contents Clin. Med.; Ei Page One; EMBASE; Eng. Index Annu.; Index IEEE Publ.; INSPEC (June 1982-); Pollut. Abstr. Indexes; Res. Alert [Full Cov.]; SCISEARCH; Soc. Sci. Cit. Index [Select. Cov.].

US/0018-9294
**IEEE TRANSACTIONS ON BIOMEDICAL ENGINEERING.** (IEEE TRANSACTIONS ON BIO-MEDICAL ENGINEERING / BIO-MEDICAL ENGINEERING GROUP.). [IEEE trans. biomed. eng.]. **Added/Corp** Institute of Electrical and Electronics Engineers. Bio-Medical Engineering Group. IEEE Engineering in Medicine and Biology Group. IEEE Engineering in Medicine and Biology Society. **VFOAT** IEEE Transactions on Biomedical Engineering; Transactions on Bio-Medical Engineering. **VAT** Institute of Electrical and Electronics Engineers Transactions on Bio-Medical Engineering. Vol. BME-11, No. 1 & 2 (Jan./April 1964)-. Academic Scholarly Publication. English. mo. $350.00. IEEE, Institution of Electrical and Electronics Engineers, Inc., 345 East 47th Street, New York NY 10017-2394. **Tel** (908)981-1393, FAX (908)981-9667. **(Subscription address:** IEEE / Institute of Electrical and Electronics Engineers, 445 Hoes Lane, PO Box 1331, Piscataway NJ 08855-1331.**) LC** R895.A1; I25. **DD** 610/.28. **NLM** W1 I223. **CODEN** IEBEAX. **[CCC]. Pr Rev.** available on microfiche. Documents available from Article Express International, The Genuine Article, BIOSIS Document Express, Ask*IEEE, CASDDS. ***Continues*** *IEEE Transactions on Bio-Medical Electronics, 0096-0616.*
**Desc:** Covers basic and applied papers dealing with biomedical engineering and applied biophysics. Papers range from practical/clinical applications through experimental science and technological development to formalized mathematical theory.
**Ind/Abst** Appl. Sci. Technol. Index; Bioeng. Abstr.; Biol. Abstr.; Biostatistica; Ceram. Abstr. (19??-); Chem. Abstr. (1964-1982); Curr. Aware. Biol. Sci., CABS; CSA Neuro. Abstr. (?-?); Curr. Contents Eng. Tech. Appl. Sci.; Curr. Contents Life Sci.; Ei Page One; EMBASE; Energy Res. Abstr.; Eng. Index Annu.; Ergon. Abstr.; Expand. Acad. Index (1992-); Health Plan. Adminis.; Index Med.; Index IEEE Publ.; INSPEC (1968-); Int. Aerosp. Abstr.; Life Sci. Collect.; Psychol. Abstr.; Res. Alert [Full Cov.]; Ref. Upd. Deluxe Ed.; Sci. Cit. Index; SCISEARCH; Soc. Sci. Cit. Index [Select. Cov.].

US/0093-3813
**IEEE TRANSACTIONS ON PLASMA SCIENCE.** [IEEE trans. plasma sci.]. **Main/Corp** IEEE Nuclear and Plasma Sciences Society. **Added/Corp** IEEE Nuclear and Plasma Sciences Society. Transactions on Plasma Science. **VFOAT** Transactions on Plasma Science; Plasma Science. Vol. PS-1 (Mar. 1973)-. Academic Scholarly Publication. English. bm. $215.00. IEEE, Institution of Electrical and Electronics Engineers, Inc., 345 East 47th Street, New York NY 10017-2394. **Tel** (908)981-1393, FAX (908)981-9667. **(Subscription address:** IEEE / Institute of Electrical and Electronics Engineers, 445 Hoes Lane, PO Box 1331, Piscataway NJ 08855-1331.**) LC** TA2001; .I18a. **DD** 621. **CODEN** ITPSBD. **[CCC]. Pr Rev.** Documents available from Article Express International, The Genuine Article, Ask*IEEE, CASDDS.
**Desc:** Covers all aspects of plasma science and engineering.
**Ind/Abst** Bioeng. Abstr.; Chem. Abstr.; Curr. Contents Phys. Chem. Earth Sci.; Ei Page One; Energy Res. Abstr. (March 1975-); Eng. Index Annu.; Expand. Acad. Index (1992-); Index IEEE Publ.; INIS Atomindex [Micro.]; INSPEC (June 1973-); Int. Aerosp. Abstr.; Math. Rev.; Res. Alert [Full Cov.]; Sci. Cit. Index; SCISEARCH.

●US/1063-6528
**IEEE TRANSACTIONS ON REHABILITATION ENGINEERING.** (TRANSACTIONS ON REHABILITATION ENGINEERING.). [IEEE trans. rehabil. eng.]. **Added/Corp** Institute of Electrical and Electronics Engineers. **VAT** Institute of Electrical and Electronics Engineers Transactions on Rehabilitation Engineering. (1993)-. Periodical. English. qt. $140.00. IEEE, Institution of Electrical and Electronics Engineers, Inc., 345 East 47th Street, New York NY 10017-2394. **Tel** (908)981-1393, FAX (908)981-9667. **(Subscription address:** IEEE / Institute of Electrical and Electronics Engineers, 445 Hoes Lane, PO Box 1331, Piscataway NJ 08855-1331.**) DD** 617. **NLM** W1; IE4463.
**Desc:** Focuses on rehabilitation aspects of biomedical engineering and covers topics including functional electrical stimulation, acoustic dynamics, human performance measurement and analysis, nerve stimulation, electromyography, motor control and stimulation, and hardware and software applications for rehabilitation engineering and assistive devices.

UK/0964-069X
**IMPACT AGBIOINDUSTRY.** ***Ceased.*** (19??)-(Jan. 1993). English. qt. CAB International Centre, Wallingford, Oxon OX10 8DE United Kingdom. **Tel** 44 491 832111, FAX 44 491 833508, telex 847964 (COMAGG G). Documents available from Documents on Demand. ***Continues*** *AgBioBusiness.*
**Ind/Abst** Abstr. BioCommer.; Environ. Abstr.

US
**INFORMATION SYSTEMS SECURITY PRODUCTS AND SERVICES CATALOGUE / PREPARED BY THE NATIONAL SECURITY AGENCY.** **Added/Corp** United States. National Security Agency. **VFOAT** Information Systems Security Products and Services Catalogue. P.Supplement. (198?)-. Bibliography. English. qt. $55.00. Superintendent of Documents, US Government Printing Office, Washington DC 20402. **Tel** (202)275-3328, FAX (202)786-2377. **LC** HD9696.C6; I542. ***Absorbed*** *Preferred Products List.*
**Desc:** A bibliographic listing of references to current articles from approximately 2,500 of the worlds' biomedical journals.

FR/0243-7228
**INNOVATION ET TECHNOLOGIE EN BIOLOGIE ET MEDECINE.** (INNOVATION ET TECHNOLOGIE EN BIOLOGIE ET MEDECINE : ITBM.). [Innov. technol. biol. med.]. **Added/Corp** Ecole Nationale pour Deficients Visuels (France). **VFOAT** ITBM. (1980)-. Periodical. French (English). bm. 420.00F France; 450.00F other. ITBM-CRDP, 3 rue Jean Bart BP 199, 59018 Lille Cedex France. **Tel** 33 20 075981, FAX 33 20 851114, telex 160.315 F. **ED** Amiel M., Barritault L., Coatrieux J., McAdams E., Morucci J.P. and Moschetto Y. **NLM** W1 IN455AM. Index available (bound in last issue). cum. index. **Circ:** 800 (ctrl). available on microfilm from University Microfilms International (UMI). Documents available from The Genuine Article.
**Desc:** Fast publication (two months) of original results either in theoretical or applied research works in the field of biomedical engineering.
**Ind/Abst** Res. Alert [Full Cov.]; Soc. Sci. Cit. Index [Select. Cov.].

US/0888-7225
**INTERNATIONAL BIOTECHNOLOGY LABORATORY.** [Int. biotechnol. lab.]. Periodical. English. qt. International Scientific Communications Inc, PO Box 870, 30 Controls Drive, Shelton CT 06484-0870. **Tel** (203)926-9300, FAX (203)926-9310, telex 964292. **ED** Brian Howard. **LC** TP248.13; .I59. **DD** 575. **NLM** W1; IN71Q. **CODEN** IBLAEK. **Circ:** 32,796.
**Ind/Abst** Abstr. BioCommer.; Anal. Abstr.; BioBusiness; Curr. Biotechnol.; Mass Spect. Bull.; PESTDOC.

US/0958-6415
**ISSUES IN REPRODUCTIVE AND GENETIC ENGINEERING : JOURNAL OF INTERNATIONAL FEMINIST ANALYSIS.** ***Ceased.*** Vol. 3 No. 1 (1990)-Vol. 5 (1992). Periodical. English. Three times a year. Pergamon Press, An Imprint of Elsevier Science Ltd., The Boulevard, Langford Lane, Kidlington, Oxford OX5 1GB United Kingdom. **Tel** 011 44 865 843000, 011 44 865 843699, FAX 011 44 865 843010. **(Subscription address:** UK/ Headington Hill Hall, Oxford OX3 0BW; Can/ 150 Consumers Road/Suite 104, Willowdale Ontario M2J 1P9; Aus-NZ/ POB 544, Potts Point NSW 2011**) ED** Jalna Hanmer and Renate Klein. **LC** RG133.5; .R46. **DD** 176/.05. **NLM** W1; IS669G. **[CCC]. Ad Acc. Circ:** 1,500. available on microfilm and microfiche from University Microfilms International (UMI). Documents available from The Genuine Article. ***Continues*** *Reproductive and Genetic Engineering, 0895-5565.*
**Desc:** Designed to facilitate the development of feminist, multidisciplinary and international analyses of new reproductive technologies and genetic engineering and impact on women.
**Ind/Abst** Altern. Press Index (199?-); Curr. Contents Soc. Behav. Sci.; Int. Bibliogr. Sociol.; Res. Alert [Full Cov.].

RU/0208-2330
**ITOGI NAUKI I TEHNIKI - VSESOUZNYJ INSTITUT NAUCNOJ I TEHNICESKOJ INFORMACII. SERIA BIOTEHNOLOGIA.** (ITOGI NAUKI I TEKHNIKI. SERIIA BIOTEKHNOLOGIIA / GOSUDARSTVENNYI KOMITET SSSR PO NAUKE I TEKHNIKE, AKADEMIIA NAUK SSSR, VSESOIUZNYI INSTITUT NAUCHNOI I TEKHNICHESKOI INFORMATSII.). [Itogi nauki teh. - Vses. inst. nauÈcn. teh. inf., Ser. biotehnol.]. **Added/Corp** Vsesoiuznyi Institut Nauchnoi i Tekhnicheskoi Informatsii (Soviet Union). **VFOAT** Seriia Biotekhnologiia; Biotekhnologiia; Itogi Nauki i Tekhniki. Biotekhnologiia. (1983)-. Monographic series. Russian. Price varies per volume. VINITI - Vsesoyuznyi Institut Nauchno-Tekhnicheskoi Informatsii, All-Union Scientific and Technical Information Institute, Baltiiskaia Ulitsa 14, 125219 Moscow Russia. **Tel** 238-46-00, FAX 9430060, telex 411160. **LC** TP248.13; .I86. **CODEN** INSBE6. Documents available from CASDDS.
**Ind/Abst** Chem. Abstr.

JA/0021-3292
**IYO DENSHI TO SEITAI KOGAKU.** [Iyo denshi to seitai kogaku]. **VFOAT** Japanese Journal of Medical Electronics and Biological Engineering. Volume 1- Feb. 1963-. Academic Scholarly Publication. Japanese (summaries and/or abstracts in English). ir. $92.00. Nihon ME Gakkai, (Japan Soc. of Medical Electronics & Biological Engineering), Dai 31 Kowa Biru 7F, 19-1, Shiroganedai 3 Chome, Minatoku, Tokyoto 108 Japan. **(Subscription address:** Maruzen Company Ltd., PO Box 5050, Import & Export Department, Tokyo 100 31 Japan.**) NLM** W1; IY585 v. 1-26; W1; BE97 v. 27-. **CODEN** IYSEAK. **Ad Acc. Circ:** 10,000 (ctrl). Documents available from Ask*IEEE, CASDDS.
**Desc:** A journal which has an object of mutual cooperation between medical science and technology.
**Ind/Abst** Chem. Abstr. (1985-); Ei Page One; EMBASE; Index Med.; INSPEC (April 1971-).

GW/0930-9152
**JAHRBUCH BIOTECHNOLOGIE.** [Jahrb. Biotechnol.]. **VFOAT** Biotechnologie Jahrbuch. (1986/1987)-. German. be. Carl Hanser Verlag, Postfach 860420, D 81631 Munich Germany. **Tel** 011 49 89 998300, FAX 011 49 89 984809. **LC** TP248.13; .J35. **DD** 660/.6/05. Documents available from The Genuine Article.
**Ind/Abst** AGRICOLA; Res. Alert [Full Cov.].

SP
**JAPANESE REPORT SERIES BIOTECHNOLOGY.** English. mo. $430.00. Newmedia International Japan, AV Infanta Carlota 123 5 A, 08029 Barcelona Spain. **Tel** 011 34 3 4195690, FAX 414 42 13. **(Subscription address:** Newmedia International Japan, Midland Bank 196 Oxford Street AC 41217380, London W1A 1 EZ England)
**Ind/Abst** PROMT [Full Txt.]; PTS Newsl. Database [Full Txt.].

●US/1058-7330
**JAPANESE TECHNOLOGY REVIEWS. SECTION E, BIOTECHNOLOGY. VFOAT** Biotechnology. (1992)-. Periodical. English. Twice a year

(1 volume). $185.00 (academic institutions), $289.00 (corporate institutions). Gordon & Breach Science Publishers, Inc., PO Box 786, Cooper Station, New York NY 10276. **Tel** (212)206-8900, FAX (212)645-2459. **[CCC].** ***Continues in part*** *Japanese Technology Reviews, 0898-5693.*

●US/1065-8483
**JOURNAL OF APPLIED BIOMECHANICS.** [J. appl. biomech.]. **Added/Corp** International Society of Biomechanics. International Society for the Biomechanics of Sport. **VFOAT** JAB. Vol. 9, No. 1 (Feb. 1993)-. Periodical. English. qt (Feb., May, Aug., Nov.). $40.00 (individual), $90.00 (institution) US; $44.00 (individual), $94.00 (institution) other. Human Kinetics Publishers Inc, 1607 North Market Street, PO Box 5076, Champaign IL 61825-5076. **Tel** (217)351-5076, FAX (217)351-2674. **ED** Robert J. Gregor. **DD** 612. **[CCC].** Index available (Included in Nov. issue). ***Continues*** *International Journal of Sport Biomechanics, 0740-2082.*
**Desc:** Devoted to the study of human biomechanics in sport, exercise, and rehabilitation. Includes research articles, clinical studies, and other pertinent information on current advance in the field.
**Ind/Abst** Soc. Sci. Cit. Index [Select. Cov.]; SPORT Discus.

US/0885-3282
**JOURNAL OF BIOMATERIALS APPLICATIONS.** [J. biomater. appl.]. **VFOAT** Biomaterials Applications. Vol. 1, No. 1 (July 1986)-. Periodical. English. qt (Jan.,Apr., July and Oct.). $285.00 (one year), $560.00 (two year), $835.00 (three year). Technomic Publishing Company, Inc., 851 New Holland Avenue, Box 3535, Lancaster PA 17604. **Tel** (717)291-5609, (800)233-9936, FAX (717)295-4538. **ED** Michael Szycher. **LC** R856.A1; J64. **DD** 610/.28. **NLM** W1; JO564KF. **[CCC].** cum. index. **Circ:** 100. available on microfilm from University Microfilms International (UMI). Documents available from Article Express International, The Genuine Article, CASDDS.
**Desc:** Contains original articles that emphasize the clinical applications of implantable biomaterials. Development, manufacture, and clinical uses of biomaterials most compatible with the human body are highlighted from a scientific viewpoint. Devoted to new and emerging technologies, particular focus is placed on the many applications under development at industrial, biomedical, and polymer research facilities, as well as ongoing activities in academic and medical research laboratories.
**Ind/Abst** Chem. Abstr.; Ei Page One; Eng. Index Annu.; Index Med.; Res. Alert [Full Cov.].

US/0148-0731
**JOURNAL OF BIOMECHANICAL ENGINEERING.** (TRANSACTIONS OF THE ASME. JOURNAL OF BIOMECHANICAL ENGINEERING.). [J. biomech. eng.]. Vol. 99, No. 1 (Feb. 1977)-. Academic Scholarly Publication. English. qt. $140.00 (nonmember), $40.00 (member) US and Canada. American Society of Mechanical Engineers, 22 Law Drive, Fairfield NJ 07007. **Tel** (201)882-1167, (212)705-7722 (editorial). **ED** Cornelia Monahan. **LC** R856.A1. **DD** 610/.28. **NLM** W1 JO564L. **CODEN** JBENDY. **[CCC]. Bk Rev. Ad Acc. Pr Rev. Circ:** 874. available on microfilm and microfiche from University Microfilms International (UMI). Documents available from Article Express International, The Genuine Article, BIOSIS Document Express, Ask*IEEE, CASDDS.
**Desc:** Bio-fluids, bio-solid mechanics, bio-materials, health care delivery systems, artificial organs and prostheses, bio-instrumentation and measurement simulation of physiological systems, etc.
**Ind/Abst** BioBusiness; Bioeng. Abstr.; Biol. Abstr. (1985-); Chem. Abstr. (1977-1986); Civ. Struct. Eng. Abstr.; Comput. Inf. Syst. Abstr. J. [Full Cov.]; Curr. Contents Life Sci.; Ei Page One; EMBASE; Energy Res. Abstr. (April 1978-); Eng. Index Annu.; Expand. Acad. Index (1992-); Fluid Abstr., Civil Eng.; Fluid Abstr. Proc. Eng.; FLUIDEX (1978-); Health Devices Alerts; Index Med.; INSPEC (Feb. 1977-); Int. Aerosp. Abstr.; Mater. Sci. Eng. Abstr.; Mech. Eng. Abstr.; Proc. Chem. Eng.; Res. Alert [Full Cov.]; Sci. Cit. Index; SCISEARCH; SportSearch; Theoret. Chem. Eng.

UK/0141-5425
**JOURNAL OF BIOMEDICAL ENGINEERING.** ***Title Change.*** [J. biomed. eng.]. **Added/Corp** Biological Engineering Society. Vol. 1 (Jan. 1979)-Vol. 15, No. 6 (Nov. 1993). Academic Scholarly Publication. English. bm. Butterworth Heinemann Publishers, Linacre House, Jordan Hill, Oxford OX2 8DP England. **Tel** 011 44 865 310366. **ED** G. H. Byford. **NLM** W1 JO564N. **CODEN** JBIEDR. **[CCC].** Index available. **Bk Rev. Ad Acc. Pr Rev.** available on microfilm and microfiche from University Microfilms International (UMI). Documents available from Article Express International, The Genuine Article, BIOSIS Document Express, Ask*IEEE, CASDDS. ***Continued by*** *Medical Engineering & Physics, 1350-4533.*
**Desc:** Provides clinicians with an awareness of technological developments which have potential applications in health care. Contributions to the journal deal not only with original progress in various disciplines, but also give speedy attention to short communications describing unique applications. Review established techniques for user's benefit.
**Ind/Abst** Appl. Sci. Technol. Index; Biol. Abstr.; Ceram. Abstr.; Chem. Abstr.; Curr. Aware. Biol. Sci., CABS; Curr. Biotechnol.; Curr. Contents Life Sci.; Ei Page One; EMBASE; Eng. Index Annu.; Index Med.; Index Vet.; INSPEC (Oct. 1979-); Pap. Board Abstr.; Ref. Upd. Deluxe Ed.; Res. Alert [Full Cov.]; Sci. Cit. Index; SCISEARCH; Soc. Sci. Cit. Index [Select. Cov.]; Vet. Bull.

NE/0168-1656
**JOURNAL OF BIOTECHNOLOGY.** [J. biotechnol.]. Vol. 1, No. 1 (May 1984)-. Academic Scholarly Publication. English. Twenty-one times a year (7 volumes). Fl3136.00. Elsevier Science Publishers BV, PO Box 211, 1000 AE Amsterdam Netherlands. **Tel** 011 31 20 5803642, FAX 011 31 20 5862696, telex 15682. **ED** A Fiechter, H Bungay, S Fukui, J Messing, and E L Winnacker. **NLM** W1; JO568H. **CODEN** JBITD4JBDITD4. **[CCC]. Pr Rev.** available on microfilm and microfiche from University Microfilms International (UMI). Documents available from Article Express International, The Genuine Article, CASDDS, ADONIS.
**Desc:** Provides a medium for the rapid publication of full articles as well as short communications on various aspects of biotechnology.
**Ind/Abst** ADONIS; AGRICOLA [Select. Cov.]; BioBusiness; Biodeter. Abstr. (1991-); Biol. Agric. Index; Biotechnol. Res. Abstr.; Chem. Abstr. (1984-); Chem. Titles; Curr. Aware. Biol. Sci., CABS; Curr. Biotechnol.; Curr. Contents, Agric. Biol. Environ. Sci.; Dairy Sci. Abstr.; Ei Page One; EMBASE; Eng. Index Annu.; Field Crop Abstr.; Food Sci. Technol. Abstr.; For. Prod. Abstr. (1991-); Genet. Abstr.; Microbiol. Abstr. Sect. B; Microbiol. Abstr. Sect. A; Microbiol. Abstr. Sect. C; Oncog. Growth Factors Abstr.; Life Sci. Collect.; PESTDOC; Plant Breed. Abstr.; Plant Genet. Resour. Abstr.; Ref. Upd. Deluxe Ed.; Res. Alert [Full Cov.]; Rev. Agric. Entomol.; Sci. Cit. Index; SCISEARCH; Seed Abstr.; Weed Abstr.; Wheat Barley Trit. Abstr.

●US/1073-7774
**JOURNAL OF CARDIOVASCULAR DIAGNOSIS AND PROCEDURES.** [J. cardiovasc. diagn. proced.]. Vol. 11, No. 2 (1993)-. Periodical. English. qt. $194.00. Mary Ann Liebert Inc., 1651 Third Avenue, New York NY 10128. **Tel** (212)289-2300, (800)M-LIEBERT, FAX (212)289-4697. **ED** Michele Nanna. **DD** 616. **NLM** W1; JO575J. ***Continues*** *Journal of Cardiovascular Technology, 1043-4356.*
**Desc:** Clinically oriented; fulfills demand for physicians who need to understand the underlying technologies of new instruments and procedures.

US/1043-4356
**JOURNAL OF CARDIOVASCULAR TECHNOLOGY (NEW YORK, N.Y.).** ***Title Change.*** (JOURNAL OF CARDIOVASCULAR TECHNOLOGY.). [J. cardiovasc. technol.]. Vol. 8, No. 1 (Spring 1989)-(1993). Periodical. English. qt. Mary Ann Liebert Inc., 1651 Third Avenue, New York NY 10128. **Tel** (212)289-2300, (800)M-LIEBERT, FAX (212)289-4697. **ED** Myron Schoenfeld and Kenneth Taylor. **DD** 616. **NLM** W1; JO577H. **CODEN** JCATE6. Documents available from The Genuine Article, BIOSIS Document Express. ***Continues*** *Journal of Cardiovascular Ultrasonography, 0730-8396.* ***Continued by*** *Journal of Cardiovascular Diagnosis and Procedures, 1073-7774.*
**Desc:** Publishes articles on all biomedical engineering applications, diagnostic and therapeutic, to cardiovascular disease.
**Ind/Abst** Biol. Abstr. (1989-); Curr. Contents Clin. Med.; EMBASE; Res. Alert [Select. Cov.]; SCISEARCH.

UK/0268-2575
**JOURNAL OF CHEMICAL TECHNOLOGY AND BIOTECHNOLOGY (1986).** **See** Chemistry-Chemical Technology.

US/0363-8855
**JOURNAL OF CLINICAL ENGINEERING.** [J. clin. eng.]. Vol. 1, No. 1 (Oct./Dec. 1976)-. Periodical. English. Six times a year (Jan., Mar., May, July, Sept., Nov.). $143.00 US; $178.00 other. Quest Publishing Company, 1351 Titan Way, Brea CA 92621. **Tel** (714)738-6400, FAX (714)525-6258. **ED** Allan F. Pacela. **LC** R856.A1; J68. **DD** 610/.28. **NLM** W1 JO588C. **CODEN** JCEND7. **[CCC].** Index available. **Bk Rev. Ad Acc. Circ:** 3,000. Documents available from Article Express International, BIOSIS Document Express, Ask*IEEE.
**Desc:** Features the latest technical and professional information in biomedical and clinical engineering.
**Ind/Abst** BioBusiness; Bioeng. Abstr.; Biol. Abstr.; Comput. Inf. Syst. Abstr. J. [Full Cov.]; Ei Page One; EMBASE; Eng. Index Annu.; Environ. Eng. Abstr.; Health Devices Alerts; Hospit. Health Admin. Index; INSPEC (Jan./March 1979-); Mech. Eng. Abstr.

●US
**JOURNAL OF MARINE BIOTECHNOLOGY, THE.** **See** Biology-Marine Biology.

UK/0957-4530
**JOURNAL OF MATERIALS SCIENCE. MATERIALS IN MEDICINE.** **VFOAT** Materials in Medicine. Vol. 1, No. 1 (June 1990)-. Academic Scholarly Publication. English. mo. $460.00 US and Canada; £270.00 Europe; £290.00 other. Chapman & Hall, 2-6 Boundary Row, London SE1 8HN England. **Tel** 011 44 71 865 0066, FAX 011 44 71 522 9623, telex 290164 Chapmag. **(Subscription address:** Chapman & Hall, Cheriton House, North Way, Andover, Hampshire, SP10 5BE England.**) LC** R857.M3; J69. **DD** 610/.28. **NLM** W1; JO748QR. **CODEN** JSMMEL. **[CCC]. Pr Rev.** Documents available from Article Express International, The Genuine Article, Ask*IEEE, CASDDS.
**Desc:** Publishes papers on the science and technology of biomaterials and their applications as medical or dental implants, prostheses and devices, and of biological materials. Publishes a wide range of topics from the basic underpinning science to clinical applications, around a central theme of materials in medicine or dentistry.
**Ind/Abst** Ceram. Abstr. (19??-); Chem. Abstr. (1990-); Curr. Contents Eng. Tech. Appl. Sci.; Ei Page One; Eng. Index Annu.; INSPEC (June 1990-); Res. Alert [Full Cov.]; SCISEARCH.

UK/0309-1902
**JOURNAL OF MEDICAL ENGINEERING & TECHNOLOGY.** [J. med. eng. technol.]. **VFOAT** Journal of Medical Engineering and Technology. Vol. 1, No. 1 (Jan. 1977)-. Academic Scholarly Publication. English. bm. £120.00 UK; $199.00 other. Taylor & Francis Ltd., Rankine Road, Basingstoke Hampshire, RG24 8PR United Kingdom. **Tel** 011 44 256 840366, FAX 011 44 256 479438, telex 858540. **(Subscription address:** Taylor & Francis Inc., 1900 Frost Road, Suite 101, Bristol PA 19007-1598.**) ED** R. E. Trotman (editor's address: Medical Physics Department, Royal Postgraduate Medical School, Ducane Road, London W12 0HS United Kingdom). **LC** R856.A1; J7. **DD** 610/.28. **NLM** W1 JO75C. **CODEN** JMTEDN. **[CCC]. Pr Rev.** available on microfilm from University Microfilms International (UMI). Documents available from Article Express International, The Genuine Article, Ask*IEEE, CASDDS, ADONIS. ***Continues*** *Biomedical Engineering (London, England), 0006-2898.*
**Desc:** An international and independent publication for engineers and scientists, physicians and surgeons, hospital administrators and industry, and all personnel concerned with the effective use of medical devices.
**Ind/Abst** ADONIS; Agric. Eng. Abstr.; BioBusiness; Bioeng. Abstr.; Chem. Abstr.; Curr. Contents Clin. Med.; Curr. Technol. Index; Ei Page One; EMBASE; Energy Res. Abstr. (March 1978-);; Eng. Index Annu.; Health Devices Alerts; Index Med.; INSPEC (Jan. 1977-); Phys. Med. Biol. (19??-19??); Res. Alert [Full Cov.]; Sci. Cit. Index; SCISEARCH.

II/0256-8551
**JOURNAL OF MICROBIAL BIOTECHNOLOGY.** [J. microb. biotechnol.]. **VFOAT** JMB. Vol. 1, No. 1 (Jan. 1986)-. Academic Scholarly Publication. English. sa. $40.00. Biotech Publications, 111/233 Harsh Nagar, Kanpur - 208, 012 UP India. **(Subscription address:** Prints India, 11 Darya Ganj, New Delhi 110002 India.**) NLM** W1; JO762B. **CODEN** JMIBES. Documents available from The Genuine Article, BIOSIS Document Express, CASDDS, Documents on Demand.
**Ind/Abst** Biocont. News Inf. (1991-); Biodeter. Abstr. (1991-); Biol. Abstr. (1987-); Chem. Abstr. (1986-); Curr. Aware. Biol. Sci., CABS; Curr. Biotechnol.; Curr. Contents, Agric. Biol. Environ. Sci.; Environ. Abstr.; PESTDOC; Res. Alert [Full Cov.]; Rev. Med. Vet. Entomol.; SCISEARCH; Sug. Indus. Abstr.

●US
**JPRS REPORT. SCIENCE & TECHNOLOGY. CENTRAL EURASIA, LIFE SCIENCES.** **Added/Corp** United States. Foreign Broadcast Information Service. United States. Joint Publications Research Service. **VFOAT** Science & Technology. Central Eurasia, Life Sciences; Science and Technology. Central Eurasia, Life Sciences; Central Eurasia, Life Sciences; Life Sciences. (14 Jan. 1992)-. Periodical. English (translations available in Russian). ***Continues*** *JPRS Report. Science & Technology. USSR, Life Sciences.*

CI/0352-1311
**JUGOSLAVENSKA MEDICINSKA BIOKEMIJA.** **VFOAT** JMB. (1982)-. Periodical. Serbo-Croatian (Roman). sa. Jugoslovenska Medicinska Biokemija, Petrova 13, 41000 Zagreb Croatia. **UDC** 577. Documents available from CASDDS.
**Ind/Abst** Chem. Abstr.; EMBASE [Select. Cov.].

BE/0368-9697
**MEDELDELINGEN VAN DE FACULTEIT LANDBOUWWETENSCHAPPEN, RIJKSUNIVERSITEIT, GENT.** [Meded. fac. landbouwwet., Rijksuniv., Gent]. **Main/Corp**

Rijksuniversiteit te Gent. Faculteit van de Landbouwwetenschappen. (1970)-. French. qt (4000.00F). Faculteit Landbouwwetenschappen, Coupure 653, B-9000 Ghent Belgium. **Tel** 011 32 91 236961. ***Continues*** *Rijksfaculteit der Landbouwwetenschappen, Ghent. Mededelingen - Rijksfaculteit Landbouwwetenschapen te Gent.*
**Ind/Abst** AGRICOLA; Field Crop Abstr.; Index Vet.; Nematol. Abstr.; Rev. Agric. Entomol.; Vitis Vitic. Enol. Abstr.; Weed Abstr.

UK/0140-0118
**MEDICAL & BIOLOGICAL ENGINEERING & COMPUTING.** [Med. biol. eng. comput.]. **Added/Corp** International Federation for Medical and Biological Engineering. **VFOAT** Medical and Biological Engineering and Computing. **VAT** Medical and Biological Engineering and Computing. Vol. 15 (Jan. 1977)-. Academic Scholarly Publication. English (French and German; summaries and/or abstracts in French and German). bm. £285.00. Peter Peregrinus Ltd, Station House, Nightingale Road, Hitchin Herts, SG5 1RJ England. **Tel** 011 44 438 313311. **(Subscription address:** Peter Prergrinus Ltd / IEE, PO Box 96, Stevenage Herts, SG1 2SD England.**) ED** C. Roberts. **LC** R895.A1; I55. **DD** 610/.28. **NLM** W1 ME168M. **CODEN** MBECDY. **[CCC]. Bk Rev. Ad Acc. Circ:** 1,500. Documents available from Article Express International, The Genuine Article, BIOSIS Document Express, Ask*IEEE, CASDDS. ***Continues*** *Medical & Biological Engineering, 0025-696X.*
**Desc:** Research level publication describing work on medical engineering topics and computer applications.
**Ind/Abst** Bioeng. Abstr.; Biol. Abstr.; Chem. Abstr.; Comput. Inf. Syst. Abstr. J. [Full Cov.]; Curr. Aware. Biol. Sci., CABS; Curr. Contents Eng. Tech. Appl. Sci.; Curr. Contents Life Sci.; Ei Page One; Elect. Comm. Abstr.; EMBASE; Energy Res. Abstr. (March 1978-); Eng. Index Annu.; Ergon. Abstr.; Index Med.; INSPEC (Jan. 1977-); Manuf. Process Eng. Abstr.; Mech. Eng. Abstr.; Life Sci. Collect.; Phys. Med. Biol. (19??-19??); Res. Alert [Full Cov.]; Sci. Cit. Index; SCISEARCH; Soc. Sci. Cit. Index [Select. Cov.].

●US/1063-1178
**MEDICAL & PHARMACEUTICAL BIOTECHNOLOGY ABSTRACTS. See** Medical Science and Technology-Abstracting, Bibliographies and Statistics.

●UK/1350-4533
**MEDICAL ENGINEERING & PHYSICS. Added/Corp** Biological Engineering Society. **VFOAT** Medical Engineering and Physics. Vol. 16, No. 1 (Jan. 1994)-. Periodical. English. Eight times a year. $529.00 The Americas; £355.00 other. Butterworth Heinemann Publishers, Linacre House, Jordan Hill, Oxford OX2 8DP England. **Tel** 011 44 865 310366. **(Subscription address:** Elsevier Science Ltd. Oxford Fulfillment Centre, PO Box 800, Kidlington, Oxford OX5 1DX United Kingdom.**) NLM** W1; ME3101M. **CODEN** MEPHEO. ***Continues*** *Journal of Biomedical Engineering, 0141-5425.*

US/0275-4940
**MEDICAL PRODUCTS MARKETERS DIRECTORY.** ***Title Change.*** (MEDICAL PRODUCTS MARKETERS DIRECTORY : MPMD.). [Med. prod. mark. dir.]. **Added/Corp** Fisher Stevens, Inc. **VFOAT** MPMD. 1st Ed. (1981)-(19??). Directory. English. an. CPS Communications Inc, 7200 West Camino Road, Suite 215, Boca Raton FL 33433. **Tel** (407)368-9301, FAX (407)368-7870. **ED** John C Banghart. **LC** HD9994.U5; M44. **DD** 681/.761/029473. **Ad Acc. Circ:** 1,800. ***Merged into*** *Pharmaceutical Marketers Directory, 0149-0885.*
**Desc:** About 9,000 individuals responsible for marketing medical equipment, instruments, services, and supplies to hospitals, medical groups and laboratories; medical advertising agencies and suppliers; publications.

NE/0047-6552
**MEDICAL PROGRESS THROUGH TECHNOLOGY.** [Med. progr. technol.]. **VFOAT** Medical Progress Technology. Vol. 1 (Mar. 1972)-. Academic Scholarly Publication. English. qt. $396.00. Kluwer Academic Publishers, Postbus 322, 3300 AH Dordrecht, The Netherlands. **Tel** 011 (31) 78 524400, FAX 011 31 78 183273, telex 20083. **ED** H Hutten. **NLM** W1 ME4198. **CODEN** MDPTBG. **[CCC].** Index available in last issue of volume--attached. **Bk Rev. Ad Acc. Pr Rev. Acid Free. Circ:** 1,000. available on microfilm and microfiche from University Microfilms International (UMI). Documents available from Article Express International, The Genuine Article, Ask*IEEE.
**Desc:** Supports the exchange of information between the medical sciences and the engineering and physical sciences. Promotes understanding of interdisciplinary problems originating from applied medicine.
**Ind/Abst** BioBusiness (-1990); Bioeng. Abstr.; Cumul. Index Nurs. Allied Health Lit.; Curr. Contents Clin. Med.; Ei Page One; EMBASE; Energy Res. Abstr. (July 1976-); Eng. Index Annu.; Index Med.; INSPEC (1974-); Life Sci. Collect.; Ref. Upd. Deluxe Ed.; Res. Alert [Full Cov.]; Sci. Cit. Index; SCISEARCH.

US/1065-996X
**MEDICAL TECHNOLOGY STOCK LETTER. See** Business-Investments.

UK/0958-2118
**MEMBRANE TECHNOLOGY.** [Membr. technol.]. (1990)-. Periodical. English. mo. $389.00 The Americas; £261.00 other. Elsevier Advanced Technology, An Imprint of Elsevier Science Ltd., The Boulevard, Langford Lane, Kidlington, Oxford OX5 1GB United Kingdom. **Tel** 011 44 865 843000, 011 44 865 843699, FAX 011 44 865 843010. **(Subscription address:** Elsevier Science Ltd. Oxford Fulfillment Centre, PO Box 800, Kidlington, Oxford OX5 1DX United Kingdom.**) ED** William Lavers. **NLM** W1; ME8937L. **[CCC]. Bk Rev.**
**Ind/Abst** Fluid Abstr., Civil Eng.; Fluid Abstr. Proc. Eng.; FLUIDEX (19??-).

UK
**METHODS IN GENE TECHNOLOGY. VFOAT** Gene Technology. Vol. 1 (1991)-. English. JAI Press Ltd., 28 High Street, Hampton Hill, Middlesex TW12 1PD England. **Tel** 011 44 81 943 9296, FAX 011 44 81 943 9317. **LC** QH442; .M478. **DD** 575.1/0724/05. **NLM** W1; ME9615KG.

UK
**MICROBIAL BIOTECHNOLOGY.** ***Ceased.*** **See** Biology-Microbiology.

●US/1073-6085
**MOLECULAR BIOTECHNOLOGY.** [Mol. biotechnol.]. (1994)-. Periodical. English. bm (6 issues). $195.00 US; $230.00 other; comes also with Applied Biochemistry and Biotechnology $755.00 US; $855.00 other. Humana Press Inc., 999 Riverview Drive, Suite 208, Totawa NJ 07512. **Tel** (201)256-1699, FAX (201)256-8341. **ED** John M. Walker. **LC** IN PROCESS. **DD** 660. **NLM** W1; MO196DB. **CODEN** MLBOEO. ***Separated from*** *Applied Biochemistry and Biotechnology, 0273-2289.*
**Desc:** Publishes the latest detailed laboratory protocols for molecular biology techniques, reviews articles and other information on the application of these techniques in the laboratory.

US/1053-6426
**MOLECULAR MARINE BIOLOGY AND BIOTECHNOLOGY. See** Biology-Marine Biology.

●UK/0958-3165
**NANOBIOLOGY : JOURNAL OF RESEARCH ON NANOSCALE LIVING SYSTEMS. See** Biology-Cytology and Histology.

CN/0384-1820
**NEWSLETTER - CANADIAN MEDICAL AND BIOLOGICAL ENGINEERING SOCIETY. Main/Corp** Canadian Medical and Biological Engineering Society. Began with Jan. 1966? issue. Newsletter. English. ir. Free. Canadian Medical and Biological Engineering Society Wellington Crescent, Winnipeg Manitoba R3M 0A8 Canada. **DD** 610.28/06/271. ctrl circ.

JA/0914-9457
**NIHON JIKI KYOMEI IGAKKAI ZASSHI.** [Nihon Jiki Kyomei Igakkai zasshi]. **VFOAT** Japanese Journal of Magnetic Resonance in Medicine. (1987)-. Academic Scholarly Publication. Multiple languages. qt. Nihon Jiki Kyomei Igakkai, (Japanese Soc. of Magnetic Resonance in Medicine), c/o Chiba Daigaku Igakubu, Hoshasen Igaku Kyoshitsu, 8-1, Inohana 1 Chome, Chibashi, Chibaken 280, Japan. **DD** 616. Documents available from CASDDS. ***Continues*** *NMR Igaku, 0286-1364.*
**Ind/Abst** Chem. Abstr.

KO/1013-9435
**NONGSA SIHOM YON'GU NONMUNJIP. SAENGMYONG KONGHAK P'YON. VFOAT** Research Reports of the Rural Development Administration. Biotechnology; Research Reports of R.D.A., B. (1988)-. Periodical. Multiple languages. ir. Rural Development Administration, Plant Environment Mycology and Farm Products Utilization, Suweon 170 Korea.
**Ind/Abst** Biocont. News Inf.; Crop Physiol. Abstr.; Hortic. Abstr.; Rev. Plant Pathol.; Rice Abstr.; Seed Abstr.

US
**NTIS ALERT. BIOMEDICAL TECHNOLOGY & HUMAN FACTORS ENGINEERING. Added/Corp** United States. National Technical Information Service. (1992)-. Periodical. English. Twenty-four times a year. $145.00 US; $210.00 other. National Technical Information Service - NTIS, Room 2027S, 5285 Port Royal Road, Springfield VA 22161. **Tel** (703)487-4630, (703)487-4660, (703)487-4650, FAX (703)321-8547, telex 89-9405. Index available. ***Continues*** *Biomedical Technology & Human Factors Engineering / NTIS, 0163-1497.*
**Desc:** Provides information on instrumentation and bioengineering, bionics and artificial intelligence, human factors engineering, tissue preservation and storage, etc.

US/0889-616X
**OLSEN'S BIOTECHNOLOGY REPORT.** ***Ceased.*** [Olsen's biotechnol. rep.]. Vol. 1, No. 1 (April 1986)-(19??). Periodical. English. mo. G V Olsen Associates, 123 Picketts Ridge Road, West Redding CT 06896. **Tel** (203)938-4188, FAX (203)938-4186. **ED** Gus Olsen. **DD** 660. **Bk Rev**, (Qty: 12). **Circ:** 150. ***Continues*** *Biotechnology.*
**Desc:** Covers engineering of plants and animals and recombinant DNA gene manipulation.

FR/1146-5034
**PASCAL. 215, BIOTECHNOLOGIES. Added/Corp** Institut de l'Information Scientifique et Technique (France). **VFOAT** Biotechnologies; Biotechnology. No. 1 (1991)-. Periodical. English (French). mo (10 issues with cumulative index). 1655.00F France; 1750.00F other. CNRS / Institut d'Information Scientifique et Technique, (Centre National de la Recherche Scientifique), 15 Quai Anatole France, Paris 75700 France. **Tel** 011 33 1 47531515, telex 299 356 F. **(Subscription address:** Institut de l'Information Scientifique et Technique Diffusion, 2 Allee du Parc de Brabois, 54514 Vandoeuvre Nancy France; (telephone: 011 33 83 504664)**) NLM** ZQ 1; B9355. Index available. cum. index. ***Continues*** *PASCAL Thema. T215, Biotechnologies.*

FR/0761-2311
**PASCAL EXPLORE. E84, GENIE BIOMEDICALE, INFORMATIQUE BIOMEDICALE.** ***Title Change.*** **Added/Corp** Centre National de la Recherche Scientifique (France). Centre de Documentation Scientifique et Technique. **VFOAT** Genie Biomedical, Informatique Biomedicale; Biomedical Engineering, Biomedical Computerized Data Processing. (1984)-. Periodical. French. mo. Institut de l'Information Scientique et Technique (INIST), 2 Allee du Parc de Brabois, 54514 Vandoeuvre Nancy Cedex France. **Tel** 011 33 83 504600, FAX 011 33 83 504650. **NLM** ZQ 1; B936RE. ***Continues*** *Bulletin Signaletique. 310, Genie Biomedical, Informatique Biomedicale, Physique Biomedicale, 0240-852X.*

US/1074-8636
**PHARMACEUTICAL & BIOTECH DAILY.** ***Title Change.*** [Pharm. biotech dly.]. **VFOAT** Pharmaceutical and Biotech Daily. Vol. 1, No. 1 (Jan. 25, 1994)-(Nov. 1994). Periodical. English. da. King Publishing Group, 627 National Press Building, Washington DC 20045. **Tel** (202)638-4260, FAX (202)662-9744. **DD** 615. **CODEN** PBDAEN. ***Formed by the union of*** *Biotech Daily, 1067-1196* ***and*** *Pharmaceutical Daily, 1071-5096.* ***Merged into*** *Washington Drug Letter, 0194-1291.*

US/1071-5096
**PHARMACEUTICAL DAILY.** ***Title Change.*** [Pharm. dly.]. Vol. 1, No. 1 (Mar. 30, 1993)-(199?). Periodical. English. da. King Publishing Group, 627 National Press Building, Washington DC 20045. **Tel** (202)638-4260, FAX (202)662-9744. **DD** 338. ***Merged with*** *Biotech Daily, 1067-1196* ***to form*** *Pharmaceutical and Biotech Daily, 1074-8636.*

PH/0117-0503
**PHILIPPINE JOURNAL OF BIOTECHNOLOGY.** [Philipp. j. biotechnol.]. (1990)-. Periodical. English. sa (June, Dec.). $40.00, $20.00 per copy. BIOTECH-UPLB, College, Lagune 4031, Philippines. **Tel** FAX 63 94 2721. **ED** Reynaldo E. Dela Cruz. **DD** 620.8. Index available. cum. index. **Bk Rev**, (Qty: varies). **Pr Rev. Acid Free. Circ:** 500.

UK/0162-2528
**PHYSICAL TECHNIQUES IN MEDICINE.** [Phys. tech. med.]. V. 1-. English. ir. John Wiley & Sons Ltd., Baffins Lane, Chichester West Sussex PO19 1UD England. **Tel** 0243 779777, FAX 0243 776128 BTG:JWP001, telex 86290 WIBOOKG. **(Subscription address:** North, South and Central America/ John Wiley & Sons, Inc., Subscription Department, 605 Third Avenue, New York, NY 10158-0012, USA; telephone: (212)850-6645; FAX: (212)850-6021**) ED** J T McMullan. **NLM** W1 PH748.

●UK/0967-3334
**PHYSIOLOGICAL MEASUREMENT. Added/Corp** Institute of Physical Sciences in Medicine (Great Britain). Vol. 14, No. 1 (Feb. 1993)-. Periodical. English. qt. $207.00. Institute of Physics, Techno House, Redcliffe Way, Bristol BS1 6NX England. **Tel** 011 44 272 297481, FAX 011 44 272 294318, telex 449149 INSTP G. **(Subscription address:** American Institute of Physics, Publishing Sales, 500 Sunnyside Blvd., Woodbury NY 11797.**) ED** D. H. Evans. **NLM** W1; PH926M. **CODEN** PMEAE3. Index available. ***Continues*** *Clinical Physics and Physiological Measurment., 0143-0815.*
**Desc:** Reports the applications of physical measurement to clinical practice and investigation, and serving the collaborative interests of biomedical engineers, medical physicists and clinical specialists.
**Ind/Abst** Sci. Cit. Index.

# Medical Science and Technology —Biotechnology

UK
**PLANT BIOTECHNOLOGY.** See Biology-Botany.

UK/0260-5902
**PLANT BIOTECHNOLOGY.** See Biology-Botany.

US/1045-4160
**PRECISION MACHINERY. INCORPORATING LIFE SUPPORT TECHNOLOGY.** [Prec. mach. inc. life support technol.]. **VFOAT** Precision Machinery. Vol. 2, No. 2 (1988)-. Periodical. English. qt. $1017.00 (academic institutions), $1586.00 (corporate institutions). Gordon & Breach Science Publishers, Inc., PO Box 786, Cooper Station, New York NY 10276. **Tel** (212)206-8900, **FAX** (212)645-2459. **LC** R856.A1; P73. **DD** 610/.28. **NLM** W1; PR334. **CODEN** PMMNEE. **[CCC]**. *Continues* Precision Machinery, Medical Engineering, and Mechaoptoelectronics, 0741-3327.

YU/0352-9193
**PREHRAMBENO-TEHNOLOSKA I BIOTEHNOLOSKA REVIJA.** See Food and Food Industry.

US/0146-146X
**PROCEEDINGS OF THE ANNUAL AAMI/FDA CONFERENCE ON MEDICAL DEVICE REGULATION.** **Main/Corp** Association for the Advancement of Medical Instrumentation. **VAT** Proceedings of the Annual Association for the Advancement of Medical Instrumentation-Food and Drug Administration Conference on Medical Device Regulation. 1st- 1974-. Proceedings. English. an. **NLM** W3 AS759.

US
**PROCEEDINGS OF THE ANNUAL INTERNATIONAL CONFERENCE OF THE IEEE ENGINEERING IN MEDICINE AND BIOLOGY SOCIETY.** **Main/Corp** IEEE Engineering in Medicine and Biology Society. Conference. 10th (1988)-. Proceedings. English. an. IEEE, Institution of Electrical and Electronics Engineers, Inc., 345 East 47th Street, New York NY 10017-2394. **Tel** (908)981-1393, **FAX** (908)981-9667. *Continues* Proceedings of the ... Annual Conference of the IEEE/Engineering in Medicine and Biology Society. **Ind/Abst** Index IEEE Publ.

UK/0954-4119
**PROCEEDINGS OF THE INSTITUTION OF MECHANICAL ENGINEERS. PART H, JOURNAL OF ENGINEERING IN MEDICINE.** [Proc. Inst. Mech. Eng., H J. eng. med.]. **Added/Corp** Institution of Mechanical Engineers (Great Britain). **VFOAT** Journal of Engineering in Medicine. Vol. 203, No. H1 (1989)-. Proceedings. English. Four times a year (Feb., May, Aug., Nov.). $289.00. Mechanical Engineering Publications, PO Box 24, Northgate Avenue, Bury St. Edmunds, Suffolk IP32 6BW England. **Tel** 011 44 284 763277, telex 817376. **(Subscription address:** Mechanical Engineering Publications / Western Hemisphere Subscriptions, Subscription Office, PO Box 361, Birmingham AL 35201-0361.**)** **ED** D. Dowson. **LC** R856.A1; P76. **NLM** W1; PR5852D. **CODEN** PIHMEQ. **[CCC]**. available on microfilm and microfiche from University Microfilms International (UMI). Documents available from Article Express International, Ask*IEEE. *Continues* Engineering in Medicine (Institution of Mechanical Engineers (Great Britain)), 0046-2039. **Desc:** Objectives of this journal are to record and encourage developments of further work in the field of engineering in medicine; report new work through the publication of research papers in good standing; publish review articles and relevant book reviews; illustrate the development and use of new and improved products and systems in the field of medicine; and much more. **Ind/Abst** Eng. Index Annu.; Health Plan. Adminis.; Hospit. Health Admin. Index (1989-); Index Med. (1989-); INSPEC (1989-).

US/0095-5876
**PROCEEDINGS OF THE SAN DIEGO BIOMEDICAL SYMPOSIUM.** **Main/Conf** San Diego Biomedical Symposium. V. 9- 1970-. Proceedings. English. an. $20.00. San Diego Biomedical Symposium, PO Box 965, San Diego CA 92112. **LC** R856; .S3. **DD** 610/.28. **NLM** W3 SA305. *Continues* San Diego Symposium for Biomedical Engineering Proceedings.

UK
**PROCESS BIOCHEMISTRY.** See Engineering-Chemical Engineering.

●US
**PROGRESS IN BIOCHEMISTRY AND BIOTECHNOLOGY.** See Biology-Biochemistry.

NE/0920-5438
**PROGRESS IN BIOMEDICAL ENGINEERING.** [Prog. biomed. eng.]. Vol. 1 (1984)-. Academic Scholarly Publication. English. ir. Price varies per volume. Elsevier Science Publishers BV, PO Box 211, 1000 AE Amsterdam Netherlands. **Tel** 011 31 20 5803642, **FAX** 011 31 20 5862696, telex 15682. **(Subscription address:** Elsevier Science Inc. / New York Books, 655 Avenue of the Americas, New York NY 10010.**)** **NLM** W1; PR666M. **CODEN** PRBEEZ. Documents available from BIOSIS Document Express, CASDDS. **Ind/Abst** Biol. Abstr.; Chem. Abstr. (1984-).

US
**RAFI COMMUNIQUE / RURAL ADVANCEMENT FUND INTERNATIONAL.** See Agriculture.

US/0196-0229
**RECOMBINANT DNA TECHNICAL BULLETIN.** Ceased. [Recomb. DNA tech. bull.]. **VAT** Recombinant Deoxyribonucleic Acid Technical Bulletin. (Summer 1977)-(1993). Academic Scholarly Publication. English. qt. Superintendent of Documents, US Government Printing Office, Washington DC 20402. **Tel** (202)275-3328, **FAX** (202)786-2377. **LC** QH442. **DD** 574.87/3282. **NLM** W1 RE1109I. **CODEN** RDTBD5. Documents available from BIOSIS Document Express, CASDDS. *Continues* Nucleic Acid Recombinant Scientific Memoranda, 0190-0714. **Desc:** Provides scientific information and reports on recent progress in DNA research in the U.S. and abroad and a periodically updated listing of hostvector systems certified by NIH. **Ind/Abst** BioBusiness; Biol. Abstr.; Biol. Dig.; Chem. Abstr.; Chem. Hazards Ind.; Curr. Biotechnol.; EMBASE; Index Med.; Lab. Hazards Bull.

CN/1183-7454
**REHABILITATION TECHNOLOGY.** [Rehabil. technol.]. **Added/Corp** University of New Brunswick. Institute of Biomedical Engineering. **VFOAT** Technologie de la Readaption. Vol. 1, No. 1 (Spring 1991)-. Periodical. English (French). sa. Limited free distribution. Institute of Biomedical Engineering, University of New Brunswick, PO Box 4400, Fredericton New Brunswick E3B 5A3 Canada. **DD** 610/.28. **NLM** W1; RE1763.

CN/1183-7454
**REHABILITATION TECHNOLOGY.** (TECHNOLOGIE DE LA READAPTION.). [Rehabil. technol.]. **Added/Corp** University of New Brunswick. Institute of Biomedical Engineering. **VFOAT** Rehabilitation Technology. Vol. 1, No 1 (Spring 1991)-. Periodical. French (English). sa. Limited free distribution. Institute of Biomedical Engineering, University of New Brunswick, PO Box 4400, Fredericton New Brunswick E3B 5A3 Canada. **DD** 610/.28.

UK/0961-6071
**REPORT / IGER.** See Agriculture.

●US/1068-3682
**RUSSIAN BIOTECHNOLOGY.** (1993)-. Periodical. English (translations available in Russian). Twelve times a year. $675.00. Allerton Press, Inc., 150 Fifth Avenue, New York NY 10011. **Tel** (212)924-3950, **FAX** (212)463-9684, telex 427441 ALPRES. **NLM** W1; BI9189. **[CCC]**. *Continues* Biotekhnologiia. English. Soviet Biotechnology, 0890-734X.

US/1052-6781
**SAAS BULLETIN, BIOCHEMISTRY AND BIOTECHNOLOGY.** [SAAS bull. biochem. biotechnol.]. **Added/Corp** Southern Association of Agricultural Scientists. Biochemistry and Biotechnology. **VFOAT** SAAS Bulletin of Biochemistry and Biotechnology. Vol. 1 (Jan. 1988)-. Bulletin. English. **DD** 630. **NLM** W1; SA104K. Documents available from CASDDS. **Ind/Abst** AgBiotech News Inf.; AGRICOLA [Select. Cov.]; Biodeter. Abstr.; Chem. Abstr.; Hortic. Abstr.; Index Vet.; Maize Abstr.; Plant Breed. Abstr.; Rev. Agric. Entomol.

KO/1016-0884
**SAENGHWAHAK NYUSU.** **VFOAT** Biochemistry News; Saenghwahak Hoe Nyusu. (19??)-. Periodical. Multiple languages. **UDC** 577.1. Documents available from CASDDS. **Ind/Abst** Chem. Abstr.

US/1053-6868
**SECOND SOURCE BIOMEDICAL.** Title Change. [Second source biomed.]. **VFOAT** Biomedical. Vol. 1, No. 1 (May 1990)-(1993). Periodical. English. bm. Second Source Publications Inc., PO Box 930, Portsmouth RI 02871. **Tel** (401)683-7470. **DD** 338. Documents available from The Genuine Article. *Continues in part* Second Source, 0892-3426. *Continued by* Biomedical Technology Management, 1073-1210. **Ind/Abst** Res. Alert.

●JA/0919-3758
**SEIBUTSU KOGAKKAI SHI / SEIBUTSU-KOGAKU KAISHI.** **Added/Corp** Nihon Seibutsu Kogakkai. **VFOAT** Seibutsu-Kogaku Kaishi. (1993)-. Periodical. Japanese (summaries and/or abstracts in English; table of contents in English). Six times a year. $326.00. Nihon Hakko Kogakkai, (Society of Fermentation Technology, Japan), Osaka Daigaku Kogakubu, 2-1, Yamadaoka, Suitashi, Osakafu 565 Japan. **(Subscription address:** Kyowa Book Company Inc., 1 38 Kanda Jinbocho Chiyoda-ku, Tokyo 101 Japan.**)** **CODEN** SEKAEA. *Continues* Hakko Kogakkai shi, 0385-6151. **Ind/Abst** Chem. Abstr.

CC/1000-3061
**SHENGWU GONGCHENG XUEBAO.** (SHENG WU KUNG CHENG HSUEH PAO.). [Shengwu gongcheng xuebao]. **Added/Corp** Chung-Kuo Wei Sheng Wu Hsueh Hui. Kuo Chia Ko Wei Sheng Wu Kung Cheng Kai Fa Chung Hsin (China). **VFOAT** Chinese Journal of Biotechnology. (198?)-. Academic Scholarly Publication. Chinese (summaries and/or abstracts in English). qt. $66.80. Science Press, 16 Donghuangchenggen North Street, Beijing 100707, People's Republic of China. **Tel** 011 86 1 4019821, 011 86 1 4010642, **FAX** 011 86 1 4012180, 011 86 1 4019810, telex 210147. **LC** IN PROCESS. **CODEN** SGXUED. **Ad Acc. Pr Rev. Circ:** 6,000. Documents available from CASDDS. **Desc:** Covers research papers on genetic, fermentation, cell and enzyme engineering. **Ind/Abst** Chem. Abstr.

CC/1000-8543
**SHENGWU HUAXUE ZAZHI.** (SHENG WU HUA HSUEH TSA CHIH.). [Shengwu huaxue zazhi]. **Added/Corp** Chung-Kuo Sheng Wu Hua Hsueh Hui. **VFOAT** Chinese Biochemical Journal. (1985)-. Periodical. Chinese (summaries and/or abstracts in English; table of contents in English). bm. Beijing Yike Daxue / Shengwu Huaxue Xi, Beijing Medical University, Department of Biochemistry, No. 38, Xueyuan Lu, Beijing 100083, People's Republic of China. **Tel** 861 2091416, **FAX** 861 2015681. **ED** C. Changying. **NLM** W1; SH287M. **CODEN** SHZAE4. **Bk Rev. Ad Acc. Pr Rev.** Documents available from BLDSC, CASDDS. **Ind/Abst** Chem. Abstr.

US/0743-8656
**SMALL COMPUTERS IN BIOMEDICAL RESEARCH.** Academic Scholarly Publication. English. mo. Elsevier Science Publishing Company Inc, Madison Square Station, PO Box 882, New York NY 10159-0882. **Tel** (212)633-3950, **FAX** (212)633-3990.

FR/0295-1967
**SPECTRA BIOLOGIE.** Vol. 14 No. 116 (Nov./Dec. 1986)-. Academic Scholarly Publication. French (summaries and/or abstracts in English). Nineteen times a year. 390.00F France; 560.00F other. Editions PCI, BP 268, 54512 Vandoeuvre Cedex France. **Tel** 011 33 83 412335, **FAX** 011 83 414353. **NLM** W1; SP314F. Documents available from CASDDS. *Continues* Spectra 2000 Biologie. **Ind/Abst** Anal. Abstr.; Chem. Abstr.

US/1055-7318
**STRATEGIC DEVELOPMENTS IN BIOTECHNOLOGY / NORTH CAROLINA BIOTECHNOLOGY CENTER.** [Strateg. dev. biotechnol.]. **Added/Corp** North Carolina Biotechnology Center. Information Division. Vol. 1, No. 1 (Feb. 1991)-. Periodical. English. mo. $250.00. North Carolina Biotechnology Center, PO Box 13547, Research Triangle Park NC 27709-3547. **DD** 620.

SZ/0253-9675
**SWISS BIOTECH.** **Added/Corp** Swiss Coordination Committee for Biotechnology. (198?)-. Periodical. English (French, Italian and Spanish). Six times a year (Feb., Apr., June, Aug., Oct., Dec.). 100.00F Switzerland; 120.00F Europe; 200.00F other. Verlag Dr Felix Wuest AG, Seestrasse 5/Postfach, CH-8700 Kuesnacht Switzerland. **Tel** 011 41 1 9110055, **FAX** (01)9106080, telex 825705. **NLM** W1; SW406G. **CODEN** SWBIED. **Desc:** Information medium of the Swiss Coordination Committee for biotechnology. **Ind/Abst** Curr. Biotechnol.; PESTDOC.

US/0741-3661
**TECHNICAL INSIGHTS ANNUAL REPORT ON GENETIC TECHNOLOGY.** [Tech. Insights annu. rep. genet. technol.]. **Added/Corp** Technical Insights, Inc. **VFOAT** Annual Report on Genetic Technology. (1984)-. English. qt. Free on request. Technical Insights Inc., PO Box 1304, Fort Lee NJ 07024-9967. **Tel** (201)568-4744, **FAX** (201)568-8247, telex 425900 SWIFT UI. **LC** TP248.6; .T42. **DD** 660/.6.

IT
**TECNOLOGIE BIOMEDICHE.** See Medical Science and Technology-Hospital Administration and Medical Centers.

UK/0140-0835
**TOPICS IN ENZYME AND FERMENTATION BIOTECHNOLOGY.** ***Ceased.*** [Top. enzyme ferment. biotechnol.]. V. 1-(1977)-Ceased with Vol 10. Academic Scholarly Publication. English. an. John Wiley & Sons Ltd., Baffins Lane, Chichester West Sussex PO19 1UD England. **Tel** 0243 779777, FAX 0243 776128 BTG:JWP001, telex 86290 WIBOOKG. **(Subscription address:** North, South and Central America/ John Wiley & Sons, Inc., PO Box 7247-8491, Philadelphia, PA 19170-8491**)** **LC** TP248.3. **DD** 660/.63. **NLM** W1 TO539LP. **CODEN** TEFBDW. Documents available from BIOSIS Document Express, CASDDS.
**Ind/Abst** AGRICOLA [Select. Cov.]; Biol. Abstr.; Biotechnol. Res. Abstr.; Chem. Abstr.; Food Sci. Technol. Abstr.; Life Sci. Collect.; PESTDOC.

CN
**TORONTO BIOSCAN.** English. qt. Toronto Biotechnology Initiative, PO Box 446, Station A, Toronto, Ontario M5W 1C2 Canada.
**Ind/Abst** Abstr. BioCommer.

●US/1051-9688
**TRANSGENICA (LEVITTOWN, PA).** (TRANSGENICA : THE JOURNAL OF CLINICAL BIOTECHNOLOGY.). [Transgenica]. **Added/Corp** Pharmaceutical Information Associates. Vol. 1, No. 1 (Spring 1994)-. Periodical. English. Four times a year. $60.00. Pharmaceutical Information Associates, Ltd., 2761 Trenton Road, Levittown PA 19056. **Tel** (215)949-0490. **DD** 660. **NLM** W1; TR228WT.

US/1061-6314
**TRENDS, BIOTECHNOLOGY : INFORMATION AND ISSUES FOR PHARMACISTS.** **See** Pharmacy and Pharmacology.

NE/0167-7799
**TRENDS IN BIOTECHNOLOGY (PERSONAL EDITION).** (TRENDS IN BIOTECHNOLOGY.). [Trends biotechnol.]. Vol. 1, No. 1 (March/April 1983)-. Academic Scholarly Publication. English. mo. 110.00. Elsevier Science Publishers BV, PO Box 211, 1000 AE Amsterdam Netherlands. **Tel** 011 31 20 5803642, FAX 011 31 20 5862696, telex 15682. **ED** J. Hodgson. **LC** TP248.13. **DD** 660/.6/05. **NLM** W1 TR3407. **CODEN** TRBIDM. **[CCC]. Bk Rev. Ad Acc. Circ:** 4,000. available in microform from University Microfilms International (UMI). Documents available from The Genuine Article, CASDDS.
**Desc:** Provides ideas and opinions on all facets of biotechnology from cell culture; gene cloning, protoplast fusion, and screening through fermentation technology, raw materials formulation and immobilization techniques, to down-stream processing and purification.
**Ind/Abst** Abstr. BioCommer.; AgBiotech News Inf.; BioBusiness; Biodeter. Abstr.; Biotechnol. Res. Abstr.; Chem. Abstr. (1983-); CSA Neuro. Abstr. (?-?); Curr. Aware. Biol. Sci., CABS; Curr. Contents, Agric. Biol. Environ. Sci.; EMBASE; Food Sci. Technol. Abstr.; Genet. Abstr.; Maize Abstr.; Microbiol. Abstr. Sect. B; Microbiol. Abstr. Sect. A; Nematol. Abstr.; Oncog. Growth Factors Abstr.; Life Sci. Collect.; Plant Breed. Abstr.; Plant Grow. Reg. Abstr.; Protozoolog. Abstr.; Res. Alert [Full Cov.]; Rice Abstr.; Sci. Cit. Index; SCISEARCH; Seed Abstr.; Soils Fert.; Soyabean Abstr.

NE/0167-9430
**TRENDS IN BIOTECHNOLOGY (REFERENCE ED.).** (TRENDS IN BIOTECHNOLOGY.). [Trends biotechnol.]. Vol. 1 (1983)-. Periodical. English. mo. $514.00 The Americas; £345.00 other. Elsevier Trends Journals, An Imprint of Elsevier Science Ltd., The Boulevard, Langford Lane, Kidlington, Oxford OX5 1GB United Kingdom. **Tel** 011 44 865 843000, 011 44 865 843699, FAX 011 44 865 843010. **(Subscription address:** Elsevier Science Ltd. Oxford Fulfillment Centre, PO Box 800, Kidlington, Oxford OX5 1DX United Kingdom.**)** **LC** TP248.13; .T743. **DD** 660/.6. **[CCC]. Pr Rev.** available on microfilm and microfiche from University Microfilms International (UMI). Documents available from Article Express International, ADONIS.
**Ind/Abst** ADONIS; AGRICOLA [Select. Cov.]; Curr. Biotechnol.; Curr. Contents, Agric. Biol. Environ. Sci.; Ei Page One; EMBASE; Eng. Index Annu. [Select. Cov.]; Index Vet.; PESTDOC; Ref. Upd. Deluxe Ed.

●US/1066-2936
**UNDERSEA & HYPERBARIC MEDICINE.** (UNDERSEA & HYPERBARIC MEDICINE : JOURNAL OF THE UNDERSEA AND HYPERBARIC MEDICAL SOCIETY.). [Undersea hyperb. med.]. **Added/Corp** Undersea and Hyperbaric Medical Society. **VFOAT** Undersea and Hyperbaric Medicine. (1993)-. Periodical. English. qt. $85.00. Undersea and Hyperbaric Medical Society, 10531 Metropolitan Avenue, Kensington MD 20895. **Tel** (301)942-2980. **DD** 616. **CODEN** UHMEE7. Documents available from BIOSIS Document Express. ***Formed by the union of*** *Undersea Biomedical Research, 0093-5387* ***and*** *Journal of Hyperbaric Medicine, 0884-1225.*
**Ind/Abst** Biol. Abstr.; Curr. Contents Life Sci.; Sci. Cit. Index; Soc. Sci. Cit. Index [Select. Cov.].

US/0093-5387
**UNDERSEA BIOMEDICAL RESEARCH.** ***Title Change.*** [Undersea biomed. res.]. **Added/Corp** Undersea Medical Society. Undersea and Hyperbaric Medical Society. Vol. 1 (Mar. 1974)-(199?). Periodical. English. qt. Undersea and Hyperbaric Medical Society, 10531 Metropolitan Avenue, Kensington MD 20895. **Tel** (301)942-2980. **ED** Hugh VanLiew. **LC** RC1000; .U5. **DD** 616.9/8022/05. **NLM** W1; UN103D. **CODEN** UBMRAY. Index available. **Bk Rev. Ad Acc. Pr Rev. Circ:** 1,800 (ctrl). available on microfilm and microfiche from University Microfilms International (UMI). Documents available from The Genuine Article, BIOSIS Document Express, CASDDS. ***Merged with*** *Journal of Hyperbaric Medicine, 0884-1225;* ***Absorbed by*** *Undersea & Hyperbaric Medicine, 1066-2936.*
**Desc:** Scientific journal covering areas of diving research, and physiology, hyperbaric medicine and oxygen therapy, submarine and naval medicine and clinical research.
**Ind/Abst** Aquat. Sci. Fish. Abstr. (Computer File); Biol. Abstr.; Chem. Abstr.; CSA Neuro. Abstr. (?-?); Curr. Contents Life Sci.; EMBASE; Energy Res. Abstr. (March 1982-); Index Med.; Ocean. Abstr.; Life Sci. Collect.; Psychol. Abstr. (1974-); PsycINFO (?-?); PsycLit; Res. Alert [Full Cov.]; Sci. Cit. Index (19??-19??); SCISEARCH; SportSearch.

US/1078-2893
**UNIVERSITY BIOMED WEEKLY.** (19??)-. English. wk (48 issues). $995.00 US, Canada and Mexico; $1195.00 other. CW Henderson, PO Box 5528, Atlanta GA 30307-0528. **Tel** (404)377-8895, FAX (404)378-5411. **(Subscription address:** CW Henderson, Subscription Office, PO Box 830409, Birmingham AL 35283-0409.**)**
**Desc:** Bridges the research tracks of academia and industry. Geared toward both university-based researchers interested in pharmaceutical industry involvement in biomedical research, as well as pharmaceutical professionals interested in biotech activities at universities.

US/1047-4730
**WORLD BIO LICENSING & PATENT REPORT.** [World bio licens. pat. rep.]. **VFOAT** World Bio Licensing and Patent Report; World Biolicensing & Patent Report; World Biolicensing and Patent Report. (198?)-. Periodical. English. mo. Deborah Mysiewicz Publishers, PO Box 2009, Oak Harbor WA 98277. **Tel** (415)689-2972. **DD** 574. **NLM** W1; NO849L. ***Continues*** *World Biolicensing Report, 0883-5527.*

UK
**WORLD BIOTECH REPORT.** English. ir. Online Publications, Blenheim House, Ash Hill Drive, Pinner Middlesex HA5 2AE England. **Tel** 011 44 81 868 4466.
**Ind/Abst** PESTDOC.

UK/0959-3993
**WORLD JOURNAL OF MICROBIOLOGY & BIOTECHNOLOGY.** **See** Biology-Microbiology.

CC/1001-8689
**ZHONGGUO KANGSHENGSU ZAZHI.** **See** Pharmacy and Pharmacology.

---

## CARDIOLOGY

---

FR/0763-7446
**ABSTRACT CARDIO PARIS.** [Abstr. cardio Paris]. **VFOAT** Abstract Cardio Hebdo. (1985)-. Periodical. French. wk. 269.34F France; 475.00F other. Abstract, 25 Bis Av Pierre Grenier, 92100 Boulogne Billanct France. **Tel** 011 33 1 49100606. **UDC** 616.12.

●US/1062-1458
**ACC CURRENT JOURNAL REVIEW.** (ACC CURRENT JOURNAL REVIEW / AMERICAN COLLEGE OF CARDIOLOGY.). [ACC curr. j. rev.]. **Added/Corp** American College of Cardiology. **VFOAT** Current Journal Review. **VAT** American College of Cardiology Current Journal Review. Vol. 1, No. 1 (Nov./Dec. 1992)-. Academic Scholarly Publication. English. bm (1 volume). $125.00 US; $165.00 other. Elsevier Science Publishing Company Inc, Madison Square Station, PO Box 882, New York NY 10159-0882. **Tel** (212)633-3950, FAX (212)633-3990. **DD** 378. **NLM** W1; AC588. **[CCC].**

US
**ACCEL.** **Added/Corp** American College of Cardiology. Vol. 4, No. 10 (1972)-. Periodical. English. Twelve times a year. $125.00 North America, $155.00 other (member); $150.00 North America, $180.00 other (non-member). American College of Cardiology, ACCEL Department, PO Box 79231, Baltimore MD 21279-9745. **Tel** (800)253-4636, (301)897-5400, FAX (301)887-9745. ***Continues*** *Access.*

US
**ACCEL. SUPPLEMENT.** (1973)-. English. ir. $12.00 (No. 53). American College of Cardiology, ACCEL Department, PO Box 79231, Baltimore MD 21279-9745. **Tel** (800)253-4636, (301)897-5400, FAX (301)887-9745.

US/1041-7974
**ACLS ALERT.** [ACLS alert]. **Added/Corp** American Health Consultants. **VAT** Advanced Cardiac Life Support Alert. (1988)-. Periodical. English. mo. $179.00 (without Continuing Medical Education credits); $229.00 (with Continuing Medical Education credits). American Health Consultants, 3525 Piedmont Road, Suite 400, Atlanta GA 30305. **Tel** (800)688-2421, (404)262-7436. **(Subscription address:** American Health Consultants, PO Box 95278, Chicago IL 60694.**)** **DD** 616. **NLM** W1; AC732.
**Desc:** Features six to ten concise articles covering the full range of acute care concerns. Enables readers to stay on top of advances in acute cardiac medicine in little more than an hour each month.

BE/0001-5385
**ACTA CARDIOLOGICA.** [Acta cardiol.]. Vol. 1 (1946)-. Academic Scholarly Publication. English. bm. 2300F (Belgium); 3100F (other). Association Soc Scientifique Med Belguim, Avenue Circulaire 138A, B 1180 Brussels Belgium. **Tel** 011 32 2 3745158, FAX 011 32 2 3749628. **ED** J Lequime, H Kesteloot. **NLM** W1 AC775. **CODEN** ACCAAQ. Index available. **Bk Rev. Ad Acc. Pr Rev. Circ:** 1,000 (ctrl). Documents available from The Genuine Article, BIOSIS Document Express, CASDDS. ***Supersedes*** *Bulletin de la Societe Belge de Cardiologie.*
**Desc:** Devoted to the study of cardiovascular diseases. Publishes original papers about physiology, anatomy and clinics.
**Ind/Abst** Biol. Abstr.; Chem. Abstr.; Curr. Contents Clin. Med.; EMBASE; Index Med.; Int. Aerosp. Abstr.; Life Sci. Collect.; PESTDOC; Res. Alert [Select. Cov.]; SCISEARCH; SportSearch.

IT/0392-9698
**ACTA CARDIOLOGICA MEDITERRANEA.** (ARCHIVIO SICILIANO DI MEDICINA E CHIRURGIA. N.3, P.ACTA CARDIOLOGICA MEDITERRANEA.). [Acta cardiol. mediterr.]. **VFOAT** Acta Cardiologica Mediterranea. (1983)-. Periodical. Italian (English). Three times a year. L40000 Italy; L60000 other. Edizioni Carbone Alfonsa, Via G Daita 29, 90139 Palermo Italy. **Tel** 011 39 91 321273, FAX 39 91 322736. **ED** A. Strano and A. Di Benedetto. **NLM** W1; AR597TB. Index available. cum. index. **Bk Rev. Ad Acc.** ctrl circ. available on diskette. ***Separated from*** *Archivio Siciliano di Medicina e Chirurgia, 0392-2049.*

BE/0373-7934
**ACTA CARDIOLOGICA. SUPPLEMENTUM.** [Acta cardiol., Suppl.]. No. 1 (1946)-. Academic Scholarly Publication. French (English). ir. Included with subscription to Acta Cardiologica. Association Soc Scientifique Med Belguim, Avenue Circulaire 138A, B 1180 Brussels Belgium. **Tel** 011 32 2 3745158, FAX 011 32 2 3749628. **NLM** W1 AC7752. **CODEN** ACRSCL. Documents available from BIOSIS Document Express, CASDDS.
**Ind/Abst** Biol. Abstr.; Chem. Abstr.; EMBASE; Health Plan. Adminis.; Index Med.; Int. Aerosp. Abstr.

FR
**ACTUALITES D'ANGEIOLOGIE.** [Actual. angeiol.]. (1978)-. French. mo (except July and Aug.). 293.83F France; 350.00F other. Editions Medicales DHR, 1 Allee des Noisetiers, Bos Postale 43, 92145 Clamart Cedex France. **Tel** 011 33 1 46428182, FAX 011 33 1 146440885. **(Subscription address:** PDG Communications, 30 rue d Armaille, 75017 Paris France.**)** ***Continues*** *Actualites d'Angeiologie et de Pathologie Vasculaire, 0397-2003.*

FR/0997-7287
**ACTUALITIES MEDICALES INTERNATIONALES. HYPERTENSION.** **VFOAT** Hypertension. Vol. 1, No. 1 (Jan. 1989)-. Periodical. French. Ten times a year (Except July & Aug.). 342.80F France; 450.00F others. Medica Press International, 14 Rue de Silly, 92000 Boulogne France. **Tel** 011 33 1 48251110. **NLM** W1; AC993R.

SP
**ACTUALIZACIONES TERAPEUTICAS EN CARDIOLOGIA.** Spanish. bm. 6360.00ptas. Aran Ediciones SA, Avda General Peron, 20 5 DCHA, 28020 Madrid Spain. **Tel** 011 34 1 5332525.

US/0889-5074
**ADVANCES IN CARDIAC SURGERY.** **See** Medical Science and Technology-Surgery.

SZ/0065-2326
**ADVANCES IN CARDIOLOGY.** [Adv. cardiol.]. Vol. 4 (1970)-. Academic Scholarly Publication. English. an. 190.00F (approx. per volume). S. Karger AG, Allschwilerstrasse 10, PO Box - Postfach - Case Postale, CH-4009 Basel Switzerland. **Tel** 011 41 61 306-1111, FAX 011 41 61 306-1234, telex CH 962 652. **ED** J. J. Kellermann. **LC** RC681.A25; A38. **NLM** W1 AD53C.

**CODEN** ACDYB2. **[CCC].** Documents available from BIOSIS Document Express, CASDDS. ***Continues*** *Fortschritte der Kardiologie.*
**Desc:** This series records international symposia devoted to problems of current importance to clinical and preventive cardiology. Each volume is a collection of critical reviews designed to distinguish current fads from genuine advances. Receiving special emphasis are diagnostic and therapeutic concerns relating to non-invasive techniques, cardiac pharmacology, coronary artery disease, congenital heart disease, drugs, diet, and exercise.
**Ind/Abst** Biol. Abstr.; Chem. Abstr. (1970-1982); Cumul. Index Nurs. Allied Health Lit.; EMBASE; Health Plan. Adminis.; Index Med.; Ref. Upd. Deluxe Ed.; SportSearch.

SZ/0378-6900
**ADVANCES IN CARDIOVASCULAR PHYSICS.** **See** Biology-Biophysics.

US/0272-9237
**ADVANCES IN CLINICAL CARDIOLOGY.** ***Ceased.*** [Adv. clin. cardiol.]. Vol. 1- ?. Academic Scholarly Publication. English. ir. Yorke Medical Books, 666 5th Avenue, New York NY 10103. **Tel** (212)605-9400. **ED** H W Heiss. **NLM** W1 AD539. **CODEN** ACCADT. Documents available from CASDDS.
**Ind/Abst** Chem. Abstr. (1980-).

●US/1056-618X
**ADVANCES IN HYPERTENSION.** [Adv. hypertens.]. **Added/Corp** American Heart Association. Council for High Blood Pressure Research (American Heart Association). (1992)-. Periodical. English. $49.95. J.B. Lippincott Company, 227 East Washington Square, Philadelphia PA 19106-3780. **Tel** (215)238-4200 or 4454, FAX (215)238-4227. **DD** 616. **NLM** W1; AD645.

SZ/0065-2938
**ADVANCES IN MICROCIRCULATION.** ***Ceased.*** [Adv. microcirc.]. Vol. 1 (1968)-(19??). English. an. S. Karger AG, Allschwilerstrasse 10, PO Box - Postfach - Case Postale, CH-4009 Basel Switzerland. **Tel** 011 41 61 306-1111, FAX 011 41 61 306-1234, telex CH 962 652. **ED** B M Altura. **LC** QP101; .A33. **DD** 574.1/1. **NLM** W1 AD682. **CODEN** ADVMBT. **[CCC].** Documents available from BIOSIS Document Express, CASDDS.
**Desc:** Creates new bases for understanding how the microcirculation is involved in various states of health and disease. Acquaints the reader with the main directions in circulatory research. Information on the various techniques now available to study the microcirculation; illustrations included.
**Ind/Abst** Biol. Abstr.; Chem. Abstr.; Ref. Upd. Deluxe Ed.

US/0146-8790
**ADVANCES IN THE MANAGEMENT OF CLINICAL HEART DISEASE.** (1976)-. Monographic series. English. ir. Price varies per volume. Futura Publishing Company Inc., 135 Bedford Road, PO Box 418, Armonk NY 10504-0418. **Tel** (914)273-1014, (800)877-8761, FAX (914)273-1015, (914)273-1016. **ED** J. I. Haft and C. P. Bailey. **LC** RC681.A1; A53. **DD** 616.1/2. **NLM** W1 AD8793.

US
**ALTSCHUL SYMPOSIA SERIES.** Vol. 1 (1991)-. Monographic series. English. ir. Price varies per volume. Plenum Press, 233 Spring Street, New York NY 10013-1578. **Tel** (212)620-8000, (800)221-9369, FAX (212)463-0742, (212)807-1047, telex 23/421139. **NLM** W1; AL996J.

US/0002-8703
**AMERICAN HEART JOURNAL, THE.** [Am. heart j.]. **Added/Corp** American Heart Association. Vol. 1 (Oct. 1925)-. Academic Scholarly Publication. English. mo. $213.00 (institutions), $109.00 (individuals) US; $243.00 (institutions), $139.00 (individuals) other. Mosby Year Book Inc., 11830 Westline Industrial Drive, St Louis MO 63146. **Tel** (800)325-4177, (314)872-8370, FAX (314)432-1380, telex 44-2402. **ED** Dean T. Mason. **LC** RC681.A1; A58. **DD** 616.1/2/005. **NLM** W1 AM423. **CODEN** AHJOA2. **[CCC].** Index available. **Ad Acc. Pr Rev. Circ:** 12,107. available on microfilm and microfiche from University Microfilms International (UMI). Documents available from The Genuine Article, BIOSIS Document Express, CASDDS, ADONIS.
**Desc:** Serves practicing cardiologists, university-affiliated clinicians who lecture and treat, and other physicians who want to keep abreast of significant developments in the diagnosis and management of cardiovascular disease.
**Ind/Abst** Abr. Index Med.; ADONIS; Annals Behav. Med.; Biol. Abstr.; Biol. Dig.; Chem. Abstr.; Curr. Aware. Biol. Sci., CABS; Curr. Contents Clin. Med.; Curr. Contents Life Sci.; Dairy Sci. Abstr.; EMBASE; Energy Res. Abstr.; Health Devices Alerts; Health Period. Database; Health Plan. Adminis.; Index Med.; INIS Atomindex [Micro.]; Int. Aerosp. Abstr.; Iowa Drug Inf. Serv. (1967-); J. Watch (-199?); Med. Abstr. Newsl.; Mod. Med.; Nutr. Abstr. Rev., Ser. B, Live Feeds and Feed.; Nutr. Abstr. Rev., Ser. A, Hum. Exp.; Nutr. Res. Newsl.; Life Sci. Collect.; PESTDOC; Physic. Medline Plus; Protozoolog. Abstr.; Ref. Upd. Basic Ed.; Ref. Upd. Clinical Ed.; Ref. Upd. Deluxe Ed.; Res. Alert [Full Cov.]; Rev. Med. Vet. Mycology; Risk Abstr.; Saf. Health Work; Sci. Cit. Index; SCISEARCH; Soc. Sci. Cit. Index [Select. Cov.]; SPORT Discus; SportSearch; Stat. Theory Method Abstr. (1959-1963); Trop. Dis. Bull.

US/0887-7971
**AMERICAN JOURNAL OF CARDIAC IMAGING.** [Am. j. card. imaging]. Vol. 1, No. 1 (Jan. 1987)-. Academic Scholarly Publication. English. qt (Jan., Apr., July, Oct.). $99.00 (individual), $123.00 (institution), $59.00 (student) US; $167.00 (individual), $176.00 (institution) other. W.B. Saunders Company, A Subsidiary of Harcourt Brace Jovanovich, Inc., The Curtis Center/Suite 300, Independence Square West, Philadelphia PA 19106-3399. **Tel** (215)238-7800 or, 5587, FAX (215)238-7883, telex 173146. **(Subscription address:** W. B. Saunders Company / North America Subscriptions, c/o Periodicals, 6277 Sea Harbour Drive, 4th Floor, Orlando FL 32887.**) ED** James V. Talano. **DD** 616. **NLM** W1; AM448Y. **CODEN** AJCIEZ. **[CCC].** Index available. cum. index. **Bk Rev. Ad Acc. Pr Rev. Circ:** 1,500. Documents available from BIOSIS Document Express, CASDDS.
**Desc:** Presents original contributions, selected case reports, and state-of-the-art review articles related to two-dimensional and Doppler echo-cardiography, digital angiography, magnetic resonance imaging, PET and CAT scanning, radionuclide techniques, and related modalities.
**Ind/Abst** Biol. Abstr. (1990-); Chem. Abstr. (?-1989); EMBASE.

US/0002-9149
**AMERICAN JOURNAL OF CARDIOLOGY, THE.** [Am. j. cardiol.]. **Added/Corp** American College of Cardiology. Vol. 1 (Jan. 1958)-. Academic Scholarly Publication. English. sm (24 issues). $125.00 (institutions), $75.00 (individuals). Excerpta Medica / US, PO Box 3085, Princeton NJ 08543-3085. **Tel** (908)874-8550, FAX (908)874-5611. **(Subscription address:** American Journal of Cardiology, PO Box 7722, Riverton NJ 08077-7722.**) ED** Margaret Phelan. **LC** RC681.A1; A565. **DD** 616.105. **NLM** W1 AM449. **CODEN** AJCDAG. **Pr Rev.** available on microfilm and microfiche from University Microfilms International (UMI). Documents available from The Genuine Article, BIOSIS Document Express, CASDDS. ***Supersedes*** *Transactions of the American College of Cardiology.*
**Desc:** Explores and highlights advances in diagnosis and treatment of cardiovascular diseases. Articles stress the practical, clinical approach to cardiology.
**Ind/Abst** Abr. Index Med.; AGRICOLA; Annals Behav. Med.; Biol. Abstr.; Biol. Dig.; Calcium Calcif. Tissue Abstr.; Chem. Abstr.; CSA Neuro. Abstr. (?-?); Cumul. Index Nurs. Allied Health Lit.; Curr. Aware. Biol. Sci., CABS; Curr. Contents Life Sci.; EMBASE; Energy Res. Abstr.; Health Devices Alerts; Health Index (1989-); Health Period. Database [Full Txt.]; Health Ref. Cent. (Jan. 1989-) [Full Cov.]; Index Med.; Int. Aerosp. Abstr.; Int. Pharm. Abstr.; Iowa Drug Inf. Serv. (1966-); J. Watch; Med. Abstr. Newsl.; Mod. Med.; Nutr. Abstr. Rev., Ser. B, Live Feeds and Feed.; Nutr. Abstr. Rev., Ser. A, Hum. Exp.; Nutr. Res. Newsl.; Life Sci. Collect.; PESTDOC; Physic. Medline Plus; Protozoolog. Abstr.; Ref. Upd. Basic Ed.; Ref. Upd. Clinical Ed.; Ref. Upd. Deluxe Ed.; Res. Alert [Full Cov.]; Saf. Health Work; Sci. Cit. Index; SCISEARCH; Soc. Sci. Cit. Index [Select. Cov.]; SPORT Discus; SportSearch; Trop. Dis. Bull.

US/0887-8005
**AMERICAN JOURNAL OF CARDIOVASCULAR PATHOLOGY, THE.** [Am. j. cardiovasc. pathol.]. Vol. 1, No. 1 (Jan. 1987)-. Periodical. English. qt. $165.00 (institutions), $115.00 (individuals). Field & Wood, Inc., 4156 Manayunk Avenue, Philadelphia PA 19128. **Tel** (215)828-4010. **(Subscription address:** Field and Wood, PO Box 975, Blue Bell PA 19422.**) ED** Colin M. Bloor. **LC** RC669.9; .A47. **DD** 616.1/005. **NLM** W1; AM449E. **CODEN** AJCPEM. Documents available from CASDDS.
**Ind/Abst** Chem. Abstr.; EMBASE; Health Plan. Adminis.; Index Med.; Ref. Upd. Deluxe Ed.

US
**AMERICAN JOURNAL OF GERIATRIC CARDIOLOGY, THE.** (199?)-. Periodical. English. Six times a year. $60.00 (individuals), $75.00 (institutions) US; $75.00 (individuals), $90.00 (institutions) other. Le Jacq Communications Inc., 777 West Putnam Avenue, Greenwich CT 06830. **Tel** (203)531-0460, FAX (203)625-0393. **NLM** W1; AM452EL. **CODEN** AJGCE3. **Pr Rev.**

US/0895-7061
**AMERICAN JOURNAL OF HYPERTENSION.** (AMERICAN JOURNAL OF HYPERTENSION : JOURNAL OF THE AMERICAN SOCIETY OF HYPERTENSION.). [Am. j. hypertens.]. **Added/Corp** American Society of Hypertension. **VFOAT** AJH. Vol. 1, No. 1 (Jan. 1988)-. Academic Scholarly Publication. English. Twelve times a year (1 volume). $235.00 US; $318.00 Europe; $340.00 Japan; $291.00 (surface*mail) other. Elsevier Science Publishing Company Inc, Madison Square Station, PO Box 882, New York NY 10159-0882. **Tel** (212)633-3950, FAX (212)633-3990. **DD** 616. **NLM** W1; AM466E. **CODEN** AJHYE6. **[CCC]. Pr Rev.** Documents available from The Genuine Article, BIOSIS Document Express, CASDDS, ADONIS. ***Continues*** *Journal of Clinical Hypertension, 0748-450X.*
**Ind/Abst** ADONIS; Anim. Breed. Abstr.; Biol. Abstr.; Biol. Dig.; Chem. Abstr.; Curr. Contents Clin. Med.; EMBASE; Health Plan. Adminis.; Index Med. (Jan. 1988-); Nutr. Abstr. Rev., Ser. A, Hum. Exp.; Nutr. Res. Newsl.; Ref. Upd. Deluxe Ed.; Res. Alert [Select. Cov.]; SCISEARCH.

SZ/0258-4425
**AMERICAN JOURNAL OF NONINVASIVE CARDIOLOGY.** [Am. j. noninvasive cardiol.]. Vol. 1, No. 1 (Jan./Feb. 1987)-. Periodical. English. bm (6 issues). $307.00. S. Karger AG, Allschwilerstrasse 10, PO Box - Postfach - Case Postale, CH-4009 Basel Switzerland. **Tel** 011 41 61 306-1111, FAX 011 41 61 306-1234, telex CH 962 652. **ED** D. H. Spodick. **NLM** W1; AM494TF. **CODEN** AJNCE4. **[CCC].** Documents available from The Genuine Article, BIOSIS Document Express.
**Desc:** Covers the full range of methodologies, instrumentation, diagnostic applications, dynamic assessment, static and ambulatory monitoring, physiology, clinical pharmacology and exercise testing as well as other cardiocirculatory challenges. Each issue is designed to meet the information needs of hospital-based and academic physicians as well as all clinicians involved in cardiology, rehabilitation medicine, critical and emergency care, and internal medicine.
**Ind/Abst** Biol. Abstr. (1987-); Curr. Contents Clin. Med.; EMBASE; Ref. Upd. Deluxe Ed.; Res. Alert [Select. Cov.]; SCISEARCH.

US/0363-6135
**AMERICAN JOURNAL OF PHYSIOLOGY : HEART AND CIRCULATORY PHYSIOLOGY.** **See** Biology-Physiology.

US/0735-1283
**AMERICAN REVIEW OF DIAGNOSTICS.** [Am. rev. diagn.]. Vol. 1, No. 1 (Nov./Dec.1982)-. Academic Scholarly Publication. English. bm. $36.00. Degram Communications Inc., PO Box 617, Encino CA 91426. **Tel** (213)501-6167. **NLM** W1 AM747. **[CCC].**
**Ind/Abst** EMBASE.

GW/0721-9318
**ANGIO : ZEITSCHRIFT DER DEUTSCHEN GESELLSCHAFT FUER GEFASSCHIRURGIE.** **Added/Corp** Deutsche Gesellschaft fuer Gefasschirurgie. (197?)-. Periodical. German (summaries and/or abstracts in English; table of contents in English). Six times a year. DM122.00. Karl Demeter Verlag, Wuermstrasse 13, Postfach 1660, W 8032 Graefelfing Germany. **Tel** 011 49 89 852033, FAX 011 49 89 9543347, telex 524068 Delta D. **NLM** W1; AN224L.
**Ind/Abst** EMBASE.

SP/0003-3170
**ANGIOLOGIA.** [Angiologia]. Vol.1 (Jan./Feb. 1949)-. Periodical. Spanish (summaries and/or abstracts in English). bm. $100.00. Editorial Rocas SA, Muntaner 393, Pral 2A Desp 4A, 08021 Barcelona Spain. **Tel** 011 34 3 200-1389. **ED** Alvaro Trevino Pedro. **NLM** W1 AN225. **CODEN** ANGOAT. Index available. **Bk Rev. Ad Acc. Circ:** 3,000. Documents available from BIOSIS Document Express, CASDDS.
**Desc:** Articles concerning the entire blood circulation, and surgery of veins and arteries.
**Ind/Abst** Biol. Abstr.; Chem. Abstr.; EMBASE; Index Med.; Indice Med. Esp.; Life Sci. Collect.

FR/0003-3928
**ANNALES DE CARDIOLOGIE ET D'ANGEIOLOGIE.** [Ann. cardiol. angeiol.]. (Jan./Mar. 1968)-. Periodical. French (summaries and/or abstracts in English and German). Ten times a year. 830.00F France; 1100.00F other. Expansion Scientifique Francaise, 31 Boulevard de la Tour-Maubourg, 75007 Paris France. **Tel** 011 33 1 40 62 64 00, 011 33 1 40626439. **ED** M. Grivaux. **NLM** W1 AN327C. **CODEN** ACAABH. **[CCC].** Index Available, published separately, free-automatically sent. **Bk Rev. Ad Acc. Pr Rev. Circ:** 2,800. Documents available from The Genuine Article, BIOSIS Document Express. ***Continues*** *Actualities Cardiologiques et Angeiologiques Internationales.*
**Ind/Abst** Biol. Abstr.; Curr. Contents Clin. Med.; EMBASE; Health Plan. Adminis.; Index Med.; Nutr. Abstr. Rev., Ser. A, Hum. Exp.; Life Sci. Collect.; Res. Alert [Select. Cov.]; SCISEARCH; Soc. Sci. Cit. Index [Select. Cov.]; SportSearch.

UK/0952-0562
**ANNUAL OF CARDIAC SURGERY.** **See** Medical Science and Technology-Surgery.

US
**ANNUAL REPORT - ARTERIOSCLEROSIS AND HYPERTENSION ADVISORY COMMITTEE, NATIONAL INSTITUTES OF HEALTH.** **Main/Corp** National Heart, Lung, and Blood Institute Arteriosclerosis and Hypertension Advisory Committee. 1975/76-. English. an. National Heart Lung and Blood Institute, Division of Heart and Vascular Diseases, Devices and Technology Branch,

9000 Rockville Pike, Bethesda MD 20014. ***Continues*** *Annual Report - Arteriosclerosis and Hypertension Advisory Committee, National Institutes of Health.*

US
**ANNUAL REPORT - CARDIOVASCULAR AND PULMONARY STUDY SECTION, NATIONAL INSTITUTES OF HEALTH.** **Main/Corp** United States. National Institutes of Health. Cardiovascular and Pulmonary Study Section. (19??)-. English. National Institutes of Health, 9000 Rockville Pike, Bethesda MD 20014. **Tel** (301)496-6975.

US/8755-707X
**ANNUAL REPORT - MARYLAND HIGH BLOOD PRESSURE COMMISSION.** (ANNUAL REPORT FOR THE FISCAL YEAR ... / MARYLAND HIGH BLOOD PRESSURE COMMISSION.). **Main/Corp** Maryland High Blood Pressure Commission. English. an. Maryland High Blood Pressure Commission, 201 West Preston Street, Baltimore MD 21201. **LC** RC685.H8; M293A. **DD** 353.97520084/1.

US/0278-0577
**ANNUAL REPORT / NATIONAL HEART, LUNG, AND BLOOD INSTITUTE.** [Annu. rep. - Natl. Heart, Lung, Blood Inst.]. **Main/Corp** National Heart, Lung, and Blood Institute. **Added/Corp** National Heart, Lung, and Blood Institute. Intramural Research. **VFOAT** Intramural Research. (19??)-. English. an. National Heart Lung and Blood Institute, Division of Heart and Vascular Diseases, Devices and Technology Branch, 9000 Rockville Pike, Bethesda MD 20014. **LC** RC666; .N29b. **DD** 616.1/0072073. **NLM** W 22 AA1 I61.

US
**AORTA (NEW YORK, N.Y.).** (AORTA.). 1 (1982)-. Periodical. English. PO Box 30A, Brooklyn NY 11202.

US/0920-5268
**APPLIED CARDIOPULMONARY PATHOPHYSIOLOGY : ACP.** [ACP, Appl. cardiopulm. pathophysiol.]. **VFOAT** ACP. No. 1 (1987)-. Academic Scholarly Publication. English. qt. $297.00. Kluwer Academic Publishers, Postbus 322, 3300 AH Dordrecht, The Netherlands. **Tel** 011 (31) 78 524400, FAX 011 31 78 183273, telex 20083. **ED** Omar Prakash. **NLM** W1; AP516C. **CODEN** AAPAED. **[CCC]. Pr Rev. Acid Free.** available on microfilm and microfiche from University Microfilms International (UMI). Documents available from The Genuine Article, CASDDS.
**Desc:** Articles start from the principle that appropriate therapy is based on understanding how normal body function is perturbed. They link the basic physiology and pharmacology with practical problems, which anesthesiologists, intensivists, pulmonologists and cardiologists are regularly faced with. Each issue covers some topics in depth by presenting a number of educational articles dealing with different aspects of the problem.
**Ind/Abst** Chem. Abstr. (1987-); Curr. Contents Clin. Med.; Curr. Contents Life Sci.; EMBASE; Ref. Upd. Deluxe Ed.; Res. Alert [Full Cov.]; Sci. Cit. Index; SCISEARCH.

SP/0214-3917
**APUNTES DE CARDIOLOGIA.** [Apunt. cardiol.]. (1983)-. Periodical. Spanish. ir. Ediciones Nacionales Especializadas, Modesto Lafuente 41, 28003 Madrid Spain. **UDC** 612.17.

FR/0003-9683
**ARCHIVES DES MALADIES DU COEUR ET DES VAISSEAUX.** [Arch. mal. coeur vaiss.]. **Added/Corp** Societe Francaise de Cardiologie. Vol. 30 (1939)-. Periodical. French (English). mo. 786.73F France; 930.00F other. JB Bailliere, 37 Avenue des Champs Elysees, 75008 Paris France. **Tel** 011 33 1 49536900. **ED** J Beytout. **NLM** W1 AR375Z. **CODEN** AMCVAN. **[CCC].** Index available. **Ad Acc. Pr Rev. Circ:** 5,000. Documents available from The Genuine Article, BIOSIS Document Express. ***Continues*** *Archives des Maladies du Coeur, des Vaisseaux et du Sang.*
**Ind/Abst** Biol. Abstr.; CSA Neuro. Abstr. (?-?); Curr. Contents Clin. Med.; EMBASE; Health Plan. Adminis.; Index Med.; Nutr. Abstr. Rev., Ser. B, Live Feeds and Feed.; Nutr. Abstr. Rev., Ser. A, Hum. Exp.; Life Sci. Collect.; Protozoolog. Abstr.; Res. Alert [Full Cov.]; Saf. Health Work; Sci. Cit. Index; SCISEARCH; Soc. Sci. Cit. Index [Select. Cov.].

MX/0020-3785
**ARCHIVOS DEL INSTITUTO DE CARDIOLOGIA DE MEXICO.** [Arch. Inst. Cardiol. Mex.]. **Added/Corp** Instituto Nacional de Cardiologia (Mexico) Sociedad Mexicana de Cardiologia. Vol. 14 (July/Aug.1944)-. Academic Scholarly Publication. Spanish (summaries and/or abstracts in English and French). Six times a year. $75.00. Instituto Nacional Cardiologia, Juan Badiano #1 Col. Seccion 16, 14080 Mexico DF Mexico. **Tel** 011 52 5 5732911, ext 297 310. **ED** Dr. Eduardo Salazar. **NLM** W1 AR712J. **CODEN** AICMA2. Index available. **Ad Acc. Pr Rev. Circ:** 2,500 (ctrl). Documents available from BIOSIS Document Express, CASDDS. ***Continues*** *Archivos Latino Americanos de Cardiologia y Hematologia.*
**Ind/Abst** Biol. Abstr.; Chem. Abstr.; EMBASE; Health Plan. Adminis.; Index Med.; SportSearch.

IT/1120-8635
**ARGOMENTI DI CARDIOLOGIA.** [Argom. cardiol.]. (1990)-. Periodical. Italian. Six times a year. L8200. Masson S.P.A, Via Statuto 2/4, 20121 Milan Italy. **Tel** 011 39 2 63671, FAX 011 39 2 6367211. **ED** Alberto Zanchetti. **UDC** 616.12. **Bk Rev. Ad Acc. Circ:** 15,000 (ctrl).

BL/0066-782X
**ARQUIVOS BRASILEIROS DE CARDIOLOGIA.** [Arq. bras. cardiol.]. Vol. 1 (Mar. 1948)-. Academic Scholarly Publication. Portuguese (summaries and/or abstracts in English). mo. $200.00. Sociedade Brasileira de Cardiologia, Rua Itapeva 574 80 Conj 81-B, 01332 Sao Paulo Brazil. **Tel** 011 55 11 289-1202. **ED** Max Grinberg. **NLM** W1 AR867. **CODEN** ABCAAJ. Index available. **Ad Acc. Circ:** 7,000. Documents available from CASDDS.
**Desc:** Official journal of the Sociedade Brasileira de Cardiologia, containing original articles, cases reports, reviews, therapeutic updates and therapeutic essays.
**Ind/Abst** Chem. Abstr.; EMBASE; Health Plan. Adminis.; Index Med.; Protozoolog. Abstr.; SportSearch.

FR/0293-5090
**ARTERES ET VEINES.** (1982)-. Periodical. French. Six times a year. 274.24F France; 340.00F other. Publications Medicales AGCF, 77 bis rue de Chesneaux, 95160 Montmorency France. **Tel** 011 33 34 176888. **UDC** 616.1.

US/1049-8834
**ARTERIOSCLEROSIS AND THROMBOSIS.** [Arterioscler. thromb.]. **Added/Corp** American Heart Association. Vol. 11, No. 1 (Jan./Feb. 1991)-. Academic Scholarly Publication. English. mo. $198.00 institution. American Heart Association, 7272 Greenville Avenue, Dallas TX 75231-4596. **Tel** (214)706-1310, (214)373-6300, FAX (214)691-6342. **(Subscription address:** American Heart Association, PO Box 843543, Dallas TX 75284-3543.**) LC** RC692; .A667. **DD** 616.1/36. **NLM** W1; AR9515E. **CODEN** ARTTE5. **[CCC].** Index available (free). **Ad Acc. Acid Free.** available on microfilm and microfiche from University Microfilms International (UMI). Documents available from The Genuine Article, BIOSIS Document Express, CASDDS. ***Continues*** *Arteriosclerosis, 0276-5047.*
**Desc:** Provides a forum for the publication of original research on the biology, prevention, and impact of vascular diseases relating to arteriosclerosis. Includes biochemistry, biophysics, cell and molecular biology, genetics, nutrition, metabolism, and pathology. For researchers and internists.
**Ind/Abst** Biol. Abstr. (1991-); Chem. Abstr. (Jan. 1991-); Curr. Aware. Biol. Sci., CABS; Curr. Contents Life Sci.; EMBASE; Health Plan. Adminis.; Index Med. (Jan. 1991-); Ref. Upd. Basic Ed.; Ref. Upd. Clinical Ed.; Ref. Upd. Deluxe Ed.; Res. Alert [Full Cov.]; Sci. Cit. Index; SCISEARCH.

AU/0250-4677
**ATHEROGENESE (WIEN).** (ATHEROGENESIS / ATHEROGENESE.). [Atherogenese]. **Added/Corp** Verband der Wissenschaftlichen Gesellschaften Oesterreichs. Austria. Bundesministerium fuer Wissenschaft und Forschung. **VFOAT** Atherogenese. (1976)-. Monographic series. English (German). ir. Price varies per volume. **NLM** W1 AT383. **CODEN** ATRGD3.

NE/0021-9150
**ATHEROSCLEROSIS.** [Atherosclerosis]. Vol. 11 (Jan./Feb. 1970)-. Academic Scholarly Publication. English (summaries and/or abstracts in German). Fourteen times a year (7 vols.). $1537.00. Elsevier Science Ireland Ltd., Bay 15, Shannon Industrial Estate, Co Clare Ireland. **Tel** 011 353 61 471944. **ED** D Kritchevsky, N B Myant, D Seidel, and C W M Adams. **NLM** W1 AT384. **CODEN** ATHSBL. **[CCC]. Pr Rev.** available on microfilm and microfiche from University Microfilms International (UMI). Documents available from The Genuine Article, BIOSIS Document Express, CASDDS, ADONIS. ***Continues*** *Journal of Atherosclerosis Research, 0368-1319.*
**Desc:** Brings together research papers related to the focal accumulation of lipids, collagen, complex carbohydrates, blood and blood products, fibrous tissue and calcium deposits in the intima of arteries, its medical complications, related phenomena and diseases.
**Ind/Abst** ADONIS; AGRICOLA [Select. Cov.]; Biol. Abstr.; Chem. Abstr.; Curr. Aware. Biol. Sci., CABS; Curr. Contents Life Sci.; Dairy Sci. Abstr.; EMBASE; Foods Adlibra; Health Plan. Adminis.; Index Med.; Index Vet.; Int. Aerosp. Abstr.; Med. Abstr. Newsl.; NAPRALERT; Nutr. Abstr. Rev., Ser. B, Live Feeds and Feed.; Nutr. Abstr. Rev., Ser. A, Hum. Exp.; Nutr. Res. Newsl.; Life Sci. Collect.; PESTDOC; Ref. Upd. Deluxe Ed.; Res. Alert [Full Cov.]; Sci. Cit. Index; SCISEARCH; Soyabean Abstr.; SportSearch; Vet. Bull.

US/0362-1650
**ATHEROSCLEROSIS REVIEWS.** [Atheroscler. rev.]. Vol. 1 (1976)-. Academic Scholarly Publication. English. ir. Price varies per volume. Raven Press, 1185 Avenue of the Americas, 37th Floor, New York NY 10036. **Tel** (212)930-9500, (212)930-9604, FAX (212)869-3495, (212)302-8507, telex 640073. **ED** Antonio M. Gotto, Jr. and Rodolfo Paoletti. **LC** RC692; .A729. **DD** 616.1/36/005. **NLM** W1 AT385. **CODEN** ATHEDF. Documents available from BIOSIS Document Express, CASDDS.
**Ind/Abst** Biol. Abstr.; Chem. Abstr.

UK/0268-1641
**ATRIAL NATRIURETIC FACTORS.** [Atrial. natriuret. factors]. (1986)-. English. Twenty-four times a year. £105.00. SUBIS, Mansion House, 19 Kingfield Road, Sheffield S11 9AS England. **Tel** 011 44 114 255 4433, FAX 011 44 114 255 4626. **DD** 016.612173. **[CCC]. Bk Rev. Ad Acc.**
**Desc:** Current awareness service for researchers and clinicians.

US/0731-1672
**BASIC AND CLINICAL CARDIOLOGY.** [Basic clin. cardiol.]. Vol. 1 (1981)-. Academic Scholarly Publication. English. ir. Price varies per volume. Marcel Dekker Inc., 270 Madison Avenue, New York NY 10016. **Tel** (212)696-9000, (800)228-1160, FAX (212)685-4540, telex 421419. **(Subscription address:** Marcel Dekker Inc, PO Box 5017, Monticello NY 12701.**) LC** UNC. **DD** 616.1/2/005. **NLM** W1 BA813ST. **CODEN** BACCDW. Documents available from CASDDS.
**Desc:** Covers various aspects of cardiology including cardiac diseases and disorders.
**Ind/Abst** Chem. Abstr. (1981-1983).

GW/0300-8428
**BASIC RESEARCH IN CARDIOLOGY.** [Basic res. cardiol.]. **Added/Corp** Deutsche Gesellschaft fuer Kreislaufforschung. Vol. 68 (Jan./Feb. 1973)-. Periodical. English (German). Six times a year. DM825.00. Dr Dietrich Steinkopff Verlag, PO Box 111442, D 64229 Darmstadt Germany. **Tel** 011 49 6151 17450. **(Subscription address:** Springer Verlag New York Inc. / for North America, 44 Hartz Way, Secaucus NJ 07096.**) ED** R. Jacob, T.H. Kenner and W. Schaper. **LC** RC633.A1; B35. **DD** 616.9/94/005. **NLM** W1 BA814N. **CODEN** BRCAB7. **[CCC]. Pr Rev.** Documents available from The Genuine Article, BIOSIS Document Express, CASDDS. ***Continues*** *Archiv fur Kreislaufforschung, 0003-9217.*
**Desc:** This journal keeps scientists in several fields abreast of results in fundamental cardiology research.
**Ind/Abst** Biol. Abstr.; Chem. Abstr.; CSA Neuro. Abstr. (?-?); Curr. Contents Life Sci.; EMBASE; Energy Res. Abstr. (Jan. 1975-); Health Plan. Adminis.; Index Med.; Nutr. Abstr. Rev., Ser. B, Live Feeds and Feed.; Nutr. Abstr. Rev., Ser. A, Hum. Exp.; Nutr. Res. Newsl.; Life Sci. Collect.; Res. Alert [Full Cov.]; Sci. Cit. Index; SCISEARCH.

SZ/0067-7906
**BIBLIOTHECA CARDIOLOGICA.** [Bibl. cardiol.]. Vol. 1 (1939)-. Monographic series. English (French and German). an. 150.00F (approx. per volume). S. Karger AG, Allschwilerstrasse 10, PO Box - Postfach - Case Postale, CH-4009 Basel Switzerland. **Tel** 011 41 61 306-1111, FAX 011 41 61 306-1234, telex CH 962 652. **ED** A. Maseri. **NLM** W1 BI396. **CODEN** BCSCAL. **[CCC].** Documents available from BIOSIS Document Express, CASDDS.
**Desc:** Records experimental and applied investigations that yield information relevant to the measurement of cardiovascular performance and the treatment of its disorders. Intended to facilitate safe and accurate assessment of cardiac function, also provides clinical cardiologists with information on how new examination methods can facilitate early diagnosis or aid evaluation of therapeutic measures.
**Ind/Abst** Biol. Abstr.; Chem. Abstr.; Cumul. Index Nurs. Allied Health Lit.; Health Plan. Adminis.; Index Med.; Ref. Upd. Deluxe Ed.

RU/0201-7369
**BIULLETEN VSESOIUZNOGO KARDIOLOGICHESKOGO NAUCHNOGO TSENTRA AMN SSSR.** **Added/Corp** Akademiia Meditsinskikh Nauk SSSR. Vsesoiuznyi Kardiologicheskii Nauchnyi Tsentr. (1978)-. Academic Scholarly Publication. Russian (summaries and/or abstracts in English; table of contents in English). sa. $28.50. Izdatelstvo Meditsina / Russian Academy of Medical Sciences, Ulitsa Solyanka 14, 109801 Moscow Russia. **Tel** 011 95 297-05-04. **(Subscription address:** Victor Kamkin, 4956 Boiling Brook Parkway, Rockville MD 20852.**) NLM** W1 BI99LU. **CODEN** BVKSDT. Documents available from BIOSIS Document Express, CASDDS.
**Ind/Abst** Biol. Abstr.; Chem. Abstr. (1984-); Index Med. (1981-).

●NO/0803-7051
**BLOOD PRESSURE.** (1992)-. Periodical. English. Six times a year. Kr955.00, $155.00. Scandinavian University Press, PO Box 2959 Toeyen, N 0608 Oslo 6 Norway. **Tel** 011 47 2 2575400, FAX 011 47 2 2575353, telex 71896 UROR N. **(Subscription address:** Scandinavian University Press, 200 Meacham Ave., Elmont NY 11003.**) ED** Lennart Hansson. **NLM** W1; BL661F. **CODEN** BLPREG. **Pr Rev.**
**Desc:** Information on blood pressure and hypertension.

UK/0007-0769
**BRITISH HEART JOURNAL.** [Br. heart j.]. **Added/Corp** British Medical Association. British Cardiac Society. International Congress of Physicians. Cardiological Section. Vol. 1 (Jan. 1939)-. Academic Scholarly Publication. English. mo. £190.00. BMJ / British Medical Journal Publishing Group, British Medical Association House, Tavistock Square, London WC1H 9JR England. **Tel** 011 44 71 3874499, FAX 011 44 71 383 6402, telex 290034 HBJ MN. **DD** 616. **NLM** W1 BR455G. **CODEN** BHJUAV. **[CCC].** cum. index. **Pr Rev.** available on microfilm and microfiche from University Microfilms International (UMI). Documents available from The Genuine Article, BIOSIS Document Express, ADONIS.
**Desc:** Original work on heart and circulation - anatomical, physiological and pathological. Features include editorials, which tie in with original papers published in areas relevant to the development of cardiology.
**Ind/Abst** Abr. Index Med. (19??-); ADONIS (19??-); Annals Behav. Med. (19??-); Biol. Abstr. (19??-); Cumul. Index Nurs. Allied Health Lit. (19??-); Curr. Aware. Biol. Sci., CABS (19??-); Curr. Contents Clin. Med. (19??-); Curr. Contents Life Sci. (19??-); EMBASE (19??-); Health Period. Database (19??-); Health Plan. Adminis. (19??-); Helminthol. Abstr. (19??-); Index Med. (19??-); Int. Aerosp. Abstr. (19??-); Iowa Drug Inf. Serv. (1966-); Med. Abstr. Newsl. (19??-); Mod. Med. (19??-); Nutr. Abstr. Rev., Ser. B, Live Feeds and Feed. (19??-); Nutr. Abstr. Rev., Ser. A, Hum. Exp. (19??-); Nutr. Res. Newsl. (19??-); Life Sci. Collect. (19??-); PESTDOC (19??-); Physic. Medline Plus (19??-); Protozoolog. Abstr. (19??-); Ref. Upd. Basic Ed. (19??-); Ref. Upd. Clinical Ed. (19??-); Ref. Upd. Deluxe Ed. (19??-); Res. Alert (19??-) [Full Cov.]; Rev. Med. Vet. Entomol. (19??-); Saf. Health Work (19??-); Sci. Cit. Index (19??-); SCISEARCH (19??-); Soc. Sci. Cit. Index (19??-) [Select. Cov.]; SportSearch (19??-); Trop. Dis. Bull. (19??-).

FR
**BULLETIN DE STIMAREC.** Bulletin. French. bm. $50.00 US; 300.00F other. Stimarec Hospital Jean Rostand, 39 rue Jean le Galleu France. **Tel** 011 33 1 46701555 ext. 254.

UK/0260-0064
**BUTTERWORTHS INTERNATIONAL MEDICAL REVIEWS. CARDIOLOGY.** [Butterworths int. med. rev. Cardiol.]. **VFOAT** Cardiology. (1982)-. Monographic series. English. ir. Price varies per volume. Butterworth Heinemann Publishers, Linacre House, Jordan Hill, Oxford OX2 8DP England. **Tel** 011 44 865 310366. **LC** UNC. **NLM** W1 BU98J. **CODEN** BMRCDL. Documents available from BIOSIS Document Express.
**Ind/Abst** Biol. Abstr. (?-1986).

US/0148-2378
**CA SELECTS: ATHEROSCLEROSIS & HEART DISEASE.** **See** Chemistry-Abstracting, Bibliographies and Statistics.

US/1051-3922
**CA SELECTS: HYPERTENSION & ANTIHYPERTENSIVES.** **See** Chemistry-Abstracting, Bibliographies and Statistics.

SP/1130-4014
**CADRIOLOGIA & HIPERTENSION.** **VFOAT** Cardiologia e Hipertension. (1990)-. Spanish. bm. Editorial Saned SA, Apolonio Morales 6, 28036 Madrid Spain. **Tel** 011 34 1 359-4092, FAX 011 34 1 457-9918.
**Ind/Abst** EMBASE [Select. Cov.].

CN/0828-282X
**CANADIAN JOURNAL OF CARDIOLOGY.** (THE CANADIAN JOURNAL OF CARDIOLOGY.). [Can. j. cardiol.]. **VFOAT** Cardiology; Journal Canadien de Cardiologie. Vol. 1, No. 1 (Jan. 1985)-. Academic Scholarly Publication. English (French). Ten times a year. $131.00 (institution), $110.00 (individual) US. Pulsus Group Inc., 2902 South Sheridan Way, Oakville Ontario L6J 7L6 Canada. **Tel** (416)829-4770, FAX (416)829-4799. **DD** 616.1/2. **NLM** W1; CA579. **CODEN** CJCAEX. **Ad Acc. Pr Rev.** Documents available from The Genuine Article, BIOSIS Document Express, CASDDS.
**Desc:** Publishes original papers, case reports and reviews pertaining to cardiovascular medicine and surgery.
**Ind/Abst** Biol. Abstr. (1985-); Chem. Abstr. (1985-); Curr. Contents Clin. Med.; EMBASE; Health Plan. Adminis.; Index Med. (1985-); Nutr. Res. Newsl.; Protozoolog. Abstr.; Res. Alert [Select. Cov.]; SCISEARCH.

CN/0843-6096
**CANADIAN JOURNAL OF CARDIOVASCULAR NURSING.** [Can. j. cardiovasc. nurs.]. **Added/Corp** Canadian Council of Cardiovascular Nurses. **VFOAT** Journal Canadien en Soins Infirmiers Cardio-Vasculaires; Revue Canadienne de Nursing Cardio-Vasculaire. Vol. 1, No. 1 (April 1989)-. Periodical. English (French). Four times a year. 42.00Can$ (institution), 28.00Can$ (individual) Canada; 52.00Can$ (institution), 35.00Can$ (individual) other; $20.00 students. Canadian Council of Cardiovascular Nursing, 200 160 George Street Maiden, Ottawa Ontario K1N 9M2 Canada. **Tel** (613)237-4361, FAX (613)234-3278. **ED** Ellen Rukholm (editor's address: School of Nursing, Laurentian University, Sudbury Ontario P3E 2C6 Canada). **DD** 610.73/691/05. **NLM** W1; CA579E. **Bk Rev. Ad Acc, Adv Mgr:** Barb Fenwick. **Pr Rev. Circ:** 700 (ctrl). ***Continues*** *Canadian Bulletin of Cardiovascular Nursing, 0831-4462.*
**Desc:** A referred journal concerned with health care issues related to cardiovascular health and illness.
**Ind/Abst** Cumul. Index Nurs. Allied Health Lit.; Health Plan. Adminis.; Int. Nurs. Index (1989-).

US/0194-2557
**CARDIAC ALERT.** [Card. alert]. Vol. 1 (1979)-. Periodical. English. Twelve times a year. $49.95 one year; $89.95 two years. Phillips Business Information, Inc., 1201 Seven Locks Road, Potomac MD 20854. **Tel** (301)424-3338, (800)777-5006, FAX (301)309-3847. **ED** Jorge C. Rios. **NLM** W1 CA763C. **[CCC].** Index available.
**Desc:** Personal advice on every aspect of heart health with emphasis on case histories, recent cardiac developments, diet, exercise, lifestyle, subscriber questions, news, studies and reviews.
**Ind/Abst** AGRICOLA.

NE
**CARDIAC IMAGING VIDEO JOURNAL.** ***Ceased.*** (19??)-(1993). English. qt. Kluwer Academic Publishers, Postbus 322, 3300 AH Dordrecht, The Netherlands. **Tel** 011 (31) 78 524400, FAX 011 31 78 183273, telex 20083.

US/0892-4082
**CARDIAC IMPULSE.** ***Ceased.*** [Card. impulse]. Vol. 1, No. 1 (March 1980)-Ceased ?. Periodical. English. bm. Matrix Communications, 120 N Oak Park Avenue, Suite 202, Oak Park IL 60301. **DD** 616. **NLM** W1; CA763H.

US/0887-9850
**CARDIAC SURGERY.** ***Ceased.*** **See** Medical Science and Technology-Surgery.

US/0742-9622
**CARDIO.** [Cardio]. Vol. 1, No. 1 (Jan. 1984)-. Periodical. English. mo. $90.00 US; $105.00 other. Miller Freeman Inc., 600 Harrison Street, San Francisco CA 94107. **Tel** (415)905-2337, FAX (415)905-2240, telex 278273. **(Subscription address:** Miller Freeman / Aurora, IL, 434 West Downer Place, Aurora IL 60506.**) ED** Joe Kornfeld. **NLM** W1; CA764T. **[CCC]. Circ:** 27,285. available on microfilm from University Microfilms International (UMI).
**Desc:** Covers the field of cardiovascular medicine; specializes in reporting news of clinical developments and research technology, drugs, regulations and legislation, meetings and conferences, and new books and literature; serves practicing cardiologists and internal medicine physicians throughout the United States.

US
**CARDIO INTERNATIONAL.** (19??)-. English. Four times a year. $65.00. Miller Freeman Inc., 600 Harrison Street, San Francisco CA 94107. **Tel** (415)905-2337, FAX (415)905-2240, telex 278273.

US
**CARDIO INTERVENTION.** (19??)-. English. bm. $45.00 US; $60.00. Miller Freeman Inc., 600 Harrison Street, San Francisco CA 94107. **Tel** (415)905-2337, FAX (415)905-2240, telex 278273. **(Subscription address:** Miller Freeman / Aurora, IL, 434 West Downer Place, Aurora IL 60506.**)**

US/0008-6355
**CARDIO-VASCULAR NURSING.** **See** Medical Science and Technology-Nursing.

SP/0213-8115
**CARDIOLOGIA ... BARCELONA.** (CARDIOLOGIA.). [Cardiologia Barc.]. (1986)-. Periodical. Spanish. qt. Ediciones Doyma SA, Travesera de Gracia 17 21, 08021 Barcelona Spain. **Tel** 011 34 3 2000711, 011 34 3 4145706, FAX 011 34 3 2091136, telex 51964 INK E. **UDC** 616.12.

IT/1120-3730
**CARDIOLOGIA PER IMMAGINI.** [Cardiol. immagini]. (1988)-. Periodical. Multiple languages. Three times a year. Includes Rays: L100000 (individuals), L120000 (institutions). Il Pensiero Scientifico Editore s.r.l., Via Bradano 3C, 00199 Rome Italy. **Tel** 011 39 6 86207158, 86207159, 86207168, 86207169, FAX 011 39 6 86207160. **ED** James V. Talano. **UDC** 612.12. **Ad Acc.** Full Page (B&W) L1.650.000. **Circ:** 1,400.
**Ind/Abst** Index Med.

IT/0393-1978
**CARDIOLOGIA (ROMA).** (CARDIOLOGIA.). [Cardiologia]. **Added/Corp** Societa Italiana di Cardiologia. Vol. 27 (1982)-. Periodical. Italian (English). mo. L120000.00. Italian Society of Cardiology, Corso Francia 197, 00197 Rome Italy. **Tel** 011 39 6 36309819, FAX 011 39 6 36308197. **ED** A Reale. **NLM** W1; CA7649. **CODEN** CARDDJ. **Bk Rev. Circ:** 3,500. Documents available from BIOSIS Document Express. ***Continues*** *Bolletino, Della Societa Italiana di Cardiologia, 0037-878X.*
**Ind/Abst** Biol. Abstr.; Health Plan. Adminis.; Index Med. (1982-).

US/0741-7454
**CARDIOLOGIC CONSULTATION.** [Cardiol. consult.]. Periodical. English. qt. Free. Hospital Practice, 10 Astor Place/7th Floor, New York NY 10003-6903. **Tel** (212)477-2727. ctrl circ.

FR/0766-3633
**CARDIOLOGIE PRATIQUE PARIS.** (CARDIOLOGIE PRATIQUE.). (1985)-. Periodical. French. wk (except during July & Aug.). 342.80F France; 350.00F other. Len Medical, 48 Bis Avenue Kleber, F-75116 Paris France. **Tel** 011 33 1 47550606. **UDC** 616.12.

GW/0179-7166
**CARDIOLOGISCH-ANGIOLOGISCHES BULLETIN.** [Cardiol.-angiol. Bull.]. Vol. 23 (1st Quarter 1986)-. Bulletin. German (English). qt. **NLM** W1; CA7699. **CODEN** CANBES. Documents available from BIOSIS Document Express. ***Continues*** *Cardiologisches Bulletin, 0084-8603.*
**Ind/Abst** Biol. Abstr. (1986-).

US/0276-4296
**CARDIOLOGIST'S COMPENDIUM OF DRUG THERAPY, THE.** (THE CARDIOLOGIST'S COMPENDIUM OF DRUG THERAPY : A PUBLICATION OF BIOMEDICAL INFORMATION CORPORATION.). [Cardiol. compend. drug ther.]. **VFOAT** Compendium of Drug Therapy. 1981/1982-. English. an. Biomedical Information Corporation, 800 Second Avenue, New York NY 10017. **Tel** (212)262-9662.

US/0741-515X
**CARDIOLOGISTS' LEGAL LETTER.** **See** Law.

SZ/0008-6312
**CARDIOLOGY.** [Cardiology]. (1970)-. Periodical. English. mo. $615.00. S. Karger AG, Allschwilerstrasse 10, PO Box - Postfach - Case Postale, CH-4009 Basel Switzerland. **Tel** 011 41 61 306-1111, FAX 011 41 61 306-1234, telex CH 962 652. **ED** J. S. Alpert, E. Ewy, S. Goldman. **LC** RC681.A1; C25. **DD** 616.1/2/005. **NLM** W1 CA77F. **CODEN** CAGYAO. **[CCC].** Index available. **Ad Acc. Pr Rev.** available on microfilm from University Microfilms International (UMI). Documents available from The Genuine Article, BIOSIS Document Express, CASDDS. ***Continues*** *Cardiologia, 0366-5313.*
**Desc:** Features high quality papers from all over the world to keep its readers regularly informed of current strategies in the prevention and treatment of heart disease. They not only describe but offer critical appraisals of new developments in non-invasive, invasive, diagnostic and therapeutic methods. The importance of experimental work is also acknowledged through reports covering the functions and metabolism of the heart and the morphology and physiology of cardiovascular disease. Special sections in a variety of subspecialty areas reinforce its value as a complete record of recent progress for all cardiologists, internists, cardiac surgeons and clinical physiologists.
**Ind/Abst** Biol. Abstr.; Chem. Abstr.; Curr. Contents Clin. Med.; Curr. Contents Life Sci.; EMBASE; Health Plan. Adminis.; Index Med.; Int. Aerosp. Abstr.; Mod. Med.; Nutr. Abstr. Rev., Ser. B, Live Feeds and Feed.; Nutr. Abstr. Rev., Ser. A, Hum. Exp.; Nutr. Res. Newsl.; Life Sci. Collect.; PESTDOC; Protozoolog. Abstr.; Ref. Upd. Clinical Ed.; Ref. Upd. Deluxe Ed.; Res. Alert [Full Cov.]; Sci. Cit. Index; SCISEARCH; SportSearch.

US/0888-8418
**CARDIOLOGY BOARD REVIEW.** [Cardiol. board rev.]. Vol. 1, No. 1 (Nov. 1984). Periodical. English. mo. $60.00 (one year), $110.00 (two year), $160.00 (three year) US; $80.00 other. MRA Publications Inc, Greenwich Office Park 3, Greenwich CT 06831-5154. **Tel** (203)629-3550. **ED** Ann Maxwell. **DD** 616. **NLM** W1; CA771FG. Index available. **Ad Acc. Pr Rev. Circ:** 67,000 (ctrl).
**Ind/Abst** EMBASE.

US/0733-8651
**CARDIOLOGY CLINICS.** [Cardiol. clin.]. Vol. 1, No. 1 (Feb. 1983)-. Periodical. English. qt. $89.00 (individual), $110.00 (institution) US; $127.00 (individual), $134.00 (institution) other. W.B. Saunders Company, A Subsidiary of Harcourt Brace Jovanovich, Inc., The Curtis Center/Suite 300, Independence Square West, Philadelphia PA 19106-3399. **Tel** (215)238-7800 or, 5587, FAX (215)238-7883, telex 173146. **(Subscription address:** W. B. Saunders Company / North America Subscriptions, c/o Periodicals, 6277 Sea Harbour Drive, 4th Floor, Orlando FL 32887.**) ED** Barbara A. Conover. **LC** RC681.A1. **DD** 616.1/2/005. **NLM** W1 CA77G. **CODEN** CACLE3. **[CCC].** Index available. **Circ:** 4,500. available on microfilm and microfiche from University Microfilms International (UMI). Documents available from BIOSIS Document Express.
**Desc:** Surveys new agents, therapeutic strategies, new instrumentation, and new ideas in providing a better basis for patient care.
**Ind/Abst** Biol. Abstr. (1987-); Cumul. Index Nurs. Allied Health Lit.; EMBASE; Health Devices Alerts; Health Plan. Adminis.; Index Med. Vol. 1, No. 1, 1983-; INIS Atomindex [Micro.].

CN/1181-9030
**CARDIOLOGY CONSULTANT.** [Cardiol. consult.]. Vol. 1, No. 1 (Aug. 1990)-. Periodical. English. qt. Limited free distribution. STA Communications Inc., 955 St. John Boulevard, Suite 306, Pt Claire, Quebec H9R 5K3 Canada. **Tel** (514)695-7623. **DD** 616.1/005.

US/0008-6347
**CARDIOLOGY DIGEST (1979).** (CARDIOLOGY DIGEST.). [Cardiol. dig.]. V. 14, No. 8/9-Aug./Sept. 1979-. Periodical. English. mo. Medical Digest, 444 Frontage Road, PO Box 8021, Northfield IL 60093. **NLM** W1 CA77H. available on microfilm from University Microfilms International (UMI); available on microfiche from University Microfilms International (UMI). ***Continues*** *Journal of Continuing Education in Cardiology, 0148-5199.*
**Desc:** Includes abstracts on medical literature.

UK/0262-5547
**CARDIOLOGY IN PRACTICE.** ***Suspended.*** [Cardiol. pract.]. Vol. 1, No. 1 (May 1982)-(19??). Periodical. English. bm. £36.00 UK; £42.00 Europe; £48.00 other. The Medical Tribune Group, Tower House, Southampton Street, London WC2E 7LS England. **Tel** (01)379-6005, FAX (01)379-6737, telex 266854. **ED** Philip Poole-Wilson and Kim Fox. **NLM** W1 CA77I. **Bk Rev. Ad Acc. Circ:** 20,000.
**Desc:** Articles on management and treatment of cardiovascular diseases, investigative procedures, research, case reports, book reviews, news for GPs and cardiologists.

●US/1061-5377
**CARDIOLOGY IN REVIEW.** [Cardiol. rev.]. Vol. 1, No. 1 (Jan. 1993)-. Periodical. English. bm. $145.00 (institution) $95.00 (individual) US; $135.00 (individual), $185.00 (institution) other. Williams & Wilkins Company, 428 East Preston Street, Baltimore MD 21202-3993. **Tel** (410)528-4000, (800)638-6423, FAX (410)528-8596, telex 87669. **(Subscription address:** Williams & Wilkins, PO Box 64380, Baltimore MD 21264.**) DD** 616. **NLM** W1; CA77IC. **[CCC].** Documents available from Quick Copies.
**Desc:** Quick-reading, authoritative reviews for the cardiologist/internist covering pathogenesis, diagnosis, clinical course, prevention, and treatment of cardiovascular disorders.

●US/1058-3661
**CARDIOLOGY IN THE ELDERLY.** [Cardiol. elder.]. Vol. 1, No. 1 (Feb. 1993)-. Periodical. English. Six times a year. $144.95 (individual); $295.00 (institution). Current Science, 20 North 3rd Street, Philadelphia PA 19106. **Tel** (215)574-2266, (800)552-5866, FAX (215)574-2270. **DD** 616. **NLM** W1; CA77ID.

US/1047-9511
**CARDIOLOGY IN THE YOUNG.** [Cardiol. young]. Vol. 1, No. 1 (Jan. 1991)-. Periodical. English. qt. $125.00. World Publishing Inc, 1811 Billabong Lane, PO Box 16086, Chapel Hill NC 27516. **Tel** (919)929-9091, FAX (919)929-5132. **ED** Prof. Robert H. Anderson. **DD** 616. **NLM** W1; CA77IE. Index available. cum. index. **Bk Rev**, (Qty: 8). **Ad Acc. Pr Rev. Circ:** 1,200 (ctrl).

●US
**CARDIOLOGY JOURNAL CLUB JOURNAL.** Vol. 1 (1995)-. Periodical. English. bm (6 issues). $80.00 (individuals), $110.00 (institutions) US; $90.00 (individuals), $120.00 (institutions) other. Raven Press, 1185 Avenue of the Americas, 37th Floor, New York NY 10036. **Tel** (212)930-9500, (212)930-9604, FAX (212)869-3495, (212)302-8507, telex 640073.

US/0892-9327
**CARDIOLOGY MANAGEMENT.** ***Ceased.*** [Cardiol. manage.]. Vol. 1, No. 1 (Feb./March 1987)-Ceased Vol. 2 No. 3. Periodical. English. bm. Macmillan Professional Journal, 30 Vreeland Road, Florham Park NJ 07932. **Tel** (201)822-1622, FAX (201)822-2498. **ED** Rebecca Morrow. **DD** 616. **NLM** W1; CA771H. Index available. **Bk Rev. Ad Acc. Circ:** 14,000 (ctrl). ***Continues*** *Applied Cardiology, 8750-0426.*
**Desc:** Primarily business-oriented; for cardiologists, cardiology directors, and cardiology administrators in private practices, hospitals, and cardiac rehabilitation centers. Includes clinical cardiology articles.
**Ind/Abst** Cumul. Index Nurs. Allied Health Lit. (?-?); Health Plan. Adminis.; Hospit. Health Admin. Index (1987-).

US/0275-0066
**CARDIOLOGY (NEW YORK, N.Y.).** (CARDIOLOGY.). [Cardiology]. (1981)-. English. an. $70.00. Butterworth Heinemann / Woburn, MA, 225 Wildwood Avenue, Unit B, Woburn MA 01801. **Tel** (800)366-2665, FAX (617)928-2620, telex 880052. **ED** William C. Roberts. **LC** RC681.A1; C252. **DD** 616.1/2/005. **NLM** W1 CA77FE. **Circ:** 5,000.
**Desc:** Publication covering the most recent developments in cardiovascular medicine and surgery.

US/0278-4157
**CARDIOLOGY TIMES.** [Cardiol. times]. Began in 1982?. Periodical. English. mo. $35.00. Office of Personnel and Training, Commandant (G-PDT-2), Women in the Coast Guard Newsletter, 2100 Second Street SW, Washington DC 20593-0001.

US/0163-1675
**CARDIOLOGY UPDATE.** [Cardiol. update]. (1979)-. Monographic series. English. ir. Price varies per volume. Elsevier Science Publishing Company Inc, Madison Square Station, PO Box 882, New York NY 10159-0882. **Tel** (212)633-3950, FAX (212)633-3990. **(Subscription address:** Elsevier Science Inc. / New York Books, 655 Avenue of the Americas, New York NY 10010.**) LC** RC681.A1; C255. **DD** 616.1/2/005. **NLM** W1 CA77KE. **Pr Rev.**

US/0883-4946
**CARDIOLOGY WORLD NEWS.** [Cardiol. world news]. (1985)-. Periodical. English. Ten times a year. $49.00. Medical Publishers Enterprises, 15 22 Fair Lawn Avenue, Fair Lawn NJ 07410. **Tel** (201)796-6500. **DD** 616. **NLM** W1; CA77KG.

US
**CARDIOPULMONARY PHYSICAL THERAPY JOURNAL.** **See** Physical Therapy.

IT/1015-5007
**CARDIOSCIENCE.** Vol. 1, No. 1 (Mar. 1990)-. Periodical. English. qt. $105.00 US; £60.00 Other. Canal Press, San Polo 2171, 30125 Venice Italy. **Tel** (041)5289310, FAX (041)719030. **(Subscription address:** Turpin Transactions Ltd., Blackhorse Road, Letchworth, Hertfordshire SG6 1HN United Kingdom; Telephone: (0462) 672555, FAX: (0462) 48-947**) ED** Peter Harris. **NLM** W1; CA77MDS. **CODEN** CRDIEG. Index available. **Bk Rev. Pr Rev. Circ:** 5,000. Documents available from The Genuine Article.
**Ind/Abst** Curr. Contents Clin. Med.; EMBASE; Res. Alert [Full Cov.]; Sci. Cit. Index; SCISEARCH.

IT
**CARDIOSTIMOLAZIONE.** **Added/Corp** Associazione Italiana di Cardiostimolazione. **VFOAT** Cardio Stimolazione. Vol. 1 No. 1 (1983)-. Periodical. Italian (summaries and/or abstracts in English). qt. L90000 (Italy); $120.00 (other). Edizioni Luigi Pozzi Srl, Via Panama 68, 00198 Rome Italy. **Tel** (06)8553548, FAX (06)8554105. **NLM** W1; CA77MDL.

US/1046-1795
**CARDIOTHORACIC AND VASCULAR ANESTHESIA UPDATE.** **See** Medical Science and Technology-Anesthesiology.

US/0893-8725
**CARDIOTHORACIC SURGERY.** [Cardiothorac. surg.]. Vol. 1 (1986)-. Monographic series. English. ir. Price varies per volume. Marcel Dekker Inc., 270 Madison Avenue, New York NY 10016. **Tel** (212)696-9000, (800)228-1160, FAX (212)685-4540, telex 421419. **(Subscription address:** Marcel Dekker Inc, PO Box 5017, Monticello NY 12701.**) DD** 617. **NLM** W1; CA77ME.

US/0174-1551
**CARDIOVASCULAR AND INTERVENTIONAL RADIOLOGY.** **See** Medical Science and Technology-Radiology.

US/0069-0384
**CARDIOVASCULAR CLINICS.** ***Ceased.*** [Cardiovasc. clin.]. (1969)-(1993). Academic Scholarly Publication. English. ir. FA Davis Company, 1915 Arch Street, Philadelphia PA 19103. **Tel** (800)523-4049, (215)568-2270, FAX (215)568-5065, telex 83-4837. **ED** Albert N Brest. **LC** RC681.A1; C27. **DD** 616.1. **NLM** W1 CA77N. **CODEN** CCLIBG. **[CCC]. Circ:** 3,000. Documents available from BIOSIS Document Express, CASDDS.
**Desc:** On-going series which extends concepts in the diagnosis and management of a wide range of cardiovascular disorders. Each book covers a topic of major interest in cardiology. Acclaimed.
**Ind/Abst** Biol. Abstr. (1987-); Chem. Abstr. (1969-1983); EMBASE (?-?); Energy Res. Abstr. (Feb. 1977-); Health Plan. Adminis.; Index Med. (?-?); INIS Atomindex [Micro.].

US/0897-3830
**CARDIOVASCULAR DRUG ALERT.** [Cardiovasc. drug alerts]. Vol. 1, No. 1 (Jan. 1988)-. Periodical. English. Twelve times a year. $59.00 US; $76.00 Canada; $83.00 other. M. J. Powers and Company Publishers, 374 Millburn Avenue, Millburn NJ 07041. **Tel** (201)467-4556. **DD** 616.

US/0897-5957
**CARDIOVASCULAR DRUG REVIEWS.** [Cardiovasc. drug rev.]. Vol. 6 (1988)-. Academic Scholarly Publication. English. Four times a year. $160.00 (institutions), $115.00 (individuals) North America; add $30.00 (surface mail) or $45.00 (airmail) other. Neva Press, PO Box 347, Branford CT 06405. **Tel** (203)272-5338, FAX (203)272-5338. **DD** 615. **NLM** W1; CA77X. **CODEN** CDREEA. **[CCC].** Documents available from The Genuine Article, BIOSIS Document Express, CASDDS. ***Continues*** *New Cardiovascular Drugs, 0891-3692.*
**Ind/Abst** Biol. Abstr. (1989-); Chem. Abstr. (1988-); EMBASE; Ref. Upd. Deluxe Ed.; Res. Alert [Full Cov.]; Sci. Cit. Index; SCISEARCH.

US/0161-5734
**CARDIOVASCULAR DRUGS.** [Cardiovasc. drugs]. V. 1-. Academic Scholarly Publication. English. Price varies per volume. University Park Press, PO Box 4034, New York NY 10163. **LC** RM345; .C3752. **DD** 615/.71. **NLM** W1 CA77V. **CODEN** CADRDP. Documents available from BIOSIS Document Express, CASDDS.
**Ind/Abst** Biol. Abstr.; Chem. Abstr. (1978-1979).

US/0920-3206
**CARDIOVASCULAR DRUGS AND THERAPY.** (CARDIOVASCULAR DRUGS AND THERAPY / SPONSORED BY THE INTERNATIONAL SOCIETY OF CARDIOVASCULAR PHARMACOTHERAPY.). [Cardiovasc. drugs ther.]. **Added/Corp** International Society of Cardiovascular Pharmacotherapy. Vol. 1, No. 1 (1987)-. Academic Scholarly Publication. English. bm (occassional free supplements). $569.00. Kluwer Academic Publishers / Massachusetts, PO Box 358, Accord Station, Hingham MA 02018. **Tel** (617)871-6600. **ED** Lionel Opie and Elliot Rapaport. **LC** RM345; .C3754. **DD** 616.1/061/05. **NLM** W1; CA77VK. **CODEN** CDTHET. **[CCC]. Bk Rev. Ad Acc. Pr Rev. Acid Free. Circ:** 1,000. available on microfilm and microfiche from University Microfilms International (UMI). Documents available from The Genuine Article, BIOSIS Document Express, CASDDS, ADONIS.
**Desc:** Provides an objective and scientifically rigorous international forum which focuses on advances in cardiac therapy and emphasizes drug treatments of heart disorders. The scope includes original clinical studies, reviews, essays on state-of-the-art therapy, discussions of controversial topics, and original laboratory investigations.
**Ind/Abst** ADONIS; Biol. Abstr. (1987-); Chem. Abstr. (?-1988); Curr. Aware. Biol. Sci., CABS; Curr. Contents Clin. Med.; Curr. Contents Life Sci.; EMBASE; Health Plan. Adminis.; Ref. Upd. Deluxe Ed.; Res. Alert [Full Cov.]; Sci. Cit. Index; SCISEARCH; Soc. Sci. Cit. Index [Select. Cov.].

IT/1120-0421
**CARDIOVASCULAR IMAGING : CI.** **VFOAT** CI. (1989)-. Italian (English). Four times a year. $110.00. CEPI, Vis Nicolo Tartaglia, 00197 Rome Italy. **Tel** 011 39 6 8082101 or 8077011, FAX 011 39 6 8072458. **ED** Armando Dagianti. **Bk Rev. Ad Acc, Adv Mgr:** Marine Buongiorno, **Tel** (06)8077011. **Pr Rev. Circ:** 2,500 (ctrl).
**Desc:** Promotes imaging as a tool for research and a link with clinical medicine. Categories of articles includes echocardiography, doppler, nuclear cardiology, cardiac-coronary angiography, vascular imaging, computer tomography, nuclear magnetic resonance, image processing, computer engineering. Readers include physicians, cardiologists, radiologists and health care professionals interested in imaging techniques.

●US/1076-4763
**CARDIOVASCULAR NETWORK NEWS.** (1994)-. Periodical. English. qt. $250.00. Mendenhall Associates, Inc., 1500 Cedar Boulevard, Ann Arbor MI 48105. **Tel** (313)741-4710, FAX (313)741-7277.

US/0747-461X
**CARDIOVASCULAR NEWS.** ***Title Change.*** [Cardiovasc. news]. Vol. 1, No. 1 (Jan. 1982)-(19??). Periodical. English. mo. McMahon Publishing Company, 148 West 24th Street, 8th Floor, New York NY 10011. **Tel** (212)620-4600, FAX (212)620-5928. **LC** Discard. ***Continued by*** *Newspaper of Cardiology.*

●US/1054-8807
**CARDIOVASCULAR PATHOLOGY.** (CARDIOVASCULAR PATHOLOGY : THE OFFICIAL JOURNAL OF THE SOCIETY FOR CARDIOVASCULAR PATHOLOGY.). [Cardiovasc. pathol.]. **Added/Corp** Society for Cardiovascular Pathology. Vol. 1, No. 1 (Jan./Mar. 1992)-. Academic Scholarly Publication. English. qt (1 volume). $174.00 US; $204.00 other. Elsevier Science Publishing Company Inc, Madison Square Station, PO Box 882, New York NY 10159-0882. **Tel** (212)633-3950, FAX (212)633-3990. **DD** 616. **NLM** W1; CA771C. **[CCC].**
**Ind/Abst** Sci. Cit. Index.

UK/0263-7243
**CARDIOVASCULAR PHARMACOLOGY.** [Cardiovasc. pharmacol.]. (1983)-. English. mo. £115.00. SUBIS, Mansion House, 19 Kingfield Road, Sheffield S11 9AS England. **Tel** 011 44 114 255 4433, FAX 011 44 114 255 4626. **DD** 016.6161061. **Bk Rev. Ad Acc.**
**Desc:** Current awareness service for researchers and clinicians.

US/0363-387X
**CARDIOVASCULAR PHYSIOLOGY (LONDON, ENGLAND).** (CARDIOVASCULAR PHYSIOLOGY.). [Cardiovasc. physiol.]. (1974)-. Periodical. English. be. University Park Press, PO Box 4034, New York NY 10163. **ED** A C Guyton. **LC** QP1; .P62 subser; QP101.2. **DD** 599/.01/1. **NLM** W1 IN834F v.9 etc. WG 102 C2672.

UK/0008-6363
**CARDIOVASCULAR RESEARCH.** [Cardiovasc. res.]. **Added/Corp** British Medical Association. British Cardiac Society. Vol. 1 (Jan. 1967)-. Academic Scholarly Publication. English. mo. £291.00. BMJ / British Medical Journal Publishing Group, British Medical Association House, Tavistock Square, London WC1H 9JR England. **Tel** 011 44 71 3874499, FAX 011 44 71 383 6402, telex 290034 HBJ MN. **ED** David J. Hearse. **DD** 616. **NLM** W1 CA772. **CODEN** CVREAU. **[CCC]. Pr Rev.** available on microfilm and microfiche from University Microfilms International (UMI). Documents available from The Genuine Article, BIOSIS Document Express, CASDDS, ADONIS.
**Desc:** The subjects covered include physiological, pathological, pharmacological, biochemical, biophysical, haemodynamic, surgical and similar advances in the study of the heart and circulation.
**Ind/Abst** ADONIS (19??-); Biol. Abstr. (19??-); Chem. Abstr. (19??-); CSA Neuro. Abstr. (?-?); Curr. Aware. Biol. Sci., CABS (19??-); Curr. Contents Life Sci. (19??-); EMBASE (19??-); Health Plan. Adminis. (19??-); Index Med. (19??-); Index Vet. (19??-); Int. Aerosp. Abstr. (19??-); Mod. Med. (19??-); Nutr. Abstr. Rev., Ser. B, Live Feeds and Feed. (19??-); Nutr. Abstr. Rev., Ser. A, Hum. Exp. (19??-); Nutr. Res. Newsl. (19??-); Life Sci. Collect. (19??-); PESTDOC (19??-); Phys. Med. Biol. (19??-19??); Pig News Inf. (19??-); Protozoolog. Abstr. (19??-); Ref. Upd. Deluxe Ed. (19??-); Res. Alert (19??-) [Full Cov.]; Sci. Cit. Index (19??-); SCISEARCH (19??-); Soc. Sci. Cit. Index [Select. Cov.]; SportSearch (19??-).

US/0271-4779
**CARDIOVASCULAR REVIEW (BALTIMORE).** (CARDIOVASCULAR REVIEW.). [Cardiovasc. rev.]. 1979-. English. an. Grune & Stratton Inc., 6277 Sea Harbor Drive, Orlando FL 32887. **Tel** (800)782-4479, (407)345-2567. **LC** RC666; .T55. **DD** 616.1/005. **NLM** W1 CA773E.

US/0197-3118
**CARDIOVASCULAR REVIEWS & REPORTS.** [Cardiovasc. rev. rep.]. **VFOAT** CVT and R; CVR&R. **VAT** Cardiovascular Reviews and Reports. Vol. 1 April (1980)-. Periodical. English. mo. $65.00 (individuals), $80.00 (institutions) US; $80.00 (individuals), $95.00 (institutions) other. Le Jacq Communications Inc., 777 West Putnam Avenue, Greenwich CT 06830. **Tel** (203)531-0460, FAX (203)625-0393. **ED** John Laragh. **DD** 616. **NLM** W1 CA773H. **Bk Rev. Ad Acc. Pr Rev. Circ:** 110,000 (ctrl). available on microfilm from University Microfilms International (UMI).
**Desc:** Features articles on the treatment of cardiovascular diseases.
**Ind/Abst** EMBASE; Nutr. Res. Newsl.

SP/0211-6553
**CARDIOVASCULAR REVIEWS & REPORTS EDICION ESPANOLA.** [Cardiovasc. rev. rep.Ed. esp.]. **VFOAT** Cardiovascular Reviews and reports (Edicion Espanola). (1980)-. Periodical. Spanish. mo (11 issues per year - July/Aug. issue combined). $66.00. Haymarket SA, Calle Aribau 168 170, 08036 Barcelona Spain. **Tel** 011 34 3 238-1742. **UDC** 616.1.

CN/0842-537X
**CARDIOVASCULAR RISK FACTORS.** [Cardiovasc. risk factors]. (1988)-. Periodical. English. Six times a year. 10.000ptas Spain; $135.00 (individual), $200.00 (institutions) other. Editorial Saned SA, Apolonio Morales 6, 28036 Madrid Spain. **Tel** 011 34 1 359-4092, FAX 011 34 1 457-9918. **ED** Azturo Fernandez-Cruz. **DD** 616.1/005. **Pr Rev. Circ:** 3,000.
**Desc:** Topics related to cardiovascular risk factors, points of view, and current concepts.
**Ind/Abst** EMBASE.

US
**CARDIOVASCULAR SURGERY. See** Medical Science and Technology-Surgery.

●UK/0967-2109
**CARDIOVASCULAR SURGERY : OFFICIAL JOURNAL OF THE INTERNATIONAL SOCIETY FOR CARDIOVASCULAR SURGERY.** **Added/Corp** International Society for Cardiovascular Surgery. Vol. 1, No. 1 (Feb. 1993)-. Periodical. English. bm. $172.00 The Americas; £115.00 other. Butterworth Heinemann Publishers, Linacre House, Jordan Hill, Oxford OX2 8DP England. **Tel** 011 44 865 310366. **(Subscription address:** Elsevier Science Ltd. Oxford Fulfillment Centre, PO Box 800, Kidlington, Oxford OX5 1DX United Kingdom.**) NLM** W1; CA773S.

US/0098-6569
**CATHETERIZATION AND CARDIOVASCULAR DIAGNOSIS.** [Catheter. cardiovasc. diagn.]. Vol. 1 (1975)-. Academic Scholarly Publication. English. mo. $744.00 US; $864.00 Canada and Mexico; $909.00 other. John Wiley & Sons, Inc., 605 Third Avenue, New York NY 10158-0012. **Tel** (212)850-6000, (212)850-6645, FAX (212)850-6088, telex 12-7063. **(Subscription address:** John Wiley & Sons / England, Baffins Lane, Chichester, West Sussex PO19 1UD England.**) ED** Frank J. Hildner. **LC** RC683; .C335. **DD** 616.1/2/0757205. **NLM** W1 CA967. **CODEN** CCDID. **[CCC]. Ad Acc. Pr Rev.** Documents available from The Genuine Article, BIOSIS Document Express.
**Desc:** Devoted primarily to invasive cardiology. Special emphasis is placed on angioplasty and the newest techniques of interventional cardiology.
**Ind/Abst** Biol. Abstr.; Curr. Contents Clin. Med.; EMBASE; Energy Res. Abstr. (Oct. 1977-); Health Devices Alerts; Health Plan. Adminis.; Index Med.; INIS Atomindex [Micro.]; Life Sci. Collect.; Res. Alert [Full Cov.]; Rev. Med. Vet. Mycology; Sci. Cit. Index; SCISEARCH.

SZ/1015-9770
**CEREBROVASCULAR DISEASES. See** Medical Science and Technology-Neurology.

US/0012-3692
**CHEST.** (CHEST : OFFICIAL PUBLICATION OF THE AMERICAN COLLEGE OF CHEST PHYSICIANS.). [Chest]. **Added/Corp** American College of Chest Physicians. Vol. 57, No. 1 (Jan. 1970)-. Academic Scholarly Publication. English. mo. $144.00 (institution), $108.00 (individual) US; $180.00 (institution), $144.00 (individual) other. American College of Chest Physicians, 3300 Dundee Road, Northbrook IL 60062. **Tel** (708)498-1400, FAX (708)498-5460. **ED** Alfred Soffer. **LC** RC705; .D5. **DD** 616.2. **NLM** W1 CH415. **CODEN** CHETBF. **Bk Rev. Ad Acc. Pr Rev. Circ:** 19,500 (ctrl). available on microfilm and microfiche from University Microfilms International (UMI). Documents available from The Genuine Article, BIOSIS Document Express, CASDDS. ***Continues** Diseases of the Chest, 0096-0217.*
**Desc:** The journal for pulmonologists, cardiologists, cardiothoracic surgeons and related specialists.
**Ind/Abst** Abr. Index Med.; Annals Behav. Med.; Biol. Abstr.; Chem. Abstr.; Coal Abstr.; Cumul. Index Nurs. Allied Health Lit.; Curr. Aware. Biol. Sci., CABS; Curr. Contents Clin. Med.; Curr. Contents Life Sci.; EMBASE; Energy Res. Abstr. (Jan. 1971-); Health Devices Alerts; Health Period. Database [Full Txt.]; Health Plan. Adminis.; Helminthol. Abstr. (19??-19??); Immunol. Abstr.; Index Med.; Index Vet.; INIS Atomindex [Micro.]; Int. Aerosp. Abstr.; Iowa Drug Inf. Serv. (1967-); Maize Abstr.; Med. Abstr. Newsl.; Microbiol. Abstr. Sect. B; Microbiol. Abstr. Sect. C; Mod. Med.; Nutr. Abstr. Rev., Ser. B, Live Feeds and Feed.; Nutr. Abstr. Rev., Ser. A, Hum. Exp.; Oncog. Growth Factors Abstr.; Life Sci. Collect.; Physic. Medline Plus; Pollut. Abstr. Indexes; Protozoolog. Abstr.; Ref. Upd. Basic Ed.; Ref. Upd. Clinical Ed.; Ref. Upd. Deluxe Ed.; Res. Alert [Full Cov.]; Rev. Agric. Entomol.; Rev. Med. Vet. Entomol.; Rev. Med. Vet. Mycology; Rev. Plant Pathol.; Saf. Health Work; Sci. Cit. Index; SCISEARCH; Soc. Sci. Cit. Index [Select. Cov.]; SportSearch; Virol. AIDS Abstr.; Wheat Barley Trit. Abstr.

US/0894-5853
**CHOICES IN CARDIOLOGY.** Vol. 1, No. 1, (1987)-. Periodical. English. bm (6 issues). $96.00. Choices Publishing Group, 129 Washington Street, Hoboken NJ 07030. **Tel** (201)792-1900. **DD** 616. **NLM** W1; CH883H.

CC/0253-3758
**CHUNG-HUA HSIN HSUEH KUAN PING TSA CHIH.** [Zhonghua xinxueguanbing zazhi]. **VFOAT** Chinese Journal of Cardiovascular Disease; Zhonghua Xinxueguanbing Zazhi. (1973)-. Academic Scholarly Publication. Chinese. qt. $34.02. Chinese Medical Association, 42 Dongsi Xidajie, 100710 Beijing, China. **Tel** (1)550394. **(Subscription address:** China International Book Trading Corporation, PO Box 399, Library Service Department, Beijing 100044 People's Republic of China.**) NLM** W1 CH9819. **CODEN** CHHCDF. Documents available from BIOSIS Document Express, CASDDS.
**Desc:** Contains information on cardiovascular diseases.
**Ind/Abst** Biol. Abstr.; Chem. Abstr.; EMBASE; Index Med. (1979-); NAPRALERT.

US/0009-7322
**CIRCULATION (NEW YORK, N.Y.).** (CIRCULATION.). [Circulation]. **Added/Corp** American Heart Association. American Heart Association. Abstracts. Vol. 1 (Jan. 1950)-. Academic Scholarly Publication. English. Twenty-four times a year. $224.00 institution. American Heart Association, 7272 Greenville Avenue, Dallas TX 75231-4596. **Tel** (214)706-1310, (214)373-6300, FAX (214)691-6342. **(Subscription address:** American Heart Association, PO Box 843543, Dallas TX 75284-3543.**) ED** Burton E. Sobel. **LC** RC681.A1; C5. **DD** 616.105. **NLM** W1 CI743. **CODEN** CIRCAZ. **[CCC].** Index available (bound in December issue). cum. index. **Bk Rev. Ad Acc. Pr Rev. Circ:** 23,000 (ctrl). available on microfilm and microfiche from University Microfilms International (UMI). Documents available from The Genuine Article, BIOSIS Document Express, CASDDS.
**Desc:** Original articles in cardiovascular clinical and laboratory investigation. Editorials, perspectives, preludes and progress, and the American Heart Association news.
**Ind/Abst** Abr. Index Med.; Annals Behav. Med.; Biol. Abstr.; Chem. Abstr.; Chicano Index; CSA Neuro. Abstr. (?-?); Curr. Aware. Biol. Sci., CABS; Curr. Contents Clin. Med.; Curr. Contents Life Sci.; EMBASE; Energy Res. Abstr.; Health Devices Alerts; Health Period. Database; Health Plan. Adminis.; Helminthol. Abstr.; Index Med.; Int. Aerosp. Abstr.; Iowa Drug Inf. Serv.; J. Watch; Med. Abstr. Newsl.; Mod. Med.; Nutr. Res. Newsl.; Life Sci. Collect.; PESTDOC; Physic. Medline Plus; Phys. Med. Biol. (19??-19??); Protozoolog. Abstr.; Ref. Upd. Basic Ed.; Ref. Upd. Clinical Ed.; Ref. Upd. Deluxe Ed.; Res. Alert [Full Cov.]; Saf. Health Work; Sci. Cit. Index; SCISEARCH; Soc. Sci. Cit. Index [Select. Cov.]; SportSearch.

US/0009-7330
**CIRCULATION RESEARCH.** (CIRCULATION RESEARCH : A JOURNAL OF THE AMERICAN HEART ASSOCIATION.). [Circ. res.]. **Added/Corp** American Heart Association. Vol. 1, No. 1 (Jan. 1953)-. Academic Scholarly Publication. English. mo. $270.00 institution. American Heart Association, 7272 Greenville Avenue, Dallas TX 75231-4596. **Tel** (214)706-1310, (214)373-6300, FAX (214)691-6342. **(Subscription address:** American Heart Association, PO Box 843543, Dallas TX 75284-3543.**) ED** Harry A. Fozzard. **LC** RC681.A1; A57137. **DD** 616.105. **NLM** W1 CI741. **CODEN** CIRUAL. **[CCC].** Index available (Index published in June). **Bk Rev. Ad Acc. Pr Rev. Acid Free. Circ:** 4,000 (ctrl). available on microfilm and microfiche from University Microfilms International (UMI). Documents available from The Genuine Article, BIOSIS Document Express, CASDDS.
**Desc:** Provides a medium for bringing together basic research on the cardiovascular system from various disciplines including biology, biochemistry, biophysics, morphology, pathology, physiology and pharmacology. Also accepts for publication manuscripts on clinical research that contribute to an understanding of fundamental problems.
**Ind/Abst** Abstr. Clin. Care Guidel.; Biol. Abstr.; Calcium Calcif. Tissue Abstr.; Chem. Abstr.; CSA Neuro. Abstr.; Curr. Aware. Biol. Sci., CABS; Curr. Contents Life Sci.; EMBASE; Energy Res. Abstr.; Health Plan. Adminis.; Index Med.; Index Vet.; INIS Atomindex [Micro.]; Int. Aerosp. Abstr.; Iowa Drug Inf. Serv. (1968-); Mod. Med.; Nutr. Res. Newsl.; Life Sci. Collect.; PESTDOC; Pig News Inf.; Ref. Upd. Basic Ed.; Ref. Upd. Deluxe Ed.; Res. Alert [Full Cov.]; Sci. Cit. Index; SCISEARCH; Vet. Bull.

US/0009-7330
**CIRCULATION RESEARCH.** (CIRCULATION RESEARCH. MICROFORM). **Added/Corp** American Heart Association. Vol. 1, No. 1 (Jan. 1953)-. Periodical. English. sa. **CODEN** CIRUAL. **[CCC].** Documents available from CASDDS. ***Continued in part by** Hypertension, 0194-911X.*
**Ind/Abst** Chem. Abstr.

US
**CIRCULATION. SUPPLEMENT. Added/Corp** American Heart Association. Circulation. Supplement. No. 1 (Apr. 1964)-. English. ir. $15.00 US; $20.00 other. American Heart Association, 7272 Greenville Avenue, Dallas TX 75231-4596. **Tel** (214)706-1310, (214)373-6300, FAX (214)691-6342. **NLM** W1 CI743A. **CODEN** CISUAQ. Documents available from CASDDS.
**Ind/Abst** Chem. Abstr.

US
**CIRCULATION. [MICROFICHE].** (19??)-. English. ir. University Microfilms International, 300 North Zeeb Road, Ann Arbor MI 48106-1346. **Tel** (313)761-4700, (800)521-0600 Exts. 2490, 2491, FAX (313)973-1540. available in print.

US/0092-6213
**CIRCULATORY SHOCK.** [Circ. shock]. Vol. 1 (March 1974)-. Academic Scholarly Publication. English. mo. $996.00 US; $1,116.00 Canada and Mexico; $1,161.00 other. John Wiley & Sons, Inc., 605 Third Avenue, New York NY 10158-0012. **Tel** (212)850-6000, (212)850-6645, FAX (212)850-6088, telex 12-7063. **(Subscription address:** John Wiley & Sons / England, Baffins Lane, Chichester, West Sussex PO19 1UD England.**) ED** James P. Filkins. **LC** RC685.C18; C56. **DD** 616/.047. **NLM** W1 CI745K. **CODEN** CRSHAG. **[CCC]. Pr Rev.** Documents available from The Genuine Article, BIOSIS Document Express, CASDDS.
**Desc:** An international journal devoted to basic and clinical research on shock and low-flow states. Publishes original contributions concerned with the biochemical, physiological, pathological, medical, and surgical aspects of circulatory shock and related states.
**Ind/Abst** Biol. Abstr.; Chem. Abstr.; CSA Neuro. Abstr. (?-?); Curr. Contents Life Sci.; EMBASE; Energy Res. Abstr. (Oct. 1980-); Health Plan. Adminis.; Index Med. (1977-); INIS Atomindex [Micro.]; Microbiol. Abstr. Sect. B; Nutr. Abstr. Rev., Ser. A, Hum. Exp.; Life Sci. Collect.; Pig News Inf.; Ref. Upd. Deluxe Ed.; Res. Alert [Full Cov.]; Sci. Cit. Index; SCISEARCH.

US/0193-7545
**CIRCULATORY SHOCK. SUPPLEMENT.** (1979)-. Monographic series. English. ir. Price varies per volume. John Wiley & Sons, Inc., 605 Third Avenue, New York NY 10158-0012. **Tel** (212)850-6000, (212)850-6645, FAX (212)850-6088, telex 12-7063. **(Subscription address:** John Wiley & Sons / England, Baffins Lane, Chichester, West Sussex PO19 1UD England.**) NLM** W1 CI745KB.
**Ind/Abst** Index Med.

IT/0392-1344
**CLINICA & TERAPIA CARDIOVASCOLARE.** [Clin. ter. cardiovasc.]. **VFOAT** Clinica e Terapia Cardiovascolare. Vol. 1, No. 1 (Jan./Febr. 1982)-. Periodical. Italian (English). bm (6 issues). L60000. CIC Edizioni Internazionali, Via L Spallanzani 11, 00161 Rome Italy. **Tel** 011 39 6 841-2673, FAX 011 39 6 844-3365, telex 622099 CIC I. **NLM** W1; CL285H. **[CCC].**
**Ind/Abst** EMBASE [Select. Cov.].

SP/0212-1808
**CLINICA CARDIOVASCULAR.** [Clin. cardiovasc.]. Vol. 1, No. 1 (Sept./Oct. 1982)-. Periodical. Spanish (summaries and/or abstracts in English). bm (6 issues). $60.00 Europe; $100.00 other. Alpe Editores SA, C Pedro Rico 27, Oficinas 11 & 12, 28029 Madrid Spain. **Tel** 011 34 1 7338811, FAX 011 34 1 3159652. **NLM** W1; CL291. **[CCC].**
**Ind/Abst** Indice Med. Esp.

SP
**CLINICA E INVESTIGACION EN ARTERIOSCLEROSIS.** Spanish. Ediciones Doyma SA, Travesera de Gracia 17 21, 08021 Barcelona Spain. **Tel** 011 34 3 2000711, 011 34 3 4145706, FAX 011 34 3 2091136, telex 51964 INK E. **NLM** W1; CL366ST.
**Ind/Abst** Indice Med. Esp.

●US/1073-1644
**CLINICAL ADVANCES IN CARDIO-RESPIRATORY CARE. See** Medical Science and Technology-Respiratory System.

●US
**CLINICAL AND APPLIED THROMBOSIS / HEMOSTATIS.** Vol. 1 (1995)-. Periodical. English. qt. $95.00 (individuals), $115.00 (institutions) US; $105.00 (individuals), $125.00 (institutions) other. Raven Press, 1185 Avenue of the Americas, 37th Floor, New York NY 10036. **Tel** (212)930-9500, (212)930-9604, FAX (212)869-3495, (212)302-8507, telex 640073.

●US/1064-1963
**CLINICAL AND EXPERIMENTAL HYPERTENSION (1993).** (CLINICAL AND EXPERIMENTAL HYPERTENSION : CHE.). [Clin. exp. hypertens.]. **VFOAT** CHE. Vol. 15, No. 1 (Jan. 1993)-. Academic Scholarly Publication. English. Eight times a year. $1,195.00 US; $1,223.00 other. Marcel Dekker Inc., 270 Madison Avenue, New York NY 10016. **Tel** (212)696-9000, (800)228-1160, FAX (212)685-4540, telex 421419. **(Subscription address:** Marcel Dekker Inc, PO Box 5017, Monticello NY 12701.**) DD** 616. **NLM** W1; CL658D. **CODEN** CEHYER. **[CCC].** Documents available from BIOSIS Document Express, CASDDS, ADONIS. ***Continues*** *Clinical and Experimental Hypertension. Part A, Theory and Practice, 0730-0077.*
**Ind/Abst** ADONIS; Biol. Abstr.; Biol. Dig.; Chem. Abstr.; Curr. Contents Life Sci.; EMBASE; Index Med. (1993-); Int. Pharm. Abstr. (19??-19??); Life Sci. Collect.; PESTDOC (?-?); Sci. Cit. Index.

US/0730-0077
**CLINICAL AND EXPERIMENTAL HYPERTENSION. PART A, THEORY AND PRACTICE.** ***Title Change.*** [Clin. exp. hypertens., Part A Theory pract.]. **VFOAT** Theory and Practice. Vol. A4, No. 1 & 2-Vol. A14, No. 6 (Nov. 1992). Academic Scholarly Publication. English. Four times a year. Marcel Dekker Inc., 270 Madison Avenue, New York NY 10016. **Tel** (212)696-9000, (800)228-1160, FAX (212)685-4540, telex 421419. **(Subscription address:** Marcel Dekker Inc, PO Box 5017, Monticello NY 12701.**) ED** Joseph P. Buckley, M. J. Antonaccio, V. Dequattro, D. Gantan, J. P. Chalmers, K. Yoshinaga. **LC** RC685.H8; C553. **DD** 616. **NLM** W1; CL658B. **CODEN** CEHADM. **Bk Rev. Ad Acc. Pr Rev.** available on microfiche. Documents available from The Genuine Article, BIOSIS Document Express, CASDDS. ***Continues in part*** *Clinical and Experimental Hypertension, 0148-3927.* ***Continued by*** *Clinical and Experimental Hypertension (New York, N.Y. : 1993), 1064-1963.*
**Desc:** Covers all aspects of human and animal hypertension, ranging from neurogenic mechanisms to circulatory control and drug development and application. Its special interdisciplinary approach contributes to the understanding and treatment of this pervasive disorder.
**Ind/Abst** Biol. Abstr.; Biol. Dig.; Calcium Calcif. Tissue Abstr.; Chem. Abstr.; CSA Neuro. Abstr.; Curr. Aware. Biol. Sci., CABS; Curr. Contents Life Sci.; EMBASE; Health Plan. Adminis.; Index Med.; Int. Pharm. Abstr. (19??-19??); Life Sci. Collect.; PESTDOC; Ref. Upd. Deluxe Ed.; Res. Alert [Full Cov.]; Sci. Cit. Index (19??-19??); SCISEARCH.

US/0730-0085
**CLINICAL AND EXPERIMENTAL HYPERTENSION. PART B, HYPERTENSION IN PREGNANCY.** ***Title Change.*** **See** Medical Science and Technology-Gynecology and Obstetrics.

US/0741-4218
**CLINICAL CARDIOLOGY ALERT.** [Clin. cardiol. alert]. (1982)-. Periodical. English. mo. $115.00 without CME; $165.00 with CME. American Health Consultants, 3525 Piedmont Road, Suite 400, Atlanta GA 30305. **Tel** (800)688-2421, (404)262-7436. **(Subscription address:** American Health Consultants, PO Box 95278, Chicago IL 60694.**)** ***Continues*** *Cardiology Alert.*
**Desc:** Each issue contains six to eight summaries of recent medical journal articles focusing on the latest developments in the field of cardiology and cardiovascular disease.
**Ind/Abst** Mod. Med.

US/0891-2092
**CLINICAL CARDIOLOGY (LOS ALTOS , CALIF.).** (CLINICAL CARDIOLOGY.). [Clin. cardiol.]. 1st Ed. (1977)-. Monographic series. English. ir (every three yeras). $37.95 (latest volume). Appleton Century Crofts, Prentice Hall, 200 Old Tappan Road, Old Tappan NJ 07675. **Tel** (201)767-5188, (800)922-0579. **ED** Maurice Sokolow and Malcolm McIlroy. **LC** RC681; .C664. **DD** 616.1/2. **[CCC].**
**Ind/Abst** Curr. Contents Clin. Med.; Rev. Med. Vet. Mycology.

US/0160-9289
**CLINICAL CARDIOLOGY (MAHWAH, N.J.).** (CLINICAL CARDIOLOGY : INTERNATIONAL JOURNAL FOR CARDIOVASCULAR DISEASES.). [Clin. cardiol.]. **Added/Corp** Foundation for Advances in Medicine and Science. **VFOAT** Clinical Cardiology. Vol. 1 (April 1978)-. Periodical. English. mo. $80.00. Foundation Advances in Medicine and Science Inc., Box 832, Mahwah NJ 07430. **Tel** (201)818-1010, FAX (201)818-0086, telex 220883 TAUR. **ED** H W Heiss. **NLM** W1 CL673. **[CCC]. Bk Rev. Ad Acc. Pr Rev. Circ:** 22,000 (ctrl). Documents available from The Genuine Article.
**Desc:** Full coverage of all aspects of cardiac physiology and treatment of diseases of the heart.
**Ind/Abst** EMBASE; Health Plan. Adminis.; Index Med. (1978-); INIS Atomindex [Micro.]; Nutr. Res. Newsl.; Protozoolog. Abstr.; Res. Alert [Full Cov.]; Sci. Cit. Index; SCISEARCH.

UK/0956-3075
**CLINICAL INTENSIVE CARE : INTERNATIONAL JOURNAL OF CRITICAL & CORONARY CARE MEDICINE.** **VFOAT** International Journal of Critical & Coronary Care Medicine. Vol. 1, No. 1 (Jan. 1990)-. Periodical. English. bm. £70.00 (individuals), £95.00 (institutions) Europe; £82.00 (individuals), £112.00 (institutions) other. Castle House Publications Ltd, 28-30 Church Road, Tunbridge Wells Kent, TN1 1JP England. **Tel** 011 44 892 539606, FAX 011 44 892 517005, telex 957565 CBJ AG. **ED** Dr. E.D. Bennett. **NLM** W1; CL715S. **CODEN** CICAEQ. Index available. **Bk Rev. Ad Acc, Adv Mgr:** Wendy Reinders. **Pr Rev.**
**Ind/Abst** EMBASE.

●US/1068-0640
**CLINICAL PULMONARY MEDICINE.** [Clin. pulm. med.]. Vol. 1, No. 1 (Jan. 1994)-. Periodical. English. bm. $84.00 (individual), $119.00 (institution) US; $109.00 (individual), $144.00 (institution) other. Williams & Wilkins Company, 428 East Preston Street, Baltimore MD 21202-3993. **Tel** (410)528-4000, (800)638-6423, FAX (410)528-8596, telex 87669. **(Subscription address:** Williams & Wilkins, PO Box 64380, Baltimore MD 21264.**) DD** 616. **NLM** W1; CL768F. Documents available from Quick Copies.
**Desc:** Focuses on key aspects of clinical practice.

US/0961-7787
**CLINICIAN'S MANUAL ON HYPERLIPIDEMIA.** [Clin. man. hyperlipid.]. **Added/Corp** International Atherosclerosis Society. (1991)-. English. an. $30.00 (individuals) North America. Current Science, 20 North 3rd Street, Philadelphia PA 19106. **Tel** (215)574-2266, (800)552-5866, FAX (215)574-2270. **ED** A. M. Gotto. **NLM** WD 200.1; C641.
**Desc:** Targeted to the general practitioner. Focuses on diagnosis, treatment and screening hyperlipidemia.

US/0069-5319
**COLLECTED WORKS ON CARDIO-PULMONARY DISEASES.** [Collect. works cardio-pulm. dis.]. **Added/Corp** Heineman Foundation Laboratories. **VFOAT** Cardiopulmonary Disease. Vol. 1/2 (Sept. 1959)-. English. Heineman Foundation Laboratories, Charlotte Memorial Hospital, Charlotte NC. **NLM** W1 CO169S. **CODEN** CWCDAR. Documents available from BIOSIS Document Express.
**Ind/Abst** Biol. Abstr. (?-1979); Energy Res. Abstr. (Aug. 1982-); Health Plan. Adminis.

US/0276-6574
**COMPUTERS IN CARDIOLOGY.** [Comput. cardiol.]. **Added/Corp** National Institutes of Health (U.S.) IEEE Computer Society. (Oct. 2-4, 1974)-. English. an. $60.00. IEEE Computer Society, 10662 Los Vaqueros Circle, PO Box 3014, Los Alamitos CA 90720-1264. **Tel** (714)821-8380, (800)272-6657, FAX (714)821-4641. **LC** RC683.5.D36; C637. **DD** 616.1/2/02854. **NLM** W3 C185. **CODEN** COCADX. **[CCC]. Bk Rev.** ctrl circ. Documents available from Article Express International, Ask*IEEE.
**Desc:** Covers engineering details of clinically useful systems for applications such as arrhythmia monitoring, intensive care, information displays, etc.
**Ind/Abst** Bioeng. Abstr.; Ei Page One; Eng. Index Annu.; Index IEEE Publ.; INSPEC.

CN/1181-9049
**CONSULTATIONS EN CARDIOLOGIE.** [Consult. cardiol.]. Vol. 1, No 1 (Aug. 1990)-. Periodical. French. qt. Limited free distribution. STA Communications Inc., 955 St. John Boulevard, Suite 306, Pt Claire, Quebec H9R 5K3 Canada. **Tel** (514)695-7623. **DD** 616.1/005.

US/0093-5166
**CONTEMPORARY PROBLEMS IN CARDIOLOGY.** V. 1- 1974-. English. Futura Publishing Company Inc., 135 Bedford Road, PO Box 418, Armonk NY 10504-0418. **Tel** (914)273-1014, (800)877-8761, FAX (914)273-1015, (914)273-1016. **NLM** W1 CO769T. **CODEN** CPCAD6. Documents available from CASDDS.
**Ind/Abst** Chem. Abstr.

XR/0010-8650
**COR ET VASA (ENGLISH ED.).** (COR ET VASA.). [Cor et vasa]. **Added/Corp** Ceskoslovenska Kardiologicka Spolecnost. **VFOAT** International Journal of Cardiology. Vol. 1 (1959)-. Academic Scholarly Publication. Multiple languages (English, French and German). bm (6 issues). $215.00. Avicenum Medical Press, Malostranske Nam 28, 11802 Prague Czech Republic. **Tel** 011 42 2 530643. **(Subscription address:** Karger Libri AG, Petersgraben 31, CH 4009 Basel 11 Switzerland; Phone: 011 41 61 3061500**) NLM** W1 CO8496. **CODEN** COVAAN. Documents available from BIOSIS Document Express, CASDDS.
**Ind/Abst** Biol. Abstr.; Chem. Abstr.; EMBASE; Health Plan. Adminis.; Index Med.; Life Sci. Collect.; SportSearch.

SP
**CORAZON Y SALUD.** Spanish. qt. Ediciones Doyma SA, Travesera de Gracia 17 21, 08021 Barcelona Spain. **Tel** 011 34 3 2000711, 011 34 3 4145706, FAX 011 34 3 2091136, telex 51964 INK E.

NE
**CORDIAAL.** Insert BV, Postbus 90053, 1006 BB Amsterdam Netherlands.

NE/0165-9405
**CORE JOURNALS IN CARDIOLOGY.** [Core j. cardiol.]. Vol. 1, No. 1 (Sept. 1980)-. English. Eleven times a year (1 volume). Fl549.00. Excerpta Medica Publishing Group, PO Box 548, 1000 AM Amsterdam Netherlands. **Tel** 011 31 20 5803243. **(Subscription address:** Excerpta Medica Journals, PO Box 85, Limerick Ireland.**) NLM** ZWG 100 C797. **CODEN** CJCADW. **[CCC].** available on microfilm from University Microfilms International (UMI).
**Desc:** Part of a series intended to optimize the busy clinician's time by providing an overview of the most significant clinical studies in his/her field.

US/0954-6928
**CORONARY ARTERY DISEASE.** [Coron. artery dis.]. Vol. 1, No. 1 (Jan./Feb. 1990)-. Periodical. English. Six times a year. $144.95 (individual); $295.00 (institution). Current Science, 20 North 3rd Street, Philadelphia PA 19106. **Tel** (215)574-2266, (800)552-5866, FAX (215)574-2270. **ED** Burton E. Sobel. **LC** RC685.C6; C6278. **DD** 616.1/23/005. **NLM** W1; CO884L. **CODEN** CADIEX. **[CCC].** Index available. **Ad Acc. Pr Rev. Circ:** 1,500. available on diskette. Documents available from The Genuine Article, BIOSIS Document Express.
**Desc:** Presents original research and clinical investigations in the expanding field of Coronary Artery Research. Presenting reviews in-depth with annotated references. Each issue features a bibliography of the current world literature published during the previous year.
**Ind/Abst** Biol. Abstr. (1991-); Curr. Contents Clin. Med.; EMBASE; Ref. Upd. Deluxe Ed.; Res. Alert [Full Cov.]; Sci. Cit. Index; SCISEARCH; Soc. Sci. Cit. Index [Select. Cov.].

US/8755-5271
**CORONARY CLUB BULLETIN, THE.** (HEARTLINE. CORONARY CLUB BULLETIN.). [Coron. Club bull.]. **Added/Corp** Coronary Club. Vol. 3, No. 2 (Sept. 1974)-. Newsletter. English. mo. $29.00 (one year) $50.00 (two year) US; $39.00 (one year), $70.00 (two year) other. Coronary Club, 9500 Euclid Avenue, One

Clinic Center, Cleveland OH 44195. **Tel** (216)444-3690, FAX (216)444-9385. **ED** Jean Rothman. **DD** 616. Index available. **Bk Rev. Circ:** 8,000 (ctrl). ***Continues*** *Bulletin - The Coronary Club, Incorporated, 8755-6308.*
**Desc:** Information on cardiac health awareness.

IT
**CUORE, IL.** Vol. 1, No. 1 (Dec. 1984)-. Periodical. Italian. qt. **NLM** W1; CU48L. **CODEN** CREEE9.
**Ind/Abst** EMBASE.

US/0163-9501
**CURRENT CARDIOLOGY.** ***Ceased.*** Vol. 1 (1979)-Vol. 2 (?). Periodical. English. ir. John Wiley & Sons, Inc., 605 Third Avenue, New York NY 10158-0012. **Tel** (212)850-6000, (212)850-6645, FAX (212)850-6088, telex 12-7063. **(Subscription address:** John Wiley & Sons / England, Baffins Lane, Chichester, West Sussex PO19 1UD England.**) LC** RC681.A1; C87. **DD** 616.1/2/005. **NLM** W1 CU71.

UK/0957-0462
**CURRENT CARDIOVASCULAR PATENTS. CARDIOVASCULAR FAST-ALERT.** ***Ceased.*** **VFOAT** Cardiovascular Fast-Alert; Cardiovascular Fast Alert; Cardiovascular Patent Fast Alert; Cardiovascular Patent Fast-Alert; Current Cardiovascular Patents. (1989)-(Apr. 1992). Periodical. English. wk. Current Science / England, Middlesex House, 34-42 Cleveland Street, London W1P 5FB England. **Tel** 011 44 71 580 8393, 011 44 71 323 0323, FAX 011 44 81 580 1938. **(Subscription address:** Current Science, 20 North 3rd Street, Philadelphia PA 19106.**) NLM** QV 772; C97572.

UK
**CURRENT MEDICAL LITERATURE-CARDIOVASCULAR MEDICINE.** **Added/Corp** European Society of Cardiology. Royal Society of Medicine (Great Britain). **VFOAT** Cardiovascular Medicine. (198?)-. Periodical. English. qt. £20.00 UK; $40.00 US; £20.00 other. Current Medical Literature Ltd., 40-42 Osnaburgh Street, London NW1 3ND England. **Tel** 011 44 71 4658377, FAX 011 44 71 4658380. **(Subscription address:** Royal Society Medicine Services, 1 Wimpole Street, London W1M 8AE England.**) NLM** ZWG 100; C976.

UK/0268-4705
**CURRENT OPINION IN CARDIOLOGY.** [Curr. opin. cardiol.]. Vol. 1, No. 1 (Jan./Feb. 1986)-. Periodical. English. bm. $134.95 (individual); $269.95 (institution). Current Science / England, Middlesex House, 34-42 Cleveland Street, London W1P 5FB England. **Tel** 011 44 71 580 8393, 011 44 71 323 0323, FAX 011 44 81 580 1938. **(Subscription address:** Current Science, 20 North 3rd Street, Philadelphia PA 19106.**) ED** Burton E Sobel. **DD** 616. **NLM** W1; CU799GC. **CODEN** COPCE3. **[CCC]. Pr Rev. Circ:** 6,500. available on diskette. Documents available from The Genuine Article, BIOSIS Document Express.
**Desc:** Directed toward researchers and practicing cardiologists. Presents review articles from an area of concentration covering an entire year's literature with annotated references. Each issue features a bibliography of the current world literature published during the previous year.
**Ind/Abst** Biol. Abstr. (1991-); Cumul. Index Nurs. Allied Health Lit.; Curr. Aware. Biol. Sci., CABS; Curr. Contents; Curr. Contents Clin. Med.; EMBASE; Res. Alert [Select. Cov.]; SCISEARCH.

UK/0957-9672
**CURRENT OPINION IN LIPIDOLOGY.** [Curr. opin. lipidol.]. Vol. 1, No. 1 (Feb. 1990)-. Periodical. English. Six times a year. $169.95 (individual); $345.50 (institution). Current Science / England, Middlesex House, 34-42 Cleveland Street, London W1P 5FB England. **Tel** 011 44 71 580 8393, 011 44 71 323 0323, FAX 011 44 81 580 1938. **(Subscription address:** Current Science, 20 North 3rd Street, Philadelphia PA 19106.**) ED** G. R. Thompson. **LC** QP751; .C87. **DD** 616.3/997/005. **NLM** W1; CU799GFL. **CODEN** COPLEU. **[CCC]. Circ:** 500. available on diskette.
**Desc:** Directed toward cardiologists involved with lipids in research and clinical practice. Presents comments on the latest developments in all areas of lipidology.
**Ind/Abst** Cumul. Index Nurs. Allied Health Lit.; EMBASE; Soc. Sci. Cit. Index [Select. Cov.].

US/0146-2806
**CURRENT PROBLEMS IN CARDIOLOGY.** [Curr. probl. cardiol.]. **VFOAT** CPC, Current Problems in Cardiology. Vol. 1, (Apr. 1976)-. Monographic series. English. mo. $110.00 (institutions), $82.00 (individuals) US; $119.00 (institutions), $91.00 (individuals) other. Mosby Year Book Inc., 11830 Westline Industrial Drive, St Louis MO 63146. **Tel** (800)325-4177, (314)872-8370, FAX (314)432-1380, telex 44-2402. **ED** Robert A. O'Rourke. **LC** UNC. **DD** 616. **NLM** W1 CU804J. **[CCC].** Index available. **Pr Rev.** available on microfilm and microfiche from University Microfilms International (UMI). Documents available from The Genuine Article.
**Desc:** Offers busy practitioners an update on a single topic in the specialty. Discussions include elements of pathophysiology, non-invasive and invasive diagnosis, drug therapy, surgical management, and rehabilitation.
**Ind/Abst** Curr. Contents Clin. Med.; EMBASE; Health Plan. Adminis.; Index Med.; Res. Alert [Full Cov.]; Sci. Cit. Index; SCISEARCH.

US/0163-7800
**CURRENT PULMONOLOGY.** Vol. 1, (1979)-. English. an. $69.95. Mosby Year Book Inc., 11830 Westline Industrial Drive, St Louis MO 63146. **Tel** (800)325-4177, (314)872-8370, FAX (314)432-1380, telex 44-2402. **LC** RC756; .C87. **DD** 616.2/4. **NLM** W1 CU807M. **[CCC].**

US/1054-917X
**CURRENTS IN EMERGENCY CARDIAC CARE.** (CURRENTS IN EMERGENCY CARDIAC CARE : AMERICAN HEART ASSOCIATION AND CITIZEN CPR FOUNDATION NEWSLETTER.). [Curr. emerg. card. care]. **Added/Corp** American Heart Association. Citizen CPR Foundation. Vol. 1, No. 1 (Spring 1990)-. Periodical. English. qt. $20.00 institution. American Heart Association, 7272 Greenville Avenue, Dallas TX 75231-4596. **Tel** (214)706-1310, (214)373-6300, FAX (214)691-6342. **DD** 362. **NLM** W1; CU828. **[CCC].**
**Desc:** Offers scientific information about important ideas, developments, and trends in emergency cardiac care.

US/0747-6124
**DATELINE HYPERTENSION.** Periodical. English. bm. $18.00 US; $24.00 other. National Hypertension Information Network, Division of World Medical Communications Organization, 5 Center Avenue, Little Falls NJ 07424. **ED** Norman M Kaplan. **DD** 616. **Ad Acc. Circ:** 55,000 (ctrl).
**Desc:** Up-to-date information on developments and techniques in the field of hypertension. Written by leaders in this field, with a tele-lecture presentation.

US/1046-6959
**DEVELOPMENTS IN CARDIOLOGY.** [Dev. cardiol.]. **Added/Corp** Dannemiller Memorial Education Foundation. (1989)-. Periodical. English. mo. $150.00 (individual), $165.00 (institution), US; $215.00 (individual), $230.00 (institution) other. W.B. Saunders Company, A Subsidiary of Harcourt Brace Jovanovich, Inc., The Curtis Center/Suite 300, Independence Square West, Philadelphia PA 19106-3399. **Tel** (215)238-7800 or, 5587, FAX (215)238-7883, telex 173146. **(Subscription address:** W. B. Saunders Company / North America Subscriptions, c/o Periodicals, 6277 Sea Harbour Drive, 4th Floor, Orlando FL 32887.**) DD** 616. ***Continues*** *Progress in Cardiology (San Antonio, Tex.), 1041-3375.*

NE/0166-9842
**DEVELOPMENTS IN CARDIOVASCULAR MEDICINE.** [Dev. cardiovasc. med.]. (1979)-. Monographic series. English. Martinus Nijhoff Publishers, Subsidiary of Kluwer Academic Publishers, Koraalrood 50, 2718 SC Zoetermeer Netherlands. **Tel** 011 31 79 684400. **LC** UNC. **NLM** W1 DE997VME. **CODEN** DCMEDM. Documents available from BIOSIS Document Express, Ask*IEEE, CASDDS.
**Ind/Abst** Biol. Abstr.; Chem. Abstr.; INSPEC.

JA/0386-2682
**DOMYAKU KOKA.** [Domyaku koka]. **VFOAT** Journal of Japan Atherosclerosis Society. (1973)-. Periodical. Multiple languages. qt. Japan Atherosclerosis Society, 2-1 Uchisaiwaicho 2-chome, Chiyoda-ku 100 Tokyo Japan. **DD** 616.1.
**Ind/Abst** EMBASE.

US/0742-2822
**ECHOCARDIOGRAPHY (MOUNT KISCO, N.Y.).** (ECHOCARDIOGRAPHY.). [Echocardiography]. Vol. 1, No. 1 (Jan. 1984)-. Periodical. English. bm (6 issues). $130.00 US & Canada; $160.00 other. Futura Publishing Company Inc., 135 Bedford Road, PO Box 418, Armonk NY 10504-0418. **Tel** (914)273-1014, (800)877-8761, FAX (914)273-1015, (914)273-1016. **ED** Vincent Friedewald. **DD** 616. **NLM** W1; EC384. **[CCC].** Index available. cum. index. **Bk Rev. Ad Acc. Circ:** 2,500. Documents available from The Genuine Article.
**Desc:** Comprehensive review journal devoted to providing a single source of current knowledge for performing and interpreting M Mode, 2-D and Doppler echocardiograms for adults and children.
**Ind/Abst** Curr. Contents Clin. Med.; EMBASE; Res. Alert [Select. Cov.]; SCISEARCH.

IT
**ECOCARDIOGRAFIA.** Ghedini Libraio, V Pezzotti 4, 20141 Milan Italy. **Tel** 011 39 2 76023133.

US/1053-8437
**ELECTROPHYSIOLOGICAL APPROACH TO THE DIAGNOSIS OF ARRHYTHMIAS, AN.** (1991)-. Monographic series. English. Price varies per volume. Futura Publishing Company Inc., 135 Bedford Road, PO Box 418, Armonk NY 10504-0418. **Tel** (914)273-1014, (800)877-8761, FAX (914)273-1015, (914)273-1016. **DD** 616. **NLM** W1; EL451U.

FR
**ENCYCLOPEDIE MEDICO-CHIRURGICALE : MEDECINE GENERALE ET SPECIALITES. COEUR VAISSEAUX.** **See** Medical Science and Technology-Surgery.

SP/0210-9697
**ESTIMULACION CARDIACA.** [Estimul. card.]. (1980)-. Periodical. Spanish. qt. Editorial Cientifico Medica / Madrid, Plaza de Santa Ana 9, 28012 Madrid Spain. **UDC** 616.1.

UK/0195-668X
**EUROPEAN HEART JOURNAL.** [Eur. heart j.]. **Added/Corp** European Society of Cardiology. Vol. 1 (Feb. 1980)-. Academic Scholarly Publication. English. mo. $405.00 US; £225.00 Europe (institution); $150.00 US; £83.00 Europe. Harcourt Brace & Company Ltd., Foots Cray, High Street, Sidcup Kent DA14 5HP England. **Tel** 011 44 81 300 3322, FAX 011 44 81 309 0807. **(Subscription address:** W. B. Saunders Company / North America Subscriptions, c/o Periodicals, 6277 Sea Harbour Drive, 4th Floor, Orlando FL 32887.**) ED** H. E. Kulbertus and D. L. Brutsaert. **NLM** W1 EU636. **CODEN** EHJODF. **[CCC]. Pr Rev.** Documents available from The Genuine Article, CASDDS.
**Desc:** A leading international publication for practicing cardiologists, publishing original papers on all aspects of cardiovascular medicine, surgery, and basic research. Features requested reviews, editorial comments, notes concerning recent developments in drug research, new techniques and other advances, correspondence, readers' comments, and book reviews.
**Ind/Abst** Chem. Abstr.; Curr. Contents Clin. Med.; EMBASE; Health Plan. Adminis.; Helminthol. Abstr. (1991-); Index Med. (Feb. 1980-); Nutr. Abstr. Rev., Ser. A, Hum. Exp.; Nutr. Res. Newsl.; Life Sci. Collect.; PESTDOC; Res. Alert [Full Cov.]; Rev. Med. Vet. Mycology; Sci. Cit. Index; SCISEARCH; Soc. Sci. Cit. Index [Select. Cov.]; SportSearch.

GW/0939-6780
**EUROPEAN JOURNAL OF CARDIAC PACING AND ELECTROPHYSIOLOGY.** Vol. 1, No. 1 (May 1991)-. Periodical. English. Four times a year. DM265.00 Europe; DM295.00 others. EBM Erdmann Brenger GmbH, Postfach 810255, D-81902 Munich 81 Germany. **Tel** 011 49 89 9305779. **NLM** W1; EU72BB.
**Ind/Abst** EMBASE.

NE/0928-0529
**EUROPEAN VIDEO JOURNAL OF CARDIOLOGY, THE.** English. bm. $695.00. Kluwer Academic Publishers, Postbus 322, 3300 AH Dordrecht, The Netherlands. **Tel** 011 (31) 78 524400, FAX 011 31 78 183273, telex 20083. **ED** Lars Ryden.
**Desc:** Provides in-depth coverage of recent important advances in the broad field of cardiology.

NE/0014-4223
**EXCERPTA MEDICA. SECTION 18. CARDIOVASCULAR DISEASES AND CARDIOVASCULAR SURGERY.** **See** Medical Science and Technology-Abstracting, Bibliographies and Statistics.

US/1067-5264
**FUNDAMENTAL AND CLINICAL CARDIOLOGY.** [Fundam. clin. cardiol.]. Vol. 1 (1991)-. Monographic series. English. ir. Price varies per volume. Marcel Dekker Inc., 270 Madison Avenue, New York NY 10016. **Tel** (212)696-9000, (800)228-1160, FAX (212)685-4540, telex 421419. **(Subscription address:** Marcel Dekker Inc., PO Box 5017, Monticello, NY 12701-5176; (telephone: (800)228-1160)**) ED** Norman M. Kaplan & C. Venkata S. Ram. **DD** 616. **NLM** W1; FU538TD. **CODEN** FCCAEH. Documents available from BIOSIS Document Express.
**Desc:** Each title presents information on cardiovascular disease, including prevention and drug and treatment.
**Ind/Abst** Biol. Abstr. (1992-).

IT/0017-0224
**GIORNALE DELL'ARTERIOSCLEROSI.** [Arterioscler.]. **Added/Corp** Societa Italiana Per lo Studio dell'Arteriosclerosi. Societa Italiana di Gerontologia e Geriatria. **VFOAT** Giornale della Arteriosclerosi. (1963)-. Academic Scholarly Publication. Italian (summaries and/or abstracts in English). Three times a year. L50000 Italy; L60000 others. Utet Periodici Scient, Viale Tunisia 37, 20124 Milan Italy. **Tel** 011 39 2 29003555. **NLM** W1 GI423C. **CODEN** GIARA5. Documents available from BIOSIS Document Express, CASDDS.
**Ind/Abst** Biol. Abstr.; Chem. Abstr.; EMBASE [Select. Cov.].

IT/0392-7679
**GIORNALE DI EMODINAMICA.** ***Ceased.*** [G. emodin.]. Vol. 1, No. 1 (Jan./June 1981)-?. Periodical. Italian (English). sa. Edizioni Minerva Medica, Corso Bramante 83-85, 10126 Turin Italy. **Tel** 011 39 11 678282, FAX 011 39 11 674502. **ED** G Biffani. **NLM** W1; GI513M. **Bk Rev. Ad Acc.**

IT
**GIORNALE DI RIABILITAZIONE CARDIOLOGICA ANGIOLOGICA RESPIRATORIA.** Edizioni Scientifiche Gioggi, Via Bra 5, 00166 Rome Italy.

IT/0392-1387
**GIORNALE ITALIANO DI ANGIOLOGIA.** [G. ital. angiol.]. Vol. 1, No. 1 (Jan./March 1981)-. Periodical. Italian (English). qt. $60.00. CIC Edizioni Internazionali, Via L Spallanzani 11, 00161 Rome Italy. **Tel** 011 39 6 841-2673, FAX 011 39 6 844-3365, telex 622099 CIC I. **ED** P. Pola. **NLM** W1; GI765. **[CCC]. Ad Acc.** ctrl circ.
**Ind/Abst** EMBASE [Select. Cov.].

IT/0046-5968
**GIORNALE ITALIANO DI CARDIOLOGIA.** [G. ital. cardiol.]. Vol. 1 (1971)-. Academic Scholarly Publication. Italian (summaries and/or abstracts in English). Twelve times a year. $200.00. Piccin Nuova Libraria, Via Altinate 107, 35121 Padua Italy. **Tel** 39 49 655566, FAX 39 49 8750693. **NLM** W1 GI767. **CODEN** GICDA7. Index available. **Bk Rev. Ad Acc. Circ:** 4,500. Documents available from BIOSIS Document Express, CASDDS. ***Formed by the union of*** *Cuore e Circolazione; Folia Cardiologica* ***and*** *Malattie Cardiovascolari.*
**Ind/Abst** Biol. Abstr.; Chem. Abstr. (1971-1981); EMBASE [Select. Cov.]; Health Plan. Adminis.; Index Med.; Index Dent. Lit.; Life Sci. Collect.; SportSearch.

RU/0236-2791
**GRUDNAIA I SERDECHNO-SOSUDISTAIA KHIRURGIIA. Added/Corp** Soviet Union. Ministerstvo Zdravookhraneniia. Vsesoiuznoe Nauchnoe Obshchestvo Khirurgov (Soviet Union). **VFOAT** Grudnaiia i Serdechno Sosudistaia Khirurgiia. (1990)-. Periodical. Russian (summaries and/or abstracts in English). Six times a year. $99.95. Izdatelstvo Meditsina / Russian Academy of Medical Sciences, Ulitsa Solyanka 14, 109801 Moscow Russia. **Tel** 011 95 297-05-04. **(Subscription address:** East View Publications Inc., 3020 Harbor Lane North, Suite 110, Minneapolis MN 55447.**) NLM** W1; GR919CK. **CODEN** GSKHEV. ***Continues*** *Grudnaia Khirurgiia (Moscow, R.S.F.S.R.), 0017-4866.*
**Ind/Abst** Index Med. (1990-).

UK
**HANDBOOK OF HYPERLIPIDAEMIA.** (19??)-. English. $35.00. Current Science, 20 North 3rd Street, Philadelphia PA 19106. **Tel** (215)574-2266, (800)552-5866, FAX (215)574-2270. **ED** G. R. Thompson.
**Desc:** Targeted to lipid and cardiovascular specialists as well as the general practitioner, the annual covers all aspects of hyperlipidemia including pathopsysiology, classification and clinical practice.

NE
**HANDBOOK OF HYPERTENSION.** Vol. 1 (1983)-. Academic Scholarly Publication. English. ir. Price varies. Elsevier Science Publishers BV, PO Box 211, 1000 AE Amsterdam Netherlands. **Tel** 011 31 20 5803642, FAX 011 31 20 5862696, telex 15682. **(Subscription address:** Elsevier Science Inc. / New York Books, 655 Avenue of the Americas, New York NY 10010.**) ED** W. H. Birkenhager and H. L. Reid. **LC** RC685.H8; H28. **DD** 616.1/32. **NLM** W1; HA51MH. Documents available from CASDDS.
**Ind/Abst** Chem. Abstr.

NE/0301-8202
**HART BULLETIN.** [Hart bull.]. Vol. 1- 1970-. Bulletin. Dutch (Dutch). Fl40.00. Uitgeversmij Vewe Bv, Postbus 50, 3640 AB Mijdrecht The Netherlands. **Tel** 011 31 2979 81251. **NLM** W1 HA599. Index Available, published separately, free-automatically sent. **Bk Rev.** ctrl circ.

US/1051-5313
**HARVARD HEART LETTER.** [Harv. heart lett.]. Vol. 1, No. 1 (Sept. 1990)-. Periodical. English. mo. $24.00 US; $30.00 Canada; $39.00 other. Harvard Medical School, 164 Longwood Avenue, 1st Floor, Boston MA 02115. **Tel** (617)432-1485, FAX (617)432-1506. **(Subscription address:** Harvard Heart Letter, PO Box 420234, Palm Coast, FL 32142-0234**) DD** 616.
**Desc:** Focuses on topics pertaining to cardiovascular health, written for the lay audience.
**Ind/Abst** Consum. Health Nutr. Index; Mag. Artic. Summar. Elite (July 1994-).

JA/0910-8327
**HEART AND VESSELS.** [Heart vessels]. **Added/Corp** Japanese Research Promotion Society for Cardiovascular Diseases. Vol. 1, No. 1 (Feb. 1985)-. Academic Scholarly Publication. English. Six times a year. DM320.00. Springer-Verlag Tokyo, 37-3 Hongo 3-Chrome, Bunkyo-ku, Tokyo 113 Japan. **Tel** 011 81 3 38120331, FAX 011 81 3 38120719, telex 26536 SREBS J. **(Subscription address:** Springer Verlag New York Inc. / for North America, 44 Hartz Way, Secaucus NJ 07096.**) ED** A. Takao. **NLM** W1; HE644M. **CODEN** HEVEEO. **[CCC]. Circ:** 1,000. available on microfilm and microfiche from University Microfilms International (UMI). Documents available from BIOSIS Document Express, CASDDS.
**Desc:** Provides a forum for those engaged in the diagnosis, treatment and understanding of a wide scope of cardiovascular diseases as well as for those involved in basic research on the cardiovascular system.
**Ind/Abst** Biol. Abstr. (1985-); Chem. Abstr. (1985); EMBASE; Index Med. (Vol. 1, No. 1, 1985-).

JA/0935-736X
**HEART AND VESSLES. SUPPLEMENT.** [Heart vessels, Suppl.]. Vol. 1 (1985)-. Monographic series. English. ir. Price varies per volume. Springer-Verlag Tokyo, 37-3 Hongo 3-Chrome, Bunkyo-ku, Tokyo 113 Japan. **Tel** 011 81 3 38120331, FAX 011 81 3 38120719, telex 26536 SREBS J. **(Subscription address:** Springer Verlag New York Inc. / for North America, 44 Hartz Way, Secaucus NJ 07096.**) NLM** W1; HE644L.
**Ind/Abst** Index Med. (1985-).

US/1058-2819
**HEART DISEASE AND STROKE.** ***Ceased.*** (HEART DISEASE AND STROKE : A JOURNAL FOR PRIMARY CARE PHYSICIANS.). [Heart dis. stroke]. **Added/Corp** American Heart Association. Vol. 1, No. 1 (Jan./Feb. 1992)-(Nov./Dec. 1994). Periodical. English. bm. American Heart Association, 7272 Greenville Avenue, Dallas TX 75231-4596. **Tel** (214)706-1310, (214)373-6300, FAX (214)691-6342. **ED** J. Willis Hurst. **DD** 616. **NLM** W1; HE654L. **CODEN** HDSTED. **[CCC].** Index available. **Ad Acc, Adv Mgr:** Krista Curnutt, **Tel** (214)706-1426. **Circ:** 75,000 (ctrl).
**Desc:** Presents practical reviews on prevention, diagnosis, treatment and management of cardiovascular and cerebrovascular diseases. Also highlights frontiers of research that affect clinical practice.

US/8755-7673
**HEART FAILURE.** [Heart fail.]. Vol. 1, No. 1 (Jan./Feb. 1985)-. Periodical. English. Six times a year. $30.00 (individuals), $45.00 (institutions) US; $40.00 (individuals), $60.00 (institutions) other. Heart Failure Inc., 777 West Putnam Ave, Greenwich CT 06830. **Tel** (203)531-0450, FAX (203)531-0533. **ED** Suzanne Del Gallo. **DD** 616. **NLM** W1; HE654M. **Pr Rev. Circ:** 72,000. available on microfilm from University Microfilms International (UMI).

UK/0953-0495
**HEART LONDON. 1987.** (HEART). [HeartLond., 1987]. (1987)-. Periodical. English. ir (1-3 issues per year). £12.00 (individuals),£60.00 (institutions) UK; £18.00 other. Coronary Prevention Group, 31 35 Fenchurch St Plantation, London EC3M 3NN England. **Tel** 011 44 71 626-4844. **ED** Jeanette Longfield. **DD** 616.12305. **Bk Rev.** ***Continues*** *Heart to Heart, 0269-1353.*
**Desc:** News and analysis on heart health issues for the general public and health workers.

US
**HEARTCARE.** ***Ceased.*** (19??)-(19??). English. bm. Heartcorps Inc., 5655 Lindero Canyon Road, Suite 701, Westlake Village CA 91362. available on an online database (file 149/Full-Text) from DIALOG.
**Ind/Abst** Health Index (1990-199?); Health Period. Database [Full Txt.]; Health Ref. Cent. (Jan. 1989-) [Full Txt.] [Full Cov.].

CN/0046-7251
**HEMOPHILIA TODAY.** (HEMOPHILIA TODAY / THE CANADIAN HEMOPHILIA SOCIETY.). [Hemophilia today]. **Added/Corp** Canadian Hemophilia Society. Vol. 1, No. 2 (March/April 1964)-. Periodical. English. qt. Free on request. Canadian Hemophilia Society, 1450 City Councillors Street, Suite 840, Montreal Quebec H3A 236 Canada. **Tel** (514)848-0503. **DD** 616.1/572/00971. ***Continues*** *Report (Canadian Hemophilia Society), 0822-6636.*

GW/0340-9937
**HERZ.** [Herz]. Vol. 1 (1976)-. Periodical. German. bm. $130.88. Urban & Vogel, Postfach 152209, D-80052 Munich Germany. **Tel** 011 49 89 53292140, FAX 089/536052, telex 521701. **NLM** W1 HE986U. **CODEN** HERZDW. **[CCC]. Pr Rev.** Documents available from The Genuine Article, BIOSIS Document Express.
**Ind/Abst** Biol. Abstr.; Curr. Contents Clin. Med.; EMBASE; Energy Res. Abstr. (May 1979-); Health Plan. Adminis.; Index Med.; Life Sci. Collect.; Res. Alert [Full Cov.]; Sci. Cit. Index; SCISEARCH.

GW/0046-7324
**HERZ-KREISLAUF.** [Herz-Kreisl.]. Vol. 1 (1969)-. Academic Scholarly Publication. German (summaries and/or abstracts in English). mo. DM85.80. Richard Pflaum Verlag Gmbh, Postfach 190737, D 80607 Munich Germany. **Tel** 011 49 89 126070, FAX 011 49 89 12607200, telex 5216075. **CODEN** HZKLAV. **[CCC]. Pr Rev.** Documents available from The Genuine Article, CASDDS.
**Ind/Abst** Chem. Abstr.; Curr. Contents Clin. Med.; EMBASE; Energy Res. Abstr. (June 1975-); Life Sci. Collect.; Res. Alert [Select. Cov.]; SCISEARCH; Soc. Sci. Cit. Index [Select. Cov.]; SportSearch.

US/1120-9879
**HIGH BLOOD PRESSURE AND CARDIOVASCULAR PREVENTION.** English. qt. L80.000 Italy; $80.00 other. Editrice Kurtis Srl, Via Luigi Zoja 30, 20153 Milan Italy. **Tel** 011 39 2 48202740, FAX 011 39 2 48201219. **Ad Acc. Acid Free.**
**Desc:** Publishes papers reporting original clinical and basic research on hypertension and other cardiovascular risk factors.

US/0164-758X
**HIGH BLOOD PRESSURE HIGHLIGHTS.** V. 1- Sept. 1978-. Periodical. English. qt. California Department of Health Services, B A Myers Director, 714 P Street, Room 1494, Sacramento CA 95814. **Tel** (916)445-1010.

SP/0212-8241
**HIPERTENSION.** [Hipertension]. (1984)-. Periodical. Spanish. Ten times a year. $48.00. IDEPSA International Ediciones Publs SA, Principe de Vergara 112 1F, 28002 Madrid Spain. **Tel** 011 34 1 5637306. **UDC** 616.12.

SP/0214-6436
**HIPERTENSION Y ARTERIOESCLEROSIS.** ***Ceased.*** (1989)-(19??). Periodical. Spanish (summaries and/or abstracts in English; table of contents in English). Six times a year. Edicomplet SA, C Apolonio Morales 6 FL, 28036 Madrid Spain. **Tel** 011 34 1 4035014. **NLM** W1; HI409S. **CODEN** HIAREK.
**Ind/Abst** EMBASE; Indice Med. Esp.

BE/0770-1276
**HYPERTENSIE IN DE HUISARTSENPRAKTIJK.** [Hypertens. huisartsenprakt.]. Began with: V. 1, 1971. Monographic series. Dutch. an. Price varies per volume. Acco Academische Cooperatief, Tiensestraat 134-136, 3000 Leuven Belgium. **Tel** 011 32 16 233520. **ED** Antoon K P C Amery. **NLM** W1 HY841L.

UK/0956-2311
**HYPERTENSION ANNUAL.** [Hypertens. annu.]. **VFOAT** ISH ... Hypertension Annual. (1987)-. English. an. £20.00. Current Science, 20 North 3rd Street, Philadelphia PA 19106. **Tel** (215)574-2266, (800)552-5866, FAX (215)574-2270. **ED** L. Hansson. **DD** 616.132. **Circ:** 2,700. ***Continues*** *Hypertension Yearbook, 0950-2319.*
**Desc:** Distinguished researchers in the field evaluate topics of current interest to update physicians not actively involved in research themselves.

US/0194-911X
**HYPERTENSION (DALLAS, TEX. 1979).** (HYPERTENSION.). [Hypertension]. **Added/Corp** American Heart Association. Council for High Blood Pressure Research (American Heart Association) Proceedings of the Council for High Blood Pressure Research. Interamerican Society of Hypertension. Scientific Meeting. Proceedings of the ... Scientific Meeting of the Interamerican Society of Hypertension. Vol. 1, No. 1 (Jan./Feb. 1979)-. Academic Scholarly Publication. English. mo. $190.00 institution. American Heart Association, 7272 Greenville Avenue, Dallas TX 75231-4596. **Tel** (214)706-1310, (214)373-6300, FAX (214)691-6342. **(Subscription address:** American Heart Association, PO Box 843543, Dallas TX 75284-3543.**) ED** Edgar Haber. **LC** RC685.H8; H767. **DD** 616.1/32/005. **NLM** W1 HY841M. **CODEN** HPRTDNHPTRDN. **[CCC]. Bk Rev. Ad Acc. Pr Rev. Acid Free. Circ:** 4,000 (ctrl). available on microfilm and microfiche from University Microfilms International (UMI). Documents available from BIOSIS Document Express, CASDDS. ***Absorbed*** *Hypertension, 0073-425X.*
**Desc:** Publishing reports of clinical and laboratory investigation in hypertension. Designed for clinicians, clinical investigators, laboratory scientists.
**Ind/Abst** Biol. Abstr.; Chem. Abstr.; Cumul. Index Nurs. Allied Health Lit.; Curr. Aware. Biol. Sci., CABS; Curr. Biotechnol.; EMBASE; Index Med.; INIS Atomindex [Micro.]; Med. Abstr. Newsl.; Nutr. Abstr. Rev., Ser. A, Hum. Exp.; Nutr. Res. Newsl.; PESTDOC; Ref. Upd. Basic Ed.; Ref. Upd. Deluxe Ed.; Sci. Cit. Index; SCISEARCH.

●US/1064-1955
**HYPERTENSION IN PREGNANCY. See** Medical Science and Technology-Gynecology and Obstetrics.

US/1044-8071
**HYPERTENSION INDEX & REVIEWS.** [Hypertens. index rev.]. **VFOAT** Hypertension Index and Reviews. Vol. 1, No. 1 (July 1989)-. Periodical. English. qt. $60.00. Hypertension Index and Reviews Knolls NJ 07927. **DD** 616.

US/0362-4323
**HYPERTENSION (NEW YORK).** (HYPERTENSION.). [Hypertension]. Periodical. English. mo. $25.00. Hypertension Publishing Company, 79 Madison Avenue, New York NY 10016. **LC** RC685.H8; A766. **DD** 616.1/32/005. Documents available from The Genuine Article.

**Ind/Abst** Curr. Contents Clin. Med.; Curr. Contents Life Sci.; Mod. Med.; Res. Alert [Full Cov.]; Soc. Sci. Cit. Index [Select. Cov.].

●JA/0916-9636
**HYPERTENSION RESEARCH, CLINICAL AND EXPERIMENTAL.** [Hypertens. res. clin. exp.]. **VFOAT** Official Journal of the Japanese Society of Hypertension. (1992)-. Academic Scholarly Publication. English. qt. $130.00 (institutions), $100.00 (individuals). Japanese Society of Hypertension, Center for Academic Societies Osaka, 14th Floor Senri Life Science Center Building, 1-4-2 Shinsenrihgashi-machi, Toyonaka 565, Japan. **Tel** 81-6-873-2301, FAX 81-6-873-2300. **(Subscription address:** Japan Publications Trading Company, Ltd., PO Box 5030, Tokyo International, Tokyo 100-31 Japan.**) Ad Acc.** Documents available from BIOSIS Document Express, CASDDS. ***Continues*** *Koketsuatsu, 0288-0032.*
**Desc:** Publishes articles on worldwide research topics of hypertension. A basic principle of this journal is to attach equal importance to both experimental and clinical studies including the disciplines of biochemistry, cellular and molecular biology, immunology, physiology, pharmacology, and epidemiology.
**Ind/Abst** Biol. Abstr.; Chem. Abstr.; Index Med.

US/0192-5385
**INDEX OF FEDERALLY SUPPORTED PROGRAMS IN HEART, BLOOD VESSEL, LUNG, AND BLOOD DISORDERS.** 1976/77-. English. an. US Department of Health and Human Services National Institutes of Health, 9000 Rockville Pike, Bethesda MD 20892. **Tel** (301)496-9291, FAX (301)496-2443. **LC** RC669; .I57. **DD** 616.1/007/2073. **NLM** W 22 AA1 I34.

II/0019-4832
**INDIAN HEART JOURNAL.** [Indian heart j.]. **Added/Corp** Cardiological Society of India. Vol. 1 (Jan. 1949)-. Academic Scholarly Publication. English. bm. $70.00. Cardiological Society of India, Bombay, India. **(Subscription address:** Prints India, 11 Darya Ganj, New Delhi, 110002 India, (Phone: 011 91 11 3268645)**) LC** RC681; .A1. **NLM** W1 IN206.
**Ind/Abst** EMBASE [Select. Cov.]; Index Med.; Sorghum Mill. Abstr.; Soyabean Abstr.; SportSearch.

II/0377-9343
**INDIAN JOURNAL OF CHEST DISEASES & ALLIED SCIENCES, THE.** [Indian j. chest dis. allied sci.]. **Added/Corp** Vallabhbhai Patel Chest Institute. Indian Association for Chest Diseases. **VAT** Indian Journal of Chest Diseases and Allied Sciences. Vol.18 (Jan. 1976)-. Periodical. English. Four times a year. $70.00. University of Delhi / VP Chest Institute, PO Box 2101, New Delhi 110007 India. **Tel** 7257102. **NLM** W1 IN206S. **[CCC]. Bk Rev**, (Qty: 12). **Ad Acc. Circ:** 1,500. ***Continues*** *Indian Journal of Chest Diseases.*
**Desc:** Advancement of knowledge in the field of cardiorespiratory diseases and allied sciences.
**Ind/Abst** Index Med.; Life Sci. Collect.

US
**INFO MEMO.** Periodical. English. National High Blood Pressure Education Program, National Heart Lung and Blood Institute Human Services, Public Health Service, National Institutes of Health, Bethesda MD 20014. **NLM** W1; IN41LS. ***Absorbed*** *Director's Memo (Bethesda, Md.).*

FR/0220-2476
**INFORMATION CARDIOLOGIQUE, L'.** [Inf. cardiol.]. **Added/Corp** Centre Cardiologique du Nord (France). Vol. 1, No. 1 (Oct. 1978)-. Periodical. French. Eleven times a year. 420.00F (France); 490.00F (other). Publications Medicales AGCF, 77 bis rue de Chesneaux, 95160 Montmorency France. **Tel** 011 33 34 176888. **NLM** W1 IN416ED. Index available. **Bk Rev. Ad Acc. Circ:** 2,750 (ctrl).
**Desc:** Covers official papers, reviews, and case reports.

IT
**INFORMAZIONE CARDIOLOGICA.** Periodical. Italian. Six times a year. L30,000. Assn Prevenzione Cardiopatie Div Cardiologia, Viale Verdi 18, 28100 Novara Italy. **Tel** 011 39 321 373236. **ED** Paolo Rossi (Editor-in-Chief). **Bk Rev**, (Qty: 6). **Ad Acc, Adv Mgr:** Sig. Boscarello Walter, **Tel** 011 39 2 29572541. **Circ:** 10,000 (ctrl).

US/0271-1141
**INTELLIGENCE REPORTS IN CARDIOVASCULAR DISEASE.** [Intell. rep. cardiovasc. dis.]. Vol. 1, No. 1 (Nov./Dec. 1980)-. Periodical. English. bm (6 issues). $30.00. Healthscan Inc., Valley Road at Copper Avenue, Upper Montclair NJ 07043. **Tel** (201)744-4755. **LC** RC666; .I57. **DD** 616.1/005.

US/0274-5542
**INTERNAL MEDICINE NEWS & CARDIOLOGY NEWS.** **See** Medical Science and Technology-Gastroenterology.

CN/0836-7884
**INTERNATIONAL ABSTRACTS IN HYPERTENSION.** [Int. abstr. hypertens.]. (July/Aug. 1987)-. Periodical. English. bm. International Abstracts in Hypertension, 640 St Paul West/Suite 302, Montreal Quebec H3C 1L9 Canada. **DD** 616.1/32/005.

US/0147-3042
**INTERNATIONAL CARDIOLOGICAL REPORTER.** Vol. 1 (1977)-. Periodical. English. mo. $47.00. International Medical Reporter, 325 Suffolk Road, Baltimore MD 21218. ***Supersedes*** *International Cardiological & Respiratory Disease Reporter.*

●US/1061-1711
**INTERNATIONAL JOURNAL OF ANGIOLOGY, THE.** (THE INTERNATIONAL JOURNAL OF ANGIOLOGY : OFFICIAL PUBLICATION OF THE INTERNATIONAL COLLEGE OF ANGIOLOGY, INC.). [Int. j. angiol.]. **Added/Corp** International College of Angiology. **VFOAT** IJA. Vol. 1, No.1 (Winter 1992)-. Periodical. English. Four times a year. $117.00. Springer-Verlag New York Inc., 175 5th Avenue, New York NY 10010. **Tel** (212)460-1500, telex 232 235 SPB UR. **(Subscription address:** Springer Verlag New York Inc. / for North America, 44 Hartz Way, Secaucus NJ 07096.**) ED** John B. Chang M.D. **DD** 616. Index available (Bound in 4th iss., in (Dec).). cum. index. **Bk Rev. Ad Acc. Pr Rev. Circ:** 1,500 (ctrl).

US/0167-9899
**INTERNATIONAL JOURNAL OF CARDIAC IMAGING.** [Int. j. card. imaging]. Vol. 1, No. 1 (1985)-. Periodical. English. qt. $388.00. Kluwer Academic Publishers, Postbus 322, 3300 AH Dordrecht, The Netherlands. **Tel** 011 (31) 78 524400, FAX 011 31 78 183273, telex 20083. **ED** G.B.J. Mancini, J.H.C. Reiber. **DD** 616. **NLM** W1; IN766BH. **[CCC]. Bk Rev. Ad Acc. Pr Rev. Acid Free. Circ:** 1,000. available on microfilm and microfiche from University Microfilms International (UMI).
**Desc:** Promotes an integrated and physiologic approach to cardiac imaging as it relates to cardiovascular disease.
**Ind/Abst** EMBASE; Index Med. (1985-); Ref. Upd. Deluxe Ed.

NE/0167-5273
**INTERNATIONAL JOURNAL OF CARDIOLOGY.** [Int. j. cardiol.]. Vol. 1, No. 1 (1981)-. Academic Scholarly Publication. English. Fifteen times a year (5 vols.). $973.00. Elsevier Science Ireland Ltd., Bay 15, Shannon Industrial Estate, Co Clare Ireland. **Tel** 011 353 61 471944. **ED** Robert H. Anderson, Michael Tynan, Chuichi Kawai, R.L. Frye, and R. Vlietstra. **NLM** W1 IN766C. **CODEN** IJCDD5. **[CCC]. Pr Rev.** available on microfilm and microfiche from University Microfilms International (UMI). Documents available from The Genuine Article, BIOSIS Document Express, CASDDS, ADONIS. ***Continues*** *European Journal of Cardiology, 0301-4711.*
**Desc:** Devoted to cardiology in the broadest sense. Both basic research and clinical papers can be submitted, but articles on the fundamental principles of cardiology will also be considered for publication.
**Ind/Abst** ADONIS; Biol. Abstr.; Chem. Abstr. (1981-1983); Curr. Aware. Biol. Sci., CABS; Curr. Contents Clin. Med.; Curr. Contents Life Sci.; Dairy Sci. Abstr.; EMBASE; Index Med.; Mod. Med.; Nutr. Res. Newsl.; Life Sci. Collect.; PESTDOC; Protozoolog. Abstr.; Ref. Upd. Deluxe Ed.; Res. Alert [Full Cov.]; Sci. Cit. Index; SCISEARCH; Soc. Sci. Cit. Index [Select. Cov.]; SportSearch.

SZ
**INTERNATIONAL SOCIETY FOR APPLIED CARDIOVASCULAR BIOLOGY.** ***Ceased.*** **Added/Corp** International Society for Applied Cardiovascular Biology. Vol. 1 (1990)-Vol. 2 (1992). Monographic series. English. an. S. Karger AG, Allschwilerstrasse 10, PO Box - Postfach - Case Postale, CH-4009 Basel Switzerland. **Tel** 011 41 61 306-1111, FAX 011 41 61 306-1234, telex CH 962 652. **ED** P P Zilla. **NLM** W1; IN8422. **CODEN** ISOAEI. Documents available from BIOSIS Document Express.
**Desc:** A problem-oriented series designed to foster collaboration leading to a better understanding and treatment of cardiovascular disease.
**Ind/Abst** Biol. Abstr.; Ref. Upd. Deluxe Ed.

●US/1063-4282
**INTERVENTIONAL CARDIOLOGY NEWSLETTER.** (INTERVENTIONAL CARDIOLOGY NEWSLETTER : ICN.). **VFOAT** ICN. Vol. 1, No. 1 (Jan. 1993)-. Newsletter. English. bm (1 volume). $98.00 US; $123.00 other. Elsevier Science Publishing Company Inc, Madison Square Station, PO Box 882, New York NY 10159-0882. **Tel** (212)633-3950, FAX (212)633-3990. **DD** 616. **NLM** W1; IN982W. **CODEN** ICANEB. **[CCC].**

●US
**INTERVENTIONAL CARDIOVASCULAR NEWSLETTER.** (1993)-. Newsletter. English. Six times a year. $75.00 institutions US (add $23.00 for postage outside the US). Elsevier Science Publishing Company Inc, Madison Square Station, PO Box 882, New York NY 10159-0882. **Tel** (212)633-3950, FAX (212)633-3990.

JA/0047-1828
**JAPANESE CIRCULATION JOURNAL.** [Jpn. circ. j.]. Vol. 24, (Jan. 1960)-. Academic Scholarly Publication. English (Japanese). Twelve times a year. $200.00. **(Subscription address:** Kyowa Book Company Inc., 1-38 Kanda Jinbo-Cho, Chiyoda-Ku Tokyo 101, Japan**) ED** Kazuo Yamada. **LC** RC681; .J35. **NLM** W1 JA949C. **CODEN** JCIRA2. Index available. **Bk Rev. Ad Acc. Pr Rev. Circ:** 10,000. Documents available from The Genuine Article, BIOSIS Document Express, CASDDS. ***Absorbed*** *Nihon Junkankigaku Shi.*
**Desc:** Comprises of the original articles in English and selected abstracts from the Japanese edition.
**Ind/Abst** Biol. Abstr.; Chem. Abstr.; CSA Neuro. Abstr. (?-?); Curr. Contents Clin. Med.; Curr. Contents Life Sci.; EMBASE; Index Med.; Mod. Med.; Nutr. Abstr. Rev., Ser. B, Live Feeds and Feed.; Nutr. Abstr. Rev., Ser. A, Hum. Exp.; Life Sci. Collect.; Res. Alert [Full Cov.]; Rev. Med. Vet. Entomol.; Sci. Cit. Index; SCISEARCH; SportSearch.

JA/0021-4868
**JAPANESE HEART JOURNAL.** [Jpn. heart j.]. **Added/Corp** Japanese Heart Journal Association. Tokyo Daigaku. Igakubu. Naikagaku Kyoshitsu (2d). Vol. 1 (Jan. 1960)-. Academic Scholarly Publication. English. bm. 517.00F (includes distribution costs). Baltzer Science Publishers BV, Asterweg 1A, 1031 HL Amsterdam Netherlands. **Tel** 011 31 20 6370061, FAX 011 31 20 6323651. **ED** H. Ueda, S. Murao, J. Takeuchi, K. Matsuda, S. Okinaka, I. Ito, T. Sakamoto, M. Ishii, T. Koide, H. Matsuo, S. Mashima. **NLM** W1 JA95. **CODEN** JHEJAR. **Bk Rev. Ad Acc. Pr Rev.** available on microfilm and microfiche from University Microfilms International (UMI). Documents available from The Genuine Article, BIOSIS Document Express, CASDDS.
**Ind/Abst** Biol. Abstr.; Chem. Abstr.; CSA Neuro. Abstr. (?-?); Curr. Contents Clin. Med.; EMBASE; Index Med.; Int. Aerosp. Abstr.; Mod. Med.; Nutr. Res. Newsl.; Life Sci. Collect.; Res. Alert [Select. Cov.]; SCISEARCH; SportSearch.

FR/0398-0499
**JOURNAL DES MALADIES VASCULAIRES.** [J. mal. vasc.]. **Added/Corp** College Francaise de Pathologie Vasculaire. Vol. 1, (1976)-. Periodical. French (summaries and/or abstracts in English). Four times a year. $190.00. Masson Editeur, Box Postale 22, 41353 Vineuil 16 France. **Tel** 011 33 54 438994. **(Subscription address:** 7A Boulevard de Perolles, CH-1701 Fribourg Switzerland**) NLM** W1 JO371M. **[CCC]. Pr Rev.** available on microfilm and microfiche from University Microfilms International (UMI). Documents available from The Genuine Article.
**Ind/Abst** Curr. Contents Clin. Med.; EMBASE; Index Med.; Res. Alert [Full Cov.]; Sci. Cit. Index; SCISEARCH.

●US/1071-9164
**JOURNAL OF CARDIAC FAILURE.** (1994)-. Periodical. English. qt. $145.00 institution, $115.00 individual. Churchill Livingstone Inc., 650 Avenue of the Americas, New York NY 10011. **Tel** (212)206-5062, FAX (212)727-7808. **(Subscription address:** Churchill Livingstone Inc., 5 South 250 Frontenac Road, Naperville, IL 60563; (telephone: (800)553-5426 or (708)416-3939)**)**

JA/0914-5087
**JOURNAL OF CARDIOLOGY.** [J. cardiol.]. **Added/Corp** Nihon Shinzobyo Gakkai. Vol. 17, No. 1 (March 1987)-. Periodical. Japanese (summaries and/or abstracts in English; table of contents in English). Four times a year. $228.00. **(Subscription address:** Kyowa Book Company Inc., 1 38 Kanda Jinbocho Chiyoda-ku, Tokyo 101 Japan.**) NLM** W1; JO574SJ. ***Continues*** *Journal of Cardiography, 0386-2887.*
**Ind/Abst** EMBASE; Energy Res. Abstr. (1987-); Index Med. (1987-).

JA
**JOURNAL OF CARDIOLOGY. SUPPLEMENT.** (1987)-. Monographic series. Japanese (summaries and/or abstracts in English). Price varies per volume. **(Subscription address:** Kyowa Book Company Inc., 1-38 Kanda Jinbo-Cho Chiyoda-Ku, Tokyo 101 Japan**) NLM** W1; JO575Sa. ***Continues*** *Journal of Cardiography. Supplement.*
**Ind/Abst** Index Med. (1987-).

US/0883-9212
**JOURNAL OF CARDIOPULMONARY REHABILITATION.** [J. cardiopulm. rehabil.]. **Added/Corp** American Association of Cardiovascular & Pulmonary Rehabilitation. **VFOAT** JCR. Vol. 5, No. 5 (May 20, 1985)-. Periodical. English. bm. $69.00 (individuals), $125.00 (institutions) US; $99.00 (individuals), $155.00 (institutions) other. J.B. Lippincott Company, 227 East Washington Square, Philadelphia PA 19106-3780. **Tel** (215)238-4200 or 4454, FAX (215)238-4227. **(Subscription address:** J.B. Lippincott, PO Box 350, Hagerstown MD 21740.**) DD** 616. **NLM** W1; JO574V. **[CCC]. Bk Rev. Ad Acc. Pr Rev. Circ:** 17,000 (ctrl). available on microfilm and microfiche from University Microfilms International (UMI). ***Continues*** *Journal of Cardiac Rehabilitation, 0275-1429.*
**Desc:** Articles on the subject of cardiovascular and

pulmonary rehabilitation.
**Ind/Abst** Cumul. Index Nurs. Allied Health Lit.; EMBASE; Mod. Med.; Phys. Educ. Index.

US/1045-3873
**JOURNAL OF CARDIOVASCULAR ELECTROPHYSIOLOGY.** [J. cardiovasc. electrophysiol.]. Vol. 1, No. 1 (Feb. 1990)-. Periodical. English. mo (12 issues). $135.00 US & Canada; $180.00 other. Futura Publishing Company Inc., 135 Bedford Road, PO Box 418, Armonk NY 10504-0418. **Tel** (914)273-1014, (800)877-8761, FAX (914)273-1015, (914)273-1016. **ED** Douglas P. Zipes. **DD** 616. **NLM** W1; JO575L. **CODEN** JCELE2. Index available. cum. index. **Bk Rev**. **Ad Acc**. **Pr Rev. Circ:** 3,285. Documents available from The Genuine Article, BIOSIS Document Express. ***Continues** Journal of Electrophysiology, 0892-1059.*
**Desc:** Devoted to the study of cardiovascular electrophysiology from proteins to channels, membranes to single cells, blood vessels to hearts, whole animals to humans. Consists of original research, scholarly reviews, editorials and unique case reports. Will also have important and timely supplements.
**Ind/Abst** Biol. Abstr. (1990-); Curr. Contents Clin. Med.; EMBASE; Res. Alert [Select. Cov.].

US/0889-4655
**JOURNAL OF CARDIOVASCULAR NURSING, THE. See** Medical Science and Technology-Nursing.

US/0160-2446
**JOURNAL OF CARDIOVASCULAR PHARMACOLOGY. See** Pharmacy and Pharmacology.

IT/0021-9509
**JOURNAL OF CARDIOVASCULAR SURGERY. See** Medical Science and Technology-Surgery.

US/0022-0736
**JOURNAL OF ELECTROCARDIOLOGY.** [J. electrocardiol.]. Vol. 1, No. 1 (1968)-. Academic Scholarly Publication. English. qt (plus supplement). $152.00 institution, $95.00 individual. Churchill Livingstone Inc., 650 Avenue of the Americas, New York NY 10011. **Tel** (212)206-5062, FAX (212)727-7808. **(Subscription address:** Churchill Livingstone Inc., 5 South 250 Frontenac Road, Naperville, IL 60563; (telephone: (800)553-5426 or (708)416-3939)) **ED** Ronald H. Startt-Selvester. **LC** RC681.A1; J6. **DD** 616.1/207547/05. **NLM** W1 JO628R. **CODEN** JECAB4. **[CCC]**. Index available (bound in Oct. issue). **Bk Rev**. **Ad Acc**. **Pr Rev. Circ:** 2,500. available on microfilm and microfiche from University Microfilms International (UMI). Documents available from The Genuine Article, BIOSIS Document Express.
**Desc:** Devoted to clinical and experimental studies of the electrical activities of the heart and contributes significantly to the accuracy of diagnosis and prognosis and to the effective treatment and prevention of heart disease. Readership: cardiologists.
**Ind/Abst** Biol. Abstr.; Curr. Aware. Biol. Sci., CABS; Curr. Contents Clin. Med.; EMBASE; Energy Res. Abstr. (July 1982-); Index Med.; INIS Atomindex [Micro.]; Int. Aerosp. Abstr.; Life Sci. Collect.; Res. Alert [Full Cov.]; Sci. Cit. Index; SCISEARCH.

●UK/0966-8519
**JOURNAL OF HEART VALVE DISEASE, THE.** (1992)-. Periodical. English. bm. £57.00 (individual), £99.00 (institution) UK; $97.00 (individual), $167.00 (institution) other. ICR Publishers, 9 West End Ct, West End Avenue, Pinner, Middlesex HA5 1BP England. **Tel** 011 44 81 8663117. **NLM** W1; JO67BW. **CODEN** JHVDEU.
**Ind/Abst** Index Med. (Sept. 1992-).

UK/0950-9240
**JOURNAL OF HUMAN HYPERTENSION.** **VFOAT** Hypertension. Vol. 1, No. 1 (June 1987)-. Periodical. English. bm. £245.00 UK and EEC; £260.00 other. Macmillan Magazines Ltd., Houndmills, Basingstoke, Hampshire RG21 2XS England. **Tel** 011 44 256 29242, FAX 011 44 256 812358, telex 858493. **ED** D. G. Beevers and Franz H. Messerli. **LC** RC685.H8; J68. **DD** 616.1/32/005. **NLM** W1; JO673VET. **[CCC]**. Index available. **Bk Rev**. **Ad Acc**. **Pr Rev. Circ:** 1,000. available on microfilm from University Microfilms International (UMI). Documents available from The Genuine Article.
**Desc:** The journal is exclusively concerned with the clinical aspects of human hypertension. It aims to perform the dual role of increasing knowledge in the field of high blood pressure, as well as improving the standard of care of patients.
**Ind/Abst** Curr. Contents Clin. Med.; EMBASE; Index Med.; Res. Alert [Select. Cov.]; SCISEARCH; Soc. Sci. Cit. Index [Select. Cov.].

US/0263-6352
**JOURNAL OF HYPERTENSION.** [J. hypertens.]. **Added/Corp** European Society of Hypertension. International Society of Hypertension. Vol. 1, No. 1 (June 1983)-. Academic Scholarly Publication. English. Twelve times a year. $160.00 (individuals); $345.00 (institutions). Current Science / England, Middlesex House, 34-42 Cleveland Street, London W1P 5FB England. **Tel** 011 44 71 580 8393, 011 44 71 323 0323, FAX 011 44 81 580 1938. **(Subscription address:** Current Science, 20 North 3rd Street, Philadelphia PA 19106.) **ED** John L. Reid. **DD** 616. **NLM** W1 JO674R. **CODEN** JOHYD3. **[CCC]**. Index available. **Ad Acc**. **Pr Rev. Circ:** 5,580. available on diskette. Documents available from The Genuine Article, BIOSIS Document Express, CASDDS.
**Desc:** For researchers and clinicians working in hypertension. Featuring rapid publication of the foremost data and research. Each issue features one review and a bibliography of the current world literature published during the previous month.
**Ind/Abst** Annals Behav. Med.; Biol. Abstr. (1988-); Chem. Abstr. (1983-); Curr. Aware. Biol. Sci., CABS; Curr. Contents Clin. Med.; Curr. Contents Life Sci.; EMBASE; Index Med. (Vol. 1, No. 1, 1983-); Mod. Med.; Nutr. Abstr. Rev., Ser. A, Hum. Exp.; Nutr. Res. Newsl.; PESTDOC; Ref. Upd. Clinical Ed.; Ref. Upd. Deluxe Ed.; Res. Alert [Full Cov.]; Sci. Cit. Index; SCISEARCH; Soc. Sci. Cit. Index [Select. Cov.]; SportSearch.

UK/0952-1178
**JOURNAL OF HYPERTENSION. SUPPLEMENT.** (JOURNAL OF HYPERTENSION. SUPPLEMENT : OFFICIAL JOURNAL OF THE INTERNATIONAL SOCIETY OF HYPERTENSION.). [J. hypertens. Suppl.]. **Added/Corp** International Society of Hypertension. Vol. 1, Suppl. 1 (Oct. 1983)-. Monographic series. English. ir. Price varies per volume. Current Science / England, Middlesex House, 34-42 Cleveland Street, London W1P 5FB England. **Tel** 011 44 71 580 8393, 011 44 71 323 0323, FAX 011 44 81 580 1938. **(Subscription address:** Current Science, 20 North 3rd Street, Philadelphia PA 19106.) **NLM** W1; JO674RA. Index available in last issue of volume--attached.
**Ind/Abst** Index Med.

US/0896-4327
**JOURNAL OF INTERVENTIONAL CARDIOLOGY.** [J. interv. cardiol.]. Vol. 1, No. 1 (Mar. 1988)-. Periodical. English. Six times a year (6 issues). $98.00 US & Canada; $136.00 other. Futura Publishing Company Inc., 135 Bedford Road, PO Box 418, Armonk NY 10504-0418. **Tel** (914)273-1014, (800)877-8761, FAX (914)273-1015, (914)273-1016. **ED** Gerald C. Timmis. **DD** 616. **NLM** W1; IN719D. Index available. cum. index. **Bk Rev**. **Ad Acc**. **Circ:** 2,100. Documents available from The Genuine Article.
**Desc:** Presents articles in areas of cardiac catheterization, angioplasty, valvuloplasty, reperfusion, laser, mechanical assist devices, thrombolytic therapy, hemodynamic monitoring techniques, diagnostic techniques and interventional electrophysiology.
**Ind/Abst** Curr. Contents Clin. Med.; Res. Alert [Select. Cov.].

US/1042-3931
**JOURNAL OF INVASIVE CARDIOLOGY, THE.** Vol. 1, No. 1 (Nov. 1988)-. Periodical. English. Nine times a year. $90.00 (one year), $160.00 (two year), $240.00 (three year) US; $126.00 (one year), $220.00 (two year), $315.00 (three year) other. Health Management Publications, 550 American Avenue, Circulation Department, King of Prussia PA 19406. **Tel** (215)337-4466, (800)237-7285, FAX (215)337-0890. **ED** Ted Parris. **DD** 616. **NLM** W1; JO725. **Ad Acc**. Documents available from The Genuine Article.
**Desc:** Includes clinical papers, long-term case studies, product reports and guest columns.
**Ind/Abst** Curr. Contents Clin. Med.; Health Devices Alerts; Res. Alert [Select. Cov.]; Soc. Sci. Cit. Index [Select. Cov.].

UK/0022-2828
**JOURNAL OF MOLECULAR AND CELLULAR CARDIOLOGY.** [J. mol. cell. cardiol.]. Vol. 1 (Mar. 1970)-. Academic Scholarly Publication. English. mo. $1100.00. Academic Press Ltd., A Division of Harcourt Brace & Company Ltd., 24-28 Oval Road, London NW1 7DX England. **Tel** 071 267 4466, FAX 071 482 2293, 071 485 4752, telex 25775 ACPRES G. **(Subscription address:** Harcourt Brace & Company, Ltd., Foots Cray, High Street, Sidcup Kent DA14 5HP England.) **ED** A. M. Katz. **LC** RC681.A1. **NLM** W1 JO772. **CODEN** JMCDAY. **[CCC]**. **Bk Rev**. **Pr Rev**. Documents available from The Genuine Article, BIOSIS Document Express, CASDDS.
**Desc:** Provides a forum for research papers dealing with the molecular biology, physiology, pharmacology, and pathophysiology of the heart and cardiovascular system. Intended mainly for reports of original research in molecular and cellular cardiology, it also publishes editorials, special articles, and book reviews that highlight important developments in these areas. By presenting a broad range of research reports, it provides investigators in the many subject areas of experimental cardiology with an overview of the latest developments in molecular and cellular cardiology.
**Ind/Abst** Biol. Abstr.; Calcium Calcif. Tissue Abstr.; Chem. Abstr.; Chem. Titles; CSA Neuro. Abstr. (?-?); Curr. Contents Life Sci.; EMBASE; Index Med.; Life Sci. Collect.; PESTDOC; Protozoolog. Abstr.; Ref. Upd. Basic Ed.; Ref. Upd. Deluxe Ed.; Res. Alert [Full Cov.]; Sci. Cit. Index; SCISEARCH.

US/1045-7984
**JOURNAL OF MYOCARDIAL ISCHEMIA, THE.** (1989)-. Periodical. English. Ten times a year (July/Aug., and Nov./Dec. issues combined). $60.00. PRR Communications Inc., 17 Prospect Street, Huntington NY 11743. **Tel** (516)424-8900, FAX (516)424-8503. **DD** 616. **NLM** W1; JO777E. **CODEN** JMYIER. **[CCC]**.

●US/1071-3581
**JOURNAL OF NUCLEAR CARDIOLOGY.** [J. nucl. cardiol.]. **Added/Corp** American Society of Nuclear Cardiology. Vol. 1, No. 1 (Jan./Feb. 1994)-. Periodical. English. Six times a year. $120.00 (institutions), $95.00 (individuals) US; $148.00 (institutions), $123.00 (individuals) other. Mosby Year Book Inc., 11830 Westline Industrial Drive, St Louis MO 63146. **Tel** (800)325-4177, (314)872-8370, FAX (314)432-1380, telex 44-2402. **DD** 616. **NLM** W1; JO795M.

US/0748-8238
**JOURNAL OF ST. LUKE'S HEART INSTITUTE.** [J. St. Luke's Heart Inst.]. **Added/Corp** St. Luke's Heart Institute (St. Louis, Mo.). **VFOAT** Journal of Saint Luke's Heart Institute. (198?)-. Periodical. English. qt. Free. St Luke's Heart Institute, St Luke's Hospitals, 5535 Delmar Boulevard, St Louis MO 63112. **DD** 616.

US/0735-1097
**JOURNAL OF THE AMERICAN COLLEGE OF CARDIOLOGY.** [J. Am. Coll. Cardiol.]. **Added/Corp** American College of Cardiology. **VFOAT** JACC; J.A.C.C. Vol. 1, No. 1 (Jan. 1983)-. Academic Scholarly Publication. English. Fourteen times a year (2 volumes). $180.00 US; $378.00 Europe; $445.00 Japan; $265.00 (surface mail) other. Elsevier Science Publishing Company Inc, Madison Square Station, PO Box 882, New York NY 10159-0882. **Tel** (212)633-3950, FAX (212)633-3990. **ED** Simon Dack. **NLM** W1 JO908K. **CODEN** JACCDI. **[CCC]**. **Bk Rev**. **Ad Acc**. **Pr Rev. Circ:** 17,400. available on an online database from BRS; available on microfilm and microfiche from University Microfilms International (UMI). Documents available from The Genuine Article, CASDDS, ADONIS.
**Desc:** Publishes original clinical and experimental reports on all aspects of cardiovascular disease, including methodology, pediatric cardiology, cooperative studies, hypertension, epidemiology, drugs, and therapy.
**Ind/Abst** Abr. Index Med.; Abstr. Clin. Care Guidel.; ADONIS; Chem. Abstr. (1983-); Cumul. Index Nurs. Allied Health Lit.; Curr. Contents Clin. Med.; Curr. Contents Life Sci.; EMBASE; Health Devices Alerts; Index Med.; INIS Atomindex [Micro.]; J. Watch; Mod. Med.; Nutr. Res. Newsl.; Life Sci. Collect.; PESTDOC; Physic. Medline Plus; Ref. Upd. Basic Ed.; Ref. Upd. Clinical Ed.; Ref. Upd. Deluxe Ed.; Res. Alert [Full Cov.]; Risk Abstr.; Sci. Cit. Index; SCISEARCH; Soc. Sci. Cit. Index [Select. Cov.]; SPORT Discus; SportSearch.

US/0894-7317
**JOURNAL OF THE AMERICAN SOCIETY OF ECHOCARDIOGRAPHY.** (JOURNAL OF THE AMERICAN SOCIETY OF ECHOCARDIOGRAPHY : OFFICIAL PUBLICATION OF THE AMERICAN SOCIETY OF ECHOCARDIOGRAPHY.). [J. Am. Soc. Echocardiogr.]. **Added/Corp** American Society of Echocardiography. Vol. 1, No. 1 (Jan./Feb. 1988)-. Periodical. English. bm. $97.00 (institutions), $72.00 (individuals) US; $112.00 (institutions), $87.00 (individuals) other. Mosby Year Book Inc., 11830 Westline Industrial Drive, St Louis MO 63146. **Tel** (800)325-4177, (314)872-8370, FAX (314)432-1380, telex 44-2402. **ED** Harvey Feigenbaum. **DD** 616. **NLM** W1; JO911B. **CODEN** JSECEJ. **[CCC]**. **Pr Rev**. available on microfilm and microfiche from University Microfilms International (UMI).
**Desc:** Information on the technical basis and clinical application of echocardiography, a primary imaging modality used by clinical cardiologists for investigation of a wide range of heart abnormalities. Sections include original articles, technologies, and legislative, legal, and regulatory issues.
**Ind/Abst** Health Plan. Adminis.; Index Med. (1988-), (Vol. 1, No. 1, 1988-).

US/0022-5223
**JOURNAL OF THORACIC AND CARDIOVASCULAR SURGERY. See** Medical Science and Technology-Surgery.

●UK/1353-8012
**JOURNAL OF VASCULAR INVESTIGATION. See** Medical Science and Technology.

US/1062-0303
**JOURNAL OF VASCULAR NURSING. See** Medical Science and Technology-Nursing.

●SZ/1018-1172
**JOURNAL OF VASCULAR RESEARCH.** (Jan./Feb. 1992)-. Periodical. English. bm. $383.00. S. Karger AG, Allschwilerstrasse 10, PO Box - Postfach - Case Postale, CH-4009 Basel Switzerland. **Tel** 011 41 61

306-1111, FAX 011 41 61 306-1234, telex CH 962 652. **ED** M.J. Mulvany. **NLM** W1; JO97BV. **CODEN** JVREE9. **[CCC].** Documents available from The Genuine Article, BIOSIS Document Express. ***Continues*** *Blood Vessels, 0303-6847.*
**Desc:** Publishes original articles and reviews of scientific excellence in vascular biology, physiology and pathophysiology. The scope of the journal covers a broad spectrum of vascular and lymphatic research including vascular structure, vascular function, haemodynamics, mechanics, cell signaling, intercellular communication, growth and differentiation. Papers employing cellular, biophysical and molecular techniques, as well as more classical approaches are welcomed.
**Ind/Abst** Biol. Abstr.; Curr. Contents Clin. Med.; Curr. Contents Life Sci.; EMBASE; Index Med.; Ref. Upd. Deluxe Ed.; Res. Alert [Full Cov.]; Sci. Cit. Index; SCISEARCH.

US/1044-4122
**JOURNAL OF VASCULAR TECHNOLOGY, THE.** (THE JOURNAL OF VASCULAR TECHNOLOGY : JVT : OFFICIAL JOURNAL OF THE SOCIETY OF NON-INVASIVE VASCULAR TECHNOLOGY.). [J. vasc. technol.]. **Added/Corp** Society of Non-Invasive Vascular Technology (U.S.) Society of Vascular Technology. **VFOAT** JVT. (Jan. 1987)-. Periodical. English. bm (6 issues). $75.00 US and Canada; $90.00 other. Society of Vascular Technology, 1101 Connecticut Avenue Northwest, Suite 700, Washington DC 20036. **Tel** (202)857-1149, FAX (202)857-1130. **DD** 616. **NLM** W1; JO97CP. **CODEN** JVTEEJ. **Ad Acc. Pr Rev.** ***Continues*** *Bruit (South Dartmouth, Mass.), 0739-8670.*
**Desc:** A peer reviewed journal published as an educational service for practicing noninvasive vascular technologists, technologists involved in supervision and/or education in a clinical setting, physicians, surgeons, researchers, manufacturers, and other health care professionals.

GW
**KAINDL-ARCHIV : MITTEILUNGEN DER RAIMUND FRIEDRICH KAINDL GESELLSCHAFT.** **VFOAT** Kaindl Archiv. Periodical. German (English). an. DM20.00 Germany; $15.00 US. Raimund Friedrich Kaindl Gesellschaft, Waldburgstrasse 247, W-7000 Stuttgart 80 Germany. **Tel** 0045-711-742721. **ED** H Mayer, G Bornemann, and K Rain. **LC** DK508.95.C543; K34. **DD** 947/.718. **Bk Rev. Circ:** 400 (ctrl).

PL/0022-9032
**KARDIOLOGIA POLSKA (1957).** (KARDIOLOGIA POLSKA.). [Kardiol. pol.]. **Added/Corp** Polskie Towarzystwo Kardiologiczne. Vol. 1 (1957)-. Periodical. Polish. mo. Price on Request. **(Subscription address:** ARS Polona, PO Box 1001, 00068 Warsaw Poland.**)** **NLM** W1 KA759.
**Ind/Abst** EMBASE [Select. Cov.]; Index Med.; SportSearch.

RU/0022-9040
**KARDIOLOGIJA.** (KARDIOLOGIIA.). [Kardiologija]. **Added/Corp** Soviet Union. Ministerstvo Zdravookhraneniia. **VFOAT** Cardiology. Vol. 1 (1961)-. Academic Scholarly Publication. Russian (summaries and/or abstracts in English). mo. $139.95. Izdatelstvo Meditsina / Russian Academy of Medical Sciences, Ulitsa Solyanka 14, 109801 Moscow Russia. **Tel** 011 95 297-05-04. **(Subscription address:** East View Publications Inc., 3020 Harbor Lane North, Suite 110, Minneapolis MN 55447.**)** **NLM** W1 KA775. **CODEN** KARDA2. **[CCC].** Index available. **Bk Rev. Pr Rev.** Documents available from The Genuine Article, BIOSIS Document Express, CASDDS.
**Ind/Abst** Biol. Abstr.; Chem. Abstr.; EMBASE; Index Med.; Int. Aerosp. Abstr.; Res. Alert [Full Cov.]; Sci. Cit. Index (19??-19??); SCISEARCH; SportSearch.

US/0899-8019
**KEY CARDIOLOGY.** [KEY cardiol.]. **VFOAT** Key. (1988)-. Periodical. English. qt. $82.00 (institutions). Mosby Year Book Inc., 11830 Westline Industrial Drive, St Louis MO 63146. **Tel** (800)325-4177, (314)872-8370, FAX (314)432-1380, telex 44-2402. **DD** 616.

JA
**KOKURITSU JUNKANKIBYO SENTA GYOSEKI NEMPO.** **Added/Corp** Kokuritsu Junkankibyo Senta (Japan). (1977/78)-. Periodical. Japanese. an. Kokuritsu Junkankibyo Senta, 5-125 Fujishirodai, Suita 565 Japan. **LC** RC666; .K64.

AI/0368-6736
**KROVOOBRASCENIE.** (KROVOOBRASHCHENIE.). [Krovoobrascenie]. **Added/Corp** Haykakan SSH Gitutyunneri Akademia. (1970)-. Periodical. Russian (Armenian; summaries and/or abstracts in Armenian and English). Three times a year. $89.95. **NLM** W1 KR599. **CODEN** KROVAO. Documents available from BIOSIS Document Express, CASDDS.
**Ind/Abst** Biol. Abstr.; Chem. Abstr.

US/0742-3896
**L.E.R.S. MONOGRAPH SERIES.** [L.E.R.S. monogr. ser.]. **Added/Corp** Laboratoires d'Etudes et de Recherches Synthelabo. **VFOAT** LERS Monograph Series. **VAT** Laboratoires d'Etudes et de Recherches-Synthelabo Monograph Series. Vol. 1 (1983)-. Academic Scholarly Publication. English. ir. Price varies per volume. Raven Press, 1185 Avenue of the Americas, 37th Floor, New York NY 10036. **Tel** (212)930-9500, (212)930-9604, FAX (212)869-3495, (212)302-8507, telex 640073. **NLM** W1; LE886. **CODEN** LMSED6. Documents available from CASDDS.
**Ind/Abst** Chem. Abstr. (1983-).

FR/0761-5035
**LETTRE DU CARDIOLOGUE, LA.** [Lett. cardiol.]. (198?)-. Periodical. French. Eighteen times a year. 538.69F France; 700.00F other. Edimark, 207 rue Gallieni, 92100 Boulogne France. **Tel** 011 33 1 48251159. **UDC** 616.12.

UK/0951-9599
**LIPID FILE.** ***Ceased.*** [Lipid file]. (1987)-Vol. 7, No. 4 (Dec. 1993). Periodical. English. qt. Current Medical Literature Ltd., 40-42 Osnaburgh Street, London NW1 3ND England. **Tel** 011 44 71 4658377, FAX 011 44 71 4658380. **Pr Rev.** ctrl circ.
**Desc:** Reviews of current articles published in the field of cardiology and lipid research.

UK/0950-5857
**LIPID REVIEW.** [Lipid rev.]. Vol. 1, No. 1 (Jan. 1987)-. Periodical. English. mo. Free. Current Medical Literature Ltd., 40-42 Osnaburgh Street, London NW1 3ND England. **Tel** 011 44 71 4658377, FAX 011 44 71 4658380. **NLM** W1; LI646. **CODEN** CMLREE. Documents available from CASDDS.
**Ind/Abst** Chem. Abstr.

SP
**MEDICAL DIGEST. CARDIOLOGIA.** Spanish. Editorial M.C.R. SA, Mallorca 310, 08037 Barcelona Spain.

US/0738-2979
**MEDIGUIDE TO CARDIOLOGY.** [Mediguide cardiol.]. Vol. 1, No. 1-. Periodical. English. qt. Dellacorte Publications, 919 3rd Avenue, New York NY 10022-3904. **Tel** (212)751-2806. **NLM** W1 ME787FKE.

US
**MEDTRONIC NEWS.** English. Twice a year. Free. Medtronic Inc., 7000 Central Avenue Northeast, Minneapolis MN 55432. **Tel** (800)328-2516, FAX (612)574-3397. **ED** Chris Trevis, (phone: (612)574-3617). **Circ:** 45,000 (ctrl).
**Desc:** It is designed to advance knowledge of the technology and practices associated with medical devices and cardiovascular therapy.

●US/1063-2468
**MEETING REPORTS, CARDIOVASCULAR.** [Meet. rep., Cardiovasc.]. **VFOAT** Cardiovascular. Vol. 1 (1992)-. Periodical. English. Four times a year. $210.00 (institutions), $115.00 (individuals) North America; add $25.00 (surface mail) or $40.00 (airmail) other. Neva Press, PO Box 347, Branford CT 06405. **Tel** (203)272-5338, FAX (203)272-5338. **ED** Alexander Scriabine, M.D. **DD** 616. **NLM** W1; ME877M. **Ad Acc.**
**Desc:** Consists of brief reports on new developments in basic medical sciences presented at recent scientific meetings. Each report is written by a scientist who attended the meeting and is known in his field.

NE/0167-725X
**METABOLIC ASPECTS OF CARDIOVASCULAR DISEASE.** [Metab. aspects cardiovasc. dis.]. Vol. 1-. Academic Scholarly Publication. English. Price varies per volume. Elsevier Science Publishing Company Inc, Madison Square Station, PO Box 882, New York NY 10159-0882. **Tel** (212)633-3950, FAX (212)633-3990. **NLM** W1 ME961KN (P). **CODEN** MACDDK. Documents available from CASDDS.
**Ind/Abst** Chem. Abstr.

IT/0026-4725
**MINERVA CARDIOANGIOLOGICA.** [Minerva cardioangiol.]. Vol. 1 (Nov./Dec. 1953)-. Periodical. Italian (Italian; summaries and/or abstracts in English). mo. $110.00 (individuals), $150.00 (institutions). Edizioni Minerva Medica, Corso Bramante 83-85, 10126 Turin Italy. **Tel** 011 39 11 678282, FAX 011 39 11 674502. **ED** F Spadaccimi. **NLM** W1 MI634. **Bk Rev. Ad Acc.** available on microfilm from University Microfilms International (UMI).
**Ind/Abst** EMBASE [Select. Cov.]; Index Med.; Life Sci. Collect.; SportSearch.

FR/0300-0702
**MISES A JOUR CARDIOLOGIQUES.** (1972)-. Periodical. French (English). bm. 300.00F France 350.00 other. Editions Medicales DHR, 1 Allee des Noisetiers, Bos Postale 43, 92145 Clamart Cedex France. **Tel** 011 33 1 46428182, FAX 011 33 1 146440885.

US/0742-1354
**MISSOURI STATE PLAN FOR HIGH BLOOD PRESSURE CONTROL.** Fiscal Year 1980-. English. an. Department of Social Services / Missouri, Broadway State Office Building, Jefferson City MO 65102. **LC** RA645.H9; M58. **DD** 362.1/9616132. ***Continues*** *Missouri State Plan for Hypertension Control, 0742-1362.*

MX
**MONOGRAFIAS DEL INSTITUTO NACIONAL DE CARDIOLOGIA.** **Added/Corp** Instituto Nacional de Cardiologia (Mexico). Periodical. Spanish. **NLM** W1; MO5423L.

US/0891-320X
**MONOGRAPH / AMERICAN HEART ASSOCIATION.** [Monogr. - Am. Heart Assoc.]. **Added/Corp** American Heart Association. No. 118 (1986)-. Monographic series. English. ir. Price varies per volume. Futura Publishing Company Inc., 135 Bedford Road, PO Box 418, Armonk NY 10504-0418. **Tel** (914)273-1014, (800)877-8761, FAX (914)273-1015, (914)273-1016. **DD** 616. Documents available from BIOSIS Document Express. ***Continues*** *American Heart Association Monograph, 0065-8499.*
**Ind/Abst** Biol. Abstr.

●CN/1193-1884
**MULTI-FACT.** [Multi-fact]. **Added/Corp** Fondation des Maladies du Coeur du Quebec. Vol. 4, No 1 (Feb 1992)-. Periodical. French. qt. Limited free distribution. Fondation des Maladies du Coeur du Quebec, Bureau 1440, 440 Ouest Boulevard Rene Levesque, (Anciennement Ouest Boulevard Dorchester), Montreal Quebec H2V 1Z7 Canada. **DD** 616.1/32/005. ***Continues*** *Tension Arterielle Quebec., 1181-9960.*

US/0164-0577
**MULTIPLE RISK FACTOR INTERVENTION TRIAL. PUBLIC ANNUAL REPORT.** **Main/Corp** National Heart, Lung, and Blood Institute. Division of Heart and Vascular Diseases. **VFOAT** Public Annual Report. English. an. National Heart Lung and Blood Institute, Division of Heart and Vascular Diseases, Devices and Technology Branch, 9000 Rockville Pike, Bethesda MD 20014. ***Continues*** *Multiple Risk Factor Intervention Trial. Public Annual Report, 0146-4884.*

NE/0921-5018
**NETHERLANDS JOURNAL OF CARDIOLOGY : THREE-MONTHLY ISSUE OF THE NETHERLANDS HEART FOUNDATION AND THE NETHERLANDS SOCIETY OF CARDIOLOGY, THE.** **Added/Corp** Nederlandse Hartstichting. Nederlandse Vereniging voor Cardiologie. (198?)-. Periodical. English. bm (6 issues). Fl26.25 Netherlands and Luxembourg; Fl35.00 other. Wegener Tijl Tijdschriften Group, Postbus 9943, 1006 AP Amsterdam Netherlands. **Tel** 011 31 20 5182828. **NLM** W1; NE229H.

US/0743-9237
**NEW CONCEPTS IN CARDIAC IMAGING.** [New concepts card. imag.]. **VFOAT** Cardiac Imaging. (1985)-. English. an. $57.50. Mosby Year Book Inc., 11830 Westline Industrial Drive, St Louis MO 63146. **Tel** (800)325-4177, (314)872-8370, FAX (314)432-1380, telex 44-2402. **DD** 616. **NLM** W1; NE372G. **[CCC].**

IT/0393-5302
**NEW TRENDS IN ARRHYTHMIAS.** [New trends arrhythm.]. Vol. 1, No. 1 (Apr./June 1985)-. Periodical. English. qt. $80.00. CIC Edizioni Internazionali, Via L Spallanzani 11, 00161 Rome Italy. **Tel** 011 39 6 841-2673, FAX 011 39 6 844-3365, telex 622099 CIC I. **NLM** W1; NE513B. **[CCC].**
**Ind/Abst** EMBASE.

US
**NEWSPAPER OF CARDIOLOGY.** (19??)-. English. Twelve times a year. $55.00 US; $79.00 others. McMahon Publishing Company, 148 West 24th Street, 8th Floor, New York NY 10011. **Tel** (212)620-4600, FAX (212)620-5928. ***Continues*** *Cardiovascular News, 0747-461X.*

GW/0939-4753
**NUTRITION, METABOLISM, AND CARDIOVASCULAR DISEASES : NMCD.** **VFOAT** NMCD. Vol. 1, No. 1 (1991)-. Periodical. English. qt. DM298.00. Springer-Verlag GmbH & Company KG, Heidelberger Platz 3, D 14197 Berlin Germany. **Tel** 011 49 30 8207223, FAX 011 49 30 8214091, telex 183 319 SPBLN D. **(Subscription address:** Springer Verlag New York Inc. / for North America, 44 Hartz Way, Secaucus NJ 07096.**)** **NLM** W1; NU888L. **[CCC].** available on microfilm and microfiche from University Microfilms International (UMI).

US/0147-8389
**PACING AND CLINICAL ELECTROPHYSIOLOGY.** (PACE. PACING AND CLINICAL ELECTROPHYSIOLOGY.). [Pacing clin. electrophysiol.]. **Added/Corp** North American Society of Pacing and Electrophysiology. International Cardiac Pacing Society. Asian-Pacific Working Group on Cardiac

Pacing. Vol. 1 (Jan. 1978)-. Periodical. English. mo (12 issues plus supplements). $160.00 US & Canada; $208.00 other. Futura Publishing Company Inc., 135 Bedford Road, PO Box 418, Armonk NY 10504-0418. **Tel** (914)273-1014, (800)877-8761, FAX (914)273-1015, (914)273-1016. **ED** Seymour Furman. **LC** RC684.P3; P18. **DD** 617/.412. **NLM** W1 P114T. **[CCC].** Index available. cum. index. **Bk Rev. Ad Acc. Pr Rev. Circ:** 4,891. Documents available from The Genuine Article.
**Desc:** Presents communications in laboratory and clinical cardiac pacing, electrophysiology and the electro-stimulation of other organs which affect the cardiovascular system.
**Ind/Abst** EMBASE; Health Devices Alerts; Index Med.; Life Sci. Collect.; Physic. Medline Plus; Res. Alert [Full Cov.]; Sci. Cit. Index; SCISEARCH.

UK/0261-7021
**PAEDIATRIC CARDIOLOGY.** **See** Medical Science and Technology-Pediatrics.

FR/1146-559X
**PASCAL. 75, CARDIOLOGIE ET APPAREIL CIRCULATOIRE.** **Added/Corp** Institut de l'Information Scientifique et Technique (France). **VFOAT** Cardiologie et Appareil Circulatoire; Cardiology and Circulatory System. No. 1 (1991)-. Periodical. English (French). Ten times a year. 1600.00F France; 1695.00F other. CNRS / Institut d'Information Scientifique et Technique, (Centre National de la Recherche Scientifique), 15 Quai Anatole France, Paris 75700 France. **Tel** 011 33 1 47531515, telex 299 356 F. **(Subscription address:** Institut d'Information Scientifique et Technique, 2 Allee du Parc de Brabois, 54514 Vandoeuvre Nancy France) **NLM** ZWG 100; P278. ***Continues*** *PASCAL. E75, Cardiologie et Appareil Circulatoire.*

SP
**PATHOS. MONOGRAFIAS DE PATOLOGIA MEDICA.** Spanish (English). mo. 5.500ptas Spain; 7.500ptas other. Jarpyo Editores SA, Antonio Lopez Aguados 4, 28029 Madrid, Spain. **Tel** 011 34 1 3144338, 011 34 1 3144458. **(Subscription address:** Antonio Lopez Aguado 1-4, 28029 Madrid Spain) **ED** Robert A O'Rourke. **Ad Acc. Circ:** 3,000.

US/0172-0643
**PEDIATRIC CARDIOLOGY.** **See** Medical Science and Technology-Pediatrics.

UK/0267-6591
**PERFUSION.** [Perfusion]. Vol. 1, No. 1 (1986)-. Periodical. English. Six times a year. $335.00 North America; £220.00 Europe; £235.00 Other. Edward Arnold, 338 Euston Road, London NW1 3BH England. **Tel** 011 44 71 873 6000, FAX 011 44 071 873 6325. **(Subscription address:** Edward Arnold, PO Box 386, Avenel NJ 07001-0386.) **ED** K. Taylor and M. Kurusz. **NLM** W1; PE786. **CODEN** PERFER. **[CCC].** Documents available from The Genuine Article, BIOSIS Document Express.
**Desc:** Provides a focus for cardiac surgeons, perfusionists, anaesthetists, bioengineers, biochemists, and haemotologists. For all who are concerned with the field of extracorporeal circulation. Carries up-to-date information on all aspects of perfusion, oxygenation, and biocompatibility, vital areas for development in perfusion science and practice. Original papers, review articles, device assessments, case assessments and case reports.
**Ind/Abst** Biol. Abstr. (1986-); Curr. Contents Clin. Med.; EMBASE; Index Med.; Res. Alert [Select. Cov.]; SCISEARCH.

CN/0828-6396
**PERSPECTIVES IN CARDIOLOGY.** [Perspect. cardiol.]. Vol. 1 No. 1 (Jan. 1985)-. Periodical. English. Six times a year. 85.00Can$ Canada; 107.50Can$ others. STA Communications Inc., 955 St. John Boulevard, Suite 306, Pt Claire, Quebec H9R 5K3 Canada. **Tel** (514)695-7623. **DD** 616.1/2/005. **NLM** W1; PE871AK. **Circ:** 24,000 (ctrl).
**Desc:** Contains state-of-the-art review articles on the diagnosis and treatment of cardiovascular diseases. Written by Canadian specialists and directed to the primary and secondary care physicians - general practitioners and specialists.

PH/0115-1029
**PHILIPPINE JOURNAL OF CARDIOLOGY.** [Philipp. j. cardiol.]. (1973)-. Periodical. English. qt. **NLM** W1 PH565S.
**Ind/Abst** Philip. Sci. Technol. Abstr.

FR/0031-8280
**PHLEBOLOGIE.** (PHLEBOLOGIE : BULLETIN DE LA SOCIETE FRANCAISE DE L'UNION INTERNATIONALE DE PHLEBOLOGIE.). [Phlebologie]. (Jan./March 1952)-. Bulletin. French. qt. 421.16F France; 565.00F other. Societe Francaise de Phlebologie, 46 rue Saint Lambert, 75015 Paris France. **Tel** 011 33 1 45330271. **(Subscription address:** Gestion Informatique Stocks, BP 5 Les Allaux, 14410 Vassy France) **NLM** W1 PH62K. **[CCC].** ***Continues*** *Bulletin of the Societe Francaise de Phlebologie.*
**Ind/Abst** EMBASE [Select. Cov.]; Index Med.; SportSearch.

GW/0939-978X
**PHLEBOLOGIE STUTTGART.** [Phlebologie Stuttg.]. (1991)-. Periodical. Multiple languages. Six times a year. DM220.00 (institutions), DM179.00 (individuals) Europe; $138.70 (institutions), $111.70 (individuals) other. F K Schattauer Verlagsgesellschaft mbH, Postfach 10 45 45, D 70040 Stuttgart Germany. **Tel** 011 49 711 2298726. **UDC** 61. ***Continues*** *Phlebologie und Proktologie, 0340-305X.*
**Ind/Abst** EMBASE.

US/1055-9086
**PLACES TO PRACTICE (INTERNAL MEDICINE/CARDIOLOGY ED.).** **See** Medical Science and Technology-Internal Medicine.

US/0361-3372
**PRACTICAL CARDIOLOGY.** ***Ceased.*** [Pract. cardiol.]. Vol. 1 (Oct. 1975)-Ceased (Jan. 1991). Academic Scholarly Publication. English. mo. Office Center, Princeton Building 1000, Plainsboro NJ 08536. **Tel** (609)275-1900. **LC** RC681.A1; P7. **DD** 616.1/2/005. **NLM** W1 PR1382. **[CCC]. Ad Acc.**
**Ind/Abst** EMBASE [Select. Cov.]; Health Ref. Cent. (Jan. 1989-) [Full Cov.]; Mod. Med.

US/0896-5463
**PRACTICAL REVIEWS IN CARDIOLOGY.** (PRACTICAL REVIEWS IN CARDIOLOGY [SOUND RECORDING].). [Pract. rev. cardiol.]. **Added/Corp** Educational Reviews, Inc. Montefiore Medical Center. **VFOAT** Practical Reviews. (197?)-. Periodical. English. mo. $175.00 Physicians/Dentists; $125.00 Residents. Educational Reviews Inc., 6801 Cahaba Valley Road, Birmingham AL 35242. **Tel** (205)991-5188, (800)633-4743, FAX (205)995-1926. **DD** 616.

US/0363-5104
**PRIMARY CARDIOLOGY.** [Prim. cardiol.]. (19??)-. Periodical. English. mo. $68.00 US; $80.00 Canada; $119.00 other. Physicians World Comm Group, 400 Plaza Drive, Secaucus NJ 07096. **Tel** (201)865-7500. **LC** RC681.A1; P73. **DD** 616.1/005. **NLM** W1 PR521R. **CODEN** PRCRDA. available on microfilm and microfiche from University Microfilms International (UMI). Documents available from BIOSIS Document Express. ***Absorbed*** *Cardiovascular Medicine (New York, N.Y. : 1984), 8756-4211.*
**Ind/Abst** Biol. Abstr. (1986-); EMBASE; Health Index (1992-).

US/0894-2285
**PRINCIPLES OF CLINICAL ELECTROCARDIOGRAPHY.** (PRINCIPLES OF CLINICAL ELECTROCARDIOGRAPHY / BY MERVIN J. GOLDMAN.). [Princ. clin. electrocardiogr.]. **VFOAT** Clinical Electrocardiography. 1st Ed. (1956)-. English (Italian, Portuguese and Spanish). ir. $24.50 (latest edition). Appleton Century Crofts, Prentice Hall, 200 Old Tappan Road, Old Tappan NJ 07675. **Tel** (201)767-5188, (800)922-0579. **ED** Mervin J. Goldman. **LC** RC683.5.E5; G62. **DD** 616.12075.
**Desc:** The basic concepts of electrophysiology, the sequences of myocardial activation, and the projection of these electrical events onto leas axes.

FR
**PROCEEDINGS - ASSOCIATION OF EUROPEAN PAEDIATRIC CARDIOLOGISTS.** **See** Medical Science and Technology-Pediatrics.

US/0894-1084
**PROCEEDINGS OF THE AMERICAN ACADEMY OF CARDIOVASCULAR PERFUSION, THE.** [Proc. Am. Acad. Cardiovasc. Perfus.]. **Main/Conf** Seminar on Cardiovascular Perfusion of the American Academy of Cardiovascular Perfusion. **Added/Corp** American Academy of Cardiovascular Perfusion. Vol. 1, No. 1 (Jan. 1980)-. English. an. $40.00. American Academy of Cardiovascular Perfusion, PO Box 100546, Birmingham AL 35210. **Tel** (205)854-2341. **ED** Mark Kurusz. **DD** 612. **NLM** W3; SE465E. **Circ:** 1,000.

US
**PROCEEDINGS OF THE MEETING ON CARDIOVASCULAR EPIDEMIOLOGY AND BIOSTATISTICS TRAINING PROGRAMS.** **Main/Conf** Meeting on Cardiovascular Epidemiology and Biostatistics Training Programs. 4th-1979-. Proceedings. English. **NLM** W3 ME427SP. ***Continues*** *Proceedings of the Workshop on Cardiovascular Epidemiology and Biostatistics Training Programs.*

US
**PROCEEDINGS OF THE U.S. PUBLIC HEALTH SERVICE COOPERATIVE STUDIES (RENAL DISEASE AND HYPERTENSION).** **Main/Corp** United States. Public Health Service Cooperative Study. **VFOAT** Renal Disease and Hypertension. Vol. 2 (Apr. 1965)-. Proceedings. English. an. Federal Center Building #3, Prince George Center, 6525 Belerest Road West, Hyattsville MD 20782. **UDC** 616.61; 616.12-008.331.1. ***Continues*** *Proceedings of the Annual Conferences of the U.S. Public Health Service Cooperative Study (Anti-Hypertensive Agents).*

SP
**PROGRESOS EN LAS ENFERMEDADES CARDIOVASCULARES.** Spanish. Editorial Cientifico Medica / Barcelona, Via Layetana 53, 08003 Barcelona Spain.

US
**PROGRESS IN CARDIOLOGY (PHILADELPHIA, PA. : 1988).** (PROGRESS IN CARDIOLOGY.). Vol. 1; 1988-. Periodical. English. sa. $49.50. Lea & Febiger, 600 Washington Square, Philadelphia PA 19106-4198. **Tel** (800)433-3850, FAX (215)629-0060. **ED** Douglas P Zipes and Derek J Rowlands. **LC** RC681.A1; P75. **DD** 616.1/2/005. ctrl circ. ***Continues*** *Progress in Cardiology.*
**Desc:** Articles in cardiology.

US/0033-0620
**PROGRESS IN CARDIOVASCULAR DISEASES.** [Prog. cardiovasc. dis.]. Vol. 1 (June 1958)-. Academic Scholarly Publication. English. bm (6 issues). $99.00 (individual), $167.00 (institution) US; $193.00 (individual), $218.00 (institution) other. W.B. Saunders Company, A Subsidiary of Harcourt Brace Jovanovich, Inc., The Curtis Center/Suite 300, Independence Square West, Philadelphia PA 19106-3399. **Tel** (215)238-7800 or, 5587, FAX (215)238-7883, telex 173146. **(Subscription address:** W. B. Saunders Company / North America Subscriptions, c/o Periodicals, 6277 Sea Harbour Drive, 4th Floor, Orlando FL 32887.) **DD** 616. **NLM** W1 PR6671. **CODEN** PCVDAN. **[CCC]. Pr Rev.** Documents available from The Genuine Article, BIOSIS Document Express, CASDDS.
**Desc:** Covers a single major topic important in today's understanding and treatment of disorders of the heart and circulation.
**Ind/Abst** Abr. Index Med.; Biol. Abstr.; Chem. Abstr.; Curr. Aware. Biol. Sci., CABS; Curr. Contents Clin. Med.; Curr. Contents Life Sci.; EMBASE; Energy Res. Abstr. (Oct. 1975-); Index Med.; Index Sci. Rev. [Full Cov.]; Mod. Med.; Nutr. Abstr. Rev., Ser. A, Hum. Exp.; Nutr. Res. Newsl.; Life Sci. Collect.; Physic. Medline Plus; Ref. Upd. Clinical Ed.; Ref. Upd. Deluxe Ed.; Res. Alert [Full Cov.]; Sci. Cit. Index; SCISEARCH; SportSearch.

US/0889-7204
**PROGRESS IN CARDIOVASCULAR NURSING.** [Prog. cardiovasc. nurs.]. Vol. 1, No. 1 (Oct./Dec. 1986)-. Periodical. English. qt. $70.00 (institutions), $50.00 (individuals). Medquest Communications Inc., 629 Euclid Avenue, Suite 500, Cleveland OH 44114. **Tel** (216)522-9700. **(Subscription address:** PO Box 20179, Cleveland, OH 44120) **ED** Marguerite Engler, Julie A. Shinn, Ericka Froelicher. **NLM** W1; PR6671E. **Pr Rev.** available on microfilm and microfiche from University Microfilms International (UMI).
**Desc:** Information specific to the needs of the cardiovascular nurse. Emphasis on research, new therapies, and technologies. Reflects current practice in caring of the cardiac patient. Special features on pharmacological developments, legal issues, complex arrhythmias, and their treatment.
**Ind/Abst** Cumul. Index Nurs. Allied Health Lit. (1988-); Int. Nurs. Index (1987-).

●US/1058-9813
**PROGRESS IN PEDIATRIC CARDIOLOGY.** (1992)-. Periodical. English. qt. $140.00 (institution), $98.00 (individual) US and Canada; $170.00 (institution), $125.00 (individual) other. Butterworth Heinemann / Woburn, MA, 225 Wildwood Avenue, Unit B, Woburn MA 01801. **Tel** (800)366-2665, FAX (617)928-2620, telex 880052. **[CCC].**
**Desc:** Presents information and experience opinion important to understanding and managing cardiovascular disease in children. Each issue presents an in-depth review of one complex or controversial subject.

UK/0144-865X
**PROGRESS IN STROKE RESEARCH.** [Prog. stroke res.]. 1-. English. **ED** R M Greenhalgh and F C Rose. **NLM** W1 PR681K.

IT/0033-0701
**PROGRESSI IN PATOLOGIA CARDIOVASCOLARE.** **VFOAT** Progress in Cardiovascular Diseases. (19??)-. Italian. Six times a year. L100000 (individuals), L140000 (institutions). Il Pensiero Scientifico Editore s.r.l., Via Bradano 3C, 00199 Rome Italy. **Tel** 011 39 6 86207158, 86207159, 86207168, 86207169, FAX 011 39 6 86207160. **ED** E.H. Sonnenblick and M. Lesch. **Ad Acc, Adv Mgr:** Dott Dalla. Full Page (B&W) L1.650.000. **Circ:** 1,750.

GW
**PSYCHOSOZIALER STRESS UND KORONARE HERZKRANKHEIT.** English (German). **NLM** W3 PS966.

UK/0951-807X
**RECENT ADVANCES IN CARDIAC ARRHYTHMIAS.** [Recent adv. card. arrhythm.]. 1-. Academic Scholarly Publication. English. ir. Price varies per volume. John Libbey & Company Ltd, 13 Smiths Yard, Summerley Street, London SW18 4HR England. **Tel** 01-947 2777, FAX 01-947 2664, telex 94013503 JOHN G. **NLM** W1; RE105SJ. **CODEN** RACAEX. Documents available from CASDDS.
**Ind/Abst** Chem. Abstr. (1983-).

UK
**RECENT ADVANCES IN CARDIOLOGY.** No. 1 (1929)-. English. ir (every 3-5 years). Price varies per volume. Churchill Livingstone, 1-3 Baxter's Place, Leith Walk, Edinburgh EH1 3AF Scotland. **Tel** 011 44 31 556 2424, FAX 011 44 31 558 1278, telex 727511. **(Subscription address:** Churchill Livingstone / US, 5 S 250 Frontenac Road, Naperville IL 60563.**) LC** RC681.A1; R4. **DD** 616.1/2. **NLM** W1 RE105SL.

US/0090-1326
**RECURRING BIBLIOGRAPHY OF HYPERTENSION.** ***Ceased.*** [Recurr. bibliogr. hypertens.]. V. 1- May/June 1969-Ceased December (1990). Bibliography. English. bm. American Heart Association, 7272 Greenville Avenue, Dallas TX 75231-4596. **Tel** (214)706-1310, (214)373-6300, FAX (214)691-6342. **ED** J Edwin Wood. **DD** 616. **NLM** ZWG 340 R311. **Bk Rev. Ad Acc. Circ:** 1,050 (ctrl).
**Desc:** Provides a rapid survey of current published developments in the field.

US/0193-7340
**REPORT OF THE DIRECTOR, NATIONAL HEART, LUNG, AND BLOOD INSTITUTE.** See Public Health and Safety.

US/0161-1917
**REPORT OF THE NATIONAL HEART, LUNG, AND BLOOD ADVISORY COUNCIL.** **Main/Corp** National Heart, Lung, and Blood Advisory Council. **VFOAT** 30 Years of Progress for the People in Heart, Lung, and Blood Disease. Began with 4th, 1976. English. an. US Department of Health and Human Services, 200 Independence Avenue Southwest, Washington DC 20201. **LC** RA645.H4; U53A. **DD** 362.1/961. **NLM** W2 A N162a. ***Continues*** *Report of the National Heart and Lung Advisory Council, 0193-2225.*

AG/0034-7000
**REVISTA ARGENTINA DE CARDIOLOGIA.** (REVISTA ARGENTINA DE CARDIOLOGIA : ORGANO DE LA SOCIEDAD ARGENTINA DE CARDIOLOGIA.). [Rev. Argent. cardiol.]. Began with: Vol. 1, published in 1934. Academic Scholarly Publication. Spanish (summaries and/or abstracts in English). bm. Sociedad Argentina de Cardiologia, Gia Larrea 1132, Buenos Aires Argentina. **NLM** W1 RE267L. **CODEN** RACDA4.
**Ind/Abst** EMBASE.

CU
**REVISTA CUBANA CARDIOLOGIA Y CIRURGIA CARDIOVASCULAR.** Vol. 1, No. 1 (Jan./June 1987)-. Periodical. Spanish. Three times a year. $21.00 North America; $23.00 South America; $28.00 other. Ediciones Cubanas, Obispo 527, Altos ESQ Bernaza, CP 10100 Havana Cuba. **Tel** 011 632980, 631942, FAX 011 631011, telex 512337, 6540. **NLM** W1; RE359BN. ***Continues*** *Boletin de Cardiologia y Cirugia Cardiovascular.*
**Desc:** Features to satisfy the demand for professional information in the field, as well as constitute and medium for the diffusion of scientific studies, national as well as foreign studies.

SP/0300-8932
**REVISTA ESPANOLA DE CARDIOLOGIA.** (REVISTA ESPANOLA DE CARDIOLOGIA : PUBLICACION OFICIAL DE LA SOCIEDAD ESPANOLA DE CARDIOLOGIA.). [Rev. esp. cardiol.]. **Added/Corp** Sociedad Espanola de Cardiologia. Vol. 1 (1947)-. Academic Scholarly Publication. Spanish (summaries and/or abstracts in English and French). mo. $79.00. Ediciones Doyma SA, Travesera de Gracia 17 21, 08021 Barcelona Spain. **Tel** 011 34 3 2000711, 011 34 3 4145706, FAX 011 34 3 2091136, telex 51964 INK E. **ED** D. E. Marin Huerta. **NLM** W1 RE531. **CODEN** RCDOAM. Index available. cum. index. **Bk Rev. Ad Acc. Pr Rev. Circ:** 4,000 (ctrl). Documents available from CASDDS.
**Desc:** Official publication of the Spanish Society of Cardiology. Consists of research studies regarding the areas of cardiology, clinical, diagnostic and therapeutic techniques, surgery, etc.
**Ind/Abst** Chem. Abstr. (1947-1983); EMBASE [Select. Cov.]; Index Med.; Indice Med. Esp.; Life Sci. Collect.; SportSearch.

SP/0210-8755
**REVISTA LATINA DE CARDIOLOGIA EUROAMERICANA.** (REVISTA LATINA DE CARDIOLOGIA.). [Rev. lat. cardiol. euroam.]. Vol. 1, No. 1 (Jan. 1980)-. Periodical. Spanish (summaries and/or abstracts in English). Six times a year. $55.00. IDEPSA International Ediciones Publs SA, Principe de Vergara 112 1F, 28002 Madrid Spain. **Tel** 011 34 1 5637306. **NLM** W1; RE59678H. **CODEN** RLCEEK.
**Ind/Abst** EMBASE [Select. Cov.]; Indice Med. Esp.

PO/0870-2551
**REVISTA PORTUGUESA DE CARDIOLOGIA.** (REVISTA PORTUGUESA DE CARDIOLOGIA : ORGAO OFICIAL DA SOCIEDADE PORTUGUESA DE CARDIOLOGIA.). [Rev. port. cardiol.]. **Added/Corp** Sociedade Portuguesa de Cardiologia. **VFOAT** Portuguese Journal of Cardiology. Vol. 1, No. 1 (June 1982)-. Periodical. English (Portuguese). bm (6 issues). Society Portuguesa de Cardiologia, Campo Grande 28 4-C, 1700 Lisbon Portugal. **NLM** W1; RE716QK. ***Continues*** *Boletim da Sociedade Portuguesa de Cardiologia, 0304-4750.*
**Ind/Abst** EMBASE [Select. Cov.]; Index Med. (Vol. 7, No. 1, 1988-).

FR
**REVUE DU CARDIOLOGUE PRATICIEN, LA.** **VFOAT** A.Revue du cardiologue. Vol. 1, No. 1 (Oct. 1989)-. Periodical. French. Eight times a year. $144.00. Masson Editeur, Box Postale 22, 41353 Vineuil 16 France. **Tel** 011 33 54 438994. **NLM** W1; RE8336.

IT/0393-2028
**RIVISTA DI CARDIOLOGIA PREVENTIVA E RIABILITATIVA : ORGANO DELL'ASSOCIAZIONE NAZIONALE DEI CENTRI PER LE MALATTIE CARDIOVASCOLARI.** **Added/Corp** Associazione Nazionale dei Centri per le Malattie Cardiovascolari. **VFOAT** Cardiologia Preventiva e Riabilitativa. (198?)-. Periodical. Italian. qt. Edizioni Minerva Medica, Corso Bramante 83-85, 10126 Turin Italy. **Tel** 011 39 11 678282, FAX 011 39 11 674502. **NLM** W1; RE519D. **Bk Rev. Pr Rev.** ctrl circ.

FR/0999-7385
**SANG, THROMBOSE, VAISSEAUX : STV.** **VFOAT** STV; Sang, Thrombose, et Vaisseaux. (198?)-. Periodical. French (summaries and/or abstracts in English). Ten times a year. 670.00F (institutions), 400.00F (individuals), 270.00F (students) EEC and Switzerland; 750.00F (institutions), 480.00F (individuals), 350.00F (students) other. John Libbey Eurotext Ltd, 6 rue Blanche, Isabelle Trope, 92120 Montrouge France. **Tel** 011 33 1 47358552. **(Subscription address:** 23 25 rue Fernand Combette, 93100 Montreuil France, Telephone: 011 33 1 48595811**) NLM** W1; SA645N.
**Ind/Abst** EMBASE.

SW/0586-9587
**SCANDINAVIAN JOURNAL OF THORACIC AND CARDIOVASCULAR SURGERY. SUPPLEMENTUM.** [Scand. j. thoracic cardiovasc. surg., Suppl.]. No. 1 (1969)-. Periodical. English. ir. Comes with Scandinavian Journal of Thoracic and Cardiovascular Surgery: $132.00. Scandinavian University Press, PO Box 2959 Toeyen, N 0608 Oslo 6 Norway. **Tel** 011 47 2 2575400, FAX 011 47 2 2575353, telex 71896 UROR N. **(Subscription address:** Scandinavian University Press, 200 Meacham Ave., Elmont NY 11003.**) NLM** W1 SC154CA. **CODEN** STCSBO. Documents available from BIOSIS Document Express.
**Ind/Abst** Biol. Abstr.; Curr. Contents Clin. Med.; Index Med.; Life Sci. Collect.

UK
**SCRIP REPORT ON HYPERTENSION.** (19??)-. English. £425.00. PJB Publications, 18-20 Hill Rise, Richmond Surrey TW10 6UA England. **Tel** 011 44 81 948 3262.

JA/0911-0836
**SHINZO PESHINGU.** **Added/Corp** Nihon Shinzo Peshingu Gakkai. **VFOAT** Cardiac Pacing. (1984)-. Periodical. Japanese (English). Five times a year. $360.00. Pesu Meka Iinka, (Japanese Society of Cardiac Pacing), Shinbashi Ekimae Biru 1 Gokan, 2-20, Shinbashi, Minatoku, Tokyoto 105 Japan. **(Subscription address:** Kyowa Book Company Inc., 1 38 Kanda Jinbocho Chiyoda-ku, Tokyo 101 Japan.**) NLM** W1; SH335F. **CODEN** SHPEEY.
**Ind/Abst** EMBASE [Select. Cov.].

●UK/1064-5969
**SLIDE ATLAS OF CURRENT CARDIOLOGY.** (SLIDE ATLAS OF CURRENT CARDIOLOGY [SLIDE].). [Slide atlas curr. cardiol.]. Update 1 (Feb. 1992)-. English. Six times a year. $298.50. Current Science / England, Middlesex House, 34-42 Cleveland Street, London W1P 5FB England. **Tel** 011 44 71 580 8393, 011 44 71 323 0323, FAX 011 44 81 580 1938. **(Subscription address:** Current Science, 20 North 3rd Street, Philadelphia PA 19106.**)**

FR/0755-1916
**SOINS. CARDIOLOGIE.** [Soins, Cardiol.]. **VFOAT** Cardiologie. No. 1 (March 83)-. Periodical. French. mo. OPISA, 33 Chemin des Hutins, 1247 Anieres Geneva Switzerland. **Tel** 011 41 22 7512347. **NLM** W1; SO8862KT.
**Ind/Abst** Int. Nurs. Index; SportSearch.

SZ/0888-0697
**SOVIET MEDICAL REVIEWS. SECTION A, CARDIOLOGY REVIEWS.** ***Ceased.*** [Sov. med. rev., A Cardiol. rev.]. **Added/Corp** Soviet Medical Reviews (Firm : Chur, Switzerland). **VFOAT** Cardiology Reviews. Vol. 1 (1987)-(1993). Periodical. English (translations available in Russian). an. Harwood Academic Publishers, PO Box 90, Reading RG1 8JL England. **Tel** 011 44 734 560080. **(Subscription address:** International Publishers Distributor at one of the following addresses: 820 Town Center Drive, Langhorne, PA 19047; or PO Box 90, Reading Berkshire RG1 8JL UK; or Kent Ridge PO Box 1180, Singapore 9111, Republic of Singapore**) LC** RC666; .S65. **DD** 616.1/2. **NLM** W1; SO996LAM. **CODEN** SRAREY. **[CCC].**

FR/0989-2192
**STIMULOGRAPHY.** (198?)-. Periodical. English (French). qt. 350.00 France; 420.00 other. College Francais de Stimulation Cardiaque, Chu Rangueil c/o Mariee Lopes, 31054 Toulouse Cedex France. **Tel** 011 33 61 521250, FAX 011 33 61 523680. **ED** P. Godin. **NLM** W1; ST512. **Ad Acc.** ctrl circ.

US/0039-2499
**STROKE (1970).** (STROKE.). [Stroke]. **Added/Corp** American Heart Association. Vol. 1 (Jan./Feb. 1970)-. Academic Scholarly Publication. English. mo. $184.00 institution. American Heart Association, 7272 Greenville Avenue, Dallas TX 75231-4596. **Tel** (214)706-1310, (214)373-6300, FAX (214)691-6342. **(Subscription address:** American Heart Association, PO Box 843543, Dallas TX 75284-3543.**) ED** Oscar M. Reinmuth. **LC** RC388.5; .S84. **DD** 616.8/1/005. **NLM** W1 ST81K. **CODEN** SJCCA7. **[CCC]. Bk Rev. Ad Acc. Pr Rev. Acid Free. Circ:** 6,000 (ctrl). available on microfilm and microfiche from University Microfilms International (UMI). Documents available from The Genuine Article, BIOSIS Document Express, CASDDS.
**Desc:** It is of interest to the practicing physician, internist, cardiologist and neurologist. Articles include clinical conferences and deal with prevention, diagnosis, treatment and rehabilitation.
**Ind/Abst** Biol. Abstr.; Chem. Abstr.; CSA Neuro. Abstr. (?-?); Cumul. Index Nurs. Allied Health Lit.; Curr. Aware. Biol. Sci., CABS; Curr. Contents Clin. Med.; Curr. Contents Life Sci.; EMBASE; Energy Res. Abstr. (1974-); Index Med.; Med. Abstr. Newsl.; Mod. Med.; Nutr. Abstr. Rev., Ser. A, Hum. Exp.; Nutr. Res. Newsl.; Life Sci. Collect.; PESTDOC; Physic. Medline Plus; Ref. Upd. Basic Ed.; Ref. Upd. Deluxe Ed.; Res. Alert [Full Cov.]; Sci. Cit. Index; SCISEARCH; Soc. Sci. Cit. Index [Select. Cov.].

KO
**SUNHWANGI.** **VFOAT** Korean Circulation Journal. Periodical. Korean (summaries and/or abstracts in English). Taehan Sunhwangi Hakhoe, 28 Yongon-dong Chongno-ku, Seoul Korea. **LC** RC666; .S92. **DD** 616.1/2/005.

US/8756-8586
**TECHNOLOGY FOR CARDIOLOGY.** [Technol. cardio.]. **Added/Corp** Emergency Care Research Institute. (198?)-. Periodical. English. mo. $95.00 US; $105.00 Canada; $125.00 other. ECRI Emergency Care Research Institute, 5200 Butler Pike, Plymouth Meeting PA 19462. **Tel** (215)825-6000, FAX (215)834-1275, telex 510-660-8023. **ED** J. Novel. **DD** 616. **[CCC]. Bk Rev.** ***Continues*** *Health Devices Update. Cardiology.*
**Desc:** A newsletter for cardiologists and cardiovascular specialists summarizing health care technology issues and reporting product recalls, hazards, and problems.

FR/0989-2672
**TENSIOLOGIE.** ***Suspended.*** (April 1984)-?. Periodical. French (summaries and/or abstracts in English and French). bm. 240.00F. Editions de l'Interligne, 47 rue de Charonne, F-75011 Paris France. **Tel** 011 33 1 48068466. **NLM** W1; TE4185.

US/0730-2347
**TEXAS HEART INSTITUTE JOURNAL.** [Texas Heart Inst. j.]. **Added/Corp** Texas Heart Institute. Cardiovascular Surgical Research Laboratories (Texas Heart Institute). Vol. 9, No. 1 (Mar. 1982)-. Periodical. English. qt. $25.00 US; $35.00 other. Texas Heart Institute, MC 1-194 PO Box 20345, Houston TX 77225. **Tel** (713)522-7060, FAX (713)630-0999. **ED** James E Bagg Jr. **NLM** W1 TE778. **CODEN** THIJDO. Index available (published annually in last issue). cum. index. **Pr Rev. Circ:** 25,000 (ctrl). available on microfilm; available on microfiche. Documents available from The Genuine Article, BIOSIS Document Express. ***Continues*** *Cardiovascular Diseases, 0093-3546.*
**Desc:** Journal that publishes all types of articles on cardiovascular diseases.
**Ind/Abst** Biol. Abstr.; Curr. Contents Clin. Med.; EMBASE; Health Devices Alerts; Helminthol. Abstr. (1991-); Index Med. (1993-); Life Sci. Collect.; Protozoolog. Abstr.; Res. Alert [Select. Cov.]; Rev. Med. Vet. Mycology; Soc. Sci. Cit. Index [Select. Cov.].

## Medical Science and Technology —Communicable Diseases

US/0049-3848
**THROMBOSIS RESEARCH.** [Thromb. res.]. Vol. 1 (Feb. 1972)-. Academic Scholarly Publication. English (French, German and Russian). sm. $1505.00 The Americas; £1010.00 other. Pergamon Press, An Imprint of Elsevier Science Ltd., The Boulevard, Langford Lane, Kidlington, Oxford OX5 1GB United Kingdom. **Tel** 011 44 865 843000, 011 44 865 843699, FAX 011 44 865 843010. **(Subscription address:** Elsevier Science Ltd. Oxford Fulfillment Centre, PO Box 800, Kidlington, Oxford OX5 1DX United Kingdom.**) ED** Birger Blomback and Colvin Redman. **DD** 616. **NLM** W1 TH94. **CODEN** THBRAA. **[CCC].** Index available. **Bk Rev. Ad Acc. Pr Rev.** available on microfilm and microfiche from University Microfilms International (UMI). Documents available from The Genuine Article, BIOSIS Document Express, CASDDS, ADONIS.
**Desc:** Serves as a world forum for the rapid dissemination of original research on thrombus information, thromboembolization, hemorrhage due to alterations of the blood vessel wall and/or defects in hemostasis, and other related hemorrheological disturbances which impair circulation.
**Ind/Abst** ADONIS; Biol. Abstr.; Chem. Abstr.; Curr. Aware. Biol. Sci., CABS; Curr. Biotechnol.; Curr. Contents Life Sci.; Dairy Sci. Abstr.; EMBASE; Energy Res. Abstr. (July 1975-); Helminthol. Abstr. (1974-); Index Med.; Life Sci. Collect.; PESTDOC; Protozoolog. Abstr.; Ref. Upd. Basic Ed.; Ref. Upd. Deluxe Ed.; Res. Alert [Full Cov.]; Sci. Cit. Index; SCISEARCH; Soyabean Abstr.; SportSearch.

JA/0440-0852
**TO SHIN, HAI.** See Medical Science and Technology.

US/1042-2455
**TODAY IN MEDICINE. CARDIOVASCULAR DISEASE.** [Today med., Cardiovasc. dis.]. **Added/Corp** Data Centrum Communications, Inc. ICI Pharma. **VFOAT** Cardiovascular Disease. (1986)-. Periodical. English. Twelve times a year. $45.00. Data Centrum Communications Inc, The Soho Building, 110 Greene Street, Suite 505, New York NY 10012. **Tel** (212)226-5252. **DD** 616. **Pr Rev.**

US/1050-1738
**TRENDS IN CARDIOVASCULAR MEDICINE.** [Trends cardiovasc. med.]. **VFOAT** TCM. Vol. 1, No. 1 (Jan./Feb. 1991)-. Academic Scholarly Publication. English. bm (1 volume). $189.00 US; $220.00 other. Elsevier Science Publishing Company Inc, Madison Square Station, PO Box 882, New York NY 10159-0882. **Tel** (212)633-3950, FAX (212)633-3990. **DD** 616. **NLM** W1; TR3407L. **CODEN** TCMDEQ. **[CCC].** Documents available from The Genuine Article.
**Desc:** Designed to help clinical cardiologists and basic researchers keep up with advances and emerging techniques in cardiovascular research.
**Ind/Abst** Curr. Aware. Biol. Sci., CABS; Curr. Contents Life Sci.; EMBASE; Ref. Upd. Deluxe Ed.; Res. Alert [Full Cov.]; Sci. Cit. Index; SCISEARCH.

TU/1016-5169
**TURK KARDIYOLOJI DERNEGI ARSIVI.** **VFOAT** Archives of the Turkish Society of Cardiology. (1972)-. Turkish. qt. Logos Yayincilik A.S., Altan Erbulak Sok., Birlik Apt. No. 7/6, Mecidiyekoy 80300, Istanbul Turkey.
**Ind/Abst** EMBASE [Select. Cov.].

US/0162-0975
**UPDATE : CARDIOLOGY.** V. 1- 1976-. Periodical. English. J.B. Lippincott Company, 227 East Washington Square, Philadelphia PA 19106-3780. **Tel** (215)238-4200 or 4454, FAX (215)238-4227. **NLM** W1 UP511.

GW/0174-2817
**VERHANDLUNGEN DER DEUTSCHEN GESELLSCHAFT FUER HERZ- UND KREISLAUFFORSCHUNG.** [Verh. Dtsch. Ges. Herz- Kreislaufforsch]. **Added/Corp** Deutsche Gesellschaft fuer Herz- und Kreislaufforschung. Vol. 45 (1979)-. Academic Scholarly Publication. German. ir. Price varies per volume. Dr Dietrich Steinkopff Verlag, PO Box 111442, D 64289 Darmstadt Germany. **Tel** 011 49 6151 17450. **ED** P. Lichtlen and F. Loogan. **LC** RC667; .D4. **NLM** W1 VE483MK. **CODEN** VDGKDB. **Ad Acc.** **Circ:** 3,000 (ctrl). Documents available from CASDDS. **Continues** Verhandlungen der Deutschen Gesellschaft fuer Kreislaufforschung, 0070-4075.
**Desc:** Publishes the contributions of the conferences of German Society of Cardiology.
**Ind/Abst** Chem. Abstr.; EMBASE; Index Med.

US/1052-2174
**VIDEO JOURNAL OF ECHOCARDIOGRAPHY.** (1991)-. Periodical. English. Four times a year. $250.00 US; $270.00 Canada and (surface mail) other; $295.00 (airmail) other. Dynamedia Inc., 2 Fulham Court, Silver Spring MD 20902. **Tel** (301)649-6886, FAX (301)649-3447. **ED** Samuel Ritter. **[CCC].** Index available in last issue of volume-attached. **Ad Acc, Adv Mgr:** M. Linzer. **Pr Rev. Circ:** 800. available on videocassette. **Continues**
Dynamic Cardiovascular Imaging, 0891-9313.
**Desc:** A multi-media medical journal on echocardiography.

US/0145-4145
**YEAR BOOK OF CARDIOLOGY, THE.** [Year book cardiol.]. (1976)-. English (Italian). an (Sept.). Price varies. Mosby Year Book Inc., 11830 Westline Industrial Drive, St Louis MO 63146. **Tel** (800)325-4177, (314)872-8370, FAX (314)432-1380, telex 44-2402. **(Subscription address:** Williams and Wilkins / Mosby, PO Box 431, Artarmon NSW 2064 Australia.**) ED** Robert C. Schlant, John J. Collins, Mary Allen Eagle, Robert L. Frye, Ray W. Gifford and Robert A. O'Rourke. **LC** RC681.A1; Y4. **DD** 616.1/2/005. **NLM** W1 YE113. available on CD-ROM from SilverPlatter (US). **Continues** Year Book of Cardiovascular Medicine, 0360-6023.

GW/0930-9225
**ZEITSCHRIFT FUER HERZ THORAX UND GEFAESSCHIRURGIE.** See Medical Science and Technology-Surgery.

GW/0300-5860
**ZEITSCHRIFT FUER KARDIOLOGIE.** (ZEITSCHRIFT FUER KARDIOLOGIE. GERMAN JOURNAL OF CARDIOLOGY.) [Z. Kardiol.]. **Added/Corp** Deutsche Gesellschaft fuer Kreislaufforschung. Berufsverband Deutcher Internisten. Sektion Kardiologie. Deutsche Gesellschaft fuer Herz- und Kreislaufforschung. **VFOAT** German Journal of Cardiology. Vol. 62 (Jan. 1973)-. Academic Scholarly Publication. German (summaries and/or abstracts in English). Twelve times a year. DM530.00. Dr Dietrich Steinkopff Verlag, PO Box 111442, D 64229 Darmstadt Germany. **Tel** 011 49 6151 17450. **(Subscription address:** Springer Verlag New York Inc. / for North America, 44 Hartz Way, Secaucus NJ 07096.**) NLM** W1 ZE42. **CODEN** ZKRDAX. **[CCC]. Pr Rev.** Documents available from The Genuine Article, BIOSIS Document Express, CASDDS, ADONIS. **Continues** Zeitschrift fuer Kreislaufforschung.
**Ind/Abst** ADONIS; Biol. Abstr.; Chem. Abstr.; Curr. Contents Clin. Med.; Curr. Contents Life Sci.; EMBASE; Energy Res. Abstr. (Oct. 1974-); Index Med.; Life Sci. Collect.; PESTDOC; Pig News Inf.; Res. Alert [Full Cov.]; Sci. Cit. Index; SCISEARCH; SportSearch.

CH/1011-6842
**ZHONGHUA MINGUO XINZANGXUE HUI ZAZHI.** **VFOAT** Acta Cardiologica Sinica. (1984)-. Periodical. Multiple languages. qt.
**Ind/Abst** EMBASE.

---

## COMMUNICABLE DISEASES

US/1054-9218
**ABSTRACTS IN INFECTIOUS DISEASE.** [Abstr. infect. dis.]. Vol. 1, No. 1 (Feb. 1991)-. English. qt (4 issues). $55.00. SCP Communications Inc, 134 West 29th Street, New York NY 10001. **Tel** (212)714-1740, FAX (212)629-3760. **DD** 616. **NLM** ZWC 100; A164.

UK/0260-5511
**ABSTRACTS ON HYGIENE AND COMMUNICABLE DISEASES.** See Public Health and Safety-Abstracting, Bibliographies and Statistics.

US/1041-4487
**ACQUIRED IMMUNE DEFICIENCY SYNDROME NEWSLETTER.** Title Change. See Medical Science and Technology-Allergy and Immunology.

UY
**ACTUALIZACIONES EN INFECTOLOGIA.** (1986)-. Periodical. Spanish (summaries and/or abstracts in English). Libreria Medica Editorial, 11000 Montevideo Uruguay. **NLM** W1; AC998N.

US/0732-0566
**ADVANCES IN HOST DEFENSE MECHANISMS.** [Adv. host def. mech.]. (1982)-. Monographic series. English. ir. Price varies per volume. Raven Press, 1185 Avenue of the Americas, 37th Floor, New York NY 10036. **Tel** (212)930-9500, (212)930-9604, FAX (212)869-3495, (212)302-8507, telex 640073. **ED** John I. Gallin and Anthony S. Fauci. **DD** 616.07/9. **CODEN** AHDMD3.

US/0884-9404
**ADVANCES IN PEDIATRIC INFECTIOUS DISEASES.** See Medical Science and Technology-Pediatrics.

●US/1066-1107
**AIDS ABSTRACTS (ATLANTA, GA.).** See Medical Science and Technology-Abstracting, Bibliographies and Statistics.

US/0887-0292
**AIDS ALERT.** Ceased. See Medical Science and Technology-Allergy and Immunology.

US/1055-0380
**AIDS & SOCIETY.** See Medical Science and Technology-Allergy and Immunology.

US
**AIDS & TB ARTICLE SUMMARIES.** Title Change. See Medical Science and Technology-Allergy and Immunology.

US
**AIDS & TB WEEKLY ABSTRACTS FROM CONFERENCE PROCEEDINGS.** See Medical Science and Technology-Allergy and Immunology.

●US
**AIDS & TB WEEKLY ARTICLE SUMMARIES.** See Medical Science and Technology-Allergy and Immunology.

US/1068-6282
**AIDS ARTICLE SUMMARIES.** Title Change. See Medical Science and Technology-Allergy and Immunology.

SA/1019-8334
**AIDS BULLETIN TYGERBERG.** [AIDS bull.Tygerb.]. **VFOAT** Acquired Immune Deficiency Syndrome Bulletin(Tygerberg). (1992)-. Periodical. English. qt (Mar., May, Aug., Dec.). R45.60 South Africa; R50.00 other. The Corporate Communication Division, MRC, PO Box 19070, 7505 Tygerberg South Africa. **Tel** 011 27 21 9380205, FAX 011 27 21 9380395. **ED** Malcolm Steinberg. **UDC** 615.37. **Bk Rev,** (Qty: 4). **Circ:** 2,000 (ctrl).

US/1043-1543
**AIDS CLINICAL CARE.** [AIDS clin. care]. **Added/Corp** Massachusetts Medical Society. American Foundation for AIDS Research. **VAT** Acquired Immune Deficiency Syndrome Clinical Care. Vol. 1, No. 1 (May 1989)-. Periodical. English. Twelve times a year. $89.00 US and US possessions; $109.35 Canada; $117.00 other. New England Journal of Medicine, 1440 Main Street, Waltham MA 02154-1649. **Tel** (617)893-3800, (800)843-6356, FAX (617)647-5785, telex 5106015660 NEJM BOS UQ. **(Subscription address:** New England Journal of Medicine, PO Box 9135, Waltham MA 02154.**) ED** Gardiner Morse. **DD** 616. **NLM** W1; AI696CHFG. Index available (December). **Ad Acc, Adv Mgr:** Carolyn Ferris, **Tel** (617)893-3800 Ext 1217. **Circ:** 25,000. available on CD-ROM from Macmillan New Media.
**Desc:** Newsletter bringing the latest developments in diagnosis and treatment of HIV-related diseases to the practicing clinician. Useful to all health care professionals who are treating AIDS patients, or to those who need to plan and prepare for the HIV health crisis.
**Ind/Abst** Trop. Dis. Bull.

●US/1065-6162
**AIDS DIRECTORY, THE.** See Medical Science and Technology-Allergy and Immunology.

US
**AIDS EPIDEMIOLOGICAL AND CLINICAL STUDIES.** (19??)-. Monographic series. English. ir. $48.00. New England Journal of Medicine, 1440 Main Street, Waltham MA 02154-1649. **Tel** (617)893-3800, (800)843-6356, FAX (617)647-5785, telex 5106015660 NEJM BOS UQ.

NE/1013-7785
**AIDS HEALTH PROMOTION, EXCHANGE.** See Medical Science and Technology-Allergy and Immunology.

US/0899-742X
**AIDS/HIV RECORD.** Ceased. See Medical Science and Technology-Allergy and Immunology.

UK/0268-8360
**AIDS NEWSLETTER (LONDON, ENGLAND).** See Medical Science and Technology-Allergy and Immunology.

US/1053-0894
**AIDS READER, THE.** See Medical Science and Technology-Allergy and Immunology.

US/1056-1080
**AIDS RESEARCH REVIEWS.** See Medical Science and Technology-Allergy and Immunology.

US/1052-4207
**AIDS TREATMENT NEWS.** See Medical Science and Technology-Allergy and Immunology.

US/1040-6247
**AIDS UPDATES.** See Medical Science and Technology-Allergy and Immunology.

US
**AIDS WATCH.** (19??)-. Periodical. English. Four times a year. L50000 institutions; L30000 individuals. Il Pensiero Scientifico Editore s.r.l., Via Bradano 3C, 00199 Rome Italy. **Tel** 011 39 6 86207158, 86207159, 86207168, 86207169, FAX 011 39 6 86207160. **ED** Giuseppe Ippolito. **Circ:** 1,200.

# Medical Science and Technology —Communicable Diseases

**US/1069-1456**
**AIDS WEEKLY. See** Medical Science and Technology-Allergy and Immunology.

**GW/0934-1129**
**AIDS WIESBADEN. Ceased. See** Medical Science and Technology-Allergy and Immunology.

**US/1059-8855**
**AIDSMONTHLY (GOVERNMENT ED.).**
*Title Change.* **See** Medical Science and Technology-Allergy and Immunology.

**US/1059-8820**
**AIDSMONTHLY (HEALTHCARE ED.).**
*Title Change.* **See** Medical Science and Technology-Allergy and Immunology.

**US/1059-8901**
**AIDSMONTHLY (INTERNATIONAL ED.).**
*Title Change.* **See** Medical Science and Technology-Allergy and Immunology.

**US/1059-8812**
**AIDSMONTHLY (JOURNAL ED.).** *Title Change.* **See** Medical Science and Technology-Allergy and Immunology.

**US/1059-8871**
**AIDSMONTHLY (LEGAL ED.). Ceased. See** Medical Science and Technology-Allergy and Immunology.

**US/1059-8863**
**AIDSMONTHLY (PSYCHOSOCIAL ED.).**
*Title Change.* **See** Medical Science and Technology-Allergy and Immunology.

**US/1059-8898**
**AIDSMONTHLY (RESEARCH ED.).** *Title Change.* **See** Medical Science and Technology-Allergy and Immunology.

**US/1059-891X**
**AIDSMONTHLY (SERVICE ORGANIZATION ED.).** *Title Change.* **See** Medical Science and Technology-Allergy and Immunology.

**US/1059-8804**
**AIDSMONTHLY (TREATMENT ED.).** *Title Change.* **See** Medical Science and Technology-Allergy and Immunology.

**US/1059-888X**
**AIDSMONTHLY (WORKPLACE ED.).** *Title Change.* **See** Medical Science and Technology-Allergy and Immunology.

**UA/1014-2347**
**AL-NASHRAH AL-WABAIYAH LI-IQLIM SHARQ AL-BAHR AL-MUTAWASSIT.**
**Added/Corp** World Health Organization. Regional Office for the Eastern Mediterranean. **VFOAT** Eastern Mediterranean Region Epidemiological Bulletin. (1985)-. Periodical. Arabic (English). qt. **NLM** W1; AL127.
**Ind/Abst** Trop. Dis. Bull.

**IT**
**ANLAIDS NOTIZIE.** (19??)-. Italian. mo. Free on request. Sedac Srl, Via Simone Martini 136, 00142 Rome Italy. **Tel** 011 39 6 5041226.

**US/0882-2239**
**ANNUAL REPORT OF INTRAMURAL ACTIVITIES - NATIONAL INSTITUTE OF ALLERGY AND INFECTIOUS DISEASES (U.S.).** (ANNUAL REPORT OF INTRAMURAL ACTIVITIES / NATIONAL INSTITUTE OF ALLERGY AND INFECTIOUS DISEASES.). **Main/Corp** National Institute of Allergy and Infectious Diseases (U.S.). English. an. US Department of Health and Human Services National Institutes of Health, 9000 Rockville Pike, Bethesda MD 20892. **Tel** (301)496-9291, FAX (301)496-2443. **LC** RC109; .N37A. **DD** 616.9/072073.

**US/0085-462X**
**ANNUAL REPORT OF THE DIRECTOR - PAN AMERICAN SANITARY BUREAU. BUREAU. Main/Corp** Pan American Sanitary Bureau. **VFOAT** Report of the Director; Annual Report of the Director of the Pan American Sanitary Bureau, Regional Office for the Americas of the World Health Organization. (1902)-. English. an. Pan American Health Organization, 525 23rd Street Northwest, Office District Sales, Washington DC 20037. **Tel** (202)293-8130, FAX (202)338-0869. **LC** RA10; .P23. **NLM** W2 MP2 P9A.
*Formed by the union of* Pan American Sanitary Bureau. Quadrennial Report of the Director of the Pan American Sanitary Bureau, Regional Office for the Americas of the World Health Organization.

**US/0730-6814**
**ANNUAL SUMMARY - IOWA. STATE DEPT. OF HEALTH. DIVISION OF DISEASE PREVENTION.** (ANNUAL SUMMARY / IOWA STATE DEPARTMENT OF HEALTH.).
**Main/Corp** Iowa. State Dept. of Health. Division of Disease Prevention. English. an. Lucas State Office Building, Des Moines IA 50319. **LC** RA643.6.I8; I58A. **DD** 312/.39/09777.

**VE**
**ANUARIO DE EPIDEMIOLOGIA Y ESTADISTICA VITAL. See** Medical Science and Technology-Abstracting, Bibliographies and Statistics.

●**US/1071-0906**
**ARCHIVES OF STD/HIV RESEARCH. See** Medical Science and Technology-Allergy and Immunology.

●**UK/1071-6564**
**BAILLIERE'S CLINICAL INFECTIOUS DISEASES. VFOAT** Clinical Infectious Diseases. (1994)-. Periodical. English. tq (3 issues). £78.00 (institution). Harcourt Brace & Company Ltd., Foots Cray, High Street, Sidcup Kent DA14 5HP England. **Tel** 011 44 81 300 3322, FAX 011 44 81 309 0807. **(Subscription address:** W. B. Saunders Company / North America Subscriptions, c/o Periodicals, 6277 Sea Harbour Drive, 4th Floor, Orlando FL 32887.) **NLM** W1; BA46ELM.

**IO**
**BERITA EPIDEMIOLOGI. Main/Corp** Indonesia. Direktorat Jenderal Pencegahan, Pembrantasan/Pembasnian Penyakit Menular. **VFOAT** Epidemiological Bulletin. Periodical. Multiple languages (English and Indonesian). mo. Surveillance Epidemiology Subdi, Coc & EH J1 Percetakan Negara 29, Jakarta 10520 Indonesia. **LC** RA643.7.I5; I53A. **NLM** W2 JI5 D5B. *Continues* Berita Epidemiologi.

**US/1058-708X**
**BETA (SAN FRANCISCO, CALIF.). See** Medical Science and Technology-Allergy and Immunology.

**VE**
**BOLETIN EPIDEMIOLOGICO SEMANAL / MINISTERIO DE SANIDAD Y ASISTENCIA SOCIAL, DIRECCION DE SALUD PUBLICA, DEPARTAMENTO DE DEMOGRAFIA Y EPIDEMIOLOGIA, DIVISION DE EPIDEMIOLOGIA. See** Medical Science and Technology-Epidemiology.

**SP**
**BOLETIN MICROBIOLOGICO SEMANAL. Added/Corp** Spain. Subdireccion General de Informacion Sanitaria y Epidemiologia. Instituto de la Salud Carlos III. **VFOAT** BMS. (19??)-. Periodical. Spanish. wk. Free. Centro Nacional de Epidemiologia, Calle Sinesio Delgado 6, 28029 Madrid Spain. **Tel** 011 34 1 3156333. **NLM** W1; BO4296.
**Ind/Abst** Trop. Dis. Bull.

**US/0898-8323**
**BROWN UNIVERSITY STD UPDATE, THE.** *Title Change.* **See** Public Health and Safety.

**FR/0245-7466**
**BULLETIN EPIDEMIOLOGIQUE HEBDOMADAIRE : BEH / REPUBLIQUE FRANCAISE, MINISTERE DE LA SOLIDARITE, DE LA SANTE ET DE LA PROTECTION SOCIALE, DIRECTION GENERALE DE LA SANTE. See** Medical Science and Technology-Epidemiology.

**IQ/0007-4845**
**BULLETIN OF ENDEMIC DISEASES. See** Public Health and Safety.

**II/0304-9515**
**BULLETIN OF HAFFKINE INSTITUTE.**
[Bull. Haffkine Inst.]. **Added/Corp** Haffkine Institute. Vol. 1 (Aug. 1973)-. Bulletin. English. Three times a year. $20.00. **(Subscription address:** Prints India, 11 Darya Ganj, New Delhi 110002 India.) **NLM** W1 BU78. **CODEN** BHFIA9. Documents available from BIOSIS Document Express, CASDDS.
**Ind/Abst** Biol. Abstr.; Chem. Abstr.; NAPRALERT; Life Sci. Collect.; Trop. Dis. Bull.

**US**
**CALIFORNIA HIV TESTING AND COUNSELING MONTHLY REPORT. See** Medical Science and Technology-Allergy and Immunology.

●**CN/1188-4169**
**CANADA COMMUNICABLE DISEASE REPORT. See** Public Health and Safety.

●**CN/1188-4169**
**CANADA COMMUNICABLE DISEASE REPORT. See** Public Health and Safety.

**CN/1180-2332**
**CANADIAN JOURNAL OF INFECTIOUS DISEASES, THE.** [Can. j. infect. dis.]. **VFOAT** Infectious Diseases; Journal Canadien des Maladies Infectieuses. Vol. 1, No. 1 (Spring 1990)-. Periodical. English (French). bm. $84.00 (institution), $61.00 (individual) US. Pulsus Group Inc., 2902 South Sheridan Way, Oakville Ontario L6J 7L6 Canada. **Tel** (416)829-4770, FAX (416)829-4799. **DD** 616.9/05. **Ad Acc.**
**Desc:** Publishes original articles in infectious disease research and therapy.

**US/1058-7888**
**CD SUMMARY.** [CD summ.]. **Added/Corp** Oregon. Office of Epidemiology & Health Statistics. **VFOAT** Current Disease Summary. Vol. 40, No. 1 (Jan. 1, 1991)-. Periodical. English. sm. Oregon Health Division, PO Box 231, Portland OR 97207. **DD** 616. *Continues* Communicable Disease Summary, 0744-7035.

**US**
**CDC HIV : AIDS PREVENTION NEWSLETTER. Added/Corp** Centers for Disease Control (U.S.) Centers for Disease Control (U.S.). Office of the Deputy Director (HIV). **VFOAT** HIV AIDS Prevention Newsletter; HIV/AIDS Prevention; CDC HIV/AIDS Prevention Newsletter. Vol. 1 No. 1 (Oct. 1990)-. Newsletter. English. Four times a year. Free on request. US Department of Health and Human Services, 1600 Clifton Road, MS E41, Atlanta GA 30333. **Tel** (404)639-0938, FAX (404)639-0943. **ED** Linda Elsner. **LC** RA644.A25; H576. **DD** 614.5/993. **Circ:** 16,500 (ctrl).
**Desc:** Current CDC research and prevention program initiatives relating to HIV/AIDS.

●**US/1058-4838**
**CLINICAL INFECTIOUS DISEASES.**
(CLINICAL INFECTIOUS DISEASES: AN OFFICIAL PUBLICATION OF THE INFECTIOUS DISEASES SOCIETY OF AMERICA.). [Clin. infect. dis.].
**Added/Corp** Infectious Diseases Society of America. Vol. 14, No. 1 (Jan. 1992)-. Academic Scholarly Publication. English. mo. $216.00 institution, $93.00 individual, $81.00 ASM and IUMS individual member, $46.00 students, interns, residents, and fellows. University of Chicago Press / Journals Division, PO Box 37005, 5720 South Woodlawn, Chicago IL 60637. **Tel** (312)753-3347, FAX (312)753-0811. **(Subscription telephone:** (312)753-8083) **LC** RC110; .R47. **DD** 616.9/05. **NLM** W1; IN715LN. **CODEN** CIDIEL. **Ad Acc. Acid Free.**
available on microfilm and microfiche from University Microfilms International (UMI). Documents available from The Genuine Article, BIOSIS Document Express, CASDDS. *Continues* Reviews of Infectious Diseases, 0162-0886.
**Desc:** The purpose is to publish review articles offering comprehensive consideration of recent literature in a particular area or on a group of related topics, and to publish thematic studies focusing on central topics in infectious diseases research.
**Ind/Abst** Biol. Abstr.; Chem. Abstr.; Curr. Aware. Biol. Sci., CABS; Curr. Contents Clin. Med.; Curr. Contents Life Sci.; Index Med. (1992-); Microbiol. Abstr. Sect. B; Life Sci. Collect.; PESTDOC (?-?); Physic. Medline Plus; Ref. Upd. Basic Ed.; Ref. Upd. Clinical Ed.; Ref. Upd. Deluxe Ed.; Res. Alert [Full Cov.]; Sci. Cit. Index; SCISEARCH; Soc. Sci. Cit. Index [Select. Cov.]; Trop. Dis. Bull.

**CN/1198-743X**
**CLINICAL MICROBIOLOGY AND INFECTIOUS DISEASES. See** Biology-Microbiology.

●**US/1062-8150**
**CLINICAL MICROBIOLOGY REPORTS.** (1992)-. Periodical. English. mo. $95.00 (individual), $139.00 (institution) US; $154.00 (individual), $197.00 (institution) other. W.B. Saunders Company, A Subsidiary of Harcourt Brace Jovanovich, Inc., The Curtis Center/Suite 300, Independence Square West, Philadelphia PA 19106-3399. **Tel** (215)238-7800 or, 5587, FAX (215)238-7883, telex 173146. **(Subscription address:** W. B. Saunders Company / North America Subscriptions, c/o Periodicals, 6277 Sea Harbour Drive, 4th Floor, Orlando FL 32887.) **ED** Irving Nachamkin. **NLM** W1; CL73S. **[CCC].**

**US**
**COMMON SENSE ABOUT AIDS. See** Medical Science and Technology-Allergy and Immunology.

**UK**
**COMMUNICABLE DISEASE STATISTICS / OFFICE OF POPULATION CENSUSES AND SURVEYS [AND] COMMUNICABLE DISEASE SURVEILLANCE CENTRE OF THE PUBLIC HEALTH LABORATORY SERVICE. See** Medical Science and Technology-Abstracting, Bibliographies and Statistics.

US/0888-7756
**CONTEMPORARY ISSUES IN INFECTIOUS DISEASES.** [Contemp. issues infect. dis.]. Vol. 1 (1984)-. Academic Scholarly Publication. English. ir. Price varies per volume. Churchill Livingstone, 1-3 Baxter's Place, Leith Walk, Edinburgh EH1 3AF Scotland. **Tel** 011 44 31 556 2424, FAX 011 44 31 558 1278, telex 727511. **(Subscription address:** US and Canada/ Churchill Livingstone Inc., 5 South 250 Frontenac Road, Naperville, IL 60563; (telephone: (800)553-5426 or (708)416-3939)) **DD** 616. **NLM** W1; CO769MQV. **CODEN** CIIDEV. Documents available from CASDDS.
**Desc:** Book series, provides a wealth of authoritative, up-to-date clinical information on the pathogenesis, diagnosis, therapy and prevention of various infectious diseases.
**Ind/Abst** Chem. Abstr. (1984-).

US/8755-4046
**CONTROL OF COMMUNICABLE DISEASES IN MAN.** [Control commun. dis. man]. 7th Ed. (1950)-. English. ir. Price varies per volume. American Public Health Association, 1015 15th Street Northwest, Washington DC 20005. **Tel** (202)789-5666. **ED** Abram S. Benenson. **LC** RA643; .C72. **DD** 614. ***Continues*** *Control of Communicable Diseases.*
**Desc:** This pocket-size reference manual covers more than 200 communicable diseases.

UK/0952-8075
**CURRENT AIDS LITERATURE. See** Medical Science and Technology-Allergy and Immunology.

UK/0951-7375
**CURRENT OPINION IN INFECTIOUS DISEASES.** [Curr. opin. infect. dis.]. Vol. 1, No. 1, (Jan./Feb. 1988)-. Periodical. English. Six times a year. $134.95 (individual); $269.95 (institution). Current Science / England, Middlesex House, 34-42 Cleveland Street, London W1P 5FB England. **Tel** 011 44 71 580 8393, 011 44 71 323 0323, FAX 011 44 81 580 1938. **(Subscription address:** Current Science, 20 North 3rd Street, Philadelphia PA 19106.**) ED** Edward W. Hook and Harold P. Lambert. **LC** RC109; .C86. **DD** 616.9/05. **NLM** W1; CU799GE. **CODEN** COIDE5. **[CCC]. Pr Rev. Circ:** 3,500. available on diskette. Documents available from The Genuine Article, BIOSIS Document Express.
**Desc:** Directed toward researchers and practicing infectious disease specialists. Presents review articles from an area of concentration covering an entire year's literature with annotated references. Each issues features a bibliography of the current world literature published during the previous year.
**Ind/Abst** Biol. Abstr.; Curr. Aware. Biol. Sci., CABS; Curr. Contents Clin. Med.; EMBASE; Helminthol. Abstr. (1991-); Immunol. Abstr.; Index Vet.; Microbiol. Abstr. Sect. B; Microbiol. Abstr. Sect. A; Microbiol. Abstr. Sect. C; Protozoolog. Abstr.; Ref. Upd. Deluxe Ed.; Res. Alert [Select. Cov.]; Rev. Med. Vet. Entomol.; Rev. Med. Vet. Mycology; SCISEARCH; Trop. Dis. Bull.; Virol. AIDS Abstr.

CN/0899-3947
**CURRENT THERAPY IN INFECTIOUS DISEASE.** [Curr. ther. infect. dis.]. (1983-1984)-. English. ir. Mosby Year Book Inc., 11830 Westline Industrial Drive, St Louis MO 63146. **Tel** (800)325-4177, (314)872-8370, FAX (314)432-1380, telex 44-2402. **ED** Edward H. Kass and Richard Platt. **LC** RC109; .C87. **DD** 616.9/005.

UK
**CURRENT TOPICS IN INFECTION.** ***Ceased.*** No. 1 (1981)-Completed Series (19??). Monographic series. English. ir. Chapman & Hall, 2-6 Boundary Row, London SE1 8HN England. **Tel** 011 44 71 865 0066, FAX 011 44 71 522 9623, telex 290164 Chapmag. **NLM** W1 CU82IM (P). **Pr Rev.**

GW/0937-2156
**CURRENT TOPICS IN INFECTIOUS DISEASES AND CLINICAL MICROBIOLOGY.** [Curr. top. infect. dis. clin. microbiol.]. Vol. 1 (1986)-. Monographic series. English. ir. Price varies per volume. Vieweg Publishing, PO Box 5829, D 65048 Wiesbaden Germany. **Tel** 011 49 611 160230, FAX 011 49 611 160229. **NLM** W1; CU82IME. **CODEN** CTIDE6. Documents available from BIOSIS Document Express.
**Ind/Abst** Biol. Abstr. (1989-); EMBASE.

US/0011-4162
**CUTIS (NEW YORK, N.Y.). See** Medical Science and Technology-Dermatology.

US/0732-8893
**DIAGNOSTIC MICROBIOLOGY AND INFECTIOUS DISEASE. See** Biology-Microbiology.

UK/0278-0240
**DISEASE MARKERS.** [Dis. markers]. Vol. 1, No. 1 (March 1983)-. Academic Scholarly Publication. English. Four times a year. $395.00 all except Europe. ASFRA BV, Voorhaven 33, 1135 BL Edam The Netherlands. **Tel** 011 31 02993 72751, FAX 011 31 02993 72877. **(Subscription address:** John Wiley & Sons, Inc., PO Box 7247-8491, Philadelphia, PA 19170-8491**) ED** C M Steel and R A Gatti. **DD** 616. **NLM** W1; DI749. **CODEN** DMARD3. **[CCC]. Pr Rev. Circ:** 800. available on microfilm and microfiche from University Microfilms International (UMI). Documents available from The Genuine Article, BIOSIS Document Express, CASDDS, ADONIS.
**Desc:** Publishes original research findings and reviews on the subject of the identification of markers associated with the disease processes whether or not they are an integral part of the pathological lesion.
**Ind/Abst** ADONIS; AgBiotech News Inf.; Biol. Abstr. (1987-); Chem. Abstr. (1983-); Curr. Aware. Biol. Sci., CABS; Curr. Contents Life Sci.; EMBASE; Genet. Abstr.; Health Plan. Adminis.; Immunol. Abstr.; Index Med. (Vol. 4, No. 1-2, 1986-); Ref. Upd. Deluxe Ed.; Res. Alert [Full Cov.]; Sci. Cit. Index; SCISEARCH; Soc. Sci. Cit. Index [Select. Cov.]; Virol. AIDS Abstr.

SP/0213-005X
**ENFERMEDADES INFECCIOSAS Y MICROBIOLOGIA CLINICA.** [Enferm. infecc. microbiol. clin.]. **Added/Corp** Sociedad Espanola de Enfermedades Infecciosas y Microbiologia Clinica. **VFOAT** Enfermedades Infecciosas. Vol. 2, No. 1 (Jan./Feb. 1984)-. Periodical. Spanish (summaries and/or abstracts in English). ir (10 issues per year). $66.00. Ediciones Doyma SA, Travesera de Gracia 17 21, 08021 Barcelona Spain. **Tel** 011 34 3 2000711, 011 34 3 4145706, FAX 011 34 3 2091136, telex 51964 INK E. **NLM** W1; EN5899. **CODEN** EIMCE2. **[CCC]. *Continues*** *Enfermedades Infecciosas.*
**Ind/Abst** EMBASE; Indice Med. Esp.

US/0251-4710
**EPI NEWSLETTER.** [EPI newsl.]. **VAT** Expanded Program on Immunization Newsletter. V. 1- May 1979-. Newsletter. English (Spanish). bm. Free. Expanded Program on Immunization Paho, 525-23rd Street NW, Washington DC 20037. **Tel** (202)861-3247. **ED** Ciro de Quadros. **NLM** W1 E42. **Bk Rev. Circ:** 6,000 (ctrl).
**Desc:** Articles on epidemiology of diseases (polio, tuberculosis, tetanus, diphtheria, measles, whooping cough) in countries of Americas. Includes vaccination coverage, data and morbidity.
**Ind/Abst** Trop. Dis. Bull.

US
**EPI NOTES. Added/Corp** North Carolina. Division of Health Services. Epidemiology Section. Report No. 86-6 (June 1986)-. Periodical. English. mo. PO Box 2091, Raleigh NC 27602. **Tel** (919)733-3421. ***Continues*** *Epidemiologic Notes & Communicable Disease Morbidity Report.*

UK/0950-2688
**EPIDEMIOLOGY AND INFECTION.** [Epidemiol. inf.]. Vol. 98, No. 1 (Feb. 1987)-. Academic Scholarly Publication. English. bm (6 issues). $326.00 US, Canada & Mexico; £176.00 other. Cambridge University Press, The Edinburgh Building, Shaftesbury Road, Cambridge CB2 2RU United Kingdom. **Tel** 011 44 223 312393, FAX 011 44 223 325959. **(Subscription address:** Cambridge University Press / North America, 110 Midland Avenue, Port Chester NY 10573.**) ED** J. R. Pattison, W. C. Noble, J. G. Cruickshank, C. R. Madeley and D. Baxby. **LC** RA421; .J88. **DD** 614.4/05. **NLM** W1; EP452PE. **CODEN** EPINEU. **Pr Rev.** available on microfilm and microfiche from University Microfilms International (UMI). Documents available from The Genuine Article, BIOSIS Document Express, CASDDS, Documents on Demand. ***Continues*** *Journal of Hygiene, 0022-1724.*
**Desc:** An international journal which publishes original reports and reviews on all aspects of infection in man and animals. Particular emphasis is given to the epidemiology, prevention and control of infectious diseases, but the field covered is broad and includes microbiology, virology, immunology, tropical infections, food hygiene, statistics and the clinical, social and public health aspects of disease.
**Ind/Abst** AgBiotech News Inf.; AGRICOLA; Biodeter. Abstr. (19??-19??); Biol. Abstr. (Feb. 1987-); Biostatistica; Chem. Abstr. (Feb. 1987-); Curr. Aware. Biol. Sci., CABS; Curr. Contents Life Sci.; Dairy Sci. Abstr.; EMBASE; Environ. Abstr. (Feb. 1987-?); Fish Rev. (Jan. 1989-July 1992); Food Sci. Technol. Abstr.; Health Plan. Adminis.; Immunol. Abstr.; Index Med. (Feb. 1987-); Index Vet.; Microbiol. Abstr. Sect. B; Microbiol. Abstr. Sect. A; Microbiol. Abstr. Sect. C; Nutr. Abstr. Rev., Ser. B, Live Feeds and Feed.; Life Sci. Collect. (1987-); Pig News Inf.; Pollut. Abstr. Indexes; Poult. Abstr.; Protozoolog. Abstr.; Res. Alert [Full Cov.]; Rev. Med. Vet. Entomol.; Rev. Med. Vet. Mycology; Sci. Cit. Index; SCISEARCH; Vet. Bull.; Trop. Dis. Bull.; Virol. AIDS Abstr.; Wildl. Rev. (Jan. 1989-July 1992).

GW/0934-9723
**EUROPEAN JOURNAL OF CLINICAL MICROBIOLOGY & INFECTIOUS DISEASES. See** Biology-Microbiology.

NE/0392-2990
**EUROPEAN JOURNAL OF EPIDEMIOLOGY. See** Medical Science and Technology-Epidemiology.

US/1047-0719
**FOCUS (SAN FRANCISCO, CALIF.). See** Medical Science and Technology-Allergy and Immunology.

GW
**GESUNDHEITSWESEN. REIHE 2, MELDEPFLICHTIGE KRANKHEITEN / HERAUSGEBER STATISTISCHES BUNDESAMT. Added/Corp** Germany (West). Statistisches Bundesamt. **VFOAT** Meldepflichtige Krankheiten; Fachserie 12. (1981)-. German. DM11.30. Metzler Poeschel Verlag Veroeffen, Statist Bundesamt Kernerstr 43, D 70182 Stuttgart Germany. **Tel** 011 49 7071 935350. **(Subscription address:** Metzler Poeschel H Leins GmbH, Postfach 1152, D 72125 Kusterdingen Germany.**) LC** RA407.5.G4; G49. **DD** 362.1/0943021. **NLM** W2; GG4 S49f. ***Absorbed*** *Gesundheitswesen. Reihe 2.1, Geschlechtskrankheiten, 0173-3834; Gesundheitswesen. Reihe 2.2, Tuberkulose, 0172-8946* ***and*** *Gesundheitswesen. Reihe 2.3, Sonstige Meldepflichtige Krankheiten.*

GW/0173-3869
**GESUNDHEITSWESEN. REIHE 2.3, SONSTIGE MELDEPFLICHTIGE KRANKHEITEN (STUTTGART. KOHLHAMMER. 1977).** (GESUNDHEITSWESEN. REIHE 2.3 : SONSTIGE MELDEPFLICHTIGE KRANKHEITEN.). **VFOAT** Sonstige Meldepflichtige Krankheiten. Periodical. German. qt. American Pomological Society, c/o Dr R M Crassweller, 103 Tyson Building, University Park PA 16802. **Tel** (814)863-6163, FAX (814)863-6139 **NLM** W2 GG4 S772GC. ***Continues*** *Bevolkerung und Kultur. Reihe 7: Gesundheitswesen. 1: Meldepflichtige Krankheiten.*

●US/1063-8423
**GLOBAL ACCESS TO STD DIAGNOSTICS.** [Glob. access STD diagn.]. **Added/Corp** Rockefeller Foundation. Program for Appropriate Technology in Health. **VAT** Global Access to Sexually Transmitted Disease Diagnostics. Vol. 1, No. 1 (May 1992)-. Periodical. English. sa. Free (qualified subscribers). PATH, 4 Nicherson, Seattle WA 98109. **DD** 616.

●SZ/1020-007X
**GLOBAL AIDSNEWS: THE NEWSLETTER OF THE WORLD HEALTH ORGANIZATION GLOBAL PROGRAMME ON AIDS. Added/Corp** Global Programme on AIDS (World Health Organization). **VFOAT** Global AIDS News; AIDS News; AIDSnews. No. 1 (1992)-. Periodical. English. qt. Free on request. World Health Organization, Distribution and Sales, 20 Avenue Appia, CH-1211 Geneva 27 Switzerland. **Tel** 011 41 22 7912111, FAX 011 41 22 7880401. **LC** RA644.A25; G562.

CN/1186-2947
**GRAND ROUNDS IN INFECTIOUS DISEASES.** [Grand rounds infect. dis.]. **Added/Corp** Thomson Healthcare Communications. Vol. 1 No. 1 Feb./Mar. (1991)-. Periodical. English. qt. Limited free distribution. **DD** 616.9/05.

US/1063-0627
**HARVARD AIDS INSTITUTE SERIES ON GENE REGULATION OF HUMAN RETROVIRUSES. See** Medical Science and Technology-Allergy and Immunology.

US/0095-3539
**HEALTH INFORMATION FOR INTERNATIONAL TRAVEL. Added/Corp** Center for Disease Control. Bureau of Epidemiology. Center for Disease Control. Quarantine Division. Center for Prevention Services (U.S.). Quarantine Division. National Center for Prevention Services (U.S.). Division of Quarantine. (1974)-. Government Publication. English. an (June). $16.00. Superintendent of Documents, US Government Printing Office, Washington DC 20402. **Tel** (202)275-3328, FAX (202)786-2377. **LC** RA783.5; .C45a. **DD** 614.4/2/02491. **NLM** W2 A C17H.

US
**HIV/AIDS UPDATE / PENNSYLVANIA DEPARTMENT OF HEALTH, BUREAU OF HIV/AIDS. See** Public Health and Safety.

FR
**INFECTIOLOGIE.** ***Title Change.*** (198?)-(19??). Periodical. French. Six times a year. Editions de l'Interligne, 47 rue de Charonne, F-75011 Paris France. **Tel** 011 33 1 48068466. **NLM** W1; IN405L. ***Merged into*** *Infectiologie Immunologie.*

FR
**INFECTIOLOGIE IMMUNOLOGIE.** (19??)-. French. Ten times a year (Except July & Aug.). 538.00F France; 738.00F EEC countries; 798.00F others. Editions

de l'Interligne, 47 rue de Charonne, 75011 Paris France. **Tel** 011 33 1 48068466. ***Continues*** *Infectiologie; Immunologie Medicale, 0755-0871.*

GW/0300-8126
**INFECTION.** [Infection]. **Added/Corp** Deutsche Gesellschaft fuer Infektiologie. Paul Ehrlich Gesellschaft. **VFOAT** Zeitschrift fur Klinik und Therapie der Infektionen; Journal for the Clinical Study and Treatment of Infections. Vol. 1 (1973)-. Academic Scholarly Publication. German (English). Six times a year (Feb., Apr., Jun., Aug., Oct., Dec.). DM207.00 (members), DM252.00 (nonmembers) Germany; DM213.00 (members), DM258.00 (nonmembers) other. MMV Medizin Verlag, Postfach 801246, Neumarkter Street 18, W-8000 Muenchen 80 F R Germany. **Tel** 011/49/89/9269070, FAX 089/48189-633, telex 522053. **NLM** W1 IN405K. **CODEN** IFTNAL. **[CCC].** cum. index (published in December). **Bk Rev**, (Qty: 6). **Ad Acc**, **Adv Mgr:** E. Caesar, **Tel** 089-43189-642. **Pr Rev. Circ:** 3,000 (ctrl). Documents available from The Genuine Article, BIOSIS Document Express, CASDDS.
**Desc:** Journal for the clinical study and treatment of infectious diseases. Contains a clinically relevant theoretical section in vitro and animal studies.
**Ind/Abst** Biol. Abstr.; Chem. Abstr.; Curr. Contents Clin. Med.; Curr. Contents Life Sci.; EMBASE; Helminthol. Abstr.; Immunol. Abstr.; Index Med.; Microbiol. Abstr. Sect. B; Microbiol. Abstr. Sect. A; Life Sci. Collect.; PESTDOC; Protozoolog. Abstr.; Ref. Upd. Clinical Ed.; Ref. Upd. Deluxe Ed.; Res. Alert [Full Cov.]; Rev. Med. Vet. Mycology; Sci. Cit. Index; SCISEARCH; Soc. Sci. Cit. Index [Select. Cov.]; Virol. AIDS Abstr.

●US/1074-2905
**INFECTION CONTROL WEEKLY.** (1993)-. English. Forty-eight times a year. $995.00 US, Canada and Mexico; $1,195.00 other. CW Henderson, PO Box 5528, Atlanta GA 30307-0528. **Tel** (404)377-8895, FAX (404)378-5411. **(Subscription address:** CW Henderson, Subscription Office, PO Box 830409, Birmingham AL 35283-0409.**)**
**Desc:** Concentrates on nosocomial infections originating in hospitals, prisons, and other sites with high risk of infection. Topics include discoveries of various acquired infections from AIDS to tuberculosis, surgical site infections, nosocomial candida infections, hospital epidemiology, hospital policies, CDC guidelines and basic and applied research.

●US/1056-2044
**INFECTIOUS AGENTS AND DISEASE.** [Infect. agents dis.]. Vol. 1, No. 1 (Feb. 1992)-. Academic Scholarly Publication. English. qt. $95.00 (individuals), $135.00 (institutions) US; $116.00 (individuals), $168.00 (institutions) other. Raven Press, 1185 Avenue of the Americas, 37th Floor, New York NY 10036. **Tel** (212)930-9500, (212)930-9604, FAX (212)869-3495, (212)302-8507, telex 640073. **ED** Bernard Roizman. **DD** 616. **NLM** W1; IN406HKP. **CODEN** IADIEV. **[CCC].** available on microfilm and microfiche from University Microfilms International (UMI). Documents available from CASDDS.
**Desc:** Features critical, invited reviews and commentary to provide the infectious disease specialist with a broader, more timely, and more cohesive view of current clinical and research issues.
**Ind/Abst** Chem. Abstr.; Curr. Aware. Biol. Sci., CABS; Curr. Contents Life Sci.; Sci. Cit. Index.

US
**INFECTIOUS DISEASE.** Monographic series. English. ir. Price varies per volume. Marcel Dekker Inc., 270 Madison Avenue, New York NY 10016. **Tel** (212)696-9000, (800)228-1160, FAX (212)685-4540, telex 421419. **(Subscription address:** Marcel Dekker Inc, PO Box 5017, Monticello NY 12701.**)**
**Desc:** Series covering topics in infectious diseases such as parasitic infections, quinolones, and herpes virus infections.

US/0739-7348
**INFECTIOUS DISEASE ALERT.** **See** Medical Science and Technology-Allergy and Immunology.

US/1043-2981
**INFECTIOUS DISEASE AND THERAPY.** [Infect. dis. ther.]. Vol. 1 (1989)-. Monographic series. English. Marcel Dekker Inc., 270 Madison Avenue, New York NY 10016. **Tel** (212)696-9000, (800)228-1160, FAX (212)685-4540, telex 421419. **(Subscription address:** Marcel Dekker Inc, PO Box 5017, Monticello NY 12701.**)** **DD** 616. **NLM** W1; IN406HMN. **CODEN** IDTHER. Documents available from BIOSIS Document Express, CASDDS.
**Ind/Abst** Biol. Abstr.; Chem. Abstr.

US/0891-5520
**INFECTIOUS DISEASE CLINICS OF NORTH AMERICA.** [Infect. dis. clin. North Am.]. **VFOAT** Infectious Disease Clinics. Vol. 1, No. 1 (March 1987)-. Periodical. English. qt. $111.00 (institutions), $89.00 (individuals) US; $123.00 (individual), $129.00 (institution) other. W.B. Saunders Company, A Subsidiary of Harcourt Brace Jovanovich, Inc., The Curtis Center/Suite 300, Independence Square West, Philadelphia PA 19106-3399. **Tel** (215)238-7800 or, 5587, FAX (215)238-7883, telex 173146. **(Subscription address:** W. B. Saunders Company / North America Subscriptions, c/o Periodicals, 6277 Sea Harbour Drive, 4th Floor, Orlando FL 32887.**)** **LC** RC109; .I53. **DD** 616.9/05. **NLM** W1; IN406HR. **CODEN** IDCAEN. **[CCC].**
**Ind/Abst** Curr. Contents Clin. Med.; EMBASE; Index Med. (1987-); Physic. Medline Plus; Sci. Cit. Index; Soc. Sci. Cit. Index [Select. Cov.].

US/1056-9251
**INFECTIOUS DISEASE NEWS.** [Infect. dis. news]. **VFOAT** Infectious Disease News for Today's Primary Care Physician. (1988)-. Periodical. English. mo. $170.00 institution, $160.00 individual (US). Slack Inc., 6900 Grove Road, Thorofare NJ 08086. **Tel** (609)848-1000, (800)257-8290, FAX (609)853-5991, telex 517108 SLACK INC VD. **DD** 617. **NLM** W1; IN406J.

US/0734-4627
**INFECTIOUS DISEASES AND ANTIMICROBIAL AGENTS.** [Infect. dis. antimicrob. agents]. (1981)-. Academic Scholarly Publication. English. ir. Price varies per volume. Marcel Dekker Inc., 270 Madison Avenue, New York NY 10016. **Tel** (212)696-9000, (800)228-1160, FAX (212)685-4540, telex 421419. **(Subscription address:** Marcel Dekker Inc, PO Box 5017, Monticello NY 12701.**)** **LC** UNC. **DD** 616.9/05. **NLM** W1 IN406L. **CODEN** IDAADC. Documents available from CASDDS.
**Desc:** Covers topics such as viral infections and fungal disease.
**Ind/Abst** Chem. Abstr. (1981-1982).

US/1044-9779
**INFECTIOUS DISEASES IN CHILDREN.** [Infect. dis. child.]. Vol. 1, No. 1 (Jan. 1988)-. Periodical. English. mo. $170.00 institution, $160.00 individual (US). Slack Inc., 6900 Grove Road, Thorofare NJ 08086. **Tel** (609)848-1000, (800)257-8290, FAX (609)853-5991, telex 517108 SLACK INC VD. **DD** 618. **NLM** W1; IN406P.

●US/1056-9103
**INFECTIOUS DISEASES IN CLINICAL PRACTICE (BALTIMORE, MD.).** (INFECTIOUS DISEASES IN CLINICAL PRACTICE : IDCP.). [Infect. dis. clin. pract.]. **VFOAT** IDCP. Vol. 1, No. 1 (Jan.-Feb. 1992)-. Periodical. English. bm. $87.00 (individual), $135.00 (institution) US; $112.00 (individual), $160.00 (institution) other. Williams & Wilkins Company, 428 East Preston Street, Baltimore MD 21202-3993. **Tel** (410)528-4000, (800)638-6423, FAX (410)528-8596, telex 87669. **(Subscription address:** Williams & Wilkins, PO Box 64380, Baltimore MD 21264.**)** **DD** 616. **NLM** W1; IN406QT. **[CCC].** Documents available from Quick Copies.
**Desc:** One-stop consolidated coverage on treatment and prevention for clinicians who manage patients with infectious diseases.
**Ind/Abst** Sci. Cit. Index; Soc. Sci. Cit. Index [Select. Cov.].

US/0278-2316
**INFECTIOUS DISEASES NEWSLETTER (NEW YORK, N.Y.).** ***Title Change.*** (INFECTIOUS DISEASES NEWSLETTER : IDN.). [Infect. dis. newsl.]. **VFOAT** IDN. Vol. 1, No. 1 (Oct. 1981)-(1993). Newsletter. English. Twelve times a year. Elsevier Science Publishing Company Inc, Madison Square Station, PO Box 882, New York NY 10159-0882. **Tel** (212)633-3950, FAX (212)633-3990. **ED** Paul D Hoeprich. **LC** Discard. **DD** 616. **NLM** W1 IN406T. **[CCC]. Circ:** 960. available on microfilm and microfiche from University Microfilms International (UMI). ***Continued by*** *Antimicrobics and Infectious Diseases Newsletter.*
**Desc:** Presents in an easily readable and digestible format summaries of recent events occurring in the area of infectious diseases.
**Ind/Abst** Trop. Dis. Bull.

MX/0185-0628
**INFECTOLOGIA.** (INFECTOLOGIA : ORGANO DE LA ASOCIACION MEXICANA DE INFECTOLOGIA, A.C.). [Infectologia]. **Added/Corp** Asociacion Mexicana de Infectologia. (1981)-. Periodical. Spanish (summaries and/or abstracts in English). Twelve times a year. $165.00. Mundo Medico SA, Ejercito Nacional 381, 11520 Mexico DF Mexico. **Tel** 011 52 5 2038111. **NLM** W1; IN406TD. **CODEN** INFTET. **Ad Acc**, **Adv Mgr:** Oscar Baqnarelli. **Circ:** 13,000 (ctrl). Documents available from CASDDS.
**Desc:** News and information on infection and infectology.
**Ind/Abst** Chem. Abstr.

SP/0212-3800
**INFECTOLOGIKA.** **See** Medical Science and Technology-Allergy and Immunology.

BU/0861-8259
**INFEKTOLOGIA.** **VFOAT** Infectology. (1964)-. Bulgarian (summaries and/or abstracts in English and Russian). bm (6 issues). 30lv. Infektologia, Bul. la. Sakuzov 26, 1504 Sofia Bulgaria.

GW/0937-1591
**INTERNATIONAL JOURNAL OF MEDICAL MICROBIOLOGY AND HYGIENE ABSTRACTS OF MICROBIOLOGY, VIROLOGY, PARASITOLOGY, PREVENTIVE MEDICINE AND ENVIRONMENTAL HYGIENE.** ***Ceased.*** **See** Biology-Microbiology.

II/0019-5138
**JOURNAL OF COMMUNICABLE DISEASES.** **See** Public Health and Safety.

US/0195-6701
**JOURNAL OF HOSPITAL INFECTION, THE.** [J. hosp. infect.]. Vol. 1 (March 1980)-. Periodical. English. mo. £199.00 (institution) UK/Europe; $358.00 (institution) other. Harcourt Brace & Company Ltd., Foots Cray, High Street, Sidcup Kent DA14 5HP England. **Tel** 011 44 81 300 3322, FAX 011 44 81 309 0807. **(Subscription address:** W. B. Saunders Company / North America Subscriptions, c/o Periodicals, 6277 Sea Harbour Drive, 4th Floor, Orlando FL 32887.**)** **NLM** W1 JO673N. **CODEN** JHINDS. **[CCC]. Bk Rev. Pr Rev.** Documents available from The Genuine Article, BIOSIS Document Express.
**Desc:** Publishes original articles in the field of hospital-acquired infection and related subjects. The journal aims to provide a forum for original observations of international significance in all aspects of hospital infection. Leading articles and review articles, editorials, letters and book reviews are also published.
**Ind/Abst** Biodeter. Abstr. (1991-); Biol. Abstr. (1985-); Chem. Hazards Ind.; Cumul. Index Nurs. Allied Health Lit.; Curr. Contents Clin. Med.; Dairy Sci. Abstr.; EMBASE; Health Plan. Adminis.; Helminthol. Abstr.; Immunol. Abstr.; Index Med.; Index Vet.; Lab. Hazards Bull.; Microbiol. Abstr. Sect. B; Microbiol. Abstr. Sect. A; Microbiol. Abstr. Sect. C; Nutr. Abstr. Rev., Ser. A, Hum. Exp.; Life Sci. Collect.; Protozoolog. Abstr.; Res. Alert [Full Cov.]; Rev. Med. Vet. Mycology; Sci. Cit. Index; SCISEARCH; Trop. Dis. Bull.; Virol. AIDS Abstr.

UK/0163-4453
**JOURNAL OF INFECTION, THE.** [J. infect.]. Vol. 1 (Mar. 1979)-. Academic Scholarly Publication. English. bm (6 issues). £144.00 UK and Europe; $266.00 other (institution). Harcourt Brace & Company Ltd., Foots Cray, High Street, Sidcup Kent DA14 5HP England. **Tel** 011 44 81 300 3322, FAX 011 44 81 309 0807. **(Subscription address:** W. B. Saunders Company / North America Subscriptions, c/o Periodicals, 6277 Sea Harbour Drive, 4th Floor, Orlando FL 32887.**)** **ED** BK Mandal, EM Dunbar, CED Taylor, JM Medlock, T Riordan and WRC Weir. **UDC** 616-022.1; 579.097. **NLM** W1 JO706M. **CODEN** JINFD2. **[CCC]. Bk Rev. Pr Rev.** Documents available from The Genuine Article, CASDDS.
**Desc:** Concentrates on all aspects of infection and its scientific basis are accepted from anywhere in the world. Publishes editorials, review articles, original articles, epidemiological studies, case reports, letters, and book reviews. Supplements are published periodically. The journal is committed to rapid publication.
**Ind/Abst** Chem. Abstr.; Curr. Aware. Biol. Sci., CABS; Curr. Contents Life Sci.; Dairy Sci. Abstr.; EMBASE; Helminthol. Abstr. (19??-19??); Index Med.; Index Vet.; Int. Pharm. Abstr.; Microbiol. Abstr. Sect. B; Microbiol. Abstr. Sect. C; Life Sci. Collect.; PESTDOC; Pig News Inf.; Poult. Abstr.; Protozoolog. Abstr.; Ref. Upd. Deluxe Ed.; Res. Alert [Full Cov.]; Rev. Med. Vet. Entomol.; Rev. Med. Vet. Mycology; Sci. Cit. Index; SCISEARCH; Small Anim. Abstr. Bibliogr.; Vet. Bull.; Trop. Dis. Bull.; Virol. AIDS Abstr.

US/0022-1899
**JOURNAL OF INFECTIOUS DISEASES, THE.** (THE JOURNAL OF INFECTIOUS DISEASES : OFFICIAL PUBLICATION OF THE INFECTIOUS DISEASES SOCIETY OF AMERICA.). [J. infect. dis.]. **Added/Corp** Memorial Institute for Infectious Diseases (Chicago, Ill.) John McCormick Institute for Infectious Diseases. John Rockefeller McCormick Memorial Fund. Infectious Diseases Society of America. Vol. 1 (Jan. 1904)-. Academic Scholarly Publication. English. mo. $216.00 institution, $93.00 individual, $46.00 ASM and IUMS individual member. University of Chicago Press / Journals Division, PO Box 37005, 5720 South Woodlawn, Chicago IL 60637. **Tel** (312)753-3347, FAX (312)753-0811. **(Subscription telephone:** (312)753-8083**)** **ED** Marvin Tuck. **LC** NOT IN LC. **NLM** W1 JO707. **CODEN** JIDIAQ. **[CCC].** cum. index. **Ad Acc. Pr Rev. Acid Free.** available on microfilm and microfiche from University Microfilms International (UMI). Documents available from The Genuine Article, BIOSIS Document Express, CASDDS.
**Desc:** Publishes original research on the pathogenesis, diagnosis, and treatment of infectious diseases; on the microbes that cause them; and on disorders of host immune mechanisms.
**Ind/Abst** Abr. Index Med.; AgBiotech News Inf.; Biol. Abstr.; Biol. Dig.; Chem. Abstr.; Cumul. Index Nurs. Allied Health Lit.; Curr. Aware. Biol. Sci., CABS; Dairy Sci. Abstr.; EMBASE; Energy Res. Abstr.; Genet. Abstr.; Health Period. Database; Health Serv. Abstr.; Helminthol. Abstr. (19??-19??); Immunol. Abstr.; Index Med.; INIS Atomindex [Micro.]; Int. Pharm. Abstr.; Iowa Drug Inf. Serv. (1969-); J. Watch; Microbiol. Abstr. Sect. B; Microbiol. Abstr. Sect. A; Microbiol. Abstr. Sect. C; Mod. Med.; Nutr. Abstr. Rev., Ser. B, Live Feeds and Feed.; Nutr. Abstr. Rev., Ser. A, Hum. Exp.; Life Sci. Collect.; PESTDOC; Physic. Medline Plus; Pig News Inf.; Protozoolog. Abstr.; Ref. Upd. Basic Ed.; Ref. Upd. Deluxe Ed.; Res. Alert [Full Cov.]; Rev. Med. Vet. Entomol.; Rev. Med. Vet. Mycology; Rev. Plant Pathol.;

Risk Abstr.; Sci. Cit. Index; SCISEARCH; Small Anim. Abstr. Bibliogr.; Soc. Sci. Cit. Index [Select. Cov.]; Trop. Dis. Bull.; Virol. AIDS Abstr.; Wildl. Rev.

●US/1074-2395
**JOURNAL OF THE PHYSICIANS ASSOCIATION FOR AIDS CARE. See** Medical Science and Technology-Allergy and Immunology.

●KO
**KOREAN JOURNAL OF PARASITOLOGY, THE. Added/Corp** Taehan Kisaengchung Hakhoe. **VFOAT** Kisaengchunghak Chapchi. Vol. 31, No. 1 (1993)-. Periodical. English (Korean). qt. Korean Department of Parasitology, 28 Yeon-Keon dong Chong-ro ku, 110799 Seoul Korea. **Tel** 011 82 2 7603317, 011 82 2 7408348, FAX 011 82 2 7656142. **NLM** W1; KO608F. ***Continues*** *Kisaengchunghak Chapchi, 0023-4001.*

KO/0023-4001
**KOREAN JOURNAL OF PARASITOLOGY.** ***Title Change.*** (KISAENGCHUNGHAK CHAPCHI / THE KOREAN JOURNAL OF PARASITOLOGY.). [Korean j. parasitol.]. **Added/Corp** Taehan Kisaengchung Hakhoe. **VFOAT** Korean Journal of Parasitology. (1963)-(1992). Academic Scholarly Publication. Korean (English). Four times a year (March, June, Sept., Dec.). Korean Department of Parasitology, 28 Yeon-Keon dong Chong-ro ku, 110799 Seoul Korea. **Tel** 011 82 2 7603317, 011 82 2 7408348, FAX 011 82 2 7656142. **ED** Soon-Hyung Lee. **LC** QL757; .K55. **NLM** W1; KI839. **CODEN** KSCHAV. Index available. cum. index. **Pr Rev. Circ:** 850. Documents available from BIOSIS Document Express, CASDDS. ***Continued by*** *Korean Journal of Parasitology.*
**Desc:** Contains original papers, case records, and a brief communications on parasites of humans or animals and their host parasite relations.
**Ind/Abst** Biol. Abstr.; Chem. Abstr.; EMBASE; Health Plan. Adminis.; Helminthol. Abstr. (1991-?); Protozoolog. Abstr.; Rev. Med. Vet. Entomol.; Trop. Dis. Bull.

US
**MALARIA SURVEILLANCE : ANNUAL SUMMARY / NATIONAL COMMUNICABLE DISEASE CENTER. Added/Corp** National Communicable Disease Center (U.S.) Center for Disease Control. Centers for Disease Control (U.S.). **VFOAT** Malaria Surveillance. (195?)-. English. an. Free. Center for Disease Control, 1600 Clifton Road, Atlanta GA 30333. **Tel** (404)639-3311, ((404)639-3534. **(Subscription address:** CDC Distribution / Georgia, c/o G. Dixon, Mail Stop A 22, Atlanta GA 30333.**)** **LC** RC156.A1; C45. **DD** 614.5/3/20973. **NLM** W2 A C7CM. available on microfiche (Vols. for (1982-) distributed to depository libraries).

US/0737-6030
**MEDIGUIDE TO INFECTIOUS DISEASES.** [Mediguide infect. dis.]. Vol. 1, Issue 1-. Periodical. English. qt. Dellacorte Publications, 919 3rd Avenue, New York NY 10022. **Tel** (212)751-2806. **NLM** W1 ME787FL.

US
**MICHIGAN HIV REPORT / DEPARTMENT OF PUBLIC HEALTH. See** Public Health and Safety.

UK/0882-4010
**MICROBIAL PATHOGENESIS.** [Microb. pathog.]. Vol. 1, No. 1 (Feb. 1986)-. Academic Scholarly Publication. English. mo. $415.00. Academic Press Ltd., A Division of Harcourt Brace & Company Ltd., 24-28 Oval Road, London NW1 7DX England. **Tel** 071 267 4466, FAX 071 482 2293, 071 485 4752, telex 25775 ACPRES G. **(Subscription address:** Harcourt Brace & Company, Ltd., Foots Cray, High Street, Sidcup Kent DA14 5HP England.**)** **ED** P. H. Makela, A. T. Haase, A. Mahmoud, M. Brahic and T. Nilsen. **LC** QR175; .M53. **DD** 616/.01. **NLM** W1; MI265. **CODEN** MIPAEV. **[CCC]. Pr Rev.** Documents available from The Genuine Article, BIOSIS Document Express, CASDDS.
**Desc:** Publishes original contributions, mini-reviews, and notes on molecular and cellular mechanisms in infectious disease. The journal aims for rapid publication of articles of high quality and significance in an international forum.
**Ind/Abst** AgBiotech News Inf.; Biol. Abstr. (1986-); Chem. Abstr. (1986-); CSA Neuro. Abstr. (?-?); Curr. Aware. Biol. Sci., CABS; Curr. Contents Life Sci.; Genet. Abstr.; Immunol. Abstr.; Index Med.; Index Vet.; Microbiol. Abstr. Sect. B; Oncog. Growth Factors Abstr.; Pig News Inf.; Poult. Abstr.; Ref. Upd. Deluxe Ed.; Res. Alert [Full Cov.]; Sci. Cit. Index; SCISEARCH; Vet. Bull.; Trop. Dis. Bull.; Virol. AIDS Abstr.

AT/1035-5693
**MIMS DISEASE INDEX.** [Mims dis. index]. (1991)-. English. be. 64.00Aus$ Australia; 81.00Aus$ New Zealand and Papua New Guinea; 90.00Aus$ other. Mims Australia, 98 Albany Street, Crows Nest NSW 2065 Australia. **Tel** 011 61 2 9067966, FAX 011 61 2 9063955. **ED** Kathryn Tuckwell; Linda Badewitz-Dodd. **DD** 616.005. Index available. **Ad Acc, Adv Mgr:** M McCathey. **Circ:** 16,000.
**Desc:** Expert discussion of disease. Articles cover epidemiology, differential diagnosis, and treatment.

AT/1030-5289
**NATIONAL AIDS BULLETIN / AUSTRALIAN FEDERATION OF AIDS ORGANISATIONS INC. Added/Corp** AIDS Council of South Australia. Australian Federation of AIDS Organisations. **VFOAT** AFAO National AIDS Bulletin. Vol. 1, No. 1 (Sept. 1987)-. Periodical. English. Ten times a year (Dec./Jan. issues combined). Free to AIDS Councils/AFAO affiliates; 60.00Aus$ (individuals) community groups, 140.00Aus$ (institutions) government & corporate Australia; 90.00Aus$ (individuals) community groups, 170.00Aus$ (institutions) government & corporate others. Australian Federation of AIDS Organisations, PO Box H274, Australian Square 2000 Australia. **Tel** 011 61 2 2312111, FAX 011 61 2 2312092. **ED** Adrian Flood. **LC** WMLC L 83/7259. **NLM** W1; NA228. **Circ:** 2,000.
**Desc:** This journal contains all of the latest national and world news, information and comments.

US
**NATIONAL AIDS INFORMATION CLEARINGHOUSE CONFERENCE CALENDAR. See** Medical Science and Technology-Allergy and Immunology.

US/0894-1769
**NEWSLETTER / NATIONAL ALOPECIA AREATA FOUNDATION, NAAF. Added/Corp** National Alopecia Areata Foundation (U.S.). **VFOAT** NAAF Newsletter; N.A.A.F. Newsletter. (19??)-. Periodical. English. Six times a year (Jan., Mar., May, July, Sept., Nov.). $30.00. National Alopecia Areata Foundation, 710 C Street, Suite 11, San Rafael CA 94901. **Tel** (415)456-4644, FAX (415)456-4274. **DD** 616. **Bk Rev**, (Qty: 5). **Ad Acc, Adv Mgr:** Carol ,Mayer. **Circ:** 6,000.

UV/0253-3901
**O.C.C.G.E. INFORMATIONS / OCCGE, SECRETARIAT GENERAL. See** Medical Science and Technology-Epidemiology.

US/1059-7913
**PAAC NOTES (CHICAGO, ILL.).** ***Title Change.*** (PAAC NOTES : A NEWS JOURNAL OF THE PHYSICIANS ASSOCIATION FOR AIDS CARE.). [PAACnotes]. **Added/Corp** Physicians Association for AIDS Care. **VFOAT** PAAC Notes. **VAT** Physicians Association for AIDS Care Notes. Vol. 1, No. 1 (Jan/Feb. 1989)-(199?). Periodical. English. Twelve times a year. Physicians Association for AIDS Care, 101 West Grand Avenue, Suite 200, Chciago IL 60610. **Tel** (312)222-1326, FAX (312)222-0329. **ED** Gordon Nary, (editor's phone: (312)222-1326). **LC** RC607.A26; P33. **DD** 362.1/969792/005. **NLM** W1; PA108. **Bk Rev**, (Qty: 3). **Ad Acc, Adv Mgr:** Gordon Nary. **Pr Rev. Circ:** 6,000. ***Continued by*** *Journal of the Physicians Association for AIDS Care, 1074-2395.*

US/0891-3668
**PEDIATRIC INFECTIOUS DISEASE JOURNAL, THE. See** Medical Science and Technology-Pediatrics.

US/1061-6047
**PERSPECTIVES GLOBALES DES LA HEPATITIS.** (1992)-. Periodical. Spanish. sa. Free. PATH, 4 Nicherson, Seattle WA 98109.

PH/0115-0324
**PHILIPPINE JOURNAL OF MICROBIOLOGY AND INFECTIOUS DISEASES, THE. See** Biology-Microbiology.

●US
**POSITIVE LIVING. See** Public Health and Safety.

US/0892-1857
**PRAEGER MONOGRAPHS IN INFECTIOUS DISEASE. See** Public Health and Safety.

UK/0269-1396
**PRATIQUE LONDON.** [Pratique Lond.]. (1974)-. Periodical. English. qt. £12.00 England; £15.00 other. Disinfected Mail Study Circle, 25 Sinclair Grove, London NW11 9JH England. **Tel** 011 44 81 455 9190. **ED** V. Denis Vandervelde. Index available. cum. index. **Bk Rev**, (Qty: 4). **Ad Acc.** Full Page (B&W) $80.00. Half Page (B&W) $45.00. **Circ:** 140.
**Desc:** Researches and publishes accounts of the treatment of mail in ways thought to prevent the spread of infectious diseases, from the fourteenth century until recent times.

UK
**PRINCIPLES & PRACTICE OF INFECTIOUS DISEASE.** English. Churchill Livingstone, 1-3 Baxter's Place, Leith Walk, Edinburgh EH1 3AF Scotland. **Tel** 011 44 31 556 2424, FAX 011 44 31 558 1278, telex 727511.

BU/0204-9155
**PROBLEMS OF INFECTIOUS AND PARASITIC DISEASES.** [Probl. infect. parasit. dis.]. **Added/Corp** Meditsinska Akademiia. (1973)-. Academic Scholarly Publication. English (Bulgarian; summaries and/or abstracts in Russian). Izdatelstvo Medicina i Fizkult, PL Slavejkov 11, 1000 Sofia Bulgaria. **NLM** W1 PR574P. **CODEN** PIPDD4. Documents available from BIOSIS Document Express, CASDDS.
**Desc:** Provides information on communicable and parasitic diseases.
**Ind/Abst** Biol. Abstr.; Chem. Abstr.; EMBASE; Trop. Dis. Bull.

PL/0033-2100
**PRZEGLAD EPIDEMIOLOGICZNY. See** Medical Science and Technology-Epidemiology.

US/1069-3637
**PWA NEWSLINE.** (PWA NEWSLINE / PEOPLE WITH AIDS COALITION.). [PWA newsline]. **Added/Corp** People with AIDS Coalition. **VFOAT** People with AIDS Newsline; PWA Coalition Newsline. (19??)-. Periodical. English. Eleven times a year. $35.00. PWA Coalition Newsline / New York, 50 West 17th Street, 8th Floor, New York NY 10011. **Tel** (212)647-1415, FAX (212)647-1419. **ED** Michael Slowm. **DD** 616. **Circ:** 15,000. ***Continues*** *PWA Coalition Newsline.*
**Desc:** A magazine that is written for and by the people who are affected with HIV/AIDS.

CN/1189-3087
**RAPPORT D'ACTIVITES / CENTRE QUEBECOIS DE COORDINATION SUR LE SIDA. See** Public Health and Safety.

UK/0144-1078
**RECENT ADVANCES IN INFECTION.** ***Ceased.*** [Recent adv. infect.]. (1979)-(Dec. 1992). Academic Scholarly Publication. English. ir (every 3 to 5 years). Churchill Livingstone, 1-3 Baxter's Place, Leith Walk, Edinburgh EH1 3AF Scotland. **Tel** 011 44 31 556 2424, FAX 011 44 31 558 1278, telex 727511. **ED** D. Reeves and A. Geddes. **LC** RC111; .R43. **DD** 616.9. **NLM** W1 RE105UMG. **CODEN** RAIFD9. Documents available from CASDDS.
**Ind/Abst** Chem. Abstr.

UK
**RECENT ADVANCES IN SEXUALLY TRANSMITTED DISEASES AND AIDS.** No. 4 (1991)-. Monographic series. English. ir. Price varies per volume. Churchill Livingstone, 1-3 Baxter's Place, Leith Walk, Edinburgh EH1 3AF Scotland. **Tel** 011 44 31 556 2424, FAX 011 44 31 558 1278, telex 727511. **(Subscription address:** Churchill Livingstone / US, 5 S 250 Frontenac Road, Naperville IL 60563.**)** **NLM** W1; RE105YJG. ***Continues*** *Recent Advances in Sexually Transmitted Diseases, 0143-6805.*

US/0161-3618
**REPORT FROM THE DIRECTOR, NATIONAL INSTITUTE OF ALLERGY AND INFECTIOUS DISEASES. Main/Corp** United States. National Institute of Allergy and Infectious Diseases. **VFOAT** NIAID Report of the Director. English. US Department of Health and Human Services National Institutes of Health, 9000 Rockville Pike, Bethesda MD 20892. **Tel** (301)496-9291, FAX (301)496-2443. **LC** RC583; .U54A. **DD** 616.07/9/072073. **NLM** W1 RE212TN.

US
**REPORT OF THE COMMITTEE ON INFECTIOUS DISEASES. Main/Corp** American Academy of Pediatrics. Committee on Infectious Diseases. **VFOAT** Red Book. 16th Ed. (1970)-. English. ir (usually published in April). $73.45. American Academy of Pediatrics, 141 Northwest Point Boulevard, Elk Grove Village IL 60009-0927. **Tel** (708)981-7903, FAX (708)228-5088. **NLM** W1 RE209R. **Ad Acc, Adv Mgr Tel** (708)981-7902. ***Continues*** *American Academy of Pediatrics. Committee on the Control of Infectious Diseases. Report of the Committee on the Control of Infectious Diseases, 0065-6909.*

US/1050-964X
**REPORT ON PEDIATRIC INFECTIOUS DISEASES, THE.** (THE REPORT ON PEDIATRIC INFECTIOUS DISEASES : AN OFFICIAL PUBLICATION OF THE PEDIATRIC INFECTIOUS DISEASES SOCIETY.). [Rep. pediatr. infect. dis.]. **Added/Corp** Pediatric Infectious Diseases Society. No. 1 (Jan. 1991)-. Periodical. English. Ten times a year. $70.00 (institution), $45.00 (individual) US. Churchill Livingstone Inc., 650 Avenue of the Americas, New York NY 10011. **Tel** (212)206-5062, FAX (212)727-7808. **(Subscription address:** Churchill Livingstone Inc., 5 South 250 Frontenac Road, Naperville, IL 60563 (telephone: (800)553-5426 or (708)416-3939)**)** **ED** Jerome Klein and Georges Peter. **DD** 618. **NLM** W1; RE212DE. **CODEN** RPIDE7. **[CCC].**
**Desc:** A publication of the Pediatric Infectious Diseases Society, this newsletter provides concise and contemporary information on issues of importance to

## Medical Science and Technology —Communicable Diseases

practicing physicians responsible for the care of infants and children. Readership: pediatricians and infectious disease specialists.

FR
**REPORT ON THE DISEASE STATUS WORLDWIDE IN ... / OFFICE INTERNATIONAL DES EPIZOOTIES.** See Veterinary Sciences.

US
**REPORTABLE DISEASE BULLETIN / N. DAK. STATE DEPARTMENT OF HEALTH. Added/Corp** North Dakota. State Dept. of Health. (19??)-. Bulletin. English. **LC** RA643.6.N9; R46. **DD** 312/.39/09784.

US/0273-5202
**REPORTED MORBIDITY AND MORTALITY IN TEXAS, ANNUAL SUMMARY.** See Public Health and Safety.

US/0731-9266
**REVIEWS OF CLINICAL INFECTIOUS DISEASES.** [Rev. clin. infect. dis.]. (1982)-. Academic Scholarly Publication. English. an. Academic Press, Inc., 6277 Sea Harbor Drive, Orlando FL 32887. **Tel** (800)543-9534, (407)345-4100, FAX (407)363-9661. **DD** 616.

BL/0304-2138
**REVISTA DA FUNDACAO SESP.** See Public Health and Safety.

●US
**RMI ... REVIEW OF HIV & AIDS RESEARCH.** See Medical Science and Technology-Allergy and Immunology.

NO/0036-5548
**SCANDINAVIAN JOURNAL OF INFECTIOUS DISEASES.** [Scand. j. infect. dis.]. Vol. 1 (1969)-. Academic Scholarly Publication. English. bm (6 issues). Kr1150.00, $187.00. Scandinavian University Press, PO Box 2959 Toeyen, N 0608 Oslo 6 Norway. **Tel** 011 47 2 2575400, FAX 011 47 2 2575353, telex 71896 UROR N. **(Subscription address:** Scandinavian University Press, 200 Meacham Ave., Elmont NY 11003.**) ED** Folke Nordbring, Stellan Bengtsson. **NLM** W1 SC15K. **CODEN** SJIDB7. **Bk Rev. Pr Rev.** Documents available from The Genuine Article, BIOSIS Document Express, CASDDS.
**Desc:** Publishes original papers on clinical aspects of infectious diseases. The topics may concern prophylaxis or therapy of infectious diseases, laboratory investigations of clinical significance, epidemiological studies of human infections and experimental infections.
**Ind/Abst** Biol. Abstr.; Biol. Dig.; Chem. Abstr.; Cumul. Index Nurs. Allied Health Lit.; Curr. Aware. Biol. Sci.; CABS; Curr. Contents Clin. Med.; Curr. Contents Life Sci.; Dairy Sci. Abstr.; EMBASE; Helminthol. Abstr. (19??-19??); Immunol. Abstr.; Index Med.; Microbiol. Abstr. Sect. B; Microbiol. Abstr. Sect. A; Microbiol. Abstr. Sect. C; Mod. Med.; Life Sci. Collect.; PESTDOC; Pig News Inf.; Protozoolog. Abstr.; Ref. Upd. Deluxe Ed.; Res. Alert [Full Cov.]; Rev. Med. Vet. Entomol.; Rev. Med. Vet. Mycology; Rev. Plant Pathol.; Sci. Cit. Index; SCISEARCH; Soc. Sci. Cit. Index [Select. Cov.]; Trop. Dis. Bull.; Virol. AIDS Abstr.

SW/0300-8878
**SCANDINAVIAN JOURNAL OF INFECTIOUS DISEASES. SUPPLEMENTUM.** [Scand. j. infect. dis., Suppl.]. (1970)-. Academic Scholarly Publication. English. ir. Comes with Scandinavian Journal of Infectious Diseases: $187.00. Scandinavian University Press, PO Box 2959 Toeyen, N 0608 Oslo 6 Norway. **Tel** 011 47 2 2575400, FAX 011 47 2 2575353, telex 71896 UROR N. **(Subscription address:** Scandinavian University Press, 200 Meacham Ave., Elmont NY 11003.**) NLM** W1 SC15L. **CODEN** SJISAH. Documents available from BIOSIS Document Express, CASDDS.
**Ind/Abst** Biol. Abstr.; Chem. Abstr.; Curr. Aware. Biol. Sci., CABS; EMBASE; Index Med.; Life Sci. Collect.

JA/0371-2761
**SCIENCE REPORTS OF THE RESEARCH INSTITUTES. SERIES C, MEDICINE, THE.** [Sci. rep. Res. Inst., Tohoku Univ., Ser. C]. **Main/Corp** Tohoku Daigaku. **VFOAT** Tohoku Daigaku Kenkyusho Hokoku, Igaku; Reports of the Research Institute for Tuberculosis and Leprosy, Hokoku University. Vol. 1 (Dec. 1949)-. Periodical. English. sm (24 issues). Research Institute for Tuberculosis and Cancer, Tohoku University, 4 1 Seiryoma, Sendai Miyagiken 980 Japan. **NLM** W1 TO182I. **CODEN** SRTCAC. Documents available from BIOSIS Document Express, CASDDS.
**Ind/Abst** Biol. Abstr.; Chem. Abstr. (1949-1982); EMBASE; Index Med.

JA/0254-8720
**SEAMIC INFORMATION RETRIEVAL ON CURRENT LITERATURE. SERIES L. VENEREAL DISEASE, GONORRHEA.** See Public Health and Safety.

US/0748-9528
**SECOND OPINION (SAN FRANCISCO, CALIF.).** *Title Change.* See Public Health and Safety.

●US
**SELECTED REPORTABLE DISEASES BY HEALTH JURISDICTION. Added/Corp** Michigan. Division of Disease Control. (1992)-. Periodical. English. wk. *Continues* Cases of Common Reportable Diseases.

US/1045-1870
**SEMINARS IN PEDIATRIC INFECTIOUS DISEASES.** [Semin. pediatr. infect. dis.]. (1990)-. Periodical. English. qt (Jan., Apr., July, Oct.). $94.00 (individual) $129.00 (institution) US; $135.00 (individual), $149.00 (institution) other. W.B. Saunders Company, A Subsidiary of Harcourt Brace Jovanovich, Inc., The Curtis Center/Suite 300, Independence Square West, Philadelphia PA 19106-3399. **Tel** (215)238-7800 or, 5587, FAX (215)238-7883, telex 173146. **(Subscription address:** W. B. Saunders Company / North America Subscriptions, c/o Periodicals, 6277 Sea Harbour Drive, 4th Floor, Orlando FL 32887.**) NLM** W1; SE489EL. **[CCC].**

UK/0888-0786
**SERODIAGNOSIS AND IMMUNOTHERAPY IN INFECTIOUS DISEASE.** See Biology-Microbiology.

US/0148-5717
**SEXUALLY TRANSMITTED DISEASES.** See Public Health and Safety.

CN/0711-8929
**SEXUALLY TRANSMITTED DISEASES IN CANADA.** See Public Health and Safety.

SP
**SIDAHORA : UN PROYECTO DEL DEPARTAMENTO DE PUBLICACIONES DEL PWA COALITION, NY.** See Medical Science and Technology-Allergy and Immunology.

US
**SIDAMERICA.** See Medical Science and Technology-Allergy and Immunology.

SA
**SOUTHERN AFRICAN JOURNAL OF EPIDEMIOLOGY & INFECTION : OFFICIAL JOURNAL OF THE SEXUALLY TRANSMITTED DISEASES, INFECTIOUS DISEASES, AND EPIDEMIOLOGICAL SOCIETIES OF SOUTHERN AFRICA, THE. VFOAT** Epidemiology & Infection; Epidemiology and Infection. (1986)-. Periodical. English. qt. R10.00. MIMS Pty Ltd., PO Box 2059, Pretoria 0001 South Africa. **Tel** 011 27 12 348-5010, FAX 011 27 12 477716. **(Subscription address:** PO Box 1038, Johannesburg 2000 South Africa**) ED** H J Koornhof. **NLM** W1; SO925H. **Bk Rev. Ad Acc. Circ:** 1,800 (ctrl).
**Desc:** Covers local scientific articles.

US/0049-2116
**STAR (CARVILLE), THE.** (THE STAR.). **Added/Corp** United States. Public Health Service. Hospital (Carville, La.). (19??)-. Academic Scholarly Publication. English. bm. $2.00 US; $5.00 other. US Public Health Service Hospital, Box 325, Carville LA 70721. **Tel** (504)642-5559. **ED** Ray Elwood. **NLM** WX 2 A5L6 M3S. **Circ:** 45,000.
**Ind/Abst** EMBASE.

●US/1065-982X
**TB WEEKLY.** [TB wkly.]. **VFOAT** Tuberculosis Weekly. (1993)-. Periodical. English. wk (48 issues). $995.00 US, Canada and Mexico; $1,195.00 other. CW Henderson, PO Box 5528, Atlanta GA 30307-0528. **Tel** (404)377-8895, FAX (404)378-5411. **(Subscription address:** CW Henderson, Subscription Office, PO Box 830409, Birmingham AL 35283-0409.**) DD** 616. **[CCC].**
**Desc:** Concentrates on tuberculosis-related news and research worldwide. Features original reporting, periodical reviews and upcoming meetings. Topics include TB programs, vaccine development, government roles and responses and more.

US
**TOTAL AIDS CASES, UTAH AND UNITED STATES.** See Public Health and Safety.

US/1050-625X
**TREATMENT ISSUES.** See Medical Science and Technology-Allergy and Immunology.

NE
**UIT HET NIEUWS GLICHT : KNIPSELKRANT.** Dutch. Ten times a year. Nederlandse Kankerbestrijding, Tavm Nijland Sophialaan 8, 1075 BR Amsterdam Netherlands. **Tel** 011 31 20 6644044. available on CD-ROM from MEDLINE.
**Desc:** Information and news about cancer.

AT
**VENEREOLOGY : OFFICIAL PUBLICATION OF THE NATIONAL VENEREOLOGY COUNCIL OF AUSTRALIA. Added/Corp** National Venereology Council of Australia. Vol. 1, No. 1 (August 1988)- Vol.6 No. 7 (Feb. 1993)-. Periodical. English. Four times a year (Feb., May, Aug., Nov.). 40.00 Aus$ (individual) Members of the state Venereology Societies of Australia & New Zealand; 70.00Aus$ (institution) Australia & New Zealand; 90.00Aus$ other. Venereology Publishing Incorporated, 580 Swanson Street, Carlton Vic 3053 Australia. **Tel** 03 347 0309, FAX 03 349 2376. **ED** David Plummer, Staff Specialist, Sydney Sexual Health Centre, Sydney Hospital, Macquarie Street, Sydney 2000 Australia; 61 2 223 7066 (Telephone). **NLM** W1; VE1783. **Bk Rev,** (Qty: 8). **Ad Acc, Adv Mgr:** Heather McDuff, **Tel** 03 347 0309. **Pr Rev. Circ:** 500 (ctrl).
**Desc:** Venereology is a non-profit journal published with the sole aim of fostering the discipline of sexual health in its broadest sense.

RU/0372-5952
**VOPROSY INFEKCIONNOJ PATOLOGII I IMMUNOLOGII.** (VOPROSY INFEKTSIONNOI PATOLOGII I IMMUNOLOGII.). [Vopr. infekc. patol. immunol.]. **Added/Corp** Akademiia Meditsinskikh Nauk SSSR. Vol. 3 (1963)-. Periodical. Russian. Izdatelstvo Meditsina / Russian Academy of Medical Sciences, Ulitsa Solyanka 14, 109801 Moscow Russia. **Tel** 011 95 297-05-04. **NLM** W1 VO628J. **Continues** Voprosy Infektsionnoi Patologii i Immunologii.

SZ/0049-8114
**WEEKLY EPIDEMIOLOGICAL RECORD.** (RELEVE EPIDEMIOLOGIQUE HEBDOMADAIRE / SECTION D'HYGIENE DU SECRETARIAT DE LA SOCIETE DES NATIONS). [Wkly. epidemiol. rec.]. **Added/Corp** League of Nations. Secretariat. Health Section. United Nations. Economic and Social Council. Interim Commission of the World Health Organization. Interim Commission of the World Health Organization. Epidemiological Information Service. Interim Commission of the World Health Organization. Sanitary Conventions and Quarantine Service. World Health Organization. Sanitary Conventions and Quarantine Service. World Health Organization. Quarantine Service. World Health Organization. Section of International Quarantine. World Health Organization. International Quarantine. World Health Organization. International Quarantine. World Health Organization. Epidemiological Surveillance and Quarantine Service. World Health Organization. Epidemiological Surveillance and Quarantine Unit. World Health Organization. Epidemiological Surveillance of Communicable Diseases. **VFOAT** Weekly Epidemiological Record. (Nov. 22, 1928)-. Academic Scholarly Publication. English (French). wk. $167.00 Surface Mail; $189.00 (airmail) Europe; $207.00 (airmail) other. World Health Organization, Distribution and Sales, 20 Avenue Appia, CH-1211 Geneva 27 Switzerland. **Tel** 011 41 22 7912111, FAX 011 41 22 7880401. **LC** RA651; .A483.
**Desc:** Serves as an instrument for the collation and dissemination of epidemiological data useful in disease surveillance on a global level. Priority is given to diseases or risk factors known to threaten international health. Additional data is specifically given at risk and prospects for vaccine development.
**Ind/Abst** EMBASE; Health Plan. Adminis.; Helminthol. Abstr. (1991-); Index Vet.; Protozoolog. Abstr.; Rev. Med. Vet. Entomol.; Rural Dev. Abstr.; Small Anim. Abstr. Bibliogr.; Trop. Dis. Bull.

US/0743-9261
**YEAR BOOK OF INFECTIOUS DISEASES, THE.** [Year b. infect. dis.]. **VFOAT** Yearbook of Infectious Diseases. (1986)-. English. an. $59.95. Mosby Year Book Inc., 11830 Westline Industrial Drive, St Louis MO 63146. **Tel** (800)325-4177, (314)872-8370, FAX (314)432-1380, telex 44-2402. **LC** RC109. **DD** 616.9. **NLM** W1; YE199F. **CODEN** YBIDEK. Documents available from BIOSIS Document Express.
**Ind/Abst** Biol. Abstr. (1986-).

AU/0175-7784
**ZEITSCHRIFT FUER STOMATOLOGIE.** (ZEITSCHRIFT FUER STOMATOLOGIE / HERAUSGEGEBEN VON DER OSTERREICHISCHEN GESELLSCHAFT FUER ZAHN-, MUND- UND KIEFERHEILKUNDE UND DER BUNDESFACHGRUPPE FUER ZAHN-, MUND- UND KIEFERHEILKUNDE DER OSTERREICHISCHEN ARZTEKAMMER.). **Added/Corp** Osterreichische Arztekammer. Bundesfachgruppe fur Zahn-, Mund- und Kieferheilkunde. Osterreichische Gesellschaft fur Zahn-, Mund- und Kieferheilkunde. Vol. 81 No. 1 (Feb. 1984)-. Academic Scholarly Publication. German (summaries and/or abstracts in English). Ten times a year. $196.50. Springer-Verlag Wien, Sachsenplatz 4 6, PO Box 89,

A-1201 Vienna Austria. **Tel** 011 43 1 3302415. **(Subscription address:** Springer Verlag New York Inc. / for North America, 44 Hartz Way, Secaucus NJ 07096.) **ED** G Watzek and M Matejka. **NLM** W1; ZE609F. **[CCC]. *Continues*** *Osterreichische Zeitschrift fur Stomatologie w (OCoLC)1761044.*
**Desc:** Contains original papers dealing with all topics related to dentistry, stomatology and orthodontics constitute the main part of this German-language journal.
**Ind/Abst** Curr. Aware. Biol. Sci., CABS; Curr. Titl. Dent.; EMBASE; Index Dent. Lit.

GW/0343-3048
**ZENTRALBLATT HAUT- UND GESCHLECHTSKRANKHEITEN. See** Medical Science and Technology-Dermatology.

CC/0254-6450
**ZHONGHUA LIUXINGBING ZAZHI.** (CHUNG-HUA LIU HSING PING HSUEH TSA CHIH.). [Zhonghua liuxingbing zazhi]. **Added/Corp** Chung-Hua i Hsueh Hui (China : 1949- ) Chung-Kuo i Hsueh k'o Hsueh Yuan. Liu Hsing Ping Hsueh Wei Sheng wu Hsueh Yen Chiu So. **VFOAT** Zhonghua Liuxingbingxue Zazhi; Chinese Journal of Epidemiology. (1981)-. Chinese (table of contents in English). qt. $20.34. **(Subscription address:** China International Book Trading Corporation, PO Box 399, Library Service Department, Beijing 100044 People's Republic of China.) **NLM** W1 CH982KJ. **CODEN** ZLZAD6. Documents available from BIOSIS Document Express. ***Continues*** *Liu Hsing Ping Hsueh Tsa Chih, 0255-6707.*
**Ind/Abst** Biol. Abstr.; Index Med. (1982-); Poult. Abstr.; Protozoolog. Abstr.

## DERMATOLOGY

US/0884-1489
**ABMS DIRECTORY OF CERTIFIED DERMATOLOGISTS.** ***Title Change.*** [ABMS dir. certif. dermatol.]. **Added/Corp** American Board of Medical Specialties. American Board of Dermatology. **VFOAT** Directory of Certified Dermatologists. **VAT** American Board of Medical Specialties Directory of Certified Dermatologists. 1st Ed. (1984)-(19??). Directory. English. be. American Board of Medical Specialties, 1 Rotary Center, Suite 805, Evanston IL 60201. **Tel** (708)491-9091. **LC** RL43; .A27. **DD** 616.5/0025/73. **NLM** WR 22.1; A1523. **Bk Rev. Ad Acc. Circ:** 600 (ctrl). ***Continued by*** *Official American Board of Medical Specialties (ABMS) Directory of Board Certified Dermatologists, 0000-1422.*
**Desc:** Biographical listing of certified medical specialists.

FR/0763-7454
**ABSTRACT DERMATO PARIS.** [Abstr. derm. Paris]. (1985)-. Periodical. French. wk. 269.34F France; 475.00F other. Abstract, 25 Bis Av Pierre Grenier, 92100 Boulogne Billanct France. **Tel** 011 33 1 49100606. **UDC** 616.5.

SW/0001-5555
**ACTA DERMATO-VENEREOLOGICA.** [Acta derm. venereol.]. Vol. 1 (1920)-. Academic Scholarly Publication. English (French and German). bm. Kr1065.00, $172.00. Scandinavian University Press, PO Box 2959 Toeyen, N 0608 Oslo 6 Norway. **Tel** 011 47 2 2575400, FAX 011 47 2 2575353, telex 71896 UROR N. **(Subscription address:** Scandinavian University Press, 200 Meacham Ave., Elmont NY 11003.) **ED** Lennart Juhlin. **NLM** W1 AC7921. **CODEN** ADVEA4. **Ad Acc. Pr Rev. Circ:** 1,500. available in microform. Documents available from The Genuine Article, BIOSIS Document Express, CASDDS.
**Desc:** A journal for clinical and experimental research. Publishes full-length manuscripts and short case reports in English. Dissertations, proceedings and extensive papers published as supplements. Advertisements announcing pertinent meetings and books are included.
**Ind/Abst** Biol. Abstr.; Chem. Abstr.; CSA Neuro. Abstr. (?-?); Curr. Aware. Biol. Sci., CABS; Curr. Contents Clin. Med.; Curr. Contents Life Sci.; Dairy Sci. Abstr.; EMBASE; Health Plan. Adminis.; Immunol. Abstr.; Index Med.; Microbiol. Abstr. Sect. B (19??-19??); Microbiol. Abstr. Sect. C; Nutr. Abstr. Rev., Ser. B, Live Feeds and Feed.; Nutr. Abstr. Rev., Ser. A, Hum. Exp.; Life Sci. Collect.; PESTDOC; Protozoolog. Abstr.; Ref. Upd. Deluxe Ed.; Res. Alert [Full Cov.]; Rev. Med. Vet. Entomol.; Rev. Med. Vet. Mycology; Rev. Plant Pathol.; Saf. Health Work; Sci. Cit. Index; SCISEARCH; Trop. Dis. Bull. (19??-19??).

FI/0365-8341
**ACTA DERMATO-VENEREOLOGICA. SUPPLEMENTUM.** [Acta derm.-venereol., Suppl.]. Vol. 1 (1929)-. Academic Scholarly Publication. English (German). Six times a year. Kr965.00 Scandinavia, Norway, Sweden, Finland, Denmark, Iceland, & Greenland; Kr1015.00 others Comes with Acta Dermato Venereologica. Scandinavian University Press, PO Box 2959 Toeyen, N 0608 Oslo 6 Norway. **Tel** 011 47 2 2575400, FAX 011 47 2 2575353, telex 71896 UROR N. **(Subscription address:** Scandinavian University Press, 200 Meacham Ave., Elmont NY 11003.) **NLM** W1 AC7922. **CODEN** AVSUAR. Index available (bound in last issue). Documents available from BIOSIS Document Express, CASDDS.
**Ind/Abst** Biol. Abstr.; Chem. Abstr.; Curr. Aware. Biol. Sci., CABS; EMBASE; Index Med.; Life Sci. Collect.

JA/0065-1176
**ACTA DERMATOLOGICA.** (HIFUKA KIYO. ACTA DERMATOLOGICA.). [Acta dermatol.]. **VFOAT** Acta Dermatologica, Dermatologia, Syphildologia et Urologia. Vol. 1 (1923)-. Academic Scholarly Publication. Japanese (English and German). qt. $74.00. Hifuka Kiyo Henshubu, (Editorial Office of Acta Dermatologica), c/o Kyoto Daigaku Igakubu, Hifuka Kyoshitsu, 54 Kawaracho,, Shogoin, Sakyoku, Kyotoshi, Kyotofu 606 Japan. **(Subscription address:** Maruzen Company Ltd., PO Box 5050, Import & Export Department, Tokyo 100 31 Japan.) **NLM** W1 HI198.
**Desc:** Each volume includes abstracts of papers presented at various Japanese Dermatological Society meetings.
**Ind/Abst** EMBASE [Select. Cov.].

SP/0001-7310
**ACTAS DERMO-SIFILOGRAFICAS.** [Actas dermo-sifiliogr.]. **Added/Corp** Academia Espanola de Dermatologia y Sifilografia. Vol. 1 (May/June 1909)-. Academic Scholarly Publication. Spanish. Twelve times a year. $123.00 Eurorpe; $134.00 Spain & others. Editorial Garsi SA, Juan Bravo 46, 28006 Madrid, Spain. **Tel** 011 34 1 4021212, telex 98358 GARSI E. **NLM** W1 AC96.
**Ind/Abst** EMBASE; Indice Med. Esp.; Life Sci. Collect.

SP/0210-279X
**ACTUALIDAD DERMATOLOGICA.** [Actual. dermatol.]. (1962)-. Periodical. Spanish. mo. Publicidad Medica Esmon, Corcega 38, 08029 Barcelona Spain. **UDC** 616.5.

US/0882-0880
**ADVANCES IN DERMATOLOGY.** [Adv. dermatol.]. Vol. 1 (1986)-. English. an. $59.95 (latest volume). Mosby Year Book Inc., 11830 Westline Industrial Drive, St Louis MO 63146. **Tel** (800)325-4177, (314)872-8370, FAX (314)432-1380, telex 44-2402. **DD** 616. **NLM** W1; AD546L. **CODEN** ADDEEK. **[CCC]. *Continues*** *Current Issues in Dermatology, 0738-7865.*
**Ind/Abst** Health Plan. Adminis.; Index Med. (1986-).

GW/0340-2541
**AKTUELLE DERMATOLOGIE.** [Aktuel. Dermatol.]. Vol. 1, (Feb. 1975)-. Periodical. German (summaries and/or abstracts in English). Twelve times a year. $182.00. Georg Thieme Verlag Stuttgart, Postfach 301120, D 70451 Stuttgart Germany. **Tel** 011 49 711 89310, FAX 011 49 711 8931298, telex 7 252 275 GTVD. **(Subscription address:** Thieme Medical Publishers Inc., 381 Park Avenue South, New York NY 10016.) **NLM** W1 AK991P. **[CCC].** available on microfilm from University Microfilms International (UMI).
**Ind/Abst** EMBASE.

US/1046-199X
**AMERICAN JOURNAL OF CONTACT DERMATITIS.** [Am. j. contact dermat.]. (March 1990)-. Periodical. English. qt (4 issues). $115.00 (individuals), $147.00 (institution) US; $159.00 (individuals), $169.00 (institutions) other. W.B. Saunders Company, A Subsidiary of Harcourt Brace Jovanovich, Inc., The Curtis Center/Suite 300, Independence Square West, Philadelphia PA 19106-3399. **Tel** (215)238-7800 or, 5587, FAX (215)238-7883, telex 173146. **(Subscription address:** W. B. Saunders Company / North America Subscriptions, c/o Periodicals, 6277 Sea Harbour Drive, 4th Floor, Orlando FL 32887.) **DD** 616. **NLM** W1; AM45LH. **[CCC].**

US/0193-1091
**AMERICAN JOURNAL OF DERMATOPATHOLOGY, THE.** [Am. j. dermatopathol.]. Vol. 1 (Spring 1979)-. Academic Scholarly Publication. English. bm. $155.00 (individuals), $235.00 (institutions) US; $194.00 (individuals), $286.00 (institutions) other. Raven Press, 1185 Avenue of the Americas, 37th Floor, New York NY 10036. **Tel** (212)930-9500, (212)930-9604, FAX (212)869-3495, (212)302-8507, telex 640073. **ED** Clifton R. White, Jr. **LC** RL95; .A47. **DD** 616.5/005. **NLM** W1 AM45NH. **CODEN** AJODDB. **[CCC]. Pr Rev.** available on microfilm and microfiche from University Microfilms International (UMI). Documents available from The Genuine Article, BIOSIS Document Express, CASDDS.
**Desc:** Selected articles survey today's rapid progress in studying skin diseases - using gross examinations, conventional microscopy, electron microscopy, histochemistry, immunopathology, and various emerging techniques. The guidelines presented enable pathologists and technicians to utilize new technologies and discoveries.
**Ind/Abst** Biol. Abstr.; Chem. Abstr. (1979-1982); Curr. Contents Clin. Med.; EMBASE; Health Plan. Adminis.; Immunol. Abstr.; Index Med. (Spring 1979-); Index Vet.; Life Sci. Collect.; Res. Alert [Full Cov.]; Rev. Med. Vet. Mycology; Sci. Cit. Index; SCISEARCH; Soc. Sci. Cit. Index [Select. Cov.].

BL/0365-0596
**ANAIS BRASILEIROS DE DERMATOLOGIA.** [An. bras. dermatol.]. (1961)-. Academic Scholarly Publication. Portuguese (summaries and/or abstracts in English and French). bm (Feb., Apr., June, Aug., Oct., Dec.). $80.00. ECN-Editora Cientifica Nacional Ltda., Caixa Postal 590, 20001-Rio de Janeiro RJ Brazil. **Tel** 011 55 21 2622825, 011 55 21 2213235, FAX 011 55 21 2521691. **ED** Ruben David Azulay. **NLM** W1 AN106. Index available. **Bk Rev. Ad Acc. Circ:** 3,000 (ctrl). ***Continues*** *Anais Brasileiros de Dermatologia e Sifilografia.*
**Desc:** Medical journal covering diseases of the skin.
**Ind/Abst** EMBASE; Helminthol. Abstr. (1991-); Nutr. Abstr. Rev., Ser. A, Hum. Exp.; Protozoolog. Abstr.; Rev. Med. Vet. Entomol.; Rev. Med. Vet. Mycology; Soils Fert.; Trop. Dis. Bull.

FR/0151-9638
**ANNALES DE DERMATOLOGIE ET DE VENEREOLOGIE.** [Ann. dermatol. venereol.]. **Added/Corp** Societe Francaise de Dermatologie et de Syphiligraphie. Association des Dermatologistes et Syphiligraphes de Langue Francaise. Vol. 104 (Jan. 1977)-. Periodical. French. Eleven times a year. $280.00. Masson Editeur, Box Postale 22, 41353 Vineuil 16 France. **Tel** 011 33 54 438994. **(Subscription address:** 7A Boulevard de Perolles, CH-1701 Fribourg Switzerland) **NLM** W1 AN334B. **CODEN** ADVED7. **[CCC]. Pr Rev.** available on microfilm and microfiche from University Microfilms International (UMI). Documents available from The Genuine Article, BIOSIS Document Express. ***Continues*** *Annales de Dermatologie et de Syphiligraphie, 0003-3979.*
**Ind/Abst** Biol. Abstr.; Chem. Hazards Ind.; Curr. Contents Clin. Med.; EMBASE; Helminthol. Abstr.; Index Med.; Index Vet.; Lab. Hazards Bull.; Life Sci. Collect.; Pig News Inf.; Protozoolog. Abstr.; Res. Alert [Full Cov.]; Rev. Med. Vet. Entomol.; Rev. Med. Vet. Mycology; Rev. Plant Pathol.; Saf. Health Work; Sci. Cit. Index; SCISEARCH.

IT/0365-169X
**ANNALI ITALIANI DI DERMATOLOGIA CLINICA E SPERIMENTALE.** [Ann. Ital. Dermatol. Clin. Sper.]. (1961)-. Periodical. Italian. Four times a year. L140000 (institutions), L80000 (individuals). Il Pensiero Scientifico Editore s.r.l., Via Bradano 3C, 00199 Rome Italy. **Tel** 011 39 6 86207158, 86207159, 86207168, 86207169, FAX 011 39 6 86207160. **ED** Paolo Lisi. **CODEN** ADRCACADRCAC. Index available in last issue of volume--attached. Full Page (B&W) L1.650.000. Documents available from FAXON Xpress. ***Continues*** *Annali Italiani di Dermatologia e Sifilologia, 0003-4703.*
**Desc:** Aimed at dermatologists, allergists, and immunologists.
**Ind/Abst** EMBASE.

KO/1013-9087
**ANNALS OF DERMATOLOGY.** [Ann. dermatol.]. **Added/Corp** Taehan Pibukwa Hakhoe. Vol. 1, No. 1 (Jan. 1989)-. Periodical. English. Twice a year. Free. Korean Dermatological Association, 40 Isindonga Jonghap-Sangka 491, Seoul 137-070 Korea. **Tel** 011 82 2 5670284. **NLM** W1; AN573L. **CODEN** ANDEEM. Documents available from BIOSIS Document Express.
**Ind/Abst** Biol. Abstr. (1991-); EMBASE; Rev. Med. Vet. Mycology.

US/8756-2243
**ANNUAL REPORT - NATIONAL PSORIASIS FOUNDATION (U.S.).** (ANNUAL REPORT / NATIONAL PSORIASIS FOUNDATION.). [Annu. rep. - Natl. Psoriasis Found. (U. S.)]. **Main/Corp** National Psoriasis Foundation (U.S.). (19??)-. English. an. National Psoriasis Foundation, 6443 SW Bvrtn Highway 210, Portland OR 97221-1164. **LC** RL321; .N37a. **DD** 616.5/26/005.

SP/0210-1300
**ANTOLOGIA DERMATOLOGICA.** [Antol. dermatol.]. (1971)-. Periodical. Spanish. mo. Editorial Garsi SA, Juan Bravo 46, 28006 Madrid, Spain. **Tel** 011 34 1 4021212, telex 98358 GARSI E. **UDC** 616.5.

GW/0340-3696
**ARCHIVES OF DERMATOLOGICAL RESEARCH.** (ARCHIVES OF DERMATOLOGICAL RESEARCH. ARCHIV FUER DERMATOLOGISCHE FORSCHUNG.). [Arch. dermatol. res.]. **VFOAT** Archiv fur Dermatologische Forschung. Vol. 261, No. 1 (1978)-. Academic Scholarly Publication. English (German). Eight times a year. DM1058.00. Springer-Verlag GmbH & Company KG, Heidelberger Platz 3, D 14197 Berlin Germany. **Tel** 011 49 30 8207223, FAX 011 49 30 8214091, telex 183 319 SPBLN D. **(Subscription address:** Springer Verlag New York Inc. / for North America, 44 Hartz Way, Secaucus NJ 07096.) **ED** E Christophers. **NLM** W1 AR452K. **CODEN** ADREDL. **[CCC].** available on microfilm from University Microfilms International (UMI). Documents available from The Genuine Article, BIOSIS Document Express, CASDDS. ***Continues*** *Archives for Dermatological Research.*
**Desc:** Publishes original contributions in the field of experimental dermatology, including papers on biochemistry, morphology, and immunology of the skin.
**Ind/Abst** Biol. Abstr.; Chem. Abstr.; Curr. Contents Life Sci.; Dairy Sci. Abstr.; EMBASE; Energy Res. Abstr. (May 1978-); Index Med.; Index Vet.; Nutr. Abstr. Rev., Ser. B, Live Feeds and Feed.; Nutr. Abstr. Rev., Ser. A, Hum. Exp.; Nutr. Res. Newsl.; Oncog. Growth Factors Abstr.;

Life Sci. Collect.; PESTDOC; Protozoolog. Abstr.; Res. Alert [Full Cov.]; Rev. Med. Vet. Mycology; Rev. Plant Pathol.; Sci. Cit. Index; SCISEARCH.

US/0003-987X
**ARCHIVES OF DERMATOLOGY.** [Arch. dermatol.]. **Added/Corp** American Medical Association. Vol. 82 (July 1960)-. Academic Scholarly Publication. English. mo. $150.00 (institution), $135.00 (individual) US. American Medical Association, 515 North State Street, Chicago IL 60610. **Tel** (312)464-5000, (800)262-2350, FAX (312)464-5831. **ED** Kenneth A. Arndt. **NLM** W1 AR452N. **CODEN** ARDEAC. **[CCC].** Index available. **Bk Rev. Ad Acc. Pr Rev. Circ:** 19,000. available on microfilm and microfiche from University Microfilms International (UMI); available on an online database (file 442/Full-Text) from DIALOG. Documents available from The Genuine Article, BIOSIS Document Express, CASDDS. ***Continues*** *A.M.A. Archives of Dermatology, 0096-5359.*
**Desc:** Published as an educational service to physicians who practice dermatology as a primary specialty, and to physicians of other specialties who treat conditions of the skin. It is oriented toward the clinician. Every issue offers new concepts and methods applicable to everyday practice.
**Ind/Abst** Abr. Index Med.; Biol. Abstr.; Chem. Abstr.; Chicano Index; Curr. Aware. Biol. Sci., CABS; Curr. Contents Clin. Med.; Curr. Contents Life Sci.; EMBASE; Energy Res. Abstr.; Health Plan. Adminis.; Helminthol. Abstr.; Immunol. Abstr.; Index Med.; Index Vet.; INIS Atomindex [Micro.]; Int. Pharm. Abstr.; Iowa Drug Inf. Serv.; Med. Abstr. Newsl.; Microbiol. Abstr. Sect. B; Microbiol. Abstr. Sect. C; Mod. Med.; Nutr. Abstr. Rev., Ser. A, Hum. Exp.; Nutr. Res. Newsl.; Oncog. Growth Factors Abstr.; Life Sci. Collect.; PESTDOC; Physic. Medline Plus; Poult. Abstr.; Protozoolog. Abstr.; Ref. Upd. Basic Ed.; Ref. Upd. Deluxe Ed.; Res. Alert [Full Cov.]; Rev. Med. Vet. Entomol.; Rev. Med. Vet. Mycology; Saf. Health Work; Sci. Cit. Index; SCISEARCH; Soc. Sci. Cit. Index [Select. Cov.]; Vet. Bull.; Trop. Dis. Bull.; Virol. AIDS Abstr.

AG/0066-6750
**ARCHIVOS ARGENTINOS DE DERMATOLOGIA.** [Arch. argent. dermatol.]. (1951)-. Academic Scholarly Publication. Spanish. bm. $140.00. Archivos Argentinos de Dermatologia, Paraguay 13074038, 1057 Buenos Aires Argentina. **Tel** 011 54 1 424698. **NLM** W1 AR6394.
**Ind/Abst** EMBASE; Rev. Med. Vet. Entomol.; Rev. Med. Vet. Mycology.

AT/0004-8380
**AUSTRALASIAN JOURNAL OF DERMATOLOGY, THE.** [Australas. j. dermatol.]. **Added/Corp** Australasian College of Dermatologists. Dermatological Association of Australia. Vol. 9 (1967)-. Periodical. English. Three times a year. 50.00Aus$. The Australasian College of Dermatologists, PO Box B65, Boronia Park 2111 Australia. **Tel** 011 61 2 8796177. **ED** David Nurse. **NLM** W1 AU248. **CODEN** AJDEBP. **Bk Rev. Ad Acc.** ctrl circ. Documents available from BIOSIS Document Express. ***Continues*** *Australian Journal of Dermatology.*
**Desc:** Original articles, case reports, and research reports in dermatology.
**Ind/Abst** Biol. Abstr.; EMBASE; Health Plan. Adminis.; Index Med.; Index Vet.; Mod. Med.; Nutr. Abstr. Rev., Ser. A, Hum. Exp.; Life Sci. Collect.; Protozoolog. Abstr.; Rev. Med. Vet. Mycology; Rev. Plant Pathol.

GW/0171-0184
**BEITRAGE ZUR DERMATOLOGIE.** v. 1-. Monographic series. German. Price varies per volume. Verlag Mr Med D Straube, W-8520 Erlangen Germany. **UDC** 616.5. **NLM** W1 BE221.

VE/0798-4618
**BOLETIN DERMATOLOGIA SANITARIO.** [Bol. dermatol. sanit.]. **Added/Corp** Venezuela. Direccion de Salud Publica. Departamento de Dermatologia Sanitaria. (1976)-. Periodical. Spanish. an. **DD** 616.500987. ***Continues*** *Boletin Leprologico.*
**Ind/Abst** Trop. Dis. Bull.

HU/0006-7768
**BORGYOGYASZATI ES VENEROLOGIAI SZEMLE.** [Borgyogyasz. venerol. szle.]. **Added/Corp** Magyar Dermatologiai Tarsulat. Orszagos Antivenereas Bizottsag. (1947)-. Academic Scholarly Publication. Hungarian. bm. $34.00 Austria, Crotia, Ukraine, Czech & Slovak Republics, Romaina, Yugoslavia, & Slovenia; $38.00 other. **(Subscription address:** Kultura, PO Box 149, H 1389 Budapest 62 Hungary (011 36 1 359370)) **NLM** W1 BO119.
**Ind/Abst** EMBASE; Nutr. Abstr. Rev., Ser. A, Hum. Exp.

UK/0007-0963
**BRITISH JOURNAL OF DERMATOLOGY (1951).** (BRITISH JOURNAL OF DERMATOLOGY.). [Br. j. dermatol.]. **Added/Corp** British Association of Dermatologists. Nederlandse Vereniging voor Dermatologie en Venereologie. Nederlandse Vereniging van Dermatologen. Vol. 63 (1951)-. Academic Scholarly Publication. English. mo (12 issues). $403.00 US & Canada; £237.50 Europe; £260.00 other. Blackwell Scientific Publications Ltd, Marston Book Services, PO Box 87, Oxford OX2 ODT UK. **Tel** 011 44 865 791155, FAX 011 44 865 791927, telex 837 515 MARDIS G. **ED** R. M. Mackie. **NLM** W1 BR526. **CODEN** BJDEAZ. **[CCC]. Bk Rev. Ad Acc. Pr Rev. Circ:** 4,100. available on microfilm and microfiche from University Microfilms International (UMI). Documents available from The Genuine Article, BIOSIS Document Express, CASDDS, ADONIS. ***Continues*** *British Journal of Dermatology and Syphilis, 0366-2845.*
**Desc:** Publishes original articles on all aspects of the biology and pathology of the skin. Attracts contributions from all countries in which research is carried out.
**Ind/Abst** ADONIS; Biol. Abstr.; Chem. Abstr.; Curr. Aware. Biol. Sci., CABS; Dairy Sci. Abstr.; EMBASE; Health Plan. Adminis.; Helminthol. Abstr. (19??-19??); Index Med.; Index Vet.; Int. Pharm. Abstr.; Iowa Drug Inf. Serv. (1969-); Mod. Med.; Nutr. Abstr. Rev., Ser. B, Live Feeds and Feed.; Nutr. Abstr. Rev., Ser. A, Hum. Exp.; Nutr. Res. Newsl.; Life Sci. Collect.; PESTDOC; Protozoolog. Abstr.; Ref. Upd. Basic Ed.; Ref. Upd. Deluxe Ed.; Res. Alert [Full Cov.]; Rev. Med. Vet. Entomol.; Rev. Med. Vet. Mycology; Rev. Plant Pathol.; Saf. Health Work; Sci. Cit. Index; SCISEARCH; Virol. AIDS Abstr.

UK/0366-077X
**BRITISH JOURNAL OF DERMATOLOGY. SUPPLEMENT.** [Br. j. dermatol. Suppl.]. **Added/Corp** British Association of Dermatologists. (1969)-. Academic Scholarly Publication. English. Included with subscription to British Journal of Dermatology. Blackwell Scientific Publications Ltd, Marston Book Services, PO Box 87, Oxford OX2 ODT UK. **Tel** 011 44 865 791155, FAX 011 44 865 791927, telex 837 515 MARDIS G. **CODEN** BJDSA9. **[CCC].** Documents available from BIOSIS Document Express, CASDDS.
**Ind/Abst** Biol. Abstr.; Chem. Abstr.; Curr. Aware. Biol. Sci., CABS; EMBASE; Life Sci. Collect.

CN/0843-4247
**CANADIAN JOURNAL OF DERMATOLOGY, THE.** [Can. j. dermatol.]. Vol. 1, No. 1 (Feb./Mar. 1989)-. Periodical. English. Five times a year. 60.00Can$. Contemporary Journals, 19180 Trans Canada, Boie d'Urfe Quebec H9X 3T9 Canada. **Tel** (514)457-2673. **DD** 616.5/005. **NLM** W1; CA586I. available on microfilm and microfiche from Micromedia Limited. ***Continues*** *Contemporary Dermatology, 0836-1207.*
**Ind/Abst** Can. Index.

XR/0009-0514
**CESKOSLOVENSKA DERMATOLOGIE.** [Cesk. dermatol.]. Vol. 22, No. 2- 1946-. Academic Scholarly Publication. Czech (summaries and/or abstracts in Russian, English and French). bm. $56.10. **(Subscription address:** Artia Pegas Press Ltd., Palac Metro Narodni Trida 25, 11210 Prague 1 Czech Republic.) **UDC** 616.5. **NLM** W1 CE879. **CODEN** CEDEAB. **[CCC].** Documents available from BIOSIS Document Express, CASDDS. ***Continues*** *Ceska Dermatologie.*
**Ind/Abst** Biol. Abstr.; Chem. Abstr. (1948-1983); EMBASE; Helminthol. Abstr.; Index Med.; Life Sci. Collect.; Protozoolog. Abstr.; Saf. Health Work.

IT/0390-5411
**CHRONICA DERMATOLOGICA.** [Chron. dermatol.]. **Added/Corp** Istituto Dermopatico dell'Immacolata, Rome. Associazione Dermatologi Ospedalieri Italiani. Vol. 1 (1970)-. Periodical. Italian (English; summaries and/or abstracts in English and French). bm (6 issues). Free on request. Chronica Dermatologica, Via Monti di Creta 104, 00167 Rome Italy. **Tel** 011 39 6 9126212. **NLM** W1 CH961. ***Supersedes*** *Cronache dell'IDI.*
**Ind/Abst** EMBASE [Select. Cov.].

CC/0412-4030
**CHUNG-HUA PI FU KO TSA CHIH.** **VFOAT** Chinese Journal of Dermatology. (1953)-. Periodical. Chinese (English; summaries and/or abstracts in English; table of contents in English). bm (6 issues). $64.62. **(Subscription address:** China International Book Trading Corporation, PO Box 399, Library Service Department, Beijing 100044 People's Republic of China.) **DD** 616.5. **Bk Rev. Ad Acc.**
**Desc:** The official organ of the Society of Dermatology, Chinese Medical Association.
**Ind/Abst** Trop. Dis. Bull.

UK/0307-6938
**CLINICAL AND EXPERIMENTAL DERMATOLOGY.** [Clin. exp. dermatol.]. **Added/Corp** St. John's Hospital Dermatological Society. Vol. 1 (March 1976)-. Academic Scholarly Publication. English. bm (6 issues). $363.00 US & Canada; £212.00 Europe; £234.00 other. Blackwell Scientific Publications Ltd, Marston Book Services, PO Box 87, Oxford OX2 ODT UK. **Tel** 011 44 865 791155, FAX 011 44 865 791927, telex 837 515 MARDIS G. **ED** W. Griffiths. **NLM** W1 CL656. **CODEN** CEDEDE. **[CCC]. Bk Rev. Ad Acc. Pr Rev. Circ:** 1,500. available on microfilm and microfiche from University Microfilms International (UMI). Documents available from The Genuine Article, BIOSIS Document Express, CASDDS, ADONIS. ***Supersedes*** *Transactions of the St. John's Hospital Dermatological Society, 0036-2891.*
**Desc:** Articles of interest to practicing dermatologists. Articles on the history of dermatology, controversies and unusual observations.
**Ind/Abst** ADONIS; Biol. Abstr.; Chem. Abstr.; Curr. Contents Clin. Med.; EMBASE; Health Plan. Adminis.; Index Med.; Microbiol. Abstr. Sect. C; Nutr. Abstr. Rev., Ser. B, Live Feeds and Feed.; Nutr. Abstr. Rev., Ser. A, Hum. Exp.; Nutr. Res. Newsl.; Life Sci. Collect.; PESTDOC; Protozoolog. Abstr.; Res. Alert [Full Cov.]; Rev. Med. Vet. Mycology; Rev. Plant Pathol.; Sci. Cit. Index; SCISEARCH; Trop. Dis. Bull.; Virol. AIDS Abstr.

US/1053-9697
**CLINICAL DERMATOLOGY.** [Clin. dermatol.]. (1989)-. Monographic series. English. ir. Price varies per volume. Marcel Dekker Inc., 270 Madison Avenue, New York NY 10016. **Tel** (212)696-9000, (800)228-1160, FAX (212)685-4540, telex 421419. **(Subscription address:** Marcel Dekker Inc, PO Box 5017, Monticello NY 12701.) **DD** 616. **NLM** W1; CL69L. **CODEN** CLDSE4.
**Desc:** Series covering topics such as dermatitis, cutaneous antifungal agents, and retinoids.

US/1043-2604
**CLINICAL DIGEST SERIES. DERMATOLOGY.** [Derm. clin. dig. ser.]. **VFOAT** Dermatology Clinical Digest Series. Vol. 1, No. 5 (May 1989)-. Periodical. English. mo. Bugamor Pharma, Inc., 36 West 44th Street Suite 1412, New York NY 10036. **DD** 616.

US/0738-081X
**CLINICS IN DERMATOLOGY.** [Clin. dermatol.]. Vol. 1, No. 1 (July/Sept. 1983)-. Academic Scholarly Publication. English. Six times a year (1 volume). $250.00 US; $290.00 other. Elsevier Science Publishing Company Inc, Madison Square Station, PO Box 882, New York NY 10159-0882. **Tel** (212)633-3950, FAX (212)633-3990. **ED** Lawrence C Parish. **LC** IN PROCESS. **DD** 616. **NLM** W1; CL831AL. **[CCC]. Pr Rev. Circ:** 825. available on microfilm and microfiche from University Microfilms International (UMI). Documents available from The Genuine Article.
**Desc:** Features practical, clinically-oriented information. Each issue focuses on a specific topic in dermatology and related specialties.
**Ind/Abst** Curr. Aware. Biol. Sci., CABS; Curr. Contents Clin. Med.; EMBASE; Health Plan. Adminis.; Index Med.; Nutr. Abstr. Rev., Ser. A, Hum. Exp.; Res. Alert [Select. Cov.]; SCISEARCH; Soc. Sci. Cit. Index [Select. Cov.].

DK/0105-1873
**CONTACT DERMATITIS.** [Contact dermatitis]. (1975)-. Academic Scholarly Publication. English. mo (monthly except June and Dec.). kr1710.00 US, Canada and Japan; kr1670.00 other. Munksgaard International Publishers Ltd, PO Box 2148, DK-1016 Copenhagen K Denmark. **Tel** 011 45 33 12 70 30, FAX 011 45 33 12 93 87, telex 19431 MUNKS DK. **ED** R J G Rycroft. **UDC** 616.5-002. **NLM** W1 CO768CH. **CODEN** CODEDG. **[CCC].** Index available. **Bk Rev. Ad Acc. Pr Rev. Circ:** 1,500 (ctrl). Documents available from The Genuine Article, BIOSIS Document Express, CASDDS.
**Desc:** Covers environmental and occupational dermatitis: allergy, clinical immunology and chemistry.
**Ind/Abst** Agrofor. Abstr. (1991-); Art Archaeol. Tech. Abstr.; BioBusiness; Biol. Abstr.; Chem. Abstr.; Chem. Hazards Ind.; Curr. Contents Clin. Med.; EMBASE; For. Prod. Abstr. (1991-); For. Abstr.; Hortic. Abstr.; Index Med.; Index Vet.; Ind. Hyg. Dig.; Lab. Hazards Bull.; Med. Abstr. Newsl.; Ornamental Hort. (1991-); Life Sci. Collect.; Res. Alert [Full Cov.]; Rev. Agric. Entomol.; Rev. Med. Vet. Entomol.; Rev. Med. Vet. Mycology; Rev. Plant Pathol.; Sci. Cit. Index; SCISEARCH; Vet. Bull.; Trop. Dis. Bull.; Weed Abstr.

NE/0167-5796
**CORE JOURNALS IN DERMATOLOGY.** **Added/Corp** Excerpta Medica (Firm). Vol. 1 (1982)-. Periodical. English. Eleven times a year (1 volume). Fl549.00. Excerpta Medica Publishing Group, PO Box 548, 1000 AM Amsterdam Netherlands. **Tel** 011 31 20 5803243. **(Subscription address:** Excerpta Medica Journals, PO Box 85, Limerick Ireland.) **NLM** ZWR 100; C793. **[CCC].** available on microfilm from University Microfilms International (UMI).

US/0199-8757
**CURRENT CONCEPTS IN SKIN DISORDERS.** [Curr. concepts skin disord.]. **Added/Corp** Continuing Professional Education (Firm). **VFOAT** Skin Disorders. Vol. 1, No. 1 (Spring 1980)-. Periodical. English. Three times a year. $39.00 US; $45.54 other. Macmillan Professional Journal, 30 Vreeland Road, Florham Park NJ 07932. **Tel** (201)822-1622, FAX (201)822-2498. **NLM** W1 CU788AZ.

●US/1068-381X
**CURRENT OPINION IN DERMATOLOGY.** [Curr. opin. dermatol.]. 1st Edition (1993)-. English. an. $99.95 (individuals); $215.95 (institutions). Current Science, 20 North 3rd Street, Philadelphia PA 19106. **Tel** (215)574-2266, (800)552-5866, FAX (215)574-2270. **DD** 616.

SZ/0070-2064
**CURRENT PROBLEMS IN DERMATOLOGY.** [Curr. probl. dermatol.]. Vol. 2 (1968)-. Monographic series. English. an. 220.00F (approx. per volume). S. Karger AG, Allschwilerstrasse 10, PO Box - Postfach - Case Postale, CH-4009 Basel Switzerland. **Tel** 011 41 61 306-1111, FAX 011 41 61 306-1234, telex CH 962 652. **ED** G. Burg. **LC** UNC. **NLM** W1 CU804L. **CODEN** APDEBX. **[CCC].** Documents available from BIOSIS Document Express, CASDDS. ***Continues*** *Aktuelle Probleme der Dermatologie.*
**Desc:** This series provides a selection of new thoughts and methods of investigation of value to the practicing dermatologist and the research worker. Editing uncovers 'the right topics and the right authors' and has produced well-referenced and timely expositions. Topics range from normal and pathological conditions of skin, hair, and nails to the progress achieved through development of new equipment and analytical techniques.
**Ind/Abst** Biol. Abstr.; Chem. Abstr. (1959-1984); Health Plan. Adminis.; Index Med.; Ref. Upd. Deluxe Ed.

US/1040-0486
**CURRENT PROBLEMS IN DERMATOLOGY (CHICAGO, ILL.).** (CURRENT PROBLEMS IN DERMATOLOGY.). [Curr. probl. dermatol.]. Vol. 1, No. 1 (Jan./Feb. 1989)-. Periodical. English. bm. $95.00 (institutions), $68.00 (individuals) US; $101.00 (institutions), $74.00 (individuals) other. Mosby Year Book Inc., 11830 Westline Industrial Drive, St Louis MO 63146. **Tel** (800)325-4177, (314)872-8370, FAX (314)432-1380, telex 44-2402. **ED** William L. Weston. **DD** 616. **NLM** W1; CU804LD. **[CCC]. Ad Acc.**
**Desc:** Geared to the needs of dermatologists in daily clinical practice. Each issue focuses on a single disease or disorder and explains etiology and presentation (pediatric, adult, and geriatric considerations), diagnosis, treatment (including medical and surgical approaches), and prognosis.

US/0011-4162
**CUTIS (NEW YORK, N.Y.).** (CUTIS.). [Cutis]. Vol. 1 (Feb. 1965)-. Academic Scholarly Publication. English. mo. $115.00 (institutions), $85.00 (physicians). Excerpta Medica / US, PO Box 3085, Princeton NJ 08543-3085. **Tel** (908)874-8550, FAX (908)874-5611. **(Subscription address:** Cutis, PO Box 3095, Denville NJ 07834.) **ED** Sharon Finch. **LC** RL1; .C8. **DD** 616.5/005. **NLM** W1 CU97. **CODEN** CUTIB. **Pr Rev.** available on microfilm and microfiche from University Microfilms International (UMI). Documents available from The Genuine Article, BIOSIS Document Express.
**Desc:** Resource for any physician whose practice is devoted to the diagnosis and treatment of conditions related to dermatology and allergy. Covers subjects of clinical significance including sexually transmitted diseases, psoriasis, contact dermatology, disease of the nails, fungal diseases, environmentally induced dermatoses, allergy and immunology.
**Ind/Abst** Biol. Abstr.; EMBASE; Energy Res. Abstr.; For. Prod. Abstr.; Index Med.; INIS Atomindex [Micro.]; Med. Abstr. Newsl.; Mod. Med.; Nutr. Abstr. Rev., Ser. B, Live Feeds and Feed.; Nutr. Abstr. Rev., Ser. A, Hum. Exp.; Nutr. Res. Newsl.; Life Sci. Collect.; Protozoolog. Abstr.; Res. Alert [Full Cov.]; Rev. Med. Vet. Entomol.; Rev. Med. Vet. Mycology; Sci. Cit. Index; SCISEARCH; Soc. Sci. Cit. Index [Select. Cov.]; Weed Abstr.

MX/0185-4038
**DERMATOLOGIA.** [Dermatologia]. (1956)-. Periodical. Spanish (summaries and/or abstracts in English). tq. Obsidiana SA de CV, Calz de Tlalpan 2365, Col. Ciudad Jardin, 04370 Mexico DF. **Tel** 011 52 5 689 91 33, FAX 011 52 5 689 59 17. **DD** 611.5.
**Ind/Abst** EMBASE.

IT/0392-1395
**DERMATOLOGIA CLINICA.** [Dermatol. clin.]. Vol. 1, No. 1 (Jan./March 1981)-. Periodical. Italian (summaries and/or abstracts in English). Four times a year. $60.00. CIC Edizioni Internazionali, Via L Spallanzani 11, 00161 Rome Italy. **Tel** 011 39 6 841-2673, FAX 011 39 6 844-3365, telex 622099 CIC I. **NLM** W1; DE485.

IT/0394-2503
**DERMATOLOGIA OGGI.** [Dermatol. oggi]. (1986)-. Periodical. Italian. sa. Esi Stampa Medica Srl, Casella Postale 42, 20097 San Donato Mil Italy. **Tel** 11 39 2 5274241, FAX 11 39 2 55600670, telex 324894. **UDC** 616.5.
**Ind/Abst** EMBASE.

MX
**DERMATOLOGIA REVISTA MEXICANA.** Spanish. bm. Free. Dermatologia Revista Mexicana, Mexico DF 06720 Mexico. **Tel** 52 5 588-9694.
**Ind/Abst** Rev. Med. Vet. Mycology; Trop. Dis. Bull.

US/0741-7489
**DERMATOLOGIC CAPSULE & COMMENT.** (DERMATOLOGIC CAPSULE & COMMENT / UPJOHN.). **Added/Corp** Upjohn Company. **VFOAT** Dermatologic Capsule and Comment. (19??)-. English. mo. Free. Hospital Practice, 10 Astor Place/7th Floor, New York NY 10003-6903. **Tel** (212)477-2727. ctrl circ.

US/0733-8635
**DERMATOLOGIC CLINICS.** [Dermatol. clin.]. Vol. 1, No. 1 (Jan. 1983)-. Periodical. English. qt (Jan., Apr., July, Oct.). $134.00 (institutions), $110.00 (individuals) US; $148.00 (institutions), $154.00 (individuals) other. W.B. Saunders Company, A Subsidiary of Harcourt Brace Jovanovich, Inc., The Curtis Center/Suite 300, Independence Square West, Philadelphia PA 19106-3399. **Tel** (215)238-7800 or, 5587, FAX (215)238-7883, telex 173146. **(Subscription address:** W. B. Saunders Company / North America Subscriptions, c/o Periodicals, 6277 Sea Harbour Drive, 4th Floor, Orlando FL 32887.) **ED** Livia Berardi. **LC** RL1; .D385. **DD** 616.5/005. **NLM** W1 DE501B. **[CCC].** Index available. **Pr Rev. Circ:** 3,500. available on microfilm and microfiche from University Microfilms International (UMI). Documents available from The Genuine Article.
**Desc:** Practical update for physicians on new advances. Each issue devoted to a single topic in patient care.
**Ind/Abst** Curr. Contents Clin. Med.; EMBASE; Health Plan. Adminis.; Index Med. (Vol. 3, No. 1, 1985-); Res. Alert [Select. Cov.]; SCISEARCH.

●US/1076-0512
**DERMATOLOGIC SURGERY.** (1995)-. Academic Scholarly Publication. English. Twelve times a year (1 volume). $140.00 US; $223.00 Europe; $245.00 Japan; $196.00 (surface mail) other. Elsevier Science Publishing Company Inc, Madison Square Station, PO Box 882, New York NY 10159-0882. **Tel** (212)633-3950, FAX (212)633-3990. ***Continues*** *Journal of Dermatologic Surgery and Oncology, 0148-0812.*

FR
**DERMATOLOGIE MALADIES SEXUELLEMENT TRANSMISSIBLES. E73.** French. ir. 969.95F France; 1010.00F other. CNRS / Institut d'Information Scientifique et Technique, (Centre National de la Recherche Scientifique), 15 Quai Anatole France, Paris 75700 France. **Tel** 011 33 1 47531515, telex 299 356 F. ***Continues*** *Pascal Explore E73, Dermatologie Maladies Sexuellement Transmissibles.*

FR/0982-8567
**DERMATOLOGIE PRATIQUE.** [Dermatol. prat.]. (1986)-. Periodical. French. Twenty times a year. 293.83F France; 300.00F other. Len Medical, 48 Bis Avenue Kleber, F-75116 Paris France. **Tel** 011 33 1 47550606. **UDC** 616.5.

BU/0417-0792
**DERMATOLOGIJA I VENEROLOGIJA.** (DERMATOLOGIIA I VENEROLOGIIA.). [Dermatol. venerol.]. **Added/Corp** Bulgaria. Ministerstvo na Narodnoto Zdrave i Sotsialnite Grizhi. Bulgaria. Ministerstvo na Narodnoto Zdrave. Bulgaria. Ministerstvo na Zdraveopazvaneto. Nauchno Druzhestvo na Dermatolozite (Bulgaria). (1962)-. Periodical. Bulgarian (table of contents in English and Russian). qt. Academy of Medicine / Bulgaria, 1 G Sofiiski Boulevard, 1431 Sofia Bulgaria. **NLM** W1 DE502L. **CODEN** DVENA3. Documents available from CASDDS.
**Ind/Abst** Chem. Abstr. (1962-1985); EMBASE [Select. Cov.]; Saf. Health Work.

GW/0011-9083
**DERMATOLOGISCHE MONATSSCHRIFT.** [Dermatol. Mon.schr.]. **Added/Corp** Dermatologische Gesellschaft der Deutschen Demokratischen Republik. Vol. 155 (1969)-. Periodical. German. mo. Hartmann Verlag GmbH, Zum Aussichsturm 16, D 91018 Marlofsstein Germany. **Tel** 011 49 9131 2105859. **NLM** W1 DE502N. **CODEN** DMONBP. Index available in last issue of volume--attached. **Bk Rev. Ad Acc.** ctrl circ. Documents available from BIOSIS Document Express, CASDDS. ***Continues*** *Dermatologische Wochenschrift, 0366-8940.*
**Desc:** Provides information about the newest state of knowledge in the field of diagnosis and therapy. Detailed minutes of proceedings inform about congresses at home and abroad. Important events are made known.
**Ind/Abst** Biol. Abstr.; Chem. Abstr.; EMBASE; Health Plan. Adminis.; Hortic. Abstr.; Index Med.; Ornamental Hort. (1991-); Life Sci. Collect.; Rev. Med. Vet. Entomol.; Rev. Med. Vet. Mycology; Rev. Plant Pathol.; Saf. Health Work.

US/0276-430X
**DERMATOLOGIST'S COMPENDIUM OF DRUG THERAPY, THE.** (THE DERMATOLOGIST'S COMPENDIUM OF DRUG THERAPY : A PUBLICATION OF BIOMEDICAL INFORMATION CORPORATION.). [Dermatol. compend. drug ther.]. **VFOAT** Compendium of Drug Therapy. 1981/1982-. English. an. Biomedical Information Corporation, 800 Second Avenue, New York NY 10017. **Tel** (212)262-9662. **UDC** 615.218; 615.2:616.5.

US/0273-2254
**DERMATOLOGY & ALLERGY.** [Dermatol. allergy]. **VFOAT** Dermatology. **VAT** Dermatology and Allergy. Began with Mar. 1980 issue. Periodical. English. mo. $20.00 US; $30.00 other. Didactic Inc, 1603 Orrington Avenue, Evanston IL 60201. **Tel** (312)869-6840. **LC** RL1. **DD** 616.5/005. **UDC** 616-056.3; 616-056.3:616.5. **NLM** W1 DE5085M. ***Continues*** *Dermatology, 0162-5446.*

●SZ/1018-8665
**DERMATOLOGY (BASEL).** (DERMATOLOGY : INTERNATIONAL JOURNAL FOR CLINICAL AND INVESTIGATIONAL DERMATOLOGY.). [Dermatology]. **Added/Corp** Schweizerische Gesellschaft fuer Dermatologie und Venereologie. Societe Belge de Dermatologie et de Syphiligraphie. (1992)-. Periodical. English. Eight times a year. $532.00. S. Karger AG, Allschwilerstrasse 10, PO Box - Postfach - Case Postale, CH-4009 Basel Switzerland. **Tel** 011 41 61 306-1111, FAX 011 41 61 306-1234, telex CH 962 652. **ED** J.H. Saurat. **NLM** W1; DE5083. **CODEN** DERAEG. **[CCC].** Documents available from The Genuine Article, BIOSIS Document Express. ***Continues*** *Dermatologica, 0011-9075.*
**Desc:** Provides a worldwide survey of clinical and investigative research in the field of dermatology. Original papers report clinical and laboratory findings. In order to inform readers of the implications of recent research, editorials and reviews prepared by invited, internationally recognized scientists are regularly featured. The journal answers the complete information needs of practitioners concerned with progress in research related to skin, clinical dermatology and therapy.
**Ind/Abst** Biol. Abstr.; Curr. Contents Clin. Med.; Index Med. (1992-); Ref. Upd. Deluxe Ed.; Res. Alert [Full Cov.]; Soc. Sci. Cit. Index [Select. Cov.].

US/1051-8258
**DERMATOLOGY (BIENNIAL).** (DERMATOLOGY : DIAGNOSIS AND THERAPY.). [Dermatology]. 1st Ed. (1991)-. English. be. $26.50. Appleton & Lange, (A Subsidiary of Simon & Schuster), 25 Van Zant Street, East Norwalk CT 06855. **Tel** (203)838-4400, (800)423-1359, FAX (203)854-9486. **DD** 616.

US/0198-6643
**DERMATOLOGY DIGEST (1979).** (DERMATOLOGY DIGEST.). [Dermatol. dig.]. V. 18, No. 8/9- Aug./Sept. 1979-. Periodical. English. mo. $27.50. Medical Digest, 444 Frontage Road, PO Box 8021, Northfield IL 60093. **UDC** 616.5. **NLM** W1 DE509G. available on microfilm and microfiche from Xerox. ***Continues*** *Journal of Continuing Education in Dermatology, 0160-7685.*
**Desc:** Includes abstracts of medical literature.

UK/0262-5504
**DERMATOLOGY IN PRACTICE (LONDON).** (DERMATOLOGY IN PRACTICE.). [Dermatol. pract.]. (198?)-. Periodical. English. bm (6 issues). £44.00 UK; £50.00 other. Hayward Medical Communications, 44 Earlham Street Covent Garden, London WC2H 9LA England. **Tel** 011 44 71 240 4493. **NLM** W1 DE509H. **Bk Rev. Ad Acc. Circ:** 20,700 (ctrl).
**Desc:** Articles on management and treatment of skin diseases, book review, news for general practitioners and dermatologists.

US/0742-3217
**DERMATOLOGY (NEW YORK, N.Y.).** (DERMATOLOGY.). [Dermatology]. Vol. 1 (1982)-. Academic Scholarly Publication. English. Price varies per volume. Marcel Dekker Inc., 270 Madison Avenue, New York NY 10016. **Tel** (212)696-9000, (800)228-1160, FAX (212)685-4540, telex 421419. **(Subscription address:** Marcel Dekker Inc, PO Box 5017, Monticello NY 12701.) **ED** Charles C. Calnan and Howard Maibach. **DD** 616. **NLM** W1 DE5084. **CODEN** DERMEI. Documents available from CASDDS.
**Desc:** Series covering various aspects of dermatology. Topics include the science of hair care and psoriasis.
**Ind/Abst** Chem. Abstr. (1985-); Curr. Aware. Biol. Sci., CABS.

US/1060-3441
**DERMATOLOGY NURSING.** (DERMATOLOGY NURSING / DERMATOLOGY NURSES' ASSOCIATION.). [Dermatol. nurs.]. **Added/Corp** Dermatology Nurses' Association (U.S.). Vol. 1, No. 1 (1989)-. Periodical. English. bm. $38.00 (institutions), $28.00 (individuals). A.J. Jannetti Inc., East Holly Avenue, Box 56, Pitman NJ 08071-0056. **Tel** (609)256-2300, FAX (609)589-7463. **DD** 610. **NLM** W1; DE509J. **Pr Rev.**
**Ind/Abst** Cumul. Index Nurs. Allied Health Lit.; Int. Nurs. Index (Apr. 1990-).

US/0196-6197
**DERMATOLOGY TIMES.** [Dermatol. times]. (1980)-. Periodical. English. mo. $95.00 US and possessions; $140.00 Canada; $185.00 other. Advanstar Communications Inc., 131 West First Street, Duluth MN 55802. **Tel** (218)723-9477, (800)346-0085. **ED** Dean Celia. **LC** Discard. **DD** 616. **CODEN** DETIEG. **[CCC]. Circ:** 6,372. available on an online database (file 16/Full-Text) from DIALOG.
**Desc:** A scientific tabloid newspaper providing accurate news of dermatology.
**Ind/Abst** BioBusiness; F&S Index Plus Text, Int. [Full Txt.] [Select. Cov.]; PROMT [Full Txt.].

US/0163-1691
**DERMATOLOGY UPDATE.** 1979- Ed. Academic Scholarly Publication. English. an. Elsevier Science Publishing Company Inc, Madison Square

Station, PO Box 882, New York NY 10159-0882. **Tel** (212)633-3950, FAX (212)633-3990. **LC** RL1; .D44. **DD** 616.5/005. **UDC** 616.5. **NLM** W1 DE509K.

●GW
**DERMATON.** (1995)-. Four times a year. $52.00. Georg Thieme Verlag Stuttgart, Postfach 301120, D 70451 Stuttgart Germany. **Tel** 011 49 711 89310, FAX 011 49 711 8931298, telex 7 252 275 GTVD. **(Subscription address:** Thieme Medical Publishers Inc., 381 Park Avenue South, New York NY 10016.**)**

●US/1078-4454
**DERMATOPATHOLOGY: PRACTICAL & CONCEPTUAL.** (1995)-. English. qt. $80.00 (individual), $100.00 (institution) US; $122.00 (individual), $142.00 (institution) other. Hanley & Belfus Inc., 210 South 13th Street, Philadelphia PA 19107. **Tel** (215)546-7293, FAX (215)790-9330.

GW/0343-2432
**DERMATOSEN IN BERUF UND UMWELT.** [Dermatosen Beruf Umwelt]. **VFOAT** Occupational and Environmental Dermatoses. Vol. 26 (1978)-. Academic Scholarly Publication. German (summaries and/or abstracts in English). bm (6 issues). DM79.00. Editio Cantor, Postfach 1255, D 88322 Aulendorf Germany. **Tel** 011 49 7525 9400, FAX 011 49 7525 9401. **ED** H. Ippen, K. H. Schulz and H. Tronnier. **NLM** W1 DE509L. **CODEN** DBUMDB. **[CCC].** Index available. **Bk Rev. Ad Acc. Circ:** 5,000. Documents available from The Genuine Article, CASDDS. ***Continues*** *Berufs-Dermatosen, 0005-9498.*
**Desc:** Journal for questions concerning skin lesions induced by occupation and environment; intended for dermatologists, industrial medical officers and specialists in internal medicine.
**Ind/Abst** Chem. Abstr.; Curr. Contents Clin. Med.; EMBASE; Energy Res. Abstr. (July 1982-); For. Prod. Abstr.; Health Plan. Adminis.; Index Med.; Ornamental Hort.; Res. Alert [Select. Cov.]; Rev. Med. Vet. Entomol.; SCISEARCH; Soc. Sci. Cit. Index [Select. Cov.].

IT
**DERMO TIME. VFOAT** Dermotime. (19??)-. Italian. Ten times a year. L35000 Italy; L60000 other. ISED SAS, Via Cipro 33, 25125 Brescia Italy. **Tel** 011 39 30 223685, FAX 011 39 30 2422060. **Bk Rev. Ad Acc. Circ:** 3,000.
**Desc:** Covers the practice of dermatology.

IT/0303-8890
**DERMOFARMACIA.** V. 1- Jan./Apr. 1974-. Periodical. Italian (summaries and/or abstracts in English). ir. Edizioni Minerva Medica, Corso Bramante 83-85, 10126 Turin Italy. **Tel** 011 39 11 678282, FAX 011 39 11 674502. **UDC** 615.2:616.5. **NLM** W1 DE509M.

GW/0340-8078
**DEUTSCHE DERMATOLOGE, DER.** [Dtsch. Dermatol.]. (1977)-. Periodical. German. mo. DM270.00. Medi A Derm Verlagsges MBH, Heidenkampsweg 24, W-2000 Hamburg 1 Germany. **Tel** 011 49 40 232334. **[CCC].** ***Continues*** *Mitteilungsblatt - Verband der Niedergelassenen Dermatologen Deutschlands e. V., 0340-806X.*

US/0278-9000
**DIRECTORY - AMERICAN ACADEMY OF DERMATOLOGY.** (DIRECTORY.). [Dir. - Am. Acad. Dermatol.]. **Main/Corp** American Academy of Dermatology. Directory. English. be. $25.00 (per copy). American Academy of Dermatology, 1567 Maple Avenue, PO Box 3116, Evanston IL 60204-3116. **Tel** (312)869-3954, FAX (312)869-4382. **ED** Thomas H Stluka. **LC** RL43; .A47A. **DD** 616.5/006/07. **UDC** 616.5(060.21)(73). **NLM** WR 22.1 A512R. **Ad Acc. Circ:** 7,600 (ctrl). ***Continues*** *American Academy of Dermatology. Roster: Bylaws, Officers, Committees, 0162-0037.*
**Desc:** Alphabetical and geographic listing of the members of the American Academy of Dermatology. Provides membership status, addresses and telephone numbers. Also includes listing of council and committee structure and by-laws.

FR
**ENCYCLOPEDIE MEDICO CHIRURGICALE. MEDECINE GENERALE & SPECIALITES. DERMATOLOGIE.** French. ir. Editions Techniques, 141 rue de Javel, 75747 Paris Cedex 15 France. **Tel** 011 33 1 45589100.

JA
**EUPHORIA ET CACOPHORIA. Added/Corp** Arudo Kasuterani Kenkyukai. No. 1 (May 1974)-. English (German). ir. Distributed complimentary. Aldo Castellani Research Institute, PO Box No 120, Gifu City 500-91 Japan. **Tel** (0582)53-2593. **LC** RL1; .E8. **DD** 616.5/005. **NLM** W1 EU51. **CODEN** EUCADT. cum. index. **Bk Rev. Pr Rev. Circ:** 2,000 (ctrl). Documents available from BIOSIS Document Express. ***Supersedes*** *Yakugaku Kenkyujo, Osaka. Bulletin of Pharmaceutical Research Institute.*
**Desc:** It contains articles on dermatology, history of medicine, and book reviews. "Aldo Castellani Memorial Bulletin".
**Ind/Abst** Biol. Abstr. (?-1979).

FR/1167-1122
**EUROPEAN JOURNAL OF DERMATOLOGY : EJD.** [EJD, Eur. j. dermatol.]. **VFOAT** EJD. Vol. 1, No. 1 (Oct. 1991)-. Academic Scholarly Publication. English. bm. John Libbey Eurotext Ltd, 6 rue Blanche, Isabelle Trope, 92120 Montrouge France. **Tel** 011 33 1 47358552. **NLM** W1; EU72DCL. **CODEN** EJDEE4. Documents available from CASDDS.
**Ind/Abst** Chem. Abstr.; Int. Pharm. Abstr.

NE/0014-4177
**EXCERPTA MEDICA. SECTION 13. DERMATOLOGY AND VENEREOLOGY.**
**See** Medical Science and Technology-Abstracting, Bibliographies and Statistics.

●DK/0906-6705
**EXPERIMENTAL DERMATOLOGY.** (1992)-. English. bm. kr1150.00 US, Canada and Japan; kr1020.00 other. Munksgaard International Publishers Ltd, PO Box 2148, DK-1016 Copenhagen K Denmark. **Tel** 011 45 33 12 70 30, FAX 011 45 33 12 93 87, telex 19431 MUNKS DK. **ED** G.L. Vejlgaard & T.A. Luger. **Ad Acc.**
**Desc:** Publishes short, complete and definitive reports and review articles covering all aspects of experimental dermatology.

●US/1072-2521
**FITZPATRICK'S JOURNAL OF CLINICAL DERMATOLOGY.** [Fitzpatrick's j. clin. dermatol.]. **VFOAT** Journal of Clinical Dermatology. (Nov./Dec. 1993)-. Periodical. English. bm. $160.00. Kenet Medical Publishing, 6 Pembroke Road, Weston MA 02193. **Tel** (617)492-9289. **DD** 616. **NLM** W1; FI815K.

SP/0367-2743
**FONTILLES.** (FONTILLES. REVISTA DE LEPROLOGIA.). [Fontilles]. **Added/Corp** Sanatorio de Fontilles. **VFOAT** Revista Fontilles. (19??)-. Periodical. Spanish. Three times a year. Sanatorio Leprologico de San Francisco de Borja, 03791 Fontilles (Alicante). **NLM** W1 FO369. **CODEN** FNTLA4. Documents available from BIOSIS Document Express. ***Continues*** *Trabajos del Sanatorio Nacional de Fontilles, 0213-5302.*
**Ind/Abst** Biol. Abstr.; Indice Med. Esp.

GW/0932-3848
**FORTSCHRITTE DER OPERATIVEN DERMATOLOGIE.** [Fortschr. oper. Dermatol.]. Periodical. German. Springer-Verlag New York Inc., 175 5th Avenue, New York NY 10010. **Tel** (212)460-1500, telex 232 235 SPB UR. **(Subscription address:** Springer Verlag New York Inc. / for North America, 44 Hartz Way, Secaucus NJ 07096.**) UDC** 616.5-089. **NLM** W1; FO86WF.

GW/0932-8661
**GIATROS DERMATOLOGIE.** [Giatros Dermatol.]. **VFOAT** Jatros Dermatologie. (1987)-. Periodical. German. mo. DM150.00. Universimed Verlag GmbH, August-Schanz Strasse 21, W-6000 Frankfurt 50 Germany. **Tel** 011 49 69 5480000, FAX 069/54 80 00-77. **UDC** 61. **Bk Rev. Ad Acc. Circ:** 4,000 (ctrl).
**Desc:** A scientific journal containing summaries of original articles, congress reports and interviews.

IT/1120-0499
**GIORNALE INTERNAZIONALE DI DERMATOLOGIA PEDIATRICA.** (1989)-. Periodical. Italian. qt. L60000. CIC Edizioni Internazionali, Via L Spallanzani 11, 00161 Rome Italy. **Tel** 011 39 6 841-2673, FAX 011 39 6 844-3365, telex 622099 CIC I. **ED** F. Rantuccio (Director). **UDC** 616.1.
**Desc:** Information on pediatric dermatology.

IT/0392-0488
**GIORNALE ITALIANO DI DERMATOLOGIA E VENEREOLOGIA.** (GIORNALE ITALIANO DI DERMATOLOGIA E VENEREOLOGIA : ORGANO UFFICIALE SOCIETA ITALIANA DI DERMATOLOGIA E SIFILOGRAFIA.). [G. ital. derm. venereol.]. **Added/Corp** Societa Italiana di Dermatologia e Sifilografia. Vol. 115, No. 1-2 (Jan./Feb. 1980)-. Academic Scholarly Publication. Italian (English and Italian). mo. $130.00 (individuals), $160.00 (institutions). Edizioni Minerva Medica, Corso Bramante 83-85, 10126 Turin Italy. **Tel** 011 39 11 678282, FAX 011 39 11 674502. **ED** G Zina. **NLM** W1 GI777A. **CODEN** GIDVDZ. Index available. **Bk Rev. Ad Acc.** Documents available from CASDDS. ***Continues*** *Giornale Italiana di Dermatologia. Minerva Dermatologica, 0533-7712.*
**Desc:** Addressed to practitioners and specialists in dermatology in Italy and abroad; deals with topics in scientific practice and research.
**Ind/Abst** Chem. Abstr. (1980-1983); EMBASE; Index Med. (1982-Dec. 1990); Index Vet.; Life Sci. Collect.; Rev. Med. Vet. Entomol.; Rev. Med. Vet. Mycology; Small Anim. Abstr. Bibliogr.

GW/0301-0481
**H + G ZEITSCHRIFT FUER HAUTKRANKHEITEN.** (ZEITSCHRIFT FUER HAUTKRANKHEITEN.). [H + G. Z. Hautkr.]. **VFOAT** H + G. Vol. 48 No. 13 (1973)-. Academic Scholarly Publication. German. mo. DM398.00. Blackwell Wissenschafts-Verlag, Kurfuerstendamm 57, D 10707 Berlin Germany. **Tel** 011 49 30 32790623, 011 49 30 32790624, FAX 011 49 30 327 90610. **ED** T. Krieg. **NLM** W1 ZE361H. **[CCC].** Index available. **Bk Rev. Ad Acc. Circ:** 2,200. ***Continues*** *Zeitschrift fuer Haut- und Geschlechtskrankheiten.*
**Ind/Abst** EMBASE; Energy Res. Abstr. (Feb. 1975-); For. Prod. Abstr.; Immunol. Abstr.; Index Med.; Microbiol. Abstr. Sect. B (19??-19??); Life Sci. Collect.; PESTDOC; Protozoolog. Abstr.; Rev. Med. Vet. Entomol.; Saf. Health Work; Virol. AIDS Abstr.

GW/0017-8470
**HAUTARZT.** (HAUTARZT, ZEITSCHRIFT FUER DERMATOLOGIE, VENEROLOGIE UND VERWANDTE GEBIETE.). [Hautarzt]. **Added/Corp** Deutsche Dermatologische Gesellschaft. (1950)-. Academic Scholarly Publication. German. Twelve times a year. DM478.00. Springer-Verlag GmbH & Company KG, Heidelberger Platz 3, D 14197 Berlin Germany. **Tel** 011 49 30 8207223, FAX 011 49 30 8214091, telex 183 319 SPBLN D. **(Subscription address:** Springer Verlag New York Inc. / for North America, 44 Hartz Way, Secaucus NJ 07096.**) ED** O Braun-Falco, D Petzoldt, U W Schneyder and K Wolff. **NLM** W1 HA899. **CODEN** HAUTAW. **[CCC]. Bk Rev. Pr Rev.** available on microfilm from University Microfilms International (UMI). Documents available from The Genuine Article, BIOSIS Document Express, CASDDS.
**Desc:** Presents original articles, letters to the editor, questions, surveys, current events, convention reports and historical notes.
**Ind/Abst** Biol. Abstr.; Chem. Abstr.; EMBASE; Energy Res. Abstr.; Health Plan. Adminis.; Helminthol. Abstr. (1991-); Index Med.; Nucl. Sci. Abstr.; Life Sci. Collect.; PESTDOC; Protozoolog. Abstr.; Res. Alert [Full Cov.]; Rev. Med. Vet. Entomol.; Rev. Med. Vet. Mycology; Sci. Cit. Index; SCISEARCH; Soc. Sci. Cit. Index [Select. Cov.].

JA/0018-1390
**HIFU. SKIN RESEARCH. Added/Corp** Nippon Hifuka Gakkai. Osaka Chihokai. Osaka Daigaku. Igakubu. Hifuka Kyoshitsu. **VFOAT** Skin Research. (195?)-. Academic Scholarly Publication. Japanese (English; summaries and/or abstracts in English). bm. Osaka Dermatological Association, 1-1-50 Fukushima, Osaka-Shi Japan. **Tel** (06)451-0051, telex (06)452-3912. **ED** Minoru Yasuhara. **NLM** W1 HI192. **CODEN** HIFUAG. Index available. **Ad Acc. Circ:** 1,400 (ctrl). Documents available from BIOSIS Document Express, CASDDS.
**Desc:** Clinical electron microscopic atlas, review and original articles focusing on all aspects of dermatology.
**Ind/Abst** Biol. Abstr.; Chem. Abstr.; EMBASE [Select. Cov.].

II/0019-5154
**INDIAN JOURNAL OF DERMATOLOGY.** [Indian j. dermatol.]. (Oct. 1955)-. Academic Scholarly Publication. English. qt. $20.00. Dermatological Society, 78 Dharamtala Street, Calcutta 13 India. **Tel** 24-4547. **(Subscription address:** Prints India, 11 Darya Ganj, New Delhi, 110002 India, (Phone: 011 91 11 3268645)**) ED** A K Dutta. **NLM** W1 IN2075. **CODEN** IJDEAA. **Bk Rev. Ad Acc. Circ:** 500. Documents available from BIOSIS Document Express.
**Desc:** Subjects include: dermatology, venereology, and leprology.
**Ind/Abst** Biol. Abstr.; EMBASE; Index Med.; Protozoolog. Abstr.; Rev. Med. Vet. Mycology.

II/0378-6323
**INDIAN JOURNAL OF DERMATOLOGY, VENEREOLOGY AND LEPROLOGY.** [Indian j. dermatol. venereol. leprol.]. **Added/Corp** Indian Association of Dermatologists, Venereologists and Leprologists. Vol. 42 (Jan./Feb. 1976)-. Periodical. English. bm. $80.00. Indian Association of Dermatology Venereology and Leprology, Department of Dermatology and Venereology, B J Medical College and Sasson General Hospital, Pune 411 001 India. **(Subscription address:** Prints India, 11 Darya Ganj, New Delhi, 110002 India, (Phone: 011 91 11 3268645)**) ED** G. Sinzh. **NLM** W1 IN208F. **CODEN** IJDLDY. Index available. **Bk Rev,** (Qty: 6-10). **Ad Acc. Circ:** 2,500. available on microfilm and microfiche from University Microfilms International (UMI). Documents available from BIOSIS Document Express. ***Continues*** *Indian Journal of Dermatology and Venereology, 0019-5162.*
**Ind/Abst** Biol. Abstr.; EMBASE; Life Sci. Collect.; Rev. Med. Vet. Mycology; Rev. Plant Pathol.

CN/0829-9935
**INTERNATIONAL ABSTRACTS IN DERMATOLOGY.** [Int. abstr. dermatol.]. **VFOAT** Dermatology. (1984)-. Periodical. English. bm (6 issues). 22.43Can$. Parkhurst Publishing, 400 McGill 3rd Floor, Montreal Quebec H2Y 2G1 Canada. **Tel** (514)397-8833, (514)397-9393. **DD** 616.5/005.

CN/0820-6880
**INTERNATIONAL HAIR ROUTE.** [Int. hair route]. **VAT** Hair Route (1981). Issue No. 6 (Feb. 1981)-. Periodical. English. qt (4 issues). $25.00 (one year), $46.00 (two year) US. International Hair Route, PO Box 313, Port Credit PO, Mississauga Ontario L5G 4L8 Canada. **Tel** (905)271-0339. **ED** Derek R. Copperthwaite and Jill Copperthwaite. **DD** 617/.47. Index available. **Bk Rev. Ad Acc. Circ:** 3,500 (ctrl). ***Continues** Hair Route, 0820-6872.*
**Desc:** Serves the profession of electrolysis, the permanent removal of superfluous hair, using the needle-type method, and related subjects; electricity, skin care, hair growth, endocrinology.

US/0011-9059
**INTERNATIONAL JOURNAL OF DERMATOLOGY.** [Int. j. dermatol.]. **Added/Corp** International Society of Tropical Dermatology. Vol. 9 (Jan./Mar. 1970)-. Academic Scholarly Publication. English (French and Spanish; summaries and/or abstracts in French and Spanish). Twelve times a year. $145.00 (institutions), $110.00 (individuals) US & Canada; $170.00 (institutions), $145.00 (individuals) other. Decker Periodicals Publishing Inc, PO Box 620, Station A, Hamilton Ontario L8N 3K7 Canada. **Tel** (416)522-7017, (800) 568-7281, FAX (416)522-7839. **ED** Lawrence Charles. **LC** RL1; .D38. **DD** 616.5/005. **NLM** W1 IN766G. **CODEN** IJDEBB. **[CCC]. Bk Rev. Ad Acc. Pr Rev. Circ:** 9,214. available on microfilm and microfiche from University Microfilms International (UMI). Documents available from The Genuine Article, BIOSIS Document Express, and A. CASDDS. ***Continues** Dermatologia Internationalis, 0096-1108.*
**Desc:** Includes new information written with clinical concerns and continuing education needs in mind. Offers a worldwide view of skin disorders and current treatment.
**Ind/Abst** Biol. Abstr.; Chem. Abstr.; Chem. Hazards Ind.; Curr. Contents Clin. Med.; Dairy Sci. Abstr.; EMBASE; Energy Res. Abstr. (May 1981-); Helminthol. Abstr. (19??-19??); Index Med.; INIS Atomindex [Micro.]; Lab. Hazards Bull.; Mod. Med.; Nutr. Res. Newsl.; Life Sci. Collect.; Pig News Inf.; Protozoolog. Abstr.; Res. Alert [Full Cov.]; Rev. Med. Vet. Entomol.; Rev. Med. Vet. Mycology; Rev. Plant Pathol.; Sci. Cit. Index; SCISEARCH; Soc. Sci. Cit. Index [Select. Cov.].

IT/0021-292X
**ITALIAN GENERAL REVIEW OF DERMATOLOGY.** **VFOAT** Revue Generale Italienne de Dermatologie. (1959)-. Periodical. Multiple languages (English and French). Three times a year. L70000 (institutions), L50000 (individuals) Italy; $60.00 (institutions), $40.00 (individuals) other. Digred Srl, Via Lapini 1, 50136 Firenze Italy. **Tel** 011 39 55 670369, FAX 011 39 55 660236. **ED** E. Panconesi. **NLM** ZWR 100 I88. **Bk Rev. Ad Acc. Circ:** 3,300 (ctrl).
**Desc:** Articles of interest to dermatologists and venereologists by investigators/reports presented at meetings held in Italy/current literature section.
**Ind/Abst** Index Med.

IT/0392-8543
**JOURNAL OF APPLIED COSMETOLOGY.** [J. appl. cosmetol.]. Vol. 1, No. 1 (Oct./Dec. 1983)-. Academic Scholarly Publication. English. Four times a year. L70000 Italy; $60.00 other. International Ediemme, Via Innocenzo XI 41, 00165 Rome Italy. **Tel** 011 39 6 39378788, FAX 011 39 6 6380839. **NLM** W1; JO541DB. **CODEN** JACOEL. Index available (bound in Dec. issue). **Bk Rev. Ad Acc, Adv Mgr:** P. Morganti. **Circ:** 5,000. Documents available from CASDDS.
**Ind/Abst** Chem. Abstr. (1983-); EMBASE [Select. Cov.].

US/0894-0061
**JOURNAL OF CUTANEOUS AGING & COSMETIC DERMATOLOGY.** ***Ceased.*** [J. cutan. aging cosmet. derm.]. **VFOAT** Journal of Cutaneous Aging and Cosmetic Dermatology. Vol. 1, No. 1 (1988)-(19??). Periodical. English. qt. Mary Ann Liebert Inc., 1651 Third Avenue, New York NY 10128. **Tel** (212)289-2300, (800)M-LIEBERT, FAX (212)289-4697. **DD** 616. **NLM** W1; JO612DQ.

DK/0303-6987
**JOURNAL OF CUTANEOUS PATHOLOGY.** [J. cutan. pathol.]. **VFOAT** Cutaneous Pathology. Vol. 1 (1974)-. Academic Scholarly Publication. English. bm. kr1790.00 (institution), kr1790.00 (individual) US, Canada and Japan; kr1780.00 (institution), kr1780.00 (individual) other. Munksgaard International Publishers Ltd, PO Box 2148, DK-1016 Copenhagen K Denmark. **Tel** 011 45 33 12 70 30, FAX 011 45 33 12 93 87, telex 19431 MUNKS DK. **ED** Evan R Farmer. **NLM** W1 JO612P. **CODEN** JCUPBN. **[CCC].** Index available. **Ad Acc. Pr Rev. Circ:** 1,600 (ctrl). Documents available from The Genuine Article, BIOSIS Document Express, CASDDS.
**Desc:** Diseases of the epidermis, dermis and cutaneous appendages, light and electron microscopy, histochemistry, microbiology, biochemistry, immunology, pharmacology, tissue culture, embryology and genetics.
**Ind/Abst** Biol. Abstr.; Chem. Abstr.; Curr. Contents Clin. Med.; Curr. Titl. Dent.; Dairy Sci. Abstr.; EMBASE; Energy Res. Abstr. (May 1978-); Index Med.; Nutr. Abstr. Rev., Ser. B, Live Feeds and Feed.; Nutr. Abstr. Rev., Ser. A, Hum. Exp.; Life Sci. Collect.; Protozoolog. Abstr.; Res. Alert [Full Cov.]; Rev. Med. Vet. Mycology; Rev. Plant Pathol.; Sci. Cit. Index; SCISEARCH.

US/0148-0812
**JOURNAL OF DERMATOLOGIC SURGERY AND ONCOLOGY, THE.** ***Title Change.*** **See** Medical Science and Technology-Surgery.

NE/0923-1811
**JOURNAL OF DERMATOLOGICAL SCIENCE.** [J. dermatol. sci.]. **Added/Corp** Japanese Society for Investigative Dermatology. Vol. 1 Issue 1 (Jan. 1990)-. Academic Scholarly Publication. English. bm (2 volumes). $361.00. Elsevier Science Ireland Ltd., Bay 15, Shannon Industrial Estate, Co Clare Ireland. **Tel** 011 353 61 471944. **ED** H. Ogawa. **NLM** W1; JO619EK. **CODEN** JDSCEI. Index available. cum. index. **Ad Acc. Pr Rev. Circ:** 1,500. available on microfilm and microfiche from University Microfilms International (UMI). Documents available from BIOSIS Document Express, CASDDS.
**Ind/Abst** Biol. Abstr. (1990-); Chem. Abstr.; Curr. Aware. Biol. Sci., CABS; EMBASE; Health Plan. Adminis.; Index Med. (1990-).

UK/0954-6634
**JOURNAL OF DERMATOLOGICAL TREATMENT, THE.** Vol. 1, No. 1 (June 1989)-. Periodical. English. bm (6 issues). £120.00 UK and EEC; £130.00 other. Macmillan Magazines Ltd., Houndmills, Basingstoke, Hampshire RG21 2XS England. **Tel** 011 44 256 29242, FAX 011 44 256 812358, telex 858493. **ED** R. Marks and A. Finlay. **NLM** W1; JO619L. **CODEN** JDTREY. **[CCC].** Index available. **Bk Rev. Ad Acc. Pr Rev. Circ:** 500. available on microfilm from University Microfilms International (UMI).
**Desc:** A forum for advances in the treatment and management of skin disorders. It includes articles on all types of treatment, including topical and systemically administered drugs, physical treatments, and surgical forms of therapy.
**Ind/Abst** EMBASE.

JA/0385-2407
**JOURNAL OF DERMATOLOGY, THE.** [J. dermatol.]. **Added/Corp** Nihon Hifuka Gakkai. Vol. 1 (March 1974)-. Academic Scholarly Publication. English. mo. $200.00. Nihon Hifuka Gakkai, (Japanese Dermatological Association), Taisei Building, 3-14-10 Hongo, Bunkyoku, Tokyoto 113 Japan. **(Subscription address:** Kyowa Book Company Inc., 1 38 Kanda Jinbocho Chiyoda-ku, Tokyo 101 Japan.**) NLM** W1 JO619R. **CODEN** JDMYAG. Documents available from BIOSIS Document Express, CASDDS. ***Supersedes** Japanese Journal of Dermatology. Ser. B.*
**Ind/Abst** Biol. Abstr.; Chem. Abstr.; EMBASE; Index Med.; SEA Abstr.

US/0022-202X
**JOURNAL OF INVESTIGATIVE DERMATOLOGY, THE.** [J. invest. dermatol.]. **Added/Corp** Society for Investigative Dermatology. European Society for Dermatological Research. Vol. 1 (Feb. 1938)-. Academic Scholarly Publication. English. mo (2 volumes). $336.00 US; $426.00 Europe; $446.00 Japan; $406.00 (surface mail) other. Elsevier Science Publishing Company Inc, Madison Square Station, PO Box 882, New York NY 10159-0882. **Tel** (212)633-3950, FAX (212)633-3990. **ED** David A Norris. **LC** RL1; .J82. **DD** 616.505. **NLM** W1 JO73. **CODEN** JIDEAE. **[CCC]. Pr Rev.** available on microfilm and microfiche from University Microfilms International (UMI). Documents available from The Genuine Article, BIOSIS Document Express, CASDDS, ADONIS. ***Absorbed** Advances in Biology of Skin, 0065-2253.*
**Desc:** Publishes original papers and reviews pertinent to the normal and abnormal function of the skin.
**Ind/Abst** ADONIS; AGRICOLA; Biol. Abstr.; Chem. Abstr.; Chem. Hazards Ind.; Curr. Aware. Biol. Sci., CABS; Curr. Contents Clin. Med.; Curr. Contents Life Sci.; Curr. Titl. Dent.; EMBASE; Energy Res. Abstr.; Index Med.; Index Vet.; INIS Atomindex [Micro.]; Int. Pharm. Abstr.; Iowa Drug Inf. Serv. (1970-); Lab. Hazards Bull.; Mod. Med.; Nutr. Abstr. Rev., Ser. B, Live Feeds and Feed.; Nutr. Abstr. Rev., Ser. A, Hum. Exp.; Life Sci. Collect.; PESTDOC; Protozoolog. Abstr.; Ref. Upd. Basic Ed.; Ref. Upd. Deluxe Ed.; Res. Alert [Full Cov.]; Rev. Med. Vet. Mycology; Rev. Plant Pathol.; Saf. Health Work; Sci. Cit. Index; SCISEARCH; Vet. Bull.; Trop. Dis. Bull.

US/0190-9622
**JOURNAL OF THE AMERICAN ACADEMY OF DERMATOLOGY.** [J. Am. Acad. Dermatol.]. **Main/Corp** American Academy of Dermatology. Vol. 1, (July 1979)-. Periodical. English. mo. $207.00 (institutions), $120.00 (individuals) US; $239.00 (institutions), $152.00 (individuals) other. Mosby Year Book Inc., 11830 Westline Industrial Drive, St Louis MO 63146. **Tel** (800)325-4177, (314)872-8370, FAX (314)432-1380, telex 44-2402. **ED** Richard L. Dobson. **LC** RL1; .A38a. **DD** 616.5/005. **NLM** W1 JO907WL. **CODEN** JAADDB. **[CCC].** Index available. cum. index. **Bk Rev. Ad Acc. Pr Rev. Circ:** 11,768. available on microfilm and microfiche from University Microfilms International (UMI). Documents available from The Genuine Article, BIOSIS Document Express. ***Continues** Bulletin of the American Academy of Dermatology, 0145-9082.*
**Desc:** Devoted exclusively to the clinical and continuing education needs of the entire dermatologic community.
**Ind/Abst** Biol. Abstr.; Curr. Aware. Biol. Sci., CABS; Curr. Contents Clin. Med.; Curr. Contents Life Sci.; Dairy Sci. Abstr.; EMBASE; Health Period. Database; Index Med.; INIS Atomindex [Micro.]; Int. Pharm. Abstr.; Med. Abstr. Newsl.; Mod. Med.; Nutr. Abstr. Rev., Ser. A, Hum. Exp.; Nutr. Res. Newsl.; Life Sci. Collect.; Physic. Medline Plus; Protozoolog. Abstr.; Ref. Upd. Basic Ed.; Ref. Upd. Deluxe Ed.; Res. Alert [Full Cov.]; Rev. Med. Vet. Entomol.; Rev. Med. Vet. Mycology; Sci. Cit. Index; SCISEARCH; Small Anim. Abstr. Bibliogr.; Soc. Sci. Cit. Index [Select. Cov.].

US/0360-4020
**JOURNAL OF THE ASSOCIATION OF MILITARY DERMATOLOGISTS.** **Added/Corp** Association of Military Dermatologists. Dome Laboratories, West Haven, Conn. Vol. 1 (1975)-. Academic Scholarly Publication. English. Interaction Projects Inc., PO Box 416, 25 Church Hill Road, Newtown CT 06470-0416. **NLM** W1 JO912K. ***Supersedes** Bulletin of the Association of Military Dermatologists, 0571-6438.*
**Ind/Abst** EMBASE [Select. Cov.].

●NE/0926-9959
**JOURNAL OF THE EUROPEAN ACADEMY OF DERMATOLOGY AND VENEREOLOGY : JEADV.** **Added/Corp** European Academy of Dermatology and Venereology. **VFOAT** JEADV. Vol. 1, No. 1 (May 1992)-. Academic Scholarly Publication. English. Six times a year (2 volumes). Fl870.00. Elsevier Science Publishers BV, PO Box 211, 1000 AE Amsterdam Netherlands. **Tel** 011 31 20 5803642, FAX 011 31 20 5862696, telex 15682. **NLM** W1; JO92Q. **CODEN** JEAVEQ. **[CCC].**

UK/0965-206X
**JOURNAL OF TISSUE VIABILITY.** **See** Biology-Cytology and Histology.

UK/0961-2033
**LUPUS.** Vol. 1, No. 1 (Nov. 1991)-. Periodical. English. Six times a year. £130.00 UK and EEC; £130.00 (surface mail), £156.00 (air mail) other. Macmillan Magazines Ltd., Houndmills, Basingstoke, Hampshire RG21 2XS England. **Tel** 011 44 256 29242, FAX 011 44 256 812358, telex 858493. **NLM** W1; LU72. **CODEN** LUPUES. Documents available from The Genuine Article.
**Ind/Abst** Curr. Aware. Biol. Sci., CABS; Curr. Contents Clin. Med.; Res. Alert [Full Cov.]; Sci. Cit. Index.

US/0732-0280
**LUPUS NEWS.** (LUPUS NEWS : LN.). [Lupus news]. **Added/Corp** Lupus Foundation of America. **VFOAT** LN. (19??)-. Periodical. English. Four times a year. $15.00 (individuals), $25.00 (families), $50.00 (sustaining), $75.00 (families sustaining), $225.00 (patron), $500.00 (life) Comes with Lupus Foundation of America membership. The Lupus Foundation of America Inc, 3741 Wasatch Avenue, Los Angeles CA 90066. **Tel** (213)391-7774.

UK/0301-7842
**MAJOR PROBLEMS IN DERMATOLOGY.** ***Ceased.*** Vol. 1 (1974). Periodical. English. ir. Lloyd Luke Medical Books Ltd, 49 Newman Street, London W1P 4BX England. **UDC** 616.5. **NLM** W1 MA492S.

US
**MEDICAL AND SURGICAL DERMATOLOGY.** English. Six times a year. $114.00. Springer-Verlag New York Inc., 175 5th Avenue, New York NY 10010. **Tel** (212)460-1500, telex 232 235 SPB UR. **(Subscription address:** Springer Verlag New York Inc. / for North America, 44 Hartz Way, Secaucus NJ 07096.**) ED** Kenneth A. Arndt, Robert S. Stern.
**Desc:** Complete critical review for the practicing clinician. Each issues contains 75-100 summaries of the most clinically significant articles drawn from a comprehensive review of the literature.

●US/0944-5196
**MEDICAL & SURGICAL DERMATOLOGY : A CRITICAL GUIDE TO THE WORLD LITERATURE.** **VFOAT** Medical and Surgical Dermatology. Vol. 1, No. 1 (1994)-. Periodical. English. bm. $114.00. Springer-Verlag New York Inc., 175 5th Avenue, New York NY 10010. **Tel** (212)460-1500, telex 232 235 SPB UR. **(Subscription address:** Springer Verlag New York Inc. / for North America, 44 Hartz Way, Secaucus NJ 07096.**) NLM** W1; ME185BL. **CODEN** MSDEEJ.

SP
**MEDICAL DIGEST. DERMATOLOGIA.** Spanish. Editorial M.C.R. SA, Mallorca 310, 08037 Barcelona Spain.

PO/0210-5187
**MEDICINA CUTANEA IBERO-LATINO-AMERICANA.** [Med. cutan. ibero-latino-am.]. **Added/Corp** Colegio Ibero Latino-Americano de Dermatologia. Vol. 1 (1973)-. Academic Scholarly Publication. Multiple languages (Portuguese and Spanish; summaries and/or abstracts in Spanish, French, German and English). bm. $105.00

Europe; $130.00 other. Editorial Garsi SA, Juan Bravo 46, 28006 Madrid, Spain. **Tel** 011 34 1 4021212, telex 98358 GARSI E. **NLM** W1 ME575CI. ***Formed by the union of*** *Dermatologia Ibero Latino-Americana, 0011-9040* ***and*** *Medicina Cutanea, 0025-7788.*
**Ind/Abst** EMBASE [Select. Cov.]; Helminthol. Abstr. (1991-); Index Med.; Indice Med. Esp.; Nutr. Abstr. Rev., Ser. A, Hum. Exp.; Protozoolog. Abstr.; Rev. Med. Vet. Mycology.

US/0737-6081
**MEDIGUIDE TO SKIN CONDITIONS.** [Mediguide skin cond.]. Vol. 1, Issue 1-. Periodical. English. bm. Dellacorte Publications, 919 3rd Avenue, New York NY 10022. **Tel** (212)751-2806. **UDC** 08527025. **NLM** W1 ME787GHD.

SZ/0259-1340
**MODELS IN DERMATOLOGY.** ***Ceased.*** Vol. 1 (1985)-(19??). Academic Scholarly Publication. English. an. S. Karger AG, Allschwilerstrasse 10, PO Box - Postfach - Case Postale, CH-4009 Basel Switzerland. **Tel** 011 41 61 306-1111, FAX 011 41 61 306-1234, telex CH 962 652. **ED** H I Maibach and N J Lowe. **NLM** W1; MO113V. **CODEN** MODEEP. **[CCC].** Documents available from BIOSIS Document Express, CASDDS.
**Desc:** Allows reference to virtually all test models currently used in the study of skin disease and in the development and screening of preparations for therapeutic or cosmetic use. Reflecting the difficulties of approximating the special conditions of human skin, the books present research protocols for a striking diversity of in vivo and in vitro human, animal and non-animal test systems. The result is the most comprehensive and authoritative work on this topic to appear during the past decade.
**Ind/Abst** Biol. Abstr. (1987-); Chem. Abstr.; Ref. Upd. Deluxe Ed.

SP/0210-5268
**MONOGRAFIA DEL COLEGIO IBERO-LATINO-AMERICANO DE DERMATOLOGIA.** [Monogr. Col. 1 bero-Latino-Am. Dermatol.]. 3.- 1977-. Monographic series. Spanish. Price varies per volume. Editorial Cientifico Medica / Barcelona, Via Layetana 53, 08003 Barcelona Spain. **NLM** W1 MO5415T. ***Continues*** *Monografia de Dermatologia Ibero Latino-Americana.*

SP/0214-4220
**MONOGRAFIAS DE DERMATOLOGIA : M.D.D.** **VFOAT** M.D.D.; MDD. (198?)-. Periodical. Spanish (summaries and/or abstracts in English). Six times a year. 3000ptas Spain; 5000ptas others. Grupo Aula Medica, Isabel Colbrand S N Alfa 3, 28050 Madrid Spain. **Tel** 011 34 1 3588657. **NLM** W1; MO5417T. **CODEN** MONDE4.
**Ind/Abst** EMBASE [Select. Cov.].

NE/0925-8604
**NEDERLANDS TIJDSCHRIFT VOOR DERMATOLOGIE & VENEREOLOGIE.** [Ned. tijdschr. dermatol. venereol.]. (1991)-. Periodical. Dutch. mo (8 issues). Fl152.83 Netherlands; Fl188.68 other. Bugamor International, De Haak 58, 1353 AE Almere Netherlands. **Tel** 011 31 36 5382297. **UDC** 616.5. ***Continues*** *Psoriasis Nieuws, 0920-4520.*

JA/0021-499X
**NIPPON HIFUKA GAKKAI ZASSHI.** [Nihon Hifuka Gakkai zasshi]. **Added/Corp** Nihon Hifuka Gakkai. **VFOAT** Japanese Journal of Dermatology; Japanese Journal of Dermatology Ser. A. No. 67 (1957)-. Academic Scholarly Publication. Japanese (summaries and/or abstracts in English). mo. ¥7000. Nihon Hifuka Gakkai, (Japanese Dermatological Association), Taisei Building, 3-14-10 Hongo, Bunkyoku, Tokyoto 113 Japan. **(Subscription address:** Kyowa Book Company Inc., 1 38 Kanda Jinbocho Chiyoda-ku, Tokyo 101 Japan.**) NLM** W1 NI902E. **CODEN** NHKZAD. Documents available from CASDDS. ***Continues*** *Hifuka Seibyoka Zasshi, 0368-3524.*
**Ind/Abst** Chem. Abstr.; Index Med.; Nutr. Abstr. Rev., Ser. A, Hum. Exp.; Rev. Med. Vet. Mycology.

JA/0386-9784
**NISHI NIHON HIFUKA.** [Nishi Nihon hifuka]. **Added/Corp** Nihon Hifuka Gakkai. Seibu Shibu. **VFOAT** Nishinihon Journal of Dermatology. (1969)-. Periodical. Japanese (summaries and/or abstracts in English; table of contents in English). bm. $130.00. Nishinihon Journal of Dermatology, 1-1 Maidashi 3-chome, Higashi-ku, 812 Fukuoka, Japan. **(Subscription address:** Kyowa Book Company Inc., 1 38 Kanda Jinbocho Chiyoda-ku, Tokyo 101 Japan.**) NLM** W1 NI983G. **CODEN** NNHIAN. Documents available from BIOSIS Document Express. ***Continues*** *Hifu to Hinyo.*
**Ind/Abst** Biol. Abstr. (-1989); EMBASE [Select. Cov.].

FR/0752-5370
**NOUVELLES DERMATOLOGIQUES, LES.** [Nouv. dermatol.]. (1982)-. Academic Scholarly Publication. French (English). Ten times a year. 390.00F France; 440.00F other. PCIM, 2 Place Golbery, 67000 Strasbourg France. **Tel** 011 33 88 604600, FAX 011 33 88 604670. **UDC** 616.5. Index available. **Ad Acc, Adv Mgr:** Frederique Nartz. **Circ:** 4,000-6,000.

FR/0996-553X
**OFFICIEL DES DERMATOLOGISTES ET VENEREOLOGISTES, L'.** (198?)-. Periodical. French (English). Ten times a year. 246.86F France; 290.00F other. Officiel des Dermatologistes et Venereologistes, 45 rue Chevereul, 94600 Choisy le Roi France. **Tel** 011 33 1 48522232. **NLM** W1; OF575.

US/0736-8046
**PEDIATRIC DERMATOLOGY.** **See** Medical Science and Technology-Pediatrics.

SZ/1011-291X
**PHARMACOLOGY AND THE SKIN.** [Pharmacol. skin]. Vol. 1 (1987)-. Monographic series. English. an. 200.00F (approx. per volume). S. Karger AG, Allschwilerstrasse 10, PO Box - Postfach - Case Postale, CH-4009 Basel Switzerland. **Tel** 011 41 61 306-1111, FAX 011 41 61 306-1234, telex CH 962 652. **ED** B. Shroot, H. Schaefer. **NLM** W1; PH283H. **CODEN** PHSKEY. **[CCC].** Index available. ctrl circ. Documents available from BIOSIS Document Express.
**Desc:** Presents in-depth coverage of particularly important themes in skin pharmacology. Individual volumes will contain both critical reviews of recent research results. They are designed to provide information on new and relevant advances in cutaneous pharmacology for basic and clinical scientists involved in dermatology, skin care and pharmacology.
**Ind/Abst** Biol. Abstr.; Ref. Upd. Deluxe Ed.

DK/0905-4383
**PHOTODERMATOLOGY, PHOTOIMMUNOLOGY & PHOTOMEDICINE.** **VFOAT** Photodermatology, Photoimmunology and Photomedicine. Vol. 7, No. 1 (Feb. 1990)-. Academic Scholarly Publication. English. Six times a year. kr1170.00 US, Canada and Japan; kr1150.00 other. Munksgaard International Publishers Ltd, PO Box 2148, DK-1016 Copenhagen K Denmark. **Tel** 011 45 33 12 70 30, FAX 011 45 33 12 93 87, telex 19431 MUNKS DK. **NLM** W1; PH661M. **CODEN** PPPHEW. **[CCC].** Documents available from The Genuine Article, CASDDS. ***Continues*** *Photodermatology, 0108-9684.*
**Ind/Abst** Chem. Abstr.; Curr. Aware. Biol. Sci., CABS; Curr. Contents Clin. Med.; EMBASE; Index Med. (1990-); Res. Alert [Full Cov.]; Rev. Med. Vet. Mycology; Sci. Cit. Index; SCISEARCH.

US/1046-7076
**PRACTICAL REVIEWS IN DERMATOLOGY.** (PRACTICAL REVIEWS IN DERMATOLOGY [SOUND RECORDING].). [Pract. rev. dermatol.]. **Added/Corp** Educational Reviews, Inc. Montefiore Medical Center. (1989)-. Periodical. English. bm. $135.00 Physicians/Dentists; $105.00 Residents. Educational Reviews Inc., 6801 Cahaba Valley Road, Birmingham AL 35242. **Tel** (205)991-5188, (800)633-4743, FAX (205)995-1926. **DD** 616. **NLM** W1; PR153P.

PL/0033-2526
**PRZEGLAD DERMATOLOGICZNY.** [Przeg. derm.]. **Added/Corp** Polskie Towarzystwo Dermatologiczne. Vol. 46 (1959)-. Academic Scholarly Publication. Polish (summaries and/or abstracts in English and Russian). bm. Price on Request. **(Subscription address:** ARS Polona, PO Box 1001, 00068 Warsaw Poland.**) NLM** W1 PR925. **CODEN** PRDEA7. Documents available from CASDDS. ***Continues*** *Przeglad Dermatologii i Wenerologii.*
**Ind/Abst** Chem. Abstr.; EMBASE [Select. Cov.]; Index Med.

IT/0033-9490
**RASSEGNA DI DERMATOLOGIA E SIFILOGRAFIA.** [Rass. dermatol. sifilogr.]. (1948)-. Periodical. Italian. L30000.00 Italy; L60000.00 other. Casa Editrice Maccari, Via Trento 53, 43100 Parma Italy. **Tel** 011 39 521 771268, FAX 011 39 521 771268. **CODEN** RDSIAI. Documents available from BIOSIS Document Express.
**Ind/Abst** Biol. Abstr. (1986-).

FR/1155-2492
**REALITES THERAPEUTIQUES EN DERMATO-VENEROLOGIE.** (1990)-. Periodical. French. mo (except July and Aug.). 300.00F France; 400.00F other. Performances Medicales, 1 Rue St Hubert, 75011 Paris France. **Tel** 011 33 1 47006714, FAX 011 33 1 47006999. **UDC** 616.5(44). **Ad Acc, Adv Mgr:** G. Koster.

UK/0309-2747
**RECENT ADVANCES IN DERMATOLOGY.** (1938)-. Periodical. English. ir (published every 3-5 years). price varies per volume. Churchill Livingstone, 1-3 Baxter's Place, Leith Walk, Edinburgh EH1 3AF Scotland. **Tel** 011 44 31 556 2424, FAX 011 44 31 558 1278, telex 727511. **(Subscription address:** Churchill Livingstone / US, 5 S 250 Frontenac Road, Naperville IL 60563.**) ED** A. J. Rook. **NLM** W1 RE105UJ.

BL/0101-9872
**REVIEW OF IBERIAN LATIN AMERICAN DERMATOLOGY.** ***Ceased.*** [Rev. iber. lat. am. dermatol.]. **VFOAT** Revista Ibero-Latino-Americana de Dermatologia. Periodical. English (Portuguese and Spanish). sa. ECN-Editora Cientifica Nacional Ltda., Caixa Postal 590, 20001-Rio de Janeiro RJ Brazil. **Tel** 011 55 21 2622825, 011 55 21 2213235, FAX 011 55 21 2521691. **NLM** ZWR 100; R454.

AG/0325-2787
**REVISTA ARGENTINA DE DERMATOLOGIA.** (1959)-. Spanish (summaries and/or abstracts in English). ir (Jan./April/July/Sept.; Supplement Nov.). 40.00Arg$ Argentina; 80.00Arg$ other. Asociacion Argentina de Dermatologia, Urquiza 609, 1221 Buenos Aires Argentina. **Tel** 011 54 1 8245441. **UDC** 61. Index available.
**Ind/Abst** EMBASE [Select. Cov.]; Int. Pharm. Abstr. (199?-); Rev. Med. Vet. Mycology.

FR
**REVUE DES MST ET DU SIDA / REVUE INTERNE DE DERMATOLOGIE ET DU SIDA.** French. Ten times a year. 500.00F France; 750.00F other. Cogemed, BP 9, 78670 Villennes Seine France. **Tel** 011 33 39 753975.

FR/1140-5325
**REVUE EUROPEENNE DE DERMATOLOGIE ET DE MST.** **VFOAT** Revue Europeenne de Dermatologie et de Maladies Sexuellement Transmissibles. (1989)-. Periodical. Multiple languages. mo (except July and Aug.). 370.00F France; 480.00F other. Litemed, 23 rue des Quatre Vents, 92380 Garches France. **Tel** 011 33 1 47415441. **UDC** 616.5. ***Continues*** *Recherche et Dermatologie, 0992-616X.*

US/0487-6520
**SCHOCH LETTER, THE.** **Added/Corp** American Academy of Dermatology. (1975)-. Periodical. English. Twelve times a year. $25.00. Schoch Letter, 17 East Grace Street, Richmond VA 23219. **Tel** (804)644-3006. **ED** Harry L. Arnold and Ervin Epstein. **NLM** W1 SC225. ***Continues*** *Current News in Dermatology, 0191-796X.*

AU/0586-7703
**SCHRIFTTUM UND PRAXIS.** [Schr. Prax. - Arztekamm. Wien, Fachgr. Dermatol.]. Began in 1969. Periodical. German. qt. **NLM** ZWR 100; S379.

US/0278-145X
**SEMINARS IN DERMATOLOGY.** [Semin. dermatol.]. Vol. 1, No. 1 (Mar. 1982)-. Periodical. English. qt (Mar., June, Sept., Dec.). $89.00 (individual), $128.00 (institution) US; $152.00 (individual), $164.00 (institution) other. W.B. Saunders Company, A Subsidiary of Harcourt Brace Jovanovich, Inc., The Curtis Center/Suite 300, Independence Square West, Philadelphia PA 19106-3399. **Tel** (215)238-7800 or, 5587, FAX (215)238-7883, telex 173146. **(Subscription address:** W. B. Saunders Company / North America Subscriptions, c/o Periodicals, 6277 Sea Harbour Drive, 4th Floor, Orlando FL 32887.**) ED** Arthur Rook and Howard Maibach. **NLM** W1; SE487M. **CODEN** SDERDN. **[CCC]. Pr Rev. Circ:** 1,124. Documents available from The Genuine Article, BIOSIS Document Express.
**Desc:** Intended as a source for publication of new concepts and research findings applicable to day-to-day practice.
**Ind/Abst** Biol. Abstr. (1984-); Curr. Contents Clin. Med.; EMBASE; Health Plan. Adminis.; Helminthol. Abstr. (1991-); Protozoolog. Abstr.; Res. Alert [Select. Cov.]; Rev. Med. Vet. Entomol.; Rev. Med. Vet. Mycology.

IT/1121-1881
**SEMINARS IN DERMATOLOGY ED. ITALIANA.** [Semin. dermatol. Ed. ital.]. (1992)-. Periodical. Italian. Four times a year. L140000 institutions; L100000 individuals. Il Pensiero Scientifico Editore s.r.l., Via Bradano 3C, 00199 Rome Italy. **Tel** 011 39 6 86207158, 86207159, 86207168, 86207169, FAX 011 39 6 86207160. **ED** Committee. **UDC** 616.5.

US/0037-6337
**SKIN & ALLERGY NEWS.** [Skin allergy news]. **VAT** Skin and Allergy News. Vol. 1 (May 1970)-. Periodical. English. mo. $70.00 US; $91.00 other. International Medical News Group, 12230 Wilkins Avenue, Rockville MD 20852. **Tel** (301)770-6170. **ED** William Rubin. **DD** 616. **NLM** W1 SK59. **CODEN** SKANB4. **Bk Rev. Ad Acc. Circ:** 35,000 (ctrl). available on microfilm from University Microfilms International (UMI).
**Desc:** Information of specific or general interest to the dermatologist, allergist, and pediatric allergist, and those GP's and FP's prescribing in these specialties.
**Ind/Abst** BioBusiness; Mod. Med.

US/0898-6525
**SKIN INC.** [Skin inc.]. (1988)-. Periodical. English. bm (6 issues). $46.00 (one year), $78.00 (two year). Allured Publishing Corporation, 362 South Schmale Road, Carol

Stream IL 60188-2787. **Tel** (708)653-2155, FAX (708)653-2192. **DD** 646. **NLM** W1; SK59PH. Index available (bound in Jan. issue).

SZ/1011-0283
**SKIN PHARMACOLOGY.** (SKIN PHARMACOLOGY : THE OFFICIAL JOURNAL OF THE SKIN PHARMACOLOGY SOCIETY.). [Skin pharmacol.]. **Added/Corp** Skin Pharmacology Society. Skin Pharmacology Society. Symposium. (1988)-. Periodical. English. Six times a year. $266.00. S. Karger AG, Allschwilerstrasse 10, PO Box - Postfach - Case Postale, CH-4009 Basel Switzerland. **Tel** 011 41 61 306-1111, FAX 011 41 61 306-1234, telex CH 962 652. **ED** H.F. Merk. **NLM** W1; SK59Q. **CODEN** SKPHEU. **[CCC].** Index available. cum. index. **Ad Acc. Circ:** 1,000 (ctrl). available on microfilm and microfiche. Documents available from The Genuine Article, BIOSIS Document Express.
**Desc:** Concentrating on a developing area of research, this journal offers a forum combining dermatologic and pharmacologic studies investigating the specific pathophysiology of the skin. Relevant findings are presented from a variety of complementary fields such as human, animal and cell pharmacology, immunopharmacology, pharmacokinetics, metabolism and toxicology. Innovative approaches and progress in both the laboratory and clinical domain are reported in original papers, reviews and short communications. Contributions from this specialized field are of particular interest to pharmacologists, dermatologists, toxicologists and experts in pharmaceutics.
**Ind/Abst** Biol. Abstr.; Curr. Contents Life Sci.; EMBASE; Health Plan. Adminis.; Index Med.; PESTDOC; Ref. Upd. Deluxe Ed.; Res. Alert [Full Cov.]; Sci. Cit. Index; SCISEARCH.

KO/0494-4739
**TAEHAN PIBU KWAHAKHOE CHI. VFOAT** Korean Journal of Dermatology. (1960)-. Periodical. Korean. Six times a year. $30.00. Korean Dermatological Association, 40 Isindonga Jonghap-Sangka 491, Seoul 137-070 Korea. **Tel** 011 82 2 5670284. **UDC** 616.5.
**Ind/Abst** EMBASE [Select. Cov.]; Rev. Med. Vet. Mycology.

RU/0042-4609
**VESTNIK DERMATOLOGII I VENEROLOGII.** [Vestn. dermatol. venerol.]. Vol. 31 (1957)-. Academic Scholarly Publication. Russian. Six times a year. $119.95. Izdatelstvo Meditsina / Russian Academy of Medical Sciences, Ulitsa Solyanka 14, 109801 Moscow Russia. **Tel** 011 95 297-05-04. **(Subscription address:** East View Publications Inc., 3020 Harbor Lane North, Suite 110, Minneapolis MN 55447.**) NLM** W1 VE821. **CODEN** VDVEAV. **[CCC]. Bk Rev. Pr Rev.** Documents available from The Genuine Article, BIOSIS Document Express, CASDDS.
**Ind/Abst** Biol. Abstr.; Chem. Abstr.; Curr. Contents Clin. Med.; EMBASE [Select. Cov.]; Index Med.; Life Sci. Collect.; Protozoolog. Abstr.; Res. Alert [Full Cov.]; Rev. Agric. Entomol.; Rev. Med. Vet. Entomol.; Rev. Med. Vet. Mycology; Sci. Cit. Index; SCISEARCH; Soils Fert.; SportSearch; Trop. Dis. Bull.

CN/1187-1164
**WOUND & SKIN CARE.** [Wound skin care]. **VFOAT** Wound and Skin Care. No. 1 (Apr. 1991)-. Periodical. English. qt. Limited free distribution. STA Communications Inc., 955 St. John Boulevard, Suite 306, Pt Claire, Quebec H9R 5K3 Canada. **Tel** (514)695-7623. **DD** 617.1/4/005. ***Continues** Wound Management (Pointe Claire, Quebec)., 0836-6098.*

●US/1059-0587
**YEAR BOOK OF DERMATOLOGIC SURGERY.** [Year book dermatol. surg.]. **VFOAT** Yearbook of Dermatologic Surgery. (1992)-. English. an. $69.95. Mosby Year Book Inc., 11830 Westline Industrial Drive, St Louis MO 63146. **Tel** (800)325-4177, (314)872-8370, FAX (314)432-1380, telex 44-2402. **DD** 616. **NLM** W1; YE119.

US/0093-3619
**YEAR BOOK OF DERMATOLOGY, THE.** (1902)-. English. an. $64.95. Mosby Year Book Inc., 11830 Westline Industrial Drive, St Louis MO 63146. **Tel** (800)325-4177, (314)872-8370, FAX (314)432-1380, telex 44-2402. **LC** RL26; .Y4. **DD** 616.5/005.

GW/0343-3048
**ZENTRALBLATT HAUT- UND GESCHLECHTSKRANKHEITEN.** [Zentralbl. Haut- Geschlechtskr.]. **Added/Corp** Deutsche Dermatologische Gesellschaft. Vol. 138, (April 1977)-. English (German). Thirteen times a year. DM2698.00. Springer-Verlag GmbH & Company KG, Heidelberger Platz 3, D 14197 Berlin Germany. **Tel** 011 49 30 8207223, FAX 011 49 30 8214091, telex 183 319 SPBLN D. **(Subscription address:** Springer Verlag New York Inc. / for North America, 44 Hartz Way, Secaucus NJ 07096.**) ED** R. Clorius and E. Landes. **NLM** ZWR 100 Z56. **[CCC]. Bk Rev. *Continues*** *Zentralblatt fur Haut- und Geschlechtskrankheiten, Sowie Deren Grenzgebieten.*
**Desc:** Reports of congresses, survey of new concepts, skin pathology, diagnostics, therapy, urogenital pathology, histology.

## EMERGENCY MEDICINE

US/0742-0366
**ABMD DIRECTORY OF CERTIFIED EMERGENCY PHYSICIANS.** ***Title Change.*** [ABMS dir. certif. emerg. phys.]. **Added/Corp** American Board of Medical Specialties. American Board of Emergency Medicine. **VFOAT** A.B.M.S. Directory of Certified Emergency Physicians. 1st Ed. (1983)-(19??). Directory. English. be. American Board of Medical Specialties, 1 Rotary Center, Suite 805, Evanston IL 60201. **Tel** (708)491-9091. **LC** RC86; .A25. **DD** 616/.025/02573. **NLM** WB 22; AA1 A15. ***Continued by*** *Official American Board of Medical Specialties (ABMS) Directory of Board Certified Emergency Medicine Physicians, 0000-1430.*

●US/1069-6563
**ACADEMIC EMERGENCY MEDICINE.** [Acad. emerg. med.]. **Added/Corp** Society for Academic Emergency Medicine (U.S.). (1994)-. Periodical. English. bm. $76.00 (US & possessions), $86.00 (other) individual; $96.00 (US & possessions), $106.00 (other) institution. Hanley & Belfus Inc., 210 South 13th Street, Philadelphia PA 19107. **Tel** (215)546-7293, FAX (215)790-9330. **DD** 616. **NLM** W1; AC33ND. **[CCC].**

UK/0952-3758
**AMBULANCE MANAGEMENT INTERNATIONAL.** [Ambulance manag. int.]. **VFOAT** AMI. (1987)-. Periodical. English. qt (4 issues). £32.25 UK. Sawell Publications Ltd., 127 Stanstead Road, Forest Hill, London SE23 1JE England. **Tel** 011 44 81 6996792. **DD** 362.18.

AT/0817-4474
**AMBULANCE WORLD (1986).** [Ambulanc. world 1986]. **Added/Corp** Ambulance Employees Association (Australia). (1986)-. Periodical. English. qt. 20.00Aus$ Austalia; 30.00Aus$ other. Ambulance World, PO Box 60, Carlton South, Victoria, 3053 Australia. **Tel** (03)3295777, FAX (03)3295533. **ED** Chris Tyler. **DD** 362.180994. **Ad Acc. *Continues*** *Australian Paramedic, 0814-5814.*
**Desc:** Contains articles on pre-hospital emergency care.

US/0735-6757
**AMERICAN JOURNAL OF EMERGENCY MEDICINE, THE.** [Am. j. emerg. med.]. **VFOAT** A.J.E.M.; AJEM. Vol. 1, No. 1 (July 1983)-. Periodical. English. bm (6 issues). $96.00 (individuals), $130.00 (institution) US; $156.00 (individuals), $171.00 (institutions) other. W.B. Saunders Company, A Subsidiary of Harcourt Brace Jovanovich, Inc., The Curtis Center/Suite 300, Independence Square West, Philadelphia PA 19106-3399. **Tel** (215)238-7800 or, 5587, FAX (215)238-7883, telex 173146. **(Subscription address:** W. B. Saunders Company / North America Subscriptions, c/o Periodicals, 6277 Sea Harbour Drive, 4th Floor, Orlando FL 32887.**) ED** J. Douglas White. **NLM** W1 AM451C. **CODEN** AJEMEN. **[CCC].** Index available (bound in issue). **Bk Rev. Ad Acc. Pr Rev. Circ:** 3,000. available on microfilm and microfiche from University Microfilms International (UMI). Documents available from The Genuine Article, BIOSIS Document Express.
**Desc:** Contains original research, work in progress, case reports, and regular features. An independent journal covering important issues and developments from many sources and perspectives.
**Ind/Abst** Biol. Abstr. (1988-); Curr. Contents Clin. Med.; Dairy Sci. Abstr.; EMBASE; Food Sci. Technol. Abstr.; Health Devices Alerts; Health Plan. Adminis.; Index Med. (Vol. 1, No. 1, 1983-); Physic. Medline Plus; Protozoolog. Abstr.; Res. Alert [Select. Cov.]; Rev. Med. Vet. Entomol.; SCISEARCH; Soc. Sci. Cit. Index [Select. Cov.].

GW/0939-2661
**ANASTHESIOLOGIE, INTENSIVMEDIZIN, NOTFALLMEDIZIN, SCHMERZTHERAPIE : AINS.** **See** Medical Science and Technology-Anesthesiology.

US/0196-0644
**ANNALS OF EMERGENCY MEDICINE.** [Ann. emerg. med.]. **Added/Corp** American College of Emergency Physicians. University Association for Emergency Medicine. Vol. 9 (Jan. 1980)-. Periodical. English. mo. $88.00 (institutions), $75.00 (individuals) US; $117.00 (institutions), $104.00 (individuals) other. Mosby Year Book Inc., 11830 Westline Industrial Drive, St Louis MO 63146. **Tel** (800)325-4177, (314)872-8370, FAX (314)432-1380, telex 44-2402. **ED** Joseph F. Waeckerle. **LC** RC86; .J2. **DD** 616/.025/05. **NLM** W1 AN574M. **CODEN** AEMED3. Index available. cum. index. **Bk Rev. Ad Acc. Pr Rev. Circ:** 18,500 (ctrl). available on microfilm and microfiche from University Microfilms International (UMI). Documents available from The Genuine Article, BIOSIS Document Express. ***Continues*** *JACEP, 0361-1124.*
**Desc:** Original clinical and research articles, case reports, methods and techniques in emergency medicine and emergency medical services.
**Ind/Abst** Abr. Index Med.; Biol. Abstr.; Chem. Hazards Ind.; Cumul. Index Nurs. Allied Health Lit.; Curr. Contents Clin. Med.; EMBASE; Energy Res. Abstr. (Aug. 1982-); Health Devices Alerts; Health Plan. Adminis.; Index Med.; Index Vet.; INIS Atomindex [Micro.]; Int. Pharm. Abstr.; Lab. Hazards Bull.; Med. Abstr. Newsl.; Mod. Med.; Nutr. Abstr. Rev., Ser. A, Hum. Exp.; Life Sci. Collect.; Physic. Medline Plus; Protozoolog. Abstr.; Res. Alert [Select. Cov.]; Rev. Med. Vet. Entomol.; Rev. Med. Vet. Mycology; SCISEARCH; Soc. Sci. Cit. Index [Select. Cov.]; SportSearch.

US
**ANNUAL REPORT - INTERAGENCY COMMITTEE ON EMERGENCY MEDICAL SERVICES, HEALTH SERVICES ADMINISTRATION. Main/Corp** United States. Interagency Committee on Emergency Medical Services. English. an. US Department of Health and Human Services, 200 Independence Avenue Southwest, Washington DC 20201.

UK/0264-4924
**ARCHIVES OF EMERGENCY MEDICINE.** ***Title Change.*** [Arch. emerg. med.]. Vol. 1, No. 1 (Mar. 1984)-(1993). Academic Scholarly Publication. English. qt. Blackwell Scientific Publications Ltd, Marston Book Services, PO Box 87, Oxford OX2 ODT UK. **Tel** 011 44 865 791155, FAX 011 44 865 791927, telex 837 515 MARDIS G. **(Subscription address:** UK/ Marston Book Services, PO Box 87, Oxford UK; US/ 3 Cambridge Center, Suite 208, Cambridge MA 02142; Aus/ 54 University Street, Carlton Victoria 3053 Australia; Germany/ Meinekestrasse 4, D-1000 Berlin 15 Germany; France/ Arnette, 2 rue Casimir Delavigne, 75006 Paris France; Austria/ Blackwell MZV, Medizinische Zeitschriftenverlags Gesellschaft, Feldgasse 13, A-1238 Vienna Austria**) NLM** W1; AR454F. **[CCC]. Pr Rev.** Documents available from The Genuine Article. ***Continued by*** *Journal of Accident and Emergency Medicine.*
**Ind/Abst** Curr. Contents Clin. Med.; EMBASE; Health Plan. Adminis.; Health Serv. Abstr.; Index Med. (1984-); Protozoolog. Abstr.; Res. Alert [Select. Cov.]; Risk Abstr. (19??-19??); SCISEARCH; Soc. Sci. Cit. Index [Select. Cov.].

US
**CATALOGUE OF EMERGENCY MEDICINE RESIDENCY PROGRAMS.** **Added/Corp** Society for Academic Emergency Medicine (U.S.). (1990/1991)-. English.

SP/0213-5353
**CIRUGIA DE URGENCIA.** ***Suspended.*** [Cir. urgencia]. (1986)-Suspended. Periodical. Spanish (English). qt. Jarpyo Editores SA, Antonio Lopez Aguados 4, 28029 Madrid, Spain. **Tel** 011 34 1 3144338, 011 34 1 3144458. **ED** Jose R. Polo. **UDC** 617.5. **Ad Acc. Circ:** 1,000.
**Ind/Abst** Indice Med. Esp.

US/0733-4354
**CLINICS IN EMERGENCY MEDICINE.** ***Ceased.*** [Clin. emerg. med.]. Vol. 1 ( )-?. Monographic series. English. ir. Churchill Livingstone Inc., 650 Avenue of the Americas, New York NY 10011. **Tel** (212)206-5062, FAX (212)727-7808. **(Subscription address:** US/ Churchill Livingstone, Fulfillment Office, PO Box 11318, Birmingham, AL 35202**) ED** Sheldon Jacobson. **NLM** W1 CL831BCP.
**Desc:** This book series effectively bridges the gap between research and the many diverse problems that actually confront the emergency room physician. Each volume presents an intensive, critical review of the latest developments in a specific area of emergency medicine, and features lucid, up-to-date contributions by recognized authorities working in the forefront of that particular specialty.

US
**COMPREHENSIVE PLAN FOR EMERGENCY MEDICAL SERVICES.** **Main/Corp** Indiana. Emergency Medical Services Commission. English. Indiana Emergency Medical Services Commission, 315 State Office Building, Indianapolis IN 46204. **LC** RA645.6.I5; I5A. **DD** 362.1/8/09772.

FR/0296-1350
**CONTACT & URGENCES 92. VFOAT** Contact et Urgences Quatre-vingt Douze. (1985)-. Periodical. French. Eleven times a year. 113.75F. Getam, 8 Allee de la Mare Jodoin, 91190 Gif-sur-Yvette France. **Tel** 011 31 1 47010909. **UDC** 658.382.3 : 614.88 (443.61).

US/0090-3493
**CRITICAL CARE MEDICINE.** [Crit. care med.]. **Added/Corp** Society of Critical Care Medicine. Vol. 1 (Jan./Feb. 1973)-. Academic Scholarly Publication. English. mo. $169.00 (institution) $109.00 (individual), US; $154.00 (individual), $214.00 (institution), other. Williams & Wilkins Company, 428 East Preston Street, Baltimore MD 21202-3993. **Tel** (410)528-4000, (800)638-6423, FAX (410)528-8596, telex 87669. **(Subscription address:** Williams & Wilkins, PO Box 64380, Baltimore MD 21264.**) ED** William C. Shoemaker. **LC** RC86; .S613. **DD** 616/.025/05. **NLM** W1 CR216K. **CODEN** CCMDC7. **[CCC]. Ad Acc. Pr Rev. Circ:** 10,100. available on CD-ROM. Documents available from

The Genuine Article, BIOSIS Document Express, Quick Copies.
**Desc:** The official journal of the Society of Critical Care Medicine. A cross-disciplinary for hospital-based specialists who treat patients in the ICU and CCU, including anaesthesiologists and critical care nurses.
**Ind/Abst** Abr. Index Med.; Biol. Abstr. (1986-); Cumul. Index Nurs. Allied Health Lit.; Curr. Contents Clin. Med.; EMBASE; Energy Res. Abstr. (July 1982-); Health Devices Alerts; Health Plan. Adminis.; Index Med.; INIS Atomindex [Micro.]; Microbiol. Abstr. Sect. B; Mod. Med.; Nutr. Abstr. Rev., Ser. A, Hum. Exp.; Life Sci. Collect.; Physic. Medline Plus; Protozoolog. Abstr.; Ref. Upd. Deluxe Ed.; Res. Alert [Full Cov.]; Rev. Med. Vet. Mycology; Risk Abstr.; Sci. Cit. Index; SCISEARCH; Soc. Sci. Cit. Index [Select. Cov.].

SA
**CRITICAL HEALTH.** $20.00 (institutions); $12.00 (individuals). Critical Health Wits Medical, PO Box 16250, 2028 Doornfontein, South Africa. **Tel** 27 484 3078.
**Ind/Abst** Hum. Rights Intern. Rep.

US/0894-2293
**CURRENT EMERGENCY DIAGNOSIS & TREATMENT.** (CURRENT EMERGENCY DIAGNOSIS & TREATMENT / EDITED BY JOHN MILLS, MARY T. HO, DONALD D. TRUNKEY.). [Curr. emerg. diagn. treat.]. **VFOAT** Current Eergency Dagnosis and Teatment. 1st Ed.(1983)-. English. be. $38.95 (latest edition). Appleton Century Crofts, Prentice Hall, 200 Old Tappan Road, Old Tappan NJ 07675. **Tel** (201)767-5188, (800)922-0579. **DD** 616.

US/0739-8573
**CURRENT EMERGENCY THERAPY.** [Curr. emerg. ther.]. (1984)-. Periodical. English. an. Appleton Century Crofts, Prentice Hall, 200 Old Tappan Road, Old Tappan NJ 07675. **Tel** (201)767-5188, (800)922-0579. **ED** Richard F. Edlich and Daniel A. Spyker. **LC** RC86; .C87. **DD** 616/.025. **NLM** W1; CU788GF.

US/0736-8070
**DISASTER MEDICINE (PHILADELPHIA, PA.).** (DISASTER MEDICINE : THE OFFICIAL JOURNAL OF THE CLUB OF MAINZ FOR EMERGENCY AND DISASTER MEDICINE WORLDWIDE AND THE INTERNATIONAL LEAGUE OF RED CROSS SOCIETIES.). [Disaster med.]. Vol. 1, No. 1 (Spring 1983)-. Monographic series. English. qt. Price varies per volume. Centrum Philadelphia, 3508 Market Street, Suite 230, Philadelphia PA 19104. **LC** RC86; .D59. **DD** 616/.025/05. **NLM** W1; DI728.

US/1044-9167
**ED MANAGEMENT.** (ED MANAGEMENT : THE MONTHLY UPDATE ON EMERGENCY DEPARTMENT MANAGEMENT.). [ED manage.]. **Added/Corp** American Health Consultants. **VAT** Emergency Department Management. (1989)-. Periodical. English. mo. $269.00 (with continuing medical education credits); $319.00 (without continuing medical credits). American Health Consultants, 3525 Piedmont Road, Suite 400, Atlanta GA 30305. **Tel** (800)688-2421, (404)262-7436. **(Subscription address:** American Health Consultants, PO Box 95278, Chicago IL 60694.**) DD** 362.
**Desc:** Keeps emergency department medical directors, administrators, physicians, and nurse supervisors on top of developments in the business and management of emergency medical care.

SP
**EMERGENCIAS.** Spanish (Spanish). bm. 3.000ptas Spain; $35.00 North America; $40.00 other. Soc Espanola Med Emergencias, Avenida de Felipe II l 8, 28009 Madrid Spain. **Tel** 91 576 7684, FAX 91 576 5488. Index available. cum. index. **Bk Rev. Ad Acc. Circ:** 3,000 (ctrl).
**Desc:** Originals, case reports, letters, and editorials related to emergency medicine.

US/8755-8467
**EMERGENCY CARE QUARTERLY.** ***Ceased.*** [Emerg. care q.]. **VFOAT** ECQ. Vol. 1, No. 1 (April 1985). Ceased (1991). Periodical. English. qt. Aspen Publishers Inc., 7201 McKinney Circle, Frederick MD 21701. **Tel** (800)234-1660, (301)698-7100, FAX (301)251-5784, telex 5106014543. **DD** 616. **NLM** W1; EM6629. **[CCC].** available on microfilm and microfiche from University Microfilms International (UMI).
**Ind/Abst** Cumul. Index Nurs. Allied Health Lit.; EMBASE.

US/0094-6575
**EMERGENCY MEDICAL SERVICES.** [Emerg. med. serv.]. Vol. 1 (Nov./Dec. 1972)-. Periodical. English. Twelve times a year. $18.95 US; $29.00 other. Emergency Medical Services, 7626 Densmore Avenue, Van Nuys CA 91406. **Tel** (818)786-4367, FAX (818)786-9246. **ED** Barbara Feiner. **NLM** W1 EM661V. Index available. cum. index. **Bk Rev. Ad Acc. Circ:** 46,000 (ctrl).
**Desc:** Professional journal with clinical features for paramedics, EMTS, physicians, nurses, rescue personnel and administrators. Covers prehospital and emergency departments.
**Ind/Abst** Cumul. Index Nurs. Allied Health Lit.; Health Devices Alerts; Health Plan. Adminis.; Hospit. Health Admin. Index.

US/0193-7448
**EMERGENCY MEDICAL SERVICES RESEARCH METHODOLOGY WORKSHOP. Added/Corp** National Center for Health Services Research. (Apr. 20/21, 1978)-. English. Vajra Bodhi Sea Publication Society, Sagely City of Ten Thousand Buddhas, Talmage CA 95481-0217. **Tel** (707)462-0939. **NLM** W3 EM51.

US/0884-4836
**EMERGENCY MEDICAL TECHNICIAN LEGAL BULLETIN.** (EMERGENGY MEDICAL TECHNICIAN LEGAL BULLETIN : EMTLB). [Emerg. med. tech. leg. bull.]. **VFOAT** EMTLB. Vol. 1, No. 1 (1976)-. Periodical. English. Four times a year. $15.00. Med/Law Publishing, PO Box 293, Westville NJ 08093. **Tel** (800)848-3721. **DD** 344.
**Ind/Abst** Cumul. Index Nurs. Allied Health Lit.

US/1064-5934
**EMERGENCY MEDICAL UPDATE.** (EMERGENCY MEDICAL UPDATE / VIDEORECORDING.). [Emerg. med. update]. Vol. 1, No. 1 (Nov. 1987)-. English. mo. $898.00. Emergency Medical Update, PO Box 11380, Bainbridge Island WA 98110. **Tel** 800 327-3841, FAX (206)842-5640. **ED** Ellen Lockert. **DD** 616. Index available. cum. index. **Bk Rev**, (Qty: 4). **Ad Acc, Adv Mgr:** Karen Douglas. ctrl circ.
**Desc:** Video based training for continuing education training in the EMS field.

US/0013-6654
**EMERGENCY MEDICINE.** [Emerg. med.]. Vol. 1 (Feb. 1969)-. Periodical. English. Sixteen times a year. $85.00 (institutions), $60.00 (individuals). Excerpta Medica / US, PO Box 3085, Princeton NJ 08543-3085. **Tel** (908)874-8550, FAX (908)874-5611. **(Subscription address:** Emergency Medicine, PO Box 3095, Denville NJ 07834.**) ED** W. E. Wagner. **LC** RC86; .E45. **DD** 616/.02. **NLM** W1 EM664. **Ad Acc. Circ:** 140,000 (ctrl). available on microfilm and microfiche from University Microfilms International (UMI).
**Desc:** Medical journal that concentrates on issues of acute medicine for the primary care physician, with an emphasis on trauma and related issues.
**Ind/Abst** Cumul. Index Nurs. Allied Health Lit.; Health Devices Alerts; Health Plan. Adminis.; Physic. Medline Plus.

US/0733-8627
**EMERGENCY MEDICINE CLINICS OF NORTH AMERICA.** [Emerg. med. clin. North Am.]. Vol. 1, No. 1 (April 1983)-. Monographic series. English. qt. $92.00 (individual), $110.00 (institution) US; $125.00 (individual), $132.00 (institution) other. W.B. Saunders Company, A Subsidiary of Harcourt Brace Jovanovich, Inc., The Curtis Center/Suite 300, Independence Square West, Philadelphia PA 19106-3399. **Tel** (215)238-7800 or, 5587, FAX (215)238-7883, telex 173146. **(Subscription address:** W. B. Saunders Company / North America Subscriptions, c/o Periodicals, 6277 Sea Harbour Drive, 4th Floor, Orlando FL 32887.**) ED** Mary K. Smith. **LC** UNC. **NLM** W1 EM661J. **CODEN** EMCAD7. **[CCC].** Index available. **Circ:** 5,100. available on microfilm and microfiche from University Microfilms International (UMI). Documents available from BIOSIS Document Express.
**Desc:** Each issue contains 13 to 17 practice applicable articles, in a symposium format, on important, current topics and review topics in emergency medicine.
**Ind/Abst** Biol. Abstr.; Cumul. Index Nurs. Allied Health Lit.; EMBASE; Health Plan. Adminis.; Index Med. (Vol. 1, No. 1, 1983-); Physic. Medline Plus.

US/1054-0725
**EMERGENCY MEDICINE NEWS.** [Emerg. med. news]. Vol. 11, No. 7 (July 1989)-. Periodical. English. mo. $90.00 (individuals), $123.00 (institutions) US; $116.00 (individuals), $162.00 (institutions) other. J.B. Lippincott Company, 227 East Washington Square, Philadelphia PA 19106-3780. **Tel** (215)238-4200 or 4454, FAX (215)238-4227. **(Subscription address:** J.B. Lippincott, PO Box 350, Hagerstown MD 21740.**) DD** 616. **NLM** W1; EM661JAF. **[CCC].** available on microfilm and microfiche from University Microfilms International (UMI). ***Continues*** *Emergency Medicine & Ambulatory Care News, 1042-7023.*

US/0887-7343
**EMERGENCY MEDICINE OBSERVER.** [Emerg. med. obs.]. Vol. 1, No. 1 (Sept. 1986)-. Periodical. English. mo. $65.00. Aspen Publishers Inc., 7201 McKinney Circle, Frederick MD 21701. **Tel** (800)234-1660, (301)698-7100, FAX (301)251-5784, telex 5106014543. **(Subscription address:** Aspen Publishers Inc., PO Box 990, Frederick MD 21701.**) DD** 616. **NLM** W1; EM661JB.

US/0746-2506
**EMERGENCY MEDICINE REPORTS.** [Emerg. med. rep.]. Vol. 4, No. 14 (July 11, 1983)-. Periodical. English. bw. $219.00 without CME; $294.00 with CME. American Health Consultants, 3525 Piedmont Road, Suite 400, Atlanta GA 30305. **Tel** (800)688-2421, (404)262-7436. **(Subscription address:** American Health Consultants, PO Box 95278, Chicago IL 60694.**) NLM** W1; EM661JF. **[CCC].** ***Continues*** *ER Reports.*
**Desc:** Features original state-of-the-art review articles on important clinical issues in emergency medicine with practical treatment recommendations.

●UK
**EMERGENCY NURSE : THE JOURNAL OF THE RCN ACCIDENT AND EMERGENCY NURSING ASSOCIATION.** **See** Medical Science and Technology-Nursing.

CN/0836-7272
**EMERGENCY PREHOSPITAL MEDICINE.** [Emerg. prehosp. med.]. Vol. 2, No. 1 (June/July/Aug. 1987)-. Periodical. English. Six times a year (Jan., Mar., May, Jul., Sep., Nov.). 35.00Can$ Canada, 45.00Can$ other (one year); 55.00Can$ Canada, 65.00Can$ other (two years); 78.99Can$ Canada, 88.99Can$ other (three years). CME Communications, Inc, 20854 Dalton Road, PO Box 507, Sutton West ONT L0E 1RO Canada. **Tel** (416)722-9839/ 800-262-1095, FAX (416)722-9687. **(Subscription address:** PO Box 507, Sutton West ONT L0E 1RO Canada**) ED** Michael Raschotte. **DD** 616/.025/05. **NLM** W1; EM664E. **Ad Acc, Adv Mgr:** John Moir, **Tel** (416)722-9839. ***Continues*** *Canadian Journal of Prehospital Medicine, 0829-5603.*
**Desc:** Focusing on the continuing emergency prehospital medical education of ambulance officers, paramedics, emergency room nurses, and most recently, firefighters.

US
**EMR ON-LINE.** (19??)-. English. American Health Consultants, 3525 Piedmont Road, Suite 400, Atlanta GA 30305. **Tel** (800)688-2421, (404)262-7436. **(Subscription address:** American Health Consultants, PO Box 95278, Chicago IL 60694.**)**
**Desc:** A user-friendly state-of-the-art emergency medical clinical infobase drawn from Emergency Medicine Reports issues 1988 through the present.

US/0275-0716
**EMS COMMUNICATOR.** ***Title Change.*** [EMS commun.]. **VAT** Emergency Medical Services Communicator. (1974)-?. Periodical. English. bm. Mosby Year Book Inc., 11830 Westline Industrial Drive, St Louis MO 63146. **Tel** (800)325-4177, (314)872-8370, FAX (314)432-1380, telex 44-2402. **ED** E. Thomas Wetzel. **Bk Rev.** ***Continued by*** *EMS Insider.*
**Desc:** News of developments in emergency medical services and emergency medicine.

US
**EMS INSIDER.** (19??)-. Periodical. English. mo. $90.00. Mosby Year Book Inc., 11830 Westline Industrial Drive, St Louis MO 63146. **Tel** (800)325-4177, (314)872-8370, FAX (314)432-1380, telex 44-2402. **(Subscription address:** JEMS Communications, PO Box 2789, Carlsbad CA 92018.**)** ***Continues*** *EMS Communicator, 0275-0716.*
**Desc:** Designed to keep administrators and other decision-makers in the emergency medical field informed of late breaking news in the industry.

US/0897-0297
**EMS LEADER, THE.** ***Ceased.*** [EMS lead.]. **VAT** Emergency Medical Services Leader. Vol. 4 No. 1 (Jan/Feb 1988)-(1992). Periodical. English. bm. Cornell Publishing and Communications, 330 Garfield Avenue, Eau Claire WI 54701. **Tel** (715)834-6046. **ED** Dixie Cornell. **DD** 362. Index available. cum. index. **Bk Rev. Circ:** 500. ***Continues*** *Ambulance Manager, 0882-150X.*
**Desc:** Management information for the busy EMS manager. Topics include: motivation of crew, recruitment, public relations, national news and the personal side.

US/1056-7062
**ENA'S NURSING SCAN IN EMERGENCY CARE.** **See** Medical Science and Technology-Nursing.

US/0098-1524
**EPLB. EMERGENCY PHYSICIAN LEGAL BULLETIN. VFOAT** Emergency Physician Legal Bulletin. Vol. 1 (1975)-. Bulletin. English. qt. $25.00. Medical Publishers Inc, PO Box 293, Westville NJ 08093. **ED** James E George. **NLM** W1 E51. ctrl circ.
**Desc:** Covers medical legal aspects of emergency care.

NZ/0113-1990
**FRONTLINE DUNEDIN.** (FRONTLINE.). [Frontline Duned.]. **VFOAT** Front Line. (1987)-. Periodical. English. bm (Feb., Apr., June, Aug., Oct., Dec.). $90.00. Frontline Subscriptions, PO Box 1679, Christchurch New Zealand. **Tel** FAX 011 64 9 8371548. **ED** Brian Copley. **DD** 362.18. **Ad Acc. Circ:** 1,200 (ctrl).

●US/1073-6506
**INSIDE AMBULATORY CARE.** [Inside ambul. care]. Vol. 1, No. 1 (Apr. 1994)-. Periodical. English. mo. $189.00. Aspen Publishers Inc., 7201 McKinney Circle, Frederick MD 21701. **Tel** (800)234-1660, (301)698-7100, FAX (301)251-5784, telex 5106014543. **(Subscription address:** Aspen Publishers Inc., PO Box 990, Frederick MD 21701.**) DD** 362.

US/0197-2510
**JEMS.** (JEMS : A JOURNAL OF EMERGENCY MEDICAL SERVICES.). [JEMS]. **VFOAT** J.E.M.S.; Journal of Emergency Medical Services. **VAT** Journal of

Emergency Medical Services. Vol. 5 No. 1 (Mar. 1980)-. Periodical. English. mo. $23.97 (one year), $42.97 (two year). Mosby Year Book Inc., 11830 Westline Industrial Drive, St Louis MO 63146. **Tel** (800)325-4177, (314)872-8370, FAX (314)432-1380, telex 44-2402. **(Subscription address:** JEMS Communications, PO Box 2789, Carlsbad CA 92018.**) ED** Dana A. Jarvis. **NLM** W1 JO637. **Bk Rev. Ad Acc. Circ:** 30,000. available on microfilm and microfiche from University Microfilms International (UMI). ***Continues** Paramedics International, 0191-6351.*
**Desc:** Serves the providers and administrators of emergency medical care and rescue with the latest news and educational information relevant to this field.
**Ind/Abst** Cumul. Index Nurs. Allied Health Lit.; Health Devices Alerts; Health Plan. Adminis.; Hospit. Health Admin. Index.

FR
**JOURNAL EUROPEEN DES URGENCIES : JEUR. VFOAT** JEUR; European Journal of Emergencies. (1988)-. Periodical. French (English). qt. $168.00. Masson Editeur, Box Postale 22, 41353 Vineuil 16 France. **Tel** 011 33 54 438994. **(Subscription address:** 7A Boulevard de Perolles, CH-1701 Fribourg Switzerland**) NLM** W1; JO37706. **CODEN** JEUREC.
**Ind/Abst** EMBASE.

●UK/1351
**JOURNAL OF ACCIDENT & EMERGENCY MEDICINE. VFOAT** Journal of Accident and Emergency Medicine. (1994)-. Academic Scholarly Publication. English. qt. $254.00 US & Canada; £149.00 Europe; £164.00 other. Blackwell Scientific Publications Ltd, Marston Book Services, PO Box 87, Oxford OX2 ODT UK. **Tel** 011 44 865 791155, FAX 011 44 865 791927, telex 837 515 MARDIS G. **NLM** W1; JO533PH. ***Continues** Archives of Emergency Medicine, 0264-4924.*

US/0886-9723
**JOURNAL OF AMBULATORY CARE MARKETING.** [J. ambul. care mark.]. Vol. 1, No. 1 (Spring/Summer 1987)-. Periodical. English. sa. $90.00 US; $126.00 other. The Haworth Press Inc, 10 Alice Street, Binghamton NY 13904-1580. **Tel** (607)722-5857, (800)3-HAWORTH, FAX (607)722-1424. **ED** Robert Sweeney (editor's address: VP Marketing and Sales, 194 Yates Road South, Memphis, TN 38120-2256). **DD** 362. **Bk Rev. Ad Acc. Pr Rev. Acid Free. Circ:** 116. available on microfilm and microfiche from University Microfilms International (UMI). Documents available from Haworth Document Delivery Service. ***Continues** Emergency Health Services Review, 0738-6192.*
**Desc:** Focuses on the marketing of traditional emergency health care, urgent/convenient care services, surgicenters, group practices providing emergency ambulatory care and new sectors of health care such as HMOS, IPAS, and PPOS that are involved in the provision of ambulatory health care services.
**Ind/Abst** EMBASE; Health Plan. Adminis.; Hospit. Health Admin. Index (1987-); Hospit. Manage. Rev.; Hum. Resour. Abstr. (?-?); Soc. Work Abstr. (1987-?).

US/0736-4679
**JOURNAL OF EMERGENCY MEDICINE, THE.** [J. emerg. med.]. Vol. 1, No. 1 (1983)-. Periodical. English. bm. $320.00 The Americas; £215.00 other. Pergamon Press, An Imprint of Elsevier Science Ltd., The Boulevard, Langford Lane, Kidlington, Oxford OX5 1GB United Kingdom. **Tel** 011 44 865 843000, 011 44 865 843699, FAX 011 44 865 843010. **(Subscription address:** Elsevier Science Ltd. Oxford Fulfillment Centre, PO Box 800, Kidlington, Oxford OX5 1DX United Kingdom.**) ED** Peter Rosen. **NLM** W1; JO638. **[CCC].** available on microfilm and microfiche from University Microfilms International (UMI).
**Desc:** Features authoritative, timely articles pertinent to the practicing emergency physician.
**Ind/Abst** Cumul. Index Nurs. Allied Health Lit.; Curr. Aware. Biol. Sci., CABS; EMBASE; Health Saf. Sci. Abstr.; Index Med. (Vol. 1, No. 1, 1983-) (Vol. 1 No. 1, 1983-); Life Sci. Collect. (1983-); Physic. Medline Plus; Pollut. Abstr. Indexes; Rev. Med. Vet. Entomol.

US/0099-1767
**JOURNAL OF EMERGENCY NURSING.** **See** Medical Science and Technology-Nursing.

IT/1120-8708
**JOURNAL OF EMERGENCY SURGERY AND INTENSIVE CARE, THE.** **See** Medical Science and Technology-Surgery.

UK
**JOURNAL OF THE BRITISH ASSOCIATION FOR IMMEDIATE CARE, THE. Added/Corp** British Association for Immediate Care. (19??)-. Periodical. English. Three times a year (Jan., July, and Nov.). £18.00 UK and Eire; £20.00 other. Basics, 7 Black Horse Lane, Ipswich Suff 1P1 2 EF England. **Tel** (0473)218407. **ED** B. Robertson. **NLM** W1 JO913M. Index available. cum. index. **Bk Rev. Ad Acc. Circ:** 2,200.
**Desc:** Aims to promote prehospital care and be a forum for original research, equipment evaluations and correspondence relevant to the immediate care field.

US/0275-2735
**MEDICAL 911. *Title Change.* Added/Corp** Emergency Care Information Center. **VAT** Medical Nine Eleven. (1974)-(19??). Periodical. English. bm. JEMS Publishing Company, 1947 Camino Vida Robleste 200, Carlsbad CA 92008. **Tel** (619)431-9797, FAX (619)481-2711. **ED** E. Thomas Wetzel. ***Continued by** Medical 911 Sourcebooks.*
**Desc:** A resource guide to reports, books, films, instructional materials, journal articles and organizations related to emergency medical services.

US
**MEDICAL 911 SOURCEBOOK.** (19??)-. Periodical. English. an. $65.95. JEMS Publishing Company, 1947 Camino Vida Robleste 200, Carlsbad CA 92008. **Tel** (619)431-9797, FAX (619)481-2711. ***Continues** Medical 911.*

US/0192-6055
**NEWSLETTER - AMBULANCE & MEDICAL SERVICES ASSOCIATION OF AMERICA. VAT** Newsletter - Ambulance and Medical Services Association of America. V. 1- July 1978-. Newsletter. English. **NLM** W1 NE997TM.

US
**NHSC HEALTH CARE PRACTITIONERS. Main/Corp** National Health Service Corps (U.S.). **VAT** National Health Service Corps Health Care Practitioners. English. US Department of Health & Human Services / Public Health Service, 200 Independence Avenue SW, Room 716G, Washington DC 20201. **Tel** (202)690-6867, FAX (202)690-6274. **NLM** W 22.AA1 N101.

GW/0177-2309
**NOTARZT, DER.** (DER NOTARZT / HERAUSGEBER, BAND (BUNDESVEREINIGUNG DER ARBEITSGEMEINSCHAFTEN NOTARZTE DEUTSCHLANDS).). [Notarzt]. **Added/Corp** Bundesvereinigung der Arbeitsgemeinschaften Notarzte Deutschlands. Vol., No. 1 (Jan. 1985)-. Periodical. German. bm. $79.00. Georg Thieme Verlag Stuttgart, Postfach 301120, D 70451 Stuttgart Germany. **Tel** 011 49 711 89310, FAX 011 49 711 8931298, telex 7 252 275 GTVD. **(Subscription address:** Thieme Medical Publishers Inc., 381 Park Avenue South, New York NY 10016.**) NLM** W1; NO701.
**Ind/Abst** EMBASE [Select. Cov.].

GW/0341-2903
**NOTFALL-MEDIZIN (ERLANGEN).** (NOTFALLMEDIZIN.). [Notfall-Med.]. Vol. 1 (Oct. 1975)-. Academic Scholarly Publication. German. Twelve times a year. DM96.00 Germany, DM109.20 others. Perimed Spitta Med Verlagsges, Marienbergstrasse 78, D 90411 Nuernberg Germany. **Tel** 011 49 911 952800. **NLM** W1 NO763P. **Bk Rev. Ad Acc. Circ:** 40,000 (ctrl).
**Desc:** First-aid measures in emergency situations and first-aid equipment.
**Ind/Abst** EMBASE [Select. Cov.].

CN/1183-1049
**ON SCENE (CALGARY).** (ON SCENE.). [On scene]. Vol. 1, No. 1 (June 1990)-. Periodical. English. Eight times a year. 24.00Can$ Canada; 34.00Can$ other. On Scene Communications, PO Box 71067, Silver Springs, Calgary Alberta T3B 5K2 Canada. **Tel** (800)663-0312. **DD** 616.02/5/05.

US/0270-207X
**OUTREACH (CHICAGO).** (OUTREACH.). [Outreach]. **Added/Corp** American Hospital Association. Center for Ambulatory Care. Vol. 1 (March/April 1980)-. English. bm. $65.00 member, $85.00 non-member. American Hospital Association, 840 North Lake Shore Drive, Chicago IL 60611. **Tel** (312)280-6000, (800)242-2626. **ED** Diane M. Howard. **NLM** W1 OU56. **Bk Rev. Circ:** 8,000 (ctrl).
**Desc:** Ambulatory care management issues into homecare hospice PPO's, HMO's ambulatory surgery and emergency services.

US/0749-5161
**PEDIATRIC EMERGENCY CARE.** [Pediatr. emerg. care]. Vol. 1, No. 1 (March 1985)-. Periodical. English. bm. $84.00 (individual) $134.00 (institution) US; $109.00 (individual), $159.00 (institution) other. Williams & Wilkins Company, 428 East Preston Street, Baltimore MD 21202-3993. **Tel** (410)528-4000, (800)638-6423, FAX (410)528-8596, telex 87669. **(Subscription address:** Williams & Wilkins, PO Box 64380, Baltimore MD 21264.**) ED** Stephen Ludwig and Gary Fleisher. **DD** 618. **NLM** W1; PE167FC. **CODEN** PECAE5. **[CCC]. Ad Acc. Circ:** 2,200. available on microfilm. Documents available from The Genuine Article, BIOSIS Document Express, Quick Copies.
**Desc:** Valuable clinical information for emergency physicians and pediatricians who care for acutely ill or injured children and adolescents.
**Ind/Abst** Biol. Abstr. (1987-); Curr. Contents Clin. Med.; EMBASE; Index Med. (1985-); Res. Alert [Select. Cov.]; SCISEARCH.

US/0896-5382
**PRACTICAL REVIEWS IN EMERGENCY MEDICINE.** (PRACTICAL REVIEWS IN EMERGENCY MEDICINE [SOUND RECORDING].). [Pract. rev. emerg. med.]. **Added/Corp** Educational Reviews, Inc. Montefiore Medical Center. **VFOAT** Practical reviews. (197?)-. Periodical. English. mo. $175.00 Physicians/Dentists; $125.00 Residents. Educational Reviews Inc., 6801 Cahaba Valley Road, Birmingham AL 35242. **Tel** (205)991-5188, (800)633-4743, FAX (205)995-1926. **DD** 616.
**Desc:** Abstract cards of articles found in the journal literature.

US/1063-3332
**PREHOSPITAL CARE REPORTS. *Ceased.* Added/Corp** American Health Consultants. (19??)-(1992). Periodical. English. mo. American Health Consultants, 3525 Piedmont Road, Suite 400, Atlanta GA 30305. **Tel** (800)688-2421, (404)262-7436. **DD** 617.
**Desc:** State-of-the-art emergency care guidelines for paramedics and other prehospital care givers.

US/0744-3471
**PROFESSIONALS. Added/Corp** Wisconsin Emergency Medical Technicians Association. **VFOAT** Ambulance, Rescue, Fire and Police. Your Community. (19??)-. Periodical. English. Six times a year. $18.00. Wisconsin Emergency Medical Technicians Association - WEMTA, 21332 Seven Mile Road, Franksville WI 53126. **Tel** (800)793-6820. **ED** Don Hunjadi (Editor's phone: (414)895-6098). **Ad Acc, Adv Mgr:** R. Seliger, **Tel** (414)895-6098. **Circ:** 2,500 (ctrl). ***Continues** WEMTA Journal, 0194-519X.*

FR
**REANIMATION D'URGENCES.** (19??)-. French. 1050.00F France; 1350.00F or $270.00 other. Blackwell Scientific Publishers / Arnette, 2 rue Casimir-Delavigne, 75006 Paris France. **Tel** 011 33 1 44860770, FAX 011 33 1 46336797.

FR/0246-1234
**REANIMATION ET MEDECINE D'URGENCE. *Ceased.*** [Reanim. med. urgence]. **VFOAT** Conferences de Reanimation et de Medecine d'Urgence de l'Hopital Raymond Poincare et de l'Hopital Henri Mondor. (1968)-?. Academic Scholarly Publication. French. an. Expansion Scientifique Francaise, 31 Boulevard de la Tour-Maubourg, 75007 Paris France. **Tel** 011 33 1 40 62 64 00, 011 33 1 40626439. **NLM** W3 RE288. **CODEN** RMDUA8. **[CCC].** Documents available from BIOSIS Document Express, CASDDS.
**Ind/Abst** Biol. Abstr.; Chem. Abstr.

US/0272-1368
**REFLECTIONS (LOS ANGELES).** (REFLECTIONS.). [Reflections]. Periodical. English. bm. Free to members. Director's Office, Emergency Medicine Center, UCLA Hospitals and Clinics, 10833 Le Conte Avenue, Los Angeles CA 90024. **NLM** W1 RE1698M. ***Continues** Weekly Reader (Los Angeles, Calif.).*

SZ/0377-8347
**SCHWEIZERISCHE ZEITSCHRIFT FUER MILITAR- UND KATASTROPHENMEDIZIN.** [Schweizer. Z. Mil. - Katastr.med.]. **Added/Corp** Schweizerische Gesellschaft der Offiziere der Sanitatstruppen. **VFOAT** Revue Suisse de Medecine Militaire et de Catastrophes; Rivista Svizzera di Medicina Militaire e di Catastrofe. Vol. 52 (May 1975)-. Periodical. Multiple languages. Four times a year. 68.00F Switzerland; 88.00F other. Medecine et Hygiene, Case Postale 456, CH-1211 Geneve 4 Switzerland. **Tel** 011 41 22 3469355, 011 41 22 3469356. **NLM** W1 SC591. ***Continues** Schweizerische Zeitschrift fuer Militarmedizin, 0036-8024.*
**Ind/Abst** EMBASE.

US/0272-555X
**STAT (SANTA MONICA).** (STAT.). [Stat]. V. 1- Spring 1979-. Periodical. English. qt. Janzen Johnston and Rockwell, PO Box 92198, Los Angeles CA 90009-2198. **LC** RC86; .S75. **DD** 616/.025. **NLM** W1 ST292B.

US/0164-2340
**TOPICS IN EMERGENCY MEDICINE.** [Top. emerg. med.]. **Added/Corp** Aspen Systems Corporation. Vol. 1 (May 1979)-. Academic Scholarly Publication. English. qt. $81.00 US and Canada. Aspen Publishers Inc., 7201 McKinney Circle, Frederick MD 21701. **Tel** (800)234-1660, (301)698-7100, FAX (301)251-5784, telex 5106014543. **(Subscription address:** Aspen Publishers Inc., PO Box 990, Frederick MD 21701.**) ED** M. Borenstein and C. G. Warner. **LC** UNC. **NLM** W1 TO539LL. **[CCC]. Pr Rev.** available on microfilm and microfiche from University Microfilms International (UMI).
**Desc:** A critical companion for emergency care procedures. An important vehicle for advanced continuing education. Designed to be your vital information link with the latest developments in emergency medicine.
**Ind/Abst** Cumul. Index Nurs. Allied Health Lit.; EMBASE; Hospit. Health Admin. Index.

GW/0177-5537
**UNFALLCHIRURG, DER.** [Unfallchirurg]. **Added/Corp** Deutsche Gesellschaft fuer Unfallheilkunde.

Vol. 88, No. 1, (Jan. 1985)-. Periodical. German (summaries and/or abstracts in English and German). Twelve times a year. DM468.00. Springer-Verlag GmbH & Company KG, Heidelberger Platz 3, D 14197 Berlin Germany. **Tel** 011 49 30 8207223, FAX 011 49 30 8214091, telex 183 319 SPBLN D. **(Subscription address:** Springer Verlag New York Inc. / for North America, 44 Hartz Way, Secaucus NJ 07096.**)** **ED** J Rehn, L Schweiberer, and H Tscherne. **LC** R51; .D28. **DD** 617. **NLM** W1; UN103Y. **CODEN** UNFAE2. **[CCC]**. **Pr Rev.** available on microfilm from University Microfilms International (UMI). Documents available from The Genuine Article, BIOSIS Document Express. ***Continues*** *Unfallheilkunde, 0341-5694.*
**Desc:** Journal for emergency medicine. Offers original articles on research, critical commentaries on procedure, and technique up-dates. Data on burns, head injuries, and legal ramifications.
**Ind/Abst** Biol. Abstr. (1985-); Curr. Contents Clin. Med.; EMBASE; Index Med. (1985-); Res. Alert [Select. Cov.].

US/0271-7964
**YEAR BOOK OF EMERGENCY MEDICINE, THE.** [Year book of emerg. med.]. **VAT** Yearbook of Emergency Medicine. (1981)-. English. an (Feb.). $64.95. Mosby Year Book Inc., 11830 Westline Industrial Drive, St Louis MO 63146. **Tel** (800)325-4177, (314)872-8370, FAX (314)432-1380, telex 44-2402. **LC** RC86; .Y4. **DD** 616/.025/05. **NLM** W1 YE143.

•GW
**YEARBOOK OF INTENSIVE CARE AND EMERGENCY MEDICINE.** (1992)-. English. Springer-Verlag GmbH & Company KG, Heidelberger Platz 3, D 14197 Berlin Germany. **Tel** 011 49 30 8207223, FAX 011 49 30 8214091, telex 183 319 SPBLN D. **(Subscription address:** Springer Verlag New York Inc. / for North America, 44 Hartz Way, Secaucus NJ 07096.**)** **NLM** W1; YE199GL. ***Continues in part*** *Update in Intensive Care and Emergency Medicine.*

## ENDOCRINOLOGY

GW/0940-5429
**ACTA DIABETOLOGICA.** [Acta diabetol.]. Vol. 28, No. 2 (1991/1992)-. Academic Scholarly Publication. English. Four times a year. DM356.00. Springer-Verlag GmbH & Company KG, Heidelberger Platz 3, D 14197 Berlin Germany. **Tel** 011 49 30 8207223, FAX 011 49 30 8214091, telex 183 319 SPBLN D. **(Subscription address:** Springer Verlag New York Inc. / for North America, 44 Hartz Way, Secaucus NJ 07096.**)** **NLM** W1; AC7927. **CODEN** ACDAEZ. Documents available from The Genuine Article, BIOSIS Document Express, CASDDS. ***Continues*** *Acta Diabetologica Latina, 0001-5563.*
**Desc:** Publishing reports of experimental and clinical research on diabetes mellitus and related metabolic diseases. Features original articles on biochemical, physiological, pathophysiological and clinical aspects of research on diabetes and metabolic diseases.
**Ind/Abst** Biol. Abstr. (1991-); Chem. Abstr. (1991-); Curr. Contents Life Sci.; EMBASE (1991-); Index Med. (1991-); Res. Alert [Full Cov.]; Sci. Cit. Index; SCISEARCH.

DK/0001-5598
**ACTA ENDOCRINOLOGICA (COPENHAGEN).** (ACTA ENDOCRINOLOGICA.). [Acta endocrinol.]. Vol. 1 (1948)-. Academic Scholarly Publication. English (French and German). mo. Kr2150.00 Scandinavia; Kr2275.00 other. Scandinavian University Press, PO Box 2959 Toeyen, N 0608 Oslo 6 Norway. **Tel** 011 47 2 2575400, FAX 011 47 2 2575353, telex 71896 UROR N. **(Subscription address:** Scandinavian University Press, 200 Meacham Ave., Elmont NY 11003.**)** **NLM** W1; AC798. **CODEN** ACENA7. **[CCC]**. Index available. **Pr Rev. Circ:** 2,000 (ctrl). Documents available from The Genuine Article, BIOSIS Document Express, CASDDS.
**Desc:** Publishes papers dealing with clinical and experimental endocrinology. The subscription price also covers supplements, comprising scientifically selected monographs and proceedings from endocrinological meetings and symposia.
**Ind/Abst** AGRICOLA; Anim. Breed. Abstr.; Annals Behav. Med.; Biol. Abstr.; Calcium Calcif. Tissue Abstr.; Chem. Abstr.; CIS Abstr.; CSA Neuro. Abstr.; Curr. Aware. Biol. Sci., CABS; Curr. Contents Life Sci.; Curr. Ref. Fish Res.; Dairy Sci. Abstr.; EMBASE; Energy Res. Abstr.; Fish Rev.; Health Plan. Adminis.; Index Med.; Index Vet.; NAPRALERT; Nucl. Sci. Abstr.; Nutr. Abstr. Rev., Ser. B, Live Feeds and Feed.; Nutr. Abstr. Rev., Ser. A, Hum. Exp.; Oncog. Growth Factors Abstr.; Life Sci. Collect.; PESTDOC; Pig News Inf.; Poult. Abstr.; Ref. Upd. Basic Ed.; Ref. Upd. Clinical Ed.; Ref. Upd. Deluxe Ed.; Res. Alert [Full Cov.]; Rev. Med. Vet. Entomol.; Saf. Health Work; Sci. Cit. Index; SCISEARCH; Small Anim. Abstr. Bibliogr.; Soc. Sci. Cit. Index [Select. Cov.]; SportSearch; Vet. Bull.; Wildl. Rev.

DK/0300-9750
**ACTA ENDOCRINOLOGICA. SUPPLEMENTUM.** [Acta endocrinol., Suppl.]. (1948)-. Academic Scholarly Publication. English (French and German). ir. Comes with Acta Endocrinologica. Scandinavian University Press, PO Box 2959 Toeyen, N 0608 Oslo 6 Norway. **Tel** 011 47 2 2575400, FAX 011 47 2 2575353, telex 71896 UROR N. **(Subscription address:** Scandinavian University Press, 200 Meacham Ave., Elmont NY 11003.**)** **LC** QP1; .A184. **NLM** W1 AC7981. **CODEN** ACEDAB. Documents available from BIOSIS Document Express, CASDDS.
**Ind/Abst** Biol. Abstr.; Chem. Abstr.; Curr. Aware. Biol. Sci., CABS; EMBASE; Energy Res. Abstr.; Index Med. (1948-1988); Life Sci. Collect.

US/1049-6734
**ADVANCES IN ENDOCRINOLOGY AND METABOLISM.** Vol. 1 (1990)-. English. an (Oct.). $69.95. Mosby Year Book Inc., 11830 Westline Industrial Drive, St Louis MO 63146. **Tel** (800)325-4177, (314)872-8370, FAX (314)432-1380, telex 44-2402. **LC** RC648.a1; A4. **DD** 616.4/005. **NLM** W1; AD552L.
**Ind/Abst** Ref. Upd. Deluxe Ed.

US/0732-8141
**ADVANCES IN PROSTAGLANDIN, THROMBOXANE, AND LEUKOTRIENE RESEARCH.** [Adv. prostaglandin thromboxane leukotriene res.]. Vol. 9 (1982)-. Academic Scholarly Publication. English. ir. Price varies per volume. Raven Press, 1185 Avenue of the Americas, 37th Floor, New York NY 10036. **Tel** (212)930-9500, (212)930-9604, FAX (212)869-3495, (212)302-8507, telex 640073. **ED** Bengt Samuelsson and Rodolfo Paoletti. **LC** QP801.P68; A36. **DD** 612/.015. **NLM** W1 AD788. **CODEN** ATLRD6. **[CCC]**. Documents available from The Genuine Article, BIOSIS Document Express, CASDDS. ***Continues*** *Advances in Prostaglandin and Thromboxane Research, 0361-5952.*
**Desc:** Information on prostaglandins, thromboxanes, leukotrienes, and lipoxygenases.
**Ind/Abst** Biol. Abstr.; Chem. Abstr.; Index Med.; Index Sci. Rev. [Full Cov.]; Mass Spect. Bull. (?-?); PESTDOC; Res. Alert [Full Cov.]; Sci. Cit. Index (19??-19??); SCISEARCH.

GW/0943-1837
**AKTUELLE ENDOKRINOLOGIE.** ***Ceased.*** (1992)-(1993). English. Four times a year. Georg Thieme Verlag Stuttgart, Postfach 301120, D 70451 Stuttgart Germany. **Tel** 011 49 711 89310, FAX 011 49 711 8931298, telex 7 252 275 GTVD. **(Subscription address:** Thieme Medical Publishers Inc., 381 Park Avenue South, New York NY 10016.**)** ***Continues*** *Aktuelle Endokrinologie und Stoffwechsel, 0172-4606.*

GW/0172-4606
**AKTUELLE ENDOKRINOLOGIE UND STOFFWECHSEL.** ***Title Change.*** [Aktuel. Endokrinol. Stoffwechsel]. Vol. 1, (Jan. 1980)-(19??). Academic Scholarly Publication. German. qt. Georg Thieme Verlag Stuttgart, Postfach 301120, D 70451 Stuttgart Germany. **Tel** 011 49 711 89310, FAX 011 49 711 8931298, telex 7 252 275 GTVD. **(Subscription address:** Thieme Medical Publishers Inc., 381 Park Avenue South, New York, NY 10016**)** **NLM** W1 AK992AE. **CODEN** AENSDG. **[CCC]**. Documents available from CASDDS. ***Continued by*** *Aktuelle Endokrinologie.*
**Ind/Abst** Chem. Abstr.; EMBASE.

US/0193-1849
**AMERICAN JOURNAL OF PHYSIOLOGY : ENDOCRINOLOGY AND METABOLISM.** **See** Biology-Physiology.

FR/0003-4266
**ANNALES D'ENDOCRINOLOGIE.** [Ann. endocrinol.]. **Added/Corp** Societe Francaise d'Endocrinologie. Vol. 1 (March 1939)-. Academic Scholarly Publication. French (English). bm. $345.00. Masson Editeur, Box Postale 22, 41353 Vineuil 16 France. **Tel** 011 33 54 438994. **(Subscription address:** 7A Boulevard de Perolles, CH-1701 Fribourg Switzerland**)** **NLM** W1 AN396H. **CODEN** ANENAG. **[CCC]**. **Pr Rev.** available on microfilm and microfiche from University Microfilms International (UMI). Documents available from The Genuine Article, BIOSIS Document Express, CASDDS.
**Ind/Abst** Anim. Breed. Abstr.; Biol. Abstr.; Chem. Abstr.; CSA Neuro. Abstr.; Curr. Contents Life Sci.; Curr. Ref. Fish Res.; Dairy Sci. Abstr.; EMBASE; Energy Res. Abstr.; Health Plan. Adminis.; Index Med.; Index Vet.; Nutr. Abstr. Rev., Ser. A, Hum. Exp.; Life Sci. Collect.; Protozoolog. Abstr.; Res. Alert [Full Cov.]; Sci. Cit. Index; SCISEARCH.

AT/1031-4709
**ANNUAL REPORT AND ACCOUNTS - HOWARD FLOREY INSTITUTE OF EXPERIMENTAL PHYSIOLOGY AND MEDICINE.** (ANNUAL REPORT AND ACCOUNTS.). [Annu. rep. acc. - Howard Florey Inst. Exp. Physiol. Med.]. **Main/Corp** Howard Florey Institute of Experimental Physiology and Medicine. (1985)-. English. **NLM** W1; AN759CDG. ***Continues*** *Annual Report and Notice of Meeting - Howard Florey Institute of Experimental Physiology and Medicine, 0314-6162.*

US
**APPENDIX TO THE DIABETES MELLITUS COORDINATING COMMITTEE ... ANNUAL REPORT TO THE DIRECTOR, NATIONAL INSTITUTES OF HEALTH.** 6th (Fiscal Year 1979)-. English. an. Diabetes Mellitus Coordinating Committee, National Institutes of Health, Bethesda MD 20205.

BL/0004-2730
**ARQUIVOS BRASILEIROS DE ENDOCRINOLOGIA E METABOLOGIA.** [Arq. bras. endocrinol. metabol.]. V. 5- 1955-. Periodical. Portuguese. ir. Inst de Endocrinologia, rua Santa Luzia 206ZC-39, Rio de Janeiro GB Brazil. **NLM** W1 AR869. **CODEN** ABENAY. Documents available from BIOSIS Document Express, CASDDS. ***Continues*** *Arquivos Brasileiros de Endocrinologia, 0301-5343.*
**Ind/Abst** Biol. Abstr.; Chem. Abstr.; EMBASE.

UK/0950-351X
**BAILLIERE'S CLINICAL ENDOCRINOLOGY AND METABOLISM.** [Bailliere's clin. endocrinol. metab.]. **VFOAT** Clinical Endocrinology and Metabolism; Endocrinology and Metabolism. Vol. 1, No. 1 (Feb. 1987)-. Periodical. English. qt (4 issues). £94.00 (institution). Harcourt Brace & Company Ltd., Foots Cray, High Street, Sidcup Kent DA14 5HP England. **Tel** 011 44 81 300 3322, FAX 011 44 81 309 0807. **(Subscription address:** W. B. Saunders Company / North America Subscriptions, c/o Periodicals, 6277 Sea Harbour Drive, 4th Floor, Orlando FL 32887.**)** **NLM** W1; BA46EE. **[CCC]**. Index available. **Pr Rev.** available on microfilm. Documents available from The Genuine Article. ***Continues in part*** *Clinics in Endocrinology and Metabolism, 0300-595X.*
**Ind/Abst** Curr. Contents Clin. Med.; Curr. Contents Life Sci.; EMBASE; Health Plan. Adminis.; Index Med. (Feb. 1987-); Res. Alert [Full Cov.]; Sci. Cit. Index; SCISEARCH; Soc. Sci. Cit. Index [Select. Cov.].

US/0277-7886
**BASIC AND CLINICAL ENDOCRINOLOGY.** [Basic clinc. endocrinol.]. (1981)-. Academic Scholarly Publication. English. ir. Price varies per volume. Marcel Dekker Inc., 270 Madison Avenue, New York NY 10016. **Tel** (212)696-9000, (800)228-1160, FAX (212)685-4540, telex 421419. **(Subscription address:** Marcel Dekker Inc, PO Box 5017, Monticello NY 12701.**)** **LC** UNC. **DD** 616.4/005. **NLM** W1 BA813T. **CODEN** BCLEDT. Documents available from BIOSIS Document Express, CASDDS.
**Desc:** Covers topics in endocrinology such as metabolism and endocrine disorders.
**Ind/Abst** Biol. Abstr. (1985-); Chem. Abstr.

CN/0710-0248
**BETA RELEASE.** (BETA RELEASE : BRINGING EDUCATION TO ALL / CANADIAN DIABETIC ASSOCIATION.). [Beta release]. **Added/Corp** Canadian Diabetic Association. Professional Health Workers Section. (1976)-. Periodical. English. Four times a year (Jan., Apr., July, Oct.). 26.75Can$. Canadian Diabetes Association, 15 Toronto Street, Suite 1001, Toronto Ontario M5C 2E3 Canada. **Tel** (416)363-3373. **DD** 616.4/62/005. **[CCC]**.
**Ind/Abst** Cumul. Index Nurs. Allied Health Lit.

NE/0169-6009
**BONE AND MINERAL.** [Bone and miner.]. **Added/Corp** International Conference on Calcium Regulating Hormones. Vol. 1, No. 1 (Feb. 1986)-. Academic Scholarly Publication. English. Twelve times a year (4 volumes). $790.00. Elsevier Science Ireland Ltd., Bay 15, Shannon Industrial Estate, Co Clare Ireland. **Tel** 011 353 61 471944. **ED** David V. Cohn. **NLM** W1; BO707CH. **CODEN** BOMIET. **[CCC]**. **Pr Rev.** available on microfilm and microfiche from University Microfilms International (UMI). Documents available from The Genuine Article, BIOSIS Document Express, CASDDS.
**Desc:** Publishes original research articles and invited reviews on work relating to the structure, function, and development of bone and on factors and hormones that regulate bone metabolism.
**Ind/Abst** Biol. Abstr. (1986-); Calcium Calcif. Tissue Abstr.; Chem. Abstr. (1986-); CSA Neuro. Abstr.; Curr. Aware. Biol. Sci., CABS; EMBASE; Health Plan. Adminis.; Index Med.; Index Vet.; Nutr. Abstr. Rev., Ser. A, Hum. Exp.; Nutr. Res. Newsl.; Ref. Upd. Deluxe Ed.; Res. Alert [Full Cov.]; Sci. Cit. Index; SCISEARCH; Vet. Bull.

US/0891-8929
**CLINICAL DIABETES.** [Clin. diabetes]. **Added/Corp** American Diabetes Association. Vol. 1, No. 1 (Jan./Feb. 1983)-. Periodical. English. bm. $40.00 (institution) North America. American Diabetes Association, National Service Center, 1660 Duke Street, Alexandria VA 22314. **Tel** (703)549-1500, (800)232-3472, FAX (703)836-2464. **(Subscription address:** American Diabetes Association, Journal Subscriptions, Department 0028, Washington DC 20073.**)** **DD** 616. **NLM** W1; CL692. **CODEN** CLDIE8. available on microfilm and microfiche from University Microfilms International (UMI); available on an online database (file 149/Full-Text) from DIALOG. Documents available from

BIOSIS Document Express.
**Ind/Abst** Biol. Abstr. (1986-); Health Index (1989-); Health Period. Database [Full Txt.]; Health Ref. Cent. (Jan. 1989-) [Full Cov.]; Mod. Med.

●US/1059-0471
**CLINICAL ENDOCRINOLOGY (NEW YORK, N.Y.,1992).** (CLINICAL ENDOCRINOLOGY.). (1992)-. Periodical. English. qt. $120.00. Mary Ann Liebert Inc., 1651 Third Avenue, New York NY 10128. **Tel** (212)289-2300, (800)M-LIEBERT, FAX (212)289-4697.

UK/0300-0664
**CLINICAL ENDOCRINOLOGY (OXFORD).** (CLINICAL ENDOCRINOLOGY.). [Clin. endocrinol.]. Vol. 1 (Jan. 1972)-. Academic Scholarly Publication. English. mo (12 issues). $595.00 US & Canada; £349.50 Europe; £384.00 other. Blackwell Scientific Publications Ltd, Marston Book Services, PO Box 87, Oxford OX2 ODT UK. **Tel** 011 44 865 791155, FAX 011 44 865 791927, telex 837 515 MARDIS G. **ED** D. C. Anderson and J. S. Jenkins. **NLM** W1 CL696. **CODEN** CLECAP. **[CCC]. Bk Rev. Ad Acc. Pr Rev. Circ:** 1,360. available on microfilm and microfiche from University Microfilms International (UMI). Documents available from The Genuine Article, BIOSIS Document Express, CASDDS, ADONIS.
**Desc:** Publishes material contributing directly to the understanding of human endocrine disorder.
**Ind/Abst** ADONIS; Biol. Abstr.; Chem. Abstr.; CSA Neuro. Abstr.; Curr. Aware. Biol. Sci., CABS; Curr. Contents Clin. Med.; Curr. Contents Life Sci.; Dairy Sci. Abstr.; EMBASE; Index Med.; Nutr. Abstr. Rev., Ser. B, Live Feeds and Feed.; Nutr. Abstr. Rev., Ser. A, Hum. Exp.; Life Sci. Collect.; PESTDOC; Protozoolog. Abstr.; Ref. Upd. Basic Ed.; Ref. Upd. Clinical Ed.; Ref. Upd. Deluxe Ed.; Res. Alert [Full Cov.]; Sci. Cit. Index; SCISEARCH; SportSearch.

JA/0918-5739
**CLINICAL PEDIATRIC ENDOCRINOLOGY.** [Clin. pediatr. endocrinol.]. (1992)-. Periodical. English. sa. ¥5000.00 (institutions), ¥2000.00 (individuals) Japan; ¥7000.00 (institutions), ¥3000.00 (individuals) other. Jeff Corporation Co. Ltd., Shiba Shimura Building 4F 2-3-12, Shib Minato-ku Tokyo 105 Japan. **ED** Jeff K. Ishiwata. **Circ:** 1,500.

US/0160-242X
**COMPREHENSIVE ENDOCRINOLOGY.** [Compr. endocrinol.]. (1979)-. Monographic series. English. ir. Price varies per volume. Raven Press, 1185 Avenue of the Americas, 37th Floor, New York NY 10036. **Tel** (212)930-9500, (212)930-9604, FAX (212)869-3495, (212)302-8507, telex 640073. **ED** Luciano Martini. ***Continues*** *Comprehensive Endocrinology Series, 0271-1850.*

US/0196-8653
**CONTEMPORARY ENDOCRINOLOGY.** [Contemp. endocrinol.]. (1979)-. Academic Scholarly Publication. English. ir. Price varies per volume. Plenum Press, 233 Spring Street, New York NY 10013-1578. **Tel** (212)620-8000, (800)221-9369, FAX (212)463-0742, (212)807-1047, telex 23/421139. **ED** Sidney H. Ingbar. **LC** QP187.A1; Y4. **DD** 612/.4/005. **NLM** W1 CO769MPE. **CODEN** CNEND7. Documents available from CASDDS. ***Supersedes*** *Year in Endocrinology, 0146-4078.*
**Ind/Abst** Chem. Abstr. (1979).

US/1070-9282
**COUNTDOWN / JUVENILE DIABETES FOUNDATION INTERNATIONAL.** [Countdown]. **Added/Corp** Juvenile Diabetes Foundation International. **VFOAT** JDF International Countdown. (19??)-. Periodical. English. qt. $25.00 (US); $30.00 (including postage) other. Juvenile Diabetes Foundation International, 432 Park Avenue South, New York NY 10016. **Tel** (212)889-7575, FAX (212)725-7259. **ED** Glenn Peterson. **DD** 616. **Bk Rev. Ad Acc, Adv Mgr:** Sandy Dylak. **Circ:** 150,000. ***Continues*** *Diabetes Countdown.*
**Desc:** From an international arena of diabetes investigators, to parents of small children with diabetes, from physicians to school teachers, pharmacists to corporate executives, readers look to Countdown for the latest news in diabetes research and treatment.

●UK/0964-8720
**CURRENT ADVANCES IN ENDOCRINOLOGY AND METABOLISM.**
**See** Medical Science and Technology-Abstracting, Bibliographies and Statistics.

UK/0265-797X
**CURRENT MEDICAL LITERATURE. DIABETES.** [Curr. med. lit., Diabetes]. (1984)-. Periodical. English. qt. £20.00. Current Medical Literature Ltd., 40-42 Osnaburgh Street, London NW1 3ND England. **Tel** 011 44 71 4658377, FAX 011 44 71 4658380. **(Subscription address:** Royal Society Medicine Services, 1 Wimpole Street, London W1M 8AE England.**)** **DD** 016.616462.

●US/1068-3097
**CURRENT OPINION IN ENDOCRINOLOGY & DIABETES.** [Curr. opin. endocrinol. diabetes]. **VFOAT** Current Opinion in Endocrinology and Diabetes. 1st Edition (1994)-. English. Six times a year. $129.95 (individuals); $259.95 (institutions). Current Science, 20 North 3rd Street, Philadelphia PA 19106. **Tel** (215)574-2266, (800)552-5866, FAX (215)574-2270. **DD** 616. **NLM** W1; CU799GCMB.

US/0091-7397
**CURRENT TOPICS IN EXPERIMENTAL ENDOCRINOLOGY.** [Curr. top. exp. endocrinol.]. Vol. 1 (1971)-. Monographic series. English. ir. Price varies per volume. Academic Press, Inc., 6277 Sea Harbor Drive, Orlando FL 32887. **Tel** (800)543-9534, (407)345-4100, FAX (407)363-9661. **ED** L. Martini and V. H. T. James. **LC** RC648.A1; C86. **DD** 616.4/027. **NLM** W1 CU82H. **CODEN** CTEEAJ. Documents available from BIOSIS Document Express, CASDDS.
**Ind/Abst** Biol. Abstr. (?-1978); Chem. Abstr.; Energy Res. Abstr. (Jan. 1974-).

GW/0723-1229
**CURRENT TOPICS IN NEUROENDOCRINOLOGY.** [Curr. tap. neuroendocrinol.]. Vol. 1 (1982)-. Academic Scholarly Publication. English. ir. Price varies per volume. Springer-Verlag GmbH & Company KG, Heidelberger Platz 3, D 14197 Berlin Germany. **Tel** 011 49 30 8207223, FAX 011 49 30 8214091, telex 183 319 SPBLN D. **(Subscription address:** Springer Verlag New York Inc. / for North America, 44 Hartz Way, Secaucus NJ 07096.**)** **ED** D. Ganten, D. Pfaff. **LC** UNC. **NLM** W1 CU82Q. **CODEN** CTNEEY. Documents available from BIOSIS Document Express, CASDDS.
**Ind/Abst** Biol. Abstr. (1985-); Chem. Abstr.

UK/0742-3616
**CURRENT TOPICS IN REPRODUCTIVE ENDOCRINOLOGY.** [Curr. top. reprod. endocrinol.]. **VFOAT** Wiley Series on Current Topics in Reproductive Endocrinology. Vol. 1-. Academic Scholarly Publication. English. Price varies per volume. John Wiley & Sons, Inc., 605 Third Avenue, New York NY 10158-0012. **Tel** (212)850-6000, (212)850-6645, FAX (212)850-6088, telex 12-7063. **(Subscription address:** John Wiley & Sons / England, Baffins Lane, Chichester, West Sussex PO19 1UD England.**)** **ED** S L Jeffcoate. **NLM** W3 CU614. **CODEN** CTENEG. Documents available from CASDDS.
**Ind/Abst** Chem. Abstr.

US/0167-6334
**DEVELOPMENTS IN ENDOCRINOLOGY (THE HAGUE).** ***Ceased.*** (DEVELOPMENTS IN ENDOCRINOLOGY.). [Dev. endocrinol.]. **Added/Corp** Commission of the European Communities. Vol. 1 (1981)-(19??). Academic Scholarly Publication. English. ir. Kluwer Academic Publishers / Massachusetts, PO Box 358, Accord Station, Hingham MA 02018. **Tel** (617)871-6600. **LC** UNC. **NLM** W1 DE997VWB. **CODEN** DVEND6. Documents available from CASDDS.
**Ind/Abst** Chem. Abstr. (1981-?).

FR/0338-1684
**DIABETE & METABOLISME.** [Diabete metab.]. **Added/Corp** Association de Langue Francaise pour l'Etude du Diabete et Des Maladies Metaboliques. Vol. 1 (1975)-. Academic Scholarly Publication. French (English). bm. $231.00. Masson Editeur, Box Postale 22, 41353 Vineuil 16 France. **Tel** 011 33 54 438994. **(Subscription address:** 7A Boulevard de Perolles, CH-1701 Fribourg Switzerland**)** **NLM** W1 DI139. **CODEN** DIMEDU. **[CCC]. Pr Rev.** Documents available from The Genuine Article, BIOSIS Document Express, CASDDS. ***Continues*** *Diabete.*
**Ind/Abst** Biol. Abstr.; Chem. Abstr.; CSA Neuro. Abstr.; Curr. Contents Life Sci.; EMBASE; Index Med.; Nutr. Abstr. Rev., Ser. B, Live Feeds and Feed.; Nutr. Abstr. Rev., Ser. A, Hum. Exp.; Life Sci. Collect.; Res. Alert [Full Cov.]; Sci. Cit. Index; SCISEARCH; Soc. Sci. Cit. Index [Select. Cov.]; SportSearch.

FR/0012-1789
**DIABETE ET NUTRITION.** [Diabete nutr.]. (1955)-. French. qt. 120.00F France; 135.00F other. Semad, 37 Ave Norman Price, 64000 Pau France. **Tel** 33 16 58802952. **ED** Pierre Massabie Semad (editor's phone: 33 16 59275285). **UDC** 613.2. **Ad Acc. Circ:** 6,000 (ctrl).

VE/0378-6277
**DIABETES (CARACAS).** (DIABETES.). Yearly V. 1- 1976-. Periodical. Spanish. **NLM** W1 DI152N.
**Ind/Abst** CSA Neuro. Abstr.; Immunol. Abstr.; Ref. Upd. Basic Ed.; Ref. Upd. Clinical Ed.; Ref. Upd. Deluxe Ed.

US/0149-5992
**DIABETES CARE.** [Diabetes care]. **Added/Corp** American Diabetes Association. Vol. 1 (Jan./Feb. 1978)-. Academic Scholarly Publication. English. Twelve times a year. $150.00 (institution) North America. American Diabetes Association, National Service Center, 1660 Duke Street, Alexandria VA 22314. **Tel** (703)549-1500, (800)232-3472, FAX (703)836-2464. **(Subscription address:** American Diabetes Association, Journal Subscriptions, Department 0028, Washington DC 20073.**)** **ED** Allan Drash. **LC** RC660.A1; D49. **DD** 616.4/62/005. **NLM** W1 DI161Q. **CODEN** DICAD2. **Bk Rev. Ad Acc. Pr Rev. Circ:** 10,300. available on microfilm and microfiche from University Microfilms International (UMI). Documents available from The Genuine Article, BIOSIS Document Express, CASDDS.
**Desc:** This journal presents research advances with clinical relevance. Articles on clinical practice, commentaries, digests of recent research reports, clinical news, clinical reviews, and policies of the American Diabetes Association of Control, Diagnosis, Diet and Therapy.
**Ind/Abst** AGRICOLA [Select. Cov.]; Annals Behav. Med.; Biol. Abstr. (1987-); Chem. Abstr.; Chicano Index; CSA Neuro. Abstr.; Cumul. Index Nurs. Allied Health Lit.; Curr. Contents Clin. Med.; Curr. Contents Life Sci.; EMBASE; Health Plan. Adminis.; Index Med. (1978-); Int. Pharm. Abstr.; Mod. Med.; Nutr. Abstr. Rev., Ser. A, Hum. Exp.; Nutr. Res. Newsl.; Physic. Medline Plus; Ref. Upd. Deluxe Ed.; Res. Alert [Full Cov.]; Sci. Cit. Index; SCISEARCH; Soc. Sci. Cit. Index [Select. Cov.]; SportSearch.

US/1055-8322
**DIABETES CONSULTANT.** [Diabetes consult.]. Vol. 1, Issue 1 (1991)-. Periodical. English. qt. Free. Dellacorte Publications, 919 3rd Avenue, New York NY 10022-3904. **Tel** (212)751-2806. **DD** 616.

UK
**DIABETES CONTENTS.** (1987)-. English. Four times a year. £14.00 UK, £16.00 other Europe; £20.00 other. British Diabetic Association, 10 Queen Anne Street, London W1M 0BD England. **Tel** 011 44 71 323 1531, FAX 011 44 71 637 3644. **ED** Katy Griggs. Index available. **Circ:** 400.

US
**DIABETES DATELINE : THE NDIC BULLETIN.** **Added/Corp** National Diabetes Information Clearinghouse (U.S.). Vol. 1, No. 1 (Sept. 1979)-. Periodical. English. Six times a year. Free. National Diabetes Information Clearinghouse, Box NDIC, Bethesda MD 20205. **Tel** (301)468-2162. **ED** Beatrice Jakubowski. **Bk Rev. Circ:** 6,000 (ctrl).
**Desc:** Announcements of meetings, new materials, research studies, and other topics relevant to diabetes care.

CN/0703-5764
**DIABETES DIALOGUE.** [Diabetes dialogue]. **Added/Corp** Canadian Diabetic Association. Canadian Diabetes Association. Vol. 24 1st Quarter (1977)-. Periodical. English. qt. 15.00Can$ Canada; 20.00Can$ other (membership to the Canadian Diabetes Association). Canadian Diabetes Association, 15 Toronto Street, Suite 1001, Toronto Ontario M5C 2E3 Canada. **Tel** (416)363-3373. **ED** R.D. Silver. **DD** 616.4/62/005. **Ad Acc.** ***Continues*** *Canadian Diabetic Association. Newsletter, 0007-8018.*
**Desc:** Presents news, information, and research findings on diabetes.

US/0145-7217
**DIABETES EDUCATOR, THE.** [Diabetes educ.]. **Added/Corp** American Association of Diabetes Educators. (19??)-. Periodical. English. bm. $45.00 (subscription) $175.00 (institutional membership), $55.00 (individual membership) US; $47.00 Canada; $52.00 other. American Association of Diabetes Educators, 444 North Michigan Avenue / Suite 1240, Chicago IL 60611. **Tel** (312)645-1710, (800)338-3633, FAX (312)661-0769. **ED** James W. Pichert and Martha Urban. **LC** RC660.A1; A494. **DD** 616.4/62/005. **NLM** W1 DI161R. **CODEN** DIEDEM. Index available. **Bk Rev. Ad Acc. Circ:** 5,660.
**Desc:** Vehicle for reaching healthcare professionals who recommend, select and purchase products and services. Targets diabetes healthcare professionals, principal providers of patient education. Serves as a reference for the science and art of diabetes management.
**Ind/Abst** AGRICOLA [Select. Cov.]; Annals Behav. Med.; Chicano Index; Cumul. Index Nurs. Allied Health Lit.; Health Plan. Adminis.; Index Med.; Int. Nurs. Index; Nutr. Res. Newsl.

US/0095-8301
**DIABETES FORECAST.** [Diabetes forecast]. **Added/Corp** American Diabetes Association. Vol. 27, No. 6 (Nov./Dec. 1974)-. Periodical. English. Twelve times a year. $24.00 US; $39.00 Mexico; $41.73 Canada (institution). American Diabetes Association, National Service Center, 1660 Duke Street, Alexandria VA 22314. **Tel** (703)549-1500, (800)232-3472, FAX (703)836-2464. **(Subscription address:** American Diabetes Association, Journal Subscriptions, Department 0028, Washington DC 20073.**)** **ED** Philip Levy. **LC** RC660.A1; A5213. **DD** 616.4/62/005. **NLM** W1 DI161T. **Ad Acc. Circ:** 215,455 (ctrl). available on an online database (file 149/Full-Text) from DIALOG. ***Continues*** *ADA Forecast, 0001-0847.*
**Desc:** The consumer publication of the American Diabetes Association. The magazine helps people with diabetes and their families lead normal, healthy lives by providing comprehensive, accurate, and timely information and support on all aspects of diabetes treatment, management and self care. With its lively upbeat tone, profiles of people with diabetes from all walks of life, recipes, diet and exercise articles, Diabetes

Forecast is the lifestyle magazine for people with diabetes.
**Ind/Abst** AGRICOLA [Select. Cov.]; Consum. Health Nutr. Index; Cumul. Index Nurs. Allied Health Lit.; Health Index (1989-); Health Period. Database [Full Txt.]; Health Ref. Cent. (Jan. 1989-) [Full Txt.] [Full Cov.].

US/0893-5939
**DIABETES IN THE NEWS : DITN.** [Diabetes news]. **VFOAT** DITN. (Jan./Feb. 1987)-. Periodical. English. bm. $12.00 (1 year), $22.00 (2 year). Miles Laboratories Inc, Ames Education Service, 1201 North Clark Street/Suite 405, Chicago IL 60610. **Tel** (312)664-9782. **ED** Morton B Stone. **DD** 616. Index available. cum. index. **Bk Rev. Ad Acc. Circ:** 110,000 (ctrl). ***Continues** DITN, 8750-1244.*
**Desc:** Consumer health related.
**Ind/Abst** Acad. Abstr. Full Text Elite (Jan. 1992-); Acad. Abstr. (Jan. 1992-); Acad. Search (Jan. 1992-); Health Period. Database [Full Txt.]; Health Ref. Cent. (Jan. 1989-) [Full Txt.] [Full Cov.]; Health Source (Jan. 1992-); INFO-SOUTH Abstr.; Mag. Search.

US/0742-4221
**DIABETES/METABOLISM REVIEWS.** [Diabetes/metab. rev.]. **VFOAT** Diabetes Metabolism Reviews. Vol. 1, No. 1 & 2 (1985)-. Academic Scholarly Publication. English. Four times a year. $325.00. John Wiley & Sons, Inc., 605 Third Avenue, New York NY 10158-0012. **Tel** (212)850-6000, (212)850-6645, FAX (212)850-6088, telex 12-7063. **(Subscription address:** John Wiley & Sons / England, Baffins Lane, Chichester, West Sussex PO19 1UD England.**) ED** D .Andreani. **DD** 616. **NLM** W1; DI163H. **CODEN** DMREEG. **[CCC]. Pr Rev.** available on microfilm and microfiche from University Microfilms International (UMI). Documents available from The Genuine Article, BIOSIS Document Express, CASDDS, ADONIS.
**Desc:** Provides an ongoing update of clinical and basic scientific advances in the most important areas of diabetes and metabolism. The areas of study include endocrinology, insulin secretion, resistance, ketone metabolism, obesity and lipid metabolism, pathogenesis and cellular action of insulin.
**Ind/Abst** ADONIS; Biol. Abstr. (1985-); Chem. Abstr. (1986-); Curr. Aware. Biol. Sci., CABS; Curr. Contents Clin. Med.; Curr. Contents Life Sci.; EMBASE; Health Plan. Adminis.; Index Med. (1985-); Nutr. Res. Newsl.; Res. Alert [Select. Cov.].

US/0012-1797
**DIABETES (NEW YORK, N.Y.).** (DIABETES.). [Diabetes]. **Added/Corp** American Diabetes Association. Vol. 1 (Jan./Feb. 1952)-. Academic Scholarly Publication. English. mo. $200.00 (institution) North America. American Diabetes Association, National Service Center, 1660 Duke Street, Alexandria VA 22314. **Tel** (703)549-1500, (800)232-3472, FAX (703)836-2464. **(Subscription address:** American Diabetes Association, Journal Subscriptions, Department 0028, Washington DC 20073.**) ED** Philip Cryer. **LC** RC660.A1; A5214. **DD** 616. **NLM** W1 DI151. **CODEN** DIAEAZ. Index available. **Pr Rev.** Documents available from The Genuine Article, CASDDS. ***Formed by the union of** Proceedings of the American Diabetes Association, 0097-1472 **and** Diabetes Abstracts.*
**Desc:** Published for researchers concerned with diabetes and related endocrine and metabolic disorders. It contains major scientific papers and review articles, editorials, and association news. Every volume is indexed by author and subject.
**Ind/Abst** Abr. Index Med.; AGRICOLA [Select. Cov.]; Biostatistica (19??-19??); Calcium Calcif. Tissue Abstr.; Chem. Abstr.; Curr. Aware. Biol. Sci., CABS; Curr. Contents Clin. Med.; Curr. Contents Life Sci.; Dairy Sci. Abstr.; EMBASE; Health Period. Database [Full Txt.]; Health Plan. Adminis.; Index Med.; INIS Atomindex [Micro.]; Int. Pharm. Abstr.; Med. Abstr. Newsl.; Mod. Med.; Nutr. Abstr. Rev., Ser. B, Live Feeds and Feed.; Nutr. Abstr. Rev., Ser. A, Hum. Exp.; Nutr. Res. Newsl.; Oncog. Growth Factors Abstr.; Life Sci. Collect.; PESTDOC; Physic. Medline Plus; Res. Alert [Full Cov.]; Sci. Cit. Index; SCISEARCH; Soc. Sci. Cit. Index [Select. Cov.]; SportSearch; Trop. Dis. Bull.

US/1048-5597
**DIABETES NEWS DIGEST. *Suspended.*** [Diabetes news dig.]. (Jan. 1990)-. Periodical. English. bm. $30.00. Medupdate, 845 Richardson, Palo Alto CA 94303. **Tel** (415)424-8208. **DD** 616.
**Desc:** Contains comprehensive coverage of research developments, available products and general diabetes news from leading journals.

SP/0213-5787
**DIABETES NEWS ED. ESPANOLA.** (DIABETES NEWS). [Diabetes newsEd. esp.]. (1980)-. Periodical. Spanish. qt. Boehringer Mannheim SA, Copernico 61-63, 08006 Barcelona Spain. **UDC** 616.379-008.64.

US/0895-0644
**DIABETES PATIENT.** (1990)-. Periodical. English. bm. Tom Jones Associates, 270 Pascack Road, Woodcliff Lake NJ 07675.

UK/1056-053X
**DIABETES, PREVENTION AND THERAPY.** (DIABETES, PREVENTION AND THERAPY : I.D.I.G. NWSLETTER.). [Diabetes prev. ther.]. **Added/Corp** International Diabetes Federation. International Diabetes Immunotherapy Group. **VFOAT** Diabetes, Prevention & Therapy. (198?)-. Periodical. English. Four times a year. $65.00. John Wiley & Sons Ltd., Baffins Lane, Chichester West Sussex PO19 1UD England. **Tel** 0243 779777, FAX 0243 776128 BTG:JWP001, telex 86290 WIBOOKG. **(Subscription address:** John Wiley / Philadelphia, PO Box 7247, Philadelphia PA 19170.**) ED** Paolo Pozzilli. **DD** 616. **NLM** W1; DI167L. **CODEN** DPTHEM.
**Desc:** Provides information and stimulates debate through the discussion and analysis of old and new issues, and the publication of proposals, statements and trials data relating to the prediction, prevention and therapy of insulin-dependent diabetes mellitus.

NE/0168-8227
**DIABETES RESEARCH AND CLINICAL PRACTICE.** [Diabetes res. clin. pract.]. **Added/Corp** International Diabetes Federation. Western Pacific Region of IDF. Vol. 1, No. 1 (1985)-. Academic Scholarly Publication. English. Twelve times a year (4 volumes). $878.00. Elsevier Science Ireland Ltd., Bay 15, Shannon Industrial Estate, Co Clare Ireland. **Tel** 011 353 61 471944. **ED** S. Baba, Y. Goto, J.J. Hoet, L.P. Krall, and J.R. Turtle. **NLM** W1; DI167T. **CODEN** DRCPE9. **Pr Rev.** available on microfilm from University Microfilms International (UMI). Documents available from The Genuine Article, BIOSIS Document Express, CASDDS.
**Desc:** Devoted to covering original research articles and high quality reviews in areas of growing interest in the field of epidemiology, experimental biology, nutrition, ecology and clinical practice, including occasional case reports.
**Ind/Abst** Biol. Abstr. (1985-); Chem. Abstr. (1985-); Curr. Contents Clin. Med.; EMBASE; Health Plan. Adminis.; Index Med. (Vol. 1, No. 1, 1985-); Nutr. Abstr. Rev., Ser. A, Hum. Exp.; Nutr. Res. Newsl. (Vol. 1, No. 1, 1985-); Protozoolog. Abstr. (1985-); Ref. Upd. Deluxe Ed.; Res. Alert [Full Cov.]; Sci. Cit. Index; SCISEARCH; Soc. Sci. Cit. Index [Select. Cov.].

NE/0168-8227
**DIABETES RESEARCH AND CLINICAL PRACTICE.** (DIABETES RESEARCH AND CLINICAL PRACTICE. SUPPLEMENT.). [Diabetes res. clin. pract.]. **Added/Corp** International Diabetes Federation. Western Pacific Region of IDF. (1985)-. Monographic series. English. Price varies per volume. Elsevier Science Ireland Ltd., Bay 15, Shannon Industrial Estate, Co Clare Ireland. **Tel** 011 353 61 471944. **NLM** W1; DI167TA. **Pr Rev.**
**Ind/Abst** Index Med.

UK/0256-5985
**DIABETES RESEARCH (EDINBURGH, LOTHIAN).** (DIABETES RESEARCH.). [Diabetes res.]. Vol. 1 No. 1 (May 1984)-. Academic Scholarly Publication. English. mo. £395.00 EEC countries; £495.00 others; $975.00 US. Teviot Scientific Publications, 82 Great King Street, Edinburgh EH3 6QU Scotland. **Tel** 011 44 31 3328764, FAX 011 44 31 3432633. **NLM** W1; DI167R. **CODEN** DIREEM. **Pr Rev.** Documents available from The Genuine Article, CASDDS.
**Ind/Abst** Chem. Abstr. (1984-); EMBASE; Health Plan. Adminis.; Index Med. (Vol. 1, No. 1, 1984-); Nutr. Abstr. Rev., Ser. A, Hum. Exp.; Protozoolog. Abstr.; Res. Alert [Select. Cov.]; Wheat Barley Trit. Abstr.

●US/1066-9442
**DIABETES REVIEWS (ALEXANDRIA, VA.).** (DIABETES REVIEWS.). [Diabet. rev.]. **Added/Corp** American Diabetes Association. Vol. 1, No. 1 (Spring 1993)-. Periodical. English. qt. $125.00 (institution) North America. American Diabetes Association, National Service Center, 1660 Duke Street, Alexandria VA 22314. **Tel** (703)549-1500, (800)232-3472, FAX (703)836-2464. **(Subscription address:** American Diabetes Association, Journal Subscriptions, Department 0028, Washington DC 20073.**) DD** 616. **NLM** W1; DI168BL.

US/0741-6253
**DIABETES SELF-MANAGEMENT.** [Diabetes self-manage.]. **VFOAT** Diabetes Self Management. (Winter 1983/84)-. Periodical. English. bm. $18.00 US; $24.00 Canada; $36.00 other. R A Rapaport Publishing Inc, 150 West 22nd Street, New York NY 10011. **Tel** (212)989-0200. **(Subscription address:** Diabetes Self-Management, PO Box 52890, Boulder, CO 80322-2890**) ED** James Hazlett. **DD** 616. **CODEN** DSMAEL. **Bk Rev. Ad Acc. Circ:** 150,000.
**Desc:** Aimed at the diabetic population, containing articles of interest to all diabetics, in subjects such as health, medication, and diet.
**Ind/Abst** Foods Adlibra.

US/1040-9165
**DIABETES SPECTRUM.** [Diabetes spectr.]. **Added/Corp** American Diabetes Association. Vol. 1, No. 1 (March/April 1988)-. Periodical. English. bm. $40.00 (institution) North America. American Diabetes Association, National Service Center, 1660 Duke Street, Alexandria VA 22314. **Tel** (703)549-1500, (800)232-3472, FAX (703)836-2464. **(Subscription address:** American Diabetes Association, Journal Subscriptions, Department 0028, Washington DC 20073.**) ED** Elizabeth A. Walker. **LC** RC660.A1; D526. **DD** 616.4/62/005. **NLM** W1; DI68BV. **Bk Rev. Ad Acc. Circ:** 12,000. available on microfilm from University Microfilms International (UMI).
**Desc:** This bimonthly magazine translates the latest diabetes research advances into practical treatment advice. Diabetes spectrum is designed for the nurse, educator, dietitian, pharmacist every member of the health care team.

US
**DIABETES. [MICROFICHE].** (19??)-. English. ir. University Microfilms International, 300 North Zeeb Road, Ann Arbor MI 48106-1346. **Tel** (313)761-4700, (800)521-0600 Exts. 2490, 2491, FAX (313)973-1540. available in print.

UK/0742-3071
**DIABETIC MEDICINE.** (DIABETIC MEDICINE : A JOURNAL OF THE BRITISH DIABETIC ASSOCIATION.). [Diabet. med.]. **Added/Corp** British Diabetic Association. Vol. 1, No. 1 (May 1984)-. Periodical. English. mo. $395.00. John Wiley & Sons Ltd., Baffins Lane, Chichester West Sussex PO19 1UD England. **Tel** 0243 779777, FAX 0243 776128 BTG:JWP001, telex 86290 WIBOOKG. **(Subscription address:** John Wiley / Philadelphia, PO Box 7247, Philadelphia PA 19170.**) ED** Andrew Boulton, Manchester Royal Infirmary, UK. **DD** 616. **NLM** W1; DI174. **CODEN** DIMEEV. **[CCC].** Index available. **Bk Rev. Ad Acc. Pr Rev. Circ:** 2,500. Documents available from The Genuine Article, ADONIS.
**Desc:** Covers all aspects of diabetes mellitus and aims to interest everyone helping diabetic patients whether through fundamental research or better health care. Includes articles on the aetiology and pathogenesis of diabetes and its complications.
**Ind/Abst** ADONIS; Annals Behav. Med.; CSA Neuro. Abstr.; Curr. Aware. Biol. Sci., CABS; Curr. Contents Clin. Med.; EMBASE; Health Plan. Adminis.; Index Med. (1984-); Nutr. Res. Newsl.; Oncog. Growth Factors Abstr.; Protozoolog. Abstr.; Res. Alert [Select. Cov.]; SCISEARCH; Soc. Sci. Cit. Index [Select. Cov.]; Sug. Indus. Abstr.

US/0899-2398
**DIABETIC TRAVELER, THE.** **See** Travel and Tourism.

GW/0012-186X
**DIABETOLOGIA.** [Diabetologia]. **Added/Corp** European Association for the Study of Diabetes. Vol. 1 (Aug. 1965)-. Academic Scholarly Publication. German (English, French and German). Twelve times a year. DM998.00. Springer-Verlag GmbH & Company KG, Heidelberger Platz 3, D 14197 Berlin Germany. **Tel** 011 49 30 8207223, FAX 011 49 30 8214091, telex 183 319 SPBLN D. **(Subscription address:** Springer Verlag New York Inc. / for North America, 44 Hartz Way, Secaucus NJ 07096.**) ED** Prof. Rune Dahlqvist (Coordinating Editor's address: Division of Clinical Pharmacology, University Hospital, S-90185 Umea, Sweden). **LC** RC660.A1; D53. **NLM** W1 DI217. **CODEN** DBTGAJ. **[CCC]. Pr Rev.** available on microfilm and microfiche from University Microfilms International (UMI). Documents available from The Genuine Article, BIOSIS Document Express, CASDDS, ADONIS.
**Desc:** Publishes reports of clinical and experimental work on all subjects, provided they have scientific merit and present important facts or new data.
**Ind/Abst** ADONIS; Annals Behav. Med.; Biol. Abstr.; Chem. Abstr.; CSA Neuro. Abstr.; Curr. Aware. Biol. Sci., CABS; Curr. Contents Clin. Med.; Curr. Contents Life Sci.; EMBASE; Energy Res. Abstr.; Health Plan. Adminis.; Immunol. Abstr.; Index Med.; Med. Abstr. Newsl.; Nutr. Abstr. Rev., Ser. A, Hum. Exp.; Nutr. Res. Newsl.; Life Sci. Collect.; PESTDOC; Ref. Upd. Basic Ed.; Ref. Upd. Deluxe Ed.; Res. Alert [Full Cov.]; Sci. Cit. Index; SCISEARCH; Soc. Sci. Cit. Index [Select. Cov.]; SportSearch.

CI/0351-0042
**DIABETOLOGIA CROATICA.** [Diabetol. Croat.]. **Added/Corp** Republicki Zavod za Zastitu Z Dravija S. R. Hrvatske. Strucni Odbor za Dijabetes. Zavod za Dijabetes Endokrinologiju i Bolesti Metabolizma "Vuk Vrhovac". Zavod za Dijabetes "Vuk Vrhovac". Vol. 1 (1972)-. Periodical. Serbo-Croatian (Roman) (English). qt. Vuk Vrhovac Institute for Diabetes, Endocrinology, and Metabolic Disorders, PO Box 958, Dugi Dol 4a, 41000 Zagreb Croatia. **NLM** W1 DI218. **CODEN** DBCRB2. Documents available from BIOSIS Document Express, CASDDS.
**Ind/Abst** Biol. Abstr.; Chem. Abstr. (?-1988); EMBASE [Select. Cov.].

GW/0171-8045
**DIABETOLOGIE-INFORMATIONEN.** [Diabetol.-Inf.]. 1.- Yearly volume; 1979-. Periodical. German. Martinus Nijhoff Publishers, Subsidiary of Kluwer Academic Publishers, Koraalrood 50, 2718 SC Zoetermeer Netherlands. **Tel** 011 31 79 684400. **NLM** W1 DI219.

US/0739-7240
**DOMESTIC ANIMAL ENDOCRINOLOGY.** [Domest. anim. endocrinol.]. Vol. 1, No. 1 (Jan. 1984)-. Academic Scholarly Publication. English. qt. $140.00 US; $170.00 other. Butterworth Heinemann / Woburn, MA, 225 Wildwood Avenue, Unit B, Woburn MA 01801. **Tel** (800)366-2665, FAX (617)928-2620, telex 880052. **(Subscription address:** Elsevier Science Inc. / New York Books, 655 Avenue of the Americas, New York NY 10010.) **ED** James L Sartin. **NLM** W1; DO656. **CODEN** DANEEE. **[CCC].** Index available. **Ad Acc. Pr Rev. Circ:** 400. Documents available from The Genuine Article, BIOSIS Document Express, CASDDS.
**Desc:** A journal to promote basic and clinical endocrine research in domestic animal species.
**Ind/Abst** AgBiotech News Inf.; AGRICOLA [Full Cov.]; Anim. Breed. Abstr.; Biol. Abstr.; Chem. Abstr. (1984-); CSA Neuro. Abstr. (?-?); Curr. Aware. Biol. Sci., CABS; Curr. Contents, Agric. Biol. Environ. Sci.; Dairy Sci. Abstr.; Index Med.; Index Vet.; Nutr. Abstr. Rev., Ser. B, Live Feeds and Feed.; Pig News Inf.; Poult. Abstr.; Ref. Upd. Deluxe Ed.; Res. Alert [Full Cov.]; Sci. Cit. Index; SCISEARCH; Vet. Bull.

SP/0212-0348
**ECYM. ENDOCRINOLOGIA CLINICA Y METABOLISMO.** [ECYM, Endocrinol. clin. metab.]. **VFOAT** Endocrinologia Clinica y Metabolismo. (1981)-. Periodical. Spanish. bm. Edimedica SA, Basilica 19, 28020 Madrid Spain. **UDC** 616.4.

GW/0934-9820
**EICOSANOIDS.** ***Ceased.*** [Eicosanoids]. Vol. 1, No. 1 (Sept. 1988)-Vol. 5 (1992). Periodical. English. Four times a year. Springer-Verlag GmbH & Company KG, Heidelberger Platz 3, D 14197 Berlin Germany. **Tel** 011 49 30 8207223, FAX 011 49 30 8214091, telex 183 319 SPBLN D. **(Subscription address:** Springer Verlag New York Inc. / for North America, 44 Hartz Way, Secaucus NJ 07096.) **ED** K Schroer and A M Lefer. **NLM** W1; EI44. **CODEN** EICOEM. **[CCC].** available on microfilm and microfiche from University Microfilms International (UMI). Documents available from The Genuine Article, CASDDS.
**Desc:** Presents reviews, original research articles, short communications and letters to the editor linked to the study of eicosanoids and their contributions to medicine and biology. Contains original clinical and experimental work in the area of farachidonic acid metabolites: prostaglandins, thromboxanes, leukotrienes and other lipid mediators derived from polyunsaturated fatty acids.
**Ind/Abst** Chem. Abstr. (?-?); Curr. Aware. Biol. Sci., CABS; Curr. Contents Life Sci.; EMBASE; Index Vet.; PESTDOC; Pig News Inf.; Ref. Upd. Deluxe Ed.; Res. Alert [Full Cov.]; Sci. Cit. Index; SCISEARCH.

●JA/0918-8959
**ENDOCRINE JOURNAL.** **Added/Corp** Nihon Naibunpi Gakkai. Vol. 40, No. 1 (Feb. 1993)-. Periodical. English. bm. £290.00. Macmillan Magazines Ltd., Houndmills, Basingstoke, Hampshire RG21 2XS England. **Tel** 011 44 256 29242, FAX 011 44 256 812358, telex 858493. **(Subscription address:** Maruzen Company Ltd., PO Box 5050, Import & Export Department, Tokyo 100 31 Japan.) **NLM** W1; EN365. ***Continues*** *Endocrinologia Japonica, 0013-7219.*
**Ind/Abst** Sci. Cit. Index.

US/1046-3976
**ENDOCRINE PATHOLOGY.** [Endocr. pathol.]. Vol. 1, No. 1 (March 1990)-. Periodical. English. qt. $320.00 US; $355.00 other. Humana Press Inc., 999 Riverview Drive, Suite 208, Totawa NJ 07512. **Tel** (201)256-1699, FAX (201)256-8341. **ED** Ricardo V. Lloyd, M.D. **LC** RC648.A1; E49. **DD** 616. **NLM** W1; EN367B. **[CCC].** available on microfilm and microfiche from University Microfilms International (UMI). Documents available from The Genuine Article.
**Ind/Abst** Curr. Aware. Biol. Sci., CABS; Curr. Contents Life Sci.; Res. Alert [Full Cov.]; Sci. Cit. Index; SCISEARCH.

US/1043-9986
**ENDOCRINE PATHOLOGY UPDATE.** [Endocr. pathol. update]. (1990)-. Monographic series. English. an. Price varies per volume. Field & Wood, 1405 Locust Street, Philadelphia PA 19102. **Tel** (215)824-4010. **NLM** W1; EN367C.

US/0732-6262
**ENDOCRINE PHYSIOLOGY.** Began with Vol. issued in 1974. English. University Park Press, PO Box 4034, New York NY 10163. **ED** S M McCann. **LC** QP1; .P62 subser. **DD** 612/.4/005.

XO/1210-0668
**ENDOCRINE REGULATIONS (BRATISLAVA).** (ENDOCRINE REGULATIONS.). [Endocr. regul.]. **Added/Corp** Ustav Experimentalnej Endokrinologie (Slovenska Akademia Vied). Vol. 25 No. 1-2 (June 1991)-. Periodical. English. Four times a year. $145.00. Bratislava, Czech and Slova Federal Republic, Veda, Basil Switzerland. **(Subscription address:** Karger Libri AG, Petersgraben 31, CH 4009 Basel 11 Switzerland.) **NLM** W1; EN367CH. **CODEN** EREGE3. Documents available from BIOSIS Document Express. ***Continues*** *Endocrinologia Experimentalis, 0013-7200.*
**Ind/Abst** Biol. Abstr. (1991-); Index Med. (1991-).

UK
**ENDOCRINE-RELATED CANCER.** (19??)-. English. qt (4 issues). $160.00 (institutions), $80.00 (individuals) North & South America; £100.00 (institutions), £50.00 (individuals) other. Journal of Endocrinology Ltd., 17 18 North Court Courtyard, Bristol BS12 4NQ England. **Tel** 011 44 454 616045, FAX 011 44 454 616071. **(Subscription address:** Turpin Distribution Services Limited, Blackhorse Road, Letchworth, Hertfordshire SG6 1HN, United Kingdom.)

US/0743-5800
**ENDOCRINE RESEARCH.** [Endocr. res.]. Vol. 10, No. 1 (1984)-. Academic Scholarly Publication. English. qt (four issues per volume). $450.00 US; $464.50 other. Marcel Dekker Inc., 270 Madison Avenue, New York NY 10016. **Tel** (212)696-9000, (800)228-1160, FAX (212)685-4540, telex 421419. **(Subscription address:** Marcel Dekker Inc, PO Box 5017, Monticello NY 12701.) **ED** Paul J. Davis, Alexander C. Brownie, Vivian Cody and Jerone Kowal. **LC** QP187.A1; E513. **DD** 599/.0142/05. **NLM** W1; EN367E. **CODEN** ENRSE8. **[CCC]. Bk Rev. Ad Acc. Pr Rev.** Documents available from The Genuine Article, CASDDS. ***Continues*** *Endocrine Research Communications, 0093-6391.*
**Desc:** Specializes in bringing the researcher up-to-the-minute laboratory findings and developments in all areas of active investigation, including artificial hormone testing in vitro and in vivo chemical effects on hormone activity and production, gland functioning, hormone synthesis and analysis, molecular structure studies, hormone enhancer and inhibitors, and hormone and gland activity studies. All articles contain fully detailed laboratory protocols and occasional reports emphasize the importance of researcher awareness of the influence of varying procedures on results.
**Ind/Abst** Anim. Breed. Abstr.; Chem. Abstr. (1984-); Curr. Aware. Biol. Sci., CABS; Curr. Contents Life Sci.; Curr. Ref. Fish Res.; Dairy Sci. Abstr.; EMBASE; Index Med.; INIS Atomindex [Micro.]; Nutr. Abstr. Rev., Ser. A, Hum. Exp.; Ref. Upd. Deluxe Ed.; Res. Alert [Full Cov.]; Sci. Cit. Index; SCISEARCH.

US/0163-769X
**ENDOCRINE REVIEWS.** [Endocr. rev.]. **Added/Corp** Endocrine Society. Vol. 1 (Winter 1980)-. Academic Scholarly Publication. English. bm (6 issues). $170.00 (institutions), $105.00 (individuals) US; $195.00 (institutions), $125.00 (individuals) other. Endocrine Society / Maryland, 9650 Rockville Pike, Bethesda MD 20814-3998. **Tel** (301)571-1802, FAX (301)571-1869. **ED** Andres Negro-Vilar, M.D. **LC** QP187.A1; E515. **DD** 612/.4. **NLM** W1 EN367R. **CODEN** ERVIDP. **Ad Acc. Pr Rev. Acid Free. Circ:** 4,400. available on microfilm. Documents available from The Genuine Article, BIOSIS Document Express, CASDDS, Documents on Demand.
**Desc:** Clinical and experimental endocrinology covered through in-depth review articles focusing on current topics of high interest.
**Ind/Abst** Anim. Breed. Abstr.; Biol. Abstr. (1986-); Chem. Abstr. (Winter 1980-); CSA Neuro. Abstr.; Curr. Aware. Biol. Sci., CABS; Curr. Contents Life Sci.; EMBASE; Environ. Abstr.; Health Plan. Adminis.; Index Med. (Winter 1980-); Ref. Upd. Basic Ed.; Ref. Upd. Clinical Ed.; Ref. Upd. Deluxe Ed.; Res. Alert [Full Cov.]; Sci. Cit. Index; SCISEARCH; Soc. Sci. Cit. Index [Select. Cov.].

US
**ENDOCRINE SOCIETY - ANNUAL MEETING, PROGRAM AND ABSTRACTS, THE.** **Main/Corp** Endocrine Society. Meeting. **Added/Corp** Endocrine Society. Program and abstracts. **VFOAT** Program and Abstracts, Annual Meeting - The Endocrine Society. 57th (1975)-. English. an (June). $65.00 (airmail), $56.00 (surface mail). Endocrine Society / Maryland, 9650 Rockville Pike, Bethesda MD 20814-3998. **Tel** (301)571-1802, FAX (301)571-1869. **NLM** W1; EN368MM. Index available. **Ad Acc. Circ:** 8,500 (ctrl). ***Continues*** *Program of the Annual Meeting - Endocrine Society, 0092-2757.*

SP/0211-2299
**ENDOCRINOLOGIA (BARCELONA).** (ENDOCRINOLOGIA : ORGANO DE LA SOCIEDAD ESPANOLA DE ENDOCRINOLOGIA.). [Endocrinologia]. **Added/Corp** Sociedad Espanola de Endocrinologia. (1953)-. Academic Scholarly Publication. English (Spanish). Ten times a year. $66.00. Ediciones Doyma SA, Travesera de Gracia 17 21, 08021 Barcelona Spain. **Tel** 011 34 3 2000711, 011 34 3 4145706, FAX 011 34 3 2091136, telex 51964 INK E. **NLM** W1 EN385T. Documents available from CASDDS.
**Ind/Abst** Chem. Abstr.

JA/0013-7219
**ENDOCRINOLOGIA JAPONICA.** ***Title Change.*** [Endocrinol. jpn.]. **Added/Corp** Nihon Naibunpi Gakkai. Nihon Naibunpi Gakkai. Tobu Bukai. Vol. 1 (Sept. 1954)-(1992). Academic Scholarly Publication. English (German and French). bm. Nihon Naibunpi Gakkai, (Japan Endocrine Society), Kyoto Furitsu Ika Daigaku, Seiren Kaikan, Kojinbashi, Nishizume Sagaru, Kamigyoku,, Kyotoshi, Kyotofu 602 Japan. **(Subscription address:** Maruzen Company Ltd., PO Box 5050, Import & Export Department, Tokyo 100 31 Japan.) **NLM** W1; EN393. **CODEN** ECJPAE. Index available in last issue of volume--attached. **Pr Rev.** Documents available from The Genuine Article, BIOSIS Document Express, CASDDS. ***Continued by*** *Endocrine Journal.*
**Ind/Abst** Biol. Abstr.; Chem. Abstr.; CSA Neuro. Abstr.; Curr. Aware. Biol. Sci., CABS; Curr. Contents Life Sci.; Curr. Ref. Fish Res.; Dairy Sci. Abstr.; EMBASE; Health Plan. Adminis.; Helminthol. Abstr. (1991-); Index Med.; Life Sci. Collect.; Protozoolog. Abstr.; Res. Alert [Full Cov.]; Sci. Cit. Index (19??-19??); SCISEARCH.

FR
**ENDOCRINOLOGIE HUMAINE ET EXPERIMENTALE ENDOCRINOPATHIES. E64.** French. ir. 1398.77F France; 1455.00F other. CNRS / Institut d'Information Scientifique et Technique, (Centre National de la Recherche Scientifique), 15 Quai Anatole France, Paris 75700 France. **Tel** 011 33 1 47531515, telex 299 356 F. ***Continues*** *Pascal Explore. E64: Endocrinologie Humaine et Experimentale Endocrinopathies.*

US/1051-2144
**ENDOCRINOLOGIST, THE.** English. bm. $86.00 (individual), $145.00 (institution), US; $106.00 (individual), $165.00 (institution) other. Williams & Wilkins Company, 428 East Preston Street, Baltimore MD 21202-3993. **Tel** (410)528-4000, (800)638-6423, FAX (410)528-8596, telex 87669. **(Subscription address:** Williams & Wilkins, PO Box 64380, Baltimore MD 21264.) **[CCC].** Documents available from Quick Copies.

US/1051-2144
**ENDOCRINOLOGIST (BALTIMORE, MD.), THE.** (THE ENDOCRINOLOGIST.). [Endocrinologist]. Vol. 1, No. 1 (Feb. 1991)-. Periodical. English. bm. $135.00 (institution) US. Williams & Wilkins Company, 428 East Preston Street, Baltimore MD 21202-3993. **Tel** (410)528-4000, (800)638-6423, FAX (410)528-8596, telex 87669. **(Subscription address:** Williams & Wilkins, PO Box 64380, Baltimore, MD 21264) **DD** 616. **NLM** W1; EN396G. **CODEN** EDOCEB. **[CCC].** Documents available from Quick Copies.
**Desc:** First journal directed exclusively to clinicians interested in practical applications of new discoveries in endocrinology, diabetes, metabolism, reproduction, growth and development.

UK/0307-157X
**ENDOCRINOLOGY.** **VFOAT** International Symposium on Endocrinology. (1971)-. English. Butterworth Heinemann Publishers, Linacre House, Jordan Hill, Oxford OX2 8DP England. **Tel** 011 44 865 310366. **NLM** W3 EN661C.
**Desc:** Consists of proceedings of the 3rd international symposium on endocrinology.
**Ind/Abst** Calcium Calcif. Tissue Abstr.; Curr. Contents Life Sci.; Health Period. Database.

US/0889-8529
**ENDOCRINOLOGY AND METABOLISM CLINICS OF NORTH AMERICA.** [Endocrinol. metab. clin. North Am.]. Vol. 16, No. 1 (March 1987)-. Periodical. English. qt (Mar., June, Sept., Dec.). $118.00 (institutions), $98.00 (individuals) US; $129.00 (individual), $135.00 (institution) other. W.B. Saunders Company, A Subsidiary of Harcourt Brace Jovanovich, Inc., The Curtis Center/Suite 300, Independence Square West, Philadelphia PA 19106-3399. **Tel** (215)238-7800 or, 5587, FAX (215)238-7883, telex 173146. **(Subscription address:** W. B. Saunders Company / North America Subscriptions, c/o Periodicals, 6277 Sea Harbour Drive, 4th Floor, Orlando FL 32887.) **ED** Diane Ramanauskas. **LC** RC648.A1; E529. **DD** 612/.4/005. **NLM** W1; EN396ST. **CODEN** ECNAER. **[CCC].** Index available. **Pr Rev. Circ:** 2,500. available on microfilm and microfiche from University Microfilms International (UMI). Documents available from The Genuine Article, BIOSIS Document Express, CASDDS. ***Continues in part*** *Clinics in Endocrinology and Metabolism, 0300-595X.*
**Desc:** Contains updates for the clinician on the latest advances. Each issue addresses a single topic in patient care.
**Ind/Abst** Biol. Abstr. (1987-); Chem. Abstr.; CSA Neuro. Abstr. (?-?); EMBASE; Health Plan. Adminis.; Index Med. March 1987-; Nutr. Abstr. Rev., Ser. A, Hum. Exp.; Ref. Upd. Basic Ed.; Ref. Upd. Clinical Ed.; Ref. Upd. Deluxe Ed.; Res. Alert [Full Cov.]; Sci. Cit. Index; SCISEARCH; Soc. Sci. Cit. Index [Select. Cov.].

●UK/1074-939X
**ENDOCRINOLOGY AND METABOLISM (LONDON, ENG.).** (ENDOCRINOLOGY AND METABOLISM.). (1994)-. Periodical. English. qt (4 issues). £95.00 (institution) UK/Europe; $170.00 (institution) other. Harcourt Brace & Company Ltd., Foots Cray, High Street, Sidcup Kent DA14 5HP England. **Tel** 011 44 81 300 3322, FAX 011 44 81 309 0807. **(Subscription address:** W. B. Saunders Company / North America Subscriptions, c/o Periodicals, 6277 Sea Harbour Drive, 4th Floor, Orlando FL 32887.)

UK/0264-0767
**ENDOCRINOLOGY AND METABOLISM SERIES.** [Endocrinol. metab. ser.]. Vol. 1-. Academic Scholarly Publication. English. Price varies per volume. Praeger, Publishing Division of Greenwood Press, PO Box 5007, Westport CT 06881. **Tel** (203)226-3571. **NLM**

W1 EN396U. **CODEN** EMSEEW. Documents available from CASDDS.
**Ind/Abst** Chem. Abstr.

US/0013-7227
**ENDOCRINOLOGY (PHILADELPHIA).** (ENDOCRINOLOGY.). [Endocrinology]. **Added/Corp** Endocrine Society. Association for the Study of Internal Secretions (U.S.). Vol. 1 (1917)-. Academic Scholarly Publication. English. mo. $360.00 (institutions), $180.00 (individuals) US; $440.00 (institutions), $240.00 (individuals) other. Endocrine Society / Maryland, 9650 Rockville Pike, Bethesda MD 20814-3998. **Tel** (301)571-1802, FAX (301)571-1869. **ED** Shlomo Melmed, M.D. **LC** QP187; .A25. **DD** 612.4005. **NLM** W1 EN396S. **CODEN** ENDOAO. cum. index. **Ad Acc. Pr Rev. Acid Free. Circ:** 6,150. available on microfilm and microfiche from University Microfilms International (UMI). Documents available from The Genuine Article, BIOSIS Document Express, CASDDS, Documents on Demand. ***Absorbed in part** American Goiter Association. Transactions of the American Goiter Association, 0096-7173.*
**Desc:** Broad-focus journal covering all aspects of research on endocrine glands and their hormones for the endocrinologist and internist.
**Ind/Abst** Abr. Index Med.; AgBiotech News Inf.; AGRICOLA; Anim. Breed. Abstr.; Biol. Abstr.; Chem. Abstr.; CSA Neuro. Abstr.; Curr. Aware. Biol. Sci., CABS; Curr. Contents Life Sci.; Curr. Ref. Fish Res.; Dairy Sci. Abstr.; EMBASE; Energy Res. Abstr.; Environ. Abstr.; Fish Rev. (Jan. 1989-July 1992); Genet. Abstr.; Health Plan. Adminis.; Helminthol. Abstr. (1991-); Index Med.; Index Vet.; INIS Atomindex [Micro.]; Int. Aerosp. Abstr.; Nucl. Acids Abstr.; Nutr. Abstr. Rev., Ser. B, Live Feeds and Feed.; Nutr. Abstr. Rev., Ser. A, Hum. Exp.; Oncog. Growth Factors Abstr.; Life Sci. Collect.; PESTDOC; Pig News Inf.; Poult. Abstr.; Protozoolog. Abstr.; Ref. Upd. Basic Ed.; Ref. Upd. Clinical Ed.; Ref. Upd. Deluxe Ed.; Res. Alert [Full Cov.]; Sci. Cit. Index; SCISEARCH; Small Anim. Abstr. Bibliogr.; Stat. Theory Method Abstr. (1959-1963); Vet. Bull.; Wildl. Rev. (Jan. 1989-July 1992).

PL/0423-104X
**ENDOKRYNOLOGIA POLSKA.** [Endokrynol. pol.]. **Added/Corp** Polskie Towarzystwo Endokrynologiczne. Vol. 1, (1950)-. Academic Scholarly Publication. Polish (summaries and/or abstracts in English, French and Russian). bm. $51.00. **(Subscription address:** ARS Polona, PO Box 1001, 00068 Warsaw Poland.**) NLM** W1 EN397. **CODEN** EDPKA2. Documents available from BIOSIS Document Express, CASDDS.
**Ind/Abst** Biol. Abstr.; Chem. Abstr. (-1988); CSA Neuro. Abstr.; EMBASE; Health Plan. Adminis.; Index Med.

●NO/0804-4643
**EUROPEAN JOURNAL OF ENDOCRINOLOGY / EUROPEAN FEDERATION OF ENDOCRINE SOCIETIES. Added/Corp** European Federation of Endocrine Societies. Vol. 130, No. 1 (Jan. 1994)-. Periodical. English. mo. Kr2200.00, $375.00. Scandinavian University Press, PO Box 2959 Toeyen, N 0608 Oslo 6 Norway. **Tel** 011 47 2 2575400, FAX 011 47 2 2575353, telex 71896 UROR N. **(Subscription address:** Scandinavian University Press, 200 Meacham Ave., Elmont NY 11003.**) LC** QP187.A1; E8. **NLM** W1; EU72DDM. **CODEN** EJOEEP. ***Continues** Acta Endocrinologica, 0001-5598.*
**Ind/Abst** Index Med. (1994-).

NE/0014-407X
**EXCERPTA MEDICA. SECTION 3. ENDOCRINOLOGY. See** Medical Science and Technology-Abstracting, Bibliographies and Statistics.

GW/0232-7384
**EXPERIMENTAL AND CLINICAL ENDOCRINOLOGY.** [Exp. clin. endocrinol.]. **Added/Corp** Gesellschaft fuer Endokrinologie und Stoffwechselkrankheiten der DDR. Vol. 81, No. 1 (Jan. 1983)-. Academic Scholarly Publication. English (German). bm (6 issues). $165.00. Johann Ambrosius Barth, Prager Strasse 16 B, D 04103 Leipzig Germany. **Tel** 011 49 341 7137570. **(Subscription address:** Huethig Publishing Inc., 29 Macintosh Drive, Oxford CT 06478.**) LC** QP187.A1; E53. **DD** 599/.01/42. **NLM** W1 EX464. **CODEN** EXCEDSENDCAC. Documents available from The Genuine Article, CASDDS. ***Continues** Endokrinologie, 0013-7251.*
**Ind/Abst** AGRICOLA [Select. Cov.]; Anim. Breed. Abstr.; Calcium Calcif. Tissue Abstr.; Chem. Abstr. (1983-); Chem. Titles; CSA Neuro. Abstr.; Curr. Aware. Biol. Sci., CABS; Curr. Contents Life Sci.; Dairy Sci. Abstr.; EMBASE; Health Plan. Adminis.; Immunol. Abstr.; Index Med.; Nutr. Abstr. Rev., Ser. B, Live Feeds and Feed.; Life Sci. Collect. (-1985); PESTDOC; Ref. Upd. Basic Ed.; Ref. Upd. Clinical Ed.; Ref. Upd. Deluxe Ed.; Res. Alert [Full Cov.]; Sci. Cit. Index; SCISEARCH; SportSearch.

SZ/0251-5342
**FRONTIERS IN DIABETES.** [Front. diabetes]. Vol. 1 (1981)-. Academic Scholarly Publication. English. an. 200.00F (approx. per volume). S. Karger AG, Allschwilerstrasse 10, PO Box - Postfach - Case Postale, CH-4009 Basel Switzerland. **Tel** 011 41 61 306-1111, FAX 011 41 61 306-1234, telex CH 962 652. **ED** F. Belfiore. **NLM** W1 FR945X. **CODEN** FDIADJ. **[CCC].** Documents available from BIOSIS Document Express, CASDDS.
**Desc:** Data at the frontiers of diabetes research are collected, systematically organized, and critically evaluated by volumes in this series. Contents are based on information presented, orally or by poster, at meetings of European, American, and international diabetes associations and until now recorded only as alphabetically ordered abstracts.
**Ind/Abst** Biol. Abstr.; Chem. Abstr.; Index Med.; Ref. Upd. Deluxe Ed.

US/0016-6480
**GENERAL AND COMPARATIVE ENDOCRINOLOGY.** [Gen. comp. endocrinol.]. Vol. 1 (April 1961)-. Academic Scholarly Publication. English. mo. $850.00 US and Canada; $965.00 other. Academic Press, Inc., 6277 Sea Harbor Drive, Orlando FL 32887. **Tel** (800)543-9534, (407)345-4100, FAX (407)363-9661. **ED** Aubrey Gorbman and Ian W. Henderson. **LC** QP187; .G37. **DD** 591.14. **NLM** W1 GE23. **CODEN** GCENA5. **[CCC]. Pr Rev.** Documents available from The Genuine Article, BIOSIS Document Express, CASDDS.
**Desc:** Devoted to basic endocrinological research. Emphasizing fundamental research, the journal also features occasional brief reviews that deal with a particular field or problem.
**Ind/Abst** AgBiotech News Inf.; AGRICOLA [Select. Cov.]; Anim. Breed. Abstr.; AQUAREF; Biocont. News Inf.; Biol. Abstr.; Calcium Calcif. Tissue Abstr.; Chem. Abstr.; Chem. Titles; CSA Neuro. Abstr.; Curr. Aware. Biol. Sci., CABS; Curr. Contents Life Sci.; Curr. Ref. Fish Res.; Dairy Sci. Abstr.; EMBASE; Energy Res. Abstr.; Entomol. Abstr.; Fish Rev.; Index Med.; Index Vet.; INIS Atomindex [Micro.]; Int. Aerosp. Abstr.; Key Word Index Wildl. Res.; Nematol. Abstr.; Nutr. Abstr. Rev., Ser. B, Live Feeds and Feed.; Nutr. Abstr. Rev., Ser. A, Hum. Exp.; Life Sci. Collect.; Poult. Abstr.; Protozoolog. Abstr.; Ref. Upd. Basic Ed.; Ref. Upd. Deluxe Ed.; Res. Alert [Full Cov.]; Rev. Agric. Entomol.; Rev. Med. Vet. Entomol.; Sci. Cit. Index; SCISEARCH; Vet. Bull.; Wildl. Rev.

IT/0391-7525
**GIORNALE ITALIANO DI DIABETOLOGIA.** [G. ital. diabetol.]. Vol. 1, No. 1 (Jan. 1981)-. Academic Scholarly Publication. Italian (summaries and/or abstracts in English and Italian). Three times a year. Pacini Editore Srl, Via A Gherardesca 1, 56121 Ospedaletto Pisa Italy. **Tel** 011 39 50 982439. **NLM** W1; GI777D. Documents available from CASDDS.
**Ind/Abst** Chem. Abstr.; EMBASE [Select. Cov.].

UK/0964-7554
**GROWTH FACTORS & CYTOKINES. See** Biology-Physiology.

JA/0533-6724
**GUNMA SYMPOSIA ON ENDOCRINOLOGY.** [Gunma symp. endocrinol.]. **Added/Corp** Gunma Daigaku. Naibunpi Kenkyujo. Gunma Daigaku. Naibunpi Kenkyujo. Annual Report of the Institute of Endocrinology, Gunma University. (1964)-. English. an. Institute of Endocrinology Gunma University, Maebashi Japan. **LC** QP187.A1; G86. **DD** 599/.0142/05. **NLM** W3 GU81. **CODEN** GUSYAU. Documents available from BIOSIS Document Express, CASDDS.
**Ind/Abst** Biol. Abstr.; Chem. Abstr.

UK/0951-3590
**GYNECOLOGICAL ENDOCRINOLOGY. Added/Corp** International Society of Gynecological Endocrinology. Vol. 1, No. 1 (March 1987)-. Periodical. English. qt. £135.00 (institutions), £72.00 (individuals). Parthenon Publishing, Casterton Hall Carnforth, Lancashire LA6 2LA England. **Tel** 011 44 5242 72084, FAX 44-5242-71587. **ED** A.R. Genazzani. **LC** RG159; .G97. **NLM** W1; GY557D. **CODEN** GYENER. Index available. **Ad Acc. Pr Rev.** Documents available from The Genuine Article.
**Ind/Abst** Curr. Aware. Biol. Sci., CABS; Curr. Contents Clin. Med.; EMBASE; Health Plan. Adminis.; Index Med. (Vol. 1, No. 1, 1987-); Res. Alert [Select. Cov.]; SCISEARCH.

GW/0018-5043
**HORMONE AND METABOLIC RESEARCH.** [Horm. metabol. res.]. **VFOAT** Hormon- und Stoffwechselforschung; Hormones et Metabolisme. Vol. 1, No. 1 (Jan. 1969)-. Academic Scholarly Publication. English (French and German). mo. $283.00. Georg Thieme Verlag Stuttgart, Postfach 301120, D 70451 Stuttgart Germany. **Tel** 011 49 711 89310, FAX 011 49 711 8931298, telex 7 252 275 GTVD. **(Subscription address:** Thieme Medical Publishers Inc., 381 Park Avenue South, New York NY 10016.**) ED** E F Pfeiffer and G M Reaven. **LC** QP801.H7; H65. **DD** 591.1/92/705. **NLM** W1 HO63P. **CODEN** HMMRA2. **[CCC]. Pr Rev. Circ:** 16,000. available on microfilm and microfiche from University Microfilms International (UMI). Documents available from The Genuine Article, BIOSIS Document Express, CASDDS, ADONIS.
**Desc:** Covers all topics of endocrinology and metabolism. Up to 50% of content can be devoted to problems of diabetology in the widest sense, emphasizing their endocrinologic 'mass disease' aspect.
**Ind/Abst** ADONIS; AGRICOLA [Select. Cov.]; Anim. Breed. Abstr.; Biol. Abstr.; Calcium Calcif. Tissue Abstr.; Chem. Abstr.; Chem. Titles; CSA Neuro. Abstr.; Curr. Aware. Biol. Sci., CABS; Curr. Contents Life Sci.; Dairy Sci. Abstr.; EMBASE; Energy Res. Abstr.; Health Plan. Adminis.; Index Med.; Index Vet.; Nutr. Abstr. Rev., Ser. B, Live Feeds and Feed.; Nutr. Abstr. Rev., Ser. A, Hum. Exp.; Oncog. Growth Factors Abstr.; Life Sci. Collect.; PESTDOC; Pig News Inf.; Poult. Abstr.; Ref. Upd. Basic Ed.; Ref. Upd. Deluxe Ed.; Res. Alert [Full Cov.]; Sci. Cit. Index; SCISEARCH; SportSearch; Vet. Bull.

GW/0170-5903
**HORMONE AND METABOLIC RESEARCH. SUPPLEMENT SERIES.** [Horm. metab. res., Suppl. ser.]. (1969)-. Monographic series. English. ir. Price varies per volume. Georg Thieme Verlag Stuttgart, Postfach 301120, D 70451 Stuttgart Germany. **Tel** 011 49 711 89310, FAX 011 49 711 8931298, telex 7 252 275 GTVD. **(Subscription address:** Thieme Medical Publishers Inc., 381 Park Avenue South, New York NY 10016.**) ED** R. Levine and E. F. Pfeiffer. **NLM** W1 HO63Q. **CODEN** HMRSAU. Documents available from CASDDS.
**Ind/Abst** Chem. Abstr.; Index Med.

SZ/0301-0163
**HORMONE RESEARCH.** [Horm. res.]. **Added/Corp** European Association of Endocrinology. Vol. 4 (1973)-. Periodical. English. Twelve times a year. $592.00. S. Karger AG, Allschwilerstrasse 10, PO Box - Postfach - Case Postale, CH-4009 Basel Switzerland. **Tel** 011 41 61 306-1111, FAX 011 41 61 306-1234, telex CH 962 652. **ED** J. Girard, M. Zachmann. **LC** QP187.A1; H64. **DD** 574.1/927/05. **NLM** W1 HO63T. **CODEN** HRMRA3. **[CCC].** Index available in last issue of volume--attached. **Bk Rev. Ad Acc. Pr Rev. Circ:** 950. available on microfilm from University Microfilms International (UMI). Documents available from The Genuine Article, BIOSIS Document Express, CASDDS. ***Continues** Hormones (Basel, Switzerland), 0367-617X.*
**Desc:** Original research papers provide a background of experimental data on the pathology, cytology, histology, biochemistry, pharmacology and regulation of hormones. This information is complemented by authoritative reports drawing on clinical experiences concerning many diagnostic and therapeutic procedures and possibilities. In particular, such topical problems as growth, diabetes, sexual development and hormone-dependent cancers are covered.
**Ind/Abst** Biol. Abstr.; Chem. Abstr.; CSA Neuro. Abstr.; Curr. Contents Life Sci.; Dairy Sci. Abstr.; EMBASE; Health Plan. Adminis.; Index Med.; Nutr. Abstr. Rev., Ser. B, Live Feeds and Feed.; Nutr. Abstr. Rev., Ser. A, Hum. Exp.; Life Sci. Collect.; PESTDOC; Ref. Upd. Deluxe Ed.; Res. Alert [Full Cov.]; Sci. Cit. Index; SCISEARCH; Soc. Sci. Cit. Index [Select. Cov.].

US/0018-506X
**HORMONES AND BEHAVIOR.** [Horm. behav.]. Vol. 1 (Apr. 1969)-. Academic Scholarly Publication. English. qt (4 issues). $241.50 US and Canada; $298.00 other. Academic Press, Inc., 6277 Sea Harbor Drive, Orlando FL 32887. **Tel** (800)543-9534, (407)345-4100, FAX (407)363-9661. **ED** Robert W. Goy and Richard W. Whalen. **LC** QP187.A1; H65. **DD** 591.1/92/705. **NLM** W1 HO656F. **CODEN** HOBEAO. **[CCC]. Pr Rev.** Documents available from The Genuine Article, BIOSIS Document Express, CASDDS.
**Desc:** Publishes a broad range of original articles dealing diversely with behavioral systems that are known to be hormonally influenced. The range extends from studies of the evolutionary significance of hormone-behavior relations to those concerned with cellular and molecular mechanisms of hormonal actions on tissues relevant to behavior.
**Ind/Abst** Abstr. Anthropol. (19??-); AGRICOLA; Anim. Behav. Abstr.; Anim. Breed. Abstr.; Biol. Abstr.; Chem. Abstr.; CSA Neuro. Abstr.; Curr. Aware. Biol. Sci., CABS; Curr. Contents Life Sci.; Dairy Sci. Abstr.; EMBASE; Energy Res. Abstr. (Aug. 1982-); Health Plan. Adminis.; Index Med.; Nutr. Abstr. Rev., Ser. B, Live Feeds and Feed.; Nutr. Abstr. Rev., Ser. A, Hum. Exp.; Life Sci. Collect.; Psychol. Abstr. (1971-); PsycINFO; PsycLit; Ref. Upd. Deluxe Ed.; Res. Alert [Full Cov.]; Sci. Cit. Index; SCISEARCH; Soc. Sci. Cit. Index [Select. Cov.].

NE
**HORMONES AND THEIR ACTIONS. PART I.** Academic Scholarly Publication. English. ir. FL110.00 Netherlands; $63.00 US (paperback), FL200.00 Netherlands; $114.00 US (hardback). Elsevier Science Publishers BV, PO Box 211, 1000 AE Amsterdam Netherlands. **Tel** 011 31 20 5803642, FAX 011 31 20 5862696, telex 15682.
**Desc:** Contains up-to-date information concerning different aspects of hormone action which includes the control of the biosynthesis of different mechanisms of action for both steroid hormones and polypeptides.

NE
**HORMONES AND THEIR ACTIONS. PART II.** Academic Scholarly Publication. English. ir. FL115.00 Netherlands; $66.00 US (paperback), FL235.00 Netherlands; $134.00 US (hardback). Elsevier Science Publishers BV, PO Box 211, 1000 AE Amsterdam Netherlands. **Tel** 011 31 20 5803642, FAX 011 31 20 5862696, telex 15682.
**Desc:** Concerned with protein and peptide hormones

and growth factors, their receptors, transducing systems, mechanisms of their release and their biological and biochemical actions.

JA/0045-7167
**HORUMON TO RINSHO.** (HORUMON TO RINSHO.). [Horumon To Rinsho]. **VFOAT** Clinical Endocrinology. Vol. 1 (April 1953)-. Periodical. Japanese (table of contents in English). mo. $354.00. Igaku No Sekaisha, 12-4, Kudan Kita 1 Chome, Chiyodaku, Tokyoto 102 Japan. **(Subscription address:** Kyowa Book Company Inc., 1 38 Kanda Jinbocho Chiyoda-ku, Tokyo 101 Japan.) **NLM** W1 HO688. **CODEN** HORIAE. Documents available from CASDDS.
**Ind/Abst** Chem. Abstr.

US/0306-4980
**IDF BULLETIN.** [IDF bull.]. **Added/Corp** International Diabetes Federation. American Diabetes Association. **VAT** International Diabetes Foundation Bulletin. Vol. 19 (April 1974)-. Periodical. English. tq. $32.00. American Diabetes Association, National Service Center, 1660 Duke Street, Alexandria VA 22314. **Tel** (703)549-1500, (800)232-3472, FAX (703)836-2464. **(Subscription address:** International Diabetes Association, 40 Washington Street, 1050 Brussels Belgium.) **ED** J. S. Bajaj. **NLM** W1 I219K. **CODEN** IDFBD6. **Bk Rev. Ad Acc. Circ:** 3,000. Documents available from BIOSIS Document Express, CASDDS. ***Continues*** *News Bulletin - International Diabetes Federation, 0534-9753.*
**Desc:** Review articles on aspects of living with diabetes. Federation and national association news.
**Ind/Abst** Biol. Abstr. (1986-); Chem. Abstr.

US/0160-7626
**INFERTILITY.** ***Ceased.*** **See** Medical Science and Technology-Gynecology and Obstetrics.

CN/0832-9958
**INFO-DIABETE : BULLETIN D'INFORMATION DE LA SECTION PROFESSIONNELLE DE L'ASSOCIATION DU DIABETE DU QUEBEC.** ***Ceased.*** [Info-diabete]. **Added/Corp** Association du Diabete du Quebec. Section Professionnelle. Association du Diabete du Quebec. Vol. 1, No 1 (Sept. 1981)-(1992). Bulletin. French. ir (3 or 4 times per year). Association du Diabete du Quebec, 5635 rue Sherbrooke EST, Montreal QUE H1N 1A3 Canada. **Tel** (514)259-3422, FAX (514)259-9286. **DD** 616.4/62/005. **Circ:** 500.

UK/0142-8144
**INSULIN AND GLUCAGON.** [Insulin glucagon]. (1979)-. English. Twenty-four times a year. £85.00. SUBIS, Mansion House, 19 Kingfield Road, Sheffield S11 9AS England. **Tel** 011 44 114 255 4433, FAX 011 44 114 255 4626. **DD** 016.61234. **[CCC]. Bk Rev. Ad Acc.**
**Desc:** Current awareness service for researchers and clinicians.

CN/0820-6880
**INTERNATIONAL HAIR ROUTE. See** Medical Science and Technology-Dermatology.

US/0161-7524
**INTERNATIONAL WORKSHOP ON DIABETES AND CAMPING.** 3rd 1976-. Periodical. English. an. American Association of Diabetes Educators, 444 North Michigan Avenue / Suite 1240, Chicago IL 60611. **Tel** (312)645-1710, (800)338-3633, FAX (312)661-0769. **NLM** W3 IN9324Q.

US/0021-972X
**JOURNAL OF CLINICAL ENDOCRINOLOGY AND METABOLISM, THE.** (THE JOURNAL OF CLINICAL ENDOCRINOLOGY & METABOLISM.). [J. clin. endocrinol. metab.]. **Added/Corp** Endocrine Society. **VFOAT** Journal of Clinical Endocrinology and Metabolism. Vol. 12 (Jan. 1952)-. Academic Scholarly Publication. English. mo (12 issues). $260.00 (institutions), $155.00 (individuals) US; $300.00 (institutions), $200.00 (individuals) other. Endocrine Society / Maryland, 9650 Rockville Pike, Bethesda MD 20814-3998. **Tel** (301)571-1802, FAX (301)571-1869. **ED** Maria I. New, M.D. **DD** 616. **NLM** W1 JO588. **CODEN** JCEMAZ. **Ad Acc. Pr Rev. Acid Free. Circ:** 9,500. available on microfilm and microfiche from University Microfilms International (UMI). Documents available from The Genuine Article, BIOSIS Document Express, CASDDS, Documents on Demand. ***Continues*** *Journal of Cclinical Endocrinology, 0368-1610;* ***Absorbed in part*** *American Goiter Association. Transactions of the American Goiter Association.*
**Desc:** The latest information on the clinical applications of endocrine research for internists, endocrinologists, obstetrics/gynecologist's physiologists.
**Ind/Abst** Abr. Index Med.; Annals Behav. Med.; Biol. Abstr.; Calcium Calcif. Tissue Abstr.; Chem. Abstr.; CSA Neuro. Abstr.; Curr. Aware. Biol. Sci., CABS; Curr. Contents Clin. Med.; Curr. Contents Life Sci.; Dairy Sci. Abstr.; EMBASE; Energy Res. Abstr.; Environ. Abstr.; Fish Rev. (Jan. 1989-July 1992); Immunol. Abstr.; Index Med.; INIS Atomindex [Micro.]; Int. Aerosp. Abstr.; Iowa Drug Inf. Serv. (1967-); Med. Abstr. Newsl.; Mod. Med.; Nutr. Abstr. Rev., Ser. B, Live Feeds and Feed.; Nutr. Abstr. Rev., Ser. A, Hum. Exp.; Oncog. Growth Factors Abstr.; Life Sci. Collect.; PESTDOC; Physic. Medline Plus; Ref. Upd. Basic Ed.; Ref. Upd. Clinical Ed.; Ref. Upd. Deluxe Ed.; Res. Alert [Full Cov.]; Sci. Cit. Index; SCISEARCH; Soc. Sci. Cit. Index [Select. Cov.]; Sorghum Mill. Abstr.; SportSearch; Wildl. Rev. (Jan. 1989-July 1992).

●US/1056-8727
**JOURNAL OF DIABETES AND ITS COMPLICATIONS.** [J. diabetes its complicat.]. Vol. 6, No. 1 (Jan./Mar. 1992)-. Academic Scholarly Publication. English. qt (1 volume). $195.00 US; $225.00 other. Elsevier Science Publishing Company Inc, Madison Square Station, PO Box 882, New York NY 10159-0882. **Tel** (212)633-3950, FAX (212)633-3990. **DD** 616. **NLM** W1; JO619VD. **CODEN** JDICE2. **[CCC].** available on microfilm and microfiche from University Microfilms International (UMI). Documents available from BIOSIS Document Express. ***Continues*** *Journal of Diabetic Complications, 0891-6632.*
**Ind/Abst** Biol. Abstr.; Index Med. (1992-).

US/0895-0652
**JOURNAL OF DIABETES MANAGEMENT.** 1989-. Periodical. English. bm. Tom Jones Associates, 270 Pascack Road, Woodcliff Lake NJ 07675.

IT/0391-4097
**JOURNAL OF ENDOCRINOLOGICAL INVESTIGATION.** [J. endocrinol. invest.]. **Added/Corp** Societa Italiana di Endocrinologia. Vol. 1 (Jan. 1978)-. Academic Scholarly Publication. English. mo (11 issues per year). $182.00. Editrice Kurtis SRL, Via Luigi Zoja 30, Milan 20153 Italy. **Tel** 011 39 2 48202740, FAX 011 39 2 48201219. **ED** Aldo Pinchera. **NLM** W1 JO641. **CODEN** JEIND7. **Bk Rev. Ad Acc. Pr Rev. Acid Free. Circ:** 4,000 (ctrl). Documents available from The Genuine Article, BIOSIS Document Express, CASDDS.
**Desc:** Studies on clinical and experimental research in endocrinology and related fields.
**Ind/Abst** Biol. Abstr.; Calcium Calcif. Tissue Abstr.; Chem. Abstr.; CSA Neuro. Abstr. (?-?); Curr. Aware. Biol. Sci., CABS; Curr. Contents Life Sci.; Dairy Sci. Abstr.; EMBASE; Index Med.; Nutr. Abstr. Rev., Ser. B, Live Feeds and Feed.; Nutr. Abstr. Rev., Ser. A, Hum. Exp.; Life Sci. Collect.; Ref. Upd. Basic Ed.; Ref. Upd. Clinical Ed.; Ref. Upd. Deluxe Ed.; Res. Alert [Full Cov.]; Sci. Cit. Index; SCISEARCH.

UK/0022-0795
**JOURNAL OF ENDOCRINOLOGY, THE.** [J. endocrinol.]. **Added/Corp** Society for Endocrinology. Vol. 1 (June 1939)-. Academic Scholarly Publication. English. mo. $470.00 North & South America; £260.00 Europe; £285.00 other. Journal of Endocrinology Ltd., 17 18 North Court Courtyard, Bristol BS12 4NQ England. **Tel** 011 44 454 616045, FAX 011 44 454 616071. **(Subscription address:** Turpin Transactions Ltd., Blackhorse Road, Letchworth, Hertfordshire SG6 1HN United Kingdom; Telephone: (0462) 672555, FAX: (1462) 480947) **ED** G. P. Vinson. **LC** QP187.A1; J6. **NLM** W1 JO642. **CODEN** JOENAK. **[CCC].** Index available. cum. index. **Bk Rev. Ad Acc. Pr Rev. Circ:** 2,200 (ctrl). Documents available from The Genuine Article, BIOSIS Document Express, CASDDS.
**Desc:** All aspects of the nature and functions of the endocrine systems.
**Ind/Abst** AgBiotech News Inf.; AGRICOLA [Select. Cov.]; Anim. Behav. Abstr.; Anim. Breed. Abstr.; Annals Behav. Med.; Biol. Abstr.; Calcium Calcif. Tissue Abstr.; Chem. Abstr.; Chem. Titles; CSA Neuro. Abstr.; Curr. Aware. Biol. Sci., CABS; Curr. Biotechnol.; Curr. Contents Life Sci.; Curr. Ref. Fish Res.; Dairy Sci. Abstr.; EMBASE; Fish Rev.; Index Med.; Key Word Index Wildl. Res.; Nutr. Abstr. Rev., Ser. B, Live Feeds and Feed.; Nutr. Abstr. Rev., Ser. A, Hum. Exp.; Oncog. Growth Factors Abstr.; Life Sci. Collect.; PESTDOC; Pig News Inf.; Poult. Abstr.; Res. Alert [Full Cov.]; Rev. Med. Vet. Mycology; Sci. Cit. Index; SCISEARCH; Small Anim. Abstr. Bibliogr.; Soc. Sci. Cit. Index [Select. Cov.]; Soyabean Abstr.; Wildl. Rev.

IT
**JOURNAL OF GYNAECOLOGICAL ENDOCRINOLOGY.** Vol. 1, N. 1/2 (1985)-. Periodical. English. SOG/SRL, Galleria Storione 2A, 35123 Padua Italy. **Tel** 011 39 49 8756900, 8758644, FAX 8750860. **NLM** W1; JO669QJ. **CODEN** JGENE2. Documents available from BIOSIS Document Express, CASDDS.
**Ind/Abst** Biol. Abstr.; Chem. Abstr.

UK/0952-5041
**JOURNAL OF MOLECULAR ENDOCRINOLOGY.** [J. mol. endocrinol.]. **Added/Corp** Society for Endocrinology. Vol. 1, No. 1 (July 1988)-. Periodical. English. mo. $280.00 North & South America; £145.00 Europe; £165.00 other. Journal of Endocrinology Ltd., 17 18 North Court Courtyard, Bristol BS12 4NQ England. **Tel** 011 44 454 616045, FAX 011 44 454 616071. **(Subscription address:** Turpin Distribution Services Limited, Blackhorse Road, Letchworth, Hertfordshire SG6 1HN, United Kingdom.) **ED** B.L. Brown. **LC** QP187.3.M64; J68. **NLM** W1; JO773G. **CODEN** JMLEEI. **[CCC]. Pr Rev.** Documents available from The Genuine Article, BIOSIS Document Express, CASDDS.
**Desc:** Publishes research papers, reviews and rapid communications in the area of cellular and molecular aspects of endocrine and related systems.
**Ind/Abst** Anim. Breed. Abstr.; Biol. Abstr. (1988-); Chem. Abstr.; Curr. Aware. Biol. Sci., CABS; Curr. Contents Life Sci.; EMBASE; Index Med. (Vol. 1, No. 1 1988-); Poult. Abstr.; Ref. Upd. Basic Ed.; Ref. Upd. Deluxe Ed.; Res. Alert [Full Cov.]; Sci. Cit. Index; SCISEARCH.

UK/0334-018X
**JOURNAL OF PEDIATRIC ENDOCRINOLOGY, THE. See** Medical Science and Technology-Pediatrics.

II/0304-4513
**JOURNAL OF THE DIABETIC ASSOCIATION OF INDIA.** [J. Diabetic Assoc. India]. **Added/Corp** Diabetic Association of India. Vol. 14 (Jan. 1974)-. Periodical. English. qt. $20.00. Diabetic Association of India, Maneckji Wadia Building, 127 Mahatma Gandhi Road, 400 001 Bombay India. **(Subscription address:** Prints India, 11 Darya Ganj, New Delhi, 110002 India, (Phone: 011 91 11 3268645)) **NLM** W1 JO9183. **CODEN** JDAIB8. ***Continues*** *tMadhumeh, 0024-9424.*

II/0970-4027
**JOURNAL OF THE DIABETIC ASSOCIATION OF INDIA. SCIENTIFIC SECTION.** [J. Diabet. Assoc. India, Sci. Sect.]. (1988)-. Periodical. English. qt. Diabetic Association of India, Maneckji Wadia Building, 127 Mahatma Gandhi Road, 400 001 Bombay India. **UDC** 616.63. ***Continues*** *Journal of the Diabetic Association of India, 0304-4513.*
**Ind/Abst** EMBASE [Select. Cov.].

FR/0075-4439
**JOURNEES ANNUELLES DE DIABETOLOGIE DE L'HOTEL-DIEU.** [Journ. annu. diabetol. hotel-Dieu]. **Added/Corp** Flammarion Medecine-Sciences. **VFOAT** Journees de Diabetologie de l'Hotel-Dieu. (1961)-. French. ir. 369.67F. Dawson France SA, BP 40, 91121 Palaiseau Cedex France. **Tel** 011 33 1 69104700, telex 220064F. **NLM** W1 JO994D. **CODEN** JDBHAC. **[CCC].** Documents available from BIOSIS Document Express, CASDDS.
**Ind/Abst** Biol. Abstr.; Chem. Abstr.; Index Med.

II
**LIFE SCIENCE ADVANCES. EXPERIMENTAL AND CLINICAL ENDOCRINOLOGY : A JOURNAL OF THE COUNCIL OF SCIENTIFIC RESEARCH INTEGRATION. VFOAT** Experimental and Clinical Endocrinology; Experimental & Clinical Endocrinology - Life Science Advances. Periodical. English. $30.00 (individuals), $60.00 (institutions). Compilers International, 1/25 Nagwa Lanka, Varanasi 221 005 India. **NLM** W1; LI4064. ***Continues in part*** *Life Science Advances, 0255-6642.*

II
**LIFE SCIENCE ADVANCES. GENERAL ENDOCRINOLOGY : A JOURNAL OF THE COUNCIL OF SCIENTIFIC RESEARCH INTEGRATION. VFOAT** General Endocrinology; General Endocrinology - Life Science Advances. Periodical. English. $30.00 (individuals), $60.00 (institutions). Compilers International, 1/25 Nagwa Lanka, Varanasi 221 005 India. ***Continues in part*** *Life Science Advances, 0255-6642.*

US/0895-397X
**LIVING WELL WITH DIABETES.** [Living well diabetes]. **VFOAT** Living Well. Periodical. English. qt. $6.00. Diabetes Center Inc, PO Box 41945, Minneapolis MN 55441. **Tel** (800)848-0614. **DD** 616.

UK/0081-136X
**MEMOIRS OF THE SOCIETY FOR ENDOCRINOLOGY.** [Mem. Soc. Endocrinol.]. **Main/Corp** Society for Endocrinology. No. 1 (July 1953)-. Monographic series. English. ir. Price varies per volume. Cambridge University Press, The Edinburgh Building, Shaftesbury Road, Cambridge CB2 2RU United Kingdom. **Tel** 011 44 223 312393, FAX 011 44 223 325959. **(Subscription address:** North America/ Cambridge University Press, 40 West 20th Street, New York, NY 10011-4211; telephone: (212)924-3900) **NLM** W1 ME895V. **CODEN** MSENAD. Documents available from BIOSIS Document Express, CASDDS.
**Ind/Abst** Biol. Abstr.; Chem. Abstr.

SZ/0378-0392
**MINERAL AND ELECTROLYTE METABOLISM. See** Medical Science and Technology-Internal Medicine.

IT/0391-1977
**MINERVA ENDOCRINOLOGICA.** [Minerva endocrinol.]. (197?)-. Academic Scholarly Publication. Italian (English). qt. $90.00 (individuals), $140.00 (institutions). Edizioni Minerva Medica, Corso Bramante

83-85, 10126 Turin Italy. **Tel** 011 39 11 678282, FAX 011 39 11 674502. **NLM** W1; MI64. **CODEN** MNREDJ. Documents available from CASDDS.
**Ind/Abst** Chem. Abstr. (-1988); Index Med. (Vol. 9, No. 1, 1984-).

IE/0303-7207
**MOLECULAR AND CELLULAR ENDOCRINOLOGY.** [Mol. cell. endocrinol.]. Vol. 1 (March 1974)-. Academic Scholarly Publication. English. Eighteen times a year (9 volumes). $1726.00. Elsevier Science Ireland Ltd., Bay 15, Shannon Industrial Estate, Co Clare Ireland. **Tel** 011 353 61 471944. **ED** B.A. Cooke and E.R. Simpson. **LC** QP187.A1; M63. **DD** 574.1/4. **NLM** W1 MO194V. **CODEN** MCEND6. **[CCC].** Index available. **Ad Acc. Pr Rev.** available on microfilm and microfiche from University Microfilms International (UMI). Documents available from The Genuine Article, BIOSIS Document Express, CASDDS.
**Desc:** Meets the demand for integrated publication on all aspects related to the biochemical effects, synthesis and secretions of extracellular signals (hormones, neurotransmitters, etc.) and to the understanding of cellular regulatory mechanisms involved in hormonal control.
**Ind/Abst** AgBiotech News Inf.; AGRICOLA; Anim. Breed. Abstr.; Biol. Abstr.; Calcium Calcif. Tissue Abstr.; Chem. Abstr.; Chem. Titles; CSA Neuro. Abstr.; Curr. Aware. Biol. Sci., CABS; Curr. Contents Life Sci.; Curr. Ref. Fish Res.; Dairy Sci. Abstr.; EMBASE; Genet. Abstr.; Health Plan. Adminis.; Index Med.; Index Vet.; Nucl. Acids Abstr.; Oncog. Growth Factors Abstr.; Life Sci. Collect.; Ref. Upd. Basic Ed.; Ref. Upd. Deluxe Ed.; Res. Alert [Full Cov.]; Rev. Agric. Entomol.; Rev. Med. Vet. Entomol.; Sci. Cit. Index; SCISEARCH; Soc. Sci. Cit. Index [Select. Cov.].

US/0888-8809
**MOLECULAR ENDOCRINOLOGY (BALTIMORE, MD.).** (MOLECULAR ENDOCRINOLOGY.). [Mol. endocrinol.]. **Added/Corp** Endocrine Society. Vol. 1, No. 1 (Jan. 1987)-. Academic Scholarly Publication. English. mo (12 issues). $260.00 (institutions), $155.00 (individuals) US; $300.00 (institutions), $200.00 (individuals) other. Endocrine Society / Maryland, 9650 Rockville Pike, Bethesda MD 20814-3998. **Tel** (301)571-1802, FAX (301)571-1869. **ED** Anthony R. Means, M.D. **LC** QP187.3.M64; M63. **DD** 591.1/42/05. **NLM** W1; MO196E. **CODEN** MOENEN. **Ad Acc. Pr Rev. Acid Free.** Documents available from The Genuine Article, BIOSIS Document Express, CASDDS.
**Desc:** Devoted to the molecular mechanisms of cellular regulation, this new interdisciplinary journal supplies a forum for the increasing number of s scientists working on molecular mechanisms of hormone action.
**Ind/Abst** AgBiotech News Inf.; Anim. Breed. Abstr.; Biol. Abstr. (1987-); Chem. Abstr. (1987-); CSA Neuro. Abstr.; Curr. Aware. Biol. Sci., CABS; Curr. Contents Life Sci.; Dairy Sci. Abstr.; EMBASE; Fish Rev. (Jan. 1989-July 1992); Genet. Abstr.; Index Med. (1987-); Index Vet.; Pig News Inf.; Poult. Abstr. (1987-); Ref. Upd. Basic Ed.; Ref. Upd. Deluxe Ed.; Res. Alert [Full Cov.]; Rev. Agric. Entomol.; Sci. Cit. Index; SCISEARCH; Vet. Bull.; Wildl. Rev. (Jan. 1989-July 1992).

US/0077-1015
**MONOGRAPHS ON ENDOCRINOLOGY.** [Monogr. endocrinol.]. Vol. 1 (1967)-. Monographic series. English. ir. Price varies per volume. Springer Verlag New York Inc., PO Box 19386 Books, Newark NJ 07195. **Tel** (201)348-4033. **(Subscription address:** North America/ Journal Fulfillment Services, 44 Hartz Way, Secaucus, NJ 07094) **LC** UNC. **NLM** W1 MO57. **CODEN** MOENBK. Documents available from BIOSIS Document Express, CASDDS.
**Desc:** Covers basic and advanced subjects in endocrinology and related fields, stressing new methods and developments in basic research and clinical investigation.
**Ind/Abst** Biol. Abstr.; Chem. Abstr.; Index Med.

GW/0172-780X
**NEURO ENDOCRINOLOGY LETTERS.** [Neuro-endocrinol. lett.]. (1979)-. Academic Scholarly Publication. English. Six times a year (Feb., Apr., June, Aug., Oct., Dec.). $270.00 Americas; DM200.00 (individual), DM350.00 (institution), Europe; DM250.00 (individual), DM400.00 (institution) other. Brain Research and Promotion, Lange Gasse 6, D 72070 Tubingen Germany. **Tel** 011 49 7071 24706. **(Subscription address:** 303 NW 12th Avenue, Deerfield Beach FL 33442; telephone: (305)428-5566) **NLM** W1 NE328E. **CODEN** NLETDU. **[CCC]. Pr Rev.** Documents available from The Genuine Article, CASDDS.
**Ind/Abst** Chem. Abstr.; EMBASE; Ref. Upd. Basic Ed.; Ref. Upd. Deluxe Ed.; Res. Alert [Full Cov.]; Sci. Cit. Index; SCISEARCH.

NE/0168-0617
**NEUROENDOCRINE PERSPECTIVES.** ***Ceased.*** [Neuroendocr. perspect.]. Vol. 1 (1982)-Vol. 5 (19??). Academic Scholarly Publication. English. an. Elsevier Science Publishers BV, PO Box 211, 1000 AE Amsterdam Netherlands. **Tel** 011 31 20 5803642, FAX 011 31 20 5862696, telex 15682. **ED** Eugenio E. Muller and Robert M. MacLeod. **LC** QP356.4; .N4773. **DD** 612/.814. **NLM** W1 NE328C. **CODEN** NEPEEQ. Documents available from BIOSIS Document Express, CASDDS.
**Ind/Abst** Biol. Abstr. (1984-); Chem. Abstr.

SZ/0028-3835
**NEUROENDOCRINOLOGY. See** Medical Science and Technology-Neurology.

UK/0143-4276
**NEUROHYPOPHYSIAL HORMONES.** ***Title Change.*** [Neurohypophysial horm.]. **VFOAT** Neurohypophyseal Hormones. (1980)-(1993). English. bw. SUBIS, Mansion House, 19 Kingfield Road, Sheffield S11 9AS England. **Tel** 011 44 114 255 4433, FAX 011 44 114 255 4626. **DD** 016.574. **[CCC]. Bk Rev. Ad Acc.** ***Continued by*** *Oxytocin and Vasopressin.*
**Desc:** Current awareness service for researchers and clinicians.

US/1054-9412
**NOVO DIABETES CARE PROFILE.** (NOVO DIABETES CARE PROFILE / NOVO NORDISK PHARMACEUTICALS INC.). [Novo diabetes care profile]. **Added/Corp** Novo Nordisk Pharmaceuticals, Inc. **VFOAT** Profile. (Spring 1991)-. Periodical. English. qt. Comed Communications, 210 West Washington Square, Philadelphia PA 19106-3512. **DD** 616.

UK/1351-5330
**OXYTOCIN AND VASOPRESSIN.** (19??)-. English. sm. £85.00. SUBIS, Mansion House, 19 Kingfield Road, Sheffield S11 9AS England. **Tel** 011 44 114 255 4433, FAX 011 44 114 255 4626. ***Continues*** *Neurohypophysial Hormones, 0143-4276.*

UK/0142-825X
**PANCREATIC AND SALIVARY SECRETION.** [Pancr. saliv. secret.]. (1979)-. English. sm. £110.00. SUBIS, Mansion House, 19 Kingfield Road, Sheffield S11 9AS England. **Tel** 011 44 114 255 4433, FAX 011 44 114 255 4626. **DD** 016.574. **[CCC]. Bk Rev. Ad Acc.**
**Desc:** Current awareness service for researchers and clinicians.

SZ/0304-4254
**PEDIATRIC AND ADOLESCENT ENDOCRINOLOGY. See** Medical Science and Technology-Pediatrics.

US/0361-0225
**PERSPECTIVES IN NEUROENDOCRINE RESEARCH.** (1975)-. Academic Scholarly Publication. English. ir. Price varies per volume. Plenum Press, 233 Spring Street, New York NY 10013-1578. **Tel** (212)620-8000, (800)221-9369, FAX (212)463-0742, (212)807-1047, telex 23/421139. **NLM** W1 PE871H. **CODEN** PNRSDQ. Documents available from CASDDS.
**Ind/Abst** Chem. Abstr.

CN/0384-7810
**PLEIN SOLEIL (MONTREAL).** (PLEIN SOLEIL.). [Plein soleil]. **Added/Corp** Association du Diabete du Quebec. Vol. 18, (Jan./Mar. 1976)-. Periodical. French. Four times a year (Feb., May, Aug., Nov.). 20.00Can$. Association du Diabete du Quebec, 5635 rue Sherbrooke EST, Montreal QUE H1N 1A3 Canada. **Tel** (514)259-3422, FAX (514)259-9286. **DD** 616.4/62/005. Index available (Bound in each iss.). **Ad Acc, Adv Mgr:** L. Bouchard, **Tel** (514)259-3422 Ext. 24. **Circ:** 15,000 (ctrl). ***Continues*** *Survivre, 0562-7087.*
**Desc:** Bulletin of medical information on diabetes in a proper manner for diabetics.
**Ind/Abst** Point Repere (1983-).

US/0897-2931
**PRACTICAL ASPECTS OF DIABETES MANAGEMENT.** ***Ceased.*** [Pract. asp. diabetes manage.]. (Feb. 1988)-(1992). Periodical. English. bm. HP Publishing Company, 55 Fifth Avenue, 14th Floor, New York NY 10003-4301. **Tel** (212)989-2100, FAX (212)989-2100. **DD** 616. **NLM** W1; PR138RP.

UK/0266-447X
**PRACTICAL DIABETES.** [Pract. diabetes]. Vol. 1, No. 1 (Sept. 1984)-. Periodical. English. bm. £34.00 (organizations and libraries), £26.00 other UK; £Europe and Republic of Ireland; £49.00 other. PMH Publications Ltd, PO Box 100 Chichester, West Sussex PO19 1XR England. **Tel** 011 44 243771111. **ED** Ak Baksi and Jane Jones. **NLM** W1; PR293T. Index available. cum. index. **Bk Rev. Ad Acc. Circ:** 10,700 (ctrl).
**Ind/Abst** EMBASE.

US/0730-3491
**PRACTICAL DIABETOLOGY.** (PRACTICAL DIABETOLOGY / THE INTERNATIONAL ASSOCIATION FOR IMPROVED DIABETES CARE.). [Pract. diabetol.]. **Added/Corp** International Association for Improved Diabetes Care. Vol. 1, No. 1 (Jan./Feb. 1982)-. Periodical. English. bm (6 issues). $48.00 (one year), $80.00 (two years), $100.00 (three years) US; $72.00 (one year), $120.00 (two years) other. R A Rapaport Publishing Inc, 150 West 22nd Street, New York NY 10011. **Tel** (212)989-0200. **NLM** W1 PR139S. **Ad Acc.**
**Desc:** Written by diabetes specialists and provides a broad array of information on the current approaches to the treatment of diabetes.

US/0895-0660
**PRIMARY DIABETOLOGY.** 1989-. Periodical. English. bm. Tom Jones Associates, 270 Pascack Road, Woodcliff Lake NJ 07675.

RU/0375-9660
**PROBLEMY ENDOKRINOLOGII.** [Probl. endokrinol.]. **Added/Corp** Soviet Union. Ministerstvo Zdravookhraneniia. Vsesoiuznoe Nauchnoe Obshchestvo Endokrinologov (Soviet Union). Vol. 13 (Jan./Feb. 1967)-. Academic Scholarly Publication. Russian. Six times a year. $99.95. Izdatelstvo Meditsina / Russian Academy of Medical Sciences, Ulitsa Solyanka 14, 109801 Moscow Russia. **Tel** 011 95 297-05-04. **(Subscription address:** East View Publications Inc., 3020 Harbor Lane North, Suite 110, Minneapolis MN 55447.) **NLM** W1 PR5784. **CODEN** PROEAS. Documents available from BIOSIS Document Express, CASDDS. ***Continues*** *Problemy Endokrinologii i Gormonoterapii.*
**Ind/Abst** Biol. Abstr.; Chem. Abstr.; CSA Neuro. Abstr. (?-?); Dairy Sci. Abstr.; EMBASE [Select. Cov.]; Index Med.; Int. Aerosp. Abstr.; Life Sci. Collect.; PESTDOC.

AT/0312-4738
**PROCEEDINGS - ENDOCRINE SOCIETY OF AUSTRALIA.** [Proc. - Endocr. Soc. Aust.]. **VFOAT** Proceedings of the Annual Meeting - Endocrine Society of Australia. Proceedings. English. an. $4.87. Endocrine Society, Royal Adelaide Hospital, Adelaide South Australia 5000 Australia. **NLM** W1 PR583W.
**Ind/Abst** EMBASE.

DK/0906-9666
**PROGRAM OF PLENARY SESSIONS AND ADVANCE ABSTRACTS OF SHORT COMMUNICATIONS. See** Medical Science and Technology-Abstracting, Bibliographies and Statistics.

US/0890-7048
**PROGRESS IN ENDOCRINE RESEARCH AND THERAPY.** [Prog. endocr. res. ther.]. Vol. 1 (1984)-. Academic Scholarly Publication. English. ir. Price varies per volume. Raven Press, 1185 Avenue of the Americas, 37th Floor, New York NY 10036. **Tel** (212)930-9500, (212)930-9604, FAX (212)869-3495, (212)302-8507, telex 640073. **ED** Dieter K. Ludecke, George P. Chrousos and George Tolis. **DD** 616. **NLM** W1; PR668QM. Documents available from CASDDS.
**Ind/Abst** Chem. Abstr.

US/1045-2001
**PROGRESS IN NEUROENDOCRINIMMUNOLOGY.** ***Ceased.*** (PROGRESS IN NEUROENDOCRINIMMUNOLOGY : PNEI.). **Added/Corp** Fidia Information Network. **VFOAT** PNEI. Vol. 1, No. 1 (Winter 1988)-(1992). Periodical. English. qt. Thieme Medical Publishers Inc., 381 Park Avenue South, Suite 1201, New York NY 10016. **Tel** (212)683-5088, (212)683-5089, FAX (212)779-9020, telex 220 862 TSINC UR. **ED** R.M. MacLeod, J. Blalock, J. Martin and U. Scapagnini. **LC** QP356.47; .P76. **DD** 616. **NLM** W1; PR672P. **CODEN** PNEIEY. Documents available from The Genuine Article, BIOSIS Document Express.
**Desc:** Dedicated to enhancing knowledge of the intricate interactions among the endocrine, immune and central nervous systems. It highlights important advances in diverse but interelated scientific disciplines and, by unifying their concepts into an intergrated whole, stimulates research to elucidate how these systems coordinate to affect the health of the host.
**Ind/Abst** Biol. Abstr. (1992-); Curr. Aware. Biol. Sci., CABS; Curr. Contents Life Sci.; Res. Alert [Full Cov.]; SCISEARCH.

SZ/0254-105X
**PROGRESS IN REPRODUCTIVE BIOLOGY AND MEDICINE. See** Biology.

UK/0142-8276
**PROLACTIN SHEFFIELD.** (PROLACTIN.). [Prolactin Sheff.]. (1979)-. English. bw. £85.00. SUBIS, Mansion House, 19 Kingfield Road, Sheffield S11 9AS England. **Tel** 011 44 114 255 4433, FAX 011 44 114 255 4626. **DD** 016.59901927. **Bk Rev. Ad Acc.**
**Desc:** Current awareness service for researchers and clinicians.

UK/0142-8284
**PROSTAGLANDINS-BIOLOGY.** Vol. 1 (1979)-. English. Twenty-four times a year. £115.00. SUBIS, Mansion House, 19 Kingfield Road, Sheffield S11 9AS England. **Tel** 011 44 114 255 4433, FAX 011 44 114 255 4626. **[CCC].**

UK/0306-4530
**PSYCHONEUROENDOCRINOLOGY.** [Psychoneuroendocrinology]. **Added/Corp** International Society of Psychoneuroendocrinology. Vol. 1 (July 1975)-. Academic Scholarly Publication. English. Eight times a year. $641.00 The Americas; £430.00 other. Pergamon Press, An Imprint of Elsevier Science Ltd., The Boulevard, Langford Lane, Kidlington, Oxford OX5 1GB United Kingdom. **Tel** 011 44 865 843000, 011 44 865

843699, FAX 011 44 865 843010. **(Subscription address:** Elsevier Science Ltd. Oxford Fulfillment Centre, PO Box 800, Kidlington, Oxford OX5 1DX United Kingdom.**)** **ED** Robert T. Rubin and Harvey Feder. **NLM** W1 PS748G. **CODEN** PSYCDE. **[CCC]. Pr Rev.** available on microfilm and microfiche from University Microfilms International (UMI). Documents available from The Genuine Article, BIOSIS Document Express, CASDDS, ADONIS.
**Desc:** Provides a critical forum for the reporting of both basic and clinical psychoneuroendocrine research.
**Ind/Abst** ADONIS; Biol. Abstr.; Chem. Abstr.; CSA Neuro. Abstr.; Cumul. Index Nurs. Allied Health Lit.; Curr. Aware. Biol. Sci., CABS; Curr. Contents Life Sci.; Dairy Sci. Abstr.; EMBASE; Index Med.; Life Sci. Collect.; PESTDOC; Psychol. Abstr. (1975-); PsycINFO; PsycLit; Res. Alert [Full Cov.]; Sci. Cit. Index; SCISEARCH; Soc. Sci. Cit. Index [Select. Cov.].

UK/0264-7397
**RECENT ADVANCES IN DIABETES.**
***Ceased.*** [Recent adv. diabetes]. No. 1-?. Periodical. English. Churchill Livingstone, 1-3 Baxter's Place, Leith Walk, Edinburgh EH1 3AF Scotland. **Tel** 011 44 31 556 2424, FAX 011 44 31 558 1278, telex 727511. **(Subscription address:** US/ Churchill Livingstone, Fulfillment Office, PO Box 11318, Birmingham, AL 35202**)** **ED** Malcolm Nattrass and Julio V Santiago. **LC** RC660.A1; R42. **DD** 616.4/62. **NLM** W1 RE105UK.

UK/0140-9123
**RECENT ADVANCES IN ENDOCRINOLOGY AND METABOLISM.**
[Recent adv. endocrinol. metab.]. No. 1 (1978)-. Academic Scholarly Publication. English. ir. Price varies. Churchill Livingstone, 1-3 Baxter's Place, Leith Walk, Edinburgh EH1 3AF Scotland. **Tel** 011 44 31 556 2424, FAX 011 44 31 558 1278, telex 727511. **(Subscription address:** Churchill Livingstone / US, 5 S 250 Frontenac Road, Naperville IL 60563.**)** **LC** RC648.A1; R43. **DD** 616.4/005. **NLM** W1 RE105UL. **CODEN** RAEMDA. Documents available from BIOSIS Document Express, CASDDS.
**Ind/Abst** Biol. Abstr.; Chem. Abstr. (-1978); Curr. Aware. Biol. Sci., CABS; Life Sci. Collect.

HU/0079-9955
**RECENT DEVELOPMENTS OF NEUROBIOLOGY IN HUNGARY.** **See** Medical Science and Technology-Neurology.

US/0079-9963
**RECENT PROGRESS IN HORMONE RESEARCH.** [Recent prog. horm. res.]. Vol. 1 (1947)-. Academic Scholarly Publication. English. ir. Price varies per volume. Academic Press, Inc., 6277 Sea Harbor Drive, Orlando FL 32887. **Tel** (800)543-9534, (407)345-4100, FAX (407)363-9661. **ED** Gregory Pincus. **LC** QP187; .R32. **DD** 612.4058. **NLM** W1 RE106E. **CODEN** RPHRA6. **[CCC].** cum. index. **Pr Rev.** Documents available from The Genuine Article, BIOSIS Document Express, CASDDS.
**Ind/Abst** AGRICOLA; Anim. Breed. Abstr.; Biol. Abstr.; Chem. Abstr.; EMBASE; Index Med.; Index Sci. Rev. [Full Cov.]; Life Sci. Collect.; Res. Alert [Full Cov.]; Sci. Cit. Index (19??-19??); SCISEARCH.

UK/0142-8314
**RELEASING HORMONES.** [Releasing horm.]. (1978)-. English. mo. £85.00. SUBIS, Mansion House, 19 Kingfield Road, Sheffield S11 9AS England. **Tel** 011 44 114 255 4433, FAX 011 44 114 255 4626. **DD** 016.574. **[CCC]. Bk Rev. Ad Acc.**
**Desc:** Current awareness service for researchers and clinicians.

FR/0994-3919
**REPRODUCTION HUMAINE ET HORMONES.** [Reprod. hum. horm.]. (1988)-. Periodical. French. mo (10 issues). 318.32F France; 433.00F other. Editions Eska, 27 rue Dunois, 75013 Paris France. **Tel** 011 33 1 44068042. **UDC** 618.

US
**RESEARCH PROGRAMS OF THE NATIONAL INSTITUTE OF CHILD HEALTH AND HUMAN DEVELOPMENT. NUTRITION AND ENDOCRINOLOGY.** **See** Nutrition and Dietetics.

CK/0120-1182
**REVISTA DE LA SOCIEDAD COLOMBIANA DE ENDOCRINOLOGIA.**
[Rev. Soc. Colomb. Endocrinol.]. **Added/Corp** Sociedad Colombiana de Endocrinologia. Vol. 1 No. 1 (Dec. 1955)-. Periodical. Spanish. sa. **NLM** W1 RE412P.

FR/0048-8062
**REVUE FRANCAISE D'ENDOCRINOLOGIE CLINIQUE, NUTRITION ET METABOLISME.** [Rev. fr. endocrinol. clin., nutr. metab.]. (Jan./Feb. 1960)-. Academic Scholarly Publication. French (summaries and/or abstracts in English). Six times a year. 600.00F. Editions de Medecine Pratique, 4 rue Louis Armand, 92600 Asnieres France. **Tel** 011 33 1 47910910. **NLM** W1 RE848N. **CODEN** RECNAS. **[CCC].** Documents available from BIOSIS Document Express, CASDDS.
**Ind/Abst** Biol. Abstr.; Chem. Abstr.; EMBASE; Saf. Health Work.

●RM
**ROMANIAN JOURNAL OF ENDOCRINOLOGY / SPONSORE [SIC] BY THE ACADEMY OF MEDICAL SCIENCES.** **Added/Corp** Academia de Stiinte Medicale. New Series, Vol. 30, Issue 1/2 (1992)-. Periodical. English (summaries and/or abstracts in Romanian). qt. DM268.00. Editura Academia Republicii Socialiste Romania, Calea Victoriei Nr 125, R-79717 Bucuresti Romania. **Tel** telex 10376 PRSFI R. **(Subscription address:** Kubon & Sagner, ABT Zeitschriftenimport, D 80328 Munich Germany.**)** **NLM** W1; RO326S. **CODEN** RJENE9. ***Continues*** *Endocrinologie, 0253-1801.*

IT
**SCIENZA E DIABETE.** (19??)-. Italian. bm (6 issues). L20000. Scienze e Diabete, Via Rucellai 46/8, 20126 Milan Italy. **Tel** 011 39 2 2570176.

NE/0167-8523
**SECRETORY PROCESS, THE.** **See** Medical Science and Technology.

US/0734-8630
**SEMINARS IN REPRODUCTIVE ENDOCRINOLOGY.** [Semin. reprod. endocrinol.]. Vol. 1, No. 1 (Feb. 1983)-. Periodical. English. qt. $137.00 (institutions), $97.00 (individuals) US; $162.00 (institutions), $122.00 (individuals) other. Thieme Medical Publishers Inc., 381 Park Avenue South, Suite 1201, New York NY 10016. **Tel** (212)683-5088, (212)683-5089, FAX (212)779-9020, telex 220 862 TSINC UR. **ED** Leon Speroff. **DD** 618. **NLM** W1 SE489H. **CODEN** SRENE8. **[CCC].** cum. index. **Bk Rev. Ad Acc. Pr Rev. Circ:** 1,200 (ctrl). available on microfilm and microfiche from University Microfilms International (UMI). Documents available from The Genuine Article, BIOSIS Document Express.
**Desc:** Topic-oriented journal for the practitioner specializing in reproductive functions and diseases.
**Ind/Abst** Biol. Abstr. (1985-); Curr. Aware. Biol. Sci., CABS; Curr. Contents Clin. Med.; EMBASE; Nutr. Abstr. Rev., Ser. A, Hum. Exp.; Res. Alert [Select. Cov.].

UK/0142-8330
**STEROID RECEPTORS.** **See** Biology-Cytology and Histology.

GW/0931-8283
**STOFFWECHSELKRANKHEITEN.**
[Stoffwechselkrankheiten]. Vol. 5, No. 1, (Feb. 1986)-. Periodical. German. bm. **NLM** W1; ST6319. ***Continues*** *Diabetes Mellitus (Frankfurt AM MAin, Germany), 0724-2573.*

US/1050-7256
**THYROID (NEW YORK, N.Y.).** (THYROID : OFFICIAL JOURNAL OF THE AMERICAN THYROID ASSOCIATION.). [Thyroid]. **Added/Corp** American Thyroid Association. Vol. 1, No. 1, (1990)-. Periodical. English. bm. $170.95. Mary Ann Liebert Inc., 1651 Third Avenue, New York NY 10128. **Tel** (212)289-2300, (800)M-LIEBERT, FAX (212)289-4697. **ED** Jerome Hershman, M.D. **DD** 616. **NLM** W1; TH959. **CODEN** THYRER. Documents available from The Genuine Article.
**Desc:** Publishes original articles and reviews reflecting the ever-expanding and broadening activities in the thyroid field, from the molecular biology of the cell to clinical management of thyroid disorders.
**Ind/Abst** Curr. Aware. Biol. Sci., CABS; Curr. Contents Life Sci.; EMBASE; Index Med. (1990-); Res. Alert [Full Cov.]; Sci. Cit. Index; SCISEARCH.

US/0190-0625
**THYROID TODAY.** [Thyroid today]. **Added/Corp** Flint Laboratories. Vol. 1 (Aug. 1977)-. Academic Scholarly Publication. English. Four times a year. Free on request. Boots Pharmaceuticals Inc, 300 Tri-State International Center, Lincolnshire IL 60069. **Tel** (708)405-7400, FAX (708)405-7505. **ED** J. Oppenheimer. **NLM** W1 TH96. **CODEN** THTODQ. ctrl circ. Documents available from CASDDS.
**Desc:** Information on the thyroid gland and thyroid diseases.
**Ind/Abst** Chem. Abstr. (1977-1983).

US/1042-2838
**TODAY IN MEDICINE DIABETOLOGY AND ENDOCRINOLOGY.** [Today med., Diabetol. endocrinol.]. **VFOAT** Diabetology and Endocrinology. Periodical. English. bm. $45.00 US; $60.00 Canada. Data Centrum Communications Inc, The Soho Building, 110 Greene Street, Suite 505, New York NY 10012. **Tel** (212)226-5252. **DD** 616.

JA/0021-437X
**TONYOBYO.** [Tonyobyo]. **Added/Corp** Nihon Tonyobyo Gakkai. **VFOAT** Journal of the Japan Diabetic Society. (1958)-. Periodical. Japanese (summaries and/or abstracts in English). Twelve times a year. $262.00. Japan Diabetes Society, Hongo Sky Building, Room 403, 3-38-11 Hongo, Bunkyo-ku, 113 Tokyo Japan. **(Subscription address:** Kyowa Book Company Inc., 1 38 Kanda Jinbocho Chiyoda-ku, Tokyo 101 Japan.**)** **CODEN** TONYA4. Documents available from BIOSIS Document Express, CASDDS.
**Ind/Abst** Biol. Abstr.; Chem. Abstr.; EMBASE [Select. Cov.].

US/1043-2760
**TRENDS IN ENDOCRINOLOGY AND METABOLISM.** (TRENDS IN ENDOCRINOLOGY AND METABOLISM : TEM.). [Trends endocrinol. metab.]. **Added/Corp** Elsevier Science Publishers. **VFOAT** TEM. Vol. 1, No. 1 (Sept./Oct. 1989)-. Academic Scholarly Publication. English. Ten times a year (1 volume). $215.00 US; $251.00 other. Elsevier Science Publishing Company Inc, Madison Square Station, PO Box 882, New York NY 10159-0882. **Tel** (212)633-3950, FAX (212)633-3990. **LC** RC648.A1; T73. **DD** 616.4/005. **NLM** W1; TR3409. **CODEN** TENME4. **[CCC]. Pr Rev.** available on microfilm and microfiche from University Microfilms International (UMI). Documents available from The Genuine Article, BIOSIS Document Express.
**Ind/Abst** Biol. Abstr. (1990-); Curr. Aware. Biol. Sci., CABS; Curr. Contents Life Sci.; EMBASE; Ref. Upd. Deluxe Ed.; Res. Alert [Full Cov.]; Sci. Cit. Index; SCISEARCH.

US/0083-6729
**VITAMINS AND HORMONES; ADVANCES IN RESEARCH AND APPLICATIONS.** [Vitam. horm.]. Vol. 1 (1943)-. Monographic series. English. ir. Price varies per volume. Academic Press, Inc., 6277 Sea Harbor Drive, Orlando FL 32887. **Tel** (800)543-9534, (407)345-4100, FAX (407)363-9661. **ED** Robert S. Harris. **LC** QP801.V5; V5. **DD** 612.05058. **NLM** W1 VI985. **CODEN** VIHOAQ. **[CCC].** cum. index. Documents available from The Genuine Article, CASDDS.
**Ind/Abst** AGRICOLA [Select. Cov.]; Chem. Abstr.; Curr. Aware. Biol. Sci., CABS; EMBASE; Energy Res. Abstr. (Aug. 1982-); Index Med.; Index Sci. Rev. [Full Cov.]; PESTDOC; Res. Alert [Full Cov.].

US/1041-8490
**VOICE OF THE DIABETIC.** (VOICE OF THE DIABETIC / THE DIABETICS DIVISION OF THE NATIONAL FEDERATION OF THE BLIND.). [Voice diabet.]. **Added/Corp** National Federation of the Blind. Diabetics Division. (1986)-. Periodical. English. qt (Jan., Apr., July, Oct.). $20.00 one year, $35.00 two year, $50.00 three year. National Federation of the Blind, 1800 Johnson Street, Baltimore MD 21230. **Tel** (410)659-9314, FAX (410)685-5653. **ED** Ed Bryant. **DD** 616. **Bk Rev. Ad Acc. Circ:** 65,000. available on audiocassette.
**Desc:** This publication provides current medical and health insurance information and dietary ideas for diabetics with a special emphasis on the diabetic blind.

US/0084-3741
**YEAR BOOK OF ENDOCRINOLOGY, THE.** [Year book endocrinol.]. (1950)-. English. an. $69.95. Mosby Year Book Inc., 11830 Westline Industrial Drive, St Louis MO 63146. **Tel** (800)325-4177, (314)872-8370, FAX (314)432-1380, telex 44-2402. **ED** John D. Bagdade. **LC** RC648; .Y4. **DD** 616.4058. **NLM** W1; YE144. **[CCC].** cum. index. ***Continues in part*** *Yearbook of Endocrinology, Metabolism and Nutrition, 0196-836X.*
**Ind/Abst** AGRICOLA.

●US/1062-371X
**YOUR PATIENT & FITNESS IN ENDOCRINOLOGY.** [Your patient fit. endocrinol.]. **VFOAT** Your Patient and Fitness in Endocrinology; Your Patient & Fitness; Your Patient and Fitness. Vol. 6, No. 2 (Mar./Apr. 1992)-. Periodical. English. bm. McGraw Hill Publishing Company, Inc., 1221 Avenue of the Americas, New York NY 10020. **Tel** (212)512-6410, (800)525-5003, FAX (212)512-6111. **DD** 616.

CC/1000-6699
**ZHONGHUA NEIFENMI DAIXIE ZAZHI.**
**VFOAT** Chinese Journal of Endocrinology and Metabolism. (1985)-. Academic Scholarly Publication. Chinese. qt. $10.00. Shanghai Institute of Endocrinology, (Shanghai-shi Neifenmi Yanjiusuo), 197 Ruijin lu Section 2, Shanghai, People's Republic of China. **Tel** 4315587. **DD** 616.4. **Ad Acc. Circ:** 10,000. Documents available from BLDSC, CASDDS.
**Ind/Abst** Chem. Abstr.

---

## EPIDEMIOLOGY

---

US
**AIDS EPIDEMIOLOGICAL AND CLINICAL STUDIES.** **See** Medical Science and Technology-Communicable Diseases.

UN/0365-3803
**AKTUAL'NYE VOPROSY EPIDEMIOLOGII.** **Added/Corp** TSentral'nyi Nauchno-Issledovatel'Skii Institut Epidemiologii. (1967)-.

Periodical. Russian. **NLM** W1 AK989G. **CODEN** AKVEAJ. Documents available from CASDDS.
**Ind/Abst** Chem. Abstr. (-1970).

UA/1014-2347
**AL-NASHRAH AL-WABAIYAH LI-IQLIM SHARQ AL-BAHR AL-MUTAWASSIT.** **See** Medical Science and Technology-Communicable Diseases.

US/0002-9262
**AMERICAN JOURNAL OF EPIDEMIOLOGY.** [Am. j. epidemiol.]. **Added/Corp** Johns Hopkins University. School of Hygiene and Public Health. Society for Epidemiologic Research (U.S.). Vol. 81 (1965)-. Academic Scholarly Publication. English. Twenty-four times a year. $225.00 (institution) US; $233.00 (institution) other. American Journal of Epidemiology, 111 Market Place, Candler Building, Suite 840, Baltimore MD 21202. **Tel** (410)223-1600, FAX (410)223-1620. **(Subscription address:** American Journal of Epidemiology, PO Box 64655, Baltimore, MD 21264**)** **ED** Moyses Szklo. **DD** 614. **NLM** W1 AM451D. **CODEN** AJEPAS. Index available (free). **Ad Acc. Pr Rev. Circ:** 5,000. Documents available from The Genuine Article, BIOSIS Document Express. ***Continues*** *American Journal of Hygiene, 0096-5294.*
**Desc:** Publishes original field and laboratory studies on the occurrence and distribution of endemic and epidemic diseases, including infectious and non-infectious acute and chronic diseases, and statistical methodology.
**Ind/Abst** Annals Behav. Med.; Biodeter. Abstr. (1991-); Biol. Abstr.; Biol. Dig.; Biostatistica; Chem. Hazards Ind.; Coal Abstr.; Curr. Aware. Biol. Sci., CABS; Curr. Contents Life Sci.; Dairy Sci. Abstr.; Dev. Med. Child Neurol.; EMBASE; Energy Res. Abstr.; Health Saf. Sci. Abstr.; Health Plan. Adminis.; Helminthol. Abstr. (19??-19??); Index Med.; Index Vet.; INIS Atomindex [Micro.]; Lab. Hazards Bull.; Med. Abstr. Newsl.; Microbiol. Abstr. Sect. B (19??-19??); Nutr. Abstr. Rev., Ser. B, Live Feeds and Feed.; Nutr. Abstr. Rev., Ser. A, Hum. Exp.; Nutr. Res. Newsl.; Life Sci. Collect.; Pollut. Abstr. Indexes; Popul. Index; Protozoolog. Abstr.; Ref. Upd. Clinical Ed.; Ref. Upd. Deluxe Ed.; Res. Alert [Full Cov.]; Rev. Med. Vet. Entomol.; Rev. Med. Vet. Mycology; Rev. Plant Pathol.; Risk Abstr.; Saf. Health Work; Sci. Cit. Index; SCISEARCH; Small Anim. Abstr. Bibliogr.; Soc. Sci. Cit. Index [Select. Cov.]; SportSearch; Vet. Bull.; Trop. Dis. Bull.; Virol. AIDS Abstr.; Wildl. Rev.

US/0196-6553
**AMERICAN JOURNAL OF INFECTION CONTROL.** [Am. j. infect. control]. **Added/Corp** Association for Practitioners in Infection Control. **VFOAT** AJIC. Vol. 8 (Feb. 1980)-. Periodical. English. bm. $126.00 (institutions), $46.00 (individuals) US; $136.00 (institutions), $56.00 (individuals) other. Mosby Year Book Inc., 11830 Westline Industrial Drive, St Louis MO 63146. **Tel** (800)325-4177, (314)872-8370, FAX (314)432-1380, telex 44-2402. **ED** Mary Castle White. **LC** RA969; .A84a. **DD** 614.4/4/05. **NLM** W1 AM468N. **[CCC].** Index available. **Bk Rev. Ad Acc. Pr Rev. Circ:** 8,355. available on microfilm and microfiche from University Microfilms International (UMI). Documents available from The Genuine Article, ADONIS. ***Continues*** *APIC Journal, 0161-6005.*
**Desc:** Serves an international network of infection control practitioners and hospital epidemiologists united by a common concern for control of infection associated with hospital, extended care facilities and other health care institutions.
**Ind/Abst** Abstr. Clin. Care Guidel.; ADONIS; Cumul. Index Nurs. Allied Health Lit.; Curr. Contents Clin. Med.; EMBASE; Health Devices Alerts; Health Plan. Adminis.; Helminthol. Abstr.; Hospit. Health Admin. Index; Index Med. (1982-); Index Vet.; INIS Atomindex [Micro.]; Int. Nurs. Index; Nurs. Abstr.; Life Sci. Collect.; Physic. Medline Plus; Protozoolog. Abstr.; Res. Alert [Select. Cov.]; SCISEARCH.

US/1047-2797
**ANNALS OF EPIDEMIOLOGY.** [Ann. epidemiol.]. **Added/Corp** American College of Epidemiology. **VFOAT** AEP. Vol. 1, No. 1 (Oct. 1990)-. Academic Scholarly Publication. English. Six times a year (1 volume). $230.00 US; $270.00 other. Elsevier Science Publishing Company Inc, Madison Square Station, PO Box 882, New York NY 10159-0882. **Tel** (212)633-3950, FAX (212)633-3990. **ED** Charles H Hennetlens. **LC** RA648.5; .A56. **DD** 614.4/05. **NLM** W1; AN574T. **CODEN** ANNPE3. **[CCC]. Ad Acc. Pr Rev.** available in microform.
**Desc:** An international journal publishing reports of original research in the epidemiology of chronic and acute diseases for clinicians as well as public health researchers.
**Ind/Abst** EMBASE; Trop. Dis. Bull.

US
**ANNUAL REPORT - EPIDEMIOLOGY & DISEASE CONTROL STUDY SECTION, NATIONAL INSTITUTES OF HEALTH.**
**Main/Corp** United States. National Institutes of Health. Epidemiology and Disease Control Study Section. **VAT** Annual Report - Epidemiology and Disease Control Study Section, National Institutes of Health. English. an. National Institutes of Health, 9000 Rockville Pike, Bethesda MD 20014. **Tel** (301)496-6975.

GW/0067-5083
**BEITRAEGE ZUR HYGIENE UND EPIDEMIOLOGIE.** [Beitr. Hyg. Epidemiol.]. Vol. 1 (1943)-. Monographic series. German. ir. Price varies per volume. Johann Ambrosius Barth, Prager Strasse 16 B, D 04103 Leipzig Germany. **Tel** 011 49 341 7137570. **DD** 613; 614. **NLM** W1 BE341. **CODEN** BHEPAP. Documents available from BIOSIS Document Express.
**Ind/Abst** Biol. Abstr. (-1971); EMBASE; Index Med.

VE
**BOLETIN EPIDEMIOLOGICO SEMANAL / MINISTERIO DE SANIDAD Y ASISTENCIA SOCIAL, DIRECCION DE SALUD PUBLICA, DEPARTAMENTO DE DEMOGRAFIA Y EPIDEMIOLOGIA, DIVISION DE EPIDEMIOLOGIA.** Periodical. Spanish. wk. Informacion de la Sanitaria Epidemiologica, Paseo del Prado 18 20, 28014 Madrid Spain. **Tel** 011 34 1 4202176. **NLM** W1; BO297RL.

IT/0021-2547
**BOLLETTINO DELL'INSTITUTO SIEROTERAPICO MILANESE.** ***Ceased.*** **See** Medical Science and Technology-Allergy and Immunology.

FR/0245-7466
**BULLETIN EPIDEMIOLOGIQUE HEBDOMADAIRE : BEH / REPUBLIQUE FRANCAISE, MINISTERE DE LA SOLIDARITE, DE LA SANTE ET DE LA PROTECTION SOCIALE, DIRECTION GENERALE DE LA SANTE.** **Added/Corp** France. Direction Generale de la Sante. **VFOAT** BEH; B.E.H. (1980)-. Bulletin. French. wk (52 issues). 244.86F France; 250.00F other. Imprimerie Nationale / France, BP 514, 59505 Douai Cedex France. **Tel** 011 33 27 937090. **NLM** W2; GF7 D5b. ***Continues*** *Bulletin Hebdomadaire d'Information Epidemiologique.*
**Ind/Abst** Trop. Dis. Bull.

US/1055-9965
**CANCER EPIDEMIOLOGY, BIOMARKERS & PREVENTION.** **See** Medical Science and Technology-Neoplasma, Neoplastic.

TR
**CAREC SURVEILLANCE REPORT.**
**Added/Corp** Caribbean Epidemiology Centre. **VFOAT** CSR. **VAT** Caribbean Epidemiology Centre Surveillance Report. Vol. 1, No. 1 (Mar. 1975)-. Periodical. English. mo. **LC** RA650.55.C27; C37. **DD** 614.4/2729/05.
**Ind/Abst** Trop. Dis. Bull.

US/0748-5093
**CATALOG OF UNIVERSITY PRESENTATIONS.** **See** Public Health and Safety.

XR/0009-0522
**CESKOSLOVENSKA EPIDEMIOLOGIE, MIKROBIOLOGIE, IMUNOLOGIE.** [Cesk. epidemiol., mikrobiol., imunol.]. (1956)-. Periodical. Czech. bm. $76.50. **(Subscription address:** Artia Pegas Press Ltd., Palac Metro Narodni Trida 25, 11210 Prague 1 Czech Republic.**)** **NLM** W1; CE879K. **CODEN** CKEMAE. **[CCC].** Documents available from CASDDS. ***Continues*** *Ceskoslovenska Hygiena, Epidemiologie, Mikrobiologie.*
**Ind/Abst** Biodeter. Abstr. (1991-); Chem. Abstr.; Helminthol. Abstr. (1991-); Index Med.; Index Vet.; Microbiol. Abstr. Sect. B; Microbiol. Abstr. Sect. A; Pig News Inf.; Protozoolog. Abstr.; Rev. Med. Vet. Entomol.; Rev. Med. Vet. Mycology; Rev. Plant Pathol.; Vet. Bull.; Trop. Dis. Bull.; Virol. AIDS Abstr.

DK/0301-5661
**COMMUNITY DENTISTRY AND ORAL EPIDEMIOLOGY.** **See** Dentistry.

SZ/0377-3574
**CONTRIBUTIONS TO EPIDEMIOLOGY AND BIOSTATISTICS.** [Contrib. epidemiol. biostat.]. Vol. 1 (1979)-. Academic Scholarly Publication. English. an. 180.00F (approx. per volume). S. Karger AG, Allschwilerstrasse 10, PO Box - Postfach - Case Postale, CH-4009 Basel Switzerland. **Tel** 011 41 61 306-1111, FAX 011 41 61 306-1234, telex CH 962 652. **ED** J. Wahrendorf. **NLM** W1 CO778RC. **CODEN** CEPBDV. **[CCC].** Documents available from BIOSIS Document Express, CASDDS.
**Desc:** Appreciation for the unique knowledge gleaned from epidemiologic studies has underscored the success of this series, which features innovative studies showing how epidemiologic and biostatistical methods can aid understanding of diseases that pose major threats to public health. Edited to provide compact digests of recent developments, individual volumes have set forth information on diseases and disorders which hold particular importance for public health and preventive medicine.
**Ind/Abst** Biol. Abstr.; Chem. Abstr.; Ref. Upd. Deluxe Ed.

XR/0139-598X
**CZECHOSLOVAK BIBLIOGRAPHY ON EPIDEMIOLOGY AND MICROBIOLOGY.** (1971)-. Bibliography. English. an. **NLM** ZWA 105 C998.
**Ind/Abst** Rev. Med. Vet. Entomol.; Trop. Dis. Bull.

FR
**DIRECTORY OF ON-GOING RESEARCH IN CANCER EPIDEMIOLOGY.** **See** Medical Science and Technology-Neoplasma, Neoplastic.

US/0732-2445
**EIS ... DIRECTORY.** [EIS dir.]. **VFOAT** E.I.S. ... Directory. Began with: 1954?. Directory. English. an. Centers for Disease Control, 1600 Clifton Road NE, Atlanta GA 30333. **Tel** (404)639-3311, FAX (404)639-3296. **LC** RA650.5. **DD** 614.4/025/73. **NLM** WA 22; AA1 E36.

IT
**EPIDEMIOLOGIA E PREVENZIONE.**
(1976)-. Periodical. Italian (summaries and/or abstracts in English). qt. L70000 Italy; L80000 other. Coop Epidemiologia Prevenzione, Via Venezian 1, 20133 Milan Italy. **Tel** 011 39 2 2390460. **NLM** W1; EP448K.
**Ind/Abst** Index Med. (March 1987-).

●IT/1121-189X
**EPIDEMIOLOGIA E PSICHIATRIA SOCIALE.** (1992)-. Periodical. Italian (English). Three times a year (Jan., May, Sept.). L70000 (individuals), L100000 (institutions). Il Pensiero Scientifico Editore s.r.l., Via Bradano 3C, 00199 Rome Italy. **Tel** 011 39 6 86207158, 86207159, 86207168, 86207169, FAX 011 39 6 86207160. **ED** M. Tansella. **UDC** 616.89. **Bk Rev. Ad Acc, Adv Mgr:** Dott Dalla, **Tel** 06-86207165. Full Page (B&W) L1.650.000. **Circ:** 1,100.
**Desc:** Covers epidemiology and research in social psychiatry.

US/0193-936X
**EPIDEMIOLOGIC REVIEWS.** [Epidemiol. rev.]. **Added/Corp** Society for Epidemiologic Research (U.S.) International Epidemiological Association. Vol. 1 (1979)-. English. an. $20.00. American Journal of Epidemiology, 111 Market Place, Candler Building, Suite 840, Baltimore MD 21202. **Tel** (410)223-1600, FAX (410)223-1620. **ED** Moyses Szklo. **LC** RA648.5; .E65. **DD** 614.4/05. **NLM** W1 EP449. **CODEN** EPIRD7. Index available. **Ad Acc. Pr Rev. Circ:** 4,800 (ctrl). available in microform. Documents available from The Genuine Article, BIOSIS Document Express.
**Desc:** Original and laboratory studies on occurrence of disease with articles on infectious and non-infectious diseases and statistical methodology.
**Ind/Abst** Biol. Abstr.; Biol. Dig.; Biostatistica; Curr. Aware. Biol. Sci., CABS; Curr. Contents Life Sci.; EMBASE; Health Plan. Adminis.; Index Med. (1979-); Index Vet.; Life Sci. Collect.; Pollut. Abstr. Indexes; Protozoolog. Abstr.; Ref. Upd. Deluxe Ed.; Res. Alert [Full Cov.]; Rev. Med. Vet. Entomol.; Sci. Cit. Index; SCISEARCH; Vet. Bull.; Trop. Dis. Bull.; Weed Abstr.

US/0256-1859
**EPIDEMIOLOGICAL BULLETIN - PAN AMERICAN HEALTH ORGANIZATION.**
(EPIDEMIOLOGICAL BULLETIN.). [Epidemiol. bull. - Pan Am. Health Organ.]. **Added/Corp** Pan American Health Organization. Vol. 1 (1980)-. Periodical. English (Spanish). Four times a year. Free. Pan American Health Organization, 525 23rd Street Northwest, Office District Sales, Washington DC 20037. **Tel** (202)293-8130, FAX (202)338-0869. **ED** Marlo Libel. **LC** RA650; .E64. **DD** 614.4/27/05. **NLM** W1 EP449P. Index available. cum. index. **Bk Rev. Circ:** 15,000. ***Supersedes*** *Weekly Epidemiological Report.*
**Desc:** Periodical publication of short accounts and comments on epidemiological activities of priority public concern and information regarding technical aspects involved in health prevention in the Region of the Americas.
**Ind/Abst** Health Plan. Adminis.; Index Vet.; Vet. Bull.

SA
**EPIDEMIOLOGICAL COMMENTS.**
**Added/Corp** South Africa. Dept. of Health. South Africa. Dept. of Health & Welfare. (19??)-. Afrikaans (English). mo. Free. Department of National Health and Population Development, Civitas Building, Private Bag X828, Pretoria 0001 South Africa. **Tel** 012 325 5100, FAX 012 325 5706. **ED** Dr. H.G.V. Kuestner. **LC** RA650.8.S6; E64. **DD** 614.4/268. Index available. cum. index. **Circ:** 1,600.
**Desc:** Publishes articles with an epidemiological flavor that are written by readers. Back issues are available on request.
**Ind/Abst** Trop. Dis. Bull.

BU
**EPIDEMIOLOGIIA, MIKROBIOLOGIIA, I INFEKTSIOZNI BOLESTI.** ***Title Change.*** **See** Biology-Microbiology.

UK/0950-2688
**EPIDEMIOLOGY AND INFECTION.** **See** Medical Science and Technology-Communicable Diseases.

US/1044-3983
**EPIDEMIOLOGY (CAMBRIDGE, MASS.).** (EPIDEMIOLOGY.). [Epidemiology]. Vol. 1, No. 1 (Jan. 1990)-. Periodical. English. bm. $119.00 (individual), $159.00 (institution) US; $149.00 (individual), $189.00 (institution) other. Williams & Wilkins Company, 428 East Preston Street, Baltimore MD 21202-3993. **Tel** (410)528-4000, (800)638-6423, FAX (410)528-8596, telex 87669. **(Subscription address:** Williams & Wilkins, PO Box 64380, Baltimore MD 21264.) **LC** RA648.5; .E655. **DD** 614.4/05. **NLM** W1; EP4520. **CODEN** EPIDEY. **[CCC].** available on microfilm and microfiche from University Microfilms International (UMI). Documents available from The Genuine Article, Quick Copies.
**Desc:** Current research and methods of data analysis for epidemiologists, public health investigators and other health professionals.
**Ind/Abst** Curr. Aware. Biol. Sci., CABS; Curr. Contents Clin. Med.; EMBASE; Health Plan. Adminis.; Index Med. (Jan. 1990-); Res. Alert [Select. Cov.]; Risk Abstr.; SCISEARCH; Soc. Sci. Cit. Index [Select. Cov.]; Trop. Dis. Bull.

US/0744-0898
**EPIDEMIOLOGY MONITOR, THE. See** Public Health and Safety.

US/1049-510X
**ETHNICITY & DISEASE.** [Ethn. dis.]. **Added/Corp** International Society on Hypertension in Blacks. **VFOAT** Ethnicity and Disease. Vol. 1, No. 1 (Winter 1991)-. Periodical. English. qt. $90.00 (institutions), $40.00 (individuals). Allen Press Inc., 810 East 10th Street, PO Box 1897, Lawrence KS 66044-8897. **Tel** (913)843-1221, (800)627-0629, FAX (913)843-1274. **DD** 616. **NLM** W1; ET44C. **CODEN** ETDIEI. **Ad Acc.**
**Desc:** An international journal on population differences in disease patterns. It provides a comprehensive source of information on casual relationships in the etiology of common illnesses through the study of ethnic patterns of disease.

NE/0392-2990
**EUROPEAN JOURNAL OF EPIDEMIOLOGY.** (1985)-. English. bm. $514.00. Kluwer Academic Publishers, Postbus 322, 3300 AH Dordrecht, The Netherlands. **Tel** 011 (31) 78 524400, FAX 011 31 78 183273, telex 20083. **ED** Claude Hannoun. **Pr Rev.**
**Desc:** Serves as a forum on the epidemiology of communicable and non-communicable diseases and their control.

IT/0393-2990
**EUROPEAN JOURNAL OF EPIDEMIOLOGY.** [Eur. j. epidemiol.]. Vol. 1, No. 1 (Mar. 1985)-. Academic Scholarly Publication. English. bm. L210000 (Italy); $248.00 (Europe), $290.00 (other). European Journal of Epidemiology, Administration Office, V Zandonai 11, 00194 Rome Italy. **Tel** 39 6 3279593. **ED** Antonio Sanna. **NLM** W1; EU72DE. **CODEN** EJEPE8. **[CCC].** Index available. **Bk Rev. Ad Acc. Pr Rev. Circ:** 2,000. Documents available from The Genuine Article, BIOSIS Document Express, CASDDS.
**Desc:** Devoted to the publication of original articles concerning the epidemiology of communicable and non-communicable diseases and their control.
**Ind/Abst** AgBiotech News Inf.; Biol. Abstr. (1985-); Chem. Abstr. (1985-); Curr. Aware. Biol. Sci., CABS; Curr. Contents Clin. Med.; Curr. Contents Life Sci.; Dairy Sci. Abstr.; EMBASE; Health Plan. Adminis.; Helminthol. Abstr. (1991-); Immunol. Abstr.; Index Med. (Vol. 1, No. 1, 1985-); Index Vet.; Microbiol. Abstr. Sect. B; Microbiol. Abstr. Sect. A; Microbiol. Abstr. Sect. C; Nutr. Res. Newsl.; Poult. Abstr.; Protozoolog. Abstr.; Res. Alert [Select. Cov.]; Rev. Med. Vet. Entomol.; Rev. Med. Vet. Mycology; Risk Abstr.; SCISEARCH; Soc. Sci. Cit. Index [Select. Cov.]; Vet. Bull.; Trop. Dis. Bull.; Virol. AIDS Abstr.

SW/1101-1262
**EUROPEAN JOURNAL OF PUBLIC HEALTH. See** Public Health and Safety.

NE
**EXCERPTA MEDICA. SECTION 17. PUBLIC HEALTH, SOCIAL MEDICINE AND EPIDEMIOLOGY. See** Medical Science and Technology-Abstracting, Bibliographies and Statistics.

US/0741-0395
**GENETIC EPIDEMIOLOGY.** [Genet. epidemiol.]. Vol. 1 No. 1 (1984)-. Periodical. English. Six times a year. $654.00 (US); $714.00 (Canada and Mexico); $736.50 (other). John Wiley & Sons, Inc., 605 Third Avenue, New York NY 10158-0012. **Tel** (212)850-6000, (212)850-6645, FAX (212)850-6088, telex 12-7063. **(Subscription address:** John Wiley & Sons / England, Baffins Lane, Chichester, West Sussex PO19 1UD England.) **ED** John J. Mulvihill and Aravinda Chakravarti. **DD** 614. **NLM** W1; GE281P. **[CCC]. Pr Rev.** Documents available from The Genuine Article.
**Desc:** A forum for research concerned with the etiology, distribution, and control of diseases in groups of relatives, and with the inherited predisposition to or causes of diseases in populations.
**Ind/Abst** Anim. Breed. Abstr.; Curr. Contents Life Sci.; EMBASE; Health Plan. Adminis.; Index Med. (Vol. 1, No. 1, 1984-); Life Sci. Collect.; Plant Breed. Abstr.; Ref. Upd. Deluxe Ed.; Res. Alert [Full Cov.]; Sci. Cit. Index; SCISEARCH; Soc. Sci. Cit. Index [Select. Cov.].

US
**GENETIC EPIDEMIOLOGY. SUPPLEMENT.** (1987)-. Monographic series. English. ir. Price varies per volume. Wiley Liss, 605 3rd Avenue, New York NY 10158. **Tel** (212)850-8800, (212)850-6645. **(Subscription address:** John Wiley / Philadelphia, PO Box 7247, Philadelphia PA 19170.) **NLM** W1; GE281PA.
**Ind/Abst** Index Med. (1987-).

HU/0300-807X
**GEOGRAPHIA MEDICA (BUDAPEST).** (GEOGRAPHIA MEDICA.). [Geogr. med.]. **Added/Corp** Magyar Foldrajzi Tarsasag. Sectio Medico-Geographica. International Geographical Union. Commission on Medical Geography. (1969/70)-. Monographic series. English (French and German). ir. Price varies per volume. Hungarian Geographical Society. **(Subscription address:** Kultura, PO Box 149, H 1389 Budapest 62 Hungary.) **LC** RA791; .G46. **NLM** W1 GE359S. **CODEN** GMDCB4. **Ad Acc. Circ:** 450 (ctrl). Documents available from BIOSIS Document Express, Documents on Demand. ***Supersedes** Geographia Medica Hungarica, 0435-3730.*
**Ind/Abst** Biol. Abstr.; Ecol. Abstr.; EMBASE; Environ. Abstr.; Geogr. Abstr. Phys. Geogr.; Geogr. Abstr. Human Geogr.; Health Plan. Adminis.; Index Med.; Int. Dev. Abstr.

HU/0866-4323
**GEOGRAPHIA MEDICA. SUPPLEMENT / GEOGRAPHIA MEDICA. SONDERBAND.** [Geogr. med., Suppl.]. **Added/Corp** Magyar Foeldrajzi Tarsasag. Sectio Medico-Geographica. IGU Working Group on Geography of Health. International Geographical Union. Commission on Geography of Health and Development. **VFOAT** Geographia Medica. Sonderband. (1988)-. English (French and German). ir. $15.00. Hungarian Geographical Society. **(Subscription address:** Kultura, PO Box 149, H 1389 Budapest 62 Hungary.) **NLM** W1; GE359Sa.
**Ind/Abst** Health Plan. Adminis.; Index Med. (1988-).

KO
**HANGUK YOK HAKHOE CHI. VFOAT** Korean Journal of Epidemiology. Periodical. Korean (summaries and/or abstracts in English). Hanguk Yok Hakhoe, 28 Yongon-dong, Chongno-ku 110, Seoul South Korea. **LC** RA648.5; .H35.

US/0899-823X
**INFECTION CONTROL AND HOSPITAL EPIDEMIOLOGY.** [Infect. control hosp. epidemiol.]. Vol. 9, No. 1 (Jan. 1988)-. Academic Scholarly Publication. English. mo. $105.00 institution, $95.00 individual (US). Slack Inc., 6900 Grove Road, Thorofare NJ 08086. **Tel** (609)848-1000, (800)257-8290, FAX (609)853-5991, telex 517108 SLACK INC VD. **LC** RA969. **DD** 614.4/4. **NLM** W1; IN406D. **CODEN** ICEPE3. **[CCC]. Pr Rev.** available on microfilm and microfiche from University Microfilms International (UMI). Documents available from The Genuine Article, BIOSIS Document Express. ***Continues** Infection Control, 0195-9417.*
**Ind/Abst** Biol. Abstr. (1988-); Chem. Hazards Ind.; Cumul. Index Nurs. Allied Health Lit.; Curr. Contents Clin. Med.; EMBASE; Health Devices Alerts; Helminthol. Abstr. (1991-); Index Med. Jan. 1988-; Int. Nurs. Index (Jan. 1988-); Lab. Hazards Bull.; Leis. Recreat. Tour. Abstr.; Microbiol. Abstr. Sect. B; Microbiol. Abstr. Sect. A; Microbiol. Abstr. Sect. C; Nurs. Abstr.; Physic. Medline Plus; Protozoolog. Abstr.; Res. Alert [Full Cov.]; Rev. Med. Vet. Entomol.; Rev. Med. Vet. Mycology; Sci. Cit. Index; SCISEARCH; Soc. Sci. Cit. Index [Select. Cov.]; Trop. Dis. Bull.; Virol. AIDS Abstr.

US/0749-6524
**INFECTIONS IN MEDICINE.** [Infect. med.]. Vol. 1, No. 1 (Sept./Oct. 1984)-. Periodical. English. Twelve times a year. $59.54 New York City; $55.00 others. SCP Communications Inc, 134 West 29th Street, New York NY 10001. **Tel** (212)714-1740, FAX (212)629-3760. **DD** 616. **NLM** W1; IN406HJ. **[CCC].**
**Ind/Abst** EMBASE [Select. Cov.]; Ref. Upd. Deluxe Ed.

UK/0300-5771
**INTERNATIONAL JOURNAL OF EPIDEMIOLOGY.** [Int. j. epidemiol.]. **Added/Corp** International Epidemiological Association. Vol. 1 (Spring 1972)-. Periodical. English. bm. £160.00 UK and Europe; $295.00 other. Oxford University Press, Walton Street, Oxford OX2 6DP England. **Tel** 011 44 865 56767, FAX 011 44 865 267773, telex 837330 OXPRES G. **(Subscription address:** Oxford University Press / USA, Journals Marketing Department, Oxford University Press, 2001 Evans Road, Cary NC 27513.) **ED** C. du Ve Florey. **LC** RA651; .A358. **DD** 614.4/05. **NLM** W1 IN766I. **CODEN** IJEPBF. **[CCC].** Index available. **Bk Rev. Ad Acc. Pr Rev. Circ:** 2,500. available on microfilm and microfiche from University Microfilms International (UMI). Documents available from The Genuine Article, BIOSIS Document Express.
**Desc:** Covers epidemiology of infectious and non-infectious diseases, with research into health services and medical care, and with new methods, statistical or otherwise, for the analysis of data used by those who practice social and preventive medicine.
**Ind/Abst** Annals Behav. Med.; Biol. Abstr.; Biol. Dig.; Biostatistica; Chem. Hazards Ind.; Curr. Contents Clin. Med.; Curr. Contents Life Sci.; Curr. Titl. Dent.; Dairy Sci. Abstr.; Dev. Med. Child Neurol.; EMBASE; Geogr. Abstr. Human Geogr.; Helminthol. Abstr. (1991-); Index Med.; Int. Dev. Abstr.; Lab. Hazards Bull.; Nutr. Abstr. Rev., Ser. A, Hum. Exp.; Nutr. Res. Newsl.; Life Sci. Collect.; Popul. Index; Protozoolog. Abstr.; Ref. Upd. Deluxe Ed.; Res. Alert [Full Cov.]; Rev. Med. Vet. Entomol.; Rural Dev. Abstr.; Saf. Health Work; Sci. Cit. Index; SCISEARCH; Soc. Sci. Cit. Index [Select. Cov.]; Trop. Dis. Bull.; Virol. AIDS Abstr.

UK/0895-4356
**JOURNAL OF CLINICAL EPIDEMIOLOGY.** [J. clin. epidemiol.]. **VFOAT** JCE. Vol. 41, No. 1 (1988)-. Academic Scholarly Publication. English. mo. $887.00 The Americas; £595.00 other. Pergamon Press, An Imprint of Elsevier Science Ltd., The Boulevard, Langford Lane, Kidlington, Oxford OX5 1GB United Kingdom. **Tel** 011 44 865 843000, 011 44 865 843699, FAX 011 44 865 843010. **(Subscription address:** Elsevier Science Ltd. Oxford Fulfillment Centre, PO Box 800, Kidlington, Oxford OX5 1DX United Kingdom.) **ED** Alvan Feinstein and Walter Spitzer. **LC** RB156; .J6. **DD** 616/.005. **NLM** W1; JO588CJ. **CODEN** JCEPEEJOCDAE. **[CCC]. Pr Rev.** available on microfilm and microfiche from University Microfilms International (UMI). Documents available from The Genuine Article, BIOSIS Document Express, CASDDS. ***Continues** Journal of Chronic Diseases, 0021-9681.*
**Ind/Abst** Abstr. Anthropol.; Annals Behav. Med.; Biol. Abstr. (1988-); Chem. Abstr. (1988-); Cumul. Index Nurs. Allied Health Lit. (1988-); Curr. Aware. Biol. Sci., CABS; Curr. Contents Clin. Med.; Curr. Contents Life Sci.; Dairy Sci. Abstr.; Dev. Med. Child Neurol.; EMBASE; Energy Res. Abstr. (1988-); High. Educ. Abstr.; Index Med. (1988-); INIS Atomindex [Micro.]; Int. Pharm. Abstr.; Iowa Drug Inf. Serv. (1988-); Leis. Recreat. Tour. Abstr.; Nutr. Abstr. Rev., Ser. A, Hum. Exp.; Nutr. Res. Newsl.; Life Sci. Collect. (1988-); Pollut. Abstr. Indexes (1988-); Ref. Upd. Deluxe Ed.; Res. Alert [Full Cov.]; Risk Abstr.; Saf. Health Work (1988-); Sci. Cit. Index; SCISEARCH; Soc. Sci. Cit. Index [Select. Cov.]; Trop. Dis. Bull.; Virol. AIDS Abstr.

UK/0143-005X
**JOURNAL OF EPIDEMIOLOGY AND COMMUNITY HEALTH (1979).** (JOURNAL OF EPIDEMIOLOGY AND COMMUNITY HEALTH.). [J. epidemiol. community health]. **Added/Corp** British Medical Association. Vol. 33, No. 2 (June 1979)-. Periodical. English. bm. £116.00. BMJ / British Medical Journal Publishing Group, British Medical Association House, Tavistock Square, London WC1H 9JR England. **Tel** 011 44 71 3874499, FAX 011 44 71 383 6402, telex 290034 HBJ MN. **ED** J.R.T. Colley. **DD** 614. **NLM** W1 JO644BQ. **CODEN** JECHDR. **[CCC]. Pr Rev.** available on microfilm and microfiche from University Microfilms International (UMI). Documents available from The Genuine Article, BIOSIS Document Express. ***Continues** Epidemiology and Community Health, 0142-467X.*
**Desc:** Original work in the field, with emphasis on epidemiological methods in medical research.
**Ind/Abst** Biol. Abstr.; Biostatistica; Chem. Hazards Ind.; Curr. Aware. Biol. Sci., CABS; Curr. Contents Clin. Med.; Curr. Contents Life Sci.; Dairy Sci. Abstr.; Dev. Med. Child Neurol.; EMBASE; Food Sci. Technol. Abstr.; Geogr. Abstr. Human Geogr.; Health Saf. Sci. Abstr.; Hospit. Health Admin. Index; Index Med.; Int. Dev. Abstr.; Lab. Hazards Bull.; Nutr. Abstr. Rev., Ser. B, Live Feeds and Feed.; Nutr. Abstr. Rev., Ser. A, Hum. Exp.; Nutr. Res. Newsl.; Life Sci. Collect.; Popul. Index; Protozoolog. Abstr.; Psychol. Abstr. (1979-); PsycINFO; PsycLit; Res. Alert [Full Cov.]; Sci. Cit. Index; SCISEARCH; Soc. Sci. Cit. Index [Select. Cov.]; Trop. Dis. Bull.

US/1053-4245
**JOURNAL OF EXPOSURE ANALYSIS AND ENVIRONMENTAL EPIDEMIOLOGY. See** Environmental Issues.

XR/0022-1732
**JOURNAL OF HYGIENE, EPIDEMIOLOGY, MICROBIOLOGY, AND IMMUNOLOGY. See** Public Health and Safety.

US
**JPRS REPORT EPIDEMIOLOGY. VFOAT** J.P.R.S. Report; Epidemiology. **VAT** Joint Publications Research Service Report. Epidemiology. JPRS-TEP-87-013 (2 June 1987)-. Periodical. English. ir. National Technical Information Service - NTIS, Room 2027S, 5285 Port Royal Road, Springfield VA 22161. **Tel** (703)487-4630, (703)487-4660, (703)487-4650, FAX (703)321-8547, telex 89-9405. **NLM** ZWA 100; E64. available on microfiche (Vols. for 1987 distributed to depository libraries). ***Continues** Worldwide Report. Epidemiology, 0740-0918.*

KG
**MATERIALY KRAEVOI EPIDEMIOLOGII I GIGIENY.** **Added/Corp** Kirgizskii Nauchno-Issledovatelskii Institut Epidemiologii, Mikrobiologii i Gigieny. (1960)-. Periodical. Russian. **NLM** W1 MA9425F.
**Desc:** Information on epidemiology, hygiene, and public health.

US/0276-6884
**MENTAL HEALTH SERVICE SYSTEM REPORTS. SERIES AN, EPIDEMIOLOGY.** (MENTAL HEALTH SERVICE SYSTEM REPORTS. SERIES AN, EPIDEMIOLOGY / U.S. DEPARTMENT OF HEALTH AND HUMAN SERVICES, PUBLIC HEALTH SERVICE, ALCOHOL, DRUG ABUSE, AND MENTAL HEALTH ADMINISTRATION.). [Ment. health serv. syst. rep., Ser. AN, Epidemiol.]. **VFOAT** Epidemiology. No. 1-. Monographic series. English. Price varies per volume. US Department of Health and Human Services National Institutes of Health, 9000 Rockville Pike, Bethesda MD 20892. **Tel** (301)496-9291, FAX (301)496-2443. **NLM** W1 ME928EN.

●US/1076-6294
**MICROBIAL DRUG RESISTANCE, MECHANISMS, EPIDEMIOLOGY, AND DISEASE.** (1994)-. Periodical. English. qt. $156.00. Mary Ann Liebert Inc., 1651 Third Avenue, New York NY 10128. **Tel** (212)289-2300, (800)M-LIEBERT, FAX (212)289-4697.

US/0740-0845
**MONOGRAPHS IN EPIDEMIOLOGY AND BIOSTATISTICS.** [Monogr. epidemiol. biostat.]. (1981)-. Monographic series. English. ir. Price varies per volume. Oxford University Press / New York, 200 Madison Avenue, New York NY 10016. **Tel** (212)679-7300, (919)677-0977, (800)451-7556, (800)445-9714, FAX (919)677-1303. **ED** Abraham M. Lilienfeld. **CODEN** MEBIEP. Documents available from BIOSIS Document Express.
**Ind/Abst** Biol. Abstr. (1985-).

US/8750-4642
**NEW MEXICO EPIDEMIOLOGY REPORT.** (NEW MEXICO EPIDEMIOLOGY REPORT / STATE OF NEW MEXICO, OFFICE OF EPIDEMIOLOGY.). [N.M. epidemiol. rep.]. Dec. 15, 1983-. Periodical. English. mo. PO Box 968, 724 Saint Michaels Drive, Crown Building, Santa Fe NM 87503. **DD** 614. ***Continues*** *New Mexico Communicable Disease Summary, 0279-1919.*

UV/0253-3901
**O.C.C.G.E. INFORMATIONS / OCCGE, SECRETARIAT GENERAL.** **Added/Corp** Organisation de Coordination et de Cooperation pour la Lutte contre les Grandes Endemies. Secretariat General. Organisation de Coordination et de Cooperation pour la Lutte contre les Grandes Endemies. Centre de Documentation et de Statistique. **VFOAT** OCCGE Informations; Informations. **VAT** Organisation de Coordination et de Cooperation pour la Lutte contre les Grandes Endemies Informations. (May/June 1982)-. Periodical. French. bm. **LC** RA650.8.B87; B85. **DD** 614.4/266/25. ***Continues*** *Bull. OCCGE-Inf.*
**Ind/Abst** Trop. Dis. Bull.

UK/0269-5022
**PAEDIATRIC AND PERINATAL EPIDEMIOLOGY.** [Paediatr. perinat. epidemiol.]. Vol. 1, No. 1 (April 1987)-. Academic Scholarly Publication. English. qt (4 issues). $135.00 US & Canada; £79.00 Europe; £87.00 other. Blackwell Scientific Publications Ltd, Marston Book Services, PO Box 87, Oxford OX2 ODT UK. **Tel** 011 44 865 791155, FAX 011 44 865 791927, telex 837 515 MARDIS G. **NLM** W1; PE163HN. **[CCC].** Index available (bound in last issue). available on microfilm and microfiche from University Microfilms International (UMI).
**Ind/Abst** Dev. Med. Child Neurol.; EMBASE; Index Med.; Trop. Dis. Bull.

US
**PROCEEDINGS OF THE MEETING ON CARDIOVASCULAR EPIDEMIOLOGY AND BIOSTATISTICS TRAINING PROGRAMS.** **See** Medical Science and Technology-Cardiology.

PL/0033-2100
**PRZEGLAD EPIDEMIOLOGICZNY.** [Prz. epidemiol.]. **Added/Corp** Polskie Towarzystwo Epidemiologow i Lekarzy Chorob Zakaznych. Panstwowy Zakad Higieny (Poland). Vol. 1 (1947)-. Periodical. Polish (summaries and/or abstracts in English and French). qt. Price on Request. **(Subscription address:** ARS Polona, PO Box 1001, 00068 Warsaw Poland.**)** **NLM** W1 PR929.
**Ind/Abst** EMBASE; Helminthol. Abstr. (1991-); Index Med.; Life Sci. Collect.; Protozoolog. Abstr.; Rev. Med. Vet. Entomol.; Trop. Dis. Bull.

FI/0357-3346
**PUBLICATIONS OF THE UNIVERSITY OF KUOPIO. COMMUNITY HEALTH. SERIES ORIGINAL REPORTS.** **See** Public Health and Safety.

US/0166-8544
**REVIEWS IN CANCER EPIDEMIOLOGY.** **See** Medical Science and Technology-Neoplasma, Neoplastic.

CU/0253-1151
**REVISTA CUBANA DE HIGIENE Y EPIDEMIOLOGIA.** [Rev. cub. hig. epidemiol.]. **Added/Corp** Centro Nacional de Informacion de Ciencias Medicas. Year 13 (Jan./August 1975)-. Academic Scholarly Publication. Spanish (summaries and/or abstracts in Spanish, French and Russian). sa. 42.58Cub$ North America; 39.92Cub$ South America; 45.24Cub$ other. Editorial Ciencias Medicas, Vedado Apartado 6520, Ciudad de la Habana 10400 Cuba. **NLM** W1 RE3596. **CODEN** RCHEDF. Index available. **Bk Rev**. **Ad Acc. Circ:** 5,000 (ctrl). Documents available from BIOSIS Document Express, CASDDS. ***Continues*** *Boletin Higiene y Epidemiologia, 0006-629X.*
**Desc:** Articles related to the development of hygiene and epidemiology. Scientific papers on epidemiology and environmental hygiene; food hygiene, labor, medicine and other related branches.
**Ind/Abst** Biocont. News Inf.; Biodeter. Abstr. (1991-); Biol. Abstr.; Chem. Abstr.; Dairy Sci. Abstr.; EMBASE [Select. Cov.]; Food Sci. Technol. Abstr.; Helminthol. Abstr.; Index Vet.; Nutr. Abstr. Rev., Ser. B, Live Feeds and Feed.; Nutr. Abstr. Rev., Ser. A, Hum. Exp.; Protozoolog. Abstr.; Rev. Agric. Entomol.; Rev. Med. Vet. Entomol.; Vet. Bull.; Trop. Dis. Bull.

US/0398-7620
**REVUE D'EPIDEMIOLOGIE ET DE SANTE PUBLIQUE.** [Rev. epidemiol. sante publique]. Vol. 24 (Jan./Feb. 1976)-. Periodical. English (French; summaries and/or abstracts in French and English; table of contents in English and French). bm. $230.00. Masson Editeur, Box Postale 22, 41353 Vineuil 16 France. **Tel** 011 33 54 438994. **(Subscription address:** 7A Boulevard de Perolles, CH-1701 Fribourg Switzerland**)** **NLM** W1 RE798R. **CODEN** RESPDF. **[CCC]. Pr Rev.** available on microfilm and microfiche from University Microfilms International (UMI). Documents available from The Genuine Article, BIOSIS Document Express. ***Continues*** *Revue d'Epidemiologie, Medecine Sociale et Sante Publique, 0035-2438.*
**Ind/Abst** Biol. Abstr.; Curr. Contents Clin. Med.; Dairy Sci. Abstr.; Dev. Med. Child Neurol.; EMBASE; Energy Res. Abstr. (March 1977-); Helminthol. Abstr. (1991-); Index Med.; Nutr. Abstr. Rev., Ser. A, Hum. Exp.; Life Sci. Collect.; Protozoolog. Abstr.; Res. Alert [Select. Cov.]; Saf. Health Work; Soc. Sci. Cit. Index [Select. Cov.]; Trop. Dis. Bull.

CN/0711-8929
**SEXUALLY TRANSMITTED DISEASES IN CANADA.** **See** Public Health and Safety.

GW/0933-7954
**SOCIAL PSYCHIATRY AND PSYCHIATRIC EPIDEMIOLOGY.** **See** Medical Science and Technology-Psychiatry.

SA
**SOUTHERN AFRICAN JOURNAL OF EPIDEMIOLOGY & INFECTION : OFFICIAL JOURNAL OF THE SEXUALLY TRANSMITTED DISEASES, INFECTIOUS DISEASES, AND EPIDEMIOLOGICAL SOCIETIES OF SOUTHERN AFRICA, THE.** **See** Medical Science and Technology-Communicable Diseases.

RU/0202-1447
**TRUDY INSTITUTA IMENI PASTERA.** **Added/Corp** Leningradskii Nauchno-Issledovatelskii Institut Epidemiologii i Mikrobiologii imeni Pastera. Vol. 43 (1975)-. Periodical. Russian. **(Subscription address:** Victor Kamkin, 4956 Boiling Brook Parkway, Rockville MD 20852.**)** **NLM** W1 TR951TI. **CODEN** TIPAE6. ***Continues*** *Trudy Leningradskogo Nauchno-Issledovatelskogo Instituta Epidemiologii I Mikrobiologii im Pastera.*
**Ind/Abst** Index Med.

SZ/0049-8114
**WEEKLY EPIDEMIOLOGICAL RECORD.** **See** Medical Science and Technology-Communicable Diseases.

CC/0254-6450
**ZHONGHUA LIUXINGBING ZAZHI.** **See** Medical Science and Technology-Communicable Diseases.

RU/0372-9311
**ZHURNAL MIKROBIOLOGII, EPIDEMIOLOGII I IMMUNOBIOLOGII.** **See** Medical Science and Technology-Allergy and Immunology.

## FAMILY PRACTICE

US/0896-6877
**AAFP REPORTER.** (AAFP REPORTER / AMERICAN ACADEMY OF FAMILY PHYSICIANS.). [AAFP report.]. **Added/Corp** American Academy of Family Physicians. American Academy of Family Physicians. Communications Division. **VAT** American Academy of Family Physicians Reporter. Vol. 1, No. 1 (Jan. 1974)-. Periodical. English. mo. Free on request. American Academy of Family Physicians, 8880 Ward Parkway, Kansas City MO 64114. **Tel** (816)333-9700 ext. 1142, FAX (816)333-0303. **DD** 610. **NLM** W1; AA101AF.
**Desc:** Of interest to family physicians or those involved with family medicine.

US/0884-643X
**ABMS DIRECTORY OF CERTIFIED FAMILY PHYSICIANS.** [ABMS dir. certif. fam. phys.]. **VAT** American Board of Medical Specialties Directory of Certified Family Physicians. 1985-. Directory. English. be. $39.95. American Board of Medical Specialties, 1 Rotary Center, Suite 805, Evanston IL 60201. **Tel** (708)491-9091. **LC** R712.A1. **DD** 610. **NLM** W 22.1; A15232.

US/0002-838X
**AMERICAN FAMILY PHYSICIAN (1970).** (AMERICAN FAMILY PHYSICIAN.). [Am. fam. phys.]. **Added/Corp** American Academy of Family Physicians. Vol. 2, No. 6 (Dec. 1970)-. Academic Scholarly Publication. English. ir (16 issues). $88.00 (institutions), $72.00 (individuals and physicians). American Academy of Family Physicians, 8880 Ward Parkway, Kansas City MO 64114. **Tel** (816)333-9700 ext. 1142, FAX (816)333-0303. **ED** Clayton R. Hasser. **LC** R11; .A44. **DD** 610. **NLM** W1 AM397T. cum. index. **Bk Rev**. **Ad Acc. Pr Rev. Circ:** 140,000 (ctrl). available on microfilm from University Microfilms International (UMI); available on an online database from BRS; and MEDLINE; available on CD-ROM. Documents available from The Genuine Article, UMI Article Clearinghouse. ***Continues*** *American Family Physician/GP, 0572-3612.*
**Desc:** A clinical publication for primary care physicians.
**Ind/Abst** Abr. Index Med.; Acad. Ind. [Computer File] (1992-); Acad. Search (July 1993-); Bus. Index (1981-Dec. 1984); CIS Abstr.; Consum. Health Nutr. Index; Cumul. Index Nurs. Allied Health Lit.; Curr. Contents Clin. Med.; Dairy Sci. Abstr.; EMBASE; Expand. Acad. Index (1989-); Gen. Sci. Index; Gen. Sci. Source (Jul. 1993-); Health Index (1989-); Health Period. Database [Full Txt.]; Health Plan. Adminis.; Health Ref. Cent. (Jan. 1989-) [Full Txt.] [Full Cov.]; Health Source (Jul. 1993-); Helminthol. Abstr. (1991-); Index Med.; INFO-SOUTH Abstr.; Int. Nurs. Index; Mag. Search; Med. Abstr. Newsl.; Microbiol. Abstr. Sect. B (19??-19??); Newsp. Period. Abstr. (1989-); Nutr. Abstr. Rev., Ser. B, Live Feeds and Feed.; Nutr. Abstr. Rev., Ser. A, Hum. Exp.; Nutr. Res. Newsl.; Life Sci. Collect.; Physic. Medline Plus; Protozoolog. Abstr.; Res. Alert [Select. Cov.]; Rev. Med. Vet. Mycology; Risk Abstr.; Saf. Health Work; SCISEARCH; Small Anim. Abstr. Bibliogr.; Soc. Sci. Cit. Index [Select. Cov.]; SPORT Discus; SportSearch; Trade Ind. Index (1981-?); Virol. AIDS Abstr.

US
**AMERICAN FAMILY PHYSICIAN. [CD-ROM].** English. an. $399.50 US; $405.00 other. Creative Multimedia Corporation, 513 Northwest Avenue, Suite 400, Portland OR 97209. **Tel** (503)241-4351. available on microfiche from University Microfilms International (UMI); available in print; available on an online database from MEDLINE.

●US/1063-3987
**ARCHIVES OF FAMILY MEDICINE.** [Arch. fam. med.]. **Added/Corp** American Medical Association. (1992)-. Periodical. English. mo. $105.00 (institution), $95.00 (individual) US. American Medical Association, 515 North State Street, Chicago IL 60610. **Tel** (312)464-5000, (800)262-2350, FAX (312)464-5831. **ED** Margorie Bowman. **DD** 616. **NLM** W1; AR455AC. **[CCC]. Ad Acc. Pr Rev.**
**Desc:** A primary source, association-based journal for the entire family practice audience. Provides the information family practitioners want and need to be effective in today's practice environment.

US/0270-9074
**ARCHIVES OF FAMILY PRACTICE.** ***Ceased.*** [Arch. fam. pract.]. Vol. 1 (1980)-Completed series. Periodical. English. an. Maxwell Macmillan Professional Business Division, 910 Sylvan Avenue, Englewood Cliffs NJ 07632-3310. **Tel** (800)431-9025. **LC** R5; .A7. **DD** 616. **NLM** W1 AR455AF.

SP/0212-6567
**ATENCION PRIMARIA.** (ATENCION PRIMARIA / SOCIEDAD ESPANOLA DE MEDICINA DE FAMILIA Y COMUNITARIA.). [Aten. prim.]. **Added/Corp** Sociedad Espanola de Medicina de Familia y Comunitaria. (1983)-. Periodical. Spanish (summaries and/or abstracts in English; table of contents in English). ir. $85.00 (all except Spain). Haymarket SA, Calle Aribau 168 170, 08036

Barcelona Spain. **Tel** 011 34 3 238-1742. **NLM** W1; AT212M. **CODEN** ATEPEY.
**Ind/Abst** Indice Med. Esp.

AT/0300-8495
**AUSTRALIAN FAMILY PHYSICIAN.** [Aust. fam. phys.]. Vol.1 (Feb. 1972). Academic Scholarly Publication. English. mo. 120.00Aus$ Australia; 161.00Aus$ other. Royal Australian College of GP Australia, 70 Jolimont Street 4th Floor, Melbourne Vic 3002, Australia. **Tel** 11 61 3 6543000, FAX (03)650 5723, telex AA 33532. **ED** John Burke, John Murtagh. **NLM** W1 AU53K. **CODEN** AFPHCX. **[CCC]**. cum. index. **Bk Rev. Ad Acc. Circ:** 19,500. Documents available from BIOSIS Document Express. ***Absorbed*** *Annals of General Practice.*
**Desc:** Emphasis on practical aspects of general practice in Australia.
**Ind/Abst** Biol. Abstr.; Cumul. Index Nurs. Allied Health Lit.; EMBASE; Index Med.; Mod. Med.; Rev. Med. Vet. Entomol.; SportSearch.

UK/0960-1643
**BRITISH JOURNAL OF GENERAL PRACTICE, THE.** [Br. j. gen. pract.]. Vol. 40, No. 330 (Jan. 1990)-. Periodical. English. mo. £110.00 UK; £125.00 other. World Wide Subscription Services, Unit 4, Gibbs Reed Farm, East Sussex TN5 7HE England. **Tel** (0580)200657, FAX (0580)200616. **NLM** W1; BR532. **CODEN** BJGPEJ. Documents available from The Genuine Article. ***Continues*** *Journal of the Royal College of General Practitioners, 0035-8797.*
**Ind/Abst** Curr. Contents Clin. Med.; EMBASE; Health Plan. Adminis.; Helminthol. Abstr. (1991-); Index Med. (1990-); Index Vet.; Nutr. Abstr. Rev., Ser. A, Hum. Exp.; Protozoolog. Abstr.; Res. Alert [Full Cov.]; Rev. Med. Vet. Entomol.; Sci. Cit. Index; SCISEARCH; Soc. Sci. Cit. Index [Select. Cov.]; Trop. Dis. Bull.

CN/0008-350X
**CANADIAN FAMILY PHYSICIAN.** [Can. fam. phys.]. **Added/Corp** College of Family Physicians of Canada. College of General Practice of Canada. **VFOAT** Medecin de Famille Canadien. Vol. 13, No. 7 (July 1967)-. Academic Scholarly Publication. English (French). mo. 80.00Can$ Canada; 90.00Can$ US; 120.00Can$ others. College of Family Physicians of Canada, 2630 Skymark Avenue, Mississauga ONT L4W 5A4 Canada. **Tel** (905) 629-0900, FAX (905)629-0893. **ED** Jo File. **NLM** W1 CA553P. Index available. **Bk Rev. Ad Acc. Pr Rev. Circ:** 25,000 (ctrl). Documents available from The Genuine Article. ***Continues*** *College of General Practice of Canada. Journal, 0315-4912.*
**Desc:** Clinical journal dedicated to the interests of family physicians.
**Ind/Abst** Can. Index (?-?); Curr. Contents Clin. Med.; EMBASE [Select. Cov.]; Health Devices Alerts; Index Med.; Microbiol. Abstr. Sect. B (19??-19??); Life Sci. Collect.; Protozoolog. Abstr.; Res. Alert [Select. Cov.]; Risk Abstr.; SCISEARCH; Soc. Sci. Cit. Index [Select. Cov.]; Virol. AIDS Abstr.

UK/0958-9376
**CURRENT MEDICAL LITERATURE. GENERAL PRACTICE / THE ROYAL SOCIETY OF MEDICINE.** ***Ceased.*** **Added/Corp** Royal Society of Medicine (Great Britain). **VFOAT** General Practice. (199?)-(199?). Periodical. English. qt. Current Medical Literature Ltd., 40-42 Osnaburgh Street, London NW1 3ND England. **Tel** 011 44 71 4658377, FAX 011 44 71 4658380. **NLM** ZWT 100; C996.

US/1055-3487
**DIRECTORY OF DIPLOMATES / AMERICAN BOARD OF FAMILY PRACTICE.** [Dir. dipl. - Am. Board Fam. Pract.]. **Added/Corp** American Board of Family Practice. Directory. English. $10.00. American Board of Family Practice, 2228 Young Drive, Lexington KY 40505. **Tel** (606)269-5626. **DD** 610. ***Continues*** *Diplomate Directory, 0732-8982.*

US/0897-182X
**DIRECTORY OF FAMILY PRACTICE RESIDENCY PROGRAMS.** [Dir. fam. pract. resid. programs]. **Added/Corp** American Academy of Family Physicians. American Medical Student Association. Ciba Pharmaceutical Company. Pfizer Laboratories. Pfizer Pharmaceuticals. Roerig Division. (1980)-. Directory. English. an. $15.00. American Academy of Family Physicians, 8880 Ward Parkway, Kansas City MO 64114. **Tel** (816)333-9700 ext. 1142, FAX (816)333-0303. **DD** 610.

UK/0046-0451
**DOCTOR GUILDFORD.** [DoctorGuildford]. (1971)-. Periodical. English. wk (48 issues per year). £75.00 UK; £102.00 Europe; £121.00 other. Reed Business Publishing Group / England, Quadrant House, Quadrant Sutton Surrey, SM2 5AS England. **Tel** 011 44 81 652-3500. **(Subscription address:** Reed Healthcare Subscriptions, 120 126 Lavender Avenue, Mitcham Surrey CR4 3HP United Kingdom.**)** **DD** 610. **[CCC]. Ad Acc. Circ:** 40,000 (ctrl). available on microfilm from University Microfilms International (UMI).
**Desc:** Newspaper for doctors in general practice community healthcare.

FR/0767-1407
**DOCUMENTS DE RECHERCHES EN MEDECINE GENERALE.** (DOCUMENTS DE RECHERCHES EN MEDECINE GENERALE / SOCIETE FRANCAISE MEDECINE GENERALE.). [Doc. rech. med. gen.]. (1982)-. Periodical. French (English). bm. **NLM** W1; DO554P.

US/0163-0512
**FACETS (CHICAGO, ILL.).** (FACETS.). [Facets]. Vol. 38, No. 3 (Summer 1977)-. Periodical. English. bm (8 no. a year). $5.00. Facets, 535 North Dearborn Street, Chicago IL 60610. **NLM** W1; FA171H.

US/0160-6379
**FAMILY & COMMUNITY HEALTH. See** Public Health and Safety.

US/0742-3225
**FAMILY MEDICINE.** [Fam. med.]. **Added/Corp** Society of Teachers of Family Medicine. Vol. 13, No. 1 (Jan./Feb. 1981)-. Periodical. English. mo (July/Aug. and Nov./Dec. issues combined). $100.00 institution, $75.00 individual. Society of Teachers of Family Medicine, 8880 Ward Parkway, PO Box 8729, Kansas City MO 64114. **Tel** (800)274-2237, (816)333-9700, FAX (816)333-3884. **ED** Barry Weiss, MD. **NLM** W1 FA45N. Index available (bound in Jan. issue). cum. index. **Bk Rev**, (Qty: 10). **Ad Acc. Pr Rev. Circ:** 4,500 (ctrl). ***Continues*** *Family Medicine Teacher.*
**Desc:** Family medicine education and research.
**Ind/Abst** Abstr. Res. Pastor. Care Couns.; Annals Behav. Med.; EMBASE; Health Plan. Adminis.; Index Med. (1985-); Int. Nurs. Index.

US/0197-6974
**FAMILY MEDICINE REVIEW, THE.** [Fam. med. rev.]. V. 1, No. 1 (Winter 1980)-. Periodical. English. qt. Editor Family Medicine Review, Department of Family Medicine North Carolina, Chapel Hill NC 27514. **NLM** W1 FA4504.

MY
**FAMILY PHYSICIAN (KUALA LUMPUR, MALAYSIA).** (FAMILY PHYSICIAN.). Vol. 1, No. 1 (April 1989)-. Periodical. English. Three times a year (April, Aug., and Dec.). College of General Practitioners of Malay, 124 Jalan Pahang, Room 7 / Fifth Floor, 53000 Kuala Lumpur Malaysia. **NLM** W1; FA4516. **Bk Rev. Ad Acc. Circ:** 2,500 (ctrl). ***Continues*** *Family Practitioner, 0301-2093.*
**Ind/Abst** Trop. Dis. Bull.

UK/0263-2136
**FAMILY PRACTICE.** [Fam. pract.]. **Added/Corp** World Organization of National Colleges, Academies, and Academic Associations of General Practitioners/Family Physicians. Vol. 1, No. 1 (March 1984)-. Periodical. English. qt. £85.00 UK and Europe; $155.00 other. Oxford University Press, Walton Street, Oxford OX2 6DP England. **Tel** 011 44 865 56767, FAX 011 44 865 267773, telex 837330 OXPRES G. **(Subscription address:** Oxford University Press / USA, Journals Marketing Department, Oxford University Press, 2001 Evans Road, Cary NC 27513.**)** **ED** J.G.R. Howie. **NLM** W1; FA454CDA. **[CCC]**. Index available. **Bk Rev. Ad Acc. Pr Rev.** available on microfilm and microfiche from University Microfilms International (UMI). Documents available from The Genuine Article.
**Desc:** Intended mainly as a means of broadening the international base of family medicine in general practice. Also covers such fields as health care delivery, epidemiology, public health and medical sociology.
**Ind/Abst** Curr. Contents Clin. Med.; EMBASE; Index Med. (Vol. 1, No. 1 1984-); Res. Alert [Select. Cov.]; Rural Dev. Abstr.; SCISEARCH; Soc. Sci. Cit. Index [Select. Cov.].

US/0899-9562
**FAMILY PRACTICE ALERT.** ***Ceased.*** [Fam. pract. alert]. (1988)-(Novermber 1992). Periodical. English. mo. American Health Consultants, 3525 Piedmont Road, Suite 400, Atlanta GA 30305. **Tel** (800)688-2421, (404)262-7436. **DD** 616.

US/0271-1362
**FAMILY PRACTICE (GLENDALE, CALIF.).** (AUDIO-DIGEST. FAMILY PRACTICE.). [Fam. pract.]. **Added/Corp** Audio-Digest Foundation. **VFOAT** Audio-Digest Family Practice; Audio Digest Family Practice. (1972)-. Periodical. English. wk (also semi-monthly). $359.52 (weekly), $179.76 (semi-monthly) US; $405.60 (weekly), $202.80 (semi-monthly) Canada; $494.88 (weekly), $247.44 (semi-monthly) other. Audio-Digest Foundation, 1577 Chevy Chase Drive, Glendale CA 91206. **Tel** (213)245-8505, (800)423-2308, FAX (818)240-7379. **ED** Claron L. Oakley. **DD** 610. **NLM** W1 AU201DF. ***Continues*** *General Practice, 0571-8619.*
**Desc:** Interactive system of audio cassette postgraduate medical education, with each one-hour program eligible for two Category I credit hours.

US/0191-2461
**FAMILY PRACTICE JOURNAL.** **Added/Corp** John F. Kennedy Medical Center (Edison, N.J.). Family Practice Residency Program. (Dec. 1977)-. Periodical. English. an. Free. John F. Kennedy Medical Center, Family Practice Residency Prog, Edison NJ 08817. **Tel** (201)321-7493. **NLM** W1 FA454CDB.

●US/1069-5648
**FAMILY PRACTICE MANAGEMENT.** **Added/Corp** American Academy of Family Physicians. (1994)-. Periodical. English. mo (10 issues). $57.00 institution, $47.00 individual. American Academy of Family Physicians, 8880 Ward Parkway, Kansas City MO 64114. **Tel** (816)333-9700 ext. 1142, FAX (816)333-0303. **NLM** W1; FA454CDM.

US/0300-7073
**FAMILY PRACTICE NEWS.** [Fam. pract. news]. Vol. 1 (Oct. 1971)-. Periodical. English. sm. $96.00 US; $138.00 other. International Medical News Group, 12230 Wilkins Avenue, Rockville MD 20852. **Tel** (301)770-6170. **DD** 610. **NLM** W1 FA454CF. available on microfilm from University Microfilms International (UMI).

US/1047-0638
**FAMILY PRACTICE PEDIATRICS.** (1991)-. Periodical. English. qt. $18.00. Riverpress Inc., PO Box 23, Jersey City NJ 07303. **Tel** (201)434-5073, FAX (201)434-7230.

US/0163-6642
**FAMILY PRACTICE RECERTIFICATION.** Vol.1 (April 1979)-. Periodical. English. mo. $60.00 (one year), $110.00 (two year), $160.00 (three year) US; $80.00 other. Medical Recertification Association, 2 Park Avenue 4th Floor, New York NY 20016. **Tel** (212)689-3777. **ED** Peggy Ann Chevalier. **LC** R11; .F35. **DD** 616/.005. **NLM** W1 FA454CM. **Bk Rev. Ad Acc.** ctrl circ.
**Desc:** Clinical journal with constantly updated articles on most frequent patient problems in family practice, keeping current departments, 20 hours Category I CME credits.

US/0270-2304
**FAMILY PRACTICE RESEARCH JOURNAL, THE.** ***Ceased.*** [Fam. pract. res. j.]. **Added/Corp** Michigan Academy of Family Physicians. Family Health Research, Education and Service Institute (Alma, Mich.). Vol. 1, No. 1 (Fall 1981)-Vol. 14, No. 4 (Dec. 1994). Periodical. English. qt. Human Sciences Press, PO Box 735, 233 Spring Street, New York NY 10013. **Tel** (212)620-8000, FAX (212)807-1047, telex 23421139. **(Subscription address:** UK & European Subscriptions: Eurospan Group, Journals & Serials Division, 3 Henrietta Street, Covent Garden, London WC2E 8LU England; Telephone: 011 44 71 240-0856 FAX: 011 44 71 379-0609**)** **ED** Leif Solberg. **LC** Discard. **NLM** W1 FA454CP. **CODEN** FPRJD5. **[CCC]. Pr Rev.** available on microfilm and microfiche from University Microfilms International (UMI).
**Desc:** Research-oriented journal provides a forum for significant experimental, historical, basic and clinical case studies. Addresses the unique problems and emerging treatment modalities of particular interest to family physicians.
**Ind/Abst** Cumul. Index Nurs. Allied Health Lit.; Health Plan. Adminis.; Index Med. (Vol. 5, No. 3, 1986-); Psychol. Abstr. (1982-); PsycINFO; PsycLit; Sage Fam. Stud. Abstr.; Soc. Work Abstr. [Select. Cov.].

●US/1063-8555
**FAMILY PRACTICE RESIDENT, THE.** ***Suspended.*** [Fam. pract. resid.]. (1992)-(Mar./Apr. 1994). Periodical. English. bm. $58.00 institution, $48.00 individual (US). Slack Inc., 6900 Grove Road, Thorofare NJ 08086. **Tel** (609)848-1000, (800)257-8290, FAX (609)853-5991, telex 517108 SLACK INC VD. **DD** 610. **NLM** W1; FA4505.

UK/0305-9669
**FAMILY PRACTITIONER SERVICES, THE.** V. 1- May 1974-. Periodical. English. mo. £1.25. **NLM** W1 FA454DF.

US/0736-1718
**FAMILY SYSTEMS MEDICINE.** [Fam. syst. med.]. Vol. 1, No. 1 (Spring 1983)-. Periodical. English. qt. $40.00 (individuals), $92.00 (institutions) US; $46.00 (individuals), $98.00 (institutions) other. Family Process Inc., 70 W Allendale Ave., Suite D, Allendale NJ 07401. **Tel** (201)236-8381. **(Subscription address:** Family Process Inc., Subscription Department, PO Box 6542, Syracuse NY 13217.**)** **ED** Donald A Bloch. **LC** R729.5.G4; F3. **NLM** W1 FA454L. Index available. **Bk Rev. Ad Acc. Circ:** 1,700. available on microfilm and microfiche from University Microfilms International (UMI).
**Desc:** Joins psychological and biomedical approaches to health care with a focus on the family as the unit of diagnosis and treatment.
**Ind/Abst** Cumul. Index Nurs. Allied Health Lit.; EMBASE; Psychol. Abstr. (1983-); PsycINFO; PsycLit; Soc. Plann. Policy Dev. Abstr.; Sociol. Abstr.

US/0015-4067
**FLORIDA FAMILY PHYSICIAN.** Vol. 1 (1951)-. English. qt. Florida Academy of Family Physicians, 1627 Rogero Road, Jacksonville FL 32211-4866. **Tel** (904)398-5667. **ED** Alexander D Brickler and Martha J Moores. **DD** 610. **Ad Acc. Circ:** 16,300 (ctrl).
**Desc:** The voice of family practice in Florida.

UK/0046-5607
**GENERAL PRACTITIONER.** **VFOAT** GP; G.P. (June 1971)-. Periodical. English. wk (50 issues). £100.00 UK; £109.00 other. Haymarket Publishing Ltd., 12 14 Ansdell Street, London W8 5TR England. **Tel** 011 44 483 733800, FAX 011 44 483 776573. **(Subscription address:** Haymarket Publishing Ltd, PO Box 219, Subscriptions Department, Woking Surrey GU21 1ZW, United Kingdom.**)** **ED** Jerry Cowhig. **NLM** W1 GE265C. **[CCC]. Bk Rev. Ad Acc. Circ:** 39,766 (ctrl). ***Continues*** *GP, 0433-0501.*
**Desc:** Caters to family doctors. Includes news, comments and scientific and general articles.
**Ind/Abst** Abstr. BioCommer.; Health Serv. Abstr.; Law Office Inf. Serv.

NZ/1039-7469
**GP GENERAL PRACTITIONER.** ***Ceased.*** (19??)-(Dec. 1994). English. sm (24 issues per year). ADIS International Ltd, 41 Centorian Drive, Private Bag 65901, Mairangi Bay, Auckland 10 New Zealand. **Tel** 011 64 9 4798100, FAX 011 64 9 4791418. ***Continues*** *Patient Management.*

●NZ/1171-347X
**GP WEEKLY.** [GP wkly.]. **VFOAT** General Practitioners Weekly; GPweekly. (1992)-. Periodical. English. wk. 83.00NZ$ New Zealand; 138.00NZ$ Pacific; 200.00NZ$ Asia, Canada & US; 227.00NZ$ UK, Europe other. ADIS International Ltd, 41 Centorian Drive, Private Bag 65901, Mairangi Bay, Auckland 10 New Zealand. **Tel** 011 64 9 4798100, FAX 011 64 9 4791418. **DD** 610.6952099305. ***Continues*** *New Zealand General Practice, 0114-2550.*

NE/0165-7054
**HUISARTS & PRAKTIJK.** (HUISARTS & I.E. EN PRAKTIJK.). **VAT** Huisarts en Praktijk. (June 1977)-. Monographic series. Dutch. mo. Price varies per volume. Samson Bedrijfsinformatie, Postbus 4, 2400 HA Alphen Rij Netherlands. **Tel** 011 31 1 72066633. **NLM** W1 HU439P. **CODEN** HUPRE9.

BE/0775-0501
**HUISARTS NU : MAANDBLAD VAN DE WETENSCHAPPELIJKE VERENIGING DER VLAAMSE HUISARTSEN : HANU.** [Huisarts nu]. **VFOAT** HANU. (1972)-. Periodical. Dutch (English). Twelve times a year. 3850F. Huisarts Nu, Hubertusstraat 58, 2600 Berchem, Belgium. **Tel** 11 32 3 2397930, FAX 11 32 3 2185184. **NLM** W1; HU44H. Index available (Jan. iss.). cum. index. **Bk Rev. Ad Acc. Adv Mgr:** Ludo Truyons, **Tel** (03)287-1616. **Circ:** 3,200 (ctrl).

●UK/1353-887X
**INFORMATION MANAGEMENT IN HEALTH CARE / PRIMARY CARE SERVICE.** **See** Medical Science and Technology.

US/0094-3509
**JOURNAL OF FAMILY PRACTICE, THE.** [J. fam. pract.]. **Added/Corp** American Academy of Family Physicians. Society of Teachers of Family Medicine. North American Primary Care Research Group. Association of Departments of Family Medicine. Vol. 1 (May 1974)-. Academic Scholarly Publication. English. mo. $135.00 institution, $84.00 individual. Appleton & Lange, (A Subsidiary of Simon & Schuster), 25 Van Zant Street, East Norwalk CT 06855. **Tel** (203)838-4400, (800)423-1359, FAX (203)854-9486. **(Subscription address:** Journal of Family Practice, PO Box 3000, Department FP, Denville NJ 07834.**)** **ED** John P. Geyman. **LC** R11; .J684. **DD** 610. **NLM** W1 JO6444. **[CCC].** (free). cum. index. **Bk Rev. Ad Acc. Pr Rev. Circ:** 74,107 (ctrl). available on microfilm and microfiche from University Microfilms International (UMI). Documents available from The Genuine Article.
**Desc:** Original articles and clinical research of interest to the family practitioner and related health professionals.
**Ind/Abst** Abr. Index Med.; Cumul. Index Nurs. Allied Health Lit.; Curr. Contents Clin. Med.; EMBASE; Energy Res. Abstr. (May 1982-); Health Devices Alerts; Health Index (1989-); Health Period. Database [Full Txt.]; Health Ref. Cent. (Jan. 1989-) [Full Txt.] [Full Cov.]; Highw. Res. Abstr.; Index Med.; INIS Atomindex [Micro.]; Int. Nurs. Index; Int. Pharm. Abstr.; J. Watch; Med. Abstr. Newsl.; Microbiol. Abstr. Sect. B (19??-19??); Mod. Med.; Nutr. Abstr. Rev., Ser. B, Live Feeds and Feed.; Nutr. Abstr. Rev., Ser. A, Hum. Exp.; Life Sci. Collect.; Physic. Medline Plus; Psychol. Abstr. (1974-); PsycINFO; PsycLit; Res. Alert [Full Cov.]; Rev. Med. Vet. Mycology; Sci. Cit. Index; SCISEARCH; Soc. Sci. Cit. Index [Select. Cov.]; SportSearch; Virol. AIDS Abstr.

II
**JOURNAL OF GENERAL MEDICINE, THE.** Vol. 1, No. 1 (Oct. 1988)-. Periodical. English. qt. $30.00. The Indian Practitioner, David Sassoon Building/3rd Floor, 143 Mahatma Gandhi Road, Bombay 400 023 India. **Tel** 27 38 09. **(Subscription address:** Prints India, 11 Darya Ganj, New Delhi 110002 India.**)** **NLM** W1; JO667L.

US/0893-8652
**JOURNAL OF THE AMERICAN BOARD OF FAMILY PRACTICE, THE.** (THE JOURNAL OF THE AMERICAN BOARD OF FAMILY PRACTICE / AMERICAN BOARD OF FAMILY PRACTICE.). [J. Am. Board Fam. Pract.]. **Added/Corp** American Board of Family Practice. Massachusetts Medical Society. **VFOAT** JABFP. Vol. 1, No. 1 (Jan./Mar. 1988)-. Periodical. English. bm (6 issues). $58.00 (institutions), $35.00 (individuals) US. American Board of Family Practice / Waltham, PO Box 9085, Waltham MA 02254. **Tel** (617)893-3800, (800)843-6356, FAX (617)893-0413, telex 510607779 NEJM BOS. **(Subscription address:** American Board of Family Practice, PO Box 9135, Subscription Department, c/o Barbara Hill, Waltham MA 02254.**)** **DD** 616. **NLM** W1; JO908FK. **CODEN** JABPEJ. **[CCC]. Bk Rev. Ad Acc.** available on microfilm and microfiche from University Microfilms International (UMI); available on CD-ROM.
**Desc:** A forum for research vital to physicians in family practice. Regular features include: clinical investigations, review articles, case reports, socioeconomic issues, book reviews and editorials.
**Ind/Abst** EMBASE [Select. Cov.]; Health Plan. Adminis.; Index Med. (1988-); J. Watch (199?-).

UK/0262-0200
**MATERNAL & CHILD HEALTH (RICHMOND, SURREY).** (MATERNAL & CHILD HEALTH.). [Matern. child health]. **VFOAT** Journal of Maternal and Child Health; Maternal and Child Health. Vol. 6, No. 3 (Mar. 1981)-. Periodical. English. Twelve times a year. £43.00 UK; £54.00 Europe; £75.00 other. Barker Publications Limited, Barker House, 539 London Road, Isleworth, Middlesex TW7 4DA United Kingdom. **Tel** 011 44 81 847 1774, FAX 011 44 81 568 2766, telex 896691 TLXIRG. **ED** D. Harvey. **NLM** W1 MA946XA. Index available. cum. index. **Bk Rev. Ad Acc. Circ:** 18,000 (ctrl). available on microfilm. ***Continues*** *Journal of Maternal and Child Health, 0308-4426.*
**Desc:** Review articles on family medicine with special emphasis on the care of women and children for medical practitioners.

UK/0260-2342
**MEDICINE IN PRACTICE.** [Med. pract.]. Periodical. English. mo. **NLM** W1; ME652J.

CN/0317-7017
**MEDIFACTS [SOUND RECORDING].** [Medifacts]. **Added/Corp** College of Family Physicians of Canada. (1971)-. Periodical. English. mo. 59.00Can$ Canada; 195.00Can$ other. Medifacts Group Ltd, 20 Camelot Drive, Suite 600, Ottawa Ontario K2A 0G3 Canada. **Tel** (613)728-4655. **ED** Les Johnson. **DD** 610. **NLM** W1 ME787FK. **Ad Acc. Circ:** 9,000 (ctrl).
**Desc:** Continuing medical education on audio cassettes for family physicians and specialists.

US/1065-061X
**NEW YORK FAMILY PHYSICIAN.** [N.Y. fam. physician]. **Added/Corp** New York State Academy of Family Physicians. Vol. 24, No. 4 (July/Aug. 1972)-. Periodical. English. qt. $10.00. New York State Academy Family Physician, 30 West State Street, Colonial Plaza, Binghampton NY 13901. **Tel** (607)722-7205. **DD** 610. ***Continues*** *New York FP.*

NZ/0110-022X
**NEW ZEALAND FAMILY PHYSICIAN, THE.** [N. Z. fam. physician]. **Added/Corp** New Zealand College of General Practitioners. Vol. 1 (Mar 1974)-. Periodical. English. Four times a year (Feb., May, Aug., Nov.). 60.00NZ$. New Zealand Family Physician - Dr. West, 33 MacPherson Street, Meadowbank Auckland, 5 New Zealand. **Tel** 011 64 9 5215602, FAX 011 64 5215602. **ED** Dr. S. R. West. **NLM** W1 NE9728P. **CODEN** NZFPDJ. **[CCC].** Index available. cum. index. **Bk Rev. Ad Acc. Circ:** 3,150 (ctrl). Documents available from CASDDS.
**Ind/Abst** Chem. Abstr.

US/0885-1131
**OFFICE PROCEDURES.** ***Ceased.*** [Off. proced.]. **VFOAT** State of the Art Reviews in Office Procedures. Vol. 1 No. 1 (Jan./Mar 1986)-(19??). Periodical. English. qt. Hanley & Belfus Inc., 210 South 13th Street, Philadelphia PA 19107. **Tel** (215)546-7293, FAX (215)790-9330. **LC** R11; .O48. **DD** 616/.025/005. **NLM** W1; ST315CF.

US/0031-305X
**PATIENT CARE.** [Patient care]. Vol. 1 (Jan. 1967)-. Periodical. English. Twenty times a year. $79.00 US; $115.00 other. Medical Economics Publishing, Five Paragon Drive, Second Floor, Montvale NJ 07645. **Tel** (800)432-4570, (201)358-2210. **(Subscription address:** Fulco Medical Economics, PO Box 3000, Denville NJ 07834.**)** **ED** Robert L. Edsall. **LC** R11; .P34. **DD** 610/.5. **NLM** W1 PA963N. **[CCC].** Index available. **Bk Rev. Ad Acc. Circ:** 113,000 (ctrl). available on an online database (files 149,648/Full-Text) from DIALOG. Documents available from UMI Article Clearinghouse.
**Desc:** Advice for the primary care physician on the diagnosis and treatment of conditions encountered in office practice.
**Ind/Abst** Acad. Ind. [Computer File] (1992-); Acad. Search (July 1993-); Bus. Index (1981-?); Cumul. Index Nurs. Allied Health Lit.; Expand. Acad. Index (1992-); Gen. Period. Index (1985-); Health Devices Alerts; Health Index (1989-); Health Period. Database [Full Txt.]; Health Ref. Cent. (Jan. 1989-) [Full Txt.] [Full Cov.]; Hospit. Health Admin. Index; INFO-SOUTH Abstr.; Mag. ASAP Plus [Full Txt.]; Mag. Index Plus (1992-); Mag. Search; Newsp. Period. Abstr. (1989-); Trade Ind. ASAP [Full Txt.]; Trade Ind. Index (1981-?).

US/0270-1553
**PATIENT CARE FLOW CHART MANUAL.** [Patient care flow chart man.]. **Main/Corp** Patient Care Publications, Inc. Special Publications Group. (19??)-. English. an. Mark Powley Associates Inc, 88 Main Street, New Canaan CT 06840. **Tel** (203)972-1902. **LC** RC59; .P37a. **DD** 616. **NLM** W1 PA963R.

UK/0959-4299
**POSTGRADUATE EDUCATION FOR GENERAL PRACTICE.** Vol. 1 (1990)-. Periodical. English. Three times a year (May, Aug., Nov.). £55.00. Radcliffe Medical Press Ltd, 15 Kings Meadow, Ferry Hinksey Oxford OX2 ODP, England. **Tel** 011 44 865 790696, FAX 011 44 865 794930. **ED** Dedan Dwyer. **NLM** W1; PO955I. Index available (Bound in 3rd issue publish in October). cum. index. **Bk Rev. Pr Rev. Circ:** 1,500 (ctrl). ***Absorbed*** *Journal (Association of Course Organisers).*
**Desc:** Educational articles for general practitioners.

US/0896-5412
**PRACTICAL REVIEWS IN FAMILY PRACTICE.** (PRACTICAL REVIEWS IN FAMILY PRACTICE [SOUND RECORDING].). [Pract. rev. fam. pract.]. **Added/Corp** Educational Reviews, Inc. Montefiore Medical Center. **VFOAT** Practical Reviews. (197?)-. Periodical. English. mo. $175.00 Physicians/Dentists; $125.00 Residents. Educational Reviews Inc., 6801 Cahaba Valley Road, Birmingham AL 35242. **Tel** (205)991-5188, (800)633-4743, FAX (205)995-1926. **DD** 610.

UK/0032-6518
**PRACTITIONER, THE.** [Practitioner]. Vol. 1 (July 1868)-. Academic Scholarly Publication. English. mo. £57.00 UK & Northern Ireland; $134.00 other. Morgan Grampian, 40 Beresford Street Woolwich, London SE18 6BQ England. **Tel** 011 44 81 855 7777, FAX 011 44 81 855 5548, telex 896238. **ED** Rachel Arthur. **NLM** W1 PR158. Index available. cum. index. **Ad Acc. Circ:** 28,600 (ctrl). available on microfilm and microfiche from University Microfilms International (UMI).
**Desc:** Monthly symposiums keep the general practitioner informed on current developments of practical interest specialty by specialty; research by general practitioners is published.
**Ind/Abst** Cumul. Index Nurs. Allied Health Lit.; EMBASE [Select. Cov.]; Health Devices Alerts; Helminthol. Abstr. (1991-); Index Med.; Int. Nurs. Index; Life Sci. Collect.; PESTDOC; Protozoolog. Abstr.; Rev. Med. Vet. Mycology; Soc. Sci. Cit. Index [Select. Cov.]; SportSearch.

US/0095-4543
**PRIMARY CARE.** [Prim. care]. Vol. 1, No. 1 (Mar. 1974)-. Academic Scholarly Publication. English. qt. $81.00 (individual), $100.00 (institution) US; $111.00 (individual), $117.00 (institution) other. W.B. Saunders Company, A Subsidiary of Harcourt Brace Jovanovich, Inc., The Curtis Center/Suite 300, Independence Square West, Philadelphia PA 19106-3399. **Tel** (215)238-7800 or, 5587, FAX (215)238-7883, telex 173146. **(Subscription address:** W. B. Saunders Company / North America Subscriptions, c/o Periodicals, 6277 Sea Harbour Drive, 4th Floor, Orlando FL 32887.**)** **ED** Barbara Cohen-Kligerman. **LC** R11; .P747. **DD** 610/.5. **NLM** W1 PR522A. **[CCC].** Index available. **Pr Rev. Circ:** 5,000. available on microfilm and microfiche from University Microfilms International (UMI). Documents available from The Genuine Article.
**Desc:** Practical updates for the clinician on the latest advances. Each issue is devoted to a single topic in patient care.
**Ind/Abst** Cumul. Index Nurs. Allied Health Lit.; Curr. Contents Clin. Med.; EMBASE; Energy Res. Abstr. (Jan. 1981-); Index Med.; Life Sci. Collect.; Res. Alert [Select. Cov.]; SCISEARCH; Soc. Sci. Cit. Index [Select. Cov.]; SportSearch.

US/0743-8176
**PRIMARY CARE & CANCER.** **See** Medical Science and Technology-Neoplasma, Neoplastic.

US/0887-2414
**PRIMARY CARE CASE MANAGEMENT NEWSLETTER.** [Prim. care case manage. newsl.]. **Added/Corp** Coastal Research Group. Vol. 1, No. 1 (June/July 1983)-. Periodical. English. Six times a year (Jan., Mar., May, July, Sept., Nov.). $30.00 (one year); $55.00 (two years); $75.00 (three years). Coastal Research Group, PO Box 2355, Granite Bay Station, Roseville CA 95746. **Tel** (916)791-1648. **DD** 362. **Circ:** 400.

US/8756-5390
**PRIMARY CARE EMERGENCY DECISIONS.** ***Ceased.*** [Prim. care emerg. decis.]. **VFOAT** Emergency Decisions. Vol. 1, No. 1 (Feb. 1985)-Ceased (Dec. 1988). Periodical. English. mo. Physicians World Communications, PO Box 1505, Secaucus NJ 07094. **Tel** (201)865-7500. **DD** 616. **NLM** W1; PR522ACM.

US/0732-1260
**PRIMARY CARE FOCUS.** [Prim. care focus]. Began with: Vol. 1, No. 1 (Mar. 1981). Periodical. English. bm. $50.00. National Association of Community Health Centers, 1625 I Street NW/Suite 403, Washington DC 20006. **NLM** W1 PR522AD.

UK/0969-4978
**PRIMARY CARE MANAGEMENT.** (19??)-. Newsletter. English. mo. £108.00 Europe; £110.00 Other (Institutions). Churchill Livingstone, 1-3 Baxter's Place, Leith Walk, Edinburgh EH1 3AF Scotland. **Tel** 011 44 31 556 2424, FAX 011 44 31 558 1278, telex 727511. **(Subscription address:** Maruzen Company Ltd., PO Box 5050, Import & Export Department, Tokyo 100 31 Japan.**)**

UK/0960-250X
**PRIMARY HEALTH CARE MANAGEMENT.** [Prim. health care manag.]. (1990)-. Periodical. English. mo. £103.00 UK; £104.00 Europe; $172.00 US; £106.00 other (institution). Churchill Livingstone, 1-3 Baxter's Place, Leith Walk, Edinburgh EH1 3AF Scotland. **Tel** 011 44 31 556 2424, FAX 011 44 31 558 1278, telex 727511. **(Subscription address:** Maruzen Company Ltd., PO Box 5050, Import & Export Department, Tokyo 100 31 Japan.**) DD** 362.1068. **[CCC].** available in microform from University Microfilms International (UMI).

UK
**QUALITY IN PRACTICE : A BULLETIN FROM THE ROYAL COLLEGE OF GENERAL PRACTITIONERS. Main/Corp** Royal College of General Practitioners. Bulletin. English. ir.

UK/0557-3912
**REPORTS FROM GENERAL PRACTICE.** [Rep. gen. pract.]. No. 1 (May 1965)-. Monographic series. English. ir. Price varies per volume. Royal College General Practitioners, 14 Princes Gate, Hyde Park, London SW7 1PU England. **Tel** 011 44 71 225 7629, 011 44 71 823 9698. **ED** Professor D.J. Pereira. cum. index. **Bk Rev. Pr Rev. Circ:** 17,500 (ctrl).
**Ind/Abst** EMBASE.

UK/0262-7043
**RESPIRATORY DISEASE IN PRACTICE. See** Medical Science and Technology-Respiratory System.

CU
**REVISTA CUBANA DE MEDICINA GENERAL INTEGRAL. VFOAT** Medicina General Integral. Periodical. Spanish. qt. $24.00 North America; $28.00 South America; $35.00 other. Ediciones Cubanas, Obispo 527, Altos ESQ Bernaza, CP 10100 Havana Cuba. **Tel** 011 632980, 631942, FAX 011 631011, telex 512337, 6540. **NLM** W1; RE362C.
**Desc:** A vehicle used by doctors to publish their experiences by means of scientific studies presented with the required quality.

IT
**RIVISTA CONSULTORIO FAMILIARE.** Italian. Three times a year. L40000 Italy; L70000 other. Associazione Culturale Cieffe, Via Ognissanti N 65, 35129 Padua Italy. **Tel** 011 39 49 8719943. **ED** Carla Rigoni.
**Desc:** Themes and problems in family medicine.

FR
**SANTE DE L'ECOLIER. See** Psychology.

SW/0107-833X
**SCANDINAVIAN JOURNAL OF PRIMARY HEALTH CARE.** [Scand. j. prim. health care]. **Added/Corp** Joint Committee of the Nordic Medical Research Councils. Hafnia Fond. Vol. 1, No. 1 (1983)-. Academic Scholarly Publication. English. qt. Kr785.00, $132.00. Scandinavian University Press, PO Box 2959 Toeyen, N 0608 Oslo 6 Norway. **Tel** 011 47 2 2575400, FAX 011 47 2 2575353, telex 71896 UROR N. **(Subscription address:** Scandinavian University Press, 200 Meacham Ave., Elmont NY 11003.**) NLM** W1; SC152D. **CODEN** SJPCD7. Documents available from BIOSIS Document Express.
**Ind/Abst** Biol. Abstr. (1988-); EMBASE; Index Med.; Int. Nurs. Index; Nutr. Res. Newsl.

SW/0281-3432
**SCANDINAVIAN JOURNAL OF PRIMARY HEALTH CARE. SUPPLEMENT.** Vol. 1 (1988)-. English. ir. Comes with Scandinavian Journal of Primary Health Care: $132.00. Scandinavian University Press, PO Box 2959 Toeyen, N 0608 Oslo 6 Norway. **Tel** 011 47 2 2575400, FAX 011 47 2 2575353, telex 71896 UROR N. **(Subscription address:** Scandinavian University Press, 200 Meacham Ave., Elmont NY 11003.**) NLM** W1; SC152D. **[CCC].** Documents available from BIOSIS Document Express.
**Ind/Abst** Biol. Abstr.; EMBASE; Index Med. (1988-).

SI/0377-5305
**SINGAPORE FAMILY PHYSICIAN, THE.** Vol. 1 (Jan./March 1975)-. Periodical. English. qt. **NLM** W1 SI52. ***Supersedes** G.P. (Singapore), 0303-7251.*

CE/0254-8623
**SRI LANKAN FAMILY PHYSICIAN.** [Sri Lankan fam. phys.]. (1978)-. Periodical. English. **NLM** W1 SR64M.

US/0098-1052
**TEXAS FAMILY PHYSICIAN.** Vol. 26 (Jan./Feb. 1975)-. Periodical. English. bm. Texas Academy of Family Physicians, 1905 North Lamar, Austin TX 78705. **NLM** W1 TE724. ***Continues** GP Press, 0098-0994.*

US/1054-8521
**TODAY IN MEDICINE. FAMILY PRACTICE.** [Today med. Fam. pract.]. **VFOAT** Family Practice. Vol. 1, No. 1 (Jan./Feb. 1991)-. Periodical. English. bm. $45.00 US; $70.00 Canada. Data Centrum Communications Inc Data Centrum Communications Inc, The Soho Building, 110 Greene Street, Suite 505, The Soho Building, 110 Greene Street, Suite 505, New York New York NY NY 10012 10012. **Tel** (212)226-5252, (212)226-5252. **DD** 610.

US
**UCLA FAMILY MEDICINE NEWS. Added/Corp** University of California, Los Angeles. Division of Family Medicine. Vol. 1, No. 1 (Winter 1990)-. Periodical. English.

UK/0301-5718
**UPDATE.** [Update]. Vol. 1 (Oct. 1968)-. Academic Scholarly Publication. English. sm (24 issues). £82.00 UK; £100.00 Europe; £107.00 other. Reed Business Publishing Group / England, Quadrant House, Quadrant Sutton Surrey, SM2 5AS England. **Tel** 011 44 81 652-3500. **NLM** W1 UP51. ***Absorbed** Update Plus.*
**Ind/Abst** EMBASE (19??-); Health Serv. Abstr. (19??-).

US
**VIRGINIA FAMILY PHYSICIAN NEWSLETTER. Added/Corp** Virginia Academy of Family Physicians. 1st Quarter (1990)-. Newsletter. English. qt. Virginia Academy of Family Physicians, 4211 Dover Road, Richmond VA 23221. **NLM** W1; VI777M. ***Continues** Virginia Family Physician, 0194-1119.*

US/0147-1996
**YEAR BOOK OF FAMILY PRACTICE, THE.** [Year book fam. pract.]. (1977)-. English. an. $72.00. Mosby Year Book Inc., 11830 Westline Industrial Drive, St Louis MO 63146. **Tel** (800)325-4177, (314)872-8370, FAX (314)432-1380, telex 44-2402. **LC** R101; .Y33. **DD** 616/.005. **NLM** W1 YE155.

GW/0044-2178
**ZEITSCHRIFT FUER ARZTLICHE FORTBILDUNG.** [Z. arztl. Fortbild.]. Vol. 1 (1904)-. Academic Scholarly Publication. German. Seven times a year. DM138.00 Germany; DM152.00 other. Gustav Fischer Verlag Jena, Postfach 100537, D 07705 Jena Germany. **Tel** 011 49 3641 27332, FAX 011 49 3641 626500. **(Subscription address:** VCH Publishers Inc., 303 Northwest 12th Avenue, Journals Department, Deerfield FL 33442.**) ED** H Berndt. **NLM** W1 ZE2302. **[CCC].** Index available. **Bk Rev. Ad Acc. Circ:** 7,580.
**Desc:** Directed at the general practitioner, particularly for use in his practice as a family doctor. Practical instructions for basic medical care imparting significant experiences of medical science and its theoretical understanding are passed on. Intended for all practitioners in clinical and hygienic disciplines of basic medical care and contributes to an efficient cooperation with the family doctor.
**Ind/Abst** EMBASE; Index Med.; Int. Nurs. Index; Saf. Health Work; SportSearch.

GW/0341-9835
**ZFA. ZEITSCHRIFT FUER ALLGEMEINMEDIZIN.** [ZFA, Z. Allgemeinmed.]. **Added/Corp** Vereinigung der Hochschullehrer und Lehrbeauftragten fuer Allgemeinmedizin. **VFOAT** Zeitschrift fuer Allgemeinmedizin. Vol. 52, (Jan. 10, 1976)-. Periodical. German. Twenty-four times a year. $152.00. Hippokrates Verlag, Postfach 102263, W 70018 Stuttgart Germany. **Tel** 011 49 711 89310. **(Subscription address:** Thieme Medical Publishers Inc., 381 Park Avenue South, New York NY 10016.**) NLM** W1 Z11. **[CCC]. *Continues** Zeitschrift fuer Allgemeinmedizin, 0300-8673.*
**Ind/Abst** EMBASE [Select. Cov.].

## FORENSIC MEDICINE, MEDICAL JURISPRUDENCE

TU/1018-5275
**ADLI TP DERGISI.** [Adli tp derg.]. **VFOAT** Journal of Forensic Medicine; ATD. Adli tp Dergisi. (1985)-. Periodical. Turkish. sa. **UDC** 63. Documents available from CASDDS.
**Ind/Abst** Chem. Abstr.

GW/0930-9535
**ADVANCES IN FORENSIC HAEMOGENETICS. See** Medical Science and Technology-Hematology.

US/0747-6353
**ADVANCES IN FORENSIC PSYCHOLOGY AND PSYCHIATRY. See** Psychology.

US/0899-1464
**AIDS LITIGATION REPORTER.** [AIDS litig. report.]. **Added/Corp** Andrews Publications, Inc. **VAT** Acquired Immune Deficiency Syndrome Litigation Reporter. (Oct. 1987)-. Periodical. English. sm (24 issues). $725.00. Andrews Publications Inc., 1646 West Chester Pike, PO Box 1000, Westtown PA 19395. **Tel** (610)399-6600, (800)345-1101, FAX (610)399-6610. **ED** Ronald V. Baker. **LC** KF3803.A54; A493. **DD** 344.73/04369792; 347.3044369792. **NLM** WA 33; A288. Index available. cum. index.
**Desc:** Publishes the latest information on the ever-changing world of AIDS-related litigation. Gives details of the events and key documents. Follows important cases in which decisions are made regarding confidentiality, HIV testing, health care, medical malpractice, estate law, libel and slander, corrections, education and criminal issues.

US/0195-7910
**AMERICAN JOURNAL OF FORENSIC MEDICINE AND PATHOLOGY, THE.** [Am. j. forensic med. pathol.]. **Added/Corp** National Association of Medical Examiners (U.S.). Vol. 1, (March 1980)-. Periodical. English. qt. $140.00 (individuals), $202.00 (institutions) US; $178.00 (individuals), $248.00 (institutions) other. Raven Press, 1185 Avenue of the Americas, 37th Floor, New York NY 10036. **Tel** (212)930-9500, (212)930-9604, FAX (212)869-3495, (212)302-8507, telex 640073. **ED** William G. Eckert. **LC** RA1001; .A58. **DD** 614/.1/05. **NLM** W1 AM451R. **[CCC]. Bk Rev. Ad Acc. Pr Rev. Circ:** 1,700. available on microfilm and microfiche from University Microfilms International (UMI). Documents available from The Genuine Article.
**Desc:** Presents a balanced, up-to-date picture of forensic medical practices worldwide.
**Ind/Abst** Chicano Index; Coal Abstr.; Crim. Justice Abstr. (March 1980-); Crim. Penol. Police Sci. Abstr.; Curr. Contents Clin. Med.; EMBASE; Health Plan. Adminis.; Index Med. March 1980-; INIS Atomindex [Micro.]; Life Sci. Collect.; Res. Alert [Select. Cov.]; Rev. Med. Vet. Entomol.; SCISEARCH; Soc. Sci. Cit. Index [Select. Cov.].

US/0733-1290
**AMERICAN JOURNAL OF FORENSIC PSYCHOLOGY, THE.** [Am. J. Forensic Psychol.]. **Added/Corp** American College of Forensic Psychology. Vol. 1, Issue 1 (1983)-. Periodical. English. Four times a year (Jan., Apr., July, Oct.). $65.00 (one year); $110.00 (two years). American College of Forensic Psychiatry, PO Box 5870, Balboa Island CA 92662. **Tel** (714)831-0236, FAX (714)675-1107. **ED** Debra Miller. **LC** K1; .M443. **DD** 347/.066; 342.766. **NLM** W1; AM451T. cum. index. **Bk Rev. Ad Acc.** available on microfilm from Williams S Hein & Co.
**Desc:** Professional journal for psychologists who testify in civil and criminal cases and for attorneys representing mental disability claimants and interested in mental disability law.
**Ind/Abst** Crim. Justice Abstr.; Psychol. Abstr. (1983-); PsycINFO (1990-).

US/0098-8588
**AMERICAN JOURNAL OF LAW & MEDICINE. See** Law.

US/0162-9417
**ANNUAL REPORT - CENTER FOR LAW AND HEALTH SCIENCES. Main/Corp** Boston University. Center for Law and Health Sciences. 1970/71-. English. an. Boston University School of Law, 765 Commonwealth Avenue, Boston MA 02215. **Tel** (617)353-3157, (617)353-3115. **NLM** W1 CE185.

IT/0392-5145
**ARCHIVIO DI MEDICINA LEGALE E DELLE ASSICURAZIONI.** (ARCHIVIO DI MEDICINA LEGALE E DELLE ASSICURAZIONI : ORGANO UFFICIALE DELLA SOCIETA LOMBARDA DI MEDICINA LEGALE E DELLE ASSICURAZIONI.). [Arch. med. leg. Assicur.]. **Added/Corp** Societa Lombarda di Medicina Legale e Delle Assicurazioni. Vol. 1, No. 1-2 (1979)-. Periodical. Italian (summaries and/or abstracts in English). qt. L40000. Societa Lombarda Medicina Legale e delle Assicurazioni, Via Mangiagalli 37, 20133 Milan Italy. **Tel** 011 39 2 2665249. **NLM** W1 AR538G. ***Continues** Archivio della Societa Lombarda di Medicina Legale e delle Assicurazioni, 0390-7317.*

GW/0343-5733
**ARZTRECHT (1977).** (ARZTRECHT.). (Sept. 1977)-. Periodical. German. Twelve times a year. DM77.27. Verlag fur Arztrecht, Schinnrainstrasse, D 76227 Karlsruhe Germany. **Tel** 011 49 721 402904. **NLM**

W1 AR996. Index available in last issue of volume--attached. ***Continues*** *Arzt + Arzneimittelrecht, 0340-5532.*

US
**ATTORNEYS' DICTIONARY OF MEDICINE.** English. an. Matthew Bender & Company Inc., 1275 Broadway, Albany NY 12204. **Tel** (800)833-9844, (518)487-3000.

US
**ATTORNEYS' TEXTBOOK OF MEDICINE.** English. ir. Matthew Bender & Company Inc., 1275 Broadway, Albany NY 12204. **Tel** (800)833-9844, (518)487-3000.

AT/0045-0618
**AUSTRALIAN JOURNAL OF FORENSIC SCIENCES, THE.** [Aust. j. forensic sci.]. **Added/Corp** Australian Academy of Forensic Sciences. (1968)-. Periodical. English. Four times a year. 60.00Aus$. McGraw Hill Book Company / Australia, 4 Barcoo Street East, Roseville NSW 2069 Australia. **Tel** 011 61 2 4174288, FAX 011 61 2 4065687, telex 120849. **ED** Dr. David Bell (phone: 011 61 2 969-5058). **LC** K1; .U78. **DD** 340/.6/05. **NLM** W1 AU611R. **CODEN** AJFSB9. Index available. cum. index. **Bk Rev**, (Qty: 4-11). **Ad Acc**, **Adv Mgr:** John Rowe. **Pr Rev. Circ:** 500 (ctrl). Documents available from CASDDS.
**Desc:** A distinguished international forum for some of the finest scholarship in forensic sciences from eminent Australian and overseas contributors.
**Ind/Abst** APAIS, Aust. Public Aff. Inf. Ser. (1977-); Aust. Leg. Mon. Dig.; Chem. Abstr. (1968-1981); Curr. Law Index (1980-); EMBASE; Leg. Resour. Index (1980-); LegalTrac (1980-).

AU/0067-5016
**BEITRAEGE ZUR GERICHTLICHEN MEDIZIN.** [Beitr. gerichtl. Med.]. (1911)-. Academic Scholarly Publication. German. an. DM3280.00. Franz Deuticke Verlagsges MbH, Helferstorferstrasse 4, PF 761, A 1011 Vienna Austria. **Tel** (0222)5331535, FAX (02236)63535240, telex 7PR46 OEBV. **LC** RA1001; .B37. **NLM** W1 BE27. **CODEN** BEGMA5. Documents available from CASDDS. ***Supersedes*** *Beytrage zur Gerichtlichen Arzneykunde.*
**Ind/Abst** Chem. Abstr.; EMBASE; Health Plan. Adminis.; Index Med.

US/0730-031X
**BIOTECHNOLOGY LAW REPORT.** **See** Medical Science and Technology-Biotechnology.

GW/0006-5250
**BLUTALKOHOL.** [Blutalkohol]. Vol. 1 (Jan. 1961)-. Academic Scholarly Publication. German. bm. DM86.00 Germany; DM86.60 Europe; DM88.90 other. Steintor Verlag Hamburg GmbH, Postfach 1228, W 2400 Luebeck 1 Germany. **Tel** 011 49 451 8900549. **DD** 340. **NLM** W1 BL962. **CODEN** BLALAL. Index available. Documents available from BIOSIS Document Express, CASDDS.
**Ind/Abst** Biol. Abstr.; Chem. Abstr.; Crim. Penol. Police Sci. Abstr.; EMBASE; Health Plan. Adminis.; Index Med. (Vol. 21, No. 1, 1984-).

CN/0008-5030
**CANADIAN SOCIETY OF FORENSIC SCIENCE JOURNAL.** [Can. Soc. Forensic Sci. j.]. **Main/Corp** Canadian Society of Forensic Science. Vol. 1 (March 1968)-. Academic Scholarly Publication. English (French). qt. 75.00Can$ Canada; 85.00Can$ other. Canadian Society of Forensic Science, 2660 Southvale Crescent, Suite 215, Ottawa Ontario K1B 4W5 Canada. **Tel** (613)731-0001. **ED** Brian T. Hodgson. **CODEN** JCFSBP. **[CCC]. Bk Rev. Ad Acc. Circ:** 1,000 (ctrl). Documents available from CASDDS. ***Supersedes*** *Canadian Society of Forensic Science. Newsletter, 0576-6117.*
**Desc:** Original papers, chemistry, blood, alcohol, analysis, toxicology, questioned documents, odontology, firearms examination, pathology, biology, law enforcement and jurisprudence.
**Ind/Abst** Art Archaeol. Tech. Abstr.; Chem. Abstr.; EMBASE.

SP/1131-5253
**CIENCIA PHARMACEUTICA.** [Cienc. pharm.]. (1991)-. Periodical. Spanish. bm. 4370 ptas Spain; $60.00 Europe; $100.00 other. Alpe Editores SA, C Pedro Rico 27, Oficinas 11 & 12, 28029 Madrid Spain. **Tel** 011 34 1 7338811, FAX 011 34 1 3159652. **CODEN** CIPHEA. ***Continues*** *Pharmaklinik, 1011-4386.*

US/1061-608X
**CLINICAL TRIALS.** ***Title Change.*** [Clin. trials]. Vol. 1, No. 1 (June 1992)-(1993). Periodical. English. mo. CTB International Publishing Inc., PO Box 218, Maplewood NJ 07040. **Tel** (201)379-7749, FAX (201)379-1158. **DD** 615. **NLM** W1; CL799J. **[CCC].** ***Continued by*** *Clinical Trials Monitor.*

●US
**CLINICAL TRIALS MONITOR : MONTHLY MONITORING OF CLINICAL TRIALS OF HUMAN PHARMACEUTICALS.** Vol. 2, No. 10 (Oct. 1993)-. Periodical. English. mo. $1137.00. CTB International Publishing Inc., PO Box 218, Maplewood NJ 07040. **Tel** (201)379-7749, FAX (201)379-1158. **NLM** W1; CL799P. ***Continues*** *Clinical Trials, 1061-608X.*

FR/0398-9119
**COLLECTION DE MEDECINE LEGALE ET DE TOXICOLOGIE MEDICALE.** [Collect. med. leg. toxicol. med.]. No. 53-. Academic Scholarly Publication. French. Price varies per volume. Editions Masson, 120 BD Street Germain, 75280 Paris Cedex 06 France. **Tel** (1)46342760, FAX (1)45872999. **NLM** W1 CO17Q. **CODEN** CMLMDW. Documents available from CASDDS.
**Ind/Abst** Chem. Abstr.; EMBASE.

US
**CONTEMPORARY PUBLIC HEALTH ISSUES.** Vol. 1 (1991)-. Monographic series. English. Price varies per volume. **NLM** W 32.5; AA1 C761.

US
**EMERGENCY LEGAL BRIEFINGS.** (19??)-. English. $159.00 without CME; $209.00 with CME. American Health Consultants, 3525 Piedmont Road, Suite 400, Atlanta GA 30305. **Tel** (800)688-2421, (404)262-7436. **(Subscription address:** American Health Consultants, PO Box 95278, Chicago IL 60694.**)**
**Desc:** Focuses exclusively on the legal aspects of practicing emergency medicine, offering specific guidelines for minimizing legal exposure while maintaining high quality patient care.

US/0098-1524
**EPLB. EMERGENCY PHYSICIAN LEGAL BULLETIN.** **See** Medical Science and Technology-Emergency Medicine.

NE/0031-0743
**EXCERPTA MEDICA. SECTION 49. FORENSIC SCIENCE ABSTRACTS.** (FORENSIC SCIENCE ABSTRACTS.). **VAT** Excerpta Medica. Section Forty-Nine. Forensic Science Abstracts. Vol. 1 (1975)-. English. Six times a year (1 volume). Fl1180.00. Excerpta Medica Publishing Group, PO Box 548, 1000 AM Amsterdam Netherlands. **Tel** 011 31 20 5803243. **(Subscription address:** Excerpta Medica Journals, PO Box 85, Limerick Ireland.**) LC** RA1001; .F653. **DD** 614/.19/05. **NLM** ZW 1 E978W. **[CCC].** available on microfilm from University Microfilms International (UMI); available on CD-ROM.
**Desc:** The contents are considerably beyond the bounds of forensic medicine.

US/0737-8726
**EXPERT AND THE LAW, THE.** **See** Law.

US/0014-9306
**FEDERATION BULLETIN (FULTON).** (FEDERATION BULLETIN.). [Fed. bull.]. **Main/Corp** Federation of State Medical Boards of the United States. Vol. 7, (Jan. 1921)-. Periodical. English. Four times a year. $35.00. Federation of State Medical Boards of the United States, 6000 West Place, Suite 707, Ft Worth TX 76107. **Tel** (817)735-8445, FAX (817)738-6629. **ED** Ray L. Casterline. **DD** 610. **NLM** W1 FE272. **[CCC]. Circ:** 3,378. available in microform. ***Continues*** *Monthly Bulletin of the Federation of State Medical Boards of the United States.*
**Desc:** Medical licensure; requirements for licensure; state board policies.
**Ind/Abst** Health Plan. Adminis.; Hospit. Health Admin. Index (Jan. 1978-Dec. 1990).

US/0888-692X
**FORENSIC REPORTS.** ***Ceased.*** [Forensic rep.]. (1988)- (1993). Periodical. English. qt. Taylor & Francis Ltd., Rankine Road, Basingstoke Hampshire, RG24 8PR United Kingdom. **Tel** 011 44 256 840366, FAX 011 44 256 479438, telex 858540. **(Subscription address:** Taylor & Francis Inc., 1900 Frost Road, Suite 101, Bristol PA 19007-1598.**) ED** Martin I Kurke (editor's address: 4519 Arendale Square, Alexandria, VA 22309). **CODEN** FOREEI. **[CCC].** Index available. cum. index. **Bk Rev. Ad Acc. Pr Rev. Circ:** 300. available on microfilm and microfiche from University Microfilms International (UMI).
**Desc:** Presents the latest advances in the practice of forensic science. Addresses your professional concerns, as well as academic interests relating to forensic practice. assessments of eyewitness testimony, accident causation studies.
**Ind/Abst** Psychol. Abstr. (1988-); PsycINFO; PsycLit.

SZ/0379-0738
**FORENSIC SCIENCE INTERNATIONAL.** [Forensic sci. int.]. Vol. 12 (July/Aug. 1978)-. Academic Scholarly Publication. English (French and German). Eighteen times a year (6 volumes). $817.00. Elsevier Science Ireland Ltd., Bay 15, Shannon Industrial Estate, Co Clare Ireland. **Tel** 011 353 61 471944. **ED** J. Voigt. **LC** RA1001; .F65. **DD** 614/.19. **NLM** W1 FO615I. **CODEN** FSINDR. **[CCC].** Index available. **Pr Rev.** available on microfilm and microfiche from University Microfilms International (UMI). Documents available from The Genuine Article, BIOSIS Document Express, CASDDS. ***Continues*** *Forensic Science, 0300-9432.*
**Desc:** An international journal for the publication of original contributions in the many different scientific disciplines pertaining to the forensic sciences.
**Ind/Abst** Anal. Abstr.; Biol. Abstr.; Chem. Abstr.; Crim. Justice Abstr.; Crim. Penol. Police Sci. Abstr. -?; CSA Neuro. Abstr. (?-?); Curr. Aware. Biol. Sci., CABS; Curr. Contents Clin. Med.; Curr. Law Index (1980-); EMBASE; Energy Res. Abstr. (Aug. 1982-); Health Saf. Sci. Abstr.; Health Plan. Adminis.; Highw. Res. Abstr.; Index Med.; Index Vet.; Leg. Resour. Index (1980-); LegalTrac (1980-); Mass Spect. Bull. (?-?); Ornamental Hort.; Life Sci. Collect.; Pollut. Abstr. Indexes; Poult. Abstr.; Ref. Upd. Deluxe Ed.; Res. Alert [Full Cov.]; Rev. Agric. Entomol.; Rev. Med. Vet. Entomol.; Sci. Cit. Index; SCISEARCH; Soc. Sci. Cit. Index [Select. Cov.]; Vet. Bull.; Toxicol. Abstr.

GW/0930-1461
**FORENSIC SCIENCE PROGRESS.** [Forensic sci. prog.]. Vol. 1 (1986)-. English. Springer-Verlag GmbH & Company KG, Heidelberger Platz 3, D 14197 Berlin Germany. **Tel** 011 49 30 8207223, FAX 011 49 30 8214091, telex 183 319 SPBLN D. **(Subscription address:** Springer Verlag New York Inc. / for North America, 44 Hartz Way, Secaucus NJ 07096.**) ED** A Maehly and R L Williams. **LC** HV8073; .F588. **DD** 363.2/5/05. **NLM** W1; FO615P. **CODEN** FSPRE7. Documents available from BIOSIS Document Express, CASDDS.
**Ind/Abst** Biol. Abstr. (1988-); Chem. Abstr.

US/1042-7201
**FORENSIC SCIENCE REVIEW.** [Forensic sci. rev.]. Vol. 1, No. 1 (June 1989)-. Periodical. English. sa. $80.00 (institutions), $60.00 (individuals), $40.00 (students) (add $15.00 postage for other). Forensic Science Review, PO Box 55802, Birmingham AL 35255. **Tel** (205)934-2069, FAX (205)934-8664. **LC** HV8073; .F589. **DD** 363.2/5/05. **NLM** W1; FO615V.

JA/0302-0029
**HANZAIGAKU ZASSHI.** **Added/Corp** Nippon Hanzai Gakkai. **VFOAT** Archiv fur Gerichtlich Medizin und Kriminologie; Acta Criminologiae et Medicinae Legalis Japonica. Vol. 1 (Sept. 1928)-. Periodical. Japanese (summaries and/or abstracts in English). bm. $55.00. Medical Research Institute, 3-10 Kandasurugadai 2-chome Chiyoda-ku, Tokyo 101 Japan. **Tel** 011 81 32919577, . **ED** Osamu Nakata. **NLM** W1 HA552. **CODEN** HAZAAY. Index available. **Bk Rev. Ad Acc. Circ:** 6 (ctrl). Documents available from BIOSIS Document Express, CASDDS.
**Desc:** Publishes a thesis on a subject following the result of a psychiatric test, an inquest, a study of blood type, etc.
**Ind/Abst** Biol. Abstr.; Chem. Abstr.

●US/1075-0606
**HEALTH LAW LITIGATION REPORTER.** [Health law litig. report.]. (Aug. 1993)-. Periodical. English. mo. $800.00. Andrews Publications Inc., 1646 West Chester Pike, PO Box 1000, Westtown PA 19395. **Tel** (610)399-6600, (800)345-1101, FAX (610)399-6610. **DD** 346. ***Continues*** *Medical Malpractice - OB/GYN Litigation Reporter, 1056-4098.*

US/0748-383X
**HEALTH MATRIX.** (HEALTH MATRIX : THE JOURNAL OF LAW-MEDICINE.). [Health matrix]. **Added/Corp** Franklin Thomas Backus School of Law. Vol. 1, No. 1 (Spring 1991)-. Periodical. English. Twice a year (Feb., May). $24.00. Case Western Reserve University School of Law, 11075 East Boulevard, Cleveland OH 44106. **Tel** (216)368-3304, FAX (216)368-6144. **ED** Dean A. Schwartz (phone: (216)368-2099). **DD** 344. **NLM** W1; HE414EM. **Ad Acc, Adv Mgr:** Carolyn Speaker, **Tel** (216)368-3304. **Circ:** 500. available on microfilm and microfiche from WESTLAW; available on CD-ROM and an online database from WESTLAW. ***Continues*** *Health Matrix (Owings Mills, Md.), 0748-383X.*

US/0883-0452
**HEALTHSPAN.** [HealthSpan]. **VFOAT** Health Span. Vol. 2, No. 1 (Jan. 1985)-. Periodical. English. Eleven times a year. $217.00. Prentice-Hall Law and Business, 270 Sylvan Avenue, Englewood Cliffs NJ 07632. **Tel** (800)223-0231, (201)894-8538, FAX (201)894-8666. **ED** Cliff Stromber and Michele L. Robinson. **LC** RA410.A1; H43. **DD** 338.4/73621/0973. **NLM** W1; HE616. **Bk Rev. Circ:** 1,100. ***Continues*** *HealthScan, 8755-2205.*
**Desc:** Provides an in-depth look at the legal and regulatory events that are shaping the nature of the health care industry.
**Ind/Abst** Health Plan. Adminis.; Hospit. Health Admin. Index (1985-).

JA/0915-9606
**HOCHUDOKU.** **VFOAT** Japanese Journal of Forensic Toxicology. (1990)-. Periodical. Multiple languages. tq. Fukuoka Nihon Hochudoku Gakkai. **DD** 614.1. Documents available from CASDDS. ***Continues*** *Hochudokugakku Nyusu.*
**Ind/Abst** Chem. Abstr.

●US/1065-2817
**HOSPITAL LAW MANUAL BULLETIN.** [Hosp. law man. bull.]. Vol. 1, No. 1 (Oct. 1992)-. Bulletin. English. Twelve times a year. $285.00 US. Aspen Publishers Inc., 7201 McKinney Circle, Frederick MD 21701. **Tel** (800)234-1660, (301)698-7100, FAX (301)251-5784, telex 5106014543. **(Subscription**

**address:** Aspen Publishers Inc., PO Box 990, Frederick MD 21701.) **DD** 344. ***Continues*** *Hospital Law Newsletter, 0738-0984.*
**Desc:** Goal is to deliver facts, strategies, and insights to ensure that decisions made in today's legal environment are informed. Addresses issues such as malpractice concerns, credentialing requirements, peer review issues, legal aspects of staff privileges, termination, and withholding of care.

US/0738-0984
**HOSPITAL LAW NEWSLETTER.** ***Title Change.*** [Hosp. law newsl.]. **Added/Corp** Aspen Systems Corporation. Vol. 1, No. 1 (July 1983)-(199?). Newsletter. English. Twelve times a year. Aspen Publishers Inc., 7201 McKinney Circle, Frederick MD 21701. **Tel** (800)234-1660, (301)698-7100, FAX (301)251-5784, telex 5106014543. **ED** Nathan Hershey, LLB. **LC** KF3825.A15; H67. **DD** 344.73/03211/05; 347.304321105. **NLM** W1; HO812IF. **Pr Rev.** ***Continued by*** *Hospital Law Manual Bulletin, 1065-2817.*
**Desc:** Goal is to deliver facts, strategies, and insights to ensure that decisions made in today's legal environment are informed. Addresses issues such as malpractice concerns, credentialing requirements, peer review issues, legal aspects of staff privileges, termination, and withholding of care.
**Ind/Abst** Health Devices Alerts; Hospit. Health Admin. Index (Nov. 1988-).

II/0970-1982
**INDIAN JOURNAL OF FORENSIC SCIENCES : THE OFFICIAL PUBLICATION OF THE FORENSIC SCIENCE SOCIETY OF INDIA.** **Added/Corp** Forensic Science Society of India. Vol. 1, No. 1 (Jan. 1987)-. Periodical. English. qt. $40.00. Forensic Science Society of India, Madras, India. **(Subscription address:** Prints India, 11 Darya Ganj, New Delhi 110002 India.) **LC** RA1001; .I53. **DD** 614/.1/05. **NLM** W1; IN208V. ***Continues*** *Journal of the Forensic Science Society of India, 0970-1974.*

GW/0937-9827
**INTERNATIONAL JOURNAL OF LEGAL MEDICINE.** Vol. 104, No. 1 (Dec. 1990)-. Periodical. English (summaries and/or abstracts in German). bm. DM894.00. Springer-Verlag GmbH & Company KG, Heidelberger Platz 3, D 14197 Berlin Germany. **Tel** 011 49 30 8207223, FAX 011 49 30 8214091, telex 183 319 SPBLN D. **(Subscription address:** Springer Verlag New York Inc. / for North America, 44 Hartz Way, Secaucus NJ 07096.) **NLM** W1; IN769N. **CODEN** IJLMEA. **[CCC].** available on microfilm from University Microfilms International (UMI). Documents available from The Genuine Article. ***Continues*** *Zeitschrift fur Rechtsmedizin.*
**Ind/Abst** Curr. Contents Clin. Med.; EMBASE; Health Plan. Adminis.; Index Med. (1990-); Res. Alert [Full Cov.]; Sci. Cit. Index; SCISEARCH; Soc. Sci. Cit. Index [Select. Cov.].

UK/0334-3049
**INTERNATIONAL JOURNAL OF MEDICINE AND LAW.** (THE INTERNATIONAL JOURNAL OF MEDICINE AND LAW : IJML.). [Int. j. med. law]. **Added/Corp** Applied Scientific Research Co. Vol. 1, No. 1 (Summer 1979)-. Periodical. English. qt. $50.00. Turtledove Publishing, 15 Kinneret Street, PO Box 1337, Ramat Gan Israel. **LC** K9; .N849. **DD** 344/.041/05. **NLM** W1 IN769S. **[CCC].**
**Ind/Abst** Bibliogr. Mission.

US/8755-4933
**INTERNATIONAL MICROFORM JOURNAL OF LEGAL MEDICINE AND FORENSIC SCIENCES.** ***Ceased.*** [Int. microform. j. leg. med. forensic sci.]. Vol. 14 (Spring 1979)-?. Periodical. Multiple languages. qt. University Microfilms International, 300 North Zeeb Road, Ann Arbor MI 48106-1346. **Tel** (313)761-4700, (800)521-0600 Exts. 2490, 2491, FAX (313)973-1540. **DD** 614. **NLM** W1; IN824R. ***Continues*** *International Microform Journal of Legal Medicine.*

FR/0249-6208
**JOURNAL DE MEDECINE LEGALE, DROIT MEDICAL.** [J. med. leg., droit med.]. **VFOAT** Medecine Legale, Droit Medical. Vol. 24, No. 1 (Jan./Feb. 1981)-. Academic Scholarly Publication. English (French). Eight times a year. 930.46F (individuals), 1,077.38F (institutions) France; 1,155.00F (individuals), 1,320.00F (institutions) others. Editions Alexandre Lacassagne, 162 Avenue Lacassagne, 69424 Lyon Cedex 03 France. **Tel** 011 33 72 334040. **(Subscription address:** 7A Boulevard de Perolles, CH-1701 Fribourg Switzerland) **LC** RA1001; .B84. **DD** 614/.1/05. **NLM** W1 JO322M. **CODEN** JMLMD7. **[CCC].** Documents available from CASDDS. ***Continues*** *Medecine Legale, Toxicologie, 0241-6751.*
**Desc:** Includes the proceedings of the meetings of the Society of Medicine and Legal Criminology in France.
**Ind/Abst** Chem. Abstr. (1981-1985); EMBASE; Life Sci. Collect.; SCISEARCH.

UK/0015-7368
**JOURNAL - FORENSIC SCIENCE SOCIETY.** (JOURNAL OF THE FORENSIC SCIENCE SOCIETY.). [J. - Forensic Sci. Soc.]. **Added/Corp** Forensic Science Society. California Association of Criminalists. Vol. 22, No. 1 (Jan. 1982)-. Academic Scholarly Publication. English. qt (Jan., Apr., July, Oct.). £80.00. Forensic Science Society, Mt. Parade Clarke House, Harrogate, North Yorkshire HG1 1BX England. **Tel** 011 44 423 506068, FAX 011 44 423 530948. **ED** Dr. Brian Caddy. **CODEN** FSSJAS. cum. index. **Bk Rev. Ad Acc. Pr Rev. Circ:** 2,500 (ctrl). Documents available from The Genuine Article, CASDDS. ***Continues*** *Journal (Forensic Science Society), 0015-7368.*
**Desc:** Contains original articles, reviews, abstracts, editorial comment and correspondence. A must for every practising forensic scientist and those in associated professions: specialist investigators, police, pathology, law, etc.
**Ind/Abst** Anal. Abstr.; Chem. Abstr.; Curr. Contents Clin. Med.; Curr. Law Index (1982-); EMBASE; Index Med.; Index Dent. Lit.; Index Vet.; Leg. Resour. Index (1982-); LegalTrac (1980-); Mass Spect. Bull.; Life Sci. Collect.; Res. Alert [Full Cov.]; Rev. Agric. Entomol.; Sci. Cit. Index; SCISEARCH; Small Anim. Abstr. Bibliogr.; Soc. Sci. Cit. Index [Select. Cov.]; Vet. Bull.

UK/1353-1131
**JOURNAL OF CLINICAL FORENSIC MEDICINE.** (19??)-. Periodical. English. Four times a year. £110.00 Europe; £111.00 Other (Institutions). Churchill Livingstone, 1-3 Baxter's Place, Leith Walk, Edinburgh EH1 3AF Scotland. **Tel** 011 44 31 556 2424, FAX 011 44 31 558 1278, telex 727511. **(Subscription address:** Maruzen Company Ltd., PO Box 5050, Import & Export Department, Tokyo 100 31 Japan.)

US/0895-173X
**JOURNAL OF FORENSIC IDENTIFICATION.** (JOURNAL OF FORENSIC IDENTIFICATION : OFFICIAL PUBLICATION OF THE INTERNATIONAL ASSOCIATION FOR IDENTIFICATION.). [J. forensic identif.]. **Added/Corp** International Association for Identification. Vol. 38, No. 1 Jan./Feb. (1988)-. Periodical. English. Six times a year (Jan., Mar., May, July, Sept., Nov.). $70.00 (individuals), $90.00 (institutions) North America; $110.00 others. International Association for Identification, PO Box 2423, Alameda CA 94501. **Tel** (510)865-2174. **ED** John P. Neilson. **LC** HV8073; .I3. **DD** 363.2/5/05. Index available. **Bk Rev. Pr Rev. Circ:** 2,500 (ctrl). available on microfilm and microfiche from University Microfilms International (UMI). ***Continues*** *Identification News, 0019-1450.*
**Ind/Abst** Crim. Justice Period. Index.

US/0022-1198
**JOURNAL OF FORENSIC SCIENCES.** [J. forensic sci.]. **Added/Corp** American Academy of Forensic Sciences. American Society for Testing and Materials. **VFOAT** Forensic Sciences. Vol. 1, No. 1 (Jan. 1956)-. Academic Scholarly Publication. English. Six times a year. $124.00 North America; $136.00 other. American Society for Testing and Materials, 1916 Race Street, Philadelphia PA 19103. **Tel** (215)299-5585, FAX (215)299-9679, telex 710 670 1037. **LC** RA1001; .A57. **DD** 340.6. **NLM** W1 JO659. **CODEN** JFSCAS. **[CCC]. Pr Rev.** available on microfilm and microfiche from University Microfilms International (UMI). Documents available from The Genuine Article, BIOSIS Document Express, CASDDS.
**Ind/Abst** Abstr. Bull. Inst. Pap. Sci. Tech.; Abstr. Anthropol. (19??-); AGRICOLA; Biol. Abstr. (1988-); Chem. Abstr.; Crim. Justice Abstr.; Crim. Justice Period. Index; Crim. Penol. Police Sci. Abstr. (1985-); Cumul. Index Nurs. Allied Health Lit.; Curr. Contents Clin. Med.; Curr. Law Index (1980-); EMBASE; Energy Res. Abstr.; Health Devices Alerts; Highw. Res. Abstr.; Index Med.; INIS Atomindex [Micro.]; Int. Aerosp. Abstr.; Leg. Resour. Index (1980-); LegalTrac (1980-); Life Sci. Collect.; Psychol. Abstr. (1989-); PsycINFO; PsycLit; Res. Alert [Full Cov.]; Rev. Med. Vet. Entomol.; Sci. Cit. Index; SCISEARCH; Soc. Sci. Cit. Index [Select. Cov.].

US/1044-6419
**JOURNAL OF LAW AND HEALTH.** [J. law health]. **Added/Corp** Cleveland-Marshall College of Law. Vol. 1, No. 1 (1985/86)-. Periodical. English. sa. $20.00. Cleveland State University / Office of Bursar, 1983 East 24th Steet, Cleveland OH 44115. **Tel** (216)687-3615. **ED** Tonda Moore & Durin Rogers. **LC** K10; .O87327. **DD** 344.73/041/05; 347.3044105. **NLM** W 32.5; AA1 JO738.
**Ind/Abst** Health Ref. Cent. (1987-) [Select. Cov.]; Index Leg. Period.; Leg. Resour. Index; LegalTrac (1980-).

US/0194-7648
**JOURNAL OF LEGAL MEDICINE (CHICAGO. 1979), THE.** (THE JOURNAL OF LEGAL MEDICINE.). [J. leg. med.]. **Added/Corp** American College of Legal Medicine. (April 1979)-. Periodical. English. qt. £81.00 UK; $134.00 other. Taylor & Francis Ltd., Rankine Road, Basingstoke Hampshire, RG24 8PR United Kingdom. **Tel** 011 44 256 840366, FAX 011 44 256 479438, telex 858540. **(Subscription address:** Taylor & Francis Inc., 1900 Frost Road, Suite 101, Bristol PA 19007-1598.) **ED** Theodore R. LeBlang, Esq (editor's address: Southern Illinois University School of Medicine, 801 N Rutledge Street, PO Box 19230, Springfield, IL 62794-9230). **LC** K10; .O8737. **DD** 344.73/041/05; 347.3044105. **NLM** W1 JO745B. **[CCC]. Bk Rev. Ad Acc. Pr Rev.** available on microfilm and microfiche from University Microfilms International (UMI). Documents available from The Genuine Article, ADONIS.
**Desc:** Includes articles and commentaries on topics of interest in legal medicine, health law and policy, professional liability, hospital law, food and drug law, medical legal research and education, the history of legal medicine, and a broad range of other related topics. The official publication of the American College of Legal Medicine.
**Ind/Abst** ADONIS; Crim. Justice Abstr.; Cumul. Index Nurs. Allied Health Lit.; Curr. Contents Soc. Behav. Sci.; Curr. Law Index (1982-); EMBASE; Health Devices Alerts; Index Med.; Index Leg. Period.; Int. Nurs. Index; Leg. Resour. Index (1982-); LegalTrac (1981-); Res. Alert [Full Cov.]; Soc. Sci. Cit. Index [Full Cov.].

US/1046-3607
**JOURNAL OF THE AMERICAN MOSQUITO CONTROL ASSOCIATION. SUPPLEMENT.** [J. Am. Mosq. Control Assoc., Suppl.]. **Added/Corp** American Mosquito Control Association. No. 1, (Dec. 1988)-. Monographic series. English. ir. Price varies per volume. American Mosquito Control Association, PO Box 5416, Lake Charles LA 70606-5416. **Tel** (318)474-2723, FAX (318)439-8615, (318)478-9434. **LC** RA640; .J69. **DD** 614.4/323. **NLM** W1; JO909TB.
**Ind/Abst** AGRICOLA [Full Cov.]; Index Med. (Dec. 1988-); PESTDOC.

II/0579-4749
**JOURNAL OF THE INDIAN ACADEMY OF FORENSIC SCIENCES.** [J. Ind. Acad. Forensic Sci.]. **Main/Corp** Indian Academy of Forensic Sciences. (19??)-. Academic Scholarly Publication. English. $20.00. Journal of Indian Academy of Forensic Sciences, 30 Gora Chand Road, Calcutta 14 India. **(Subscription address:** Prints India, 11 Darya Ganj, New Delhi 110002 India.) **NLM** W1 JO93N. **CODEN** JIFSAW. **Bk Rev. Ad Acc. Circ:** 600 (ctrl). Documents available from CASDDS.
**Ind/Abst** Chem. Abstr.; EMBASE.

BE/0775-0803
**JUS MEDICUM.** [Jus med.]. **Main/Conf** World Congress on Medical Law. **Added/Corp** Rijksuniversiteit te Gent. Centrum voor Medisch Recht. (1976)-. Monographic series. Dutch (English, French and German). ir. Price varies per volume. Rijksuniversiteit van Gent, Medisch Recht Apotheekstraat 5, B-9000 Geny Belgium. **Tel** 3291253116. **NLM** W3; WO541D. ***Continues*** *World Meeting on Medical Law. Jus Medicum.*

US
**LAWS RELATING TO THE PRACTICE OF PHYSICIANS AND SURGEONS, PODIATRISTS, DISPENSING OPTICIANS, SPEECH LANGUAGE PATHOLOGISTS, AUDIOLOGISTS, PHYSICAL THERAPISTS, PSYCHOLOGISTS, HEARING AID DISPENSERS, PHYSICIANS' ASSISTANTS, ACUPUNCTURISTS, RESPIRATORY THERAPISTS, RESEARCH PSYCHOANALYSTS AND MEDICAL ASSISTANTS / MEDICAL BOARD OF CALIFORNIA.** **Main/Corp** California. **Added/Corp** Medical Board of California. **VFOAT** BMQA--Laws. (1991)-. English. Medical Board of California, 1430 Howe Avenue/Suite 85A, Sacramento CA 95825. **Tel** (916)920-6393. ***Continues*** *Laws Relating to the Practice of Medicine and Surgery, Podiatry, Dispensing Opticians, Speech Pathology, Audiology, Physical Therapy, Psychology, Hearing Aid Dispensers, Physicians' Assistants and Acupuncture, Respiratory Therapy, Research Psychoanalysts and Medical Assistants.*

US/1056-4748
**MALPRACTICE BI-WEEKLY NEWSLETTER INDEX OF FRAUD, MEDICAL MISTAKES, DIAGNOSTIC ERRORS, AND ADVERSE REACTIONS, INCLUDING ILLNESSES AND DISEASES CAUSED BY DOCTORS.** (1991)-. Newsletter. English. bw. $240.00. Abbe Publishers Association, Virginia Division, 4111 Gallows Road, Annandale VA 22003.

US/1056-4098
**MEDICAL MALPRACTICE - OB/GYN LITIGATION REPORTER.** ***Title Change.*** [Med. malpract. - ob/gyn litig. report.]. **VFOAT** Medical Malpractice - OB GYN Litigation Reporter; OB/GYN Litigation Reporter. (Apr. 1991)-(July 1993). Periodical. English. mo. Andrews Publications Inc., 1646 West Chester Pike, PO Box 1000, Westtown PA 19395. **Tel** (610)399-6600, (800)345-1101, FAX (610)399-6610. **LC** KF2910.G943; A496. **DD** 346.7303/32/0269;

347.3063320269. ***Continues*** *OB/GYN Litigation Reporter, 0735-9551;* ***Absorbed*** *Medical Malpractice Litigation Reporter.* ***Continued by*** *Health Law Litigation Reporter, 1075-0606.*
**Desc:** This reporter keeps attorneys and medical professionals abreast of the latest medical malpractice, obstetrical and gynecological-related litigation.

US/0025-7591
**MEDICAL TRIAL TECHNIQUE QUARTERLY.** [Med. trial tech. q.]. V. 1- Sept. 1954-. Periodical. English. qt. $100.00. Clark Boardman Callaghan, 155 Pfingsten Road, Deerfield IL 60015. **Tel** (800)323-8067. **ED** Fred Lane. **DD** 614/.1/05. **UDC** 616-091. **NLM** W1 ME5278. cum. index.
**Desc:** Journal on medical-legal subjects, designed for the practicing attorney; litigation issue oriented.
**Ind/Abst** Curr. Law Index (1980-); Energy Res. Abstr. (Aug. 1982-); Index Leg. Period.; Leg. Resour. Index (1980-); LegalTrac (1980-).

GW/0723-1393
**MEDICINE AND LAW.** [Med. law]. Vol. 1, No. 1 (June 1982)-. Periodical. English. qt. $100.00 (one year); $180.00 (two year). International Center Medicine and Law, PO Box 6975, Mmabatho 8681, Bophuthatswana South Africa. **Tel** 011 27 140 842470, FAX 011 27 140 24894. **LC** K13; .E28. **DD** 344/.041/05; 342.4105. **NLM** W1 ME649F. **[CCC]. Bk Rev. Ad Acc.** available on microfilm from University Microfilms International (UMI).
**Desc:** Dealing with medico-legal issues. Contains articles, court-decisions, and legislation on medical law, forensic medicine, medicine and law, psychiatry and law, psychology and law, and more.
**Ind/Abst** Crim. Penol. Police Sci. Abstr.; EMBASE; Index Med.

UK/0025-8024
**MEDICINE, SCIENCE, AND THE LAW.** [Med., sci. law]. **Added/Corp** British Academy of Forensic Sciences. Vol. 1, No. 1 Oct. (1960)-. Academic Scholarly Publication. English. Four times a year (Jan., Apr., July, Oct.). £55.00 UK & Ireland; £65.00 others. Chiltern Publishing, 18 Burgess Wood Road, Beaconsfield Bucks HP9 1EQ England. **Tel** 011 44 494 673062, FAX 011 44 494 678914. **LC** K13; .E3. **DD** 614/.1/05. **NLM** W1 ME655. **CODEN** MDSLA6. **[CCC].** Index available in last issue of volume--attached. **Bk Rev**, (Qty: 10). **Ad Acc, Adv Mgr:** Alex Reeve. **Pr Rev. Acid Free. Circ:** 2,000. Documents available from The Genuine Article, CASDDS.
**Desc:** Academic journal featuring topics associated with forensic science: medicine, science, law, forensic odontology, etc. Contains information on recent cases of coronership and pathology.
**Ind/Abst** Arts Humanit. Citation Index [Select. Cov.]; Chem. Abstr. (1960-1983); Coal Abstr.; Crim. Penol. Police Sci. Abstr.; Curr. Contents Clin. Med.; Curr. Contents Soc. Behav. Sci.; Curr. Law Index (1980-); EMBASE; Index Med.; Leg. Resour. Index (1980-); LegalTrac (1980-); Life Sci. Collect.; Res. Alert [Full Cov.]; Rev. Med. Vet. Entomol.; Saf. Health Work; Sci. Cit. Index; SCISEARCH; Soc. Sci. Cit. Index [Full Cov.]; SportSearch.

UK/0025-8172
**MEDICO-LEGAL JOURNAL, THE.** [Med.-legal j.]. **Added/Corp** Medico-Legal Society (Great Britain). **VFOAT** Medico Legal Journal. Vol. 15, No. 1 (Jan./March 1947)-. Academic Scholarly Publication. English. Four times a year (Mar., June, Sept., Dec.). £30.00. Dramrite Printers Limited, 129 Long Lane Southwark, London SE1 4PL England. **Tel** 011 44 71 407 4077, FAX 011 44 71 378 1538. **DD** 614/.1/05. **NLM** W1 ME768P. ***Continues*** *Medico-Legal and Criminological Review, 0302-1637.*
**Ind/Abst** Appl. Soc. Sci. Index Abstr.; Cumul. Index Nurs. Allied Health Lit.; EMBASE; Index Med.; Leg. Resour. Index; LegalTrac (1980-).

US
**MEDICOLEGAL-GRAM / OFFICE OF THE CHIEF MEDICAL EXAMINER.** Vol. 1, No. 1 (July 1980)-. Periodical. English. qt. Free. Board of Medicolegal Investigations, Office of the Chief Medical Examiner, 901 North Stonewall, Oklahoma City OK 73117. **Tel** (405)239-7141. **ED** Fred B Jordan and Bettye Davenport. **LC** RA1001; .M54. **DD** 614/.1/05. **UDC** 613.98. **Circ:** 960. ***Continues*** *Oklahoma Journal of Forensic Medicine, 0363-2679.*
**Desc:** Published for the edification of county medical examiners and law enforcement personnel. Different subjects are written about including drug abuse, and unusual deaths.

GW/0176-7151
**MEDICOLEGAL LIBRARY.** [Med.leg. libr.]. Vol. 1 (1984)-. Monographic series. English. sa. Price varies per volume. Springer-Verlag GmbH & Company KG, Heidelberger Platz 3, D 14197 Berlin Germany. **Tel** 011 49 30 8207223, FAX 011 49 30 8214091, telex 183 319 SPBLN D. **(Subscription address:** Springer Verlag New York Inc. / for North America, 44 Hartz Way, Secaucus NJ 07096.**) ED** A. Carmi. **NLM** W1; ME768TR. **CODEN** MEMEEY. Documents available from BIOSIS Document Express.
**Ind/Abst** Biol. Abstr. (1985-).

GW/0176-4284
**MEDIZIN IN RECHT UND ETHIK.** Vol. 12 (1983)-. Monographic series. German. ir. Price varies per volume. Ferdinand Enke Verlag, Ruedigerstrasse 14, D-70469 Stuttgart Germany. **Tel** 011 49 711 8931124, 011 49 711 893123. **ED** Albin Eser and Eduard Seidler. **NLM** W1 ME811F. ***Continues*** *Medizin und Recht, 0340-9511.*

GW/0723-8886
**MEDIZINRECHT.** (MEDIZINRECHT : MEDR.). [Medizinrecht]. **Added/Corp** Deutsche Gesellschaft fuer Medizinrecht. **VFOAT** MedR. Vol. 1, 1 (Jan./Feb. 1983)-. Periodical. German. Twelve times a year. DM558.00. Springer-Verlag GmbH & Company KG, Heidelberger Platz 3, D 14197 Berlin Germany. **Tel** 011 49 30 8207223, FAX 011 49 30 8214091, telex 183 319 SPBLN D. **(Subscription address:** Springer Verlag New York Inc. / for North America, 44 Hartz Way, Secaucus NJ 07096.**) ED** F Laufs and H Narr. **LC** KK6206.A13; M43. **DD** 344.43/041/05; 344.3044105. **NLM** W1 ME856. **[CCC].** available on microfilm and microfiche from University Microfilms International (UMI).
**Desc:** Covers medicine as related to and affected by law in areas such as rights of patients and of hospital administrators, medical ethics, medical taxes and welfare patients.

IT/0026-4849
**MINERVA MEDICOLEGALE : ORGANO UFFICIALE DELLA SOCIETA ITALIANA DI MMEDICINA LEGALE E DELLE ASSICURAZIONI. Added/Corp** Societa Italiana di Medicina Legale e delle Assicurazioni. Associazione Italiana di Medicina Legale e delle Assicurazioni. Vol. 70 (May 1950)-. Italian. qt. $90.00 (individuals), $140.00 (institutions). Edizioni Minerva Medica, Corso Bramante 83-85, 10126 Turin Italy. **Tel** 011 39 11 678282, FAX 011 39 11 674502. **ED** T Oliaro. **LC** HV6004; .A7. **NLM** W1 MI648. **Bk Rev. Ad Acc.** available on microfilm from University Microfilms International (UMI). ***Continues*** *Archivio di Antropologia Criminale, Psichiatria, e Medicina Legale.*
**Desc:** Journal addressed to practitioners and specialists in forensic medicine and criminal anthropology in Italy and abroad. It deals with topics in scientific practice and research.
**Ind/Abst** CIS Abstr.; Saf. Health Work.

US/0749-1042
**NATIONAL FORENSIC JOURNAL.** [Natl. forensic j.]. **Added/Corp** National Forensic Association. Vol. 1, No. 1 (Spring 1983)-. Periodical. English. sa (Apr. and Oct.). $10.00. Suffolk University / Communications, Department of Communications, 41 Temple Street, Boston MA 02114. **Tel** (617)573-8504. **ED** Sheryl A. Freidley. **LC** WMLC 93/1529. **DD** 808. **Bk Rev. Ad Acc. Circ:** 325 (ctrl).
**Desc:** Encourages contributions from authors who represent all aspects of forensics including readers' theatre and debate.

US/0363-2679
**OKLAHOMA JOURNAL OF FORENSIC MEDICINE.** English. ir. Board of Medicolegal Investigations, Office of the Chief Medical Examiner, 901 North Stonewall, Oklahoma City OK 73117. **Tel** (405)239-7141. **LC** RA1001; .O37. **DD** 614/.19. **UDC** 340.6.

US/0741-7470
**ORTHOPEDIC SURGEONS' LEGAL LETTER.** [Orthoped. surg. leg. lett.]. **VFOAT** Legal Letter. Periodical. English. Free. Merck Sharp and Dohme / NJ, PO Box 2000, Rahway NJ 07065. **LC** KF2910.O78; A136. **DD** 344.73/0412; 347.304412. **UDC** 617.3:614.25(73).

UK/0308-0242
**POLICE SURGEON, THE.** (THE POLICE SURGEON : JOURNAL OF THE ASSOCIATION OF POLICE SURGEONS OF GREAT BRITAIN.). [Police surg.]. Periodical. English. sa. $20.00. Association Police Surgeons Great Britain, Creaton House, Creaton Nhmptn NN6 NN6 8ND England. **NLM** W1; PO198C.
**Ind/Abst** EMBASE.

BE
**PROCEEDINGS / CONGRESS OF THE INTERNATIONAL ACADEMY OF FORENSIC AND SOCIAL MEDICINE.** 12th (1982)-. Proceedings. English. 39 rue Dos Fanchon, B-4020 Liege Belgium. **Tel** 87 22 21 98. ***Continues*** *Acta Medicinae Legalis et Socialis.*
**Ind/Abst** Index Med.

GW/0172-116X
**RECHT UND MEDIZIN.** [Recht Med.]. **VFOAT** Recht & Medizin. Vol. 1, (1979)-. Monographic series. German. ir. Price varies per volume. **ED** E. Deutsch, A. Laufs, and H. L. Schreiber. **LC** UNC. **NLM** W1 RE1093.

GW/0937-9819
**RECHTSMEDIZIN BERLIN.** [Rechtsmedizin Berl.]. (1991)-. Periodical. German (summaries and/or abstracts in English). Four times a year. DM266.00. Springer-Verlag GmbH & Company KG, Heidelberger Platz 3, D 14197 Berlin Germany. **Tel** 011 49 30 8207223, FAX 011 49 30 8214091, telex 183 319 SPBLN D. **(Subscription address:** Springer Verlag New York Inc. / for North America, 44 Hartz Way, Secaucus NJ 07096.**) ED** M Staak. **UDC** 340.6. **[CCC].** Index available. **Bk Rev. Ad Acc.** ctrl circ. available on microfilm and microfiche from University Microfilms International (UMI).
**Desc:** A forum for scientific information and critical discussion in all areas of forensic medicine. Includes toxicological, serological, and psychopathological articles, and contributions on malpractice and medical insurance issues.

CK/0120-0097
**REVISTA DEL INSTITUTO NACIONAL DE MEDICINA LEGAL DE COLOMBIA.** [Rev. Inst. Nac. Med. Leg. Colomb.]. **Main/Corp** Instituto Nacional de Medicina Legal de Colombia. Began in 1975. Academic Scholarly Publication. Spanish. sa. Carrera 13 No 7-46, Bogota Colombia. **LC** RA1001. **DD** 614/.19/05. **UDC** 340.6; 616-091. **NLM** W1 RE513EI. **CODEN** RINCDD. Documents available from CASDDS. ***Continues*** *Revista de Medicina Legal de Colombia.*
**Ind/Abst** Chem. Abstr. (1975-1979); EMBASE.

SP/0377-4732
**REVISTA ESPANOLA DE MEDICINA LEGAL.** (1974)-. Periodical. Spanish. Asociacion Nacional de Medicos Forenses, Goya 99, 28009 Madrid Spain. **NLM** W1 RE544N.
**Ind/Abst** Indice Med. Esp.

IT
**RIVISTA ITALIANA DI MEDICINA LEGALE : DOTTRINA, CASISTICA, RICERCA SPERIMENTALE, GIURISPRUDENZE E LEGISLAZIONE.** (19??)-. Academic Scholarly Publication. Italian. Four times a year. L130000.00 Italy; L195000.00 other. Giuffre Editore SPA, Via Busto Arsizio 40, 20151 Milan Italy. **Tel** 011 398 2 38089200. **ED** Francesco Introna.
**Desc:** Presents information on the general problems of doctrine and method. Includes contributions on disciplines which have a bearing on questions of forensic medicine, in regard to application and interpretation of laws.
**Ind/Abst** EMBASE.

US/0276-3079
**SPECIALTY LAW DIGEST. HEALTH CARE (ANNUAL).** ***Ceased.*** (SPECIALTY LAW DIGEST. HEALTH CARE.). [Spec. law dig., Health care]. **VFOAT** Health Care; Specialty Law Digest. Health Care Cases; Specialty Digest. Health Care Law. Digest V. 1, Mar. (1979)-?. English. mo. Specialty Digest Publications, PO Box 24439, Minneapolis MN 55424. **Tel** (612)823-4220. **LC** KF3821.A59. **DD** 344.73/041/02648; 347. 3044102648. **UDC** 351.84:614.2(73). **NLM** W 32.5 AA1; S7sa.

US
**SPECIALTY LAW DIGEST. HEALTH CARE LAW. VFOAT** Health Care Law; Specialty Law Digest. Health Care; Specialty Digest. Health Care. No. 149 (July 1991)-. Periodical. English. mo. $390.00 US; $411.00 Canada and Mexico; $422.00 other. Specialty Digest Publications, PO Box 24439, Minneapolis MN 55424. **Tel** (612)823-4220. **NLM** W 32.5; AA1 S7s. Index available (bound in all issues). ***Continues*** *Specialty Law Digest : Health Care, 0198-8788.*
**Ind/Abst** Hospit. Health Admin. Index.

RU/0039-4521
**SUDEBNO-MEDICINSKAJA EKSPERTIZA.** (SUDEBNOMEDITSINSKAIA EKSPERTIZA.). [Sud.-med. ekspert.]. **Added/Corp** Soviet Union. Ministerstvo Zdravookhraneniia. Vol. 1 (1958)-. Academic Scholarly Publication. Russian (summaries and/or abstracts in English). Four times a year. $69.95. Izdatelstvo Meditsina / Russian Academy of Medical Sciences, Ulitsa Solyanka 14, 109801 Moscow Russia. **Tel** 011 95 297-05-04. **(Subscription address:** East View Publications Inc., 3020 Harbor Lane North, Suite 110, Minneapolis MN 55447.**) NLM** W1 SU167. **CODEN** SMEZA5. Documents available from BIOSIS Document Express, CASDDS.
**Ind/Abst** Biol. Abstr.; Chem. Abstr.; EMBASE; Index Med.

US/0564-1470
**TRAUMA (NEW YORK, N.Y.).** (TRAUMA.). [Trauma]. Vol. 1 (June 1959)-. Periodical. English. bm (6 issues). $260.00 US; $290.00 Canada. Matthew Bender & Company Inc., 1275 Broadway, Albany NY 12204. **Tel** (800)833-9844, (518)487-3000. **ED** M. Houts. **LC** RA1001; .T7. **DD** 340.6. **NLM** W1 TR257. cum. index.
**Ind/Abst** Curr. Law Index (1980-); Leg. Resour. Index (1980-); LegalTrac (1980-).

RU
**VOPROSY TRAVMATOLOGII, TOSIKOLOGII, SKOROPOSTIZHNOI SMERTI I DEONTOLOGII V EKSPERTNOI PRAKTIKE. Added/Corp** Moscow. Biuro Sudebnomeditsinskoi Ekspertizy. (1966)-.

Russian. Izdatelstvo Meditsina / Russian Academy of Medical Sciences, Ulitsa Solyanka 14, 109801 Moscow Russia. **Tel** 011 95 297-05-04. **NLM** W1 VO644Y. ***Continues*** *Voprosy Travmatologii, Skoropostizh Skoropostizhnoi Smerti i Deontologii V Ekspertnoi Praktike.*

US/1055-0305
**WOUND BALLISTICS REVIEW. See** Law-Law Enforcement and Criminology.

GW/0722-3056
**ZENTRALBLATT RECHTSMEDIZIN.** [Zentralbl. Rechtsmed.]. **Added/Corp** Deutsche Gesellschaft fur Rechtsmedizin. **VFOAT** Rechtsmedizin; Legal Medicine. Vol. 24, No. 1 (1982)-. English (German). Twenty-six times a year. DM4898.00. Springer-Verlag GmbH & Company KG, Heidelberger Platz 3, D 14197 Berlin Germany. **Tel** 011 49 30 8207223, FAX 011 49 30 8214091, telex 183 319 SPBLN D. **(Subscription address:** Springer Verlag New York Inc. / for North America, 44 Hartz Way, Secaucus NJ 07096.**) ED** J B Dalgaard, J Gerchow, G Schmidt, F Schwarzfischer, and M Valverius. **LC** RA1001; .Z46. **DD** 614/.1. **NLM** ZW 700 Z56. **[CCC]. *Continues*** *Zentralblatt fur die Gesamte Rechtsmedizin und Ihre Grenzgebiete, 0044-4154.*
**Desc:** Covers deaths by suicide, traffic accidents, murder; criminology, industrial medicine, insurance, liability; psychology and psychiatry; and symposia proceedings.

## GASTROENTEROLOGY

BE/0001-5644
**ACTA GASTRO-ENTEROLOGICA BELGICA.** [Acta gastro-enterol. belg.]. **Added/Corp** Societe Royale Belge de Gastro-Enterologie. Vol. 9 (1946)-. Academic Scholarly Publication. French (Dutch and German; summaries and/or abstracts in English, French, Dutch and German). Six times a year. 2700F Belgium; 3000F others. Association for the Society of Scientifique Medica Belgique, Avenue Circulaire 138A, B-1180 Brussels Belgium. **Tel** 011 32 2 3745158. **NLM** W1 AC804. Index Available, published separately, free-automatically sent. **Pr Rev.** Documents available from The Genuine Article. ***Continues*** *Journal Belge de Gastro-Enterologie, 0301-7354.*
**Ind/Abst** Curr. Contents Clin. Med.; EMBASE; Health Plan. Adminis.; Index Med.; Life Sci. Collect.; Protozoolog. Abstr.; Res. Alert [Select. Cov.]; SCISEARCH.

BO/0253-5513
**ACTA GASTROENTEROLOGICA BOLIVIANA.** (ACTA GASTROENTEROLOGICA BOLIVIANA : PUBLICACION OFICIAL DE LOS INSTITUTOS DE GASTROENTEROLOGIA BOLIVIANO-JAPONES.). [Acta gastroenterol. Boliv.]. **Added/Corp** Institutos de Gastroenterologia Boliviano-Japones. Vol. 1, No. 1 (Jan./April 1981)-. Academic Scholarly Publication. English (Spanish; summaries and/or abstracts in Spanish). Three times a year. $b22.20 institutions, $b24.00 individuals Bolivia; $b24.20 institutions, $b26.00 individuals other. Administrador Acta Gastroenterologica, Japones Catilla 8578, La Paz Bolivia. **NLM** W1 AC804G. **CODEN** AGBODQ. Documents available from CASDDS.
**Ind/Abst** Chem. Abstr.

US/0002-9270
**AMERICAN JOURNAL OF GASTROENTEROLOGY, THE.** (THE AMERICAN JOURNAL OF GASTROENTEROLOGY : OFFICIAL PUBLICATION OF THE NATIONAL GASTROENTEROLOGICAL ASSOCIATION.). [Am. j. gastroenterol.]. **Added/Corp** National Gastroenterological Association (U.S.) American College of Gastroenterology. Vol. 21, No. 1 (Jan. 1954)-. Academic Scholarly Publication. English. mo. $199.00 (institution), $149.00 (individual) US; $244.00 (institution), $194.00 (individual), other. Williams & Wilkins Company, 428 East Preston Street, Baltimore MD 21202-3993. **Tel** (410)528-4000, (800)638-6423, FAX (410)528-8596, telex 87669. **(Subscription address:** Williams & Wilkins, PO Box 64380, Baltimore MD 21264.**) ED** Arthur E. Lindner. **LC** RC799; .N33. **NLM** W1 AM452. **CODEN** AJGAAR. **[CCC]. Ad Acc. Pr Rev. Circ:** 4,500. available on microfilm and microfiche from University Microfilms International (UMI). Documents available from The Genuine Article, BIOSIS Document Express, CASDDS, Quick Copies. ***Continues*** *Review of Gastroenterology, 0096-2929.*
**Desc:** Practical, clinically oriented original articles and major reviews of current topics in gastroenterology, for gastroenterologists and internists.
**Ind/Abst** Annals Behav. Med.; Biol. Abstr.; Chem. Abstr.; Curr. Aware. Biol. Sci., CABS; Curr. Contents Clin. Med.; EMBASE; Energy Res. Abstr.; Health Devices Alerts; Health Plan. Adminis.; Helminthol. Abstr. (1991-); Immunol. Abstr.; Index Med.; INIS Atomindex [Micro.]; Iowa Drug Inf. Serv.; Maize Abstr.; Microbiol. Abstr. Sect. B; Microbiol. Abstr. Sect. C; Mod. Med.; Nutr. Res. Newsl.; Life Sci. Collect.; PESTDOC; Physic. Medline Plus; Protozoolog. Abstr.; Ref. Upd. Clinical Ed.; Ref. Upd. Deluxe Ed.; Res. Alert [Full Cov.]; Rev. Agric. Entomol.; Rev. Med. Vet. Entomol.; Rev. Med. Vet. Mycology; Sci. Cit. Index; SCISEARCH; Soc. Sci. Cit. Index [Select. Cov.]; Sug. Indus. Abstr.; Virol. AIDS Abstr.

US/0193-1857
**AMERICAN JOURNAL OF PHYSIOLOGY : GASTROINTESTINAL AND LIVER PHYSIOLOGY. See** Biology-Physiology.

FR/0066-2070
**ANNALES DE GASTROENTEROLOGIE ET D'HEPATOLOGIE.** [Ann. gastroenterol. hepatol.]. (1970)-. Academic Scholarly Publication. French. bm. 1050.00F France; 1460.00F other. Expansion Scientifique Francaise, 31 Boulevard de la Tour-Maubourg, 75007 Paris France. **Tel** 011 33 1 40 62 64 00, 011 33 1 40626439. **NLM** W1 AN335K. **CODEN** AGHPBN. **[CCC]. Pr Rev.** Documents available from The Genuine Article, BIOSIS Document Express. ***Continues*** *Actualites Hepato-Gastro-Enterologiques.*
**Ind/Abst** Biol. Abstr.; Curr. Contents Clin. Med.; EMBASE; Energy Res. Abstr. (Jan. 1971-); Health Plan. Adminis.; Helminthol. Abstr.; Index Med.; Nutr. Abstr. Rev., Ser. A, Hum. Exp.; Life Sci. Collect.; Res. Alert [Select. Cov.]; Soc. Sci. Cit. Index [Select. Cov.].

UK/0952-6293
**ANNUAL OF GASTROINTESTINAL ENDOSCOPY.** (1988)-. English. an (May). $95.00. Current Science / England, Middlesex House, 34-42 Cleveland Street, London W1P 5FB England. **Tel** 011 44 71 580 8393, 011 44 71 323 0323, FAX 011 44 81 580 1938. **(Subscription address:** Current Science, 20 North 3rd Street, Philadelphia PA 19106.**) ED** P. B. Cotton, G. N. J. Tytgat and C. B. Williams. **NLM** W1; AN756F. **Circ:** 7,500.
**Desc:** Targeted to physicians, endoscopists, surgeons, radiologists and others interested in gastroenterology and gastrointestinal imaging or therapy. Reviews the most important papers of each year.

BG/0253-5386
**ANNUAL REPORT - INTERNATIONAL CENTRE FOR DIARRHOEAL DISEASE RESEARCH.** (ANNUAL REPORT / INTERNATIONAL CENTRE FOR DIARRHOEAL DISEASE RESEARCH, BANGLADESH.). [Annu. rep. - Int. Cent. Diarrhoeal Dis. Res.]. **Main/Corp** International Centre for Diarrhoeal Disease Research, Bangladesh. 1979-. English. an. **NLM** W1 IN719R. ***Continues*** *Annual Report of the Cholera Research Laboratory.*

IT/1120-8651
**ARGOMENTI DI GASTROENTEROLOGIA CLINICA.** [Argom. gastroenterol. clinic.]. (1988)-. Italian. Eight times a year. L12000 Italy. Masson S.P.A, Via Statuto 2/4, 20121 Milan Italy. **Tel** 011 39 2 63671, FAX 011 39 2 6367211.

BL/0004-2803
**ARQUIVOS DE GASTROENTEROLOGIA.** (ARQUIVOS DE GASTROENTEROLOGIA. ARCHIVES OF GASTROENTEROLOGY.). [Arq. gastroenterol.]. **Added/Corp** Instituo Brasileiro de Estudos e Pesquisas de Gastroenterologia. **VFOAT** Archives of Gastroenterology. Vol. 1 (Jan./March 1964)-. Academic Scholarly Publication. Portuguese (English). qt (Jan., Apr., July, Oct.). $50.00. Arquivos de Gastroenterologia, IBEPEGE, Rua Dr. Seng, 320, CP 6209, 01331-020 Sao Paulo, Brazil. **Tel** 55 11 289-2768, FAX 55 11 289-5057. **ED** Nelson Henrique Michelsohn. **NLM** W1 AR901M. **CODEN** ARQGAF. Index available. **Bk Rev**, (Qty: 12-15). **Ad Acc, Adv Mgr:** Jarbas Antonio de Godoy. **Circ:** 2,500. available in microform from University Microfilms International (UMI). Documents available from UMI Article Clearinghouse, CASDDS.
**Desc:** A medical journal covering research and studies on the function and disorders of the digestive system, with corollary articles on pediatric gastroenterology and clinical progress reports.
**Ind/Abst** Chem. Abstr. (1964-1982); EMBASE; Health Plan. Adminis.; Helminthol. Abstr. (1991-); Index Med. (Jan. 1978-); Nutr. Abstr. Rev., Ser. B, Live Feeds and Feed.; Nutr. Abstr. Rev., Ser. A, Hum. Exp.; Protozoolog. Abstr.; Rev. Med. Vet. Entomol.; Soyabean Abstr.; Trop. Dis. Bull.

UK/0950-3528
**BAILLIERE'S CLINICAL GASTROENTEROLOGY.** [Bailliere's clin. gastroenterol.]. **VFOAT** Clinical Gastroenterology; Gastroenterology. Vol. 1, No. 1 (Jan. 1987)-. Academic Scholarly Publication. English. qt (4 issues). £94.00 (institution). Harcourt Brace & Company Ltd., Foots Cray, High Street, Sidcup Kent DA14 5HP England. **Tel** 011 44 81 300 3322, FAX 011 44 81 309 0807. **(Subscription address:** W. B. Saunders Company / North America Subscriptions, c/o Periodicals, 6277 Sea Harbour Drive, 4th Floor, Orlando FL 32887.**) NLM** W1; BA46EJ. **[CCC].** Index available. **Pr Rev.** available on microfilm. Documents available from The Genuine Article, BIOSIS Document Express, CASDDS. ***Continues in part*** *Clinics in Gastroenterology, 0300-5089.*
**Ind/Abst** Biol. Abstr. (1987-); Chem. Abstr. (1987-); CSA Neuro. Abstr. (?-?); Curr. Contents Clin. Med.; EMBASE; Health Plan. Adminis.; Index Med. (Jan. 1987-); Life Sci. Collect. (1987-); Protozoolog. Abstr.; Res. Alert [Full Cov.]; Sci. Cit. Index; SCISEARCH; Trop. Dis. Bull.

US/0736-7120
**BIBLIOGRAPHY OF DIARRHOEAL DISEASES.** (BIBLIOGRAPHY OF ACUTE DIARRHOEAL DISEASES / PROGRAMME FOR CONTROL OF DIARRHOEAL DISEASES.). Vol. 1, No. 1 (Second Half, 1981)-. Bibliography. English. sa. National Library of Medicine, 8600 Rockville Pike, Bethesda MD 20894. **Tel** (301)496-6308. **NLM** ZWI 407 B581.

CN/0835-7900
**CANADIAN JOURNAL OF GASTROENTEROLOGY, THE.** [Can. j. gastroenterol.]. **VFOAT** Journal Canadien de Gastroenterologie. Vol. 1, No. 1 (Oct. 1987)-. Periodical. English (French). bm. $84.00 (institution), $61.00 (individual) US; $122.00 (institution), $94.00 (individual) other except Canada. Pulsus Group Inc., 2902 South Sheridan Way, Oakville Ontario L6J 7L6 Canada. **Tel** (416)829-4770, FAX (416)829-4799. **ED** Abr Thomson and Cn Williams. **DD** 616.3/3/005. **NLM** W1; CA586Y. Index available. **Bk Rev. Ad Acc. Pr Rev. Circ:** 18,500 (ctrl). Documents available from The Genuine Article.
**Desc:** Publishes original papers, case reports and reviews pertaining to gastroenterology and hepatology.
**Ind/Abst** Curr. Contents Clin. Med.; EMBASE; Nutr. Res. Newsl.; Res. Alert [Select. Cov.]; SCISEARCH.

IT/0009-4765
**CHIRURGIA GASTROENTEROLOGICA.** [Chir. gastroenterol.]. **Added/Corp** Collegium Internationale Chirirgiae Digestivae. Vol. 1 (Jan./March 1967)-. Periodical. Italian (summaries and/or abstracts in English). qt. L90000 Italy; $90.00 other. Chirurgia Gastroenterologica, Casella Postale 4236, 00100 Rome Appio Italy. **Tel** 011 39 6 70454246, FAX 011 39 6 7883156. **DD** 617. **NLM** W1 CH8186. **Bk Rev. Ad Acc.**
**Desc:** Articles concerning gastroenterological surgery.
**Ind/Abst** EMBASE.

GW/0177-9990
**CHIRURGISCHE GASTROENTEROLOGIE MIT INTERDISZIPLINAREN GESPRACHEN.** [Chir. Gastroenterol. interdiszip. Gespr.]. Nr. 1 (Apr. 1985)-. Periodical. German (English). qt. $100.00. S. Karger AG, Allschwilerstrasse 10, PO Box - Postfach - Case Postale, CH-4009 Basel Switzerland. **Tel** 011 41 61 306-1111, FAX 011 41 61 306-1234, telex CH 962 652. **ED** A. Akovbiantz, H. Denck, K.J. Paquet, C.E. Zockler. **NLM** W1; CH834H.
**Ind/Abst** Index Med.; Ref. Upd. Deluxe Ed.

US/1046-7165
**CLINICAL ADVANCES IN GASTROENTEROLOGY.** (CLINICAL ADVANCES IN GASTROENTEROLOGY [SOUND RECORDING].). [Clin. adv. gastroenterol.]. **Added/Corp** American College of Gastroenterology. (1989)-. Periodical. English. bm. $145.00 Physicians, $105.00 Residents (members); $160.00 Physicians, $105.00 Residents (nonmembers). Educational Reviews Inc., 6801 Cahaba Valley Road, Birmingham AL 35242. **Tel** (205)991-5188, (800)633-4743, FAX (205)995-1926. **DD** 616.

NE/0165-8719
**CORE JOURNALS IN GASTROENTEROLOGY.** [Core j. gastroenterol.]. (1980)-. English. Eleven times a year (1 volume). Fl549.00. Excerpta Medica Publishing Group, PO Box 548, 1000 AM Amsterdam Netherlands. **Tel** 011 31 20 5803243. **(Subscription address:** Excerpta Medica Journals, PO Box 85, Limerick Ireland.**) NLM** ZWI 100 C797. **CODEN** CJGADI. **[CCC].** available on microfilm from University Microfilms International (UMI).
**Desc:** Part of a series abstracting service of international literature. It is intended to optimize the busy clinician's time by providing an overview of the most significant clinical studies in his/her field.

US/0363-6526
**CURRENT CONCEPTS IN GASTROENTEROLOGY.** ***Suspended.*** Vol. 1 (May 1976)-?. Periodical. English. bm. $50.00. Macmillan Professional Journal, 30 Vreeland Road, Florham Park NJ 07932. **Tel** (201)822-1622, FAX (201)822-2498. **LC** RC799; .C87. **DD** 616.3/005. **NLM** W1 CU7877.

US/0198-8085
**CURRENT GASTROENTEROLOGY.** [Curr. gastroenterol.]. Vol. 1, (1980)-. Academic Scholarly Publication. English. an. $75.00. Mosby Year Book Inc., 11830 Westline Industrial Drive, St Louis MO 63146. **Tel** (800)325-4177, (314)872-8370, FAX (314)432-1380, telex 44-2402. **LC** RC799; .C88. **DD** 616.3. **NLM** W1 CU788JAD. **CODEN** CUGADR. **[CCC].** Documents available from CASDDS.
**Ind/Abst** Chem. Abstr. (1980-1983).

UK/0263-2659
**CURRENT MEDICAL LITERATURE. GASTROENTEROLOGY / THE ROYAL SOCIETY OF MEDICINE. Added/Corp** Royal Society of Medicine (Great Britain). **VFOAT**

Gastroenterology. (198?)-. Periodical. English. qt. £20.00 UK; $40.00 US; £20.00 other (journal or disk). Current Medical Literature Ltd., 40-42 Osnaburgh Street, London NW1 3ND England. **Tel** 011 44 71 4658377, FAX 011 44 71 4658380. **(Subscription address:** Royal Society Medicine Services, 1 Wimpole Street, London W1M 8AE England.**)** **NLM** ZWI 100; C9755.

UK/0267-1379
**CURRENT OPINION IN GASTROENTEROLOGY.** [Curr. opin. gastroenterol.]. Vol. 1, No. 1 (Jan./Feb. 1985)-. Academic Scholarly Publication. English. Six times a year. $134.95 (individual); $269.95 (institution). Current Science / England, Middlesex House, 34-42 Cleveland Street, London W1P 5FB England. **Tel** 011 44 71 580 8393, 011 44 71 323 0323, FAX 011 44 81 580 1938. **(Subscription address:** Current Science, 20 North 3rd Street, Philadelphia PA 19106.**)** **ED** Ian AD Bouchier. **NLM** W1; CU799GD. **CODEN** COGAEK. **[CCC]. Pr Rev. Circ:** 10,000. available on diskette. Documents available from The Genuine Article, CASDDS.
**Desc:** Directed toward researchers and practicing gastroenterologists. Presents review articles from an entire year's literature with annotated references. Each issue features a bibliography of the current world literature published during the previous year.
**Ind/Abst** Chem. Abstr. (1985-); Cumul. Index Nurs. Allied Health Lit.; Curr. Aware. Biol. Sci., CABS; Curr. Contents Clin. Med.; EMBASE; Helminthol. Abstr. (1991-); Protozoolog. Abstr.; Res. Alert [Select. Cov.]; SCISEARCH; Trop. Dis. Bull.

SZ/0012-2823
**DIGESTION.** [Digestion]. Vol. 1 (1968)-. Academic Scholarly Publication. English. bm (6 issues). $547.00. S. Karger AG, Allschwilerstrasse 10, PO Box - Postfach - Case Postale, CH-4009 Basel Switzerland. **Tel** 011 41 61 306-1111, FAX 011 41 61 306-1234, telex CH 962 652. **ED** R. Arnold. **LC** QP141.A1; D5. **DD** 616.3/005. **NLM** W1 DI57. **CODEN** DIGEBW. **[CCC]. Ad Acc. Pr Rev.** available on microfilm and microfiche from University Microfilms International (UMI). Documents available from The Genuine Article, BIOSIS Document Express, CASDDS. ***Supersedes*** *Gastroenterologia.*
**Desc:** Publishes research reports on diseases and pathophysiology of the gastrointestinal tract, liver and pancreas and on gastrointestinal endocrinology. Papers cover investigative physiology in humans and animals, metabolic studies, and extensive clinical work on the etiology, diagnosis, and therapy of human diseases. The journal's coverage of studies on the metabolism and effects of therapeutic drugs carries considerable value for clinicians and investigators beyond the immediate field of gastroenterology.
**Ind/Abst** AGRICOLA [Select. Cov.]; Biol. Abstr.; Chem. Abstr.; Curr. Aware. Biol. Sci., CABS; Curr. Contents Clin. Med.; Curr. Contents Life Sci.; Dairy Sci. Abstr.; EMBASE; Health Plan. Adminis.; Index Med.; Nutr. Abstr. Rev., Ser. B, Live Feeds and Feed.; Nutr. Abstr. Rev., Ser. A, Hum. Exp.; Nutr. Res. Newsl.; Life Sci. Collect.; Pig News Inf.; Protozoolog. Abstr.; Ref. Upd. Clinical Ed.; Ref. Upd. Deluxe Ed.; Res. Alert [Full Cov.]; Sci. Cit. Index; SCISEARCH.

US
**DIGESTIVE DISEASES. VFOAT** NIAMDD Research Advances; NIADDK Research Advances. (1979)-. English. an. $140.00. National Institutes of Health, 9000 Rockville Pike, Bethesda MD 20014. **Tel** (301)496-6975. **NLM** W1 DI572. available on microfiche (Vols. for (1986-) distributed to depository libraries). Documents available from The Genuine Article.
**Desc:** Offers brief reviews that summarize and synthesize new knowledge on normal and abnormal functions of the digestive tract.
**Ind/Abst** Curr. Contents Clin. Med.; Helminthol. Abstr. (1991-); Nutr. Abstr. Rev., Ser. A, Hum. Exp.; Nutr. Res. Newsl.; Res. Alert [Select. Cov.]; SCISEARCH.

US/0163-2116
**DIGESTIVE DISEASES AND SCIENCES.** [Dig. dis. sci.]. New Ser., Vol. 24 (Jan. 1979)-. Academic Scholarly Publication. English. Twelve times a year. $445.00 institutions, $87.00 individuals US; $520.00 institutions, $102.00 individuals other. Plenum Press, 233 Spring Street, New York NY 10013-1578. **Tel** (212)620-8000, (800)221-9369, FAX (212)463-0742, (212)807-1047, telex 23/421139. **ED** Richard L. Wechsler. **LC** RC799; .A63. **DD** 616.3/005. **NLM** W1 DI573. **CODEN** DDSCDJ. **[CCC].** Index available. **Pr Rev.** available on microfilm and microfiche from University Microfilms International (UMI). Documents available from The Genuine Article, BIOSIS Document Express, CASDDS, ADONIS. ***Continues*** *American Journal of Digestive Diseases, 0002-9211.*
**Ind/Abst** Abr. Index Med.; ADONIS; AGRICOLA [Select. Cov.]; Annals Behav. Med.; Biol. Abstr.; Chem. Abstr.; CSA Neuro. Abstr. (?-?); Curr. Aware. Biol. Sci., CABS; Curr. Contents Clin. Med.; Curr. Contents Life Sci.; Dairy Sci. Abstr.; EMBASE; Energy Res. Abstr. (Feb. 1981-); Health Period. Database; Health Plan. Adminis.; Helminthol. Abstr. (19??-19??); Immunol. Abstr.; Index Med. (Jan. 1979-); Index Vet.; INIS Atomindex [Micro.]; Iowa Drug Inf. Serv. (1966-); Microbiol. Abstr. Sect. B; Mod. Med.; Nutr. Abstr. Rev., Ser. B, Live Feeds and Feed.; Nutr. Abstr. Rev., Ser. A, Hum. Exp.; Nutr. Res. Newsl.; Life Sci. Collect.; PESTDOC; Physic. Medline Plus; Pig News Inf.; Protozoolog. Abstr.; Ref. Upd. Basic Ed.; Ref. Upd. Clinical Ed.; Ref. Upd. Deluxe Ed.; Res. Alert [Full Cov.]; Rev. Med. Vet. Mycology; Sci. Cit. Index; SCISEARCH; Soc. Sci. Cit. Index [Select. Cov.]; SportSearch; Virol. AIDS Abstr.

SZ/0257-2753
**DIGESTIVE DISEASES (BASEL).** (DIGESTIVE DISEASES.). [Dig. dis.]. (April 1986)-. Academic Scholarly Publication. English. Six times a year (one volume per year). $335.00. S. Karger AG, Allschwilerstrasse 10, PO Box - Postfach - Case Postale, CH-4009 Basel Switzerland. **Tel** 011 41 61 306-1111, FAX 011 41 61 306-1234, telex CH 962 652. **ED** S.R. Achem. **NLM** W1; DI57D. **CODEN** DIDIEW. **[CCC].** Index available. cum. index. **Ad Acc. Pr Rev. Circ:** 600 (ctrl). available on microfilm; available on microfiche; available in microform. Documents available from BIOSIS Document Express, CASDDS. ***Continues*** *Survey of Digestive Diseases, 0253-4398.*
**Desc:** Covers both clinical and basic science topics in gastrointestinal function disorders. In original and peer-reviewed articles, noted experts synthesize current thinking and practice with their own extensive experience. The contributions encompass a variety of disciplines including medicine, surgery, nutrition, pathology, and the basic sciences. Strives to bridge the communication gap between advances made in the academic setting and their application in patient care.
**Ind/Abst** Biol. Abstr. (1986-); Chem. Abstr. (1986-); Health Plan. Adminis.; Index Med. (1986-); Ref. Upd. Deluxe Ed.; Soc. Sci. Cit. Index [Select. Cov.].

JA/0915-5635
**DIGESTIVE ENDOSCOPY : OFFICIAL JOURNAL OF THE JAPAN GASTROENTEROLOGICAL ENDOSCOPY SOCIETY. Added/Corp** Nihon Shokaki Naishikyo Gakkai. Vol. 1, No. 1 (October 1989)-. Periodical. English. qt. $70.00. Japan Gastroenterological Endoscopy Society, Taimei Building, 22,3 Chome Kanda Ogawa Machi, Chiyoda-ku Tokyo 101 Japan. **Tel** 011 81 3 3291 4111, FAX 011 81 3 3291 5568. **NLM** W1; DI57AL. **Ad Acc, Adv Mgr:** Y. Matsumoto. **Circ:** 1,000.
**Desc:** Study and investigation relating to the various endoscopic techniques used in diagnosis and treatment of digestive diseases.
**Ind/Abst** EMBASE.

SZ/0253-4886
**DIGESTIVE SURGERY.** **See** Medical Science and Technology-Surgery.

US/0012-3706
**DISEASES OF THE COLON & RECTUM.** [Dis. colon rectum]. **Added/Corp** American Society of Colon and Rectal Surgeons. American Proctologic Society. **VAT** Diseases of the Colon and Rectum. Vol. 1 (Jan./Feb. 1958)-. Academic Scholarly Publication. English. mo. $188.00 (institutions), $125.00 (individual) US; $165.00 (individual), $228.00 (institution) other. Williams & Wilkins Company, 428 East Preston Street, Baltimore MD 21202-3993. **Tel** (410)528-4000, (800)638-6423, FAX (410)528-8596, telex 87669. **(Subscription address:** Williams & Wilkins, PO Box 64380, Baltimore MD 21264.**)** **DD** 616.3. **NLM** W1 DI755. **CODEN** DICRAG. **[CCC]. Bk Rev. Ad Acc. Pr Rev. Circ:** 4,379. available on microfilm and microfiche from University Microfilms International (UMI). Documents available from The Genuine Article, BIOSIS Document Express, Quick Copies.
**Desc:** Primarily for surgeons, but also of value to gastroenterologists and internists concerned with surgical management of lower GI tract disorders.
**Ind/Abst** Annals Behav. Med.; Biol. Abstr.; Cumul. Index Nurs. Allied Health Lit.; Curr. Aware. Biol. Sci., CABS; Curr. Contents Clin. Med.; EMBASE; Energy Res. Abstr.; Health Plan. Adminis.; Index Med.; INIS Atomindex [Micro.]; Med. Abstr. Newsl.; Mod. Med.; Nutr. Abstr. Rev., Ser. B, Live Feeds and Feed.; Nutr. Abstr. Rev., Ser. A, Hum. Exp.; Nutr. Res. Newsl.; Life Sci. Collect.; Physic. Medline Plus; Protozoolog. Abstr.; Ref. Upd. Clinical Ed.; Ref. Upd. Deluxe Ed.; Res. Alert [Full Cov.]; Risk Abstr. (19??-19??); Sci. Cit. Index; SCISEARCH; Sug. Indus. Abstr.

GR/1012-0424
**ELLENIKE GASTROENTEROLOGIA.** (HELLENIC JOURNAL OF GASTROENTEROLOGY.). [Ell. gastroenterol.]. (1988)-. Periodical. Multiple languages. qt. $35.00. Hellenic Society of Gastroenterology, 20 22 Ipsilantou St, 106 706 Athens Greece. **Tel** 011 30 1 7232302.
**Ind/Abst** Trop. Dis. Bull.

GW/0013-726X
**ENDOSCOPY.** [Endoscopy]. Vol. 1 (April 1969)-. Academic Scholarly Publication. English (German; summaries and/or abstracts in German). Nine times a year. $274.00. Georg Thieme Verlag Stuttgart, Postfach 301120, D 70451 Stuttgart Germany. **Tel** 011 49 711 89310, FAX 011 49 711 8931298, telex 7 252 275 GTVD. **(Subscription address:** Thieme Medical Publishers Inc., 381 Park Avenue South, New York NY 10016.**)** **ED** M Classen, D L Carr-Locke, K Kawai, R Ottenjann, N Soehendra. **NLM** W1 EN42. **CODEN** ENDCAM. **[CCC]. Pr Rev. Circ:** 1,900. available on microfilm and microfiche from University Microfilms International (UMI). Documents available from The Genuine Article, BIOSIS Document Express.
**Desc:** An interdisciplinary and professional approach to keep users abreast of latest developments and critical discussions of controversial issues in the field. Of interest to: internists, gynecologists, urologists, surgeons, gastroenterologists, otorhinolaryngologists, anesthesiologists, and pulmonologists.
**Ind/Abst** Biol. Abstr.; Curr. Contents Clin. Med.; Curr. Contents Life Sci.; EMBASE; Energy Res. Abstr. (July 1980-); Health Plan. Adminis.; Helminthol. Abstr. (19??-19??); Index Med.; Nutr. Abstr. Rev., Ser. B, Live Feeds and Feed.; Nutr. Abstr. Rev., Ser. A, Hum. Exp.; Protozoolog. Abstr.; Res. Alert [Full Cov.]; Sci. Cit. Index; SCISEARCH.

US/8756-968X
**ENDOSCOPY REVIEW.** [Endosc. rev.]. (1984)-. Periodical. English. mo (Jan./Feb., July/Aug., Nov./Dec. issues combined). $49.00 (one year), $89.00 (two year), $149.00 (three year). Island Publishing Group Inc, PO Box 598, Lawrence NY 11559. **Tel** (516)295-3188. **ED** Harold Jacob. **DD** 616. **NLM** W1; EN422. **Bk Rev. Ad Acc. Circ:** 13,000 (ctrl).
**Desc:** A guide to techniques and products in the application of diagnostic and therapeutic endoscopy to the science of gastroenterology.

GW/0174-1616
**ERGEBNISSE DER GASTROENTEROLOGIE.** Monographic series. German. Price varies per volume. Karl Demeter Verlag, Wuermstrasse 13, Postfach 1660, W 8032 Graefelfing Germany. **Tel** 011 49 89 852033, FAX 011 49 89 9543347, telex 524068 Delta D. **NLM** W1 ZE356B Nr.8 etc.
**Desc:** Consists of congress proceedings of the Deutsche Gesellschaft fur Verdauungs- und Stoffwechselkrankheiten.

UK/0954-691X
**EUROPEAN JOURNAL OF GASTROENTEROLOGY & HEPATOLOGY.** [Eur. j. gastroenterol. hepatol.]. **Added/Corp** European Association for Gastroenterology and Endoscopy. **VFOAT** European Journal of Gastroenterology and Hepatology; Gastroenterology & Hepatology; Gastroenterology and Hepatology. Vol. 1, No. 1 (Aug. 1989)-. Periodical. English. Twelve times a year. $144.95 (individual); $295.00 (institution). Current Science / England, Middlesex House, 34-42 Cleveland Street, London W1P 5FB England. **Tel** 011 44 71 580 8393, 011 44 71 323 0323, FAX 011 44 81 580 1938. **(Subscription address:** Current Science, 20 North 3rd Street, Philadelphia PA 19106.**)** **ED** J. J. Misiewicz. **NLM** W1; EU77DED. **CODEN** EJGHES. **[CCC].** Index available. **Ad Acc. Pr Rev.** available on diskette. Documents available from The Genuine Article.
**Desc:** Directed toward researchers and clinicians involved with gasteroenterology and hepatology. Featuring rapid publication of the foremost data and research. Each issue features a bibliography of the current world literature publishing during the previous month.
**Ind/Abst** Curr. Aware. Biol. Sci., CABS; Curr. Contents Clin. Med.; EMBASE; Helminthol. Abstr. (1991-); Nutr. Abstr. Rev., Ser. A, Hum. Exp.; Res. Alert [Select. Cov.]; SCISEARCH; Soc. Sci. Cit. Index [Select. Cov.].

US/0353-9245
**EXPERIMENTAL AND CLINICAL GASTROENTEROLOGY. Added/Corp** Sveuciliste u Zagrebu. Medicinski Fakultet. **VFOAT** Experimental and Clinical Gastroenterology. Vol. 1, No. 1 (Jan./Mar. 1991)-. Periodical. English. qt. $281.00 The Americas; £188.00 other. Pergamon Press, An Imprint of Elsevier Science Ltd., The Boulevard, Langford Lane, Kidlington, Oxford OX5 1GB United Kingdom. **Tel** 011 44 865 843000, 011 44 865 843699, FAX 011 44 865 843010. **(Subscription address:** Elsevier Science Ltd. Oxford Fulfillment Centre, PO Box 800, Kidlington, Oxford OX5 1DX United Kingdom.**)** **ED** Predrag Sikiric and Gyula Moszik. **NLM** W1; EX464E. **CODEN** ECGAEQ. **[CCC].** available on microfilm and microfiche from University Microfilms International (UMI).
**Ind/Abst** Curr. Aware. Biol. Sci., CABS.

SZ/0302-0665
**FRONTIERS OF GASTROINTESTINAL RESEARCH.** [Front. gastrointest. res.]. Vol. 1 (1975)-. English. an. 250.00F (approx. per volume). S. Karger AG, Allschwilerstrasse 10, PO Box - Postfach - Case Postale, CH-4009 Basel Switzerland. **Tel** 011 41 61 306-1111, FAX 011 41 61 306-1234, telex CH 962 652. **ED** P. Rozen, C. Scarpignato, I.M. Modlin. **NLM** W1 FR946E. **CODEN** FGREDT. Documents available from BIOSIS Document Express, CASDDS. ***Supersedes*** *Bibliotheca Gastroenterologica, 0067-7949.*
**Desc:** This series is designed for both the physician active in the clinical practice of gastroenterology and the gastroenterologist or student engaged in research. Each volume offers a ready reference guide to current progress and a review of past achievement in a particular area of gastrointestinal study. The series covers structural, pathological, and surgical considerations relating to the digestive system, as well as the latest techniques and instrumentation used in the management of gastrointestinal disorders.
**Ind/Abst** Biol. Abstr.; Chem. Abstr. (1975-1984)(19??); Health Plan. Adminis.; Index Med.; Ref. Upd. Deluxe Ed.

UK/0142-8098
**GASTRIC SECRETION.** (1979)-. English. Twenty-four times a year. £115.00. SUBIS, Mansion House, 19 Kingfield Road, Sheffield S11 9AS England. **Tel** 011 44 114 255 4433, FAX 011 44 114 255 4626. **DD** 016.6123. **Bk Rev. Ad Acc.**
**Desc:** Current awareness service for researchers and clinicians.

IT/1120-3757
**GASTROENTEROLOGIA CLINICA.** [Gastroenterol. clin.]. (1986)-. Periodical. Multiple languages. Six times a year. L100000 (individuals) L140000 (institutions). Il Pensiero Scientifico Editore s.r.l., Via Bradano 3C, 00199 Rome Italy. **Tel** 011 39 6 86207158, 86207159, 86207168, 86207169, FAX 011 39 6 86207160. **UDC** 616.3. **Ad Acc, Adv Mgr:** Dott Dalla, **Tel** 06-86207165. Full Page (B&W) L1.650.000. **Circ:** 1,000. ***Continues*** *Clinica Moderna. Serie Gastroenterologia Clinica, 0391-9536.*

JA/0435-1339
**GASTROENTEROLOGIA JAPONICA.** ***Title Change.*** [Gastroenterol. Jpn.]. **Added/Corp** Japanese Society of Gastroenterology. (1966)-. Academic Scholarly Publication. English. bm. Japanese Society of Gastroenterology, G Orient Building 9-13, Ginza 8 chome Chuo-ku, Tokyo 104 Japan. **Tel** 03-573-4297, FAX 03-289-2359. **ED** Hisaaki Shimazu. **NLM** W1 GA455N. **CODEN** GAJABC. Index available. **Ad Acc. Circ:** 3,700. Documents available from The Genuine Article, BIOSIS Document Express, CASDDS. ***Continued by*** *Journal of Gastroenterology, 0944-1174.*
**Desc:** Original articles on gastroenterology, including case records, short communications, editorials, proceedings, etc.
**Ind/Abst** Biol. Abstr.; Chem. Abstr.; Curr. Contents Clin. Med.; EMBASE; Health Plan. Adminis.; Index Med.; Res. Alert [Select. Cov.]; SCISEARCH; Soc. Sci. Cit. Index [Select. Cov.].

SP/0210-5705
**GASTROENTEROLOGIA Y HEPATOLOGIA.** [Gastroenterol. hepatol.]. (1978)-. Academic Scholarly Publication. Spanish (summaries and/or abstracts in English). Ten times a year. $66.00 (surface mail); $86.00 Europe, $105.00 others (airmail). Ediciones Doyma SA, Travesera de Gracia 17 21, 08021 Barcelona Spain. **Tel** 011 34 3 2000711, 011 34 3 4145706, FAX 011 34 3 2091136, telex 51964 INK E. **ED** D. Juan Rodes Teixidor. **NLM** W1; GA456. **CODEN** GHEPDF. **[CCC]. Circ:** 6,000. Documents available from BIOSIS Document Express.
**Desc:** A publication that features with strict scientific exigency the evolved concepts of the pathology on the areas of gastroenterology and liver diseases. Original and leading articles and clinical observations.
**Ind/Abst** Biol. Abstr. (1986-); EMBASE; Indice Med. Esp.

JA/0387-1207
**GASTROENTEROLOGICAL ENDOSCOPY.** [Gastroenterol. endosc.]. **VFOAT** Nihon Shokaki Naishikyo Gakkai Zasshi; Nihon; Naishikyo Gakkaishi. (1959)-. Periodical. Multiple languages. Twelve times a year. $230.00. Japan Gastroenterological Endoscopy Society, Taimei Building, 22,3 Chome Kanda Ogawa Machi, Chiyoda-ku Tokyo 101 Japan. **Tel** 011 81 3 3291 4111, FAX 011 81 3 3291 5568. **(Subscription address:** Kyowa Book Company Inc., 1 38 Kanda Jinbocho Chiyoda-ku, Tokyo 101 Japan.**) DD** 616.3.
**Ind/Abst** EMBASE [Select. Cov.].

FR/0399-8320
**GASTROENTEROLOGIE CLINIQUE ET BIOLOGIQUE.** [Gastroenterol. clin. biol.]. **Added/Corp** Societe Nationale Francaise de Gastro-Enterologie. Vol. 1 (Jan. 1977)-. Academic Scholarly Publication. Multiple languages (English and French). Ten times a year. $257.00. Masson Editeur, Box Postale 22, 41353 Vineuil 16 France. **Tel** 011 33 54 438994. **(Subscription address:** 7A Boulevard de Perolles, CH-1701 Fribourg Switzerland**) NLM** W1 GA456L. **CODEN** GCBIDC. **[CCC]. Pr Rev.** available on microfilm and microfiche from University Microfilms International (UMI). Documents available from The Genuine Article, BIOSIS Document Express, CASDDS. ***Formed by the union of*** *Archives Francaises des Maladies de l'Appareil Digestif, 0003-9772* ***and*** *Biologie et Gastro-Enterologie, 0006-3258.*
**Desc:** Includes the reports of the Society National France Gastroenterology and its subdivisions.
**Ind/Abst** Biol. Abstr.; Chem. Abstr.; Curr. Contents Clin. Med.; Curr. Contents Life Sci.; Dairy Sci. Abstr.; EMBASE; Helminthol. Abstr. (1991-); Hortic. Abstr.; Index Med.; Nutr. Abstr. Rev., Ser. B, Live Feeds and Feed.; Nutr. Abstr. Rev., Ser. A, Hum. Exp.; Life Sci. Collect.; Protozoolog. Abstr.; Res. Alert [Full Cov.]; Rev. Med. Vet. Mycology; Sci. Cit. Index; SCISEARCH; Soc. Sci. Cit. Index [Select. Cov.].

SZ/0302-9255
**GASTROENTEROLOGISCHE FORTBILDUNGSKURSE FUER DIE PRAXIS.** ***Ceased.*** [Gastroenterol. Fortbild.-kurse Prax.]. (19??)-Series Complete with Volume 5. Monographic series. German. ir. S. Karger AG, Allschwilerstrasse 10, PO Box - Postfach - Case Postale, CH-4009 Basel Switzerland. **Tel** 011 41 61 306-1111, FAX 011 41 61 306-1234, telex CH 962 652.
**Ind/Abst** Health Plan. Adminis.

●US/1065-2477
**GASTROENTEROLOGIST (BOSTON, MASS.), THE.** (THE GASTROENTEROLOGIST.). [Gastroenterol.]. (1993)-. Periodical. English. qt. $151.00 (institutions), $87.00 (individuals) US; $169.00 (institutions), $105.00 (individuals) Canada; $182.00 (institutions), $116.00 (individuals) other. Little Brown & Company, 34 Beacon Street, Boston MA 02108. **Tel** (617)227-0730, (800)759-0190. **(Subscription address:** Little Brown and Company, PO Box 7671, Riverton NJ 08077-7671.**) DD** 616. **NLM** W1; GA457N. **[CCC].**

US/1042-5713
**GASTROENTEROLOGIST'S CLINICAL UPDATE.** (GASTROENTEROLOGIST'S CLINICAL UPDATE / SPONSORED BY ALBERT EINSTEIN COLLEGE OF MEDICINE/MONTEFIORE MEDICAL CENTER.). [Gastroenterol. clin. update]. **Added/Corp** Albert Einstein College of Medicine. Montefiore Medical Center. Vol. 1, No. 1 (Jan. 1989)-. Periodical. English. mo. $135.00 Physicians, $95.00 Residents US; $150.00 Physicians, $110.00 Residents Other. Educational Reviews Inc., 6801 Cahaba Valley Road, Birmingham AL 35242. **Tel** (205)991-5188, (800)633-4743, FAX (205)995-1926. **DD** 616.

NE
**GASTROENTEROLOGY.** Vol. 1 (Apr. 1971)-. English. Sixteen times a year (2 vols.). Fl1868.00. Excerpta Medica Publishing Group, PO Box 548, 1000 AM Amsterdam Netherlands. **Tel** 011 31 20 5803243. **(Subscription address:** Excerpta Medica Journals, PO Box 85, Limerick Ireland.**) LC** RC799; .G29. **DD** 616.3/005. available on microfilm from University Microfilms International (UMI).
**Desc:** This journal covers the entire digestive system from the mouth to the rectum, including the liver and bilary system, the pancreas, the peritoneum, mesentery and omentum, the diseases of the oropharynx, esophagus, and small and large intestine, including malabsorption syndromes, the appendix and proctology, gastrointestinal hemorrhage, gastrointestinal infections, and various parts of the digestive tract.
**Ind/Abst** Ref. Upd. Basic Ed.; Ref. Upd. Clinical Ed.; Ref. Upd. Deluxe Ed.

US/0883-8348
**GASTROENTEROLOGY & ENDOSCOPY NEWS.** [Gastroenterol. endosc. news]. **VFOAT** Gastroenterology and Endoscopy News. Vol. 36, No. 3 (March 1985)-. Academic Scholarly Publication. English. mo. $55.00 US; $79.00 other. McMahon Publishing Company, 148 West 24th Street, 8th Floor, New York NY 10011. **Tel** (212)620-4600, FAX (212)620-5928. **ED** Mary Joe Krey. **LC** RC864.A1; I5. **DD** 616.3/3/005. **Bk Rev. Ad Acc. Pr Rev. Circ:** 6,000 (ctrl). ***Continues*** *American Journal of Proctology, Gastroenterology & Colon & Rectal Surgery, 0162-6566.*
**Desc:** Literature review and meeting coverage in news format plus original papers, CME series, features, news items in gastroenterology, endoscopy and colorectal surgery.
**Ind/Abst** EMBASE; Life Sci. Collect.

UK/0959-3314
**GASTROENTEROLOGY & RHEUMATOLOGY IN PRACTICE.** **VFOAT** Gastroenterology and Rheumatology in Practice. Vol. 1, No. 1 (Feb./Mar. 1990)-. Periodical. English. bm. Medical News Tribune, Tower House, Southampton Street, London WC2E 7LS England. **Tel** (01)379-6005, FAX 01379 6737, telex 266854. **NLM** W1; GA458D. ***Formed by the union of*** *Rheumatology in Practice, 0262-5512* ***and*** *Gastroenterology in Practice, 0264-7478.*

US/0889-8553
**GASTROENTEROLOGY CLINICS OF NORTH AMERICA.** [Gastroenterol. clin. North Am.]. **VFOAT** Gastroenterology. Vol. 16, No. 1 (March 1987)-. Academic Scholarly Publication. English. qt (4 issues). $99.00 (individuals), $118.00 (institution) US; $128.00 (individuals), $135.00 (institutions) other. W.B. Saunders Company, A Subsidiary of Harcourt Brace Jovanovich, Inc., The Curtis Center/Suite 300, Independence Square West, Philadelphia PA 19106-3399. **Tel** (215)238-7800 or, 5587, FAX (215)238-7883, telex 173146. **(Subscription address:** W. B. Saunders Company / North America Subscriptions, c/o Periodicals, 6277 Sea Harbour Drive, 4th Floor, Orlando FL 32887.**) ED** Melissa Mitchell. **LC** RC799. **DD** 616. **NLM** W1; GA458G. **CODEN** GCNAEF. **[CCC].** Index available. **Pr Rev. Circ:** 4,000. available on microfilm and microfiche from University Microfilms International (UMI). Documents available from The Genuine Article, BIOSIS Document Express, CASDDS. ***Continues in part*** *Clinics in Gastroenterology, 0300-5089.*
**Ind/Abst** Biol. Abstr. (1987-); Chem. Abstr. (March 1987-); Curr. Contents Clin. Med.; EMBASE (March 1987-); Index Med. (March 1987-); INIS Atomindex [Micro.]; Nutr. Abstr. Rev., Ser. A, Hum. Exp.; Life Sci. Collect. (March 1987-); Physic. Medline Plus; Res. Alert [Full Cov.]; Sci. Cit. Index; SCISEARCH; Soc. Sci. Cit. Index [Select. Cov.].

US/0892-9386
**GASTROENTEROLOGY (GLENDALE, CALIF.).** (GASTROENTEROLOGY. SOUND RECORDING.). [Gastroenterol.]. **Added/Corp** Audio-Digest Foundation. **VFOAT** Audio-Digest Gastroenterology; Audio Digest Gastroenterology. Vol. 1, No. 1 (April 30, 1987)-. Periodical. English. mo. $89.88 US; $101.40 Canada; $123.72 other. Audio-Digest Foundation, 1577 Chevy Chase Drive, Glendale CA 91206. **Tel** (213)245-8505, (800)423-2308, FAX (818)240-7379. **DD** 616. **NLM** W1; GA457T. Index available.
**Desc:** Interactive system of audio cassette postgraduate medical education, with each one-hour program eligible for two Category I credit hours.

UK/0264-7478
**GASTROENTEROLOGY IN PRACTICE.** ***Title Change.*** [Gastroenterol. pract.]. -(1989). Periodical. English. **NLM** W1; GA455EE. ***Merged with*** *Rheumatologu in Practive, 0262-5512* ***to form*** *Gastroenterology & Rheumatology in Practice.*

IT/0950-5911
**GASTROENTEROLOGY INTERNATIONAL.** Vol. 1, No. 1 (Sept. 1988)-. Periodical. English. Four times a year (Mar., June, Dept., Dec.). 130000.00L (institutions), 80000.00L (individuals) Italy; $130.00 (institutions), $80.00 (individuals) other. International University Press Srl, Via Monte Delle Giole 22, 00199 Rome Italy. **Tel** 011 39 6 86211027 or 28. **NLM** W1; GA458K.
**Ind/Abst** Curr. Aware. Biol. Sci., CABS; EMBASE.

US
**GASTROENTEROLOGY JOURNAL CLUB.** English. Four times a year. $41.60 US; $50.32 other. Macmillan Professional Journal, 30 Vreeland Road, Florham Park NJ 07932. **Tel** (201)822-1622, FAX (201)822-2498.

●US/1063-1291
**GASTROENTEROLOGY MEDICINE TODAY.** (1992)-. Periodical. English. qt. Bugamor Pharma, Inc., 36 West 44th Street Suite 1412, New York NY 10036.

US/0016-5085
**GASTROENTEROLOGY (NEW YORK, N.Y. 1943).** (GASTROENTEROLOGY.). [Gastroenterology]. **Added/Corp** American Gastroenterological Association. Vol. 1 (Jan. 1943)-. Academic Scholarly Publication. English. mo (Plus one supplement). $258.00 (institutions), $165.00 (individuals) US; $323.00 (institutions), $258.00 (individuals), other. W.B. Saunders Company, A Subsidiary of Harcourt Brace Jovanovich, Inc., The Curtis Center/Suite 300, Independence Square West, Philadelphia PA 19106-3399. **Tel** (215)238-7800 or, 5587, FAX (215)238-7883, telex 173146. **(Subscription address:** W. B. Saunders Company / North America Subscriptions, c/o Periodicals, 6277 Sea Harbour Drive, 4th Floor, Orlando FL 32887.**) ED** Raj K. Goyal. **LC** RC799; .A634. **DD** 616.305. **NLM** W1 GA458. **CODEN** GASTAB. **[CCC].** cum. index. **Bk Rev. Ad Acc. Pr Rev. Circ:** 15,000. available on microfilm and microfiche from University Microfilms International (UMI). Documents available from The Genuine Article, BIOSIS Document Express, CASDDS.
**Desc:** Covers all aspects of the digestive tract and liver in clinical and basic science articles, brief reviews, and clinical case reports.
**Ind/Abst** Abr. Index Med.; Annals Behav. Med.; Biol. Abstr.; Chem. Abstr.; Dairy Sci. Abstr.; EMBASE; Energy Res. Abstr.; Health Period. Database; Health Plan. Adminis.; Helminthol. Abstr. (1991-); Index Med.; Index Vet.; INIS Atomindex [Micro.]; Iowa Drug Inf. Serv. (1968-); Med. Abstr. Newsl.; Mod. Med.; Nutr. Res. Newsl.; Life Sci. Collect.; PESTDOC; Physic. Medline Plus; Pig News Inf.; Poult. Abstr.; Protozoolog. Abstr.; Res. Alert [Full Cov.]; Saf. Health Work; Sci. Cit. Index; SCISEARCH; Soc. Sci. Cit. Index [Select. Cov.]; Soyabean Abstr.; Sug. Indus. Abstr.; Trop. Dis. Bull.

US/0892-1601
**GASTROENTEROLOGY (NEW YORK, N.Y. : 1983).** (GASTROENTEROLOGY.). [Gastroenterology]. Vol. 1 (1983)-. Monographic series. English. ir. Price varies per volume. Marcel Dekker Inc., 270 Madison Avenue, New York NY 10016. **Tel** (212)696-9000, (800)228-1160, FAX (212)685-4540, telex 421419. **(Subscription address:** Marcel Dekker Inc, PO Box 5017, Monticello NY 12701.**) LC** UNC. **DD** 616.

US/1042-895X
**GASTROENTEROLOGY NURSING.** **See** Medical Science and Technology-Nursing.

US
**GASTROINTESTINAL CARCINOGENESIS.** **See** Medical Science and Technology-Neoplasma, Neoplastic.

●US/1061-6004
**GASTROINTESTINAL DISEASES TODAY.** [Gastrointes. dis. today]. **Added/Corp** American Gastroenterological Association. (1992)-. Periodical. English. bm. W.B. Saunders Company, A Subsidiary of Harcourt Brace Jovanovich, Inc., The Curtis Center/Suite 300, Independence Square West, Philadelphia PA 19106-3399. **Tel** (215)238-7800 or, 5587, FAX (215)238-7883, telex 173146. **(Subscription address:** W. B. Saunders Company / North America Subscriptions, c/o Periodicals, 6277 Sea Harbour Drive, 4th Floor, Orlando FL 32887.**)** **DD** 616. **NLM** W1; GA458T.

US/0016-5107
**GASTROINTESTINAL ENDOSCOPY.** [Gastroint. endosc.]. **Added/Corp** American Society for Gastrointestinal Endoscopy. Vol. 12 (Aug. 1965)-. Academic Scholarly Publication. English. mo. $144.00 (institutions), $108.00 (individuals) US; $189.00 (institutions), $153.00 (individuals) other. Mosby Year Book Inc., 11830 Westline Industrial Drive, St Louis MO 63146. **Tel** (800)325-4177, (314)872-8370, FAX (314)432-1380, telex 44-2402. **LC** RC804.E6; G37. **DD** 616.3/307544. **NLM** W1 GA459E. **CODEN** GAENBQ. **[CCC]. Ad Acc. Pr Rev. Circ:** 6,350. available on microfilm and microfiche from University Microfilms International (UMI). Documents available from The Genuine Article, BIOSIS Document Express. ***Continues*** *Bulletin of Gastrointestinal Endoscopy, 1051-7472.*
**Desc:** Clinical journal, publishing papers in fiberoptic endoscopy for gastroenterologists and general surgeons.
**Ind/Abst** Biol. Abstr.; Curr. Contents Clin. Med.; EMBASE; Energy Res. Abstr.; Health Devices Alerts; Health Plan. Adminis.; Helminthol. Abstr. (19??-19??0; Index Med.; INIS Atomindex [Micro.]; Nutr. Abstr. Rev., Ser. A, Hum. Exp.; Life Sci. Collect.; Physic. Medline Plus; Ref. Upd. Clinical Ed.; Ref. Upd. Deluxe Ed.; Res. Alert [Full Cov.]; Rev. Med. Vet. Mycology; Sci. Cit. Index; SCISEARCH.

US/1052-5157
**GASTROINTESTINAL ENDOSCOPY CLINICS OF NORTH AMERICA.** [Gastrointest. endosc. clin. N. Am.]. Vol. 1, No. 1 (May 1991)-. Periodical. English. qt (4 issues). $99.00 (individual), $111.00 (institution) US; $128.00 (individual), $134.00 (institution) other. W.B. Saunders Company, A Subsidiary of Harcourt Brace Jovanovich, Inc., The Curtis Center/Suite 300, Independence Square West, Philadelphia PA 19106-3399. **Tel** (215)238-7800 or, 5587, FAX (215)238-7883, telex 173146. **(Subscription address:** W. B. Saunders Company / North America Subscriptions, c/o Periodicals, 6277 Sea Harbour Drive, 4th Floor, Orlando FL 32887.**)** **DD** 616. **NLM** W1; GA459L.

UK/0142-8101
**GASTROINTESTINAL HORMONES.** [Gastrointest. horm.]. (1977)-. English. Twenty-four times a year. £105.00. SUBIS, Mansion House, 19 Kingfield Road, Sheffield S11 9AS England. **Tel** 011 44 114 255 4433, FAX 011 44 114 255 4626. **DD** 016.61233. **[CCC].**

US/0364-2356
**GASTROINTESTINAL RADIOLOGY.** ***Title Change.*** **See** Medical Science and Technology-Radiology.

GW/0323-4762
**GASTRONOMIE.** (19??)-. Trade Publication. German. Ten times a year. DM85.00 Germany; DM114.00 others. Verlag die Wirtschaft Berlin, Am Friedrichshain 22, D 10407 Berlin Germany. **Tel** 011 49 30 42870. **(Subscription address:** Verlag Wirtschaft Huss GmbH, Am Friedrichshain 22, D 10407 Berlin Germany.**)**
**Desc:** A trade journal which helps chefs, caterers, food-service personnel and managers to upgrade and deepen their professional knowledge. Techniques aimed at achieving higher productivity at restaurants and mass-catering establishments are described in detail.

SP/0211-058X
**GASTRUM.** [Gastrum]. (1977)-. Monographic series. Spanish. mo. Price varies per volume. Jarpyo Editores SA, Antonio Lopez Aguados 4, 28029 Madrid, Spain. **Tel** 011 34 1 3144338, 011 34 1 3144458. **(Subscription address:** Antonio Lopez Aguado 1-4, 28029 Madrid Spain**)** **ED** Jose Maria Pajares Garcia. **UDC** 616.3. **Ad Acc. Circ:** 3,000 (ctrl).

VE/0016-3503
**GEN, GASTROENTEROLOGIA, ENDOCRINOLOGIA I NUTRICION.** (G. E. N. : ORGANO OFICIAL DE LA SOCIEDAD VENEZOLANA DE GASTROENTEROLOGIA, ENDOCRINOLOGIA Y NUTRICION.). [GEN, Gastroenterol., Endocrinol. Nutr.]. **Added/Corp** Sociedad Venezolana de Gastroenterologia, Endocrinologia y Nutricion. Sociedad Venezolana de Gastroenterologia. **VFOAT** GEN. **VAT** Gastroenterologia, Endocrinologia y Nutricion. Vol. 1 No. 1 (July/Aug./Sept. 1946)-. Academic Scholarly Publication. Spanish (English and Portuguese). qt. $50.00. Apartado 51890, Sabana Grande, Caracas 1050-A Venezuela. **Tel** 979-9380. **ED** Miguel A Garassini. **NLM** W1 G425. Index available. cum. index. **Bk Rev. Ad Acc. Circ:** 1,900.
**Desc:** Original papers and review articles concerning all aspects of gastroenterology and hepatology.
**Ind/Abst** EMBASE; Helminthol. Abstr. (1991-); Index Med.; Life Sci. Collect.; Protozoolog. Abstr.

UK/0017-5749
**GUT.** (GUT : JOURNAL OF THE BRITISH SOCIETY OF GASTROENTEROLOGY.). [Gut]. **Added/Corp** British Society of Gastroenterology. British Medical Association. Vol. 1 (March 1960)-. Academic Scholarly Publication. English. mo. £191.00. BMJ / British Medical Journal Publishing Group, British Medical Association House, Tavistock Square, London WC1H 9JR England. **Tel** 011 44 71 3874499, FAX 011 44 71 383 6402, telex 290034 HBJ MN. **ED** R.N. Allan. **NLM** W1 GU821. **CODEN** GUTTAK. **[CCC]. Pr Rev.** available on microfilm and microfiche from University Microfilms International (UMI). Documents available from The Genuine Article, BIOSIS Document Express, CASDDS, ADONIS.
**Desc:** A journal of physicians, surgeons, radiologists and pathologists, carrying authoritative articles on all aspects of gastroenterology. Clinical topics include epidemiology, medicine, surgery, radiology and histology.
**Ind/Abst** Abr. Index Med.; ADONIS; Annals Behav. Med.; Biol. Abstr.; Chem. Abstr.; Curr. Aware. Biol. Sci., CABS; Curr. Contents Clin. Med.; Curr. Contents Life Sci.; Dairy Sci. Abstr.; EMBASE; Health Period. Database; Health Plan. Adminis.; Helminthol. Abstr.; Immunol. Abstr.; Index Med.; Microbiol. Abstr. Sect. B; Mod. Med.; Nutr. Abstr. Rev., Ser. B, Live Feeds and Feed.; Nutr. Abstr. Rev., Ser. A, Hum. Exp.; Nutr. Res. Newsl.; Life Sci. Collect.; PESTDOC; Physic. Medline Plus; Pig News Inf.; Protozoolog. Abstr.; Ref. Upd. Basic Ed.; Ref. Upd. Clinical Ed.; Ref. Upd. Deluxe Ed.; Res. Alert [Full Cov.]; Rev. Med. Vet. Mycology; Sci. Cit. Index; SCISEARCH; Soc. Sci. Cit. Index [Select. Cov.]; Sug. Indus. Abstr.; Trop. Dis. Bull.; Wheat Barley Trit. Abstr.

GW/0172-6390
**HEPATO-GASTROENTEROLOGY.** [Hepato-gastroenterol.]. Vol. 27 (Feb. 1980)-. Academic Scholarly Publication. English. bm (6 issues). $204.00. Georg Thieme Verlag Stuttgart, Postfach 301120, D 70451 Stuttgart Germany. **Tel** 011 49 711 89310, FAX 011 49 711 8931298, telex 7 252 275 GTVD. **(Subscription address:** Thieme Medical Publishers Inc., 381 Park Avenue South, New York NY 10016.**)** **ED** N J Lygidakis, E Moreno Gonzales, R Mizumoto, M Classen, J R Siewart, G Biarchi Porro, S Raptis and J F Riemann. **NLM** W1 HE91. **CODEN** HEGAD4. **[CCC]. Pr Rev. Circ:** 1,350. available on microfilm and microfiche from University Microfilms International (UMI). Documents available from The Genuine Article, CASDDS, ADONIS. ***Continues*** *Acta Hepato-Gastroenterologica, 0300-970X.*
**Desc:** Concerned with the vast area of gastroenterology and hepatology. Communicates primarily through original papers but also by way of editorials, abstracts and critical reviews on subjects topical at the time of publication.
**Ind/Abst** ADONIS; Chem. Abstr.; Curr. Aware. Biol. Sci., CABS; Curr. Contents Clin. Med.; Curr. Contents Life Sci.; EMBASE; Energy Res. Abstr. (Feb. 1983-); Health Plan. Adminis.; Helminthol. Abstr. (1991-); Index Med.; Life Sci. Collect.; Res. Alert [Full Cov.]; Sci. Cit. Index; SCISEARCH; Sug. Indus. Abstr.

US/0270-9139
**HEPATOLOGY (BALTIMORE, MD.). See** Medical Science and Technology-Internal Medicine.

●UK/1352-8513
**ILLUSTRATED CASE REPORTS IN GASTROENTEROLOGY.** (1994)-. Periodical. English. Four times a year. $245.00 US and Canada; £130.00 Europe; £155.00 Other. Chapman & Hall, 2-6 Boundary Row, London SE1 8HN England. **Tel** 011 44 71 865 0066, FAX 011 44 71 522 9623, telex 290164 Chapmag. **(Subscription address:** Chapman & Hall, Cheriton House, North Way, Andover, Hampshire, SP10 5BE England.**)**

II/0254-8860
**INDIAN JOURNAL OF GASTROENTEROLOGY.** (INDIAN JOURNAL OF GASTROENTEROLOGY : OFFICIAL JOURNAL OF THE INDIAN SOCIETY OF GASTROENTEROLOGY.). [Indian j. gastroenterol.]. **Added/Corp** Indian Society of Gastroenterology. Vol. 1, No. 1 (April 1982)-. Periodical. English. qt (Jan., Apr., July, Oct.). $50.00 India; $70.00 (air mail) other. Indian Society of Gastroenterology, Bombay Mutual TE, 534 Sandhurst, Bombay 400 007 India. **Tel** 011 55 22 3613344, 3613333. **(Subscription address:** Prints India, 11 Darya Ganj, New Delhi 110002 India.**)** **ED** Prof. S. R. Naik. **NLM** W1; IN208W. **[CCC].** Index available (Included in Oct. issue). cum. index. **Bk Rev. Ad Acc. Circ:** 1,250 (ctrl).
**Desc:** Includes original articles of clinical investigations.
**Ind/Abst** EMBASE [Select. Cov.]; Index Med.; Trop. Dis. Bull.

US/0274-5542
**INTERNAL MEDICINE NEWS & CARDIOLOGY NEWS.** [Intern. med. news cardiol. news]. **VFOAT** Internal Medicine and Cardiology News; Internal Medicine & Cardiology News. **VAT** Internal medicine News and Cardiology News. Vol. 13, No. 9 (May 1, 1980)-. Periodical. English. sm. $96.00 US; $138.00 other. International Medical News Group, 12230 Wilkins Avenue, Rockville MD 20852. **Tel** (301)770-6170. **ED** William Rubin. **DD** 616. **NLM** W1; IN699G. **Bk Rev. Ad Acc. Circ:** 72,500 (ctrl). available on microfilm and microfiche from ABC Database. ***Continues*** *Internal Medicine News, 0099-152X.*
**Desc:** Coverage of clinical meetings, symposia, and conventions to report clinical developments in internal medicine, cardiology, gastroenterology, and pulmonary disease.

●CN/1188-4525
**INTERNATIONAL SEMINARS IN PAEDIATRIC GASTROENTEROLOGY AND NUTRITION.** [Int. semin. paediatr. gastroenterol. nutr.]. Vol. 1, No. 1 (Mar. 1992)-. Periodical. English. qt. $78.00 (institutions), $52.00 (individuals) US & Canada; $105.00 (institutions), $79.00 (individuals) other. Decker Periodicals Publishing Inc, PO Box 620, Station A, Hamilton Ontario L8N 3K7 Canada. **Tel** (416)522-7017, (800) 568-7281, FAX (416)522-7839. **DD** 618.92/33. **NLM** W1; IN835IM.

UK/0261-4995
**INTESTINAL FUNCTION.** [Intest. funct.]. Vol. 1, No. 1 (Jan. 1982)-. English. Twenty-four times a year. £115.00. SUBIS, Mansion House, 19 Kingfield Road, Sheffield S11 9AS England. **Tel** 011 44 114 255 4433, FAX 011 44 114 255 4626. **DD** 016.59113205. ***Continues*** *Intestinal Absorption, 0306-3003.*

IT/0392-0623
**ITALIAN JOURNAL OF GASTROENTEROLOGY, THE.** [Ital. j. gastroenterol.]. **Added/Corp** Associazione Italiana per lo Studio del Fegato. Societa Italiana di Gastroenterologia. Vol. 10 (Apr. 1978)-. Academic Scholarly Publication. English (summaries and/or abstracts in Italian). Nine times a year. $200.00 institutions; $130.00 individuals. International University Press Srl, Via Monte Delle Giole 22, 00199 Rome Italy. **Tel** 011 39 6 86211027 or 28. **ED** Aldo Torsoli. **NLM** W1 IT1355. **CODEN** ITJGDH. **Bk Rev. Ad Acc. Pr Rev. Circ:** 2,000 (ctrl). available on microfilm and microfiche from University Microfilms International (UMI). Documents available from The Genuine Article, CASDDS. ***Continues*** *Rendiconti di Gastro-Enterologia, 0390-4849.*
**Desc:** Official organ of the Societa Italiana di Gastroenterologia (Italian Association of Gastroenterology) and of the Italian Association for the Study of the Liver.
**Ind/Abst** Chem. Abstr.; Curr. Contents Clin. Med.; EMBASE; Protozoolog. Abstr.; Res. Alert [Full Cov.]; Sci. Cit. Index; SCISEARCH; Sug. Indus. Abstr.

CN/1197-4982
**JOURNAL / CROHN'S AND COLITIS FOUNDATION OF CANADA, THE.** [J. - Crohn's Colitis Found. Can.]. **Added/Corp** Crohn's and Colitis Foundation of Canada. Crohn's and Colitis Foundation of Canada. National Education Committee. **VFOAT** Journal. **VAT** Journal - Fondation Canadienne des Maladies Inflammatoires de l'Intestin. Feb. (1993)-. Periodical. English (French). qt. Free to members. Crohn's and Colitis Foundation of Canada, 21 St. Clair Avenue East, Suite 301, Toronto ONT M4T 1L9 Canada. **Tel** (416)920-5035, FAX (416)929-0364. **ED** Barbara Victor. **DD** 616.3/445. **Bk Rev**, (Qty: 3-4). **Circ:** 11,000 (ctrl). ***Continues*** *Journal (Canadian Foundation for Ileitis and Colitis)., 0827-4681.*
**Desc:** Current information on research of IBD -- questions answered by a gastroenterologist, member's perspectives, and reviews of IBD literature.

FR/1161-9147
**JOURNAL DE PATHOLOGIE DIGESTIVE. VFOAT** JPD. Vol. 1 No. 1 (May 1991)-. Periodical. French. bm. **NLM** W1; JO326RL.

US/0192-0790
**JOURNAL OF CLINICAL GASTROENTEROLOGY.** [J. clin. gastroenterol.]. Vol. 1, (Mar. 1979)-. Periodical. English. Eight times a year. $124.00 (individuals), $224.00 (institutions) US; $176.00 (individuals), $266.00 (institutions) other. Raven Press, 1185 Avenue of the Americas, 37th Floor, New York NY 10036. **Tel** (212)930-9500, (212)930-9604, FAX (212)869-3495, (212)302-8507, telex 640073. **ED** Howard M. Spiro. **LC** RC799; .J68. **DD** 616.3/005. **NLM** W1 JO588CM. **[CCC]. Pr Rev.** available on microfilm and microfiche from University Microfilms International (UMI). Documents available from The Genuine Article.
**Desc:** Helps practitioners keep pace with advances in those areas of digestive diseases that are essential to clinical practice and have a direct bearing on patient care problems.
**Ind/Abst** Curr. Aware. Biol. Sci., CABS; Curr. Contents Clin. Med.; EMBASE; Index Med.; Mod. Med.; Nutr. Res. Newsl.; Life Sci. Collect.; Protozoolog. Abstr.; Ref. Upd. Clinical Ed.; Ref. Upd. Deluxe Ed.; Res. Alert [Full Cov.]; Sci. Cit. Index; SCISEARCH; Soc. Sci. Cit. Index [Select. Cov.].

SP/0214-2880
**JOURNAL OF CLINICAL NUTRITION & GASTROENTEROLOGY, THE.** ***Ceased.*** [J. clin. nutr. gastroenterol.]. **VFOAT** Journal of Clinical Nutrition and Gastroenterology. Vol. 1, No. 1 (Jan./Feb.

1986)-(19??). Periodical. English (summaries and/or abstracts in Spanish). bm. Cempro, Plaza Conde Valle Suchil 20, 28015 Madrid Spain. **Tel** 011 34 1 4462050, 011 34 1 4472700. **NLM** W1; JO894E. Documents available from CASDDS.
**Ind/Abst** Chem. Abstr. (?-?); EMBASE; Indice Med. Esp.

BG/0253-8768
**JOURNAL OF DIARRHOEAL DISEASES RESEARCH.** [J. diarrhoeal dis. res.]. **Added/Corp** International Centre for Diarrhoeal Disease Research, Bangladesh. Vol. 1, No. 1 (March 1983)-. Periodical. English. qt. $70.00 countries of the South Asian Association for Regional Cooperation; $100.00 other. International Center of Diarrhoeal Diseases, GPO Box 128, Dacca 1000 Bangladesh. **Tel** 011 880 2 600171 78, FAX 011 880 2 883116, telex 675612. **ED** Dilip Mahalanabis. **NLM** W1 JO622C. **CODEN** JDDREM. **[CCC].** Index available. **Bk Rev. Ad Acc. Circ:** 600 (ctrl). Documents available from The Genuine Article, BIOSIS Document Express.
**Ind/Abst** Biol. Abstr. (1985-); Curr. Contents Clin. Med.; EMBASE [Select. Cov.]; Helminthol. Abstr. (19??-19??); Index Med. (Vol. 1, No. 1, 1983-); Index Vet.; Pig News Inf.; Protozoolog. Abstr.; Res. Alert [Select. Cov.]; Rev. Med. Vet. Entomol.; Rural Dev. Abstr.; SCISEARCH; Vet. Bull.; Trop. Dis. Bull.

●JA/0944-1174
**JOURNAL OF GASTROENTEROLOGY.** (1994)-. English. Six times a year. DM280.00. Springer-Verlag Tokyo, 37-3 Hongo 3-Chrome, Bunkyo-ku, Tokyo 113 Japan. **Tel** 011 81 3 38120331, FAX 011 81 3 38120719, telex 26536 SREBS J. **(Subscription address:** Springer Verlag New York Inc. / for North America, 44 Hartz Way, Secaucus NJ 07096.) ***Continues*** *Gastroenterologia Japonica, 0435-1339.*

AT/0815-9319
**JOURNAL OF GASTROENTEROLOGY AND HEPATOLOGY.** [J. gastroenterol. hepatol.]. Vol. 1, No. 1 (Jan./Feb. 1986)-. Academic Scholarly Publication. English. Six times a year. 358.00Aus$ Australia; $251.00 other. Blackwell Scientific Publications Australia, 54 University Street, PO Box 378, Carlton Victoria 3053 Australia. **Tel** 011 61 3 3470300, FAX 011 61 3 3475001, telex 10716421. **(Subscription address:** UK/ Marston Book Services, PO Box 87, Oxford UK; US/ 3 Cambridge Centre, Suite 208, Cambridge MA 02142; Germany/ Meinekestrasse 4, D-1000 Berlin 15 Germany; France/ Arnette, 2 rue Casimir Delavigne, 75006 Paris France; Austria/ Blackwell MZV, Medizinische Zeitschriftenverlags Gesellschaft, Feldgasse 13, A-1238 Vienna Austria) **ED** S.K. Lam, K. Okuda, L. Powell, and D.J. Shearman. **NLM** W1; JO663J. **CODEN** JGHEEO. **[CCC]. Pr Rev.** available on microfilm and microfiche from University Microfilms International (UMI). Documents available from The Genuine Article, BIOSIS Document Express, CASDDS, ADONIS.
**Desc:** Review articles, editorial comments, original contributions and case reports concerned with clinical practice and research in the fields of hepatology and gastroenterology.
**Ind/Abst** ADONIS; Biol. Abstr.; Chem. Abstr. (1986-); Curr. Aware. Biol. Sci., CABS; Curr. Contents Clin. Med.; Curr. Contents Life Sci.; EMBASE; Health Plan. Adminis.; Helminthol. Abstr. (19??-19??); Index Vet.; Nutr. Abstr. Rev., Ser. A, Hum. Exp.; Poult. Abstr.; Protozoolog. Abstr.; Res. Alert [Full Cov.]; Rev. Med. Vet. Mycology; Sci. Cit. Index; SCISEARCH; Soyabean Abstr.; Vet. Bull.

US/1043-4518
**JOURNAL OF GASTROINTESTINAL MOTILITY.** ***Title Change.*** [J. gastrointest. motil.]. Vol. 1, No. 1 (Sept. 1989)-(1993). Academic Scholarly Publication. English. qt. Blackwell Scientific Publications Ltd, Marston Book Services, PO Box 87, Oxford OX2 ODT UK. **Tel** 011 44 865 791155, FAX 011 44 865 791927, telex 837 515 MARDIS G. **(Subscription address:** UK/ Marston Book Services, PO Box 87, Oxford UK; Aus/ 54 University Street, Carlton Victoria 3053 Australia; Germany/ Meinekestrasse 4, D-1000 Berlin 15 Germany; France/ Arnette, 2 rue Casimir Delavigne, 75006 Paris France; Austria/ Blackwell MZV, Medizinische Zeitschriftenverlags Gesellschaft, Feldgasse 13, A-1238 Vienna Austria) **DD** 616. **NLM** W1; JO663L. **CODEN** JGMOEB. **[CCC].** available on microfilm and microfiche from University Microfilms International (UMI). ***Continued by*** *Neurogastroenterology & Motility.*
**Ind/Abst** Curr. Aware. Biol. Sci., CABS; EMBASE.

●US
**JOURNAL OF INFLAMMATORY BOWEL DISEASE.** Vol. 1 (1995)-. Periodical. English. qt. $85.00 (individuals), $105.00 (institutions) US; $95.00 (individuals), $115.00 (institutions) other. Raven Press, 1185 Avenue of the Americas, 37th Floor, New York NY 10036. **Tel** (212)930-9500, (212)930-9604, FAX (212)869-3495, (212)302-8507, telex 640073.

CN/0827-4681
**JOURNAL / THE CANADIAN FOUNDATION FOR ILEITIS AND COLITIS.** ***Title Change.*** [J. - Can. Found. Ileitis Colitis]. **Added/Corp** Canadian Foundation for Ileitis and Colitis. Canadian Foundation for Ileitis and Colitis. Educational Committee. **VFOAT** Journal. **VAT** Journal - Fondation Canadienne Pour l'Ileite et la Colite. May (1979)-(1992). Periodical. English (French). ir (3 or 4 per year). Crohn's and Colitis Foundation of Canada, 21 St. Clair Avenue East, Suite 301, Toronto ONT M4T 1L9 Canada. **Tel** (416)920-5035, FAX (416)929-0364. **ED** Barbara Victor. **DD** 616.3/445. **Bk Rev**, (Qty: 3-4). **Circ:** 11,000 (ctrl). ***Continued by*** *Journal (Crohn's and Colitis Foundation of Canada), 1197-4982.*
**Desc:** Current information on research of IBD -- questions answered by a gastroenterologist, member's perspectives, and reviews of IBD literature.

GW/0940-9092
**KONTINENZ.** (1992)-. Periodical. German. Six times a year. $81.00. Georg Thieme Verlag Stuttgart, Postfach 301120, D 70451 Stuttgart Germany. **Tel** 011 49 711 89310, FAX 011 49 711 8931298, telex 7 252 275 GTVD. **(Subscription address:** Thieme Medical Publishers Inc., 381 Park Avenue South, New York NY 10016.)

GW/0300-8622
**LEBER, MAGEN, DARM.** [Leber, Magen, Darm]. Vol. 1 (June 1971)-. Academic Scholarly Publication. German (English). Six times a year. DM120.60 Germany; DM129.60 other. Richard Pflaum Verlag Gmbh, Postfach 190737, D 80607 Munich Germany. **Tel** 011 49 89 126070, FAX 011 49 89 12607200, telex 5216075. **ED** M. Classeu, V. Schusdziarra, J. R. Siewert. **NLM** W1 LE324. **CODEN** LBMDAT. **[CCC].** Index available. cum. index. **Bk Rev. Ad Acc. Pr Rev.** ctrl circ. available on microfilm and microfiche from University Microfilms International (UMI). Documents available from The Genuine Article, BIOSIS Document Express, CASDDS.
**Ind/Abst** Biol. Abstr. (1985-); Chem. Abstr. (1971-1983); Curr. Contents Clin. Med.; Curr. Contents Eng. Tech. Appl. Sci.; EMBASE; Index Med.; Life Sci. Collect.; Res. Alert [Select. Cov.]; SCISEARCH.

IT
**MINERVA GASTROENTEROLOGICA E DIETOLOGICA.** Vol. 37, 1 (Jan./Mar. 1991)-. Periodical. Italian (summaries and/or abstracts in English; table of contents in English). qt. $90.00 (individuals), $140.00 (institutions). Edizioni Minerva Medica, Corso Bramante 83-85, 10126 Turin Italy. **Tel** 011 39 11 678282, FAX 011 39 11 674502. **NLM** W1; MI642K. **CODEN** MGADEJ. ***Continues*** *Minerva Dietologica e Gastroenterologica, 0391-1993.*
**Ind/Abst** Index Med. (1991-).

FR/1146-5603
**PASCAL. E 76, GASTROENTEROLOGIE, FOIE, PANCREAS, ABDOMEN. VFOAT** PASCAL. E 76, Gastroenterology, Liver, Pancreas, Abdomen; PASCAL. E Soixante-seize, Gastroenterologie, Foie, Pancreas, Abdomen. (1990)-. Periodical. Multiple languages. Eleven times a year. 1600.00F France; 1695.00F other. CNRS / Institut d'Information Scientifique et Technique, (Centre National de la Recherche Scientifique), 15 Quai Anatole France, Paris 75700 France. **Tel** 011 33 1 47531515, telex 299 356 F. **UDC** 011. ***Continues*** *Pascal Explore. E76 : Gastroenterologie Foie Pancreas Abdomen.*

US/0196-9781
**PEPTIDES (NEW YORK, N.Y, : 1980).** **See** Biology-Biochemistry.

US/0277-4208
**PRACTICAL GASTROENTEROLOGY.** [Pract.gastroenterol.]. Vol. 4, No. 9 (Oct. 1980)-. Periodical. English. Ten times a year. $115.00 US; $160.00 other. Shugar Publishing Inc., 32 Mill Road, West Hampton Beach NY 11978. **Tel** (516)288-4404, FAX (516)288-4435. **DD** 616. **NLM** W1 PR141N. **CODEN** PRGAEE. **[CCC]. Bk Rev. Ad Acc.** available on microfilm from University Microfilms International (UMI). Documents available from BIOSIS Document Express. ***Continues*** *Primary Care Physician's Guide to Practical Gastroenterology, 0163-7894.*
**Ind/Abst** Biol. Abstr. (1985-); EMBASE [Select. Cov.].

US/0896-5439
**PRACTICAL REVIEWS IN GASTROENTEROLOGY.** (PRACTICAL REVIEWS IN GASTROENTEROLOGY [SOUND RECORDING].). [Pract. rev. gastroenterol.]. **Added/Corp** Educational Reviews, Inc. Albert Einstein College of Medicine. Montefiore Medical Center. **VFOAT** Practical Reviews. (198?)-. Periodical. English. mo. $175.00 Physicians/Dentists; $125.00 Residents. Educational Reviews Inc., 6801 Cahaba Valley Road, Birmingham AL 35242. **Tel** (205)991-5188, (800)633-4743, FAX (205)995-1926. **DD** 616.

US/0079-6271
**PROGRESS IN GASTROENTEROLOGY.** ***Ceased.*** [Prog. gastroenterol.]. (1968)-(19??). English. Grune & Stratton Inc., 6277 Sea Harbor Drive, Orlando FL 32887. **Tel** (800)782-4479, (407)345-2567. **ED** G B J Glass. **LC** RC801; .P76. **DD** 616.3. **NLM** W1 PR668W. **CODEN** PGGAAZ. Documents available from BIOSIS Document Express, CASDDS.
**Ind/Abst** Biol. Abstr.; Chem. Abstr.; Life Sci. Collect.

UK/0141-5581
**RECENT ADVANCES IN GASTROENTEROLOGY.** (1965)-. Academic Scholarly Publication. English. ir (Published every three to five years). Price varies. Churchill Livingstone, 1-3 Baxter's Place, Leith Walk, Edinburgh EH1 3AF Scotland. **Tel** 011 44 31 556 2424, FAX 011 44 31 558 1278, telex 727511. **(Subscription address:** Churchill Livingstone / US, 5 S 250 Frontenac Road, Naperville IL 60563.) **ED** John Badenoch and Bryan N. Brooke. **LC** RC799; .R43. **DD** 616.3/3/005. **NLM** W1 RE105ULA. **CODEN** RAGADI. Documents available from CASDDS.
**Ind/Abst** Chem. Abstr. (1965-1976).

MX/0375-0906
**REVISTA DE GASTROENTEROLOGIA DE MEXICO.** [Rev. gastroenterol. Mex.]. **Added/Corp** Asociacion Mexicana de Gastro-Enterologia. Vol. 1 (1935)-. Periodical. Spanish (summaries and/or abstracts in English). qt. $80.00. Asociacion Mexicana Gastroenterologia, Avenida Veracruz 93-301, 06140 Mexico DF Mexico. **Tel** 011 52 5 5531711, FAX 011 52 5 5535362. **(Subscription address:** Obsidiana SA de CV, Calzada de Tlalpan 2365, CP 04370 Mexico DF Mexico.) **NLM** W1 RE398F. Index available in last issue of volume--attached.
**Ind/Abst** Index Med.

SP/1130-0108
**REVISTA ESPANOLA DE ENFERMEDADES DIGESTIVAS.** **Added/Corp** Sociedad Espanola de Patologia Digestiva. Vol. 77, No. 1 (Jan. 1990)-. Periodical. Spanish (summaries and/or abstracts in English). mo. $73.94 Spain; $128.00 Europe; $150.00 other. Editorial Garsi SA, Juan Bravo 46, 28006 Madrid, Spain. **Tel** 011 34 1 4021212, telex 98358 GARSI E. **ED** Francisco Vilardell. **CODEN** REDIEM. Index available. cum. index. **Bk Rev. Ad Acc. Pr Rev. Circ:** 2,500 (ctrl). Documents available from The Genuine Article, BIOSIS Document Express, CASDDS. ***Continues*** *Revista Espanola de las Enfermedades del Aparato Digestivo.*
**Desc:** Publishes papers on clinical and research subjects of medical and surgical gastroenterology, including the liver.
**Ind/Abst** Biol. Abstr. (1990-); Chem. Abstr.; Curr. Contents Clin. Med.; EMBASE [Select. Cov.]; Res. Alert [Select. Cov.].

FR/0035-2888
**REVUE FRANCAISE DE GASTRO-ENTEROLOGIE.** [Rev. fr. gastro-enterol.]. (1964)-. Periodical. French. mo (10 issues). 254.65F France; 340.00F other. Galliena Promotion, 58 A rue du Dessous des Berges, 75013 Paris France. **Tel** 011 33 1 45849766. **UDC** 616.34.
**Ind/Abst** EMBASE.

IT/0035-6255
**RIVISTA DI GASTRO-ENTEROLOGIA.** [Riv. gastro-enterol.]. (1949)-. Periodical. Italian. bm. L30000.00 Italy; L60000.00 other. Casa Editrice Maccari, Via Trento 53, 43100 Parma Italy. **Tel** 011 39 521 771268, FAX 011 39 521 771268. **NLM** W1 RI469.

NO/0036-5521
**SCANDINAVIAN JOURNAL OF GASTROENTEROLOGY.** [Scand. j. gastroenterol.]. Vol. 1 (Sept. 1966)-. Academic Scholarly Publication. English. mo. Kr2650.00, $459.00. Scandinavian University Press, PO Box 2959 Toeyen, N 0608 Oslo 6 Norway. **Tel** 011 47 2 2575400, FAX 011 47 2 2575353, telex 71896 UROR N. **(Subscription address:** Scandinavian University Press, 200 Meacham Ave., Elmont NY 11003.) **ED** E. Gjone and J. Myren. **NLM** W1 SC149G. **CODEN** SJGRA4. **[CCC].** cum. index. **Ad Acc. Pr Rev. Circ:** 1,800 (ctrl). available on microfilm and microfiche from University Microfilms International (UMI). Documents available from The Genuine Article, BIOSIS Document Express, CASDDS.
**Desc:** Presents research within the field of gastroenterology.
**Ind/Abst** Biol. Abstr.; Chem. Abstr.; Curr. Aware. Biol. Sci., CABS; Curr. Contents Clin. Med.; Curr. Contents Life Sci.; Dairy Sci. Abstr.; EMBASE; Energy Res. Abstr.; Helminthol. Abstr. (1991-); Index Med.; Iowa Drug Inf. Serv. (1968-); Maize Abstr.; Nutr. Abstr. Rev., Ser. B, Live Feeds and Feed; Nutr. Abstr. Rev., Ser. A, Hum. Exp.; Nutr. Res. Newsl.; Life Sci. Collect.; PESTDOC; Pig News Inf.; Poult. Abstr.; Protozoolog. Abstr.; Ref. Upd. Basic Ed.; Ref. Upd. Deluxe Ed.; Res. Alert [Full Cov.]; Sci. Cit. Index; SCISEARCH; Sug. Indus. Abstr.

NO/0085-5928
**SCANDINAVIAN JOURNAL OF GASTROENTEROLOGY. SUPPLEMENT.** [Scand. j. gastroenterol., Suppl.]. **VFOAT** Supplement; Supplementum. Vol. 1 (1968)-. Academic Scholarly Publication. English. mo. Kr2650.00, $459.00. Scandinavian University Press, PO Box 2959 Toeyen, N 0608 Oslo 6 Norway. **Tel** 011 47 2 2575400, FAX 011 47 2 2575353, telex 71896 UROR N. **(Subscription address:** Scandinavian University Press, 200 Meacham Ave., Elmont NY 11003.) **NLM** W1 SC149GA. **CODEN** SJGSB8. **[CCC].** available on microfilm and microfiche from University Microfilms International (UMI). Documents available from BIOSIS

Document Express, CASDDS.
**Ind/Abst** Biol. Abstr.; Chem. Abstr.; Curr. Aware. Biol. Sci., CABS; EMBASE; Helminthol. Abstr. (1991-); Index Med.; Leis. Recreat. Tour. Abstr.; Microbiol. Abstr. Sect. B (19??-19??); Nutr. Abstr. Rev., Ser. A, Hum. Exp.; Life Sci. Collect.; Protozoolog. Abstr.

US/1049-5118
**SEMINARS IN GASTROINTESTINAL DISEASE.** [Semin. gastrointest. dis.]. Vol. 1, Issue 1 (Oct. 1990)-. Periodical. English. qt. $98.00 (individual), $123.00 (institution), $69.00 (student) US; $136.00 (individual), $152.00 (institution) other. W.B. Saunders Company, A Subsidiary of Harcourt Brace Jovanovich, Inc., The Curtis Center/Suite 300, Independence Square West, Philadelphia PA 19106-3399. **Tel** (215)238-7800 or, 5587, FAX (215)238-7883, telex 173146. **(Subscription address:** W. B. Saunders Company / North America Subscriptions, c/o Periodicals, 6277 Sea Harbour Drive, 4th Floor, Orlando FL 32887.**)** **DD** 616. **NLM** W1; SE488P. **CODEN** SGDIED. **[CCC].**

CN/1188-0244
**SEMINARS IN PEDIATRIC GASTROENTEROLOGY AND NUTRITION.** **See** Medical Science and Technology-Pediatrics.

US/1057-9095
**SGNA NEWS.** [SGNA news]. **Added/Corp** Society of Gastroenterology Nurses and Associates. **VAT** Society of Gastroenterology Nurses and Associates News. (19??)-. Periodical. English. Six times a year. $90.00 active membership; $75.00 affiliate membership. Society of Gastroenterology Nurses and Associates, 1070 Sibley Tower, Rochester NY 14604. **Tel** (800)245-7462, (716)546-7241. **DD** 616.

JA/0389-3626
**SHOKA TO KYUSHU.** [ShÂoka to kyÂushÂu]. **Added/Corp** Nihon Shoka Kyushu Gakkai. **VFOAT** Digestion and Absorption; Digestion & Absorption. (1978)-. Academic Scholarly Publication. Japanese. Nihon Shoka Kyushu Gakkai, (Japanese Soc. of Digestion & Absorption), 2-8, Shinkawa 1 Chome, Chuoku, Tokyoto 104, Japan. **CODEN** SHKYEZ. Documents available from CASDDS.
**Ind/Abst** Chem. Abstr. (1985-).

JA/0387-2645
**SHOKAKI GEKA.** **VFOAT** Gastroenterological Surgery. (1978)-. Periodical. Japanese (table of contents in English). Thirteen times a year. $414.00. **(Subscription address:** Japan Publications Trading Company, Ltd., PO Box 5030, Tokyo International, Tokyo 100-31 Japan.**)** **NLM** W1; SH502E.

US/0730-2681
**SURGICAL GASTROENTEROLOGY.** ***Title Change.*** [Surg. gastroenterol.]. Vol. 1, No. 1 (1982)-?. Periodical. English. qt. Masson SA, Avenue Beauregard 12, CH-1701 Fribourg Switzerland. **Tel** 011 41 37 249585, FAX 011 41 37 247559, telex 942658 SEMI CH. **(Subscription address:** 7A Boulevard de Perolles, CH-1701 Fribourg Switzerland**)** **NLM** W1 SU765K. ***Continued by*** *Digestive Surgery.*
**Ind/Abst** Index Med. (Vol. 3, No. 1, 1984-).

JA/0536-2180
**TO CHO, I.** **Added/Corp** Soki Igan Kenkyukai. **VFOAT** Stomach and Intestine. (1966)-. Periodical. Japanese (summaries and/or abstracts in English). mo. $370.00. Igaku Shoin Ltd., 5-24-3 Hongo Bunkyo-ku, Tokyo 113 Japan. **Tel** 011 81 3 817 5670. **(Subscription address:** Maruzen Company Ltd., PO Box 5050, Import & Export Department, Tokyo 100 31 Japan.**)** **NLM** W1 I471TH. **CODEN** ITCHAG. Documents available from BIOSIS Document Express.
**Ind/Abst** Biol. Abstr.; EMBASE [Select. Cov.].

UK/0307-6598
**TOPICS IN GASTROENTEROLOGY.** [Top. gastroenterol.]. Vol. 1 (1973)-. Academic Scholarly Publication. English. ir. Blackwell Scientific Publications Ltd, Marston Book Services, PO Box 87, Oxford OX2 ODT UK. **Tel** 011 44 865 791155, FAX 011 44 865 791927, telex 837 515 MARDIS G. **ED** D.P. Jewell and P.R. Gibson. **LC** RC799; .T66. **DD** 616.3/3. **NLM** W1 TO539MG. **CODEN** TOGAD2. Each issue contains an index to its own contents (no volume index)--loose. Documents available from CASDDS.
**Ind/Abst** Chem. Abstr. (1973-1977).

GW/0174-738X
**VERDAUUNGSKRANKHEITEN.** [Verdauungskrankheiten]. Vol. 1, No. 1 (1983)-. Academic Scholarly Publication. German. bm (6 issues). DM116.00. Dustri-Verlag, Dr Karl Feistle, Postfach 49, D 82032 Deisenhofen Germany. **Tel** 011 49 89 6138610, FAX 011 49 89 6135412. **NLM** W1; VE26. **CODEN** VERDEJ. Documents available from CASDDS.
**Ind/Abst** Chem. Abstr.; EMBASE.

US
**VIEWPOINTS ON DIGESTIVE DISEASES.** ***Ceased.*** **Added/Corp** American Gastroenterological Association. Digestive Disease Foundation (India). Vol. 1 (April 1969)-(1992). Periodical. English. qt. **NLM** W1 VI48.

US/0360-7666
**WARREN-TEED G.I. TRACT.** **VFOAT** G.I. Tract. **VAT** Warren-Teed Gastrointestinal Tract; Gastrointestinal Tract. V. 1- 1970-. Periodical. English. qt. $5.00. 582 West Goodale Street, Columbus OH 43215. **NLM** W1 WA265.

GW/0044-2771
**ZEITSCHRIFT FUER GASTROENTEROLOGIE.** [Z. Gastroenterol.]. Vol. 1 (1963)-. Academic Scholarly Publication. German. Twelve times a year. DM180.00. Karl Demeter Verlag, Wuermstrasse 13, Postfach 1660, W 8032 Graefelfing Germany. **Tel** 011 49 89 852033, FAX 011 49 89 9543347, telex 524068 Delta D. **ED** N. Henning. **NLM** W1 ZE356. **CODEN** ZGASAX. **Bk Rev. Ad Acc. Pr Rev. Circ:** 2,400. Documents available from The Genuine Article, BIOSIS Document Express, CASDDS.
**Ind/Abst** Biol. Abstr.; Chem. Abstr.; CSA Neuro. Abstr. (?-?); Curr. Contents Clin. Med.; EMBASE; Energy Res. Abstr.; Index Med.; Nutr. Abstr. Rev., Ser. B, Live Feeds and Feed.; Nutr. Abstr. Rev., Ser. A, Hum. Exp.; Life Sci. Collect.; Protozoolog. Abstr.; Res. Alert [Full Cov.]; Sci. Cit. Index; SCISEARCH.

CH/1013-7696
**ZHONGHUA MINGUO XIAOHUA XIYI XUEHUI ZAZHI.** **VFOAT** Chinese Journal of Gastroenterology. (1984)-. Periodical. English. qt. Free to medical institutions. Gastroenterological Society of the Republic of China, Taita Jing-Fu Alumni Building, 2nd Floor, 7 Chung Shan South Road, Taipei Taiwan. **Tel** 011 886 2 3119062.
**Ind/Abst** EMBASE.

CC/0254-1432
**ZHONGHUA XIAOHUA ZAZHI.** (CHUNG-HUA HSIAO HUA TSA CHIH.). [Zhonghua xiaohua zazhi]. **VFOAT** Chinese Journal of Digestion. Vol. 1 (1981)-. Periodical. Chinese (summaries and/or abstracts in Chinese and English). bm. $48.22. Chinese Medical Association / Shanghai Branch, 1623 Beijing Xilu, Shanghai 200040 People's Republic of China. **Tel** 2531885. **ED** J. Shaoji. **NLM** W1 CH9818M. **Circ:** 13,000. Documents available from BLDSC.

---

## GERIATRICS

---

●US/1061-3056
**1992 DIRECTORY OF AGING RESOURCES.** **See** Sociology-Social Services and Welfare.

US/1047-4862
**ABSTRACTS IN SOCIAL GERONTOLOGY.** **See** Medical Science and Technology-Abstracting, Bibliographies and Statistics.

JA/0001-5768
**ACTA GERONTOLOGICA JAPONICA.** (YOKUFUKAI CHOSA KENKYU KIYO.). **VFOAT** Acta Gerontologica Japonica. Week 56 Nov. 1972-. Periodical. Japanese. Yokufukai Byoin, (Yokufukai Hospital), 12-1, Takaido Nishi 1 Chome, Suginamiku, Tokyoto 168, Japan. **UDC** 613.98. **NLM** W1 YO675A. ***Continues*** *Acta Gerontologica Japonica, 0001-5768.*

US/0192-4788
**ACTIVITIES, ADAPTATION & AGING.** [Act., adapt., aging]. **VAT** Activities, Adaptation, and Aging. Vol. 1, No. 1 (Fall 1980)-. Periodical. English. qt. $200.00 US; $280.00 other. The Haworth Press Inc, 10 Alice Street, Binghamton NY 13904-1580. **Tel** (607)722-5857, (800)3-HAWORTH, FAX (607)722-1424. **ED** Phyllis M. Foster (editor's address: Activities Program Consultant, 6549 South Lincoln Street, Littleton, CO 80121). **LC** RC952.5; .A24. **DD** 362.6/05. **NLM** W1 AC9802. **CODEN** AADADK. **Bk Rev. Ad Acc. Pr Rev. Acid Free. Circ:** 383. available on microfilm and microfiche from University Microfilms International (UMI). Documents available from BIOSIS Document Express, Haworth Document Delivery Service.
**Desc:** Provides timely and useful case studies, program evaluations, research and theory for activities directors/coordinators in nursing homes and community centers as well as other professionals concerned with the enhancement of the lifestyles of the aged. All articles are peer reviewed or refereed.
**Ind/Abst** Abstr. Soc. Gerontol.; Abstr. Res. Pastor. Care Couns. (19??-); Biol. Abstr.; Commun. Abstr. (?-?); Cumul. Index Nurs. Allied Health Lit.; Index Period. Lit. Aging; Leis. Recreat. Tour. Abstr.; Linguist. Lang. Behav. Abstr.; Psychol. Abstr. (1980-); PsycINFO; PsycLit; Ref. Z.; Soc. Plann. Policy Dev. Abstr.; Soc. Work Abstr. [Select. Cov.]; Sociol. Abstr.; SPORT Discus; SportSearch.

AT/0725-3249
**ACTIVITIES DIGEST.** ***Ceased.*** (1980)-(June 1993). Periodical. English. bm. Activities Digest, PO Box 5227D Newcastle West, New South Wales 2302 Australia. **Tel** 11 61 49 621069.
**Desc:** Information for activity co-ordinators for the aged and disabled.

UK/0261-2763
**ADVANCED GERIATRIC MEDICINE.** [Adv. geriatr. med.]. **VFOAT** Geriatric Medicine. 1-. English. Pitman Books Ltd, 39 Parker Street, London WC2B 51B England. **ED** F I Caird and J Grimley Evans. **UDC** 616-053.9. **NLM** W1 AD404.

UK/0002-0729
**AGE AND AGEING.** [Age ageing]. **Added/Corp** British Geriatrics Society. British Society for Research on Ageing. Vol. 1 (Feb. 1972)-. Academic Scholarly Publication. English. bm. £95.00 UK and Europe; $165.00 other. Oxford University Press, Walton Street, Oxford OX2 6DP England. **Tel** 011 44 865 56767, FAX 011 44 865 267773, telex 837330 OXPRES G. **(Subscription address:** Oxford University Press / USA, Journals Marketing Department, Oxford University Press, 2001 Evans Road, Cary NC 27513.**)** **ED** J. Grimley Evans. **LC** RC952; .A13. **DD** 618.97/005. **NLM** W1 AG31. **CODEN** AANGAH. **[CCC].** Index available. **Bk Rev. Ad Acc. Pr Rev.** available on microfilm and microfiche from University Microfilms International (UMI). Documents available from The Genuine Article, BIOSIS Document Express, UMI Article Clearinghouse, CASDDS.
**Desc:** Biological gerontology and geriatrics, including research on ageing and the clinical, epidemiological and psychological aspects of medicine in old age.
**Ind/Abst** Acad. Abstr. Full Text Elite (July 1990-); Acad. Abstr. (July 1990-); Acad. Search (July 1990-); Appl. Soc. Sci. Index Abstr.; Biol. Abstr.; Chem. Abstr. (1972-1982); Curr. Aware. Biol. Sci., CABS; Curr. Contents Clin. Med.; EMBASE; Expand. Acad. Index (1989-); Health Plan. Adminis.; Health Source (Jul. 1990-); Index Med.; Index Period. Lit. Aging; INFO-SOUTH Abstr.; Mag. Search; Med. Abstr. Newsl.; Mod. Med.; Newsp. Period. Abstr. (1990-); Nutr. Abstr. Rev., Ser. A, Hum. Exp.; Nutr. Res. Newsl. (1972-1982); Life Sci. Collect.; Res. Alert [Full Cov.]; Sci. Cit. Index; SCISEARCH; Soc. Sci. Source (Jul. 1990-); Soc. Sci. Cit. Index [Select. Cov.]; Soc. Sci. Index; Soc. Sci. Index Fulltext (July 1988-) [Full Txt.]; Trop. Dis. Bull.

US/0161-9152
**AGE (OMAHA).** (AGE : THE JOURNAL OF THE AMERICAN AGING ASSOCIATION.). [Age]. **Added/Corp** American Aging Association. Vol. 1, No. 1 (Jan. 1978)-. Academic Scholarly Publication. English. Four times a year. $35.00 (members), $50.00 (non-members) US & Canada; $40.00 (members), $55.00 (non-members) others Comes with America Aging Association membership. American Aging Association, 2129 Providence Avenue, Chester PA 19013. **Tel** (610)876-0200, FAX (610)876-1981. **ED** Arthur K. Balin (editor's phone: (215)874-7550). **NLM** W1 AG299. **CODEN** AGEEDB. Index available. cum. index. **Bk Rev,** (Qty: Varies). **Pr Rev. Circ:** 400. Documents available from The Genuine Article, BIOSIS Document Express, CASDDS.
**Desc:** Papers pertinent to biomedical aging research. Subject areas include effect of age on DNA, RNA hormones, mitochondria, connective tissue, lipid metabolism, central nervous system, etc.
**Ind/Abst** Biol. Abstr.; Chem. Abstr.; Curr. Aware. Biol. Sci., CABS; EMBASE; Int. Aerosp. Abstr.; Life Sci. Collect.; Res. Alert [Full Cov.]; Sci. Cit. Index; SCISEARCH; Soc. Sci. Cit. Index [Select. Cov.].

UK/0144-686X
**AGEING AND SOCIETY.** [Ageing soc.]. **Added/Corp** Centre for Policy on Ageing (London, England) British Society of Gerontology. Vol. 1, Pt. 1 (March 1981)-. Academic Scholarly Publication. English. qt (March, June, September and December). $126.00 US, Canada & Mexico; £72.00 other. Cambridge University Press, The Edinburgh Building, Shaftesbury Road, Cambridge CB2 2RU United Kingdom. **Tel** 011 44 223 312393, FAX 011 44 223 325959. **(Subscription address:** Cambridge University Press / North America, 110 Midland Avenue, Port Chester NY 10573.**)** **ED** Peter G. Coleman. **LC** HQ1060; .A3. **DD** 305.2/6/05. **NLM** W1 AG343T. **[CCC]. Bk Rev.** available on microfilm and microfiche from University Microfilms International (UMI). Documents available from The Genuine Article, UMI Article Clearinghouse.
**Desc:** An interdisciplinary and international journal devoted to publishing papers, particularly from the social sciences and humanitites, which further the understanding of all aspects of human ageing. In addition to the original articles, an extensive book review section, review symposia and an invaluable abstracts section of relevant articles in other journals is featured. A recent feature is the Forum section devoted to controversial and speculative articles.
**Ind/Abst** Abstr. Soc. Gerontol.; Acad. Search (Jan. 1994-); Am. Hist. Life (1985-); Appl. Soc. Sci. Index Abstr.; Curr. Contents Soc. Behav. Sci.; Expand. Acad. Index (1989-); Geogr. Abstr. Human Geogr.; Health Source (Jul. 1993-); Index Period. Lit. Aging; INFO-SOUTH Abstr.; Int. Bibliogr. Sociol.; Int. Polit. Sci. Abstr.; J. Plan. Lit.; Linguist. Lang. Behav. Abstr.; Mag. Search; Newsp. Period. Abstr. (1991-); PAIS Int. Print; Res. Alert [Full Cov.]; Soc. Plann. Policy Dev. Abstr.; Soc. Sci. Source (Jul. 1993-); Soc. Sci. Cit. Index [Full Cov.]; Soc. Sci. Index; Soc. Sci. Index Fulltext (Dec. 1987-) [Full Txt.]; Sociol. Abstr.

US/0890-278X
**AGHE EXCHANGE.** (AGHE EXCHANGE : NEWSLETTER OF THE ASSOCIATION FOR

GERONTOLOGY IN HIGHER EDUCATION.). [AGHE exch.]. **Added/Corp** Association for Gerontology in Higher Education. **VFOAT** AGHExchange; AGHE Xchange. **VAT** Association for Gerontology in Higher Education Exchange. (19??)-. Periodical. English. Four times a year (Jan., Apr., Sept., Nov.). $25.00 US; $30.00 others. Association for Gerontology in Higher Education - AGHE, 1001 Connecticut Avenue Northwest, Suite 410, Washington DC 20036-5504. **Tel** (202)429-9277. **ED** Leslie Morgan, Ph.D. **DD** 305.
**Desc:** News and information of annual meetings, new books of interest, geriatrics, conferences and summer institutes. It describes the varied dimensions of aging, effects on behavior, and successful strategies for aging.

UK/0268-1544
**AGING.** (19??)-. English. Twenty-four times a year. £110.00. SUBIS, Mansion House, 19 Kingfield Road, Sheffield S11 9AS England. **Tel** 011 44 114 255 4433, FAX 011 44 114 255 4626. **[CCC]**. **Bk Rev**. available on diskette.
**Desc:** A medium for sharing information about programs and activities among interested individuals, agencies, and organizations in the field of geriatrics.

US/0002-0966
**AGING.** ***Ceased.*** (AGING / FEDERAL SECURITY AGENCY.). [Aging]. No. 1 (June 18, 1951)-Issue 367 (1994). Government Publication. English. bm. Superintendent of Documents, US Government Printing Office, Washington DC 20402. **Tel** (202)275-3328, FAX (202)786-2377. **ED** Priscilla Jones (Editors Phone: (202)619-1352). **LC** HV1457; .A65. **NLM** W1 AG342. available on microfilm and microfiche from University Microfilms International (UMI). Documents available from UMI Article Clearinghouse. ***Continues*** *Aging (United States Office of Aging), 0002-0966.*
**Desc:** A medium for sharing information about programs and activities among interested individuals, agencies, and organizations in the field of geriatrics.
**Ind/Abst** Acad. Abstr. Full Text Elite (Feb. 1984-Dec. 1993) [Full Txt.]; Acad. Abstr. (Feb. 1984-Dec. 1993); Acad. Search (Feb. 1984-Dec. 1993); Book Rev. Index; Gen. Period. Index (1985-); Health Plan. Adminis.; Health Ref. Cent. (1987-) [Full Txt.] [Select. Cov.]; Health Source (Feb. 1984-); Hospit. Health Admin. Index; INFO-SOUTH Abstr.; Mag. Artic. Summar. Elite (Feb. 1984-Dec. 1993) [Full Txt.]; Mag. Artic. Summar. Select (Feb. 1984-) [Full Txt.]; Mag. Artic. Summar. CD-ROM (Feb. 1984-Dec. 1993); Mag. Search; Newsp. Period. Abstr. (1988-); Read. Guide Period. Lit.; Soc. Sci. Source (Jul. 1993-) [Full Txt.]; Mag. Index (1977-); Urban Aff. Abstr.; Vocat. Search (Feb. 1984-) [Full Txt.].

UK/0959-1346
**AGING AND AGING DISORDERS.** ***Ceased.*** **Added/Corp** Stiftelsen Gamla Tjanarinnor (Stockholm, Sweden). No. 1 (1990)-(199?). Monographic series. English. Smith Gordon and Company Ltd, 16 Gunter Grove, No. 1, London SE1 0UJ England. **Tel** 011 44 71 3517042, FAX 011 44 71 3511250. **NLM** W1; AG326E.

US/0194-455X
**AGING & LEISURE LIVING.** **Added/Corp** Modern Life Systems. National Geriatrics Society. **VAT** Aging and Leisure Living. Vol. 1 (Nov. 1978)-. Periodical. English. mo. **NLM** W1 AG326D. ***Supersedes*** *Concern in Care of the Aging.*
**Ind/Abst** Index Period. Lit. Aging.

US
**AGING AND SENSORY CHANGE : AN ANNOTATED BIBLIOGRAPHY.** Bibliography. English. $12.50. Gerontological Society of America, 1275 K Street Northwest, Suite 350, Washington DC 20005. **Tel** (202)842-1275, FAX (202)842-1150.
**Desc:** A new state-of-the-art synthesis of works published on aging and sensory change: vision, hearing, chemosensory, somotosensory, multiple/interactive conditions, and rehabilitation.

US/0272-3808
**AGING (GUILFORD, CONN.).** (AGING.). [Aging]. **VFOAT** Annual Editions: Aging. (1980)-. Periodical. English. an. $10.95. Dushkin Publishing Group Inc., Sluice Dock, Guilford CT 06437. **Tel** (203)453-4351, (800)243-6532, FAX (203)453-6000. **ED** Harold Cox. **LC** HQ1060; .A57. **DD** 305.2/6. ***Continues*** *Focus. Aging, 0162-3621.*
**Desc:** Includes articles from the biological sciences, medicine, nursing, psychology, sociology, and social work. Articles are taken from the public press, government publications, and scientific journals and represent a wide cross section of authors, perspectives, and issues related to the aging process.

IT/0394-9532
**AGING (MILAN, ITALY).** (AGING : CLINICAL AND EXPERIMENTAL RESEARCH.). Vol. 1, No. 1 (Sept. 1989)-. Periodical. English. bm. L10000 Italy; $100.00 other. Editrice Kurtis Srl, Via Luigi Zoja 30, 20153 Milan Italy. **Tel** 011 39 2 48202740, FAX 011 39 2 48201219. **NLM** W1; AG326CH. **Ad Acc**. Documents available from The Genuine Article.
**Desc:** Offers a multidisciplinary forum on the field of gerontology and geriatrics.
**Ind/Abst** Curr. Contents Clin. Med.; EMBASE; Health Plan. Adminis.; Index Med. (1989-); Res. Alert [Select. Cov.]; Soc. Sci. Cit. Index [Select. Cov.].

US/0160-2721
**AGING (NEW YORK, N.Y.).** (AGING.). [Aging]. **VFOAT** Aging Series. Vol. 1 (1975)-. Academic Scholarly Publication. English. ir. Price varies per volume. Raven Press, 1185 Avenue of the Americas, 37th Floor, New York NY 10036. **Tel** (212)930-9500, (212)930-9604, FAX (212)869-3495, (212)302-8507, telex 640073. **LC** UNC. **DD** 612. **NLM** W1 AG342E. **CODEN** AGNYDE. Documents available from BIOSIS Document Express, CASDDS.
**Ind/Abst** Biol. Abstr.; Chem. Abstr.; Mag. ASAP Plus [Full Txt.]; Mag. ASAP Sel. [Full Txt.]; Mag. Index Plus (1989-); Mag. Index. Sel. (1986-); Nutr. Res. Newsl.; Read. Guide Abstr. Select Ed.; Read. Guide Period. Lit.; Soc. Work Abstr. [Select. Cov.].

US/0888-6830
**AGING RESEARCH & TRAINING NEWS.** [Aging res. train. news]. **VFOAT** Aging Research and Training News. (198?)-. Periodical. English. Twenty-four times a year. $240.00. Business Publishers Inc., 951 Pershing Drive, Silver Spring MD 20910-4464. **Tel** (301)587-6300, (800)274-0122, FAX (301)585-9075. **LC** HQ1060; .A34. **DD** 305.2/6/072073. **[CCC]**. ***Continues*** *Aging News, 0197-4017.*
**Desc:** The only grants newsletter exclusively covering gerontology and geriatrics. Keeps you updated on the most current gerontological research.

US/0734-6026
**AMERICAN ASSOCIATION FOR GERIATRIC PSYCHIATRY NEWSLETTER.** **See** Medical Science and Technology-Psychiatry.

US/1064-7481
**AMERICAN JOURNAL OF GERIATRIC PSYCHIATRY, THE.** [Am. j. geriatr. psychiatry]. **Added/Corp** American Association for Geriatric Psychiatry. American Psychiatric Press. (199?)-. Periodical. English. qt. $135.00 US; $150.00 other (institution). American Psychiatric Press Inc., 1400 K Street Northwest, Suite 1101, Washington DC 20005. **Tel** (202)682-6222, FAX (202)789-2648. **DD** 616. **NLM** W1; AM452EQ. **Bk Rev**. **Ad Acc**. **Pr Rev**.
**Desc:** This journal will be the leading source of scientific and clinical information for the rapidly developing field of geriatric psychiatry. Regular features include clinical concepts and case reports, editorials and perspectives, book reviews, abstracts, and letters to the editor, as well as AAGP news and announcements.

US
**ANDERSON PLANNER, THE.** **See** Recreation, Leisure-Games and Amusements.

FR/0184-6531
**ANNEES. DOCUMENTS CLEIRPPA.** [Annees, Doc. CLEIRPPA]. **VFOAT** Annees. Documents Centre de Liaison, d'Etude, d'Information et de Recherche sur les Problemes des Personnes Agees. (1971)-. Periodical. French. bm (6 issues). 293.83F France; 350.00F other. CLEIRPPA, 15 Rue Chateaubraind, 75008 Paris France. **Tel** 011 33 1 42257878, FAX 011 33 1 42564826. **UDC** 36. ***Continues*** *Documents CLEIRPPA (Paris), 0991-9244.* ***Continued in part by*** *CLEIRPPA Infos (Paris), 1146-2965.*

US
**ANNUAL REPORT - ADULT DEVELOPMENT AND AGING RESEARCH COMMITTEE, NATIONAL INSTITUTES OF HEALTH.** **Main/Corp** National Institute of Child Health and Human Development. Adult Development and Aging Research Committee. English. an. National Institute of Child Health and Human Development, 9000 Rockville Pike, Bethesda MD 20014.

US
**ANNUAL REPORT / IOWA DEPARTMENT OF ELDER AFFAIRS.** **Main/Corp** Iowa. Dept. of Elder Affairs. **VFOAT** Partners in Aging. (1987)-. English. Commission on the Aging, 415 10th Street, Des Moines IA 50319. **LC** HV1468.I8; I65a. **DD** 353.97770084/6/06. ***Continues*** *Annual Report - Iowa. Commission on the Aging.*

US/0743-0981
**ANNUAL REPORT / KANSAS ADVISORY COUNCIL ON AGING.** [Annu. rep. - Kansas Advis. Counc. Aging]. **Main/Corp** Kansas Advisory Council on Aging. **Added/Corp** Kansas. Department on Aging. (1979)-. English. an. **LC** PAR. **DD** 362.6/09781.

US
**ANNUAL REPORT / SOUTH CAROLINA GENERAL ASSEMBLY. STUDY COMMITTEE ON AGING.** ***Ceased.*** **Main/Corp** South Carolina. General Assembly. Study Committee on Aging. 17th (1986)-(19??). English. Director of Research and Administration, Joint Legislative Study Committee on Aging, PO Box 142, 305 Gressette Building, Columbia SC 29202. **LC** HQ1064.U6; S62a. **DD** 362.6/09757/05. ***Continues*** *Annual Report of the Committee to Conduct Continuing Studies of Public and Private Services Programs and Facilities for the Aging.*

US/0198-8794
**ANNUAL REVIEW OF GERONTOLOGY & GERIATRICS.** [Annu. rev. gerontol. geriatr.]. **VFOAT** Annual Review of Gerontology and Geriatrics. **VAT** Annual review of gerontology and geriatrics. Vol. 1 (1980)-. English. an. $46.00 US; $51.00 other (volume 13). Springer Publishing Company, 536 Broadway, New York NY 10012-3955. **Tel** (212)431-4370, FAX (212)941-7842. **ED** Powell Lawton. **LC** RC952.A1; A56. **DD** 362.5/05. **NLM** W1 AN772.
**Ind/Abst** Abstr. Soc. Gerontol.; Health Plan. Adminis.; Index Med.

US/0191-7854
**AOA OCCASIONAL PAPERS IN GERONTOLOGY.** **VAT** Administration on Aging Occasional Papers in Gerontology. No. 1-. Monographic series. English. ir. Price varies per volume. Administration for Children & Families, 370 L'Enfant Promenade SW, 6th Floor, Washington DC 20447. **Tel** (202)401-9200, FAX (202)252-4683. **UDC** 613.98. **NLM** W1 A14V.

NE/0167-4943
**ARCHIVES OF GERONTOLOGY AND GERIATRICS.** [Arch. gerontol. geriatr.]. Vol. 1, No. 1 (May 1982)-. Academic Scholarly Publication. English. bm (2 vols.). $673.00. Elsevier Science Ireland Ltd., Bay 15, Shannon Industrial Estate, Co Clare Ireland. **Tel** 011 353 61 471944. **ED** I Zs Nagy, R Cutler, S Hoyer, K Kitani and L S Libow. **LC** QP86; .A73. **DD** 305.2/6/05. **NLM** W1 AR455AL. **CODEN** AGGEDL. **Pr Rev.** available on microfilm and microfiche from University Microfilms International (UMI). Documents available from The Genuine Article, CASDDS.
**Desc:** Provides a medium for the publication of papers from the fields of experimental gerontology and clinical and social geriatrics.
**Ind/Abst** Chem. Abstr.; Curr. Aware. Biol. Sci., CABS; Curr. Contents Life Sci.; EMBASE; Health Plan. Adminis.; Index Med. (May 1980-1989); Index Period. Lit. Aging; Int. Aerosp. Abstr. (1983-); Nutr. Res. Newsl.; Life Sci. Collect.; Psychol. Abstr. (1982-); PsycINFO; PsycLit; Ref. Upd. Deluxe Ed.; Res. Alert [Full Cov.]; Sci. Cit. Index; SCISEARCH; Soc. Sci. Cit. Index [Select. Cov.]; SportSearch.

NE/0924-7947
**ARCHIVES OF GERONTOLOGY AND GERIATRICS. SUPPLEMENT.** [Arch. gerontol. geriatr., Suppl.]. Vol. 1 (1989)-. Monographic series. English. Price varies per volume. Elsevier Science Ireland Ltd., Bay 15, Shannon Industrial Estate, Co Clare Ireland. **Tel** 011 353 61 471944. **LC** RC952.A1; A73. **NLM** W1; AR455ALa.
**Ind/Abst** Health Plan. Adminis.; Index Med. (1989-).

IT/1120-6888
**ARGOMENTI DI GERONTOLOGIA.** [Argom. gerontol.]. (1989)-. Periodical. Italian. ir (6 issues). L8100. Masson S.P.A, Via Statuto 2/4, 20121 Milan Italy. **Tel** 011 39 2 63671, FAX 011 39 2 6367211. **UDC** 613.98.

●US
**AUDIO-VISUAL GUIDE, RESOURCES IN GERONTOLOGY & GERIATRICS.** **Added/Corp** Pacific Geriatric Education Center. **VFOAT** Resources in Gerontology & Geriatrics; Resources in Gerontology and Geriatric Education; Audio-Visual Guide, Resources for Gerontology and Geriatric Education. 4th Ed. (1991/1992)-. English. **LC** HQ1060; .A92. ***Continues*** *Audio-Visual Resources for Gerontological and Geriatric Education.*

AT/0726-4240
**AUSTRALIAN JOURNAL ON AGEING.** **Added/Corp** Australian Council on the Ageing. **VFOAT** Australian Journal of Ageing. Vol. 1, No. 1 (Feb. 1982)-. Periodical. English. Four times a year (Feb., May, Aug., Nov.). 48.00Aus$ Australia; 54.00Aus$ News Zealand & Pacific Islands; 60.00Aus$ others. Australian Council on the Ageing, VACC House, 464 Kilda Road, 3rd Floor, Melbourne Victoria 3004 Australia. **Tel** 011 61 3 8202655. **ED** Cliff Picton. **NLM** W1; AU6267. Index available. cum. index. **Bk Rev**. **Ad Acc**. **Circ:** 1,000.
**Ind/Abst** APAIS, Aust. Public Aff. Inf. Ser.

US/1049-085X
**BEHAVIOR, HEALTH AND AGING.** [Behav. health aging]. Vol. 1, No. 1 (Spring 1990)-. Periodical. English. qt. $40.00 (1 year, individuals), $72.00 (2 year, individuals), $77.00 (1 year, institutions), $129.00 (2 year, institutions) US; $45.00 (1 year, individuals), $82.00 (2 year, individuals), $86.00 (1 year, institutions), $149.00 (2 year, institutions) other. Springer Publishing Company, 536 Broadway, New York NY 10012-3955. **Tel** (212)431-4370, FAX (212)941-7842. **ED** Carl Eisdorfer. **LC** RC952.A1; B44. **DD** 618.97. **NLM** W1; BE124L. **CODEN** BHAGEG.
**Desc:** Addresses health issues in aging, focusing on lifestyles and behavior. Provides a forum for the interchange of ideas, reports on clinical practice, and advances in research; explorations of biopsychosocial implications of health conscious aging starting in mid-life.
**Ind/Abst** Abstr. Soc. Gerontol.; Annals Behav. Med.; Cumul. Index Nurs. Allied Health Lit.; Psychoanal. Abstr.; Psychol. Abstr. (1990-); PsycINFO; PsycScan: Appl. Exp.

Eng. Psych.; PsycScan: LD/MR; PsycScan: Neuropsych.; Sage Fam. Stud. Abstr.; Soc. Plann. Policy Dev. Abstr.; Sociol. Abstr.

US/0743-7560
**BIBLIOGRAPHIES AND INDEXES IN GERONTOLOGY.** [Bibliogr. indexes gerontol.]. (1985)-. Monographic series. English. ir. Price varies per volume. Greenwood Press Inc., PO Box 5007, Westport CT 06881-5007. **Tel** (203)226-3571, FAX (203)222-1502. **DD** 362. **NLM** ZWT 100; B5824.

US/0149-0966
**BIORESEARCH TODAY. HUMAN & ANIMAL AGING.** ***Ceased.*** **VFOAT** Human & Animal Aging. **VAT** BioResearch Today. Human and Animal Aging. Ceased (Dec. 1991). Periodical. English. mo. BioSciences Information Service, Biological Abstracts / BIOSIS, 2100 Arch Street, Philadelphia PA 19103-1399. **Tel** (800)523-4806 US, (215)587-4800 Pennsylvania and worldwide, FAX (215)587-2016, telex 831739. **UDC** 591.139; 612.67.
**Desc:** Current awareness journal including abstracts and content summaries of studies involving human and animal aging.

●US/1067-7372
**BROWN UNIVERSITY GERIATRIC RESEARCH APPLICATION DIGEST, THE.** (THE BROWN UNIVERSITY GERIATRIC RESEARCH APPLICATION DIGEST : GRAD.). [Brown Univ. geriatr. res. appl. dig.]. **Added/Corp** Brown University. Center for Gerontology and Health Care Research. **VFOAT** GRAD; Geriatric Research Application Digest. Vol. 1, No. 1 (Jan. 1993)-. Periodical. English. mo. $129.00 (institutions), $99.00 (individuals) US; $139.00 (institutions), $109.00 (individuals) Canada; $149.00 (institutions), $119.00 (individuals) other. Manisses Communications Group Inc., PO Box 3357, Providence RI 02906-0757. **Tel** (401)831-6020, (800)333-7771, FAX (401)861-6370. **ED** Vincent Mor. **DD** 617. Index available.

CN/0845-2970
**CANADIAN JOURNAL OF GERIATRICS, THE.** [Can. j. geriatr.]. **VFOAT** Geriatrics. Vol. 3 No. 5 (Oct./Nov. 1987)-. Periodical. English. ir (8 issues). 68.00Can$ Canada; 86.00Can$ other. STA Communications Inc., 955 St. John Boulevard, Suite 306, Pt Claire, Quebec H9R 5K3 Canada. **Tel** (514)695-7623. **DD** 618.97/005. **NLM** W1; CA588F. **Circ:** 24,000 (ctrl). ***Continues*** *Perspectives in Geriatrics, 0828-640X.*
**Desc:** Contains essential, practical clinical review articles on the day-to-day medical and social treatment of our aging population. Articles written by distinguished experts from various specialties, directed to the primary care physician.
**Ind/Abst** Can. Period. Index.

CN/0008-4174
**CANADIAN JOURNAL OF OCCUPATIONAL THERAPY (1939). See** Medical Science and Technology-Psychiatry.

CN/0714-9808
**CANADIAN JOURNAL ON AGING.** [Can. j. aging]. **Added/Corp** Canadian Association on Gerontology. **VFOAT** Revue Canadienne du Vieillissement. Vol. 1, No. 1/2 (1982)-. Periodical. English (summaries and/or abstracts in French). qt (4 issues). 58.00Can$ (institutions), 43.00Can$ (individuals) Canada; 67.00Can$ (institutions), 52.00Can$ (individuals) other; Comes also with Canadian Association on Gerontology membership. University of Guelph / Business Office, Room 039, Mackinnon Building, Guelph, Ontario N1G 2W1 Canada. **Tel** (519)824-4120 ext. 6925, FAX (519)837-9953. **ED** J. Rosemary Vanderkamp (editor's telephone: (519)824-4120 ext. 3330). **DD** 612.6/7/05. **Bk Rev. Ad Acc, Adv Mgr:** same as editor. **Pr Rev.** Documents available from The Genuine Article.
**Ind/Abst** Abstr. Soc. Gerontol.; Can. Index (?-?); Can. Period. Index (19??-); Curr. Contents Soc. Behav. Sci.; Curr. Index J. Educ.; EMBASE; Linguist. Lang. Behav. Abstr.; Psychol. Abstr. (1982-); PsycINFO; PsycLit; Res. Alert [Full Cov.]; Sage Fam. Stud. Abstr. (?-?); Soc. Plann. Policy Dev. Abstr.; Soc. Sci. Cit. Index [Full Cov.]; Soc. Work Abstr. (Spring, Summer 1987-) [Select. Cov.]; Sociol. Abstr.

US
**CAPSULE. See** Senior Citizens.

●US/1058-3661
**CARDIOLOGY IN THE ELDERLY. See** Medical Science and Technology-Cardiology.

UK/0955-4262
**CARE OF THE ELDERLY.** Vol. 1, No. 1 (May 1989)-. Periodical. English. mo (10 issues). £45.00 UK; £67.50 Europe; $115.00 US & Canada; £63.50 other. Macmillan Magazines Ltd., Houndmills, Basingstoke, Hampshire RG21 2XS England. **Tel** 011 44 256 29242, FAX 011 44 256 812358, telex 858493. **NLM** W1; CA778.

US/0738-467X
**CARING (WASHINGTON, D.C.).** (CARING : NATIONAL ASSOCIATION FOR HOME CARE MAGAZINE.). [Caring]. **Added/Corp** National Association for Home Care (U.S.). (Oct. 1982)-. Periodical. English. mo. $45.00. National Association for Home Care, 519 C Street Northeast, Stanton Park, Washington DC 20002. **Tel** (202)547-7424, FAX (202)547-3540. **ED** Christopher E Laxton and Rebecca Staebler. **NLM** W1 CA789J. **CODEN** CARGET. Index available. **Ad Acc. Circ:** 4,000.
**Desc:** Features articles on the wide variety of health care services provided in the home. Profiles of service providers, case studies of patients, technical and clinical coverage, legislative, legal, accounting and management issues.
**Ind/Abst** Abstr. Clin. Care Guidel.; Cumul. Index Nurs. Allied Health Lit.; Hospit. Health Admin. Index; Int. Nurs. Index; Int. Pharm. Abstr.

FR/1146-2965
**CLEIRPPA INFOS PARIS.** (CLEIRPPA INFOS.). **VFOAT** Centre de Liaison, d'Etude, d'Information et de Recherche sur les Problemes des Personnes Agees Infos (Paris). (19??)-. Periodical. French. mo. 146.91F France; 195.00F other. CLEIRPPA, 15 Rue Chateaubraind, 75008 Paris France. **Tel** 011 33 1 42257878, FAX 011 33 1 42564826. **UDC** 308-053.88. ***Continues in part*** *Annees. Documents CLEIRPPA, 0184-6531.*

US/0731-7115
**CLINICAL GERONTOLOGIST.** [Clin. gerontol.]. Vol. 1, No. 1 (Fall 1982)-. Periodical. English. qt. $240.00 US; $343.00 other. The Haworth Press Inc, 10 Alice Street, Binghamton NY 13904-1580. **Tel** (607)722-5857, (800)3-HAWORTH, FAX (607)722-1424. **ED** Terry Brink (editor's address: 1103 Church Street, Redlands, CA 92374). **NLM** W1 CL71D. **Bk Rev. Ad Acc. Pr Rev. Acid Free. Circ:** 459. available on microfilm and microfiche from University Microfilms International (UMI). Documents available from Haworth Document Delivery Service. ***Absorbed*** *Aged Care & Services Review, 0161-1151.*
**Desc:** This journal presents timely material which is relevant to the needs of mental health professionals and all practitioners who deal with the aged client and the problems found later in life.
**Ind/Abst** Abstr. Soc. Gerontol.; Abstr. Res. Pastor. Care Couns. (19??-); Annals Behav. Med.; Cumul. Index Nurs. Allied Health Lit.; EMBASE; Health Plan. Adminis.; Health Serv. Abstr.; Hospit. Health Admin. Index; Hum. Resour. Abstr.; Index Period. Lit. Aging; Linguist. Lang. Behav. Abstr.; Mod. Med.; Life Sci. Collect.; Pollut. Abstr. Indexes; Psychol. Abstr. (1982-); PsycINFO; PsycLit; Ref. Z.; Sage Fam. Stud. Abstr. (?-?); Soc. Plann. Policy Dev. Abstr.; Soc. Work Abstr. (Summer 1987-) [Select. Cov.]; Sociol. Abstr.

US/0749-0690
**CLINICS IN GERIATRIC MEDICINE.** [Clin. geriatr. med.]. **VFOAT** Geriatric Clinics. Vol. 1, No. 1 (Feb. 1985)-. Periodical. English. qt. $87.00 (individual), $111.00 (institution) US; $124.00 (individual), $131.00 (institutions) other. W.B. Saunders Company, A Subsidiary of Harcourt Brace Jovanovich, Inc., The Curtis Center/Suite 300, Independence Square West, Philadelphia PA 19106-3399. **Tel** (215)238-7800 or, 5587, FAX (215)238-7883, telex 173146. **(Subscription address:** W. B. Saunders Company / North America Subscriptions, c/o Periodicals, 6277 Sea Harbour Drive, 4th Floor, Orlando FL 32887.) **ED** Christine Battle. **LC** RC952.A1. **DD** 618.97/005. **UDC** 616-053.9. **NLM** W1; CL831BGC. **[CCC].** Index available. **Circ:** 1,500. available on microfilm and microfiche from University Microfilms International (UMI).
**Desc:** Updates for clinicians on the latest advances. Each issue addresses a single topic in patient care.
**Ind/Abst** Cumul. Index Nurs. Allied Health Lit.; EMBASE; Health Plan. Adminis.; Index Med. (1985-); Physic. Medline Plus; Soc. Sci. Cit. Index [Select. Cov.].

US/0748-2760
**CONTEMPORARY GERIATRIC MEDICINE.** [Contemp. geriatr. med.]. (1983)-. Monographic series. English. ir. Price varies per volume. Plenum Press, 233 Spring Street, New York NY 10013-1578. **Tel** (212)620-8000, (800)221-9369, FAX (212)463-0742, (212)807-1047, telex 23/421139. **ED** Steven R. Gambert. **LC** RC952.A1; C66. **DD** 618.97/005. **NLM** W1 CO769MPJ.

●US/1069-0840
**CONTEMPORARY GERONTOLOGY.** (1994)-. Periodical. English. qt. $36.00 (individuals, 1 year), $62.00 (individuals, 2 year), $70.00 (institutions, 1 year), $109.00 (institutions, 2 year) US; $40.00 (individuals, 1 year), $74.00 (individuals, 2 year), $79.00 (institutions, 1 year), $119.00 (institutions, 2 year) other. $18.00 (1 year), $31.00 (2 year) US; $20.00 (1 year), $37.00 (2 year) other, ASA members. Springer Publishing Company, 536 Broadway, New York NY 10012-3955. **Tel** (212)431-4370, FAX (212)941-7842. **ED** Robert C. Atchley, PhD.

CN/0824-1384
**CONTINUING CARE RESOURCES. See** Medical Science and Technology-Hospital Administration and Medical Centers.

US/0732-085X
**CONTRIBUTIONS TO THE STUDY OF AGING.** [Contrib. stud. aging]. No. 1 (1982)-. Monographic series. English. ir. Price varies per volume. Greenwood Press Inc., PO Box 5007, Westport CT 06881-5007. **Tel** (203)226-3571, FAX (203)222-1502. **LC** UNC. **NLM** W1 CO778W.

UK/0953-2501
**CURRENT MEDICAL LITERATURE-GERIATRICS.** (CURRENT MEDICAL LITERATURE. GERIATRICS/THE ROYAL SOCIETY OF MEDICINE.). **Added/Corp** Royal Society of Medicine (Great Britain) Imperial Chemical Industries, ltd. Pharmaceuticals Division. **VFOAT** Geriatrics. (198?)-. Periodical. English. qt. £20.00 UK; 40.00 US;; £20.00 other. Current Medical Literature Ltd., 40-42 Osnaburgh Street, London NW1 3ND England. **Tel** 011 44 71 4658377, FAX 011 44 71 4658380. **(Subscription address:** Royal Society Medicine Services, 1 Wimpole Street, London W1M 8AE England.) **NLM** ZWT 100; C9765.

NE
**DENKBEELD.** Versluys Uitgeverij BJ, Ranstad 21-25, 1314 BE Almere Netherlands.

US/1056-1951
**DIGEST OF GERIATRICS.** ***Ceased.*** [Dig. geriatr.]. Vol. 1, No. 1 (June 1991)-Vol. 3, No. 12, (Dec. 1993). Periodical. English. mo. W.B. Saunders Company, A Subsidiary of Harcourt Brace Jovanovich, Inc., The Curtis Center/Suite 300, Independence Square West, Philadelphia PA 19106-3399. **Tel** (215)238-7800 or, 5587, FAX (215)238-7883, telex 173146. **(Subscription address:** W. B. Saunders Company / North America Subscriptions, c/o Periodicals, 6277 Sea Harbour Drive, 4th Floor, Orlando FL 32887.) **DD** 618.

US/0745-
**DIRECTORY OF GERIATRIC PUBLICATIONS, THE.** (19??)-. Directory. English. an. $89.00 US; (add $15.00 postage) other. DRS Geriatric Publishing Co, 7435 Southeast 71st Street, Mercer Island WA 98040. **Tel** (206)232-9689. **ED** Frances Greer. **LC** Z7164.O4; D5. **NLM** ZWT 100; D598. Index available. **Bk Rev. Circ:** 1,000. ***Continues*** *Geriatric Guide to Pertinent Publications.*
**Desc:** Instant easy access to all printed sources on every aspect of geriatric care.

NZ/1170-229X
**DRUGS & AGING. See** Pharmacy and Pharmacology.

UK
**EDUCATION & AGEING.** (19??)-. English. Twice a year (Apr., & Oct.). £12.00 UK; £13.00 Europe; £14.50 others. Association for Educational Gerontology, Center for Social Gerontology, University of Keele, Staff ST5 5BG England. **Tel** 0782-584063. **Bk Rev. Circ:** 350. ***Continues*** *Journal of Educational Gerontology.*

US
**ELDER VOICES. See** Ethnic Interests.

●SP
**EUROPEAN JOURNAL OF GERONTOLOGY : THE JOURNAL OF THE EUROPEAN REGION OF THE INTERNATIONAL ASSOCIATION OF GERONTOLOGY.** ***Suspended.*** **Added/Corp** International Association of Gerontology. European Region. Vol. 1 No. 1 (Sept. 1991)-(19??). Periodical. English. Eight times a year. $180.00. SANED SA, Paseo de la Habana 202 Bis, 28036 Madrid Spain. **Tel** 011 34 1 5553508. **NLM** W1; EU77DEJ. **CODEN** EJGEEJ.

NE/0014-424X
**EXCERPTA MEDICA. SECTION 20. GERONTOLOGY AND GERIATRICS. See** Medical Science and Technology-Abstracting, Bibliographies and Statistics.

US/0361-073X
**EXPERIMENTAL AGING RESEARCH.** [Exp. aging res.]. Vol. 1 (Sept. 1975)-. Periodical. English. qt (published within the seasons, starting with Spring issue). £92.00 UK; $152.00 other. Taylor & Francis Ltd., Rankine Road, Basingstoke Hampshire, RG24 8PR United Kingdom. **Tel** 011 44 256 840366, FAX 011 44 256 479438, telex 858540. **(Subscription address:** Taylor & Francis Inc., 1900 Frost Road, Suite 101, Bristol PA 19007-1598.) **ED** Merrill F. Elias. **LC** QP86; .E84. **NLM** W1 EX46. **CODEN** EAGRDS. **Bk Rev. Ad Acc. Pr Rev. Circ:** 1,000 (ctrl). available on microfilm and microfiche from University Microfilms International (UMI). Documents available from The Genuine Article, BIOSIS Document Express, CASDDS.
**Desc:** A behavioral, behavioral-medical and bio-behavioral journal dealing with the scientific study of aging and the elderly. Submissions can be from any discipline as long as behavior is a predictor or criterion variable. Original research, book reviews, monographs, special symposia, notes and news are published. Emphasis on rapid, critical, and objective scientific review of manuscripts.

**Ind/Abst** Abstr. Soc. Gerontol.; Annals Behav. Med.; Biol. Abstr.; Chem. Abstr.; Cumul. Index Nurs. Allied Health Lit.; Curr. Contents Life Sci.; EMBASE; Energy Res. Abstr. (Aug. 1982-); Health Plan. Adminis.; Hospit. Health Admin. Index; Index Med.; Index Period. Lit. Aging; INIS Atomindex [Micro.]; Nutr. Res. Newsl.; Life Sci. Collect.; Protozoolog. Abstr. (?-1987); Psychol. Abstr. (1975-); PsycINFO (1975-); PsycLit; Res. Alert [Full Cov.]; Sci. Cit. Index; SCISEARCH; Soc. Sci. Cit. Index [Select. Cov.]; SportSearch.

UK/0531-5565
**EXPERIMENTAL GERONTOLOGY.** [Exp. gerontol.]. Vol. 1 (July 1964)-. Academic Scholarly Publication. English. bm. $582.00 The Americas; £390.00 other. Pergamon Press, An Imprint of Elsevier Science Ltd., The Boulevard, Langford Lane, Kidlington, Oxford OX5 1GB United Kingdom. **Tel** 011 44 865 843000, 011 44 865 843699, FAX 011 44 865 843010. **(Subscription address:** Elsevier Science Ltd. Oxford Fulfillment Centre, PO Box 800, Kidlington, Oxford OX5 1DX United Kingdom.**) ED** Leonard Hayflick. **LC** QP86; .E85. **DD** 612.6/7/05. **NLM** W1 EX504D. **CODEN** EXGEAB. **[CCC]. Pr Rev.** available on microfilm and microfiche from Microfilms International Marketing Corp. Documents available from The Genuine Article, BIOSIS Document Express, CASDDS.
**Desc:** Devoted to the publication of results of research that elucidate the processes of biological aging in plants, animals and humans from the molecular level to that of the whole organism.
**Ind/Abst** AGRICOLA; Anim. Breed. Abstr.; Appl. Soc. Sci. Index Abstr.; Biol. Abstr.; Chem. Abstr.; CSA Neuro. Abstr. (?-?); Curr. Aware. Biol. Sci., CABS; Curr. Contents Life Sci.; EMBASE; Index Med.; Index Vet.; INIS Atomindex [Micro.]; Int. Aerosp. Abstr.; Nematol. Abstr.; Nutr. Res. Newsl.; Life Sci. Collect.; Protozoolog. Abstr.; Res. Alert [Full Cov.]; Rev. Med. Vet. Entomol.; Sci. Cit. Index; SCISEARCH; Soc. Sci. Cit. Index [Select. Cov.]; Vet. Bull.

●US
**FACTS AND RESEARCH IN GERONTOLOGY.** (1992)-. English. an. $44.95 (hardcover). Springer Publishing Company, 536 Broadway, New York NY 10012-3955. **Tel** (212)431-4370, FAX (212)941-7842. **LC** RC952.A1; F3.

CN/0827-3103
**FIT THIRD AGE.** (A FIT THIRD AGE / SECRETARIAT FOR FITNESS IN THE THIRD AGE.). [Fit third age]. **Added/Corp** Secretariat for Fitness in the Third Age. **VFOAT** Troisieme Age en Forme. **VAT** Troisieme Age en Forme. No. 1 (1984)-. Periodical. English (French). Three times a year. Free. Secretariat for Fitness in the Third Age, 333 River Road, Vanier Ontario K1L 8H9 Canada. **Tel** (613)748-5651. **ED** Harry F Kerrison. **DD** 613.7/0971. **Bk Rev. Circ:** 6,000 (ctrl).
**Desc:** Normally about trends and philosophies relating to physical activity and the aging process.
**Ind/Abst** Leis. Recreat. Tour. Abstr.

US/0892-7103
**FOCUS ON GERIATRIC CARE & REHABILITATION.** [Focus geriatr. care rehabil.]. **VFOAT** Focus on Geriatric Care and Rehabilitation. (1987)-. Periodical. English. Ten times a year (Jul./Aug. and Nov./Dec. issues combined). $75.00 US. Aspen Publishers Inc., 7201 McKinney Circle, Frederick MD 21701. **Tel** (800)234-1660, (301)698-7100, FAX (301)251-5784, telex 5106014543. **(Subscription address:** Aspen Publishers Inc., PO Box 990, Frederick MD 21701.**) ED** Joan K. Glickstein, PhD. **DD** 362.
**Desc:** Practical reports for direct caregivers in geriatric setting. Special emphasis given to tips and strategies that can be implemented immediately to improve patient well being.

US/0271-955X
**FRONTIERS IN AGING SERIES.** [Front. aging ser.]. Vol. 1 (1980)-. Monographic series. English. ir. Price varies per volume. Human Sciences Press, PO Box 735, 233 Spring Street, New York NY 10013. **Tel** (212)620-8000, FAX (212)807-1047, telex 23421139. **ED** Gari Lesnoff-Caravaglia. **LC** UNC. **NLM** W1 FR945T. **CODEN** FROAEC. **Pr Rev.** available in reprints from University Microfilms International (UMI); available in microform from University Microfilms International (UMI). Documents available from BIOSIS Document Express.
**Ind/Abst** Biol. Abstr.; Health Plan. Adminis.; Hospit. Health Admin. Index.

SZ/1011-2901
**GERATRIE FUER DIE TAEGLICHE PRAXIS.** [Geriatr. Tagl. Prax.]. (1988)-. Monographic series. German. an. 30.00F (approx. per volume). S. Karger AG, Allschwilerstrasse 10, PO Box - Postfach - Case Postale, CH-4009 Basel Switzerland. **Tel** 011 41 61 306-1111, FAX 011 41 61 306-1234, telex CH 962 652. **ED** W. Meier-Ruge. **CODEN** GTPREP. Index available. cum. index. available on microfilm and microfiche. Documents available from BIOSIS Document Express.
**Ind/Abst** Biol. Abstr.

AT/1032-4410
**GERIACTION.** [Geriaction]. **Added/Corp** Australian Association for Geriatric Nursing Care. (1970)-. Periodical. English. qt. 60.00Aus$. Geriaction Inc., 282 Victoria Avenue, Suite 401, Chatswood New South Wales, 2067 Australia. **Tel** 11 61 2 4122145. **DD** 610.736505.

UK/0951-5216
**GERIATRIC CARDIOVASCULAR MEDICINE.** [Geriatr. cardiovasc. med.]. Began in 1988. Periodical. English. ir. $80.00 (personal); $135.00 (institutions). Gower Academic Journals, c/o J Robinson, 34 Cleveland Street, London W1P 5FB England. **NLM** W1; GE455R.

US
**GERIATRIC CARE.** Periodical. English. mo. $87.50 (25 copies monthly). Eymann Publications, PO Box 3577, Reno NV 89505. **Tel** (702)333-6651. **Circ:** 1,000 (ctrl).

US/1048-7514
**GERIATRIC CARE NEWS.** [Geriatr. care news]. Vol. 14, No. 7 (July 1989)-. Periodical. English. mo. $69.00 (one year), $128.00 (two year), $189.00 (three year). DRS Geriatric Publ Corp, 7435 SE 71st Street, Mercer Island WA 98040. **DD** 618. ***Continues*** *Geriatric & Residential Care News, 0745-5070.*

US/0745-1202
**GERIATRIC CONSULTANT.** ***Ceased.*** [Geriatr. consult.]. Vol. 1, No. 1 (July/Aug. 1982)-(Nov./Dec. 1993). Periodical. English. bm. Medical Publishers Enterprises, 15 22 Fair Lawn Avenue, Fair Lawn NJ 07410. **Tel** (201)796-6500. **DD** 618. **NLM** W1; GE456L.

US/0891-2173
**GERIATRIC LENGTH OF STAY BY DIAGNOSIS AND OPERATION, UNITED STATES.** [Geriatr. length stay diagn. oper. U. S.]. **Added/Corp** Commission on Professional and Hospital Activities. **VFOAT** Length of Stay by Diagnosis, by Operation, United States, Geriatric; Length of Stay, Geriatric. (1981)-. English. an. $165.89 Connecticut; $166.26 Illinois; $164.40 South Carolina & Maryland; $162.91 Michigan; $168.72 Washington; $156.95 others. HCIA, 300 East Lombard Street, Baltimore MD 21202. **Tel** (410)576-9600, (800)568-3282. **LC** RA981.A2; G4. **DD** 362.1/1/0973021. **NLM** W1; GE457AF. **Circ:** 8,000. ***Continues*** *Geriatric Length of Stay in PAS Hospitals, by Diagnosis and Operation, United States.*

US/0882-4614
**GERIATRIC MEDICINE ANNUAL.** ***Ceased.*** [Geriatr. med. annu.]. (1986)-(1989). English. an. Medical Economics Data, Five Paragon Drive, PO Box 27, Montvale NJ 07645. **Tel** (800)442-6657, (201)358-7200. **LC** RC952.A1; G468. **DD** 618.97/005. **UDC** 616-053.9(058). **NLM** W1; GE457BH.
**Desc:** Contents: geriatric medicine: a practical methodology.

US/0890-7811
**GERIATRIC MEDICINE CURRENTS.** [Geriatr. med. curr.]. **Added/Corp** Ross Laboratories. Vol. 1, No. 1 (May/June 1980)-. Periodical. English. qt. Free (to health care professionals). Ross Laboratories, 625 Cleveland Avenue, Columbus OH 43216. **Tel** (614)227-3333. **DD** 618.
**Ind/Abst** Index Period. Lit. Aging.

UK/0268-201X
**GERIATRIC MEDICINE (HORTON KIRBY. 1985).** (GERIATRIC MEDICINE.). [Geriatr. med.]. Vol. 15, No. 1 (Jan. 1985)-. Periodical. English. mo. £43.00 UK; £59.00 other. Findlay Publications Ltd, Franks Hall, Horton Kirby, Kent DA4 9LL England. **Tel** 011 44 (0322)222222, FAX 011 44 (0322)289577. **NLM** W1; GE457AR. ***Continues*** *Geriatrics for GPS, 0267-8675.*

NE/0924-8455
**GERIATRIC NEPHROLOGY AND UROLOGY. See** Medical Science and Technology-Urology and Nephrology.

US/0197-4572
**GERIATRIC NURSING (NEW YORK). See** Medical Science and Technology-Nursing.

SZ/1011-4831
**GERIATRICA.** Vol. 1, No. 1 (Feb. 1988)-. Periodical. French. bm (6 issues). Keller and Company, Baselstrasse 11, CH-6002 Luzern Switzerland. **Tel** 041 281111, FAX 041 222253. **NLM** W1; GE457CIB. **Circ:** 3,000.

US/0016-867X
**GERIATRICS.** [Geriatrics]. **Added/Corp** American Geriatrics Society. Vol. 1 (Jan. 1946)-. Academic Scholarly Publication. English. mo. $55.00 US and possessions; $80.00 Canada; $115.00 other. Advanstar Communications Inc., 131 West First Street, Duluth MN 55802. **Tel** (218)723-9477, (800)346-0085. **ED** Richard L Peck. **LC** RC952.A1; G47. **DD** 618.97/005. **NLM** W1 GE457H. **CODEN** GERTAZ. **[CCC]. Ad Acc. Pr Rev. Circ:** 55,525 (ctrl). available on microfilm and microfiche from University Microfilms International (UMI). Documents available from The Genuine Article, BIOSIS Document Express, UMI Article Clearinghouse, CASDDS.
**Desc:** A medical journal for physicians who treat older patients.
**Ind/Abst** Abr. Index Med.; Abstr. Soc. Gerontol.; Acad. Search (July 1993-); Biol. Abstr.; Chem. Abstr.; Cumul. Index Nurs. Allied Health Lit.; Curr. Contents Clin. Med.; EMBASE; Energy Res. Abstr.; Expand. Acad. Index (1992-); Gen. Sci. Index; Gen. Sci. Source (Jul. 1993-); Health Plan. Adminis.; Index Med.; INFO-SOUTH Abstr.; INIS Atomindex [Micro.]; Int. Pharm. Abstr.; Iowa Drug Inf. Serv. (1969-); Mag. Search; Newsp. Period. Abstr. (1989-); Nutr. Abstr. Rev., Ser. A, Hum. Exp.; Nutr. Res. Newsl.; Life Sci. Collect.; PESTDOC; Physic. Medline Plus; Res. Alert [Full Cov.]; Sci. Cit. Index; SCISEARCH; Soc. Sci. Cit. Index [Select. Cov.]; SportSearch; Vocat. Search (July 1993-).

IT/0392-9663
**GERIATRICS ED. ITALIANA.** (GERIATRICS.). [Geriatrics Ed. ital.]. (1984)-. Periodical. Italian. Ten times a year. L30000 Italy; L42000 Europe; L55000 Western Hemisphere and Asia; L50000 Africa; L65000 other. Esi Stampa Medica Srl, Casella Postale 42, 20097 San Donato Mil Italy. **Tel** 11 39 2 5274241, FAX 11 39 2 55600670, telex 324894. **UDC** 616 - 053.9. Index available in last issue of volume--attached. cum. index. **Ad Acc, Adv Mgr:** Uff. Marketing. **Circ:** 70,000 (ctrl).

GW
**GERIATRIE & REHABILITATION / IM AUFTRAG DER DEUTSCHEN GESELLSCHAFT FUER GERIATRIE UND IN ZUSAMMENARBEIT MIT DER DEUTSCHEN GESELLSCHAFT FUER MEDIZINISCHE PSYCHOLOGIE UND PSYCHOPATHOMETRIE. VFOAT** Geriatrie und Rehabilitation. Periodical. English (French and German). qt. **NLM** W1; GE457KD. ***Continues*** *Geriatrics, Pregeriatrics Rehabilitation.*
**Ind/Abst** EMBASE.

SP/0212-9744
**GERIATRIKA.** [Geriatrika]. **Added/Corp** Sociedad Levantina de Geriatria. Liga de Geriatras y Gerontologos de Lengua Latina. (198?)-. Periodical. Spanish. mo (10 issues per year). $80.00 Europe; $120.00 other. Alpe Editores SA, C Pedro Rico 27, Oficinas 11 & 12, 28029 Madrid Spain. **Tel** 011 34 1 7338811, FAX 011 34 1 3159652. **NLM** W1; GE457KE. **CODEN** GERIE5. Documents available from BIOSIS Document Express.
**Ind/Abst** Biol. Abstr. (1986-); EMBASE [Select. Cov.]; Indice Med. Esp.

US/0734-0664
**GERODONTOLOGY.** ***Suspended.*** [Gerodontology]. Vol. 1, No. 1 (Summer 1982)-Suspended Jan 1991. Academic Scholarly Publication. English. qt. $199.00. Beech Hill Publishing Company, PO Box 40, Mt Desert ME 04660. **Tel** (207)667-5048, FAX (207)667-5048. **ED** Edgar A Tohna. **UDC** 616.314-053.9. **NLM** W1 GE569. **CODEN** GRDND6. **Bk Rev. Ad Acc. Circ:** 1,000 (ctrl). available on microfilm from University Microfilms International (UMI). Documents available from CASDDS.
**Desc:** The first international journal with original research articles, clinical studies, reviews of the literature, book reviews, recent symposia, and news on the aging patient, dentition, oral tissue and bone.
**Ind/Abst** Chem. Abstr. (1982-1986); Curr. Titl. Dent.; Dent. Abstr. (-1991); EMBASE; Health Plan. Adminis.; Index Dent. Lit. (Vol. 3, No. 2, 1984-); Mod. Med.; Nutr. Res. Newsl.; Life Sci. Collect.; SCISEARCH.

US/0736-4342
**GERONTOLOGICAL ABSTRACTS.** ***Ceased.* See** Medical Science and Technology-Abstracting, Bibliographies and Statistics.

FR
**GERONTOLOGIE.** **Added/Corp** Amis de la Revue de la Gerontologie. No. 1 (Nov. 1970)-. Periodical. French. Four times a year. 323.21F France; 360.00F French Overseas Department; 420.00F other. Gerontologie, 14 Passage Duguesclin, 75015 Paris France. **Tel** 011 33 1 47346463. **LC** WMLC 91/1321. **NLM** W1 GE579G.

FR/0151-0193
**GERONTOLOGIE ET SOCIETE (PARIS).** (GERONTOLOGIE ET SOCIETE : CAHIERS DE LA FONDATION NATIONALE DE GERONTOLOGIE.). [Gerontol. soc.]. **Added/Corp** Fondation Nationale de Gerontologie (France). No. 5 (1978)-. Periodical. French. qt. Fondation Nationale de Gerontologie, 49 rue Mirabeau, 75016 Paris France. **LC** HQ1064.F7; C32. **DD** 305.26/0944/05. ***Continues*** *Cahiers de la Fondation Nationale de Gerontologie, 0241-5771.*
**Ind/Abst** Point Repere (1991-).

US/0016-9013
**GERONTOLOGIST, THE.** [Gerontologist]. **Added/Corp** Gerontological Society. Vol. 1 (Mar. 1961)-. Academic Scholarly Publication. English. Six times a year. $60.00 (individual), $94.00 (institution) US; $70.00 (individual), $104.00 (institution) other. Gerontological Society of America, 1275 K Street Northwest, Suite 350, Washington DC 20005. **Tel** (202)842-1275, FAX (202)842-1150. **ED** Rose C. Gibson. **LC** HQ1060; .G4. **DD** 305.2/6/05. **NLM** W1 GE583. **CODEN** GRNTA3. **Bk Rev. Ad Acc. Pr Rev. Circ:** 10,373 (ctrl). available on microfilm and microfiche from University Microfilms

International (UMI). Documents available from The Genuine Article, UMI Article Clearinghouse.
**Desc:** Practical and clinical aspects of management in medical and behavioral care of the aging population; practice concepts, book reviews, and audiovisual reviews. Multidisciplinary.
**Ind/Abst** Abstr. Soc. Gerontol.; Abstr. Res. Pastor. Care Couns.; Acad. Abstr. Full Text Elite (Jan. 1991-); Acad. Abstr. (Jan. 1991-); Acad. Ind. [Computer File] (1988-); Acad. Search (Jan. 1991-); AGRICOLA; Annals Behav. Med.; Appl. Soc. Sci. Index Abstr.; Chicano Index; Commun. Abstr.; Crim. Justice Abstr.; Cumul. Index Nurs. Allied Health Lit.; Curr. Contents Soc. Behav. Sci.; Curr. Index J. Educ.; EMBASE; Energy Res. Abstr. (March 1979-); Ergon. Abstr.; Expand. Acad. Index (1988-); Gen. Sci. Source (Jul. 1990-); Health Index (1989-); Health Period. Database; Health Plan. Adminis.; Health Source (Jul. 1990-); High. Educ. Abstr. (1982-19??); Index Med.; Index Period. Lit. Aging; INFO-SOUTH Abstr.; Int. Pharm. Abstr.; Leis. Recreat. Tour. Abstr.; Mag. Search; Middle East Abstr. Index; Newsp. Period. Abstr. (1987-); Nutr. Res. Newsl.; Life Sci. Collect.; Psychol. Abstr. (1961-); PsycINFO; PsycLit; Res. Alert [Full Cov.]; Soc. Sci. Source (Jul. 1990-); Soc. Sci. Cit. Index [Full Cov.]; Soc. Sci. Index; Soc. Sci. Index Fulltext (Oct. 1988-) [Full Txt.]; Soc. Work Abstr. [Full Cov.]; SportSearch; Women Stud. Abstr.

US/0270-1960
**GERONTOLOGY & GERIATRICS EDUCATION.** [Gerontol. geriatr. educ.]. **VAT** Gerontology and Geriatrics Education. Vol. 1, No. 1 (Fall 1980)-. Academic Scholarly Publication. English. qt (Published during the academic year). $160.00 US; $224.00 other. The Haworth Press Inc, 10 Alice Street, Binghamton NY 13904-1580. **Tel** (607)722-5857, (800)3-HAWORTH, FAX (607)722-1424. **ED** John F. Santos and Grace D. Dawson (editor's address: The Geras Center, G170 Hesburgh Library, University of Notre Dame, Notre Dame, IN 46556). **LC** RC952.5; .G447. **DD** 362.6/05. **NLM** W1 GE585KF. **[CCC]. Bk Rev. Ad Acc. Pr Rev. Acid Free. Circ:** 430. available on microfilm and microfiche from University Microfilms International (UMI). Documents available from Haworth Document Delivery Service.
**Desc:** A source of practical curriculum information for educators, trainers and supervisors in the aging field.
**Ind/Abst** Cumul. Index Nurs. Allied Health Lit.; EMBASE; Health Plan. Adminis.; Index Med.; Index Dent. Lit.; Index Period. Lit. Aging; Psychol. Abstr. (1984-); PsycINFO; PsycLit; Soc. Plann. Policy Dev. Abstr.; Soc. Work Abstr. [Select. Cov.]; Sociol. Abstr.

SZ/0304-324X
**GERONTOLOGY (BASEL).** (GERONTOLOGY.). [Gerontology (Basel)]. Vol. 22 (1976)-. Academic Scholarly Publication. English (French). bm. $276.00. S. Karger AG, Allschwilerstrasse 10, PO Box - Postfach - Case Postale, CH-4009 Basel Switzerland. **Tel** 011 41 61 306-1111, FAX 011 41 61 306-1234, telex CH 962 652. **ED** W. Meier-Ruge. **NLM** W1 GE585K. **CODEN** GERNDJ. **[CCC].** Index available. **Ad Acc.** available on microfilm; available on microfiche. Documents available from The Genuine Article, BIOSIS Document Express, CASDDS. ***Continues*** *Gerontologia, 0016-898X; Gerontologia Clinica, 0016-8998.*
**Desc:** As the ratio of people over sixty-five continues to rise, understanding the basic mechanisms of aging and age-related diseases has become a matter of urgent necessity. The journal responds to this need by drawing experimental contributions from diverse medical, biological and behavioral disciplines to provide a primary source of papers covering all aspects of aging in man, animals and plants. Recent research on the clinical problems of aging and the practical applications of laboratory results is also included to support the fundamental goals of extending active life and enhancing its quality.
**Ind/Abst** Abstr. Res. Pastor. Care Couns.; Appl. Soc. Sci. Index Abstr.; Biol. Abstr.; Chem. Abstr.; CSA Neuro. Abstr. (?-?); EMBASE; Ergon. Abstr. (?-?); Health Saf. Sci. Abstr.; Index Med.; Middle East Abstr. Index; Nutr. Abstr. Rev., Ser. B, Live Feeds and Feed.; Nutr. Abstr. Rev., Ser. A, Hum. Exp.; Nutr. Res. Newsl.; Life Sci. Collect.; Protozoolog. Abstr.; Psychoanal. Abstr.; Psychol. Abstr. (1990-); PsycINFO; PsycLit; PsycScan: Appl. Exp. Eng. Psych.; PsycScan: LD/MR; PsycScan: Neuropsych.; Ref. Upd. Deluxe Ed.; Res. Alert [Full Cov.]; Rev. Agric. Entomol.; Sci. Cit. Index; SCISEARCH; Soc. Sci. Cit. Index [Select. Cov.]; SportSearch.

US/0279-4101
**GERONTOLOGY SPECIAL INTEREST SECTION NEWSLETTER.** [Gerontol. Spec. Interest Sect. newsl.]. **Added/Corp** American Occupational Therapy Association. Gerontology Special Interest Section. (19??)-. Newsletter. English. qt. $20.00. American Occupational Therapy Association, 1383 Piccard Drive, PO Box 1725, Rockville MD 20849. **Tel** (301)948-9626, FAX (301)948-5512. **ED** Karen Barney. **Bk Rev. Circ:** 4,800 (ctrl). ***Continues*** *Newsletter - Gerontology Specialty Section, American Occupational Therapy Association, 0194-6366.*
**Desc:** Studies sensory integration and deprivation and their effects on activities of daily living among aged, and mentally ill patients. Also studies sensory disorders.

IT/0017-0305
**GIORNALE DI GERONTOLOGIA.** [G. gerontol.]. **Added/Corp** Societa Italiana di Gerontologia e Geriatria. (1953)-. Academic Scholarly Publication. Italian. mo. L200000 Italy; L280000 other. Societa Italiana di Gerontologiae, Via G C Vanini N 5, 50129 Florence Italy. **Tel** 011 39 55 4743300. **NLM** W1 GI515. **CODEN** GIGEAU. Documents available from BIOSIS Document Express, CASDDS.
**Ind/Abst** Biol. Abstr.; Chem. Abstr.; EMBASE [Select. Cov.]; Life Sci. Collect.; Protozoolog. Abstr.

US
**GUIDELINES FOR PREPARATION OF GRANT APPLICATIONS. RESEARCH AND DEVELOPMENT PROJECTS IN AGING, TITLE IV-B OF THE OLDER AMERICANS ACT.** **Main/Corp** United States. Administration on Aging. **VFOAT** Research and Development Projects in Aging, Title IV-B of the Older Americans Act. 1978-. English. Administration on Aging, 330 Independence Avenue SW, Washington DC 20201. ***Continues*** *Guidelines for Preparation of Grant Applications. Research and Development Projects in Aging, Title IV-B of the Older Americans Act.*

US/1054-1373
**ILLNESS CRISIS & LOSS. See** Ethics.

US
**INDEX OF CURRENT RESEARCH GRANTS AND CONTRACTS ADMINISTERED BY THE NATIONAL INSTITUTE ON AGING.** **Main/Corp** National Institute on Aging. Program Analysis Office. **Added/Corp** National Institutes of Health (U.S.). (19??)-. Periodical. English. wk. free. National Institute on Aging, National Institutes of Health, Room B4NB08 Building 31, Bethesda MD 20205. **Tel** (301)496-1789.

II/0019-5219
**INDIAN JOURNAL OF GERONTOLOGY.** **Added/Corp** Indian Gerontological Association. (Jan. 1969)-. Periodical. English. qt. $50.00. Aalekh Printers, Jaipur, India. **(Subscription address:** Prints India, 11 Darya Ganj, New Delhi, 110002 India, (Phone: 011 91 11 3268645)) **LC** RC952. **DD** 618.97/005. **NLM** W1 IN208X.

SZ
**INFORMATION GERONTOLOGIQUE INTERNATIONALE BULLETIN.** (19??)-. Bulletin. French. qt. 14.00F. Information Gerontologique Internationale, BP 22, 1010 Lausanne Switzerland. **Tel** 011 41 21379003, FAX 011 41 21 6526911. **ED** Armine L. Scherler.

SZ/0074-1132
**INTERDISCIPLINARY TOPICS IN GERONTOLOGY.** [Interdiscip. top. gerontol.]. Vol. 1 (1968)-. Monographic series. English. an. 150.00F (approx. per volume). S. Karger AG, Allschwilerstrasse 10, PO Box - Postfach - Case Postale, CH-4009 Basel Switzerland. **Tel** 011 41 61 306-1111, FAX 011 41 61 306-1234, telex CH 962 652. **ED** H. P. Von Hahn. **LC** HQ1060; .I53. **NLM** W1 IN679. **CODEN** ITGEAR. **[CCC].** Documents available from BIOSIS Document Express, CASDDS.
**Desc:** This series is aimed at a comprehensive and integrated approach to the problems of aging as a whole and presents pertinent data from studies in animal and human gerontology. In order to provide a forum for a unified concept of gerontology, both the bioexperimental foundations and the clinical and sociological consequences of aging in man are presented.
**Ind/Abst** Biol. Abstr.; Chem. Abstr.; Ref. Upd. Deluxe Ed.

GW/0723-8800
**INTERDISZIPLINARE GERONTOLOGIE.** (1981)-. Academic Scholarly Publication. German. Price varies per volume. **NLM** W1 IN681. **CODEN** INGRDR. Documents available from CASDDS.
**Ind/Abst** Chem. Abstr.

US/0730-6695
**INTERNATIONAL JOURNAL OF BEHAVIORAL GERIATRICS.** [Int. j. behav. geriatr.]. Vol. 1, No. 1 (Spring 1982)-. Academic Scholarly Publication. English. qt. $96.00. Van Nostrand Reinhold Company Inc., 115 5th Avenue, New York NY 10003. **Tel** (212)254-3232, FAX (212)673-1239, telex 272562. **LC** RC451.4.A5; I55. **DD** 618.97/689/005. **NLM** W1; IN7655M. available on microfilm from University Microfilms International (UMI).
**Ind/Abst** Cumul. Index Nurs. Allied Health Lit.; EMBASE; Index Period. Lit. Aging; Life Sci. Collect.; Psychol. Abstr. (1982-).

UK/0885-6230
**INTERNATIONAL JOURNAL OF GERIATRIC PSYCHIATRY.** [Int. j. geriatr. psychiatry]. **VFOAT** Geriatric Psychiatry. Vol. 1, No. 1 July (1986)-. Periodical. English. mo. $445.00. John Wiley & Sons Ltd., Baffins Lane, Chichester West Sussex PO19 1UD England. **Tel** 0243 779777, FAX 0243 776128 BTG:JWP001, telex 86290 WIBOOKG. **(Subscription address:** John Wiley / Philadelphia, PO Box 7247, Philadelphia PA 19170.) **ED** Elaine Murphy and George S. Alexopoulos. **LC** RC451.4.A5; I56. **DD** 618.97/689/005. **NLM** W1; IN766M. **CODEN** IJGPES. **[CCC]. Pr Rev.** available on microfilm and microfiche from University Microfilms International (UMI). Documents available from The Genuine Article, BIOSIS Document Express.
**Desc:** Communicates the results of original research in the causes, treatment and care of all forms of mental disorder which affect the elderly. The journal is of interest to psychiatrists, psychologists, social scientists, nurses and others engaged in therapeutic professions together with basic neurobiological researchers.
**Ind/Abst** Abstr. Soc. Gerontol.; Biol. Abstr. (1986-); EMBASE; Psychol. Abstr. (1987-); PsycINFO (1990-); PsycLit; Res. Alert [Full Cov.]; Sage Fam. Stud. Abstr.; Soc. Sci. Cit. Index [Full Cov.].

US/0891-4478
**INTERNATIONAL JOURNAL OF TECHNOLOGY & AGING.** ***Ceased.*** [Int. j. technol. aging]. **VFOAT** International Journal of Technology and Aging; Technology and Aging. **VAT** Technology & Aging. Vol. 1, No. 1 (Spring/Summer 1988)-Vol 5, Issue 2 (1992). Periodical. English. sa. Human Sciences Press, PO Box 735, 233 Spring Street, New York NY 10013. **Tel** (212)620-8000, FAX (212)807-1047, telex 23421139. **LC** HQ1060. **DD** 362.6/05. **NLM** W1; IN791MB. **CODEN** IJTAEE. **[CCC].**
**Desc:** Designed to serve the burgeoning group of researchers, academicians, health care professionals, and government and industry personnel who are addressing a major new phenomenon: the convergence of the dramatic new advances in technology with an aging population.
**Ind/Abst** Abstr. Anthropol.; Abstr. Soc. Gerontol.; Ergon. Abstr.; Person. Manage. Abstr.; Psychol. Abstr. (1988-); PsycINFO (1990-); PsycLit; Soc. Plann. Policy Dev. Abstr.

US/1041-6102
**INTERNATIONAL PSYCHOGERIATRICS / IPA.** [Int. psychogeriatr.]. **Added/Corp** International Psychogeriatric Association. Vol. 1, No. 1 (Spring 1989)-. Periodical. English. sa. $59.00 (1 year, individuals), $99.00 (2 year, individuals), $104.00 (1 year, institutions), $169.00 (2 year, institutions) US; $64.00 (1 year, individuals), $115.00 (2 year, individuals), $119.00 (1 year, institutions), $189.00 (2 year, institutions) other. Springer Publishing Company, 536 Broadway, New York NY 10012-3955. **Tel** (212)431-4370, FAX (212)941-7842. **ED** Gene Cohen, Manfred Bergener, Sanford Finkel, and Kazuo Hasegawa. **LC** WMLC 93/1066. **DD** 618. **NLM** W1; IN827VL. **CODEN** INPSE8. **[CCC]. Pr Rev.** available on microfilm and microfiche from University Microfilms International (UMI).
**Desc:** A multi-disciplinary, peer-reviewed journal offering contributions from the mental health field, as well as the health professions in general. Serves as a global forum for advances in practice, research, service development, and education.
**Ind/Abst** Abstr. Soc. Gerontol.; Health Plan. Adminis.; Index Med. (spring 1989-); Int. Nurs. Index; Psychoanal. Abstr.; Psychol. Abstr. (1989-); PsycINFO; PsycScan: Appl. Exp. Eng. Psych.; PsycScan: LD/MR; PsycScan: Neuropsych.; Sage Fam. Stud. Abstr. (?-?); Sage Urban Stud. Abstr (?-?); Soc. Plann. Policy Dev. Abstr.; Soc. Work Abstr. [Select. Cov.]; Sociol. Abstr.

SA/1017-2572
**JARD. JOURNAL OF AGE RELATED DISORDERS.** [JARD, J. age relat. disord.]. **VFOAT** Journal of Age Related Disorders. (1989)-. Periodical. English. Six times a year. R39.60 South Africa; R54.50 others. Medical Media CC, PO Box 581, 9 Glenavon Park, Aston Manor, 1620 Kempton Park, South Africa. **Tel** 011 27 11 9756439. **UDC** 616-053.9. ***Continues*** *Geriatrx, 1012-8182.*
**Ind/Abst** EMBASE.

US/0093-7320
**JOURNAL FOR GERIATRIC CARE STAFF MEMBER.** **Added/Corp** Nebraska Association of Homes for the Aging. Vol. 1 (Feb. 1974)-. Periodical. English. mo. American Geriatrics Society, 770 Lexington Avenue, Suite 400, New York NY 10021. **Tel** (212)308-1414. **NLM** W1 JO38M.

US/0898-2643
**JOURNAL OF AGING AND HEALTH.** [J. aging health]. **VFOAT** Aging and Health. (1989)-. Periodical. English. qt (Feb., May, Aug., Nov.). $135.00. SAGE Periodical Press, 2455 Teller Road, Thousand Oaks CA 91320. **Tel** (805)499-0721, FAX (805)499-0871, telex 100799. **ED** Kyriakos S. Markides. **LC** RA564.8; .J68. **DD** 362.1/9897/005. **NLM** W1; JO534BH. **CODEN** JAHEEG. Index available. cum. index. **Ad Acc. Acid Free. Circ:** 990. available on microfilm and microfiche from University Microfilms International (UMI).
**Desc:** Deals with social and behavioral factors related to aging and health, emphasizing health and quality of life.
**Ind/Abst** Abstr. Soc. Gerontol.; Annals Behav. Med.; EMBASE; Health Plan. Adminis.; Hospit. Health Admin. Index; Psychol. Abstr. (1989-); PsycINFO (1990-); PsycLit; Soc. Plann. Policy Dev. Abstr.

●US/1063-8652
**JOURNAL OF AGING AND PHYSICAL ACTIVITY.** (1993)-. Periodical. English. qt (Jan., Apr., July, Oct.). $40.00 (individual), $90.00 (institution) US; $44.00 (individual), $94.00 (institution) other. Human Kinetics Publishers Inc, 1607 North Market Street, PO Box 5076, Champaign IL 61825-5076. **Tel** (217)351-5076, FAX (217)351-2674. **ED** Wojtek Chodzko-Zajko, Ph.D. **NLM** W1; JO534BJ. Index available (Included in Oct. issue).
**Desc:** Focuses on the impact of physical activity on the physiological, psychological, and social well-being of older adults and examines the effect of the aging process on physical activity among older adults.

US/0733-4648
**JOURNAL OF APPLIED GERONTOLOGY.** (JOURNAL OF APPLIED GERONTOLOGY : THE OFFICIAL JOURNAL OF THE SOUTHERN GERONTOLOGICAL SOCIETY.). [J. appl. gerontol.]. **Added/Corp** Southern Gerontological Society (U.S.). **VFOAT** J.A.G.; Applied Gerontology; JAG. Vol. 1 (June 1982)-. English. qt (Jan., Apr., July, Oct.). $150.00. SAGE Periodical Press, 2455 Teller Road, Thousand Oaks CA 91320. **Tel** (805)499-0721, FAX (805)499-0871, telex 100799. **ED** William J. McAuley. **LC** HQ1061; .J66. **DD** 362.6/042. **NLM** W1; JO541G. **[CCC].** Index available. **Bk Rev. Ad Acc. Acid Free. Circ:** 725. available on microfilm and microfiche from University Microfilms International (UMI).
**Desc:** Strives to consistently publish articles in all subdisciplines of aging whose findings, conclusions, or suggestions have clear and sometimes immediate applicability to the problems encountered by older persons.
**Ind/Abst** Abstr. Soc. Gerontol.; EMBASE; Health Plan. Adminis.; Hum. Resour. Abstr.; Psychol. Abstr. (1982-); PsycINFO; PsycLit; Sage Fam. Stud. Abstr.; Soc. Plann. Policy Dev. Abstr.; Soc. Sci. Cit. Index [Full Cov.].

US/0192-1193
**JOURNAL OF CLINICAL AND EXPERIMENTAL GERONTOLOGY.** ***Ceased.*** [J. clin. exp. gerontol.]. **VFOAT** Gerontology. Vol. 1 (1979)-(1992). Academic Scholarly Publication. English. qt. Marcel Dekker Inc., 270 Madison Avenue, New York NY 10016. **Tel** (212)696-9000, (800)228-1160, FAX (212)685-4540, telex 421419. **(Subscription address:** Marcel Dekker Inc, PO Box 5017, Monticello NY 12701.**) ED** F. I. Caird. **LC** RC952.A1. **DD** 618.97/005. **NLM** W1 JO5852. **CODEN** JCEGDK. **[CCC]. Bk Rev. Ad Acc. Pr Rev.** ctrl circ. available on microfiche. Documents available from The Genuine Article, BIOSIS Document Express, CASDDS.
**Desc:** Emphasizing the biology of aging and its clinical applications, the 'Journal of Clinical and Experimental Gerontology' bypasses the usual administrative and organizational concerns of other journals to focus on scientific explorations critical to the field. Ranging across experimental and human gerontology and geriatric medicine, this journal transmits the latest research on all aspects of human aging - including anatomical, physiological, and psychological changes and problems of disease in the aged.
**Ind/Abst** Biol. Abstr.; Chem. Abstr.; Curr. Contents Clin. Med.; EMBASE; Hum. Resour. Abstr. (?-?); Index Period. Lit. Aging; Int. Pharm. Abstr.; Med. Abstr. Newsl.; Nutr. Res. Newsl.; Psychol. Abstr. (1985-); PsycINFO; PsycLit; Ref. Upd. Deluxe Ed.; Res. Alert [Select. Cov.]; Sage Fam. Stud. Abstr.; SCISEARCH.

●US
**JOURNAL OF CLINICAL GEROPSYCHOLOGY.** See Psychology.

NE/0169-3816
**JOURNAL OF CROSS-CULTURAL GERONTOLOGY.** [J. cross-cult. gerontol.]. **VFOAT** Journal of Cross Cultural Gerontology. Vol. 1, No. 1 (1986)-. Academic Scholarly Publication. English. qt. $349.00. Kluwer Academic Publishers, Postbus 322, 3300 AH Dordrecht, The Netherlands. **Tel** 011 (31) 78 524400, FAX 011 31 78 183273, telex 20083. **ED** Cynthia M Beall, Melvyn C Goldstein, Charlotte Ikels. **NLM** W1; JO612BL. **CODEN** JCCGEB. Index available. **Bk Rev. Ad Acc. Pr Rev. Acid Free. Circ:** 1,000 (ctrl). available on microfilm and microfiche from University Microfilms International (UMI). Documents available from BIOSIS Document Express.
**Desc:** An international and interdisciplinary journal providing a forum for scholarly discussion of the aging process and the problems of the aged throughout the world. Emphasizes discussions of research findings, theoretical issues and applied approaches dealing with non-Western populations.
**Ind/Abst** Abstr. Soc. Gerontol.; Anthropol. Lit.; Biol. Abstr. (1986-); Int. Bibliogr. Sociol.; Soc. Plann. Policy Dev. Abstr.

UK/0268-9987
**JOURNAL OF EDUCATIONAL GERONTOLOGY.** ***Title Change.*** [J. educ. gerontol.]. (1986)-(19??). Periodical. English. sa. Association for Educational Gerontology, Center for Social Gerontology, University of Keele, Staff ST5 5BG England. **Tel** 0782-584063. **ED** Dr. F. Glenndenning. **Bk Rev. Pr Rev.** ***Continued by*** *Education & Ageing.*
**Ind/Abst** Br. Educ. Index.

US/8756-4629
**JOURNAL OF GERIATRIC DRUG THERAPY.** [J. geriatr. drug ther.]. Vol. 1, No. 1 (Fall 1986)-. Periodical. English. qt (Published during the academic year). $160.00 US; $224.00 other. The Haworth Press Inc, 10 Alice Street, Binghamton NY 13904-1580. **Tel** (607)722-5857, (800)3-HAWORTH, FAX (607)722-1424. **ED** James Cooper (editor's address: Department of Pharmacy Practice, College of Pharmacy, University of Georgia, Athens, GA 30602). **DD** 618. **NLM** W1; JO669LH. **CODEN** JGDTEF. **Bk Rev. Ad Acc. Pr Rev. Acid Free. Circ:** 175. available on microfilm and microfiche from University Microfilms International (UMI). Documents available from BIOSIS Document Express, Haworth Document Delivery Service.
**Desc:** Devoted specifically to drug therapy and related issues in the geriatric population. Publishes important findings and controversial, innovative views related to geripharmacotherapy.
**Ind/Abst** Abstr. Soc. Gerontol.; Appl. Soc. Sci. Index Abstr.; Biol. Abstr. (1986-); EMBASE; Hum. Resour. Abstr. (?-?); Int. Pharm. Abstr.; Mod. Med.; Psychol. Abstr. (1986-); PsycINFO; PsycLit; Soc. Plann. Policy Dev. Abstr.; Soc. Work Abstr. [Select. Cov.].

US/0022-1414
**JOURNAL OF GERIATRIC PSYCHIATRY.** See Medical Science and Technology-Psychiatry.

US/0891-9887
**JOURNAL OF GERIATRIC PSYCHIATRY AND NEUROLOGY.** [J. geriatr. psychiatry neurol.]. **VFOAT** Geriatric Psychiatry and Neurology. Vol. 1, No. 1 (Jan. 1988)-. Periodical. English. qt. $112.00 (institutions), $77.00 (individuals) US & Canada; $132.00 (institutions), $97.00 (individuals) other. Decker Periodicals Publishing Inc, PO Box 620, Station A, Hamilton Ontario L8N 3K7 Canada. **Tel** (416)522-7017, (800) 568-7281, FAX (416)522-7839. **ED** Michael A. Jenike. **DD** 618. **NLM** W1; JO669ND. **CODEN** JGPNEN. **[CCC].** Index available. **Bk Rev. Ad Acc. Pr Rev. Circ:** 1,000. ***Continues*** *Topics in Geriatrics, 0732-1139.*
**Desc:** Presents results of investigations of clinical research studies pertaining to the care of elderly patients. Articles consider all aspects of psychiatric and neurologic care of aging patients including: age-related biologic, neurologic, and psychiatric illness; psychosocial problems; forensic issues; and family care.
**Ind/Abst** EMBASE; Health Plan. Adminis.; Index Med. (1988-); Psychol. Abstr. (1988-); PsycINFO; PsycLit; Soc. Sci. Cit. Index [Select. Cov.].

US/0022-1422
**JOURNAL OF GERONTOLOGY (KIRKWOOD).** (JOURNAL OF GERONTOLOGY.). [J. gerontol.]. **Added/Corp** Gerontological Society. **VFOAT** Journals of Gerontology. Vol. 1 No. 1 Pt. 1 (Jan. 1946)-. Academic Scholarly Publication. English. bm. $65.00 US. Gerontological Society of America, 1275 K Street Northwest, Suite 350, Washington DC 20005. **Tel** (202)842-1275, FAX (202)842-1150. **(Subscription address:** Department 5018, Washington, DC 20061-5018**) ED** Vincent J Cristofalo, Harvey Jay Cohen, George C Myers and K Warner Schaie. **LC** HQ1060; .J6. **DD** 301.435. **NLM** W1 JO669P. **CODEN** JOGEA3. Index available. **Bk Rev. Ad Acc. Pr Rev. Circ:** 9,362 (ctrl). available on microfilm and microfiche from University Microfilms International (UMI). Documents available from BIOSIS Document Express, UMI Article Clearinghouse, CASDDS.
**Desc:** Reports original research in the biological, medical, psychological and social sciences.
**Ind/Abst** Abr. Index Med.; Abstr. Anthropol.; Abstr. Soc. Gerontol.; Acad. Search (July 1993-); Anim. Breed. Abstr.; Appl. Soc. Sci. Index Abstr.; Biol. Abstr.; Book Rev. Index (1984-); Chem. Abstr.; Chicano Index; CSA Neuro. Abstr. (?-?); Cumul. Index Nurs. Allied Health Lit.; Curr. Index J. Educ.; Curr. Titl. Dent.; Dairy Sci. Abstr.; EMBASE; Energy Res. Abstr.; Ergon. Abstr.; Expand. Acad. Index (1989-); Health Index (1989-); Health Period. Database; Health Ref. Cent. (Jan. 1989-) [Full Cov.]; Index Med.; Index Period. Lit. Aging; Index Vet.; INFO-SOUTH Abstr.; Int. Aerosp. Abstr.; Med. Abstr. Newsl.; Middle East Abstr. Index; Nematol. Abstr.; Newsp. Period. Abstr. (1991-); Nutr. Res. Newsl.; Life Sci. Collect.; Physic. Medline Plus; Protozoolog. Abstr.; Psychol. Abstr. (1946-); PsycLit; Ref. Upd. Deluxe Ed.; Soc. Sci. Source (Jul. 1993-); Soc. Sci. Index; Soc. Sci. Index Fulltext (Nov. 1988-) [Full Txt.]; Soc. Work Abstr. (Summer 1987-) [Select. Cov.]; Soyabean Abstr.; SPORT Discus; SportSearch; Women Stud. Abstr.; Work Relat. Abstr. (-19??).

●US
**JOURNAL OF GERONTOLOGY: PSYCHOLOGICAL SCIENCES AND SOCIAL SCIENCES, THE.** (1995)-. English. bm. $62.00 (individual), $95.00 (institution) US; $72.00 (individual), $105.00 (institution) other. Gerontological Society of America, 1275 K Street Northwest, Suite 350, Washington DC 20005. **Tel** (202)842-1275, FAX (202)842-1150. **(Subscription address:** Gerontological Society of America, Department 5018, Washington DC 20061-5018.**)** ***Continues in part*** *Journals of Gerontology.*

US/1050-2289
**JOURNAL OF RELIGIOUS GERONTOLOGY.** [J. relig. gerontol.]. **Added/Corp** National Interfaith Coalition on Aging. Vol. 7 No. 1/2 (1990)-. Periodical. English. qt. $125.00 US; $175.00 other. The Haworth Press Inc, 10 Alice Street, Binghamton NY 13904-1580. **Tel** (607)722-5857, (800)3-HAWORTH, FAX (607)722-1424. **ED** William M. Clements (editor's address: Professor Pastor Care and Counseling, School of Theology at Claremont, 1325 North College Avenue, Claremont, CA 91711). **LC** BV4435; .J68. **DD** 261.8/3426/05. **CODEN** JRGEES. **Bk Rev. Ad Acc. Pr Rev. Acid Free. Circ:** 803. available on microfilm and microfiche from University Microfilms International (UMI). Documents available from Haworth Document Delivery Service. ***Continues*** *Journal of Religion & Aging, 0738-6184.*
**Desc:** An interdisciplinary, interfaith professional journal in which the needs, aspirations, and resources of elderly constituencies come clearly into focus. Combines practical innovation and scholarly insight to offer timely information and probing articles on religion and aging issues.
**Ind/Abst** Abstr. Soc. Gerontol.; Abstr. Res. Pastor. Care Couns. (19??-); Christ. Period. Index (199?-); Commun. Abstr. (?-?); Hum. Resour. Abstr. (?-?); Index Book Rev. Relig.; Relig. Index One Period.; Relig. Theol. Abstr. (199?-); Soc. Plann. Policy Dev. Abstr.; Soc. Work Abstr. [Select. Cov.].

US/0002-8614
**JOURNAL OF THE AMERICAN GERIATRICS SOCIETY.** [J. Am. Geriatr. Soc.]. **Added/Corp** American Geriatrics Society. American Therapeutic Society. Texas Geriatrics Society. Vol. 1 (Jan. 1953)-. Academic Scholarly Publication. English. mo. $109.00 (individual), $184.00 (institution) US; $144.00 (institution), $74.00 (individual) other. Williams & Wilkins Company, 428 East Preston Street, Baltimore MD 21202-3993. **Tel** (410)528-4000, (800)638-6423, FAX (410)528-8596, telex 87669. **(Subscription address:** Williams & Wilkins, PO Box 64380, Baltimore MD 21264.**) ED** Gene H. Stollerman and John P. Blass. **CODEN** JAGSAF. **[CCC].** Index available. **Bk Rev. Ad Acc. Pr Rev. Circ:** 9,300. available on microfilm and microfiche from University Microfilms International (UMI). Documents available from The Genuine Article, BIOSIS Document Express, CASDDS, Quick Copies. ***Absorbed*** *Transactions of the American Therapeutic Society, 0096-686X.*
**Desc:** Geriatricians, internists, cardiologists, gastroeneterologists, rheumatologists, and other specialists who treat older patients look to this source for information on all aspects of geriatric health care.
**Ind/Abst** Abr. Index Med.; Abstr. Soc. Gerontol.; Abstr. Clin. Care Guidel.; AGRICOLA; Annals Behav. Med.; Appl. Soc. Sci. Index Abstr.; Biol. Abstr.; Chem. Abstr.; Chicano Index; CIS Abstr.; Cumul. Index Nurs. Allied Health Lit.; Curr. Contents Clin. Med.; Curr. Contents Soc. Behav. Sci.; EMBASE; Energy Res. Abstr.; Index Med.; INIS Atomindex [Micro.]; Int. Aerosp. Abstr.; Int. Nurs. Index; Int. Pharm. Abstr.; Iowa Drug Inf. Serv. (1966-); J. Watch (199?-); Leis. Recreat. Tour. Abstr.; Med. Abstr. Newsl.; Mod. Med.; Nucl. Sci. Abstr.; Nutr. Abstr. Rev., Ser. A, Hum. Exp.; Nutr. Res. Newsl.; Life Sci. Collect.; PESTDOC; Physic. Medline Plus; Psychol. Abstr. (1953-); PsycINFO; PsycLit; Ref. Upd. Deluxe Ed.; Res. Alert [Full Cov.]; Rev. Med. Vet. Entomol.; Rural Dev. Abstr.; Saf. Health Work; Sci. Cit. Index; SCISEARCH; Soc. Plann. Policy Dev. Abstr.; Soc. Sci. Cit. Index [Full Cov.]; Soc. Welf. Soc. Plan./Policy Soc. Dev.; Soc. Work Abstr. (?-?); Sociol. Abstr.; SportSearch; Women Stud. Abstr.; World Agric. Econ.

US
**JOURNALS OF GERONTOLOGY.** ***Title Change.*** (1993)-(1995). English. bm (Jan., Mar., May, Jul., Sep., Nov.). Gerontological Society of America, 1275 K Street Northwest, Suite 350, Washington DC 20005. **Tel** (202)842-1275, FAX (202)842-1150. **(Subscription address:** Gerontological Society of America, Department 5018, Washington, DC 20061; telephone: (202)842-1275**)** available in microform from University Microfilms International (UMI). ***Split into*** *The Journal of Gerontology: Biological Sciences and Medical Sciences* ***and*** *The Journal of Gerontology: Psychological Sciences and Social Sciences.*
**Ind/Abst** Sci. Cit. Index; Soc. Sci. Cit. Index [Full Cov.].

●US
**JOURNALS OF GERONTOLOGY: BIOLOGICAL SCIENCES AND MEDICAL SCIENCES, THE.** (1995)-. English. bm. $95.00 (individual), $145.00 (institution) US; $105.00 (individual), $155.00 (institution) other. Gerontological Society of America, 1275 K Street Northwest, Suite 350, Washington DC 20005. **Tel** (202)842-1275, FAX (202)842-1150. **(Subscription address:** Gerontological Society of America, Department 5018, Washington DC 20061-5018.**)** ***Continues in part*** *Journals of Gerontology.*

UK
**LECTURES ON GERONTOLOGY.** Vol. 1-. Monographic series. English. Price varies per volume. Each issue contains an index to its own contents (no volume index)--loose.

US/0191-1864
**LONG LIFE MAGAZINE.** V. 2, No. 2- (Issue No. 7-); March/April 1978-. Periodical. English. bm. $9.00. Society for Life Extension, 627 West Berry 3-N, Chicago IL 60657. **NLM** W1 LO73. ***Continues** Life Extension Magazine.*

US/0895-8254
**LONGEVITY (NEW YORK, N.Y. : 1988).** (LONGEVITY.). **VFOAT** Omni Longevity. Vol. 1, No. 1 (Oct. 1988)-. Periodical. English. mo. $24.00. General Media Publishing Company, 1965 Broadway, New York NY 10023. **Tel** (212)496-6100. **(Subscription address:** CDS Agency Hard Copy, PO Box 4966, Des Moines IA 50340.) **LC** RA776.75; .L66. **DD** 612.6/8/05. **CODEN** LONGE2. ***Continues** Longevity (New York, N.Y. : 1986), 0895-8254.*
**Ind/Abst** Consum. Health Nutr. Index; Foods Adlibra.

MX
**MADUREZ.** Spanish (summaries and/or abstracts in English and French). **LC** RC952.A1.

●US/1063-035X
**MANAGING SENIORCARE.** **See** Sociology-Social Services and Welfare.

IE/0378-5122
**MATURITAS.** [Maturitas]. Vol. 1 (June 1978)-. Academic Scholarly Publication. English. Nine times a year (3 volumes). $459.00. Elsevier Science Ireland Ltd., Bay 15, Shannon Industrial Estate, Co Clare Ireland. **Tel** 011 353 61 471944. **ED** P.A. van Keep, F. Riphagen and W.H. Utian. **NLM** W1 MA99. **CODEN** MATUDK. **[CCC]. Pr Rev.** available on microfilm and microfiche from University Microfilms International (UMI). Documents available from The Genuine Article, BIOSIS Document Express, CASDDS, ADONIS.
**Desc:** Provides a critical medium for the exchange of information and ideas concerning the important changes in many physiological, psychological and sociological functions occurring in the middle years.
**Ind/Abst** ADONIS; Biol. Abstr.; Chem. Abstr.; CSA Neuro. Abstr. (?-?); Curr. Aware. Biol. Sci., CABS; Curr. Contents Clin. Med.; Curr. Contents Life Sci.; EMBASE; Index Med.; Nutr. Abstr. Rev., Ser. A, Hum. Exp.; Life Sci. Collect.; Ref. Upd. Deluxe Ed.; Res. Alert [Full Cov.]; Sci. Cit. Index; SCISEARCH; Soc. Sci. Cit. Index [Select. Cov.].

SZ/0047-6374
**MECHANISMS OF AGEING AND DEVELOPMENT.** **See** Biology-Physiology.

IT/0391-4844
**MEDICINA GERIATRICA.** (MEDICINA GERIATRICA : ORGANO UFFICIALE DELLA ASSOCIAZIONENA ZIONALE ITALIANA MEDICI E OPERATORI GERIATRICI.). [Med. geriatr.]. **Added/Corp** Associazione Nazionale Italiana Medici e Operatori Geriatrici. (1969)-. Academic Scholarly Publication. Italian. bm. L50000 (Italy); L60000 (other). Casa Editrice Mattioli, Via Codura 1B, 43036 Fidenza PR Italy. **Tel** 39 524 84547. **CODEN** MGRCAT. Documents available from BIOSIS Document Express.
**Ind/Abst** Biol. Abstr.; EMBASE.

US/0275-360X
**MODERN AGING RESEARCH.** ***Ceased.*** [Mod. aging res.]. Vol. 1 (1980)- Completed Series with Vol. 8 (19??). Academic Scholarly Publication. English. ir. John Wiley & Sons, Inc., 605 Third Avenue, New York NY 10158-0012. **Tel** (212)850-6000, (212)850-6645, FAX (212)850-6088, telex 12-7063. **(Subscription address:** John Wiley & Sons / England, Baffins Lane, Chichester, West Sussex PO19 1UD England.) **ED** Richard Adelman, George Baker III, Vincent Cristofalo, and Jay Roberts. **LC** UNC. **NLM** W1 MO117. **CODEN** MARDDR. **[CCC]. Bk Rev. Ad Acc.** Documents available from BIOSIS Document Express, CASDDS.
**Desc:** Covering aspects of aging such as visual functions, intervention in aging process, comparative pathobiology of major age related diseases, altered endocrine status, etc.
**Ind/Abst** Biol. Abstr.; Chem. Abstr.

US/0148-4508
**NATIONAL DIRECTORY OF EDUCATIONAL PROGRAMS IN GERONTOLOGY AND GERIATRICS.** **Added/Corp** Association for Gerontology in Higher Education. 5th Ed. (1991)-. Directory. English. ir (Published every three years). $55.00 members, $85.00 non-members. Association for Gerontology in Higher Education - AGHE, 1001 Connecticut Avenue Northwest, Suite 410, Washington DC 20036-5504. **Tel** (202)429-9277. **ED** Joy C. Lobenstine, Pamela F. Wendt and David A. Peterson. **LC** HQ1060; .N35. **NLM** WT 22; AA1 N277. ***Continues** National Directory of Educational Programs in Gerontology.*
**Desc:** This lists over 1,000 gerontology programs at more than 500 institutions of higher education. Listing provide information on the name of the program organizational unit, area of study, educational level, type of credential awarded, number of students in the program, the year the program begin, and the contact person's full address, phone, fax, and e-mail numbers.

US
**NEWSLETTER.** **Main/Corp** American Geriatrics Society. Vol. 1 (1972)-. Newsletter. English. mo. comes with Journal of the American Geriatrics Society. American Geriatrics Society, 770 Lexington Avenue, Suite 400, New York NY 10021. **Tel** (212)308-1414.

JA/0300-9173
**NIHON RONEN IGAKKAI ZASSHI.** [Nihon Ronen Igakkai zasshi]. **Main/Corp** Nihon Ronen Igakkai. **VFOAT** Japanese Journal of Geriatrics. Vol. 1 (1964)-. Periodical. Japanese (summaries and/or abstracts in English). bm. Japan Geriatrics Society Tokyo, Daigaku Igakubu Hongo 3 1 7, Bunkyoku Tokyo 113 Japan. **NLM** W1 NI93G. **CODEN** NIRZAL. Documents available from BIOSIS Document Express.
**Ind/Abst** Biol. Abstr.; EMBASE; Index Med.

US
**NURSE AIDE VIP.** English. mo (12 issues). $18.00. Eymann Publications, PO Box 3577, Reno NV 89505. **Tel** (702)333-6651.

US/1070-1370
**NURSING HOME MEDICINE.** **See** Medical Science and Technology-Hospital Administration and Medical Centers.

US/0738-9639
**OLDER AMERICAN (BOSTON, MASS.), THE.** (THE OLDER AERICAN.). **Added/Corp** Massachusetts Association of Older Americans. (1975)-. Periodical. English. Six times a year. $15.00. Massachusetts Association of Older Americans, 110 Arlington Street, Boston MA 02116. **Tel** (617)426-0805.

US/0096-2740
**PERSPECTIVE ON AGING.** **Added/Corp** National Council on the Aging. Vol. 1 (Spring 1972)-. Periodical. English. bm. comes with membership. National Council on the Aging, Department 5087, Washington DC 20061. **Tel** (202)479-1200. **ED** William Oriol and Louise Cleveland. **LC** HQ1060; .P47. **DD** 301.43/5/05. **NLM** W1 PE8705E. **Ad Acc. Circ:** 7,000 (ctrl).
**Ind/Abst** Abstr. Soc. Gerontol.; AGRICOLA.

CN/0831-7445
**PERSPECTIVES - GERONTOLOGICAL NURSING ASSOCIATION.** **See** Medical Science and Technology-Nursing.

US/0270-3181
**PHYSICAL & OCCUPATIONAL THERAPY IN GERIATRICS.** **See** Physical Therapy.

US
**PLAN FOR DEPARTMENT ON AGING.** **Added/Corp** Illinois. Dept. on Aging. (1979)-. English. 2401 West Jefferson Street, Springfield IL 62706. **LC** HV1468.I3; I443a. **DD** 362.6/09773. ***Continues** State plan on aging.*

BG/1012-9197
**PROBIN HITAISHI.** [Probin hitaishi]. **Added/Corp** Bangladesh Association for the Aged. **VFOAT** Bangladesh Journal of Geriatrics; Prabina Hitaishi. (1980)-. Periodical. Bengali (English). sa. TK10.00 Bangladesh; $2.00 other. Bangladesh Association for the Aged, Institute of Geriatric Medicine, Agargaon Sher-e-Bangla Nagar, Dhaka 1207 Bangladesh. **Tel** 32 85 59. **NLM** W1 PR552G. **Ad Acc. Circ:** 500. ***Continues** Pakistan Journal of Geriatrics.*

AT/0311-9297
**PROCEEDINGS OF THE AUSTRALIAN ASSOCIATION OF GERONTOLOGY.** **Main/Corp** Australian Association of Gerontology. Vol. 1 (1969)-. Proceedings. English. ir. 30.00Aus$. Australian Association of Gerontology, 191 Royal Parade, Parkville 3052 Australia. **Tel** 011 61 33472570. **NLM** W1 PR5845.
**Desc:** Consists of proceedings of the association's annual conference.

US/0882-7974
**PSYCHOLOGY AND AGING.** **See** Psychology.

IT/0486-0306
**RASSEGNA GERIATRICA.** (1965)-. Periodical. Italian. qt. Casa Editrice Libraria Idelson Gnocchi, via Alcide De Gasperi 55, 80133 Naples Italy. **Tel** 011 39 81 5524733. **UDC** 613.98.
**Ind/Abst** EMBASE.

UK/0144-0519
**RECENT ADVANCES IN GERIATRIC MEDICINE.** ***Ceased.*** [Recent adv. geriatr. med.]. **VFOAT** Geriatric Medicine. No. 1-?. Academic Scholarly Publication. English. ir. Churchill Livingstone, 1-3 Baxter's Place, Leith Walk, Edinburgh EH1 3AF Scotland. **Tel** 011 44 31 556 2424, FAX 011 44 31 558 1278, telex 727511. **(Subscription address:** US/ Churchill Livingstone, Fulfillment Office, PO Box 11318, Birmingham, AL 35202) **ED** B Isaacs. **NLM** W1 RE105ULB. **CODEN** RAGMDK. Documents available from CASDDS.
**Ind/Abst** Chem. Abstr.

US/0278-517X
**REPORT FROM THE WHITE HOUSE CONFERENCE ON AGING.** **Main/Conf** White House Conference on Aging. Began with: No. 1 (April 1980). Periodical. English. mo. The White House Conference on Aging, 330 Independence Avenue SW, Washington DC 20201. **NLM** W1 RE209BQC.

US
**REPORT ON THE ... ANNUAL MEETING OF THE NIA GERIATRIC MEDICINE ACADEMIC AWARDEES.** 1st (June 16-17, 1980)-. English. an. National Institute of Aging, National Institutes of Health, Bethesda MD 20205. **LC** RC952.5; .R46. **DD** 618.97/007/11. **NLM** W1 RE212HD.

US/0499-9797
**RESEARCH HIGHLIGHTS IN AGING.** **Main/Corp** United States. National Institutes of Health. Center for Aging Research. 1959-. Periodical. English. an. National Institutes of Health / Aging, Center for Aging Research, Bethesda MD 20014. **LC** QP86; .U57. **DD** 612.67072.

US/0164-0275
**RESEARCH ON AGING.** [Res. aging]. Vol. 1 (March 1979)-. Periodical. English. qt (Mar., June, Sept., Dec.). $160.00. SAGE Periodical Press, 2455 Teller Road, Thousand Oaks CA 91320. **Tel** (805)499-0721, FAX (805)499-0871, telex 100799. **ED** Rhonda J. V. Montgomery (University of Kansas). **LC** HQ1060; .R38. **DD** 301.43/5/0973. **NLM** W1 RE232L. **[CCC]. Pr Rev. Acid Free.** available on microfilm and microfiche from University Microfilms International (UMI). Documents available from The Genuine Article, UMI Article Clearinghouse.
**Desc:** A journal of interdisciplinary research on current issues and methodological and research problems in the study of the aged.
**Ind/Abst** Abstr. Soc. Gerontol.; Acad. Search (Jan. 1994-); AGRICOLA; Annals Behav. Med.; Crim. Justice Abstr.; Curr. Contents Soc. Behav. Sci.; EMBASE; Expand. Acad. Index (1989-); Hum. Resour. Abstr.; Index Med. (Vol. 6, No. 1, 1984-); Index Period. Lit. Aging; INFO-SOUTH Abstr.; Int. Nurs. Index; J. Plan. Lit.; Mag. Search; Newsp. Period. Abstr. (1991-); Nutr. Res. Newsl.; Psychol. Abstr. (1983-); PsycINFO; PsycLit; Res. Alert [Full Cov.]; Sage Fam. Stud. Abstr.; Soc. Plann. Policy Dev. Abstr.; Soc. Sci. Source (Jul. 1993-); Soc. Sci. Cit. Index [Full Cov.]; Soc. Sci. Index; Soc. Sci. Index Fulltext (Sept. 1988-) [Full Txt.]; Soc. Work Abstr. (Spring, Summer 1987-) [Select. Cov.]; Sociol. Abstr.

CN/1195-4167
**RESIDENTIAL CARE FACILITIES, AGED / STATISTICS CANADA, CANADIAN CENTRE FOR HEALTH INFORMATION.** **Added/Corp** Canadian Centre for Health Information. **VFOAT** Etablissements de Soins Speciaux pour Beneficiaires Internes, Agees. (1990/1991)-. English (French). 15.00Can$ Canada; $18.00 US; $21.00 other. Statistics Canada, Publications Sales & Services, Main Building Room 1710, Ottawa Ontario K1A 0T6 Canada. **Tel** (613)951-5078, (800)267-6677, FAX (613)951-1584, telex 053-3585. **LC** RA998.C3; H42. **DD** 362.1/6/0971021. ***Continues** Health Reports. Supplement. Residential Care Facilities, Aged, 1181-8794.*

US/0736-5055
**REVIEW OF BIOLOGICAL RESEARCH IN AGING.** [Rev. biol. res. aging]. (1983)-. Academic Scholarly Publication. English. ir. Price varies per volume. John Wiley & Sons, Inc., 605 Third Avenue, New York NY 10158-0012. **Tel** (212)850-6000, (212)850-6645, FAX (212)850-6088, telex 12-7063. **(Subscription address:** John Wiley & Sons / England, Baffins Lane, Chichester, West Sussex PO19 1UD England.) **ED** Morton Rothstein. **LC** QP86; .R485. **DD** 599/.0372. **NLM** W1 RE252N. **CODEN** RBRADC. **[CCC].** Documents available from BIOSIS Document Express, CASDDS.
**Ind/Abst** Biol. Abstr.; Chem. Abstr. (1983-).

UK/0959-2598
**REVIEWS IN CLINICAL GERONTOLOGY.** [Rev. clin. gerontol.]. **VFOAT** Clinical Gerontology. Vol. 1, No. 1 (Feb. 1991)-. Periodical. English. qt. $230.00 US, Canada and Mexico. Edward Arnold, 338 Euston Road, London NW1 3BH England. **Tel** 011 44 71 873 6000, FAX 011 44 071 873 6325. **(Subscription address:** Turpin Distribution Services Limited, Blackhorse Road, Letchworth, Hertfordshire SG6 1HN, United Kingdom.) **ED** Raymond Tallis. **LC** RC952.A1; R48. **DD** 618.97/005. **NLM** W1; RE257CEGJ. **CODEN** RCGEEB. **[CCC]. Ad Acc. Pr Rev.**
**Desc:** Dedicated to the advancement of knowledge and clinical practice in the health care of the elderly, this new international journal will bring together specially commissioned reviews on recent developments in geriatric medicine. Thorough coverage of the field will

include biological gerontology, clinical geriatrics, psychiatry of old age, rehabilitation, and psychological and social gerontology. All the major topics of interest will be reviewed during the course of a unique three-year, 12-issue cycle.
**Ind/Abst** Abstr. Soc. Gerontol.; EMBASE; Psychol. Abstr.; PsycINFO; PsycLit.

SP
**REVISTA DE MEDICINA GERIATRICA.** Spanish. Editorial Saned SA, Apolonio Morales 6, 28036 Madrid Spain. **Tel** 011 34 1 359-4092, FAX 011 34 1 457-9918.
**Ind/Abst** EMBASE.

SP/0211-139X
**REVISTA ESPANOLA DE GERIATRIA Y GERONTOLOGIA.** [Rev. esp. geriatr. gerontol.]. Vol.15 (Jan./Feb. 1980)-. Periodical. Spanish. bm. 4900.00ptas. Editorial Garsi SA, Juan Bravo 46, 28006 Madrid, Spain. **Tel** 011 34 1 4021212, telex 98358 GARSI E. **NLM** W1 RE534G. **CODEN** REGGDU. **Bk Rev. Ad Acc. Pr Rev. Circ:** 1,250. Documents available from BIOSIS Document Express. ***Continues*** *Revista Espanola de Gerontologia y Geriatria, 0210-6175.*
**Ind/Abst** Biol. Abstr. (1987-); EMBASE [Select. Cov.]; Indice Med. Esp.

FR/0397-7927
**REVUE DE GERIATRIE, LA.** [Rev. geriatr.]. Vol. 1 (Sept. 1976)-. Periodical. French. Ten times a year. 300.00F France; 400.00F others. Edimedica, 146 Boulevard Voltaire, 92600 Asnieres France. **Tel** 011 33 1 47935603. **NLM** W1 RE778EN. ***Supersedes*** *Revue de Gerontologie d'Expresion Francaise, 0035-2896.*
**Ind/Abst** EMBASE.

RM/0254-2307
**ROMANIAN JOURNAL OF GERONTOLOGY AND GERIATRICS.** (ROMANIAN JOURNAL OF GERONTOLOGY AND GERIATRICS / THE NATIONAL INSTITUTE OF GERONTOLOGY AND GERIATRICS, BUCHAREST.). [Rom. j. gerontol. geriatr.]. **Added/Corp** Institutul National de Gerontologie si Geriatrie (Romania). (1980)-. Academic Scholarly Publication. English (French). Four times a year. DM340.00. **(Subscription address:** Kubon & Sagner, ABT Zeitschriftenimport, D 80328 Munich Germany.**)** **NLM** W1 RO327. **CODEN** RJGGDV. Documents available from CASDDS.
**Desc:** Contains articles and speciality studies with medical, biological and sociological character.
**Ind/Abst** Abstr. Anthropol. (19??-); Chem. Abstr.; EMBASE [Select. Cov.].

GW/0172-1364
**SCRIPTUM GERIATRICUM.** Periodical. German. Urban & Schwarzenberg, Landwehrstr 61, W-8 Munchen 2 Germany. **NLM** W3 SC65.
**Desc:** Consists of the proceedings of the Internationaler Fortbildungskurs fur Geriatrie, 2d?- 1957?- .

UK/0267-0348
**SELECTED BIBLIOGRAPHIES ON AGEING.** See Medical Science and Technology-Abstracting, Bibliographies and Statistics.

SA/0037-2234
**SENIOR NEWS.** See Senior Citizens.

US
**SENIOR SPECTRUM.** See Senior Citizens.

US
**SOUTHWEST JOURNAL ON AGING, THE.** (1992)-. English. ir. Southwest Society on Aging, PO Box 13346, University of North Texas, Denton TX 76203. **Tel** (817)565-2823.

US/0272-5835
**SPRINGER SERIES ON ADULTHOOD AND AGING.** ***Ceased.*** Vol. 1 (1978)-Completed Series (19??). Monographic series. English. ir. Springer Publishing Company, 536 Broadway, New York NY 10012-3955. **Tel** (212)431-4370, FAX (212)941-7842. **ED** L. F. Jarvik and B. D. Starr. **NLM** W1 SP685N.
**Desc:** Interdisciplinary and cross-cultural in scope. Addresses broad concerns in psychology, sociology, medicine, health sciences, as well as educational, social, and recreational services.

●US/1071-0000
**STATE-OF-THE-ART RESEARCH SUMMARIES.** [State-of-the-art res. summ.]. **Added/Corp** Association for Gerontology in Higher Education. **VFOAT** State of the Art Research Summaries. (1992)-. Monographic series. English. ir. $7.00 members, $10.00 non-members. Association for Gerontology in Higher Education - AGHE, 1001 Connecticut Avenue Northwest, Suite 410, Washington DC 20036-5504. **Tel** (202)429-9277. **DD** 362.
**Desc:** These publications is to provide a series of research summaries which link current research findings in a sub-field of gerontology or geriatrics with teaching objectives and outcomes. The summaries are intended to provide technical expertise as well as resources to instructors.

SZ/1011-3738
**TEACHING AND TRAINING IN GERIATRIC MEDICINE.** [Teach. train. geriatr. med.]. (1987)-. Monographic series. English. an. 30.00F (approx. per volume). S. Karger AG, Allschwilerstrasse 10, PO Box - Postfach - Case Postale, CH-4009 Basel Switzerland. **Tel** 011 41 61 306-1111, FAX 011 41 61 306-1234, telex CH 962 652. **ED** W. Meier-Ruge. **NLM** W1; TE129L. **CODEN** TTGME6. **[CCC].** Index available. ctrl circ. available in microform. Documents available from BIOSIS Document Express.
**Desc:** The growth of the elderly population has resulted in an accretion in the need for up-to-date knowledge on age-related diseases. Psychogeriatric medicine holds a place of particular importance among the clinical problems that are common in elderly patients - chronic illnesses of the elderly involve the brain most of all. This new series of handbooks takes a clinical-practical orientation and proposes to fulfil a teaching role.
**Ind/Abst** Biol. Abstr.; Ref. Upd. Deluxe Ed.

NE/0167-9228
**TIJDSCHRIFT VOOR GERONTOLOGIE EN GERIATRIE.** [Tijdschr. gerontol. geriatr.]. **Added/Corp** Nederlandse Vereniging voor Gerontologie. Nederlands Instituut voor Gerontologie. (1982)-. Periodical. Dutch (summaries and/or abstracts in English). Six times a year. Fl120.00. LSOB Nig Abonnementen Administratie, Postbus 220, 3980 CE Bunnik Netherlands. **Tel** 03405 71999. **NLM** W1 TI653M. **CODEN** NDGEA4. ***Continues*** *Gerontologie (Deventer, Netherlands), 0168-8677.*
**Ind/Abst** EMBASE [Select. Cov.]; Index Med.; Psychol. Abstr. (1982-); PsycINFO (1970-); PsycLit.

JA
**TOKYO-TO ROJIN SOGO KENKYUJO NEMPO.** **Main/Corp** Tokyo-to Rojin Sogo Kenkyujo. Japanese. an. Free. Tokyo-To Rojin Sogo Kenkyujo, 35-2 Sakaecho, Itabashi-ku 173 Tokyo Japan. **Tel** 03(964)1131, FAX 813-579-4776, telex 02722468 JIG J. **ED** Toru Tsumita. **LC** RC952; .T63A. **Circ:** 1,000 (ctrl). ***Continues*** *Kenkyu Kiyo - Tokyo-To Rojin Sogo Kenkyujo, Tokyo-To Yoikuin Fuzoku Byoin.*
**Desc:** This is the report of Tokyo Metropolitan Institute of Gerontology which is conducting basic research on aging in the sphere from biomedical to sociological aspects.

US/0882-7524
**TOPICS IN GERIATRIC REHABILITATION.** [Top. geriatr. rehabil.]. **Added/Corp** Aspen Systems Corporation. **VFOAT** TGR. Vol. 1, No. 1 (Oct. 1985)-. Periodical. English. qt. $66.00 US and Canada. Aspen Publishers Inc., 7201 McKinney Circle, Frederick MD 21701. **Tel** (800)234-1660, (301)698-7100, FAX (301)251-5784, telex 5106014543. **(Subscription address:** Aspen Publishers Inc., PO Box 990, Frederick MD 21701.**)** **ED** Carole B. Lewis. **LC** RC952.5; .T66. **DD** 016.61897. **NLM** W1; TO539MK. **[CCC]. Bk Rev. Ad Acc. Pr Rev.** ctrl circ.
**Desc:** Presents clinical, basic, and applied research, as well as theoretical information, consolidated into a clinically relevant from and provides a resource for the health care professional practicing in the area of geriatric rehabilitation.
**Ind/Abst** Abstr. Soc. Gerontol.; EMBASE.

FR
**VOIX DU RETRAITE.** French. ir. 85.00F France; 96.00F other. Societe Presse Edition et Info, 44 rue Vielle du Temple, 75004 Paris France.

US
**VOLUNTEER & VISITOR'S GUIDE.** English. ir (12 issues). $29.00. Eymann Publications, PO Box 3577, Reno NV 89505. **Tel** (702)333-6651.

●US/1071-2275
**WISER NOW.** [Wiser now]. Vol. 1, Issue 1 (Sept. 1992)-. Periodical. English (Spanish). Twelve times a year. $31.95 US; $33.95 Canada. Better Directions Multi-Media, PO Box 6484, Vero Beach FL 32961. **Tel** (800)999-0795, (407)563-0011, FAX (407)563-0022. **ED** Kathy Pickell. **DD** 616. Index available. cum. index. **Bk Rev**, (Qty: 10). **Circ:** 3,000 (ctrl).
**Desc:** Publication intended for caregivers of people with Alzheimer's Disease. Provides helpful information for family members as well as professional and private caregivers.

US/0894-2757
**YEAR BOOK OF GERIATRICS AND GERONTOLOGY.** [Year b. geriatr. gerontol.]. **Added/Corp** Year Book Medical Publishers. **VFOAT** Yearbook of Geriatrics and Gerontology; Geriatrics and Gerontology. (1988)-. Periodical. English. an. $59.95. Mosby Year Book Inc., 11830 Westline Industrial Drive, St Louis MO 63146. **Tel** (800)325-4177, (314)872-8370, FAX (314)432-1380, telex 44-2402. **LC** RC952.A1; Y43. **DD** 618.97/005. **NLM** ZWT 100; Y39.

GW/0044-281X
**ZEITSCHRIFT FUER GERONTOLOGIE.** [Z. Gerontol.]. **Added/Corp** Deutsche Gesellschaft fuer Gerontologie. Osterreichische Gesellschaft fuer Geriatrie. Vol. 1 (Jan./Feb. 1968)-. Academic Scholarly Publication. German (summaries and/or abstracts in English). Six times a year. DM318.00. Dr Dietrich Steinkopff Verlag, PO Box 111442, D 64229 Darmstadt Germany. **Tel** 011 49 6151 17450. **(Subscription address:** Springer Verlag New York Inc. / for North America, 44 Hartz Way, Secaucus NJ 07096.**)** **ED** I. Falck and U. Lehr. **LC** RC952; .A485. **NLM** W1 ZE357T. **CODEN** ZGERAG. **[CCC]. Bk Rev. Ad Acc. Pr Rev. Circ:** 1,500 (ctrl). Documents available from The Genuine Article, BIOSIS Document Express, CASDDS. ***Absorbed*** *Aktuelle Gerontologie.*
**Desc:** European journal for geriatrics and gerontology, regarding all disciplines.
**Ind/Abst** Biol. Abstr. (1987-); Chem. Abstr. (1968-1982); Curr. Contents Clin. Med.; Curr. Contents Soc. Behav. Sci.; EMBASE; Index Med.; Int. Nurs. Index; Nutr. Abstr. Rev., Ser. A, Hum. Exp.; Life Sci. Collect.; Psychol. Abstr. (1968-); PsycINFO (1968-); PsycLit; Res. Alert [Full Cov.]; Soc. Sci. Cit. Index [Full Cov.].

SZ/1011-6877
**ZEITSCHRIFT FUER GERONTOPSYCHOLOGIE & -PSYCHIATRIE.** **VFOAT** Zeitschrift fuer Gerontopsychologie und -Psychiatrie. (March 1988)-. Periodical. German (English). qt. 103.00F. Verlag Hans Huber Ag Bern, Laenggass Strasse 76, CH 3000 Bern 9 Switzerland. **Tel** 011 41 31 3004500. **ED** W. Oswald, S. Kanowski, U.M. Fleischmann. **NLM** W1; ZE357U. **Circ:** 800.

CC/0254-9026
**ZHONGHUA LAONIAN YIXUE ZAZHI.** (CHUNG-HUA LAO NIEN I HSUEH TSA CHIH.). [Zhonghua laonian yixue zazhi]. **Added/Corp** Chung-hua I Hsueh Hui (China : 1949- ). Lao Nien I Hsueh Hsueh Hui. **VFOAT** Chinese Journal of Geriatrics. (Feb. 1982)-. Periodical. Chinese (summaries and/or abstracts in English). qt. $2.50 (per issue). Zhonghua Yixuehui / Chinese Society of Medical Sciences, Beijing Yiyuan (Beijing Hospital), Dongdan, Beijing 100730, People's Republic of China. **Tel** 5126611. **ED** W. Xinde. **NLM** W1 CH982KD. Documents available from BLDSC.

## GYNECOLOGY AND OBSTETRICS

CN/0824-8230
**A L'AUTRE, UNE.** ***Ceased.*** (L'UNE A L'AUTRE : LE JOURNAL DE NAISSANCE-RENAISSANCE.). [Une autre]. Vol. 1, No 1 (Winter 1983)-(199?). Periodical. French. qt. Naissance-Renaissance, 1493 Rachel E 1, Montreal Quebec H2J 2K3 Canada. **Tel** (514)525-5895. **DD** 612/.63/05. Index available. **Bk Rev. Ad Acc. Circ:** 2,000 (ctrl).
**Desc:** Information on birth humanization, issues and rights of women on the legalization of midwifery and holistics medicine.

US/0884-1535
**ABMS DIRECTORY OF CERTIFIED OBSTETRICIANS AND GYNECOLOGISTS.** [ABMS dir. certif. obstet. gynecol.]. **VFOAT** Directory of Certified Obstetricians and Gynecologists. **VAT** American Board of Medical Specialties Directory of Certified Obstetricians and Gynecologists. 1985-. Directory. English. be. $44.95. American Board of Medical Specialties, 1 Rotary Center, Suite 805, Evanston IL 60201. **Tel** (708)491-9091. **LC** RG33.U6. **DD** 618.1/0025/73. **NLM** WQ 22.1; A1523. **Bk Rev. Ad Acc.** ctrl circ.

UK/0262-7299
**ABORTION REVIEW.** [Abortion rev.]. (1981)-. Newsletter. English. Four times a year (Mar., June, Sept., Dec.). £15.00. Birth Control Trust, 27 Mortimer Street, London W1N 7RJ England. **Tel** 011 44 71 5809360, FAX 011 44 71 8371378. **DD** 363.460942.
**Desc:** Legislation news and other information on abortion from around the world.

FR/0296-9947
**ABSTRACT GYNECO PARIS.** [Abstr. gyneco Paris]. (1985)-. Periodical. French. sm. 177.46F France; 295.00F other. Abstract, 25 Bis Av Pierre Grenier, 92100 Boulogne Billanct France. **Tel** 011 33 1 49100606. **UDC** 618.

US/0897-1471
**ACOG CURRENT JOURNAL REVIEW.** (ACOG CURRENT JOURNAL REVIEW / AMERICAN COLLEGE OF OBSTETRICIANS AND GYNECOLOGISTS.). [ACOG curr. j. rev.]. **Added/Corp** American College of Obstetricians and Gynecologists. **VAT** American College of Obstetricians and Gynecologists Current Journal Review. Vol. 1, No. 1 (1987)-. Academic Scholarly Publication. English. bm (1 volume). $125.00 US; $165.00 other. Elsevier Science Publishing Company Inc, Madison Square Station, PO Box 882, New York NY 10159-0882. **Tel** (212)633-3950, FAX (212)633-3990. **DD** 618. **[CCC].**

US/0400-048X
**ACOG NEWSLETTER.** [ACOG newsl.]. **VFOAT** ACOG. **VAT** American College of Obstetricians and

Gynecologists Newsletter. (1956)-. Newsletter. English. mo. **NLM** W1 A103. ***Continues*** *AAOG Newsletter.*
**Ind/Abst** Curr. Lit. Fam. Plan.

US/1074-8628
**ACOG TECHNICAL BULLETIN.** [ACOG tech. bull.]. **Added/Corp** American College of Obstetricians and Gynecologists. **VFOAT** American College of Obstetricians and Gynecologists Technical Bulletin. No. 1 (Jan. 1965)-. Periodical. English. ir. $50.00 ACOG Technical Bulletin; $80.00 Comes with combination with ACOG Committee Opinions. American College of Obstetricians and Gynecologists, 409 12th Street Southwest, Washington DC 20024. **Tel** (202)638-5577. **DD** 618. **NLM** W1 A1136S. Index Available in first issue of next volume--loose-unpaged. cum. index.

US
**ACOG UPDATE (AUDIO CASSETTE).** English. $170.00 members; $195.00 nonmembers. Medical Information Systems, 2 Sealview Blvd., Port Washington NY 11050. **Tel** (516)621-7200.

SP/0001-5776
**ACTA GINECOLOGICA.** [Acta Ginecol.]. (1950)-. Periodical. Spanish. sm. 8000ptas Sapin. Editores Medicos SA, Calle Gabriela Mistral 2, 28035 Madrid Spain. **Tel** 011 34 1 3860033, 34 1 3860366, FAX 34 1 3739907. **UDC** 618. **CODEN** ACGLA.

SP/0210-9832
**ACTA OBSTETRICA Y GINECOLOGICA HISPANO-LUSITANA.** [Acta obstet. ginecol. hisp. - lusit.]. (1968)-. Periodical. Spanish. mo. Manuel Usandizaga, Santalo 11, 28001 Madrid Spain. **UDC** 618. ***Continues*** *Acta Obstetrica y Ginecologica Hispano-Lusitana. Suplemento, 0300-8940.*

SW/0001-6349
**ACTA OBSTETRICIA ET GYNECOLOGICA SCANDINAVICA.** [Acta obstet. gynecol. Scand.]. Vol. 4 (1926)-. Academic Scholarly Publication. English. Ten times a year. kr1910.00 US, Canada and Japan; kr1860.00 other. Munksgaard International Publishers Ltd, PO Box 2148, DK-1016 Copenhagen K Denmark. **Tel** 011 45 33 12 70 30, FAX 011 45 33 12 93 87, telex 19431 MUNKS DK. **ED** J. Jocksson. **NLM** W1 AC8731. **CODEN** AOGSAE. **[CCC].** Index available. cum. index. **Bk Rev. Ad Acc. Pr Rev. Circ:** 2,200 (ctrl). available on microfilm and microfiche from University Microfilms International (UMI). Documents available from The Genuine Article, BIOSIS Document Express, CASDDS, ADONIS. ***Continues*** *Acta Gynecologica Scandinavica.*
**Desc:** Covers all aspects of obstetrics and gynecology and publishes contributions concerned with clinical and experimental research work in the field, including perinatology, gynecologic endocrinology, female urology and gynecological oncology.
**Ind/Abst** ADONIS; Biol. Abstr.; Chem. Abstr.; Curr. Contents Clin. Med.; Curr. Lit. Fam. Plan.; Dairy Sci. Abstr.; Dev. Med. Child Neurol.; EMBASE; Energy Res. Abstr.; Health Plan. Adminis.; Index Med.; Med. Abstr. Newsl.; Nutr. Abstr. Rev., Ser. B, Live Feeds and Feed.; Nutr. Abstr. Rev., Ser. A, Hum. Exp.; Life Sci. Collect.; PESTDOC; Protozoolog. Abstr.; Ref. Upd. Deluxe Ed.; Res. Alert [Full Cov.]; Rev. Med. Vet. Mycology; Risk Abstr.; Sci. Cit. Index; SCISEARCH; Soc. Sci. Cit. Index [Select. Cov.]; SPORT Discus.

SW/0300-8835
**ACTA OBSTETRICIA ET GYNECOLOGICA SCANDINAVICA. SUPPLEMENTUM.** [Acta obstet. gynecol. Scand. Suppl.]. (1926)-. Academic Scholarly Publication. English (French and German). kr1910.00 US, Canada & Japan; kr1860.00 other'(included with Acta Anaesthesiologica Scandinavica). Munksgaard International Publishers Ltd, PO Box 2148, DK-1016 Copenhagen K Denmark. **Tel** 011 45 33 12 70 30, FAX 011 45 33 12 93 87, telex 19431 MUNKS DK. **NLM** W1 AC8732. **CODEN** AGSSAI. **[CCC].** Documents available from BIOSIS Document Express, CASDDS.
**Ind/Abst** Biol. Abstr.; Chem. Abstr.; EMBASE; Health Plan. Adminis.; Index Med.; Life Sci. Collect.

SP/1132-029X
**ACTUALIDAD OBSTETRICO GINECOLOGICA MADRID.** [Actual. obstet. ginecol. Madr.]. (1989)-. Periodical. Spanish. Six times a year. 5300ptas Spain; 5000ptas others. Nuevas Creaciones Medicas, C Santillana del Mar, 3 Chalet 44, 28660 Boadilla del Monte Madrid Spain. **Tel** 011 34 1 6321544, 011 34 1 6321608, FAX 011 34 1 6321544. **UDC** 618.

FR/0223-4661
**ACTUALITES GYNECOLOGIQUES (PARIS. 1971).** (ACTUALITES GYNECOLOGIQUES.). [Actual. gynecol.]. (197?)-. Academic Scholarly Publication. French. bm. Masson SA / Spain, La Llagosta 6 8, 08120 Barcelona Spain. **Tel** 011 34 3 5741135. **CODEN** ACGYBH. Documents available from CASDDS.
**Ind/Abst** Chem. Abstr.

US/0932-8610
**ADOLESCENT AND PEDIATRIC GYNECOLOGY.** [Adolesc. pediatr. gynecol.]. **Added/Corp** North American Society for Pediatric and Adolescent Gynecology. Vol. 1, No. 1 (1988)-. Periodical. English. Four times a year. $173.00. Springer-Verlag New York Inc., 175 5th Avenue, New York NY 10010. **Tel** (212)460-1500, telex 232 235 SPB UR. **(Subscription address:** Springer Verlag New York Inc. / for North America, 44 Hartz Way, Secaucus NJ 07096.**) ED** Joseph S Sanfilippo. **LC** RJ478; .A34. **DD** 618.92/098. **NLM** W1; AD37E. **[CCC]. Pr Rev.** available on microfilm and microfiche from University Microfilms International (UMI). Documents available from The Genuine Article.
**Desc:** Serves as an international source of information for physicians and other health professionals working in pediatric and adolescent gynecology. Scope includes all aspects of clinical and basic science research in pediatric and adolescent gynecology, as well as in molecular biology as applied to the field.
**Ind/Abst** Comb. Cumul. Index Pediatr. (199?-); Curr. Contents Clin. Med.; EMBASE; Res. Alert [Select. Cov.]; SCISEARCH.

II
**ADVANCES IN GYNAECOLOGICAL ONCOLOGY.** English. $65.00. S O G S R L, Galleria Storione 2A, 35128 Padua Italy. **Tel** 011 39 49 8756900.

UK
**ADVANCES IN GYNECOLOGICAL AND OBSTETRIC RESEARCH SERIES.** Vol. 1 (1990)-. Monographic series. English. Price varies per volume. Parthenon Publishing, Casterton Hall Carnforth, Lancashire LA6 2LA England. **Tel** 011 44 5242 72084, FAX 44-5242-71587. **NLM** W1; AD621L.

●US/1070-5392
**ADVANCES IN OBSTETRICS AND GYNECOLOGY (ST. LOUIS, MO.).** (ADVANCES IN OBSTETRICS AND GYNECOLOGY.). **VFOAT** Advances in Obstetrics and Gynecology. (1994)-. English. $79.95. Mosby Year Book Inc., 11830 Westline Industrial Drive, St Louis MO 63146. **Tel** (800)325-4177, (314)872-8370, FAX (314)432-1380, telex 44-2402. **NLM** W1; AD685NT.

US/0731-1400
**ADVANCES IN PERINATAL MEDICINE.** [Adv. perinat. med.]. Vol. 1 (1981)-. Academic Scholarly Publication. English. ir. Price varies per volume. Plenum Press, 233 Spring Street, New York NY 10013-1578. **Tel** (212)620-8000, (800)221-9369, FAX (212)463-0742, (212)807-1047, telex 23/421139. **ED** Aubrey Milunsky, Emanuel A. Friedman, and Louis Gluck. **DD** 618.3/2. **NLM** W1 AD73T. **CODEN** APMDD9. Documents available from CASDDS.
**Ind/Abst** Chem. Abstr. (1981-1983).

RU/0002-3906
**AKUSERSTVO I GINEKOLOGIJA (MOSKVA).** (AKUSHERSTVO I GINEKOLOGIIA.). [Akus. ginekol.]. **Added/Corp** Soviet Union. Ministerstvo Zdravookhraneniia. Soviet Union. Narodnyi Komissariat Zdravookhraneniia. (1936)-. Academic Scholarly Publication. Russian. Six times a year. $69.95. Izdatelstvo Meditsina / Russian Academy of Medical Sciences, Ulitsa Solyanka 14, 109801 Moscow Russia. **Tel** 011 95 297-05-04. **(Subscription address:** East View Publications Inc., 3020 Harbor Lane North, Suite 110, Minneapolis MN 55447.**) NLM** W1 AK998. **CODEN** AKGIAO. Documents available from CASDDS. ***Formed by the union of*** *Zhurnal Akusherstva i Zhenskikh Boleznei* ***and*** *Ginekologiia i Akusherstva.*
**Ind/Abst** Chem. Abstr.; EMBASE [Select. Cov.]; Index Med.

BU/0324-0959
**AKUSHERSTVO I GINEKOLOGIIA.** [Akus. ginekol.]. **Added/Corp** Bulgaria. Ministerstvo na Naradnoto Zdrave i Sofsialnite Grizhi. Vol. 1 (1962)-. Periodical. Bulgarian (summaries and/or abstracts in English and Russian; table of contents in Russian and English). Six times a year. DM109.00. **(Subscription address:** Kubon & Sagner, ABT Zeitschriftenimport, D 80328 Munich Germany.**) NLM** W1 AK998E. **CODEN** AKGIBP. Documents available from CASDDS.
**Ind/Abst** Chem. Abstr.; EMBASE; Index Med.

US/0279-490X
**AMERICAN BABY'S CHILDBIRTH EDUCATOR.** ***Ceased.*** [Am. baby's childbirth educ.]. **Added/Corp** American Baby, Inc. **VFOAT** Childbirth Educator. Vol. 1, No. 1 (Fall 1981)-(199?). Periodical. English. qt. Childbirth Educator, 475 Park Avenue South 5th Floor, New York NY 10016. **Tel** (212)689-3600, (800)525-0643. **ED** Marsha Rehns. **LC** RG651; .A46. **DD** 618.4/05. **[CCC]. Bk Rev. Ad Acc. Circ:** 22,000 (ctrl). available on microfilm from University Microfilms International (UMI).
**Desc:** Labor and birth, fetal development, pregnancy, child care, and teaching techniques for teachers of childbirth classes.

US
**AMERICAN DIRECTORY OF OBSTETRICIANS AND GYNECOLOGISTS.** 1st Edition (1954/55)-. Directory. English. be. American Directory of Obstetricians and Gynecologists, 5710 Kingston Pike, Knoxville TN 37919.

US/0895-3643
**AMERICAN JOURNAL OF GYNECOLOGIC HEALTH, THE.** ***Ceased.*** [Am. j. gynecol. health]. Vol. 1, No. 1 (July/Sept. 1987)-Vol. 7. Periodical. English. bm. Macor Publishing Company, 116 West 32nd Street/8th Floor, New York NY 10001. **Tel** (212)736-6688, FAX (212)564-1763. **DD** 618. **NLM** W1; AM452FC. **[CCC].**
**Ind/Abst** Curr. Lit. Fam. Plan.

US/0002-9378
**AMERICAN JOURNAL OF OBSTETRICS AND GYNECOLOGY.** [Am. j. obstet. gynecol.]. **Added/Corp** American Gynecological Society. Vol. 1 (Oct. 1920)-. Academic Scholarly Publication. English. mo. $222.00 (institutions), $124.00 (individuals) US; $255.00 (institutions), $157.00 (individuals) other. Mosby Year Book Inc., 11830 Westline Industrial Drive, St Louis MO 63146. **Tel** (800)325-4177, (314)872-8370, FAX (314)432-1380, telex 44-2402. **ED** John I. Brewer, E.J. Quilligan, Frederick P. Zuspan, and Albert B. Gerbie. **LC** RG1; .A62. **DD** 618. **NLM** W1 AM496E. **CODEN** AJOGAH. **[CCC].** Index available. cum. index. **Ad Acc. Pr Rev. Circ:** 20,532. available on microfilm and microfiche from University Microfilms International (UMI). Documents available from The Genuine Article, BIOSIS Document Express, CASDDS, Documents on Demand, ADONIS. ***Continues*** *American Journal of Obstetrics and Diseases of Women and Children, 0894-5543.*
**Desc:** Edited for physicians specializing in obstetrics and gynecology and those in general practice. Scientific material published represents original contributions. Clinical and investigative reports are also published.
**Ind/Abst** Abr. Index Med.; ADONIS; Anim. Breed. Abstr.; Annals Behav. Med.; Biol. Abstr.; Biol. Dig.; Calcium Calcif. Tissue Abstr.; Chem. Abstr.; Comb. Cumul. Index Ob./Gyn.; CSA Neuro. Abstr. (?-?); Cumul. Index Nurs. Allied Health Lit.; Curr. Aware. Biol. Sci., CABS; Curr. Contents Clin. Med.; Curr. Contents Life Sci.; Curr. Lit. Fam. Plan.; Dairy Sci. Abstr.; Dev. Med. Child Neurol.; EMBASE; Energy Inf. Abstr.; Energy Res. Abstr.; Environ. Abstr.; Health Devices Alerts; Health Index (1989-); Health Period. Database; Health Plan. Adminis.; Health Ref. Cent. (Jan. 1989-) [Full Cov.]; Immunol. Abstr.; Index Med.; Index Vet.; Int. Aerosp. Abstr.; Int. Pharm. Abstr.; Iowa Drug Inf. Serv. (1966-); Maize Abstr.; Med. Abstr. Newsl.; Microbiol. Abstr. Sect. B; Microbiol. Abstr. Sect. C; Mod. Med.; Nutr. Abstr. Rev., Ser. B, Live Feeds and Feed.; Nutr. Abstr. Rev., Ser. A, Hum. Exp.; Nutr. Res. Newsl.; Oncog. Growth Factors Abstr.; Life Sci. Collect.; PESTDOC; Physic. Medline Plus; Protozoolog. Abstr.; Ref. Upd. Basic Ed.; Ref. Upd. Deluxe Ed.; Res. Alert [Full Cov.]; Rev. Med. Vet. Mycology; Rev. Plant Pathol.; Risk Abstr.; Sci. Cit. Index; SCISEARCH; Soc. Sci. Cit. Index [Select. Cov.]; SportSearch; Vet. Bull.; Virol. AIDS Abstr.

US/0735-1631
**AMERICAN JOURNAL OF PERINATOLOGY.** [Am. j. perinatol.]. Vol. 1, No. 1 (Oct. 1983)-. Periodical. English. bm (Jan., Mar., May, July, Sep., Nov.). $105.00 (individuals), $147.00 (institutions) US; $130.00'(individuals), $172.00 (institutions) other. Thieme Medical Publishers Inc., 381 Park Avenue South, Suite 1201, New York NY 10016. **Tel** (212)683-5088, (212)683-5089, FAX (212)779-9020, telex 220 862 TSINC UR. **ED** P A M Auld, A N Krauss, J R Niebyl. **LC** RG600; .A47. **DD** 618.3/2/005. **NLM** W1; AM498BP. **[CCC]. Bk Rev. Ad Acc. Pr Rev. Circ:** 1,500 (ctrl). available on microfilm and microfiche from University Microfilms International (UMI). Documents available from The Genuine Article, BIOSIS Document Express.
**Desc:** Offers a timely forum of ideas on perinatal care. Presents articles on all aspects of clinical practice and critical care management. Original articles will concern themselves with pediatrics, obstetrics, neonatology, pediatric neurology, labor and delivery and intensive care for infants. Each issue includes case reports and state-of-the-art review articles.
**Ind/Abst** Biol. Abstr. (1985-); Curr. Contents Clin. Med.; Dairy Sci. Abstr.; Dev. Med. Child Neurol.; EMBASE; Health Plan. Adminis.; Index Med. (Vol. 1, No. 1, 1983-); Int. Nurs. Index; Ref. Upd. Deluxe Ed.; Res. Alert [Select. Cov.]; Rev. Med. Vet. Mycology; SCISEARCH; Soc. Sci. Cit. Index [Select. Cov.].

FI/0355-9521
**ANNALES CHIRURGIAE ET GYNAECOLOGIAE.** [Ann. chir. gynaecol.]. Vol. 65 (1976)-. Academic Scholarly Publication. English. qt. $200.00 (Denmark, Iceland, Norway, & Sweden); $220.00 (rest of Europe); $230.00 (other). The Finnish Surgical Society, Makelankatu 2 A, SF-00500 Helsinki Finland. **Tel** 358-03930768. **ED** Jorma Sipponen, Peter Roberts, Pertti Myllynen, Juha Niinikoski, Matti Lempinen. **UDC** 616-089.888; 618.1-089.8. **NLM** W1 AN3094. **CODEN** ACGYDJ. Index available. cum. index. **Ad Acc. Pr Rev. Circ:** 2,000 (ctrl). available on microfilm from

University Microfilms International (UMI). Documents available from The Genuine Article, BIOSIS Document Express, CASDDS. ***Continues** Annales Chirurgiae et Gynaecologiae Fenniae, 0003-3855.*
**Desc:** Surgical research and closely related topics in operative gynecology and obstetrics as well as anesthesiology.
**Ind/Abst** Biol. Abstr.; Chem. Abstr. (1976-1982); Curr. Contents Clin. Med.; EMBASE; Index Med.; Life Sci. Collect.; Res. Alert [Select. Cov.]; SCISEARCH; Soc. Sci. Cit. Index [Select. Cov.]; SportSearch.

FI/0355-9874
**ANNALES CHIRURGIAE ET GYNAECOLOGIAE. SUPPLEMENTUM.** [Ann. chir. gynaecol., Suppl.]. No. 192 (1976)-. Monographic series. ir. Price varies per volume. Finnish Surgical Society, Makelankatu 2, SF 00550 Helsinki Finland. **NLM** W1 AN30951A. Documents available from BIOSIS Document Express. ***Continues** Annales Chirurgiae et Gynaecologiae Fenniae. Supplementum.*
**Ind/Abst** Biol. Abstr.; Calcium Calcif. Tissue Abstr.; Health Plan. Adminis.; Index Med.

IT/0300-0087
**ANNALI DI OSTETRICIA, GINECOLOGIA, MEDICINA PERINATALE.** [Ann. ostet. ginecol. med. perinat.]. Vol. 93 (Jan. 1972)-. Academic Scholarly Publication. Italian (summaries and/or abstracts in English, French and German; table of contents in English). Six times a year. L95000 Italy; L125000 Europe; L150000 other. Istituti Clinici d'Perfezionamento AMM, Riviste V Daverio 6, 20122 Milan Italy. **Tel** 011 39 2 57992033. **NLM** W1 AN501. **CODEN** AOGMAU. Index available. **Ad Acc. Circ:** 500. Documents available from CASDDS. ***Continues** Annali di Ostetricia e Ginecologia, 0003-4657.*
**Ind/Abst** Chem. Abstr.; EMBASE; Health Plan. Adminis.; Index Med.; Life Sci. Collect.

GW/0932-0067
**ARCHIVES OF GYNECOLOGY AND OBSTETRICS.** [Arch. gynecol. obstet.]. **Added/Corp** Deutsche Gesellschaft fuer Gynakologie und Geburtshilfe. Vol. 241, No. 1 (July 1987)-. Periodical. English. Eight times a year. DM996.00. Springer-Verlag GmbH & Company KG, Heidelberger Platz 3, D 14197 Berlin Germany. **Tel** 011 49 30 8207223, FAX 011 49 30 8214091, telex 183 319 SPBLN D. **(Subscription address:** Springer Verlag New York Inc. / for North America, 44 Hartz Way, Secaucus NJ 07096.**) ED** H A Hirsch, F E Loeffler, H Ludwig, and K H Wulf. **NLM** W1; AR455AR. **CODEN** AGOBEJ. **[CCC].** Index available. **Bk Rev. Ad Acc.** available on microfilm from University Microfilms International (UMI). Documents available from The Genuine Article, BIOSIS Document Express, CASDDS. ***Continues** Archives of Gynecology, 0170-9925.*
**Desc:** Informs the gynecological researcher about the latest advances in the field.
**Ind/Abst** Anim. Breed. Abstr.; Biol. Abstr. (1987-); Chem. Abstr.; Curr. Contents Clin. Med.; Curr. Contents Life Sci.; EMBASE; Health Plan. Adminis.; Index Med. (1987-); Res. Alert [Full Cov.]; Sci. Cit. Index; SCISEARCH; Soc. Sci. Cit. Index [Select. Cov.].

IT/0004-0126
**ARCHIVIO DI OSTETRICIA E GINECOLOGIA.** [Arch. ostet. ginecol.]. **VFOAT** AOG. Vol. 1 (1894)-. Periodical. Italian (French; summaries and/or abstracts in English, German and Spanish). Six times a year. $90.00. Clinical Ostetrica Ginecologica, LGO Madonna Grazie 1 Martella, 80138 Naples Italy. **Tel** 011 39 81 459849, 011 39 81 444445. **NLM** W1 AR547. **CODEN** AOGNAX. Documents available from CASDDS.
**Ind/Abst** Chem. Abstr. (1894-1981); Index Med.

CI/0004-1289
**ARHIV ZA ZASTITU MAJKE I DJETETA.** **VFOAT** Archives for Mother and Child Health. (1957)-. Multiple languages. ir. Institute for Mother and Child Health, Klaiceva 16, 41000 Zagreb Croatia. **(Subscription address:** Mladost Export Import, PO Box 1028, Ilica 30, 41000 Zagreb Croatia.**) CODEN** A.613.9A.618.
**Ind/Abst** EMBASE [Select. Cov.].

PO/0871-4592
**ARQUIVOS DA MATERNIDADE DR. ALFREDO DA COSTA.** **Added/Corp** Maternidade Dr. Alfredo da Costa. (198?)-. Periodical. Portuguese (English). sa. Free on request. Maternidade Dr A. da Costa, Rua Virato, 1000 Lisbon Portugal. **Tel** 011 351 1 541030. **(Subscription address:** Roussel, Rua Joao de Deus 19 Venda Nova, 2701 Amadora Codex Portugal.**) NLM** W1; AR89QH. **CODEN** AMACES. ***Continues** Arquivo Clinico da Maternidade Dr. Alfredo da Costa, 0302-4326.*
**Ind/Abst** EMBASE [Select. Cov.].

JA/0389-2328
**ASIA-OCEANIA JOURNAL OF OBSTETRICS AND GYNAECOLOGY.** (ASIA-OCEANIA JOURNAL OF OBSTETRICS AND GYNAECOLOGY / AOFOG.). [Asia-Oceania j. obstet. gynaecol.]. **Added/Corp** Asia and Oceania Federation of Obstetrics and Gynaecology. Vol. 6, No. 1 (Sept. 1980)-. Academic Scholarly Publication. English. Four times a year (Mar., June, Sept., Dec.). Y8000 Japan; Y10000 other. Asia-Oceania Journal Obstetrics & Gynaecology, Juntendo University, 211 Hongo Bunkyo, Tokyo 113 Japan. **Tel** 011 81 3 38133111, FAX 011 81 3 58024876. **ED** Professor Yoshinori Kuwabara. **NLM** W1 AS138. **CODEN** AOJGDU. Index available (Bound in 4th iss. (Dec.)). **Bk Rev. Ad Acc. Circ:** 4,000 (ctrl). Documents available from CASDDS. ***Continues** Journal of the Asian Federation of Obstetrics and Gynaecology.*
**Ind/Abst** Chem. Abstr. (1975-1987); Health Plan. Adminis.; Index Med. (1982-).

US
**ASPO/LAMAZE MEMBERSHIP DIRECTORY.** **Main/Corp** American Society for Psychoprophylaxis in Obstetrics. **VFOAT** Membership Directory. (1990)-. Directory. English. 1411 K Street NW, Washington DC 20005. **NLM** WQ 22; AA1 A6d. ***Continues** Who's Who in Childbirth Education, 0163-5492.*

US/1051-2446
**ASSISTED REPRODUCTIVE REVIEWS.** [Assist. reprod. rev.]. Vol. 1, No. 1 (Apr. 1991)-. Periodical. English. qt. $158.00 (individual) $180.00 (institution) US; $188.00 (individual), $210.00 (institution) other. Williams & Wilkins Company, 428 East Preston Street, Baltimore MD 21202-3993. **Tel** (410)528-4000, (800)638-6423, FAX (410)528-8596, telex 87669. **(Subscription address:** Williams & Wilkins, PO Box 64380, Baltimore MD 21264.**) DD** 618. **NLM** W1; AS363H. **CODEN** AEPEEJ. **[CCC].** Documents available from Quick Copies.
**Desc:** Publishes reviews covering advances in reproductive medicine directory to ob/gyns, urologists, endocrinologists, embryologists, and biologists.

UK
**ASSOCIATION OF CHARTERED PHYSIOTHERAPISTS IN OBSTETRICS AND GYNAECOLOGY NEWSLETTER.** (19??)-. Newsletter. English. sa. £20.00. ACPOG, The Cottage, 15 Grange Court Westbury, Bristol BS9 HDP England.

US/0571-8635
**AUDIO-DIGEST. OBSTETRICS AND GYNECOLOGY.** (19??)-. Periodical. English. sm (24 issues). $179.76 US; $202.80 Canada; $247.44 other (audiocassette). Audio-Digest Foundation, 1577 Chevy Chase Drive, Glendale CA 91206. **Tel** (213)245-8505, (800)423-2308, FAX (818)240-7379. **ED** Claron L. Oakley. Index available. ctrl circ.
**Desc:** Interactive system of audio cassette postgraduate medical education, with each one-hour program eligible for two Category I credit hours.

AT/0004-8666
**AUSTRALIAN AND NEW ZEALAND JOURNAL OF OBSTETRICS AND GYNAECOLOGY.** [Aust. N.Z. j. obstet. gynaecol.]. **VFOAT** Journal of Obstetrics & Gynaecology; Australian and New Zealand Journal of Obstetrics and Gynaecology. Vol. 1 March (1961)-. Academic Scholarly Publication. English. qt. 70.00Aus$ Australia, New Zealand and Papua New Guinea; 75.00Aus$ other. Australian & New Zealand Journal of Obstetrics and Gynecology, 254 Albert Street, College House, East Melbourne, 3002 Victoria Australia. **Tel** 011 61 3 4171699. **ED** N. A. Beischer. **DD** 618.05. **UDC** 618. **NLM** W1 AU497. **CODEN** AZOGBS. Index available. **Bk Rev. Ad Acc. Pr Rev. Circ:** 3,000 (ctrl). Documents available from The Genuine Article, BIOSIS Document Express, CASDDS.
**Desc:** The only Australasian journal specializing in this field, and the official organ of the Royal Australian College of Obstetricians and Gynaecologists.
**Ind/Abst** Biol. Abstr.; Chem. Abstr. (1961-1982); Curr. Contents Clin. Med.; EMBASE; Health Plan. Adminis.; Helminthol. Abstr. (1991-); Index Med. (1978-); Nutr. Abstr. Rev., Ser. B, Live Feeds and Feed.; Nutr. Abstr. Rev., Ser. A, Hum. Exp.; Nutr. Res. Newsl.; Life Sci. Collect.; Protozoolog. Abstr.; Res. Alert [Select. Cov.]; SCISEARCH; Soc. Sci. Cit. Index [Select. Cov.].

SP/0210-7171
**AVANCES EN OBSTETRICIA Y GINECOLOGIA.** [Av. obstet. ginecol.]. (1975)-. Periodical. Spanish. SALVAT, Antonio Lopez Aguado 1 Loc DCH, 28029 Madrid Spain. **Tel** 011 34 1 2473359. **ED** J Gonzalez-Merlo and I Burzaco. **NLM** W3 AV13. **CODEN** AOGIEM. Documents available from BIOSIS Document Express.
**Ind/Abst** Biol. Abstr. (1988-).

US/1066-3614
**AWHONN'S CLINICAL ISSUES IN PERINATAL AND WOMEN'S HEALTH NURSING.** ***Title Change.*** [AWHONN's clin. issues perinat. women's health nurs.]. **Added/Corp** Association of Women's Health, Obstetric, and Neonatal Nurses. **VFOAT** Clinical Issues in Perinatal and Women's Health Nursing. **VAT** Association of Women's Health, Obstetric, and Neonatal Nurses Clinical Issues in Perinatal and Women's Hhealth Nursing. Vol. 4, No. 1 (1993)-(1993). Periodical. English. qt. J.B. Lippincott Company, 227 East Washington Square, Philadelphia PA 19106-3780. **Tel** (215)238-4200 or 4454, FAX (215)238-4227. **DD** 618. **NLM** W1; AW946M. ***Continues** NAACOG's Clinical Issues in Perinatal and Women's Health Nursing, 1046-7475. **Merged into** Journal of Obstetric Gynecologic and Neonatal Nursing.*
**Ind/Abst** Int. Nurs. Index (1993-).

US/0749-971X
**BABY TALK (1977).** **See** Medical Science and Technology-Pediatrics.

UK/0950-3552
**BAILLIERE'S CLINICAL OBSTETRICS AND GYNAECOLOGY.** [Bailliere's clin. obstet. gynaecol.]. **VFOAT** Clinical Obstetrics and Gynaecology. Vol. 1, No. 1 (March 1987)-. Periodical. English. qt (4 issues). £94.00 (institution). Harcourt Brace & Company Ltd., Foots Cray, High Street, Sidcup Kent DA14 5HP England. **Tel** 011 44 81 300 3322, FAX 011 44 81 309 0807. **(Subscription address:** W. B. Saunders Company / North America Subscriptions, c/o Periodicals, 6277 Sea Harbour Drive, 4th Floor, Orlando FL 32887.**) NLM** W1; BA46EP. Index available. **Pr Rev.** available on microfilm. Documents available from The Genuine Article. ***Continues in part** Clinics in Obstetrics and Gynaecology, 0306-3356.*
**Ind/Abst** Curr. Contents Clin. Med.; Dev. Med. Child Neurol.; EMBASE; Health Plan. Adminis.; Index Med. (1987-); Res. Alert [Full Cov.]; Sci. Cit. Index; SCISEARCH; Soc. Sci. Cit. Index [Select. Cov.].

GW/0722-9852
**BERICHTE GYNAKOLOGIE, GEBURTSHILFE.** **Added/Corp** Deutsche Gesellschaft fuer Gynakologie und Geburtshilfe. **VFOAT** Gynaecology, Obstetrics. Vol. 118, No. 1 (1982)-. Periodical. German (English and German). Thirteen times a year. DM5196.00. Springer-Verlag GmbH & Company KG, Heidelberger Platz 3, D 14197 Berlin Germany. **Tel** 011 49 30 8207223, FAX 011 49 30 8214091, telex 183 319 SPBLN D. **(Subscription address:** Springer Verlag New York Inc. / for North America, 44 Hartz Way, Secaucus NJ 07096.**) ED** H Ludwig and W Kuenzel and E Koschade. **NLM** ZWP 100 B511. **[CCC]. Bk Rev.** ***Continues** Berichte uber die Gesamte Gynakologie und Geburtshilfe Sowie Deren Grenzgebiete, 0005-9064.*
**Desc:** Reports on conferences and offers general articles in the field. Topics include eugenics, x-ray diagnosis, oncology, neonatology, pregnancy, pathology, and instructional texts.

US/0730-7659
**BIRTH (BERKELEY, CALIF.).** (BIRTH.). [Birth]. Vol. 9 (Spring 1982)-. Academic Scholarly Publication. English. qt. $95.00 (institution), $40.00 (individual) US; $125.00 (institution), $65.00 (individual) other. Blackwell Scientific Publishers, 238 Main Street, Cambridge MA 02142. **Tel** (617)547-7110, (800)835-6770, FAX (617)547-0789. **ED** Madeleine H Shearer. **LC** RG651; .B54. **DD** 618.1/005. **NLM** W1 BI963B. **[CCC]. Bk Rev. Ad Acc. Pr Rev. Circ:** 6,000. available on microfilm and microfiche from University Microfilms International (UMI). Documents available from The Genuine Article. ***Continues** Birth and the Family Journal, 0098-860X.*
**Desc:** Issues in perinatal care and education such as obstetric practices, childbirth, parent education, contraception and abortion, breastfeeding, and family life.
**Ind/Abst** Cumul. Index Nurs. Allied Health Lit.; Curr. Contents Soc. Behav. Sci.; Health Plan. Adminis.; Int. Nurs. Index; Nutr. Res. Newsl.; Life Sci. Collect.; Physic. Medline Plus; Psychol. Abstr. (1982-); Res. Alert [Full Cov.]; Risk Abstr. (19??-19??); SCISEARCH; Soc. Sci. Cit. Index [Full Cov.].

US/0547-6844
**BIRTH DEFECTS ORIGINAL ARTICLE SERIES.** [Birth defects orig. artic. ser.]. **Added/Corp** National Foundation. **VFOAT** Birth Defects. Vol. 1 (1965)-. Academic Scholarly Publication. English. mo. Price varies per volume. John Wiley & Sons, Inc., 605 Third Avenue, New York NY 10158-0012. **Tel** (212)850-6000, (212)850-6645, FAX (212)850-6088, telex 12-7063. **(Subscription address:** John Wiley & Sons / England, Baffins Lane, Chichester, West Sussex PO19 1UD England.**) ED** D Bergsma. **LC** RG626; .B63. **DD** 616/.043/05; 611. **NLM** W1 BI966. **CODEN** BTHDAK. **[CCC].** cum. index. **Bk Rev. Ad Acc.** Documents available from BIOSIS Document Express, CASDDS.
**Desc:** A scholarly book series concerning birth defects.
**Ind/Abst** Biol. Abstr.; Chem. Abstr.; EMBASE; Genet. Abstr.; Index Med.; Life Sci. Collect.

US/0890-3255
**BIRTH GAZETTE, THE.** [Birth gaz.]. **Added/Corp** Religious and Educational Fund (Walden, Tenn.). (1986)-. Periodical. English. qt. $30.00 (1 year), $50.00 (2 year), (institutions), $25.00 (1 year), $45.00 (2 year) (individuals) US; $33.00 (1 year), $53.00 (2 year), (institutions), $28.00 (1 year), $48.00 (2 year) (individuals) Canada; $35.00 (1 year), $55.00 (2 year), (institutions), $30.00 (1 year), $50.00 (2 year) (individuals) other. The Birth Gazette, 42 The Farm, Summertown TN 38483. **Tel** (615)964-2519. **ED** Ina May Gaskin. **DD** 618. **NLM** W1; BI966D. **Bk Rev. Ad Acc. Circ:** 2,000. available on microfiche. ***Continues** Practicing Midwife, 0733-8317.*
**Desc:** Articles, interviews, news items, pictures, opinions, reviews, advertisements and other features of

interest to midwives, physicians, nurses, childbirth educators, parents, and students.
**Ind/Abst** Int. Nurs. Index (1992-).

US/0734-3124
**BIRTH PSYCHOLOGY BULLETIN.** [Birth psychol. bull.]. Vol. 1, No. 1 (Jan. 1980)-. Bulletin. English. sa. $8.00 US; $9.00 other. Association for Birth Psychology, 444 East 82nd Street, New York NY 10028. **ED** Leslie Feher. **LC** RG658; .B57. **DD** 618.2/001/9. **UDC** 618.2. **Ad Acc.**
**Desc:** Theoretical, clinical and empirical papers on perinatal issues.
**Ind/Abst** Psychol. Abstr. (1980-); PsycINFO; PsycLit.

US/0892-7227
**BIRTH TRAUMA.** **See** Law.

US/1043-321X
**BREAST DISEASES.** [Breast dis.]. Vol. 1, No. 1 (1990)-. Periodical. English. qt. $112.50 (institutions), $75.00 (individuals) US; $116.50 (institutions), $79.00 (individuals) Canada; $126.50 (institutions), $89.00 (individuals) other. Mosby Year Book Inc., 11830 Westline Industrial Drive, St Louis MO 63146. **Tel** (800)325-4177, (314)872-8370, FAX (314)432-1380, telex 44-2402. **ED** Charles M. Balch. **DD** 616. **NLM** ZWP 840; B828. **Ad Acc.**
**Desc:** Provides an interdisciplinary perspective on advances in the treatment, screening, diagnosis and management of breast diseases. Includes more than 40 abstracts accompanied by editorial commentary; articles are selected from the 900 journals surveyed by the editorial staff.

●UK/0960-9776
**BREAST : OFFICIAL JOURNAL OF THE EUROPEAN SOCIETY OF MASTOLOGY, THE.** **Added/Corp** European Society of Mastology. Vol. 1, No. 1 (Mar. 1992)-. Periodical. English. qt. £186.00 Europe; £188.00 Other (Institutions). Churchill Livingstone, 1-3 Baxter's Place, Leith Walk, Edinburgh EH1 3AF Scotland. **Tel** 011 44 31 556 2424, FAX 011 44 31 558 1278, telex 727511. **(Subscription address:** Maruzen Company Ltd., PO Box 5050, Import & Export Department, Tokyo 100 31 Japan.**)** **NLM** W1; BR191L.
**Desc:** The official journal of the European Society of Mastology.
**Ind/Abst** Curr. Aware. Biol. Sci., CABS; Med. Abstr. Newsl.

US/0896-4572
**BREASTFEEDING ABSTRACTS.** **See** Medical Science and Technology-Abstracting, Bibliographies and Statistics.

UK
**BRITISH JOURNAL OF MIDWIFERY.** (19??)-. Periodical. English. Twelve times a year. £80.00 (institutions), £40.00 (individuals) UK and EIRE; £100.00 (institutions), £70.00 (individuals) other. Mark Allen Publishing Ltd., Croxped Mews, 288 Croxped Road, London SE24 9DA England. **Tel** 011 44 1 671 7521.

UK/0306-5456
**BRITISH JOURNAL OF OBSTETRICS AND GYNAECOLOGY.** [Br. j. obstet. gynaecol.]. **Added/Corp** Royal College of Obstetricians and Gynaecologists (Great Britain). Vol. 82 (Jan. 1975)-. Academic Scholarly Publication. English. mo (12 issues). $205.00 US & Canada; £120.00 Europe; £132.00 other. Blackwell Scientific Publications Ltd, Marston Book Services, PO Box 87, Oxford OX2 ODT UK. **Tel** 011 44 865 791155, FAX 011 44 865 791927, telex 837 515 MARDIS G. **ED** F. Hytten. **NLM** W1 BR586. **CODEN** BJOGAS. **[CCC].** Index available. **Bk Rev. Ad Acc. Pr Rev. Circ:** 4,700 (ctrl). available on microfilm and microfiche from University Microfilms International (UMI). Documents available from The Genuine Article, BIOSIS Document Express, CASDDS, ADONIS. ***Continues*** *Journal of Obstetrics and Gynaecology of the British Commonwealth, 0022-3204.*
**Desc:** An international journal aimed at both the practicing clinician and research scientist.
**Ind/Abst** Abr. Index Med.; ADONIS; Biol. Abstr.; Chem. Abstr.; Cumul. Index Nurs. Allied Health Lit.; Curr. Aware. Biol. Sci., CABS; Curr. Contents Clin. Med.; Curr. Contents Life Sci.; Dairy Sci. Abstr.; Dev. Med. Child Neurol.; EMBASE; Health Period. Database; Health Serv. Abstr.; Helminthol. Abstr.; Index Med.; Iowa Drug Inf. Serv. (1969-); Microbiol. Abstr. Sect. B (19??-19??); Nutr. Abstr. Rev., Ser. B, Live Feeds and Feed.; Nutr. Abstr. Rev., Ser. A, Hum. Exp.; Nutr. Res. Newsl.; Life Sci. Collect.; PESTDOC; Physic. Medline Plus; Phys. Med. Biol. (19??-19??); Protozoolog. Abstr.; Ref. Upd. Basic Ed.; Ref. Upd. Deluxe Ed.; Res. Alert [Full Cov.]; Risk Abstr. (19??-19??); Sci. Cit. Index; SCISEARCH; Soc. Sci. Cit. Index [Select. Cov.]; SportSearch.

UK/0140-7686
**BRITISH JOURNAL OF OBSTETRICS AND GYNAECOLOGY. SUPPLEMENT.** [Br. j. obstet. gynaecol. Suppl.]. (1977)-. Monographic series. English. ir. Included with subscription to British Journal of Obstetrics and Gynaecology. Blackwell Scientific Publications Ltd, Marston Book Services, PO Box 87, Oxford OX2 ODT UK. **Tel** 011 44 865 791155, FAX 011 44 865 791927, telex 837 515 MARDIS G.
**Ind/Abst** EMBASE.

GW/0068-337X
**BUCHEREI DES FRAUENARZTES.** German. ir. DM39.60. Ferdinand Enke Verlag, Ruedigerstrasse 14, D-70469 Stuttgart Germany. **Tel** 011 49 711 8931124, 011 49 711 893123. **ED** G Martius and M Schmidt-Gollwitzer.
**Desc:** Deals with practical and clinical relevant subjects from the whole subject of gynecology and obstetrics. The volumes are supplements of the journal "Zeitschrift fur Geburtshilfe und Perinatologie".

FR
**BULLETIN OFFICIEL DE LA SOCIETE FRANCAISE DE PSYCHO-PROPHYLAXIE OBSTETRIQUE.** (June 1963)-. Bulletin. French. qt. Soc Franc Psycho Prophylaxie Obstet, 7 Ave Henri Barbusse, 93156 Le Blanc Mesnil France. **NLM** W1; BU901H. ***Continues*** *Bulletin Trimestriel - Societe Francaise de Psycho-Prophylaxie Obstetrique.*

FR/0037-9468
**BULLETIN OFFICIEL DE LA SOCIETE INTERNATIONALE DE PSYCHO-PROPHYLAXIE OBSTETRICALE.** **Added/Corp** Societe Internationale de Psycho-Prophylaxie Obstetricale. Vol. 1 (Oct./Dec. 1959)-. Periodical. French (summaries and/or abstracts in English, Spanish and German). ir. 120.00F France; 150.00F other. Editions de Medecine Pratique, 4 rue Louis Armand, 92600 Asnieres France. **Tel** 011 33 1 47910910. **NLM** W1 BU901J. **Ad Acc.**

CN/1183-2517
**CANADIAN JOURNAL OF OB/GYN & WOMEN'S HEALTH CARE, THE.** [Can. j. ob/gyn women's health care]. **VFOAT** Ob/Gyn & Women's Health Care. (June 1991)-. Periodical. English. bm. $67.00 US; Free to interns and residentsin Canada; 60.00Can$ Canada; 90.00Can$ other. Canadian Journal of Ob Gyn, 19180 Trans Canada, Baire d'Urfe Quebec H9X 3T9 Canada. **Tel** (514)457-2673. **DD** 618. **NLM** W1; CA596TG. available on microfilm and microfiche from Micromedia Limited. ***Continues*** *The Canadian Journal of Ob/Gyn., 0843-4255.*
**Ind/Abst** Can. Index.

US
**CAPSULES AND COMMENTS IN MATERNITY AND GYNECOLOGIC NURSING.** **See** Medical Science and Technology-Nursing.

IT/0393-3512
**CERVIX AND THE LOWER FEMALE GENITAL TRACT, THE.** [Cervix low. female genit. tract]. **Added/Corp** Societa Italiana di Colposcopia e Patologia Cervico-Vaginale. Vol. 1, No. 1 (Jan./Apr. 1983)-. Periodical. English (Italian). tq. Societa Milanese di Studi Ginecologici, Via L.B. Alberti 10, 20149 Milan, Italy. **Tel** (2)311075. **NLM** W1; CE65.
**Ind/Abst** EMBASE.

●XR
**CESKA GYNEKOLOGIE / CESKA LEKARSKA SPOLECNOST J EV. PURKYNE.** **VFOAT** Czech Gynaecology. (1994)-. Periodical. Czech. ir. **(Subscription address:** Artia Pegas Press Ltd., Palac Metro Narodni Trida 25, 11210 Prague 1 Czech Republic.**)** ***Continues*** *Czeskoslovenska Gynekologie, 0374-6852.*

XR/0374-6852
**CESKOSLOVENSKA GYNAEKOLOGIE.** ***Title Change.*** [Cesk. gynaekol.]. **Added/Corp** Ceskoslovenska Spolecnost Gynekologicka Porodnicka. **VFOAT** Cesko-Slovenska Gynekologie. Vol. 1 (Jan. 1936)-(1993). Periodical. Czech. ir. **(Subscription address:** Artia Pegas Press Ltd., Palac Metro Narodni Trida 25, 11210 Prague 1 Czech Republic.**)** **NLM** W1; CE885F. **[CCC].** ***Supersedes in part*** *Rozhledy v Chirurgii a Gynaekologii.* ***Continued by*** *Ceska Gynekologie.*
**Ind/Abst** EMBASE (?-?); Index Med. (?-?); SportSearch (?-?).

CN/0705-3215
**C'EST POUR QUAND.** V. 1- March 1978-. Periodical. French. sa. Free. Les Publications Mon Bebe Inc., Suite 204, 6841, Rue St-Hubert, Montreal Quebec H2S 2M8. **DD** 612.6/3/05. **UDC** 612.63. ctrl circ.

CC/0529-567X
**CHUNG-HUA FU CHAN KO TSA CHIH.** [Chung-hua fu chan ko tsa chih]. **VFOAT** Chinese Journal of Obstetrics and Gynecology. (1953)-. Academic Scholarly Publication. Chinese (English; summaries and/or abstracts in English; table of contents in English). bm (6 issues). $34.02. **(Subscription address:** China International Book Trading Corporation, PO Box 399, Library Service Department, Beijing 100044 People's Republic of China.**)** **DD** 618. **NLM** W1 CH982. **CODEN** CHFCA2. Documents available from CASDDS.
**Ind/Abst** Chem. Abstr.; Index Med. (1979-); NAPRALERT.

SP/0210-573X
**CLINICA E INVESTIGACION EN GINECOLOGIA Y OBSTETRICIA.** [Clin. invest. ginecol. obstet.]. (1974)-. Academic Scholarly Publication. Spanish (summaries and/or abstracts in English). Ten times a year. $66.00. Ediciones Doyma SA, Travesera de Gracia 17 21, 08021 Barcelona Spain. **Tel** 011 34 3 2000711, 011 34 3 4145706, FAX 011 34 3 2091136, telex 51964 INK E. **ED** Juan Esteban Altirriba. **NLM** W1 CL366T. **CODEN** CIGODJ. Index available. cum. index. **Bk Rev. Ad Acc. Pr Rev. Circ:** 5,000 (ctrl). Documents available from BIOSIS Document Express.
**Desc:** Advanced specialization in gynecology and obstetrics. Dedicated to the precocious detection of gynecologic diseases, the optimalization of methods of family planning, treatment of sterility and infertility and vigilance of pregnancy.
**Ind/Abst** Biol. Abstr. (?-1983); EMBASE; Indice Med. Esp.

IT/0529-9608
**CLINICA GINECOLOGICA, LA.** **Added/Corp** Universita di Catania. Clinica Ostetrica e Ginecologica. Vol. 1 (1959)-. Periodical. Italian (summaries and/or abstracts in English). bm. Clinica Ginecologica, Via Del Plebiscito 632, 90124 Catania Italy. **NLM** W1 CL386.
**Ind/Abst** Index Med.

US/0730-0085
**CLINICAL AND EXPERIMENTAL HYPERTENSION. PART B, HYPERTENSION IN PREGNANCY.** ***Title Change.*** [Clin. exp. hypertens., B, Hypertens. pregnancy]. **Added/Corp** International Society for the Study of Hypertension in Pregnancy. **VFOAT** Hypertension in Pregnancy. Vol. B1, No. 1 (1982)-Vol. B11, No. 2 & 3 (1992). Academic Scholarly Publication. English. qt. Marcel Dekker Inc., 270 Madison Avenue, New York NY 10016. **Tel** (212)696-9000, (800)228-1160, FAX (212)685-4540, telex 421419. **(Subscription address:** Marcel Dekker Inc, PO Box 5017, Monticello NY 12701.**)** **ED** Henk C. S. Wallenburg, William M. Barron, Fiona Broughton Pipkin. **LC** RG580.H9; C58. **DD** 618.3. **NLM** W1 CL658C. **CODEN** CEHBDP. **[CCC]. Bk Rev. Ad Acc. Pr Rev.** ctrl circ. available on microfiche. Documents available from The Genuine Article, BIOSIS Document Express, CASDDS. ***Continues in part*** *Clinical and Experimental Hypertension, 0148-3927.* ***Continued by*** *Hypertension in Pregnancy, 1064-1955.*
**Desc:** Provides an exclusive forum for in-depth, state-of-the-art reviews of the most common and serious antenatal complication of pregnancy - induced hypertension. All of the important and vital issues relating to the safe and effective management of pregnancy in induced hypertension are thoroughly covered.
**Ind/Abst** Biol. Abstr.; Chem. Abstr.; Curr. Aware. Biol. Sci., CABS; Curr. Contents Life Sci.; EMBASE; Health Plan. Adminis.; Life Sci. Collect.; PESTDOC; Ref. Upd. Deluxe Ed.; Res. Alert [Full Cov.]; Sci. Cit. Index (19??-19??); SCISEARCH.

IT/0390-6663
**CLINICAL AND EXPERIMENTAL OBSTETRICS & GYNECOLOGY.** [Clin. exp. obstet. gynecol.]. **Added/Corp** Universita di Padova. Clinica Ostetrica Ginecologica. Proceedings. **VAT** Clinical and Experimental Obstetrics and Gynecology. Vol. 1 (Jan. 1974)-. Academic Scholarly Publication. English. qt. $250.00 (institutions), $150.00 (individuals). SOG/SRL, Galleria Storione 2A, 35123 Padua Italy. **Tel** 011 39 49 8756900, 8758644, FAX 8750860. **ED** A. Onnis. **NLM** W1 CL664C. **CODEN** CEOGA4. **[CCC]. Bk Rev. Ad Acc. Acid Free. Circ:** 500 (ctrl). Documents available from BIOSIS Document Express, CASDDS.
**Desc:** Experimental and clinical research in every field of obstetrics and gynecology. Includes neonatology and family planning.
**Ind/Abst** Biol. Abstr.; Chem. Abstr.; EMBASE; Health Plan. Adminis.; Index Med. (1980-).

US/1043-0660
**CLINICAL CONSULTATIONS IN OBSTETRICS AND GYNECOLOGY.** [Clin. consult. obstet. gynecol.]. (Sept. 1989)-. Monographic series. English. qt (4 issues). $93.00 (individual), $113.00 (institution) US; $117.00 (individual), $124.00 (institution) other. W.B. Saunders Company, A Subsidiary of Harcourt Brace Jovanovich, Inc., The Curtis Center/Suite 300, Independence Square West, Philadelphia PA 19106-3399. **Tel** (215)238-7800 or, 5587, FAX (215)238-7883, telex 173146. **(Subscription address:** W. B. Saunders Company / North America Subscriptions, c/o Periodicals, 6277 Sea Harbour Drive, 4th Floor, Orlando FL 32887.**)** **DD** 618. **NLM** W1; CL69G. **[CCC].**

US/0892-7081
**CLINICAL DECISIONS IN OBSTETRICS AND GYNECOLOGY.** ***Ceased.*** [Clin. decis. obstet. gynecol.]. ( )-(1988). Periodical. English. mo. Aspen Publishers Inc., 7201 McKinney Circle, Frederick MD 21701. **Tel** (800)234-1660, (301)698-7100, FAX (301)251-5784, telex 5106014543. **DD** 618. **UDC** 618.

SP
**CLINICAL GINECOLOGICA (BARCELONA, SPAIN).** (CLINICA GINECOLOGICA.). (1975)-. Monographic series. Spanish. Three times a year. Price varies per volume. Salvat Editores SA, Calle Mallorca 45-49, Barcelona 08029 Spain. **Tel** 011 34 3 2010911, FAX 011 34 3 321-0565, telex SAEDI E 53132. **(Subscription address:** Salvat Publicaciones Cientificas SA, Avda Burgos 19 50 D, Madrid 28036 Spain**) NLM** W1; CL387W.

US/0009-9201
**CLINICAL OBSTETRICS AND GYNECOLOGY.** [Clin. obstet. gynecol.]. Vol. 1 (Mar. 1958)-. Academic Scholarly Publication. English (Spanish and Italian). qt. $114.00 (individuals), $199.00 (institutions) US; $149.00 (individuals), $229.00 (institutions) other. J.B. Lippincott Company, 227 East Washington Square, Philadelphia PA 19106-3780. **Tel** (215)238-4200 or 4454, FAX (215)238-4227. **(Subscription address:** J.B. Lippincott, PO Box 350, Hagerstown MD 21740.**) ED** James R. Scott and Roy M. Pitkin. **LC** RG101; .C68. **DD** 618/.05. **NLM** W1 CL742. **CODEN** COGYAK. **[CCC]. Pr Rev. Circ:** 11,600. available on microfilm and microfiche from University Microfilms International (UMI). Documents available from The Genuine Article, BIOSIS Document Express, CASDDS.
**Desc:** Clinical topics permanently bound in hard cover.
**Ind/Abst** Biol. Abstr.; Chem. Abstr.; Comb. Cumul. Index Ob./Gyn.; Cumul. Index Nurs. Allied Health Lit.; Curr. Contents Clin. Med.; Curr. Lit. Fam. Plan.; Dev. Med. Child Neurol.; EMBASE; Energy Res. Abstr.; Health Plan. Adminis.; Index Med.; INIS Atomindex [Micro.]; Life Sci. Collect.; Physic. Medline Plus; Res. Alert [Full Cov.]; Sci. Cit. Index; SCISEARCH; Soc. Sci. Cit. Index [Select. Cov.]; SportSearch; Virol. AIDS Abstr.

US/1043-3198
**CLINICAL PRACTICE OF GYNECOLOGY.** ***Suspended.*** [Clin. pract. gynecol.]. Vol. 1, No. 1 (1989)-(19??). Academic Scholarly Publication. English. Three times a year. $62.00 (institutions) US, (add $21.00 for postage) other. Elsevier Science Publishing Company Inc, Madison Square Station, PO Box 882, New York NY 10159-0882. **Tel** (212)633-3950, FAX (212)633-3990. **ED** Michael S Baggish. **LC** IN PROCESS. **DD** 618. **NLM** W1; CL767JH. **CODEN** CPGYEV. **[CCC]. Circ:** 600. Documents available from BIOSIS Document Express.
**Ind/Abst** Biol. Abstr.

US/0095-5108
**CLINICS IN PERINATOLOGY.** [Clin. perinatol.]. Vol. 1 (March 1974)-. Academic Scholarly Publication. English. qt (4 issues). $94.00 (institution), $77.00 (individual), US; $109.00 (institution), $103.00 (individual) other. W.B. Saunders Company, A Subsidiary of Harcourt Brace Jovanovich, Inc., The Curtis Center/Suite 300, Independence Square West, Philadelphia PA 19106-3399. **Tel** (215)238-7800 or, 5587, FAX (215)238-7883, telex 173146. **(Subscription address:** W. B. Saunders Company / North America Subscriptions, c/o Periodicals, 6277 Sea Harbour Drive, 4th Floor, Orlando FL 32887.**) ED** Mary K. Smith. **NLM** W1 CL831CH. **CODEN** CLPEDL. **[CCC]. Pr Rev. Circ:** 4,000. available on microfilm and microfiche from University Microfilms International (UMI). Documents available from The Genuine Article, BIOSIS Document Express, CASDDS.
**Desc:** Practical updates for the clinician on the latest advances. Each issue is devoted to a single topic in patient care.
**Ind/Abst** Biol. Abstr.; Chem. Abstr.; Cumul. Index Nurs. Allied Health Lit.; Curr. Contents Clin. Med.; Dev. Med. Child Neurol.; EMBASE; Energy Res. Abstr. (June 1978-); Index Med.; INIS Atomindex [Micro.]; Life Sci. Collect.; Physic. Medline Plus; Protozoolog. Abstr.; Ref. Upd. Basic Ed.; Ref. Upd. Deluxe Ed.; Res. Alert [Full Cov.]; Sci. Cit. Index; SCISEARCH; Soc. Sci. Cit. Index [Select. Cov.].

US/0443-9058
**COLLECTED LETTERS OF THE INTERNATIONAL CORRESPONDENCE SOCIETY OF OBSTETRICIANS, GYNECOLOGISTS.** [Collect. lett. Int. Corresp. Soc. Obstet. Gynecol.]. **Main/Corp** International Correspondence Society of Obstetricians and Gynecologists. **VFOAT** Collected Letters; Collected Letters - International Correspondence Society of Obstetricians & Gynecologists; International Correspondence Society of Obstetricians & Gynecologists Collected Letters. (1960)-. Periodical. English. mo. Comes with International Correspondence Society of Obstetricians and Gynecologists membership. Laux Company Inc, 63 Great Road, Maynard MA 01754. **Tel** (508)897-5552, FAX (508)897-6824. **ED** Terry Brown. **DD** 618. **NLM** W1 CO169D. **[CCC]. Bk Rev. Circ:** 2,000.
**Desc:** Ob/Gyn medical letters.

US/0884-8092
**COMBINED CUMULATIVE INDEX TO OBSTETRICS AND GYNECOLOGY.** **See** Medical Science and Technology-Abstracting, Bibliographies and Statistics.

US/8756-9582
**COMPENDIUM OF DRUG & PATIENT INFORMATION.** **Added/Corp** Biomedical Information Corporation. **VFOAT** Compendium of Drug and Patient Information; Obstetrician's and Gynecologist's Compendium of Drug & Patient Information; Obstetrician's & Gynecologist's Compendium of Drug & Patient Information. (1985/1986)-. English. Biomedical Information Corporation, 800 Second Avenue, New York NY 10017. **Tel** (212)262-9662. **LC** RG131; .O27. **DD** 615.5/8. ***Continues** Obstetrician's & Gynecologist's Compendium of Drug Therapy.*

CN/0829-8564
**COMPLEAT MOTHER, THE.** (Winter 1985)-. Periodical. English. Four times a year. $12.00. The Compleat Mother, PO Box 209, Minot ND 58702. **Tel** (701)852-2822. **ED** Jody McLoughlin, Catherine Yoleng. **DD** 618.2/005. **Bk Rev**, (Qty: 8-10). **Ad Acc. Circ:** 15,000 (ctrl).
**Desc:** Promotes breast feeding and maternal instincts.

US/0092-5594
**CONGENITAL MALFORMATIONS SURVEILLANCE.** (CONGENITAL MALFORMATIONS SURVEILLANCE / CENTER FOR DISEASE CONTROL.). **Added/Corp** Center for Disease Control. Centers for Disease Control (U.S.) United States. Public Health Service. (19??)-. Periodical. English. qt. Centers for Disease Control, 1600 Clifton Road NE, Atlanta GA 30333. **Tel** (404)639-3311, FAX (404)639-3296. **LC** RG627; .C44a. **DD** 616/.043/05. **NLM** W2 A C15C. Documents available from Documents on Demand. ***Continues** Metropolitan Atlanta Congenital Defects Program, 0190-2504.*
**Ind/Abst** Am. Stat. Index; Curr. Lit. Fam. Plan.

US/0893-8822
**CONTEMPORARY ISSUES IN FETAL AND NEONATAL MEDICINE.** [Contempor. issues fetal neonatal med.]. Vol. 1 (1985)-. Academic Scholarly Publication. English. ir. Price varies per volume. Blackwell Publishers, 238 Main Street, Cambridge MA 02142. **Tel** (617)547-7110, (800)835-6770, FAX (617)547-0789. **DD** 618. **NLM** W1; CO769MQP. **CODEN** CIFME9. Documents available from CASDDS.
**Ind/Abst** Chem. Abstr. (1985-).

US/1050-9615
**CONTEMPORARY MANAGEMENT IN OBSTETRICS AND GYNECOLOGY.** ***Ceased.*** **VFOAT** CMOG. (1992)-(1993). Monographic series. English. qt. Churchill Livingstone Inc., 650 Avenue of the Americas, New York NY 10011. **Tel** (212)206-5062, FAX (212)727-7808. **ED** Joe Leigh Simpson. **[CCC].**

US/0090-3159
**CONTEMPORARY OB/GYN.** [Contemp. ob/gyn]. **VAT** Contemporary Obstetrics-Gynecology. Vol. 1 (Jan. 1973)-. Periodical. English. mo (with 3 special issues). $85.00 US; $115.00 other. Medical Economics Publishing, Five Paragon Drive, Second Floor, Montvale NJ 07645. **Tel** (800)432-4570, (201)358-2210. **(Subscription address:** Fulco Medical Economics, PO Box 3000, Denville NJ 07834.**) ED** James Swan. **LC** RG1; .C65. **DD** 618/.05. **NLM** W1 CO769NK. **[CCC]. Ad Acc. Circ:** 31,000 (ctrl).
**Desc:** Offers clinical reporting on obstetric and gynecological procedures, problems, and thought.
**Ind/Abst** Curr. Lit. Fam. Plan.; EMBASE; Health Devices Alerts; Life Sci. Collect.

UK/0953-9182
**CONTEMPORARY REVIEWS IN OBSTETRICS AND GYNAECOLOGY.** Vol. 1, No. 1 (Sept. 1988)-. Periodical. English. qt. £100.00 institutions; £50.00 individuals. Parthenon Publishing, Casterton Hall Carnforth, Lancashire LA6 2LA England. **Tel** 011 44 5242 72084, FAX 44-5242-71587. **NLM** W1; CO769WK. **CODEN** CROGEV. **[CCC].**
**Ind/Abst** EMBASE.

SZ/0304-4246
**CONTRIBUTIONS TO GYNECOLOGY AND OBSTETRICS.** [Contrib. gynecol. obstet.]. Vol. 1 (1976)-. Academic Scholarly Publication. English. an. 150.00F (approx. per volume). S. Karger AG, Allschwilerstrasse 10, PO Box - Postfach - Case Postale, CH-4009 Basel Switzerland. **Tel** 011 41 61 306-1111, FAX 011 41 61 306-1234, telex CH 962 652. **ED** P. J. Keller, G. Zador. **LC** UNC. **NLM** W1 CO778RG. **CODEN** CGOBD6. **[CCC].** Documents available from BIOSIS Document Express, CASDDS. ***Continues** Fortschritte der Geburtshilfe und Gynakologie.*
**Desc:** This international series is devoted to current problems in all fields of gynecology including endocrinology, reproductive biology, oncology, and perinatal medicine. Volumes, authored by one or several notable specialists, are designed to give comprehensive coverage to a particular subject. Readers will find original data and reviews of current information, often integrated for the first time in a single publication.
**Ind/Abst** Biol. Abstr.; Chem. Abstr. (1976-1982); EMBASE; Health Plan. Adminis.; Index Med.; Life Sci. Collect.; Ref. Upd. Deluxe Ed.

NE/0376-5059
**CORE JOURNALS IN OBSTETRICS/GYNECOLOGY.** [Core j. obstet./gynecol.]. Vol. 1 (1977)-. Academic Scholarly Publication. English. Eleven times a year (1 volume). Fl549.00. Excerpta Medica Publishing Group, PO Box 548, 1000 AM Amsterdam Netherlands. **Tel** 011 31 20 5803243. **(Subscription address:** Excerpta Medica Journals, PO Box 85, Limerick Ireland.**) NLM** ZWP 100 C797. **CODEN** CJOGD8. **[CCC].** available on microfilm from University Microfilms International (UMI). Documents available from CASDDS.
**Desc:** This publication is intended to optimize the busy clinician's time by providing an overview of the most significant clinical studies in his/her field.
**Ind/Abst** Chem. Abstr.

SP/1132-0273
**CUADERNOS DE MEDICINA PSICOSOMATICA.** (1987)-. Periodical. Multiple languages. Four times a year. 4000ptas. Nuevas Creaciones Medicas, C Santillana del Mar, 3 Chalet 44, 28660 Boadilla del Monte Madrid Spain. **Tel** 011 34 1 6321544, 011 34 1 6321608, FAX 011 34 1 6321544. **UDC** 613.88. ***Continues** Cuadernos de Medicina Psicosomatica y Sexologia, 1132-0281.*

US/0733-8643
**CURRENT LITERATURE REVIEW IN OBSTETRICS & GYNECOLOGY.** [Curr. lit. rev. obstet. gynecol.]. **VFOAT** Current Literature Review in Obstetrics and Gynecology. 1980-. English. an. Appleton Century Crofts, Prentice Hall, 200 Old Tappan Road, Old Tappan NJ 07675. **Tel** (201)767-5188, (800)922-0579. **UDC** 618.

UK/0953-6787
**CURRENT MEDICAL LITERATURE. BREAST AND PROSTRATE CANCER/THE ROYAL SOCIETY OF MEDICINE.** English. qt. £15.00 UK; $40.00 overseas. Royal Society of Medicine Press, 1 Wimpole Street, London W1M 8AE England. **Tel** 011 44 71 2902928. **NLM** ZWP 870; C976.

UK/0956-6511
**CURRENT MEDICAL LITERATURE-BREAST CANCER.** (CURRENT MEDICAL LITERATURE. BREAST CANCER/THE ROYAL SOCIETY OF MEDICINE.). [Curr. med. lit., Breast cancer]. **Added/Corp** Royal Society of Medicine (Great Britain). (1989)?-. Periodical. English. qt. £20.00 UK; $40.00 US; £20.00 other (journal or disk). Royal Society of Medicine Press, 1 Wimpole Street, London W1M 8AE England. **Tel** 011 44 71 2902928. **CODEN** CMBCEL.

US/0197-582X
**CURRENT OBSTETRIC & GYNECOLOGIC DIAGNOSIS & TREATMENT.** [Curr. obstet. gynecol. diagn. treat.]. **VFOAT** Current Obstetric and Gynecologic Diagnosis and Treatment; Current Obstetric Gynecologic Treatment. **VAT** Current Obstetric and Gynecologic Diagnosis and Treatment. 1st (1976)-. English. ir. $41.95. Appleton Century Crofts, Prentice Hall, 200 Old Tappan Road, Old Tappan NJ 07675. **Tel** (201)767-5188, (800)922-0579. **ED** Martin Pernoll and Ralph C. Benson. **LC** RG1; .C87. **DD** 618. **NLM** W1 CU799G.
**Desc:** Discusses basic information and recent developments affecting the diagnosis and treatment of all diseases and disorders of women and of the female generative organs.

US/1051-077X
**CURRENT OBSTETRIC MEDICINE.** [Curr. obstet. med.]. Vol. 1 (1991)-. English. an. $69.95. Mosby Year Book Inc., 11830 Westline Industrial Drive, St Louis MO 63146. **Tel** (800)325-4177, (314)872-8370, FAX (314)432-1380, telex 44-2402. **LC** RG1; .C874. **DD** 618.2/005. **NLM** W1; CU799GAH.

UK/0957-5847
**CURRENT OBSTETRICS AND GYNAECOLOGY.** **VFOAT** Current Obstetrics & Gynecology. Vol. 1, No. 1 (March 1991)-. Periodical. English. qt. £139.00 Europe; £140.00 Other (Institutions). Churchill Livingstone, 1-3 Baxter's Place, Leith Walk, Edinburgh EH1 3AF Scotland. **Tel** 011 44 31 556 2424, FAX 011 44 31 558 1278, telex 727511. **(Subscription address:** Maruzen Company Ltd., PO Box 5050, Import & Export Department, Tokyo 100 31 Japan.**) NLM** W1; CU799GAL. **[CCC].**

US/1040-872X
**CURRENT OPINION IN OBSTETRICS & GYNECOLOGY.** [Curr. opin. obstet. gynecol.]. **VFOAT** Current Opinion in Obstetrics and Gynecology. Vol. 1, No. 1 (Oct. 1989)-. Periodical. English. Six times a year. $134.95 (individual); $269.95 (institution). Current Science, 20 North 3rd Street, Philadelphia PA 19106. **Tel** (215)574-2266, (800)552-5866, FAX (215)574-2270. **ED** Edward E. Wallach. **LC** RG1; .C88. **DD** 618/.05. **NLM** W1; CU799GGB. **CODEN** COOGEA. **[CCC].** Documents available from The Genuine Article.
**Desc:** Directed toward researchers and practicing

obstetricians and gynecologists. Presents review articles from an area of concentration covering an entire year's literature with annotated references. Each issue features a bibliography of the current world literature published during the previous year.
**Ind/Abst** Cumul. Index Nurs. Allied Health Lit.; Curr. Aware. Biol. Sci., CABS; Curr. Contents Clin. Med.; EMBASE; Health Plan. Adminis.; Index Med. (1989-); Res. Alert [Select. Cov.]; SCISEARCH; Soc. Sci. Cit. Index [Select. Cov.].

US/0361-9249
**CURRENT PRACTICE IN OBSTETRIC AND GYNECOLOGIC NURSING.** [Curr. pract. obstetr. gynecol. nurs.]. Vol. 1 (1976)-. Periodical. English. **ED** Editors: v. 1- L. K. McNall and J. T. Galeener. **NLM** W1 CU803BG.
**Ind/Abst** Health Plan. Adminis.

US/8756-0410
**CURRENT PROBLEMS IN OBSTETRICS, GYNECOLOGY AND FERTILITY.** [Curr. probl. obstet. gynecol. fertil.]. **VFOAT** CPO. Vol. 8, No. 1 (Jan. 1985)-. Academic Scholarly Publication. English. bm. $95.00 (institutions), $71.00 (individuals) US; $101.00 (institutions), $77.00 (individuals) other. Mosby Year Book Inc., 11830 Westline Industrial Drive, St Louis MO 63146. **Tel** (800)325-4177, (314)872-8370, FAX (314)432-1380, telex 44-2402. **DD** 618. **NLM** W1; CU804NF. **CODEN** CPOIEN. **[CCC].** Documents available from CASDDS. ***Continues*** *Current Problems in Obstetrics and Gynecology, 0147-1988.*
**Desc:** Focuses on clinical problems commonly seen by obstetricians and gynecologists, Particular emphasis is devoted to the management of fertility and other endocrine problems, as well as high-risk obstetrics.
**Ind/Abst** Chem. Abstr. (1986-1988); EMBASE.

US/0882-2441
**CURRENT RESEARCH UPDATES. OBSTETRICS & GYNECOLOGY.** **See** Medical Science and Technology-Abstracting, Bibliographies and Statistics.

US/0899-3882
**CURRENT THERAPY OF INFERTILITY.** [Curr. ther. infertil.]. 1982-83-. Periodical. English. be. B C Decker Inc, 3 Belmont Circle, Trenton NJ 08618. **ED** Celso-Ramon Garcia. **LC** RC889; .C88. **UDC** 616.697; 618.177. **NLM** W1; CU8192.

SZ/0379-8305
**DEVELOPMENTAL PHARMACOLOGY AND THERAPEUTICS.** ***Ceased.*** **See** Pharmacy and Pharmacology.

US/0167-8302
**DEVELOPMENTS IN OBSTETRICS AND GYNECOLOGY.** ***Ceased.*** [Dev. obstet. gynecol.]. (1980)-(19??). Academic Scholarly Publication. English. ir. Kluwer Academic Publishers / Massachusetts, PO Box 358, Accord Station, Hingham MA 02018. **Tel** (617)871-6600. **(Subscription address:** Kluwer Academic Publishers / Netherlands, PO Box 322, 3300 AH Dordrecht Netherlands.**)** **CODEN** DOGYDY. Documents available from BIOSIS Document Express, CASDDS.
**Ind/Abst** Biol. Abstr. (?-1981); Chem. Abstr. (?-?).

NE/0167-6385
**DEVELOPMENTS IN PERINATAL MEDICINE.** ***Ceased.*** [Dev. perinat. med.]. **Added/Corp** Commission of the European Communities. Vol. 1 (1981)-(19??). Academic Scholarly Publication. English. ir. Kluwer Academic Publishers, Postbus 322, 3300 AH Dordrecht, The Netherlands. **Tel** 011 (31) 78 524400, FAX 011 31 78 183273, telex 20083. **LC** UNC. **DD** 618.3/2. **NLM** W1; DE998NI. **CODEN** DPMDD8. Documents available from CASDDS.
**Ind/Abst** Chem. Abstr. (?-?).

US
**DIRECTORY OF WOMEN'S HEALTH CARE CENTERS / EDITED AND COMPILED BY THE ORYX PRESS IN COOPERATION WITH THE NATIONAL ASSOCIATION OF WOMEN'S HEALTH PROFESSIONALS.** ***Ceased.*** **Added/Corp** National Association of Women's Health Professionals. **VFOAT** Women's Health Care Centers. (1989)-(19??). Directory. English. ir. Oryx Press, 4041 North Central Avenue, #700, Phoenix AZ 85012-3397. **Tel** (800)279-ORYX, (602)265-2651, FAX (602)265-6250, (800)279-4663, (800)279-6799.
**Desc:** Information on women's maternal health services .

NE/0378-3782
**EARLY HUMAN DEVELOPMENT.** [Early hum. dev.]. Vol. 1 (June 1977)-. Academic Scholarly Publication. English. Nine times a year (3 vols.). $563.00. Elsevier Science Ireland Ltd., Bay 15, Shannon Industrial Estate, Co Clare Ireland. **Tel** 011 353 61 471944. **ED** David R. Harvey, John Dobbing, Heinz F.R. Prechtl, C.R. Rosenfield and John C. Sinclair. **LC** RG600; .E27. **DD** 618.3/005. **NLM** W1 EA753. **CODEN** EHDEDN. **[CCC].** **Bk Rev. Ad Acc. Pr Rev. Circ:** 350. available on microfilm and microfiche from University Microfilms International (UMI). Documents available from The Genuine Article, BIOSIS Document Express, CASDDS.
**Desc:** Provides a unique opportunity for researchers and clinicians to bridge the communications gap between disciplines.
**Ind/Abst** AGRICOLA; Biol. Abstr.; Chem. Abstr.; Cumul. Index Nurs. Allied Health Lit.; Curr. Contents Clin. Med.; Curr. Contents Life Sci.; Dairy Sci. Abstr.; Dev. Med. Child Neurol.; EMBASE; Index Med. (1977-); Med. Abstr. Newsl.; Nutr. Abstr. Rev., Ser. B, Live Feeds and Feed.; Nutr. Abstr. Rev., Ser. A, Hum. Exp.; Life Sci. Collect.; Psychol. Abstr. (1979-); PsycINFO; PsycLit; Ref. Upd. Deluxe Ed.; Res. Alert [Full Cov.]; Sci. Cit. Index; SCISEARCH; Soc. Sci. Cit. Index [Select. Cov.]; Trop. Dis. Bull.

●UK/1354-4195
**EARLY PREGNANCY: BIOLOGY AND MEDICINE.** (March 1995)-. English. qt. £150.00 (institution), £85.00 (individual). Parthenon Publishing, Casterton Hall Carnforth, Lancashire LA6 2LA England. **Tel** 011 44 5242 72084, FAX 44-5242-71587.

US
**EMBRYO TRANSFER NEWSLETTER.** **Added/Corp** International Embryo Transfer Society. Vol. 1, No. 1 (April 1982)-. Newsletter. English. qt. $60.00. International Embryo Transfer Society, 309 West Clark Street, Champaign IL 61820. **Tel** (217)356-3182, FAX (217)398-4119. **Ad Acc.**

FR
**ENCYCLOPEDIE MEDICO CHIRURGICALE: MEDECINE GENERALE AND SPECIALITES. OBSTETRIQUE.** (19??)-. Academic Scholarly Publication. French. ir. 280.00F. Editions Techniques, 141 rue de Javel, 75747 Paris Cedex 15 France. **Tel** 011 33 1 45589100.

FR
**ENCYCLOPEDIE MEDICO CHIRURGICALE / TECHNIQUES CHIRURGICALES. GYNECOLOGIE.** French. Editions Techniques, 141 rue de Javel, 75747 Paris Cedex 15 France. **Tel** 011 33 1 45589100.

US/0897-1870
**ENDOMETRIOSIS ASSOCIATION NEWSLETTER.** **Added/Corp** Endometriosis Association. Vol. 9, No. 1 (1988)-. Newsletter. English. Six times a year. $25.00 (regular) one year; $30.00 (associates) one year. Endometriosis Association, 8585 North 76th place, Milwaukee WI 53223. **Tel** (414)355-2200. **DD** 618. ***Continues*** *Endometriosis Association, 0899-2967.*
**Desc:** A highly-acclaimed newsletter articles, facts sheets, research reviews, and other materials of the Association. A must read book for every woman with endometriosis.

US/0145-9937
**ENDOMETRIUM.** 1976-. English. an. Scientia Press, Box 154, Thornhill Ontario L3T 5B4 Canada. **Tel** (416)889-7411. **LC** RG316; .E63. **DD** 618.1/4. **UDC** 611.664; 618.14. **NLM** ZWP 400 E56.

IT/0392-2936
**EUROPEAN JOURNAL OF GYNAECOLOGICAL ONCOLOGY.** **See** Medical Science and Technology-Neoplasma, Neoplastic.

NE/0301-2115
**EUROPEAN JOURNAL OF OBSTETRICS, GYNECOLOGY AND REPRODUCTIVE BIOLOGY.** [Eur. j. obstet., gynecol. reprod. biol.]. **Added/Corp** Nederlandse Vereniging voor Obstetrie en Gynaecologie. Societe Royale Belge de Gynecologie et d'Obstetrique. Vol. 3 (1973)-. Academic Scholarly Publication. English. Twelve times a year (6 vols.). $1226.00. Elsevier Science Ireland Ltd., Bay 15, Shannon Industrial Estate, Co Clare Ireland. **Tel** 011 353 61 471944. **ED** T.K.A.B. Eskes. **NLM** W1 EU72DK. **CODEN** EOGRAL. **[CCC].** **Pr Rev.** available on microfilm and microfiche from University Microfilms International (UMI). Documents available from The Genuine Article, BIOSIS Document Express, CASDDS. ***Continues*** *European Journal of Obstetrics and Gynecology, 0028-2243.*
**Desc:** Studies, case reports and reviews in the field of general obstetrics and gynecology, pediatric gynecology, perinatology, reproductive endocrinology, female and male sterility and fertility and oncology of the reproductive organs, as well as reports on basic biochemical, physiological, and pharmacological research related to human reproduction are accepted.
**Ind/Abst** Biol. Abstr.; Chem. Abstr.; Curr. Contents Clin. Med.; Dairy Sci. Abstr.; Dev. Med. Child Neurol.; EMBASE; Health Plan. Adminis.; Index Med.; Nutr. Abstr Rev., Ser. B, Live Feeds and Feed.; Nutr. Abstr. Rev., Ser. A, Hum. Exp.; Nutr. Res. Newsl.; Life Sci. Collect.; Protozoolog. Abstr.; Ref. Upd. Deluxe Ed.; Res. Alert [Full Cov.]; Sci. Cit. Index; SCISEARCH; Soc. Sci. Cit. Index [Select. Cov.]; Vet. Bull.

NE/0014-4142
**EXCERPTA MEDICA. SECTION 10. OBSTETRICS AND GYNECOLOGY.** **See** Medical Science and Technology-Abstracting, Bibliographies and Statistics.

RU/0014-9772
**FELDSER I AKUSERKA.** ***Title Change.*** (FELDSHER I AKUSHERKA.). [Feldser akus.]. **Added/Corp** Soviet Union. Narodnyi Komissariat Zdravookhraneniia. Soviet Union. Ministerstvo Zdravookhraneniia. (1940)-(1992). Periodical. Russian. mo. **(Subscription address:** Victor Kamkin, 4956 Boiling Brook Parkway, Rockville MD 20852.**)** ***Merged with*** *Meditsinskaia Sestra, 0025-8342* ***to form*** *Meditsinskaia Pomoshch, 0869-7760.*
**Ind/Abst** Int. Nurs. Index; SportSearch.

US/0888-2398
**FEMALE PATIENT. PRACTICAL ADVICE FOR PRIMARY CARE, THE.** [Female patient, Pract. advice prim. care]. (July 1981)-. Periodical. English. mo. $75.00 (institutions), $55.00 (individuals). Excerpta Medica / US, PO Box 3085, Princeton NJ 08543-3085. **Tel** (908)874-8550, FAX (908)874-5611. **(Subscription address:** Female Patient, PO Box 3000, Denville NJ 07834.**)** **DD** 616. **NLM** W1; FE543F. **CODEN** FPPCE9. **[CCC].** ***Continues in part*** *Female Patient, 0364-1198.*
**Desc:** Strives to provide timely and practical clinical information to clinicians involved in providing health care to women.

US/0888-2401
**FEMALE PATIENT. PRACTICAL OB/GYN MEDICINE, THE.** [Female patient, Pract. ob/gyn med.]. Vol. 6, No. 7 (July 1981)-. Periodical. English. mo. $75.00 (institutions), $55.00 (individuals). Excerpta Medica / US, PO Box 3085, Princeton NJ 08543-3085. **Tel** (908)874-8550, FAX (908)874-5611. **(Subscription address:** Female Patient, PO Box 3000, Denville NJ 07834.**)** **DD** 618. **NLM** W1; FE546. **CODEN** FPPME5. **[CCC].** ***Continues in part*** *Female Patient, 0364-1198.*
**Desc:** Strives to provide timely and practical clinical information to clinicians involved in providing health care to women.

GW/0179-1796
**FERTILITAT.** [Fertilitat]. Vol. 1, No. 1 (Sept. 1985)-. Academic Scholarly Publication. German (English; summaries and/or abstracts in English). Four times a year. DM268.00. Springer-Verlag GmbH & Company KG, Heidelberger Platz 3, D 14197 Berlin Germany. **Tel** 011 49 30 8207223, FAX 011 49 30 8214091, telex 183 319 SPBLN D. **(Subscription address:** Springer Verlag New York Inc. / for North America, 44 Hartz Way, Secaucus NJ 07096.**)** **ED** L Mettler and H W Michelmann. **NLM** W1; FE838K. **CODEN** FSIKEJ. **[CCC].** available on microfilm and microfiche from University Microfilms International (UMI). Documents available from CASDDS.
**Desc:** Publishes original articles and brief surveys from research and clinical areas relevant to fertility, sterility, contraception, in-vitro and embryo transfer. New drugs, instruments and methodology are also discussed.
**Ind/Abst** Chem. Abstr. (1986-).

US
**FERTILITY OF AMERICAN WOMEN ... ADVANCE REPORT / U.S. DEPARTMENT OF COMMERCE, BUREAU OF THE CENSUS.** Began with June 1977. Government Publication. English. an. US Department of Commerce, 14th Street & Constitution Avenue NW, Washington DC 20230. **Tel** (202)482-2000, FAX (202)482-3772. **UDC** 618.179(047.1)(73). ***Continues*** *Prospects for American Fertility.*

●UK/0965-5395
**FETAL AND MATERNAL MEDICINE REVIEW.** Vol. 4, No. 1 (Jan. 1992)-. Academic Scholarly Publication. English. Four times a year. $144.00 US, Canada & Mexico; £80.00 other. Cambridge University Press, The Edinburgh Building, Shaftesbury Road, Cambridge CB2 2RU United Kingdom. **Tel** 011 44 223 312393, FAX 011 44 223 325959. **(Subscription address:** Cambridge University Press / North America, 110 Midland Avenue, Port Chester NY 10573.**)** **ED** William Dunlop. **NLM** W1; FE843K. **CODEN** FMMREI. **Pr Rev.** ***Continues*** *Fetal Medicine Review.*
**Desc:** Publishes high quality reviews drawn from all relevant disciplines in this rapidly expanding specialty. Each issue brings together and synthesizes the substantial amount of new information from an impressive group of international contributors.

SZ/1015-3837
**FETAL DIAGNOSIS AND THERAPY.** **Added/Corp** International Fetal Medicine and Surgery Society. Vol. 5 (Jan. 1990)-. Periodical. English. bm. $335.00. S. Karger AG, Allschwilerstrasse 10, PO Box - Postfach - Case Postale, CH-4009 Basel Switzerland. **Tel** 011 41 61 306-1111, FAX 011 41 61 306-1234, telex CH 962 652. **ED** M. Michejda, S. Uzan. **NLM** W1; FE843T. **CODEN** FDTHES. **[CCC].** Index available. cum. index. **Circ:** 600 (ctrl). Documents available from The Genuine Article, BIOSIS Document Express. ***Continues*** *Fetal*

*Therapy, 0257-2788.*
**Desc:** Provides a wide range of biomedical specialists with a unique single source of reports aimed at ameliorating and/or preventing congenital abnormalities. Original papers cover both basic research and clinical investigations into all aspects of fetal diagnosis and therapy, including relevant technical advances and procedures. Attention is also given to the controversial moral and ethical issues involved in intrauterine intervention, the legal rights of the fetus and new concepts of fetal behaviour.
**Ind/Abst** Biol. Abstr.; Curr. Contents Clin. Med.; EMBASE; Health Plan. Adminis.; Index Med. (1991-); Ref. Upd. Deluxe Ed.; Res. Alert [Select. Cov.]; Soc. Sci. Cit. Index [Select. Cov.].

US/1057-137X
**FETUS (NASHVILLE, TENN.), THE.** (THE FETUS.). [Fetus]. (19??)-. Periodical. English. bm (Feb., Apr., June, Aug., Oct., Dec.). $120.00. Vanderbilt University Department of Radiology, 21st & Garland, Nashville TN 37232. **Tel** (615)343-4890 or, 322-3274, FAX (615)322-3764. **ED** Philippe Jeanty, Roberto Romero, Rafael Elejalde, Robert Lebel, David Dyberg. **DD** 618. Index available. cum. index. **Bk Rev**, (Qty: 6). **Ad Acc. Pr Rev. Circ:** 400.
**Desc:** Dedicated to the timely publication of original articles dealing with all aspects of prenatal diagnosis. This material can be used to recognize unusual anomalies, suggest differential diagnoses, evaluate prognoses, assess recurrence risk, assist in patient management.

GW/0344-6204
**FORTSCHRITTE DER FERTILITATSFORSCHUNG.** Monographic series. German. Price varies per volume. Grosse Verlag, Kurfuerstenstrasse 112/113, W-1000 Berlin 30 Germany. **UDC** 612.663. **NLM** W1 FO853S.

GW
**FRAUENARZT.** (19??)-. German. ir (9 issues). DM180.00. Karl Demeter Verlag, Wuermstrasse 13, Postfach 1660, W 8032 Graefelfing Germany. **Tel** 011 49 89 852033, FAX 011 49 89 9543347, telex 524068 Delta D.

BG/0253-5475
**FRP REPORT.** [FRP rep.]. **Added/Corp** Johns Hopkins University. Fertility Research Project. **VFOAT** F.R.P. Report. **VAT** Fertility Research Project Report. No. 1 (Jan. 1975)-. Monographic series. English. ir. Price varies per volume. MacDonald Communications / London, 281 City Road, Rococo House, London EC1V 1LA England. **Tel** 011 44 250-1234 UK, (713)-266-0610 US. **LC** UNC. **DD** 363.9/6. **NLM** W1 FR946I.

GW/0016-5751
**GEBURTSHILFE UND FRAUENHEILKUNDE.** (GEBURTSHILFE UND FRAUENHEILKUNDE : ERGEBNISSE DER FORSCHUNG FUER DIE PRAXIS.). [Geburtshilfe Frauenheilkd.]. Vol. 1 (Jan. 1939)-. Academic Scholarly Publication. German (summaries and/or abstracts in English and Spanish). mo. $234.00. Georg Thieme Verlag Stuttgart, Postfach 301120, D 70451 Stuttgart Germany. **Tel** 011 49 711 89310, FAX 011 49 711 8931298, telex 7 252 275 GTVD. **(Subscription address:** Thieme Medical Publishers Inc., 381 Park Avenue South, New York NY 10016.**) NLM** W1 GE103. **CODEN** GEFRA2. **[CCC]. Pr Rev.** available on microfilm from University Microfilms International (UMI). Documents available from The Genuine Article, CASDDS.
**Ind/Abst** Chem. Abstr.; Curr. Contents Clin. Med.; Dev. Med. Child Neurol.; EMBASE; Energy Res. Abstr.; Health Plan. Adminis.; Index Med.; Nutr. Abstr. Rev., Ser. A, Hum. Exp.; Life Sci. Collect.; PESTDOC; Protozoolog. Abstr.; Res. Alert [Full Cov.]; Sci. Cit. Index; SCISEARCH; Soc. Sci. Cit. Index [Select. Cov.].

US/0744-0596
**GENESIS (WASHINGTON, D.C.).** (GENESIS.). [Genesis]. **Added/Corp** American Society for Psychoprophylaxis in Obstetrics. (19??)-. Periodical. English. bm. $30.00 libraries and institutions. ASPO Lamaze, 1101 Connecticut Avenue Northwest, Suite 700, Washington DC 20036. **Tel** (202)857-1128. **ED** Alice Berman and Katharine M. Roberts. **Bk Rev. Ad Acc. Circ:** 6,200 (ctrl).
**Desc:** Membership magazine of ASPO/Lamaze. Serves to keep childbirth educators, physicians and parents informed regarding the world of childbirth, child health and maternal health.

GW/0177-9109
**GIATROSGYNAKOLOGIE.** [Giatrosgynakologie]. **VFOAT** Jatrosgynakologie. (1985)-. Periodical. German. mo. DM150.00. Universimed Verlag GmbH, August-Schanz Strasse 21, W-6000 Frankfurt 50 Germany. **Tel** 011 49 69 5480000, FAX 069/54 80 00-77. **UDC** 618. **Bk Rev. Ad Acc. Pr Rev. Circ:** 8,200 (ctrl).

SP/0211-6901
**GINE-DIPS.** (GINE DIPS : ORGANO COLABORADOR DEL DEPARTAMENTO DE OBSTETRICIA Y GINECOLOGIA DE LA FACULTAD DE MEDICINA DE BARCELONA.). [Gine-Dips]. **VFOAT** G.I.N.E. D.I.P.S.; D.I.P.S. G.I.N.E.; DIPS GINE. (1970)-. Periodical. Spanish. mo. Editorial Rocas SA, Muntaner 393, Pral 2A Desp 4A, 08021 Barcelona Spain. **Tel** 011 34 3 200-1389. **NLM** W1 GI159.
**Ind/Abst** Indice Med. Esp.

IT/0392-2944
**GINECOLOGIA CLINICA.** [Ginecol. clin.]. (1980)-. Periodical. Italian (summaries and/or abstracts in English and Italian). qt. L80000. S O G S R L, Galleria Storione 2A, 35128 Padua Italy. **Tel** 011 39 49 8756900. **NLM** W1; GI212F. **CODEN** GICLDY. Documents available from BIOSIS Document Express.
**Ind/Abst** Biol. Abstr. (1989).

IT/0393-5337
**GINECOLOGIA DELL'INFANZIA E DELL'ADOLESCENZA.** ***Ceased.*** (1985)-(Oct. 1991). Periodical. Italian. qt. CIC Edizioni Internazionali, Via L Spallanzani 11, 00161 Rome Italy. **Tel** 011 39 6 841-2673, FAX 011 39 6 844-3365, telex 622099 CIC I. **ED** M. Maneschi. **UDC** 618.3. **CODEN** 3-053.6. **Ad Acc.**

MX/0300-9041
**GINECOLOGIA Y OBSTETRICIA DE MEXICO.** [Ginecol. obstet. Mex.]. **Added/Corp** Asociacion Mexicana de Ginecologia y Obstetricia. Vol. 1 (Jan./March 1946)-. Academic Scholarly Publication. Spanish (English). Twelve times a year. $125.00 (institutions), $110.00 (individuals). Federacion Mexicana Association of Ginecologia & Obstetricia, Amsterdam No. 214-PH2, 06100 Mexico DF Mexico. **Tel** 011 52 5 5645463. **ED** Carlos Espinosa Flores. **NLM** W1 GI214. **CODEN** GOMEAY. **Bk Rev. Ad Acc. Circ:** 4,000 (ctrl). Documents available from CASDDS.
**Desc:** Publishes articles in cardiovascular diseases, geriatrics, endocrinology, preservatives, etc., in relation to gynecology and obstetrics.
**Ind/Abst** Chem. Abstr. (1946-1982); EMBASE; Health Plan. Adminis.; Index Med.

SP
**GINECOLOGIA Y OBSTETRICIA : TEMAS ACTUALES.** (19??)-. Spanish. McGraw Hill, Interamericana de Espana SA, Manuel Ferrero 13, 28036 Madrid Spain.

PL
**GINEKOLOGIA POLSKA. SUPLEMENT.** **Added/Corp** Instytut Matki i Dziecka. Zakad Ochrony Zdrowia Matki. No. 1 (1972)-. Periodical. Polish (summaries and/or abstracts in English and Russian). Panstwowe Wydawn Naukowe, Miodowa 10, PO Box 391, 00251 Warsaw Poland. **(Subscription address:** ARS Polona, PO Box 1001, 00068 Warsaw Poland.**) NLM** W1 GI212U.

IT/0391-9013
**GIORNALE ITALIANO DI OSTETRICIA E GINECOLOGIA.** [G. ital. ostet. ginecol.]. Vol. 1, No. 1 (Sept.-Oct. 1979)-. Periodical. Italian (English). mo. $90.00. CIC Edizioni Internazionali, Via L Spallanzani 11, 00161 Rome Italy. **Tel** 011 39 6 841-2673, FAX 011 39 6 844-3365, telex 622099 CIC I. **ED** M. Maneschi. **UDC** 618. **NLM** W1; GI812H. **[CCC]. Bk Rev. Ad Acc.** ctrl circ. ***Continues*** *Aggiornamenti in Ostetricia e Ginecologia.*
**Ind/Abst** EMBASE [Select. Cov.].

●UK/0962-1091
**GYNAECOLOGICAL ENDOSCOPY.** **Added/Corp** British Society for Gynaecological Endoscopy. Australian Gynaecological Endoscopy Society. **VFOAT** Gynecological Endoscopy. Vol. 1, No. 1 (1992)-. Academic Scholarly Publication. English. qt (4 issues). $220.00 US & Canada; £130.00 Europe; £142.00 other. Blackwell Scientific Publications Ltd, Marston Book Services, PO Box 87, Oxford OX2 ODT UK. **Tel** 011 44 865 791155, FAX 011 44 865 791927, telex 837 515 MARDIS G. **NLM** W1; GY54P. **[CCC].**

GW/0017-5994
**GYNAKOLOGE (BERLIN).** (GYNAEKOLOGE.). [Gynaekologe]. Vol. 1 (1968)-. Academic Scholarly Publication. German. Six times a year. DM358.00. Springer-Verlag GmbH & Company KG, Heidelberger Platz 3, D 14197 Berlin Germany. **Tel** 011 49 30 8207223, FAX 011 49 30 8214091, telex 183 319 SPBLN D. **(Subscription address:** Springer Verlag New York Inc. / for North America, 44 Hartz Way, Secaucus NJ 07096.**) ED** L Beck, H G Bender, V Friedberg, O Kaser, W Kunzel, and E J Plotz. **NLM** W1 GY554. **CODEN** GYNKAP. **[CCC]. Pr Rev.** available on microfilm from University Microfilms International (UMI). Documents available from The Genuine Article, BIOSIS Document Express, CASDDS.
**Desc:** Serves as information and professional development source for the practicing gynecologist; primary goal is to report on the newest results from research and practice in gynecology and related fields such as internal medicine, urology, and surgery.
**Ind/Abst** Anim. Breed. Abstr.; Arts Humanit. Citation Index [Select. Cov.]; Biol. Abstr.; Chem. Abstr.; Curr. Contents; EMBASE; Energy Res. Abstr. (March 1982-); Health Plan. Adminis.; Index Med.; Res. Alert [Select. Cov.]; SCISEARCH.

●SZ/1018-8843
**GYNAKOLOGISCH-GEBURTSHILFLICHE RUNDSCHAU.** **Added/Corp** Osterreiche Gesellschaft fuer Gynakologie und Geburtshilfe. Vol. 32, No. 1 (1992)-. Periodical. German (summaries and/or abstracts in English). qt. $238.00. S. Karger AG, Allschwilerstrasse 10, PO Box - Postfach - Case Postale, CH-4009 Basel Switzerland. **Tel** 011 41 61 306-1111, FAX 011 41 61 306-1234, telex CH 962 652. **ED** U. Haller, H. Hepp and E. Reinold. **NLM** W1; GY555T. **CODEN** GGRUEL. Documents available from BIOSIS Document Express. ***Continues*** *Gynakologische Rundschau, 0017-6001.*
**Desc:** Offers abstracts of works from foreign journals along with original contributions on obstetrics and gynecology.
**Ind/Abst** Biol. Abstr.; Index Med.; Ref. Upd. Deluxe Ed.

GW/0341-0481
**GYNAKOLOGISCHE PRAXIS.** [Gynaekol. Prax.]. Vol. 1 (1977)-. Academic Scholarly Publication. German. qt. Hans Marseille Verlag GmbH, Buerkleinstrasse 12, D 80538 Munich Germany. **Tel** 011 49 89 227988, FAX 011 49 89 2904643. **NLM** W1 GY555I.
**Ind/Abst** EMBASE.

SZ/0378-7346
**GYNECOLOGIC AND OBSTETRIC INVESTIGATION.** [Gynecol. obstet. invest.]. Vol. 9 (1978)-. Academic Scholarly Publication. English. Eight times a year. $614.00. S. Karger AG, Allschwilerstrasse 10, PO Box - Postfach - Case Postale, CH-4009 Basel Switzerland. **Tel** 011 41 61 306-1111, FAX 011 41 61 306-1234, telex CH 962 652. **ED** G. Zador. **NLM** W1 GY556U. **CODEN** GOBIDS. **[CCC]. Ad Acc.** available on microfilm and microfiche. Documents available from The Genuine Article, BIOSIS Document Express, CASDDS. ***Continues*** *Gynecologic Investigation, 0017-5986.*
**Desc:** Covers the most active and promising areas of current research in gynecology and obstetrics. Invited reviews keep readers in touch with the general framework and direction of international study. Original papers report selected experimental and clinical investigations in all fields related to gynecology, obstetrics and reproduction. Short communications are published to allow immediate discussion of new data. The international and interdisciplinary character of this periodical provides an avenue to less accessible sources and to worldwide research for investigators and practitioners.
**Ind/Abst** Anim. Breed. Abstr.; Biol. Abstr.; Chem. Abstr.; CSA Neuro. Abstr. (?-?); Curr. Contents Life Sci.; Dairy Sci. Abstr.; EMBASE; Health Plan. Adminis.; Index Med.; Nutr. Res. Newsl.; Life Sci. Collect.; Ref. Upd. Deluxe Ed.; Res. Alert [Full Cov.]; Rev. Med. Vet. Mycology; Sci. Cit. Index; SCISEARCH.

US/0090-8258
**GYNECOLOGIC ONCOLOGY.** **See** Medical Science and Technology-Neoplasma, Neoplastic.

UK/0951-3590
**GYNECOLOGICAL ENDOCRINOLOGY.** **See** Medical Science and Technology-Endocrinology.

FR/0301-2204
**GYNECOLOGIE.** ***Title Change.*** [Gynecologie]. **Added/Corp** Societe francaise de gynecologie. International Federation of Infantile and Juvenile Gynecology. (1973)-(1993). Periodical. French. bm. Masson SA, Avenue Beauregard 12, CH-1701 Fribourg Switzerland. **Tel** 011 41 37 249585, FAX 011 41 37 247559, telex 942658 SEMI CH. **NLM** W1; GY558K. **[CCC].** available on microfilm and microfiche from University Microfilms International (UMI). ***Continues*** *Gynecologie Pratique, 0017-6028.* ***Merged with*** *Revue du Gynecologue Obstetricien* ***and*** *Gynecologie (Paris, France : 1993)* ***to form*** *Gynecologie: Revue du Gynecologue.*
**Ind/Abst** EMBASE (19??)-(19??); Health Plan. Adminis. (19??)-(19??).

FR
**GYNECOLOGIE, OBSTETRIQUE, ANDROLOGIE. E82.** French. ir. 1163.94F France; 1210.00F other. Institut de l'Information Scientifique et Technique (INIST), 2 Allee du Parc de Brabois, 54514 Vandoeuvre Nancy Cedex France. **Tel** 011 33 83 504600, FAX 011 33 83 504650. ***Continues*** *Pascal Explore. E82: Gynecologie, Obstetrique, Andrologie.*

FR/0988-6990
**GYNECOLOGIE OBSTETRIQUE PRATIQUE.** (1988)-. Periodical. French. mo (10 issues). 244.86F France; 195.89F other EEC; 320.00F other. Len Medical, 48 Bis Avenue Kleber, F-75116 Paris France. **Tel** 011 33 1 47550606. **UDC** 618.

●FR
**GYNECOLOGIE : REVUE DU GYNECOLOGUE.** **Added/Corp** Societe Francaise de Gynecologie. **VFOAT** Revue du Gynecologue. Vol. 1 (1993)-. Periodical. French (summaries and/or abstracts in English; table of contents in English). ir. $170.00. Masson Editeur, Box Postale 22, 41353 Vineuil 16

France. **Tel** 011 33 54 438994. **NLM** W1; GY558Q. ***Formed by the union of*** *Gynecologie, 0301-2204* ***and*** *Revue du Gynecologue Obstetricien.*

GW
**GYNLIT.** (19??)-. an. $72.00. Georg Thieme Verlag Stuttgart, Postfach 301120, D 70451 Stuttgart Germany. **Tel** 011 49 711 89310, FAX 011 49 711 8931298, telex 7 252 275 GTVD. **(Subscription address:** Thieme Medical Publishers Inc., 381 Park Avenue South, New York NY 10016.**)**

●US/1062-5704
**HANDBOOK OF GYNECOLOGY & OBSTETRICS.** [Handb. gynecol. obste.]. **VFOAT** Handbook of Gynecology and Obstetrics. 1st Ed. (1993)-. Monographic series. English (Spanish, Italian, Portuguese and Polish). te. $22.95 (latest edition). Appleton Century Crofts, Prentice Hall, 200 Old Tappan Road, Old Tappan NJ 07675. **Tel** (201)767-5188, (800)922-0579. **LC** RG1; .H35. **DD** 618. ***Continues*** *Handbook of Obstetrics & Gynecology, 0891-2041.*

●US/1070-910X
**HARVARD WOMEN'S HEALTH WATCH.** [Harv. women's health watch]. **Added/Corp** Harvard Medical School. **VFOAT** Women's Health Watch. Vol. 1, No. 1 (Sept. 1993)-. Periodical. English. mo. $24.00 US; $30.00 Canada; $39.00 other. Harvard Medical School, 164 Longwood Avenue, 1st Floor, Boston MA 02115. **Tel** (617)432-1485, FAX (617)432-1506. **DD** 362. **NLM** W1; HA695.
**Ind/Abst** Mag. Artic. Summar. Elite (July 1994-).

US/0739-9332
**HEALTH CARE FOR WOMEN INTERNATIONAL.** [Health care women int.]. Vol. 5, No. 1-3 (1984)-. Periodical. English. bm. £106.00 UK; $175.00 other. Taylor & Francis Ltd., Rankine Road, Basingstoke Hampshire, RG24 8PR United Kingdom. **Tel** 011 44 256 840366, FAX 011 44 256 479438, telex 858540. **(Subscription address:** Taylor & Francis Inc., 1900 Frost Road, Suite 101, Bristol PA 19007-1598.**) ED** Phyllis Noerager Stern. **DD** 362. **UDC** 613.99. **NLM** W1; HE299KG. **CODEN** HCWIDQ. **[CCC]**. Index available. **Bk Rev. Ad Acc. Pr Rev. Circ:** 800. available on microfilm and microfiche from University Microfilms International (UMI). Documents available from BIOSIS Document Express. ***Continues*** *Issues in Health Care of Women, 0161-5246.*
**Desc:** Provides an interdisciplinary approach to health care and related topics that concern women. Focusing on the newest theories, skills, and procedures, the journal spans nursing, health care, psychology, sociology, and anthropology - topics such as cultural differences, alternative lifestyles, wife abuse, problems of aging, psychological challenges, childbearing and childrearing, and ethical issues.
**Ind/Abst** Biol. Abstr. (1986-); Cumul. Index Nurs. Allied Health Lit.; Int. Nurs. Index; J. Abstr. Artic. Int. Educ.; Multicult. Educ. Abstr.; Nurs. Abstr.; Nutr. Res. Newsl.; Sage Fam. Stud. Abstr. (?-?); Soc. Plann. Policy Dev. Abstr.; Spec. Educ. Needs Abstr.; Stud. Women Abstr.

●US/1075-0606
**HEALTH LAW LITIGATION REPORTER.** **See** Medical Science and Technology-Forensic Medicine, Medical Jurisprudence.

CN/1180-3088
**HEALTH REPORTS. SUPPLEMENT. BIRTHS.** (HEALTH REPORTS. NO. 14, SUPPLEMENT. BIRTHS / STATISTICS CANADA, CANADIAN CENTRE FOR HEALTH INFORMATION.). [Health rep., Suppl., Births]. **Added/Corp** Canadian Centre for Health Information. **VFOAT** Births; Naissances; Statistique Canada. No 14, Naissances. (1987/1988)-. English (French). an. 20.00Can$ Canada; $24.00 US; $28.00 other. Statistics Canada, Publications Sales & Services, Main Building Room 1710, Ottawa Ontario K1A 0T6 Canada. **Tel** (613)951-5078, (800)267-6677, FAX (613)951-1584, telex 053-3585. **LC** HB939; .H43. **DD** 304.6/3/0971021. ***Continues in part*** *Births and Deaths, Vital Statistics, Volume I, 0825-2971.*

GW/0932-8122
**HEBAMME, DIE.** Vol. 1, No. 1 (May 1988)-. Periodical. German. qt. $48.00. Ferdinand Enke Verlag, Ruedigerstrasse 14, D-70469 Stuttgart Germany. **Tel** 011 49 711 8931124, 011 49 711 893123. **(Subscription address:** Thieme Medical Publishers Inc., 381 Park Avenue South, New York NY 10016.**) ED** G. Martins and J.W. Dudenhausen. **NLM** W1; HE649L.

US/0892-628X
**HERS NEWSLETTER.** (HERS NEWSLETTER / HYSTERECTOMY EDUCATIONAL RESOURCES AND SERVICES.). [HERS newsl.]. **VAT** Hysterectomy Educational Resources and Services Newsletter. (198?)-. Newsletter. English. qt. $20.00. HERS Newsletter, 422 Bryn Mawr Avenue, Bala Cynwyd PA 19004. **Tel** (215)667-7757, (215) 667-7758. **ED** Helen E. Plotkin. **DD** 618. **UDC** 618.14-089.85. Index available. **Bk Rev. Circ:** 10,000 (ctrl). available on audiocassette; available on videocassette.
**Desc:** HERS provides information about the alternative to and consequences of hysterectomy. All counseling is by telephone, and is free. HERS also provides referral to doctors for second opinion. Counseling and referrals are throughout the U.S. and Europe.

NE/0165-7100
**HUMAN REPRODUCTIVE MEDICINE.** [Hum. reprod. med.]. V. 1-. Academic Scholarly Publication. English. Price varies per volume. Elsevier Science Publishing Company Inc, Madison Square Station, PO Box 882, New York NY 10159-0882. **Tel** (212)633-3950, FAX (212)633-3990. **ED** S E Hafez. **UDC** 612.6; 618. **NLM** W1 HU462. **CODEN** HRMEDZ. Documents available from BIOSIS Document Express, CASDDS.
**Ind/Abst** Biol. Abstr.; Chem. Abstr. (1977-1980).

●US/1064-1955
**HYPERTENSION IN PREGNANCY.** (HYPERTENSION IN PREGNANCY : OFFICIAL JOURNAL OF THE INTERNATIONAL SOCIETY FOR THE STUDY OF HYPERTENSION IN PREGNANCY.). [Hypertens. pregnancy]. **Added/Corp** International Society for the Study of Hypertension in Pregnancy. Vol. 12, No. 1 (1993)-. Academic Scholarly Publication. English. Three times a year. $415.00 US; $425.50 other. Marcel Dekker Inc., 270 Madison Avenue, New York NY 10016. **Tel** (212)696-9000, (800)228-1160, FAX (212)685-4540, telex 421419. **(Subscription address:** Marcel Dekker Inc, PO Box 5017, Monticello NY 12701.**) LC** RG580.H9; C58. **DD** 618.3. **NLM** W1; HY8423. **CODEN** HYPPEV. Documents available from CASDDS, ADONIS. ***Continues*** *Clinical and Experimental Hypertension. Part B, Hypertension in Pregnancy, 0730-0085.*
**Desc:** Provides and exclusive forum for in-depth, state-of-the-art reviews of the most common and serious antenatal complication of pregnancy- including hypertension. All of the important and vital issues relating to the safe and effective management of pregnancy in induced hypertension are thoroughly covered.
**Ind/Abst** ADONIS; Chem. Abstr.; EMBASE; Life Sci. Collect.; PESTDOC (?-?); Sci. Cit. Index.

II/0253-7184
**INDIAN JOURNAL OF SEXUALLY TRANSMITTED DISEASES.** **See** Public Health and Safety.

US
**INFECTIOUS AND MEDICAL DISEASE LETTERS FOR OBSTETRICS AND GYNECOLOGY, THE.** Vol. 8, No. 1 (Jan./March 1986)-. Periodical. English. Six times a year. $48.00 US; $60.00 other. IDI Publishing, PO Box 1029, Bellevue NE 68005. **Tel** (402)280-4410. **ED** Gilles R.G. Monif, (402)280-4424. **NLM** W1; IN406HL. Index available in last issue of volume--attached. cum. index. **Ad Acc. Circ:** 500. ***Continues*** *Infectious Disease Letters for Obstetrics, Gynecology, 0196-500X.*

●US/1064-7449
**INFECTIOUS DISEASES IN OBSTETRICS AND GYNECOLOGY.** [Infect. dis. obstet. gynecol.]. (1993)-. Periodical. English. Six times a year. $95.00 (US); $135.00 (Canada & Mexico); $177.50 (other). John Wiley & Sons, Inc., 605 Third Avenue, New York NY 10158-0012. **Tel** (212)850-6000, (212)850-6645, FAX (212)850-6088, telex 12-7063. **(Subscription address:** John Wiley & Sons / England, Baffins Lane, Chichester, West Sussex PO19 1UD England.**) ED** Sebastian Faro. **DD** 618. **CODEN** IDOGEX. **Pr Rev.**
**Desc:** Publishes original papers on both clinical and research work pertaining to the study or treatment of infectious disease in the obstetric patient or the female reproductive organs.

US/0160-7626
**INFERTILITY.** ***Ceased.*** [Infertility]. Vol. 1-Ceased Vol. 13, No. 3/4. Academic Scholarly Publication. English. qt. Taylor & Francis Ltd., Rankine Road, Basingstoke Hampshire, RG24 8PR United Kingdom. **Tel** 011 44 256 840366, FAX 011 44 256 479438, telex 858540. **(Subscription address:** Taylor & Francis Inc., 1900 Frost Road, Suite 101, Bristol PA 19007-1598.**) ED** Louis A Mucelli (editor's address: 601 Madison Avenue, 7th Floor, New York, NY 10022). **LC** RC889. **DD** 618.1/78/005. **UDC** 618.177. **NLM** W1 IN408K. **CODEN** INFEDH. **[CCC]**. Index available. **Bk Rev. Ad Acc. Circ:** 500. Documents available from BIOSIS Document Express, CASDDS.
**Desc:** An interdisciplinary journal devoted to the rapid communication of problems devoted to human infertility. Areas of coverage are gynecology, urology, endocrinology, genetrics, immunology, and others as they may relate to infertility.
**Ind/Abst** Biol. Abstr.; Chem. Abstr.; EMBASE; Int. Pharm. Abstr.

US/1047-9422
**INFERTILITY AND REPRODUCTIVE MEDICINE CLINICS OF NORTH AMERICA.** [Infertil. reprod. med. clin. North Am.]. Vol. 1, No. 1 (Oct. 1990)-. Periodical. English. qt. $81.00 (individual), $105.00 (institution) US; $129.00 (individual), $136.00 (institution) other. W.B. Saunders Company, A Subsidiary of Harcourt Brace Jovanovich, Inc., The Curtis Center/Suite 300, Independence Square West, Philadelphia PA 19106-3399. **Tel** (215)238-7800 or, 5587, FAX (215)238-7883, telex 173146. **(Subscription address:** W. B. Saunders Company / North America Subscriptions, c/o Periodicals, 6277 Sea Harbour Drive, 4th Floor, Orlando FL 32887.**) LC** RG133.5; .I54. **DD** 616.6/92/005. **NLM** W1; IN408M.
**Ind/Abst** Cumul. Index Nurs. Allied Health Lit.

FR
**INSEMINATION ARTIFICIELLE EN FRANCE, L'.** **VFOAT** Elevage Insemination. Statistiques. 1967-. Periodical. French. **UDC** 612.613; 618.177-089.888.11.

US
**INSIDE OUTSIDE MAGAZINE.** ***Ceased.*** (19??)-(1992). English. Four times a year. Institute for Women and Children, 4680 Lake Underhill Road, Orlando FL 32807. **Tel** (407)277-1942. ***Continues*** *Heartbeat.*

CN/0824-5401
**INTERIM (TORONTO).** (THE INTERIM.). [Interim]. Vol. 1, No. 1 (Mar. 1983)-. Periodical. English (French; summaries and/or abstracts in French). Twelve times a year. 15.00Can$ Canada; 22.00Can$ US; 24.00Can$ others. Interim Canada, 53 Dundas Street East, Suite 306, Toronto ONT M5B 1C6 Canada. **Tel** (416)368-0250. **DD** 179/.76/0971.

US/0887-8625
**INTERNATIONAL JOURNAL OF CHILDBIRTH EDUCATION, THE.** (THE INTERNATIONAL JOURNAL OF CHILDBIRTH EDUCATION : THE OFFICIAL PUBLICATION OF THE INTERNATIONAL CHILDBIRTH EDUCATION ASSOCIATION.). [Int. j. childbirth educ.]. **Added/Corp** International Childbirth Education Association. **VFOAT** IJCE. Vol. 1, No. 1 (May 1986)-. Periodical. English. Four times a year. $25.00. International Childbirth Education Association, PO Box 20048, Minneapolis MN 55420-0048. **Tel** (612)854-8660. **DD** 618. **NLM** W1; IN766DEH. **Bk Rev. Ad Acc. Circ:** 12,000 (ctrl). ***Formed by the union of*** *ICEA News; ICEA Forum/Sharing* ***and*** *ICEA Review.*
**Desc:** Official journal of the International Childbirth Education Association. Covers topics of interest for those dedicated to the health of the childbearing family.
**Ind/Abst** Cumul. Index Nurs. Allied Health Lit.

●US/1069-3130
**INTERNATIONAL JOURNAL OF FERTILITY AND MENOPAUSAL STUDIES.** **Added/Corp** United States International Foundation for Studies in Reproduction. Scandinavian Association for Studies in Fertility. Falloppius International Society. International Society of Reproductive Medicine. World Menopause Foundation. **VFOAT** International Journal of Fertility. Vol. 38, No. 1 (Jan./Feb. 1993)-. Academic Scholarly Publication. English. bm. $55.00 surface mail; $91.00 air mail. Medical Science Publishing, 403 Main Street, Port Washington NY 11050. **Tel** (516)944-7340, FAX (516)944-8663. **ED** Kathleen M. Yasas. **DD** 612. **NLM** W1; IN766JD. Documents available from BIOSIS Document Express, CASDDS, Documents on Demand. ***Continues*** *International Journal of Fertility, 0020-725X.*
**Desc:** A medium for the presentation of clinical and experimental work concerning reproduction.
**Ind/Abst** AGRICOLA; Biol. Abstr.; Chem. Abstr.; EMBASE; Energy Inf. Abstr.; Environ. Abstr.; Index Med. (1993-); Life Sci. Collect.; PESTDOC.

GW/0933-0445
**INTERNATIONAL JOURNAL OF FETO-MATERNAL MEDICINE.** Vol. 1, No. 1 (1988)-. Periodical. English. Four times a year (Jan., Apr., July, Oct.). DM202.00 Europe; DM212.00 other. Medifact Publishing House, Marchioninistrasse 15, 86899 Munich 70 Germany. **Tel** 011 49 819159639. **(Subscription address:** Agentur Mrugalla, Schlesierstr 32A, W 8910 Landsberg Lech Germany**) ED** E R Weisenbacher. **NLM** W1; IN766JE. **Ad Acc. Circ:** 1,500 (ctrl).
**Desc:** Publishes high quality articles covering all aspects of feto-maternal medicine, including drug evaluation and drug use during pregnancy as well as epidemiological studies.
**Ind/Abst** EMBASE.

IE/0020-7292
**INTERNATIONAL JOURNAL OF GYNAECOLOGY AND OBSTETRICS.** (INTERNATIONAL JOURNAL OF GYNAECOLOGY AND OBSTETRICS : THE OFFICIAL ORGAN OF THE INTERNATIONAL FEDERATION OF GYNAECOLOGY AND OBSTETRICS.). [Int. j. gynaecol. obstet.]. **Added/Corp** International Federation of Gynecology and Obstetrics International Fertility Research Program. Family Health International (Organization). **VFOAT** International Journal of Gynaecology & Obstetrics; International Journal of Gynecology & Obstetrics; International Journal of Gynecology and Obstetrics. Vol. 7, No. 1 (Feb. 1969)-. Academic Scholarly Publication. English. Twelve times a year (4 vols.). $762.00. Elsevier Science Ireland Ltd., Bay 15, Shannon Industrial Estate, Co Clare Ireland. **Tel** 011 353 61 471944. **ED** J.J. Sciarra, L. Hamberger and W. Kuhn. **LC** RG1; .I57. **NLM** W1;

IN766T. **CODEN** IJGOAL. **[CCC].** Index available. **Ad Acc. Pr Rev.** available on microfilm and microfiche from University Microfilms International (UMI). Documents available from The Genuine Article, BIOSIS Document Express, CASDDS. ***Continues*** *International Federation of of Gynaecology and Obstetrics. Journal.*
**Desc:** Publishes articles on basic and clinical research in the fields of obstetrics and gynaecology and related subjects, with emphasis on matters of worldwide interest.
**Ind/Abst** Biol. Abstr.; Chem. Abstr.; Curr. Contents Clin. Med.; Curr. Lit. Fam. Plan.; EMBASE; Energy Res. Abstr. (Oct. 1981-); Health Plan. Adminis.; Hospit. Health Admin. Index; Index Med.; Mod. Med.; Nutr. Res. Newsl.; Ref. Upd. Deluxe Ed.; Res. Alert [Full Cov.]; Rural Dev. Abstr.; Sci. Cit. Index; SCISEARCH; Soc. Sci. Cit. Index [Select. Cov.].

US/1048-891X
**INTERNATIONAL JOURNAL OF GYNECOLOGICAL CANCER. See** Medical Science and Technology-Neoplasma, Neoplastic.

US/0277-1691
**INTERNATIONAL JOURNAL OF GYNECOLOGICAL PATHOLOGY. See** Medical Science and Technology-Pathology.

UK/0959-289X
**INTERNATIONAL JOURNAL OF OBSTETRIC ANESTHESIA.** (1991)-. Periodical. English. Four times a year. £103.00 Europe; £104.00 Other (Institutions). Churchill Livingstone, 1-3 Baxter's Place, Leith Walk, Edinburgh EH1 3AF Scotland. **Tel** 011 44 31 556 2424, FAX 011 44 31 558 1278, telex 727511. **(Subscription address:** Maruzen Company Ltd., PO Box 5050, Import & Export Department, Tokyo 100 31 Japan.**) ED** Felicity Reynolds and David Dewan. **NLM** W1; IN77PN. **CODEN** IOANER. Index available. **Bk Rev. Ad Acc. Pr Rev.**
**Desc:** Research in obstetric anesthesia and related topics, also perinatal physiology and pharmacology maternal - fetal exchange. Serious medical and obstetric disorders in pregnancy, fetal and neonatal welfare, and consumer views.

UK/0937-3462
**INTERNATIONAL UROGYNECOLOGY JOURNAL.** Vol. 1, No. 1 (Mar. 1990)-. Periodical. English. Six times a year. £180.00. Springer-Verlag London Ltd., Springer House, 8 Alexandra Road Wimbledon, London SW19 7JZ England. **Tel** 011 44 81 9471280, or 9475885, FAX 011 44 81 9474651, telex 21531 SPRGB G. **(Subscription address:** North America: Springer Verlag, Journal Fulfillment Department, 44 Hartz Way, Secaucus, NJ 07096; Outside North America: Springer Verlag, Postfach 311340, D 10643 Berlin Germany**) ED** O C Ortiz. **NLM** W1; IN928D. **CODEN** IUJOEF.

AT/1030-4711
**IVF AND GIFT PREGNANCIES AUSTRALIA AND NEW ZEALAND / NATIONAL PERINATAL STATISTICS UNIT; FERTILITY SOCIETY OF AUSTRALIA. Added/Corp** National Perinatal Statistics Unit (Australia) Fertility Society of Australia. (1986)-. English. an. National Perinatal Statistics Unit / Fertility Society of Australia, Sydney NSW Australia. **NLM** W2; KA8 N3i. ***Continues*** *In Vitro Fertilization Pregnancies Australia and New Zealand.*

SW/0021-7468
**JORDEMODERN.** [Jordemodern]. (1888)-. Academic Scholarly Publication. Swedish. mo. Kr230.00. SV Barnmorskeforbundet, Ostermalmsgatan 19, S 114 26 Stockholm, Sweden. **Tel** 011 46 8 107088, FAX 011 46 8 212106. **ED** Anita Karlsson. **UDC** 362.15. **Bk Rev**, (Qty: 10). **Ad Acc. Circ:** 6,700 (ctrl).
**Desc:** Contains information about midwifery.

BL/0368-1416
**JORNAL BRASILEIRO DE GINECOLOGIA.** [J. bras. ginecol.]. **Added/Corp** Universidade Federal do Rio de Janeiro. Centro de Estudos da Maternidade-Escola. Centro Brasileiro de Dinamica Populacional e Reproducao Humana. **VAT** JBG. Vol. 69 (Jan. 1970)-. Periodical. Portuguese (English and French; summaries and/or abstracts in English and French). ir. $5.05 Brazil; $180.00 other. Cidade Editora Cientifica Ltda, rue Mexico 90, 2 Andar CEP, 20031 Rio de Janeiro Brazil. **Tel** 011 55 21 2404578, 011 55 21 2404728. **NLM** W1 JO193P. **CODEN** JBGCA8. Documents available from BIOSIS Document Express. ***Continues*** *Anais Brasileiros de Ginecologia.*
**Ind/Abst** Biol. Abstr.; EMBASE [Select. Cov.].

FR/0368-2315
**JOURNAL DE GYNECOLOGIE, OBSTETRIQUE ET BIOLOGIE DE LA REPRODUCTION.** [J. gynecol. obstet. biol. reprod.]. **Added/Corp** Federation des Societes de Gynecologie et d'Obstetrique de Langue Francaise. Vol. 1 (Jan./Feb. 1972)-. Academic Scholarly Publication. French. Eight times a year. $212.00. Masson Editeur, Box Postale 22, 41353 Vineuil 16 France. **Tel** 011 33 54 438994. **(Subscription address:** 7A Boulevard de Perolles, CH-1701 Fribourg Switzerland**) NLM** W1 JO308. **CODEN** JGOBAC. **[CCC].** available on microfilm and microfiche from University Microfilms International (UMI). Documents available from BIOSIS Document Express, CASDDS. ***Formed by the union of*** *Gynecologie et Obstetrique, 0017-601X* ***and*** *Bulletin de la Federation des Societes de Gynecologie et d'Obstetrique de Langue Francaise, 0046-3515.*
**Ind/Abst** Biol. Abstr.; Chem. Abstr.; EMBASE; Index Med.; Nutr. Abstr. Rev., Ser. B, Live Feeds and Feed.; Nutr. Abstr. Rev., Ser. A, Hum. Exp.; Life Sci. Collect.

●US/1058-0468
**JOURNAL OF ASSISTED REPRODUCTION AND GENETICS.** [J. assist. reprod. genet.]. **Added/Corp** International Working Group on Preimplantation Genetics. **VFOAT** Assisted Reproduction. Vol. 9, No. 1 (Feb. 1992)-. Periodical. English. Ten times a year. $425.00 institutions, $99.00 individuals US; $495.00 institutions, $116.00 individuals other. Plenum Press, 233 Spring Street, New York NY 10013-1578. **Tel** (212)620-8000, (800)221-9369, FAX (212)463-0742, (212)807-1047, telex 23/421139. **LC** RG135; .J68. **DD** 618.1/78/005. **NLM** W1; JO544R. **CODEN** JARGE4. **[CCC].** available on microfilm and microfiche from University Microfilms International (UMI). Documents available from The Genuine Article. ***Continues*** *Journal of In Vitro Fertilization and Embryo Transfer, 0740-7769.*
**Ind/Abst** Curr. Aware. Biol. Sci., CABS; Curr. Contents Clin. Med.; INIS Atomindex [Micro.]; Res. Alert [Select. Cov.]; SCISEARCH.

UK/0141-9846
**JOURNAL OF DEVELOPMENTAL PHYSIOLOGY.** [J. dev. physiol]. **VFOAT** Developmental Physiology. Vol. 1 (Feb. 1979)-. Academic Scholarly Publication. English. mo. £236.25 UK and Europe; $457.80 other. Caxton Communications Limited, Unit 8 Central Park Business Centre, Bellfield Road Bucks HP13 5HG, England. **Tel** 0494 473405, FAX 0494 535573. **ED** C. T. Jones. **UDC** 612.63. **NLM** W1 JO619V. **CODEN** JDPHDH. **[CCC].** Index available. **Bk Rev. Ad Acc. Pr Rev. Circ:** 500. available on microfilm and microfiche from University Microfilms International (UMI). Documents available from The Genuine Article, BIOSIS Document Express, CASDDS.
**Desc:** Papers describing the result of original research on aspects of the scientific study of the pregnancy, the fetus, or the neonate of man or experimental animals.
**Ind/Abst** AGRICOLA [Select. Cov.]; Biol. Abstr.; Chem. Abstr.; Curr. Contents Life Sci.; Curr. Ref. Fish Res.; Dev. Med. Child Neurol.; EMBASE; Index Med.; Index Vet.; Life Sci. Collect.; Ref. Upd. Deluxe Ed.; Res. Alert [Full Cov.]; Sci. Cit. Index; SCISEARCH; Soc. Sci. Cit. Index [Select. Cov.]; Vet. Bull.

IT/0392-9507
**JOURNAL OF FOETAL MEDICINE.** [J. foetal med.]. (198?)-. Academic Scholarly Publication. English. Four times a year. $150.00 (individuals), $250.00 (institutions). SOG/SRL, Galleria Storione 2A, 35123 Padua Italy. **Tel** 011 39 49 8756900, 8758644, FAX 8750860. **ED** A. Onnis. **NLM** W1; JO65PD. **CODEN** JFMED7. **[CCC]. Bk Rev. Ad Acc. Circ:** 150. Documents available from CASDDS.
**Ind/Abst** Chem. Abstr. (1981-1986); EMBASE.

IT
**JOURNAL OF GYNAECOLOGICAL ENDOCRINOLOGY. See** Medical Science and Technology-Endocrinology.

US/1042-4067
**JOURNAL OF GYNECOLOGIC SURGERY.** [J. gynecol. surg.]. **Added/Corp** Gynecologic Laser Society (U.S.) International Society for Gynecologic Endoscopy. British Society for Cervical Pathology. Vol. 5 (1989)-. Periodical. English. qt. $169.00. Mary Ann Liebert Inc., 1651 Third Avenue, New York NY 10128. **Tel** (212)289-2300, (800)M-LIEBERT, FAX (212)289-4697. **ED** Michael S. Baggish, M.D. **DD** 618. **NLM** W1; JO669QM. **CODEN** JGYSEF. **Pr Rev.** Documents available from The Genuine Article, BIOSIS Document Express. ***Continues*** *Colposcopy & Gynecologic Laser Surgery, 0741-6113.*
**Desc:** Publishes original papers, review articles, point and counter-point, abstracts from selected meetings, and selected letters. The designated central forum for clinical articles dealing with aspects of operative and office gynecology, including colposcopy, endoscopy, hysteroscopy and laparascopy, laser surgery, conventional surgery, female urology, microsurgery and in vitro fertilization.
**Ind/Abst** Biol. Abstr.; Curr. Contents Clin. Med.; EMBASE; Res. Alert [Full Cov.]; Sci. Cit. Index; SCISEARCH.

●US/1069-2673
**JOURNAL OF GYNECOLOGIC TECHNIQUES.** (1994)-. Periodical. English. Four times a year. $135.00 (Institutions), $89.00 (Individuals). Churchill Livingstone Inc., 650 Avenue of the Americas, New York NY 10011. **Tel** (212)206-5062, FAX (212)727-7808. **(Subscription address:** Churchill Livingstone Inc., 5 South 250 Frontenac Road, Naperville, IL 60563; (telephone: (800)553-5426 or (708)416-3939)**)**

US/0890-3344
**JOURNAL OF HUMAN LACTATION.** (JOURNAL OF HUMAN LACTATION : OFFICIAL JOURNAL OF INTERNATIONAL LACTATION CONSULTANT ASSOCIATION.). [J. hum. lact.]. **Added/Corp** International Lactation Consultant Association. **VFOAT** JHL. (June 1985)-. Periodical. English. qt. $185.00 US; $215.00 other. Human Sciences Press, PO Box 735, 233 Spring Street, New York NY 10013. **Tel** (212)620-8000, FAX (212)807-1047, telex 23421139. **(Subscription address:** Eurospan Ltd., Journals and Serials Division, 3 Henrietta Street, Covent Garden, London WC2E 8LU England.**) ED** Kathleen G. Auerbach. **DD** 649. **NLM** W1; JO673VL. **CODEN** JHLAE5. **[CCC].** Index available. **Bk Rev. Ad Acc. Pr Rev. Circ:** 2,000.
**Desc:** Provides a specialized channel of communication in the interdisciplinary field of lactation consulting, including its application to medicine and nursing.
**Ind/Abst** Cumul. Index Nurs. Allied Health Lit.; Health Plan. Adminis.; Int. Nurs. Index.

US/0939-6322
**JOURNAL OF MATERNAL-FETAL INVESTIGATION : THE OFFICIAL JOURNAL OF FRENCH SOCIETY OF ULTRASOUND IN MEDICINE AND BIOLOGY ... [ET AL.]. Added/Corp** French Society of Ultrasound in Medicine and Biology. Vol. 1 (1991)-. Periodical. English. qt. $151.00. Springer-Verlag New York Inc., 175 5th Avenue, New York NY 10010. **Tel** (212)460-1500, telex 232 235 SPB UR. **(Subscription address:** Springer Verlag New York Inc. / for North America, 44 Hartz Way, Secaucus NJ 07096.**) ED** Dev Maulik. **NLM** W1; JO748RJ. **[CCC].** available in microform from University Microfilms International (UMI). Documents available from The Genuine Article.
**Desc:** Features basic and clinical investigations concerning the physiology and pathology of conception, early pregnancy loss, physical adaptation in pregnancy, immunology of pregnancy, and medical diseases in pregnancy.
**Ind/Abst** Res. Alert [Select. Cov.]; SCISEARCH.

●US/1057-0802
**JOURNAL OF MATERNAL-FETAL MEDICINE, THE.** [J. matern.-fetal med.]. **VFOAT** Journal of Maternal Fetal Medicine. (1992)-. Periodical. English. bm. $125.00 US; $185.00 Canada and Mexico; $207.50 other. John Wiley & Sons, Inc., 605 Third Avenue, New York NY 10158-0012. **Tel** (212)850-6000, (212)850-6645, FAX (212)850-6088, telex 12-7063. **(Subscription address:** John Wiley & Sons / England, Baffins Lane, Chichester, West Sussex PO19 1UD England.**) ED** Roy H. Petrie and Hung N. Winn. **DD** 618. **NLM** W1; JO748RM. **CODEN** JMFIEY.
**Desc:** Provides expert coverage of the pathophysiology of the placenta, the pregnant patient, the fetus, and the neonate in both normal and abnormal states.

US/0091-2182
**JOURNAL OF NURSE-MIDWIFERY. See** Medical Science and Technology-Nursing.

US/0884-2175
**JOURNAL OF OBSTETRIC, GYNECOLOGIC, AND NEONATAL NURSING : JOGNN. See** Medical Science and Technology-Nursing.

UK/0144-3615
**JOURNAL OF OBSTETRICS AND GYNAECOLOGY.** [J. obstet. gynaecol.]. **Added/Corp** University of London. Institute of Obstetrics and Gynaecology. Vol. 1, No. 1 (Aug. 1980)-. Academic Scholarly Publication. English. Six times a year. £110.00 EC; $198.00 US; £118.00 other. Carfax Publishing Company, PO Box 25 Abingdon, Oxfordshire OX14 3UE England. **Tel** 011 44 235 555335, FAX (0279)31067, telex 817484. **(Subscription address:** US and Canada/ PO Box 2025, Dunnellon, FL 34430-2025; telephone:(904)489-6996**) ED** D. F. Hawkins. **NLM** W1 JO798M. **CODEN** JOGYDW. **[CCC]. Bk Rev. Ad Acc.** ctrl circ. available on microfilm and microfiche from University Microfilms International (UMI). Documents available from BIOSIS Document Express, CASDDS.
**Desc:** Publishes original material, with breadth of coverage from laboratory work to practical midwifery. A typical issue will include: reports on developments in clinical practice in obstetrics, gynaecology, infertility work and contraception, selected papers on laboratory and scientific topics, which provide the background for future clinical progress, selected case reports and correspondence from readers.
**Ind/Abst** Abr. Index Med.; Biol. Abstr. (1985-); Chem. Abstr.; EMBASE; Helminthol. Abstr. (1991-); Protozoolog. Abstr.

II/0022-3190
**JOURNAL OF OBSTETRICS AND GYNAECOLOGY OF INDIA.** [J. obstet. gynaecol. India]. **Added/Corp** Federation of Obstetric and Gynaecological Societies of India. (1951)-. Periodical. English. bm. $45.00. Federation of Obstetric & Gynaecological Societies of India, Bombay, India. **(Subscription address:** Prints India, 11 Darya Ganj,

New Delhi 110002 India.) **NLM** W1 JO799. **CODEN** JOBYA4. Documents available from CASDDS.
**Ind/Abst** Chem. Abstr.; Health Plan. Adminis.; Life Sci. Collect.

HK/1012-8875
**JOURNAL OF PAEDIATRICS, OBSTETRICS, AND GYNAECOLOGY.** **See** Medical Science and Technology-Pediatrics.

US/8756-6206
**JOURNAL OF PEDIATRIC & PERINATAL NUTRITION.** ***Ceased.*** **See** Medical Science and Technology-Pediatrics.

US/0893-2190
**JOURNAL OF PERINATAL & NEONATAL NURSING, THE.** **See** Medical Science and Technology-Nursing.

●US/1058-1243
**JOURNAL OF PERINATAL EDUCATION, THE.** (THE JOURNAL OF PERINATAL EDUCATION : AN ASPO/LAMAZE PUBLICATION.). [J. perinat. educ.]. **Added/Corp** American Society for Psychoprophylaxis in Obstetrics. Vol. 1, No. 1 (Spring 1992)-. Periodical. English. Four times a year (Spring, Summer, Fall, Winter). $140.00 (institutions), $95.00 (individuals); $39.00 (individuals), $140.00 (institutions) non-members, $85.00 (members), Comes with ASPO Lamaze membership. Jones and Bartlett Publishing Inc., One Exeter Plaza, Boston MA 02116. **Tel** (617)859-3900, (800)832-0034. **(Subscription address:** ASPO/Lamaze, 1101 Connecticut Avenue Northwest, Suite 700, Washington, DC 20036, phone: (202)857-1128 or (800)368-4404**) ED** Francine H. Nichols. **LC** RG973; .J68. **DD** 618.4/071/1. **NLM** W1; JO828HT. Index available (published separately). **Bk Rev**, (Qty: 4). **Ad Acc, Adv Mgr:** Megan Thompson, **Tel** (202)857-1128. **Pr Rev. Circ:** 5,000.
**Desc:** A professional organization of childbirth educators, physicians, nurses, nurse-midwives, and other health professionals and concerned parents dedicated to developing and promoting standards for perinatal education and family-centered maternity care.

GW/0300-5577
**JOURNAL OF PERINATAL MEDICINE.** [J. perinat. med.]. Vol. 1, (1973)-. Academic Scholarly Publication. English (summaries and/or abstracts in German and French). bm. $332.20. Walter de Gruyter Inc., PO Box 303421, D 10728 Berlin Germany. **Tel** 011 49 30 260050, FAX 011 49 30 26005251. **ED** J. W. Dudenhausen. **NLM** W1 JO828I. **CODEN** JPEMAO. **[CCC]. Ad Acc. Pr Rev. Circ:** 2,000. Documents available from The Genuine Article, BIOSIS Document Express, CASDDS.
**Desc:** The journal features contributions from specialists worldwide in this new and developing field of perinatal medicine.
**Ind/Abst** Biol. Abstr.; Chem. Abstr.; Curr. Contents Clin. Med.; Dev. Med. Child Neurol.; EMBASE; Index Med.; Nutr. Abstr. Rev., Ser. A, Hum. Exp.; Life Sci. Collect.; Res. Alert [Full Cov.]; Sci. Cit. Index; SCISEARCH; Soc. Sci. Cit. Index [Select. Cov.].

GW/0936-174X
**JOURNAL OF PERINATAL MEDICINE SUPPLEMENT.** [J. perinat. med., Suppl.]. (19??)-. English. ir. Walter de Gruyter Inc., PO Box 303421, D 10728 Berlin Germany. **Tel** 011 49 30 260050, FAX 011 49 30 26005251. **UDC** 618.
**Ind/Abst** EMBASE.

US/0743-8346
**JOURNAL OF PERINATOLOGY.** (JOURNAL OF PERINATOLOGY : OFFICIAL JOURNAL OF THE CALIFORNIA PERINATAL ASSOCIATION.). [J. perinatol.]. **Added/Corp** California Perinatal Association. National Perinatal Association (U.S.). Vol. 4, No. 3 (Summer 1984)-. Periodical. English. Six times a year. $92.00 (institutions), $55.00 (individuals) US; $105.00 (institutions), $68.00 (individuals) other. Mosby Year Book Inc., 11830 Westline Industrial Drive, St Louis MO 63146. **Tel** (800)325-4177, (314)872-8370, FAX (314)432-1380, telex 44-2402. **DD** 618. **NLM** W1; JO828J. **CODEN** JOPEEI. **[CCC].** available on microfilm and microfiche from University Microfilms International (UMI). ***Continues*** *Journal of the California Perinatal Association, 0733-334X.*
**Desc:** Provides information to all who work in the interdisciplinary specialty of perinatology.
**Ind/Abst** Cumul. Index Nurs. Allied Health Lit. (Vol. 7, No. 1, 1987-); Index Med. (Vol. 7 No. 1, 1987-); Int. Nurs. Index.

NE/0167-482X
**JOURNAL OF PSYCHOSOMATIC OBSTETRICS AND GYNAECOLOGY.** [J. psychsom. obstet. gynaecol.]. **Added/Corp** International Society of Psychosomatic Obstetrics and Gynecology. **VFOAT** Journal of Psychosomatic Obstetrics and Gynecology. Vol. 1, No. 1 (May 1982)-. Periodical. English. qt. £145.00 (institutions), £72.00 (individulas). Parthenon Publishing, Casterton Hall Carnforth, Lancashire LA6 2LA England. **Tel** 011 44 5242 72084, FAX 44-5242-71587. **ED** Eylard V. Van Hall, Lorraine Dennerstein, and John J. LaFerla. **NLM** W1 JO858VF. **[CCC]. Pr Rev.** Documents available from The Genuine Article.
**Desc:** Brings together information in the field of psychosomatic medicine related to obstetrics and gynaecology. Provides a forum for the many disciplines involved such as ethology, gynaecology, gynaecology oncology, nursing and nurse midwifery, obstetrics, perinatology, psychiatry, psychology and reproductive endocrinology, and will therefore publish clinical and basic information of multidisciplinary interest.
**Ind/Abst** Curr. Contents Clin. Med.; Curr. Contents Soc. Behav. Sci.; EMBASE; PsycINFO; Res. Alert [Full Cov.]; SCISEARCH; Soc. Sci. Cit. Index [Full Cov.].

UK/0264-6838
**JOURNAL OF REPRODUCTIVE AND INFANT PSYCHOLOGY.** [J. reprod. infant psychol.]. **Added/Corp** Society for Reproductive and Infant Psychology (Great Britain). **VFOAT** JRIP. Vol. 1, Pt. 1 (May 1983)-. Periodical. English. qt. £75.00 UK; £78.00 (surface mail), £85.00 (air mail) other. Society for for Reproductive and Infant Psychology, University of Dundee, Department of Psychology, Dundee DD1 4HN Scotland. **Tel** 011 44 38223181 ext.4630. **(Subscription address:** North, South and Central America/ John Wiley & Sons, Inc., PO Box 7247-8491, Philadelphia, PA 19170-8491**) ED** Sandre Elliott, Peter Stratton, and Michael O'Hara. **DD** 155. **NLM** W1; JO868L. **CODEN** JRIPE3. **[CCC].**
**Desc:** Reports and reviews outstanding research on psychological, behavioural, medical and social aspects of human reproduction, pregnancy, and infancy. Medical interests center mainly on obstetrics and gynaecology, paediatrics and psychiatry, though relevant aspects of medical communication and medical sociology are included.
**Ind/Abst** Psychol. Abstr. (1983-); PsycINFO; PsycLit; Soc. Plann. Policy Dev. Abstr.

US/0024-7758
**JOURNAL OF REPRODUCTIVE MEDICINE.** [J. reprod. med.]. **Added/Corp** Chicago Lying-in Hospital and Dispensary. Vol. 2 (Jan. 1969)-. Periodical. English. mo. $105.00 (individual), $145.00 (institition) US; $131.00 (individual), $187.00 (institution) other. Science Printers and Publishers Inc., PO Drawer 12425, 8342 Olive Boulevard, St Louis MO 63132-2814. **Tel** (314)991-4440, FAX (314)991-4654. **ED** George L. Wied. **LC** RG1; .L9. **DD** 618/.05. **NLM** W1 JO868S. **CODEN** JRPMAP. **[CCC].** Index available. cum. index. **Bk Rev. Ad Acc. Pr Rev. Circ:** 30,447 (ctrl). available on microfilm and microfiche from University Microfilms International (UMI). Documents available from The Genuine Article, BIOSIS Document Express, CASDDS. ***Continues*** *Lying-In, 0096-7033.*
**Desc:** Clinical obstetrics and gynecology. Original articles and review articles including invitational symposia with in-depth coverage of a clinical topic.
**Ind/Abst** AgBiotech News Inf.; Biol. Abstr.; Chem. Abstr.; Comb. Cumul. Index Ob./Gyn.; Cumul. Index Nurs. Allied Health Lit.; Curr. Contents Clin. Med.; Curr. Lit. Fam. Plan.; EMBASE; Energy Res. Abstr. (Oct. 1975-); Health Devices Alerts; Index Med.; Med. Abstr. Newsl.; Microbiol. Abstr. Sect. B (19??-19??); NAPRALERT; Nutr. Res. Newsl.; Life Sci. Collect.; Protozoolog. Abstr.; Ref. Upd. Deluxe Ed.; Res. Alert [Full Cov.]; Sci. Cit. Index; SCISEARCH; Soc. Sci. Cit. Index [Select. Cov.].

UK/0955-2839
**JOURNAL OF THE ASSOCIATION OF OBSTETRIC AND GYNAECOLOGICAL PHYSIOTHERAPISTS.** [J. Assoc. Obstet. Gynaecol. Physiother.]. (19??)-. Periodical. English. sa. £20.00. ACPOG, The Cottage, 15 Grange Court Westbury, Bristol BS9 HDP England. **Circ:** 550.

●US/1071-5576
**JOURNAL OF THE SOCIETY FOR GYNECOLOGIC INVESTIGATION.** **Added/Corp** Society for Gynecologic Investigation. (1994)-. Academic Scholarly Publication. English. Six times a year (1 volume). $179.00 US; $219.00 other. Elsevier Science Publishing Company Inc, Madison Square Station, PO Box 882, New York NY 10159-0882. **Tel** (212)633-3950, FAX (212)633-3990. **ED** Rogerio A. Lobo, MD. **NLM** W1; JO954LM. **Ad Acc, Adv Mgr:** Andrea Cernichiari, **Tel** (212)633-3813.
**Desc:** Publishes scientific papers in all aspects of reproductive biology, including the disciplines of perinatology, obstetrics, gynecology, reproductive endocrinology, infertility, gynecologic oncology, and related fields.

YU/0352-5562
**JUGOSLAVENSKA GINEKOLOGIJA I PERINATOLOGIJA.** [Jugosl. ginekol. perinatol.]. V. 25, Nos. 1-2 (Jan./April 1985)-. Periodical. Serbo-Croatian (Roman). bm. $98.00. **(Subscription address:** Jugoslovenska Knjiga, PO Box 36, YU 11001 Belgrade Yugoslovia.**) UDC** 618. **NLM** W1; JU6246. ***Continues*** *Jugoslavenska Ginekologija I Opstetricija.*
**Ind/Abst** EMBASE [Select. Cov.]; Index Med. (1985-).

IO
**KEADAAN KESEHATAN ANAK DAN IBU : HASIL SURVEI SOSIAL EKONOMI NASIONAL.** **VFOAT** Health Conditions of the Children and Mothers : Results of National Socio-Economic Survey; Health Conditions of the Children and Mothers. Indonesian (English). an. Rp1,000 Indonesia; $.75 US. Central Bureau of Statistics / Indonesia, c/o Dr. Sutomo, 8 Jalan, PO Box 3, Jakarta Indonesia. **Tel** 372808 374908 Ext.342. **LC** RG965.I5; K42. **DD** 362.1/982/0099598. **UDC** 613.95(594); 364.4(594). ctrl circ.

US/0896-4467
**KEY OBSTETRICS AND GYNECOLOGY.** [Key obstet. gynecol.]. **VFOAT** Obstetrics and Gynecology. Vol. 1, No. 1 (2nd Quarter 1988)-. Periodical. English. qt. $112.50 (institutions), $75.00 (individuals) US; $116.50 (institutions), $79.00 (individuals) Canada; $126.50 (institutions), $89.00 (individuals) other. Mosby Year Book Inc., 11830 Westline Industrial Drive, St Louis MO 63146. **Tel** (800)325-4177, (314)872-8370, FAX (314)432-1380, telex 44-2402. **ED** Daniel R. Mishell Jr. **DD** 618. **[CCC].**
**Desc:** Provides abstracts from scientific literature covering new diagnostic techniques, new therapeutic approaches, and new issues, trends, discoveries, and developments. Topics include: estrogen replacement and breast cancer, hypertension, and gallstones; genital condylomata in pregnancy; ovarian remnent syndrome.

SW/0348-8365
**KVINNOVETENSKAPLIG TIDSKRIFT.** V. 1, No. 1-. Periodical. Swedish (English). qt. Kr90.00. Kvinnovetenskaplig Tidskrift, Klostergatan 9, 222, 22 Lund. **LC** HQ1104; .K84.

US/0362-3173
**LACTATION REVIEW, THE.** ***Suspended.*** **Added/Corp** Human Lactation Center. Vol. 1 (1976)-Suspended (1982). Periodical. English. ir. $35.00. Human Lactation Center, 666 Sturges Highway, Westport CT 06880. **Tel** (203)259-5995. **ED** Dana Raphael. **NLM** W1 LA245. **Bk Rev. Ad Acc. Circ:** 5,000.
**Desc:** Books and research articles on breastfeeding, infant feeding practices, family planning, women in development, nutrition and cultural patterns.

CN/0714-3680
**LAMAZE IN ONTARIO.** [Lamaze Ont.]. Periodical. English. bm. $10.00. Lamaze Childbirth Association of Ontario, 48 Drakefield Road Canada. **DD** 618.4/5/05. **UDC** 618.4.

FR/0759-1594
**LETTRE DU GYNECOLOGUE, LA.** [Lett. gynecol.]. **VFOAT** C.S. (1984)-. Periodical. French. Ten times a year. 205.68F France; 300.00F other. Edimark, 207 rue Gallieni, 92100 Boulogne France. **Tel** 011 33 1 48251159. **UDC** 618.

HU/0025-021X
**MAGYAR NOORVOSOK LAPJA.** [M. noorv. lapja]. **Added/Corp** Budapesti Orvosegyesulet. Gynaekologiai Szakosztaly. Budapest. Tudomany-Egetem. Noi Klinika (2d). Magyar-Noorvosok Tarsasaga. Magyar Orvosok Szabad Szakszervezete. Nogyogyasz Szakcsoport. Orvos- Egeszsegugyi Szakszervezet. Nogyogyasz Szakcsoport. (1938)-. Periodical. Hungarian. Six times a year. $56.60. Ifjusagi Lap -es Konyvkiado Vallalat, Revay u. 16, H-1374, Budapest, 6 Hungary. **(Subscription address:** Kultura, PO Box 149, H 1389 Budapest 62 Hungary.**) NLM** W1 MA404N. **CODEN** MNLAA8. Documents available from CASDDS.
**Ind/Abst** Chem. Abstr.; EMBASE [Select. Cov.]; Energy Res. Abstr. (Feb. 1980-).

US/0738-1948
**MALPRACTICE REPORTER. OB/GYN, THE.** **See** Law.

UK/0262-0200
**MATERNAL & CHILD HEALTH (RICHMOND, SURREY).** **See** Medical Science and Technology-Family Practice.

US
**MATERNAL AND CHILD HEALTH STATISTICS : NORTH CAROLINA.** **See** Medical Science and Technology-Abstracting, Bibliographies and Statistics.

US/0090-0702
**MATERNAL-CHILD NURSING JOURNAL.** **See** Medical Science and Technology-Nursing.

CN/0820-6465
**MATERNAL HEALTH NEWS.** [Matern. health news]. **Added/Corp** Maternal Health Committee (Vancouver, B.C.). Maternal Health Society (Vancouver, B.C.). (1976)-. Periodical. English. qt. 9.00Can$. Maternal Health Society, Box 74561 Kitsilano Postal Outlet, Vancouver British Columbia V6K 1R2 Canada. **Tel** (604)433-5827. **DD** 362.1/982/009711.

US/0190-0757
**MATERNAL/NEWBORN ADVOCATE.** ***Ceased.*** **Added/Corp** National Foundation. **VAT** Maternal Newborn Advocate. Vol. 1 (July 1974)-(19??). Periodical. English. qt. March of Dimes Birth Defects Foundation, PO Box 1657, Wilkes Barre PA 18703. **Tel** 800 367-6630. **ED** Linda Pagano. **NLM** W1 MA947MC.

SP
**MEDICAL DIGEST. GINECOLOGIA. OBSTETRICA.** Spanish. Editorial M.C.R. SA, Mallorca 310, 08037 Barcelona Spain.

US/0091-4223
**MEDICAL EXAMINATION REVIEW BOOK. OBSTETRICS AND GYNECOLOGY SPECIALTY BOARD REVIEW.** [Med. exam. rev. book obstet. gynecol. spec. board rev.]. **VFOAT** Obstetrics and Gynecology Specialty Board Review. 1st- Ed. English. ir. Medical Exam Publishing Company, 52 Vanderbilt Avenue Elsevier, New York NY 10017-3808. **Tel** (212)463-1052. **UDC** 618.

US/1056-4098
**MEDICAL MALPRACTICE - OB/GYN LITIGATION REPORTER.** ***Title Change.*** **See** Medical Science and Technology-Forensic Medicine, Medical Jurisprudence.

DK/0904-1966
**MEDICINSK FDSELS- OG MISDANNELSESSTATISTIK / SUNDHEDSSTYRELSEN.** 1986-. Danish (summaries and/or abstracts in English). an. **LC** RG503.2.D4; M43. ***Formed by the union of*** *Medicinsk Fdseksstatustuj. Denmark. Sundhedsstryrelsen.* ***and*** *Misdannelsesregister, 0109-5331.*

US/0738-2987
**MEDIGUIDE TO OB/GYN.** (MEDIGUIDE TO OB/GYN / PROVIDED AS A PROFESSIONAL SERVICE BY MILES PHARMACEUTICALS.). [Mediguide ob/gyn]. **Added/Corp** Miles Pharmaceuticals. **VAT** Mediguide to Obstetrics Gynecology. Vol. 1 Iss 1 (1982)-. English. qt. Dellacorte Publications, 919 3rd Avenue, New York NY 10022. **Tel** (212)751-2806. **NLM** W1 ME787FLC.

US/0196-3163
**MEMBERSHIP DIRECTORY - NATIONAL ABORTION FEDERATION.** **Main/Corp** National Abortion Federation (U.S.). (19??)-. Directory. English. National Abortion Federation, 110 East 59th Street, Suite 1019, New York NY 10022. **LC** HQ767.5.U5; N37a. **DD** 363.4/6/02573.

US/1061-4397
**MENOPAUSE NEWS.** [Menopause news]. (1991)-. Periodical. English. Six times a year. $30.00 (institutions), $23.00 (individuals). Menopause News, 2074 Union Street, Suite 10, San Francisco CA 94123. **Tel** (415)567-2368. **DD** 612.

UK/0961-5555
**MIDIRS MIDWIFERY DIGEST.** [MIDIRS midwifery dig.]. **VFOAT** Midwives Information and Resource Service Midwifery Digest. (1991)-. Periodical. English. qt. £55.00 UK; £60.00 other. Institute of Child Health / England, Royal Hospital, St Michaels Hills, Bristol BS2 8BJ England. **Tel** 011 44 272 251 791. **DD** 610.73678. ***Continues*** *MIDIRS Information Pack, 0955-8683.*

US/0740-6150
**MIDLIFE WELLNESS.** ***Suspended.*** Vol. 1, No. 3 (1983)-. Periodical. English. qt. $12.00. University of Florida / Gainesville, 901 NW 8th Avenue Suite B, Gainesville FL 32601. **Tel** (904)373-0440. **LC** RG186; .M53. **DD** 613/.04244. **UDC** 618.173. ***Continues*** *Menopause Update, 0734-9009.*

UK/0266-6138
**MIDWIFERY.** [Midwifery]. Vol. 1, No. 1 (Spring 1985)-. Periodical. English. qt. £105.00 Europe; £106.00 Other (Institutions). Churchill Livingstone, 1-3 Baxter's Place, Leith Walk, Edinburgh EH1 3AF Scotland. **Tel** 011 44 31 556 2424, FAX 011 44 31 558 1278, telex 727511. **(Subscription address:** Maruzen Company Ltd., PO Box 5050, Import & Export Department, Tokyo 100 31 Japan.**)** **ED** Ann M Thomson. **NLM** W1; MI331T. **[CCC].** available on microfilm and microfiche from University Microfilms International (UMI).
**Desc:** Enhances the quality of care for childbearing women and their families and to promote continuing education by publishing original papers, review articles and significant preliminary communications covering the clinical, epidemiological, education, managerial and technological aspects of midwifery.
**Ind/Abst** Cumul. Index Nurs. Allied Health Lit.; Health Serv. Abstr.; Int. Nurs. Index (1986-).

US/0891-7701
**MIDWIFERY TODAY.** ***Title Change.*** [Midwifery today]. Vol. 1, No. 1 (Winter 1987)-(1992). Periodical. English. qt. Midwifery Today, Box 2672-EB, Eugene OR 97402. **Tel** (503)344-7438, (800)743-0974, FAX (503)344-9919. **ED** Jan Tritten. **DD** 618. Index available. **Bk Rev**. **Ad Acc. Circ:** 2,500. ***Continued by*** *Midwifery Today and Childbirth Education.*
**Desc:** Publication of interest to birth practitioners, childbirth educators and interested consumers. Includes columns for midwifery and childbirth educator networking and feature articles, both scientific and spiritual.

●US
**MIDWIFERY TODAY AND CHILDBIRTH EDUCATION.** **VFOAT** Midwifery Today. (1992)-. Periodical. English. qt (Mar., June, Sept., Dec.). $30.00 US; $40.00 Canada & Mexico; $50.00 (airmail) other. Midwifery Today, Box 2672-EB, Eugene OR 97402. **Tel** (503)344-7438, (800)743-0974, FAX (503)344-9919. **ED** Jan Tritten. **NLM** W1; MI332L. Index available. cum. index. **Bk Rev**, (Qty: 25-35). **Ad Acc, Adv Mgr:** Nicole Van DeVeere. **Circ:** 3,000. ***Continues*** *Midwifery Today, 0891-7701.*
**Desc:** Directed to birth practitioners, childbirth educators and parents-to-be. Emphasis is on safe, natural childbirth, networking, education, and the physiology of birth. The aim is to foster communication between practitioners and families, and to promote responsible midwifery and childbirth education.

UK/0026-3524
**MIDWIVES CHRONICLE AND NURSING NOTES.** [Midwives chron. nurs. notes]. **Added/Corp** Royal College of Midwives (Great Britain). **VFOAT** Midwives Chronicle; Midwives Chronicle & Nursing Notes. (19??)-. Periodical. English. Twelve times a year. £20.50 UK; £26.00 Europe; £43.00 Australia, New Zealand, Japan, China and Malaysia; £38.00 other. TG Scott Subscriber Services, 6 Bourne Enterprise Center, Wrotham Road, Borough Green, Kent TN15 8DG England. **Tel** 011 44 01 732 884023, FAX 011 44 01 732 884034. **ED** Ann Graveley. **NLM** W1 MI333. Index available. **Bk Rev. Ad Acc. Circ:** 36,000 (ctrl). available on microfilm and microfiche from University Microfilms International (UMI). ***Continues*** *Midwives Chirurgical Nursing.*
**Desc:** Up-to-date in all matters relating to midwifery education, research, practice, maternity services, topical news, appointments and courses.
**Ind/Abst** Cumul. Index Nurs. Allied Health Lit.; Int. Nurs. Index.

IT/0026-4784
**MINERVA GINECOLOGICA.** [Minerva ginecol.]. Vol. 1 (Oct. 1949)-. Academic Scholarly Publication. Italian. mo. $110.00 (individuals), $150.00 (institutions). Edizioni Minerva Medica, Corso Bramante 83-85, 10126 Turin Italy. **Tel** 011 39 11 678282, FAX 011 39 11 674502. **ED** T Oliaro. **NLM** W1 MI643. **Bk Rev. Ad Acc.** available on microfilm from University Microfilms International (UMI). ***Formed by the union of*** *Folia Gynaecologica; Folia Gynaecologica* ***and*** *Ginecologia.*
**Desc:** Addressed to practitioners and specialists in gynecology and obstetrics in Italy and abroad; deals with topics in scientific practice and research.
**Ind/Abst** EMBASE [Select. Cov.]; Index Med.

US/0745-8371
**MOTHERS TODAY.** [Mothers today]. Vol. 19, No. 1 (Jan./Feb. 1983)-. Periodical. English. bm. $1.00 single issue. Mothers Today, PO Box 56, Wynnewood PA 19096-0056. **LC** RG525; .M65. **DD** 649/.1/05. **UDC** 649.1. ***Continues*** *Mothers Manual (Franklin Lakes, N.J.), 0027-1551.*

US/0889-0579
**NAACOG NEWSLETTER.** ***Title Change.*** **See** Medical Science and Technology-Nursing.

US/1046-7475
**NAACOG'S CLINICAL ISSUES IN PERINATAL AND WOMEN'S HEALTH NURSING.** ***Title Change.*** [NAACOG's clin. issues perinat. women's health nurs.]. **Added/Corp** NAACOG (Organization). **VFOAT** Clinical Issues in Perinatal and Women's Health Nursing. **VAT** Nurse's Association of the American College of Obstetricians and Gynecologists' Clinical Issues in Perinatal and Women's Health Nursing. Vol. 1 No. 1 (1990)-Vol. 3 No. 4 (1992). Periodical. English. qt. J.B. Lippincott Company, 227 East Washington Square, Philadelphia PA 19106-3780. **Tel** (215)238-4200 or 4454, FAX (215)238-4227. **DD** 618. **NLM** W1; N103M. **[CCC].** cum. index. ***Continued by*** *AWHONN's Clinical Issues in Perinatal and Women's Health Nursing, 1066-3614.*
**Ind/Abst** Cumul. Index Nurs. Allied Health Lit.; Health Plan. Adminis.; Int. Nurs. Index (1990-).

FR
**NAISSANCE & PETITE ENFANCE.** **VFOAT** Naissance et Petite Enfance; Naissance. No 1 (Mar/April 1991)-. Periodical. French. bm. **NLM** W1; NA119J.

US/0273-3730
**NAPSAC DIRECTORY OF ALTERNATIVE BIRTH SERVICES AND CONSUMER GUIDE.** **Main/Corp** National Association of Parents & Professionals for Safe Alternatives in Childbirth. **VAT** National Association of Parents & Professionals for Safe Alternatives in Childbirth Directory of Alternative Birth Services and Consumer Guide. 2nd- Ed.; 1980-. Directory. English. an. $5.95. NAPSAC International, Rt 1 Box 646, Marble Hill MO 63764. **Tel** (314)238-2010. **ED** Lee Stewart. **LC** RG661; .N37A. **DD** 362.1/984/0973. **UDC** 613.95. Index available. **Ad Acc. Circ:** 2,000 (ctrl).
**Desc:** Covers birth, pregnancy, nutrition, midwifery, obstetrics, homebirth, breastfeeding, parenting, pediatrics, medical politics, legal issues, health rights, legislation.

US
**NATASHA. [CD-ROM].** English. an. $495.00. Sociometrics Corporation, 170 State Street, Suite 260, Los Altos CA 94022. **Tel** (415)949-3282.
**Desc:** Provides instant access to over 39,000 individually identified variables from 109 data sets and 82 major studies pertaining to adolescent fertility.

US
**NATIONAL ADVISORY COUNCIL ON MATERNAL, INFANT, AND FETAL NUTRITION ... BIENNIAL REPORT.** ***Title Change.*** **Main/Corp** United States. National Advisory Council on Maternal, Infant, and Fetal Nutrition. **Added/Corp** United States. Food and Nutrition Service. (19??)-(198?). English. be. US Department of Agriculture, 14th Street and Independence Avenue SW, Washington DC 20250. **Tel** (202)720-5457. ***Continued by*** *United States. National Advisory Council on Maternal, Infant, and Fetal Nutrition.; Biennial Report on the Special Supplemental Food Program for Women, Infants, and Children, and on the Commodity Supplemental Food Program.*

US/1062-2454
**NEONATAL INTENSIVE CARE.** (NEONATAL INTENSIVE CARE : THE JOURNAL OF PERINATOLOGY-NEONATOLOGY.). [Neonatal intensive care]. (198?)-. Periodical. English. bm. $60.00. Goldstein and Associates, 1150 Yale Street, Suite 12, Santa Monica CA 90403. **Tel** (310)828-1309, FAX (310)829-1169. **DD** 618. **NLM** W1; NE198W.

US/0747-6132
**NEONATOLOGY LETTER.** [Neonatol. lett.]. **Added/Corp** National Neonatology Information Network (U.S.). (198?)-. Periodical. English. bm. $18.00 (U.S.), $24.00 (foreign). Neonatology Letter, 150 River Road/Building G, Montville NJ 07045-9441. **Tel** (201)334-0041. **ED** John W. Scanlon. **DD** 618. **Bk Rev. Ad Acc.** ctrl circ.
**Desc:** Up-to-date information on developments and techniques in the fields of neonatology and obstetrics/gynecology, written by leaders in these fields, with tele-lecture presentation.

US/0897-6295
**NEONATOLOGY (NORWALK, CONN.).** (NEONATOLOGY.). (1988/89)-. Periodical. English. be. Appleton & Lange, (A Subsidiary of Simon & Schuster), 25 Van Zant Street, East Norwalk CT 06855. **Tel** (203)838-4400, (800)423-1359, FAX (203)854-9486. **DD** 618.

II
**NEW SURGICAL TRENDS AND INTEGRATED THERAPIES IN ENDOMETRIAL, VULVAR, TROPHOBLASTIC NEOPLASIAS, ACTUALITY OF SURGICAL STAGING IN GYNAECOLOGICAL MALIGNANCIES-A.** (19??)-. English. $60.00. S O G S R L, Galleria Storione 2A, 35128 Padua Italy. **Tel** 011 39 49 8756900.

IT
**NEW SURGICAL TRENDS AND INTEGRATED THERAPIES IN GYNAECOLOGIC ONCOLOGY: OVARIAN CERVICAL BREAST CANCER-A.** (19??)-. English. $60.00. S O G S R L, Galleria Storione 2A, 35128 Padua Italy. **Tel** 011 39 49 8756900.

JA/0285-8096
**NIHON SANKA FUJINKA GAKKAI KANTO RENGO CHIHO BUKAI KAIHO.** [Nippon Sanka Fujinka Gakkai Kanto Rengo Chiho Bukai kaiho]. **Added/Corp** Nihon Sanka Fujinka Gakkai (1949-). Kanto Rengo Chiho Bukai. **VFOAT** Kanto Journal of Obstetrics and Gynecology. (1964)-. Academic Scholarly Publication. Japanese. sa. Nihon Sanka Fujinka Gakkai Kanto Rengo Chiho Bukai, (Kanto Branch, Japan Soc. of Obstetrics & Gynecology), Hoken Kaikan Bekkan, 1-1, Ichigaya Sadoharacho, Shinjukuku, Tokyoto 162, Japan. **CODEN** NKRKES. Documents available from CASDDS.
**Ind/Abst** Chem. Abstr. (1986-).

JA/0029-0386
**NIHON SHINSEIJI GAKKAI ZASSHI.** **VFOAT** Acta Neonatologica Japonica. (1965)-. Periodical. Multiple languages. qt. $138.00. Japan Society of Neonatology, 5-8 Hatanodai 1-chome, Shinagawa-ku 142 Tokyo Japan. **(Subscription address:** Kyowa Book Company Inc., 1 38 Kanda Jinbocho Chiyoda-ku, Tokyo 101 Japan.**)** **DD** 618.92.
**Ind/Abst** EMBASE [Select. Cov.].

JA/0029-0629
**NIPPON FUNIN GAKKAI ZASSHI.** [Nippon Funin Gakkai zasshi]. **VFOAT** Japanese Journal of Fertility and Sterility. Vol. 1 (1956)-. Academic Scholarly Publication. Japanese (English). qt. $162.00. **(Subscription address:** Kyowa Book Company Inc., 1 38 Kanda Jinbocho Chiyoda-ku, Tokyo 101 Japan.**) NLM** W1 NI893. **CODEN** NFGZAD. Documents available from BIOSIS Document Express, CASDDS.
**Ind/Abst** Biol. Abstr.; Chem. Abstr.; EMBASE; Health Plan. Adminis.

JA/0300-9165
**NIPPON SANKA FUJINKA GAKKAI ZASSHI.** (NIPPON SANKA FUJINKA GAKKAI ZASSHI. ACTA OBSTETRICA ET GYNECOLOGICA JAPONICA.). [Nippon Sanka Fujinka Gakkai zasshi]. **Main/Corp** Nippon Sanka Fujinka Gakkai. **VFOAT** Acta Obstetrica et Gynecologica Japonica. Vol. 29 No. 1 (Jan. 1977)-. Academic Scholarly Publication. Japanese (English; summaries and/or abstracts in English). mo. $294.00. **(Subscription address:** Kyowa Book Company Inc., 1-38 Kanda Jinbo-Cho, Chiyoda-Ku Tokyo 101, Japan**) CODEN** NISFAY. Documents available from BIOSIS Document Express, CASDDS. ***Formed by the union of*** *Nippon Sanka Fujinka Gakkai Zasshi* ***and*** *Acta Obstetrica et Gynecologica Japonica.*
**Ind/Abst** Biol. Abstr.; Chem. Abstr.; EMBASE; Health Plan. Adminis.; Index Med.; Life Sci. Collect.; SportSearch.

US/1069-8787
**OB/GYN ANNALS.** ***Ceased.*** **VFOAT** OB GYN Annals. **VAT** Obstetrics/Gynecology Annals. (1994)-(1994). Periodical. English. bm. Slack Inc., 6900 Grove Road, Thorofare NJ 08086. **Tel** (609)848-1000, (800)257-8290, FAX (609)853-5991, telex 517108 SLACK INC VD.

US/0743-8354
**OB/GYN CLINICAL ALERT.** [OB/GYN clin. alert]. **VFOAT** OBGYN Clinical Alert; O.B./G.Y.N. Clinical Alert. Vol. 1, No. 1 (May 1984)-. Periodical. English. mo. $115.00 without CME; $165.00 with CME; $79.00 nurses and midwife. American Health Consultants, 3525 Piedmont Road, Suite 400, Atlanta GA 30305. **Tel** (800)688-2421, (404)262-7436. **(Subscription address:** American Health Consultants, PO Box 95278, Chicago IL 60694.**) ED** Leon Speroff. **DD** 618. ***Continues*** *Advances in Reproductive Medicine, 0741-420X.*
**Desc:** Brings you six to eight abstracts of the most clinically relevant studies in female reproductive medicine, as well as interpretive clinical commentary.

US/0029-7437
**OB. GYN. NEWS.** [Ob. gyn. news]. **VAT** Obstetrics Gynecology News. (19??)-. Periodical. English. sm. $96.00 US;$138.00 other. International Medical News Group, 12230 Wilkins Avenue, Rockville MD 20852. **Tel** (301)770-6170. **ED** William Rubin. **LC** RG1; .O13. **DD** 618. **NLM** W1 OB402P. **Bk Rev. Ad Acc. Circ:** 28,000 (ctrl). available on microfilm from University Microfilms International (UMI).
**Desc:** Coverage of clinical meetings, symposia, and conventions to report clinical developments in the fields of obstetrics and gynecology.
**Ind/Abst** Curr. Lit. Fam. Plan.

US/0029-7445
**OB-GYN OBSERVER.** V. 1- Dec. 1961-. Periodical. English. bm. Science & Medicine Publishing Company, 909 3rd Avenue, New York NY 10022. **UDC** 618. **NLM** W1 OB4024.

●US/1058-1677
**OB/GYN RESIDENT, THE.** [OB/GYN resid.]. **VFOAT** OB GYN Resident. **VAT** Obstetrics Gynecology Resident. (Jan/Feb 1992)-. Periodical. English. bm. $58.00 institution, $48.00 individual (US). Slack Inc., 6900 Grove Road, Thorofare NJ 08086. **Tel** (609)848-1000, (800)257-8290, FAX (609)853-5991, telex 517108 SLACK INC VD. **DD** 618. **NLM** W1; O1234.

US/1055-5595
**OB/GYN ROUNDS.** [OB/GYN rounds]. **Added/Corp** Gardiner-Caldwell SynerMed. American Academy of Family Physicians. **VFOAT** OB GYN Rounds. **VAT** Obstetrics, Gynecology Rounds. Vol. 1, No. 1 (Feb. 1991)-. Periodical. English. Free. Gardiner-Caldwell Synermed, Route 513 and Trimmer Road, PO Box 458, Califon NJ 07830. **DD** 616. **NLM** W1; OB402RG.

US/0883-492X
**OB/GYN TRENDS AT MOUNT SINAI SCHOOL OF MEDICINE.** [Ob/gyn trends Mount Sinai Sch. Med.]. **Added/Corp** Mount Sinai School of Medicine. **VFOAT** Ob/Gyn Trends. **VAT** Obstetrics Gynecology Trends at Mount Sinai School of Medicine. Vol. 1, No. 1 (Mar. 1985)-. Periodical. English. qt. $19.00. Medical Publishers Enterprises, 15 22 Fair Lawn Avenue, Fair Lawn NJ 07410. **Tel** (201)796-6500. **DD** 618.

US/0738-3029
**OBG DIAGNOSIS.** [OBG diagn.]. **VFOAT** O.B.G. Diagnosis. **VAT** Obstetrics Gynecology Diagnosis. Vol. 1, No. 1. Periodical. English. qt. Free. Dellacorte Publications, 919 3rd Avenue, New York NY 10022-3904. **Tel** (212)751-2806. **UDC** 618-07. **NLM** W1 OB402KF.

US/1044-307X
**OBG MANAGEMENT.** [OBG manage.]. **VAT** Obstetrics, Gynecology Management. (Sept. 1989)-. Periodical. English. mo. $65.00. Dowden Publishing Company, 110 Summit Avenue, Montvale NJ 07645. **Tel** (201)391-9100, FAX (201)391-2778. **ED** Carroll Dowden. **DD** 658. **NLM** W1; OB402KN. **Ad Acc. Circ:** 31,000 (ctrl).
**Desc:** Addresses the issues of the latest on malpractice insurance and the option of dropping obstetrical patients. In addition, other management issues, such as collecting more from the party billing, taxes, government-import fee controls, obstetrical and gynecological equipment and personal finance will be covered.

US/0275-665X
**OBSTETRIC ANESTHESIA DIGEST.** **See** Medical Science and Technology-Anesthesiology.

FI/0358-4844
**OBSTETRICA ET GYNECOLOGICA (OULU).** (OBSTETRICA ET GYNECOLOGICA.). No. 1-. Monographic series. English (Finnish). ir. Price varies per volume. Professor Sakari Piha, University of Oulu, 90100 Oulu 10 Finland. **Tel** 358-81-332133. **ED** Leo Hirvonen. **UDC** 618. **NLM** W1 AC954NM no.8 etc. **Ad Acc. Circ:** 500 (ctrl).
**Desc:** Monographs, reviews and dissertations in the field of obstetrics and gynecology.

US/0029-7828
**OBSTETRICAL & GYNECOLOGICAL SURVEY.** [Obstet. gynecol. surv.]. **VAT** Obstetrical and Gynecological Survey. Vol. 1 (Feb. 1946)-. Academic Scholarly Publication. English. mo. $99.00 (individual), $154.00 (institution) US; $139.00 (individual), $194.00 (institution) other. Williams & Wilkins Company, 428 East Preston Street, Baltimore MD 21202-3993. **Tel** (410)528-4000, (800)638-6423, FAX (410)528-8596, telex 87669. **(Subscription address:** Williams & Wilkins, PO Box 64380, Baltimore MD 21264.**) ED** E. Stewart Taylor. **LC** RG1; .O17. **DD** 618.1. **NLM** ZWP 100 O14. **CODEN** OGSUA8. **[CCC].** cum. index. **Ad Acc. Circ:** 12,100. Documents available from BIOSIS Document Express, CASDDS, Quick Copies.
**Desc:** Review articles and condensations of obstetric/gynecology articles from nearly 100 US and international journals.
**Ind/Abst** Biol. Abstr.; Chem. Abstr. (1946-1983); Comb. Cumul. Index Ob./Gyn.; Curr. Lit. Fam. Plan.; EMBASE; Energy Res. Abstr. (Jan. 1981-); Index Med.; Life Sci. Collect.; Physic. Medline Plus.

AG/0029-7836
**OBSTETRICIA Y GINECOLOGIA LATINO-AMERICANAS.** (1943)-. Academic Scholarly Publication. Spanish. qt. $90.00. Obstetricia y Gynecologia, Pichincha 2129 1249, Buenos Aires Argentina. **NLM** W1 OB483. **CODEN** OGLAAF. Index available. cum. index. **Ad Acc. Circ:** 2,800 (ctrl). Documents available from CASDDS.
**Desc:** Original articles and updates of the different societies whom this journal serves as an organ of communication.
**Ind/Abst** Chem. Abstr. (1943-1983).

CN/0824-7404
**OBSTETRICS AND GYNAECOLOGY (OTTAWA).** (OBSTETRICS AND GYNAECOLOGY SOUND RECORDING / SPECIALIST DIVISION.). [Obstet. gynaecol.]. Periodical. English. Medifacts Group Ltd, 20 Camelot Drive, Suite 600, Ottawa Ontario K2A 0G3 Canada. **Tel** (613)728-4655. **DD** 618/.05. **UDC** 618.
**Ind/Abst** Iowa Drug Inf. Serv.

US/0889-8545
**OBSTETRICS AND GYNECOLOGY CLINICS OF NORTH AMERICA.** [Obstet. gynecol. clin. North Am.]. **VFOAT** Obstetrics and Gynecology. Vol. 14, No. 1 (March 1987)-. Monographic series. English. qt. $94.00 (individual), $119.00 (institutions) US; $129.00 (individual), $137.00 (institution) other. W.B. Saunders Company, A Subsidiary of Harcourt Brace Jovanovich, Inc., The Curtis Center/Suite 300, Independence Square West, Philadelphia PA 19106-3399. **Tel** (215)238-7800 or, 5587, FAX (215)238-7883, telex 173146. **(Subscription address:** W. B. Saunders Company / North America Subscriptions, c/o Periodicals, 6277 Sea Harbour Drive, 4th Floor, Orlando FL 32887.**) ED** Livia Berardi. **DD** 618. **UDC** 618. **NLM** W1; OB493. **CODEN** OGCAE8. **[CCC].** Index available. **Pr Rev. Circ:** 2,000. available on microfilm and microfiche from University Microfilms International (UMI). Documents available from The Genuine Article, BIOSIS Document Express. ***Continues in part*** *Clinics in Obstetrics and Gynaecology, 0306-3356.*
**Desc:** Practical updates for the clinician on the latest advances in ob/gyn written by experts in the field.
**Ind/Abst** Biol. Abstr. (March 1987-); Cumul. Index Nurs. Allied Health Lit.; Curr. Contents Clin. Med.; Dev. Med. Child Neurol.; EMBASE; Index Med. (1987-); Life Sci. Collect. (March 1987-); Res. Alert [Full Cov.]; Sci. Cit. Index; SCISEARCH; Soc. Sci. Cit. Index [Select. Cov.].

US/0029-7844
**OBSTETRICS AND GYNECOLOGY (NEW YORK. 1953).** (OBSTETRICS AND GYNECOLOGY.). [Obstet. gynecol.]. **Added/Corp** American College of Obstetricians and Gynecologists. American Academy of Obstetrics and Gynecology. Vol. 1 (Jan. 1953)-. Academic Scholarly Publication. English. Twelve times a year (2 volumes). $210.00 US; $365.00 Europe; $398.00 Japan; $295.00 (surface mail) other. Elsevier Science Publishing Company Inc, Madison Square Station, PO Box 882, New York NY 10159-0882. **Tel** (212)633-3950, FAX (212)633-3990. **ED** Roy M Pitkin. **LC** RG1; .A382. **DD** 618.05. **NLM** W1 OB488. **CODEN** OBGNAS. **[CCC].** cum. index. **Bk Rev. Ad Acc. Pr Rev. Circ:** 30,075. available on microfilm and microfiche from University Microfilms International (UMI). Documents available from The Genuine Article, BIOSIS Document Express, CASDDS, ADONIS.
**Desc:** Features original research studies and case reports on new medical and surgical techniques, obstetric management, clinical evaluation of drugs and instruments as well as other timely topics.
**Ind/Abst** Abr. Index Med.; ADONIS; Annals Behav. Med.; Biol. Abstr.; Chem. Abstr.; Comb. Cumul. Index Ob./Gyn.; CSA Neuro. Abstr. (?-?); Cumul. Index Nurs. Allied Health Lit.; Curr. Aware. Biol. Sci., CABS; Curr. Contents Clin. Med.; Curr. Contents Life Sci.; Dev. Med. Child Neurol.; EMBASE; Energy Res. Abstr.; Health Devices Alerts; Health Period. Database; Index Med.; Int. Pharm. Abstr.; J. Watch (199?-); Med. Abstr. Newsl.; Microbiol. Abstr. Sect. B (19??-19??); Nutr. Abstr. Rev., Ser. A, Hum. Exp.; Nutr. Res. Newsl.; Life Sci. Collect.; PESTDOC; Physic. Medline Plus; Protozoolog. Abstr.; Ref. Upd. Deluxe Ed.; Res. Alert [Full Cov.]; Rev. Med. Vet. Mycology; Sci. Cit. Index; SCISEARCH; Soc. Sci. Cit. Index [Select. Cov.]; SportSearch; Virol. AIDS Abstr.

US/0078-298X
**OBSTETRICS & GYNECOLOGY (NEW YORK. 1970).** (OBSTETRICS & GYNECOLOGY.). [Obstet. gynecol.]. **VAT** Obstetrics and Gynecology. (19??)-. Periodical. English. an. Medical World News, 299 Park Avenue, New York NY 10017. **LC** RG1; .O356. **DD** 618/.05.

US/1060-507X
**OBSTETRICS & GYNECOLOGY REVIEW.** [Obstet. gynecol. rev.]. **VFOAT** Obstetrics and Gynecology Review. (1991)-. Periodical. English. Pergamon Press, An Imprint of Elsevier Science Ltd., The Boulevard, Langford Lane, Kidlington, Oxford OX5 1GB United Kingdom. **Tel** 011 44 865 843000, 011 44 865 843699, FAX 011 44 865 843010. **DD** 618. **NLM** WP 18; O135. ***Continues*** *Obstetrics & Gynecology (New York, N.Y.), 0957-3038.*

IT
**ONCOLOGIA GINECOLOGICA.** Vol. 1, No. 1 (May 1982)-. Periodical. Italian. qt. L30000. Contraccezione Fertilita Sess, Piazzale Ungheria 73, 90141 Palermo Italy. **Tel** 011 39 91 321922. **NLM** W1; ON105M.

FR/0761-229X
**PASCAL EXPLORE. E82, GYNECOLOGIE, OBSTETRIQUE, ANDROLOGIE.** ***Title Change.*** **VFOAT** Gynecologie, Obstetrique, Andrologie; Gynecology, Obstetrics, Andrology. (1984)-?. Periodical. French. mo. Institut de l'Information Scientique et Technique (INIST), 2 Allee du Parc de Brabois, 54514 Vandoeuvre Nancy Cedex France. **Tel** 011 33 83 504600, FAX 011 33 83 504650. **NLM** ZQ 1; P27793. ***Continues in part*** *Bulletin Signaletique. 361, Reproduction, Gynecologie, Obstetrique, Embryologie, Endocrinologie, 0245-9884.* ***Continued by*** *Gynecologie, Obstetrique, Andrologie. E82.*

IT/0304-0313
**PATOLOGIA E CLINICA OSTETRICA E GINECOLOGICA.** ***Ceased.*** [Patol. clin. ostet. ginecol.]. Vol. 1 (1973)-No. 6 (1993). Academic Scholarly Publication. Italian (summaries and/or abstracts in English). bm. Edizioni Luigi Pozzi Srl, Via Panama 68, 00198 Rome Italy. **Tel** (06)8553548, FAX (06)8554105. **UDC** 618. **NLM** W1 PA969G. **Circ:** 2,087. ***Supersedes*** *Clinica Ostetrica e Ginecologica, 0009-9031.*
**Desc:** Italian translation of the American Journal Clinical Obstetrics and Gynecology.
**Ind/Abst** EMBASE [Select. Cov.]; Life Sci. Collect.

US/0160-3701
**PERINATAL CARE.** V. 1- June 1977-. Periodical. English. mo. $25.00. Perinatal Care, 666 5th Avenue, New York NY 10019. **LC** RG1; .P46. **DD** 618.2/005. **UDC** 618.2. **NLM** W1 PE788B.

UK/0893-6293
**PERINATAL PRACTICE.** [Perinat. pract.]. **VFOAT** Wiley Series on Perinatal Practice. Vol. 1 (1984)-. Monographic series. English. ir. Price varies per volume. J Schweitzer Verlag KG, Geibelstrasse 8, W-8000 Munchen 80 Germany. **ED** Geoffrey Chamberlain and Forrester Cockburn. **DD** 618. **NLM** W1; PE788F.

US/0160-7219
**PERINATAL PRESS.** [Perinat. press]. (Jan. 1977)-. Periodical. English. Six times a year. $20.00 US; $30.00 US and Canada; $35.00 other. Perinatal Press Inc., PO Box 710698, Sacramento CA 92171. **Tel** (619)541-6875, 541-6870. **ED** K. Mulligan. **UDC** 616-053.3. **NLM** W1 PE788H. Index available. **Bk Rev. Circ:** 5,000 (ctrl).
**Desc:** Practical information for those caring for the pregnant woman, fetus and newborn.
**Ind/Abst** Cumul. Index Nurs. Allied Health Lit.

GW/0936-7160
**PERINATALMEDIZIN : OFFIZIELLES MITTEILUNGSBLATT DER DEUTSCHEN GESELLSCHAFT FUER PERINATALE MEDIZIN.** **Added/Corp** Deutsche Gesellschaft fuer Perinatale Medizin. **VFOAT** Perinatal Medizin. Vol. 1, No. 1 (1989)-. Periodical. German. Four times a year. DM122.00. Springer-Verlag GmbH & Company KG, Heidelberger Platz 3, D 14197 Berlin Germany. **Tel** 011 49 30 8207223, FAX 011 49 30 8214091, telex 183 319 SPBLN D. **(Subscription address:** Springer Verlag New York Inc. / for North America, 44 Hartz Way, Secaucus NJ 07096.**) ED** J W Dudenhausen. **NLM** W1; PE788D. **[CCC].** available on microfilm and microfiche from University Microfilms International (UMI).
**Desc:** Addresses obstetricians, neonatologists, and scientists who research perinatal medicine and work in theoretical institutes.

SP
**PERINATOLOGIA CLINICA.** Monographic series. Spanish. an. Price varies per volume. McGraw Hill, Interamericana de Espana SA, Manuel Ferrero 13, 28036 Madrid Spain. **NLM** W3 PE535L.

US
**PMS ACCESS.** See Women's Interests.

US/0194-3898
**POSTGRADUATE OBSTETRICS & GYNECOLOGY.** [Postgrad. obstet. & gynecol.]. (1979)-. Monographic series. English. Twenty-six times a year. $175.00 US; $225.00 other. Postgraduate Obstetrics & Gynecology, PO Box 23263, Baltimore MD 21203-5263. **Tel** (410)955-3669, FAX (410)955-0035. Index available. cum. index. ctrl circ.
**Desc:** Continuing medical education lesson featuring a state-of-the-art review of a pertinent topic in obstetrics, gynecology and related subjects.

US/0896-5390
**PRACTICAL REVIEWS IN OB/GYN.** (PRACTICAL REVIEWS IN OB/GYN [SOUND RECORDING].). [Pract. rev. OB/GYN]. **Added/Corp** Educational Reviews, Inc. Montefiore Medical Center. **VFOAT** Practical Reviews; Practical Reviews in Obstetrics and Gynecology. (197?)-. Periodical. English. mo. $175.00 Physicians/Dentists; $125.00 Residents. Educational Reviews Inc., 6801 Cahaba Valley Road, Birmingham AL 35242. **Tel** (205)991-5188, (800)633-4743, FAX (205)995-1926. **DD** 618.

US/0883-3095
**PRE- AND PERI-NATAL PSYCHOLOGY JOURNAL.** (PRE-AND PERI-NATAL PSYCHOLOGY JOURNAL : OFFICIAL JOURNAL OF THE PRE AND PERI-NATAL PSYCHOLOGY ASSOCIATION OF NORTH AMERICA (PPPANA).). [Pre- peri-nat. psychol. j.]. **Added/Corp** Pre and Peri-natal Psychology Association of North America. **VAT** Pre and Peri Natal Psychology Journal. Vol. 1, Issue 1 (Fall 1986)-. Periodical. English. qt. £42.00 (individuals), £160.00 (institutions) UK; $195.00 US; $230.00 other. Human Sciences Press, PO Box 735, 233 Spring Street, New York NY 10013. **Tel** (212)620-8000, FAX (212)807-1047, telex 23421139. **(Subscription address:** Eurospan Ltd., Journals and Serials Division, 3 Henrietta Street, Covent Garden, London WC2E 8LU England.**) ED** Charles Laughlin. **LC** RG635; .P74. **DD** 618.2/001/9. **NLM** W1; PR33K. **CODEN** PPPJE4PPNYJ1. **[CCC].** available on microfilm from University Microfilms International (UMI).
**Desc:** At the cutting edge of rapidly growing science of pre-and peri-natal psychology, contributions provide in-depth exploration of the psychological dimensions of human reproduction and pregnancy and the mental and emotional development of the unborn child.
**Ind/Abst** Psychol. Abstr. (1986-); PsycINFO (1990-); PsycLit; Sage Fam. Stud. Abstr.

UK/0197-3851
**PRENATAL DIAGNOSIS.** [Prenat. diagn.]. Vol. 1, No. 1 (Jan. 1981)-. Academic Scholarly Publication. English. Thirteen times a year. $745.00. John Wiley & Sons Ltd., Baffins Lane, Chichester West Sussex PO19 1UD England. **Tel** 0243 779777, FAX 0243 776128 BTG:JWP001, telex 86290 WIBOOKG. **(Subscription address:** John Wiley / Philadelphia, PO Box 7247, Philadelphia PA 19170.**) ED** M. A. Ferguson-Smith and M. M. Kaback and C. H. Rodeck. **DD** 618. **NLM** W1 PR397M. **CODEN** PRDIDM. **[CCC]. Bk Rev. Ad Acc. Pr Rev. Circ:** 1,000. available on microfilm and microfiche from University Microfilms International (UMI). Documents available from The Genuine Article, BIOSIS Document Express, CASDDS, ADONIS.
**Desc:** Communicates the results of original research with 'in utero' diagnosis of fetal abnormality in man (and animal models) resulting from genetic and environmental factors.
**Ind/Abst** ADONIS; Biol. Abstr.; Chem. Abstr.; Curr. Aware. Biol. Sci., CABS; Curr. Contents Clin. Med.; Curr. Contents Life Sci.; Dev. Med. Child Neurol.; EMBASE; Genet. Abstr.; Hum. Genome Abstr.; Index Med.; Res. Alert [Full Cov.]; Sci. Cit. Index; SCISEARCH; Soc. Sci. Cit. Index [Select. Cov.].

US/1051-4171
**PRESCRIBING REFERENCE FOR OBSTETRICIANS & GYNECOLOGISTS.** (1991)-. Periodical. English. sa. $20.00. Prescribing Reference Inc, PO Box 844, Pearl River NY 10965. **Tel** (800)436-9269, FAX (212)732-2360.

●US/1068-607X
**PRIMARY CARE UPDATE FOR OB/GYNS.** **VFOAT** Primary Care Update for Ob Gyns. **VAT** Primary Care Update for Obstetricians/Gynecologists. (1994)-. Academic Scholarly Publication. English. bm (1 volume). $105.00 US; $145.00 other. Elsevier Science Publishing Company Inc, Madison Square Station, PO Box 882, New York NY 10159-0882. **Tel** (212)633-3950, FAX (212)633-3990. **ED** Vicki L. Seltzer, MD. **NLM** W1; PR522AN. **[CCC]. Ad Acc. Pr Rev. Acid Free.**
**Desc:** Presents practical clinical information pertaining to the diagnosis, treatment, and management of non-ob/gyn disorders in women.

CN/0715-4356
**PRO-LIFE NEWS.** [Pro-life news]. **Added/Corp** Alliance for Life. **VFOAT** Pro-Life News Canada. (1976)-. Periodical. English. bm. 15.42Can$. Alliance Non Profit Prolife, B1-90 Garry Street, Winnipeg Manitoba R3C 4H1 Canada. **Tel** (204)943-5273, FAX (204)943-9283. **ED** Barbara LeBow. **DD** 363.4/6/05. **Bk Rev. Ad Acc. Circ:** 50,000 (ctrl).
**Desc:** Promotes the right to life. Discusses fetal development, bioethical questions, discrimination of handicapped, dignity and rights of each person.

UK/0964-4156
**PROFESSIONAL CARE OF MOTHER AND CHILD.** Vol. 1, No. 1 (Sept. 1991)-. Periodical. English. mo. Newbourne Group, Hampstead Road, Greater London House, London NW1 7QP England. **Tel** 011 44 1 388 3171. **NLM** W1; PR5884. ***Continues Midwife, Health Visitor & Community Nurse, 0306-9699.***
**Ind/Abst** Cumul. Index Nurs. Allied Health Lit.

SP/0304-5013
**PROGRESOS DE OBSTETRICIA Y GINECOLOGIA.** [Prog. obstet. ginecol.]. (1958)-. Periodical. Spanish (English). Ten times a year. $69.72 Spain; $104.00 other Europe; $129.00 other. Salvat Editores SA, Calle Mallorca 45-49, Barcelona 08029 Spain. **Tel** 011 34 3 2010911, FAX 011 34 3 321-0565, telex SAEDI E 53132. **(Subscription address:** Editorial Garsi, C Juan Bravo, 28006 Madrid Spain.**) ED** Gonzalez Merlo and Santiago Dexeus. **UDC** 618. Index available. **Bk Rev. Ad Acc. Circ:** 2,000.
**Desc:** Update in gynecology and obstetrics.
**Ind/Abst** EMBASE; Indice Med. Esp.

SP/1130-0523
**PROGRESOS EN DIAGNOSTICO PRENATAL.** [Prog. diagn. prenat.]. **Added/Corp** Ociacion Espa*f*nola de Diagnostico Prenatal. **VFOAT** Progress in Prenatal Diagnosis. (1989)-. Periodical. Spanish (English). qt. $33.10 Spain; $51.00 other Europe; $58.00 other. Salvat Editores SA, Calle Mallorca 45-49, Barcelona 08029 Spain. **Tel** 011 34 3 2010911, FAX 011 34 3 321-0565, telex SAEDI E 53132. **(Subscription address:** Editorial Garsi, C Juan Bravo, 28006 Madrid Spain.**) ED** Jose Maria Carrera. **UDC** 616-07-053.13. Index available. **Bk Rev. Ad Acc. Circ:** 2,000.
**Desc:** Progress in prenatal diagnosis.

UK/0261-0140
**PROGRESS IN OBSTETRICS AND GYNAECOLOGY.** [Prog. obstet. gynaecol.]. (1981)-. Monographic series. English. an. Price varies per volume. Churchill Livingstone, 1-3 Baxter's Place, Leith Walk, Edinburgh EH1 3AF Scotland. **Tel** 011 44 31 556 2424, FAX 011 44 31 558 1278, telex 727511. **(Subscription address:** Churchill Livingstone / US, 5 S 250 Frontenac Road, Naperville IL 60563.**) ED** John Studd. **NLM** W1 PR675P.
**Ind/Abst** Ref. Upd. Deluxe Ed.

IT
**PROPHYLAXIS AND PREVENTION IN GYNAECOLOGIC ONCOLOGY NEW TRENDS.** English. $40.00. S O G S R L, Galleria Storione 2A, 35128 Padua Italy. **Tel** 011 39 49 8756900.

IT/0033-491X
**QUADERNI DI CLINICA OSTETRICA E GINECOLOGICA.** [Quad. clin. ostet. ginecol.]. (1946)-. Periodical. Italian. Six times a year. L60000.00 Italy; L120000.00 other. Casa Editrice Maccari, Via Trento 53, 43100 Parma Italy. **Tel** 011 39 521 771268, FAX 011 39 521 771268. **NLM** W1 QU122.
**Ind/Abst** Life Sci. Collect.

UK/1351-8402
**RCOG DIPLOMATE, THE.** (19??)-. English. qt. £35.00. Parthenon Publishing, Casterton Hall Carnforth, Lancashire LA6 2LA England. **Tel** 011 44 5242 72084, FAX 44-5242-71587.

UK/0143-6848
**RECENT ADVANCES IN OBSTETRICS AND GYNAECOLOGY.** [Recent adv. obstet. gynaecol.]. (1926)-. Periodical. English. ir (Publishes every 3 to 5 years). $69.00 (latest volume). Churchill Livingstone, 1-3 Baxter's Place, Leith Walk, Edinburgh EH1 3AF Scotland. **Tel** 011 44 31 556 2424, FAX 011 44 31 558 1278, telex 727511. **(Subscription address:** Churchill Livingstone / US, 5 S 250 Frontenac Road, Naperville IL 60563.**) LC** RG1; .R42. **DD** 618/.05. **NLM** W1 RE105YJ.

UK/0264-2417
**RECENT ADVANCES IN PERINATAL MEDICINE.** [Recent adv. perinat. med.]. (1983)-. English. ir. Longman Group Ltd., Fourth Avenue, Longman House, Harlow Essex CM19 5SR England. **Tel** 011 44 279 429655, FAX 011 44 279 431059, telex 81259. **LC** RG626; .R42. **DD** 618.3/2/005. **NLM** W1 RE105XR.

SP/0303-5220
**REPRODUCCION (MADRID).** (REPRODUCCION.). [Reproduccion]. **Added/Corp** Sociedad Argentina de Esterilidad y Fertilidad. Sociedad Espanola para el Estudio de la Esterilidad. Sociedade Brasileira de Reproducao Humana. (1974)-. Academic Scholarly Publication. Multiple languages (Portuguese and Spanish; summaries and/or abstracts in English). qt. **NLM** W1 RE213K. **CODEN** RDCNBM. Documents available from BIOSIS Document Express, CASDDS.
**Ind/Abst** Biol. Abstr. (-1983); Chem. Abstr. (1974-1984); EMBASE; Health Plan. Adminis.; Index Med.; Life Sci. Collect.

US/0732-1279
**REPRODUCTIVE MEDICINE.** [Reprod. med.]. Vol. 1 (1980)-. Monographic series. English. ir. Price varies per volume. Marcel Dekker Inc., 270 Madison Avenue, New York NY 10016. **Tel** (212)696-9000, (800)228-1160, FAX (212)685-4540, telex 421419. **(Subscription address:** Marcel Dekker Inc, PO Box 5017, Monticello NY 12701.**) LC** UNC. **DD** 618/.05. **NLM** W1 RE213P.
**Desc:** Covers topics in reproductive medicine such as diagnostic procedure in obstetrics and gynecology and the basis of perinatology.

●UK/0962-2799
**REPRODUCTIVE MEDICINE REVIEW.** Vol. 1, No. 1 (1992)-. Periodical. English. Three times a year. $137.50 North America; £80.00 Europe; £90.00 Other. Edward Arnold, 338 Euston Road, London NW1 3BH England. **Tel** 011 44 71 873 6000, FAX 011 44 071 873 6325. **(Subscription address:** Edward Arnold, PO Box 386, Avenel NJ 07001-0386.**) ED** S. K. Smith. **LC** QP251; .R44454. **DD** 612.6/005. **NLM** W1; RE213PC.
**Desc:** Dedicated to the advancement of knowledge and clinical practice in this expanding specialty. It will provide an up-to-date, authoritative reference source in reproductive medicine. Subjects include gynecological endocrinology, menopause, menstrual dysfunction, andrology, infertility, and assisted conception.
**Ind/Abst** EMBASE.

AT
**RESEARCH LIBRARY JOURNAL OF ABSTRACTS.** **Added/Corp** Right to Life Association. South Australia Division. Research Committee. Autumn (1975)-. English. 8.00Aus$. **LC** HQ767; .R36. **DD** 301.

US/0198-9774
**RESOURCES IN HUMAN NURTURING MONOGRAPH.** [Resour. hum. nurtur. monogr.]. **VFOAT** RHNI Monograph. No. 1-. Monographic series. English. ir. Price varies per volume. Lact-Aid International, PO Box 1066, Athens TN 37303. **Tel** (615)744-9090. **ED** Jimmie Lynne Avery. **NLM** W1 RE248BM. Index available.

US/0362-5699
**REVIEWS IN PERINATAL MEDICINE.** [Rev. perinat. med.]. (1976)-. Academic Scholarly Publication. English. ir. $141.50. Raven Press, 1185 Avenue of the Americas, 37th Floor, New York NY 10036. **Tel** (212)930-9500, (212)930-9604, FAX (212)869-3495, (212)302-8507, telex 640073. **ED** Emile M. Scarpelli and Ermelando V. Cosmi. **LC** RG600; .R47. **DD** 618.3/2/05. **NLM** W1 RE257CG. **CODEN** PPMED7. Documents available from BIOSIS Document Express, CASDDS.
**Ind/Abst** Biol. Abstr.; Chem. Abstr.

CL/0048-766X
**REVISTA CHILENA DE OBSTETRICIA Y GINECOLOGIA.** [Rev. chil. obstet. ginecol.]. **Added/Corp** Sociedad Chilena de Obstetricia y Ginecologia. Vol. 26, No. 1 (Jan./Feb. 1961)-. Periodical. Spanish. Six times a year. $80.00. Societe Chilena Obstetrics Ginecologia, Casilla 1 Correo 27 las Condes, Santiago Chile. **Tel** 011 56 2 2113774. **NLM** W1 RE3502.

***Continues*** *Boletin de la Sociedad Chilena de Obstetricia y Ginecologia.*
**Ind/Abst** Index Med.

CK/0034-7434
**REVISTA COLOMBIANA DE OBSTETRICIA Y GINECOLOGIA.** [Rev. colomb. obstet. ginecol.]. **Added/Corp** Sociedad Colombiana de Obstetricia y Ginecologia. (19??)-. Periodical. Spanish. qt. $45.00 South America; $50.00 other. Societe Colombiana de Obstetricia y Ginecologia Revista, Carrera 23 No 39-82, Bogota Colombia. **Tel** 011 57 1 2681485. **ED** Enrique Archila. **NLM** W1 RE357. Index available. **Bk Rev. Ad Acc. Pr Rev. Circ:** 1,200 (ctrl).
**Ind/Abst** EMBASE [Select. Cov.].

CU
**REVISTA CUBANA DE OBSTETRICIA Y GINECOLOGIA.** **Added/Corp** Centro Nacional de Informacion de Ciencias Medicas. Vol. 1 (Jan./April 1975)-. Periodical. Spanish (summaries and/or abstracts in English, French and Russian). qt. $24.00 North America; $28.00 South America; $35.00 other. Ediciones Cubanas, Obispo 527, Altos ESQ Bernaza, CP 10100 Havana Cuba. **Tel** 011 632980, 631942, FAX 011 631011, telex 512337, 6540. **NLM** W1 RE363F. **Circ:** 3,000 (ctrl).
**Desc:** Articles on obstetrics, gynecology and other related specialities. It contains original papers, reviews of topics and the presentation of cases, mainly by Cuban authors.
**Ind/Abst** Energy Res. Abstr. (July 1982-).

AG/0037-8542
**REVISTA DE LA SOCIEDAD DE OBSTETRICIA Y GINECOLOGIA DE BUENOS AIRES.** [Rev. Soc. obstet. ginecol. B. Aires]. (1961)-. Periodical. Spanish. mo. $90.00. Society Obstetricia Ginecologia, Buenos Aires, Pichincha 2129, 1249 Buenos Aires Argentina. **Tel** 011 54 1 271177, FAX 011 54 1 843190. **UDC** 618. **CODEN** RSOGA. Index available. cum. index. **Pr Rev. Circ:** 3,000 (ctrl).
***Continues*** *Boletin de la Sociedad de Obstetricia y Ginecologia de Buenos Aires, 0327-5191.*

RM/0377-4961
**REVISTA DE PEDIATRIE, OBSTETRICA SI GINECOLOGIE. OBSTETRICA SI GINECOLOGIE.** [Rev. pediatr., obstet. ginecol., Obstet. ginecol.]. **Added/Corp** Societatea de Obstetrica si Ginecologie. **VFOAT** Obstetrica si Ginecologia. Vol. 22, No. 4 (July/Sept. 1974)-. Periodical. Romanian (summaries and/or abstracts in English, French, German and Russian). qt. DM225.00. **(Subscription address:** Kubon & Sagner, ABT Zeitschriftenimport, D 80328 Munich Germany.**)** **NLM** W1 RE458R. **CODEN** RPOGDB. Documents available from BIOSIS Document Express, CASDDS. ***Continues*** *Obstetrica si Ginecologia, 0029-781X.*
**Desc:** Publishes articles on obstetric and surgical technique.
**Ind/Abst** Biol. Abstr.; Chem. Abstr.; EMBASE.

SP/0034-9445
**REVISTA ESPANOLA DE OBSTETRICIA Y GINECOLOGIA.** [Rev. esp. obstet. ginecol.]. (1944)-. Academic Scholarly Publication. Spanish. Six times a year. $40.00. Editoral Facta, Avellanas 4, 46003 Valencia Spain. **Tel** 011 34 96 3323842 3794. **NLM** W1 RE5465. **CODEN** REOGAX. **[CCC].** Documents available from CASDDS.
**Ind/Abst** Chem. Abstr.; EMBASE; Indice Med. Esp.

SP
**REVISTA IBEROAMERICANA DE FERTILIDAD Y REPRODUCCION HUMANA : OORH.** **VFOAT** OORH; Fertilidad. (198?)-. Periodical. Spanish (summaries and/or abstracts in English; table of contents in English). Six times a year. 6890ptas Spain; 6500ptas others. Nuevas Creaciones Medicas, C Santillana del Mar, 3 Chalet 44, 28660 Boadilla del Monte Madrid Spain. **Tel** 011 34 1 6321544, 011 34 1 6321608, FAX 011 34 1 6321544. **NLM** W1; RE593RF.

MX/0034-9984
**REVISTA MEXICANA DE CIRUGIA, GINECOLOGIA Y CANCER.** [Rev. mex. cir. ginecol. cancer]. Yearly V. 1- August 1933-. Periodical. Spanish. bm. **UDC** 618.14-006. **NLM** W1 RE6828.

VE/0048-7732
**REVISTA OBSTETRICIA Y GINECOLOGIA DE VENEZUELA.** [Rev. obstet. ginecol. Venez.]. **Added/Corp** Sociedad de Obstetricia y Ginecologia de Venezuela. **VFOAT** Revista de Obstetricia y Ginecologia de Venezuela. Vol. 20 (1960)-. Periodical. Spanish. qt (Mar., June, Sept., Dec.). Soc Obst Y Ginic de Venezuela, Apartado 20081 San Martin, Caracas Venezuela. **Tel** 011 58 2 4622076. **NLM** W1 RE4534. ***Continues*** *Revista de Obstetricia y Ginecologia.*
**Ind/Abst** EMBASE [Select. Cov.].

FR/1141-5886
**REVUE DU GYNECOLOGUE OBSTETRICIEN.** ***Title Change.*** **VFOAT** Revue du Gynecologue-Obstetricien. Vol. 1, No. 1 (June 1989)-(1993). Periodical. French. Eight times a year. Masson SA, Avenue Beauregard 12, CH-1701 Fribourg Switzerland. **Tel** 011 41 37 249585, FAX 011 41 37 247559, telex 942658 SEMI CH. **NLM** W1; RE799R. ***Merged with*** *Gynecologie, 0301-2204* ***to form*** *Gynecologie (Paris, France : 1993).*

FR/0035-290X
**REVUE FRANCAISE DE GYNECOLOGIE ET D'OBSTETRIQUE.** [Rev. fr. gynecol. obstet.]. Vol. 14, No. 8 (Aug. 1919)-. Academic Scholarly Publication. French (summaries and/or abstracts in English). mo (10 issues per year). 1000.00F France; 1270.00F other. Expansion Scientifique Francaise, 31 Boulevard de la Tour-Maubourg, 75007 Paris France. **Tel** 011 33 1 40 62 64 00, 011 33 1 40626439. **ED** Y. Malinas and J. Seneze. **NLM** W1 RE845C. **CODEN** RFGOAO. **[CCC]. Bk Rev. Ad Acc. Circ:** 5,000. available on microfilm from University Microfilms International (UMI). Documents available from CASDDS. ***Continues*** *Revue Mensuelle de Gynecologie, d'Obstetrique, et de Pediatrie, 0301-8458.*
**Ind/Abst** Chem. Abstr.; EMBASE; Index Med.; Life Sci. Collect.

JA/0386-9865
**RINSHO FUJINKA SANKA.** [Rinsho fujinka sanka]. **VFOAT** Clinical Gynecology and Obstetrics. (1946)-. Periodical. Japanese. mo. Igaku Shoin, (Igaku Shoin Ltd.), 24-3, Hongo 5 Chome, Bunkyoku, Tokyoto 113-9, Japan. **CODEN** RFUSA4. Documents available from CASDDS.
**Ind/Abst** Chem. Abstr.

IT/0391-0970
**RIVISTA DI OSTETRICIA GINECOLOGIA PRATICA E MEDICINA PERINATALE.** ***Suspended.*** **Added/Corp** Associazione Regionale Lombarda Ostetrici- Ginecologi, Anestesisti, Pediatri. Vol. 54 (Jan. 1973/74)-Suspended (Apr. 1994). Academic Scholarly Publication. Italian (English; summaries and/or abstracts in English, French and German). Four times a year. Ariete Edizioni SRL, Via G Stephenson 33, 20157 Milan Italy. **Tel** 011 39 2 332141. **ED** A. Zacutti. **NLM** W1 RI574I. **Ad Acc.** ctrl circ. ***Continues*** *Rivista d'Ostetricia e Ginecologia Pratica e di Medicina Perinatale, 0391-0970.*
**Ind/Abst** EMBASE.

FR/0180-0612
**SAGES FEMMES.** ***Ceased.*** [Sages femmes]. **Added/Corp** Societe SOPEPHARM. Vol. 1 (1977)-(1993). Periodical. French. Eleven times a year. Societe Sopepharm, 15 Rue Du Nord, 95100 Argenteuil France. **Tel** 011 33 1 39820202. **NLM** W1 SA127.

JA/0558-471X
**SANFUJINKA CHIRYO.** [Sanfujinka chiryo]. **VFOAT** Obstetrical and Gynecological Therapy. (1960)-. Academic Scholarly Publication. Japanese. Twelve times a year. $255.00. Nagai Shoten Company Ltd, 21-15 8-Chome Fukushima, Fukushima Osaka 553 Japan. **Tel** 06-452-1881, FAX 06-452-1882. **ED** Tadao Nagai. **CODEN** SACHAR. **Circ:** 10,000. Documents available from CASDDS.
**Ind/Abst** Chem. Abstr.; Curr. Biotechnol.

JA/0386-9873
**SANFUJINKA NO SEKAI.** [Sanfujinka no sekai]. **VFOAT** World of Obstetrics & Gynecology; World of Obstetrics and Gynecology. (1949)-. Academic Scholarly Publication. Japanese. mo. $266.50. Igaku No Sekaisha, 12-4, Kudan Kita 1 Chome, Chiyodaku, Tokyoto 102 Japan. **(Subscription address:** Japan Publications Trading Company, Ltd., PO Box 5030, Tokyo International, Tokyo 100-31 Japan.**)** **UDC** 618. **CODEN** SASEAU. Documents available from CASDDS.
**Ind/Abst** Chem. Abstr.

●NE/0925-6164
**SCREENING: JOURNAL OF THE INTERNATIONAL SOCIETY OF NEONATAL SCREENING.** **Added/Corp** International Society of Neonatal Screening. Vol. 1, No. 1 (Jan./Mar. 1992)-. Academic Scholarly Publication. English. Four times a year (1 volume). $215.00. Elsevier Science Ireland Ltd., Bay 15, Shannon Industrial Estate, Co Clare Ireland. **Tel** 011 353 61 471944. **NLM** W1; SC9273. **[CCC].**
**Ind/Abst** Curr. Aware. Biol. Sci., CABS.

US/0146-0005
**SEMINARS IN PERINATOLOGY.** [Semin. perinatol.]. Vol. 1 (Jan. 1977)-. Periodical. English. bm. $151.00 (institutions), $99.00 (individuals) US; $188.00 (institutions), $171.00 (individuals) other. W.B. Saunders Company, A Subsidiary of Harcourt Brace Jovanovich, Inc., The Curtis Center/Suite 300, Independence Square West, Philadelphia PA 19106-3399. **Tel** (215)238-7800 or, 5587, FAX (215)238-7883, telex 173146. **(Subscription address:** W. B. Saunders Company / North America Subscriptions, c/o Periodicals, 6277 Sea Harbour Drive, 4th Floor, Orlando FL 32887.**)** **ED** Robert K. Creasy and Joseph B. Warshaw. **DD** 618. **NLM** W1 SE489F. **CODEN** SEMPDU. **[CCC]. Pr Rev. Circ:** 3,652. Documents available from The Genuine Article, BIOSIS Document Express.
**Desc:** Tailored to the interest of professionals who care for the mother, the fetus, and the newborn.
**Ind/Abst** Biol. Abstr.; Curr. Contents Clin. Med.; Dev. Med. Child Neurol.; EMBASE; Energy Res. Abstr. (Aug. 1982-); Index Med.; Index Sci. Rev. [Full Cov.]; Life Sci. Collect.; Res. Alert [Full Cov.]; Sci. Cit. Index; SCISEARCH; Soc. Sci. Cit. Index [Select. Cov.].

US/0734-8630
**SEMINARS IN REPRODUCTIVE ENDOCRINOLOGY.** **See** Medical Science and Technology-Endocrinology.

GW/0341-4884
**SEXUALMEDIZIN.** ***Ceased.*** Vol. 1 (Jan. 1972)-(19??). Periodical. German (summaries and/or abstracts in English). ir. Medical Tribune, Rheinstrasse 19, W-62 Wiesbaden 1 Germany. **NLM** W1 SE99W.

CC/0253-357X
**SHENGZHI YU BIYUN.** **See** Birth Control.

SI/0129-3273
**SINGAPORE JOURNAL OF OBSTETRICS & GYNAECOLOGY.** [Sing. J. Obstet. Gynaecol.]. **Added/Corp** Obstetrical and Gynaecological Society, Singapore. **VAT** Singapore Journal of Obstetrics and Gynaecology. Vol. 8 (1977)-. Academic Scholarly Publication. English. Three times a year (Mar., July, Nov.). S$30.00 Singapore; $25.00 US. Obstetrics-Gynecology Society of Singapore, National University Hospital, Lower Kent Ridge Road, Singapore 0511 Singapore. **Tel** 011 65 7724267. **(Subscription address:** Department of Obstetrics and Gynaecology, National University Hospital, Lower Kent Ridge Road, 0511 Singapore) **ED** A. P. Ariffeen Bongoo, (editor's address: 3C #06-04 Tanglin Park, Ridley Road, Singapore 1024, phone: 772-4129 (office)). **NLM** W1 SI52M. **CODEN** SJOGDE. Index available. **Bk Rev**, (Qty: 1-2). **Ad Acc. Circ:** 750 (ctrl). Documents available from BIOSIS Document Express, CASDDS. ***Continues*** *Proceedings of the Obstetrical and Gynaecological Society, Singapore, 0377-2942.*
**Desc:** Studies and editorials relevant to the practice of obstetrics and gynecology mainly from Asia and Africa in general, and Singapore and Malaysia in particular.
**Ind/Abst** Biol. Abstr. (1986-); Chem. Abstr.; Life Sci. Collect.

FR/0766-1193
**SOINS. GYNECOLOGIE, OBSTETRIQUE, PUERICULTURE, PEDIATRIE.** [Soins, Gynecol. obstet. pueric. pediatr.]. **VFOAT** Gynecologie, Obstetrique, Puericulture, Pediatrie. 7 (Nov. 1981)-. Academic Scholarly Publication. French. Ten times a year. 518.00F. OPISA, 33 Chemin des Hutins, 1247 Anieres Geneva Switzerland. **Tel** 011 41 22 7512347. **(Subscription address:** Canada/ 2307 rue Frontenac, Montreal Quebec H2K 2Z8**)** **UDC** 618. **NLM** W1 SO8862S. Documents available from CASDDS. ***Continues*** *Soins. Gynecologie, Obstetrique, Puericulture, 0151-6655.*
**Ind/Abst** Chem. Abstr.; Int. Nurs. Index.

FR
**SOINS. GYNECOLOGIE PUERICULTRICE.** French. mo (10 issues). 367.29F France; 375.00F other. Intereditions, 7 rue de L Laromiguiere, 75005 Paris France. **Tel** 011 33 1 46342160.

CN/0700-8279
**SPOKESWOMAN FOR ABORTION LAW REPEAL.** **See** Law.

US/0276-6787
**STANDARDS FOR OBSTETRIC, GYNECOLOGIC, AND NEONATAL NURSING.** [Stand. obstet. gynecol. neonatal nurs.]. English. ir. $10.00. Nurses Association of the American College of Obstetrics and Gynecology, 409 12th Street SW, Washington DC 20024-2191. **Tel** (202)638-0026.
**Ind/Abst** Abstr. Clin. Care Guidel.

IE/0924-8447
**SUPPLEMENT TO INTERNATIONAL JOURNAL OF GYNECOLOGY AND OBSTETRICS.** [Suppl. Int. j. gynecol. obstet.]. **VFOAT** International Journal of Gynecology and Obstetrics. Supplement. Suppl. 1 (1989)-. Monographic series. English. ir. Price varies per volume. Photoart Printers Pte Ltd., Blk 3, 10 02 Pasir Panjang Road, Singapore 0511. **Tel** 011 65 273 0256. **NLM** W1; IN766TA.
**Ind/Abst** Helminthol. Abstr. (1991-); Index Med. (1989); Nutr. Abstr. Rev., Ser. A, Hum. Exp.

US/0039-6087
**SURGERY, GYNECOLOGY & OBSTETRICS.** ***Title Change.*** **See** Medical Science and Technology-Surgery.

US/0743-6173
**SURGICAL STERILIZATION SURVEILLANCE. TUBAL STERILIZATION AND HYSTERECTOMY IN WOMEN AGED 15-44.** **VFOAT** Tubal Sterilization and Hysterectomy in Women Aged 15-44. 1979/1980-. English. be. US Department of Health and Human Services, 200 Independence Avenue Southwest, Washington DC 20201. **LC** RG138; .S974. **DD** 363.9/7/0973. **UDC** 618.14-089. available on microfiche (Vols. for (1980-) distributed to depository libraries). ***Formed by the union of*** *Centers for Disease Control Surgical Sterilization Surveillance. Hysterectomy in Women Aged 15-44, 0277-3430* ***and*** *Tubal Sterilization, 0743-6165.*
**Ind/Abst** Curr. Lit. Fam. Plan.

●US/1060-5681
**TELINDE'S OPERATIVE GYNECOLOGY UPDATES.** [TeLinde's oper. gynecol. updates]. (1992)-. Periodical. English. mo. $125.00. J.B. Lippincott Company, 227 East Washington Square, Philadelphia PA 19106-3780. **Tel** (215)238-4200 or 4454, FAX (215)238-4227. **DD** 618. **NLM** W1; TE298R.

SP
**TEMAS DE GINECOLOGIA DE NORTEAMERICA.** Spanish. qt. 17384.00ptas. McGraw Hill Publishing Company, Inc., 1221 Avenue of the Americas, New York NY 10020. **Tel** (212)512-6410, (800)525-5003, FAX (212)512-6111.

CN/1195-4078
**THERAPEUTIC ABORTIONS - CANADIAN CENTRE FOR HEALTH INFORMATION.** (THERAPEUTIC ABORTIONS / STATISTICS CANADA, CANADIAN CENTRE FOR HEALTH INFORMATION / LES AVORTEMENTS THERAPEUTIQUES / STATISTIQUE CANADA, CENTRE CANADIEN D'INFORMATION SUR LA SANTE.). [Ther. abort. - Can. Cent. Health Inf.]. **Added/Corp** Canadian Centre for Health Information. **VFOAT** Avortements Therapeutiques. (1991)-. Statistical Publication. English (French). an. Statistics Canada, Publications Sales & Services, Main Building Room 1710, Ottawa Ontario K1A 0T6 Canada. **Tel** (613)951-5078, (800)267-6677, FAX (613)951-1584, telex 053-3585. **DD** 363.4/6/09711021. ***Continues*** *Health Reports. Supplement. Therapeutic Abortions, 1180-3061.*

SP/0040-8867
**TOKO-GINECOLOGIA PRACTICA.** [Toko-Ginecol. pract.]. (1936)-. Periodical. Spanish. Ten times a year. $37.32 Spain; $69.00 other Europe; $79.00 other. Editorial Garsi SA, Juan Bravo 46, 28006 Madrid, Spain. **Tel** 011 34 1 4021212, telex 98358 GARSI E. **UDC** 618.

US/0892-1962
**TRANSACTIONS OF THE AMERICAN GYNECOLOGICAL AND OBSTETRICAL SOCIETY.** [Trans. Am. Gynecol. Obstet. Soc.]. **Main/Corp** American Gynecological and Obstetrical Society. Vol. 1 (1982)-. Monographic series. English. ir. Price varies per volume. Mosby Year Book Inc., 11830 Westline Industrial Drive, St Louis MO 63146. **Tel** (800)325-4177, (314)872-8370, FAX (314)432-1380, telex 44-2402. **LC** RG1; .A42a. **DD** 618/.05. **NLM** W1; TR224V. **Circ:** 320. ***Continues*** *American Gynecological Society. Transactions of the American Gynecological Society, American Association of Obstetricians and Gynecologists, 0738-6257.*
**Desc:** A published record of the annual meeting of the American Gynecological and Obstetrical Society, including scientific papers presented and meeting minutes.

US/0078-7442
**TRANSACTIONS OF THE PACIFIC COAST OBSTETRICAL AND GYNECOLOGICAL SOCIETY.** [Trans. Pac. Coast Obstet. Gynecol. Soc.]. **Main/Corp** Pacific Coast Obstetrical and Gynecological Society. Vol. 14 (1944/46)-. English. an. $33.50. Mosby Year Book Inc., 11830 Westline Industrial Drive, St Louis MO 63146. **Tel** (800)325-4177, (314)872-8370, FAX (314)432-1380, telex 44-2402. **LC** RG1; .P3. **DD** 618/.05. **NLM** W1 TR227A. ***Continues*** *Pacific Coast Society of Obstetrics and Gynecology. Transactions.*
**Ind/Abst** Energy Res. Abstr.

IT/0393-7801
**ULTRASONICA.** (ULTRASONICA : ORGANO UFFICIALE DI SOCIETA ITALIANA DI ECOGRAFIA OSTETRICO-GINECOLOGICA ... ET AL.). [Ultrasonica]. **Added/Corp** Societa Italiana di Ecografia Ostetrico-Ginecologica. Vol. 2, No. 1-2 (Jan./June 1987)-. Periodical. Italian (summaries and/or abstracts in English). qt. L60000 Italy; $42.64 other. CIC Edizioni Internazionali, Via L Spallanzani 11, 00161 Rome Italy. **Tel** 011 39 6 841-2673, FAX 011 39 6 844-3365, telex 622099 CIC I. **ED** Andrea Salvati. **NLM** W1; UL745E. **Circ:** 2,000. available on videocassette. ***Continues*** *Ultrasuoni in Ostetricia e Ginecologia, 0392-7741.*

UK/0960-7692
**ULTRASOUND IN OBSTETRICS AND GYNAECOLOGY.** **Added/Corp** International Society of Ultrasound in Obstetrics and Gynecology. **VFOAT** Ultrasound in Obstetrics and Gynecology. Vol.1, No. 1 (Jan. 1991)-. Periodical. English. bm. £150.00 (institutions), £105.00 (individuals). Parthenon Publishing, Casterton Hall Carnforth, Lancashire LA6 2LA England. **Tel** 011 44 5242 72084, FAX 44-5242-71587. **NLM** W1; UL751G. Documents available from The Genuine Article.
**Ind/Abst** Curr. Contents Clin. Med.; Res. Alert [Select. Cov.]; SCISEARCH; Soc. Sci. Cit. Index [Select. Cov.].

●US/1066-2944
**VOICES (WASHINGTON, D.C.).** **See** Medical Science and Technology-Nursing.

CN/0710-5479
**VOIE LACTEE.** (LA VOIE LACTEE.). [Voie lactee]. **Added/Corp** Ligue Internationale de la Leche. Ligue la Leche du Canada. Vol. 1, No. 1 (Jan./Feb. 1978)-. Periodical. French. bm. $10.00 Canada; $12.00 other. Ligue la Leche, CP 874, Montreal Quebec H4L 4W3 Canada. **Tel** (514)327-6714, FAX (514)747-6667. **ED** Denise Gingras. **DD** 649/.3. **Bk Rev**, (Qty: 5). **Ad Acc. Circ:** 1,100.
**Desc:** Breastfeeding information.

US/0363-0242
**WOMEN & HEALTH.** [Women health]. **Added/Corp** State University of New York/College at Old Westbury. Biological Sciences Program. **VAT** Women and Health. Vol. 1 (Jan./Feb. 1976)-. Academic Scholarly Publication. English. qt (4 issues). $225.00 US; $315.00 other. The Haworth Press Inc, 10 Alice Street, Binghamton NY 13904-1580. **Tel** (607)722-5857, (800)3-HAWORTH, FAX (607)722-1424. **ED** Jeanne Stellman (editor's address: 600 West 168th Street, New York, NY 10032). **LC** RG1; .W64. **DD** 613/.04/24405. **NLM** W1 WO478. **CODEN** WOHEDI. **Bk Rev. Ad Acc. Pr Rev. Acid Free. Circ:** 800. available on microfilm and microfiche from University Microfilms International (UMI). Documents available from The Genuine Article, BIOSIS Document Express, UMI Article Clearinghouse, Haworth Document Delivery Service.
**Desc:** Widely accepted as the standard reference source for specialists in the field. Contains information that is useful for all women - consumers as well as providers of health care.
**Ind/Abst** Abstr. Soc. Gerontol. (?-?); Acad. Search (July 1993-); Altern. Press Index; Biol. Abstr.; Biol. Dig.; Chicano Index; Commun. Abstr.; Cumul. Index Nurs. Allied Health Lit.; Curr. Contents Soc. Behav. Sci.; Curr. Lit. Fam. Plan. (19??-199?); EMBASE; Expand. Acad. Index (1988-); Gen. Sci. Index; Gen. Sci. Source (Jul. 1993-); Health Index (1989-); Health Period. Database; Health Plan. Adminis.; Health Ref. Cent. (Jan. 1989-) [Full Cov.]; Health Source (Jul. 1993-); Hospit. Health Admin. Index; Index Med.; INFO-SOUTH Abstr.; Mag. Search; Multicult. Educ. Abstr.; Newsp. Period. Abstr. (1991-); Nutr. Res. Newsl.; PAIS Int. Print; Psychol. Abstr. (1979-); PsycINFO; PsycLit; Res. Alert [Full Cov.]; Sage Fam. Stud. Abstr.; Soc. Plann. Policy Dev. Abstr.; Soc. Sci. Source (Jul. 1993-); Soc. Sci. Cit. Index [Full Cov.]; Soc. Sci. Index; Soc. Sci. Index Fulltext (1988-) [Full Txt.]; Soc. Work Abstr. (Summer 1987) [Select. Cov.]; Sociol. Abstr.; SportSearch; Stud. Women Abstr.; Trop. Dis. Bull.; Women Stud. Abstr.

●US/1070-308X
**WOMEN'S HEALTH NURSING SCAN (1993).** **See** Medical Science and Technology-Nursing.

US/8756-7849
**WOMEN'S HEALTH UPDATE.** ***Ceased.*** [Women's health update]. Vol. 1, No. 1 (Jan./Feb. 1985)-Vol. 1, No. 3 (1985). Periodical. English. bm. Pat Camillo, PO Box 303, Hurley NY 12443. **DD** 618. **NLM** ZWP 100; W872.

US/1071-9075
**WORKSHOPS FOR LEGAL ASSISTANTS. LITIGATION, LEGAL RESEARCH AND WRITING, ENVIRONMENTAL LAW AND TOXIC TORT LITIGATION.** [Workshops legal assist., Litig. Legal res. writ. Environ. law toxic tortlitig.]. **Added/Corp** Practising Law Institute. **VFOAT** Litigation, Legal Research and Writing, Environmental Law and Toxic Tort litigation; Litigation; Legal Research and Writing; Environmental Law and Toxic Tort Litigation. (1991)-. English. Practising Law Institute, 810 Seventh Avenue, New York NY 10019-5818. **Tel** (212)765-5700, FAX (212)581-4670 general correspondence, (212)265-4742 orders and billing inquiries. **DD** 346. ***Continues in part*** *Legal Assistants, 0730-3068.*

US/0892-614X
**WORLD MEDICAL REVIEWS IN PERINATOLOGY.** **See** Medical Science and Technology-Pediatrics.

US/1044-4890
**YEAR BOOK OF NEONATAL AND PERINATAL MEDICINE, THE.** [Year book neonatal perinat. med.]. **Added/Corp** Year Book Medical Publishers. **VFOAT** Yearbook of Neonatal and Perinatal Medicine; Neonatal and Perinatal Medicine. (1989)-. English. an. $59.95. Mosby Year Book Inc., 11830 Westline Industrial Drive, St Louis MO 63146. **Tel** (800)325-4177, (314)872-8370, FAX (314)432-1380, telex 44-2402. **LC** RG631; .Y43. **DD** 618.3/2/005. **NLM** W1; YE1994H. ***Continues*** *Year Book of Perinatal/Neonatal Medicine, 8756-5005.*

US/0084-3911
**YEAR BOOK OF OBSTETRICS AND GYNECOLOGY, THE.** [Year book obstet gynecol.]. (1933)-. English (Spanish). an. $69.95. Mosby Year Book Inc., 11830 Westline Industrial Drive, St Louis MO 63146. **Tel** (800)325-4177, (314)872-8370, FAX (314)432-1380, telex 44-2402. **ED** Daniel R. Mishell, Thomas H. Kirschbaum, and C. Paul Morrow. **LC** RG26; .Y4. **DD** 610.58 S. **UDC** 618(058). **NLM** W1 YE282. **CODEN** YOBGAD. Documents available from BIOSIS Document Express. ***Continues*** *Obstetrics. Gynecology.*
**Ind/Abst** Biol. Abstr. (1985-).

GW/0300-967X
**ZEITSCHRIFT FUER GEBURTSHILFE UND PERINATOLOGIE.** [Z. geburtshilfe perinatol.]. **VFOAT** Geburtshilfe und Perinatologie. (1972)-. Academic Scholarly Publication. German (summaries and/or abstracts in English). bm. $234.00. Ferdinand Enke Verlag, Ruedigerstrasse 14, D-70469 Stuttgart Germany. **Tel** 011 49 711 8931124, 011 49 711 893123. **(Subscription address:** Thieme Medical Publishers Inc., 381 Park Avenue South, New York NY 10016.**)** **LC** RG1; .G35. **DD** 618.2/005. **NLM** W1 ZE357C. **CODEN** ZGPRA3. **[CCC]. Pr Rev.** available on microfilm from University Microfilms International (UMI). Documents available from The Genuine Article, BIOSIS Document Express, CASDDS, ADONIS. ***Continues*** *Zeitschrift fur Geburtshilfe und Gynakologie.*
**Ind/Abst** ADONIS; Biol. Abstr.; Chem. Abstr.; Curr. Contents Clin. Med.; EMBASE; Energy Res. Abstr. (May 1980-); Index Med.; Life Sci. Collect.; Res. Alert [Full Cov.]; Sci. Cit. Index; SCISEARCH.

GW/0044-4197
**ZENTRALBLATT FUER GYNAKOLOGIE.** [Zentralbl. gynaekol.]. **Added/Corp** Gesellschaft fuer Gynakologie und Geburtshilfe der DDR. Vol. 27 (Jan. 1903)-. Academic Scholarly Publication. German (summaries and/or abstracts in English and German). sm (24 issues). DM306.00. Johann Ambrosius Barth, Prager Strasse 16 B, D 04103 Leipzig Germany. **Tel** 011 49 341 7137570. **(Subscription address:** Huethig Publishing Inc., 29 Macintosh Drive, Oxford CT 06478.**)** **NLM** W1 ZE777N. **CODEN** ZEGYAX. **Pr Rev.** available on microfilm from University Microfilms International (UMI). Documents available from BIOSIS Document Express, CASDDS. ***Continues*** *Central Blatt fur Gynakologie.*
**Ind/Abst** Biol. Abstr.; Chem. Abstr.; EMBASE; Energy Res. Abstr.; Index Med.; Life Sci. Collect.; Protozoolog. Abstr.

## HEMATOLOGY

US/8756-6095
**AABB NEWS BRIEFS.** (AAB NEWS BRIEFS / AMERICAN ASSOCIATION OF BLOOD BANKS.). [AABB news briefs]. **Added/Corp** American Association of Blood Banks. **VFOAT** News Briefs. **VAT** American Association of Blood Banks News Briefs. (19??)-. Periodical. English. mo (11 issues). Comes with American Association of Blood Banks membership. American Association of Blood Banks, 8101 Glenbrook Road, Bethesda MD 20814. **Tel** (301)907-6977. **ED** Jackie Campbell. **DD** 616. **Ad Acc. Circ:** 10,000.
**Desc:** Blood banking and transfusion therapy news and information regarding technical and administrative aspects, government regulation, and continuing education as well as research.

SZ/0001-5792
**ACTA HAEMATOLOGICA.** [Acta haematol.]. **Added/Corp** International Society of Hematology. European Division. European Society of Haematology. Vol. 1 (1948)-. Academic Scholarly Publication. English (French and German; summaries and/or abstracts in French and German). Eight times a year. $532.00. S. Karger AG, Allschwilerstrasse 10, PO Box - Postfach - Case Postale, CH-4009 Basel Switzerland. **Tel** 011 41 61 306-1111, FAX 011 41 61 306-1234, telex CH 962 652. **ED** B Ramot, I Ben-Bassat. **NLM** W1 AC807. **CODEN** ACHAAH. **[CCC].** cum. index. **Bk Rev. Ad Acc. Pr Rev.** available on microfilm from University Microfilms International (UMI). Documents available from The Genuine Article, BIOSIS Document Express, CASDDS.
**Desc:** Features balanced, wide-ranging coverage of current hematology research. A wealth of information on such problems as anemia, leukemia, lymphoma, multiple myeloma, hereditary disorders and blood coagulation is contained in basic and clinical papers. In particular, the journal has established itself as a special platform for case reports of practical value to the clinical hematologist. These are supplemented by short communications, reviews and correspondence as well as occasional special issues devoted to 'hot topics' in hematology.
**Ind/Abst** Biol. Abstr.; Chem. Abstr.; Curr. Contents Clin.

Med.; Curr. Contents Life Sci.; EMBASE; Genet. Abstr.; Health Plan. Adminis.; Immunol. Abstr.; Index Med.; Index Vet.; Nutr. Abstr. Rev., Ser. B, Live Feeds and Feed.; Nutr. Abstr. Rev., Ser. A, Hum. Exp.; Oncog. Growth Factors Abstr.; Life Sci. Collect.; Ref. Upd. Basic Ed.; Ref. Upd. Clinical Ed.; Ref. Upd. Deluxe Ed.; Res. Alert [Full Cov.]; Rev. Med. Vet. Mycology; Sci. Cit. Index; SCISEARCH; Vet. Bull.

GW/0930-9535
**ADVANCES IN FORENSIC HAEMOGENETICS.** [Adv. forensic haemogenet.]. **Main/Corp** Society for Forensic Haemogenetics. Congress. (1986)-. English. an. DM68.00 (latest volume). Springer-Verlag GmbH & Company KG, Heidelberger Platz 3, D 14197 Berlin Germany. **Tel** 011 49 30 8207223, FAX 011 49 30 8214091, telex 183 319 SPBLN D. **(Subscription address:** Springer Verlag New York Inc. / for North America, 44 Hartz Way, Secaucus NJ 07096.**) LC** RA1061; .S63a. **DD** 612/.1182. **NLM** W1; AD603. **CODEN** AFHAE8. Documents available from BIOSIS Document Express, CASDDS.
**Ind/Abst** Biol. Abstr.; Chem. Abstr.

US/0887-6193
**ADVANCES IN LOW-TEMPERATURE PLASMA CHEMISTRY, TECHNOLOGY, APPLICATIONS.** [Adv. low-temp. plasma chem. technol. appl.]. **VFOAT** Advances in Low Temperature Plasma Chemistry, Technology, Applications. Vol. 1 (1984)-. Periodical. English. Technomic Publishing Company, Inc., 851 New Holland Avenue, Box 3535, Lancaster PA 17604. **Tel** (717)291-5609, (800)233-9936, FAX (717)295-4538. **LC** QD581; .A335. **DD** 541/.0424. **CODEN** ALPAEM. Documents available from CASDDS.
**Ind/Abst** Chem. Abstr.

US/0361-8609
**AMERICAN JOURNAL OF HEMATOLOGY.** [Am. j. hematol.]. Vol. 1 (1976)-. Periodical. English. mo. $1,092.00 US; $1,121.00 Canada and Mexico; $1,257.00 other. John Wiley & Sons, Inc., 605 Third Avenue, New York NY 10158-0012. **Tel** (212)850-6000, (212)850-6645, FAX (212)850-6088, telex 12-7063. **(Subscription address:** John Wiley & Sons / England, Baffins Lane, Chichester, West Sussex PO19 1UD England.**) ED** Ananda S. Prasad. **LC** QP91; .A55. **DD** 616.1/5/05. **NLM** W1 AM452J. **CODEN** AJHEDD. **[CCC]. Pr Rev.** Documents available from The Genuine Article, BIOSIS Document Express, CASDDS, ADONIS.
**Desc:** Provides broad coverage of both human and animal hematologic topics and publishes contributions from investigators and clinicians in hematology and related areas such as immunology, blood banking, genetics, chemotherapy, and cell biology.
**Ind/Abst** ADONIS; Biol. Abstr.; Chem. Abstr.; CSA Neuro. Abstr. (?-?); Curr. Contents Life Sci.; EMBASE; Energy Res. Abstr. (Oct. 1978-); Genet. Abstr.; Immunol. Abstr.; Index Med.; INIS Atomindex [Micro.]; Nutr. Abstr. Rev., Ser. B, Live Feeds and Feed.; Nutr. Abstr. Rev., Ser. A, Hum. Exp.; Oncog. Growth Factors Abstr.; Life Sci. Collect.; Protozoolog. Abstr.; Ref. Upd. Basic Ed.; Ref. Upd. Clinical Ed.; Ref. Upd. Deluxe Ed.; Res. Alert [Full Cov.]; Rev. Med. Vet. Mycology; Sci. Cit. Index; SCISEARCH; Soc. Sci. Cit. Index [Select. Cov.]; SportSearch; Trop. Dis. Bull.; Virol. AIDS Abstr.

GW/0939-5555
**ANNALS OF HEMATOLOGY. Added/Corp** Deutsche Gesellschaft fur Hamatologie und Onkologie. Vol. 62, No. 1 (Feb. 1991)-. Academic Scholarly Publication. English. mo. DM1320.00. Springer-Verlag GmbH & Company KG, Heidelberger Platz 3, D 14197 Berlin Germany. **Tel** 011 49 30 8207223, FAX 011 49 30 8214091, telex 183 319 SPBLN D. **(Subscription address:** Springer Verlag New York Inc. / for North America, 44 Hartz Way, Secaucus NJ 07096.**) ED** R Willemze. **NLM** W1; AN592. **CODEN** ANHEE8. **[CCC].** available on microfilm from University Microfilms International (UMI). Documents available from The Genuine Article, BIOSIS Document Express, CASDDS. ***Continues*** *Blut, 0006-5242.*
**Desc:** Continues to be a journal for general hematologists. Covers the whole spectrum of clinical and experimental hematology, hemostasiology, immunohematology and blood transfusion, including the diagnosis and treatment of hematopoietic and lymphatic neoplasias and of bone marrow transplantation.
**Ind/Abst** Biol. Abstr. (1991-); Chem. Abstr. (1991-); Curr. Contents Clin. Med.; Curr. Contents Life Sci.; EMBASE; Health Plan. Adminis.; Index Med. (1991-); Ref. Upd. Deluxe Ed.; Res. Alert [Full Cov.]; Sci. Cit. Index; SCISEARCH.

UK/0950-3536
**BAILLIERE'S CLINICAL HAEMATOLOGY.** [Bailliere's clin. haematol.]. **VFOAT** Clinical Haematology; Haematology. Vol. 1, No. 1 (March 1987)-. Periodical. English. qt (4 issues). £94.00 (institution). Harcourt Brace & Company Ltd., Foots Cray, High Street, Sidcup Kent DA14 5HP England. **Tel** 011 44 81 300 3322, FAX 011 44 81 309 0807. **(Subscription address:** W. B. Saunders Company / North America Subscriptions, c/o Periodicals, 6277 Sea Harbour Drive, 4th Floor, Orlando FL 32887.**) NLM** W1; BA46EG. Documents available from The Genuine Article. ***Continues in part*** *Clinics in Haematology, 0308-2261.*
**Ind/Abst** EMBASE; Health Plan. Adminis.; Hum. Genome Abstr.; Index Med. (1987-); Res. Alert [Full Cov.]; Sci. Cit. Index.

UK
**BERGAMO SPRING CONFERENCES ON HAEMATOLOGY.** Monographic series. English. Price varies per volume. **NLM** W1; BE589D.

YU/0350-2023
**BILTEN ZA HEMATOLOGIJU I TRANSFUZIJU.** [Bilt. hematol. transfuz.]. **Added/Corp** Udruzenje Hematologa i Transfuziologa Jugoslavije. Zavod za Transfuziju Krvi SRS. (1973)-. Periodical. Serbo-Croatian (Roman) (English; summaries and/or abstracts in English and German). Three times a year. 100.00 Din (individuals), 200.00 Din (institutions). Zavod za Transfuziju Krvi, Belgradesvetsavska 39, Belgrad Yugoslavia. **Tel** 0114442 651, telex ZTK SRS 72997. **ED** Stanoje Stefanovic, M Ristic, Radmila Bakiaja, P Cvetkovic, G Bogdanovic. **NLM** W1 BI618L. **Bk Rev. Ad Acc. Pr Rev. Circ:** 2,000 (ctrl). ***Supersedes*** *Bilten Transfuzije, 0523-6150.*
**Desc:** Yugoslavian journal for transfusion and hematology.
**Ind/Abst** Index Med.

SP/0210-895X
**BIOLOGIA & CLINICA HEMATOLOGICA.** [Biol. clin. hematol.]. **Added/Corp** Hospital de la Santa Cruz y San Pablo. Servicio de Hematologia. Hospital de la Santa Cruz y San Pablo. Unidad de Hematologia Clinica. Hospital de la Santa Cruz y San Pablo. Servicio de Hemoterapia. Universidad Autonoma de Barcelona. Unidad Docente. **VAT** Biologia y Clinica Hematologica. Vol. 1 (Jan./March 1979)-. Academic Scholarly Publication. Spanish (English; summaries and/or abstracts in English). qt. 4600.00ptas. Springer Verlag Iberica SA, Avinguda Diagonal 468 4 C, 08006 Barcelona Spain. **Tel** 011 34 3 4157620, 011 34 3 4157621. **(Subscription address:** Springer Verlag New York Inc. / for North America, 44 Hartz Way, Secaucus NJ 07096.**) ED** Manuel Sanchez Moya. **NLM** W1 BI671T. **CODEN** BCHED9. **Bk Rev. Ad Acc. Circ:** 1,500 (ctrl). Documents available from CASDDS.
**Ind/Abst** Chem. Abstr.; EMBASE; Indice Med. Esp.

US/0006-4971
**BLOOD.** [Blood]. Vol. 1 (Jan. 1946)-. Academic Scholarly Publication. English. sm (24 issues). $366.00 (individual), $430.00 (institution) US; $445.00 (individual), $497.00 (institution) other. W.B. Saunders Company, A Subsidiary of Harcourt Brace Jovanovich, Inc., The Curtis Center/Suite 300, Independence Square West, Philadelphia PA 19106-3399. **Tel** (215)238-7800 or, 5587, FAX (215)238-7883, telex 173146. **(Subscription address:** W. B. Saunders Company / North America Subscriptions, c/o Periodicals, 6277 Sea Harbour Drive, 4th Floor, Orlando FL 32887.**) ED** Arthur W. Nienhuis. **LC** RB145; .B56. **DD** 616. **NLM** W1 BL661. **CODEN** BLOOAW. **[CCC].** Index available (bound in issue). **Pr Rev.** Documents available from The Genuine Article, BIOSIS Document Express, CASDDS.
**Desc:** Provides an international forum for the publication of original articles describing basic laboratory and clinical investigations encompassed in the discipline of hematology.
**Ind/Abst** Abr. Index Med.; AgBiotech News Inf.; Anim. Breed. Abstr.; Biol. Abstr.; Chem. Abstr.; CSA Neuro. Abstr. (?-?); Curr. Aware. Biol. Sci., CABS; Curr. Biotechnol.; Curr. Contents Clin. Med.; Curr. Contents Life Sci.; Dairy Sci. Abstr.; EMBASE; Energy Res. Abstr.; Genet. Abstr.; Health Plan. Adminis.; Immunol. Abstr.; Index Med.; Index Vet.; INIS Atomindex [Micro.]; Int. Aerosp. Abstr.; Iowa Drug Inf. Serv.; Microbiol. Abstr. Sect. C; Mod. Med.; Nutr. Abstr. Rev., Ser. B, Live Feeds and Feed.; Nutr. Abstr. Rev., Ser. A, Hum. Exp.; Oncog. Growth Factors Abstr.; Life Sci. Collect.; PESTDOC; Physic. Medline Plus; Pig News Inf.; Protozoolog. Abstr.; Ref. Upd. Basic Ed.; Ref. Upd. Clinical Ed.; Ref. Upd. Deluxe Ed.; Res. Alert [Full Cov.]; Rev. Med. Vet. Mycology; Sci. Cit. Index; SCISEARCH; Small Anim. Abstr. Bibliogr.; Soc. Sci. Cit. Index [Select. Cov.]; Vet. Bull.; Trop. Dis. Bull.; Virol. AIDS Abstr.

US/0747-2420
**BLOOD BANK WEEK.** (BLOOD BANK WEEK / AMERICAN ASSOCIATION OF BLOOD BANKS.). [Blood bank week]. **Added/Corp** American Association of Blood Banks. **VFOAT** AABB Blood Bank Week. Vol. 1, No. 1 (Mar. 9, 1984)-. Periodical. English. ir (48 issues). $98.00 (AABB members), $128.00 (non-members). American Association of Blood Banks, 8101 Glenbrook Road, Bethesda MD 20814. **Tel** (301)907-6977. **ED** Eileen R. Church. **DD** 362. **NLM** W1; BL649. **Ad Acc. Circ:** 1,500. ***Continues*** *Federal Register Excerpts Program.*
**Desc:** Newsletter concerning events in blood banking and transfusion medicine, including scientific, administrative and sociopolitical news. Also included are scientific references.

US
**BLOOD CELL BIOCHEMISTRY.** Vol. 1 (1991)-. Monographic series. English. ir. Price varies per volume. Plenum Press, 233 Spring Street, New York NY 10013-1578. **Tel** (212)620-8000, (800)221-9369, FAX (212)463-0742, (212)807-1047, telex 23/421139. **ED** J.R. Harris (editor's address: University of Mainz, Germany). **NLM** W1; BL649L. ***Continues in part*** *Sub-Cellular Biochemistry, 0306-0225.*
**Desc:** Devoted to all aspects of blood cell biochemistry, development, immunology, and ultrastructure.

GW
**BLOOD CELLS (1978).** ***Title Change.*** (BLOOD CELLS.). Vol. 4 (1978)-Vol. 20 (1994). Periodical. English. Three times a year. Springer-Verlag New York Inc., 175 5th Avenue, New York NY 10010. **Tel** (212)460-1500, telex 232 235 SPB UR. **(Subscription address:** Springer Verlag New York Inc. / for North America, 44 Hartz Way, Secaucus NJ 07096.**) ED** B. S. Bull and D. Orlic. Documents available from The Genuine Article, CASDDS, ADONIS. ***Continues in part*** *Nouvelle Revue Francaise d'Hematologie; Blood Cells.* ***Continued by*** *Blood Cells, Molecules and Diseases.*
**Desc:** Indispensable to researchers involved in physiology, ultrastructure, immunology, and biophysics of blood cells. The journal also appeals to the hematologist who observes the cellular components of the blood with admiration and curiosity, and is creative in his methods of problem-solving.
**Ind/Abst** ADONIS; Chem. Abstr.; Curr. Aware. Biol. Sci., CABS; Curr. Contents Life Sci.; EMBASE; Immunol. Abstr.; Index Med.; Protozoolog. Abstr.; Ref. Upd. Basic Ed.; Ref. Upd. Deluxe Ed.; Res. Alert [Full Cov.]; Sci. Cit. Index; SCISEARCH.

SZ/0253-5068
**BLOOD PURIFICATION.** [Blood purif.]. **Added/Corp** International Society of Hemofiltration. (Sept. 1983)-. Academic Scholarly Publication. English. bm (6 issues). $296.00. S. Karger AG, Allschwilerstrasse 10, PO Box - Postfach - Case Postale, CH-4009 Basel Switzerland. **Tel** 011 41 61 306-1111, FAX 011 41 61 306-1234, telex CH 962 652. **ED** LW Henderson, TA Golper, KML Loinissen. **NLM** W1; BL661G. **CODEN** BLPUDO. **[CCC]. Ad Acc. Pr Rev.** available in microform. Documents available from The Genuine Article, BIOSIS Document Express, CASDDS.
**Desc:** Practical information on hemodialysis, hemofiltration, peritoneal dialysis and plasma filtration is featured in this journal. Recognizing the critical importance of equipment and procedures, particular emphasis has been placed on reports, drawn from a wide range of fields, describing technical advances and improvements in methodology. Papers reflect the search for cost-effective solutions which increase not only patient survival but also comfort through prevention or correction of undesirable effects. Advances in vascular access and blood anti-coagulation as well as problems associated with exposure of blood to foreign surfaces also receive attention.
**Ind/Abst** Biol. Abstr.; Chem. Abstr. (1983-); Curr. Contents Clin. Med.; EMBASE; Health Plan. Adminis.; Index Med. (Vol. 3, No. 1, 1985-); Life Sci. Collect.; Ref. Upd. Deluxe Ed.; Res. Alert [Full Cov.]; SCISEARCH.

UK/0268-960X
**BLOOD REVIEWS.** [Blood rev.]. Vol. 1, No. 1 (March 1987)-. Periodical. English. Four times a year. £125.00 Europe; £126.00 Other (Institution). Churchill Livingstone, 1-3 Baxter's Place, Leith Walk, Edinburgh EH1 3AF Scotland. **Tel** 011 44 31 556 2424, FAX 011 44 31 558 1278, telex 727511. **(Subscription address:** Maruzen Company Ltd., PO Box 5050, Import & Export Department, Tokyo 100 31 Japan.**) ED** D W Golde and D Linch. **NLM** W1; BL661L. **CODEN** BLOREB. **[CCC]. Pr Rev.** available on microfilm from University Microfilms International (UMI). Documents available from The Genuine Article, BIOSIS Document Express.
**Desc:** Provides comprehensive coverage of all the branches of haematology - diagnosis, clinical management, routine laboratory practice, transfusion serology, haemostasis, pharmacology and assessments of both basic and clinical research.
**Ind/Abst** Biol. Abstr. (1987-); Curr. Aware. Biol. Sci., CABS; Curr. Contents Life Sci.; EMBASE; Health Plan. Adminis.; Index Med. (Vol. 1, No. 1, 1987-); Ref. Upd. Deluxe Ed.; Res. Alert [Full Cov.]; Sci. Cit. Index; SCISEARCH; Trop. Dis. Bull.

II/0006-5005
**BLOOD THERAPY JOURNAL INTERNATIONAL.** [Blood ther. j., Int.]. Vol. 1, No. 1 (Jan. 1980)-. Periodical. English. bm. $4.50 (single issue). BTJ Verlag and Scientific News Service, 4 Pusa Road, PO Box 2544, New Delhi 110005 India. **NLM** W1 BL6615B. ***Continues*** *Blood Therapy Journal.*

●US/1065-6073
**BLOOD WEEKLY.** (BLOOD WEEKLY.). [Blood wkly.]. (1993)-. Periodical. English. wk (48 issues). $995.00 US, Canada and Mexico; $1,195.00 other. CW Henderson, PO Box 5528, Atlanta GA 30307-0528. **Tel** (404)377-8895, FAX (404)378-5411. **(Subscription address:** CW Henderson, Subscription Office, PO Box 830409, Birmingham AL 35283-0409.**) DD** 612. **[CCC].**
**Desc:** Concentrates solely on blood-related news and research. Features original reporting, research, periodical reviews and upcoming meetings. Topics include blood products and substitutes, blood-related disease, tissue transplants and more.

BL/0046-9963
**BOLETIM DO INSTITUTO ESTADUAL DE HEMATOLOGIA ARTHUR DE SEQUERIA CAVALCANTI.** [Bol. Inst. Estad. Hematol. Arthur Sequeira Cavalcanti]. Vol. 1 (Jan./June 1971)-. Bulletin. Portuguese. sa. **NLM** W1 BO163F.
**Ind/Abst** EMBASE.

UK/0007-1048
**BRITISH JOURNAL OF HAEMATOLOGY.** [Br. j. haematol.]. Vol. 1 (Jan. 1955)-. Academic Scholarly Publication. English. mo (12 issues). $463.00 US & Canada; £272.00 Europe; £299.00 other. Blackwell Scientific Publications Ltd, Marston Book Services, PO Box 87, Oxford OX2 ODT UK. **Tel** 011 44 865 791155, FAX 011 44 865 791927, telex 837 515 MARDIS G. **ED** M. Worwood. **NLM** W1 BR535. **CODEN** BJHEAL. **[CCC]. Pr Rev. Circ:** 300 (ctrl). available on microfilm and microfiche from University Microfilms International (UMI). Documents available from The Genuine Article, BIOSIS Document Express, CASDDS, ADONIS.
**Desc:** Covers clinical laboratory and experimental hematology.
**Ind/Abst** ADONIS; Anim. Breed. Abstr.; Biol. Abstr.; Chem. Abstr.; Curr. Aware. Biol. Sci., CABS; Curr. Contents Clin. Med.; Curr. Contents Life Sci.; Dairy Sci. Abstr.; EMBASE; Genet. Abstr.; Health Plan. Adminis.; Hum. Genome Abstr.; Immunol. Abstr.; Index Med.; Index Vet.; Int. Aerosp. Abstr.; Nutr. Abstr. Rev., Ser. B, Live Feeds and Feed.; Nutr. Abstr. Rev., Ser. A, Hum. Exp.; Oncog. Growth Factors Abstr.; Life Sci. Collect.; PESTDOC; Protozoolog. Abstr.; Ref. Upd. Basic Ed.; Ref. Upd. Clinical Ed.; Ref. Upd. Deluxe Ed.; Res. Alert [Full Cov.]; Rev. Med. Vet. Mycology; Sci. Cit. Index; SCISEARCH; Vet. Bull.; Trop. Dis. Bull.; Virol. AIDS Abstr.

UK/0141-9854
**CLINICAL AND LABORATORY HAEMATOLOGY.** [Clin. lab. haematol.]. Vol. 1 (1979)-. Academic Scholarly Publication. English. qt (4 issues). $289.00 US & Canada; £169.50 Europe; £186.50 other. Blackwell Scientific Publications Ltd, Marston Book Services, PO Box 87, Oxford OX2 ODT UK. **Tel** 011 44 865 791155, FAX 011 44 865 791927, telex 837 515 MARDIS G. **ED** J. M. England. **NLM** W1 CL664L. **CODEN** CLHAD3. **[CCC].** Index available. **Bk Rev. Ad Acc. Pr Rev. Circ:** 700 (ctrl). available on microfilm and microfiche from University Microfilms International (UMI). Documents available from The Genuine Article, CASDDS, ADONIS.
**Desc:** Publishes a broad spectrum of work related to the practice of hematology and blood transfusion.
**Ind/Abst** ADONIS; Chem. Abstr.; Curr. Contents Clin. Med.; EMBASE; Health Plan. Adminis.; Index Med. (1979-); Nutr. Abstr. Rev., Ser. A, Hum. Exp.; Protozoolog. Abstr.; Ref. Upd. Deluxe Ed.; Res. Alert [Full Cov.]; Rev. Med. Vet. Mycology; Sci. Cit. Index; SCISEARCH.

UK/0960-3964
**CLINICAL AND LABORATORY HAEMATOLOGY. SUPPLEMENT.** [Clin. lab. haematol., Suppl.]. (1990)-. Academic Scholarly Publication. English. sa. Blackwell Scientific Publications Ltd, Marston Book Services, PO Box 87, Oxford OX2 ODT UK. **Tel** 011 44 865 791155, FAX 011 44 865 791927, telex 837 515 MARDIS G. **DD** _a616.15.
**Ind/Abst** EMBASE.

US/0271-5198
**CLINICAL HEMORHEOLOGY.** [Clin. hemorheol.]. **Added/Corp** International Society of Biorheology. Vol. 1, No. 1 (1981)-. Academic Scholarly Publication. English. bm. $522.00 The Americas; £350.00 other. Pergamon Press, An Imprint of Elsevier Science Ltd., The Boulevard, Langford Lane, Kidlington, Oxford OX5 1GB United Kingdom. **Tel** 011 44 865 843000, 011 44 865 843699, FAX 011 44 865 843010. **(Subscription address:** Elsevier Science Ltd. Oxford Fulfillment Centre, PO Box 800, Kidlington, Oxford OX5 1DX United Kingdom.**) ED** S. Witte and J. F. Stoltz. **LC** QP105; .C57. **DD** 612/.1181. **NLM** W1 CL71F. **CODEN** CLHEDF. **[CCC]. Bk Rev. Ad Acc. Pr Rev.** available on microfilm and microfiche from University Microfilms International (UMI). Documents available from The Genuine Article, BIOSIS Document Express, CASDDS.
**Desc:** Deals with the clinical aspects of hemorheology. Includes pathogenesis, symtomatology, diagnostic methods, prophylactic and therapeutic measures. The aims of this journal are: (1) to be of service to clinical investigations and to hemorheological testing in the clinical laboratory or in blood transfusion centers, (2) to acquaint physicians and surgeons with hemorheology.
**Ind/Abst** Biol. Abstr. (1987-); Chem. Abstr.; Curr. Aware. Biol. Sci., CABS; Curr. Contents Clin. Med.; Curr. Contents Life Sci.; EMBASE; Res. Alert [Full Cov.]; Sci. Cit. Index; SCISEARCH.

US/0894-1025
**CLINICAL HEMOSTASIS REVIEW.** See Medical Science and Technology.

UK/0938-7714
**COMPARATIVE HAEMATOLOGY INTERNATIONAL.** Vol. 1, No. 1 Feb. (1991)-. Periodical. English. qt. £140.00. Springer-Verlag London Ltd., Springer House, 8 Alexandra Road Wimbledon, London SW19 7JZ England. **Tel** 011 44 81 9471280, or 9475885, FAX 011 44 81 9474651, telex 21531 SPRGB G. **(Subscription address:** North America: Springer Verlag, Journal Fulfillment Department, 44 Hartz Way, Secaucus, NJ 07096; Outside North America: Springer Verlag, Postfach 311340, D 10643 Berlin Germany**) NLM** W1; CO435J. **CODEN** CHAIEX. available on microfilm and microfiche from University Microfilms International (UMI). Documents available from The Genuine Article.
**Desc:** Publishes papers encompassing the entire spectrum of comparative haematology.
**Ind/Abst** Curr. Contents Life Sci.; Index Vet.; Res. Alert [Full Cov.]; Sci. Cit. Index; Small Anim. Abstr. Bibliogr.

US/0197-3649
**CONTEMPORARY HEMATOLOGY/ONCOLOGY.** [Contemp. hematol./oncol.]. **VAT** Contemporary Hematology, Oncology. Vol. 1 (1980)-. Academic Scholarly Publication. English. ir. Price varies per volume. Plenum Press, 233 Spring Street, New York NY 10013-1578. **Tel** (212)620-8000, (800)221-9369, FAX (212)463-0742, (212)807-1047, telex 23/421139. **ED** Albert S. Gordon, Robert Silber and Joseph LoBue. **LC** RB145; .C58. **DD** 616.1/5/005. **NLM** W1 CO769MQ. **CODEN** CHONDF. Documents available from BIOSIS Document Express, CASDDS. ***Supersedes** Year in Hematology, 0160-7014.*
**Ind/Abst** Biol. Abstr. (-1984); Chem. Abstr. (1980-1984).

US/1040-8428
**CRITICAL REVIEWS IN ONCOLOGY/HEMATOLOGY.** See Medical Science and Technology-Neoplasma, Neoplastic.

US/0739-4810
**CURRENT HEMATOLOGY AND ONCOLOGY.** [Curr. hematl. oncol.]. **Added/Corp** Fairbanks, Virgil F., 1930-. Vol. 3 (1984)-. Academic Scholarly Publication. English. an. Mosby Year Book Inc., 11830 Westline Industrial Drive, St Louis MO 63146. **Tel** (800)325-4177, (314)872-8370, FAX (314)432-1380, telex 44-2402. **LC** RC633.A1; C87. **DD** 616.1/5/005. **NLM** W1; CU788JAP. **CODEN** CHONEG. **[CCC].** Documents available from CASDDS. ***Continues** Current Hematology, 0272-085X.*
**Ind/Abst** Chem. Abstr. (1984-).

UK/0961-2246
**CURRENT MEDICAL LITERATURE. THROMBOSIS.** [Curr. med. lit., Thromb.]. (1991)-. Periodical. English. qt. £20.00 UK; $40.00 other. Current Medical Literature Ltd., 40-42 Osnaburgh Street, London NW1 3ND England. **Tel** 011 44 71 4658377, FAX 011 44 71 4658380. **(Subscription address:** Royal Society Medicine Services, 1 Wimpole Street, London W1M 8AE England.**) DD** 616.135.

●US/1065-6251
**CURRENT OPINION IN HEMATOLOGY.** [Curr. opin. hematol.]. Vol. 1, No. 1 (1993)-. Periodical. English. Six times a year. $323.95 (institutions), $159.95 (individulas). Current Science, 20 North 3rd Street, Philadelphia PA 19106. **Tel** (215)574-2266, (800)552-5866, FAX (215)574-2270. **LC** RC633.A1; C88. **DD** 616.1/5/005. **NLM** W1; CU799GDF.

SZ/0258-0330
**CURRENT STUDIES IN HEMATOLOGY AND BLOOD TRANSFUSION.** [Curr. stud. hematol. blood transfus.]. No. 52 (1986)-. Academic Scholarly Publication. English. an. 230.00F (approx. per volume). S. Karger AG, Allschwilerstrasse 10, PO Box - Postfach - Case Postale, CH-4009 Basel Switzerland. **Tel** 011 41 61 306-1111, FAX 011 41 61 306-1234, telex CH 962 652. **ED** J. Leikola, P. Lundsgaard-Hansen. **LC** UNC. **NLM** W1; CU8105. **CODEN** CSHTE8. **[CCC].** Documents available from BIOSIS Document Express, CASDDS. ***Continues** Bibliotheca Haematologica.*
**Desc:** Experimental and clinical papers, many presented at specially organized symposia, cover recent therapeutic and methodologic advances and do much to define the limitations and possibilities of specific techniques. Each volume offers well edited and stimulating material and justifies study by researchers and clinicians working in the field of hematology.
**Ind/Abst** Biol. Abstr. (1986-); Chem. Abstr.; EMBASE; Index Med. (1986-); Ref. Upd. Deluxe Ed.

US/0190-1486
**CURRENT TOPICS IN HEMATOLOGY.** [Curr. top. hematol.]. Vol. 1 (1978)-. Periodical. English. Alan R Liss, Inc., 41 East 11th Street, New York NY 10003. **LC** RB145; .C83. **DD** 616.1/5/005. **NLM** W1 CU82HN. **CODEN** CTHED3. Documents available from BIOSIS Document Express, CASDDS.
**Ind/Abst** Biol. Abstr.; Chem. Abstr.

NE/0167-8418
**DEVELOPMENTS IN HEMATOLOGY AND IMMUNOLOGY.** [Dev. hematol. immunol.]. **Added/Corp** Commission of the European Communities. (1982)-. Academic Scholarly Publication. English. ir. Price varies per volume. Kluwer Academic Publishers, Postbus 322, 3300 AH Dordrecht, The Netherlands. **Tel** 011 (31) 78 524400, FAX 011 31 78 183273, telex 20083. **LC** UNC. **NLM** W1; DE997VZK. **CODEN** DHIMDR. Documents available from BIOSIS Document Express, CASDDS. ***Continues** Developments in Hematology, 0167-448X.*
**Ind/Abst** Biol. Abstr. (1988-); Chem. Abstr.

US
**DIRECTORY FOR THE NATIONAL BLOOD EXCHANGE : A PROGRAM OF THE AMERICAN ASSOCIATION OF BLOOD BANKS.** **Main/Corp** National Blood Exchange (U.S.). **Added/Corp** American Association of Blood Banks. **VFOAT** NBE Directory for the National Blood Exchange; NBE Directory. 13th Ed. (March 1988)-. English. American Association of Blood Banks, 8101 Glenbrook Road, Bethesda MD 20814. **Tel** (301)907-6977. **NLM** WH 22; AA1 N277d. ***Continues** Directory for the National Clearinghouse Lifeline Program of the American Association of Blood Banks, 0748-7703.*

DK/0902-4441
**EUROPEAN JOURNAL OF HAEMATOLOGY.** [Eur. j. haematol.]. **VFOAT** Haematology. Vol. 38, No. 1 (Jan. 1987)-. Academic Scholarly Publication. English. Ten times a year. kr2470.00 US, Canada and Japan; kr2390.00 other. Munksgaard International Publishers Ltd, PO Box 2148, DK-1016 Copenhagen K Denmark. **Tel** 011 45 33 12 70 30, FAX 011 45 33 12 93 87, telex 19431 MUNKS DK. **ED** Inge Olsson. **NLM** W1; EU72DFC. **CODEN** EJHAEC. **[CCC].** Index available. **Bk Rev. Ad Acc. Pr Rev. Circ:** 1,400 (ctrl). Documents available from The Genuine Article, BIOSIS Document Express, CASDDS, ADONIS. ***Continues** Scandinavian Journal of Haematology.*
**Desc:** Original articles on clinical and experimental haematology and related subjects.
**Ind/Abst** ADONIS; Biol. Abstr. (1987-); Chem. Abstr. (1987-); Curr. Aware. Biol. Sci., CABS; EMBASE; Energy Res. Abstr. (1987-); Health Plan. Adminis.; Index Med. (1987-); Life Sci. Collect. (1987-); Ref. Upd. Basic Ed.; Ref. Upd. Deluxe Ed.; Res. Alert [Full Cov.]; Sci. Cit. Index; SCISEARCH.

DK/0902-4506
**EUROPEAN JOURNAL OF HAEMATOLOGY. SUPPLEMENTUM.** [Eur. j. haematol., Suppl.]. No. 47 (1987)-. Academic Scholarly Publication. English. kr2470.00 US, Canada and Japan; kr2390.00 other (comes with subscription to European Journal of Haematology). Munksgaard International Publishers Ltd, PO Box 2148, DK-1016 Copenhagen K Denmark. **Tel** 011 45 33 12 70 30, FAX 011 45 33 12 93 87, telex 19431 MUNKS DK. **NLM** W1; EU72DFE. Documents available from BIOSIS Document Express, CASDDS. ***Continues** Scandinavian Journal of Haematology. Supplementum.*
**Ind/Abst** Biol. Abstr. (1987-); Chem. Abstr. (1987-); EMBASE; Energy Res. Abstr. (1987-); Health Plan. Adminis.; Index Med. (1987-); Life Sci. Collect. (1987-).

NE/0014-4290
**EXCERPTA MEDICA. SECTION 25. HEMATOLOGY.** See Medical Science and Technology-Abstracting, Bibliographies and Statistics.

US/0301-472X
**EXPERIMENTAL HEMATOLOGY.** [Exp. hematol.]. **Added/Corp** International Society for Experimental Hematology. Vol. 1 (1973)-. Academic Scholarly Publication. English. mo. $313.00. Kluge, Carden & Jennings, 853 West Main Street, Charlottesville VA 22903. **Tel** (804)979-4913, FAX (804)979-4025. **ED** Peter J. Quesenberry. **NLM** W1 EX504K. **CODEN** EXHMA6. **[CCC]. Pr Rev.** Documents available from The Genuine Article, BIOSIS Document Express, CASDDS. ***Supersedes** Experimental Hematology (Oak Ridge), 0531-5573.*
**Desc:** Publishes papers related to international experimentation in hematology. Also contains periodic supplements dealing with thematic issues such as bone marrow transplantation.
**Ind/Abst** Biol. Abstr.; Chem. Abstr.; Curr. Contents Life Sci.; EMBASE; Health Plan. Adminis.; Helminthol. Abstr. (1991-); Index Med.; INIS Atomindex [Micro.]; Oncog. Growth Factors Abstr.; Life Sci. Collect.; Ref. Upd. Basic Ed.; Ref. Upd. Deluxe Ed.; Res. Alert [Full Cov.]; Sci. Cit. Index; SCISEARCH.

GW
**FORSCHUNGSBERICHT / INSTITUT FUER PLASMAFORSCHUNG DER UNIVERSITAT STUTTGART.** **Added/Corp** Universitat Stuttgart. Institut fur Plasmaforschung. (19??)-. German. an. **LC** QC717.6; .F67. **DD** 530.4/4/07204347. Documents available from CASDDS.
**Ind/Abst** Chem. Abstr.

RU
**GEMATOLOGIYA I TRANSFUZIOLOGIYA.** [Gematol. transfuziol.]. **Added/Corp** Vsesoiuznoe Obshchestvo Gematologov i Transfuziologov (Soviet Union). Vol. 1 (1983)-. Academic Scholarly Publication. Russian (summaries and/or abstracts in English). Six times a year. $89.95. Izdatelstvo

Meditsina / Russian Academy of Medical Sciences, Ulitsa Solyanka 14, 109801 Moscow Russia. **Tel** 011 95 297-05-04. **(Subscription address:** East View Publications Inc., 3020 Harbor Lane North, Suite 110, Minneapolis MN 55447.**) ED** Audrey Vorobyov and Valery Kotelnikov (editors' address: Kotelnikov VM MD, Novozykovskypr 42, 125167 Moscow USSR). **NLM** W1 GE14P. **CODEN** GETRE8. Index available. cum. index. **Bk Rev. Ad Acc. Circ:** 4,500 (ctrl). Documents available from The Genuine Article, BIOSIS Document Express, CASDDS. ***Continues*** *Problemy Gematologii i Perelivaniia Krovi, 0552-2080.*
**Ind/Abst** Biol. Abstr.; Chem. Abstr. (1983-); Curr. Contents Clin. Med.; EMBASE; Index Med.; Nutr. Abstr. Rev., Ser. A, Hum. Exp.; Res. Alert [Select. Cov.]; SCISEARCH.

HU/0133-4883
**HAEMATOLOGIA (BUDAPEST. 1976. SOROZAT).** (HAEMATOLOGIA.). Vol. 1 (1976)-. Academic Scholarly Publication. English. ir. Price varies per volume. Akademiai Kiado, Publishing House of the Hungarian Academy of Sciences, Prielle Kornelia u. 19-35, H-1117 Budapest Hungary. **Tel** 011 36 1 1811991, FAX 011 36 1 1811991, telex 22-6228 AKNYO H. **NLM** W1 HA155R. Documents available from The Genuine Article.
**Ind/Abst** Curr. Contents Clin. Med.; Res. Alert [Select. Cov.].

IT/0390-6078
**HAEMATOLOGICA (ROMA).** (HAEMATOLOGICA.). [Haematologica]. **Added/Corp** Societa Italiana di Ematologia. Vol. 59 (Mar. 1974)-. Academic Scholarly Publication. Multiple languages (Italian and English). Six times a year. L160000 (institutions), L125000 (individuals). Il Pensiero Scientifico Editore s.r.l., Via Bradano 3C, 00199 Rome Italy. **Tel** 011 39 6 86207158, 86207159, 86207168, 86207169, FAX 011 39 6 86207160. **ED** Edoardo Ascari. **CODEN** HAEMAX. Index available. **Bk Rev. Ad Acc, Adv Mgr:** Dott Dalla, **Tel** 06-86207165. Full Page (B&W) L1.650.000. **Pr Rev. Circ:** 2,000. Documents available from The Genuine Article, BIOSIS Document Express, CASDDS. ***Continues*** *Haematologica; Archivio.*
**Desc:** Contents include original papers, editorials, case reports, reviews, short communications, and letters.
**Ind/Abst** Biol. Abstr.; Chem. Abstr.; Curr. Aware. Biol. Sci., CABS; Curr. Contents Life Sci.; EMBASE; Health Plan. Adminis.; Immunol. Abstr.; Index Med.; Oncog. Growth Factors Abstr.; Life Sci. Collect.; Protozoolog. Abstr.; Ref. Upd. Deluxe Ed.; Res. Alert [Full Cov.]; Rev. Med. Vet. Mycology; Sci. Cit. Index; SCISEARCH; Virol. AIDS Abstr.

GW/0171-7111
**HAEMATOLOGY AND BLOOD TRANSFUSION.** [Haematol. blood transfus.]. **Added/Corp** Deutsche Gesellschaft fur Hamatologie. Deutsche Gesellschaft fur Hamatologie und Onkologie. Deutsche Gesellschaft fur Bluttransfusion und Immunhamatologie. Osterreichische Gesellschaft fur Hamatologie. Osterreichische Gesellschaft fur Hamatologie und Onkologie. **VFOAT** Hamatologie und Bluttransfusion. Vol. 20 (1977)-. Academic Scholarly Publication. English (German). ir. Price varies per volume. Springer Verlag New York Inc., PO Box 19386 Books, Newark NJ 07195. **Tel** (201)348-4033. **(Subscription address:** North America/ Journal Fulfillment Services, 44 Hartz Way, Secaucus, NJ 07094**) NLM** W1 HA1655; W1 HA1655. **CODEN** HBTRDV. **[CCC].** Documents available from CASDDS. ***Continues*** *Hamatologie und Bluttransfusion, 0440-0607.*
**Ind/Abst** Chem. Abstr.; Index Med.

●US/1067-2370
**HEM/ONC ANNALS.** [Hem/onc ann.]. **VFOAT** Hem Onc Annals; Hematology Oncology Annals. Vol. 1, No. 1 (May/June 1993)-. Periodical. English. bm. $135.00 institution, $124.00 individual (US). Slack Inc., 6900 Grove Road, Thorofare NJ 08086. **Tel** (609)848-1000, (800)257-8290, FAX (609)853-5991, telex 517108 SLACK INC VD. **DD** 616. **NLM** W1; HE879.

UK/0278-0232
**HEMATOLOGICAL ONCOLOGY.** [Hematol. oncol.]. Vol. 1, No. 1 (Jan./Mar. 1983)-. Academic Scholarly Publication. English. Six times a year. $450.00. John Wiley & Sons Ltd., Baffins Lane, Chichester West Sussex PO19 1UD England. **Tel** 0243 779777, FAX 0243 776128 BTG:JWP001, telex 86290 WIBOOKG. **(Subscription address:** John Wiley / Philadelphia, PO Box 7247, Philadelphia PA 19170.**) ED** J. W. Parker, G. P. Canellos, J. M. A. Whitehouse and R. J. Lukes. **DD** 616. **NLM** W1 HE87E. **CODEN** HAONDL. **[CCC]. Bk Rev. Ad Acc. Pr Rev. Circ:** 850. available on microfilm and microfiche from University Microfilms International (UMI). Documents available from The Genuine Article, BIOSIS Document Express, CASDDS, ADONIS.
**Desc:** Publishes a variety of clinical and scientific specialities concerned with neoplastic disease of the hemopoietic system and any neoplastic or related process which may directly or indirectly involve the hemopoietic system.
**Ind/Abst** ADONIS; Biol. Abstr. (1987-); Chem. Abstr. (1983-); Curr. Aware. Biol. Sci., CABS; Curr. Contents Life Sci.; EMBASE; Health Plan. Adminis.; Immunol. Abstr.; Index Med.; Ref. Upd. Deluxe Ed.; Res. Alert [Full Cov.]; Sci. Cit. Index; SCISEARCH; Soc. Sci. Cit. Index [Select. Cov.].

US/0091-2336
**HEMATOLOGY CASE STUDIES.** V. 1- 1973-. English. Medical Exam Publishing Company, 52 Vanderbilt Avenue Elsevier, New York NY 10017-3808. **Tel** (212)463-1052. **LC** RC633.A1; H475. **DD** 616.1/5/0905.
**Desc:** Provides the logical work-up of a patient throughout the course of the disease. A question-and-answer section with references follows each case.

US/0891-9763
**HEMATOLOGY (NEW YORK, N.Y.).** (HEMATOLOGY.). [Hematology]. Vol. 1 (1985)-. Monographic series. English. ir. Price varies per volume. Marcel Dekker Inc., 270 Madison Avenue, New York NY 10016. **Tel** (212)696-9000, (800)228-1160, FAX (212)685-4540, telex 421419. **(Subscription address:** Marcel Dekker Inc, PO Box 5017, Monticello NY 12701.**) DD** 616. **NLM** W1; HE873. **[CCC].**
**Desc:** Series covering topics such as bone marrow transplantation, hematopoietic stem cells, and plasma fibronectin.

US/0889-8588
**HEMATOLOGY/ONCOLOGY CLINICS OF NORTH AMERICA.** [Hematol./oncol. clin. North Am.]. **VFOAT** Hematology, Oncology Clinics of North America. Vol. 1, No. 1 (March 1987)-. Periodical. English. bm. $111.00 (individual), $129.00 (institution) US; $124.00 (individual), $131.00 (institution) other. W.B. Saunders Company, A Subsidiary of Harcourt Brace Jovanovich, Inc., The Curtis Center/Suite 300, Independence Square West, Philadelphia PA 19106-3399. **Tel** (215)238-7800 or, 5587, FAX (215)238-7883, telex 173146. **(Subscription address:** W. B. Saunders Company / North America Subscriptions, c/o Periodicals, 6277 Sea Harbour Drive, 4th Floor, Orlando FL 32887.**) ED** Barbara Conover. **LC** RB145. **DD** 616.1/5. **NLM** W1; HE87EG. **[CCC].** Index available. **Pr Rev. Circ:** 5,000. Documents available from The Genuine Article, BIOSIS Document Express. ***Formed by the union of*** *Clinics in Haematology, 0308-2261* ***and*** *Clinics in Oncology, 0261-9873.*
**Desc:** Each issue is devoted to a single topic in patient care, including updates for the clinician on the latest advances.
**Ind/Abst** Biol. Abstr.; Cumul. Index Nurs. Allied Health Lit.; EMBASE; Index Med. (1987-); Ref. Upd. Clinical Ed.; Ref. Upd. Deluxe Ed.; Res. Alert [Full Cov.]; Sci. Cit. Index; SCISEARCH.

SZ/0882-8083
**HEMATOLOGY REVIEWS AND COMMUNICATIONS.** [Hematol. rev. commun.]. Vol. 1, No. 1 (1986)-. Periodical. English. Eight times a year. $373.00 (academic institutions), $582.00 (corporate institutions). Harwood Academic Publishers, PO Box 90, Reading RG1 8JL England. **Tel** 011 44 734 560080. **(Subscription address:** International Publishers Distributor at one of the following addresses: 820 Town Center Drive, Langhorne, PA 19047; or PO Box 90, Reading Berkshire RG1 8JL UK; or Kent Ridge PO Box 1180, Singapore 9111, Republic of Singapore**) DD** 616. **NLM** W1; HE8748. **CODEN** HRCOEG. **[CCC].**
**Ind/Abst** Dairy Sci. Abstr.; EMBASE.

CN/0822-5974
**HEMOPHILIA ONTARIO.** (HEMOPHILIA ONTARIO / THE CANADIAN HEMOPHILIA SOCIETY, ONTARIO CHAPTER.). **Added/Corp** Canadian Hemophilia Society. Ontario Chapter. Vol. 15, No. 2 (June 1983)-. Periodical. English. Four times a year. Canadian Hemophilia Society - Ontario Chapter, 1643 Yonge Street, Toronto Ontario M4T 2A1 Canada. **Tel** (416)488-2244. **ED** Frank Terpstra. **DD** 616.1/572/009713. **Bk Rev. Circ:** 2,000 (ctrl). ***Continues*** *Canadian Hemophilia Society. Ontario Chapter. Ontario Chapter Bulletin, 0045-4923.*
**Desc:** Medical and informational articles to inform hemophiliacs, families, medical personnel and interested people in Ontario.

US/0360-7607
**HEMOSTASIS AND THROMBOSIS.** (HEMOSTASIS AND THROMBOSIS; A BIBLIOGRAPHY.). V. 11, No. 7- July 1975-. Bibliography. English. mo. $39.50 US; $49.40 other. US Department of Health & Human Services / Public Health Service, 200 Independence Avenue SW, Room 716G, Washington DC 20201. **Tel** (202)690-6867, FAX (202)690-6274. **LC** Z6664.B5; F5; RC647.C55. **NLM** ZWH 310 F443. ***Continues*** *Fibrinolysis, Thrombolysis, and Blood Clotting, 0071-4690.*

US/0894-203X
**IMMUNOHEMATOLOGY.** (IMMUNOHEMATOLOGY / AMERICAN RED CROSS.). [Immunohematology]. **Added/Corp** American Red Cross. Vol. 1, No. 1 (Sept. 1984)-. Periodical. English. Four times a year (Mar., June, Sept., Dec.). $25.00 US; $30.00 others. American Red Cross, 15601 Crabbs Branch Way, Rockville MD 20855. **Tel** (301)738-0526, FAX (301)738-0666. **ED** Delores Mallory, (phone: (301)738-0505). **DD** 616. **NLM** W1; IM485I. **CODEN** IMMUEQ. Index available. **Bk Rev**, (Qty: 1). **Ad Acc. Pr Rev. Circ:** 2,500.
**Desc:** Provides a forum for exchanging ideas, disseminating information, and keeping abreast of the latest developments in the field. Each issue offers current and original articles, many by recognized experts in the discipline. Also featured are case reports with pertinent serology, helpful tech tips, up-to-date blood group system reviews, and timely papers on the use of computers in the blood bank.
**Ind/Abst** EMBASE.

US
**INFOLINE (BETHESDA, MD.). See** Sociology-Social Services and Welfare.

●SZ/1019-8466
**INFUSIONSTHERAPIE UND TRANSFUSIONSMEDIZIN.** [Infus.ther. Transfus.med.]. **Added/Corp** Deutsche Gesellschaft fuer Transfusionsmedizin und Immunhamatologie. (Feb. 1992)-. Periodical. German (English). Six times a year. $94.00. S. Karger AG, Allschwilerstrasse 10, PO Box - Postfach - Case Postale, CH-4009 Basel Switzerland. **Tel** 011 41 61 306-1111, FAX 011 41 61 306-1234, telex CH 962 652. **ED** H. Reissigl. **NLM** W1; IN447CE. **CODEN** IFTRE3. Documents available from The Genuine Article, BIOSIS Document Express. ***Continues*** *Infusionstherapie (Basel, Switzerland), 1011-6966.*
**Desc:** An interdisciplinary forum covering basic research and clinical application in the fields of parenteral and enteral nutrition as well as blood transfusion, blood substitutes and their various application techniques.
**Ind/Abst** Biol. Abstr.; Curr. Contents Clin. Med.; Index Med.; Ref. Upd. Deluxe Ed.; Res. Alert [Full Cov.]; Sci. Cit. Index.

US/0742-7719
**INTERNATIONAL BLOOD/PLASMA NEWS.** **Added/Corp** Marketing Research Bureau. **VFOAT** International Blood, Plasma News. (198?)-. Periodical. English. mo. $350.00 US and Canada; $375.00 other. Marketing Research Bureau Inc., 352 3rd Street/ Suite 308, Laguna Beach CA 92651. **Tel** (714)497-6522, FAX (714)497-6525, telex 294559. **ED** Jack Reasor. Index available. **Bk Rev. Ad Acc. Circ:** 200 (ctrl).
**Desc:** Covers business and general information regarding happenings around the world about blood/plasma/genetic subjects. Lists a patent section covering blood/plasma products and a list of meetings.

NE/0925-5710
**INTERNATIONAL JOURNAL OF HEMATOLOGY.** **Added/Corp** Nihon Ketsueki Gakkai. Vol. 54, No. 1 (Feb. 1991)-. Academic Scholarly Publication. English. Eight times a year (2 volumes). $320.00. Elsevier Science Ireland Ltd., Bay 15, Shannon Industrial Estate, Co Clare Ireland. **Tel** 011 353 61 471944. **NLM** W1; IN768G. **CODEN** IJHEEY. **[CCC].** Documents available from The Genuine Article, CASDDS. ***Continues*** *Nihon Ketsueki Gakkai Zasshi, 0001-5806.*
**Ind/Abst** Chem. Abstr. (1991-); Curr. Aware. Biol. Sci., CABS; Curr. Contents Clin. Med.; EMBASE; Index Med.; Res. Alert [Select. Cov.]; SCISEARCH; Soc. Sci. Cit. Index [Select. Cov.].

CN/0715-8602
**JOURNAL - CANADIAN RED CROSS SOCIETY. BLOOD PROGRAMME. See** Sociology-Social Services and Welfare.

US/0162-9360
**JOURNAL OF CLINICAL HEMATOLOGY AND ONCOLOGY.** ***Ceased.*** [J. clin. hematol. oncol.]. Vol. 7 (19??)-(19??). Academic Scholarly Publication. English. qt. Wadley Institution Molecular Medicine, 9000 Harry Hines Boulevard, Dallas TX 75232. **Tel** (214)351-8571. **ED** Amanullah Khan. **UDC** 616.15; 616-006. **NLM** W1 JO588D. **CODEN** JCHODP. **Bk Rev. Circ:** 9,000 (ctrl). Documents available from BIOSIS Document Express, CASDDS. ***Continues*** *Wadley Medical Bulletin, 0097-5427.*
**Desc:** All articles pertaining to hematology and oncology and reviewed for publication in the journal.
**Ind/Abst** Biol. Abstr. (1975-1985); Chem. Abstr. (1975-1985); EMBASE; Life Sci. Collect.

US/0022-1058
**JOURNAL OF EXTRA-CORPOREAL TECHNOLOGY, THE.** [J. extra-corpor. technol.]. **Added/Corp** American Society of Extra-Corporeal Technology. Vol. 1 (1968)-. Academic Scholarly Publication. English. Four times a year (Mar., June, Sept., Dec.). $40.00 US; $55.00 other. American Society of Extra Corporeal Technology, 11480 Sunset Hills Road, Suite 100E, Reston VA 22090. **Tel** (703)435-8556, FAX (703)435-0056. **ED** Kurt Larrick. **LC** QP110.A7; J68. **DD** 617/.412059. **NLM** W1 J06442. **CODEN** JEXCBD. Index available. cum. index. **Bk Rev**, (Qty: 4-8). **Pr Rev. Circ:** 3,000 (ctrl). Documents available from CASDDS. ***Absorbed*** *AmSECT Proceedings, 0162-2560.* ***Continued in part by*** *American Society of Extra-Corporeal Technology. International Conference., 1045-6988.*
**Desc:** International scientific articles on case studies and

techniques on extracorporeal (perfusion) technology. **Ind/Abst** Chem. Abstr.; Cumul. Index Nurs. Allied Health Lit.; EMBASE; Health Devices Alerts.

US/1045-7984
**JOURNAL OF MYOCARDIAL ISCHEMIA, THE.** **See** Medical Science and Technology-Cardiology.

●US
**JOURNAL OF PEDIATRIC HEMATOLOGY / ONCOLOGY.** (1995)-. Periodical. English. qt. $140.00 (individuals), $202.00 (institutions) US; $178.00 (individuals), $252.00 (institutions) other. Raven Press, 1185 Avenue of the Americas, 37th Floor, New York NY 10036. **Tel** (212)930-9500, (212)930-9604, FAX (212)869-3495, (212)302-8507, telex 640073. ***Continues*** *The American Journal of Pediatric Hematology/Oncology.*

●US
**JOURNAL : THE JOURNAL OF THE AMERICAN BLOOD RESOURCES ASSOCIATION, THE.** **Added/Corp** American Blood Resources Association. **VFOAT** Journal of the American Blood Resources Association. Vol. 1, No. 1 (Spring 1992)-. Periodical. English. qt. $75.00. American Blood Resources Association, PO Box 669, Annapolis MD 21403. **Tel** (410)263-8296. **NLM** W1; JO22DG. ***Continues*** *Plasmapheresis, 0894-6779.*

JA/0386-9717
**KETSUEKI TO MYAKUKAN.** (KETSUEKI TO MYAKKAN : NIHON KESSEN SHIKETSU GAKKAISHI.). [Ketsueki to myakukan]. **Added/Corp** Nihon Kessen Shiketsu Gakkai. **VFOAT** Blood & Vessel; Blood and Vessel. (1970)-. Academic Scholarly Publication. Japanese. qt. Nihon Kessen Shiketsu Gakkai, (Japanese Soc. on Thrombosis & Hemostasis), 2-11, Kanda Tacho, Chiyodaku, Tokyoto 101 Japan. **CODEN** KTMYA3. Documents available from CASDDS.
**Ind/Abst** Chem. Abstr. (?-1989).

US
**KIDNEY, UROLOGY, AND HEMATOLOGY.** ***Ceased.*** **See** Medical Science and Technology-Urology and Nephrology.

US/0024-7766
**LYMPHOLOGY.** [Lymphology]. **Added/Corp** International Society of Lymphology. Vol. 1, (March 1968)-. Academic Scholarly Publication. English. Four times a year (Mar., June, Sept., Dec.). $75.00 (institutions), $55.00 (individuals). International Society of Lymphology, 1501 North Campbell Avenue, Tucson AZ 85724. **Tel** (602)626-6118, FAX (602)626-0822. **LC** RC646; .L95. **NLM** W1 LY528. **CODEN** LYMPBN. **[CCC]. Pr Rev.** available on microfilm from University Microfilms International (UMI). Documents available from The Genuine Article, BIOSIS Document Express, CASDDS.
**Ind/Abst** Biol. Abstr.; Chem. Abstr. (-1988); Curr. Aware. Biol. Sci., CABS; Curr. Contents Life Sci.; EMBASE; Energy Res. Abstr.; Index Med.; Life Sci. Collect.; Ref. Upd. Deluxe Ed.; Res. Alert [Full Cov.]; Sci. Cit. Index; SCISEARCH.

US/0277-8599
**METHODS IN HEMATOLOGY.** ***Ceased.*** [Methods hematol.]. Vol. 1-?. Academic Scholarly Publication. English. ir. Churchill Livingstone Inc., 650 Avenue of the Americas, New York NY 10011. **Tel** (212)206-5062, FAX (212)727-7808. **(Subscription address:** US/ Churchill Livingstone, Fulfillment Office, PO Box 11318, Birmingham, AL 35202**) NLM** W1 ME9615L. **CODEN** MHEMD4. Documents available from CASDDS.
**Ind/Abst** Chem. Abstr.

US/0026-2862
**MICROVASCULAR RESEARCH.** [Microvascular res.]. **VFOAT** MVR. Vol. 1 (June 1968)-. Academic Scholarly Publication. English. bm (6 issues). $470.00 US and Canada; $559.00 other. Academic Press, Inc., 6277 Sea Harbor Drive, Orlando FL 32887. **Tel** (800)543-9534, (407)345-4100, FAX (407)363-9661. **ED** David Shepro and Benjamin W. Zweifach. **LC** RC681.A1; M5. **DD** 612/.135/072. **NLM** W1 MI313N. **CODEN** MIVRA6MIVRAG. **[CCC]. Pr Rev.** Documents available from The Genuine Article, BIOSIS Document Express, CASDDS.
**Desc:** Dedicated to the dissemination of fundamental information related to the microvasular field. Full-length articles presenting the results of original research and brief communications are featured.
**Ind/Abst** Biol. Abstr.; Chem. Abstr.; CSA Neuro. Abstr. (?-?); Curr. Contents Life Sci.; EMBASE; Energy Res. Abstr. (Jan. 1971-); Index Med.; Index Vet.; Life Sci. Collect.; Ref. Upd. Deluxe Ed.; Res. Alert [Full Cov.]; Sci. Cit. Index; SCISEARCH; Vet. Bull.

GW/0029-4810
**NOUVELLE REVUE FRANCAISE D'HEMATOLOGIE.** [Nouv. rev. fr. hematol.]. **VFOAT** Journal of Experimental and Clinical Hematology. Vol. 20, No. 1 (1978)-. Academic Scholarly Publication. French (English). Six times a year. 1960.00F. Springer-Verlag France, 26 rue des Carmes, F 75005 Paris France. **Tel** 011 33 1 44411599, FAX 011 33 43250225. **(Subscription address:** Springer Verlag New York Inc. / for North America, 44 Hartz Way, Secaucus NJ 07096.**) ED** J.L. Binet and J.P. Cazenave. **NLM** W1 NO834LB. **CODEN** NRFHA4. **[CCC].** available on microfilm from University Microfilms International (UMI). Documents available from The Genuine Article, BIOSIS Document Express, CASDDS. ***Continues in part*** *Nouvelle Revue Francaise d'Hematologie, Blood Cells.*
**Desc:** Includes original articles, up-dates on research and chronicles current happenings in the field at an international level.
**Ind/Abst** Biol. Abstr.; Chem. Abstr.; EMBASE; Energy Res. Abstr. (1978-); Index Med.; Life Sci. Collect.; Res. Alert [Full Cov.]; Sci. Cit. Index; SCISEARCH; Virol. AIDS Abstr.

US/0093-9404
**OVERVIEW OF BLOOD.** [Overv. blood]. English. Blood Information Service, 508 Getzuille Road, Buffalo NY 14226. **Tel** (716)832-7997. **ED** C Bishop. **LC** RC633.A1; O94. **DD** 612/.11/05.

US/0888-0018
**PEDIATRIC HEMATOLOGY AND ONCOLOGY.** [Pediatr. hematol. oncol.]. Vol. 3, No. 1 (1986)-. Academic Scholarly Publication. English. bm (6 issues). £175.00 UK; $289.00 other. Taylor & Francis Ltd., Rankine Road, Basingstoke Hampshire, RG24 8PR United Kingdom. **Tel** 011 44 256 840366, FAX 011 44 256 479438, telex 858540. **(Subscription address:** Taylor & Francis Inc., 1900 Frost Road, Suite 101, Bristol PA 19007-1598.**) ED** Jorgen Cohn (editor's address: University of Tromso, Department of Pediatrics, PO Box 8, N-9038 Tromso, Norway). **DD** 618. **NLM** W1; PE167P. **CODEN** PHONEN. **[CCC].** Index available. **Bk Rev. Ad Acc. Pr Rev. Circ:** 600. available on microfilm and microfiche from University Microfilms International (UMI). Documents available from The Genuine Article, BIOSIS Document Express, CASDDS. ***Continues*** *European Paediatric Haematology and Oncology, 0800-2789.*
**Desc:** The journal deals with immunology, pathology, and pharmacology in relation to blood diseases and cancer in children and shows how basic experimental research can contribute to the understanding of clinical problems. Articles from all over the world are considered for publication in the journal. The journal is not dependent on or connected with any organization or society.
**Ind/Abst** Biol. Abstr. (1986-); Chem. Abstr. (1986-); Curr. Aware. Biol. Sci., CABS; Curr. Contents Clin. Med.; Curr. Contents Clin. Pract.; EMBASE; Health Plan. Adminis.; Index Med. (1986-); Int. Nurs. Index; Res. Alert [Full Cov.]; Rev. Med. Vet. Mycology; Sci. Cit. Index; SCISEARCH; Soc. Sci. Cit. Index [Select. Cov.].

US/0747-3079
**PERFUSION LIFE.** **Added/Corp** American Society of Extra-Corporeal Technology. (Jan. 1984)-. Periodical. English. Ten times a year (Except Apr. and Dec.). $35.00. American Society of Extra Corporeal Technology, 11480 Sunset Hills Road, Suite 100E, Reston VA 22090. **Tel** (703)435-8556, FAX (703)435-0056. **ED** Kurt Larrick (phone: (703)435-8556). **LC** RD598.35.A77; P47. **DD** 617.4/1. **Bk Rev**, (Qty: 1-10). **Ad Acc. Circ:** 3,000 (ctrl).
**Desc:** In-depth backgrounders on key issues, resources, events, and professional development opportunities for perfusionists.

UK/0953-7104
**PLATELETS.** **Added/Corp** British Library. Medical Information Service. Vol. 1 (1990)-. Periodical. English. Six times a year. £227.00 Europe; £228.00 Other (Institutions). Churchill Livingstone, 1-3 Baxter's Place, Leith Walk, Edinburgh EH1 3AF Scotland. **Tel** 011 44 31 556 2424, FAX 011 44 31 558 1278, telex 727511. **(Subscription address:** Maruzen Company Ltd., PO Box 5050, Import & Export Department, Tokyo 100 31 Japan.**) ED** S Heptinstall. **NLM** W1; PL235. **CODEN** PLTEEF. **[CCC].** available on microfilm and microfiche from University Microfilms International (UMI).
**Desc:** Devoted to platelet-related research. Containing original articles, review articles, short communications and correspondence on all aspects of platelet-related research, including vascular disease, cerebral and myocardial ischaemia, asthma, inflammation, platelet biochemistry, growth factors, pathology and morphology of platelets.
**Ind/Abst** EMBASE; Sci. Cit. Index.

UK/0142-8268
**PLATELETS SHEFFIELD.** (PLATELETS.). [PlateletsSheff.]. (1976)-. English. Twenty-four times a year. £110.00. SUBIS, Mansion House, 19 Kingfield Road, Sheffield S11 9AS England. **Tel** 011 44 114 255 4433, FAX 011 44 114 255 4626. **DD** 016.612117. **[CCC]. Bk Rev. Ad Acc.** available on diskette.
**Desc:** Current awareness service for researchers in clinical and life sciences.

JA/0915-1699
**PROCEEDINGS OF JAPANESE SYMPOSIUM ON PLASMA CHEMISTRY.** **See** Chemistry.

FR/0246-0149
**PROGRES EN HEMATOLOGIE.** [Prog. hematol.]. 1 (Oct. 1980)-. Monographic series. French. Price varies per volume. Doin Editeurs, 8 Place de l'Odeon, F 75006 Paris France. **Tel** 011 33 1 46332237. **NLM** W1 PR64M.

US/0362-6350
**PROGRESS IN HEMOSTASIS AND THROMBOSIS.** [Prog. hemostasis thromb.]. Vol. 1 (1972)-. Monographic series. English. ir. Price varies per volume. Grune & Stratton Inc., 6277 Sea Harbor Drive, Orlando FL 32887. **Tel** (800)782-4479, (407)345-2567. **LC** RB144; .P75. **DD** 616.1/57/005. **NLM** W1 PR67F. **CODEN** PGHTAT. Documents available from BIOSIS Document Express, CASDDS.
**Ind/Abst** Biol. Abstr.; Chem. Abstr.; Energy Res. Abstr. (Aug. 1982-); Index Med.; Index Sci. Rev. [Full Cov.]; Ref. Upd. Clinical Ed.; Ref. Upd. Deluxe Ed.

US/0146-1540
**PROGRESS IN PEDIATRIC HEMATOLOGY/ONCOLOGY.** [Prog. pediatr. hematol./oncol.]. V. 1-. Academic Scholarly Publication. English. Price varies per volume. Publishing Sciences Group Inc, 545 Great Road, Littleton MA 01460. **Tel** (617)486-8971. **ED** C Pochedly and D R Miller. **UDC** 616-006-053.2; 616.15-053.2. **NLM** W1 PR677E. **CODEN** PPHODC. Documents available from CASDDS.
**Ind/Abst** Chem. Abstr. (1976-1980).

UK/0268-2613
**PROGRESS IN TRANSFUSION MEDICINE.** [Prog. transfus. med.]. Vol. 1 (1986)-. Academic Scholarly Publication. English. ir. Churchill Livingstone, 1-3 Baxter's Place, Leith Walk, Edinburgh EH1 3AF Scotland. **Tel** 011 44 31 556 2424, FAX 011 44 31 558 1278, telex 727511. **LC** RM171; .P76. **DD** 615/.65/005. **NLM** W1; PR684E. **CODEN** PTMEE2. Documents available from CASDDS.
**Ind/Abst** Chem. Abstr. (1986-).

UK/0143-697X
**RECENT ADVANCES IN HAEMATOLOGY.** [Recent adv. haematol.]. **VFOAT** Haematology. No. 1 (1971)-. Academic Scholarly Publication. English. ir (every 3-5 years). $69.00. Churchill Livingstone, 1-3 Baxter's Place, Leith Walk, Edinburgh EH1 3AF Scotland. **Tel** 011 44 31 556 2424, FAX 011 44 31 558 1278, telex 727511. **(Subscription address:** Churchill Livingstone / US, 5 S 250 Frontenac Road, Naperville IL 60563.**) ED** A. Goldbert and M.C. Brain. **LC** RC633.A1; R43. **DD** 616.1/5/005. **NLM** W1 RE105UM. **CODEN** RAHADN. Documents available from CASDDS.
**Ind/Abst** Chem. Abstr.

CN/0824-6882
**REFERENCE SERIES. HEMATOLOGY.** [Ref. ser., Hematol.]. HE-1-. Monographic series. English. Price varies per volume. Toronto Institute of Medical Technology, 222 St Patrick Street, Toronto Ontario M5T 1V4 Canada. **DD** 616.1/5.

US/0161-1917
**REPORT OF THE NATIONAL HEART, LUNG, AND BLOOD ADVISORY COUNCIL.** **See** Medical Science and Technology-Cardiology.

US/0272-507X
**REVIEWS OF HEMATOLOGY.** [Rev. hematol.]. (1980)-. Academic Scholarly Publication. English. ir. Price varies per volume. PJD Publications Ltd., PO Box 966, Westbury NY 11590. **Tel** (516)626-0650, FAX (516)626-5546. **ED** Julian L. Ambrus. **LC** RB145; .R48. **NLM** W1; RE257DE. **CODEN** REHEDT. Documents available from CASDDS.
**Ind/Abst** Chem. Abstr.

PO/0871-4649
**REVISTA PORTUGUESA DE HEMORREOLOGIA : ORGAO OFICIAL DA SOCIEDADE PORTUGUESA DE HEMORREOLOGIA / SOCIEDADE PORTUGUESA DE HEMORREOLOGIA.** **Added/Corp** Sociedade Portuguesa de Hemorreologia. Vol. 1, No. 1 (1987)-. Periodical. English (Portuguese). Twice a year. 60$00 Portugal; 16$00 Europe; 32$00 others. Portuguese Society of Haemorheology, PO Box 4098, P-1052 Lisbon Portugal. **Tel** 011 351 1 7931813. **NLM** W1; RE717F.
**Ind/Abst** EMBASE.

FR/1140-4639
**REVUE FRANCAISE DE TRANSFUSION ET D'HEMOBIOLOGIE : BULLETIN DE LA SOCIETE NATIONALE DE TRANSFUSION SANGUINE.** ***Title Change.*** [Rev. fr. transfus. hemobiol.]. **Added/Corp** Societe Nationale de Transfusion Sanguine (France). (Feb. 1989)-(Dec. 1993). Bulletin. French (summaries and/or abstracts in English). bm. Blackwell Scientific Publishers / Arnette, 2 rue Casimir-Delavigne, 75006 Paris France. **Tel** 011 33 1 44860770, FAX 011 33 1 46336797. **NLM** W1; RE848DK. **CODEN** RFTHE4. available on microfilm from University Microfilms International (UMI). Documents available from The Genuine Article, BIOSIS Document Express. ***Continues*** *Revue Francaise de Transfusion et Immuno-Hematologie, 0338-4535.* ***Continued by*** *Transfusion Clinique et Biologique.*

**Ind/Abst** Biol. Abstr. (?-?); Curr. Contents Clin. Med. (?-?); Index Med. (1989-?); Res. Alert (?-?) [Full Cov.]; Sci. Cit. Index (?-?); SCISEARCH (?-?).

JA/0485-1439
**RINSHO KETSUEKI.** [Rinsho ketsueki]. **VFOAT** Japanese Journal of Clinical Hematology. (Jan. 1960)-. Academic Scholarly Publication. Japanese. Twelve times a year. **(Subscription address:** Kyowa Book Company Inc., 1 38 Kanda Jinbocho Chiyoda-ku, Tokyo 101 Japan.**)** **NLM** W1 RI21654.
**Ind/Abst** EMBASE; Index Med.

FR/0999-7385
**SANG, THROMBOSE, VAISSEAUX : STV.** See Medical Science and Technology-Cardiology.

SP/0036-4355
**SANGRE.** [Sangre]. Vol. 1 (1956)-. Academic Scholarly Publication. Spanish (English, French and Spanish). bm (February, April, June, August, October, and December). 6360ptas Spain; $80.00 other. Sangre, Apartado Postal 687, 50080 Zaragoza Spain. **Tel** 011 34 976 222638, FAX 011 34 976 222638. **ED** A. Raichs and M. Giralt. **LC** RC633.A1; S34. **NLM** W1 SA6455. **CODEN** SNGRAW. Index available. **Bk Rev. Ad Acc. Circ:** 2,000. Documents available from BIOSIS Document Express, CASDDS.
**Desc:** Official organ of the Spanish Society of Hematology, Blood Transfusions, and Latinoamerican Hematological Societies.
**Ind/Abst** Biol. Abstr.; Chem. Abstr.; EMBASE [Select. Cov.]; Index Med.; Indice Med. Esp.

US/0037-1963
**SEMINARS IN HEMATOLOGY.** [Semin. hematol.]. Vol. 1, No. 1 (Jan. 1964)-. Academic Scholarly Publication. English. qt. $92.00 (individual), $123.00 (institution), $58.00 (student) US; $144.00 (individual) $158.00 (institution), other. W.B. Saunders Company, A Subsidiary of Harcourt Brace Jovanovich, Inc., The Curtis Center/Suite 300, Independence Square West, Philadelphia PA 19106-3399. **Tel** (215)238-7800 or, 5587, FAX (215)238-7883, telex 173146. **(Subscription address:** W. B. Saunders Company / North America Subscriptions, c/o Periodicals, 6277 Sea Harbour Drive, 4th Floor, Orlando FL 32887.**)** **ED** Peter A. Miescher and Ernst R. Jaffe. **LC** RC633.A1; S44. **DD** 616.1505. **NLM** W1 SE489. **CODEN** SEHEA3. **[CCC]. Pr Rev. Circ:** 7,580. Documents available from The Genuine Article, BIOSIS Document Express, CASDDS.
**Desc:** Focuses on subjects of current importance in clinical hematology and related fields. Devoted to making the present status of such topics and the results of new investigations readily available to the practicing physician.
**Ind/Abst** Biol. Abstr.; Chem. Abstr.; Curr. Aware. Biol. Sci., CABS; Curr. Contents Clin. Med.; Curr. Contents Life Sci.; EMBASE; Energy Res. Abstr.; Immunol. Abstr.; Index Med.; Life Sci. Collect.; Physic. Medline Plus; Ref. Upd. Basic Ed.; Ref. Upd. Clinical Ed.; Ref. Upd. Deluxe Ed.; Res. Alert [Full Cov.]; Sci. Cit. Index; SCISEARCH; Virol. AIDS Abstr.

US/0094-6176
**SEMINARS IN THROMBOSIS AND HEMOSTASIS.** [Semin. thromb. hemost.]. Vol. 1 (July 1974)-. Academic Scholarly Publication. English. qt (Jan., Apr., July, Oct.). $135.00 (institutions), $99.00 (individuals) US; $160.00˚(institutions), $124.00 (individuals) other. Thieme Medical Publishers Inc., 381 Park Avenue South, Suite 1201, New York NY 10016. **Tel** (212)683-5088, (212)683-5089, FAX (212)779-9020, telex 220 862 TSINC UR. **ED** Eberbard F Mammen. **NLM** W1 SE489P. **CODEN** STHMBV. **[CCC].** cum. index. **Bk Rev. Ad Acc. Pr Rev. Circ:** 1,500 (ctrl). available on microfilm and microfiche from University Microfilms International (UMI). Documents available from The Genuine Article, BIOSIS Document Express, CASDDS, ADONIS.
**Desc:** Focuses on hemostasis and thrombosis. Topic-oriented journal for the practitioner specializing in areas of vascular diseases, blood clots and metabolism.
**Ind/Abst** ADONIS; Biol. Abstr.; Chem. Abstr.; Curr. Contents Clin. Med.; Curr. Contents Life Sci.; Dairy Sci. Abstr.; EMBASE; Energy Res. Abstr. (Nov. 1980-); Index Med.; Life Sci. Collect.; Ref. Upd. Clinical Ed.; Ref. Upd. Deluxe Ed.; Res. Alert [Full Cov.]; Sci. Cit. Index; SCISEARCH; Soc. Sci. Cit. Index [Select. Cov.].

SZ/0888-3920
**SOVIET MEDICAL REVIEWS. SECTION C, HEMATOLOGY REVIEWS.** ***Ceased.*** [Sov. med. rev., C Hematol. rev.]. **Added/Corp** Soviet Medical Reviews (Firm : Chur, Switzerland). **VFOAT** Hematology Reviews. Vol. 1 (1987)-(1993). Periodical. English. an. Harwood Academic Publishers, PO Box 90, Reading RG1 8JL England. **Tel** 011 44 734 560080. **(Subscription address:** International Publishers Distributor at one of the following addresses: 820 Town Center Drive, Langhorne, PA 19047; or PO Box 90, Reading Berkshire RG1 8JL UK; or Kent Ridge PO Box 1180, Singapore 9111, Republic of Singapore**)** **LC** RC633.A1; S65. **DD** 616.1/5. **CODEN** SMCRE9. **[CCC].**

US/0730-6865
**STANDARDS FOR BLOOD BANKS AND TRANSFUSION SERVICES.** (STANDARDS FOR BLOOD BANKS AND TRANSFUSION SERVICES / PREPARED BY COMMITTEE ON STANDARDS, AMERICAN ASSOCIATION OF BLOOD BANKS.). [Stand. blood blanks transfus. serv.]. **Added/Corp** American Association of Blood Banks. Committee on Standards. (19??)-. English. ir (every two to three years). Price varies per volume. American Association of Blood Banks, 8101 Glenbrook Road, Bethesda MD 20814. **Tel** (301)907-6977. **ED** Paul V. Holland. **LC** RM172; .S7. **DD** 615/.39. **NLM** W1 ST149. Index available. **Circ:** 40,000. ***Continues*** *Standards for a Blood Transfusion Service, 0272-2038.*
**Desc:** Used throughout the world as a basis for maintaining and improving the quality, safety and effectiveness of human blood transfusions.
**Ind/Abst** Abstr. Clin. Care Guidel.

KO
**TAEHAN HYORAEK HAKHOE CHI. VFOAT** Korean Journal of Hematology. (1986)-. Periodical. Korean (summaries and/or abstracts in English). sa. Taehan Choksipcha SA, 175-1 Tohwa-dong, Mapo-ku, Seoul Korea. **LC** RB145; .T28. ***Continues*** *Taehan Hyoraek Hakhoe Chapchi, 0301-4045.*

US/0896-0569
**THROMBOSIS RESEARCH. SUPPLEMENT.** [Thromb. res., Suppl.]. No. 1 (June 1974)-. Monographic series. English. ir. Price varies per volume. Elsevier Applied Science, An Imprint of Elsevier Science Ltd., The Boulevard, Langford Lane, Kidlington, Oxford OX5 1GB United Kingdom. **Tel** 011 44 865 843000, 011 44 865 843699, FAX 011 44 865 843010. **(Subscription address:** Elsevier Science Inc., 660 White Plains Rd., Tarrytown NY 10591.**)** **DD** 616. **NLM** W1 TH945. Documents available from ADONIS.
**Ind/Abst** ADONIS; Index Med.

AU/0934-9669
**THROMBOTIC AND HAEMORRHAGIC DISORDERS.** ***Ceased.*** **Added/Corp** Danubian League Against Thrombosis and Haemorrhagic Disorders. University of Sheffield. Biomedical Information Service. Vol. 1, No. 1 (1990)-Vol. 8, No. 2 (Dec. 1993). Periodical. English. qt. Springer-Verlag Wien, Sachsenplatz 4 6, PO Box 89, A-1201 Vienna Austria. **Tel** 011 43 1 3302415. **(Subscription address:** Springer Verlag New York Inc. / for North America, 44 Hartz Way, Secaucus NJ 07096.**)** **NLM** W1; TH94L. **[CCC].**

FR/1246-7820
**TRANSFUSION CLINIQUE ET BIOLOGIQUE.** (1993)-. Bulletin. French. bm. 959.84F France; 1240.00F other. Blackwell Scientific Publishers / Arnette, 2 rue Casimir-Delavigne, 75006 Paris France. **Tel** 011 33 1 44860770, FAX 011 33 1 46336797. ***Continues*** *Revue Francaise de Transfusion et d'Hemobiologie, 1140-4639.*

UK/0960-5592
**TRANSFUSION MEDICINE. SUPPLEMENT.** [Transfus. med. Suppl.]. (1990)-. English. **DD** 615.39.
**Ind/Abst** Curr. Aware. Biol. Sci., CABS.

US/0041-1132
**TRANSFUSION (PHILADELPHIA).** (TRANSFUSION.). [Transfusion]. **Added/Corp** American Association of Blood Banks. Vol. 1 (Jan./Feb. 1961)-. Academic Scholarly Publication. English. mo (11 issues). $195.00 (institutions) US, $335.00 (institutions) other. American Association of Blood Banks, 8101 Glenbrook Road, Bethesda MD 20814. **Tel** (301)907-6977. **ED** Thomas F. Zuck. **LC** RC633.A1; T7. **DD** 615. **NLM** W1 TR228W. **CODEN** TRANAT. Index available (bound in Nov. issue). **Bk Rev. Ad Acc. Pr Rev. Circ:** 12,450. available on microfilm and microfiche from University Microfilms International (UMI). Documents available from The Genuine Article, BIOSIS Document Express, CASDDS. ***Continues*** *Bulletin - American Association of Blood Banks, 0360-9197.*
**Desc:** Original manuscripts and reports in all fields relating to transfusion blood groups, immunology, genetics and anthropology. Also contains Association news.
**Ind/Abst** Biol. Abstr.; Chem. Abstr.; Curr. Aware. Biol. Sci., CABS; Curr. Contents Clin. Med.; Curr. Contents Life Sci.; EMBASE; Energy Res. Abstr.; Index Med.; Life Sci. Collect.; Ref. Upd. Basic Ed.; Ref. Upd. Deluxe Ed.; Res. Alert [Full Cov.]; Rev. Med. Vet. Entomol.; Sci. Cit. Index; SCISEARCH; Soc. Sci. Cit. Index [Select. Cov.]; Virol. AIDS Abstr.

SZ/0042-9007
**VOX SANGUINIS.** [Vox sang.]. **Added/Corp** International Society of Blood Transfusion. League of Red Cross Societies. Nederlandse Stichting voor Bloedgroepenonderzoek. Vol. 3-5, (March 1953)-. Academic Scholarly Publication. English (Dutch, French and German; summaries and/or abstracts in Dutch and French). Eight times a year. $360.00. S. Karger AG, Allschwilerstrasse 10, PO Box - Postfach - Case Postale, CH-4009 Basel Switzerland. **Tel** 011 41 61 306-1111, FAX 011 41 61 306-1234, telex CH 962 652. **ED** C. P. Engelfriet. **DD** 616.1. **NLM** W1 VO87. **CODEN** VOSAAD. **[CCC].** Index available in last issue of volume--attached. **Ad Acc. Pr Rev.** available on microfilm from University Microfilms International (UMI). Documents available from The Genuine Article, BIOSIS Document Express, CASDDS. ***Continues*** *Bulletin van het Centraal Laboratorium van de Bloedtransfusiedienst van het Nederlandse Rode Kruis.*
**Desc:** Original papers and review articles are published on new techniques in blood transfusion and plasma exchange, as well as on preparation procedures for blood cell concentrates, plasma derivatives and coagulation factors, clinical application and storage. Articles dealing with immunohematology, immunogenetics, immune diagnosis and histocompatibility are also included.
**Ind/Abst** AGRICOLA; Biol. Abstr.; Chem. Abstr.; Curr. Aware. Biol. Sci., CABS; Curr. Contents Life Sci.; EMBASE; Immunol. Abstr.; Index Med.; Life Sci. Collect.; Protozoolog. Abstr.; Ref. Upd. Basic Ed.; Ref. Upd. Deluxe Ed.; Res. Alert [Full Cov.]; Sci. Cit. Index; SCISEARCH; Soc. Sci. Cit. Index [Select. Cov.]; Trop. Dis. Bull.

US/0882-5998
**YEAR BOOK OF HEMATOLOGY, THE.** [Year book hematol.]. **Added/Corp** Year Book Medical Publishers. **VFOAT** Yearbook of Hematology; Hematology. (1987)-. English. an. $69.95. Mosby Year Book Inc., 11830 Westline Industrial Drive, St Louis MO 63146. **Tel** (800)325-4177, (314)872-8370, FAX (314)432-1380, telex 44-2402. **LC** RB145; .Y39. **DD** 616.1/5/005. **NLM** W1; YE199CN. **CODEN** YBHEEI. Documents available from BIOSIS Document Express.
**Ind/Abst** Biol. Abstr. (1988-).

CC/0253-2727
**ZHONGHUA XUEYEXUE ZAZHI.** (CHUNG-HUA HSUEH YEH HSUEH TSA CHIH.). [Zhonghua xueyexue zazhi]. **Added/Corp** Chung-kuo I Hsueh k'o Hsueh Yuan. **VFOAT** Zhonghua Xueyexue Zazhi; Chinese Journal of Hematology. (19??)-. Academic Scholarly Publication. Chinese. mo. Zhongguo Yixue Kexueyuan / Xueye Yanjiusuo, Chinese Academy of Medical Sciences, Institute of Hematology, 288 Nanjing lu, Tianjin 300020, People's Republic of China. **Tel** 86 22 704167, FAX 86 22 706542. **ED** Chen Wen-Chich. **NLM** W1 CH9819H. **CODEN** CHTCD7. **Bk Rev. Ad Acc. Circ:** 15,000. Documents available from CASDDS.
**Desc:** Publishing the articles on clinical or experimental hematology, including editorial writings, case reports, brief reports, methods and experiences, reviews, lectures CPC and coherent accounts, etc.
**Ind/Abst** Chem. Abstr.; NAPRALERT.

## HOMEOPATHY

US/0747-606X
**AMERICAN HOMEOPATHY (1984).** (AMERICAN HOMEOPATHY.). [Am. homeopath.]. **Added/Corp** United States Homeopathic Association. Vol. 1 No. 1 (July/Aug. 1984)-. Periodical. English. ir. $20.00. United States Homeopathic Association, 5305 Lee Highway, Springfield VA 22207. **ED** Kathy Duggan. **DD** 615. **Bk Rev. Ad Acc. Circ:** 12,000. ***Formed by the union of*** *American Homeopathy (Consumer Edition), 0741-6857; American Homeopathy (Professional Edition), 0741-6865* ***and*** *American Homeopathy (Affiliate Edition), 0741-6873.*

US/0733-2661
**BIOLOGICAL THERAPY.** [Biol. ther.]. No. 1 (Jan. 1983)-. Periodical. English (French and German). qt. Free to medical universities; $12.50 other. Menaco Publishing Company, PO Box 13677, Albuquerque NM 87192. **Tel** (505)293-3843. **ED** Lex E O'Brient. **DD** 615. **NLM** W1; B176. **Bk Rev. Ad Acc. Circ:** 2,000 (ctrl).
**Desc:** Articles relating to various homeopathic combined remedies as well as other holistic forms of medical treatment.

FR/0007-9782
**CAHIERS DE KINESITHERAPIE.** See Medical Science and Technology-Sports Medicine.

CN/0824-0698
**COMMON GROUND (VANCOUVER).** (COMMON GROUND.). [Common ground]. Issue No. 1 (Winter 1982/83)-. Periodical. English. Six times a year (Aug., Oct., Dec., Feb., April, June). 27.00Can$. Common Ground, PO Box 34090 Station D, Vancouver British Columbia, V6J 4M1 Canada. **Tel** (604)733-2215. **ED** Joseph Roberts (editor's address: 201-3091 West Broadway, Vancouver BC V6K 2G9 Canada). **DD** 615.8/025/711. **Bk Rev. Ad Acc. Circ:** 90,000.
**Desc:** Directory to resources and services, from events, arts an and music to health and bodywork, counselling and spiritual resources.

FR
**HOMEOPATHIE FRANCAISE, L'.** French. mo. 150.00F France; 170.00F other. L'Homeopathie Francaise, 228 Boulevard Raspail, 75014 Paris France.

US/0363-2776
**HOMEOTHERAPY.** **Added/Corp** California State Homoeopathic Medical Society. Los Angeles County Homoeopathic Medical Society. San Francisco County Homoeopathic Medical Society. Vol. 1 Aug. (1974)-. Periodical. English. bm. $16.00. Hahnemann Foundation,

Box 9008, San Diego CA 92109. **Tel** (714)270-3064. **NLM** W1 HO519C. ***Supersedes*** *Pacific Coast Homeopathic Bulletin, 0363-2784.*

●UK
**JOURNAL OF INTERPROFESSIONAL CARE.** Vol. 6, No. 1 (Spring 1992)-. Periodical. English. tq. £118.00. Carfax Publishing Company, PO Box 25 Abingdon, Oxfordshire OX14 3UE England. **Tel** 011 44 235 555335, FAX (0279)31067, telex 817484. **(Subscription address:** US and Canada/ PO Box 2025, Dunnellon, FL 34430-2025; telephone:(904)489-6996**)** **NLM** W1; JO719D. available on microfiche. ***Continues*** *Holistic Medicine, 0884-3988.*
**Desc:** Dedicated to the furtherance of whole person care within the community, primary health, hospital and other institutional settings.

US/0002-8967
**JOURNAL OF THE AMERICAN INSTITUTE OF HOMEOPATHY.** [J. Am. Inst. Homeopat.]. **Added/Corp** American Institute of Homeopathy. Vol. 1, (Jan. 1909)-. Academic Scholarly Publication. English. Four times a year (Mar., June, Sept., Dec.). $35.00. American Institute of Homeopathy, 1585 Glencoe Street, Suite 44, Denver CO 80220. **Tel** (303)898-5477. **ED** Karl Robinson. **LC** RX1; .A53. **DD** 615.5/32/0973. **NLM** W1 JO909I. Index available. **Bk Rev**. **Ad Acc. Circ:** 500 (ctrl). ***Continues*** *American Institute of Homeopathy. Transactions of the Session of the American Ins, 0893-1518;* ***Absorbed*** *Homeopathic Recorder.*
**Desc:** A scholarly journal containing articles written by homeopathic practitioners on unusual cases and treatments, philosophy, research, education and recent developments in the field.

●II
**NATIONAL JOURNAL OF HOMOEOPATHY : NJH.** **VFOAT** NJH; Homoeopathy. Vol. 1, No. 1 (Jan./Feb. 1992)-. Periodical. English. bm. $20.00. **(Subscription address:** Prints India, 11 Darya Ganj, New Delhi 110002 India.**)** **NLM** W1; NA486SG.

GW/0931-1513
**NATURA & MED.** **VFOAT** Natura-Med. (198?)-. Periodical. German. Eleven times a year. DM84.00 Germany; DM96.00 other. Verlag Kirchheim & Co GmbH, Kaiserstrasse 41, W-6500 Mainz Germany. **Tel** 061 31 67 10 81, FAX 061 31 31 63 88 43. **ED** Verlag Kircheim. **NLM** W1; NA799N. cum. index. **Bk Rev**. **Ad Acc. Circ:** 20,000.

BE/0035-0885
**REVUE BELGE D'HOMOEOPATHIE.** (REVUE BELGE D'HOMOPATHIE.). [Rev. belge homoeopath.]. **Added/Corp** Association Homopathique Belge. Societe Royale Belge d'Homopathie. (19??)-. Academic Scholarly Publication. French. Four times a year. 1800F Belgium; 2000F other. Revue Belge d'Homopathie, Boulevard Louis Schimdt 117 BTE 6, 1040 Brussels Belgium. **Tel** 011 32 2 7353525. **CODEN** RBHOD4. Documents available from CASDDS.
**Ind/Abst** Chem. Abstr.

US
**TODAY'S HERBS.** English. mo. $15.00. Woodlands Health Books, PO Box 1422, Provo UT 84603. **Tel** (801)785-8100, , FAX (801)785-8511. **ED** Louise and Deanne Tenney. cum. index. **Bk Rev**, (Qty: 12). **Circ:** 5,000.
**Desc:** Subjects relative to natural health, insights into new products and breakthroughs in the use of natural foods, vitamins, herbs, herbal combinations, and formulas.

GW
**ZEITSCHRIFT FUER KLASSISCHE HOMOOPATHIE : KH.** **VFOAT** KH. Vol. 31, No. 1 (Jan./Feb. 1987)-. Periodical. German. bm (6 issues). DM201.00. Karl F Haug Verlag GmbH and Company, Postfach 102840, D 69018 Heidelberg Germany. **Tel** 011 49 6221 40620. **NLM** W1; ZE43S. ***Continues*** *Zeitschrift fuer Klassische Homopathie und Arzneipotenzierung.*

---

## HOSPITAL ADMINISTRATION AND MEDICAL CENTERS

---

US/0744-6748
**1ST READING (SACRAMENTO, CALIF.).** **See** Law.

US/0012-6535
**1199 NEWS.** **See** Economics-Labor.

FR/0339-8854
**A.D.P.H.S.O.** **VFOAT** Association pour le Developpement de la Pharmacie Hospitaliere du Sud-Ouest. (1976)-. Periodical. French. qt. 250.00F. ADPHSO, CTR Hospital, J. Rougier BP 269, 46005 Cahors France. **Tel** 011 33 1 65205048, FAX 011 33 1 65205096. **UDC** 61. cum. index. **Bk Rev**, (Qty: 4). **Ad Acc. Circ:** 800 (ctrl).

US/1054-5913
**AAPPO JOURNAL.** (AAPPO JOURNAL : THE JOURNAL OF THE AMERICAN ASSOCIATION OF PREFERRED PROVIDER ORGANIZATIONS.). [AAPPO j.]. **Added/Corp** American Association of Preferred Provider Organizations. **VFOAT** Managed Healthcare AAPPO Journal; Journal of the American Association of Preferred Provider Organizations. **VAT** American Association of Preferred Provider Organizations Journal. Vol. 1, No. 1 (Feb./Mar. 1991)-. Periodical. English. Six times a year. $50.00. Health Care Communications Inc., One Bridge Plaza, Suite 350, Fort Lee NJ 07024. **Tel** (201)947-5545. **LC** RA413.5.U5; A533. **DD** 362.1/0425. **NLM** W1; AA101AX.
**Desc:** Offers timely, accurate reports of current developments within the managed healthcare field derived from the proceedings of meetings of the AAPPO as well as original articles and reader survey research results.
**Ind/Abst** Int. Pharm. Abstr.

●US/1078-0076
**ACCREDITATION MANUAL FOR HEALTH CARE NETWORKS. VOL. 1, STANDARDS.** [Accredit. man. health care netw., Vol. 1 Stand.]. **Added/Corp** Joint Commission on Accreditation of Healthcare Organizations. (1994)-. Periodical. English. be. $85.00. Joint Commission on Accreditation of Hospitals, 1 Renaissance Boulevard, Headquarters Center, Oakbrook Terrace IL 60181. **Tel** (708)916-5800. **DD** 362.
**Desc:** Focuses on functions performed in health care networks and presents a framework for improving the performance of those functions.

●US/1077-9817
**ACCREDITATION MANUAL FOR HEALTH CARE NETWORKS. VOL. 2, SCORING GUIDELINES.** [Accredit. man. health care netw., Vol. 2 Scoring guidel.]. **Added/Corp** Joint Commission on Accreditation of Healthcare Organizations. (1994)-. Periodical. English. be. $85.00. Joint Commission on Accreditation of Hospitals, 1 Renaissance Boulevard, Headquarters Center, Oakbrook Terrace IL 60181. **Tel** (708)916-5800.

US/1059-7409
**ACCREDITATION MANUAL FOR HOSPITALS / THE JOINT COMMISSION.** [Accredit. man. hosp.]. **Main/Corp** Joint Commission on Accreditation of Healthcare Organizations. **VFOAT** AMH. (1989)-. English. an. $16.50. Joint Commission on Accreditation of Hospitals, 1 Renaissance Boulevard, Headquarters Center, Oakbrook Terrace IL 60181. **Tel** (708)916-5800. **LC** RA981.A2; J59a. **DD** 362. ***Continues*** *Joint Commission on Accreditation of Hospitals. Accreditation Manual for Hospitals, 1059-7409.*

US
**ACCREDITATION MANUAL FOR LONG TERM CARE.** (19??)-. Periodical. English. be. $85.00 (per volume); $140.00 (set). Joint Commission on Accreditation of Hospitals, 1 Renaissance Boulevard, Headquarters Center, Oakbrook Terrace IL 60181. **Tel** (708)916-5800.
**Desc:** Information on how to prepare for a survey and how to use the Joint Commission long term care standards as a measure for providing high quality care.

BE/0044-6009
**ACTA HOSPITALIA.** [Acta hosp.]. **Added/Corp** Louvain Universite Catholique. Centre de Sciences Hospitalieres. (19??)-. Periodical. Dutch (English and French; summaries and/or abstracts in English and French). Four times a year (Mar., June, Sept., Dec.). 15000.00F Belgium and The Netherlands; 1900.00F other. Katholieke Univesiteit Leuven, Kapucijnenvoer 35, B-3000 Leuven Belgium. **Tel** 32 16 336973, FAX 011 32 16 216970. **ED** P. Quaethoven. **NLM** W1 AC811. Index available. cum. index (Yearly in last issue). **Bk Rev**, (Qty: 50-60). **Ad Acc. Circ:** 1,200.
**Desc:** News covering the health care management and the health care financing.
**Ind/Abst** EMBASE; Health Plan. Adminis.; Hospit. Health Admin. Index (winter 1977-1992); Int. Nurs. Index.

US
**ACTION KIT FOR HOSPITAL LAW.** **See** Law.

SZ/0254-0819
**ACUTE CARE.** ***Ceased.*** **See** Medical Science and Technology-Nursing.

US/0147-524X
**ADMINISTRATIVE BRIEFS.** **Added/Corp** American College of Hospital Administrators. Committee on Publications and Public Information. Vol. 1 (1967)-. Periodical. English. qt. American College of Hospital Administrators, Chicago IL.

NE
**ADRESBOEKJE VAN DE AMSTERDAMSE GENEESKUNDIGEN.** (19??)-. Dutch. Three times a year. F80.19. F Van Rossen BV, Laurierstraat 246, 1016 PT Amsterdam Netherlands. **Tel** 011 31 20 6240593.

CN/0847-1495
**AGENDA - ONTARIO HOSPITAL ASSOCIATION.** ***Ceased.*** (AGENDA : NEWSLETTER OF THE ONTARIO HOSPITAL ASSOCIATION.). [Agenda - Ont. Hosp. Assoc.]. **Added/Corp** Ontario Hospital Association. Vol. 1, no. 1 (Sept. 1989)-Vol. 4, No. 6 (June 1992). Periodical. English. mo. Ontario Hospital Association, 150 Ferrand Drive, Don Mills Ontario M3C 1H6 Canada. **Tel** (905)429-2661 ext. 7736. **DD** 362.1/1/09713. ***Continues*** *Ontario Hospitals Today, 0829-3791.*

US/0891-6608
**AHA NEWS (CHICAGO, ILL.).** (AHA NEWS / AMERICAN HOSPITAL ASSOCIATION.). [AHA news]. **Added/Corp** American Hospital Association. **VAT** American Hospital Association News. (Jan. 12, 1987)-. Periodical. English. wk (except Christmas and Thanksgiving). $100.00 (non-member); $45.00 (member of AHA). American Hospital Publishing Inc., (A Subsidiary of the American Hospital Association), PO Box 92683, Chicago IL 60675. **Tel** (312)440-6836, (800)621-6902, FAX (312)951-8491. **(Subscription address:** American Hospital Publishing Inc, PO Box 92567, Chicago, IL 60675; telephone: (800)621-6902**)** **ED** Barbara J Varro. **DD** 362. **NLM** W1; AH28. **Ad Acc. Circ:** 40,000 (ctrl). ***Formed by the union of*** *Aging and Long-Term Care, 0891-8139; Hospital Week, 0149-6352; Interact (Chicago, Ill.); Metropolitan Hospital, 0888-2657; Newsletter / American Hospital Association. Section for Rehabilitation Hospitals and Programs; Psychiatric Services; Small or Rural Hospital Report* ***and*** *Washington Memo (American Hospital Association), 0746-472X.*
**Desc:** Business news related to hospitals, legal/regulatory issues affecting hospitals.

DK
**AKTIVITETEN I SYGEHUSVSENET / SUNDHEDSSTYRELSEN.** **Added/Corp** Denmark. Sundhedsstyrelsen. (1979)-. Danish. **LC** RA989.D4; A75.

US/1053-0649
**ALLIANCE ALERT. MEDICAL/HEALTH.** [Alliance alert, Med./health]. **Added/Corp** Venture Economics, Inc. **VFOAT** Medical/Health; Medical/Health, Industry Alliances. **VAT** Medical, Health, Industry Alliances. Vol. 1, Issue 1 (Apr. 1990)-. Periodical. English. qt (Jan., Apr., Jul., Oct.). $395.00. Securities Data Company, 40 West 57th Street, 11th Floor, New York NY 10019. **Tel** (212)765-5311. **LC** HD9994.U5; A45. **DD** 338.7/613621/02573. available on an online database (files 16,636) from DIALOG.
**Ind/Abst** PROMT [Full Txt.]; PTS Newsl. Database [Full Txt.].

●US
**AMAHC : ACCREDITATION MANUAL FOR AMBULATORY HEALTH CARE.** **Added/Corp** Joint Commission on Accreditation of Healthcare Organizations. **VFOAT** Accreditation Manual for Ambulatory Healthcare.; Accreditation Manual for Ambulatory Health Care. (1992)-. Periodical. English. be. $85.00. Joint Commission on Accreditation of Hospitals, 1 Renaissance Boulevard, Headquarters Center, Oakbrook Terrace IL 60181. **Tel** (708)916-5800. ***Continues in part*** *Ambulatory Health Care Standards Manual, 0898-7351.*

AG/0326-0674
**AMBIENTE MEDICO : REVISTA DEL HOSPITAL J.A. FERNANDEZ.** **Added/Corp** Hospital Fernandez (Buenos Aires, Argentina) Hospital Fernandez (Buenos Aires, Argentina). Asociacion de Profesionales. Comite de Docencia e Investigacion. Universidad de Buenos Aires. Unidad Docente Hospitalaria "R" Fernandez. (198?)-. Periodical. Spanish (summaries and/or abstracts in English; table of contents in English). sa. Free, Argentina; $5.00 other. Hospital Ja Fernandez, Direc PC 3356, First Floor, CP 1425, Cap Fed Buenos Aires Argentina. **Tel** 011 54 1 801-0020, FAX 011 53 1 801-4011. **ED** Dr. Jorge Daniel Lemus. **NLM** W1; AM103D. **Pr Rev. Circ:** 500 (ctrl).

US/0894-3672
**AMBULATORY CARE.** [Ambul. care]. **Added/Corp** National Association for Ambulatory Care (U.S.). Vol. 4, No. 10 (Oct. 1984)-. Periodical. English. mo (within the seasons). $96.00. National Association for Ambulatory Care, 5151 Belt Line Road, Suite 1017, Dallas TX 75240. **Tel** (214)788-2456. **DD** 362. **NLM** W1; AM107B. ***Continues*** *Emergence, 0894-1017.*
**Ind/Abst** Hospit. Health Admin. Index (1987).

US/0898-7351
**AMBULATORY HEALTH CARE STANDARDS MANUAL.** ***Title Change.*** [Ambul. health care stand. man.]. **Added/Corp** Joint Commission on Accreditation of Hospitals. Accreditation Council for Ambulatory Health Care. Accreditation Manual for Ambulatory Health Care. (1985)-(19??). English. an. Joint

# Medical Science and Technology —Hospital Administration and Medical Centers

Commission on Accreditation of Hospitals, 1 Renaissance Boulevard, Headquarters Center, Oakbrook Terrace IL 60181. **Tel** (708)916-5800. **DD** 362. **NLM** WX 15; A497. *Continued by* Accreditation Manual for Ambulatory Health Care.

US/1057-753X
### AMBULATORY RECORD MONITOR. Title Change. (AMBULATORY RECORD MONITOR : ARM.).
[Ambul. rec. monit.]. **VFOAT** ARM. (1991)-(1993). Periodical. English. mo. United Communications Group, 11300 Rockville Pike, Suite 1100, Rockville MD 20852. **Tel** (301)816-8950 ext. 223, FAX (301)816-8945. **ED** Margaret Stewart. **DD** 651. cum. index. **Bk Rev**, (Qty: 4). **Circ:** 500 (ctrl). *Merged into* Med Rec Automation & Management Report.
 **Desc:** Provides information on health record documentation.

US
### AMERICAN HOSPITAL ASSOCIATION HOSPITAL STATISTICS. *See* Medical Science and Technology-Abstracting, Bibliographies and Statistics.

US/0002-9289
### AMERICAN JOURNAL OF HOSPITAL PHARMACY. *See* Pharmacy and Pharmacology.

●US/1062-8606
### AMERICAN JOURNAL OF MEDICAL QUALITY. (AMERICAN JOURNAL OF MEDICAL QUALITY : THE OFFICIAL JOURNAL OF THE AMERICAN COLLEGE OF MEDICAL QUALITY.). [Am. j. med. qual.]. **Added/Corp** American College of Medical Quality. Vol. 7, No. 3 (Fall 1992)-. Periodical. English. qt. $107.00 (individual), $122.00 (institution); US $127.00 (individual), $142.00 (institution) other. Williams & Wilkins Company, 428 East Preston Street, Baltimore MD 21202-3993. **Tel** (410)528-4000, (800)638-6423, FAX (410)528-8596, telex 87669. (Subscription address: Williams & Wilkins, PO Box 64380, Baltimore MD 21264.) **DD** 610. **Pr Rev.** Documents available from , , Quick Copies. *Continues* Quality Assurance and Utilization Review, 0885-713X.
 **Desc:** Articles on utilization review, quality assurance, cost containment, diagnosis related groups, and risk management.

US
### AMH : ACCREDITATION MANUAL FOR HOSPITALS / THE JOINT MISSION.
**Main/Corp** Joint Commission on Accreditation of Healthcare Organizations. **VFOAT** Accreditation Manual for Hospitals. (1991)-. English. Joint Commission on Accreditation of Healthcare Organizations, One Renaissance Boulevard, Headquarters Center, Oakbrook Terrace IL 60181. **Tel** (708)916-5800. *Continues* Joint Commission on Accreditation of Health Care Organizations Accreditation Manual for Hospitals.

BE/0583-8142
### ANNALES DE LA SOCIETE BELGE D'HISTOIRE DES HOPITAUX. (ANNALES DE LA SOCIETE BELGE D'HISTOIRE DES HOPITAUX. ANNALEN VAN DE BELGISCHE VERENIGING VOOR HOSPITAAL-GESCHIEDENIS.). **Main/Corp** Societe Belge d'Histoire des Hopitaux. **VFOAT** Annalen van de Belgische Vereniging voor Hospitaal-Geschiedenis. (1963)-. French (Dutch). ir. 1200.00F (Vols. 26 and 27). Societe Belge d'Histoire Hospital, rue Haute 298A, B-1000 Brussels Belgium. **Tel** 32 2 5353028. **LC** RA989.B4; S6.

US
### ANNUAL FINANCIAL REPORT - TEXAS HEALTH FACILITIES COMMISSION.
**Main/Corp** Texas Health Facilities Commission. **Added/Corp** Texas Health Facilities Commission. Audit Report. **VFOAT** Audit Report - Texas Health Facilities Commission. (19??)-. English. an. Texas Health Facilities Commission, 111 East 17th/Room 1116, Austin TX 78701. **LC** RA981.T4; T35b. **DD** 353.97640072/31.

US/0277-9579
### ANNUAL HOSPITAL REPORT. (ANNUAL HOSPITAL REPORT / SOUTH DAKOTA DEPARTMENT OF HEALTH, STATE CENTER FOR HEALTH STATISTICS.). **Added/Corp** South Dakota. State Center for Health Statistics. **VFOAT** South Dakota Annual Hospital Report. (19??)-. English. an. South Dakota Department of Health, 523 East Capitol, Pierre SD 57501. **Tel** (605)773-3361. **LC** RA981.S62; A56. **DD** 362.1/1/09783.

US
### ANNUAL NURSING HOME SURVEY / SOUTH DAKOTA DEPARTMENT OF HEALTH, STATE CENTER FOR HEALTH STATISTICS. **Added/Corp** South Dakota. State Center for Health Statistics. **VFOAT** South Dakota Annual Nursing Home Report. (19??)-. English. an. South Dakota Department of Health, 523 East Capitol, Pierre SD 57501. **Tel** (605)773-3361. **LC** RA997.5.S8; A74. **DD** 362.1/6/09783.

US
### ANNUAL REPORT. **Main/Corp** Warm Springs State Hospital. (19??)-. English. an. Warm Springs State Hospital, Warm Springs MT 59756. **LC** RC445.M9; W36. **DD** 362.1/1/0978687.

US
### ANNUAL REPORT. **Main/Corp** Massachusetts General Hospital. Vol. 1 (1814)-. English. an. Massachusetts General Hospital, Department of Preventive Medicine, Boston MA 02114. **Tel** (617)726-5908. **LC** RA982.B7; M4.

US/0362-6849
### ANNUAL REPORT - ALASKA NATIVE MEDICAL CENTER. **Main/Corp** Alaska Native Medical Center. (19??)-. English. an. PO Box 7-741, Anchorage AK 99510. **LC** RA982.A382; A42a. **DD** 362.8/4.

US/0737-0601
### ANNUAL REPORT AND FINANCIAL STATEMENTS / ALASKA MEDICAL FACILITY AUTHORITY. [Annu. rep. financ. statements - Alsk. Med. Facil. Auth.]. **Main/Corp** Alaska Medical Facility Authority. (19??)-. English. an. Alaska Medical Facility Authority, c/o Alaska Department of Revenue, Treasury Division, Pouch SB, Juneau AK 99811. **LC** RA981.A58; A55a. **DD** 353.0084/1.

US
### ANNUAL REPORT FOR FISCAL YEAR ... / VERMONT STATE HOSPITAL. **Main/Corp** Vermont State Hospital. (19??)-. English. an. Vermont Department of Mental Health, Osgood Building, 103 South Main Street, Waterbury VT 05676. **LC** RC445.V43; V47a. **DD** 362.2/1/09743.

US
### ANNUAL REPORT FOR THE FISCAL YEAR ... / SOUTH CAROLINA STATE BOARD OF EXAMINERS FOR NURSING HOME ADMINISTRATORS. **Main/Corp** South Carolina State Board of Examiners for Nursing Home Administrators. (19??)-. English. an. South Carolina State Board of Examiners for Nursing Home Administrators, 221 Devine Street/Suite 201, PO Box 11477. **LC** RA997.5.S6; S66a. **DD** 353.97570082/43.

US
### ANNUAL REPORT - GENERAL CLINICAL RESEARCH CENTERS COMMITTEE, NATIONAL INSTITUTES OF HEALTH. **Main/Corp** National Institutes of Health. General Clinical Research Centers Committee. (19??)-. English. an. National Institutes of Health, 9000 Rockville Pike, Bethesda MD 20014. **Tel** (301)496-6975.

AT
### ANNUAL REPORT - HOSPITALS AND HEALTH SERVICES COMMISSION.
**Main/Corp** Australia. Hospitals and Health Services Commission. (1973/74)-. English. Hospitals and Health Services Commission, PO Box 392, Woden Canberra Australian Capital Territory 2600 Australia. **LC** J905; .L3 subser; RA371. **DD** 354/.994/0084105.

US
### ANNUAL REPORT - ILLINOIS HEALTH FACILITIES AUTHORITY. **Main/Corp** Illinois Health Facilities Authority. (19??)-. English. Illinois Health Facilities Authority, 35 East Wacker Drive, Chicago IL 60601. **LC** RA981.I4; I44a. **DD** 353.9/773/00841.

US
### ANNUAL REPORT / ILLINOIS HEALTH FINANCE AUTHORITY. **Main/Corp** Illinois Health Finance Authority. (1979)-. English. an. Illinois Health Finance Authority, 524 South 2nd Street, Room 577, Springfield IL 62706. **LC** RA981.I4; I45a. **DD** 353.97730084/1045.

US/0145-773X
### ANNUAL REPORT - NEW CASTLE STATE HOSPITAL. **Main/Corp** New Castle State Hospital. (19??)-. English. an. New Castle State Hospital, New Castle IN. **LC** HV3006.I62; N485. **DD** 362.2/1/0977264.

US/0361-4018
### ANNUAL REPORT - NEW YORK STATE MEDICAL CARE FACILITIES FINANCE AGENCY. **Main/Corp** New York State Medical Care Facilities Finance Agency. (1973)-. English. an. New York State Medical Care Facilities, Finance Agency, 1250 Broadway, New York NY 10001. **LC** RA981.N7; N48a. **DD** 353.9/747/008243.

US
### ANNUAL REPORT - NURSING HOME OMBUDSMEN OFFICE. **Main/Corp** Connecticut. Nursing Home Ombudsmen Office. (1977/1978)-. English. an. **LC** RA997.5.C8; C666a. **DD** 353.97460084/6.

CN/0713-1887
### ANNUAL REPORT ... OF ALBERTA HEALTH FACILITIES REVIEW COMMITTEE. [Annu. rep. Alta. Health Facil. Rev. Comm.]. **Main/Corp** Alberta Health Facilities Review Committee. (1979)-. English. an. Alberta Health Facilities Review Committee, 9942 - 108 Street, Edmonton Alberta Canada. **LC** RA983.A4; A422. **DD** 354.71230084/1. *Continues* Alberta Hospital Visitors Committee. Annual Report, 0706-9804.

US
### ANNUAL REPORT OF THE WASHINGTON STATE HOSPITAL COMMISSION. **Main/Corp** Washington State Hospital Commission. (19??)-. English. an. Free. Washington State Hospital Commission, 206 Evergreen Plaza, 711 Capitol Way, Olympia WA 98504. **Tel** (206)753-1990. **LC** RA981.W2; W33a. **DD** 353.97970084/1. **Circ:** 1,000.
 **Desc:** Summary of the activities of the Hospital Commission which reviews and approves budgets and rates of all licensed hospitals in Washington State. Contains financial and patient discharge summary information.

US/0464-5685
### ANNUAL REPORT - PINELAND HOSPITAL & TRAINING CENTER.
**Main/Corp** Pineland Hospital and Training Center. (19??)-. English. an. Box C, Pownal ME 04069. **LC** RJ506.M4; P55a. **DD** 362.2/1/0974191.

US
### ANNUAL REPORT: STATE HOSPITALS FOR THE MENTALLY DISORDERED. **Main/Corp** California. Center for Health Statistics. **Added/Corp** California. Center for Health Statistics. State Hospitals for the Mentally Disordered. (19??)-. English. an. 744 P Street, Room 777, Sacramento CA 95814. **LC** RC445.C178; C45a. **DD** 362.2/1/09794. **NLM** W2 AC2 C3A.

US/0098-4167
### ANNUAL REPORT - STATE OF CONNECTICUT HEALTH & EDUCATIONAL FACILITIES AUTHORITY. **Main/Corp** Connecticut. Health and Educational Facilities Authority. **VAT** Annual Report - State of Connecticut Health and Educational Facilities Authority. (19??)-. English. an. Connecticut Health & Educational Facilities Authority, 60 Washington Street, Hartford CT 06106. **LC** RA981.C6; C66a. **DD** 353.9/746/00841.

US
### ANNUAL REPORT / TERRELL STATE HOSPITAL. **Main/Corp** Terrell State Hospital. (19??)-. English. an. Terrell State Hospital, Box 70, Terrell TX 75160. **LC** RC445.T4; T27a. **DD** 362.2/1/09764277.

US/0277-0571
### ANNUAL REPORT / TEXAS BOARD OF LICENSURE FOR NURSING HOME ADMINISTRATORS. **Main/Corp** Texas Board of Licensure for Nursing Home Administrators. (Aug. 31, 1979)-. English. an. Texas Board of Licensure For Nursing Home Administrators, PO Box 9706, Austin TX 78766. **LC** RA997.5.T4; T46a. **DD** 353.97640072/2368243. **NLM** W2; AT4 B6a.

US/0146-7077
### ANNUAL REPORT TO THE GOVERNOR AND GENERAL ASSEMBLY - STATE OF CONNECTICUT, COMMISSION ON HOSPITALS & HEALTH CARE. (ANNUAL REPORT TO THE GOVERNOR AND GENERAL ASSEMBLY.). **Main/Corp** Commission on Hospitals and Health Care. **VAT** Annual Report to the Governor and General Assembly - State of Connecticut, Commission on Hospitals and Health Care. (1973/1974)-. English. an. Commission on Hospitals & Health Care, 340 Capitol Avenue, Hartford CT 06115. **LC** RA395.A4; C83. **NLM** W2 AC8 C75A.

US
### ANNUAL REPORT TO THE GOVERNOR AND LEGISLATURE / STATE OF FLORIDA, HEALTH CARE COST CONTAINMENT BOARD. **Main/Corp** Florida. Health Care Cost Containment Board. **VFOAT** Annual Report. (1988)-. English. an. Larson Building, 200 East Gaines Street, Tallahassee FL 32301. **LC** RA981.F4; F56c. **DD** 338.4/33621/09759. *Continues* Florida. Hospital Cost Containment Board. Annual Report ... to the Governor and Legislature, 0735-4118.

US
### ANNUAL STATISTICAL REPORT / EMILY P. BISSELL HOSPITAL. *See* Medical Science and Technology-Abstracting, Bibliographies and Statistics.

EC
**ANUARIO DE ESTADISTICAS HOSPITALARIAS.** **Added/Corp** Instituto Nacional de Estadistica (Ecuador). (19??)-. Statistical Publication. Spanish. an. Instituto Nacional de Estadistica y Censos, Avda 10 de Agosto 229, Quito Ecuador. **Tel** 51.95.97/51.93.20, telex 21421 INFEC ED. **LC** RA407.5.E2; A57. ***Continues*** *Estadisticas Hospitalarias.*

●US
**AOHA PROGRESS : A PUBLICATION OF THE AMERICAN OSTEOPATHIC HOSPITAL ASSOCIATION.** **Added/Corp** American Osteopathic Hospital Association. **VFOAT** American Osteopathic Hospital Association Progress. Vol. 1, No. 1 (Aug. 1992)-. Periodical. English. Twelve times a year (with special issues). $25.00. American Osteopathic Hospital Association, 5301 Wisconsin Avenue Northwest, Suite 630, Washington DC 20015. **Tel** (202)686-1700. **ED** Susan Sagosti and Betty Lynn Sprinkle. **NLM** W1; AO616. **Circ:** 1,200 (ctrl). ***Continues*** *AOHA, 1058-6385.*
**Desc:** Includes information about AOHA, its members, and related organizations. Covers topics of interest to CEOs and trustees of osteopathic hospitals including legislative news, national trends and marketing ideas.
**Ind/Abst** Hospit. Health Admin. Index (1992-).

US/1044-1980
**AOHA TODAY!.** ***Title Change.*** [AOHA today]. **Added/Corp** American Osteopathic Hospital Association. **VAT** American Osteopathic Hospital Association Today. Vol. 33, No. 2 (Apr. 1989)-. Periodical. English. mo. American Osteopathic Hospital Association, 5301 Wisconsin Avenue Northwest, Suite 630, Washington DC 20015. **Tel** (202)686-1700. **DD** 362. **NLM** W1; A062. ***Continues*** *Osteopathic Hospital Leadership, 8750-9202.* ***Continued by*** *AOHA Progress.*
**Ind/Abst** Health Plan. Adminis.; Hospit. Health Admin. Index.

●US/1072-5067
**AONE'S LEADERSHIP PROSPECTIVES.** **See** Medical Science and Technology-Nursing.

CN/0823-4124
**ARTERE (MONTREAL).** (ARTERE / ASSOCIATION DES HOPITAUX DU QUEBEC.). [Artere]. **Added/Corp** Association des Hopitaux du Quebec. (Oct. 1983)-. Periodical. French. mo (Jan./Feb. and Jul./Aug. issues combined). 60.00Can$ non-member; 45.00Can$ member. Association des Hopitaux du Quebec, 505 Maisonneuve Boulevard West, Suite 400, Montreal Quebec H3A 32C Canada. **Tel** (514)842-4861, FAX (514)842-0321. **ED** Charles Meunier. **DD** 362.1/1/068. **Ad Acc, Adv Mgr:** Michel Lauzier. **Circ:** 6,800.
**Desc:** A French publication distributed to all senior executives in the Quebec hospital sector with a capital expenditure of over one billion dollars.

HK/1011-596X
**ASIAN HOSPITAL.** [Asian hosp.]. (1987)-. Periodical. English. qt. $100.00 Hong Kong; $25.00 other. Techni-Press Asia Ltd, PO Box 20494, Hennessy Road, Hong Kong Hong Kong. **Tel** 011 852 5 278399 278682, FAX 011 852 5 278399 278682, telex 780 72727. **ED** A. W. Neill. **UDC** 61. **Bk Rev. Ad Acc. Circ:** 5,000 (ctrl).
**Desc:** Clinical and administrative management of hospitals in Asia.

IT/0392-050X
**ASSISTENZA SANITARIA, L'.** [Assistenza sanit.]. **Added/Corp** Federazione Nazionale Tecnici Ospedalieri. Associazione dei Segretari Generali e Degli Altri Dirigenti di Enti Sanitari. Centro Studi. **VFOAT** Tecnologia Sanitaria. Vol. 28 (Jan. 1978)-. Periodical. Italian. Ten times a year. L30000 Comes with Unione Nazionale Utenti Strutture membership. Unione Nazionale Utenti Strutture Sanitarie, Via Monte Bianco 63, 20149 Milan Italy. **Tel** 011 39 2 4692934. **NLM** W1 AS364CB. ***Continues*** *Assistenza Ospedaliera, 0004-5179.*

CN/0820-9995
**ASSOCIATION DES STOMISES DES BASSES LAURENTIDES.** (ASSOCIATION DES STOMISES DES BASSES LAURENTIDES : BULLETIN.). **Added/Corp** Association des Stomises des Basses Laurentides. Vol. 1, No. 1 (June 1983)-. Bulletin. French. qt. Free to Members. Association des Stomises des Basses Laurentides, 126 31E Avenue, St-Eustache Quebec J7P 2X4 Canada. **DD** 362.1/97554.

US
**AUDIT REPORT, HARLINGEN STATE CHEST HOSPITAL.** **Main/Corp** Harlingen State Chest Hospital. **Added/Corp** Texas. Office of the State Auditor. (19??)-. English. an. **LC** RA982.H19; H34a. **DD** 362.1/9754/09764495.

US
**AUDIT REPORT. TEXAS BOARD OF LICENSURE FOR NURSING HOME ADMINISTRATORS.** **Main/Corp** Texas Board of Licensure for Nursing Home Administrators. **Added/Corp** Texas. Office of the State Auditor. **VFOAT** Texas Board of Licensure for Nursing Home Administrators. (19??)-. English. State Auditor, John H Reagan, State Office Building, PO Box 12067, Austin TX 78711. **LC** RA997.5.T4; T46b. **DD** 353.97640084/1.

AT/0156-5788
**AUSTRALIAN HEALTH REVIEW.** (AUSTRALIAN HEALTH REVIEW : A PUBLICATION OF THE AUSTRALIAN HOSPITAL ASSOCIATION.). [Aust. health rev.]. **Added/Corp** Australian Hospital Association. (1978)-. Periodical. English. Four times a year (Feb., May, Aug., Nov.). 50.00Aus$ Australia; 80.00Aus$ other. Australian Hospital Association, 42 Thesiger Court, Deakin Act 2600 Australia. **Tel** 011 61 62851488, FAX 011 61 6 2822395. **ED** Peter Bauldevstone. **NLM** W1 AU453T. Index available. **Bk Rev. Circ:** 1,000 (ctrl).
**Desc:** For hospital administrators, medical and nursing directors, students in health administration, and anyone interested in keeping informed in the health field, in particular, management.
**Ind/Abst** APAIS, Aust. Public Aff. Inf. Ser.; EMBASE; Health Plan. Adminis.; Hospit. Health Admin. Index.

AT
**AUSTRALIAN HOSPITAL.** No. 167 (1991)-. Periodical. English. bm. 75.00Aus$ Australia; 90.00Aus$ Pacific Region; 96.00Aus$ other. Peter Isaacson Publications, 46-50 Porter Street, Prahran Victoria, 3181 Australia. **Tel** 011 61 3 2457777, FAX 011 61 3 2457605. **NLM** W1; AU532L. ***Continues*** *Health Professional.*

AT/0727-730X
**AUSTRALIAN HOSPITAL ENGINEER.** [Aust. hosp. eng.]. (1978)-. Periodical. English. qt. 30.00Aus$. Chevron Publishing, 40 Errol Stree, First Floor, North Melbourne, 3051 Australia. **Tel** 011 61 3 3295844, FAX 011 661 3 3281333. **DD** 690.5510994. **Ad Acc. Circ:** 4,500.

AT/0817-3907
**AUSTRALIAN MEDICAL RECORD JOURNAL / MEDICAL RECORD ASSOCIATION OF AUSTRALIA.** **Added/Corp** Medical Record Association of Australia. **VFOAT** AMR Journal. (1983)-. Periodical. English. Four times a year (Mar., June, Sept., Dec.). 50.00Aus$ Australia; 70.00Aus$ others. Australian Medical Record, GPO Box 4119, Sydney NSW 2001 Australia. **NLM** W1; AU628D. Index available (Bound in 1st iss. (Mar.).). cum. index. **Bk Rev. Ad Acc. Pr Rev. Circ:** 1,200. ***Continues*** *Australian Medical Record.*

US
**BRIEFINGS ON HOSPITAL SAFETY.** (19??)-. Periodical. English. Twelve times a year. $177.00. Medical Records Briefing, PO Box 1168, Marblehead MA 01945. **Tel** (617)639-1872.

FR/0583-8517
**BULLETIN.** **Main/Corp** Societe Francaise d'Histoire des Hopitaux. **Added/Corp** Les Amis de l'Assistance Publique, Paris. No. 1 (1959)-. Bulletin. French. ir (1 to 4 times a year). 200.00F. Musee des Hospices Civiles, 1 rue de l'Hopital, 69002 Lyon France. **Tel** 11 33 78 373646.

US/0045-9550
**BULLETIN OF THE MEDICAL STAFF OF THE METHODIST HOSPITALS OF DALLAS.** [Bull. med. staff Methodist Hosp. Dallas]. **Main/Corp** Methodist Hospitals of Dallas. **VFOAT** Bulletin - Methodist Hospitals of Dallas Medical Staff. (19??)-. Academic Scholarly Publication. English. sa. $5.00. Methodist Hospital of Dallas, PO Box 225999, Dallas TX 75265. **Tel** (214)944-8457. **NLM** W1 BU857GB. **CODEN** BMSDDT. Documents available from CASDDS.
**Ind/Abst** Chem. Abstr.

US/0199-1256
**BULLETIN - UNIVERSITY OF KANSAS MEDICAL CENTER, THE.** [Bull. - Univ. Kan. Med. Cent.]. **Main/Corp** Kansas. University. Medical Center. Bulletin. English. qt. Free. University of Kansas Medical Center, 39th Rainbow Boulevard, Kansas City KS 66103.
**Desc:** Contains material on programs, activities and people of interest to Kansas medical personnel and university alumni.

●US/1072-1932
**BUSINESS OF MANAGED CARE.** (1994)-. English. $87.00. Mosby Year Book Inc., 11830 Westline Industrial Drive, St Louis MO 63146. **Tel** (800)325-4177, (314)872-8370, FAX (314)432-1380, telex 44-2402.

JA
**BYOIN KANRI KENKYUJO. ANNUAL REPORT OF THE NATIONAL INSTITUTE OF HOSPITAL ADMINISTRATION.** **Main/Corp** Byoin Kanri Kenkyujo. **Added/Corp** Byoin Kanri Kenkyujo. Annual Report of the National Institute of Hospital Administration. **VFOAT** Annual Report of the National Institute of Hospital Administration. (19??)-. Japanese. Byoin Kanri Kenkyujo, 1 Toyamamachi, Shinjuku-ku 162, Tokyo Japan. **LC** RA971; .B94a.

JA
**BYOIN YORAN.** **Added/Corp** Japan. Koseisho. Imukyoku. Somuka. **VFOAT** Japanese Hospital Directory. (19??)-. Japanese (Japanese). ¥8500. Igaku Shoin Ltd., 5-24-3 Hongo Bunkyo-ku, Tokyo 113 Japan. **Tel** 011 81 3 817 5670. **LC** RA990.J3; B96. **NLM** WX 22 JJ3 QB9.

CN/0226-5923
**C. H. A. C. REVIEW.** [C.H.A.C. rev.]. **Main/Corp** Catholic Health Association of Canada. **VAT** Catholic Health Association of Canada Review. Vol. 8, No. 1 (Jan./Feb. 1980)-. Periodical. English. Three times a year (Mar., Jul., Nov.). 30.00Can$ Canada; 35.00Can$ other. Catholic Health Association of Canada, 1247 Killborn Place, Ottawa Ontario K1H 6K9 Canada. **Tel** (613)731-7148, FAX (613)731-7797. **ED** Freda Fraser. **DD** 362.1/1/0971. **NLM** W1 C342. Index available. cum. index. **Ad Acc, Adv Mgr:** Martine Leroux. **Circ:** 1,500 (ctrl). ***Continues*** *Catholic Hospital, 0008-8099.* ***Continued in part by*** *CHAC Info., 0822-8426.*
**Ind/Abst** Hospit. Health Admin. Index.

BL
**CADASTRO HOSPITALAR BRASILEIRO.** **Main/Corp** Brazil. Coordenacao de Assistencia Medica e Hospitalar. (19??)-. Portuguese. **LC** RA984.B8; B72a.

BL
**CADASTROS: ESTABLECIMENTOS HOSPITALARES, ESTABLECIMENTOS PARA-HOSPITALARES, ESTABLECIMENTOS DE SERVICOS OFICIAIS DE SAUDE PUBLICA.** **Added/Corp** Minas Gerais (Brazil). Instituto Estadual de Estatistica. (19??)-. Portuguese. Instituto Estadual de Estatistica, Av Afonso Pena 867 - 200 Andar, Belo Horizonte Brazil. **LC** RA984.B83; M553.

US/0896-7997
**CAHHS INSIGHT.** [CAHHS insight]. **Added/Corp** California Association of Hospitals and Health Systems. **VAT** California Association of Hospitals and Health Systems Insight. Vol. 10, No. 18 (Dec. 17, 1986)-. Periodical. English. bm. $40.00 non-member; $20.00 member CAHHS. California Association of Hospitals and Health Systems, PO Box 1100, Sacramento CA 95812. **Tel** (916)443-7401. **DD** 362. cum. index. ***Continues*** *CHA Insight.*
**Ind/Abst** Hospit. Manage. Rev.

FR/0295-4591
**CAHIERS HOSPITALIERS: PERSONNEL AND FORMATION.** (1986)-. Periodical. French. mo. 490.00F. Editions Berger-Levrault, BP 50, 54840 Velaine en Haye France. **Tel** 011 33 1 1683916808, FAX 011 33 1 1683232492. **UDC** 61.35. **CODEN** 35.

US/0896-2766
**CALIFORNIA HOSPITALS.** [Calif. hosp.]. **Added/Corp** California Hospital Association. California Association of Hospitals and Health Systems. Vol. 1, No. 1 (Oct./Nov. 1986)-. Periodical. English. bm (Jan., Mar., May, Jul., Sep., Nov.). $40.00 non-member, $20.00 member CAHHS. California Association of Hospitals and Health Systems, PO Box 1100, Sacramento CA 95812. **Tel** (916)443-7401. **DD** 362. **NLM** W1; CA371F. **Ad Acc.** ctrl circ.
**Ind/Abst** Health Plan. Adminis.; Hospit. Manage. Rev.

CN
**CANADIAN HEALTH CARE MANAGEMENT.** English. Twelve times a year. 187.00Can$. MPL Communications, 133 Richard Street West, Suite 700, Toronto Ontario M5H 3M8 Canada. **Tel** (416)869-1177, FAX (416)869-0456.
**Desc:** Provides current information for health care administrators. Provides reference articles written by health care professors, management and other professionals.

CN
**CANADIAN HEALTHCARE MANAGER.** (19??)-. English. Four times a year. 40.00Can$ Canada. MacLean Hunter Ltd. Business Publishers / Canada, Box 9100, Station A, Toronto ONT M5W 1A5 Canada. **Tel** (416)946-8420, (800)567-0444. **(Subscription address:** Indas, 35 Riviera Drive, Building 17, Markham Ontario L3R 8N4 Canada.**)**

CN/0228-8907
**CANADIAN HOSPITAL ASSOCIATION COMMITTEE RESEARCH REPORT.** [Comm. res. rep. - Can. Hosp. Assoc.]. **Added/Corp** Canadian Hospital Association (Founded 1931). (1971)-. Monographic series. English. Price varies per volume. **NLM** W1 CA563.

CN/0068-8932
**CANADIAN HOSPITAL DIRECTORY.** ***Title Change.*** (CANADIAN HOSPITAL DIRECTORY. ANNUAIRE DES HOPITAUX DU CANADA.). [Can. hosp. dir.]. **Added/Corp** Canadian Hospital Association. **VFOAT** Annuaire des Hopitaux du Canada. Vol.1 (1953)-(199?). Directory. English (French). an. Canadian Hospital Association, 17 York Street, Suite 100, Ottawa Ontario K1N 9J6 Canada. **Tel** (613)238-8005. **ED** Tess

Radford. **DD** 362.1/1/02571. **NLM** WX 22 DC2 C2. **Bk Rev.** **Ad Acc. Circ:** 4,500 (ctrl). ***Merged into*** *Guide to Canadian Health Care Facilities.*
**Desc:** Lists over 1,200 hospitals, health centers and nursing stations, 1,000 companies who manufacture or distribute to health, a statistical compendium, bed distribution tables, etc.

CN/0821-2236
**CANADIAN HOSPITAL ENGINEERING JOURNAL.** [Can. hosp. eng. j.]. **Added/Corp** Canadian Hospital Engineering Society. **VFOAT** Journal Canadien d'Ingenierie Hospitaliere; CHES Quarterly Journal; Journal Trimestriel SCIH; SCIH Journal Trimestriel. **VAT** Quarterly Journal - Canadian Hospital Engineering Society; Canadian Hospital Engineering Society Quarterly Journal; Societe Canadien d'Ingenierie Hospitaliere. Vol. 1, No. 1 (Oct. 1981)-. Periodical. English (French; summaries and/or abstracts in French). qt (Jan., Apr., Jul., Oct.). 60.00Can$ US; 40.00Can$ other. Canadian Hospital Engineering Society, PO Box 3456, Station C, Ottawa Ontario M4P 2G9 Canada. **Tel** (613)596-2861. **DD** 362.1/1/0682.

CN/1187-3779
**CANADIAN HOSPITAL FORUM.** [Can. hosp. forum]. **Added/Corp** Thomson Healthcare Communications. **VFOAT** Hospital Forum. Vol. 1, No. 1 (Winter 1991)-. Periodical. English. sa. Thomson Healthcare, 1120 Birchmount Road, Suite 200, Scarborough Ontario M1K 5G4 Canada. **Tel** (905)750-8900. **DD** 338.4/76151/0971.

CN/0847-5520
**CANADIAN NURSING HOME.** [Can. nurs. home]. Vol. 1, No. 1 (Feb./Mar. 1990)-. Periodical. English. qt. 18.00Can$ Canada; 20.00Can$ US. Health Media Inc, 14453 29A Avenue, White Rock BC V4A 9K8 Canada. **Tel** (604)535-7933, FAX (604)535-9000. **DD** 362.1/6/09713. ***Continues*** *Ontario Nursing Home Journal., 0829-6340.*

CN/0715-9471
**CANADIAN PALLIATIVE CARE DIRECTORY, THE.** [Can. palliat. care dir.]. **Added/Corp** Palliative Care Foundation. Royal Victoria Hospital (Montreal, Quebec). Palliative Care Service. **VFOAT** Repertoire Canadien de Soins Palliatifs. (1983)-. Directory. English (French). Palliative Care Foundation, 228 Bloor Street West, Toronto Ontario M5S 1V8 Canada. **DD** 362.1/75/02571.

US/0163-2213
**CARCH NEWS.** **Main/Corp** California Association of Residential Care Homes. **VAT** California Association of Residential Care Homes News. (19??)-. Periodical. English. mo. California Association of Residential Care Homes, 1600 Sacramento Inn Way Suite 110, Sacramento CA 95815-3458. **ED** Charles W Skoien Jr. **Circ:** 6,000.

US/1053-5500
**CASE MANAGEMENT ADVISOR.** [Case manage. advis.]. **Added/Corp** American Health Consultants. (1990)-. Periodical. English. mo. $199.00. American Health Consultants, 3525 Piedmont Road, Suite 400, Atlanta GA 30305. **Tel** (800)688-2421, (404)262-7436. **(Subscription address:** American Health Consultants, PO Box 95278, Chicago IL 60694.**)** **DD** 610. **NLM** W1; CA901M. **[CCC].**
**Desc:** Provides practical, concise information needed to provide the highest quality, yet cost-effective, care for clients.
**Ind/Abst** Cumul. Index Nurs. Allied Health Lit.

US/0193-9394
**CASE STUDIES IN HEALTH ADMINISTRATION.** **Added/Corp** American College of Hospital Administrators. Vol. 1 (1978)-. Monographic series. English. **ED** Editor: v. 1- J. O. Hepner. **LC** UNC. **NLM** W1 CA901PH.
**Ind/Abst** Health Plan. Adminis.

US
**CATALOG OF HEALTHCARE INFORMATION AND MANAGEMENT SYSTEMS PUBLICATIONS / AHA.** **Main/Corp** Healthcare Information and Management Systems Society. **Added/Corp** American Hospital Association. (1988)-. Catalog. English. an. Included with Healthcare Information & Management Systems Society membership. American Hospital Association, 840 North Lake Shore Drive, Chicago IL 60611. **Tel** (312)280-6000, (800)242-2626. **NLM** ZWX 150; C623c. ***Continues*** *Hospital Management Systems Society. Catalog of Hospital Management Systems Publications, 0888-7071.*

US/8756-4068
**CATHOLIC HEALTH WORLD.** (CATHOLIC HEALTH WORLD / CATHOLIC HEALTH ASSOCIATION OF THE UNITED STATES.). [Cathol. health world]. **Added/Corp** Catholic Health Association of the United States. Vol. 1, No. 1 (Feb. 15, 1985)-. Periodical. English. Twenty-four times a year (bi-monthly on 1st & 15th of each month). $24.00 US; $28.00 other. Catholic Health Association of the US, 4455 Woodson Road, St Louis MO 63134. **Tel** (314)427-2500, FAX (314)427-0029. **ED** Michael McCauley, Suzy Farren and Sandy Gilfillan. **DD** 362. **Ad Acc. Circ:** 6,500.
**Desc:** Contains national and regional news, human interest features, health care legislation stories, and people photos. Interesting to administrators, management, and religious ownership of U.S. Catholic hospitals and long-term care facilities.

CN/0712-3108
**CENTRES HOSPITALIERS. GUIDE BUDGETAIRE.** (CENTRES HOSPITALIERS : GUIDE BUDGETAIRE ... : STANDARDS BUDGETAIRES.). [Cent. hosp., Guide budg.]. **Main/Corp** Quebec (Province). Ministere des Affaires Sociales. **VFOAT** Guide Budgetaire. (198?)-. French. an. Gouvernement du Quebec, 600 St Amable 4E Etage, Quebec Quebec G1R 4Z1 Canada. **DD** 362.1/1/0681.

CN/0828-0967
**CERTIFIED PUBLIC HOSPITAL LIST.** [Certif. public hosp. list]. **Added/Corp** Canada. Customs and Excise. Canada. Excise Branch. **VFOAT** Liste des Hopitaux Publics Certifies. (May 1971)-. English (French). an. Technical Information Section Excise, Department of National Revenue/Customs and Excise, Ottawa Ontario K1A 0L5 Canada. **LC** RA983.A1; C47. **DD** 362.1/1/02571. **Circ:** 450 (ctrl).
**Desc:** Contains the names and addresses of hospitals that have been certified as bona fide public hospitals by the Department of National Health and Welfare for the purposes of the Excise Tax Act and the Excise Act.

UK
**CHARLES BELL JOURNAL, THE.** English. Three times a year. £5.00. Mortimer Street, London W1 England. **Tel** 071-387-7050 ext. 2169, FAX 071-380-7193. **Bk Rev.** **Ad Acc. Circ:** 1,000. ***Continues*** *Middlesex Hospital Journal, 0026-3222.*

US/0739-9154
**CHFC REPORT.** **Added/Corp** California Health Facilities Commission. **VFOAT** C.H.F.C. **VAT** California Health Facilities Commission Report. (19??)-. Monographic series. English. Price varies per volume. 717 K Street, Suite 100, Sacramento CA 95814. **LC** RA981.C3; C47. **DD** 338.4/33621/109794.

US/0069-4428
**CLARK'S DIRECTORY OF SOUTHERN HOSPITALS.** ***Title Change.*** (19??)-(198?). Directory. English. ir. Clarks Publishing Company, PO Box 88, Greenville SC 29602. **Tel** (404)955-5656. **ED** Jeanine Glinski. **LC** RA977; .C56. **DD** 362.1/1/02575. **Ad Acc. Circ:** 4,000. ***Merged into*** *Hospital Blue Book, 1047-6903.*
**Desc:** Directory of (16 Southeastern states) hospitals, number of beds, key personnel and titles, average daily census; number of outpatient visits.

IT
**CLINICA MEDICA DEL NORD AMERICA.** (19??)-. Italian. bm (6 issues). $180.00 all, except Italy; L180000.00 Italy. Piccin Editore, Via Altinate 107, 35121 Padua Italy. **Tel** 011 39 49 655566, FAX 011 39 49 8750693.

US
**CLINICAL OUTCOMES : MANAGING PATIENTS AND THE TOTAL COST OF CARE.** **VFOAT** Managing Patients and the Total Cost of Care. (19??)-. Periodical. English. qt. $35.00. Health Sciences Institute, 350 Main Street #315, Doylestown PA 18901. **Tel** (215)340-9602. **NLM** W1; CL761ME.
**Ind/Abst** Hospit. Manage. Rev. (19??-).

US/0896-5765
**CLINICAL RC MANAGER.** [Clin. RC manager]. **VAT** Clinical Respiratory Care Manager. (Dec. 1984)-. Periodical. English. Six times a year. $90.00. Hospital Features, PO Box 9452, St Louis MO 63117. **Tel** (314)569-6363. **ED** Anthony McDonald. **DD** 362. Index available (published in Jan. issue). cum. index. **Circ:** 800 (ctrl).
**Desc:** Articles make recommendations for managing a respiratory care (hospital) department from a clinical and managerial standpoint.

US/0742-9800
**CODING CLINIC FOR ICD-9-CM.** **Added/Corp** American Hospital Association. Central Office on ICD-9-CM. **VFOAT** Coding Clinic. Began with: Vol. 1, No. 1 (May/June 1984)-. Periodical. English. qt. $105.00 member; $160.00 nonmember. American Hospital Publishing Inc., (A Subsidiary of the American Hospital Association), PO Box 92683, Chicago IL 60675. **Tel** (312)440-6836, (800)621-6902, FAX (312)951-8491. **(Subscription address:** American Hospital Publishing Inc, PO Box 92567, Chicago, IL 60675; telephone: (800)621-6902**)** **DD** 651. **NLM** W1; CO106L.
**Desc:** This publication provides up-to-the-minute coding information for hospital and health-related organizations nationwide that are interested in and dedicated to improving the accuracy and uniformity of coding. It provides advice on achieving coding consistency, maintaining coding integrity, determining accepted coding standards, compiling reliable data for trends analysis, assigning ICD-9-CM codes for new technologies, supplementing hospital inservice training of coders, and expanding coder's basic knowledge of medical science. All coding advice proposed for publication in Coding Clinic for ICD-9-CM requires the written approval of the representatives of the cooperating parties for the Central Office on ICD-9-CM. The cooperating parties are the National Center for Health Statistics, American Medical Record Association, Health Care Financing Administration, and the American Hospital Association.

US/0742-5937
**COMPENSATION REPORT, MANAGEMENT EMPLOYEES IN HOSPITAL & NURSING HOME MANAGEMENT COMPANIES.** **See** Business-Personnel Management.

US
**COMPENSATION SURVEY FOR CHICAGO AREA HOSPITALS / CHICAGO HOSPITAL COUNCIL.** **Added/Corp** Chicago Hospital Council. Chicago Hospital Personnel Management Association. (19??)-. English. Chicago Hospital Council, 840 North Lake Shore Drive, Chicago IL 60611. **LC** RA982.C45; C65. **DD** 331.2/8136211/0977311021.

US/0745-1075
**COMPUTERS IN HEALTHCARE.** ***Title Change.*** **See** Computers.

US/0889-8707
**CONNECTICUT HEALTH CARE.** (CONNECTICUT HEALTH CARE : JOURNAL OF THE CONNECTICUT HOSPITAL ASSOCIATION.). [Conn. health care]. **Added/Corp** Connecticut Hospital Association. (198?)-. Periodical. English. bm. $10.00. Connecticut Hospital Association, PO Box 90, Wallingford CT 06492. **DD** 362.

US
**CONNECTICUT'S PRIVATE MENTAL HOSPITALS : INPATIENT STATISTICS FOR YEAR ENDING ... / PREPARED BY STATISTICS SECTION, CONNECTICUT STATE DEPARTMENT OF MENTAL HEALTH.** **See** Medical Science and Technology-Abstracting, Bibliographies and Statistics.

US/1071-5320
**CONSENT MANUAL (SACRAMENTO, CALIF.).** (CALIFORNIA HOSPITAL ASSOCIATION CONSENT MANUAL.). [Consent man.]. **Added/Corp** California Hospital Association. California Association of Hospitals and Health Systems. (1960)-. English (Spanish). an. $110.00 (members of California Hospital Association); $225.00 other. California Association of Hospitals and Health Systems, PO Box 1100, Sacramento CA 95812. **Tel** (916)443-7401. **DD** 344.

US
**CONSOLIDATED STANDARDS MANUAL FOR CHILD, ADOLESCENT, AND ADULT PSYCHIATRIC, ALCOHOLISM, AND DRUG ABUSE FACILITIES.** ***Title Change.*** **Added/Corp** Joint Commission on Accreditation of Hospitals. (1979)-(19??). Periodical. English. an. Joint Commission on Accreditation of Hospitals, 1 Renaissance Boulevard, Headquarters Center, Oakbrook Terrace IL 60181. **Tel** (708)916-5800. ***Continued by*** *Mental Health Manual.*

CN/0824-1384
**CONTINUING CARE RESOURCES.** [Contin. care resour.]. Vol. 1, No. 1 (Nov. 1984)-. Periodical. English. Twelve times a year. 24.00Can$ Canada; 26.00Can$ other. Armour Health Associates Ltd., PO Box 80688, South Burnaby BC V5H 3Y1 Canada. **Tel** (604)438-1950. **ED** Shelagh A. Armour Godbolt, M.S.W., R.S.W. **DD** 326.1/6/09711. Index available (free - bound in Feb. issue). **Bk Rev**, (Qty: 3-4). **Ad Acc. Circ:** 175.
**Desc:** Contains information on geriatric nursing, care for impaired or disabled persons at home and activity and volunteer programs.

●US/1064-4571
**COST SURVEY (1992).** (COST SURVEY / MEDICAL GROUP MANAGEMENT ASSOCIATION.). [Cost surv.]. **Added/Corp** Medical Group Management Association. (1992)-. English. $195.00 (non-members). Medical Group Management Association, 104 Inverness Terrace East, Englewood CO 80112. **Tel** (303)397-7879, FAX (303)799-1683. **DD** 338. ***Continues in part*** *Cost and Production Survey Report, 0741-9287.*

US/0146-2814
**COTH REPORT.** **Added/Corp** Council of Teaching Hospitals. **VAT** Council of Teaching Hospitals Report. Vol. 1 (July 1967)-. Periodical. English. mo. $36.00; Also comes with membership. Association of American Medical Colleges, 2450 North Street Northwest, Washington DC 20037-1126. **Tel** (202)828-0400, (202)828-0416, FAX (202)828-1123. **NLM** W1 C544T.

US
**COUNCIL OF TEACHING HOSPITALS SURVEY OF HOUSESTAFF STIPENDS, BENEFITS, AND FUNDING / PREPARED BY: ASSOCIATION OF AMERICAN MEDICAL COLLEGES, DIVISION OF CLINICAL SERVICES.** **Added/Corp** Council of Teaching Hospitals. Association of American Medical Colleges. Division of Clinical Services. **VFOAT** Survey of Housestaff Stipends, Benefits, and Funding; COTH Survey of Housestaff Stipends, Benefits, and Funding. (1990)-. English. Association of the American Medical Colleges, 2450 North Street Northwest, Washington DC 20037. **Tel** (202)828-0400. **NLM** W1; CO963H. ***Continues*** *COTH Survey of House Staff Stipends, Benefits, and Funding, 0272-9148.*

US/0749-0704
**CRITICAL CARE CLINICS.** [Crit. care clin.]. Vol. 1, No. 1 (March 1985)-. Periodical. English. qt (Jan., Apr., Jul., Oct.). $110.00 (institution), $89.00 (individual) US; $131.00 (institution), $124.00 (individual) other. W.B. Saunders Company, A Subsidiary of Harcourt Brace Jovanovich, Inc., The Curtis Center/Suite 300, Independence Square West, Philadelphia PA 19106-3399. **Tel** (215)238-7800 or, 5587, FAX (215)238-7883, telex 173146. **(Subscription address:** W. B. Saunders Company / North America Subscriptions, c/o Periodicals, 6277 Sea Harbour Drive, 4th Floor, Orlando FL 32887.**)** **ED** Barbara Cohen-Kligerman. **LC** RC86; .C74. **DD** 616.028. **NLM** W1; CR216F. **CODEN** CCCLEH. **[CCC].** Index available. **Pr Rev. Circ:** 3,000. available on microfilm and microfiche from University Microfilms International (UMI). Documents available from The Genuine Article, BIOSIS Document Express.
**Desc:** Practical updates for the clinician on the latest advances. Each issue addresses a single topic in patient care.
**Ind/Abst** Biol. Abstr. (1986-); Cumul. Index Nurs. Allied Health Lit.; Curr. Contents Clin. Med.; EMBASE; Health Plan. Adminis.; Index Med. (Vol.1, No. 1, 1985-); Res. Alert [Select. Cov.]; SCISEARCH; Soc. Sci. Cit. Index [Select. Cov.].

US/0517-2160
**CUMULATIVE INDEX OF HOSPITAL LITERATURE.** ***Title Change.*** **Main/Corp** Library of the American Hospital Association, Asa S. Bacon Memorial. **Added/Corp** American Hospital Association. (1945/49)-(1994). English. an. American Hospital Association, 840 North Lake Shore Drive, Chicago IL 60611. **Tel** (312)280-6000, (800)242-2626. **DD** 362; 016. **NLM** ZWX 100 C971. ***Continued by*** *Hospital and Health Administration Index.*
**Desc:** Contains the references that have appeared in the Hospital Literature Index.

US
**CURRENT CHARGES FOR SELECTED HOSPITAL SERVICES ... / STATE OF FLORIDA, HOSPITAL COST CONTAINMENT BOARD.** **Main/Corp** Florida. Hospital Cost Containment Board. **Added/Corp** Florida. Hospital Cost Containment Board. Annual Report, Current Charges for Selected Services. **VFOAT** Annual Report, Current Charges for Selected Services. (19??)-. English. an. Florida Hospital Cost, Containment Board/Larson Building, Tallahassee FL 32301. **LC** RA981.F4; F56b. **DD** 338.4/336211/09759.

US/1057-0098
**DIRECT CONTRACTING & HOSPITAL MANAGED CARE.** ***Title Change.*** [Direct contract. hosp. managed care]. **VFOAT** Direct Contracting and Hospital Managed Care. (1991-1992). Periodical. English. mo. Aspen Publishers Inc., 7201 McKinney Circle, Frederick MD 21701. **Tel** (800)234-1660, (301)698-7100, FAX (301)251-5784, telex 5106014543. **DD** 362. **NLM** W1; DI658P. ***Continued by*** *Hospital Managed Care & Direct Contracting, 1061-7620.*

US
**DIRECTORY / AMERICAN COLLEGE OF HEALTHCARE EXECUTIVES.** **Main/Corp** American College of Healthcare Executives. (1986)-. English. an (published in even years). $150.00. American College of Healthcare Executives, 840 North Lake Shore Drive, c/o J. Flory, Chicago IL 60611. **Tel** (312)943-0544 ext. 3000, FAX (312)943-3791. **(Subscription address:** FDN American College of Healthcare Executives, Order Processing Center, 1951 Cornell Avenue, Melrose Park IL 60160.**)** **LC** RA977; .A57a. **DD** 362.1/068. ***Continues*** *American College of Hospital Administrators. Directory - American College of Hospital Administrators, 0065-7794.*

US/0098-2377
**DIRECTORY - AMERICAN GROUP PRACTICE ASSOCIATION.** **Main/Corp** American Group Practice Association. **Added/Corp** American Group Practice Association. AGPA Directory. **VFOAT** AGPA Directory. 17th Ed. (1974)-. Directory. English. an (Mar.). $125.00. American Group Practice Association, 1422 Duke Street, Alexandria VA 22313-3430. **Tel** (703)838-0033, FAX (703)548-1890. **ED** Susan Bautch. **LC** RA977; .A56a. **DD** 362.1/2/02573. **NLM** WX 22 AA1 A45D. **Ad Acc, Adv Mgr:** Fred Haag. **Circ:** 26,000 (ctrl). ***Continues*** *Directory - American Association of Medical Clinics, 0569-2679.*
**Desc:** A directory of the AGPA members.

US/0276-6590
**DIRECTORY - ASSOCIATION OF ACADEMIC HEALTH CENTERS (U.S.).** ***Title Change.*** (DIRECTORY / ASSOCIATION OF ACADEMIC HEALTH CENTERS.). [Dir. - Assoc. Acad. Heal. Cent. (U.S.)]. **Main/Corp** Association of Academic Health Centers (U.S.). (1981)-(1993). English. an (Jan.). Association of Academic Health Centers, 1400 16th Street Northwest, Suite 410, Washington DC 20036. **Tel** (202)265-9600, FAX (202)265-7514. **LC** RA977; .A88a. **DD** 610/.7/1173. **NLM** WX 22; AA1 A849d. ctrl circ. ***Continued by*** *Association of Academic Health Centers (U.S.). Membership Directory.*

US/0884-3368
**DIRECTORY. HOSPITAL EQUIPMENT & SUPPLIES.** **Added/Corp** American Business Directories, Inc. **VFOAT** Directory. Hospital Equipment and Supplies; Hospital Equipment & Supplies; Hospital Equipment and Supplies; Hospital Equipment Directory. (19??)-. Directory. English. an. American Business Directory, 5711 South 86th Circle, Omaha NE 68127. **Tel** (402)593-4600, FAX (402)331-5481. **LC** HD9995.H63; U543. **DD** 381/.45681761/02573.
**Ind/Abst** Nonwovens Abstr.

US/1059-7220
**DIRECTORY, INVESTOR-OWNED HOSPITALS, RESIDENTIAL TREATMENT FACILITIES AND CENTERS, HOSPITAL MANAGEMENT COMPANIES, HEALTH SYSTEMS.** [Dir. investor-owned hosp. resid. treat. facil. cent. hosp. manage. co. health syst.]. **Added/Corp** Federation of American Health Systems. **VFOAT** Directory of Investor-Owned Hospitals, Residential Treatment Facilities and Centers, Hospital Management Companies and Health Systems; Federation of American Health Systems ... Directory. (1991)-. Directory. English. an (Nov.). $60.00 (member); $100.00 (non-member). Federation of American Health Systems, 1405 North Pierce, Suite 311, Little Rock AR 72207. **Tel** (501)661-9555, FAX (501)663-4903. **LC** RA977; .D474. **DD** 362.1/1/02573. ***Continues*** *Directory of Investor-Owned Hospitals, Hospital Management Companies and Health Systems.*

US/0363-2563
**DIRECTORY: LICENSED & CERTIFIED HEALTH CARE FACILITIES.** **Added/Corp** Minnesota. Dept. of Health. Minnesota. Division of Health Systems. **VAT** Directory, Licensed and Certified Health Care Facilities. (19??)-. English. Minnesota Department of Health, 717 Southeast Delaware Street, Minneapolis MN 55440. **Tel** (612)623-5000. **LC** RA981.M6; D56. **DD** 362.1/025/776. **NLM** WX 22 AM6 D4M. ***Continues*** *Directory: Licensed Hospitals and Related Institutions.*

US/0272-0892
**DIRECTORY, LICENSED HOSPITALS AND AMBULATORY SURGICAL TREATMENT CENTERS IN TENNESSEE.** **Added/Corp** Tennessee. Board for Licensing Health Care Facilities. **VFOAT** Licensed Hospitals and Ambulatory Surgical Treatment Centers in Tennessee. No. 1 (1978)-. Directory. English. an. Board for Licensing Health Care Facilities, 283 Plus Park Boulevard, Nashville TN 37217. **Tel** (615)741-6393. **LC** RA977.5.T2; D57. **DD** 362.1/1/025768. **NLM** WX 22 AT2 D6LA. ***Continues*** *Directory, Licensed Hospitals in Tennessee.*

US/8755-593X
**DIRECTORY OF FACILITIES OBLIGATED TO PROVIDE UNCOMPENSATED SERVICES BY STATE AND CITY.** (DIRECTORY OF FACILITIES OBLIGATED TO PROVIDE UNCOMPENSATED SERVICES BY STATE AND CITY AS OF JANUARY L ...). **Added/Corp** United States. Bureau of Health Maintenance Organizations and Resources Development. Assurances Data and Analysis Branch. (1984)-. Directory. English. an. US Department of Health and Human Services, 200 Independence Avenue Southwest, Washington DC 20201. **LC** RA977; .D46. **DD** 362.1/1/02573. **NLM** WX 22; AA1 D5985.

US/0098-6135
**DIRECTORY OF HEALTH CARE FACILITIES.** **Added/Corp** Illinois. Division of Health Facilities. (19??)-. Directory. English. an. Illinois Department of Public Health, 535 West Jefferson Street, 5th Floor, Springfield IL 62761. **Tel** (217)785-8830. **LC** RA981.I4; D57. **DD** 362.1/025/773. **NLM** WX 22 AI3 B8da. ***Continues*** *Directory of Health Care Facilities and Approved Schools of Nursing, 0536-3942.*

US/1064-8496
**DIRECTORY OF HEALTH CARE GROUP PURCHASING ORGANIZATIONS.** (DIRECTORY OF HEALTH CARE GROUP PURCHASING ORGANIZATIONS : PUBLICATION OF MCKNIGHT MEDICAL COMMUNICATIONS, CO.). [Dir. health care group purch. organ.]. **Added/Corp** McKnight Medical Communications, Co. Medical Economics Data (Firm). **VFOAT** Directory of Healthcare Group Purchasing Organizations. 4th Ed., (1984)-. Directory. English. an. $306.50. Medical Economics Data, Five Paragon Drive, PO Box 27, Montvale NJ 07645. **Tel** (800)442-6657, (201)358-7200. **LC** RA971.33; .D58. **DD** 362.1/068/7. **NLM** WX 22; AA1 D5988. ***Continues*** *Hospital Group Purchasing Directory.*

US/0885-9671
**DIRECTORY OF HOSPITAL PERSONNEL, THE.** [Dir. hosp. pers.]. **Added/Corp** Whole World Publishing (Deerfield, Ill.). (1986)-. Directory. English. an. $317.50. Medical Economics Data, Five Paragon Drive, PO Box 27, Montvale NJ 07645. **Tel** (800)442-6657, (201)358-7200. **LC** RA977; .D4718. **DD** 362.1/1/02573. **NLM** WX 22; AA1 D5992.

II
**DIRECTORY OF HOSPITALS IN INDIA.** **Added/Corp** India. Central Bureau of Health Intelligence. (19??)-. Directory. English. ir. Central Bureau of Health Intelligence, Directorate General of Health Services, Nirman Bhavan, New Delhi 110011 India. **Tel** 3019544. **LC** RA978.I4; D57. **DD** 362.1/1/02554. **NLM** WX 22 JI4 D5. **Bk Rev. Circ:** 3,000.

UK/0260-8820
**DIRECTORY OF INDEPENDENT HOSPITALS AND HEALTH SERVICES, THE.** **Added/Corp** Association of Independent Hospitals and Kindred Organisations (Great Britain). (1987)-. Directory. English. an. Price varies per volume. Longman Group Ltd., Fourth Avenue, Longman House, Harlow Essex CM19 5SR England. **Tel** 011 44 279 429655, FAX 011 44 279 431059, telex 81259. **NLM** WX 22; FA1 A8y. ***Continues*** *Directory of Private Hospitals and Health Services.*

US/0147-3921
**DIRECTORY OF INPATIENT FACILITIES FOR THE MENTALLY RETARDED.** (1976)-. Directory. English. an. US Directory Service, 655 NW 128 Street, PO Box 68-1700, Miami FL 33168. **Tel** (305)769-1700. **NLM** WM 22 AA1 D36.
**Desc:** Source of information for the names, locations, and admission policies of all inpatient facilities for the mentally retarded in the United States. Geographical arrangement.

CN/0226-5419
**DIRECTORY OF LONG TERM CARE CENTRES IN CANADA.** ***Title Change.*** (DIRECTORY OF LONG TERM CARE CENTRES IN CANADA. REPERTOIRE DES CENTRES DE SERVICES DE SANTE A LONG TERME AU CANADA.). [Dir. long term care cent. Can.]. **Added/Corp** Canadian Hospital Association. **VFOAT** Repertoire des Centres de Services de Sante A Long Terme au Canada; Annuaire des Centres de Sante a Long-Terme au Canada. Vol. 1 (1980)-(199?). Directory. English (French). an. Canadian Hospital Association, 17 York Street, Suite 100, Ottawa Ontario K1N 9J6 Canada. **Tel** (613)238-8005. **ED** Tess Radford and Indra Seegobin. **DD** 362.1/6/02571. **Ad Acc. Circ:** 2,000 (ctrl). ***Merged into*** *Guide to Canadian Health Care Facilities.*
**Desc:** Lists definitions of special long-term care, information on 3,500 facilities, a buyers' guide, association list and educational programs for long-term care personnel.

US/0894-1114
**DIRECTORY OF MEDICAL FACILITIES. REGION VIII, DENVER.** [Dir. med. facil., Reg. VIII Denver]. **Added/Corp** United States. Division of Health Standards and Quality. **VFOAT** Directory of Medical Facilities. Region 8, Denver; Region VIII, Denver; Denver; DMF. (Oct. 1, 1984)-. Directory. English. Health Care Financing Administration Region 8, 1961 Stout Street, Room 1185, Denver CO 80294. **Tel** (303)844-2111, FAX (303)844-3753. **DD** 362. **NLM** WX 22; AA1 D5993. ***Continues in part*** *Directory of Medical Facilities. All Regions, 0272-4049.*

US/0191-2879
**DIRECTORY OF NURSING HOME ADMINISTRATORS LICENSED AND REGISTERED IN TENNESSEE.** **Added/Corp** Tennessee. Division of Health Related Boards. Tennessee. State Licensing Board for the Healing Arts. Tennessee. State Licensing Board for the Healing Arts Act. Tennessee. Nursing Home Administrators Practice Act. (1976)-. Directory. English. an. **LC** WMLC L 83/7255. **NLM** WX 22 AT2 D5. ***Continues*** *Directory of Nursing Home Administrators Licensed in Tennessee, 0164-2596.*

US/0888-7624
**DIRECTORY OF NURSING HOMES (PHOENIX, ARIZ.).** (DIRECTORY OF NURSING HOMES.). [Dir. nurs. homes]. 1st Ed. (1982)-. Directory. English. ir. $256.95. HCIA, 300 East Lombard Street, Baltimore MD 21202. **Tel** (410)576-9600, (800)568-3282. **ED** Sam Mongeau. **LC** RA997.A2; D49. **DD**

362.1/6/02573. **NLM** WX 22; AA1 D7.
**Desc:** Describes nearly 18,000 licensed nursing homes nationwide, listing new or changed contract names and addresses and information on personnel, licensure, admission requirements, amenities, activities, and ownership.

US/1062-1946
**DIRECTORY OF U.S. HOSPITALS.** [Dir. U.S. hosp.]. **Added/Corp** Health Care Investment Analysts, Inc. **VFOAT** Directory of US Hospitals. **VAT** Directory of United States Hospitals. 1st Ed. (1991)-. Directory. English. an. $226.95. Health Care Investment Analysts Inc, 300 East Lonbart Street, Baltimore MD 21202. **Tel** 800 568-3282, (410)576-9600. **DD** 362. **NLM** WX 22; AA1 D735.

US/0276-4652
**DISCHARGE PLANNING UPDATE.** [Disch. plann. update]. **Added/Corp** American Hospital Association. Society for Hospital Social Work Directors. **VFOAT** Discharge Planning. Began with: Vol. 1, No. 1 (Fall 1980)-. Periodical. English. bm (Jan., Mar., May, Jul., Sep., Nov.). $66.00 member; $86.00 non-member. American Hospital Association, 840 North Lake Shore Drive, Chicago IL 60611. **Tel** (312)280-6000, (800)242-2626. **NLM** W1 DI742V.
**Desc:** This is a multidisciplinary publication for persons interested in the hospital discharge planning process and/or the delivery of posthospital care. In addition to highlighting a single patient-focused subject, each issue of Update includes features such as the Washington Report, Legal Qs and As, the Discharge Dilemma, plus a special column directed to small and rural hospitals.
**Ind/Abst** Hospit. Health Admin. Index.

●US/1062-1679
**DUN'S HEALTHCARE REFERENCE BOOK.** [Dun's healthc. ref. book]. **Added/Corp** Dun's Marketing Services. **VFOAT** Dun's Health Care Reference Book; Healthcare Reference Book. (1992)-. English. an (Aug.). $425.00. Dun & Bradstreet Information Services, 3 Sylvan Way, Parsippany NJ 07054. **Tel** (201)605-6000, (800)526-0651. **LC** HD9994.U5; D86. **DD** 338.7/681761/02573. **NLM** W 22; AA1 D95. ***Continues*** *Duns's Guide to Healthcare Companies, 0887-5103.*
**Desc:** Information on medical instruments and apparatus, health facilities, and dental instruments and apparatus.

US
**DYNAMIC SUPERVISION IN THE HOSPITAL.** ***Ceased.*** **Added/Corp** Bureau of Business Practice (Waterford, Conn.). ( )-(Sept. 1988). Periodical. English. sm. Bureau of Business Practice, 24 Rope Ferry Road, Waterford CT 06386. **Tel** (800)243-0876, (203)442-4365, (800)876-9105, FAX (203)443-1123.

US
**ECONOMIC TRENDS.** **Added/Corp** American Hospital Association. Office of Public Policy Analysis. Hospital Research and Educational Trust. Vol. 1, No. 1 (Spring 1985)-. Periodical. English. qt (Jan., Apr., Jul., Oct.). $85.00 (AHA member); $135.00 (non-member). American Hospital Association, 840 North Lake Shore Drive, Chicago IL 60611. **Tel** (312)280-6000, (800)242-2626. ***Continues*** *Trends (Chicago, Ill.).*

US/1044-9167
**ED MANAGEMENT.** **See** Medical Science and Technology-Emergency Medicine.

GW/0992-4663
**EJHP, EUROPEAN JOURNAL OF HOSPITAL PHARMACY.** **See** Pharmacy and Pharmacology.

CN/0705-5005
**ENSEMBLE (LACHINE).** (ENSEMBLE.). **Added/Corp** Centre Hospitalier de Lachine. Vol. 1 (Feb. 1977)-. Periodical. French. mo. Centre Hospitalier de Lachine, 650-16E Avenue, Lachine Quebec H8S 3N5 Canada. **DD** 362.1/1/0971428.

SP/0210-4598
**ESTADISTICA DE ESTABLECIMIENTOS SANITARIOS CON REGIMEN DE INTERNADO.** **Added/Corp** Spain. Instituto Nacional de Estadistica. (1976)-. Statistical Publication. Spanish. Instituto Nacional de Estadistica, Avda Generalisimo 91, Madrid 91 Spain. **NLM** W2 GS6 I46EC. ***Continues*** *Instituto Nacional de Estadistica (Spain). Estadistica de Establecimientos Sanitarios con Regimen Interno.*

BL/0101-3033
**ESTATISTICAS DA SAUDE. ASSISTENCIA MEDICO-SANITARIA.** **Added/Corp** Fundacao Instituto Brasileiro de Geografia e Estatistica. **VFOAT** Assistencial Medico-Sanitaria. Vol. 1 (1976)-. Portuguese. an. Instituto Brasileiro de Geografia e Estatistica, Rua General Canabarro 666 AN2, 20271 Rio de Janeiro RJ Brazil. **Tel** 011 55 21 2847690, 011 55 21 2342043. **LC** RA984.B8; E8. **DD** 362.1/0981/021.
**Desc:** Data presented in this publication result from a co-operative venture of IBGE and the ministry of health, with the object of continual improvement of health statistics in municipalities.

US/0094-9361
**EUROHEALTH HANDBOOK.** **VFOAT** Statistical Health and Hospital Data for Fourteen West European Countries. (1971)-. Periodical. English. an. Robert First, Inc., 405 Lexington Avenue, New York NY 10017. **NLM** W1 EU578.

NE/0920-2153
**EUROPEAN NEWSLETTER ON QUALITY ASSURANCE.** [Eur. newsl. qual. assur.]. (1984)-. Periodical. English. qt. Free. CBO, PO Box 20064, Churchillaan 11, 3502 LB Utrecht Netherlands. **Tel** 011 31 30 960647, FAX 011 31 30 943644. **UDC** 614. **CODEN** NU054.
**Ind/Abst** Trop. Dis. Bull.

NE
**EXCERPTA MEDICA. SECTION 36. HEALTH POLICY, ECONOMICS, AND MANAGEMENT.** **See** Medical Science and Technology-Abstracting, Bibliographies and Statistics.

GW/0175-4548
**F & W, FUHREN UND WIRTSCHAFTEN IM KRANKENHAUS.** (FUHREN UND WIRTSCHAFTEN IM KRANKENHAUS : F&W : OFFIZIELLES ORGAN DES BUNDESVERBANDES DEUTSCHER PRIVATKRANKENANSTALTEN UND DES VEREINS DER LEITENDEN ARZTE DEUTSCHER PRIVATKRANKENANSTALTEN.). [F & w, Fuehr. wirtsch. Krankenh.]. **Added/Corp** Bundesverband Deutscher Privatkrankenanstalten. Verein der Leitenden Arzte Deutscher Privatkrankenanstalten. **VFOAT** F&W; F und W. (1984)-. Periodical. German. bm. Bibliomed Medizinische Verlag, Postfach 150 Nuernberger St 10, W 34201 Melsungen F R Germany. **Tel** 011 49 5661 6001, FAX 011 49 5661 8360. **NLM** W1; FU493. ***Continues*** *Privatkrankenanstalt.*

US
**FACTS ABOUT HOSPITALS IN METROPOLITAN CHICAGO.** **Main/Corp** Chicago Hospital Council. **Added/Corp** American Hospital Association. (19??)-. English. **LC** RA982.C45; C47a. **DD** 362.1/1/0977311.

US/0192-2211
**FEDERAL MEDICAL CENTERS, HOSPITALS, AND MEDICAL CLINICS WITH REPORTED MORBIDITY DATA.** **Added/Corp** Association of Military Surgeons of the United States. **VFOAT** Federal Medical Centers, Hospitals, and Clinics with Selected Statistical Data for Fiscal Year ... . (19??)-. English. an. Association of Military Surgeons of the United States, 9320 Old Georgetown Road, Bethesda MD 20814. **Tel** (301)897-8800. **LC** UH463; .F43. **DD** 355.3/45/0973.

US
**FIRST AND READMISSIONS TO STATE AND COUNTY PSYCHIATRIC HOSPITALS BY COUNTY, MUNICIPALITY OF RESIDENCE, AND SERVICE AREA.** **Main/Corp** New Jersey. Bureau of Statistical Analysis and Social Research. (1975/1976)-. English. an. **LC** RC445.N48; N48b. **DD** 362.2/1/09749.

US
**FIVE YEAR MEDICAL FACILITY DEVELOPMENT PLAN.** ***Title Change.*** **Main/Corp** United States. Veterans Administration. Office of Facilities. **VFOAT** FY ... Five Year Medical Facility Development Plan. (1991-1992). English. an. VA Office of Facilities, Washington DC 20420. **LC** UB369; .U57d. available on microfiche (Vols. for FY 1987-FY 1991 distributed to depository libraries). ***Continues*** *United States. Veterans Administration. Dept. of Medicine and Surgery.; Five Year Medical Facility Construction needs Assessment, 0749-274x.* ***Continued by*** *United States. Dept. of Veterans Affairs. Office of Facilities.; FY ... Five Year Medical Facility Development Plan.*

US
**FORUM / RISK MANAGEMENT FOUNDATION.** **Added/Corp** Risk Management Foundation. Vol. 1, No. 1 (June/July 1980)-. Periodical. English. bm (6 issues). $95.00; $150.00 combined subscription with Resource. Risk Management Foundation, 840 Memorial Drive, Cambridge MA 02139. **Tel** (617)495-5100, FAX (617)495-9711. **ED** Jock Hoffman (editor's telephone: (617)495-5700). **NLM** W1; FO943T. Index available. cum. index. **Circ:** 9,000.
**Desc:** Critically written journal offers workable solutions for health care risk management problems.

US/0016-8106
**GEORGETOWN MEDICAL BULLETIN.** [Georgetown med. bull.]. **Added/Corp** Georgetown University. School of Medicine. Vol. 13 (August 1959)-. Bulletin. English. ir (3 issues). Free. Georgetown University School of Medicine, 3800 Reservoir Road Northwest, Washington DC 20007. **Tel** (202)784-2000. **ED** Karen M. Jones and R. Scott Klappenbach. **LC** R11; .G43. **NLM** W1 GE434. **CODEN** GTMBAQ. **Bk Rev. Circ:** 9,000 (ctrl). Documents available from BIOSIS Document Express, CASDDS. ***Continues*** *Bulletin - Georgetown University Medical Center, 0097-1006.*
**Desc:** Editorials written by the Dean of the School of Medicine, Georgetown University, on issues affecting the school. Features medical center activities, faculty publications and alumni news and activities related to Georgetown's School of Medicine.
**Ind/Abst** Biol. Abstr.; Chem. Abstr.

GW
**GESCHICHTE DES HOSPITALS.** Vol. 2 (1971)-. Monographic series. German. Price varies per volume. **ED** D Jetter. **NLM** W1 GE693. ***Continues*** *Geschichte des Hospitals.*

FR/0016-9218
**GESTIONS HOSPITALIERES.** [Gest. hosp.]. (1960)-. Periodical. French. ir (10 issues). 500.00F France; 620.00F other. Gestions Hospitalieres, 44 rue Jules Ferry, 94400 Vitry Sur Seine France. **Tel** 011 46 825300, FAX 011 46 825515. **ED** Sylvie Cheroutre-Bonneau. **UDC** 362. **[CCC]**. **Ad Acc, Adv Mgr:** J. Ganavat. **Circ:** 3,600 (ctrl).

NE/0921-8343
**GGD-NIEWS (GRAVENHAGE).** **See** Public Health and Safety.

US
**GRANT$ FOR HOSPITALS, MEDICAL CARE, & RESEARCH.** **See** Philanthropy.

US/0199-5103
**GROUP PRACTICE JOURNAL.** [Group pract. j.]. **Added/Corp** American Group Practice Association. Vol. 29 (Jan. 1980)-. Academic Scholarly Publication. English. Six times a year (Jan., Mar., May, July, Sept., Nov.). $65.00 (one year); $120.00 (two years). American Group Practice Association, 1422 Duke Street, Alexandria VA 22313-3430. **Tel** (703)838-0033, FAX (703)548-1890. **ED** Laura Johnson. **DD** 610. **NLM** W1 GR8586F. Index available (bound in issues). cum. index. **Bk Rev**, (Qty: 2). **Ad Acc, Adv Mgr:** Fred Haag. **Circ:** 48,000 (ctrl). ***Continues*** *Group Practice, 0017-4726.*
**Desc:** A magazine that concentrates on the socioeconomic, political business, and legal aspects of medical care by group practices, HMOS, PPOS, and other managed care organizations.
**Ind/Abst** EMBASE; Health Plan. Adminis.; Hospit. Health Admin. Index; Hospit. Manage. Rev.

US/0190-440X
**GROUP PRACTICE (NEWSLETTER).** (GROUP PRACTICE.). **Added/Corp** American Group Practice Association. (197?)-. Periodical. English. sm. American Group Practice Association, 1422 Duke Street, Alexandria VA 22313-3430. **Tel** (703)838-0033, FAX (703)548-1890. **ED** Timothy A Stalker. **Ad Acc. Circ:** 40,000 (ctrl).
**Desc:** Medical journal for physicians practicing in medical group practices.

CN
**GUIDE TO CANADIAN HEALTH CARE FACILITIES.** English. an (Oct.). $112.95. Canadian Hospital Association, 17 York Street, Suite 100, Ottawa Ontario K1N 9J6 Canada. **Tel** (613)238-8005. ***Absorbed*** *Canadian Hospital Directory & Directory of Long Term Care Centers in Canada.*

UK/C017-5870
**GUY'S HOSPITAL GAZETTE.** ***Title Change.*** (1872)-(199?). Periodical. English. ir. Gazette Office, 238 St. Thomas Street, London SE1 9RT England. ***Continued by*** *Guy's Gazette, 0017-5870.*
**Ind/Abst** Index Med.

US
**HANDBOOK FOR STAFF PHYSICIANS / CLINICAL CENTER, NATIONAL INSTITUTES OF HEALTH.** **Main/Corp** National Institutes of Health (U.S.). Clinical Center. (19??)-. English. an. US Department of Health and Human Services National Institutes of Health, 9000 Rockville Pike, Bethesda MD 20892. **Tel** (301)496-9291, FAX (301)496-2443.

US/1046-8900
**HEALTH & MEDICAL CARE DIRECTORY.** ***Title Change.*** [Health med. care dir.]. **Added/Corp** Yellow Pages of America, Inc. International Association for Medical Assistance to Travellers. **VFOAT** Health and Medical Care Directory. (198?)-(19??). Directory. English. an. Business Yellow Pages, PO Box 2010, Niagara Falls NY 14302. **Tel** (716)282-2209. **LC** RA981.A2; H36. **DD** 362.1/025/73. **NLM** W 22; AA1 H434. available on CD-ROM from Innotech Inc. ***Continued by*** *Medi Press.*

US
**HEALTH & MEDICAL CARE DIRECTORY ON CD-ROM.** ***Ceased.*** (19??)-(19??). Directory. English. ir. Innotech Inc, 2001 Sheppard Avenue East 118, North York, Ontario M2J 4Z7 Canada. **Tel** (416)492-3838. available in print.
**Desc:** Contains data of more than 1,000,000 American health-related businesses from coast to coast. Well

organized and informative directory that minimizes search for medical organizations and services, telephones and addresses.

US
**HEALTH CARE FACILITIES : HILL-BURTON STATE PLAN DATA. EXISTING AND NEEDED.** **Added/Corp** United States. Health Care Facilities Service. Office of Program Planning and Analysis. United States. Health Care Facilities Service. Program Planning and Analysis Branch. (1969)-. English. an. US Department of Health and Human Services, 200 Independence Avenue Southwest, Washington DC 20201. **DD** 362.1/0973. ***Continues*** *Hill-Burton State Plan Data : A National Summary.*

US/0893-6099
**HEALTH CARE LAW NEWSLETTER. See** Law.

UK/0269-2104
**HEALTH CARE MANAGEMENT. *Title Change.*** Vol. 1, No. 1 (1986)-?. Periodical. English. Five times a year. MCB University Press, 60 62 Toller Lane, Bradford West Yorkshire BD8 9BX England. **Tel** 011 44 274 499821, FAX 011 44 274 547143, telex 51317 MCBUNI G. **ED** Robin Gourlay. Index available in last issue of volume--attached. **Ad Acc. *Continued by*** *International Journal of Health Care Quality Assurance.*
**Desc:** Aims to improve the quality of health care management. Provides a forum for the development of policies and good management practices. It is concerned with innovation and in particular the sharing ideas. Analyses theories and practices both in and out of health care and considers their relevance and application for managers in health care.

●US/1069-6571
**HEALTH CARE MANAGEMENT.** (HEALTH CARE MANAGEMENT : STATE OF THE ART REVIEWS.). (1994)-. Periodical. English. Twice a year. $59.00 (US & possessions); $69.00 (other). Hanley & Belfus Inc., 210 South 13th Street, Philadelphia PA 19107. **Tel** (215)546-7293, FAX (215)790-9330.

US/0361-6274
**HEALTH CARE MANAGEMENT REVIEW.** [Health care manage. rev.]. **Added/Corp** Aspen Systems Corporation. **VFOAT** HCM Review. Vol. 1 (Winter 1976)-. Academic Scholarly Publication. English. qt. $120.00 US. Aspen Publishers Inc., 7201 McKinney Circle, Frederick MD 21701. **Tel** (800)234-1660, (301)698-7100, FAX (301)251-5784, telex 5106014543. **(Subscription address:** Aspen Publishers Inc., PO Box 990, Frederick MD 21701.**) ED** Montague Brown, MBA. **LC** RA393; .H4. **DD** 658/.91/3621. **NLM** W1 HE299M. **[CCC]. Bk Rev. Pr Rev. Circ:** 5,300. available on microfilm and microfiche from University Microfilms International (UMI); available on an online database (file 15/Full-Text) from DIALOG. Documents available from UMI Article Clearinghouse.
**Desc:** Key aspects of health care finance, marketing, management policy, operations, regulations, and more are addressed by leading authorities in health care management. Addresses the full range of challenges and concerns that busy hospital executives face every day.
**Ind/Abst** ABI/INFORM Glob. Ed.; ABI Inform Ondisc (Spring 1979-); Acad. Search (July 1993-); Bus. ASAP (1992-) [Full Txt.]; Bus. Index (1985-); Bus. Period. Index; Bus. Source (Jul. 1993-); Cumul. Index Nurs. Allied Health Lit.; EMBASE; Gen. BusinessFile (1985-); Gen. Period. Index (1985-); Health Serv. Abstr.; Health Source (Jul. 1993-); Hospit. Health Admin. Index; Hospit. Manage. Rev.; Index Med.; INFO-SOUTH Abstr.; Int. Pharm. Abstr.; Mag. Search; Physic. Medline Plus; Trade Ind. ASAP [Full Txt.]; Trade Ind. Index [Full Txt.]; UMI ABI/Inform--Bus. Period. Ondisc (Spring 1987-) [Full Txt.]; Wilson Bus. Abstr.

●US/1071-460X
**HEALTH-CARE MEDIA SOURCE. See** Business-Advertising and Public Relations.

US/0742-1478
**HEALTH CARE STRATEGIC MANAGEMENT.** [Health care strateg. manage.]. **VFOAT** HCSM. Vol. 1, No. 1 (Oct. 1983)-. Periodical. English. mo. $207.00 US; $213.00 Canada; $225.00 other. Business Word Inc., 5350 South Roslyn Street, Suite 400, Englewood CA 80111-2125. **Tel** (303)290-8500, FAX (303)290-9025. **ED** Donald E. L. Johnson. **DD** 362. **NLM** W1; HE302M. Index available (published in Dec. issue). **Bk Rev. Ad Acc. Circ:** 2,000. available on microfilm and microfiche from University Microfilms International (UMI); available on an online database (file 15/Full-Text) from DIALOG. Documents available from UMI Article Clearinghouse.
**Desc:** Professional journal for hospital administrators, planners, and marketing department directors. Includes articles on timely topics, interviews with health care leaders, case studies, and meeting reviews.
**Ind/Abst** ABI/INFORM Glob. Ed.; ABI Inform Ondisc (Jan. 1991-); Hospit. Health Admin. Index; Hospit. Manage. Rev.; Int. Nurs. Index; Int. Pharm. Abstr.

US/0731-3381
**HEALTH CARE SUPERVISOR, THE.** [Health care superv.]. **Added/Corp** Aspen Systems Corporation. (Oct. 1982)-. Periodical. English. qt. $104.00 US. Aspen Publishers Inc., 7201 McKinney Circle, Frederick MD 21701. **Tel** (800)234-1660, (301)698-7100, FAX (301)251-5784, telex 5106014543. **(Subscription address:** Aspen Publishers Inc., PO Box 990, Frederick MD 21701.**) ED** Charles R. McConnell. **LC** RA971; .H386. **DD** 362.1/068. **NLM** W1; HE302R. **[CCC]. Bk Rev. Pr Rev. Circ:** 4,400. available on microfilm and microfiche from University Microfilms International (UMI). Documents available from UMI Article Clearinghouse.
**Desc:** This journal, written for every health care professional in a supervisory role, focuses on strengthening your supervisory skills-the people skills that can ensure your own success and the effectiveness of your team.
**Ind/Abst** ABI/INFORM Glob. Ed.; ABI Inform Ondisc (Jan. 1984-); Cumul. Index Nurs. Allied Health Lit.; Health Plan. Adminis.; Hospit. Health Admin. Index; UMI ABI/Inform--Bus. Period. Ondisc (Apr. 1987-) [Full Txt.].

UK/0261-0736
**HEALTH EQUIPMENT INFORMATION.** [Health equip. inf.]. (1974)-. Periodical. English. ir. £80.00. Department of Health and Social Security Library, PO Box 21, Stanmore, Middlesex HA7 1AY England. **Tel** 011 44 71 9722000, 9728161. ***Continues*** *Hospital Equipment Information.*

UK/0957-7742
**HEALTH ESTATE JOURNAL : JOURNAL OF THE INSTITUTE OF HOSPITAL ENGINEERING.** **Added/Corp** Institute of Hospital Engineering. Vol. 44, No. 1 (Feb. 1990)-. Periodical. English. Ten times a year (monthly except January and August). £48.00 UK; £53.00 other. Institute of Hospital Engineering, 2 Abingdon House, Cumberland Business Center, Portsmouth PO5 1DS England. **Tel** 011 44 705 823186, FAX 011 44 705 815927. **ED** Sandy Ratcliffe. **NLM** W1; HE329H. Index available. cum. index. **Bk Rev. Ad Acc. Circ:** 4,000 (ctrl). ***Continues*** *Journal of the Institute of Hospital Engineering.*
**Desc:** Covers hospital engineering and facilities management.
**Ind/Abst** Health Plan. Adminis.; Hospit. Health Admin. Index (1990-).

US/0361-2929
**HEALTH FACILITIES DIRECTORY (SACRAMENTO). *Title Change.*** (HEALTH FACILITIES DIRECTORY.). **Added/Corp** California. Dept. of Health. Facilities Licensing Section. California. Dept. of Health. Licensing and Certification Division. **VFOAT** Directory of Health Facilities; Health Facilities Licensed by Department of Health Services, Licensing and Certification Division. (Mar. 1975)-(19??). Directory. English. qt. Sacramento Department of Health Facilities Licensing Section, 744 P Street/Room 440, Sacramento CA 95814. **LC** RA981.C3; H4. **DD** 362.1/025/794. **NLM** WX 22 AC2 H4. ***Continued by*** *Health Facilities Licensed and Certified by Department of Health Services, Licensing and Certification.*

US/0272-8443
**HEALTH FACILITIES ENERGY REPORT. *Title Change.* See** Energy.

●US/1062-4562
**HEALTH FACILITIES REPORT.** [Health facil. rep.]. Vol. 1, No.1 Feb. (1992)-. Periodical. English. mo. $180.00. Safety Publications, Inc., PO Box 2573, Waco TX 76702. **DD** 363.

US/0270-3343
**HEALTH LAW VIGIL. *Ceased.* See** Law.

US/0891-3250
**HEALTH MANAGEMENT QUARTERLY.** (HEALTH MANAGEMENT QUARTERLY : HMQ.). [Health manage q.]. **Added/Corp** American Hospital Supply Corporation Foundation. Baxter Foundation. **VFOAT** HMQ. (Fall 1984)-. Periodical. English. qt. Free on request. The Baxter Foundation, 1 Baxter Parkway, Deerfield IL 60015. **Tel** (708)948-2000, FAX (708)948-2887. **ED** Philip J Smith, George N Couch, Rebecca S Carino. **LC** RA971; .H396. **DD** 362.1/068. **NLM** W1; HE413Q. **CODEN** HMAQEB. Index available. cum. index. **Bk Rev. Circ:** 24,000 (ctrl). ***Continues*** *Hospital Management Quarterly, 0891-9941.*
**Desc:** Discusses issues that are of concern to top managers of health care organizations.
**Ind/Abst** Hospit. Health Admin. Index; Hospit. Manage. Rev.

●US/1065-0679
**HEALTH PLANNING AND ADMINISTRATION. See** Medical Science and Technology-Abstracting, Bibliographies and Statistics.

US
**HEALTH PLANNING AND ADMINISTRATION DATABASE (HEALTH).** (1978)-. English. an. American Hospital Association, 840 North Lake Shore Drive, Chicago IL 60611. **Tel** (312)280-6000, (800)242-2626. available on CD-ROM.
**Desc:** HEALTH is a computerized bibliographic file that provides access to worldwide literature concerned with all aspects of health care delivery. It is available online through subscribing hospitals, medical schools, universities, government agencies, and health related commercial organizations in the U.S. and abroad. These online centers subscribe to HEALTH through one of the following sources: BRS Information Technologies, DIALOG, NLM, Australian MEDLARS Center, FRG MEDLARS Center, or Pan American Health Organization (Brazil).

US/0882-1577
**HEALTH PROGRESS (SAINT LOUIS, MO.).** (HEALTH PROGRESS.). [Health prog.]. **Added/Corp** Catholic Health Association of the United States. Vol. 65, No. 8 (Sept. 1984)-. Periodical. English. Ten times a year (Jan./Feb., July/Aug. combined). $35.00 US; $40.00 other. Catholic Health Association of the US, 4455 Woodson Road, St Louis MO 63134. **Tel** (314)427-2500, FAX (314)427-0029. **ED** Judy Cassidy. **LC** RA960; .C3. **DD** 362.1/05. **NLM** W1; HE486. Index available. **Bk Rev. Ad Acc. Pr Rev. Circ:** 14,000 (ctrl). ***Continues*** *Hospital Progress, 0018-5817.*
**Desc:** Edited for administrative personnel in Catholic health care facilities. Featured are articles on management concepts, legislative and regulatory trends, and theological, sociological, ethical and technical issues.
**Ind/Abst** Abstr. Soc. Gerontol.; Abstr. Res. Pastor. Care Couns.; Cumul. Index Nurs. Allied Health Lit.; Health Devices Alerts; Hospit. Health Admin. Index; Hospit. Manage. Rev.; Abr. Cathol. Period. Lit. Index; Cathol. Period. Lit. Index.

CN/1180-2456
**HEALTH REPORTS. SUPPLEMENT. HOSPITAL STATISTICS, PRELIMINARY ANNUAL REPORT.** (HEALTH REPORTS. SUPPLEMENT. HOSPITAL STATISTICS, PRELIMINARY ANNUAL REPORT / STATISTICS CANADA, CANADIAN CENTRE FOR HEALTH INFORMATION.). [Health rep., Suppl., Hosp. stat. prelim. annu. rep.]. **Added/Corp** Canadian Centre for Health Information. **VFOAT** Hospital Statistics, Preliminary Annual Report; Statistique Hospitaliere, Rapport Annuel Preliminaire; Rapports sur la Sante. Statistique Hospitaliere, Rapport Annuel Preliminaire. (1987)-. English (French). an. 15.00Can$. Statistics Canada, Publications Sales & Services, Main Building Room 1710, Ottawa Ontario K1A 0T6 Canada. **Tel** (613)951-5078, (800)267-6677, FAX (613)951-1584, telex 053-3585. **LC** RA983.A1; H43. **DD** 362.1/1/0971021. ***Continues*** *Hospital Statistics, Preliminary Annual Report, 0381-8802.*

CN/1180-2391
**HEALTH REPORTS. SUPPLEMENT. LIST OF CANADIAN HOSPITALS.** (HEALTH REPORTS. SUPPLEMENT. LIST OF CANADIAN HOSPITALS / STATISTICS CANADA, CANADIAN CENTRE FOR HEALTH INFORMATION.). [Health rep., Suppl., List Can. hosp.]. **Added/Corp** Canadian Centre for Health Information. **VFOAT** List of Canadian Hospitals; Liste des Hopitaux au Canada; Rapports sur la Sante. Liste des Hopitaux au Canada. (1988)-. English (French). an. 23.00Can$ Canada; $24.00 other. Statistics Canada, Publications Sales & Services, Main Building Room 1710, Ottawa Ontario K1A 0T6 Canada. **Tel** (613)951-5078, (800)267-6677, FAX (613)951-1584, telex 053-3585. **LC** RA983.A1; H44. **DD** 362.1/1/02571. ***Continues*** *List of Canadian Hospitals, 0831-7313.*

US/0731-6607
**HEALTH SERVICES DIRECTORY.** [Health serv. dir.]. (1981)-. English. ir. Gale Research Inc., 835 Penobscot Building, Detroit MI 48226. **Tel** (800)877-GALE, (313)961-2242, FAX (313)961-6083, telex TWX 810-221-7086. **ED** Anthony T. Kruzas. **LC** RA977; .H43. **DD** 362.1/025/73. **NLM** W 22 AA1 H55.

UK/0953-8534
**HEALTH SERVICES MANAGEMENT.** ***Ceased.*** [Health serv. manag.]. **Added/Corp** Institute of Health Services Management. Vol. 84, No. 3 (June 1988)-(July 1994). Periodical. English. Ten times a year. Institute of Health Services Management, 75 Portland Place, London W1N 4AN England. **Tel** 011 44 71 5805041, FAX 011 44 71 2551289. **ED** Hazel Coad. **NLM** W1; HE576BG. **CODEN** HSEMER. **Bk Rev. Ad Acc. Circ:** 10,000. ***Continues*** *Hospital and Health Services Review, 0308-0234.*
**Ind/Abst** EMBASE; Health Plan. Adminis.; Hospit. Health Admin. Index (June 1988-); Manage. Market. Abstr.

UK/0951-4848
**HEALTH SERVICES MANAGEMENT RESEARCH : AN OFFICIAL JOURNAL OF THE ASSOCIATION OF UNIVERSITY PROGRAMS IN HEALTH ADMINISTRATION.** **Added/Corp** Association of University Programs in Health Administration. University of Birmingham. Health Services Management Centre. **VFOAT** HSMR. Vol. 1, No. 1 (March 1988)-. Periodical. English. qt (Feb., May, Aug., Nov.). £77.00 Europe; £83.00 Other (Institutions). Longman Group Ltd., Fourth Avenue, Longman House, Harlow Essex CM19 5SR

England. **Tel** 011 44 279 429655, FAX 011 44 279 431059, telex 81259. **ED** Peter Spurgeon, Peggy Leatt. **LC** RA440.6; .H42. **NLM** W1; HE576BGK. **CODEN** HSRMEO. **[CCC].** Index available. **Bk Rev. Ad Acc. Circ:** 700. available on microfilm and microfiche from University Microfilms International (UMI).
**Desc:** Provides information for making decisions on management and administration, evaluating health systems.
**Ind/Abst** EMBASE; Hospit. Health Admin. Index (1988-).

US/0361-0195
**HEALTH SYSTEMS MANAGEMENT.** Vol. 1 (1974)-. Monographic series. English. ir. Price varies per volume. Spectrum, Inc., 714 Ninth Avenue, Suite 447, New York NY 10019. **NLM** W1 HE588F.
**Ind/Abst** Hospit. Health Admin. Index (1980-).

US/1055-7466
**HEALTH SYSTEMS REVIEW.** [Health syst. rev.]. **Added/Corp** Federation of American Health Systems. Vol. 24, No. 1 (Jan./Feb. 1991)-. Academic Scholarly Publication. English. bm (Jan., Mar., May, July, Sept., Nov.). $20.00 US; $25.00 Canada and Mexico; $45.00 other. Federation of American Health Systems, 1405 North Pierce, Suite 311, Little Rock AR 72207. **Tel** (501)661-9555, FAX (501)663-4903. **DD** 362. **NLM** W1; HE589FB. available on an online database (file 15,Full-Text) from DIALOG. ***Continues*** *Review (Federation of American Health Systems), 0891-0200.*
**Desc:** In-depth analysis of a wide-ranging set of health care policy issues, including government regulations, finance, law, hospital operation and ethics. The magazine is written for all top-level health system executives, as well as the administration and their respective staffs.
**Ind/Abst** EMBASE; Hospit. Health Admin. Index (1991-); Hospit. Manage. Rev. (199?-).

UK
**HEALTH TECHNICAL MEMORANDUM / DEPARTMENT OF HEALTH AND SOCIAL SECURITY ; WELSH OFFICE.** **Added/Corp** Great Britain. Dept. of Health and Social Security. Great Britain. Welsh Office. (197?)-. Monographic series. English. Price varies per volume. Her Majesty's Stationery Office, 51 Nine Elms Lane, London SW8 5DR England. **Tel** 011 44 71 873 8459, 011 44 71 873 8499, FAX 011 44 71 873 8499, 011 44 71 873 8456, telex 297138. **NLM** W1; HE589FD.
**Ind/Abst** Archit. Period. Index (Jan. 1978-June 1978).

●CN/1197-4710
**HEALTHCARE ADVOCATE (EDMONTON).** (HEALTHCARE ADVOCATE : THE JOURNAL OF THE ALBERTA HEALTHCARE ASSOCIATION.). [Healthc. advocate]. **Added/Corp** Alberta Healthcare Association. Vol. 1, No. 1 (Apr. 1993)-. Periodical. English. Ten times a year (Jan./Feb. & July/Aug. issues combined). 20.00Can$. Alberta Healthcare Association, 10009 108th Street, 5th Floor, Edmonton, Alberta T5J 3C5 Canada. **Tel** (403)498-8400, FAX (403)498-8465. **ED** Clay Adams. **DD** 362.1/1/097123. **Ad Acc, Adv Mgr:** Jan Henry, **Tel** (403)484-3895. Full Page (B&W) $696.00. Half Page (B&W) $495.00. **Circ:** 2,800 (ctrl). ***Continues*** *HospitAlta (1991)., 1187-7405.*
**Desc:** Published by the Alberta Healthcare Association, is distributed to healthcare administrators, Board Chairmen, trustees, managers, staff, purchasing agents and other professionals within the provinces acute care, long term care and specialty care facilities. It is also distributed to government MLAs, media, health units and other provincial and national health organizations.

US/1062-032X
**HEALTHCARE BOTTOM LINE.** [Healthc. bottom line]. Vol. 3, No. 5 (June 1986)-. Periodical. English. Eleven times a year (July/Aug. issues combined). $115.00 (one year); $205.00 (two years); $290.00 (three years). CHIPS, 445 King Avenue, Columbus OH 43201. **Tel** (800)859-2447, FAX (614)421-1491. **ED** William O. Cleverley. **DD** 647. **NLM** W1; HE303G. **Circ:** 500. ***Continues*** *Hospital Bottom Line.*
**Desc:** Taking place in communities that have historically had low levels of managed care business and are associated with traditional indemnity plans.

CN/0842-5353
**HEALTHCARE COMPUTING & COMMUNICATIONS CANADA.** [Healthc. comput. commun. Can.]. **Added/Corp** Canadian Organization for Advancement of Computers in Health. **VFOAT** Health Care Computing & Communications Canada. **VAT** Healthcare Computing and Communications Canada. (1987)-. Periodical. English. Five times a year (Jan., Fe., April, July, Oct.). 39.00Can$ Canada; $39.00 US; $43.00 other. Healthcare Computing & Communications Canada, Suite 216 10458 Mayfield Road, Edmonton Alberta T5P 4P4 Canada. **Tel** (403)489-4521, FAX (403)489-3290. **DD** 362.1/1/0684.

US/0883-5381
**HEALTHCARE EXECUTIVE.** [Healthc. exec.]. **Added/Corp** American College of Healthcare Executives. Foundation. PSSI (Firm). **VFOAT** Health Care Executive. Vol. 1, No. 1 (Nov./Dec. 1985)-. Periodical. English. Six times a year (Jan., Mar., May, July, Sept., Nov.). $45.00 US; $60.00 others. American College of Healthcare Executives, 840 North Lake Shore Drive, c/o J. Flory, Chicago IL 60611. **Tel** (312)943-0544 ext. 3000, FAX (312)943-3791. **(Subscription address:** FDN American College of Healthcare Executives, Order Processing Center, 1951 Cornell Avenue, Melrose Park IL 60160.) **ED** Walter Wachel and Esther Vital Freilich. **LC** RA971; .H45. **DD** 362.1/068/8. **NLM** W1; HE607K. **CODEN** HEEXEU. **[CCC].** Index available. **Ad Acc. Circ:** 23,500 (ctrl). available on microfilm and microfiche from University Microfilms International (UMI); available on an online database (file 15/Full-Text) from DIALOG. Documents available from UMI Article Clearinghouse. ***Continues*** *Executive News.*
**Desc:** Magazine focusing on critical professional development issues in healthcare management. Designed for executives, trustees, physicians, executives, staff and business leaders.
**Ind/Abst** ABI/INFORM Glob. Ed.; ABI Inform Ondisc (Jan. 1991-); Health Plan. Adminis.; Hospit. Health Admin. Index (1986-); Hospit. Manage. Rev.; Work Relat. Abstr.

US/0735-0732
**HEALTHCARE FINANCIAL MANAGEMENT.** (HEALTHCARE FINANCIAL MANAGEMENT: JOURNAL OF THE HEALTHCARE FINANCIAL MANAGEMENT ASSOCIATION.). [Healthc. financ. manage.]. **Added/Corp** Healthcare Financial Management Association (U.S.). **VFOAT** H.F.M.; Health Care Financial Management; HFM. Vol. 36, No. 6 (June 1982)-. Periodical. English. mo. $75.00 US; $120.00 Canada; $130.00 other. HFMA - Healthcare Financial Management Association, 2 Westbrook Corporation Center, Suite 700, Westchester IL 60154-5700. **Tel** (708)531-9600, (800)252-4362. **ED** Ronald E. Keener. **LC** HF5686.H7; A48. **DD** 362.1/068/1. **NLM** W1 HE608. **CODEN** HFMAD7. **Bk Rev. Ad Acc. Circ:** 27,000 (ctrl). available on microfilm and microfiche from University Microfilms International (UMI); available on an online database (files 15,485,648/Full-Text) from DIALOG. Documents available from UMI Article Clearinghouse, Ask*IEEE. ***Continues*** *Hospital Financial Management, 0018-5639.*
**Desc:** Accounting and financial management of hospitals and healthcare providers. Covers issues related to the theory and practice of healthcare financial management including topics such as the practical applications of professional and technical advances, legislative and regulatory changes, strategic planning, patient accounts management, and management issues.
**Ind/Abst** ABI/INFORM Glob. Ed.; ABI Inform Ondisc (June 1982-); Acad. Search (Jan. 1994-); Account. Tax Datab. (Mar. 1973-) [Full Txt.]; Account. Art.; Anbar Account. Finan. Abstr. [Full Txt.]; Anbar Mark. Distr. Abstr. [Full Txt.]; Anbar Top Manage. Abstr. [Full Txt.]; Bibliogr. Mission. (June 1982-); Bus. ASAP (1990-) [Full Txt.]; Bus. Index (1985-); Bus. Period. Index; Bus. Source (Jul. 1993-); Cumul. Index Nurs. Allied Health Lit.; EMBASE; Fed. Tax Artic.; Gen. BusinessFile (1985-); Gen. Period. Index (1985-); Health Source (Jul. 1993-); Hospit. Health Admin. Index; Hospit. Manage. Rev.; INFO-SOUTH Abstr.; INSPEC (July 1982-); Int. Pharm. Abstr. (19??-19??); Mag. Search; Manage. Bibliogr. Rev.; Oper. Prod. Manage. Abstr. [Full Txt.]; Person. Train. Abstr. [Full Txt.]; Trade Ind. ASAP [Full Txt.]; Trade Ind. Index [Full Txt.]; UMI ABI/Inform--Bus. Period. Ondisc (Dec. 1987-) [Full Txt.]; Wilson Bus. Abstr.; Women Manage. Rev. [Full Txt.].

US/0899-9287
**HEALTHCARE FORUM JOURNAL, THE.** **See** Medical Science and Technology.

US
**HEALTHCARE FUND RAISING NEWSLETTER.** (Jan. 1979)-. Newsletter. English. Six times a year. $137.00 (one year), $244.00 (two years), $350.00 (three years), $97.00 (intriductory subscription). Health Resources Publishing, 3100 Highway 138, Wall Township NJ 07719-1442. **Tel** (908)681-1133, FAX (908)681-0490. ***Continues*** *Hospital Fund Raising Newsletter.*
**Desc:** Contains reliable and timely information plus all the latest news, ideas and tips in healthcare fund raising from across the country.

US/0193-9939
**HEALTHCARE FUNDRAISING NEWSLETTER.** (Jan. 1979)-. Newsletter. English. Six times a year. $77.00. Health Resources Publishing, 3100 Highway 138, Wall Township NJ 07719-1442. **Tel** (908)681-1133, FAX (908)681-0490. **ED** Robert K. Jenkins. **[CCC].** Index available. cum. index.
**Desc:** Brings you reliable and timely information plus all the latest news, ideas, and tips in hospital fund raising from across the country.

US/1050-9135
**HEALTHCARE INFORMATICS.** (HEALTHCARE INFORMATICS : THE BUSINESS MAGAZINE FOR INFORMATION AND COMMUNICATION SYSTEMS.). [Healthc. inform.]. **Added/Corp** Health Data Analysis Inc. **VFOAT** Health Care Informatics. Vol. 7, No. 2 (Feb. 1990)-. Periodical. English. mo. $28.00 (one year), $48.00 (two year). Health Data Analysis Inc., 2902 Highway 74, Suite 100, Box 2830, Evergreen CO 80439. **Tel** (303)674-2774. **ED** Karol Marlowe and Bill W Childs. **DD** 362. **NLM** W1; HE608RD. **Bk Rev. Ad Acc. Circ:** 25,000 (ctrl). ***Continues*** *U.S. Healthcare, 1040-3973.*
**Desc:** Serves the healthcare industry in matters dealing with computerization and communications, etc.
**Ind/Abst** Hospit. Health Admin. Index (1990-); Hospit. Manage. Rev. (199?-).

US
**HEALTHCARE INFORMATION MANAGEMENT.** **Added/Corp** Healthcare Information and Management Systems Society. **VFOAT** Journal of the Healthcare Information and Management Systems Society. Vol. 1, No. 4 (Nov. 1987)-. Periodical. English. qt. Included with Healthcare Information and Management Systems Society membership. American Hospital Association, 840 North Lake Shore Drive, Chicago IL 60611. **Tel** (312)280-6000, (800)242-2626. **ED** Andrew Pasternack. **NLM** W1; HE298PN. **Bk Rev. Pr Rev. Circ:** 4,000 (ctrl). ***Continues*** *Health Care Systems, 0149-2888.*
**Desc:** Articles cover professional development issues in healthcare communications, information systems, and management engineering.

CN/0840-4704
**HEALTHCARE MANAGEMENT FORUM.** [Healthc. manage. forum]. **Added/Corp** Canadian College of Health Services Executives. **VFOAT** Forum Gestion des Soins de Sante. Vol. 1, No. 1 (Spring 1988)-. Periodical. English (French). qt. 65.00Can$ Canada; 80.00Can$ US; 95.00Can$ other. Canadian College of Health Service Executives, 17 York Street 201, Ottawa, Ontario K1N 5S7 Canada. **Tel** (613)235-7218. **DD** 362.1/068. **NLM** W1; HE608RM. ***Continues*** *Health Management Forum, 0712-5046.*
**Ind/Abst** Health Plan. Adminis.; Hospit. Health Admin. Index (Spring 1988-).

US/0741-9368
**HEALTHCARE MARKETING REPORT.** [Healthc. mark. rep.]. **VFOAT** Health Care Marketing Report. (Oct 1983)-. Periodical. English. mo. $135.00. Healthcare Marketing Report, PO Box 76002, Atlanta GA 30358. **Tel** (404)457-6105, FAX (404)457-0049. **ED** Richard Cohen (404)457-6160. **DD** 362. **Ad Acc. Circ:** 1,500 (ctrl).
**Desc:** Covers the advertising and marketing aspects of the healthcare field.
**Ind/Abst** F&S Index Plus Text, Int. [Select. Cov.]; Hospit. Manage. Rev.; Mark. Advert. Ref. Serv.; PROMT.

US/0737-6219
**HEALTHCARE MICROCOMPUTING NETWORK.** **See** Computers-Microcomputers, Personal Computers.

●US
**HEALTHCARE PR & MARKETING NEWS.** **VFOAT** Healthcare PR and Marketing News; Healthcare Public Relations & Marketing News; Healthcare PR News. (1993)-. Periodical. English. bw (25 issues). $397.00 US; $430.00 other. Phillips Business Information, Inc., 1201 Seven Locks Road, Potomac MD 20854. **Tel** (301)424-3338, (800)777-5006, FAX (301)309-3847. ***Continues*** *Healthcare PR News, 1068-0403.*

US/1068-0403
**HEALTHCARE PR NEWS.** ***Title Change.*** [Healthc. PR news]. **VAT** Healthcare Public Relations News. (1992)-(1993). Periodical. English. bw (25 issues). Phillips Business Information, Inc., 1201 Seven Locks Road, Potomac MD 20854. **Tel** (301)424-3338, (800)777-5006, FAX (301)309-3847. **DD** 659. available on an online database (file 636/Full-Text) from DIALOG. ***Continued by*** *Healthcare PR & Marketing News, 1072-3684.*

US/1055-9183
**HEALTHCARE STAFFING MANAGEMENT.** ***Ceased.*** [Healthc. staff. manage.]. Vol. 1, No. 1 (Apr. 1991)-(199?). Periodical. English. mo. Healthcare Staffing Management, PO Box 88062, Atlanta GA 30356-8062. **DD** 362.

US/0894-7961
**HEALTHCARE TRENDS REPORT.** [Healthc. trends rep.]. **VFOAT** Health Care Trends Report. Vol. 1, No. 1 (July 1987)- Vol. 7 No. 1 (Jan. 1993)-. Periodical. English. mo. $204.75 Maryland; $195.00 other. Health Trends, PO Box 151026, Chevy Chase MD 20815. **Tel** (301)652-8937. **ED** Sylvia F Moore. **DD** 362. Index Bound in First Issue (Bound in 12th issued in December). **Circ:** 1650. available on diskette.
**Desc:** A digest of business and public policy news related to the health services industry.

US/1048-4167
**HEALTHTEXAS (AUSTIN, TEX.).** (HEALTHTEXAS / TEXAS HOSPITAL ASSOCIATION.). [HealthTexas]. **Added/Corp** Texas Hospital Association. **VFOAT** Health Texas. (Jan. 1989)-. Periodical. English. Eleven times a year. $26.00 (THA members); $36.00 (nonmembers) US; $53.00 (nonmembers) other. Texas Hospital Association, PO Box 15587, Austin TX 78761. **Tel** (512)465-1000, FAX (512)465-1090. **ED** Margaret Harrist (editor's address: 6225 US Highway 290 East,

Austin, TX 78761-5587). **DD** 362. **NLM** W1; HE589T. **Ad Acc, Adv Mgr:** Martin Bevins. **Circ:** 7,000. available on microfilm and microfiche from University Microfilms International (UMI). ***Continues*** *Texas Hospitals, 0040-4357.*
**Desc:** Covers managerial aspects of health care. Its purpose is to aid health care professionals in maintaining and improving management skills and keeping abreast of new trends.
**Ind/Abst** Health Plan. Adminis.; Hospit. Health Admin. Index (1989-); Hospit. Manage. Rev. (19??-).

CN/0707-204X
**HEBDO A H P Q. Main/Corp** Association des Hopitaux de la Province de Quebec. **VAT** Hebdo. Association des Hopitaux de la Province de Quebec. Vol. 1 (Dec. 17, 1976)-. Periodical. French. wk. Free to Members. Association Des Hopitaux De La Province De Quebec, 324, 276, Rue Saint-Jacques, Montreal Quebec H2Y 1N3. **DD** 362.1/1/09714.

NE/0956-2737
**HEC FORUM.** (HEC FORUM: AN INTERDISCIPLINARY JOURNAL ON HOSPITALS' ETHICAL AND LEGAL ISSUES.). [HEC forum]. **VFOAT** Hospital Ethics Committee Forum. Vol. 1, No. 1 (1989)-. Periodical. English. bm. $233.00. Kluwer Academic Publishers, Postbus 322, 3300 AH Dordrecht, The Netherlands. **Tel** 011 (31) 78 524400, FAX 011 31 78 183273, telex 20083. **ED** Stuart Spicker and Judith Wilson Ross. **LC** R724; .H38. **DD** 174/.2/05. **NLM** W1; HE682H. **CODEN** HEFOE8. **[CCC]. Pr Rev. Acid Free.** available on microfilm and microfiche from University Microfilms International (UMI).
**Desc:** Provides for the rapid communication of information on the ethical and legal issues confronting today's hospitals and health care providers.
**Ind/Abst** Health Plan. Adminis.; Hospit. Health Admin. Index (1989-); Int. Nurs. Index.

GW/0440-9043
**HISTORIA HOSPITALIUM. Added/Corp** Deutsche Gesellschaft fuer Krankenhausgeschichte. No. 1 (March 1966)-. Periodical. German. sa. Konrad Triltsch Druck & Verlagsanstalt, PF 6660, D 97016 Wuerzburg Germany. **Tel** 011 49 931 308030. **NLM** W1 HI78.
**Ind/Abst** Am. Hist. Life (1983-); BHA : Biblio. Hist. Art.

US/1050-902X
**HMO MANAGERS LETTER.** (HMO MANAGERS LETTER / GROUP HEALTH ASSOCIATION OF AMERICA, INC.). [HMO managers lett.]. **Added/Corp** Group Health Association of America. **VFOAT** HML. **VAT** Health Maintenance Organization Managers Letter. Vol. 1, No. 1 (Sept. 17, 1984)-. Periodical. English. Twenty-two times a year. $125.00 (one years); $175.00 (two years); $235.00 (three years) Comes with HMO Magazine. Group Health Association of America, Department 0612, Washington DC 20073. **Tel** (202)778-3247, FAX (202)331-7487. **DD** 362. **CODEN** HMALEU.

CN/0229-415X
**HOMES FOR THE AGED.** [Homes aged]. **Added/Corp** Community Information Centre of Metropolitan Toronto. (1978)-. English. be. Community Information Centre of Metropolitan Toronto, 590 Jarvis Street, Toronto Ontario M4Y 2J4 Canada. **Tel** (416)392-4575, FAX (416)392-4404. **DD** 362.6/1/025713541.

FR/0018-4861
**HOPITAL A PARIS, L'. *Suspended.*** **Added/Corp** Amis de l'Assistance Publique a Paris. Vol. 1 (Jan./Feb. 1960)-(19??). Periodical. Multiple languages (French; summaries and/or abstracts in English, German and Spanish). bm. 250.00F France; 350.00F other. Association des Amis de l'Assistance Publique a Paris, 7 rue des Minimes, 75003 Paris France. **Tel** 40 27 50 75, FAX 40 27 50 74. ***Continues*** *Revue de l'Assistance Publique a Paris.*

US/0193-6816
**HOSPICE LETTER.** (1979)-. Periodical. English. Twelve times a year. $157.00 (one year), $284.00 (two years), $400.00 (three years); $97.00 (introductory subscription). Health Resources Publishing, 3100 Highway 138, Wall Township NJ 07719-1442. **Tel** (908)681-1133, FAX (908)681-0490. **ED** Robert K Jenkins. **Bk Rev. Ad Acc. Circ:** 1,000.
**Desc:** Monthly newsletter reporting the latest developments in the rapidly expanding hospice concept of caring for the terminally ill. Read by administrators and directors who follow Medicare reimbursement and hospice accreditation; how hospices are raising money and staging community events; new legislation and regulations; and the latest on nursing care, volunteers, and counseling programs.

•US/1065-3155
**HOSPICE SALARY & BENEFITS REPORT.** [Hosp. salary benefits rep.]. **Added/Corp** Hospital & Healthcare Compensation Service. **VFOAT** Hospice Salary and Benefits Report. (1992)-. English. an (Published in October). $195.00. Hospital & Healthcare Compensation Service, PO Box 376, 69 Minnehaha Blvd., Oakland NJ 07436. **Tel** (201)405-0075, FAX (201)405-1258. **DD** 331.
**Desc:** Covers salary and bonus data on sixty-three management, nursing, therapy, and clerical jobs.

US/0018-5485
**HOSPITAL, EL.** [Hospital]. Vol. 1 (July 1945)-. Periodical. English (Spanish). bm. Free on request. Salud Publications International Inc, 5790 Eaglesridge Lane, Cincinnati OH 45230. **Tel** (513)232-0511, (513)232-0518. **ED** Nigel Sylvester. **NLM** W1 HO812. **Bk Rev. Ad Acc. Circ:** 15,235 (ctrl).
**Desc:** Contains information about recent medical research, techniques and equipment of interest to the Spanish-speaking world.

SP/0214-2422
**HOSPITAL 2000. *Suspended.* See** Architecture.

US
**HOSPITAL ACCESS MANAGEMENT.** (199?)-. English. mo. $269.00. American Health Consultants, 3525 Piedmont Road, Suite 400, Atlanta GA 30305. **Tel** (800)688-2421, (404)262-7436. **(Subscription address:** American Health Consultants, PO Box 95278, Chicago IL 60694.**)** ***Continues*** *Hospital Admitting Monthly, 0745-1466.*

II/0018-5531
**HOSPITAL ADMINISTRATION (NEW DELHI).** (HOSPITAL ADMINISTRATION.). [Hosp. adm.]. **Added/Corp** Indian Hospital Association. Vol. 1 (1964)-. Academic Scholarly Publication. English. qt. $50.00. Indian Hospital Association, B 401 404 Sarita Vihar Dr Gei, New Delhi 110044 Inia. **Tel** 011 91 11 6835648. **(Subscription address:** Prints India, 11 Darya Ganj, New Delhi, 110002 India, (Phone: 011 91 11 3268645)**) ED** A K Khokhar and P Ghei. **NLM** W1 HO7S. **Circ:** 1,000.
**Desc:** Deals with hospital and health administration aspects, particularly in planning, management, evaluation and primary health care.
**Ind/Abst** EMBASE; Health Plan. Adminis.

US/0745-1466
**HOSPITAL ADMITTING MONTHLY. *Title Change.*** **Added/Corp** American Health Consultants. Vol. 1, No. 1 (July 1982)-(199?). Periodical. English. mo. American Health Consultants, 3525 Piedmont Road, Suite 400, Atlanta GA 30305. **Tel** (800)688-2421, (404)262-7436. **NLM** W1 HO71K. ***Continued by*** *Hospital Access Management.*
**Ind/Abst** Health Plan. Adminis.

•US/1077-1719
**HOSPITAL AND HEALTH ADMINISTRATION INDEX. See** Medical Science and Technology-Abstracting, Bibliographies and Statistics.

US
**HOSPITAL AND HEALTH ADMINISTRATION INDEX. ANNUAL CUMULATION. See** Medical Science and Technology-Abstracting, Bibliographies and Statistics.

US/0146-7360
**HOSPITAL AND HEALTH CARE REPORT. Main/Corp** American Management Association. Executive Compensation Service. 1st Ed. (1976/1977)-. English. ir. American Management Association, 135 West 50th Street, New York NY 10020-1201. **Tel** (212)586-8100, (212)903-8375 (periodicals), FAX (212)903-8168, (212)903-8083 (periodicals). **(Subscription address:** CDS-SIFD Agency Control, 1901 Bell Avenue, Des Moines, IA 50315; (telephone: (515)246-6924)**) LC** RA981.A2; E96a. **DD** 331.2/81/362110973. **NLM** W1; HO71MN.

US/8750-3735
**HOSPITAL & HEALTH SERVICES ADMINISTRATION.** (HOSPITAL & HEALTH SERVICES ADMINISTRATION : QUARTERLY JOURNAL OF THE AMERICAN COLLEGE OF HOSPITAL ADMINISTRATORS.). [Hosp. health serv. adm.]. **Added/Corp** American College of Hospital Administrators. American College of Hospital Administrators. Foundation. American College of Healthcare Executives. Foundation. **VFOAT** Hospital and Health Services Administration; ACHA Journal. Vol. 21 (Winter 1976)-. Periodical. English. Four times a year (Feb., May, Aug., Nov.). $55.00. American College of Healthcare Executives, 840 North Lake Shore Drive, c/o J. Flory, Chicago IL 60611. **Tel** (312)943-0544 ext. 3000, FAX (312)943-3791. **(Subscription address:** FDN American College of Healthcare Executives, Order Processing Center, 1951 Cornell Avenue, Melrose Park IL 60160.**) ED** Samuel Levey and Rebecca McDermott. **LC** RA971; .H583. **DD** 362.1/1/068. **NLM** W1 HO71PY; HO71PY. **[CCC]. Bk Rev. Pr Rev. Circ:** 24,000 (ctrl). available on microfilm and microfiche from University Microfilms International (UMI); available on an online database (files 149,648/Full-Text) from DIALOG. Documents available from The Genuine Article, UMI Article Clearinghouse. ***Continues*** *Hospital Administration, 0018-5523.*
**Desc:** Publishes articles on new developments, innovations and trends in healthcare management. Subject areas include strategy planning and policy, board/medical staff administrative relations and others.
**Ind/Abst** ABI/INFORM Glob. Ed.; ABI Inform Ondisc (Jan. 1984-); Acad. Search (Jan. 1993-); Bus. Index (1985-); Cumul. Index Nurs. Allied Health Lit.; Curr. Contents Soc. Behav. Sci.; EMBASE; Gen. BusinessFile (1985-); Gen. Period. Index (1985-); Health Index (1989-); Health Period. Database [Full Txt.]; Health Ref. Cent. (Jan. 1989-) [Full Txt.] [Full Cov.]; Hospit. Health Admin. Index; Hospit. Manage. Rev.; INFO-SOUTH Abstr.; Int. Pharm. Abstr.; Mag. Search; Person. Manage. Abstr.; Res. Alert [Full Cov.]; Soc. Sci. Cit. Index [Full Cov.]; Trade Ind. ASAP [Full Txt.]; Trade Ind. Index [Full Txt.]; UMI ABI/Inform--Bus. Period. Ondisc (Feb. 1987-) [Full Txt.]; Vocat. Search (Jan. 1993-); Work Relat. Abstr.

UK/0308-0234
**HOSPITAL AND HEALTH SERVICES REVIEW, THE.** V. 1- 1904-. Periodical. English. bm. £31.00 UK; $61.00 US; £35.00 other. Longman Group Ltd., Fourth Avenue, Longman House, Harlow Essex CM19 5SR England. **Tel** 011 44 279 429655, FAX 011 44 279 431059, telex 81259. **(Subscription address:** PO Box 1584, Birmingham, AL 35201**) [CCC].** available on microfilm and microfiche from University Microfilms International (UMI).
**Ind/Abst** Hospit. Health Admin. Index.

AT/0813-7471
**HOSPITAL & HEALTHCARE AUSTRALIA.** [Hosp. health. Aust.]. **VFOAT** Hospital and Healthcare Australia. (1983)-. Periodical. English. mo. 38.00Aus$ Australia; 105.00Aus$ other. Yaffa Publishing Group Pty Ltd., GPO Box 606, Sydney NSW 2001 Australia. **Tel** 011 61 2 2812333, FAX 011 61 2 2812750. **ED** Tony Burrett. **NLM** W1; HO71ML. **Bk Rev. Ad Acc. Circ:** 3,919 (ctrl). ***Continues*** *Hospital Journal of Australia, 0312-8490.*
**Desc:** Covers latest government, labour and legal matters. Also an update on technological equipment and new products for hospitals.

SA
**HOSPITAL AND NURSING YEAR BOOK OF SOUTHERN AFRICA (JOHANNESBURG (SOUTH AFRICA) : 1971)).** (HOSPITAL AND NURSING YEARBOOK OF SOUTHERN AFRICA.). **Added/Corp** Harold MacCarthy Publications (Pty.) Ltd. **VFOAT** Hospital & Nursing Year Book. (19??)-. English. an (Aug.). R230.00 South Africa; R255.00 other. H. Englehardt & Co, PO Box 3551, Cape Town 8000 South Africa. **Tel** 011 27 21 4193794, FAX 011 27 21 4197038. **LC** RA991.S7; H6. **DD** 362.1/1/0968. **NLM** W1 HO73E. **Circ:** 1,500 (ctrl). ***Continues*** *Hospital and Nursing Year Book of South Africa.*

UK
**HOSPITAL AND PRIMARY HEALTH CARE.** English. ir. £5.00. International Hospital Federation, 4 Abbots Place, London NW6 4NP England. **Tel** 011 44 71 372-7181, FAX 011 44 71 328-7433.
**Desc:** Describes noteworthy hospital-linked innovations in such fields as health promotion, family planning, acccident prevention, rehabilitation, integrated hospital and community care, training and administrative support for primary care.

UK/0959-2512
**HOSPITAL BED USE STATISTICS / WELSH OFFICE [AND] WELSH HEALTH COMMON SERVICES AUTHORITY. Added/Corp** Great Britain. Welsh Office. Health Intelligence Unit. Welsh Health Common Services Authority. (1988/1989)-. English. Health Intelligence Unit, Welsh Office, Cathays Park, Cardiff CF1 3NQ. **LC** RA987.W2; G72a. **DD** 362.1/1/09429021. ***Continues*** *Great Britain. Welsh Office. Bed Use Statistics, 0140-2706.*

US/1047-6903
**HOSPITAL BLUE BOOK (OFFICIAL NATIONAL ED.).** (HOSPITAL BLUE BOOK.). [Hosp. blue book]. **VFOAT** Official National Hospital Blue Book. (198?)-. English. an. $149.50. Billian Publishing Inc., 2100 Powers Ferry Road, Atlanta GA 30339. **Tel** (404)955-5656, FAX (404)952-0669. **LC** RA981.A2; H56. **DD** 362.1/1/02573. **NLM** WX 22; AA1 H8285.

US/0740-3674
**HOSPITAL/COMMUNITY RELATIONS PROFESSIONAL.** [Hosp./community relat. prof.]. **Added/Corp** Hospital/Community Associates. **VFOAT** Hospital, Community Relations Professional. (Aug. 1983)-. Periodical. English. mo. $50.00. Hospital/Community Relations Professional, PO Box 590, Naperville IL 60566.

US/0734-0028
**HOSPITAL CONTRACTS MANUAL. See** Law.

US/1045-1765
**HOSPITAL COST MANAGEMENT AND ACCOUNTING.** [Hosp. cost manage. account.]. Vol. 1, No. 1 (April 1989)-. Periodical. English. mo. $215.00 US. Aspen Publishers Inc., 7201 McKinney Circle, Frederick MD 21701. **Tel** (800)234-1660, (301)698-7100,

FAX (301)251-5784, telex 5106014543. **(Subscription address:** Aspen Publishers Inc., PO Box 990, Frederick MD 21701.**)** **ED** Steven A. Finkler PhD, CPA, CCA. **DD** 362. **NLM** W1; HO754LM. **Pr Rev.** ***Continues*** *Hospital Cost Accounting Advisor, 8756-7288.*
**Desc:** Brings together the latest techniques, tested strategies, procedures, and insights for controlling expenses and maximizing reimbursement under DRGs. The newsletter provides up-to-the-minute systems for tracking patient costs and innovative budgeting for cost allocation.
**Ind/Abst** Hospit. Health Admin. Index (1992-).

UK/0300-5720
**HOSPITAL DEVELOPMENT.** [Hosp. dev.]. **VFOAT** HD Hospital Development; HD. Vol. 1 (Jan./Feb. 1973)-. Academic Scholarly Publication. English. Eleven times a year. $134.00 US and Canada; £52.00 UK. Wilmington Publishing Ltd., PO Box 200, Field End Road, Ruislip Middx HA4 OSY England. **Tel** 011 44 81 841 3970, FAX 011 44 81 841 9676. **NLM** W1 HO77T. ***Supersedes*** *Hospital Building & Engineering, 0018-5582.*
**Ind/Abst** Archit. Period. Index (19??-); EMBASE (19??-); Health Plan. Adminis. (19??-); Hospit. Health Admin. Index (19??-); Int. Build. Serv. Abstr. (19??-).

US/0744-6470
**HOSPITAL EMPLOYEE HEALTH.** [Hosp. empl. health]. Vol. 1, No. 1 (Jan. 1982)-. Periodical. English. mo. $289.00. American Health Consultants, 3525 Piedmont Road, Suite 400, Atlanta GA 30305. **Tel** (800)688-2421, (404)262-7436. **(Subscription address:** American Health Consultants, PO Box 95278, Chicago IL 60694.**)** **NLM** W1; HO772D. **[CCC].**
**Ind/Abst** Cumul. Index Nurs. Allied Health Lit.

US
**HOSPITAL ENGINEERING BULLETIN / AMERICAN SOCIETY FOR HOSPITAL ENGINEERING OF THE AMERICAN HOSPITAL ASSOCIATION.** **Added/Corp** American Society for Hospital Engineering. American Hospital Association. Vol. 1, No. 1 (Jan. 1983)-. Periodical. English. Twelve times a year. $75.00 (members); $105.00 (non-members) Comes with American Society for Hospital Engineering membership. American Society of Hospital Engineering, 840 North Lake Shore Drive, Chicago IL 60611. **Tel** (312)280-6615. **NLM** W1; HO772T.
**Ind/Abst** Health Devices Alerts.

UK/0018-5620
**HOSPITAL EQUIPMENT & SUPPLIES.** [Hosp. equip. supplies]. **VFOAT** Hospital Equipment and Supplies. (1955)-. Periodical. English. mo. $214.00 US; £44.00 UK. Wilmington Publishing Ltd., PO Box 200, Field End Road, Ruislip Middx HA4 OSY England. **Tel** 011 44 81 841 3970, FAX 011 44 81 841 9676.
**Ind/Abst** Health Plan. Adminis. (19??-).

US/0271-406X
**HOSPITAL FINANCIAL MANAGEMENT ASSOCIATION ANNUAL REPORT.** [Hosp. Financ. Manage. Assoc. annu. rep.]. **Main/Corp** Hospital Financial Management Association (U.S.). **Added/Corp** Hospital Financial Management Association (U.S.). Annual Report. (1979)-. English. an. **NLM** W1 HO776D.

US/0046-7979
**HOSPITAL FOOD SERVICE.** **Added/Corp** American Society for Hospital Food Service Administrators. Vol. 1 (Nov. 1967)-. Periodical. English. qt. Comes with American Society of Hospital Food Service Administration membership. American Society of Hospital Food Services Administration, 840 North Lake Shore Drive, Chicago IL 60611. **Tel** (312)280-6029. **NLM** W1 HO777L.

US/0193-9939
**HOSPITAL FUND RAISING NEWSLETTER.** ***Title Change.*** (1979)-(19??). Newsletter. English. bm. Hospital Fund Raising, PO Box 1442, Wall Township NJ 07719. **Tel** (201)681-1133. **ED** Robert K Jenkins. **[CCC].** **Bk Rev.** **Ad Acc.** ***Continued by*** *Healthcare Fund Raising Newsletter.*
**Desc:** Summary of ways to raise funds to meet competitive pressures and demands for services.

US/0739-3466
**HOSPITAL GRAPHICS.** ***Title Change.*** **See** The Arts-Graphic Arts.

US
**HOSPITAL LAW MANUAL. ADMINISTRATORS VOLUME.** **See** Law.

US/0018-5728
**HOSPITAL LAW MANUAL. ATTORNEYS VOLUME.** **See** Law.

US
**HOSPITAL LAW MANUAL. NEWSLETTER AND QUARTERLY SUPPLEMENT.** **See** Law.

US/0018-5736
**HOSPITAL LITERATURE INDEX.** ***Title Change.*** **See** Medical Science and Technology-Abstracting, Bibliographies and Statistics.

US/1048-5201
**HOSPITAL LITIGATION REPORTER.** **See** Law.

UK
**HOSPITAL MAGAZINE.** (19??)-. Periodical. English. Eleven times a year. £56.00 (institutions), £34.00 (individuals) UK; £56.00 (institutions), £44.00 (individuals) other. Mark Allen Publishing Ltd., Croxped Mews, 288 Croxped Road, London SE24 9DA England. **Tel** 011 44 1 671 7521.

●US/1061-7620
**HOSPITAL MANAGED CARE & DIRECT CONTRACTING.** [Hosp. managed care direct contract.]. **VFOAT** Hospital Managed Care and Direct Contracting. Vol. 1, No. 10 (Apr. 1992)-. Periodical. English. mo. $261.00 US. Aspen Publishers Inc., 7201 McKinney Circle, Frederick MD 21701. **Tel** (800)234-1660, (301)698-7100, FAX (301)251-5784, telex 5106014543. **(Subscription address:** Aspen Publishers Inc., PO Box 990, Frederick MD 21701.**)** **ED** Allan Fine. **DD** 362. **NLM** W1; HO816. ***Continues*** *Direct Contracting & Hospital Managed Care, 1057-0098.*
**Desc:** Provides the information needed to identify, plan, and set up profitable direct contracting agreements, which can pay off big in improving cash flow and quality of care, and improving your payor mix and increasing your market share. The journal has insider information that will help hospital executives to capitalize on new, creative approaches to managed care.

UK/0953-9743
**HOSPITAL MANAGEMENT INTERNATIONAL / INTERNATIONAL HOSPITAL FEDERATION.** **Added/Corp** International Hospital Federation. **VFOAT** Gestion Hospitaliere dans le Monde; Administracion Hospitalaria en el Mundo. (1989)-. English (French and Spanish). an. £28.00. International Hospital Federation, 4 Abbots Place, London NW6 4NP England. **Tel** 011 44 71 372-7181, FAX 011 44 71 328-7433. **ED** Leslie Paine. **NLM** W1; HO817CI. **Ad Acc.** ***Continues*** *Official Yearbook (International Hospital Federation).*
**Desc:** This publication results from several years of information collection on health services around the world; how systems are financed, organized and administered and provides a basic overview of the health services of 60 nations.

US/0737-903X
**HOSPITAL MANAGEMENT REVIEW.** **See** Medical Science and Technology-Abstracting, Bibliographies and Statistics.

US/0363-390X
**HOSPITAL MANAGEMENT SERIES.** **Added/Corp** Catholic Hospital Association. (1975)-. Monographic series. English. Price varies per volume. American Catholic Hospital Association, 1438 South Grand Boulevard, St. Louis MO 63104. **NLM** W1 HO817CM.

US/0888-3068
**HOSPITAL MATERIALS MANAGEMENT.** [Hosp. mater. manage.]. **VFOAT** Hospital Materials Management. Vol. 11, No. 3 (March 1986)-. Academic Scholarly Publication. English. mo. $207.00 US; $213.00 Canada; $225.00 other. Business Word Inc., 5350 South Roslyn Street, Suite 400, Englewood CA 80111-2125. **Tel** (303)290-8500, FAX (303)290-9025. **ED** Donald E. L. Johnson. **DD** 610. **NLM** W1; HO817EF. Index available (published in Dec. issue). **Bk Rev.** **Ad Acc.** **Circ:** 2,000. available on microfilm and microfiche from University Microfilms International (UMI); available on an online database (file 15/Full-Text) from DIALOG. ***Continues*** *Hospital Purchasing Management, 0163-1322.*
**Desc:** Newsletter for group purchasing and materials management covering major price trends, VA product evaluations, special industry issues, market reports, healthcare purchasing law, group purchasing organizations and purchasing management. Price indexes are produced.
**Ind/Abst** Bibliogr. Mission. (1986-); EMBASE (1986-); Health Devices Alerts; Hospit. Health Admin. Index (March 1986-); Hospit. Manage. Rev.; Int. Pharm. Abstr.

US/0749-6672
**HOSPITAL MATERIALS MANAGEMENT NEWS.** (HOSPITAL MATERIALS MANAGEMENT NEWS : THE BIMONTHLY NEWSLETTER OF ASHMM REPRESENTING PURCHASING MANAGEMENT, LOGISTICS MANAGEMENTS, AND INVENTORY AND DISTRIBUTION MANAGEMENT SECTIONS / AMERICAN SOCIETY FOR HOSPITAL MATERIALS MANAGEMENT OF THE AMERICAN HOSPITAL ASSOCIATION.). [Hosp. mater. manage. news]. **Added/Corp** American Society for Hospital Materials Management. Vol. 27, No. 1 (Jan./Feb. 1983)-. Newsletter. English. bm. Comes with membership. American Hospital Association, 840 North Lake Shore Drive, Chicago IL 60611. **Tel** (312)280-6000, (800)242-2626. **ED** Cheryl L Ritzi. **DD** 362. **Bk Rev.** **Circ:** 1,800 (ctrl). ***Continues*** *Hospital Purchasing (Chicago, Ill.).*
**Desc:** A membership newsletter which includes industry developments and changes.

US/0192-2262
**HOSPITAL MATERIEL MANAGEMENT QUARTERLY.** [Hosp. mater. manage. q.]. **Added/Corp** Aspen Systems Corporation. **VFOAT** HMMQ. Vol. 1 (Aug. 1979)-. Academic Scholarly Publication. English. qt. $110.00 US. Aspen Publishers Inc., 7201 McKinney Circle, Frederick MD 21701. **Tel** (800)234-1660, (301)698-7100, FAX (301)251-5784, telex 5106014543. **(Subscription address:** Aspen Publishers Inc., PO Box 990, Frederick MD 21701.**)** **ED** Charles E. Housley. **LC** RA971.33; .H66. **DD** 362.1/1/0687. **NLM** W1 HO817E. **[CCC].** **Ad Acc.** **Circ:** 2,100. available on microfilm and microfiche from University Microfilms International (UMI). Documents available from UMI Article Clearinghouse.
**Desc:** Addresses and explores, on a timely basis, conceptual and practical issues in the rapidly expanding field of hospital material management. Every three months it focuses objectively on one subject of interest to material management professionals, defining the issues, clarifying alternatives, weighing the pros and cons, and pinpointing appropriate solutions.
**Ind/Abst** ABI/INFORM Glob. Ed.; ABI Inform Ondisc (Nov. 1980-); EMBASE; Gen. BusinessFile (1992-); Health Plan. Adminis.; Hospit. Health Admin. Index; Int. Pharm. Abstr.; UMI ABI/Inform--Bus. Period. Ondisc (Feb. 1990-) [Full Txt.].

CN/1195-4000
**HOSPITAL MORBIDITY - CANADIAN CENTRE FOR HEALTH INFORMATION.** **See** Medical Science and Technology-Abstracting, Bibliographies and Statistics.

US/1056-3040
**HOSPITAL NEWS FOR HEALTHCARE PROVIDERS. (EASTERN MASS/BOSTON ED.).** (HOSPITAL NEWS FOR HEALTHCARE PROVIDERS.). [Hosp. news healthc. provid.]. **VFOAT** Hospital News; Hospital News, Eastern Mass/Bosotn. Vol. 1, No. 7 (Jan. 1991)-. Periodical. English. mo. $18.00. Hospital News, PO Box 3796, Nashua NH 03061-3796. **DD** 362. ***Continues*** *Eastern Massachusetts Hospital News.*

US/1056-3032
**HOSPITAL NEWS FOR HEALTHCARE PROVIDERS (NORTHERN NEW ENGLAND ED.).** (HOSPITAL NEWS FOR HEALTHCARE PROVIDERS.). [Hosp. news healthc. provid.]. **VFOAT** Hospital News; Hospital News, Northern New England. Vol. 4, No. 4 (Jan. 1991)-. Periodical. English. mo. $18.00. Hospital News, PO Box 3796, Nashua NH 03061-3796. **DD** 362. ***Continues*** *Vermont Hospital News.*

US/1071-0582
**HOSPITAL NEWS (PITTSBURGH, PA. 1986).** (HOSPITAL NEWS.). [Hosp. news]. **VFOAT** Pittsburgh Hospital News. (Dec. 1986)-. Periodical. English. Twelve times a year. $25.44 Pennsylvania; $24.00 others. Medical Publications Inc., 300 Mt. Lebanon Boulevard, Suite 201-A, Pittsburgh PA 15234. **Tel** (412)341-1775, FAX (412)341-2028. **ED** Nancy Carrou. **DD** 362. **Ad Acc, Adv Mgr:** Bob Milie, **Tel** (412)341-1775. **Circ:** 14,000 (ctrl).
**Desc:** An trade publication for health care professionals.

US/1062-9947
**HOSPITAL NEWS. WISCONSIN.** [Hosp. news, Wis.]. (1991)-. Periodical. English. mo. $24.95. Niche Publications, 3989 Central Avenue NE, Minneapolis MN 55421. **DD** 362.

US/1048-4477
**HOSPITAL PATIENT RELATIONS REPORT.** [Hosp. patient relat. rep.]. **Added/Corp** Business Publishers. Vol. 4, No. 11 (Nov. 1989)-. Periodical. English. mo. $276.00. Business Publishers Inc., 951 Pershing Drive, Silver Spring MD 20910-4464. **Tel** (301)587-6300, (800)274-0122, FAX (301)585-9075. **DD** 362. **NLM** W1; HO862. **[CCC].** ***Continues*** *Hospital Guest Relations Report, 0899-8957;* ***Absorbed*** *Hospital Patient Relations Advisor, 0892-709X.*
**Desc:** Stresses immediate operational concerns and addresses daily problems through case studies, interviews, and innovative ideas that are working for hospitals. Deals with patient satisfaction, involvement of middle managers and physicians with customer service programs, and the doctor/patient relationship, i.e. protecting confidentiality, accomodating families of patients and their needs, and dealing with complaints and threats of suits.
**Ind/Abst** Health Plan. Adminis.; Hospit. Health Admin. Index (Nov. 1989-); Hospit. Manage. Rev. (19??-).

US/1074-8334
**HOSPITAL PAYMENT & INFORMATION MANAGEMENT.** ***Ceased.*** (HOSPITAL PAYMENT & INFORMATION MANAGEMENT / AMERICAN

HEALTH CONSULTANTS.). [Hosp. paym. inf. manag.]. **Added/Corp** American Health Consultants. **VFOAT** Hospital Payment and Information Management. Vol. 15, No. 1 (Jan. 1994)-(Dec. 1994). Periodical. English. mo. American Health Consultants, 3525 Piedmont Road, Suite 400, Atlanta GA 30305. **Tel** (800)688-2421, (404)262-7436. **DD** 368. ***Continues*** *Hospital's Medicare Policy & Payment Report, 1060-7838.*

US/0149-2632
**HOSPITAL PEER REVIEW.** Vol. 1 (Aug. 1976)-. Periodical. English. mo. $249.00. American Health Consultants, 3525 Piedmont Road, Suite 400, Atlanta GA 30305. **Tel** (800)688-2421, (404)262-7436. **(Subscription address:** American Health Consultants, PO Box 95278, Chicago IL 60694.**) NLM** W1 HO864. **[CCC].** available on microfilm and microfiche from University Microfilms International (UMI).
**Ind/Abst** Health Plan. Adminis.; Hospit. Manage. Rev.

US/0278-5153
**HOSPITAL PHONE BOOK, THE.** [Hosp. phone book]. **Added/Corp** U.S. Directory Service. (1980/1981)-. English. an. $89.95. Reed Reference Publishing, 121 Chanlon Road, New Providence NJ 07974. **Tel** (908)464-6800, (800)521-8110 Ext. 3387, (800)223-1797, FAX (908)665-3560. **LC** RA981.A2; H5767. **DD** 362.1/102573. **NLM** WX 22 AA1 H8392. **Circ:** 250,000.
**Desc:** A complete, accurate and up-to-date name, address and phone book of hospitals in the US.

US/8755-4542
**HOSPITAL PRACTICE (HOSPITAL ED.).** (HOSPITAL PRACTICE.). [Hosp. pract.]. (198?)-. Periodical. English. Twelve times a year. HP Publishing Company, 55 Fifth Avenue, 14th Floor, New York NY 10003-4301. **Tel** (212)989-2100, FAX (212)989-2100. **DD** 616. ***Continues in part*** *Hospital Practice, 0018-5809.*
**Ind/Abst** Health Index (1992-); Health Ref. Cent. (Jan. 1989-) [Full Cov.]; Helminthol. Abstr. (1991-); Hospit. Health Admin. Index; Index Med.; Int. Pharm. Abstr.; Physic. Medline Plus.

US
**HOSPITAL PRODUCT COMPARISON SYSTEM. VFOAT** Hospital PCS; ECRI Hospital Product Comparison System. (19??)-. English. mo. $595.00. ECRI Emergency Care Research Institute, 5200 Butler Pike, Plymouth Meeting PA 19462. **Tel** (215)825-6000, FAX (215)834-1275, telex 510-660-8023.

US
**HOSPITAL PRODUCT LINE REPORT.** **VFOAT** Product Line Report; Product Line. (19??)-. Periodical. English. mo. St Anthony Hospital Publications, 801 Pennsylvania Avenue SE/Suite 001, Washington DC 20003.
**Ind/Abst** Hospit. Manage. Rev. (19??-19??).

US/0279-4799
**HOSPITAL PURCHASING NEWS.** (HOSPITAL PURCHASING NEWS : HPN.). [Hosp. purch. news]. **VFOAT** HPN. Vol. 5, No. 9 (Sept. 1981)-. Periodical. English. mo. $44.95. McKnight Medical Communications Inc, 1419 Lake Cook Road, Suite 110, Deerfield IL 60015. **Tel** (708)647-0259, (800)451-7838. **(Subscription address:** Hallmark Data Systems, PO Box 1165, Skokie IL 60076.**) ED** Mark Thill and John Hall. **[CCC]. Ad Acc. Circ:** 22,000 (ctrl). ***Continues*** *Purchasing Administration, 0192-4311.*
**Desc:** For materials management professionals at every hospital. Reaches materials managers, purchasing directors and central service managers.
**Ind/Abst** Health Devices Alerts; Hospit. Health Admin. Index (1981-1986).

US/1052-8733
**HOSPITAL REVENUE REPORT.** [Hosp. revenue rep.]. **Added/Corp** United Communications Group. Vol. 8, No. 9 (Sept. 1990)-. Periodical. English. Twenty-four times a year. $419.00 (one year), $828.00 (two year). United Communications Group, 11300 Rockville Pike, Suite 1100, Rockville MD 20852. **Tel** (301)816-8950 ext. 223, FAX (301)816-8945. **DD** 362. **NLM** W1; HO876N. ***Formed by the union of*** *Part A News and Health Care Marketer, 0896-1204.*
**Ind/Abst** Health Plan. Adminis.; Hospit. Health Admin. Index (1990-Dec. 2, 1991).

US/0199-6312
**HOSPITAL RISK MANAGEMENT. See** Business-General Management.

US/0276-2323
**HOSPITAL SAFETY INFORMATION SERVICE.** [Hosp. saf. inf. serv.]. Vol. 1, No. 1 (Mar./Apr. 1979)-. Periodical. English. Six times a year. $110.00 (one year), $210.00 (two years). Scientific Enterprises Inc, 5104 Randolph Road, North Little Rock AR 72116. **Tel** (501)771-1775, FAX (501)771-1775. **ED** James O. Wear. **NLM** W1 HO877. Index Available published separately, bound from publisher, free-automatically sent.
**Desc:** The only newsletter focusing on hospital safety for the patient, employee, and visitor. It is a resource to administrators, safety coordinators, risk managers, hospital engineers, and clinical / biomedical engineers. Topics such as JCAHO and OSHA information, FDA recalls, hazards, questions and answers, off-the-job safety, and special features are in each issue. Sample policy statements and material for employee bulletins are published periodically. Over 30 pages per issue and a binder is furnished with the first issue each year.

US/0277-2353
**HOSPITAL SALARY SURVEY REPORT.** **Added/Corp** Hospital Compensation Service. (1991)-. English. an. $250.00. Hospital & Healthcare Compensation Service, PO Box 376, 69 Minnehaha Blvd., Oakland NJ 07436. **Tel** (201)405-0075, FAX (201)405-1258. **LC** RA981.A2; H577. **DD** 331.2/8136211/0973. **NLM** W1; HO879L. Index available. ***Continues*** *Hospital Salary Survey Report on Department Head Positions, 0277-2353.*
**Desc:** Covers salaries and bonuses for 140 hospital positions including m,anagement, nursing, therapy, laboratory, radiological rehabilitation, dietary, pharmacy, technical and clerical.

US
**HOSPITAL SALARY SURVEY REPORT.** English. an (published in July). $255.00. Hospital & Healthcare Compensation Service, PO Box 376, 69 Minnehaha Blvd., Oakland NJ 07436. **Tel** (201)405-0075, FAX (201)405-1258. **ED** Rosanne Goffe.

US/0745-1148
**HOSPITAL SECURITY AND SAFETY MANAGEMENT.** [Hosp. secur. safety manage.]. Vol. 3, No. 5 (Sept. 1982)-. Periodical. English. mo. $169.00 (one year), $298.00 (two year). Rusting Publications, PO Box 190, Port Washington NY 11050. **Tel** (516)883-1440. **ED** Robert R. Rusting. **NLM** W1; HO881N. Index available. cum. index. **Bk Rev. Circ:** 1,100. ***Continues*** *Health Care Security and Safety Management, 0279-3466.*
**Desc:** Programs, ideas, and trends for preventing, reducing, and dealing with employee theft, violent crime, accidents and fires in hospitals.
**Ind/Abst** Hospit. Health Admin. Index (1982-).

CN/0383-574X
**HOSPITAL STATISTICS. VOLUME 1. BEDS, SERVICES, PERSONNEL. See** Medical Science and Technology-Abstracting, Bibliographies and Statistics.

US/1040-6263
**HOSPITAL STRATEGY REPORT.** [Hosp. strategy rep.]. Vol. 1, No. 1 (Nov. 1988)-. Periodical. English. mo. $199.00 US. Aspen Publishers Inc., 7201 McKinney Circle, Frederick MD 21701. **Tel** (800)234-1660, (301)698-7100, FAX (301)251-5784, telex 5106014543. **(Subscription address:** Aspen Publishers Inc., PO Box 990, Frederick MD 21701.**) ED** Russell C. Coile Jr. **DD** 610. **NLM** W1; HO591P. ***Continues*** *Hospital Entrepreneurs' Newsletter, 8756-7253.*
**Desc:** Written exclusively for strategic hospital planners and executives who are determined to survive and prosper through turbulent times ahead in health care. You will be in the know on the most important trends and issues that will affect your hospital over the next 3 to 5 years. Each issue is devoted to one or two specific strategic challenges that could dramatically affect your hospital's financial future.
**Ind/Abst** Health Plan. Adminis.; Hospit. Health Admin. Index (Nov. 1988-); Hospit. Manage. Rev.

US/0018-585X
**HOSPITAL SUPERVISOR'S BULLETIN. See** Business-Personnel Management.

US/0887-672X
**HOSPITAL TECHNOLOGY ALERTS.** [Hosp. technol. alerts]. **Added/Corp** American Hospital Association. Division of Management and Technology. **VFOAT** AHA Hospital Technology Alerts; TIM Hospital Technology Alerts. Vol. 3, No. 3 (March 1984)-. Periodical. English. mo. $125.00 (one year), $240.00 (two year). Ross Publications, PO Box 80, Boston MA 02113. **Tel** (617)720-4556. **DD** 610. ***Continues*** *AHA Hospital Technology Alerts, 0735-4479.*
**Ind/Abst** Health Devices Alerts.

US/0888-711X
**HOSPITAL TECHNOLOGY SERIES.** [Hosp. technol. ser.]. **Added/Corp** American Hospital Association. Division of Management and Technology. **VFOAT** Executive Briefing; Technology Scanner; Guideline Report; Hospital Technology Series. Executive Briefing; Hospital Technology Series. Technology Scanner; Hospital Technology Series. Guideline Report. Vol. 2, No. 25, (1983)-. Periodical. English. mo. $195.00 (members), $295.00 (nonmembers). American Hospital Association, 840 North Lake Shore Drive, Chicago IL 60611. **Tel** (312)280-6000, (800)242-2626. **(Subscription address:** American Hospital Publishing Inc., PO Box 92567, Chicago, IL 60675 USA**) ED** Dianne Spenner. **DD** 610. **NLM** W1; HO892. Index available. **Circ:** 1,800. ***Continues*** *AHA Hospital Technology Series, 0735-4681.*
**Desc:** A four-part series for hospital executives covering trends and developments in clinical services and technology.
**Ind/Abst** Hospit. Health Admin. Index (Vol. 2, No. 25, 1983-).

US/0018-5868
**HOSPITAL TOPICS.** [Hosp. top.]. Vol. 29, No. 9 (Sept. 1951)-. Periodical. English. qt. $55.00 (institution), $30.00 (individual). Heldref Publications, 1319 Eighteenth Street Northwest, Washington DC 20036-1802. **Tel** (202)296-6267, (800)365-9753, FAX (202)296-5149. **ED** Mark E Celmer, Kurt Darr, and Dennis S Palkon. **DD** 362. **NLM** W1 HO893. **[CCC]. Bk Rev. Ad Acc. Circ:** 4,000. available on microfilm and microfiche from University Microfilms International (UMI). ***Continues*** *Hospital Topics and Buyer's Guide, 0093-173X.*
**Desc:** Specialized in short, practical articles to help hospital administrators and department heads stay up-to-date on the latest techniques and systems. Successful managers working in the pharmacy, operating room, central service, purchasing, infection control, business office, and other hospital departments share their expertise in feature articles, question-and-answer columns, and news briefs.
**Ind/Abst** Appl. Soc. Sci. Index Abstr.; Cumul. Index Nurs. Allied Health Lit.; Energy Res. Abstr. (Aug. 1982-); Health Plan. Adminis.; Hospit. Health Admin. Index; Index Med.; Int. Pharm. Abstr.; Life Sci. Collect.

US
**HOSPITAL TOPICS. [MICROFICHE].** (19??)-. English. ir. University Microfilms International, 300 North Zeeb Road, Ann Arbor MI 48106-1346. **Tel** (313)761-4700, (800)521-0600 Exts. 2490, 2491, FAX (313)973-1540. available in print.

CN/0704-0407
**HOSPITAL TRUSTEE.** ***Title Change.*** [Hosp. trustee]. **Added/Corp** Canadian Hospital Association. Vol. 1 (May 1977)-(19??). Periodical. English. bm. Canadian Hospital Association, 17 York Street, Suite 100, Ottawa Ontario K1N 9J6 Canada. **Tel** (613)238-8005. **ED** Ruta Klicius. **DD** 658.4/2. **NLM** W1 HO894D. **Ad Acc. Circ:** 6,000. available on microfilm and microfiche from University Microfilms International (UMI). ***Merged into*** *Leadership in Health Services, 1188-3669.*
**Desc:** Material to help members of hospital governing boards to conduct their business.
**Ind/Abst** Can. Index (?-?); Cumul. Index Nurs. Allied Health Lit.; Hospit. Health Admin. Index.

US
**HOSPITAL UTILIZATION DATA, WISCONSIN. Main/Corp** Wisconsin. Bureau of Health Statistics. **VFOAT** Hospitals, Wisconsin. (1974)-. English. an. Center for Health Statistics / Wisconsin, PO Box 309, Madison WI 53701. **Tel** (608)266-0633. ***Continues*** *Wisconsin. Bureau of Health Statistics. Hospital Inventory and Utilization Data, Wisconsin.*
**Desc:** Source of data is the Annual survey of hospitals.

US/0198-6384
**HOSPITAL WAGE, SALARY, AND BENEFITS SURVEY. Main/Corp** Kentucky Hospital Research and Education Foundation. **Added/Corp** Kentucky Hospital Association. Kentucky Hospital Association. Board of Directors. (19??)-. English. Kentucky Hospital Association, 1951 Bishop Lane/Suite 407, Louisville KY 40218. **LC** RA981.K4; K46a. **DD** 331.2/8136211/09769.

●US/1068-8838
**HOSPITALS & HEALTH NETWORKS.** (HOSPITALS & HEALTH NETWORKS / AHA.). [Hosp. health netw.]. **Added/Corp** American Hospital Association. **VFOAT** Hospitals and Health Networks. Vol. 67, No. 11 (June 5, 1993)-. Periodical. English. sm (24 issues per year). $65.00 US; $125.00 other. American Hospital Publishing Inc., (A Subsidiary of the American Hospital Association), PO Box 92683, Chicago IL 60675. **Tel** (312)440-6836, (800)621-6902, FAX (312)951-8491. **LC** RA960; .H6. **DD** 362.1/1/0973. **NLM** W1; HO934H. **CODEN** HHNEE5. Index available. ***Continues*** *Hospitals (Chicago, Ill. : 1936), 0018-5973.*
**Desc:** Information on hospitals and health facilities.
**Ind/Abst** Acad. Search (June 1993-); Soc. Sci. Cit. Index [Full Cov.].

US
**HOSPITALS & HEALTH NETWORKS.** (HOSPITALS & HEALTH NETWORKS [MICROFORM] / AHA.). [Hosp. health netw.]. **Added/Corp** American Hospital Association. **VFOAT** Hospitals and Health Networks. Vol. 67, No. 11 (June 5, 1993)-. Academic Scholarly Publication. English. ir. University Microfilms International, 300 North Zeeb Road, Ann Arbor MI 48106-1346. **Tel** (313)761-4700, (800)521-0600 Exts. 2490, 2491, FAX (313)973-1540. **LC** RA960; .H6. available in print. ***Continues*** *Hospitals (Chicago, Ill. : 1936), 0018-5973.*
**Ind/Abst** Account. Index, Suppl.; Cumul. Index Nurs. Allied Health Lit.; EMBASE; Energy Res. Abstr.; Hospit. Health Admin. Index; Index Med.; Manage. Contents; Life Sci. Collect.; Trade Ind. Index.

UK/0300-5968
**HOSPITALS & HEALTH SERVICES YEAR BOOK AND DIRECTORY OF HOSPITAL SUPPLIERS, THE.** [Hosp. health serv. yearb. dir. hosp. suppl.]. **VFOAT** Hospitals and Health Services Year Book and Directory of Hospital Suppliers. (1973). Directory. English. an. £70.00 UK; £77.00 US; $84.00 other. Institute Health Service

Management, 75 Portland Place, London W1N 4AN England. **Tel** 01-580-5041, FAX 01-255-1289. **ED** Hazel Coad. **LC** RA986; .H65. **DD** 362.1/1/02541. **NLM** WX 22 FA1 H9. **Ad Acc, Adv Mgr:** M. Nasser. **Circ:** 6,000 (ctrl). ***Continues*** *Hospitals Year Book and Directory of Hospitals Suppliers, 0300-8479.*
**Desc:** A comprehensive directory of health authorities in the UK and the hospitals they manage. Government departments, statutous bodies and other organizations concerned with health care and other related information.

AT
**HOSPITALS & HEALTH SERVICES YEARBOOK AUSTRALIA. Added/Corp** University of New South Wales. School of Health Administration. **VAT** Hospitals and Health Services Yearbook Australia. (197?)-. English. an. 105.00Aus$. Peter Isaacson Publications, 46-50 Porter Street, Prahran Victoria, 3181 Australia. **Tel** 011 61 3 2457777, FAX 011 61 3 2457605. **ED** John Ross. **Bk Rev. Ad Acc. Circ:** 2,500. ***Continues*** *Australian Hospitals and Health Services Yearbook.*
**Desc:** Source of information for anyone connected with hospitals and health services.

US/0018-5973
**HOSPITALS (CHICAGO, ILL. 1936).** ***Title Change.*** (HOSPITALS : THE JOURNAL OF THE AMERICAN HOSPITAL ASSOCIATION.). [Hospitals]. **Added/Corp** American Hospital Association. Vol. 10, No. 1 (Jan. 1936)-Vol. 67, No. 10 (May 20, 1993). Academic Scholarly Publication. English. sm. American Hospital Publishing Inc., (A Subsidiary of the American Hospital Association), PO Box 92683, Chicago IL 60675. **Tel** (312)440-6836, (800)621-6902, FAX (312)951-8491. **LC** RA960; .H6. **DD** 362.1/1/0973. **NLM** W1 HO934. **Pr Rev.** Documents available from The Genuine Article, UMI Article Clearinghouse. ***Continues*** *Bulletin of the American Hospital Association;* ***Absorbed*** *American Hospital Directory.* ***Continued in part by*** *American Hospital Association. Hospital Statistics, 0090-6662* ***and*** *AHA Guide to the Health Care Field;* ***Continued by*** *Hospitals & Health Networks, 1068-8838.*
**Ind/Abst** ABI/INFORM Glob. Ed. (19??-19??); ABI Inform Ondisc (March 1988-); ABI/INFORM Ondisc: Expr. Ed. (19??-19??); Abr. Index Med. (19??-19??); Abstr. Res. Pastor. Care Couns. (1974-19??); Acad. Search (Jan. 1993-June 1993); Archit. Period. Index (19??-19??); Bus. ASAP (1990-199?) [Full Txt.]; Bus. Index (1986-19??); Bus. Period. Index (19??-19??); Bus. Source (Jul. 1993-1993); Cumul. Index Nurs. Allied Health Lit. (19??-19??); EMBASE (19??-19??); Energy Res. Abstr. (19??-19??); Expand. Acad. Index (1992-1993); Gen. BusinessFile (198?-19??); Gen. Period. Index (1986-19??); Health Plan. Adminis. (19??-19??); Health Ref. Cent. (1987-19??) [Select. Cov.]; Hospit. Health Admin. Index (19??-19??); Hospit. Manage. Rev. (1981-19??); Index Med. (19??-19??); INFO-SOUTH Abstr. (19??-19??); INIS Atomindex [Micro.] (19??-19??); Int. Pharm. Abstr. (19??-19??); Mag. Search (19??-19??); Mark. Advert. Ref. Serv. (19??-19??); Newsp. Period. Abstr. (1992-1993); Life Sci. Collect. (19??-19??); Physic. Medline Plus (19??-19??); Res. Alert (19??-19??) [Full Cov.]; Soc. Sci. Cit. Index (19??-19??) [Full Cov.]; Stat. Ref. Index (19??-19??); Trade Ind. ASAP (19??-19??) [Full Txt.]; Trade Ind. Index (1981-19??) [Full Txt.]; UMI ABI/Inform--Bus. Period. Ondisc (Mar. 1988-19??) [Full Txt.]; Wilson Bus. Abstr. (19??-19??).

US/1060-7838
**HOSPITAL'S MEDICARE POLICY & PAYMENT REPORT, THE.** ***Title Change.*** [Hosp. Medicare policy paym. rep.]. **Added/Corp** American Health Consultants. **VFOAT** Hospital's Medicare Policy and Payment Report; Medicare Policy and Payment Report; Medicare Policy & Payment Report. Vol. 10, No. 1 (Jan. 1992)-(1993). Periodical. English. mo. American Health Consultants, 3525 Piedmont Road, Suite 400, Atlanta GA 30305. **Tel** (800)688-2421, (404)262-7436. **LC** RA971.32; .H68. **DD** 368.4/2. **NLM** W1; HO936H. ***Continues*** *Prospective Payment Survival, 0746-4703.* ***Continued by*** *Hospital Payment & Information Management, 1074-8334.*
**Ind/Abst** Hospit. Manage. Rev. (199?-199?).

US/0094-9833
**HOSPITALS, NURSING HOMES AND RELATED HEALTH FACILITIES.** (HOSPITALS, NURSING HOMES AND RELATED HEALTH FACILITIES LICENSED BY THE STATE OF CALIFORNIA, DEPARTMENT OF HEALTH, HEALTH QUALITY SYSTEMS, FACILITIES LICENSING SECTION.). **Added/Corp** California. Dept. of Health. Facilities Licensing Section. (1973)-. Periodical. English. an. California Department of Health Services, B A Myers Director, 714 P Street, Room 1494, Sacramento CA 95814. **Tel** (916)445-1010. **NLM** WX 22 AC2 H8. ***Continues*** *Hospitals, Nursing Homes and Related Health Facilities Licensed by the State of California, Department of Public Health, Bureau of Health Facilities Licensing and Certification, 0094-9833.*

CN/0821-2465
**HUMBER HIGHLIGHTS.** (HUMBER HIGHLIGHTS / HUMBER MEMORIAL HOSPITAL.). [Humber highlights]. **Added/Corp** Humber Memorial Hospital. (19??)-. Periodical. English. qt. Free. Humber Highlights/Humber Memorial Hospital, 200 Church Street, Weston Ontario M9N 1N8 Canada. **Tel** (416)243-4595. **ED** Judy Keenan. **DD** 362.1/1/09713541. **Circ:** 3,500 (ctrl).
**Desc:** For employees and friends of this 352-bed acute care community hospital.

US/1068-5286
**IDEA LETTER FOR HEALTH CARE MANAGERS, THE.** (THE IDEA LETTER FOR HEALTH CARE MANAGERS / AMERICAN HEALTH CONSULTANTS.). [Idea lett. health care manag.]. **Added/Corp** American Health Consultants. (199?)-. Periodical. English. mo. $129.00. American Health Consultants, 3525 Piedmont Road, Suite 400, Atlanta GA 30305. **Tel** (800)688-2421, (404)262-7436. **(Subscription address:** American Health Consultants, PO Box 95278, Chicago IL 60694.**)** **DD** 362.

US/0889-8561
**IMMUNOLOGY AND ALLERGY CLINICS OF NORTH AMERICA. See** Medical Science and Technology-Allergy and Immunology.

IT/0393-0394
**IMPEGNO OSPEDALIERO. See** Economics-Labor.

CR/0379-7015
**INFORMACIONES ESTADISTICAS.** **Added/Corp** Costa Rica. Ministerio de Salud. Unidad Sectorial de Planificacion. Costa Rica. Ministerio de Salud. Departamento de Estadistica. (1900)-. Statistical Publication. Spanish. **LC** RA191.C8; I53. **DD** 614.4/27286/021. **NLM** W2 DC8 M63I.

●UK/1353-8888
**INFORMATION MANAGEMENT IN HEALTH CARE / HOSPITAL SYSTEMS SERVICE.** (1994)-. Periodical. English. Three times a year. £125.00 (Institutions). Churchill Livingstone, 1-3 Baxter's Place, Leith Walk, Edinburgh EH1 3AF Scotland. **Tel** 011 44 31 556 2424, FAX 011 44 31 558 1278, telex 727511. **(Subscription address:** Maruzen Company Ltd., PO Box 5050, Import & Export Department, Tokyo 100 31 Japan.**)**

●UK/1353-8861
**INFORMATION MANAGEMENT IN HEALTH CARE / IM & T SERVICE. See** Medical Science and Technology.

FR/0763-0387
**INFORMATIONS HOSPITALIERES.** [Inf. hosp.]. (1984)-. Periodical. French. bm. 300.00F. Direction Hopitaux, 8 rue de Segur, 75007 Paris France. **Tel** 011 33 1 4056 4374, FAX 011 33 1 40564963. **UDC** 61.

CN/0705-0828
**INTERBLOCS. Added/Corp** Hopital Sainte-Justine. No. 1 (Oct. 1977)-. Periodical. French. ir. Limited free distribution. Hopital Sainte-Justine Cise, 3175 Cote Ste-Catherine, Montreal, Quebec H3T 1C5 Canada. **Tel** (514)731-4931. **DD** 362.1/1/09714281. ctrl circ.

US/0272-4308
**INTERNATIONAL JOURNAL OF PARTIAL HOSPITALIZATION.** ***Ceased.*** [Int. j. partial hosp.]. **VFOAT** Partial Hospitalization. Vol. 1, No. 1 (Jan. 1982)-Vol. 8 (1992). Academic Scholarly Publication. English. sa. Plenum Press, 233 Spring Street, New York NY 10013-1578. **Tel** (212)620-8000, (800)221-9369, FAX (212)463-0742, (212)807-1047, telex 23/421139. **ED** Raymond F Luber. **NLM** W1 IN771ND. **CODEN** IPHOD3. **[CCC].** Index available. available on microfilm and microfiche from University Microfilms International (UMI).
**Desc:** Has the primary intent of stimulating and communicating information regarding research programming and administrative issues in all types of partial hospitalization as well as other community based residential or rehabilitation settings.
**Ind/Abst** Cumul. Index Nurs. Allied Health Lit.; EMBASE; Health Plan. Adminis.; Hospit. Health Admin. Index; Psychol. Abstr. (1982-); PsycINFO; PsycLit.

US
**INVENTORY OF HOSPITAL FACILITIES.** **Added/Corp** Metropolitan Health Planning Corporation. (196?)-. English. an. 908 Standard Building, Cleveland OH 44113. **LC** Discard.

CN/0831-4411
**JASMU : JOURNAL POUR L'AVANCEMENT DES SOINS MEDICAUX D'URGENCE.** ***Ceased.*** [JASMU, J. av. soins med. urgence]. **VFOAT** Journal pour l'Avancement des Soins Medicaux d'Urgence. Vol. 1, No. 1 (June 1986)-Ceased Oct. 1988. Periodical. French. ir. CP 826, Succ Tour de la Bourse Canada. **DD** 362.1/1/09714.

US/1065-0881
**JENKS HEALTHCARE BUSINESS REPORT.** [Jenks healthc. bus. rep.]. **Added/Corp** Jenks Enterprises, Inc. (199?)-. Periodical. English. sm. $245.00. Jenks Enterprises, PO Box 7664, Atlanta GA 30357. **Tel** (404)872-9546, FAX (404)872-5269. **ED** Alan Jenks. **DD** 338. **Circ:** 5,000.

US/0888-7675
**JOHNS HOPKINS STUDIES IN HEALTH CARE FINANCE AND ADMINISTRATION.** [Johns Hopkins stud. health care finance admin.]. (1984)-. Monographic series. English. ir. Price varies per volume. Johns Hopkins University Press, 2715 North Charles Street, Baltimore MD 21218-4319. **Tel** (410)516-6987, FAX (410)516-6968. **DD** 338. **NLM** W1; JO159H.

●US/1070-3241
**JOINT COMMISSION JOURNAL ON QUALITY IMPROVEMENT, THE.** [Joint Comm. j. qual. improv.]. **Added/Corp** Joint Commission on Accreditation of Healthcare Organizations. (1993)-. Periodical. English. mo. $115.00 US; $130.00 other. Mosby Year Book Inc., 11830 Westline Industrial Drive, St Louis MO 63146. **Tel** (800)325-4177, (314)872-8370, FAX (314)432-1380, telex 44-2402. **DD** 362. **NLM** W1; JO1786B. ***Continues*** *QRB. Quality Review Bulletin, 0097-5990.*
**Ind/Abst** Cumul. Index Nurs. Allied Health Lit.; Hospit. Health Admin. Index; Index Med.; Soc. Work Abstr.

US/1044-4017
**JOINT COMMISSION PERSPECTIVES.** [Jt. Comm. perspect.]. **Main/Corp** Joint Commission on Accreditation of Healthcare Organizations. **VFOAT** Perspectives. Vol. 7, No. 9/10 (Sept./Oct. 1987)-. Periodical. English. bm (Feb., Apr., Jun., Aug., Oct., Dec.). $80.00 US; $90.00 other. Mosby Year Book Inc., 11830 Westline Industrial Drive, St Louis MO 63146. **Tel** (800)325-4177, (314)872-8370, FAX (314)432-1380, telex 44-2402. **DD** 362. **NLM** W1; JO1786C. ***Continues*** *Joint Commission on Accreditation of Hospitals. JCAH Perspectives, 0277-8327;* ***Absorbed*** *Joint Commission on Accreditation of Healthcare Organizations. Agenda for Change Update.*
**Ind/Abst** Hospit. Health Admin. Index (Sept./Oct. 1987-).

II/0970-9452
**JOURNAL / ACADEMY OF HOSPITAL ADMINISTRATION. Added/Corp** Academy of Hospital Administration (India). **VFOAT** JAHA; Journal of Academy of Hospital Administration. Vol. 1, No. 1 (Jan. 1989)-. Periodical. English. sa. $25.00. Academy of Hospital Administration, New Delhi, India. **(Subscription address:** Prints India, 11 Darya Ganj, New Delhi, 110002 India, (Phone: 011 91 11 3268645)**)** **NLM** W1; JO222K.
**Ind/Abst** Health Plan. Adminis.; Hospit. Health Admin. Index (1991-).

US/1061-7655
**JOURNAL - ASSOCIATION FOR HEALTHCARE PHILANTHROPY (U.S.).** (JOURNAL / ASSOCIATION FOR HEALTHCARE PHILANTHROPY.). [Journal - Assoc. Healthc. Philanthr. (U.S.)]. **Added/Corp** Association for Healthcare Philanthropy (U.S.). **VFOAT** AHP Journal. (Spring 1991)-. Periodical. English. sa. $38.00. Association for Healthcare Philanthropy, 313 Park Avenue 400, Falls Church VA 22046. **Tel** (703)532-6243. **DD** 362. **NLM** W1; JO2223. ***Continues*** *Journal (National Association for Hospital Development (U.S.)), 0196-4933.*
**Ind/Abst** Hospit. Health Admin. Index (1991-).

US/1060-5487
**JOURNAL OF AHIMA.** (JOURNAL OF AHIMA / AMERICAN HEALTH INFORMATION MANAGEMENT ASSOCIATION.). [J. AHIMA]. **Added/Corp** American Health Information Management Association. **VFOAT** Journal of American Health Information Management Association; Journal of the American Health Information Management Association; JAHIMA. (Nov. 1991)-. Academic Scholarly Publication. English. mo. $72.00. American Health Information Management Association, Order Unit, PO Box 97349, Chicago IL 60690-7349. **Tel** (312) 787-2672, FAX (312) 787-5926, (312) 787-9793. **LC** RA976; .J68. **DD** 651.5/04261/05. **NLM** W1; JO534JF. **CODEN** JAHIES. ***Continues*** *Journal (American Medical Record Association), 0273-9976.*
**Ind/Abst** Cumul. Index Nurs. Allied Health Lit. (1991-); EMBASE; Hospit. Health Admin. Index; Life Sci. Collect.

US/0148-9917
**JOURNAL OF AMBULATORY CARE MANAGEMENT, THE.** [J. ambul. care manage.]. **VFOAT** Ambulatory Care Management. Vol. 1 (Jan. 1978)-. Periodical. English. qt. $115.00 US. Aspen Publishers Inc., 7201 McKinney Circle, Frederick MD 21701. **Tel** (800)234-1660, (301)698-7100, FAX (301)251-5784, telex 5106014543. **(Subscription address:** Aspen Publishers Inc., PO Box 990, Frederick MD 21701.**)** **ED** Seth B. Goldsmith and Norbert Goldfield. **LC** RA411; .J68. **DD** 362.1/2. **NLM** W1 JO535CM. **[CCC]. Bk Rev. Ad Acc. Pr Rev.** ctrl circ. available on microfilm and microfiche from University Microfilms International (UMI).
**Desc:** Gives complete coverage of topics encompassing

all facets of ambulatory care management. You will gain valuable insights from the industry's leading thinkers and practitioners. Learn from actual case studies and current research from the fields. Contains comprehensive, straight-to-the-point articles that cover everything you need to know to boost productivity.
**Ind/Abst** Cumul. Index Nurs. Allied Health Lit.; EMBASE; Health Plan. Adminis.; Hospit. Health Admin. Index.

●US/1061-3706
**JOURNAL OF CASE MANAGEMENT.** [J. case manag.]. **Added/Corp** Connecticut Community Care, Inc. Case Management Institute. Vol. 1, No. 1 (Spring 1992)-. Periodical. English. qt. $39.00 (individuals), $78.00 (institutions) US; $44.00 (individuals), $87.00 (institutions) other. Springer Publishing Company, 536 Broadway, New York NY 10012-3955. **Tel** (212)431-4370, FAX (212)941-7842. **ED** Joan Quinn, RN, CMI, (editor's address: 43 Enterprise Dr., Bristol, CT 06011-2360, phone: (203)589-6226). **LC** HV43; .J68. **DD** 361.3/2/05. **NLM** W1; JO577JK. **CODEN** JCMNEE. Index available (bound in 4th iss. in Dec.). cum. index. **Bk Rev**, (Qty: 6-12). **Ad Acc**, **Adv Mgr:** Linda Mappleback. **Pr Rev. Acid Free. Circ:** 700.
**Desc:** Provides editorials, articles, reviews of books, articles and other media, and calendars of events that disseminate relevant information pertinent to the field of case management. Articles are applicable to practice including reviews of current programs, explanations of procedures or systems, case studies, and innovative ideas.
**Ind/Abst** Int. Nurs. Index (Spring 1992-).

US/0090-1091
**JOURNAL OF CLINICAL COMPUTING.** [J. clin. comput.]. Vol. 1 (1971)-. Academic Scholarly Publication. English. bm (6 issues). $40.00. Journal of Clinical Computing, 4 Cambridge Center, Cambridge MA 02142. **Tel** (617)494-0909. **ED** Kathleen E. Seibold and E.R. Gabrieli. **NLM** W1 JO587K. **CODEN** JCLCB. **Bk Rev. Ad Acc. Circ:** 500. Documents available from Ask*IEEE.
**Desc:** Covers office management, hospital information systems, medical privacy, computerized medical text processing and standardization of medical text.
**Ind/Abst** ACM Guide Comput. Lit.; Comput. Rev.; EMBASE; Health Plan. Adminis.; Hospit. Health Admin. Index; Inf. Sci. Abstr.; INSPEC (1977-).

US/1046-4360
**JOURNAL OF HEALTH AND HOSPITAL LAW : A PUBLICATION OF THE AMERICAN ACADEMY OF HOSPITAL ATTORNEYS OF THE AMERICAN HOSPITAL ASSOCIATION.** **See** Law.

US/0885-4726
**JOURNAL OF HEALTH CARE CHAPLAINCY.** **See** Religion and Theology.

US
**JOURNAL OF HEALTH CARE FINANCE.**
**See** Business-Banking and Finance.

US/0889-2482
**JOURNAL OF HEALTHCARE MATERIAL MANAGEMENT.** [J. healthc. mat. manage.]. **VFOAT** Journal HMM. Vol. 3, No. 5 (Sept./Oct. 1985)-. Periodical. English. mo. $39.00 (one year), $68.00 (two year) US; $50.00 (one year), $90.00 (two year) Canada; $98.00 other. Mayworm Associates Inc, 507 North Milwaukee Avenue, Libertyville IL 60048. **Tel** (708)680-7878, FAX (708)680-8180. **ED** Marilyn Ferdinand. **DD** 362. **NLM** W1; JO67BP. cum. index. **Bk Rev. Ad Acc. Pr Rev. Circ:** 23,167. ***Continues** Journal of Hospital Supply, Processing, and Distribution, 0738-2928.*
**Desc:** Serves the educational needs of hospital personnel charged with the responsibility of purchasing, reprocessing, storing and distributing equipment and supplies within the facility.
**Ind/Abst** Hospit. Health Admin. Index (Sept.-Oct. 1985-).

US/0891-7930
**JOURNAL OF HEALTHCARE PROTECTION MANAGEMENT.** (JOURNAL OF HEALTHCARE PROTECTION MANAGEMENT : PUBLICATION OF THE INTERNATIONAL ASSOCIATION FOR HOSPITAL SECURITY.). [J. healthc. prot. manage. nurs. educ.]. **Added/Corp** International Association for Hospital Security. Vol. 1, No. 1 (1984)-. Periodical. English. sa. $25.00. Rusting Publications, PO Box 190, Port Washington NY 11050. **Tel** (516)883-1440. **DD** 610. **NLM** W1; JO67BR. **Bk Rev. Circ:** 1,800.
**Ind/Abst** Index Med. (1984-).

US/0883-7570
**JOURNAL OF HOSPITAL MARKETING.** [J. hosp. mark.]. Vol. 1, No. 1/2 (Fall/Winter 1986)-. Periodical. English. sa (Published during the academic year). $135.00 US; $189.00 other. The Haworth Press Inc, 10 Alice Street, Binghamton NY 13904-1580. **Tel** (607)722-5857, (800)3-HAWORTH, FAX (607)722-1424. **ED** William J. Winston (editor's address: Management and Marketing Consultant, PO Box 8566, Berkeley, CA 94707). **LC** RA965.5; .J68. **DD** 362.1/1/0688. **NLM** W1; JO673P. **Bk Rev. Ad Acc. Pr Rev. Acid Free. Circ:** 119. available on microfilm and microfiche from University Microfilms International (UMI). Documents available from Haworth Document Delivery Service.
**Desc:** Presents new and effective ways of marketing hospital services. Shares current marketing applications and methodologies by professional hospital marketing consultants and educators.
**Ind/Abst** EMBASE; Health Plan. Adminis.; Hospit. Health Admin. Index (1986-); Hospit. Manage. Rev.

II/0520-5085
**JOURNAL OF J J GROUP OF HOSPITALS AND GRANT MEDICAL COLLEGE.** **Main/Corp** Bombay. J J Group of Hospitals. **Added/Corp** J J Group of Hospitals and Grant Medical College. Journal. (1956)-. Periodical. English. qt. $22.00. **(Subscription address:** Prints India, 11 Darya Ganj, New Delhi 110002 India.**)**

US/0093-4445
**JOURNAL OF LONG TERM CARE ADMINISTRATION, THE.** [J. long term care adm.]. **Added/Corp** American College of Nursing Home Administrators. American College of Health Care Administrators. **VFOAT** Journal of Long-Term Care Administration; Long Term Care Administration. (197?)-. Periodical. English. Four times a year (Feb., June, Aug., Nov.). $70.00. American College of Health Care Administrators, 325 South Patrick Street, Alexandria VA 22314. **Tel** (703)549-5822, (703)739-7913, FAX (703)739-7901. **ED** Jan Lamoglia. **LC** RA997.A1; A35. **DD** 362.1/6/05. **NLM** W1 JO746. **CODEN** JLTAD4. **[CCC].** Index available (Winter issue). **Bk Rev**, (Qty: 12-15). **Ad Acc**, **Adv Mgr:** Jan Lamoglia, **Tel** (703)739-7913. **Pr Rev. Circ:** 6,500. available on microfilm and microfiche from University Microfilms International (UMI); available on an online database; available on CD-ROM from SilverPlatter (US). Documents available from BIOSIS Document Express. ***Continues** American College of Nursing Home Administrators. Journal.*
**Desc:** This professional journal features research reports and articles that address the foremost concerns of long-term care administrators. The journal contains articles covering a wide range of areas, including the latest research trends, practical information and technology in long-term care.
**Ind/Abst** Abstr. Soc. Gerontol.; Biol. Abstr.; Cumul. Index Nurs. Allied Health Lit.; Health Plan. Adminis.; Hospit. Health Admin. Index; Index Med.; Index Period. Lit. Aging; Int. Pharm. Abstr.; Soc. Work Abstr. (Summer 1987-) [Select. Cov.].

US/0148-5598
**JOURNAL OF MEDICAL SYSTEMS.** [J. med. syst.]. Vol. 1 (1977)-. Periodical. English. Six times a year. $335.00 institutions, $56.00 individuals US; $390.00 institutions, $66.00 individuals other. Plenum Press, 233 Spring Street, New York NY 10013-1578. **Tel** (212)620-8000, (800)221-9369, FAX (212)463-0742, (212)807-1047, telex 23/421139. **ED** Ralph R. Grams. **LC** R858.A1; J677. **DD** 362.1/028/54. **NLM** W1 JO756T. **CODEN** JMSYDA. **[CCC].** Index available. available on microfilm and microfiche from University Microfilms International (UMI). Documents available from The Genuine Article, BIOSIS Document Express. ***Supersedes** Journal of Medical Systems.*
**Desc:** Designed to provide a forum for presentation and discussion of the increasingly extensive applications of new systems techniques and methods in hospitals, clinics and doctors' office administrations.
**Ind/Abst** ACM Guide Comput. Lit.; Biol. Abstr.; Comput. Rev.; CSA Neuro. Abstr. (?-?); Cumul. Index Nurs. Allied Health Lit.; EMBASE; Energy Res. Abstr. (Dec. 1981-); Health Plan. Adminis.; Hospit. Health Admin. Index; Index Med.; Inf. Sci. Abstr.; INIS Atomindex [Micro.]; Res. Alert [Full Cov.]; Soc. Sci. Cit. Index [Select. Cov.].

US
**KENTUCKY HOSPITAL FACTS.** **Added/Corp** Kentucky Research and Education Foundation. Kentucky Hospital Association. (19??)-. English. an. Kentucky Hospital Association, 1951 Bishop Lane/Suite 407, Louisville KY 40218. **LC** RA981.K4; K45. **DD** 362.1/1/09769.

US
**KENTUCKY HOSPITALS MAGAZINE.** **Added/Corp** Kentucky Hospital Association. **VFOAT** Kentucky Hospitals. Vol. 6, Issue 1 (Winter 1989)-. Periodical. English. qt. $25.00. Kentucky Hospital Service Corporation, 1302 Clear Spring Trace, Louisville KY 40224. **Tel** (800)292-6573, FAX (502)426-6226. **NLM** W1; KE687R. ***Continues** Kentucky Hospitals.*

JA
**KOKURITSU RYOYOJO YORAN.** **Added/Corp** Japan. Koseisho. Kokuritsu Ryoyojoka. (19??)-. Japanese. Koseisho Imukyoku Kokuritsu Ryoyojoka, 2-2 Kasumigaseki 1, Chiyoda-ku 100, Tokyo Japan. **LC** RA990.J4; K62.

AU/0075-7063
**KRANKENHAUS (WIEN).** (KRANKENHAUS.). **VFOAT** Theorie und Praxis im Krankenhauswesen. Vol. 1 (1970)-. Periodical. German. mo. DM220.00. **ED** R.M. Tornar. **NLM** W1 KR257D. ***Continues** Unser Krankenhaus; Jahrbuch des Osterreichischen Krankenhauswesens.*
**Desc:** Professional journal for hospital concerns.

GW/0720-3977
**KRANKENHAUSTECHNIK.** (197?)-. Periodical. German. mo. DM96.00 Germany; DM115.00 other. Ecomed Verlagsgesellschaft GmbH, Postfach 1752, D 86895 Landsberg Germany. **Tel** 011 49 8191 125544, FAX 011 49 8191 125513. **ED** Maria Thalmaya. **UDC** 615.478. Index available. cum. index. **Ad Acc. Pr Rev. Circ:** 9,000 (ctrl).
**Desc:** All points concerning hospital engineering from medical high-tech to communication systems, fire prevention, construction, heating, kitchen, laundry, laboratories, and environment.

GW/0023-4508
**KRANKENHAUSUMSCHAU.** **VFOAT** Aku. Krankenhausumschau. (1957)-. Periodical. German. Twelve times a year. DM234.00 Germany; DM246.00 others. Baumann GmBH. & Co. KG, PO Box 1149, D 95301 Kulmbach Germany. **Tel** 011 49 9221 9490, FAX 011 49 9221 949377. **ED** Angelika Beyer-Rehfeld, (editor's address: Hagdorn 27/29 D-45468 Mulheim, Germany, phone: 011 49 0208 35121). **UDC** 725.51. **CODEN** 615.478. Index available (Bound in issue). **Bk Rev. Ad Acc**, **Adv Mgr:** Mr. Geist, **Tel** 011 49 9221 949234.
**Desc:** News and information on hospital management.

SP/0211-8262
**LABOR HOSPITALARIA.** (1948)-. Periodical. Spanish. qt. 1850.00ptas. Hospital San Juan de Dios, Carretera Esplugas S/N, 08034 Barcelona Spain. **Tel** 011 34 3 2034000. **ED** Miguel Martin. **UDC** 271. **Ad Acc. Pr Rev. Circ:** 3,000 (ctrl).
**Desc:** Hospital care, bioethics, prenatal diagnosis, geriatric engineering, and transplants.

CN
**LABOUR RELATIONS BULLETIN.** **See** Economics-Labor.

US
**LDI MANAGEMENT DISCUSSION PAPER.** **Added/Corp** Leonard Davis Institute of Health Economics. No. 47 (June 1983)-. Monographic series. English. Price varies per volume. **NLM** W1; LD432H. ***Continues** Discussion Paper (Leonard Davis Institute of Health Economics), 0892-7898.*

●CN/1188-3669
**LEADERSHIP IN HEALTH SERVICES.** [Leadersh. health serv.]. **Added/Corp** Canadian Hospital Association. **VFOAT** Leadership dans les Services de Ante. Vol. 1, No. 1 (Jan./Feb. 1992)-. Periodical. English (French). bm. 40.00Can$ Canada; $50.00 US. Canadian Hospital Association, 17 York Street, Suite 100, Ottawa Ontario K1N 9J6 Canada. **Tel** (613)238-8005. **ED** James D. Godsoe and Marilyn Laidlaw. **DD** 362.1. **NLM** W1; LE11. **Ad Acc**, **Adv Mgr:** Michelle Garneau. ***Formed by the union of** Dimensions in Health Service, 0317-7645 **and** Hospital Trustee, 0704-0407.*
**Ind/Abst** Can. Period. Index; Cumul. Index Nurs. Allied Health Lit.; Hospit. Health Admin. Index; Index Med.; Int. Pharm. Abstr.

US/0895-9846
**LENGTH OF STAY BY DIAGNOSIS AND OPERATION, NORTH CENTRAL REGION.** [Length stay diagn. oper. north central reg.]. **Added/Corp** Commission on Professional and Hospital Activities. (1986)-. English. an. $85.00. HCIA, 300 East Lombard Street, Baltimore MD 21202. **Tel** (410)576-9600, (800)568-3282. **LC** RA981.M52; L45. **DD** 362.1/1/0977021. **NLM** W1; LE772JAL. **Circ:** 8,000. ***Formed by the union of** Length of Stay by Diagnosis, North Central Region, 0891-2165 **and** Length of Stay by Operation, North Central Region, 0891-222X.*

US/0895-9838
**LENGTH OF STAY BY DIAGNOSIS AND OPERATION, NORTHEASTERN REGION.** [Length stay diagn. oper. northeast. reg.]. **Added/Corp** Commission on Professional and Hospital Activities. (1986)-. English. an. HCIA, 300 East Lombard Street, Baltimore MD 21202. **Tel** (410)576-9600, (800)568-3282. **LC** RA981.N86; L45. **DD** 362.1/1/0974021. **NLM** W1; LE772JAM. ***Formed by the union of** Length of Stay by Diagnosis, Northeastern Region, 0891-2122 **and** Length of Stay by Operation, Northeastern Region, 0888-2673.*

US/0895-9854
**LENGTH OF STAY BY DIAGNOSIS AND OPERATION, SOUTHERN REGION.** [Length stay diagn. oper. south. reg.]. **Added/Corp** Commission on Professional and Hospital Activities. (1986)-. English. an. HCIA, 300 East Lombard Street, Baltimore MD 21202. **Tel** (410)576-9600, (800)568-3282. **LC** RA981.S63; L45. **DD** 362.1/1/0975021. **NLM** W1; LE772JAN. **Circ:** 8,000. ***Formed by the union of** Length of Stay by Diagnosis, Southern Region, 0891-2130 **and** Length of Stay by Operation, Southern Region, 0891-219X.*

US/0895-982X
**LENGTH OF STAY BY DIAGNOSIS AND OPERATION, UNITED STATES.** [Length stay diagn. oper. U.S.]. **Added/Corp** Commission on Professional and Hospital Activities. (1986)-. English. an. Price varies. HCIA, 300 East Lombard Street, Baltimore MD 21202. **Tel** (410)576-9600, (800)568-3282. **LC** RA407.3; .L45. **DD** 362.1/1/0973021. **NLM** W1; LE772JAO. **Circ:** 8,000. ***Formed by the union of*** *Length of Stay by Diagnosis, United States, 0891-2149* ***and*** *Length of Stay by Operation, United States, 0891-2203.*
**Desc:** Length of stay in short-term general hospitals published for the US and four census regions, also by geriatric and pediatric.

US/0895-9862
**LENGTH OF STAY BY DIAGNOSIS AND OPERATION, WESTERN REGION.** [Length stay diagn. oper. west. reg.]. **Added/Corp** Commission on Professional and Hospital Activities. (1986)-. English. an. HCIA, 300 East Lombard Street, Baltimore MD 21202. **Tel** (410)576-9600, (800)568-3282. **LC** RA981.W36; L45. **DD** 362.1/1/0978021. **NLM** W1; LE772JAP. **Circ:** 8,000. ***Formed by the union of*** *Length of Stay by Diagnosis, Western Region, 0891-2157* ***and*** *Length of Stay by Operation, Western Region, 0891-2211.*

US/0096-1329
**LENGTH OF STAY IN PAS HOSPITALS, UNITED STATES, EASTERN REGION.**
***Title Change.*** **Main/Corp** Commission on Professional and Hospital Activities. **VAT** Length of Stay in Professional Activity Study Hospitals, United States, Eastern Region. (1973)-(19??). Periodical. English. an. Commission on Professional and Hospital Activities, 1968 Green Road, PO Box 1809, Ann Arbor MI 48106. **Tel** (313)769-6511. **LC** RA981.N86; C65a. **DD** 362.1/1/0974. **NLM** W1 LE772NR. ***Continues in part*** *Length of Stay in PAS Hospitals, United States, Regional, 0097-904X.* ***Merged into*** *Length of Stay by Diagnosis & Operation, United States.*

CN/0843-2457
**LIST OF ACCREDITED HEALTH CARE FACILITIES.** (LIST OF ACCREDITED HEALTH CARE FACILITIES AT CONCLUSION OF ... SURVEY YEAR.). [List accred. health care facil.]. **Added/Corp** Canadian Council on Health Facilities Accreditation. **VFOAT** Liste des Etablissements de Sante Agrees a la Conclusion du Programme Pour l'Annee ... . (1987)-. English (French). Canadian Council on Hospital Accreditation, 1815 Alta Vista Drive, Ottawa Ontario K1G 3Y6 Canada. **DD** 362.1/1/02571. ***Continues*** *List of Accredited Hospitals and Other Health Care Institutions at Conclusion ... Survey Year., 0710-4936.*

US/0192-7701
**LONG TERM CARE.** Vol. 1 (Sept. 1, 1972)-. English. wk. $187.00. National Press Building, Washington DC 20045. **NLM** W1 LO789.

US/0146-275X
**LONG-TERM CARE ADMINISTRATOR.** [Long-term care adm.]. **Added/Corp** American College of Health Care Administrators. American College of Nursing Home Administrators. Vol. 9, No. 2 (Feb. 1975)-. Periodical. English. Eight times a year (published monthly except Feb., Apr., Aug., & Nov.). $45.00. American College of Health Care Administrators, 325 South Patrick Street, Alexandria VA 22314. **Tel** (703)549-5822, (703)739-7913, FAX (703)739-7901. **ED** Jan Lamoglia. **NLM** W1 LO7899. **[CCC].** Index available. **Ad Acc**, **Adv Mgr:** J. Lamoglia. **Circ:** 6,200. ***Continues*** *Newsletter - American College of Nursing Home Administrators.*
**Desc:** Contains practical tips and information about long-term care administration. Includes legislative reports and education calendar.

US/0891-8104
**LONG-TERM CARE QUARTERLY.** ***Ceased.*** [Long-term care q.]. Vol. 1, No. 1 (Spring 1986)-?. Periodical. English. qt. National Council of State Boards of Nursing Inc, 676 North Saint Clair Street, Suite 550, Chicago IL 60611. **Tel** (312)787-6555. **DD** 614. **NLM** W1; LO792.
**Ind/Abst** Cumul. Index Nurs. Allied Health Lit.; Int. Nurs. Index (Spring 1986-).

US
**MAINE HEALTH FACILITIES, RESOURCES, AND UTILIZATION / PREPARED BY BUREAU OF HEALTH PLANNING AND DEVELOPMENT, MAINE DEPARTMENT OF HUMAN SERVICES.** **Added/Corp** Maine. Bureau of Health Planning and Development. (1979)-. English. an. $10.00. Office of Data and Research and Vital Statistics, Department of Human Services, Station 11/State House, Augusta ME 04333. **Tel** (207)289-3001. **ED** Deborah Smiley. **LC** RA981.M2; M335. **DD** 362.1/1/09741. ctrl circ.

US/0193-6166
**MALPRACTICE PREVENTION FOR HOSPITALS.** See Law.

●US/1062-3388
**MANAGED CARE (LANGHORNE, PA.).** (MANAGED CARE.). [Manag. care]. (1992)-. Periodical. English. mo. $72.00. Stezzi Communications, Inc., 301 Oxford Valley Road, Suite 603B, Yardley PA 19067. **Tel** (215)321-6663, FAX (215)321-6670. **ED** Carroll V. Dowden. **DD** 610. **NLM** W1; MA559G. **Ad Acc**, **Adv Mgr:** Timothy Search. **Circ:** 77,000 (ctrl).
**Desc:** This is a guide for physicians which helps them adapt and adjust to their entry into managed care.

US/0896-6567
**MANAGED CARE OUTLOOK.** [Managed care outlook]. Vol. 1, No. 1 (Jan. 8, 1988)-. Periodical. English. sm. $399.00. Capitol Publications, 1101 King Street, Suite 444, Alexandria VA 22314. **Tel** (703)683-4100, (800)655-5597. **(Subscription address:** Capitol Publications, PO Box 1453, Alexandria VA 22313.**) ED** Pam Taulbee, Russ Jackson. **LC** RA413.5.U5; M36. **DD** 362. **[CCC].** available on an online database (file 636/Full-Text) from DIALOG. ***Absorbed*** *Managed Care Report.*
**Desc:** Covers inside news of the prepaid healthcare movement and its impact on employee benefit plans.
**Ind/Abst** Hospit. Manage. Rev.; PROMT [Full Txt.]; PTS Newsl. Database [Full Txt.].

US/1056-7461
**MANAGED CARE WEEK.** [Manag. care week]. **Added/Corp** Atlantic Information Services. (1991)-. Periodical. English. ir (69 issues). $379.00. Atlantic Information Services Inc., 1050 17th Street Northwest, Suite 480, Washington DC 20036. **Tel** (202)775-9008, (800)521-4323, FAX (202)331-9542. **DD** 362. **[CCC].** available on an online database (file 636/Full-Text) from DIALOG.

US/1072-2815
**MANAGED HEALTH CARE DIRECTORY.** (MANAGED HEALTH CARE DIRECTORY / AMCRA.). [Manag. health care dir.]. **Added/Corp** American Managed Care and Review Association. **VFOAT** AMCRA's ... Managed Health Care Directory. (1991)-. Directory. English. an. $195.00. American Managed Care and Review Association, 1227 25th St. NW, Suite 610, Washington DC 20037-1156. **Tel** (202)728-0506, FAX (202)728-0609. **LC** RA413.5.U5; M3634. **DD** 362. **NLM** W 22; AA1 M266. Index available. **Circ:** 500. ***Formed by the union of*** *Directory of Preferred Provider Organizations and the Industry Report on PPO Development, 0894-9891* ***and*** *Directory of Health Maintenance Organizations, 0894-9905.*

UK
**MANAGING CLINICAL DIRECTORATES.** (19??)-. Periodical. English. sa. £52.00 Europe; £55.00 Other (Institutions). Longman Group Ltd., Fourth Avenue, Longman House, Harlow Essex CM19 5SR England. **Tel** 011 44 279 429655, FAX 011 44 279 431059, telex 81259.

●US/1059-4531
**MATERIALS MANAGEMENT IN HEALTH CARE.** [Mater. manag. health care]. **VFOAT** Materials Management. Vol. 1, No. 1 (Mar. 1992)-. Periodical. English. mo. $30.00 US; $50.00 other. American Hospital Publishing Inc., (A Subsidiary of the American Hospital Association), PO Box 92683, Chicago IL 60675. **Tel** (312)440-6836, (800)621-6902, FAX (312)951-8491. **DD** 362. **NLM** W1; MA94K.
**Ind/Abst** Hospit. Health Admin. Index (Mar. 1992-).

US/1048-3314
**MCKNIGHT'S LONG-TERM CARE NEWS.** See Sociology-Social Services and Welfare.

US/0735-4436
**MD/PC.** See Law.

US
**MED-REC AUTOMATION & MANAGEMENT REPORT.** (1993)-. English. sm. $277.00 (one year), $544.00 (two year). United Communications Group, 11300 Rockville Pike, Suite 1100, Rockville MD 20852. **Tel** (301)816-8950 ext. 223, FAX (301)816-8945. ***Continues*** *Ambulatory Record Monitor : ARM, 1057-753X.*
**Desc:** Provides information on health record documentation.

US/1066-825X
**MEDICAL CARE PRODUCTS.** [Med. care prod.]. (1982)-. Periodical. English. bm (7 issues). $24.00 US, Canada & Mexico; $34.00 (surface mail), $60.00 (airmail) other. Cahners Publishing Company, 249 West 17th Street, New York NY 10011. **Tel** (212)645-0067, FAX (212)242-6987. **(Subscription address:** Gordon Publications, Inc., Paid Circulation Department, 301 Gibraltar Drive, Box 650, Morris Plains NJ 07950-0650.**) DD** 610.
**Desc:** Serves nursing supervisors, medical department heads, purchasing and materials management directors, and physician administrators responsible for patient care in hospitals, nursing homes and medical clinics.

US/0745-4910
**MEDICAL CENTER.** (MEDICAL CENTER / UNIVERSITY OF ALABAMA IN BIRMINGHAM.). [Med. cent.]. **Added/Corp** University of Alabama. Medical Center. **VFOAT** UAB Medical Center. Vol. 16, No.3 (March 1972)-. Periodical. English. qt. UAB Medical Center, University Station, Birmingham AL 35294. ***Continues*** *University of Alabama Medical Center News Bulletin.*

US/0278-808X
**MEDICAL DEVISE REGISTER.** [Medic. device regist.]. **Added/Corp** Directory Systems, Inc. United States. Food and Drug Administration. Medical Economics Data (Firm). **VFOAT** MDR. (1981)-. English. an. $295.00. Medical Economics Data, Five Paragon Drive, PO Box 27, Montvale NJ 07645. **Tel** (800)442-6657, (201)358-7200. **ED** Heidi Garrett. **LC** R856.48; .M42. **DD** 681/.761/0294. **[CCC].** Each issue contains an index to its own contents (no volume index)--loose. **Ad Acc. Circ:** 11,000.
**Desc:** The official directory of hospital suppliers, a 2,300 page hard cover book with complete information on medical equipment, supplies and their suppliers.

US/1040-2306
**MEDICAL GROUP MANAGEMENT WASHINGTON REPORT.** (MEDICAL GROUP MANAGEMENT WASHINGTON REPORT : MGMA'S LEGISLATIVE UPDATE.). [Med. group manage. Wash. rep.]. **Added/Corp** Medical Group Management Association. **VFOAT** Washington Report. (198?)-. Periodical. English. mo. $30.00 (members), $35.00 (MGMA affiliates), $40.00 (nonmembers). Medical Group Management Association, 104 Inverness Terrace East, Englewood CO 80112. **Tel** (303)397-7879, FAX (303)799-1683. **DD** 344. ***Continues*** *Inside the Arena, 0741-4293.*

US/1052-4894
**MEDICAL OFFICE MANAGER.** [Med. off. manager]. (Nov. 1987)-. Periodical. English. Twelve times a year. $152.00. Ardmore Publishing Company, PO Box 52843, Atlanta GA 30355. **Tel** (404)319-8105, FAX (404)436-4618. **ED** Susan Crawford. **DD** 610. **NLM** W1; ME407E. Index available (In Jan. issue). **Bk Rev**, (Qty: 2 or 3). **Circ:** 3,500 (ctrl).
**Desc:** Covers all aspects of management of physician office.
**Ind/Abst** Hospit. Manage. Rev. (19??-).

●US/1069-1944
**MEDICAL PRACTICE MANAGEMENT NEWS.** [Med. pract. manag. news]. **VFOAT** A.Medical practice management. (1993)-. Periodical. English. Twenty-two times a year. $240.00 US; $265.00 other. Williams & Wilkins Company, 428 East Preston Street, Baltimore MD 21202-3993. **Tel** (410)528-4000, (800)638-6423, FAX (410)528-8596, telex 87669. **(Subscription address:** Williams & Wilkins, PO Box 64380, Baltimore MD 21264.**) DD** 658. Documents available from Quick Copies.
**Desc:** For practice managers and health administrators, features the latest on-line reports and inside information on issues concerning the health care industry.

●US/1061-4192
**MEDICAL RECORD RISKS, CLAIMS & LITIGATION.** See Law.

US/1052-4924
**MEDICAL RECORDS BRIEFING.** [Med. rec. brief.]. **VFOAT** MRB. Vol. 1, No. 1 (Oct. 1986)-. Newsletter. English. mo (12 issues). $157.00 (one year), $257.00 (two year). Medical Records Briefing, PO Box 1168, Marblehead MA 01945. **Tel** (617)639-1872. **ED** Susan Crawford. **DD** 651. Index available. **Circ:** 2,400 (ctrl).
**Desc:** Covers medical records management.
**Ind/Abst** Hospit. Manage. Rev. (19??-).

US
**MEDICAL STAFF BRIEFING.** (19??)-. Periodical. English. mo. $237.00. Medical Records Briefing, PO Box 1168, Marblehead MA 01945. **Tel** (617)639-1872.
**Ind/Abst** Hospit. Manage. Rev. (19??-).

US/0735-2514
**MEDICAL STAFF FORUM.** (MEDICAL STAFF FORUM / AHA, AMERICAN HOSPITAL ASSOCIATION.). [Med. staff forum]. **Added/Corp** American Hospital Association. Division of Medical Affairs. Vol. 1, No. 1 (July/Aug. 1981)-. Periodical. English. bm. $25.00. American Hospital Association, 840 North Lake Shore Drive, Chicago IL 60611. **Tel** (312)280-6000, (800)242-2626. **ED** Daniel Schechter. **Circ:** 20,000.
**Desc:** News and analysis related to the relationship between hospitals and their medical staffs.

US
**MEDICARE HOSPITAL MANUAL.** See Insurance.

US
**MEDICARE/MEDICAID NURSING HOME INFORMATION. NEW JERSEY.** **Added/Corp** United States. Health Care Financing Administration.

**VFOAT** Medicare, Medicaid Nursing Home Information. New Jersey; Nursing Home Information. New Jersey. (1987/1988)-. English.

US
**MEDPRO MONTH.** (1991)-. Periodical. English. mo. $696.00 (one year), $1,260.00 (two year), $1,692.00 (three year). Medical Data International Inc., 2 Park Plaza, Suite 750, Irvine CA 92714. **Tel** (714)251-2780, FAX (714)251-2781. **NLM** W1; ME86F.
**Ind/Abst** Hospit. Manage. Rev. (19??-).

●US
**MEMBERSHIP DIRECTORY. Main/Corp** Association of Academic Health Centers (U.S.). (1994)-. Directory. English. an (Jan.). Free (members); $10.00 (non-members). Association of Academic Health Centers, 1400 16th Street Northwest, Suite 410, Washington DC 20036. **Tel** (202)265-9600, FAX (202)265-7514. **LC** RA977; .A88a. **DD** 610/.7/1173. ***Continues*** *Association of Academic Health Centers (U.S.). Directory, 0276-6590.*

US/0190-1672
**MENTAL HEALTH AUDIT CRITERIA SERIES. See** Public Health and Safety.

US/0094-291X
**MENTAL HEALTH, RETARDATION AND HOSPITALS (CRANSTON).** (MENTAL HEALTH, RETARDATION AND HOSPITALS.). **Main/Corp** Rhode Island. Dept. of Mental Health, Retardation and Hospitals. (1970/1971)-. English. an. A J Forand Buildings, 600 New London Avenue, Cranston RI 02920. **LC** RA790.65.R4; R45a. **DD** 362.2/09745.

US/0026-220X
**MICHIGAN HOSPITALS.** [Mich. hosp.]. **Added/Corp** Michigan Hospital Association. Vol. 1 (1965)-. Periodical. English. bm (six issues per year). $18.00 one year, $32.00 two year, $45.00 three year. Michigan Hospitals Association, 6215 West Street, St Joseph Highway, Lansing MI 48917. **Tel** (517)323-3443. **ED** Maryanne Butt. **DD** 610. **NLM** W1 MI203. Index available. **Bk Rev. Ad Acc. Circ:** 2,400. available on microfilm and microfiche from University Microfilms International (UMI).
**Desc:** Each edition examines in detail a timely health care issue affecting hospitals.
**Ind/Abst** Health Plan. Adminis.; Hospit. Health Admin. Index; Hospit. Manage. Rev.

US
**MILESTONES.** Vol. 3, No. 1 (Jan. 1990)-. English. bm. Healthcare Professional Publishing, 105 Main Street, Hackensack NJ 07601. **Tel** (201)342-6511. **ED** Katherine Piatt. **Bk Rev. Circ:** 22,000 (ctrl).
**Desc:** Healthcare publication geared to administrators of hospitals, nursing homes and HMO's.

AT/0159-9100
**MIMS HOSPITAL EQUIPMENT AND SUPPLIES.** (MIMS HOSPITAL EQUIPMENT AND SUPPLIES DIRECTORY.). (1978)-. Directory. English. an (September). 114.00Aus$ Australia; 119.00Aus$ New Zealand & Papus New Guinea; 146.00Aus$ other. Mims Australia, 98 Albany Street, Crows Nest NSW 2065 Australia. **Tel** 011 61 2 9067966, FAX 011 61 2 9063955. **ED** Marian Borland. **Ad Acc, Adv Mgr:** G. Hard, **Tel** 02 438-3558. **Circ:** 4,000.
**Desc:** Comprehensive listing of products and series for use by the hospital and medical industries. Information supplied by manufacturers of hospital equipment and supplies.

CN/0384-9481
**MINUTES OF ANNUAL MEETING - BRITISH COLUMBIA ASSOCIATION OF HOSPITALS AND HEALTH ORGANIZATIONS. Main/Corp** British Columbia Association of Hospitals and Health Organizations. (1974)-. Periodical. English. an. British Columbia Association of Hospitals and Health Organizations, 440 Cambie Street, Vancouver British Columbia V6B 2N6 Canada. **NLM** W1 MI7804B. ***Continues*** *Minutes of Annual Meeting and Conference - British Columbia Hospitals' Association, 0317-3755.*

US
**MISSISSIPPI STATE PLAN FOR CONSTRUCTION OF HOSPITALS AND MEDICAL FACILITIES. Added/Corp** Mississippi. Commission on Hospital Care. (19??)-. English. an. **LC** WMLC L 83/1305.

US/0192-6543
**MISSOURI HOSPITAL PROFILES.** (MISSOURI HOSPITAL PROFILES / MISSOURI DEPARTMENT OF SOCIAL SERVICES, DIVISION OF HEALTH, MISSOURI CENTER FOR HEALTH STATISTICS.). **Added/Corp** Missouri Center for Health Statistics. (1978)-. English. an. $25.00. Missouri Department of Health, Financial Services, PO Box 570, Jefferson City MO 65102. **Tel** (314)751-6279, (314)751-6400. **LC** RA981.M8; M59. **DD** 362.1/1/09778. **NLM** W2 AM8 B8M. **Circ:** 350. ***Continues*** *Missouri Hospital Profiles for ... .*
**Desc:** Contains statistical summary and agency-specific information for each licensed hospital in the state.

US
**MISSOURI NURSING HOME AND RESIDENTIAL CARE FACILTIY [I.E. FACILITY] PROFILES / MISSOURI DEPARTMENT OF HEALTH, STATE CENTER FOR HEALTH STATISTICS. Added/Corp** Missouri. State Center for Health Statistics. **VFOAT** Missouri Nursing Home and Residential Care Facility Profiles. (1984)-. English. an. $17.50. Missouri Department of Health, Financial Services, PO Box 570, Jefferson City MO 65102. **Tel** (314)751-6279, (314)751-6400. **LC** RA997.5.M8; M57. **DD** 362.1/609778021. **NLM** W2; AM8 M67. **Circ:** 1,000. ***Continues*** *Missouri Nursing Home and Boarding Home Profiles.*
**Desc:** Contains statistical summary and agency-specific information for each licensed nursing home and residential care facility in the state.

US/0160-7480
**MODERN HEALTHCARE (1977).** (MODERN HEALTHCARE.). [Mod. healthc.]. Vol. 6, No. 2, Aug. (1976)-. Periodical. English. wk. $110.00 US and possessions; $158.00 other (surface mail). Crain Communications Inc., 1400 Woodbridge, Detroit MI 48207. **Tel** (313)446-6000, (800)992-9970. **ED** Clark Bell. **LC** RA960; .M685. **DD** 338.4/7/36210973. **NLM** W1 MO132T. **[CCC].** Index available. cum. index. **Ad Acc. Circ:** 90,000 (ctrl). available on microfilm and microfiche from University Microfilms International (UMI). Documents available from UMI Article Clearinghouse. ***Formed by the union of*** *Modern Healthcare, 0093-7053* ***and*** *Modern Healthcare, 0093-7061.*
**Desc:** Business news magazine for healthcare management, edited to keep healthcare executives current with news and trends in the field. Circulation is concentrated among those with purchasing responsibility in hospitals and nursing homes, primarily administrators, purchasing and financial officers and board officers.
**Ind/Abst** ABI/INFORM Glob. Ed.; ABI Inform Ondisc (July 1985-); Acad. Search (Jan. 1994-); Archit. Period. Index; Bus. Index (1985-); Cumul. Index Nurs. Allied Health Lit.; Energy Res. Abstr. (Aug. 1982-); F&S Index Plus Text, Int. [Full Txt.] [Select. Cov.]; Gen. BusinessFile (1985-); Health Source (Jul. 1993-); Hospit. Health Admin. Index; Hospit. Manage. Rev.; Int. Pharm. Abstr. (19??-19??); Mag. Search; Mod. Med.; PROMT [Full Txt.]; Soc. Work Abstr. (?-?); Trade Ind. Index; UMI ABI/Inform--Bus. Period. Ondisc (Jan. 1987-) [Full Txt.].

US/0093-9900
**MODERN NURSING HOME DIRECTORY OF NURSING HOMES IN THE UNITED STATES, U.S. POSSESSIONS AND CANADA. VFOAT** Directory of Nursing Homes in the United States, U.S. Possessions and Canada. **VAT** Directory of Nursing Homes in the United States, United States Possessions and Canada. (19??)-. Directory. English. McGraw Hill Publishing Company, Inc., 1221 Avenue of the Americas, New York NY 10020. **Tel** (212)512-6410, (800)525-5003, FAX (212)512-6111. **LC** RA997.A2; D5. **DD** 362.1/6/02573. ***Continues*** *Directory of Nursing Homes in the United States, U.S. Territories, and Canada.*

US
**MONDAY REPORT.** English. Forty-eight times a year. $61.00. Massachusetts Hospital Association, 5 New England Executive Park, Burlington MA 01803. **Tel** (617)272-8000, FAX (617)272-0466. **ED** Lisa Derbyshire. **Circ:** 5,500 (ctrl).

IT
**MONDO SANITARIO COMMISSIONI GRUPPI STUDI E LAVORO.** ir. L500000. IDMA SRL, Via Gradisca 8, 20151 Milan Italy. **Tel** 39 2 3087137.

FR/0993-9199
**MONITEUR HOSPITALIER, LE.** (198?)-. Periodical. French. Eleven times a year. 450.00F France & French overseas departments and territories; 530.00F other. Moniteur Pharmac Laboratoires, 11 17 rue Godefroy Cavaignac, 75541 Paris Cedex 11 France. **Tel** 011 33 1 43790630, FAX 011 33 1 43791775. **UDC** 615.

US/1057-3526
**NAHAM MANAGEMENT JOURNAL, THE.** [NAHAM manage. j.]. **Added/Corp** National Association of Healthcare Access Management. **VAT** National Association of Healthcare Access Management Journal. Vol. 16, No. 3 (Winter 1991)-. Periodical. English. qt. $90.00. National Association of Healthcare Access Management, 1101 Connecticut Avenue NW, Suite 700, Washington DC 20036. **DD** 362. **NLM** W1; NA1157N. ***Continues*** *Admitting Management Journal.*
**Ind/Abst** Hospit. Health Admin. Index (1991-).

IT
**NASCITA ATTIVA.** tq (3 issues per year). L300000 Italy; L4000000 other. Centro Studi Nascita Attiva, Via San Giovanni Cantone 72, 41100 Modena Italy. **Tel** 011 39 59 313144.

US
**NATIONAL DIRECTORY OF OCCUPATIONAL HEALTH PROVIDERS.** (19??)-. Directory. English. an. $175.00. Datalink Research Group, PO Box 141, Fair Oaks CA 95628. **Tel** (916)987-1486. **ED** Mary Rucker. **Ad Acc. Circ:** 200.
**Desc:** Lists physicians, clinics, and hospitals who offer occupational health series, including drug screening, employment physicals, workers compensation evaluations.

US
**NATIONAL HOSPITAL DISCHARGE SURVEY. ANNUAL SUMMARY. Added/Corp** National Center for Health Statistics (U.S.). **VFOAT** Annual Summary. (1987)-. English. an. US Department of Health and Human Services, 200 Independence Avenue Southwest, Washington DC 20201. ***Continues*** *Utilization of Short-Stay Hospitals. United States ... Annual Summary, 0748-4798.*

US/0895-2728
**NATIONAL MEDICAL CARE UTILIZATION AND EXPENDITURE SURVEY. SERIES B, DESCRIPTIVE REPORT.** (SERIES B--DESCRIPTIVE REPORT.). [Natl. Med. Care Util. Expend. Surv., Ser. B Descr. rep.]. **Added/Corp** United States. Health Care Financing Administration. Office of Research and Demonstrations. National Center for Health Statistics (U.S.). **VFOAT** Descriptive Report. No. 1 (1986)-. English. **DD** 610. **NLM** W2; A N2237n.
**Ind/Abst** Health Plan. Adminis.; Hospit. Health Admin. Index (n1,1980-).

US/0895-2671
**NATIONAL MEDICAL CARE UTILIZATION AND EXPENDITURE SURVEY. SERIES C, ANALYTICAL REPORT.** [Natl. Med. Care Util. Expend. Surv., Ser. C Anal. rep.]. **Added/Corp** National Center for Health Statistics (U.S.) United States. Health Care Financing Administration. Office of Research and Demonstrations. No. 1 (1985)-. English. Health Resources Administration, Office of the Administrator, DMS Committee Management Branch, 5600 Fishers Lane, Rockville MD 20857. **DD** 610. **NLM** W2; A N224n.
**Ind/Abst** Health Plan. Adminis.; Hospit. Health Admin. Index (1985-).

US/0270-7950
**NCI FACT BOOK. See** Medical Science and Technology-Neoplasma, Neoplastic.

US/0148-9321
**NEBRASKA HEALTH MANPOWER REPORTS: NURSING HOME ADMINISTRATORS. Main/Corp** Nebraska. Division of Health Data and Statistical Research. **Added/Corp** Nebraska. Bureau of Examining Boards. (19??)-. English. an. Nebraska State Department of Health, PO Box 95007, Lincoln NE 68509. **Tel** (402)471-2133, FAX (402)471-0383. **LC** RA997.5.N2; N43a. **DD** 331.1/1. **NLM** W2 AN1 D34NN.

US
**NEW JERSEY STATE PLAN FOR THE CONSTRUCTION AND MODERNIZATION OF HOSPITALS AND OTHER MEDICAL FACILITIES. Main/Corp** New Jersey. Bureau of Medical Facility Construction and Planning. **VFOAT** New Jersey State Plan for the Construction and Modernization of Hospitals and Related Medical Facilities. (19??)-. English. an. Bureau of Medical Facility Construction and Planning, PO Box 1540, John Fitch Plaza, Trenton NJ 08625. **LC** RA981.N5; A35. **DD** 362.1/1/09749. ***Continues*** *New Jersey State Plan for the Construction of Hospitals and Related Medical Facilities.*

NZ/0114-3727
**NEW ZEALAND HEALTH & HOSPITAL. Added/Corp** Hospital Boards' Association of New Zealand. **VFOAT** New Zealand Health and Hospital. Vol. 41, No. 2 (March/April 1989)-. Periodical. English. bm (6 issues per year). 35.00NZ$ New Zealand 50.00NZ$ other. Hospital Boards Association of New Zealand, PO Box 3541, Wellington 1 New Zealand. **Tel** 767-318. **NLM** W1; NE9728T. ***Continues*** *New Zealand Hospital.*
**Ind/Abst** Health Plan. Adminis.; Hospit. Health Admin. Index (1989-).

US
**NEWS / CALIFORNIA ASSOCIATION OF HOSPITALS AND HEALTH SYSTEMS. Added/Corp** California Association of Hospitals and Health Systems. Vol. 18, No. 33 (Dec. 5, 1986)-. Periodical. English. wk (published each Friday). $80.00 non-members; $40.00 members of CAHHS. California

Association of Hospitals and Health Systems, PO Box 1100, Sacramento CA 95812. **Tel** (916)443-7401. ***Continues*** *CHA News.*

US/1066-9078
**NEWS - HEALTHCARE INFORMATION AND MANAGEMENT SYSTEMS SOCIETY.** (NEWS / HEALTHCARE INFORMATION AND MANAGEMENT SYSTEMS SOCIETY OF THE AMERICAN HOSPITAL ASSOCIATION.). [News - Healthc. Inf. Manag. Syst. Soc.]. **Added/Corp** Healthcare Information and Management Systems Society. **VFOAT** HIMSS News. Vol. 1, No. 1 (June 1990)-. Periodical. English. mo. Free (members). American Hospital Association, 840 North Lake Shore Drive, Chicago IL 60611. **Tel** (312)280-6000, (800)242-2626. **DD** 610. **NLM** W1; NE992L.

US/0018-5574
**NEWS - HOSPITAL ASSOCIATION OF NEW YORK STATE.** **Main/Corp** Hospital Association of New York State. (1970)-. Periodical. English. wk. $150.00 (non-members), $50.00 (members). Hospital Association of New York State, 74 North Pearl Street, Albany NY 12207. **Tel** (518)431-7600, FAX (518)431-7915. **Circ:** 2,000 (ctrl).
**Desc:** Information of current interest concerning health care institutions.

US/0027-8637
**NEWSLETTER (NATIONAL ASSOCIATION OF PRIVATE PSYCHIATRIC HOSPITALS).** (NEWSLETTER / NATIONAL ASSOCIATION OF PRIVATE PSYCHIATRIC HOSPITALS.). **Added/Corp** National Association of Private Psychiatric Hospitals. Began publication in (1950)-. Newsletter. English. bm (6 issues). National Association of Private Psychiatric Hospitals, 1319 F Street NW/Suite 1000, Washington DC 20004. **Tel** (202)393-6700.

JA/0385-9363
**NIPPON BYOINKAI ZASSHI.** [Nihon Byoinkai zasshi]. **Added/Corp** Nihon Byoinkai. **VFOAT** Journal of Japan Hospital Association; Nihon Byoinkai Zasshi. Vol. 22 (Jan. 1975)-. Periodical. Japanese. mo (12 issues). $218.00. **(Subscription address:** Kyowa Book Company Inc., 1 38 Kanda Jinbocho Chiyoda-ku, Tokyo 101 Japan.**)** **NLM** W1 NI8833. ***Continues*** *Nippon Byoin Kyokai Zasshi, 0385-9355.*

CN/0704-8815
**NOTRE HOPITAL.** **Added/Corp** Hotel-Dieu de Montreal. First Issue, Dec. (1965)-. Periodical. French. Free. Hotel-Dieu de Montreal, Centre de Documentation, 3840 rue Saint-Urbain, Montreal Quebec H2W 1T8 Canada. **Tel** (514)843-2638. **DD** 362.1/1/09714281. **Ad Acc**. ctrl circ.

FR/0029-4853
**NOUVELLES ARCHIVES HOSPITALIERES.** [Nouv. arch. hosp.]. **Added/Corp** Societe des Amis de Felix d'Herelle. Societe Medico-Chirurgicale des Hopitaux Libres de France. Vol. 36, No. 6, June (1964)-. Periodical. French. qt. 30.00F. Societe des Amis de Felix d'Herelle, 11 rue Boissiere, 75116 Paris France. **NLM** W1 NO835N. Index available. **Bk Rev**. **Ad Acc**. available with charts; available with illustrations. ***Continues*** *Archives Hospitaleres.*

●US
**NTIS ALERT. HEALTH CARE / PREPARED BY THE NATIONAL TECHNICAL INFORMATION SERVICE, U.S. DEPARTMENT OF COMMERCE, TECHNOLOGY ADMINISTRATION.** **See** Public Health and Safety.

US/1070-1370
**NURSING HOME MEDICINE.** [Nurs. home med.]. Vol. 1, No. 1 (Mar./Apr. 1993)-. Periodical. English. Ten times a year. $50.00, medical professionals; $75.00 other, US and Canada; $125.00 other. Multimedia Healthcare Inc., 300 Buckelew Avenue, Suite 202, Jamesburg NJ 08831. **Tel** (908)521-8282. **DD** 618.

US
**NURSING HOME PRACTITIONER.** **See** Sociology-Social Services and Welfare.

US/0275-1070
**NURSING HOME SALARY & BENEFITS REPORT.** **Added/Corp** Hospital Compensation Service. **VAT** Nursing Home Salary and Benefits Report. (1979)-. English. an (Publishes in April). $240.00 (prepaid), $250.00 (billed). Hospital & Healthcare Compensation Service, PO Box 376, 69 Minnehaha Blvd., Oakland NJ 07436. **Tel** (201)405-0075, FAX (201)405-1258. **LC** RA997.A1; N88. **DD** 331.2/81362160973. **NLM** W1; NU6093. Index available.
**Desc:** Covers salary and bonus data on fifty-two management, nursing, therapy, dietary, and clerical positions.

US/1061-4753
**NURSING HOMES (1991).** (NURSING HOMES : LONG TERM CARE MANAGEMENT.). [Nurs. homes]. **VFOAT** Nursing Homes and Senior Citizen Care. Vol. 40, No. 6 (Nov./Dec. 1991)-. Periodical. English. mo (9 issues). $50.00 US; $75.00 Canada and Mexico; $95.00 other. Medquest Communications Inc., 629 Euclid Avenue, Suite 500, Cleveland OH 44114. **Tel** (216)522-9700. **(Subscription address:** PO Box 20179, Cleveland, OH 44120**)** **DD** 610. **NLM** W1; NU6096. ***Continues*** *Nursing Homes and Senior Citizen Care, 0896-6915.*
**Ind/Abst** Bus. ASAP (199?-) [Full Txt.]; Bus. Index (1991-); Bus. Period. Index (Nov./Dec. 1991-); Cumul. Index Nurs. Allied Health Lit. (Nov./Dec. 1991-); Gen. BusinessFile (1991-); Gen. Period. Index (1991-); Health Index (1991-); Int. Pharm. Abstr.; Trade Ind. ASAP [Full Txt.]; Trade Ind. Index [Full Txt.].

US/0278-7059
**NURSING HOMES IN WASHINGTON STATE.** (NURSING HOMES IN WASHINGTON STATE / CENTER FOR HEALTH STATISTICS.). **Added/Corp** Washington (State). Center for Health Statistics. **VFOAT** Report, Nursing Homes in Washington State. (19??)-. English. Center for Health Statistics / Washington, MS LL-15 Health Services Division, Department of Social and Health Services, Olympia WA 98504. **LC** RA997.5.W3; N87. **DD** 362.1/6/09797.

CN/0712-1342
**NURSING HOMES (TORONTO).** (NURSING HOMES.). [Nurs. homes]. **Added/Corp** Community Information Centre of Metropolitan Toronto. **VFOAT** Nursing Homes in Metropolitan Toronto. (1978)-. Periodical. English. be. $3.00 per issue. Community Information Centre of Metropolitan Toronto, 590 Jarvis Street, Toronto Ontario M4Y 2J4 Canada. **Tel** (416)392-4575, FAX (416)392-4404. **DD** 362.6/1.
**Ind/Abst** Gen. Period. Index (1985-1989); Trade Ind. Index (1981-?)(1981-).

CN/0843-5901
**OHLA NEWSLINE.** **See** Library and Information Sciences.

US/1046-3356
**ONCOLOGY ISSUES.** **See** Medical Science and Technology-Neoplasma, Neoplastic.

CN/0826-6808
**ONTARIO HOSPITALS DIRECTORY.** [Ont. hosp. dir.]. **Added/Corp** Ontario. Ministry of Health. (198?)-. Directory. English. Ontario Government Bookstore, 880 Bay Street, Toronto Ontario M7A 1N8 Canada. **LC** RA978.C2; O57. **DD** 362.1/1/025713.

CN/0829-6340
**ONTARIO NURSING HOME JOURNAL.** ***Ceased.*** [Ont. nurs. home j.]. Vol. 1, No. 1 (Sept. 1985)-?. Periodical. English. ir (five issues per year). Health Media Inc, 14453 29A Avenue, White Rock BC V4A 9K8 Canada. **Tel** (604)535-7933, FAX (604)535-9000. **ED** Frank Fagan. **DD** 362.1/6/09713. Index available. **Ad Acc**. **Circ:** 4,500 (ctrl).
**Desc:** Provides continuing educational, technical and professional information to management personnel of long term care facilities.

CN/0712-9971
**ONTARIO NURSING HOMES.** [Ont. nurs. homes]. **Added/Corp** Ontario Nursing Home Association. Vol. 5, No. 12 (Autumn 1974)-. Periodical. English. ir (5 times a year). $6.00. Ontario Nursing Home Association, 6075 Yonge Street Canada. **DD** 362.6/1/09713. ***Continues*** *Ontario Nursing Home News.*

IT/0394-283X
**ORGANIZZAZIONE SANITARIA.** [Organ. sanit.]. (1977)-. Periodical. Italian. bm. L100000. Secup Srl, Via E Quirino Visconti 20, 00193 Rome Italy. **Tel** 011 39 6 3217056, FAX 011 39 6 3211751. **UDC** 614.2. **Bk Rev**, (Qty: 6). **Ad Acc**.

JA/0386-4103
**OSAKA-SHI IGAKKAI ZASSHI.** [Osaka-shi Igakkai zasshi]. **Added/Corp** Osaka-Shi Igakkai. **VFOAT** Journal of the Osaka City Medical Center. (1975)-. Periodical. Japanese (summaries and/or abstracts in English). qt. Osaka City Medical Center, 4-54 Asahimachi, 1-chome Abeno-ku, 545 Osaka Japan. ***Continues*** *Osaka Shiritsu Daigaku Igaku Zasshi.*
**Ind/Abst** EMBASE [Select. Cov.]; Energy Res. Abstr. (Sept. 1980-); Nutr. Abstr. Rev., Ser. A, Hum. Exp.

IT/0030-6231
**OSPEDALE.** [Ospedale]. **VFOAT** Periodico dell'Associazione Nazionale Medici Direzioni Ospedaliere. (1948)-. Periodical. Italian. Nine times a year (monthly with Jan./Feb., April/May, July/Aug. and Oct./Nov. issues combined). L48000.00 Italy, L60000.00 other. Ospedale Presso IST d Igiene, Via Santena 5 BIS, 10126 Turin, Italy. **Tel** 39 11 6502203 or 6502204. **ED** Silvio Moro. **UDC** 362. **Bk Rev**. **Ad Acc**. ctrl circ.

IT/0369-7843
**OSPEDALE MAGGIORE.** [Osp. magg.]. **Added/Corp** Ospedale Maggiore di Milano. (1906)-. Academic Scholarly Publication. Italian. qt. L76000. Masson S.P.A, Via Statuto 2/4, 20121 Milan Italy. **Tel** 011 39 2 63671, FAX 011 39 2 6367211. **NLM** W1 OS527.
**Ind/Abst** EMBASE.

IT
**OSPEDALI DELLA VITA, GLI.** (19??)-. Italian. Six times a year. Free on request. Gli Ospedali della Vita, Usl 27, V Calori 2G, 40122 Bologna Italy.

IT
**OSPEDALITA PRIVATA.** Free. AIOP, Via Lucrezio Caro 67, 00197 Rome Italy.

IT
**OSSERVATORE SANITARIO.** Osservatore Sanitario, Casella Postale 61, 16043 Chiavari Italy.

US/0195-7775
**PATIENT ACCOUNTS.** [Patient acc.]. **Added/Corp** Hospital Financial Management Association (U.S.). Vol. 1, No. 1 (Feb. 10, 1978)-. Periodical. English. mo (12 issues). $55.00 (members), $98.00 (non-members). HFMA - Healthcare Financial Management Association, 2 Westbrook Corporation Center, Suite 700, Westchester IL 60154-5700. **Tel** (708)531-9600, (800)252-4362. **NLM** W1 PA963M.
**Desc:** Covers healthcare regulatory and legislative news as well as the latest healthcare management trends.
**Ind/Abst** Hospit. Health Admin. Index; Hospit. Manage. Rev.

US/0147-3913
**PATIENT CARE REVIEW.** V. 1- Aug. 1975-. Periodical. English. mo. Illinois Hospital Association, 1200 Jorie Blvd., Oak Brook IL 60521. **NLM** W1 PA9632.

US/0147-0957
**PATIENT ORIGIN DATA FOR NORTH DAKOTA HOSPITALS AND NURSING HOMES.** **Main/Corp** North Dakota. Division of Health Facilities. English. North Dakota Division of Health Facilities, 1200 Missouri Avenue, Bismarck ND 58505. **LC** RA981.N85; N64A. **DD** 362.1/09784. **NLM** W2 AN8 D65P.

●US/1069-6520
**PATIENT OUTCOMES.** [Patient outcomes]. (1993)-. Periodical. English. Ten times a year. $75.00 (indiviual), $125.00 (institution) US; $105.00 (indiidual), $155.00 (institution) other. Williams & Wilkins Company, 428 East Preston Street, Baltimore MD 21202-3993. **Tel** (410)528-4000, (800)638-6423, FAX (410)528-8596, telex 87669. **(Subscription address:** Williams & Wilkins, PO Box 64380, Baltimore MD 21264.**)** **DD** 610. Documents available from Quick Copies.
**Desc:** An guide through the issues concerning managed care for primary care physicians and medical directors responsible for case management.

CN/0847-8090
**PATIENT UPDATE.** ***Suspended.*** [Patient update]. **Added/Corp** Ontario Medical Association. **VFOAT** OMA Patient Update. **VAT** Ontario Medical Association Patient Update. (Spring 1989)-(19??). Periodical. English. qt. 10 00Can$. Ontario Medical Association, 525 University Avenue, Suite 300, Toronto Ontario M5G 2K7, Canada. **Tel** (416)599-2580. **ED** Jeff Henry and Elizabeth Petruccelli. **DD** 613/.05. **Ad Acc**, **Adv Mgr:** K. Secord. **Pr Rev**. **Circ:** 6,000 (ctrl).
**Desc:** Provides current medical information of interest to patients.

US/0744-5636
**PENNSYLVANIA HOSPITALS.** [Pa. hosp.]. **Added/Corp** Hospital Association of Pennsylvania. Hospital Association of Pennsylvania. Membership Directory. Vol. 1, No. 1 (Spring 1982)-. Periodical. English. qt. (comes with PA Organization of Nurse Execs membership). Hospital Association of Pennsylvania, 4750 Lindle Road, Harrisburg PA 17105. **Tel** (717)564-9200. **DD** 362. **NLM** W2; AP4 P5. **Bk Rev**. **Circ:** 6,000 (ctrl). ***Continues*** *Hospital Issues & Trends, 0164-520X.*
**Ind/Abst** Health Devices Alerts; Hospit. Manage. Rev.

US/0890-4421
**PERSPECTIVES ON STAFFING & SCHEDULING.** [Perspect. staff./sched.]. **Added/Corp** Nursing Management Services Inc. (Montclair, N.J.). **VFOAT** Perspectives on Staffing, Scheduling; Perspectives on Staffing & Scheduling; Perspectives on Staffing and Scheduling; Staffing/Scheduling. (198?)-. Periodical. English. Six times a year. $50.00. Lawrenz Madden & Association Inc., 24 South Mountain Avenue, Montclair NJ 07042. **Tel** (201)746-5232, FAX (201)746-8321. **ED** Eunice Lawrenz (phone: (201)746-5232). **DD** 610. **NLM** W1; PE872K. cum. index. **Circ:** 500.
**Desc:** A newsletter specifically with the staffing and scheduling issues which face hospitals and nursing homes today. You will receive helpful information and strategies you can use in your setting as well as actual case studies of how hospitals solve specific staffing problems.

CN/1187-5011
**PERSPECTIVES - ST. BONIFACE GENERAL HOSPITAL.** (PERSPECTIVES.). [Perspect. - St. Boniface Gen. Hosp.]. **Main/Corp** Hospital

General de Saint-Boniface. Vol. 1, No. 1 (Oct. 1991)-. Periodical. French (English). qt. Free. Hopital General de Saint-Boniface, 409 Avenue Tache, Winnipeg Manitoba R2H 2A6 Canada. **DD** 362.1/1/0971274305. ***Continues*** *Hopital General de Saint-Boniface. Newslines.*

CN/1187-5011
**PERSPECTIVES - ST. BONIFACE GENERAL HOSPITAL.** (PERSPECTIVES.). [Perspect. - St. Boniface Gen. Hosp.]. **Main/Corp** St. Boniface General Hospital. Vol. 1, No. 1 (Oct. 1991)-. Periodical. English (French). qt. Free. St Boniface General Hospital, Public Relations Department, 409 Tache Avenue, Winnipeg Manitoba R2H 2A6 Canada. **Tel** (204)235-3229. **DD** 362.1/1/0971274305. ***Continues*** *Newslines., 0822-8132.*

FR/0369-9579
**PHARMACIE HOSPITALIERE FRANCAISE, LA.** [Pharm. hosp. fr.]. **Added/Corp** Syndicat National des Pharmaciens Residents Monoappartenants ou Universitaires des Etablissements Francais d'Hospitalisation de Soins et de Cure Publics. (19??)-. Academic Scholarly Publication. French. qt (Mar., June, Sep., Dec.). 316.50F France; 360.00F other. Chru, BP 69, 63003 Clermont Ferrand, Cedex France. **Tel** 33 73 625702, FAX 33 73 625694. **ED** Mme Christine Dupont. **CODEN** PHHFAS. **Bk Rev. Circ:** 1,200 (ctrl). Documents available from CASDDS.
**Ind/Abst** Chem. Abstr.; EMBASE; Int. Pharm. Abstr.

US/1055-1603
**PHYSICIAN MANAGER.** [Phys. manag.]. **Added/Corp** Atlantic Information Services. (Nov. 1990)-. Periodical. English. mo. $231.00. Atlantic Information Services Inc., 1050 17th Street Northwest, Suite 480, Washington DC 20036. **Tel** (202)775-9008, (800)521-4323, FAX (202)331-9542. **LC** RA972; .P495. **DD** 362.1/068. **NLM** W1; PH776M.
**Ind/Abst** Hospit. Manage. Rev. (199?-).

US
**PHYSICIANS FEE GUIDE / AS COMPILED BY HEALTHCARE CONSULTANTS, INC.** ***Title Change.*** **Added/Corp** HealthCare Consultants, Inc. (1990)-(199?). English. **NLM** W1; PH787P. ***Continued by*** *Physicians Fee & Coding Guide.*

CN/1188-1771
**PHYSICIAN'S GUIDE FOR TRAVEL & MEDICAL CONVENTION PLANNING.** [Physician's guide trav. med. conv. plan.]. **Added/Corp** Thomson Healthcare Communications. **VFOAT** Physician's Guide; Physician's Guide for Travel & Medical Conference Planning. Vol. 1, No. 1 (Nov./Dec. 1991)-. Periodical. English. Four times a year. 40.00Can$. Thomson Healthcare, 1120 Birchmount Road, Suite 200, Scarborough Ontario M1K 5G4 Canada. **Tel** (905)750-8900. **DD** 610/.25.

US/1061-0219
**PREPAID HEALTHCARE ASSEMBLY DIRECTORY : ... REPORT BASED ON ... DATA / MEDICAL GROUP MANAGEMENT ASSOCIATION.** **Added/Corp** Medical Group Management Association. Center for Research in Ambulatory Health Care Administration (U.S.). (1991)-. Directory. English. $65.00. CRAHCA, 104 Inverness Terrace East, Englewood CO 80112-5306. **DD** 362.

US
**PRIMER SERIES FOR HEALTH CARE PROFESSIONALS.** **See** Law.

US/0162-9913
**PRIVATE PSYCHIATRIC HOSPITALS.** **Main/Corp** United States. National Institute of Mental Health. English. National Institute of Mental Health, 9000 Rockville Pike, Rockville MD 20892. **Tel** (301)496-9291. **LC** RC443; .U54C. **DD** 362.2/1/0973.

US/1065-1489
**PROCEDURAL SKILLS AND OFFICE TECHNOLOGY BULLETIN.** [Proced. skills off. technol. bull.]. (19??)-. Bulletin. English. ir (Nine issues per volume). $40.00 (one year), $75.00 (two year). PSOT Bulletin, 1843 Brooksedge, Memphis TN 38138. **Tel** (901)448-5467. **ED** William MacMillan Rodney, MD (Editor's telephone: (901)448-7282). **DD** 616.
**Desc:** Medical literature for the practicing physician who is developing skills in GI endoscopy, OB ultrasound, colposcopy, and other outpatient services.

US/0193-0486
**PROCEEDINGS OF THE ... ANNUAL CONFERENCE OF THE HOSPITAL MANAGEMENT SYSTEMS SOCIETY.** **Main/Corp** Hospital Management Systems Society. Conference. **Added/Corp** National Cooperative Services Center for Hospital Management Engineering. Center for Hospital Management Engineering (U.S.) Clearinghouse for Hospital Management Engineering (U.S.). Began with: 1st (1972)-. Proceedings. English. an. Price varies. American Hospital Association, 840 North Lake Shore Drive, Chicago IL 60611. **Tel** (312)280-6000, (800)242-2626. **LC** RA971; .H594a. **DD** 658/.91/36211. **NLM** W3 HO823R.

US/1048-8987
**PROCEEDINGS OF THE ANNUAL HEALTH CARE INFORMATION AND MANAGEMENT SYSTEMS CONFERENCE.** [Proc. annu. Health Care Inf. Manage. Syst. Conf.]. **Main/Conf** Health Care Information and Management Systems Conference. **Added/Corp** Society for Health Systems. **VFOAT** Proceedings of the ... Annual HIMSS Conference. **VAT** Proceedings of the Annual Health Care Information and Management Systems Conference. (1990)-. Periodical. English. an. Included with Healthcare Information and Management Systems Society membership. American Hospital Association, 840 North Lake Shore Drive, Chicago IL 60611. **Tel** (312)280-6000, (800)242-2626. **DD** 362. ***Continues*** *Proceedings of the ... Annual Health Care Systems Conference.*

US/0098-1559
**PROGRAM NOTES - ASSOCIATION OF UNIVERSITY PROGRAMS IN HEALTH ADMINISTRATION.** [Program notes - Assoc. Univ. Programs Health Adm.]. **Main/Corp** Association of University Programs in Health Administration. No. 54 (June 1973)-. Periodical. English. Association of University Programs in Health Administration, 1911 North Fort Myer Drive, Suite 503, Arlington VA 22209. **Tel** (703)524-5500, FAX (703)525-4791. **NLM** W1 PR633. ***Continues*** *Association of University Programs in Hospital Administration. Program Notes - Association of University Programs in Hospital Administration, 0098-1567.*
**Ind/Abst** Health Plan. Adminis.

US
**PROGRAM STATUS REPORT ... TO THE GOVERNOR AND LEGISLATURE / STATE OF FLORIDA, HOSPITAL COST CONTAINMENT BOARD.** **Main/Corp** Florida. Hospital Cost Containment Board. **Added/Corp** Florida. Hospital Cost Containment Board. Annual Report, Program Status. **VFOAT** Annual Report, Program Status. (19??)-. English. an. $8.50. Florida Hospital Cost, Containment Board/Larson Building, Tallahassee FL 32301. **LC** RA981.F4; F56a. **DD** 362.1.

US/0737-5913
**PROSPECTIVE REIMBURSEMENT SYSTEM BASED ON PATIENT CASE-MIX FOR NEW JERSEY HOSPITALS, A.** (A PROSPECTIVE REIMBURSEMENT SYSTEM BASED ON PATIENT CASE-MIX FOR NEW JERSEY HOSPITALS .... ANNUAL REPORT.). **Main/Corp** New Jersey. State Dept. of Health. **VFOAT** Annual Report. (1977)-. English. an. New Jersey Department of Health, John Fitch Plaza, CN-360, Trenton NJ 08625. **Tel** (609)292-7837, FAX (609)984-5474. **LC** RA981.N5; N476a. **DD** 362.1/1/0681.

US/0885-7717
**PSYCHIATRIC HOSPITAL, THE.** ***Ceased.*** [Psychiatr. hosp.]. Vol. 13, No. 2 (Spring 1982)-(1993). Periodical. English. qt. The Psychiatric Hospital, 1319 F Street NW/Suite 1000, Washington DC 20004. **Tel** (202)393-6700. **ED** Freida Eastman. **DD** 362. **NLM** W1; PS257. Index available. **Bk Rev. Ad Acc. Circ:** 8,500 (ctrl). ***Continues*** *Journal - National Association of Private Psychiatric Hospitals, 0027-8629.*
**Desc:** Clinical papers on hospital- based psychiatric care.
**Ind/Abst** EMBASE; Hospit. Health Admin. Index; Psychol. Abstr. (1982-); PsycINFO.

US/0898-0543
**PSYCHIATRIC LENGTH OF STAY BY DIAGNOSIS, UNITED STATES.** [Psychiatr. length stay diagn. U. S.]. **Added/Corp** Commission on Professional and Hospital Activities. **VFOAT** LOS. (1986)-. English. an. $85.00 (per volume). Healthcare Knowledge Systems Publications, 1968 Green Road, Box 1809, Ann Arbor MI 48106. **Tel** (800)521-6210. **LC** RC443; .P76. **DD** 362.2/1/0973021. **Ad Acc.**

US/0898-249X
**PSYCHIATRIC LENGTH OF STAY BY DIAGNOSIS, UNITED STATES, NORTH CENTRAL REGION.** [Psychiatr. length stay diagn. U. S. north cent. reg.]. **VFOAT** LOS. (1986)-. English. an. $55.00. Healthcare Knowledge Systems Publications, 1968 Green Road, Box 1809, Ann Arbor MI 48106. **Tel** (800)521-6210. **LC** RC445.M53; P89. **DD** 362.2/1/0977021.

US/0898-0527
**PSYCHIATRIC LENGTH OF STAY BY DIAGNOSIS, UNITED STATES, NORTHEASTERN REGION.** [Psychiatr. length stay diagn. U. S. northeast. reg.]. **VFOAT** LOS. (1986)-. English. an. $85.00 (per volume). Healthcare Knowledge Systems Publications, 1968 Green Road, Box 1809, Ann Arbor MI 48106. **Tel** (800)521-6210. **LC** RC445.N94; P89. **DD** 362.2/1/0974021. **Ad Acc.**

US/0898-0519
**PSYCHIATRIC LENGTH OF STAY BY DIAGNOSIS, UNITED STATES, SOUTHERN REGION.** [Psychiatr. length stay diagn. U. S. south. reg.]. **VFOAT** LOS. (1986)-. English. an. $85.00 (per volume). Healthcare Knowledge Systems Publications, 1968 Green Road, Box 1809, Ann Arbor MI 48106. **Tel** (800)521-6210. **LC** RC445.S89; P89. **DD** 362.2/1/0975021. **Ad Acc.**

US/0898-0535
**PSYCHIATRIC LENGTH OF STAY BY DIAGNOSIS. UNITED STATES, WESTERN REGION.** [Psychiatr. length stay diagn. U. S. west. reg.]. **VFOAT** LOS. (1986)-. English. an. $85.00 (per volume). Healthcare Knowledge Systems Publications, 1968 Green Road, Box 1809, Ann Arbor MI 48106. **Tel** (800)521-6210. **LC** RC445.W36; P89. **DD** 362.2/1/0978021. **Ad Acc.**

US/0270-8973
**PUBLIC SECTOR HEALTH CARE RISK MANAGEMENT.** ***Title Change.*** **VFOAT** Health Care Risk Management. (June 1980)-?. Periodical. English. mo. Cox Publications, PO Box 20316, Billings MT 59104-0316. **Tel** (406)256-8822. **ED** Meridith B Cox. **NLM** W1 PU638F. Index available. **Circ:** 425. ***Continued by*** *Health Insurance/Medical Records Risk Management Reporter, 0883-6671.*
**Desc:** Designed for health care professionals, risk managers and others dealing with complex health care issues in the public sector.
**Ind/Abst** Hospit. Health Admin. Index.

US/0569-5090
**PUBLICATIONS CATALOG - AMERICAN HOSPITAL ASSOCIATION.** (PUBLICATIONS CATALOG.). [Publ. cat. - Am. Hosp. Assoc.]. **Main/Corp** American Hospital Association. (19??)-. Catalog. English. an. $40.00 student member; $75.00 (individuals) Food Service Management employed by an member institutions of AHA; $105.00 (individuals) Food Service Management employed by an non-member institutions of AHA; $200.00 Chief Executive Officer non-member institutions retired active member; Includes Hospital Food Service AHA Publications Catalog. American Society Hospital Food Service Administration, 840 North Lakeshore Drive, Chicago IL 60611. **Tel** (312)280-6029.

US/0097-5990
**QRB. QUALITY REVIEW BULLETIN.** ***Title Change.*** [QRB, Qual. rev. bull.]. **Added/Corp** Joint Commission on Accreditation of Hospitals. Quality Review Center. **VFOAT** Quality Review Bulletin. Vol. 1 (Sept. 1974)-(19??). Academic Scholarly Publication. English. mo. Mosby Year Book Inc., 11830 Westline Industrial Drive, St Louis MO 63146. **Tel** (800)325-4177, (314)872-8370, FAX (314)432-1380, telex 44-2402. **NLM** W1 Q65. **Pr Rev.** available in microform from University Microfilms International (UMI). ***Continued by*** *Joint Commission Journal on Quality Improvement, 1070-3241.*
**Ind/Abst** Abstr. Clin. Care Guidel.; Cumul. Index Nurs. Allied Health Lit.; EMBASE; Health Plan. Adminis.; Health Serv. Abstr.; High. Educ. Abstr.; Hospit. Health Admin. Index; Hospit. Manage. Rev.; Index Med.; Int. Pharm. Abstr.; Nurs. Abstr.; Physic. Medline Plus; Soc. Plann. Policy Dev. Abstr.; Soc. Work Abstr. [Select. Cov.].

US/0747-7384
**QRC ADVISOR.** [QRC advis.]. **VFOAT** Q.R.C. Advisor. **VAT** Quality, Risk, Cost Advisor. Vol. 1, No. 1 (May 1984)-. Periodical. English. mo. $199.00 US and Canada. Aspen Publishers Inc., 7201 McKinney Circle, Frederick MD 21701. **Tel** (800)234-1660, (301)698-7100, FAX (301)251-5784, telex 5106014543. **(Subscription address:** Aspen Publishers Inc., PO Box 990, Frederick MD 21701.) **ED** Julie L. Hopkins, MA, MBA. **DD** 362. **NLM** W1; Q67.
**Desc:** Offers sound, authoritative, state-of-the-art for effectively handling your official quality assurance, risk management and cost control issues. Each issue is brimming with the valuable insights of seasoned professionals in the field.
**Ind/Abst** Health Plan. Adminis.; Hospit. Health Admin. Index (Nov. 1988-).

IT/1120-7906
**QTGO. QUADERNI DI TECNICA E GESTIONE OSPEDALIERA.** ***Ceased.*** [QTGO, Quad. tec. gest. osp.]. **VFOAT** Quaderni di Tecnica e Gestione Ospedaliera. (1991)-(Dec. 1993). Periodical. Italian. qt. Il Pensiero Scientifico Editore s.r.l., Via Bradano 3C, 00199 Rome Italy. **Tel** 011 39 6 86207158, 86207159, 86207168, 86207169, FAX 011 39 6 86207160. **UDC** 61. **Bk Rev. Ad Acc, Adv Mgr:** Dott Dalla, **Tel** 06-86207165. **Circ:** 500.

US/1047-5311
**QUALITY LETTER FOR HEALTHCARE LEADERS, THE.** [Qual. lett. healthc. lead.]. **VFOAT** Quality Letter. (1989)-. Periodical. English. Ten times a year. $279.00. Bader & Associates Inc, PO Box 2106, Rockville MD 20847. **Tel** (301)468-1610, FAX (301)770-4919. **ED** Reggi Veatch. **DD** 362. **NLM** W1; QU158LA. ctrl circ.
**Ind/Abst** Hospit. Manage. Rev. (19??-).

●US/1063-8628
**QUALITY MANAGEMENT IN HEALTH CARE.** **See** Business-General Management.

US
**QUALITY MANAGEMENT UPDATE.** **See** Medical Science and Technology.

SP
**RAMON Y CAJAL. REVISTA MEDICA DEL HOSPITAL RAMON Y CAJAL.**
Spanish. Etxegaray SA, Conde de Aranda 10, 28024 Madrid Spain.

US/1060-0418
**RECEIVABLES REPORT, THE.** **See** Business-Banking and Finance.

US/0034-317X
**REGAN REPORT ON HOSPITAL LAW, THE.** **See** Law.

●US/1062-7340
**REGISTER OF NORTH AMERICAN HOSPITALS.** (1992)-. Periodical. English. $78.95. American Preeminent Registry, 510 Oldbridge Turnpike, South River NJ 08882. **NLM** WX 22; AA1 R34r.

US/1043-2752
**REGULATORY AFFAIRS.** [Regul. aff.]. **Added/Corp** Regulatory Affairs Professionals Society. (Spring 1989)-. Periodical. English. Four times a year. $120.00 (institution) US and Canada. Regulatory Affairs Professional Society, 12300 Twinbrook Parkway, Suite 630, Rockville MD 20852. **Tel** (301)770-2920, FAX (301)770-2924. **ED** Margaret Deegan. **LC** K18; .E64. **DD** 344.73/041; 347.30441. **NLM** W1; RE173JE. **Pr Rev.** ctrl circ.
**Desc:** Provides a worldwide forum for communication, education, and development for health care regulatory professionals in industry and government. It publishes scholarly articles on matters relating to pharmaceutical, medical device, food and cosmetic products, and the related products of biotechnology and radiological health.

US/1054-2280
**REHABILITATION TODAY.** [Rehab. today]. Vol. 1, Issue 1 (Jan. 1991)-. Periodical. English. mo. $65.00 (one year), $120.00 (two year). Club Industry and Rehabilitation Today, 101 Witmer Road, Horsham PA 19044. **Tel** (215)957-4260. **LC** RM735.A1; R44. **DD** 362.1/786/05.

US/0884-2795
**REIMBURSEMENT ADVISOR.** [Reimburse. advis.]. Vol. 1, No. 1 (Sept. 1985)-. Periodical. English. mo. $220.00 US and Canada. Aspen Publishers Inc., 7201 McKinney Circle, Frederick MD 21701. **Tel** (800)234-1660, (301)698-7100, FAX (301)251-5784, telex 5106014543. **(Subscription address:** Aspen Publishers Inc., PO Box 990, Frederick MD 21701.**) ED** Dennis Barry, Esq. **DD** 362.
**Desc:** Offers strategies to minimize the adverse effects of DRGs and to maximize your hospital's reimbursement.

CN/1181-8824
**RELIEF (MONTREAL).** (LE RELIEF / CENTRE HOSPITALIER NOTRE-DAME-DE-LA-MERCI.). [Relief]. **Added/Corp** Centre Hospitalier Notre-Dame-de-la-Merci. Vol. 1, No 1 (Dec. 1990)-. Periodical. French. qt. Limited free distribution. Centre Hospitalier Notre-Dame-de-la-Merci, 555 Ouest Boulevard Gouin, Montreal, Quebec H3L 1K5 Canada. **DD** 362.1/1/097142805.

US/0045-7590
**REPORT - COMMISSION ON ACCREDITATION OF REHABILITATION FACILITIES.** **Added/Corp** Commission on Accreditation of Rehabilitation Facilities (U.S.). **VFOAT** CARF Report. (June 1968)-. Periodical. English. Commission on Accreditation of Rehabilitation Facilities, 6610 North Clark, Chicago IL 60626. **NLM** W1 RE209AN.
**Desc:** Each issue contains a revised list called Accredited Rehabilitation Facilities.
**Ind/Abst** Hospit. Health Admin. Index (1978-1984).

NZ/0110-6929
**REPORT - HOSPITAL DESIGN AND EVALUATION UNIT, DEPARTMENT OF HEALTH.** (REPORT - HOSPITAL DESIGN AND EVALUATION UNIT, DEPARTMENT OF HEALTH, NEW ZEALAND.). [Rep. - Hosp. Des. Eval. Unit, Dep. Health]. **Added/Corp** New Zealand. Hospital Design and Evaluation Unit. No. 1, (1972)-. Monographic series. English. ir. Price varies per volume. **NLM** W1 RE209CJ.

US/0147-2607
**REPORT OF THE MISSISSIPPI STATE HOSPITAL COMMISSION.** **Main/Corp** Mississippi. State Hospital Commission. (1970)-. English. an. Mississippi State University / State Hospital Commission, Mississippi State MS 39762. **LC** RA981.M7; M57a. **DD** 338.4/3. ***Continues*** *Biennial Report of the Mississippi State Hospital Commission.*

US
**REPORT OF THE OHIO NURSING HOME COMMISSION TO THE GOVERNOR AND OHIO GENERAL ASSEMBLY.** **Main/Corp** Ohio Nursing Home Commission. 1978-. English. an. Ohio Nursing Home Commission, Statehouse, Columbus OH 43210. **LC** RA997.5.O3; O38A. **DD** 362.1/6/09771.

●US/1071-006X
**REPORT ON HEALTHCARE INFORMATION MANAGEMNET.** (1993)-. Periodical. English. mo. $325.00. Capitol Publications, 1101 King Street, Suite 444, Alexandria VA 22314. **Tel** (703)683-4100, (800)655-5597. **(Subscription address:** Capitol Publications, PO Box 1453, Alexandria, VA 22313)

CN/0384-0883
**REPORTS - BRITISH COLUMBIA ASSOCIATION OF HOSPITALS AND HEALTH ORGANIZATIONS.** **Main/Corp** British Columbia Association of Hospitals and Health Organizations. (1973/1974)-. English. an. British Columbia Association of Hospitals and Health Organizations, 440 Cambie Street, Vancouver British Columbia V6B 2N6 Canada. **DD** 362.1/06/2711.

AT
**RETIREMENT INDUSTRY JOURNAL, THE.** **See** Senior Citizens.

CN/0226-5931
**REVUE A. C. C. S.** [Rev. A.C.C.S.]. **Main/Corp** Association Catholique Canadienne de la Sante. **VAT** Revue Association Catholique Canadienne de la Sante. Vol. 8, No 1 (Jan./Feb. 1980)-. Periodical. French. Three times a year. 30.00Can$ Canada; 35.00Can$ other. Catholic Health Association of Canada, 1247 Killborn Place, Ottawa Ontario K1H 6K9 Canada. **Tel** (613)731-7148, FAX (613)731-7797. **ED** Freda Fraser. **DD** 362.1/1/0971. Index available. **Ad Acc, Adv Mgr:** Martine Leroux. **Circ:** 500 (ctrl). ***Continues*** *Hopital Catholique, 0315-4858.* ***Continued in part by*** *Info ACCS., 0822-8426.*

FR/0397-4626
**REVUE HOSPITALIERE DE FRANCE.** [Rev. hosp. Fr.]. (1936)-. Academic Scholarly Publication. French. ir. price varies per volume. Revue Hospitaliere de France, 33 A 87 Avenue d'Italie, 75013 Paris France. **Tel** 011 33 1 44068444. **NLM** W1 RE865. ctrl circ.
**Desc:** Hospital science in France.
**Ind/Abst** EMBASE; Saf. Health Work.

IT
**RIVISTA DELL'INFERMIERE.** (198?)-. Periodical. Italian (summaries and/or abstracts in English and Italian). Four times a year. L60000 individuals; L70000 institutions. Il Pensiero Scientifico Editore s.r.l., Via Bradano 3C, 00199 Rome Italy. **Tel** 011 39 6 86207158, 86207159, 86207168, 86207169, FAX 011 39 6 86207160. **ED** Paola Di Giulio. **NLM** W1; RE5149N. **Bk Rev. Ad Acc, Adv Mgr:** Dott Dalla, **Tel** 06-86207165. Full Page (B&W) L1.650.000. **Circ:** 3,200.

CN/0847-1398
**RRM REPORT.** [RRM rep.]. **VFOAT** Rozovsky Risk Management Report. Vol. 1, No. 1 (Apr. 1989)-. Periodical. English. mo. $150.00 per year. Lefar Health Associates, PO Box 308 Station M, Halifax NS B3J 2N7 Canada. **Tel** (902)420-1321. **DD** 346.03/32/05.

●US/1063-9004
**SATISFACTION (EVANS, GA.).** (SATISFACTION : HOSPITAL EXECUTIVE FORUM.). [Satisfaction]. Vol. 1, No. 1 (Oct. 1992)-. Periodical. English. mo. $118.00. ScanEx, 4771 Bass Drive, Evans GA 30809. **DD** 362.

SZ/0304-4432
**SCHWEIZER SPITAL.** [Schweiz. Spital]. **Added/Corp** Vereinigung Schweizerischer Krankenhauser. **VFOAT** Hopital Suisse; Ospedale Svizzero. 44. Vol. (1980/1)-. Academic Scholarly Publication. French (German). mo (12 issues). 80.00 Italy, Yugoslavia, Luxembourg, Malta, Netherlands, Norway, Austria, Portugal, Sweden, Spain, Turkey and Cypress; 90.00F Egypt, Albania, Algeria, Belgium, Bulgaria, Gibraltar, UK, Ireland, Israel, Jordan, Lebanon, Libya, Marocco, Marino, Syria, USSR, Czechoslovakia, Tunisia, Hungary, Vatican; 100.00F other. Verlag Schweizer Spital, Postfach 4202, Rain 32, CH-5001 Aarau Switzerland. **Tel** 064 24 12 22, FAX 064 22 33 35. **NLM** W1; SC399. Index available. **Bk Rev. Ad Acc. Circ:** 3,000. ***Continues*** *Veska.*
**Desc:** Management in health care hospitals.
**Ind/Abst** EMBASE.

FR/0037-1777
**SEMAINE DES HOPITAUX.** (LA SEMAINE DES HOPITAUX DE PARIS.). [Sem. hop.]. **Added/Corp** Association d'Enseignement Medical des Hopitaux. College de Medecine des Hopitaux de Paris. **VFOAT** La Semaine des Hopitaux. Vol. 1 (Jan. 2, 1925)-. Academic Scholarly Publication. French (English). ir (44 issues). 1770.00F France, 2270.00F other (institutions). Semaine de Hopitaux, 31 Boulevard de la Tour-Maubourg, 75007 Paris, France. **Tel** 011 33 1 40 62 64 00. **ED** L. Justin Besancon. **NLM** W1 SE39. **CODEN** SHPAAI. **Pr Rev.** Documents available from The Genuine Article, BIOSIS Document Express, CASDDS.
**Ind/Abst** Biol. Abstr.; Bull. Signal.; Chem. Abstr.; CIS Abstr.; EMBASE [Select. Cov.]; Energy Res. Abstr.; Helminthol. Abstr. (1991-); Index Med.; Nutr. Abstr. Rev., Ser. A, Hum. Exp.; Life Sci. Collect.; PESTDOC; Protozoolog. Abstr.; Res. Alert [Select. Cov.]; Rev. Med. Vet. Entomol.; Saf. Health Work; Soc. Sci. Cit. Index [Select. Cov.]; SportSearch.

FR/0302-9271
**SEMAINE DES HOPITAUX. THERAPEUTIQUE.** (LA SEMAINE DES HOPITAUX. THERAPEUTIQUE.). **Added/Corp** College de Medecine des Hopitaux de Paris. (Jan. 1973)-. Periodical. French. ir. Expansion Scientifique Francaise, 31 Boulevard de la Tour-Maubourg, 75007 Paris France. **Tel** 011 33 1 40 62 64 00, 011 33 1 40626439. **NLM** W1 SE416D. ***Continues*** *Therapeutique.*
**Ind/Abst** Curr. Contents Clin. Med.

US
**SMG MARKET LETTER.** English. mo. $150.00. SMG Marketing Group, 1342 North LaSalle Drive, Chicago IL 60610. **Tel** (312)642-3026.
**Ind/Abst** Hospit. Manage. Rev. (19??-).

US/1059-5023
**SOLUTIONS FOR LONG-TERM CARE ADMINISTRATION.** [Solut. long-term care adm.]. **VFOAT** Solutions for Long Term Care Administration; Solutions. (1991)-. Periodical. English. mo. $125.00. National Health Publishing, 428 East Preston Street, Baltimore MD 21202-3923. **Tel** (301)363-6400. **DD** 362. **NLM** W1; SO887JD.

US/0038-4178
**SOUTHERN HOSPITALS.** ***Ceased.*** [South. hosp.]. (1942)-(19??). Periodical. English. bm. Billan Publishing Company, 2100 Powers Ferry Road, Atlanta GA 30339. **Tel** (404)955-5656, FAX (404)952-0669. **ED** Angela Counts. **DD** 658. **NLM** W1 SO953E. **Bk Rev. Ad Acc. Circ:** 16,435 (ctrl). ***Continues*** *Southern Hospital.*
**Desc:** Addresses the unique needs, concerns, opportunities and news makers of health care in the 16 state sun belt region. News, information, techniques and strategies for administrators, professional and service department heads. Presents timely profiles, surveys and news articles on people and events of the south that are shaping the future of health care. Impact of national issues on the south are also examined.
**Ind/Abst** Cumul. Index Nurs. Allied Health Lit.; Health Plan. Adminis.; Hospit. Health Admin. Index.

US/1064-4636
**SRDS MEDIA & MARKET PLANNER. HEALTHCARE MARKETS.** ***Title Change.*** **See** Business-Advertising and Public Relations.

UK/0263-3507
**ST. THOMAS'S HOSPITAL GAZETTE (1981).** (ST. THOMAS'S HOSPITAL GAZETTE.). **Added/Corp** St. Thomas's Hospital (London, England). **VFOAT** Saint Thomas's Hospital Gazette. Vol. 78, No. 3 (Winter 1980)-. Periodical. English. Three times a year. $25.00. St Thomas Hospital Medical School, c/o Medical School Library/MS Bonner, London SE1 7EH England. **Tel** 11 44 71 9289292 Ext. 2367. **ED** D O'Regan. **NLM** W1 ST121. **Bk Rev. Ad Acc. Circ:** 700 (ctrl). ***Continues*** *STH Gazette.*
**Desc:** Articles on medical education, history of medicine relating particularly to St. Thomas Hospital and medical school.

US/0162-2374
**STATE MENTAL HOSPITALS.** OMH 1.13-1971-. English. an. Department of Public Welfare / Pennsylvania, Harrisburg PA 17120. **NLM** W2 AP4 O3S. ***Continues*** *State Mental Hospital Patients.*

US/0081-2692
**STATE PLAN FOR CONSTRUCTION AND MODERNIZATION OF HOSPITAL AND MEDICAL FACILITIES (COLUMBIA).** (SOUTH CAROLINA STATE PLAN FOR CONSTRUCTION AND MODERNIZATION OF HOSPITAL AND MEDICAL FACILITIES.). **Main/Corp** South Carolina State Board of Health. 1965/66-. English. an. South Carolina State Plan, Hospital and Medical Facilities Construction, 725-PL, 482 with Amendments, Columbia SC. **LC** RA981.S6; A3. **DD** 362.1/1/09757. **NLM** W2 AS6 S7S. ***Continues*** *South Carolina State Plan: Hospital and Medical Facilities Construction Program, P. L. 725-P. L. 482 with Amendments.*

US/0091-1585
**STATE PLAN FOR HOSPITAL AND MEDICAL FACILITIES CONSTRUCTION.** [State plan hosp. med. facil. constr.]. **Main/Corp** North Dakota. State Dept. of Health. (19??)-. Periodical. English. North Dakota State Department of Health & Consolidated Laboratories, 600 East Boulevard Avenue, Bismarck ND 58505. **Tel** (701)224-2372, FAX (701)224-3000. **LC** RA981.N85; N67a. **DD** 362.1/09784.

US/0098-8057
**STATISTICAL REPORT - LOUISIANA, HEALTH AND SOCIAL AND REHABILITATION SERVICES ADMINISTRATION (ANNUAL).** **See** Medical Science and Technology-Abstracting, Bibliographies and Statistics.

CN/0524-5354
**STATISTICS OF HOSPITAL CASES DISCHARGED. BRITISH COLUMBIA.** **See** Medical Science and Technology-Abstracting, Bibliographies and Statistics.

CN/0524-5451
**STATISTICS OF HOSPITALIZED ACCIDENTS : BRITISH COLUMBIA.** **See** Medical Science and Technology-Abstracting, Bibliographies and Statistics.

US/0749-5153
**STRATEGIC HEALTH CARE MARKETING.** [Strateg. health care mark.]. Vol. 1, No. 1 (Oct. 1984)-. Periodical. English. mo. $229.00 US; $239.00 Canada; $254.00 other. Health Care Communications, 211 Midland Avenue, PO Box 594, Rye NY 10580. **Tel** (914)967-6741. **ED** Michele von Dambrowski. **DD** 362. **[CCC].** Index available. **Bk Rev.**
**Desc:** Newsletter includes marketing news, case histories and applications in hospitals, group practices, HMOS and other settings.

US/1058-7829
**STRATEGIES FOR HEALTHCARE EXCELLENCE.** (STRATEGIES FOR HEALTHCARE EXCELLENCE : ORGANIZATIONAL PRODUCTIVITY, QUALITY AND EFFECTIVENESS.). [Strateg. healthc. excell.]. (19??)-. Periodical. English. mo. $197.00 (one year), $344.00 (two year) US and Canada; $209.00 (one year) other. COR Healthcare Resources, (A Division of COR Research Inc.), PO Box 40959, Santa Barbara CA 93140. **Tel** (805)564-2177, FAX (805)564-2146. **DD** 362. **NLM** W1; ST788. **[CCC].** ***Continues*** *Healthcare Productivity Report, 1043-1306.*
**Ind/Abst** Hospit. Health Admin. Index (Jan. 1992-); Hospit. Manage. Rev. (19??-).

US/0039-6109
**SURGICAL CLINICS OF NORTH AMERICA, THE.** **See** Medical Science and Technology-Surgery.

US
**TACTICS.** English. Twelve times a year. $40.00. Chicago Hospital Risk Pooling Program, 222 South Riverside Plaza, Chicago IL 60606. **Tel** (312)906-6000.

IT/0392-4831
**TECNICA OSPEDALIERA MILANO.** [Tec. osp.Milano]. (1971)-. Periodical. Italian. mo. L85000.00 Italy; L150000.00 Europe except Italy; L210000.00 other. Tecniche Nuove SPA, Via Ciro Menotti 14, 20129 Milan Italy. **Tel** 011 39 2 75701, FAX 011 39 2 7610351, telex 334647 TECHS I. **UDC** 362.

IT
**TECNOLOGIE BIOMEDICHE.** Italian. Twice a year. L100000 Italy; L120000 Europe; L135000 other. Edizioni Protezione Civile SPA, Via dell Acqua Traversa 187/189, 00135 Rome Italy. **Tel** 011 39 6 3313000, FAX 011 39 6 3313212, telex 626462 EPCINFI. Index available. cum. index. **Circ:** 5,000. ***Continues*** *Elettromedicali.*

DK/0040-702X
**TIDSSKRIFT FOR DANSKE SYGEHUSE.** [Tidsskr. dan. sygehuse]. **Added/Corp** Sygehusinspektrforeningen i Danmark. Central-arkiv for Danske sygehuse. Foreningen af Sygehusadministratorer i Danmark. (1925)-. Periodical. Danish. mo. Kr740.00. Forlaget John Vabo, Hartmannsvej 47-49, 2920 Charlottenlund Denmark. **Tel** 011 45 1 38338000, FAX 011 45 2 383382. **NLM** W1; TI105. ***Continues*** *Samvirke.*

●NE/0928-2998
**TIJDSCHRIFT VOOR HYGIENE EN INFEKTIEPREVENTIE.** [Tijdschr. hyg. infekt.prev.]. **VFOAT** ZIP. (1992)-. Periodical. Dutch. bm. Fl48.00. Mevr Gerritsen, Tijdsch Zip Kennedy Straat 4A, 6921 CW Duiven The Netherlands. **Tel** 011 31 8367 63743. **UDC** 616.9 :613. ***Continues*** *Ziekenhuishygiene en Infektiepreventie, 0168-6976.*

US/1054-5204
**TODAY'S HEALTHCARE MANAGER.** [Today's healthc. manager]. **VFOAT** Today's Health Care Manager. Vol. 1, No. 1 (Jan. 1991)-. Periodical. English. bm (Jan., Mar., May, July, Sept., Nov.). $47.00. Management Transformation Inc, PO Box 5225, Englewood CO 80155-5225. **ED** John F. Talbot (phone: (303)220-8351). **DD** 363. **Bk Rev**, (Qty: 4-6). **Circ:** 750 (ctrl).
**Desc:** Provides information relevant to healthcare management and and synopses of articles, interviews and book reviews.

SP
**TODO HOSPITAL.** (Nov./Dec. 1982)-. Periodical. Spanish (summaries and/or abstracts in English, French and German). Ten times a year. 8050ptas Spain; 10000ptas other Europe; 11000ptas other. Puntex SA, Via Laietana 30 4 F, 08003 Barcelona Spain. **Tel** 011 34 3 2680444. **NLM** W1; TO172T. ***Continues*** *Estudios Sobre Hospitales.*
**Ind/Abst** Indice Med. Esp.

US/0095-3814
**TOPICS IN HEALTH CARE FINANCING.** ***Title Change.*** **See** Business-Banking and Finance.

US/0270-5230
**TOPICS IN HEALTH INFORMATION MANAGEMENT.** ***Title Change.*** [Top. health rec. manage.]. **Added/Corp** Aspen Systems Corporation. **VFOAT** THRM. (1980-1992). Periodical. English. qt. Aspen Publishers Inc., 7201 McKinney Circle, Frederick MD 21701. **Tel** (800)234-1660, (301)698-7100, FAX (301)251-5784, telex 5106014543. **ED** Melanie M Brodnik. **DD** 651. **NLM** W1; TO539MP. **[CCC]. Bk Rev. Pr Rev. Circ:** 3,581. available on microfilm and microfiche from University Microfilms International (UMI). ***Continued by*** *Topics in Health Information Management, 1065-0989.*
**Desc:** Covers every area of the fast-changing field of medical records fully and authoritatively, with informative, indepth articles by nationally recognized leaders.
**Ind/Abst** Cumul. Index Nurs. Allied Health Lit.; Health Plan. Adminis.; Hospit. Health Admin. Index.

US/0041-3674
**TRUSTEE.** [Trustee]. **Added/Corp** American Hospital Association. Vol. 1 (Oct. 1947)-. Periodical. English. mo. $25.00 US; $40.00 other. American Hospital Publishing Inc., (A Subsidiary of the American Hospital Association), PO Box 92683, Chicago IL 60675. **Tel** (312)440-6836, (800)621-6902, FAX (312)951-8491. **LC** RA960; .A513. **DD** 362.11. **NLM** W1 TR985. **CODEN** TRSTB. available on microfilm and microfiche from University Microfilms International (UMI); available on an online database (file 15/Full-Text) from DIALOG. Documents available from UMI Article Clearinghouse.
**Ind/Abst** ABI/INFORM Glob. Ed.; ABI Inform Ondisc (Jan. 1988-); Health Plan. Adminis.; Hospit. Health Admin. Index; Hospit. Manage. Rev.; Int. Nurs. Index; Int. Pharm. Abstr.; UMI ABI/Inform--Bus. Period. Ondisc (Jan. 1988-) [Full Txt.].

US/0095-1129
**TUBERCULOSIS BEDS IN HOSPITALS.** **See** Medical Science and Technology-Respiratory System.

US/0091-8393
**U.S. MEDICAL DIRECTORY.** **Added/Corp** U.S. Directory Service. (1972)-. Directory. English. ir. $150.00. Reed Reference Publishing, 121 Chanlon Road, New Providence NJ 07974. **Tel** (908)464-6800, (800)521-8110 Ext. 3387, (800)223-1797, FAX (908)665-3560. **LC** R712.A1; U5. **DD** 610/.25/73. **NLM** W 22 AA1 U57.
**Desc:** Provides information on thousands of medical doctors, hospitals, nursing facilities, laboratories, medical information sources, poison control centers, and U.S. medical schools.

US/1059-6100
**UNIQUE OPPORTUNITIES.** (UNIQUE OPPORTUNITIES : UO : THE MAGAZINE FOR PHYSICIAN RECRUITMENT). [Unique oppor.]. **VFOAT** UO. Vol. 1, No. 1 (Nov./Dec. 1991)-. Periodical. English. bm. $30.00. Unique Opportunities Inc., 455 South 4th Avenue, Louisville KY 40202. **DD** 362.
**Desc:** An independent, full-color, national magazine offering professional guidance to physicians, enabling them to make informed decisions concerning practice opportunities. Extensive editorial provides physician perspectives and in-depth, timely information about all aspects of the search process. Physicians may utilize a convenient business-reply card to request information on specific opportunities.

●US
**UPMC FORUM / UNIVERSITY OF PITTSBURGH MEDICAL CENTER.** **Added/Corp** University of Pittsburgh. Medical Center. **VFOAT** Forum. Vol. 3, No. 1 (February/March 1992)-. Periodical. English. bm.

US/0748-5816
**UTILIZATION OF SHORT-TERM GENERAL AND SPECIALTY HOSPITALS IN METROPOLITAN CHICAGO FOR THE ... QUARTER OF ... .** [Util. short-term gen. spec. hosp. metrop. Chic. quart.]. **VFOAT** C.H.C. Utilization Report, Metro Chicago; CHC Utilization Report, Metro Chicago. English. qt. Chicago Hospital Council, 840 North Lake Shore Drive, Chicago IL 60611. **LC** RA982.C45; U85. **DD** 362.1/1/0977311.

US/0882-6943
**UTILIZATION OF SHORT-TERM GENERAL AND SPECIALTY HOSPITALS IN METROPOLITAN CHICAGO FOR THE YEAR ENDING DECEMBER 31 ... .** 1982-. English. an. Chicago Hospital Council, 840 North Lake Shore Drive, Chicago IL 60611. **LC** RA982.C45; U86. **DD** 362.1/0977311021.

US/0883-5721
**VA PRACTITIONER.** (VA PRACTITIONER : THE MAGAZINE FOR PHYSICIANS AND PHARMACISTS OF THE VETERANS ADMINISTRATION.). [VA pract.]. **VAT** Veterans Administration Practitioner. Vol. 1, No. 1 (Jan. 1984)-. Periodical. English. mo. $70.00 (institutions), $55.00 (individuals). Excerpta Medica / US, PO Box 3085, Princeton NJ 08543-3085. **Tel** (908)874-8550, FAX (908)874-5611. **(Subscription address:** VA Practitioner, PO Box 10500, Riverton NJ 07076.**)** **DD** 610. **NLM** W1; VA12. available on microfilm and microfiche from University Microfilms International (UMI).
**Desc:** A journal specifically geared to the needs of the health care professional working in the Veterans Administration medical system.

DK/0903-8086
**VIRKSOMHEDEN VED SYGEHUSE ... / SUNDHEDSSTYRELSEN.** **Added/Corp** Denmark. Sundhedsstyrelsen. (1986)-. Danish. **LC** RA989.D4; V57.

US/0889-3543
**VOICE (FRANKLIN, WIS.), THE.** (THE VOICE / WISCONSIN MEDICAL CREDIT ASSOCIATION.). [Voice]. **Added/Corp** Wisconsin Medical Credit Association. **VFOAT** WMCA Voice. (196?)-. Periodical. English. Six times a year (Feb., April, June, Aug., Oct., Dec.). $50.00. Wisconsin Medical Credit Association, c/o Reedsburg Memorial Hospital, 2000 North Dewey, Reedsburg WI 53959. **Tel** (608)524-6487. **ED** Dennis Schommer. **DD** 338. **Ad Acc. Circ:** 500 (ctrl).

US/0005-1861
**VOLUNTEER LEADER, THE.** [Volunt. lead.]. **Added/Corp** American Hospital Association. Vol. 10, (1969)-. Periodical. English. qt. $8.00 US; $12.00 other. American Hospital Publishing Inc., (A Subsidiary of the American Hospital Association), PO Box 92683, Chicago IL 60675. **Tel** (312)440-6836, (800)621-6902, FAX (312)951-8491. **NLM** W1 VO597K. available on microfilm and microfiche from University Microfilms International (UMI). ***Continues*** *Auxiliary Leader.*
**Ind/Abst** Health Plan. Adminis.; Hospit. Health Admin. Index.

US
**VOLUNTEER NEWSPAPER / CALIFORNIA HOSPITAL ASSOCIATION, DIVISION OF VOLUNTEER SERVICES.** Periodical. English. qt. California Association of Hospitals and Health Systems, PO Box 1100, Sacramento CA 95812. **Tel** (916)443-7401.

US/0091-7311
**WASHINGTON REPORT ON LONG TERM CARE.** Periodical. English. sm. $287.00. McGraw Hill Publishing Company, Inc., 1221 Avenue of the Americas, New York NY 10020. **Tel** (212)512-6410, (800)525-5003, FAX (212)512-6111. **ED** Donna M Jablonski. **NLM** W1 WA619L. **Bk Rev.**
**Desc:** Congressional, administration, state, legal, and business developments affecting long term health care.

UK/0266-0776
**WELSH HOSPITAL WAITING LIST BULLETIN / WELSH OFFICE / BWLETIN RHESTR AROS YSBYTAI CYMRU / Y SWYDDFA GYMREIG.** **Added/Corp** Great Britain. Welsh Office. **VFOAT** Bwletin Rhestr Aros Ysbytai Cymru. No. 1 (1984)-. Bulletin. English. sa. Welsh Office Publications Unit, Crown Building, Cathay's Park, Cardiff CF1 3NQ Wales. **Tel** 011 44 222 825111. **LC** RA987.W2; W44. **DD** 362.1/1/09429021.

US/8755-1519
**WISCONSIN MEDICAL ALUMNI QUARTERLY.** **See** College and School Publications-Alumni.

UK/0512-3135
**WORLD HOSPITALS.** [World hosp.]. **Added/Corp** International Hospital Federation. **VFOAT** Hopital dans le Monde. Vol. 1 July (1964)-. Academic Scholarly Publication. English (summaries and/or abstracts in French and Spanish). tq. £59.00. International Hospital Federation, 4 Abbots Place, London NW6 4NP England. **Tel** 011 44 71 372-7181, FAX 011 44 71 328-7433. **ED** Errol Pickering. **NLM** W1 WO88C. cum. index. **Bk Rev. Ad Acc. Circ:** 2,500. available on microfilm and microfiche from University Microfilms International (UMI).
**Desc:** Contains reprints of health care articles from around the world, interviews with prominent health professionals, reports on major speeches and book

review reviews.
**Ind/Abst** Appl. Soc. Sci. Index Abstr.; Archit. Period. Index; Cumul. Index Nurs. Allied Health Lit.; EMBASE; Health Plan. Adminis.; Hospit. Health Admin. Index; Int. Pharm. Abstr.

KO
**YONBO. Main/Corp** Soul Choksipcha Pyongwon. **VFOAT** Annual Report; Soul Choksipcha Pyongwon Yonbo. V. 1- (1981)-. Korean (English). an. Soul Choksipcha Pyongwon, 32 3-ka Namsan-dong, Chung-ku, Seoul South Korea. **LC** RA990.K64; S477A.

NE/0044-4715
**ZIEKENHUIS, HET.** [Het Ziekenh.]. **Added/Corp** Nationale Ziekenhuisraad (Netherlands). Vol. 1 (1971)-. Periodical. Dutch. Twenty-four times a year. Fl155.66 Netherlands; Fl167.77 Belgium; Fl212.26 others. Misset Uitgeverij, Postbus 1110, 3600 BC Maarssen Netherlands. **Tel** 011 31 3465 58222. **NLM** W1 ZI431H. Index available. **Bk Rev**. **Ad Acc**.
**Desc:** Journal for managers in the health care field.
**Ind/Abst** EMBASE.

NE
**ZIEKENHUIS MANAGEMENT MAGAZINE.** WYT Uitgeefgrouep, Postbus 6438, 3000 AG Rotterdam Netherlands. **Tel** 011 31 10 4762566, 4255944.

NE/0169-2720
**ZIEKENHUISFARMACIE. See** Pharmacy and Pharmacology.

NE/0168-6976
**ZIEKENHUISHYGIENE EN INFEKTIEPREVENTIE.** ***Title Change.*** [Ziekenh.hyg. infekt.prev.]. **VFOAT** ZIP. (1982)-(1992). Periodical. Dutch. bm. Mevr Gerritsen, Tijdsch Zip Kennedy Straat 4A, 6921 CW Duiven The Netherlands. **Tel** 011 31 8367 63743. **UDC** 616.9 :613. ***Continued by*** *Tijdschrift voor Hygiene en Infektiepreventie, 0928-2998.*

## INTERNAL MEDICINE

US/0884-6448
**ABMS DIRECTORY OF CERTIFIED INTERNISTS. VFOAT** Directory of Certified Internists. 1985-. Directory. English. be. $59.95. American Board of Medical Specialties, 1 Rotary Center, Suite 805, Evanston IL 60201. **Tel** (708)491-9091. **LC** R712.A1. **DD** 616/.002573. **UDC** 616-051. **NLM** W 22.1; A15234.

US/1056-8751
**ACP JOURNAL CLUB.** [ACP j. club]. **Added/Corp** American College of Physicians. **VAT** American College of Physicians Journal Club. Vol. 114, Supplement 1 (Jan./Feb. 1991)-. Periodical. English. bm. $50.00. American College of Physicians, 6th Street and Race Street, Independence Mall West, Philadelphia PA 19106-1572. **Tel** (215)351-2600, (800)523-1546. **(Subscription address:** American College of Physicians, PO Box 7777 R 0320, Philadelphia PA 19175.**) DD** 616. **NLM** ZW 1; A185. **CODEN** AIMEAS.

FR/0240-642X
**ACTA ENDOSCOPICA.** [Acta endosc.]. **Added/Corp** Societe Medicale Internationale d'Endoscopie et de Radio-Cinema. Societe Nationale Francaise d'Endoscopie Digestive. Sociedad Colombiana de Endoscopia Digestiva. Societe Belge d'Endoscopie Digestive. Societa Italiana di Endoscopia Digestiva. Vol. 8 (1978)-. Periodical. English (French and Spanish). bm. 675.81F France; 885.00F US; 930.00F other. Endoscopica, 127 rue St Dizier, 54000 Nancy France. **Tel** 011 33 83 374438, FAX 8335.34.53. **ED** F. Vicari. **NLM** W1 AC8012G. **CODEN** AENDD5. **[CCC].** Index available. cum. index. **Bk Rev**. **Ad Acc**. **Circ:** 5,000. Documents available from BIOSIS Document Express. ***Continues*** *Acta Endoscopica et Radiocinematographica.*
**Desc:** Original articles about endoscopy in its medical and surgical applications- experimental studies of endoscopic instrumentation, bibliographical analysis, and confrontations with other techniques.
**Ind/Abst** Biol. Abstr.; EMBASE.

AG/0300-9033
**ACTA GASTROENTEROLOGICA LATINOAMERICANA.** [Acta gastroenterol. latinoam.]. (1969)-. Academic Scholarly Publication. Spanish (English and Portuguese). qt. 50.00Arg$. Acta Gastroenterologica Latino Americana, Juncal 2134 PB B, 1125 Buenos Aires Republica Argentina. **Tel** 011 54 1 8250050. **ED** Jaime Katz. **NLM** W1 AC804H. **CODEN** AGLTBL. Index available. cum. index. **Bk Rev**. **Ad Acc**. **Pr Rev. Circ:** 2,500 (ctrl). Documents available from BIOSIS Document Express, CASDDS.
**Desc:** Covers gastrointestinal, hepatic, pancreatic and bile duct diseases, metabolic and neoplastic disease, nutrition, medical and surgical treatment, and progress in physiopathological and pharmacological knowledges.
**Ind/Abst** Biol. Abstr.; Chem. Abstr.; EMBASE; Health Plan. Adminis.; Helminthol. Abstr.; Index Med.

PL/0001-5814
**ACTA HAEMATOLOGICA POLONICA.** (ACTA HAEMATOLOGICA POLONICA : ORGAN POLSKIEGO TOWARZYSTWA HEMATOLOGOW I TRANSFUZJOLOGOW I INSTYTUTU HEMATOLOGII.). [Acta haematol. pol.]. **Added/Corp** Polskie Towarzystwo Hematologow i Transfuzjologow i Instytutu Hematologii. (1970)-. Academic Scholarly Publication. Polish (summaries and/or abstracts in English and Russian). sa. Price on Request. **(Subscription address:** ARS Polona, PO Box 1001, 00068 Warsaw Poland.**) CODEN** AHPLBO. Documents available from BIOSIS Document Express, CASDDS.
**Ind/Abst** Biol. Abstr.; Chem. Abstr.; EMBASE; Health Plan. Adminis.; Index Med.

AU/0303-8173
**ACTA MEDICA AUSTRIACA.** [Acta med. Austriaca]. **Added/Corp** Oesterreichische Gesellschaft fËur Innere Medizin. Vol. 1 (1974)-. Periodical. German (summaries and/or abstracts in English). Five times a year. S1300.00 Austria; S1330.00 other. Medizinische Verlagsgesellschaft mbH, Feldgasse 13, A-1238 Vienna Austria. **Tel** 011 43 1 8893646, FAX 011 43 1 889364724, telex 8893647. **ED** G. Geyer, F. Kaindl, E. Deutsch and M. Weissel. **NLM** W1 AC831K. **CODEN** AMAUBB. Index available. **Bk Rev**. **Ad Acc**. **Pr Rev. Circ:** 1,500. available on microfilm and microfiche from University Microfilms International (UMI). Documents available from The Genuine Article, BIOSIS Document Express, ADONIS. ***Supersedes*** *Weiner Zeitschrift fur Innere Medizin und Ihre Grenzgebiete, 0043-5376.*
**Desc:** Austrian internal medicine.
**Ind/Abst** ADONIS; Biol. Abstr.; Curr. Contents Clin. Med.; EMBASE; Index Med.; Nutr. Abstr. Rev., Ser. B, Live Feeds and Feed.; Nutr. Abstr. Rev., Ser. A, Hum. Exp.; Life Sci. Collect.; Res. Alert [Full Cov.]; Sci. Cit. Index; SCISEARCH; SportSearch.

AU/0303-8181
**ACTA MEDICA AUSTRIACA. SUPPLEMENT.** [Acta med. Austriaca, Suppl.]. No. 1 (June 1974)-. Periodical. German (English; summaries and/or abstracts in English and German). ir. S1200.00. Medizinische Verlagsgesellschaft mbH, Feldgasse 13, A-1238 Vienna Austria. **Tel** 011 43 1 8893646, FAX 011 43 1 889364724, telex 8893647. **NLM** W1 AC831KA. **CODEN** AMEAD7. Documents available from BIOSIS Document Express.
**Ind/Abst** Biol. Abstr.; Health Plan. Adminis.; Index Med.

FR/0567-8757
**ACTUALITIES HEMATOLOGIQUES.** [Actual. hematol.]. (1967)-. Periodical. French. ir. Masson SA / Spain, La Llagosta 6 8, 08120 Barcelona Spain. **Tel** 011 34 3 5741135. **NLM** W1 AC992A. **CODEN** ACHEBU. Documents available from CASDDS.
**Ind/Abst** Chem. Abstr.

US/1052-0465
**ADVANCES IN EATING DISORDERS. See** Medical Science and Technology-Psychiatry.

US/1055-808X
**ADVANCES IN GASTROINTESTINAL RADIOLOGY.** [Adv. gastrointest. radiol.]. Vol. 1 (1991)-. English. $69.95. Mosby Year Book Inc., 11830 Westline Industrial Drive, St Louis MO 63146. **Tel** (800)325-4177, (314)872-8370, FAX (314)432-1380, telex 44-2402. **DD** 616. **NLM** W1; AD609.

US/0065-2822
**ADVANCES IN INTERNAL MEDICINE.** [Adv. intern. med.]. Vol. 1 (1942)-. English. an. Price varies. Mosby Year Book Inc., 11830 Westline Industrial Drive, St Louis MO 63146. **Tel** (800)325-4177, (314)872-8370, FAX (314)432-1380, telex 44-2402. **ED** J. M. Steele. **LC** RC46; .A2. **DD** 616. **NLM** W1 AD653. **CODEN** AIMNAL. **[CCC].** available on microfilm from University Microfilms International (UMI). Documents available from The Genuine Article, CASDDS.
**Desc:** Covers advances in AIDS and HIV infections, displacement of bone marrow transplantation and immunoprophylaxis for genetic diseases, just to name a few, plus much more.
**Ind/Abst** Chem. Abstr.; Energy Res. Abstr.; Health Plan. Adminis.; Index Med.; Index Sci. Rev. [Full Cov.]; INIS Atomindex [Micro.]; Ref. Upd. Clinical Ed.; Ref. Upd. Deluxe Ed.; Res. Alert [Full Cov.]; SCISEARCH.

CK/0120-2448
**AMC. ACTA MEDICA COLOMBIANA.** (ACTA MEDICA COLOMBIANA : AMC : ORGANO DE LA ASOCIACION COLOMBIANA DE MEDICINA INTERNA.). [AMC, Acta med. Colomb.]. **Added/Corp** Asociacion Colombiana de Medicina Interna. **VFOAT** AMC. (1976)-. Academic Scholarly Publication. Spanish. bm. 6.000Col$ Colombia; $40.00 other. ACTA Medica Colombiana, Apartado Aereo 57241, Bogota 2 Colombia. **Tel** 57 1 2573463, FAX 57 1 6105137. **(Subscription address:** CRA 16 A No 77-11, Oficina 403, Bogota DE Colombia**) ED** Fernando Chalem. **NLM** W1 AC833R. **CODEN** AAMCD3. Index available. **Ad Acc. Circ:** 3,000 (ctrl). Documents available from CASDDS.
**Desc:** Original articles, presentation of cases, actualizations and reviews.
**Ind/Abst** Chem. Abstr.

US/0898-672X
**AMERICAN SOCIETY OF HYPERTENSION SYMPOSIUM SERIES.** [Am. Soc. Hypertens. symp. ser.]. **Added/Corp** American Society of Hypertension. **VFOAT** Symposium Series. Vol. 1 (1987)-. Monographic series. English. ir. Price varies per volume. Raven Press, 1185 Avenue of the Americas, 37th Floor, New York NY 10036. **Tel** (212)930-9500, (212)930-9604, FAX (212)869-3495, (212)302-8507, telex 640073. **ED** Barry M. Brenner and John H. Laragh. **DD** 616. **NLM** W1; AM787. **CODEN** ASHSEH. Documents available from BIOSIS Document Express, CASDDS.
**Ind/Abst** Biol. Abstr.; Chem. Abstr.

SP/0212-7199
**ANALES DE MEDICINA INTERNA : ORGANO OFICIAL DE LA SOCIEDAD ESPANOLA DE MEDICINA INTERNA.** **Added/Corp** Sociedad Espanola de Medicina Interna. (1984)-. Periodical. Spanish (summaries and/or abstracts in English; table of contents in English). Twelve times a year. 170ptas. Aran Ediciones SA, Avda General Peron, 20 5 DCHA, 28020 Madrid Spain. **Tel** 011 34 1 5332525. **NLM** W1; AN156F.
**Ind/Abst** Index Med. (1989-).

US/0003-3197
**ANGIOLOGY.** [Angiology]. **Added/Corp** American College of Angiology. International College of Angiology. Angiology Research Foundation. Vol. 1 (Feb. 1950)-. Academic Scholarly Publication. English. mo. $130.00 (individual), $145.00 (institution), US; $170.00 (individual), $185.00 (institution) other. Westminister Publications Inc., 708 Glen Cove Avenue, Glen Head NY 11545. **Tel** (516)759-0025. **LC** RC691; .A543. **DD** 616.105. **NLM** W1 AN227. **CODEN** ANGIAB. **Pr Rev.** Documents available from The Genuine Article, BIOSIS Document Express, CASDDS. ***Absorbed*** *Vascular Diseases.*
**Ind/Abst** Biol. Abstr.; Chem. Abstr.; Curr. Contents Clin. Med.; EMBASE; Energy Res. Abstr.; Health Plan. Adminis.; Index Med.; INIS Atomindex [Micro.]; Life Sci. Collect.; PESTDOC; Res. Alert [Full Cov.]; Rev. Med. Vet. Mycology; Saf. Health Work; Sci. Cit. Index; SCISEARCH.

FR/0003-410X
**ANNALES DE MEDECINE INTERNE.** [Ann. med. interne]. **Added/Corp** Societe Medicale de Hopitaux de Paris. Vol. 120 (Jan. 1969)-. Academic Scholarly Publication. French. Eight times a year. $345.00. Masson Editeur, Box Postale 22, 41353 Vineuil 16 France. **Tel** 011 33 54 438994. **NLM** W1 AN352N. **CODEN** AMDIBO. **[CCC]. Pr Rev.** available on microfilm and microfiche from University Microfilms International (UMI). Documents available from The Genuine Article, CASDDS. ***Continues*** *Bulletins et Memoires de la Societe Medicale des Hopitaux de Paris, 0366-1334.*
**Ind/Abst** Chem. Abstr.; Curr. Contents Clin. Med.; EMBASE; Energy Res. Abstr. (Jan. 1971-); Health Plan. Adminis.; Helminthol. Abstr. (1991-); Index Med.; Nutr. Abstr. Rev., Ser. A, Hum. Exp.; Life Sci. Collect.; Protozoolog. Abstr.; Res. Alert [Full Cov.]; Rev. Med. Vet. Entomol.; Rev. Med. Vet. Mycology; Rev. Plant Pathol.; Saf. Health Work; Sci. Cit. Index; SCISEARCH; Soc. Sci. Cit. Index [Select. Cov.].

IT
**ANNALI ITALIANI DI MEDICINA INTERNA : ORGANO UFFICIALE DELLA SOCIETA ITALIANA DI MEDICINA INTERNA. Added/Corp** Societa Italiana di Medicina Interna. **VFOAT** Medicina Interna; Italian Annals of Internal Medicine. Vol. 1, No. 1 (Mar. 1986)-. Periodical. Italian (English). Four times a year. L60.000.00 Italy, L80.00 other (one year). CEPI, Vis Nicolo Tartaglia, 00197 Rome Italy. **Tel** 011 39 6 8082101 or 8077011, FAX 011 39 6 8072458. **ED** Eugenia Pasquinelli. **NLM** W1; AN5427. **CODEN** AIMIEA. cum. index. **Bk Rev**, (Qty: 15). **Ad Acc, Adv Mgr:** Marine Buongiorno, **Tel** (06)8077011. **Pr Rev. Circ:** 6,000 (ctrl).
**Ind/Abst** EMBASE; Health Plan. Adminis.

US/0003-4819
**ANNALS OF INTERNAL MEDICINE.** [Ann. intern. med.]. **Added/Corp** American College of Physicians. Vol. 1 (July 1927)-. Academic Scholarly Publication. English. sm. $92.00 US and US possessions; $119.00 Canada; $159.00 Japan; $150.00 western Europe; $145.00 other. American College of Physicians, 6th Street and Race Street, Independence Mall West, Philadelphia PA 19106-1572. **Tel** (215)351-2600, (800)523-1546. **(Subscription address:** American College of Physicians, PO Box 7777 R 0320, Philadelphia PA 19175.**) ED** Edward J. Huth and Kathleen Case. **LC** R11; .A84. **NLM** W1 AN605. **CODEN** AIMEAS. **[CCC].** Index available. cum. index. **Bk Rev**. **Ad Acc**. **Pr Rev. Circ:** 91,000. available on microfilm from University Microfilms International (UMI); available on CD-ROM from Maxwell Electronic Publishing. Documents available from The Genuine Article, BIOSIS Document Express, CASDDS. ***Supersedes*** *Annals of Clinical Medicine, 0095-9944.*
**Desc:** Official journal of American College of Physicians. Covers internal medicine and its sub-specialties,

emphasizing the latest developments in medical science and practice. Includes original research articles, NIH/UCLA clinical staff conferences, clinical reports, and comprehensive review articles.
**Ind/Abst** Abr. Index Med.; Abstr. Anthropol.; Abstr. Clin. Care Guidel.; Annals Behav. Med.; Biol. Abstr.; Calcium Calcif. Tissue Abstr.; Chem. Abstr.; Coal Abstr.; CSA Neuro. Abstr. (?-?); Cumul. Index Nurs. Allied Health Lit.; Curr. Aware. Biol. Sci., CABS; Curr. Contents Clin. Med.; Curr. Contents Life Sci.; Dairy Sci. Abstr.; EMBASE; Energy Res. Abstr.; Health Devices Alerts; Health Index (1989-); Health Period. Database; Health Plan. Adminis.; Health Ref. Cent. (Jan. 1989-) [Full Cov.]; Health Serv. Abstr.; Helminthol. Abstr. (1991-); Immunol. Abstr.; Index Med.; Index Vet.; INIS Atomindex [Micro.]; Int. Pharm. Abstr.; Iowa Drug Inf. Serv. (1966-); J. Watch; Med. Abstr. Newsl.; Microbiol. Abstr. Sect. B; Microbiol. Abstr. Sect. C; Mod. Med.; Nutr. Abstr. Rev., Ser. B, Live Feeds and Feed.; Nutr. Abstr. Rev., Ser. A, Hum. Exp.; Nutr. Res. Newsl.; Life Sci. Collect.; PESTDOC; Physic. Medline Plus; Protozoolog. Abstr.; Ref. Upd. Basic Ed.; Ref. Upd. Clinical Ed.; Ref. Upd. Deluxe Ed.; Res. Alert [Full Cov.]; Rev. Med. Vet. Entomol.; Rev. Med. Vet. Mycology; Rev. Plant Pathol.; Risk Abstr.; Saf. Health Work; Sci. Cit. Index; SCISEARCH; Small Anim. Abstr. Bibliogr.; Soc. Sci. Cit. Index [Select. Cov.]; SportSearch; Trop. Dis. Bull.; Virol. AIDS Abstr.

US
**ANNALS OF INTERNAL MEDICINE. CD-ROM.** (19??)-. English. an. $505.00 (institution) US; 525.00 (institution) other (1986-1993 backfile). Appleton & Lange, (A Subsidiary of Simon & Schuster), 25 Van Zant Street, East Norwalk CT 06855. **Tel** (203)838-4400, (800)423-1359, FAX (203)854-9486. available in print.

US/0891-8465
**ANNUAL REPORT OF THE DIGESTIVE DISEASES COORDINATING COMMITTEE TO THE SECRETARY, U.S. DEPARTMENT OF HEALTH AND HUMAN SERVICES.** [Annu. rep. Dig. Dis. Coord. Comm. Secr. U. S. Dep. Health Hum. Serv.]. **Main/Corp** United States. Digestive Diseases Coordinating Committee. 2nd (Fiscal year 1978)-. English. an. National Institute of Arthritis Metabolism and Digestive Diseases, National Institutes of Health, 9000 Rockville Pike, Bethesda MD 20014. **DD** 616. **NLM** W2; A D507. ***Continues** Annual Report of the Digestive Diseases Coordinating Committee to the Secretary, U.S. Department of Health, Education, and Welfare, 0193-6506.*

US/0003-9926
**ARCHIVES OF INTERNAL MEDICINE (1960).** (ARCHIVES OF INTERNAL MEDICINE.). [Arch. intern. med.]. **Added/Corp** American Medical Association. Vol. 106 (July 1960)-. Academic Scholarly Publication. English. Twenty-four times a year. $135.00 (institution), $115.00 (individual) US. American Medical Association, 515 North State Street, Chicago IL 60610. **Tel** (312)464-5000, (800)262-2350, FAX (312)464-5831. **ED** James E. Dalen. **DD** 616. **NLM** W1 A126. **CODEN** AIMDAP. **[CCC].** Index available (free). **Ad Acc. Pr Rev. Circ:** 83,000. available on microfilm and microfiche from University Microfilms International (UMI); available on an online database (file 442/Full-Text) from DIALOG; and MEDIS. Documents available from The Genuine Article, BIOSIS Document Express, CASDDS. ***Continues** A.M.A. Archives of Internal Medicine, 0888-2479.*
**Desc:** Published as an educational service for physicians who practice internal medicine as a primary specialty, and to physicians of other specialties who are engaged in primary care. Edited to present information understandable to all practitioners, it contains articles of immediate clinical applicability.
**Ind/Abst** Abr. Index Med.; Biol. Abstr.; Biol. Dig.; Calcium Calcif. Tissue Abstr.; Chem. Abstr.; Cumul. Index Nurs. Allied Health Lit.; Curr. Aware. Biol. Sci., CABS; Curr. Contents Clin. Med.; Curr. Contents Life Sci.; Dairy Sci. Abstr.; EMBASE; Energy Res. Abstr.; Health Devices Alerts; Health Index (1989-); Health Period. Database; Health Plan. Adminis.; Health Ref. Cent. (Jan. 1989-) [Full Cov.]; Helminthol. Abstr.; Immunol. Abstr.; Index Med.; Index Vet.; INIS Atomindex [Micro.]; Int. Pharm. Abstr.; Iowa Drug Inf. Serv. (1967-); J. Watch (199?-); Med. Abstr. Newsl.; Microbiol. Abstr. Sect. B; Microbiol. Abstr. Sect. C; Mod. Med.; Nutr. Abstr. Rev., Ser. B, Live Feeds and Feed.; Nutr. Abstr. Rev., Ser. A, Hum. Exp.; Nutr. Res. Newsl.; Life Sci. Collect.; PESTDOC; Physic. Medline Plus; Protozoolog. Abstr.; Ref. Upd. Basic Ed.; Ref. Upd. Clinical Ed.; Ref. Upd. Deluxe Ed.; Res. Alert [Full Cov.]; Rev. Med. Vet. Entomol.; Rev. Med. Vet. Mycology; Rev. Plant Pathol.; Risk Abstr.; Saf. Health Work; Sci. Cit. Index; SCISEARCH; Soc. Sci. Cit. Index [Select. Cov.]; Trop. Dis. Bull.; Virol. AIDS Abstr.

IT/0004-010X
**ARCHIVIO DI MEDICINA INTERNA PARMA.** [Arch. med. interna Parma]. (1949)-. Periodical. Italian. bm. L60000.00 Italy; L120000.00. Casa Editrice Maccari, Via Trento 53, 43100 Parma Italy. **Tel** 011 39 521 771268, FAX 011 39 521 771268. **UDC** 611.
**Ind/Abst** EMBASE [Select. Cov.].

US/0098-6127
**ARTERY.** [Artery]. (Dec. 1974)-. Academic Scholarly Publication. English. Six times a year (Jan., Mar., May, July, Sept., Nov.). $75.00 US; $80.00 others. Artery, 13998 West Avenue East, Fulton MI 49052. **Tel** (616)496-8308. **ED** Charles E. Day. **LC** RC691; .A79. **DD** 616.1/3/005. **NLM** W1 AR9515K. **CODEN** ARTEDR. Index available. **Bk Rev. Pr Rev. Circ:** 300. Documents available from The Genuine Article, BIOSIS Document Express, CASDDS.
**Desc:** Publishes manuscripts on any topic related to arteries in both health and disease, including biochemistry, morphology, physiology and pharmacology.
**Ind/Abst** ARTbibliogr. Mod.; Biol. Abstr.; Chem. Abstr.; CSA Neuro. Abstr. (?-?); Curr. Contents Life Sci.; Dairy Sci. Abstr.; EMBASE; Health Plan. Adminis.; Index Med. (Jan. 1979-); Nutr. Abstr. Rev., Ser. B, Live Feeds and Feed.; Nutr. Abstr. Rev., Ser. A, Hum. Exp.; Life Sci. Collect.; Res. Alert [Full Cov.]; Sci. Cit. Index; SCISEARCH.

CN/0844-0506
**ASSOCIATION NEWS - INDUSTRIAL FIRST AID ATTENDANTS ASSOCIATION OF BRITISH COLUMBIA.** (ASSOCIATION NEWS.). [Assoc. news - Ind. First Aid Attend. Assoc. B.C.]. Dec. 1986-Sept./Oct. 1987-. Periodical. English. bm. Free to members. I.F.A.A.A. of British Columbia, Vancouver BC V6R 4G5 Canada. **DD** 616.02/52/05. **Ad Acc. Circ:** 500 (ctrl). ***Continues** Vital Sign, 0826-0303.*

AT/0004-8291
**AUSTRALIAN AND NEW ZEALAND JOURNAL OF MEDICINE.** [Aust. N. Z. j. med.]. **Added/Corp** Royal Australasian College of Physicians. **VFOAT** Journal of Medicine. Vol. 1 (Feb. 1971)-. Periodical. English. bm. 180.00Aus$ Australia; 206.00Aus$ New Zealand, Papua & New Guinea; 217.00Aus$ Fiji, Indonesia & Malaysia; 227.00Aus$ India, Hong Kong, Japan, & Korea; 240.00Aus$ US, Israel & Canada; 252.00Aus$ UK, Europe & South Africa. ADIS International Ltd, 41 Centorian Drive, Private Bag 65901, Mairangi Bay, Auckland 10 New Zealand. **Tel** 011 64 9 4798100, FAX 011 64 9 4791418. **(Subscription address:** Adis International Pty. Ltd., 9 Rodborough Road, Frenchs Forest, N.S.W. 2086 Australia.**) ED** Michael F. O'Rourke. **NLM** W1 AU495. **CODEN** ANZJB8. **[CCC].** Index available. **Bk Rev. Ad Acc. Pr Rev. Circ:** 6,000 (ctrl). available on microfilm and microfiche from University Microfilms International (UMI). Documents available from The Genuine Article, BIOSIS Document Express, CASDDS. ***Continues** Australasian Annals of Medicine, 0571-9283.*
**Desc:** Accounts of original research in internal medicine and the biomedical sciences.
**Ind/Abst** Arts Humanit. Citation Index [Select. Cov.]; Biol. Abstr.; Chem. Abstr.; Curr. Aware. Biol. Sci., CABS; Curr. Contents Clin. Med.; Curr. Contents Life Sci.; Dairy Sci. Abstr.; EMBASE; Health Plan. Adminis.; Index Med.; Index Vet.; Int. Pharm. Abstr.; Microbiol. Abstr. Sect. B (19??-19??); Mod. Med.; Nutr. Abstr. Rev., Ser. B, Live Feeds and Feed.; Nutr. Abstr. Rev., Ser. A, Hum. Exp.; Nutr. Res. Newsl.; Life Sci. Collect.; PESTDOC; Protozoolog. Abstr.; Ref. Upd. Deluxe Ed.; Res. Alert [Full Cov.]; Rev. Med. Vet. Entomol.; Rev. Med. Vet. Mycology; Rev. Plant Pathol.; Sci. Cit. Index; SCISEARCH; SportSearch; Vet. Bull.; Trop. Dis. Bull.; Virol. AIDS Abstr.

SP/0304-873X
**AVANCES EN MEDICINA INTERNA.** Vol. 1 (1974)-. Spanish. an. Aran Ediciones SA, Avda General Peron, 20 5 DCHA, 28020 Madrid Spain. **Tel** 011 34 1 5332525. **NLM** W1 AV217.

UK/0957-5235
**BLOOD COAGULATION & FIBRINOLYSIS : AN INTERNATIONAL JOURNAL IN HAEMOSTASIS AND THROMBOSIS.** [Blood coagul. fibrinolysis]. **VFOAT** Blood Coagulation and Fibrinolysis. Vol. 1, No. 1 (March/April 1990)-. Periodical. English. Eight times a year. $625.00 US; £365.00 other. Rapid Communications of Oxford Ltd, The Old Malthouse, Paradise Street, Oxford OX1 1LD England. **Tel** 011 44 0865 790447, FAX 011 44 0865 244012, telex 9403712. **ED** Dr J Francis, Dr S Gordon. **NLM** W1; BL657. **CODEN** BLFIE7. **[CCC].** Index available. cum. index. **Bk Rev. Ad Acc. Pr Rev.** Documents available from The Genuine Article, BIOSIS Document Express, CASDDS.
**Desc:** Features review and original research articles on all clinical laboratory and experimental aspects of haemostasis and thrombosis. The journal is devoted to significant developments around the world in blood coagulation, fibrinolysis, thrombosis, platelets and the kininogen-kinin system as well as dealing with those aspects of blood rheology relevant to haemostasis and the effects of drugs on haemostasis components.
**Ind/Abst** Biol. Abstr.; Chem. Abstr.; Curr. Aware. Biol. Sci., CABS; Curr. Contents Life Sci.; Health Plan. Adminis.; Index Med.; Res. Alert [Full Cov.]; Sci. Cit. Index; SCISEARCH.

UK/0261-4596
**BLOOD TRANSFUSION.** [Blood transfus.]. (1982)-. English. mo. £80.00. SUBIS, Mansion House, 19 Kingfield Road, Sheffield S11 9AS England. **Tel** 011 44 114 255 4433, FAX 011 44 114 255 4626. **Ad Acc.**
**Desc:** Current awareness service for researchers and clinicians.

SP/0210-1262
**BOLETIN DE LA ASOCIACION ESPANOLA DE ENDOSCOPIA DIGESTIVA.** [Bol. Asoc. Esp. Endosc. Dig.]. (1974)-. Periodical. Spanish. bm. Editorial Garsi SA, Juan Bravo 46, 28006 Madrid, Spain. **Tel** 011 34 1 4021212, telex 98358 GARSI E. **UDC** 616.3.

SP/0213-3954
**BRITISH MEDICAL JOURNAL ED. ESPANOLA.** [Br. med. j.Ed. esp.]. **VFOAT** BMJ. (1986)-. Periodical. Spanish. mo (11 issues per year). $47.89 Spain; $69.00 other Europe; $77.00 other. Salvat Editores SA, Calle Mallorca 45-49, Barcelona 08029 Spain. **Tel** 011 34 3 2010911, FAX 011 34 3 321-0565, telex SAEDI E 53132. **(Subscription address:** Editorial Garsi, C Juan Bravo, 28006 Madrid Spain.**) UDC** 61. **Ad Acc. Circ:** 5,000. ***Continues** British Medical Journal (Edicion Espanola).*
**Desc:** Various articles about internal medicine: editorials, papers and audit in practice.

CN/0226-2347
**CANDID FACTS.** [Candid facts]. **VFOAT** A Propos. Began publication in 1960. Periodical. English (French). Free. Canadian Cystic Fibrosis Foundation, 2221 Young Street/Suite 601, Toronto Ontario M4S 2B4 Canada. **Tel** (416)485-9149. **DD** 616.3/7. ctrl circ.

US/1047-6059
**CE/Q MEDICAL NEWSLETTER.** [CE/Q med. newsl.]. **VFOAT** CE Q Medical Newsletter; CE/Q. Vol. 1, No. 1 (Feb. 1990)-. Newsletter. English. mo. $175.00. CE - Q Publishers Inc, PO Box 50399, Palo Alto CA 94303. **Tel** (800)926-1121. **ED** Harvey Knoernschied - telephone:(408)298-1080. **DD** 616.
**Desc:** Indentifies from the current medical literature significant ways in which health care can be provided in a more cost-efficient manner without reducing quality or outcome.

●US/0963-6897
**CELL TRANSPLANTATION.** [Cell transp.]. **Added/Corp** Cell Transplant Society. Vol. 1, No. 1 (1992)-. Periodical. English. Six times a year. $351.00 The Americas; £235.00 other. Pergamon Press, An Imprint of Elsevier Science Ltd., The Boulevard, Langford Lane, Kidlington, Oxford OX5 1GB United Kingdom. **Tel** 011 44 865 843000, 011 44 865 843699, FAX 011 44 865 843010. **(Subscription address:** Elsevier Science Ltd. Oxford Fulfillment Centre, PO Box 800, Kidlington, Oxford OX5 1DX United Kingdom.**) ED** P. Sanberg. **NLM** W1; CE1283G. **CODEN** CTRAE8. **[CCC].**
**Desc:** Articles on the subject of cell transplantation and its application to human diseases. Articles will deal with a wide range of topics including physiological, medical, preclinical, tissue engineering and device-oriented aspects of transplantation of nervous system, endocrine, growth-factor secreting, bone-marrow, epithelial, endothelial and genetically engineered cells among others.
**Ind/Abst** Curr. Aware. Biol. Sci., CABS; Sci. Cit. Index.

XR/0009-0565
**CESKOSLOVENSKA GASTROENTEROLOGIA A VYZIVA.** [Cesk. gastroenterol. vyz.]. Vol. 9 (1955)-. Periodical. Czech. ir. $86.00. **(Subscription address:** Artia Pegas Press Ltd., Palac Metro Narodni Trida 25, 11210 Prague 1 Czech Republic.**) NLM** W1 CE885C. **CODEN** CKGAAM. **[CCC].** Documents available from BIOSIS Document Express, CASDDS. ***Continues** Sbornik Pro Pathofysiologii Traveni a Vyzivu.*
**Ind/Abst** Biol. Abstr.; Chem. Abstr.; Dairy Sci. Abstr.; EMBASE; Food Sci. Technol. Abstr.; Helminthol. Abstr.; Saf. Health Work.

IT/0390-0037
**CHRONOBIOLOGIA.** [Chronobiologia]. **Added/Corp** International Society for Chronobiology. Vol. 1-18 (Jan./Mar. 1974)-. Academic Scholarly Publication. English (Italian). Four times a year. $220.00 Comes with Associated Chronobiologia Researchers membership. Associated Chronobiologia Researchers, via R di Lauria 12 A, 20149 Milan Italy. **Tel** 011 39 2 324750, FAX 011 39 2 70635425. **LC** QP84.6; .C44. **DD** 574.1. **NLM** W1 CH972. **CODEN** CBLGA2. Index available. **Bk Rev. Pr Rev.** available on microfilm from University Microfilms International (UMI). Documents available from The Genuine Article, BIOSIS Document Express, CASDDS.
**Desc:** Publishes results of original research, didactic material concerning patho-physiological and statistical evaluation of rhythms, growth, development, aging and other predictable changes in life forms.
**Ind/Abst** Anim. Breed. Abstr.; Biocont. News Inf.; Biol. Abstr.; Chem. Abstr.; CSA Neuro. Abstr. (?-?); Curr. Contents, Agric. Biol. Environ. Sci.; EMBASE; Index Med.; Index Vet.; Nutr. Abstr. Rev., Ser. B, Live Feeds and Feed.; Nutr. Abstr. Rev., Ser. A, Hum. Exp. (1977-); Life Sci. Collect.; Protozoolog. Abstr.; Psychol. Abstr. (1977-); PsycINFO; PsycLit; Res. Alert [Select. Cov.]; Rev. Med. Vet. Mycology; SCISEARCH; Soils Fert.; Vet. Bull.

US/0092-6213
**CIRCULATORY SHOCK.** **See** Medical Science and Technology-Cardiology.

●US/1064-1963
**CLINICAL AND EXPERIMENTAL HYPERTENSION (1993).** **See** Medical Science and Technology-Cardiology.

US/0164-0852
**CLINICAL EXERCISES IN INTERNAL MEDICINE.** V. 1 (1978)-. Monographic series. English. ir. Price varies per volume. W.B. Saunders Company, A Subsidiary of Harcourt Brace Jovanovich, Inc., The Curtis Center/Suite 300, Independence Square West, Philadelphia PA 19106-3399. **Tel** (215)238-7800 or, 5587, FAX (215)238-7883, telex 173146. **(Subscription address:** W. B. Saunders Company / North America Subscriptions, c/o Periodicals, 6277 Sea Harbour Drive, 4th Floor, Orlando FL 32887.**)** **NLM** WB 18 C641.

GW
**CLINICAL INVESTIGATION.** ***Title Change.*** (1992)-(1992). English. mo. Springer-Verlag GmbH & Company KG, Heidelberger Platz 3, D 14197 Berlin Germany. **Tel** 011 49 30 8207223, FAX 011 49 30 8214091, telex 183 319 SPBLN D. **(Subscription address:** Springer Verlag New York Inc. / for North America, 44 Hartz Way, Secaucus NJ 07096.**)** Documents available from The Genuine Article. ***Continues*** *Klinische Wochenschrift.* ***Continued by*** *Clinical Investigator, 0941-0198.*
**Ind/Abst** EMBASE; Res. Alert [Full Cov.]; Sci. Cit. Index (19??-19??); SCISEARCH.

US/0275-4541
**CLINICAL ULTRASOUND REVIEW.** (CLINICAL ULTRASOUND REVIEW / FRED WINSBERG.). [Clin. ultrasound rev.]. **VFOAT** Clinical Ultrasound Reviews. Vol. 1 (1981)-. Periodical. English. an. **LC** RC78.7.U4; W57. **DD** 616.07/543. **NLM** W1 CL799R. **[CCC].**
**Ind/Abst** Helminthol. Abstr. (1991-).

US/0883-0339
**CLINICAL UPDATE IN NEPHROLOGY.** [Clin. update nephrol.]. Periodical. English. bw. $245.00. Nassau Publications Inc., 11 Forest Street, New Canaan CT 06840. **DD** 616.

US/8756-9523
**COMPENDIUM OF DRUG THERAPY.** **VFOAT** Internist's Compendium of Drug Therapy. (1983)-. English. an. $40.00. Core Publishing Division, 105 Raider Boulevard, Belle Mead NJ 08502. **Tel** (908)874-8550. ***Continues*** *Internist's Compendium of Drug Therapy, 0276-4342.*

SP/0211-528X
**COMUNICACIONES UROLOGICAS.** [Comun. urol.]. (1978)-. Monographic series. Spanish. ir. Price varies per volume. Reycosa, Orense 39/ 1-C, 28020 Madrid Spain. **UDC** 616.6.

US/8755-8823
**CONN'S CURRENT THERAPY.** [Conn's curr. ther.]. (1984)-. English. an. $55.00. W.B. Saunders Company, A Subsidiary of Harcourt Brace Jovanovich, Inc., The Curtis Center/Suite 300, Independence Square West, Philadelphia PA 19106-3399. **Tel** (215)238-7800 or, 5587, FAX (215)238-7883, telex 173146. **(Subscription address:** W. B. Saunders Company / North America Subscriptions, c/o Periodicals, 6277 Sea Harbour Drive, 4th Floor, Orlando FL 32887.**)** **ED** R. E. Rakel. **LC** RM101; .C87. **DD** 615.5/05. **NLM** W1; CO728H. **Circ:** 40,000. ***Continues*** *Current Therapy, 0070-2102.*
**Desc:** Latest approved methods of treatment for the practicing physician.

US/1042-9646
**CONTEMPORARY INTERNAL MEDICINE.** [Contemp. intern. med.]. (April 1989)-. Periodical. English. Twelve times a year. $85.00. Aegean Communications Inc., 666 Glenbrook Road, Stamford CT 06906. **Tel** (203)353-0111, FAX (203)353-1975. **ED** Lucy Labson. **DD** 616. **NLM** W1; CO769MQB. Index available (published separately in Dec.). cum. index. **Ad Acc, Adv Mgr:** Mark Branca. **Pr Rev. Circ:** 90,000 (ctrl).
**Desc:** This journal offers the internal medicine group of special ties high-quality, practical authoritative review information in areas of immediate interest to clinical practice. Article and departments are highly readable and include excellent illustrative and other graphic materials.

US/1050-9607
**CONTEMPORARY MANAGEMENT IN INTERNAL MEDICINE.** ***Suspended.*** [Contemp. manag. intern. med.]. **VFOAT** CMIM. Vol. 1, No. 1 (1990)-?. Monographic series. English. bm. Price varies per volume. Churchill Livingstone, 1-3 Baxter's Place, Leith Walk, Edinburgh EH1 3AF Scotland. **Tel** 011 44 31 556 2424, FAX 011 44 31 558 1278, telex 727511. **DD** 616. **NLM** W1; CO769MU. **[CCC].**
**Ind/Abst** EMBASE.

US/0198-8093
**CURRENT HEPATOLOGY.** [Curr. hepatol.]. Vol. 1, (1980)-. English. an. $79.95. Mosby Year Book Inc., 11830 Westline Industrial Drive, St Louis MO 63146. **Tel** (800)325-4177, (314)872-8370, FAX (314)432-1380, telex 44-2402. **LC** RC845; .C88. **DD** 616.3/62/005. **NLM** W1 CU788JAN. **CODEN** CUHEDA. **[CCC].** Documents available from BIOSIS Document Express.
**Ind/Abst** Biol. Abstr. (1985-).

UK/0950-8724
**CURRENT MEDICAL LITERATURE / REVERSIBLE OBSTRUCTIVE AIRWAYS DISEASE.** **See** Medical Science and Technology-Respiratory System.

UK/0961-2246
**CURRENT MEDICAL LITERATURE. THROMBOSIS.** **See** Medical Science and Technology-Hematology.

US/0899-6865
**CURRENT THERAPY IN INTERNAL MEDICINE.** [Curr. ther. intern. med.]. (1984/85)-. English. qt. Mosby Year Book Inc., 11830 Westline Industrial Drive, St Louis MO 63146. **Tel** (800)325-4177, (314)872-8370, FAX (314)432-1380, telex 44-2402. **LC** RC39; .C88. **DD** 616.

IT
**DIALISI OGGI.** Abetre Edizioni, Via Arzaga 4, 20146 Milan Italy.

UK/0950-0235
**DIALOGUE ON DIARRHOEA.** [Dialogue diarrhoea]. **Added/Corp** Appropriate Health Resources & Technologies Action Group. (198?)-. Periodical. English (French, Spanish, Portuguese, Arabic and Tamil). qt. £10.00 or $20.00. AHRTAG, 1 London Bridge Street, 3 Castle, London SE1 9SG England. **Tel** 011 44 71 378 1403, FAX 011 44 71 403 6003, telex 912881 TXG. **CODEN** DDIAEW. Documents available from BIOSIS Document Express. ***Continues*** *Diarrhoea Dialogue.*
**Desc:** Newsletter for health workers and educators concerned with all aspects of diarrhoeal diseases.
**Ind/Abst** Biol. Abstr. (1985-1989); Dairy Sci. Abstr.; Trop. Dis. Bull.

US
**DISEASES OF THE LIVER AND BILIARY SYSTEM.** (19??)-. Academic Scholarly Publication. English. ir. $89.50 (latest edition). Blackwell Scientific Publishers, 238 Main Street, Cambridge MA 02142. **Tel** (617)547-7110, (800)835-6770, FAX (617)547-0789. **ED** Sheila Sherlock.

GW/0340-3238
**DOKUMENTATION ARBEITSMEDIZIN.** ***Title Change.*** (DOKUMENTATION: ARBEITSMEDIZIN. DOCUMENTATION: OCCUPATIONAL HEALTH.). **Added/Corp** Institut fuer Dokumentation und Information ueber Sozialmedizin und Oeffentliches Gesundheitswesen. Bundesanstalt fuer Arbeitsschutz und Unfallforschung. DIMDI. Germany (West). Bundesministerium fuer Arbeit und Sozialordnung. Germany (West). Bundesministerium fuer Jugend, Familie und Gesundheit. North Rhine-Westphalia (Germany). Ministerium fuer Arbeit, Gesundheit und Soziales. **VFOAT** Documentation: Occupational Health. Vol. 1 (Jan. 1975)-(19??). German (English). mo. Idis Oeffentl Gesundheitswesen, Postfach 201012, D33548 Bielefeld F R Germany. **Tel** 011 49 521 86033. **NLM** ZWA 400; D658. ***Continued by*** *IDIS-Literaturliste. Arbeitsmedizin.*
**Ind/Abst** Ind. Hyg. Dig. (19??-).

UK/0792-5077
**DRUG METABOLISM AND DRUG INTERACTIONS.** [Drug metab. drug interact.]. **VFOAT** Reviews on Drug Metabolism and Drug Interactions. Vol. 6, No. 1 (1988)-. Periodical. English. qt. $220.00. Freund Publishing House Ltd, PO Box 35010, 61 Nachmani Street, Tel Aviv 61350 Israel. **Tel** 011 972 3 5662925, FAX 011 972 3 5605335. **(Subscription address:** Freund Publishing House Ltd., Suite 500 Chesham House, 150 Regent Street, London W1R 5FA England.**)** **ED** N. Kingsley. **NLM** W1; DR533J. **CODEN** DMDIEQ. Documents available from BIOSIS Document Express, CASDDS. ***Continues*** *Reviews on Drug Metabolism and Drug Interactions, 0334-2190.*
**Ind/Abst** Biol. Abstr.; Chem. Abstr.; EMBASE; Health Plan. Adminis.; Index Med. (1989-); PESTDOC.

UA/0301-8849
**EGYPTIAN JOURNAL OF BILHARZIASIS.** [Egypt. j. bilharz.]. **Added/Corp** Egyptian Society of Tropical Medicine and Parasitology. General Society for Combat of Bilharziasis. Markaz al-Qawmi lil-Ilam wa-al-Tawthiq. Vol. 1 (1974)-. Academic Scholarly Publication. English (summaries and/or abstracts in Arabic). sa. National Information & Documentation Center, A1-Tahrir St Dokki AGWAF, Cairo Egypt. **Tel** 011 20 2 701696, telex 93069. **NLM** W1 EG913K. **CODEN** EJBLAB. Documents available from CASDDS.
**Ind/Abst** Chem. Abstr.; Health Plan. Adminis.

BE/0301-150X
**ELECTROMYOGRAPHY AND CLINICAL NEUROPHYSIOLOGY.** [Electromyogr. clin. neurophysiol.]. (1972)-. Academic Scholarly Publication. English (summaries and/or abstracts in German and French). Eight times a year. $100.00. Nauwelaerts Publishing, rue de L'Eglise St-Sulpice 19, B-5998 Beauvechain Belgium. **Tel** 7518470, FAX 7517408. **ED** N Rosselle and W T Liberson. **LC** RC77.5. **DD** 616.7/4/0754. **NLM** W1 EL332E. **CODEN** EMCNA9. Index available. cum. index. **Bk Rev. Ad Acc. Circ:** 1,250. Documents available from BIOSIS Document Express, Ask*IEEE. ***Continues*** *Electromyography.*
**Desc:** An international journal which contains original articles dealing with the different clinical and basic scientific aspects of electromyography and related neurophysiological techniques. Editors welcome contributions concerning the clinical application of established and new electrophysiological techniques in the practice of rehabilitation medicine.
**Ind/Abst** Biol. Abstr.; EMBASE; Health Plan. Adminis.; Index Med.; INSPEC (Jan.-March 1972-).

IT
**EPATOLOGIA E MALATTIE DEL RICAMBIO.** ***Ceased.*** Vol. 31, (Jan./Apr. 1985)-(1993). Periodical. Italian (English). qt. Societa Editrice Universo, Via GB Morgagni 1, 00161 Rome Italy. **Tel** 011 39 6 44231171. **NLM** W1; EP393E. ***Continues*** *Epatologia, 0013-9475.*
**Ind/Abst** EMBASE [Select. Cov.].

GW/0071-111X
**ERGEBNISSE DER INNEREN MEDIZIN UND KINDERHEILKUNDE.** [Ergeb. inn. Med. Kinderheilkd.]. Vol. 1-65 (1908-1945); New Ser. 1 (1949)-. Periodical. German. ir. Price varies per volume. Springer-Verlag GmbH & Company KG, Heidelberger Platz 3, D 14197 Berlin Germany. **Tel** 011 49 30 8207223, FAX 011 49 30 8214091, telex 183 319 SPBLN D. **(Subscription address:** Springer Verlag New York Inc. / for North America, 44 Hartz Way, Secaucus NJ 07096.**)** **NLM** W1 ER281.
**Desc:** Advances in internal medicine and pediatrics.
**Ind/Abst** Health Plan. Adminis.; Index Med.

UK/0953-6205
**EUROPEAN JOURNAL OF INTERNAL MEDICINE.** **Added/Corp** Association Europeenne de Medecine Interne d'Ensemble. Vol. 1, No. 1 (May 1989)-. Periodical. English. qt. $200.00. Edizioni Luigi Pozzi Srl, Via Panama 68, 00198 Rome Italy. **Tel** (06)8553548, FAX (06)8554105. **NLM** W1; EU72DHK. available on microfilm and microfiche from University Microfilms International (UMI).
**Ind/Abst** EMBASE.

NE/0014-410X
**EXCERPTA MEDICA. SECTION 6. INTERNAL MEDICINE.** **See** Medical Science and Technology-Abstracting, Bibliographies and Statistics.

IT/0014-9659
**FEGATO, IL.** ***Suspended.*** (1955)-Vol. 36 No. 2/3. Periodical. Multiple languages (English, French, German, Italian and Spanish; summaries and/or abstracts in English). Three times a year. Terme di Chianciano, Via delle Rose 12, 53042 Chianciano Terme Italy. **Tel** 011 39 578-39011. Documents available from CASDDS.
**Ind/Abst** Chem. Abstr. (?-?).

US
**FOCUS & OPINION : INTERNAL MEDICINE.** English. Six times a year. $68.00 (individuals), $112.50 (institutions), $106.90 (government) US; $72.00 (individuals), $116.50 (institutions) Canada; $82.00 (individuals), $126.50 (institutions) other. Mosby Year Book Inc., 11830 Westline Industrial Drive, St Louis MO 63146. **Tel** (800)325-4177, (314)872-8370, FAX (314)432-1380, telex 44-2402.

●US/1072-0863
**FOCUS & OPINION, INTERNAL MEDICINE.** [Focus & opin., intern. med.]. **VFOAT** Focus and Opinion, Internal Medicine; Focus & Opinion; Focus and Opinion; Internal Medicine. Vol. 1, No. 1 (Jan.-Feb. 1994)-. Periodical. English. bm. $112.50 (institutions), $68.00 (individuals) US; $116.50 (institutions), $72.00 (individuals) Canada; $126.50 (institutions), $82.00 (individuals) other. Mosby Year Book Inc., 11830 Westline Industrial Drive, St Louis MO 63146. **Tel** (800)325-4177, (314)872-8370, FAX (314)432-1380, telex 44-2402. **DD** 616.

IT
**GIORNALE ITALIANO DI ENDOSCOPIA DIGESTIVA : ORGANO UFFICIALE DELLA SOCIETA ITALIANA DI ENDOSCOPIA DIGESTIVA.** **Added/Corp** Societa Italiana di Endoscopia Digestiva. Vol. 4, No. 1 (1981)-. Periodical. Italian (summaries and/or abstracts in English). qt. L87200 Italy. Masson S.P.A, Via Statuto 2/4, 20121 Milan Italy. **Tel** 011 39 2 63671, FAX 011 39 2

6367211. **NLM** W1; GI777L. **CODEN** GIEDEL. ***Continues*** *Giornale di Gastroenterologia ed Endoscopia.* **Ind/Abst** EMBASE.

US/1049-2771
**GLOBAL PERSPECTIVES ON HEPATITIS : NEWSLETTER OF THE INTERNATIONAL TASK FORCE ON HEPATITIS B IMMUNIZATION.** Vol. 1, No. 1 (April 1990)-. Newsletter. English. Three times a year. Free. Program for Appropriate Technology in Health, 4 Nickerson Street, Seattle WA 98109. **Tel** (206)285-3500, FAX (206)285-6619, telex 4740049. **DD** 616. **NLM** W1; GL362TG.

HU/0017-6559
**HAEMATOLOGIA.** (HAEMATOLOGIA. INTERNATIONAL QUARTERLY OF HAEMATOLOGY.). [Haematologia]. Vol. 1 (1967)-. Academic Scholarly Publication. English (French, German and Russian). qt. DM290.00. VSP International Science Publishers, Godfried van Seystlaan 47, 3703 BR Zeist Netherlands. **Tel** 011 31 3404 25790, FAX 011 31 3404 32081, telex 40217 USP NL. **(Subscription address:** VSP International Science Publishers, PO Box 346, 3700 AH Zeist Netherlands.**) ED** S. R. Hollan. **NLM** W1 HA155P. **CODEN** HAEMBY. Index available. **Bk Rev. Ad Acc. Pr Rev. Circ:** 300. Documents available from BIOSIS Document Express, CASDDS. ***Supersedes*** *Haematologia Hungarica, 0367-5599.*
**Desc:** Journal publishing papers in haematology and related fields such as immunology, blood transfusion, transplantation and oncology.
**Ind/Abst** Biol. Abstr.; Chem. Abstr.; EMBASE; Health Plan. Adminis.; Index Med.

●US/1061-5318
**HEMATOPOIETIC THERAPY. Added/Corp** World Medical Communications Organization. (1992)-. Periodical. English. qt. $60.00. World Medical Communications Organizations, 7 Ridgedale Avenue, Cedar Knolls NJ 07927. **Tel** (201)455-1121. **NLM** ZWH 140; H487.

US/0363-0269
**HEMOGLOBIN.** [Hemoglobin]. Vol. 1 (1976)-. Academic Scholarly Publication. English. bm. $665.00 US; $686.00 other. Marcel Dekker Inc., 270 Madison Avenue, New York NY 10016. **Tel** (212)696-9000, (800)228-1160, FAX (212)685-4540, telex 421419. **(Subscription address:** Marcel Dekker Inc, PO Box 5017, Monticello NY 12701.**) ED** T.H.J. Huisman, R.T. Jones, D. Loukopoulos and Y. Ohba. **LC** RC641.7.H35; H44. **DD** 616.1/5. **NLM** W1 HE878. **CODEN** HEM0D8. **[CCC]. Bk Rev. Ad Acc. Pr Rev.** ctrl circ. available on microfiche. Documents available from The Genuine Article, BIOSIS Document Express, CASDDS.
**Desc:** Emphasizes several topic areas: normal, modified, and abnormal human hemoglobins including new variants, structure-function relationships, physicochemical characteristics, physiological properties, biosynthetic analyses, the thalassemias, and new therapeutic approaches; the genetic aspects of the hemoglobinopathies, including family and population studies; International Hemoglobins Information Center reports of all published hemoglobin variants; and reviews of hemoglobin abnormalities in selected countries and continents.
**Ind/Abst** AgBiotech News Inf.; Biol. Abstr.; Chem. Abstr.; Curr. Contents Life Sci.; EMBASE; Energy Res. Abstr. (Dec. 1981-); Genet. Abstr.; Health Plan. Adminis.; Hum. Genome Abstr.; Index Med.; Life Sci. Collect.; Ref. Upd. Deluxe Ed.; Res. Alert [Full Cov.]; Sci. Cit. Index; SCISEARCH; Soc. Sci. Cit. Index [Select. Cov.].

GW/0171-6123
**HEPATOLOGY. Added/Corp** Falk Foundation. **VFOAT** Hepatology Rapid Literature Review. (1978)-. Periodical. English (German). mo. DM290.00. Falk Foundation EV, PO Box 6529, D 79041 Freiburg Germany. **Tel** 011 49 761 130340, telex 772458 FALK D. **NLM** ZWI 700; H528. Index available. **Bk Rev.**
**Ind/Abst** Curr. Contents Clin. Med.; Curr. Contents Life Sci.

US/0270-9139
**HEPATOLOGY (BALTIMORE, MD.).** (HEPATOLOGY : OFFICIAL JOURNAL OF THE AMERICAN ASSOCIATION FOR THE STUDY OF LIVER DISEASES.). [Hepatology]. **Added/Corp** American Association for the Study of Liver Diseases. Vol. 1, No. 1 (Jan./Feb. 1981)-. Academic Scholarly Publication. English. mo. $338.00 (institutions), $215.00 (individuals) US; $378.00 (institutions), $255.00 (individuals) other. W.B. Saunders Company, A Subsidiary of Harcourt Brace Jovanovich, Inc., The Curtis Center/Suite 300, Independence Square West, Philadelphia PA 19106-3399. **Tel** (215)238-7800 or, 5587, FAX (215)238-7883, telex 173146. **(Subscription address:** W. B. Saunders Company / North America Subscriptions, c/o Periodicals, 6277 Sea Harbour Drive, 4th Floor, Orlando FL 32887.**) ED** Steven Schenker. **LC** RC845; .H45a. **DD** 616.3/62/005. **NLM** W1 HE912. **CODEN** HPTLD9. **[CCC]. Ad Acc. Pr Rev. Circ:** 4,350. available on microfilm and microfiche from University Microfilms International (UMI). Documents available from The Genuine Article, BIOSIS Document Express, CASDDS.
**Desc:** Publishes original articles concerning liver structure, function, and disease. Serves physicians in the fields of hepatology, gastroenterology, internal medicine, pathology, general surgery, and pediatrics.
**Ind/Abst** Biol. Abstr.; Chem. Abstr.; Curr. Aware. Biol. Sci., CABS; EMBASE; Health Plan. Adminis.; Helminthol. Abstr. (1991-); Index Med.; INIS Atomindex [Micro.]; Ref. Upd. Basic Ed.; Ref. Upd. Clinical Ed.; Ref. Upd. Deluxe Ed.; Res. Alert [Full Cov.]; Sci. Cit. Index; SCISEARCH; Soc. Sci. Cit. Index [Select. Cov.]; Trop. Dis. Bull.

US/1050-9631
**HIPPOCAMPUS (NEW YORK, N.Y.).** (HIPPOCAMPUS.). [Hippocampus]. Vol. 1, No. 1 (Jan. 1991)-. Periodical. English. bm (6 issues). $345.00 US; $405.00 Canada and Mexico; $427.50 other. John Wiley & Sons, Inc., 605 Third Avenue, New York NY 10158-0012. **Tel** (212)850-6000, (212)850-6645, FAX (212)850-6088, telex 12-7063. **(Subscription address:** John Wiley & Sons / England, Baffins Lane, Chichester, West Sussex PO19 1UD England.**) ED** David G. Amaral and Menno P. Witter. **DD** 616. **NLM** W1; HI416. **CODEN** HIPPEL. **[CCC].** Documents available from The Genuine Article.
**Desc:** The hippocampus is a brain region that is one of the most frequently studied structures of the central nervous system. This journal publishes papers dealing with hippocampal structure and function and will be of interest to both researchers and clinicians. Readership: neuroscientists.
**Ind/Abst** Curr. Aware. Biol. Sci., CABS; Curr. Contents Life Sci.; Ref. Upd. Deluxe Ed.; Res. Alert [Full Cov.]; Sci. Cit. Index; Soc. Sci. Cit. Index [Select. Cov.].

US/0887-3712
**HLB NEWSLETTER, THE.** [HLB newsl.]. **VAT** Heart, Lung, Blood Newsletter. (1985)-. Periodical. English. Twenty-four times a year. $296.00. British Trading Company Ltd., 821 Delaware Avenue Southwest, Washington DC 20024. **Tel** (202)488-7533. **ED** Nathaniel Polster. **DD** 616. Index available.
**Desc:** Primarily covering policy development at the National Heart, Lung & Blood Institute; also providing news from other government scientific organizations from when that news influences the flow of NHLBI research grant and contract funds.

US
**IBD WATCH.** (19??)-. Periodical. English. Four times a year. Il Pensiero Scientifico Editore s.r.l., Via Bradano 3C, 00199 Rome Italy. **Tel** 011 39 6 86207158, 86207159, 86207168, 86207169, FAX 011 39 6 86207160.
**Desc:** Research and findings on intestinal inflammatory disease.

GW/0932-2876
**IDIS-LITERATURLISTE. ARBEITSMEDIZIN / IDIS. Added/Corp** Institut fuer Dokumentation und Information ueber Sozialmedizin und Oeffentliches Gesundheitswesen. **VFOAT** Arbeitsmedizin. (1987)-. Monographic series. German (English). ir. Price varies per volume. Idis Oeffentl Gesundheitswesen, Postfach 201012, D33548 Bielefeld F R Germany. **Tel** 011 49 521 86033. **NLM** ZWA 400; I19. ***Continues*** *Dokumentation: Arbeitsmedizin, 0340-3238.*

GW/0938-0922
**IN-VITRO-DIAGNOSTICA-NACHRICHTEN.** [In-vitro-Diagn.-Nachr.]. **VFOAT** Diagnostica-Nachrichten. (1990)-. Periodical. German. Twelve times a year. DM248.00. Blackwell Wissenschafts-Verlag, Kurfuerstendamm 57, D 10707 Berlin Germany. **Tel** 011 49 30 32790623, 011 49 30 32790624, FAX 011 49 30 327 90610. **UDC** 61.

II/0367-8326
**INDIAN JOURNAL OF MALARIOLOGY.** [Indian j. malariol.]. **Added/Corp** Indian Research Fund Association. Indian Council of Medical Research. Malaria Institute of India. Vol. 1, No. 1 (March 1947)-. Academic Scholarly Publication. English. qt. $20.00. Indian Research Fund Association, Calcutta, India. **(Subscription address:** Prints India, 11 Darya Ganj, New Delhi 110002 India.**) LC** RC164.I3; M322. **NLM** W1 IN212. **CODEN** IJMAA9. Documents available from BIOSIS Document Express. ***Continues*** *Journal of the Malaria Institute of India.*
**Ind/Abst** Agrofor. Abstr. (1991-); Biocont. News Inf. (1991-); Biol. Abstr. (1985-); EMBASE [Select. Cov.]; For. Prod. Abstr. (19??-19??); Health Plan. Adminis.; Index Med. (1984-); Nematol. Abstr.; Protozoolog. Abstr.; Rev. Med. Vet. Entomol.; Trop. Dis. Bull.

GW/0303-4305
**INNERE MEDIZIN.** [Inn. Med.]. Vol. 1 (May 1974)-. Academic Scholarly Publication. German (summaries and/or abstracts in English). Six times a year. DM113.40 Germany; DM117.60 other. Richard Pflaum Verlag Gmbh, Postfach 190737, D 80607 Munich Germany. **Tel** 011 49 89 126070, FAX 011 49 89 12607200, telex 5216075. **NLM** W1 IN454N. **[CCC]. Pr Rev.** Documents available from The Genuine Article.
**Ind/Abst** EMBASE; Energy Res. Abstr. (Nov. 1979-); Res. Alert [Select. Cov.]; SCISEARCH.

●JA
**INTERNAL MEDICINE. Added/Corp** Nihon Naika Gakkai. Vol. 31, No. 1 (Jan. 1992)-. Periodical. English. mo. $270.00. Japanese Society of Internal Medicine, 34 3 3 Chome Hongo Bunkyo Ku, Tokyo 113 Japan. **Tel** 011 81 3 38135991, FAX 011 81 3 38181556. **(Subscription address:** Japan Publications Trading Company, Ltd., PO Box 5030, Tokyo International, Tokyo 100-31 Japan.**) NLM** W1; IN698T. **CODEN** IEDIEP. ***Continues*** *Japanese Journal of Medicine.*
**Ind/Abst** Index Med. (1992-).

US/0897-6309
**INTERNAL MEDICINE.** 1988/89-. English. be. $20.00 per issue. University of Texas Department of Medicine, Health Science Center, San Antonio TX 78285. **DD** 616. Documents available from The Genuine Article.
**Ind/Abst** Curr. Contents Clin. Med.; Res. Alert [Select. Cov.].

US/0195-315X
**INTERNAL MEDICINE ALERT.** [Intern. med. alert]. Vol. 1 (Mar. 15, 1979)-. Periodical. English. sm. $116.00 (without CME); $191.00 (with CME credits). American Health Consultants, 3525 Piedmont Road, Suite 400, Atlanta GA 30305. **Tel** (800)688-2421, (404)262-7436. **(Subscription address:** American Health Consultants, PO Box 95278, Chicago IL 60694.**) DD** 616. **NLM** W1 IN698M. **[CCC].**
**Desc:** Brings six to eight abstracts of the most recent clinical studies in internal and family medicine, followed by interpretive commentary from our team of over 12 distinguished physician editors.

US/1065-9498
**INTERNAL MEDICINE BULLETIN.** ***Ceased.*** [Intern. med. bull.]. (1993)-Vol. 2 (1994). Bulletin. English. bw. W.B. Saunders Company, A Subsidiary of Harcourt Brace Jovanovich, Inc., The Curtis Center/Suite 300, Independence Square West, Philadelphia PA 19106-3399. **Tel** (215)238-7800 or, 5587, FAX (215)238-7883, telex 173146. **(Subscription address:** W. B. Saunders Company / North America Subscriptions, c/o Periodicals, 6277 Sea Harbour Drive, 4th Floor, Orlando FL 32887.**) ED** Dr. Malcolm S. Thaler. **DD** 616. **[CCC].**
**Desc:** Reviews articles from professional literature dealing with internal medicine and family practice.

US/0271-1303
**INTERNAL MEDICINE (GLENDALE, CALIF.).** (INTERNAL MEDICINE [SOUND RECORDING].). [Intern. med.]. **Added/Corp** Audio-Digest Foundation. **VFOAT** Audio-Digest Internal Medicine; Audio Digest Internal Medicine. (1954)-. Periodical. English. sm (24 issues). $179.76 US; $202.80 Canada; $247.44 other (audiocassette). Audio-Digest Foundation, 1577 Chevy Chase Drive, Glendale CA 91206. **Tel** (213)245-8505, (800)423-2308, FAX (818)240-7379. **ED** Claron L. Oakley. **DD** 616. **NLM** W1 AU201DI. Index available (Free).
**Desc:** An interactive system of audio cassette postgraduate medical education, with each one-hour program eligible for two Category I credit hours.

US/1056-9286
**INTERNAL MEDICINE (PLAINSBORO, N.J.).** (INTERNAL MEDICINE.). [Intern. med.]. **VFOAT** IM. Vol. 12, No. 1 (Jan. 1991)-. Periodical. English. mo. $75.00 US; $99.00 other. Medical Economics Publishing, Five Paragon Drive, Second Floor, Montvale NJ 07645. **Tel** (800)432-4570, (201)358-2210. **(Subscription address:** Fulco Medical Economics, PO Box 3000, Denville NJ 07834.**) LC** R11; .I57. **DD** 616. **NLM** W1; IN698P. **CODEN** IMEIEI. ***Continues*** *Internal Medicine for the Specialist, 0273-6608.*
**Ind/Abst** EMBASE [Select. Cov.].

●US/1058-1685
**INTERNAL MEDICINE RESIDENT.** (1992)-. Periodical. English. bm. $58.00 institution, $48.00 individual (US). Slack Inc., 6900 Grove Road, Thorofare NJ 08086. **Tel** (609)848-1000, (800)257-8290, FAX (609)853-5991, telex 517108 SLACK INC VD. **NLM** W1; IN699V.

US/1078-2869
**INTERNAL MEDICINE WEEKLY.** (19??)-. English. wk (48 issues). $995.00 US, Canada and Mexico; $1195.00 other. CW Henderson, PO Box 5528, Atlanta GA 30307-0528. **Tel** (404)377-8895, FAX (404)378-5411. **(Subscription address:** CW Henderson, Subscription Office, PO Box 830409, Birmingham AL 35283-0409.**)**
**Desc:** A comprehensive resource for the internist focusing on maintaining clinical skills and lifelong learning. With a balance of topics from the most common to the most obscure of nonsurgical diseases, it emphasizes the clinical aspects of treatment and patient management.

UK
**INTERNATIONAL BACK PAIN NEWS.** (1986)-. English. Three times a year. £30.00. Congress Team International Ltd, 15 Bedford Raod, Northwood, Middlesex, HA6 2BA England. **Tel** 011 44 81 206 0426, FAX 011 44 81 206 0427.

●NE/0928-4346
**INTERNATIONAL HEPATOLOGY COMMUNICATIONS. Added/Corp** Nihon Kanzo Gakkai. Vol. 1, No. 1 (Mar. 15, 1993)-. Academic

Scholarly Publication. English. Twelve times a year (2 vols.). $506.00. Elsevier Science Ireland Ltd., Bay 15, Shannon Industrial Estate, Co Clare Ireland. **Tel** 011 353 61 471944. **NLM** W1; IN764FM. **[CCC]. Bk Rev. Ad Acc. Pr Rev. Acid Free.** available on diskette (Must be forward by the editor for submission of the disk).
**Desc:** An international journal devoted to the rapid dissemination of concise original reports concerned with basic and clinical research in the field of hepatology.

IT/0391-3988
**INTERNATIONAL JOURNAL OF ARTIFICIAL ORGANS, THE.** [Int. j. artif. organs.]. Vol. 1 (Jan. 1978)-. Academic Scholarly Publication. English. mo. $300.00 US. Wichtig Editore, Via Friuli 72 74, 20135 Milan Italy. **Tel** 011 39 2 55195443. **(Subscription address:** Wichtig Editore, Subscription Office, PO Box 830350, Birmingham AL 35283-0350.**) ED** Diego Brancaccio and George Dunea. **LC** RD130 Db .I576. **NLM** W1 IN7655H. **CODEN** IJAODS. **[CCC].** Index available (bound in Nov. issue). cum. index. **Bk Rev. Ad Acc. Pr Rev. Circ:** 2,000. Documents available from The Genuine Article, CASDDS.
**Desc:** Reports on the latest research and discoveries in dialysis and artificial kidneys, gas exchange and artificial lungs, liver-assist devices and detoxification and other pertinent information.
**Ind/Abst** Chem. Abstr.; Curr. Contents Clin. Med.; EMBASE; Index Med.; Life Sci. Collect.; Ref. Upd. Deluxe Ed.; Res. Alert [Full Cov.]; Sci. Cit. Index; SCISEARCH; Soc. Sci. Cit. Index [Select. Cov.].

US/0276-3478
**INTERNATIONAL JOURNAL OF EATING DISORDERS, THE.** [Int. j. eat. disord.]. Vol. 1, No. 1 Autumn (1981)-. Periodical. English. Eight times a year. $512.00 (US); $592.00 (Canada and Mexico); $622.00 (other). John Wiley & Sons, Inc., 605 Third Avenue, New York NY 10158-0012. **Tel** (212)850-6000, (212)850-6645, FAX (212)850-6088, telex 12-7063. **(Subscription address:** John Wiley & Sons / England, Baffins Lane, Chichester, West Sussex PO19 1UD England.**) ED** Michael Strober. **LC** RC552.A72; I57. **DD** 616.89. **NLM** W1; IN766GB. **CODEN** INDIDJ. **[CCC]. Ad Acc. Pr Rev. Circ:** 1,300. available on microfilm and microfiche from University Microfilms International (UMI). Documents available from The Genuine Article, BIOSIS Document Express.
**Desc:** Considers the full range of eating disorders from environmentally induced dietary abnormalities to genetically or disease-induced disorders. Covers the scope of treatment, symptoms, causation and long-term effects for such disorders as anorexia nervosa, bulimia, obesity and infantile rumination.
**Ind/Abst** AGRICOLA [Select. Cov.]; Biol. Abstr.; Curr. Contents Clin. Med.; Curr. Contents Soc. Behav. Sci.; EMBASE; Health Saf. Sci. Abstr.; Nutr. Abstr. Rev., Ser. A, Hum. Exp.; Nutr. Res. Newsl.; Life Sci. Collect.; Pollut. Abstr. Indexes; Psychol. Abstr. (1981-); PsycINFO; PsycLit; Res. Alert [Full Cov.]; SCISEARCH; Soc. Sci. Cit. Index [Full Cov.]; Spec. Educ. Needs Abstr.

NE/0167-6865
**INTERNATIONAL JOURNAL OF MICROCIRCULATION: CLINICAL AND EXPERIMENTAL.** (INTERNATIONAL JOURNAL OF MICROCIRCULATION, CLINICAL AND EXPERIMENTAL.). [Int. j. microcirc., clin. exp.]. **Added/Corp** European Society for Microcirculation. **VFOAT** Microcirculation, Clinical and Experimental. Vol. 1, No. 1 (1982)-. Academic Scholarly Publication. English. bm (6 issues). $333.00. S. Karger AG, Allschwilerstrasse 10, PO Box - Postfach - Case Postale, CH-4009 Basel Switzerland. **Tel** 011 41 61 306-1111, FAX 011 41 61 306-1234, telex CH 962 652. **ED** K. Messmer, B. Fagrell. **LC** QP106.6; .I56. **DD** 599/.01. **NLM** W1 IN769Z. **CODEN** IMCEDT. **[CCC]. Bk Rev. Ad Acc. Pr Rev. Acid Free. Circ:** 300. available on microfilm and microfiche from University Microfilms International (UMI). Documents available from The Genuine Article, BIOSIS Document Express, CASDDS.
**Desc:** Publishes papers describing theoretical, experimental and clinical work which have as their focus the terminal blood vessels, the blood circulating through them, the fluid and materials exchanged across their walls, the tissues supplied by them or the lymphatics draining these tissues.
**Ind/Abst** Biol. Abstr. (1987-); Chem. Abstr.; Curr. Aware. Biol. Sci., CABS; Curr. Contents Life Sci.; Index Med.; Ref. Upd. Deluxe Ed.; Res. Alert [Full Cov.]; Sci. Cit. Index; SCISEARCH.

NE/0169-4197
**INTERNATIONAL JOURNAL OF PANCREATOLOGY.** (INTERNATIONAL JOURNAL OF PANCREATOLOGY : OFFICIAL JOURNAL OF THE INTERNATIONAL ASSOCIATION OF PANCREATOLOGY.). [Int. j. pancreatol.]. **Added/Corp** International Association of Pancreatology. Vol. 1/1 (May 1986)-. Academic Scholarly Publication. English. bm (6 issues). $360.00 US; $410.00 other. Humana Press Inc., 999 Riverview Drive, Suite 208, Totawa NJ 07512. **Tel** (201)256-1699, FAX (201)256-8341. **ED** Parviz Pour, M.D. **NLM** W1; IN771H. **CODEN** IJPNEX. **[CCC]. Pr Rev.** Documents available from The Genuine Article, BIOSIS Document Express, CASDDS.
**Desc:** A multidisciplinary communication medium covering basic and clinical research on both the exocrine and endocrine pancreas, including endocrine-exocrine interactions in health and diseases states.
**Ind/Abst** Biol. Abstr. (1986-); Chem. Abstr. (1986-); Curr. Aware. Biol. Sci., CABS; Curr. Contents Life Sci.; EMBASE; Index Med. (Vol. 1, No. 1, 1986-); Ref. Upd. Deluxe Ed.; Res. Alert [Full Cov.]; Sci. Cit. Index; SCISEARCH.

GW/0020-9554
**INTERNIST (BERLIN), DER.** (INTERNIST.). [Internist]. **Added/Corp** Berufsverband Deutscher Internisten. (1960)-. Academic Scholarly Publication. German. Twelve times a year. DM398.00. Springer-Verlag GmbH & Company KG, Heidelberger Platz 3, D 14197 Berlin Germany. **Tel** 011 49 30 8207223, FAX 011 49 30 8214091, telex 183 319 SPBLN D. **(Subscription address:** Springer Verlag New York Inc. / for North America, 44 Hartz Way, Secaucus NJ 07096.**) ED** E. Buchborn, M. Classen, W. Doelle, J. van de Loo, G. Riecker, H. P Schuster, P. C. Scriba, W. Siegenthaler, P. von Wichert. **NLM** W1 IN962. **CODEN** INTEAG. **[CCC].** cum. index. **Pr Rev.** available on microfilm from University Microfilms International (UMI). Documents available from The Genuine Article, BIOSIS Document Express, CASDDS, ADONIS. ***Supersedes*** *Aertzliche Wochenschrift.*
**Desc:** Covers all areas of internal medicine. Each issue is dedicated to one specific area. Articles are coordinated for a comprehensive coverage of the subject. Diagnosis and therapy take priority.
**Ind/Abst** ADONIS; Biol. Abstr.; Chem. Abstr.; CIS Abstr.; Curr. Contents Clin. Med.; EMBASE; Energy Res. Abstr.; Helminthol. Abstr. (19??-19??); Index Med.; Nucl. Sci. Abstr.; Nutr. Abstr. Rev., Ser. B, Live Feeds and Feed.; Nutr. Abstr. Rev., Ser. A, Hum. Exp.; PESTDOC; Protozoolog. Abstr.; Res. Alert [Full Cov.]; Saf. Health Work; Sci. Cit. Index; SCISEARCH.

GW/0344-4201
**INTERNISTISCHE WELT.** [Internist. Welt]. Vol. 1 (Jan. 1978)-. Academic Scholarly Publication. German. Comes with Die Medizinische Welt. F K Schattauer Verlagsgesellschaft mbH, Postfach 10 45 45, D 70040 Stuttgart Germany. **Tel** 011 49 711 2298726. **ED** H. G. Lasch, P. Matis, and G. Oehler. **NLM** W1 IN968C. **[CCC].** Index available. **Ad Acc.**
**Ind/Abst** EMBASE; Energy Res. Abstr. (Nov. 1981-).

JA
**ISHOKU. Added/Corp** Nippon Ishoku Gakkai. **VFOAT** Transplantation Journal; Japanese Journal of Transplantation. (1966)-. Periodical. Japanese. bm (6 issues). $180.00. **(Subscription address:** Kyowa Book Company Inc., 1 38 Kanda Jinbocho Chiyoda-ku, Tokyo 101 Japan.**) NLM** W1 IS405. ***Continues*** *Nippon Ishoku Gakkai Zasshi.*
**Ind/Abst** Energy Res. Abstr. (Dec. 1979-).

US/0360-5914
**JOHNS HOPKINS UNIVERSITY SCHOOL OF MEDICINE POSTGRADUATE COURSE IN INTERNAL MEDICINE, THE.** (THE JOHNS HOPKINS UNIVERSITY SCHOOL OF MEDICINE POSTGRADUATE COURSE IN INTERNAL MEDICINE. KIT.). [Johns Hopkins Univ. Sch. Med. postgrad. course intern. med.]. **VFOAT** Johns Hopkins Postgraduate Course in Internal Medicine; Postgraduate Course in Internal Medicine. V. 1- (Program 1- April 1975)-. Periodical. English. mo. Johns Hopkins University / Medicine, School of Medicine, 1721 East Madison Street, Baltimore MD 21205. **Tel** (301)338-6990. **NLM** W1 JO159D.
**Desc:** Each program consists of cassettes, 35mm slides or flipcards, a study syllabus, and a Physician's Assessment.

US/1045-4861
**JOURNAL OF APPLIED BIOMATERIALS.** (JOURNAL OF APPLIED BIOMATERIALS : AN OFFICIAL JOURNAL OF THE SOCIETY FOR BIOMATERIALS.). [J. appl. biomater.]. **Added/Corp** Society for Biomaterials. (1990)-. Periodical. English. Four times a year. $196.00 (US); $236.00 (Canada and Mexico); $251.00 (other). John Wiley & Sons, Inc., 605 Third Avenue, New York NY 10158-0012. **Tel** (212)850-6000, (212)850-6645, FAX (212)850-6088, telex 12-7063. **(Subscription address:** John Wiley & Sons / England, Baffins Lane, Chichester, West Sussex PO19 1UD England.**) ED** Harold Alexander. **LC** IN PROCESS. **DD** 610. **NLM** W1; JO539X. **CODEN** JABIEW. **[CCC].** available on microfilm and microfiche from University Microfilms International (UMI). Documents available from Article Express International, The Genuine Article.
**Desc:** Covers medical device development, implant retrieval and analysis, details on government regulations, liability and legal issues, and much more.
**Ind/Abst** Curr. Contents Life Sci.; Ei Page One; Eng. Index Annu.; Res. Alert [Full Cov.]; Sci. Cit. Index; SCISEARCH.

US/0884-8734
**JOURNAL OF GENERAL INTERNAL MEDICINE.** (JOURNAL OF GENERAL INTERNAL MEDICINE : OFFICIAL JOURNAL OF THE SOCIETY FOR RESEARCH AND EDUCATION IN PRIMARY CARE INTERNAL MEDICINE.). [J. gen. intern. med.]. **Added/Corp** Society for Research and Education in Primary Care Internal Medicine. Vol. 1, No. 1 (Jan./Feb. 1986)-. Periodical. English. mo. $78.00 (US & possessions), $88.00 (other) individual; $98.00 (US & possessions), $108.00 (other) institution. Hanley & Belfus Inc., 210 South 13th Street, Philadelphia PA 19107. **Tel** (215)546-7293, FAX (215)790-9330. **ED** Robert Fletcher and Suzanne Fletcher (Editor's address: The University of North Carolina at Chapel Hill, Box 7110, 5039 Old Clinic Building, Chapel Hill, NC 27599-7110; (919)966-3521). **LC** R11; .J686. **DD** 616/.005. **NLM** W1; JO667F. **CODEN** JGIMEJ. **[CCC].** Index available. cum. index. **Bk Rev. Ad Acc. Pr Rev. Circ:** 4,000. Documents available from The Genuine Article, BIOSIS Document Express.
**Desc:** Covers common medical problems of general internal medicine, including original research and reviews.
**Ind/Abst** Annals Behav. Med.; Biol. Abstr. (1986-); Cumul. Index Nurs. Allied Health Lit.; Curr. Contents Clin. Med.; EMBASE; Index Med. (Vol. 1, No. 1, 1986-); J. Watch; Mod. Med.; Res. Alert [Select. Cov.]; SCISEARCH; Soc. Sci. Cit. Index [Select. Cov.].

●US/1061-6128
**JOURNAL OF HEMATOTHERAPHY.** [J. hematother.]. **Added/Corp** International Society for Hematotherapy and Graft Engineering. Vol. 1, No. 1 (Spring 1992)-. Periodical. English. qt. $124.00. Mary Ann Liebert Inc., 1651 Third Avenue, New York NY 10128. **Tel** (212)289-2300, (800)M-LIEBERT, FAX (212)289-4697. **ED** Adrian Gee and Nancy Collins. **DD** 615. **NLM** W1; JO67D. **CODEN** JOEMEL. **Pr Rev.**
**Desc:** Focuses on ex vivo manipulation of hematopoietic cells for in vivo therapy. Developments in conventional therapy that impact on ex vivo technology are included. Contains papers on the basic and clinical science of marrow graft engineering, cellular immunotherapy, gene therapy, immunoengineering, and ex vivo hematopoiesis. Covers the transition of these technologies from basic research through to early clinical applications to demonstrate efficacy.

NE/0168-8278
**JOURNAL OF HEPATOLOGY.** (JOURNAL OF HEPATOLOGY : THE JOURNAL OF THE EUROPEAN ASSOCIATION FOR THE STUDY OF THE LIVER.). [J. hepatol.]. **Added/Corp** European Association for the Study of the Liver. Vol. 1, No. 1 (1985)-. Academic Scholarly Publication. English. Twelve times a year. kr4650.00 (institutions), kr1250.00 (individuals) US, Canada and Japan; kr4550.00 (institutions), kr1150.00 (individuals) other. Munksgaard International Publishers Ltd, PO Box 2148, DK-1016 Copenhagen K Denmark. **Tel** 011 45 33 12 70 30, FAX 011 45 33 12 93 87, telex 19431 MUNKS DK. **ED** Dame Sheila Sherlock, J. P. Benhamon Clichy, R. Preisig, J. Rodes and J. A. Summerfield. **NLM** W1; JO67E. **CODEN** JOHEEC. **[CCC]. Pr Rev.** available on microfilm and microfiche from University Microfilms International (UMI). Documents available from The Genuine Article, BIOSIS Document Express, CASDDS, ADONIS. ***Absorbed*** *Journal of Hepatology. Supplement, 0169-5185.*
**Desc:** Publishes original papers and reviews concerned with practice and research in the field of hepatology. Papers may cover the medical, surgical, radiological, pathological, biochemical or historical aspects.
**Ind/Abst** ADONIS; Biol. Abstr. (1985-); Chem. Abstr. (1985-); CSA Neuro. Abstr. (?-?); Curr. Aware. Biol. Sci., CABS; Curr. Contents Clin. Med.; Curr. Contents Life Sci.; EMBASE; Index Med. (Vol. 1, No. 1, 1985-)( 1985-); Nutr. Abstr. Rev., Ser. A, Hum. Exp.; Ref. Upd. Clinical Ed.; Ref. Upd. Deluxe Ed.; Res. Alert [Full Cov.]; Rev. Med. Vet. Mycology; Sci. Cit. Index; SCISEARCH.

UK/0141-8955
**JOURNAL OF INHERITED METABOLIC DISEASE.** [J. inherit. metab. dis.]. **Added/Corp** Society for the Study of Inborn Errors of Metabolism. **VFOAT** Inherited Metabolic Disease. Vol. 1 (1978)-. Academic Scholarly Publication. English. bm. $631.00. Kluwer Academic Publishers, Postbus 322, 3300 AH Dordrecht, The Netherlands. **Tel** 011 (31) 78 524400, FAX 011 31 78 183273, telex 20083. **ED** R A Harkness, R J Pollitt, G M Addison and T N Besley. **NLM** W1 JO709. **CODEN** JIMDDP. **[CCC].** cum. index. **Bk Rev. Ad Acc. Pr Rev. Acid Free. Circ:** 1,000. available on microfilm and microfiche from University Microfilms International (UMI). Documents available from The Genuine Article, BIOSIS Document Express, CASDDS.
**Desc:** Provides a medium for disseminating research information in this rapidly growing subject.
**Ind/Abst** Anim. Breed. Abstr.; Biol. Abstr.; Chem. Abstr.; Curr. Aware. Biol. Sci., CABS; Curr. Biotechnol.; Curr. Contents Life Sci.; Dairy Sci. Abstr.; Dev. Med. Child Neurol.; EMBASE; Index Med.; Index Vet.; Int. Nurs. Index; Nutr. Abstr. Rev., Ser. A, Hum. Exp.; Life Sci. Collect.; Ref. Upd. Deluxe Ed.; Res. Alert [Full Cov.]; Sci. Cit. Index; SCISEARCH; Small Anim. Abstr. Bibliogr.; Soc. Sci. Cit. Index [Select. Cov.].

UK/0954-6820
**JOURNAL OF INTERNAL MEDICINE.** [J. intern. med.]. Vol. 225, No. 1 (Jan. 1989)-. Academic Scholarly Publication. English. mo. $316.00 US & Canada; £204.00 other. Blackwell Scientific Publications Ltd, Marston Book Services, PO Box 87, Oxford OX2 ODT UK. **Tel** 011 44 865 791155, FAX 011 44 865

791927, telex 837 515 MARDIS G. **ED** L. E. Bottiger. **NLM** W1; JO716N. **CODEN** JINMEO. **[CCC]. Pr Rev.** available on microfilm and microfiche from University Microfilms International (UMI). Documents available from The Genuine Article, BIOSIS Document Express, CASDDS, ADONIS. ***Continues*** *Acta Medica Scandinavica, 0001-6101.*
**Desc:** Presents leading clinical research in internal medicine.
**Ind/Abst** ADONIS; Biol. Abstr.; Chem. Abstr.; Curr. Aware. Biol. Sci., CABS; Curr. Contents Clin. Med.; Curr. Contents Life Sci.; EMBASE; Index Med. (1989-); Iowa Drug Inf. Serv.; Nutr. Abstr. Rev., Ser. A, Hum. Exp.; Nutr. Res. Newsl.; PESTDOC; Protozoolog. Abstr.; Ref. Upd. Basic Ed.; Ref. Upd. Deluxe Ed.; Res. Alert [Full Cov.]; Sci. Cit. Index; SCISEARCH; Soc. Sci. Cit. Index [Select. Cov.]; Soyabean Abstr.

UK/0955-7873
**JOURNAL OF INTERNAL MEDICINE. SUPPLEMENT.** [J. intern. med., Suppl.]. (1989)-. Monographic series. English. ir. Comes with subscription to Journal of Internal Medicine. Blackwell Scientific Publications Ltd, Marston Book Services, PO Box 87, Oxford OX2 ODT UK. **Tel** 011 44 865 791155, FAX 011 44 865 791927, telex 837 515 MARDIS G. **NLM** W1; JO716NA. **CODEN** JIMSE3. Documents available from BIOSIS Document Express, CASDDS. ***Continues*** *Acta Medica Scandinavica. Supplementum, 0365-463X.*
**Ind/Abst** Biol. Abstr. (1989-); Chem. Abstr.; EMBASE; Health Plan. Adminis.; Index Med. (1989-).

US/0741-5400
**JOURNAL OF LEUKOCYTE BIOLOGY.** [J. leukoc. biol.]. **Added/Corp** Reticuloendothelial Society. Federation of American Societies for Experimental Biology. Society for Leukocyte Biology. Vol. 35, No. 1 (Jan. 1984)-. Academic Scholarly Publication. English. mo (plus supplement). $696.00 (institution), $105.00 (individual) US; $716.00 (institution), $125.00 (individual) Canada and Mexico; $744.00 (institution), $153.00 (individual) other. Federation of American Societies for Experimental Biology, Room L-2310, 9650 Rockville Park, Bethesda MD 20814-3998. **Tel** (301)530-7027. **ED** Carleton C Stewart. **LC** QP185; .R47. **DD** 599/.01/13. **NLM** W1; J0745H. **CODEN** JLBIE7. **[CCC]. Pr Rev.** Documents available from The Genuine Article, BIOSIS Document Express, CASDDS. ***Continues*** *Reticuloendothelial Society. Res. Journal of the Reticuloendothelial Society, 0033-6890.*
**Desc:** Presents manuscripts of original investigations on the orgins, including developmental biology and functions, of granulocytes, lymphocytes, and mononuclear phagocytes; their mechanisms of inter-cellular communication; and the ways effector molecules recognize and destroy infectious organisms, foreign tissue, or neoplastic cells.
**Ind/Abst** Biol. Abstr.; Chem. Abstr. (1984-); Chemorecept. Abstr.; Curr. Aware. Biol. Sci., CABS; Curr. Contents Life Sci.; EMBASE; Immunol. Abstr.; Index Med.; Index Vet.; INIS Atomindex [Micro.]; NAPRALERT; Oncog. Growth Factors Abstr.; Life Sci. Collect.; Pig News Inf.; Poult. Abstr.; Protozoolog. Abstr.; Ref. Upd. Basic Ed.; Ref. Upd. Deluxe Ed.; Res. Alert [Full Cov.]; Rev. Med. Vet. Mycology; Sci. Cit. Index; SCISEARCH; Small Anim. Abstr. Bibliogr.; Soc. Sci. Cit. Index [Select. Cov.]; Vet. Bull.; Virol. AIDS Abstr.

II
**JOURNAL OF THE ASSOCIATION OF PHYSICIANS OF INDIA.** (19??)-. English. Twelve times a year. $200.00. Association of Physicians of India, Laud Mansion, 21 M Karve Road / 3rd, Bombay 400004 India. **Tel** 3829348. **(Subscription address:** Prints India, 11 Darya Ganj, New Delhi 110002 India.) **ED** Dr. P. J. Mehta (editor's address: Commissariat Building, 3rd Floor, 231 D. N. Road, Bombay, 400001 India, phone: 2611719). **Bk Rev. Ad Acc, Adv Mgr Tel** 2611719. **Pr Rev. Circ:** 7,500 (ctrl).

DK/0905-9199
**JOURNAL OF TRANSPLANT COORDINATION : OFFICIAL PUBLICATION OF THE NORTH AMERICAN TRANSPLANT COORDINATORS ORGANIZATION (NATCO).** **Added/Corp** North American Transplant Coordinators Organization. Vol. 1, Issue 1 (Apr. 1991)-. Academic Scholarly Publication. English. Three times a year. kr590.00 (institution), kr435.00 (individual) US and Canada; kr650.00 (institution), kr495.00 (individual) other. Munksgaard International Publishers Ltd, PO Box 2148, DK-1016 Copenhagen K Denmark. **Tel** 011 45 33 12 70 30, FAX 011 45 33 12 93 87, telex 19431 MUNKS DK. **ED** Barbara A. Elick. **LC** RD129.5; .J68. **DD** 362.1/783. **NLM** W1; JO966M. **[CCC]. Ad Acc. Pr Rev. Circ:** 2,000.
**Ind/Abst** EMBASE (1993-).

●US
**JOURNAL : THE JOURNAL OF THE AMERICAN BLOOD RESOURCES ASSOCIATION, THE.** See Medical Science and Technology-Hematology.

JA
**KOKU IGAKU JIKKENTAI KENKYU SEIKA GAIYO.** **Main/Corp** Japan. Kioku Igaku Jikkentai. (19??)-. Periodical. Japanese. Kioku Igaku Jikkentai, 2-10 Sakaecho 1, Tachikawa Japan. **LC** RC1050; .J35a.

JA/0452-3458
**KOKYU TO JUNKAN.** [Kokyu to junkan]. **VFOAT** Respiration and Circulation. (1953)-. Periodical. Japanese. mo. $208.70. Igaku Shoin Ltd., 5-24-3 Hongo Bunkyo-ku, Tokyo 113 Japan. **Tel** 011 81 3 817 5670. **CODEN** KOJUA9. Documents available from BIOSIS Document Express, CASDDS.
**Ind/Abst** Biol. Abstr.; Chem. Abstr.; EMBASE [Select. Cov.]; Index Med.

JA/0009-3378
**KYOTO DAIGAKU KEKKAKU KYOBU SHIKKAN KENKYUJO KIYO.** [Kyoto Daigaku Kekkaku Kyobu Shikkan Kenkyujo Kiyo]. **Main/Corp** Kyoto Daigaku. Kekkuku Kyobu Shikkan Kenkyujo. **VFOAT** Bulletin of the Chest Disease Research Institute, Kyoto University. Vol. 1 (March 1968)-. Academic Scholarly Publication. Japanese (English). an. Free on request. Chest Disease Research Institute, Library Kyoto Institute Sakyo KU 606, Koyoto Japan. **NLM** W1 BU845A. **CODEN** KDKBBH. Documents available from CASDDS. ***Supersedes*** *Acta Tuberculosa Japonica; Kyoto Daigaku Kekkaku Kenkyujo Kiyo.*
**Ind/Abst** Chem. Abstr.; EMBASE; Health Plan. Adminis.; Index Med.; Trop. Dis. Bull.

DK/0106-9543
**LIVER (COPENHAGEN).** (LIVER.). [Liver]. Vol. 1, No. 1 (Mar. 1981)-. Periodical. English. bm. kr1240.00 US, Canada and Japan; kr1210.00 other. Munksgaard International Publishers Ltd, PO Box 2148, DK-1016 Copenhagen K Denmark. **Tel** 011 45 33 12 70 30, FAX 011 45 33 12 93 87, telex 19431 MUNKS DK. **ED** Hemming Poulsen and Per Christoffersen. **NLM** W1 LI919N. **CODEN** LIVEDR. **[CCC].** Index available. **Bk Rev. Ad Acc. Pr Rev. Circ:** 800 (ctrl). Documents available from The Genuine Article, BIOSIS Document Express.
**Desc:** Liver pathology, hepatology and diseases of the liver.
**Ind/Abst** Biol. Abstr.; Curr. Aware. Biol. Sci., CABS; Curr. Contents Clin. Med.; Curr. Contents Life Sci.; EMBASE; Helminthol. Abstr. (1991-); Index Med.; Res. Alert [Select. Cov.]; Rev. Med. Vet. Mycology; Sci. Cit. Index; SCISEARCH.

US/0163-9021
**LIVER, NORMAL FUNCTION AND DISEASE.** [Liver: norm. func. dis.]. Vol. 1 (1978)-. Academic Scholarly Publication. English. ir. Price varies per volume. Marcel Dekker Inc., 270 Madison Avenue, New York NY 10016. **Tel** (212)696-9000, (800)228-1160, FAX (212)685-4540, telex 421419. **(Subscription address:** Marcel Dekker Inc, PO Box 5017, Monticello NY 12701.) **LC** UNC. **NLM** W1 LI921. **CODEN** LNFDDD. Documents available from CASDDS.
**Desc:** Covers the various aspects of the liver and liver disease. Topics include jaundice and hepatitis.
**Ind/Abst** Chem. Abstr.

US/0025-6196
**MAYO CLINIC PROCEEDINGS.** [Mayo Clin. proc.]. **Main/Corp** Mayo Clinic. **Added/Corp** Mayo Foundation for Medical Education and Research. Mayo Association. Mayo Clinic. Proceedings. Vol. 39 (Jan. 1964)-. Academic Scholarly Publication. English. mo. Free (physicians and third year medical students); 99.00Can$ Canada, $72.00 other. Mayo Clinic Proceedings, 200 First Street Southwest, Rochester MN 55905. **Tel** (507)284-2094, FAX (507)284-0252. **ED** P.J. Palumbo. **NLM** W1 MA997V. **CODEN** MACPAJ. **[CCC].** Index available. cum. index. **Bk Rev. Ad Acc. Pr Rev. Circ:** 126,000 (ctrl). available on microfilm and microfiche from University Microfilms International (UMI). Documents available from The Genuine Article, BIOSIS Document Express, CASDDS. ***Continues*** *Proceedings of the Staff Meetings of the Mayo Clinic, 0092-699X.*
**Desc:** New information about clinical and research activities of the Mayo Clinic and Mayo Foundation, plus review articles and reports written by Mayo Clinic staff members.
**Ind/Abst** Abr. Index Med.; Biol. Abstr.; Chem. Abstr.; Cumul. Index Nurs. Allied Health Lit.; Curr. Aware. Biol. Sci., CABS; Curr. Contents Clin. Med.; Curr. Contents Life Sci.; EMBASE; Energy Res. Abstr.; Health Devices Alerts; Index Med.; Index Vet.; Ind. Hyg. Dig.; Int. Pharm. Abstr.; Iowa Drug Inf. Serv. (1968-); J. Watch (199?-); Med. Abstr. Newsl.; Mod. Med.; Nutr. Abstr. Rev., Ser. A, Hum. Exp.; Nutr. Res. Newsl.; Life Sci. Collect.; Physic. Medline Plus; Ref. Upd. Basic Ed.; Ref. Upd. Clinical Ed.; Ref. Upd. Deluxe Ed.; Res. Alert [Full Cov.]; Rev. Med. Vet. Mycology; Sci. Cit. Index; SCISEARCH; Soc. Sci. Cit. Index [Select. Cov.]; SportSearch; Trop. Dis. Bull.

RM
**MEDICINA INTERNA (BUCHAREST, ROMANIA : 1991).** (19??)-. Periodical. Romanian (summaries and/or abstracts in English, French, German and Russian). Four times a year. DM260.00. Uniunea Societ Stiinte Medical, Str Progresului 8, Bucharest Romania. **(Subscription address:** Kubon & Sagner, ABT Zeitschriftenimport, D 80328 Munich Germany.) ***Continues*** *Revista de Medicina Interna, Neurologie, Psyhiatrie, Neurochirurgie, Dermato-Veneralogie. Medicina Interna, 1220-0905.*

US
**MEDICINE.** English. an. John Wiley & Sons, Inc., 605 Third Avenue, New York NY 10158-0012. **Tel** (212)850-6000, (212)850-6645, FAX (212)850-6088, telex 12-7063. **(Subscription address:** John Wiley & Sons / England, Baffins Lane, Chichester, West Sussex PO19 1UD England.) **LC** R5; .M45. **DD** 610/.5.
**Desc:** Vols. for 1976 contain proceedings of the Symposium on Advanced Medicine.

SP
**MEDICINE. TRATADO DE MEDICINA INTERNA.** Spanish. sa. 13500.00ptas. IDEPSA International Ediciones Publs SA, Principe de Vergara 112 1F, 28002 Madrid Spain. **Tel** 011 34 1 5637306.

IT/0026-0509
**METABOLISMO.** ***Ceased.*** Vol. 1 (1965)-?. Periodical. Italian. bm. CEPI, Vis Nicolo Tartaglia, 00197 Rome Italy. **Tel** 011 39 6 8082101 or 8077011, FAX 011 39 6 8072458. **LC** RC620.A1; M4. ***Continues*** *Archivo del Ricambio.*

IT
**METABOLISMO OGGI.** Italian. Three times a year. Free. Servier Italia/Sig G Galliano, Via Aldobrandeschi 75, 00163 Rome Italy. **Tel** 011 39 6 6806241.

US/0898-3127
**MIND BODY HEALTH DIGEST.** ***Ceased.*** [Mind body health dig.]. Periodical. English. Institute for the Advancement of Health, 16 East 53rd Street, New York NY 10022. **Tel** (212)832-8282. **ED** Sheldon Lewis. **DD** 616. **Bk Rev. Ad Acc. Circ:** 5,000 (ctrl).

SZ/0378-0392
**MINERAL AND ELECTROLYTE METABOLISM.** [Miner. electrolythe metab.]. Vol. 1 (1978)-. Academic Scholarly Publication. English. bm. $412.00. S. Karger AG, Allschwilerstrasse 10, PO Box - Postfach - Case Postale, CH-4009 Basel Switzerland. **Tel** 011 41 61 306-1111, FAX 011 41 61 306-1234, telex CH 962 652. **ED** S. G. Massry. **NLM** W1 MI624E. **CODEN** MELMDI. **[CCC].** Index available. **Ad Acc. Pr Rev.** available on microfilm and microfiche. Documents available from The Genuine Article, BIOSIS Document Express, CASDDS.
**Desc:** Provides valuable clinical and experimental research data on the normal physiology and disorders of mineral and electrolyte homeostasis. Concise reports present new findings concerning calcium, potasium, sodium, magnesium, phosphorous, acid-base and water metabolism as well as hormones, trace metals and vitamins.
**Ind/Abst** Biol. Abstr.; Calcium Calcif. Tissue Abstr.; Chem. Abstr.; Curr. Aware. Biol. Sci., CABS; Curr. Contents Life Sci.; EMBASE [Select. Cov.]; Index Med.; Nutr. Res. Newsl.; Life Sci. Collect.; Ref. Upd. Basic Ed.; Ref. Upd. Deluxe Ed.; Res. Alert [Full Cov.]; Sci. Cit. Index; SCISEARCH; Soc. Sci. Cit. Index [Select. Cov.].

IT/0391-3627
**MINERVA ANGIOLOGICA.** (MINERVA ANGIOLOGICA : ORGANO UFFICIALE DELLA SOCIETA ITALIANA DI PATOLOGIA VASCOLARE.). [Minerva angiol.]. **Added/Corp** Societa Italiana di Patologia Vascolare. (19??)-. Periodical. Italian. qt. $90.00 (individuals), $140.00 (institutions). Edizioni Minerva Medica, Corso Bramante 83-85, 10126 Turin Italy. **Tel** 011 39 11 678282, FAX 011 39 11 674502. **NLM** W1; MI631D.

IT/0026-4806
**MINERVA MEDICA.** [Minerva med.]. (1909)-. Academic Scholarly Publication. Italian. Twelve times a year. $110.00 (individuals), $150.00 (institutions). Edizioni Minerva Medica, Corso Bramante 83-85, 10126 Turin Italy. **Tel** 011 39 11 678282, FAX 011 39 11 674502. **ED** A Oliaro. **LC** R61; .M48. **NLM** W1 MI646. **CODEN** MIMEAO. **Bk Rev. Ad Acc.** available on microfilm from University Microfilms International (UMI). Documents available from CASDDS.
**Desc:** Journal addressed to practitioners and specialists in internal medicine in Italy and abroad. It deals with topics in medicine, scientific practice and research.
**Ind/Abst** Chem. Abstr.; CIS Abstr.; EMBASE; Index Med.; Life Sci. Collect.; PESTDOC; Saf. Health Work; SportSearch.

AU
**MITTEILUNGEN OESTERREICHISCHEN GESELLSCHAFT TROPENMEDIZIN UND PARASITOLOGIE.** Vol. 12 (1990)-. German. an. Free. Oesterreichischer Gesellschaft, Absatzwirtschaft Augasse 2 6, A 1090 Vienna Austria. **Tel** 011 43 1 313364400.
**Ind/Abst** Dairy Sci. Abstr.

SP/0212-1514
**MTA. MEDICINA INTERNA.** [MTA, Med. interna]. **VFOAT** Metodos Terapeutico-Diagnosticos de Actualidad. Medicina Interna; MTA. Metodos

Terapeutico-Diagnosticos de Actualidad. Medicina Interna. (1983)-. Periodical. Spanish. mo. $75.00. Prous Science Publishers, Apartado de Correos 540, 08080 Barcelona Spain. **Tel** 011 34 3 4592220, FAX 011 34 3 4581535. **UDC** 616.

JA/0547-1729
**NAIKA.** (NAIKA INTERNAL MEDICINE.). **VFOAT** Internal Medicine. (1955)-. Periodical. Japanese. Twelve times a year. $435.00. Nankodo, (Nankodo Co., Ltd.), 42-6, Hongo 3 Chome, Bunkyoku, Tokyoto 113 Japan. **(Subscription address:** Maruzen Company Ltd., PO Box 5050, Import & Export Department, Tokyo 100 31 Japan.**) NLM** W1 NA11695. Index available. **Bk Rev. Ad Acc. Circ:** 13,300.

JA/0021-4809
**NAIKA HOKAN.** [Naika hokan]. **Added/Corp** Kyoto Daigaku. Igakubu. Naikagaku Kyoshitsu. Kyoto. University. Dept. of Internal Medicine. **VFOAT** Japanese Archives of Internal Medicine. Vol. 1 (Sept. 1954)-. Academic Scholarly Publication. Japanese (summaries and/or abstracts in English, French and German). mo. $105.00. Naika Hokan Kankokai, (Society for Publication of Japanese Archives of Internal Medicine), c/o Kyoto Daigaku Igakubu, Naikagaku Kyoshitsu, 54 Shogoin Kawaracho, Sakyoku, Kyotoshi, Kyotofu 606 Japan. **(Subscription address:** Japan Publications Trading Company, Ltd., PO Box 5030, Tokyo International, Tokyo 100-31 Japan.**) NLM** W1 NA117. **CODEN** NAHOAI. Documents available from BIOSIS Document Express, CASDDS.
**Ind/Abst** Biol. Abstr.; Chem. Abstr.; EMBASE [Select. Cov.].

NE/0300-2977
**NETHERLANDS JOURNAL OF MEDICINE.** [Neth. j. med.]. **Added/Corp** Netherlands Association of Internal Medicine. Nederlandsche Internisten Vereeniging. Vol. 16 (1973)-. Academic Scholarly Publication. English. Twelve times a year (2 vols.). Fl984.00. Elsevier Science Publishers BV, PO Box 211, 1000 AE Amsterdam Netherlands. **Tel** 011 31 20 5803642, FAX 011 31 20 5862696, telex 15682. **ED** P W de Leeuw. **NLM** W1 NE229J. **CODEN** NLJMAV. **[CCC]. Pr Rev.** available on microfilm and microfiche from University Microfilms International (UMI). Documents available from The Genuine Article, BIOSIS Document Express, CASDDS. ***Continues** Folia Medica Neerlandica, 0015-5624.*
**Desc:** Publishes original research, reviews, editorials and case reports in all fields of interest to the general and specialist internist.
**Ind/Abst** Biol. Abstr.; Chem. Abstr.; Curr. Contents Clin. Med.; EMBASE; Helminthol. Abstr. (1991-); Index Med.; Index Vet.; Nutr. Abstr. Rev., Ser. A, Hum. Exp.; Nutr. Res. Newsl.; Life Sci. Collect.; PESTDOC; Protozoolog. Abstr.; Res. Alert [Full Cov.]; Rev. Med. Vet. Mycology; Sci. Cit. Index; SCISEARCH; Small Anim. Abstr. Bibliogr.

CN/0715-3236
**NEWSLETTER / NORTHWESTERN SOCIETY OF INTESTINAL RESEARCH.** [Newsl. - Northwest. Soc. Intest. Res.]. **Added/Corp** Northwestern Society of Intestinal Research. (1978)-. Newsletter. English. ir. Free to members. Northwestern Society of Intestinal Research, Box 80838, South Burnaaby BC V5H 3Y1. **DD** 616.3/4/005. ***Continues** Newsletter to all Members (Northwestern Society of Intestinal Research), 0715-3228.*

JA/0385-3667
**NIHON KYOBU RINSHO.** [Nihon kyobu rinsho]. **VFOAT** Japanese Journal of Chest Diseases. (19??)-. Academic Scholarly Publication. Japanese. mo. $382.00. Kokuseido Shuppan K.K., (Kokuseido Publishing Co., Ltd.), 23-5-202, Hongo 3 Chome, Bunkyoku, Tokyoto 113 Japan. **(Subscription address:** Kyowa Book Company Inc., 1 38 Kanda Jinbocho Chiyoda-ku, Tokyo 101 Japan.**) NLM** W1 NI921. **CODEN** NKYRAC. Documents available from BIOSIS Document Express, CASDDS.
**Ind/Abst** Biol. Abstr.; Chem. Abstr. (1940-1983); EMBASE [Select. Cov.]; Saf. Health Work.

JA/0301-1542
**NIHON KYOBU SHIKKAN GAKKAI ZASSHI.** [Nihon Kyobu Shikkan Gakkai zasshi]. **Added/Corp** Nihon KyÂobu Shikkan Gakkai. **VFOAT** Japanese Journal of Thoracic Diseases. (196?)-. Periodical. Japanese (summaries and/or abstracts in English). Thirteen times a year. $176.00. **(Subscription address:** Kyowa Book Company Inc., 1 38 Kanda Jinbocho Chiyoda-ku, Tokyo 101 Japan.**) CODEN** NKYZA2. Documents available from BIOSIS Document Express.
**Ind/Abst** Biol. Abstr.; EMBASE; Index Med.

JA/0021-5384
**NIHON NAIKA GAKKAI ZASSHI.** (NIHON NAIKA GAKKAI ZASSHI. THE JOURNAL OF THE JAPANESE SOCIETY OF INTERNAL MEDICINE.). [Nippon Naika Gakkai zasshi]. **Added/Corp** Nihon Naika Gakkai. **VFOAT** The Journal of the Japanese Society of Internal Medicine. Vol. 1 (July 1913)-. Academic Scholarly Publication. Japanese (summaries and/or abstracts in English). mo. $232.60 North America; $214.10 Asia & Oceania; $251.10 other. Nihon Naika Gakkai, (Japanese Soc. of Internal Medicine), 34-3, Hongo 3 Chome, Bunkyoku, Tokyoto 113, Japan. **(Subscription address:** Japan Publications Trading Company, Ltd., PO Box 5030, Tokyo International, Tokyo 100-31 Japan.**) NLM** W1 NI923P. **CODEN** NNGAAS. Index available in last issue of volume--attached. Documents available from CASDDS. ***Supersedes** Nihon Naika Gakkaishi.*
**Ind/Abst** Chem. Abstr.; Index Med.

JA/0446-6586
**NIHON SHOKAKIBYO GAKKAI ZASSHI.** [Nippon Shokakibyo Gakkai zasshi]. **Added/Corp** Nihon ShÂokakibyÂo Gakkai. **VFOAT** Japanese Journal of Gastroenterology. (1902)-. Academic Scholarly Publication. Japanese (summaries and/or abstracts in English). Thirteen times a year. $226.00. **(Subscription address:** Kyowa Book Company Inc., 1 38 Kanda Jinbocho Chiyoda-ku, Tokyo 101 Japan.**) CODEN** NIPAA4. Documents available from BIOSIS Document Express, CASDDS.
**Ind/Abst** Biol. Abstr. (1986-); Chem. Abstr.; EMBASE; Index Med.

SZ/1019-1291
**OSTEOLOGIE.** (1992)-. German. Four times a year. 260.00F. Verlag Hans Huber Ag Bern, Laenggass Strasse 76, CH 3000 Bern 9 Switzerland. **Tel** 011 41 31 3004500. **(Subscription address:** Hogrefe & Huber Publishers, Seattle Office, Box 2487, Kirkland WA 98083.**) ED** H.G. Willert, E. Keck, S. Perren, E. Willvonseder, A. Roessner.

US/0885-3177
**PANCREAS.** [Pancreas]. Vol. 1, No. 1 (1986)-. Academic Scholarly Publication. English. Eight times a year. $345.00 (individuals), $560.00 (institutions) US; $426.00 (individuals), $610.00 (institutions) other. Raven Press, 1185 Avenue of the Americas, 37th Floor, New York NY 10036. **Tel** (212)930-9500, (212)930-9604, FAX (212)869-3495, (212)302-8507, telex 640073. **ED** Vay Liang. **DD** 616. **NLM** W1; PA465. **CODEN** PANCE4. **[CCC]. Pr Rev.** available on microfilm and microfiche from University Microfilms International (UMI). Documents available from The Genuine Article, BIOSIS Document Express, CASDDS.
**Desc:** Provides a central forum for communication of original works involving both basic and clinical research on the exocrine and endocrine pancreas and their interrelationships and consequences in disease states.
**Ind/Abst** Biol. Abstr. (1987-); Chem. Abstr. (1986-); Curr. Aware. Biol. Sci., CABS; Curr. Contents Life Sci.; EMBASE; Index Med. (1986-); Ref. Upd. Clinical Ed.; Ref. Upd. Deluxe Ed.; Res. Alert [Select. Cov.]; Sci. Cit. Index; SCISEARCH.

US/0896-8608
**PERITONEAL DIALYSIS INTERNATIONAL.** (PERITONEAL DIALYSIS INTERNATIONAL : JOURNAL OF THE INTERNATIONAL SOCIETY FOR PERITONEAL DIALYSIS.). [Perit. dial. int.]. **Added/Corp** International Society for Peritoneal Dialysis. **VFOAT** PDI. Vol. 8, No. 1 (1988)-. Periodical. English. Five times a year. $160.00 (institutions); $110.00 (physicians); $65.00 (nurses/residents). Multimed Publications Inc., 1120 Finch Avenue West Suite 601, Toronto Ontario M3J 3H7 Canada. **Tel** (416)650-0610, FAX (416)650-0639. **DD** 617. **NLM** W1; PE802. **[CCC].** Index available. **Ad Acc. Pr Rev. Circ:** 3,800. Documents available from The Genuine Article. ***Continues** Peritoneal Dialysis Bulletin, 0226-8787.*
**Desc:** A publication dedicated to peritoneal dialysis. Includes papers on clinical subjects, reviews and original research related to peritoneal dialysis written by scientists working peritoneal dialysis and related fields.
**Ind/Abst** Curr. Contents Clin. Med.; EMBASE; Health Devices Alerts; Health Plan. Adminis.; Index Med. (1989-); Protozoolog. Abstr.; Res. Alert [Full Cov.]; Rev. Med. Vet. Mycology; Sci. Cit. Index; SCISEARCH.

PH/0556-0071
**PHILIPPINE JOURNAL OF INTERNAL MEDICINE.** [Philipp. J. Intern. Med.]. English. Philippine College of Physicians, Facilities Centre Condominium Building, 548 Shaw Boulevard, Mandaluyong, Metro Manila, Philippines. **CODEN** PJIMB.
**Ind/Abst** EMBASE [Select. Cov.].

GW/0340-305X
**PHLEBOLOGIE UND PROKTOLOGIE.** ***Title Change.*** [Phlebol. Proktol.]. Vol. 1, No. 1 (1972)-(19??). Academic Scholarly Publication. German. bm. F K Schattauer Verlagsgesellschaft mbH, Postfach 10 45 45, D 70040 Stuttgart Germany. **Tel** 011 49 711 2298726. **NLM** W1 PH62M. **[CCC].** Index available. **Bk Rev. Ad Acc. *Continued by** Phlebologie (Stuttgart), 0939-978X.*
**Desc:** The journal of the German Society of Phlebology and Proctology.
**Ind/Abst** EMBASE.

UK/0268-3555
**PHLEBOLOGY / VENOUS FORUM OF THE ROYAL SOCIETY OF MEDICINE.** **Added/Corp** Royal Society of Medicine (Great Britain). Venous Forum. (19??)-. Periodical. English. qt. £104.00. Springer-Verlag France, 26 rue des Carmes, F 75005 Paris France. **Tel** 011 33 1 44411599, FAX 011 33 43250225. **(Subscription address:** Springer Verlag New York Inc. / for North America, 44 Hartz Way, Secaucus NJ 07096.**) NLM** W1; PH62P. **CODEN** PHLEEF. **[CCC].** available on microfilm from University Microfilms International (UMI). Documents available from The Genuine Article.
**Desc:** Publishes papers on all aspects of disease of the venous system, case reports, and descriptions of special techniques of investigation and treatment.
**Ind/Abst** Curr. Contents Clin. Med.; EMBASE; Res. Alert [Full Cov.]; Sci. Cit. Index.

US/1055-9086
**PLACES TO PRACTICE (INTERNAL MEDICINE/CARDIOLOGY ED.).** (PLACES TO PRACTICE.). [Places pract.]. (Spring 1991)-. Periodical. English. qt. MD Publications Inc, 3 East 54th Street, New York NY 10022. **Tel** (212)355-5432, FAX (212)838-1083. **DD** 616.

PL/0032-3772
**POLSKIE ARCHIWUM MEDYCYNY WEWNETRZNEJ.** (POLSKIE ARCHIWUM MEDYCYNY WEWNETRZNEJ. ARCHIVES POLONAISES DE MEDECINE INTERNE. POLISH ARCHIVES OF INTERNAL MEDICINE.). [Pol. arch. med. wew.]. **Added/Corp** Towarzystwo Internistow Polskich. **VFOAT** Archives Polonaises de Medecine Interne; Polish Archives of Internal Medicine. Vol. 1 (1923)-. Academic Scholarly Publication. Polish (summaries and/or abstracts in English, French and Russian). mo. Price on Request. **(Subscription address:** ARS Polona, PO Box 1001, 00068 Warsaw Poland.**) NLM** W1 PO292. **CODEN** PAMWAL. Documents available from BIOSIS Document Express, CASDDS.
**Ind/Abst** Biol. Abstr.; Chem. Abstr.; EMBASE [Select. Cov.]; Index Med.

US/0896-5323
**PRACTICAL REVIEWS IN INTERNAL MEDICINE (1984).** (PRACTICAL REVIEWS IN INTERNAL MEDICINE [SOUND RECORDING].). [Pract. rev. intern. med.]. **Added/Corp** Educational Reviews, Inc. Montefiore Medical Center. **VFOAT** Practical Reviews. Vol. 18, No. 1 (1984)-. Periodical. English. mo. $195.00 Physicians/Dentists; $140.00 Residents. Educational Reviews Inc., 6801 Cahaba Valley Road, Birmingham AL 35242. **Tel** (205)991-5188, (800)633-4743, FAX (205)995-1926. **DD** 616. ***Continues** Internist's Journal Outreach.*

US/0147-5258
**PROCEEDINGS - ANNUAL CONTRACTOR'S CONFERENCE OF THE ARTIFICIAL KIDNEY PROGRAM OF THE NATIONAL INSTITUTE OF ARTHRITIS, METABOLISM, AND DIGESTIVE DISEASES.** (ANNUAL CONTRACTOR'S CONFERENCE OF THE ARTIFICIAL KIDNEY PROGRAM OF THE NATIONAL INSTITUTE OF ARTHRITIS, METABOLISM, AND DIGESTIVE DISEASES.). **Main/Conf** Contractor's Conference of the Artificial Kidney Program of the National Institute of Arthritis, Metabolism, and Digestive Diseases. English. an. US National Institutes of Health, 9000 Rockville Pike, Bethesda MD 20814. **Tel** (301)496-6975. **LC** RC901.7.A7; C63. **DD** 617/.461. **NLM** W1 PR583CGB. ***Continues** Contractor's Conference of the Artificial Kidney Program of the National Institute of Arthritis and Metabolic Diseases. Annual Contractor's Conference.*

US/0894-7708
**PROCEEDINGS OF THE ANNUAL VETERINARY MEDICAL FORUM. See** Veterinary Sciences.

●US/1060-913X
**PROGRESS IN LIVER DISEASES (PHILADELPHIA, PA.).** (PROGRESS IN LIVER DISEASE.). (1992)-. Periodical. English. an. $94.00 (individual), $116.00 (institution) US; $135.00 (individual), $143.00 (institution) other. W.B. Saunders Company, A Subsidiary of Harcourt Brace Jovanovich, Inc., The Curtis Center/Suite 300, Independence Square West, Philadelphia PA 19106-3399. **Tel** (215)238-7800 or, 5587, FAX (215)238-7883, telex 173146. **(Subscription address:** W. B. Saunders Company / North America Subscriptions, c/o Periodicals, 6277 Sea Harbour Drive, 4th Floor, Orlando FL 32887.**) [CCC].**
**Ind/Abst** Index Sci. Rev. [Full Cov.].

US/0270-4137
**PROSTATE, THE.** [Prostate]. Vol. 1, No. 1 (1980)-. Academic Scholarly Publication. English. mo. $69.00 US; $816.00 Canada and Mexico; $861.00 other. John Wiley & Sons, Inc., 605 Third Avenue, New York NY 10158-0012. **Tel** (212)850-6000, (212)850-6645, FAX (212)850-6088, telex 12-7063. **(Subscription address:** John Wiley & Sons / England, Baffins Lane, Chichester, West Sussex PO19 1UD England.**) ED** Avery A. Sandberg and Gerald P. Murphy. **LC** RC899; .P69. **DD** 616. **NLM** W1; PR77V. **CODEN** PRSTDS. **[CCC]. Pr Rev.** Documents available from The Genuine Article, BIOSIS Document Express, CASDDS.
**Desc:** Dedicated to studies of the prostate and male accessory glands. Serves as the central publication medium for these studies, presenting a forceful, cogent view of its field.
**Ind/Abst** Biol. Abstr.; Chem. Abstr.; Curr. Contents Life

Sci.; EMBASE; Index Med.; Index Vet.; Life Sci. Collect.; Ref. Upd. Deluxe Ed.; Res. Alert [Full Cov.]; Sci. Cit. Index; SCISEARCH; Vet. Bull.

IT
**RASSEGNA DI MEDICINA INTERNA.** (1980)-. Periodical. Italian (summaries and/or abstracts in English). bm. Editoriale Bios s.a.s., PO Box 528, 87100, Cosenza, Italy. **Tel** (984)28172. **NLM** W1; RA661Q.
**Ind/Abst** EMBASE [Select. Cov.].

UK/0264-7532
**RECENT ADVANCES IN HEPATOLOGY.** [Recent adv. hepat.]. (1983)-. English. ir. Churchill Livingstone, 1-3 Baxter's Place, Leith Walk, Edinburgh EH1 3AF Scotland. **Tel** 011 44 31 556 2424, FAX 011 44 31 558 1278, telex 727511. **(Subscription address:** Churchill Livingstone / US, 5 S 250 Frontenac Road, Naperville IL 60563.**) ED** Howard C. Thomas and Roderick N.M. MacSween. **LC** RC845; .R36. **DD** 616.3/62/005. **NLM** W1; RE105UMB.

IT/0034-1193
**RECENTI PROGRESSI IN MEDICINA.** [Recent. prog. med.]. Vol. 1 (Oct. 1946)-. Academic Scholarly Publication. Italian (English and French; summaries and/or abstracts in English). mo. L150000 (institutions), L85000 (individuals). Il Pensiero Scientifico Editore s.r.l., Via Bradano 3C, 00199 Rome Italy. **Tel** 011 39 6 86207158, 86207159, 86207168, 86207169, FAX 011 39 6 86207160. **ED** L. Bonomo. **NLM** W1 RE106R. **CODEN** RPMDAN. Index available (bound in Jan. issue). **Bk Rev. Ad Acc, Adv Mgr:** Dott Dalla, **Tel** 06-86207165. Full Page (B&W) L2.000.000. **Circ:** 4,000. Documents available from CASDDS.
**Desc:** Contains original papers, case reports, pharmacology and therapy articles, reviews, books and journal reviews.
**Ind/Abst** Chem. Abstr.; EMBASE [Select. Cov.]; Index Med.

US
**REFERENCE UPDATE CLINICAL EDITION [COMPUTER FILE].** See Medical Science and Technology-Abstracting, Bibliographies and Statistics.

US/0098-9223
**REFLECTIONS (OKLAHOMA CITY).** (REFLECTIONS.). Periodical. English. qt. $10.00. Oklahoma Institute of Ultrasound in Medicine, PO Box 26901, Oklahoma City OK 73190. **LC** RC78.7.U4; R43. **DD** 616.07/54.
**Ind/Abst** Archit. Period. Index.

US/0197-7423
**REPORT OF THE PATIENT REGISTRY.** [Rep. patient regist.]. **Main/Corp** Cystic Fibrosis Foundation. (1977)-. English. ir. Free. Cystic Fibrosis Foundation, 6000 Executive Blvd., Suite 309, Rockville MD 20852. **Tel** (301)881-9130. **LC** RC858.C95; C95a. **DD** 614.5/937. **NLM** W1 CY751F. ***Continues*** *Report on Survival Studies of Patients with Cystic Fibrosis, 0161-472X.*

MX/0034-8376
**REVISTA DE INVESTIGACION CLINICA.** [Rev. invest. clin.]. **Added/Corp** Instituto Nacional de la Nutricion (Mexico). Vol. 1 (1948)-. Academic Scholarly Publication. Spanish (English; summaries and/or abstracts in English and Spanish). Four times a year (Mar., June, Sept., Dec.). $20.00 one year; $40.00 two year. Instituto Nacional de la Nutricion, Ave San Fernando Y VIA Ducto, Mexico 22 DF Mexico. **Tel** 011 52 5 5731200 Ext. 2305, FAX 011 52 5 6551076. **ED** Ruben Lisker and Alvar Loria. **NLM** W1; RE403T. **CODEN** RICLAG. Index Available, published separately, free-automatically sent. **Bk Rev. Ad Acc. Circ:** 1,500 (ctrl). Documents available from The Genuine Article, CASDDS.
**Desc:** Most papers relate to clinical research in internal medicine. Case reports, review articles, medical education, and quality control is generally included.
**Ind/Abst** Chem. Abstr.; Curr. Contents Clin. Med.; EMBASE [Select. Cov.]; Helminthol. Abstr. (1991-); Index Med.; Nutr. Abstr. Rev., Ser. A, Hum. Exp.; Life Sci. Collect.; Res. Alert [Select. Cov.]; Soc. Sci. Cit. Index [Select. Cov.].

SP/0213-1463
**REVISTA DE LA ASOCIACION CASTELLANA DE APARATO DIGESTIVO.** [Rev. Asoc. Castell. Apar. Dig.]. **Added/Corp** Ociacion Castellana de Aparato Digestivo. Madrid. **VFOAT** Revista ACAD; ACAD. (1985)-. Periodical. Spanish. qt. 2.000ptas Spain. Jarpyo Editores SA, Antonio Lopez Aguados 4, 28029 Madrid, Spain. **Tel** 011 34 1 3144338, 011 34 1 3144458. **(Subscription address:** Antonio Lopez Aguado 1-4, 28029 Madrid Spain**) ED** Jose Maria Pajares Garcia. **UDC** 616.3. **Ad Acc. Circ:** 2,000 (ctrl).
**Desc:** Journal of the Spanish Association of the Digestive System.
**Ind/Abst** Indice Med. Esp.

SP
**REVISTA ESPANOLA DE ESTOMATOLOGIA.** ***Title Change.*** Spanish. bm. Graficas Fomento, C Peligro 8, 08012 Barcelona Spain. **Tel** 011 34 3 2580425. ***Continued by*** *Revista Europea de Odonto-Estomatologia.*

CL/0034-9887
**REVISTA MEDICA DE CHILE.** [Rev. med. Chile]. **Added/Corp** Sociedad Medica de Santiago. Vol. 1, (July 1872)-. Periodical. Spanish (summaries and/or abstracts in English). mo. $195.00 (surface mail); $240.00 (air mail Europe); $233.00 (airmail South America). Revista Medica de Chile, Clasificador 1 Correo 27, Santiago Chile. **Tel** 11 56 2 2202887, 2202866, FAX 11 56 2 2128510. **ED** Alejandro Goic G. **NLM** W1 RE616L. **CODEN** RMCHAW. **Bk Rev. Ad Acc. Pr Rev. Circ:** 2,000 (ctrl). Documents available from The Genuine Article, CASDDS.
**Desc:** Dedicated to the research concerning internal medicine and its special fields.
**Ind/Abst** Chem. Abstr.; Curr. Contents Clin. Med.; Dairy Sci. Abstr.; Helminthol. Abstr. (1991-); Index Med.; Index Vet.; Microbiol. Abstr. Sect. B (19??-19??); Microbiol. Abstr. Sect. C; Nutr. Abstr. Rev., Ser. A, Hum. Exp.; Life Sci. Collect.; Protozoolog. Abstr.; Res. Alert [Full Cov.]; Rev. Med. Vet. Mycology; Sci. Cit. Index; SCISEARCH; Soc. Sci. Cit. Index [Select. Cov.]; SportSearch; Vet. Bull.; Trop. Dis. Bull.

FR/0248-8663
**REVUE DE MEDECINE INTERNE, LA.** (LA REVUE DE MEDECINE INTERNE / FONDEE ... PAR LA SOCIETE NATIONALE FRANCAISE DE MEDECINE INTERNE.). [Rev. med. interne]. **Added/Corp** Societe Nationale Francaise de Medecine Interne. Vol. 1 No. 1 (June 1980)-. Academic Scholarly Publication. French (summaries and/or abstracts in English). Twelve times a year. 1250.00F France; 1400.00F other. Editions Scientifique Elsevier, 141 rue de Javel, 75747 Paris Cedex 15 France. **Tel** 011 33 1 47 07 11 22, FAX 011 33 1 43 36 80 93. **(Subscription address:** Editions Scientifiques Elsevier / for North America, PO Box 7247-7576, Philadelphia PA 19170-7576.**) ED** Bernard Devulder. **NLM** W1 RE795G. **CODEN** RMEIDE. **[CCC]. Ad Acc. Pr Rev.** Documents available from The Genuine Article, BIOSIS Document Express. ***Continues*** *Coeur et Medecine Interne, 0010-0234.*
**Ind/Abst** Biol. Abstr.; Curr. Contents Clin. Med.; EMBASE; Helminthol. Abstr.; Index Med.; Nutr. Abstr. Rev., Ser. A, Hum. Exp.; Life Sci. Collect.; Protozoolog. Abstr.; Res. Alert [Select. Cov.]; Rev. Med. Vet. Entomol.; Rev. Med. Vet. Mycology; Saf. Health Work; Soc. Sci. Cit. Index [Select. Cov.].

RM/1220-4749
**REVUE ROUMAINE DE MEDECINE INTERNE (1990).** (ROMANIAN JOURNAL OF INTERNAL MEDICINE / REVUE ROUMAINE DE MEDECINE INTERNE.). [Rev. roum. m,ed. interne]. **Added/Corp** Institutul de Medicina Interna "Nicolae Gh. Lupu." Academia de Stiinte Medicale. **VFOAT** Revue Roumaine de Medecine Interne. Vol. 29, 1/2 (Jan./June 1991)-. Periodical. English (summaries and/or abstracts in Romanian). Four times a year. $55.00. Uniunea Societ Stiinte Medical, Str Progresului 8, Bucharest Romania. **NLM** W1; RO327F. ***Continues*** *Medecine Interne, 0377-1202.*
**Ind/Abst** Index Med. (1991-).

RU
**RUSSIAN ARCHIVES OF INTERNAL MEDICINE.** ***Ceased.*** (19??)-(19??). English. bm. MAIK Nauka / Interperiodica, Ulitsa Profsoyuznaya 90, Moscow 117864 Russia. ***Continues*** *Soviet Archives of Internal Medicine.*

SP
**SCANDINAVIAN JOURNAL OF GASTROENTEROLOGY (EDICION ESPANOLA).** Editorial Saned SA, Apolonio Morales 6, 28036 Madrid Spain. **Tel** 011 34 1 359-4092, FAX 011 34 1 457-9918.

SZ/1013-2058
**SCHWEIZERISCHE RUNDSCHAU FUER MEDIZIN PRAXIS.** [Schweiz. Rundsch. Med. Prax.]. **VFOAT** Revue Suisse de Medecine Praxis; Praxis. Vol. 59 (Jan. 6, 1970)-. Academic Scholarly Publication. German (French; summaries and/or abstracts in English and Italian). wk. 210.60F Germany; 180.00F Switzerland; 243.00F other. Hallwag AG, Nordring 4, CH-3001 Bern Switzerland. **Tel** 011 41 31 3323131, FAX 031/414133, telex 912661 HAWA CH. **NLM** W1; SC618. **CODEN** SRMPDJ. **Bk Rev. Ad Acc. Circ:** 4,500 (ctrl). Documents available from BIOSIS Document Express, CASDDS. ***Continues*** *Praxis, 0369-8394.*
**Desc:** Editorials, original articles with bibliographies, question-answer page, CPC, book and journal reviews.
**Ind/Abst** Biol. Abstr. (1986-); Chem. Abstr.; EMBASE [Select. Cov.]; Index Med.; Life Sci. Collect.; PESTDOC; Rev. Med. Vet. Entomol.; Saf. Health Work.

JA/1012-8646
**SEAMIC INFORMATION RETRIEVAL ON CURRENT LITERATURE. SERIES J, VIRAL DIARRHEA.** See Public Health and Safety.

JA/1012-8654
**SEAMIC INFORMATION RETRIEVAL ON CURRENT LITERATURE. SERIES K, DYSENTERY, BACILLARY.** See Public Health and Safety.

US/0272-8087
**SEMINARS IN LIVER DISEASE.** [Semin. liver dis.]. Vol. 1, No. 1 (Feb. 1981)-. Periodical. English. qt. $135.00 (institutions), $99.00 (individuals) US; $160.00 (institutions), $124.00 (individuals) other. Thieme Medical Publishers Inc., 381 Park Avenue South, Suite 1201, New York NY 10016. **Tel** (212)683-5088, (212)683-5089, FAX (212)779-9020, telex 220 862 TSINC UR. **ED** M A Rothschild. **DD** 616. **NLM** W1 SE489C. **CODEN** SLDIEE. **[CCC]. Bk Rev. Ad Acc. Pr Rev. Circ:** 2,000 (ctrl). available on microfilm and microfiche from University Microfilms International (UMI). Documents available from The Genuine Article, BIOSIS Document Express.
**Desc:** Provides up-to-date critical and comprehensive reviews of current techniques and evaluations of new developments in the rapidly evolving and exciting field. Designed for both physicians and academicians, this periodical offers summaries of opinions. Each issue includes illustrations and graphics.
**Ind/Abst** Biol. Abstr. (1985-); Curr. Contents Clin. Med.; EMBASE; Index Med.; Index Sci. Rev. [Full Cov.]; Nutr. Abstr. Rev., Ser. A, Hum. Exp.; Ref. Upd. Clinical Ed.; Ref. Upd. Deluxe Ed.; Res. Alert [Full Cov.]; Sci. Cit. Index; SCISEARCH.

US/0097-6008
**SONIX.** [Sonix]. V. 1- Apr. 1975-. Periodical. English. mo. $2.00. Norman House, 1569 South Pearl, Denver CO 80210. **LC** RC78.7.U4; S65. **DD** 616.07/54. **NLM** W1 SO88845. **CODEN** SONIDG.

US/1054-6596
**SOVIET ARCHIVES OF INTERNAL MEDICINE.** ***Title Change.*** **VFOAT** Terapevticheskii Arkhiv. (1991)-(19??). Periodical. English (Russian). bm. MAIK Nauka / Interperiodica, Ulitsa Profsoyuznaya 90, Moscow 117864 Russia. **ED** Eugene Chazov. **Circ:** 45,000. ***Continued by*** *Russian Archives of Internal Medicine.*
**Desc:** Articles are written by physicians in the field of therapeutic medicine and include examples of medical case histories. Each issue of the journal is usually dedicated to one common subject.

BG/0255-7126
**SPECIAL PUBLICATION / INTERNATIONAL CENTRE FOR DIARRHOEAL DISEASE RESEARCH, BANGLADESH.** [Spec. publ. - Int. Cent. Diarrheal Dis. Res. Bangladesh]. **Added/Corp** International Centre for Diarrhoeal Disease Research, Bangladesh. No. 4 (1980)-. Monographic series. English. Price varies per volume. **NLM** W1 SP295DL. ***Continues*** *Special Publications (International Centre for Diarrhoeal Disease Research, Bangladesh).*

JA/0913-0071
**SUIZO.** [Suizo]. **VFOAT** Journal of Japan Pancreas Society. (1986)-. Academic Scholarly Publication. Multiple languages. qt. Nihon Suizo Gakkai, (Japan Pancreas Soc.), Kansai Ika Daigaku, Daisan Naikagaku Kyoshitsu, 1, Fumizonocho, Moriguchishi, Osakafu 570 Japan. **DD** 616.37. Documents available from CASDDS.
**Ind/Abst** Chem. Abstr.

US/0887-4476
**SYNAPSE (NEW YORK, N.Y.).** (SYNAPSE.). [Synapse]. Vol. 1, No. 1 (1987)-. Academic Scholarly Publication. English. Twelve times a year. $972.00 (US); $1,092.00 (Canada and Mexico); $1,137.00 (other). John Wiley & Sons, Inc., 605 Third Avenue, New York NY 10158-0012. **Tel** (212)850-6000, (212)850-6645, FAX (212)850-6088, telex 12-7063. **(Subscription address:** John Wiley & Sons / England, Baffins Lane, Chichester, West Sussex PO19 1UD England.**) ED** John E. Johnson, Jr. **LC** QP364; .S94. **DD** 612/.81/05. **NLM** W1; SY507E. **CODEN** SYNAET. **[CCC].** Documents available from The Genuine Article, BIOSIS Document Express, CASDDS.
**Desc:** A forum for the presentation of new basic and clinical research pertaining to all aspects of synaptic structure and function, including attention to practical clinical considerations.
**Ind/Abst** Biol. Abstr. (1988-); Chem. Abstr. (1987-); CSA Neuro. Abstr.; Curr. Aware. Biol. Sci., CABS; Curr. Contents Life Sci.; EMBASE; Index Med. (1987-); Ref. Upd. Deluxe Ed.; Res. Alert [Full Cov.]; Sci. Cit. Index; SCISEARCH; Soc. Sci. Cit. Index [Select. Cov.].

FR/0040-5922
**THERAPEUTIQUE.** (1969)-. Periodical. French. **Circ:** 9,000 (ctrl).

GW/0340-6245
**THROMBOSIS AND HAEMOSTASIS.** [Thromb. haemostasis]. **Added/Corp** International Society on Thrombosis and Haemostasis. Vol. 35 (Feb. 29, 1976)-. Academic Scholarly Publication. English. Twelve times a year. DM604.00 (institutions), DM480.00 (individuals) Europe; $360.00 (institutions), $280.00 (individuals) other. F K Schattauer Verlagsgesellschaft

mbH, Postfach 10 45 45, D 70040 Stuttgart Germany. **Tel** 011 49 711 2298726. **ED** J. J. Sixma, B. N. Bouma, and J. W. N. Akkerman. **NLM** W1 TH923. **CODEN** THHADQ. **[CCC].** Index available. **Bk Rev. Ad Acc. Pr Rev.** ctrl circ. Documents available from The Genuine Article, BIOSIS Document Express, CASDDS. ***Continues*** *Thrombosis et Diathesis Haemorrhagica, 0340-5338.*
**Desc:** Publishes original papers that contribute new information about any aspect of thrombosis and haemostasis. Also contains papers with laboratory or clinical orientation and review articles.
**Ind/Abst** Biol. Abstr.; Chem. Abstr.; Curr. Contents Life Sci.; EMBASE; Energy Res. Abstr. (May 1979-); Index Med.; Index Vet.; Nutr. Abstr. Rev., Ser. A, Hum. Exp.; Life Sci. Collect.; PESTDOC; Ref. Upd. Basic Ed.; Ref. Upd. Deluxe Ed.; Res. Alert [Full Cov.]; Rev. Med. Vet. Entomol.; Sci. Cit. Index; SCISEARCH; Small Anim. Abstr. Bibliogr.; SportSearch; Vet. Bull.; Virol. AIDS Abstr.

IT
**THYROIDOLOGY.** Vol. 1, No. 1 (April 1989)-. Periodical. Italian. Three times a year. $40.00. Pacini Editore Srl, Via A Gherardesca 1, 56121 Ospedaletto Pisa Italy. **Tel** 011 39 50 982439. **NLM** W1; TH97.
**Ind/Abst** Index Med. (1988-).

BE/0371-683X
**TIJDSCHRIFT VOOR GENEESKUNDE.** [Tijdschr. geneeskd.]. Vol. 22 (1966). Academic Scholarly Publication. Dutch. sm (24 issues per year). 1100.00F Belgium; 1400.00F other. Tijdschrift Voor Geneeskunde, Minderbroedersstraat 12, 3000 Louvain Belgium. **Tel** 011 32 16 216600. **ED** I Leusen and J Lauweryns. **NLM** W1 TI653C. Index available. cum. index. **Bk Rev,** (Qty: 150-160/yr). **Ad Acc. Pr Rev. Circ:** 8,500. ***Formed by the union of*** *Belgisch Tijdschrift voor Geneeskunde, 0366-368X* ***and*** *Luevens Geneeskunde Tijdschrift.*
**Desc:** Journal of medicine, internal medicine, and general practice.
**Ind/Abst** EMBASE [Select. Cov.].

DK/0001-2815
**TISSUE ANTIGENS.** [Tissue antigens]. Vol. 1 (Jan. 1971)-. Academic Scholarly Publication. English. Ten times a year (monthly except June and Dec.). kr2010.00 US, Canada and Japan; kr1960.00 other. Munksgaard International Publishers Ltd, PO Box 2148, DK-1016 Copenhagen K Denmark. **Tel** 011 45 33 12 70 30, FAX 011 45 33 12 93 87, telex 19431 MUNKS DK. **ED** Flemming Kissmeyer-Nielsen. **LC** QR180; .T55. **DD** 591.2/92/05. **NLM** W1 TI827K. **CODEN** TSANA2TSANAZ. **[CCC].** Index available. **Bk Rev. Ad Acc. Pr Rev. Circ:** 1,000 (ctrl). Documents available from The Genuine Article, BIOSIS Document Express, CASDDS.
**Desc:** Presents original full length articles, brief communications and occasional reviews on research in: immunogenetics of cell surface antigens, immunogentics of cell interactions, functional aspects of cell surface antigens and their natural ligands. Emphasis is on leukocyte differentiation antigens and transplantation antigens.
**Ind/Abst** AgBiotech News Inf.; Anim. Breed. Abstr.; Biol. Abstr.; Chem. Abstr.; Curr. Aware. Biol. Sci., CABS; Curr. Contents Life Sci.; EMBASE; Energy Res. Abstr. (Dec. 1973-); Genet. Abstr.; Immunol. Abstr.; Index Med.; Life Sci. Collect.; Res. Alert [Full Cov.]; Rev. Med. Vet. Mycology; Sci. Cit. Index; SCISEARCH; Small Anim. Abstr. Bibliogr.; Trop. Dis. Bull.; Virol. AIDS Abstr.

UK/0958-7578
**TRANSFUSION MEDICINE. Added/Corp** British Blood Transfusion Society. (1991)-. Academic Scholarly Publication. English. Four times a year. $153.00 US & Canada; £90.00 Europe; £99.00 other. Blackwell Scientific Publications Ltd, Marston Book Services, PO Box 87, Oxford OX2 ODT UK. **Tel** 011 44 865 791155, FAX 011 44 865 791927, telex 837 515 MARDIS G. **ED** A. H. Waters. **NLM** W1; TR228WAL. **[CCC].** available on microfilm and microfiche from University Microfilms International (UMI). Documents available from The Genuine Article.
**Desc:** Publishes articles on transfusion medicine in its widest context, including blood transfusion practice (blood procurement, pharmaceutical, clinical, scientific, computing and documentary aspects), immunohaematology, immunogenetics, medico-legal applications, and related molecular biology and biotechnology.
**Ind/Abst** Curr. Aware. Biol. Sci., CABS; Curr. Contents Life Sci.; Res. Alert [Full Cov.]; Sci. Cit. Index; SCISEARCH.

UK/0960-5592
**TRANSFUSION MEDICINE. SUPPLEMENT.** See Medical Science and Technology-Hematology.

IT/0041-1787
**TRASFUSIONE DEL SANGUE.** (LA TRASFUSIONE DEL SANGUE : REVISTA DELLA SOCIETA ITALIANA DI IMMUNOEMATOLOGIA, ASSOCIAZIONE ITALIANA DEI CENTRI TRASFUSIONALI.). [Trasfus. sang.]. **Added/Corp** Societa Italiana di Immunoematologia. Associazione Italiana dei Centri Trasfusionali. (19??)-. Academic Scholarly Publication. Italian (English). Six times a year. L100000 (individuals), L130000 (institutions) Italy; L180000 others. Societa Italiana Immunoematologia e Trasfusione Associazione, Italiana Centri Trasfusionali, via Rocca Sinibalda 71, 00199 Rome Italy. **Tel** 011 39 6 86203724. **CODEN** TRSABD. Index available. **Bk Rev. Ad Acc. Circ:** 1,000. Documents available from CASDDS.
**Desc:** Official organ of the Italian Society of Blood Transfusion Centers.
**Ind/Abst** Chem. Abstr. (1956-1982); EMBASE.

US
**TREATMENT IN GENERAL PRACTICE.** 1st Ed. (1930)-. English. ir. W.B. Saunders Company, A Subsidiary of Harcourt Brace Jovanovich, Inc., The Curtis Center/Suite 300, Independence Square West, Philadelphia PA 19106-3399. **Tel** (215)238-7800 or, 5587, FAX (215)238-7883, telex 173146. **(Subscription address:** W. B. Saunders Company / North America Subscriptions, c/o Periodicals, 6277 Sea Harbour Drive, 4th Floor, Orlando FL 32887.**) LC** RC46; .B4. **DD** 616.

IT
**TUTTO DIABETE. VFOAT** Tuttodiabete. (19??)-. Italian. bm. L15000. Medikal Press, Via Luigi Zoja 30, 20153 Milan Italy. **Tel** 011 39 2 4526378.

US/0161-7346
**ULTRASONIC IMAGING.** [Ultrason. imag.]. Vol. 1 (Jan. 1979)-. Academic Scholarly Publication. English. qt (4 issues). $151.00 US and Canada; $198.00 other. Academic Press, Inc., 6277 Sea Harbor Drive, Orlando FL 32887. **Tel** (800)543-9534, (407)345-4100, FAX (407)363-9661. **ED** Melvin Linzer. **LC** RC78.7.U4; U43. **DD** 616.07/54. **NLM** W1 UL745. **CODEN** ULIMD4. **[CCC]. Pr Rev.** Documents available from The Genuine Article, Ask*IEEE.
**Desc:** Provides rapid publication for original and exceptional articles concerned with the development and application of ultrasonic techniques, with emphasis on medical diagnosis.
**Ind/Abst** Curr. Contents Eng. Tech. Appl. Sci.; EMBASE; Index Med.; INSPEC (Jan. 1980-); Int. Aerosp. Abstr.; Phys. Med. Biol. (19??-19??); Res. Alert [Full Cov.]; Sci. Cit. Index; SCISEARCH.

SZ/0301-1526
**VASA.** (VASA. ZEITSCHRIFT FUER GEFASSKRANKHEITEN. JOURNAL FOR VASCULAR DISEASES.). [VASA]. **Added/Corp** Schweizerische Gesellschaft fuer Angiologie. Schweizerische Gesellschaft fuer Phlebologie. Deutsche Gesellschaft fuer Angiologie. Oesterreichische Gesellschaft fuer Angiologie. Oesterreichische Gesellschaft fuer Gefaesschirurgie. Oesterreichische Arbeitsgemeinschaft fuer Morphologische und Funktionelle Atherosklerosforschung. Niederlaendische Gesellschaft fuer Gefaesschirurgie. Societas Phlebologica Scandinavica. **VFOAT** Journal for Vascular Diseases.; Zeitschrift fuer Gefaesskrankheiten. Vol. 1 (1972)-. Academic Scholarly Publication. German (English). qt. 134.00F. Verlag Hans Huber Ag Bern, Laenggass Strasse 76, CH 3000 Bern 9 Switzerland. **Tel** 011 41 31 3004500. **ED** H.J. Leu. **NLM** W1 V101C. **CODEN** VASAAH. **[CCC]. Bk Rev. Ad Acc. Pr Rev. Circ:** 1,200. Documents available from The Genuine Article, BIOSIS Document Express. ***Supersedes*** *Zentralblatt fuer Phlebologie.*
**Desc:** Covers vascular diseases. Directed at angiologists, phlebologists and circulation physiologists, but also toward general and specialty physicians frequently confronted with vascular problems.
**Ind/Abst** Biol. Abstr.; EMBASE; Index Med.; Life Sci. Collect.; Res. Alert [Full Cov.]; Sci. Cit. Index; SCISEARCH.

SZ/0251-1029
**VASA. SUPPLEMENTUM.** [VASA, Suppl.]. (1973)-. German (English). Verlag Hans Huber Ag Bern, Laenggass Strasse 76, CH 3000 Bern 9 Switzerland. **Tel** 011 41 31 3004500. **NLM** W1; VA911H. **CODEN** VASUDC. **[CCC].** Documents available from BIOSIS Document Express.
**Ind/Abst** Biol. Abstr. (19??-); Index Med. (1973-).

UK/0954-2582
**VASCULAR MEDICINE REVIEW.** (1990)-. Periodical. English. Four times a year. $190.00 North America; £115.00 Europe; £130.00 Other. Edward Arnold, 338 Euston Road, London NW1 3BH England. **Tel** 011 44 71 873 6000, FAX 011 44 071 873 6325. **(Subscription address:** Edward Arnold, PO Box 386, Avenel NJ 07001-0386.**) ED** John E. Tooke. **NLM** W1; VA92P. **CODEN** VMEREI. **[CCC]. Bk Rev.**
**Desc:** New, multi-disciplinary review journal which covers arterial, venous and lymphatic disease of all the major systems with particular emphasis on those areas of clinical relevance. Physicians with an interest in vascular medicine, specialist angiologists, vascular physiologists, postgraduate doctors in training, and vascular laboratory technical and nursing staff will benefit from authoritative articles on the latest developments in pathophysiology, diagnosis and clinical management. In each issue an impressive group of international contributors will bring together and synthesize the substantial amount of new information in the field. Includes information on new products, a calendar of meetings, book review, journals abstracts and reports of medical interest.
**Ind/Abst** EMBASE.

GW/0070-4067
**VERHANDLUNGEN DER DEUTSCHEN GESELLSCHAFT FUER INNERE MEDIZIN.** [Verh. Dtsch. Ges. Inn. Med.]. **Added/Corp** Deutsche Gesellschaft fur Innere Medizin. Deutsche Gesellschaft fur Rheumabekampfung. Gesellschaft Deutscher Hamatologen. (1921)-. Academic Scholarly Publication. German. ir. $107.10 (vol. 95). Springer Verlag New York Inc., PO Box 19386 Books, Newark NJ 07195. **Tel** (201)348-4033. **(Subscription address:** North America/ Journal Fulfillment Services, 44 Hartz Way, Secaucus, NJ 07094; telephone: (030)8207-1**) NLM** W1 VE483Q. **CODEN** VDGIA2. **[CCC].** cum. index. Documents available from BIOSIS Document Express, CASDDS. ***Continues*** *Deutscher Kongress fur Innere Medizin. Verhandlungen.*
**Desc:** Annual congress.
**Ind/Abst** Biol. Abstr.; Chem. Abstr.; EMBASE [Select. Cov.]; Index Med.

XR/0042-773X
**VNITRNI LEKARSTVI.** [Vnitr. lek.]. **Added/Corp** Ceskoslovenska Spolecnost Pro Vnitrni Lekarstvi. Ceskoslovenska Lekarska Spolecnost J.E. Purkyne. (1955)-. Academic Scholarly Publication. Czech (summaries and/or abstracts in Russian, English and French; table of contents in Russian, English and French). mo. $142.00. Artia Pegas Press Ltd., Palac Metro Narodni TR 25, 11000 Prague 1 Czech Republic. **Tel** 011 42 2 24196265 or 24196266, 24196266. **NLM** W1 VN872. **CODEN** VNLEAH. **[CCC].** Documents available from CASDDS. ***Continues*** *Lekarske Listy.*
**Ind/Abst** Chem. Abstr. (19??-); EMBASE (19??-) [Select. Cov.]; Index Med. (19??-); Protozoolog. Abstr. (19??-); Rev. Med. Vet. Mycology (19??-); Saf. Health Work (19??-).

US/0739-5930
**YEAR BOOK OF DIGESTIVE DISEASES, THE.** [Year book dig. dis.]. (1984)-. Periodical. English. an. $69.95. Mosby Year Book Inc., 11830 Westline Industrial Drive, St Louis MO 63146. **Tel** (800)325-4177, (314)872-8370, FAX (314)432-1380, telex 44-2402. **LC** RC799; .Y43. **DD** 616.3/3/005. **NLM** W1; YE122T.

GW
**ZENTRALBLATT INNERE MEDIZIN.** ***Ceased.*** **Added/Corp** Deutsche Gesellschaft fuer Innere Medizin. **VFOAT** Internal Medicine. Vol. 336, No. 1 (1986)-(Dec. 1991). Periodical. German (summaries and/or abstracts in English). mo. Springer-Verlag GmbH & Company KG, Heidelberger Platz 3, D 14197 Berlin Germany. **Tel** 011 49 30 8207223, FAX 011 49 30 8214091, telex 183 319 SPBLN D. **(Subscription address:** Springer Verlag New York Inc. / for North America, 44 Hartz Way, Secaucus NJ 07096.**) NLM** ZW 1; Z56. ***Formed by the union of*** *Zentralblatt Praktische Innere Medizin, 0722-9860; Zentralblatt Kardiologie-Nephrologie, 0301-5858; Zentralblatt Pneumonologie-Tuberkulose; Zentralblatt Immunologie, Klinische Rheumatologie, 0722-3048; Zentralblatt Haematologie-Klinische Onkologie, 0341-2598* ***and*** *Zentralblatt Gastroenterologie-Stoffwechsel-Endokrinologie.*

## MUSCULOSKELETAL SYSTEM

FR/0295-2556
**ABSTRACT RHUMATO PARIS.** [Abstr. rhumato Paris]. (1985)-. Periodical. French. sm. 181.19F France; 295.00F other. Abstract, 25 Bis Av Pierre Grenier, 92100 Boulogne Billanct France. **Tel** 011 33 1 49100606. **UDC** 616.7.

GW/0341-051X
**AKTUELLE RHEUMATOLOGIE.** [Aktuel. Rheumatol.]. Vol. 1, (Sept. 1976)-. Periodical. German (summaries and/or abstracts in English). bm (6 issues). $137.00. Georg Thieme Verlag Stuttgart, Postfach 301120, D 70451 Stuttgart Germany. **Tel** 011 49 711 89310, FAX 011 49 711 8931298, telex 7 252 275 GTVD. **(Subscription address:** Thieme Medical Publishers Inc., 381 Park Avenue South, New York NY 10016.**) NLM** W1 AK996. **CODEN** AKRHDB. **[CCC]. Pr Rev.** Documents available from The Genuine Article, BIOSIS Document Express.
**Ind/Abst** Biol. Abstr. (1986-); Curr. Contents Clin. Med.; EMBASE; Energy Res. Abstr. (July 1979-); Life Sci. Collect.; Protozoolog. Abstr.; Res. Alert [Select. Cov.]; SCISEARCH.

CN/0715-3139
**ALS NEWS.** (ALS NEWS / AMYOTROPHIC LATERAL SCLEROSIS SOCIETY OF CANADA.). [ALS news]. **VAT** Amyotrophic Lateral Sclerosis News. Vol. 4, No. 1 (Spring 1981)-. Periodical. English. Amyotrophic Lateral Sclerosis Society of Canada, Suite 305, 234 Eglinton Avenue East, Toronto Ontario M4P 1K5 Canada. **DD** 616.8/3. ***Continues*** *ALSSOC News, 0715-3147.*

UK/0003-4967
**ANNALS OF THE RHEUMATIC DISEASES.** [Ann. rheum. dis.]. **Added/Corp** Empire Rheumatism Council. British Medical Association. Vol. 1, No. 2 (1939)-. Periodical. English. mo. £233.00. BMJ / British Medical Journal Publishing Group, British Medical Association House, Tavistock Square, London WC1H 9JR England. **Tel** 011 44 71 3874499, FAX 011 44 71 383 6402, telex 290034 HBJ MN. **ED** Michael Doherty. **DD** 616. **NLM** W1 AN627. **CODEN** ARDIAO. **[CCC].** available on microfilm and microfiche from University Microfilms International (UMI). Documents available from The Genuine Article, BIOSIS Document Express, CASDDS, ADONIS. ***Continues*** *Rheumatic Diseases.*
**Desc:** Publishes work on aspects of rheumatology and disorders of connective tissue. Leaders and review articles are commissioned to cover the wider aspects of rheumatology. Other features include clinical, epidemiological and laboratory and clinical reports, hypothesis articles, and Masterclass clinical teaching. Letters, including brief case reports are encouraged.
**Ind/Abst** ADONIS; Annals Behav. Med.; Biol. Abstr.; Chem. Abstr.; Cumul. Index Nurs. Allied Health Lit.; Health Index (1989-); Health Plan. Adminis.; Index Med.; Med. Abstr. Newsl.; Nucl. Sci. Abstr.; Res. Alert [Full Cov.]; Sci. Cit. Index; SCISEARCH; Soc. Sci. Cit. Index [Select. Cov.].

IT/0390-7368
**ARCHIVIO DI ORTOPEDIA E REUMATOLOGIA. Added/Corp** Istituto ortopedico "Gaetano Pini.". Vol. 87 (1974)-. Periodical. Italian (summaries and/or abstracts in English). qt. L160000 Italy; L220000 Europe & the Mediterranean; L280000 other. Grafiche Zanini, Via Emilia Ponente 41/E, 40011 Anzola Bo Italy. **Tel** 39 51 765562, 39 51 733594, FAX 39 51 766060. **NLM** W1 AR546E. Index available (bound in fourth issue). **Bk Rev. Ad Acc. Circ:** 3,000 (ctrl). ***Continues*** *Archivio di Ortopedia, 0004-0118.*

PO/0871-4304
**ARQUIVOS DE REUMATOLOGIA E DOENCAS OSTEO-ARTICU-LARES.** Vol. 1, Num. 1 (1980)-. Periodical. Portuguese (summaries and/or abstracts in English). mo. $45.00. Mediedicoes - Soc. Com. Editora Ltd., Avenida Almirante Reis 89-F, 1100, Lisbon Portugal. **Tel** (1)576631. **NLM** W1; AR9193.
**Ind/Abst** EMBASE [Select. Cov.].

US/0004-3591
**ARTHRITIS AND RHEUMATISM.** [Arthritis rheum.]. **Added/Corp** American College of Rheumatology. American Rheumatism Association. Arthritis Foundation. American Rheumatism Association. Proceedings of the Interim Scientific Session. American Rheumatism Association. Proceedings of the Annual Meeting. **VFOAT** Arthritis & Rheumatism. Vol. 1 (Feb. 1958)-. Academic Scholarly Publication. English. mo. $122.00 (individuals), $180.00 (institutions) US; $175.00 (individuals), $225.00 (institutions) other. J.B. Lippincott Company, 227 East Washington Square, Philadelphia PA 19106-3780. **Tel** (215)238-4200 or 4454, FAX (215)238-4227. **(Subscription address:** J.B. Lippincott, PO Box 350, Hagerstown MD 21740.**) ED** William J. Koopman. **LC** RC927.A1; A7. **DD** 616.706273. **NLM** W1 AR95163. **CODEN** ARHEAW. **[CCC].** Index available. **Bk Rev. Ad Acc. Pr Rev. Circ:** 8,000. available on microfilm and microfiche from University Microfilms International (UMI). Documents available from The Genuine Article, BIOSIS Document Express, CASDDS.
**Desc:** Publishes juried original articles on the research and clinical aspects of the rheumatic diseases. Topics include immunology, biochemistry, radiology, and case reports. Contains articles relevant to practitioners and researchers who desire knowledge of current trends in treatment and investigation of all forms of arthritis.
**Ind/Abst** Abr. Index Med.; Annals Behav. Med.; Biol. Abstr.; Calcium Calcif. Tissue Abstr.; Chem. Abstr.; Curr. Aware. Biol. Sci., CABS; Curr. Contents Clin. Med.; Curr. Contents Life Sci.; EMBASE; Energy Res. Abstr.; Genet. Abstr.; Health Period. Database; Health Plan. Adminis.; Immunol. Abstr.; Index Med.; INIS Atomindex [Micro.]; Int. Pharm. Abstr.; Oncog. Growth Factors Abstr.; Life Sci. Collect.; PESTDOC; Physic. Medline Plus; Res. Alert [Full Cov.]; Saf. Health Work; Sci. Cit. Index; SCISEARCH; Soc. Sci. Cit. Index [Select. Cov.]; Virol. AIDS Abstr.

NE/0014-4355
**ARTHRITIS AND RHEUMATISM.** Vol. 1 (1965)-. English. Eight times a year (1 volume). Fl1114.00. Excerpta Medica Publishing Group, PO Box 548, 1000 AM Amsterdam Netherlands. **Tel** 011 31 20 5803243. **(Subscription address:** Excerpta Medica Journals, PO Box 85, Limerick Ireland.**) LC** RC933.A1; A68. **DD** 616.7/2. **NLM** ZW 1 E978K. **[CCC].** available on microfilm from University Microfilms International (UMI).
**Desc:** Contains abstracts from the clinical and basic research of rheumatoid arthritis, rheumatic fever, non-articular rheumatism and the collagen diseases, and also on connective tissue disorders, arthroses and other disorders of the bones and joints.
**Ind/Abst** Int. Pharm. Abstr.; Iowa Drug Inf. Serv.; Microbiol. Abstr. Sect. B (19??-19??); Mod. Med.; Ref. Upd. Basic Ed.; Ref. Upd. Clinical Ed.; Ref. Upd. Deluxe Ed.

US/0893-7524
**ARTHRITIS CARE AND RESEARCH.** [Arthritis care res.]. **Added/Corp** Arthritis Health Professions Association. Vol. 1 (1988)-. Periodical. English. Four times a year. $115.00 US and Canada; $139.00 other. Arthritis Foundation, 1314 Spring Street Northwest, Atlanta GA 30309. **Tel** (404)872-7100, FAX (404)872-9559. **(Subscription address:** Arthritis Care and Research, PO Box 1897, Lawrence KS 66044-8897.**) ED** Donna J. Hawley. **LC** RC933.A1; A69. **DD** 616.7/22/005. **NLM** W1; AR953D. **CODEN** ARCREG. **Pr Rev.**
**Desc:** Publication of rheumatology and rheumatology-related papers. Publishes original manuscripts concerning clinical problems as well as articles analyzing economic, educational, and social issues important to health care professionals.
**Ind/Abst** Annals Behav. Med.; Cumul. Index Nurs. Allied Health Lit.; EMBASE; Health Plan. Adminis.; Psychol. Abstr. (1988-); PsycINFO; PsycLit; Ref. Upd. Deluxe Ed.

US/0191-2836
**ARTHRITIS FOUNDATION ANNUAL REPORT. Main/Corp** Arthritis Foundation. (1964/65)-. English. an. Arthritis Foundation, 1314 Spring Street Northwest, Atlanta GA 30309. **Tel** (404)872-7100, FAX (404)872-9559. **ED** Cindy McDaniel. **NLM** W1 AR953H. **Circ:** 15,000 (ctrl). ***Continues*** *Interim Report - Arthritis Foundation.*
**Desc:** Review of highlights from the Arthritis Foundation's programs and financial activities for the previous year.

US/0198-7216
**ARTHRITIS INTERAGENCY COORDINATING COMMITTEE ANNUAL REPORT TO THE SECRETARY, U.S. DEPARTMENT OF HEALTH, EDUCATION, AND WELFARE. Main/Corp** United States. Arthritis Interagency Coordinating Committee. **VFOAT** Annual Report to the Secretary, U.S. Department of Health, Education, and Welfare. **VAT** Arthritis Interagency Coordinating Committee Annual Report to the Secretary, United States Department of Health, Education, and Welfare. English. an. US Department of Health and Human Services National Institutes of Health, 9000 Rockville Pike, Bethesda MD 20892. **Tel** (301)496-9291, FAX (301)496-2443. **LC** RC933.A1; U52A. **DD** 362.1/96722. **NLM** W2 A A6R.

CN/0820-9006
**ARTHRITIS NEWS (TORONTO).** (ARTHRITIS NEWS : AN INFORMATION PUBLICATION OF THE ARTHRITIS SOCIETY.). [Arthritis news]. **Added/Corp** Arthritis Society (Canada). Vol. 3, No. 4 (Sept. 1981)- Vol. 4, No. 5 (Sept. 1982)-. Periodical. English. Four times a year (Mar., June, Sept., Dec.). 10.00Can$ Canada; 20.00Can$ others. Arthritis Society, 250 Bloor Street East, Suite 901, Toronto Ontario M4W 3P2 Canada. **Tel** (416)967-1414, FAX (416)967-7171. **ED** Dennis Jeanes. **DD** 616.7/22/006071. **Ad Acc. Circ:** 16,000. ***Continues*** *Arthritis Society News, 0227-8146.*
**Desc:** It provides clear in-depth articles about arthritis, its treatment and the latest research as well as coping strategies that makes everyday life a bit easier.

US
**ARTHRITIS, RHEUMATIC DISEASES, AND RELATED DISORDERS. Main/Corp** National Institute of Arthritis, Metabolism, and Digestive Diseases. English. an. National Institute of Arthritis Metabolism and Digestive Diseases, National Institutes of Health, 9000 Rockville Pike, Bethesda MD 20014. **NLM** W1 AR953W.

US/0890-1120
**ARTHRITIS TODAY.** (ARTHRITIS TODAY: PUBLICATION OF THE ARTHRITIS FOUNDATION.). [Arthritis today]. **Added/Corp** Arthritis Foundation. Vol. 1, No. 1, Jan./Feb. (1987)-. Periodical. English. bm. $20.00. Arthritis Foundation (Texas), PO Box 870384, Dallas TX 75287. **Tel** (800)933-0032. **(Subscription address:** PO Box 96012, Washington, DC 20090-6012**) ED** Cindy T McDaniel. **DD** 616. Index available. **Ad Acc. Circ:** 600,000 (ctrl). ***Continues*** *National Arthritis News, 0882-9705.*
**Desc:** Contains inspirational and practical articles to help the person with arthritis live a more productive, independent and pain-free life.
**Ind/Abst** Acad. Abstr. Full Text Elite (Jan. 1992-); Acad. Abstr. (Jan. 1992-); Acad. Search (Jan. 1992-); Consum. Health Nutr. Index; Health Index (1989-); Health Period. Database [Full Txt.]; Health Ref. Cent. (Jan. 1989-) [Full Txt.] [Full Cov.]; Health Source (Jan. 1992-); INFO-SOUTH Abstr.; Mag. Search.

CN
**ARTHRO EXPRESS.** (19??)-. English (French). Four times a year. $20.00 US. Societe d'Arthrite du Canada, 250 Brool Street East #901, Toronto Ontario M4W 3P2 Canada. **Tel** (416)967-1414, FAX (416)967-7171. **ED** Dennis Jeanes. **Ad Acc, Adv Mgr Tel** same as publisher. **Circ:** 16,000. ***Continues*** *Communique / Societe d'Arthrite du Canada, 0824-4154.*
**Desc:** Official journal of The Arthritis Society. Provides in-depth articles about arthritis, its treatment and the latest research, as well as coping strategies that make everyday life a bit easier.

CN/0712-9122
**BACK TO BACK (TORONTO, ONT.).** (BACK TO BACK.). [Back back]. V. 1, Issue 1 (June 15, 1981)-. Periodical. English. qt. Free to members, $12.00 others. Back Association of Canada, Concourse Level, 111 Avenue Road, Toronto Ontario M5R 3J8. **DD** 616.7/3/06071.

UK/0950-3579
**BAILLIERE'S CLINICAL RHEUMATOLOGY.** [Bailliere's clin. rheumatol.]. **VFOAT** Clinical Rheumatology; Rheumatology. Vol. 1, No. 1 (April 1987)-. Periodical. English. qt (4 issues). £94.00 (institution). Harcourt Brace & Company Ltd., Foots Cray, High Street, Sidcup Kent DA14 5HP England. **Tel** 011 44 81 300 3322, FAX 011 44 81 309 0807. **(Subscription address:** W. B. Saunders Company / North America Subscriptions, c/o Periodicals, 6277 Sea Harbour Drive, 4th Floor, Orlando FL 32887.**) NLM** W1; BA46EM. **Pr Rev.** Documents available from The Genuine Article. ***Continues in part*** *Clinics in Rheumatic Diseases, 0307-742X.*
**Ind/Abst** Curr. Contents Clin. Med.; EMBASE; Health Plan. Adminis.; Index Med. (April 1987-); Protozoolog. Abstr.; Res. Alert [Full Cov.]; Sci. Cit. Index; SCISEARCH; Soc. Sci. Cit. Index [Select. Cov.].

IT/1120-9992
**BASIC AND APPLIED MYOLOGY : BAM. VFOAT** BAM. Vol. 1 (1991)-. Periodical. English. Four times a year. $180.00 (institutions), $130.00 (individuals). Unipress Padova, Via C Battisti 231, 35121 Padova Italy. **Tel** 11 39 49 8752542, FAX 11 39 49 8752542. **NLM** W1; BA813J. Index available (bound in last issue). **Bk Rev**, (Qty: 2). **Ad Acc, Adv Mgr:** G. L. Borgato. **Circ:** 120.
**Desc:** BAM covers skeletal muscle basic research and its applications. Special attention is paid to reports on experimental studies in large mammals to test hypotheses on ethiology, pathogenesis and managements of muscles and non-muscle diseases.

US/0888-7721
**BIBLIO-PROFILE.** [Biblio-profile]. Began with: No. 1, published 1983. Monographic series. English. ir. Price varies per volume. Arthritis Information Clearinghouse, PO Box 9782, Arlington VA 22209. **DD** 616. **NLM** ZWE 300; B582.

US
**BIENNIAL REPORT OF EXAMINING AND LICENSING BOARDS. Main/Corp** Minnesota State Board of Chiropractic Examiners. (19??)-. English. be. Board of Chiropractic Examiners, 717 Delaware Street SE, Department of Health, Minneapolis MN 55414.

●US/1063-0295
**BONE & JOINT DISEASES.** (BONE & JOINT DISEASES: INDEX & REVIEWS.). **Added/Corp** World Medical Communications Organization. **VFOAT** Bone and Joint Diseases. (1992)-. Periodical. English. bm. $60.00. World Medical Communications Organizations, 7 Ridgedale Avenue, Cedar Knolls NJ 07927. **Tel** (201)455-1121.

NE/0168-051X
**BONE AND MINERAL RESEARCH.** [Bone miner. res.]. V. 1 (1983)-. Academic Scholarly Publication. English. an. $73.00. Elsevier Science Publishers BV, PO Box 211, 1000 AE Amsterdam Netherlands. **Tel** 011 31 20 5803642, FAX 011 31 20 5862696, telex 15682. **ED** William A Peck. **NLM** W1 BO707D. **CODEN** BMRSDZ. Documents available from CASDDS.
**Ind/Abst** Chem. Abstr. (1983-); Curr. Contents Life Sci.

US/8756-3282
**BONE (NEW YORK, N.Y.).** (BONE.). [Bone]. Vol. 6, No. 1 (1985)-. Academic Scholarly Publication. English. bm. $790.00 The Americas; £530.00 other. Elsevier Science Publishing Company Inc, Madison Square Station, PO Box 882, New York NY 10159-0882. **Tel** (212)633-3950, FAX (212)633-3990. **ED** Roland Baron. **DD** 616. **NLM** W1; BO707C. **CODEN** BONEDL. **[CCC]. Pr Rev.** available on microfilm and microfiche from University Microfilms International (UMI). Documents available from The Genuine Article, BIOSIS Document Express, CASDDS. ***Continues*** *Metabolic Bone Disease & Related Research, 0221-8747.*
**Desc:** Provides an interdisciplinary forum for the rapid publication of original experimental and clinical studies and review articles dealing with both normal and pathological processes which occur in bone or other tissues affecting bone metabolism. Particular attention is placed on the application of experimental studies to clinical practice.
**Ind/Abst** Biol. Abstr. (1985-); Calcium Calcif. Tissue Abstr.; Chem. Abstr. (1985-); Curr. Aware. Biol. Sci., CABS; Curr. Contents Clin. Med.; Curr. Contents Life Sci.; EMBASE; Health Plan. Adminis.; Index Med. (1985-); Nutr. Abstr. Rev., Ser. A, Hum. Exp.; Nutr. Res. Newsl.; Oncog. Growth Factors Abstr.; Ref. Upd. Deluxe Ed.; Res. Alert [Full Cov.]; Sci. Cit. Index; SCISEARCH.

UK/0263-7103
**BRITISH JOURNAL OF RHEUMATOLOGY.** [Br. j. rheumatol.]. **Added/Corp** British Association for Rheumatology and Rehabilitation. Vol. 22, No. 1 (Feb. 1983)-. Periodical. English. mo. £190.00 UK and Europe; $335.00 other. Oxford University Press, Walton Street, Oxford OX2 6DP England. **Tel** 011 44 865 56767, FAX 011 44 865 267773, telex 837330 OXPRES G. **(Subscription address:** Oxford University Press / USA, Journals Marketing Department, Oxford University Press, 2001 Evans Road, Cary NC 27513.**) ED** H. A. Bird, D. L. Scott and M. Walport. **CODEN** BJRHDF. **[CCC]. Bk Rev. Ad Acc. Pr Rev. Circ:** 2,600. available on microfilm and microfiche from University Microfilms International (UMI). Documents available from The Genuine Article, BIOSIS Document Express. ***Continues*** *Rheumatology and Rehabilitation.*
**Desc:** International clinical laboratory research, editorials, correspondence. The official journal of the British Society for Rheumatology.
**Ind/Abst** Abr. Index Med.; Annals Behav. Med.; Biol. Abstr. (1985-); Biol. Dig.; Curr. Aware. Biol. Sci., CABS; Curr. Contents Clin. Med.; EMBASE; Health Plan. Adminis.; Helminthol. Abstr.; Index Med.; Mod. Med.; Nutr. Abstr. Rev., Ser. A, Hum. Exp.; Life Sci. Collect.; PESTDOC; Protozoolog. Abstr.; Res. Alert [Full Cov.]; Sci. Cit. Index; SCISEARCH; Soc. Sci. Cit. Index [Select. Cov.].

●US/0018-5647
**BULLETIN / HOSPITAL FOR JOINT DISEASES. Added/Corp** Hospital for Joint Diseases (New York, N.Y.). Vol. 52, No. 1 (Summer 1992)-. Bulletin. English. qt. $40.00 US; $45.00 other. Hospital for Joint Diseases, Orthopaedic Institute, 301 East 17th Street, New York NY 10003. **Tel** (212)460-0158. **NLM** W1; BU478HCGD. **CODEN** BHJDEI. **[CCC]. *Continues*** *Bulletin of the Hospital for Joint Diseases Orthopaedic Institute, 0883-9344.*
**Ind/Abst** Health Plan. Adminis.; Index Med. (1992-).

US/0007-5248
**BULLETIN ON THE RHEUMATIC DISEASES.** [Bull. rheum. dis.]. **Added/Corp** Arthritis Foundation. (Sept. 1966)-. Academic Scholarly Publication. English. bm (6 issues). Free to US; $15.00 other. Arthritis Foundation, 1314 Spring Street Northwest, Atlanta GA 30309. **Tel** (404)872-7100, FAX (404)872-9559. **ED** John S. Sergent, M.D. **LC** RC927; .B83. **DD** 616.7/23/005. **NLM** W1 BU903J. **CODEN** BRDIAZ. **[CCC].** Index available. cum. index. **Pr Rev. Acid Free. Circ:** 40,000. available on microfilm and microfiche from University Microfilms International (UMI). Documents available from The Genuine Article, BIOSIS Document Express, CASDDS. ***Continues*** *Bulletin on Rheumatic Diseases, 0007-5248.*
**Desc:** Geared for primary care physicians. Contains a discussion by an authority on current topics in management and research in rheumatic diseases.
**Ind/Abst** Biol. Abstr. (19??-); Chem. Abstr. (1950-1983); Curr. Contents Clin. Med. (19??-); EMBASE (19??-); Energy Res. Abstr. (19??-); Health Plan. Adminis. (19??-); Index Med. (19??-); Life Sci. Collect. (19??-); Res. Alert (19??-) [Full Cov.]; Sci. Cit. Index (19??-); SCISEARCH (19??-).

US/0277-9552
**CATALOG (ARTHRITIS INFORMATION CLEARINGHOUSE (U.S.).** (CATALOG / ARTHRITIS INFORMATION CLEARINGHOUSE.). [Cat., Arthritis Inf. Clgh. (U.S.)]. 1979-. Catalog. English. an. Arthritis Information Clearinghouse, PO Box 9782, Arlington VA 22209. **LC** Z6664.A74; C37; RC933.A1. **DD** 016.6167/22. **NLM** ZWE 344 C357C.

US/0196-2728
**CHAIRMAN'S REPORT - NATIONAL ARTHRITIS ADVISORY BOARD. Main/Corp** United States. National Arthritis Advisory Board. English. National Arthritis Advisory Board, 1801 Rockville Pike, Suite 500, Rockville MD 20852. **LC** RC933.A1; U54B. **DD** 362.1/96722.

US/0897-6058
**CHIROPRACTIC (FORT WAYNE, IND.).**
**See** Physical Therapy.

US/0899-6938
**CHIROPRACTIC RESEARCH JOURNAL.** (CHIROPRACTIC RESEARCH JOURNAL : CRJ : A PUBLICATION OF THE SID. E. WILLIAMS RESEARCH CENTER, LIFE CHIROPRACTIC COLLEGE.). [Chiropr. res. j.]. **Added/Corp** Sid. E. Williams Research Center. Life Chiropractic College. **VFOAT** CRJ. Vol. 1, No. 1 (Spring 1988)-. Periodical. English. qt. $40.00 US; $50.00 other. Chiropractic Research Journal, 1269 Barclay Circle, Marietta GA 30060. **Tel** (800)358-9737. **ED** John Grostic. **DD** 615. **NLM** W1; CH8144. **Pr Rev. Circ:** 3,000 (ctrl).

●US
**CHIROPRACTIC TECHNIQUE.** Vol. 4, No. 2 (May 1992)-. Periodical. English. qt. $89.00 (institution) US. Williams & Wilkins Company, 428 East Preston Street, Baltimore MD 21202-3993. **Tel** (410)528-4000, (800)638-6423, FAX (410)528-8596, telex 87669. **(Subscription address:** Williams & Wilkins, PO Box 64380, Baltimore, MD 21264-4380**) NLM** W1; CH8145M. Documents available from , , Quick Copies. ***Continues*** *Journal of Chiropractic Technique, 1062-9920.*
**Desc:** Deals exclusively with chiropractic techniques. Issues focus on traditional, time-tested procedures as well as new and innovative concepts in manipulative and physiological therapeutics.

FR/0009-7209
**CINESIOLOGIE.** (1962)-. Periodical. French. bm. 445.50F France; 570.00F other. Cinesiologie, c/o Dr A. Monroche, rue d Alsace, 49100 Angers France. **Tel** 011 33 1 41883535. **UDC** 61:796. **CODEN** 796:61. **[CCC].**
**Ind/Abst** SPORT Discus.

BE/0770-3198
**CLINICAL RHEUMATOLOGY.** [Clin. rheumatol.]. Vol. 1, No. 1 (March 1982)-. Academic Scholarly Publication. English. bm (6 issues). 5000F Belgium; 5100F other. Association for the Society of Scientifique Medica Belgique, Avenue Circulaire 138A, B-1180 Brussels Belgium. **Tel** 011 32 2 3745158. **NLM** W1 CL779L. **CODEN** CLRHD6. **Pr Rev.** Documents available from The Genuine Article, BIOSIS Document Express, CASDDS. ***Continues*** *Acta Rhumatologica, 0250-4642.*
**Ind/Abst** Biol. Abstr. (1984-); Chem. Abstr.; Curr. Contents Clin. Med.; EMBASE; Health Plan. Adminis.; Index Med. (1982-); Res. Alert [Select. Cov.]; SCISEARCH; Soc. Sci. Cit. Index [Select. Cov.].

US/1055-9361
**CLINIGUIDE TO RHEUMATOLOGY.** [Cliniguide rheumatol.]. Vol. 1, Issue 1 (1991)-. Periodical. English. qt. Free. Dellacorte Publications, 919 3rd Avenue, New York NY 10022-3904. **Tel** (212)751-2806. **DD** 616. **NLM** W1; CL85.

CN/0824-4154
**COMMUNIQUE - SOCIETE D'ARTHRITE. *Title Change.*** (COMMUNIQUE.). [Commun. - Soc. arthrite]. **Added/Corp** Societe d'Arthrite (Canada). Vol. 1 (Dec. 1982)-(19??). Periodical. French. Four times a year. Societe d'Arthrite du Canada, 250 Brool Street East #901, Toronto Ontario M4W 3P2 Canada. **Tel** (416)967-1414, FAX (416)967-7171. **ED** Dennis Jeanes. **DD** 616.7/22/006071. ctrl circ. ***Continued by*** *Arthro Express.*

UK
**CONFERENCE PROCEEDINGS (ARTHRITIS AND RHEUMATISM COUNCIL FOR RESEARCH IN GREAT BRITAIN AND THE COMMONWEALTH).** (CONFERENCE PROCEEDINGS / THE ARTHRITIS & RHEUMATISM COUNCIL FOR RESEARCH.). Proceedings. English. ir. Price varies per volume. **NLM** W1; CO4799.

IT
**CONNECTIVE TISSUE DISEASES / LE MALATTIE DEL TESSUTO CONNETTIVO. Added/Corp** Societa Napoletana "Carlo Curzio" per lo Studio delle Malattie del Tessuto Connettivo. **VFOAT** Malattie del Tessuto Connettivo. Vol. 1, No. 1 (Jan./June 1982)-. Periodical. English (Italian). bm (6 issues). $70.00. Casa Editrice Libr Idelson Gnocchi, Via Alcide de Gasperi 55, 80133 Naples Italy. **Tel** 011 39 81 552-4733. **NLM** W1; CO727K.

UK/0261-3360
**CURRENT MEDICAL LITERATURE. RHEUMATOLOGY.** [Curr. med. lit. Rheumatol.]. (1982)-. Periodical. English. bm. £20.00 UK; $40.00 US; £20.00 other. Current Medical Literature Ltd., 40-42 Osnaburgh Street, London NW1 3ND England. **Tel** 011 44 71 4658377, FAX 011 44 71 4658380. **(Subscription address:** Royal Society Medicine Services, 1 Wimpole Street, London W1M 8AE England.**)**

US/1040-8711
**CURRENT OPINION IN RHEUMATOLOGY.** [Curr. opin. rheumatol.]. Vol. 1, No. 1 (June 1989)-. Periodical. English. Six times a year. $269.95 (institutions), $134.95 (individuals). Current Science, 20 North 3rd Street, Philadelphia PA 19106. **Tel** (215)574-2266, (800)552-5866, FAX (215)574-2270. **ED** Daniel J. McCarthy. **LC** RC925.A1; C87. **DD** 616.7/23/005. **NLM** W1; CU799GHL. **CODEN** CORHES. **[CCC].** Documents available from BIOSIS Document Express.
**Desc:** Directed toward researchers and practicing rheumatologists covering an entire year's literature with annotated references. Each issue features a bibliography of the current world literature published during the previous year.
**Ind/Abst** Biol. Abstr. (1990-); Cumul. Index Nurs. Allied Health Lit.; Curr. Aware. Biol. Sci., CABS; EMBASE; Health Plan. Adminis.

US
**CYSTIC FIBROSIS FOUNDATION ANNUAL REPORT FOR THE FISCAL YEAR ... . Main/Corp** Cystic Fibrosis Foundation. Began with: 1975. Periodical. English. an. **NLM** W1 CY751C. ***Continues*** *National Cystic Fibrosis Research Foundation. Report.*

US/1041-469X
**D.C. TRACTS.** [D.C. tracts]. **Added/Corp** American Chiropractic Association. **VAT** Data Trace Tracts. Vol. 1, No. 1 (Feb. 1989)-. Periodical. English. Four times a year. $195.00 (institutions). Data Trace Publishing Group, PO Box 1239, Brooklandville MD 21022. **Tel** (410)494-4994, (800)342-0454, FAX (410)494-0515. **(Subscription address:** Data Trace Chiropractic Publishers, Inc., PO Box 1239, Brooklandville MD 21022.**) [CCC].**

SP/0214-1485
**DOLOR & INFLAMACION : FARMACOTERAPIA, INVESTIGACION Y CLINICA MEDICA / PATROCINADA POR LIGA REUMATOLOGICA ESPANOLA (LIRE). Added/Corp** Liga Reumatologica Espanola. **VFOAT** Dolor e Inflamacion. (19??)-. Periodical. Spanish. ir. 3500.00ptas Spain; 7000.00ptas other. Editorial Saned SA, Apolonio Morales 6, 28036 Madrid Spain. **Tel** 011 34 1 359-4092, FAX 011 34 1 457-9918. **NLM** W1; DO648.
**Ind/Abst** Indice Med. Esp.

SP
**ESCOLIOSIS.** Spanish. Ediciones Epiome SA, Paseo de Bonanova 10/4th Floor, Barcelona Spain.

SZ/0253-0333
**EULAR BULLETIN. MONOGRAPH SERIES.** [Eular bull., Monogr. ser.]. **Added/Corp** European League against Rheumatism. **VFOAT** Monograph Series. (1978)-. Monographic series. English (French and German). qt. Price varies per volume. Eular Verlag, Missionsstrasse 36, CH-4012 Basel Switzerland. **Tel** 011 41 61 2611317, FAX 011 41 61 256213, telex 963 755 REIN CH. **ED** K. Chlud. **NLM** W1 EU471. **Bk Rev. Ad Acc. Circ:** 22,000.
**Desc:** Official journal of the European League against Rheumatism.

●NO/0803-5288
**EUROPEAN JOURNAL OF EXPERIMENTAL MUSCULOSKELETAL RESEARCH.** Vol. 1 No. 1 (1992)-. Academic Scholarly Publication. English. qt. Kr740.00, $120.00. Scandinavian University Press, PO Box 2959 Toeyen, N 0608 Oslo 6 Norway. **Tel** 011 47 2 2575400, FAX 011 47 2 2575353, telex 71896 UROR N. **(Subscription address:** Scandinavian University Press, 200 Meacham Ave., Elmont NY 11003.**) ED** John Sevastik. **NLM** W1; EU73. **CODEN** EJEREE. Documents available from CASDDS.
**Desc:** A new interdisciplinary journal publishing original papers, short communication and review articles on experimental research into the physiology and pathology of the locomotor system. Addresses itself to a wide international audience of physicians, dentists, veterinarians, biochemists, biomechanics and pathologists.
**Ind/Abst** Chem. Abstr.

UK/0140-1610
**EUROPEAN JOURNAL OF RHEUMATOLOGY AND INFLAMMATION (ENGLISH EDITION).** (EUROPEAN JOURNAL OF RHEUMATOLOGY AND INFLAMMATION.). [Eur. j. rheumatol. inflammation]. Vol. 1 (Jan. 1978)-. Academic Scholarly Publication. English. qt. $80.00. Charterhouse Conf. and Comm. Company, 35 Cloth Fair, London EC1A 7JQ England. **Tel** 011 44 71 606 2435. **ED** E C Huskisson. **NLM** W1 EU72EM. **CODEN** EJRIDH. **Bk Rev.** Documents available from BIOSIS Document Express, CASDDS.
**Desc:** Original work reviews and other material that represents a useful contribution to the literature.
**Ind/Abst** Biol. Abstr.; Chem. Abstr.; EMBASE; Health Plan. Adminis.; Index Med.; PESTDOC.

GW/0258-2015
**FUNKTIONSKRANKHEITEN DES BEWEGUNGSAPPARATES.** [Funkt.krankh. Beweg.appar.]. Vol. 1, No. 1 (May 1986)-. Periodical. German (English; summaries and/or abstracts in English). Twice a year. DM102.00 Germany; DM106.00 other. Gustav Fischer Verlag Stuttgart, Postfach 720143, Wollgrasweg 49, D 70577 Stuttgart Germany. **Tel** 011 49 711 458030, FAX 0711-4580334, telex 2627-7111488. **(Subscription address:** VCH Publishers Inc., 303 Northwest 12th Avenue, Journals Department, Deerfield FL 33442.**) ED** Alois Brigger and C H Zurich. **NLM** W1; FU566U. **[CCC].** Index available. **Bk Rev. Ad Acc. Circ:** 1,200.
**Desc:** Covers the medical and physiotherapeutical field of orthopedics.

IT/1120-7000
**HIP INTERNATIONAL : THE JOURNAL OF CLINICAL AND EXPERIMENTAL RESEARCH ON HIP PATHOLOGY AND THERAPY.** Vol. 1, No 1 (Mar. 1991)-. Periodical. English. qt. $140.00. Wichtig Editore, Via Friuli 72 74, 20135 Milan Italy. **Tel** 011 39 2 55195443. **NLM** W1; HI409P.

US/0882-8318
**INDEX TO CHIROPRACTIC LITERATURE.** [Index chiropr. lit.]. **Added/Corp** Chiropractic Library Consortium. Canadian Memorial Chiropractic College. (1980)-. English. an (current year ed. in May following year). $20.00. Chiropractic Library Consortium, 2900 Northeast 132nd Avenue/WSCC, Portland OR 97230. **Tel** (503)251-5757. **ED** Kay Irvine. **LC** Z6675.C55; I5; RZ241. **DD** 016.6155/34. **NLM** ZWB 905; I38. Index available. cum. index. **Circ:** 40.
**Desc:** This literature of chiropractic medicine and a guide to chiropractic therapeutics and alternative healing techniques.

IT
**INFORMAZIONI RIABILITAZIONE.**
***Suspended.*** (19??)-(Dec. 1991). Italian. bm. L20000 Italy; L25000 other. Centro St Consul Invalidi, Via Gozzadini 7, 20148 Milan Italy. **Tel** 011 39 2 4038339.

NE/0169-1163
**JAPANESE JOURNAL OF RHEUMATOLOGY.** [Jpn. j. rheumatol.]. **Added/Corp** Nihon Ryumachi Gakkai. Vol. 1, No. 1 (1987)-. Periodical. English. qt. DM220.00. VSP International Science Publishers, Godfried van Seystlaan 47, 3703 BR Zeist Netherlands. **Tel** 011 31 3404 25790, FAX 011 31 3404 32081, telex 40217 USP NL. **(Subscription address:** VSP International Science Publishers, PO Box 346, 3700 AH Zeist Netherlands.**) ED** T. Azuma. **NLM** W1; JA975HG.
**Desc:** Provides dissemination of current Japanese research in rheumatology and associated areas such as pathology, physiology, clinical immunology, microbiology, biochemistry, experimental animal models and pharmacology.
**Ind/Abst** EMBASE.

SP/0210-8240
**JORNADAS DE TRABAJO SOBRE SUSTITUCIONES ARTICULARES.**
Spanish. an. Ministerio de Trabajo y Seguridad Social, Calle 20 No 8-18, Bogota Colombia. **NLM** W3 JO528K.

US/1053-8127
**JOURNAL OF BACK AND MUSCULOSKELETAL REHABILITATION.** **VFOAT** JBMR; Back and Musculoskeletal Rehabilitation. Vol. 1, No. 1 (Spring 1991)-. Periodical. English. qt. $105.00 (institution), $75.00 (individual) US and Canada; $125.00 (institution), $90.00 (individual) other. Butterworth Heinemann / Woburn, MA, 225 Wildwood Avenue, Unit B, Woburn MA 01801. **Tel** (800)366-2665, FAX (617)928-2620, telex 880052. **DD** 616. **NLM** W1; JO549. **[CCC].**

US/0884-0431
**JOURNAL OF BONE AND MINERAL RESEARCH.** (JOURNAL OF BONE AND MINERAL RESEARCH : THE OFFICIAL JOURNAL OF THE AMERICAN SOCIETY FOR BONE AND MINERAL RESEARCH.). [J. bone miner. res.]. **Added/Corp** American Society for Bone and Mineral Research. Vol. 1, No. 1 (Feb. 1986)-. Academic Scholarly Publication. English. mo. $300.00 US; $350.00 other. Blackwell Scientific Publishers, 238 Main Street, Cambridge MA 02142. **Tel** (617)547-7110, (800)835-6770, FAX (617)547-0789. **ED** Lawrence G. Raisz. **DD** 616. **NLM** W1; JO57BJ. **CODEN** JBMREJ. **Pr Rev.** Documents available from The Genuine Article, BIOSIS Document Express, CASDDS.
**Desc:** Provides a forum for papers dealing with all areas of calcium regulation, skeletal physiology, and metabolic bone diseases. It is the official journal of the American Society for Bone and Mineral Research and co-sponsored by the National Osteoporosis Foundation.
**Ind/Abst** Biol. Abstr. (1988-); Chem. Abstr. (1986-); Curr. Contents Life Sci.; Curr. Titl. Dent. (1986-); Dairy Sci. Abstr.; EMBASE; Health Plan. Adminis.; Index Med. (Vol. 1 No. 1, 1986-);; Nutr. Abstr. Rev., Ser. A, Hum. Exp.; Ref. Upd. Deluxe Ed.; Res. Alert [Full Cov.]; Rev. Med. Vet. Mycology; Sci. Cit. Index; SCISEARCH; Soc. Sci. Cit. Index [Select. Cov.].

US/1042-5055
**JOURNAL OF CHIROPRACTIC EDUCATION, THE.** [J. chiropr. educ.]. **VFOAT** JCE. Vol. 1, No. 1 (June 1987)-. Periodical. English. qt (Mar., June, Sept., Dec.). $30.00 (institutions), $25.00 (individuals). Journal of Chiropractic Education, 12570 Portland Avenue South, Suite 313, Burnsville MN 55337. **Tel** (612)882-1585, FAX (612)882-1585. **ED** Grace Jacobs. **DD** 615. **NLM** W1; JO5842D. **Bk Rev**, (Qty: 1-2). **Pr Rev. Circ:** 1,000.

US/1062-9920
**JOURNAL OF CHIROPRACTIC TECHNIQUE.** ***Title Change.*** [J. chiropr. tech.]. **VFOAT** Chiropractic Technique. Vol. 3, No. 2 (May 1991)-Vol. 4, No. 1 (Feb. 1992). Periodical. English. qt. Williams & Wilkins Company, 428 East Preston Street, Baltimore MD 21202-3993. **Tel** (410)528-4000, (800)638-6423, FAX (410)528-8596, telex 87669. **(Subscription address:** Williams & Wilkins, PO Box 64380, Baltimore, MD 21264-4380**) DD** 615. **NLM** W1; JO5843L. Documents available from Quick Copies.
***Continues*** *Chiropractic Technique, 0899-3467.*
***Continued by*** *Chiropractic Technique (Baltimore, Md. : 1992).*

DK/0270-4145
**JOURNAL OF CRANIOFACIAL GENETICS AND DEVELOPMENTAL BIOLOGY.** [J. craniofac. genet. dev. biol.]. **Added/Corp** Society of Craniofacial Genetics. Vol. 1, No. 1 (1981)-. Academic Scholarly Publication. English. qt. kr1250.00 US & Canada; kr1300.00 other. Munksgaard International Publishers Ltd, PO Box 2148, DK-1016 Copenhagen K Denmark. **Tel** 011 45 33 12 70 30, FAX 011 45 33 12 93 87, telex 19431 MUNKS DK. **ED** Michael Melnick and Harold C Slavkin. **LC** QL991; .J68. **DD** 612/.640191/05. **NLM** W1 JO602T. **CODEN** JCGBDF. **[CCC]. Bk Rev. Pr Rev.** Documents available from The Genuine Article, BIOSIS Document Express, CASDDS.
**Ind/Abst** AGRICOLA; Anim. Breed. Abstr.; Biol. Abstr.; Chem. Abstr.; Curr. Contents Life Sci.; Curr. Titl. Dent.; EMBASE; Index Med.; Index Dent. Lit.; Life Sci. Collect.; Res. Alert [Full Cov.]; Sci. Cit. Index; SCISEARCH.

UK/1050-6411
**JOURNAL OF ELECTROMYOGRAPHY AND KINESIOLOGY.** (JOURNAL OF ELECTROMYOGRAPHY AND KINESIOLOGY : OFFICIAL JOURNAL OF THE INTERNATIONAL SOCIETY OF ELECTROPHYSIOLOGICAL KINESIOLOGY.). [J. electromyogr. kinesiol.]. **Added/Corp** International Society of Electrophysiological Kinesiology. Vol. 1, No. 1 (Mar. 1991)-. Periodical. English. qt. $179.00 The Americas; £120.00 other. Butterworth Heinemann Publishers, Linacre House, Jordan Hill, Oxford OX2 8DP England. **Tel** 011 44 865 310366. **(Subscription address:** Elsevier Science Ltd. Oxford Fulfillment Centre, PO Box 800, Kidlington, Oxford OX5 1DX United Kingdom.**) LC** QP321; .J67. **DD** 612. **NLM** W1; JO628VH. **CODEN** JEKIE3. **[CCC].** available on microfilm and microfiche from University Microfilms International (UMI). Documents available from The Genuine Article.
**Desc:** Original articles on the study of muscle contraction and human motion through combined mechanical and electrical detection techniques. Topics include: control of movement; muscle fatique; muscle/nerve properties; joint biomechanics; eletrical stimulation.
**Ind/Abst** Curr. Contents Clin. Med.; EMBASE; Phys. Educ. Index (1991-); Res. Alert [Full Cov.]; SCISEARCH; Soc. Sci. Cit. Index [Select. Cov.].

US/1053-2137
**JOURNAL OF HUMAN MUSCLE PERFORMANCE.** ***Ceased.*** [J. hum. muscle perform.]. Vol. 1, No. 1 (June 1991)- Ceased with Vol. 1, No. 4 (March 1992). Periodical. English. qt. Aspen Publishers Inc., 7201 McKinney Circle, Frederick MD 21701. **Tel** (800)234-1660, (301)698-7100, FAX (301)251-5784, telex 5106014543. **LC** QP321; .J64. **DD** 612.7/4/05. **NLM** W1; JO673VP. **[CCC].**

US/0899-2517
**JOURNAL OF MUSCULOSKELETAL MEDICINE.** [J. musculoskelet. med.]. Vol. 1 No. 1 (Dec. 1983)-. Periodical. English. mo. $70.00 US; $90.00 other. Cliggott Publishing Company, 55 Holly Hill Lane, Box 4010, Greenwich CT 06830. **Tel** (203)661-0600, (212)993-0440. **DD** 616. **NLM** W1; JO775RF. **[CCC].**
**Desc:** Contains information that is both practical and authoritative on the diagnosis and management of a wide variety of common musculoskeletal disorders. Clinical information is drawn from diverse specialties, including rheumatology, orthopedics, cardiology, gastroenterology, sports medicine, emergency medicine, occupational medicine, as well as physical medicine and rehabilitation.

●US/1058-2452
**JOURNAL OF MUSCULOSKELETAL PAIN.** [J. musculoskelet. pain]. Vol. 1, No. 1 (1993)-. Periodical. English. qt. $75.00 US; $105.00 other. The Haworth Press Inc, 10 Alice Street, Binghamton NY 13904-1580. **Tel** (607)722-5857, (800)3-HAWORTH, FAX (607)722-1424. **ED** I. Jon Russell. **LC** RC927.3; .J68. **DD** 616.7. **NLM** W1; JO775RK. **CODEN** JMPAEQ. **Acid Free.** available on microfiche. Documents available from Haworth Document Delivery Service.
**Desc:** A fervent goal of the journal would be to foster quality research and meaningful communication between investigators and clinicians. Publishes original work on musculoskeletal pain problems, but would focus on those conditions currently categorized under the term "non-articular rheumatism."

CN/0315-162X
**JOURNAL OF RHEUMATOLOGY, THE.** [J. rheumatol.]. **VFOAT** Perspectives in Pediatric Rheumatology. Vol. 1 (March 1974)-. Academic Scholarly Publication. English. mo. 170.00Can$ (individuals), 190.00Can$ (institutions), 50.00Can$ (trainees) Canada; $160.00 (individuals), $180.00 (institutions), $50.00 (trainees) other. Journal of Rheumatology, 920 Yonge Street, Suite 115, Toronto Ontario M4W 3C7 Canada. **Tel** (416)967-5155. **ED** Duncan A. Gordon, M.D. **NLM** W1 JO87H. **CODEN** JRHUA9. **[CCC].** Index available. **Bk Rev. Ad Acc. Pr Rev. Circ:** 3,000. available on microfilm and microfiche from University Microfilms International (UMI). Documents available from The Genuine Article, BIOSIS Document Express, CASDDS.
**Desc:** Original research and clinical reports on rheumatology and related disorders irrespective of the geographical origin.
**Ind/Abst** Annals Behav. Med.; Biol. Abstr.; Calcium Calcif. Tissue Abstr.; Chem. Abstr.; Cumul. Index Nurs. Allied Health Lit.; Curr. Aware. Biol. Sci., CABS; Curr. Contents Clin. Med.; Curr. Contents Life Sci.; EMBASE; Helminthol. Abstr. (1991-); Immunol. Abstr.; Index Med.; Index Vet.; Microbiol. Abstr. Sect. B; Mod. Med.; Life Sci. Collect.; PESTDOC; Protozoolog. Abstr.; Ref. Upd. Basic Ed.; Ref. Upd. Clinical Ed.; Ref. Upd. Deluxe Ed.; Res. Alert [Full Cov.]; Rev. Med. Vet. Entomol.; Rev. Med. Vet. Mycology; Sci. Cit. Index; SCISEARCH; Soc. Sci. Cit. Index [Select. Cov.]; Vet. Bull.; Virol. AIDS Abstr.

CN/0380-0903
**JOURNAL OF RHEUMATOLOGY. SUPPLEMENT, THE.** [J. rheumatol. Suppl.]. No. 1- 1974-. Academic Scholarly Publication. English. 140.00Can$ (libraries and institutions), 120.00Can$ (individuals) Canada; $140.00 (libraries and institutions), $120.00 (individuals) other. Journal of Rheumatology, 920 Yonge Street, Suite 115, Toronto Ontario M4W 3C7 Canada. **Tel** (416)967-5155. **DD** 616.7/2/005. **NLM** W1 JO87HD. **CODEN** JRSUDX. Documents available from CASDDS.
**Ind/Abst** Chem. Abstr.; Index Med.

JA/0916-8737
**JOURNAL OF SMOOTH MUSCLE RESEARCH.** **Added/Corp** Nihon Heikatsukin Gakkai. **VFOAT** Nihon Heikatsukin Gakkai Kikanshi. Vol. 27, No. 1 (Feb. 1991)-. Periodical. English (Japanese). bm. Journal of Smooth Muscle Research, Ika Daigalu Dai 1 Geka Kyoshi, 840 Shijocho Kashihara Japan. **NLM** W1; JO877LK. ***Continues*** *Nippon Heikatsukin Gakkai Zasshi.*
**Ind/Abst** EMBASE; Index Med. (1991-).

US/0895-0385
**JOURNAL OF SPINAL DISORDERS.** [J. spinal disord.]. Vol. 1, No. 1 (1988)-. Periodical. English. bm (6 issues). $120.00 (individuals), $155.00 (institutions) US; $148.00 (individuals), $190.00 (institutions) other. Raven Press, 1185 Avenue of the Americas, 37th Floor, New York NY 10036. **Tel** (212)930-9500, (212)930-9604, FAX (212)869-3495, (212)302-8507, telex 640073. **DD** 616. **NLM** W1; JO902P. **CODEN** JSDIEW. **[CCC].** available on microfilm and microfiche from University Microfilms International (UMI). Documents available from The Genuine Article.
**Desc:** Features original articles on the diagnosis, management, and clinically relevant laboratory investigations of spinal disorders.
**Ind/Abst** Curr. Contents Clin. Med.; EMBASE; Index Med. (1988-); Res. Alert [Select. Cov.]; SCISEARCH.

CN/0008-3194
**JOURNAL OF THE CANADIAN CHIROPRACTIC ASSOCIATION, THE.** [J. Can. Chiropr. Assoc.]. **VFOAT** Journal de l'Association Chiropratique Canadienne; JCCA. (196?)-. Periodical. English (French). Four times a year (Mar., June, Sept., Dec.). 74.00Can$. Canadian Chiropractic Association, 1396 Eglington Avenue W, Toronto Ontario M6C 3E4 Canada. **Tel** (416)781-5656. **ED** Allan Gotlib. **DD** 615.5/34/0971. **NLM** W1 J223RB. **[CCC].** Index available. **Bk Rev. Ad Acc. Circ:** 3,300 (ctrl). available on microfilm and microfiche from University Microfilms International (UMI). ***Continues*** *Canadian Chiropractic Journal, 0410-8795.*
**Desc:** Covers scientific articles and papers related to the principles and clinical applications of chiropractic, cultivates professional dialogue and awareness through the publication of information and enhances continuing education of the practising chiropractor.

●US/1067-8239
**JOURNAL OF THE NEUROMUSCULOSKELETAL SYSTEM.** (JOURNAL OF THE NEUROMUSCULOSKELETAL SYSTEM : JNMS : A JOURNAL OF THE AMERICAN CHIROPRACTIC ASSOCIATION, INC.). [J. neuromusculoskel. syst.]. **Added/Corp** American Chiropractic Association. **VFOAT** JNMS. Vol. 1, No. 1 (Spring 1993)-. Periodical. English. qt. $118.00 (institution). Data Trace Publishing Group, PO Box 1239, Brooklandville MD 21022. **Tel** (410)494-4994, (800)342-0454, FAX (410)494-0515. **(Subscription address:** Data Trace Chiropractic Publishers, Inc., PO Box 1239, Brooklandville MD 21022.**) DD** 616. **NLM** W1; JO941WM. **Pr Rev.**
**Desc:** Publishes original articles on all aspects of disorders of the neuromusculoskeletal system, with an amphasis on non-operative care and management. Articles cover biomechanics and clinical anatomy; manual therapy, occupational health, orthopedics, and more. Targeted toward osteopaths, allopaths, physical therapists, chiropractors, medicine practitioners, and others.

JA/0389-7079
**KETSUGO SOSHIKI.** [Ketsugo soshiki]. **Added/Corp** Nihon Ketsugo Soshiki Gakkai. **VFOAT** Connective Tissue. (1969)-. Periodical. Japanese (English). tq. Nihon Ketsugo Soshiki Gakkai, (Japanese Soc. for Connective Tissue Research), Tokyo Ika Daigaku Byorigaku, Kyoshitsu, 1-1, Shinjuku 6 Chome,

Shinjukuku, Tokyoto 160 Japan. **CODEN** KESOD3. Documents available from CASDDS.
**Ind/Abst** Chem. Abstr.

FR/0297-6005
**KINESITHERAPEUTE PRATICIEN.** [Kinesither. prat.]. **VFOAT** K.P. (1985)-. Periodical. French. qt. 150.00F. Edi Pro Sante, 42 Rue Theodore Lenotre, 31500 Toulouse France. **Tel** 011 33 61 584772. **UDC** 615.825 (448.6). ***Continues*** *Keo, 0751-2619.*

●UK/0968-0160
**KNEE, THE.** (1994)-. English. Four times a year. $187.00 The Americas; £125.00 other. Butterworth Heinemann Publishers, Linacre House, Jordan Hill, Oxford OX2 8DP England. **Tel** 011 44 865 310366. **(Subscription address:** Elsevier Science Ltd. Oxford Fulfillment Centre, PO Box 800, Kidlington, Oxford OX5 1DX United Kingdom.**)**

FR
**LETTRE DU RHUMATOLOGUE.** French. 270.00F France; 330.00F other. Edimark, 207 rue Gallieni, 92100 Boulogne France. **Tel** 011 33 1 48251159.

US/8750-2321
**MDA NEWSMAGAZINE / MUSCULAR DYSTROPHY ASSOCIATION.** ***Title Change.*** [MDA newsmag.]. **Added/Corp** Muscular Dystrophy Association. **VFOAT** MDA News Magazine; M.D.A. Newsmagazine. **VAT** Muscular Dystrophy Association Newsmagazine. Vol. 1, No. 1 (Aug. 1984)-(199?). Periodical. English. qt. Muscular Dystrophy Association / Arizona, 3561 East Sunrise Drive, Tucson AZ 85718. **Tel** (602)529-2000. **ED** Cathy Carlson. **LC** RC935.M7; M33. **DD** 362.1/96748/005. **Bk Rev. Circ:** 90,000. ***Continues*** *MDA News, 0279-0742.* ***Continued by*** *MDA Reports, 1061-4370.*
**Desc:** A magazine serving all those interested in neuromuscular diseases, featuring patient profiles, association news, special features and research information in lay language.
**Ind/Abst** Consum. Health Nutr. Index (?-?); Health Index (1989-); Health Period. Database; Health Ref. Cent. (Jan. 1989-) [Full Cov.].

US/0738-3002
**MEDIGUIDE TO RHEUMATOLOGY.** [Mediguide rheumatol.]. Vol. 1, Issue 1-. Periodical. English. qt. Dellacorte Publications, 919 3rd Avenue, New York NY 10022-3904. **Tel** (212)751-2806. **NLM** W1; ME787GHC.

●UK/1355-3224
**MUSCULOSKELETAL MANAGEMENT.** (199?)-. Academic Scholarly Publication. English. Twice a year. $68.00 US & Canada; £40.00 Europe; £44.00 other. Blackwell Scientific Publications Ltd, Marston Book Services, PO Box 87, Oxford OX2 ODT UK. **Tel** 011 44 865 791155, FAX 011 44 865 791927, telex 837 515 MARDIS G.

US/0277-3007
**MUSCULOSKELETAL UPDATE.** Periodical. English. qt. Biomedical Information Corporation, 800 Second Avenue, New York NY 10017. **Tel** (212)262-9662.

●US
**NATIONAL DIRECTORY OF CHIROPRACTIC, THE.** 2nd Ed. (1991/1992)-. Directory. English. **NLM** WB 22; AA1 N277. ***Continues*** *One Directory of Chiropractic.*

UK/0261-8412
**NEUROMUSCULAR DISEASES. See** Medical Science and Technology-Neurology.

UK/0960-8966
**NEUROMUSCULAR DISORDERS : NMD.** **VFOAT** NMD. Vol. 1, No. 1, (1991)-. Periodical. English. bm. $358.00 The Americas; £240.00 other. Pergamon Press, An Imprint of Elsevier Science Ltd., The Boulevard, Langford Lane, Kidlington, Oxford OX5 1GB United Kingdom. **Tel** 011 44 865 843000, 011 44 865 843699, FAX 011 44 865 843010. **(Subscription address:** Elsevier Science Ltd. Oxford Fulfillment Centre, PO Box 800, Kidlington, Oxford OX5 1DX United Kingdom.**) ED** Victor Dubowitz. **NLM** W1; NE337GB. **CODEN** NEDIEC. **[CCC].** available on microfilm and microfiche from University Microfilms International (UMI). Documents available from The Genuine Article.
**Ind/Abst** Curr. Aware. Biol. Sci., CABS; EMBASE; Index Med. (1991-); Res. Alert [Full Cov.].

US
**NEWSLETTER - FLORIDA ARTHRITIS FOUNDATION.** **Main/Corp** Florida. Arthritis Foundation. (19??)-. Newsletter. English. qt. Free on request. Florida Arthritis Foundation, 5211 Manatee Avenue W, Bradenton FL 33529. **Tel** (813)748-3010.

CN/0827-7389
**ONTARIO LUPUS ASSOCIATION NEWSLETTER (1985).** (ONTARIO LUPUS ASSOCIATION NEWSLETTER.). [Ont. Lupus Assoc. newsl.]. **Main/Corp** Ontario Lupus Association. **VFOAT** OLA Newsletter. Vol. 5, No. 3 (1985)-. Periodical. English. Ontario Lupus Association, 250 Bloor Street East/Suite 401, Toronto Ontario M4W 3P2 Canada. **DD** 616.7/7/0060713. ***Continues*** *Ontario Lupus Association. OLA Newsletter., 0225-5634.*

●UK/1063-4584
**OSTEOARTHRITIS AND CARTILAGE.** (1993)-. English. qt (4 issues). £96.00 (institution), £64.00 (individual) UK/Europe; $172.00 (institution), $117.00 (individual). Harcourt Brace & Company Ltd., Foots Cray, High Street, Sidcup Kent DA14 5HP England. **Tel** 011 44 81 300 3322, FAX 011 44 81 309 0807. **(Subscription address:** W. B. Saunders Company / North America Subscriptions, c/o Periodicals, 6277 Sea Harbour Drive, 4th Floor, Orlando FL 32887.**) ED** R. D. Altman. **NLM** W1; OS792.
**Desc:** The official journal of the Osteoarthritis Research Society. It serves as a focal point and a forum for the exchange of ideas for the many kinds of specialists and practitioners concerned with osteoarthritis.

UK/0937-941X
**OSTEOPOROSIS INTERNATIONAL : A JOURNAL ESTABLISHED AS RESULT OF COOPERATION BETWEEN THE EUROPEAN FOUNDATION FOR OSTEOPOROSIS AND THE NATIONAL OSTEOPOROSIS FOUNDATION OF THE USA.** **Added/Corp** European Foundation for Osteoporosis. National Osteoporosis Foundation. Vol. 1, No. 1 (Oct. 1990)-. Periodical. English. Six times a year. £156.00. Springer-Verlag London Ltd., Springer House, 8 Alexandra Road Wimbledon, London SW19 7JZ England. **Tel** 011 44 81 9471280, or 9475885, FAX 011 44 81 9474651, telex 21531 SPRGB G. **(Subscription address:** North America: Springer Verlag, Journal Fulfillment Department, 44 Hartz Way, Secaucus, NJ 07096; Outside North America: Springer Verlag, Postfach 311340, D 10643 Berlin Germany**) ED** P J Meunier and R Lindsay. **NLM** W1; OS912L. **CODEN** OSINEP. **[CCC].** Documents available from The Genuine Article.
**Desc:** Devoted to the clinical aspects of osteoporosis management. Reports progress in all areas of osteoporosis and related disorders.
**Ind/Abst** Curr. Contents Clin. Med.; EMBASE; Index Med. (Oct. 1990-); Res. Alert [Full Cov.]; Sci. Cit. Index; Soc. Sci. Cit. Index [Select. Cov.].

UK
**PHYSICIAN'S RESOURCE MANUAL ON OSTEOPOROSIS.** (1987)-. Periodical. English. National Osteoporosis Foundation, 2100 M Street NW, Suite 602, Washington DC 20037. **Tel** (202)223-2226. **Circ:** 25,000 (ctrl).

US/0742-745X
**PROGRESS IN CLINICAL RHEUMATOLOGY.** [Prog. clin. rheumatol.]. Vol. 1 (1984)-. Periodical. English. ir. $33.00. Grune & Stratton Inc., 6277 Sea Harbor Drive, Orlando FL 32887. **Tel** (800)782-4479, (407)345-2567. **ED** Alan S. Cohen. **LC** RC927; .P69. **DD** 616.7/23/005. **NLM** W1; PR668HF 1984.

UK/0309-2283
**RECENT ADVANCES IN RHEUMATOLOGY.** [Recent adv. rheumatol.]. (1976)-. Academic Scholarly Publication. English. ir (every 3 to 5 years). Price varies per volume. Churchill Livingstone, 1-3 Baxter's Place, Leith Walk, Edinburgh EH1 3AF Scotland. **Tel** 011 44 31 556 2424, FAX 011 44 31 558 1278, telex 727511. **ED** W.W. Buchanan and W.C. Dick. **NLM** W1 RE105YH. **CODEN** RARHDQ. Documents available from CASDDS.
**Ind/Abst** Chem. Abstr.

FR/0294-0922
**REEDUCATION POSTURALE GLOBALE.** [Reeduc. posturale glob.]. (1983)-. Periodical. French. Four times a year. 180.00F. Editorial Le Pousoe, Philippe Souchard, 32400 Saint-Mont France. **Tel** 011 33 62696318, FAX 011 33 62696193. **ED** Philippe Souchard. **UDC** 615.8. **Ad Acc. Circ:** 1,000 (ctrl).
**Desc:** Founded on method of reeducation in global postural kinesitherapy.

US/0193-9998
**REPORT TO THE SECRETARY, DEPARTMENT OF HEALTH, EDUCATION, AND WELFARE (U.S. ARTHRITIS INTERAGENCY COORDINATING COMMITTEE).** (REPORT TO THE SECRETARY, DEPARTMENT OF HEALTH, EDUCATION, AND WELFARE.). **Main/Corp** United States. Arthritis Interagency Coordinating Committee. 1976-. Periodical. English. US Department of Health and Human Services National Institutes of Health, 9000 Rockville Pike, Bethesda MD 20892. **Tel** (301)496-9291, FAX (301)496-2443. **NLM** W2 A A6R.

UK/0957-0381
**REPORTS ON RHEUMATIC DISEASES (1985).** (REPORTS ON RHEUMATIC DISEASES. TOPICAL REVIEWS / THE ARTHRITIS AND RHEUMATISM COUNCIL.). [Rep. rheum. dis.]. **Added/Corp** Arthritis and Rheumatism Council for Research in Great Britain and the Commonwealth. Vol. 1 (July 1985)-. Periodical. English. Free on request. Arthritis & Rheumatism Council, PO Box 177, Chesterfield S41 7TQ England. **Tel** 011 44 246 558033, FAX 011 44 246 558007. Documents available from BIOSIS Document Express. ***Continues in part*** *Rheumatic Diseases.*
**Ind/Abst** Biol. Abstr. (1985-).

UK/0957-0381
**REPORTS ON RHEUMATIC DISEASES (1985).** (REPORTS ON RHEUMATIC DISEASES. PRACTICAL PROBLEMS / THE ARTHRITIS AND RHEUMATISM COUNCIL.). [Rep. rheum. dis.]. **Added/Corp** Arthritis and Rheumatism Council for Research in Great Britain and the Commonwealth. **VFOAT** Practical Problems. Vol. 1 (July 1985)-. Periodical. English. Three times a year (Jan., May, Sept.). Free on request. Arthritis & Rheumatism Council, PO Box 177, Chesterfield S41 7TQ England. **Tel** 011 44 246 558033, FAX 011 44 246 558007. **NLM** W1; RE213B. **CODEN** RRDPEW. Documents available from BIOSIS Document Express. ***Continues in part*** *Rheumatic Diseases.*
**Ind/Abst** Biol. Abstr. (1985-).

IT/0048-7449
**REUMATISMO.** [Reumatismo]. (1949)-. Periodical. Italian. Four times a year (end of Mar., Jun., Sept. and Dec.). $115.00. SIR - Societa Italiana di Reumatologia, Corso Plebisciti 9, 20129 Milan Italy. **Tel** (02)7387945, FAX (02)7385763, telex 33215 BOFFIS I. **ED** Prof. Bruno Colombo (Scientific Director). **CODEN** REUMADREUMAD.
**Desc:** Official journal of the Italian Rheumatology Society.
**Ind/Abst** EMBASE.

CI
**REUMATIZAM.** Vol. 11, No. 3 (1964)-. Serbo-Croatian (Roman). DM200.00 (institutions), DM100.00 (individuals). Reumatizam, Jurjevska Ul 25 1, 41000 Zagreb Croatia. ***Continues*** *Praxis Medici Reumatizam.*
**Ind/Abst** Index Med.

IT/0391-8963
**REUMATOLOGO : PUBBLICA IL BOLLETTINO DELLA SOCIETA ITALIANA DI REUMATOLOGIA, IL.** **Added/Corp** Societa Italiana di Reumatologia. Vol. 1, No. 1 (Jan./Feb. 1980)-. Periodical. Italian. bm. L25000 Italy; $17.77 US. CIC Edizioni Internazionali, Via L Spallanzani 11, 00161 Rome Italy. **Tel** 011 39 6 841-2673, FAX 011 39 6 844-3365, telex 622099 CIC I. **ED** C. Cervini. **NLM** W1; RE251LD. **Bk Rev. Ad Acc.**

SP/0304-4815
**REVISTA ESPANOLA DE REUMATOLOGIA : ORGANO OFICIAL DE LA SOCIEDAD ESPANOLA DE REUMATOLOGIA.** **Added/Corp** Sociedad Espanola de Reumatologia. (197?)-. Periodical. Spanish (summaries and/or abstracts in English; table of contents in English). bm. $63.00. Ediciones Doyma SA, Travesera de Gracia 17 21, 08021 Barcelona Spain. **Tel** 011 34 3 2000711, 011 34 3 4145706, FAX 011 34 3 2091136, telex 51964 INK E. **NLM** W1; RE549.
**Ind/Abst** EMBASE; Indice Med. Esp.

FR/0035-2659
**REVUE DU RHUMATISME ET DES MALADIES OSTEO-ARTICULAIRES.** ***Title Change.*** [Rev. rhum. mal. osteo-artic.]. **Added/Corp** Societe Francaise de Rhumatologie. Ligue Francaise Contre le Rhumatisme. No. 1 (Jan. 1946)-(Dec. 1992). Academic Scholarly Publication. French (summaries and/or abstracts in English, German and Spanish). mo (10 issues per year). Expansion Scientifique Francaise, 31 Boulevard de la Tour-Maubourg, 75007 Paris France. **Tel** 011 33 1 40 62 64 00, 011 33 1 40626439. **NLM** W1; RE841. **CODEN** RRMOA2. **[CCC].** Index Available, published separately, free-automatically sent. cum. index. **Bk Rev. Ad Acc. Pr Rev. Circ:** 4,000. available on microfilm from University Microfilms International (UMI). Documents available from The Genuine Article, CASDDS. ***Continues*** *Revue du Rhumatisme, 0301-8474.* ***Continued by*** *Revue du Rhumatisme (Ed. Francaise : 1993).*
**Desc:** Information on arthritis and rheumatic diseases.
**Ind/Abst** Chem. Abstr. (1934-1986); EMBASE; Helminthol. Abstr.; Index Med.; Nutr. Abstr. Rev., Ser. A, Hum. Exp.; Life Sci. Collect.; Protozoolog. Abstr.; Res. Alert [Full Cov.]; Rev. Med. Vet. Entomol.; Saf. Health Work; Sci. Cit. Index (19??-19??); SCISEARCH.

●FR/0035-2659
**REVUE DU RHUMATISME : MALADIES DES OS ET DES ARTICULATIONS.** **Added/Corp** Societe Francaise de Rhumatologie. (1993)-. Periodical. French (summaries and/or abstracts in English; table of contents in English). mo (10 issues). 1100.00F France; 1325.00F other. Expansion Scientifique Francaise, 31 Boulevard de la Tour-Maubourg, 75007 Paris France. **Tel** 011 33 1 40 62 64 00, 011 33 1 40626439. **NLM** W1; RE8396. **[CCC].** ***Continues*** *Revue du Rhumatisme et des Maladies*

*Osteo-Articulaires, 0035-2659.*
**Desc:** Information on arthritis and rheumatic diseases.
**Ind/Abst** Sci. Cit. Index.

FR/0294-474X
**REVUE INTERNATIONALE DE RHUMATOLOGIE.** ***Ceased.*** [Rev. int. rhumatol.]. **VFOAT** Revue Internationale de Rhumatologie et des Maladies de l'Appareil locomoteur; R; Revue Internationale de Rhumatologie "R". (1982)-(1992). Academic Scholarly Publication. French (English and Spanish). bm. Revue Internationale de Rhumatologie, 15 rue Turgot, 78100 St. Germain Laye France. **Tel** 011 33 81 534167. **NLM** W1; RE889C. **CODEN** RIRHDE. Documents available from CASDDS. ***Continues*** *Rhumatologie, 0003-4929.*
**Ind/Abst** Chem. Abstr. (?-1987); EMBASE (1983-?).

US/0889-857X
**RHEUMATIC DISEASE CLINICS OF NORTH AMERICA.** [Rheum. dis. clin. North Am.]. **VFOAT** Rheumatic Disease Clinics. Vol. 13, No. 1 (April 1987)-. English. qt. $100.00 (individual) $123.00 (institution) US; $135.00 (individual), $141.00 (institution). W.B. Saunders Company, A Subsidiary of Harcourt Brace Jovanovich, Inc., The Curtis Center/Suite 300, Independence Square West, Philadelphia PA 19106-3399. **Tel** (215)238-7800 or, 5587, FAX (215)238-7883, telex 173146. **(Subscription address:** W. B. Saunders Company / North America Subscriptions, c/o Periodicals, 6277 Sea Harbour Drive, 4th Floor, Orlando FL 32887.**) ED** Barbara A. Conover. **DD** 616. **NLM** W1; RH281. **CODEN** RDCAEK. **[CCC].** Index available. **Pr Rev. Circ:** 2,000. available on microfilm and microfiche from University Microfilms International (UMI). Documents available from The Genuine Article, BIOSIS Document Express. ***Continues in part*** *Clinics in Rheumatic Diseases, 0307-742X.*
**Desc:** Surveys new drugs, diagnostic techniques, and management. Each issue addresses a single topic in patient care.
**Ind/Abst** Biol. Abstr. (1987-); Cumul. Index Nurs. Allied Health Lit.; Curr. Contents Clin. Med.; EMBASE; Index Med. (1987-); Res. Alert [Full Cov.]; Sci. Cit. Index; SCISEARCH; Soc. Sci. Cit. Index [Select. Cov.].

SZ/0080-2727
**RHEUMATOLOGY.** [Rheumatology]. Vol. 1 (1966)-. Periodical. English. an. 200.00F (approx. per volume). S. Karger AG, Allschwilerstrasse 10, PO Box - Postfach - Case Postale, CH-4009 Basel Switzerland. **Tel** 011 41 61 306-1111, FAX 011 41 61 306-1234, telex CH 962 652. **ED** M. Schattenkirchner, F. W. Hagena. **LC** RC927.A1; R5. **NLM** W1; RH42G. **CODEN** RHEUBD. **[CCC].** Documents available from BIOSIS Document Express, CASDDS.
**Desc:** Features extensive reviews covering clinical and pathophysiologic aspects of rheumatology. Efforts to understand and treat the rheumatic diseases is evident in the titles of volumes published in this series. Individual volumes, each focused on a particular approach or specific disease entity, are reference works of particular value to rheumatologists, dermatologists, immunologists, and physicians treating arthritis.
**Ind/Abst** Biol. Abstr.; Chem. Abstr.; Index Med. (1969-1975); Ref. Upd. Deluxe Ed.

UK/0268-747X
**RHEUMATOLOGY FORUM.** Periodical. English. **NLM** W1; RH39K.

GW/0172-8172
**RHEUMATOLOGY INTERNATIONAL.** [Rheumatol. int.]. Vol. 1, No. 1 (1981)-. Academic Scholarly Publication. English. Six times a year. DM480.00. Springer-Verlag GmbH & Company KG, Heidelberger Platz 3, D 14197 Berlin Germany. **Tel** 011 49 30 8207223, FAX 011 49 30 8214091, telex 183 319 SPBLN D. **(Subscription address:** Springer Verlag New York Inc. / for North America, 44 Hartz Way, Secaucus NJ 07096.**) ED** B Bresnihan, E G L Bywaters, K Fehr, J R Kalden, E -M Lennel, K D Muirden, J B Natvig, C Steffen, R Winchester and M Ziff. **NLM** W1 RH42H. **CODEN** RHINDE. **[CCC]. Pr Rev.** available on microfilm and microfiche from University Microfilms International (UMI). Documents available from The Genuine Article, CASDDS.
**Desc:** An independent journal reflecting world-wide progress in the research, diagnosis and treatment of the various rheumatic diseases. It is designed to serve the international and interdisciplinary group of workers involved in problems of rheumatic diseases.
**Ind/Abst** Chem. Abstr.; Curr. Contents Clin. Med.; Curr. Contents Life Sci.; EMBASE; Index Med.; Res. Alert [Full Cov.]; Sci. Cit. Index; SCISEARCH.

UK/0958-2584
**RHEUMATOLOGY REVIEW (EDINBURGH).** (RHEUMATOLOGY REVIEW.). [Rheumatol. rev. Edinb.]. (Sept. 1991)-. Periodical. English. qt. £125.00 UK; $208.00 US; £126.00 other (institution). Churchill Livingstone, 1-3 Baxter's Place, Leith Walk, Edinburgh EH1 3AF Scotland. **Tel** 011 44 31 556 2424, FAX 011 44 31 558 1278, telex 727511. **(Subscription address:** Maruzen Company Ltd., PO Box 5050, Import & Export Department, Tokyo 100 31 Japan.**) ED** Roger Sturrock and Matthew Liang. **DD** 616.723005. **[CCC].**
**Desc:** Review journal publishing specially commissioned articles on the actiopathogenesis, diagnosis and treatment of all major rheumatological conditions. All the topics will be covered systematically in a three-year cycle and the journal will provide invaluable information for qualified and trainee rheumatologists as well as general physicians and practitioners.

FR/0249-7581
**RHUMATOLOGIE (AIX-LES-BAINS).** (RHUMATOLOGIE.). [Rhumatologie]. (1949)-. Periodical. French. Ten times a year. 520.00F (France); 60.00F (other). France Regions Publications, 38 rue Pascal, 75013 Paris France. **Tel** 11 33 1 43315727.
**Ind/Abst** EMBASE; Saf. Health Work.

JA/0300-9157
**RYUMACHI.** (RYUMACHI / THE RYUMACHI : OFFICIAL JOURNAL OF THE JAPAN RHEUMATISM ASSOCIATION.). [Ryumachi]. **Added/Corp** Nihon Ryumachi Gakkai. **VFOAT** Ryumachi. (1958)-. Academic Scholarly Publication. Japanese (summaries and/or abstracts in English). bm. $178.00. Japan Rheumatism Association, 401 Pare-Nogizaka, 9-5-26 Akasa, Minato-ku Tokyo 107 Japan. **NLM** W1 RY659. **CODEN** RYMCAF. Documents available from CASDDS.
**Ind/Abst** Chem. Abstr.; EMBASE; Index Med.

SW/0300-9742
**SCANDINAVIAN JOURNAL OF RHEUMATOLOGY.** [Scand. j. rheumatol.]. **Added/Corp** Scandinavian Society of Rheumatologists. Vol. 1 (1972)-. Academic Scholarly Publication. English. Six times a year. Kr895.00, $152.00. Scandinavian University Press, PO Box 2959 Toeyen, N 0608 Oslo 6 Norway. **Tel** 011 47 2 2575400, FAX 011 47 2 2575353, telex 71896 UROR N. **(Subscription address:** Scandinavian University Press, 200 Meacham Ave., Elmont NY 11003.**) ED** Eimar Munthe. **LC** RC927; .S3. **DD** 616.7/2/005. **NLM** W1 SC154B. **CODEN** SJRHAT. **Bk Rev. Ad Acc. Pr Rev. Circ:** 1,500 (ctrl). Documents available from The Genuine Article, BIOSIS Document Express, CASDDS. ***Supersedes*** *Acta Rheumatologica Scandinavica.*
**Desc:** Covers the clinical, experimental and laboratory, diagnostic, epidemiological, social and therapeutic aspects of rheumatic diseases.
**Ind/Abst** Annals Behav. Med.; Biol. Abstr.; Chem. Abstr.; Curr. Aware. Biol. Sci., CABS; Curr. Contents Clin. Med.; EMBASE; Energy Res. Abstr. (Feb. 1975-); Index Med.; Life Sci. Collect.; PESTDOC; Ref. Upd. Basic Ed.; Ref. Upd. Deluxe Ed.; Res. Alert [Full Cov.]; Rev. Med. Vet. Entomol.; Sci. Cit. Index; SCISEARCH; Soc. Sci. Cit. Index [Select. Cov.]; Sug. Indus. Abstr.

SW/0301-3847
**SCANDINAVIAN JOURNAL OF RHEUMATOLOGY. SUPPLEMENT.** [Scand. j. rheumatol., Suppl.]. (1973)-. Academic Scholarly Publication. English. Kr895.00, $152.00. Scandinavian University Press, PO Box 2959 Toeyen, N 0608 Oslo 6 Norway. **Tel** 011 47 2 2575400, FAX 011 47 2 2575353, telex 71896 UROR N. **(Subscription address:** Scandinavian University Press, 200 Meacham Ave., Elmont NY 11003.**) NLM** W1 SC154BA. **CODEN** SJRSAS. Documents available from BIOSIS Document Express, CASDDS. ***Supersedes*** *Acta Rheumatologica Scandinavica. Supplementum, 0065-163X.*
**Ind/Abst** Biol. Abstr.; Chem. Abstr.; Curr. Aware. Biol. Sci., CABS; EMBASE; Index Med.; Life Sci. Collect.

US/0049-0172
**SEMINARS IN ARTHRITIS AND RHEUMATISM.** [Semin. arthritis rheum.]. **VFOAT** Arthritis and Rheumatism. Vol. 1 (May 1971)-. Academic Scholarly Publication. English. bm. $116.00 (individual) $174.00 (institution) US; $197.00 (individual), $216.00 (institution) other. W.B. Saunders Company, A Subsidiary of Harcourt Brace Jovanovich, Inc., The Curtis Center/Suite 300, Independence Square West, Philadelphia PA 19106-3399. **Tel** (215)238-7800 or, 5587, FAX (215)238-7883, telex 173146. **(Subscription address:** W. B. Saunders Company / North America Subscriptions, c/o Periodicals, 6277 Sea Harbour Drive, 4th Floor, Orlando FL 32887.**) ED** Roy D. Altman. **LC** RC933.A1. **DD** 616.7/2/005. **NLM** W1 SE487. **CODEN** SAHRBF. **[CCC]. Pr Rev. Circ:** 3,696. Documents available from The Genuine Article, BIOSIS Document Express, CASDDS.
**Desc:** Provides a broad interpretation of the field, including aspects of general medicine and orthopedics. Presents review articles focusing on one or more topics in rheumatology.
**Ind/Abst** Annals Behav. Med.; Biol. Abstr.; Chem. Abstr.; Curr. Contents Clin. Med.; EMBASE; Energy Res. Abstr. (March 1982-); Index Med.; Mod. Med.; Life Sci. Collect.; Res. Alert [Full Cov.]; Sci. Cit. Index; SCISEARCH; Soc. Sci. Cit. Index [Select. Cov.].

US/0364-2348
**SKELETAL RADIOLOGY.** **See** Medical Science and Technology-Radiology.

CN/0840-8386
**SMDI INTERNATIONAL NEWSLETTER.** (SMDI INTERNATIONAL NEWSLETTER / SOCIETY FOR MUSCULAR DYSTROPHY INFORMATION INTERNATIONAL.). [SMDI Int. newsl.]. **Added/Corp** Society for Muscular Dystrophy Information International. **VFOAT** SMDI(I) Newsletter. **VAT** Society for Muscular Dystrophy Information International Newsletter. Vol. 1, No. 1 (1987)-. Periodical. English. Four times a year. $35.00. Society for Muscular Dystrophy Information International, PO Box 479, Bridgewater Nova Scotia B4V 2X6 Canada. **Tel** (902)682-3086. **DD** 616.7/48/005.
**Desc:** Neuromuscular international non-technical publication by and for those concerned with muscular dystrophy or the allied disorders. Based mainly on international neuromuscular organization publication/information exchange. Research reports, reviews, articles, disability information, information sources and addresses, Muscular Dystrophy Association/allied disorders groups directory, etc.

UK/0261-4928
**SMOOTH MUSCLE.** [Smooth muscle]. (1982)-. English. mo. £75.00. SUBIS, Mansion House, 19 Kingfield Road, Sheffield S11 9AS England. **Tel** 011 44 114 255 4433, FAX 011 44 114 255 4626. **DD** 016.61274. **Ad Acc.**
**Desc:** Current awareness service for researchers and clinicians.

US/0160-9475
**SPINA BIFIDA THERAPY.** Vol. 1, No. 1 (July 1978)-. Periodical. English. Four times a year. $30.00. Eterna Press, PO Box 157941, Chicago IL 60615. **Tel** (312)969-0318. **ED** Stephen B. Parrish. **NLM** W1 SP466.
**Ind/Abst** PsycINFO (?-?); PsycLit.

US
**SPINAL MANIPULATION. Added/Corp** Foundation for Chiropractic Education and Research (U.S.). Vol. 2, No. 1 (April 1986)-. Periodical. English. qt. $50.00 (one year), $90.00 (two year) nonmembers, $45.00 (one year) $85.00 (two year) members. Foundation for Chiropractic Education and Research, 1701 Clarendon Boulevard, Arlington VA 22209. **Tel** (703)276-7445, (800)637-6244. **NLM** ZWB 905; S757. ***Continues*** *Literature Review (Virginia Beach, Va.).*

●US/1073-2837
**TOPICS IN CLINICAL CHIROPRACTIC.** (1994)-. English. qt. $58.00. Aspen Publishers Inc., 7201 McKinney Circle, Frederick MD 21701. **Tel** (800)234-1660, (301)698-7100, FAX (301)251-5784, telex 5106014543. **(Subscription address:** Aspen Publishers Inc., PO Box 990, Frederick MD 21701.**) NLM** W1; TO539LBM.

US
**VENTILATORS & MUSCULAR DYSTROPHY.** (1987)-. Periodical. English. $6.00 US; $7.35 Canada/Mexico and Overseas. Gazette International Networking Institute, 5100 Oakland Avenue, Number 206, St Louis MO 63110. **Tel** (314)534-0475, FAX (314)534-5070. **ED** Nancy C Schock and Agatha P Colbert.
**Desc:** Discusses the option of mechanical ventilation for persons with Duchenne muscular dystrophy to improve the prognosis for life expectancy.

GW/0070-4121
**VERHANDLUNGEN DER DEUTSCHEN GESELLSCHAFT FUER RHEUMATOLOGIE.** ***Ceased.*** [Verh. Dtsch. Ges. Rheumatol.]. **Main/Corp** Deutsche Gesellschaft fur Rheumatologie. **VFOAT** Zeitschrift fur Rheumatologie Supplement. Vol. 1 (1969)-(19??). Academic Scholarly Publication. German (summaries and/or abstracts in English and French). Dr Dietrich Steinkopff Verlag, PO Box 111442, D 64229 Darmstadt Germany. **Tel** 011 49 6151 17450. **NLM** W1 VE483MR. **CODEN** VDGRAT. **[CCC].** Documents available from CASDDS.
**Ind/Abst** Chem. Abstr. (?-?); EMBASE (?-?); Index Med. (?-?).

●US
**YEAR BOOK OF CHIROPRACTIC.** (1993)-. English. an. $59.95. Mosby Year Book Inc., 11830 Westline Industrial Drive, St Louis MO 63146. **Tel** (800)325-4177, (314)872-8370, FAX (314)432-1380, telex 44-2402. **NLM** W1; YE114AF.

GW/0340-1855
**ZEITSCHRIFT FUER RHEUMATOLOGIE.** [Z. Rheumatol.]. **Added/Corp** Deutsche Gesellschaft fuer Rheumatologie. Schweizerische Gesellschaft fuer Rheumatologie. Osterreichische Rheumaliga. Berufsverband Deutscher Rheumatologen. Schweizerische Gesellschaft fuer Physikalische Medizin und Rheumatologie. Osterreichische Liga zur Bekaempfung des Rheumatismus. Vol. 33 (1974)-. Academic Scholarly Publication. German (summaries and/or abstracts in English and French). Six times a year. DM340.00. Dr Dietrich Steinkopff Verlag, PO Box 111442, D 64229 Darmstadt Germany. **Tel** 011 49 6151 17450. **(Subscription address:** Springer Verlag New York Inc. / for North America, 44 Hartz Way, Secaucus NJ 07096.**) ED** W.H. Hauss, V.R. Ott and K.L. Schmidt. **NLM** W1 ZE583. **CODEN** ZRHMBQ. **[CCC]. Pr Rev.** Documents available from The Genuine Article, BIOSIS Document Express, CASDDS, ADONIS. ***Continues*** *Zeitschrift fur Rheumaforschung.*
**Desc:** Official organ of the German Society of Rheumatology, the Austrian Society of Rheumatology, the Swiss Society of Rheumatology, and the German Association of Practicing Rheumatologists.
**Ind/Abst** ADONIS; Biol. Abstr.; Chem. Abstr.; Curr. Contents Clin. Med.; EMBASE; Energy Res. Abstr. (Oct. 1975-); Index Med.; Life Sci. Collect.; PESTDOC; Res. Alert [Full Cov.]; Sci. Cit. Index; SCISEARCH; Soc. Sci. Cit. Index [Select. Cov.].

## NEOPLASMA, NEOPLASTIC

SP/0001-6381
**ACTA ONCOLOGICA.** [Acta oncol.]. (1962)-. Periodical. Spanish. tq. Asociacion Espanola Contra El Cancer, Maiquez 7, 28009 Madrid Spain. **UDC** 616 - 006.

BL/0100-3127
**ACTA ONCOLOGICA BRASILEIRA.** [Acta Oncol. Bras.]. **Added/Corp** Instituto Central - Hospital A. C. Camargo, Sao Paulo, Brazil. Vol. 1 July/Sept. (1977)-. Academic Scholarly Publication. Portuguese (summaries and/or abstracts in English). Instituto Central-Hospital, A.C. Camargo, Rua Prof. Antonio Prudente, 211 Caixa Postal, 5271 Liberdade, Sao Paula, SP Brazil. **NLM** W1 AC877E. Documents available from BIOSIS Document Express.
**Ind/Abst** Biol. Abstr.; EMBASE.

IT/0393-7542
**ACTA ONCOLOGICA PADOVA.** [Acta oncol.Padova]. (1980)-. Periodical. Multiple languages (English). bm. $125.00. Piccin Editore, Via Altinate 107, 35121 Padua Italy. **Tel** 011 39 49 655566, FAX 011 39 49 8750693. **UDC** 616-006.

SW/0284-186X
**ACTA ONCOLOGICA (STOCKHOLM, SWEDEN).** (ACTA ONCOLOGICA.). [Acta oncol.]. **Added/Corp** European Organization for Research on Treatment of Cancer. Education Branch. (1987-1992). Periodical. English (French and German). Eight times a year. Kr1715.00, $280.00. Scandinavian University Press, PO Box 2959 Toeyen, N 0608 Oslo 6 Norway. **Tel** 011 47 2 2575400, FAX 011 47 2 2575353, telex 71896 UROR N. **(Subscription address:** Scandinavian University Press, 200 Meacham Ave., Elmont NY 11003.**)** **ED** Lars-Gunnar Larsson. **NLM** W1; AC877CK. **CODEN** ACTOEL. **Ad Acc. Circ:** 2,500 (ctrl). Documents available from The Genuine Article, BIOSIS Document Express, Ask*IEEE. ***Continues*** *Acta Radiologica. Oncology, 0349-652X.* ***Continued in part by*** *Reviews in Oncology.*
**Desc:** A journal for the clinical oncologist. Publishes articles within all fields of clinical cancer research including cancer nursing and psychological and social aspects of cancer.
**Ind/Abst** Biol. Abstr. (1987-); Curr. Aware. Biol. Sci., CABS; Curr. Contents Clin. Med.; Curr. Contents Life Sci.; Ei Page One; EMBASE; Health Plan. Adminis.; Index Med. (1987-); INSPEC (1987-); PESTDOC; Ref. Upd. Deluxe Ed.; Res. Alert [Full Cov.]; Rev. Med. Vet. Mycology; Sci. Cit. Index; SCISEARCH; Soc. Sci. Cit. Index [Select. Cov.].

US
**ACTIVATION AND METABOLISM OF CARCINOGENS.** **Main/Corp** International Cancer Research Date Bank. (197?)-. Periodical. English. US Department of Health and Human Services National Institutes of Health, 9000 Rockville Pike, Bethesda MD 20892. **Tel** (301)496-9291, FAX (301)496-2443.

US/0190-4817
**ADVANCES IN CANCER CHEMOTHERAPY.** [Adv. cancer chemother.]. Vol. 1, (1979)-. Academic Scholarly Publication. English. ir. Price varies per volume. Marcel Dekker Inc., 270 Madison Avenue, New York NY 10016. **Tel** (212)696-9000, (800)228-1160, FAX (212)685-4540, telex 421419. **(Subscription address:** Marcel Dekker Inc, PO Box 5017, Monticello NY 12701.**)** **LC** RC271.C5; A238. **DD** 616.9/94/061. **NLM** W1 AD511M. **CODEN** ACEMD7. Documents available from BIOSIS Document Express, CASDDS.
**Desc:** This is an ongoing series. Each title covers a different topic.
**Ind/Abst** Biol. Abstr. (-1979); Chem. Abstr.; PESTDOC.

US/0065-230X
**ADVANCES IN CANCER RESEARCH.** [Adv. cancer res.]. Vol. 1 (1953)-. Academic Scholarly Publication. English. ir. Price varies per volume. Academic Press, Inc., 6277 Sea Harbor Drive, Orlando FL 32887. **Tel** (800)543-9534, (407)345-4100, FAX (407)363-9661. **ED** George Klein and George F. Vande Woude. **LC** RC267; .A45. **DD** 616.99/4. **NLM** W1 AD512. **CODEN** ACRSAJ. **[CCC]. Pr Rev.** Documents available from The Genuine Article, CASDDS.
**Ind/Abst** AGRICOLA [Select. Cov.]; Chem. Abstr.; EMBASE; Energy Res. Abstr.; Health Plan. Adminis.; Index Med.; Index Sci. Rev. [Full Cov.]; Index Vet.; INIS Atomindex [Micro.]; NAPRALERT; Life Sci. Collect.; PESTDOC; Physic. Medline Plus; Ref. Upd. Basic Ed.; Ref. Upd. Clinical Ed.; Ref. Upd. Deluxe Ed.; Res. Alert [Full Cov.]; Sci. Cit. Index; SCISEARCH; Vet. Bull.

US
**ADVANCES IN TUMOUR PREVENTION, DETECTION AND CHARACTERIZATION.** V.1 (1974)-. Monographic series. English. ir. Price varies per volume. Elsevier Science Publishing Company Inc, Madison Square Station, PO Box 882, New York NY 10159-0882. **Tel** (212)633-3950, FAX (212)633-3990.

US/0735-0104
**ADVANCES IN VIRAL ONCOLOGY.** [Adv. viral oncol.]. Vol. 1 (1982)-. Academic Scholarly Publication. English. ir. Price varies per volume. Raven Press, 1185 Avenue of the Americas, 37th Floor, New York NY 10036. **Tel** (212)930-9500, (212)930-9604, FAX (212)869-3495, (212)302-8507, telex 640073. **NLM** W1 AD888. **CODEN** AVONDN. Documents available from BIOSIS Document Express, CASDDS.
**Ind/Abst** Biol. Abstr.; Chem. Abstr.; Oncog. Growth Factors Abstr.; Life Sci. Collect.

US/0277-3732
**AMERICAN JOURNAL OF CLINICAL ONCOLOGY.** (AMERICAN JOURNAL OF CLINICAL ONCOLOGY : CANCER CLINICAL TRIALS.). [Am. j. clin. oncol.]. **Added/Corp** American Radium Society. **VFOAT** AJCO. Vol. 5, No. 1 (Feb. 1982)-. Academic Scholarly Publication. English. bm. $152.00 (individuals), $218.00 (institutions) US; $190.00 (individuals), $262.00 (institutions) other. Raven Press, 1185 Avenue of the Americas, 37th Floor, New York NY 10036. **Tel** (212)930-9500, (212)930-9604, FAX (212)869-3495, (212)302-8507, telex 640073. **ED** Luther W. Brady. **DD** 616. **NLM** W1 AM45K. **CODEN** AJCODI. **[CCC]. Pr Rev.** available on microfilm and microfiche from University Microfilms International (UMI). Documents available from The Genuine Article, BIOSIS Document Express, CASDDS. ***Continues*** *Cancer Clinical Trials, 0190-1206.*
**Desc:** Covers ongoing research in cancer treatment, presenting the latest pathologic, surgical, and clinical data related to end-results in medical and surgical treatment of metastatic and neoplastic diseases and localized tumors.
**Ind/Abst** Biol. Abstr.; Chem. Abstr. (-1988); Curr. Aware. Biol. Sci., CABS; Curr. Contents Clin. Med.; EMBASE; Index Med.; INIS Atomindex [Micro.]; Nutr. Res. Newsl.; Life Sci. Collect.; PESTDOC; Res. Alert [Full Cov.]; Sci. Cit. Index; SCISEARCH; Soc. Sci. Cit. Index [Select. Cov.].

US/0192-8562
**AMERICAN JOURNAL OF PEDIATRIC HEMATOLOGY/ONCOLOGY, THE.** ***Title Change.*** **See** Medical Science and Technology-Pediatrics.

NE/0923-7534
**ANNALS OF ONCOLOGY : OFFICIAL JOURNAL OF THE EUROPEAN SOCIETY FOR MEDICAL ONCOLOGY.** [Annals oncol.]. (1990)-. Periodical. English. Ten times a year. $658.00. Kluwer Academic Publishers, Postbus 322, 3300 AH Dordrecht, The Netherlands. **Tel** 011 (31) 78 524400, FAX 011 31 78 183273, telex 20083. **ED** F. Cavalli. **NLM** W1; AN617D. **CODEN** ANONE2. **[CCC].** available on microfilm and microfiche from University Microfilms International (UMI). Documents available from The Genuine Article.
**Desc:** Devoted to the rapid circulation of scientific communications in oncology, particularly medical oncology. Its character, however, is multidisciplinary, to reflect the proliferation of activities and interests in Europe. Contributions on clinically oriented laboratory research, surgery and radiotherapy are assured by the presence of representatives of these disciplines on the Editorial Committee and Board.
**Ind/Abst** Curr. Aware. Biol. Sci., CABS; Curr. Contents Clin. Med.; EMBASE; Health Plan. Adminis.; Res. Alert [Full Cov.]; Sci. Cit. Index; SCISEARCH; Soc. Sci. Cit. Index [Select. Cov.].

US/0197-016X
**ANNUAL MEETING OF THE AMERICAN ASSOCIATION FOR CANCER RESEARCH PROCEEDINGS.** [Annu. meet. Am. Assoc. Cancer Res., Proc.]. **Main/Corp** American Association for Cancer Research. **VFOAT** Annual Meeting of the American Society of Clinical Oncology. Vol. 15 (March 1974)-. Academic Scholarly Publication. English. an (Mar.). $35.00. American Association of Cancer Research, 620 Chestnut Street, Pub Ledger Building, Philadelphia PA 19106. **Tel** (215)440-9300. **(Subscription address:** Fulco, 30 Broad Street, Denville NJ 07834.**)** **DD** 616. **NLM** W1 PR583HR. Documents available from Quick Copies. ***Continues*** *Annual Meeting. Proceedings of the American Association for Cancer Research, 0197-0151.* ***Continued in part by*** *Directory of Members, 0277-3414; Proceedings - American Society of Clinical Oncology. Meeting, 0736-7589.*
**Ind/Abst** EMBASE; PESTDOC; Risk Abstr. (19??-19??).

UK
**ANNUAL REPORT.** **Main/Corp** Cancer Research Campaign. 48th (1970)-. Corporate Report. English. an. Free. Cancer Research Campaign, 10 Cambridge Terrace, London NW1 4JL England. **Tel** 011 44 71 935 1546. **ED** Susan Osborne. Documents available from BLDSC. ***Continues*** *British Empire Cancer Campaign for Research. Annual Report.*

US
**ANNUAL REPORT - DIAGNOSTIC RESEARCH ADVISORY GROUP, NATIONAL INSTITUTES OF HEALTH.** **Main/Corp** National Cancer Institute. Diagnostic Research Advisory Committee. (19??)-. Periodical. English. an. National Cancer Institute, NCI Building Room, 10A 18, Bethesda MD 20892. **Tel** (800)422-6237, (301)496-8774.

US
**ANNUAL REPORT - DIVISION OF CANCER CONTROL AND REHABILITATION.** **Main/Corp** National Cancer Institute (U.S.). Division of Cancer Control and Rehabilitation. (19??)-. English. an. National Cancer Institute, NCI Building Room, 10A 18, Bethesda MD 20892. **Tel** (800)422-6237, (301)496-8774.

AT/0819-8756
**ANNUAL REPORT FOR THE PERIOD ... / CANCER FOUNDATION OF WESTERN AUSTRALIA INC.** [Annu. rep. period - Cancer Found. West. Aust.]. **Main/Corp** Cancer Foundation of Western Australia. 3rd Jan. 1983 to 31st Dec. 1983-. English. an. **NLM** W1; CA679UC. ***Continues*** *Cancer Council of Western Australia. Annual Report.*

US/0148-8333
**ANNUAL REPORT - NATIONAL CANCER INSTITUTE, DIVISION OF CANCER BIOLOGY AND DIAGNOSIS.** (ANNUAL REPORT / DIVISION OF CANCER BIOLOGY AND DIAGNOSIS.). English. an. US Department of Health and Human Services, 200 Independence Avenue Southwest, Washington DC 20201. **LC** RC267; .U542C. **DD** 616.9/94/0072073. available on microfiche (Vols. for (1982/1983-) distributed to depository libraries).

US
**ANNUAL REPORT / NATIONAL CANCER INSTITUTE, DIVISION OF CANCER TREATMENT.** **Main/Corp** National Cancer Institute (U.S.) Division of Cancer Treatment. **VFOAT** DCT ... Annual Report; Division of Cancer Treatment ... Annual Report. English. an. National Cancer Institute, NCI Building Room, 10A 18, Bethesda MD 20892. **Tel** (800)422-6237, (301)496-8774. **LC** RC261.A1; U54A. **DD** 616.99/4061/072073. **NLM** W2 A N1475A. available on microfiche (Vols. for (1982/1983-) distributed to depository libraries). ***Continues*** *Report of the Division of Cancer Treatment, NCI, 0145-7268.*

US/0883-3176
**ANNUAL REPORT - NATIONAL CANCER INSTITUTE (U.S.). DIVISION OF CANCER PREVENTION AND CONTROL.** (ANNUAL REPORT / DIVISION OF CANCER PREVENTION AND CONTROL.). [Annu. rep. - Natl. Cancer Inst. (U.S.), Div. Cancer Prev. Control]. **Main/Corp** National Cancer Institute (U.S.). Division of Cancer Prevention and Control. 1984-. English. an. National Cancer Institute, NCI Building Room, 10A 18, Bethesda MD 20892. **Tel** (800)422-6237, (301)496-8774. **ED** Peter Greenwald. **LC** RC267; .N37B. **DD** 614.5/999. **Circ:** 300. available on microfiche (Vols. for (1984-) distributed to depository libraries). ***Continues*** *National Cancer Institute (U.S.). Division of Resources, Centers, and Community Activities. Annual Report, 0730-1650.*

US/0738-0372
**ANNUAL REPORT - NATIONAL CANCER INSTITUTE (U.S.). DIVISION OF EXTRAMURAL ACTIVITIES.** (ANNUAL REPORT / DIVISION OF EXTRAMURAL ACTIVITIES.). **Main/Corp** National Cancer Institute (U.S.). Division of Extramural Activities. **Added/Corp** National Cancer Institute (U.S.). (19??)-. English. an. National Cancer Institute, NCI Building Room, 10A 18, Bethesda MD 20892. **Tel** (800)422-6237, (301)496-8774. **LC** RC261.A1; N37a. **DD** 353/.0084/1. **NLM** W2; A N14765a. available on microfiche (Vols. for (1981/1982-) distributed to depository libraries).

US/0730-6911
**ANNUAL REPORT - NATIONAL CANCER INSTITUTE (U.S.). FIELD STUDIES AND STATISTICS PROGRAM.** (ANNUAL REPORT / FIELD STUDIES AND STATISTICS PROGRAM.). **Main/Corp** National Cancer Institute U.S. Field Studies and Statistics Program. Oct. 1, 1980 through Sept. 30, 1981-. English. an. National Cancer Institute, NCI Building Room, 10A 18, Bethesda MD 20892. **Tel** (800)422-6237, (301)496-8774. **LC** RC276; .N35A. **DD** 614.5/999. ***Continues*** *Report of the Field Studies and Statistics Program, 0277-8629.*

US/0888-7713
**ANNUAL REPORT OF CANCER INCIDENCE IN MASSACHUSETTS.** [Annu. rep. cancer incid. Mass.]. **VFOAT** Annual Report, Cancer Incidence in Massachusetts. 1982-. English. an. Massachusetts Department of Public Health, Division of Health Statistics and Research, Boston MA. **LC** RC277.M4. **DD** 614.5/999/09744. **NLM** W2; AM4 C53a.

US/0272-2836
**ANNUAL REPORT ON CARCINOGENS.** [Annu. rep. carcinog.]. 1st (1980)-. English. an. Public Information Office / North Carolina, National Toxicology Program, PO Box 12233, Research Triangle Park NC

Medical Science and Technology —Neoplasma, Neoplastic

27709. **LC** RC268.6; .N38A. **DD** 616.99/4071. **NLM** W1 AN762T. available on microfiche (Vols. for (1981-) distributed to depository libraries).

SW/0348-8799
**ANNUAL REPORT ON THE RESULTS OF TREATMENT IN GYNECOLOGICAL CANCER.** **Added/Corp** American Cancer Society. International Federation of Gynaecology and Obstetrics. Vol. 17 (1969/72)-. English. te. $45.00. International Federation of Gynecology & Obstetrics, Radiumhemmet, S104 01 Stockholm 60 Sweden. **Tel** 46 8 328752. **ED** Folke Pettersson. **NLM** W1 AN768BD. **Ad Acc. Circ:** 2,000 (ctrl). ***Continues*** *Annual Report on the Results of Treatment in Carcinoma of the Uterus, Vagina, and Ovary, 0346-7503.*
**Desc:** Presentation of five-year results of treatment in gynecological cancer.

US
**ANNUAL REPORT - THE FRANKLIN MCLEAN MEMORIAL RESEARCH INSTITUTE.** **Main/Corp** Franklin McLean Memorial Research Institute. 1975-. Periodical. English. an.

UK/0266-9536
**ANTI-CANCER DRUG DESIGN.** [Anti-cancer drug des.]. **Added/Corp** Cancer Research Campaign (Great Britain). **VAT** Anticancer Drug Design. Vol. 1, No. 1 (Oct. 1985)-. Academic Scholarly Publication. English. bm. £195.00 UK and Europe; $325.00 other. Oxford University Press, Walton Street, Oxford OX2 6DP England. **Tel** 011 44 865 56767, FAX 011 44 865 267773, telex 837330 OXPRES G. **(Subscription address:** Oxford University Press / USA, Journals Marketing Department, Oxford University Press, 2001 Evans Road, Cary NC 27513.**)** **ED** Stephen Neidle, Stanley T. Crooke and Shigeru Tsukagoshi. **NLM** W1; AN859H. **CODEN** ACDDEA. **[CCC].** Index available. **Ad Acc. Pr Rev. Circ:** 500. available on microfilm from University Microfilms International (UMI). Documents available from The Genuine Article, BIOSIS Document Express, CASDDS.
**Desc:** Concentrates on the rational scientific principles involved in the development of new anti-cancer agents and features both experimental and clinically oriented research papers. These papers reflect increasing importance of the tools of structural and molecular biology, as well as the more traditional methodologies of pharmacology, chemistry and biophysics.
**Ind/Abst** Biol. Abstr. (1985-); Chem. Abstr. (1985-); Curr. Aware. Biol. Sci., CABS; Curr. Contents Life Sci.; EMBASE; Index Med. (Vol. 1, No. 1, 1985-); PESTDOC; Protozoolog. Abstr.; Res. Alert [Full Cov.]; Sci. Cit. Index; SCISEARCH.

US/0892-7049
**ANTIBODY, IMMUNOCONJUGATES, AND RADIOPHARMACEUTICALS.** Vol. 1, No. 1 (1987)-. Periodical. English. qt. $158.00. Mary Ann Liebert Inc., 1651 Third Avenue, New York NY 10128. **Tel** (212)289-2300, (800)M-LIEBERT, FAX (212)289-4697. **ED** Stanley Order. **LC** RM282.I44; A58. **DD** 616.07/93. **NLM** W1; AN859F. **Pr Rev.** Documents available from The Genuine Article, CASDDS.
**Desc:** Publishes papers and review articles in the holistic science that involves the use of antibody, immunoconjugates and radiopharmaceuticals in the diagnosis and treatment of cancer.
**Ind/Abst** Chem. Abstr.; Curr. Contents Life Sci.; Res. Alert [Full Cov.]; Sci. Cit. Index; SCISEARCH.

GR/0250-7005
**ANTICANCER RESEARCH.** [Anticancer res.]. Vol. 1, No. 1 (1981)-. Academic Scholarly Publication. English. bm. $723.00 (Europe); $757.00 (other) institution; $380.00 (Europe); $345.00 (other) individual. Anticancer Research, c/o Dr Delinassios, 5 Argyropoulou Street, Kato Patissia Athens Gr-111 45 Greece. **Tel** 011 30 1 2016380, 011 30 1 8171209, FAX 011 30 1 2016380. **ED** John G Delinassios. **NLM** W1 AN859T. **CODEN** ANTRD4. **[CCC].** Index available. cum. index. **Bk Rev. Ad Acc. Pr Rev. Circ:** 1200. Documents available from The Genuine Article, BIOSIS Document Express, CASDDS.
**Desc:** Rapid publication within 1-3 months of original high quality works and reviews on all aspects of experimental and clinical cancer research.
**Ind/Abst** Biol. Abstr.; Chem. Abstr.; Curr. Aware. Biol. Sci., CABS; Curr. Contents Life Sci.; Curr. Titl. Dent.; Dairy Sci. Abstr.; EMBASE; Genet. Abstr.; Health Plan. Adminis.; Immunol. Abstr.; Index Med.; NAPRALERT; Nutr. Abstr. Rev., Ser. A, Hum. Exp.; Nutr. Res. Newsl.; Oncog. Growth Factors Abstr.; Life Sci. Collect.; Pollut. Abstr. Indexes; Protozoolog. Abstr.; Ref. Upd. Deluxe Ed.; Res. Alert [Full Cov.]; Sci. Cit. Index; SCISEARCH.

IT/0004-0266
**ARCHIVIO ITALIANO DI PATOLOGIA E CLINICA DEI TUMORI.** (1957)-. Italian. sa. Archivio Italiano di Patologia, 20129 Italy. **NLM** W1 AR5953. **CODEN** AIPUAN. Documents available from BIOSIS Document Express.
**Ind/Abst** Biol. Abstr.; Index Med. (?-1972).

IT
**ARGOMENTI DI ONCOLOGIA.** (19??)-. Italian. qt. L9000000 Italy; L10000000 other. Casa Editrice Ambrosiana, Via G Frua 6, 20146 Milan Italy. **Tel** 011 39 2 463936.

US/0160-6344
**ATLAS OF TUMOR PATHOLOGY.** [Atlas tumor pathol.]. **Added/Corp** Armed Forces Institute of Pathology (U.S.) Universities Associated for Research and Education in Pathology. (1949)-. Monographic series. English. Price varies per volume. Armed Forces Institute of Pathology, GPO Sales Office, Room G 134, Washington DC 20306. **Tel** (205)576-2940. **(Subscription address:** American Registry of Pathology / Sales Office, AFIP Room 1077, Washington DC 20306.**)** **DD** 616.

●US/1073-0028
**BASIC AND CLINICAL ONCOLOGY.** [Basic clin. oncol.]. (1993)-. Monographic series. English. ir. Price varies per volume. Marcel Dekker Inc., 270 Madison Avenue, New York NY 10016. **Tel** (212)696-9000, (800)228-1160, FAX (212)685-4540, telex 421419. **(Subscription address:** Marcel Dekker Inc, PO Box 5017, Monticello NY 12701.**)** **DD** 616.

SZ/0250-3220
**BEITRAEGE ZUR ONKOLOGIE.** (CONTRIBUTIONS TO ONCOLOGY.). [Beitr. Onkol.]. Vol. 1 (1979)-. Academic Scholarly Publication. German (English and German). an. 120.00F (approx. per volume). S. Karger AG, Allschwilerstrasse 10, PO Box - Postfach - Case Postale, CH-4009 Basel Switzerland. **Tel** 011 41 61 306-1111, FAX 011 41 61 306-1234, telex CH 962 652. **ED** J. H. Holzner, W. Queisser. **NLM** W1 BE444N. **CODEN** COONEVBEONDH. **[CCC].** Documents available from BIOSIS Document Express, CASDDS.
**Desc:** Reports of basic investigation, review articles and Congress proceedings which demonstrate the steady progress in the knowledge of the factors involved in oncogenesis, epidemiology and prevention, management by radio- and chemotherapy, and the psychosocial impact of cancer.
**Ind/Abst** Biol. Abstr.; Chem. Abstr. (1979-1983,19??-); Ref. Upd. Deluxe Ed.

FR
**BIENNIAL REPORT / WORLD HEALTH ORGANIZATION, INTERNATIONAL AGENCY FOR RESEARCH ON CANCER.** **Added/Corp** International Agency for Research on Cancer. (1986/1987)-. English. be. World Health Organization, Distribution and Sales, 20 Avenue Appia, CH-1211 Geneva 27 Switzerland. **Tel** 011 41 22 7912111, FAX 011 41 22 7880401. **LC** RC267; .I5257a. **DD** 616.99/4/005. **NLM** W1; BI529. ***Continues*** *International Agency for Research on Cancer. Annual Report -International Agency for Research on Cancer.*

US/1056-3903
**BIOLOGIC THERAPY OF CANCER UPDATES.** [Biol. ther. cancer updat.]. Vol. 1, No. 1 (May/June 1991)-. Periodical. English. bm. $60.00 (institutions, U.S.). J.B. Lippincott Company, 227 East Washington Square, Philadelphia PA 19106-3780. **Tel** (215)238-4200 or 4454, FAX (215)238-4227. **DD** 616. **NLM** W1; BO671PL.

US/0736-7414
**BIOLOGICAL RESPONSES IN CANCER.** (BIOLOGICAL RESPONSES IN CANCER : PROGRESS TOWARD POTENTIAL APPLICATIONS.). [Biol. responses cancer]. (1982)-. Academic Scholarly Publication. English. an. Price varies per volume. Plenum Press, 233 Spring Street, New York NY 10013-1578. **Tel** (212)620-8000, (800)221-9369, FAX (212)463-0742, (212)807-1047, telex 23/421139. **ED** Enrico Mihich. **NLM** W1 BI754PB. **CODEN** BRECDP. Documents available from CASDDS.
**Ind/Abst** Chem. Abstr.

US
**BIOMEDICAL ADVANCES IN CARCINOGENESIS.** Vol. 1, (1984)-. Monographic series. English. ir. Price varies per volume. **ED** Merle Mizell. **NLM** W1; BI853T (P).

GW
**BIOMUDULATION UND BIOTHERAPIE DES KREBSES.** Vol. 1 (1986)-. Periodical. German. Verlag fuer Medizin VFM, Postfach 105767, W-6900 Heidelberg 1 Germany. **Tel** 011 49 6221 406248, FAX 011 49 6221 400727, telex 461683HVVFM D. **NLM** W1; BI862M.

US/0149-1016
**BIORESEARCH TODAY. CANCER A. CARCINOGENESIS.** ***Ceased.*** **VFOAT** Cancer A. Carcinogenesis. **VAT** BioResearch Today. Cancer A - Carcinogenesis. Ceased (Dec. 1991). English. mo. BioSciences Information Service, Biological Abstracts / BIOSIS, 2100 Arch Street, Philadelphia PA 19103-1399. **Tel** (800)523-4806 US, (215)587-4800 Pennsylvania and worldwide, FAX (215)587-2016, telex 831739.
**Desc:** Current awareness journal including abstracts and content summaries of studies involving carcinogenesis.

US/0149-1024
**BIORESEARCH TODAY. CANCER B. ANTICANCER AGENTS.** ***Ceased.*** **VFOAT** Cancer B. Anticancer Agents. **VAT** BioResearch Toady. Cancer B - Anticancer Agents. Ceased (Dec. 1991). English. mo. BioSciences Information Service, Biological Abstracts / BIOSIS, 2100 Arch Street, Philadelphia PA 19103-1399. **Tel** (800)523-4806 US, (215)587-4800 Pennsylvania and worldwide, FAX (215)587-2016, telex 831739.
**Desc:** Current awareness journal including abstracts and content summaries of studies involving cancer and anticancer agents.

US/0149-1032
**BIORESEARCH TODAY. CANCER C. IMMUNOLOGY.** ***Ceased.*** **VFOAT** Cancer C. Immunology. **VAT** BioResearch Today. Immunology. Ceased (Dec. 1991). English. mo. BioSciences Information Service, Biological Abstracts / BIOSIS, 2100 Arch Street, Philadelphia PA 19103-1399. **Tel** (800)523-4806 US, (215)587-4800 Pennsylvania and worldwide, FAX (215)587-2016, telex 831739.
**Desc:** Current awareness journal including abstracts and content summaries of studies involving cancer and immunology.

US/0161-0112
**BREAST CANCER.** [Breast cancer]. (1977)-. Academic Scholarly Publication. English. Plenum Press, 233 Spring Street, New York NY 10013-1578. **Tel** (212)620-8000, (800)221-9369, FAX (212)463-0742, (212)807-1047, telex 23/421139. **ED** W.L. McGuire. **LC** RC280.B8; B66. **DD** 616.9/94/49. **NLM** W1 BR191. **CODEN** BCATDJ. Documents available from CASDDS.
**Ind/Abst** Chem. Abstr. (1977-1981).

NE/0167-6806
**BREAST CANCER RESEARCH AND TREATMENT.** [Breast cancer res. treat.]. Vol. 1, No. 1 (1981)-. Academic Scholarly Publication. English. mo (12 issues). $1,248.00. Kluwer Academic Publishers / Massachusetts, PO Box 358, Accord Station, Hingham MA 02018. **Tel** (617)871-6600. **ED** Mark E. Lippman. **NLM** W1 BR191R. **CODEN** BCTRD6. **[CCC]. Pr Rev. Acid Free.** available on microfilm and microfiche from University Microfilms International (UMI). Documents available from The Genuine Article, BIOSIS Document Express, CASDDS, ADONIS.
**Desc:** Provides the surgeon, radiotherapist, medical oncologist, endocrinologist, epidemiologist, immunologist or cell biologist investigating problems in breast cancer a single forum for communication.
**Ind/Abst** ADONIS; Biol. Abstr. (1985-); Chem. Abstr.; CSA Neuro. Abstr. (?-?); Curr. Aware. Biol. Sci., CABS; Curr. Contents Clin. Med.; Curr. Contents Life Sci.; EMBASE; Health Plan. Adminis.; Index Med. (1981-); INIS Atomindex [Micro.]; Oncog. Growth Factors Abstr.; Ref. Upd. Deluxe Ed.; Res. Alert [Full Cov.]; Sci. Cit. Index; SCISEARCH.

UK/0007-0920
**BRITISH JOURNAL OF CANCER.** (THE BRITISH JOURNAL OF CANCER / CANCER RESEARCH CAMPAIGN.). [Br. j. cancer]. **Added/Corp** Cancer Research Campaign (Great Britain). Vol. 1 (March 1947)-. Academic Scholarly Publication. English. mo. £385.00 UK and EEC; £420.00 (surface mail), £504.00 (airmail) other. Macmillan Magazines Ltd., Houndmills, Basingstoke, Hampshire RG21 2XS England. **Tel** 011 44 256 29242, FAX 011 44 256 812358, telex 858493. **ED** Peter Twentyman, Peter Selby and David Harnden. **NLM** W1 BR509. **CODEN** BJCAAI. **[CCC].** Index available. **Ad Acc. Pr Rev. Circ:** 2,000. available on microfilm and microfiche from University Microfilms International (UMI). Documents available from The Genuine Article, BIOSIS Document Express, CASDDS.
**Desc:** Publishes papers and short communications from scientists, researchers and oncologists throughout the world. In addition, publishes reports on selected national and international conferences and symposia. Each month's issue includes correspondence from readers and an international calendar of events.
**Ind/Abst** Anim. Breed. Abstr.; Biol. Abstr.; Chem. Abstr.; Curr. Aware. Biol. Sci., CABS; Curr. Biotechnol.; Curr. Contents Clin. Med.; Curr. Contents Life Sci.; Dairy Sci. Abstr.; EMBASE; Genet. Abstr.; Health Saf. Sci. Abstr.; Health Plan. Adminis.; Helminthol. Abstr.; Immunol. Abstr.; Index Med.; Index Vet.; NAPRALERT; Nutr. Abstr. Rev., Ser. B, Live Feeds and Feed.; Nutr. Abstr. Rev., Ser. A, Hum. Exp.; Nutr. Res. Newsl.; Oncog. Growth Factors Abstr.; Life Sci. Collect.; PESTDOC; Ref. Upd. Basic Ed.; Ref. Upd. Clinical Ed.; Ref. Upd. Deluxe Ed.; Res. Alert [Full Cov.]; Rev. Med. Vet. Mycology; Rev. Plant Pathol.; Saf. Health Work; Sci. Cit. Index; SCISEARCH; Small Anim. Abstr. Bibliogr.; Soc. Sci. Cit. Index [Select. Cov.]; Vet. Bull.; Trop. Dis. Bull.; Virol. AIDS Abstr.

UK/0306-9443
**BRITISH JOURNAL OF CANCER. SUPPLEMENT, THE.** [Br. j. cancer. Suppl.]. **Added/Corp** Cancer Research Campaign. No. 1 (1973)-. Monographic series. English. ir. Price varies per volume.

Macmillan Magazines Ltd., Houndmills, Basingstoke, Hampshire RG21 2XS England. **Tel** 011 44 256 29242, FAX 011 44 256 812358, telex 858493. **DD** 616.9. **NLM** W1 BR509A. **CODEN** BJCSB5. Documents available from CASDDS.
**Ind/Abst** Chem. Abstr.; Health Plan. Adminis.; Index Med.

FR/0753-7417
**BULLETIN DE LA SOCIETE FRANCAISE DE CANCEROLOGIE PRIVEE.** [Bull. Soc. fr. cancerol. priv.]. (1982)-. Periodical. French. ir (4-5 issues per year). 500.00F. Societe Francaise Cancerologie Privee, 87 Bis Av de Wagram, 75017 Paris France. **Tel** 011 33 1 46223547. **UDC** 616-006.

FR/0007-4551
**BULLETIN DU CANCER.** [Bull. cancer]. **Added/Corp** Association Francaise pour l'Etude du Cancer. Societe Francaise du Cancer. Vol. 53 (1966)-. Academic Scholarly Publication. French. mo. 1375.00F (regular subscription), 2003.00F (combined subscription with Bulletin du Cancer/Radiotherapie) France; 1600.00F (regular subscription), 2295.00F (combined subscription with Bulletin du Cancer/Radiotherapie) other. Editions Scientifique Elsevier, 141 rue de Javel, 75747 Paris Cedex 15 France. **Tel** 011 33 1 47 07 11 22, FAX 011 33 1 43 36 80 93. **(Subscription address:** Editions Scientifiques Elsevier / for North America, PO Box 7247-7576, Philadelphia PA 19170-7576.**) ED** P. Burtin and G. Mathieu. **NLM** W1; BU647K. **CODEN** BUCABS. **[CCC].** available on microfilm and microfiche from University Microfilms International (UMI). Documents available from The Genuine Article, BIOSIS Document Express, CASDDS, ADONIS. ***Continues*** *Bulletin de l'Association Francaise pour l'Etude du Cancer, 0004-5497.* ***Continued in part by*** *Bulletin du Cancer. Radiotherapie.*
**Ind/Abst** ADONIS; Biol. Abstr.; Chem. Abstr.; Curr. Aware. Biol. Sci., CABS; Curr. Contents Clin. Med.; Curr. Contents Life Sci.; EMBASE; Energy Res. Abstr.; Health Plan. Adminis.; Index Med.; Index Vet.; NAPRALERT; Nutr. Abstr. Rev., Ser. B, Live Feeds and Feed.; Nutr. Abstr. Rev., Ser. A, Hum. Exp.; Life Sci. Collect.; PESTDOC; Res. Alert [Full Cov.]; Sci. Cit. Index; SCISEARCH; Soc. Sci. Cit. Index [Select. Cov.]; Vet. Bull.

FR/0924-4212
**BULLETIN DU CANCER. RADIOTHERAPIE : JOURNAL DE LA SOCIETE FRANCAISE DU CANCER.** **Added/Corp** Societe Francaise du Cancer. Societe Francaise de Radiotherapie Oncologique. **VFOAT** Radiotherapie. Vol. 77, No. 1 (Feb. 1990)-. Academic Scholarly Publication. French (summaries and/or abstracts in English; table of contents in English). qt (1 volume). 850.00F (regular subscription), 2003.00F (combined subscription with Bulletin du Cancer) France; 950.00F (regular subscription), 2295.00F (combined subscription with Bulletin du Cancer) other. Editions Scientifique Elsevier, 141 rue de Javel, 75747 Paris Cedex 15 France. **Tel** 011 33 1 47 07 11 22, FAX 011 33 1 43 36 80 93. **(Subscription address:** Editions Scientifiques Elsevier / for North America, PO Box 7247-7576, Philadelphia PA 19170-7576.**) NLM** W1; BU647L. **CODEN** BCRAEE. **[CCC].** available on microfilm and microfiche from University Microfilms International (UMI). Documents available from ADONIS. ***Continues in part*** *Bulletin du Cancer, 0007-4551.*
**Ind/Abst** ADONIS; EMBASE; Index Med. (1990-).

US/0007-9235
**CA.** [Ca]. **Added/Corp** American Cancer Society. Vol. 1 (Nov. 1950)-. Academic Scholarly Publication. English. bm. $65.00 (individuals), $95.00 (institutions). American Cancer Society International Activities, 1599 Clifton Avenue Northeast, Atlanta GA 30329. **Tel** (404)329-7680, 320-3333. **(Subscription address:** J.B. Lippincott, PO Box 350, Hagerstown MD 21740.**) ED** C.S. Cameron. **LC** RC261; .C2. **DD** 616.99405. **NLM** W1 C103. **CODEN** CAMCAM. **Pr Rev.** available on microfilm and microfiche from University Microfilms International (UMI). Documents available from The Genuine Article, BIOSIS Document Express, CASDDS.
**Desc:** Cancer journal for clinicians.
**Ind/Abst** Abr. Index Med.; Biol. Abstr.; Chem. Abstr.; Cumul. Index Nurs. Allied Health Lit.; Curr. Contents Clin. Med.; EMBASE; Energy Res. Abstr.; Health Index (1989-); Health Period. Database [Full Txt.]; Health Plan. Adminis.; Health Ref. Cent. (Jan. 1989-) [Full Txt.] [Full Cov.]; Index Med.; INIS Atomindex [Micro.]; Med. Abstr. Newsl.; Life Sci. Collect.; Physic. Medline Plus; Res. Alert [Select. Cov.].

FR
**CAHIERS DE CANCEROLOGIE. BIOLOGIE CLINIQUE THERAPEUTIQUE.** French. Eleven times a year. 500.00F France; 750.00F other. Cogemed, BP 9, 78670 Villennes Seine France. **Tel** 011 33 39 753975.

●FR/0941-3804
**CAHIERS D'ONCOLOGIE.** (1992)-. French. Six times a year. 650.00F. Springer-Verlag France, 26 rue des Carmes, F 75005 Paris France. **Tel** 011 33 1 44411599, FAX 011 33 43250225. **(Subscription address:** Springer Verlag New York Inc. / for North America, 44 Hartz Way, Secaucus NJ 07096.**) NLM** W1; CA143EE. available on microfilm and microfiche from University Microfilms International (UMI).

CN/1183-2509
**CANADIAN JOURNAL OF ONCOLOGY, THE.** [Can. j. oncol.]. Vol. 1, No. 1 (Sept. 1991)-. Periodical. English. qt. Limited free distribution. Rodar Publishing Inc., 1918 Trans-Canada Highway, Baie-D'Urfe Quebec H9X 3T9 Canada. **DD** 616.9/9061. **NLM** W1; CA597J.

CN/1181-912X
**CANADIAN ONCOLOGY NURSING JOURNAL.** See Medical Science and Technology-Nursing.

CN/1181-912X
**CANADIAN ONCOLOGY NURSING JOURNAL.** See Medical Science and Technology-Nursing.

US/0008-543X
**CANCER.** (CANCER; DIAGNOSIS, TREATMENT, RESEARCH.). [Cancer]. **Added/Corp** American Cancer Society. Vol. 1 (May 1948)-. Academic Scholarly Publication. English. sm. $135.00 (individuals), $220.00 (institutions) US; $220.00 (individuals), $350.00 (institutions) other. J.B. Lippincott Company, 227 East Washington Square, Philadelphia PA 19106-3780. **Tel** (215)238-4200 or 4454, FAX (215)238-4227. **(Subscription address:** J.B. Lippincott, PO Box 350, Hagerstown MD 21740.**) ED** Jonathan E. Rhods. **LC** RC261; .A22. **DD** 616.99405. **NLM** W1 CA671K. **CODEN** CANCAR. **[CCC].** cum. index. **Ad Acc. Pr Rev. Circ:** 21,216. available on microfilm and microfiche from University Microfilms International (UMI). Documents available from The Genuine Article, BIOSIS Document Express, CASDDS.
**Desc:** Contains original articles oriented toward clinical research seeking to bridge the gap between the investigator and the clinician.
**Ind/Abst** Abr. Index Med.; Annals Behav. Med.; Biol. Abstr.; Biol. Dig.; Chem. Abstr.; Curr. Biotechnol.; Curr. Contents Clin. Med.; Curr. Contents Life Sci.; EMBASE; Health Period. Database; Health Plan. Adminis.; Health Ref. Cent. (Jan. 1989-) [Full Cov.]; Helminthol. Abstr. (1991-); Index Med.; Index Vet.; INIS Atomindex [Micro.]; Int. Aerosp. Abstr.; Med. Abstr. Newsl.; Oncog. Growth Factors Abstr.; Life Sci. Collect.; PESTDOC (?-?); Physic. Medline Plus; Poult. Abstr.; Res. Alert [Full Cov.]; Rev. Med. Vet. Mycology; Saf. Health Work; Sci. Cit. Index; Soc. Sci. Cit. Index [Select. Cov.].

NE/0167-7659
**CANCER AND METASTASIS REVIEWS.** [Cancer metastasis rev.]. Vol. 4, No. 1 (1985)-. Academic Scholarly Publication. English. qt. $446.00. Kluwer Academic Publishers / Massachusetts, PO Box 358, Accord Station, Hingham MA 02018. **Tel** (617)871-6600. **ED** Robert Kerbel. **DD** 616. **NLM** W1; CA6722J. **CODEN** CMRED4. **[CCC]. Pr Rev. Acid Free.** Documents available from The Genuine Article, CASDDS. ***Continues*** *Cancer Metastasis Reviews, 0167-7659.*
**Desc:** Features articles on both basic research and clinical studies and includes such topics as the identification and characterization of tumor promoters and carciongens; epidemiologic studies; the mechanism of action of carcinogens; the functional role of oncogenes in normal and neoplastic cells; molecular and biochemical correlates of tumorigenitity and metastasis; mechanisms of tumor progression; the generation and control of cellular diversity with neoplasms; host factors distribution of metastases; tumor models for studies of the pathogenesis, diagnosis and treatment of neoplasitic disease; new strategies for development of diagnostic therapeutic agents; drug delivery systems and strategies for drug targeting; and the clinical management of cancer, with particular reference to metastatic disease.
**Ind/Abst** Chem. Abstr. (1985-); Curr. Aware. Biol. Sci., CABS; Index Med. (1985-); Index Sci. Rev. [Full Cov.]; Index Vet.; Ref. Upd. Deluxe Ed.; Res. Alert [Full Cov.]; Sci. Cit. Index; SCISEARCH; Small Anim. Abstr. Bibliogr.

US/0305-7232
**CANCER BIOCHEMISTRY BIOPHYSICS.** [Cancer biochem. biophys.]. Vol. 1 (Nov. 1974)-. Periodical. English. ir (1 volume). $678.00 (academic institutions), $1057.00 (corporate institutions). Gordon & Breach Science Publishers, Inc., PO Box 786, Cooper Station, New York NY 10276. **Tel** (212)206-8900, FAX (212)645-2459. **(Subscription address:** Gordon & Breach Science Publishers / England, PO Box 90, Reading RG1 8JL England.**) ED** H. D. Brown. **LC** RC261.A1; C37. **DD** 599/.01/9024616. **NLM** W1 CA673. **CODEN** CABCD4. **[CCC]. Bk Rev. Ad Acc. Pr Rev.** Documents available from The Genuine Article, BIOSIS Document Express, CASDDS.
**Ind/Abst** Biol. Abstr. (-1984); Chem. Abstr.; Curr. Aware. Biol. Sci., CABS; Curr. Contents Life Sci.; Dairy Sci. Abstr.; EMBASE; Index Med. (1976-); NAPRALERT; Nutr. Abstr. Rev., Ser. A, Hum. Exp.; Life Sci. Collect.; PESTDOC; Protozoolog. Abstr.; Ref. Upd. Deluxe Ed.; Res. Alert; Sci. Cit. Index; SCISEARCH.

US/0363-017X
**CANCER BIOLOGY. Added/Corp** Given Institute of Pathobiology. (1976)-. Monographic series. English. an. Price varies per volume. Stratton Intercontinental Medical Book Corporation, 381 Park Avenue South, New York NY 10016. **LC** RC254; .C352. **DD** 616.9/94. **NLM** W1 AD716 v.2 etc.

●US/1062-8401
**CANCER BIOTHERAPY.** [Cancer biother.]. Vol. 8, No. 1 (Spring 1993)-. Academic Scholarly Publication. English. qt. $131.00. Mary Ann Liebert Inc., 1651 Third Avenue, New York NY 10128. **Tel** (212)289-2300, (800)M-LIEBERT, FAX (212)289-4697. **ED** Robert Oldham. **DD** 616. **NLM** W1; CA6746. **CODEN** CNBTEB. Documents available from BIOSIS Document Express, CASDDS. ***Continues*** *Selective Cancer Therapeutics, 1043-0733.*
**Desc:** Reports on investigations of methods to improve cancer therapy. This includes more selective delivery of drugs, biologicals, radiopharmaceuticals, or other agents, and advances in delivery instrumentation and technology, with the aim of increasing the efficacy of therapy and/or decreasing toxicity or improving the convenience of therapy.
**Ind/Abst** Biol. Abstr. (1993-); Chem. Abstr. (1993-); Index Med. (1993-); Life Sci. Collect. (1993-); Sci. Cit. Index.

US
**CANCER BULLETIN - M.D. ANDERSON CANCER CENTER, THE.** (THE CANCER BULLETIN / THE UNIVERSITY OF TEXAS M.D. ANDERSON CANCER CENTER.). [Cancer bull. - M.D. Anderson Cancer Cent.]. **Added/Corp** University of Texas M.D. Anderson Cancer Center. Vol. 40, No. 2 (Mar./Apr. 1988)-. Bulletin. English. bm (Feb., Apr., June, Aug., Oct., Dec.). $55.00 US; $65.00 other. Educational Publishing Service, 1515 Holcombe Blouvard, Houston TX 77030. **Tel** (713)792-6014, FAX (713)792-6016. **ED** Stephen P. Tomsavic, Phd & Martin N. Raber M.D. Index available. ***Continues*** *Cancer Bulletin of the University of Texas M.D. Anderson Hospital and Tumor Institute at Houston, 0740-820X.*
**Ind/Abst** EMBASE [Select. Cov.].

UK/0957-5243
**CANCER CAUSES & CONTROL : CCC.** **VFOAT** Cancer Causes and Control; CCC. Vol. 1, No. 1 (July 1990)-. Periodical. English. bm. $499.00 US; £295.00 other. Rapid Communications of Oxford Ltd, The Old Malthouse, Paradise Street, Oxford OX1 1LD England. **Tel** 011 44 0865 790447, FAX 011 44 0865 244012, telex 9403712. **ED** Dr Brian MacMahon. **NLM** W1; CA677BE. **CODEN** CCCNEN. **[CCC].** Index available. cum. index. **Bk Rev. Ad Acc. Pr Rev. Acid Free.** Documents available from The Genuine Article.
**Desc:** Comprehensive coverage of studies on control and prevention of cancer in the population. Scope includes epidemiology, cancer biology, medical statistics and economcis.
**Ind/Abst** Curr. Aware. Biol. Sci., CABS; Curr. Contents Clin. Med.; Health Plan. Adminis.; Index Med.; Res. Alert [Select. Cov.]; Risk Abstr.; SCISEARCH.

US/1045-7410
**CANCER (CD-ROM ED.).** (CANCER : [COMPUTER FILE]. A JOURNAL OF THE AMERICAN CANCER SOCIETY). [Cancer]. **Added/Corp** American Cancer Society. **VFOAT** Cancer on Disc!. Vol. 61 and 62 (1988)-. Academic Scholarly Publication. English. $195.00. Creative Multimedia Corporation, 513 Northwest Avenue, Suite 400, Portland OR 97209. **Tel** (503)241-4351. **DD** 616. Documents available from BIOSIS Document Express, CASDDS.
**Ind/Abst** Biol. Abstr.; Chem. Abstr.; EMBASE; Index Med.; Int. Aerosp. Abstr.; Life Sci. Collect.; PESTDOC; Physic. Medline Plus; Ref. Upd. Basic Ed.; Ref. Upd. Clinical Ed.; Ref. Upd. Deluxe Ed.

NE/0921-4410
**CANCER CHEMOTHERAPY AND BIOLOGICAL RESPONSE MODIFIERS.** (1987)-. Academic Scholarly Publication. English. an. Price varies. Elsevier Science Publishers BV, PO Box 211, 1000 AE Amsterdam Netherlands. **Tel** 011 31 20 5803642, FAX 011 31 20 5862696, telex 15682. **(Subscription address:** Elsevier Science Inc. / New York Books, 655 Avenue of the Americas, New York NY 10010.**) NLM** W1; CA677BS. **CODEN** CCBAED. Documents available from BIOSIS Document Express. ***Continues*** *Cancer Chemotherapy (European Organization for Research on Treatment of Cancer), 0167-7853.*
**Ind/Abst** Biol. Abstr. (1991-); Health Plan. Adminis.; Index Med. (1987-); Int. Nurs. Index.

GW/0344-5704
**CANCER CHEMOTHERAPY AND PHARMACOLOGY.** [Cancer chemother. pharmacol.]. Vol. 1 (1978)-. Academic Scholarly Publication. English. Twelve times a year. DM2128.00. Springer-Verlag GmbH & Company KG, Heidelberger Platz 3, D 14197 Berlin Germany. **Tel** 011 49 30 8207223, FAX 011 49 30 8214091, telex 183 319 SPBLN D. **(Subscription address:** Springer Verlag New York Inc. / for North America, 44 Hartz Way, Secaucus NJ 07096.**) ED** A H Calvert, S K Carter, M J Egorin, D R Newell. **NLM** W1 CA677C. **CODEN** CCPHDZ. **[CCC]. Pr Rev.** available on microfilm and microfiche from University Microfilms International (UMI). Documents

available from The Genuine Article, CASDDS, ADONIS.
**Desc:** A pre-eminent journal in the field. The primary focus on this rapid publication medium is on new chemical agents, their extraction or synthesis, experimental screening, preclinical toxicology and pharmacology, single and combined drug application modalities, and clinical phases I, II, and III.
**Ind/Abst** ADONIS; Chem. Abstr.; Curr. Aware. Biol. Sci., CABS; Curr. Contents Clin. Med.; Curr. Contents Life Sci.; EMBASE; Energy Res. Abstr. (Nov. 1982-); Health Plan. Adminis.; Index Med. (1978-); NAPRALERT; Life Sci. Collect.; PESTDOC; Ref. Upd. Deluxe Ed.; Res. Alert [Full Cov.]; Sci. Cit. Index; SCISEARCH.

UK
**CANCER CHEMOTHERAPY REPORT.** (19??)-. English. ir. £495.00. PJB Publications, 18-20 Hill Rise, Richmond Surrey TW10 6UA England. **Tel** 011 44 81 948 3262.

US/1044-6508
**CANCER CHRONICLES, THE.** [Cancer chron.]. Vol. 1, No. 1 (Summer 1989)-. Periodical. English. bm. $25.00 US; $30.00 Canada; $35.00 other. Equinox Press, 144 St. John's Place, Brooklyn NY 11217. **Tel** (718)636-1679, FAX (718)636-0186. **DD** 616.

US/0191-3794
**CANCER CONTROL JOURNAL.** **Added/Corp** Cancer Control Society. Vol. 1 (May/June 1973)-. Periodical. English. Six times a year. $25.00 Comes with Cancer Control Society membership. Cancer Control Society, 2043 North Berendo Street, Los Angeles CA 90027. **Tel** (310)663-7801. **NLM** W1 CA6779. Index available. **Circ:** 5,000.
**Desc:** Journals based on theme: alternative non-toxic natural therapies and nutrition for cancer and other degenerative diseases.

NZ/0548-9415
**CANCER DATA.** (CANCER DATA / NEW ZEALAND.). [Cancer data]. **Added/Corp** New Zealand. Medical Statistics Branch. National Health Statistics Centre (N.Z.). **VFOAT** New Zealand Cancer Data. (1965)-. Periodical. English. an. $17.50. National Health Statistics Centre, Department of Health, Wellington New Zealand. **Tel** 844 167. **LC** RC279.N47; C36. **DD** 312/.39/94009931. **NLM** W2 KN4 N24C. Index available. **Ad Acc. Circ:** 450.
**Desc:** New Zealand cancer data.

US/0361-090X
**CANCER DETECTION AND PREVENTION.** [Cancer detec. prev.]. **Added/Corp** International Study Group for the Detection and Prevention of Cancer International Society for Preventive Oncology. Vol. 1 (1976)-. Academic Scholarly Publication. English. Six times a year. $400.00 (institution), $125.00 (individual) US; $450.00 (institution), $175.00 (individual) other. Blackwell Scientific Publishers, 238 Main Street, Cambridge MA 02142. **Tel** (617)547-7110, (800)835-6770, FAX (617)547-0789. **ED** H. E. Nieburgs. **LC** RC268; .C35. **DD** 616.9/94/05. **NLM** W1 CA6785K. **CODEN** CDPRD4. **[CCC]. Pr Rev.** Documents available from The Genuine Article, BIOSIS Document Express, CASDDS.
**Desc:** A multidisciplinary, primary journal devoted to predictive and preventive oncology indentifying avoidable risk factors and effects of cofactorial exposure for prognostic assessment of incipient human oncogenesis and utilization of interventions for prevention and detection of early curable neoplasms.
**Ind/Abst** Biodeter. Abstr.; Biol. Abstr. (1991-); Chem. Abstr.; EMBASE; Health Plan. Adminis.; Index Med. (1980-); Index Vet.; INIS Atomindex [Micro.]; Life Sci. Collect.; Physic. Medline Plus; Res. Alert [Select. Cov.]; Rev. Med. Vet. Mycology; SCISEARCH; Soc. Sci. Cit. Index [Select. Cov.]; Vet. Bull.; Trop. Dis. Bull.

US/1043-6995
**CANCER DETECTION AND PREVENTION. SUPPLEMENT.** [Cancer detect. prev., Suppl.]. Vol. 1 (1987)-. Monographic series. English. Six times a year. $7.95 per issue. CRC Press Inc., 2000 Corporate Boulevard Northwest, Boca Raton FL 33431. **Tel** (407)994-0555, (800)272-7737, FAX (407)998-9784, telex 568689. **DD** 616. **NLM** W1; CA679P. **[CCC].**
**Ind/Abst** Index Med. (1987-); Physic. Medline Plus.

US/1053-9611
**CANCER ECONOMICS.** [Cancer econ.]. (1987)-. Periodical. English. Twelve times a year. $225.00 US, Canada, Mexico & Caribbean; $250.00 others Comes with Cancer Letter. The Cancer Letter Inc., PO Box 15189, Washington DC 20003. **Tel** (202)543-7665. **DD** 616.

PR/0896-9566
**CANCER EN PUERTO RICO / ESTADO LIBRE ASOCIADO DE PUERTO RICO, DEPARTAMENTO DE SALUD, PROGRAMA CONTROL DEL CANCER, REGISTRO CENTRAL DEL CANCER.** [Cancer P. R.]. English (Spanish). an. Central Cancer Registry, Department of Health, PO Box 9342, Santurce PR 00908. **LC** RC279.P8; C36. **DD** 614.5/999. **NLM** W2 DP8 C3C.

US/1055-9965
**CANCER EPIDEMIOLOGY, BIOMARKERS & PREVENTION.** (CANCER EPIDEMIOLOGY, BIOMARKERS & PREVENTION : A PUBLICATION OF THE AMERICAN ASSOCIATION FOR CANCER RESEARCH / COSPONSORED BY THE AMERICAN SOCIETY OF PREVENTIVE ONCOLOGY.). [Cancer epidemiol. biomark. prev.]. **Added/Corp** American Association for Cancer Research. American Society of Preventive Oncology. **VFOAT** Cancer Epidemiology, Biomarkers, and Prevention. Vol. 1, No. 1 (Nov./Dec. 1991)-. Academic Scholarly Publication. English. Eight times a year. $180.00 institution; $90.00 individual. American Association of Cancer Research, 620 Chestnut Street, Pub Ledger Building, Philadelphia PA 19106. **Tel** (215)440-9300. **(Subscription address:** Fulco, 30 Broad Street, Denville NJ 07834.**) LC** RC268.48; .C364. **DD** 614.5/999/05. **NLM** W1; CA679PK. **CODEN** CEBPE4. **Ad Acc. Acid Free.** Documents available from The Genuine Article, CASDDS.
**Desc:** Original research on the causes and prevention of cancer in humans. The journal also presents investigations on the use of biomarkers to study the neoplastic and preneoplastic processes, research on chemoprevention and related clinical trials, and studies on the role of behavioral factors in prevention.
**Ind/Abst** Chem. Abstr.; Curr. Contents Clin. Med.; Res. Alert [Full Cov.]; Soc. Sci. Cit. Index [Select. Cov.].

US/0069-0147
**CANCER FACTS AND FIGURES.** **VFOAT** Cancer Facts & Figures. English. an. American Cancer Society Institute Activities, 1599 Clifton Road Northeast, Atlanta GA 30329. **NLM** W1 CA679S.
**Ind/Abst** Stat. Ref. Index.

AT/0311-306X
**CANCER FORUM.** **Added/Corp** Australian Cancer Society. (Autumn 1974)-. Periodical. English. Three times a year (Mar., July, Nov.). Free. Australian Cancer Society, General Post Office Box 4708, Sydney New South Wales 2001 Australia. **Tel** 011 61 2 3582066, FAX 011 61 2 3564558. **ED** L. A. Wright. **NLM** W1 CA679U. Index available. cum. index. **Bk Rev. Pr Rev. Circ:** 4,000 (ctrl).
**Desc:** Presents original and reprinted reports on cancer research education and patient welfare in the field of cancer.

●US/0929-1903
**CANCER GENE THERAPY.** Vol. 1, No. 1 (Mar. 1994)-. Periodical. English. qt. $190.00 institution; $85.00 individual. Appleton & Lange, (A Subsidiary of Simon & Schuster), 25 Van Zant Street, East Norwalk CT 06855. **Tel** (203)838-4400, (800)423-1359, FAX (203)854-9486. **(Subscription address:** Cancer Gene Therapy, PO Box 3000, Denville NJ 07834.**) NLM** W1; CA679UCJ.

US/0165-4608
**CANCER GENETICS AND CYTOGENETICS.** [Cancer genet. cytogenet.]. Vol. 1 (July 1979)-. Academic Scholarly Publication. English. Fourteen times a year (7 volumes). $1421.00 US; $1523.00 other. Elsevier Science Publishing Company Inc, Madison Square Station, PO Box 882, New York NY 10159-0882. **Tel** (212)633-3950, FAX (212)633-3990. **ED** A A Sandberg, H van den Berghe, A W Block, J J Cassiman and C Turc-Carel. **LC** RC268.4; .C35. **DD** 616.99/4042. **NLM** W1 CA697UD. **CODEN** CGCYDF. **[CCC]. Ad Acc. Pr Rev. Circ:** 500. available on microfilm and microfiche from University Microfilms International (UMI). Documents available from The Genuine Article, BIOSIS Document Express, CASDDS.
**Desc:** Original articles on human, animal, molecular, population and biomedical genetics and cytogenetics as they relate to broad fields of cancer.
**Ind/Abst** Biol. Abstr.; Chem. Abstr.; Curr. Aware. Biol. Sci., CABS; Curr. Contents Life Sci.; EMBASE; Genet. Abstr.; Health Plan. Adminis.; Hum. Genome Abstr.; Immunol. Abstr.; Index Med. (1981-); Oncog. Growth Factors Abstr.; Life Sci. Collect.; Ref. Upd. Basic Ed.; Ref. Upd. Deluxe Ed.; Res. Alert [Full Cov.]; Sci. Cit. Index; SCISEARCH.

GW/0340-7004
**CANCER IMMUNOLOGY AND IMMUNOTHERAPY.** (CANCER IMMUNOLOGY, IMMUNOTHERAPY : CII.). [Cancer immunol. immunother.]. **VFOAT** CII; C.I.I.; Cancer Immunology and Immunotherapy. Vol. 13, No. 1 (1982)-. Periodical. English. Twelve times a year. DM1738.00. Springer-Verlag GmbH & Company KG, Heidelberger Platz 3, D 14197 Berlin Germany. **Tel** 011 49 30 8207223, FAX 011 49 30 8214091, telex 183 319 SPBLN D. **(Subscription address:** Springer Verlag New York Inc. / for North America, 44 Hartz Way, Secaucus NJ 07096.**) ED** R W Baldwin and E Mihich. **NLM** W1; CA679UL. **[CCC]. Pr Rev.** Documents available from The Genuine Article. ***Continues** Cancer Immunology and Immunotherapy, 0340-7004.*
**Desc:** Staying abreast of the latest research results and clinical findings in the fields of oncology and immunology is one of the primary purposes of this publication.
**Ind/Abst** EMBASE; Index Med. (1982-); Life Sci. Collect.; PESTDOC; Protozoolog. Abstr.; Ref. Upd. Basic Ed.; Ref. Upd. Deluxe Ed.; Res. Alert [Full Cov.]; Sci. Cit. Index.

CN/1195-406X
**CANCER IN CANADA (1989).** (CANCER IN CANADA / STATISTICS CANADA, CANADIAN CENTRE FOR HEALTH INFORMATION / LE CANCER AU CANADA / STATISTIQUE CANADA, CENTRE CANADIEN D'INFORMATION SUR LA SANTE.). **VFOAT** Cancer au Canada. (1989)-. Statistical Publication. French (English). an. Statistics Canada, Publications Sales & Services, Main Building Room 1710, Ottawa Ontario K1A 0T6 Canada. **Tel** (613)951-5078, (800)267-6677, FAX (613)951-1584, telex 053-3585. ***Continues** Health Reports. Supplement. Cancer in Canada, 1180-3053.*

US/0277-7215
**CANCER IN ILLINOIS.** Began with: 1976. English. an. American Cancer Society Institute Activities, 1599 Clifton Road Northeast, Atlanta GA 30329. **LC** RC277.I3. **DD** 312.3994009773. **NLM** W1; CA679UR.

AT/0157-2547
**CANCER IN NEW SOUTH WALES : INCIDENCE AND MORTALITY.** **Added/Corp** New South Wales. Central Cancer Registry. (1972)-. English. Health Commission of New South Wales / New South Wales Central Cancer Registry, Sydney NSW Australia. **NLM** W2 KA8.1 N5C3C. ***Continues** Interim Report - New South Wales Cancer Registry.*

US/0735-7907
**CANCER INVESTIGATION.** [Cancer invest.]. Vol. 1, No. 1 (Jan./Feb. 1983)-. Academic Scholarly Publication. English. bm (6 issues). $595.00 US; $616.00 other. Marcel Dekker Inc., 270 Madison Avenue, New York NY 10016. **Tel** (212)696-9000, (800)228-1160, FAX (212)685-4540, telex 421419. **(Subscription address:** Marcel Dekker Inc, PO Box 5017, Monticello NY 12701.**) ED** Yashar Hirshaut. **LC** RC261.A1; C378. **DD** 616.99/4/005. **NLM** W1; CA6798R. **CODEN** CINVD7. **[CCC]. Bk Rev. Ad Acc. Pr Rev.** ctrl circ. available on microfiche. Documents available from The Genuine Article, BIOSIS Document Express, CASDDS, ADONIS.
**Desc:** Designed to provide workers in both the basic and clinical sciences who need to keep informed about the current state of progress in the cancer field with the broad background of reliable information necessary for effective decision making. In addition to presenting original papers of fundamental significance, it also publishes reviews, essays, specialized presentations of controversies, considerations of new technologies and their applications to specific laboratory problems, discussions of public issues, miniseries on major topics, and letters to the editor.
**Ind/Abst** ADONIS; Biol. Abstr.; Biol. Dig.; Chem. Abstr. (1984-); Curr. Biotechnol.; Curr. Contents Clin. Med.; Curr. Contents Life Sci.; EMBASE; Health Plan. Adminis.; Immunol. Abstr.; Index Med. (1983-); Nutr. Res. Newsl.; Oncog. Growth Factors Abstr.; Ref. Upd. Deluxe Ed.; Res. Alert [Full Cov.]; Sci. Cit. Index; SCISEARCH; Soc. Sci. Cit. Index [Select. Cov.].

FR/0765-7846
**CANCER JOURNAL (VILLEJUIF), THE.** (THE CANCER JOURNAL / LE JOURNAL DU CANCER / EL DIARIO DEL CANCER.). [Cancer j.]. **Added/Corp** Association pour le Developpement de la Communication Cancerologique (France). **VFOAT** Journal du Cancer; Diario del Cancer. Vol. 1, No. 1 (May 1986)-. Academic Scholarly Publication. English (French and Spanish). Five times a year. 440.00F (individuals); 500.00F (individuals) Western Euorpe; 1200.00F (institution) others. CNRS CEMAT, 7 rue Guy Mocquet BP 8, 94802 Villjuif Cedex France. **Tel** 011 33 1 47264658 ext. 582, FAX 011 33 1 47268091. **ED** J. C. Salomon. **NLM** W1; CA6788RE. **CODEN** CANJEI. Index available. **Ad Acc.** Documents available from The Genuine Article, CASDDS.
**Ind/Abst** Chem. Abstr. (1986-); Curr. Aware. Biol. Sci., CABS; Curr. Contents Life Sci.; EMBASE; Oncog. Growth Factors Abstr.; Res. Alert [Full Cov.]; Sci. Cit. Index; SCISEARCH; Soc. Sci. Cit. Index [Select. Cov.].

US/0096-3917
**CANCER LETTER, THE.** [Cancer lett.]. Vol. 1 (Jan. 3, 1975)-. Periodical. English. wk (48 issues per year). $225.00 US, Canada, Mexico and Caribbean; $250.00 other; (includes monthly Cancer Economics). Cancer Letter Inc., PO Box 15189, Washington DC 20003. **Tel** (202)543-7665, FAX (202)543-6879. **ED** Jerry Boyd. **DD** 616. **NLM** W1 CA68. Index available (annual index free to subscribers). **Bk Rev. Circ:** 1,200. available via fax (as The Cancer Letter FAX) from the publisher. ***Supersedes** Cancer Newsletter.*
**Desc:** Program and policy development of cancer research. Back issues available.
**Ind/Abst** Food Sci. Technol. Abstr.; NAPRALERT.

NE/0304-3835
**CANCER LETTERS.** [Cancer lett.]. Vol. 1 (Sept. 1975)-. Academic Scholarly Publication. English. Eighteen times a year (9 vols.). $1639.00. Elsevier Science Ireland Ltd., Bay 15, Shannon Industrial Estate, Co Clare Ireland. **Tel** 011 353 61 471944. **ED** D. Clayson, P. Shubik, and T. Sugimura. **LC** RC261.A1; C38. **DD** 616.9/94/005. **NLM** W1 CA68E. **CODEN** CALEDQ. **[CCC]. Pr Rev.** available on microfilm from University Microfilms International (UMI). Documents available from The Genuine Article, BIOSIS Document Express, CASDDS.
**Desc:** Provides a means of rapid publication for

important scientific contributions in all fields of cancer research.
**Ind/Abst** Art Archaeol. Tech. Abstr.; Biol. Abstr.; Chem. Abstr.; Chem. Hazards Ind.; Chem. Titles; CSA Neuro. Abstr. (?-?); Curr. Contents Life Sci.; Dairy Sci. Abstr.; EMBASE; Health Plan. Adminis.; Helminthol. Abstr. (1991-); Immunol. Abstr.; Index Med.; Lab. Hazards Bull.; Med. Abstr. Newsl.; Nutr. Abstr. Rev., Ser. B, Live Feeds and Feed.; Nutr. Abstr. Rev., Ser. A, Hum. Exp.; Nutr. Res. Newsl.; Oncog. Growth Factors Abstr.; Life Sci. Collect.; Protozoolog. Abstr.; Ref. Upd. Basic Ed.; Ref. Upd. Deluxe Ed.; Res. Alert [Full Cov.]; Rev. Med. Vet. Mycology; Sci. Cit. Index; SCISEARCH.

US/0193-1415
**CANCER MANAGEMENT.** (1978)-. Monographic series. English. ir. Price varies per volume. Mosby Year Book Inc., 11830 Westline Industrial Drive, St Louis MO 63146. **Tel** (800)325-4177, (314)872-8370, FAX (314)432-1380, telex 44-2402. **NLM** W1 CA68S.

AT
**CANCER MORTALITY TRENDS IN AUSTRALIA / EPIDEMIOLOGY BRANCH, HEALTH DEPARTMENT OF WESTERN AUSTRALIA.** **Added/Corp** Western Australia. Health Dept. Epidemiology Branch. (19??)-. English. Western Australia Department of Health / Epidemiology Branch, Perth WA Australia. **LC** RC279.A79; C35. **DD** 614.5/999/0994.

US/0008-5464
**CANCER NEWS (NEW YORK, N.Y.).** (CANCER NEWS.). [Cancer news]. Vol. 1, No. 1 (Jan. 1947)-. Periodical. English. Three times a year. Free on request. American Cancer Society Initiative Activities, 1599 Clifton Road Northeast, Atlanta GA 30329. **ED** Adele Paroni and Antionette Alesi. **LC** RC261; .A224. **DD** 616. **NLM** W1 CA683. **CODEN** CANEAX. **Circ:** 150,000 (ctrl). available on an online database (file 149/Full-Text) from DIALOG. ***Continues in part** Bulletin of the American Cancer Society, Inc.; Field Army News.*
**Desc:** A national publication of the American Cancer Society, Inc. Its purpose is to stimulate and inform a broad, primarily lay audience by putting into perspective the many and diverse aspects of the cancer problem.
**Ind/Abst** Acad. Abstr. Full Text Elite (Jan. 1992-); Acad. Abstr. (Jan. 1992-); Acad. Search (Jan. 1992-); Gen. Sci. Source (Jan. 1992-); Health Index (1989-); Health Period. Database [Full Txt.]; Health Ref. Cent. (Jan. 1989-) [Full Txt.] [Full Cov.]; Health Source (Jan. 1992-); INFO-SOUTH Abstr.; Mag. Search.

US/0276-3974
**CANCER NEWSLINE.** [Cancer newsline]. V. 1-Sept. 1976-. Periodical. English. qt. Minnesota Cancer Council, 2750 Park Avenue, Minneapolis MN 55407.

US/0162-220X
**CANCER NURSING.** **See** Medical Science and Technology-Nursing.

US/0734-1873
**CANCER NURSING NEWS.** **See** Medical Science and Technology-Nursing.

US/1013-3097
**CANCER PAIN RELEASE.** (CANCER PAIN RELEASE : WORLD HEALTH ORGANIZATION COLLABORATING CENTER FOR SYMPTOM EVALUATION IN CANCER CARE.). [Cancer pain release]. **Added/Corp** World Health Organization. Collaborating Center for Symptom Evaluation in Cancer Care. (1987)-. Periodical. English (Spanish and Italian). Four times a year (Jan., Apr., July, Oct.). $12.00 US; $17.00 other. Cancer Pain Release, 1900 University Avenue, Madison WI 53705. **Tel** (608)263-0727, FAX (608)263-0259. **ED** Sophie M. Colleau. **DD** 616. **NLM** W1; CA6846. **Circ:** 10,000.
**Desc:** Designed to support efforts nationally and internationally to alleviate needless suffering from cancer pain.

NE/0920-7848
**CANCER PHARMACOLOGY ANNUAL, THE.** [Cancer pharmacol. annu.]. 1983-. Academic Scholarly Publication. English. an. Elsevier Science Publishers BV, PO Box 211, 1000 AE Amsterdam Netherlands. **Tel** 011 31 20 5803642, FAX 011 31 20 5862696, telex 15682. **ED** B A Chabner and H M Pinedo. **LC** RC271.C5. **DD** 616.99/4061. **NLM** W1; CA6884F. **CODEN** CPANE2. Documents available from BIOSIS Document Express.
**Ind/Abst** Biol. Abstr. (1987-).

●US/1065-4704
**CANCER PRACTICE.** [Cancer pract.]. **Added/Corp** American Cancer Society. (May/June 1993)-. Periodical. English. bm. $35.00 (individuals), $75.00 (institutions) US; $49.00 (individuals), $85.00 (institutions) other. J.B. Lippincott Company, 227 East Washington Square, Philadelphia PA 19106-3780. **Tel** (215)238-4200 or 4454, FAX (215)238-4227. **(Subscription address:** J.B. Lippincott, PO Box 350, Hagerstown MD 21740.**)** **DD** 616. **NLM** W1; CA6849AM.
**Desc:** A resource from the American Cancer Society for oncology nurses and their associates.

US/1043-8491
**CANCER PREVENTION (BALTIMORE, MD.).** ***Ceased.*** (CANCER PREVENTION.). [Cancer prev.]. (1990)-Ceased Vol. 1, No.3. Periodical. English. qt. Williams & Wilkins Company, 428 East Preston Street, Baltimore MD 21202-3993. **Tel** (410)528-4000, (800)638-6423, FAX (410)528-8596, telex 87669. **(Subscription address:** US/ PO Box 64380, Baltimore, MD 21264-4380; Japan/ Igaku-Shoin MYW Ltd, 1-28-36 Hongo, Bunkyo-ku Tokyo 113 Japan; European/ The Broadway House, 2-6 Fulham Broadway, London SW6 1AA England; telephone: (800)638-6423**)** **LC** RC268; .C364. **NLM** W1; CA6849B. **Pr Rev.** Documents available from Quick Copies.
**Desc:** Articles focus on strategies for the management of malignant disease.

US/0190-5112
**CANCER REPORT (NEW YORK).** (CANCER REPORT.). **Added/Corp** New York University. Medical Center. No. 1 (March 1977)-. Periodical. English. ir. Cancer Report, New York University Medical Center, Room 1WS/Bellevue, 550 First Avenue, New York NY 10016. **NLM** W1 CA687E.

US/0008-5472
**CANCER RESEARCH (BALTIMORE).** (CANCER RESEARCH : THE OFFICIAL ORGAN OF THE AMERICAN ASSOCIATION FOR CANCER RESEARCH, INC.). [Cancer res.]. **Added/Corp** American Association for Cancer Research. International Cancer Research Foundation. William H. Donner Foundation. Vol. 1 (Jan. 1941)-. Academic Scholarly Publication. English. sm. $495.00 institution; $460.00 individual. American Association of Cancer Research, 620 Chestnut Street, Pub Ledger Building, Philadelphia PA 19106. **Tel** (215)440-9300. **(Subscription address:** Fulco, 30 Broad Street, Denville NJ 07834.**)** **LC** RC261; .A274. **DD** 616.99405. **NLM** W1 CA688. **CODEN** CNREA8. **[CCC].** Index available. cum. index (Published in December). **Ad Acc. Pr Rev.** available on microfilm and microfiche from University Microfilms International (UMI). Documents available from The Genuine Article, BIOSIS Document Express, CASDDS. ***Continues** American Journal of Cancer.*
**Desc:** Devoted to the publication of significant, original research in the fields of cancer research and cancer-related biomedical science.
**Ind/Abst** Biol. Abstr.; Chem. Abstr.; Curr. Aware. Biol. Sci., CABS; Curr. Biotechnol.; Curr. Contents Clin. Med.; Curr. Contents Life Sci.; EMBASE; Energy Res. Abstr.; Health Plan. Adminis.; Helminthol. Abstr. (1991-); Immunol. Abstr.; Index Med.; Index Vet.; INIS Atomindex [Micro.]; Int. Pharm. Abstr.; Iowa Drug Inf. Serv. (1969-); Med. Abstr. Newsl.; Nucl. Acids Abstr.; Oncog. Growth Factors Abstr.; Life Sci. Collect.; PESTDOC; Res. Alert [Full Cov.]; Rev. Med. Vet. Mycology; Risk Abstr.; Sci. Cit. Index; SCISEARCH; Small Anim. Abstr. Bibliogr.; Soc. Sci. Cit. Index [Select. Cov.]; Stat. Theory Method Abstr. (1969); Wheat Barley Trit. Abstr.

●SZ/1064-0525
**CANCER RESEARCH, THERAPY & CONTROL.** (CANCER RESEARCH, THERAPY, AND CONTROL.). [Cancer res. ther. control]. **VFOAT** Cancer Research, Therapy and Control. Vol. 3 No. 1 (Nov. 1992)-. Periodical. English. ir. $288.00 (academic institutions), $449.00 (corporate institutions). Harwood Academic Publishers / New York, PO Box 786, Cooper Station, New York NY 10276. **Tel** (212)206-8900, (201)643-7500. **(Subscription address:** International Publishers Distributor at one of the following addresses: 820 Town Center Drive, Langhorne, PA 19047; or PO Box 90, Reading Berkshire RG1 8JL UK; or Kent Ridge PO Box 1180, Singapore 9111, Republic of Singapore**)** **DD** 616. **NLM** W1; CA692CB. **CODEN** CRTCEA. **[CCC].** ***Continues** Cancer Therapy and Control, 0896-5080.*

●US/1071-7226
**CANCER RESEARCHER WEEKLY.** [Cancer res. wkly.]. (May 3, 1993)-. Periodical. English. wk (48 issues). $995.00 US, Canada & Mexico; $1,195.00 other. CW Henderson, PO Box 5528, Atlanta GA 30307-0528. **Tel** (404)377-8895, FAX (404)378-5411. **(Subscription address:** CW Henderson, Subscription Office, PO Box 830409, Birmingham AL 35283-0409.**)** **DD** 616. ***Continues** Cancerweekly, 1071-7218.*

US/0069-0171
**CANCER SEMINAR.** V. 1-4, No. 2; Sept. 1950-1972; N.S. V. 1- 1976-. Periodical. English. University of South Florida, CPR 472, Tampa FL 33620-5600. **Tel** (813)974-2617.

US/1050-849X
**CANCER SURVEY (COLD SPRINGS HARBOR, N.Y.).** (CANCER SURVEY.). (1991)-. Academic Scholarly Publication. English. Three times a year. $72.00. Cold Spring Harbor Laboratory, 10 Skyline Drive, Plainview NY 11803. **Tel** (516)349-1930, (800)843-4388, FAX (516)349-1946. **Acid Free.**
**Desc:** Provides a comprehensive survey of the present state of, and future developments in, well-defined areas in oncology. Each issue deals with a specific topic and has guest editors with an expert knowledge of the subject.
**Ind/Abst** Curr. Contents Life Sci.; EMBASE; Index Med.

US/0261-2429
**CANCER SURVEYS.** [Cancer. surv.]. **Added/Corp** Imperial Cancer Research Fund (Great Britain). Vol. 1, No. 1 (Spring 1982)-. Monographic series. English. Three times a year. $72.00. Cold Spring Harbor Laboratory, 10 Skyline Drive, Plainview NY 11803. **Tel** (516)349-1930, (800)843-4388, FAX (516)349-1946. **ED** L M Franks. **DD** 616. **NLM** W1 CA692D. **CODEN** CASUD7. **[CCC].** Index available. **Bk Rev. Ad Acc. Pr Rev. Circ:** 375. Documents available from The Genuine Article, BIOSIS Document Express.
**Desc:** Comprehensive review of oncology including new research findings relative to epidemiology and laboratory research to clinical problems. This is of interest to clinicians and laboratory workers.
**Ind/Abst** Biol. Abstr. (1986-); Curr. Aware. Biol. Sci., CABS; Curr. Contents Life Sci.; EMBASE; Genet. Abstr.; Health Plan. Adminis.; Index Med. (Vol. 4, No. 1, 1985-);; Oncog. Growth Factors Abstr.; Ref. Upd. Deluxe Ed.; Res. Alert [Full Cov.]; Sci. Cit. Index; SCISEARCH; Trop. Dis. Bull.

SZ/0896-5080
**CANCER THERAPY AND CONTROL.** ***Title Change.*** [Cancer ther. control]. **VFOAT** Cancer Therapy & Control. Vol. 1, No. 1-(1989)-(199?). Periodical. English. qt. Harwood Academic Publishers / New York, PO Box 786, Cooper Station, New York NY 10276. **Tel** (212)206-8900, (201)643-7500. **(Subscription address:** International Publishers Distributor at one of the following addresses: 820 Town Center Drive, Langhorne, PA 19047; or PO Box 90, Reading Berkshire RG1 8JL UK; or Kent Ridge PO Box 1180, Singapore 9111, Republic of Singapore**)** **ED** E T Bucovaz. **LC** RC261.A1; C394. **DD** 616.99/406/05. **NLM** W1; CA692N. **CODEN** CTCOE9. **[CCC].** ***Continued by** Cancer Research, Therapy & Control, 1064-0525.*
**Desc:** An international journal which publishes original observations and investigations related to all aspects of human oncobiology, including its research, treatment and management.
**Ind/Abst** Curr. Aware. Biol. Sci., CABS.

US/1050-9992
**CANCER THERAPY REPORTS.** ***Ceased.*** (1991)-Ceased (Jan. 1991). Periodical. English. bm. Williams & Wilkins Company, 428 East Preston Street, Baltimore MD 21202-3993. **Tel** (410)528-4000, (800)638-6423, FAX (410)528-8596, telex 87669. **(Subscription address:** US/ PO Box 64380, Baltimore, MD 21264-4380; Japan/ Igaku-Shoin MYW Ltd, 1-28-36 Hongo, Bunkyo-ku Tokyo 113 Japan; European/ The Broadway House, 2-6 Fulham Broadway London SW6 1AA England; telephone: (800)638-6423**)** Documents available from Quick Copies.
**Desc:** For medical oncologists, hematologists, and radiation therapists interested in early reports on clinical and preclinical trials covering all aspects of cancer treatment.

US/0924-6533
**CANCER THERAPY UPDATE.** ***Ceased.*** (19??)-Vol 12 (Dec. 1992). Periodical. English. bm. Kluwer Academic Publishers / Massachusetts, PO Box 358, Accord Station, Hingham MA 02018. **Tel** (617)871-6600. **ED** Franco Muggia and Kenneth Norris Jr. **NLM** W1; CA692NN. **[CCC]. Pr Rev. Acid Free.** available on microfilm and microfiche from University Microfilms International (UMI).
**Desc:** Has provided critical commentaries on various aspects of cancer treatment.

SP/0212-2618
**CANCER TOPICS. VERSION ESPANOLA.** [Cancer top., Version esp.]. (1981)-. Periodical. Spanish. bm. Graficas Enar SA, Pedro Muguruza 3/1, 28016 Madrid Spain. **UDC** 616-006.

NE/0927-3042
**CANCER TREATMENT AND RESEARCH.** **VFOAT** CTAR. Vol. 1 (1981)-. Monographic series. English. ir. Price varies per volume. Kluwer Academic Publishers, Postbus 322, 3300 AH Dordrecht, The Netherlands. **Tel** 011 (31) 78 524400, FAX 011 31 78 183273, telex 20083. **LC** UNC. **NLM** W1; CA693.
**Ind/Abst** Life Sci. Collect.

UK/0305-7372
**CANCER TREATMENT REVIEWS.** [Cancer treat. rev.]. Vol. 1 (March 1974)-. Academic Scholarly Publication. English. bm (Jan., Apr., July, Oct.). £110.00 (institution), £55.00 (individual) UK & Europe; $198.00 (institution), $99.00 (individual) other. Harcourt Brace & Company Ltd., Foots Cray, High Street, Sidcup Kent DA14 5HP England. **Tel** 011 44 81 300 3322, FAX 011 44 81 309 0807. **(Subscription address:** W. B. Saunders Company / North America Subscriptions, c/o Periodicals, 6277 Sea Harbour Drive, 4th Floor, Orlando FL 32887.**)** **ED** K Hellmann. **NLM** W1 CA695. **CODEN** CTREDJ. **[CCC].** Index available. **Pr Rev.** Documents available from The Genuine Article, BIOSIS Document Express, CASDDS.
**Desc:** Devoted to important advances in the field of cancer treatment. Publishes critical, concise, and authoritative state-of-the-art reviews that represent current thinking and practice in cancer treatment research. These surveys are especially valuable in areas where concepts as well as treatments change rapidly.

Provides an especially valuable forum for physicians and oncologists by publishing the opinions of leading experts on recent developments in the therapy of specific cancers and in related basic sciences.
**Ind/Abst** Biol. Abstr.; Chem. Abstr. (1984-); Curr. Contents Clin. Med.; EMBASE; Health Plan. Adminis.; Index Med.; Index Sci. Rev. [Full Cov.]; Life Sci. Collect.; Res. Alert [Full Cov.]; Sci. Cit. Index; SCISEARCH; Soc. Sci. Cit. Index [Select. Cov.].

US/0891-0766
**CANCER VICTORS JOURNAL.** (CANCER VICTORS JOURNAL / INTERNATIONAL ASSOCIATION OF CANCER VICTIMS AND FRIENDS.). [Cancer victors j.]. **Added/Corp** International Association of Cancer Victims and Friends. Vol. 20, No. 1 (Spring 1986)-. Periodical. English. Four times a year. $20.00. International Association of Cancer Victims and Friends, 515 West Sycamore, El Secundo CA 90245. **Tel** (310)822-5032, (310)822-5132. **ED** Ann L. Cinquina. **DD** 616. **NLM** W1; CA697. **Ad Acc, Adv Mgr:** Suzanne Landon. **Circ:** 4,000 (ctrl). available on microfilm; available on an online database. ***Continues*** *Cancer News Journal, 0099-2372.*

●US/1059-3802
**CANCER WATCH.** [Cancer watch]. Vol. 1, No. 1 (Jan. 1992)-. Periodical. English. Twelve times a year. $30.00 (individuals), $55.00 (institutions) US; $40.00 (individuals), $65.00 (institutions) Canada & Mexico; $50.00 (individuals), $75.00 (institutions) others. Adenine Press, PO Box 355/340, Guilderland NY 12084. **Tel** (518)456-0784, FAX (518)452-4955. **ED** M. H. Sarma. **DD** 616. **NLM** W1; CA703. Index available (bound in Dec. issue).

US/1057-588X
**CANCERGRAM. SERIES CB19, ANTITUMOR AND ANTIVIRAL AGENTS MECHANISM OF ACTION.** ***Ceased.*** **VFOAT** Mechanism of Action; Antitumor and Antiviral Agents. Mechanism of Action. (Sept. 1988)-(Dec. 1993). Government Publication. English. mo. Superintendent of Documents, US Government Printing Office, Washington DC 20402. **Tel** (202)275-3328, FAX (202)786-2377. **NLM** ZQV 269; I35. available on microfiche (Vols. for 1988- distributed to depository libraries). ***Continues*** *ICRDB Cancergram. Series CB19, Antitumor and Antiviral Agents. Mechanisms of Action.*
**Desc:** Current awareness bulletin containing 30 to 100 abstracts of recent publications from over 3,000 sources. Active researchers in the subject area select and categorize the abstracts for a quick reference to the current cancer literature.

US/1057-5898
**CANCERGRAM. SERIES CB20 ANTITUMOR AND ANTIVIRAL AGENTS EXPERIMENTAL THERAPEUTICS TOXICOLOGY PHARMACOLOGY.** ***Ceased.*** **VFOAT** Antitumor and Antiviral Agents; Experimental Therapeutics, Toxicology, Pharmacology. (Sept. 1988)-(Dec. 1993). Government Publication. English. mo. Superintendent of Documents, US Government Printing Office, Washington DC 20402. **Tel** (202)275-3328, FAX (202)786-2377. **NLM** ZQZ 267; I11AC. available on microfiche (Vols. for (Nov. 1988-) distributed to depository libraries). ***Continues*** *ICRDB Cancergram. Series CB20, Antitumor and Antiviral Agents. Experimental Therapeutics, Toxicology, Pharmacology, 0164-193X.*
**Desc:** Current awareness bulletin containing 30 to 100 abstracts of recent publications from over 3,000 sources. Active researchers in the subject select and categorize the abstracts for a quick reference.

US/1057-5901
**CANCERGRAM. SERIES CT01 CANCER DETECTION AND MANAGEMENT BIOLOGICAL MARKERS.** ***Ceased.*** **VFOAT** Cancer Detection and Management. Biological Markers. (Oct. 1988)-(Dec. 1993). Government Publication. English. mo. Superintendent of Documents, US Government Printing Office, Washington DC 20402. **Tel** (202)275-3328, FAX (202)786-2377. **NLM** ZQZ 206; I11BB. available on microfiche (Vols. for 1988 distributed to depository libraries). ***Continues*** *ICRDB Cancergram. Series CT01, Cancer Detection and Management. Biological Markers, 0190-3438.*
**Desc:** Current awareness bulletin containing 30 to 100 abstracts of recent publications from 30 to 100 abstracts of recent publications from over 3,000 sources. Active researchers in each subject area select and categorize the abstracts for a quick reference to the current cancer literature.

US/1057-591X
**CANCERGRAM. SERIES CT02 CANCER DETECTION AND MANAGEMENT NUCLEAR MEDICINE.** ***Ceased.*** **VFOAT** Cancer Detection and Management. Nuclear Medicine. (Sept. 1988)-(Dec. 1993). Government Publication. English. mo. Superintendent of Documents, US Government Printing Office, Washington DC 20402. **Tel** (202)275-3328, FAX (202)786-2377. **NLM** ZQZ 241; C24N. available on microfiche (Vols. for (Nov. 1988-) distributed to depository libraries). ***Continues*** *ICRDB Cancergram. Series CT02, Cancer Detection and Management. Nuclear Medicine, 0164-1980.*
**Desc:** Current awareness bulletin containing 30 to 100 abstracts of recent publications from over 3,000 sources. Active researchers in each subject area select and categorize the abstracts for quick reference to the current cancer literature.

US/1057-5936
**CANCERGRAM. SERIES CT05 LYMPHOMAS DIAGNOSIS TREATMENT.** ***Ceased.*** **VFOAT** Lymphomas. Diagnosis, Treatment. (Sept. 1988)-(Dec. 1993). Government Publication. English. mo. Superintendent of Documents, US Government Printing Office, Washington DC 20402. **Tel** (202)275-3328, FAX (202)786-2377. **NLM** ZWH 525; I11L. ***Continues*** *ICRDB Cancergram. Series CT05, Lymphomas. Diagnosis, Treatment, 0164-2464.*
**Desc:** Current awareness bulletin containing 30 to 100 abstracts of recent publications from over 3,000 sources. Active researchers in each subject area select and categorize the abstracts for quick reference to the current cancer literature.

US/1057-5944
**CANCERGRAM. SERIES CT06, CLINICAL CANCER IMMUNOLOGY AND BIOLOGICAL THERAPY.** ***Ceased.*** **Added/Corp** National Cancer Institute (U.S.). International Cancer Research Data Bank. Cancer Information Dissemination and Analysis Center for Diagnosis and Therapy. **VFOAT** Clinical Cancer Immunology and Biological Therapy. (Oct. 1988)-(Dec. 1993). Government Publication. English. mo. Superintendent of Documents, US Government Printing Office, Washington DC 20402. **Tel** (202)275-3328, FAX (202)786-2377. **NLM** ZQZ 266 C24I. ***Continues*** *ICRDB Cancergram. Series CT06, Clinical Cancer Immunology and Biological Therapy, 0894-3664.*
**Desc:** Current awareness bulletins in cancer-related subject areas.

US/1057-5960
**CANCERGRAM. SERIES CT08 LUNG CANCER. DIAGNOSIS TREATMENT.** ***Ceased.*** [Cancergram, Ser. CT08 Lung cancer, Diagn. treat.]. **Added/Corp** National Cancer Institute (U.S.) International Cancer Research Data Bank. Cancer Information Dissemination and Analysis Center for Diagnosis and Therapy. **VFOAT** Lung Cancer. Diagnosis, Treatment. (Sept. 1988)-(Dec. 1993). Government Publication. English. mo. Superintendent of Documents, US Government Printing Office, Washington DC 20402. **Tel** (202)275-3328, FAX (202)786-2377. **DD** 616. **NLM** ZWF 658; C23TD. available on microfiche (Vols. for (Nov. 1988-) distributed to depository libraries). ***Continues*** *ICRDB Cancergram. Series CT08, Lung Cancer. Diagnosis, Treatment, 0164-2359.*
**Desc:** Current awareness bulletin containing 30 to 100 abstracts of recent publications from over 3,000 sources. Active researchers in each subject area select and categorize the abstracts for quick reference to the current cancer literature.

US/1057-5979
**CANCERGRAM. SERIES CT09 BREAST CANCER DIAGNOSIS TREATMENT PRE-CLINICAL BIOLOGY.** ***Ceased.*** **VFOAT** Breast Cancer; Diagnosis, Treatment, Pre-Clinical Biology. (Sept. 1988)-(Dec. 1993). Government Publication. English. mo. Superintendent of Documents, US Government Printing Office, Washington DC 20402. **Tel** (202)275-3328, FAX (202)786-2377. **NLM** ZWP 870; I11DP. available on microfiche (Vols. for (Nov. 1988-) distributed to depository libraries). ***Continues*** *ICRDB Cancergram. Series CT09, Breast Cancer. Diagnosis, Treatment, Pre-Clinical Biology, 0164-1956.*
**Desc:** Current awareness bulletin containing 30 to 100 abstracts of recent publications from over 3,000 sources. Active researchers in each subject area select and categorize the abstracts for quick reference to the current cancer literature.

US/1057-9087
**CANCERGRAM. SERIES CT10 PEDIATRIC ONCOLOGY.** ***Ceased.*** **VFOAT** Pediatric Oncology. (Oct. 1988)-(Dec. 1993). Government Publication. English. mo. Superintendent of Documents, US Government Printing Office, Washington DC 20402. **Tel** (202)275-3328, FAX (202)786-2377. **NLM** ZQZ 200; C23C. available on microfiche (Vols. for (Nov. 1988-) distributed to depository libraries). ***Continues*** *ICRDB Cancergram. Series CT10, Pediatric Oncology, 0164-2308.*
**Desc:** Current awareness bulletin containing 30 to 100 abstracts of recent publications from over 3,000 sources. Active researchers in each subject area select and categorize the abstracts for quick reference to the current cancer literature.

US/1057-9079
**CANCERGRAM. SERIES CT11 NEOPLASIA OF THE HEAD AND NECK DIAGNOSIS TREATMENT.** ***Ceased.*** **VFOAT** Neoplasia of the Head and Neck. Diagnosis, Treatment. (Sept. 1988)-(Dec. 1993). Government Publication. English. mo. Superintendent of Documents, US Government Printing Office, Washington DC 20402. **Tel** (202)275-3328, FAX (202)786-2377. **NLM** ZWE 707; C23N. available on microfiche (Vols. for (Nov. 1988-) distributed to depository libraries). ***Continues*** *ICRDB Cancergram. Series CT11, Neoplasia of the Head and Neck. Diagnosis, Treatment, 0164-2170.*
**Desc:** Current awareness bulletin containing 30 to 100 abstracts of recent publications from over 3,000 sources. Active researchers in each subject area select and categorize the abstracts for quick reference to the current cancer literature.

US/1057-9060
**CANCERGRAM. SERIES CT12 SARCOMAS AND RELATED TUMORS. DIAGNOSIS TREATMENT.** ***Ceased.*** **Added/Corp** National Cancer Institute (U.S.) International Cancer Research Data Bank. Cancer Information Dissemination and Analysis Center for Diagnosis and Therapy. **VFOAT** Diagnosis, Treatment; Sarcomas and Related Tumors. Diagnosis, Treatment. (Sept. 1988)-(Dec. 1993). Periodical. English. mo. US Department of Health and Human Services, 200 Independence Avenue Southwest, Washington DC 20201. **DD** 616. **NLM** ZQZ 345; I11D. ***Continues*** *ICRDB Cancergram. Series CT12, Sarcomas and Related Tumors. Diagnosis, Treatment, 0164-2219.*
**Desc:** Current awareness bulletin containing 30 to 100 abstracts of recent publications from over 3,000 sources. Active researchers in the subject select and categorize the abstracts for quick reference to the current cancer literature.

US/1057-5928
**CANCERGRAM. SERIES CT14 CANCER DETECTION AND MANAGEMENT DIAGNOSTIC RADIOLOGY.** ***Ceased.*** **VFOAT** Cancer Detection and Management. Diagnostic Radiology. (Sept. 1988)-(Dec. 1993). Periodical. English. mo. US Department of Health and Human Services, 200 Independence Avenue Southwest, Washington DC 20201. **NLM** ZQZ 241; I11C. ***Continues*** *ICRDB Cancergram. Series CT14, Cancer Detection and Management. Diagnostic Radiology, 0164-1964.*
**Desc:** Current awareness bulletin containing 30 to 100 abstracts of recent publications from over 3,000 sources . Active researchers in the subject select and categorize the abstracts for quick reference to the current cancer literature.

US/1057-9052
**CANCERGRAM. SERIES CT15, CLINICAL TREATMENT OF CANCER. RADIATION THERAPY.** ***Ceased.*** [Cancergram. Ser. CT15 Clin. treat. cancer, Radiat. ther.]. **Added/Corp** National Cancer Institute (U.S.) International Cancer Research Data Bank. Cancer Information Dissemination and Analysis Center for Diagnosis and Therapy. **VFOAT** Clinical Treatment of Cancer. Radiation Therapy; Radiation Therapy. (Oct. 1988)-(Dec. 1993). Government Publication. English. mo. Superintendent of Documents, US Government Printing Office, Washington DC 20402. **Tel** (202)275-3328, FAX (202)786-2377. **DD** 616. **NLM** ZQZ 269; I11CR. ***Continues*** *ICRDB Cancergram. Series CT15, Clinical Treatment of Cancer. Radiation Therapy, 0164-2146.*
**Desc:** Current awareness bulletins in cancer-related subject areas.

US/1057-9109
**CANCERGRAM. SERIES CT16, GENITO-URINARY CANCERS. DIAGNOSIS, TREATMENT.** ***Ceased.*** **VFOAT** Genito-Urinary Cancers. Diagnosis, Treatment. (Oct 1988)-(Dec. 1993). Government Publication. English. mo. Superintendent of Documents, US Government Printing Office, Washington DC 20402. **Tel** (202)275-3328, FAX (202)786-2377. **NLM** ZWJ 160; I11DG. available on microfiche (Vols. for (Nov. 1988-) distributed to depository libraries). ***Continues*** *ICRDB Cancergram. Series CT16, Genito-Urinary Cancers. Diagnosis, Treatment, 0164-243X.*
**Desc:** Current awareness bulletin containing 30 to 100 abstracts of recent publications from over 3,000 sources. Active researchers in the subject select and categorize the abstracts for quick reference to the current cancer literature.

US/1057-9117
**CANCERGRAM. SERIES CT17 GYNECOLOGIC TUMORS. DIAGNOSIS TREATMENT.** ***Ceased.*** [Cancergram, Ser. CT17 Gynecol. tumors, Diagn. treat.]. **Added/Corp** National Cancer Institute (U.S.) International Cancer Research Data Bank. Cancer Information Dissemination and Analysis Center for Diagnosis and Therapy. **VFOAT** Diagnosis, Treatment; Gynecologic Tumors. Diagnosis, Treatment. (Sept. 1988)-(Dec. 1993). Periodical. English. mo. US Department of Health and Human Services, 200 Independence Avenue Southwest, Washington DC 20201. **DD** 616. **NLM** ZWP 145; I11G. ***Continues*** *ICRDB Cancergram. Series CT17, Gynecologic Tumors. Diagnosis, Treatment, 0164-2367.*
**Desc:** Current awareness bulletin containing 30 to 100 abstracts of recent publications from over 3,000 sources.

Active researchers in the subject select and categorize the abstracts for quick reference to the current cancer literature.

US/1057-9125
**CANCERGRAM. SERIES CT18, NERVOUS SYSTEM MALIGNANCIES. DIAGNOSIS, TREATMENT.** ***Ceased.*** **VFOAT** Nervous System Malignancies. Diagnosis, Treatment; Diagnosis, Treatment. (1989)-(Dec. 1993). Periodical. English. mo. National Technical Information Service - NTIS, Room 2027S, 5285 Port Royal Road, Springfield VA 22161. **Tel** (703)487-4630, (703)487-4660, (703)487-4650, FAX (703)321-8547, telex 89-9405. **NLM** ZWL 358; I11. available on microfiche (Vols. for June 1989- distributed to depository libraries). ***Continues*** *Cancergram. Series CT18, CNS Malignancies. Diagnosis, Treatment.*

US
**CANCERGRAM. SERIES CT19, UPPER GASTRINTESTINAL TUMORS DIAGNOSIS, TREATMENT.** ***Ceased.*** (Sept. 1988)-(Dec. 1993). Government Publication. English. mo. Superintendent of Documents, US Government Printing Office, Washington DC 20402. **Tel** (202)275-3328, FAX (202)786-2377. **NLM** ZWI 149; IIIU. available on microfiche (Vols. for (Nov. 1988-) distributed to depository libraries). ***Continues*** *ICRDB Cancergram. Series CT19, Upper Gastrointestinal Tumors. Diagnosis, Treatment, 0190-4477.*
**Desc:** Current awareness bulletin containing 30 to 100 abstracts of recent publications from over 3,000 sources. Active researchers in the subject select and categorize the abstracts for quick reference to the current cancer literature.

US
**CANCERGRAM. SERIES CT20 REHABILITATION AND SUPPORTIVE CARE.** ***Ceased.*** **VFOAT** Rehabilitation and Supportive Care. (Oct. 1988)-(Dec. 1993). Periodical. English. mo. **NLM** ZQZ 200.3; I11. ***Continues*** *ICRDB Cancergram. Rehabilitation and Supportive Care, 0198-9502.*
**Desc:** Current awareness bulletin containing 30 to 100 abstracts of recent publications from over 3,000 sources. Active researchers in the subject select and categorize the abstracts for quick reference to the current cancer literature.

US/1057-9133
**CANCERGRAM. SERIES CT21 ENDOCRINE TUMORS. DIAGNOSIS TREATMENT PATHOPHYSIOLOGY.** ***Ceased.*** **VFOAT** Endocrine Tumors. Diagnosis, Treatment, Pathophysiology. (Sept. 1988)-(Dec. 1993). Periodical. English. mo. US Department of Health and Human Services, 200 Independence Avenue Southwest, Washington DC 20201. **NLM** ZWK 100.3; I11. available on microfiche (Vols. for (Nov. 1988-) distributed to depository libraries). ***Continues*** *ICRDB Cancergram. Series CT21, Endocrine Tumors. Diagnosis, Treatment, Pathophysiology, 0191-6661.*
**Desc:** Current awareness bulletin containing 30 to 100 abstracts of recent publications from over 3,000 sources. Active researchers in the subject select and categorize the abstracts for quick reference to the current cancer literature.

US/1057-9141
**CANCERGRAM. SERIES CT22 MELANOMA AND OTHER SKIN CANCER DIAGNOSIS TREATMENT.** ***Ceased.*** **VFOAT** Melanoma and other Skin Cancer. Diagnosis, Treatment. (Oct 1988)-(Dec. 1993). Government Publication. English. mo. Superintendent of Documents, US Government Printing Office, Washington DC 20402. **Tel** (202)275-3328, FAX (202)786-2377. **NLM** ZWR 500; I11. available on microfiche (Vols. for (Nov. 1988-) distributed to depository libraries). ***Continues*** *ICRDB Cancergram. Series CT22, Melanoma and other Skin Cancer. Diagnosis, Treatment, 0191-667X.*
**Desc:** Current awareness bulletin containing 30 to 100 abstracts of recent publications from over 3,000 sources. Active researchers in the subject select and categorize the abstracts for quick reference to the current cancer literature.

US/1057-915X
**CANCERGRAM. SERIES CT23, LEUKEMIAS AND MULTIPLE MYELOMA. DIAGNOSIS, TREATMENT.** ***Ceased.*** **Added/Corp** National Cancer Institute (U.S.) International Cancer Research Data Bank. Cancer Information Dissemination and Analysis Center for Diagnosis and Therapy. **VFOAT** Leukemias and Multiple Myeloma. Diagnosis, Treatment; Diagnosis, Treatment. (January 1990)-(Dec. 1993). Periodical. English. mo. **NLM** ZWH 250; I102. ***Formed by the union of*** *Cancergram. Series CT03, Acute and Chronic Leukemia. Diagnosis, Treatment* ***and*** *Cancergram. Series CT13, Clinical Evaluation and Treatment of Multiple Myeloma and Other Gammopathies.*

US/1059-8960
**CANCERMONTHLY (AIDS RELATED CANCER ED.).** ***Title Change.*** (CANCERMONTHLY.). [Cancermonthly]. **VFOAT** Cancer Monthly. (Jan. 1992)-(199?). Periodical. English. mo. Cancer Weekly, PO Box 830409, Birmingham AL 35283-0409. **Tel** (800)633-4931, (205)995-1567. **DD** 616. ***Merged with*** *Cancer Weekly.*

●US/1059-8928
**CANCERMONTHLY (BREAST CANCER ED.).** (CANCERMONTHLY.). [Cancermonthly]. **VFOAT** Cancer Monthly. Jan. (1992)-. Periodical. English. mo. $95.00. Reference Press, Inc., 6448 Highway 290 East, Suite E-104, Austin TX 78723-9828. **Tel** (800)486-8666, (512)454-7778, FAX (512)454-9401. **DD** 616.

US/1059-9029
**CANCERMONTHLY (BUSINESS AND FINANCE ED.).** ***Title Change.*** (CANCERMONTHLY.). [Cancermonthly]. **VFOAT** Cancer Monthly. (Jan. 1992)-(19??). Periodical. English. mo. Cancer Weekly, PO Box 830409, Birmingham AL 35283-0409. **Tel** (800)633-4931, (205)995-1567. **DD** 362. ***Merged into*** *Cancer Weekly.*

US/1059-8979
**CANCERMONTHLY (CANCER TREATMENT/GENE THERAPY ED.).** ***Title Change.*** (CANCERMONTHLY.). [Cancermonthly]. **VFOAT** Cancer Monthly. (Jan. 1992)-(19??). Periodical. English. Twelve times a year. Cancer Weekly, PO Box 830409, Birmingham AL 35283-0409. **Tel** (800)633-4931, (205)995-1567. **DD** 616. ***Merged into*** *Cancer Weekly.*

●US/1059-8944
**CANCERMONTHLY (CARCINOGENESIS AND EPIDEMIOLOGY ED.).** (CANCERMONTHLY.). [Cancermonthly]. **VFOAT** Cancer Monthly. (Jan. 1992)-. Periodical. English. mo. $95.00. Cancer Weekly, PO Box 830409, Birmingham AL 35283-0409. **Tel** (800)633-4931, (205)995-1567. **DD** 616.

US/1059-9010
**CANCERMONTHLY (EDUCATION AND HEALTHCARE ED.).** ***Title Change.*** **See** Public Health and Safety.

US/1059-9037
**CANCERMONTHLY (INTERNATIONAL ACTIVITIES ED.).** ***Title Change.*** (CANCERMONTHLY.). [Cancermonthly]. **VFOAT** Cancer Monthly. (Jan. 1992)-(19??). Periodical. English. mo. Cancer Weekly, PO Box 830409, Birmingham AL 35283-0409. **Tel** (800)633-4931, (205)995-1567. **DD** 616. ***Merged into*** *Cancer Weekly.*

●US/1059-8987
**CANCERMONTHLY (JOURNAL ED.).** (CANCERMONTHLY.). [Cancermonthly]. **VFOAT** Cancer Monthly. Jan. (1992)-. Periodical. English. mo. $95.00. Cancer Weekly, PO Box 830409, Birmingham AL 35283-0409. **Tel** (800)633-4931, (205)995-1567. **DD** 616.

US/1059-9002
**CANCERMONTHLY (LEUKEMIA/LYMPHOMA ED.).** ***Title Change.*** (CANCERMONTHLY.). [Cancermonthly]. **VFOAT** Cancer Monthly. (Jan. 1992)-(19??). Periodical. English. mo. Cancer Weekly, PO Box 830409, Birmingham AL 35283-0409. **Tel** (800)633-4931, (205)995-1567. **DD** 616. ***Merged into*** *Cancer Weekly, 1071-7218.*

●US/1059-8995
**CANCERMONTHLY (RESEARCH ED.).** (CANCERMONTHLY.). [Cancermonthly]. **VFOAT** Cancer Monthly. (1992)-. Periodical. English. mo. $95.00. Cancer Weekly, PO Box 830409, Birmingham AL 35283-0409. **Tel** (800)633-4931, (205)995-1567. **DD** 616.

●US/1059-8936
**CANCERMONTHLY (SMOKING AND LUNG CANCER ED.).** (CANCERMONTHLY.). [Cancermonthly]. **VFOAT** Cancer Monthly. (Jan. 1992)-. Periodical. English. mo. $95.00. Cancer Weekly, PO Box 830409, Birmingham AL 35283-0409. **Tel** (800)633-4931, (205)995-1567. **DD** 616.

US/1059-8952
**CANCERMONTHLY (SOLID TUMOR ED.).** ***Title Change.*** (CANCERMONTHLY.). [Cancermonthly]. **VFOAT** Cancer Monthly. (Jan. 1992)-(19??). Periodical. English. mo. Cancer Weekly, PO Box 830409, Birmingham AL 35283-0409. **Tel** (800)633-4931, (205)995-1567. **DD** 616. ***Merged into*** *Cancer Weekly.*

FR/0220-7346
**CANCEROLOGIE.** [Cancerologie]. 1976-. Periodical. French. Editions du CNRS, 22 rue Saint Armand, F 75015 Paris France. **Tel** 011 33 1 45075050. **ED** A Demaille. **NLM** W3 CA699N.
**Desc:** Based on post-university teaching at the Centre Oscar Lambret ... .

US/1071-7218
**CANCERWEEKLY (ATLANTA, GA.).** ***Title Change.*** (CANCERWEEKLY : NCI CANCER WEEKLY.). [Cancerweekly]. **VFOAT** Cancer Weekly. (Jan. 7, 1991)-(1993). Periodical. English. wk. Cancer Weekly, PO Box 830409, Birmingham AL 35283-0409. **Tel** (800)633-4931, (205)995-1567. **DD** 616. **NLM** W1; CA699T. ***Continues*** *NCI Cancer Weekly, 0896-7385; Cancermonthly;* ***Absorbed*** *Cancermonthly International Editions; Cancermonthly (Business and Finance Ed), 1059-9029.* ***Continued by*** *Cancer Researcher Weekly, 1071-7226.*
**Ind/Abst** Health Index (1991-); Health Period. Database [Full Txt.]; Health Ref. Cent. (Jan. 1989-) [Full Txt.] [Full Cov.]; PTS Newsl. Database [Full Txt.].

●US/1066-4114
**CAPSULES AND COMMENTS IN ONCOLOGY NURSING.** **See** Medical Science and Technology-Nursing.

US/0147-4006
**CARCINOGENESIS. A COMPREHENSIVE SURVEY.** [Carcinog.]. (1976)-. Academic Scholarly Publication. English. ir. $128.50. Raven Press, 1185 Avenue of the Americas, 37th Floor, New York NY 10036. **Tel** (212)930-9500, (212)930-9604, FAX (212)869-3495, (212)302-8507, telex 640073. **LC** RC268.5; .C36. **DD** 616.9/94/07105. **NLM** W1 CA7624. **CODEN** CCSUDL. **[CCC].** Documents available from BIOSIS Document Express, CASDDS.
**Ind/Abst** Biol. Abstr.; Chem. Abstr.; Index Med. (1980-); Life Sci. Collect.

US/0143-3334
**CARCINOGENESIS (NEW YORK).** (CARCINOGENESIS.). [Carcinogenesis]. **Added/Corp** Information Retrieval Limited. Vol. 1 (Jan. 1980)-. Academic Scholarly Publication. English. mo. £315.00 UK and Europe; $540.00 other. Oxford University Press, Walton Street, Oxford OX2 6DP England. **Tel** 011 44 865 56767, FAX 011 44 865 267773, telex 837330 OXPRES G. **(Subscription address:** Oxford University Press / USA, Journals Marketing Department, Oxford University Press, 2001 Evans Road, Cary NC 27513.**) ED** A. Dipple, R. C. Garner and C. C. Harris. **LC** RC268.5; .C34. **DD** 616.99/4071. **NLM** W1 CA7623. **CODEN** CRNGDP. **[CCC]. Bk Rev. Ad Acc. Pr Rev. Circ:** 800. available on microfilm and microfiche from University Microfilms International (UMI). Documents available from The Genuine Article, BIOSIS Document Express, CASDDS.
**Desc:** A multidisciplinary journal covering all aspects of research leading ultimately to the prevention of cancer in man: viral, physical, chemical carcinogenesis and mutagenesis and modifying factors.
**Ind/Abst** Anal. Abstr.; Biol. Abstr.; Chem. Abstr.; Chem. Hazards Ind.; Chem. Titles; CSA Neuro. Abstr. (?-?); Curr. Aware. Biol. Sci., CABS; Curr. Contents Life Sci.; Curr. Titl. Dent.; Dairy Sci. Abstr.; EMBASE; Energy Res. Abstr. (Sept. 1980-); Food Sci. Technol. Abstr.; Genet. Abstr.; Health Plan. Adminis.; Helminthol. Abstr. (1991-); Index Med. (Jan. 1980-); Index Vet.; Lab. Hazards Bull.; Maize Abstr.; Microbiol. Abstr. Sect. C; Nucl. Acids Abstr.; Nutr. Abstr. Rev., Ser. B, Live Feeds and Feed.; Nutr. Abstr. Rev., Ser. A, Hum. Exp.; Nutr. Res. Newsl.; Oncog. Growth Factors Abstr.; Life Sci. Collect.; Pig News Inf.; Ref. Upd. Basic Ed.; Ref. Upd. Deluxe Ed.; Res. Alert [Full Cov.]; Rev. Agric. Entomol.; Rev. Med. Vet. Entomol.; Rev. Med. Vet. Mycology; Sci. Cit. Index; SCISEARCH; Vet. Bull.; Toxicol. Abstr.; Virol. AIDS Abstr.

US
**CARCINOGENICITY OF NITROSO COMPOUNDS.** **Main/Corp** International Cancer Research Data Bank. Periodical. English. US Department of Health and Human Services National Institutes of Health, 9000 Rockville Pike, Bethesda MD 20892. **Tel** (301)496-9291, FAX (301)496-2443.

US/1058-4986
**CHANGING VIEWS IN SURGICAL ONCOLOGY.** (1991)-. Periodical. English. Three times a year. Miniscus Health Care Communications, 1623 Spruce Street, Philadelphia PA 19103.

GW/0940-6735
**CHEMOTHERAPIE-JOURNAL.** (1992)-. German. qt. DM84.00. Wissenschaftliche Verlagsgesellschaft mbH, Postfach 101061, D 70009 Stuttgart Germany. **Tel** 011 49 711 2582200, FAX 011 49 711 2582290, telex 723636 DAZ D. **ED** B. Wiedemann, K.G. Naber.

SZ/0009-3157
**CHEMOTHERAPY (BASEL).** (CHEMOTHERAPY.). [Chemotherapy]. **Added/Corp** International Society of Chemotherapy. Vol. 13, No. 1 (1968)-. Academic Scholarly Publication. English. bm (6 issues). $354.00. S. Karger AG, Allschwilerstrasse 10, PO Box - Postfach - Case Postale, CH-4009 Basel Switzerland. **Tel** 011 41 61 306-1111, FAX 011 41 61 306-1234, telex CH 962 652. **ED** H. Schonfeld. **DD** 615. **NLM** W1 CH399. **CODEN** CHTHBK. **[CCC]. Ad Acc. Pr Rev.** available on microfilm and microfiche from

University Microfilms International (UMI). Documents available from The Genuine Article, BIOSIS Document Express, CASDDS. ***Continues*** *Chemotherapia, 0366-7170.*
**Desc:** Publishes the results of investigations into the mode of action and pharmacologic properties of antibacterial, antiviral and antitumor substances used in chemotherapy. Although experimental work predominates, clinical studies are included. Papers selected for the journal offer data concerning the efficacy, toxicology, and interaction of new drugs in single and combined applications. The journal also publishes studies designed to determine pharmacokinetic properties or evaluate the comparative efficacy of similar preparations. The growth of chemotherapeutic applications is well served through the large number of contributions published in each issue.
**Ind/Abst** Biol. Abstr.; Chem. Abstr.; Chem. Titles; Curr. Aware. Biol. Sci., CABS; Curr. Contents Life Sci.; Dairy Sci. Abstr.; EMBASE; Health Plan. Adminis.; Immunol. Abstr.; Index Med.; Index Dent. Lit.; Index Vet.; Int. Pharm. Abstr.; Iowa Drug Inf. Serv. (1966-); Microbiol. Abstr. Sect. B; Microbiol. Abstr. Sect. A; Microbiol. Abstr. Sect. C; NAPRALERT; Life Sci. Collect.; PESTDOC; Protozoolog. Abstr.; Ref. Upd. Deluxe Ed.; Res. Alert [Full Cov.]; Rev. Med. Vet. Mycology; Rev. Plant Pathol.; Sci. Cit. Index; SCISEARCH; Small Anim. Abstr. Bibliogr.; Vet. Bull.

JA/0009-3165
**CHEMOTHERAPY (TOKYO).** (NIHON KAGAKU RYOHO GAKKAI ZASSHI.). [Chemotherapy]. **Added/Corp** Nihon Kagaku Ryoho Gakkai. **VFOAT** Chemotherapy. Vol. 1, No. 1 (Sept. 1953)-. Academic Scholarly Publication. Japanese (summaries and/or abstracts in English). mo. $206.00. Nihon Kagaku Ryoho Gakkai, (Japan Soc. of Chemotherapy), 20-8, Kamiosaki 2 Chome, Shinagawaku, Tokyoto 141, Japan. **(Subscription address:** Kyowa Book Company, Inc., 1-38 Kanda Jinbo-Cho, Chiyoda-Ku Tokyo 101, Japan**) NLM** W1 NI918D. **CODEN** NKRZAZ. available on microfilm and microfiche from University Microfilms International (UMI). Documents available from CASDDS.
**Ind/Abst** Chem. Abstr.; EMBASE; NAPRALERT; Life Sci. Collect.; PESTDOC.

JA
**CHIBA-KEN GAN SENTA NEMPO.**
**Main/Corp** Chiba-Ken Gan Senta. No. 1- ; 1972/73-. Japanese. Chiba-ken Gan Senta, 666-2 Nitonacho, Chiba Japan. **LC** RC267; .C45A.

UK/0262-0898
**CLINICAL & EXPERIMENTAL METASTASIS.** [Clin. exp. metastasis]. **VFOAT** Clinical and Experimental Metastasis. Vol. 1, No. 1 (Jan./March 1983)-. Academic Scholarly Publication. English. bm. $499.00 US; £295.00 other. Rapid Communications of Oxford Ltd, The Old Malthouse, Paradise Street, Oxford OX1 1LD England. **Tel** 011 44 0865 790447, FAX 011 44 0865 244012, telex 9403712. **ED** Kurt Hellmann, G. Nicolson, L. Milas, and S. Eccles. **NLM** W1; CL664BH. **CODEN** CEXMD2. **[CCC].** Index available. **Bk Rev. Ad Acc. Pr Rev. Acid Free. Circ:** 230. available on microfilm and microfiche from University Microfilms International (UMI). Documents available from The Genuine Article, BIOSIS Document Express, CASDDS, ADONIS.
**Desc:** An international journal publishing the latest research into all aspects of clinical and experimental metastasis.
**Ind/Abst** ADONIS; Biol. Abstr.; Chem. Abstr. (1983-); CSA Neuro. Abstr.; Curr. Aware. Biol. Sci., CABS; Curr. Contents Life Sci.; EMBASE; Health Plan. Adminis.; Index Med. (Vol. 1, No. 1, 1983-); Oncog. Growth Factors Abstr.; Life Sci. Collect.; Res. Alert [Full Cov.]; Sci. Cit. Index; SCISEARCH.

US/0164-985X
**CLINICAL CANCER LETTER, THE.** Vol. 1, No. 1 (Jan. 1978)-. Periodical. English. mo. $65.00 US, Canada, Mexico and the Caribbean; $77.00 other. Cancer Letter Inc., PO Box 15189, Washington DC 20003. **Tel** (202)543-7665, FAX (202)543-6879. **ED** Jerry Boyd. **NLM** W1; CL671F. Index available (annual index free to subscribers). **Circ:** 2,000.
**Desc:** Advances in clinical cancer research. Back issues available.

UK/0936-6555
**CLINICAL ONCOLOGY : A JOURNAL OF THE ROYAL COLLEGE OF RADIOLOGISTS. Added/Corp** Royal College of Radiologists (Great Britain). Vol. 1, No. 1 (Sept. 1989)-. Periodical. English. Six times a year. £160.00. Springer-Verlag London Ltd., Springer House, 8 Alexandra Road Wimbledon, London SW19 7JZ England. **Tel** 011 44 81 9471280, or 9475885, FAX 011 44 81 9474651, telex 21531 SPRGB G. **(Subscription address:** North America: Springer Verlag, Journal Fulfillment Department, 44 Hartz Way, Secaucus, NJ 07096; Outside North America: Springer Verlag, Postfach 311340, D 10643 Berlin Germany**) NLM** W1; CL538. **CODEN** CLIOEH. **[CCC].** available on microfilm and microfiche from University Microfilms International (UMI).
**Desc:** A new journal convering all aspects of the clinical management of cancer patients, reflecting the current multidisciplinary approach to therapy.
**Ind/Abst** Health Plan. Adminis.; Index Med. (Sept. 1989-); Int. Nurs. Index.

US/0886-7186
**CLINICAL ONCOLOGY ALERT.** [Clin. oncol. alert]. Vol. 1, No. 1 (Jan. 1986)-. Periodical. English. mo. $115.00 without CME; $165.00 with CME. American Health Consultants, 3525 Piedmont Road, Suite 400, Atlanta GA 30305. **Tel** (800)688-2421, (404)262-7436. **(Subscription address:** American Health Consultants, PO Box 95278, Chicago IL 60694.**) ED** Dan L Lango. **DD** 616.

JA/0077-3662
**COLLECTED PAPERS FROM THE NATIONAL CANCER RESEARCH INSTITUTE. Added/Corp** Kokuritsu Gan Senta. Kenkyusho. Vol. 1 (1962/65)-. Periodical. English. an. Koseisho Kokuritsu Gan Senta Toshokan, (National Cancer Center Library), 1-1 Tsukiji 5-Chome Chuoku, Tokyoto 104 Japan. **Tel** (03)271 2511. **NLM** W1; CO169E. Index available. **Circ:** 300 (ctrl).
**Desc:** Collected papers of journal articles published in the former year.

CN/0707-5995
**COMMUNIQUE - MANITOBA DIVISION, CANADIAN CANCER SOCIETY. Main/Corp** Canadian Cancer Society. Manitoba Division. Began publication with Jan. 1978 issue?. Periodical. English. qt. Free. Canadian Cancer Society, 10 Alcorn Avenue, Suite 200, Toronto ONT M4V 3B1 Canada. **Tel** (416)961-7223. **DD** 362.1/9/69940097127. ***Continues*** *Cancer Comment, 0707-5987.*

US/0197-3649
**CONTEMPORARY HEMATOLOGY/ONCOLOGY. See** Medical Science and Technology-Hematology.

US/0892-0079
**CONTEMPORARY ISSUES IN CLINICAL ONCOLOGY.** [Contemp. issues clin. oncol.]. **VFOAT** Contemporary Issues in Oncology. Vol. 1 (1983)-. Monographic series. English. ir. Price varies per volume. Churchill Livingstone, 1-3 Baxter's Place, Leith Walk, Edinburgh EH1 3AF Scotland. **Tel** 011 44 31 556 2424, FAX 011 44 31 558 1278, telex 727511. **DD** 616. **NLM** W1; CO769MQHD.
**Desc:** An ongoing, authoritative book series that deals fully with the latest knowledge, thinking, advances and developments pertinent to malignant disease. Includes highly practical material on the newest techniques and approaches in cancer diagnosis, assessment, pathology and management. Each volume presents state-of-the-art contributions by experts on an oncological area of current significance.

US/1061-0383
**CONTEMPORARY ONCOLOGY.** [Contemp. oncol.]. (March/ April 1991)-. Periodical. English. mo. $69.00 US; $89.00 other. Medical Economics Publishing, Five Paragon Drive, Second Floor, Montvale NJ 07645. **Tel** (800)432-4570, (201)358-2210. **(Subscription address:** Fulco Medical Economics, PO Box 3000, Denville NJ 07834.**) DD** 616. **NLM** W1; CO769NLH.

US/1043-8637
**COPING (FRANKLIN, TENN.).** (COPING.). [Coping]. **VFOAT** Coping Magazine. (198?)-. Periodical. English. Six times a year (Jan., mar., May, July, Sept., Nov.). $18.00 one year; $32.00 two years. Media America Inc., 2019 North Carothers Road, Franklin TN 37064. **Tel** (615)790-2400. **LC** RC261.A1; C67. **DD** 616.99/4/005.

US/0893-9675
**CRITICAL REVIEWS IN ONCOGENESIS.** [Crit. rev. oncog.]. Vol. 1, Issue 1 (1989)-. Periodical. English. Six times a year. $297.00 (institutions), $99.95 (individuals). Begell House Inc., PO Box 1109, Pearl River NY 10965. **Tel** (212)725-1999. **ED** Enrique Pimentel. **DD** 616. **NLM** W1; CR216ZE. **CODEN** CRONEI. **[CCC].** Index available. **Pr Rev.** Documents available from BIOSIS Document Express.
**Desc:** Offers a selection of extensive reviews on topics of current interest in the field of basic oncology.
**Ind/Abst** Biol. Abstr. (1991-); Curr. Aware. Biol. Sci., CABS; Curr. Contents Life Sci.; Index Med. (1989-); Sci. Cit. Index.

US/1040-8428
**CRITICAL REVIEWS IN ONCOLOGY/HEMATOLOGY.** [Crit. rev. oncol./hematol.]. **Added/Corp** Chemical Rubber Company. **VFOAT** CRC Critical Reviews in Oncology/Hematology. **VAT** Chemical Rubber Company Critical Reviews in Oncology/Hematology. Vol. 1, Issue 1 (1983)-. Academic Scholarly Publication. English. Nine times a year (3 volumes). $667.00. Elsevier Science Ireland Ltd., Bay 15, Shannon Industrial Estate, Co Clare Ireland. **Tel** 011 353 61 471944. **LC** RC254.A1; C73. **DD** 616.99/2/005. **NLM** W1; CR1244. **CODEN** CCRHEC. **[CCC].** Documents available from The Genuine Article. ***Continues*** *CRC Critical Reviews in Oncology/Hematology, 0737-9587.*
**Desc:** Provides timely, critical, and analytical evaluations in the areas of etiology, epidemiology, diagnosis, treatment, pathophysiology, immunology, and cell biology.
**Ind/Abst** Curr. Aware. Biol. Sci., CABS; Curr. Contents Clin. Med.; EMBASE; Health Plan. Adminis.; Index Med.; Index Sci. Rev. [Full Cov.]; Life Sci. Collect.; Ref. Upd. Deluxe Ed.; Res. Alert [Full Cov.]; Sci. Cit. Index; SCISEARCH.

UK/0895-9803
**CURRENT ADVANCES IN CANCER RESEARCH. See** Medical Science and Technology-Abstracting, Bibliographies and Statistics.

●US/1074-2816
**CURRENT CANCER THERAPEUTICS.** [Curr. cancer ther.]. 1st Edition (1994)-. English. an. $39.95. Current Science, 20 North 3rd Street, Philadelphia PA 19106. **Tel** (215)574-2266, (800)552-5866, FAX (215)574-2270. **DD** 616.

●UK/0969-692X
**CURRENT CLINICAL CANCER.** Vol. 1 (1993)-. English. mo. £180.00 UK; $360.00 US. Carfax Publishing Company, PO Box 25 Abingdon, Oxfordshire OX14 3UE England. **Tel** 011 44 235 555335, FAX (0279)31067, telex 817484. **(Subscription address:** US and Canada/ PO Box 2025, Dunnellon, FL 34430-2025; telephone:(904)489-6996**)** Index available. available on microfiche; available on diskette.

US/0199-4697
**CURRENT CONCEPTS IN ONCOLOGY.** ***Suspended.*** [Curr. concepts oncol.]. Periodical. English. qt. Macmillan Publishing Company, 866 3rd Avenue, New York NY 10022. **Tel** (212)702-2000, (800)257-5755. **(Subscription address:** Front and Brown Street, Riverside, NJ 08370**) NLM** W1 CU788ASB.

US/0739-4810
**CURRENT HEMATOLOGY AND ONCOLOGY. See** Medical Science and Technology-Hematology.

US/0743-930X
**CURRENT ONCOLOGY.** [Curr. oncol.]. Began in 1984. Academic Scholarly Publication. English. an. Elsevier Science Publishing Company Inc, Madison Square Station, PO Box 882, New York NY 10159-0882. **Tel** (212)633-3950, FAX (212)633-3990. **DD** 616.

US/1040-8746
**CURRENT OPINION IN ONCOLOGY.** [Curr. opin. oncol.]. Vol. 1, No. 1 (Oct. 1989)-. Periodical. English. Six times a year (Feb., Apr., June, Aug., Oct., Dec.). $169.95 (individuals); $345.50 (institutions). Current Science, 20 North 3rd Street, Philadelphia PA 19106. **Tel** (215)574-2266, (800)552-5866, FAX (215)574-2270. **ED** Martin D. Abeloff. **LC** RC254.A1; C87. **DD** 616.99/2/005. **NLM** W1; CU799GGBL. **CODEN** CUOOE8. **[CCC].** available on diskette; available on microfilm from University Microfilms International (UMI). Documents available from BIOSIS Document Express.
**Desc:** Directed toward researchers and practicing oncologists. Each presents review articles from an area of concentration covering an entire year's literature with annotated references. Each issue features a bibliography of the current world literature published during the previous year.
**Ind/Abst** Biol. Abstr. (1991-); Cumul. Index Nurs. Allied Health Lit.; Curr. Aware. Biol. Sci., CABS; EMBASE; Health Plan. Adminis.; Index Med. (1989-).

US/0147-0272
**CURRENT PROBLEMS IN CANCER.** [Curr. probl. cancer]. **VFOAT** CPCA. Current Problems in Cancer. Vol. 1, (July 1976)-. Monographic series. English. bm. $95.00 (institutions), $68.00 (individuals) US; $101.00 (institutions), $74.00 (individuals) other. Mosby Year Book Inc., 11830 Westline Industrial Drive, St Louis MO 63146. **Tel** (800)325-4177, (314)872-8370, FAX (314)432-1380, telex 44-2402. **ED** Charles M. Haskell. **DD** 616. **NLM** W1 CU804HI. **CODEN** CPRCDJ. **[CCC].** Index available. **Pr Rev.** available on microfilm and microfiche from University Microfilms International (UMI). Documents available from The Genuine Article, BIOSIS Document Express.
**Desc:** Addressed to physicians who treat patients with neoplastic disease - surgeons, medical oncologists, radiation therapists, and practitioners in surgical subspecialties. Each issue is a single topic discussion that generally focuses on the integrated management of a particular type of cancer or a particular problem faced in a wide variety of malignancies.
**Ind/Abst** Biol. Abstr.; Curr. Contents Clin. Med.; Energy Res. Abstr. (April 1982-); Health Plan. Adminis.; Index Med.; INIS Atomindex [Micro.]; Res. Alert [Full Cov.]; Sci. Cit. Index; SCISEARCH.

US
**DETECTION, DIAGNOSIS, AND THERAPY, AND PRE-CLINICAL BIOLOGY OF BREAST CANCER, THE.**
**Main/Corp** International Cancer Research Data Bank. Periodical. English. US Department of Health and Human Services National Institutes of Health, 9000 Rockville Pike, Bethesda MD 20892. **Tel** (301)496-9291, FAX (301)496-2443.

Medical Science and Technology —Neoplasma, Neoplastic

US
**DETECTION, DIAGNOSIS, AND THERAPY OF LUNG CANCER, THE.** **Main/Corp** International Cancer Research Data Bank. Periodical. English. US Department of Health and Human Services National Institutes of Health, 9000 Rockville Pike, Bethesda MD 20892. **Tel** (301)496-9291, FAX (301)496-2443.

GW/0931-0037
**DEUTSCHE ZEITSCHRIFT FUER ONKOLOGIE.** **Added/Corp** Deutsche Gesellschaft feur Onkologie. **VFOAT** DZO. Vol. 19 No. 1 (Feb. 1987)-. Periodical. German (English). Six times a year (Feb., Apr., June, Aug., Oct., Dec.). DM111.00. Verlag fuer Medizin VFM, Postfach 105767, W-6900 Heidelberg 1 Germany. **Tel** 011 49 6221 406248, FAX 011 49 6221 400727, telex 461683HVVFM D. **NLM** W1; DE906. Index available. cum. index. **Bk Rev.** **Ad Acc.** **Circ:** 4,500. ***Continues*** *Krebsgeschehen, 0340-5672.*
**Ind/Abst** EMBASE [Select. Cov.].

US/0163-6146
**DEVELOPMENTS IN CANCER RESEARCH.** [Dev. cancer res.]. Vol. 1 (1979)-. Academic Scholarly Publication. English. ir. Price varies per volume. Elsevier Science Publishing Company Inc, Madison Square Station, PO Box 882, New York NY 10159-0882. **Tel** (212)633-3950, FAX (212)633-3990. **(Subscription address:** Elsevier Science Inc. / New York Books, 655 Avenue of the Americas, New York NY 10010.**)** **NLM** W1 DE997VM. **CODEN** DCREDD. **Pr Rev.** Documents available from CASDDS.
**Ind/Abst** Chem. Abstr.

NE/0167-4927
**DEVELOPMENTS IN ONCOLOGY.** [Dev. oncol.]. (1980)-. Academic Scholarly Publication. English. ir. Price varies per volume. Kluwer Academic Publishers, Postbus 322, 3300 AH Dordrecht, The Netherlands. **Tel** 011 (31) 78 524400, FAX 011 31 78 183273, telex 20083. **LC** UNC. **NLM** W1 DE998N. **CODEN** DEOND5. Documents available from BIOSIS Document Express, CASDDS.
**Ind/Abst** Biol. Abstr. (1987-); Chem. Abstr.

US
**DIAGNOSIS AND TREATMENT OF HODGKIN'S DISEASE.** **Main/Corp** International Cancer Research Data Bank. Periodical. English. US Department of Health and Human Services National Institutes of Health, 9000 Rockville Pike, Bethesda MD 20892. **Tel** (301)496-9291, FAX (301)496-2443.

US
**DIAGNOSIS AND TREATMENT OF SARCOMAS AND RELATED TUMORS.** **Main/Corp** International Cancer Research Data Bank. Periodical. English. US Department of Health and Human Services National Institutes of Health, 9000 Rockville Pike, Bethesda MD 20892. **Tel** (301)496-9291, FAX (301)496-2443.

SZ/1013-8129
**DIAGNOSTIC ONCOLOGY.** Vol. 1 (Jan./Feb. 1991)-. Periodical. English. bm (6 issues). $387.00. S. Karger AG, Allschwilerstrasse 10, PO Box - Postfach - Case Postale, CH-4009 Basel Switzerland. **Tel** 011 41 61 306-1111, FAX 011 41 61 306-1234, telex CH 962 652. **ED** A. Malkin. **NLM** W1; DI258JP. **CODEN** DIONEY. Index available. cum. index. **Ad Acc.** **Pr Rev.** **Circ:** 1,000. available on microfilm; available on microfiche. Documents available from The Genuine Article, BIOSIS Document Express.
**Desc:** Forum for the latest developments in cancer diagnosis. Multidisciplinary in scope, the journal features clinically relevant contributions from the fields of medical, surgical and radiation oncology, pathology, tumor immunology, and diagnostic imaging. In addition to original papers, reviews, and case reports there are regular interdisciplinary symposia on specific organ systems which serve to enhance the journal's permanent reference value. Places emphasis on the practical evaluation of new diagnostic technology and monitoring techniques.
**Ind/Abst** Biol. Abstr.; Curr. Contents Clin. Med.; Ref. Upd. Deluxe Ed.; Res. Alert [Select. Cov.]; SCISEARCH.

US/0883-0312
**DIRECTIONS IN ONCOLOGY.** [Dir. oncol.]. (198?)-. Periodical. English. bw. $295.00. Nassau Publications Inc., 11 Forest Street, New Canaan CT 06840. **DD** 616.

AG
**DIRECTORIO ONCOLOGICO LATINOAMERICANO / FLASCA, FEDERACION LATINOAMERICANA DE SOCIEDADES DE CANCEROLOGIA.** **Added/Corp** Federacion Latinoamericana de Sociedades de Cancerologia. **VFOAT** Directorio de Oncologos Latinoamericanos. (1986)-. Periodical. Spanish. ir (every 3 years). Federal Latinoamerican Society of Cancer Fund, Paraguay 5190, Buenos Aires 1425 Argentina. **Tel** 771-2543. **NLM** QZ 22; DA4 D5.

US/0090-7359
**DIRECTOR'S REPORT - PAPANICOLAOU CANCER RESEARCH INSTITUTE AT MIAMI FLORIDA.** (DIRECTOR'S REPORT.). [Dir. rep. - Papanicolaou Cancer Res. Inst. Miami Fla.]. **Main/Corp** Papanicolaou Cancer Research Institute. English. Papanicolaou Cancer Research Institute, Miami FL 33135. **LC** RC261; .A4225. **DD** 616.9/94/0072075938.

FR
**DIRECTORY OF AGENTS BEING TESTED FOR CARCINOGENICITY.** **Added/Corp** International Agency for Research on Cancer. (1990)-. Directory. English. be. International Agency for Research on Cancer, 150 cours Albert Thomas, 69372 Lyon Cedex 08 France. **Tel** 72.73.84.85, FAX 72 738 575, telex 380023. **(Subscription address:** World Health Organizations, Avenue Appia, 1211 Geneva 27, Switzerland**)** **ED** Ghess MJ and Wilbourn. **NLM** QZ 22.1; I43. Index available. ***Continues*** *Information Bulletin on the Survey of Chemicals Being Tested for Carcinogenicity, 0258-1043.*
**Desc:** This directory gives data received from 82 institutes in 21 countries on 796 chemicals, and agents tested..

US/0277-3414
**DIRECTORY OF MEMBERS / AMERICAN ASSOCIATION FOR CANCER RESEARCH.** [Dir. memb. - Am. Assoc. Cancer Res.]. **Main/Corp** American Association for Cancer Research. **VFOAT** A.A.C.R. Directory of Members; AACR Directory of Members. 1980-1981-. Directory. English. **LC** RC261.A1. **DD** 616.99/4027/02573. **NLM** QZ 22 AA1 A51D. ***Continues in part*** *Annual Meeting of the American Association for Cancer Research. Proceedings, 0197-106X.*

US
**DIRECTORY OF MEMBERS - AMERICAN FEDERATION OF CLINICAL ONCOLOGIC SOCIETIES.** **Main/Corp** American Federation of Clinical Oncologic Societies. Began with Vol. for 1973/74. Directory. English. American Federation of Clinical Oncologic Societies, 219 East 42nd Street, New York NY 10017. **Tel** (212)371-2900. **LC** RC276; .A74A. **DD** 616.9/92/002573. **NLM** QZ 22 AA1 A52.

FR
**DIRECTORY OF ON-GOING RESEARCH IN CANCER EPIDEMIOLOGY.** **Added/Corp** International Agency for Research on Cancer. International Cancer Research Data Bank. Deutsches Krebsforschungszentrum Heidelberg. National Cancer Institute (U.S.). International Cancer Information Center. **VFOAT** Directory of Ongoing Research in Cancer Epidemiology; PROSE. (1976)-. English. ir. Price varies per volume. Oxford University Press, Walton Street, Oxford OX2 6DP England. **Tel** 011 44 865 56767, FAX 011 44 865 267773, telex 837330 OXPRES G. **(Subscription address:** Oxford University Press / USA, Journals Marketing Department, Oxford University Press, 2001 Evans Road, Cary NC 27513.**)** **ED** M.P. Coleman and J. Wahrendorf. **LC** RC267; .D57. **DD** 616.99/4071/072. **NLM** W1 I21K no.17 etc. available on diskette; available with illustrations.

UN/0204-3564
**EKSPERIMENTALNAJA ONKOLOGIJA.** (EKSPERIMENTALNAIA ONKOLOGIIA.). [Eksp. onkol.]. **Added/Corp** Akademiia Nauk SSSR. Otdelenie Fiziologii. Akademiia Nauk Ukrainskoi RSR. Otdelenie Biokhimii, Fiziologii i Teoreticheskoi Meditsiny. **VFOAT** Experimental Oncology. (1979)-. Academic Scholarly Publication. Russian (summaries and/or abstracts in English). Six times a year. $109.95. Izdatelstvo Naukova Dumka / Ukrainian Academy of Sciences, Vladimirskaia Ulitsa 54, 252601 Kiev Ukraine. **Tel** 225-63-66, telex 131376. **(Subscription address:** East View Publications Inc., 3020 Harbor Lane North, Suite 110, Minneapolis MN 55447.**)** **NLM** W1; EK482G. **CODEN** EKSODD. **Pr Rev.** Documents available from The Genuine Article, BIOSIS Document Express, CASDDS.
**Ind/Abst** Biol. Abstr.; Chem. Abstr.; Energy Res. Abstr. (Sept. 1982-); Health Plan. Adminis.; Immunol. Abstr.; Index Med. (Vol. 6, No. 1, 1984-); Index Vet.; Oncog. Growth Factors Abstr.; Life Sci. Collect.; Res. Alert [Full Cov.]; Rev. Med. Vet. Entomol.; Sci. Cit. Index; SCISEARCH; Vet. Bull.

US/8756-1689
**ENDOCURIETHERAPY / HYPERTHERMIA ONCOLOGY.** (ENDOCURIETHERAPY / HYPERTHERMIA ONCOLOGY: THE OFFICIAL JOURNAL OF THE AMERICAN ENDOCURIETHERAPY SOCIETY.). **Added/Corp** American Endocurietherapy Society. Endocurietherapy Research Foundation. **VFOAT** Endocurietherapy Hyperthermia Oncology. Vol. 1, No. 1 (Jan. 1985)-. Periodical. English. qt. $70.00 (individiual), $150.00 (insitution) US; $80.00 (individual), $160.00 (institution) Canada & Europe; $85.00 (individual), 170.00 (institution) other. ECHO/ Department of Radiation Oncology, 2801 Atlantic Avenue, Long Beach CA 90801. **Tel** (213)933-2929, FAX (310)933-2913. **ED** Nisar Syed, Khalid M A Sheikh, Basil S Hilaris and Ajmel A Puthawala. **DD** 616. **NLM** W1; EN396SW. **Bk Rev.** **Ad Acc, Adv Mgr:** Khalid Sheikh, PhD. **Pr Rev.** **Circ:** 1500.
**Desc:** Publishes information on the techniques and clinical application of interstitial, intraluminal, intracavity irradiation and hyperthermia in the management of cancer patients including laboratory and experimental research relevant to clinical practice.

US/0882-8164
**ENVIRONMENTAL CARCINOGENESIS REVIEWS.** ***Title Change.*** (ENVIRONMENTAL CARCINOGENESIS REVIEWS : PART C OF JOURNAL OF ENVIRONMENTAL SCIENCE AND HEALTH.). [Environ. carcinog. rev.]. **VFOAT** Part C of Journal of Environmental Science and Health; Journal of Environmental Science and Health. Vol. C3, No. 1 (1985)-(199?). Academic Scholarly Publication. English. tq. Marcel Dekker Inc., 270 Madison Avenue, New York NY 10016. **Tel** (212)696-9000, (800)228-1160, FAX (212)685-4540, telex 421419. **(Subscription address:** Marcel Dekker Inc, PO Box 5017, Monticello NY 12701.**)** **ED** Joseph C Arcos, Mary F Argus, Yin-Tak Woo. **LC** RC268.5; .J68. **DD** 616.99/4071/05. **NLM** W1; EN981GF. **CODEN** ECRVE8. Index available. cum. index. **Bk Rev.** **Ad Acc.** **Pr Rev.** Documents available from CASDDS, Documents on Demand. ***Continues*** *Journal of Environmental Science and Health. Part C, Environmental Carcinogenesis Reviews, 0736-3001.* ***Continued by*** *Journal of Environmental Science and Health. Part C, Environmental Carcinogenesis & Ecotoxicology Reviews, 1059-0501.*
**Desc:** A multidisciplinary journal for the rapid publication of integrative, critical reviews on timely and important subjects in various areas of environmental carcinogenesis. Among the subjects covered are synergism and antagonism; theoretical models; inhibition of carcinogenesis; interaction of physical, chemical, and biological factors; and others.
**Ind/Abst** AGRICOLA [Select. Cov.]; Chem. Abstr. (1985-); EMBASE; Energy Res. Abstr. (1985-); Environ. Abstr.; Environ. Period. Bibliogr. (?-?); Index Sci. Rev. [Full Cov.]; Nutr. Res. Newsl.; Life Sci. Collect.; Ref. Upd. Deluxe Ed.

GW/0720-3462
**ERGEBNISSE DER CHIRURGISCHEN ONKOLOGIE.** (ERGEBNISSE DER CHIRURGISCHEN ONKOLOGIE : VERHANDLUNGEN DER CHIRURGISCHEN ARBEITSGEMEINSCHAFT FUR ONKOLOGIE (CAO) DER DEUTSCHEN GESELLSCHAFT FUR CHIRURGIE E.V.). 1-. German. Ferdinand Enke Verlag, Ruedigerstrasse 14, D-70469 Stuttgart Germany. **Tel** 011 49 711 8931124, 011 49 711 893123. **NLM** W1 ER264D.

GW/0932-3279
**ERGEBNISSE DER INTERNISTISCHEN ONKOLOGIE.** [Ergeb. internist. Onkol.]. (1986)-. Periodical. German. Ferdinand Enke Verlag, Ruedigerstrasse 14, D-70469 Stuttgart Germany. **Tel** 011 49 711 8931124, 011 49 711 893123. **NLM** W1; ER281P.

US
**ETIOLOGY OF CANCER IN THE GENERAL POPULATION.** **Main/Corp** International Cancer Research Data Bank. (197?)-. Periodical. English. Price upon application. US Department of Health and Human Services National Institutes of Health, 9000 Rockville Pike, Bethesda MD 20892. **Tel** (301)496-9291, FAX (301)496-2443.

NE/0921-3732
**EUROPEAN CANCER NEWS.** [Eur. cancer news]. **Added/Corp** European Society for Medical Oncology. Vol. 1, No. 1 (Sept. 1987)-. Periodical. English. Ten times a year (10 issues per year). $239.00. Kluwer Academic Publishers, Postbus 322, 3300 AH Dordrecht, The Netherlands. **Tel** 011 (31) 78 524400, FAX 011 31 78 183273, telex 20083. **ED** J. Gordon McVie. **NLM** W1; EU613. **CODEN** ECNEE5. **[CCC].** **Pr Rev.** **Acid Free.** available on microfilm and microfiche from University Microfilms International (UMI).
**Desc:** Has the highly respected reputation of providing up-to-date information on the research and treatment of cancer, not only in Europe, but also around the world.
**Ind/Abst** Ref. Upd. Deluxe Ed.; Trop. Dis. Bull.

UK/0959-8049
**EUROPEAN JOURNAL OF CANCER (1990).** (EUROPEAN JOURNAL OF CANCER.). [Eur. j. cancer]. **Added/Corp** European Organization for Research on Treatment of Cancer. European Association for Cancer Research. European School of Oncology. Federation of European Cancer Societies. **VFOAT** European Journal of Cancer. Part A; EJC. Vol. 26, No. 1 (Jan. 1990)-Vol. 28, No. 2/3 (Feb./Mar. 1992) Vol. 28A, No. 4/5 (Apr./May 1992)-. Periodical. English. Fourteen times a year. $1431.00 (regular subscription), $1587.00 (combined subscription with Part B) The Americas; £960.00 (regular subscription), £1065.00 (combined subscription with Part B) other. Pergamon Press, An Imprint of Elsevier Science Ltd., The Boulevard, Langford Lane, Kidlington, Oxford OX5 1GB United Kingdom. **Tel** 011 44 865 843000, 011 44 865 843699, FAX 011 44 865 843010. **(Subscription address:** Elsevier Science Ltd. Oxford Fulfillment Centre, PO Box 800, Kidlington, Oxford

OX5 1DX United Kingdom.) **LC** RC261.A1; E88. **NLM** W1; EU72BA. **CODEN** EJCAEL. available on microfilm and microfiche from University Microfilms International (UMI). Documents available from BIOSIS Document Express, CASDDS, Documents on Demand. ***Continues*** *European Journal of Cancer & Clinical Oncology, 0277-5379.* ***Continued in part by*** *European Journal of Cancer. Part B, Oral Oncology.*
**Ind/Abst** Biol. Abstr.; Chem. Abstr.; EMBASE; Energy Res. Abstr. (1990-); Environ. Abstr.; Immunol. Abstr.; Index Med. (1990-); INIS Atomindex [Micro.]; Med. Abstr. Newsl.; NAPRALERT; Life Sci. Collect.; PESTDOC; Pollut. Abstr. Indexes; Ref. Upd. Basic Ed.; Ref. Upd. Clinical Ed.; Ref. Upd. Deluxe Ed.; Rev. Med. Vet. Mycology.

UK/0961-5423
**EUROPEAN JOURNAL OF CANCER CARE / THE OFFICIAL JOURNAL OF THE EUROPEAN ONCOLOGY NURSING SOCIETY.** **See** Medical Science and Technology-Nursing.

●UK/0964-1955
**EUROPEAN JOURNAL OF CANCER. PART B : ORAL ONCOLOGY.** [Eur. j. cancer, Part B Oral oncol.]. **Added/Corp** European Organization for Research on Treatment of Cancer. European Association for Cancer Research. European School of Oncology. Federation of European Cancer Societies. **VFOAT** Oral Oncology; EJC. Oral Oncology; European Journal of Cancer. Oral Oncology. Vol. 28B, No. 1 (July 1992)-. Periodical. English. Fourteen times a year. $380.00 (regular subscription), $1587.00 (combined subscription with Part A) The Americas; £255.00 (regular subscription), £1065.00 (combined subscription with Part A) other. Pergamon Press, An Imprint of Elsevier Science Ltd., The Boulevard, Langford Lane, Kidlington, Oxford OX5 1GB United Kingdom. **Tel** 011 44 865 843000, 011 44 865 843699, FAX 011 44 865 843010. **(Subscription address:** Elsevier Science Ltd. Oxford Fulfillment Centre, PO Box 800, Kidlington, Oxford OX5 1DX United Kingdom.) **ED** Crispian Scully. **NLM** W1; EU72BAD. **[CCC]. *Separated from*** *European Journal of Cancer (Oxford, England : 1990), 0959-8049.*
**Ind/Abst** Curr. Aware. Biol. Sci., CABS; Ref. Upd. Basic Ed.; Ref. Upd. Clinical Ed.; Ref. Upd. Deluxe Ed.; Sci. Cit. Index.

UK/0959-8278
**EUROPEAN JOURNAL OF CANCER PREVENTION.** (19??)-. English. bm. $445.00 US; £260.00 other. Rapid Communications of Oxford Ltd, The Old Malthouse, Paradise Street, Oxford OX1 1LD England. **Tel** 011 44 0865 790447, FAX 011 44 0865 244012, telex 9403712. **[CCC]. Ad Acc. Acid Free.**
**Desc:** Aims to promote an increased awareness of all aspects of cancer prevention and to stimulate new ideas and innovations. The journal has a wide ranging scope, covering such aspects as descriptive and metabolic epidemiology, histopathology, genetics, biochemistry, molecular biology, microbiology, clinical medicine, intervention trials and public education, basic laboratory studies and special group studies.
**Ind/Abst** Curr. Aware. Biol. Sci., CABS.

IT/0392-2936
**EUROPEAN JOURNAL OF GYNAECOLOGICAL ONCOLOGY.** [Eur. j. gynaecol. oncol.]. Vol. 1, No. 1 (1980)-. Periodical. English. bm (6 issues). $200.00 (individuals), $300.00 (institutions). SOG/SRL, Galleria Storione 2A, 35123 Padua Italy. **Tel** 011 39 49 8756900, 8758644, FAX 8750860. **ED** A. Onnis. **NLM** W1 EU72DF. **CODEN** EJGODE. **[CCC]. Bk Rev. Ad Acc. Circ:** 500 (ctrl). Documents available from BIOSIS Document Express.
**Desc:** Clinical and experimental research in the field of gynecological oncology with particular reference to multimodality approaches to the treatment of cancer and clinical treatment.
**Ind/Abst** Biol. Abstr.; EMBASE; Health Plan. Adminis.; Index Med.; Nutr. Res. Newsl.

UK/0748-7983
**EUROPEAN JOURNAL OF SURGICAL ONCOLOGY.** [Eur. j. surg. oncol.]. Vol. 11, No. 1 (Mar. 1985)-. Periodical. English. bm (6 issues). £128.00 (institution), £90.00 (individual) UK/Europe; $230.00 (institution), $168.00 (individual) other. Harcourt Brace & Company Ltd., Foots Cray, High Street, Sidcup Kent DA14 5HP England. **Tel** 011 44 81 300 3322, FAX 011 44 81 309 0807. **(Subscription address:** W. B. Saunders Company / North America Subscriptions, c/o Periodicals, 6277 Sea Harbour Drive, 4th Floor, Orlando FL 32887.) **ED** I. Burn, I. S. Besznyak, J. A. van Dongen, F. Gall and P. J. Roberts. **DD** 616. **NLM** W1; EU72J. **[CCC]. Pr Rev. *Continues*** *Clinical Oncology, 0305-7399.*
**Desc:** Original articles and state-of-the-art reviews of interest to surgeons treating patients with cancer. In addition, papers are published on aspects of radiotherapy, chemotherapy, epidemiology, and pathology of cancer.
**Ind/Abst** EMBASE; Health Plan. Adminis.; Index Med.; Life Sci. Collect.; SCISEARCH.

NE/0014-4207
**EXCERPTA MEDICA. SECTION 16. CANCER.** **See** Medical Science and Technology-Abstracting, Bibliographies and Statistics.

NE/0304-3789
**EXCERPTA MEDICA. SECTION 65. CANCER IMMUNOLOGY. LITERATURE INDEX.** **See** Medical Science and Technology-Abstracting, Bibliographies and Statistics.

GW/0722-7566
**FAC, FORTSCHRITTE DER ANTIMIKROBIELLEN UND ANTINEOPLASTISCHEN CHEMOTHERAPIE.** (FORTSCHRITTE DER ANTIMIKROBIELLEN UND ANTINEOPLASTISCHEN CHEMOTHERAPIE.). [FAC, Fortschr. antimikrob. antineoplast. Chemother.]. **VFOAT** Fortschritte FAC der Antimikrobiellen und Antineoplastischen Chemotherapie; FAC. (1982)-. Academic Scholarly Publication. German. ir. Price varies per volume. Futuramed GmbH, Postfach 830358, D 830358 Munich Germany. **Tel** 011 49 59 674047. **NLM** W1; FO829R. **CODEN** FAACEX. Documents available from CASDDS.
**Ind/Abst** Chem. Abstr. (1982-).

US
**FLORIDA CANCER NEWS.** ***Ceased.*** Vol. 1 (1960)-(19??). English. qt. American Cancer Society Institute Activities, 1599 Clifton Road Northeast, Atlanta GA 30329.

IT/0392-047X
**FOLIA ONCOLOGICA.** [Folia oncol.]. (1978)-. Italian (English). Libreria Universitaria, Via Garruba 39, 70122 Bari Italy. **NLM** W1 FO265.
**Ind/Abst** EMBASE.

US/0162-7260
**FOREFRONT (NEW YORK).** (FOREFRONT.). [Forefront]. V. 1- Spring 1976-. Periodical. English. Three times a year. Forefront, Memorial Sloan-Kettering Cancer Center, 1275 York Avenue, New York NY 10021. **NLM** W1 FO558I.

US/0071-9676
**FRONTIERS OF RADIATION THERAPY AND ONCOLOGY.** [Front. radiat. ther. oncol.]. Vol. 1 (1968)-. Monographic series. English. an. 250.00F (approx. per volume). S. Karger AG, Allschwilerstrasse 10, PO Box - Postfach - Case Postale, CH-4009 Basel Switzerland. **Tel** 011 41 61 306-1111, FAX 011 41 61 306-1234, telex CH 962 652. **ED** J. L. Meyer. **LC** UNC. **NLM** W3 FR935. **CODEN** FRTOA7. **[CCC].** Documents available from BIOSIS Document Express, CASDDS.
**Desc:** In the field of oncology, research activities have accelerated and clinicians have sometimes been left far behind. The aim of this series is to communicate the results of laboratory investigations to a wider circle of physicians involved in the fight against cancer. Volumes are designed to acquaint health professionals with important advances in cancer management made possible through progress in such areas as therapeutic instrumentation, basic physiology, pharmaceutics, and psychology and patient counseling.
**Ind/Abst** Biol. Abstr.; Chem. Abstr. (1968-1983); Health Plan. Adminis.; Index Med.; Ref. Upd. Deluxe Ed.

SP
**FUNDACION CIENTIFICA DE LA ASOCIACION ESPANOLA CONTRA EL CANCER INFORMA.** **Added/Corp** Asociacion Espanola Contra el Cancer. Fundacion Cientifica. (19??)-. Periodical. Spanish. an. **LC** RC261.A1; F85. **DD** 616.99/4/005.

US/0739-7364
**FUNDAMENTALS OF CANCER MANAGEMENT.** [Fundam. cancer manage.]. (1983)-. Monographic series. English. ir. Price varies per volume. Marcel Dekker Inc., 270 Madison Avenue, New York NY 10016. **Tel** (212)696-9000, (800)228-1160, FAX (212)685-4540, telex 421419. **(Subscription address:** Marcel Dekker Inc, PO Box 5017, Monticello NY 12701.) **NLM** W1 FU5395.
**Desc:** Each title covers a different topic in cancer management.

JA/0021-4949
**GAN NO RINSHO.** [Gan no rinsho]. **VFOAT** Japanese Journal of Cancer Clinics. Vol. 1 (1954)-. Academic Scholarly Publication. Japanese. Twelve times a year. $343.50. Shinohara Shuppan K.K., (Shinohara Publishers, Inc.), 11-7, Hongo 2 Chome, Bunkyoku, Tokyoto 113 Japan. **(Subscription address:** Japan Publications Trading Company, Ltd., PO Box 5030, Tokyo International, Tokyo 100-31 Japan.) **NLM** W1 GA41E. **CODEN** GANRAE. Documents available from CASDDS.
**Ind/Abst** Chem. Abstr.; Index Med.; Life Sci. Collect.

JA/0385-0684
**GAN TO KAGAKU RYOHO.** (GAN TO KAGAKU RYOHO. CANCER & CHEMOTHERAPY.). [Gan to Kagaku ryoho]. **VFOAT** Cancer & Chemotherapy. (1974)-. Academic Scholarly Publication. Japanese (summaries and/or abstracts in English). Fourteen times a year. $454.00. Gan To Kagaku Ryohosha, 8-9, Yaesu 1 Chome, Chuoku, Tokyoto 103 Japan. **(Subscription address:** Kyowa Book Company Inc., 1-38 Kanda Jinbo-Cho, Chiyoda-Ku Tokyo 101, Japan) **NLM** W1 GA411. **CODEN** GTKRDX. Documents available from CASDDS.
**Ind/Abst** Chem. Abstr.; EMBASE; Health Plan. Adminis.; Index Med.

JA
**GANN MONOGRAPH ON CANCER RESEARCH.** **Added/Corp** Nihon Gan Gakkai. Vol. 11 (1971)-. Academic Scholarly Publication. English. Price varies per volume. University of Tokyo Press, 7 3 1 Hongo Bunkyo-ku, Tokyo 113 Japan. **Tel** 011 81 3 3811 0964. **NLM** W3 GA163. **CODEN** GMCRDC. Documents available from BIOSIS Document Express, CASDDS. ***Continues*** *Gann Monograph, 0072-0151.*
**Desc:** Consists of the proceedings of international conference and symposia.
**Ind/Abst** Biol. Abstr.; Chem. Abstr.; EMBASE; GeoRef.

US
**GASTROINTESTINAL CARCINOGENESIS.** **Main/Corp** International Cancer Research Data Bank. Periodical. English. US Department of Health and Human Services National Institutes of Health, 9000 Rockville Pike, Bethesda MD 20892. **Tel** (301)496-9291, FAX (301)496-2443.

US/1045-2257
**GENES, CHROMOSOMES & CANCER.** **See** Biology-Genetics.

●US/1064-9700
**GI CANCER.** **VFOAT** Gastrointestinal Cancer. (1993)-. Periodical. English. Four times a year. Harwood Academic Publishers / New York, PO Box 786, Cooper Station, New York NY 10276. **Tel** (212)206-8900, (201)643-7500. **(Subscription address:** Harwood Academic Publishers, PO Box 786, Cooper Station, New York NY 10276.) **[CCC].**
**Desc:** Features multidisciplinary clinical and laboratory data on gastrointestinal oncology.

IT/0392-128X
**GIORNALE ITALIANO DI ONCOLOGIA.** Vol. 1, No. 1 (Jan.-March 1981)-. Periodical. Italian (English). qt. $60.00. CIC Edizioni Internazionali, Via L Spallanzani 11, 00161 Rome Italy. **Tel** 011 39 6 841-2673, FAX 011 39 6 844-3365, telex 622099 CIC I. **ED** L. Caldarola, C. Moltoni. **NLM** W1; GI812F. **[CCC]. Bk Rev. Ad Acc.** ctrl circ.
**Ind/Abst** EMBASE [Select. Cov.]; Index Med.

US/0090-8258
**GYNECOLOGIC ONCOLOGY.** [Gynecol. oncol.]. **Added/Corp** Society of Gynecologic Oncology. Vol. 1 (Nov. 1972)-. Academic Scholarly Publication. English. mo. $805.00 US and Canada; $950.00 other. Academic Press, Inc., 6277 Sea Harbor Drive, Orlando FL 32887. **Tel** (800)543-9534, (407)345-4100, FAX (407)363-9661. **ED** David Gershenson, Larry Copeland, William Hoskins and Karl Podratz. **LC** RC280.G5; G88. **DD** 616.9/92/6505. **NLM** W1 GY557N. **CODEN** GYNOA3. **[CCC]. Pr Rev.** Documents available from The Genuine Article, BIOSIS Document Express, CASDDS.
**Desc:** Provides comprehensive coverage of the latest developments in the diagnosis, treatment, etiology, and histogenesis of tumors of the female reproductive tract.
**Ind/Abst** Biol. Abstr.; Chem. Abstr.; Curr. Contents Clin. Med.; EMBASE; Energy Res. Abstr. (Feb. 1976-); Health Plan. Adminis.; Index Med.; INIS Atomindex [Micro.]; Med. Abstr. Newsl.; Nutr. Res. Newsl.; Life Sci. Collect.; Res. Alert [Full Cov.]; Sci. Cit. Index; SCISEARCH.

JA/0386-9628
**HAIGAN.** [Haigan]. **VFOAT** Lung Cancer. (1969)-. Periodical. Multiple languages. qt. Japan Lung Cancer Society, 8-1 Inihana 1-chome, 280 Chiba Japan. **DD** 616.994. ***Continues*** *Haigan Kenkyukai Kiji.*
**Ind/Abst** EMBASE.

GW/0170-3064
**HAMBURGER KREBSDOKUMENTATION.** **Added/Corp** Hamburg (Germany). Statistisches Landesamt. (19??)-. German. Statistisches Landesamt, Steckelhorn 12, W-2000 Hamburg 11 Germany. **LC** RC279.G3; H35. **DD** 614.5/999/0943515021.

US/0736-8674
**HANDBOOK OF CANCER IMMUNOLOGY, THE.** [Handb. cancer immunol.]. **VFOAT** Cancer Immunology. Vol. 1 (1978)-. English. ir. **ED** Harold Waters. **LC** RC268.3; .H35. **DD** 616.99/4/079.
**Desc:** Comprehensive reference guide to cancer immunology.

CN/1180-3053
**HEALTH REPORTS. SUPPLEMENT. CANCER IN CANADA.** ***Title Change.*** (HEALTH REPORTS. SUPPLEMENT. CANCER IN CANADA / STATISTICS CANADA, CANADIAN CENTRE FOR HEALTH INFORMATION.). [Health rep., Suppl., Cancer Can.]. **Added/Corp** Centre Canadien d'Information sur la Sante. **VFOAT** Cancer in Canada; Cancer au Canada;

Medical Science and Technology —Neoplasma, Neoplastic

Rapports sur la Sante. Le Cancer au Canada. (1984)-(199?). French (English). an. Statistics Canada, Publications Sales & Services, Main Building Room 1710, Ottawa Ontario K1A 0T6 Canada. **Tel** (613)951-5078, (800)267-6677, FAX (613)951-1584, telex 053-3585. **DD** 614.5/999/0971021. ***Continues*** *Cancer in Canada, 0227-1788.* ***Continued by*** *Cancer in Canada (Centre Canadien d'Information sur la Sante), 1195-406X.*

●US/1067-2370
**HEM/ONC ANNALS.** See Medical Science and Technology-Hematology.

UK/0278-0232
**HEMATOLOGICAL ONCOLOGY.** See Medical Science and Technology-Hematology.

US/0889-8588
**HEMATOLOGY/ONCOLOGY CLINICS OF NORTH AMERICA.** See Medical Science and Technology-Hematology.

FR/0254-9719
**IARC INTERNAL TECHNICAL REPORT.** [IARC intern. tech. rep.]. **VAT** International Agency for Research on Cancer Internal Technical Report. Began in 1970?. Monographic series. English (French). Price varies per volume. **NLM** W1 I21E.

FR/1017-1606
**IARC MONOGRAPHS ON THE EVALUATION OF CARCINOGENIC RISKS TO HUMANS.** [IARC monogr. eval. carcinog. risks hum.]. **Added/Corp** International Agency for Research on Cancer. **VFOAT** IARC Monographs. **VAT** International Agency for Research on Cancer Monographs on the Evalutaion of Carcinogenic Risks to Humans. Vol. 43 (1988)-. Monographic series. English. ir. Price varies per volume. World Health Organization, Distribution and Sales, 20 Avenue Appia, CH-1211 Geneva 27 Switzerland. **Tel** 011 41 22 7912111, FAX 011 41 22 7880401. **(Subscription address:** Canadian Public Health Association, 1565 Carling Avenue, Suite 400, Ottawa ONT K1Z 8R1 Canada.) **LC** RC268.6; .I28a. **DD** 616.99/4071. **NLM** W1; IA21I. **CODEN** IMCHE5. Index available. cum. index. **Circ:** 3,500. ***Continues*** *IARC Monographs on the Evaluation of the Carcinogenic Risk of Chemicals to Man, 0250-9555.*
**Desc:** Reviews and evaluates scientific data on the carcinogenic risk to humans of a particular group of suspected carcinogenic agents.
**Ind/Abst** EMBASE; Index Med. (1988-); Trop. Dis. Bull.

FR/1014-711X
**IARC MONOGRAPHS ON THE EVALUATION OF CARCINOGENIC RISKS TO HUMANS. SUPPLEMENT.** (IARC MONOGRAPHS ON THE EVALUATION OF CARCINOGENIC RISKS TO HUMANS. SUPPLEMENT / WORLD HEALTH ORGANIZATION, INTERNATIONAL AGENCY FOR RESEARCH ON CANCER.). [IARC monogr. eval. carcinog. risks hum., Suppl.]. **Added/Corp** International Agency for Research on Cancer. **VFOAT** IARC Monographs. Supplement. **VAT** International Agency for Research on Cancer Monographs on the Evaluation of Carcinogenic Risks to Humans. Supplement. (1987)-. Monographic series. English. ir. Price varies per volume. World Health Organization, Distribution and Sales, 20 Avenue Appia, CH-1211 Geneva 27 Switzerland. **Tel** 011 41 22 7912111, FAX 011 41 22 7880401. **NLM** W1; IA21Ia. **CODEN** IMESEE. Documents available from BIOSIS Document Express. ***Continues*** *IARC Monographs. Supplement, 1014-4307.*
**Ind/Abst** Biol. Abstr.; Index Med. (1987-).

US/0883-5896
**IMPORTANT ADVANCES IN ONCOLOGY.** [Important adv. oncol.]. (1985)-. Academic Scholarly Publication. English. an. $79.50. J.B. Lippincott Company, 227 East Washington Square, Philadelphia PA 19106-3780. **Tel** (215)238-4200 or 4454, FAX (215)238-4227. **ED** Vincent T. Devita Jr., Samuel Hellman and Steven A. Rosenberg. **LC** RC261; .I44. **DD** 616.99/4/005. **NLM** W1; IM615. **CODEN** IAONEX. Documents available from BIOSIS Document Express, CASDDS.
**Ind/Abst** Biol. Abstr. (1988-); Chem. Abstr. (1985-1988); Health Plan. Adminis.; Index Med. (Vol. 1, 1985-).

II/0019-509X
**INDIAN JOURNAL OF CANCER.** [Indian j. cancer]. Vol. 1 (Oct. 1963)-. Academic Scholarly Publication. English. qt. Rs180.00 India, $55.00 other. Indian Cancer Society, 74 Jerbai Wadia Road, Parel Bombay 400 012 India. **Tel** 412 5238. **(Subscription address:** Prints India, 11 Darya Ganj, New Delhi 110002 India.) **ED** D. J. Jussawalla. **NLM** W1 IN206PT. **CODEN** IJCAAR. Index available. **Bk Rev. Ad Acc. Circ:** 1,000. available on microfilm from University Microfilms International (UMI). Documents available from BIOSIS Document Express, CASDDS.
**Desc:** Preventive oncology and cancer treatment.
**Ind/Abst** Biol. Abstr.; Chem. Abstr. (1963-1986); EMBASE; Index Med.; Life Sci. Collect.

II/0970-2563
**INDIAN JOURNAL OF CANCER CHEMOTHERAPY.** (INDIAN JOURNAL OF CANCER CHEMOTHERAPY : THE OFFICIAL ORGAN OF INDIAN ASSOCIATION OF CANCER CHEMOTHERAPISTS.). [Indian j. cancer chemother.]. **Added/Corp** Indian Association of Cancer Chemotherapists. Vol. 1, No. 1 (Oct./Dec. 1979)-. Periodical. English. sa. $10.00. **NLM** W1; IN206PU. **CODEN** ICCHD2. Documents available from CASDDS.
**Ind/Abst** Chem. Abstr.

SZ
**INTERNATIONAL DIRECTORY OF CANCER INSTITUTES AND ORGANIZATIONS.** **Added/Corp** International Union against Cancer. Committee on International Collaborative Activities. **VFOAT** UICC International Directory of Cancer Institutes and Organizations. 5th Ed. (1990)-. English. ir. $20.00. UICC International Union Against Cancer, 3 Rue Du Conseil General, CH 1205 Geneva Switzerland. **Tel** 011 41 22 3201811. **LC** RC261.A1; I574. **DD** 362.1/96994/0025 2 20. **NLM** QZ 22.1; I61. ***Continues*** *International Directory of Specialized Cancer Research and Treatment Establishments.*

IT/0393-6155
**INTERNATIONAL JOURNAL OF BIOLOGICAL MARKERS, THE.** [Int. j. biol. markers]. Vol. 1, No. 1 (Jan./Apr. 1986)-. Periodical. English. qt. $150.00. Wichtig Editore, Via Friuli 72 74, 20135 Milan Italy. **Tel** 011 39 2 55195443. **(Subscription address:** Wichtig Editore, Subscription Office, PO Box 830350, Birmingham AL 35283-0350.) **ED** Diego Brancaccio. **NLM** W1; IN76553H. **CODEN** IBMAEP. cum. index. **Bk Rev. Ad Acc. Pr Rev. Circ:** 1,000. Documents available from BIOSIS Document Express, CASDDS.
**Desc:** Reports on all the latest developments in tumor markers. It covers in-depth news and research on immunochemistry, immunoscintigraphy and immunotherapy methods, including approaches that will improve the diagnostic and therapeutic methods now available to oncologists.
**Ind/Abst** Biol. Abstr. (1990-); Chem. Abstr.; EMBASE; Index Med. (1986-); Ref. Upd. Deluxe Ed.

US/0020-7136
**INTERNATIONAL JOURNAL OF CANCER.** [Int. j. cancer]. **Added/Corp** International Union against Cancer. **VFOAT** Journal International du Cancer. Vol. 1 (Jan. 1966)-. Academic Scholarly Publication. English (French). Thirty times a year. 1,012.00. John Wiley & Sons, Inc., 605 Third Avenue, New York NY 10158-0012. **Tel** (212)850-6000, (212)850-6645, FAX (212)850-6088, telex 12-7063. **(Subscription address:** John Wiley & Sons / England, Baffins Lane, Chichester, West Sussex PO19 1UD England.) **ED** N. Odartchenko, P. Cerutti, and S. Carrel. **LC** RC261; .A34. **DD** 616.9/94/005. **NLM** W1 IN766B. **CODEN** IJCNAW. **[CCC].** Index available. **Bk Rev. Ad Acc. Pr Rev.** Documents available from The Genuine Article, BIOSIS Document Express, CASDDS, ADONIS. ***Supersedes*** *Acta - Unio Internationalis Contra Cancrum, 0365-3056.*
**Desc:** Publishes articles on all topics relevant to experimental and clinical cancer research, with an emphasis on fundamental studies that have relevance to the understanding of human cancer.
**Ind/Abst** ADONIS; Biol. Abstr.; Chem. Abstr.; CSA Neuro. Abstr. (?-?); Curr. Aware. Biol. Sci., CABS; Curr. Biotechnol.; Curr. Contents Life Sci.; Dairy Sci. Abstr.; EMBASE; Genet. Abstr.; Hum. Genome Abstr.; Immunol. Abstr.; Index Med.; Med. Abstr. Newsl.; NAPRALERT; Nutr. Abstr. Rev., Ser. A, Hum. Exp.; Nutr. Res. Newsl.; Oncog. Growth Factors Abstr.; Life Sci. Collect.; PESTDOC; Pollut. Abstr. Indexes; Ref. Upd. Basic Ed.; Ref. Upd. Deluxe Ed.; Res. Alert [Full Cov.]; Rev. Med. Vet. Mycology; Risk Abstr.; Sci. Cit. Index; SCISEARCH; Soc. Sci. Cit. Index [Select. Cov.]; Soyabean Abstr.; Trop. Dis. Bull.; Virol. AIDS Abstr.

US/0898-6924
**INTERNATIONAL JOURNAL OF CANCER. SUPPLEMENT.** [Int. j. cancer, Suppl.]. **VFOAT** Journal International du Cancer. Vol. 1 (1987)-. Periodical. English. $646.00. John Wiley & Sons, Inc., 605 Third Avenue, New York NY 10158-0012. **Tel** (212)850-6000, (212)850-6645, FAX (212)850-6088, telex 12-7063. **(Subscription address:** John Wiley & Sons / England, Baffins Lane, Chichester, West Sussex PO19 1UD England.) **LC** RC261.A1. **DD** 616. **NLM** W1; IN766BE.
**Ind/Abst** Index Med. (1987-).

GW/0933-0453
**INTERNATIONAL JOURNAL OF EXPERIMENTAL AND CLINICAL CHEMOTHERAPY.** [Int. j. exp. clin. chemother.]. Vol. 1 No. 1 (1988)-. Academic Scholarly Publication. English. qt. DM144.00 Germany; DM180.00 other. Medifact Publishing House, Marchioninistrasse 15, 86899 Munich 70 Germany. **Tel** 011 49 819159639. **(Subscription address:** Agentur Mrugalla, Schlesierstr 32A, D 86899 Landsberg Lech Germany.) **ED** E.R. Weissenbacher. **NLM** W1; IN766IN. **CODEN** IJECED. Documents available from BIOSIS Document Express, CASDDS.
**Desc:** Presents a worldwide forum for original basic and clinical research work, interpretative reviews, actual clinical experience and new methodological and technical procedures in the range of fields comprising chemotherapy.
**Ind/Abst** Biol. Abstr. (1989-); Chem. Abstr.; EMBASE.

US/1048-891X
**INTERNATIONAL JOURNAL OF GYNECOLOGICAL CANCER.** [Int. j. gynecol. cancer]. (1990)-. Academic Scholarly Publication. English. bm. $270.00 (institution), $190.00 (individual) US; $320.00 (institution), $190.00 (individual) other. Blackwell Scientific Publishers, 238 Main Street, Cambridge MA 02142. **Tel** (617)547-7110, (800)835-6770, FAX (617)547-0789. **ED** H Fox. **DD** 616. **NLM** W1; IN766TL. **[CCC].** available on microfilm and microfiche from University Microfilms International (UMI). Documents available from The Genuine Article.
**Desc:** Aims to draw together specialists from the various fields that contribute to our present understanding of gynecological cancer.
**Ind/Abst** Curr. Aware. Biol. Sci., CABS; Curr. Contents Clin. Med.; Res. Alert [Full Cov.]; Sci. Cit. Index; SCISEARCH.

GR/1019-6439
**INTERNATIONAL JOURNAL OF ONCOLOGY.** **Added/Corp** International Center for Cancer Research. Ethnikon Hidryma Ereunon (Greece). (199?)-. Periodical. English. mo. $300.00 (individuals), $500.00 (institutions) Europe; $350.00 (individuals), $550.00 (institutions) others. National Hellenic Research Foundation, 48 Vas Constatinou Avenue, Athens 11635 Greece. **Tel** 011 30 1 7241505, FAX 011 30 1 7241505. **ED** D. A. Spandidos. **NLM** W1; IN77TF. **CODEN** IJONES. **[CCC].** Index available (Bound in 6th iss.). **Bk Rev. Ad Acc. Pr Rev. Circ:** 1,000.
**Desc:** This journal is consisted of experts in cancer research who are member of The Editorial Academy.
**Ind/Abst** Sci. Cit. Index.

US/0360-3016
**INTERNATIONAL JOURNAL OF RADIATION- ONCOLOGY, BIOLOGY, PHYSICS.** [Int. j. radiat. oncol. biol. phys.]. **Added/Corp** American Society of Therapeutic Radiologists. International Society for Radiation Oncology. American Society for Therapeutic Radiology and Oncology. Circulo de Radioterapeutas Ibero-Latinoamericanos. Vol. 1 (Oct./Nov. 1975)-. Periodical. English. Fifteen times a year. $1594.00 The Americas; £1070.00 other. Pergamon Press, An Imprint of Elsevier Science Ltd., The Boulevard, Langford Lane, Kidlington, Oxford OX5 1GB United Kingdom. **Tel** 011 44 865 843000, 011 44 865 843699, FAX 011 44 865 843010. **(Subscription address:** Elsevier Science Ltd. Oxford Fulfillment Centre, PO Box 800, Kidlington, Oxford OX5 1DX United Kingdom.) **ED** Phillip Rubin. **LC** RC271.R3; I54. **DD** 616.9/94/064205. **NLM** W1 IN785R. **CODEN** IOBPD3. **[CCC]. Pr Rev.** available on microfilm and microfiche from University Microfilms International (UMI). Documents available from The Genuine Article, BIOSIS Document Express, Ask*IEEE, CASDDS.
**Desc:** Provides an international forum for the latest work and developments in radiation oncology, and it is specifically devoted to defining and chronicling the contribution of the discipline to cancer management and cancer research.
**Ind/Abst** Biol. Abstr.; Chem. Abstr.; CSA Neuro. Abstr. (?-?); Curr. Contents Clin. Med.; Curr. Contents Life Sci.; Dairy Sci. Abstr.; Ei Page One; EMBASE; Energy Res. Abstr. (March 1977-); Health Saf. Sci. Abstr.; Health Plan. Adminis.; Index Med.; INIS Atomindex [Micro.]; INSPEC (Nov./Dec. 1976-); Life Sci. Collect.; Pollut. Abstr. Indexes; Protozoolog. Abstr.; Ref. Upd. Basic Ed.; Ref. Upd. Deluxe Ed.; Res. Alert [Full Cov.]; Sci. Cit. Index; SCISEARCH; Soc. Sci. Cit. Index [Select. Cov.]; Toxicol. Abstr.

US/0167-6997
**INVESTIGATIONAL NEW DRUGS.** [Invest. new drugs]. **VFOAT** Journal of New Anticancer Agents. Vol. 1, No. 1 (1983)-. Academic Scholarly Publication. English. qt. $446.00. Kluwer Academic Publishers / Massachusetts, PO Box 358, Accord Station, Hingham MA 02018. **Tel** (617)871-6600. **ED** Daniel D Von Hoff. **NLM** W1 IN949R. **CODEN** INNDDK. **[CCC]. Pr Rev. Acid Free.** available on microfilm and microfiche from University Microfilms International (UMI). Documents available from The Genuine Article, CASDDS.
**Desc:** Provides a forum for the rapid dissemination of information on new anticancer agents which the medicinal chemist, toxicologist, pharmacist, pharmacologist, biostatistician and clinical oncologist may utilize for efficient communication and exchange of data.
**Ind/Abst** Chem. Abstr. (1983-); Curr. Aware. Biol. Sci., CABS; Curr. Contents Life Sci.; EMBASE; Index Med. (1983-); PESTDOC; Ref. Upd. Deluxe Ed.; Res. Alert [Full Cov.]; Sci. Cit. Index; SCISEARCH.

JA/0910-5050
**JAPANESE JOURNAL OF CANCER RESEARCH : GANN.** [Jpn. j. cancer res. (Gann)]. **Added/Corp** Nihon Gan Gakkai. **VFOAT** Japanese Journal of Cancer Research (Gann); Gann. Vol. 76, No. 1

(Jan. 1985)-. Academic Scholarly Publication. English. mo (1 volume). $527.00. Elsevier Science Ireland Ltd., Bay 15, Shannon Industrial Estate, Co Clare Ireland. **Tel** 011 353 61 471944. **ED** T. Sugimura. **NLM** W1; JA95P. **CODEN** JJCREP. **[CCC]. Pr Rev.** available on microfilm and microfiche from University Microfilms International (UMI). Documents available from The Genuine Article, BIOSIS Document Express, CASDDS. ***Continues** Gann, 0016-450x.*
**Desc:** The official organ of the Japanese Cancer Association and publishes articles describing original observations on all aspects of cancer, including both laboratory and clinical research.
**Ind/Abst** Biol. Abstr. (1985-); Chem. Abstr. (1985-); CSA Neuro. Abstr. (?-?); Curr. Aware. Biol. Sci., CABS; Curr. Contents Life Sci.; EMBASE; Genet. Abstr.; Helminthol. Abstr.; Immunol. Abstr.; Index Med.; NAPRALERT; Nutr. Res. Newsl.; Oncog. Growth Factors Abstr.; Ref. Upd. Deluxe Ed.; Res. Alert [Full Cov.]; Sci. Cit. Index; SCISEARCH; Soc. Sci. Cit. Index [Select. Cov.].

JA/0368-2811
**JAPANESE JOURNAL OF CLINICAL ONCOLOGY.** [Jpn. j. clin. oncol.]. **Added/Corp** Foundation of Clinical Oncology. Gan Kenkyu Shinkokai. Vol. 1 (Jan. 1971)-. Periodical. English. bm. $221.50. Gan Kenkyu Shinko Zaidan, (Foundation for Promotion of Cancer Research), Kokuritsu Gan Senta, 1-1, Tsukiji 5 Chome, Chuoku, Tokyoto 104 Japan. **(Subscription address:** Maruzen Company Ltd., PO Box 5050, Import & Export Department, Tokyo 100 31 Japan.**) NLM** W1 JA95R. **CODEN** JJCOAC. **Pr Rev.** Documents available from The Genuine Article, BIOSIS Document Express.
**Ind/Abst** Biol. Abstr.; Curr. Contents Clin. Med.; Index Med.; Nutr. Res. Newsl.; Life Sci. Collect.; Res. Alert [Select. Cov.]; SCISEARCH; Soc. Sci. Cit. Index [Select. Cov.].

IR/0378-2360
**JOURNAL OF CANCER.** [J. cancer]. **VFOAT** Taj Pahlavi Cancer Bulletin. Academic Scholarly Publication. English. **UDC** 616-006.6. **NLM** W1 JO572J. **CODEN** JCANDL. Documents available from CASDDS. ***Continues** Cancer Bulletin, 0304-145X.*
**Ind/Abst** Chem. Abstr.

●UK/0960-9768
**JOURNAL OF CANCER CARE.** (March 1992)-. Periodical. English. qt. £95.00 Europe; £97.00 Other (Institutions). Churchill Livingstone, 1-3 Baxter's Place, Leith Walk, Edinburgh EH1 3AF Scotland. **Tel** 011 44 31 556 2424, FAX 011 44 31 558 1278, telex 727511. **(Subscription address:** Maruzen Company Ltd., PO Box 5050, Import & Export Department, Tokyo 100 31 Japan.**) ED** Ann Faulkner and Irene Scott. **NLM** W1; JO573E. **Bk Rev.**
**Desc:** Covers cancer care in hospitals, homes, and hospices. As well as original research papers and review articles, the journal will also contain reports on international practice, including news and developments from the USA, case reports, an extensive bibliography, book reviews, a news section, reports from conferences, a calendar of international events and a timetable of further education courses.

US/0885-8195
**JOURNAL OF CANCER EDUCATION, THE.** (THE JOURNAL OF CANCER EDUCATION : THE OFFICIAL JOURNAL OF THE AMERICAN ASSOCIATION FOR CANCER EDUCATION.). [J. cancer educ.]. **Added/Corp** American Association for Cancer Education. Vol. 1, No. 1 (1986)-. Periodical. English. qt. $150.00 (US & possessions), $175.00 (other) institution; $80.00 (US & possessions), $90.00 (other) individual. Hanley & Belfus Inc., 210 South 13th Street, Philadelphia PA 19107. **Tel** (215)546-7293, FAX (215)790-9330. **(Subscription address:** UK/ Headington Hill Hall, Oxford OX3 0BW; Can/ 150 Consumers Road/Suite 104, Willowdale Ontario M2J 1P9; Aus-NZ/ PO Box 544, Potts Point NSW 2011**) ED** Richard Bakemeier. **DD** 616. **NLM** W1; JO573H. **[CCC]. Bk Rev. Ad Acc. Pr Rev.** available on microfilm and microfiche from University Microfilms International (UMI).
**Desc:** An international journal dedicated to the publication of original contributions dealing with the varied aspects of cancer education for physicians, dentists, nurses, students, social workers and other allied health professionals, patients, and the general public. Discusses current problems and techniques in cancer education.
**Ind/Abst** Cumul. Index Nurs. Allied Health Lit.; Curr. Aware. Biol. Sci., CABS; EMBASE; Health Plan. Adminis.; Index Med.

GW/0171-5216
**JOURNAL OF CANCER RESEARCH AND CLINICAL ONCOLOGY.** [J. cancer res. clin. oncol.]. **Added/Corp** Deutsche Krebsgesellschaft. **VFOAT** Cancer Research and Clinical Oncology. Vol. 93 (1979)-. Academic Scholarly Publication. English (German). Twelve times a year. DM1958.00. Springer-Verlag GmbH & Company KG, Heidelberger Platz 3, D 14197 Berlin Germany. **Tel** 011 49 30 8207223, FAX 011 49 30 8214091, telex 183 319 SPBLN D. **(Subscription address:** Springer Verlag New York Inc. / for North America, 44 Hartz Way, Secaucus NJ 07096.**) ED** E Grundmann, E Hecker, F J Cleton, K Abe, H Fujiki, G T Bowden. **NLM** W1 JO574E. **CODEN** JCROD7. **[CCC].** Index available in last issue of volume--attached. **Pr Rev.** available on microfilm from University Microfilms International (UMI). Documents available from The Genuine Article, BIOSIS Document Express, CASDDS, ADONIS. ***Continues** Zeitschrift fur Krebsforschung und Klinische Onkologie, 0084-5353.*
**Desc:** Contains significant and up-to-date articles within the fields of experimental and clinical oncology and is chiefly devoted to original papers, editorials, and guest editorials of current, controversial topics.
**Ind/Abst** ADONIS; Biol. Abstr.; Chem. Abstr.; Curr. Contents; Curr. Contents Life Sci.; Dairy Sci. Abstr.; EMBASE; Energy Res. Abstr. (Feb. 1981-); Index Med.; Index Vet.; NAPRALERT; Nutr. Abstr. Rev., Ser. A, Hum. Exp.; Nutr. Res. Newsl.; Life Sci. Collect.; PESTDOC; Poult. Abstr.; Res. Alert [Full Cov.]; Rev. Med. Vet. Mycology; Sci. Cit. Index; SCISEARCH; Soc. Sci. Cit. Index [Select. Cov.]; Vet. Bull.; Virol. AIDS Abstr.

US/0733-2459
**JOURNAL OF CLINICAL APHERESIS.** [J. clin. apher.]. Vol. 1, No. 1 (1982)-. Periodical. English. qt. $272.00 US; $312.00 Canada and Mexico; $327.00 other. John Wiley & Sons, Inc., 605 Third Avenue, New York NY 10158-0012. **Tel** (212)850-6000, (212)850-6645, FAX (212)850-6088, telex 12-7063. **(Subscription address:** John Wiley & Sons / England, Baffins Lane, Chichester, West Sussex PO19 1UD England.**) ED** Harvy G. Klein and Alvaro A. Pineda. **NLM** W1 JO587AG. **CODEN** JCAPES. **[CCC].** Documents available from BIOSIS Document Express.
**Desc:** Offers a multidisciplinary approach to this rapidly progressing area of medicine. Publishes original research articles on all topics relevant to apheresis: plasmapheresis, lymphoplasmapheresis, and cytapheresis, as well as experimental and technical developments.
**Ind/Abst** Biol. Abstr. (1988-); EMBASE; Index Med. (Vol. 2, No. 1, 1984-); Life Sci. Collect.

US/0162-9360
**JOURNAL OF CLINICAL HEMATOLOGY AND ONCOLOGY.** ***Ceased.* See** Medical Science and Technology-Hematology.

US/0732-183X
**JOURNAL OF CLINICAL ONCOLOGY.** (JOURNAL OF CLINICAL ONCOLOGY : OFFICIAL JOURNAL OF THE AMERICAN SOCIETY OF CLINICAL ONCOLOGY.). [J. clin. oncol.]. **Added/Corp** American Society of Clinical Oncology. Vol. 1, No. 1 (Jan. 1983)-. Academic Scholarly Publication. English. mo. $190.00 (individual), $243.00 (institution), $76.00 (student) US; $247.00 (individual), $290.00 (institution), $88.00 (student) other. W.B. Saunders Company, A Subsidiary of Harcourt Brace Jovanovich, Inc., The Curtis Center/Suite 300, Independence Square West, Philadelphia PA 19106-3399. **Tel** (215)238-7800 or, 5587, FAX (215)238-7883, telex 173146. **(Subscription address:** W. B. Saunders Company / North America Subscriptions, c/o Periodicals, 6277 Sea Harbour Drive, 4th Floor, Orlando FL 32887.**) ED** George P. Canellos. **DD** 616. **NLM** W1 JO5895. **CODEN** JCONDN. **[CCC]. Pr Rev.** Documents available from The Genuine Article, CASDDS.
**Desc:** Provides a medium for the publication of original, international articles in the English language. The scope covers all aspects of oncology including prevention, diagnosis, management, and treatment.
**Ind/Abst** Chem. Abstr.; Cumul. Index Nurs. Allied Health Lit.; Curr. Aware. Biol. Sci., CABS; Curr. Contents Clin. Med.; Curr. Contents Life Sci.; EMBASE; Helminthol. Abstr. (1991-); Index Med.; INIS Atomindex [Micro.]; J. Watch (199?-); Mod. Med.; Nutr. Res. Newsl.; Oncog. Growth Factors Abstr.; PESTDOC; Physic. Medline Plus; Ref. Upd. Basic Ed.; Ref. Upd. Clinical Ed.; Ref. Upd. Deluxe Ed.; Res. Alert [Full Cov.]; Rev. Med. Vet. Mycology; Sci. Cit. Index; SCISEARCH; Soc. Sci. Cit. Index [Select. Cov.].

US/0731-8898
**JOURNAL OF ENVIRONMENTAL PATHOLOGY, TOXICOLOGY AND ONCOLOGY.** (JOURNAL OF ENVIRONMENTAL PATHOLOGY, TOXICOLOGY AND ONCOLOGY : OFFICIAL ORGAN OF THE INTERNATIONAL SOCIETY FOR ENVIRONMENTAL TOXICOLOGY AND CANCER.). [J. environ. pathol. toxicol. oncol.]. **Added/Corp** International Society for Environmental Toxicology and Cancer. **VFOAT** JEPTO. Vol. 5, No. 4/5 (July 1984)-. Academic Scholarly Publication. English. qt. $210.00 (institution); $84.00 (individual). Begell House Inc., PO Box 1109, Pearl River NY 10965. **Tel** (212)725-1999. **ED** Edgar M. Moran. **LC** RA1190; .J66. **DD** 615.9/02. **NLM** W1; JO644BFD. **CODEN** JEPOEC. **[CCC].** Index available. **Bk Rev. Ad Acc.** available on microfiche (back issues) from Chem-Orbital; available on microfilm and microfiche from University Microfilms International (UMI). Documents available from BIOSIS Document Express, CASDDS. ***Continues** Journal of Environmental Pathology and Toxicology, 0146-4779.*
**Desc:** Publishes research on the ecologic effects on the structure and function of cells and tissues with an emphasis on the environmental effects on carcinogenesis.
**Ind/Abst** AGRICOLA [Select. Cov.]; Biol. Abstr. (1985-); Chem. Abstr. (1984-); Chemorecept. Abstr.; EMBASE; Fish Rev.; GeoRef; Health Saf. Sci. Abstr.; Health Period. Database; Index Med.; INIS Atomindex [Micro.]; Pollut. Abstr. Indexes; Toxicol. Abstr.; Wildl. Rev.

IT/0392-9078
**JOURNAL OF EXPERIMENTAL & CLINICAL CANCER RESEARCH : CR.** [J. exp. clin. cancer res.]. **VFOAT** Journal of Experimental and Clinical Cancer Research; CR; C.R. Vol.1, No.1 (Jan./Mar. 1982)-. Periodical. English. Four times a year (Mar., June, Sept., Dec.). L100.00. Apsit Professor Ercole Sega, Viale Regina Elena 291, 00161 Rome Italy. **Tel** 011 39 6 4985536, FAX 011 39 6 4180173. **ED** Ercole Sega. **NLM** W1 JO44FR. Index available. **Bk Rev. Ad Acc. Pr Rev.** ctrl circ. Documents available from The Genuine Article, CASDDS.
**Desc:** Contains original articles with new scientific data on immunological, epidemiological, pathological, biological, and clinical aspects of oncology.
**Ind/Abst** Chem. Abstr.; Curr. Aware. Biol. Sci., CABS; Curr. Contents Clin. Med.; EMBASE; Nutr. Res. Newsl.; Res. Alert [Select. Cov.]; SCISEARCH.

US/1060-0051
**JOURNAL OF INFUSIONAL CHEMOTHERAPY, THE.** (JOURNAL OF INFUSIONAL CHEMOTHERAPY.). [J. infus. chemother.]. Vol. 1, No. 1 (Oct. 1991)-. Periodical. English. qt (Winter, Spring, Summer, Fall). $65.00 (individual), $95.00 (institution), $45.00 (student) US; $85.00 (individual), $115.00 (institution), $65.00 (student) other. Curaflex Health Services, 328 East Guasti Road, Suite 700, Ontario CA 91761. **Tel** (800)444-2872, (714)460-2400. **(Subscription address:** Williams & Wilkins, 428 East Preston Street, Baltimore, MD 21202-3993, USA**) ED** Jacob Lokich (address: The Cancer Center, 125 Parker Hill Avenue, Boston, MA 02120) (phone: (617)739-6605). **DD** 615. **NLM** W1; JO708. **Ad Acc, Adv Mgr:** Charles Healy, **Tel** (619)320-0118. **Circ:** 4,500.
**Desc:** The journal will serve as a resource for information and new data in the field of Cancer Chemotherapy, based upon, but not limited to clinical trials in optimizing anti-neoplastic therapy by continuous infusion.

JA/1040-9564
**JOURNAL OF JASTRO : THE OFFICIAL JOURNAL OF THE JAPANESE SOCIETY FOR THERAPEUTIC RADIOLOGY AND ONCOLOGY, THE. VFOAT** Nihon Hoshasen Shuyo Gakkai Shi; Journal of the Japanese Society for Therapeutic Radiology and Oncology. **VAT** Journal of the Japanese Society for Therapeutic Radiology and Oncology. (1989)-. Periodical. English (summaries and/or abstracts in Japanese and English). qt. ¥24000.00. Kyoiku Kohosha, Zaikyo Building, 30 2 Sanbancho, Tokyo 102 Japan. **Tel** 011 81 3 32639926. **ED** H. Tsunemoto. **DD** 615. **NLM** W1; JO732L. **[CCC].** available on microfilm and microfiche from University Microfilms International (UMI).
**Ind/Abst** Curr. Aware. Biol. Sci., CABS.

US/0167-594X
**JOURNAL OF NEURO-ONCOLOGY.** [J. neuro-oncol.]. Vol. 1, No. 1 (1983)-. Academic Scholarly Publication. English. mo. $1,248.00. Kluwer Academic Publishers / Massachusetts, PO Box 358, Accord Station, Hingham MA 02018. **Tel** (617)871-6600. **ED** Paul Kornblith. **DD** 616. **NLM** W1; JO789T. **CODEN** JNODD2. **[CCC]. Pr Rev. Acid Free.** available on microfilm and microfiche from University Microfilms International (UMI). Documents available from The Genuine Article, BIOSIS Document Express, CASDDS.
**Desc:** Serves as a primary medium for the dissemination of information regarding human CNS tumors.
**Ind/Abst** Biol. Abstr. (1985-1989); Chem. Abstr. (1983-); Curr. Aware. Biol. Sci., CABS; Curr. Contents Clin. Med.; EMBASE; Index Med.; Ref. Upd. Deluxe Ed.; Res. Alert [Full Cov.]; Sci. Cit. Index; SCISEARCH.

●US/1061-9364
**JOURNAL OF ONCOLOGY MANAGEMENT, THE.** (THE JOURNAL OF ONCOLOGY MANAGEMENT : THE OFFICIAL JOURNAL OF THE AMERICAN COLLEGE OF ONCOLOGY ADMINISTRATORS.). [J. oncol. manag.]. **Added/Corp** American College of Oncology Administrators. Vol. 1, No. 1 (May/June 1992)-. Periodical. English. bm (6 issues). $45.00. Knolls Publishing Group, 201 Littleton Road, Morris Plains NJ 07950. **Tel** (201)285-0855. **DD** 616. **NLM** W1; JO803E.

●US
**JOURNAL OF PEDIATRIC HEMATOLOGY / ONCOLOGY. See** Medical Science and Technology-Hematology.

US/1043-4542
**JOURNAL OF PEDIATRIC ONCOLOGY NURSING. See** Medical Science and Technology-Nursing.

US/0734-7332
**JOURNAL OF PSYCHOSOCIAL ONCOLOGY.** [J. psychosoc. oncol.]. Vol. 1, No. 1 (Spring 1983)-. Periodical. English. qt. $225.00 US; $315.00 other. The Haworth Press Inc, 10 Alice Street, Binghamton NY 13904-1580. **Tel** (607)722-5857, (800)3-HAWORTH, FAX (607)722-1424. **ED** Grace H. Christ (editor's address: 853 7th Avenue, New York, NY 10019). **LC** RC261.A1; J666. **DD** 362.1/96994/0019.

**NLM** W1 JO858VC. **Bk Rev. Ad Acc. Pr Rev. Acid Free. Circ:** 741. available on microfilm and microfiche from University Microfilms International (UMI). Documents available from Haworth Document Delivery Service.
**Desc:** Multidisciplinary journal published specifically for health professional responsible for the psychosocial needs of cancer patients and their families.
**Ind/Abst** Abstr. Res. Pastor. Care Couns. (19??-); Annals Behav. Med.; Cumul. Index Nurs. Allied Health Lit.; EMBASE; Health Saf. Sci. Abstr.; Life Sci. Collect.; Pollut. Abstr. Indexes; Psychol. Abstr. (1983-); PsycINFO; PsycLit; Soc. Plann. Policy Dev. Abstr.; Soc. Work Abstr. [Select. Cov.]; Spec. Educ. Needs Abstr.

US/0022-4790
**JOURNAL OF SURGICAL ONCOLOGY.** [J. surg. oncol.]. **VFOAT** Surgical Oncology. Vol. 1 (1969)-. Academic Scholarly Publication. English. mo. $888.00 US; $1,008.00 Canada and Mexico; $1,053.00 other. John Wiley & Sons, Inc., 605 Third Avenue, New York NY 10158-0012. **Tel** (212)850-6000, (212)850-6645, FAX (212)850-6088, telex 12-7063. **(Subscription address:** John Wiley & Sons / England, Baffins Lane, Chichester, West Sussex PO19 1UD England.**) ED** Gerald P. Murphy. **LC** RD651; .J64. **DD** 616.9/94/06. **NLM** W1 JO905M. **CODEN** JSONAU. **[CCC].** Index available. **Bk Rev. Ad Acc. Pr Rev.** available on microfilm and microfiche from University Microfilms International (UMI). Documents available from The Genuine Article, BIOSIS Document Express, CASDDS.
**Desc:** Source of original articles on topics in cancer surgery. Provides broad coverage of the field, encompassing today's surgical approaches and presenting studies of related topics such as radiotherapy, chemotherapy, and immunotherapy.
**Ind/Abst** Biol. Abstr.; Chem. Abstr.; Curr. Contents Clin. Med.; EMBASE; Energy Res. Abstr.; Health Plan. Adminis.; Helminthol. Abstr. (1991-); Index Med.; Life Sci. Collect.; Protozoolog. Abstr.; Res. Alert [Full Cov.]; Sci. Cit. Index; SCISEARCH.

US/1046-7416
**JOURNAL OF SURGICAL ONCOLOGY. SUPPLEMENT.** [J. surgi. oncol., Suppl.]. (1989)-. Monographic series. English. ir. Price varies per volume. Wiley Liss, 605 3rd Avenue, New York NY 10158. **Tel** (212)850-8800, (212)850-6645. **(Subscription address:** John Wiley / Philadelphia, PO Box 7247, Philadelphia PA 19170.**) DD** 616. **NLM** W1; JO905MA.
**Ind/Abst** Index Med. (1989-).

US/0027-8874
**JOURNAL OF THE NATIONAL CANCER INSTITUTE.** (JOURNAL OF THE NATIONAL CANCER INSTITUTE : JNCI.). [J. Natl. Cancer Inst.]. **Added/Corp** National Cancer Institute (U.S.) National Institutes of Health (U.S.). **VFOAT** JNCI. Vol. 1, No. 1 (Aug. 1940)-. Academic Scholarly Publication. English. sm. Free to members; $100.00 Membership. National Cancer Institute Member Services, Building 82, Room 123, Bethesda MD 20892. **Tel** (301)496-2794. **DD** 616. **NLM** W1 JO941C. **CODEN** JNCIEQJNCIAMJJIND8. cum. index. **Pr Rev.** available on microfilm and microfiche from University Microfilms International (UMI). Documents available from The Genuine Article, BIOSIS Document Express, CASDDS. ***Absorbed** Cancer Treatment Reports, 0361-5960.*
**Desc:** An up-to-the minute, reliable and comprehensive source of critical news and information on the latest developments in cancer research and treatment, including: prevention, clinical trials, immunology, molecular and tumor cell biology, biochemistry, carcinogenesis, epidemiology, biological response modifiers, cancer control, drug development, pharmacology, and many other fields.
**Ind/Abst** Anim. Breed. Abstr.; Annals Behav. Med.; Biol. Abstr. (1987-); Chem. Abstr.; Chem. Hazards Ind.; Cumul. Index Nurs. Allied Health Lit.; Curr. Aware. Biol. Sci., CABS; Curr. Biotechnol.; Curr. Contents Clin. Med.; Curr. Contents Life Sci.; Dairy Sci. Abstr.; EMBASE; Energy Res. Abstr. (Feb. 1981-); Food Sci. Technol. Abstr.; Foods Adlibra; Genet. Abstr.; Health Index (1992-); Hum. Genome Abstr.; Immunol. Abstr.; Index Med.; Index Vet.; Int. Aerosp. Abstr.; Int. Pharm. Abstr.; Iowa Drug Inf. Serv.; Lab. Hazards Bull.; Maize Abstr.; Med. Abstr. Newsl.; NAPRALERT; Nutr. Abstr. Rev., Ser. B, Live Feeds and Feed.; Nutr. Abstr. Rev., Ser. A, Hum. Exp.; Nutr. Res. Newsl.; Oncog. Growth Factors Abstr.; PESTDOC; Physic. Medline Plus; Protozoolog. Abstr.; Ref. Upd. Basic Ed.; Ref. Upd. Clinical Ed.; Ref. Upd. Deluxe Ed.; Res. Alert [Full Cov.]; Rev. Med. Vet. Mycology; Rev. Plant Pathol.; Risk Abstr.; Saf. Health Work; Sci. Cit. Index; SCISEARCH; Small Anim. Abstr. Bibliogr.; Soc. Sci. Cit. Index [Select. Cov.]; Stat. Theory Method Abstr. (1961-1963); Vet. Bull.; Trop. Dis. Bull.; Virol. AIDS Abstr.; Weed Abstr.

GW/0344-595X
**KLINISCH-ONKOLOGISCHES SEMINAR.** V. 1-. Monographic series. German. Price varies per volume. Georg Thieme Verlag Stuttgart, Postfach 301120, D 70451 Stuttgart Germany. **Tel** 011 49 711 89310, FAX 011 49 711 8931298, telex 7 252 275 GTVD. **(Subscription address:** Thieme Medical Publishers Inc., 381 Park Avenue South, New York NY 10016.**) UDC** 616-006. **NLM** W3 KL61.

JA
**KOKURITSU GAN SENTA NEMPO.** **Main/Corp** Kokuritsu Gan Senta. (19??)-. Japanese. an. Kokuritsu Gan Senta, 1-1 Tsukiji 5-chome Chuo-ku, Tokyo 104 Japan. **Tel** (03)542-2511. **LC** RC267; .K64a. **NLM** W2 JJ3 K86N. **Circ:** 500 (ctrl).
**Desc:** Report of National Cancer Center, Tokyo Japan.

GW/0342-8907
**KREBSBEKAMPFUNG.** V. 1-. Monographic series. German. ir. Price varies per volume. VCH Publishers Inc, 220 East 23rd Street, New York NY 10010. **Tel** (212)683-8333, , FAX (212)481-0897. **(Subscription address:** VCH Publishers Inc., 303 Northwest 12th Avenue, Journals Department, Deerfield FL 33442.**) ED** E Grundmann. **UDC** 616-006.6. **NLM** W1 KR339L.

UK/0887-6924
**LEUKEMIA.** (LEUKEMIA : OFFICIAL JOURNAL OF THE LEUKEMIA SOCIETY OF AMERICA, LEUKEMIA RESEARCH FUND, U.K.). [Leukemia]. **Added/Corp** Leukemia Society of America. Leukaemia Research Fund. Sven-Aage Killmann Leukemia Foundation. Vol. 1, No. 1 (Jan. 1987)-. Academic Scholarly Publication. English. mo. £435.00 UK and EEC; £435.00 (surface mail), £522.00 (air mail) other. Macmillan Magazines Ltd., Houndmills, Basingstoke, Hampshire RG21 2XS England. **Tel** 011 44 256 29242, FAX 011 44 256 812358, telex 858493. **DD** 616. **NLM** W1; LE905. **CODEN** LEUKED. Index available (bound in Jan. issue). **Ad Acc. Pr Rev. Circ:** 500. available on microfilm and microfiche from University Microfilms International (UMI). Documents available from The Genuine Article, BIOSIS Document Express, CASDDS.
**Desc:** The official journal of the Leukemia Society of America and the Leukemia Research Fund, U.K., is primary source of current and comprehensive information on all facets of leukemia, related diseases, and normal hemopoiesis leading to diagnosis, treatment, and research in these fields.
**Ind/Abst** Biol. Abstr. (1987-); Chem. Abstr. (1987-); Curr. Aware. Biol. Sci., CABS; Curr. Contents Life Sci.; EMBASE; Genet. Abstr.; Hum. Genome Abstr.; Immunol. Abstr.; Index Med. (Vol. 1, No. 1, 1987-); Index Vet.; Oncog. Growth Factors Abstr.; Poult. Abstr.; Ref. Upd. Deluxe Ed.; Res. Alert [Full Cov.]; Sci. Cit. Index; SCISEARCH; Small Anim. Abstr. Bibliogr.; Vet. Bull.

UK/1042-8194
**LEUKEMIA & LYMPHOMA.** [Leuk. lymphoma]. **VFOAT** Leukemia and Lymophoma. Vol. 1 No. 1 (1989)-. Periodical. English. ir. $400.00 (university and hospital libraries); $602.00 other. Harwood Academic Publishers, PO Box 90, Reading RG1 8JL England. **Tel** 011 44 734 560080. **ED** Aaron Polliack. **DD** 616. **NLM** W1; LE926. **CODEN** LELYEA. **[CCC].** Documents available from The Genuine Article, BIOSIS Document Express.
**Desc:** Includes clinical and laboratory data and lymphomas, leukemias and allied disorders. Publishes full-length papers, communications and reviews on clinical and therapeutic practice, laboratory diagnosis, pathology, cytology, ultrastructure, cytogenetics, and cellular and molecular immunology, with a strong clinical-pathologic correlation.
**Ind/Abst** Biol. Abstr. (1991-); Curr. Aware. Biol. Sci., CABS; Curr. Contents Clin. Med.; EMBASE; Helminthol. Abstr. (1991-); Ref. Upd. Deluxe Ed.; Res. Alert [Select. Cov.]; SCISEARCH.

●SZ/1060-6815
**LEUKEMIA & LYMPHOMA REVIEWS.** **VFOAT** Leukemia and Lymphoma Reviews. (1992)-. Periodical. English. Harwood Academic Publishers, PO Box 90, Reading RG1 8JL England. **Tel** 011 44 734 560080. **(Subscription address:** International Publishers Distributor at one of the following addresses: 820 Town Center Drive, Langhorne, PA 19047; or PO Box 90, Reading Berkshire RG1 8JL UK; or Kent Ridge PO Box 1180, Singapore 9111, Republic of Singapore**)**

UK/0145-2126
**LEUKEMIA RESEARCH.** [Leuk. res.]. Vol. 1 (1977)-. Academic Scholarly Publication. English. mo. $1006.00 The Americas; £675.00 other. Pergamon Press, An Imprint of Elsevier Science Ltd., The Boulevard, Langford Lane, Kidlington, Oxford OX5 1GB United Kingdom. **Tel** 011 44 865 843000, 011 44 865 843699, FAX 011 44 865 843010. **(Subscription address:** Elsevier Science Ltd. Oxford Fulfillment Centre, PO Box 800, Kidlington, Oxford OX5 1DX United Kingdom.**) ED** Terry Hamblin and Peter Reizenstein. **NLM** W1 LE928. **CODEN** LEREDD. **[CCC]. Pr Rev.** available on microfilm and microfiche from University Microfilms International (UMI). Documents available from The Genuine Article, BIOSIS Document Express, CASDDS.
**Desc:** Publishes articles which further the understanding of leukemia and related diseases.
**Ind/Abst** AgBiotech News Inf.; Biol. Abstr.; Chem. Abstr.; Curr. Contents Life Sci.; EMBASE; Genet. Abstr.; Immunol. Abstr.; Index Med.; Oncog. Growth Factors Abstr.; Life Sci. Collect.; Ref. Upd. Basic Ed.; Ref. Upd. Deluxe Ed.; Res. Alert [Full Cov.]; Rev. Med. Vet. Mycology; Sci. Cit. Index; SCISEARCH; Virol. AIDS Abstr.

US/0737-7673
**LEUKEMIA REVIEWS INTERNATIONAL.** Vol. 1-. English. ir. Marcel Dekker Inc., 270 Madison Avenue, New York NY 10016. **Tel** (212)696-9000, (800)228-1160, FAX (212)685-4540, telex 421419. **(Subscription address:** Marcel Dekker Inc, PO Box 5017, Monticello NY 12701.**) ED** Marvin A. Rich. **LC** RC643; .L436. **DD** 616.99/419. **UDC** 616-006.446; 616.155.392. **NLM** W1 LE928H.

CI/0300-8142
**LIBRI ONCOLOGICI.** [Libri oncol.]. **Added/Corp** Liga za Borbu Protiv Raka SR Hrvatske. Zbor Lijecnika Hrvatske. Kanceroloska Sekcija. Vol. 1 (1972)-. Academic Scholarly Publication. Serbo-Croatian (Roman) (summaries and/or abstracts in English and German; table of contents in English). ir. Mladost Export Import, PO Box 1028, Ilica 30, 41000 Zagreb Croatia. **Tel** 011 385 41 422425, 011 385 41 453222, FAX 011 385 41 424 434 878, telex 21 263 MLADZG RH. **NLM** W1 LI231D. **CODEN** LBOCB3. Documents available from BIOSIS Document Express, CASDDS.
**Ind/Abst** Biol. Abstr. (-1984); Chem. Abstr. (-1986); EMBASE [Select. Cov.].

AT/0737-142X
**LUDWIG SYMPOSIA.** [Ludwig symp.]. **Added/Corp** Ludwig Institute for Cancer Research. (1981)-. Monographic series. English. ir. Price varies per volume. Academic Press, Inc., 6277 Sea Harbor Drive, Orlando FL 32887. **Tel** (800)543-9534, (407)345-4100, FAX (407)363-9661. **NLM** W3 LU96D.

NE/0169-5002
**LUNG CANCER (AMSTERDAM, NETHERLANDS).** (LUNG CANCER : JOURNAL OF THE INTERNATIONAL ASSOCIATION FOR THE STUDY OF LUNG CANCER.). **Added/Corp** International Association for the Study of Lung Cancer. Vol. 1, No. 1-2 (Aug. 1985)-. Academic Scholarly Publication. English. bm (2 volumes). $442.00. Elsevier Science Ireland Ltd., Bay 15, Shannon Industrial Estate, Co Clare Ireland. **Tel** 011 353 61 471944. **NLM** W1; LU64. **[CCC].** available on microfilm and microfiche from University Microfilms International (UMI).
**Desc:** Covers all aspects of cancer. Reports on new findings, and advances in therapy, etiology and related aspects.
**Ind/Abst** Curr. Aware. Biol. Sci., CABS; EMBASE.

US
**MACROMOLECULAR ALTERATION AND REPAIR IN CARCINOGENESIS.** **Main/Corp** International Cancer Research Data Bank. Periodical. English. US Department of Health and Human Services National Institutes of Health, 9000 Rockville Pike, Bethesda MD 20892. **Tel** (301)496-9291, FAX (301)496-2443. **UDC** 576.385.5.

HU/0025-0244
**MAGYAR ONKOLOGIA.** [M. onkol.]. **Added/Corp** Magyar Onkologusok Tarsasaga. Orvos-Egeszseguegyi Szakszervezet (Hungary). Onkologus Szakcsoport. Vol. 1 (Oct. 1957)-. Academic Scholarly Publication. Hungarian (summaries and/or abstracts in English, German and Russian). qt (4 issues). $34.00. **(Subscription address:** Kultura, PO Box 149, H 1389 Budapest 62 Hungary.**) NLM** W1; MA4045. **CODEN** MGONAD. Index Available in last issue of each volume--loose separately paged. Documents available from CASDDS.
**Ind/Abst** Chem. Abstr.; EMBASE [Select. Cov.].

●UK/0962-0605
**MAMMOGRAPH ABSTRACTS : BREAST CANCER SCREENING REFERENCES.** **Added/Corp** University of Bristol. Health Care Evaluation Unit. (1992)-. Periodical. English. qt. University of Bristol / Health Care, Health Care Evaluation Unit, Dept of Epidemiology and Public Health Medicine, Bristol BS8 1TD England. **NLM** ZWP 815; M265.

US/0736-0088
**MASSON MONOGRAPHS IN PEDIATRIC HEMATOLOGY/ONCOLOGY.** **See** Medical Science and Technology-Pediatrics.

●US/1070-597X
**MCGRAW-HILL'S CANCER & GENETICS REPORT.** [McGraw-Hill's cancer genet. rep.]. **Added/Corp** McGraw-Hill, inc. **VFOAT** McGraw-Hill's Cancer and Genetics Report; Cancer and Genetics Report; Cancer & Genetics Report. (June 1993)-. Newsletter. English. mo. $425.00 US and Canada; $475.00 other. McGraw Hill Publishing Company, Inc., 1221 Avenue of the Americas, New York NY 10020. **Tel** (212)512-6410, (800)525-5003, FAX (212)512-6111. **DD** 616. **NLM** W1; MC998DM.

US
**MD ANDERSON ONCOLOG / THE UNIVERSITY OF TEXAS, MD ANDERSON CANCER CENTER.** **Added/Corp** University of Texas M.D. Anderson Cancer Center. **VFOAT** M D Anderson Oncolog. Vol. 36, No. 1 (Jan./Mar. 1991)-. Periodical. English. qt. University of Texas MD Anderson Hospital, Research Medical Library, Houston TX 77030. **Tel** (713)792-2282. **NLM** W1; MD999. ***Continues** Oncolog.*

US/0098-1532
**MEDICAL AND PEDIATRIC ONCOLOGY.** **See** Medical Science and Technology-Pediatrics.

US/0740-8226
**MEDICAL AND PEDIATRIC ONCOLOGY. SUPPLEMENT.** **See** Medical Science and Technology-Pediatrics.

UK/0736-0118
**MEDICAL ONCOLOGY AND TUMOR PHARMACOTHERAPY.** [Med. oncol. tumor pharmacother.]. Vol. 1, No. 1 (1984)-. Academic Scholarly Publication. English. qt. £135.00 (institution), £48.30 (individual) UK; $270.00 (institution), $96.60 (individual) US. Chapman & Hall, 2-6 Boundary Row, London SE1 8HN England. **Tel** 011 44 71 865 0066, FAX 011 44 71 522 9623, telex 290164 Chapmag. **(Subscription address:** International Thomson Publishing Svcs. Ltd., Subscription Department North Way Andover, Hampshire SP10 5BE England.**)** **NLM** W1; ME408D. **CODEN** MOTPE2. **[CCC].** available in microform. Documents available from The Genuine Article, BIOSIS Document Express, CASDDS, ADONIS.
**Ind/Abst** ADONIS; Biol. Abstr. (1989-); Chem. Abstr. (1984-); Curr. Aware. Biol. Sci., CABS; Curr. Contents Clin. Med.; EMBASE; Immunol. Abstr.; Index Med. (Vol. 1, No. 1, 1984-); Nutr. Abstr. Rev., Ser. A, Hum. Exp.; Life Sci. Collect.; PESTDOC; Res. Alert [Select. Cov.]; Risk Abstr.; SCISEARCH.

US/0278-2480
**MEDIGUIDE TO ONCOLOGY.** (MEDIGUIDE TO ONCOLOGY / PROVIDED AS A PROFESSIONAL SERVICE BY LEDERLE, A DIVISION OF AMERICAN CYANAMID.). **Added/Corp** Lederle Laboratories (New York, N.Y.). Vol. 1, Issue 1 (1981)-. Periodical. English. bm (6 issues). $24.00. Dellacorte Publications, 919 3rd Avenue, New York NY 10022. **Tel** (212)751-2806. **LC** Discard. **NLM** W1 ME787FM.

UK/0960-8931
**MELANOMA RESEARCH.** Vol. 1, No. 1 (Apr./May 1991)-. Periodical. English. bm (6 issues). $445.00 US; £260.00 other. Rapid Communications of Oxford Ltd, The Old Malthouse, Paradise Street, Oxford OX1 1LD England. **Tel** 011 44 0865 790447, FAX 011 44 0865 244012, telex 9403712. **NLM** W1; ME8879TG. **CODEN** MREEEH. **[CCC].** **Ad Acc.** **Acid Free.** Documents available from The Genuine Article, ADONIS.
**Desc:** Provides an international forum for the rapid dissemination of research on melanoma both at the basic and clinical levels. The journal seeks to present a coherent and up to date account of investigations pertinent to melanoma. It aims to encourage an informed and balanced view of experimental and clinical research. The intention is also to stimulate and extend communication and exchange of knowledge in the hope that the sharing of information relating to this unusual tumor will enhance cooperation and promote novel approaches to its prevention and therapy.
**Ind/Abst** ADONIS; Curr. Aware. Biol. Sci., CABS; Curr. Contents Clin. Med.; EMBASE; Res. Alert [Select. Cov.].

US/0146-0447
**MONOGRAPH SERIES OF THE EUROPEAN ORGANIZATION FOR RESEARCH ON TREATMENT OF CANCER.** [Monogr. ser. Eur. Organ. Res. Treat. Cancer]. **Main/Corp** European Organization for Research on Treatment of Cancer. (1975)-. Academic Scholarly Publication. English. ir. Price varies per volume. Raven Press, 1185 Avenue of the Americas, 37th Floor, New York NY 10036. **Tel** (212)930-9500, (212)930-9604, FAX (212)869-3495, (212)302-8507, telex 640073. **DD** 616. **NLM** W1 MO559U. **CODEN** MSECDH. Documents available from BIOSIS Document Express, CASDDS.
**Ind/Abst** Biol. Abstr.; Chem. Abstr.

US
**MONOGRAPHS NATIONAL CANCER INSTITUTE.** (19??)-. Government Publication. English. ir. Price varies per volume. Superintendent of Documents, US Government Printing Office, Washington DC 20402. **Tel** (202)275-3328, FAX (202)786-2377. ***Continues*** *Journal of the National Cancer Institute Monographs.*

US/1052-6773
**MONOGRAPHS - NATIONAL CANCER INSTITUTE (U.S.).** ***Title Change.*** (MONOGRAPHS : JOURNAL OF THE NATIONAL CANCER INSTITUTE.). [J. Natl. Cancer Inst. monographs]. **Added/Corp** National Cancer Institute (U.S.). **VFOAT** Journal of the National Cancer Institute Monographs. No. 10 (1990)-(19??). Monographic series. English. ir. US Department of Health and Human Services National Institutes of Health, 9000 Rockville Pike, Bethesda MD 20892. **Tel** (301)496-9291, FAX (301)496-2443. **LC** RC261.A2; J68. **DD** 616.99/4/005. **NLM** W1; MO567BZ. **CODEN** JNCME4. Documents available from BIOSIS Document Express. ***Continues*** *NCI Monographs, 0893-2751.* ***Continued by*** *Monographs National Cancer Institute.*
**Ind/Abst** Biol. Abstr.; Health Ref. Cent. [Full Cov.]; Index Med. (1990-).

US/0270-7950
**NCI FACT BOOK.** (NCI FACT BOOK / NATIONAL CANCER INSTITUTE.). **Main/Corp** National Cancer Institute (U.S.). **VFOAT** N.C.I. Fact Book. **VAT** National Cancer Institute Fact Book. Began with (1979)-. English. an. Free upon request. National Cancer Institute, NCI Building Room, 10A 18, Bethesda MD 20892. **Tel** (800)422-6237, (301)496-8774. **LC** RC267; .U542e. **DD** 353.0084/1. available on microfiche (Vols. for 1980-1983 distributed to depository libraries). ***Continues*** *National Cancer Institute Fact Book, 0196-8149.*

US/0272-9695
**NCI GRANTS AWARDED.** **VFOAT** N.C.I. Grants Awarded; National Cancer Institute ... Grants. **VAT** National Cancer Institute Grants Awarded. Began with 1977/78. English. an. National Cancer Institute, NCI Building Room, 10A 18, Bethesda MD 20892. **Tel** (800)422-6237, (301)496-8774. **UDC** 616-006.6. **NLM** QZ 22 AA1 N14.

SP/0212-9787
**NEOPLASIA.** (NEOPLASIA. ONCOLOGIA MULTIDISCIPLINARIA.). [Neoplasia]. (1984)-. Periodical. Spanish. bm. $53.00. Ediciones Doyma SA, Travesera de Gracia 17 21, 08021 Barcelona Spain. **Tel** 011 34 3 2000711, 011 34 3 4145706, FAX 011 34 3 2091136, telex 51964 INK E. **UDC** 616.
**Ind/Abst** Indice Med. Esp.

XO/0028-2685
**NEOPLASMA.** [Neoplasma]. **Added/Corp** Slovenska Akademia Vied. **VFOAT** Journal of Experimental and Clinical Oncology. Vol. 4 (1957)-. Academic Scholarly Publication. Multiple languages (English and German; summaries and/or abstracts in Czech, Russian and Slovak). bm. $245.00. Slovenska Akademia Vied / Slovak Academy of Sciences, PO Box 57, 81005 Bratislava Slovakia. **Tel** 011 42 7 3782715, 011 42 7 3782925, FAX 011 42 7 496849, telex 93261. **(Subscription address:** Karger Libri AG, Petersgraben 31, CH 4009 Basel 11 Switzerland.**)** **NLM** W1 NE199F. **CODEN** NEOLA4. **Pr Rev.** Documents available from The Genuine Article, BIOSIS Document Express, CASDDS. ***Continues*** *Ceskoslovenska Onkologia.*
**Ind/Abst** Biol. Abstr.; Chem. Abstr.; Curr. Aware. Biol. Sci., CABS; Curr. Contents Life Sci.; EMBASE; Index Med.; NAPRALERT; Nutr. Res. Newsl.; Life Sci. Collect.; Res. Alert [Full Cov.]; Saf. Health Work; Sci. Cit. Index; SCISEARCH; Weed Abstr.

JA/0021-4671
**NIHON GAN CHIRYO GAKKAI SHI.** (NIPPON GAN CHIRYO GAKKAI SHI.). [Nihon Gan Chiryo Gakkai shi]. **Added/Corp** Nippon Gan Chiryo Gakkai. **VFOAT** Journal of Japan Society for Cancer Therapy. Vol. 1 (1966)-. Academic Scholarly Publication. Japanese (English; summaries and/or abstracts in Japanese and English). Eleven times a year. $190.00. **(Subscription address:** Kyowa Book Company Inc., 1 38 Kanda Jinbocho Chiyoda-ku, Tokyo 101 Japan.**)** **ED** Yovinovi Higasa. **NLM** W1 NI895E. **CODEN** NGCJAK. **Circ:** 6,800 (ctrl). Documents available from BIOSIS Document Express, CASDDS.
**Desc:** Monographs about cancer therapy, and reports of the Society's activity.
**Ind/Abst** Biol. Abstr.; Chem. Abstr.; EMBASE [Select. Cov.]; Index Med.

PL/0029-540X
**NOWOTWORY.** [Nowotwory]. **Added/Corp** Polskie Towarzystwo Onkologiczne. Vol. 1 (1950)-. Academic Scholarly Publication. Polish (summaries and/or abstracts in English and Russian). qt. Price on Request. **(Subscription address:** ARS Polona, PO Box 1001, 00068 Warsaw Poland.**)** **NLM** W1 NO979. **CODEN** NOWOAL. Documents available from BIOSIS Document Express, CASDDS.
**Ind/Abst** Biol. Abstr.; Chem. Abstr.; EMBASE [Select. Cov.]; Index Med.

US
**NUCLEAR MEDICINE IN CANCER DIAGNOSIS AND MANAGEMENT.** **See** Medical Science and Technology-Nuclear Medicine.

US/0163-5581
**NUTRITION AND CANCER.** **See** Nutrition and Dietetics.

US/0897-5639
**ONCODISC (PHILADELPHIA, PA.).** (ONCODISC [COMPUTER FILE].). [OncoDisc]. Vol. 1, No. 1; July 1988-. Periodical. English. bm. $1,950. J.B. Lippincott Company, 227 East Washington Square, Philadelphia PA 19106-3780. **Tel** (215)238-4200 or 4454, FAX (215)238-4227. **(Subscription address:** Journal Fulfillment Department, Lippincott/Harper, Downsville Pike, Route 3, Box 20-B, Hagerstown, MD 21740; telephone: (800)638-3030**)** **DD** 616. **Pr Rev.** **Circ:** 250.
**Desc:** An integrated oncology library as a single CD-ROM. The one essential information source for the cancer professional.

UK/0950-9232
**ONCOGENE.** [Oncogene]. Vol. 1, No. 1 (March 1987)-. Academic Scholarly Publication. English. Twenty-four times a year. £850.00 UK and EEC; £900.00 (surface mail), £1050.00 (airmail) other. Macmillan Magazines Ltd., Houndmills, Basingstoke, Hampshire RG21 2XS England. **Tel** 011 44 256 29242, FAX 011 44 256 812358, telex 858493. **ED** John Jenkins, Graham Currie and E. Premkumar Reddy. **NLM** W1; ON102H. **CODEN** ONCNES. **[CCC].** Index available. **Ad Acc.** **Pr Rev.** **Circ:** 1,000. available on microfilm from University Microfilms International (UMI). Documents available from The Genuine Article, BIOSIS Document Express, CASDDS, ADONIS.
**Desc:** Publishes detailed papers and short communications on all aspects of oncogene research including: cellular oncogenes and their mechanisms of activation; the structure and functional aspects of their encoded proteins; oncogenes in RNA and DNA tumor viruses; the presence of oncogenes in human tumors; relevance and biology; cell cycle control; immortalisation and cellular senescence; regulatory genes and "immortalization."
**Ind/Abst** ADONIS; AgBiotech News Inf.; Anim. Breed. Abstr.; Biol. Abstr. (1987-); Chem. Abstr. (1987-); CSA Neuro. Abstr. (?-?); Curr. Aware. Biol. Sci., CABS; Curr. Contents Life Sci.; EMBASE; Genet. Abstr.; Hum. Genome Abstr.; Index Med. (1987-); Index Vet.; Nucl. Acids Abstr.; Oncog. Growth Factors Abstr.; Poult. Abstr.; Ref. Upd. Basic Ed.; Ref. Upd. Deluxe Ed.; Res. Alert [Full Cov.]; Sci. Cit. Index; SCISEARCH; Vet. Bull.; Virol. AIDS Abstr.

US/0890-6467
**ONCOGENE RESEARCH.** ***Ceased.*** [Oncog. res.]. (1987)-Volume 6 Issue 1. Periodical. English. mo. Harwood Academic Publishers / New York, PO Box 786, Cooper Station, New York NY 10276. **Tel** (212)206-8900, (201)643-7500. **(Subscription address:** International Publishers Distributor at one of the following addresses: 820 Town Center Drive, Langhorne, PA 19047; or PO Box 90, Reading Berkshire RG1 8JL UK; or Kent Ridge PO Box 1180, Singapore 9111, Republic of Singapore**)** **ED** Claudio Basilico, Hidesaburo Hanafusa, Lionel Crawford, Francois Cuzin, Thomas Graf, Charles D Stiles, Inder M Verma, and Michael H Wigler. **UDC** 616-006. **NLM** W1; ON102HR. **CODEN** ONCGE7. **[CCC].** **Pr Rev.**
**Ind/Abst** Curr. Aware. Biol. Sci., CABS; EMBASE; Index Med. (Vol. 1, No. 1, 1987-); Poult. Abstr.; Ref. Upd. Deluxe Ed.; Sci. Cit. Index (19??-19??); SCISEARCH.

US/1043-8963
**ONCOGENES AND GROWTH FACTORS ABSTRACTS.** **See** Medical Science and Technology-Abstracting, Bibliographies and Statistics.

SP/0378-4835
**ONCOLOGIA (BARCELONA).** (ONCOLOGIA.). [Oncologia (Barcelona)]. **Added/Corp** Sociedad Espanola de Oncologia. (1976)-. Academic Scholarly Publication. Spanish (summaries and/or abstracts in English). mo. $85.00 Spain; $100.00 Europe; $130.00 other. Alpe Editores SA, C Pedro Rico 27, Oficinas 11 & 12, 28029 Madrid Spain. **Tel** 011 34 1 7338811, FAX 011 34 1 3159652. **NLM** W1 ON102T. **CODEN** NCLGDV. Documents available from CASDDS.
**Ind/Abst** Chem. Abstr.; EMBASE; Indice Med. Esp.

PO/0871-5718
**ONCOLOGIA PORTO.** **VFOAT** Revista Oncologia. (1989)-. Portuguese. qt. Sociedade Portuguesa de Oncologia, Estrada Interior da Circunvalacao 6657, 4200, Porto, Portugal.
**Ind/Abst** EMBASE [Select. Cov.].

●US/1070-0900
**ONCOLOGIST'S POCKET GUIDE, THE.** [Oncol. pocket guide]. 1st Ed. (1993)-. English. an. $21.00 US; $31.00 other. W.B. Saunders Company, A Subsidiary of Harcourt Brace Jovanovich, Inc., The Curtis Center/Suite 300, Independence Square West, Philadelphia PA 19106-3399. **Tel** (215)238-7800 or, 5587, FAX (215)238-7883, telex 173146. **(Subscription address:** W. B. Saunders Company / North America Subscriptions, c/o Periodicals, 6277 Sea Harbour Drive, 4th Floor, Orlando FL 32887.**)** **DD** 616.

SZ/0030-2414
**ONCOLOGY.** [Oncology]. Vol. 21 (1967)-. Academic Scholarly Publication. English (French, German and Italian). bm. $567.00. S. Karger AG, Allschwilerstrasse 10, PO Box - Postfach - Case Postale, CH-4009 Basel Switzerland. **Tel** 011 41 61 306-1111, FAX 011 41 61 306-1234, telex CH 962 652. **ED** P. P. Carbone. **LC** RC261; .A4215. **NLM** W1 ON107. **CODEN** ONCOBS. **[CCC].** cum. index. **Bk Rev.** **Ad Acc.** **Circ:** 1,125. available on microfilm from University Microfilms International (UMI). Documents available from The Genuine Article, BIOSIS Document Express, CASDDS. ***Continues*** *Oncologia.*
**Desc:** Following a phase of specialization, experimental and clinical cancer research are now enjoying closer interaction. Nonetheless, the advances contributed at so many basic levels remain remote from direct medical application. Through the quality of its contributions, this journal works to accelerate the adaptation of experimental results to clinical application. In each issue, findings from basic research are integrated with current theoretic knowledge and discussed in terms of their relevance to the detection and treatment of cancer. The importance of the journal's distinct function has been demonstrated through a steady increase in the number of readers.
**Ind/Abst** Biol. Abstr.; Chem. Abstr.; CSA Neuro. Abstr. (?-?); Curr. Aware. Biol. Sci., CABS; EMBASE; Index

Med.; Index Vet.; Int. Aerosp. Abstr.; Nutr. Res. Newsl.; Oncog. Growth Factors Abstr.; Life Sci. Collect.; Ref. Upd. Clinical Ed.; Ref. Upd. Deluxe Ed.; Res. Alert [Full Cov.]; Sci. Cit. Index; SCISEARCH; Vet. Bull.

US/0891-8147
**ONCOLOGY DATA BASE FOCUS.** [Oncol. data base focus]. Vol. 1, No. 1 (March 1985)-. Periodical. English. qt. Data Centrum Communications Inc, The Soho Building, 110 Greene Street, Suite 505, New York NY 10012. **Tel** (212)226-5252. **DD** 616. **NLM** W1; ON107H.

US/1046-3356
**ONCOLOGY ISSUES.** (ONCOLOGY ISSUES : THE JOURNAL OF CANCER PROGRAM MANAGEMENT /ASSOCIATION OF COMMUNITY CANCER CENTERS.). [Oncol. issues]. **Added/Corp** Association of Community Cancer Centers. Vol. 3, No. 3 (Summer 1988)-. Periodical. English. Six times a year (Jan., Mar., May, July, Sept., Nov.). $20.00 health care providers; $40.00 non-health care providers. Association of Community Cancer Centers, 11600 Nebel Street, Suite 201, Rockville MD 20852. **Tel** (301)984-9496, FAX (301)770-1949. **ED** Lee Mortenson DPM. **DD** 610. **NLM** W1; ON107HF. **Ad Acc. Circ:** 13,900 (ctrl). ***Continues*** *Journal of Cancer Program Management, 0898-6053.*
**Desc:** These issues are devoted to the policy, management, and financing issues of concern to cancer care providers. Readership includes the physicians, administrators, nurses, pharmacists, medical directors, who comprise the multidisciplinary cancer care team.

US
**ONCOLOGY JOURNAL / ALLEGHENY GENERAL HOSPITAL.** **Added/Corp** Allegheny General Hospital (Pittsburgh, Pa.). Vol. 1, No. 1 (Summer 1990)-. Periodical. English. ir. Allegheny General Hospital, Physician Referral & Support Services, 320 East North Avenue, Pittsburgh PA 15212. **NLM** W1; ON107HJ.

●US/1065-2957
**ONCOLOGY NEWS INTERNATIONAL.** [Oncol. news int.]. Vol. 1, No. 1 (May 1992)-. Periodical. English. Ten times a year (July/Aug., and Nov./Dec. issues combined). $70.00. PRR Communications Inc., 17 Prospect Street, Huntington NY 11743. **Tel** (516)424-8900, FAX (516)424-8503. **DD** 616. **NLM** W1; ON107LN. **[CCC].**

US/0190-535X
**ONCOLOGY NURSING FORUM.** **See** Medical Science and Technology-Nursing.

GR/1021-335X
**ONCOLOGY REPORTS.** English. Six times a year. $90.00 (individuals), $180.00 (institutions) Europe; $100.00 (individuals), $220.00 (institutions) other. National Hellenic Research Foundation, 48 Vas Constatinou Avenue, Athens 11635 Greece. **Tel** 011 30 1 7241505, FAX 011 30 1 7241505. **ED** D.A. Spandidos.

●US/0965-0407
**ONCOLOGY RESEARCH.** [Oncol. res.]. Vol. 4, No. 1 (1992)-. Academic Scholarly Publication. English. mo. $529.00 The Americas; £355.00 other. Pergamon Press, An Imprint of Elsevier Science Ltd., The Boulevard, Langford Lane, Kidlington, Oxford OX5 1GB United Kingdom. **Tel** 011 44 865 843000, 011 44 865 843699, FAX 011 44 865 843010. **(Subscription address:** Elsevier Science Ltd. Oxford Fulfillment Centre, PO Box 800, Kidlington, Oxford OX5 1DX United Kingdom.**)** **ED** Alan Sartorelli. **DD** 616. **NLM** W1; ON107P. **CODEN** ONREE8. **[CCC].** Documents available from The Genuine Article, BIOSIS Document Express, CASDDS. ***Continues*** *Cancer Communications, 0955-3541.*
**Ind/Abst** Biol. Abstr. (1992-); Chem. Abstr. (1992-); Curr. Aware. Biol. Sci., CABS; Curr. Contents Life Sci.; Index Med. (1992-); Res. Alert [Full Cov.]; Sci. Cit. Index.

US/0276-2234
**ONCOLOGY TIMES.** [Oncol. times]. Vol. 1 (1979)-. Periodical. English. mo. $90.00 (individuals), $123.00 (institutions) US; $121.00 (individuals), $151.00 (institutions) other. J.B. Lippincott Company, 227 East Washington Square, Philadelphia PA 19106-3780. **Tel** (215)238-4200 or 4454, FAX (215)238-4227. **(Subscription address:** J.B. Lippincott, PO Box 350, Hagerstown MD 21740.**)** **DD** 616. **NLM** W1 ON107R. **[CCC]. Circ:** 21,000. available on microfilm and microfiche from University Microfilms International (UMI).
**Desc:** For specialists in cancer research and practice.
**Ind/Abst** AGRICOLA [Select. Cov.]; Biol. Dig.

US/0883-4903
**ONCOLOGY UPDATE.** [Oncol. update]. (1984)-. English. an. Medical Publishing Enterprises, 15 22 Fair Lawn Avenue, Fair Lawn NJ 07410. **Tel** (201)796-6500. **DD** 616.

US/0890-9091
**ONCOLOGY (WILLISTON PARK, N.Y.).** (ONCOLOGY.). [Oncology]. Vol. 1, No. 1 (Mar. 1987)-. Periodical. English. Twelve times a year. $75.00. PRR Communications Inc., 17 Prospect Street, Huntington NY 11743. **Tel** (516)424-8900, FAX (516)424-8503. **LC** RC254.A1; O53. **DD** 616.99/4/005. **NLM** W1; ON106K. **CODEN** OCLGE9. **[CCC].**
**Ind/Abst** EMBASE [Select. Cov.]; Health Plan. Adminis.; Ref. Upd. Deluxe Ed.

SZ/0378-584X
**ONKOLOGIE.** [Onkologie]. Vol. 1 (Feb. 1978)-. Academic Scholarly Publication. German (summaries and/or abstracts in English). bm (Feb., Apr., June, Aug., Oct., Dec.). $94.00. S. Karger AG, Allschwilerstrasse 10, PO Box - Postfach - Case Postale, CH-4009 Basel Switzerland. **Tel** 011 41 61 306-1111, FAX 011 41 61 306-1234, telex CH 962 652. **ED** H. Huber, W. Queisser. **NLM** W1 ON167. **CODEN** ONKOD2. **[CCC].** Index available. cum. index. **Bk Rev. Ad Acc. Pr Rev. Circ:** 20,000. Documents available from The Genuine Article, BIOSIS Document Express, CASDDS. ***Supersedes*** *Osterreichische Zeitschrift fur Onkologie, 0377-2004.*
**Desc:** An overview of all aspects of cancer and cancer treatment containing contributions to all problems of cancer: from basic research to clinical questions, prevention, early detection, psychological counseling and chemotherapy.
**Ind/Abst** Biol. Abstr.; Chem. Abstr.; Curr. Contents Clin. Med.; EMBASE; Index Med.; Life Sci. Collect.; Ref. Upd. Deluxe Ed.; Res. Alert [Full Cov.]; Sci. Cit. Index; SCISEARCH; Soc. Sci. Cit. Index [Select. Cov.].

UN/0369-7436
**ONKOLOGIJA (KIEV).** (ONKOLOGIIA.). [Onkol.]. **Added/Corp** Ukrainian S.S.R. Ministerstvo Okhorony Zdorovia. (1971)-. Monographic series. Russian. mo. $242.00. **(Subscription address:** Victor Kamkin, 4956 Boiling Brook Parkway, Rockville, MD 20852**)** **LC** UNC. **NLM** W1 ON172E. **CODEN** OKLGAR. Documents available from CASDDS.
**Ind/Abst** Chem. Abstr. (1971-1979).

GW/0936-1502
**ONKOLOGISCHE KLINIK.** Vol. 1, No. 1 (April 1989)-. Periodical. German. Six times a year. DM66.00. Universimed Verlag GmbH, August-Schanz Strasse 21, W-6000 Frankfurt 50 Germany. **Tel** 011 49 69 5480000, FAX 069/54 80 00-77. **NLM** W1; ON176C.

GW/0932-2760
**ONKOLOGISCHES JOURNAL / INFORMATIONSDIENST, BEHRINGWERKE AG.** **Added/Corp** Behringwerke AG. Informationsdienst. Vol. 1 No. 1 (July 1987)-. Periodical. German. **NLM** W1; ON176J.

RU
**OPUKHOLI OPORNO-DVIGATELNOGO APPARATA.** (1960)-. Periodical. Russian. **NLM** W1 OP938.

FR/1146-5697
**PASCAL. E 89, CANCER.** **VFOAT** PASCAL. E 89, Cancer; PASCAL. E Quatre-Vingt-Neuf, Cancer. (1990)-. Periodical. French. Eleven times a year. 1490.00F France; 1580.00F other. CNRS / Institut d'Information Scientifique et Technique, (Centre National de la Recherche Scientifique), 15 Quai Anatole France, Paris 75700 France. **Tel** 011 33 1 47531515, telex 299 356 F. **UDC** 011/016. ***Continues*** *Pascal Explore, E89: Cancer.*

US/0888-0018
**PEDIATRIC HEMATOLOGY AND ONCOLOGY.** **See** Medical Science and Technology-Hematology.

CN/0714-735X
**PLEINE FORME / SOCIETE CANADIENNE DU CANCER.** [Pleine forme]. Vol. 1, No 1 (Hiver 1981)-. Periodical. French. ir. Societe Canadienne Du Cancer, Bureau 1001, 130 Ouest, Rue Bloor, Toronto Ontario M5S 2V7. **DD** 613.8/5/05. **UDC** 616-006.6. ***Formed by the union of*** *Route au Tabac (Societe Canadienne du Cancer), 0227-6895* ***and*** *Souffle Nouveau, 0229-5075.*

US/0191-2232
**POLYNUCLEAR AROMATIC HYDROCARBONS.** (1976)-. Monographic series. English. ir. Price varies per volume. Raven Press, 1185 Avenue of the Americas, 37th Floor, New York NY 10036. **Tel** (212)930-9500, (212)930-9604, FAX (212)869-3495, (212)302-8507, telex 640073. **ED** Peter W. Jones and Ralph I. Freudenthal. **LC** RC268.7.H9; P66. **DD** 616.9/94/071. **NLM** W3 IN921K.

US/0896-5307
**PRACTICAL REVIEWS IN CANCER MANAGEMENT.** (PRACTICAL REVIEWS IN CANCER MANAGEMENT [SOUND RECORDING].). [Pract. rev. cancer manage.]. **Added/Corp** Educational Reviews, Inc. Albert Einstein College of Medicine. Montefiore Medical Center. **VFOAT** Practical Reviews. Vol. 1 (1975)-. Periodical. English. mo. $175.00 Physicians/Dentists; $125.00 Residents. Educational Reviews Inc., 6801 Cahaba Valley Road, Birmingham AL 35242. **Tel** (205)991-5188, (800)633-4743, FAX (205)995-1926. **DD** 616. **NLM** ZQZ 200 P895.
**Desc:** Summary: Abstract cards of articles found in the journal literature ... .

US/0743-8176
**PRIMARY CARE & CANCER.** [Prim. care cancer]. **VFOAT** Primary Care and Cancer. Vol. 4, No. 7 (July 1984)-. Periodical. English. Ten times a year (July/Aug., and Nov./Dec. issues combined). $60.00. PRR Communications Inc., 17 Prospect Street, Huntington NY 11743. **Tel** (516)424-8900, FAX (516)424-8503. **ED** Robert E. Wittes and John H. Raaf. **LC** RC261.A1; Y68. **DD** 616.99/4/005. **NLM** W1; PR522AC. **[CCC].** Index available. **Ad Acc. Circ:** 107,000 (ctrl). available on microfilm and microfiche from University Microfilms International (UMI). ***Continues*** *Your Patient & Cancer, 0272-6955.*
**Desc:** Presents information on methods of the prevention, early detection, management and follow-up of cancer.
**Ind/Abst** Mod. Med.

BU/0323-9209
**PROBLEMI NA ONKOLOGIIATA.** [Probl. onkol.]. **Added/Corp** Meditsinska Akademiia. (1973)-. Academic Scholarly Publication. Bulgarian (summaries and/or abstracts in English and Russian). an. **NLM** W1 PR572FM. **CODEN** POKLA8. Documents available from BIOSIS Document Express, CASDDS.
**Ind/Abst** Biol. Abstr. (1984-); Chem. Abstr.

US
**PROGRAM/ PROCEEDINGS / AMERICAN SOCIETY OF CLINICAL ONCOLOGY.** **Main/Corp** American Society of Clinical Oncology. Meeting. **Added/Corp** American Society of Clinical Oncology. **VFOAT** Program Proceedings; Program/Proceedings of the American Society of Clinical Oncology. Vol. 9 (Mar. 1990)-. Proceedings. English. an. $23.00. American Society of Oncology, 435 North Michigan Avenue, Suite 1717, Chicago IL 60611-4067. **Tel** (312)644-0828, FAX (312)644-8557. **NLM** W1; AM785MG. ***Continues*** *American Society of Clinical Oncology. Meeting. Proceedings, 0736-7589.*

CN/0319-3071
**PROGRESS AGAINST CANCER (TORONTO).** (PROGRESS AGAINST CANCER; NATIONAL NEWSLETTER.). **Added/Corp** Canadian Cancer Society. (1???)-. Newsletter. English. qt. Free on request. Canadian Cancer Society, 10 Alcorn Avenue, Suite 200, Toronto ONT M4V 3B1 Canada. **Tel** (416)961-7223. **DD** 616.9/94/0072071.

US/0145-3726
**PROGRESS IN CANCER RESEARCH AND THERAPY.** [Prog. cancer res. ther.]. Vol. 1 (1976)-. Academic Scholarly Publication. English. ir. Price varies per volume. Raven Press, 1185 Avenue of the Americas, 37th Floor, New York NY 10036. **Tel** (212)930-9500, (212)930-9604, FAX (212)869-3495, (212)302-8507, telex 640073. **NLM** W1 PR667M. **CODEN** PCRTDK. Documents available from BIOSIS Document Express, CASDDS.
**Ind/Abst** Biol. Abstr.; Chem. Abstr.; Life Sci. Collect.

SZ/0079-6263
**PROGRESS IN EXPERIMENTAL TUMOR RESEARCH.** [Prog. exp. tumor res.]. **VFOAT** Experimental Tumor Research; Fortschritte der Experimentellen Tumorforschung. (1960)-. Monographic series. English. an. 200.00F (approx. per volume). S. Karger AG, Allschwilerstrasse 10, PO Box - Postfach - Case Postale, CH-4009 Basel Switzerland. **Tel** 011 41 61 306-1111, FAX 011 41 61 306-1234, telex CH 962 652. **ED** C. Unger. **LC** RC254; .A335. **NLM** W1 PR668T. **CODEN** PEXTAR. **[CCC].** Documents available from The Genuine Article, BIOSIS Document Express, CASDDS.
**Desc:** Combining review information with the personal experience of the authors, these books provide detailed coverage of topics selected as either representing controversial problems or belonging to areas where the speed of developments necessitates the kind of assistance offered by integrative, critical reviews.
**Ind/Abst** Biol. Abstr.; Chem. Abstr.; Index Med.; Index Sci. Rev. [Full Cov.]; NAPRALERT; Life Sci. Collect.; Ref. Upd. Deluxe Ed.; Res. Alert [Full Cov.]; Saf. Health Work; Sci. Cit. Index (19??-19??); SCISEARCH.

US/0146-1540
**PROGRESS IN PEDIATRIC HEMATOLOGY/ONCOLOGY.** **See** Medical Science and Technology-Hematology.

SZ
**PROGRESS IN PUBLIC EDUCATION ABOUT CANCER.** **Added/Corp** International Union Against Cancer. Vol. 1, No. 1 (1989)-. Monographic series. English. ir. Price varies per volume. UICC International Union Against Cancer, 3 Rue Du Conseil General, CH 1205 Geneva Switzerland. **Tel** 011 41 22 3201811. **(Subscription address:** Hogrefe & Huber Publishers, Seattle Office, PO Box 2487, Kirkland WA 98083.**)** **NLM** W1; PR680. ***Continues*** *Public Education About Cancer.*

Medical Science and Technology —Neoplasma, Neoplastic

US/0278-5382
**PROGRESS REPORT / THE UNITED STATES-JAPAN COOPERATIVE CANCER RESEARCH PROGRAM.** [Prog. rep. - U.S.-Jpn. Coop. Cancer Res. Program]. **Main/Corp** U.S.-Japan Cooperative Cancer Research Program. Began with 1976/77. English. an. National Cancer Institute, NCI Building Room, 10A 18, Bethesda MD 20892. **Tel** (800)422-6237, (301)496-8774. **LC** RC267. **DD** 616.99/4/0072073. **UDC** 616-006.6(047.1)(520:73). **NLM** W1 UN63703. ***Continues*** *U.S.-Japan Cooperative Cancer Research Program. Report.*

US/0924-1914
**PROSTAGLANDINS, LEUKOTRIENES, AND CANCER.** [Prostaglandins leukot. cancer]. (1985)-. Monographic series. English. ir. Price varies per volume. Martinus Nijhoff Publishers, Subsidiary of Kluwer Academic Publishers, Koraalrood 50, 2718 SC Zoetermeer Netherlands. **Tel** 011 31 79 684400. **(Subscription address:** Kluwer Academic Publishers / US Subscriptions, PO Box 253, Accord Station, Hingham MA 02018.**) NLM** W1; PR77TG.
**Ind/Abst** Nutr. Abstr. Rev., Ser. A, Hum. Exp.

●UK/1057-9249
**PSYCHO-ONCOLOGY (CHICHESTER, ENGLAND).** (PSYCHO-ONCOLOGY.). [Psycho-oncol.]. **VFOAT** Psycho-oncology. (1992)-. Periodical. English. qt. $225.00. John Wiley & Sons Ltd., Baffins Lane, Chichester West Sussex PO19 1UD England. **Tel** 0243 779777, FAX 0243 776128 BTG:JWP001, telex 86290 WIBOOKG. **(Subscription address:** John Wiley / Philadelphia, PO Box 7247, Philadelphia PA 19170.**) ED** Jimmie C. Holland MD and Maggie Watson PhD. **LC** RC261.A1; P88. **DD** 616.99/4/0019. **NLM** W1; PS749F. **CODEN** POJCEE.
**Desc:** Concerned with the psychological, social, behavioral, and ethical aspects of cancer. This subspeciality addresses the two major psychological dimensions of cancer: the psychological responses of patients to cancer at all stages of the disease, and that of their families and caretakers; and the psychological, behavioral and social factors that may influence the disease process.

●US/1065-7541
**RADIATION ONCOLOGY INVESTIGATIONS.** [Radiat. oncol. investig.]. (1993)-. Periodical. English. bm. $240.00 US; $300.00 Canada and Mexico; $322.50 other. John Wiley & Sons, Inc., 605 Third Avenue, New York NY 10158-0012. **Tel** (212)850-6000, (212)850-6645, FAX (212)850-6088, telex 12-7063. **(Subscription address:** John Wiley & Sons / England, Baffins Lane, Chichester, West Sussex PO19 1UD England.**) ED** Rupert K. Schmidt-Ullrich. **DD** 616. **CODEN** ROINEU.
**Desc:** Focuses on investigational aspects of clinical and basic research in radiation therapy and the related specialties of radiobiology, cancer biology and medical physics. Gives priority to the publication of laboratory observations with significant implications for radiation therapy and to clinical studies that indicate new approaches for basic research.

NE/0167-8140
**RADIOTHERAPY AND ONCOLOGY.** (RADIOTHERAPY AND ONCOLOGY : JOURNAL OF THE EUROPEAN SOCIETY FOR THERAPEUTIC RADIOLOGY AND ONCOLOGY.). [Radiother. oncol.]. **Added/Corp** European Society for Therapeutic Radiology and Oncology. Vol. 1, No. 1 (Aug. 1983)-. Academic Scholarly Publication. English. Twelve times a year (4 vols.). $1029.00. Elsevier Science Ireland Ltd., Bay 15, Shannon Industrial Estate, Co Clare Ireland. **Tel** 011 353 61 471944. **ED** E. van der Schueren. **NLM** W1; RA371T. **CODEN** RAONDT. **[CCC]. Bk Rev. Ad Acc. Pr Rev. Circ:** 900. available on microfilm and microfiche from University Microfilms International (UMI). Documents available from The Genuine Article, CASDDS, ADONIS.
**Desc:** Covers areas of interest relating to radiation oncology. This includes: clinical radiotherapy, combined modality treatment, experimental work in radiobiology, chemobiology, hyperthermia and tumor biology, as well as physical aspects relevant to oncology, particularly in the field of imaging, dosimetry, and radiation therapy planning.
**Ind/Abst** ADONIS; Chem. Abstr. (1983-); Curr. Aware. Biol. Sci., CABS; Curr. Contents Clin. Med.; Curr. Contents Life Sci.; EMBASE; Index Med. (Vol. 1, No. 1, 1983-); Life Sci. Collect.; Ref. Upd. Deluxe Ed.; Res. Alert [Full Cov.]; Sci. Cit. Index; SCISEARCH; Soc. Sci. Cit. Index [Select. Cov.].

GW/0080-0015
**RECENT RESULTS IN CANCER RESEARCH.** [Recent results cancer res.]. **VFOAT** Fortschritte der Krebsforschung; Progres dans les Recherches sur le Cancer. Vol. 1 (1965)-. Monographic series. English. Price varies per volume. Springer Verlag New York Inc., PO Box 19386 Books, Newark NJ 07195. **Tel** (201)348-4033. **ED** P Rentchnick. **LC** RC261; .R35. **NLM** W1 RE106P. **CODEN** RRCRBU. **[CCC]. Circ:** 500. Documents available from CASDDS.
**Desc:** Contains articles on various types of cancer, such as breast, ovary and leukemia.
**Ind/Abst** Chem. Abstr.; EMBASE; Index Med.

GW/0935-0411
**REGIONAL CANCER TREATMENT.** ***Ceased.*** Vol. 1, No. 1 (Oct. 1988)- (1992). Periodical. English. Six times a year. Springer-Verlag GmbH & Company KG, Heidelberger Platz 3, D 14197 Berlin Germany. **Tel** 011 49 30 8207223, FAX 011 49 30 8214091, telex 183 319 SPBLN D. **(Subscription address:** Springer Verlag New York Inc. / for North America, 44 Hartz Way, Secaucus NJ 07096.**) ED** K R Aigner, E T Krementz, F O Stephens and Y Z Patt. **NLM** W1; RE173BJ. **[CCC]. Ad Acc.** available on microfilm and microfiche from University Microfilms International (UMI).
**Desc:** Publishes articles on clinical experience and fundamental research in locoregional cancer therapy.
**Ind/Abst** EMBASE.

US
**REPORT - FLORIDA. UNIVERSITY, GAINESVILLE. CANCER RESEARCH LABORATORY.** **Main/Corp** Florida. University, Gainesville. Cancer Research Laboratory. (1949/52)-. English. University of Florida Cancer Research Laboratory, Gainesville FL 32601. **LC** RC261; .A29. **DD** 616.994072.

US/0090-2403
**REPORT OF THE CARCINOGENESIS PROGRAM.** **Main/Corp** United States. National Cancer Institute. Division of Cancer Cause and Prevention. **VFOAT** Carcinogenesis Program. 1974/75-. English. National Cancer Institute, NCI Building Room, 10A 18, Bethesda MD 20892. **Tel** (800)422-6237, (301)496-8774. **LC** RC268.5; .U55. **DD** 616.9/94/071. **UDC** 576.385.5. ***Continues*** *Report of the Carcinogenesis Program, 0090-2403.*

US/0739-9987
**REPORT OF THE CHAIRMAN - UNITED STATES. PRESIDENT'S CANCER PANEL.** (REPORT OF THE CHAIRMAN / PRESIDENT'S CANCER PANEL.). [Rep. Chairm. - U. S., Pres. Cancer Panel]. **Main/Corp** United States. President's Cancer Panel. Oct. 1981-Oct. 1982-. English. National Institutes of Health, 9000 Rockville Pike, Bethesda MD 20014. **Tel** (301)496-6975. **LC** RC267. **DD** 616.99/4/0072073. **UDC** 616-006.6(047.1)(73). **NLM** W2; A P6n. available on microfiche (Vols. for (Oct.-Sept. 1984-) distributed to depository libraries). ***Continues*** *Report of the President's Cancer Panel Submitted to the President of the United States.*

US
**RESEARCH REPORT / UNIVERSITY OF TEXAS, MD ANDERSON CANCER CENTER.** **Added/Corp** M.D. Anderson Cancer Center. English. Free. University of Texas MD Anderson Cancer Center / Box 82, 1515 Holcombe Boulevard, Houston TX 77030. **Tel** (800)932-7362, (713)792-7362. **ED** Diane S Rivera. **LC** RC267; .R47. **NLM** W1; RE234HPO. **Circ:** 4,800 (ctrl). ***Continues*** *Research Report (M.D. Anderson Hospital and Tumor Institute : 1987).*
**Desc:** Compendium of research accomplished at the center.

US/0894-0983
**RESEARCH SAFETY MONOGRAPH SERIES.** [Res. saf. monogr. ser.]. Monographic series. English. an. Price varies per volume. US Department of Health and Human Services National Institutes of Health, 9000 Rockville Pike, Bethesda MD 20892. **Tel** (301)496-9291, FAX (301)496-2443. **DD** 363. **NLM** W1; RE234VE. ***Continues*** *Cancer Research Safety Monograph Series, 0190-2466.*

US/0166-8544
**REVIEWS IN CANCER EPIDEMIOLOGY.** [Rev. cancer epidemiol.]. Vol. 1-. Academic Scholarly Publication. English. Elsevier Science Publishing Company Inc, Madison Square Station, PO Box 882, New York NY 10159-0882. **Tel** (212)633-3950, FAX (212)633-3990. **ED** A M Lilienfeld. **LC** RC261.A1; R47. **DD** 614.5/999/05. **UDC** 616-006.6-036.2. **NLM** W1 RE257CEF.

NE/0377-7855
**REVIEWS IN LEUKAEMIA AND LYMPHOMA.** **VFOAT** Leukaemia and Lymphoma. Vol. 1-. Monographic series. English. ir. Price varies per volume. Elsevier Science Publishing Company Inc, Madison Square Station, PO Box 882, New York NY 10159-0882. **Tel** (212)633-3950, FAX (212)633-3990. **UDC** 616-006.441; 616-006.446; 616.155.392. **NLM** W1 RE251CF.

NE/0304-419X
**REVIEWS ON CANCER.** [Rev. cancer]. Vol. CR1, No. 1 (1974)-. Academic Scholarly Publication. English. Three times a year (1 volume). Fl429.00; Fl14355.00 combination subscription to all sections. Elsevier Science Publishers BV, PO Box 211, 1000 AE Amsterdam Netherlands. **Tel** 011 31 20 5803642, FAX 011 31 20 5862696, telex 15682. **ED** P Borst, P Cohen, K van Dam, L L M van Deenen, E P Kennedy, G K Radda, and E C Slater. **LC** QD1; .B55. **[CCC].** available on microfilm and microfiche from University Microfilms International (UMI). Documents available from ADONIS.
**Ind/Abst** ADONIS; Curr. Aware. Biol. Sci., CABS; EMBASE; Index Vet.; PESTDOC; Ref. Upd. Basic Ed.; Ref. Upd. Deluxe Ed.

SP
**REVISIONES EN CANCER.** Spanish. Aran Ediciones SA, Avda General Peron, 20 5 DCHA, 28020 Madrid Spain. **Tel** 011 34 1 5332525.
**Ind/Abst** EMBASE [Select. Cov.]; Indice Med. Esp.

CU
**REVISTA CUBANA DE ONCOLOGIA.** Spanish (summaries and/or abstracts in English, French and Russian). Three times a year. Ediciones Cubanas, Obispo 527, Altos ESQ Bernaza, CP 10100 Havana Cuba. **Tel** 011 632980, 631942, FAX 011 631011, telex 512337, 6540.
**Ind/Abst** EMBASE; Ind. Hyg. Dig.

RM/0377-4724
**REVISTA DE CHIRURGIE ONCOLOGIE, RADIOLOGIE, O.R.L., OFTALMOLOGIE, STOMATOLOGIE. ONCOLOGIA.** [Rev. chir., oncol., radiol., o.r.l., oftalmol., stomatol. Oncol.]. **Added/Corp** Societatea de Oncologie. **VFOAT** Oncologia. Vol. 13, No. 4 (July/Sept. 1974)-. Periodical. Romanian (summaries and/or abstracts in English and Russian). qt. $20.00. Uniunea Societatilor de Stiinte Medicale din Romania, Str. Progresului Nr. 10, Bucurest Romania. **(Subscription address:** Orion Press SRL, SPL Independentei 202-A, Bucharest 6 Romania.**) NLM** W1 RE378FJ. **CODEN** ONCODU. Index available. **Bk Rev. Ad Acc.** available with charts; available with illustrations. Documents available from BIOSIS Document Express, CASDDS. ***Continues in part*** *Oncologia si Radiologia, 0030-2406.*
**Desc:** Review of information and orientation on subjects in the speciality.
**Ind/Abst** Biol. Abstr.; Chem. Abstr.; EMBASE.

MX/0076-7131
**REVISTA DEL INSTITUTO NACIONAL DE CANCEROLOGIA.** [Rev. Inst. Nac. Concerol.]. **Added/Corp** Instituto Nacional de Cancerologia (Mexico). (1954)-. Periodical. Spanish. GETLAC, Av. San Fernando 22, 14000 D.F. Tlalpan, Mexico. **Tel** 6551437.
**Ind/Abst** EMBASE [Select. Cov.].

SP/0214-3429
**REVISTA ESPANOLA DE QUIMIOTERAPIA : PUBLICACION OFICIAL DE LA SOCIEDAD ESPANOLA DE QUIMIOTERAPIA.** **Added/Corp** Sociedad Espanola de Quimioterapia. Vol. 1, No. 1 (Nov. 1988)-. Periodical. Spanish (English). qt. $75.00. Prous Science Publishers, Apartado de Correos 540, 08080 Barcelona Spain. **Tel** 011 34 3 4592220, FAX 011 34 3 4581535. **NLM** W1; RE5473H.
**Ind/Abst** EMBASE; Indice Med. Esp.

SP/0482-640X
**REVISTA ESPANOLA ONCOLOGIA.** [Rev. esp. oncol.]. Began with 1952 issue. Periodical. English. qt. $7.25 Spain; $7.60 other. Inst Nacional de Oncologia, Ciudad Universitaria, Madrid 3 Spain. **LC** RC261.A1. **DD** 616.99/4/005. **UDC** 616-006.
**Ind/Abst** Index Med.; Indice Med. Esp.

MX/0034-9984
**REVISTA MEXICANA DE CIRUGIA, GINECOLOGIA Y CANCER.** **See** Medical Science and Technology-Gynecology and Obstetrics.

US/0270-2118
**ROLE OF VIRUSES IN HUMAN CANCER, THE.** (THE ROLE OF VIRUSES IN HUMAN CANCER : PROCEEDINGS OF THE ... INTERNATIONAL CONGRESS OF VIRAL ONCOLOGY OF THE T. AND L. DE BEAUMONT BONELLI FOUNDATION FOR CANCER RESEARCH.). [Role viruses human cancer]. **Main/Conf** International Congress of Viral Oncology. V. 1 (1979)-. Proceedings. English. te. Elsevier Science Publishing Company Inc, Madison Square Station, PO Box 882, New York NY 10159-0882. **Tel** (212)633-3950, FAX (212)633-3990. **UDC** 616.988:616-006.6. **NLM** W3 IN588.

GW
**SAARLANDISCHE KREBSDOKUMENTATION.** **Main/Corp** Saarland. Statistisches Amt. German. DM9.00. Ger Statistisches Amt, Hardenbergstrasse 3, W-6600 Saarbrucken 1 Germany. **Tel** (0681)505-969. **LC** HA1320; .S244 subser; RC279.G3. **UDC** 616-006.6(430.1). **Ad Acc.** ctrl circ.
**Desc:** The number of cases of human cancer in the Saarland and incidence rates and data about mortality of cancer in this region are published for all sites.

US/1040-0303
**SCIENTIFIC REPORT - FOX CHASE CANCER CENTER.** (SCIENTIFIC REPORT.). [Sci. rep. - Fox Chase Cancer Cent.]. 1983/84-. English.

an. Fox Chase Cancer Center, 7701 Burholme Avenue, Philadelphia PA 19111. **DD** 616. ***Continues*** *Scientific Report - Institute for Cancer Research, 0091-7087.*

US/1044-579X
**SEMINARS IN CANCER BIOLOGY.** [Semin. cancer biol.]. **VFOAT** Cancer Biology. Vol. 1, Issue 1 (Feb. 1990)-. Academic Scholarly Publication. English. bm (6 issues). $185.00. Academic Press Ltd., A Division of Harcourt Brace & Company Ltd., 24-28 Oval Road, London NW1 7DX England. **Tel** 071 267 4466, FAX 071 482 2293, 071 485 4752, telex 25775 ACPRES G. **(Subscription address:** Harcourt Brace & Company, Ltd., Foots Cray, High Street, Sidcup Kent DA14 5HP England.**) DD** 574. **NLM** W1; SE487C. **CODEN** SECBE7. **[CCC].** Documents available from CASDDS.
**Desc:** Presents topical issues that review the current state of investigations. Guest editors prepare each issue, which brings together seven or eight reviews in a single area of interest to investigators.
**Ind/Abst** Chem. Abstr. (1990-); Index Med. (Feb. 1990-); Sci. Cit. Index.

US/0093-7754
**SEMINARS IN ONCOLOGY.** [Semin. oncol.]. Vol. 1 (Mar. 1974)-. Academic Scholarly Publication. English. bm. $116.00 (individual) $163.00 (institution) US; $183.00 (individual), $202.00 (institution) other. W.B. Saunders Company, A Subsidiary of Harcourt Brace Jovanovich, Inc., The Curtis Center/Suite 300, Independence Square West, Philadelphia PA 19106-3399. **Tel** (215)238-7800 or, 5587, FAX (215)238-7883, telex 173146. **(Subscription address:** W. B. Saunders Company / North America Subscriptions, c/o Periodicals, 6277 Sea Harbour Drive, 4th Floor, Orlando FL 32887.**) ED** John W. Yarbro. **LC** RC261. **DD** 616.9/92/005. **UDC** 616-006. **NLM** W1 SE489E. **CODEN** SOLGAV. **[CCC]. Pr Rev. Circ:** 8,300. Documents available from The Genuine Article, BIOSIS Document Express, CASDDS.
**Desc:** Source of advice and information that can be immediately applied to patient treatment. Provides a complete, in-depth discussion of one major topic.
**Ind/Abst** Biol. Abstr.; Chem. Abstr.; Cumul. Index Nurs. Allied Health Lit.; Curr. Contents Clin. Med.; Curr. Contents Life Sci.; EMBASE; Energy Res. Abstr. (Aug. 1982-); Index Med.; Mod. Med.; Nutr. Res. Newsl.; Life Sci. Collect.; Physic. Medline Plus; Protozoolog. Abstr.; Ref. Upd. Deluxe Ed.; Res. Alert [Full Cov.]; Rev. Med. Vet. Mycology; Sci. Cit. Index; SCISEARCH; Soc. Sci. Cit. Index [Select. Cov.].

US/0749-2081
**SEMINARS IN ONCOLOGY NURSING.** **See** Medical Science and Technology-Nursing.

US/1053-4296
**SEMINARS IN RADIATION ONCOLOGY.** [Semin. radiat. oncol.]. (1991)-. Periodical. English. qt (Jan., Apr., July, Oct.). $93.00 (individual), $111.00 (institution) US; $126.00 (individual), $134.00 (institutions) other. W.B. Saunders Company, A Subsidiary of Harcourt Brace Jovanovich, Inc., The Curtis Center/Suite 300, Independence Square West, Philadelphia PA 19106-3399. **Tel** (215)238-7800 or, 5587, FAX (215)238-7883, telex 173146. **(Subscription address:** W. B. Saunders Company / North America Subscriptions, c/o Periodicals, 6277 Sea Harbour Drive, 4th Floor, Orlando FL 32887.**) DD** 616. **NLM** W1; SE489GL. **CODEN** SRONEO. **[CCC].**

US/8756-0437
**SEMINARS IN SURGICAL ONCOLOGY.** [Sem. surg. oncol.]. Vol. 1, No. 1 (1985)-. Academic Scholarly Publication. English. Six times a year. $348.00 (US); $408.00 (Canada and Mexico); $430.50 (other). John Wiley & Sons, Inc., 605 Third Avenue, New York NY 10158-0012. **Tel** (212)850-6000, (212)850-6645, FAX (212)850-6088, telex 12-7063. **(Subscription address:** John Wiley & Sons / England, Baffins Lane, Chichester, West Sussex PO19 1UD England.**) ED** Gerald P. Murphy. **LC** RD651; .I57. **DD** 616.99/4059. **NLM** W1; SE489LT. **CODEN** SSONEV. **Ad Acc. Pr Rev.** Documents available from The Genuine Article, BIOSIS Document Express, CASDDS. ***Continues*** *International Advances in Surgical Oncology, 0190-1575.*
**Desc:** Dedicated to reviewing important advances in diagnosis, therapy, and disease management in the field of surgical oncology. Each issue of the journal focuses on a particular disease entity or therapeutic approach.
**Ind/Abst** Biol. Abstr. (1985-); Chem. Abstr.; Curr. Contents Clin. Med.; EMBASE; Index Med.; Res. Alert [Select. Cov.].

FR/0395-0506
**SENOLOGIA.** [Senologia]. V. 1-. Academic Scholarly Publication. French. Masson SA, Avenue Beauregard 12, CH-1701 Fribourg Switzerland. **Tel** 011 41 37 249585, FAX 011 41 37 247559, telex 942658 SEMI CH. **(Subscription address:** 7A Boulevard de Perolles, CH-1701 Fribourg Switzerland**) NLM** W1 SE58. **CODEN** SENODW. Documents available from CASDDS.
**Ind/Abst** Chem. Abstr.

PO/0871-2549
**SKIN CANCER LISBOA.** [Skin cancer Lisb.]. **VFOAT** Official Organ of the Portuguese Association of Skin Cancer. (1986)-. Periodical. Multiple languages. qt. Revismedica - Revistas Medicas e Congressos Lda, Av. Marques de Tomar, 102 2o-Esq., 1000 Lison Portugal. **UDC** 616-006.
**Ind/Abst** EMBASE.

US/0882-4398
**SOCIAL ONCOLOGY NETWORK ... NEWSLETTER.** **See** Sociology.

SZ/0888-0700
**SOVIET MEDICAL REVIEWS. SECTION F, ONCOLOGY REVIEWS.** ***Ceased.*** [Sov. med. rev., F Oncol. rev.]. **Added/Corp** Soviet Medical Reviews (Firm : Chur, Switzerland). **VFOAT** Oncology Reviews; Oncology; Soviet Medical Reviews. Oncology. Vol. 1 (1987)-(1993). English. an. Harwood Academic Publishers, PO Box 90, Reading RG1 8JL England. **Tel** 011 44 734 560080. **(Subscription address:** International Publishers Distributor at one of the following addresses: 820 Town Center Drive, Langhorne, PA 19047; or PO Box 90, Reading Berkshire RG1 8JL UK; or Kent Ridge PO Box 1180, Singapore 9111, Republic of Singapore**) LC** RC261.A1; S68. **DD** 616.99/2/005. **NLM** W1; SO996LDC. **CODEN** SMFREO. **[CCC].**

GW/0179-7158
**STRAHLENTHERAPIE UND ONKOLOGIE.** [Strahlenther. Onkol.]. **Added/Corp** Deutsche Roentgengesellschaft. Vol. 162, No. 1 (Jan. 1986)-. Academic Scholarly Publication. German (English; summaries and/or abstracts in French). Twelve times a year. DM664.80 non-members, DM514.80 members, Germany; DM708.00 non-members other. Urban & Vogel, Postfach 152209, D-80052 Munich Germany. **Tel** 011 49 89 53292140, FAX 089/536052, telex 521701. **NLM** W1; ST797R. **CODEN** STONE4. Documents available from BIOSIS Document Express, CASDDS. ***Continues*** *Strahlentherapie, 0039-2073.*
**Ind/Abst** Biol. Abstr. (1986-); Chem. Abstr. (1986-); Curr. Contents Clin. Med. (1986-); EMBASE; Energy Res. Abstr. (1986-); Index Med. (1986-); Life Sci. Collect. (1986-); Phys. Med. Biol. (19??-19??).

US/0278-2529
**SUBJECT INDEX OF EXTRAMURAL RESEARCH ADMINISTERED BY THE NATIONAL CANCER INSTITUTE.** **VFOAT** Subject Index, Extramural Research Administered by the NCI. Began with 1977-78. English. an. National Institutes of Health, 9000 Rockville Pike, Bethesda MD 20014. **Tel** (301)496-6975. **LC** RC267; .S89. **DD** 016.61699/4/0072073. **UDC** 016:616-006.6(73). **NLM** QZ 22 AA1 S9. ***Continues*** *Subject Index of Current Extramural Research Administered by the National Cancer Institute, 0160-2160.*

UK
**SUPPLEMENT ... TO THE JOURNAL MEDICAL ONCOLOGY AND TUMOR PHARMACOTHERAPY.** **VFOAT** Medical Oncology and Tumor Pharmacotherapy; Supplement to Medical Oncology and Tumor Pharmacotherapy. (1988)-. Monographic series. English. ir. Price varies per volume. Science and Technology Letters, PO Box 81, Northwood, Middlesex, HA6 3DN UK. **Tel** 11 44 9238 23586, FAX 11 44 9238 25066. **NLM** W1; SU692G.
**Ind/Abst** Index Med. (1988-).

●GW/0941-4355
**SUPPORTIVE CARE IN CANCER : OFFICIAL JOURNAL OF THE MULTINATIONAL ASSOCIATION OF SUPPORTIVE CARE IN CANCER.** **Added/Corp** Multinational Association of Supportive Care in Cancer. (1993)-. Periodical. English. Six times a year. DM275.00. Springer-Verlag GmbH & Company KG, Heidelberger Platz 3, D 14197 Berlin Germany. **Tel** 011 49 30 8207223, FAX 011 49 30 8214091, telex 183 319 SPBLN D. **(Subscription address:** Springer Verlag New York Inc. / for North America, 44 Hartz Way, Secaucus NJ 07096.**) ED** N.K. Aaronson. **NLM** W1; SU695. **[CCC].**
**Ind/Abst** Sci. Cit. Index; Soc. Sci. Cit. Index [Select. Cov.].

●UK/0960-7404
**SURGICAL ONCOLOGY.** Vol. 1, No. 1 (Feb. 1992)-. Academic Scholarly Publication. English. bm (6 issues). $265.00 (institutions), $115.00 (individuals) US & Canada; £155.50 (institutions), £67.50 (individuals) Europe; £171.00 (institutions), £74.00 (individuals) other. Blackwell Scientific Publications Ltd, Marston Book Services, PO Box 87, Oxford OX2 ODT UK. **Tel** 011 44 865 791155, FAX 011 44 865 791927, telex 837 515 MARDIS G. **NLM** W1; SU767FF. **CODEN** SUOCEC. **[CCC].** available on microfilm and microfiche from University Microfilms International (UMI).
**Ind/Abst** Curr. Aware. Biol. Sci., CABS.

●US/1055-3207
**SURGICAL ONCOLOGY CLINICS OF NORTH AMERICA.** (1992)-. Periodical. English. qt. $89.00 (individual), $102.00 (institution) US; $114.00 (individual), $120.00 (institution) other. W.B. Saunders Company, A Subsidiary of Harcourt Brace Jovanovich, Inc., The Curtis Center/Suite 300, Independence Square West, Philadelphia PA 19106-3399. **Tel** (215)238-7800 or, 5587, FAX (215)238-7883, telex 173146. **(Subscription address:** W. B. Saunders Company / North America Subscriptions, c/o Periodicals, 6277 Sea Harbour Drive, 4th Floor, Orlando FL 32887.**) NLM** W1; SU767FFG.

FI/0356-3081
**SYOPA.** (SYOPA. CANCER.). **Added/Corp** Suomen Syopayhdistys. **VFOAT** Cancer. Vol. 9 (1977)-. Periodical. Finnish (summaries and/or abstracts in English and Swedish). Five times a year. Free to physicians, 750.00Fmk others. Suomen Syopayhdistys, Liisankatu 21 B, 00170 Helsinki 17 Finland. **Tel** 358 0 135331, FAX 358 0 1351093. **ED** Seppo Pyrhonen. **NLM** W1 SY66Q. **Circ:** 130,000. ***Continues*** *Syovantorjunta, 0049-2787.*

US/0270-3211
**TERATOGENESIS, CARCINOGENESIS, AND MUTAGENESIS.** [Teratog., carcinog., mutagen.]. Vol. 1, No. 1- (1980)-. Academic Scholarly Publication. English. Six times a year. $446.00 (US); $506.00 (Canada and Mexico); $528.50 (other). John Wiley & Sons, Inc., 605 Third Avenue, New York NY 10158-0012. **Tel** (212)850-6000, (212)850-6645, FAX (212)850-6088, telex 12-7063. **(Subscription address:** John Wiley & Sons / England, Baffins Lane, Chichester, West Sussex PO19 1UD England.**) ED** Philippe Shubik. **NLM** W1 TE5697. **CODEN** TCMUD8. **[CCC]. Pr Rev.** Documents available from The Genuine Article, BIOSIS Document Express, CASDDS, ADONIS.
**Desc:** Publishes reports of original research concerned with the detection, classification, and evaluation of risk associated with exposure to environmental agents that induce or promote teratogenesis, carcinogenesis, or mutagenesis, in vitro or in vivo analyses of these toxic substances, and new techniques aiding this basic research work.
**Ind/Abst** ADONIS; Biol. Abstr.; Chem. Abstr.; Chem. Hazards Ind.; Curr. Aware. Biol. Sci., CABS; Curr. Contents Life Sci.; EMBASE; Index Med.; Lab. Hazards Bull.; NAPRALERT; Nutr. Res. Newsl.; Life Sci. Collect.; PESTDOC; Ref. Upd. Deluxe Ed.; Res. Alert [Full Cov.]; Rev. Agric. Entomol.; Rev. Med. Vet. Entomol.; Sci. Cit. Index; SCISEARCH; Toxicol. Abstr.

US
**TEXAS CANCER MORTALITY STATISTICS / TEXAS DEPARTMENT OF HEALTH, BUREAU OF DISEASE CONTROL AND EPIDEMIOLOGY, CANCER REGISTRY DIVISION.** **Added/Corp** Texas. Cancer Registry Division. (1987)-. English. Texas Department of Health, 1100 West 49th Street, Austin TX 78756-3180. **Tel** (512)458-7550, FAX (512)458-7407. **LC** RC277.T4; C36. **DD** 614.5/999. ***Continues*** *Cancer Mortality Statistics, 0748-7762.*

NE/0166-3925
**TIJDSCHRIFT KANKER.** **Added/Corp** Koningin Wilhelmina Fonds Nederlandse Vereniging voor Oncologie. Koningin Wilhelmina Fonds. (1977)-. Periodical. Dutch. Six times a year. Fl45.00. Van Den Boogaard Oisterwijk BV, Postbus 24, 5060 AA Oisterwijk Netherlands. **Tel** 011 31 4242 16665. **NLM** W1 TI563.

SZ/1010-4283
**TUMOR BIOLOGY.** [Tumor biol.]. (1987)-. Periodical. English. bm (6 issues). $335.00. S. Karger AG, Allschwilerstrasse 10, PO Box - Postfach - Case Postale, CH-4009 Basel Switzerland. **Tel** 011 41 61 306-1111, FAX 011 41 61 306-1234, telex CH 962 652. **ED** A.M. Neville. **[CCC].** ***Continues*** *Tumour Biology, 0289-5447.*
**Desc:** Focuses on the basic biology of tumor markers, the crucial indicators of the onset of cancer. It reflects new approaches analyzing the structural and functional properties, differentiation status and lineage derivation of individual cells in normal and neoplastic populations.

JA/0041-4093
**TUMOR RESEARCH.** [Tumor res.]. Vol. 1 (1966)-. Periodical. Japanese. an. Free. Sapporo Medical College, South 1, West 17, Sapporo, Japan 060. **NLM** W1 TU722. **CODEN** TUREA6. Documents available from BIOSIS Document Express, CASDDS.
**Ind/Abst** Biol. Abstr.; Chem. Abstr.; Curr. Aware. Biol. Sci., CABS; EMBASE.

GW/0722-219X
**TUMORDIAGNOSTIK & THERAPIE.** [TumorDiagn. Ther.]. **VFOAT** Tumordiagnostik und Therapie; Tumor Diagnostik & Therapie. Vol. 3, No. 1, (1982)-. Periodical. English (German). bm. $126.00. Georg Thieme Verlag Stuttgart, Postfach 301120, D 70451 Stuttgart Germany. **Tel** 011 49 711 89310, FAX 011 49 711 8931298, telex 7 252 275 GTVD. **(Subscription address:** Thieme Medical Publishers Inc., 381 Park Avenue South, New York NY 10016.**) NLM** W1; TU722KC. **[CCC].** Documents available from The Genuine Article. ***Continues*** *Tumordiagnostik, 0173-086X.*
**Ind/Abst** Curr. Contents Clin. Med.; EMBASE; Energy Res. Abstr. (Aug. 1982-); Life Sci. Collect.; Res. Alert [Full Cov.]; Sci. Cit. Index; SCISEARCH.

IT/0300-8916
**TUMORI.** [Tumori]. **Added/Corp** Istituto Nazionale per lo Studio e la Cura dei Tumori. Societa Italiana di

Cencerologia. Vol. 1 (July-Aug. 1911)-. Academic Scholarly Publication. Italian. bm. L105000.00 Italy; L150000.00 other. Casa Editrice Ambrosiana, Via G Frua 6, 20146 Milan Italy. **Tel** 011 39 2 463936. **NLM** W1 TU723. **CODEN** TUMOAB. **Bk Rev**. **Pr Rev. Circ:** 2,000. available on microfilm and microfiche from University Microfilms International (UMI). Documents available from The Genuine Article, BIOSIS Document Express, CASDDS.
**Desc:** Clinical and experimental aspects of oncology.
**Ind/Abst** Biol. Abstr.; Chem. Abstr.; Curr. Aware. Biol. Sci., CABS; Curr. Contents Life Sci.; EMBASE; Index Med.; Life Sci. Collect.; Res. Alert [Full Cov.]; Sci. Cit. Index; SCISEARCH.

UK/0955-5102
**TUMOUR MARKER UPDATE.** **Added/Corp** University of Leeds. Oncology Information Service. Pharmacia Diagnostics AB. (198?)-. Periodical. English. Six times a year. £49.00 (individuals), £68.00 (institutions) UK & Europe; $100.00 (individuals), $140.00 (institutions) US; £62.00 (individuals), £84.00 (institutions) other. Leeds Medical Information, University of Leeds, Leeds LS2 9JT England. **Tel** 011 44 532 335550. **(Subscription address:** Royal Society Medicine Services, 1 Wimpole Street, London W1M 8AE England.**)** **NLM** ZQZ 241; T925. **Ad Acc. Circ:** 450.
**Desc:** An index to international literature of the clinical applications of biological markers of cancer.

GW/0074-9214
**UICC MONOGRAPH SERIES.** Monographic series. English. ir. Price varies per volume. Springer-Verlag New York Inc., 175 5th Avenue, New York NY 10010. **Tel** (212)460-1500, telex 232 235 SPB UR. **(Subscription address:** Springer Verlag New York Inc. / for North America, 44 Hartz Way, Secaucus NJ 07096.**)** **UDC** 616-006. **NLM** W1 U412.

SZ
**UICC NEWS : INTERNATIONAL UNION AGAINST CANCER NEWSLETTER.** **Added/Corp** International Union Against Cancer. **VAT** International Union Against Cancer News. (1990)-. Newsletter. English. Four times a year. Free on request. UICC International Union Against Cancer, 3 Rue Du Conseil General, CH 1205 Geneva Switzerland. **Tel** 011 41 22 3201811. **NLM** W1; UI27. ***Continues** Cancer Magazine.*

RU
**VOPROSY EPIDEMIOLOGII ZLOKACHESTVENNYKH OPUKHOLEI.** Vol. 1 (1967)-. Periodical. Russian. an. **ED** A M Merkov. **NLM** W1 NA962N vyp.6 etc.

RU/0507-3758
**VOPROSY ONKOLOGIJ.** (VOPROSY ONKOLOGII.). [Vopr. onkol.]. Vol. 1 (1955)-. Academic Scholarly Publication. Russian (summaries and/or abstracts in English). mo. $139.95. **(Subscription address:** East View Publications Inc., 3020 Harbor Lane North, Suite 110, Minneapolis MN 55447.**)** **NLM** W1 VO6405. **CODEN** VOONAW. **[CCC]**. **Pr Rev.** Documents available from The Genuine Article, BIOSIS Document Express, CASDDS.
**Ind/Abst** Biol. Abstr.; Chem. Abstr.; EMBASE; Index Med.; Index Dent. Lit.; Maize Abstr.; Nutr. Abstr. Rev., Ser. A, Hum. Exp.; Life Sci. Collect.; PESTDOC; Res. Alert [Full Cov.]; Sci. Cit. Index; SCISEARCH.

RU
**VOPROSY RADIOBIOLOGII I BIOLOGICHESKOGO DEISTVIIA TSITOSTATICHESKIKH PREPARATOV.** **Added/Corp** Tomskii Meditsinskii Institut. Tsentralnaia Nauchno-Issledovatelskaia Laboratoriia. Tomskii Meditsinskii Institut. Institut Mediko-Biologicheskikh Problem (Russia). Vol. 1 (1969)-. Academic Scholarly Publication. Russian. Izdatelstvo Tomskogo Universiteta / Tomsk State University, Prospekt Lenina 36, 634050 Tomsk Russia. **Tel** 23-44-65, FAX 22-24-66, telex 128258. **LC** QP82.2.R3; V63. **CODEN** VRBDAQ. Documents available from CASDDS.
**Ind/Abst** Chem. Abstr. (?-1977).

UK/0749-5935
**WILEY SERIES ON CANCER INVESTIGATION AND MANAGEMENT.** [Wiley ser. cancer invest. manage.]. **VFOAT** Cancer Investigation and Management. Vol. 1-. Monographic series. English. Price varies per volume. John Wiley & Sons Ltd., Baffins Lane, Chichester West Sussex PO19 1UD England. **Tel** 0243 779777, FAX 0243 776128 BTG:JWP001, telex 86290 WIBOOKG. **(Subscription address:** North, South and Central America/ John Wiley & Sons, Inc., Subscription Department, 605 Third Avenue, New York, NY 10158-0012, USA; telephone: (212)850-6645; FAX: (212)850-6021**)** **ED** J M A Whitehouse, C J Williams, and G Canellos. **DD** 616. **UDC** 616-006.6. **NLM** W1 WI53H (P).

UK/0737-7290
**WILEY SERIES ON NEW HORIZONS IN ONCOLOGY.** [Wiley ser. new horiz. oncol.]. **VFOAT** New Horizons in Oncology. Vol. 1 (1982)-. Academic Scholarly Publication. English. ir. Price varies per volume. John Wiley & Sons Ltd., Baffins Lane, Chichester West Sussex PO19 1UD England. **Tel** 0243 779777, FAX 0243 776128 BTG:JWP001, telex 86290 WIBOOKG. **(Subscription address:** North, South and Central America/ John Wiley & Sons, Inc., Subscription Department, 605 Third Avenue, New York, NY 10158-0012, USA; telephone: (212)850-6645; FAX: (212)850-6021**)** **ED** Basil A Stoll. **NLM** W1; WI53R. **CODEN** WSNOD4. Documents available from CASDDS.
**Ind/Abst** Chem. Abstr. (?-1982).

US/1040-1741
**YEAR BOOK OF ONCOLOGY.** [Year b. oncol.]. **VFOAT** Yearbook of Oncology; Oncology. (1989)-. English. an. Price varies. Mosby Year Book Inc., 11830 Westline Industrial Drive, St Louis MO 63146. **Tel** (800)325-4177, (314)872-8370, FAX (314)432-1380, telex 44-2402. **LC** RC261; .A4496. **DD** 616.99/2/005. **NLM** W1; YE199N. **CODEN** YEONEX. available on CD-ROM from SilverPlatter (US). Documents available from BIOSIS Document Express. ***Continues** Year Book of Cancer, 0084-3679.*
**Ind/Abst** Biol. Abstr. (1989-).

JA
**ZENKUKU HAIGAN KANJA TOROKU.** Japanese. Koseisho Kokuritsu Gan Senta, (National Cancer Center, Ministry of Health & Welfare), 1-1, Tsukiji 5 Chome, Chuoku, Tokyoto 104, Japan. **LC** RC280.L8; Z46.

CC/1000-8179
**ZHONGGUO ZHONGLIU LINCHUANG.** (CHUNG-KUO CHUNG LIU LIN CHUANG.). [Zhongguo zhongliu linchuang]. **VFOAT** Chinese Journal of Clinical Oncology; Zhongguo Zhongliu Linchuang. (19??)-. Periodical. Chinese. bm. $17.31. Tianjin Cancer Institute, Huan-Hu-Xi Road, Ti-Yuan-Bei, 300060 Tianjin, People's Republic of China. **Tel** (22)31-9929 ext. 205. **(Subscription address:** China National Publishers / Industry & Trade, PO Box 782, Beijing, China.**)** **CODEN** ZZLIEP. Documents available from BIOSIS Document Express.
**Ind/Abst** Biol. Abstr. (1987-); EMBASE.

CC/0253-3766
**ZHONGHUA ZHONGLIU ZAZHI.** (CHUNG-HUA CHUNG LIU TSA CHIH.). [Zhonghua zhongliu zazhi]. **Added/Corp** China (People's Republic of China, 1949-) Wei Sheng pu. Chung liu Fang Chih yen Chiu pan Kung Shih. Chung-hua Chung liu tsa Chih Pien chi wei Yuan hui. Chung-hua i Hsueh hui, Peiping. **VFOAT** Chinese Journal of Oncology. Vol. 1 (1979)-. Academic Scholarly Publication. Chinese (summaries and/or abstracts in English). bm. $44.82. Chinese Medical Association, 42 Dongsi Xidajie, 100710 Beijing, China. **Tel** (1)550394. **(Subscription address:** China International Book Trading Corporation, PO Box 399, Library Service Department, Beijing 100044 People's Republic of China.**)** **NLM** W1 CH979ID. **CODEN** CCLCDY. Documents available from BIOSIS Document Express, BIOSIS Document Express, CASDDS.
**Ind/Abst** Biol. Abstr.; Chem. Abstr.; EMBASE; Index Med. (1979-); NAPRALERT.

## NEUROLOGY

US/0884-1500
**ABMS DIRECTORY OF CERTIFIED NEUROLOGISTS.** [ABMS dir. certif. neurol.]. **VFOAT** Directory of Certified Neurologists. **VAT** American Board of Medical Specialties Directory Certified Neurologists. 1st Ed.-. Directory. English. be. $29.95. American Board of Medical Specialties, 1 Rotary Center, Suite 805, Evanston IL 60201. **Tel** (708)491-9091. **LC** RC335. **DD** 616.8/02573. **UDC** 616.8(060.21)(73). **NLM** WL 22.1; A15235.

FR/0296-9955
**ABSTRACT NEURO ET PSY PARIS.** [Abstr. neuro psy Paris]. (1985)-. Periodical. French. sm. 181.19F France; 295.00F. Abstract, 25 Bis Av Pierre Grenier, 92100 Boulogne Billanct France. **Tel** 011 33 1 49100606. **UDC** 616.8.

US/0190-5295
**ABSTRACTS - SOCIETY FOR NEUROSCIENCE.** [Abstr. - Soc. Neurosci.]. **Main/Corp** Society for Neuroscience. Vol. 3 (1977)-. English. an. $34.00d (non-members), $32.00 (members). Society for Neuroscience, 11 Dupont Circle, Suite 500, Washington DC 20036. **Tel** (202)462-6688. **LC** QP351; .S56716. **DD** 599/.01/8805. **NLM** W1 AB891. ***Continues** Neuroscience Abstracts, 0148-8791.*

NE
**ACTA NEURO PSYCHIATRICA.** Dutch. qt. Reed Healthcare Communications Leiderdorp, Postbus 1126, 1000 BC Amsterdam Netherlands. **Tel** 011 31 20 5153352.

PL/0065-1400
**ACTA NEUROBIOLOGIAE EXPERIMENTALIS.** [Acta neurobiol. exp.]. **Added/Corp** Instytut Biologii Doswiadczalnej im. M. Nenckiego. Vol. 30 (1970)-. Academic Scholarly Publication. English. Four times a year. $90.00. **(Subscription address:** ARS Polona, PO Box 1001, 00068 Warsaw Poland.**)** **LC** QP351; .A43. **NLM** W1 AC8655. **CODEN** ANEXAC. Documents available from The Genuine Article, BIOSIS Document Express, CASDDS. ***Continues** Acta Biologiae Experimentalis.*
**Ind/Abst** Anim. Behav. Abstr.; Biol. Abstr.; Chem. Abstr.; CSA Neuro. Abstr.; EMBASE; Health Plan. Adminis.; Index Med.; Life Sci. Collect.; Psychol. Abstr. (1970-); PsycINFO (1990-); PsycLit; Res. Alert [Full Cov.]; Sci. Cit. Index (19??-19??); SCISEARCH; Soc. Sci. Cit. Index [Select. Cov.].

AU/0001-6268
**ACTA NEUROCHIRURGICA.** See Medical Science and Technology-Surgery.

IT/0001-6276
**ACTA NEUROLOGICA.** ***Ceased.*** [Acta neurol.]. **Added/Corp** Universita di Napoli. Clinica delle Malattie del Sistema Nervoso. Universita di Napoli. Clinica Neurologica. Vol. 33, No. 6 (Dec. 1978); New Series, Vol. 1, No. 1 (Feb. 1979)-(Dec. 1994). Periodical. English (Italian). Six times a year (Feb., Apr., June, Aug., Oct. Dec.). Acta Neurologica, Piazza S Pasquale A Chiaia 10, 80121 Naples Italy. **Tel** 011 39 81 7463103. **ED** G. A. Buscaino. **NLM** W1 AC871. **CODEN** ACNLAC. cum. index. **Bk Rev**. **Ad Acc. Circ:** 300. Documents available from The Genuine Article, BIOSIS Document Express, CASDDS.
**Desc:** Reports in all areas in the field of neurosciences: neurology, neurobiology, neurochemistry, neuropathology, neuropharmacology, neurophysiology, neuropsychology and behavioral sciences.
**Ind/Abst** Biol. Abstr.; Chem. Abstr.; EMBASE; Health Plan. Adminis.; Index Med.; Life Sci. Collect.; Psychol. Abstr. (1969-); PsycINFO; PsycLit; Res. Alert [Full Cov.]; Soc. Sci. Cit. Index [Select. Cov.].

BE/0300-9009
**ACTA NEUROLOGICA BELGICA.** [Acta neurol. Belg.]. **Added/Corp** Societe Belge de Neurologie. Vol. 70 (1970)-. Academic Scholarly Publication. French (English and French; summaries and/or abstracts in English). Five times a year. 2200F, 650F (single issue) Belgium; 2500F, 700F (single issue) other. Association for the Society of Scientifique Medica Belgique, Avenue Circulaire 138A, B-1180 Brussels Belgium. **Tel** 011 32 2 3745158. **ED** A. Capon. **LC** RC321; .A24. **DD** 616.8/05. **NLM** W1 AC872B. **CODEN** ANUBBR. **Bk Rev**. **Ad Acc. Pr Rev. Circ:** 500. available on microfilm and microfiche from University Microfilms International (UMI). Documents available from The Genuine Article, BIOSIS Document Express, CASDDS. ***Continues in part** Acta Neurologica et Psychiatrica Belgica, 0001-6284.*
**Desc:** Neurological sciences-clinical and research.
**Ind/Abst** Biol. Abstr.; Chem. Abstr.; EMBASE [Select. Cov.]; GeoRef; Health Plan. Adminis.; Index Med.; Life Sci. Collect.; Psychol. Abstr.; Res. Alert [Full Cov.]; Rev. Med. Vet. Mycology; SCISEARCH; Soc. Sci. Cit. Index [Select. Cov.].

DK/0001-6314
**ACTA NEUROLOGICA SCANDINAVICA.** [Acta neurol. Scand.]. Vol. 37 (1961)-. Academic Scholarly Publication. English (French and German). mo. kr2480.00 US, Canada and Japan; kr2400.00 other. Munksgaard International Publishers Ltd, PO Box 2148, DK-1016 Copenhagen K Denmark. **Tel** 011 45 33 12 70 30, FAX 011 45 33 12 93 87, telex 19431 MUNKS DK. **ED** H H Pakkenberg. **LC** RC321. **UDC** 616.8. **NLM** W1 AC872I. **CODEN** ANRSAS. **[CCC]**. Index available. **Bk Rev**. **Ad Acc. Pr Rev. Circ:** 1,350 (ctrl). Documents available from The Genuine Article, BIOSIS Document Express, CASDDS, ADONIS. ***Continues in part** Acta Psychiatrica et Neurologica Scandinavica, 0365-5598.*
**Desc:** Publishes original papers on neurology, neurosurgery, and the basic neurological sciences.
**Ind/Abst** ADONIS; Biol. Abstr.; Chem. Abstr.; CSA Neuro. Abstr. (?-?); Curr. Aware. Biol. Sci., CABS; Curr. Contents Life Sci.; Curr. Ref. Fish Res.; Dairy Sci. Abstr.; Dev. Med. Child Neurol.; EMBASE; Energy Res. Abstr.; Health Plan. Adminis.; Helminthol. Abstr. (1991-); Index Med.; INIS Atomindex [Micro.]; Microbiol. Abstr. Sect. C; Nutr. Abstr. Rev., Ser. B, Live Feeds and Feed.; Nutr. Abstr. Rev., Ser. A, Hum. Exp.; Life Sci. Collect.; PESTDOC; Psychol. Abstr. (1964-); PsycINFO; PsycLit; Res. Alert [Full Cov.]; Sci. Cit. Index; SCISEARCH; Soc. Sci. Cit. Index [Select. Cov.]; Virol. AIDS Abstr.

DK/0065-1427
**ACTA NEUROLOGICA SCANDINAVICA. SUPPLEMENTUM.** [Acta neurol. Scand. Suppl.]. (1962)-. Academic Scholarly Publication. English (French and German). kr2480.00 US, Canada and Japan; kr2400.00 other°(included in subscription to Acta Neurologica°Scandinavica). Munksgaard International Publishers Ltd, PO Box 2148, DK-1016 Copenhagen K Denmark. **Tel** 011 45 33 12 70 30, FAX 011 45 33 12 93 87, telex 19431 MUNKS DK. **NLM** W1 AC872IA. **CODEN** ANSLAC. Documents available from BIOSIS Document Express, CASDDS. ***Continues in part** Acta Psychiatrica et Neurologica Scandinavica. Supplement, 0365-5067.*
**Ind/Abst** Biol. Abstr.; Chem. Abstr.; Curr. Aware. Biol. Sci., CABS; EMBASE; Energy Res. Abstr.; Health Plan. Adminis.; Index Med.; Life Sci. Collect.

GW/0001-6322
**ACTA NEUROPATHOLOGICA.** **See** Medical Science and Technology-Pathology.

NE/0924-2708
**ACTA NEUROPSYCHIATRICA.** [Acta neuropsychiatr.]. **Added/Corp** Interdisciplinair Genootschap voor Biologische Psychiatrie. (1989)-. Periodical. Dutch. qt. F70.75 Netherlands; F56.60 others. Reed Healthcare Communications Leiderdorp, Postbus 1126, 1000 BC Amsterdam Netherlands. **Tel** 011 31 20 5153352. **UDC** 616.89.
**Ind/Abst** EMBASE; Soc. Sci. Cit. Index [Select. Cov.].

SP/0300-5062
**ACTAS LUSO-ESPANOLAS DE NEUROLOGIA, PSIQUIATRIA Y CIENCIAS AFINES.** [Actas luso esp. neurol., psiquiatr. cienc. afines]. Vol. 1 (1972)-. Academic Scholarly Publication. Spanish (Portuguese; summaries and/or abstracts in Spanish and English). Six times a year. 37.32ptas Spain, $68.00 Europe; $78.00 others. Editorial Garsi SA, Juan Bravo 46, 28006 Madrid, Spain. **Tel** 011 34 1 4021212, telex 98358 GARSI E. **NLM** W1 AC965N. **CODEN** ALNPAJ. ***Continues Actas, Luso-Espanolas de Nuerologia y Psiquiatria.***
**Ind/Abst** EMBASE; Health Plan. Adminis.; Index Med.; Indice Med. Esp.; Psychol. Abstr. (1972-); PsycINFO (1990-); Soc. Sci. Cit. Index [Select. Cov.].

US/0095-4829
**ADVANCES AND TECHNICAL STANDARDS IN NEUROSURGERY.** **See** Medical Science and Technology-Surgery.

UK/0965-1802
**ADVANCES IN ALS/MND.** [Adv. ALS/MND]. **VFOAT** Advances in Amyotrophic Lateral Sclerosis/Motor Neuron Disease. (1990)-. Monographic series. English. ir. Price varies per volume. Smith Gordon and Company Ltd, 16 Gunter Grove, No. 1, London SE1 0UJ England. **Tel** 011 44 71 3517042, FAX 011 44 71 3511250. **ED** Frank Clifford Rose.

GW/0935-0195
**ADVANCES IN APPLIED NEUROLOGICAL SCIENCES.** [Adv. appl. neurol. sci.]. (1985)-. Monographic series. English. ir. Price varies per volume. Springer-Verlag GmbH & Company KG, Heidelberger Platz 3, D 14197 Berlin Germany. **Tel** 011 49 30 8207223, FAX 011 49 30 8214091, telex 183 319 SPBLN D. **(Subscription address:** Springer Verlag New York Inc. / for North America, 44 Hartz Way, Secaucus NJ 07096.**) ED** R.J. Joynt and A. Weindl. **NLM** W1; AD436AH.
**Desc:** The air of the book series is to provide a means of transfer for the progresses made in basic neurological sciences to clinical neurology and related disciplines.

US/0065-2229
**ADVANCES IN BIOCHEMICAL PSYCHOPHARMACOLOGY.** [Adv. biochem. psychopharmacol.]. **Added/Corp** American College of Neuropsychopharmacology. Vol. 1 (1969)-. Monographic series. English. ir. Price varies per volume. Raven Press, 1185 Avenue of the Americas, 37th Floor, New York NY 10036. **Tel** (212)930-9500, (212)930-9604, FAX (212)869-3495, (212)302-8507, telex 640073. **ED** E. Costa and P. Greengard. **LC** RM315; .A4. **DD** 615/.78. **NLM** W1 AD437. **CODEN** ABPYBL. **[CCC].** Documents available from The Genuine Article, BIOSIS Document Express, CASDDS.
**Ind/Abst** Biol. Abstr.; Chem. Abstr.; Energy Res. Abstr. (Aug. 1982-); Health Plan. Adminis.; Immunol. Abstr.; Index Med.; Index Sci. Rev. [Full Cov.]; Res. Alert [Full Cov.]; SCISEARCH; Virol. AIDS Abstr.

●US/0940-8606
**ADVANCES IN CHILD NEUROPSYCHOLOGY.** **See** Psychology.

US/0748-4410
**ADVANCES IN CLINICAL NEUROPSYCHOLOGY.** (1984)-. Monographic series. English. ir. Price varies per volume. Plenum Press, 233 Spring Street, New York NY 10013-1578. **Tel** (212)620-8000, (800)221-9369, FAX (212)463-0742, (212)807-1047, telex 23/421139. **ED** Gerald Goldstein. **LC** QP360; .A325. **DD** 616.89/07/05. **NLM** W1; AD54M.

US
**ADVANCES IN CNS DRUG-RECEPTOR INTERACTIONS.** **See** Pharmacy and Pharmacology.

US/0892-726X
**ADVANCES IN EPILEPTOLOGY.** **Added/Corp** International League against Epilepsy. Congress. International Bureau for Epilepsy. Symposium. (1977)-. Academic Scholarly Publication. English. ir. Price varies per volume. Raven Press, 1185 Avenue of the Americas, 37th Floor, New York NY 10036. **Tel** (212)930-9500, (212)930-9604, FAX (212)869-3495, (212)302-8507, telex 640073. **LC** RC372.A1; E618a. **DD** 616.8/53. **NLM** W1 AD556M. **CODEN** ADEPDN. Documents available from CASDDS.
**Desc:** Includes the proceedings of the Congress of the International League against Epilepsy and the Symposium of the International Bureau for Epilepsy.
**Ind/Abst** Chem. Abstr.

US/8755-0032
**ADVANCES IN NEURAL AND BEHAVIORAL DEVELOPMENT.** ***Ceased.*** [Adv. neural behav. dev.]. Vol. 1 (1985)-Vol. 4, (1994). English. ir. Ablex Publishing Corporation, 355 Chestnut Street, Norwood NJ 07648. **Tel** (201)767-8450, (201)767-8455 (Customer Service), FAX (201)767-6717. **ED** Richard N. Aslin. **LC** QP363.5; .A38. **DD** 599/.0188. **NLM** W1; AD684C.
**Desc:** Provides integrating reviews on recent findings organized around a particular species, modality or developmental issue.

US/1074-7575
**ADVANCES IN NEURAL SCIENCE.** [Adv. neural sci.]. Vol. 1 (1993)-. Periodical. English. $90.25. JAI Press Inc., 55 Old Post Road, Suite 2, PO Box 1678, Greenwich CT 06836-1678. **Tel** (203)661-7602, FAX (203)661-0792. **ED** Suudarshan Malhotra. **LC** IN PROCESS; QP351; .A465. **DD** 599. **CODEN** ANUSED.

US/0098-6089
**ADVANCES IN NEUROCHEMISTRY.** [Adv. neurochem.]. Vol. 1 (1975)-. Monographic series. English. ir. Price varies per volume. Plenum Press, 233 Spring Street, New York NY 10013-1578. **Tel** (212)620-8000, (800)221-9369, FAX (212)463-0742, (212)807-1047, telex 23/421139. **LC** QP356.3; .A37. **DD** 612/.8/042. **NLM** W1 AD684E. **CODEN** ADNEDZ. Documents available from CASDDS.
**Ind/Abst** Chem. Abstr.

US/0272-0787
**ADVANCES IN NEUROGERONTOLOGY.** [Adv. neurogerontol.]. Vol. 1 (1980)-. Academic Scholarly Publication. English. ir. Price varies per volume. Greenwood Press Inc., PO Box 5007, Westport CT 06881-5007. **Tel** (203)226-3571, FAX (203)222-1502. **NLM** W1 AD684F. **CODEN** ANEUD6. Documents available from CASDDS.
**Ind/Abst** Chem. Abstr.

UK/0960-5428
**ADVANCES IN NEUROIMMUNOLOGY.** Vol. 1, No. 1 (Jan. 1991)-. Periodical. English. Four times a year (1 volume). $321.00 The Americas; £215.00 other. Pergamon Press, An Imprint of Elsevier Science Ltd., The Boulevard, Langford Lane, Kidlington, Oxford OX5 1GB United Kingdom. **Tel** 011 44 865 843000, 011 44 865 843699, FAX 011 44 865 843010. **(Subscription address:** Elsevier Science Ltd. Oxford Fulfillment Centre, PO Box 800, Kidlington, Oxford OX5 1DX United Kingdom.**) LC** QP356.47; .A38. **NLM** W1; AD684G. **CODEN** ADNIEE. **[CCC].** Index available. cum. index. **Bk Rev. Ad Acc. Pr Rev. Circ:** 500 (ctrl). Documents available from The Genuine Article.
**Desc:** Publishes current and comprehensive reviews on significant research into the interactions between the nervous and immune systems.
**Ind/Abst** Curr. Aware. Biol. Sci., CABS; Curr. Contents Life Sci.; Res. Alert [Full Cov.]; Sci. Cit. Index; SCISEARCH; Soc. Sci. Cit. Index [Select. Cov.].

US/0091-3952
**ADVANCES IN NEUROLOGY.** [Adv. neurol.]. Vol. 1 (1973)-. Monographic series. English. ir. Price varies per volume. Raven Press, 1185 Avenue of the Americas, 37th Floor, New York NY 10036. **Tel** (212)930-9500, (212)930-9604, FAX (212)869-3495, (212)302-8507, telex 640073. **ED** John A. Kessler and Stuart Apfel. **LC** RC321; .A276. **DD** 616.8/05. **NLM** W1 AD684H. **CODEN** ADNRA3. **[CCC].** Documents available from BIOSIS Document Express, CASDDS.
**Ind/Abst** Biol. Abstr.; Chem. Abstr.; Energy Res. Abstr. (April 1982-); Genet. Abstr.; Health Plan. Adminis.; Index Med.; Life Sci. Collect.; Ref. Upd. Basic Ed.; Ref. Upd. Deluxe Ed.; SportSearch.

US
**ADVANCES IN NEUROPSYCHIATRY AND PSYCHOPHARMACOLOGY.** Vol. 1 (1991)-. Monographic series. English. ir. Price varies per volume. Raven Press, 1185 Avenue of the Americas, 37th Floor, New York NY 10036. **Tel** (212)930-9500, (212)930-9604, FAX (212)869-3495, (212)302-8507, telex 640073. **ED** Jay D. Amsterdam. **NLM** W1; AD684I.

US/0741-8957
**ADVANCES IN NEUROPSYCHOLOGY AND BEHAVIORAL NEUROLOGY.** [Adv. neuropsychology behav. neurol.]. Vol. 1 (1983)-. Monographic series. English. ir. Price varies per volume. Guilford Publications Inc., 72 Spring Street, New York NY 10012. **Tel** (212)431-9800, (800)365-7006, FAX (212)966-6708. **ED** Kenneth M. Heilman and Paul Satz. **LC** QP401; .A38. **DD** 612/.8. **NLM** W1 AD684J.

US/1059-1540
**ADVANCES IN NEUROSCIENCE.** [Adv. neurosci.]. Vol. 1 (1991)-. Monographic series. English. ir. Price varies per volume. Raven Press, 1185 Avenue of the Americas, 37th Floor, New York NY 10036. **Tel** (212)930-9500, (212)930-9604, FAX (212)869-3495, (212)302-8507, telex 640073. **DD** 612. **NLM** W1; AD684L. **CODEN** ANEUE7. Documents available from CASDDS.
**Ind/Abst** Chem. Abstr.

US/0146-0722
**ADVANCES IN PAIN RESEARCH AND THERAPY.** [Adv. pain res. ther.]. Vol. 1 (1976)-. Academic Scholarly Publication. English. ir. Price varies per volume. Raven Press, 1185 Avenue of the Americas, 37th Floor, New York NY 10036. **Tel** (212)930-9500, (212)930-9604, FAX (212)869-3495, (212)302-8507, telex 640073. **ED** John J. Bonica. **LC** UNC. **NLM** W1 AD706. **CODEN** APRTDE. Documents available from The Genuine Article, BIOSIS Document Express, CASDDS.
**Desc:** Proceedings of the World Congress on Pain.
**Ind/Abst** Biol. Abstr.; Chem. Abstr.; Index Sci. Rev. [Full Cov.]; Res. Alert [Full Cov.]; Sci. Cit. Index (19??-19??); SCISEARCH.

SZ
**ADVANCES IN STEREOENCEPHALOTOMY.** Vol. 1 (1962)-. Monographic series. English. ir. Price varies per volume. S. Karger AG, Allschwilerstrasse 10, PO Box - Postfach - Case Postale, CH-4009 Basel Switzerland. **Tel** 011 41 61 306-1111, FAX 011 41 61 306-1234, telex CH 962 652. **ED** P. L. Gildenberg. **NLM** W1 AD874 (P). **CODEN** AVSEAD. Documents available from BIOSIS Document Express.
**Desc:** Volumes acquaint specialists with fundamental information on the techniques, procedures, and clinical applications of stereotactic and functional neurosurgery. Discusses novel approaches to the management of intractable pain, movement disorders, epilepsy, visual disorders, and various forms of neurologic disease.
**Ind/Abst** Biol. Abstr. (-1986); Index Med.

KE
**AFRICAN JOURNAL OF NEUROLOGICAL SCIENCES : OFFICIAL ORGAN OF THE PAN AFRICAN ASSOCIATION OF NEUROLOGICAL SCIENCES, THE.** **Added/Corp** Pan African Association of Neurological Sciences. Vol. 1, No. 1 (Jan. 1982)-. Periodical. English (French). sa. Pan African Association of Neurological Sciences, PO Box 20413, Nairobi Kenya. **Tel** 011 02 722487. **LC** WMLC 93/2097. **NLM** W1; AF524L.
**Ind/Abst** EMBASE.

SZ/0082-4917
**AKTUELLE FRAGEN DER PSYCHIATRIE UND NEUROLOGIE.** **See** Medical Science and Technology-Psychiatry.

GW/0302-4350
**AKTUELLE NEUROLOGIE.** [Aktuel. neurol.]. No. 1 (Feb. 1974)-. Periodical. English. bm (6 issues). $181.00. Georg Thieme Verlag Stuttgart, Postfach 301120, D 70451 Stuttgart Germany. **Tel** 011 49 711 89310, FAX 011 49 711 8931298, telex 7 252 275 GTVD. **(Subscription address:** Thieme Medical Publishers Inc., 381 Park Avenue South, New York NY 10016.**) NLM** W1 AK995GN. **[CCC]. Pr Rev.** available on microfilm from University Microfilms International (UMI). Documents available from The Genuine Article.
**Ind/Abst** Curr. Contents Clin. Med.; EMBASE; Energy Res. Abstr. (Nov. 1978-); Life Sci. Collect.; Res. Alert [Full Cov.]; SCISEARCH; Soc. Sci. Cit. Index [Select. Cov.].

FR/0299-2507
**ALZHEIMER ACTUALITES.** (1986)-. Periodical. French. mo. 100.00F. Fondation Ipsen, 30 rue Cambronne, 75015 Paris France. **Tel** 011 33 1 47341095, FAX 011 33 1 47348321. **ED** Motsieur Yves Christen. **UDC** 616-053.9. **Circ:** 16,000.
**Desc:** Review of current data published in the domain of Alzheimer's disease for researchers and medical doctors.

US/0893-0341
**ALZHEIMER DISEASE AND ASSOCIATED DISORDERS.** [Alzheimer dis. assoc. disord.]. **Added/Corp** Western Geriatric Research Institute (Lawrence, Kan.). **VFOAT** ADAD. Vol. 1, Issue 1 (1987)-. Academic Scholarly Publication. English. qt. $106.00 (individuals), $158.00 (institutions) US; $130.00 (individuals), $185.00 (institutions) other. Raven Press, 1185 Avenue of the Americas, 37th Floor, New York NY 10036. **Tel** (212)930-9500, (212)930-9604, FAX (212)869-3495, (212)302-8507, telex 640073. **ED** Peter J. Whitehouse. **LC** RC523; .A376. **DD** 616.8/31/005. **NLM** W1; AL999. **CODEN** ADADE2. **[CCC]. Pr Rev.** available on microfilm and microfiche from University Microfilms International (UMI). Documents available from The Genuine Article, BIOSIS Document Express, CASDDS.
**Desc:** Aims to be an international medium for publication of authoritative and original contributions with primary emphasis on Alzheimer disease and associated disorders. Rigorous peer review of articles is ensured by an international Editorial Advisory Board of scientists and clinicians.
**Ind/Abst** Biol. Abstr.; Chem. Abstr. (1987-); Curr. Aware. Biol. Sci., CABS; Curr. Contents Clin. Med.; Curr.

Contents Life Sci.; EMBASE; Health Plan. Adminis.; Index Med. (1987-); Res. Alert [Full Cov.]; Sci. Cit. Index; SCISEARCH; Soc. Sci. Cit. Index [Select. Cov.].

US/0895-5336
**AMERICAN JOURNAL OF ALZHEIMER'S CARE AND RELATED DISORDERS & RESEARCH.** [Am. j. Alzheimer's care relat. disord. res.]. **VFOAT** American Journal of Alzheimer's Care and Related Disorders. **VAT** American Journal of Alzheimer's Care and Related Disorders and Research. (1987)-. Periodical. English. Six times a year. $66.00 (individual), $86.00 (institution) US; $76.00 (individual), $96.00 (institution); $86.00 (individual), $106.00 (institution). Prime National Publishing Corporation, 470 Boston Post Road, Weston MA 02193. **Tel** (617)899-2702. **DD** 616. **NLM** W1; AM447L. **Pr Rev.** ***Continues*** *American Journal of Alzheimer's Care and Research.*
**Desc:** National journal on Alzheimer's disease designed to serve the needs of both professional and layperson caregivers. Articles cover family issues, patient care, research, diagnosis and health policy.
**Ind/Abst** Abstr. Soc. Gerontol. (?-?).

US/0002-9238
**AMERICAN JOURNAL OF EEG TECHNOLOGY, THE.** [Am. j. E.E.G. technol.]. **Added/Corp** American Society of Electroencephalographic Technologists. American Society of Electroencephalograph Technicians. American Society of Electroneurodiagnostic Technologists. **VAT** American Journal of Electroencephalography Technology. Vol. 1 (March 1961)-. Academic Scholarly Publication. English. Four times a year (March, June, Sep., Dec.). $60.00 US; $70.00 other. American Society of Electroneurodiagnostic Technologists, 204 West 7th, Carroll IA 51401. **Tel** (712)792-2978, FAX (712)792-6962. **ED** Janet Ghigo. **LC** RC386.5; .A4. **NLM** W1 AM451. **CODEN** AJETA6. Index available. cum. index. **Bk Rev. Ad Acc. Acid Free. Circ:** 3,200 (ctrl). Documents available from The Genuine Article, Ask*IEEE.
**Desc:** Presents papers on clinical and scientific levels and book reviews on EEG, evoked potential, and related neurodiagnostic topics.
**Ind/Abst** Ei Page One; EMBASE; Health Plan. Adminis.; Hospit. Health Admin. Index; INSPEC (Sept. 1971-); Psychol. Abstr. (1967-); PsycINFO; PsycLit; Res. Alert [Full Cov.]; Soc. Sci. Cit. Index [Select. Cov.].

US/0195-6108
**AMERICAN JOURNAL OF NEURORADIOLOGY.** (AJNR, AMERICAN JOURNAL OF NEURORADIOLOGY.). [Am. j. neuroradiol.]. **Added/Corp** American Society of Neuroradiology. American Roentgen Ray Society. **VFOAT** American Journal of Neuroradiology; AJNR. Vol. 1 (Jan./Feb. 1980)-. Periodical. English. Ten times a year. $210.00 (institution), $185.00 (individual) US; $265.00 (institution), $240.00 (individual) other. American Society of Neuroradiology, 2210 Midwest Road, Suite 850, Oak Brook IL 60521. **Tel** (708)574-0220, telex (708)574-0661. **(Subscription address:** Fulco, 30 Broad Street, Denville NJ 07834.**) ED** Juan Taveras. **LC** RC349.R3; A17. **DD** 616.8/04757. **NLM** W1 A117GE. **Ad Acc. Pr Rev. Circ:** 4,200. available on microfilm. Documents available from The Genuine Article.
**Desc:** Original clinical articles on imaging diagnosis of the CNS, including the spine, for radiologists, neuroradiologists, neurosurgeons, and neurologists.
**Ind/Abst** CSA Neuro. Abstr. (?-?); Curr. Contents Clin. Med.; Curr. Contents Life Sci.; Dev. Med. Child Neurol.; EMBASE; Health Plan. Adminis.; Helminthol. Abstr. (1991-); Index Med. (Jan./Feb. 1980-); INIS Atomindex [Micro.]; Life Sci. Collect.; Res. Alert [Full Cov.]; Rev. Med. Vet. Mycology; Sci. Cit. Index; SCISEARCH; Soc. Sci. Cit. Index [Select. Cov.].

US/0364-5134
**ANNALS OF NEUROLOGY.** [Ann. neurol.]. **Added/Corp** American Neurological Association. Child Neurology Society. Vol. 1 (Jan. 1977)-. Academic Scholarly Publication. English. mo. $229.00 (institutions), $152.00 (individuals) US; $262.00 (institutions), $181.00 (individuals) Canada; $304.00 (institutions), $220.00 (individuals) other. Little Brown & Company, 34 Beacon Street, Boston MA 02108. **Tel** (617)227-0730, (800)759-0190. **(Subscription address:** Little Brown and Company, PO Box 7671, Riverton NJ 08077-7671.**) ED** Arthur K. Asbury. **LC** RC321; .A62. **DD** 616.8/005. **NLM** W1 AN6151. **CODEN** ANNED3. **[CCC]. Bk Rev. Ad Acc. Pr Rev. Circ:** 8,800. available on microfilm and microfiche from University Microfilms International (UMI). Documents available from The Genuine Article, BIOSIS Document Express, CASDDS.
**Desc:** For the community of physicians and scientists interested in the human nervous and neuromuscular systems and their diseases.
**Ind/Abst** Annals Behav. Med.; Biol. Abstr.; Biol. Dig.; Chem. Abstr.; CSA Neuro. Abstr.; Curr. Contents Clin. Med.; Curr. Contents Life Sci.; Curr. Ref. Fish Res.; Dev. Med. Child Neurol.; EMBASE; Energy Res. Abstr. (Jan. 1981-); Health Period. Database; Immunol. Abstr.; Index Med.; Index Vet.; INIS Atomindex [Micro.]; Int. Nurs. Index; Iowa Drug Inf. Serv. (1969-); Med. Abstr. Newsl.; Mod. Med.; Nutr. Abstr. Rev., Ser. B, Live Feeds and Feed.; Nutr. Abstr. Rev., Ser. A, Hum. Exp.; Life Sci. Collect.; Physic. Medline Plus; Psychol. Abstr. (1989-); PsycINFO; PsycLit; Ref. Upd. Basic Ed.; Ref. Upd. Deluxe Ed.; Res. Alert [Full Cov.]; Rev. Med. Vet. Mycology; Rev. Plant Pathol.; Sci. Cit. Index; SCISEARCH; Soc. Sci. Cit. Index [Select. Cov.]; Vet. Bull.; Virol. AIDS Abstr.

US
**ANNUAL REPORT - EPILEPSY ADVISORY COMMITTEE, NATIONAL INSTITUTES OF HEALTH.** **Main/Corp** National Institute of Neurological and Communicative Disorders and Stroke. Epilepsy Advisory Committee. English. an. National Institute of Neurological and Communicative Disorders and Stroke, National Institutes of Health, 9000 Rockville Pike, Bethesda MD 20014. **UDC** 616.853(047.1)(73). ***Continues*** *Annual Report - Epilepsy Advisory Committee, National Institutes of Health.*

US
**ANNUAL REPORT - NATIONAL MULTIPLE SCLEROSIS SOCIETY.**
**Main/Corp** National Multiple Sclerosis Society. (1951)-. Periodical. English. ir (3 issues). Free upon request. National Multiple Sclerosis Society, 6100 Building Estgate Center, Suite 4800, Chattanooga TN 37411. **Tel** (615)954-9700. **ED** Shirley Silverlerg. **LC** RC377.A1; N3. **Circ:** 400,000 (ctrl).
**Desc:** A report on the services provided by and the financial status within a given fiscal year of the National Multiple Sclerosis Society.

US/0147-006X
**ANNUAL REVIEW OF NEUROSCIENCE.** [Annu. rev. neurosci.]. Vol. 1 (1978)-. Academic Scholarly Publication. English. an (March). $47.00 US; $52.00 other. Annual Reviews Inc., 4139 El Camino Way, PO Box 10139, Palo Alto CA 94303-0139. **Tel** (415)493-4400, (800)523-8635, FAX (415)855-9815. **ED** W. Maxwell Cowan. **LC** QP351; .A68. **DD** 591.1/88/05. **NLM** W1 AN778B. **CODEN** ARNSD5. **[CCC].** Index available. cum. index. **Pr Rev.** ctrl circ. available on microfilm and microfiche from University Microfilms International (UMI). Documents available from The Genuine Article, BIOSIS Document Express, Ask*IEEE, CASDDS.
**Desc:** Comprehensive, thorough coverage of latest advances in neuroscience, written by acknowledged experts in the field. Extensive literature citations included.
**Ind/Abst** AGRICOLA [Select. Cov.]; Biol. Abstr.; Chem. Abstr.; CSA Neuro. Abstr.; Curr. Aware. Biol. Sci., CABS; Curr. Contents Life Sci.; EMBASE; Health Period. Database; Index Med. (1978-); Index Sci. Rev. [Full Cov.]; INSPEC; Nutr. Abstr. Rev., Ser. A, Hum. Exp.; Life Sci. Collect.; Psychol. Abstr. (1978-); PsycINFO; PsycLit; Ref. Upd. Basic Ed.; Ref. Upd. Deluxe Ed.; Res. Alert [Full Cov.]; Rev. Agric. Entomol.; Sci. Cit. Index; SCISEARCH; Soc. Sci. Cit. Index [Select. Cov.].

US/0883-2013
**APHASIA, APRAXIA, AGNOSIA.**
**Added/Corp** Biolinguistics Clinical Institutes. Biolinguistics Clinical Education Center. **VFOAT** Aphasia-Apraxia-Agnosia. Vol. 1, No. 1 (Jan. 1979)-. Academic Scholarly Publication. English. ir. $29.50 (individuals); $36.50 (institutions). Biolinguistics, PO Box 11356, Chicago IL 60611. **LC** RC425; .A62. **DD** 616.85/52/005. **NLM** W1 AP17.
**Ind/Abst** EMBASE.

US/0887-6177
**ARCHIVES OF CLINICAL NEUROPSYCHOLOGY.** (ARCHIVES OF CLINICAL NEUROPSYCHOLOGY : THE OFFICIAL JOURNAL OF THE NATIONAL ACADEMY OF NEUROPSYCHOLOGISTS.). [Arch. clin. neuropsychol.]. **Added/Corp** National Academy of Neuropsychologists (U.S.). Vol. 1, No. 1 (1986)-. Periodical. English. Six times a year. $234.00 The Americas; £158.00 other. Pergamon Press, An Imprint of Elsevier Science Ltd., The Boulevard, Langford Lane, Kidlington, Oxford OX5 1GB United Kingdom. **Tel** 011 44 865 843000, 011 44 865 843699, FAX 011 44 865 843010. **(Subscription address:** Elsevier Science Ltd. Oxford Fulfillment Centre, PO Box 800, Kidlington, Oxford OX5 1DX United Kingdom.**) ED** Raymon S. Dean (editor's address: Neuropsychology laboratory, TC-521, Ball State University, Muncie IN 47306). **DD** 616. **NLM** W1; AR451V. **[CCC].** Documents available from The Genuine Article.
**Desc:** Publishes original contributions dealing with psychological aspects of the etiology, diagnosis and treatment of disorders arising out of dysfunction of the central nervous system.
**Ind/Abst** Child Dev. Abstr. Bibliogr.; Curr. Aware. Biol. Sci., CABS; Curr. Contents Soc. Behav. Sci.; EMBASE; Psychol. Abstr. (1986-); PsycINFO; PsycLit; Res. Alert [Full Cov.]; Soc. Sci. Cit. Index [Full Cov.].

US/0003-9942
**ARCHIVES OF NEUROLOGY (CHICAGO).** (ARCHIVES OF NEUROLOGY.). [Arch. neurol.]. **Added/Corp** American Medical Association. American Neurological Association. Canadian Neurological Society. Vol. 3 (July 1960)-. Academic Scholarly Publication. English. mo. $175.00 (institution), $145.00 (individual) US. American Medical Association, 515 North State Street, Chicago IL 60610. **Tel** (312)464-5000, (800)262-2350, FAX (312)464-5831. **ED** Robert J. Joynt. **LC** RC321; .A67. **DD** 616. **NLM** W1 AR455E. **CODEN** ARNEAS. **[CCC].** Index available (free). **Bk Rev. Ad Acc. Pr Rev. Circ:** 19,800. available on microfilm and microfiche from University Microfilms International (UMI); available on an online database (file 442/Full-Text) from DIALOG; and MEDIS. Documents available from The Genuine Article, BIOSIS Document Express, CASDDS. ***Continues*** *A.M.A. Archives of Neurology, 0375-8540.*
**Desc:** Published as an editorial service for physicians who practice neurology as a primary specialty, and to physicians of other specialties who treat conditions of the central nervous system. It is oriented toward the clinician. Every issue offers new concepts and methods applicable to everyday practice.
**Ind/Abst** Abr. Index Med.; Biol. Abstr.; Biostatistica (19??-19??); Chem. Abstr.; CSA Neuro. Abstr. (?-?); Cumul. Index Nurs. Allied Health Lit.; Curr. Aware. Biol. Sci., CABS; Curr. Contents Clin. Med.; Curr. Contents Life Sci.; Curr. Ref. Fish Res.; Dev. Med. Child Neurol.; EMBASE; Energy Res. Abstr.; Health Period. Database; Health Plan. Adminis.; Helminthol. Abstr. (1991-); Index Med.; INIS Atomindex [Micro.]; Int. Aerosp. Abstr.; Int. Nurs. Index; Med. Abstr. Newsl.; Mod. Med.; Nutr. Abstr. Rev., Ser. B, Live Feeds and Feed.; Nutr. Abstr. Rev., Ser. A, Hum. Exp.; Life Sci. Collect.; PESTDOC; Physic. Medline Plus; Protozoolog. Abstr.; Psychol. Abstr. (1960-); PsycINFO; PsycLit; Ref. Upd. Basic Ed.; Ref. Upd. Deluxe Ed.; Res. Alert [Full Cov.]; Rev. Med. Vet. Mycology; Sci. Cit. Index; SCISEARCH; Soc. Sci. Cit. Index [Select. Cov.]; Virol. AIDS Abstr.

IT/0004-0150
**ARCHIVIO DI PSICOLOGIA, NEUROLOGIA E PSICHIATRIA.** **See** Psychology.

SP/0004-0576
**ARCHIVOS DE NEUROBIOLOGIA.** [Arch. neurobiol.]. 2nd Series, Vol. 16 (1936)-. Academic Scholarly Publication. Spanish (summaries and/or abstracts in English). Six times a year (Jan., Mar., May, July, Sept., Nov.). $39.44 Spain; $73.00 Europe; $91.00 others. Editorial Garsi SA, Juan Bravo 46, 28006 Madrid, Spain. **Tel** 011 34 1 4021212, telex 98358 GARSI E. **NLM** W1 AR697. **CODEN** ARNBBK. **[CCC]. Ad Acc. Pr Rev. Circ:** 575. Documents available from The Genuine Article.
**Ind/Abst** EMBASE; Health Plan. Adminis.; Index Med.; Indice Med. Esp.; Linguist. Lang. Behav. Abstr.; Life Sci. Collect.; Psychol. Abstr. (1966-); PsycINFO; PsycLit; Res. Alert [Full Cov.]; Soc. Plann. Policy Dev. Abstr.; Soc. Sci. Cit. Index [Select. Cov.]; Sociol. Abstr.

VE
**ARCHIVOS VENEZOLANOS DE PSIQUIATRIA Y NEUROLOGIA.** **See** Medical Science and Technology-Psychiatry.

IT/1120-866X
**ARGOMENTI DI NEUROLOGIA.** [Argom. neurolog.]. (1991)-. Periodical. Italian. Six times a year. L8300. Masson S.P.A, Via Statuto 2/4, 20121 Milan Italy. **Tel** 011 39 2 63671, FAX 011 39 2 6367211. **UDC** 616.8.

BL/0004-282X
**ARQUIVOS DE NEURO-PSIQUIATRIA.** [Arq. neuro-psiquiatr.]. **Added/Corp** Escola Paulista de Medicina. Catedra de Neurologia. Universidade de Sao Paulo. Faculdade de Medicina. Catedra de Neurologia. Faculdade de Medicina de Sorocaba. Faculdade de Medicina de Ribeirao Preto. Faculdade de Medicina de Campinas. Vol. 1 (1943)-. Portuguese (English, French, Italian and Spanish; summaries and/or abstracts in English, French, Italian and Spanish). Four times a year (Mar., June, Sept., Dec.). $80.00. Associacao Arquivos de Neuro-Psiquiatria, Caixa Postal 8877, 01065 970 Sao Paulo, SP Brazil. **Tel** 11 55 11 2898824, FAX 11 55 11 2898879. **ED** Dr. Antonio Spina-Franca Netto. **NLM** W1 AR917. **CODEN** ANPIAM. **[CCC].** Index available in last issue of volume--attached. cum. index (vols. 1-40). **Ad Acc, Adv Mgr:** Marilia L. Spina Franca. **Circ:** 1,500 (ctrl). available on microfilm from University Microfilms International (UMI); available on CD-ROM from BIREME.
**Desc:** Original papers on neurology, psychiatry and neurosciences.
**Ind/Abst** EMBASE; Health Plan. Adminis.; Index Med.; Psychol. Abstr. (1943-); PsycINFO; PsycLit.

CN/0229-3587
**AUBE.** (L'AUBE / FONDATION PARKINSON DU QUEBEC.). [Aube]. No. 1 (Jan. 1981)-. Periodical. French (English). qt. Free. Fondation Parkinson du Quebec, 110 Ouest Av des Pins, Montreal Quebec H2W 1R7 Canada. **Tel** (514)842-1481, telex 055-60398 CRIM-MTL. **DD** 616.8/33/060714. **UDC** 616.858; 616-05.8; 616.89-008.441.33.

UK/1047-5125
**AUTONOMIC NERVOUS SYSTEM, THE.** (1991)-. Monographic series. English. Harwood Academic Publishers, PO Box 90, Reading RG1 8JL England. **Tel** 011 44 734 560080. **(Subscription address:** International Publishers Distributor at one of the following addresses: 820 Town Center Drive, Langhorne, PA 19047; or PO Box 90, Reading Berkshire RG1 8JL UK; or Kent Ridge PO Box 1180, Singapore 9111, Republic of Singapore**)**

CN/0834-7824
**AXONE (DARTMOUTH).** See Medical Science and Technology-Nursing.

●UK/0961-0421
**BAILLIERE'S CLINICAL NEUROLOGY.** **VFOAT** Clinical Neurology; Neurology. Vol. 1, No. 1 (Apr. 1992)-. Monographic series. English. tq (3 issues). £71.00 (institution). Harcourt Brace & Company Ltd., Foots Cray, High Street, Sidcup Kent DA14 5HP England. **Tel** 011 44 81 300 3322, FAX 011 44 81 309 0807. **(Subscription address:** W. B. Saunders Company / North America Subscriptions, c/o Periodicals, 6277 Sea Harbour Drive, 4th Floor, Orlando FL 32887.**)** **NLM** W1; BA46EN.
**Ind/Abst** Sci. Cit. Index; Soc. Sci. Cit. Index [Select. Cov.].

BG
**BANGLADESH JOURNAL OF NEUROSCIENCE.** **Added/Corp** Institute of Postgraduate Medicine and Research (Bangladesh). Dept. of Neurology. (198?)-. Periodical. English. qt. University of Dhaka / College of Medicine, Shahbag Avenue, 1000 Dacca Bangladesh. **NLM** W1; BA642M.
**Ind/Abst** EMBASE.

GW/0941-9772
**BASIC AND CLINICAL ASPECTS OF NEUROSCIENCE.** [Basic clin. asp. neurosci.]. Vol. 1 (1985)-. Academic Scholarly Publication. English. ir. Price varies per volume. Springer-Verlag GmbH & Company KG, Heidelberger Platz 3, D 14197 Berlin Germany. **Tel** 011 49 30 8207223, FAX 011 49 30 8214091, telex 183 319 SPBLN D. **(Subscription address:** Springer Verlag New York Inc. / for North America, 44 Hartz Way, Secaucus NJ 07096.**)** **ED** C. Weil, E.W. Fluckiger. **NLM** W1; BA813S. **CODEN** BCLNEN. Documents available from BIOSIS Document Express, CASDDS.
**Ind/Abst** Biol. Abstr. (1987-); Chem. Abstr.

NE/0166-4328
**BEHAVIOURAL BRAIN RESEARCH.** [Behav. brain res.]. Vol. 1, No. 1 (Feb. 1980)-. Academic Scholarly Publication. English. Twelve times a year (6 vols.). Fl2958.00. Elsevier Science Publishers BV, PO Box 211, 1000 AE Amsterdam Netherlands. **Tel** 011 31 20 5803642, FAX 011 31 20 5862696, telex 15682. **ED** I Steele Russell, M A Berkley, and M W van Hof. **NLM** W1 BE135DE. **CODEN** BBREDI. **[CCC].** **Pr Rev.** available on microfilm and microfiche from University Microfilms International (UMI). Documents available from The Genuine Article, BIOSIS Document Express, CASDDS.
**Desc:** Provides rapid publication of articles in the neurosciences, where the principal emphasis of the research is concerned with neural mechanisms of behaviour.
**Ind/Abst** Biol. Abstr.; Chem. Abstr.; Chemorecept. Abstr.; CSA Neuro. Abstr.; Curr. Aware. Biol. Sci., CABS; Curr. Contents Life Sci.; Dev. Med. Child Neurol.; EMBASE; Health Plan. Adminis.; Index Med. (Jan. 1980-); Life Sci. Collect.; Psychol. Abstr. (1980-); PsycINFO; PsycLit; Ref. Upd. Deluxe Ed.; Res. Alert [Full Cov.]; Sci. Cit. Index; SCISEARCH; Soc. Sci. Cit. Index [Select. Cov.].

UK/0953-4180
**BEHAVIOURAL NEUROLOGY.** Vol. 1, No. 1 (Spring 1988)-. Periodical. English. qt. $275.00 US; £165.00 other. Rapid Communications of Oxford Ltd, The Old Malthouse, Paradise Street, Oxford OX1 1LD England. **Tel** 011 44 0865 790447, FAX 011 44 0865 244012, telex 9403712. **ED** Dr A.J. Lees. **NLM** W1; BE135F. **CODEN** BNEUEI. **[CCC].** Index available. cum. index. **Bk Rev.** **Ad Acc.** **Acid Free.** Documents available from ADONIS.
**Desc:** Publishes original papers and case reports dealing with disordered human behavior. These embrace the fields of organic and biological psychiatry and neurological disorders of the cerebral cortex. Thus, the journal clearly rehearses matters of interest to behavioral neurologists, and it caters explicitly for neuropsychiatrists and neurologists with a special interest in the cerebral cortex.
**Ind/Abst** ADONIS; Psychoanal. Abstr.; Psychol. Abstr. (1988-); PsycINFO; PsycScan: Appl. Exp. Eng. Psych.; PsycScan: LD/MR; PsycScan: Neuropsych.; Soc. Sci. Cit. Index [Select. Cov.].

GW/0138-5097
**BEITRAEGE ZUR KLINISCHEN NEUROLOGIE UND PSYCHIATRIE.** [Beitr. klin. Neurol. Psychiatr.]. Bd. 49-. German (English). an. Buchexport, Postfach 160, DDR-7010 Leipzig Germany. **Tel** 011 37 41 71370. **ED** Karl Seidel. **UDC** 616.8. **NLM** W1 BE35TH. ***Continues*** *Sammlung Zwangloser Abhandlungen aus dem Gebiete der Psychiatrie und Neurologie, 0558-373X.*
**Ind/Abst** Index Med.

AG
**BIBLIOTECA DE NEUROLOGIA Y CONDUCTA.** (19??)-. Monographic series. Spanish. ir. Price varies per volume. **NLM** W1 BI336B.

GW/0932-6588
**BILDGEBENDE VERFAHREN IN DER NEURORADIOLOGIE.** [Bildgeb. Verfahr. Neuroradiol.]. **VFOAT** New Imaging in Neuroradiology. (1986)-. German. Georg Thieme Verlag Stuttgart, Postfach 301120, D 70451 Stuttgart Germany. **Tel** 011 49 711 89310, FAX 011 49 711 8931298, telex 7 252 275 GTVD. **(Subscription address:** Thieme Medical Publishers Inc., 381 Park Avenue South, New York NY 10016.**)** **NLM** W1; BI615N.

US/1048-1826
**BIORESEARCH TODAY. ALZHEIMER'S DISEASE & SENILE DEMENTIAS.** ***Ceased.*** **VFOAT** BioResearch Today. Alzheimer's Disease & Senile Dementias; Alzheimer's Disease and Senile Dementias. Vol. 1, No. 1-2 (Jan./Feb. 1990)-Ceased (Dec. 1991). English. mo. BioSciences Information Service, Biological Abstracts / BIOSIS, 2100 Arch Street, Philadelphia PA 19103-1399. **Tel** (800)523-4806 US, (215)587-4800 Pennsylvania and worldwide, FAX (215)587-2016, telex 831739. **DD** 616. **CODEN** BTDDE4.
**Desc:** Current awareness journal including abstracts and content summaries of studies involving Alzheimer's Disease and Senile Dementias.

MX/0067-9666
**BOLETIN DE ESTUDIOS MEDICOS Y BIOLOGICOS.** See Biology.

IT/0394-560X
**BOLLETINO - LEGA ITALIANA CONTRO L'EPILESSIA.** (BOLLETINO.). [Boll. - Lega ital. contro epilessia]. (1987)-. Periodical. Italian. qt. Lega Italiana Contro L'Epilessia, Via della Commenda 9, 21035 Milan Italy. **Tel** (2)55180283. **UDC** 616.853.
**Ind/Abst** EMBASE.

UK/0006-8950
**BRAIN.** (BRAIN : A JOURNAL OF NEUROLOGY.). [Brain]. Vol. 1 (1878)-. Academic Scholarly Publication. English. bm. £130.00 UK and Europe; $250.00 other. Oxford University Press, Walton Street, Oxford OX2 6DP England. **Tel** 011 44 865 56767, FAX 011 44 865 267773, telex 837330 OXPRES G. **(Subscription address:** Oxford University Press / USA, Journals Marketing Department, Oxford University Press, 2001 Evans Road, Cary NC 27513.**)** **ED** P. K. Thomas. **LC** RC321; .B79. **DD** 616.8005; B814. **NLM** W1 BR112. **CODEN** BRAIAK. **[CCC].** Index available. **Bk Rev.** **Ad Acc.** **Pr Rev.** available on microfilm and microfiche from University Microfilms International (UMI). Documents available from The Genuine Article, BIOSIS Document Express, CASDDS.
**Desc:** Original papers in clinical neurology and related disciplines, and in the basic neurological sciences where they are relevant to clinical problems.
**Ind/Abst** Biol. Abstr.; Chem. Abstr. (1878-1982); CSA Neuro. Abstr.; Curr. Aware. Biol. Sci., CABS; Dev. Med. Child Neurol.; EMBASE; Health Period. Database; Health Plan. Adminis.; Index Med.; Linguist. Lang. Behav. Abstr.; Life Sci. Collect.; PESTDOC; Ref. Upd. Basic Ed.; Ref. Upd. Deluxe Ed.; Res. Alert [Full Cov.]; Sci. Cit. Index; SCISEARCH; Soc. Plann. Policy Dev. Abstr.; Soc. Sci. Cit. Index [Select. Cov.]; Sociol. Abstr.

US/0278-2626
**BRAIN AND COGNITION.** See Psychology.

JA/0387-7604
**BRAIN & DEVELOPMENT (TOKYO. 1979).** (BRAIN & DEVELOPMENT.). [Brain dev.]. **Added/Corp** Nihon Shoni Shinkeigaku Kenkyukai. **VFOAT** Brain and Development. Vol. 1 (1979)-. Academic Scholarly Publication. English. bm (one volume). Fl420.00. Elsevier Science Publishers BV, PO Box 211, 1000 AE Amsterdam Netherlands. **Tel** 011 31 20 5803642, FAX 011 31 20 5862696, telex 15682. **ED** Yukio Fukuyama. **NLM** W1 BR112H. **[CCC].** **Pr Rev.** Documents available from The Genuine Article.
***Supersedes*** *No To Hattatsu, 0029-0831.*
**Desc:** Covers the field of child neurology and related sciences.
**Ind/Abst** Curr. Aware. Biol. Sci., CABS; Curr. Contents Life Sci.; Dev. Med. Child Neurol. (1983-); EMBASE; Health Plan. Adminis.; Index Med. (1979-); Ref. Upd. Deluxe Ed.; Res. Alert [Full Cov.]; Sci. Cit. Index; SCISEARCH; Soc. Sci. Cit. Index [Select. Cov.].

US/0093-934X
**BRAIN AND LANGUAGE.** [Brain lang.]. Vol. 1 (Jan. 1974)-. Academic Scholarly Publication. English. mo. $422.50 US and Canada; $520.50 other. Academic Press, Inc., 6277 Sea Harbor Drive, Orlando FL 32887. **Tel** (800)543-9534, (407)345-4100, FAX (407)363-9661. **ED** Harry A. Whitaker and Andre Roch Lecours. **LC** RC423.A1; B68. **DD** 612/.78/05. **NLM** W1 BR112L. **CODEN** BRLGA. **[CCC].** **Bk Rev.** **Pr Rev.** Documents available from The Genuine Article.
**Desc:** A journal publishing original theoretical, clinical, and experimental papers on human language and communication; speech, hearing, reading, writing, higher language functions, and nonverbal communication as they relate to brain structure and function.
**Ind/Abst** Curr. Contents Life Sci.; Curr. Contents Soc. Behav. Sci.; Dev. Med. Child Neurol.; EMBASE; Health Plan. Adminis.; Index Med.; INIS Atomindex [Micro.]; Linguist. Lang. Behav. Abstr. (1974-) [Full Cov.]; MLA Int. Bibl. Books Artic. Mod. Lang. Lit.; Life Sci. Collect.; Psychol. Abstr. (1974-); PsycINFO; PsycLit; Res. Alert [Full Cov.]; Sci. Cit. Index; SCISEARCH; Soc. Plann. Policy Dev. Abstr.; Soc. Sci. Cit. Index [Full Cov.]; Sociol. Abstr.

SZ/0006-8977
**BRAIN, BEHAVIOR AND EVOLUTION.** [Brain behav. evol.]. Vol. 1 (1968)-. Periodical. English. mo. $978.00. S. Karger AG, Allschwilerstrasse 10, PO Box - Postfach - Case Postale, CH-4009 Basel Switzerland. **Tel** 011 41 61 306-1111, FAX 011 41 61 306-1234, telex CH 962 652. **ED** R. Glenn Northcutt and Mary Sue Northcutt. **LC** QL750; .B48. **DD** 596/.01/8. **NLM** W1 BR113. **CODEN** BRBEBE. **[CCC].** **Bk Rev.** **Pr Rev.** available on microfilm and microfiche from University Microfilms International (UMI). Documents available from The Genuine Article, BIOSIS Document Express.
**Desc:** Understanding the evolution of nervous systems and how they subserve behavior is the aim of this journal. Comparative neurobiological studies focus on the morphology, physiology, and histochemistry of various neural structures, as well as aspects of psychology, ecology, and ethology in both vertebrates and invertebrates. In addition to original research reports, the journal contains review and theory papers as well book reviews.
**Ind/Abst** Anim. Behav. Abstr.; Biol. Abstr.; CSA Neuro. Abstr.; Curr. Aware. Biol. Sci., CABS; Curr. Contents Life Sci.; EMBASE; GeoRef; Immunol. Abstr.; Index Med.; Life Sci. Collect.; Psychol. Abstr. (1971-); PsycINFO; PsycLit; Ref. Upd. Deluxe Ed.; Res. Alert [Full Cov.]; Sci. Cit. Index; SCISEARCH; Soc. Sci. Cit. Index [Select. Cov.].

US/0889-1591
**BRAIN, BEHAVIOR, AND IMMUNITY.** [Brain behav. immun.]. Vol. 1, No. 1 (Mar. 1987)-. Academic Scholarly Publication. English. qt (4 issues). $208.00 US and Canada; $234.00 other. Academic Press, Inc., 6277 Sea Harbor Drive, Orlando FL 32887. **Tel** (800)543-9534, (407)345-4100, FAX (407)363-9661. **ED** Robert Ader. **LC** QP356.47; .B73. **DD** 599/.0188/05. **NLM** W1; BR113B. **CODEN** BBIMEW. **[CCC].** Documents available from The Genuine Article, BIOSIS Document Express, CASDDS.
**Desc:** Presents research concerned with the interactions between the nervous system and the immune system at the molecular, cellular, and organismic levels. The journal features basic research in subhuman animals and clinical and experimental studies in humans.
**Ind/Abst** Biol. Abstr. (1987-); Chem. Abstr.; CSA Neuro. Abstr.; Curr. Aware. Biol. Sci., CABS; Curr. Contents Life Sci.; EMBASE; Health Plan. Adminis.; Index Med. (Vol. 1, No. 1, 1987-); Psychol. Abstr. (1987-); PsycINFO; PsycLit; Res. Alert [Full Cov.]; Sci. Cit. Index; SCISEARCH; Soc. Sci. Cit. Index [Select. Cov.].

SZ/0259-1278
**BRAIN DYSFUNCTION.** ***Title Change.*** [Brain dysfunct.]. **Added/Corp** OASI Institute for Research and Prevention of Mental Retardation (Troina, Italy) OASI Istituto per la Ricerca sul Ritardo Mentale e l'Involuzione Cerebrale. (Jan./Feb. 1988)-(1992). Periodical. English. Six times a year (one volume per year). S. Karger AG, Allschwilerstrasse 10, PO Box - Postfach - Case Postale, CH-4009 Basel Switzerland. **Tel** 011 41 61 306-1111, FAX 011 41 61 306-1234, telex CH 962 652. **ED** U. Scapagnini, R. Ferri, A. Schinzel, Y. Suzuki, J. R. Villablanca, M. Cioni. **NLM** W1; BR113C. **CODEN** BRDYEJ. **[CCC].** Index available. cum. index. **Ad Acc.** **Circ:** 1,200 (ctrl). available on microfilm; available on microfiche; available in microform. Documents available from The Genuine Article, BIOSIS Document Express.
***Continued by*** *Developmental Brain Dysfunction.*
**Desc:** The journal serves as a forum for scientific reports within the broad field of abnormal brain function particularly during development and aging (and including normal aging and development). Papers, either basic or clinical, on the genetic, anatomical, pathophysiological, biochemical or metabolic bases of impaired brain function as well as relating to responses of the nervous system to experimental interventions or pathologies and any attempts at experimentally modifying those responses are considered. Overriding criteria for acceptance of papers are sound scientific methodology, novelty, substantial experimental or clinical relevance, and interest to a multidisciplinary audience.
**Ind/Abst** Biol. Abstr. (1988-); EMBASE; Psychol. Abstr. (1988-); PsycINFO; PsycLit; Res. Alert [Full Cov.]; Soc. Sci. Cit. Index [Select. Cov.].

UK/0269-9052
**BRAIN INJURY.** (BRAIN INJURY : BI.). [Brain inj.]. **VFOAT** BI. Vol. 1, No. 1 (July-Sept. 1987)-. Periodical. English. Eight times a year. $428.00 North America; £259.00 UK. Taylor & Francis Ltd., Rankine Road, Basingstoke Hampshire, RG24 8PR United Kingdom. **Tel** 011 44 256 840366, FAX 011 44 256 479438, telex 858540. **(Subscription address:** Taylor & Francis Inc., 1900 Frost Road, Suite 101, Bristol PA 19007-1598.**)** **ED** Henry H. Stonnington, Dr. Nathan Cope, Takashi Tsubokawa and William W. McKinlay. **LC** RC387.5; .B72. **DD** 617/.481044/05. **NLM** W1; BR113E. **CODEN** BRAIEO. **[CCC].** available on microfilm and microfiche from University Microfilms International (UMI). Documents available from The Genuine Article, BIOSIS Document Express.
**Desc:** Covers all aspects of brain injury, ranging through basic scientific research, epidemiology, neuropathology,

neurosurgical and other medical procedures, assessment methods, rehabilitation and outcome.
**Ind/Abst** Biol. Abstr.; EMBASE; Health Plan. Adminis.; Index Med. (1986-); Linguist. Lang. Behav. Abstr.; Res. Alert [Full Cov.]; Soc. Plann. Policy Dev. Abstr.; Soc. Sci. Cit. Index [Select. Cov.]; Sociol. Abstr.

SZ/1015-6305
**BRAIN PATHOLOGY.** **Added/Corp** International Society of Neuropathology. Vol. 1, No. 1 (Sept. 1990)-. Periodical. English. qt (Jan., Apr., July, Oct.). 150.00F. International Society of Neuropathology, PO Box CH-8033, Zurich Switzerland. **Tel** 011 41 1 2552107, FAX 011 41 1 3637164. **NLM** W1; BR114M. **CODEN** BRPAE7. Documents available from The Genuine Article.
**Ind/Abst** Curr. Aware. Biol. Sci., CABS; Curr. Contents Life Sci.; Res. Alert; Sci. Cit. Index; SCISEARCH.

NE/0006-8993
**BRAIN RESEARCH.** [Brain res.]. Vol. 1 (Jan. 1966)-. Academic Scholarly Publication. English. ir (108 issues per year). FI19345.00. Elsevier Science Publishers BV, PO Box 211, 1000 AE Amsterdam Netherlands. **Tel** 011 31 20 5803642, FAX 011 31 20 5862696, telex 15682. **ED** D P Purpura. **LC** QP376; .B72. **DD** 599. **NLM** W1 BR114S. **CODEN** BRREAP. **[CCC].** available on microfilm and microfiche from University Microfilms International (UMI). Documents available from The Genuine Article, BIOSIS Document Express, CASDDS, ADONIS. ***Continued in part by*** *Brain Research. Cognitive Brain Research, 0926-6410.*
**Ind/Abst** ADONIS; Anim. Behav. Abstr.; Biol. Abstr.; Calcium Calcif. Tissue Abstr.; Chem. Abstr.; Chem. Titles; Chemorecept. Abstr.; CSA Neuro. Abstr.; Curr. Aware. Biol. Sci., CABS; Curr. Contents Life Sci.; Curr. Primate Ref.; Dairy Sci. Abstr.; EMBASE; Fish Rev. (Jan. 1989-19??); Helminthol. Abstr. (1991-); Index Med.; Index Vet.; Int. Aerosp. Abstr.; Nutr. Abstr. Rev., Ser. B, Live Feeds and Feed.; Nutr. Abstr. Rev., Ser. A, Hum. Exp.; Oncog. Growth Factors Abstr.; Life Sci. Collect.; PESTDOC; Protozoolog. Abstr.; Psychol. Abstr. (1970-); PsycINFO; PsycLit; Ref. Upd. Basic Ed.; Ref. Upd. Deluxe Ed.; Res. Alert [Full Cov.]; Rev. Agric. Entomol.; Rev. Med. Vet. Entomol.; Sci. Cit. Index; Small Anim. Abstr. Bibliogr.; Soc. Sci. Cit. Index [Select. Cov.]; SportSearch; Vet. Bull.; Toxicol. Abstr.; Virol. AIDS Abstr.; Wildl. Rev. (Jan. 1989-19??).

US/0361-9230
**BRAIN RESEARCH BULLETIN.** [Brain res. bull.]. Vol. 1 (Jan./Feb. 1976)-. Academic Scholarly Publication. English. Eighteen times a year. $1528.00 The Americas; £1025.00 other. Pergamon Press, An Imprint of Elsevier Science Ltd., The Boulevard, Langford Lane, Kidlington, Oxford OX5 1GB United Kingdom. **Tel** 011 44 865 843000, 011 44 865 843699, FAX 011 44 865 843010. **(Subscription address:** Elsevier Science Ltd. Oxford Fulfillment Centre, PO Box 800, Kidlington, Oxford OX5 1DX United Kingdom.**) ED** Matthew J. Wayner. **LC** QP376; .B725. **DD** 599/.01/88. **NLM** W1 BR1141. **CODEN** BRBUDU. **[CCC]. Bk Rev. Ad Acc. Pr Rev.** ctrl circ. available on microfilm and microfiche from University Microfilms International (UMI). Documents available from The Genuine Article, BIOSIS Document Express, CASDDS. ***Absorbed*** *Journal of Electrophysiological Techniques, 0361-0209.*
**Desc:** Publishes original reports on all aspects of the nervous system: biochemistry, physiology, anatomy, ultrastructure, electrophysiology, neurology, pathology and behavior. Features rapid communications and laboratory instrumentation and computing sections.
**Ind/Abst** Anim. Behav. Abstr.; Biol. Abstr.; Chem. Abstr.; Chemorecept. Abstr.; CSA Neuro. Abstr. (?-?); Curr. Contents Life Sci.; Curr. Primate Ref.; EMBASE; Energy Res. Abstr. (May 1981-); Health Plan. Adminis.; Index Med.; Index Vet.; INIS Atomindex [Micro.]; Int. Aerosp. Abstr.; Nutr. Abstr. Rev., Ser. B, Live Feeds and Feed.; Nutr. Abstr. Rev., Ser. A, Hum. Exp.; Life Sci. Collect.; Pig News Inf.; Protozoolog. Abstr.; Psychol. Abstr. (1976-); PsycINFO; PsycLit; Ref. Upd. Basic Ed.; Ref. Upd. Deluxe Ed.; Res. Alert [Full Cov.]; Sci. Cit. Index; SCISEARCH; Small Anim. Abstr. Bibliogr.; Soc. Sci. Cit. Index [Select. Cov.].

NE
**BRAIN RESEARCH REVIEWS.** (BRAIN RESEARCH. BRAIN RESEARCH REVIEWS.). [Brain res. rev.]. Vol. 14, No. 1 (Jan./March 1989)-. Academic Scholarly Publication. English. Six times a year (2 vols.). FI860.00; FI19345.00 combination subscription with Developmental Brain Research and Molecular Brain Research. Elsevier Science Publishers BV, PO Box 211, 1000 AE Amsterdam Netherlands. **Tel** 011 31 20 5803642, FAX 011 31 20 5862696, telex 15682. **NLM** W1; BR114T. **CODEN** BRERD2. available on microfilm from University Microfilms International (UMI). Documents available from ADONIS. ***Continues*** *Brain Research Reviews, 0165-0173.*
**Ind/Abst** ADONIS; Index Med. (1989-).

US/0896-0267
**BRAIN TOPOGRAPHY.** [Brain topogr.]. Vol. 1, No. 1 (Fall 1988)-. Periodical. English. qt. £79.00 (individuals), £255.00 (institutions) UK & Europe; $345.00 US; $405.00 other. Human Sciences Press, PO Box 735, 233 Spring Street, New York NY 10013. **Tel** (212)620-8000, FAX (212)807-1047, telex 23421139. **(Subscription address:** Eurospan Ltd., Journals and Serials Division, 3 Henrietta Street, Covent Garden, London WC2E 8LU England.**) ED** Peter Wong. **DD** 616. **NLM** W1; BR116Q. **CODEN** BRTOEZ. **[CCC].** available on microfilm from University Microfilms International (UMI). Documents available from BIOSIS Document Express.
**Desc:** Devoted entirely to applications of topographic techniques in clinical neurophysiology and functional localization. Emphasizes both fundamental theory and clinical applications of EEG and evoked potential mapping.
**Ind/Abst** Biol. Abstr.; Curr. Aware. Biol. Sci., CABS; EMBASE; Psychol. Abstr. (1989-); PsycINFO (1990-); PsycLit.

UK/0268-8697
**BRITISH JOURNAL OF NEUROSURGERY.** [Br. j. neurosurg.]. Vol. 1, No. 1 (1987)-. Periodical. English. bm. £198.00. Carfax Publishing Company, PO Box 25 Abingdon, Oxfordshire OX14 3UE England. **Tel** 011 44 235 555335, FAX (0279)31067, telex 817484. **(Subscription address:** US and Canada/ PO Box 2025, Dunnellon, FL 34430-2025; telephone:(904)489-6996**) ED** Robert Maurice-Williams. **NLM** W1; BR582. **CODEN** BJNEEL. **[CCC]. Pr Rev.** available on microfiche. Documents available from The Genuine Article, BIOSIS Document Express.
**Desc:** Publishes original, independently refereed articles that reflect current neurosurgical practice throughout the world. Its mixture of material on all aspects of case assessment and surgical practice has proved to be just the sort of publication that busy surgeons want and need to read.
**Ind/Abst** Biol. Abstr. (1987-); Curr. Contents Clin. Med.; Dev. Med. Child Neurol.; EMBASE; Health Plan. Adminis.; Index Med. (1987-); Res. Alert [Full Cov.]; SCISEARCH.

CN/0836-6845
**BULLETIN / THE NATIONAL EATING DISORDER INFORMATION CENTRE.** [Bull. - Natl. Eat. Disord. Inf. Cent.]. **Added/Corp** National Eating Disorder Information Centre. Vol. 1, No. 1 (April/May 1986)-. Bulletin. English. Five times a year. 20.00Can$. National Eating Disorder Information Centre, 200 Elizabeth Street, CW 1-304, Toronto Ontario M5G 2C4 Canada. **Tel** (416)340-4188, (416)340-4156. **ED** Merryl Bear. **DD** 616.85/2. **Bk Rev. Circ:** 900.
**Desc:** Funded by the Community Mental health Branch, Ministry of Health and sponsored by the Toronto Hospital.

US/1047-8183
**CA SELECTS: ALZHEIMER'S DISEASE & RELATED MEMORY DYSFUNCTIONS.** **See** Chemistry-Abstracting, Bibliographies and Statistics.

CN/0317-1671
**CANADIAN JOURNAL OF NEUROLOGICAL SCIENCES.** (THE CANADIAN JOURNAL OF NEUROLOGICAL SCIENCES. LE JOURNAL CANADIEN DES SCIENCES NEUROLOGIQUES.). [Can. j. neurol. sci.]. **Added/Corp** Canadian Neurological Society. Canadian Neurosurgical Society. Canadian Society of Electroencephalographers, Electromyographers, and Clinical Neurophysiologists Canadian Society of Clinical Neurophysiologists Canadian Association for Child Neurology. **VFOAT** Journal Canadien des Sciences Neurologiques. Vol. 1 (Feb. 1974)-. Periodical. English (French; summaries and/or abstracts in French). Four times a year (also supplements). 75.00Can$ Canada; $78.00 other. Canadian Journal of Neurological Sciences, PO Box 4220 Station C, Calgary Alberta T2T 5N1 Canada. **Tel** (403)229-9575, FAX (403)229-1661. **ED** R. G. Lee. **LC** RC321; .C28. **DD** 616.8/05. **NLM** W1 CA596I. **CODEN** CJNSA2. **[CCC]. Ad Acc. Pr Rev. Circ:** 1,400. available on microfilm and microfiche from University Microfilms International (UMI). Documents available from The Genuine Article, BIOSIS Document Express, CASDDS.
**Desc:** A peer-reviewed journal which publishes original work in clinical and basic neuroscience.
**Ind/Abst** Biol. Abstr.; Chem. Abstr.; CSA Neuro. Abstr. (?-?); Curr. Contents Clin. Med.; Curr. Contents Life Sci.; Dev. Med. Child Neurol.; EMBASE; Index Med.; Nutr. Abstr. Rev., Ser. B, Live Feeds and Feed.; Nutr. Abstr. Rev., Ser. A, Hum. Exp.; Life Sci. Collect.; Ref. Upd. Deluxe Ed.; Res. Alert [Full Cov.]; Sci. Cit. Index; SCISEARCH.

US/1057-9125
**CANCERGRAM. SERIES CT18, NERVOUS SYSTEM MALIGNANCIES. DIAGNOSIS, TREATMENT.** ***Ceased.*** **See** Medical Science and Technology-Neoplasma, Neoplastic.

US/0272-4340
**CELLULAR AND MOLECULAR NEUROBIOLOGY.** [Cell. mol. neurobiol.]. Vol. 1, No. 1 (March 1981)-. Academic Scholarly Publication. English. Six times a year. $355.00 institutions, $75.00 individuals US; $415.00 institutions, $88.00 individuals other. Plenum Press, 233 Spring Street, New York NY 10013-1578. **Tel** (212)620-8000, (800)221-9369, FAX (212)463-0742, (212)807-1047, telex 23/421139. **ED** Juan M. Saavedra. **LC** QP351; .C37. **DD** 599.01/88. **NLM** W1 CE1287. **CODEN** CMNEDI. **[CCC].** Index available. **Pr Rev.** available on microfilm and microfiche from University Microfilms International (UMI). Documents available from The Genuine Article, BIOSIS Document Express, CASDDS.
**Desc:** Publishes original research abstracts on neuronal and brain function at the cellular or subcellular levels. Articles use anatomic, physiologic, pharmacologic, and biochemical approaches.
**Ind/Abst** Biol. Abstr.; Chem. Abstr.; CSA Neuro. Abstr.; Curr. Aware. Biol. Sci., CABS; Curr. Contents Life Sci.; Dairy Sci. Abstr.; EMBASE; Index Med. (1981-); INIS Atomindex [Micro.]; Life Sci. Collect.; Ref. Upd. Deluxe Ed.; Res. Alert [Full Cov.]; Rev. Med. Vet. Entomol.; Sci. Cit. Index; SCISEARCH.

NO/0333-1024
**CEPHALALGIA.** (CEPHALALGIA : AN INTERNATIONAL JOURNAL OF HEADACHE.). [Cephalalgia]. (March 1981)-. Academic Scholarly Publication. English. bm. Kr1250.00, $220.00. Scandinavian University Press, PO Box 2959 Toeyen, N 0608 Oslo 6 Norway. **Tel** 011 47 2 2575400, FAX 011 47 2 2575353, telex 71896 UROR N. **(Subscription address:** Scandinavian University Press, 200 Meacham Ave., Elmont NY 11003.**) ED** Marcia Wilkinson. **NLM** W1 CE565. **CODEN** CEPHDF. **[CCC].** cum. index. **Ad Acc. Pr Rev. Circ:** 800 (ctrl). available on microfilm and microfiche from University Microfilms International (UMI). Documents available from The Genuine Article, BIOSIS Document Express, CASDDS.
**Desc:** Provides an international forum for original research papers, review articles, and short communications on every aspect of headache. The official journal of the International Headache Society (IHS).
**Ind/Abst** Biol. Abstr.; Chem. Abstr. (1981-1983); Curr. Contents Clin. Med.; EMBASE; Health Plan. Adminis.; Index Med. (1981-); Nutr. Res. Newsl.; Res. Alert [Full Cov.]; SCISEARCH; Soc. Sci. Cit. Index [Select. Cov.].

US/1047-3211
**CEREBRAL CORTEX (NEW YORK, N.Y. 1991).** (CEREBRAL CORTEX.). [Cereb. cortex]. Vol. 1, No. 1 (Jan./Feb. 1991)-. Periodical. English. bm (6 issues). $206.00 institutions, $130.00 individuals US; $240.00 institutions, $137.00 individuals other. Oxford University Press / New York, 200 Madison Avenue, New York NY 10016. **Tel** (212)679-7300, (919)677-0977, (800)451-7556, (800)445-9714, FAX (919)677-1303. **(Subscription address:** Oxford University Press / USA, Journals Marketing Department, Oxford University Press, 2001 Evans Road, Cary NC 27513.**) LC** QP383; .C455. **DD** 599/.0188. **NLM** W1; CE569V. **[CCC]. Bk Rev. Ad Acc. Acid Free.** available on microfilm and microfiche from University Microfilms International (UMI). Documents available from The Genuine Article.
**Desc:** The journal is multidisciplinary and covers the large variety of modern neurobiological and neuropsychological techniques, including anatomy, biochemistry, molecular neurobiology, electrophysiology, behavior, artificial intelligence, and theoretical modelling. In addition to research articles, the journal includes special features such as brief reviews, book reviews, and commentaries.
**Ind/Abst** Curr. Aware. Biol. Sci., CABS; Ref. Upd. Deluxe Ed.; Res. Alert [Full Cov.].

SZ/1015-9770
**CEREBROVASCULAR DISEASES.** Vol. 1 (Jan./Feb. 1991)-. Periodical. English. bm (6 issues). $345.00. S. Karger AG, Allschwilerstrasse 10, PO Box - Postfach - Case Postale, CH-4009 Basel Switzerland. **Tel** 011 41 61 306-1111, FAX 011 41 61 306-1234, telex CH 962 652. **ED** J. Bogousslavsky, M. G. Hennerici. **NLM** W1; CE584. **CODEN** CDISE7. Index available. cum. index. **Ad Acc. Pr Rev. Circ:** 1,000. available on microfilm and microfiche. Documents available from BIOSIS Document Express.
**Desc:** Aims to meet the growing need for a new international forum providing the readers with the most sophisticated, up-to-date scientific information on clinical data, diagnostic testing, and therapeutic issues, dealing with all aspects of stroke and cerebrovascular diseases. The journal's scope encompasses all aspects related to clinical advances in the field, while purely experimental work appears if directly relevant to clinical issues.
**Ind/Abst** Biol. Abstr.; Curr. Aware. Biol. Sci., CABS; Ref. Upd. Deluxe Ed.

XR/0301-0597
**CESKOSLOVENSKA NEUROLOGIE A NEUROCHIRURGIE.** [Cesk. neurol. neurochir.]. Vol. 36 (Jan. 1973)-. Academic Scholarly Publication. Czech (summaries and/or abstracts in Russian and English; table of contents in Russian and English). bm. $86.00. **(Subscription address:** Artia Pegas Press Ltd., Palac Metro Narodni Trida 25, 11210 Prague 1 Czech Republic.**) NLM** W1 CE897E. **[CCC].** Documents available from The Genuine Article. ***Continues*** *Ceskoslovenska Neurologie, 0009-0581.*
**Ind/Abst** EMBASE; Index Med.; Res. Alert [Full Cov.]; Saf. Health Work.

NE/0929-7049
**CHILD NEUROPSYCHOLOGY.** **See** Medical Science and Technology-Psychiatry.

GW/0256-7040
**CHILD'S NERVOUS SYSTEM.** **See** Medical Science and Technology-Pediatrics.

CC/0412-4057
**CHUNG-HUA SHEN CHING CHING SHEN K'O TSA CHIH.** [Chung-Hua Shen Ching Ching Shen K'o Tsa Chih]. **VFOAT** Chinese Journal of Neurology and Psychiatry; Zhonghua Shenjing-Jingshenke Zazhi. (1955)-. Chinese. bm. $20.85. China National Publ Industry Trade, PO Box 782, Beijing, People's Republic of China. **Tel** 011 86 1 4215031. **CODEN** CHSCAX.

US/0196-6383
**CLINICAL AND EXPERIMENTAL NEUROLOGY.** [Clin. exp. neurol.]. Vol. 14 (1977)-. Academic Scholarly Publication. English. an. 50.00Aus$. Australian Association of Neurologists, Westmead Hospital, Department of Neurology, NSW 2145 Australia. **Tel** 011 61 2 6336960. **LC** QP351; .A8512. **DD** 616.8/05. **UDC** 616.8. **NLM** W1 CL664BN. Documents available from CASDDS.
**Ind/Abst** Chem. Abstr.; Health Plan. Adminis.; Index Med. (1978-1987).

US/0195-7015
**CLINICAL APHASIOLOGY.** (CLINICAL APHASIOLOGY : PROCEEDINGS OF THE CONFERENCE.). **Main/Conf** Conference on Clinical Aphasiology. (1972)-. Proceedings. English. an. $49.00 (Vol. 22). Pro-Ed Inc., 8700 Shoal Creek Boulevard, Austin TX 78757-6897. **Tel** (512)451-3246, FAX (512)451-8542. **ED** Gerald Wallace. **LC** RC425; .C64a. **DD** 616.85/52/005. **NLM** W1; CL668F. **[CCC]. Circ:** 500.
**Desc:** Covers the diagnosis and treatment of neurologically-based speech and language disorders.

US/0009-9155
**CLINICAL EEG ELECTROENCEPHALOGRAPHY.** (CLINICAL ELECTROENCEPHALOGRAPHY.). [Clin. EEG electroencephalogr.]. **Added/Corp** American Medical Electroencephalographic Association. **VFOAT** Clinical EEG Electroencephalography. Vol. 1 (Jan. 1970)-. Academic Scholarly Publication. English. qt. $50.00 US; $55.00 Canada Caribbean, Central America & Mexico; $59.00 other. American Medical Electroencephalographic Association, 850 Elm Grove Road, Suite 11, Elm Grove WI 53122. **Tel** (414)797-7800, FAX (414)782-8788. **ED** Miles Drake. **NLM** W1 CL695. **CODEN** CEEGA. Index available. **Ad Acc. Pr Rev. Circ:** 2,000. available on microfilm and microfiche from University Microfilms International (UMI). Documents available from The Genuine Article, BIOSIS Document Express.
**Desc:** The goal of this journal is to convey clinically relevant research and development in electroencephalography to physicians, EEG labs, hospitals and medical libraries.
**Ind/Abst** Biol. Abstr.; Curr. Contents Clin. Med.; Dev. Med. Child Neurol.; EMBASE; Health Plan. Adminis.; Index Med. (1978-); Life Sci. Collect.; Res. Alert [Full Cov.]; Sci. Cit. Index; SCISEARCH; Soc. Sci. Cit. Index [Select. Cov.].

NE/0303-8467
**CLINICAL NEUROLOGY AND NEUROSURGERY.** [Clin. neurol. neurosurg.]. **Added/Corp** Nederlandse Vereniging voor Neurochirurgen. Nederlandse Vereniging voor Neurologie. Vol. 77 (Sept. 1974)-. Academic Scholarly Publication. English. qt (1 volume). Fl350.00. Elsevier Science Publishers BV, PO Box 211, 1000 AE Amsterdam Netherlands. **Tel** 011 31 20 5803642, FAX 011 31 20 5862696, telex 15682. **ED** J M Minderhoud. **NLM** W1 CL731Q. **CODEN** CNNSBV. **[CCC]. Bk Rev. Ad Acc. Pr Rev. Circ:** 1,250 (ctrl). Documents available from The Genuine Article, BIOSIS Document Express. ***Continues in part*** *Psychiatria, Neurologia, Neurochirurgia, 0033-2666.*
**Desc:** An international journal publishing papers and reports on the clinical aspects of neurology and neurosurgery.
**Ind/Abst** Biol. Abstr.; CSA Neuro. Abstr. (?-?); Curr. Contents Clin. Med.; Dev. Med. Child Neurol.; EMBASE; Helminthol. Abstr.; Index Med.; Life Sci. Collect.; Res. Alert [Full Cov.]; SCISEARCH.

NE/0923-084X
**CLINICAL NEUROPHYSIOLOGY UPDATES.** (1989)-. Monographic series. English. Price varies per volume. Elsevier Science Publishers BV, PO Box 211, 1000 AE Amsterdam Netherlands. **Tel** 011 31 20 5803642, FAX 011 31 20 5862696, telex 15682. **NLM** W1; CL731UC.

NE/0920-1637
**CLINICAL NEUROPSYCHOLOGIST, THE.** [Clin. neuropsychol.]. **VFOAT** TCN. Vol. 1, No. 1 (Jan. 1987)-. Periodical. English. qt. Fl1675.00 (all four groups) (Institutions). Swets & Zeitlinger BV, Heereweg 347B PO Box 825, 2160 SZ Lisse Holland. **Tel** 011 31 2521 35111, FAX 02521-15888, telex 41325. **(Subscription address:** Swets Publishing Service, PO Box 825, 2160 SZ Lisse The Netherlands**) ED** Byron P. Rourke, Kenneth M. Adams. **NLM** W1; CL731UK. **CODEN** CLNEEC. **[CCC].** Documents available from The Genuine Article.
**Desc:** The following areas are of particular interest: Descriptions and Evaluations of Educational and Training Programs, Clinical Issues, Professional Issues, Publication and Test Reviews. Comments on previously published work in the journal or any other matter that is judged to be of importance to the practicing clinical neuropsychologist.
**Ind/Abst** EMBASE; Except. Child Educ. Resour.; Linguist. Lang. Behav. Abstr.; Psychol. Abstr. (1987-); PsycINFO (1990-); PsycLit; Res. Alert [Full Cov.]; Soc. Plann. Policy Dev. Abstr.; Soc. Sci. Cit. Index [Select. Cov.]; Sociol. Abstr.

●US/1065-6766
**CLINICAL NEUROSCIENCE (NEW YORK, N.Y.).** (CLINICAL NEUROSCIENCE.). [Clin. neurosci.]. (1993)-. Periodical. English. qt. $192.00 US; $252.00 Canada and Mexico; $274.50 other. John Wiley & Sons, Inc., 605 Third Avenue, New York NY 10158-0012. **Tel** (212)850-6000, (212)850-6645, FAX (212)850-6088, telex 12-7063. **(Subscription address:** John Wiley & Sons / England, Baffins Lane, Chichester, West Sussex PO19 1UD England.**) ED** Ivan Bodis-Wollner and Robert C. Collins. **DD** 616. **NLM** W1; CL731WH. **CODEN** CINUE5.
**Desc:** Professional periodical devoted to serving as an educational forum and to promoting information exchange among basic and clinical researchers and practitioners in neurobiology, neurology and psychiatry.
**Ind/Abst** Soc. Sci. Cit. Index [Select. Cov.].

US/0069-4827
**CLINICAL NEUROSURGERY. See** Medical Science and Technology-Surgery.

UK/0069-4835
**CLINICS IN DEVELOPMENTAL MEDICINE.** [Clin. dev. med.]. **Added/Corp** Spastics Society. Medical Education and Information Unit. Spastics International Medical Publications. No. 13 (1964)-. Monographic series. English. qt. $137.00 US, Canada & Mexico; £92.00 other. Cambridge University Press, The Edinburgh Building, Shaftesbury Road, Cambridge CB2 2RU United Kingdom. **Tel** 011 44 223 312393, FAX 011 44 223 325959. **(Subscription address:** Cambridge University Press / North America, 110 Midland Avenue, Port Chester NY 10573.**) ED** Martin C. O. Bax. **NLM** W1 CL831B. **CODEN** CDVMAG. Documents available from BIOSIS Document Express. ***Continues*** *Little Club Clinics in Developmental Medicine.*
**Desc:** Covers the wide range of circumstances affecting child development. Each thematic volume provides a comprehensive study of the theoretical and clinical aspects of a specific childhood condition or disorder. The volumes primarily offer a practical approach to understanding and managing conditions affecting children's physical and mental development. Subject matter of considerable physiological and research interest are also addressed.
**Ind/Abst** Biol. Abstr. (1987-).

●NZ/1172-7047
**CNS DRUGS : THE CLINICAL REVIEW OF DRUGS AND THERAPEUICS IN PSYCHIATRY AND NEUROLOGY. See** Pharmacy and Pharmacology.

●NE/0926-6410
**COGNITIVE BRAIN RESEARCH. VFOAT** Cognitive Brain Research. (1992)-. Academic Scholarly Publication. English. qt (1 volume). Fl409.00. Elsevier Science Publishers BV, PO Box 211, 1000 AE Amsterdam Netherlands. **Tel** 011 31 20 5803642, FAX 011 31 20 5862696, telex 15682. **LC** IN PROCESS; QP360.5; .B72. **NLM** W1; BR114SL. **CODEN** CBRREZ. **[CCC].** ***Continues*** *Brain Research, 0006-8993.*
**Ind/Abst** Curr. Aware. Biol. Sci., CABS; Ref. Upd. Deluxe Ed.

US/0361-3267
**COLLABORATIVE STUDY ON CEREBRAL PALSY, MENTAL RETARDATION, & OTHER NEUROLOGICAL & SENSORY DISORDERS OF INFANCY & CHILDHOOD.** No. 6- July 1972/June 1973-. Periodical. English. US National Institute of Neurological Disease & Strokes. **Tel** (301)496-4000. **NLM** ZWS 340 B582. ***Continues*** *Bibliography: The Collaborative Study on Cerebral Palsy, Mental Retardation, and Other Neurological and Sensory Disorders of Infancy and Childhood, 0361-3259.*
**Desc:** Compilation of Collaborative Perinatal Research Project publications.

US/0896-5099
**COMMENTS ON DEVELOPMENTAL NEUROBIOLOGY.** ***Ceased.*** [Comments dev. neurobiol.]. (1989)-Volume 1 Issue 6. Periodical. English. bm. Gordon & Breach Science Publishers, Inc., PO Box 786, Cooper Station, New York NY 10276. **Tel** (212)206-8900, FAX (212)645-2459. **(Subscription address:** International Publishers Distributor at one of the following addresses: 820 Town Center Drive, Langhorne, PA 19047; or PO Box 90, Reading Berkshire RG1 8JL UK; or Kent Ridge PO Box 1180, Singapore 9111, Republic of Singapore**) NLM** W1; CO375H. **CODEN** CDNEEO. **[CCC].**

SI/0129-0568
**CONCEPTS IN NEUROSCIENCE.** ***Ceased.*** Vol. 1, No. 1 (June 1990)-Vol. 4 No. 2 (Dec. 1993). Periodical. English. sa. World Scientific Publishing Company, PO Box 128, Farrer Road, Singapore 9128 Singapore. **Tel** 011 65 3825663, FAX 011 65 3825919, telex RS 28561 WSPC. **LC** QP351; .C578. **DD** 612.8/2/05. **NLM** W1; CO459RJ. **CODEN** CNEVEW. **[CCC].** Documents available from The Genuine Article.
**Ind/Abst** Res. Alert [Full Cov.]; Soc. Sci. Cit. Index [Select. Cov.].

SZ/0251-2068
**CONCEPTS IN PEDIATRIC NEUROSURGERY. See** Medical Science and Technology-Pediatrics.

US/0069-9446
**CONTEMPORARY NEUROLOGY SERIES.** [Contemp. neurol. ser.]. Vol. 1 (1966)-. Academic Scholarly Publication. English. ir. Price varies per volume. FA Davis Company, 1915 Arch Street, Philadelphia PA 19103. **Tel** (800)523-4049, (215)568-2270, FAX (215)568-5065, telex 83-4837. **ED** Fred Plum. **DD** 616.8. **NLM** W1 CO769N. **CODEN** CNRSAG. **Circ:** 5,000. Documents available from BIOSIS Document Express, CASDDS.
**Desc:** Presents the latest therapeutic and management methods as well as the most up-to-date research and clinical findings on the major diseases and disorders confronting neurology.
**Ind/Abst** Biol. Abstr. (1987-); Chem. Abstr.; Energy Res. Abstr. (Aug. 1982-); Health Plan. Adminis.

US/0069-9454
**CONTEMPORARY NEUROLOGY SYMPOSIA.** Vol. 1 (1964)-. Monographic series. English. ir. Price varies per volume. FA Davis Company, 1915 Arch Street, Philadelphia PA 19103. **Tel** (800)523-4049, (215)568-2270, FAX (215)568-5065, telex 83-4837. **DD** 616.8.

NE/0165-1056
**CORE JOURNALS IN CLINICAL NEUROLOGY.** [Core j. clin. neurol.]. Vol. 1, No. 1 (Jan. 1978)-. Periodical. English. Eleven times a year (1 volume). Fl549.00. Excerpta Medica Publishing Group, PO Box 548, 1000 AM Amsterdam Netherlands. **Tel** 011 31 20 5803243. **(Subscription address:** Excerpta Medica Journals, PO Box 85, Limerick Ireland.**) NLM** ZWL 100 C797. **[CCC].** available on microfilm from University Microfilms International (UMI).
**Desc:** Part of a series abstracting service of international literature. Intended to optimize the busy clinician's time by providing an overview of the most significant clinical studies in his/her field.

US/1042-0398
**CORRELATIVE NEUROANATOMY (EAST NORWALK, CONN.).** (CORRELATIVE NEUROANATOMY.). [Correl. neuroanat.]. **VFOAT** Neuroanatomy. 20th Ed. (1988)-. English. ir. $27.50 (latest edition). Appleton Century Crofts, Prentice Hall, 200 Old Tappan Road, Old Tappan NJ 07675. **Tel** (201)767-5188, (800)922-0579. **LC** RC346; .C59. **DD** 616.8. ***Continues*** *Correlative Neuroanatomy & Functional Neurology, 0892-1237.*

IT/0010-9452
**CORTEX.** (CORTEX; A JOURNAL DEVOTED TO THE STUDY OF THE NERVOUS SYSTEM AND BEHAVIOR.). [Cortex]. Vol. 1 (June 1964)-. Periodical. English (French, German, Italian and Spanish). qt. L246000 (institution) Italy. Masson S.P.A, Via Statuto 2/4, 20121 Milan Italy. **Tel** 011 39 2 63671, FAX 011 39 2 6367211. **NLM** W1 CO911U. **CODEN** CRTXAX. **Pr Rev.** available on microfilm and microfiche from University Microfilms International (UMI). Documents available from The Genuine Article, BIOSIS Document Express.
**Ind/Abst** Biol. Abstr.; CSA Neuro. Abstr. (?-?); Curr. Contents Life Sci.; Dev. Med. Child Neurol.; EMBASE; Ergon. Abstr.; Health Plan. Adminis.; Index Med.; Life Sci. Collect.; Psychol. Abstr. (1964-); PsycINFO; PsycLit; Res. Alert [Full Cov.]; Sci. Cit. Index; SCISEARCH; Soc. Sci. Cit. Index [Select. Cov.].

CN/0712-3086
**COURANT, LE.** [Courant]. Periodical. French. bm. Association de Paralysie Cerebrale du Quebec / Trois-Rivieres, Chapitre Mauricie, Bureau 030/1055 Boulevard des Forges, Trois-Rivieres Quebec G8Z 4J8 Canada. **DD** 362.1/96836/0060714465.

GW/0939-0146
**CRITICAL REVIEWS IN NEUROSURGERY : CR. See** Medical Science and Technology-Surgery.

US/0141-7711
**CSA NEUROSCIENCES ABSTRACTS. See** Medical Science and Technology-Abstracting, Bibliographies and Statistics.

UK/0741-1677
**CURRENT ADVANCES IN NEUROSCIENCE. See** Medical Science and Technology-Abstracting, Bibliographies and Statistics.

UK/0267-0445
**CURRENT MEDICAL LITERATURE. NEUROLOGY.** [Curr. med. lit., Neurol.]. (1984)-. Periodical. English. qt. £20.00 UK; $40.00 other. Current Medical Literature Ltd., 40-42 Osnaburgh Street, London NW1 3ND England. **Tel** 011 44 71 4658377, FAX 011 44 71 4658380. **(Subscription address:** Royal Society Medicine Services, 1 Wimpole Street, London W1M 8AE England.**)** **DD** 016.6168.

US/0161-780X
**CURRENT NEUROLOGY.** [Curr. neurol.]. Vol. 1 (1978)-. Academic Scholarly Publication. English. an. $69.95. Mosby Year Book Inc., 11830 Westline Industrial Drive, St Louis MO 63146. **Tel** (800)325-4177, (314)872-8370, FAX (314)432-1380, telex 44-2402. **LC** RC321; .C87. **DD** 616.8/05. **NLM** W1 CU799F. **CODEN** CNEUDS. **[CCC].** Documents available from CASDDS.
**Ind/Abst** Chem. Abstr.

UK/0959-4388
**CURRENT OPINION IN NEUROBIOLOGY.** See Biology.

●US/1350-7540
**CURRENT OPINION IN NEUROLOGY.** (1993)-. English. Six times a year. $169.95 (individual); $345.50 (institution). Current Science, 20 North 3rd Street, Philadelphia PA 19106. **Tel** (215)574-2266, (800)552-5866, FAX (215)574-2270. ***Continues*** *Current Opinion in Neurology and Neurosurgery, 0951-7383.*
**Ind/Abst** Soc. Sci. Cit. Index [Select. Cov.].

UK/0951-7383
**CURRENT OPINION IN NEUROLOGY AND NEUROSURGERY.** ***Title Change.*** [Curr. opin. neurol. neurosurg.]. **Added/Corp** World Federation of Neurology. Research Group on Neurological Education. Vol. 1, No. 1 (Jan./Feb. 1988)-(19??). Periodical. English. bm. Current Science / England, Middlesex House, 34-42 Cleveland Street, London W1P 5FB England. **Tel** 011 44 71 580 8393, 011 44 71 323 0323, FAX 011 44 81 580 1938. **(Subscription address:** Current Science, 20 North 3rd Street, Philadelphia PA 19106.**)** **ED** Lord Walton. **DD** 616. **NLM** W1; CU799GG. **CODEN** CNENE8. **[CCC]. Pr Rev. Circ:** 4,000. available on diskette. Documents available from The Genuine Article. ***Continued by*** *Current Opinion in Neurology, 1350-7540.*
**Desc:** Directed toward researchers and practicing neurologists and neurosurgeons. Presents review articles from an area of concentration covering an entire year's literature with annotated references. Each issue features a bibliography of the current world literature published during the previous year.
**Ind/Abst** Curr. Aware. Biol. Sci., CABS; Curr. Contents Clin. Med.; EMBASE; Index Vet.; Res. Alert [Full Cov.]; SCISEARCH; Soc. Sci. Cit. Index [Select. Cov.].

UK/0950-4591
**CURRENT PROBLEMS IN EPILEPSY.** [Curr. probl. epilepsy]. 1-. Academic Scholarly Publication. English. Price varies per volume. **NLM** W1; CU804MC. **CODEN** CPEPES. Documents available from CASDDS.
**Ind/Abst** Chem. Abstr. (1983-).

UK/0268-6252
**CURRENT PROBLEMS IN NEUROLOGY.** [Curr. probl. neurol.]. (1986)-. Monographic series. English. Price varies per volume. John Libbey Eurotext Ltd, 6 rue Blanche, Isabelle Trope, 92120 Montrouge France. **Tel** 011 33 1 47358552. **NLM** W1; CU804ND.

CN/0899-3963
**CURRENT THERAPY IN NEUROLOGICAL SURGERY.** [Curr. ther. neurol. surg.]. (1985/1986)-. English. ir. Mosby Year Book Inc., 11830 Westline Industrial Drive, St Louis MO 63146. **Tel** (800)325-4177, (314)872-8370, FAX (314)432-1380, telex 44-2402. **ED** Donlin M. Long. **LC** RD593; .C844. **DD** 617/.48.

US/0093-4747
**CURRENT TOPICS IN NEUROBIOLOGY.** [Curr. top. neurobiol.]. Vol. 1 (1973)-. Monographic series. English. ir. Price varies per volume. Plenum Press, 233 Spring Street, New York NY 10013-1578. **Tel** (212)620-8000, (800)221-9369, FAX (212)463-0742, (212)807-1047, telex 23/421139. **DD** 574. **NLM** W1 CU82P. **CODEN** CTNEDX. Documents available from BIOSIS Document Express, CASDDS.
**Ind/Abst** Biol. Abstr.; Chem. Abstr.

SZ/1013-7424
**DEMENTIA (BASEL, SWITZERLAND).** (DEMENTIA.). Vol. 1, No. 1 (Jan/Feb. 1990)-. Periodical. English. bm (6 issues). $470.00. S. Karger AG, Allschwilerstrasse 10, PO Box - Postfach - Case Postale, CH-4009 Basel Switzerland. **Tel** 011 41 61 306-1111, FAX 011 41 61 306-1234, telex CH 962 652. **ED** V. Chan-Palay. **NLM** W1; DE133. **CODEN** DEMNEU. **[CCC].** Index available. **Ad Acc. Pr Rev. Circ:** 1,000. available on microfilm. Documents available from The Genuine Article, BIOSIS Document Express.
**Desc:** Devoted exclusively to the study of cognitive dysfunction, concentrates on Alzheimer's and Parkinson's disease, Huntington's chorea and other neurodegenerative diseases. Draws from diverse related research disciplines such as psychogeriatrics, neuropsychology, clinical neurology, morphology, physiology, genetic molecular biology, pathology, biochemistry, immunology, pharmacology and pharmaceutics. Strong emphasis is placed on the publication of research findings from animal studies which are complemented by clinical and therapeutic experience to give an overall appreciation of the field.
**Ind/Abst** Biol. Abstr.; Curr. Contents Clin. Med.; Curr. Contents Life Sci.; EMBASE; Psychoanal. Abstr.; Psychol. Abstr. (1990-); PsycINFO; PsycLit; PsycScan: Appl. Exp. Eng. Psych.; PsycScan: LD/MR; PsycScan: Neuropsych.; Ref. Upd. Deluxe Ed.; Res. Alert [Full Cov.]; Sci. Cit. Index; Soc. Sci. Cit. Index [Select. Cov.].

●UK/0961-0898
**DENDRON : AN INTERNATIONAL BIOMEDICAL JOURNAL FOR RESEARCH IN NEUROSCIENCE.** ***Suspended.*** Vol. 1, No. 1 (1992)-(July 1993). Periodical. English. qt. £150.00. Faculty Press, 88 Regent Street, Cambridge CB2 1DP England. **Tel** FAX 44 553 840695. **NLM** W1; DE136PK. Documents available from The Genuine Article.
**Ind/Abst** Curr. Aware. Biol. Sci., CABS; Res. Alert [Full Cov.].

●SZ/1019-5815
**DEVELOPMENTAL BRAIN DYSFUNCTION.** **Added/Corp** OASI Istituto per la Ricerca sul Ritardo Mentale e l'Involuzione Cerebrale. (Jan./June 1993)-. Periodical. English. bm (6 issues). $276.00. S. Karger AG, Allschwilerstrasse 10, PO Box - Postfach - Case Postale, CH-4009 Basel Switzerland. **Tel** 011 41 61 306-1111, FAX 011 41 61 306-1234, telex CH 962 652. **ED** R. Ferri. **NLM** W1; DE997NBP. **CODEN** DBDYEV. **Pr Rev.** Documents available from BIOSIS Document Express. ***Continues*** *Brain Dysfunction, 0259-1278.*
**Desc:** An international interdisciplinary journal which publishes original, high quality research papers in the fields of neurology, pediatric neurology, neuropathology, neuropharmacology and genetics. The journal serves as a forum for scientific reports on abnormal brain function during development, with a focus on clinical research, experimental models and genetics.
**Ind/Abst** Biol. Abstr.; Ref. Upd. Deluxe Ed.

NE/0165-3806
**DEVELOPMENTAL BRAIN RESEARCH.** (BRAIN RESEARCH. DEVELOPMENTAL BRAIN RESEARCH.). [Dev. brain res.]. Vol. 44, No. 1 (Nov. 1, 1988)-. Academic Scholarly Publication. English. Fourteen times a year (7 vols.). Fl2884.00; Fl19345.00 combination subscription with Brain Research Reviews and Molecular Brain Research. Elsevier Science Publishers BV, PO Box 211, 1000 AE Amsterdam Netherlands. **Tel** 011 31 20 5803642, FAX 011 31 20 5862696, telex 15682. **LC** QP356.25; .B73. **DD** 599.01/88. **NLM** W1; BR1143. **[CCC]. Pr Rev.** available on microfilm from University Microfilms International (UMI). Documents available from ADONIS. ***Continues*** *Developmental Brain Research, 0165-3806.*
**Ind/Abst** ADONIS; Index Med. (1989-).

UK/0012-1622
**DEVELOPMENTAL MEDICINE & CHILD NEUROLOGY.** See Medical Science and Technology-Abstracting, Bibliographies and Statistics.

UK/0419-0238
**DEVELOPMENTAL MEDICINE AND CHILD NEUROLOGY. SUPPLEMENT.** [Dev. med. child neurol. Supp.]. **Added/Corp** National Spastics Society (Great Britain). Medical Education and Information Unit. Spastics Society. Medical Education and Information Unit. Spastics International Medical Publications. MacKeith Press. American Academy for Cerebral Palsy. American Academy for Cerebral Palsy & Developmental Medicine. British Paediatric Neurology Association. **VFOAT** Developmental Medicine & Child Neurology. Supplement. Vol. 5 (1962)-. Monographic series. English. ir. Comes with Developmental Medicine and Child Neurology. Cambridge University Press, The Edinburgh Building, Shaftesbury Road, Cambridge CB2 2RU United Kingdom. **Tel** 011 44 223 312393, FAX 011 44 223 325959. **(Subscription address:** Cambridge University Press / North America, 110 Midland Avenue, Port Chester NY 10573.**)** **LC** RJ1; .D48. **DD** 616.8. **NLM** W1 DE997U. **[CCC].** ***Continues*** *Cerebral Palsy Bulletin. Supplement.*
**Ind/Abst** Health Plan. Adminis.; Index Med.; Life Sci. Collect.

SZ/0378-5866
**DEVELOPMENTAL NEUROSCIENCE.** [Dev. neurosci.]. Vol. 1 (1978)-. Academic Scholarly Publication. English. bm. $451.00. S. Karger AG, Allschwilerstrasse 10, PO Box - Postfach - Case Postale, CH-4009 Basel Switzerland. **Tel** 011 41 61 306-1111, FAX 011 41 61 306-1234, telex CH 962 652. **ED** A.T. Campagnoni. **NLM** W1 DE997UN. **CODEN** DENED7. **[CCC]. Ad Acc. Pr Rev.** available on microfilm; available on microfiche. Documents available from The Genuine Article, BIOSIS Document Express, CASDDS.
**Desc:** A multidisciplinary journal publishing neuroscience papers covering all stages of invertebrate, vertebrate and human development. Prime emphasis is kept on basic experimental studies, but clinical work contributing to the understanding of mechanisms of normal and abnormal development is also presented. The journal thus provides valuable information for both physicians and biologists. To meet the complete information needs of its readers, the journal combines original papers recording the rapid progress of these fields with concise minireviews giving a quick overview of new developments and ongoing controversies.
**Ind/Abst** Biol. Abstr.; Chem. Abstr.; CSA Neuro. Abstr. (?-?); Curr. Aware. Biol. Sci., CABS; Curr. Contents Life Sci.; Curr. Ref. Fish Res.; Dev. Med. Child Neurol.; EMBASE; Index Med. (1978-); Life Sci. Collect.; Protozoolog. Abstr.; Ref. Upd. Basic Ed.; Ref. Upd. Deluxe Ed.; Res. Alert [Full Cov.]; Sci. Cit. Index; SCISEARCH.

NE/0165-7003
**DEVELOPMENTS IN NEUROSCIENCE.** ***Ceased.*** Vol. 1 (1977)-Vol. 18. Academic Scholarly Publication. English. Elsevier Science Publishing Company Inc, Madison Square Station, PO Box 882, New York NY 10159-0882. **Tel** (212)633-3950, FAX (212)633-3990. **NLM** W1 DE998K. **CODEN** DNEUD5. Documents available from CASDDS.
**Ind/Abst** Chem. Abstr.

US/0012-2769
**DIGEST OF NEUROLOGY AND PSYCHIATRY.** **Added/Corp** Hartford. Institute of Living. (194?)-. Periodical. English. Four times a year. $25.00. Institute of Living, 400 Washington Street, Hartford CT 06106. **Tel** (203)241-6818. **LC** RC321; .H3. Index available in last issue of volume--attached. available on microfilm and microfiche from University Microfilms International (UMI). ***Continues*** *Abstracts and Translations from the Science Library.*

US/0196-6421
**DIRECTORY OF CERTIFIED PSYCHIATRISTS AND NEUROLOGISTS.** See Medical Science and Technology-Psychiatry.

SZ/0254-8852
**DISCUSSIONS IN NEUROSCIENCES.** [Discuss. neurosci.]. **Added/Corp** Fondation pour l'Etude du Systeme Nerveux Central et Peripherique. **VFOAT** Discussions in Neuroscience. Vol. 1, No. 1 (Jan. 1984)-. Monographic series. English. qt (1 volume). Fl300.00. Elsevier Science Publishers BV, PO Box 211, 1000 AE Amsterdam Netherlands. **Tel** 011 31 20 5803642, FAX 011 31 20 5862696, telex 15682. **LC** QP351; .D59. **NLM** W1; DI745C. **CODEN** DISNEK. **[CCC].** available on microfilm and microfiche from University Microfilms International (UMI). Documents available from The Genuine Article, ADONIS.
**Ind/Abst** ADONIS; Curr. Aware. Biol. Sci., CABS; Res. Alert [Full Cov.].

US
**DOWN SYNDROME PAPERS AND ABSTRACTS FOR PROFESSIONALS.** English. qt. $45.00. Children's Brain Research Clinic, 2525 Belmont Road NW, Washington DC 20008.
**Desc:** Reviews, highlights, and in some cases analyzes recent professional literature pertaining to Down's Syndrome.

CN
**EDMONTON AUTISM SOCIETY UPDATE.** English. qt (Mar., June, Sept., Dec.). 20.00Can$. Edmonton Autism Society, 11720 Kingsway Avenue, Edmonton Alberta T5B4J1 Canada. **Tel** (403)453-3971. **ED** Shiela Court. **Bk Rev**, (Qty: 6). **Circ:** 850 (ctrl).
**Desc:** News and information on autism.

GW/0170-8287
**EEG-LABOR, DAS.** [EEG-Lab.]. Vol. 1 (1979)-. Academic Scholarly Publication. German (English; summaries and/or abstracts in English). qt. DM136.00 Germany; DM144.00 other. Gustav Fischer Verlag Stuttgart, Postfach 720143, Wollgrasweg 49, D 70577 Stuttgart Germany. **Tel** 011 49 711 458030, FAX 0711-4580334, telex 2627-7111488. **(Subscription address:** VCH Publishers Inc., 303 Northwest 12th Avenue, Journals Department, Deerfield FL 33442.**)** **NLM** W1 E22L. **[CCC].**
**Ind/Abst** EMBASE.

IE/0013-4694
**ELECTROENCEPHALOGRAPHY AND CLINICAL NEUROPHYSIOLOGY.** [Electroencephalogr. clin. neurophysiol.]. **Added/Corp** International Federation of Societies for Electroencephalography and Clinical Neurophysiology. International Federation of Clinical Neurophysiology. **VFOAT** Electroencephalography and Clinical Neurophysiology. Evoked Potentials; EEG Journal; Electroencephalography and Clinical Neurophysiology. Electromyography & Motor. Vol. 1 (Feb. 1949)-. Academic Scholarly Publication. English (French and Spanish). Twenty-four times a year (4 volumes). $400.00. Elsevier Science Ireland Ltd., Bay 15, Shannon Industrial Estate, Co Clare Ireland. **Tel** 011 353 61 471944. **ED** F.

Mauguiere and T.A. Pedley. **LC** RC321; .E43. **DD** 616.8/047547. **NLM** W1 EL325. **CODEN** ECNEAZ. **[CCC]. Pr Rev.** available on microfilm from University Microfilms International (UMI). Documents available from The Genuine Article, BIOSIS Document Express, Ask*IEEE, CASDDS, ADONIS. ***Absorbed*** *Electroencephalography and Clinical Neurophysiology: Index to Current Literature.*
**Desc:** Provides coverage of research into the electrical activity in the central nervous system.
**Ind/Abst** ADONIS; Biol. Abstr.; Chem. Abstr.; CSA Neuro. Abstr.; Curr. Aware. Biol. Sci., CABS; Curr. Contents Life Sci.; Dev. Med. Child Neurol.; EMBASE; Ergon. Abstr. (?-?); Health Plan. Adminis.; Index Med.; INSPEC (July 1985-); Int. Aerosp. Abstr.; Life Sci. Collect.; Psychoanal. Abstr.; Psychol. Abstr. (1950-); PsycINFO; PsycLit; PsycScan: Appl. Exp. Eng. Psych.; PsycScan: LD/MR; PsycScan: Neuropsych.; Ref. Upd. Deluxe Ed.; Res. Alert [Full Cov.]; Saf. Health Work; Sci. Cit. Index; SCISEARCH; Soc. Sci. Cit. Index [Select. Cov.].

IE/0924-980X
**ELECTROENCEPHALOGRAPHY AND CLINICAL NEUROPHYSIOLOGY/ ELECTROMYOGRAPHY AND MOTOR CONTROL.** (19??)-. Academic Scholarly Publication. English. bm (1 volume). $120.00. Elsevier Science Ireland Ltd., Bay 15, Shannon Industrial Estate, Co Clare Ireland. **Tel** 011 353 61 471944. **ED** F. Maugiere and G.G. Celesia. **[CCC].** Documents available from ADONIS.
**Desc:** Covers all clinical applications of EMB, reflexology, premotor evoked potentials and brain stimulation as well as experimental studies of human motor physiology.
**Ind/Abst** ADONIS; Psychol. Abstr. (1991-); PsycINFO; PsycLit; Ref. Upd. Deluxe Ed.

NE/0424-8155
**ELECTROENCEPHALOGRAPHY AND CLINICAL NEUROPHYSIOLOGY. SUPPLEMENT.** [Electroenceph. clin. neurophysiol., Suppl.]. **Added/Corp** International Federation of Societies for Electroencephalography and Clinical Neurophysiology. **VFOAT** Supplement ... to Electroencephalography and Clinical Neurophysiology. No. 1 (1950)-. Monographic series. English. ir. Price varies per volume. Elsevier Science Ireland Ltd., Bay 15, Shannon Industrial Estate, Co Clare Ireland. **Tel** 011 353 61 471944. **NLM** W1 EL3251. **CODEN** EECSB3. Documents available from BIOSIS Document Express, CASDDS.
**Ind/Abst** Biol. Abstr. (-1973); Chem. Abstr. (-1987); Index Med.; Life Sci. Collect.

BE/0301-150X
**ELECTROMYOGRAPHY AND CLINICAL NEUROPHYSIOLOGY.** **See** Medical Science and Technology-Internal Medicine.

US
**EMISSARY, THE.** **Added/Corp** Texas Research Institute of Mental Sciences. (19??)-. Periodical. English. mo. Texas Research Institute of Mental Sciences, 1300 Moursund Street, Houston TX 77030.

FR/0013-7006
**ENCEPHALE.** (L'ENCEPHALE.). [Encephale]. **Added/Corp** Societe de Psychiatrie de Paris. Yearly Vol. 1-62 (Jan./Feb. 1906-1973). New Series (1973)-. Academic Scholarly Publication. French (summaries and/or abstracts in English; table of contents in English). bm (6 issues). $135.00. Doin Editeurs, 8 Place de l'Odeon, F 75006 Paris France. **Tel** 011 33 1 46332237. **(Subscription address:** Subscription Office, PO Box 830399, Birmingham, AL 35283-0399; telephone: (800)633-4931 or (205)991-6920 (outside US and Canada); FAX: (205)995-1588**) ED** P. Deniker, H. Loo, J. P. Olie and M. Vincent. **NLM** W1 EN223. **CODEN** ENCEAN. **[CCC].** Index available. **Bk Rev. Ad Acc. Circ:** 1,700. available on microfilm from University Microfilms International (UMI). Documents available from BIOSIS Document Express, CASDDS.
**Desc:** The principle French journal devoted to biological and therapeutic psychiatry and publishes the reports of the French Biological Psychiatry Association.
**Ind/Abst** Biol. Abstr.; Chem. Abstr.; EMBASE; Health Plan. Adminis.; Index Med.; Psychol. Abstr. (1951-); PsycINFO; PsycLit; Soc. Plann. Policy Dev. Abstr.

US/0191-6955
**ENCEPHALITIS SURVEILLANCE.** (ENCEPHALITIS SURVEILLANCE, ANNUAL SUMMARY / CENTER FOR DISEASE CONTROL.). **Added/Corp** Center for Disease Control. Centers for Disease Control (U.S.). **VFOAT** Encephalitis Surveillance; Center for Disease Control Encephalitis Surveillance. (1976)-. English. an. Free. Centers for Disease Control, 1600 Clifton Road NE, Atlanta GA 30333. **Tel** (404)639-3311, FAX (404)639-3296. **(Subscription address:** CDC Distribution / Georgia, c/o G. Dixon, Mail Stop A 22, Atlanta GA 30333.**) LC** RA644.E52; C45a. **DD** 614.5/9832. **NLM** W2 A C2M. ***Continues*** *Neurotropic Viral Diseases Surveillance. Encephalitis, Annual Summary, 0566-7003.*

NE/0013-9580
**EPILEPSIA (COPENHAGEN).** (EPILEPSIA : THE JOURNAL OF THE INTERNATIONAL LEAGUE AGAINST EPILEPSY.). [Epilepsia]. **Added/Corp** International League against Epilepsy. (1909)-. Academic Scholarly Publication. English (summaries and/or abstracts in French). mo. $240.00 (individuals), $385.00 (institutions) US; $285.00 (individuals), $460.00 (institutions) other. Raven Press, 1185 Avenue of the Americas, 37th Floor, New York NY 10036. **Tel** (212)930-9500, (212)930-9604, FAX (212)869-3495, (212)302-8507, telex 640073. **ED** James J. Cereghino and Timothy A. Pedley. **LC** RC395; .A25. **DD** 616.85305. **NLM** W1 EP453. **CODEN** EPILAK. **[CCC].** cum. index. **Pr Rev.** available on microfilm and microfiche from University Microfilms International (UMI). Documents available from The Genuine Article, BIOSIS Document Express, CASDDS.
**Desc:** Provides comprehensive coverage of current clinical and research results. Each issue features articles on the diagnosis, treatment, and management of epilepsy, written by the foremost experts worldwide. Articles encompass the entire range of epileptology, including clinical neurology, neurobiology, neurochemistry, neuropharmacology, neurophysiology, neuropsychology, and neurosurgery.
**Ind/Abst** Biol. Abstr.; Chem. Abstr.; CSA Neuro. Abstr. (?-?); Curr. Aware. Biol. Sci., CABS; Curr. Contents Life Sci.; Dev. Med. Child Neurol.; EMBASE; Health Plan. Adminis.; Helminthol. Abstr. (1991-); Index Med.; Int. Nurs. Index; Iowa Drug Inf. Serv. (1967-); Life Sci. Collect.; PESTDOC; Psychol. Abstr.; Ref. Upd. Deluxe Ed.; Res. Alert [Full Cov.]; Sci. Cit. Index; SCISEARCH; Soc. Sci. Cit. Index [Select. Cov.].

UK/0141-965X
**EPILEPSY.** [Epilepsy]. **VFOAT** Perspectives on Epilepsy. '78-. English. an. British Epilepsy Association, Crowthorne House, New Wokingham Road, Wokingham Berkshire England. **NLM** W1 EP454.

US/0894-6590
**EPILEPSY ADVANCES IN CLINICAL EXPERIMENTAL RESEARCH.** [Epilepsy adv. clin. exp. res.]. **VFOAT** Epilepsy Advances. Vol. 1, No. 1 (Dec. 1985)-. Periodical. English. qt. Epilepsy Foundation of America, 4351 Garden City Drive, Landover MD 20785. **Tel** (301)459-3700. **DD** 616. **NLM** W1; EP454T.

NE/0920-1211
**EPILEPSY RESEARCH.** [Epilepsy res.]. Vol. 1, No. 1 (Jan. 1987)-. Academic Scholarly Publication. English. Nine times a year (3 vols.). Fl1629.00. Elsevier Science Publishers BV, PO Box 211, 1000 AE Amsterdam Netherlands. **Tel** 011 31 20 5803642, FAX 011 31 20 5862696, telex 15682. **ED** D Schmidt, W I Loscher, I E Leppik and R W Olsen. **NLM** W1; EP455KE. **CODEN** EPIRE8. **[CCC]. Pr Rev.** available on microfilm and microfiche from University Microfilms International (UMI). Documents available from The Genuine Article, BIOSIS Document Express, CASDDS.
**Desc:** Provides for rapid publication of high quality articles in both experimental and clinical epileptology, where the principal emphasis of the research is concerned with brain mechanisms in epilepsy.
**Ind/Abst** Biol. Abstr. (1987-); Chem. Abstr. (1987-); Curr. Aware. Biol. Sci., CABS; Curr. Contents Life Sci.; Dev. Med. Child Neurol.; EMBASE; Health Plan. Adminis.; Index Med. (1987-); Ref. Upd. Deluxe Ed.; Res. Alert [Full Cov.]; Sci. Cit. Index; SCISEARCH; Soc. Sci. Cit. Index [Select. Cov.].

US/1060-9369
**EPILEPSY USA.** (EPILEPSY USA : A PUBLICATION OF THE EPILEPSY FOUNDATION OF AMERICA.). [Epilepsy USA]. **Added/Corp** Epilepsy Foundation of America. **VFOAT** Epilepsy U S A; EpilepsyUSA. Vol. 24, No. 3 (April-May 1991)-. Periodical. English. mo (10 issues). $20.00. Epilepsy Foundation of America, 4351 Garden City Drive, Landover MD 20785. **Tel** (301)459-3700. **DD** 362. ***Continues*** *National Spokesman, 0091-2387.*

UK/0147-0205
**ESSAYS IN NEUROCHEMISTRY AND NEUROPHARMACOLOGY.** [Essays neurochem. neuropharmacol.]. Vol. 1 (1977)-. Academic Scholarly Publication. English. ir. price varies per volume. John Wiley & Sons Ltd., Baffins Lane, Chichester West Sussex PO19 1UD England. **Tel** 0243 779777, FAX 0243 776128 BTG:JWP001, telex 86290 WIBOOKG. **(Subscription address:** John Wiley / Philadelphia, PO Box 7247, Philadelphia PA 19170.**) ED** M. B. H. Youdim. **NLM** W1 ES674ST. **CODEN** ENNEDD. Documents available from BIOSIS Document Express, CASDDS.
**Ind/Abst** Biol. Abstr.; Chem. Abstr. (1977-1980); Index Med. (1977-).

GW/0940-1334
**EUROPEAN ARCHIVES OF PSYCHIATRY AND CLINICAL NEUROSCIENCE.** **See** Medical Science and Technology-Psychiatry.

UK/1351-5101
**EUROPEAN JOURNAL OF NEUROLOGY.** (19??)-. English. bm. $330.00 US; £195.00 other. Rapid Communications of Oxford Ltd, The Old Malthouse, Paradise Street, Oxford OX1 1LD England. **Tel** 011 44 0865 790447, FAX 011 44 0865 244012, telex 9403712.

UK/0953-816X
**EUROPEAN JOURNAL OF NEUROSCIENCE, THE.** [Eur. j. neurosci.]. **Added/Corp** European Neuroscience Association. Vol. 1, No. 1 (Jan. 1989)-. Periodical. English. mo. £395.00 UK and Europe; $695.00 other. Oxford University Press, Walton Street, Oxford OX2 6DP England. **Tel** 011 44 865 56767, FAX 011 44 865 267773, telex 837330 OXPRES G. **(Subscription address:** Oxford University Press / USA, Journals Marketing Department, Oxford University Press, 2001 Evans Road, Cary NC 27513.**) NLM** W1; EU72DIF. **CODEN** EJONEI. **[CCC]. Pr Rev.** available on microfilm and microfiche from University Microfilms International (UMI). Documents available from The Genuine Article, BIOSIS Document Express, ADONIS.
**Ind/Abst** ADONIS; Biol. Abstr. (1991-); Curr. Aware. Biol. Sci., CABS; Curr. Contents Life Sci.; EMBASE; Ref. Upd. Deluxe Ed.; Res. Alert [Full Cov.]; Rev. Agric. Entomol.; Sci. Cit. Index; SCISEARCH; Soc. Sci. Cit. Index [Select. Cov.].

SZ/0014-3022
**EUROPEAN NEUROLOGY.** [Eur. neurol.]. Vol. 1, No. 1 (1968)-. Academic Scholarly Publication. English. bm (6 issues). $423.00. S. Karger AG, Allschwilerstrasse 10, PO Box - Postfach - Case Postale, CH-4009 Basel Switzerland. **Tel** 011 41 61 306-1111, FAX 011 41 61 306-1234, telex CH 962 652. **ED** J. Bogusslavsky. **NLM** W1 EU721L. **CODEN** EUNEAP. **[CCC]. Ad Acc. Pr Rev.** available on microfilm and microfiche from University Microfilms International (UMI). Documents available from The Genuine Article, BIOSIS Document Express, CASDDS. ***Supersedes in part*** *Psychiatria et Neurologia.*
**Desc:** Papers presented in this journal cover clinical aspects of diseases of the nervous system and muscles, as well as their neuropathological, biochemical, and electrophysiological basis. New diagnostic probes, pharmacological and surgical treatments are evaluated from clinical evidence and basic investigative studies. In addition to original papers representing general neurology and the range related fields, the journal also publishes preliminary communications, reports on new techniques, review papers, and exceptional case reports.
**Ind/Abst** Biol. Abstr.; Chem. Abstr.; CSA Neuro. Abstr. (?-?); Curr. Aware. Biol. Sci., CABS; Curr. Contents Clin. Med.; Curr. Contents Life Sci.; Curr. Ref. Fish Res.; Dev. Med. Child Neurol.; EMBASE; Health Plan. Adminis.; Helminthol. Abstr. (1991-); Index Med.; Nutr. Abstr. Rev., Ser. B, Live Feeds and Feed.; Nutr. Abstr. Rev., Ser. A, Hum. Exp.; Life Sci. Collect.; Protozoolog. Abstr.; Psychoanal. Abstr.; Psychol. Abstr. (1990-); PsycINFO; PsycLit; PsycScan: Appl. Exp. Eng. Psych.; PsycScan: LD/MR; PsycScan: Neuropsych.; Ref. Upd. Basic Ed.; Ref. Upd. Deluxe Ed.; Res. Alert [Full Cov.]; Rev. Med. Vet. Mycology; Sci. Cit. Index; SCISEARCH; Soc. Sci. Cit. Index [Select. Cov.].

NE/0924-977X
**EUROPEAN NEUROPSYCHOPHARMACOLOGY : THE JOURNAL OF THE EUROPEAN COLLEGE OF NEUROPSYCHOPHARMACOLOGY.** **Added/Corp** European College of Neuropsychopharmacology. Vol. 1, No. 1 (Nov. 1990)-. Academic Scholarly Publication. English. qt (1 volume). Fl535.00. Elsevier Science Publishers BV, PO Box 211, 1000 AE Amsterdam Netherlands. **Tel** 011 31 20 5803642, FAX 011 31 20 5862696, telex 15682. **ED** J M van Ree and S A Montgomery. **NLM** W1; EU721Q. **CODEN** EURNE8. **[CCC].** available on microfilm and microfiche from University Microfilms International (UMI). Documents available from The Genuine Article.
**Desc:** Provides a medium for the prompt publication of articles in the field of neuropsychopharmacology. Its scope encompasses clinical and basic research relevant to the effects of centrally acting agents in its broadest sense.
**Ind/Abst** Curr. Aware. Biol. Sci., CABS; Index Med. (Nov. 1990-); Res. Alert [Full Cov.]; Soc. Sci. Cit. Index [Select. Cov.].

NE/0014-4126
**EXCERPTA MEDICA. SECTION 8. NEUROLOGY AND NEUROSURGERY.** **See** Medical Science and Technology-Abstracting, Bibliographies and Statistics.

NE/0303-8459
**EXCERPTA MEDICA. SECTION 50. EPILEPSY ABSTRACTS.** **See** Medical Science and Technology-Abstracting, Bibliographies and Statistics.

GW/0014-4819
**EXPERIMENTAL BRAIN RESEARCH.** [Exp. brain res.]. **VFOAT** Experimentelle Hirnforschung; Experimentation Cerebale. Vol. 1 (1966)-. Academic Scholarly Publication. English (French and German). Fifteen times a year. DM4600.00. Springer-Verlag GmbH & Company KG, Heidelberger Platz 3, D 14197 Berlin Germany. **Tel** 011 49 30 8207223, FAX 011 49 30

8214091, telex 183 319 SPBLN D. **(Subscription address:** Springer Verlag New York Inc. / for North America, 44 Hartz Way, Secaucus NJ 07096.**) ED** O Creutzfeldt. **NLM** W1 EX485. **CODEN** EXBRAP. **[CCC]. Pr Rev.** available on microfilm and microfiche from University Microfilms International (UMI). Documents available from The Genuine Article, BIOSIS Document Express, CASDDS, ADONIS.
**Desc:** Covers the whole field of experimental brain research such as neurophysiology, sensory physiology, neuroanatomy, developmental neurobiology, neuropharmacology, histochemistry, neuroplasticity, neuroendocrinology, behavioural sciences, and neuropsychology.
**Ind/Abst** ADONIS; Biol. Abstr.; Chem. Abstr.; Chemorecept. Abstr.; CSA Neuro. Abstr.; Curr. Primate Ref.; Dairy Sci. Abstr.; EMBASE; Health Plan. Adminis.; Index Med.; Int. Aerosp. Abstr.; Nucl. Sci. Abstr.; Nutr. Abstr. Rev., Ser. B, Live Feeds and Feed.; Nutr. Abstr. Rev., Ser. A, Hum. Exp.; Life Sci. Collect.; Psychol. Abstr. (1983-); PsycINFO; PsycLit; Ref. Upd. Basic Ed.; Ref. Upd. Deluxe Ed.; Res. Alert [Full Cov.]; Sci. Cit. Index; SCISEARCH; Soc. Sci. Cit. Index [Select. Cov.].

GW/0932-4011
**EXPERIMENTAL BRAIN RESEARCH SERIES.** [Exp. brain res. ser.]. (1986)-. Monographic series. English. ir. Price varies per volume. Springer-Verlag GmbH & Company KG, Heidelberger Platz 3, D 14197 Berlin Germany. **Tel** 011 49 30 8207223, FAX 011 49 30 8214091, telex 183 319 SPBLN D. **(Subscription address:** Springer Verlag New York Inc. / for North America, 44 Hartz Way, Secaucus NJ 07096.**) NLM** W1; EX4855. **CODEN** EBRSEQ. Documents available from BIOSIS Document Express, CASDDS. ***Continues*** *Experimental Brain Research. Supplementum, 0172-9039.*
**Ind/Abst** Biol. Abstr.; Chem. Abstr.

US/0014-4886
**EXPERIMENTAL NEUROLOGY.** [Exp. neurol.]. Vol. 1 (Apr. 1959)-. Academic Scholarly Publication. English. mo. $904.00 US and Canada; $1120.00 other. Academic Press, Inc., 6277 Sea Harbor Drive, Orlando FL 32887. **Tel** (800)543-9534, (407)345-4100, FAX (407)363-9661. **ED** John R. Sladek. **LC** RC321; .E94. **DD** 612.8072. **NLM** W1 EX507. **CODEN** EXNEAC. **[CCC]. Pr Rev.** Documents available from The Genuine Article, BIOSIS Document Express, CASDDS.
**Desc:** Publishes the results and conclusions of original research in neuroscience with a particular emphasis on novel findings in neural development, regeneration, plasticity, and transplantation. Emphasis is also placed on basic mechanisms underlying or related to neurological disorders. In addition to original manuscripts, the journal publishes electron micrographs and other graphic material, brief communications, and critical reviews of important and timely topics.
**Ind/Abst** Biol. Abstr.; Chem. Abstr.; CSA Neuro. Abstr.; Curr. Aware. Biol. Sci., CABS; Curr. Contents Life Sci.; Curr. Ref. Fish Res.; EMBASE; Energy Res. Abstr.; Health Plan. Adminis.; Index Med.; INIS Atomindex [Micro.]; Int. Aerosp. Abstr.; Nutr. Abstr. Rev., Ser. B, Live Feeds and Feed.; Nutr. Abstr. Rev., Ser. A, Hum. Exp.; Oncog. Growth Factors Abstr.; Life Sci. Collect.; Protozoolog. Abstr.; Psychol. Abstr.; Ref. Upd. Basic Ed.; Ref. Upd. Deluxe Ed.; Res. Alert [Full Cov.]; Sci. Cit. Index; SCISEARCH; Soc. Plann. Policy Dev. Abstr.; Sociol. Abstr. (?-?).

US/0278-2502
**FACT BOOK / NATIONAL INSTITUTE OF NEUROLOGICAL AND COMMUNICATIVE DISORDERS AND STROKE. Main/Corp** National Institute of Neurological and Communicative Disorders and Stroke. Began with 1979. English. an. National Institute of Neurological and Communicative Disorders and Stroke, National Institutes of Health, 9000 Rockville Pike, Bethesda MD 20014. **NLM** W2 A N2052F.

US/1040-0451
**FIDIA RESEARCH FOUNDATION SYMPOSIUM SERIES.** [Fidia Res. Found. symp. ser.]. **Added/Corp** Fidia Research Foundation. Vol. 1 (1989)-. Monographic series. English. ir. Price varies per volume. Raven Press, 1185 Avenue of the Americas, 37th Floor, New York NY 10036. **Tel** (212)930-9500, (212)930-9604, FAX (212)869-3495, (212)302-8507, telex 640073. **DD** 616. **NLM** W1; FI321F. **CODEN** FRFSEL. Documents available from BIOSIS Document Express, CASDDS.
**Ind/Abst** Biol. Abstr. (1989-); Chem. Abstr.

●PL
**FOLIA NEUROPATHOLOGICA / ASSOCIATION OF POLISH NEUROPATHOLOGISTS AND MEDICAL RESEARCH CENTRE, POLISH ACADEMY OF SCIENCES. Added/Corp** Stowarzyszenie Neuropatologow Polskich. Instytut Centrum Medycyny Doswiadczalnej i Klinicznej (Polska Akademia Nauk). Vol. 32, No. 1 (1994)-. Periodical. English (summaries and/or abstracts in Polish). qt. **(Subscription address:** ARS Polona, PO Box 1001, 00068 Warsaw Poland.**) NLM** W1; FO259M. ***Continues*** *Neuropatologia Polska, 0028-3894.*

SP/0211-2558
**FOLIA NEUROPSIQUIATRICA GRANADA. VFOAT** Folia Neuropsiquiatrica del Sur de Espana; Folia Neuropsiquiatrica del Sur y Este de Espana. (1966)-. Periodical. Spanish. an. 705.00ptas Spain; 684.00 other. Universidad de Granada / Campus de Cartuja, 18071 Granada Spain. **Tel** 011 34 58 243930, 243931. **UDC** 616.8.
**Ind/Abst** EMBASE [Select. Cov.]; Soc. Sci. Cit. Index [Select. Cov.].

GW
**FORENSIA JAHRBUCH. See** Medical Science and Technology-Psychiatry.

GW/0720-4299
**FORTSCHRITTE DER NEUROLOGIE, PSYCHIATRIE.** [Fortschr. Neurol. Psychiatr.]. Vol. 49, No. 1 (Jan. 1981)-. Periodical. German (summaries and/or abstracts in English). mo. $212.00. Georg Thieme Verlag Stuttgart, Postfach 301120, D 70451 Stuttgart Germany. **Tel** 011 49 711 89310, FAX 011 49 711 8931298, telex 7 252 275 GTVD. **(Subscription address:** Thieme Medical Publishers Inc., 381 Park Avenue South, New York NY 10016.**) NLM** W1 FO86G. **CODEN** FNPSE9. **[CCC]. Pr Rev.** available on microfilm from University Microfilms International (UMI). Documents available from The Genuine Article, BIOSIS Document Express. ***Continues*** *Fortschritte der Neurologie, Psychiatrie und Ihrer Grenzgebiete.*
**Ind/Abst** Arts Humanit. Citation Index [Select. Cov.]; Biol. Abstr. (1989-); Curr. Contents Clin. Med.; EMBASE; Index Med.; Index Vet.; Life Sci. Collect.; Psychol. Abstr. (1981-); PsycINFO; PsycLit; Res. Alert [Full Cov.]; Sci. Cit. Index; SCISEARCH; Soc. Sci. Cit. Index [Select. Cov.].

US
**FOUNDATIONS OF NEUROLOGY.** (1990)-. Monographic series. English. **NLM** W1; FO99I.
**Ind/Abst** Helminthol. Abstr. (1991-); Protozoolog. Abstr.

US/0887-3658
**FRONTIERS OF CLINICAL NEUROSCIENCE.** [Front. clin. neurosci.]. Vol. 1 (1984)-. Monographic series. English. Price varies per volume. Wiley Liss, 605 3rd Avenue, New York NY 10158. **Tel** (212)850-8800, (212)850-6645. **(Subscription address:** John Wiley & Sons Inc., PO Box 7247 8402, Philadelphia, PA 19170**) DD** 616. **NLM** W1; FR946DM. **CODEN** FCNEEG.

IT/0393-5264
**FUNCTIONAL NEUROLOGY.** Vol. 1, No. 1 (Jan./March 1986)-. Monographic series. English. te. Price varies per volume. John Libbey CIC srl, Via Spallanzani 11, 00161 Rome Italy. **Tel** (06)8412673-8542783, FAX (06)8443365, telex 622099 CIC I. **NLM** W1; FU581H; SR0060290. Documents available from The Genuine Article.
**Ind/Abst** Curr. Aware. Biol. Sci., CABS; EMBASE; Health Plan. Adminis.; Index Med. (1986-); Res. Alert [Full Cov.]; Soc. Sci. Cit. Index [Select. Cov.].

IT/0392-4483
**GIORNALE DI NEUROPSICHIATRIA DELL'ETA EVOLUTIVA : ORGANO UFFICIALE DELLA SOCIETA ITALIANA DI NEUROPSICHIATRIA INFANTILE. Added/Corp** Societa Italiana di Neuropsichiatria Infantile. Vol. 1, No. 1 (Oct. 1981)-. Periodical. Italian (summaries and/or abstracts in English). qt. L86000 Italy. Masson S.P.A, Via Statuto 2/4, 20121 Milan Italy. **Tel** 011 39 2 63671, FAX 011 39 2 6367211. **NLM** W1; GI618P. cum. index. Documents available from The Genuine Article.
**Ind/Abst** Res. Alert [Full Cov.]; Soc. Sci. Cit. Index [Select. Cov.].

US/0894-1491
**GLIA (NEW YORK, N.Y.).** (GLIA.). [Glia]. Vol. 1, No. 1 (1988)-. Periodical. English. Twelve times a year. $792.00 US; $912.00 Canada and Mexico; $957.00 other. John Wiley & Sons, Inc., 605 Third Avenue, New York NY 10158-0012. **Tel** (212)850-6000, (212)850-6645, FAX (212)850-6088, telex 12-7063. **(Subscription address:** John Wiley & Sons / England, Baffins Lane, Chichester, West Sussex PO19 1UD England.**) ED** Bruce R. Ransom and Helmut Kettenmann. **LC** QP363.2; .G56. **DD** 599/.0188/05. **NLM** W1; GL362R. **CODEN** GLIAEJ. **Pr Rev.** Documents available from The Genuine Article.
**Desc:** An international journal devoted primarily to the study of the form and function of neuroglial cells in health and disease. Covers a broad range of experimental topics related to research of interest to neurobiologists.
**Ind/Abst** CSA Neuro. Abstr.; Curr. Aware. Biol. Sci., CABS; Curr. Contents Life Sci.; Index Med.; Ref. Upd. Deluxe Ed.; Res. Alert [Full Cov.]; Rev. Med. Vet. Entomol.; Sci. Cit. Index; SCISEARCH.

US/0194-0880
**HANDBOOK OF BEHAVIORAL NEUROBIOLOGY.** (1978)-. Monographic series. English. ir. Price varies per volume. Plenum Press, 233 Spring Street, New York NY 10013-1578. **Tel** (212)620-8000, (800)221-9369, FAX (212)463-0742, (212)807-1047, telex 23/421139. **LC** UNC. **NLM** W1 HA51I. **CODEN** HBNEEV.

NE
**HANDBOOK OF CLINICAL NEUROLOGY.** Vol. 1 (1968)-. Academic Scholarly Publication. English. ir. Elsevier Science Publishing Company Inc, Madison Square Station, PO Box 882, New York NY 10159-0882. **Tel** (212)633-3950, FAX (212)633-3990. **ED** P J Vinken, G W Bruyn, and Harold L Klawans. **NLM** WL 100 H236.

US
**HANDBOOK OF NEUROCHEMISTRY.** (1970)-. Monographic series. English. ir. Price varies per volume. Plenum Press, 233 Spring Street, New York NY 10013-1578. **Tel** (212)620-8000, (800)221-9369, FAX (212)463-0742, (212)807-1047, telex 23/421139. **ED** Abel Lajtha.

US/0017-8748
**HEADACHE.** [Headache]. **Added/Corp** American Association for the Study of Headache. Vol. 1 (April 1961)-. Academic Scholarly Publication. English. Ten times a year. $95.00 US; $110.00 other. American Association of the Study of Headaches, 875 Kings Highway, Suite 200, Woodbury NJ 08096. **Tel** (609)845-0322, FAX (609)853-0411. **(Subscription address:** Headache, PO Box 1897, Lawrence KS 66044-8897.**) ED** John Edmeads. **LC** RC392; .H4. **DD** 616.07/2. **NLM** W1 HE13. **CODEN** HEADAE. cum. index. **Bk Rev. Ad Acc. Pr Rev. Circ:** 5,000 (ctrl). available on microfilm and microfiche from University Microfilms International (UMI). Documents available from The Genuine Article, BIOSIS Document Express, CASDDS.
**Desc:** Contains original articles, papers, and abstracts on diagnosis and treatment of headache and related pain.
**Ind/Abst** Annals Behav. Med.; Biol. Abstr.; Chem. Abstr.; Curr. Aware. Biol. Sci., CABS; Curr. Contents Clin. Med.; Curr. Titl. Dent.; Dev. Med. Child Neurol.; EMBASE; Energy Res. Abstr. (Aug. 1982-); Health Plan. Adminis.; Index Med.; Mod. Med.; Nutr. Abstr. Rev., Ser. B, Live Feeds and Feed.; Nutr. Abstr. Rev., Ser. A, Hum. Exp.; Nutr. Res. Newsl.; Psychol. Abstr. (1983-); PsycINFO; PsycLit; Res. Alert [Full Cov.]; Sci. Cit. Index; SCISEARCH; Soc. Sci. Cit. Index [Select. Cov.].

US/1059-7565
**HEADACHE QUARTERLY.** [Headache q.]. **VFOAT** Headache Quarterly, Current Treatment and Research. Vol. 1, No. 1 (1990)-. Periodical. English. qt. $77.25 (institutions), $51.50 (individuals) US; $122.00 (institutions), $96.00 (individuals) other. International Universities Press Inc., 59 Boston Post Road, PO Box 1524, Madison CT 06443-1524. **Tel** (203)245-4000, FAX (203)245-0775, telex 282986 IUP BK. **ED** Seymour Diamond, M.D. **LC** RC392; .H46. **DD** 616. **NLM** W1; HE13L. **CODEN** HQUAEN. **Bk Rev. Pr Rev.** Documents available from The Genuine Article.
**Desc:** Papers on all aspects of headache as well as invited review articles, and abstracts of headache and pain literature. In addition, each issue reports on research currently in progress, futuristic therapies, and theories about headache.
**Ind/Abst** EMBASE; Psychol. Abstr. (1990-); PsycINFO; PsycLit; Res. Alert [Full Cov.]; SCISEARCH; Soc. Sci. Cit. Index [Select. Cov.].

XR/0960-7560
**HOMEOSTASIS IN HEALTH AND DISEASE : INTERNATIONAL JOURNAL DEVOTED TO INTEGRATIVE BRAIN FUNCTIONS AND HOMEOSTATIC SYSTEMS. Added/Corp** Collegium Internationale Activitatis Nervosae Superioris. **VFOAT** Homeostasis. Vol. 33, No. 1-2 (Apr. 1991)-. Periodical. English. Six times a year. $125.00. CIANS, IHE Srobarova 48, CS-100 42 Prague, Czech Republic. **ED** M. Horvath. **LC** QP351.S65; A2. **DD** 612/.022. **NLM** W1; HO519B. **CODEN** HOMOEB. **[CCC].** Documents available from The Genuine Article. ***Continues*** *Activitas Nervosa Superior, 0001-7604.*
**Desc:** Devoted to studies of integrated brain functions in homeostasis, their adaptation to environment and psychosocial conditions, and underlying mechanisms ranging from molecular to systemic processes and behavior.
**Ind/Abst** Curr. Contents Life Sci.; Index Med. (1991-); Res. Alert [Full Cov.]; Sci. Cit. Index; SCISEARCH; Soc. Sci. Cit. Index [Select. Cov.].

●US/1065-9471
**HUMAN BRAIN MAPPING.** [Hum. brain mapp.]. (1993)-. Periodical. English. Four times a year. $190.00 (US); $230.00 (Canada & Mexico); $245.00 (other). John Wiley & Sons, Inc., 605 Third Avenue, New York NY 10158-0012. **Tel** (212)850-6000, (212)850-6645, FAX (212)850-6088, telex 12-7063. **(Subscription address:** John Wiley & Sons / England, Baffins Lane, Chichester, West Sussex PO19 1UD England.**) ED** Peter T. Fox. **DD** 612. **NLM** W1; HU444WD.
**Desc:** Publishes basic, clinical, technical and theoretical research in the interdisciplinary and rapidly expanding field of human brain mapping. Also endorses the propagation of methodological standards and encourages database developments in this field.

UK/0742-504X
**IBRO HANDBOOK SERIES.** [IBRO handb. ser.]. **Added/Corp** International Brain Research Organization. **VAT** International Brain Research Organisation Handbook Series. Vol. 1 (1982)-. Monographic series. English. John Wiley & Sons Inc / New Jersey, 1 Wiley Drive, Somerset NJ 08875. **Tel** (800)225-5945, (908)469-4400. **NLM** W1; IB127. Documents available from CASDDS.
**Ind/Abst** Chem. Abstr.

US/0361-0713
**IBRO NEWS.** (IBRO NEWS / INTERNATIONAL BRAIN RESEARCH ORGANIZATION.). [IBRO news]. **Added/Corp** International Brain Research Organization. **VFOAT** I.B.R.O. News. **VAT** International Brain Research Organization News. (Jan. 1973)-. Periodical. English. ir. Free. IBRO News, University Laboratory of Physiology, Parks Road,, Oxford OX1 3PT England. **Tel** 011 44 865 511501, FAX 011 44 865 511501. **ED** Colin Blakemore and Andree Blakemore. **LC** QP376; .I27. **DD** 591.1/88. **NLM** W1 IN71R. **Ad Acc.** ***Continues*** *IBRO Bulletin, 0536-1192.*

US/0739-9774
**INSIDE MS.** (INSIDE MS : OFFICIAL PUBLICATION OF THE NATIONAL MULTIPLE SCLEROSIS SOCIETY.). [Inside MS]. **VFOAT** Inside M.S. **VAT** Inside Multiple Sclerosis. (1983)-. Periodical. English. qt. Free with membership. National Multiple Sclerosis Society, 6100 Building Estgate Center, Suite 4800, Chattanooga TN 37411. **Tel** (615)954-9700. **Bk Rev. Ad Acc. Circ:** 400,000 (ctrl). available on an online database (file 149/Full-Text) from DIALOG.
**Desc:** Magazine directed primarily toward people with multiple sclerosis. Research, medical services, coping, legislation, general news, volunteer activities and information.
**Ind/Abst** Acad. Abstr. Full Text Elite (Jan. 1992-); Acad. Abstr. (Jan. 1992-); Acad. Search (Jan. 1992-); Health Index (1989-); Health Period. Database [Full Txt.]; Health Ref. Cent. (Jan. 1989-) [Full Cov.]; Health Source (Jan. 1992-); INFO-SOUTH Abstr.; Mag. Search.

●US/1065-7320
**INSIDE VIEW (IRVING, TEX.).** (INSIDE VIEW.). **Added/Corp** Centre for Neuro Skills. (1992)-. Periodical. English. Three times a year. Centro for Neuro Skills, 3501 North MacArthur Boulevard, Number 200, Irving TX 75062.

UK/0736-5748
**INTERNATIONAL JOURNAL OF DEVELOPMENTAL NEUROSCIENCE.** (INTERNATIONAL JOURNAL OF DEVELOPMENTAL NEUROSCIENCE : THE OFFICIAL JOURNAL OF THE INTERNATIONAL SOCIETY FOR DEVELOPMENTAL NEUROSCIENCE.). [Int. j. dev. neurosci.]. **Added/Corp** International Society for Developmental Neuroscience. Vol. 1 No. 1 (1983)-. Academic Scholarly Publication. English. Eight times a year. $760.00 The Americas; £510.00 other. Pergamon Press, An Imprint of Elsevier Science Ltd., The Boulevard, Langford Lane, Kidlington, Oxford OX5 1GB United Kingdom. **Tel** 011 44 865 843000, 011 44 865 843699, FAX 011 44 865 843010. **(Subscription address:** Elsevier Science Ltd. Oxford Fulfillment Centre, PO Box 800, Kidlington, Oxford OX5 1DX United Kingdom.) **ED** Regino Perez-Polo. **LC** QP363.5; .I56. **DD** 591.1/88/05. **NLM** W1; IN766GBD. **CODEN** IJDND6. **[CCC]. Pr Rev.** available on microfilm and microfiche from University Microfilms International (UMI). Documents available from The Genuine Article, BIOSIS Document Express, CASDDS.
**Ind/Abst** Biol. Abstr. (1985-); Chem. Abstr. (1983-); CSA Neuro. Abstr.; Curr. Aware. Biol. Sci., CABS; Curr. Contents Life Sci.; Dev. Med. Child Neurol.; EMBASE; Index Med.; Life Sci. Collect.; Psychol. Abstr. (1983-); PsycINFO; PsycLit; Ref. Upd. Deluxe Ed.; Res. Alert [Full Cov.]; Sci. Cit. Index; SCISEARCH.

UY/0020-7446
**INTERNATIONAL JOURNAL OF NEUROLOGY.** [Int. j. neurol.]. **VFOAT** Internationale Zeitschrift fur Neurologie; Revista Internacional de Neurologia; Revue International de Neurologie. Vol. 1, No. 1 (Dec. 1959)-. Periodical. English (French, German and Spanish). qt. $80.00. International Journal of Neurology, Calle Buenos Aires 363, Montevideo Uruguay. **NLM** W1 IN77. **CODEN** IJONAO. Documents available from BIOSIS Document Express, CASDDS.
**Ind/Abst** Biol. Abstr.; Chem. Abstr. (1959-1981); Index Med.

US/0020-7454
**INTERNATIONAL JOURNAL OF NEUROSCIENCE.** [Int. j. neurosci.]. **VFOAT** Neuroscience. Vol. 1 (Oct. 1970)-. Academic Scholarly Publication. English. qt. $4494.00 (academic institutions), $7008.00 (corporate institutions). Gordon & Breach Science Publishers, Inc., PO Box 786, Cooper Station, New York NY 10276. **Tel** (212)206-8900, FAX (212)645-2459. **(Subscription address:** International Publishers Distributor at one of the following addresses: 820 Town Center Drive, Langhorne, PA 19047; or PO Box 90, Reading Berkshire RG1 8JL UK; or Kent Ridge PO Box 1180, Singapore 9111, Republic of Singapore) **ED** Mark Donato. **LC** QP351; .I775. **DD** 612/.8/05. **NLM** W1 IN77K. **CODEN** IJNUB7. **[CCC]. Pr Rev.** Documents available from The Genuine Article, BIOSIS Document Express, CASDDS.
**Desc:** Covers a broad range of studies such as electrophysiology and neuromagnetism, including basic and applied work, new recording and analytical techniques and theoretical papers.
**Ind/Abst** Biol. Abstr. (?-1984); Chem. Abstr. (1970-1986); CSA Neuro. Abstr. (?-?); Curr. Aware. Biol. Sci., CABS; Curr. Contents Life Sci.; Curr. Ref. Fish Res.; EMBASE; Index Med.; Index Vet.; Int. Aerosp. Abstr.; Math. Rev.; Life Sci. Collect.; Psychol. Abstr. (1983-); PsycINFO; PsycLit; Ref. Upd. Deluxe Ed.; Res. Alert [Full Cov.]; Sci. Cit. Index; SCISEARCH; Small Anim. Abstr. Bibliogr.; Soc. Sci. Cit. Index [Select. Cov.].

US/0074-7742
**INTERNATIONAL REVIEW OF NEUROBIOLOGY.** **See** Biology.

IT/0392-0461
**ITALIAN JOURNAL OF NEUROLOGICAL SCIENCES.** [Ital. j. neurol. sci.]. **Added/Corp** Societa Italiana di Neurologia. **VFOAT** Neurological Sciences. Vol. 1 (Nov. 1979)-. Academic Scholarly Publication. English. Nine times a year. L155000 Italy. Masson S.P.A, Via Statuto 2/4, 20121 Milan Italy. **Tel** 011 39 2 63671, FAX 011 39 2 6367211. **NLM** W1 IT357. **CODEN** IJNSD3. **Pr Rev.** available on microfilm and microfiche from University Microfilms International (UMI). Documents available from The Genuine Article, CASDDS.
**Ind/Abst** Chem. Abstr. (1979-1983); Curr. Contents Clin. Med.; EMBASE [Select. Cov.]; Index Med.; Life Sci. Collect.; Protozoolog. Abstr.; Res. Alert [Full Cov.]; SCISEARCH.

JA/0912-2036
**JAPANESE JOURNAL OF PSYCHIATRY AND NEUROLOGY, THE.** **See** Medical Science and Technology-Psychiatry.

BL
**JORNAL DA LIGA BRASILEIRA DE EPILEPSIA.** **Added/Corp** Liga Brasileira de Epilepsia. Vol. 1, No. 1 (1988)-. Periodical. Portuguese (English and Spanish). tq. US$70.00 (non-members) Brazil; US$120.00 Other. Liga Brasileira Epilepsia, Hospital Sao Lucas da Puc, Sala 322, Av. Ipiranga 6690, 90610 Porto Alegre, Brazil. **Tel** (512)243-092, FAX (051)336-0090. **ED** Jaderson costa da Costa, M.D. and Magda Lahorgue Nunes, M.D. **NLM** W1; JO195K. Index available. cum. index (First issue of the year). **Ad Acc, Adv Mgr:** Magda Nunes. Full Page (Color) $1500.00. Half Page (Color) $500-$1000. **Pr Rev. Circ:** 600 (ctrl). Documents available. ***Continues*** *Boletim da Liga Brasileira de Epilepsia.*
**Desc:** Publishes voluntary articles or articles requested by the editors on topics related to epilepsy.
**Ind/Abst** EMBASE [Select. Cov.].

BL
**JOURNAL BRASILEIRO DE NEUROCIRURGIA.** **Added/Corp** Academia Brasileira de Neurocirurgia. Vol. 1, No. 1 (1989)-. Periodical. Portuguese (summaries and/or abstracts in English). qt. Sears Medica Neurocirurgica, Caixa Postal 20-389, 04034 Sao Paulo SP Brazil. **NLM** W1; JO19392. ***Continues*** *Seara Medica Neurocirurgica, 0037-0169.*

GW/0021-8359
**JOURNAL FUER HIRNFORSCHUNG.** ***Title Change.*** [J. Hirnforsch.]. **Added/Corp** Cecile und Oskar Vogt Institut fuer Hirnforschung. World Federation of Neurology. Problem Commission of Neuroanatomy. Institut fuer Hirnforschung und Allgemeine Biologie (Neustadt im Schwarzwald, Germany). Vol. 1, (1954)-(19??). Academic Scholarly Publication. German (English and French). qt. Akademie-Verlag GmbH, Muehlenstrasse 33 34, D 13162 Berlin Germany. **Tel** 011 49 30 47889300, FAX 011 49 30 47889357. **(Subscription address:** VCH Publishers Inc., 303 Northwest 12th Avenue, Journals Department, Deerfield FL 33442.) **ED** C. Vogt and O. Vogt. **NLM** W1; JO449. **Pr Rev.** Documents available from The Genuine Article. ***Supersedes*** *Journal fuer Psychologie und Neurologie.* ***Continued by*** *Journal of Brain Research.*
**Ind/Abst** Curr. Contents Life Sci.; EMBASE; Energy Res. Abstr. (Feb. 1982-); Index Med.; Index Vet.; Res. Alert [Full Cov.]; Sci. Cit. Index; SCISEARCH; Vet. Bull.

GW
**JOURNAL OF BRAIN RESEARCH.** (19??)-. Academic Scholarly Publication. English. qt. $585.00. Akademie-Verlag GmbH, Muehlenstrasse 33 34, D 13162 Berlin Germany. **Tel** 011 49 30 47889300, FAX 011 49 30 47889357. **(Subscription address:** VCH Publishers Inc., 303 Northwest 12th Avenue, Journals Department, Deerfield FL 33442.) **ED** E. Winkelmann. ***Continues*** *Journal fuer Hirnforschung.*
**Desc:** Publishes a wide range of investigations covering the field of neuromorphology in its entirety.
**Ind/Abst** Curr. Contents, Agric. Biol. Environ. Sci.; Curr. Contents Life Sci.; EMBASE.

US/0890-2739
**JOURNAL OF CARNIOMANDIBULAR DISORDERS, THE.** ***Title Change.*** [J. craniomandib. disord.]. **Added/Corp** American Academy of Craniomandibular Disorders. European Academy of Craniomandibular Disorders. Vol. 1, No. 1 (Spring 1987)-(1992). Periodical. English. qt. Quintessence Publishing Company Inc., 551 North Kimberly Drive, Carol Stream IL 60188-1881. **Tel** (708)682-3223, (800)621-0387, FAX (708)682-3288. **DD** 616. **NLM** W1; JO602VR. **CODEN** JCDIEM. **[CCC].** Documents available from BIOSIS Document Express. ***Continued by*** *Journal of Orofacial Pain, 1064-6655.*
**Ind/Abst** Biol. Abstr. (1987-); Dent. Abstr.; Index Dent. Lit. (1987-).

UK/0891-0618
**JOURNAL OF CHEMICAL NEUROANATOMY.** (JOURNAL OF CHEMICAL NEUROANATOMY.). [J. chem. neuroanat.]. Vol. 1 (1988)-. Academic Scholarly Publication. English. Eight times a year (2 vols.). Fl1070.00. Elsevier Science Publishers BV, PO Box 211, 1000 AE Amsterdam Netherlands. **Tel** 011 31 20 5803642, FAX 011 31 20 5862696, telex 15682. **(Subscription address:** North, South and Central America/ John Wiley & Sons, Inc., Subscription Department, 605 Third Avenue, New York, NY 10158-0012, USA; telephone: (212)850-6645; FAX: (212)850-6021) **ED** H W M Steinbusch and A Claudio Cuello. **DD** 616. **NLM** W1; JO581G. **CODEN** JCNAEE. **[CCC].** Index available. **Bk Rev. Ad Acc.** available on microfilm and microfiche from University Microfilms International (UMI). Documents available from The Genuine Article, BIOSIS Document Express, CASDDS.
**Desc:** Publishes papers dealing with any aspect of the nervous system, including development, evolution, aging, behavioral aspects related to one or more neuronal systems. Discusses methods used in immunohistochemistry, hybridocytochemistry, receptor autoradiography, transplantation studies, tissue culture experiments and more.
**Ind/Abst** Biol. Abstr. (1990-); Chem. Abstr.; CSA Neuro. Abstr.; Curr. Aware. Biol. Sci., CABS; Curr. Contents Life Sci.; EMBASE; Index Med. (1988-); Ref. Upd. Deluxe Ed.; Res. Alert [Full Cov.]; Sci. Cit. Index; SCISEARCH.

US/0883-0738
**JOURNAL OF CHILD NEUROLOGY.** **See** Medical Science and Technology-Pediatrics.

NE/0168-8634
**JOURNAL OF CLINICAL AND EXPERIMENTAL NEUROPSYCHOLOGY.** (JOURNAL OF CLINICAL AND EXPERIMENTAL NEUROPSYCHOLOGY : OFFICIAL JOURNAL OF THE INTERNATIONAL NEUROPSYCHOLOGICAL SOCIETY.). [J. clin. exp. neuropsychol.]. **Added/Corp** International Neuropsychological Society. Vol. 7, No. 1 (Feb. 1985)-. Periodical. English. bm. Fl1675.00 (all four groups) (Institutions). Swets & Zeitlinger BV, Heereweg 347B PO Box 825, 2160 SZ Lisse Holland. **Tel** 011 31 2521 35111, FAX 02521-15888, telex 41325. **(Subscription address:** Swets Publishing Service, PO Box 825, 2160 SZ Lisse The Netherlands) **ED** L Costa and B P Rourke. **NLM** W1; JO586. **CODEN** JCENE8. **[CCC]. Bk Rev. Ad Acc. Pr Rev. Circ:** 3,000. Documents available from The Genuine Article, BIOSIS Document Express, ADONIS. ***Continues*** *Journal of Clinical Neuropsychology, 0165-0475.*
**Desc:** Publishes original articles dealing with research and the theory in the broad field of behavioral impairment associated with dysfunction at the level of the cerebral hemispheres.
**Ind/Abst** ADONIS; Annals Behav. Med.; Biol. Abstr. (1985-); Child Dev. Abstr. Bibliogr.; Curr. Contents Clin. Med.; Curr. Contents Soc. Behav. Sci.; EMBASE; Except. Child Educ. Resour.; Index Med.; Psychol. Abstr. (1979-); PsycINFO (1990-); PsycLit; PsycScan: Clin. Psych.; Ref. Upd. Deluxe Ed.; Res. Alert [Full Cov.]; Sci. Cit. Index; SCISEARCH; Soc. Plann. Policy Dev. Abstr.; Soc. Sci. Cit. Index [Full Cov.].

US/0736-0258
**JOURNAL OF CLINICAL NEUROPHYSIOLOGY.** (JOURNAL OF CLINICAL NEUROPHYSIOLOGY : OFFICIAL PUBLICATION OF THE AMERICAN ELECTROENCEPHALOGRAPHIC SOCIETY.). [J. clin. neurophysiol.]. **Added/Corp** American Electroencephalographic Society. Vol. 1, No. 1 (Jan. 1984)-. Periodical. English. bm (6 issues). $145.00 (individuals), $260.00 (institutions) US; $196.00 (individuals), $314.00 (institutions) other. Raven Press, 1185 Avenue of the Americas, 37th Floor, New York NY 10036. **Tel** (212)930-9500, (212)930-9604, FAX (212)869-3495, (212)302-8507, telex 640073. **ED** Cosimo Ajmone-Marsan. **DD** 616. **NLM** W1; JO5893P. **[CCC]. Pr Rev.** available on microfilm and microfiche from University Microfilms International (UMI). Documents available from The Genuine Article. ***Continues*** *Journal of the American EEG Society.*
**Desc:** The journal features reviews on topics that provide comprehensive coverage of key concerns in electroencephalography and evoked potentials, clinical neurology, neurosurgery, and psychiatry, and of experimental research on the central nervous system.
**Ind/Abst** Curr. Aware. Biol. Sci., CABS; Curr. Contents Clin. Med.; Dev. Med. Child Neurol.; EMBASE; Index

Med. (Vol. 1, No. 1, 1984-); Life Sci. Collect. (Vol. 1, No. 1, 1984-); Res. Alert [Full Cov.]; SCISEARCH; Soc. Sci. Cit. Index [Select. Cov.].

US/0898-929X
**JOURNAL OF COGNITIVE NEUROSCIENCE, THE.** [J. cogn. neurosci.]. **Added/Corp** Cognitive Neuroscience Institute (Norwich, Vt.). Vol. 1, No. 1 (Winter 1989)-. Periodical. English. qt. $58.00 (individuals), $156.00 (institutions). Massachusetts Institute of Technology (MIT) Press, 55 Hayward Street, Cambridge MA 02142-1399. **Tel** (617)253-2889, (617)625-8481, FAX (617)258-6779. **ED** Michael S. Gazzaniga. **LC** QP360; .J695. **DD** 612.8/05. **NLM** W1; JO5926F. **CODEN** JCONEO. **[CCC]. Ad Acc. Pr Rev. Circ:** 800. available on microfilm and microfiche from University Microfilms International (UMI). Documents available from The Genuine Article, UMI Article Clearinghouse.
**Desc:** Provides a forum for research involving the interaction of brain and behavior.
**Ind/Abst** Curr. Aware. Biol. Sci., CABS; Curr. Contents Life Sci.; EMBASE; Expand. Acad. Index (1992-); Linguist. Lang. Behav. Abstr.; Newsp. Period. Abstr. (1992-); Psychol. Abstr. (1989-); PsycINFO; PsycLit; Res. Alert [Full Cov.]; Sci. Cit. Index; SCISEARCH; Soc. Plann. Policy Dev. Abstr.; Soc. Sci. Cit. Index [Select. Cov.].

US/1062-2969
**JOURNAL OF COGNITIVE REHABILITATION, THE.** [J. cogn. rehabil.]. **VFOAT** Cognitive Rehabilitation. Vol. 9, Issue 1 (Jan.-Feb. 1991)-. Periodical. English. bm. $35.00 (individuals), $70.00 (institutions) US; $40.00 (individuals), $75.00 (institutions), Canada; $50.00 (individuals), $85.00 (institutions) other. Neuroscience Publishers, 6555 Carrollton Avenue, Indianapolis IN 46220. **Tel** (317)257-9672. **LC** RC387.5; .C65. **DD** 616. ***Continues*** *Cognitive Rehabilitation, 0738-1069.*
**Ind/Abst** Cumul. Index Nurs. Allied Health Lit.

US/0021-9924
**JOURNAL OF COMMUNICATION DISORDERS.** [J. commun. disord.]. Vol. 1 (May 1967)-. Academic Scholarly Publication. English. Four times a year (1 volume). $265.00 US; $295.00 other. Elsevier Science Publishing Company Inc, Madison Square Station, PO Box 882, New York NY 10159-0882. **Tel** (212)633-3950, FAX (212)633-3990. **ED** R W Rieber. **LC** RC423.A1; J64. **DD** 616.85/5/005. **NLM** W1 JO593N. **CODEN** JCDIAIJCDAIA. **[CCC]. Ad Acc. Pr Rev.** available on microfilm and microfiche from University Microfilms International (UMI). Documents available from The Genuine Article, BIOSIS Document Express.
**Desc:** Provides up-to-date information on clinical and research advances in a wide range of hearing and speech disorders.
**Ind/Abst** Abstr. Anthropol.; Appl. Soc. Sci. Index Abstr.; Biol. Abstr.; Curr. Contents Soc. Behav. Sci.; Curr. Index J. Educ.; Dev. Med. Child Neurol.; EMBASE; Except. Child Educ. Resour.; Index Med.; Linguist. Lang. Behav. Abstr. (1977-) [Full Cov.]; Middle East Abstr. Index; Psychol. Abstr. (1967-); PsycINFO; PsycLit; Res. Alert [Full Cov.]; Soc. Plann. Policy Dev. Abstr.; Soc. Sci. Cit. Index [Full Cov.].

US/0021-9967
**JOURNAL OF COMPARATIVE NEUROLOGY (1911).** (JOURNAL OF COMPARATIVE NEUROLOGY.). [J. comp. neurol.]. **Added/Corp** Wistar Institute of Anatomy and Biology. Vol. 21, No. 1 (March 1911)-. Academic Scholarly Publication. English (summaries and/or abstracts in English). Fifty-two times a year. $7,956.00 US; $8,476.00 Canada and Mexico; $8,671.00 other. John Wiley & Sons, Inc., 605 Third Avenue, New York NY 10158-0012. **Tel** (212)850-6000, (212)850-6645, FAX (212)850-6088, telex 12-7063. **(Subscription address:** John Wiley & Sons / England, Baffins Lane, Chichester, West Sussex PO19 1UD England.**) ED** Sanford L. Palay. **LC** QL1; .J83. **DD** 616. **NLM** W1 JO595E. **CODEN** JCNEAM. **[CCC].** cum. index. **Pr Rev.** Documents available from The Genuine Article, BIOSIS Document Express, CASDDS. ***Continues*** *Journal of Comparative Neurology and Psychology, 0092-7015.*
**Desc:** Publishes original articles on the anatomy and physiology of the nervous system. Preference is given to papers that deal descriptively or experimentally with the nervous system, its structure, growth and function.
**Ind/Abst** Biol. Abstr.; Chem. Abstr.; Chemorecept. Abstr.; CSA Neuro. Abstr.; Curr. Aware. Biol. Sci., CABS; Curr. Contents Life Sci.; Curr. Primate Ref.; Curr. Ref. Fish Res.; EMBASE; Energy Res. Abstr.; Entomol. Abstr.; Fish Rev.; Helminthol. Abstr. (1991-); Index Med.; INIS Atomindex [Micro.]; Int. Aerosp. Abstr.; Nematol. Abstr.; Life Sci. Collect.; Postharvest News Inf.; Protozoolog. Abstr.; Ref. Upd. Basic Ed.; Ref. Upd. Deluxe Ed.; Res. Alert [Full Cov.]; Rev. Med. Vet. Entomol.; Sci. Cit. Index; SCISEARCH; Small Anim. Abstr. Bibliogr.

GW/0340-7594
**JOURNAL OF COMPARATIVE PHYSIOLOGY. A, SENSORY, NEURAL, AND BEHAVIORAL PHYSIOLOGY. See** Biology-Physiology.

NE/0929-5313
**JOURNAL OF COMPUTATIONAL NEUROSCIENCE.** (19??)-. English. qt. $471.00. Kluwer Academic Publishers, Postbus 322, 3300 AH Dordrecht, The Netherlands. **Tel** 011 (31) 78 524400, FAX 011 31 78 183273, telex 20083.

●US
**JOURNAL OF DRUG THERPAY IN NEUROLOGICAL DISORDERS.** (Effective July 1995)-. English. Four times a year. $96.00 US; $134.40 other. The Haworth Press Inc, 10 Alice Street, Binghamton NY 13904-1580. **Tel** (607)722-5857, (800)3-HAWORTH, FAX (607)722-1424. Documents available from Haworth Document Delivery Service.

US/0896-6974
**JOURNAL OF EPILEPSY.** [J. epilepsy]. **Added/Corp** Epilepsy Foundation of America. Vol. 1, No. 1 (1988)-. Periodical. English. qt. $170.00 US; $200.00 other. Butterworth Heinemann / Woburn, MA, 225 Wildwood Avenue, Unit B, Woburn MA 01801. **Tel** (800)366-2665, FAX (617)928-2620, telex 880052. **(Subscription address:** Elsevier Science Inc. / New York Books, 655 Avenue of the Americas, New York NY 10010.**) ED** Allen R Wyler, Bruce Hermann, Gregory Holmes, Susan Spencer, and Christian E Elger. **DD** 616. **NLM** W1; JO644BT. **CODEN** JOEPEU. **[CCC].** Index available. **Bk Rev. Ad Acc. Pr Rev. Circ:** 1,800. Documents available from The Genuine Article.
**Desc:** Addresses the needs of the broad range of specialists involved in caring for the patient with epilepsy.
**Ind/Abst** Curr. Aware. Biol. Sci., CABS; Curr. Contents, Agric. Biol. Environ. Sci.; Curr. Contents Clin. Med.; Dev. Med. Child Neurol.; EMBASE; Psychoanal. Abstr.; Psychol. Abstr. (1988-); PsycINFO; PsycScan: Appl. Exp. Eng. Psych.; PsycScan: LD/MR; PsycScan: Neuropsych.; Res. Alert [Full Cov.]; SCISEARCH; Soc. Sci. Cit. Index [Select. Cov.].

US/0895-8696
**JOURNAL OF MOLECULAR NEUROSCIENCE.** (JOURNAL OF MOLECULAR NEUROSCIENCE : MN.). [J. mol. neurosci.]. **VFOAT** MN; Journal of Molecular Neuroscience MN. Vol. 1, No. 1 (1989)-. Academic Scholarly Publication. English. qt (4 issues). $185.00 US; $220.00 other. Humana Press Inc., 999 Riverview Drive, Suite 208, Totawa NJ 07512. **Tel** (201)256-1699, FAX (201)256-8341. **ED** P. Michael Conn. **LC** QP356.2; .J68. **DD** 591.1/88. **NLM** W1; JO7737. **CODEN** JMNEES. **[CCC]. Pr Rev.** Documents available from The Genuine Article, BIOSIS Document Express, CASDDS.
**Desc:** Provides a comprehensive medium for studies dealing with the synthesis of nervous system proteins at the genetic and post-translational level as well as the functional and developmental aspect of these proteins. Designed to integrate and provide balanced coverage of studies involving nucleic acids and the protein products. Seeks to cover all aspects of molecular neurobiology.
**Ind/Abst** Biol. Abstr. (1990-); Chem. Abstr. (1989-); Curr. Aware. Biol. Sci., CABS; Curr. Contents Life Sci.; Res. Alert [Full Cov.]; Sci. Cit. Index; SCISEARCH.

US/0022-3018
**JOURNAL OF NERVOUS AND MENTAL DISEASE, THE.** [J. of nerv. ment. dis.]. **Added/Corp** American Neurological Association. New York Neurological Association. Philadelphia Neurological Society. Chicago Neurological Society. Boston Society of Psychiatry and Neurology. Vol. 3 (1876)-. Academic Scholarly Publication. English. mo. $98.00 (individual), $175.00 (institution) US; $131.00 (individual), $208.00 (institutions) other. Williams & Wilkins Company, 428 East Preston Street, Baltimore MD 21202-3993. **Tel** (410)528-4000, (800)638-6423, FAX (410)528-8596, telex 87669. **(Subscription address:** Williams & Wilkins, PO Box 64380, Baltimore MD 21264.**) NLM** W1 JO778. **CODEN** JNMDAN. **[CCC]. Ad Acc. Pr Rev. Circ:** 2,520. available on microfilm. Documents available from , The Genuine Article, BIOSIS Document Express, CASDDS, , ADONIS, Quick Copies. ***Continues*** *Chicago Journal of Nervous and Mental Disease, 1060-1694.*
**Desc:** Studies in the social, behavioral, and neurological sciences relevant to the clinical practice of psychiatry.
**Ind/Abst** Abr. Index Med.; ADONIS; Appl. Soc. Sci. Index Abstr.; Biol. Abstr. (?-1985); Chem. Abstr.; Crim. Penol. Police Sci. Abstr.; CSA Neuro. Abstr. (?-?); Curr. Aware. Biol. Sci., CABS; Curr. Contents Clin. Med.; Curr. Contents Life Sci.; Curr. Contents Soc. Behav. Sci.; EMBASE; Energy Res. Abstr.; Except. Child Educ. Resour. (19??-19??); Health Period. Database; Index Med.; Index Period. Artic. Relat. Law; INIS Atomindex [Micro.]; Int. Pharm. Abstr.; Med. Abstr. Newsl.; Middle East Abstr. Index; MLA Int. Bibl. Books Artic. Mod. Lang. Lit.; Nucl. Sci. Abstr.; Nutr. Abstr. Rev., Ser. B, Live Feeds and Feed.; Nutr. Abstr. Rev., Ser. A, Hum. Exp.; Life Sci. Collect.; PESTDOC; Physic. Medline Plus; Psychol. Abstr. (1929-); PsycINFO; PsycLit; PsycScan: Clin. Psych.; Ref. Upd. Deluxe Ed.; Res. Alert [Full Cov.]; Risk Abstr.; Sci. Cit. Index; SCISEARCH; Soc. Sci. Cit. Index [Full Cov.]; Women Stud. Abstr.

AU/0300-9564
**JOURNAL OF NEURAL TRANSMISSION. GENERAL SECTION : JNT.** [J. neural transm.]. Vol. 78, No. 1 (1989)-. Periodical. English. mo. DM1340.00. Springer-Verlag Wien, Sachsenplatz 4 6, PO Box 89, A-1201 Vienna Austria. **Tel** 011 43 1 3302415. **(Subscription address:** Springer Verlag New York Inc. / for North America, 44 Hartz Way, Secaucus NJ 07096.**) NLM** W1; JO781F. **CODEN** JNGSE8. **[CCC]. Pr Rev.** available on microfilm and microfiche from University Microfilms International (UMI). Documents available from The Genuine Article, BIOSIS Document Express, CASDDS, ADONIS. ***Continues in part*** *Journal of Neural Transmission, 0300-9564.*
**Ind/Abst** ADONIS; Biol. Abstr.; Chem. Abstr.; Curr. Aware. Biol. Sci., CABS; Curr. Contents Life Sci.; EMBASE; Fish Rev. (Jan. 1989-July 1992); Index Med. (1989-); Res. Alert [Full Cov.]; Sci. Cit. Index; SCISEARCH; Soc. Sci. Cit. Index [Select. Cov.]; Wildl. Rev. (Jan. 1989-July 1992).

AU/0936-3076
**JOURNAL OF NEURAL TRANSMISSION. PARKINSON'S DISEASE AND DEMENTIA SECTION.** [J. neural transm., Parkinson's dis. dement. sect.]. Vol. 1, No. 1-2 (1989)-. Periodical. English. bm. DM670.00. Springer-Verlag Wien, Sachsenplatz 4 6, PO Box 89, A-1201 Vienna Austria. **Tel** 011 43 1 3302415. **(Subscription address:** Springer Verlag New York Inc. / for North America, 44 Hartz Way, Secaucus NJ 07096.**) ED** A Carlsson. **NLM** W1; JO781H. **CODEN** JNPSEJ. **Pr Rev.** available on microfilm and microfiche from University Microfilms International (UMI). Documents available from The Genuine Article, BIOSIS Document Express, CASDDS, ADONIS. ***Continues in part*** *Journal of Neural Transmission.*
**Desc:** Covers topics dealing with clinical investigation focusing on the pathogenic factors of neurological and psychiatric disorders.
**Ind/Abst** ADONIS; Biol. Abstr.; Chem. Abstr.; Curr. Aware. Biol. Sci., CABS; Curr. Contents Life Sci.; EMBASE; Health Plan. Adminis.; Index Med. (Vol. 1, No. 1-2, 1989-); PESTDOC; Ref. Upd. Deluxe Ed.; Res. Alert [Full Cov.]; Sci. Cit. Index; SCISEARCH.

AU/0303-6995
**JOURNAL OF NEURAL TRANSMISSION. SUPPLEMENTUM.** [J. neural. transm., Suppl.]. **Added/Corp** International Society for Neurovegetative Research. Vol. 11, (1974)-. Academic Scholarly Publication. Multiple languages (English and German; summaries and/or abstracts in English and German). ir. Price varies per volume. Springer Verlag New York Inc., PO Box 19386 Books, Newark NJ 07195. **Tel** (201)348-4033. **(Subscription address:** North America/ Journal Fulfillment Services, 44 Hartz Way, Secaucus, NJ 07094**) ED** A. Carlsson. **NLM** W1; JO781A. **CODEN** JNTSD4. available on microfilm from University Microfilms International (UMI). Documents available from CASDDS. ***Continues*** *Journal of Neuro-Visceral Relations. Supplementum, 0075-4323.*
**Desc:** Clinical neuropharmacology and basic principles of the brain's neurotransmission including receptor biochemistry.
**Ind/Abst** Chem. Abstr.; EMBASE; Index Med.

UK/0792-8483
**JOURNAL OF NEURAL TRANSPLANTATION & PLASTICITY.** **VFOAT** Journal of Neural Transplantation and Plasticity; Journal of Neural Transplantation. Vol. 2, No. 1 (1991)-. Periodical. English. ir. $240.00. Freund Publishing House Ltd, PO Box 35010, 61 Nachmani Street, Tel Aviv 61350 Israel. **Tel** 011 972 3 5662925, FAX 011 972 3 5605335. **(Subscription address:** Freund Publishing House Ltd., Suite 500 Chesham House, 150 Regent Street, London W1R 5FA England.**) ED** W.J. Freed. **NLM** W1; JO781M. **CODEN** JNPLEW. Documents available from The Genuine Article, BIOSIS Document Express. ***Continues*** *Journal of Neural Transplantation.*
**Ind/Abst** Biol. Abstr.; Curr. Aware. Biol. Sci., CABS; Curr. Contents Life Sci.; EMBASE; Index Med. (1991-); Psychoanal. Abstr.; Psychol. Abstr. (1989-); PsycINFO; PsycLit; PsycScan: Appl. Exp. Eng. Psych.; PsycScan: LD/MR; PsycScan: Neuropsych.; Ref. Upd. Deluxe Ed.; Res. Alert [Full Cov.]; Sci. Cit. Index.

●US/1069-7438
**JOURNAL OF NEURO-AIDS. VFOAT** Journal of Neuro Aids. (1994)-. Periodical. English. Four times a year (Published during the academic year). $75.00 US; $105.00 other. The Haworth Press Inc, 10 Alice Street, Binghamton NY 13904-1580. **Tel** (607)722-5857, (800)3-HAWORTH, FAX (607)722-1424. **ED** Richard W. Price. **Acid Free.** Documents available from Haworth Document Delivery Service.
**Desc:** Focuses broadly on the neurology and neurobiology of HIV-1 infection and AIDS.

US/0167-594X
**JOURNAL OF NEURO-ONCOLOGY. See** Medical Science and Technology-Neoplasma, Neoplastic.

●US/1070-8022
**JOURNAL OF NEURO-OPHTHALMOLOGY. See** Medical Science and Technology-Ophthalmology.

US/0022-3034
**JOURNAL OF NEUROBIOLOGY.** [J. neurobiol.]. Vol. 1 (1969)-. Periodical. English. mo.

$1,080.00 US; $1,200.00 Canada and Mexico; $1,245.00 other. John Wiley & Sons, Inc., 605 Third Avenue, New York NY 10158-0012. **Tel** (212)850-6000, (212)850-6645, FAX (212)850-6088, telex 12-7063. **(Subscription address:** John Wiley & Sons / England, Baffins Lane, Chichester, West Sussex PO19 1UD England.**) ED** Darcy B. Kelley and Eduardo Macagno. **LC** QP351; .J55. **DD** 612/.8/05. **NLM** W1 JO784. **CODEN** JNEUBZ. **[CCC]. Ad Acc. Pr Rev. Circ:** 750. available on microfilm and microfiche from University Microfilms International (UMI). Documents available from The Genuine Article, BIOSIS Document Express, CASDDS.
**Desc:** Provides a forum for experimental studies of the function and development of the nervous system and how it generates behavior. Publishes papers covering a wide range of neuroscience from molecular, genetic and cellular approaches. Vertebrate and invertebrate nervous systems are examined at the levels of the individual cell, the ensemble and overall behavior.
**Ind/Abst** AGRICOLA; Biol. Abstr.; Chem. Abstr.; CSA Neuro. Abstr.; Curr. Contents Life Sci.; Curr. Ref. Fish Res.; EMBASE; Energy Res. Abstr. (July 1975-); Entomol. Abstr.; Index Med.; Life Sci. Collect.; Protozoolog. Abstr.; Ref. Upd. Basic Ed.; Ref. Upd. Deluxe Ed.; Res. Alert [Full Cov.]; Rev. Agric. Entomol.; Sci. Cit. Index; SCISEARCH.

US/0022-3042
## JOURNAL OF NEUROCHEMISTRY.
[J. neurochem.]. **Added/Corp** International Society for Neurochemistry. Vol. 1 (May 1956)-. Academic Scholarly Publication. English. mo. $405.00 (individuals), $1360.00 (institutions). Raven Press, 1185 Avenue of the Americas, 37th Floor, New York NY 10036. **Tel** (212)930-9500, (212)930-9604, FAX (212)869-3495, (212)302-8507, telex 640073. **ED** M. B. Lees and K. F. Tipton. **LC** QP351; .J57. **NLM** W1 JO786. **CODEN** JONRA9. **[CCC]. Pr Rev.** available on microfilm from Microfilms International Marketing Corp.; available on microfilm and microfiche from University Microfilms International (UMI). Documents available from The Genuine Article, BIOSIS Document Express, CASDDS.
**Desc:** Official journal of the International Society for Neurochemistry.
**Ind/Abst** Anim. Breed. Abstr.; Biol. Abstr.; Calcium Calcif. Tissue Abstr.; Chem. Abstr.; Chem. Titles; CSA Neuro. Abstr.; Curr. Aware. Biol. Sci., CABS; Curr. Contents Life Sci.; Curr. Ref. Fish Res.; Dairy Sci. Abstr.; EMBASE; Helminthol. Abstr. (1991-); Index Med.; Int. Aerosp. Abstr.; Nematol. Abstr.; Nutr. Abstr. Rev., Ser. B, Live Feeds and Feed.; Nutr. Abstr. Rev., Ser. A, Hum. Exp.; Life Sci. Collect.; PESTDOC; Pig News Inf.; Ref. Upd. Basic Ed.; Ref. Upd. Deluxe Ed.; Res. Alert [Full Cov.]; Rev. Agric. Entomol.; Sci. Cit. Index; SCISEARCH; Small Anim. Abstr. Bibliogr.; Soc. Sci. Cit. Index [Select. Cov.].

UK/0953-8194
## JOURNAL OF NEUROENDOCRINOLOGY.
[J. neuroendocrinol.]. Vol. 1, No. 1 (1989)-. Academic Scholarly Publication. English. Twelve times a year. $612.00 US & Canada; £360.00 Europe; £395.00 other. Blackwell Scientific Publications Ltd, Marston Book Services, PO Box 87, Oxford OX2 ODT UK. **Tel** 011 44 865 791155, FAX 011 44 865 791927, telex 837 515 MARDIS G. **NLM** W1; JO787C. **CODEN** JOUNE2. **[CCC]. Pr Rev.** available on microfilm and microfiche from University Microfilms International (UMI). Documents available from The Genuine Article, BIOSIS Document Express, CASDDS.
**Ind/Abst** Anim. Breed. Abstr.; Biol. Abstr. (1991-); Chem. Abstr.; Curr. Aware. Biol. Sci., CABS; Curr. Contents Life Sci.; Dairy Sci. Abstr.; EMBASE; Ref. Upd. Deluxe Ed.; Res. Alert [Full Cov.]; Sci. Cit. Index; SCISEARCH.

SZ/0167-7063
## JOURNAL OF NEUROGENETICS.
See Biology-Genetics.

US/1051-2284
## JOURNAL OF NEUROIMAGING.
(JOURNAL OF NEUROIMAGING : OFFICIAL JOURNAL OF THE AMERICAN SOCIETY OF NEUROIMAGING.). **Added/Corp** American Society of Neuroimaging. Vol. 1, No. 1 (Feb. 1991)-. Periodical. English. qt. $209.00 (institutions), $131.00 (individuals) US; $231.00 (institutions), $144.00 (individuals) Canada; $252.00 (institutions), $169.00 (individuals) other. Little Brown & Company, 34 Beacon Street, Boston MA 02108. **Tel** (617)227-0730, (800)759-0190. **(Subscription address:** Little Brown and Company, PO Box 7671, Riverton NJ 08077-7671.**) DD** 616. **NLM** W1; JO787J. **[CCC].** available on microfilm and microfiche from University Microfilms International (UMI). Documents available from The Genuine Article.
**Ind/Abst** EMBASE; Res. Alert [Full Cov.].

NE/0165-5728
## JOURNAL OF NEUROIMMUNOLOGY.
[J. neuroimmunol.]. Vol. 1, No. 1 (March 1981)-. Academic Scholarly Publication. English. Sixteen times a year (8 vols.). Fl3696.00. Elsevier Science Publishers BV, PO Box 211, 1000 AE Amsterdam Netherlands. **Tel** 011 31 20 5803642, FAX 011 31 20 5862696, telex 15682. **ED** Cedric S Raine and Peter O Behan. **NLM** W1 JO787M. **CODEN** JNRIDW. **[CCC]. Bk Rev. Ad Acc. Pr Rev.** available on microfilm and microfiche from University Microfilms International (UMI). Documents available from The Genuine Article, BIOSIS Document Express, CASDDS.
**Desc:** A forum for the publication of works applying immunologic methodology to the furtherance of the neurological sciences.
**Ind/Abst** Biol. Abstr.; Chem. Abstr.; CSA Neuro. Abstr.; Curr. Aware. Biol. Sci., CABS; Curr. Contents Life Sci.; EMBASE; Immunol. Abstr.; Index Med.; Index Vet.; Life Sci. Collect.; Protozoolog. Abstr.; Psychol. Abstr. (1981-); PsycINFO; PsycLit; Ref. Upd. Basic Ed.; Ref. Upd. Deluxe Ed.; Res. Alert [Full Cov.]; Sci. Cit. Index; SCISEARCH; Vet. Bull.; Virol. AIDS Abstr.

US/0888-4390
## JOURNAL OF NEUROLOGIC REHABILITATION.
[J. neurol. rehabil.]. **VFOAT** J Neuro Rehab. Vol. 1, No. 1 (1987)-. Periodical. English. qt. $135.00 (institutions), $95.00 (individuals) US and Canada; $155.00 (institutions), $115.00 (individuals) other. Demos Publications Inc, 386 Park Avenue South, Suite 201, New York NY 10016. **Tel** (800)532-8663, (212)683-0072, FAX (212)683-0118. **DD** 616. **NLM** W1; JO7874. **Bk Rev. Ad Acc.**
**Desc:** Addresses the needs of all professionals who manage neurologically impaired patients, including neurologists, psychiatrists, occupational and physical therapists, and rehabilitation nurses.
**Ind/Abst** Psychol. Abstr. (1988-); PsycINFO; PsycLit.

US/0890-6599
## JOURNAL OF NEUROLOGICAL & ORTHOPAEDIC MEDICINE & SURGERY, THE.
See Medical Science and Technology-Surgery.

GW/0340-5354
## JOURNAL OF NEUROLOGY.
(JOURNAL OF NEUROLOGY. ZEITSCHRIFT FUER NEUROLOGIE.). [J. neurol.]. **Added/Corp** Deutsche Gesellschaft fuer Neurochirurgie. Deutsche Gesellschaft fuer Neurologie. **VFOAT** Zeitschrift fuer Neurologie. Vol. 207 (May 9, 1974)-. Academic Scholarly Publication. English (German). Ten times a year. DM1498.00. Springer-Verlag GmbH & Company KG, Heidelberger Platz 3, D 14197 Berlin Germany. **Tel** 011 49 30 8207223, FAX 011 49 30 8214091, telex 183 319 SPBLN D. **(Subscription address:** Springer Verlag New York Inc. / for North America, 44 Hartz Way, Secaucus NJ 07096.**) ED** A Compston and K Poeck. **NLM** W1 JO789. **CODEN** JNRYA9. **[CCC]. Pr Rev.** available on microfilm and microfiche from University Microfilms International (UMI). Documents available from The Genuine Article, BIOSIS Document Express, CASDDS. ***Continues** Zeitschrift fur Neurologie, 0012-1037.*
**Desc:** Publishes original investigations comprising full papers on clinical neurology and related basic research.
**Ind/Abst** Biol. Abstr.; Chem. Abstr.; CSA Neuro. Abstr. (?-?); Curr. Aware. Biol. Sci., CABS; Curr. Contents; Curr. Contents Life Sci.; Curr. Ref. Fish Res.; Dev. Med. Child Neurol.; EMBASE; Energy Res. Abstr. (Jan. 1976-); Helminthol. Abstr. (19??-19??); Index Med.; Life Sci. Collect.; Protozoolog. Abstr.; Res. Alert [Full Cov.]; Sci. Cit. Index; SCISEARCH; Soc. Sci. Cit. Index [Select. Cov.].

UK/0022-3050
## JOURNAL OF NEUROLOGY, NEUROSURGERY AND PSYCHIATRY.
[J. neurol., neurosurg. psychiatry]. **Added/Corp** British Medical Association. (Jan. 1938)-. Academic Scholarly Publication. English. mo. £187.00. BMJ / British Medical Journal Publishing Group, British Medical Association House, Tavistock Square, London WC1H 9JR England. **Tel** 011 44 71 3874499, FAX 011 44 71 383 6402, telex 290034 HBJ MN. **(Subscription telephone:** (800)654-2452**) ED** R.A.C. Hughes. **LC** RC321; .J833. **DD** 616.8/005. **CODEN** JNNPAV. **[CCC]. Pr Rev.** available on microfilm and microfiche from University Microfilms International (UMI). Documents available from The Genuine Article, BIOSIS Document Express, CASDDS. ***Supersedes** Journal of Neurology and Psychopathology.*
**Desc:** Original articles on current research, throwing light on practice in neurology, neurosurgery and psychiatry. Each issue contains an editorial concerning a recent advance or area of current controversy. The journal includes the proceedings of the meetings of the Society of British Neurological Surgeons, and of the Association of British Neurologists.
**Ind/Abst** Annals Behav. Med.; Biol. Abstr.; Chem. Abstr.; CSA Neuro. Abstr. (?-?); Cumul. Index Nurs. Allied Health Lit.; Curr. Aware. Biol. Sci., CABS; Curr. Contents Clin. Med.; Curr. Contents Life Sci.; Dev. Med. Child Neurol.; EMBASE; Helminthol. Abstr. (19??-19??); Index Med.; Int. Aerosp. Abstr.; Nutr. Abstr. Rev., Ser. B, Live Feeds and Feed.; Nutr. Abstr. Rev., Ser. A, Hum. Exp.; Life Sci. Collect.; Physic. Medline Plus; Psychol. Abstr. (1950-); PsycINFO; PsycLit; Ref. Upd. Basic Ed.; Ref. Upd. Deluxe Ed.; Res. Alert [Full Cov.]; Rev. Agric. Entomol.; Rev. Med. Vet. Entomol.; Rev. Med. Vet. Mycology; Sci. Cit. Index; SCISEARCH; Soc. Sci. Cit. Index [Select. Cov.].

GW/0939-1517
## JOURNAL OF NEUROLOGY SUPPLEMENT.
[J. naurol., Suppl.]. (?985)-. English. ir. DM1260.00. Springer-Verlag GmbH & Company KG, Heidelberger Platz 3, D 14197 Berlin Germany. **Tel** 011 49 30 8207223, FAX 011 49 30 8214091, telex 183 319 SPBLN D. **(Subscription address:** Springer Verlag New York Inc. / for North America, 44 Hartz Way, Secaucus NJ 07096.**) UDC** 61.
**Ind/Abst** EMBASE.

US/0022-3069
## JOURNAL OF NEUROPATHOLOGY AND EXPERIMENTAL NEUROLOGY.
[J. neuropathol. exp. neurol.]. Vol. 1 (Jan. 1942)-. Academic Scholarly Publication. English. bm (Jan., Mar., May, July, Sept., Nov.). $80.00 US; $86.00 Canada, Mexico, South & Central America; $92.00 other. American Association of Neuropathologists. **(Subscription address:** Journal of Neuropathology and Experimental Neurology, PO Box 1897, Lawrence KS 66044-8897.**) ED** John and Yvonne Moossy. **LC** RC321; .J835. **DD** 616.805. **NLM** W1 JO793. **CODEN** JNENAD. Index available. cum. index. **Bk Rev. Ad Acc. Pr Rev. Acid Free. Circ:** 1,600 (ctrl). available on microfilm and microfiche from University Microfilms International (UMI). Documents available from The Genuine Article, BIOSIS Document Express, CASDDS.
**Desc:** The journal publishes original articles on neuropathology and experimental neurology, letters, and news of the Association.
**Ind/Abst** Biol. Abstr.; Chem. Abstr.; CSA Neuro. Abstr.; Curr. Aware. Biol. Sci., CABS; Curr. Contents Life Sci.; EMBASE; Energy Res. Abstr.; Helminthol. Abstr.; Index Med.; Int. Aerosp. Abstr.; Life Sci. Collect.; Ref. Upd. Basic Ed.; Ref. Upd. Deluxe Ed.; Res. Alert [Full Cov.]; Sci. Cit. Index; SCISEARCH; Small Anim. Abstr. Bibliogr.; Soc. Sci. Cit. Index [Select. Cov.].

US/0022-3077
## JOURNAL OF NEUROPHYSIOLOGY.
[J. neurophysiol.]. **Added/Corp** American Physiological Society (1887- ). **VFOAT** Neurophysiology. Vol. 1 (Jan. 1938)-. Academic Scholarly Publication. English. mo. $479.00 US; $519.00 Canada and Mexico; $549.00 other*(non-member, institution). American Physiological Society, 9650 Rockville Pike, Bethesda MD 20814. **Tel** (301)530-7180, FAX (301)571-1814. **ED** G.M. Shepherd. **LC** QP351; .J6. **DD** 612.805. **NLM** W1 JO794. **CODEN** JONEA4. **[CCC]. Ad Acc. Pr Rev. Circ:** 1,740 (ctrl). available on microfilm and microfiche from University Microfilms International (UMI). Documents available from The Genuine Article, BIOSIS Document Express, CASDDS.
**Desc:** Publishes original articles on the function of the nervous system.
**Ind/Abst** Biol. Abstr.; Chem. Abstr.; Chemorecept. Abstr.; CSA Neuro. Abstr.; Curr. Aware. Biol. Sci., CABS; Curr. Contents Life Sci.; Curr. Primate Ref. (1938-); Curr. Ref. Fish Res.; EMBASE; Energy Res. Abstr.; Index Med.; INIS Atomindex [Micro.]; Int. Aerosp. Abstr.; Life Sci. Collect.; PESTDOC; Psychol. Abstr. (1938-); PsycINFO; PsycLit; Ref. Upd. Basic Ed.; Ref. Upd. Deluxe Ed.; Res. Alert [Full Cov.]; Sci. Cit. Index; SCISEARCH; Soc. Sci. Cit. Index [Select. Cov.].

US/0895-0172
## JOURNAL OF NEUROPSYCHIATRY AND CLINICAL NEUROSCIENCES, THE.
See Medical Science and Technology-Psychiatry.

FR/0150-9861
## JOURNAL OF NEURORADIOLOGY.
[J. neuroradiol.]. **Added/Corp** Societe Francaise de Neuroradiologie. **VFOAT** Journal de Neuroradiologie. Vol. 3 (March 1976)-. Periodical. English (French; summaries and/or abstracts in French). qt. $260.00. Masson Editeur, Box Postale 22, 41353 Vineuil 16 France. **Tel** 011 33 54 438994. **(Subscription address:** 7A Boulevard de Perolles, CH-1701 Fribourg Switzerland**) NLM** W1 JO795BK. **CODEN** JNEUD3. **[CCC].** available on microfilm and microfiche from University Microfilms International (UMI). Documents available from The Genuine Article, BIOSIS Document Express. ***Continues** Journal de Neuroradiologie, 0335-0800.*
**Ind/Abst** Biol. Abstr.; CSA Neuro. Abstr. (?-?); Curr. Contents Clin. Med.; Dev. Med. Child Neurol.; EMBASE; Index Med.; Life Sci. Collect.; Res. Alert [Full Cov.]; SCISEARCH.

US/0270-6474
## JOURNAL OF NEUROSCIENCE, THE.
(THE JOURNAL OF NEUROSCIENCE : THE OFFICIAL JOURNAL OF THE SOCIETY FOR NEUROSCIENCE.). [J. neurosci.]. **Added/Corp** Society for Neuroscience. **VFOAT** Neuroscience. Vol. 1, No. 1 (Jan. 1981)-. Academic Scholarly Publication. English. Twelve times a year. $880.00 US; $995.00 other. Oxford University Press / New York, 200 Madison Avenue, New York NY 10016. **Tel** (212)679-7300, (919)677-0977, (800)451-7556, (800)445-9714, FAX (919)677-1303. **(Subscription address:** Oxford University Press / USA, Journals Marketing Department, Oxford University Press, 2001 Evans Road, Cary NC 27513.**) ED** W. Maxwell Cowan. **LC** QP351; .J65. **DD** 599.01/88/05. **NLM** W1 JO795BN. **CODEN** JNRSDS. **[CCC]. Ad Acc. Pr Rev. Acid Free. Circ:** 3,400. available on microfilm and microfiche from University Microfilms International (UMI). Documents available from The Genuine Article, BIOSIS Document Express, CASDDS.
**Desc:** A broad-focus, interdisciplinary journal bringing together findings in neural systems and all areas of neuroscience: molecular, cellular, developmental, and behavioral.
**Ind/Abst** AgBiotech News Inf.; Anim. Behav. Abstr.; Anim. Breed. Abstr.; Biol. Abstr. (1985-); Chem. Abstr.;

Chemorecept. Abstr.; CSA Neuro. Abstr.; Curr. Aware. Biol. Sci., CABS; Curr. Contents Life Sci.; Curr. Ref. Fish Res.; EMBASE; Entomol. Abstr.; Helminthol. Abstr.; Index Med.; Index Vet.; Nematol. Abstr.; Oncog. Growth Factors Abstr.; Life Sci. Collect.; Ref. Upd. Basic Ed.; Ref. Upd. Deluxe Ed.; Res. Alert [Full Cov.]; Rev. Agric. Entomol.; Rev. Med. Vet. Entomol.; Sci. Cit. Index; SCISEARCH; Soc. Sci. Cit. Index [Select. Cov.]; Vet. Bull.

NE/0165-0270
**JOURNAL OF NEUROSCIENCE METHODS.** [J. neurosci. methods]. Vol. 1 (March 1979)-. Academic Scholarly Publication. English. Twelve times a year (6 vols.). Fl2742.00. Elsevier Science Publishers BV, PO Box 211, 1000 AE Amsterdam Netherlands. **Tel** 011 31 20 5803642, FAX 011 31 20 5862696, telex 15682. **ED** J S Kelly, V E Dionne, E M Glaser, J P Huston, R N McBurney, J L Roberts, and F J L Vandesande. **NLM** W1 JO795BS. **CODEN** JNMEDT. **[CCC]. Bk Rev. Ad Acc. Pr Rev.** available on microfilm and microfiche from University Microfilms International (UMI). Documents available from The Genuine Article, BIOSIS Document Express, Ask*IEEE, CASDDS.
**Desc:** Publishes research papers dealing with new methods or significant developments in recognized methods used to investigate the organization and fine structure, biochemistry, histo- and cytochemistry, physiology, biophysics, and pharmacology of receptors, neurones, synapsis and glial cells in the nervous system of man, vertebrates and invertebrates, or applicable to the clinical and behavioural sciences.
**Ind/Abst** Biol. Abstr.; Chem. Abstr.; CSA Neuro. Abstr.; Curr. Aware. Biol. Sci., CABS; Curr. Contents Life Sci.; EMBASE; Index Med.; INSPEC (March 1979-); Mass Spect. Bull.; Life Sci. Collect.; Ref. Upd. Basic Ed.; Ref. Upd. Deluxe Ed.; Res. Alert [Full Cov.]; Sci. Cit. Index; SCISEARCH.

US/0888-0395
**JOURNAL OF NEUROSCIENCE NURSING, THE. See** Medical Science and Technology-Nursing.

US/0360-4012
**JOURNAL OF NEUROSCIENCE RESEARCH.** [J. neurosci. res.]. Vol. 1 (1975)-. Periodical. English. Eighteen times a year. $2,286.00 US; $2,466.00 Canada and Mexico; $2,533.50 other. John Wiley & Sons, Inc., 605 Third Avenue, New York NY 10158-0012. **Tel** (212)850-6000, (212)850-6645, FAX (212)850-6088, telex 12-7063. **(Subscription address:** John Wiley & Sons / England, Baffins Lane, Chichester, West Sussex PO19 1UD England.**) ED** Bernard Haber. **LC** QP351; .J64. **DD** 599/.01/8805. **NLM** W1 JO795C. **CODEN** JNREDK. **[CCC]. Bk Rev. Pr Rev.** Documents available from The Genuine Article, BIOSIS Document Express, CASDDS.
**Desc:** Publishes basic research reports on molecular, cellular, and subcellular aspects of the neurosciences. Features full-length papers, short communications, book reviews, and mini-reviews on emerging areas of interest to neurobiologists.
**Ind/Abst** Biol. Abstr.; Chem. Abstr.; Chem. Titles; CSA Neuro. Abstr.; Curr. Contents Life Sci.; Curr. Ref. Fish Res.; EMBASE; Energy Res. Abstr. (April 1981-); Fish Rev. (Jan. 1989-July 1992); Genet. Abstr.; Immunol. Abstr.; Index Med.; Oncog. Growth Factors Abstr.; Life Sci. Collect.; Ref. Upd. Basic Ed.; Ref. Upd. Deluxe Ed.; Res. Alert [Full Cov.]; Sci. Cit. Index; SCISEARCH; Wildl. Rev. (Jan. 1989-July 1992).

US/0022-3085
**JOURNAL OF NEUROSURGERY.** [J. neurosurg.]. **Added/Corp** American Association of Neurological Surgeons. Harvey Cushing Society. Vol. 1 (Jan. 1944)-. Periodical. English. mo. $145.00 (institutions), $120.00 (individuals), $70.00 (student) US; $130.00 (individual), $155.00 (institution), $75.00 (student) Canada, South & Central America; $155.00 (individual), $180.00 (institution), $90.00 (student) Japan, Australia, & New Zealand; $145.00 (individual), $170.00 (institution), $85.00 (student) other, surface mail. American Finance Association, New York University, 44 West 4th Street, New York NY 10012. **Tel** (212)998-0355. **(Subscription address:** Fulco, 30 Broad Street, Denville NJ 07834.**) LC** RD1; .J66. **DD** 617.4805. **NLM** W1 JO795E. **CODEN** JONSAC. **Pr Rev.** available on microfilm and microfiche from University Microfilms International (UMI). Documents available from The Genuine Article, BIOSIS Document Express, CASDDS.
**Desc:** Published works relating primarily to neurosurgery, including studies in clinical neurophysiology, organic neurology, opthamology, radiology and pathology.
**Ind/Abst** Abr. Index Med.; Anim. Behav. Abstr.; Biol. Abstr.; Chem. Abstr.; CSA Neuro. Abstr.; Curr. Contents Clin. Med.; Curr. Contents Life Sci.; Dev. Med. Child Neurol.; EMBASE; Energy Res. Abstr.; Helminthol. Abstr. (1991-); Index Med.; INIS Atomindex [Micro.]; Mod. Med.; Life Sci. Collect.; Physic. Medline Plus; Protozoolog. Abstr.; Ref. Upd. Basic Ed.; Ref. Upd. Deluxe Ed.; Res. Alert [Full Cov.]; Rev. Med. Vet. Mycology; Sci. Cit. Index; SCISEARCH; Virol. AIDS Abstr.

US/0897-7151
**JOURNAL OF NEUROTRAUMA.** [J. neurotrauma]. **Added/Corp** Neurotrauma Society. Vol. 5, No. 1 (1988)-. Periodical. English. bm. $154.00. Mary Ann Liebert Inc., 1651 Third Avenue, New York NY 10128. **Tel** (212)289-2300, (800)M-LIEBERT, FAX (212)289-4697. **ED** John Povlishock. **DD** 616. **NLM** W1; NE795EN. **CODEN** JNEUE4. Documents available from The Genuine Article, BIOSIS Document Express. ***Continues*** *Central Nervous System Trauma, 0737-5999.*
**Desc:** Dedicated to publication of papers on advances in the mechanisms and treatments of neurotrauma of the central and peripheral nervous systems.
**Ind/Abst** Biol. Abstr. (1988-); Curr. Contents Life Sci.; EMBASE; Index Med. (1988-); Ref. Upd. Deluxe Ed.; Res. Alert [Full Cov.]; Sci. Cit. Index.

●UK
**JOURNAL OF NEUROVIROLOGY.** (1994)-. Periodical. English. bm. £135.00 UK and EEC countries; £145.00 (surface mail), £174.00 (air mail) other. Macmillan Magazines Ltd., Houndmills, Basingstoke, Hampshire RG21 2XS England. **Tel** 011 44 256 29242, FAX 011 44 256 812358, telex 858493.

●US/1064-6655
**JOURNAL OF OROFACIAL PAIN.** [J. orofac. pain]. **Added/Corp** American Academy of Orofacial Pain. European Academy of Craniomandibular Disorders. (1993)-. Periodical. English. Four times a year. $68.00 North America; $88.00 other. Quintessence Publishing Company Inc., 551 North Kimberly Drive, Carol Stream IL 60188-1881. **Tel** (708)682-3223, (800)621-0387, FAX (708)682-3288. **DD** 616. **CODEN** JOROEO. **[CCC].** ***Continues*** *Journal of Craniomandibular Disorders, 0890-2739.*

CN/1180-4882
**JOURNAL OF PSYCHIATRY & NEUROSCIENCE. See** Medical Science and Technology-Psychiatry.

US/1052-3057
**JOURNAL OF STROKE AND CEREBROVASCULAR DISEASES.** (JOURNAL OF STROKE AND CEREBROVASCULAR DISEASES : THE OFFICIAL JOURNAL OF NATIONAL STROKE ASSOCIATION / NSA.). [J. stroke cerebrovasc. dis.]. **Added/Corp** National Stroke Association (U.S.). (1991)-. Periodical. English. Four times a year. $115.00 (institutions), $80.00 (individuals) US; $135.00 (institutions), $100.00 (individuals) other. National Stroke Association, 8480 East Orchard Road, Suite 1000, Englewood CO 80111-5015. **Tel** (303)771-1700, FAX (303)771-1886. **ED** Clark H. Millikan, M.D. (editor's address: Creighton University, School of Medicine, Omaha, NE 68178). **LC** RC388.5; .J68. **DD** 616.8/1. **NLM** W1; JO904TJ. Index available. cum. index. **Bk Rev. Ad Acc. Pr Rev.**
**Desc:** Multidisciplinary clinical journal devoted to all aspects of managing stroke in the acute and rehabilitative phases.

NE/0165-1838
**JOURNAL OF THE AUTONOMIC NERVOUS SYSTEM.** [J. auton. nerv. syst.]. Vol. 1, No. 1 (Oct. 1979)-. Academic Scholarly Publication. English. Fifteen times a year (5 vols.). Fl2225.00. Elsevier Science Publishers BV, PO Box 211, 1000 AE Amsterdam Netherlands. **Tel** 011 31 20 5803642, FAX 011 31 20 5862696, telex 15682. **ED** G Burnstock, J Furness, G Gabella, C De Groat, K Koizumi and C McC Brooks. **NLM** W1 JO912VD. **CODEN** JASYDS. **[CCC]. Pr Rev.** available on microfilm and microfiche from University Microfilms International (UMI). Documents available from The Genuine Article, BIOSIS Document Express, CASDDS.
**Desc:** The aim of the journal is to stimulate, publish and disseminate original investigations on the autonomic nervous system; this includes the nerves of blood vessels and viscera, autonomic ganglia, efferent and afferent autonomic pathways, and autonomic nuclei and pathways in the central nervous system.
**Ind/Abst** Biol. Abstr.; Chem. Abstr.; CSA Neuro. Abstr.; Curr. Aware. Biol. Sci., CABS; Curr. Contents Life Sci.; EMBASE; Index Med.; Life Sci. Collect.; Protozoolog. Abstr.; Ref. Upd. Basic Ed.; Ref. Upd. Deluxe Ed.; Res. Alert [Full Cov.]; Sci. Cit. Index; SCISEARCH.

NE/0022-510X
**JOURNAL OF THE NEUROLOGICAL SCIENCES.** [J. neurol. sci.]. **Added/Corp** World Federation of Neurology. Vol. 1 (Jan./Feb. 1964)-. Academic Scholarly Publication. English (French and German; summaries and/or abstracts in Russian and Spanish). Sixteen times a year (8 volumes). Fl2948.00. Elsevier Science Publishers BV, PO Box 211, 1000 AE Amsterdam Netherlands. **Tel** 011 31 20 5803642, FAX 011 31 20 5862696, telex 15682. **ED** G W Bruyn and J M B V de Jong. **LC** RC321; .J865. **NLM** W1 JO941U. **CODEN** JNSCAG. **[CCC]. Pr Rev.** available on microfilm and microfiche from University Microfilms International (UMI). Documents available from The Genuine Article, BIOSIS Document Express, CASDDS.
**Desc:** An interdisciplinary medium for original contributions on clinical themes and experimental work. The journal publishes in all of those sciences which underlie modern concepts of nervous structure and function.
**Ind/Abst** Biol. Abstr.; Chem. Abstr.; CSA Neuro. Abstr.; Curr. Contents Life Sci.; Curr. Ref. Fish Res.; Dev. Med. Child Neurol.; EMBASE; Index Med.; Int. Nurs. Index; Nutr. Abstr. Rev., Ser. B, Live Feeds and Feed.; Nutr. Abstr. Rev., Ser. A, Hum. Exp.; Life Sci. Collect.; Protozoolog. Abstr.; Ref. Upd. Basic Ed.; Ref. Upd. Deluxe Ed.; Res. Alert [Full Cov.]; Sci. Cit. Index; SCISEARCH; Soc. Sci. Cit. Index [Select. Cov.]; Virol. AIDS Abstr.

●US/1067-8239
**JOURNAL OF THE NEUROMUSCULOSKELETAL SYSTEM. See** Medical Science and Technology-Musculoskeletal System.

UK/0963-0880
**JOURNAL OF TROPICAL & GEOGRAPHICAL NEUROLOGY : THE OFFICIAL JOURNAL OF THE RESEARCH GROUP ON TROPICAL NEUROLOGY OF THE WORLD FEDERATION OF NEUROLOGY.** ***Ceased.*** **Added/Corp** World Federation of Neurology. Research Group on Tropical Neurology. **VFOAT** Journal of Tropical and Geographical Neurology. (1991)-Vol. 2, No. 4 (1992). Periodical. English (summaries and/or abstracts in French and Spanish). qt. Royal Society of Medicine Press, 1 Wimpole Street, London W1M 8AE England. **Tel** 011 44 71 2902928. **NLM** W1; JO966S. **Pr Rev.** Documents available from The Genuine Article.
**Desc:** Publishes peer-reviewed papers on diseases of the nervous system that are generally prevalent in tropical and subtropical areas and neurological problems that appear to be modified by geographical factors.
**Ind/Abst** Res. Alert [Full Cov.]; Trop. Dis. Bull.

US/0886-8018
**KEY NEUROLOGY AND NEUROSURGERY.** [Key neurol. neurosurg.]. **VFOAT** Neurology and Neurosurgery. Vol. 1, No. 1 (1st Quarter 1986)-. Periodical. English. qt. $112.50 (institutions), $75.00 (individuals) US; $116.50 (institutions), $79.00 (individuals) Canada; $126.50 (institutions), $89.00 (individuals) other. Mosby Year Book Inc., 11830 Westline Industrial Drive, St Louis MO 63146. **Tel** (800)325-4177, (314)872-8370, FAX (314)432-1380, telex 44-2402. **ED** Robert D. Currier and Robert M. Crowell. **DD** 616. **NLM** ZWL 100; K44. **[CCC].**
**Desc:** Surveys more than 800 medical publications, finds the relevant articles, and condenses each article to a summary. An editorial commentary highlights each article's significance and impact on clinical medicine.

JA
**KOKURITSU MUSASHI RYOYOJO SHINKEI SENTA NENPO. Main/Corp** Kokuritsu Musashi Ryoyojo (Japan). Shinkei Senta. Japanese. an. Kokuritsu Musashi Ryoyojo Shinkei Senta, 2620 Ogawa Higashicho, Kodaira-shi 187 Japan. **LC** RC321; .K64A.

FR/0223-9434
**LETTRE DU PSYCHIATRE PARIS, LA. See** Medical Science and Technology-Psychiatry.

US
**LINK (WOODLAND HILLS).** (LINK.). English. qt. Free. Amyotropic Lateral Sclerosis Association, 21021 Ventura Boulevard, Suite 321, Woodland Hills CA 91364. **Tel** (818)340-7500. **Bk Rev. Pr Rev. Circ:** 62,000 (ctrl).
**Desc:** Purpose is to raise public awareness about Amyotropic Laterial Sclerosis; patient information, and research updates.

CN/1181-8212
**LUMINA (MONTREAL).** (LUMINA / EPILEPSY CANADA.). [Lumina]. **Added/Corp** Epilepsy Canada. **VFOAT** Lumina. Vol. 8, No. 2 (Nov. 1990)-. Periodical. English (French). sa. Free (with Epilepsy Canada membership, 20.00Can$). Epilepsy Canada, 1470 Peel, Suite 745, Montreal Quebec H3A 1T1 Canada. **Tel** (514)845-7855, FAX (514)845-7866. **ED** Heather Pengelley. **DD** 616.8/53/0097105. **Circ:** 11,000 (ctrl). ***Continues*** *Epilepsy Canada News., 0821-4255.*
**Desc:** Concerned with medical and social aspects and developments of epilepsy. Intended for doctors, neurologists, health care and social workers, libraries, institutions, epilepsy associations, patients, and interested persons.

CN/0707-0934
**M S ONTARIO. VAT** Multiple Sclerosis Ontario. No. 1- Feb. 1977-. Periodical. English. ir. Free. Multiple Sclerosis Society of Canada, Ontario Division, 250 Bloor Street East Suite 1000, Toronto Ontario M4W 3P9 Canada. **Tel** (416)922-6065, FAX (416)922-7538. **DD** 616.8/34/0062713.

UK/0301-5602
**MAJOR PROBLEMS IN NEUROLOGY.** [Major prob. neurol.]. (1973)-. Monographic series. English. ir. Price varies per volume. W.B. Saunders Company, A Subsidiary of Harcourt Brace Jovanovich, Inc., The Curtis Center/Suite 300, Independence Square West, Philadelphia PA 19106-3399. **Tel** (215)238-7800 or, 5587, FAX (215)238-7883, telex 173146. **(Subscription address:** W. B. Saunders Company / North America Subscriptions, c/o Periodicals, 6277 Sea Harbour Drive, 4th Floor, Orlando FL 32887.**) NLM** W1 MA492U.

US/0090-7073
**MEDICAL EXAMINATION REVIEW BOOK. NEUROLOGY SPECIALTY BOARD REVIEW.** **VFOAT** Neurology Specialty Board Review. 1st- Ed. English. ir. Medical Exam Publishing Company, 52 Vanderbilt Avenue Elsevier, New York NY 10017-3808. **Tel** (212)463-1052.

•US/1063-245X
**MEETINGS REPORTS. CNS.** [Meet. rep., CNS]. **VFOAT** CNS. Vol. 1, No. 1 (1992)-. Periodical. English. qt (seasonal). $210.00 (institution); $115.00 (individual); $55.00 (single issue). Neva Press, PO Box 347, Branford CT 06405. **Tel** (203)272-5338, FAX (203)272-5338. **DD** 616. **NLM** W1; ME877N.

US/0885-7490
**METABOLIC BRAIN DISEASE.** [Metab. brain dis.]. Vol. 1, No. 1 (March 1986)-. Academic Scholarly Publication. English. Four times a year. $325.00 institutions, $77.00 individuals US; $380.00 institutions, $90.00 individuals other. Plenum Press, 233 Spring Street, New York NY 10013-1578. **Tel** (212)620-8000, (800)221-9369, FAX (212)463-0742, (212)807-1047, telex 23/421139. **ED** David W. McCandless. **LC** RC394.M48; M48. **DD** 616.8. **NLM** W1; ME961LM. **CODEN** MBDIEE. **[CCC]. Pr Rev.** available on microfilm and microfiche from University Microfilms International (UMI). Documents available from The Genuine Article, BIOSIS Document Express, CASDDS.
**Ind/Abst** Biol. Abstr. (1986-); Chem. Abstr. (1986-); CSA Neuro. Abstr.; Curr. Aware. Biol. Sci., CABS; Curr. Contents Life Sci.; EMBASE; Index Med. (1986); Res. Alert [Full Cov.]; Rev. Med. Vet. Mycology; Sci. Cit. Index; SCISEARCH.

US/1043-9471
**METHODS IN NEUROSCIENCES.** [Methods neurosci.]. Vol. 1 (1989)-. Academic Scholarly Publication. English. ir. Price varies per volume. Academic Press, Inc., 6277 Sea Harbor Drive, Orlando FL 32887. **Tel** (800)543-9534, (407)345-4100, FAX (407)363-9661. **DD** 591. **NLM** W1; ME9616K. **CODEN** MENEE5. **[CCC].** Documents available from BIOSIS Document Express, CASDDS.
**Ind/Abst** Biol. Abstr. (1991-); Chem. Abstr.

GW
**MINIMALLY INVASIVE NEUROSURGERY.** Volume 1 (Sept. 1994)-. English. qt. $172.00. Georg Thieme Verlag Stuttgart, Postfach 301120, D 70451 Stuttgart Germany. **Tel** 011 49 711 89310, FAX 011 49 711 8931298, telex 7 252 275 GTVD. **(Subscription address:** Thieme Medical Publishers Inc., 381 Park Avenue South, New York NY 10016.) **ED** A. Perneczky.
**Desc:** Covers the latest advances and innovations in neurosurgery. Strives to cover the whole spectrum of modern neurosurgery; sections include microsurgery, keyhole surgery, endoscopy and more.

NE
**MODERN APPROACHES TO THE DIAGNOSIS AND INSTRUCTION OF MULTI-HANDICAPPED CHILDREN.** English. ir. Swets & Zeitlinger BV, Heereweg 347B PO Box 825, 2160 SZ Lisse Holland. **Tel** 011 31 2521 35111, FAX 02521-15888, telex 41325. **ED** Dirk J Bakker. **NLM** W1 MO12.
**Desc:** Series of monographs devoted to speech pathology and speech physiology, with special emphasis on neurological disorders that entail language disturbances.

US/1044-7431
**MOLECULAR AND CELLULAR NEUROSCIENCES.** [Mol. cell. neurosci.]. Vol. 1, No. 1 (Aug. 1990)-. Academic Scholarly Publication. English. bmtq (6 issues). $307.00 US and Canada; $338.00 other. Academic Press, Inc., 6277 Sea Harbor Drive, Orlando FL 32887. **Tel** (800)543-9534, (407)345-4100, FAX (407)363-9661. **ED** P. Michael Conn, Lothar Jennes and Robert A. Steiner. **LC** QP356.2; .M62. **DD** 591.1/88. **NLM** W1; MO195B. **CODEN** MOCNED. **[CCC]. Ad Acc. Pr Rev.** ctrl circ. Documents available from The Genuine Article, BIOSIS Document Express, CASDDS.
**Desc:** Provides a unique forum in a fast-growing discipline. Publishes manuscripts describing novel and original results in the areas of neurobiology, neuropharmacology, neuroendocrinology, neurochemistry, and neuroanatomy at the molecular, cellular, and tissue levels. Articles present studies performed in animal and human model systems so long as the fundamental observations relate to basic science (as contrasted with clinical science). Topics of considerable broad interest to the neuroscience community are also included.
**Ind/Abst** Biol. Abstr. (1990-); Chem. Abstr.; Curr. Aware. Biol. Sci., CABS; Curr. Contents Life Sci.; EMBASE; Res. Alert [Full Cov.]; Sci. Cit. Index.

US/1044-7393
**MOLECULAR AND CHEMICAL NEUROPATHOLOGY.** (MOLECULAR AND CHEMICAL NEUROPATHOLOGY / SPONSORED BY THE INTERNATIONAL SOCIETY FOR NEUROCHEMISTRY AND THE WORLD FEDERATION OF NEUROLOGY AND RESEARCH GROUPS ON NEUROCHEMISTRY AND CEREBROSPINAL FLUID.). [Mol. chem. neuropathol.]. **Added/Corp** International Society for Neurochemistry. World Federation of Neurology. Vol. 10, No. 1 (Feb. 1989)-. Academic Scholarly Publication. English. Nine times a year. $365.00 US; $425.00 other. Humana Press Inc., 999 Riverview Drive, Suite 208, Totawa NJ 07512. **Tel** (201)256-1699, FAX (201)256-8341. **ED** Lloyd A. Horrocks, Allan J. Yates. **DD** 574. **NLM** W1; MO194VK. **CODEN** MCHNEM. **[CCC].** Index available. cum. index. **Bk Rev. Ad Acc. Pr Rev. Circ:** 150. Documents available from The Genuine Article, BIOSIS Document Express, CASDDS. ***Continues** Neurochemical Pathology, 0734-600X.*
**Desc:** Editorial for neurologists, neurochemists and anyone interested in the neurology field.
**Ind/Abst** Biol. Abstr. (1989-); Chem. Abstr.; Curr. Aware. Biol. Sci., CABS; Curr. Contents; Curr. Contents Life Sci.; EMBASE; Index Med. (Feb. 1989-); Res. Alert [Full Cov.]; Sci. Cit. Index; SCISEARCH.

NE/0169-328X
**MOLECULAR BRAIN RESEARCH.** (BRAIN RESEARCH. MOLECULAR BRAIN RESEARCH.). [Mol. brain res.]. Vol. 5, No. 1 (Jan. 1989)-. Academic Scholarly Publication. English. Fourteen times a year (7 volumes). FI3010.00; FI19345.00 combination subscription with Brain Research Reviews and Developmental Brain Research. Elsevier Science Publishers BV, PO Box 211, 1000 AE Amsterdam Netherlands. **Tel** 011 31 20 5803642, FAX 011 31 20 5862696, telex 15682. **ED** D P Purpura. **LC** QP356.2; .B73. **DD** 599/.0188. **NLM** W1; BR116G. **CODEN** MBREE4. **[CCC].** Index available. cum. index. **Ad Acc. Pr Rev.** available on microfilm from University Microfilms International (UMI). Documents available from ADONIS. ***Continues** Molecular Brain Research, 0169-328X.*
**Desc:** Prompt publication of studies in molecular mechanisms of neuronal synoptic and related processes that underlie the structure and function in the brain.
**Ind/Abst** ADONIS; EMBASE; Index Med. (1989-); Nucl. Acids Abstr.

US/0893-7648
**MOLECULAR NEUROBIOLOGY.** [Mol. neurobiol.]. Vol. 1, No. 1/2 (Spring/Summer 1987)-. Academic Scholarly Publication. English. Six times a year. $310.00 US; $350.00 other. Humana Press Inc., 999 Riverview Drive, Suite 208, Totawa NJ 07512. **Tel** (201)256-1699, FAX (201)256-8341. **ED** Nicholas G. Bazan, Jacques Mallet. **LC** QP365.2; .M64. **DD** 591.1/88/05. **NLM** W1; MO196P. **CODEN** MONBEW. **[CCC].** Index available. **Pr Rev. Circ:** 200. Documents available from The Genuine Article, CASDDS.
**Desc:** Published for neuroscientists needing to stay in touch with progress in brain research today.
**Ind/Abst** Chem. Abstr.; Curr. Aware. Biol. Sci., CABS; Curr. Contents Life Sci.; Index Med. (1987-); Ref. Upd. Deluxe Ed.; Res. Alert [Full Cov.]; Sci. Cit. Index; SCISEARCH.

UK/0959-5244
**MOLECULAR NEUROPHARMACOLOGY.** ***Ceased.*** **Added/Corp** British Pharmacological Society. Vol. 1, No. 1 (July 1990)-(1993). Academic Scholarly Publication. English. Four times a year. Macmillan Magazines Ltd., Houndmills, Basingstoke, Hampshire RG21 2XS England. **Tel** 011 44 256 29242, FAX 011 44 256 812358, telex 858493. **NLM** W1; MO196T. **CODEN** MOLNEO. available on microfilm and microfiche from University Microfilms International (UMI). Documents available from The Genuine Article, CASDDS.
**Ind/Abst** Chem. Abstr.; Curr. Aware. Biol. Sci., CABS; EMBASE; Res. Alert [Full Cov.].

GW/0077-0671
**MONOGRAPHIEN AUS DEM GESAMTGEBIETE DER PSYCHIATRIE.** [Monogr. Gesamtgeb. Psychiatr.]. Monographic series. German. ir. Price varies per volume. Springer-Verlag GmbH & Company KG, Heidelberger Platz 3, D 14197 Berlin Germany. **Tel** 011 49 30 8207223, FAX 011 49 30 8214091, telex 183 319 SPBLN D. **(Subscription address:** Springer Verlag New York Inc. / for North America, 44 Hartz Way, Secaucus NJ 07096.) **NLM** W1 MO561B. **CODEN** MGGPBE. Documents available from CASDDS. ***Continues in part** Monographien aus dem Gesamtgebiete der Neurologie und Psychiatrie, 0376-0464.*
**Desc:** Contains articles on neurology and psychiatry.
**Ind/Abst** Chem. Abstr. (1970-1982); Index Med.; Psychol. Abstr. (1972-).

SZ/0300-5186
**MONOGRAPHS IN NEURAL SCIENCES.** [Monogr. neural sci.]. Vol. 1 (1973)-. Academic Scholarly Publication. English. an. 180.00F (approx. per volume). S. Karger AG, Allschwilerstrasse 10, PO Box - Postfach - Case Postale, CH-4009 Basel Switzerland. **Tel** 011 41 61 306-1111, FAX 011 41 61 306-1234, telex CH 962 652. **ED** A. Korczyn. **NLM** W1 MO568C. **CODEN** MNUSB6. **[CCC].** Documents available from BIOSIS Document Express, CASDDS.
**Desc:** Covering topics from the broad range of interdisciplinary neurological sciences, this series makes fundamental and vital information available to clinicians active in the diagnosis, evaluation, and treatment of neurological diseases. In order to provide precise guidance in the management of such disorders as cerebral tumors, epilepsy, hydrocephalus, and neuroimmunologic diseases, each volume emphasizes a critical, comparative approach to the subject in question and couples review material with current investigative information.
**Ind/Abst** Biol. Abstr.; Chem. Abstr.; Index Med. (1973-1987); Ref. Upd. Deluxe Ed.

FR/0245-5919
**MOTRICITE CEREBRALE, READAPTATION, NEUROLOGIE DU DEVELOPPEMENT.** [Mot. cereb.]. **Added/Corp** Cercle de Documentation et d'Information Pour la Reeducation des Infirmes Moteurs Cerebraux. Vol. 1 (1980)-. Academic Scholarly Publication. French. qt. $94.00. Masson Editeur, Box Postale 22, 41353 Vineuil 16 France. **Tel** 011 33 54 438994. **(Subscription address:** 7A Boulevard de Perolles, CH-1701 Fribourg Switzerland) **NLM** W1 MO949N. **[CCC].** available on microfilm and microfiche from University Microfilms International (UMI). ***Supersedes** Cahier du Cercle de Documentation et d'Information pour la Reeducation des Infirmes Moteurs Cerebraux, 0150-0511.*
**Ind/Abst** EMBASE.

US/0885-3185
**MOVEMENT DISORDERS.** (MOVEMENT DISORDERS : OFFICIAL JOURNAL OF THE MOVEMENT DISORDER SOCIETY.). [Mov. disord.]. **Added/Corp** Movement Disorder Society. Vol. 1, No. 1, (1986)-. Periodical. English. bm (plus videocassette). $258.00 (individuals), $342.00 (institutions) US; $335.00 (individuals), $440.00 (institutions) other. Raven Press, 1185 Avenue of the Americas, 37th Floor, New York NY 10036. **Tel** (212)930-9500, (212)930-9604, FAX (212)869-3495, (212)302-8507, telex 640073. **DD** 616. **NLM** W1; MO973P. **CODEN** MOVDEA. **[CCC]. Pr Rev.** available on microfilm and microfiche from University Microfilms International (UMI). Documents available from The Genuine Article.
**Desc:** Provides a forum for the exchange of information on movement disorders among neurologists, neurosurgeons, pharmacologists and psychiatrists.
**Ind/Abst** Curr. Aware. Biol. Sci., CABS; Curr. Contents Clin. Med.; Curr. Contents Life Sci.; EMBASE; Index Med. (Vol. 1, No. 1 1986-); Protozoolog. Abstr.; Res. Alert [Select. Cov.]; Sci. Cit. Index; SCISEARCH; Soc. Sci. Cit. Index [Select. Cov.].

CN/0315-1131
**MS CANADA.** **Added/Corp** Multiple Sclerosis Society of Canada. **VFOAT** SP Canada. **VAT** Multiple Sclerosis Canada. (Feb. 1974)-. Periodical. English (French). Four times a year (Jan., Apr., July, Oct.). 12.00Can$. Multiple Sclerosis Society of Canada, Ontario Division, 250 Bloor Street East Suite 1000, Toronto Ontario M4W 3P9 Canada. **Tel** (416)922-6065, FAX (416)922-7538. **ED** Deanna Groetzinger. **Bk Rev**, (Qty: 1-2). **Circ:** 26,000.
**Desc:** Newsletters for members of Multiple Sclerosis (MS) Society of Canada. Contains information about MS research, services and society activities.

US/0738-3967
**MS QUARTERLY REPORT.** [MS q. rep.]. **Added/Corp** Eastern Paralyzed Veterans Association (U.S.). **VFOAT** M.S. Quarterly Report. **VAT** Multiple Sclerosis Quarterly Report. (19??)-. Periodical. English. qt. $16.00 US and Canada; $29.95 other. Demos Publications Inc, 386 Park Avenue South, Suite 201, New York NY 10016. **Tel** (800)532-8663, (212)683-0072, FAX (212)683-0118. **ED** Caroline Jaffe. cum. index. **Bk Rev. Circ:** 6,000 (ctrl). ***Continues** MS Quarterly, 0195-2285.*

•UK
**MULTIPLE SCLEROSIS.** (1994)-. English. qt. £135.00 UK and EEC countries; £145.00 (surface mail), £174.00 (air mail) other. Macmillan Magazines Ltd., Houndmills, Basingstoke, Hampshire RG21 2XS England. **Tel** 011 44 256 29242, FAX 011 44 256 812358, telex 858493.

US/0897-0270
**MULTIPLE SCLEROSIS RESEARCH REPORTS.** [Mult. scler. res. rep.]. **Added/Corp** International Federation of Multiple Sclerosis Societies. Vol. 1, No. 1 (1987)-. Periodical. English. qt. $39.50. Demos Publications Inc, 386 Park Avenue South, Suite 201, New York NY 10016. **Tel** (800)532-8663, (212)683-0072, FAX (212)683-0118. **DD** 616. **NLM** ZWL 360; M962. ***Continues** Multiple Sclerosis Indicative Abstracts, 0360-0017.*

US/0148-639X
**MUSCLE & NERVE.** [Muscle nerve]. **Added/Corp** American Association of Electromyography and Electrodiagnosis. American Association of Electrodiagnostic Medicine. **VFOAT** Muscle and Nerve. Vol. 1 (Jan./Feb. 1978)-. Academic Scholarly Publication. English. mo. $648.00 US; $768.00 Canada and Mexico; $813.00 other. John Wiley & Sons, Inc., 605 Third Avenue, New York NY 10158-0012. **Tel** (212)850-6000, (212)850-6645, FAX (212)850-6088, telex 12-7063. **(Subscription address:** John Wiley & Sons / England, Baffins Lane, Chichester, West Sussex PO19 1UD England.) **ED** Jun Kimura. **LC** RC925.A1; M78. **DD**

616.7/4. **NLM** W1 MU925. **CODEN** MUNEDE. **[CCC]. Ad Acc. Pr Rev. Circ:** 3,200. available on microfilm and microfiche from University Microfilms International (UMI). Documents available from The Genuine Article, BIOSIS Document Express, CASDDS.
**Desc:** Devoted to studies concerning muscle, the peripheral motor and sensory neurons and the neuromuscular junction in both health and disease. Covers a variety of disciplines including neurophysiology, clinical chemistry, histopathology, immunology, rheumatology, neuropharmacology and genetics.
**Ind/Abst** Biol. Abstr.; Chem. Abstr.; CSA Neuro. Abstr.; Curr. Aware. Biol. Sci., CABS; Curr. Contents Life Sci.; Dev. Med. Child Neurol.; EMBASE; Index Med.; Life Sci. Collect.; Ref. Upd. Basic Ed.; Ref. Upd. Deluxe Ed.; Res. Alert [Full Cov.]; Sci. Cit. Index; SCISEARCH; SportSearch.

US/0892-6972
**NATIONAL DIRECTORY OF HEAD INJURY REHABILITATION SERVICES.** **See** Medical Science and Technology.

US/0091-2387
**NATIONAL SPOKESMAN.** ***Title Change.*** [Natl. spokesman]. **Added/Corp** Epilepsy Foundation of America. Vol. 4 No. 2 (Spring 1971)-(19??). Periodical. English. mo. Epilepsy Foundation of America, 4351 Garden City Drive, Landover MD 20785. **Tel** (301)459-3700. ***Continues*** *National News (Epilepsy Foundation of America).* ***Continued by*** *Epilepsy USA.*

●US/1063-7664
**NDTA NETWORK.** [NDTA netw.]. **Added/Corp** Neuro-Developmental Treatment Association. **VFOAT** Neuro Developmental Treatment Association Network. **VAT** Neuro-Developmental Treatment Association Network. (1992)-. Periodical. English. bm. $9.50. NDTA Network, 1029 Lake Street, Oak Park IL 60301. **DD** 616.

SZ/0749-4300
**NEIROKHIMIIA.** (NEUROCHEMISTRY.). [Neurochemistry]. Vol. 3, No. 1 (1985)-. Periodical. English (translations available in Russian). qt (3 volumes). $798.00 (academic institutions), $1244.00 (corporate institutions). Harwood Academic Publishers, PO Box 90, Reading RG1 8JL England. **Tel** 011 44 734 560080. **LC** QP356.3; .N4. **DD** 591.1/88. **NLM** W1; NE3236. **CODEN** NECHE4. **[CCC].**

UN/0028-2561
**NEJROFIZIOLOGIJA (KIEV, 1969).** (NEIROFIZIOLOGIIA. NEUROPHYSIOLOGY.). [Nejrofiziologija]. **Added/Corp** Instytut Fiziolohii im. O.O. Bohomoltsia. **VFOAT** Neurophysiology. Vol. 1, (July/Aug. 1969)-. Academic Scholarly Publication. Russian (summaries and/or abstracts in English). Six times a year. $126.00 US; $129.00 others. **(Subscription address:** East View Publications Inc., 3020 Harbor Lane North, Suite 110, Minneapolis MN 55447.**) LC** QP361; .N45. **NLM** W1 NE195K. **CODEN** NEFZB2. Documents available from BIOSIS Document Express, CASDDS.
**Ind/Abst** Biol. Abstr.; Chem. Abstr.; EMBASE; Index Med.; Int. Aerosp. Abstr.

UN/0131-6842
**NEJROHIRURGIJA.** **See** Medical Science and Technology-Surgery.

GW/0028-2804
**NERVENARZT.** (NERVENARZT; MONATSSCHRIFT FUER ALLE GEBIETE NERVENARZTLICHER FORCHUNG UND PRAXIS.). [Nervenarzt]. **Added/Corp** Deutschen Gesellschaft fur Psychiatrie und Nervnenheilkunde. Deutschen Gesellschaft fur Neurologie. Vol. 1 (1928)-. Academic Scholarly Publication. German. Twelve times a year. DM398.00. Springer-Verlag GmbH & Company KG, Heidelberger Platz 3, D 14197 Berlin Germany. **Tel** 011 49 30 8207223, FAX 011 49 30 8214091, telex 183 319 SPBLN D. **(Subscription address:** Springer Verlag New York Inc. / for North America, 44 Hartz Way, Secaucus NJ 07096.**) ED** T Brandt, P A Fischer, W Hacke, H Helmchen, S O Hoffmann, W Janzarik and H Lauter. **NLM** W1 NE207H. **CODEN** NERVAF. **[CCC]. Bk Rev. Pr Rev.** available on microfilm from University Microfilms International (UMI). Documents available from The Genuine Article, BIOSIS Document Express, CASDDS.
**Desc:** Informs doctors and scientists in all fields of neurology, neurosurgery, neuropathology, psychiatry, and psychotherapy. Instructional articles, research reports, brief up-dates and conference reports.
**Ind/Abst** Biol. Abstr.; Chem. Abstr.; Dev. Med. Child Neurol.; EMBASE; Energy Res. Abstr.; Helminthol. Abstr.; Index Med.; Nucl. Sci. Abstr.; Nutr. Abstr. Rev., Ser. A, Hum. Exp.; Life Sci. Collect.; PESTDOC; Protozoolog. Abstr.; Psychol. Abstr. (1929-); PsycINFO; PsycLit; Res. Alert [Full Cov.]; Rev. Med. Vet. Entomol. (1929-); Sci. Cit. Index; SCISEARCH; Soc. Sci. Cit. Index [Select. Cov.].

GW/0722-1541
**NERVENHEILKUNDE.** [Nervenheilkunde]. (Feb. 1982)-. Academic Scholarly Publication. German. Seven times a year. DM158.00 Europe; $96.40 other. F K Schattauer Verlagsgesellschaft mbH, Postfach 10 45 45, D 70040 Stuttgart Germany. **Tel** 011 49 711 2298726. **ED** D. Soyka and E. Lungershausen. **NLM** W1 NE207J. **[CCC].** Index available. **Bk Rev. Ad Acc. Pr Rev.** Documents available from The Genuine Article.
**Ind/Abst** Curr. Contents Clin. Med.; EMBASE; Nutr. Abstr. Rev., Ser. A, Hum. Exp.; Res. Alert [Full Cov.]; SCISEARCH; Soc. Sci. Cit. Index [Select. Cov.].

US
**NERVLINE. A MICROCOMPUTER INFORMATION RETRIEVAL SYSTEM IN THE CLINICAL NEUROSCIENCES.** **See** Computers-Microcomputers, Personal Computers.

RU/0470-6625
**NERVNAJA SISTEMA.** (NERVNAIA SISTEMA / LENINGRADSKII ORDENA LENINA GOSUDARSTVENNYI UNIVERSITET IMENI A.A. ZHDANOVA, FIZIOLOGICHESKII INSTITUT IMENI AKAD. A.A. UKHTOMSKOGO.). [Nervn. sist.]. **Added/Corp** Leningradskii Gosudarstvennyi Universitet Imeni A.A. Zhdanova. Russian S.F.S.R. Ministerstvo Vysshego i Srednego Spetsialnogo Obrazovaniia. Fiziologicheskii Institut Imeni A.A. Ukhtomskogo. Vol. 1 (1960)-. Academic Scholarly Publication. Russian. Price varies per volume. St Petersburg State University / Izdatelstvo Leningradskogo Universiteta, Universitetskaia Nab 7/9, 199034 St Petersburg Russia. **Tel** 011 95 218-97-88, FAX 011 95 218-51-52, telex 121481. **LC** QP351; .N4. **NLM** W1 NE208. **CODEN** NSLFAZ. Documents available from CASDDS.
**Ind/Abst** Chem. Abstr.; Index Med. (1965-1991); Int. Aerosp. Abstr.

US
**NERVOUS SYSTEM AND ELECTRIC CURRENTS : PROCEEDINGS OF THE ... ANNUAL NATIONAL CONFERENCE OF THE NEUROELECTRIC SOCIETY, THE.** **Main/Corp** Neuro-Electric Society. **Added/Corp** Neuroelectric Society. (1970)-. Proceedings. English. Plenum Press, 233 Spring Street, New York NY 10013-1578. **Tel** (212)620-8000, (800)221-9369, FAX (212)463-0742, (212)807-1047, telex 23/421139. **ED** N.L. Wulfsohn and A. Sances Jr. **LC** QP341; .N47. **NLM** W1 NE216.

IT
**NEU.** (19??)-. Italian (summaries and/or abstracts in English). Four times a year. L50000 Italy; L70000 other. Neu, Rivista dell Anin, Musso S Raffaele, via Olgettina #60, 20122 Milan Italy. **Tel** 011 39 2 2642332. Index available. cum. index. **Bk Rev. Ad Acc.** ctrl circ. ***Continues*** *Infermieristica Neurochirurgica, 0391-4445.*
**Desc:** Contains information on neurosurgery.

UK/0941-0643
**NEURAL COMPUTING & APPLICATIONS.** **VFOAT** Neural Computing and Applications. Vol. 1, No. 1 (1993)-. Periodical. English. qt. £136.00. Springer-Verlag London Ltd., Springer House, 8 Alexandra Road Wimbledon, London SW19 7JZ England. **Tel** 011 44 81 9471280, or 9475885, FAX 011 44 81 9474651, telex 21531 SPRGB G. **NLM** W1; NE32T. **[CCC].**
**Ind/Abst** CSA Neuro. Abstr.

FR/0028-3770
**NEURO-CHIRURGIE.** **See** Medical Science and Technology-Surgery.

NE/0165-8107
**NEURO-OPHTHALMOLOGY (AMSTERDAM : AEOLUS PRESS. 1980).** **See** Medical Science and Technology-Ophthalmology.

AU/0177-7955
**NEURO-ORTHOPEDICS.** **VFOAT** Neuroorthopedics. Vol. 1 No. 1 (1986)-. Periodical. English. Twice a year. $230.00. Springer-Verlag Wien, Sachsenplatz 4 6, PO Box 89, A-1201 Vienna Austria. **Tel** 011 43 1 3302415. **(Subscription address:** Springer Verlag New York Inc. / for North America, 44 Hartz Way, Secaucus NJ 07096.**) ED** H. Verbiest and P.F. van Akkerveeken. **NLM** W1; NE337KM. **[CCC].**
**Desc:** Takes a unique approach to disorders and injuries of the musculo-skeletal system in conjunction with the nervous system, and includes articles on applied research as well as diagnosis and clinical management.
**Ind/Abst** EMBASE.

FR/0296-3981
**NEURO-PSY.** [Neuro-psy]. No. 1 (June 1985)-. Periodical. French. mo (10 issues). 538.69F. Editions de l'Interligne, 47 rue de Charonne, 75011 Paris France. **Tel** 011 33 1 48068466. **NLM** W1; NE399H.
**Desc:** Information on neuropsychology.

BL/0028-3800
**NEUROBIOLOGIA (RECIFE).** (NEUROBIOLOGIA.). [Neurobiologia]. **Added/Corp** Sociedade de Psiquiatria, Neurologia e Higiene Mental do Nordeste Brasileiro. Vol. 1 (June 1938)-. Periodical. Portuguese (English, French and Spanish). qt. $55.00. Neurobiologia/Revista de Neurologia Psiquiatria E Neurocirurgica, Caixa Postal 651, 50001 Recife Brazil. **Tel** 55 81 2224359. **ED** A Codeceira Jr. **LC** RC321; .N26. **NLM** W1 NE323G. **CODEN** NURBAX. Index available. **Bk Rev. Ad Acc. Circ:** 500. Documents available from BIOSIS Document Express.
**Desc:** Original papers on neurobiology, psychiatry, and neurosurgery.
**Ind/Abst** Biol. Abstr.; Psychol. Abstr. (1962-); PsycINFO; PsycLit.

●HU
**NEUROBIOLOGY.** **Added/Corp** Magyar Tudomanyos Akademia. Vol. 1, No. 1 (1993)-. Academic Scholarly Publication. English. Four times a year. $84.00. Akademiai Kiado, Publishing House of the Hungarian Academy of Sciences, Prielle Kornelia u. 19-35, H-1117 Budapest Hungary. **Tel** 011 36 1 1811991, FAX 011 36 1 1811991, telex 22-6228 AKNYO H. **LC** QP351; .N4273. **DD** 591.1/88. **NLM** W1; NE323KB. **CODEN** NROBEZ. Documents available from CASDDS. ***Continues*** *Acta Biochimica et Biophysica Hungarica, 0237-6261.*
**Ind/Abst** Chem. Abstr.; Index Med. (1993-).

US/0197-4580
**NEUROBIOLOGY OF AGING.** [Neurobiol. aging]. Vol. 1 (Summer 1980)-. Academic Scholarly Publication. English. Six times a year. $753.00 The Americas; £505.00 other. Pergamon Press, An Imprint of Elsevier Science Ltd., The Boulevard, Langford Lane, Kidlington, Oxford OX5 1GB United Kingdom. **Tel** 011 44 865 843000, 011 44 865 843699, FAX 011 44 865 843010. **(Subscription address:** Elsevier Science Ltd. Oxford Fulfillment Centre, PO Box 800, Kidlington, Oxford OX5 1DX United Kingdom.**) ED** Paul Coleman. **LC** QP376; .N47. **DD** 618.97/8047. **NLM** W1 NE323R. **CODEN** NEAGDO. **[CCC]. Bk Rev. Ad Acc. Pr Rev.** ctrl circ. available on microfilm and microfiche from University Microfilms International (UMI). Documents available from The Genuine Article, BIOSIS Document Express, CASDDS, ADONIS.
**Desc:** Publishes the results of multidisciplinary studies in physiology, endocrinology, biochemistry, neurology, anatomy, pharmacology, and behavior in which the primary emphasis involves CNS changes with age.
**Ind/Abst** ADONIS; Biol. Abstr.; Chem. Abstr.; CSA Neuro. Abstr.; Curr. Aware. Biol. Sci., CABS; Curr. Contents Life Sci.; EMBASE; Index Med.; Life Sci. Collect.; Psychol. Abstr. (1980-); PsycINFO; PsycLit; Ref. Upd. Deluxe Ed.; Res. Alert [Full Cov.]; Sci. Cit. Index; SCISEARCH; Soc. Sci. Cit. Index [Select. Cov.].

●US/1074-7427
**NEUROBIOLOGY OF LEARNING AND MEMORY.** **See** Biology.

UK/1355-4794
**NEUROCASE.** (19??)-. English. Six times a year. £195.00 UK and Europe; $295.00 other. Oxford University Press, Walton Street, Oxford OX2 6DP England. **Tel** 011 44 865 56767, FAX 011 44 865 267773, telex 837330 OXPRES G. **(Subscription address:** Oxford University Press / USA, Journals Marketing Department, Oxford University Press, 2001 Evans Road, Cary NC 27513.**)**

US/0364-3190
**NEUROCHEMICAL RESEARCH.** [Neurochem. res.]. Vol. 1 (Feb. 1976)-. Academic Scholarly Publication. English. Twelve times a year. $775.00 US; $905.00 other. Plenum Press, 233 Spring Street, New York NY 10013-1578. **Tel** (212)620-8000, (800)221-9369, FAX (212)463-0742, (212)807-1047, telex 23/421139. **ED** Abel Lajtha. **LC** QP356.3; .N456. **DD** 591.1/88. **NLM** W1 NE3235. **CODEN** NEREDZ. **[CCC].** Index available. **Pr Rev.** available on microfilm and microfiche from University Microfilms International (UMI). Documents available from The Genuine Article, BIOSIS Document Express, CASDDS.
**Desc:** Devoted to the rapid publication of studies which use neurochemical methodology in research of the nervous system; serves as a bridge between neurochemistry and all other fields.
**Ind/Abst** Biol. Abstr.; Calcium Calcif. Tissue Abstr.; Chem. Abstr.; Chem. Titles; CSA Neuro. Abstr.; Curr. Contents Life Sci.; EMBASE; Energy Res. Abstr. (Feb. 1982-); Index Med.; Life Sci. Collect.; Ref. Z.; Ref. Upd. Basic Ed.; Ref. Upd. Deluxe Ed.; Res. Alert [Full Cov.]; Sci. Cit. Index; SCISEARCH.

US/0197-0186
**NEUROCHEMISTRY INTERNATIONAL.** [Neurochem. int.]. (1980)-. Academic Scholarly Publication. English. mo. $626.00 The Americas; £420.00 other. Pergamon Press, An Imprint of Elsevier Science Ltd., The Boulevard, Langford Lane, Kidlington, Oxford OX5 1GB United Kingdom. **Tel** 011 44 865 843000, 011 44 865 843699, FAX 011 44 865 843010. **(Subscription address:** Elsevier Science Ltd. Oxford Fulfillment Centre, PO Box 800, Kidlington, Oxford OX5 1DX United Kingdom.**) ED** Neville Osborne. **LC** QP356.3; .N465. **DD** 599.01/88. **NLM** W1 NE3237. **CODEN** NEUIDS. **[CCC]. Pr Rev.** available on microfilm and microfiche from University Microfilms International (UMI). Documents available from The Genuine Article, BIOSIS Document Express, CASDDS.
**Ind/Abst** Biol. Abstr.; Chem. Abstr.; Chem. Titles; CSA Neuro. Abstr.; Curr. Aware. Biol. Sci., CABS; Curr. Contents Life Sci.; EMBASE; Index Med. (Jan. 1992-); Life Sci. Collect.; Psychol. Abstr.; PsycINFO; PsycLit; Ref. Upd. Deluxe Ed.; Res. Alert [Full Cov.]; Sci. Cit. Index; SCISEARCH.

●US/1055-8330
**NEURODEGENERATION (PHILADELPHIA, PA.).**
(NEURODEGENERATION.). (1992)-. Academic Scholarly Publication. English. qt (4 issues). $195.00. Academic Press Ltd., A Division of Harcourt Brace & Company Ltd., 24-28 Oval Road, London NW1 7DX England. **Tel** 071 267 4466, FAX 071 482 2293, 071 485 4752, telex 25775 ACPRES G. **(Subscription address:** Harcourt Brace & Company, Ltd., Foots Cray, High Street, Sidcup Kent DA14 5HP England.**) ED** J. W. Langston and D. M. A. Mann. **NLM** W1; NE328AE. Documents available from The Genuine Article.
**Desc:** International forum for original research reports on work in neurodegenerative disorders.
**Ind/Abst** Res. Alert [Full Cov.].

SZ/0028-3835
**NEUROENDOCRINOLOGY.**
[Neuroendocrinology]. **Added/Corp** International Society of Neuroendocrinology. Vol. 1 (1965/1966)-. Academic Scholarly Publication. English (summaries and/or abstracts in French and German). mo. $1134.00. S. Karger AG, Allschwilerstrasse 10, PO Box - Postfach - Case Postale, CH-4009 Basel Switzerland. **Tel** 011 41 61 306-1111, FAX 011 41 61 306-1234, telex CH 962 652. **ED** C. Kordon. **LC** QP187.A1; N4. **DD** 616.4/005. **NLM** W1 NE328D. **CODEN** NUNDAJ. **[CCC]. Ad Acc. Pr Rev.** available on microfilm and microfiche from University Microfilms International (UMI). Documents available from The Genuine Article, BIOSIS Document Express, CASDDS.
**Desc:** Publishes papers reporting original research in basic and clinical neuroendocrinology. Topics range through the multiple, complex interactions between the endocrine system and the nervous system that occur in all parts of the body. The editorial board stresses a strong commitment to rapid, thorough review and expeditious publication devotes a rapid communication section to new important findings.
**Ind/Abst** AGRICOLA; Anim. Breed. Abstr.; Biol. Abstr.; Chem. Abstr.; Chem. Titles; CSA Neuro. Abstr.; Curr. Aware. Biol. Sci., CABS; Curr. Contents Life Sci.; Dairy Sci. Abstr.; EMBASE; Index Med.; Int. Aerosp. Abstr.; Nutr. Abstr. Rev., Ser. B, Live Feeds and Feed.; Nutr. Abstr. Rev., Ser. A, Hum. Exp.; Life Sci. Collect.; PESTDOC; Pig News Inf.; Poult. Abstr.; Ref. Upd. Basic Ed.; Ref. Upd. Deluxe Ed.; Res. Alert [Full Cov.]; Sci. Cit. Index; SCISEARCH.

SZ/0251-5350
**NEUROEPIDEMIOLOGY.**
[Neuroepidemiology]. **Added/Corp** World Federation of Neurology. Research Committee on Neuroepidemiology. Vol. 1 (April 1982)-. Periodical. English. bm. $296.00. S. Karger AG, Allschwilerstrasse 10, PO Box - Postfach - Case Postale, CH-4009 Basel Switzerland. **Tel** 011 41 61 306-1111, FAX 011 41 61 306-1234, telex CH 962 652. **ED** M. Alter, H. Lee. **NLM** W1 NE328F. **CODEN** NEEPD3. **[CCC]. Ad Acc. Pr Rev.** available on microfilm and microfiche. Documents available from The Genuine Article, BIOSIS Document Express.
**Desc:** The journal contains data of interest to many branches of neuroscience. Original articles discuss the classification, natural history and frequency of neurologic disease in different populations. Reports are published of new analytic methods and of research on environmental and genetic factors affecting risk of neurologic disease. The journal also features timely, critical reviews by invited authorities in neuroepidemiology giving readers current and comprehensive information from around the world.
**Ind/Abst** Biol. Abstr.; Curr. Aware. Biol. Sci., CABS; Curr. Contents Life Sci.; EMBASE; Index Med.; Index Vet.; Life Sci. Collect.; Ref. Upd. Deluxe Ed.; Res. Alert [Full Cov.]; SCISEARCH.

●UK
**NEUROGASTROENTEROLOGY & MOTILITY.** (199?)-. Academic Scholarly Publication. English. Four times a year (Mar., June, Sept., Dec.). $191.00 (institutions), $124.00 (individuals) US & Canada; £112.00 (institutions), £73.00 (individuals) Europe; £123.00 (institutions), £80.00 (individuals) other. Blackwell Scientific Publications Ltd, Marston Book Services, PO Box 87, Oxford OX2 ODT UK. **Tel** 011 44 865 791155, FAX 011 44 865 791927, telex 837 515 MARDIS G.

●US/1053-8119
**NEUROIMAGE (SAN DIEGO, CALIF.).**
(NEUROIMAGE.). [NeuroImage]. (1992)-. Academic Scholarly Publication. English. qt (4 issues). $270.00 US and Canada. Academic Press, Inc., 6277 Sea Harbor Drive, Orlando FL 32887. **Tel** (800)543-9534, (407)345-4100, FAX (407)363-9661. **DD** 616. **NLM** W1; NE328GH. **[CCC].**
**Desc:** Focuses on the visualization of all neuroscientific data. Intended to advance the state of knowledge of nervous system structure and function through the publication of articles describing neurobiological insights revealed through the use of imaging. The scope of research includes all types of imaging, image synthesis, and image analysis applied to basic research.

US/1052-5149
**NEUROIMAGING CLINICS OF NORTH AMERICA.** [Neuroimaging clin. N. Am.]. **VFOAT** Neuroimaging Clinics. Vol. 1, No. 1 (Sept. 1991)-. Periodical. English. qt. $100.00 (individual), $118.00 (institution) US; $132.00 (individual), $140.00 (institution) other. W.B. Saunders Company, A Subsidiary of Harcourt Brace Jovanovich, Inc., The Curtis Center/Suite 300, Independence Square West, Philadelphia PA 19106-3399. **Tel** (215)238-7800 or, 5587, FAX (215)238-7883, telex 173146. **(Subscription address:** W. B. Saunders Company / North America Subscriptions, c/o Periodicals, 6277 Sea Harbour Drive, 4th Floor, Orlando FL 32887.**) DD** 616. **NLM** W1; NE328GL.

SZ/1021-7401
**NEUROIMMUNOMODULATION.** (19??)-. English. Six times a year. $461.00. S. Karger AG, Allschwilerstrasse 10, PO Box - Postfach - Case Postale, CH-4009 Basel Switzerland. **Tel** 011 41 61 306-1111, FAX 011 41 61 306-1234, telex CH 962 652. **ED** S.M. McCann. **Pr Rev.**
**Desc:** Explores the way in which the nervous system interacts with the immune system via neural, hormonal, and paracrine actions. Basic investiagations consider all neural and humoral interactions from molecular genetics through cell regulation to integrative systems of the body. Also aims to clarify the basic mechanisms involved in the pathogenesis of the CNS pathology in AIDS patients and in various neurodegenerative diseases.

SP/0213-4853
**NEUROLOGIA (BARCELONA, SPAIN).**
(NEUROLOGIA : PUBLICACION OFICIAL DE LA SOCIEDAD ESPANOLA DE NEUROLOGIA.). **Added/Corp** Sociedad Espanola de Neurologia. (198?)-. Periodical. Spanish (summaries and/or abstracts in English; table of contents in English). Ten times a year. $63.00. Ediciones Doyma SA, Travesera de Gracia 17 21, 08021 Barcelona Spain. **Tel** 011 34 3 2000711, 011 34 3 4145706, FAX 011 34 3 2091136, telex 51964 INK E. **NLM** W1; NE328L. **CODEN** NERLEN.
**Ind/Abst** EMBASE; Index Med. Nov./Dec. 1987-; Indice Med. Esp.

CI/0353-8842
**NEUROLOGIA CROATICA : GLASILO UDRUZENJA NEUROLOGA JUGOSLAVIJE, OFFICIAL JOURNAL OF YUGOSLAV NEUROLOGICAL ASSOCIATION.** **Added/Corp** Udruzenje Neurohirurga Jugoslavije. Sveuciliste u Zagrebu. Klinicki Bolubicki Centar. Neurolska Klinika. Sveuciliste u Zagrebu. Zavod za Neuropatologiju. Vol. 40, No. 1 (1991)-. Periodical. English (Serbo-Croatian (Roman)). Four times a year (Mar., June, Sept., Dec.). $25.00 one year. Casopis Neurologiju Granicna, 410000 Zagreb Neuroloska Klini, Bolnica Rebro Croatia. **Tel** 38 41 235595, FAX 011 38 41 233 233 363. **ED** Z. Mubrin. **NLM** W1; NE328N. Index available (Bound in 4th iss.). cum. index. **Bk Rev**, (Qty: 20). **Ad Acc. Pr Rev. Circ:** 1,000 (ctrl). ***Continues** Neurologija, 0350-9559.*
**Desc:** Covers clinical neurology, basic neuroscience and other related fields, in addition to full communication, case reports, preliminary reports and reviews, and historical articles.
**Ind/Abst** Index Med. (1991-)(1991-1992);(1991-1992); Soc. Sci. Cit. Index [Select. Cov.].

CK/0120-1034
**NEUROLOGIA EN COLOMBIA.**
**Added/Corp** Fundacion Instituto Neurologico de Colombia. Vol. 1 (1977)-. Periodical. Spanish (Spanish; summaries and/or abstracts in English). ir. $25.00. Fundacion Institute of Neurologia in Colombia, PO Box 90303, Bogota 8 Colombia. **Tel** (91) 232-61-31. **ED** Edwin Ruiz Alarcon. **NLM** W1 NE328P. **Bk Rev. Circ:** 2,000 (ctrl).
**Desc:** Neurosurgery, clinical neurology, neuropsychiatric advances and new trends in neurosciences. Also covers Neuropathology infections of central nervous system, epilepsy, brain tumors and immunotherapy.

GR/0253-9446
**NEUROLOGIA ET PSYCHIATRIA.** [Neurol. psychiatr.]. Periodical. English (Greek, Modern and German). qt. **NLM** W1 NE328R.

PL/0028-3843
**NEUROLOGIA I NEUROCHIRURGIA POLSKA.** [Neurol. neurochir. pol.]. **Added/Corp** Polskie Towarzystwo Neurochirurgow. Polskie Towarzystwo Neurologiczne (Founded 1966). Vol. 1 (1967)-. Academic Scholarly Publication. Polish (summaries and/or abstracts in English and Russian). bm. Price on Request. **(Subscription address:** ARS Polona, PO Box 1001, 00068 Warsaw Poland.**) NLM** W1 NE328T. **CODEN** NNPOBE. Index Available, published separately, free-automatically sent. Documents available from CASDDS. ***Continues** Neurologia, Neurochirurgia I Psychiatria Polska.*
**Ind/Abst** Chem. Abstr.; EMBASE; Index Med.; SportSearch.

JA/0470-8105
**NEUROLOGIA MEDICO-CHIRURGICA.**
[Neurol. med.-chir.]. **Added/Corp** Japan Neurosurgical Society. Nippon No-Shinkeigeka Gakkai. Vol. 1 (1959)-. Academic Scholarly Publication. English. mo. $252.00. **(Subscription address:** Kyowa Book Company Inc., 1 38 Kanda Jinbocho Chiyoda-ku, Tokyo 101 Japan.**) NLM** W1 NE3285. **CODEN** NMCHBN. Documents available from BIOSIS Document Express.
**Desc:** Contains the proceedings of the 12th annual meeting of the Japan Neurosurgical Society.
**Ind/Abst** Biol. Abstr.; EMBASE; Index Med.

IT
**NEUROLOGIA PSICHIATRIA SCIENZE UMANE.** **See** Medical Science and Technology-Psychiatry.

US/0733-8619
**NEUROLOGIC CLINICS.** [Neurol. clin.]. Vol. 1, No. 1 (Feb. 1983)-. Periodical. English. qt. $98.00 (individual), $120.00 (institution) US; $132.00 (individual), $140.00 (institution) other. W.B. Saunders Company, A Subsidiary of Harcourt Brace Jovanovich, Inc., The Curtis Center/Suite 300, Independence Square West, Philadelphia PA 19106-3399. **Tel** (215)238-7800 or, 5587, FAX (215)238-7883, telex 173146. **(Subscription address:** W. B. Saunders Company / North America Subscriptions, c/o Periodicals, 6277 Sea Harbour Drive, 4th Floor, Orlando FL 32887.**) ED** Brenda Frank. **LC** RC321. **DD** 616.8/005. **NLM** W1 NE329T. **[CCC].** Index available. **Pr Rev. Circ:** 6,250. available on microfilm and microfiche from University Microfilms International (UMI). Documents available from The Genuine Article.
**Desc:** Practical update for physicians on latest advances. Each issue devoted to single topic in patient care.
**Ind/Abst** Cumul. Index Nurs. Allied Health Lit.; Curr. Contents Clin. Med.; Dev. Med. Child Neurol.; EMBASE; Index Med. (Vol. 1, No. 1, 1983-); Psychol. Abstr. (1987-); PsycINFO; PsycLit; Res. Alert [Full Cov.]; SCISEARCH; Soc. Sci. Cit. Index [Select. Cov.].

IT
**NEUROLOGIC CLINICS (ITALIAN EDITION).** Editrice McGraw Hill Italia, Piazza Emilia 5, 20129 Milan Italy. **Tel** 011 39 2 76110226, 76110248.

US/0736-9263
**NEUROLOGIC ILLNESS: DIAGNOSIS & TREATMENT.** (NEUROLOGIC ILLNESS.). [Neurol. illn.: diagn. treat.]. Vol. 1-. Monographic series. English. Price varies per volume. Spectrum Publications Inc, 175-20 Wexford Terrace, Jamaica NY 11432. **Tel** (718)658-0888. **ED** Michael I Weintraub. **NLM** W1 NE329V.
**Desc:** Clinical monographs in neurological illness: diagnosis and treatment.

US/1058-7535
**NEUROLOGICAL DISEASE AND THERAPY.** [Neurol. dis. ther.]. Vol. 2 (1989)-. Monographic series. English. ir. Price varies per volume. Marcel Dekker Inc., 270 Madison Avenue, New York NY 10016. **Tel** (212)696-9000, (800)228-1160, FAX (212)685-4540, telex 421419. **(Subscription address:** Marcel Dekker Inc, PO Box 5017, Monticello NY 12701.**) DD** 616. **NLM** W1; NE33LD. **CODEN** NDTHEE.
**Desc:** Series covering topics such as sleep disorders, Parkinson's Disease, and Alzheimer's Disease.

UK/0161-6412
**NEUROLOGICAL RESEARCH (NEW YORK).** (NEUROLOGICAL RESEARCH.). [Neurol. res.]. Vol. 1 (1979)-. Academic Scholarly Publication. English. bm (6 issues). $500.00 US & Canada; £295.00 other. Forefront Publishing Group, 5 River Road, Suite 113, Wilton CT 06897. **Tel** (203)221-9949. **(Subscription address:** Neurological Research, Celtic House, 33 Johns Mews, London WC1N 2QL England.**) LC** RC321; .N38. **DD** 612.8/05. **NLM** W1 NE33N. **CODEN** NRESDZ. **[CCC].** Index available. **Bk Rev. Ad Acc.** available on microfilm and microfiche from University Microfilms International (UMI). Documents available from The Genuine Article, CASDDS.
**Desc:** Contains original fundamental, basic and clinical research in neurosurgery and the neurosciences underlying medical disciplines.
**Ind/Abst** Chem. Abstr.; CSA Neuro. Abstr. (?-?); Curr. Aware. Biol. Sci., CABS; EMBASE; Index Med.; Life Sci. Collect.; Ref. Upd. Deluxe Ed.; Res. Alert [Full Cov.]; Soc. Sci. Cit. Index [Select. Cov.].

US/1073-8584
**NEUROLOGIST, THE.** English. bm. $97.00 (individual), $195.00 (institution), US; $117.00 (individual), $215.00 (institution). Williams & Wilkins Company, 428 East Preston Street, Baltimore MD 21202-3993. **Tel** (410)528-4000, (800)638-6423, FAX (410)528-8596, telex 87669. **(Subscription address:** Williams & Wilkins, PO Box 64380, Baltimore MD 21264.**)** Documents available from Quick Copies.

●US/1074-7931
**NEUROLOGIST (BALTIMORE, MD.), THE.** (THE NEUROLOGIST.). (1995)-. Periodical. English. bm. $130.00 (institutions), $95.00 (individuals) US; $160.00 (institution), $125.00 (individual) other. Williams & Wilkins Company, 428 East Preston Street, Baltimore MD 21202-3993. **Tel** (410)528-4000, (800)638-6423, FAX (410)528-8596, telex 87669. **(Subscription address:** Williams & Wilkins, PO Box 64380, Baltimore MD 21264.**)** Documents available from Quick Copies.

US/0028-3878
**NEUROLOGY.** [Neurology]. **Added/Corp** American Academy of Neurology. Vol. 1 (Jan./Feb. 1951)-. Academic Scholarly Publication. English. mo. $200.00 US and possessions and Canada; $250.00 other. Advanstar Communications Inc., 131 West First Street, Duluth MN 55802. **Tel** (218)723-9477, (800)346-0085. **LC** RC321; .A47. **DD** 616.8/05. **NLM** W1 NE337. **CODEN** NEURAI. **[CCC]. Pr Rev.** available on microfilm and microfiche from University Microfilms International (UMI). Documents available from The Genuine Article, BIOSIS Document Express, CASDDS.
**Desc:** Includes American Academy of Neurology newsletter.
**Ind/Abst** Abr. Index Med.; Annals Behav. Med.; Biol. Abstr.; Chem. Abstr.; CSA Neuro. Abstr. (?-?); Curr. Aware. Biol. Sci., CABS; Dev. Med. Child Neurol.; EMBASE; Health Period. Database; Helminthol. Abstr.; Index Med.; Int. Aerosp. Abstr.; Iowa Drug Inf. Serv. (1967-); Med. Abstr. Newsl.; Life Sci. Collect.; Physic. Medline Plus; Protozoolog. Abstr.; Psychol. Abstr. (1951-); PsycINFO; PsycLit; Ref. Upd. Basic Ed.; Ref. Upd. Deluxe Ed.; Res. Alert [Full Cov.]; Risk Abstr.; Saf. Health Work; Sci. Cit. Index; SCISEARCH; Soc. Plann. Policy Dev. Abstr.; Soc. Sci. Cit. Index [Select. Cov.]; Sociol. Abstr.; SportSearch; Virol. AIDS Abstr.

US/0741-4234
**NEUROLOGY ALERT.** [Neurol. alert]. **Added/Corp** Warren, Gorham & Lamont, Inc. American Health Consultants. Vol. 1, No. 1 (Sept. 1982)-. Periodical. English. mo. $128.00 without CME; $178.00 with CME. American Health Consultants, 3525 Piedmont Road, Suite 400, Atlanta GA 30305. **Tel** (800)688-2421, (404)262-7436. **(Subscription address:** American Health Consultants, PO Box 95278, Chicago IL 60694.**)** **DD** 616. Index Available, published separately, free-automatically sent. cum. index.
**Desc:** Presents abstracts of the most recent clinical studies in neurology, neuroscience, clinical pharmacology and brain behavior, followed by authoritative commentary by our distinguished physician editors.

US/0736-4563
**NEUROLOGY AND NEUROBIOLOGY.** [Neurol neurobiol.]. (1982)-. Academic Scholarly Publication. English. ir. Price varies per volume. John Wiley & Sons, Inc., 605 Third Avenue, New York NY 10158-0012. **Tel** (212)850-6000, (212)850-6645, FAX (212)850-6088, telex 12-7063. **(Subscription address:** John Wiley & Sons / England, Baffins Lane, Chichester, West Sussex PO19 1UD England.**)** **ED** Victoria Chan-Palay and Sanford Paylay. **NLM** W1 NE337B. **CODEN** NEUND9. **[CCC]. Bk Rev. Ad Acc.** Documents available from BIOSIS Document Express, CASDDS.
**Desc:** A scholarly book series covering topics such as sensorimotor activity, catecholamines, nervous systems, excitable cells, and anorexia nervosa.
**Ind/Abst** Biol. Abstr.; Chem. Abstr.

US/1060-4197
**NEUROLOGY CHRONICLE.** [Neurol. chron.]. (1991)-. Periodical. English. mo (10 issues). $135.00 (institutions); $110.00 (individuals). Adams Publishing Group, Box 263 Prudential Center, Newton MA 02199. **Tel** (617)965-8448. **DD** 616. **NLM** W1; NE337BE.

II/0028-3886
**NEUROLOGY, INDIA.** [Neurol. India]. **Added/Corp** Neurological Society of India. Vol. 12, (Jan/Mar. 1964)-. Academic Scholarly Publication. English. Four times a year (Jan., Apr., July, October). $90.00 US; $110.00 other. Neurological Society of India, 2 Central Street Kilpauk Garden Co, Madras 600 010 India. **Tel** 11 91 44 611233. **(Subscription address:** Prints India, 11 Darya Ganj, New Delhi 110002 India.**)** **ED** J. S. Chopra. **NLM** W1 NE337D. Index Available, published separately, free-automatically sent. **Bk Rev** (Qty: 2-5). **Ad Acc. Pr Rev. Circ:** 1,300. ***Continues*** *Neurology.*
**Ind/Abst** EMBASE; Life Sci. Collect.

GW/0941-9500
**NEUROLOGY, PSYCHIATRY AND BRAIN RESEARCH.** ***Ceased.*** **VFOAT** Neurology, Psychiatry & Brain Research. Vol. 1, No. 1 (Aug. 1992)-Vol. 2. Periodical. English. qt. Springer-Verlag GmbH & Company KG, Heidelberger Platz 3, D 14197 Berlin Germany. **Tel** 011 49 30 8207223, FAX 011 49 30 8214091, telex 183 319 SPBLN D. **(Subscription address:** Springer Verlag New York Inc. / for North America, 44 Hartz Way, Secaucus NJ 07096.**)** **NLM** W1; NE337DL. **[CCC].**
**Ind/Abst** Soc. Sci. Cit. Index [Select. Cov.].

US/0893-2336
**NEUROMETHODS.** [Neuromethods]. (1985)-. Monographic series. English. ir. Price varies per volume. Humana Press Inc., 999 Riverview Drive, Suite 208, Totawa NJ 07512. **Tel** (201)256-1699, FAX (201)256-8341. **LC** RC337; .N475. **DD** 612.8/028. **NLM** W1; NE337G. **CODEN** NUROE8. **[CCC].**

UK/0261-8412
**NEUROMUSCULAR DISEASES.** (19??)-. English. mo. £80.00. SUBIS, Mansion House, 19 Kingfield Road, Sheffield S11 9AS England. **Tel** 011 44 114 255 4433, FAX 011 44 114 255 4626. **Ad Acc.**
**Desc:** Current awareness service for researchers and clinicians.

UK/0960-8966
**NEUROMUSCULAR DISORDERS : NMD.** **See** Medical Science and Technology-Musculoskeletal System.

US/0896-6273
**NEURON (CAMBRIDGE, MASS.).** **See** Biology.

NE/0166-3518
**NEUROONCOLOGY.** [Neurooncology]. V. 1-. Academic Scholarly Publication. English. Price varies per volume. Elsevier Science Publishers Ltd, Crown House, Linton Road, Barking Essex IG11 8JU England. **Tel** 011 44 81 5947272, FAX 081-594-5942, telex 896950. **NLM** W1 NE337J. **CODEN** NRNCDW. Documents available from CASDDS.
**Ind/Abst** Chem. Abstr. (-1979).

UK/0305-1846
**NEUROPATHOLOGY AND APPLIED NEUROBIOLOGY.** **See** Medical Science and Technology-Pathology.

PL/0028-3894
**NEUROPATOLOGIA POLSKA.** ***Title Change.*** [Neuropatol. Pol.]. **Added/Corp** Polska Akademia Nauk. Wydzia VI--Nauk Medycznych. (1963)-(1993). Academic Scholarly Publication. Polish (Polish; summaries and/or abstracts in English and Russian; table of contents in English and Russian). qt. **(Subscription address:** ARS Polona, PO Box 1001, 00068 Warsaw Poland.**)** **NLM** W1; NE337P. **CODEN** NUPOBT. Documents available from CASDDS.
***Continued by*** *Folia Neuropathologica.*
**Ind/Abst** Chem. Abstr.; EMBASE [Select. Cov.]; Index Med.

GW/0174-304X
**NEUROPEDIATRICS.** [Neuropediatrics]. **VFOAT** Journal of Pediatric Neurobiology, Neurology and Neurosurgery. Vol. 11, No. 3 (Aug. 1980)-. Academic Scholarly Publication. English (German). bm. $242.00. Hippokrates Verlag, Postfach 102263, W 70018 Stuttgart Germany. **Tel** 011 49 711 89310. **(Subscription address:** Thieme Medical Publishers Inc., 381 Park Avenue South, New York NY 10016.**)** **ED** F.J. Schulte. **NLM** W1 NE337SD. **CODEN** NRPDDB. **[CCC]. Pr Rev. Circ:** 1,500. Documents available from The Genuine Article, CASDDS. ***Continues*** *Neuropadiatrie, 0028-3797.*
**Desc:** Journal of pediatric neurobiology, neurology and neurosurgery. Of interest to pediatricans, neurologists, neurosurgeons, neurobiologists. Journal for science, training, and continuing education.
**Ind/Abst** Chem. Abstr. (1980-1985); Curr. Contents Clin. Med.; Curr. Contents Life Sci.; Dev. Med. Child Neurol.; EMBASE; Energy Res. Abstr. (Dec. 1982-); Index Med.; Life Sci. Collect.; Res. Alert [Full Cov.]; Sci. Cit. Index; SCISEARCH.

UK/0143-4179
**NEUROPEPTIDES (EDINBURGH).** (NEUROPEPTIDES.). [Neuropeptides]. Vol. 1, No. 1 (July 1980)-. Academic Scholarly Publication. English. mo. £436.00 Europe; £438.00 Other (Institutions). Churchill Livingstone, 1-3 Baxter's Place, Leith Walk, Edinburgh EH1 3AF Scotland. **Tel** 011 44 31 556 2424, FAX 011 44 31 558 1278, telex 727511. **(Subscription address:** Maruzen Company Ltd., PO Box 5050, Import & Export Department, Tokyo 100 31 Japan.**)** **ED** M J Brownstein and J Hughes. **LC** Discard. **NLM** W1 NE337SL. **CODEN** NRPPDD. **[CCC]. Bk Rev. Ad Acc. Pr Rev.** available on microfilm and microfiche from University Microfilms International (UMI). Documents available from The Genuine Article, BIOSIS Document Express, CASDDS, ADONIS.
**Desc:** Publishes original research and reviews articles on the structure, distribution, actions and functions of peptides in the central and peripheral nervous systems.
**Ind/Abst** ADONIS; Biol. Abstr. (1986-); Chem. Abstr.; Chem. Titles; CSA Neuro. Abstr.; Curr. Aware. Biol. Sci., CABS; Curr. Contents Life Sci.; EMBASE; Index Med.; Nutr. Abstr. Rev., Ser. A, Hum. Exp.; Life Sci. Collect.; Res. Alert [Full Cov.]; Sci. Cit. Index; SCISEARCH.

UK/0142-8233
**NEUROPEPTIDES (SHEFFIELD).** (NEUROPEPTIDES.). **Added/Corp** University of Sheffield. Biomedical Information Service. (19??)-. Periodical. English. Twenty-four times a year. £120.00. SUBIS, Mansion House, 19 Kingfield Road, Sheffield S11 9AS England. **Tel** 011 44 114 255 4433, FAX 011 44 114 255 4626. **[CCC]. Bk Rev. Ad Acc.** available on diskette.
**Desc:** Current awareness service for researchers in clinical and life sciences.
**Ind/Abst** Curr. Contents Life Sci.; Ref. Upd. Basic Ed.; Ref. Upd. Deluxe Ed.

NE/0987-7053
**NEUROPHYSIOLOGIE CLINIQUE.** [Neurophysiol. clin.]. **Added/Corp** Societe d'Electroencephalographie et de Neurophysiologie Clinique de Langue Francaise. **VFOAT** Clinical Neurophysiology. Vol. 18, No. 1 (Feb. 1988)-. Academic Scholarly Publication. French (summaries and/or abstracts in English). Six times a year (1 volume). 1200.00F France; 1395.00F other. Editions Scientifique Elsevier, 141 rue de Javel, 75747 Paris Cedex 15 France. **Tel** 011 33 1 47 07 11 22, FAX 011 33 1 43 36 80 93. **(Subscription address:** Editions Scientifiques Elsevier / for North America, PO Box 7247-7576, Philadelphia PA 19170-7576.**)** **ED** A. Avtret and Chu Bretonneau. **NLM** W1; NE337U. **CODEN** NCLIE4. **[CCC].** Index available. **Bk Rev. Ad Acc. Circ:** 3,000 (ctrl). available on microfilm and microfiche from University Microfilms International (UMI). Documents available from The Genuine Article, BIOSIS Document Express. ***Continues*** *Revue d'Electroencephalographie et de Neurophysiologie Clinique, 0370-4475.*
**Ind/Abst** Biol. Abstr.; EMBASE; Index Med. (Feb. 1988-); Res. Alert [Full Cov.]; Soc. Sci. Cit. Index [Select. Cov.].

US/0090-2977
**NEUROPHYSIOLOGY (NEW YORK).** (NEUROPHYSIOLOGY.). [Neurophysiology]. **Added/Corp** Consultants Bureau. Vol. 1 (July/Aug. 1969)-. Academic Scholarly Publication. English (Russian). bm (6 issues). $1145.00 US; $1340.00 other. Consultants Bureau, A Division of Plenum Publishing Corporation, 233 Spring Street, New York NY 10013. **Tel** (212)620-8000, (212)620-8466, FAX (212)463-0742, telex 23/421139. **ED** V. I. Skok. **NLM** W1 NE337V. **CODEN** NPHYBI. **[CCC].** available on microfilm and microfiche from University Microfilms International (UMI). Documents available from The Genuine Article, BIOSIS Document Express, CASDDS.
**Ind/Abst** Biol. Abstr. (1984); Chem. Abstr.; CSA Neuro. Abstr.; Curr. Contents Life Sci.; EMBASE; Index Med.; Life Sci. Collect.; Psychol. Abstr. (1979); Res. Alert [Full Cov.]; Sci. Cit. Index.

●US/1058-6741
**NEUROPROTOCOLS (ORLANDO, FLA.).** (NEUROPROTOCOLS : A COMPANION TO METHODS IN NEUROSCIENCES.). [NeuroProtocols]. Vol. 1, No. 1 (Aug. 1992)-. Academic Scholarly Publication. English. bm (6 issues). $170.00 US and Canada. Academic Press, Inc., 6277 Sea Harbor Drive, Orlando FL 32887. **Tel** (800)543-9534, (407)345-4100, FAX (407)363-9661. **ED** P. Michael Conn. **DD** 616. **NLM** W1; NE337VL. **CODEN** NEPREV. **[CCC].** Documents available from CASDDS.
**Desc:** The articles in these topic-oriented issues will provide methodology of central significance to the neurosciences. Techniques presented will range from molecular biology to whole animal physiology.
**Ind/Abst** Chem. Abstr.

IT/0028-3916
**NEUROPSICHIATRIA.** (1929)-. Periodical. Italian. mo. Instituto Psichiatrico, Via Redipuglia 95, Genoa Italy.

IT/0394-9540
**NEUROPSICOFARMACOLOGIA DEL COMPORTAMENTO.** **See** Pharmacy and Pharmacology.

GW
**NEUROPSYCHIATRIE.** **See** Medical Science and Technology-Psychiatry.

FR/0222-9617
**NEUROPSYCHIATRIE DE L'ENFANCE ET DE L'ADOLESCENCE.** [Neuropsychiatr. enfance adolesc.]. **Added/Corp** Societe Francaise de Psychiatrie de l'Enfant et de l'Adolescent. (Jan./Feb. 1979)-. Periodical. French (summaries and/or abstracts in English, German and Spanish). Eight times a year. 850.00F France; 1145.00F other. Expansion Scientifique Francaise, 31 Boulevard de la Tour-Maubourg, 75007 Paris France. **Tel** 011 33 1 40 62 64 00, 011 33 1 40626439. **NLM** W1 NE339L. **[CCC].** Documents available from The Genuine Article. ***Continues*** *Revue de Neuropsychiatrie Infantile et d'Hygiene Mentale de l'Enfance, 0035-1628.*
**Ind/Abst** EMBASE; Index Med.; Psychol. Abstr. (1979-); PsycINFO; PsycLit; Res. Alert [Full Cov.]; Soc. Plann. Policy Dev. Abstr.

US/0894-878X
**NEUROPSYCHIATRY, NEUROPSYCHOLOGY, BEHAVIORAL NEUROLOGY.** [Neuropsychiatry neuropsychol. behav. neurol.]. Vol. 1, No. 1 (Spring 1988)-. Periodical. English. qt. $106.00 (individuals); 155.00 (institutions) US; $145.00 (individuals), $192.00 (institutions) other. Raven Press, 1185 Avenue of the Americas, 37th Floor, New York NY 10036. **Tel** (212)930-9500, (212)930-9604, FAX (212)869-3495, (212)302-8507, telex 640073. **ED** Michael Alan Taylor. **DD** 616. **NLM** W1; NE341G. **CODEN** NNNEEB. **[CCC].** available on microfilm and microfiche from University Microfilms International (UMI). Documents available from The Genuine Article.
**Desc:** Presents original articles on basic brain processes, critical review articles, case reports, and brief reports on preliminary studies and clinical issues. Emphasis will be the neurological and neuropsychological correlates of psychopathological phenomena and mental syndromes.

**Ind/Abst** Curr. Contents Clin. Med.; EMBASE; Psychol. Abstr. (1988-); PsycINFO; PsycLit; Res. Alert [Full Cov.]; Soc. Sci. Cit. Index [Select. Cov.].

SZ/0302-282X
**NEUROPSYCHOBIOLOGY.** [Neuropsychobiology]. Vol. 1 (1975)-. Academic Scholarly Publication. English. Eight times a year. $516.00. S. Karger AG, Allschwilerstrasse 10, PO Box - Postfach - Case Postale, CH-4009 Basel Switzerland. **Tel** 011 41 61 306-1111, FAX 011 41 61 306-1234, telex CH 962 652. **ED** J. Mendlewicz, B. Saletu, P. Netter, W.M. Herrmann. **NLM** W1 NE3412. **CODEN** NPBYAL. **[CCC]. Ad Acc. Pr Rev.** Documents available from The Genuine Article, BIOSIS Document Express, CASDDS. ***Absorbed*** *International Pharmacopsychiatry, 0020-8272.*
**Desc:** The biological approach to mental disorders continues to yield innovative findings of immense clinical importance. In four separately edited but closely related sections, this journal facilitates immediate comparison of data resulting from various experimental and clinical approaches. It features original and fundamental data on the relationship between neurophysiology, neurochemistry, neuroendocrinology, genetics and between normal and abnormal behavior. The reader will also find pharmacoelectroencephalographic studies and extensive information on how psychotropic compounds effect both normal and abnormal psychologic states.
**Ind/Abst** Biol. Abstr.; Chem. Abstr.; CSA Neuro. Abstr. (?-?); Cumul. Index Nurs. Allied Health Lit.; Curr. Contents Life Sci.; Dairy Sci. Abstr.; EMBASE; Index Med.; Life Sci. Collect.; PESTDOC; Psychol. Abstr. (1975-); PsycINFO; PsycLit; Ref. Upd. Deluxe Ed.; Res. Alert [Full Cov.]; Sci. Cit. Index; SCISEARCH; Soc. Sci. Cit. Index [Select. Cov.].

UK/0028-3932
**NEUROPSYCHOLOGIA.** [Neuropsychologia]. Vol. 1 (1963)-. Academic Scholarly Publication. English (French and German). mo. $1155.00 The Americas; £775.00 other. Pergamon Press, An Imprint of Elsevier Science Ltd., The Boulevard, Langford Lane, Kidlington, Oxford OX5 1GB United Kingdom. **Tel** 011 44 865 843000, 011 44 865 843699, FAX 011 44 865 843010. **(Subscription address:** Elsevier Science Ltd. Oxford Fulfillment Centre, PO Box 800, Kidlington, Oxford OX5 1DX United Kingdom.**)** **ED** M. Jeeves. **LC** RC321; .N435. **DD** 616.805. **NLM** W1 NE342. **CODEN** NUPSA6. **[CCC]. Pr Rev.** available on microfilm and microfiche from University Microfilms International (UMI). Documents available from The Genuine Article, BIOSIS Document Express.
**Desc:** Devoted to promoting the study and understanding of human behavior from a neurological point of view, and to integrating clinical, genetic and experimental contributions into its field.
**Ind/Abst** Annals Behav. Med.; Biol. Abstr.; CSA Neuro. Abstr. (?-?); Curr. Aware. Biol. Sci., CABS; Curr. Contents Life Sci.; Curr. Contents Soc. Behav. Sci.; Dev. Med. Child Neurol.; EMBASE; Index Med.; Int. Aerosp. Abstr.; Life Sci. Collect.; Psychol. Abstr. (1967-); PsycINFO; PsycLit; Ref. Upd. Deluxe Ed.; Res. Alert [Full Cov.]; Sci. Cit. Index; SCISEARCH; Soc. Sci. Cit. Index [Full Cov.]; SportSearch.

UK/0960-2011
**NEUROPSYCHOLOGICAL REHABILITATION.** **See** Psychology.

US/0894-4105
**NEUROPSYCHOLOGY.** **See** Psychology.

US/1040-7308
**NEUROPSYCHOLOGY REVIEW.** [Neuropsychol. rev.]. Vol. 1 No. 1 (Mar. 1990)-. Periodical. English. Four times a year. $130.00 institutions, $39.00 individuals US; $150.00 institutions, $46.00 individuals other. Plenum Press, 233 Spring Street, New York NY 10013-1578. **Tel** (212)620-8000, (800)221-9369, FAX (212)463-0742, (212)807-1047, telex 23/421139. **ED** Gerald Goldstein and Antonio Gerald Goldstein. **LC** QP360; .N498. **DD** 612.8/2/05. **NLM** W1; NE342E. **CODEN** NERVEJ. **[CCC].** available on microfilm and microfiche from University Microfilms International (UMI). Documents available from BIOSIS Document Express.
**Desc:** Comprehensive, scholarly reviews integrate and interpret topics of interest to clinical or research neuropsychologists and behavioral neurologists.
**Ind/Abst** Biol. Abstr. (1991-); EMBASE; Psychoanal. Abstr.; PsycScan: Appl. Exp. Eng. Psych.; PsycScan: LD/MR; PsycScan: Neuropsych.; Soc. Sci. Cit. Index [Select. Cov.]; Soc. Work Abstr. [Select. Cov.].

US/0893-133X
**NEUROPSYCHOPHARMACOLOGY (NEW YORK, N.Y.).** (NEUROPSYCHOPHARMACOLOGY : OFFICIAL PUBLICATION OF THE AMERICAN COLLEGE OF NEUROPSYCHOPHARMACOLOGY.). [Neuropsychopharmacology]. **Added/Corp** American College of Neuropsychopharmacology. Vol. 1, No. 1 (Dec. 1987)-. Academic Scholarly Publication. English. Eight times a year (2 volumes). $398.00 US; $443.00 other. Elsevier Science Publishing Company Inc, Madison Square Station, PO Box 882, New York NY 10159-0882. **Tel** (212)633-3950, FAX (212)633-3990. **ED** J. Christian Gillin. **DD** 615. **NLM** W1; NE342F. **CODEN** NEROEW. **[CCC]. Pr Rev.** Documents available from The Genuine Article, BIOSIS Document Express, CASDDS, ADONIS.
**Desc:** Focuses on clinical and basic science contributions to the field, encompassing biological and psychological sciences relevant to the effects of centrally acting agents. Regular topics include the effects of these agents and the molecular, cellular, physiological and psychological bases of their actions.
**Ind/Abst** ADONIS; Biol. Abstr.; Chem. Abstr.; Curr. Aware. Biol. Sci., CABS; Curr. Contents Life Sci.; EMBASE; Health Plan. Adminis.; Index Med. (1987-); Int. Nurs. Index; PESTDOC; Psychol. Abstr. (1987-); PsycINFO (1990-); PsycLit; Ref. Upd. Deluxe Ed.; Res. Alert [Full Cov.]; Sci. Cit. Index; SCISEARCH; Soc. Sci. Cit. Index [Select. Cov.].

GW/0028-3940
**NEURORADIOLOGY.** [Neuroradiology]. Vol. 1 (April 1970)-. Academic Scholarly Publication. German (English). Eight times a year. DM798.00. Springer-Verlag GmbH & Company KG, Heidelberger Platz 3, D 14197 Berlin Germany. **Tel** 011 49 30 8207223, FAX 011 49 30 8214091, telex 183 319 SPBLN D. **(Subscription address:** Springer Verlag New York Inc. / for North America, 44 Hartz Way, Secaucus NJ 07096.**)** **ED** T. Naidich. **LC** RC349.R3; N4. **DD** 616.8/047/5705. **NLM** W1 NE342K. **[CCC]. Pr Rev.** available on microfilm and microfiche from University Microfilms International (UMI). Documents available from The Genuine Article.
**Desc:** Covers a wide variety of imaging techniques pertaining to the neurosciences, while also including aspects of treatment falling into the field of "interventional radiology."
**Ind/Abst** Curr. Contents Clin. Med.; Curr. Contents Life Sci.; Dev. Med. Child Neurol.; EMBASE; Energy Res. Abstr. (July 1974-); Helminthol. Abstr. (1991-); Index Med.; Life Sci. Collect.; Res. Alert [Full Cov.]; Rev. Med. Vet. Mycology; Sci. Cit. Index; SCISEARCH.

US/1053-8135
**NEUROREHABILITATION (READING, MASS.).** (NEUROREHABILITATION.). **VFOAT** Neuro Rehabilitation. Vol. 1, No. 1 (Feb. 1991)-. Periodical. English. qt. $105.00 (institution), $75.00 (individual) US and Canada; $125.00 (institution), $90.00 (individual) other. Butterworth Heinemann / Woburn, MA, 225 Wildwood Avenue, Unit B, Woburn MA 01801. **Tel** (800)366-2665, FAX (617)928-2620, telex 880052. **DD** 615. **NLM** W1; NE342KG. **[CCC]. Bk Rev. Pr Rev.**
**Desc:** Provides multidisciplinary rehabilitation teams with the most current clinical information for treating patients with cerebrovascular disease, or patients who have sustained traumatic brain injury.

UK/0959-4965
**NEUROREPORT.** **VFOAT** Neuro Report. Vol. 1, No. 1 (Sept. 1990)-. Periodical. English. Eighteen times a year. $1250.00 US; £735.00 other. Rapid Communications of Oxford Ltd, The Old Malthouse, Paradise Street, Oxford OX1 1LD England. **Tel** 011 44 0865 790447, FAX 011 44 0865 244012, telex 9403712. **(Subscription address:** Rapid Communications of Oxford Ltd, ITPS, Cheriton Cheriton House, North Way, Andover Mants SP10 5BE UK**)** **ED** D Ottoson, C Blakemore, M Saitama, and M Mishkin. **NLM** W1; NE432L. **CODEN** NERPEZ. **[CCC].** Index available. cum. index. **Bk Rev. Ad Acc. Pr Rev. Acid Free.** Documents available from The Genuine Article.
**Desc:** Covers all aspects of sensory and motor systems, cellular, molecular and developmental neuroscience and behavioral, integrative and clinical neuroscience.
**Ind/Abst** CSA Neuro. Abstr.; Curr. Aware. Biol. Sci., CABS; Curr. Contents Life Sci.; EMBASE; Health Plan. Adminis.; Index Med. (Sept. 1990-); Res. Alert [Full Cov.]; Sci. Cit. Index; SCISEARCH; Soc. Sci. Cit. Index [Select. Cov.].

UK/0306-4522
**NEUROSCIENCE.** [Neuroscience]. **Added/Corp** International Brain Research Organization. Vol. 1 (1976)-. Academic Scholarly Publication. English. Twenty-four times a year. $3487.00 The Americas; £2340.00 other. Pergamon Press, An Imprint of Elsevier Science Ltd., The Boulevard, Langford Lane, Kidlington, Oxford OX5 1GB United Kingdom. **Tel** 011 44 865 843000, 011 44 865 843699, FAX 011 44 865 843010. **(Subscription address:** Elsevier Science Ltd. Oxford Fulfillment Centre, PO Box 800, Kidlington, Oxford OX5 1DX United Kingdom.**)** **ED** P. G. Kostyuk, R. Llinas and A. D. Smith. **LC** QP351; .N43. **DD** 591.1/88/05. **NLM** W1 NE342M. **CODEN** NRSCDNNRSCD. **[CCC]. Pr Rev.** available on microfilm and microfiche from University Microfilms International (UMI). Documents available from The Genuine Article, BIOSIS Document Express, CASDDS, ADONIS.
**Desc:** Publishes papers describing the results of original research on any aspect of the scientific study of the nervous system.
**Ind/Abst** ADONIS; Anim. Behav. Abstr.; Biol. Abstr.; Calcium Calcif. Tissue Abstr.; Chem. Abstr.; Chemorecept. Abstr.; CSA Neuro. Abstr.; Curr. Aware. Biol. Sci., CABS; Curr. Contents Life Sci.; Curr. Ref. Fish Res.; EMBASE; Index Med.; Life Sci. Collect.; PESTDOC; Ref. Upd. Basic Ed.; Ref. Upd. Deluxe Ed.; Res. Alert [Full Cov.]; Sci. Cit. Index; SCISEARCH; Soc. Sci. Cit. Index [Select. Cov.].

US/0097-0549
**NEUROSCIENCE AND BEHAVIORAL PHYSIOLOGY.** **See** Biology-Physiology.

US/0149-7634
**NEUROSCIENCE AND BIOBEHAVIORAL REVIEWS.** [Neurosci. biobehav. rev.]. **VFOAT** Neuroscience & Biobehavioral Reviews. Vol. 2 (Spring 1978)-. Academic Scholarly Publication. English. qt. $552.00 The Americas; £370.00 other. Pergamon Press, An Imprint of Elsevier Science Ltd., The Boulevard, Langford Lane, Kidlington, Oxford OX5 1GB United Kingdom. **Tel** 011 44 865 843000, 011 44 865 843699, FAX 011 44 865 843010. **(Subscription address:** Elsevier Science Ltd. Oxford Fulfillment Centre, PO Box 800, Kidlington, Oxford OX5 1DX United Kingdom.**)** **ED** Matthew J. Wayner. **LC** QP360; .B55. **DD** 599/.01/88. **NLM** W1 NE342PB. **CODEN** NBREDE. **[CCC]. Bk Rev. Ad Acc. Pr Rev.** ctrl circ. available on microfilm and microfiche from University Microfilms International (UMI). Documents available from The Genuine Article, BIOSIS Document Express, CASDDS. ***Continues*** *Biobehavioral Reviews, 0147-7552.*
**Desc:** Publishes original reviews in anatomy, biochemistry, embryology, endocrinology, genetics, pharmacology, physiology, and all aspects of biological sciences when relevant to problems of the nervous system or the investigation of behavior is clearly established.
**Ind/Abst** Anim. Behav. Abstr.; Biol. Abstr.; Chem. Abstr.; CSA Neuro. Abstr.; Curr. Aware. Biol. Sci., CABS; Curr. Contents Life Sci.; EMBASE; Index Med.; Index Sci. Rev. [Full Cov.]; Nutr. Res. Newsl.; Life Sci. Collect.; Psychol. Abstr. (1978-); PsycINFO; PsycLit; Ref. Upd. Deluxe Ed.; Res. Alert [Full Cov.]; Sci. Cit. Index; SCISEARCH; Soc. Sci. Cit. Index [Select. Cov.].

US/1057-6096
**NEUROSCIENCE CITATION INDEX.** (NEUROSCIENCE CITATION INDEX [COMPUTER FILE].). [Neurosci. cit. index]. **Added/Corp** Institute for Scientific Information. (July-Aug. 1991)-. English. bm. $1469.00. Institute for Scientific Information, 3501 Market Street, Philadelphia PA 19104. **Tel** (215)386-0100, (800)523-1850, FAX (215)386-6362, telex 84-5305. **(Subscription address:** Institute for Scientific Information, PO Box 71416, Chicago IL 60694.**)** **DD** 016.

US/1056-7186
**NEUROSCIENCE FACTS.** (NEUROSCIENCE FACTS / FIDIA RESEARCH FOUNDATION.). [Neurosci. facts]. **Added/Corp** Fidia Research Foundation. Vol. 1, No. 1 (Thursday, 13 Sept. 1990)-. Periodical. English. bw. Fidia Research Foundation, 1640 Wisconsin Ave. NW, Suite 3, Washington DC 20007. **DD** 574.

NE/0304-3940
**NEUROSCIENCE LETTERS.** [Neurosci. lett.]. Vol. 1 (July 1975)-. Academic Scholarly Publication. English. Thirty-eight times a year (19 volumes). $3090.00. Elsevier Science Ireland Ltd., Bay 15, Shannon Industrial Estate, Co Clare Ireland. **Tel** 011 353 61 471944. **ED** M. Zimmermann. **LC** QP351; .N432. **DD** 599.01/88. **NLM** W1 NE342S. **CODEN** NELED5. **[CCC].** Index available. **Ad Acc. Pr Rev.** available on microfilm and microfiche from University Microfilms International (UMI). Documents available from The Genuine Article, BIOSIS Document Express, CASDDS, ADONIS.
**Desc:** Provides rapid publication of short, complete reports, but not preliminary communications, in all areas in the fields of neuroanatomy, neuroendocrinology, neurophysiology, neurochemistry, neuropharmacology, neurotoxicology, molecular neurobiology, behavioural sciences, biocybernetics and and clinical neurobiology.
**Ind/Abst** ADONIS; Biol. Abstr.; Calcium Calcif. Tissue Abstr.; Chem. Abstr.; Chemorecept. Abstr.; CSA Neuro. Abstr.; Curr. Contents Life Sci.; Curr. Ref. Fish Res.; EMBASE; Index Med.; Oncog. Growth Factors Abstr.; Life Sci. Collect.; Ref. Upd. Basic Ed.; Ref. Upd. Deluxe Ed.; Res. Alert [Full Cov.]; Rev. Agric. Entomol.; Rev. Med. Vet. Entomol.; Sci. Cit. Index; SCISEARCH; Soc. Sci. Cit. Index [Select. Cov.]; Toxicol. Abstr. (19??-19??).

IE/0167-6253
**NEUROSCIENCE LETTERS. SUPPLEMENT.** [Neurosci. lett., Suppl.]. Vol. 1 (1978)-. Monographic series. English. ir. Price varies per volume. Elsevier Science Ireland Ltd., Bay 15, Shannon Industrial Estate, Co Clare Ireland. **Tel** 011 353 61 471944. **NLM** W1 NE342SA. **CODEN** NLSUE2. Documents available from BIOSIS Document Express.
**Ind/Abst** Biol. Abstr. (1985-); Index Med.

●US/1064-8712
**NEUROSCIENCE NEWSLETTER (COLLEGE STATION, TEX.).** (NEUROSCIENCE NEWSLETTER / COLLEGE OF MEDICINE, TEXAS A&M UNIVERSITY HEALTH SCIENCE CENTER.). [Neurosci. newsl.]. **Added/Corp** Texas A & M University. College of Medicine. Texas A & M University Health Science Center. Vol. 1, No. 1 (Mar. 1992)-. Newsletter. English. mo. $15.00. Neuroscience Newsletter, College of Medicine, Texas A&M University, College Station TX 77843-1114. **DD** 616.

IE/0168-0102
**NEUROSCIENCE RESEARCH.** [Neurosci. res.]. **Added/Corp** Nihon Shinkei Kagaku Kyokai. **VFOAT** Shinkei Kagaku. Vol. 1, No. 1 (Feb. 1984)-. Academic Scholarly Publication. English. Twelve times a year (3 vols.). $634.00. Elsevier Science Ireland Ltd., Bay 15, Shannon Industrial Estate, Co Clare Ireland. **Tel** 011 353

61 471944. **ED** M. Ito. **LC** RC337; .N48. **NLM** W1; NE342T. **CODEN** NERADN. **[CCC].** Index available. **Ad Acc. Pr Rev.** available on microfilm and microfiche from University Microfilms International (UMI). Documents available from The Genuine Article, BIOSIS Document Express, CASDDS.
**Desc:** Covers the entire field of neuroscience, from the molecular to behavioural levels.
**Ind/Abst** Biol. Abstr.; Chem. Abstr. (1984-); Curr. Aware. Biol. Sci., CABS; Curr. Contents Life Sci.; EMBASE; Index Med. (1984-); Life Sci. Collect.; PESTDOC; Psychol. Abstr.; PsycINFO; PsycLit; Ref. Upd. Deluxe Ed.; Res. Alert [Full Cov.]; Rev. Med. Vet. Entomol.; Sci. Cit. Index; SCISEARCH; Soc. Sci. Cit. Index [Select. Cov.].

UK/0893-6609
**NEUROSCIENCE RESEARCH COMMUNICATIONS.** [Neurosci. res. commun.]. Vol. 1 No. 1 (July/Aug. 1987)-. Academic Scholarly Publication. English. bm. $425.00. John Wiley & Sons Ltd., Baffins Lane, Chichester West Sussex PO19 1UD England. **Tel** 0243 779777, FAX 0243 776128 BTG:JWP001, telex 86290 WIBOOKG. **(Subscription address:** John Wiley / Philadelphia, PO Box 7247, Philadelphia PA 19170.) **ED** W. H. Gispen. **LC** RC346; .N457. **DD** 616.8/05. **NLM** W1; NE342TB. **CODEN** NRCOEE. **[CCC]. Pr Rev.** available on microfilm and microfiche from University Microfilms International (UMI). Documents available from The Genuine Article, BIOSIS Document Express, CASDDS.
**Desc:** Publishes important and original contributions to the neurosciences, the journal is international and multidisciplinary. It comprises short papers, selected mini-reviews and timely comments by leading authorities on current topics.
**Ind/Abst** Biol. Abstr. (1990-); Chem. Abstr.; CSA Neuro. Abstr.; Curr. Aware. Biol. Sci.; CABS; Curr. Contents Life Sci.; EMBASE; Ref. Upd. Deluxe Ed.; Res. Alert [Full Cov.]; Rev. Agric. Entomol.; Sci. Cit. Index; SCISEARCH; Soc. Sci. Cit. Index [Select. Cov.].

IE/0921-8696
**NEUROSCIENCE RESEARCH. SUPPLEMENT.** [Neurosci. res., Suppl.]. **Added/Corp** Nihon Shinkei Kagaku Kyokai. (1985)-. Monographic series. English. ir. Price varies per volume. Elsevier Science Ireland Ltd., Bay 15, Shannon Industrial Estate, Co Clare Ireland. **Tel** 011 353 61 471944. **LC** RC321; .N481. **NLM** W1; NE342TA. **CODEN** NRSUEA. Documents available from BIOSIS Document Express.
**Ind/Abst** Biol. Abstr. (1990-).

JA/0388-7448
**NEUROSCIENCES (KOBE. 1975).** (NO KENKYUKAI KAISHI. JAPANESE JOURNAL OF THE NEUROSCIENCES RESEARCH ASSOCIATION.). [Neurosciences]. **Added/Corp** No Kenkyukai. **VFOAT** Japanese Journal of the Neurosciences Research Association; Neurosciences. Maki 1 (Nigatsu 1975)-. Academic Scholarly Publication. Japanese. Nihon No Kenkyukai, (Japan Neurosciences Research Assoc.), Okayama Daigaku Igakubu No, Taisha Kenkyu Shisetsu Kino, Seikagaku Bumon, 5-1, Shikatacho, 2 Chome, Okayamashi, Okayamaken 700 Japan. **NLM** W1 NO101CS. **CODEN** NUOCDO. Documents available from The Genuine Article, CASDDS.
**Ind/Abst** Chem. Abstr.; Res. Alert.

US/0148-396X
**NEUROSURGERY.** See Medical Science and Technology-Surgery.

US/1042-3680
**NEUROSURGERY CLINICS OF NORTH AMERICA.** See Medical Science and Technology-Surgery.

US/1050-6438
**NEUROSURGERY QUARTERLY.** See Medical Science and Technology-Surgery.

US/1045-6694
**NEUROSURGICAL CONSULTATIONS.** ***Ceased.*** [Neurosurg. consult.]. Vol. 1, Issue 1 (1990)-Vol. 4, No. 26 (1994). Periodical. English. bw. Williams & Wilkins Company, 428 East Preston Street, Baltimore MD 21202-3993. **Tel** (410)528-4000, (800)638-6423, FAX (410)528-8596, telex 87669. **DD** 617. **NLM** W1; NE343V. **[CCC].** Documents available from Quick Copies.
**Desc:** This 26-week series provides an ongoing forum for professional dialogue on current modes of diagnosis and treatment.

US/1051-1490
**NEUROSURGICAL OPERATIVE ATLAS.** See Medical Science and Technology-Surgery.

US/0892-0362
**NEUROTOXICOLOGY AND TERATOLOGY.** [Neurotoxicol. teratol.]. **Added/Corp** Behavioral Toxicology Society. Neurobehavioral Teratology Society. **VFOAT** Neurotoxicology & Teratology. Vol. 9, No. 1 (Jan./Feb. 1987)-. Academic Scholarly Publication. English. bm. $634.00 The Americas; £425.00 other. Pergamon Press, An Imprint of Elsevier Science Ltd., The Boulevard, Langford Lane, Kidlington, Oxford OX5 1GB United Kingdom. **Tel** 011 44 865 843000, 011 44 865 843699, FAX 011 44 865 843010. **(Subscription address:** Elsevier Science Ltd. Oxford Fulfillment Centre, PO Box 800, Kidlington, Oxford OX5 1DX United Kingdom.) **ED** Donald Hutchings. **DD** 616. **NLM** W1; NE3494HI. **CODEN** NETEEC. **[CCC].** available on microfilm and microfiche from University Microfilms International (UMI). Documents available from The Genuine Article, BIOSIS Document Express, CASDDS, Documents on Demand, ADONIS. ***Continues*** *Neurobehavioral Toxicology and Teratology, 0275-1380.*
**Desc:** Emphasizing the nervous system and behavior, this journal publishes original reports of studies in the areas of neural toxicology and teratology.
**Ind/Abst** ADONIS; Biol. Abstr. (Jan./Feb. 1987-); Chem. Abstr. (Jan./Feb. 1987-); CSA Neuro. Abstr.; Curr. Aware. Biol. Sci., CABS; Curr. Contents Life Sci. (1987-); Dairy Sci. Abstr.; Dev. Med. Child Neurol.; EMBASE; Environ. Abstr.; Health Saf. Sci. Abstr.; Index Med. (1987-); Index Vet.; Nutr. Abstr. Rev., Ser. A, Hum. Exp.; Life Sci. Collect. (Jan./Feb. 1987-); Pollut. Abstr. Indexes; Psychol. Abstr. (Jan./Feb. 1987-); PsycINFO (1990-); PsycLit; Res. Alert [Full Cov.]; Rev. Agric. Entomol.; Rev. Med. Vet. Entomol.; Rev. Med. Vet. Mycology; Risk Abstr.; Sci. Cit. Index (Jan./Feb. 1987-); SCISEARCH; Soc. Sci. Cit. Index [Select. Cov.]; Toxicol. Abstr.

US/0161-813X
**NEUROTOXICOLOGY (PARK FOREST SOUTH).** (NEUROTOXICOLOGY.). [Neurotoxicology]. **VFOAT** Neuro Toxicology. Vol. 1 (1979)-. Academic Scholarly Publication. English (Japanese and Russian). Four times a year. $129.00 (institutions), $59.00 (individuals) US; add $26.00 postage other. Intox Press Publishers, PO Box 24865, Little Rock AR 72221-4865. **Tel** (501)227-8622, FAX (501)224-1947. **ED** Joan M. Cranmer, Department of Pediatrics, #512, UAMS/Arkansas Children's Hospital, 800 Marshall-South Campus 207, Little Rock, AR 72202; Telephone: (501)320-2986, Fax: (501)320-3947. **LC** RC321; .N437. **DD** 616.8. **NLM** W1 NE3494HB. **CODEN** NRTXDN. Index available in last issue of volume--attached. cum. index. **Bk Rev. Ad Acc. Pr Rev. Circ:** 1,000 (ctrl). Documents available from The Genuine Article, BIOSIS Document Express, CASDDS, Documents on Demand.
**Desc:** Covers all aspects of the effects of toxic substance on the nervous system of man and animals.
**Ind/Abst** AGRICOLA [Select. Cov.]; Biol. Abstr.; Biol. Dig.; Chem. Abstr.; CSA Neuro. Abstr. (?-?); Curr. Aware. Biol. Sci., CABS; EMBASE; Environ. Abstr.; Index Med.; Nutr. Res. Newsl.; Life Sci. Collect.; Ref. Upd. Deluxe Ed.; Res. Alert [Full Cov.]; Sci. Cit. Index; SCISEARCH.

US/0733-2467
**NEUROUROL. URODYN.** (NEUROUROLOGY AND URODYNAMICS.). (1982)-. Academic Scholarly Publication. English. bm. $486.00 US; $546.00 Canada and Mexico; $568.00 other. John Wiley & Sons, Inc., 605 Third Avenue, New York NY 10158-0012. **Tel** (212)850-6000, (212)850-6645, FAX (212)850-6088, telex 12-7063. **(Subscription address:** John Wiley & Sons / England, Baffins Lane, Chichester, West Sussex PO19 1UD England.) **ED** Jerry G. Blaivas. **NLM** W1 NE3495M. **[CCC]. Pr Rev.** Documents available from The Genuine Article, CASDDS.
**Desc:** Provides multidisciplinary coverage of recent developments in the study of the urinary tract function.
**Ind/Abst** Chem. Abstr.; Curr. Contents Clin. Med.; EMBASE; Life Sci. Collect.; Res. Alert [Select. Cov.]; SCISEARCH.

FR
**NEVRAXE : REVUE DE NEUROLOGIE.** (19??)-. French. qt. 489.72F France; 600.00F other. Edimedica, 146 Boulevard Voltaire, 92600 Asnieres France. **Tel** 011 33 1 47935603.

BU/0548-3794
**NEVROLOGIJA, PSIHIATRIJA I NEVROHIRURGIJA.** (NEVROLOGIIA, PSIKHIATRIIA I NEVROKHIRURGIIA.). [Nevrol. psihiatr. nevrohir.]. **Added/Corp** Bulgaria. Ministerstvo na Narodnoto Zdrave i Sotsialnite Grizhi. (1964)-. Periodical. Bulgarian (summaries and/or abstracts in English and Russian). bm (6 issues). $7.00. Medicina i Fizkultura, 11 Slaveikov Square, 1000 Sofia Bulgaria. **Tel** 879111. **ED** V. Ivanov. **NLM** W1 NE352B. **CODEN** NPNMAB. **Circ:** 1,360. Documents available from CASDDS. ***Continues*** *Nevrologiia i Psikhiatriia.*
**Ind/Abst** Chem. Abstr.; EMBASE [Select. Cov.].

IT/0393-5345
**NEW TRENDS IN CLINICAL NEUROPHARMACOLOGY : OFFICIAL JOURNAL OF THE EUROPEAN ASSOCIATION FOR CLINICAL NEUROPHARMACOLOGY. Added/Corp** European Association for Clinical Neuropharmacology. Vol. 1, No. 1 (Jan./March 1987)-. Periodical. English. qt. $80.00. CIC Edizioni Internazionali, Via L Spallanzani 11, 00161 Rome Italy. **Tel** 011 39 6 841-2673, FAX 011 39 6 844-3365, telex 622099 CIC I. **ED** A. Agnoli. **NLM** W1; NE513EE. **CODEN** NTCNEP. **Ad Acc.**
**Ind/Abst** EMBASE.

US/8750-0728
**NEWSLETTER (SPINAL CORD SOCIETY (U.S.)).** (NEWSLETTER / SPINAL CORD SOCIETY.). [Newsl. - Spinal Cord Soc. (U.S.)]. **Added/Corp** Spinal Cord Society (U.S.). **VFOAT** SPC. (19??)-. Newsletter. English. mo. comes with membership. Spinal Cord Society, RR 5 Box 22A, Fergus Falls MN 56537. **Tel** (218)739-5252. **ED** Chas Carson. ***Continues*** *Spinal Cord Society, 0279-1137.*

II
**NIMHANS JOURNAL.** See Medical Science and Technology-Psychiatry.

US
**NINCDS NEUROMUSCULAR DISORDERS RESEARCH PROGRAM, THE. Main/Corp** National Institute of Neurological and Communicative Disorders and Stroke. **VAT** National Institute of Neurological and Communicative Disorders and Stroke Neuromuscular Disorders Research Program. (19??)-. Periodical. English. an. US Department of Health and Human Services National Institutes of Health, 9000 Rockville Pike, Bethesda MD 20892. **Tel** (301)496-9291, FAX (301)496-2443. ***Continues*** *NINCDS Muscular Dystrophy and the Neuromuscular Disorders Research Program, 0161-3057.*

US
**NINCDS RESEARCH PROGRAM. EPILEPSY, THE. Main/Corp** National Institute of Neurological and Communicative Disorders and Stroke. **VFOAT** Epilepsy. **VAT** National Institute of Neurological and Communicative Disorders and Stroke Research Program. Epilepsy. 1980-. English. an. National Institute of Neurological and Communicative Disorders and Stroke, National Institutes of Health, 9000 Rockville Pike, Bethesda MD 20014. ***Continues*** *NINCDS Epilepsy Research Program, 0161-3014.*

US/0888-8035
**NINCDS RESEARCH PROGRAM. MULTIPLE SCLEROSIS, THE.** [NINCDS res. program, Mult. scler.]. **VFOAT** Multiple Sclerosis. **VAT** National Institute of Neurological and Communicative Disorders and Stroke Research Program. Multiple Sclerosis. Began with 1980. English. an. National Institutes of Health, 9000 Rockville Pike, Bethesda MD 20014. **Tel** (301)496-6975. **DD** 616. **NLM** W2; A N2052NL. ***Continues*** *NINCDS Multiple Sclerosis Research Program, 0161-3030.*

US
**NINCDS RESEARCH PROGRAM. MUSCULAR DYSTROPHY AND OTHER NEUROMUSCULAR DISORDERS, THE. Main/Corp** National Institute of Neurological and Communicative Disorders and Stroke. **VFOAT** Muscular Dystrophy and Other Neuromuscular Disorders. **VAT** National Institute of Neurological and Communicative Disorders and Stroke Research Program. Muscular Dystrophy and Other Neuromuscular Disorders. (1980)-. English. an. National Institute of Neurological and Communicative Disorders and Stroke, National Institutes of Health, 9000 Rockville Pike, Bethesda MD 20014. ***Continues*** *NINCDS Muscular Dystrophy and the Neuromuscular Disorders Research Program, 0161-3057.*

US/0892-7863
**NINCDS RESEARCH PROGRAM. STROKE, THE.** [NINCDS res. program, Stroke]. **VFOAT** Stroke. **VAT** National Institute of Neurological and Communicative Disorders and Stroke Research Program. Stroke. Began with 1980. English. an. National Institutes of Health, 9000 Rockville Pike, Bethesda MD 20014. **Tel** (301)496-6975. **DD** 616. **NLM** W2; A N2052nt. ***Continues*** *NINCDS Stroke Research Program, 0161-3006.*

US/1012-9871
**NINS. NEW ISSUES IN NEUROSCIENCES.** ***Ceased.*** [NINS, New issues neurosci.]. **VFOAT** New Issues in Neurosciences. (1988)-Vol. 4 (1992). Periodical. English. Three times a year. Thieme Medical Publishers Inc., 381 Park Avenue South, Suite 1201, New York NY 10016. **Tel** (212)683-5088, (212)683-5089, FAX (212)779-9020, telex 220 862 TSINC UR. **ED** A Bignami, C L Bolis, R S J Frackowiak, H Hippius, J Kimura, U Lindblom, P J Magistretti, G Serratrice and PK Thomas.
**Desc:** Provides perspectives on particular neurological diseases or topics in light of new advances in neuroscience. Each issue is devoted to a special topic with an emphasis on the correlation between research and practical applications in the interest of clinical neurologists and other medical practitioners.

JA/0301-2603
**NO SHINKEI GEKA.** [No shinkei geka]. **VFOAT** Neurological Surgery. (1973)-. Academic Scholarly Publication. Japanese (summaries and/or abstracts in English; table of contents in English). mo. $375.00. Igaku Shoin Ltd., 5-24-3 Hongo Bunkyo-ku, Tokyo 113 Japan. **Tel** 011 81 3 817 5670. **(Subscription address:** Maruzen Company Ltd., PO Box 5050, Import & Export Department, Tokyo 100 31 Japan.) **NLM** W1 NO101G.

**CODEN** NOKGB6. Documents available from BIOSIS Document Express, CASDDS.
**Ind/Abst** Biol. Abstr.; Chem. Abstr.; EMBASE; Index Med.

JA/0006-8969
**NO TO SHINKEI.** (BRAIN AND NERVE. NO TO SHINKEI.). [No To Shinkei]. **VFOAT** No To Shinkei. Vol. 1 (Nov. 1948)-. Academic Scholarly Publication. English (Japanese). mo. ¥28320. Igaku Shoin Ltd., 5-24-3 Hongo Bunkyo-ku, Tokyo 113 Japan. **Tel** 011 81 3 817 5670. **NLM** W1 NO102K. **CODEN** BRNED8. **Bk Rev. Ad Acc. Circ:** 5,000. Documents available from The Genuine Article, BIOSIS Document Express, CASDDS.
**Desc:** Devoted to the publication of work relating primarily to neurology, including studies in clinical neurophysiology, organic neurology, neuroradiology, and neuropathology.
**Ind/Abst** Biol. Abstr.; Chem. Abstr.; EMBASE; Index Med.; Res. Alert [Full Cov.].

IT
**NUOVA RIVISTA DI NEUROLOGIA.** **VFOAT** Rivista di Neurologia. Vol. 61, No. 1 (Jan/Feb 1991)-. Periodical. Italian (English). Six times a year. L140000 (institution); L80000 (individual). Il Pensiero Scientifico Editore s.r.l., Via Bradano 3C, 00199 Rome Italy. **Tel** 011 39 6 86207158, 86207159, 86207168, 86207169, FAX 011 39 6 86207160. **ED** V. Floris. **NLM** W1; NU373E. **CODEN** NRNUEJ. **Bk Rev. Ad Acc, Adv Mgr:** Dott Dalla, **Tel** 06-49914735. Full Page (B&W) L1.650.000. **Circ:** 1,200. Documents available from BIOSIS Document Express. ***Continues*** *Rivista di Neurologia, 0035-6344.*
**Ind/Abst** Biol. Abstr. (1991-); Index Med. (1991-).

US/0149-2667
**NUTRITION AND THE BRAIN. See** Nutrition and Dietetics.

SZ/0255-3910
**PAIN AND HEADACHE.** [Pain headache]. Vol. 7 (1985)-. Academic Scholarly Publication. English. an. 200.00F (approx. per volume). S. Karger AG, Allschwilerstrasse 10, PO Box - Postfach - Case Postale, CH-4009 Basel Switzerland. **Tel** 011 41 61 306-1111, FAX 011 41 61 306-1234, telex CH 962 652. **ED** P. L. Gildenberg. **NLM** W1; PA293. **[CCC].** Documents available from BIOSIS Document Express, CASDDS. ***Continues*** *Research and Clinical Studies in Headache, 0080-1453.*
**Desc:** This series brings information on the latest advances in pain research and treatment to the attention of researchers, specialists in neurology and related fields, internists and general practitioners. Volumes are a mix of original research, new approaches to therapy, clinical studies, and laboratory experimentation.
**Ind/Abst** Biol. Abstr.; Chem. Abstr. (1985-); Index Med. (1985-1989); Ref. Upd. Deluxe Ed.

FR/1146-562X
**PASCAL. E 78, NEUROLOGIE. VFOAT** PASCAL. E 78, Neurology; PASCAL. E Soixante-Dix-Huit, Neurologie. (1990)-. Periodical. Multiple languages. Eleven times a year. 1750.00F France; 1855.00F other. CNRS / Institut d'Information Scientifique et Technique, (Centre National de la Recherche Scientifique), 15 Quai Anatole France, Paris 75700 France. **Tel** 011 33 1 47531515, telex 299 356 F. **(Subscription address:** Institut d'Information Scientifique et Technique Diffusion, 2 Allee du Parc de Brabois, 54514 Vandoeuvre Nancy France.**) UDC** 011.

FR/1146-5670
**PASCAL. E 83, ANESTHESIE ET REANIMATION.** (ANESTHESIE & REANIMATION (E83).). **VFOAT** PASCAL. E 83, Anesthesiology and Resuscitation; PASCAL. E Quatre-Vingt-Trois, Anesthesie et Reanimation. (1990)-. Periodical. French. Eleven times a year. 1085.00F France; 1155.00F other. CNRS / Institut d'Information Scientifique et Technique, (Centre National de la Recherche Scientifique), 15 Quai Anatole France, Paris 75700 France. **Tel** 011 33 1 47531515, telex 299 356 F. **UDC** 011/016. cum. index.

US/0887-8994
**PEDIATRIC NEUROLOGY. See** Medical Science and Technology-Pediatrics.

SZ/1016-2291
**PEDIATRIC NEUROSURGERY. See** Medical Science and Technology-Pediatrics.

US/1045-3733
**PERSPECTIVES IN NEUROLOGICAL SURGERY. See** Medical Science and Technology-Surgery.

SP
**PHRONESIS. REVISTA DE NEUROLOGIA, NEUROCIRUGIA Y PSIQUIATRIA.** (1972)-. Periodical. Spanish.
**Ind/Abst** Indice Med. Esp.

FR/0292-9651
**PRATIQUES CORPORELLES.** (PRATIQUES CORPORELLES : BULLETIN DE LA SFERPM.). [Prat. corp.]. **Added/Corp** Societe Francaise d'Education et de Reeducation Psychomotrice. No. 48-49 (Nov. 1980)-. Bulletin. French. qt. 240.00F (institutions), 190.00F (individuals) France; 300.00F (institutions), 240.00F (individuals) other. Societe Francaise d'Education et de Reeducation Psychomotrice, Les Aires Causses et Veyran, 34490 Murviel / Beziers France. **Tel** 011 33 67 895454. **NLM** W1; PR304. ***Continues*** *Bulletin de la SFERPM, 0223-3282.*

NE/0069-5769
**PROCEEDINGS - INTERNATIONAL CONGRESS OF NEURO-PSYCHOPHARMACOLOGY.** **Main/Corp** International Congress of Neuro-Psychopharmacology. 1st- 1958-. Proceedings. English (French, German and Italian). International Congress of Neuro-Psychopharmacology, Elsevier Publishing Company, PO Box 211, 1000 AE Amsterdam Netherlands. **LC** RC327. **DD** 615.780631.

NE/0079-6123
**PROGRESS IN BRAIN RESEARCH.** [Prog. brain res.]. Vol. 1 (1963)-. Academic Scholarly Publication. English. ir. Price varies per volume. Elsevier Science Publishers BV, PO Box 211, 1000 AE Amsterdam Netherlands. **Tel** 011 31 20 5803642, FAX 011 31 20 5862696, telex 15682. **LC** QP376; .P96. **NLM** W1 PR667J. **CODEN** PBRRA4. **[CCC]. Pr Rev.** Documents available from The Genuine Article, BIOSIS Document Express, CASDDS.
**Ind/Abst** Biol. Abstr.; Chem. Abstr.; CSA Neuro. Abstr. (?-?); EMBASE; Index Med.; Index Sci. Rev. [Full Cov.]; Life Sci. Collect.; Res. Alert [Full Cov.]; Sci. Cit. Index; SCISEARCH; Soc. Sci. Cit. Index [Select. Cov.].

SZ/0378-4045
**PROGRESS IN CLINICAL NEUROPHYSIOLOGY.** ***Ceased.*** [Prog. clin. neurophysiol.]. Vol. 1 (1977)-?. Academic Scholarly Publication. English. S. Karger AG, Allschwilerstrasse 10, PO Box - Postfach - Case Postale, CH-4009 Basel Switzerland. **Tel** 011 41 61 306-1111, FAX 011 41 61 306-1234, telex CH 962 652. **ED** J E Desmedt. **NLM** WL 102 P963. **CODEN** PCNEDN. **[CCC].** Documents available from BIOSIS Document Express, CASDDS.
**Desc:** Volumes covering one of the most promising areas now under study in the neurological sciences.
**Ind/Abst** Biol. Abstr.; Chem. Abstr. (-1983).

UK/0262-6330
**PROGRESS IN MIGRAINE RESEARCH.** [Progr. migraine res.]. 1-. Academic Scholarly Publication. English. Price varies per volume. **NLM** W1 PR6718. **CODEN** PMIRD5. Documents available from CASDDS.
**Ind/Abst** Chem. Abstr.

UK/0301-0082
**PROGRESS IN NEUROBIOLOGY.** [Prog. neurobiol.]. Vol. 1 (1973)-. English. Eighteen times a year. $1267.00 The Americas; £850.00 other. Pergamon Press, An Imprint of Elsevier Science Ltd., The Boulevard, Langford Lane, Kidlington, Oxford OX5 1GB United Kingdom. **Tel** 011 44 865 843000, 011 44 865 843699, FAX 011 44 865 843010. **(Subscription address:** Elsevier Science Ltd. Oxford Fulfillment Centre, PO Box 800, Kidlington, Oxford OX5 1DX United Kingdom.**) ED** G. A. Kerkut. **LC** QP356; .P73. **DD** 612/.8/05. **NLM** W1 PR672K. **CODEN** PGNBA5PNNEA. **[CCC]. Pr Rev.** available on microfilm and microfiche from University Microfilms International (UMI). Documents available from The Genuine Article, BIOSIS Document Express, CASDDS, ADONIS.
**Desc:** Helps scientists keep abreast of advances in knowledge in the field of neurosciences.
**Ind/Abst** ADONIS; Biol. Abstr.; Chem. Abstr.; CSA Neuro. Abstr.; Curr. Contents Life Sci.; EMBASE; Fish Rev. (Jan. 1989-July 1992); Index Med.; Index Sci. Rev. [Full Cov.]; Life Sci. Collect.; Ref. Upd. Basic Ed.; Ref. Upd. Deluxe Ed.; Res. Alert [Full Cov.]; Sci. Cit. Index; SCISEARCH; Wildl. Rev. (Jan. 1989-July 1992).

US/0099-9016
**PROGRESS IN NEUROPATHOLOGY.** [Prog. neuropathol.]. (1971)-. Monographic series. English. ir. Price varies per volume. Raven Press, 1185 Avenue of the Americas, 37th Floor, New York NY 10036. **Tel** (212)930-9500, (212)930-9604, FAX (212)869-3495, (212)302-8507, telex 640073. **ED** Harry M. Zimmerman. **LC** RC347; .P762. **DD** 616.8/047. **NLM** W1 PR674K. **CODEN** PRNPAM. Documents available from BIOSIS Document Express, CASDDS.
**Ind/Abst** Biol. Abstr.; Chem. Abstr.

JA/0033-2658
**PSYCHIATRIA ET NEUROLOGIA JAPONICA. See** Medical Science and Technology-Psychiatry.

GW
**PSYCHIATRIE, NEUROLOGIE UND MEDIZINISCHE PSYCHOLOGIE. BEIHEFTE. See** Medical Science and Technology-Psychiatry.

●US/1058-6660
**PSYCSCAN. NEUROPSYCHOLOGY. See** Psychology-Abstracting, Bibliographies and Statistics.

IT
**QUADERNI DI NEUROPATOLOGIA.** Centro Scientifico Torinese, Via Borgone 57, 10139 Turin Italy. **Tel** 011 39 11 331493.

SZ
**RECENT ACHIEVEMENTS IN RESTORATIVE NEUROLOGY. Added/Corp** Institute for Rehabilitation and Research (Houston, Tex.). Dept. of Clinical Neurophysiology. Baylor College of Medicine. Dept. of Rehabilitation. Vivian L. Smith Foundation for Restorative Neurology. (1985)-. Academic Scholarly Publication. English. an. 250.00F (approx. per volume). S. Karger AG, Allschwilerstrasse 10, PO Box - Postfach - Case Postale, CH-4009 Basel Switzerland. **Tel** 011 41 61 306-1111, FAX 011 41 61 306-1234, telex CH 962 652. **ED** M. R. Dimitrijevic. **NLM** W1; RE105PM. **CODEN** RARNEB. Documents available from BIOSIS Document Express, CASDDS.
**Desc:** The purpose of this series is to review achievements in restorative procedures that could modify impaired functions in chronic neurological disorders and facilitate the use of these procedures. It also aims to further the development of clinical neurophysiological techniques essential for the selection of patients and the evaluation of therapeutic procedures. In addition, the volumes will review the latest advances in related neurosciences, evaluate their possible application to clinical problems, and consider how neuroscientists can contribute to still unsolved clinical problems.
**Ind/Abst** Biol. Abstr. (1985-); Chem. Abstr. (1985-); Ref. Upd. Deluxe Ed.

UK/0307-7403
**RECENT ADVANCES IN CLINICAL NEUROLOGY.** (1975)-. Periodical. English. ir (every 3-5 years). $59.00. Churchill Livingstone, 1-3 Baxter's Place, Leith Walk, Edinburgh EH1 3AF Scotland. **Tel** 011 44 31 556 2424, FAX 011 44 31 558 1278, telex 727511. **(Subscription address:** US/ Churchill Livingstone, Fulfillment Office, PO Box 11318, Birmingham, AL 35202**) ED** W.B. Matthews. **NLM** W1 RE105T. ***Supersedes*** *Recent Advances in Neurology and Neuropsychiatry.*

UK/0264-7400
**RECENT ADVANCES IN EPILEPSY.** No. 1-. Periodical. English. Churchill Livingstone, 1-3 Baxter's Place, Leith Walk, Edinburgh EH1 3AF Scotland. **Tel** 011 44 31 556 2424, FAX 011 44 31 558 1278, telex 727511. **(Subscription address:** US/ Churchill Livingstone, Fulfillment Office, PO Box 11318, Birmingham, AL 35202**) ED** Timothy A Pedley and Brian S Meldrum. **LC** RC372.A1; R43. **DD** 616.8/53. **NLM** W1 RE105ULAH.

UK/0144-0535
**RECENT ADVANCES IN NEUROPATHOLOGY.** [Recent adv. neuropathol.]. No. 1 (1979)-. Academic Scholarly Publication. English. Churchill Livingstone, 1-3 Baxter's Place, Leith Walk, Edinburgh EH1 3AF Scotland. **Tel** 011 44 31 556 2424, FAX 011 44 31 558 1278, telex 727511. **ED** W T Smith and J B Cavanagh. **NLM** W1 RE105VH. **CODEN** RADND8. Documents available from CASDDS.
**Ind/Abst** Chem. Abstr.

HU/0079-9955
**RECENT DEVELOPMENTS OF NEUROBIOLOGY IN HUNGARY.** [Recent dev. neurobiol. Hung.]. **Added/Corp** Akademiai Kiado. (1967)-. Academic Scholarly Publication. English. ir. Price varies per volume. Vieweg Publishing, PO Box 5829, D 65048 Wiesbaden Germany. **Tel** 011 49 611 160230, FAX 011 49 611 160229. **LC** RC346; .R4. **DD** 616.8,05. **NLM** W1 RE106B. **CODEN** RDNHAO. Documents available from BIOSIS Document Express, CASDDS.
**Ind/Abst** Biol. Abstr. (-1983); Chem. Abstr. (1967-1982).

US
**REPORT OF THE ADVISORY PANEL ON ALZHEIMER'S DISEASE. Main/Corp** Advisory Panel on Alzheimer's Disease (U.S.). English. an. US Department of Health and Human Services, 200 Independence Avenue Southwest, Washington DC 20201. **LC** RC523; .A344A. **DD** 362.1/96831/00973. **NLM** W2; A D218a.

US/0277-3090
**RESEARCH GRANTS, TRAINING AWARDS, SUMMARY TABLES.** (RESEARCH GRANTS, TRAINING AWARDS ... SUMMARY TABLES / NATIONAL INSTITUTE OF NEUROLOGICAL AND COMMUNICATIVE DISORDERS AND STROKE.). [Res. grants, train. awards, summ. tables]. **VFOAT** Research Grants, Training Awards, Fellowship Awards. FY 1980-. English. an. Office of Data Analysis and Reports, NINCDS Extramural Activities Program, National Institute of Neurological and Communicative Disorders and Stroke, National Institutes of Health, Bethesda MD 20205. **LC** RC321; .R374. **DD** 616.8/0072073. available on microfiche (Vols. for (1982-) distributed to depository libraries).

US/0096-2902
**RESEARCH METHODS IN NEUROCHEMISTRY.** [Res. methods neurochem.]. Vol. 1 (1972)-. Monographic series. English. ir. Price varies per volume. Plenum Press, 233 Spring Street, New York NY 10013-1578. **Tel** (212)620-8000, (800)221-9369, FAX (212)463-0742, (212)807-1047, telex 23/421139. **LC** QP356.3; .R46. **DD** 612/.8/042. **NLM** W1 RE232D. **CODEN** RMNUBP. **[CCC].** Documents available from BIOSIS Document Express, CASDDS.
**Ind/Abst** Biol. Abstr. (-1974); Chem. Abstr.

US/0939-4818
**RESEARCH NOTES IN NEURAL COMPUTING.** [Res. notes neural comput.]. Vol. 1 (1989)-. Monographic series. English. Price varies per volume. Springer-Verlag New York Inc., 175 5th Avenue, New York NY 10010. **Tel** (212)460-1500, telex 232 235 SPB UR. **(Subscription address:** Springer Verlag New York Inc. / for North America, 44 Hartz Way, Secaucus NJ 07096.**)** **NLM** W1; RE232KJ.
**Ind/Abst** Zentralbl. Math. Ihre Grenzgeb.

US/0091-7443
**RESEARCH PUBLICATIONS - ASSOCIATION FOR RESEARCH IN NERVOUS AND MENTAL DISEASE.** [Res. publ. - Assoc. Res. Nerv. Ment. Dis.]. **Main/Corp** Association for Research in Nervous and Mental Disease. Vol. 20 (1939)-. Monographic series. English. ir. Price varies per volume. Raven Press, 1185 Avenue of the Americas, 37th Floor, New York NY 10036. **Tel** (212)930-9500, (212)930-9604, FAX (212)869-3495, (212)302-8507, telex 640073. **ED** Richard W. Perry and Samuel W. Perry, III. **NLM** W1 RE233P. **CODEN** RPARA5. Documents available from BIOSIS Document Express, CASDDS. ***Continues*** *Association for Research in Nervous and Mental Disease. Series of Research Publications.*
**Ind/Abst** Biol. Abstr.; Chem. Abstr.; Index Med.

NE/0169-0833
**RESTORATIVE NEUROLOGY.** [Restor. neurol.]. Vol. 1 (1985)-. Monographic series. English. Price varies per volume. Elsevier Science Publishers BV, PO Box 211, 1000 AE Amsterdam Netherlands. **Tel** 011 31 20 5803642, FAX 011 31 20 5862696, telex 15682. **NLM** W1; RE248W. **CODEN** RETNEF. Documents available from BIOSIS Document Express.
**Ind/Abst** Biol. Abstr. (1991-).

NE/0922-6028
**RESTORATIVE NEUROLOGY AND NEUROSCIENCE.** Vol. 1, No. 1 (Nov. 1989)-. Academic Scholarly Publication. English. Eight times a year (2 vols.). $600.00. Elsevier Science Ireland Ltd., Bay 15, Shannon Industrial Estate, Co Clare Ireland. **Tel** 011 353 61 471944. **NLM** W1; RE248WL. **[CCC].** available on microfilm and microfiche from University Microfilms International (UMI). Documents available from The Genuine Article.
**Ind/Abst** CSA Neuro. Abstr.; Curr. Aware. Biol. Sci., CABS; Curr. Contents Life Sci.; EMBASE; Ref. Upd. Deluxe Ed.; Res. Alert [Full Cov.]; Sci. Cit. Index; SCISEARCH.

UK/0334-1763
**REVIEWS IN THE NEUROSCIENCES.** [Rev. neurosci.]. Vol. 1, No. 1 (Oct./Dec. 1986)-. Periodical. English. qt. $220.00. Freund Publishing House Ltd, PO Box 35010, 61 Nachmani Street, Tel Aviv 61350 Israel. **Tel** 011 972 3 5662925, FAX 011 972 3 5605335. **(Subscription address:** Freund Publishing House Ltd., Suite 500 Chesham House, 150 Regent Street, London W1R 5FA England.**)** **ED** J.P. Huston. **NLM** W1; RE253JNJ. **CODEN** RNEUEO. Documents available from The Genuine Article, CASDDS.
**Ind/Abst** Chem. Abstr.; EMBASE; Res. Alert [Full Cov.]; Soc. Sci. Cit. Index [Select. Cov.].

BL/0101-8469
**REVISTA BRASILEIRA DE NEUROLOGIA : ORGAO OFICIAL DO INSTITUTO DE NEUROLOGIA DEOLINDO COUTO, UNIVERSIDADE FEDERAL DO RIO DE JANEIRO.** **Added/Corp** Instituto de Neurologia Deolindo Couto. (19??)-. Periodical. Portuguese (summaries and/or abstracts in English). bm. Editora Cientifica Nacional Ltda., PO Box 590, Av. Almirante Barroso 97, Grupos 1205-1210, 20031, Rio de Janeiro, Brazil. **Tel** (21)262-2825. **NLM** W1; RE343KC.
**Ind/Abst** EMBASE [Select. Cov.].

CL/0034-7388
**REVISTA CHILENA DE NEURO-PSIQUIATRIA.** **See** Medical Science and Technology-Psychiatry.

RM/0377-497X
**REVISTA DE MEDICINA-INTERNA, NEUROLOGIE, PSIHIATRIE, NEUROCHIRURGIE, DERMATO-VENEROLOGIE. NEUROLOGIE, PSIHIATRIE, NEUROCHIRURGIE.** **See** Medical Science and Technology-Psychiatry.

PE/0034-8597
**REVISTA DE NEURO-PSIQUIATRIA.** **Added/Corp** Universidad Nacional Mayor de San Marcos Universidad Nacional Mayor de San Marcos Catedra de Neurologia. Universidad Nacional Mayor de San Marcos Catedra de Psiquiatria. Vol.1 (March 1938). Periodical. Spanish (summaries and/or abstracts in English, French and German). Four times a year. $50.00. Revista De Neuro-Psiquiatria, Casilla 1589, Lima Peru. **Tel** FAX 51 14 458583. **ED** Dr. Javier Mariategui. **NLM** W1 RE447. **CODEN** RVNPA4. Index available. cum. index. **Ad Acc, Adv Mgr:** Jose C. Mariategui, **Tel** 51 14 907207. **Pr Rev. Circ:** 1000. Documents available from BIOSIS Document Express.
**Ind/Abst** Biol. Abstr.; Index Med.

SP/0210-0010
**REVISTA DE NEUROLOGIA.** [Rev. neurol.]. Vol. 1 (1973)-. Periodical. Spanish. bm. Publicidad Permanyer SA, Mallorc 310, 08037 Barcelona Spain. **NLM** W1 RE446E.
**Ind/Abst** EMBASE.

EC/1019-8113
**REVISTA ECUATORIANA DE NEUROLOGIA.** [Rev. ecuat. neurol.]. (1992)-. Periodical. Multiple languages. sa. **UDC** 616.8. Documents available from The Genuine Article.
**Ind/Abst** Res. Alert.

SP/0213-4241
**REVISTA ESPANOLA DE EPILEPSIA.** ***Ceased.*** [Rev. esp. epilepsia]. **VFOAT** Epilepsia (Madrid). (1986)-(19??). Periodical. Spanish. qt. SANED SA, Paseo de la Habana 202 Bis, 28036 Madrid Spain. **Tel** 011 34 1 5553508. **UDC** 616.853.
**Ind/Abst** Indice Med. Esp.

SP
**REVISTA ESPANOLA DE FONIATRIA.** **Added/Corp** Sociedad Medica Espanola de Foniatria. (1988)-. Periodical. Spanish (Spanish; summaries and/or abstracts in English; table of contents in English). sa. **NLM** W1; RE543D.

SP/0213-4233
**REVISTA ESPANOLA DE NEUROLOGIA.** Vol. 1 (1986)-. Periodical. Spanish (summaries and/or abstracts in English; table of contents in English). Six times a year. 5800ptas Spain; 6000ptas others. Editorial Saned SA, Apolonio Morales 6, 28036 Madrid Spain. **Tel** 011 34 1 359-4092, FAX 011 34 1 457-9918. **NLM** W1; RE545B. **CODEN** RESNEA.
**Ind/Abst** EMBASE; Indice Med. Esp.

SP/0034-9453
**REVISTA ESPANOLA DE OTO-NEURO-OFTALMOLOGIA Y NEUROCIRUGIA.** ***Ceased.*** [Rev. esp. oto-neuro-oftalmol. neurocir.]. Vol. 1 (1944)-Ceased ?. Academic Scholarly Publication. Spanish. ir. Editorial Facta, Avellanas 4, 46003 Valencia Spain. **Tel** 011 34 96 3323842 3794. **NLM** W1 RE5469.
**Ind/Abst** EMBASE.

AG/0325-0938
**REVISTA NEUROLOGICA ARGENTINA.** [Rev. neurol. argent.]. **Added/Corp** Sociedad Neurologica Argentina. Vol. 1 (1974)-. Academic Scholarly Publication. Spanish (summaries and/or abstracts in English). Twenty-six times a year. Americana de Publicaciones, Cerrito 512 2 Piso, 1010 Bueno Aires Argentina. **Tel** 011 54 1 3826600. **NLM** W1 RE696H. ***Supersedes*** *Revista Neurologica de Buenos Aires, 0370-6494.*
**Ind/Abst** EMBASE [Select. Cov.].

FR/1155-4452
**REVUE DE NEUROPSYCHOLOGIE / SOCIETE DE NEUROPSYCHOLOGIE DE LANGUE FRANCAISE.** **Added/Corp** Societe de Neuropsychologie de Langue Francaise. (199?)-. Periodical. French (summaries and/or abstracts in English; table of contents in English). qt. 521.33F France; 550.00F other. ADRSC, IBHOP Traverse Charles Susini, 13388 Marseille CDX 13 France. **Tel** 011 33 91 660069, FAX 011 33 91 611420. **ED** Michel Habib and Eric Sieroff. **NLM** W1; RE7969. cum. index. **Ad Acc. Circ:** 400 (ctrl).
**Desc:** Articles in neuropsychology.

CN/0847-5733
**REVUE FRANCOPHONE DE LA DEFICIENCE INTELLECTUELLE.** [Rev. francoph. defic. intellect.]. Vol. 1, No. 1 (June 1990)-. Periodical. French. Twice a year (June & Dec.). 25.20Can$ (individuals), 36.00Can$ (institutions) Canada; 31.00Can$ (individuals), 41.00Can$ (institutions) others. Revue Francophone de la Deficience Intellectuelle, 3958 rue Dandurand, Montreal Quebec H1X 1P7 Canada. **Tel** (418)228-2051, FAX (418)228-3072. **ED** Hubert Gascon. **DD** 616.8/588/005. Index available. cum. index. **Ad Acc, Adv Mgr:** H. Gascon, **Tel** (418)228-2051. **Pr Rev. Circ:** 650 (ctrl).

FR/0035-3787
**REVUE NEUROLOGIQUE.** [Rev. neurol.]. **Added/Corp** Societe Francaise de Neurologie. Societe de Neurologie de Paris. Vol. 1 (Feb. 1893)-. Academic Scholarly Publication. French (summaries and/or abstracts in English). Ten times a year. $272.00. Masson Editeur, Box Postale 22, 41353 Vineuil 16 France. **Tel** 011 33 54 438994. **(Subscription address:** 7A Boulevard de Perolles, CH-1701 Fribourg Switzerland**)** **NLM** W1 RE943. **CODEN** RENEAM. **[CCC].** Index Available, published separately, free-automatically sent. **Pr Rev.** available on microfilm and microfiche from University Microfilms International (UMI). Documents available from The Genuine Article, BIOSIS Document Express.
**Ind/Abst** Biol. Abstr.; Curr. Contents Clin. Med.; Curr. Contents Life Sci.; Curr. Ref. Fish Res.; Dev. Med. Child Neurol.; EMBASE; Helminthol. Abstr. (1991-); Index Med.; Index Vet.; Life Sci. Collect.; Protozoolog. Abstr.; Res. Alert [Full Cov.]; Rev. Med. Vet. Entomol.; Rev. Med. Vet. Mycology; Saf. Health Work; Sci. Cit. Index; SCISEARCH; Soc. Sci. Cit. Index [Select. Cov.].

RM/1017-5644
**REVUE ROUMAINE DE NEUROLOGIE ET PSYCHIATRIE (1990).** (ROMANIAN JOURNAL OF NEUROLOGY AND PSYCHIATRY.). [Rev. roum. neurol. psychiat.]. **Added/Corp** Academia de Stiinte Medicale. **VFOAT** Revue Roumaine de Neurologie et Psychiatrie. Vol. 28, No. 1 (Jan./March 1990)-. Periodical. English. qt. DM268.00. **(Subscription address:** Kubon & Sagner, ABT Zeitschriftenimport, D 80328 Munich Germany.**)** **NLM** W1; RO327K. ***Continues*** *Neurologie et Psychiatrie, 0377-502X.*
**Ind/Abst** Index Med. (1990-).

JA/0009-918X
**RINSHO SHINKEIGAKU.** **Added/Corp** Nihon Shinkei Gakkai. **VFOAT** Clinical Neurology. Vol. 1 (1960)-. Periodical. Japanese (English). mo. $252.00. Japanese Society of Neurology, Ichimaru Building 2-31-21 Yushima, Bunkyo-ku Tokyo 113 Japan. **Tel** (03)815-1080, FAX (03)815-1931. **(Subscription address:** Kyowa Book Company Inc., 1-38 Kanda Jinbo-Cho, Chiyoda-Ku Tokyo 101, Japan**)** **ED** Katsuhiko Hamaguchi and Shunsaku Hirai. **NLM** W1 RI2167R. cum. index. **Ad Acc. Pr Rev. Circ:** 5,800 (ctrl). Documents available from BIOSIS Document Express.
**Desc:** A journal of clinical neurology containing original articles of research, case reports, and diagnosis and treatment for neurological diseases.
**Ind/Abst** Biol. Abstr.; EMBASE; Index Med.

IT/0035-6336
**RIVISTA DI NEUROBIOLOGIA.** [Riv. neurobiol.]. **Added/Corp** Ospedale Neuropsichiatrico Provincale di Arezzo. Vol. 1 (Jan./March 1955)-. Academic Scholarly Publication. Multiple languages (Italian and French; summaries and/or abstracts in Italian and English). Six times a year. L100000 Italy; L200000 other. Editrice IL Ventaglio, via Cagliari 42, 00198 Rome Italy. **Tel** 011 39 6 8415621. **NLM** W1 RI544. **CODEN** RNBLAC. **Bk Rev. Ad Acc.** Documents available from BIOSIS Document Express.
**Desc:** Clinical neurology, neuroradiology and neurosurgery.
**Ind/Abst** Biol. Abstr.; EMBASE; Index Med.

IT/0035-6352
**RIVISTA DI NEUROPSICHIATRIA E SCIENZE AFFINI.** [Riv. neuropsichiatr. sci. affini]. (1955)-. Periodical. Italian. qt. L60000.00 Italy; L120000.00 other. Casa Editrice Maccari, Via Trento 53, 43100 Parma Italy. **Tel** 011 39 521 771268, FAX 011 39 521 771268.
**Ind/Abst** Life Sci. Collect.

IT
**RIVISTA DI NEURORADIOLOGIA.** (1988)-. Periodical. Italian (English and French). bm. L200000. Edizioni Centauro, Via Pietro Calvi 3, 20129 Milan Italy. **Tel** (011) 39 2 76110615, FAX (011)39 2 76110615. **NLM** W1; RI555D. Index available. cum. index. **Bk Rev**, (Qty: 2-4). **Ad Acc, Adv Mgr:** M. Leonardi. **Pr Rev. Circ:** 1,800 (ctrl).
**Ind/Abst** Arts Humanit. Citation Index [Select. Cov.]; EMBASE.

GW/0080-715X
**SCHRIFTENREIHE NEUROLOGIE.** [Schriftenr. Neurol.]. **VFOAT** Neurology Series. Vol. 1 (1969)-. Periodical. German. ir. DM108.00 (vol. 32). Springer Verlag New York Inc., PO Box 19386 Books, Newark NJ 07195. **Tel** (201)348-4033. **(Subscription address:** North America/ Journal Fulfillment Services, 44 Hartz Way, Secaucus, NJ 07094**)** **NLM** W1 SC344. ***Supersedes in part*** *Monographien aus dem Gesamtgebiete der Neurologie und Psychiatrie.*
**Desc:** Numbered series.
**Ind/Abst** Index Med.

SZ
**SCHWEIZER ARCHIV FUR NEUROLOGIE UND PSYCHIATRIE (ZURICH, SWITZERLAND : 1985).** (SCHWEIZER ARCHIV FUER NEUROLOGIE UND PSYCHIATRIE.). **Added/Corp** Schweizerische Neurologische Gesellschaft. Schweizerische Gesellschaft fuer Psychiatrie. **VFOAT** Archives Suisses de Neurologie et de Psychiatrie; Archivio Svizzero di Neurologia e Psichiatria. Vol. 136, No. 1 (1985)-. Periodical. German

(French and Italian; summaries and/or abstracts in English). bm (6 issues). 210.00F Switzerland; 234.00F other. Zuerichsee Zeitschriftenverlag, Seestrasse 86, CH 8712 Staefa Switzerland. **Tel** 011 41 1 9285611. **NLM** W1; SC392Z. ***Continues*** *Schweizer Archiv fur Neurologie, Neurochirurgie und Psychiatrie.*
**Ind/Abst** EMBASE; Index Med. (Vol. 136, No. 1, 1985-); PsycINFO (1990-); PsycLit.

●UK/1059-1311
**SEIZURE (LONDON, ENGLAND).** (SEIZURE.). (1992)-. Periodical. English. qt (4 issues). £99.00 (institution), £50.00 (individual)*UK/Europe; $178.00 (institution), $90.00*(individual). Harcourt Brace & Company Ltd., Foots Cray, High Street, Sidcup Kent DA14 5HP England. **Tel** 011 44 81 300 3322, FAX 011 44 81 309 0807. **(Subscription address:** W. B. Saunders Company / North America Subscriptions, c/o Periodicals, 6277 Sea Harbour Drive, 4th Floor, Orlando FL 32887.**)** **ED** T. Betts. **Pr Rev.**
**Desc:** Provides an international forum for the publication of papers related to epilepsy.

US/0271-8235
**SEMINARS IN NEUROLOGY.** [Semin. neurol.]. Vol. 1, No. 1 (Mar. 1981)-. Periodical. English. qt (Mar., June, Sep., Dec.). $135.00 (institutions), $99.00 (individuals) US; $160.00*(institutions), $124.00 (individuals) other. Thieme Medical Publishers Inc., 381 Park Avenue South, Suite 1201, New York NY 10016. **Tel** (212)683-5088, (212)683-5089, FAX (212)779-9020, telex 220 862 TSINC UR. **ED** David Goldblatt. **NLM** W1 SE489CS. **CODEN** SEMNEP. **[CCC].** cum. index. **Bk Rev. Ad Acc. Circ:** 1,800 (ctrl). available on microfilm and microfiche from University Microfilms International (UMI). Documents available from The Genuine Article, BIOSIS Document Express.
**Desc:** Topic-oriented journal devoted to case reports and subjects in neurology and designed for the practitioner.
**Ind/Abst** Biol. Abstr. (1984-); Curr. Contents Clin. Med.; Dev. Med. Child Neurol.; EMBASE; Index Med. (Vol. 6, No. 1, 1986-); Res. Alert [Full Cov.].

US/1044-5765
**SEMINARS IN NEUROSCIENCES.** [Semin. neurosci.]. (1989)-. Academic Scholarly Publication. English. bm (6 issues). $185.00. Academic Press Ltd., A Division of Harcourt Brace & Company Ltd., 24-28 Oval Road, London NW1 7DX England. **Tel** 071 267 4466, FAX 071 482 2293, 071 485 4752, telex 25775 ACPRES G. **(Subscription address:** Harcourt Brace & Company, Ltd., Foots Cray, High Street, Sidcup Kent DA14 5HP England.**)** **NLM** W1; SE489LT. **[CCC].** Documents available from The Genuine Article.
**Desc:** Covers the rapidly developing work in the neurosciences. Consists of topical reviews of single topics that form each issue.
**Ind/Abst** CSA Neuro. Abstr.; Res. Alert [Full Cov.]; Soc. Sci. Cit. Index [Select. Cov.].

●US/1071-9091
**SEMINARS IN PEDIATRIC NEUROLOGY.** (1994)-. Periodical. English. qt. $89.00 (individual), $109.00 (institutions); $129.00 (institution), $109.00 (individual) other. W.B. Saunders Company, A Subsidiary of Harcourt Brace Jovanovich, Inc., The Curtis Center/Suite 300, Independence Square West, Philadelphia PA 19106-3399. **Tel** (215)238-7800 or, 5587, FAX (215)238-7883, telex 173146. **(Subscription address:** W. B. Saunders Company / North America Subscriptions, c/o Periodicals, 6277 Sea Harbour Drive, 4th Floor, Orlando FL 32887.**)**

CC/1000-2464
**SHENJING JINGSHEN JIBING ZAZHI.** (SHEN CHING CHING SHEN CHI PING TSA CHIH.). [Shenjing jingshen jibing zazhi]. **Added/Corp** Chung-Shan i Hsueh Yuan (Canton, China). **VFOAT** Journal of Nervous and Mental Diseases. (197?)-. Periodical. Chinese (table of contents in English). Six times a year. $14.77. **(Subscription address:** China International Book Trading Corporation, PO Box 399, Library Service Department, Beijing 100044 People's Republic of China.**)** **NLM** W1; SH28.

JN/0386-9709
**SHINKEI NAIKA.** [Shinkei naika]. **VFOAT** Neurological Medicine. (1974)-. Periodical. Japanese (summaries and/or abstracts in English). mo. $354.00. **(Subscription address:** Kyowa Book Company Inc., 1-38 Kanda Jinbo-Cho, Chiyoda-Ku Tokyo 101, Japan**)** **NLM** W1 SH3305I.

JA/0388-7588
**SHINKEI SEISHIN YAKURI.** [Shinkei seishin yakuri]. **VFOAT** Japanese Journal of Neuropsychopharmacology. (1979)-. Periodical. Japanese. Twelve times a year. $318.00. Seiwa Shoten Co. Ltd., 2-5 Kamitakaido 1-chome, Suginami-ku 168 Tokyo Japan. **(Subscription address:** Kyowa Book Company Inc., 1 38 Kanda Jinbocho Chiyoda-ku, Tokyo 101 Japan.**)** **NLM** W1; SH3305M. **CODEN** SSYAD7. Documents available from CASDDS.
**Ind/Abst** Chem. Abstr.; EMBASE; Soc. Sci. Cit. Index [Select. Cov.].

SA/0379-8046
**SOUTH AFRICAN JOURNAL OF COMMUNICATION DISORDERS.** (THE SOUTH AFRICAN JOURNAL OF COMMUNICATION DISORDERS.). [S. Afr. j. commun. disord.]. **Added/Corp** South African Speech and Hearing Association. **VFOAT** Die Suid-Afrikaanse Tydskrif vir Kommunikasieafwykings. Vol. 24 (1977)-. English (Afrikaans). an. R7.50. South Africa Speech & Hearing Association, PO Box 31782, Braamfontein 2017 South Africa. **Tel** 011 716-2374. **ED** Brenda Louw. **LC** RC423.A1; S62a. **DD** 616.8/55/005. **NLM** W1 SO9044M. **CODEN** SAJDDJ. **Ad Acc. Circ:** 700 (ctrl). Documents available from BIOSIS Document Express. ***Continues*** *Journal of the South African Speech and Hearing Association, 0300-9874.*
**Desc:** Academic research and therapeutic applications in the field of speech pathology and audiology.
**Ind/Abst** Biol. Abstr.; Index Med.; Index Dent. Lit.

SZ/0896-8306
**SOVIET MEDICAL REVIEWS. SECTION G, NEUROPHARMACOLOGY REVIEWS.** ***Ceased.*** **See** Pharmacy and Pharmacology.

US/0038-559X
**SOVIET NEUROLOGY & PSYCHIATRY.** ***Title Change.*** [Sov. neurol. psych.]. **Added/Corp** International Arts and Sciences Press. **VFOAT** Soviet Neurology and Psychiatry. **VAT** Soviet Neurology and Psychiatry. Vol. 1 (Spring 1968)-(1991). Academic Scholarly Publication. English (translations available in Russian). qt. M. E. Sharpe Inc., 80 Business Park Drive, Armonk NY 10504. **Tel** (914)273-1800, (800)541-6563, FAX (914)273-2106. **ED** Gordon Mangan. **LC** RC321; .S67. **DD** 616.8/005. **NLM** W1 SO996M. **Ad Acc. Circ:** 150. available on microfilm from University Microfilms International (UMI). Documents available from BIOSIS Document Express. ***Continues in part*** *Soviet Psychology and Psychiatry, 0584-5610.* ***Continued by*** *Jornal of Russian and East European Psychiatry, 1061-0413.*
**Desc:** Reflects current developments in Soviet psychiatric and neurological theory and practice.
**Ind/Abst** Biol. Abstr.; EMBASE; Psychol. Abstr. (1980-); PsycINFO; PsycLit.

CN/0822-5702
**SP QUEBEC.** (MS QUEBEC / MULTIPLE SCLEROSIS SOCIETY OF CANADA, QUEBEC DIVISION.). [SP Que.]. **Added/Corp** Multiple Sclerosis Society of Canada. Quebec Division. **VFOAT** SP Quebec. **VAT** Sclerose en Plaques Quebec; Multiple Sclerosis Quebec. Vol. 6, No. 18 (Spring 1981)-. Periodical. English (French). qt. Free. Multiple Sclerosis Society of Canada, Ontario Division, 250 Bloor Street East Suite 1000, Toronto Ontario M4W 3P9 Canada. **Tel** (416)922-6065, FAX (416)922-7538. **DD** 616.8/34/0060714. ctrl circ. ***Continues*** *SP Quebec., 0822-5702.*

SZ/1011-6125
**STEREOTACTIC AND FUNCTIONAL NEUROSURGERY.** **See** Medical Science and Technology-Surgery.

BU/0204-4560
**STROEZ I FUNKCII NA MOZKA.** (STROEZH I FUNKTSII NA MOZUKA / BULGARSKA AKADEMIIA NA NAUKITE, TSENTRALNA LABORATORIIA ZA IZUCHAVANE NA MOZUKA.). [Stroez funkc. mozuka]. **Added/Corp** TSentralna Laboratoriia za Izuchavane na Mozuka (Bulgarska Akademiia na Naukite). **VFOAT** Structure and Functions of the Brain. (1976)-. Academic Scholarly Publication. Bulgarian (English, French, German and Russian). 1.10lv. Izdatelstvo No Ban, Ul Akad G Bonchev Por No 33, 1113 Sofia Bulgaria. **Tel** 72-09-22. **ED** A. Varbanova. **LC** QP376; .S83. **DD** 612/.82/05. **CODEN** SFMODY. **Bk Rev. Ad Acc. Circ:** 500 (ctrl). Documents available from CASDDS.
**Desc:** Research of functions, structure, and disease of the brain.
**Ind/Abst** Chem. Abstr.

US/0039-2499
**STROKE (1970).** **See** Medical Science and Technology-Cardiology.

GW/0172-5742
**STUDIES OF BRAIN FUNCTION.** Vol. 1 (1977)-. Monographic series. English. ir. Price varies per volume. Springer-Verlag GmbH & Company KG, Heidelberger Platz 3, D 14197 Berlin Germany. **Tel** 011 49 30 8207223, FAX 011 49 30 8214091, telex 183 319 SPBLN D. **(Subscription address:** Springer Verlag New York Inc. / for North America, 44 Hartz Way, Secaucus NJ 07096.**)** **NLM** W1 ST937KF.
**Desc:** Studies operation of the visual cortex, and vision in drosophila.

BU/0324-0258
**SUVREMENNI PROBLEMI NA NEVROMORFOLOGIIATA.** [Suvrem. probl. neuromorfol.]. **Added/Corp** Bulgarska Akademiia na Naukite, Sofia. Tsentralna Laboratoriia po Regeneratsiia. **VFOAT** Contemporary Problems of Neuromorphology. Vol. 1 (1973)-. Academic Scholarly Publication. Bulgarian (summaries and/or abstracts in English and Russian). Bulgarska Akademiia na Naukite, 7 Noemvri 1, Sofia Bulgaria. **LC** QP355.2; .S96. **NLM** W1 SU931. **CODEN** SPNEDB. Documents available from CASDDS.
**Ind/Abst** Chem. Abstr. (1973-1983).

IT
**SYMPOSIA IN NEUROSCIENCE.** **Added/Corp** FIDIA. Vol. 1 (1983)-. Academic Scholarly Publication. English. Price varies per volume. Liviana Medicina SRL, Via A de Gasperi 55, 80133 Naples Italy. **Tel** 011 39 81 5524733, FAX 011 39 81 5518295. **NLM** W1; SY432F. **CODEN** SYNEE7. Documents available from BIOSIS Document Express, CASDDS.
**Ind/Abst** Biol. Abstr. (1986-); Chem. Abstr. (1986-).

FR/0762-7475
**SYNAPSE.** (1984)-. Periodical. French. Ten times a year. 250.00F France; 450.00F other. NHA Communications, 217 rue Saint Honore, F-75001 Paris France. **Tel** 33 1 40209300, FAX 33 1 40209142. **ED** Michel Reynaud. **UDC** 159.9. **Bk Rev. Ad Acc.** ctrl circ.

JA
**TANIGUCHI SYMPOSIA ON BRAIN SCIENCES.** ***Ceased.*** (19??)- (19??). Monographic series. English. an. S. Karger AG, Allschwilerstrasse 10, PO Box - Postfach - Case Postale, CH-4009 Basel Switzerland. **Tel** 011 41 61 306-1111, FAX 011 41 61 306-1234, telex CH 962 652. **ED** Osamu Hayaishi. **NLM** W1; TA549. **CODEN** TSBSEQ. Documents available from BIOSIS Document Express.
**Desc:** Based on the Taniguchi Symposia on Brain Sciences, this series highlights original in vitro and in vivo studies into numerous physiological aspects of the brain. Neural programming and cellular and molecular analyses of brain aging and Alzheimer's disease are examples of the topical subjects dealt with in individual titles in this series.
**Ind/Abst** Biol. Abstr. (1987-); Ref. Upd. Deluxe Ed.

US
**TECHNIQUES IN NEUROSURGERY.** Vol. 1 (1995)-. Periodical. English. qt. $95.00 (individuals), $115.00 (institutions) US; $105.00 (individuals), $130.00 (institutions) other. Raven Press, 1185 Avenue of the Americas, 37th Floor, New York NY 10036. **Tel** (212)930-9500, (212)930-9604, FAX (212)869-3495, (212)302-8507, telex 640073.

NE/0921-0709
**TECHNIQUES IN THE BEHAVIORAL AND NEURAL SCIENCES.** **See** Psychology.

JA
**TENKAN KENKYU / NIHON TENKAN GAKKAI.** [Tenkan kenkyu]. **Added/Corp** Nihon Tenkan Gakkai. **VFOAT** Journal of the Japan Epilepsy Society; JES. (1983)-. Periodical. Japanese (summaries and/or abstracts in English; table of contents in English). Twice a year. $94.00. Japan Epilepsy Society, 1-1 Ogawa Higashicho 4-chome, Kodaira-shi 187 Tokyo Japan. **(Subscription address:** Kyowa Book Company Inc., 1 38 Kanda Jinbocho Chiyoda-ku, Tokyo 101 Japan.**)** **NLM** W1; TE415E. **CODEN** TENKDV. Documents available from CASDDS.
**Ind/Abst** Chem. Abstr.; EMBASE.

FR/0154-473X
**THERAPIE ET REEDUCATION PSYCHOMOTRICE.** [Ther. reeduc. psychomot.]. French. an. Editions Maloine, 27 rue de l'Ecole de Medecine, F-75006 Paris France. **Tel** 011 33 1 43256045, FAX 011 33 1 46340589, telex 203215 F. **ED** J Defontaine. **NLM** W1 TH644I.

UK
**TINS PRODUCT DIRECTORY.** **VFOAT** Trends in Neurosciences Product Directory. (1987/88)-. Directory. English. Elsevier Science Publishers Ltd, Crown House, Linton Road, Barking Essex IG11 8JU England. **Tel** 011 44 81 5947272, FAX 081-594-5942, telex 896950.

JA/0301-5041
**TOKYO-TO SHINKEI KAGAKU SOGO KENKYUJO NEMPO.** **Main/Corp** Tokyo-to Shinkei Kagaku Sogo Kenkyujo. Vol. 1, No. 47 (1972)-. Japanese. 6 Ban Musashidai 2-chome Fuchushi, Tokyo Japan. **LC** RC329; .T64a. **NLM** W1 TO2145E.

UK/0952-2638
**TOPICS IN NEUROCHEMISTRY AND NEUROPHARMACOLOGY.** ***Ceased.*** [Top. neurochem. neuropharmacol.]. Vol. 1 (1987)-(19??). Academic Scholarly Publication. English. ir. Taylor & Francis Ltd., Rankine Road, Basingstoke Hampshire, RG24 8PR United Kingdom. **Tel** 011 44 256 840366, FAX 011 44 256 479438, telex 858540. **(Subscription address:** Taylor & Francis Inc., 1900 Frost Road, Suite 101, Bristol PA 19007-1598.**)** **NLM** W1; TO54D. **CODEN** TNNEE9. Documents available from BIOSIS Document Express, CASDDS.
**Ind/Abst** Biol. Abstr. (1988)-(19??); Chem. Abstr. (?-1989).

US/0897-3946
**TOPICS IN THE NEUROSCIENCES.** [Top. neurosci.]. (1986)-. Monographic series. English. ir. Price varies per volume. Kluwer Academic Publishers /

Massachusetts, PO Box 358, Accord Station, Hingham MA 02018. **Tel** (617)871-6600. **DD** 591. **NLM** W1; TO54VF.
**Ind/Abst** CSA Neuro. Abstr. (?-?).

SP/0211-8343
**TRABAJOS DEL INSTITUTO CAJAL.** ***Suspended.*** **See** Biology-Cytology and Histology.

US
**TRAINING AWARDS, FELLOWSHIP AWARDS ... DATA BOOK / NATIONAL INSTITUTE OF NEUROLOGICAL AND COMMUNICATIVE DISORDERS AND STROKE.** **Main/Corp** National Institute of Neurological and Communicative Disorders and Stroke. **Added/Corp** Extramural Activities Program (National Institute of Neurological and Communicative Disorders and Stroke). Office of Data Analysis and Reports. National Institute of Neurological and Communicative Disorders and Stroke. Management Information and Data Section. **VFOAT** NINCDS Training and Fellowship Awards; Training Awards & Fellowship Awards. (19??)-. English. an. National Institute of Neurological and Communicative Disorders and Stroke, National Institutes of Health, 9000 Rockville Pike, Bethesda MD 20014.

US/0066-0132
**TRANSACTIONS OF THE AMERICAN SOCIETY FOR NEUROCHEMISTRY.** [Trans. Am. Soc. Neurochem.]. **Main/Corp** American Society for Neurochemistry. Vol. 1 (1970)-. English. an (Mar.). $30.00. American Society for Neurochemistry, University of Texas Medical Branch, 200 University Boulevard, Suite 519, Galveston TX 77555-0843. **Tel** (409)772-2108, FAX (409)762-9382. **LC** QP356.3; .A46a. **DD** 596/.01/88. **NLM** W1 TR225D. Index available. **Ad Acc. Circ:** 1,200 (ctrl).
**Desc:** Contains abstracts of papers delivered at each annual meeting.

UK/0378-5912
**TRENDS IN NEUROSCIENCES (REFERENCE ED.).** (TRENDS IN NEUROSCIENCES.). [Trends neurosci.]. **VFOAT** TINS. Vol. 1 (1978)-. Academic Scholarly Publication. English. an. £514.00. Elsevier Science Publishers Ltd, Crown House, Linton Road, Barking Essex IG11 8JU England. **Tel** 011 44 81 5947272, FAX 081-594-5942, telex 896950. **ED** David Bousfield. **LC** QP351; .T692. **[CCC].** available on microfilm from University Microfilms International (UMI). Documents available from CASDDS, ADONIS.
**Desc:** Covers six major areas: molecular neurobiology, cellular neuroscience, developmental neuroscience, sensory and motor systems, neurology, and the behavioral sciences.
**Ind/Abst** ADONIS; Chem. Abstr.; CSA Neuro. Abstr.; Index Med.; Index Vet.; Psychol. Abstr. (1979-); PsycINFO; PsycLit; Ref. Upd. Basic Ed.; Ref. Upd. Deluxe Ed.; Sci. Cit. Index; SCISEARCH.

NE/0166-2236
**TRENDS IN NEUROSCIENCES (REGULAR ED.).** (TRENDS IN NEUROSCIENCES.). [Trends neurosci.]. **VFOAT** TINS. (July 1978)-. Academic Scholarly Publication. English. mo. $514.00 The Americas; £345.00 other. Elsevier Trends Journals, An Imprint of Elsevier Science Ltd., The Boulevard, Langford Lane, Kidlington, Oxford OX5 1GB United Kingdom. **Tel** 011 44 865 843000, 011 44 865 843699, FAX 011 44 865 843010. **(Subscription address:** Elsevier Science Ltd. Oxford Fulfillment Centre, PO Box 800, Kidlington, Oxford OX5 1DX United Kingdom.**)** **LC** QP351; .T69. **NLM** W1 TR341D. **CODEN** TNSCDR. **[CCC].** available on microfilm and microfiche from University Microfilms International (UMI). Documents available from The Genuine Article, BIOSIS Document Express, UMI Article Clearinghouse, CASDDS, ADONIS.
**Ind/Abst** ADONIS; Biol. Abstr.; Chem. Abstr. (1979-); Curr. Aware. Biol. Sci., CABS; Curr. Contents Life Sci.; EMBASE; Energy Res. Abstr. (Aug. 1980-); Newsp. Period. Abstr. (1992-); Life Sci. Collect.; Psychol. Abstr. (1979-); Res. Alert [Full Cov.]; Soc. Sci. Cit. Index [Select. Cov.].

RU/0455-6550
**TRUDY LENINGRADSKOGO NAUCHNO-ISSLEDOVATELSKOGO PSIKHONEVROLOGICHESKOGO INSTITUTA IM. V. M. BEKHTEREVA.** [Tr. Leningr. naucno-issled. psihonevrol. inst. im. V. M. Behtereva]. **Added/Corp** Leningradskii Nauchno-Issledovatelskii Psikhonevrologicheskii Institut Imeni V. M. Bekhtereva. **VFOAT** Proceedings of the Leningrad V. M. Bekhterev Psychoneurological Research Institute. Vol. 58 (1971)-. Monographic series. Russian (summaries and/or abstracts in English). Price varies per volume. Leningrad V M Bekhterev, Psychoneurological Research Institute, Tipografiya No. 2 Lenyprizdata Liteinyi Pr. 55, 191104 St. Petersburg Russia. **NLM** W1 TR957BN. Documents available from CASDDS. ***Continues*** *Trudy Instituta - Leningradskii Nauchno-Issledovatelskii Psikhonevrologicheskii Institut Imeni V. M. Bekhtereva.*
**Ind/Abst** Chem. Abstr.; Psychol. Abstr. (1980-?); PsycINFO (1980-); PsycLit.

TU/1019-5149
**TURKISH NEUROSURGERY.** (1990)-. Turkish. Inkilap Sokak, 24/2 Kizilay, Ankara, Turkey.
**Ind/Abst** EMBASE.

GW/0935-3224
**TW NEUROLOGIE, PSYCHIATRIE.** **VFOAT** Neurologie, Psychiatrie. (198?)-. Periodical. German (summaries and/or abstracts in English). bm. G Braun Verlag, Postfach 1709, D 76006 Karlsruhe Germany. **Tel** 011 49 721 165392. **NLM** W1; TW455.
**Ind/Abst** EMBASE [Select. Cov.].

US/0952-5238
**VISUAL NEUROSCIENCE.** [Vis. neurosci.]. Vol. 1, No. 1 (1988)-. Academic Scholarly Publication. English. Six times a year. $385.00 US, Canada & Mexico; £248.00 other. Cambridge University Press / New York, 40 West 20th Street, New York NY 10011-4211. **Tel** (212)924-3900, (800)221-4512. **(Subscription address:** Cambridge University Press / Outside of North America, Journal Fulfillment Department, The Edinburgh Building, Cambridge CB2 2RU United Kingdom.**)** **ED** James T. Mcilwain. **LC** QP474; .V54. **NLM** W1; VI911E. **CODEN** VNEUEY. **Pr Rev.** available on microfilm from University Microfilms International (UMI). Documents available from The Genuine Article, BIOSIS Document Express.
**Desc:** Devoted to the prompt publication of research and theoretical articles in basic visual neuroscience, with primary emphasis on retinal and brain mechanisms that underlie visually-guided behaviors and visual perception. The major goal is to bring together in one journal a broad range of studies which reflect the exciting diversity and originality of contemporary research in basic visual neuroscience. Methodologies are drawn from neuroanatomy, neurophysiology, neurochemistry, neuroimmunology, and behavioral science, as well as computational models and computer-assisted formulations. Molecular, cellular, local-circuit, and systems-level analyses in both vertebrate and invertebrate species are presented.
**Ind/Abst** Biol. Abstr. (1991-); Curr. Aware. Biol. Sci., CABS; Curr. Contents Life Sci.; Index Med. (1988-); Psychoanal. Abstr.; Psychol. Abstr. (1986-); PsycINFO; PsycScan: Appl. Exp. Eng. Psych.; PsycScan: LD/MR; PsycScan: Neuropsych.; Ref. Upd. Deluxe Ed.; Res. Alert [Full Cov.]; Sci. Cit. Index; SCISEARCH; Soc. Sci. Cit. Index [Select. Cov.].

US/0899-9465
**WORLD NEUROLOGY (NEW YORK, N.Y.).** (WORLD NEUROLOGY : THE NEWSLETTER OF THE WORLD FEDERATION OF NEUROLOGY.). [World neurol.]. **Added/Corp** World Federation of Neurology. (Apr. 1986)-. Newsletter. English. Four times a year (Jan., Apr., Aug., Oct.). $25.00 (individuals), $46.00 (institutions). Smith Gordon and Company Ltd, 16 Gunter Grove, No. 1, London SE1 0UJ England. **Tel** 011 44 71 3517042, FAX 011 44 71 3511250. **DD** 616. Index available (Back issues). **Bk Rev. Ad Acc, Adv Mgr:** Clare Parker.

US/0513-5117
**YEAR BOOK OF NEUROLOGY AND NEUROSURGERY, THE.** [Year b. neurol. neurosurg.]. **VFOAT** Yearbook of Neurology and Neurosurgery. (1969)-. English (Italian). an. $59.95. Mosby Year Book Inc., 11830 Westline Industrial Drive, St Louis MO 63146. **Tel** (800)325-4177, (314)872-8370, FAX (314)432-1380, telex 44-2402. **ED** Russell N DeJong, Robert D Currier and Robert M Crowell. **LC** RC329; .Y42. **DD** 616.8. **NLM** W1 YE276N. ***Continues in part*** *Yearbook of Neurology, Psychiatry and Neurosurgery (Chicago, Ill. : 1953).*

SZ/1016-264X
**ZEITSCHRIFT FUER NEUROPSYCHOLOGIE.** **See** Psychology.

GW/0722-3064
**ZENTRALBLATT NEUROLOGIE, PSYCHIATRIE.** **Added/Corp** Gesellschaft Deutscher Neurologen und Psychiater. **VFOAT** Neurology, Psychiatry. **VAT** Zentralblatt Neurologie-Psychiatrie. Vol. 238, No. 1 (1982)-. German (English). Fifty-two times a year. DM9180.00. Springer-Verlag GmbH & Company KG, Heidelberger Platz 3, D 14197 Berlin Germany. **Tel** 011 49 30 8207223, FAX 011 49 30 8214091, telex 183 319 SPBLN D. **(Subscription address:** Springer Verlag New York Inc. / for North America, 44 Hartz Way, Secaucus NJ 07096.**)** **ED** O Hallen and G Huber. **NLM** ZWL 100; Z56. **[CCC].** ***Continues*** *Zentralblatt fur die Gesamte Neurologie und Psychiatrie, 0044-412X.*
**Desc:** Reports of conventions, neurological and psychiatric diagnostics, psychoanalysis, bioclimatology, EEG, epilepsy endogenous psychosis, ethics, and child psychology.

RU/0044-4677
**ZHURNAL VYSSHEI NERVNOI DEIATELNOSTI IMENI I. P. PAVLOVA.** [Z. vyss. nervn. dejat. I P Pavlova]. **Added/Corp** Akademiia Nauk SSSR. Vol. 1, (Jan./Feb. 1951)-. Academic Scholarly Publication. Russian (summaries and/or abstracts in English). bm. $179.95. Izdatelstvo Nauka / Akademiia Nauk, Publishing House of the Russian Academy of Sciences, Leninskii Porspekt 14, 117901 Moscow Russia. **Tel** 011 95 954-21-53, FAX 011 95 938-21-44, telex 411964. **(Subscription address:** East View Publications Inc., 3020 Harbor Lane North, Suite 110, Minneapolis MN 55447.**)** **NLM** W1; ZH425. **CODEN** ZVNDAM. **[CCC].** Index available. cum. index. **Bk Rev. Pr Rev.** Documents available from The Genuine Article, BIOSIS Document Express, CASDDS.
**Ind/Abst** Biol. Abstr.; Chem. Abstr.; CSA Neuro. Abstr. (?-?); Curr. Contents Life Sci.; EMBASE [Select. Cov.]; Index Med.; Int. Aerosp. Abstr.; Life Sci. Collect.; Psychol. Abstr. (1951-); PsycINFO (1951-); PsycLit; Res. Alert [Full Cov.]; Sci. Cit. Index; SCISEARCH; Soc. Sci. Cit. Index [Select. Cov.].

RU/0044-4588
**ZURNAL NEVROPATOLOGII I PSIHIATRII IM S.S. KORSAKOVA.** ***Ceased.*** (ZHURNAL NEVROPATOLOGII I PSIKHIATRII IMENI S.S. KORSAKOVA / MINISTERSTVO ZDRAVOOKHRANENIIA SOIUZA SSR.). [Z. nevropatol. psihiatr. S.S. Korsakova]. **Added/Corp** Soviet Union. Ministerstvo Zdravookhraneniia. Vsesoiuznoe Nauchnoe Meditsinskoe Obshchestvo Nevropatologov i Psikhiatrov (Soviet Union). (1952)-(1993). Academic Scholarly Publication. Russian (summaries and/or abstracts in English and French). Six times a year. Izdatelstvo Meditsina / Russian Academy of Medical Sciences, Ulitsa Solyanka 14, 109801 Moscow Russia. **Tel** 011 95 297-05-04. **(Subscription address:** Victor Kamkin, 4956 Boiling Brook Parkway, Rockville, MD 20852**)** **NLM** W1; ZH422. **CODEN** ZNPIAP. **[CCC]. Pr Rev.** Documents available from The Genuine Article, BIOSIS Document Express, CASDDS. ***Continues*** *Nevropatologiia i Psikhiatriia.*
**Ind/Abst** Biol. Abstr.; Chem. Abstr.; Dev. Med. Child Neurol.; EMBASE; Index Med. (1960-); Int. Aerosp. Abstr.; Life Sci. Collect.; PESTDOC; Psychol. Abstr. (1952-); PsycINFO (1928-); PsycLit; Res. Alert [Full Cov.].

---

## NUCLEAR MEDICINE

---

US/0193-5224
**ANNUAL PROGRESS REPORT - UNIVERSITY OF CALIFORNIA, LABORATORY OF NUCLEAR MEDICINE AND RADIATION BIOLOGY.** **Main/Corp** University of California, Los Angeles. Laboratory of Nuclear Medicine and Radiation Biology. Periodical. English. an. **NLM** W1 AN7581.

US
**ANNUAL REPORT - THE FRANKLIN MCLEAN MEMORIAL RESEARCH INSTITUTE.** **See** Medical Science and Technology-Neoplasma, Neoplastic.

US/0160-9963
**APPLIED RADIOLOGY (1976).** **See** Medical Science and Technology-Radiology.

US/1057-591X
**CANCERGRAM. SERIES CT02 CANCER DETECTION AND MANAGEMENT NUCLEAR MEDICINE.** ***Ceased.*** **See** Medical Science and Technology-Neoplasma, Neoplastic.

US/0363-9762
**CLINICAL NUCLEAR MEDICINE.** [Clin. nucl. med.]. Vol. 1 (June 1976)-. Periodical. English. mo. $129.00 (individuals), $193.00 (institutions) US; $163.00 (individuals), $223.00 (institutions) other. J.B. Lippincott Company, 227 East Washington Square, Philadelphia PA 19106-3780. **Tel** (215)238-4200 or 4454, FAX (215)238-4227. **(Subscription address:** J.B. Lippincott, PO Box 350, Hagerstown MD 21740.**)** **ED** Sheldon Baum. **LC** R895.A1; C55. **DD** 616.07/575/05. **NLM** W1 CL739. **CODEN** CNMEDK. **[CCC]. Bk Rev. Ad Acc. Pr Rev. Circ:** 3,166. available on microfilm and microfiche from University Microfilms International (UMI). Documents available from The Genuine Article, BIOSIS Document Express.
**Desc:** Original manuscripts involving scanning, imaging, and related subjects; also meeting announcements.
**Ind/Abst** Biol. Abstr.; Curr. Contents Clin. Med.; EMBASE; Energy Res. Abstr. (Oct. 1980-); Health Plan. Adminis.; Helminthol. Abstr. (1991-); Index Med. (1978-); INIS Atomindex [Micro.]; Iowa Drug Inf. Serv. (1981-); Life Sci. Collect.; Phys. Med. Biol. (19??-19??); Protozoolog. Abstr.; Res. Alert [Full Cov.]; Rev. Med. Vet. Mycology; Sci. Cit. Index; SCISEARCH; SportSearch.

US/0895-996X
**CONTEMPORARY ISSUES IN NUCLEAR IMAGING.** [Contemp. issues nucl. imaging]. Vol. 1 (1985)-. Monographic series. English. ir. Price varies per volume. Churchill Livingstone, 1-3 Baxter's Place, Leith Walk, Edinburgh EH1 3AF Scotland. **Tel** 011 44 31 556 2424, FAX 011 44 31 558 1278, telex 727511. **(Subscription address:** US and Canada/

Churchill Livingstone Inc., 5 South 250 Frontenac Road, Naperville, IL 60563; (telephone: (800)553-5426 or (708)416-3939)) **DD** 616. **NLM** W1; CO769MRC.

US/0167-9074
**DEVELOPMENTS IN NUCLEAR MEDICINE.** [Dev. nucl. med.]. Vol. 1 (1981)-. Academic Scholarly Publication. English. ir. Price varies per volume. Kluwer Academic Publishers / Massachusetts, PO Box 358, Accord Station, Hingham MA 02018. **Tel** (617)871-6600. **NLM** W1; DE998KF. **CODEN** DNMDDS. Documents available from CASDDS.
**Ind/Abst** Chem. Abstr.

US/0194-2514
**DIAGNOSTIC IMAGING (SAN FRANCISCO, CALIF.).** See Medical Science and Technology-Radiology.

GW/0340-6997
**EUROPEAN JOURNAL OF NUCLEAR MEDICINE.** [Eur. j. nucl. med.]. **Added/Corp** European Nuclear Medicine Society. Vol. 1 (1976)-. Academic Scholarly Publication. English. Twelve times a year. DM1200.00. Springer-Verlag GmbH & Company KG, Heidelberger Platz 3, D 14197 Berlin Germany. **Tel** 011 49 30 8207223, FAX 011 49 30 8214091, telex 183 319 SPBLN D. **(Subscription address:** Springer Verlag New York Inc. / for North America, 44 Hartz Way, Secaucus NJ 07096.**)** **ED** P J Ell, V R McCready, E K J Pauwels, O Schober, and H Sochor. **NLM** W1 EU72DJ. **CODEN** EJNMD9. **[CCC].** **Pr Rev.** available on microfilm and microfiche from University Microfilms International (UMI). Documents available from The Genuine Article, Ask*IEEE, CASDDS.
**Desc:** Covers the most important developments in nuclear medicine, including original articles on such vital topics as diagnosis, therapy with 'open' radionuclides, in-vitro investigations, and methods of radiobiological and radiation protection studies.
**Ind/Abst** Chem. Abstr.; Coal Abstr.; Curr. Contents Clin. Med.; Curr. Contents Life Sci.; EMBASE; Energy Res. Abstr. (March 1977-); Index Med.; INSPEC (1979-); Life Sci. Collect.; Phys. Med. Biol. (19??-19??); Protozoolog. Abstr.; Res. Alert [Full Cov.]; Sci. Cit. Index; SCISEARCH.

NE/0014-4274
**EXCERPTA MEDICA. SECTION 23. NUCLEAR MEDICINE.** See Medical Science and Technology-Abstracting, Bibliographies and Statistics.

US/1041-0090
**IN SERVICE REVIEWS IN NUCLEAR MEDICINE.** (IN SERVICE REVIEWS IN NUCLEAR MEDICINE [SOUND RECORDING].). [In serv. rev. nucl. med.]. **VFOAT** In Service Reviews in Nuclear Medicine Technology; In-Service Reviews in Nuclear Medicine Technology. (19??)-. Periodical. English. mo. $175.00. Educational Reviews Inc., 6801 Cahaba Valley Road, Birmingham AL 35242. **Tel** (205)991-5188, (800)633-4743, FAX (205)995-1926. **DD** 616.

UK/0883-2897
**INTERNATIONAL JOURNAL OF RADIATION APPLICATIONS AND INSTRUMENTATION. PART B, NUCLEAR MEDICINE AND BIOLOGY.** ***Title Change.*** See Biology.

FR/0221-0363
**JOURNAL DE RADIOLOGIE.** See Medical Science and Technology-Radiology.

FR/0992-3039
**JOURNAL OF MEDECINE NUCLEAIRE ET BIOPHYSIQUE.** ***Title Change.*** See Biology-Biophysics.

US/0161-5505
**JOURNAL OF NUCLEAR MEDICINE (1978), THE.** (THE JOURNAL OF NUCLEAR MEDICINE.). [J. nucl. med.]. **Added/Corp** Society of Nuclear Medicine (1953)-. **VFOAT** JNM. Vol. 19 (Jan. 1978)-. Academic Scholarly Publication. English. mo (12 issues). $180.00 institution; $120.00 individual; (includes supplements). Society of Nuclear Medicine, 136 Madison Avenue/8th Floor, New York NY 10016. **Tel** (212)889-0717, FAX (212)545-0221. **ED** Stanley J. Goldsmith. **LC** RM845; .J78. **DD** 616.07/57/05. **NLM** W1 JO796D. **CODEN** JNMEAQ. **[CCC].** Index available (bound in Dec. issue). cum. index. **Bk Rev.** **Ad Acc.** **Pr Rev.** **Circ:** 13,700. available on microfilm and microfiche from University Microfilms International (UMI). Documents available from The Genuine Article, BIOSIS Document Express, Ask*IEEE, CASDDS. ***Continues*** *JNM. Journal of Nuclear Medicine, 0097-9031.*
**Desc:** Publishes original articles in the clinical and basic sciences of nuclear medicine. Covers a broad range of subjects including diagnostic nuclear medicine, radiochemistry and radiopharmaceuticals.
**Ind/Abst** Biol. Abstr.; Chem. Abstr.; Curr. Aware. Biol. Sci., CABS; Curr. Contents Clin. Med.; Curr. Contents Life Sci.; Dairy Sci. Abstr.; EMBASE; Energy Res. Abstr.; Index Med.; Index Vet.; INIS Atomindex [Micro.]; INSPEC (Jan. 1978-); Int. Pharm. Abstr.; Iowa Drug Inf. Serv.; Med. Abstr. Newsl.; Nutr. Abstr. Rev., Ser. B, Live Feeds and Feed.; Nutr. Abstr. Rev., Ser. A, Hum. Exp.; Life Sci. Collect.; Physic. Medline Plus; Phys. Med. Biol. (19??-19??); Protozoolog. Abstr.; Ref. Upd. Basic Ed.; Ref. Upd. Deluxe Ed.; Res. Alert [Full Cov.]; Risk Abstr.; Sci. Cit. Index; SCISEARCH; Small Anim. Abstr. Bibliogr.; Soc. Sci. Cit. Index [Select. Cov.]; Vet. Bull.

US/0075-4315
**JOURNAL OF NUCLEAR MEDICINE. SUPPLEMENT.** [J. nucl. med., Suppl.]. **Added/Corp** Society of Nuclear Medicine (1953)-. Medical Internal Radiation Dose Committee. (1968)-. English. ir. comes with Journal of Nuclear Medicine. Society of Nuclear Medicine, 136 Madison Avenue/8th Floor, New York NY 10016. **Tel** (212)889-0717, FAX (212)545-0221. **ED** H. William Strauss. **DD** 616. Index available. cum. index. **Ad Acc.** **Circ:** 12,912. available on microfilm.
**Ind/Abst** Energy Res. Abstr.

US/0091-4916
**JOURNAL OF NUCLEAR MEDICINE TECHNOLOGY.** [J. nucl. med. technol.]. **Added/Corp** Society of Nuclear Medicine (1953- ). Technologist Section. Vol. 1 (March 1973)-. Periodical. English. qt (Mar., June, Sept., Dec.). $70.00 (also comes with membership). Society of Nuclear Medicine, 136 Madison Avenue/8th Floor, New York NY 10016. **Tel** (212)889-0717, FAX (212)545-0221. **ED** Susan C. Weiss. **LC** R895.A1; J68. **DD** 616.07/575/05. **NLM** W1 JO796E. **CODEN** JNMTB4. **[CCC].** Index available (bound in Dec. issue). **Bk Rev.** **Ad Acc.** **Pr Rev.** **Circ:** 5,600. available on microfilm and microfiche from University Microfilms International (UMI). Documents available from BIOSIS Document Express, Ask*IEEE, CASDDS.
**Desc:** Devoted to the practice of nuclear medicine technology. Publishes original contributions to professionals in their daily practice.
**Ind/Abst** Biol. Abstr.; Chem. Abstr.; EMBASE; Energy Res. Abstr. (Oct. 1982-); Health Devices Alerts; INSPEC (March 1974-); Int. Pharm. Abstr.

JA/0022-7854
**KAKU IGAKU.** (KAKU IGAKU. THE JAPANESE JOURNAL OF NUCLEAR MEDICINE.). [Kaku igaku]. **Added/Corp** Nihon Kaku Igakkai. **VFOAT** The Japanese Journal of Nuclear Medicine. Vol. 1 (1964)-. Academic Scholarly Publication. English. mo. $301.00. Japanese Society of Nuclear Medicine, 28 45 2 Chome Hon Komagome, Bunkyo Ku Tokyo Japan. **(Subscription address:** Japan Publications Trading Company, Ltd., PO Box 5030, Tokyo International, Tokyo 100-31 Japan.**)** **NLM** W1 KA411H. **CODEN** KAIGBZ. Documents available from BIOSIS Document Express, CASDDS.
**Ind/Abst** Biol. Abstr.; Chem. Abstr.; EMBASE; Energy Res. Abstr.; Index Med.

FR
**MEDECINE NUCLEAIRE.** (199?)-. Academic Scholarly Publication. French. Nine times a year (1 volume). 960.00F France; 1075.00F other. Editions Scientifique Elsevier, 141 rue de Javel, 75747 Paris Cedex 15 France. **Tel** 011 33 1 47 07 11 22, FAX 011 33 1 43 36 80 93. **(Subscription address:** Editions Scientifiques Elsevier / for North America, PO Box 7247-7576, Philadelphia PA 19170-7576.**)** ***Continues*** *Journal de Medecine Nucleaire et Biophysique.*

●US/1064-9689
**MRI CLINICS OF NORTH AMERICA.** See Medical Science and Technology-Radiology.

AT/0159-8376
**NEWSLETTER - AUSTRALIAN AND NEW ZEALAND SOCIETY OF NUCLEAR MEDICINE.** (1979)-. Periodical. English. Four times a year (Mar., June, Sept., Dec.). 70.00Aus$. Australian & New Zealand Society of Nuclear Medicine, Private Mail Bag 1, Darlinghurst New South Wales, 2010 Australia. **Tel** 011 61 2 3316920. **ED** Peter John Frederick Newton (editor's address: 2 Carieville Street, Balmain, New South Wales, 2041 Australia, phone: 011 61 2 8101133). **Bk Rev**, (Qty: varies). **Ad Acc**, **Adv Mgr:** S. Bass. **Pr Rev.** **Circ:** 850 (ctrl).

GW/0344-3752
**NUC COMPACT : COMPACT NEWS IN NUCLEAR MEDICINE.** ***Ceased.*** [NUC compact, compact news nucl. med.]. **VFOAT** N.U.C. Compact; Compact News in Nuclear Medicine; NUCCompact; NUC-Compact. (1970)-(Jan. 1992). Academic Scholarly Publication. English (German). Six times a year. GIT Verlag GmbH, Roblerstrabe 90, Postfach 110564, D 64220 Darmstadt Germany. **Tel** 011 49 6151 8090-0, FAX 011 49 6151 8090-45. **ED** Jorg Mahloledt. **NLM** W1; NU108. **CODEN** CNNMAC. **Pr Rev.** **Circ:** 5,000. Documents available from The Genuine Article, CASDDS.
**Ind/Abst** Chem. Abstr.; EMBASE; Energy Res. Abstr. (May 1979-); Res. Alert [Select. Cov.]; SCISEARCH.

GW/0029-5566
**NUCLEAR MEDICINE.** **Added/Corp** Gesellschaft fuer Nuklearmedizin. **VFOAT** Nuklearmedizin. Vol. 23/1 (Feb. 1984)-. Academic Scholarly Publication. English (German). bm (Feb., Apr., June, Aug., Oct., Dec.). DM328.00 (institutions), DM238.00 (individuals) Europe; $201.70 (institutions), $142.70 (individuals) other. F K Schattauer Verlagsgesellschaft mbH, Postfach 10 45 45, D 70040 Stuttgart Germany. **Tel** 011 49 711 2298726. **CODEN** NUMEEL. **[CCC].** Documents available from CASDDS. ***Continues*** *Nuklearmedizin.*
**Ind/Abst** Chem. Abstr. (1984-).

●UK
**NUCLEAR MEDICINE AND BIOLOGY.** **VFOAT** NMB. Vol. 20, No. 1 (Jan. 1993)-. Academic Scholarly Publication. English. Eight times a year. $634.00 The Americas; £425.00 other. Pergamon Press, An Imprint of Elsevier Science Ltd., The Boulevard, Langford Lane, Kidlington, Oxford OX5 1GB United Kingdom. **Tel** 011 44 865 843000, 011 44 865 843699, FAX 011 44 865 843010. **(Subscription address:** Elsevier Science Ltd. Oxford Fulfillment Centre, PO Box 800, Kidlington, Oxford OX5 1DX United Kingdom.**)** **LC** R895.A1; I56. **DD** 616.07/57/05. **NLM** W1; NU124L. Documents available from The Genuine Article, CASDDS, ADONIS. ***Continues*** *International Journal of Radiation Applications and Instrumentation. Part B, Nuclear Medicine and Biology, 0883-2897.*
**Ind/Abst** ADONIS; Chem. Abstr.; Curr. Aware. Biol. Sci., CABS; Index Med. (1993-); PESTDOC; Res. Alert [Full Cov.]; Sci. Cit. Index; SCISEARCH.

US/0272-0108
**NUCLEAR MEDICINE ANNUAL.** [Nucl. med. annu.]. (1980)-. Academic Scholarly Publication. English. an. Price varies per volume. Raven Press, 1185 Avenue of the Americas, 37th Floor, New York NY 10036. **Tel** (212)930-9500, (212)930-9604, FAX (212)869-3495, (212)302-8507, telex 640073. **ED** Leonard M. Freeman. **LC** R895.A1; N73. **DD** 616.07/57. **NLM** W1 NU124M. **CODEN** NMANDX. Documents available from BIOSIS Document Express, CASDDS.
**Ind/Abst** Biol. Abstr.; Chem. Abstr.; Ref. Upd. Deluxe Ed.

UK/0143-3636
**NUCLEAR MEDICINE COMMUNICATIONS.** [Nucl. med. commun.]. **Added/Corp** British Nuclear Medicine Society. Vol. 1, No. 1 (March 1980)-. Academic Scholarly Publication. English. mo. $670.00 US and Canada; £390.00 Europe; £425.00 other. Chapman & Hall, 2-6 Boundary Row, London SE1 8HN England. **Tel** 011 44 71 865 0066, FAX 011 44 71 522 9623, telex 290164 Chapmag. **(Subscription address:** Chapman & Hall, Cheriton House, North Way, Andover, Hampshire, SP10 5BE England.**)** **ED** K. Britton, J. H. McKillop, L. K. Harding, I. R. McDougall. **NLM** W1 NU124P. **CODEN** NMCODC. **[CCC].** Index available. **Bk Rev.** **Ad Acc.** **Pr Rev.** available on microfilm and microfiche from University Microfilms International (UMI). Documents available from The Genuine Article, BIOSIS Document Express, CASDDS, ADONIS.
**Desc:** Clinical application of nuclear medicine, radiopharmacy, radiochemistry, interdisciplinary studies which include the use of a nuclear medicine procedure, physics of nuclear medicine, nuclear medicine instrumentation and computing, conceptual and theoretical matters relevant to nuclear medicine, clinical application of in vitro radionuclide techniques, etc.
**Ind/Abst** ADONIS; Biol. Abstr.; Chem. Abstr.; CSA Neuro. Abstr. (?-?); Curr. Contents Clin. Med.; EMBASE; Energy Res. Abstr. (Aug. 1980-); Health Saf. Sci. Abstr.; Index Med. (Vol. 5, No. 1, 1984-); Life Sci. Collect.; Pollut. Abstr. Indexes; Protozoolog. Abstr.; Res. Alert [Select. Cov.]; SCISEARCH.

US
**NUCLEAR MEDICINE IN CANCER DIAGNOSIS AND MANAGEMENT.** **Main/Corp** International Cancer Research Data Bank. Periodical. English. US Department of Health and Human Services National Institutes of Health, 9000 Rockville Pike, Bethesda MD 20892. **Tel** (301)496-9291, FAX (301)496-2443. **UDC** 616-006.6-085.849; 615.849:616-006.6.

GW/0550-3175
**NUCLEAR-MEDIZIN. SUPPLEMENTUM.** (NUKLEARMEDIZIN. SUPPLEMENTUM.). [Nuclearmedizin, Suppl.]. **Added/Corp** Society of Nuclear Medicine (1963- ). Society of Nuclear Medicine, Europe. **VFOAT** Nuclear Medicine. (1977)-. Academic Scholarly Publication. English (French, German and Spanish). Available only to subscribers of Nuclear Medicine. F K Schattauer Verlagsgesellschaft mbH, Postfach 10 45 45, D 70040 Stuttgart Germany. **Tel** 011 49 711 2298726. **LC** R895.A1; N82. **DD** 616.07/575/05. **NLM** W1 NU183A. **CODEN** NMBSAGNUSUDU. Documents available from CASDDS. ***Continues*** *Nuclear-Medizin. Supplementum, 0550-3775.*
**Ind/Abst** Chem. Abstr.; Energy Res. Abstr. (1977-).

GW/0723-7065
**NUKLEARMEDIZINER, DER.** (DER NUKLEARMEDIZINER : ORGAN DES BERUFSVERBANDES DEUTSCHER NUKLEARMEDIZINER.). [Nuklearmediziner]. Began with March 1977. Academic Scholarly Publication. English

(German). qt. **NLM** W1; NU183F. **CODEN** NKLZD8. Documents available from The Genuine Article, CASDDS. **Ind/Abst** Chem. Abstr.; Energy Res. Abstr. (July 1981-); Res. Alert [Select. Cov.]; SCISEARCH.

•US/0000-1457
**OFFICIAL AMERICAN BOARD OF MEDICAL SPECIALTIES (ABMS) DIRECTORY OF BOARD CERTIFIED NUCLEAR MEDICINE SPECIALISTS, THE.** [Off. Am. Board Med. Spec. (ABMS) dir. board certif. nucl. med. spec.]. **Added/Corp** American Board of Medical Specialties. American Board of Nuclear Medicine. **VFOAT** Directory of Board Certified Nuclear Medicine Specialists; Nuclear Medicine Specialists; Official ... ABMS Directory of Board Certified Nuclear Medicine Specialists. 5th Ed. (1992)-. Directory. English. be. $79.95. Marquis Who's Who, A Reed Reference Publishing Company, Part of Reed International PLC, 121 Chanlon Road, New Providence NJ 07974. **Tel** (908)464-6800, (800)521-8110, FAX (908)665-6688, telex 138 755. **DD** 616. **NLM** WN 22.1; A152. ***Continues*** *ABMS Directory of Certified Nuclear Medicine Specialists, 0884-1454.*

US
**PHYSICIANS' DESK REFERENCE FOR RADIOLOGY AND NUCLEAR MEDICINE.** **See** Medical Science and Technology-Radiology.

PL/0860-1089
**POLSKI PRZEGLAD RADIOLOGII.** (POLSKI PRZEGLAD RADIOLOGII / POLSKIE LEKARSKIE TOWARZYSTWO RADIOLOGICZNE.). [Pol. prz. radiol.]. **Added/Corp** Polskie Lekarskie Towarzystwo Radiologiczne. **VFOAT** Polish Review of Radiology. Vol 47 No 1 (Jan/Feb 1983)-. Academic Scholarly Publication. Polish (summaries and/or abstracts in Russian and English). mo. **(Subscription address:** ARS Polona, PO Box 1001, 00068 Warsaw Poland.**)** **NLM** W1; PO2878. ***Continues*** *Polski Przeglad Radiologii I Medycyny Nuklearnej, 0137-7183.*
**Ind/Abst** EMBASE.

US/0896-5331
**PRACTICAL REVIEWS IN NUCLEAR MEDICINE.** (PRACTICAL REVIEWS IN NUCLEAR MEDICINE [SOUND RECORDING].). [Pract. rev. nucl. med.]. **Added/Corp** Educational Reviews, Inc. Montefiore Medical Center. **VFOAT** Practical Reviews. Vol. 1 (1975)-. Periodical. English. mo. $175.00 Physicians/Dentists; $125.00 Residents. Educational Reviews Inc., 6801 Cahaba Valley Road, Birmingham AL 35242. **Tel** (205)991-5188, (800)633-4743, FAX (205)995-1926. **DD** 616.
**Desc:** Summary: Abstract cards of articles found in the journal literature.

US/0741-160X
**RADIOLOGY & IMAGING LETTER.** [Radiol. imag. lett.]. **VFOAT** Radiology and Imaging Letter. Vol. 4, No. 1 (Jan. 1, 1984)-. Periodical. English. sm (published once during January and August). $266.00 US, Canada, Mexico; $300.00 other. Quest Publishing Company, 1351 Titan Way, Brea CA 92621. **Tel** (714)738-6400, FAX (714)525-6258. **ED** Allan F. Pacela. **NLM** W1; RE369F. **[CCC].** Index available. **Bk Rev**. Documents available from UMI Article Clearinghouse. ***Continues*** *Radiology Letter, 0273-4958.*
**Desc:** Written for professionals concerned with radiology, medical imaging, radiation therapy, ultrasound and nuclear medicine.
**Ind/Abst** Health Devices Alerts; Pharm. News Index (Dec. 1987-).

US/0748-6111
**RADIOPHARMACY AND RADIOPHARMACOLOGY YEARBOOK.** [Radiopharm. radiopharmacol. yearb.]. **VFOAT** Radiopharmacy & Radiopharmacology Yearbook. 1-. English. an. $47.00. Gordon & Breach Science Publishers, Inc., PO Box 786, Cooper Station, New York NY 10276. **Tel** (212)206-8900, FAX (212)645-2459. **(Subscription address:** International Publishers Distributor at one of the following addresses: 820 Town Center Drive, Langhorne, PA 19047; or PO Box 90, Reading Berkshire RG1 8JL UK; or Kent Ridge PO Box 1180, Singapore 9111, Republic of Singapore**)** **ED** Peter M Cox and C M King. **DD** 615. **NLM** W1; RA369R.

UK/0308-2458
**RECENT ADVANCES IN CLINICAL NUCLEAR MEDICINE.** [Recent adv. clin. nucl. med.]. No. 1 (1975)-. Academic Scholarly Publication. English. ir. Churchill Livingstone, 1-3 Baxter's Place, Leith Walk, Edinburgh EH1 3AF Scotland. **Tel** 011 44 31 556 2424, FAX 011 44 31 558 1278, telex 727511. **(Subscription address:** Longman Group Ltd., Subscription Office, PO Box 1584, Birmingham AL 35201-1584.**)** **ED** W.R. Greig and F.C. Gillespie. **NLM** W1 RE105TL. **CODEN** RACMDY. Documents available from CASDDS.
**Ind/Abst** Chem. Abstr.

US/0883-8291
**REVIEWS OF MAGNETIC RESONANCE IN MEDICINE.** ***Title Change.*** [Rev. magn. reson. med.]. Vol. 1, No. 1- (1986)-. Periodical. English. Twice a year. Pergamon Press Inc., 660 White Plains Road, Tarrytown NY 10591-5153. **Tel** (914)524-9200, FAX (914)333-2444, telex 13-7328. **(Subscription address:** UK/ Headington Hill Hall, Oxford OX3 0BW; Can/ 150 Consumers Road/Suite 104, Willowdale Ontario M2J 1P9; Aus-NZ/ POB 544, Potts Point NSW 2011**)** **ED** John Gore. **DD** 610. **NLM** W1; RE257DK. **[CCC].** available on microfilm and microfiche from University Microfilms International (UMI). ***Continued by*** *Magnetic Resonance Imaging, 0730-725X.*
**Ind/Abst** Curr. Aware. Biol. Sci., CABS.

AG
**REVISTA DE BIOLOGIA Y MEDICINA NUCLEAR.** Periodical. Multiple languages (English, Spanish and Portuguese). Three times a year. Revista de Biologia y Medicina Nuclear, Casilla de Correo No 13 Suc, 53 Buenos Aires Argentina. **LC** R895.A1; R46.

SP
**REVISTA ESPANOLA DE MEDICINA NUCLEAR.** (198?)-. Periodical. Spanish. Three times a year. $42.25. Editorial Garsi SA, Juan Bravo 46, 28006 Madrid, Spain. **Tel** 011 34 1 4021212, telex 98358 GARSI E.
**Ind/Abst** EMBASE; Indice Med. Esp.

SP/0213-814X
**REVISTA ESPANOLA DE MEDICINA NUCLEAR. SUPLEMENTO.** (1986)-. Periodical. Multiple languages. ir. Editorial Garsi SA, Juan Bravo 46, 28006 Madrid, Spain. **Tel** 011 34 1 4021212, telex 98358 GARSI E. **UDC** 61 :621.039.
**Ind/Abst** EMBASE.

US/0001-2998
**SEMINARS IN NUCLEAR MEDICINE.** [Semin. nucl. med.]. **VFOAT** Nuclear Medicine. Vol. 1 (Jan. 1971)-. Academic Scholarly Publication. English. qt. $104.00 (individual), $147.00 (institution), $69.00 (student) US; $164.00 (individual), $180.00 (institution) other. W.B. Saunders Company, A Subsidiary of Harcourt Brace Jovanovich, Inc., The Curtis Center/Suite 300, Independence Square West, Philadelphia PA 19106-3399. **Tel** (215)238-7800 or, 5587, FAX (215)238-7883, telex 173146. **(Subscription address:** W. B. Saunders Company / North America Subscriptions, c/o Periodicals, 6277 Sea Harbour Drive, 4th Floor, Orlando FL 32887.**)** **ED** Leonard M Freeman and M Donald Blaufox. **DD** 616. **NLM** W1 SE489D. **CODEN** SMNMAB. **[CCC]. Pr Rev. Circ:** 6,610. Documents available from The Genuine Article, BIOSIS Document Express, Ask*IEEE, CASDDS.
**Desc:** A source for newer concepts and techniques developed in nuclear medicine. The clinically oriented oriented articles provide a ready reference for all those involved in the performance and interpretation of nuclear medicine procedures.
**Ind/Abst** Biol. Abstr.; Chem. Abstr.; Curr. Aware. Biol. Sci., CABS; Curr. Contents Clin. Med.; EMBASE; Energy Res. Abstr. (Jan. 1971-); Index Med.; INSPEC (Jan. 1971-); Iowa Drug Inf. Serv. (1981-); Mod. Med.; Life Sci. Collect.; Phys. Med. Biol. (19??-19??); Res. Alert [Full Cov.]; Sci. Cit. Index; SCISEARCH.

IS
**TRANSACTIONS - THE ISRAEL NUCLEAR SOCIETY, THE ISRAEL HEALTH PHYSICS SOCIETY, RADIATION RESEARCH SOCIETY OF ISRAEL, THE ISRAEL SOCIETY OF MEDICAL PHYSICS, THE ISRAEL SOCIETY OF NUCLEAR MEDICINE.** **See** Physics-Nuclear Physics.

US/0084-3903
**YEAR BOOK OF NUCLEAR MEDICINE, THE.** [Year book nucl. med.]. **VFOAT** Nuclear Medicine. Vol. 1, (1966)-. English. an. $69.95. Mosby Year Book Inc., 11830 Westline Industrial Drive, St Louis MO 63146. **Tel** (800)325-4177, (314)872-8370, FAX (314)432-1380, telex 44-2402. **ED** Paul B. Hoffer, John C. Gore, Alexander Gottschalk, Dirk Sostman and Barry L. Zaret. **LC** RC93.A1; Y4. **DD** 616. **NLM** W1 YE279. **CODEN** YNUMAH. Documents available from BIOSIS Document Express.
**Ind/Abst** Biol. Abstr. (1985-).

CC/0253-9780
**ZHONGHUA HEYIXUE ZAZHI.** (CHUNG-HUA HO I HSUEH TSA CHIH.). [Zhonghua heyixue zazhi]. **VFOAT** Chinese Journal of Nuclear Medicine. 1981-. Academic Scholarly Publication. Chinese. qt. $3.60. Science Press, 16 Donghuangchenggen North Street, Beijing 100707, People's Republic of China. **Tel** 011 86 1 4019821, 011 86 1 4010642, FAX 011 86 1 4012180, 011 86 1 4019810, telex 210147. **UDC** 615.849.2. **NLM** W1 CH9817D. **CODEN** CITCDE. Documents available from CASDDS.
**Ind/Abst** Chem. Abstr.; NAPRALERT; SPIN (1982-).

## NURSING

CN/0001-0197
**A A R N NEWSLETTER.** [A A R N newsl.]. **Main/Corp** Alberta Association of Registered Nurses. (Sept. 1945)-. Newsletter. English. Eleven times a year (July and August issues combined). 35.00Can$ Canada; 40.00Can$ other. AARN News Letter, 11620-168 Street, Edmonton Alberta T5M 4A6 Canada. **Tel** (403)451-0043, FAX (403)452-3276. **ED** Evelyn Henderson. **NLM** W1 A1028. **[CCC]. Bk Rev**, (Qty: 4-6). **Ad Acc, Adv Mgr:** Jan Henry, **Tel** (403)484-3895. **Circ:** 25,000.
**Desc:** Official publication of the registered nurses of Alberta. Nursing topics/information in specific interest to registered nurses. Health promotion and illness prevention.
**Ind/Abst** Cumul. Index Nurs. Allied Health Lit.; Int. Nurs. Index.

US/1046-7467
**AACN CLINICAL ISSUES IN CRITICAL CARE NURSING.** [AACN clin. issues crit. care nurs.]. **Added/Corp** American Association of Critical-Care Nurses. **VFOAT** Clinical Issues in Critical Care Nursing. **VAT** American Association of Critical-Care Nurses Clinical Issues in Critical Care Nursing; American Association of Critical Care Nurses Clinical Issues in Critical Care Nursing. Vol. 1, No. 1 (May 1990)-. Periodical. English. qt. $62.00 (individuals), $110.00 (institutions) US; $75.00 (individuals), $125.00 (institutions) other. J.B. Lippincott Company, 227 East Washington Square, Philadelphia PA 19106-3780. **Tel** (215)238-4200 or 4454, FAX (215)238-4227. **DD** 610. **NLM** W1; AA101AP. cum. index. **Pr Rev.**
**Ind/Abst** Cumul. Index Nurs. Allied Health Lit.; Health Plan. Adminis.; Int. Nurs. Index (Vol. 1, No. 1, 1990-).

US/1055-8349
**AACN NURSING SCAN IN CRITICAL CARE.** [AACN nurs. scan crit. care]. **Added/Corp** American Association of Critical-Care Nurses. **VAT** American Association of Critical-Care Nurses Nursing Scan in Critical Care. Vol. 1, No. 1 (May/June 1991)-. Periodical. English. bm (6 issues). $63.00 (institutions), $43.00 (individuals) US; $74.00 (institutions), $54.00 (individuals) other. NURSECOM Inc., 1211 Locust Street, Philadelphia PA 19107. **Tel** (215)545-7222, (800)242-6757, FAX (215)545-8107. **ED** Gayle R. Whitman, RN, MSN. **DD** 610. **NLM** W1; AA96. **Pr Rev. Circ:** 6258. available on an online database, CD-ROM, magnetic tape, and microfilm from University Microfilms International (UMI).
**Desc:** A professional resource journal containing synopsis and commentary of articles surveyed from nursing, medical and professional periodicals as well as other current sources that relate to all aspects of critical care nursing. The abstracts are annotated with remarks and opinion by nurses known and respected for their involvement in critical care.

US/0094-6354
**AANA JOURNAL.** [A. A. N. A. j.]. **Added/Corp** American Association of Nurse Anesthetists. Vol. 42 (Feb. 1974)-. Academic Scholarly Publication. English. bm. $24.00. American Association of Nurse Anesthetists, 222 South Prospect Avenue, Park Ridge IL 60068. **Tel** (708)692-7050 ext. 314, FAX (708)692-6968. **ED** Betty A. Colitti Stuffers. **NLM** W1 A1026T. **CODEN** ANJOEE. Index available. cum. index. **Bk Rev. Ad Acc. Pr Rev. Circ:** 24,000 (ctrl). available on microfilm and microfiche from University Microfilms International (UMI). ***Continues*** *Journal of the American Association of Nurse Anesthetists, 0002-7448.*
**Desc:** Focuses on the clinical in the form of both practical and theoretical editorial matter provided by various specialists (principally in nursing and medicine).
**Ind/Abst** Cumul. Index Nurs. Allied Health Lit.; EMBASE [Select. Cov.]; Health Plan. Adminis.; Index Med.; Int. Nurs. Index.

US/0199-2554
**AANA NEWSBULLETIN.** **Main/Corp** American Association of Nurse Anesthetists. **VFOAT** A. A. N. A. News Bulletin. **VAT** American Association of Nurse Anesthetists News Bulletin. V. 1- Sept. 1947-. Periodical. English. mo. American Association of Nurse Anesthetists, 222 South Prospect Avenue, Park Ridge IL 60068. **Tel** (708)692-7050 ext. 314, FAX (708)692-6968. **ED** Betty Colitti. **Circ:** 24,000 (ctrl).

US/0891-0162
**AAOHN JOURNAL.** (AAOHN JOURNAL : OFFICAL JOURNAL OF THE AMERICAN ASSOCIATION OF OCCUPATIONAL HEALTH NURSES.). [AAOHN j.]. **VAT** American Association of Occupational Health Nurses Journal. Vol. 34, No. 1 (Jan. 1986)-. Periodical. English. mo. $49.00 (individuals), $62.00 (institutions) US. Slack Inc., 6900 Grove Road, Thorofare NJ 08086. **Tel** (609)848-1000, (800)257-8290, FAX (609)853-5991, telex 517108 SLACK INC VD. **LC** RC966. **DD** 610.73/46/05. **NLM** W1; AA101D. **[CCC]. Pr Rev.** available on microfilm and microfiche from University Microfilms International (UMI). Documents available. ***Continues*** *Occupational Health Nursing, 0029-7933.*

**Ind/Abst** Chem. Hazards Ind.; Cumul. Index Nurs. Allied Health Lit.; EMBASE; Ind. Hyg. Dig.; Int. Nurs. Index; Lab. Hazards Bull.; Nurs. Abstr.; Work Relat. Abstr.

US/0746-620X
**AAOHN NEWS / AMERICAN ASSOCIATION OF OCCUPATIONAL HEALTH NURSES, INC.** [AAOHN news]. **Added/Corp** American Association of Occupational Health Nurses. **VFOAT** A.A.O.H.N. News. **VAT** American Association of Occupational Health Nurses News. (198?)-. Periodical. English. mo. $12.00. American Association of Occupational Health Nurses, 50 Lenox Pointe, Atlanta GA 30324. **Tel** (800)241-8014, (404)262-1162. **ED** Kriste L. Roof. **Bk Rev. Ad Acc. Pr Rev. Circ:** 13,000 (ctrl). ***Continues*** *AAOHN Newsletter, 0745-4376.*

US/1046-7041
**ABNF JOURNAL, THE.** [ABNF j.]. **Added/Corp** Association of Black Nursing Faculty in Higher Education. **VAT** Association of Black Nursing Faculty Journal. Vol. 1, No. 1 (Spring 1990)-. Periodical. English. bm (6 issues). $125.00 institution, $75.00 individual. Tucker Publications Inc., PO Box 580, Lisle IL 60532. **Tel** (708)969-3809, FAX (708)969-3895. **ED** Dr. Sallie Tucker-Allen (editor's address: 5823 Queens Cove, Lisle, IL 60532). **DD** 610. **NLM** W1; AB855F. Index available (bound in 6th issue). **Bk Rev**, (Qty: 6-8). **Ad Acc**, **Adv Mgr Tel** same as publisher. **Pr Rev. Circ:** 500.
**Desc:** Focuses on minority health issues, especially those dealing with African-American patients, families, communities, faculty and students.
**Ind/Abst** Cumul. Index Nurs. Allied Health Lit.; Int. Nurs. Index.

US/1062-0249
**ACADEMIC NURSE, THE.** **See** Occupations and Careers.

CN/1182-8897
**ACCESS / ARNN, ASSOCIATION OF REGISTERED NURSES OF NEWFOUNDLAND.** [Access - Assoc. Regist. Nurses Nfld.]. **Added/Corp** Association of Registered Nurses of Newfoundland. **VFOAT** ARNN Access. Vol. 10, No. 4 (May/Nov. 1990)-. Periodical. English. qt. Free to members. Association of Registered Nurses of Newfoundland, ARNN House, PO Box 6116, St John's Newfoundland A1C 5X8 Canada. **Tel** (709)753-6040, FAX (709)753-4940. **DD** 610.73/06/0718. ***Continues*** *ARNN News News News., 0822-7160.*

●UK/0965-2302
**ACCIDENT AND EMERGENCY NURSING.** Vol. 1, No. 1 (Jan. 1993)-. Periodical. English. qt (4 issues). £106.00 Europe; £107.00 Other (Institutions). Churchill Livingstone, 1-3 Baxter's Place, Leith Walk, Edinburgh EH1 3AF Scotland. **Tel** 011 44 31 556 2424, FAX 011 44 31 558 1278, telex 727511. **(Subscription address:** Maruzen Company Ltd., PO Box 5050, Import & Export Department, Tokyo 100 31 Japan.**)** **NLM** W1; AC701.

AT/1031-1017
**ACORN JOURNAL.** [Acorn j.]. **Added/Corp** Australian Confederation of Operating Room Nurses. **VFOAT** Australian Confederation of Operating Room Nurses Journal. (1987)-. Periodical. English. qt. 50.00Aus$ Australia; 60.00Aus$ other. Australian Confederation of Operating Room Nurses, PO Box 733, Petersham, NSW 2049 Australia. **ED** Lynne Redknap. **DD** 610.736770994. **Bk Rev**, (Qty: 3-4). **Ad Acc. Pr Rev. Circ:** 3,500. ***Continues*** *Forceps, Snippets, Acorn News, 0819-1964.*
**Ind/Abst** Cumul. Index Nurs. Allied Health Lit.

AT/0156-3491
**ACORN JOURNAL : OFFICIAL JOURNAL OF THE AUSTRALIAN CONFEDERATION OF OPERATING ROOM NURSES.** **Added/Corp** Australian Confederation of Operating Room Nurses. **VFOAT** Australian Confederation of Operating Room Nurses Journal. (1988)-. Periodical. English. Four times a year (Jan., June, Sept., Dec.). 50.00Aus$ Australia; 60.00Aus$ other. Acorn Journal Account, PO Box 733, Petersham 2049 Australia. **Tel** 011 61 2 5168565, FAX 011 61 2 9014306. **ED** Lynne Redknap, (phone: 011 61 2 7366729). **NLM** W1; AC734. **Bk Rev. Ad Acc, Adv Mgr:** K. Collins, **Tel** 02 212 2780. **Pr Rev. Circ:** 3,500 (ctrl). ***Continues*** *Forceps, Snippets & ACORN News.*

SZ/0254-0819
**ACUTE CARE.** ***Ceased.*** [Acute care]. 10/1/83-84 (Sept. 1984)-Ceased Vol. 15, Dec. 1989. Academic Scholarly Publication. English. qt. S. Karger AG, Allschwilerstrasse 10, PO Box - Postfach - Case Postale, CH-4009 Basel Switzerland. **Tel** 011 41 61 306-1111, FAX 011 41 61 306-1234, telex CH 962 652. **ED** M. H. Weil and E. C. Rackow. **LC** QH324.9.B5; I552. **NLM** W1; AC999W. **[CCC].** Index available. **Ad Acc.** available on microfilm; available on microfiche. Documents available from Article Express International, BIOSIS Document Express, Ask*IEEE. ***Continues*** *Biotelemetry and Patient Monitoring, 0378-309X.*
**Desc:** Features state-of-the-art reviews selected for their value in aiding medical decisions or guiding the introduction of newly developed techniques and instruments. New diagnostic, monitoring and therapeutic devices evaluated in terms of existing procedures, patient-risk, noninvasive qualities and cost-effectiveness are also included.
**Ind/Abst** Bioeng. Abstr.; Biol. Abstr. (1984-?); Ei Page One; EMBASE; Energy Res. Abstr. (1984-?); Eng. Index Annu.; Health Plan. Adminis. (?-?); Index Med. (Vol. 10, No. 1, 1983-?); INSPEC (1984-?); Int. Aerosp. Abstr.; Life Sci. Collect.

US/0899-9112
**ADDICTION NURSING NETWORK.** ***Title Change.*** [Addict. nurs. netw.]. Vol. 1, No. 1 (Apr. 1989)-(19??). Periodical. English. qt. Mary Ann Liebert Inc., 1651 Third Avenue, New York NY 10128. **Tel** (212)289-2300, (800)M-LIEBERT, FAX (212)289-4697. **ED** Madeline A. Naegle. **DD** 610. **NLM** W1; AD132. ***Continued by*** *Addictions Nursing.*
**Desc:** Recognizes the roles of nurses in identifying and intervening with drug and alcohol abuse. It provides information on these health problems and the specialty of addictions nursing.
**Ind/Abst** Cumul. Index Nurs. Allied Health Lit.

●US/1073-886X
**ADDICTIONS NURSING.** [Addict. nurs.]. Vol. 6, No. 1 (Spring 1994)-. Periodical. English. qt. $104.00. Mary Ann Liebert Inc., 1651 Third Avenue, New York NY 10128. **Tel** (212)289-2300, (800)M-LIEBERT, FAX (212)289-4697. **DD** 610. ***Continues*** *Addictions Nursing Network, 0899-9112.*

US/0161-9268
**ADVANCES IN NURSING SCIENCE.** (ANS, ADVANCES IN NURSING SCIENCE.). [Adv. nurs. sci.]. **VFOAT** Advances in Nursing Science. Vol. 1 (Oct. 1978)-. Periodical. English. qt. $68.00. Aspen Publishers Inc., 7201 McKinney Circle, Frederick MD 21701. **Tel** (800)234-1660, (301)698-7100, FAX (301)251-5784, telex 5106014543. **(Subscription address:** Aspen Publishers Inc., PO Box 990, Frederick MD 21701.**)** **ED** Peggy L. Chinn RN, PhD. **LC** RT1; .A16. **DD** 174/.2. **NLM** W1 A14SH. **[CCC]. Pr Rev.** available on microfilm and microfiche from University Microfilms International (UMI). Documents available from The Genuine Article.
**Desc:** A journal of knowledge, ethics, theory and research to support today's professional nurse. The primary purposes of ANS are to stimulate the development of nursing science and promote application and practice of emerging theories and research findings.
**Ind/Abst** Annals Behav. Med.; Cumul. Index Nurs. Allied Health Lit.; Curr. Contents Soc. Behav. Sci.; Health Plan. Adminis.; Index Med. (1981-); Int. Nurs. Index; Nurs. Abstr.; Psychol. Abstr. (1984-); PsycINFO (1990-); PsycLit; Res. Alert [Full Cov.]; Soc. Sci. Cit. Index [Full Cov.].

JA
**AICHI KENRITSU KANGO TANKI DAIGAKU ZASSHI.** **Main/Corp** Aichi Kenritsu Kango Tanki Daigaku. No. 1 (1970)-. Periodical. Japanese. an. Kenritsu Kango Tanki Daigaku, Oaza Kami-Shidami Moriyama-ku, Nagoya Japan. **LC** RT1; .A35a.

●FR
**AIDE-SOIGNANTE, L'.** **VFOAT** AS. (1992)-. Periodical. French. Eleven times a year. 245.00F France; 290.00F other. Expansion Scientifique Francaise, 31 Boulevard de la Tour-Maubourg, 75007 Paris France. **Tel** 011 33 1 40 62 64 00, 011 33 1 40626439. **NLM** W1; AI69663. ***Continues*** *AS Revue de l'Aide-Soignante, 0987-8947.*

US
**AJN CAREER GUIDE FOR ... .** **Added/Corp** American Journal of Nursing Company. **VFOAT** American Journal of Nursing Career Guide for ... . (1993)-. English. an (Jan.). Free on request. American Journal of Nursing Company, 555 West 57th Street, New York NY 10019-2961. **Tel** (212)582-8820, FAX (212)586-5462. **LC** RT82; .A56. ***Continues*** *AJN Guide to Nursing Career Opportunities.*

US
**AJN GUIDE TO NURSING CAREER OPPORTUNITIES, THE.** ***Title Change.*** **Added/Corp** American Journal of Nursing Company. **VFOAT** AJN Guide. (198?)-(1992). English. American Journal of Nursing Company, 555 West 57th Street, New York NY 10019-2961. **Tel** (212)582-8820, FAX (212)586-5462. ***Continues*** *AJN Guide, 0898-4046.* ***Continued by*** *AJN Career Guide for ... .*

US
**AJN/MOSBY ... NURSING BOARDS REVIEW FOR THE NCLEX-RN EXAMINATION.** **VFOAT** American Journal of Nursing/Mosby. ... Nursing Boards Review for the NCLEX-RN Examination; Nursing Boards Review. (1991)-. English. an (Nov.). $27.95 (latest edition). Mosby Year Book Inc., 11830 Westline Industrial Drive, St Louis MO 63146. **Tel** (800)325-4177, (314)872-8370, FAX (314)432-1380, telex 44-2402. **LC** RT52; .A37. **NLM** WY 18; A312. ***Continues*** *AJN Nursing Boards Review for the NCLEX-RN Examination, 0737-3058.*

US/0002-4317
**ALABAMA NURSE, THE.** [Ala. nurse]. **Added/Corp** Alabama State Nurses' Association. (19??)-. English. ir. Free on request. Alabama State Nurses Association, 229 Profession Center, Montgomery AL 36104. **Tel** (205) 262-8321. **NLM** W1 AL161. ***Supersedes*** *Alabama State Nurses' Association. Bulletin.*
**Ind/Abst** Health Plan. Adminis.; Int. Nurs. Index.

US/0002-4546
**ALASKA NURSE, THE.** [Alsk. nurse]. **Added/Corp** Alaska Nurses' Association. (1951)-. Periodical. English. bm. $15.00. Alaska Nurses Association, 237 East 3rd Avenue, Anchorage AK 99501. **Tel** (907)274-0827. **ED** Kathy North. **DD** 610. **NLM** W1 AL194. **Ad Acc. Circ:** 500 (ctrl).
**Desc:** Pertains to nursing topics.
**Ind/Abst** Health Plan. Adminis.; Int. Nurs. Index.

US/0149-2608
**ALUMNI MAGAZINE - ALUMNI ASSOCIATION OF THE JOHNS HOPKINS HOSPITAL SCHOOL OF NURSING, THE.** **See** College and School Publications-Alumni.

US/0898-4093
**ALUMNI MAGAZINE / COLUMBIA UNIVERSITY-PRESBYTERIAN HOSPITAL SCHOOL OF NURSING ALUMNI ASSOCIATION, INC.** [Alumni mag. - Columbia Univ.-Presbyt. Hosp. School Nurs. Alumni Assoc.]. **Added/Corp** Columbia University-Presbyterian Hospital School of Nursing Alumni Association. Vol. 80, No. 1 (Winter 1985)-. Periodical. English. Three times a year. Columbia University / Presbyterian Hospital Nursing Association, 179 Fort Washington, New York NY 10032. **Tel** (212)694-3193. **DD** 610. **NLM** W1; AL996U. ***Continues*** *Alumnae Magazine (Columbia University-Presbyterian Hospital School of Nursing Alumnae Association), 0069-634X.*
**Ind/Abst** Int. Nurs. Index (Winter 1985-).

●US/1062-3264
**AMERICAN JOURNAL OF CRITICAL CARE.** [Am. j. crit. care]. **Added/Corp** American Association of Critical Care Nurses. **VFOAT** Critical Care. (1992)-. Periodical. English. bm (6 issues). $110.00 (institutions), $45.00 (individuals) US. American Association Critical Care Nurses, 101 Columbia, Alisa Veijo CA 92655. **Tel** (714)362-2000. **(Subscription address:** American Journal of Critical Care, PO Box 626, Holmes, PA 19043; (telephone: (800)345-8112)**)** **ED** Kathleen Dracup and Christopher Bryan-Brown. **DD** 610. **NLM** W1; AM45LN. **Ad Acc. Pr Rev. Acid Free. Circ:** 74,000. available on CD-ROM from SilverPlatter (US).
**Desc:** Multidisciplinary and publishes the latest research in the field of critical care.
**Ind/Abst** Cumul. Index Nurs. Allied Health Lit.; Index Med.

US/0002-936X
**AMERICAN JOURNAL OF NURSING, THE.** [Am. j. nurs.]. **Added/Corp** American Nurses' Association. Nurses' Associated Alumnae of the United States. **VFOAT** AJN. Vol. 1 (Oct. 1900)-. Periodical. English. mo. $45.00 institution, $23.00 indiviudal. American Journal of Nursing Company, 555 West 57th Street, New York NY 10019-2961. **Tel** (212)582-8820, FAX (212)586-5462. **(Subscription address:** American Journal of Nursing, PO Box 50480, Boilder CO 80322-0480.**)** **LC** RT1; .A5. **DD** 610. **NLM** W1 AM495. Index available (free). cum. index. available on microfilm and microfiche from University Microfilms International (UMI). Documents available from The Genuine Article, UMI Article Clearinghouse. ***Continued in part by*** *Proceedings of the Convention of the American Nurses' Association, 0191-3778.*
**Desc:** Directed to highly qualified nurses practicing in all settings. Combines authoritative articles on clinical practice, issues, and trends with fast-paced broad news coverage.
**Ind/Abst** Abr. Index Med.; Acad. Abstr. Full Text Elite (July 1990-); Acad. Abstr. (July 1990-); Acad. Ind. [Computer File] (1989-); Acad. Search (July 1990-); AGRICOLA; Appl. Soc. Sci. Index Abstr.; Cumul. Index Nurs. Allied Health Lit.; Curr. Lit. Fam. Plan.; Expand. Acad. Index (1989-); Gen. Sci. Index; Gen. Sci. Source (Jul. 1990-); Health Devices Alerts; Health Index (1989-); Health Period. Database; Health Plan. Adminis.; Health Ref. Cent. (Jan. 1989-) [Full Cov.]; Hospit. Manage. Rev.; Index Med.; INFO-SOUTH Abstr.; Int. Nurs. Index; Int. Pharm. Abstr.; Mag. Artic. Summar. Elite (July 1990-); Mag. Artic. Summar. Select (July 1990-); Mag. Artic. Summar. CD-ROM (July 1990-); Mag. Search; Newsp. Period. Abstr. (1986-); Nurs. Abstr.; Nutr. Res. Newsl.; Life Sci. Collect.; Physic. Medline Plus; Res. Alert [Full Cov.]; Rev. Med. Vet. Entomol.; Sci. Cit. Index (19??-19??); SCISEARCH; Soc. Sci. Cit. Index [Full Cov.]; Soc. Work Abstr. [Select. Cov.]; SportSearch; Stud. Women Abstr.; Vocat. Search (July 1990-); Women Stud. Abstr.

US/0098-1486
**AMERICAN NURSE, THE.** [Am. nurse]. **Added/Corp** American Nurses' Association. Vol. 4, No. 1

(Feb. 1972)-. Periodical. English. mo (10 issues per year - July/Aug & Nov/Dec issues combined). $20.00. American Nurses Association, 600 Maryland Avenue Southwest, Suite 100, Washington DC 20024. **Tel** (202)554-4444. **(Subscription address:** American Nurses Association, PO Box 2244, Waldof MD 20604.**)** **ED** Patricia McCarty. **NLM** W1 AM6635. **Ad Acc. Circ:** 200,000. available on microfilm and microfiche from University Microfilms International (UMI). ***Continues*** *American Nurses' Association. ANA in Action, 0587-3053.*
**Desc:** A broad range of professional, economic, political, ethical and legal issues and events that affect nursing.
**Ind/Abst** Cumul. Index Nurs. Allied Health Lit.; Hospit. Health Admin. Index; Int. Nurs. Index; Nurs. Abstr.

●US/1066-8977
**AMERICAN SOCIETY OF POST ANESTHESIA NURSES (ASPAN).** (AMERICAN SOCIETY OF POST ANESTHESIA NURSES (ASPAN) : [JOURNAL].). **Added/Corp** American Society of Post Anesthesia Nurses. **VFOAT** American Society of Post Anesthesia Nurses. (1993)-. Periodical. English. bm. $49.00 (individual), $85.00 (institution) US; $100.00 other. W.B. Saunders Company, A Subsidiary of Harcourt Brace Jovanovich, Inc., The Curtis Center/Suite 300, Independence Square West, Philadelphia PA 19106-3399. **Tel** (215)238-7800 or, 5587, FAX (215)238-7883, telex 173146. **(Subscription address:** W. B. Saunders Company / North America Subscriptions, c/o Periodicals, 6277 Sea Harbour Drive, 4th Floor, Orlando FL 32887.**)** **NLM** W1; PO934D. **[CCC].**

US/0065-9495
**ANA CLINICAL SESSIONS.** 1966-. Periodical. English. be. Appleton Century Crofts, Prentice Hall, 200 Old Tappan Road, Old Tappan NJ 07675. **Tel** (201)767-5188, (800)922-0579. **LC** RT3; .A5. **DD** 610.73. **NLM** W1 A1398P.
**Desc:** Consists of papers present at clinical sessions of the annual conventions of the American Nurses' Association.

BL/0102-2334
**ANAIS DO CBEN.** [An. CBEN]. **Added/Corp** Associacao Brasileira de Enfermagem. **VFOAT** Anais do Congresso Brasileiro de Enfermagem,. Vol. 29 (1977)-. Portuguese. ir. Price varies. Associacion Brasileira Enfermagem, Sgan Avenue L2 Norte Q 603 Mod B, Brazilia 70830 DF Brazil. **Tel** 226-0653, 225-4473. **NLM** W1 AN1096R. ***Continues*** *Revista Brasileira de Enfermagem.*

US/8750-0779
**ANNA JOURNAL.** (ANNA JOURNAL / AMERICAN NEPHROLOGY NURSES' ASSOCIATION.). [ANNA j.]. **Added/Corp** American Nephrology Nurses' Association. **VFOAT** A.N.N.A. Journal. **VAT** American Nephrology Nurses Association Journal. Vol. 11, No. 4 (June 1984)-. Periodical. English. bm. $40.00 (institutions), $28.00 (individuals). A.J. Jannetti Inc., East Holly Avenue, Box 56, Pitman NJ 08071-0056. **Tel** (609)256-2300, FAX (609)589-7463. **LC** RC902.A1; A55. **DD** 616. **NLM** W1; AN27. **[CCC].** ***Continues*** *AANNT Journal, 0744-1479.*
**Ind/Abst** Cumul. Index Nurs. Allied Health Lit.; Health Plan. Adminis.; Int. Nurs. Index (Vol. 11, No. 4, 1984-); Nurs. Abstr.

US/0360-4624
**ANNUAL REPORT - BOARD OF NURSE REGISTRATION AND NURSING EDUCATION.** **Main/Corp** Oklahoma. Board of Nurse Registration and Nursing Education. English. an. Oklahoma Board of Nurse Registration and Nursing Education, 2915 North Classen Boulevard 524, Oklahoma City OK 73106-5437. **LC** RT5.O5; B63A. **DD** 610.73/09766.

US
**ANNUAL REPORT TO THE GOVERNOR OF THE STATE OF LOUISANA.** **Main/Corp** Louisiana State Board of Nursing. Jan. (1986)-. English. State Board of Nursing / Louisiana, 907 Pere Marquette Building, 150 Baronne Street, New Orleans LA 70112. **NLM** W2; AL6 L2a. ***Continues*** *Report - Louisiana State Board of Nursing, 0149-0346.*

US/0098-2679
**ANNUAL REPORT - WYOMING STATE BOARD OF NURSING.** **Main/Corp** Wyoming. State Board of Nursing. English. an. $5.00 (per issue). Wyoming State Board of Nursing, Barrett Building/4th Floor, 2301 Central Avenue, Cheyenne WY 82002. **Tel** (307)777-7601. **LC** RT81.U6; W94A. **DD** 353.9/787/008416. ctrl circ.
**Desc:** Provides information about the depth and scope of activities of the Wyoming State Board of Nursing from July 1, 1986 through June 30, 1987.

US/0739-6686
**ANNUAL REVIEW OF NURSING RESEARCH.** [Annu. rev. nurs. res.]. **VFOAT** Review of Nursing Research. Vol. 1 (1983)-. English. an. $41.00 (volume 10). Springer Publishing Company, 536 Broadway, New York NY 10012-3955. **Tel** (212)431-4370, FAX (212)941-7842. **ED** Joyce Fitzpatrick, Roma Lee Taunton, and Ada Jacox. **LC** RT81.5; .A55. **DD** 610.73/072. **NLM** W1; AN778CF.
**Ind/Abst** Cumul. Index Nurs. Allied Health Lit.; Health Plan. Adminis.; Index Med.; Int. Nurs. Index.

SA
**ANNUAL RREPORT / REPUBLIC OF BOPHUTHATSWANA, DEPARTMENT OF HEALTH AND SOCIAL WELFARE, NURSING DIVISION.** **Main/Corp** Bophuthatswana (South Africa) Nursing Division. Vol. 1 (1980)-. English. an. **LC** RT97; .B6a. **DD** 354.682/9400841.

CN/0825-2815
**ANNUAL SALARIES, NURSES, MAJOR HOSPITAL AGREEMENTS, CANADA.** [Annu. salaries nurses major hosp. agreem. Can.]. **Added/Corp** Canadian Nurses' Association. Dept. of Work Life Affairs. **VFOAT** Salaires Annuels, Infirmieres et Infirmieres, Conventions Signees dans les Principaux Hopitaux, Canada. (1983)-. Periodical. English (French). ir. $3.00. Canadian Nurses Association, 50 The Driveway, Ottawa Ontario K2P 1E2 Canada. **Tel** (613)237-2133, FAX (613)237-3520. **DD** 331.2/8161073/0971.

PH/0065-0676
**ANPHI PAPERS, THE.** (ANPHI PAPERS.). [Anphi pap.]. **Main/Corp** Academy of Nursing of the Philippines. **VAT** A P PHI Papers. (1966)-. Periodical. English. sa (2 issues). $10.00. Academy of Nursing of the Philippines, College of Nursing, University of the Philippines, Padre Faura Emita 1000, Manila Philippines. **ED** Cecilia M. Laurente. **NLM** W1 A14S. cum. index. ctrl circ. available on microfilm from University Microfilms International (UMI).
**Ind/Abst** Cumul. Index Nurs. Allied Health Lit.; Philip. Sci. Technol. Abstr.

●US/1072-5067
**AONE'S LEADERSHIP PROSPECTIVES.** [AONE's leadersh. prospect.]. **Added/Corp** American Association of Nurse Executives. **VFOAT** Leadership Perspectives. **VAT** American Association of Nurse Executives' Leadership Prospectives. Vol. 1, No. 1 (Nov./Dec. 1993)-. Periodical. English. bm (6 issues). $63.00 (institutions), $43.00 (individuals) US; $74.00 (institutions), $54.00 (individuals) other. NURSECOM Inc., 1211 Locust Street, Philadelphia PA 19107. **Tel** (215)545-7222, (800)242-6757, FAX (215)545-8107. **DD** 610. ***Continues*** *Nursing Scan in Administration, 1056-3091.*

US/0001-2092
**AORN JOURNAL.** [AORN j.]. **Main/Corp** Association of Operating Room Nurses. **Added/Corp** Association of Operating Room Nurses. Journal. **VAT** Association of Operating Room Nurses Journal. Vol. 1 (Jan./Feb. 1963)-. Periodical. English. mo. $50.00 US; $60.00 other. Association of Operating Room Nurses, Inc., 2170 South Parker Road, Suite 300, Denver CO 80231-5711. **Tel** (303)755-6300, (303)755-6304. **ED** Patricia N. Palmer. **LC** RD99.A1; O22. **NLM** W1; A142. **CODEN** AOJOEL. **[CCC].** Index available. **Bk Rev. Ad Acc. Pr Rev. Circ:** 39,659 (ctrl). available on microfilm and microfiche from University Microfilms International (UMI). ***Supersedes*** *OR Nursing.*
**Ind/Abst** Cumul. Index Nurs. Allied Health Lit.; Health Devices Alerts; Health Plan. Adminis.; Health Serv. Abstr.; Index Med. (July 1978-); Int. Nurs. Index; Int. Pharm. Abstr.; Nurs. Abstr.

US/0001-2092
**AORN JOURNAL.** **Main/Corp** Association of Operating Room Nurses. **VAT** Association of Operating Room Nurses Journal. Vol. 1 (Jan./Feb. 1963)-. Periodical. English. mo. University Microfilms International, 300 North Zeeb Road, Ann Arbor MI 48106-1346. **Tel** (313)761-4700, (800)521-0600 Exts. 2490, 2491, FAX (313)973-1540. **LC** RD99.A1; O22. **[CCC].** ***Continues*** *OR Nursing.*

US/0897-1897
**APPLIED NURSING RESEARCH : ANR.** [Appl. nurs. res.]. **VFOAT** ANR. Vol. 1, No. 1 (May 1988)-. Periodical. English. qt (4 issues). $44.00 (individual), $76.00 (institution) US; $113.00 (indvidual), $121.00 (institution), other. W.B. Saunders Company, A Subsidiary of Harcourt Brace Jovanovich, Inc., The Curtis Center/Suite 300, Independence Square West, Philadelphia PA 19106-3399. **Tel** (215)238-7800 or, 5587, FAX (215)238-7883, telex 173146. **(Subscription address:** W. B. Saunders Company / North America Subscriptions, c/o Periodicals, 6277 Sea Harbour Drive, 4th Floor, Orlando FL 32887.**)** **DD** 610. **NLM** W1; AP516D. **CODEN** ANUREA. **[CCC]. Pr Rev.**
**Ind/Abst** Cumul. Index Nurs. Allied Health Lit.; Health Plan. Adminis.; Int. Nurs. Index.

US/0883-9417
**ARCHIVES OF PSYCHIATRIC NURSING.** [Arch. psychiatr. nurs.]. **VFOAT** APN. Vol. 1, No. 1 (Feb. 1987)-. Periodical. English. bm. $47.00 (individual), $65.00 (institution) other US; $77.00 (individual), $85.00 (institution) other. W.B. Saunders Company, A Subsidiary of Harcourt Brace Jovanovich, Inc., The Curtis Center/Suite 300, Independence Square West, Philadelphia PA 19106-3399. **Tel** (215)238-7800 or, 5587, FAX (215)238-7883, telex 173146. **(Subscription address:** W. B. Saunders Company / North America Subscriptions, c/o Periodicals, 6277 Sea Harbour Drive, 4th Floor, Orlando FL 32887.**)** **ED** Judith B Krauss. **DD** 610. **NLM** W1; AR477ME. **[CCC].** Index available. cum. index. **Bk Rev. Ad Acc. Pr Rev. Circ:** 2,000. available on microfilm.
**Desc:** Disseminates knowledge that directs psychiatric and mental health nursing practice. The field is considered in its broadest perspective, including theory practice and research applications related to all ages, special populations, settings, interdisciplinary collaborations, and both the public and private sectors.
**Ind/Abst** Abstr. Res. Pastor. Care Couns. (19??-); Cumul. Index Nurs. Allied Health Lit.; Health Plan. Adminis.; Index Med.; Int. Nurs. Index (1987-); Nurs. Abstr.; Psychol. Abstr. (1988-); PsycINFO; PsycLit.

US/0004-1599
**ARIZONA NURSE.** [Ariz. nurse]. **Added/Corp** Arizona Nurses' Association. Arizona State Nurses' Association. (1947)-. Periodical. English. Six times a year (Jan., Mar., May, July, Sept., Oct.). $30.00. Arizona State Nurses Association, 1850 East Southern Avenue, Suite 1, Tempe AZ 85282. **Tel** (602)831-0404, FAX (602)839-4780. **ED** Jennifer McAfes, (phone: (602)831-0404). **DD** 610. **NLM** W1 AR797. **Ad Acc. Circ:** 1.300 (ctrl). available on microfilm and microfiche from University Microfilms International (UMI).
**Desc:** Continuing education for nurses, state legislation, organization activities, clinical articles, resources, book reviews.
**Ind/Abst** Cumul. Index Nurs. Allied Health Lit.; Int. Nurs. Index.

US/0272-586X
**ARKANSAS HEALTH MANPOWER STATISTICS : LICENSED PRACTICAL NURSES.** **See** Medical Science and Technology-Abstracting, Bibliographies and Statistics.

US/0272-5878
**ARKANSAS HEALTH MANPOWER STATISTICS : REGISTERED NURSES.** **See** Medical Science and Technology-Abstracting, Bibliographies and Statistics.

US
**ARKANSAS NURSING NEWS.** (19??)-. English. Four times a year (Jan., Apr., July, Oct.). $20.00. Arkansas State Nurses Association, 117 South Cedar Street, Little Rock AR 72205. **Tel** (501)664-5853. **ED** Joanne DeJanovich, (editor's address: 117 South Cedar, Little Rock, AR 72205, phone: (501)664-5853). **Ad Acc.** Full Page (B&W) $350.00. Half Page (B&W) $210.00. **Circ:** 1,000 (ctrl).

●US/1061-4338
**ASORN NEWS.** [ASORN news]. **Added/Corp** American Society of Ophthalmic Registered Nurses. **VAT** American Society of Ophthalmic Registered Nurses News. (Feb. 1992)-. Periodical. English. bm. Glen Erin Publishing, PO Box 193030, San Francisco CA 94119. **DD** 617.

US/0883-9743
**ASPEN'S ADVISOR FOR NURSE EXECUTIVES.** ***Title Change.*** (THE ASPEN ADVISOR FOR NURSE EXECUTIVES.). [Aspen's advis. nurse exec.]. **Added/Corp** Aspen Systems Corporation. **VFOAT** Aspen's Advisor; Advisor. Vol. 1, No. 1 (Oct. 1985)-(19??). Periodical. English. mo. Aspen Publishers Inc., 7201 McKinney Circle, Frederick MD 21701. **Tel** (800)234-1660, (301)698-7100, FAX (301)251-5784, telex 5106014543. **DD** 610. **NLM** W1; AS346M. ***Continued by*** *Aspen's Nurse Executive Network.*
**Desc:** Newsletter for nurse executives focusing on the business side of nursing.
**Ind/Abst** Health Plan. Adminis.; Int. Nurs. Index (Vol. 4, No. 1, 1988-).

●US/1064-8119
**ASPEN'S NURSE EXECUTIVE NETWORK.** **VFOAT** A.Nurse executive network. (1992)-. Periodical. English. mo. $161.00 US. Aspen Publishers Inc., 7201 McKinney Circle, Frederick MD 21701. **Tel** (800)234-1660, (301)698-7100, FAX (301)251-5784, telex 5106014543. **(Subscription address:** Aspen Publishers Inc., PO Box 990, Frederick MD 21701.**)** **ED** Tim Porter. ***Continues*** *Aspen's Advisor for Nurse Executives, 0883-9743.*
**Desc:** Eight fact-filled pages, focusing on your needs-with key insights needed by every busy nurse executive. Packed into a time-saving format, this newsletter offers authoritative, professionally sound guidance you can rely on.

●AT/1036-7314
**AUSTRALIAN CRITICAL CARE : OFFICIAL JOURNAL OF THE CONFEDERATION OF AUSTRALIAN CRITICAL CARE NURSES.** **Added/Corp** Confederation of Australian Critical Care Nurses. Vol. 5, No.1 Mar. (1991)-. Periodical. English. qt (Mar., June, Sept., Dec.). 60.00Aus$ (institution), 50.00Aus$ (individual) Australia; 70.00Aus$ (other). Confederation of Australian Critical Care, PO Box 143, No Stratford NSW,

2137 Australia. **Tel** 11 61 2 4761411, FAX 11 61 2 4761411. **ED** Sally Robertson. **NLM** W1; AU238. cum. index. **Bk Rev. Ad Acc, Adv Mgr:** Jane Perkins. **Circ:** 2,600. ***Continues*** *Confederation of Australian Critical Care Nurses Journal.*
**Ind/Abst** Cumul. Index Nurs. Allied Health Lit.

AT/0813-0531
**AUSTRALIAN JOURNAL OF ADVANCED NURSING.** (THE AUSTRALIAN JOURNAL OF ADVANCED NURSING : A QUARTERLY PUBLICATION OF THE ROYAL AUSTRALIAN NURSING FEDERATION.). [Aust. j. adv. nurs.]. **Added/Corp** Royal Australian Nursing Federation. **VFOAT** AJAN. Vol. 1, No. 1 (Sept.-Nov. 1983)-. Periodical. English. qt (4 issues). 55.00Aus$ (non-members) Australia; 35.00 (members) Australia; 65.00Aus$ (institutions and libraries and others). Royal Australian Nursing Federation, 373-375 St Georges Road, North Fitzroy Victoria 3068 Australia. **Tel** 011 61 3 4822722, FAX 011 61 3 4822330. **ED** Shirley Russell. **NLM** W1; AU554. **Bk Rev. Ad Acc. Circ:** 1,500.
**Ind/Abst** Aust. Educ. Index; Cumul. Index Nurs. Allied Health Lit.; Int. Nurs. Index.

AT/0045-0758
**AUSTRALIAN NURSES' JOURNAL.** ***Title Change.*** (THE AUSTRALIAN NURSES' JOURNAL.). [Aust. nurses j.]. **Added/Corp** Royal Australian Nursing Federation. Vol. 1 (July 1971)-(19??). Periodical. English. mo (except combined Dec./Jan.). Royal Australian Nursing Federation, 373-375 St Georges Road, North Fitzroy Victoria 3068 Australia. **Tel** 011 61 3 4822722, FAX 011 61 3 4822330. **ED** Shirley Russell. **NLM** W1; AU643A. Index available. cum. index. **Bk Rev. Ad Acc. Circ:** 42,000 (ctrl). available on microfilm and microfiche from University Microfilms International (UMI). ***Absorbed*** *UNA.* ***Continued by*** *Australian Nursing Journal.*
**Desc:** The official publication of the sole national organization representing nursing at both the professional and industrial levels, the Royal Australian Nursing Federation.
**Ind/Abst** Cumul. Index Nurs. Allied Health Lit.; Int. Nurs. Index.

AT
**AUSTRALIAN NURSING JOURNAL, THE.** ***Title Change.*** (1993)-(1993). English. Royal Australian Nursing Federation, 373-375 St Georges Road, North Fitzroy Victoria 3068 Australia. **Tel** 011 61 3 4822722, FAX 011 61 3 4822330. **NLM** W1; AU643BK. ***Continues*** *Australian Nurses Journal, 0045-0758.* ***Continued by*** *Australian Nursing Journal (July 1993).*

●AT
**AUSTRALIAN NURSING JOURNAL (JULY 1993).** (AUSTRALIAN NURSING JOURNAL : ANJ.). (1993)-. English. ir (11 issues). 33.00Aus$ Australia; 50.00Aus$ other. Royal Australian Nursing Federation, 373-375 St Georges Road, North Fitzroy Victoria 3068 Australia. **Tel** 011 61 3 4822722, FAX 011 61 3 4822330. **NLM** W1; AU643BJ. Index available (bound in Oct. issue). ***Continues*** *The Australian Nursing Journal.*

AT/1036-5060
**AUSTRALIAN PAEDIATRIC NURSE.** (THE AUSTRALIAN PAEDIATRIC NURSE.). (1991)-. English. Queensland Paediatric Nurses Association. ***Continues*** *Queensland Paediatric Nurses Association, 1035-2600.*
**Ind/Abst** Cumul. Index Nurs. Allied Health Lit.

FR/0240-6411
**AVENIR & SANTE.** [Avenir sante]. **VFOAT** Avenir et Sante. (1979)-. Periodical. French. ir (10 issues). 783.55F. FNI Informations, 7 rue Godot de Mauroy, F-75009 Paris France. **Tel** 011 33 1 47429413. **UDC** 61. ***Continues*** *Les Dossiers de Notre Profession, 0397-2291.*

CN/0834-7824
**AXONE (DARTMOUTH).** (L'AXONE / THE CANADIAN ASSOCIATION OF NEUROSCIENCE NURSES.). [Axone]. **Added/Corp** Canadian Association of Neurological and Neurosurgical Nurses. **VFOAT** Axon. (1979)-. Periodical. English. qt. 25.00Can$ Canada; 40.00Can$ US; 50.00Can$ other. Canadian Association of Neuroscience Nurses, 2411 Agricola Street, Halifax, N.S. B3K 4C1 Canada. **Tel** (902)423-2679, FAX (902)422-3706. **ED** Wendy Blackburn (Editor's Adress: 449 Wilkins Street London, Ontario N6Z 5B5 (Phone: (519)452-4437)). **DD** 610.73/68. **Ad Acc, Adv Mgr:** Sera Nicosia, **Tel** (416)547-8822. **Pr Rev. Circ:** 500 (ctrl).
**Desc:** Distributed to neuroscience nurses. Article content based on research and cases regarding neuroscience.
**Ind/Abst** Cumul. Index Nurs. Allied Health Lit.

US/0145-9694
**BACCALAUREATE EDUCATION IN NURSING. KEY TO A PROFESSIONAL CAREER IN NURSING.** ***Ceased.*** (BACCALAUREATE EDUCATION IN NURSING.). **VFOAT** Key to a Professional Career in Nursing. (1974)-?. Periodical. English. an. National League for Nursing, 350 Hudson Street, New York NY 10014. **Tel** (212)989-9393, (800)669-1656. **LC** RT79; .B33. **DD** 610.73/071173. **NLM** WY 22 AA1 B11.

US/0270-7799
**BAYLOR NURSING EDUCATOR.** [Baylor nurs. educ.]. V. 1-. English. Baylor University / School of Nursing, 3616 Worth Street, Dallas TX 75246. **NLM** W1 BA964.
**Ind/Abst** Cumul. Index Nurs. Allied Health Lit.

US/1071-2984
**BEGINNINGS : THE OFFICIAL NEWSLETTER OF THE AMERICAN HOLISTIC NURSES' ASSOCIATION.** [Beginnings]. **Added/Corp** American Holistic Nurses' Association. (1981)-. Newsletter. English. mo. $16.00 (1 year), $28.00 (2 year) US; $19.50 (1 yer), 35.00 (2 year) other. American Holistic Nurses Association, 4101 Lake Boonetrail Suite 201, Raleigh NC 27607. **Tel** (919)787-5181, FAX (919)787-4916. **ED** Susan Rexer. **DD** 610. **NLM** W1; BE117. **Bk Rev**, (Qty: 6). **Ad Acc. Circ:** 3,500.
**Desc:** Covers holistic healing techniques, American Holistic Nurses' Association news, health and wellness events.
**Ind/Abst** Int. Nurs. Index (1992-).

US
**BIENNIAL REPORT OF EXAMINING AND LICENSING BOARDS - MINNESOTA BOARD OF NURSING.** **Main/Corp** Minnesota Board of Nursing. 1974-6-. English. be. Minnesota Board of Nursing, 717 Delaware Street SE, Minneapolis MN 55414. **LC** RT5.M6; M53A. **DD** 353.97760084/1. ***Continues*** *Minnesota Board of Nursing. Biennial Report to Governor, State of Minnesota.*

PR/0145-6245
**BOLETIN - COLEGIO DE PROFESIONALES DE LA ENFERMERIA DE PUERTO RICO.** [Bol. - Col. Prof. Enferm. P. R.]. **VFOAT** Boletin del Colegio de Profesionales de la Enfermeria de Puerto Rico. (Vol. 1- ); March 1975-. Periodical. Spanish (English). Colegio Profes de Enfermeria, GOP Box 3647, San Juan 00936 Puerto Rico. **Tel** (809)753-7197. **NLM** W1 BO207P. ***Supersedes*** *Puerto Rico y su Enfermeria, 0145-6652.*

●UK/0966-0461
**BRITISH JOURNAL OF NURSING : BJN.** **VFOAT** BJN. Vol. 1, No. 1 (Apr. 23, 1992)-. Periodical. English. Twenty-two times a year. £90.00 (institution), £54.00 (individual) UK; £120.00 (institution), £100.00 (individual) other. Mark Allen Publishing Limited, Robjohns Farm, Vicarage Road, Finchingfield CM7 4LJ England. **Tel** 11 44 371 810433. **LC** RT1; .B74. **NLM** W1; BR58H. ***Continues*** *Nursing, 0142-0372.*
**Ind/Abst** Cumul. Index Nurs. Allied Health Lit.; Int. Nurs. Index (1992-).

UK
**BRITISH JOURNAL OF THEATRE NURSING : NATNEWS : THE OFFICIAL JOURNAL OF THE NATIONAL ASSOCIATION OF THEATRE NURSES, THE.** **Added/Corp** National Association of Theatre Nurses (Great Britain). **VFOAT** NATNews; NATN News. (1991)-. Periodical. English. Twelve times a year. £30.00 UK; £40.00. National Association of Theatre Nurses, 22 Mount Parade, Harrogate N Yorkshire, HG1 1BX England. **Tel** 011 44 423 506603, 508079, FAX 011 44 423 531613. **ED** Kate Nightingale. **NLM** W1; BR642. **Ad Acc, Adv Mgr:** John Matthews, Pam Noble, **Tel** 0831-224771, 062 082 3383. **Circ:** 7,000 (ctrl). ***Continues*** *NATNews.*
**Ind/Abst** Cumul. Index Nurs. Allied Health Lit.; Int. Nurs. Index (1991-).

US/0898-6622
**BULLETIN / AMERICAN ASSOCIATION FOR THE HISTORY OF NURSING.** [Bull. - Am. Assoc. Hist. Nurs.]. **Added/Corp** American Association for the History of Nursing. **VFOAT** American Association for the History of Nursing Bulletin; Bulletin of the American Association for the History of Nursing. No. 1 (Fall 1982)-. Bulletin. English. Four times a year (Winter, Spring, Summer & Fall). Memberships to the American Association for the History of Nursing / AAHN: $60.00 (regular membership); $75.00 (individual agencies or supporting memberships). American Association for the History of Nursing, PO Box 90803, Washington DC 20090. **Tel** (202)543-2127. **ED** Dr. Alma S. Wooley (editor's address: Georgetown University School of Nursing, 3700 Reservoir Road, NW, Washington, DC 20007; phone: (202)687-5517; FAX: (202)687-5553). **DD** 610. **NLM** W1; BU478HA. **Bk Rev**, (Qty: 2-4). **Circ:** 400 (ctrl).
**Desc:** Includes Association news, short research reports, author's queries.

FR/0007-9820
**CAHIERS DE LA PUERICULTRICE.** [Cah. pueric.]. (1964)-. Periodical. English (French). qt. 500.00F France; 520.00F other. Association Nationale Puericultrices, 132 av du General Leclerc, 75014 Paris France. **Tel** 011 33 1 45399762. **UDC** 613.95.

US/0008-1310
**CALIFORNIA NURSE.** [Calif. nurse]. **Added/Corp** California Nurses Association. Vol. 65, No. 7 (July/Aug. 1969)-. Periodical. English. Ten times a year (July/Aug. and Nov./Dec. issues combined). $30.00 US and Possessions; $35.00 other. California Nurses Association, 1145 Market Street, Suite 1100, San Francisco CA 94103. **Tel** (415)864-4141, (415)861-0670, FAX (415)431-1011. **ED** Jennifer Watson (phone: (415)864-4141 ext.860). **NLM** W1 CA402V. **Bk Rev. Ad Acc. Circ:** 26,000. available on microfilm and microfiche from University Microfilms International (UMI). ***Continues*** *CNA Bulletin.*
**Desc:** Topics of interest to nurses and general health related coverage.
**Ind/Abst** Calif. Period. Index (19??-); Calif. Period. Microfi. (19??-); Cumul. Index Nurs. Allied Health Lit.; Int. Nurs. Index.

US/1060-8532
**CANA, INC.** (CANA, INC. : NEWS BULLETIN.). [CANA Inc.]. **Added/Corp** California Association of Nurse Anesthetists. **VFOAT** News Bulletin; CANA, Inc. News Bulletin; California Association of Nurse Anesthetists, Inc. **VAT** California Association of Nurse Anesthetists, Inc. Vol. 46, No. 1 (Oct. 1991)-. Bulletin. English. qt. California Association Nurse Anesthetists, PO Box 5128, Eureka CA 95502. **Tel** (707)442-3621. **DD** 610. ***Continues*** *CANA, 0196-2752.*
**Ind/Abst** Int. Nurs. Index.

CN/0826-6778
**CANADIAN CRITICAL CARE NURSING JOURNAL.** ***Ceased.*** [Can. crit. care nurs. j.]. **VFOAT** Critical Care. Vol. 1, No. 1 (Sept. 1984)-Ceased Vol. 9, No. 8 (March 1992). Periodical. English. ir (four issues per year). Health Media Inc, 14453 29A Avenue, White Rock BC V4A 9K8 Canada. **Tel** (604)535-7933, FAX (604)535-9000. **ED** Agnes Fagan. **DD** 610.73/61/05. Index available. **Bk Rev. Ad Acc. Circ:** 4,500 (ctrl).
**Desc:** Critical care nursing, intensive care, cardial care, post anaesthetic, etc.
**Ind/Abst** Cumul. Index Nurs. Allied Health Lit. (?-?); Health Plan. Adminis.; Int. Nurs. Index (?-?).

CN/0838-2948
**CANADIAN JOURNAL OF NURSING ADMINISTRATION.** [Can. j. nurs. adm.]. Vol. 1, No. 1 (March/April 1988)-. Periodical. English. qt. 28.00Can$ Canada; 35.00Can$ US; 45.00Can$ other. Health Media Inc, 14453 29A Avenue, White Rock BC V4A 9K8 Canada. **Tel** (604)535-7933, FAX (604)535-9000. **ED** Jan Dick. **DD** 362.1/73/068. **NLM** W1; CA596M. Index available. cum. index. **Bk Rev. Ad Acc. Pr Rev. Circ:** 4,100.
**Ind/Abst** Cumul. Index Nurs. Allied Health Lit.; Health Plan. Adminis.; Int. Nurs. Index (Mar. 1988-).

CN/0844-5621
**CANADIAN JOURNAL OF NURSING RESEARCH, THE.** [Can. j. nurs. res.]. **VFOAT** Nursing Papers; Revue Canadienne de Recherche en Sciences Infirmieres. Vol. 20, No. 1 (Spring 1988)-. Periodical. English (French). qt (4 issues). 85.00Can$ institution, 40.00Can$ individual. McGill University / School of Nursing, Wilson Hall, 3506 University Street, Montreal Quebec H3A 2A7 Canada. **Tel** (514)398-4160, FAX (514)398-8455. **ED** Dr. Laurie Gottlieb. **DD** 610.73/0971. **NLM** W1; CA596N. Index available. cum. index (published in last issue). **Bk Rev**, (Qty: varies). **Ad Acc. Pr Rev. Circ:** 1000. ***Continues*** *Nursing Papers, 0318-1006.*
**Desc:** Primary mandate is to publish nursing research that develops basic knowledge for the discipline and examines the application of the knowledge in practice. Also accepts research related to education and history and welcomes methodological, theory and review papers that advance nursing science.
**Ind/Abst** Cumul. Index Nurs. Allied Health Lit.; Int. Nurs. Index (1988-); Point Repere (1988-).

CN/0008-4581
**CANADIAN NURSE (1924).** (THE CANADIAN NURSE.). [Can. nurse]. **Added/Corp** Canadian Nurses' Association. **VFOAT** Infirmiere Canadienne. Vol. 20, No. 10 (Oct. 1924)-. Periodical. English (French). mo. 36.00Can$ Canada; 50.00Can$ US; 60.00Can$ other. Canadian Nurses Association, 50 The Driveway, Ottawa Ontario K2P 1E2 Canada. **Tel** (613)237-2133, FAX (613)237-3520. **ED** Judith A. Banning. **DD** 610.73/0971. **NLM** W1 CA63F. **[CCC]**. Index available (bound in Dec. issue). cum. index. **Bk Rev. Ad Acc. Pr Rev. Circ:** 110,000. available on microfilm and microfiche from University Microfilms International (UMI). ***Continues*** *Canadian Nurse and Hospital Review, 0315-1018;* ***Absorbed*** *Infirmiere Canadienne, 0019-9605.*
**Desc:** Articles on health care and nursing in Canada.
**Ind/Abst** Can. Index (?-?); Can. Period. Index; Cumul. Index Nurs. Allied Health Lit.; Health Plan. Adminis.; Int. Nurs. Index; Nurs. Abstr.; Life Sci. Collect.; Point Repere (19??-19??).

CN
**CANADIAN NURSING MANAGEMENT.** English. Twelve times a year. 93.00Can$. MPL Communications, 133 Richard Street West, Suite 700, Toronto Ontario M5H 3M8 Canada. **Tel** (416)869-1177, FAX (416)869-0456.

**Desc:** News service for nurse managers. Provides in-depth, must-have information for all nursing professionals.

CN/1181-912X
**CANADIAN ONCOLOGY NURSING JOURNAL.** (CANADIAN ONCOLOGY NURSING JOURNAL = REVUE CANADIENNE DE NURSING ONCOLOGIQUE.). [Can. oncol. nurs. j.]. **Added/Corp** Association Canadienne des Infirmieres en Oncologie. **VFOAT** Revue Canadienne de Nursing Oncologique. (1991)-. Periodical. French (English). Four times a year (Feb., May, Aug., Nov.). 44.94Can$ (individuals); 64.20Can$ (institutions); 75.00Can$ others. Canadian Association of Nurses in Oncology, 184 Edelweiss Drive Northwest, Calgary ALTA T3A 3P9 Canada. **Tel** (613)735-0954, FAX (613)735-7983. **ED** Beverly Page (phone: (416)425-8067 home and (416)480-5942 work. **DD** 610.73. Index available (Bound in 1st iss.). cum. index. **Bk Rev**, (Qty: 4-6). **Ad Acc**, **Adv Mgr:** Pappin, **Tel** (613)735-0952. **Pr Rev. Circ:** 1,200.
**Desc:** This journal is directed to the professional nurse caring for patients with cancer.

CN/1181-912X
**CANADIAN ONCOLOGY NURSING JOURNAL.** (CANADIAN ONCOLOGY NURSING JOURNAL = REVUE CANADIENNE DE NURSING ONCOLOGIQUE.). [Can. oncol. nurs. j.]. **Added/Corp** Canadian Association of Nurses in Oncology. **VFOAT** Revue Canadienne de Nursing Oncologique. No. 1 (1991)-. Periodical. English (French). Four times a year (Feb., May, Aug., Nov.). 44.94Can$ (individuals); 64.20Can$ (institutions); 75.00Can$ others. Canadian Association of Nurses in Oncology, 184 Edelweiss Drive Northwest, Calgary ALTA T3A 3P9 Canada. **Tel** (613)735-0954, FAX (613)735-7983. **ED** Beverly Page (phone: (416)425-8067 home and (416)480-5942 work. **DD** 610.73. **NLM** W1; CA633. Index available (Bound in 1st iss.). cum. index. **Bk Rev**, (Qty: 4-6). **Ad Acc**, **Adv Mgr:** Pappin, **Tel** (613)735-0952. **Pr Rev. Circ:** 1,200.
**Desc:** This journal is directed to the professional nurse caring for patients with cancer.

CN/0712-6778
**CANADIAN OPERATING ROOM NURSING JOURNAL.** [Can. oper. room nurs. j.]. **VFOAT** Operating Room Nursing Journal. Vol. 1, No. 1 (Feb. 1983)-. Periodical. English (French). qt. 16.00Can$ Canada; 22.00Can$ US; 26.00Can$ other. Health Media Inc, 14453 29A Avenue, White Rock BC V4A 9K8 Canada. **Tel** (604)535-7933, FAX (604)535-9000. **ED** Frank Fagan. **DD** 610.73/677/05. **NLM** W1; CA634. Index available. cum. index. **Ad Acc. Circ:** 5,000 (ctrl).
**Desc:** Operating room technology, procedures and asepsis.
**Ind/Abst** Cumul. Index Nurs. Allied Health Lit.; Health Plan. Adminis.; Index Med.; Int. Nurs. Index.

US/0162-220X
**CANCER NURSING.** [Cancer nurs.]. **Added/Corp** International Society of Nurses in Cancer Care. European Oncology Nursing Society. Vol. 1 (Feb. 1978)-. Periodical. English. bm (6 issues). $44.00 (individuals), $84.00 (institutions) US; $62.00 (individuals), $106.00 (institutions) other. Raven Press, 1185 Avenue of the Americas, 37th Floor, New York NY 10036. **Tel** (212)930-9500, (212)930-9604, FAX (212)869-3495, (212)302-8507, telex 640073. **ED** Carol Reed Ash. **LC** RC266; .C35. **DD** 610.73/6. **NLM** W1 CA683NG. **[CCC]. Pr Rev.** available on microfilm and microfiche from University Microfilms International (UMI). Documents available from The Genuine Article.
**Desc:** The official publication of the International Society of Nurses in Cancer Care and The European Oncology Nursing Society. Addresses the whole spectrum of problems arising in the care and support of cancer patients.
**Ind/Abst** Cumul. Index Nurs. Allied Health Lit.; EMBASE; Index Med. Vol. 9, No. 4, 1986-; Int. Nurs. Index; Nurs. Abstr.; Res. Alert [Full Cov.]; SCISEARCH; Soc. Sci. Cit. Index [Full Cov.].

US/0734-1873
**CANCER NURSING NEWS.** (CANCER NURSING NEWS : AMERICAN CANCER SOCIETY NEWSLETTER FOR NURSES.). [Cancer nurs. news]. **Added/Corp** American Cancer Society. Vol. 1, No. 1 (Sept./Oct. 1982)-. Newsletter. English. qt. Free. American Cancer Society Institute Activities, 1599 Clifton Road Northeast, Atlanta GA 30329.
**Desc:** Information on cancer nursing.

US
**CAPITAL NURSING. Added/Corp** District of Columbia Nurses' Association. Vol. 1, No. 1 (May 1984)-. Periodical. English. Four times a year. District of Columbia Nursing Association, 5100 Wisconsin Avenue NW, Washington DC 20016. **Tel** (202)244-2705. **ED** Nancy Kofie. **Ad Acc.** ctrl circ.
**Desc:** Covers the activities of the District of Columbia Nurses Association. Presents issues of interest to DC nurses.
**Ind/Abst** Int. Nurs. Index (Vol. 1, No. 7, 1984-).

US
**CAPITAL UPDATE. Main/Corp** American Nurses Association. English. sm. $75.00 (nonmeembers), $25.00 (American Nurses Association council affiliate), $50.00 (state nurses association member). American Nurses Association, 600 Maryland Avenue Southwest, Suite 100, Washington DC 20024. **Tel** (202)554-4444. Index available.

●US/1066-4815
**CAPSULES AND COMMENTS IN CRITICAL CARE NURSING.** [Capsul. comments crit. care nurs.]. **VFOAT** Capsules and Comments in Critical Care Nursing. (1993)-. Periodical. English. qt. $52.50 (institutions), $34.95 (individuals) US; $59.50 (institutions), $41.95 (individuals) Canada; $67.05 (institutions), $49.50 (individuals) other. Mosby Year Book Inc., 11830 Westline Industrial Drive, St Louis MO 63146. **Tel** (800)325-4177, (314)872-8370, FAX (314)432-1380, telex 44-2402. **DD** 610.

US
**CAPSULES AND COMMENTS IN MATERNITY AND GYNECOLOGIC NURSING.** (19??)-. Periodical. English. qt. $59.95 (institutions), $39.95 (individuals) US; $66.95 (institutions), $46.95 (individuals) Canada; $74.50 (institutions), $54.50 (individuals) other. Mosby Year Book Inc., 11830 Westline Industrial Drive, St Louis MO 63146. **Tel** (800)325-4177, (314)872-8370, FAX (314)432-1380, telex 44-2402.

●US/1068-6088
**CAPSULES & COMMENTS IN NURSING LEADERSHIP & MANAGEMENT.** [Capsul. comments nurs. leadersh. manag.]. **VFOAT** Capsules and Comments in Nursing Leadership and Management. Vol. 1, Issue 1 (Spring 1993)-. Periodical. English. qt. $59.95 (institutions), $39.95 (individuals) US; $66.95 (institutions), $46.95 (individuals) Canada; $74.50 (institutions), $54.50 (individuals) other. Mosby Year Book Inc., 11830 Westline Industrial Drive, St Louis MO 63146. **Tel** (800)325-4177, (314)872-8370, FAX (314)432-1380, telex 44-2402. **DD** 610.

●US/1066-4114
**CAPSULES AND COMMENTS IN ONCOLOGY NURSING.** [Capsul. comments oncol. nurs.]. **VFOAT** Capsules and Comments in Oncology Nursing. (1993)-. Periodical. English. qt. $59.95 (institutions), $39.95 (individuals) US; $66.95 (institutions), $46.95 (individuals) Canada; $74.50 (institutions), $54.50 (individuals) other. Mosby Year Book Inc., 11830 Westline Industrial Drive, St Louis MO 63146. **Tel** (800)325-4177, (314)872-8370, FAX (314)432-1380, telex 44-2402. **DD** 616.

●US
**CAPSULES & COMMENTS IN PEDIATRIC NURSING. VFOAT** Capsules and Comments in Pediatric Nursing. (June 1994)-. Periodical. English. qt. $59.95 (institutions), $39.95 (individuals) US; $66.95 (institutions), $46.95 (individuals) Canada; $74.50 (institutions), $54.50 (individuals) other. Mosby Year Book Inc., 11830 Westline Industrial Drive, St Louis MO 63146. **Tel** (800)325-4177, (314)872-8370, FAX (314)432-1380, telex 44-2402.

US
**CAPSULES AND COMMENTS IN PERIOPERATIVE NURSING.** (19??)-. English. Four times a year. $52.45 (institutions), $34.95 (individuals) US; $59.45 (institutions), $41.95 (individuals) Canada; $67.00 (institutions), $49.50 (individuals) other. Mosby Year Book Inc., 11830 Westline Industrial Drive, St Louis MO 63146. **Tel** (800)325-4177, (314)872-8370, FAX (314)432-1380, telex 44-2402.

●US
**CAPSULES AND COMMENTS IN PSYCHIATRIC NURSING.** (1994)-. English. qt (4 issues). $52.45 (institutions), $34.95 (individuals) US; $59.45 (institutions), $41.95 (individuals) Canada; $67.00 (institutions), $49.50 (individuals) other. Mosby Year Book Inc., 11830 Westline Industrial Drive, St Louis MO 63146. **Tel** (800)325-4177, (314)872-8370, FAX (314)432-1380, telex 44-2402. **NLM** ZWY 160; C254.

US/0008-6355
**CARDIO-VASCULAR NURSING.** [Cardio-vasc. nurs.]. **Added/Corp** American Heart Association. **VFOAT** Cardiovascular Nursing. Vol. 1 (Winter 1965)-. Periodical. English. bm (6 issues). $11.00 (institutions), $6.00 (individuals) US. American Heart Association, 7272 Greenville Avenue, Dallas TX 75231-4596. **Tel** (214)706-1310, (214)373-6300, FAX (214)691-6342. **(Subscription address:** American Heart Association, PO Box 843543, Dallas TX 75284-3543.**) ED** Elizabeth Winslow. **DD** 610. **NLM** W1 CA771. **[CCC]. Ad Acc.** available on microfilm and microfiche from University Microfilms International (UMI).
**Desc:** Discusses developments in care for patients with heart disease.
**Ind/Abst** Cumul. Index Nurs. Allied Health Lit.; Health Plan. Adminis.; Int. Nurs. Index; Nurs. Abstr.

CN/0843-9966
**CARE CONNECTION, THE.** [Care connect.]. **Added/Corp** Ontario Association of Registered Nursing Assistants. Vol. 4, Issue 3 (June/July 1989)-. Periodical. English. Four times a year (Mar., June, Sept., Dec.). 23.50Can$ Canada; 29.00Can$ others. Registered Practical Nurses Association of Ontario / RPNAO, 5025 Orbitor Drive, Building 4, Suite 200, Mississauga Ontario L4W 4Y5 Canada. **Tel** (905)602-4664, FAX (905)602-4666. **ED** Kelly Zimmer. **DD** 610.73/06/93. **Ad Acc.** Full Page (B&W) $425.00. Half Page (B&W) $235.00. **Pr Rev. Circ:** 5,000 (ctrl). ***Continues** Bedside Specialist., 0835-6203.*
**Desc:** Contains information about current membership, nursing and health care issues, as well as educational articles.

UK/0309-2399
**CAREERS IN NURSING AND OTHER HEALTH SERVICE PROFESSIONS.** [Careers nurs. other health serv. prof.]. Periodical. English. **NLM** W1 CA786C. ***Continues** Careers in Nursing, 0309-2327.*

US/0069-2778
**CHART (CHICAGO. 1956).** (CHART.). [Chart]. **Added/Corp** Illinois Nurses Association. Vol. 53, No. 6 (June/July 1956)-. Periodical. English. mo. $20.00. Illinois Nurses Association, 20 North Wacker Drive/Suite 2520, Chicago IL 60606. **Tel** (312)236-9708. **ED** Pamela Towne. **DD** 610. **NLM** W1 CH147L. **Ad Acc. Circ:** 10,000. available on microfilm. ***Continues** ISNA.*
**Desc:** Professional publication which covers health care and professional issues of importance to all nurses.
**Ind/Abst** Cumul. Index Nurs. Allied Health Lit.; Int. Nurs. Index.

CN/1197-4729
**CHCG PULSE. Main/Corp** Canadian Health Care Guild. (19??)-. English. ir (20-25 issues per year). 16.00Can$. Canadian Health Care Guild, 17410 107th Avenue, Edmonton Alberta, T5S 1E9 Canada. **Tel** (403)483-8126. ***Continues** AARNA Pulse: Alberta Association of Registered Nursing Assistants, 0706-2192.*

US/0199-2066
**CHICAGO NURSE.** Periodical. English. bm (varies). $5.00. Chicago Nurses Association, 180 North Michigan/Suite 1510, Chicago IL 60601. **Tel** (312)263-2708. **Bk Rev. Ad Acc.** ctrl circ.
**Desc:** Informational newsletter sent to memberships and other subscribers.

US
**CHILDREN'S NURSE.** (Fall/Winter 1987)-. English. Twice a year. Free on request. Children's Hospital of Wisconsin, PO Box 1997, Milwaukee WI 53201. **Tel** (414)931-4043.

CN
**CINA : OFFICIAL JOURNAL OF THE CANADIAN INTRAVENOUS NURSES ASSOCIATION.** (19??)-. Periodical. English. qt (4 issues). 37.45Can$ Canada; 42.80Can$ US; 48.15Can$ other. Canadian Intravenous Nurses Association, 4433 Sheppard Avenue East, Suite 200, Agincourt Ontario M1S 1V3, Canada. **Tel** (905)292-0687, FAX (905)292-1038.
**Ind/Abst** Cumul. Index Nurs. Allied Health Lit.

US
**CINAHL NEWS. Added/Corp** Cumulative Index to Nursing & Allied Health Literature (Firm). **VFOAT** Cumulative Index to Nursing & Allied Health Literature News. (198?)-. Periodical. English. qt (4 issues). Free on request. CINAHL Information Systems, 1509 Wilson Terrace, Glendale CA 91209. **Tel** (818)409-8005. **(Subscription address:** CINAHL Information Systems, PO Box 871, Glendale, CA 91209**) LC** RT41; .C82.
**Desc:** The official newsletter from CINAHL featuring news, interviews, updates, tips and more.

●US
**CINAHL (PEABODY, MASS.).** **See** Medical Science and Technology-Abstracting, Bibliographies and Statistics.

US/0197-6958
**CLINICAL AND SCIENTIFIC SESSIONS.** (CLINICAL AND SCIENTIFIC SESSIONS (AMERICAN NURSES' ASSOCIATION).). [Clin. sci. sess.]. **Main/Corp** American Nurses' Association. English. American Nurses Association, 600 Maryland Avenue Southwest, Suite 100, Washington DC 20024. **Tel** (202)554-4444. **LC** RT3; .A517. **DD** 610.73. **NLM** W1 CL664R.

US/0887-6274
**CLINICAL NURSE SPECIALIST.** (CLINICAL NURSE SPECIALIST : CNS.). [Clin. nurse spec.]. **VFOAT** CNS. Vol. 1, No. 1 (Spring 1987)-. Periodical. English. bm. $95.00 (institution), $74.00 (individual), US; $99.00 (individual), $120.00 (institution) other. Williams & Wilkins Company, 428 East Preston Street, Baltimore MD 21202-3993. **Tel** (410)528-4000, (800)638-6423, FAX (410)528-8596, telex 87669. **(Subscription address:** Williams & Wilkins, PO Box 64380, Baltimore MD 21264.**) DD** 610. **[CCC]. Pr Rev.** Documents available from , , Quick Copies.
**Desc:** Role-oriented information for the clinician, researcher, consultant, executive and peer and patient educator.
**Ind/Abst** Cumul. Index Nurs. Allied Health Lit.; Health Plan. Adminis.; Int. Nurs. Index (1987-); Nurs. Abstr.

•US/1054-7738
**CLINICAL NURSING RESEARCH.** [Clin. nurs. res.]. Vol. 1, No. 1 (Feb. 1992)-. Periodical. English. qt (Feb., May, Aug., Nov.). $123.00. SAGE Periodical Press, 2455 Teller Road, Thousand Oaks CA 91320. **Tel** (805)499-0721, FAX (805)499-0871, telex 100799. **ED** Marilynn J. Wood and Patricia Hayes (University of Alberta). **LC** RT81.5; .C539. **DD** 610. **NLM** W1; CL739EM. Index available. cum. index. **Bk Rev. Ad Acc. Pr Rev. Acid Free.** available on microfilm.
**Desc:** Designed to meet the increasing demand for an international forum of scholarly research focused on clinical practice.

CN/1188-1887
**CNA TODAY.** (AIIC AUJOURD'HUI.). [CNA today]. **Added/Corp** Association des Infirmieres et Infirmiers du Canada. **VFOAT** Association des Infirmieres et Infirmiers du Canada Aujourd'Hui; CNA Today. **VAT** Canadian Nurses' Association Today. Vol. 1, No 1 (Aug 1991)-. Periodical. French (English). qt. Association des Infirmieres et Infirmiers du Canada, 50 The Driveway, Ottawa Ontario K2P 1E2 Canada. **DD** 610.73.

CN/1188-1887
**CNA TODAY.** [CNA today]. **Added/Corp** Canadian Nurses' Association. **VFOAT** Canadian Nurses' Association Today; AIIC Aujourd'Hui. Vol. 1, No. 1 (Aug. 1991)-. Periodical. English (French). qt. Canadian Nurses Association, 50 The Driveway, Ottawa Ontario K2P 1E2 Canada. **Tel** (613)237-2133, FAX (613)237-3520. **DD** 610.73.

US/8750-846X
**COLORADO NURSE (1985).** (COLORADO NURSE : OFFICIAL BULLETIN OF THE COLORADO NURSES' ASSOCIATION.). [Colo. nurse]. **Added/Corp** Colorado Nurses' Association. Vol. 1, No. 4 (Feb. 25, 1985)-. Periodical. English. Four times a year. $20.00. Colorado Nurses' Association, 5453 East Evans Place, Denver CO 80222. **Tel** (303)757-7483. **ED** Alison Biggs. **DD** 610. **NLM** W1; CO25W. **Bk Rev. Ad Acc. Circ:** 2,000 (ctrl). ***Continues*** *Colorado Nurse Update, 8750-8451.*
**Desc:** Contains association activities, nursing issues, legislative reports, continuing education listings.
**Ind/Abst** Cumul. Index Nurs. Allied Health Lit. (1985-); Int. Nurs. Index (1985-).

US/0160-1652
**COMMUNICATING NURSING RESEARCH.** [Commun. nurs. res.]. **Added/Corp** Western Interstate Commission for Higher Education. Western Institute of Nursing (U.S.) Western Society for Research in Nursing (U.S.). Vol. 1 (1968)-. Monographic series. English. ir. Price varies per volume. Western Interstate Commission Higher Education, PO Drawer P, Boulder CO 80301-9752. **Tel** (303)541-0290, FAX (303)541-0291. **ED** Jeanne M. Kearns. **DD** 610. **NLM** W3 C1746. **Circ:** 650.
**Desc:** Contains keynote and award papers, abstracts of podium symposia, and poster presentations presented at the annual Communicating Nursing Research Conference, sponsored by the Western Society for Research in Nursing of the Western Institute of Nursing.
**Ind/Abst** Cumul. Index Nurs. Allied Health Lit.; Health Plan. Adminis.; Int. Nurs. Index.

US/0887-4557
**COMMUNIQUE (MILWAUKEE, WIS.), THE.** (THE COMMUNIQUE.). [Communique]. Began publication with issue for Spring, 1979?. Periodical. English. qt. Wisconsin League for Nursing, 9040 North Rexleigh Drive, Milwaukee WI 53217. **DD** 610. ***Continues*** *Newsletter (Wisconsin League for Nursing).*
**Ind/Abst** Int. Nurs. Index.

UK/0262-8759
**COMMUNITY OUTLOOK.** [Community outlook]. **VFOAT** Nursing Times Community Outlook. (Aug. 1977)-. Periodical. English. mo (12 issues). £37.00 UK; $110.00 US & Canada; £50.00 other. Macmillan Magazines Ltd., Houndmills, Basingstoke, Hampshire RG21 2XS England. **Tel** 011 44 256 29242, FAX 011 44 256 812358, telex 858493. **NLM** W1 CO429U.
**Ind/Abst** Cumul. Index Nurs. Allied Health Lit.; Int. Nurs. Index; SportSearch.

UK/0265-7007
**COMMUNITY PSYCHIATRIC NURSING JOURNAL.** ***Title Change.*** [Community psychiatr. nurs. j.]. (1984)-(19??). Periodical. English. bm. CPNA Publications, 44 Dartford Road, Sevenoaks Kent TN133TQ England. **Tel** 011 44 732 455244, FAX 011 44 732 457542, telex 957592. **DD** 610.73680941. ***Continues*** *CPNA Journal, 0264-5483.* ***Continued by*** *Mental Health Nursing.*

•UK/1353-6117
**COMPLEMENTARY THERAPIES IN NURSING AND MIDWIFERY. See** Medical Science and Technology.

US/0736-8593
**COMPUTERS IN NURSING.** [Comput. nurs.]. **VFOAT** C.I.N. Vol. 1, No. 1 (March 1983)-. Periodical. English. bm (6 issues). $50.00 (individuals), $110.00 (institutions) US; $79.00 (individuals), $150.00 (institutions) other. J.B. Lippincott Company, 227 East Washington Square, Philadelphia PA 19106-3780. **Tel** (215)238-4200 or 4454, FAX (215)238-4227. **(Subscription address:** J.B. Lippincott, PO Box 350, Hagerstown MD 21740.**) ED** Gary D. Hales (editor's address: PO Box 36369, Birmingham, AL, 35236, telephone: (205)733-1659). **NLM** W1; CO4572BC. **[CCC].** Index available. **Bk Rev. Ad Acc, Adv Mgr:** Susan Edison, **Tel** (215)238-4492. **Pr Rev. Circ:** 4,473. available on microfilm and microfiche from University Microfilms International (UMI). Documents available from The Genuine Article.
**Desc:** Deals with the selection and application of computers in the field of nursing. Facts and evaluations of hardware, software, and the latest technological developments are presented. Contains information on current applications of computers in nursing.
**Ind/Abst** Cumul. Index Nurs. Allied Health Lit.; Health Plan. Adminis.; Index Med. (Vol. 4, No. 5, 1986-); Inf. Sci. Abstr. (Vol. 4, No. 5, 1986-); Int. Nurs. Index (March 1983-); Nurs. Abstr.; Res. Alert [Full Cov.]; Soc. Sci. Cit. Index [Select. Cov.].

CN/0708-6474
**CONA JOURNAL.** [CONA j.]. **Main/Corp** Canadian Orthopaedic Nurses' Association. Vol. 1 (Dec. 1978)-. Periodical. English (French). qt (Mar., June, Sept., Dec.). 50.00Can$ Canada; 55.00Can$ other. Canadian Orthopaedic Nurses Association, 43 Wellesley Street East, Toronto Ontario M4Y 1H1 Canada. **Tel** (416)967-8622. **ED** Susie Thibeault. **DD** 610.73/677. **Ad Acc. Circ:** 400 (ctrl).
**Desc:** This publication reflects current trends in orthopedic nursing and related fields in Canada.
**Ind/Abst** Cumul. Index Nurs. Allied Health Lit.

CN/0836-7310
**CONCERN (REGINA).** (CONCERN / SASKATCHEWAN RN ASSOCIATION.). [Concern]. **Added/Corp** Saskatchewan Registered Nurses' Association. Vol. 16, No. 3 or 4 (1987)-. Periodical. English. Six times a year. 15.00Can$ Canada; 25.00Can$ other. SRNA / Saskatchewan Registered Nurses Association, 2066 Retallack Street, Regina Saskatchewan S4T 2K2 Canada. **Tel** (306)757-4643, (800)667-9945. **ED** Joy Johnson. **DD** 610.73/06/07124. **NLM** W1; CO459RW. Index available (published separately). cum. index. **Bk Rev**, (Qty: 6/year). **Ad Acc, Adv Mgr:** Judi Horning, **Tel** (306)565-3808. **Circ:** 10,500 (ctrl). ***Continues*** *News Bulletin - Saskatchewan Registered Nurses' Association, 0319-8499.*
**Desc:** Presents clinical articles, research reports and letters on nurses' concerns. Includes association council reports, member profiles, health-related news, a bulletin board of upcoming nursing-related conferences and workshops, and career and professional opportunities.
**Ind/Abst** Br. Educ. Index; Cumul. Index Nurs. Allied Health Lit.

US/0278-4092
**CONNECTICUT NURSING NEWS (1980).** (CONNECTICUT NURSING NEWS.). [Conn. nurs. news]. **Added/Corp** Connecticut Nurses' Association. (Feb 1980)-. Periodical. English. Ten times a year (Nov./Dec. and June/July issues combined). $20.00 (US); $50.00 (other). Connecticut Nurses Association, 377 Research Parkway, Suite 2D, Meriden CT 06450-7160. **Tel** (203)238-1207, FAX (203) 238-3437. **ED** Marylou Welch. **DD** 610. **Ad Acc. Circ:** 1,700 (ctrl). available on microfilm and microfiche from University Microfilms International (UMI). ***Continues*** *Nursing News, 0029-652X.*
**Desc:** Contains information about nursing issues; aimed at professional nurses' concerns.
**Ind/Abst** Cumul. Index Nurs. Allied Health Lit.; Int. Nurs. Index.

•AT/1037-6178
**CONTEMPORARY NURSE : A JOURNAL FOR THE AUSTRALIAN NURSING PROFESSION.** Vol. 1, No. 1 (Apr. 1992)-. Periodical. English. qt. £77.00 Europe; £70.00 Other (Institutions). Churchill Livingstone / Australia, 95 Coventry Street, South Melbourne Victoria, 3205 Australia. **Tel** 03 6970671, FAX 03 6965205. **(Subscription address:** Maruzen Company Ltd., PO Box 5050, Import & Export Department, Tokyo 100 31 Japan.**) ED** Susan Tregining. **NLM** W1; CO769NDE. **Bk Rev. Ad Acc, Adv Mgr:** J. Chandler. **Circ:** 1,000.
**Ind/Abst** Cumul. Index Nurs. Allied Health Lit.; Int. Nurs. Index (1992-).

CN/1183-7985
**CONTINUING EDUCATION IN NURSING, A DIRECTORY.** [Contin. educ. nurs. dir.]. **Added/Corp** Canadian Nurses' Association. **VFOAT** Formation Continue en Soins Infirmiers, Repertoire. (1991)-. English (French). $20.00. Canadian Nurses Association, 50 The Driveway, Ottawa Ontario K2P 1E2 Canada. **Tel** (613)237-2133, FAX (613)237-3520. **DD** 610.73.
**Desc:** Guide to short-term, post-basic nursing courses in Canada. Lists over 500 programs ranging from refresher courses in various specialties to post-RN baccalaureate programs.

CN/1183-7985
**CONTINUING EDUCATION IN NURSING, A DIRECTORY.** [Contin. educ. nurs. dir.]. **Added/Corp** Association des Infirmieres et Infirmiers du Canada. **VFOAT** Formation Continue en Soins Infirmiers, Repertoire. (1991)-. Directory. French (English). 20.00Can$ per volume. Association des Infirmieres et Infirmiers du Canada, 50 The Driveway, Ottawa Ontario K2P 1E2 Canada. **DD** 610.73.

US
**CREATIVE NURSING.** (19??)-. Periodical. English. bm. $25.00. Creative Nursing Management, 614 East Grant Street, Minneapolis MN 55404. **Tel** (612)339-7766, FAX (612)339-2065. **ED** Claire Mantley Haukkala. **Bk Rev**, (Qty: 5-10). **Ad Acc, Adv Mgr:** Eric Haukkala. **Circ:** 2,000. ***Continues*** *Primarily Nursing, 0739-4446.*
**Desc:** Forum for discussion and renewal of the values of nursing.

US/0279-5442
**CRITICAL CARE NURSE.** [Crit. care nurse]. **Added/Corp** Simms Associates. American Association of Critical-Care Nurses. **VFOAT** Critical Care Nurse Magazine. Vol. 1, No. 1 (Nov./Dec. 1980)-. Periodical. English. bm (6 issues). $45.00 (institutions); $27.00 (individuals) US. American Association Critical Care Nurses, 101 Columbia, Alisa Veijo CA 92655. **Tel** (714)362-2000. **(Subscription address:** Critical Care Nurse, PO Box 611, Holmes, PA 19043; (telephone: (800)345-8112)**) ED** JoAnn Grif Alspach. **NLM** W1 CR216N. **CODEN** CCNUEV. **[CCC].** Index available (free on request). **Bk Rev. Ad Acc. Pr Rev. Circ:** 95,000 (ctrl). available on microfilm and microfiche from University Microfilms International (UMI).
**Desc:** For critical care nursing professionals. Covers the latest advances in critical care, the newest clinical techniques, information on cardiac care, pharmacology, nutrition, pulmonary care, and neurology.
**Ind/Abst** Cumul. Index Nurs. Allied Health Lit.; Hospit. Health Admin. Index; Int. Nurs. Index; Nurs. Abstr.

US/0899-5885
**CRITICAL CARE NURSING CLINICS OF NORTH AMERICA.** [Crit. care nurs. clin. North Am.]. **VFOAT** Critical Care Nursing Clinics. Vol. 1, No. 1 (March 1989)-. Periodical. English. qt. $58.00 (individual), $75.00 (institution) US; $87.00 (individual), $91.00 (institution) other. W.B. Saunders Company, A Subsidiary of Harcourt Brace Jovanovich, Inc., The Curtis Center/Suite 300, Independence Square West, Philadelphia PA 19106-3399. **Tel** (215)238-7800 or, 5587, FAX (215)238-7883, telex 173146. **(Subscription address:** W. B. Saunders Company / North America Subscriptions, c/o Periodicals, 6277 Sea Harbour Drive, 4th Floor, Orlando FL 32887.**) ED** Sandra Masse. **DD** 610. **NLM** W1; CR216NC. Index available. **Circ:** 3,500. available on microfilm.
**Ind/Abst** Cumul. Index Nurs. Allied Health Lit.; Health Plan. Adminis.; Int. Nurs. Index; Nurs. Abstr.

US/0887-9303
**CRITICAL CARE NURSING QUARTERLY.** [Crit. care nurs. q.]. **VFOAT** CCNQ. Vol. 9, No. 4 (March 1987)-. Periodical. English. qt. $66.00 US. Aspen Publishers Inc., 7201 McKinney Circle, Frederick MD 21701. **Tel** (800)234-1660, (301)698-7100, FAX (301)251-5784, telex 5106014543. **(Subscription address:** Aspen Publishers Inc., PO Box 990, Frederick MD 21701.**) ED** Janet M. Barber, RN, MS. **DD** 610. **NLM** W1; CR216NE. **CODEN** CCNQEJ. **[CCC]. Pr Rev.** available in microform from University Microfilms International (UMI). Documents available from BIOSIS Document Express. ***Continues*** *Critical Care Quarterly, 0160-2551.*
**Desc:** Each valuable issue focuses on one central key subject that is crucial to true professionalism in critical care so you can keep pace with all major developments and advances in your fast changing specialty.
**Ind/Abst** Biol. Abstr. (March 1987-); Cumul. Index Nurs. Allied Health Lit. (March 1987-); EMBASE; Health Devices Alerts; Health Plan. Adminis.; Hospit. Health Admin. Index (March 1987-); Int. Nurs. Index; Nurs. Abstr.; PsycINFO.

US/1048-2687
**CRNA. See** Medical Science and Technology-Anesthesiology.

US/0146-5554
**CUMULATIVE INDEX TO NURSING & ALLIED HEALTH LITERATURE. See** Medical Science and Technology-Abstracting, Bibliographies and Statistics.

US
**CUMULATIVE INDEX TO NURSING & ALLIED HEALTH LITERATURE. [MICROFICHE]. See** Medical Science and Technology-Abstracting, Bibliographies and Statistics.

SA/0379-8577
**CURATIONIS (PRETORIA).** (CURATIONIS.). [Curationis]. **Added/Corp** South African Nursing Association. Vol. 1, No. 1 (June 1978)-. Periodical. Afrikaans (English). Four times a year. $40.00. University

Natal / South African Nursing Association, King George V Avenue, Durban 4001 South Africa. **Tel** 011 27 31 8161431. **ED** Lilian Medlen. **NLM** W1 CU485. Index available. **Pr Rev. Circ:** 500. available on microfiche. ***Continues*** *S. A. Nursing Journal.*
**Desc:** Research journal of South African nursing.
**Ind/Abst** Cumul. Index Nurs. Allied Health Lit.; Int. Nurs. Index.

US
**CURRENT PERSPECTIVES IN NURSING MANAGEMENT.** (1979)-. English. Mosby Year Book Inc., 11830 Westline Industrial Drive, St Louis MO 63146. **Tel** (800)325-4177, (314)872-8370, FAX (314)432-1380, telex 44-2402. **NLM** WY 105 C976.

US
**CURRENT PRACTICE IN GERONTOLOGICAL NURSING.** Vol. 1 (1979)-. English. $10.50. Mosby Year Book Inc., 11830 Westline Industrial Drive, St Louis MO 63146. **Tel** (800)325-4177, (314)872-8370, FAX (314)432-1380, telex 44-2402.

US/0190-6771
**CURRENT PRACTICE IN NURSING CARE OF THE ADULT.** V. 1- 1979-. Periodical. English. Mosby Year Book Inc., 11830 Westline Industrial Drive, St Louis MO 63146. **Tel** (800)325-4177, (314)872-8370, FAX (314)432-1380, telex 44-2402. **NLM** W1 CU803AZ.

US/0164-310X
**CURRENT REVIEWS FOR NURSE ANESTHETISTS. See** Medical Science and Technology-Anesthesiology.

US/0896-1182
**CURRENT REVIEWS FOR POST ANESTHESIA CARE NURSES.** [Curr. rev. post anesth. care nurses]. Vol. 9, Lesson 1 (1987)-. Periodical. English. Twenty-two times a year. $150.00. Current Reviews, 7480 Fairway Drive, Suite 106, Miami Lakes FL 33014. **Tel** (305)822-1415, FAX (305)823-9367. **ED** Joaquin Aldrete M.D., S. G. Hershey M.D., Susan B. Christoph M.D., Phillip W. Watson M. D., Howard S. Goldman M.D., and S. H. Wittels M.D. **DD** 610. **NLM** W1; CU8093KH. ***Continues*** *Current Reviews for Recovery Room Nurses, 0164-3118.*
**Desc:** Contains news and different topics of the latest techniques in the field of post anesthesia care. Also listed are the educational lessons that you can study at home and learn at your own pace.
**Ind/Abst** Cumul. Index Nurs. Allied Health Lit. (1987-).

GW/0012-074X
**DEUTSCHE KRANKENPFLEGEZEITSCHRIFT.** [Dtsch. Krankenpfl.-z.]. Vol. 24; (1971)-. Periodical. German. mo. DM88.00. W Kohlhammer Verlag GmbH, Postfach 800430, D 70549 Stuttgart Germany. **Tel** 011 49 711 78631, FAX 011 49 711 7863263, telex 7-255820. **ED** Antje Grauhan and Paul W Schreiner. **NLM** W1 DE735R. **[CCC]. Bk Rev. Ad Acc. Circ:** 20,000 (ctrl). ***Continues*** *Deutsche Schwesternzeitung.*
**Desc:** All aspects of nursing: administration, legislation, research. Each issue contains a supplement with a larger comprehensive article.
**Ind/Abst** Int. Nurs. Index.

US/0730-4625
**DIMENSIONS OF CRITICAL CARE NURSING.** (DIMENSIONS OF CRITICAL CARE NURSING : DCCN.). [Dimens. crit. care nurs.]. **VFOAT** DCCN; D.C.C.N. Vol. 1, No. 1 (Jan./Feb. 1982)-. Periodical. English. bm. $45.00 (individuals), $78.00 (institutions) US; $57.00 (individuals), $90.00 (institutions) Canada; $98.00 (institutions), $65.00 (individuals) other. Hall Johnson Communications Inc, 9737 West Ohio Avenue, Lakewood CO 80226. **Tel** (303)988-0056. **ED** Suzanne Hall Johnson. **NLM** W1 DI594. **[CCC]. Bk Rev. Ad Acc. Pr Rev. Circ:** 5,742. available on microfilm and microfiche from University Microfilms International (UMI).
**Desc:** Articles discuss new techniques, medication and equipment in all areas of critical care nursing; also features editorials, book reviews, product news and research abstracts.
**Ind/Abst** Cumul. Index Nurs. Allied Health Lit.; Health Plan. Adminis.; Int. Nurs. Index; Nurs. Abstr.

US/0272-5940
**DIRECTORY - COUNCIL OF SPECIALISTS IN PSYCHIATRIC AND MENTAL HEALTH NURSING.** [Dir. - Counc. Spec. Psychiatr. Ment. Heal. Nurs.]. **Main/Corp** American Nurses' Association. Council of Specialists in Psychiatric and Mental Health Nursing. 1979-. Directory. English. be. ANA, 2420 Pershing Road, Kansas City MO 64108. **NLM** WY 22 AA1 A3D.

US
**DIRECTORY OF CERTIFIED NURSES. Main/Corp** American Nurses' Association. **VFOAT** ANA Directory of Certified Nurses. 1975?-. Directory. English. ir. American Nurses Association, 600 Maryland Avenue Southwest, Suite 100, Washington DC 20024. **Tel** (202)554-4444.

US
**DIRECTORY OF EDUCATIONAL SOFTWARE FOR NURSING. Added/Corp** National League for Nursing. (1987)-. Directory. English. be. $79.95. National League for Nursing, 350 Hudson Street, New York NY 10014. **Tel** (212)989-9393, (800)669-1656. **NLM** WY 18; D598.

US
**DIRECTORY OF EXPANDED ROLE PROGRAMS FOR REGISTERED NURSES, A.** (197?)-. Directory. English. Dividion of Nursing, HRSA, BHPr, Parklawn Building/Room 5C-26, 5600 Fishers Lane, Rockville Maryland 20857. **NLM** WY 22 AA1 D6. ***Continues*** *Directory of Programs Preparing Registered Nurses for Expanded Roles, 0160-4449.*

AT
**DIRECTORY OF HIGHER EDUCATION NURSING COURSES.** [Dir. high. educ. nurs. courses]. (1984)-. Directory. English. an. 20.00Aus$ (members); 25.00Aus$ (non-members). Royal College Nursing Australia, 2 Slater Street, Melbourne VIC 3004 Australia. **Tel** 011 61 3 8202055, FAX 011 61 3 8201954. **DD** 610.73071194.

US
**DIRECTORY OF SOUTH DAKOTA REGISTERED NURSES AND LICENSED PRACTICAL NURSES.** Directory. English. South Dakota State Board of Nursing, 301 Western Building, Mitchell SD 57301. **LC** RT5.S8; D57. **DD** 610.73/025/783. **NLM** WY 22 AS8 D5.

US
**DNA REPORTER. Added/Corp** Delaware Nurses' Association. **VFOAT** Reporter. **VAT** Delaware Nurses' Association Reporter. Vol. 10, No. 8 (Oct. 1986)-. Periodical. English. Ten times a year (July/Aug. & Nov./Dec. issues combined). $15.00 US; $25.00 Canada and Mexico. Delaware Nurses Association, 2634 Capitol Trail, Suite C, Newark DE 19711. **Tel** (302)368-2333, FAX (302)366-1775. **ED** Karen Morin. **Bk Rev**, (Qty: 4). **Ad Acc, Adv Mgr:** Delaware Nurses Assoc., **Tel** (302)368-2333. **Pr Rev. Circ:** 700 (ctrl). ***Continues*** *Reporter (Wilmington, Del.), 0418-5412.*
**Desc:** Nursing issues in the state of Delaware. Continuing education, upcoming events, legislative nursing information and Board of Nursing updates.

CN/1187-7669
**EDUNEUF (OTTAWA).** (EDUNEUF.). [Eduneuf]. **Added/Corp** Association des Infirmieres et Infirmiers du Canada. Vol. 1, No 1 (Jun 1991)-. Periodical. French. bm. Free for members. Association des Infirmieres et Infirmiers du Canada, 50 The Driveway, Ottawa Ontario K2P 1E2 Canada. **DD** 610.73.

●UK
**ELDERLY CARE.** Vol. 5, No. 1 (Jan./Feb. 1993)-. Periodical. English. bm. £25.00 Europe and UK; £50.00 other. Royal College of Nursing, Department A Glynteg House, STA House, Ely Cardiff CF5 4XG England. **Tel** 011 44 71 222 553411. **(Subscription address:** Royal College of Nursing, Glynteg House Station Terrace, Ely Cardiff CF5 4XG England.**) NLM** W1; EL289. ***Continues*** *Nursing the Elderly.*

●UK
**EMERGENCY NURSE : THE JOURNAL OF THE RCN ACCIDENT AND EMERGENCY NURSING ASSOCIATION. Added/Corp** RCN Accident and Emergency Nursing Association. (Mar. 25, 1992)-. Periodical. English. sa. **NLM** W1; EM664DN.
**Ind/Abst** Int. Nurs. Index (1992-).

US/0886-7143
**EMPHASIS, NURSING.** (EMPHASIS, NURSING / LOS ANGELES COUNTY, HARBOR-UCLA MEDICAL CENTER, NURSING DEPARTMENT.). Vol. 1, No. 1-. Periodical. English. sa. Free. Harbor-UCLA Medical Center, 1000 West Carson, Department of Nursing, Torrance CA 90509. **Tel** (310)533-3413, FAX (310)212-4280. **ED** Paula Siler. **DD** 610. **NLM** W1; EM679T. Index available. cum. index. **Pr Rev. Circ:** 5,000.
**Ind/Abst** Cumul. Index Nurs. Allied Health Lit.; Int. Nurs. Index.

US/1056-7062
**ENA'S NURSING SCAN IN EMERGENCY CARE.** [ENA's nurs. scan emerg. care]. **Added/Corp** Emergency Nurses Association. **VFOAT** Nursing Scan in Emergency Care. Vol. 1, No. 1 (Sept./Oct. 1991)-. Periodical. English. bm (6 issues). $63.00 (institutions), $43.00 (individuals) US; $74.00 (institutions), $54.00 (individuals) other. NURSECOM Inc., 1211 Locust Street, Philadelphia PA 19107. **Tel** (215)545-7222, (800)242-6757, FAX (215)545-8107. **ED** Patricia A. Lenaghan, RN, MS. **DD** 610. **NLM** ZWY 101; E56. **Pr Rev. Circ:** 2404. available on an online database, CD-ROM, magnetic tape, and microfilm from University Microfilms International (UMI).
**Desc:** A professional resource journal containing synopsis and commentary of articles surveyed from nursing, medical and professional periodicals as well as other current sources that relate to all aspects of emergency care nursing. The abstracts are annotated with remarks and opinion by nurses known and respected for their involvement in the field of emergency care.

MX/0185-0970
**ENFERMERA AL DIA.** [Enf. dia]. (1975)-. Periodical. Spanish. mo. $50.00. Intersistemas SA de CV, Fernando Alencastre #110, Mexico City DF Mexico. **Tel** 011 52 5 5202073, 011 52 5 5405600. **ED** Martha Castilleja. **NLM** W1 EN593. **Bk Rev. Ad Acc. Circ:** 15,800.
**Desc:** Continuous education for nurses: general practice, emergencies, and general information.

SP/0211-9005
**ENFERMERIA CIENTIFICA.** (198?)-. Periodical. Spanish. mo. 6748.00ptas. Graficas Alberdi SA, D Francisca Armada 38, 28047 Madrid Spain. **Tel** 011 34 1 4637017. **NLM** W1; EN636.
**Ind/Abst** Indice Med. Esp.

SP
**ENFERMERIA INTEGRAL.** Spanish. Colegio de ATS-DUE, Dr. Zamenhoff 11, 46008 Valencia Spain.

US/0098-1516
**ENLB, EMERGENCY NURSE LEGAL BULLETIN.** [ENLB, emerg. nurse legal bull.]. **VFOAT** Emergency Nurse Legal Bulletin. Vol. 1 (1975)-. Periodical. English. Four times a year (Jan., Apr., July, Oct.). $20.00. Medical Law Publishing, PO Box 293, Westville NJ 08093. **Tel** (800)848-3721. **ED** James E. George. **LC** KF2915.N8; A132. **DD** 344/.73/041. **NLM** W1 E385. ctrl circ.
**Desc:** Covers medicolegal aspects of emergency nursing.
**Ind/Abst** Cumul. Index Nurs. Allied Health Lit.; Int. Nurs. Index.

CN/0710-2976
**ENTRANCE REQUIREMENTS FOR DIPLOMA SCHOOLS OF NURSING AND SCHOOLS OF PRACTICAL NURSING.** (ENTRANCE REQUIREMENTS FOR DIPLOMA SCHOOLS OF NURSING AND SCHOOLS OF PRACTICAL NURSING / CANADIAN NURSES' ASSOCIATION.). **Added/Corp** Canadian Nurses' Association. **VFOAT** Conditions d'Admission aux Ecoles Decernant de Diplome d'Infirmiere et d'Infirmiere Auxiliaire. (1981/1982)-. English (French). an. 5.00Can$. Canadian Nurses Association, 50 The Driveway, Ottawa Ontario K2P 1E2 Canada. **Tel** (613)237-2133, FAX (613)237-3520. **DD** 610.73/07/1171. ***Continues*** *General Entrance Requirements for Schools of Nursing and Schools of Practical Nursing, 0706-3865.*
**Desc:** Lists entrance requirements, by province, for Canadian diploma schools of nursing and of practical nursing.

SP
**ESCUELA DE ENFERMERIA.** Spanish. SANED SA, Paseo de la Habana 202 Bis, 28036 Madrid Spain. **Tel** 011 34 1 5553508.

UK/0961-5423
**EUROPEAN JOURNAL OF CANCER CARE / THE OFFICIAL JOURNAL OF THE EUROPEAN ONCOLOGY NURSING SOCIETY. Added/Corp** European Oncology Nursing Society. Vol. 1, No. 1 (1991)-. Academic Scholarly Publication. English (German, Spanish and Italian). qt (4 issues). $136.00 (institutions), $58.00 (individuals) US & Canada; £69.00 (institutions), £39.50 (individuals) Europe; £76.00 (institutions), £37.50 (individuals) other. Blackwell Scientific Publications Ltd, Marston Book Services, PO Box 87, Oxford OX2 ODT UK. **Tel** 011 44 865 791155, FAX 011 44 865 791927, telex 837 515 MARDIS G. **NLM** W1; EU72BAH. available on microfilm and microfiche from University Microfilms International (UMI).

US/0071-3651
**FACTS ABOUT NURSING. Added/Corp** American Nurses' Association. Nursing Information Bureau. National League of Nursing Education (U.S.) National Organization for Public Health Nursing (U.S.). (1935)-. English. ir. $48.50. American Nurses Association, 600 Maryland Avenue Southwest, Suite 100, Washington DC 20024. **Tel** (202)554-4444. **LC** RT1; .A67. **DD** 362.1/73/0973021.
**Ind/Abst** Stat. Ref. Index.

US
**FACULTY SALARIES IN BACCALAUREATE AND GRADUATE PROGRAMS IN NURSING / INSTITUTE DATA SYSTEMS. Added/Corp** American Association of Colleges of Nursing. Institutional Data Systems. (199?)-. English. American Association of Colleges of Nursing, One Dupont Circle NW / Suite 530, Washington DC 20036. **Tel** (202)463-6930. **LC** RT79;

.R45. **DD** 331.2/8161073/071173. **NLM** W1; FA199G. ***Continues*** *Report on Faculty Salaries in Baccalaureate and Graduate Programs in Nursing, 1055-6958.*

NO/0802-9768
### FAG TIDSSKRIFTET SYKEPLEIEN.
**Added/Corp** Norsk Sykepleierforbund. **VFOAT** Fagtidsskriftet Sykepleien; Sykepleien. Vol. 77, No. 16/89 (Sept. 1989)-. Periodical. Norwegian. Thirty times a year (21 plus 9 issues). $595.00. Norwegian Nurses Association, PO Box 2633 SF Hanshaugen, 0131 Oslo 1 Norway. **Tel** 011 47 2 382000, FAX 011 47 2 353663. **NLM** W1; FA199L. cum. index. **Ad Acc.** ctrl circ. ***Continues in part*** *Sykepleien, 0039-7628.*
**Ind/Abst** Int. Nurs. Index (1989-).

US/0273-3544
### FAMILY-CENTERED COMMUNITY NURSING.
[Fam.-cent. community nurs.]. **VAT** Family Centered Community Nursing. V. 2-. English. Mosby Year Book Inc., 11830 Westline Industrial Drive, St Louis MO 63146. **Tel** (800)325-4177, (314)872-8370, FAX (314)432-1380, telex 44-2402. **ED** A M Reinhardt and M D Quinn. **NLM** W1 FA432BN. ***Continues*** *Current Practice in Family-Centered Community Nursing.*

US/0732-9644
### FLESCHNER SERIES IN CRITICAL CARE NURSING, THE.
[Fleschner ser. crit. care nurs.]. Began with: 1 (1981). Monographic series. English. Price varies per volume. Fleschner Publishing Company, 270 Amity Road, New Haven CT 06525-2205. **DD** 610.73/61. **NLM** W1 FL627.

US/0015-4199
### FLORIDA NURSE, THE.
(THE FLORIDA NURSE : OFFICIAL BULLETIN OF THE FLORIDA NURSES ASSOCIATION.). [Fla. nurse]. **Added/Corp** Florida Nurses Association. (1955)-. Bulletin. English. mo (Except July and Dec.). $15.00 (US); $20.00 (other) includes postage. Florida Nurses Association, 1235 East Concord Street, PO Box 6985, Orlando FL 32803. **Tel** (407)896-3261. **ED** Paula Massey and Karen Rogers. **DD** 610. **NLM** W1 FL882. **Bk Rev. Ad Acc. Circ:** 7,400 (ctrl). available on microfiche; available on microfilm. ***Continues*** *Bulletin of the Florida State Nurses Association.*
**Desc:** Information, trends and news relevant to health care and nursing.
**Ind/Abst** Cumul. Index Nurs. Allied Health Lit.; Health Plan. Adminis.; Int. Nurs. Index.

US/0887-5006
### FLORIDA NURSING REVIEW.
[Fla. nurs. rev.]. **Added/Corp** University of Florida. College of Nursing. Vol. 1, No. 1 (July 1, 1986)-. Periodical. English. qt. Free. Florida Nursing Update, 2750 Southwest 140 Terrace, Davie FL 33330. **ED** Diane R. LaRochelle and Lois J. Malasanos. **DD** 610. **Circ:** 7,000.

US/0736-3605
### FOCUS ON CRITICAL CARE. *Ceased.*
[Focus crit. care]. Vol. 10, No. 1 (Feb. 1983)-Ceased (April 1992). Periodical. English. bm. Mosby Year Book Inc., 11830 Westline Industrial Drive, St Louis MO 63146. **Tel** (800)325-4177, (314)872-8370, FAX (314)432-1380, telex 44-2402. **ED** Marguerite Kinney. **NLM** W1 FO1003H. **[CCC]. Bk Rev. Ad Acc. Pr Rev. Circ:** 58,198. available on microfilm and microfiche from University Microfilms International (UMI). ***Continues*** *Focus on AACN.*
**Desc:** Provides clinically relevant information for critical-care nurses, pediatric practitioners, educators, managers, and other members of the critical-care nursing community. Covers newsworthy issues that affect nursing in general and critical care in particular.
**Ind/Abst** Cumul. Index Nurs. Allied Health Lit. (?-?); Health Plan. Adminis.; Int. Nurs. Index (?-?); Nurs. Abstr. (?-?).

US/0016-2116
### FRONTIER NURSING SERVICE QUARTERLY BULLETIN.
[Front. Nurs. Serv. q. bull.]. **Added/Corp** Frontier Nursing Service, Inc. **VFOAT** Annual Report - Frontier Nursing Service. Vol. 4 (June 1928)-. Bulletin. English. Four times a year (Mar., June, Sept., Dec.). $10.00. Frontier Nursing Service Inc, PO Box 4, C/O Mae Irvin, Wendover KY 41775. **Tel** (606)672-2312, FAX (606)672-3022. **ED** David M. Watfield. **NLM** W1 FR945K. **Circ:** 6,200 (ctrl). available on microfilm and microfiche from University Microfilms International (UMI). ***Continues*** *Quarterly Bulletin of the Kentucky Committee for Mothers and Babies.*
**Desc:** Articles on activities of frontier nursing service: rural health care, nurse-midwifery, nursing education, etc.
**Ind/Abst** Cumul. Index Nurs. Allied Health Lit.; Int. Nurs. Index.

US/1042-895X
### GASTROENTEROLOGY NURSING.
(GASTROENTEROLOGY NURSING : THE OFFICIAL JOURNAL OF THE SOCIETY OF GASTROENTEROLOGY NURSES AND ASSOCIATES.). [Gastroenterol. nurs.]. **Added/Corp** Society of Gastroenterology Nurses and Associates. Vol. 11, No. 4 (Spring 1989)-. Periodical. English. bm. $69.00 (individual), $99.00 (institution) US; $104.00 (individual), $134.00 (institutions) other. Williams & Wilkins Company, 428 East Preston Street, Baltimore MD 21202-3993. **Tel** (410)528-4000, (800)638-6423, FAX (410)528-8596, telex 87669. **(Subscription address:** Williams & Wilkins, PO Box 64380, Baltimore MD 21264.**) DD** 616. **NLM** W1; GA458KH. **CODEN** GANUER. **[CCC].** Documents available from , BIOSIS Document Express, , Quick Copies. ***Continues*** *SGA Journal (Society of Gastrointestinal Assistants (U.S.)), 0744-1126.*
**Desc:** The official journal of the Society of Gastroenterology Nurses and Associates. Specifically for gastroenterology nurses, describes new procedures, techniques, and equipment.
**Ind/Abst** Biol. Abstr. (1989-); Cumul. Index Nurs. Allied Health Lit. (1989-); Health Plan. Adminis.; Int. Nurs. Index (Summer 1989-).

US/0016-8335
### GEORGIA NURSING.
[Georgia nurs.]. **Added/Corp** Georgia Nurses' Association. Vol. 1 (Aug. 1945)-. Periodical. English. bm. $25.00. Georgia Nurses Association, 1362 West Peachtree Street NW, Atlanta GA 30309. **Tel** (404)876-4624, FAX (404)876-4621. **ED** Susan Williamson and Sylvia Smith. **NLM** W1 GE444. **Ad Acc. Circ:** 3,500 (ctrl).
**Desc:** Provides up-to-date coverage of the latest nursing news and issues in the state of Georgia.
**Ind/Abst** Cumul. Index Nurs. Allied Health Lit.; Health Plan. Adminis.; Int. Nurs. Index.

US/0197-4572
### GERIATRIC NURSING (NEW YORK).
(GERIATRIC NURSING.). [Geriatr. nurs.]. **Added/Corp** American Journal of Nursing Company. Vol. 1 (May/June 1980)-. Periodical. English. bm. $48.00 (institutions), $31.00 (individuals) US; $59.00 (institutions), $42.00 (individuals) other. Mosby Year Book Inc., 11830 Westline Industrial Drive, St Louis MO 63146. **Tel** (800)325-4177, (314)872-8370, FAX (314)432-1380, telex 44-2402. **LC** RC954; .G45. **DD** 610.73/65/05. **NLM** W1 GE457CB. **[CCC].** cum. index. **Bk Rev. Ad Acc. Pr Rev. Circ:** 30,000. available on microfilm and microfiche from University Microfilms International (UMI).
**Desc:** Presents articles by professionals on clinical problems of the old, with drug/nutrition columns, relevant legislation, profiles of outstanding elders, letters and editorials, and a management section.
**Ind/Abst** Cumul. Index Nurs. Allied Health Lit.; Hum. Resour. Abstr. (?-?); Index Med. (Vol. 7, No. 6, 1986-); Index Period. Lit. Aging; Int. Nurs. Index; Int. Pharm. Abstr. (19??-19??); Nurs. Abstr.; Nutr. Res. Newsl.; Physic. Medline Plus; Psychol. Abstr. (1983-); PsycINFO; PsycLit.

SP/0214-8919
### GESTION HOSPITALARIA.
[Gest. hosp.]. **VFOAT** GH (Madrid); GH. Gestion Hospitalaria. (1989)-. Periodical. Spanish. Four times a year. $50.00 Europe; $80.00 other. Alpe Editores SA, C Pedro Rico 27, Oficinas 11 & 12, 28029 Madrid Spain. **Tel** 011 34 1 7338811, FAX 011 34 1 3159652. **UDC** 364.44.046.6.

US/1047-4749
### HAWAII NURSE, THE.
(THE HAWAII NURSE : THE OFFICIAL MONTHLY NEWSLETTER OF THE HAWAII NURSES' ASSOCIATION.). [Hawaii nurse]. **Added/Corp** Hawaii Nurses' Association. (198?)-. Newsletter. English. mo. $15.00. Hawaii Nurses Association, 677 ala Moana Boulevard, #601, Honolulu HI 96813. **DD** 610. **NLM** W1; HA965. ***Continues*** *Hawaii Nurses Pipeline, 0146-2784.*
**Ind/Abst** Health Plan. Adminis.; Int. Nurs. Index (May 1989-).

UK/0017-9140
### HEALTH VISITOR : THE JOURNAL OF THE HEALTH VISITORS' ASSOCIATION.
[Health visit.]. **Added/Corp** Health Visitors' Association (Great Britain). (1964)-. Periodical. English. mo. £54.00. Professional & Scientific Publishers, Tavistock House, East Tavistock Square, London WC1H 9JR England. **Tel** 011 44 71 387-4499, telex 005311. **(Subscription address:** Professional & Scientific Publishers, PO Box 294, London WC1H 9TB England.**) ED** Nick Robin. **LC** RT97; .H43. **NLM** W1 HE604. **Bk Rev. Ad Acc. Circ:** 16,000 (ctrl). available on microfilm and microfiche from University Microfilms International (UMI). ***Continues*** *Woman Health Officer.*
**Desc:** It publishes news coverage, and regular columns of reviews, advice and information. Also new legislation, front line changes and analysis from behind the lines are discussed.
**Ind/Abst** Appl. Soc. Sci. Index Abstr.; Cumul. Index Nurs. Allied Health Lit.; Int. Nurs. Index; Spec. Educ. Needs Abstr.

US/0147-9563
### HEART & LUNG.
[Heart lung]. **Added/Corp** American Association of Critical-Care Nurses. **VFOAT** Heart and Lung. Vol. 1 (Jan./Feb. 1972)-. Academic Scholarly Publication. English. bm. $114.00 (institutions), $36.00 (individuals) US; $127.00 (institutions), $49.00 (individuals) other. Mosby Year Book Inc., 11830 Westline Industrial Drive, St Louis MO 63146. **Tel** (800)325-4177, (314)872-8370, FAX (314)432-1380, telex 44-2402. **ED** Kathleen Dracup and Christopher W. Bryan-Brown. **LC** RC681.A1; H38. **DD** 616.1/2. **NLM** W1 HE644J. **CODEN** HELUAI. **[CCC].** Index available. **Bk Rev. Ad Acc. Pr Rev. Circ:** 63,776. available on microfilm and microfiche from University Microfilms International (UMI). Documents available from The Genuine Article, BIOSIS Document Express, CASDDS, ADONIS.
**Desc:** Concerned with the nurse's role and responsibility in the care and management of critically ill patients. Also emphasizes collaborative practice in critical care. Articles are intended to increase those skills required in ICUs - decision-making ability, administrative skills, knowledge of procedure and equipment, teaching and training skills.
**Ind/Abst** Abr. Index Med.; ADONIS; Annals Behav. Med.; Biol. Abstr.; Chem. Abstr.; Cumul. Index Nurs. Allied Health Lit.; Curr. Contents Clin. Med.; EMBASE; Energy Res. Abstr. (May 1977-); Health Devices Alerts; Health Period. Database; Hospit. Health Admin. Index; Index Med.; INIS Atomindex [Micro.]; Int. Nurs. Index; Nurs. Abstr.; Nutr. Abstr. Rev., Ser. B, Live Feeds and Feed.; Nutr. Abstr. Rev., Ser. A, Hum. Exp.; Life Sci. Collect.; Physic. Medline Plus; Res. Alert [Select. Cov.]; Rev. Med. Vet. Mycology; SCISEARCH; Soc. Sci. Cit. Index [Select. Cov.]; SportSearch.

UK
### HISTORY OF NURSING BULLETIN.
**Added/Corp** Royal College of Nursing (Great Britain). History of Nursing Group. **VFOAT** Bulletin of History of Nursing. Vol. 2, No. 1 (1987)-. Bulletin. English. ir (3 issues). £10.00. Royal College of Nursing / England, 20 Cavendish Square, London W1M 0AB England. **Tel** 011 44 71 409-3333 ext. 239, FAX 011 44 71 408-0190. **NLM** W1; HI85N. ***Continues*** *Bulletin (Royal College of Nursing (Great Britain). History of Nursing Group).*

FI/0786-5686
### HOITOTIEDE.
**Added/Corp** Sairaanhoitajien Koulutussaatio (Finland). **VFOAT** Hoito Tiede. Vol. 1, No. 1-(1989)-. Periodical. Finnish (summaries and/or abstracts in English). sa. **NLM** W1; HO464. ***Continues*** *Sairaanhoidon Vuosikirja.*
**Ind/Abst** Health Plan. Adminis.; Index Dent. Lit.; Int. Nurs. Index.

US/0887-9311
### HOLISTIC NURSING PRACTICE.
[Holist. nurs. pract.]. **VFOAT** HNP. Vol. 1, No. 1 (Nov. 1986)-. Periodical. English. qt. $75.00 US. Aspen Publishers Inc., 7201 McKinney Circle, Frederick MD 21701. **Tel** (800)234-1660, (301)698-7100, FAX (301)251-5784, telex 5106014543. **(Subscription address:** Aspen Publishers Inc., PO Box 990, Frederick MD 21701.**) ED** Doris Sutterley, MSN, RN and Gloria F. Donnely PhD, RN. **DD** 610. **NLM** W1; HO491QE. **[CCC]. Pr Rev.** available on microfilm and microfiche from University Microfilms International (UMI). ***Continues*** *Topics in Clinical Nursing, 0164-0534.*
**Desc:** Offers nurse clinicians and nurse researchers the opportunity to explore emerging holistic models of clinical practice in a continuous forum. It will reinforce your training and update your skills in vital subject areas such as human abuse, nursing process, and holistic sexuality-with an emphasis on health-oriented, biobehavioral research, and the controversies inherent in holistic nursing practice.
**Ind/Abst** Cumul. Index Nurs. Allied Health Lit. (1986-); Health Plan. Adminis.; Hospit. Health Admin. Index (1986-); Int. Nurs. Index (1986-); Nurs. Abstr. (1986-).

CN/0847-2378
### HOME CARE TODAY. *Ceased.*
**See** Sociology-Social Services and Welfare.

●US/1075-2188
### HOME HEALTH FOCUS.
(1994)-. Newsletter. English. mo. $55.00 (institutions), $39.95 (individuals) US; $62.00 (institutions), $46.95 (individuals) Canada; $69.55 (institutions), $54.50 (individuals) other. Mosby Year Book Inc., 11830 Westline Industrial Drive, St Louis MO 63146. **Tel** (800)325-4177, (314)872-8370, FAX (314)432-1380, telex 44-2402.

US/0884-741X
### HOME HEALTHCARE NURSE.
[Home healthc. nurse]. **VFOAT** Home Health Care Nurse. Vol. 1, No. 1 (Sept./Oct. 1983)-. Periodical. English. bm. $34.00 (individuals), $85.00 (institutions) US; $59.00 (individuals), $105.00 (institutions) other. J.B. Lippincott Company, 227 East Washington Square, Philadelphia PA 19106-3780. **Tel** (215)238-4200 or 4454, FAX (215)238-4227. **(Subscription address:** J.B. Lippincott, PO Box 350, Hagerstown MD 21740.**) ED** Joan E. Caserta. **DD** 610. **NLM** W1; H0503G. **CODEN** HHNUEJ. **[CCC]. Bk Rev. Ad Acc. Circ:** 10,000 (ctrl). available on microfilm and microfiche from University Microfilms International (UMI). ***Absorbed*** *Nephrology Nurse, 0164-4386.*
**Desc:** Geared to the professional nurse working in the home health, community health and public health areas. Keeps readers abreast of new development and procedures in such areas as preventive medicine, quality assurance, managed health care and family care.
**Ind/Abst** Abstr. Clin. Care Guidel.; Chicano Index; Cumul. Index Nurs. Allied Health Lit.; Int. Nurs. Index; Nurs. Abstr.

HK
### HONG KONG NURSING JOURNAL.
English. Twice a year. Hong Kong Nurses Association, Hong Kong.

US/0195-5713
**HOUSE OF DELEGATES REPORTS (1966).** (HOUSE OF DELEGATES REPORTS.). **Main/Corp** American Nurses' Association. (1966/1968)-. English. an. American Nurses Association, 600 Maryland Avenue Southwest, Suite 100, Washington DC 20024. **Tel** (202)554-4444. **NLM** W1 AM6639C. **Circ:** 1,500. ***Continues*** *House of Delegates, Sections Reports, 0195-5721.*
**Desc:** Summary of proceedings of the annual house of delegates meeting.

US/0743-5150
**IMAGE--THE JOURNAL OF NURSING SCHOLARSHIP.** [Image j. nurs. scholarsh.]. **Added/Corp** Sigma Theta Tau. **VFOAT** Image, The Journal of Nursing Scholarship. Vol. 15, No. 1 (Winter 1983)-. Periodical. English. Four times a year (Mar., June, Sept., Dec.). $21.00 (individuals), $30.00 (institutions) Canada & Mexico, $16.00 (individiual), $25.00 (institutions) US, $26.00 (individuals), $35.00 (institutions) others; $25.00 (individuals), $35.00 (institutions) Canada & Mexico, $20.00 (individuals), $30.00 (institutions) others Comes with combination of Reflections. Sigma Theta Tau International, 550 West North Street, Indianapolis IN 46202. **Tel** (317)634-8171, FAX (317)634-8188. **ED** Donna Diers. **DD** 610. **NLM** W1 IM457H. **CODEN** IMNSEP. Index available. cum. index. **Bk Rev**. **Ad Acc**. **Pr Rev. Circ:** 73,000 (ctrl). ***Continues*** *Image, 0363-2792.*
**Desc:** The official journal of Sigma Theta Tau International, Honor Society of Nursing. Contains manuscripts in the areas of clinical scholarship, policy and nursing education. Book reviews and "state-of-the-science" articles are also published.
**Ind/Abst** Cumul. Index Nurs. Allied Health Lit.; Health Plan. Adminis.; Index Med. (spring 1993-); Int. Nurs. Index (winter 1983-); Nurs. Abstr.; Psychol. Abstr. (1983-); PsycINFO.

US/1055-1476
**IMAGES (RESTON, VA.). See** Medical Science and Technology-Radiology.

US/0019-3062
**IMPRINT (NEW YORK, NEW YORK).** (IMPRINT.). [Imprint]. **Added/Corp** National Student Nurses' Association (U.S.). Vol. 15 (Jan. 1968)-. Periodical. English. qt (five no. a year). $15.00 North America; $20.00 other. National Student Nurses Association, 555 West 57th Street, New York NY 10019. **Tel** (212)581-2221. **ED** Diana Gallagher. **DD** 610. **NLM** W1 IM66. Index available. **Bk Rev**. **Ad Acc. Circ:** 25,000 (ctrl). ***Continues*** *NSNA Newsletter.*
**Desc:** Association news and articles on current issues and trends in nursing and nursing education. Features include reports on legislation, career planning, clinical news, highlights, etc.
**Ind/Abst** Cumul. Index Nurs. Allied Health Lit.; Energy Res. Abstr. (Aug. 1982-); Int. Nurs. Index.

US/0749-5102
**INDUSTRY WAGE SURVEY. NURSING AND PERSONAL CARE FACILITIES. See** Economics-Labor.

●CN/1195-2695
**INFIRMIERE DU QUEBEC.** (L'INFIRMIERE DU QUEBEC : REVUE OFFICIEL DE L'ORDRE DES INFIRMIERES ET INFIRMIERS DU QUEBEC.). (1993)-. French (English). bm (Jan., Mar., May, July, Sept., Nov.). 36.00Can$ (individuals), 47.00Can$ (institutions) US; 21.07 (individuals), 30.71 (institutions) Quebec; 24.30Can$ (individuals), 34.58Can$ (institutions) Canada; 46.00Can$ (individuals), 57.00Can$ (institutions) other. Order of Nurses of Quebec, 4200 Dorchester Street West, Montreal Quebec H3Z 1V4 Canada. **Tel** (514)935-2501 ext.256, FAX (514)935-1799. **ED** G. Chabot. **NLM** W1; IN409J. ***Continues*** *Nursing Quebec, 0381-6419.*

FR/0981-0560
**INFIRMIERE MAGAZINE, L'.** No. 1 (Feb. 1987)-. Periodical. French. mo. 550.00F (institutions), 445.00F (individuals) Africa, Middle East and French overseas departments; 490.00F (institutions), 380.00F (individuals) Europe; 382.98F (institutions), 279.14F (individuals) France; 685.00F (institutions), 580.00F (individuals) other. Editions Lamarre Poinat, 26 Avenue de l'Europe, 78141 Velizy, France. **Tel** 011 33 1 34633333. **NLM** W1; IN409R. ***Continues*** *Lettre de l'Infirmiere Francaise.*
**Ind/Abst** Int. Nurs. Index (Feb. 1987-).

CN/0842-3210
**INFO - NURSES ASSOCIATION OF NEW BRUNSWICK.** ***Title Change.*** (INFO.). [Info - Nurses Assoc. N.B.]. **Added/Corp** Nurses Association of New Brunswick. **VAT** Info - Association des Infirmieres et Infirmiers du Nouveau-Brunswick. Vol. 15, No. 4 (Aug. 1984)-v. 19, no. 5 (Nov. 1988). Periodical. English (French). ir. Nurses Association of New Brunswick, 231 Saunders Street, Fredericton New Brunswick E3B 1N6 Canada. **Tel** (506)458-8731. **DD** 610.73/06/0715. ***Continues*** *Info, 0382-5574.* ***Continued by*** *Info Nursing, 0846-524X.*

GW/0932-4313
**INFORMATIONEN FRESENIUS FUR KRANKENSCHWESTERN UND KRANKENPFLEGER.** [Inf. Fresenius Krankenschwestern Krankenpfl.]. (1973)-. German. **NLM** W1; IN43I.

AT/0812-9304
**INFORUM. Added/Corp** Royal Adelaide Hospital. Nursing Dept. (19??)-. Periodical. English. Nursing Department, Royal Adelaide Hospital, Nursing Administration, North Terrace, Adelaide SA 5000 Australia. **NLM** W1; IN444E.
**Ind/Abst** Cumul. Index Nurs. Allied Health Lit.; Int. Nurs. Index (July 1986-).

US/1058-0166
**INNOVATIONS IN UROLOGY NURSING.** [Innov. urol. nurs.]. (1990)-. Periodical. English. Three times a year. Meniscus Health Care Communications, 1623 Spruce Street, Philadelphia PA 19103. **DD** 616.

US/1060-135X
**INSIGHT (SAN FRANSISCO, CALIF.).** (INSIGHT / AMERICAN SOCIETY OF OPHTHALMIC REGISTERED NURSES, INC.). [Insight (San Franc. Calif.)]. **Added/Corp** American Society of Ophthalmic Registered Nurses. (19??)-. Periodical. English. Four times a year (Apr., June, Oct., Dec.). $35.00 (one year), $60.00 (two years), $85.00 (three years). American Society of Ophthalmic Nurses, PO Box 193030, San Francisco CA 94119. **Tel** (415)561-8513, FAX (415)561-8575. **ED** Kay McCoy, (editor's address: PO Box B, Drake, CO 80515, phone: (303)667-1680). **DD** 617. **NLM** W1; IN45769. cum. index. **Bk Rev**, (Qty: 2-4). **Ad Acc**, **Adv Mgr:** Robin Brandes, **Tel** (213)624-0900. **Pr Rev. Circ:** 1,800 (ctrl).
**Desc:** Serves as a forum for the dissemination of information on clinical topics, and professional issues for ophthalmic registered nurses. Also informative for operating room nurses, allied health personnel working in ophthalmology, and to physicians.
**Ind/Abst** Cumul. Index Nurs. Allied Health Lit.; Int. Nurs. Index (Dec. 1987-).

US
**INSTITUTIONAL FOOD SERVICE AND NUTRITIONAL CARE.** English. ir. EPSCO / Educational Planning Services Corporation, Box 930, East Sandwich MA 02537. **Tel** (508)888-3257, FAX (508)888-3257.

●UK/0964-3397
**INTENSIVE & CRITICAL CARE NURSING : THE OFFICIAL JOURNAL OF THE BRITISH ASSOCIATION OF CRITICAL CARE NURSES. Added/Corp** British Association of Critical Care Nurses. **VFOAT** Intensive and Critical Care Nursing. Vol. 8, No. 1 (Mar. 1992)-. Periodical. English. Six times a year. £147.00 Europe; £148.00 Other (Institutions). Churchill Livingstone, 1-3 Baxter's Place, Leith Walk, Edinburgh EH1 3AF Scotland. **Tel** 011 44 31 556 2424, FAX 011 44 31 558 1278, telex 727511. **(Subscription address:** Maruzen Company Ltd., PO Box 5050, Import & Export Department, Tokyo 100 31 Japan.**)** ***Continues*** *Intensive Care Nursing, 0266-612X.*
**Ind/Abst** Cumul. Index Nurs. Allied Health Lit.

US/0091-9462
**INTERNATIONAL DIRECTORY OF NURSES WITH DOCTORAL DEGREES.** 1973 Ed.-. Directory. English. an. American Nurses' Foundation, 10 Columbus Circle, New York NY 10019. **LC** RT25.A2; I58. **DD** 610.73/092/2; B. **NLM** WY 22 I613.

UK/0965-8335
**INTERNATIONAL JOURNAL OF HEALTH INFORMATICS.** [Int. j. health inform.]. (1990)-. Periodical. English. Four times a year (Mar., June, Sept., Dec.). $39.84 (individuals), $79.66 (institutions), EEC Countries; $47.80 (individuals), $87.63 (institutions) others. Media Medica, Index House, Midhurts Road, Liphook Hants GU30 7AZ England. **DD** 610.285.

AT/1322-7114
**INTERNATIONAL JOURNAL OF NURSING PRACTICE.** (19??)-. Academic Scholarly Publication. English. an. 60.00Aus$ (institutions), 30.00Aus$ (individuals) Australia; 86.00Aus$ (institutions), 43.00Aus$ (individuals) other. Blackwell Scientific Publications Australia, 54 University Street, PO Box 378, Carlton Victoria 3053 Australia. **Tel** 011 61 3 3470300, FAX 011 61 3 3475001, telex 10716421.

UK/0020-7489
**INTERNATIONAL JOURNAL OF NURSING STUDIES.** [Int. j. nurs. studies]. Vol. 1 (1963)-. Periodical. Multiple languages (English, French and German; summaries and/or abstracts in Russian and Spanish). bm. $373.00 The Americas; £250.00 other. Pergamon Press, An Imprint of Elsevier Science Ltd., The Boulevard, Langford Lane, Kidlington, Oxford OX5 1GB United Kingdom. **Tel** 011 44 865 843000, 011 44 865 843699, FAX 011 44 865 843010. **(Subscription address:** Elsevier Science Ltd. Oxford Fulfillment Centre, PO Box 800, Kidlington, Oxford OX5 1DX United Kingdom.**) ED** Rosemary Crow. **LC** RT1; .I63. **NLM** W1 IN77N. **CODEN** IJNUA6. **[CCC]. Pr Rev.** available on microfilm and microfiche from University Microfilms International (UMI). Documents available from The Genuine Article.
**Desc:** Publishes material of interest to an international readership of nurses and others interested in nursing topics.
**Ind/Abst** Cumul. Index Nurs. Allied Health Lit.; Curr. Aware. Biol. Sci., CABS; Curr. Contents Soc. Behav. Sci.; Index Med.; Int. Nurs. Index; Psychol. Abstr. (1982-); PsycINFO; PsycLit; Res. Alert [Full Cov.]; Soc. Sci. Cit. Index [Full Cov.].

UK
**INTERNATIONAL JOURNAL OF PALLIATIVE NURSING.** (19??)-. Periodical. English. Four times a year. £60.00 (institutions), £40.00 (individuals) UK; £90.00 (institutions), £60.00 (individuals) other. Mark Allen Publishing Limited, Robjohns Farm, Vicarage Road, Finchingfield CM7 4LJ England. **Tel** 11 44 371 810433.

●US/1075-4210
**INTERNATIONAL JOURNAL OF TRAUMA NURSING.** (1995)-. Periodical. English. qt. $68.00 (institutions), $36.00 (individuals) US; $88.00 (institutions), $56.00 (individuals) other. Mosby Year Book Inc., 11830 Westline Industrial Drive, St Louis MO 63146. **Tel** (800)325-4177, (314)872-8370, FAX (314)432-1380, telex 44-2402. **ED** Judith Stoner Halpern.
**Desc:** Review of trauma nursing practice. Encompasses facets of care, including flight, emergency, perioperative, medical/surgical, anesthesia, critical care, and rehabilitation nursing.

US/0020-8124
**INTERNATIONAL NURSING INDEX. See** Medical Science and Technology-Abstracting, Bibliographies and Statistics.

SZ/0020-8132
**INTERNATIONAL NURSING REVIEW (LONDON, ENGLAND).** (INTERNATIONAL NURSING REVIEW : OFFICIAL JOURNAL OF THE INERNATIONAL COUNCIL OF NURSES.). [Int. nurs. rev.]. **Added/Corp** International Council of Nurses. **VFOAT** Revue Internationale des Infirmieres; Internationale Schwesternumschau; Revista de Enfermeria. Vol. 1, (April 1954)-. Academic Scholarly Publication. English (French, German and Spanish). bm. 50.00F surface mail; 65.00F (air mail) Europe; 80.00F (air mail) other. International Council of Nurses, 3 Place Jean-Marteau, CH 1201 Geneva Switzerland. **Tel** 011 41 22 7312960, FAX 011 41 22 7381036. **ED** Nancy J Vatre. **LC** RT1; .I673. **DD** 610.7305. **NLM** W1 IN827A. Index available. cum. index. **Bk Rev**. **Ad Acc. Circ:** 2,500. available on microfilm and microfiche from University Microfilms International (UMI). ***Continues*** *International Nursing Bulletin, 0141-5557;* ***Absorbed*** *ICN Calling.*
**Desc:** Includes news of nursing throughout the world; articles of global interest involving nurses.
**Ind/Abst** Appl. Soc. Sci. Index Abstr.; Cumul. Index Nurs. Allied Health Lit.; EMBASE; Index Med.; Int. Nurs. Index; LABORDOC.

CK/0120-5307
**INVESTIGACION Y EDUCACION EN ENFERMERIA : REVISTA DE LA FACULTAD DE ENFERMERIA, UNIVERSIDAD DE ANTIOQUIA.** **Added/Corp** Universidad de Antioquia. Facultad de Enfermeria. Asociacion de Enfermeras de Antioquia. (1983)-. Periodical. Spanish. Twice a year (Mar., Nov.). $20.00. Univeridad de Antioquia, Apartado 1226, Facultad de Enfermeria, Medellin Columbia. **Tel** 011 57 4 2630970. **NLM** W1; IN994G.

US/0885-0046
**ISSUES (CHICAGO, ILL.).** (ISSUES / NATIONAL COUNCIL OF STATE BOARDS OF NURSING.). [Issues]. **Added/Corp** National Council of State Boards of Nursing (U.S.). Vol. 1, No. 1 (Spring 1980)-. Periodical. English. Six times a year. Free. National Council of State Boards of Nursing Inc, 676 North Saint Clair Street, Suite 550, Chicago IL 60611. **Tel** (312)787-6555. **DD** 610. **NLM** W1; IS667T.
**Ind/Abst** Cumul. Index Nurs. Allied Health Lit.

US/0146-0862
**ISSUES IN COMPREHENSIVE PEDIATRIC NURSING.** [Issues compr. pediatr. nurs.]. (May/June 1976)-. Monographic series. English. qt (4 issues). £60.00 UK; $99.00 other. Taylor & Francis Ltd., Rankine Road, Basingstoke Hampshire, RG24 8PR United Kingdom. **Tel** 011 44 256 840366, FAX 011 44 256 479438, telex 858540. **(Subscription address:** Taylor & Francis Inc., 1900 Frost Road, Suite 101, Bristol PA 19007-1598.**) ED** Chandice Covington. **DD** 610. **NLM** W1 IS6675. **CODEN** ICNUDS. **[CCC].** Index available (bound in last issue). **Bk Rev. Ad Acc. Pr Rev. Circ:** 1,800. available on microfilm and microfiche from University Microfilms International (UMI).
**Desc:** Provides vital information to practitioners, educators, and students. Because of certification and

increased specialization, it is imperative that members of the nursing profession periodically update their knowledge base and state-of-the-art awareness. Devoted to examining the specific needs of children and their families as identified by nurses and other health care providers.
**Ind/Abst** Cumul. Index Nurs. Allied Health Lit.; Int. Nurs. Index; J. Abstr. Artic. Int. Educ.; Psychol. Abstr. (1981-); PsycINFO; PsycLit; Soc. Plann. Policy Dev. Abstr.

US/0161-2840
**ISSUES IN MENTAL HEALTH NURSING.** [Issues ment. health nurs.]. **VFOAT** Mental Health Nursing. Vol. 1 (Spring 1978)-. Periodical. English. bm (6 issues). £90.00 UK; $149.00 other. Taylor & Francis Ltd., Rankine Road, Basingstoke Hampshire, RG24 8PR United Kingdom. **Tel** 011 44 256 840366, FAX 011 44 256 479438, telex 858540. **(Subscription address:** Taylor & Francis Inc., 1900 Frost Road, Suite 101, Bristol PA 19007-1598.**)** **ED** Mary Swanson Crockett (editor's address: School of Nursing, University of Texas at Austin, 1700 Red River, Austin, TX 78701-1499). **NLM** W1 IS669. **CODEN** IHNUDT. **[CCC].** Index available. **Bk Rev. Ad Acc. Pr Rev. Circ:** 700. available on microfilm and microfiche from University Microfilms International (UMI).
**Desc:** The practical information vital to working with psychosocial and mental health aspects of nursing is here. Emphasizes innovative approaches to client care, analysis of current issues, and nursing research findings, all presented by authorities at the leading edge of developments.
**Ind/Abst** Cumul. Index Nurs. Allied Health Lit.; Int. Nurs. Index (No. 1, 1987-);; J. Abstr. Artic. Int. Educ.; Nurs. Abstr.; Psychol. Abstr. (1981-); PsycINFO; PsycLit; Soc. Plann. Policy Dev. Abstr.

JM/0021-4140
**JAMAICAN NURSE.** ***Suspended.*** [Jam. nurse]. Periodical. English. qt. $15.00. Nurses Association of Jamaica, 72 Arnold Road, Kingston 5 Jamaica. **NLM** W1 JA74.
**Ind/Abst** Cumul. Index Nurs. Allied Health Lit.; Int. Nurs. Index.

●US/1062-2551
**JOURNAL FOR HEALTHCARE QUALITY.** (JOURNAL FOR HEALTHCARE QUALITY : OFFICIAL PUBLICATION OF THE NATIONAL ASSOCIATION FOR HEALTHCARE QUALITY.). [J. healthc. qual.]. **Added/Corp** National Association for Healthcare Quality (U.S.). **VFOAT** Journal for Health Care Quality; JHQ. Vol. 14, No.1 (Jan.-Feb. 1992)-. Periodical. English. bm. $90.00. National Association Healthcare Quality, 5700 Old Orchard Rd, 1st Floor, Skokie IL 60077-1057. **Tel** (708) 966-9392, FAX (708) 966-9418. **DD** 610. **NLM** W1; JO38MC. ***Continues*** *Journal of Quality Assurance, 1062-0273.*
**Ind/Abst** Hospit. Health Admin. Index (1992-).

UK/0309-2402
**JOURNAL OF ADVANCED NURSING.** [J. adv. nurs.]. Vol. 1, No. 1 (1976)-. Academic Scholarly Publication. English. mo (12 issues). $460.00 (institutions), $110.00 (individuals) US & Canada; £270.00 (institutions), £65.00 (individuals) Europe; £297.00 (institutions), £71.00 (individuals) other. Blackwell Scientific Publications Ltd, Marston Book Services, PO Box 87, Oxford OX2 ODT UK. **Tel** 011 44 865 791155, FAX 011 44 865 791927, telex 837 515 MARDIS G. **ED** J. P. Smith. **NLM** W1 JO533U. **[CCC]. Bk Rev. Ad Acc. Pr Rev. Circ:** 2,000 (ctrl). available on microfilm and microfiche from University Microfilms International (UMI). Documents available from The Genuine Article.
**Desc:** Publishes scholarly contributions on all aspects of nursing care and nursing education, management and research which have a sound scientific, theoretical or philosophical base.
**Ind/Abst** Annals Behav. Med.; Appl. Soc. Sci. Index Abstr.; Cumul. Index Nurs. Allied Health Lit.; Curr. Contents Soc. Behav. Sci.; EMBASE; Health Serv. Abstr.; Index Med.; Int. Nurs. Index; Res. Alert [Full Cov.]; Res. High. Educ. Abstr.; Soc. Sci. Cit. Index [Full Cov.].

UK/0960-9857
**JOURNAL OF ADVANCES IN HEALTH AND NURSING CARE.** [J. adv. health nurs. care]. (1991)-. Periodical. English. bm. £23.60 (individuals), £35.45 (institutions) UK; £25.00 (individuals), £37.50 (institutions) Europe; £27.50 (individuals), £41.25 (institutions) other. Quay Publishing, Nereus House New Quay Road, Lancaster LA1 5SA England. **Tel** 011 44 524843038, FAX 0524 844629. **ED** I C Henry (editor's address: Dean of Faculty of Health, Lancashire Polytechnic, Livesey House, Heatley Street Preston England; telephone: 0772 201201). **DD** 362.10941. Index available. cum. index. **Bk Rev. Ad Acc. Pr Rev.**
**Desc:** Publishes papers on topics related to the latest advances in technology, applied psychology, health community care, techniques, ethics and the educational needs of the nursing and health care professionals.

US/0889-4655
**JOURNAL OF CARDIOVASCULAR NURSING, THE.** [J. cardiovasc. nurs.]. **VFOAT** Cardiovascular Nursing; JCN. Vol. 1, Issue 1 (Nov. 1986)-. Periodical. English. qt. $68.00 US. Aspen Publishers Inc., 7201 McKinney Circle, Frederick MD 21701. **Tel** (800)234-1660, (301)698-7100, FAX (301)251-5784, telex 5106014543. **(Subscription address:** Aspen Publishers Inc., PO Box 990, Frederick MD 21701.**)** **DD** 616. **NLM** W1; JO575R. **[CCC]. Pr Rev.** available on microfilm and microfiche from University Microfilms International (UMI).
**Desc:** Focuses on the physiological, psychological, and social responses of patients in every setting with every article reflecting the present state of the art in cardiovascular nursing. It goes far beyond the medical model to include a holistic, family-oriented orientation.
**Ind/Abst** Cumul. Index Nurs. Allied Health Lit.; Int. Nurs. Index; Nurs. Abstr.

US/0897-9685
**JOURNAL OF CHILD AND ADOLESCENT PSYCHIATRIC AND MENTAL HEALTH NURSING.** ***Title Change.*** **See** Medical Science and Technology-Psychiatry.

●US/1073-6077
**JOURNAL OF CHILD AND ADOLESCENT PSYCHIATRIC NURSING.** (JOURNAL OF CHILD AND ADOLESCENT PSYCHIATRIC NURSING : OFFICIAL PUBLICATION OF THE ASSOCIATION OF CHILD AND ADOLESCENT PSYCHIATRIC NURSES, INC.). **VFOAT** JCAPN. (1994)-. English. qt. $70.00 (institutions), $40.00 (individuals) US; $82.00 (institutions), $52.00 (individuals) other. NURSECOM Inc., 1211 Locust Street, Philadelphia PA 19107. **Tel** (215)545-7222, (800)242-6757, FAX (215)545-8107. **NLM** W1; JO583JI.

US/0743-2550
**JOURNAL OF CHRISTIAN NURSING.** (JOURNAL OF CHRISTIAN NURSING : A QUARTERLY PUBLICATION OF NURSES CHRISTIAN FELLOWSHIP.). [J. Christ. nurs.]. **Added/Corp** Nurses Christian Fellowship (U.S.). Vol. 1, No. 1 (Spring 1984)-. Periodical. English. qt. $17.95 US; $20.45 other. Journal of Christian Nursing, PO Box 1650, Downers Grove IL 60515. **Tel** (708)964-5747, FAX (708)964-1251. **ED** Melodee Yohe. **NLM** W1; JO5843T. Index available. cum. index. **Bk Rev. Ad Acc. Pr Rev. Circ:** 11,000. available on microfilm and microfiche from University Microfilms International (UMI). ***Continues*** *Nurses Lamp, 0885-5854.*
**Desc:** Deals with patient's spiritual needs and spiritual care, missions and cross-cultural ethical, bioethical issues, personal and spiritual growth, and professional nursing issues.
**Ind/Abst** Christ. Period. Index (19??-); Cumul. Index Nurs. Allied Health Lit. (1984-); Int. Nurs. Index; Nurs. Abstr.

●UK/0962-1067
**JOURNAL OF CLINICAL NURSING.** Vol. 1, No. 1 (Jan. 1992)-. Academic Scholarly Publication. English. bm (6 issues). $196.00 (institutions), $60.00 (individuals) US & Canada; £115.00 (institutions), £35.00 (individuals) Europe; £126.50 (institutions), £38.50 (individuals) other. Blackwell Scientific Publications Ltd, Marston Book Services, PO Box 87, Oxford OX2 ODT UK. **Tel** 011 44 865 791155, FAX 011 44 865 791927, telex 837 515 MARDIS G. **NLM** W1; JO5893U. available on microfilm and microfiche from University Microfilms International (UMI).

US/0737-0016
**JOURNAL OF COMMUNITY HEALTH NURSING.** [J. commun. health nurs.]. Vol. 1, No. 1 (1984)-. Periodical. English. qt. $185.00 US & Canada; $210.00 other. Lawrence Erlbaum Associates, 365 Broadway, Suite 102, Hillsdale NJ 07642. **Tel** (201)666-4110, (800)926-6579, FAX (201)666-2394. **ED** Arlene Cairns and Alice Schroeder. **DD** 610. **NLM** W1; JO593R. **Ad Acc. Pr Rev.** available on microfilm and microfiche from University Microfilms International (UMI).
**Ind/Abst** Cumul. Index Nurs. Allied Health Lit. (1984-); EMBASE; Health Plan. Adminis.; Hospit. Health Admin. Index (1984-); Index Med. (1993-); Int. Nurs. Index (1984-).

UK
**JOURNAL OF COMMUNITY NURSING.** English. mo. £30.00 UK; £55.00 other. PTM Publishers Limited, 282 High Street, Sutton Surrey SM1 1PQ England. **Tel** 011 44 81 6420162.

US/0022-0124
**JOURNAL OF CONTINUING EDUCATION IN NURSING, THE.** [J. contin. educ. nurs.]. **VFOAT** Continuing Education in Nursing; JCEN. Vol. 1 (May 1970)-. Periodical. English. bm. $57.00 institution, $47.00 individual (US). Slack Inc., 6900 Grove Road, Thorofare NJ 08086. **Tel** (609)848-1000, (800)257-8290, FAX (609)853-5991, telex 517108 SLACK INC VD. **LC** RT90; .J6. **DD** 610.73/071/1. **NLM** W1 JO595X. available on microfilm and microfiche from University Microfilms International (UMI).
**Ind/Abst** Contents Pages Educ.; Cumul. Index Nurs. Allied Health Lit.; Curr. Index J. Educ.; Educ. Index; Health Plan. Adminis.; Hospit. Health Admin. Index; Int. Nurs. Index; Nurs. Abstr.

US/0099-1767
**JOURNAL OF EMERGENCY NURSING.** (JOURNAL OF EMERGENCY NURSING : JEN.). [J. emerg. nurs.]. **Added/Corp** Emergency Department Nurses Association. Emergency Nurses Association. **VFOAT** JEN. Vol. 1, (Jan./Feb. 1975)-. Periodical. English. bm. $126.00 (institutions), $46.00 (individuals) US; $136.00 (institutions), $56.00 (individuals) other. Mosby Year Book Inc., 11830 Westline Industrial Drive, St Louis MO 63146. **Tel** (800)325-4177, (314)872-8370, FAX (314)432-1380, telex 44-2402. **ED** Gail Pisarcik-Lenehan. **LC** RT120.E4; J24. **DD** 610.73/6. **NLM** WI; J26. **[CCC].** Index available. **Bk Rev. Ad Acc. Pr Rev. Circ:** 18,237. available on microfilm and microfiche from University Microfilms International (UMI).
**Desc:** Provides developments in emergency care. Covers professional, political, administrative, and educational aspects of emergency nursing through columns edited by professionals in the field.
**Ind/Abst** Cumul. Index Nurs. Allied Health Lit.; Health Plan. Adminis.; Hospit. Health Admin. Index; Int. Nurs. Index; Nurs. Abstr.

US/1055-3045
**JOURNAL OF ET NURSING.** ***Title Change.*** (JOURNAL OF ET NURSING : OFFICIAL PUBLICATION, INTERNATIONAL ASSOCIATION FOR ENTEROSTOMAL THERAPY.). [J. ET nurs.]. **Added/Corp** International Association for Enterostomal Therapy. **VAT** Journal of Enterostomal Therapy Nursing. Vol. 18, No. 3 (May/June 1991)-(1993). Periodical. English. bm. Mosby Year Book Inc., 11830 Westline Industrial Drive, St Louis MO 63146. **Tel** (800)325-4177, (314)872-8370, FAX (314)432-1380, telex 44-2402. **LC** RD540.6; .J68. **DD** 617/.554. **NLM** W1; JO644CG. **[CCC]. Pr Rev.** available on microfilm and microfiche from University Microfilms International (UMI). ***Continues*** *Journal of Enterostomal Therapy, 0270-1170.*
**Desc:** Provides valuable clinical information to an international network of ET nurses and other specialty nurses.
**Ind/Abst** Cumul. Index Nurs. Allied Health Lit.; Health Plan. Adminis.; Int. Nurs. Index.

●US/1074-8407
**JOURNAL OF FAMILY NURSING.** (Feb. 1995)-. Periodical. English. qt (Feb., May, Aug., Nov.). $125.00. SAGE Periodical Press, 2455 Teller Road, Thousand Oaks CA 91320. **Tel** (805)499-0721, FAX (805)499-0871, telex 100799. **ED** Janice M. Bell (Faculty of Nursing, University of Calgary). **Pr Rev. Acid Free.**
**Desc:** Publishes empirical and theoretical analysis and scholarly work on nursing research, practice, education and policy issues pertaining to family health and illness.

US/0098-9134
**JOURNAL OF GERONTOLOGICAL NURSING.** [J. gerontol. nurs.]. (1975)-. Periodical. English. mo. $51.00 institution, $39.00 individual (US). Slack Inc., 6900 Grove Road, Thorofare NJ 08086. **Tel** (609)848-1000, (800)257-8290, FAX (609)853-5991, telex 517108 SLACK INC VD. **ED** Edna M. Stilwell. **LC** RC954; .J67. **DD** 610.73/65/05. **NLM** W1 JO669NG. **[CCC].** Index available. **Bk Rev. Ad Acc. Pr Rev. Circ:** 13,000. available on microfilm and microfiche from University Microfilms International (UMI).
**Desc:** Covers gerontology- and nursing-care aspects of clinical research, with how-to columns on pharmacology, skin care and nutrition. Concerned with well-elderly topics, social issues and health promotion.
**Ind/Abst** Abstr. Soc. Gerontol.; Cumul. Index Nurs. Allied Health Lit.; Energy Res. Abstr. (Aug. 1982-); Int. Nurs. Index; Int. Pharm. Abstr.; Nurs. Abstr.; Psychol. Abstr. (1983-); PsycINFO; PsycLit.

US/0098-9134
**JOURNAL OF GERONTOLOGICAL NURSING.** (JOURNAL OF GERONTOLOGICAL NURSING [MICROFORM].). Vol. 1, No. 1 (Mar., Apr. 1975)-. Periodical. English. ir. $25.50. University Microfilms International, 300 North Zeeb Road, Ann Arbor MI 48106-1346. **Tel** (313)761-4700, (800)521-0600 Exts. 2490, 2491, FAX (313)973-1540. **[CCC]. Pr Rev.** available in print.

US/0898-0101
**JOURNAL OF HOLISTIC NURSING.** (JOURNAL OF HOLISTIC NURSING : OFFICIAL JOURNAL OF THE AMERICAN HOLISTIC NURSES' ASSOCIATION.). [J. holist. nurs.]. **Added/Corp** American Holistic Nurses' Association. Vol. 1, No. 1 (March 1983)-. Periodical. English. qt (Mar., June, Sept., Dec.). $93.00. SAGE Periodical Press, 2455 Teller Road, Thousand Oaks CA 91320. **Tel** (805)499-0721, FAX (805)499-0871, telex 100799. **ED** Imelda Clements. **LC** RT42; .J68. **DD** 610. **NLM** W1; JO671H. **Acid Free. Circ:** 1,800 (ctrl).
**Desc:** Offers a holistic nursing foundation for practitioners and educators through shared research and clinical experience, publishes original work and disseminates the ideals of holistic nursing to the health community.
**Ind/Abst** Acad. Abstr. Full Text Elite (Jan. 1992-); Acad. Abstr. (Jan. 1992-); Acad. Search (Jan. 1992-); Health Source (Jan. 1992-); INFO-SOUTH Abstr.; Mag. Search.

US/0896-5846
**JOURNAL OF INTRAVENOUS NURSING.** (JOURNAL OF INTRAVENOUS NURSING : THE OFFICIAL PUBLICATION OF THE INTRAVENOUS NURSES SOCIETY.). [J. intraven. nurs.]. **Added/Corp** Intravenous Nurses Society. **VFOAT** JIN. Vol. 11, No. 1 (Jan./Feb. 1988)-. Periodical. English. bm. $65.00 (individuals), $110.00 (institutions) US; $80.00 (individuals), $135.00 (institutions) other. J.B. Lippincott Company, 227 East Washington Square, Philadelphia PA 19106-3780. **Tel** (215)238-4200 or 4454, FAX (215)238-4227. **(Subscription address:** J.B. Lippincott, PO Box 350, Hagerstown MD 21740.) **ED** Mary Larkin. **DD** 610. **NLM** W1; JO7199J. **[CCC]. Bk Rev. Ad Acc. Pr Rev. Circ:** 8000 (ctrl). available on microfilm and microfiche from University Microfilms International (UMI). ***Continues** NITA, 0160-3930.*
**Ind/Abst** Cumul. Index Nurs. Allied Health Lit.; Health Devices Alerts; Int. Nurs. Index (1988-); Int. Pharm. Abstr.; Nurs. Abstr.

US/0885-6028
**JOURNAL OF NATIONAL BLACK NURSES' ASSOCIATION : JNBNA.** [J. Natl. Black Nurses' Assoc.]. **VFOAT** JNBNA; JNBNA Journal. Vol. 1, No. 1; Spring 1986-. Periodical. English. sa. $15.00 (individuals), $25.00 (institutions). Journal of National Black Nurses' Association, 1011 North Capital Street NE, Washington DC 20002. **LC** RT1; .J64. **DD** 610/.8996073.
**Ind/Abst** Cumul. Index Nurs. Allied Health Lit.; Int. Nurs. Index (1986-); Soc. Work Abstr. [Select. Cov.].

US/0888-0395
**JOURNAL OF NEUROSCIENCE NURSING, THE.** [J. neurosci. nurs.]. **Added/Corp** American Association of Neuroscience Nurses. Vol. 18, No. 1 (Feb. 1986)-. Periodical. English. Six times a year (Feb., Apr., June, Aug., Oct., Dec). $52.00 (institution), $39.00 (individual). American Association of Neuroscience Nurses, 224 North Des Plaines, Suite 601, Chicago IL 60661. **Tel** (312)993-0043. **ED** Christina Stewart-Amidei. **LC** RC350.5; .J6. **DD** 610.73/68. **NLM** W1; JO795BT. **CODEN** JNNUEF. **[CCC].** Index available. cum. index. **Bk Rev. Ad Acc. Pr Rev. Circ:** 5,000 (ctrl). available on microfilm and microfiche from University Microfilms International (UMI). Documents available from The Genuine Article. ***Continues** Journal of Neurosurgical Nursing, 0047-2603.*
**Desc:** Covers advances in neurosurgical and neurological techniques as they affect nursing practice and offers articles for CE credit.
**Ind/Abst** Cumul. Index Nurs. Allied Health Lit.; Hospit. Health Admin. Index; Index Med. (1986-); Int. Nurs. Index (1986-); Nurs. Abstr.; Res. Alert [Full Cov.].

US/0091-2182
**JOURNAL OF NURSE-MIDWIFERY.** [J. nurse-midwifery]. **Added/Corp** American College of Nurse-Midwives. Vol. 18, No. 1 (Spring 1973)-. Academic Scholarly Publication. English. bm (1 supplement). $150.00 US; $190.00 other. Elsevier Science Publishing Company Inc, Madison Square Station, PO Box 882, New York NY 10159-0882. **Tel** (212)633-3950, FAX (212)633-3990. **ED** Mary Ann Shah. **NLM** W1 JO796K. **CODEN** JNUMEQ. **[CCC]. Bk Rev. Ad Acc. Pr Rev.** available on microfilm and microfiche from University Microfilms International (UMI). Documents available from The Genuine Article. ***Continues** Bulletin of the American College of Nurse-Midwives.*
**Desc:** Promotes the writing and publication of timely, relevant and provocative literature on and for nurse-midwifery which is consistent with the philosophy, objectives, policies and positions of the American College of Nurse-Midwives.
**Ind/Abst** Appl. Soc. Sci. Index Abstr.; Cumul. Index Nurs. Allied Health Lit.; Curr. Contents Soc. Behav. Sci.; Index Med.; Int. Nurs. Index; Med. Abstr. Newsl.; Nurs. Abstr.; Res. Alert [Full Cov.]; Soc. Sci. Cit. Index [Full Cov.].

CH/0047-262X
**JOURNAL OF NURSING.** (19??)-. Chinese. qt. $35.00. Nurses Association of the Republic of China, 12 Fl 315 Sec 5 Hsin I Rd, Taipei 10666 Taiwan. **Tel** 011 886 2 7552291, FAX 011 886 2 7019817. **ED** Ms. Ming-Rong Lee. (In Dec.). cum. index. **Ad Acc. Circ:** 15,000 (ctrl).

US/0002-0443
**JOURNAL OF NURSING ADMINISTRATION, THE.** [J. nurs. adm.]. **VFOAT** JNA. Vol. 1 (Jan. 1971)-. Academic Scholarly Publication. English. Eleven times a year. $60.00 (individuals), $155.00 (institutions) US; $95.00 (individuals), $199.00 (institutions) other. J.B. Lippincott Company, 227 East Washington Square, Philadelphia PA 19106-3780. **Tel** (215)238-4200 or 4454, FAX (215)238-4227. **(Subscription address:** J.B. Lippincott, PO Box 350, Hagerstown MD 21740.) **ED** Suzanne Smith Coletta. **LC** RT89. **DD** 610.73/05. **NLM** W1 JO796R. **CODEN** JNUAA. **[CCC]. Ad Acc. Pr Rev. Circ:** 14,751. available on microfilm and microfiche from University Microfilms International (UMI). Documents available from The Genuine Article.
**Desc:** Provides knowledge, strategies, and ideas for nurse administrators. Contents are aimed at upper level nursing executives.
**Ind/Abst** Abr. Index Med.; Cumul. Index Nurs. Allied Health Lit.; Curr. Contents Soc. Behav. Sci.; Curr. Index J. Educ.; EMBASE; Health Serv. Abstr.; Hospit. Manage. Rev.; Index Med.; Int. Nurs. Index; Nurs. Abstr.; Physic. Medline Plus; Res. Alert [Full Cov.]; Soc. Sci. Cit. Index [Full Cov.].

US/1057-3631
**JOURNAL OF NURSING CARE QUALITY.** [J. nurs. care qual.]. **VFOAT** JNCQ. Vol. 6, Issue 1 (Oct. 1991)-. Periodical. English. qt. $81.00 US. Aspen Publishers Inc., 7201 McKinney Circle, Frederick MD 21701. **Tel** (800)234-1660, (301)698-7100, FAX (301)251-5784, telex 5106014543. **(Subscription address:** Aspen Publishers Inc., PO Box 990, Frederick MD 21701.) **ED** Patricia Schroeder, MSN, RN. **LC** RT85.5; .J68. **DD** 610. **NLM** W1; JO796UJ. **[CCC].** available on microfilm and microfiche from University Microfilms International (UMI). ***Continues** Journal of Nursing Quality Assurance, 0889-4647.*
**Desc:** Provides practicing nurses as well as nurses who have leadership roles in nursing care quality programs with useful information regarding the application of quality principles and concepts in the practice setting. The journal offers a forum for the scholarly discussion of "real world" implementations of quality activities.
**Ind/Abst** Cumul. Index Nurs. Allied Health Lit.; Health Plan. Adminis.; Int. Nurs. Index (Oct. 1991-); Nurs. Abstr. (Oct. 1991-).

US/0148-4834
**JOURNAL OF NURSING EDUCATION, THE.** [J. nurs. educ.]. **VFOAT** JNE. Vol. 1, No. 1 (Jan. 1962)-. Periodical. English. Nine times a year. $100.00 institution, $85.00 individual (US). Slack Inc., 6900 Grove Road, Thorofare NJ 08086. **Tel** (609)848-1000, (800)257-8290, FAX (609)853-5991, telex 517108 SLACK INC VD. **LC** RT1. **NLM** W1 JO797. **Bk Rev. Ad Acc. Pr Rev.** available on microfilm and microfiche from University Microfilms International (UMI).
**Ind/Abst** Cumul. Index Nurs. Allied Health Lit.; Educ. Index; Gen. Sci. Index; Index Med.; Int. Nurs. Index; Nurs. Abstr.

US
**JOURNAL OF NURSING ETHICS, THE.**
***Suspended.* See** Ethics.

US/1055-3088
**JOURNAL OF NURSING JOCULARITY.** (JOURNAL OF NURSING JOCULARITY : THE HUMOR MAGAZINE FOR NURSES.). Vol. 1, No. 1 (Spring 1991)-. Periodical. English. Four times a year (Feb., May, Aug., Nov.). $16.00. JNJ Publishing, PO Box 40416, Mesa AZ 85274. **Tel** (602)835-6165, FAX (602)835-6922. **(Subscription address:** Pub Data, 5615 West Cermak Road, Cicero IL 60650.) **ED** Fran London. **DD** 610. **NLM** W1; JO797CE. **Bk Rev**, (Qty: 8). **Circ:** 30,000.
**Desc:** Filled with satire, cartoons, and jokes related to nursing and the field of health care. Its purpose it to benefit not only nurses but also their patients, providing nurses tips on how to use humor therapeutically.

●UK/0966-0429
**JOURNAL OF NURSING MANAGEMENT.** Vol. 1, No. 1 (Jan. 1993)-. Academic Scholarly Publication. English. bm (6 issues). $169.00 (institutions), $54.00 (individuals) US & Canada; £99.00 (institutions), £31.50 (individuals) Europe; £109.00 (institutions), £35.00 (individuals) other. Blackwell Scientific Publications Ltd, Marston Book Services, PO Box 87, Oxford OX2 ODT UK. **Tel** 011 44 865 791155, FAX 011 44 865 791927, telex 837 515 MARDIS G. **NLM** W1; JO797CG.

●US/1061-3749
**JOURNAL OF NURSING MEASUREMENT.** [J. nurs. meas.]. (1993)-. Periodical. English. sa. $29.00 (individuals, 1 year), $52.00 (individuals, 2 year), $55.00 (institutions, 1 year), $99.00 (institutions, 2 year), US; $34.00 (individuals, 1 year), $59.00 (individuals, 2 year), $64.00 (institutions, 1 year), $115.00 (institutions, 2 year) other. Springer Publishing Company, 536 Broadway, New York NY 10012-3955. **Tel** (212)431-4370, FAX (212)941-7842. **ED** Ora L. Strickland,RN and Ada Sue Hinshaw,RN. **DD** 610.
**Desc:** Will serve as a forum for the dissemination of information on instruments, tools, approaches, and procedures developed for or utilized in measuring variables in nursing practice, education, and research.

US/1046-4972
**JOURNAL OF NURSING RESEARCH.** (1990)-. Periodical. English. bm. $21.00 (institution). SAGE Periodical Press, 2455 Teller Road, Thousand Oaks CA 91320. **Tel** (805)499-0721, FAX (805)499-0871, telex 100799. **Acid Free. *Continues** Western Journal of Nursing Research, 0193-9459.*

US/0882-0627
**JOURNAL OF NURSING STAFF DEVELOPMENT : JNSD.** [J. nurs. staff dev.]. **VFOAT** JNSD. (Spring 1985)-. Periodical. English. bm. $54.00 (individuals), $129.00 (institutions) US; $79.00 (individuals), $154.00 (institutions) other. J.B. Lippincott Company, 227 East Washington Square, Philadelphia PA 19106-3780. **Tel** (215)238-4200 or 4454, FAX (215)238-4227. **(Subscription address:** J.B. Lippincott, PO Box 350, Hagerstown MD 21740.) **DD** 610. **NLM** W1; JO797K. **[CCC]. Pr Rev.** available on microfilm and microfiche from University Microfilms International (UMI).
**Ind/Abst** Cumul. Index Nurs. Allied Health Lit.; Health Plan. Adminis.; Int. Nurs. Index (Spring 1985-).

US/0884-2175
**JOURNAL OF OBSTETRIC, GYNECOLOGIC, AND NEONATAL NURSING : JOGNN.** [J. obstet. gynecol. neonatal nurs.]. **Added/Corp** NAACOG (Organization) Association of Women's Health, Obstetric, and Neonatal Nurses. **VFOAT** JOGNN. Vol. 14, No. 1 (Jan./Feb. 1985)-. Academic Scholarly Publication. English. Nine times a year. $60.00 (individuals), $155.00 (institutions) US; $95.00 (individuals), $185.00 (institutions) other. J.B. Lippincott Company, 227 East Washington Square, Philadelphia PA 19106-3780. **Tel** (215)238-4200 or 4454, FAX (215)238-4227. **(Subscription address:** J.B. Lippincott, PO Box 350, Hagerstown MD 21740.) **LC** RG951; .J15. **DD** 610.73/678/05. **NLM** W1; JO978LR. **CODEN** JOGNEY. **Pr Rev.** available on microfilm and microfiche from University Microfilms International (UMI). ***Continues** JOGN Nursing, 0090-0311; **Absorbed** AWHONNS Clinical Issues in Perinatal and Women's Health Nursing.*
**Ind/Abst** Cumul. Index Nurs. Allied Health Lit. (1985-); Curr. Lit. Fam. Plan.; EMBASE (1985-); Index Med. (1985-); Int. Nurs. Index (1985-); Nurs. Abstr.; Physic. Medline Plus.

US/0744-7132
**JOURNAL OF OPHTHALMIC NURSING & TECHNOLOGY.** [J. ophthalmic nurs. technol.]. **VFOAT** Journal of Ophthalmic Nursing and Technology; JONT; J.O.N.T. Vol. 1, No. 1 (May 1982)-. Periodical. English. bm. $51.00 institution, $39.00 individual (US). Slack Inc., 6900 Grove Road, Thorofare NJ 08086. **Tel** (609)848-1000, (800)257-8290, FAX (609)853-5991, telex 517108 SLACK INC VD. **DD** 617. **NLM** W1 JO803I. **Bk Rev. Ad Acc.**
**Ind/Abst** Cumul. Index Nurs. Allied Health Lit.; Int. Nurs. Index; Nurs. Abstr.

US/0882-5963
**JOURNAL OF PEDIATRIC NURSING.** [J. pediatr. nurs.]. Vol. 1, No. 1 (Feb. 1986)-. Periodical. English. bm (6 issues). $49.00 (individual), $79.00 (institution) US; $93.00 (individual), $110.00 (institutions) other. W.B. Saunders Company, A Subsidiary of Harcourt Brace Jovanovich, Inc., The Curtis Center/Suite 300, Independence Square West, Philadelphia PA 19106-3399. **Tel** (215)238-7800 or, 5587, FAX (215)238-7883, telex 173146. **(Subscription address:** W. B. Saunders Company / North America Subscriptions, c/o Periodicals, 6277 Sea Harbour Drive, 4th Floor, Orlando FL 32887.) **DD** 610. **UDC** 616-053.2-083. **NLM** W1; JO828EJ. **CODEN** JLPNEO. **[CCC]. Pr Rev.**
**Ind/Abst** Cumul. Index Nurs. Allied Health Lit.; Int. Nurs. Index (Feb. 1986-); Nurs. Abstr.

US/1043-4542
**JOURNAL OF PEDIATRIC ONCOLOGY NURSING.** (JOURNAL OF PEDIATRIC ONCOLOGY NURSING : OFFICIAL JOURNAL OF THE ASSOCIATION OF PEDIATRIC ONCOLOGY NURSES.). [J. pediatr. oncol. nurs.]. (1989)-. Periodical. English. qt (4 issues). $49.00 (indivdual), $73.00 (institution) US; $94.00 (individual), $100.00 (institution) other. W.B. Saunders Company, A Subsidiary of Harcourt Brace Jovanovich, Inc., The Curtis Center/Suite 300, Independence Square West, Philadelphia PA 19106-3399. **Tel** (215)238-7800 or, 5587, FAX (215)238-7883, telex 173146. **(Subscription address:** W. B. Saunders Company / North America Subscriptions, c/o Periodicals, 6277 Sea Harbour Drive, 4th Floor, Orlando FL 32887.) **DD** 618. **NLM** W1; JO828EP. **CODEN** JONUEM. **[CCC]. Pr Rev. *Continues** Journal of the Association of Pediatric Oncology Nurses, 0748-1802.*
**Ind/Abst** Cumul. Index Nurs. Allied Health Lit. (1989-); Health Plan. Adminis.

US/0893-2190
**JOURNAL OF PERINATAL & NEONATAL NURSING, THE.** [J. perinat. neonatal nurs.]. **VFOAT** Journal of Perinatal and Neonatal Nursing; JPNN. Vol. 1, No. 1 (July 1987)-. Periodical. English. qt. $67.00 US. Aspen Publishers Inc., 7201 McKinney Circle, Frederick MD 21701. **Tel** (800)234-1660, (301)698-7100, FAX (301)251-5784, telex 5106014543. **(Subscription address:** Aspen Publishers Inc., PO Box 990, Frederick MD 21701.) **ED** Diane J. Angelini and Mary E. Lynch. **DD** 610. **NLM** W1; JO828HP. **CODEN** JPNNE8. **[CCC]. Bk Rev. Ad Acc. Pr Rev. Circ:** 3,688 (ctrl). available on microfilm and microfiche from University Microfilms International (UMI).
**Desc:** Provides practicing nurses with practical, comprehensive, up to date, and reliable information from top clinicians on perinatal and neonatal nursing.
**Ind/Abst** Cumul. Index Nurs. Allied Health Lit.; Int. Nurs. Index (1987-); Nurs. Abstr.

US/0883-9433
**JOURNAL OF POST ANESTHESIA NURSING.** [J. post anesth. nurs.]. Vol. 1, No. 1 (Feb. 1986)-. Periodical. English. bm (6 issues). $58.00 (indivdual), $89.00 (institution) US; $114.00 (individual), $120.00 (institution) other. W.B. Saunders Company, A Subsidiary of Harcourt Brace Jovanovich, Inc., The Curtis Center/Suite 300, Independence Square West,

Philadelphia PA 19106-3399. **Tel** (215)238-7800 or, 5587, FAX (215)238-7883, telex 173146. **(Subscription address:** W. B. Saunders Company / North America Subscriptions, c/o Periodicals, 6277 Sea Harbour Drive, 4th Floor, Orlando FL 32887.**) ED** Denise O'Brien. **DD** 610. **UDC** 616-083:616-089.5. **NLM** W1; JO837WC. **[CCC]. Pr Rev.**
**Desc:** Designed primarily for nurses engaged in the practice of post-surgical nursing and management of patients in the post anesthesia care unit. Contents of this journal include a broad range of topics of interest to health care providers in a variety of settings.
**Ind/Abst** Cumul. Index Nurs. Allied Health Lit.; Int. Nurs. Index (1986-).

US/0022-3867
**JOURNAL OF PRACTICAL NURSING, THE.** [J. pract. nurs.]. **Added/Corp** National Association for Practical Nurse Education and Service. (196?)-. Periodical. English. qt. $15.00 US; $25.00 other. Journal of Practical Nursing, 1400 Spring Street/Suite 310, Silver Spring MD 20910. **Tel** (301)588-2491. **ED** Mary Beth Ryan. **NLM** W1 JO842M. Index available. **Bk Rev. Ad Acc. Circ:** 10,000 (ctrl). available on microfilm and microfiche from University Microfilms International (UMI). ***Continues** Practical Nursing.*
**Desc:** This publication provides information and education for licensed practical nurses.
**Ind/Abst** Cumul. Index Nurs. Allied Health Lit.; Health Plan. Adminis.; Hospit. Health Admin. Index; Int. Nurs. Index.

US/8755-7223
**JOURNAL OF PROFESSIONAL NURSING.** [J. prof. nurs.]. **Added/Corp** American Association of Colleges of Nursing. Vol. 1, No. 1 (Jan./Feb. 1985)-. Periodical. English. Six times a year (Jan., Mar., May, July, Sept., Nov.). $65.00 (individual), $115.00 (institution) US; $134.00 (individual), $139.00 (institutions) others. W.B. Saunders Company, A Subsidiary of Harcourt Brace Jovanovich, Inc., The Curtis Center/Suite 300, Independence Square West, Philadelphia PA 19106-3399. **Tel** (215)238-7800 or, 5587, FAX (215)238-7883, telex 173146. **(Subscription address:** W. B. Saunders Company / North America Subscriptions, c/o Periodicals, 6277 Sea Harbour Drive, 4th Floor, Orlando FL 32887.**) ED** Laurel Archer Copp. **DD** 610. **NLM** W1; JO8443F. **CODEN** JPNUET. **[CCC].** Index available. **Ad Acc. Pr Rev. Circ:** 5,000. available on microfilm and microfiche from University Microfilms International (UMI).
**Desc:** Covers the practice, research, policy-making roles of nurses with baccalaureate and graduate degrees. Relevant for nurse educators, students, and practicing nurses concerned with above.
**Ind/Abst** Cumul. Index Nurs. Allied Health Lit.; Curr. Index J. Educ. (March 1990); Index Med. (Vol. 3, No. 5, 1986-);; Int. Nurs. Index (Jan.-Feb. 1985-); Nurs. Abstr.

UK/1351-0126
**JOURNAL OF PSYCHIATRIC AND MENTAL HEALTH NURSING. See** Medical Science and Technology-Psychiatry.

US/0279-3695
**JOURNAL OF PSYCHOSOCIAL NURSING AND MENTAL HEALTH SERVICES.** [J. psychosoc. nurs. ment. health serv.]. Vol. 19, No. 8 (Aug. 1981)-. Periodical. English. mo. $58.00 institution, $48.00 individual (US). Slack Inc., 6900 Grove Road, Thorofare NJ 08086. **Tel** (609)848-1000, (800)257-8290, FAX (609)853-5991, telex 517108 SLACK INC VD. **ED** Shirley A. Smoyak. **LC** RC440; .J65. **DD** 610.73/68/05. **NLM** W1 JO858V. **Bk Rev. Ad Acc. Circ:** 12,000. available on microfilm and microfiche from University Microfilms International (UMI). ***Continues** Journal of Psychiatric Nursing and Mental Health Services, 0360-5973.*
**Desc:** Clinical information for psychosocial nurses and other mental health professionals.
**Ind/Abst** Cumul. Index Nurs. Allied Health Lit.; Index Med.; Int. Nurs. Index; Middle East Abstr. Index; Nurs. Abstr.; Physic. Medline Plus; PsycINFO.

US/1059-8405
**JOURNAL OF SCHOOL NURSING, THE.** (THE JOURNAL OF SCHOOL NURSING : THE OFFICIAL PUBLICATION OF THE NATIONAL ASSOCIATION OF SCHOOL NURSES.). [J. sch. nurs.]. **Added/Corp** National Association of School Nurses (U.S.). Vol. 7, No. 3 (Oct. 1991)-. Periodical. English. Four times a year. $60.00. National Association School Nurses Inc, PO Box 1300, Scarborough ME 04074. **Tel** (207)883-2117, FAX (207)883-2683. **ED** Carole Passarelli. **DD** 371. **NLM** W1; JO8737. ***Continues** School Nurse, 0048-945X.*

US/1041-2972
**JOURNAL OF THE AMERICAN ACADEMY OF NURSE PRACTITIONERS.** [J. Am. Acad. Nurse Pract.]. **Added/Corp** American Academy of Nurse Practitioners. Vol. 1, No. 1 (Jan./March 1989)-. Periodical. English. mo. $45.00 institution, $30.00 individual (US). Slack Inc., 6900 Grove Road, Thorofare NJ 08086. **Tel** (609)848-1000, (800)257-8290, FAX (609)853-5991, telex 517108 SLACK INC VD. **ED** Jan Towers and Donna G. Nativio. **LC** RT82.8; .J68. **DD** 610. **NLM** W1; JO907XC. **CODEN** JANPEB. **[CCC]. Pr Rev.** available on microfilm and microfiche from University Microfilms International (UMI).
**Desc:** Recognized experts report on emerging trends in clinical practice, management, education, research, and legislation. All facets of the nurse practitioner specialties.
**Ind/Abst** Cumul. Index Nurs. Allied Health Lit.; Health Plan. Adminis.; Int. Nurs. Index (1989-).

US
**JOURNAL OF THE AMERICAN PSYCHIATRIC NURSING ASSOCIATION.** (Feb. 1995)-. Periodical. English. bm. $69.00. Mosby Year Book Inc., 11830 Westline Industrial Drive, St Louis MO 63146. **Tel** (800)325-4177, (314)872-8370, FAX (314)432-1380, telex 44-2402. **ED** Nikki Polis.
**Desc:** Covers mental health and psychiatric nursing practice and theory.

US/1055-3290
**JOURNAL OF THE ASSOCIATION OF NURSES IN AIDS CARE, THE.** (THE JOURNAL OF THE ASSOCIATION OF NURSES IN AIDS CARE : JANAC.). [J. Assoc. Nurses AIDS Care]. **Added/Corp** Association of Nurses in AIDS Care. **VFOAT** JANAC. Vol. 1, No. 1 (Aug. 1989)-. Periodical. English. bm. $57.00 (institutions), $46.00 (individuals) US; $69.00 (institutions), $58.00 (individuals) other. NURSECOM Inc., 1211 Locust Street, Philadelphia PA 19107. **Tel** (215)545-7222, (800)242-6757, FAX (215)545-8107. **ED** Jeanne Kalinoski, (editor's phone: (212)274-7207). **DD** 362. **NLM** W1; JO912KK. **Bk Rev**, (Qty: 5-10). **Ad Acc, Adv Mgr:** Joseph Braden, **Tel** (215)545-7222. **Pr Rev. Circ:** 3,000. available on microfilm.
**Desc:** A professional nursing journal committed to publishing information that will provide the highest quality care for people with HIV/AIDS. JANAC publishes articles on clinical practice, health services, education, research, and social issues.
**Ind/Abst** Cumul. Index Nurs. Allied Health Lit.; Health Plan. Adminis.; Index Med. (July-Aug. 1992-); Int. Nurs. Index (1989-).

US/0028-7644
**JOURNAL OF THE NEW YORK STATE NURSES ASSOCIATION, THE.** [J. New York State Nurses Assoc.]. **Main/Corp** New York State Nurses Association. (1970)-. Academic Scholarly Publication. English. qt. $24.00 (one year), $46.00 (two year) US; $29.30 (one year), $56.60 (two year) Canada and Mexico; $38.75 (one year), $75.50 (two year) other. New York State Nurses Association, 2113 Western Avenue, Guilderland NY 12084. **Tel** (518)456-5371, FAX (518)456-0697. **ED** Anne Schott. **NLM** W1 JO942W. **CODEN** JNYNA. **Bk Rev**, (Qty: 4-6/yr). **Ad Acc. Pr Rev. Circ:** 36,000. available on CD-ROM; available on microfilm and microfiche from University Microfilms International (UMI).
**Desc:** Publishes research reports and scholarly articles of interest to registered nurses.
**Ind/Abst** Cumul. Index Nurs. Allied Health Lit.; Int. Nurs. Index; Soc. Work Abstr. [Select. Cov.].

US
**JOURNAL OF THE WOCN.** English. Six times a year. $46.00 (individuals), $115.00 (institutions), $109.25 (government) US; $56.00 (individuals), $125.00 (institutions) other. Mosby Year Book Inc., 11830 Westline Industrial Drive, St Louis MO 63146. **Tel** (800)325-4177, (314)872-8370, FAX (314)432-1380, telex 44-2402. ***Continues** Journal of ET Nursing.*

US/1043-6596
**JOURNAL OF TRANSCULTURAL NURSING.** [J. transcult. nurs.]. Vol. 1, No. 1 (Summer 1989)-. Periodical. English. sa. $48.00 (institutions), $65.00 (member). Transcultural Nursing Society, Production Manager, Ronald Jordan, DeskToppers, 25107 W Warren Avenue, Dearborn Heights MI 48127. **Tel** (313)561-7320, FAX (313)561-7321. **DD** 610. **NLM** W1; JO966KN. **Ad Acc. Pr Rev.**
**Desc:** Devoted entirely to the field of transcultural nursing - the study of cultures and cultural differences and how they influence nursing care.
**Ind/Abst** Cumul. Index Nurs. Allied Health Lit.; Health Plan. Adminis.; Int. Nurs. Index (1989-).

US/0738-7350
**JOURNAL OF UROLOGICAL NURSING. See** Medical Science and Technology-Urology and Nephrology.

US/1062-0303
**JOURNAL OF VASCULAR NURSING.** (JOURNAL OF VASCULAR NURSING : OFFICIAL PUBLICATION OF THE SOCIETY FOR PERIPHERAL VASCULAR NURSING.). [J. vasc. nurs.]. **Added/Corp** Society for Peripheral Vascular Nursing. Vol. 8, No. 3 (Sept. 1990)-. Periodical. English. Four times a year. $70.00 (institutions), $45.00 (individuals) US; $78.00 (institutions), $53.00 (individuals) other. Mosby Year Book Inc., 11830 Westline Industrial Drive, St Louis MO 63146. **Tel** (800)325-4177, (314)872-8370, FAX (314)432-1380, telex 44-2402. **DD** 617. **NLM** W1; JO97BP. **[CCC]. Pr Rev. *Continues** SPVN.*
**Ind/Abst** Cumul. Index Nurs. Allied Health Lit.; Int. Nurs. Index (Sept. 1990-).

●US/1071-5754
**JOURNAL OF WOUND, OSTOMY, AND CONTINENCE NURSING.** (JOURNAL OF WOUND, OSTOMY, AND CONTINENCE NURSING : WOCN.). [J. wound ostomy continence nurs.]. **VFOAT** Journal of WOCN; WOCN. (1994)-. Periodical. English. bm (6 issues). $120.00 (institutions), $46.00 (individuals) US; $130.00 (institutions), $56.00 (individuals) other. Mosby Year Book Inc., 11830 Westline Industrial Drive, St Louis MO 63146. **Tel** (800)325-4177, (314)872-8370, FAX (314)432-1380, telex 44-2402. **DD** 617. **NLM** W1; JO9734. **[CCC].** Index available (bound in Nov. issue). ***Continues** Journal of ET Nursing, 1055-3045.*

CN/0828-542X
**JOURNAL - ONTARIO OCCUPATIONAL HEALTH NURSES ASSOCIATION.** (JOURNAL : THE OFFICIAL PUBLICATION OF THE ONTARIO OCCUPATIONAL HEALTH NURSES ASSOCIATION.). [J. - Ont. Occup. Health Nurses Assoc.]. **Added/Corp** Ontario Occupational Health Nurses Association. Vol. 5, No. 2 (June 1984)-. Periodical. English. Three times a year (Feb., June, Oct.). $20.00. Ontario Occupational Health Nurses Association, 302 The East Mall, Suite 6055, Etobicoke ONT M9B 6C7 Canada. **Tel** (416)239-6462. **ED** Kenneth Dykeman (phone: (416)983-9414). **DD** 610.73/46/05. **Bk Rev**, (Qty: 1-3). **Ad Acc. Circ:** 1,100 (ctrl). ***Continues** Commoohnacator, 0228-6009.*
**Desc:** This magazine is to provide services to our members that will help occupational health nurses work more effectively for and with employers and people in the workplace, and to enhance the image of the profession.

NO
**JOURNALEN SYKEPLEIEN.** Vol. 77, No. 16 (Sept, 28, 1989)-. Periodical. Norwegian. Thirty times a year. Kr450.00. Norwegian Nurses Association, PO Box 2633 SF Hanshaugen, 0131 Oslo 1 Norway. **Tel** 011 47 2 382000, FAX 011 47 2 353663. **ED** Vidar Kildahl. **NLM** W1; JO99L. **Bk Rev. Ad Acc. Circ:** 43,500 (ctrl). ***Continues in part** Sykepleien, 0039-7628.*
**Desc:** Covers nursing.
**Ind/Abst** Int. Nurs. Index (1989-).

JA
**KAIIN JITTAI CHOSA. Main/Corp** Nihon Kango Kyokai. **VFOAT** Report on Status of Member of Japanese Nursing Association. 1977-. Japanese (summaries and/or abstracts in English). ir (issued every four years). ¥1,300 Japan; $9.30 US. Nihen Kango Kyokai, 8-2 Jingymae 5-chome Shibuya-ku, Tokyo 150 Japan. **LC** RT1; .N52A subser; RT13.J3. Index available. cum. index. **Ad Acc. Circ:** 1,339.

JA
**KANGO GIJUTSU: JAPANESE JOURNAL OF NURSING ART.** Japanese. mo. $202.00. Mejikaru Furendosha, (Medical Friend Co., Ltd.), 2-4, Kudan Kita 3 Chome, Chiyodaku, Tokyoto 102, Japan. **(Subscription address:** Japan Publications Trading Company, Ltd., PO Box 5030, Tokyo International, Tokyo 100-31 Japan.**)**

JA/0385-549X
**KANGO TENBO.** (KANGO TENBO. THE JAPANESE JOURNAL OF NURSING SCIENCE.). [Kango tenbÃo]. **VFOAT** Japanese Journal of Nursing Science. (1976)-. Periodical. Japanese. mo (13 issues). $268.00. **(Subscription address:** Kyowa Book Company Inc., 1-38 Kanda Jinbo-Cho, Chiyoda-Ku Tokyo 101, Japan**) NLM** W1 KA442J.

US/0022-8710
**KANSAS NURSE, THE.** [Kansas nurse]. **Added/Corp** Kansas Nurses' Association. Vol. 15 (1941)-. Periodical. English. Twelve times a year. $24.00. Kansas State Nurses Association, 700 SW Jackson Street, Suite 601, Topeka KS 66603-3731. **Tel** (913)233-8638. **ED** Nancy J Davis. **NLM** W1 KA58. **Ad Acc. Circ:** 2,500 (ctrl). available on microfilm and microfiche from University Microfilms International (UMI). ***Continues** Bulletin / Kansas State Nurses' Association.*
**Desc:** The official publication of the Kansas State Nurses' Association. Criteria for publication is timely topics, relevant to nurses in Kansas.
**Ind/Abst** Cumul. Index Nurs. Allied Health Lit.; Int. Nurs. Index.

US/0742-8367
**KENTUCKY NURSE.** [Ky. nurse]. **Added/Corp** Kentucky Nurses Association. Vol. 31, No. 1 (Jan./Feb. 1983)-. Periodical. English. Four times a year. $18.00 US; $24.00 other. Kentucky Nurses Association, PO Box 2616, Louisville KY 40201. **Tel** (502)637-2546, FAX (502)637-8236. **ED** Barbara Dermody (editor's address: 1400 South 1st Street, Louisville, KY 40208). **NLM** W1 KE69T. **Ad Acc, Adv Mgr:** Spectrum Publications, **Tel** (800)728-4101. **Circ:** 2,000 (ctrl). available on microfilm. ***Continues** Newsletter (Kentucky Nurses' Association : 1978).*
**Desc:** News regarding nurses, the nursing profession,

# Medical Science and Technology — Nursing

and health care in general.
**Ind/Abst** Cumul. Index Nurs. Allied Health Lit.; Int. Nurs. Index.

SZ/0253-0465
**KRANKENPFLEGE.** [Krankenpflege]. **Added/Corp** Schweizer Berufsverband der Krankenschwestern und Krankenpflege. **VFOAT** Soins Infirmiers. (July 1979)-. German (French and Italian). mo. 79.00F Switzerland; 96.00F other. Schweizer Berufsverband der Krankenschwestern und Krankenpflege (SBK), Choisystrasse 1, CH-3001 Bern Switzerland. **Tel** 011 41 31 256427. **ED** Helga Veitel. **NLM** W1 KR263M. Index available (bound in Jan. issue). **Bk Rev. Ad Acc. Circ:** 30,000 (ctrl). **Continues** Zeitschrift fuer Krankenpflege, 0044-2941.
**Ind/Abst** Int. Nurs. Index.

GW/0174-108X
**KRANKENPFLEGE JOURNAL.** *Title Change.* [Krankenpfl.-J.]. (1980)-(1993). Periodical. German. Eleven times a year. DBFK Verlag, Postfach, D 65746 Eschborn Germany. **Tel** 011 49 6173 65086. **NLM** W1 KR263I. **Continues** Schwestern Revue. **Continued by** Pflege Aktuell, 0944-8918.
**Ind/Abst** Int. Nurs. Index.

JA/0388-5585
**KURINIKARU SUTADI.** [Kurinikaru sutadi]. **VFOAT** Clinical Study. Began with: V. 1, No. 1, (April 1980). Periodical. Japanese. mo. Mejikaru Furendosha, (Medical Friend Co., Ltd.), 2-4, Kudan Kita 3 Chome, Chiyodaku, Tokyoto 102, Japan. **NLM** W1 KU706LC.
**Ind/Abst** Int. Nurs. Index.

AT/0047-3936
**LAMP, THE.** [Lamp]. **Added/Corp** New South Wales Nurses' Association. Vol. 1 (1943)-. Periodical. English. Eleven times a year. 24.00Aus$ (individuals), 40.00Aus$ (institutions) Australia; 55.00Aus$ other. New South Wales Nurses Association, PO Box 40, 43 Australia Street, Camperdown New South Wales 2050 Australia. **Tel** 011 61 2 550 3244, FAX 011 61 2 550 3667, telex AA72339. **ED** Patricia Staunton and Peter Schwab. **NLM** W1 LA444. **Bk Rev. Ad Acc. Circ:** 33,000 (ctrl). available on microfiche.
**Desc:** Covers nursing issues, industrial issues, award matters, medical issues, inter-union matters and wage indexes.
**Ind/Abst** Cumul. Index Nurs. Allied Health Lit.; Film Lit. Index (1984-1986); Int. Nurs. Index.

UK/0266-8769
**LAMPADA.** [Lampada]. **Added/Corp** Royal College of Nursing (Great Britain). No. 1 (Fall 1984)-. Periodical. English. mo. comes with Royal College of Nursing Membership. Royal College of Nursing / England, 20 Cavendish Square, London W1M 0AB England. **Tel** 011 44 71 409-3333 ext. 239, FAX 011 44 71 408-0190. **NLM** W1; LA44D.
**Ind/Abst** Int. Nurs. Index (Summer 1985-).

US/0888-6075
**LASER NURSING.** *Title Change.* [Laser nurs.]. Vol. 1, No. 1 (1987)-(19??). Periodical. English. qt. Mary Ann Liebert Inc., 1651 Third Avenue, New York NY 10128. **Tel** (212)289-2300, (800)M-LIEBERT, FAX (212)289-4697. **ED** Kay Ball. **DD** 610. **NLM** W1; LA78TD. **Pr Rev. Continued by** Minimally Invasive Surgical Nursing, 1068-5685.
**Desc:** The central source for nursing information including safety, administration, material on diagnostic and clinical applications, responsibilities pertaining to pre-operative and post-operative patient care. Provides important and timely information for nurses who work with various types of patients who experience laser surgery.
**Ind/Abst** Cumul. Index Nurs. Allied Health Lit.

US/8756-0054
**LEGISLATIVE NETWORK FOR NURSES.** See Law.

CN/0711-7418
**LIEN (HULL).** (LE LIEN.). [Lien]. V. 5, No. 2, (Aug. 1980)-. Periodical. French (English). Free to Members. Lien, c/o Ciiro, CP 271 Succursale A, Hull Quebec J8Y 6M9 Canada. **DD** 610.73/06/07142. **Continues** Link (Hull, Quebec), 0714-3753.

US/0025-0767
**MAINE NURSE, THE.** (THE MAINE NURSE / MAINE STATE NURSES ASSOCIATION.). [Maine nurse]. **Added/Corp** Maine State Nurses Association. (1970)-. Periodical. English. Four times a year (Feb., May, Aug., Nov.). $25.00. Maine State Nurse's Association, 283 Water Street, PO Box 2240, Augusta ME 04338-2240. **Tel** (207)622-1057. **DD** 610. **Ad Acc.** ctrl circ.
**Ind/Abst** Cumul. Index Nurs. Allied Health Lit.; Int. Nurs. Index.

US/0278-9450
**MAINLINES (INDIANAPOLIS, IND.).** (MAINLINES : THE NEWSLETTER FOR THE MIDWEST ALLIANCE IN NURSING.). **Added/Corp** Midwest Alliance in Nursing. **VFOAT** Main Lines. (1980)-. Periodical. English. qt (Jan., Apr., July, Oct.). $45.00. Midwest Alliance In Nursing, 2511 E 46th St/Suite E-3, Indianapolis IN 46205. **Tel** (317)541-3600, FAX (317)541-3609. **ED** Krystine D. Hanson. **NLM** W1; MA49N. **Bk Rev,** (Qty: 1). **Ad Acc, Adv Mgr:** J Spain, **Tel** (317)541-3600. **Pr Rev. Circ:** 650 (ctrl).
**Desc:** Regional nursing news related to clinical practice, education and research in nursing. Health care and legislative issues related to improving health care in the Midwest.

US/0047-6080
**MARYLAND NURSE, THE.** [MD. nurse]. **Added/Corp** Maryland Nurses Association. Vol. 1 (July/Aug. 1970)-. Periodical. English. Eight times a year. $12.00. Maryland Nurses Association, 849 International Drive, Airport Square XX1, Suite 255, Linthicum MD 21090. **Tel** (410)859-3000, FAX (410)859-3001. **ED** Nancy McCaslin. **NLM** W1 MA76SD. **Bk Rev,** (Qty: 8). **Ad Acc. Circ:** 10,000 (ctrl). **Supersedes** Maryland Nursing News.
**Desc:** News and views of Maryland nurses and the Maryland Nurses Association.
**Ind/Abst** Cumul. Index Nurs. Allied Health Lit.; Int. Nurs. Index.

US/0163-0784
**MASSACHUSETTS NURSE, THE.** [Mass. nurse]. **Added/Corp** Massachusetts Nurses Association. Massachusetts Nurses Association. Bulletin. **VFOAT** MNA Bulletin. **VAT** Massachusetts Nurses Association Bulletin. Vol. 45 (March 1976)-. Periodical. English. Ten times a year (except June/July and Oct./Nov. issues combined). $12.00. Massachusetts Nurses Association, 340 Turnpike Street, Canton MA 02021. **Tel** (617)821-4625, FAX (617)821-4445. **ED** Lynette Aznavourian. **DD** 610. **NLM** W1 MA913. **Bk Rev. Ad Acc. Pr Rev. Circ:** 18,000 (ctrl). **Continues** Bulletin of the Massachusetts Nurses Association, 0025-4843.
**Desc:** Covers health care, legislation and a broad range of nursing issues confronting nurses in Massachusetts. Also contains nursing history articles.
**Ind/Abst** Cumul. Index Nurs. Allied Health Lit.; Int. Nurs. Index.

US/0090-0702
**MATERNAL-CHILD NURSING JOURNAL.** [Matern.-child nurs. j.]. **Added/Corp** University of Pittsburgh. Dept. of Obstetrical Nursing. University of Pittsburgh. Dept. of Pediatric Nursing. University of Pittsburgh. Dept. of Obstetrical and Pediatric Nursing. University of Pittsburgh. Graduate Program in Maternity Nursing. University of Pittsburgh. Graduate Program in Nursing Care of Children. **VFOAT** Maternal Child Nursing Journal; MCNJ. Vol. 1 (Spring 1972)-. Periodical. English. qt $47.00 (institutions), $40.00 (individuals) US; $59.00 (institutions), $52.00 (institutions) other. NURSECOM Inc., 1211 Locust Street, Philadelphia PA 19107. **Tel** (215)545-7222, (800)242-6757, FAX (215)545-8107. **ED** Corinne M. Barnes and Olive J. Rich. **LC** RJ245; .M36. **DD** 610.73/62/05. **NLM** W1 MA947M. **CODEN** MCNJA2. Index available. cum. index. **Bk Rev. Circ:** 1,500. available on microfilm and microfiche from University Microfilms International (UMI).
**Desc:** Descriptive case studies, literature reviews, and research reports furthering professional knowledge of the expert nurse practitioner/clinician in care of mothers and children.
**Ind/Abst** Cumul. Index Nurs. Allied Health Lit.; EMBASE; Energy Res. Abstr. (Aug. 1982-); Index Med.; Int. Nurs. Index; Nurs. Abstr.; Psychol. Abstr. (1972-); PsycINFO; PsycLit; Sage Fam. Stud. Abstr. (?-?).

US/0361-929X
**MCN, THE AMERICAN JOURNAL OF MATERNAL CHILD NURSING.** [MCN, Am. j. matern. child nursing]. **VFOAT** American Journal of Maternal Child Nursing. **VAT** Maternal Child Nursing, the American Journal of Maternal Child Nursing. Vol. 1 (Jan./Feb. 1976)-. Periodical. English. bm. $35.00 (institution), $23.00 (individual) US. American Journal of Nursing Company, 555 West 57th Street, New York NY 10019-2961. **Tel** (212)582-8820, FAX (212)586-5462. (**Subscription address:** MCN, The American Journal of Maternal Child Nursing, PO Box 53435, Boulder CO 80322-3435.) **ED** Barbara E. Bishop. **LC** RG951; .M13. **DD** 610.73/678. **NLM** W1 M225. **CODEN** MCNNEI. Index available. **Bk Rev. Ad Acc. Circ:** 35,000. available on microfilm and microfiche from University Microfilms International (UMI).
**Desc:** Covers every facet of maternal/child nursing. Reaches nurses in ob/gyn, neonatology, pediatrics, family planning, schools, and community health.
**Ind/Abst** Cumul. Index Nurs. Allied Health Lit.; Hospit. Health Admin. Index; Index Med.; Int. Nurs. Index; Nurs. Abstr.

US/1062-7537
**MED-SURG NURSING QUARTERLY.** Ceased. [Med-surg nurs. q.]. **VFOAT** Med Surg Nursing Quarterly. Vol. 1, No. 1 (Summer 1992)-Vol. 1, No. 4, (Spring 1993). Periodical. English. qt. Springhouse Corporation, 1111 Bethlehem Pike, Springhouse PA 19477. **Tel** (215)646-8700. **DD** 616. **NLM** W1; ME86K.

US/0730-7942
**MEDICARE, USE OF SKILLED NURSING FACILITIES.** See Insurance.

RU/0025-8342
**MEDICINSKAJA SESTRA.** *Title Change.* (MEDITSINSKAIA SESTRA.). [Med. sestra]. **Added/Corp** Soviet Union. Narodnyi Komissariat Zdravookhraneniia. Soviet Union. Ministerstvo Zdravookhraneniia. Russian S.F.S.R. Ministerstvo Zdravookhraneniia. (1942)-(1992). Academic Scholarly Publication. Russian (table of contents in English). mo. Izdatelstvo Meditsina / Russian Academy of Medical Sciences, Ulitsa Solyanka 14, 109801 Moscow Russia. **Tel** 011 95 297-05-04. **NLM** W1 ME803. **CODEN** MESEAQ. Index available in last issue of volume-attached. **Bk Rev.** Documents available from CASDDS. **Continued by** Meditsinskaia Pomoshch, 0869-7760.
**Ind/Abst** Chem. Abstr. (?-1984); Int. Nurs. Index (?-?); SportSearch (?-?).

UK
**MENTAL HEALTH NURSING.** (19??)-. Periodical. English. bm. £40.00. CPNA Publications, 44 Dartford Road, Sevenoaks Kent TN133TQ England. **Tel** 011 44 732 455244, FAX 011 44 732 457542, telex 957592. **ED** Catherine Jackson and Mick Robin. **Ad Acc, Adv Mgr:** Graham Watt, **Tel** 011 44 532 730973. ctrl circ. **Continues** Community Psychiatric Nursing Journal.

US/0026-2366
**MICHIGAN NURSE.** [Mich. nurse]. **VFOAT** Michigan Nurse Newsletter. (1928)-. Periodical. English. Eleven times a year (Except July). $33.00 North America; $50.00 other. Michigan Nurses Association, 2310 Jolly Oak Road, Okemos MI 48864. **Tel** (517)349-5640, FAX (517)349-5818. **ED** Andrea Shea Ralph. **NLM** W1 MI221. **Ad Acc, Adv Mgr Tel** (517)349-5640. **Circ:** 7,400. available on microfilm from University Microfilms International (UMI).
**Desc:** Designed to promote communications among and between nurses in Michigan about profession nursing.
**Ind/Abst** Cumul. Index Nurs. Allied Health Lit.; Int. Nurs. Index.

US/1048-499X
**MIDWEST ALLIANCE IN NURSING JOURNAL / MAIN.** [Midwest Alliance Nurs. j.]. **Added/Corp** Midwest Alliance in Nursing. **VFOAT** MAIN Journal. Vol. 1, no. 1 (summer 1989)-. Periodical. English. Three times a year. $35.00 (nonmembers), $31.50 (members), $45.00 (libraries). Midwest Alliance In Nursing, 2511 E 46th St/Suite E-3, Indianapolis IN 46205. **Tel** (317)541-3600, FAX (317)541-3609. **ED** Marian Pettengill (phone: (317)541-3607). **DD** 610. **NLM** W1; MI33P. **Ad Acc, Adv Mgr:** J. Spain, **Tel** (317)541-3600. **Pr Rev. Circ:** 233.
**Desc:** Contains publication of nursing research, as well as articles on nursing-related topics pertinent to the Midwest.

US/0026-4369
**MILWAUKEE PROFESSIONAL NURSE.** Periodical. English. qt. $4.00. Milwaukee District Nurses Association, 904 S 104 Street West, Allis WI 53214. **Tel** (414)453-8436. **ED** Genee Brukwitzki. **Bk Rev. Ad Acc. Circ:** 800 (ctrl). available on microfilm and microfiche from University Microfilms International (UMI).
**Desc:** Nursing and health care issues, particularly those with local (Milwaukee) ramifications.

●US/1068-5685
**MINIMALLY INVASIVE SURGICAL NURSING.** [Minim. invasive surg. nurs.]. Vol. 7, No. 1 (Spring 1993)-. Periodical. English. qt. $82.00. Mary Ann Liebert Inc., 1651 Third Avenue, New York NY 10128. **Tel** (212)289-2300, (800)M-LIEBERT, FAX (212)289-4697. **DD** 610. **NLM** W1; MI662. **Continues** Laser Nursing, 0888-6075.

●US/1071-9946
**MINORITY NURSE NEWSLETTER.** [Minor. nurse newsl.]. Vol. 1, No. 1 (Jan. 1994)-. Periodical. English. Six times a year. $60.00 (individuals), $110.00 (institutions). Tucker Publications Inc., PO Box 580, Lisle IL 60532. **Tel** (708)969-3809, FAX (708)969-3895. **ED** Monique N. Allen (editor's address: 5823 Queens Cove, Lisle, IL 60532). **DD** 610. **Bk Rev,** (Qty: 6-10). **Ad Acc. Circ:** 1,000.

US/0026-6388
**MISSISSIPPI RN, THE.** [Mississippi RN]. **Added/Corp** Mississippi Nurses' Association. **VAT** Mississippi Registered Nurse. Vol. 1 (1969)-. Periodical. English. Six times a year. $18.00. Mississippi Nurses Association, 135 Bound Street, Suite 100, Jackson MS 39206. **Tel** (601)982-9182. **ED** Christy Montgomery. **DD** 610. **NLM** W1 MI828. **Bk Rev. Ad Acc. Pr Rev. Circ:** 2,000 (ctrl).
**Desc:** Covers nursing issues, clinical topics and other health care related information. Research articles and features are regular items.
**Ind/Abst** Cumul. Index Nurs. Allied Health Lit.; Int. Nurs. Index.

US/0026-6655
**MISSOURI NURSE, THE.** [MO. nurse]. **Added/Corp** Missouri Nurses' Association. (1932)-. Periodical. English. Six times a year (Jan., Mar., May, July, Sept., Nov.). $25.00. Missouri Nurses Association, 206 East Dunklin, PO Box 325, Jefferson City MO 65101. **Tel** (314)636-4623, FAX (314)636-9576. **ED** Kay Fulwider, RSN, RN. **NLM** W1 MI882. **Ad Acc. Circ:** 2,500 (ctrl).
**Desc:** Educational information for registered professional

nurses.
**Ind/Abst** Cumul. Index Nurs. Allied Health Lit.; Int. Nurs. Index.

US/0026-5586
**MNA ACCENT.** [M.N.A. accent]. **Main/Corp** Minnesota Nurses Association. **Added/Corp** Minnesota Nurses Association. Accent. **VFOAT** Minnesota Nursing Accent. **VAT** Minnesota Nurses Association. Accent. (197?)-. Periodical. English. Ten times a year. $25.00. Minnesota Nurses Association, 1295 Bandana Boulevard, Suite 140, St Paul MN 55108. **Tel** (612)646-4807. **ED** Sonja Mevrholz and Hope Caldeen. **DD** 610. **NLM** W1; MI699N. **Ad Acc. Circ:** 11,500 (ctrl). ***Continues*** *Minnesota Nursing Accent.*
**Desc:** Nursing issues in Minnesota.
**Ind/Abst** Cumul. Index Nurs. Allied Health Lit.; Int. Nurs. Index.

US/0147-5223
**MONOGRAPH - SIGMA THETA TAU.** (MONOGRAPH.). **Added/Corp** Sigma Theta Tau. Series 75, No. 1 (1976)-. Monographic series. English. ir. Price varies per volume. Sigma Theta Tau International, 550 West North Street, Indianapolis IN 46202. **Tel** (317)634-8171, FAX (317)634-8188. **LC** UNC. **NLM** W1 MO56K.

US/0889-0579
**NAACOG NEWSLETTER.** ***Title Change.*** [NAACOG newsl.]. **Added/Corp** American College of Obstetricians and Gynecologists. Nurses' Association. NAACOG (Organization). **VAT** Nurses Association of the American College of Obstetricians and Gynecologists Newsletter. (1982)-(199?). Newsletter. English. mo. NAACOG, c/o Tina Lynch, 600 Maryland Avenue SW/Suite 200 E, Washington DC 20024. **Tel** (202)863-2499. **ED** Nancy J Rhodes. **DD** 610. **NLM** W1; NA10. Index available. **Ad Acc. Circ:** 22,000 (ctrl). ***Continues*** *Bulletin / American College of Obstetricians and Gynecologists. Nurses' Association, 0095-2982.* ***Continued by*** *AWHONN Voice, 1066-2944.*
**Ind/Abst** Int. Nurs. Index (Nov. 1985-).

US/1055-3533
**NAACOG'S WOMEN'S HEALTH NURSING SCAN.** ***Title Change.*** [NAACOG's women's health nurs. scan]. **Added/Corp** NAACOG (Organization). **VFOAT** Women's Health Nursing Scan; Nurses' Association of the American College of Obstetricians and Gynecologists' Women's Health Nursing Scan. **VAT** Nurses' Association of the American College of Obstetricians and Gynecologists' Women's Health Nursing Scan. Vol. 5, No. 1 (Jan./Feb. 1991)-(1992). Periodical. English. bm. NURSECOM Inc., 1211 Locust Street, Philadelphia PA 19107. **Tel** (215)545-7222, (800)242-6757, FAX (215)545-8107. **ED** Shannon E. Perry. **LC** RA778.A1; N875. **DD** 610. **Pr Rev. Circ:** 2374. available on microfilm and microfiche from University Microfilms International (UMI). ***Continues*** *Women's Health Nursing Scan, 0897-1722.* ***Continued by*** *Women's Health Nursing Scan (Philadelphia, Pa. : 1993), 1070-308X.*
**Desc:** Health Nursing Scan is a professional nursing journal committed to publishing information concerning all aspects of women's health--physical, emotional, and social. A panel of nurse leaders across the country survey over one hundred publications and provide a concise summary of relevant articles, annotated with remarks and opinion that apply that information to clinical nursing practice.

CN/0848-9947
**NATIONAL NETWORK.** [Natl. netw.]. Issue No. 1 (Dec. 1984)-. Periodical. English. Three times a year. Free to members of the Victorian Order of Nurses. Victorian Order of Nurses for Canada, 5 Blackburn Avenue, Ottawa Ontario K1N 8A2 Canada. **DD** 610.73/06/071. ***Continues*** *National Office Newsletter - Victorian Order of Nurses for Canada, 0228-0906.*

US/0028-1921
**NEBRASKA NURSE.** [Nebr. nurse]. **Added/Corp** Nebraska Nurses' Association. Nebraska State Nurses' Association. Vol. 1 (June 1946)-. Periodical. English. Four times a year (Feb., May, Aug., Nov.). $10.00. Nebraska Nurses Association, 941 O Street, Lincoln NE 68508. **Tel** (402)475 3859, FAX 9402)475-3961. **ED** Donna R. Baker. **NLM** W1 NE117. **Bk Rev. Ad Acc, Adv Mgr:** Arthur Davis Company, **Tel** (319)277-2414. **Circ:** 24,000 (ctrl).
**Desc:** Nursing practice, nursing education, legislation and professional association issues and information on the economic and general welfare of nurses.
**Ind/Abst** Cumul. Index Nurs. Allied Health Lit.; Int. Nurs. Index.

US/8756-0356
**NEHW HEALTH WATCH.** [NEHW health watch]. **Added/Corp** Nurses' Environmental Health Watch. **VFOAT** Health Watch. **VAT** Nurses' Environmental Health Watch Health Watch. (19??)-. Periodical. English. qt (4 issues). $20.00. Nurses Environmental Health Watch, 181 Marshall Street, Duxbury MA 02332. **ED** Diane J. Mancino. **DD** 610. **NLM** W1; NE193RS. **Bk Rev. Circ:** 1,000 (ctrl).
**Desc:** Issues related to environmental health nursing including air and water pollution; solid waste and toxic waste disposal; radioactive materials; and occupational health hazards.
**Ind/Abst** Health Plan. Adminis.; Int. Nurs. Index.

US/0730-0832
**NEONATAL NETWORK.** **See** Medical Science and Technology-Pediatrics.

IT
**NEONATOLOGICA INFERMIERISTICA.** Ediz Medico Scientiche Sas, c/o Tipogr Viscontea, V Riviera 39, 27100 Pavia Italy.

US/0273-4117
**NEVADA RNFORMATION.** [Nev. RNformation]. **Added/Corp** Nevada Nurses' Association. **VAT** Nevada Registered Nurse Information. (19??)-. Periodical. English. qt (Feb., May., Aug., Nov.). $15.00 North America; $20.00 other. Nevada Nurses Association, 3660 Baker Lane/Suite 104, Reno NV 89509. **Tel** (702)825-3555, FAX (702)825-3555. **ED** Maury Astley. cum. index. **Ad Acc. Circ:** 600 (ctrl).
**Ind/Abst** Cumul. Index Nurs. Allied Health Lit.; Int. Nurs. Index.

NR/0794-4373
**NEW ERA NURSING IMAGE INTERNATIONAL.** (NEW ERA NURSING IMAGE INTERNATIONAL : NENI.). [New era nurs. image int.]. **VFOAT** NENI. Periodical. English. Oyo State of Nigeria, Government Printer, Ibadan Nigeria. **NLM** W1; NE374JD.
**Ind/Abst** Int. Nurs. Index (1986-).

US/0196-4895
**NEW JERSEY NURSE (1978).** (NEW JERSEY NURSE.). [N.J. nurse]. **Added/Corp** New Jersey State Nurses' Association. Vol. 8 (Feb./Mar. 1978)-. Periodical. English. mo. $20.00. New Jersey State Nurses Association, 320 West State Street, Trenton NJ 08618. **Tel** (609)392-4884. **ED** Barbara W. Wright. **NLM** W1 NE446T. **Bk Rev. Ad Acc.** ctrl circ. ***Continues*** *NJSNA Newsletter.*
**Desc:** Publication for all members of the New Jersey State Nurses Association. Covers all areas affecting nursing in New Jersey.
**Ind/Abst** Cumul. Index Nurs. Allied Health Lit.; Int. Nurs. Index.

US/0362-7438
**NEW MEXICO BOARD OF NURSING ANNUAL REPORT TO GOVERNOR.** (ANNUAL REPORT TO GOVERNOR.). **Main/Corp** New Mexico. Board of Nursing. English. an. New Mexico Board of Nursing, 505 Marquette, NW, Albuquerque NM 87102. **LC** RT5.N44; N48A. **DD** 331.1/1.

US/0028-6273
**NEW MEXICO NURSE.** [N.M. nurse]. **Added/Corp** New Mexico Nurses' Association. (19??)-. Periodical. English. qt (Jan., Apr., July, Oct.). $12.00. New Mexico Nurses Association, 909 Virginia NE/Suite 101, Albuquerque NM 87108. **Tel** (505)268-7744. **ED** Cynde Brandou (phone: 272-1272). **NLM** W1 NE461. **Ad Acc. Circ:** 675 (ctrl).
**Ind/Abst** Cumul. Index Nurs. Allied Health Lit.; Int. Nurs. Index.

●IE
**NEW WORLD OF IRISH NURSING : OFFICIAL JOURNAL OF IRISH NURSES ORGANISATION AND NATIONAL COUNCIL OF NURSES, THE.** **Added/Corp** Irish Nurses' Organisation. National Council of Nurses of Ireland. Vol. 1, (Jan./Feb. 1993)-. Periodical. English. bm. Maxwell Publicity Ltd., 11 Fitzwilliam Place, Dublin 2 Ireland. **NLM** W1; NE513P. ***Continues*** *World of Irish Nursing, 0332-3056.*
**Ind/Abst** Int. Nurs. Index (1993-).

NZ/0110-7968
**NEW ZEALAND NURSING FORUM.** [N.Z. nurs. forum]. **Added/Corp** Nurses Society of New Zealand. **VFOAT** Nursing Forum; NZ Nursing Forum. Vol. 5 (Apr./May 1977)-. Periodical. English. Four times a year (Feb., May, Aug., Nov.). 43.00NZ$. Nurses Society of New Zealand, PO Box 3195, Auckland 1 New Zealand. **Tel** 011 64 9 8178412, FAX 011 64 9 893591. **ED** David J. Wills. **NLM** W1 NE977P. **Bk Rev. Ad Acc. Pr Rev. Circ:** 12,500 (ctrl). ***Continues*** *Nursing Forum, 0110-0890.*
**Desc:** Journal for original papers on nursing and related areas, abstracts and reviews.
**Ind/Abst** Cumul. Index Nurs. Allied Health Lit.; Int. Nurs. Index.

NZ/0028-8535
**NEW ZEALAND NURSING JOURNAL, THE.** ***Title Change.*** [N.Z. nurs. j.]. **Added/Corp** NZ Nurses Association. **VFOAT** Kai Tiaki, The New Zealand Nursing Journal; Kaitiaki, The New Zealand Nursing Journal. Vol. 22, No. 3 (1929)-Vol. 86, No. 2 (Mar. 1993). Periodical. English. mo (except combined Dec./Jan.). New Zealand Nurses Association 181-183 Willis Street, Wellington New Zealand. **Tel** 64-04-850847, FAX 64-04-829993. **ED** Claire O'Brien and Kathy Stoddart. **[CCC].** Index available. **Bk Rev. Ad Acc. Circ:** 22,300 (ctrl). ***Continues*** *Kai Tiaki.* ***Merged with*** *NZNU News* ***to form*** *Nursing New Zealand, 1172-1979.*
**Desc:** Articles relating to professional and industrial welfare nursing issues. Information from the New Zealand Nurses Association head office to its members.
**Ind/Abst** Cumul. Index Nurs. Allied Health Lit.; Int. Nurs. Index.

NR
**NIGERIAN NURSE.** (1968)-. Periodical. English. sa. N32.00. National Association Niger Nurse Midwives, Box 3857, Ikeja Post Office, Lagos Nigeria. **Tel** 01 962512.
**Ind/Abst** Cumul. Index Nurs. Allied Health Lit.

JA/0911-0844
**NIHON KANGO KYOKAI CHOSA KENKYU HOKOKU.** **Main/Corp** Nihon Kango Kyokai. Japanese (English). ir. ¥1,500 Japan; $9.30 US. Nihon Kango Kyokai, 8-2 Jingumae 5 Shibuya-ku, Tokyo 150 Japan. **Tel** 03(400)8331, telex 03(400)8336. **LC** RT1; .N52A. Index available. cum. index. **Bk Rev. Ad Acc. Circ:** 1,500 (ctrl).
**Desc:** The result of the Survey Research Section's research work about nursing, status of nursing staff, etc., in Japan.

US/0161-5513
**NJPC BULLETIN.** **Added/Corp** National Joint Practice Commission (U.S.). **VAT** National Joint Practice Commission Bulletin. Vol. 1 (May 1975)-. Bulletin. English. **NLM** W1 N145.
**Ind/Abst** Health Plan. Adminis.

GR
**NOSELEUTIKE.** (Jan./Feb. 1979)-. Periodical. Greek, Modern. qt. **NLM** W1; NO683C. ***Continues*** *Hellenis Adelphe.*
**Ind/Abst** Int. Nurs. Index (1979-).

US/0896-8047
**NOTES ON NURSING SCIENCE.** (NOTES ON NURSING SCIENCE : THE NEWSLETTER OF THE NIGHTINGALE SOCIETY.). [Notes on nurs. sci.]. **Added/Corp** Nightingale Society (Carmel, Calif.). Vol. 1, No. 1 (Winter 1988)-. Newsletter. English. qt. $19.00. Nightingale Society, 225 The Crossroads, Carmel CA 93923. **DD** 610. **NLM** W1; NO747.

CN/0849-1593
**NOUVEAU DIALOGUE EN BREF.** (NOUVEAU DIALOGUE EN BREF / LES INFIRMIERES ET INFIRMIERS UNIS INC.). [Nouv. dialogue bref]. **Added/Corp** Infirmieres et Infirmiers Unis. **VFOAT** Nouveau Dialogue les Infirmieres et Infirmiers Unis Inc. Vol. 22, No 2 (Mar 1990)-. Periodical. French. United Nurses, Suite 200, 400 St.-Jacques West, Montreal, Quebec H2Y 1S1 Canada. **DD** 610.73/06/071428. ***Continues in part*** *Nouveau Dialogue (Infirmieres et Infirmiers Unis)., 0836-8686.*

SP/0210-8275
**NUEVA ENFERMERIA.** [Nueva enferm.]. **Added/Corp** Consejo General de Ayudantes Tecnicos Sanitarios (Spain). (1979)-. Periodical. Spanish. mo. Nueva Enfermeria, Cuesta de Santo Domingo, 6-20 Madrid 13 Spain. **NLM** W1 NU143. ***Continues*** *Boletin Cultural e Informativo de A.T.S.*
**Ind/Abst** Int. Nurs. Index.

CN/0382-8476
**NURSCENE.** **Added/Corp** Manitoba Association of Registered Nurses. Vol. 1, (July 1974)-. Periodical. English. Six times a year (Jan., Mar., May, Aug., Oct., Dec.). 30.00Can$ Canada; 40.00Can$ other. Manitoba Association of Register Nurses, 647 Broadway, Winnipeg Manitoba R3C 0X2 Canada. **Tel** (204)774-3477, FAX (204)775-6052. **ED** Mary Jane MacLennan. **DD** 610,73/.06/27127. Index available (Bound in next iss.). **Bk Rev**, (Qty: 2). **Ad Acc. Circ:** 11,000 (ctrl). ***Supersedes*** *M A R News, 0382-8484.*
**Desc:** Coverage includes articles on healthcare and profiles of nurses in Manitoba and elsewhere who are prominent because of their activities both within the healthcare industry and within their communities.

US/0897-7437
**NURSE ANESTHESIA.** ***Ceased.*** **See** Medical Science and Technology-Anesthesiology.

US/1054-2353
**NURSE AUTHOR & EDITOR.** [Nurse author ed.]. **VFOAT** Nurse Author and Editor. Vol. 1, Issue 1 (Winter 1991)-. Periodical. English. qt. $38.00 US; $48.00 Canada; $56.00 other. Hall Johnson Communications Inc, 9737 West Ohio Avenue, Lakewood CO 80226. **Tel** (303)988-0056. **ED** Suzanne Hall Johnson. **LC** RT24; .N88. **DD** 808. **[CCC].** Index available (Dec. issue).
**Ind/Abst** Cumul. Index Nurs. Allied Health Lit.; Int. Nurs. Index (spring 1992-).

UK/0260-6917
**NURSE EDUCATION TODAY.** [Nurse educ. today]. (198?)-. Periodical. English. bm. £165.00 Europe; £167.00 Other (Institutions). Churchill Livingstone, 1-3 Baxter's Place, Leith Walk, Edinburgh EH1 3AF Scotland. **Tel** 011 44 31 556 2424, FAX 011 44 31 558 1278, telex 727511. **(Subscription address:** Maruzen Company Ltd., PO Box 5050, Import & Export Department, Tokyo 100 31 Japan.) **ED** J Walker. **NLM** W1; NU5523. **[CCC].** available on microfilm and microfiche from University

Microfilms International (UMI).
**Desc:** Promotes the continuing of all nurses, midwives and health visitors.
**Ind/Abst** Cumul. Index Nurs. Allied Health Lit.; Int. Nurs. Index; Spec. Educ. Needs Abstr.; Stud. Women Abstr.; Tech. Educ. Train. Abstr.

US/0363-3624
**NURSE EDUCATOR.** [Nurse educ.]. Vol. 1 (May/June 1976)-. Periodical. English. bm. $49.00 (individuals), $99.00 (institutions) US; $79.00 (individuals), $129.00 (institutions) other. J.B. Lippincott Company, 227 East Washington Square, Philadelphia PA 19106-3780. **Tel** (215)238-4200 or 4454, FAX (215)238-4227. **(Subscription address:** J.B. Lippincott, PO Box 350, Hagerstown MD 21740.**) ED** Suzanne Smith Blancett. **LC** RT71; .N74. **DD** 610.73/07/11. **NLM** W1 NU5524. **CODEN** NUEDEC. **[CCC]. Bk Rev. Ad Acc. Circ:** 4,300. available on microfilm and microfiche from University Microfilms International (UMI).
**Desc:** Resource for academic educators on the practical and theoretical aspects of nursing education.
**Ind/Abst** Cumul. Index Nurs. Allied Health Lit.; Curr. Index J. Educ.; Educ. Index (1992-); Hospit. Health Admin. Index; Int. Nurs. Index; Nurs. Abstr.

US/0361-1817
**NURSE PRACTITIONER, THE.** [Nurse pract.]. **VFOAT** NP. Vol. 1, (Sept./Oct. 1975)-. Academic Scholarly Publication. English. Twelve times a year (1 volume). $75.00 US; $94.00 other. Elsevier Science Publishing Company Inc, Madison Square Station, PO Box 882, New York NY 10159-0882. **Tel** (212)633-3950, FAX (212)633-3990. **LC** RT1; .N756. **DD** 610.73/05. **NLM** W1 NU555. **[CCC].** Index available. **Bk Rev. Ad Acc. Pr Rev. Circ:** 12,500 (ctrl). available on microfilm and microfiche from University Microfilms International (UMI).
**Desc:** Addresses advanced primary care nursing, especially research, diagnosis, management of acute or chronic illnesses; outlines new developments, approaches in health maintenance; provides management protocols, specific to an ambulatory population, of an acute symptom or chronic condition.
**Ind/Abst** Cumul. Index Nurs. Allied Health Lit.; Curr. Lit. Fam. Plan.; Energy Res. Abstr. (1982-); Index Med.; Int. Nurs. Index; Int. Pharm. Abstr.; Nurs. Abstr.

US/1045-5485
**NURSE PRACTITIONER FORUM.** [Nurse pract. forum]. (June 1990)-. Periodical. English. qt (4 issues). $45.00 (individual), $59.00 (institution) US; $83.00 (individual), $88.00 (institution) other. W.B. Saunders Company, A Subsidiary of Harcourt Brace Jovanovich, Inc., The Curtis Center/Suite 300, Independence Square West, Philadelphia PA 19106-3399. **Tel** (215)238-7800 or, 5587, FAX (215)238-7883, telex 173146. **(Subscription address:** W. B. Saunders Company / North America Subscriptions, c/o Periodicals, 6277 Sea Harbour Drive, 4th Floor, Orlando FL 32887.**) DD** 616. **NLM** W1; NU555L. **[CCC]. Pr Rev.**
**Ind/Abst** Cumul. Index Nurs. Allied Health Lit.

US/0893-4738
**NURSE SEARCH.** (NURSE SEARCH [COMPUTER FILE].). [Nurse search]. **VFOAT** NurseSearch. (1985)-. Periodical. English. Three times a year. $165.00. Cumulative Index to Nursing and Allied Health Literature, PO Box 871, Glendale CA 91209. **DD** 610.
**Desc:** A personal computer based search system enabling nurses to search 60 important nursing journals. Floppy disk software program.

US/0196-6790
**NURSE, THE PATIENT & THE LAW, THE. See** Law.

CN/0849-3383
**NURSE TO NURSE.** [Nurse nurse]. **Added/Corp** Registered Nurses Association of Nova Scotia. Vol. 1, No. 1 (Feb. 1990)-. Periodical. English. bm. Free to members. Registered Nurses' Association of Nova Scotia, 120 Eileen Stubbs Avenue, Suite 104, Dartmouth, Nova Scotia, B3B 1Y1 Canada. **Tel** (902)423-6156, FAX (902)423-8214. **DD** 610.73/06/0716. ***Continues*** *R N A N S Bulletin., 0319-4604.*

US/0364-0698
**NURSE TRAINING.** (NURSE TRAINING : REPORT TO THE CONGRESS.). **Main/Corp** United States. Bureau of Health Resources Development. Division of Nursing. English. US Department of Health and Human Services National Institutes of Health, 9000 Rockville Pike, Bethesda MD 20892. **Tel** (301)496-9291, FAX (301)496-2443. **LC** RT79; .U53A. **DD** 610.73/07/1173.

US
**NURSEREVIEW : A CLINICAL UPDATE SYSTEM. Added/Corp** Springhouse Corporation. **VFOAT** Nurse Review; Nurse Review Series. (1986)-. English. Twelve times a year. $235.00 (12 sections) US. Springhouse Corporation, 1111 Bethlehem Pike, Springhouse PA 19477. **Tel** (215)646-8700.

US/0191-2291
**NURSES' DRUG ALERT.** [Nurses' drug alert]. Vol. 1, (Sept. 1976)-. Periodical. English. Twelve times a year. $24.00 US; $30.00 Canada; $35.00 other. M. J. Powers and Company Publishers, 374 Millburn Avenue, Millburn NJ 07041. **Tel** (201)467-4556. Index available (Free).
**Ind/Abst** Cumul. Index Nurs. Allied Health Lit.

●US/1062-9092
**NURSES' DRUG GUIDE.** [Nurses' drug guide]. **VFOAT** Govoni & Hayes Nurses' Drug Guide; Govoni & Hayes, Wilson & Shannon Nurses' Drug Guide. (1993)-. English. ir. $22.95 (latest edition). Appleton & Lange, (A Subsidiary of Simon & Schuster), 25 Van Zant Street, East Norwalk CT 06855. **Tel** (203)838-4400, (800)423-1359, FAX (203)854-9486. **DD** 615.

US/0360-4039
**NURSING.** [Nurs.]. Vol. 1 (Nov. 1971)-. Periodical. English. mo. $42.00 US; $45.00 other except New Guinea, Australia, New Zealand, Pacific Isles, Papau and Canada. Springhouse Corporation, 1111 Bethlehem Pike, Springhouse PA 19477. **Tel** (215)646-8700. **(Subscription address:** Fulfillment Corporation of America / Marion Ohio, 205 West Center Street, Marion OH 43302.**) LC** RT1; .N76. **DD** 610.73/05. **NLM** W1 NU584K. **[CCC]. Ad Acc.** available on microfilm and microfiche from University Microfilms International (UMI). Documents available from UMI Article Clearinghouse. ***Absorbed*** *Nursing Update; NursingLife.*
**Ind/Abst** Acad. Search (July 1993-); Cumul. Index Nurs. Allied Health Lit.; Energy Res. Abstr. (Aug. 1978-); Gen. Period. Index (1985-); Gen. Sci. Source (Jul. 1993-); Health Plan. Adminis.; Hospit. Health Admin. Index; Int. Nurs. Index; Int. Pharm. Abstr.; Mag. Search; Newsp. Period. Abstr. (1989-); Nurs. Abstr.; Physic. Medline Plus; Trade Ind. Index (1981-).

US/0195-3354
**NURSING ABSTRACTS. See** Medical Science and Technology-Abstracting, Bibliographies and Statistics.

US/0363-9568
**NURSING ADMINISTRATION QUARTERLY.** [Nursing adm. q.]. **Added/Corp** Aspen Systems Corporation. Vol. 1 (Fall 1976)-. Periodical. English. qt. $97.00 US. Aspen Publishers Inc., 7201 McKinney Circle, Frederick MD 21701. **Tel** (800)234-1660, (301)698-7100, FAX (301)251-5784, telex 5106014543. **(Subscription address:** Aspen Publishers Inc., PO Box 990, Frederick MD 21701.**) ED** Barbara J. Brown. **LC** RT89; .N78. **DD** 658/.91/3621. **NLM** W1 NU585. **[CCC]. Bk Rev. Ad Acc, Adv Mgr:** Frances S. Ray, **Tel** (301)417-7584. **Pr Rev. Circ:** 5,934. available on microfilm and microfiche from University Microfilms International (UMI).
**Desc:** Provides nursing administrators with practical, up-to-date information on the effective management of nursing services in modern health care facilities.
**Ind/Abst** Cumul. Index Nurs. Allied Health Lit.; Health Plan. Adminis.; Hospit. Health Admin. Index; Int. Nurs. Index; Nurs. Abstr.

US
**NURSING & ALLIED HEALTH CINAHL CAMBRIDGE. CD-ROM. See** Medical Science and Technology-Abstracting, Bibliographies and Statistics.

US
**NURSING & ALLIED HEALTH (CINAHL)-CD [COMPUTER FILE]. See** Medical Science and Technology-Abstracting, Bibliographies and Statistics.

US/0888-0530
**NURSING & ALLIED HEALTH (CINAHL) ... SUBJECT HEADING LIST.** [Nurs. allied health (CINAHL) subj. head. list]. **VFOAT** Subject Heading List; Nursing and Allied Health (CINAHL) ... Subject Heading List. **VAT** Nursing and Allied Health (Cumulative Index to Nursing and Allied Health Literature) ... Subject Heading List. (1986)-. English. an. $35.00 US, (add $3.00 for postage) other. CINAHL, Glendale Adventist Medical Center, PO Box 871, Glendale CA 91209. **Tel** (818)409-8005, FAX (818)546-5679. **ED** DeLauna Lockwood. **LC** Z695.1.N8; N87. **DD** 025.4/961073. Index available. cum. index. **Ad Acc. Circ:** 7,500. ***Continues*** *CINAHL Subject Headings, 0747-6361.*
**Desc:** Lists subject headings used in all formats of the cumulative index to nursing and allied health literature.

US/0276-5284
**NURSING & HEALTH CARE.** (NURSING & HEALTH CARE : OFFICIAL PUBLICATION OF THE NATIONAL LEAGUE FOR NURSING.). [Nurs. health care]. **Added/Corp** National League for Nursing. **VFOAT** Nursing and Health Care. Vol. 1, No. 1 (July/Aug. 1980)-. Periodical. English. mo (except July and Aug.). $40.00 (one year), $65.00 (two year) individuals; $65.00 (one year), $105.00 (two year) institutions. National League for Nursing, 350 Hudson Street, New York NY 10014. **Tel** (212)989-9393, (800)669-1656. **ED** Laura Clark. **LC** RT1; .N763. **DD** 610.73/05. **NLM** W1 NU5853. Index available in last issue of volume--attached. cum. index. **Bk Rev. Ad Acc. Pr Rev. Circ:** 20,000 (ctrl). available on microfilm and microfiche from University Microfilms International (UMI). ***Continues*** *NLN News.*
**Desc:** Reports on nursing education, management, practice and research, as well as political, social, and economic issues affecting health care.
**Ind/Abst** Cumul. Index Nurs. Allied Health Lit.; Curr. Index J. Educ. (March 1990); Hospit. Health Admin. Index; Int. Nurs. Index; Nurs. Abstr.; Stat. Ref. Index.

US/0740-3992
**NURSING AND HEALTH CARE (SHERMAN OAKS, CALIF.).** (NURSING AND HEALTH CARE.). [Nurs. health care]. Vol. 1, No. 1 (Aug. 1983)-. Periodical. English. mo. $11.00. Crowder-Courtland Publications, 15445 Venture Boulevard, Suite 29, Sherman Oaks CA 91403.
**Ind/Abst** Hospit. Health Admin. Index.

AT/1033-6273
**NURSING AND HEALTH SCIENCE EDUCATION REVIEW.** (19??)-. English. Twice a year (July & Dec.). £60.00 UK; 98.00Aus$ Australia & New Zealand; $120.00 others. James Nicholas Publishers, PO Box 244, Albert Park 3206 Australia. **Tel** 011/61/3/6965545, FAX 011/61/3/6992040. **ED** Rea Zajda. Index available. cum. index. **Bk Rev. Ad Acc. Pr Rev.** ctrl circ.
**Desc:** Concerned with all current trends in nursing and health science education. Focuses on current and innovative health in theory and practice in major areas of nursing and health science education.

US/0892-7669
**NURSING ASSISTANT : OFFICIAL PUBLICATION OF THE AMERICAN ASSOCIATION OF NURSING ASSISTANTS.** [Nurs. assist.]. Began with: Vol. 1, No. 1 (Jan./March 1983). Periodical. English. qt. $17.00. American Association of Nursing Assistants, Circulation Department, 145 East 84th Street, New York NY 10028. **DD** 610. **NLM** W1; NU585F.

CN/1185-3638
**NURSING BC.** [Nurs. BC]. **Added/Corp** Registered Nurse's Association of British Columbia. **VAT** Nursing British Columbia. Vol. 23, No. 1 (Mar. 1991)-. Periodical. English. Five times a year (Jan., Mar., May, Aug., Nov.). 15.00Can$ (individual); 18.00Can$ (one year); 50.00Can$ (corporate). Registered Nurse's Association of British Columbia, 2855 Arbutus Street, Vancouver British Columbia V6J 3Y8 Canada. **Tel** (604)736-7331, FAX (604)738-2272. **ED** Bruce Wells. **DD** 610.73. **NLM** W1; NU5858. **Bk Rev**, (Qty: 3-5). **Ad Acc, Adv Mgr:** Doug Davison, **Tel** (604)688-6819. **Circ:** 36,000 (ctrl). ***Continues*** *Registered Nurse's Association of British Columbia. RNABC News, 0048-7104.*
**Desc:** Primarily professional nursing issues and health issues of interest to nurses in British Columbia.
**Ind/Abst** Cumul. Index Nurs. Allied Health Lit.; Int. Nurs. Index (1991-).

US/0885-7091
**NURSING BUSINESS NEWS.** ***Ceased.*** **See** Business.

US/0192-2394
**NURSING CAREER DIRECTORY.** [Nurs. career dir.]. (1979)-. English. an. $2.00. Customer Service, 132 Welsh Road, Horsham PA 19044. **LC** RT82; .N86. **DD** 610.73/02473. **NLM** WY 22 AA1 N9.

US/0029-6465
**NURSING CLINICS OF NORTH AMERICA, THE.** [Nurs. clin. North Am.]. Vol. 1, No. 1 (March 1966)-. Periodical. English. qt. $57.00 (individual), $77.00 (institutions) US; $87.00 (individual), $91.00 (institution), other. W.B. Saunders Company, A Subsidiary of Harcourt Brace Jovanovich, Inc., The Curtis Center/Suite 300, Independence Square West, Philadelphia PA 19106-3399. **Tel** (215)238-7800 or, 5587, FAX (215)238-7883, telex 173146. **(Subscription address:** W. B. Saunders Company / North America Subscriptions, c/o Periodicals, 6277 Sea Harbour Drive, 4th Floor, Orlando FL 32887.**) ED** Carole Wolfe. **LC** RT1; .N77. **DD** 610.73/05. **NLM** W1 NU587G. **CODEN** NCNAAK. **[CCC].** Index available. **Pr Rev. Circ:** 6,200. available on microfilm and microfiche from University Microfilms International (UMI). Documents available from The Genuine Article, CASDDS.
**Desc:** Practical updates for the clinician on the latest advances plus topics of current interest.
**Ind/Abst** Abr. Index Med.; Chem. Abstr.; Cumul. Index Nurs. Allied Health Lit.; Curr. Contents Soc. Behav. Sci.; EMBASE; Energy Res. Abstr. (1975-); Index Med.; Int. Nurs. Index; Nurs. Abstr.; Life Sci. Collect.; Physic. Medline Plus; Res. Alert [Full Cov.]; Soc. Sci. Cit. Index [Full Cov.]; SportSearch.

US/0894-3656
**NURSING DATA REVIEW.** [Nurs. data rev.]. **Added/Corp** National League for Nursing. Division of Public Policy and Research. National League for Nursing. Division of Research. (1985)-. English. an. $33.95 members; $37.95 nonmembers. National League for Nursing, 350 Hudson Street, New York NY 10014. **Tel** (212)989-9393, (800)669-1656. **LC** RT79; .N58. **DD** 610.73/07/1173021. **NLM** WY 18.3; N101. ***Continues in part*** *NLN Nursing Data Book, 0748-5573.*
**Desc:** Compiles all the data from the Annual Survey of Nursing Education Programs and the Biennial Nurse

Faculty Census. Provides complete statistics on faculty and students in practical and vocational nursing programs. Covers RN, LPN/LVN, and graduate nursing programs - includes over 200 tables, figures, and maps, providing national, regional, and state indices on the nursing profession.

US
**NURSING DATASOURCE : A RESEARCH REPORT.** **Added/Corp** National League for Nursing. Division of Research. **VFOAT** Nursing Data Source. (1990)-. English. Three times a year. $31.50 members; $35.00 nonmembers. National League for Nursing, 350 Hudson Street, New York NY 10014. **Tel** (212)989-9393, (800)669-1656. **LC** RT79; .N93. **NLM** WY 18; N9736.
**Desc:** A comprehensive analysis of nursing education based on NLN's Annual Survey of Nursing Education Programs. Devoted to contemporary nursing education, graduate education, and practical/vocational nursing, respectively. Includes graphs, tables, and summaries.

●US/1066-6184
**NURSING DEPARTMENT COMPENSATION REPORT.** [Nurs. dep. compens. rep.]. **Added/Corp** Hospital & Healthcare Compensation Service. (1993)-. English. an (Published in November). $195.00. Hospital & Healthcare Compensation Service, PO Box 376, 69 Minnehaha Blvd., Oakland NJ 07436. **Tel** (201)405-0075, FAX (201)405-1258. **DD** 331.
**Desc:** Covers salary data on nursing positions in hospitals, home care, and nursing homes.

US/1046-7459
**NURSING DIAGNOSIS.** (NURSING DIAGNOSIS : ND : THE OFFICIAL JOURNAL OF THE NORTH AMERICAN NURSING DIAGNOSIS ASSOCIATION.). [Nurs. diagn.]. **Added/Corp** North American Nursing Diagnosis Association. **VFOAT** ND. Vol. 1, No. 1 (Jan./March 1990)-. Periodical. English. qt (4 issues). $72.00 (institutions), $42.00 (individuals) US; $84.00 (institutions), $54.00 (individuals) other. NURSECOM Inc., 1211 Locust Street, Philadelphia PA 19107. **Tel** (215)545-7222, (800)242-6757, FAX (215)545-8107. **LC** RT48.6; .N8. **DD** 610. **NLM** W1; NU587JL. **[CCC].** cum. index. **Pr Rev.** ***Continues*** *Nursing Diagnosis Newsletter, 0890-7188.*
**Desc:** The official publication of the North American Nursing Diagnosis Association.
**Ind/Abst** Cumul. Index Nurs. Allied Health Lit.; Health Plan. Adminis.; Int. Nurs. Index (1990-).

US/0890-7188
**NURSING DIAGNOSIS NEWSLETTER.** ***Title Change.*** [Nurs. diagn. newsl.]. **Added/Corp** National Group for Classification of Nursing Diagnosis. North American Nursing Diagnosis Association. (197?)-. Newsletter. English. qt. North American Nursing Diagnosis Association, St. Louis University, Department of Nursing, St Louis MO 63104. **Tel** (314)577-8954 ext 675. **DD** 610; 610. ***Continued by*** *Nursing Diagnosis, 1046-7459.*

US/0731-5961
**NURSING DIMENSIONS EDUCATION SERIES.** [Nurs. dimens. educ. ser.]. Began with: Vol. 1, No. 1. Monographic series. English. qt. Price varies per volume. Nursing Resources Inc, 12 Lakeside Park/607 North Avenue, Wakefield MA 01880. **NLM** W1 NU587R.

US/0273-320X
**NURSING ... DRUG HANDBOOK.** [Nurs. drug. handb.]. **VFOAT** Drug Handbook. (1981)-. English (French). an (Oct.). $29.45. Springhouse Direct, PO Box 908, Trade & Technical Department, Springhouse PA 19477. **Tel** (215)646-8700 or, 800 666-5597, FAX (215)646-8716. **LC** RM301.12; .N87. **DD** 615/.1. **NLM** QV 39; N9735. ***Continues*** *Nurse's Guide to Drugs.*

US/0746-1739
**NURSING ECONOMIC$.** (NURSING ECONOMIC$.). [Nurs. econ.]. **VFOAT** Nursing Economics. Vol. 1, No. 1 (July/Aug. 1983)-. Periodical. English. bm (6 issues). $45.00 (institutional), $30.00 (individual) US; $58.00 (institutional), $43.00 (individual) other. A.J. Jannetti Inc., East Holly Avenue, Box 56, Pitman NJ 08071-0056. **Tel** (609)256-2300, FAX (609)589-7463. **ED** Karen Mitchell. **NLM** W1; NU588. **[CCC]. Bk Rev. Ad Acc. Pr Rev. Circ:** 7,000 (ctrl).
**Desc:** Journal for nurse executives regarding practical approaches to nursing economics.
**Ind/Abst** Cumul. Index Nurs. Allied Health Lit.; Int. Nurs. Index; Nurs. Abstr.; Nurs. Allied Health Index.

SP/0212-5382
**NURSING. EDICION ESPANOLA.** [Nursing, Ed. esp.]. **VFOAT** Nursing. Edicion en Espanol. (1983)-. Periodical. Spanish. Ten times a year. $63.00. Ediciones Doyma SA, Travesera de Gracia 17 21, 08021 Barcelona Spain. **Tel** 011 34 3 2000711, 011 34 3 4145706, FAX 011 34 3 2091136, telex 51964 INK E. **UDC** 614.253.5.

US
**NURSING EDUCATION VIDEO NEWSLETTER.** Vol. 1, No. 1 (Apr. 1990)-. Newsletter. English. **NLM** W1; NU5953.

US/0893-1356
**NURSING EDUCATORS MICROWORLD.** [Nurs. educ. microworld]. **VFOAT** Microworld. Vol. 1 (1987)-. Periodical. English. bm. $37.00 (one year), $67.00 (two year) nurse educators; $74.00 (one year), $127.00 (two year) other, US; $47.00 (one year), $87.00 (two year) nurse educators; $83.00 (one year), $145.00 (two year) other, Canada; $83.00 (1 year), $165.00 (2 year) other, other. Nursing Educators Microworld, 13740 Harleigh Court, Saratoga CA 95070. **Tel** (408)741-0156, FAX (408)741-5987. **ED** Christine Bolwell. **LC** RT50.5; .N865. **DD** 610. **NLM** W1; NU5954. Index available. **Circ:** 1,000. ***Continues*** *Nurse Educator's Microworld, 0889-3632.*
**Desc:** For academic and hospital-based nursing educators using or planning to use microcomputers. News, collegial opinions and experiences, networking.
**Ind/Abst** Cumul. Index Nurs. Allied Health Lit.; Int. Nurs. Index (Apr.-May 1988-).

●UK/0969-7330
**NURSING ETHICS.** (1994/95)-. English. qt. $110.00 (institution), $52.00 (individual) North America; £70.00 (institution), £29.50 (individual) Europe; £75.00 (institution), £32.00 (individual) other. Edward Arnold, 338 Euston Road, London NW1 3BH England. **Tel** 011 44 71 873 6000, FAX 011 44 071 873 6325. **(Subscription address:** Turpin Distribution Services Limited, Blackhorse Road, Letchworth, Hertfordshire SG6 1HN, United Kingdom.**) ED** Verena Tschudin.
**Desc:** Emphasizes ethics and law in relation to actual everyday practice and professional development. Includes studies concerning ethical and legal issues, conceptual analysis of modes of thought in health care, comparative and cross-cultural studies, ethics in the nursing curriculum, and analyses of official documents and codes of conduct.
**Ind/Abst** Appl. Soc. Sci. Index Abstr. (19??-); Cumul. Index Nurs. Allied Health Lit. (19??-).

US
**NURSING EXAMINATION REVIEW BOOK.** (1964)-. English. ir. Medical Exam Publishing Company, 52 Vanderbilt Avenue Elsevier, New York NY 10017-3808. **Tel** (212)463-1052.

US/8756-7598
**NURSING EXECUTIVE (HOSPITAL ED.).** ***Ceased.*** (NURSING EXECUTIVE.). [Nurs. exec.]. Vol. 1, No. 1 (May 1985)-?. Periodical. English. mo. Springhouse Corporation, 1111 Bethlehem Pike, Springhouse PA 19477. **Tel** (215)646-8700. **ED** William J Moran. **DD** 610. **Bk Rev.**
**Desc:** News and information that helps nurse executives contain health care costs, improve productivity, and add revenues.

US/0029-6473
**NURSING FORUM (HILLSDALE).** (NURSING FORUM.). Vol. 1 (Winter 1961/1962)-. Academic Scholarly Publication. English. qt. $52.00 (institutions), $40.00 (individuals) US; $64.00 (institutions), $52.00 (individuals) other. NURSECOM Inc., 1211 Locust Street, Philadelphia PA 19107. **Tel** (215)545-7222, (800)242-6757, FAX (215)545-8107. **ED** Phyllis Kritek, RN, PhD. **LC** RT1; .N78. **NLM** W1 NU597. **CODEN** NUFOA. **Bk Rev,** (Qty: 12). **Ad Acc, Adv Mgr:** Joseph M Braden. **Pr Rev. Circ:** 1776. available on an online database, CD-ROM, magnetic tape, and microfilm from University Microfilms International (UMI).
**Desc:** Offers an open discussion of the philosophies, theories and scientific endeavors that shape and change the discipline of contemporary nursing. Provided are a diverse array of articles designed to stimulate thinking and increase knowledge about nursing practice, nursing scholarship and the contexts of nursing. These may be philosophical, theoretical, practical or empirical in character.
**Ind/Abst** Cumul. Index Nurs. Allied Health Lit.; EMBASE; Index Med.; Int. Nurs. Index.

●US/1062-8061
**NURSING HISTORY REVIEW.** (1993)-. English. an (Nov. or Dec.). $75.00 Comes with American Assoication for the History of Nursing membership. American Association for the History of Nursing, PO Box 90803, Washington DC 20090. **Tel** (202)543-2127. **(Subscription address:** AAHN, PO Box 90803, Washington DC 20090.**) ED** Joan E. Lynaugh (editor's address: Center for the Study of the History of Nursing, University of Pennsylvania School of Nursing, 307 Nursing Education Building, Philadelphia, PA 19104-6096). **NLM** W1; NU597L. **Pr Rev.**
**Ind/Abst** Soc. Sci. Cit. Index [Full Cov.].

US/1040-2373
**NURSING ... I.V. DRUG HANDBOOK.** [Nurs. I.V. drug handb.]. **VFOAT** Nursing IV Drug Handbook. **VAT** Nursing Intravenous Drug Handbook. (1989)-. English. an. $26.95. Springhouse Direct, PO Box 908, Trade & Technical Department, Springhouse PA 19477. **Tel** (215)646-8700 or, 800 666-5597, FAX (215)646-8716. **DD** 615. **NLM** QV 39; N9745.

AT/1320-7881
**NURSING INQUIRY.** (19??)-. Academic Scholarly Publication. English. Four times a year. 175.00Aus$ Australia; $165.00 other. Blackwell Scientific Publications Australia, 54 University Street, PO Box 378, Carlton Victoria 3053 Australia. **Tel** 011 61 3 3470300, FAX 011 61 3 3475001, telex 10716421.

US
**NURSING JOB GUIDE.** **VFOAT** Guide issue, Nursingworld Journal; Nursingworld Journal Nursing Job Guide to Over 7,000 U.S. Hospitals. (1984)-. English. an. $75.00 US; $85.00 other. Prime National Publishing Corporation, 470 Boston Post Road, Weston MA 02193. **Tel** (617)899-2702. ***Continues*** *Nursing Job News Nursing Job Guide to over 7,000 Hospitals.*

II/0029-6503
**NURSING JOURNAL OF INDIA.** [Nurs. j. India]. **Added/Corp** Trained Nurses' Association of India. (1912)-. Periodical. English. mo. $15.00. Trained Nurses Association, L-17 Green Park, New Delhi 110016 India. **Tel** 666665. **(Subscription address:** Prints India, 11 Darya Ganj, New Delhi 110002 India.**) ED** Narender Nagpal. **LC** RT13. **NLM** W1 NU632. Index available. cum. index. **Bk Rev. Ad Acc. Circ:** 30,000 (ctrl). available on microfilm and microfiche from University Microfilms International (UMI).
**Desc:** The organ of the Trained Nurses Association of India, educates nurses and mothers who form its largest readership. It is popular in the nursing and medical profession.
**Ind/Abst** Cumul. Index Nurs. Allied Health Lit.; Int. Nurs. Index.

US/0738-8292
**NURSING JOURNALS INDEX, THE.** [Nurs. j. index]. Vol 1, No. 1-. English. ir. Thomason Publishing Company, PO Box 121225, Nashville TN 37212. **ED** Alice R Thomason. **LC** Z6675.N7; N867; RT41. **DD** 016.61073.

UK
**NURSING MANAGEMENT.** (19??)-. English. Ten times a year. £40.00 UK and Europe; £60.00 other. Royal College of Nursing, Department A Glynteg House, STA House, Ely Cardiff CF5 4XG England. **Tel** 011 44 71 222 553411. ***Continues*** *Senior Nurse, 0265-9999.*

US/0744-6314
**NURSING MANAGEMENT.** [Nurs. manage.]. Vol. 12, No. 9 (Sept. 1981)-. Periodical. English. mo. $47.00 hospitals and libraries. Springhouse Corporation, 1111 Bethlehem Pike, Springhouse PA 19477. **Tel** (215)646-8700. **NLM** W1 NU641N. **[CCC].** available on microfilm and microfiche from University Microfilms International (UMI); available on an online database (file 15/Full-Text) from DIALOG. Documents available from UMI Article Clearinghouse. ***Continues*** *Supervisor Nurse, 0039-5870.*
**Desc:** Covers administrative/managerial articles directed to: nursing services in health care facilities, costing nursing services, marketing health care, legal trends and professional issues.
**Ind/Abst** ABI/INFORM Glob. Ed.; ABI Inform Ondisc (Dec. 1987-); Abstr. Res. Pastor. Care Couns.; Cumul. Index Nurs. Allied Health Lit.; Hospit. Health Admin. Index; Hospit. Manage. Rev. (19??-); Int. Nurs. Index; Nurs. Abstr.; Physic. Medline Plus.

US/0272-9512
**NURSING MATTERS.** [Nurs. matters]. Vol. 1 (Nov. 1980)-. Periodical. English. Twelve times a year. $25.00. Sagittarius Communications Inc., 6117 Monona Drive, Monona WI 53716. **Tel** (608)221-8879. **ED** Sheila Farrell. **Bk Rev. Ad Acc, Adv Mgr:** Kaye Lillesand.

UK
**NURSING MIRROR INCORPORATING MIDWIVES JOURNAL & QUEENS NURSING JOURNAL.** Vol. 144, No. 26 (June 30, 1977)-. Periodical. English. wk. Reed Business Publishing / West Sussex, England, Perrymount Road, Haywards Heath, West Sussex RH16 3DH England. **Tel** 011 44 81 6523500. ***Continues*** *Nursing Mirror Incorporating Midwives Journal.*

CN/0710-6157
**NURSING MONTREAL.** [Nurs. Montr.]. Vol. 1, No. 1 (June 76)-. Periodical. English (French). Three times a year. 5.00Can$ Canada; $7.00 US. Corporation of Nurses of the Montreal District, Suite 1004/666 Sherbrooke Street West, Montreal Quebec H3A 1E7 Canada. **Tel** 288-5388. **DD** 610.73/06/0714281. **NLM** W1 NU642F. **Circ:** 17,000 (ctrl).
**Desc:** Informs our membership of what its corporation does for them, how it helps its members and informs them of conferences.
**Ind/Abst** Cumul. Index Nurs. Allied Health Lit.; Int. Nurs. Index.

●NZ/1172-1979
**NURSING NEW ZEALAND.** **Added/Corp** New Zealand Nurses Organisation. Vol. 1, No. 1 (Apr. 1993)-. Periodical. English. Eleven times a year (Dec./Jan. issues combined). $50.00. New Zealand Nurse Organization, PO Box 2128, Wellington New Zealand. **Tel** 011 64 4 3850847, FAX 011 64 4 3829993. **ED** Teresa O'Connor and Kathy Stodent. **NLM** W1; NU642J. **Ad Acc.** ctrl circ. ***Formed by the union of*** *New Zealand Nursing Journal, 0028-8535* ***and*** *NZNU News.*

US
## NURSING OPPORTUNITIES. *Title Change.*
**Added/Corp** Medical Economics Company. **VFOAT** RN Presents Nursing Opportunities; RN Nursing Opportunities. (19??)-(19??). Periodical. English. an. Medical Economics Data, Five Paragon Drive, PO Box 27, Montvale NJ 07645. **Tel** (800)442-6657, (201)358-7200. **NLM** WY 22 AA1 N21. ***Continued by** RN Nursing Opportunities.*

US/0029-6554
## NURSING OUTLOOK. [Nurs. outl.]. **Added/Corp**
National League for Nursing. Vol. 1 (Jan. 1953)-. Academic Scholarly Publication. English. bm. $48.00 (institutions), $34.00 (individuals) US; $59.00 (institutions), $45.00 (individuals) other. Mosby Year Book Inc., 11830 Westline Industrial Drive, St Louis MO 63146. **Tel** (800)325-4177, (314)872-8370, FAX (314)432-1380, telex 44-2402. **LC** RT1; .N273. **DD** 610.7305. **NLM** W1 NU655. **[CCC]**. cum. index. **Bk Rev**. **Ad Acc**. **Pr Rev**. **Circ:** 17,000. available on microfilm and microfiche from University Microfilms International (UMI). Documents available from The Genuine Article. ***Supersedes** Public Health Nursing.*
**Desc:** Focuses on issues and trends vital to key nurses in public health, education and and administration.
**Ind/Abst** Abr. Index Med.; Appl. Soc. Sci. Index Abstr.; Cumul. Index Nurs. Allied Health Lit.; Curr. Contents Soc. Behav. Sci.; Curr. Index J. Educ.; EMBASE; Hum. Resour. Abstr. (?-?); Index Med.; Int. Nurs. Index; Int. Pharm. Abstr.; Med. Rev. Dig.; Nurs. Abstr.; Physic. Medline Plus; Res. Alert [Full Cov.]; Saf. Health Work; Soc. Sci. Cit. Index [Full Cov.]; Soc. Work Abstr. [Select. Cov.].

UK/0142-0372
## NURSING (OXFORD). *Title Change.*
(NURSING.). [Nursing]. 1st Series (Apr. 1979)-Vol. 5, No. 7 (Apr. 9/22, 1992). Periodical. English. mo. Mark Allen Publishing Limited, Robjohns Farm, Vicarage Road, Finchingfield CM7 4LJ England. **Tel** 11 44 371 810433. **ED** Scilla Erskine. **NLM** W1 NU584D. **[CCC]**. **Bk Rev**. **Ad Acc**. **Circ:** 20,000. available on microfilm and microfiche from University Microfilms International (UMI). ***Continued by** British Journal of Nursing (London, England : 1992).*
**Desc:** Add-on clinical nursing text.
**Ind/Abst** Cumul. Index Nurs. Allied Health Lit.; Health Period. Database; Health Ref. Cent. (Jan. 1989-) [Full Cov.]; Int. Nurs. Index.

CN/0828-4660
## NURSING PRACTICE. [Nurs. pract.]. Vol. 1, No.
1 (June 1983)-. Periodical. English. qt. Free. Hotel Dieu Hospital Nursing Department, 123 Sydenham Street, Kingston Ontario K7L 3H6 Canada. **DD** 610.73/09713/72. ctrl circ.
**Ind/Abst** Cumul. Index Nurs. Allied Health Lit.

NZ/0112-7438
## NURSING PRAXIS IN NEW ZEALAND INC.
(1985)-. Periodical. English. tq (March, July, Nov.). 45.00NZ$ New Zealand; 69.95NZ$ other. Nursing Praxis in New Zealand, 15 Guy Avenue, Palmerstown North New Zealand. **Tel** 64 6 3576344. **NLM** W1; NU657V.
**Ind/Abst** Cumul. Index Nurs. Allied Health Lit.

CN/0229-7345
## NURSING PROGRAMS AND ENTRANCE REQUIREMENTS AT CANADIAN UNIVERSITIES.
(NURSING PROGRAMS AND ENTRANCE REQUIREMENTS AT CANADIAN UNIVERSITIES / CANADIAN NURSES' ASSOCIATION.). **Added/Corp** Canadian Nurses' Association. **VFOAT** Programmes des Sciences Infirmieres et Conditions d'Admission aux Universites du Canada. (1981/1982)-. English (French). an. 10.00Can$ U.S. Canadian Nurses Association, 50 The Driveway, Ottawa Ontario K2P 1E2 Canada. **Tel** (613)237-2133, FAX (613)237-3520. **DD** 610.73/07/1171. ***Formed by the union of** Nursing Programs Offered at Canadian Universities, 0706-3873 **and** Outline of General Academic Entrance Requirements for Basic Programs in Nursing at Canadian Universities, 0708-7683.*
**Desc:** Includes descriptions of the 27 Canadian universities offering programs in nursing.

US/1055-6818
## NURSING QUALITY CONNECTION. [Nurs.
qual. connect.]. **VFOAT** Quality Connection. (July/Aug. 1991)-. Periodical. English. bm. $65.00 (institutions), $49.95 (individuals) US; $70.00 (institutions), $54.95 (individuals) other. Mosby Year Book Inc., 11830 Westline Industrial Drive, St Louis MO 63146. **Tel** (800)325-4177, (314)872-8370, FAX (314)432-1380, telex 44-2402. **DD** 610. **NLM** W1; NU657W.
**Desc:** Designed for nurses involved in quality assurance and improvement in all health care settings. Offers practical tips, strategies, tactics and techniques for improving quality in every aspect of the nursing program.
**Ind/Abst** Int. Nurs. Index (Jul./Aug. 1992-).

CN/0381-6419
## NURSING QUEBEC. *Title Change.* [Nurs. Que.].
Vol. 1, No. 1 (June 1976)-Vol. 13, No. 4 (Aug. 1993). Periodical. English (French). Order of Nurses of Quebec, 4200 Dorchester Street West, Montreal Quebec H3Z 1V4 Canada. **Tel** (514)935-2501 ext.256, FAX (514)935-1799. **ED** G. Chabot. **DD** 610.73/0692/09714. **Ad Acc**. **Circ:** 65,983. ***Supersedes** Order of Nurses of Quebec. Notes et Nouvelles de l'Ordre des Infirmieres et Infirmiers du Qu,ebec, 0319-2636. **Continued by** L'Infirmiere du Quebec.*
**Desc:** Expectations and needs of Quebec nursing population; scope of the nurse's concerns and work; report on health issues; priorities and preoccupations of the Ordre des Infirmieres et Infirmiers du Quebec.
**Ind/Abst** Can. Period. Index (19??-); Int. Nurs. Index; Point Repere (1983-).

US/1051-4341
## NURSING RECRUITMENT & RETENTION.
[Nurs. recruit. retent.]. **VFOAT** Nursing Recruitment and Retention. (1989)-. Periodical. English. mo. $339.00. Business Publishers Inc., 951 Pershing Drive, Silver Spring MD 20910-4464. **Tel** (301)587-6300, (800)274-0122, FAX (301)585-9075. **DD** 610. **NLM** W1; NU659. **[CCC]**.

UK/0141-3899
## NURSING RESEARCH ABSTRACTS.
[Nurs. res. abstr.]. **Added/Corp** Index of Nursing Research. Vol. 1 (1978)-. English. qt. £20.00; £22.56 other Europe; £25.76 other. Department of Health and Social Security Library, PO Box 21, Stanmore, Middlesex HA7 1AY England. **Tel** 011 44 71 9722000, 9728161. **ED** Mrs L Bennett. **NLM** ZWY 100.3 N974. **[CCC]**. cum. index. **Bk Rev**. **Ad Acc**. **Circ:** 800.
**Desc:** Gives details of published and ongoing UK nursing research.

US/0098-0358
## NURSING RESEARCH (BOSTON).
(NURSING RESEARCH.). [Nurs. res.]. Vol. 1 (1975)-. Periodical. English. Little Brown & Company, 34 Beacon Street, Boston MA 02108. **Tel** (617)227-0730, (800)759-0190. **ED** P J Verhonick. **LC** RT81.5; .N86. **DD** 610.73/07/2. **NLM** W1 NU751C.
**Ind/Abst** Curr. Contents Soc. Behav. Sci.; Life Sci. Collect.; PsycINFO (1990-); PsycLit; Soc. Sci. Cit. Index [Full Cov.].

US/0029-6562
## NURSING RESEARCH (NEW YORK).
(NURSING RESEARCH.). [Nurs. res.]. **Added/Corp** Association of Collegiate Schools of Nursing. National League for Nursing. Vol. 1 (June 1952)-. Academic Scholarly Publication. English. bm. $90.00 (institution), $40.00 (individual). American Journal of Nursing Company, 555 West 57th Street, New York NY 10019-2961. **Tel** (212)582-8820, FAX (212)586-5462. **(Subscription address:** Nursing Research, PO Box 58766, Boulder CO 80322-8766.**) ED** Florence S. Downs. **LC** RT1; .N8. **DD** 610.73. **NLM** W1 NU751. **CODEN** NURNA. cum. index. **Bk Rev**. **Ad Acc**. **Pr Rev**. **Circ:** 13,000. available on microfilm and microfiche from University Microfilms International (UMI). Documents available from The Genuine Article.
**Desc:** Results of clinical, educational, administrative, and research studies in nursing by means of articles, letters, news, items, and abstracts.
**Ind/Abst** Annals Behav. Med.; Chicano Index; Cumul. Index Nurs. Allied Health Lit.; EMBASE; Energy Res. Abstr.; Index Med.; Int. Nurs. Index; Int. Pharm. Abstr.; Psychol. Abstr. (1952-); Res. Alert [Full Cov.]; Sci. Cit. Index; SCISEARCH; Soc. Work Abstr. [Select. Cov.]; Spec. Educ. Needs Abstr.; SportSearch; Stud. Women Abstr.

SA/0258-1647
## NURSING RSA. [Nurs. RSA]. **Added/Corp** South
African Nursing Association. **VFOAT** Verpleging RSA; Nursing RSA Verpleging. **VAT** Nursing Republic of South Africa. Vol. 1, No. 1 (Feb. 1986)-. Periodical. English (Afrikaans; summaries and/or abstracts in English). mo. R80.00 South Africa; R95.00 other. Medical Association of South Africa, Private Bag X1, 7430 Pinelands South Africa. **Tel** 011 27 21 5313081, FAX 534126, telex 5-20378 CT. **ED** Lilian Medlen. **NLM** W1; NU756E. Index available. cum. index. **Bk Rev**. **Ad Acc**. **Pr Rev**. **Circ:** 12,000. available on microfiche.
**Desc:** All aspects of South African Nursing and the health care industry in South Africa. Includes articles from abroad and from independent states in Southern Africa.
**Ind/Abst** Cumul. Index Nurs. Allied Health Lit.; Int. Nurs. Index (Feb. 1986-).

US/1056-3091
## NURSING SCAN IN ADMINISTRATION.
***Title Change.*** [Nurs. scan adm.]. Vol. 5, No. 1 (Jan./Feb. 1990)-(199?). Periodical. English. bm. NURSECOM Inc., 1211 Locust Street, Philadelphia PA 19107. **Tel** (215)545-7222, (800)242-6757, FAX (215)545-8107. **ED** Beverly J McElmurry, EdD. **DD** 610. **Pr Rev**. **Circ:** 1955. available on an online database, CD-ROM, magnetic tape, and microfilm from University Microfilms International (UMI). ***Continues** Jona's Nursing Scan in Administration, 0888-6288. **Continued by** AONE's Leadership Prospectives.*
**Desc:** A professional resource journal that contains synopsis and commentary of articles surveyed from nursing, medical and professional periodicals as well as other current sources, that relate to all aspects of nursing administration.

US/0897-5647
## NURSING SCAN IN RESEARCH. [Nurs. scan
res.]. Vol. 1, No. 1 (May/June 1988)-. Periodical. English. bm (6 issues). $63.00 (institutions), $43.00 (individuals) US; $74.00 (institutions), $54.00 (individuals) other. NURSECOM Inc., 1211 Locust Street, Philadelphia PA 19107. **Tel** (215)545-7222, (800)242-6757, FAX (215)545-8107. **ED** Judith Beal, RN, DNSc. **LC** RT81.5; .N8. **DD** 610. **Pr Rev**. **Circ:** 1331. available on magnetic tape, an online database, and CD-ROM from University Microfilms International (UMI); available on microfilm and microfiche from University Microfilms International (UMI).
**Desc:** Abstracts of timely research articles on topics related to nursing practice, with commentary by members of the editorial board. Themes include: patient care intervention; nurse/patient relationships; research from other disciplines; health care delivery systems; professional and organizational dynamics; technology/products; legal/ethical issues; human resources.

US/0894-3184
## NURSING SCIENCE QUARTERLY. [Nurs.
sci. q.]. Vol. 1, No. 1 (Feb. 1988)-. Periodical. English. qt. $70.00 institutions, $50.00 individuals US; $80.00 institutions, $60.00 individuals other. Chestnut House Publications, PO Box 22492, Pittsburgh PA 15222. **Tel** (412)391-8585, FAX (412)391-8458. **DD** 610. **NLM** W1; NU757B. **Pr Rev**.
**Desc:** Unites theory research and practice under one cover. Feature articles on theory development, research studies and theory based practice. Reviews, relevant theory/research books, and reports of theory/research conferences. Includes three regular columns.
**Ind/Abst** Cumul. Index Nurs. Allied Health Lit.; Int. Nurs. Index (Feb. 1988-).

US
## NURSING SPECTRUM. English. sm (24 issues).
Free to registered nurses in Illinois; $39.95 other. Nursing Spectrum, 333 West State Road, Route 176, Island Lake IL 60042. **Tel** (708)526-1919.

●US/1057-8323
## NURSING STAFF DEVELOPMENT INSIDER.
[Nurs. staff dev. insider]. (1992)-. Newsletter. English. bm. $55.00 (institutions), $39.95 (individuals) US; $62.00 (institutions), $46.95 (individuals) Canada; $69.55 (institutions), $54.50 (individuals) other. Mosby Year Book Inc., 11830 Westline Industrial Drive, St Louis MO 63146. **Tel** (800)325-4177, (314)872-8370, FAX (314)432-1380, telex 44-2402. **DD** 610. **NLM** W1; NU758E.
**Desc:** Designed for staff development specialists, clinical/ nurse educators, and nurse managers in all health care settings.
**Ind/Abst** Int. Nurs. Index (Jan.-Feb. 1992-).

UK/0029-6570
## NURSING STANDARD. [Nurs. stand.].
**Added/Corp** Royal College of Nursing (Great Britain). Vol. 1, Issue 1 (Sept. 12, 1987)-. Periodical. English. wk (52 issues per year). £70.00. Database Direct, Junction 8 BC, Rosscliffe Road, Ellesmere Port, South Wirral, L65 3EB England. **Tel** 011 44 51 3572858. **NLM** W1; NU758H. **CODEN** NSTAEU. ***Continues** Nursing Standard, 0029-6570.*

US
## NURSING STUDIES INDEX. **Added/Corp** Yale
University. School of Nursing. (1963)-. English. J.B. Lippincott Company, 227 East Washington Square, Philadelphia PA 19106-3780. **Tel** (215)238-4200 or 4454, FAX (215)238-4227.

US
## NURSING SUBJECT HEADINGS. See
Library and Information Sciences.

UK/0956-8115
## NURSING THE ELDERLY : IN HOSPITAL, HOMES AND THE COMMUNITY.
***Title Change.*** Vol. 1, No. 1 (June 1989)- Vol.4 (1992). Periodical. English. bm. Scutari Projects Ltd / Essex, Robjohns Farm, Vicarage Road, Finchingfield Essex CM7 4LJ England. **Tel** 011 44 371 810433. **NLM** W1; NU759N. ***Continues** Geriatric Nursing and Home Care, 0269-9079. **Merged into** Elderly Care.*
**Ind/Abst** Health Plan. Adminis. (?-?); Int. Nurs. Index (1989-?).

UK/0954-7762
## NURSING TIMES (1987). (NURSING TIMES :
NT.). [Nurs. times]. **VFOAT** NT; Nursing Times/Nursing Mirror; NT, NM. Vol. 83, No. 36 (Sept. 1987)-. Periodical. English. wk (published on Wed.; last two weeks in Dec. combined). £58.00 UK; $164.00 US & Canada; £88.00 other. Macmillan Magazines Ltd., Houndmills, Basingstoke, Hampshire RG21 2XS England. **Tel** 011 44 256 29242, FAX 011 44 256 812358, telex 858493. Index available (free). ***Continues** Nursing Times, Nursing Mirror, 0269-7289.*

US
## NURSING TIMES [MICROFORM] : NT.
**VFOAT** NT; Nursing Times/Nursing Mirror; NT, NM. Vol. 83, No. 36 (Sept. 9-15, 1987)-. Periodical. English. ir. University Microfilms International, 300 North Zeeb Road,

Ann Arbor MI 48106-1346. **Tel** (313)761-4700, (800)521-0600 Exts. 2490, 2491, FAX (313)973-1540. available in print. ***Continues** Nursing Times, Nursing Mirror.*

US/0895-2809
**NURSINGCONNECTIONS (WASHINGTON, D.C.).** (NURSINGCONNECTIONS.). [NursingConnections]. **Added/Corp** Washington Hospital Center. Division of Nursing. **VFOAT** Nursing Connections. Vol. 1, No. 1 (Spring 1988)-. Periodical. English. qt (Feb., May, Aug., Nov.). $75.00 (institutions), $58.00 (individuals). Nursingconnections, 110 Irving Street Northwest, Washington DC 20010. **Tel** (202)877-3048, FAX (202)877-6757. **ED** Molly Billingsley. **DD** 610. **NLM** W1; NU7943. **Ad Acc. Pr Rev. Circ:** 1,500.
**Desc:** This publication is committed to promoting collaboration among nurses in practice, education, research and administration.
**Ind/Abst** Cumul. Index Nurs. Allied Health Lit. (1988-); Int. Nurs. Index (Vol. 1, No. 1, 1988-).

US/0745-8630
**NURSINGWORLD JOURNAL.** [Nursingworld j.]. **VFOAT** Nursing World Journal. (19??)-. Periodical. English. mo. $37.30 US; $41.40 Canada; $76.00 other. Prime National Publishing Corporation, 470 Boston Post Road, Weston MA 02193. **Tel** (617)899-2702. **(Subscription address:** 470 Boston Post Road, Weston, MA 02193) **ED** Randy Gates. **DD** 610. **Bk Rev**, (Qty: 8-12). **Ad Acc, Adv Mgr:** Richard DeVito. **Circ:** 45,000 (ctrl). ***Formed by the union of** Nursing Job News, 0163-223X **and** Nursingworld Digest, 0733-317X.*
**Desc:** Reviews of all nursing literature.

UK/0029-7917
**OCCUPATIONAL HEALTH.** See Industrial Health and Safety.

US/0893-6595
**OFFICE NURSE, THE.** [Off. nurse]. **Added/Corp** American Association of Office Nurses. Vol. 1, No. 1 (April/May 1988)-. Periodical. English. bm. $25.97 US; $31.97 Canada and Mexico; $37.97 other. Medical Economics Publishing, Five Paragon Drive, Second Floor, Montvale NJ 07645. **Tel** (800)432-4570, (201)358-2210. **(Subscription address:** Office Nurse, PO Box 3000, Denville NJ 07834.) **ED** Mary Ann Jones. **DD** 610. **NLM** W1; OF454D. **Ad Acc, Adv Mgr:** Tom Jones, **Tel** (201)391-6306. **Circ:** 75,000 (ctrl).

US/0360-2850
**OFFICIAL DIRECTORY OF REGISTERED NURSES AND LICENSED PRACTICAL NURSES.** Directory. English. National Council of Jewish Women of Canada, Suite 401, 1111 Finch Avenue, Downsview Ontario M3J 2E5. **LC** RT5.N3; A3. **DD** 610.73/025/793. ***Continues** Official Directory of Registered Professional Nurses and Licensed Practical Nurses Holding Licenses Permitting Practice in the State of Nevada.*

US/0030-0993
**OHIO NURSES' REVIEW.** [Ohio nurses' rev.]. **Added/Corp** Ohio Nurses Association. (19??)-. Periodical. English. ir. $15.00 (members); $25.00 (non-members). Ohio Nurses Association, 4000 East Main Street, Colombus OH 43213. **Tel** (614)237-5414. **DD** 610. **NLM** W1 OH418.
**Ind/Abst** Cumul. Index Nurs. Allied Health Lit.; Int. Nurs. Index.

US/0030-1787
**OKLAHOMA NURSE, THE.** [Okla. nurse]. **Added/Corp** Oklahoma Nurses Association. (19??)-. Periodical. English. Four times a year. $16.00. Oklahoma Nurses Association, 6414 North Santa Fe, Suite A, Oklahoma City OK 73116. **Tel** (405)840-3476. **ED** Frances I. Waddle. **NLM** W1 OK615. **Ad Acc. Circ:** 1,200 (ctrl). available in microform from University Microfilms International (UMI).
**Desc:** Professional association for RNs; activities include nursing practice, legislation, nursing education, convention and conferences, focus on nursing leaders.
**Ind/Abst** Cumul. Index Nurs. Allied Health Lit.; Int. Nurs. Index.

SW/0280-4123
**OMVARDAREN.** [Omvardaren]. 1/82-. Periodical. Swedish. ir (5 issues a year). Omvardaren, Gamla Brogatan 32, S 111 20 Stockholm Sweden. **NLM** W1; OM98. ***Continues** Tidskrift for Sjukvardspedagoger, 0364-2722.*
**Ind/Abst** Int. Nurs. Index.

US/0190-535X
**ONCOLOGY NURSING FORUM.** [Oncol. nurs. forum]. **Added/Corp** Oncology Nursing Society. Vol. 4, No. 4 (Oct. 1977)-. Periodical. English. Ten times a year. $60.00 (institutions), $42.00 (individuals) US; $75.00 (institutions), $57.00 (individuals) other. Oncology Nursing Society, 501 Holiday Drive, Pittsburgh PA 15220. **Tel** (412)921-7373, FAX (412)921-6565. **(Subscription address:** Oncology Nursing Press Inc., Dept. 8847, Pittsburgh, PA 15278; telephone: (412)921-7373) **ED** Susan B. Baird. **NLM** W1 ON107N. Index available. cum. index. **Bk Rev. Ad Acc. Pr Rev. Circ:** 18,000 (ctrl). available on microfilm and microfiche from University Microfilms International (UMI). ***Continues** Oncology Nursing Society Newsletter.*
**Desc:** Its mission is to convey news related to developments in practice, technology, and research to promote a positive image of professional specialized nursing, print timely papers, and stimulate nursing issues in oncology.
**Ind/Abst** Chicano Index; Cumul. Index Nurs. Allied Health Lit.; Index Med. (July-Aug. 1990-); Int. Nurs. Index (Oct. 1977-); Nurs. Abstr.

US/0890-5215
**ONS NEWS.** (ONS NEWS / ONCOLOGY NURSING SOCIETY.). [ONS news]. **Added/Corp** Oncology Nursing Society. **VAT** Oncology Nursing Society news. Vol. 1, No. 1 (Aug. 1986)-. Periodical. English. Twelve times a year. $7.00. Oncology Nursing Society, 501 Holiday Drive, Pittsburgh PA 15220. **Tel** (412)921-7373, FAX (412)921-6565. **DD** 610. **NLM** W1; ON366L.
**Ind/Abst** Int. Nurs. Index (Oct. 1988-).

●US/1062-5720
**ONS NURSING SCAN IN ONCOLOGY.** [ONS nurs. scan oncol.]. **Added/Corp** Oncology Nursing Society. **VFOAT** Nursing Scan in Oncology. **VAT** Oncology Nursing Society Nursing Scan in Oncology. Vol. 1, No. 1 (May/June 1992)-. Periodical. English. bm (6 issues). $63.00 (institutions), $43.00 (individuals) US; $74.00 (institutions), $54.00 (individuals) other. NURSECOM Inc., 1211 Locust Street, Philadelphia PA 19107. **Tel** (215)545-7222, (800)242-6757, FAX (215)545-8107. **ED** Karen Hasey Dow, (editor's phone: (617)492-8633). **DD** 616. **NLM** ZWY 156; O59. **Pr Rev. Circ:** 1735. available on an online database, CD-ROM, magnetic tape, and microfilm from University Microfilms International (UMI).
**Desc:** A professional resource journal containing synopsis and commentary of articles surveyed from nursing, medical and professional periodicals as well as other current sources that relate to all aspects of oncology nursing. The abstracts are annotated with remarks and opinion by nurses known and respected for their involvement in the field of oncology.

US/8756-8047
**OR MANAGER.** [OR manager]. Vol. 1, No. 1 (April 1985)-. Periodical. English. Twelve times a year. $68.00 US; $74.00 Canada; $78.00 others. OR Manager Inc, PO Box 17487, Boulder CO 80308-7487. **Tel** (303)442-1661, FAX (303)442-5960. **ED** Patricia Patterson. **NLM** W1; O524H. **[CCC].** Index available (Bound in Dec. iss.). **Bk Rev. Ad Acc, Adv Mgr:** John Schmes, **Tel** (609)589-2319. **Circ:** 3,000.
**Desc:** News and information relating to management of the surgical suite. Topics include finance, personnel, equipment and supplies, standards and regulations and technology.
**Ind/Abst** Cumul. Index Nurs. Allied Health Lit.; Health Plan. Adminis.; Hospit. Health Admin. Index (1986-).

US/0030-4751
**OREGON NURSE.** [Or. nurse]. **Added/Corp** Oregon Nurses Association. Oregon State Nurses' Association. Vol. 1 (1931)-. Periodical. English. Four times a year (Feb., June, Sept., Dec.). $16.00. Oregon Nurses Association, 9600 Southwest Oak Street, Suite 550, Portland OR 97223-6588. **Tel** (503)293-0011, FAX (503)293-0013. **ED** Sandra Marron. **LC** RT1; .O7. **DD** 610. **NLM** W1 OR531. **Ad Acc, Adv Mgr:** Cathi, **Tel** (503)293-0011. **Circ:** 4,800 (ctrl).
**Desc:** News and information about and for registered nurses in Oregon. Includes educational offerings and reports.
**Ind/Abst** Cumul. Index Nurs. Allied Health Lit.; Int. Nurs. Index.

US/0744-6020
**ORTHOPEDIC NURSING / NATIONAL ASSOCIATION OF ORTHOPEDIC NURSES.** See Medical Science and Technology-Orthopedics.

CN/0829-5131
**OSMOSE (MONTREAL).** (OSMOSE / ASSOCIATION DES INFIRMIERES ET INFIRMIERS EN SANTE DU TRAVAIL DU QUEBEC.). [Osmose]. **Added/Corp** Association des Infirmieres et Infirmiers en Sante du Travail du Quebec. Vol. 6, No. 1 (March 1985)-. Periodical. French. Four times a year (Seasonally). 38.50Can$. Association des Infirmieres et Infirmiers en Sante du Travail du Quebec, CP 160, Succursale Delorimier, Montreal Quebec H2H 2N6 Canada. **Tel** (514)526-2733, FAX (514)528-6298. **DD** 610.73/06/9209714. Index available. cum. index. **Ad Acc. Pr Rev. Circ:** 1,000 (ctrl). ***Continues** Association des Infirmieres et Infirmiers en Sante du Travail du Quebec. A. I. I. S. T. Q., 0708-2347.*
**Desc:** Scientific articles and up-to-date information in occupational health.

UK
**PAEDIATRIC NURSING.** Vol. 1, No. 1 (Mar. 1989)-. Periodical. English. Ten times a year. £25.00 UK & Europe; £50.00 other. Royal College of Nursing, Department A Glynteg House, STA House, Ely Cardiff CF5 4XG England. **Tel** 011 44 71 222 553411. **ED** Rosemary Rogers. **NLM** W1; PA263M. **Ad Acc.**
**Desc:** This journal aimed specifically at nurses working with children, covers all issues related to the treatment and care of children.

US/0730-5524
**PATIENT CARE LAW.** See Law.

US/0097-9805
**PEDIATRIC NURSING.** [Pediatr. nursing]. **Added/Corp** National Association of Pediatric Nurse Associates and Practitioners. Vol. 1 (Jan./Feb. 1975)-. Periodical. English. bm. $28.00 (institutions), $21.00 (individuals) US; $41.00 (institutions), $34.00 (individuals) other. A.J. Jannetti Inc., East Holly Avenue, Box 56, Pitman NJ 08071-0056. **Tel** (609)256-2300, FAX (609)589-7463. **ED** Veronica D. Feeg, Gus A. Ostrum. **LC** RJ245; .P4. **DD** 610.73/62/05. **NLM** W1 PE169D. **[CCC].** Index available. **Bk Rev. Ad Acc. Pr Rev. Circ:** 12,000. available on microfilm and microfiche from University Microfilms International (UMI).
**Desc:** Provides current information on practice, policy, and research for pediatric nurses. Emphasis is placed on the changing role of the pediatric nurse practitioner/clinical specialist.
**Ind/Abst** Cumul. Index Nurs. Allied Health Lit.; Index Dent. Lit.; Int. Nurs. Index; Nurs. Abstr.; Physic. Medline Plus.

US/0097-9805
**PEDIATRIC NURSING [MICROFORM].** **Added/Corp** National Association of Pediatric Nurse Associates and Practitioners. Vol. 1 (Jan./Feb. 1975)-. Periodical. English. ir. University Microfilms International, 300 North Zeeb Road, Ann Arbor MI 48106-1346. **Tel** (313)761-4700, (800)521-0600 Exts. 2490, 2491, FAX (313)973-1540. **[CCC]. Pr Rev.** available in print.

US/0031-4161
**PELICAN NEWS.** [Pelican news]. **Added/Corp** Louisiana State Nurses Association. (1933)-. Periodical. English. Six times a year. $20.00. Louisiana State Nurses Association, 712 Transcontinental Drive, Metairie LA 70001. **DD** 610. **NLM** W1 PE255.
**Ind/Abst** Cumul. Index Nurs. Allied Health Lit.; Int. Nurs. Index.

US/0031-4617
**PENNSYLVANIA NURSE, THE.** [Pa. nurse]. **Added/Corp** Pennsylvania Nurses Association. Pennsylvania State Nurses' Association. Vol. 1 (1946)-. Periodical. English. mo (11 issues - Nov./Dec. combined issue). $15.00. Pennsylvania Nurses Association, PO Box 68525, Jackie Mullen, Harrisburg PA 17106. **Tel** (717)657-1222, FAX (717)657-3796. **ED** Christine E. Finnegan, APR. **NLM** W1 PE411. **Bk Rev**, (Qty: varies). **Ad Acc. Circ:** 9,200 (ctrl).
**Desc:** Official publication of the nursing organization in Pennsylvania. News, features of interest to nurses, especially members.
**Ind/Abst** Cumul. Index Nurs. Allied Health Lit.; Int. Nurs. Index.

CN/0710-2437
**PERIODICAL HOLDINGS / HELEN K. MUSSALLEM LIBRARY, CANADIAN NURSES ASSOCIATION.** [Period. hold. - Helen K. Mussallem Libr., Can. Nurses Assoc.]. **Main/Corp** Helen K. Mussallem Library. **VFOAT** Liste des Periodiques. **VAT** Liste des Periodiques - Bibliotheque Helen K. Mussallem. Association des Infirmieres et Infirmiers du Canada. (June 1981)-. English (French). be. 15.00Can$ US. Canadian Nurses Association, 50 The Driveway, Ottawa Ontario K2P 1E2 Canada. **Tel** (613)237-2133, FAX (613)237-3520. **DD** 016.61073/05. ***Continues** Canadian Nurses' Association. Library. Periodical Holdings, 0383-0101.*
**Desc:** List of periodical holdings of the Helen K Mussallem Library of the Canadian Nurses Association.

CN/0831-7445
**PERSPECTIVES - GERONTOLOGICAL NURSING ASSOCIATION.** (PERSPECTIVES.). [Perspect. - Gerontol. Nurs. Assoc.]. **Added/Corp** Gerontological Nursing Association (Canada). (Spring 1977)-. Periodical. English. Four times a year. 29.50Can$ (one year), 55.00Can$ (two years). Gerontological Nursing Association, PO Box 368, Station K, Toronto Ontario M4P 2G7 Canada. **Tel** (416)480-5835, FAX (416)480-5893. **ED** Erin Hughes. **DD** 610.73/65/06071. **NLM** W1; PE8705F. **Bk Rev**, (Qty: 4). **Ad Acc, Adv Mgr:** HLR & Associates, **Tel** (613)623-6975. **Circ:** 1,600.
**Desc:** Contains current information and knowledgeable in gerontological nursing practice.
**Ind/Abst** Cumul. Index Nurs. Allied Health Lit.; Health Plan. Adminis.; Int. Nurs. Index (Vol. 8, No. 1, 1984-).

US/0894-1076
**PERSPECTIVES IN NURSING.** [Perspect. nurs.]. **Added/Corp** National League for Nursing. (1983/1985)-. Proceedings. English. be. $25.95 members; $28.95 nonmembers. National League for Nursing, 350 Hudson Street, New York NY 10014. **Tel** (212)989-9393, (800)669-1656. **LC** RT3; .P47. **DD** 610.73. **NLM** W1; PE871CJ.
**Desc:** Proceedings from the biennial convention of the National League for Nursing.

US/0031-5990
**PERSPECTIVES IN PSYCHIATRIC CARE.** [Perspect. psychiatr. care]. Vol. 1, (Jan./Feb. 1963)-. Academic Scholarly Publication. English. qt. $52.00 (institutions), $40.00 (individuals) US; $64.00 (institutions), $52.00 (individuals) other. NURSECOM Inc., 1211 Locust Street, Philadelphia PA 19107. **Tel** (215)545-7222, (800)242-6757, FAX (215)545-8107. **ED** Norine J. Kerr, RN, MN. **LC** RC475; .P47. **NLM** W1 PE871E. **CODEN** PEPYA. **Bk Rev**, (Qty: 12). **Ad Acc, Adv Mgr:** Joseph M Braden. **Pr Rev. Circ:** 2580. available on an online database, CD-ROM, magnetic tape, and microfilm from University Microfilms International (UMI).
**Desc:** A continuing education vehicle with a multidisciplinary approach, designed to upgrade the care of the mentally ill by means of selected clinical, educational and research articles directed to psychiatric/mental health nurses and other mental health professionals.
**Ind/Abst** Cumul. Index Nurs. Allied Health Lit.; EMBASE; Index Med. (1964-1989); Int. Nurs. Index; Psychol. Abstr. (1972-); PsycINFO; PsycLit.

US/1057-1639
**PERSPECTIVES ON ADDICTIONS NURSING.** [Perspect. addict. nurs.]. **Added/Corp** National Nurses Society on Addictions (U.S.). (Apr. 1990)-. Periodical. English. Four times a year (Mar., June, Sept., Dec.). $20.00. National Nurses Society on Addictions, 5700 old Orchard Road, First Floor, Skokie IL 60077. **ED** Christine Vouvakis (phone: (708)966-5010). **DD** 610. **NLM** W1; PE872C. **Bk Rev**, (Qty: 8-16). **Ad Acc, Adv Mgr:** Kathy Checea, **Tel** (708)966-5010. ***Continues** NNSA news.*
**Desc:** Considerable hospital resources, including nursing staff resources, are necessary to manage the care of patients who are in severe withdrawal from alcohol and or other central nervous system depressants.

US/1060-4243
**PERTINENT LEGISLATION AFFECTING NURSES : PLAN.** **VFOAT** Plan. (1991)-. Periodical. English. mo. $40.00. Pertinent Legislation Affecting Nurses, PO Box 895, Medford MA 02155. **DD** 362. **NLM** W1; PE877.

●US/1073-7820
**PETERSON'S GUIDE TO NURSING PROGRAMS.** [Peterson's guide nurs. programs]. **Added/Corp** Peterson's Guides, Inc. American Association of Colleges of Nursing. **VFOAT** Guide to Nursing Programs; Nursing Programs. (1994)-. English. be. $21.95. Peterson's Guides, 202 Carnegie Center, Department 2342, Princeton NJ 08543. **Tel** (800)338-3282, FAX (609)452-0966. **DD** 610. **NLM** WY 22; AA1 P4.

SZ
**PFLEGE.** Vol. 1, No. 1 (April 1988)-. Periodical. German. Four times a year. 84.00F. Verlag Hans Huber Ag Bern, Laenggass Strasse 76, CH 3000 Bern 9 Switzerland. **Tel** 011 41 31 3004500. **NLM** W1; PF472.
**Ind/Abst** Health Plan. Adminis.

●GW/0944-8918
**PFLEGE AKTUELL / DBFK, DEUTSCHER BERUFSVERBAND FUER PFLEGEBERUFE.** (1993)-. German. Eleven times a year. DM69.00. DBFK Verlag, Postfach, D 65746 Eschborn Germany. **Tel** 011 49 6173 65086. ***Continues** Krankenpflege.*

US/0737-8882
**PHARMACOLOGY IN NURSING.** (PHARMACOLOGY IN NURSING / BY ELSIE E. KRUG AND HUGH ALISTER MCGUIGAN.). [Pharmacol. nurs.]. 7th Ed. (1955)-. English. ir. Mosby Year Book Inc., 11830 Westline Industrial Drive, St Louis MO 63146. **Tel** (800)325-4177, (314)872-8370, FAX (314)432-1380, telex 44-2402. **ED** E.E. Krug and B.S. Bergersen. **LC** RM125; .B45. **DD** 615.1. ***Continues** Introduction to Materia Medica and Pharmacology.*

PH/0048-3818
**PHILIPPINE JOURNAL OF NURSING, THE.** [Philipp. j. nurs.]. **Added/Corp** Philippine Nurses Association. Filipino Nurses' Association. Vol. 23, No. 1 (Jan./March 1954)-. Periodical. English. Four times a year (Apr., July, Oct. Dec.). P15.00. Philippine Nurses Association, 1663 F T Benitez Street, Malate Manila Philippines. **Tel** 011 63 2 583092 or 501545. **NLM** W1 PH569. ***Continues** Filipino Nurse.*
**Ind/Abst** Cumul. Index Nurs. Allied Health Lit.; Int. Nurs. Index.

US/0741-5206
**PLASTIC SURGICAL NURSING.** (PLASTIC SURGICAL NURSING : OFFICIAL JOURNAL OF THE AMERICAN SOCIETY OF PLASTIC AND RECONSTRUCTIVE SURGICAL NURSES.). [Plas. surg. nurs.]. **Added/Corp** American Society of Plastic and Reconstructive Surgical Nurses. Vol. 3, No. 1 (Spring 1983)-. Periodical. English. qt. $35.00 (institutions), $28.00 (individuals). A.J. Jannetti Inc., East Holly Avenue, Box 56, Pitman NJ 08071-0056. **Tel** (609)256-2300, FAX (609)589-7463. **NLM** W1; PL118D. **CODEN** PSNUEE. **[CCC]. *Continues*** *Journal of Plastic and Reconstructive Surgical Nursing, 0273-3285.*
**Ind/Abst** Cumul. Index Nurs. Allied Health Lit.; Int. Nurs. Index.

US/0145-8981
**PN. PRACTICAL NURSING CAREER.** ***Suspended.*** (PRACTICAL NURSING CAREER.). **Added/Corp** National League for Nursing. Dept. of Practical Nursing Programs. National League for Nursing. Council of Practical Nursing Programs. Division of Research. (1973/74)-Suspended. English. ir. National League for Nursing, 350 Hudson Street, New York NY 10014. **Tel** (212)989-9393, (800)669-1656. **LC** RT74; .P72. **NLM** WY 22 AA1 P8. ***Continues** Let's be Practical about a Nursing Career.*

US/0098-4345
**POINT OF VIEW (SOMERVILLE).** (POINT OF VIEW.). [Point view]. (196?)-. Periodical. English. Twenty-six times a year. Free. Ethicon Inc., PO Box 151, Sommerville NJ 08876. **NLM** W1 PO18.
**Ind/Abst** Cumul. Index Nurs. Allied Health Lit.

UK/0883-4504
**POLITICAL ISSUES IN NURSING.** [Polit. issues nurs.]. Vol. 1 (1985)-. Monographic series. English. ir. Price varies per volume. Scutari Projects Ltd / Essex, Robjohns Farm, Vicarage Road, Finchingfield Essex CM7 4LJ England. **Tel** 011 44 371 810433. **(Subscription address:** Ishiyaku Euro America, Inc., 716 Hanley Industrial Court, St. Louis MO 63144.**) LC** RT86.5; .P62. **DD** 362.1/73. **NLM** W1; PO241J.

UK/0953-6612
**PRACTICE NURSE.** [Pract. nurse]. (1988)-. Periodical. English. Eleven times a year. £35.00 UK; £57.00 other, except US and Canada. Reed Business Publishing / West Sussex, England, Perrymount Road, Haywards Heath, West Sussex RH16 3DH England. **Tel** 011 44 81 6523500. **ED** Caley Montgomery. **DD** 610.730941. Index available. **Ad Acc. Pr Rev. Circ:** 6,500.
**Desc:** Journal aimed at the nurse working alongside the GP and is an invaluable source of up-to-date information on patient care and management for all those involved in primary care.

UK/0964-9271
**PRACTICE NURSING.** [Pract. nurs.]. (1990)-. Periodical. English. Twenty times a year. £84.00 (institutions), £50.00 (individuals) UK; £110.00 (institutions), £80.00 (individuals) other. Mark Allen Publishing Ltd., Croxped Mews, 288 Croxped Road, London SE24 9DA England. **Tel** 011 44 1 671 7521. **DD** 610.73.

US/0032-6666
**PRAIRIE ROSE, THE.** [Prairie rose]. 1931. Periodical. English. qt (Mar., Jun., Sep., Dec.). $10.00 US, $30.00 other (1 year); $25.00 US, $75.00 other (3 year). North Dakota Nurses Association, 212 North 4th Green Tree Square, Bismarck ND 58501-4005. **Tel** (701)223-1385. **ED** Executive Administrator. **NLM** W1 PR2418. **Ad Acc, Adv Mgr Tel** (319)277-2414. **Circ:** 12,000 (ctrl).
**Desc:** Publication sent to all licensed nurses, student nurses and legislators in North Dakota. Quarterly periodical of the North Dakota Nurses Association. Tab size, 24 pages.
**Ind/Abst** Cumul. Index Nurs. Allied Health Lit.; Int. Nurs. Index.

US/0739-4446
**PRIMARILY NURSING.** ***Title Change.*** (198?)-(19??). Periodical. English. bm. Creative Nursing Management, 614 East Grant Street, Minneapolis MN 55404. **Tel** (612)339-7766, FAX (612)339-2065. **ED** Claire Mantley. **Bk Rev**, (Qty: 45). **Ad Acc, Adv Mgr:** Eric Haukkala, **Tel** (612)339-7766. **Circ:** 2,000. ***Continued by** Creative Nursing.*
**Desc:** Covers all non-clinical aspects of the nursing profession on a national and local scale. Written for nurses of all levels and all settings.

●US/1068-476X
**PRISM (NEW YORK, N.Y., 1993).** (PRISM : THE NLN RESEARCH & POLICY QUARTERLY.). [Prism]. **Added/Corp** National League for Nursing. Division of Research. Vol. 1, No. 1 (Mar. 1993)-. Periodical. English. Four times a year. $45.00 (members), $50.00 (nonmembers) one year; $80.00 (members), $89.00 (nonmembers) two years. National League for Nursing, 350 Hudson Street, New York NY 10014. **Tel** (212)989-9393, (800)669-1656. **DD** 610.
**Desc:** Each volume is dedicated to one newly emerging issue from the nursing and health care arena. Covers topics such as: recruitment and retention; foreign-educated nurses; nursing salaries and compensation; and newly-licensed LPNs/LVNs. Features charts, graphs, articles, and case studies.

US/1044-4025
**PRO NE NATA : PRN.** ***Title Change.*** [Pro re nata]. **VFOAT** PRN. (198?)-(19??). Periodical. English. qt. Utah State Nurses Association, 1058 East 9th South, Salt Lake City UT 84105. **Tel** (801)322-3439. **DD** 610. **NLM** W1; PR511L. ***Continues** One on One, 0270-6628.* ***Continued by** Utah Nurse.*
**Ind/Abst** Cumul. Index Nurs. Allied Health Lit.; Int. Nurs. Index (Nov./Dec. 1986-).

●UK
**PROFESSIONAL NURSE. DRUG UPDATE.** **See** Pharmacy and Pharmacology.

UK/0266-8130
**PROFESSIONAL NURSE (LONDON, ENGLAND).** (THE PROFESSIONAL NURSE.). (198?)-. Periodical. English. Twelve times a year. £33.50 UK, £37.00 Europe (individuals); £49.00 Europe (institutions); £70.50 others. Macmillan Magazines Ltd., Houndmills, Basingstoke, Hampshire RG21 2XS England. **Tel** 011 44 256 29242, FAX 011 44 256 812358, telex 858493. **(Subscription address:** Austen Cornish Ltd., Hainault Road Little Health, Romford Essex RM6 5NP England.**) LC** RT1; .P76. **NLM** W1; PR5933.
**Desc:** The quality nursing journal for nurses working in every healthcare setting.
**Ind/Abst** Cumul. Index Nurs. Allied Health Lit.; Int. Nurs. Index (July 1986-).

IT/0033-0205
**PROFESSIONI INFERMIERISTICHE.** [Prof. inferm.]. (1948)-. Periodical. Italian. Four times a year. L65000.00 Italy; L140000.00 other. Professioni Infermieristiche, Via Arno 62, 00198 Rome Italy. **Tel** 011 39 6 8840654, FAX 011 39 6 8840654. **UDC** 610.73. Index available. cum. index. **Bk Rev. Ad Acc. Circ:** 5,000 (ctrl).

US/0734-1431
**PROGRAM PLANS. NURSING BASIC SERIES.** **VFOAT** Nursing Basic Series. (1979)-. Periodical. English. mo. $76.00 (one year), $139.00 (two year), $190.00 (three year) US; $84.00 (one year), $152.00 (two year), $210.00 (three year) other. EPSCO / Educational Planning Services Corporation, Box 930, East Sandwich MA 02537. **Tel** (508)888-3257, FAX (508)888-3257. **ED** Jessica D. Terrill. **[CCC]. Circ:** 2,000.
**Desc:** Prepared inservice education programs for nursing staff. Each program is thirty minutes in length, written for presentation by the training director.

US/0889-7204
**PROGRESS IN CARDIOVASCULAR NURSING.** **See** Medical Science and Technology-Cardiology.

●UK/0969-9260
**PROGRESS IN PALLIATIVE CARE.** **Added/Corp** Leeds Medical Information. Vol. 1, no. 1 (Oct. 1993)-. Periodical. English. bm. $168.00 (institution), $76.00 (individual) US; £84.00 (institution), £38.00 (individual) UK & Europe; £94.00 (institution), £42.00 (individual) other. Royal Society of Medicine Press, 1 Wimpole Street, London W1M 8AE England. **Tel** 011 44 71 2902928. **NLM** W1; PR677CM. ***Continues in part** Pain and Pain Relief **and** Nursing and Palliative Care.*

BE
**PSYCHIATRIE EN VERPLEGING.** **See** Medical Science and Technology-Psychiatry.

US/0737-1209
**PUBLIC HEALTH NURSING (BOSTON, MASS.).** (PUBLIC HEALTH NURSING.). [Public health nurs.]. Vol. 1, No. 1 (Mar. 1984)-. Academic Scholarly Publication. English. bm. $135.00 (institution), $55.00 (individual) US; $170.00 (institution), $80.00 (individual) other. Blackwell Scientific Publishers, 238 Main Street, Cambridge MA 02142. **Tel** (617)547-7110, (800)835-6770, FAX (617)547-0789. **ED** Katherine J Young-Graham. **DD** 362. **NLM** W1; PU532. **[CCC].** Index available. **Ad Acc. Pr Rev. Circ:** 1,000. available on microfilm and microfiche from University Microfilms International (UMI). Documents available from The Genuine Article.
**Desc:** Public health nursing publishers original material having application in the areas of public health nursing practice, research, theory development, and education.
**Ind/Abst** Cumul. Index Nurs. Allied Health Lit.; Curr. Contents Soc. Behav. Sci.; Index Med. (Vol. 3, No. 4, 1986-); Int. Nurs. Index; Nurs. Abstr.; Res. Alert [Full Cov.]; Rev. Med. Vet. Entomol.; Soc. Sci. Cit. Index [Full Cov.]; World Agric. Econ.

●US/1064-7988
**QUALITY OF LIFE.** (QUALITY OF LIFE : A NURSING CHALLENGE.). (1992)-. Periodical. English. qt. Free. Meniscus Health Care Communications, 107 North 22nd Street, Suite 200, Philadelphia PA 19103-1302. **Tel** (215)564-5555. **NLM** W1; QU158LBM.

AT/0815-936X
**QUEENSLAND NURSE, THE.** [Qld. nurse]. **Added/Corp** Royal Australian Nursing Federation. Queensland Branch. Union of Employees. (198?)-. Periodical. English. Six times a year. 26.00Aus$ Australia; $36.00Aus$ others. Queensland Nurses Union, 495 499 Boundary Street, Spring Hill Queensland 4000 Australia. **Tel** 839-1411. **NLM** W1; QU693.
**Ind/Abst** Int. Nurs. Index.

CN/0822-4048
**R.P.N.A.M. UPDATE.** [R.P.N.A.M. update]. **VAT** Registered Psychiatric Nurses Association of Manitoba Update. Feb. 1983-. Periodical. English. qt. $15.00 Canada; $25.00 other. Registered Psychiatric Nurses Association of Manitoba, 1854 Portage Avenue, Winnipeg Manitoba R3J 0G9 Canada. **Tel** (204)888-4841. **ED** Annette D Osted. **DD** 610.73/68/0607127. **Circ:** 1,500 (ctrl). ***Continues*** *Prism, 0380-2442.*
**Desc:** Newsletter for members of the association.

UK/0144-6592
**RECENT ADVANCES IN NURSING.** ***Ceased.*** [Recent adv. nurs.]. 1-Ceased (1990). Monographic series. English. qt. Churchill Livingstone, 1-3 Baxter's Place, Leith Walk, Edinburgh EH1 3AF Scotland. **Tel** 011 44 31 556 2424, FAX 011 44 31 558 1278, telex 727511. **ED** Lisbeth Hockey and Alison McClymont. **NLM** W1 RE105VN. **[CCC].** available on microfilm and microfiche from University Microfilms International (UMI).
**Ind/Abst** Cumul. Index Nurs. Allied Health Lit.; Int. Nurs. Index.

FR/0297-2964
**RECHERCHE EN SOINS INFIRMIERS.** [Rech. soins infirm.]. **VFOAT** Recherches en Soins Infirmiers. (1985)-. Periodical. French. Four times a year (Mar., June, Sept., Dec.). 509.00F France; 620.00F others. Mallet Conseil, 2 Place Antonin Jutard, 69003 Lyon France. **Tel** 011 33 1 1678951011, FAX 011 33 1 1678605090. **UDC** 614.253.5. **Circ:** 900.

US/0278-2766
**RECRUIT & RETAIN.** [Recruit retain]. **VAT** Recruit and Retain. Periodical. English. mo. $35.00. Health Manpower Data Corporation, 15923 Green Hills Station, Nashville TN 37215.
**Ind/Abst** Int. Nurs. Index.

US/1044-0666
**RECRUITMENT & RETENTION REPORT.** ***Title Change.*** [Recruit. retent. rep.]. **VFOAT** Recruitment and Retention Report. Vol. 1, No. 1 (July 1988)-Vol. 7, No. 3 (Mar. 1994). Periodical. English. mo. Hall Johnson Communications Inc, 9737 West Ohio Avenue, Lakewood CO 80226. **Tel** (303)988-0056. **DD** 610. **NLM** W1; RE1138. **[CCC].** ***Continued by*** *Recruitment, Retention & Restructuring Report.*
**Ind/Abst** Int. Nurs. Index (1992-).

●US/1044-0666
**RECRUITMENT, RETENTION, & RESTRUCTURING REPORT.** **VFOAT** Recruitment, Retention, and Restructuring Report; RR and R Report; RR & R Report. (1994)-. English. mo. $128.00. Hall Johnson Communications Inc, 9737 West Ohio Avenue, Lakewood CO 80226. **Tel** (303)988-0056. **[CCC].** ***Continues*** *Recruitment & Retention Report.*
**Ind/Abst** Int. Nurs. Index.

US/0885-8144
**REFLECTIONS (INDIANAPOLIS, IND.).** (REFLECTIONS / SIGMA THETA TAU.). [Reflections]. **Added/Corp** Sigma Theta Tau. Sigma Theta Tau International. Vol. 1 (1975)-. Periodical. English. Four times a year (Mar., June, Sept., Dec.). Free to members of Sigma Theta Tau; $5.00 (non-members). Sigma Theta Tau International, 550 West North Street, Indianapolis IN 46202. **Tel** (317)634-8171, FAX (317)634-8188. **ED** Cheryl Chestnut. **DD** 610. **NLM** W1; RE1698MM. **Circ:** 73,000 (ctrl).
**Desc:** Internal newsletter of Sigma Theta Tau International, honor society of nursing. Presents organizational news to the society's members.
**Ind/Abst** Cumul. Index Nurs. Allied Health Lit.; Int. Nurs. Index (1991-).

US/0034-3196
**REGAN REPORT ON NURSING LAW, THE.** **See** Law.

CN/0840-8831
**REGISTERED NURSE (TORONTO).** (THE REGISTERED NURSE.). [Regist. nurse]. **Added/Corp** Registered Nurses' Association of Ontario. Vol. 1, No. 1 (Feb. 1989)-. Periodical. English. bm. 42.00Can$ US; 36.00Can$ Canada; 48.00Can$ other. Kenilworth Publishing Inc., 80 West Beaver Creek Suite 18, Richmond Hill ONT L4B 1H3 Canada. **Tel** (416)771-7333, FAX (416)771-7336. **ED** Ken Larone. **DD** 610.73/09713. **NLM** W1; RE173CQ. **Ad Acc, Adv Mgr:** Ellen Kral. **Pr Rev. Circ:** 26,000 (ctrl).
**Desc:** Informs and enlightens on ethical, legal, moral, professional and economic issues within the nursing profession.
**Ind/Abst** Cumul. Index Nurs. Allied Health Lit.; Int. Nurs. Index (Vol. 1, No. 1, 1989-199?).

US/0278-4807
**REHABILITATION NURSING.** [Rehabil. nurs.]. **Added/Corp** Association of Rehabilitation Nurses. Vol. 6, No. 1 (Jan/Feb 1981)-. Periodical. English. bm (6 issues). $75.00 (institution) US. Rehabilitation Nursing Corporation, 5700 Old Orchard Road, First Floor, Skokie IL 60077-1057. **Tel** (708)966-3433, FAX (708)966-9418. **(Subscription address:** RNC, # 259705401, PO Box 468, Des Plaines IL 60016-0468.**)** **ED** Belinda E. Puetz. **LC** RT120.R4; A85a. **DD** 617. **NLM** W1 RE1479D. Index available (published in issue number 6 of each volume). **Bk Rev. Ad Acc. Pr Rev. Circ:** 7,500 (ctrl). available on microfilm and microfiche from University Microfilms International (UMI). ***Continues*** *ARN Journal, 0362-3505.*
**Desc:** Provides scientific and professional data to nurses working with physically or emotionally disabled clients. Features cover nursing care techniques, nursing process, rehabilitation team functions, research and education.
**Ind/Abst** Abstr. Clin. Care Guidel.; Cumul. Index Nurs. Allied Health Lit.; Int. Nurs. Index; Nurs. Abstr.

US
**REHABILITATION NURSING CONCEPTS & PRACTICE.** (19??)-. Periodical. English. ir (every 4-5 years). $85.00 softcover; $100.00 hardcover. Rehabilitation Nursing Corporation, 5700 Old Orchard Road, First Floor, Skokie IL 60077-1057. **Tel** (708)966-3433, FAX (708)966-9418.

●US/1070-5767
**REHABILITATION NURSING RESEARCH.** [Rehabil. nurs. res.]. **Added/Corp** Association of Rehabilitation Nurses. Vol. 1, No. 1 (Fall 1992)-. Periodical. English. qt (4 issues). $85.00 institution, $65.00 individual, $45.00 member. Rehabilitation Nursing Corporation, 5700 Old Orchard Road, First Floor, Skokie IL 60077-1057. **Tel** (708)966-3433, FAX (708)966-9418. **(Subscription address:** RNC, # 259705401, PO Box 468, Des Plaines IL 60016-0468.**)** **DD** 610. **NLM** W1; RE1749E.

US
**REPORT OF NURSE POPULATION IN OKLAHOMA / OKLAHOMA BOARD OF NURSE REGISTRATION AND NURSING EDUCATION.** **See** Economics-Labor.

US
**REPORT OF THE WEST VIRGINIA BOARD OF EXAMINERS FOR REGISTERED PROFESSIONAL NURSES TO THE GOVERNOR ... FOR THE BIENNIUM PERIOD ENDING DECEMBER 31 ... .** **Main/Corp** West Virginia Board of Examiners for Registered Professional Nurses. **VFOAT** West Virginia Board of Registered Professional Nursing Biennium Report ... to the Governor ... of the State of West Virginia. English. be. West Virginia Board of Examiners for Registered Professional Nurses, Suite 309/Embleton Building, 922 Quarrier Street, Charleston WV 25301. **LC** RT5.W4; W47A. **DD** 362.1/73/09754. ***Continues*** *Report of the West Virginia Board of Examiners for Registered Nurses, 0362-1855.*

US
**REPORT ON SALARIES OF ADMINISTRATIVE FACULTY IN NURSING, EXCLUDING DEANS.** **Added/Corp** American Association of Colleges of Nursing. (19??)-. English. be. American Association of Colleges of Nursing, One Dupont Circle NW / Suite 530, Washington DC 20036. **Tel** (202)463-6930.

US/0749-3746
**REPORT - VIRGINIA. STATE BOARD OF NURSING.** (REPORT / COMMONWEALTH OF VIRGINIA, DEPARTMENT OF HEALTH REGULATORY BOARDS, STATE BOARD OF NURSING.). **Main/Corp** Virginia. State Board of Nursing. July 1, 1978-June 30, 1981-. English. Commonwealth of Virginia / Richmond, PO Box 406, Richmond VA 23203. **Tel** (804)786-6526. **LC** RT5.V8; V57A. **DD** 353.97550084/1. ***Continues*** *Virginia. State Board of Nursing. Annual Report, 0749-3738.*

US/0160-6891
**RESEARCH IN NURSING & HEALTH.** [Res. nurs. health]. **VAT** Research in Nursing and Health. Vol. 1 (Apr. 1978)-. Periodical. English. bm. $294.00 US; $354.00 Canada and Mexico; $376.50 other. John Wiley & Sons, Inc., 605 Third Avenue, New York NY 10158-0012. **Tel** (212)850-6000, (212)850-6645, FAX (212)850-6088, telex 12-7063. **(Subscription address:** John Wiley & Sons / England, Baffins Lane, Chichester, West Sussex PO19 1UD England.**)** **ED** Marilyn T. Oberst. **LC** RT81.5; .R46. **DD** 610.73/05. **NLM** W1 RE227IC. **[CCC]. Ad Acc. Pr Rev. Circ:** 1,800. available on microfilm and microfiche from University Microfilms International (UMI). Documents available from The Genuine Article.
**Desc:** Provides a forum for research in the areas of nursing practice, education and administration. Health issues relevant to nursing as well as investigations of the applications of research findings in clinical settings, are thoroughly covered.
**Ind/Abst** Annals Behav. Med.; Cumul. Index Nurs. Allied Health Lit.; Curr. Contents Soc. Behav. Sci.; Energy Res. Abstr. (Aug. 1982-); Index Med.; Int. Nurs. Index; Nurs. Abstr.; Psychol. Abstr. (1980-); PsycINFO; PsycLit; Res. Alert [Full Cov.]; Risk Abstr.; Soc. Plann. Policy Dev. Abstr.; Soc. Sci. Cit. Index [Full Cov.].

CU
**REVISTA CUBANA DE ENFERMERIA.** **Added/Corp** Centro Nacional de Informacion de Ciencias Medicas. Vol. 1, No. 1 (Enero-Marzo 1985)-. Periodical. Spanish (summaries and/or abstracts in English, French and Russian; table of contents in English). wk. Ediciones Cubanas, Obispo 527, Altos ESQ Bernaza, CP 10100 Havana Cuba. **Tel** 011 632980, 631942, FAX 011 631011, telex 512337, 6540. **LC** RT7.C9; R4. **NLM** W1; RE359H.
**Ind/Abst** Int. Nurs. Index.

SP/0210-5020
**REVISTA ROL DE ENFERMERIA.** (REVISTA DE ENFERMERIA / ROL.). [Rev. ROL enferm.]. **VFOAT** Revista ROL de Enfermeria,. No. 1, (July 1978)-. Monographic series. Spanish. ir. Price varies per voluem. Ediciones Rol SA, Marco Aurelio 8, 08006 Barcelona Spain. **Tel** 011 34 3 2008033, FAX 011 34 3 2002762. **NLM** W1 RE394J. cum. index. **Ad Acc, Adv Mgr:** Tomas Lavandeira, **Tel** (93)200.80.33. **Circ:** 25,000 (ctrl).
**Ind/Abst** Indice Med. Esp.; Int. Nurs. Index.

US/1059-0927
**REVOLUTION (STATEN ISLAND, N.Y.).** (REVOLUTION : THE JOURNAL OF NURSE EMPOWERMENT.). [Revolution]. **VFOAT** Journal of Nurse Empowerment. Vol. 1, No. 1 (Winter 1991)-. Periodical. English. Four times a year (Apr., July, Oct., Dec.). $44.95 (institution); $24.95 (individual). AD Von Publishers Inc., 56 McArthur Avenue, Staten Island NY 10312. **Tel** (800)331-6534, FAX (718)317-0858. **ED** Joan Swirsky. **DD** 610. **NLM** W1; RE74M. **Bk Rev**, (Qty: 4). **Ad Acc, Adv Mgr:** Roe, **Tel** (800)331-6534. **Pr Rev. Circ:** 50,000.
**Desc:** News and information concerning nursing.

FR/0397-7897
**REVUE DE L'INFIRMIERE. INFORMATIONS.** [Rev. infirm., Inf.]. **VFOAT** Informations. (June 1974)-. Periodical. French. ir (20 issues per year). 390.00F France; 615.00F other. Expansion Scientifique Francaise, 31 Boulevard de la Tour-Maubourg, 75007 Paris France. **Tel** 011 33 1 40 62 64 00, 011 33 1 40626439. **NLM** W1 RE789H.
**Desc:** An efficient tool containing articles on nursing care, it is an introduction to health care. Precise information, a permanent almanac for health care.
**Ind/Abst** Int. Nurs. Index; Point Repere (1983-19??).

US/0033-7021
**RN.** [RN]. **VFOAT** RN Magazine. **VAT** Registered Nurse. Vol. 1 (Oct. 1937)-. Periodical. English. mo. $35.00 US; $50.00 other. Medical Economics Publishing, Five Paragon Drive, Second Floor, Montvale NJ 07645. **Tel** (800)432-4570, (201)358-2210. **(Subscription address:** Neodata / Colorado, PO Box 2606, Boulder Boulder CO 80322.**)** **ED** James A. Reynolds. **LC** RT1; .R2. **DD** 610.7305. **NLM** W1 R118. **[CCC].** cum. index. **Ad Acc. Circ:** 275,000 (ctrl). available on microfilm from University Microfilms International (UMI); available on an online database (files 149,648/Full-Text) from DIALOG. Documents available from UMI Article Clearinghouse.
**Desc:** Clinical and professional information, with emphasis on events and current developments.
**Ind/Abst** Acad. Abstr. Full Text Elite (Jan. 1992-); Acad. Abstr. (Jan. 1992-); Acad. Ind. [Computer File] (1989-); Acad. Search (Jan. 1992-); Bus. Index (1981-?); Cumul. Index Nurs. Allied Health Lit.; Expand. Acad. Index (1989-); Gen. Period. Index (1985-); Gen. Sci. Index; Gen. Sci. Source (Jan. 1992-); Health Index (1989-); Health Period. Database [Full Txt.]; Health Plan. Adminis.; Health Ref. Cent. (Jan. 1989-) [Full Txt.] [Full Cov.]; Health Source (Jan. 1992-); Hospit. Health Admin. Index; INFO-SOUTH Abstr.; Int. Nurs. Index; Mag. Search; Newsp. Period. Abstr. (1988-); Nurs. Abstr.; Physic. Medline Plus; Trade Ind. Index (1981-?); Vocat. Search (Jan. 1992-).

US/1049-8966
**RN-AIDSLINE.** ***Ceased.*** (RN-AIDSLINE : A QUARTERLY NURSING RESOURCE ON AIDS.). [RN-aidsline]. **VFOAT** RN Aidsline. **VAT** Registered Nurse Aidsline. (1989)-(19??). Periodical. English. qt. University of Phoenix, c/o B Copland, 4614 E Elmwood Street, Center Nursing, Phoenix AZ 85040. **Tel** (602) 966-7400. **DD** 616. **Pr Rev.** ***Continues*** *Aidsline.*

US/0192-298X
**RN IDAHO.** [RN Ida.]. **Added/Corp** Idaho Nurses' Association. **VAT** Registered Nurse Idaho. (1977)-. Periodical. English. qt. $25.00. Idaho Nurses Association, 200 North 4th Street/Suite 20, Boise ID 83702-6001. **Tel** (208)323-0500. **ED** Nancy Leslie. **NLM** W1 R118D. **Ad Acc. Circ:** 700 (ctrl). ***Supersedes*** *Gem State RN News Letter, 0072-0569.*
**Desc:** Newspaper sent to RN's in Idaho schools of nursing, and libraries. Current issues of interest to health professionals.
**Ind/Abst** Int. Nurs. Index.

US
**RN MAGAZINE-NCLEX REVIEW.** (19??)-. English. an. $25.95. Pelmar Publishers, 2 Computer Drive West, Box 15015, Albany NY 12212. **Tel** (201)469-4400 Ext. 2497.

US
**RN NURSING OPPORTUNITIES : THE ... JOB MARKET.** **VFOAT** Nursing Opportunities; R N Nursing Opportunities; Job Market. (19??)-. Periodical.

English. an. $9.95 US; $15.00 other. Medical Economics Publishing, Five Paragon Drive, Second Floor, Montvale NJ 07645. **Tel** (800)432-4570, (201)358-2210. **(Subscription address:** Medical Economics Publishing / Colorado, 833 West South Boulder Road, Louisville CO 80027.) ***Continues*** *Nursing Opportunities.*

US/1050-9089
**ROGERIAN NURSING SCIENCE NEWS.** (ROGERIAN NURSING SCIENCE NEWS : NEWSLETTER OF THE SOCIETY OF ROGERIAN SCHOLARS.). [Rogerian nurs. sci. news]. **Added/Corp** Society of Rogerian Scholars. Vol. 1, No. 1 (June 1988)-. Newsletter. English. qt. $150.00 library, and institutions; $45.00 other. Rogerian Nursing Science News, 437 Twin Bay Drive, Pensacola FL 32504. **Tel** (904)474-9793. **ED** V. Malinski and S. Cheema. **DD** 610. **NLM** W1; RO288.
**Ind/Abst** Health Plan. Adminis.; Int. Nurs. Index (1988-).

CN/1187-0400
**RPNABC PROFILE.** (THE RPNABC PROFILE : A NEWSLETTER FOR MEMBERS OF THE REGISTERED PSYCHIATRIC NURSES ASSOCIATION OF BRITISH COLUMBIA.). [RPNABC profile]. **Added/Corp** Registered Psychiatric Nurses' Association of British Columbia. **VFOAT** Registered Psychiatric Association of British Columbia Profile. Vol. 1, No. 1 (Spring 1991)-. Newsletter. English. qt. Registered Psychiatric Association of British Columbia, Suite 102, Deer Lake Centre II, 4940 Canada Way, Burnaby British Columbia V5G 4H7 Canada. **DD** 610.73/68/060711. ***Continues*** *Intercom (Registered Psychiatric Nurses' Association of British Columbia)., 0822-5842.*

FI/0785-7527
**SAIRAANHOITAJA / SUOMEN SAIRAANHOITAJALIITTO RY. Added/Corp** Suomen Sairaanhoitajaliitto. **VFOAT** Sjukskoterskan. (1991)-. Periodical. Finnish (Swedish; summaries and/or abstracts in English). bm. **NLM** W1; SA237. ***Separated from*** *Tehy, 0358-4038.*
**Ind/Abst** Int. Nurs. Index (1991-).

CN/1180-3983
**SANTE QUEBEC : REVUE DE LA CORPORATION PROFESSIONNELLE DES INFIRMIERES ET INFIRMIERS AUXILIAIRES DU QUEBEC.** [Sante Que.]. **Added/Corp** Corporation Professionnelle des Infirmieres et Infirmiers Auxiliaires du Quebec. Vol. 1, No. 1 (1990)-. Periodical. French (English). Three times a year. 15.00Can$ Canada; 20.00Can$ other. Corporation Professionelle des Infirmieres Auxilliaires du Quebec, 531 Sherbrooke Est, Montreal Quebec H2L 1K2 Canada. **Tel** (514)282-9511, FAX (514)282-0631. **DD** 610.73/06/9305.

PH
**SANTO TOMAS NURSING JOURNAL.** v. 1- ; 1962-. Periodical. English. sa. University of Santo Tomas College of Nursing, Manila Philippines.

SW/0283-9318
**SCANDINAVIAN JOURNAL OF CARING SCIENCES.** Vol. 1, No. 1 (1987)-. Periodical. English. qt. Kr745.00, $122.00. Scandinavian University Press, PO Box 2959 Toeyen, N 0608 Oslo 6 Norway. **Tel** 011 47 2 2575400, FAX 011 47 2 2575353, telex 71896 UROR N. **(Subscription address:** Scandinavian University Press, 200 Meacham Ave., Elmont NY 11003.) **ED** Anne Christina Ek. **NLM** W1; SC147.
**Desc:** Aims to communicate health field research to nurses, occupational therapists, physiotherapists, physicians, and social workers. Aspects of practice, service and education are covered. Scientific quality and relevance guaranteed by a well developed international referee system.
**Ind/Abst** Cumul. Index Nurs. Allied Health Lit.; Int. Nurs. Index (1987-); Psychoanal. Abstr.; Psychol. Abstr. (1990-); PsycScan: Appl. Exp. Eng. Psych.; PsycScan: LD/MR; PsycScan: Neuropsych.

IT
**SCENARIO : IL NURSING DELLA SOPRAVVIVENZA.** ***Ceased.*** (19??)-(1993). Italian. Aniarti, c/o Drigo Elio, Via del Pozzo 19, 33100 Udine Italy. **Tel** 011 39 432 501461.
**Desc:** The official journal of the National Association of Critical Area Nurses. It contains scientific articles and clinical experiences in critical area nursing focusing mostly on Italy.

US/0889-7182
**SCHOLARLY INQUIRY FOR NURSING PRACTICE.** [Sch. inq. nurs. pract.]. Vol. 1, No. 1 (Spring 1987)-. Periodical. English. qt. $42.00 (1 year, individuals), $75.00 (2 year, individuals), $79.00 (1 year, institutions), $129.00 (2 year, institutions) US; $47.00 (1 year, individuals), $85.00 (2 year, individuals), $87.00 (1 year, institutions), $149.00 (2 year, institutions) other. Springer Publishing Company, 536 Broadway, New York NY 10012-3955. **Tel** (212)431-4370, FAX (212)941-7842. **ED** Harriet Feldman, Ruth Hyman, Barbara Kos-Munson, Carol Ann Mitchell, and Pierre Woog. **LC** WMLC 93/3162. **DD** 610. **NLM** W1; SC228. **Pr Rev.**
**Desc:** Designed to facilitate the integration of theory, research, and practice. It publishes original manuscripts concerned with the development and testing or theory relevant to nursing practice. Articles are accompanied by an invited response from a well-known scholar, who provides a constructive examination of the paper's relevance to practice.
**Ind/Abst** Annals Behav. Med.; Cumul. Index Nurs. Allied Health Lit.; Index Med. (spring 1993-); Int. Nurs. Index (1987-); Psychol. Abstr. (1987-); PsycINFO (1990-); PsycLit.

US/0891-7884
**SCHOLARSHIPS AND LOANS FOR NURSING EDUCATION.** [Scholarsh. loans nurs. educ.]. **Added/Corp** National League for Nursing. (1984/1985)-. English. an. $12.95 members; $14.95 nonmembers. National League for Nursing, 350 Hudson Street, New York NY 10014. **Tel** (212)989-9393, (800)669-1656. **DD** 610. **NLM** WY 18; S368. ***Continues*** *Scholarships and Loans for Beginning Education in Nursing.*

US/1048-3896
**SCHOOL HEALTH ALERT. See** Education.

US/0888-8299
**SCI NURSING.** (SCI NURSING : A PUBLICATION OF THE AMERICAN ASSOCIATION OF THE SPINAL CORD INJURY NURSES.). [SCI nurs.]. Vol. 1, No. 1 (1984)-. Periodical. English. qt (Jan., Apr., July, Oct.). comes with membership. American Association of the Spinal Cord Injury Nurses, 75 20 Astoria Boulevard, Jackson Heights NY 11370. **Tel** (718)803-3782. **DD** 610. **NLM** W1; SC652M.
**Ind/Abst** Cumul. Index Nurs. Allied Health Lit.; Int. Nurs. Index (Vol. 1, No. 4, 1984-).

US
**SELECTED LIST OF NURSING BOOKS AND JOURNALS.** (1979)-. English. American Journal of Nursing Company, 555 West 57th Street, New York NY 10019-2961. **Tel** (212)582-8820, FAX (212)586-5462.

●US/1066-3851
**SEMINARS FOR NURSE MANAGERS.** [Semin. nurse manag.]. (1993)-. English. qt. $49.00 (individual), $66.00 (institutions) US; $85.00 (individual), $99.00 (institution) other. W.B. Saunders Company, A Subsidiary of Harcourt Brace Jovanovich, Inc., The Curtis Center/Suite 300, Independence Square West, Philadelphia PA 19106-3399. **Tel** (215)238-7800 or, 5587, FAX (215)238-7883, telex 173146. **(Subscription address:** W. B. Saunders Company / North America Subscriptions, c/o Periodicals, 6277 Sea Harbour Drive, 4th Floor, Orlando FL 32887.) **DD** 610. **NLM** W1; SE486BL.

US/0749-2081
**SEMINARS IN ONCOLOGY NURSING.** [Sem. oncol. nurs.]. Vol. 1, No. 1 (Feb. 1985)-. Periodical. English. qt (Feb., May, Aug., Nov.). $52.00 (individual), $92.00 (institution) US; $104.00 (individual), $119.00 (institution) other. W.B. Saunders Company, A Subsidiary of Harcourt Brace Jovanovich, Inc., The Curtis Center/Suite 300, Independence Square West, Philadelphia PA 19106-3399. **Tel** (215)238-7800 or, 5587, FAX (215)238-7883, telex 173146. **(Subscription address:** W. B. Saunders Company / North America Subscriptions, c/o Periodicals, 6277 Sea Harbour Drive, 4th Floor, Orlando FL 32887.) **ED** Henke Yarbro. **DD** 616. **NLM** W1; SE489F. **[CCC]. Pr Rev.**
**Desc:** For the dissemination of current knowledge in the complex field of cancer nursing. It contains topical reviews carefully prepared by selected experts.
**Ind/Abst** Index Med.; Int. Nurs. Index; Nurs. Abstr.

●US/1056-8670
**SEMINARS IN PERIOPERATIVE NURSING.** Vol. 1, No. 1 (Jan. 1992)-. Periodical. English. qt. 52.00 (individual), $73.00 (institution) US; $99.00 (individual), $89.00 (institution) other. W.B. Saunders Company, A Subsidiary of Harcourt Brace Jovanovich, Inc., The Curtis Center/Suite 300, Independence Square West, Philadelphia PA 19106-3399. **Tel** (215)238-7800 or, 5587, FAX (215)238-7883, telex 173146. **(Subscription address:** W. B. Saunders Company / North America Subscriptions, c/o Periodicals, 6277 Sea Harbour Drive, 4th Floor, Orlando FL 32887.) **DD** 610. **NLM** W1; SE489FP. **[CCC].**

UK/0265-9999
**SENIOR NURSE.** ***Title Change.*** [Sr. nurse]. Vol. 1, No. 1 (Apr. 4, 1984)-(1994). Periodical. English. wk. Royal College of Nursing, Department A Glynteg House, STA House, Ely Cardiff CF5 4XG England. **Tel** 011 44 71 222 553411. **NLM** W1; SE497. available on microfilm and microfiche from University Microfilms International (UMI). ***Continues*** *Nursing Focus.* ***Continued by*** *Nursing Management.*
**Ind/Abst** Cumul. Index Nurs. Allied Health Lit.

US/0895-4364
**SERIES ON NURSING ADMINISTRATION.** [Ser. nurs. adm.]. **Added/Corp** University of Iowa. College of Nursing. **VFOAT** Iowa Nursing Administration Series. Vol. 1 (1988)-. Monographic series. English. an. Price varies per volume. Mosby Year Book Inc., 11830 Westline Industrial Drive, St Louis MO 63146. **Tel** (800)325-4177, (314)872-8370, FAX (314)432-1380, telex 44-2402. **DD** 610. **NLM** W1; SE72Q.
**Ind/Abst** Health Plan. Adminis.; Int. Nurs. Index.

US/0886-9278
**SOCIETY FOR NURSING HISTORY GAZETTE, THE.** [Soc. Nurs. Hist. gaz.]. Began with: Vol. 1, No. 1 (Spring 1981). Periodical. English. sa. $20.00. Society for Nursing History, PO Box 150 Teachers College, Columbia University, New York NY 10027. **ED** Aurelie Krapik and Pamella Hosang. **DD** 610. **NLM** W1; SO8547.
**Ind/Abst** Cumul. Index Nurs. Allied Health Lit.; Int. Nurs. Index (Spring 1981-).

●FR/1163-4723
**SOINS. FORMATION, PEDAGOGIE, ENCADREMENT : AVEC LA PARTICIPATION DU CEEIEC. Added/Corp** Comite d'Entente des Ecoles d'Infirmieres et des Ecoles de Cadres. **VFOAT** Formation, Pedagogie, Encadrement. No. 1 (1992)-. Periodical. French. Four times a year. 313.42F France; 320.00F other. Intereditions, 7 rue de L Laromiguiere, 75005 Paris France. **Tel** 011 33 1 46342160. **NLM** W1; SO8862NL. ***Continues*** *Infirmiere Enseignante.*
**Ind/Abst** Int. Nurs. Index (1992-).

FR/0038-0814
**SOINS PARIS.** (1956)-. Periodical. French. mo (10y). 145.00F (individuals), 210.00F (institutions) Switzerland; 230.00F (individuals), 290.00F (institutions) other. Intereditions, 7 rue de L Laromiguiere, 75005 Paris France. **Tel** 011 33 1 46342160. **(Subscription address:** OPI SA, 33 Chemin des Hutins, 1247 Aniere Geneva Switzerland.) **UDC** 61. **Bk Rev. Ad Acc. Circ:** 2,500.
**Ind/Abst** Point Repere (1979-).

US/1046-7394
**SOUTH CAROLINA NURSE, THE.** (THE SOUTH CAROLINA NURSE / SOUTH CAROLINA NURSES' ASSOCIATION.). [South Carol. nurse]. **Added/Corp** South Carolina Nurses' Association. **VFOAT** SC Nurse; S.C. Nurse. Vol. 1, No. 1 (Jan./Feb. 1986)-. Periodical. English. Four times a year. $24.00. South Carolina Nurses Association, 1821 Gadsden Street, Columbia SC 29201. **Tel** (803)252-4781, FAX (803)779-3870. **ED** Jan Bellack. **DD** 616. **NLM** W1; SO915. **Bk Rev**, (Qty: 2-3). **Ad Acc, Adv Mgr:** Art Davis, **Tel** (319)277-2414. **Pr Rev. Circ:** 2,000 (ctrl). ***Continues*** *South Carolina Nurses' Association. SCNA Newsletter, 0199-3399.*
**Desc:** A newsletter designed for the South Carolina nursing community. Updates on health issues, legislation regulation, workshops, education trends and policy issues.
**Ind/Abst** Cumul. Index Nurs. Allied Health Lit.; Health Plan. Adminis.; Int. Nurs. Index (Spring 1989-).

US/0038-335X
**SOUTH DAKOTA NURSE, THE.** [S. D. nurse]. **Added/Corp** South Dakota Nurse's Association. (19??)-. Periodical. English. Four times a year (Mar., June, Sept., Dec.). $12.00. South Dakota Nurses Association, 1505 South Minnesota, Suite 6, Sioux Falls SD 57105. **Tel** (605)338-1401. **LC** NOT IN LC. **DD** 610.
**Ind/Abst** Int. Nurs. Index.

US/0276-6787
**STANDARDS FOR OBSTETRIC, GYNECOLOGIC, AND NEONATAL NURSING. See** Medical Science and Technology-Gynecology and Obstetrics.

US/0038-9986
**STAT.** [Stat]. **Added/Corp** Wisconsin Nurses Association. (1933)-. Periodical. English. Twenty-four times a year. $45.00 US; $50.00 Canada; $52.00 other. Wisconsin Nurses Association, 6117 Monona Drive, Madison WI 53716. **Tel** (608)251-1462. **ED** Susan P Carter, (608)221-0383. **Ad Acc. Circ:** 2,500 (ctrl). ***Continues*** *Wisconsin State Nurses' Association. Bulletin.*
**Desc:** Membership information; legislative and nursing issues.
**Ind/Abst** Cumul. Index Nurs. Allied Health Lit.; Int. Nurs. Index.

US/0081-4423
**STATE-APPROVED SCHOOLS OF NURSING, L.P.N./L.V.N. Main/Corp** National League for Nursing. **Added/Corp** National League for Nursing. Research and Studies Service. National League for Nursing. Research and Development. National League for Nursing. Division of Public Policy and Research. National League for Nursing. Division of Research. **VFOAT** State-Approved Schools of Nursing, LPN/LVN. **VAT** State Approved Schools of Nursing, L.P.N./L.V.N. 9th Ed. (1967)-. English. an. $23.95 members; $27.95 nonmembers. National League for Nursing, 350 Hudson Street, New York NY 10014. **Tel** (212)989-9393, (800)669-1656. **LC** RT74; .S7. **DD** 610.73/071/173. **NLM** WY 22 AA1 S66. available on diskette. ***Continues*** *State-Approved Schools of Practical and Vocational Nursing, 0095-6570.*
**Ind/Abst** Stat. Ref. Index.

US/0081-4431
**STATE-APPROVED SCHOOLS OF NURSING-R.N. Added/Corp** National League for Nursing. Division of Research. National League for Nursing. Division of Public Policy and Research. **VAT** State Approved Schools of Nursing Registered Nurse. 25th Ed. (1967)-. English. an. $23.95 members; $39.70 nonmembers. National League for Nursing, 350 Hudson Street, New York NY 10014. **Tel** (212)989-9393, (800)669-1656. **NLM** WY 22 AA1 S7. available on diskette. ***Continues*** *State Approved Schools of Professional Nursing.*

US/0891-8341
**STATE NURSING LEGISLATION QUARTERLY.** ***Ceased.*** **See** Law.

●US/1076-4747
**STN'S JOURNAL OF TRAUMA NURSING. Added/Corp** Society for Trauma Nurses. **VFOAT** Journal of Trauma Nursing. (1994)-. Periodical. English. qt. $52.00 (institutions), $42.00 (individuals) US; $64.00 (institutions), $54.00 (individuals) other. NURSECOM Inc., 1211 Locust Street, Philadelphia PA 19107. **Tel** (215)545-7222, (800)242-6757, FAX (215)545-8107.

US
**SUID-AFRIKAANSE TEATERSUSTER.** English. Four times a year (Mar., June, Sept., Dec.). R35.00. South African Theatre Sister, PO Box 231, Panorama 7506 South Africa. **Tel** 011 27 21 920363, FAX 011 27 21 924302. **ED** G. Espost. **Bk Rev. Ad Acc, Adv Mgr:** G. Espost. **Circ:** 1,000.
**Desc:** This journal is about the nurses and or nursing in the operating room.

US/0744-2580
**SUMMARY OF PROCEEDINGS / AMERICAN NURSES' ASSOCIATION ... CONVENTION. Main/Corp** American Nurses' Association. Convention. 51st (1978)-. Proceedings. English. be. American Nurses Association, 600 Maryland Avenue Southwest, Suite 100, Washington DC 20024. **Tel** (202)554-4444. **LC** RT1; .A6235. **DD** 610.73/06/073. ***Continues*** *American Nurses' Association. Convention. Summary Proceedings.*

UK/0954-8947
**SURGICAL NURSE.** (Oct. 1988)-. Periodical. English. Six times a year (Feb., Apr., June, Aug., Oct., Dec.). £24.90 (individuals), £42.00 (institutions) UK; £30.00 others. Medicine Group (Journals) Ltd., Publishing House / United Kingdom, 62 Stert Street, Abingdon Oxon OX14 3UQ England. **Tel** 011 44 235 555770, FAX 011 44 235 554691, telex 85183147. **NLM** W1; SU767SD.

DK/0106-8350
**SYGEPLEJERSKEN.** [Sygeplejersken]. **Added/Corp** Dansk Sygeplejerad. Vol. 72 (Jan. 1972)-. Periodical. Danish. wk. kr782.00. Dansk Sygeplejeraad, Vimmelskaftet 38 Postbox 1084, 1008 Copenhagen Denmark. **Tel** 011 45 33151555. **ED** Peter Hjorth. **NLM** W1 SY424. **Bk Rev. Ad Acc. Circ:** 65,000 (ctrl). ***Continues*** *Tiksskrift for Sygeplejersker, 0049-3856.*
**Ind/Abst** Index Med.; Int. Nurs. Index.

KO
**TAEHAN KANHO. VFOAT** The Korean Nurse. Periodical. Korean (Korean). Taehan Kanho Hyophoe, 88-7 Sang Lim Dong, Choong ku, Seoul Korea. **LC** RT1; .T33. **NLM** W1 TA392R.
**Ind/Abst** Int. Nurs. Index.

US/0039-9620
**TAR HEEL NURSE.** [Tar heel nurse]. **Added/Corp** North Carolina Nurses Association. North Carolina State Nurses' Association. Vol. 1 (1939)-. Periodical. English. Six times a year (Feb., Apr., June, Aug., Oct., Dec.). $25.00. North Carolina Nurses Association, PO Box 12025, Raleigh NC 27605. **Tel** (919)821-4250. **ED** Cindy Barker. **DD** 610. **NLM** W1 TA597. **Ad Acc. Circ:** 4,000 (ctrl). available on microfilm and microfiche from University Microfilms International (UMI).
**Desc:** Information about nursing in North Carolina, including educational programs and legislative reviews.
**Ind/Abst** Cumul. Index Nurs. Allied Health Lit.; Int. Nurs. Index.

US/1055-9620
**TECHNOLOGY FOR CRITICAL CARE NURSES.** ***Ceased.*** (TECHNOLOGY FOR CRITICAL CARE NURSES : AN OFFICIAL PUBLICATION OF THE AMERICAN ASSOCIATION OF CRITICAL-CARE NURSES.). [Technol. crit. care nurses]. **Added/Corp** American Association of Critical-Care Nurses. Vol. 1, No. 1 (May 1991)-(Sept./Oct. 1994). Periodical. English. bm. ECRI Emergency Care Research Institute, 5200 Butler Pike, Plymouth Meeting PA 19462. **Tel** (215)825-6000, FAX (215)834-1275, telex 510-660-8023. **DD** 362.

US/1059-454X
**TECHNOLOGY FOR EMERGENCY CARE NURSES.** ***Ceased.*** (TECHNOLOGY FOR EMERGENCY CARE NURSES : AN OFFICIAL PUBLICATION OF THE EMERGENCY NURSES ASSOCIATION.). [Technol. emerg. care nurses]. **Added/Corp** Emergency Nurses Association. (1991)-(Aug. 1994). Periodical. English. bm. ECRI Emergency Care Research Institute, 5200 Butler Pike, Plymouth Meeting PA 19462. **Tel** (215)825-6000, FAX (215)834-1275, telex 510-660-8023. **DD** 610. **NLM** W1; TE211DE.

US/0890-9059
**TECHNOLOGY FOR NURSING.** ***Ceased.*** [Technol. nurs.]. Vol. 1, No. 1, Nov. (1986)-Ceased with Vol.6, Feb. (1991). Periodical. English. mo. ECRI Emergency Care Research Institute, 5200 Butler Pike, Plymouth Meeting PA 19462. **Tel** (215)825-6000, FAX (215)834-1275, telex 510-660-8023. **DD** 610. **NLM** W1; TE211F. **[CCC].**
**Desc:** A valuable self-teaching aid, designed to guide nurses through the growing complexity of medical devices.

FI/0358-4038
**TEHY.** [Tehy]. **Added/Corp** Terveydenhuoltoalan Ammattijarjesto Tehy (Finland) Suomen Sairaanhoitajaliitto. **VFOAT** Terveydenhuoltoalan Ammattijarjesto Tehy Ry:N Aanenkannattaja. (1981)-. Periodical. Finnish. ir. Fmk350.00 Finland; Fmk500.00 other. TEHY, Asemamiehenkatu 4, Helsink 00520 Finland. **Tel** 011 358 0 1552700. **DD** 331. **NLM** W1 TE29. ***Formed by the union of*** *Laboratoriohoitaja; Lastenhoitajalehti* ***and*** *Sairaanhoitaja.*

US/1055-3134
**TENNESSEE NURSE.** [Tenn. nurse]. **Added/Corp** Tennessee Nurses Association. Vol. 53 No. 6 (Dec. 1990)-. Periodical. English. Six times a year. $20.00. Tennessee Nurses Association, 545 Mainstream Drive, Suite 405, Nashville TN 37228-1201. **Tel** (615)254-0350. **ED** Anita Daugherty. **DD** 610. **NLM** W1; TE417AG. **Ad Acc. Circ:** 2600 (ctrl). available on microfilm from University Microfilms International (UMI). ***Continues*** *Tennessee Nurses Association. Bulletin - Tennessee Nurses Association, 0040-3342.*
**Desc:** A multi-purpose communications device containing an analysis of issues and events facing the nursing profession.
**Ind/Abst** Cumul. Index Nurs. Allied Health Lit.; Int. Nurs. Index (Dec. 1990-).

US
**TEST SERVICES FOR SCHOOLS OF NURSING. Added/Corp** National League for Nursing. Dept. of Evaluation Services. (1978/79)-. English. ir. Free on request. National League for Nursing, 350 Hudson Street, New York NY 10014. **Tel** (212)989-9393, (800)669-1656.

US/0095-036X
**TEXAS NURSING.** [Texas nurs.]. Vol. 47, No. 4 (April 1973)-. Periodical. English. mo. $25.00 North America; $30.00 other. Texas Nurses Association, 300 East Highland Mall Boulevard #300, Austin TX 78752-3718. **Tel** (512)452-0645. **ED** John L Brown. **NLM** W1 TE789. Index available. cum. index. **Ad Acc. Circ:** 6,000 (ctrl). available on microfilm and microfiche from University Microfilms International (UMI). ***Continues*** *Bulletin - Texas Nurses Association, 0040-4500.*
**Desc:** News about Association members, developments in nursing in Texas, health related issues, entry level nursing, etc.
**Ind/Abst** Cumul. Index Nurs. Allied Health Lit.; Int. Nurs. Index.

US/0194-5181
**TODAY'S OR NURSE.** [Today's OR nurse]. **VAT** Today's Operating Room Nurse. Vol. 1 (Mar. 1979)-. Periodical. English. bm. $43.00 institution, $33.00 individual (US). Slack Inc., 6900 Grove Road, Thorofare NJ 08086. **Tel** (609)848-1000, (800)257-8290, FAX (609)853-5991, telex 517108 SLACK INC VD. **NLM** W1 TO172I. **Ad Acc.** available on microfilm and microfiche from University Microfilms International (UMI).
**Ind/Abst** Cumul. Index Nurs. Allied Health Lit.; Int. Nurs. Index; Nurs. Abstr.

NE/0922-1611
**TRIAKEL GRONINGEN.** (TRIAKEL.). [Triakel Gron.]. **Added/Corp** ademisch Ziekenhuis Groningen. (1988)-. Periodical. Dutch. Eight times a year. Fl50.00. Buro Voorlichting, Academische Ziekenhuis Groningen, POB 30001, 9700 RB Groningen Netherlands. **Tel** 011 31 50 612200. **UDC** 61.

NE/0303-6456
**TVZ : VAKBLAD VOOR DE VERPLEGKUNDIGEN.** [Tijdschr. ziekenverpl.]. **VFOAT** Tijdschrift voor Zeikenverpleging. Vol. 42, No. 1 (Jan. 7, 1988)-. Periodical. Dutch. sm. Fl99.50. Uitgeversmaatschappij de Tijdstroom BV, Noorderwal 38, Postbus 14, 7240 BA Lochem Netherlands. **Tel** 011 31 5730 53651, FAX 011 31 5730 56724. **ED** T Van de Pasch. **NLM** W1; TV88. cum. index. **Bk Rev. Ad Acc. Circ:** 20,000. ***Continues*** *Tijdschrift voor Ziekenverpleging, 0303-6456.*
**Ind/Abst** Int. Nurs. Index (1988-).

US/1053-816X
**UROLOGIC NURSING.** [Urol. nurs.]. **Added/Corp** American Urological Association Allied. Vol. 9, No. 1 (July/Sept. 1988)-. Periodical. English. qt. $60.00 (institutions), $38.00 (individuals) US; 68.00 (institutions), $46.00 (individuals) other. Mosby Year Book Inc., 11830 Westline Industrial Drive, St Louis MO 63146. **Tel** (800)325-4177, (314)872-8370, FAX (314)432-1380, telex 44-2402. **ED** Patricia Bates. **DD** 610. **NLM** W1; UR636L. **CODEN** URNUES. **[CCC].** Index available. cum. index. **Bk Rev. Ad Acc. Pr Rev. Circ:** 2,000. ***Continues*** *AUAA Journal, 0882-9594.*
**Desc:** Disseminates information about urologic disease, urologic nursing, and information appropriate for the care of the urologic patient.
**Ind/Abst** Int. Nurs. Index (1988-); Nurs. Abstr.

FR/0396-8669
**V.S.T. See** Medical Science and Technology-Psychiatry.

NO/0107-4083
**VARD I NORDEN. Added/Corp** Sygeplejerskers Samarbejde i Norden. (1981)-. Periodical. Danish (English, Norwegian and Swedish; summaries and/or abstracts in English). qt. Sygeplejerskernes Samarejde, Postboks 2681, N-0131 Oslo 1 Norway. **Tel** 011 47 2 2383768. **NLM** W1; VA12T.
**Ind/Abst** Cumul. Index Nurs. Allied Health Lit. (19??-); Int. Nurs. Index (1981-).

US/0191-1880
**VERMONT REGISTERED NURSE.** [Vt. regist. nurse]. **Added/Corp** Vermont State Nurses Association. (1962)-. Periodical. English. qt (Mar., June, Sept., and Dec.). $15.00. Vermont State Nurses Association, 1 Main St. 26, Winooski VT 05404. **Tel** (802)864-9390. **ED** Bonnie Stiles. **NLM** W1 VE682. **Bk Rev. Ad Acc. Circ:** 500 (ctrl).
**Desc:** Local, state, and national news. Feature articles of interest to professional nurses.
**Ind/Abst** Cumul. Index Nurs. Allied Health Lit. (19??-); Int. Nurs. Index (19??-).

NE/0920-3273
**VERPLEEGKUNDE.** (1986)-. Periodical. Dutch (summaries and/or abstracts in English). qt. Fl103.00. Uitgeversmaatschappij de Tijdstroom BV, Noorderwal 38, Postbus 14, 7240 BA Lochem Netherlands. **Tel** 011 31 5730 53651, FAX 011 31 5730 56724. **(Subscription address:** Infolio BV, Postbus 16500, 2500 DM Den Haag Netherlands.) **NLM** W1; VE785D.
**Ind/Abst** Int. Nurs. Index (May 1993-).

NE/0167-4706
**VERPLEEGKUNDIGE STUDIES. VFOAT** Reeks Verpleegkundige Studies. V. 1-. Monographic series. Dutch. Price varies per volume. De Tijdstroom, Postbus 14, 7240 BA Lochem Netherlands. **NLM** W1 VE785S.

BE
**VERPLEEGKUNDIGEN EN GEMEENSCHAPSZORG.** (19??)-. Dutch. Five times a year. 250F (each issue). N V K V V, Vergote Square 43, B-1040 Brussels Belgium. **Tel** 02 7321050, FAX 02 7348460. Index available. cum. index. **Ad Acc, Adv Mgr:** Michel Foulon. Full Page (B&W) 880F. Half Page (B&W) 600F. Full Page (Color) 1315F. Half Page (Color) 902F.

UK
**VETERINARY NURSING JOURNAL.** (19??)-. English. Six times a year (Jan., Mar., May, July, Sept., Nov.). £37.00 UK; £42.00 Africa; £47.50 others. British Veterinary Nursing Association, Sheedbed Centre, Coldharbor Road, Harlow Essex CM19 5AF England. **Tel** 011 441 279 20181. **(Subscription address:** TG Scott Subscriber Services, 6 Bourne Enterprise Centre, Kent TN15 8DG United Kingdom.)
**Desc:** Presenting up-to-date information for the fast developing role of the veterinary nursing profession. Specializes in continuing education and clinical to commercial nursing.

US/0270-7780
**VIRGINIA NURSE.** ***Title Change.*** [Va. nurse]. **Added/Corp** Virginia Nurses' Association. Vol. 45 [i.e. Vol. 44]- (1976)-(19??). Periodical. English. tq (Mar., June, Sept.). Virginia Nurses Association, 1311 High Point Avenue, Richmond VA 23230. **Tel** (804)353-7311. **ED** Veronica Arikian. **NLM** W1; VI81K. **Bk Rev. Ad Acc, Adv Mgr:** Pat Taylor. **Circ:** 3,000 (ctrl). ***Continues*** *Virginia Nurse Quarterly.* ***Continued by*** *Virginia Nurses Today.*
**Desc:** Information on nursing issues, health care, activities of the association and news in the state, national and international nursing community.
**Ind/Abst** Cumul. Index Nurs. Allied Health Lit. (?-?); Int. Nurs. Index (?-?).

US
**VIRGINIA NURSES TODAY. Added/Corp** Virginia Nurses' Association. Vol. 1, No. 1 (June/July 1983)-. Periodical. English. bm. $30.00. Virginia Nurses Association, 1311 High Point Avenue, Richmond VA 23230. **Tel** (804)353-7311. **NLM** W1; VI81T. ***Continues*** *Virginia Nurse, 0270-7780.*
**Ind/Abst** Int. Nurs. Index (1993-).

●US/1066-2944
**VOICES (WASHINGTON, D.C.).** (VOICES : PUBLICATION OF AWHONN, ASSOCIATION OF

WOMEN'S HEALTH, OBSTETRIC, AND NEONATAL NURSING.). [AWHONN voice]. **Added/Corp** Association of Women's Health, Obstetric, and Neonatal Nursing. **VFOAT** Voice. (1993)-. Periodical. English. mo. $35.00 US and Canada. Association of Women's Health, Obstetric, and Neonatal Nursing, 700 14th St. NW, Suite 600, Washington DC 20005. **Tel** (202)863-2441. **DD** 610. **NLM** W1; AW946G. Index available (Bound in last issue). ***Continues*** *NAACOG Newsletter, 0889-0579.*
**Ind/Abst** Int. Nurs. Index (1993-).

US/0734-5666
**WASHINGTON NURSE, THE.** [Wash. nurse]. **Added/Corp** Washington State Nurses Association. Vol. 7, No. 2 (June 1977)-. Periodical. English. Six times a year. $20.00 US; $26.00 Canada & Mexico; $39.00 other. Washington State Nurses Association, 2505 2nd Avenue, Suite 500, Seattle WA 98121-1464. **Tel** (206)443-9762, FAX (206)728-2074. **ED** Dennis Burnside. **NLM** W1 WA611M. **Bk Rev. Ad Acc. Circ:** 7,500. ***Continues*** *WSNA Mini Journal.*
**Desc:** Information on nursing education, clinical information, health care legislation, economic and general welfare.
**Ind/Abst** Cumul. Index Nurs. Allied Health Lit.; Int. Nurs. Index.

US/0043-1664
**WEATHER VANE (CHARLESTON, W. VA.), THE.** ***Title Change.*** (THE WEATHER VANE.). [Weather vane]. **Added/Corp** West Virginia Nurses Association. (19??)-(1992). Periodical. English. qt. West Virginia Nurses Association, PO Box 1946, Charleston WV 25327-1946. **Tel** (304)342-1169. **ED** Carol S. Fulks. **DD** 610. **NLM** W1 WE119. **Ad Acc. Pr Rev. Circ:** 1,500. ***Continued by*** *West Virginia Nurses Association. West Virginia Nurse, 1074-8091.*
**Desc:** Professional nursing journal.
**Ind/Abst** Cumul. Index Nurs. Allied Health Lit.; Int. Nurs. Index.

●US/1074-8091
**WEST VIRGINIA NURSE.** (WEST VIRGINIA NURSE : THE OFFICIAL PUBLICATION OF THE WEST VIRGINIA NURSES ASSOCIATION, INC.). [W. Va. nurse]. **Added/Corp** West Virginia Nurses Association. (1992)-. Periodical. English. Four times a year (Mar., June, Sept., Dec.). $25.00. West Virginia Nurses Association, PO Box 1946, Charleston WV 25327-1946. **Tel** (304)342-1169. **DD** 610. **NLM** W1; WE456M. ***Continues*** *Weather Vane, 0043-1664.*
**Desc:** A professional nurse and nursing journal.
**Ind/Abst** Cumul. Index Nurs. Allied Health Lit.; Int. Nurs. Index (1992-).

US/0193-9459
**WESTERN JOURNAL OF NURSING RESEARCH.** [West. j. nursing res.]. **VFOAT** WJNR. Vol. 1 (Winter 1979)-. Academic Scholarly Publication. English. bm (Feb., Apr., June, Aug., Oct., Dec.). $194.00. SAGE Periodical Press, 2455 Teller Road, Thousand Oaks CA 91320. **Tel** (805)499-0721, FAX (805)499-0871, telex 100799. **ED** Pamela J. Brink (University of Alberta). **DD** 610. **NLM** WI WE635. **[CCC]. Ad Acc. Acid Free.** available on microfilm and microfiche from University Microfilms International (UMI).
**Desc:** An innovative forum for scholarly debate, as well as for research and theoretical papers. Clinical studies have commentaries and rebuttals. Departments deal with current issues in nursing research.
**Ind/Abst** Annals Behav. Med.; Cumul. Index Nurs. Allied Health Lit.; Hum. Resour. Abstr.; Index Med. (Vol. 8, No. 4, 1986-); Int. Nurs. Index; Sage Fam. Stud. Abstr.; SportSearch.

UK/0737-6065
**WILEY SERIES ON DEVELOPMENTS IN NURSING RESEARCH.** [Wiley ser. dev. nurs. res.]. **VFOAT** Developments in Nursing Research. Vol. 1-. Monographic series. English. Price varies per volume. John Wiley & Sons Ltd., Baffins Lane, Chichester West Sussex PO19 1UD England. **Tel** 0243 779777, FAX 0243 776128 BTG:JWP001, telex 86290 WIBOOKG. **(Subscription address:** North, South and Central America/ John Wiley & Sons, Inc., Subscription Department, 605 Third Avenue, New York, NY 10158-0012, USA; telephone: (212)850-6645; FAX: (212)850-6021**)** **NLM** W1 WI53LF.

●US/1070-308X
**WOMEN'S HEALTH NURSING SCAN (1993).** (WOMEN'S HEALTH NURSING SCAN / AWHONN.). [Women's health nurs. scan]. **Added/Corp** Association of Women's Health, Obstetric, and Neonatal Nurses. **VFOAT** AWHONN's Women's Health Nursing Scan. Vol. 7, No. 1 (Jan./Feb. 1993)-. Periodical. English. bm (6 issues). $63.00 (institutions), $43.00 (individuals) US; $74.00 (institutions), $54.00 (individuals) other. NURSECOM Inc., 1211 Locust Street, Philadelphia PA 19107. **Tel** (215)545-7222, (800)242-6757, FAX (215)545-8107. **LC** RA778.A1; N875. **DD** 610. ***Continues*** *NAACOG's Women's Health Nursing Scan, 1055-3533.*

IE/0332-3056
**WORLD OF IRISH NURSING.** ***Title Change.*** [World Ir. nurs.]. **Added/Corp** Irish Nurses' Organisation. National Council of Nurses of Ireland. Vol. 1 (Jan. 1972)-Vol. 22 (Dec. 1992). Periodical. English. bm. Maxwell Publicity Ltd., 11 Fitzwilliam Place, Dublin 2 Ireland. **NLM** W1; WO8974. ***Supersedes*** *Irish Nurses Journal; Irish Nurse* ***and*** *Irish Nurses' Magazine.* ***Continued by*** *New World of Irish Nursing.*
**Ind/Abst** Cumul. Index Nurs. Allied Health Lit.; Int. Nurs. Index.

US
**WYOMING NURSE.** (19??)-. English. Four times a year. $15.00. Wyoming Nurses Association, 1603 Capital Avenue, Majestic Building, Suite 305, Cheyenne WY 82001. **Tel** (307)635-3955. **ED** Kathy Watkins. **Ad Acc, Adv Mgr:** Mark Miller, **Tel** (319)277-2414. **Circ:** 8,000 (ctrl).

ZA/0044-1740
**ZAMBIA NURSE (KITWE, ZAMBIA : 1978).** (THE ZAMBIA NURSE.). [Zamb. nurse]. 1978-. Periodical. English. Three times a year. K150.00 Zambia; $15.00 other. Zambia Nurses Association, PO Box 50375, Lusaka Zambia. **NLM** W1 ZA756V. **Bk Rev. Ad Acc.** ctrl circ. ***Continues*** *Zambia Nurse Journal.*
**Ind/Abst** Cumul. Index Nurs. Allied Health Lit.; Int. Nurs. Index.

CC/0254-1769
**ZHONGHUA HULI ZAZHI.** (CHUNG-HUA HU LI TSA CHIH.). [Zhonghua huli zazhi]. **VFOAT** Chinese Journal of Nursing. (1954)-. Periodical. Chinese (English). bm. **(Subscription address:** China International Book Trading Corporation, PO Box 399, Library Service Department, Beijing 100044 People's Republic of China.**)** **NLM** W1 CH9819M.
**Ind/Abst** Index Med. (1985-); Int. Nurs. Index.

RH/1012-9103
**ZIMBABWE NURSE, THE.** [Zimb. nurse]. 1980-. English. an. Zimbabwe Nurses Association, PO Box 3502, Harare Zimbabwe. **Tel** 011 79 16 31. **NLM** W1; ZI437. ***Continues*** *Zimbabwe Rhodesia Nurse.*

---

## OPHTHALMOLOGY

---

GW/0567-4921
**ABHANDLUNGEN AUS DEM GEBIETE DER AUGENHEILKUNDE.** [Abh. Geb. Augenheilkd.]. Vol. 34 (1967)-. Academic Scholarly Publication. German. ir. Price varies per volume. Georg Thieme Verlag Stuttgart, Postfach 301120, D 70451 Stuttgart Germany. **Tel** 011 49 711 89310, FAX 011 49 711 8931298, telex 7 252 275 GTVD. **(Subscription address:** Thieme Medical Publishers Inc., 381 Park Avenue South, New York NY 10016.**)** **ED** K. Velhagen. **NLM** W1 AB458. **Bk Rev.** ***Continues*** *Sammlung Zwangloser Abhandlungen aus dem Gebiete der Augenheilkunde, 0487-1154.*
**Ind/Abst** EMBASE.

US/8756-9175
**ABMS DIRECTORY OF CERTIFIED OPHTHALMOLOGISTS.** ***Title Change.*** [ABMS dir. certif. ophthalmol.]. **Added/Corp** American Board of Medical Specialties. American Board of Ophthalmology. **VFOAT** Directory of Certified Ophthalmologists. **VAT** American Board of Medical Specialties Directory of Certified Ophthalmologists. 1st Ed.-(1984)-(19??). Directory. English. be. American Board of Medical Specialties, 1 Rotary Center, Suite 805, Evanston IL 60201. **Tel** (708)491-9091. **LC** RE22; .A25. **DD** 617.7/002/73. **NLM** WW 22.1; A1523. ***Continued by*** *Official American Board of Medical Specialties (ABMS) Directory of Board Certified Ophthalmologists, 0000-1465.*

DK/0105-6255
**ACTA CAMPANOLOGICA. See** Medical Science and Technology.

SP/0210-4695
**ACTA ESTRABOLOGICA.** [Acta estrabol.]. (1973)-. Periodical. Spanish. an. Sociedad Espanola de Estrabologia, Donoso Cortes 73, 28015 Madrid Spain. **UDC** 617.7.
**Ind/Abst** Indice Med. Esp.

DK/0001-639X
**ACTA OPHTHALMOLOGICA.** [Acta ophthalmol.]. Vol. 1, (1923)-. Academic Scholarly Publication. English. Six times a year (Feb., Apr., June, Aug., Oct., Dec.). kr990.00 Scandinavia; kr1190.00 Europe; kr1240.00 other. Scriptor Publisher APS, Valbygardsvej 64, 2500 Valby Copenhagen Denmark. **Tel** 011 45 1 31174113, FAX 011 45 1 31171947. **ED** Niels Ehlers. **NLM** W1 AC8811. **CODEN** ACOPAT. Index available. **Bk Rev. Ad Acc. Pr Rev. Circ:** 2,000 (ctrl). Documents available from The Genuine Article, BIOSIS Document Express, CASDDS.
**Ind/Abst** Biol. Abstr.; Chem. Abstr.; Curr. Contents Clin. Med.; EMBASE; Energy Res. Abstr.; Health Plan. Adminis.; Helminthol. Abstr. (1991-); Index Med.; INIS Atomindex [Micro.]; Mod. Med.; Life Sci. Collect.; Protozoolog. Abstr.; Res. Alert [Full Cov.]; Rev. Med. Vet. Mycology; Sci. Cit. Index; SCISEARCH; Soc. Sci. Cit. Index [Select. Cov.].

DK
**ACTA OPHTHALMOLOGICA. SUPPLEMENT.** 170 (1985)-. Monographic series. English. Price varies per volume. Scriptor Publisher APS, Valbygardsvej 64, 2500 Valby Copenhagen Denmark. **Tel** 011 45 1 31174113, FAX 011 45 1 31171947. ***Continues*** *Acta Ophthalmologica. Supplementum, 0065-1451.*

●US/1060-5991
**ADMINISTRATIVE OPHTHALMOLOGY.** (ADMINISTRATIVE OPHTHALMOLOGY : AO.). [Adm. ophthalmol.]. **Added/Corp** American Society of Ophthalmic Administrators. **VFOAT** AO. Vol. 1, No. 1 (Spring 1992)-. Periodical. English. qt (Jan., Apr., Jul., Oct.). $45.00 (1 year), $75.00 (2 year), $95.00 (3 year). American Society of Opthalmic Administrators, 4000 Legato Road, Suite 850, Fairfax VA 22033-4003. **Tel** (703)591-2222, FAX (703)591-0614. **(Subscription address:** Fulco, 30 Broad Street, Denville NJ 07834.**)** **DD** 617. **NLM** W1; AD344A.

●US/1070-5384
**ADVANCES IN CLINICAL OPHTHALMOLOGY.** [Adv. clin. ophthalmol.]. Vol. 1 (1994)-. English. an. $87.50. Mosby Year Book Inc., 11830 Westline Industrial Drive, St Louis MO 63146. **Tel** (800)325-4177, (314)872-8370, FAX (314)432-1380, telex 44-2402. **DD** 617.

US/0276-3508
**ADVANCES IN OPHTHALMIC PLASTIC AND RECONSTRUCTIVE SURGERY. See** Medical Science and Technology-Surgery.

II/0254-0517
**AFRO-ASIAN JOURNAL OF OPHTHALMOLOGY.** [Afro-asian j. ophthalmol.]. **VFOAT** Ophthalmology. Vol. 1, No. 1 (June 1982)-. Academic Scholarly Publication. English. qt. $40.00. A K Verma, 16 B 22 Dev Nagar, New Delhi 110005 India. **(Subscription address:** Prints India, 11 Darya Ganj, New Delhi 110002 India.**)** **NLM** W1 AF629. **CODEN** AAJODO. Documents available from CASDDS.
**Ind/Abst** Chem. Abstr.; EMBASE.

IT/0002-0915
**AGGIORNAMENTI DI TERAPIA OFTALMOLOGICA.** 1- 1949-. Periodical. Italian. qt. Via Carmignani 2, Pisa 56100 Italy. **Tel** 050/48531. **Circ:** 4,600.

GW/0942-5276
**AKTUELLE AUGENHEILKUNDE.** (1992)-. English. Six times a year. DM98.00. Georg Thieme Verlag Stuttgart, Postfach 301120, D 70451 Stuttgart Germany. **Tel** 011 49 711 89310, FAX 011 49 711 8931298, telex 7 252 275 GTVD. **(Subscription address:** Thieme Medical Publishers Inc., 381 Park Avenue South, New York NY 10016.**)** ***Continues*** *Folia Ophthalmological, 0323-4932.*

SY
**AL-KAHHAL. VFOAT** Alkahhal. Journal 1- Festival Year 1980-. Periodical. Arabic. qt. 35.00 medical students, 75.00 others. Majallat Al-Kahhal, Ittihad Al-Kuttab Al-Arab, Dimashq Syria. **LC** RE1; .K33.

US/0002-9394
**AMERICAN JOURNAL OF OPHTHALMOLOGY.** [Am. j. ophthalmol.]. Vol. 1 (1884)-. Academic Scholarly Publication. English. Twelve times a year. $91.00 (institutions), $66.00 (individuals) US; $134.00 (institutions), $99.00 (individuals) other. Ophthalmic Publishing Company, 77 West Wacker Drive, Suite 660, Chicago IL 60601. **Tel** (312)629-1690, FAX (312)629-1744. **ED** Frank W. Newell. **LC** RE1; .A36. **CODEN** AJOPAA. Index available. cum. index. **Bk Rev. Ad Acc. Pr Rev. Circ:** 18,000 (ctrl). available on microfilm and microfiche from University Microfilms International (UMI). Documents available from The Genuine Article, BIOSIS Document Express, CASDDS. ***Absorbed*** *Annals of Ophthalmology; Ophthalmic Record; Annals of Oftamologia; Ophthalmology; Ophthalmic Yearbook; Ophthalmic Literature.*
**Desc:** Original articles written and reviewed by ophthalmologists. Contains letters, book reviews, correspondence, clip and file abstracts from other publications and news items.
**Ind/Abst** Abr. Index Med.; Biol. Abstr.; Chem. Abstr.; Chem. Hazards Ind.; Curr. Contents Clin. Med.; Curr. Contents Life Sci.; Dairy Sci. Abstr.; EMBASE; Energy Res. Abstr.; Health Period. Database [Full Txt.]; Health Plan. Adminis.; Helminthol. Abstr. (1991-); Index Med.; Index Vet.; Int. Aerosp. Abstr.; Iowa Drug Inf. Serv. (1967-); Lab. Hazards Bull.; Microbiol. Abstr. Sect. B; Microbiol. Abstr. Sect. C; Mod. Med.; Nutr. Abstr. Rev., Ser. B, Live Feeds and Feed.; Nutr. Abstr. Rev., Ser. A, Hum. Exp.; Life Sci. Collect.; PESTDOC; Physic. Medline Plus; Protozoolog. Abstr.; Ref. Upd. Basic Ed.; Ref. Upd. Deluxe Ed.; Res. Alert [Full Cov.]; Rev. Med. Vet. Entomol.; Rev. Med. Vet. Mycology; Risk Abstr. (19??-19??); Sci. Cit. Index; SCISEARCH; Soc. Sci. Cit. Index [Select. Cov.]; SportSearch; Vet. Bull.; Virol. AIDS Abstr.

US/0065-955X
**AMERICAN ORTHOPTIC JOURNAL.** [Am. orthopt. j.]. **Added/Corp** American Association of Orthoptic Technicians. American Academy of Ophthalmology and Otolaryngology. American Association of Certified Orthoptists. Vol. 1 (1951)-. Periodical. English. an. $22.00 (one year), $44.00 (two year), $66.00 (three year) individuals; $57.00 (one year), $112.00 (two year), $166.00 (three year) institutions.

University of Wisconsin Press, Journal Division, 114 North Murray Street, Madison WI 53715. **Tel** (608)262-4952, FAX (608)262-8909. **NLM** W1 AM674. **CODEN** AOJTAW. **[CCC].** cum. index. **Ad Acc, Adv Mgr Tel** (608)262-5839. available on microfilm and microfiche from University Microfilms International (UMI). Documents available from BIOSIS Document Express.
**Desc:** The journal serves as a forum for orthoptists and ophthalmologists to present new material in the fields of amblyopia and strabismus.
**Ind/Abst** Biol. Abstr. (1969-1977); EMBASE; Energy Res. Abstr. (Aug. 1982-); Health Plan. Adminis.

CN/0710-1368
**AMIS DE LA BANQUE D'YEUX DU QUEBEC.** (LES AMIS DE LA BANQUE D'YEUX DU QUEBEC : JOURNAL.). [Amis Banque yeux Que.]. Vol. 1, No. 1 (Jan. 1981)-. Periodical. French. qt. Free. Banque d'Yeux du Quebec, 5689 Boul Rosemont, Montreal Quebec G1T 2H1 Canada. **DD** 362.1/7. ctrl circ.

SP/0210-0681
**ANALES DE LA SOCIEDAD ERGOFTALMOLOGICA ESPANOLA.** [An. Soc. Ergoftalmol. Esp.]. (1971)-. Periodical. Spanish. bm. Audiovisual y Marketing SA, Donoso Cortes 73/1, 28015 Madrid Spain. **UDC** 617.7.
**Ind/Abst** Indice Med. Esp.

SP/0020-3645
**ANALES DEL INSTITUTO BARRAQUER.** Vol. 1 (Sept. 1959)-. Periodical. Multiple languages (Spanish, French, Italian, Portuguese, German, English, Japanese and Greek, Modern). Instituto Barraquer, Laforja 188, 08021 Barcelona Spain. **NLM** W1 AN171B. ***Supersedes*** *Estudios e Informaciones Oftalmologicas.*
**Ind/Abst** Indice Med. Esp.

IT/0003-4665
**ANNALI DI OTTALMOLOGIA E CLINICA OCULISTICA.** [Ann. ottalmol. clin. ocul.]. **VFOAT** Annali di Oftalmologia e Clinica Oculistica. Vol. 45 (1917)-. Periodical. Italian (summaries and/or abstracts in English). mo. L140000.00 Italy; L280000.00 other. Casa Editrice Maccari, Via Trento 53, 43100 Parma Italy. **Tel** 011 39 521 771268, FAX 011 39 521 771268. **NLM** W1; AN502. **CODEN** AOCOAG. Documents available from BIOSIS Document Express. ***Formed by the union of*** *Annali di Ottalmologia* ***and*** *Clinica Oculista.*
**Ind/Abst** Biol. Abstr. (1985-); EMBASE; Life Sci. Collect.

US/0003-4886
**ANNALS OF OPHTHALMOLOGY (BIRMINGHAM).** (ANNALS OF OPHTHALMOLOGY.). [Ann. ophthalmol.]. **Added/Corp** American Society of Contemporary Ophthalmology. International Association of Ocular Surgeons. (June/July 1969)-. Periodical. English. Six times a year. $90.00 (surface mail) US; $95.00 (airmail) others. Altier Maynard Communications, 59 Oakwood Drive, Madison CT 06443. **Tel** (203)421-3494, FAX (203)421-3250. **ED** John Bellows. **LC** RE1; .A54. **DD** 617/.7/005. **NLM** W1 AN617G. **CODEN** ANOPB5. **Bk Rev. Pr Rev.** ctrl circ. Documents available from The Genuine Article, BIOSIS Document Express. ***Absorbed*** *Journal of Ocular Therapy & Surgery, 0730-0883* ***and*** *Glaucoma, 0164-4645.*
**Desc:** A journal that contains clinical papers that cover this field, with articles on medicine and surgery.
**Ind/Abst** Biol. Abstr.; Curr. Contents Clin. Med.; EMBASE; Energy Res. Abstr. (July 1975-); Health Plan. Adminis.; Helminthol. Abstr. (1991-); Index Med.; INIS Atomindex [Micro.]; Mod. Med.; Life Sci. Collect.; Protozoolog. Abstr.; Res. Alert [Full Cov.]; Rev. Med. Vet. Entomol.; Rev. Med. Vet. Mycology; Sci. Cit. Index; SCISEARCH; SportSearch.

US/0161-7699
**ANNUAL REPORT / NATIONAL EYE INSTITUTE.** **Main/Corp** National Eye Institute. Began with 1969/70. English. an. National Eye Institute, National Institute of Health, Building 31/Room 6A-32, 9000 Rockville Pike, Bethesda MD 20205. **LC** RE1; .N27A. **DD** 353.0084/1. **NLM** W2 A N157A. available on microfiche (Vols. for (1981-) distributed to depository libraries).

SP
**APOTEKARIS.** Spanish. ir. Colegio Oficial de Farmaceuticos de Baleares, Arco de la Merced 4, 07002 Palma de Mallorca Spain.

GW
**ARBEITSMEDIZINISCHE FRAGEN IN DER OPHTHALMOLOGIE.** **VFOAT** Problemes de la Medecine du Travail de l'Ophtalmologie; Problems of Industrial Medicine in Ophthalmology. (1968)-. Monographic series. English (German). ir. Price varies per volume. **DD** 617.7. **NLM** W1 AR125R.

GR/0471-6981
**ARCHEIA OPHTHALMOLOGIKES HETAIREIAS BOREIOU HELLADOS.** **VFOAT** Archives de la Societe d'Ophthalmologie de la Grece du Nord. V. 1- 1952-. Periodical. Greek, Modern (summaries and/or abstracts in French). **NLM** W1 AR158D.

US/0003-9950
**ARCHIVES OF OPHTHALMOLOGY.** [Arch. ophthalmol.]. **Added/Corp** American Medical Association. Vol. 64 (July 1960)-. Academic Scholarly Publication. English. mo. $125.00 (institution), $110.00 (individual) US. American Medical Association, 515 North State Street, Chicago IL 60610. **Tel** (312)464-5000, (800)262-2350, FAX (312)464-5831. **ED** Morton F. Goldberg. **LC** RE1; .A62. **DD** 617. **NLM** W1 AR457CC. **CODEN** AROPAW. **[CCC].** Index available (free). cum. index. **Bk Rev. Ad Acc. Pr Rev. Circ:** 240,000. available on microfilm and microfiche from University Microfilms International (UMI); available on an online database (file 442/Full-Text) from DIALOG; and MEDIS. Documents available from The Genuine Article, BIOSIS Document Express, CASDDS. ***Continues*** *A.M.A. Archives of Ophthalmology, 0096-6339.*
**Desc:** Published as an educational service for physicians who practice ophthalmology as a primary specialty, and to physicians of other specialties who treat conditions of the eye. It provides clinicians with a broadly diversified fund of knowledge upon which to base their clinical judgment and technical decisions.
**Ind/Abst** Abr. Index Med.; Biol. Abstr.; Chem. Abstr.; Curr. Contents Clin. Med.; Curr. Contents Life Sci.; EMBASE; Energy Res. Abstr.; Health Plan. Adminis.; Helminthol. Abstr. (19??-19??); Highw. Res. Abstr.; Index Med.; Index Vet.; INIS Atomindex [Micro.]; Iowa Drug Inf. Serv. (1968-); Med. Abstr. Newsl.; Microbiol. Abstr. Sect. B (19??-19??); Microbiol. Abstr. Sect. C; Mod. Med.; Nutr. Abstr. Rev., Ser. B, Live Feeds and Feed.; Nutr. Abstr. Rev., Ser. A, Hum. Exp.; Life Sci. Collect.; PESTDOC; Physic. Medline Plus; Protozoolog. Abstr.; Ref. Upd. Basic Ed.; Ref. Upd. Deluxe Ed.; Res. Alert [Full Cov.]; Rev. Med. Vet. Mycology; Rev. Plant Pathol.; Saf. Health Work; Sci. Cit. Index; SCISEARCH; Soc. Sci. Cit. Index [Select. Cov.]; Vet. Bull.; Virol. AIDS Abstr.

SP/1130-5134
**ARCHIVES OF OPTHALMOLOGY ED. ESPANOLA. BARCELONA.** [Arch. ophthalmol. Ed. esp., Barc.]. **Added/Corp** American Medical Association. (1990)-. Periodical. Spanish. bm (6 issues). $61.00. Ediciones Doyma SA, Travesera de Gracia 17 21, 08021 Barcelona Spain. **Tel** 011 34 3 2000711, 011 34 3 4145706, FAX 011 34 3 2091136, telex 51964 INK E. **UDC** 617.7.

SP/0211-2698
**ARCHIVOS DE LA SOCIEDAD CANARIA DE OFTALMOLOGIA.** [Arch. Soc. Canar. Oftalmol.]. No. 1- 1976-. Academic Scholarly Publication. Spanish. an. **NLM** W1 AR678.
**Ind/Abst** EMBASE.

SP
**ARCHIVOS DE LA SOCIEDAD ESPANOLA DE OFTALMOLOGIA.** (1971)-. Spanish. mo. Sociedad Espanola de Oftalmologia, C Donoso Cortes 73, 28003 Madrid Spain. **Tel** 011 34 1 5445879, 011 34 1 5448035.
**Ind/Abst** EMBASE [Select. Cov.].

AG/0066-6777
**ARCHIVOS DE OFTALMOLOGIA DE BUENOS AIRES.** [Arch. oftalmol. B. Aires]. **Added/Corp** Sociedad Argentina de Oftalmologia. Vol. 1 (Nov. 1925)-. Periodical. Spanish. Three times a year. $30.00. Society Argentina Oftalmologia Buenos Aires Argentina, Viamonte 1464 1 2, 1055 Buenos Aires Argentina. **Tel** 46-0527. **NLM** W1 AR704. **Ad Acc. Circ:** 2,000 (ctrl).
**Desc:** Papers on investigation in ophthalmology.
**Ind/Abst** EMBASE.

CK/0037-8364
**ARCHIVOS - SOCIEDAD AMERICANA DE OFTALMOLOGIA Y OPTOMETRIA.** (ARCHIVOS DE LA SOCIEDAD AMERICANA DE OFTALMOLOGIA Y OPTOMETRIA.). [Arch. - Soc. Am. Oftalmol. Optom.]. **Main/Corp** Sociedad Americana de Oftalmologia y Optometria. (1958)-. Academic Scholarly Publication. Spanish (English and French). ir. Sociedad Americana de Oftalmologia y Optometria, Apartado Aereo 091019, Bogota DE 8 Colombia. **Tel** 011 57 236 6033. **DD** 617.7. **NLM** W1 SO14.
**Ind/Abst** EMBASE.

US/0194-8172
**ARGUS (SAN FRANCISCO).** (ARGUS.). **Added/Corp** American Academy of Ophthalmology. (19??)-. Periodical. English. mo. $36.00; Also comes with membership. American Academy of Ophthalmology, 655 Beach Street, San Francisco CA 94120. **Tel** (415)561-8500. **ED** Bruce E. Spivey. **Bk Rev. Ad Acc. Circ:** 14,000 (ctrl).
**Desc:** Presents news, trends, opinions, and features affecting ophthalmology. Also serves as the official member publication for the American Academy of Ophthalmology.

BL/0004-2749
**ARQUIVOS BRASILEIROS DE OFTALMOLOGIA.** [Arq. bras. oftalmol.]. Vol. 1 (June 1938)-. Periodical. Portuguese. Four times a year. $100.00. Conselho Brasileiro de Oftalmologia, Caixa Postal 20318, 04034 Sao Paulo SP Brazil. **NLM** W1 AR8786. **CODEN** AQBOAP. Documents available from BIOSIS Document Express.
**Ind/Abst** Biol. Abstr.; EMBASE [Select. Cov.].

US/1067-9812
**AUDIOVISUAL JOURNAL OF CATARACT & IMPLANT SURGERY.** (AUDIOVISUAL JOURNAL OF CATARACT & IMPLANT SURGERY [VIDEORECORDING].). [Audiov. j. cataract implant surg.]. **Added/Corp** Cincinnati Eye Institute. **VFOAT** Audiovisual Journal of Cataract and Implant Surgery; Audio Visual Journal of Cataract & Implant Surgery. Vol. 1, No. 1 (1985)-. Periodical. English. qt. $220.00 US; $250.00 other. Audiovisual Journal of Cataract and Implant Surgery, 10494 Montgomery Road, Cincinnati OH 45242. **Tel** (513)984-5133, FAX (513)984-4240. **DD** 617.
**Desc:** Emphasizes surgical techniques, intraocular lenses, complication management, and controversies in cataract surgery.

GW/0004-7929
**AUGENOPTIKER, DER.** **Added/Corp** Zentralverband der Augenoptiker. Wissenschaftlichen Vereinigung fuer Augenoptik und Optometrie. Bundesverband Nichtselbstandiger Augenoptiker. Bundesverband der Fach-Grosshandler fuer Optik und Feinmechanik. (1953)-. Periodical. German. mo. DM106.60 Germany; DM121.55 other. Konradin Verlags Gruppe, Robert Kohlhammer GmbH, D-70765 Leinfelden Germany. **Tel** 011 49 711 7594370, 011 49 711 7594229. **ED** Konrad Kohlhammer. **DD** 617.7. **Bk Rev. Ad Acc. Circ:** 12,466 (ctrl).
**Desc:** Specialized journal for ophthalmic optics and optometry.

AT/0814-9763
**AUSTRALIAN AND NEW ZEALAND JOURNAL OF OPHTHALMOLOGY.** [Aust. N. Z. j. ophthalmol.]. Vol. 13, No. 1 (Feb. 1985)-. Academic Scholarly Publication. English. qt. 60.00Aus$. Royal Australian College of Ophthalmologists, 27 Commonwealth Street, Sydney 2010 Australia. **Tel** 61 2 267 7006, FAX 61 2 267 6534. **ED** Ian C Francis and Richard S Clemett. **NLM** W1; AU497D. **CODEN** ANZOEQ. Index available. **Bk Rev. Ad Acc. Pr Rev. Circ:** 1,200. Documents available from The Genuine Article, BIOSIS Document Express, CASDDS. ***Formed by the union of*** *Australian Journal of Ophthalmology, 0310-1177* ***and*** *Transactions of the Ophthalmological Society of New Zealand, 0300-8983.*
**Desc:** Ophthalmology and related subjects.
**Ind/Abst** Biol. Abstr. (1985-); Chem. Abstr.; Curr. Contents Clin. Med.; EMBASE; Health Plan. Adminis.; Helminthol. Abstr. (1991-); Index Med. (Vol. 13, No. 1, 1985-); Res. Alert [Full Cov.]; Rev. Med. Vet. Mycology; Rev. Plant Pathol.; Sci. Cit. Index; SCISEARCH; Soc. Sci. Cit. Index [Select. Cov.].

AT/0814-0936
**AUSTRALIAN ORTHOPTIC JOURNAL.** **Added/Corp** Orthoptic Association of Australia. (1967)-. English. an (June). 33.00Aus$ Australia; 44.00Aus$ other. Orthoptic Association of Australia Incorporated, PO Box 79, Hampton, Victoria 3188 Australia. **Tel** 11 61 3 5980371, 3 5970979, FAX 11 61 3 5970990. **ED** Elaine Cornell. **NLM** W1 AU643G. cum. index. **Bk Rev. Ad Acc. Circ:** 1,500.
**Desc:** Orthoptics, binocular vision, ocular motility, strabismus, heterophoria, diplopia, visual acuity, amblyopia, electro diagnostic techniques, research case studies, visual screening and visual rehabilitation.

US
**BINOCULAR VISION & EYE MUSCLE SURGERY QUARTERLY.** **VFOAT** Binocular Vision and Eye Muscle Surgery Quarterly; Binocular Vision Quarterly. Vol. 6, No. 4 (Fall 1991)-. Periodical. English. Four times a year (Jan., Mar., June, Sept.). $78.00 (individuals); $108.00 (institutions). Binoculus, 2500 Northwest 23rd Terrace, Gainesville FL 32605-2811. **Tel** (904)378-1129. **NLM** W1; BI619JL. Index available (Bound in 4th iss.). **Bk Rev**, (Qty: 4-6). **Ad Acc, Adv Mgr:** Judy, **Tel** (904)378-1129. **Circ:** 800-1,000. ***Continues*** *Binocular Vision, 0749-386X.*
**Desc:** This journal is for eye care professionals, with special interest in eye muscle surgery strabismus, amblyopia, eye movement & coordination, in infants, children, and adults.

US/0732-3484
**BIOMEDICAL FOUNDATIONS OF OPHTHALMOLOGY.** (1982)-. Periodical. English. an. $360.00 US; $374.00 Canada; $449.00 other. J.B. Lippincott Company, 227 East Washington Square, Philadelphia PA 19106-3780. **Tel** (215)238-4200 or 4454, FAX (215)238-4227. **(Subscription address:** J.B. Lippincott, PO Box 350, Hagerstown MD 21740.**)**

IT/0006-677X
**BOLLETTINO DI OCULISTICA.** [Boll. ocul.]. Began with Yearly V. 51, published 1972. Periodical. Italian (summaries and/or abstracts in English, French and German). bm. L60000 Italy; $60.00 other. GEM Srl Nuova Cappelli, Via Farini 14, 40124 Bologna Italy. **Tel** 011 39 51 239060. **ED** France Derme. **NLM** W1; BO562T. Index available. cum. index. **Bk Rev. Ad Acc.** ctrl circ. Documents available from BIOSIS Document Express. ***Continues*** *Bollettino d'Oculistica, 0006-677X.*
**Ind/Abst** Biol. Abstr.

UK/0007-1161
**BRITISH JOURNAL OF OPHTHALMOLOGY.** [Br. j. ophthalmol.]. **Added/Corp** British Medical Association. Institute of Ophthalmology (London, England). Vol. 1 (1917)-. Academic Scholarly Publication. English. mo. £206.00. BMJ / British Medical Journal Publishing Group, British Medical Association House, Tavistock Square, London WC1H 9JR England. **Tel** 011 44 71 3874499, FAX 011 44 71 383 6402, telex 290034 HBJ MN. **ED** J.V. Forrester. **DD** 617. **NLM** W1 BR589. **CODEN** BJOPAL. **[CCC].** cum. index. **Pr Rev.** available on microfilm and microfiche from University Microfilms International (UMI). Documents available from The Genuine Article, BIOSIS Document Express. ***Formed by the union of*** *Ophthalmoscope; Ophthalmic Review* ***and*** *Reports. Royal London Ophthalmic Hospital.*
**Desc:** Designed for the clinician and research worker and includes original articles, case notes, information on new appliances, and book reviews. In addition to original articles and case reports, a series of didactic teaching material in the form of 'mini-reviews' has been a new feature.
**Ind/Abst** Biol. Abstr.; Curr. Aware. Biol. Sci., CABS; Curr. Contents Clin. Med.; Curr. Contents Life Sci.; Dairy Sci. Abstr.; EMBASE; Health Period. Database; Health Plan. Adminis.; Helminthol. Abstr. (1991-); Hospit. Health Admin. Index; Index Med.; Index Vet.; Microbiol. Abstr. Sect. B (19??-19??); Mod. Med.; Life Sci. Collect.; Protozoolog. Abstr.; Ref. Upd. Basic Ed.; Ref. Upd. Deluxe Ed.; Res. Alert [Full Cov.]; Rev. Med. Vet. Entomol.; Rev. Med. Vet. Mycology; Rev. Plant Pathol.; Sci. Cit. Index; SCISEARCH; Small Anim. Abstr. Bibliogr.; Soc. Sci. Cit. Index [Select. Cov.].

UK/0068-2314
**BRITISH ORTHOPTIC JOURNAL.** [Br. orthopt. j.]. **Added/Corp** British Orthoptic Society. British Orthoptic Journal. No. 1, (Dec. 1939)-. Periodical. English. an (June). £26.50 UK; £27.00 other. British Orthoptic Society, Tavistock House North, Tavistock Square, London WC1H 9HX England. **Tel** 011 44 71 3877992, FAX 011 44 71 3832584. **ED** A. Horwood. **NLM** W1 BR746. Index available. cum. index. **Bk Rev. Ad Acc. Circ:** 1,600 (ctrl).
**Desc:** The learned journal of the British Orthoptic Society. Articles on the management, treatment and diagnosis of squints and other eye conditions.
**Ind/Abst** EMBASE.

GW/0068-3361
**BUCHEREI DES AUGENARZTES.** Vol. 1 (1938)-. German. ir. DM68.40 (Volume 130). Ferdinand Enke Verlag, Ruedigerstrasse 14, D-70469 Stuttgart Germany. **Tel** 011 49 711 8931124, 011 49 711 893123. **(Subscription address:** Georg Thieme Verlag Stuttgart, Postfach 301120, D 70451 Stuttgart Germany; telephone: 011 49 711 89310**)** **ED** G.O.H. Naumann, H.J. Merte, F. Hollwich and B. Gloor.
**Desc:** Deals with practical and clinical relevant subjects from the whole subject of ophthalmology. The volumes are supplements of the journal "Klinische Monatsblatter fuer Augenheilkunde".

UA/0078-5342
**BULLETIN. Main/Corp** Ophthalmological Society of Egypt. (1902)-. Bulletin. English.
**Ind/Abst** Health Plan. Adminis.

BE/0081-0746
**BULLETIN DE LA SOCIETE BELGE D'OPHTALMOLOGIE.** (BULLETIN.). [Bull. Soc. Belge Ophtalmol.]. **Main/Corp** Societe Belge d'Ophtalmologie. (1896)-. Bulletin. French. $141.01. Societe Belge d Ophtalmologie, Avenue des Jardins 24, Gillis 1030 Brussels Belgium. **NLM** W1 BU51.
**Ind/Abst** Health Plan. Adminis.; Index Med.

FR/0081-1270
**BULLETIN DES SOCIETES D'OPHTALMOLOGIE DE FRANCE.** [Bull. soc. ophtalmol. Fr.]. **Added/Corp** Societe d'Ophtalmologie de Paris. (1949)-. Academic Scholarly Publication. French. Twelve times a year. 750.00F France; 775.00F other. Librairie D L E S / Diffusion Litteraire et Scientifique, 11 rue Moliere, 13001 Marseille France. **Tel** 011 33 91 335791. **(Subscription address:** DLES, BP 47, 13262 Marseille Cedex 07 France; telephone: 011 33 91 335791**)** **NLM** W1 BU612. **CODEN** BSOFAK. Documents available from BIOSIS Document Express, CASDDS. ***Supersedes*** *Bulletin de la Societe d'Ophtalmologie de Paris, 0366-3485.*
**Ind/Abst** Biol. Abstr.; Chem. Abstr.; Index Med.

FR/0081-1092
**BULLETINS ET MEMOIRES.** ***Title Change.*** **Main/Corp** Societe Francaise d'Ophtalmologie. (1883)-(19??). French (English). an. Scientific & Medical Publishers of France, 100 East 42nd Street, Suite 1002, New York NY 10017-5613. **Tel** (212)983-6278. cum. index. **Circ:** 2,000. ***Continued by*** *Ophtalmologie, 0989-3105.*
**Ind/Abst** Health Plan. Adminis.; Index Med.

CN/0008-4182
**CANADIAN JOURNAL OF OPHTHALMOLOGY.** [Can. j. ophthalmol.]. **Added/Corp** Canadian Ophthalmological Society. **VFOAT** Journal Canadien d'Ophthalmologie. Vol. 1 (Jan. 1966)-. Academic Scholarly Publication. English (French; summaries and/or abstracts in French). Seven times a year. 70.00Can$ Canada; 80.00Can$ US; 90.00Can$ other. Canadian Ophthalmological Society, 1525 Carling Avenue/Suite 610, Ottawa Ontario K1Z 8R9 Canada. **Tel** (613)729-6779, FAX (613)729-7209. **ED** David J Addison. **NLM** W1 CA598. **CODEN** CAJOBA. **[CCC]. Bk Rev. Ad Acc. Pr Rev. Circ:** 1,500. available on microfilm and microfiche from University Microfilms International (UMI). Documents available from The Genuine Article, BIOSIS Document Express, CASDDS. ***Supersedes*** *Transactions of the Canadian Ophthalmological Society Annual Meeting, 0068-9408.*
**Desc:** Publishes scientific papers on ophthalmology and the related basic sciences.
**Ind/Abst** Biol. Abstr.; Chem. Abstr.; Curr. Contents Clin. Med.; EMBASE; Health Plan. Adminis.; Index Med.; Mod. Med.; Life Sci. Collect.; Protozoolog. Abstr.; Res. Alert [Full Cov.]; Rev. Med. Vet. Entomol.; Rev. Med. Vet. Mycology; Rev. Plant Pathol.; Sci. Cit. Index; SCISEARCH; SportSearch.

US/0740-6967
**CATARACT (NEW YORK, N.Y.).** ***Ceased.*** (CATARACT.). [Cataract]. (Nov. 1983)-?. Periodical. English. bm (eight no. a year). Park Row Publishers, 1457 Broadway/Suite 901, New York NY 10036. **NLM** W1; CA958H.

XR/0009-059X
**CESKOSLOVENSKA OFTALMOLOGIE.** [Cesk. oftalmol.]. **Added/Corp** Ceskoslovenska Oftalmologicka Spolecnost. Oftalmologicka Spolecnost. Vol. 1 (1933)-. Periodical. Czech (summaries and/or abstracts in English, Russian, French and German). bm. $81.90. **(Subscription address:** Artia Pegas Press Ltd., Palac Metro Narodni Trida 25, 11210 Prague 1 Czech Republic.**)** **NLM** W1 CE897P. **[CCC].**
**Ind/Abst** EMBASE; Index Med.

SP/0212-3940
**CHIBRET INTERNATIONAL JOURNAL OF OPHTHALMOLOGY EDICION ESPANOLA.** (ESPANOLA).). [Chibret int. j. ophthalmol.Ed. esp.]. (1983)-. Periodical. Spanish. ir. M.S.D., Josefa Valcarcel 38, 28027 Madrid Spain. **UDC** 617.7.

US/0748-9501
**CHIBRET INTERNATIONAL JOURNAL OF OPHTHALMOLOGY (ENGLISH ED.).** (CHIBRET INTERNATIONAL JOURNAL OF OPHTHALMOLOGY.). [Chibret Int. j. ophthalmol.]. **Added/Corp** Chibret International. (1983)-. Periodical. English (summaries and/or abstracts in French, German, Portuguese and Japanese). qt. Chibret International, Ophthalmic Group, PO Box 2000, Rahway NJ 07065. **Tel** (201)594-4000. **DD** 617. **NLM** W1; CH43P.
**Ind/Abst** EMBASE.

CC/0412-4081
**CHUNG-HUA YEN K'O TSA CHIH.** [Chung-hua yen k'o tsa chih]. (1951)-. Periodical. Chinese. bm (6 issues). $32.02. **(Subscription address:** China International Book Trading Corporation, PO Box 399, Library Service Department, Beijing 100044 People's Republic of China.**)** **DD** 617.7. **NLM** W1 CH985E.
**Ind/Abst** Index Med. (1979-).

US/0733-8902
**CLAO JOURNAL, THE.** [CLAO j.]. **Added/Corp** Contact Lens Association of Ophthalmologists. **VFOAT** C.L.A.O. Journal. **VAT** Contact Lens Association of Ophthalmologists Journal. Vol. 9, No. 1 (Jan/Mar. 1983)-. Academic Scholarly Publication. English. Four times a year (Jan., Apr., July, Oct.). $76.00 US; $98.00 other. Kellner and McCaffery Associates, 150 Fifth Avenue, Suite 322, New York NY 10011. **Tel** (212)741-0280, FAX (212)929-2174. **ED** W. M. Curtis. **LC** RE977.C6; C555. **DD** 617.7/523/05. **NLM** W1 CL113. **CODEN** CLAJEU. Index available (Bound in 4th iss. in (Oct).). **Bk Rev. Ad Acc. Circ:** 3,200. available on microfilm and microfiche from University Microfilms International (UMI). Documents available from CASDDS. ***Continues*** *Contact and Intraocular Lens Medical Journal, 0360-1358.*
**Desc:** Contact Lenses, anterior segment ophthalmology, cornea and corneal diseases, refractive surgery, are some of the related topics.
**Ind/Abst** Chem. Abstr.; EMBASE; Health Plan. Adminis.; Index Med.

US/0953-4431
**CLINICAL EYE AND VISION CARE.** [Clin. eye vis. care]. Vol. 1, No. 1 (Dec. 1988)-. Periodical. English. qt. $160.00 (institution), $90.00 (individual) US and Canada; $190.00 (institution), $100.00 (individual) other. Butterworth Heinemann / Woburn, MA, 225 Wildwood Avenue, Unit B, Woburn MA 01801. **Tel** (800)366-2665, FAX (617)928-2620, telex 880052. **NLM** W1; CL705L. **CODEN** CEVCEV. **[CCC]. Ad Acc.** available on microfilm and microfiche from University Microfilms International (UMI).

US/0883-0320
**CLINICAL OPHTHALMOLOGY UPDATE.** [Clin. ophthalmol. update]. (198?)-. Periodical. English. an. $542.00 US; $565.00 Canada; $690.00 other. J.B. Lippincott Company, 227 East Washington Square, Philadelphia PA 19106-3780. **Tel** (215)238-4200 or 4454, FAX (215)238-4227. **(Subscription address:** J.B. Lippincott, PO Box 350, Hagerstown MD 21740.**)** **DD** 617.

US
**CLINICAL RESEARCH REPORT.** **Main/Corp** Detroit. Optometric Research Institute. No. 1 (1937)-. Periodical. English. Optometric Research Institute, Detroit MI 48219. **LC** RE46; .D5. **DD** 617.7072.

FR/0009-9368
**CLINIQUE OPHTALMOLOGIQUE PARIS, LA.** [Clin. ophtalmol. Paris]. (193?)-. Periodical. French. qt. 420.00F. Laboratoires Martinet, 222 Boulevard Pereire, 75017 Paris France. **Tel** 011 33 1 45841122, FAX 011 33 1 45742063, telex 644 265F. **UDC** 617.7. **Bk Rev. Ad Acc. Pr Rev.** ctrl circ.
**Desc:** Articles written by opthmalmologists.

GW/0934-215X
**COLLECTION CONTACTOLOGIA.** Vol. 1 (1988)-. Periodical. French (French). Ferdinand Enke Verlag, Ruedigerstrasse 14, D-70469 Stuttgart Germany. **Tel** 011 49 711 8931124, 011 49 711 893123. **NLM** W1; CO17H.

UK/0953-6833
**COMMUNITY EYE HEALTH.** 1988-. Periodical. English. **NLM** W1; CO428M.
**Ind/Abst** Trop. Dis. Bull.

US/0096-2716
**CONTACT LENS JOURNAL.** [Contact lens j.]. V. 8- June 1974-. Periodical. English. qt. £36.00 UK; $75.00 US. The Contact Lens Journal, 90 Bagby Drive, Birmingham AL 35209. **Tel** (01)0303-62272, FAX 0303-62269. **ED** L Hines. **LC** RE977.C6; C559. **DD** 617.7/523/05. **NLM** W1 CO768D. Index available. cum. index. **Bk Rev. Ad Acc. Pr Rev. Circ:** 2,000. ***Continues*** *Journal - Contact Lens Society of America, 0589-5065.*
**Desc:** Learned articles relating to contact lens fitting and development problems; presents personalities, abstracts, social effects on wearers, general contact lens news, etc.

US/0591-0307
**CONTACT LENS MEDICAL SEMINAR.** (CONTACT LENS MEDICAL SEMINAR PROCEEDINGS.). [Contact Lens Med. Sem.]. **VFOAT** ISBA. V. 1- 1968-. Proceedings. English. be. C C Thomas, 301-327 East Lawrence Avenue, Springfield IL 62717. **ED** W G Sampson. **LC** RE977.C6; C57. **DD** 617.5/523/05. **NLM** W3 CO978SH.

US/0885-9264
**CONTACT LENS UPDATE.** [Contact lens update]. (1982)-. Periodical. English. bm (6 issues). $69.00 US; $79.00 Canada & Mexico; $84.00 other. Anadem Inc, 3620 North High Street, Columbus OH 43214. **Tel** (614)262-2539, (800)633-0055. **ED** John Schoessler. **DD** 617. Index available.
**Desc:** Covers medical and optometry journal articles about contact lens practice.

GW/0936-1235
**CONTACTOLOGIA.** Vol. 1, No. 1 (Mar. 1989)-. Periodical. English. qt. $97.00. Georg Thieme Verlag Stuttgart, Postfach 301120, D 70451 Stuttgart Germany. **Tel** 011 49 711 89310, FAX 011 49 711 8931298, telex 7 252 275 GTVD. **(Subscription address:** Thieme Medical Publishers Inc., 381 Park Avenue South, New York NY 10016.**)** **NLM** W1; CO769ET. **[CCC].**

GW/0171-9602
**CONTACTOLOGIA ED. FRANCAISE.** [Contactologia Ed. fr.]. (1979)-. Periodical. French. Four times a year. $97.00. Georg Thieme Verlag Stuttgart, Postfach 301120, D 70451 Stuttgart Germany. **Tel** 011 49 711 89310, FAX 011 49 711 8931298, telex 7 252 275 GTVD. **(Subscription address:** Thieme Medical Publishers Inc., 381 Park Avenue South, New York NY 10016.**)** **UDC** 617.7-089.243.

UK/0888-7691
**CONTEMPORARY ISSUES IN OPHTHALMOLOGY.** [Contemp. issues ophthalmol.]. Vol. 1 (1984)-. Monographic series. English. an. Price varies per volume. Churchill Livingstone, 1-3 Baxter's Place, Leith Walk, Edinburgh EH1 3AF Scotland. **Tel** 011 44 31 556 2424, FAX 011 44 31 558 1278, telex 727511. **(Subscription address:** US and Canada/ Churchill Livingstone Inc., 5 South 250 Frontenac Road, Naperville, IL 60563; (telephone: (800)553-5426 or (708)416-3939)**)** **ED** Frederick C. Blodi. **DD** 617. **NLM** W1; CO769MRM.

NE/0165-1005
**CORE JOURNALS IN OPHTHALMOLOGY. Added/Corp** Excerpta Medica (Firm). Vol. 1 (1978)-. Periodical. English. Eleven times a year (1 volume). Fl549.00. Excerpta Medica Publishing Group, PO Box 548, 1000 AM Amsterdam Netherlands. **Tel** 011 31 20 5803243. **(Subscription address:** Excerpta Medica Journals, PO Box 85, Limerick Ireland.**)** **NLM** ZWW 100; C797. **[CCC].** available on microfilm from University Microfilms International (UMI).

US/0277-3740
**CORNEA.** [Cornea]. Vol. 1, No. 1 (1982)-. Academic Scholarly Publication. English. bm (6 issues). $176.00 (individuals), $246.00 (institutions) US; $226.00 (individuals), $300.00 (institutions) other. Raven Press,

1185 Avenue of the Americas, 37th Floor, New York NY 10036. **Tel** (212)930-9500, (212)930-9604, FAX (212)869-3495, (212)302-8507, telex 640073. **ED** H. Dwight Cavanagh. **NLM** W1 CO8595M. **CODEN** CORNDB. **[CCC]. Pr Rev.** available on microfilm and microfiche from University Microfilms International (UMI). Documents available from The Genuine Article, CASDDS.
**Desc:** Brings together the latest clinical and basic research on the cornea and the anterior segment microsurgical procedures and the advantages and potential drawbacks of promising new surgical techniques.
**Ind/Abst** Chem. Abstr.; Curr. Contents Clin. Med.; EMBASE; Health Plan. Adminis.; Index Med. (Vol. 3, No. 1, 1984-); Protozoolog. Abstr.; Res. Alert [Select. Cov.]; Rev. Med. Vet. Mycology; SCISEARCH.

FR/0987-0113
**COUP D'OEIL GRANDVILLIERS.** (1987)-. Periodical. French. Six times a year (Feb., Apr., June, Sept., Oct., Dec.). 350.00F France; 400.00F ECC & Tunisia; 450.00F Europe; 500.00F North America & Middle East; 550.00F others. Editions et Regarde Attentivem, 68 BLD Des Poilus, 44300 Nantes France. **Tel** 011 1 33 40689606, FAX 011 33 40689876. **UDC** 63 (443.5). Index available (Bound in Dec. iss.). cum. index. **Bk Rev**, (Qty: 6). **Ad Acc. Circ:** 1,000 (ctrl).

UK/0271-3683
**CURRENT EYE RESEARCH.** [Curr. eye res.]. Vol. 1, No. 1 (1981)-. Academic Scholarly Publication. English. mo. £295.00 UK and Europe; $495.00 other. Oxford University Press, Walton Street, Oxford OX2 6DP England. **Tel** 011 44 865 56767, FAX 011 44 865 267773, telex 837330 OXPRES G. **(Subscription address:** Oxford University Press / USA, Journals Marketing Department, Oxford University Press, 2001 Evans Road, Cary NC 27513.**) ED** C. A. Paterson and N. A. Delamere. **LC** QP476; .C86. **DD** 599.01/823. **NLM** W1 CU788H. **CODEN** CEYRDM. **[CCC]. Bk Rev. Ad Acc. Pr Rev. Circ:** 450. available on microfilm and microfiche from University Microfilms International (UMI). Documents available from The Genuine Article, BIOSIS Document Express, CASDDS.
**Desc:** Clinical and basic research on the anatomy, physiology, biophysics, biochemistry, pharmacology, developmental biology, microbiology and immunology of the eye.
**Ind/Abst** Anim. Breed. Abstr.; Biol. Abstr.; Chem. Abstr.; Curr. Contents Life Sci.; EMBASE; Health Plan. Adminis.; Index Med. (1981-); Index Vet.; Life Sci. Collect.; Ref. Upd. Deluxe Ed.; Res. Alert [Full Cov.]; Sci. Cit. Index; SCISEARCH; Vet. Bull.

UK/0963-0112
**CURRENT MEDICAL LITERATURE / OPHTHALMOLOGY.** [Curr. med. lit. Ophthalmol.]. (1991)-. English. qt. £20.00 UK; $40.00 other. Current Medical Literature Ltd., 40-42 Osnaburgh Street, London NW1 3ND England. **Tel** 011 44 71 4658377, FAX 011 44 71 4658380. **(Subscription address:** Royal Society Medicine Services, 1 Wimpole Street, London W1M 8AE England.**) DD** 016.6177.

US
**CURRENT OCULAR THERAPY.** Vol. 1 (1980)-. English. ir. price varies per volume. W.B. Saunders Company, A Subsidiary of Harcourt Brace Jovanovich, Inc., The Curtis Center/Suite 300, Independence Square West, Philadelphia PA 19106-3399. **Tel** (215)238-7800 or, 5587, FAX (215)238-7883, telex 173146. **(Subscription address:** W. B. Saunders Company / North America Subscriptions, c/o Periodicals, 6277 Sea Harbour Drive, 4th Floor, Orlando FL 32887.**) LC** RE991; .C79. **DD** 617.7/06. **NLM** W1; CU799GA.

US/1040-8738
**CURRENT OPINION IN OPHTHALMOLOGY.** [Curr. opin. ophthalmol.]. Vol. 1, No. 1 (1990)-. Periodical. English. Six times a year. $449.95 (institutions), $224.95 (individuals). Current Science, 20 North 3rd Street, Philadelphia PA 19106. **Tel** (215)574-2266, (800)552-5866, FAX (215)574-2270. **ED** George W. Weinstein. **DD** 617. **NLM** W1; CU799GGC. **CODEN** COOTEF. **[CCC]. Circ:** 500. available on diskette. Documents available from The Genuine Article.
**Desc:** Directed toward researchers and practicing ophthalmologists. Presents review articles from an area of concentration covering an entire year's literature with annotated references. Each issue features a bibliography of the current world literature published during the previous year.
**Ind/Abst** Cumul. Index Nurs. Allied Health Lit.; Curr. Aware. Biol. Sci., CABS; Curr. Contents Clin. Med.; EMBASE; Res. Alert [Select. Cov.]; SCISEARCH.

GW/0173-7082
**CURRENT RESEARCH IN OPHTHALMIC ELECTRON MICROSCOPY.** [Curr. res. ophthalmic electron microsc.]. Began with: 1 (1977). English. Springer-Verlag New York Inc., 175 5th Avenue, New York NY 10010. **Tel** (212)460-1500, telex 232 235 SPB UR. **(Subscription address:** Springer Verlag New York Inc. / for North America, 44 Hartz Way, Secaucus NJ 07096.**) NLM** W1 CU8092.

GW/0344-7103
**DEUTSCHE OPTIKERZEITUNG.** (DOZ, DEUTSCHE OPTIKERZEITUNG.). [Dtsch. Optikerztg.]. No. 1 (Jan. 15, 1978)-. Academic Scholarly Publication. German. mo. DM81.00 Germany; $50.00 US. Optische Fachveroffentlichung GmbH, Postfach 104443, Rohrbacher Str 57, 6900 Heidelberg Germany. **Tel** (06221)14081, FAX (06221)13996. **LC** RE1. **DD** 617.7/52. **NLM** W1 D129E. **CODEN** DDOPD4. Index available. **Bk Rev. Ad Acc. Circ:** 9,500 (ctrl). Documents available from CASDDS. ***Continues** SOZ, Suddeutsche Optikerzeitung, 0344-7170.*
**Desc:** Journal content covers economics, contact lenses, physiology, workshop equipment, practice, shop design, contact lens chemics, interviews with VIPs, etc.
**Ind/Abst** Chem. Abstr.

SZ/0250-3751
**DEVELOPMENTS IN OPHTHALMOLOGY.** [Dev. ophthalmol.]. Vol. 1 (1981)-. Academic Scholarly Publication. English. ir. 200.00F (approx. per volume). S. Karger AG, Allschwilerstrasse 10, PO Box - Postfach - Case Postale, CH-4009 Basel Switzerland. **Tel** 011 41 61 306-1111, FAX 011 41 61 306-1234, telex CH 962 652. **ED** H. Kaiser. **NLM** W1 DE998NG. **CODEN** DEOPDB. **[CCC].** Documents available from BIOSIS Document Express, CASDDS. ***Formed by the union of** Advances in Ophthalmology, 0065-3004; Bibliotheca Ophthalmologica **and** Modern Problems in Ophthalmology, 0077-0078.*
**Desc:** Provides ophthalmologists, ophthalmic surgeons, and practicing optometrists with expert summaries of international developments vital to progress in this field. Innovative procedures are presented with the appropriate technical information required to encourage rapid introduction into clinical practice.
**Ind/Abst** Biol. Abstr.; Chem. Abstr.; Index Med.; Ref. Upd. Deluxe Ed.

NE/0012-4486
**DOCUMENTA OPHTHALMOLOGICA.** [Doc. ophthalmol.]. Vol. 1 (1938)-. Academic Scholarly Publication. English (German, Italian and French). mo. $1,467.00. Kluwer Academic Publishers, Postbus 322, 3300 AH Dordrecht, The Netherlands. **Tel** 011 (31) 78 524400, FAX 011 31 78 183273, telex 20083. **ED** L. Missotten and G. Fishman. **LC** RE14; .D6. **NLM** W1 DO489. **CODEN** DOOPAA. **[CCC]. Bk Rev. Ad Acc. Pr Rev. Acid Free. Circ:** 1,000. available on microfilm and microfiche from University Microfilms International (UMI). Documents available from The Genuine Article, BIOSIS Document Express, Ask*IEEE, CASDDS.
**Desc:** Publishes original articles in the field of ophthalmology. One issue per year is devoted to articles on the history of ophthalmology.
**Ind/Abst** Biol. Abstr.; Chem. Abstr.; Curr. Contents Phys. Chem. Earth Sci.; EMBASE; Health Plan. Adminis.; Helminthol. Abstr. (19??-19??); Index Med.; INSPEC (1985-); Nutr. Abstr. Rev., Ser. B, Live Feeds and Feed. (1985-); Nutr. Abstr. Rev., Ser. A, Hum. Exp. (1985-); Life Sci. Collect.; Protozoolog. Abstr. (?-1988); Ref. Upd. Deluxe Ed.; Res. Alert [Full Cov.]; Rev. Med. Vet. Mycology; Sci. Cit. Index; SCISEARCH; Soc. Sci. Cit. Index [Select. Cov.].

NE/0303-6405
**DOCUMENTA OPHTHALMOLOGICA. PROCEEDINGS SERIES.** [Doc. ophthalmol., Proc. ser.]. Vol. 1 (1973)-. Proceedings. English. $1,467.00. Kluwer Academic Publishers, Postbus 322, 3300 AH Dordrecht, The Netherlands. **Tel** 011 (31) 78 524400, FAX 011 31 78 183273, telex 20083. **ED** H E Henkes. **NLM** W3 DO637. **CODEN** DOPSBP. Documents available from BIOSIS Document Express, CASDDS.
**Ind/Abst** Biol. Abstr.; Chem. Abstr.; Psychol. Abstr. (1982-).

FR
**ENCYCLOPEDIE MEDICO CHIRURGICALE / MEDECINE GENERALE & SPECIALITES. OPHTHALMOLOGIE.** French. Editions Techniques, 141 rue de Javel, 75747 Paris Cedex 15 France. **Tel** 011 33 1 45589100.

FR/0955-3681
**EUROPEAN JOURNAL OF IMPLANT AND REFRACTIVE SURGERY, THE.** [Eur. j. implant refract. surg.]. **Added/Corp** European Intraocular Implantlens Council. European Society of Cataract and Refractive Surgeons. **VFOAT** Implant, Ocular Microsurgery; Implant, Microchirurgie Oculaire. Vol. 4, No. 3 (June/July 1986)-. Periodical. English (French). bm (6 issues). £120.00 (institution), £78.00 (individual) UK/Europe; $216.00 (institution), $120.00 (individual) other. Harcourt Brace & Company Ltd., Foots Cray, High Street, Sidcup Kent DA14 5HP England. **Tel** 011 44 81 300 3322, FAX 011 44 81 309 0807. **(Subscription address:** W. B. Saunders Company / North America Subscriptions, c/o Periodicals, 6277 Sea Harbour Drive, 4th Floor, Orlando FL 32887.**) ED** Emanuel Rosen. **LC** RE451; .E9. **NLM** W1; EU72DGM. **CODEN** EJISE3. **[CCC].** Index available. **Bk Rev. Ad Acc. Pr Rev.** ***Continues** Implant, 0765-6211.*
**Desc:** Publishes original full papers and rapid communications dealing with all aspects of ocular implants, refractive surgery, and topics of related interest. Features European meeting reports and newsletters, letters from the USA, letters from Japan, implant and refractive surgery in developing countries, European medical economics/politics, litigation, book reviews, and correspondence.
**Ind/Abst** EMBASE.

IT/1120-6721
**EUROPEAN JOURNAL OF OPHTHALMOLOGY.** Vol. 1, No. 1 (Jan.-Mar. 1991)-. Periodical. English. qt. $140.00. Wichtig Editore, Via Friuli 72 74, 20135 Milan Italy. **Tel** 011 39 2 55195443. **(Subscription address:** Wichtig Editore, Subscription Office, PO Box 830350, Birmingham AL 35283-0350.**) NLM** W1; EU72DM. **CODEN** EJOOEL.
**Desc:** Presents current research and case studies in clinical ophthalmology. Articles cover relevant research topics such as retinopathy, transplantations, surgical procedures and more.
**Ind/Abst** Index Med. (1991-).

NE/0014-4169
**EXCERPTA MEDICA. SECTION 12. OPHTHALMOLOGY.** **See** Medical Science and Technology-Abstracting, Bibliographies and Statistics.

PO/0253-0643
**EXPERIENTIA OPHTHALMOLOGICA.** [Exp. ophthalmol.]. **VFOAT** Experientia Ophthalmologica (Coimbra). Academic Scholarly Publication. English (Portuguese). **NLM** W1 EX23R.
**Ind/Abst** EMBASE.

UK/0014-4835
**EXPERIMENTAL EYE RESEARCH.** [Exp. eye res.]. Vol. 1 (Sept. 1961)-. Academic Scholarly Publication. English. mo. $945.00. Academic Press Ltd., A Division of Harcourt Brace & Company Ltd., 24-28 Oval Road, London NW1 7DX England. **Tel** 071 267 4466, FAX 071 482 2293, 071 485 4752, telex 25775 ACPRES G. **(Subscription address:** Harcourt Brace & Company, Ltd., Foots Cray, High Street, Sidcup Kent DA14 5HP England.**) ED** J. G. Hollyfield. **LC** QP474. **NLM** W1 EX504. **CODEN** EXERA6. **[CCC]. Pr Rev.** Documents available from The Genuine Article, BIOSIS Document Express, CASDDS.
**Desc:** Publishes original research papers on all aspects of the anatomy, physiology, biochemistry, biophysics, molecular biology, biophysics, pharmacology, develpmental biology, microbiology, and immunology of the eye. The journal is subdivided into three sections: general, retina, and lens.
**Ind/Abst** Biol. Abstr.; Chem. Abstr.; Chem. Titles; CSA Neuro. Abstr. (?-?); Curr. Contents Life Sci.; EMBASE; Health Plan. Adminis.; Index Med.; Index Vet.; Nutr. Abstr. Rev., Ser. B, Live Feeds and Feed.; Nutr. Abstr. Rev., Ser. A, Hum. Exp.; Life Sci. Collect.; Ref. Upd. Basic Ed.; Ref. Upd. Deluxe Ed.; Res. Alert [Full Cov.]; Sci. Cit. Index; SCISEARCH; Small Anim. Abstr. Bibliogr.; Vet. Bull.

UK/0950-222X
**EYE (LONDON, ENGLAND).** (EYE / OPHTHALMOLOGICAL SOCIETY OF THE UNITED KINGDOM.). [Eye]. **Added/Corp** Ophthalmological Society of the United Kingdom. Vol. 1, Pt. 1 (1987)-. Periodical. English. bm. £188.00. Professional & Scientific Publishers, Tavistock House, East Tavistock Square, London WC1H 9JR England. **Tel** 011 44 71 387-4499, telex 005311. **ED** P.G. Watson. **NLM** W1; EY409. **CODEN** EYEEEC. Documents available from The Genuine Article, BIOSIS Document Express. ***Continues** Ophthalmological Society of the United Kingdom. Transactions of the Ophthalmological Societies of the United Kingdom, 0078-5334.*
**Desc:** Presents to the practising ophthalmologist and those interested in the sciences related to ophthalmology a journal which strives to contain the latest information available, so that they can keep abreast of the rapid advances which are taking place on this subject.
**Ind/Abst** Biol. Abstr. (1987-); Curr. Aware. Biol. Sci., CABS; EMBASE; Health Plan. Adminis.; Index Med. (1987-); Protozoolog. Abstr.; Res. Alert [Full Cov.]; Rev. Med. Vet. Mycology; Sci. Cit. Index; SCISEARCH.

US/0891-8260
**FOCAL POINTS.** (FOCAL POINTS : CLINICAL MODULES FOR OPHTHALMOLOGISTS / AMERICAN ACADEMY OF OPHTHALMOLOGY.). **Added/Corp** American Academy of Ophthalmology. **VFOAT** Clinical Modules for Ophthalmologists. (1983)-. Monographic series. English. mo (12 times per year mailed quarterly). $95.00 (member), $125.00 (nonmember). American Academy of Ophthalmology, 655 Beach Street, San Francisco CA 94120. **Tel** (415)561-8500. **DD** 617. **NLM** W1; FO1001PE.

GW/0323-4932
**FOLIA OPHTHALMOLOGICA.** ***Title Change.*** [Folia ophthalmol.]. **Added/Corp** Gesellschaft der Augenaerzte der DDR. (Feb. 1976)-(19??). Academic Scholarly Publication. German. qt. Georg Thieme Verlag Stuttgart, Postfach 301120, D 70451 Stuttgart Germany. **Tel** 011 49 711 89310, FAX 011 49 711 8931298, telex 7 252 275 GTVD. **(Subscription address:** Thieme Medical Publishers Inc., 381 Park Avenue South, New York NY 10016.**) NLM** W1 FO268. **CODEN** FOOPDZ. **[CCC].**

Documents available from BIOSIS Document Express, CASDDS. ***Continued by*** *Aktuelle Augenheilkunde.*
**Ind/Abst** Biol. Abstr.; Chem. Abstr.; EMBASE.

JA
**GANKI. Added/Corp** Nihon Ganka Kiyo Kai. **VFOAT** Nihon Ganka Kiyo; Folia Ophthalmologica Japonica. Vol. 38, No. 1 (Jan. 1987)-. Periodical. Japanese (summaries and/or abstracts in English; table of contents in English). mo. $312.00. **(Subscription address:** Kyowa Book Company Inc., 1 38 Kanda Jinbocho Chiyoda-ku, Tokyo 101 Japan.**) NLM** W1; GA418M. ***Continues*** *Nippon Ganka Kiyo, 0015-5667.*

US/0891-2084
**GENERAL OPHTHALMOLOGY.** [Gen. ophthalmol.]. 1st Ed. (1958)-. English (Italian, Portuguese, Spanish and Polish). ir (every three years). $33.00 (latest edition). Appleton Century Crofts, Prentice Hall, 200 Old Tappan Road, Old Tappan NJ 07675. **Tel** (201)767-5188, (800)922-0579. **LC** RE1; .G43. **DD** 617.7/005.

●GW/0941-2921
**GERMAN JOURNAL OF OPHTHALMOLOGY. Added/Corp** Deutsche Ophthalmologische Gesellschaft. Vol. 1, No. 1 (1992)-. Periodical. English. bm. DM160.00. Springer-Verlag GmbH & Company KG, Heidelberger Platz 3, D 14197 Berlin Germany. **Tel** 011 49 30 8207223, FAX 011 49 30 8214091, telex 183 319 SPBLN D. **(Subscription address:** Springer Verlag New York Inc. / for North America, 44 Hartz Way, Secaucus NJ 07096.**) ED** M. Spitznas. **NLM** W1; GE457R. **CODEN** GJOPEC. ***Continues in part*** *Fortschritte der Ophthalmologie, 0723-8045.*
**Desc:** Publishes original articles on clinical and basic ophthalmic research.
**Ind/Abst** Index Med. (1992-).

FR
**GLAUCOMA ABSTRACTS INTERNATIONAL. Added/Corp** Chibret International. European Glaucoma Society. American Glaucoma Society. Japanese Glaucoma Society. Vol. 1, No. 1 (1990)-. Periodical. English. tq. Documentation Center, MSD-Chibret, 200 Boulevard Etienne Clementel, 63100 Clermont-Ferrand France. **NLM** ZWW 290; G552. ***Continues*** *Glaucoma Abstracts, 0755-9348.*

US/0164-4645
**GLAUCOMA (MIAMI).** ***Title Change.*** (GLAUCOMA.). [Glaucoma]. **Added/Corp** International Glaucoma Congress. American Society of Contemporary Ophthalmology. Vol. 1, (Feb. 1979)-(19??). Periodical. English. Six times a year. Altier Maynard Communications, 59 Oakwood Drive, Madison CT 06443. **Tel** (203)421-3494, FAX (203)421-3250. **LC** RE871; .G54. **DD** 617.7/41/005. **NLM** W1 GL359. **CODEN** GLAUD4. **Bk Rev. Ad Acc. Pr Rev. Circ:** 15,000 (ctrl). Documents available from BIOSIS Document Express. ***Merged into*** *Annals of Ophthalmology and Glaucoma.*
**Desc:** An ophthalmic journal for practicing ophthalmologists which concentrates on glaucoma.
**Ind/Abst** Biol. Abstr.

GW/0721-832X
**GRAEFE'S ARCHIVE FOR CLINICAL AND EXPERIMENTAL OPHTHALMOLOGY.** [Graefe's arch. clin. exp. ophthalmol.]. **Added/Corp** Club Jules Gonin. **VFOAT** Albrecht von Graefes Archiv fur Klinische und Experimentelle Ophthalmologie. Vol. 218 No. 1 (Jan. 1982)-. Academic Scholarly Publication. English (German). Twelve times a year. DM928.00. Springer-Verlag GmbH & Company KG, Heidelberger Platz 3, D 14197 Berlin Germany. **Tel** 011 49 30 8207223, FAX 011 49 30 8214091, telex 183 319 SPBLN D. **(Subscription address:** Springer Verlag New York Inc. / for North America, 44 Hartz Way, Secaucus NJ 07096.**) ED** S M Drance, W R Lee, R Machemer, M Spitznas, and R Sundmacher. **NLM** W1 GR139M. **CODEN** GACODL. **[CCC]. Pr Rev.** available on microfilm from University Microfilms International (UMI). Documents available from The Genuine Article, BIOSIS Document Express, CASDDS. ***Continues*** *Albrecht von Graefes Archiv fur Klinische und Experimentelle Ophthalmologie, 0065-6100.*
**Desc:** International journal that presents original clinical reports and clinically relevant experimental studies.
**Ind/Abst** Biol. Abstr.; Chem. Abstr.; Curr. Contents Clin. Med.; EMBASE; Health Plan. Adminis.; Index Med.; Life Sci. Collect.; Protozoolog. Abstr.; Res. Alert [Full Cov.]; Rev. Med. Vet. Mycology; Sci. Cit. Index; SCISEARCH; Soc. Sci. Cit. Index [Select. Cov.].

PN
**HIGHLIGHTS OF OPHTHALMOLOGY LETTER (MINI-HIGHLIGHTS) / BENJAMIN F. BOYD. VFOAT** Mini-Highlights. (1984)-. Periodical. English. mo. $85.00 (one year), $170.00 (two year), $255.00 (three year). Highlights of Ophthamology, PO Box 1189, Panama 1 Panama. **Tel** 011 507 609914. **ED** Professor Benjamin Boyd, M.D. ***Continues*** *Boyd, Benjamin F. Highlights of Ophthalmology Tri-Weekly Letter (Mini-Highlights).*

II/0301-4738
**INDIAN JOURNAL OF OPHTHALMOLOGY.** [Indian j. ophthalmol.]. **Added/Corp** All India Ophthalmological Society. (1971)-. Academic Scholarly Publication. English. qt. $90.00. Indian Books & Periodicals Syndicate, B-5/62 Dev Nagar P L Road Karol Bagh, New Delhi 110005 India. **Tel** 660110/243. **(Subscription address:** Prints India, 11 Darya Ganj, New Delhi 110002 India.**) ED** Madan Mohan. **NLM** W1 IN223N. **CODEN** IJOMBM. **Bk Rev. Ad Acc. Circ:** 2,400. Documents available from CASDDS. ***Continues*** *Journal of The All-India Ophthalmological Society, 0044-7307.*
**Desc:** Ophthalmic scientific Indian national journal--clinical and experimental.
**Ind/Abst** Chem. Abstr.; EMBASE [Select. Cov.]; Index Med.

US/1060-135X
**INSIGHT (SAN FRANSISCO, CALIF.). See** Medical Science and Technology-Nursing.

US/0892-8967
**INTERNATIONAL CONTACT LENS CLINIC (1987). See** Optometry.

US/1040-9912
**INTERNATIONAL LOW VISION DIRECTORY.** [Int. low vis. dir.]. 1988-. Directory. English. an. Free City Books, 210 Locust Street/Suite 24B, Philadelphia PA 19106. **LC** RE91; .I56. **DD** 362.4/1/025.

US/0145-370X
**INTERNATIONAL OPHTHALMOLOGICAL REPORTER.** Vol. 1 (1976)-. English. ir. $31.50. Intercontinental Publications, PO Box 5017, Westport CT 06880. **Tel** (203)226-7463, FAX (203)222-8793. **NLM** Z 6669 I61.

NE/0165-5701
**INTERNATIONAL OPHTHALMOLOGY.** [Int. ophthalmol.]. Vol. 1 (Sept. 1978)-. Academic Scholarly Publication. English. bm. $746.00. Kluwer Academic Publishers, Postbus 322, 3300 AH Dordrecht, The Netherlands. **Tel** 011 (31) 78 524400, FAX 011 31 78 183273, telex 20083. **ED** A. F. Deutman, E. L. Greve and J. J. de Lacey. **LC** RE1; .I57. **NLM** W1 IN827D. **CODEN** INOPDR. **[CCC]. Bk Rev. Ad Acc. Pr Rev. Acid Free. Circ:** 1,000. available on microfilm and microfiche from University Microfilms International (UMI). Documents available from The Genuine Article, BIOSIS Document Express, CASDDS.
**Desc:** Aims at providing clinician articles on all sub-specialties in ophthalmology relevant to clinicians.
**Ind/Abst** Biol. Abstr.; Chem. Abstr.; Curr. Contents Clin. Med.; EMBASE; Energy Res. Abstr. (Dec. 1980-); Helminthol. Abstr. (19??-19??); Index Med.; Life Sci. Collect.; Protozoolog. Abstr.; Ref. Upd. Deluxe Ed.; Res. Alert [Full Cov.]; Rev. Med. Vet. Entomol.; Sci. Cit. Index; SCISEARCH.

US/0020-8167
**INTERNATIONAL OPHTHALMOLOGY CLINICS.** [Int. ophthalmol. clin.]. Vol. 1 (1961)-. Academic Scholarly Publication. English. qt. $150.00 (institutions), $135.00 (individuals) US; $168.00 (institutions), $150.00 (individuals) Canada; $198.00 (institutions), $165.00 (individuals) other. Little Brown & Company, 34 Beacon Street, Boston MA 02108. **Tel** (617)227-0730, (800)759-0190. **(Subscription address:** Little Brown and Company, PO Box 7671, Riverton NJ 08077-7671.**) ED** Carmen D. Wiseman. **LC** UNC. **DD** 617.7/005. **NLM** W1 IN827E. **CODEN** IOPCAV. **[CCC]. Pr Rev. Circ:** 2,600. available on microfilm and microfiche from University Microfilms International (UMI). Documents available from The Genuine Article, BIOSIS Document Express.
**Desc:** Features guest editors and contributors who focus on one topic per issue that is of clinical importance in ophthalmology.
**Ind/Abst** Biol. Abstr.; Curr. Contents Clin. Med.; EMBASE; Energy Res. Abstr.; Helminthol. Abstr. (1991-); Index Med.; INIS Atomindex [Micro.]; Nucl. Sci. Abstr.; Life Sci. Collect.; Res. Alert [Select. Cov.]; Rev. Med. Vet. Entomol.; SCISEARCH.

US/0146-0404
**INVESTIGATIVE OPHTHALMOLOGY & VISUAL SCIENCE.** [Invest. ophthalmol. visual sci.]. **Added/Corp** Association for Research in Vision and Ophthalmology. **VFOAT** Investigative Ophthalmology and Visual Science; IOVS. **VAT** Investigative Ophthalmology and Visual Science. Vol. 16 (Jan. 1977)-. Academic Scholarly Publication. English. mo. $170.00 (individuals), $235.00 (institutions) US; $235.00 (individuals), $280.00 (institutions) other. J.B. Lippincott Company, 227 East Washington Square, Philadelphia PA 19106-3780. **Tel** (215)238-4200 or 4454, FAX (215)238-4227. **(Subscription address:** J.B. Lippincott, PO Box 350, Hagerstown MD 21740.**) LC** RE1; .I65. **DD** 617.7/005. **NLM** W1 IN994Z. **CODEN** IOVSDA. **[CCC].** available on microfilm and microfiche from University Microfilms International (UMI). Documents available from The Genuine Article, BIOSIS Document Express, CASDDS. ***Continues*** *Investigative Ophthalmology, 0020-9988.*
**Ind/Abst** Biol. Abstr.; Chem. Abstr.; CSA Neuro. Abstr. (?-?); Curr. Contents Life Sci.; Curr. Primate Ref.; EMBASE; Energy Res. Abstr. (Oct. 1978-); Helminthol. Abstr. (19??-19??); Immunol. Abstr.; Index Med.; Index Vet.; INIS Atomindex [Micro.]; Iowa Drug Inf. Serv. (1967-); Mod. Med.; Life Sci. Collect.; Protozoolog. Abstr.; Ref. Upd. Basic Ed.; Ref. Upd. Deluxe Ed.; Res. Alert [Full Cov.]; Rev. Med. Vet. Mycology; Sci. Cit. Index; SCISEARCH; Soc. Sci. Cit. Index [Select. Cov.]; Vet. Bull.

IT
**ITALIAN JOURNAL OF OPHTHALMOLOGY. Added/Corp** Societa Oftalmologica Italiana. Vol. 1, No. 1 (May 1986)-. Academic Scholarly Publication. English. Four times a year. L100000.00 Italy; L165000.00 other. Ghedini Libraio, V Pezzotti 4, 20141 Milan Italy. **Tel** 011 39 2 76023133. **NLM** W1; IT3577. **CODEN** ITJOE8. Documents available from CASDDS.
**Ind/Abst** Chem. Abstr. (-1988); EMBASE.

JA/0021-5155
**JAPANESE JOURNAL OF OPHTHALMOLOGY.** [Jpn. j. opthalmol.]. **Added/Corp** Tokyo Daigaku. Ganka Kyoshitsu. Vol. 1, No. 1 (April 1957)-. Academic Scholarly Publication. English. qt. $100.00. Business Center for Academic Societies Japan, Hon-Komagome 5-16-9, Bunkyo-ku, Tokyo 113 Japan. **Tel** 011 81 3 3817 5811. **(Subscription address:** Maruzen Company Ltd., PO Box 5050, Import & Export Department, Tokyo 100 31 Japan.**) NLM** W1 JA97J. **CODEN** JJOPA7. **Pr Rev.** available on microfilm and microfiche from University Microfilms International (UMI). Documents available from The Genuine Article, CASDDS.
**Desc:** Presents the latest papers.
**Ind/Abst** Chem. Abstr.; CSA Neuro. Abstr. (?-?); Curr. Contents Clin. Med.; EMBASE; Index Med.; Life Sci. Collect.; Res. Alert [Full Cov.]; Sci. Cit. Index; SCISEARCH.

FR/0240-7914
**JOURNAL FRANCAIS D'ORTHOPTIQUE.** [J. fr. orthopt.]. (1969)-. Periodical. French. an (April). 250.00F France; 280.00F other. Association Francaise D Orthoptique, 50 Rue Chaziere, 69004 Lyon France. **Tel** 011 33 78 290502. **UDC** 615.8.

FR/0181-5512
**JOURNAL FRANCAIS D'OPHTALMOLOGIE.** [J. fr. ophtalmol.]. Vol. 1 (Jan. 1978)-. Periodical. Multiple languages (French; summaries and/or abstracts in English). mo (except July and Aug.). $281.00. Masson Editeur, Box Postale 22, 41353 Vineuil 16 France. **Tel** 011 33 54 438994. **(Subscription address:** 7A Boulevard de Perolles, CH-1701 Fribourg Switzerland**) NLM** W1 JO442F. **[CCC]. Pr Rev.** available on microfilm and microfiche from University Microfilms International (UMI). Documents available from The Genuine Article. ***Formed by the union of*** *Archives d'Ophtalmologie, 0399-4236* ***and*** *Annales d'Oculistique, 0003-4371.*
**Ind/Abst** Curr. Contents Clin. Med.; EMBASE; Index Med.; Life Sci. Collect.; Protozoolog. Abstr.; Res. Alert [Select. Cov.]; Rev. Med. Vet. Mycology; SCISEARCH.

US/0886-3350
**JOURNAL OF CATARACT AND REFRACTIVE SURGERY.** [J. cataract and refract. surg.]. **Added/Corp** American Society of Cataract and Refractive Surgery. **VFOAT** Journal of Cataract & Refractive Surgery. Vol. 12, No. 1 (Jan. 1986)-. Academic Scholarly Publication. English. bm. $60.00 (one year), $90.00 (two year), $110.00 (three year) surface mail. American Society of Cataracr and Refractive Surgery, 4000 Legato Road, Suite 850, Fairfax VA 22033-4003. **Tel** (703)591-2220, telex (703)591-0614. **(Subscription address:** Fulco, 30 Broad Street, Denville NJ 07834.**) ED** Stephen Obstbaum. **DD** 616. **NLM** W1; JO578F. **CODEN** JCSUEV. Index available. cum. index. **Ad Acc. Pr Rev. Circ:** 7,000. Documents available from The Genuine Article, BIOSIS Document Express, CASDDS. ***Continues*** *Journal (American Intra-Ocular Implant Society), 0146-2776.*
**Desc:** Clinical papers on cataract surgery, intraocular lens implantation, radial keratotomy, epikeratophakia and epikeratoplasty.
**Ind/Abst** Biol. Abstr. (1986-); Chem. Abstr. (1986-); Curr. Contents Clin. Med.; EMBASE; Health Devices Alerts; Index Med. (1986-); INIS Atomindex [Micro.]; Mod. Med.; Res. Alert [Select. Cov.]; SCISEARCH.

US/0272-846X
**JOURNAL OF CLINICAL NEURO-OPHTHALMOLOGY.** ***Title Change.*** [J. clin. neuro-ophthalmol.]. Vol. 1, No. 1 (Mar. 1981)-(1994). Periodical. English. qt. Raven Press, 1185 Avenue of the Americas, 37th Floor, New York NY 10036. **Tel** (212)930-9500, (212)930-9604, FAX (212)869-3495, (212)302-8507, telex 640073. **ED** J. Lawton Smith. **DD** 617. **NLM** W1; JO5893N. **[CCC]. Pr Rev.** available on microfilm and microfiche from University Microfilms International (UMI). Documents available from The Genuine Article. ***Continued by*** *Journal of*

*Neuro-Ophthalmology, 1070-8022.*
**Desc:** Covers important advances in the neurologic and ophthalmologic sciences.
**Ind/Abst** EMBASE; Index Med.; Index Vet.; Res. Alert [Full Cov.]; SCISEARCH; Small Anim. Abstr. Bibliogr.

●US/1057-0829
**JOURNAL OF GLAUCOMA.** [J. glaucoma]. Vol. 1, No. 1 (Spring 1992)-. Periodical. English. bm (6 issues). $120.00 (individuals), $160.00 (institutions) US; $140.00 (individuals), $182.00 (institutions) other. Raven Press, 1185 Avenue of the Americas, 37th Floor, New York NY 10036. **Tel** (212)930-9500, (212)930-9604, FAX (212)869-3495, (212)302-8507, telex 640073. **DD** 617. **NLM** W1; JO669PB. **CODEN** JOGLES. available on microfilm and microfiche from University Microfilms International (UMI).

●US/1070-8022
**JOURNAL OF NEURO-OPHTHALMOLOGY.** (1994)-. Periodical. English. qt. $122.00 (individuals), $178.00 (institutions) US; $155.00 (individuals), $215.00 (institutions) other. Raven Press, 1185 Avenue of the Americas, 37th Floor, New York NY 10036. **Tel** (212)930-9500, (212)930-9604, FAX (212)869-3495, (212)302-8507, telex 640073. **NLM** W1; JO789WM. ***Continues*** *Journal of Clinical Neuro-ophthalmology, 0272-846X.*

US/8756-3320
**JOURNAL OF OCULAR PHARMACOLOGY.** [J. ocul. pharmacol.]. Vol. 1, No. 1 (Spring 1985)-. Periodical. English. qt. $152.00. Mary Ann Liebert Inc., 1651 Third Avenue, New York NY 10128. **Tel** (212)289-2300, (800)M-LIEBERT, FAX (212)289-4697. **ED** George C. Y. Chiou. **DD** 617. **NLM** W1; JO802PD. **CODEN** JOPHER. **Bk Rev. Ad Acc. Pr Rev. Circ:** 500. Documents available from The Genuine Article, CASDDS.
**Desc:** Publishes research on aspects of drug activity pertaining to preventing or controlling diseases of the eye. Centralizes all significant research findings in this interdisciplinary field.
**Ind/Abst** Chem. Abstr.; Curr. Contents Life Sci.; EMBASE; Index Med. (Vol. 1 No. 1, 1985-); PESTDOC; Res. Alert [Select. Cov.]; SCISEARCH.

US/0730-0883
**JOURNAL OF OCULAR THERAPY & SURGERY.** [J. ocul. ther. surg.]. **VFOAT** Journal of Ocular Therapy and Surgery; Ocular Therapy & Surgery; Ocular Therapy and Surgery. Vol. 1, No. 1A (Jan./Feb. 1982)-. Academic Scholarly Publication. English. bm. $37.00 US; $57.00 other. Colonial Publishing Inc, 501 Colonial Drive, St Joseph MI 49085. **DD** 617. **NLM** W1 JO802PF.
**Ind/Abst** EMBASE.

US/0744-7132
**JOURNAL OF OPHTHALMIC NURSING & TECHNOLOGY.** **See** Medical Science and Technology-Nursing.

US/0198-6155
**JOURNAL OF OPHTHALMIC PHOTOGRAPHY, THE.** [J. ophthalmic photogr.]. **Added/Corp** Ophthalmic Photographers' Society (New York, N.Y.). (1978)-. Periodical. English. sa (Apr., Oct.). $18.00. Ophthalmic Photographers Socitey, 25 Whitney Place, Buffalo NY 14201. **Tel** (716)852-6008. **ED** Richard Hackel (Editor's address: Wake Forest Eye Center, Winston-Salem, NC 27157; Editor's telephone: (910)716-2929). **LC** RE79.P54; J68. **DD** 617.7/1545. **NLM** W1; JO803IE. **Ad Acc. Pr Rev. Circ:** 1,200.
**Desc:** Dedicated to the advancement of photography as applied to ophthalmology and visual sciences.

US/0191-3913
**JOURNAL OF PEDIATRIC OPHTHALMOLOGY AND STRABISMUS.** **See** Medical Science and Technology-Pediatrics.

US
**JOURNAL OF REFRACTIVE & CORNEAL SURGERY.** English. bm (Jan., Mar., May, July, Sept., Nov.). $110.00 (individuals); $120.00 (institutions). Slack Inc., 6900 Grove Road, Thorofare NJ 08086. **Tel** (609)848-1000, (800)257-8290, FAX (609)853-5991, telex 517108 SLACK INC VD.

US/1055-5161
**JOURNAL OF THE AMERICAN SOCIETY OF OCULARISTS, THE.** [J. Am. Soc. Ocul.]. **Added/Corp** American Society of Ocularists. (1975)-. English. an. $15.00. Journal of the American Society of Ocularists, 313 South 17th Street, Philadelphia PA 19103. **Tel** (215)545-0442, FAX (215)545-5312. **ED** Joseph LeGrand. **DD** 617. **NLM** W1; JO911C. **Ad Acc, Adv Mgr:** Ted Johnson. **Circ:** 2,000. ***Continues*** *Todays Ocularist.*

UK/0141-7037
**JOURNAL OF THE BRITISH CONTACT LENS ASSOCIATION.** (THE JOURNAL OF THE B.C.L.A.). [J. Br. Contact Lens Assoc.]. **Main/Corp** British Contact Lens Association. **VFOAT** Journal of the British Contact Lens Association. Vol. 1 (1978)-. Periodical. English. Four times a year (Jan., Apr., July, Oct.). £45.00 (individuals); £65.00 (institutions). Mosby Year Book Europe Ltd., 2 16 Torrington Place, Brook HS, London WC1E 7LT England. **Tel** 011 44 71 6364622. **(Subscription address:** Mosby Year Book Europe Ltd., Hainault Road Little Heath, Romford Essex RM6 5NP England.**) ED** Judith A. Morris. **LC** RE977.C6; J6. **NLM** W1; JO913B. **Bk Rev. Ad Acc. Pr Rev. Circ:** 1,200 (ctrl). ***Absorbed*** *British Contact Lens Association. Clinical Conference. Transactions of the British Contact Lens Association Annual Clinical Conference; Scientific Meetings (British Contact Lens Association).*
**Desc:** Refereed papers on contact lens related subjects. Also available conference transactions and scientific meeting reports of the British contact Lens Association.

US/1041-0384
**JOURNAL OF VISION REHABILITATION (LINCOLN, NEB.).** (JOURNAL OF VISION REHABILITATION.). [J. vis. rehabil.]. **VFOAT** Journal of Visual Rehabilitation; J. of Visual Rehabilitation. Vol. 1, No. 1 (Jan. 1987)-. Periodical. English. qt. $50.00 (one year), $90.00 (two year) US; $57.50 (one year), $105.00 (two years) Canada; $70.00 (one year), $130.00 (two years) airmail other; $60.00 (one year), $110.00 (two years) surface mail other. Media Division Westport Publishers Inc, 2440 O Street, Suite 202, Lincoln NE 68510-1125. **Tel** (402)474-2676, FAX (402)474-5104. **ED** Randall Jose, Joseph Zahn and Eleanor E Faye. **DD** 617. **NLM** W1; JO9703. cum. index. **Bk Rev. Ad Acc. Pr Rev. Circ:** 450. available on microfiche; available on microfilm; available in microform. ***Continues*** *Journal of Vision Rehabilitation (Houston, Tex.), 1041-0384.*
**Desc:** A multidisciplinary journal that contains articles and papers dealing with low vision, its evaluation, instrumentation and rehabilitation.

US/0886-8026
**KEY OPTHALMOLOGY.** [Key ophthalmol.]. Vol. 1, No. 1 (1st Quarter 1986)-. Periodical. English. Four times a year. $112.50 (institutions), $75.00 (individuals) US; $116.50 (institutions), $79.00 (individuals) Canada; $126.50 (institutions), $89.00 (individuals) other. Mosby Year Book Inc., 11830 Westline Industrial Drive, St Louis MO 63146. **Tel** (800)325-4177, (314)872-8370, FAX (314)432-1380, telex 44-2402. **ED** Peter R. Laibson and the Wills Eye Hospital Editorial Board. **DD** 617. **NLM** W1; KE77K. **[CCC]. Pr Rev.**
**Desc:** Contains clinically applicable articles from nearly 700 medical and allied health journals published within the preceding 6-8 months. Articles are condensed and evaluated by a group of specialists who supply commentary highlighted in the margins. Illustrations and tables from the original articles are included.

PL/0023-2157
**KLINIKA OCZNA.** (KLINIKA OCZNA : ORGAN TOWARZYSTWA OKULISTOW POLSKICH.). [Klin. ocz.]. **Added/Corp** Towarzystwo Okulistow Polskich. Polskie Towarzystwo Okulistyczne. **VFOAT** Acta Ophthalmologica Polonica. Vol. 25 (1923)-. Academic Scholarly Publication. Polish (summaries and/or abstracts in English and Russian). mo. Price on Request. **(Subscription address:** ARS Polona, PO Box 1001, 00068 Warsaw Poland.**) NLM** W1 KL303. **CODEN** KOAOAE. Documents available from CASDDS. ***Continues*** *Postep Okulistyczny, 0208-5844.*
**Ind/Abst** Chem. Abstr.; EMBASE [Select. Cov.]; Index Med.

GW/0023-2165
**KLINISCHE MONATSBLATTER FUER AUGENHEILKUNDE.** [Klin. Monatsbl. Augenheilkund.]. (1963)-. Academic Scholarly Publication. German. mo. $329.00. Ferdinand Enke Verlag, Ruedigerstrasse 14, D-70469 Stuttgart Germany. **Tel** 011 49 711 8931124, 011 49 711 893123. **(Subscription address:** Thieme Medical Publishers Inc., 381 Park Avenue South, New York NY 10016.**) NLM** W1; KL47. **CODEN** KMAUAI. **[CCC]. Pr Rev.** Documents available from The Genuine Article, BIOSIS Document Express, CASDDS. ***Continues*** *Klinische Monatsblatter fuer Augenheilkunde und fuer Augenarztliche Fortbildung, 0344-6360.*
**Ind/Abst** Biol. Abstr.; Chem. Abstr.; Curr. Contents Clin. Med.; EMBASE; Energy Res. Abstr.; Helminthol. Abstr. (1991-); Index Med.; Life Sci. Collect.; Protozoolog. Abstr.; Res. Alert [Full Cov.]; Rev. Med. Vet. Entomol.; Sci. Cit. Index; SCISEARCH; Soc. Sci. Cit. Index [Select. Cov.].

KO
**KOREAN JOURNAL OF OPHTHALMOLOGY : KJO.** **VFOAT** KJO. Vol. 1, No. 1 (June 1987)-. Periodical. English. Twice a year (June and December). $20.00. Seoul National University / Department of Ophthalmology, 28 Yeongun Dong Chongroku, Seoul 110 744 Korea. **Tel** 011 82 2 7601-2437, FAX 011 82 2 7413187, telex SENUH K 25501. **ED** Dong Ho Youn M.D. and Jaeheung Lee M. D. (phone: 011 82 2 760-2430). **NLM** W1; KO608E. **Ad Acc.**
**Ind/Abst** Index Med. (Vol. 1, No. 1, 1987-).

NE/0922-5307
**LASERS AND LIGHT IN OPHTHALMOLOGY.** **VFOAT** LLO. Vol. 2, No. 1 (April 1988)-. Periodical. English. Four times a year. $165.00 The Americas; Fl295.00 Netherlands. Kugler Publications BV / Amsterdam, PO Box 11188, 1001 GD Amsterdam Netherlands. **Tel** 011 31 20 6278070. **(Subscription address:** Kugler Publications, PO Box 1498, New York, NY 10009**) ED** J Marshall. **NLM** W1; LA78E. Index available. **Ad Acc. Pr Rev. Circ:** 400. ***Continues*** *Lasers in Ophthalmology.*
**Ind/Abst** EMBASE.

UK/0309-2410
**MAJOR PROBLEMS IN OPHTHALMOLOGY.** ***Ceased.*** [Major probl. ophthalmol.]. (1975)-(19??). Monographic series. English. W.B. Saunders Company, A Subsidiary of Harcourt Brace Jovanovich, Inc., The Curtis Center/Suite 300, Independence Square West, Philadelphia PA 19106-3399. **Tel** (215)238-7800 or, 5587, FAX (215)238-7883, telex 173146. **(Subscription address:** W. B. Saunders Company / North America Subscriptions, c/o Periodicals, 6277 Sea Harbour Drive, 4th Floor, Orlando FL 32887.**) ED** P D Trevor-Roper. **NLM** W1 MA492W.

SP
**MEDICAL DIGEST. OFTALMOLOGIA.** Spanish. Editorial M.C.R. SA, Mallorca 310, 08037 Barcelona Spain.

US/1056-330X
**MEDIGUIDE TO SPECIAL PROBLEMS IN OPHTHALMOLOGY.** [Mediguide spec. probl. ophthalmol.]. Vol. 1, Issue 1 (1991)-. Periodical. English. qt. Dellacorte Publications, 919 3rd Avenue, New York NY 10022-3904. **Tel** (212)751-2806. **DD** 617.

US/0882-889X
**METABOLIC, PEDIATRIC AND SYSTEMIC OPHTHALMOLOGY (1985).** (METABOLIC, PEDIATRIC, AND SYSTEMIC OPHTHALMOLOGY.). [Metab. pediatr. system. ophthalmol.]. **Added/Corp** International Society on Metabolic Eye Disease. International Society of Pediatric Ophthalmology. World Society on Systemic Ophthalmology. Vol. 8, No. 2 & 3 (1985)-. Academic Scholarly Publication. English. Four times a year. $165.00. Opto Education Inc, 1125 Park Avenue, New York NY 10128. **Tel** (212)289-8024, FAX (212)360-7009. **ED** H. M. Haddad, MD, (phone: (212)427-1246). **DD** 617. **NLM** W1; ME961MW. **Bk Rev**, (Qty: 30). **Ad Acc. Circ:** 300. available on microfiche from University Microfilms International (UMI). Documents available from CASDDS. ***Continues*** *Metabolic Ophthalmology, Pediatric and Systemic, 0883-9522.*
**Ind/Abst** Chem. Abstr. (1985-); EMBASE; Index Med. (1984-); Life Sci. Collect. (1985-).

IT/0026-4903
**MINERVA OFTALMOLOGICA.** [Minerva oftalmol.]. Vol. 1 (July/Sept. 1959)-. Academic Scholarly Publication. Italian. qt. $90.00 (individuals), $140.00 (institutions). Edizioni Minerva Medica, Corso Bramante 83-85, 10126 Turin Italy. **Tel** 011 39 11 678282, FAX 011 39 11 674502. **ED** T Oliado. **NLM** W1 MI6489. **Bk Rev. Ad Acc.** available on microfilm and microfiche from University Microfilms International (UMI).
**Desc:** Journal addressed to practitioners and specialists in ophthalmology in Italy and abroad. It deals with topics in scientific practice and research.
**Ind/Abst** EMBASE.

US/0192-771X
**MINUTES OF MEETING / NATIONAL ADVISORY EYE COUNCIL.** **Main/Corp** National Advisory Eye Council (U.S.). Meeting. (April 3, 1969)-. Periodical. English. National Institutes of Health, 9000 Rockville Pike, Bethesda MD 20014. **Tel** (301)496-6975. **NLM** W1 MI7806.

UK
**MODERN TRENDS IN OPHTHALMOLOGY.** V. 1-. English. Butterworth Heinemann Publishers, Linacre House, Jordan Hill, Oxford OX2 8DP England. **Tel** 011 44 865 310366. **ED** F Ridley and A Sorsby. **LC** RE45. **DD** 617.7. **NLM** W1 MO1750.

NE/0165-8107
**NEURO-OPHTHALMOLOGY (AMSTERDAM : AEOLUS PRESS. 1980).** (NEURO-OPHTHALMOLOGY.). [Neuro-ophthalmology]. Vol. 1, No. 1 (Sept. 1980)-. Periodical. English. bm. $258.00. Aeolus Press, PO Box 740, 4116 ZJ Buren The Netherlands. **Tel** 011 31 3447-2055. **ED** A Huber, A Neetens, J T W Van Dalen. **NLM** W1; NE337JC. **[CCC].** Index available. cum. index. **Bk Rev. Ad Acc. Pr Rev. Circ:** 800 (ctrl). available on microfilm from University Microfilms International (UMI). Documents available from The Genuine Article.

**Desc:** Diagnostic and methods in neuro-ophthalmology. **Ind/Abst** Curr. Contents Clin. Med.; EMBASE; Res. Alert [Full Cov.]; Sci. Cit. Index; SCISEARCH.

IT
**NEW TRENDS IN OPHTHALMOLOGY.** English. te. L60000 Italy; $70.00 other. John Libbey CIC srl, Via Spallanzani 11, 00161 Rome Italy. **Tel** (06)8412673-8542783, FAX (06)8443365, telex 622099 CIC I.
**Ind/Abst** EMBASE.

JA/0374-9851
**NIHON KONTAKUTO RENZU GAKKAI KAISHI.** [Nihon Kontakuto Renzu Gakkai Kaishi]. **VFOAT** Journal of Japan Contact Lens Society. (1950)-. Academic Scholarly Publication. Japanese. mo. **CODEN** NSIZB. Documents available from CASDDS.
**Ind/Abst** Chem. Abstr.

JA/0029-0203
**NIPPON GANKA GAKKAI ZASSHI.** [Nihon Ganka Gakkai zasshi]. **Main/Corp** Nippon Ganka Gakkai. **Added/Corp** Nihon Ganka Gakkai. Acta Societatis Ophthalmologicae Japonicae. Nihon Ganka Gakkai. Journal of Japanese Ophthalmological Society. **VFOAT** Acta Societatis Ophthalmologicae Japonicae. Vol. 1 (April 1897)-. Academic Scholarly Publication. Japanese (summaries and/or abstracts in English and German). mo. $198.00. **(Subscription address:** Kyowa Book Company Inc., 1 38 Kanda Jinbocho Chiyoda-ku, Tokyo 101 Japan.) **ED** Tsamu Tsukahara. **NLM** W1; NI896M. **CODEN** NGZAA6. **Circ:** 8,000 (ctrl). Documents available from BIOSIS Document Express, CASDDS. ***Supersedes*** *Ganka Zasshi.*
**Desc:** The organ of Societas Ophthalmologica Japonica introduces dissertations and reports of activity.
**Ind/Abst** Biol. Abstr.; Chem. Abstr.; EMBASE; Health Plan. Adminis.; Index Med.

US
**OAA NEWS.** **Added/Corp** Opticians Association of America. (1987)-. Periodical. English. $16.00. Opticians Association of America, 10341 Democracy Lane, Fairfax VA 22030. **Tel** (703)691-8355. **NLM** W1; OA114. ***Continues*** *Dispensing Optician (Washington, D.C.), 0194-2174.*

US/1047-9120
**OCULAR SURGERY NEWS INTERNATIONAL EDITION.** See Medical Science and Technology-Surgery.

DK/0108-5344
**OFTALMOLOG.** See Medical Science and Technology.

RM
**OFTALMOLOGIA.** **Added/Corp** Societatea Romana de Oftalomolgie. Uniunea Societatilor de Stiinte Medicale. Vol. 34, No. 1 (Jan./Mar. 1990)-. Periodical. Romanian (summaries and/or abstracts in English and Russian; table of contents in English and Russian). qt. DM223.00. Uniunea Societ Stiinte Medical, Str Progresului 8, Bucharest Romania. **(Subscription address:** Kubon & Sagner, ABT Zeitschriftenimport, D 80328 Munich Germany.) **NLM** W1; OF838. ***Continues*** *Revista de Chirurgie, Oncologie, Radiologie, O. R. L., Oftalmologie, Stomatologie. Seria: Oftalmologie, 0377-7863.*
**Ind/Abst** Index Med. (1990-).

SP
**OFTALMOLOGIA. REVISTA D'OR.** (19??)-. Spanish. ir. Publicaciones d'Or Medico Cientificas, Aribau 254 B/6, 08006 Barcelona Spain.

UN/0030-0675
**OFTALMOLOGICESKIJ ZURNAL (KIEV).** (OFTALMOLOGICHESKII ZHURNAL.). [Oftalmol. z.]. (1946)-. Academic Scholarly Publication. Russian. Six times a year (six issues per year). $89.95 US & Canada; $99.95 Europe; $114.95 others. **(Subscription address:** East View Publications Inc., 3020 Harbor Lane North, Suite 110, Minneapolis MN 55447.) **NLM** W1 OF892. **CODEN** OFZHAV. Documents available from CASDDS.
**Ind/Abst** Chem. Abstr.; EMBASE [Select. Cov.]; Index Med.

BU/0374-2105
**OFTALMOLOGIJA.** (OFTALMOLOGIIA.). [Oftalmologija]. **Added/Corp** Naucnho Druzhestvo na Oftalmolozite. Vol. 12 (1964)-. Academic Scholarly Publication. Bulgarian (summaries and/or abstracts in English; table of contents in English). Three times a year. $42.50. Izdatelstvo Medicina i Fizkult, PL Slavejkov 11, 1000 Sofia Bulgaria. **(Subscription address:** Hemus Foreign Trade Organization, 6 Tzar Osvoboditel Boulevard, 1000 Sofia Bulgaria.) **NLM** W1 OF895. **CODEN** OPTMAI. Documents available from CASDDS. ***Continues*** *Oftalmologischen Pregled.*
**Ind/Abst** Chem. Abstr. (1964-1984); EMBASE; Saf. Health Work.

FR
**OPHTALMOLOGIE E71.** French. 929.11F France; 960.00F other. Institut de l'Information Scientifique et Technique Technologie Medecine, 2 Allee du Parc de Brabois, 54514 Vandoeuvre Nancy France. **Tel** 011 33 83 504664. cum. index. ***Continues*** *Pascal Explore : E71, Ophtalmologie.*

FR/0989-3105
**OPHTALMOLOGIE (PARIS).** (OPHTALMOLOGIE : ORGANE DE LA SOCIETE FRANCAISE D'OPHTALMOLOGIE.). [Ophtalmologie]. **Added/Corp** Societe Francaise d'Ophtalmologie. Vol. 1, No. 1 (Jan./March 1987)-. Periodical. French. qt. $130.00. Scientific & Medical Publishers of France, 100 East 42nd Street, Suite 1002, New York NY 10017-5613. **Tel** (212)983-6278. **(Subscription address:** Masson SA, 7A Boulevard de Perolles,, CH-1701 Fribourg Switzerland.) **NLM** W1; OP17. **[CCC].** ***Continues*** *Bulletins et Memoires de la Societe Francaise d'Ophtalmologie, 0081-1092.*
**Ind/Abst** EMBASE [Select. Cov.]; Index Med. Jan./March 1987.

US/1043-1780
**OPHTHALMIC DRUG FACTS.** (OPHTHALMIC DRUG FACTS : ODF.). [Ophthalmic drug facts]. **Added/Corp** J.B. Lippincott Company. Facts and Comparisons Division. **VFOAT** ODF. (1990)-. English. an. $41.95 (hardbound edition) US; $52.50 (hardbound edition) other. Facts and Comparisons Inc, 111 West Port Plaza, Suite 400, St Louis MO 63146-3098. **Tel** (314)878-2515, (800)223-0554, FAX (314)878-5563. **DD** 615. **NLM** W 39; O61.
**Desc:** A compendium of information that focuses entirely on ophthalmic drugs. It gives prescribing information on all drugs of specific interest to the eye care professional.

UK/0030-3720
**OPHTHALMIC LITERATURE.** **VFOAT** New Ophthalmic Literature of ...; New Ophthalmic Literature. Vol. 1 (June 1947)-. Periodical. English. qt. $276.00 The Americas; £185.00 other. Butterworth Heinemann Publishers, Linacre House, Jordan Hill, Oxford OX2 8DP England. **Tel** 011 44 865 310366. **(Subscription address:** Elsevier Science Ltd. Oxford Fulfillment Centre, PO Box 800, Kidlington, Oxford OX5 1DX United Kingdom.) **ED** J. H. Kelsey. **LC** Z6669; .O6. **DD** 016.6177. **NLM** ZWW 100 O56. Index available. **Bk Rev**. **Ad Acc**. available on microfilm and microfiche from University Microfilms International (UMI). ***Continues in part*** *British Journal of Ophthalmology.*
**Desc:** Abstracts ophthalmology and related sciences.

US/0743-6378
**OPHTHALMIC OBSERVER.** [Ophthalmic obs.]. Periodical. English. qt. Free to Medical Personnel. Ophthalmic Observer, POB 19587, Irvine CA 92713.

US/0740-9303
**OPHTHALMIC PLASTIC AND RECONSTRUCTIVE SURGERY.** [Ophthalmic plastic reconstr. surg.]. **Added/Corp** American Society of Ophthalmic Plastic and Reconstructive Surgery. Vol. 1, No. 1 (1985)-. Periodical. English. qt. $130.00 (individuals), $196.00 (institutions) US; $158.00 (individuals), $235.00 (institutions) other. Raven Press, 1185 Avenue of the Americas, 37th Floor, New York NY 10036. **Tel** (212)930-9500, (212)930-9604, FAX (212)869-3495, (212)302-8507, telex 640073. **DD** 617. **NLM** W1; OP236. **[CCC].** available on microfilm and microfiche from University Microfilms International (UMI). Documents available from The Genuine Article.
**Ind/Abst** Curr. Contents Clin. Med.; EMBASE; Health Plan. Adminis.; Index Med. (1984-); Res. Alert [Select. Cov.]; SCISEARCH.

CN/0832-9869
**OPHTHALMIC PRACTICE.** [Ophthalmic pract.]. **VFOAT** Practical Phacoemulsification. Vol. 5, No. 1 (March 1987)-. Periodical. English. Six times a year (Feb., Apr., June, Aug., Oct., Dec.). $60.00 Canada; $72.00 US; $94.00 other. Medicopea International, 3333 Cote Vertu Boulevard, Suite 300, Montreal QUE H4R 2N1 Canada. **Tel** (514)331-4561, FAX (514)336-1129. **ED** Inara Palieps. **DD** 617/.7/005. **NLM** W1; OP237. Index available. cum. index. **Bk Rev**, (Qty: 10-12). **Ad Acc**, **Adv Mgr:** Sara Wilkins. **Circ:** 1,300 (ctrl). ***Continues*** *Current Canadian Ophthalmic Practice, 0823-4744.*
**Desc:** A journal that issues focuses on multiple areas of ophthalmology. Includes subjects such has IOL implantation, trauma, cataracts and surgical techniques. Regular departments includes, case reports, & A, book reviews and new product news.

SZ/0030-3747
**OPHTHALMIC RESEARCH.** [Ophthalmic res.]. Vol. 1 (1970)-. Academic Scholarly Publication. English. bm. $383.00. S. Karger AG, Allschwilerstrasse 10, PO Box - Postfach - Case Postale, CH-4009 Basel Switzerland. **Tel** 011 41 61 306-1111, FAX 011 41 61 306-1234, telex CH 962 652. **ED** G.F.J.M. Vrensen. **LC** RE58; .O54. **DD** 617/.7/005. **NLM** W1 OP238P. **CODEN** OPRSAQ. **[CCC].** **Pr Rev.** available on microfilm from University Microfilms International (UMI). Documents available from The Genuine Article, BIOSIS Document Express, CASDDS.
**Desc:** Features original papers reporting basic and clinical experimental studies. Authors from throughout the world cover morphologic, physiologic, and biochemical aspects of ophthalmology. Articles on methodological problems are included as well as a number of contributions by non-ophthalmologists working in related scientific fields. The results of new experimental research are also interpreted in light of their importance to the clinical work of the eye specialist. This journal provides a record of international research for both researchers and clinicians in ophthalmology.
**Ind/Abst** Biol. Abstr.; Chem. Abstr.; Curr. Contents Life Sci.; EMBASE; Index Med.; Int. Aerosp. Abstr.; Life Sci. Collect.; Ref. Upd. Deluxe Ed.; Res. Alert [Full Cov.]; Sci. Cit. Index; SCISEARCH.

US
**OPHTHALMIC REVIEWS.** English. be (published odd years). $60.00 US; $65.00 other. Survey of Ophthalmology Inc, 7 Kent Street/Suite 4, Brookline MA 02146. **Tel** (617)566-2138, FAX (617)566-4019.

US
**OPHTHALMIC STAFF REPORT.** English. Four times a year. $40.00 US; $48.72 other. Macmillan Professional Journal, 30 Vreeland Road, Florham Park NJ 07932. **Tel** (201)822-1622, FAX (201)822-2498.

US/0022-023X
**OPHTHALMIC SURGERY.** See Medical Science and Technology-Surgery.

●GW/0941-293X
**OPHTHALMOLOGE : ZEITSCHRIFT DER DEUTSCHEN OPHTHALMOLOGISCHEN GESELLSCHAFT, DER.** **Added/Corp** Deutsche Ophthalmologische Gesellschaft. (1992)-. Academic Scholarly Publication. German (English). bm. DM228.00. Springer-Verlag GmbH & Company KG, Heidelberger Platz 3, D 14197 Berlin Germany. **Tel** 011 49 30 8207223, FAX 011 49 30 8214091, telex 183 319 SPBLN D. **(Subscription address:** Springer Verlag New York Inc. / for North America, 44 Hartz Way, Secaucus NJ 07096.) **NLM** W1; OP334P. **CODEN** OHTHEJ. Documents available from CASDDS. ***Continues in part*** *Fortschritte der Ophthalmologie, 0723-8045.*
**Ind/Abst** Chem. Abstr.

●CI/0353-9881
**OPHTHALMOLOGIA CROATICA.** **Added/Corp** Hrvatsko Oftalmolosko Drustvo. Vol. 1, No. 1 (Jan. 1992)-. Periodical. Serbo-Croatian (Roman) (English). qt. $80.00. BTS Knjiga Trgovina, Kaptol 25, 4100 Zagreb Croatia. **Tel** 011 385 41 271925 271692. **NLM** W1; OP334V.

SZ/0030-3755
**OPHTHALMOLOGICA (BASEL).** (OPHTHALMOLOGICA.). [Ophthalmologica]. **Added/Corp** Nederlands Oogheelkundig Gezelschap. Schweizerische Opthalmologische Gesellschaft. **VFOAT** International Journal of Ophthalmology. Vol. 96 (1938)-. Academic Scholarly Publication. German (English, French and German; summaries and/or abstracts in English and French). bm. $461.00. S. Karger AG, Allschwilerstrasse 10, PO Box - Postfach - Case Postale, CH-4009 Basel Switzerland. **Tel** 011 41 61 306-1111, FAX 011 41 61 306-1234, telex CH 962 652. **ED** Ch. Ohrloff. **LC** RE1; .O438. **NLM** W1 OP337. **CODEN** OPHTAD. **[CCC].** cum. index. **Bk Rev**. **Ad Acc**. **Pr Rev**. available on microfilm from University Microfilms International (UMI). Documents available from The Genuine Article, BIOSIS Document Express, CASDDS. ***Continues*** *Zeitschrift fuer Augenheilkunde.*
**Desc:** Focuses on practical problems. Each issue contains a selection of patient-oriented reports covering the etiology of eye diseases, diagnostic techniques, and advances in medical and surgical treatment. Also features book reviews and a section headed 'Clinicopathologic Case Report'.
**Ind/Abst** Biol. Abstr.; Chem. Abstr.; Curr. Contents Clin. Med.; EMBASE; Index Med.; Mod. Med.; Life Sci. Collect.; Ref. Upd. Deluxe Ed.; Res. Alert [Full Cov.]; Rev. Med. Vet. Entomol.; Rev. Med. Vet. Mycology; Sci. Cit. Index; SCISEARCH; Soc. Sci. Cit. Index [Select. Cov.].

FI/0358-4852
**OPHTHALMOLOGICA ET OTO-RHINO-LARYNGOLOGICA (OULU).** (OPHTHALMOLOGICA ET OTO-RHINO-LARYNGOLOGICA.). No. 1-. Monographic series. English (Finnish). ir. Price varies per volume. Professor Leo Hirvonen, University of Oulu, 90100 Oulu 10 Finland. **Tel** 358-81-332133. **ED** Leo Hirvonen. **NLM** W1 AC954NM no. 18 etc. cum. index. **Ad Acc. Circ:** 450 (ctrl).
**Desc:** Monographs, reviews, and dissertations in the fields of ophthalmology and otorhinolaryngology.

GW/0943-898X
**OPHTHALMOLOGISCHE NACHRICHTEN.** Twelve times a year. $69.00. Georg Thieme Verlag Stuttgart, Postfach 301120, D 70451 Stuttgart Germany. **Tel** 011 49 711 89310, FAX 011 49 711 8931298, telex 7 252 275 GTVD. **(Subscription address:** Thieme Medical Publishers Inc., 381 Park Avenue South, New York NY 10016.)

US/1047-0808
**OPHTHALMOLOGY ALERT.** ***Ceased.*** (OPHTHALMOLOGY.). [Ophthalmol. alert]. **Added/Corp** American Health Consultants. Vol. 1, No. 1 (Jan. 1990)-?. Periodical. English. mo. American Health Consultants,

3525 Piedmont Road, Suite 400, Atlanta GA 30305. **Tel** (800)688-2421, (404)262-7436. **DD** 617. **NLM** W1; OP371Q. ***Continues*** *Ocular Therapy Report, 0896-6133.*

US/0896-1549
**OPHTHALMOLOGY CLINICS OF NORTH AMERICA.** [Ophthalmol. clin. North Am.]. (Sept. 1988)-. Periodical. English. qt. $100.00 (individual), $134.00 (institutions) US; $152.00 (individual), $160.00 other. W.B. Saunders Company, A Subsidiary of Harcourt Brace Jovanovich, Inc., The Curtis Center/Suite 300, Independence Square West, Philadelphia PA 19106-3399. **Tel** (215)238-7800 or, 5587, FAX (215)238-7883, telex 173146. **(Subscription address:** W. B. Saunders Company / North America Subscriptions, c/o Periodicals, 6277 Sea Harbour Drive, 4th Floor, Orlando FL 32887.**) LC** RE1; .O49. **DD** 617.7/005. **NLM** W1; OP371S. **[CCC].**

US/0048-1955
**OPHTHALMOLOGY DIGEST (1979).** (OPHTHALMOLOGY DIGEST.). [Ophthalmol. dig.]. V. 4L, No. 8/9- Aug./Sept. 1979-. Periodical. English. mo. $27.50. Medical Digest, 444 Frontage Road, PO Box 8021, Northfield IL 60093. **NLM** W1 OP371T. ***Continues*** *Journal of Continuing Education in Ophthalmology, 0149-4260.*
**Desc:** Includes abstracts of medical literature.

US/0271-1281
**OPHTHALMOLOGY (GLENDALE, CALIF.).** (OPHTHALMOLOGY [SOUND RECORDING].). [Ophthalmol.]. **Added/Corp** Audio-Digest Foundation. **VFOAT** Audio-Digest Ophthalmology; Audio Digest Ophthalmology. (1963)-. Periodical. English. sm. $179.76 US; $202.80 Canada; $247.44 other (audiocassette). Audio-Digest Foundation, 1577 Chevy Chase Drive, Glendale CA 91206. **Tel** (213)245-8505, (800)423-2308, FAX (818)240-7379. **ED** Claron L. Oakley. **DD** 617. **NLM** W1 AU201DS. Index available.
**Desc:** An interactive system of audio cassette postgraduate medical education, with each one-hour program eligible for two Category I credit hours.

US/0746-1070
**OPHTHALMOLOGY MANAGEMENT.** [Ophthalmol. manage.]. Vol. 1, No. 1 (April 1983)-. Periodical. English. ir (ten issues per year). $18.00 US; $24.00 other. Ophthalmology Management, 1515 Broadway, New York NY 10036. **Tel** (212)869-1300. **ED** Herve M Byron. **DD** 617. Index available. **Ad Acc. Circ:** 15,339 (ctrl).
**Desc:** Practice management magazine for opthamologists; offers sophisticated hands-on information and guidelines for handling the business aspects of a medical practice.

US/1044-1557
**OPHTHALMOLOGY REPORT.** (1991)-. Periodical. English. qt. $54.50 (institutions and individuals), $27.25 (students and residents) US; $62.00 (institutions and individuals), $34.75 (students and residents) other. Mosby Year Book Inc., 11830 Westline Industrial Drive, St Louis MO 63146. **Tel** (800)325-4177, (314)872-8370, FAX (314)432-1380, telex 44-2402. **ED** Andrew P Schachat.
**Desc:** Several different clinical topics are addressed in each issue. The first issue includes articles on sedation for ophthalmic surgery, ophthalmic manifestations of AIDS, glare testing, enucleation surgery, management of naturally occurring and post cataract astigmatism, use of cyclosporine for treating eye infections, and soft contact lenses versus rigid gas permeable lenses.

US/1067-2346
**OPHTHALMOLOGY RESIDENT, THE.** ***Ceased.*** (1993)-(March/April 1994). Periodical. English. bm. Slack Inc., 6900 Grove Road, Thorofare NJ 08086. **Tel** (609)848-1000, (800)257-8290, FAX (609)853-5991, telex 517108 SLACK INC VD.

US/0161-6420
**OPHTHALMOLOGY (ROCHESTER, MINN.).** (OPHTHALMOLOGY.). [Ophthalmology]. **Added/Corp** American Academy of Ophthalmology. American Academy of Ophthalmology and Otolaryngology. Vol. 81, No. 3 (May/June 1976)-. Academic Scholarly Publication. English. mo. $120.00 (individuals), $175.00 (institutions) US; $155.00 (individuals), $210.00 (institutions) other. J.B. Lippincott Company, 227 East Washington Square, Philadelphia PA 19106-3780. **Tel** (215)238-4200 or 4454, FAX (215)238-4227. **(Subscription address:** J.B. Lippincott, PO Box 350, Hagerstown MD 21740.**) ED** Paul Lichter and Randall S. Wallach. **DD** 617. **NLM** W1 OP371P. **CODEN** 0PHTDG. **[CCC].** Index available. cum. index. **Bk Rev. Ad Acc. Pr Rev. Circ:** 20,723. available on microfilm and microfiche from University Microfilms International (UMI). Documents available from The Genuine Article, BIOSIS Document Express, CASDDS. ***Continues*** *Transactions - American Academy of Ophthalmology and Otolaryngology, 0161-6978.*
**Desc:** Articles based on clinical studies and basic research in all areas of ophthalmology.
**Ind/Abst** Biol. Abstr.; Chem. Abstr.; Cumul. Index Nurs. Allied Health Lit.; EMBASE; Energy Res. Abstr. (Aug. 1981-); Health Devices Alerts; Helminthol. Abstr. (1991-); Index Med.; Index Vet.; Med. Abstr. Newsl.; Mod. Med.; Life Sci. Collect.; Protozoolog. Abstr.; Ref. Upd. Deluxe Ed.; Res. Alert [Full Cov.]; Rev. Med. Vet. Entomol.; Rev. Med. Vet. Mycology; Sci. Cit. Index; SCISEARCH; Small Anim. Abstr. Bibliogr.; Soc. Sci. Cit. Index [Select. Cov.].

US
**OPHTHALMOLOGY. SOURCEBOOK AND REFERENCE GUIDE / THE AMERICAN ACADEMY OF OPHTHALMOLOGY.** **Added/Corp** American Academy of Ophthalmology. (1991)-. English. J.B. Lippincott Company, 227 East Washington Square, Philadelphia PA 19106-3780. **Tel** (215)238-4200 or 4454, FAX (215)238-4227. **NLM** WW 22; AA1 O6.

US/0193-032X
**OPHTHALMOLOGY TIMES.** [Ophthalmol. times]. (1976)-. Periodical. English. sm. $190.00 US and possessions; $215.00 Canada; $290.00 other. Advanstar Communications Inc., 131 West First Street, Duluth MN 55802. **Tel** (218)723-9477, (800)346-0085. **ED** Dean Celia. **LC** Discard. **DD** 617. **[CCC]. Ad Acc. Circ:** 14,553 (ctrl). available on an online database (file16/Full-Text) from DIALOG.
**Desc:** A scientific tabloid providing news of ophthalmology.
**Ind/Abst** Biol. Dig.; F&S Index Plus Text, Int. [Full Txt.] [Select. Cov.]; PROMT [Full Txt.].

US/1077-8292
**OPHTHALMOLOGY WORLD NEWS.** (19??)-. Periodical. English. mo. $80.00 (individuals), $111.00 (institutions) US; $105.00 (individuals), $148.00 (institutions) other. J.B. Lippincott Company, 227 East Washington Square, Philadelphia PA 19106-3780. **Tel** (215)238-4200 or 4454, FAX (215)238-4227. **(Subscription address:** J.B. Lippincott, PO Box 350, Hagerstown MD 21740.**)**

●UK
**OPTICAL PRACTITIONER.** Vol. 1, No. 1 (Apr. 1992)-. Periodical. English. Eight times a year (Feb., Apr., May, June, Aug., Sep., Oct., Dec.). £35.00 UK; $90.00 (surface mail), $135.00 (airmail) US; £45.00 (surface mail), £55.00 (airmail) other. Optical World Ltd, 200 London Road, Essex SS1 1PJ England. **Tel** 011 44 702 345443, FAX 011 44 702 431806. **ED** Gerald Ward. **NLM** W1; OP821E.

UK
**OPTICAL WORLD.** **VFOAT** Optische Welt. No. 1 (March, 1972)-. Periodical. English (French and German; summaries and/or abstracts in French and German). Ten times a year (Jan./Feb. and July/Aug. issues combined). $135.00 (surface), $170.00 (airmail) US; £60.00 UK and EEC; £85.00 (surface), £105.00 (airmail) other. Optical World Ltd, 200 London Road, Essex SS1 1PJ England. **Tel** 011 44 702 345443, FAX 011 44 702 431806. **DD** 338.4/7/6177505.

BE
**OPTO MAGAZINE.** (19??)-. Newsletter. French (Dutch). Six times a year. 1200F. Association Professionnelle des Opticiens de Belgique, 26 rue Capitaine Crespel, 1050 Brussels Belgium. **Tel** 2/512 55 26, FAX 2/502 34 02. **ED** Ph Carlier. **Ad Acc, Adv Mgr:** B. Denis. **Circ:** 2,500 (ctrl).
**Desc:** Technical, scientifical information for opticians and optometrists.

●US/1062-6395
**OPTOMETRIC BUSINESS STRATEGIST.** (1992)-. Periodical. English. bm. $69.00. Anadem Inc, 3620 North High Street, Columbus OH 43214. **Tel** (614)262-2539, (800)633-0055.

NE/0167-6830
**ORBIT (AMSTERDAM).** (ORBIT.). [Orbit]. Vol. 1, No. 1 (Jan. 1982)-. Periodical. English. Four times a year (Mar., June, Sept., Dec.). $191.00 US & Canada; F330.00 European Community Countries; F345.00 others. Aeolus Press, PO Box 740, 4116 ZJ Buren The Netherlands. **Tel** 011 31 3447-2055. **ED** Gabe M. Bleeker. **NLM** W1 OR146M. **[CCC].** Index available. cum. index. **Bk Rev. Ad Acc. Circ:** 600 (ctrl). available on microfilm from University Microfilms International (UMI).
**Desc:** Orbital disorders and facial reconstructive surgery.
**Ind/Abst** EMBASE.

PH/0031-7659
**PHILIPPINE JOURNAL OF OPHTHALMOLOGY.** [Philipp. j. ophthalmol.]. **Added/Corp** Philippine Society of Ophthalmology. Vol. 1, No. 1 (Jan.-March 1969)-. Academic Scholarly Publication. English. qt. Philippine Ophthalmology Society, Philippine General Hospital, Taft Avenue, Manila D-406 Philippines. **ED** Romeo V. Fajardo. **NLM** W1 PH57T. **Bk Rev. Ad Acc. Circ:** 1,000. available on microfilm from University Microfilms International (UMI).
**Desc:** Contains original articles, case reports, clinical and book reviews, and society proceedings.
**Ind/Abst** EMBASE.

US/0091-6803
**PHYSICIANS' DESK REFERENCE FOR OPHTHALMOLOGY.** [Physician desk ref. ophthalmol.]. **VFOAT** PDR for Ophthalmology. 1st Ed. (1972)-. English. an. $42.95. Medical Economics Data, Five Paragon Drive, PO Box 27, Montvale NJ 07645. **Tel** (800)442-6657, (201)358-7200. **(Subscription address:** Physicians' Desk Reference, Box 10688, Trade Department KL Grove, Des Moines, IA 50336**) LC** RE994; .P57. **DD** 617.7/061/05. **NLM** QV 772 P576.
**Desc:** A complete directory of product information relating to optometry and ophthalmology, this indispensable guide offers a wealth of information for the care and treatment of the eye. Features data on specialized instrumentation, equipment and lenses often with product photographs...a detailed encyclopedia of pharmaceuticals in ophthalmology...six complete indices...an extensive bibliography and information on lens types, uses and care.

●UK/1350-9462
**PROGRESS IN RETINAL AND EYE RESEARCH.** **VFOAT** Retinal and Eye Research. Vol. 13, No. 1 (1994)-. English. Twice a year. $395.00 (regular subscription), $1625.00 (combination subscription with Vision Research) The Americas; £265.00 (regular subscription), £1090.00 (combination subscription with Vision Research) other. Pergamon Press, An Imprint of Elsevier Science Ltd., The Boulevard, Langford Lane, Kidlington, Oxford OX5 1GB United Kingdom. **Tel** 011 44 865 843000, 011 44 865 843699, FAX 011 44 865 843010. **(Subscription address:** Elsevier Science Ltd. Oxford Fulfillment Centre, PO Box 800, Kidlington, Oxford OX5 1DX United Kingdom.**) LC** QP479; .P76. **DD** 591.1/823. **NLM** W1; PR681BF. **CODEN** PRTRES. **[CCC].** ***Continues*** *Progress in Retinal Research, 0278-4327.*

UK/0309-2437
**RECENT ADVANCES IN OPHTHALMOLOGY.** [Recent adv. ophthalmol.]. No. 1 (1927)-. Periodical. English. ir. Price varies per volume. Churchill Livingstone, 1-3 Baxter's Place, Leith Walk, Edinburgh EH1 3AF Scotland. **Tel** 011 44 31 556 2424, FAX 011 44 31 558 1278, telex 727511. **(Subscription address:** Churchill Livingstone / US, 5 S 250 Frontenac Road, Naperville IL 60563.**) ED** W. S. Duke-Elder and A. J. B. Goldsmith. **NLM** W1 RE105VP.

US/0146-4582
**RED BOOK OF OPHTHALMOLOGY, THE.** 32d Ed. (1977)-. English. be. $65.00. Butterworth Heinemann / Woburn, MA, 225 Wildwood Avenue, Unit B, Woburn MA 01801. **Tel** (800)366-2665, FAX (617)928-2620, telex 880052. **ED** Marsheela Evans. **LC** RE22; .R3. **DD** 617.7/0025/73. **NLM** WW 22 AA1 R3. **Ad Acc. Circ:** 3,000. ***Continues*** *Red Book of Eye, Ear, Nose and Throat Specialists, 0146-4590.*
**Desc:** Listing of names and addresses of American and Canadian Ophthalmologists.

US/1042-962X
**REFRACTIVE & CORNEAL SURGERY.** ***Title Change.*** **Added/Corp** International Society of Refractive Keratoplasty. European Refractive Surgery Society. **VFOAT** Refractive and Corneal Surgery. Vol. 5 No. 1 (Jan/Feb 1989)-(1994). Periodical. English. bm. Slack Inc., 6900 Grove Road, Thorofare NJ 08086. **Tel** (609)848-1000, (800)257-8290, FAX (609)853-5991, telex 517108 SLACK INC VD. **DD** 617. **NLM** W1; RE717XJ. **CODEN** RCSUEH. ***Continues*** *Journal of Refractive Surgery, 0883-0444.* ***Continued by*** *Journal of Refractive & Corneal Surgery.*
**Ind/Abst** Health Plan. Adminis. (?-?); Index Med. (Jan./Feb. 1989-?).

US/0270-4234
**REPORT - NATIONAL SOCIETY TO PREVENT BLINDNESS.** [Rep. - Natl. Soc. Prev. Blind.]. **Main/Corp** National Society to Prevent Blindness. 1977/78-. English. an. National Society to Prevent Blindness, 500 East Remington Road, Schaumburg IL 60173. **Tel** (212)684-3505. **LC** RE1; .N31. **DD** 362.1/9712/006073. **NLM** W1 NA752. ***Continues*** *National Society for the Prevention of Blindness. Report for the Year Ending ..., 0891-9062.*

MX
**RETINA.** **VFOAT** Retina; Sintesis y Enfoque Informativo. Vol. 1, No. 1 (August 1978)-. Periodical. Spanish. mo. Impresora Monterrey, Condomino Acero Monterrey, Zaragoza 1000 Sur, Despacho 1405, Monterrey NL Mexico.

US/0275-004X
**RETINA (PHILADELPHIA, PA.).** (RETINA.). [Retina]. **Added/Corp** Ophthalmic Communications Society (U.S.). Vol. 1, No. 1 (Winter 1981)-. Academic Scholarly Publication. English. bm. $120.00 (individuals), $195.00 (institutions) US; $156.00 (individuals), $225.00 (institutions) other. J.B. Lippincott Company, 227 East Washington Square, Philadelphia PA 19106-3780. **Tel** (215)238-4200 or 4454, FAX (215)238-4227. **(Subscription address:** J.B. Lippincott, PO Box 350, Hagerstown MD 21740.**) ED** Alexander J. Brucker. **LC** RE501; .R47. **NLM** W1 RE2498. **CODEN** RETIDX. **[CCC]. Ad Acc. Pr Rev. Circ:** 2,107. available on microfilm and microfiche from University Microfilms International (UMI). Documents available from The Genuine Article, BIOSIS Document Express.
**Desc:** Features articles on surgical and other techniques and an office reference system of abstracts from current

literature.
**Ind/Abst** Biol. Abstr. (1988-); Curr. Contents Clin. Med.; EMBASE; Index Med.; Res. Alert [Select. Cov.].

NE/0168-8375
**REVIEWS OF OCULOMOTOR RESEARCH.** [Rev. oculomot. res.]. (1985)-. Monographic series. English. ir. Price varies per volume. Elsevier Science Publishers BV, PO Box 211, 1000 AE Amsterdam Netherlands. **Tel** 011 31 20 5803642, FAX 011 31 20 5862696, telex 15682. **NLM** W1; RE253JNM. **[CCC].**

BL/0034-7280
**REVISTA BRASILEIRA DE OTTALMOLOGIA.** Vol. 1 (1942)-. Periodical. Portuguese. qt. $32.00. Revista Brasileira de rue Sao Salvador, 107 Laranjers, Rio de Janeiro Gua ZC01 Brazil.
**Ind/Abst** EMBASE [Select. Cov.].

CU
**REVISTA CUBANA DE OFTALMOLOGIA.** ***Ceased.*** (19??)-Ceased (19??). Spanish. Three times a year. Ediciones Cubanas, Obispo 527, Altos ESQ Bernaza, CP 10100 Havana Cuba. **Tel** 011 632980, 631942, FAX 011 631011, telex 512337, 6540.

FR/0338-9987
**REVUE CHIBRET D'OPHTALMOLOGIE.** Monographic series. French. Price varies per volume. Laboratoires Chibret, 100 Boulevard Clementel, 63018 Clermont-Fer France. **NLM** W1 RE7455D. ***Continues*** *Revue Chibret, 0338-9979.*

FR
**REVUE DE L'OPHTALMOLOGIE FRANCAISE & ANNUELLE.** French. Five times a year. 60.00F France; 90.00F other. Syndicat Natl Ophtalmologistes, 1 rue des Pucelles, 67000 Strasbourg France. **Tel** 88 78 51 43. **ED** Jean-Luc Seegmuller.
**Desc:** Professional information of general interest for the daily practice.

FR/0246-0831
**REVUE INTERNATIONALE DU TRACHOME ET DE PATHOLOGIE OCULAIRE TROPICALE ET SUBTROPICALE ET DE SANTE PUBLIQUE.** [Rev. int. trach. pathol. ocul. trop. subtrop. sante publique]. **Added/Corp** International Organization against Trachoma. Ligue Contre le Trachome. (1981)-. Academic Scholarly Publication. French (English). qt. Free. Laboratoires H Faure, BP 131, 07104 Annonay France. **Tel** 011 33 7 5332421, FAX 011 33 7 5670174, telex 345023. **NLM** W1 RE899LA. **CODEN** RITPEF. Documents available from BIOSIS Document Express. ***Continues*** *Revue Internationale du Trachome et de Pathologie Oculaire Tropicale et Subtropicale, 0249-7026.*
**Ind/Abst** Biol. Abstr. (1984-); EMBASE; Helminthol. Abstr. (1991-); Index Med.; Nutr. Abstr. Rev., Ser. A, Hum. Exp.; Rev. Med. Vet. Entomol.; Trop. Dis. Bull.

JA/0370-5579
**RINSHO GANKA.** (RINSHO GANKA. JAPANESE JOURNAL OF CLINICAL OPHTHALMOLOGY.). [Rinsho ganka]. **VFOAT** Japanese Journal of Clinical Ophthalmology; Journal of Clinical Opthalmology. (1947)-. Periodical. Japanese. Thirteen times a year. $380.00. Igaku Shoin Ltd., 5-24-3 Hongo Bunkyo-ku, Tokyo 113 Japan. **Tel** 011 81 3 817 5670. **NLM** W1 RI21623. **CODEN** RIGAA3. Documents available from BIOSIS Document Express.
**Ind/Abst** Biol. Abstr.; EMBASE.

SU
**SAUDI BULLETIN OF OPHTHALMOLOGY : OFFICIAL JOURNAL OF THE SAUDI OPHTHALMOLOGICAL SOCIETY.** **Added/Corp** Saudi Ophthalmological Society. (198?)-. Periodical. English. Four times a year (Mar., June, Sept., Dec.). $100.00. Saudi Ophthalmology Society, PO Box 55307, Riyadh 11534 Saudi Arabia. **Tel** 011 966 1 488 1234 ext. 3739, FAX 011 966 1 477 5791. **ED** Najwa Tabbara. **NLM** W1; SA965. **Ad Acc. Pr Rev. Circ:** 2,000.
**Desc:** A scientific journal covering all aspects of ophthalmology.

US/0882-0538
**SEMINARS IN OPHTHALMOLOGY.** [Sem. ophthalmol.]. Vol. 1, No. 1 (Mar. 1986)-. Periodical. English. qt (Mar., June, Sept., Dec.). $99.00 (individual), $125.00 (institution) US; $152.00 (individual), $164.00 (institutions) other. W.B. Saunders Company, A Subsidiary of Harcourt Brace Jovanovich, Inc., The Curtis Center/Suite 300, Independence Square West, Philadelphia PA 19106-3399. **Tel** (215)238-7800 or, 5587, FAX (215)238-7883, telex 173146. **(Subscription address:** W. B. Saunders Company / North America Subscriptions, c/o Periodicals, 6277 Sea Harbour Drive, 4th Floor, Orlando FL 32887.**) ED** Miles Galin, K. B. Mills, and E. S. Rosen. **DD** 617. **NLM** W1; SE489EE. **CODEN** SEOPE7. **[CCC].**

**Desc:** Devoted to the dissemination of high-level clinical reviews for trainee and practicing ophthalmologists.
**Ind/Abst** EMBASE.

JA/0289-7024
**SHINKEI GANKA.** [Shinkei ganka]. **VFOAT** Neuro-Ophthalmology Japan. (1984)-. Periodical. Multiple languages. qt. Neuro-Ophthalmology Society of Japan, 15-1-1 Kitasato, Sagamihara 228 Kanagawa Japan. **DD** 617.7.
**Ind/Abst** EMBASE.

UK/1055-6575
**SLIDE ATLAS OF CURRENT OPHTHALMOLOGY.** (SLIDE ATLAS OF CURRENT OPHTHALMOLOGY [SLIDES].). [Slide atlas curr. ophthalmol.]. Update 1 (Feb. 1991)-. Periodical. English. Six times a year. $299.95. Current Science / England, Middlesex House, 34-42 Cleveland Street, London W1P 5FB England. **Tel** 011 44 71 580 8393, 011 44 71 323 0323, FAX 011 44 81 580 1938. **(Subscription address:** Current Science, 20 North 3rd Street, Philadelphia PA 19106.**)**

●US/1064-5446
**SLIDE ATLAS OF OPHTHALMIC LASER SURGERY.** (SLIDE ATLAS OF OPHTHALMIC LASER SURGERY [SLIDE].). (1992)-. English. Current Medicine, 20 North Third Street, Philadelphia PA 19106.

SA/0301-2131
**SOUTH AFRICAN ARCHIVES OF OPHTHALMOLOGY.** (SOUTH AFRICAN ARCHIVES OF OPHTHALMOLOGY. SUID-AFRIKAANSE ARGIEF VIR OFTALMOLOGIE.). [S. Afr. arch. ophthalmol.]. **Added/Corp** Blindness Research Foundation. **VFOAT** Suid-Afrikaanse Argief vir Oftalmologie. Vol. 1 (Jan./March 1973)-. Academic Scholarly Publication. English. Twice a year. $10.00. South African Archives of Ophthalmology, University of Witwatersrand Medical School, 2193 Parktown South Africa. **Tel** 011 27 11 6472549, 6472451. **NLM** W1 SO894N. Index available in last issue of volume--attached.
**Ind/Abst** EMBASE.

AU/0930-4282
**SPEKTRUM DER AUGENHEILKUNDE : ZEITSCHRIFT DER OSTERREICHISCHEN OPHTHALMOLOGISCHEN GESELLSCHAFT, OOG.** **Added/Corp** Osterreichische Ophthalmologische Gesellschaft. (1987)-. Periodical. German (summaries and/or abstracts in English). bm. $143.50. Springer-Verlag Wien, Sachsenplatz 4 6, PO Box 89, A-1201 Vienna Austria. **Tel** 011 43 1 3302415. **(Subscription address:** Springer Verlag New York Inc. / for North America, 44 Hartz Way, Secaucus NJ 07096.**) NLM** W1; SP39. **[CCC].**

SP
**STUDIUM OPTHALMOLOGICUM.** Spanish. Three times a year. 4500.00ptas. Sociedad Espanola de Oftalmologia, C Donoso Cortes 73, 28003 Madrid Spain. **Tel** 011 34 1 5445879, 011 34 1 5448035.

US/0039-6257
**SURVEY OF OPHTHALMOLOGY.** [Surv. ophthalmol.]. Vol. 1 (Feb. 1956)-. Academic Scholarly Publication. English. bm. $75.00 (1 year), 140.00 (2 year) (institutions), $55.00 (1 year), $105.00 (2 year) (individuals) US; $85.00 (1 year), $160.00 (2 year) (institutions), $65.00 (1 year), $125.00 (2 year) (individuals) Canada; $115.00 (1 year), $220.00 (2 year) (institutions), $95.00 (1 year), $185.00 (2 year) (individuals) other. Survey of Ophthalmology Inc, 7 Kent Street/Suite 4, Brookline MA 02146. **Tel** (617)566-2138, FAX (617)566-4019. **ED** Bernard Schwartz. **DD** 617. **NLM** ZWW 100 S963. **CODEN** SUOPAD. **[CCC].** Index available. cum. index. **Bk Rev. Ad Acc. Pr Rev. Circ:** 8,350. available on microfilm and microfiche from University Microfilms International (UMI). Documents available from The Genuine Article, BIOSIS Document Express, CASDDS.
**Desc:** A review journal directed to practical needs of clinical ophthalmologists.
**Ind/Abst** Biol. Abstr.; Chem. Abstr.; CSA Neuro. Abstr. (?-?); Curr. Contents Clin. Med.; EMBASE; Energy Res. Abstr.; Index Med.; Index Sci. Rev. [Full Cov.]; Mod. Med.; Nucl. Sci. Abstr.; Life Sci. Collect.; Physic. Medline Plus; Res. Alert [Full Cov.]; Sci. Cit. Index; SCISEARCH.

US/0082-0873
**SYMPOSIUM ON OCULAR THERAPY.** [Symp. Ocul. Ther.]. V. 3- 1967-. English. John Wiley & Sons, Inc., 605 Third Avenue, New York NY 10158-0012. **Tel** (212)850-6000, (212)850-6645, FAX (212)850-6088, telex 12-7063. **(Subscription address:** John Wiley & Sons / England, Baffins Lane, Chichester, West Sussex PO19 1UD England.**) LC** RE991; .O33. **DD** 617.7/061/05. **NLM** W3 SY5365. **CODEN** SYOTAJ. Documents available from CASDDS. ***Continues*** *Ocular Therapy, Complications and Management, 0473-775X.*
**Ind/Abst** Chem. Abstr. (1966-1979).

US
**TODAY IN MEDICINE. OPHTHALMOLOGY.** **VFOAT** Ophthalmology. (1990)-. Periodical. English. bm. $45.00 US; $60.00 Canada. Data Centrum Communications Inc, The Soho Building, 110 Greene Street, Suite 505, New York NY 10012. **Tel** (212)226-5252.

US/0065-9533
**TRANSACTIONS OF THE AMERICAN OPHTHALMOLOGICAL SOCIETY ANNUAL MEETING.** [Trans. Am. Ophthalmol. Soc. annu. meet.]. **Main/Corp** American Ophthalmological Society. Vol. 1 (1864)-. Academic Scholarly Publication. English. an. $50.00. Johnson Printing Company, PO Box 1177, Rochester MN 55903. **Tel** (507)288-7788. **ED** Robert B Welch. **LC** RE1; .A45. **DD** 617.706273. **NLM** W1 TR2247. **CODEN** TAOSAT. cum. index. **Circ:** 500 (ctrl). Documents available from BIOSIS Document Express, CASDDS.
**Desc:** Includes membership listing, papers, theses, minutes of annual meeting, American Ophthalmological Society.
**Ind/Abst** Biol. Abstr.; Chem. Abstr.; EMBASE; Energy Res. Abstr.; Index Med.

US/0077-8605
**TRANSACTIONS OF THE NEW ORLEANS ACADEMY OF OPHTHALMOLOGY.** [Trans. New Orleans Acad. Ophthalmol.]. **Main/Corp** New Orleans Academy of Ophthalmology. (1956)-. Academic Scholarly Publication. English. ir. Price varies per volume. New Orleans Academy of Ophthalmology, 2626 Napoleon Avenue, New Orleans LA 70115. **Tel** (504)899-9955. **(Subscription address:** Kugler Publications, PO Box 1498, New York NY 10009.**) NLM** W1 TR226S. **CODEN** TNOOA6. Documents available from CASDDS.
**Ind/Abst** Chem. Abstr.; Index Med.

RU/0042-465X
**VESTNIK OFTALMOLOGII.** [Vestn. oftalmol.]. **Added/Corp** Soviet Union. Narodnyi Komissariat Zdravookhraneniia. Soviet Union. Ministerstvo Zdravookhraneniia. (1937)-. Academic Scholarly Publication. Russian (summaries and/or abstracts in English). Four times a year. $69.95. Izdatelstvo Meditsina / Russian Academy of Medical Sciences, Ulitsa Solyanka 14, 109801 Moscow Russia. **Tel** 011 95 297-05-04. **(Subscription address:** East View Publications Inc., 3020 Harbor Lane North, Suite 110, Minneapolis MN 55447.**) NLM** W1 VE841. **CODEN** VEOFA6. Index available. **Bk Rev. Pr Rev.** Documents available from The Genuine Article, CASDDS. ***Continues*** *Sovetskii Vestnik Oftalmologii.*
**Ind/Abst** Chem. Abstr.; Curr. Contents Clin. Med.; EMBASE [Select. Cov.]; Helminthol. Abstr. (19??-19??); Index Med.; Int. Aerosp. Abstr.; Res. Alert [Full Cov.]; Rev. Med. Vet. Mycology; Sci. Cit. Index; SCISEARCH.

US/0882-469X
**VIEWS & VISIONS.** (VIEWS & VISIONS : THE PUBLICATION OF THE HERMANN EYE CENTER.). [Views vis.]. **VFOAT** Views and Visions. Periodical. English. qt. Free. Hermann Eye Center, 1203 Ross Sterling Avenue, Houston TX 77030. **DD** 617.

UK/0892-9726
**VISION AND VISUAL HEALTH CARE.** [Vis. vis. health care]. Vol. 1 (1986)-. Monographic series. English. ir. Price varies per volume. Pergamon Press, An Imprint of Elsevier Science Ltd., The Boulevard, Langford Lane, Kidlington, Oxford OX5 1GB United Kingdom. **Tel** 011 44 865 843000, 011 44 865 843699, FAX 011 44 865 843010. **DD** 617. **NLM** W1; VI838N.

UK/0042-6989
**VISION RESEARCH (OXFORD).** (VISION RESEARCH.). [Vis. res.]. **Added/Corp** Association for Research in Vision and Ophthalmology. Vol. 1 (June 1961)-. Academic Scholarly Publication. English (French and German). Twenty-four times a year. $1409.00 (regular subscription), $1625.00 (combination subscription with Progress in Retinal and Eye Research) The Americas; £945.00 (regular subscription), £1090.00 (combination subscription with Progress in Retinal and Eye Research) other. Pergamon Press, An Imprint of Elsevier Science Ltd., The Boulevard, Langford Lane, Kidlington, Oxford OX5 1GB United Kingdom. **Tel** 011 44 865 843000, 011 44 865 843699, FAX 011 44 865 843010. **(Subscription address:** Elsevier Science Ltd. Oxford Fulfillment Centre, PO Box 800, Kidlington, Oxford OX5 1DX United Kingdom.**) ED** Henk Spekreijse. **LC** QP474; .V5. **DD** 591.18. **NLM** W1 VI84. **CODEN** VISRAM. **[CCC].** Index available. **Pr Rev.** available on microfilm and microfiche from University Microfilms International (UMI). Documents available from The Genuine Article, BIOSIS Document Express, Ask*IEEE, CASDDS.
**Desc:** Provides a single avenue for communication in the expanding field of vision research including such areas as: biochemistry and molecular and cellular biology of the eye; electrophysiology; morphology, psychophysics; depth and motion perception; eye movements; and physiological optics.
**Ind/Abst** Annals Behav. Med.; Biol. Abstr.; Chem. Abstr.; CSA Neuro. Abstr.; Curr. Aware. Biol. Sci., CABS; Curr. Contents Life Sci.; Curr. Ref. Fish Res.; EMBASE; Ergon.

Abstr.; Index Med.; INSPEC (1968-); Int. Aerosp. Abstr.; Life Sci. Collect.; Psychol. Abstr. (1963-); PsycINFO; PsycLit; Ref. Upd. Deluxe Ed.; Res. Alert [Full Cov.]; Rev. Med. Vet. Entomol.; Sci. Cit. Index; SCISEARCH; Small Anim. Abstr. Bibliogr.; Soc. Sci. Cit. Index [Select. Cov.]; Vet. Bull.

US/1054-7665
**VISIONMONDAY (NEW YORK, N.Y.). See** Optometry.

US
**WELLCOME TRENDS IN OPHTHALMOLOGY. Added/Corp** Burroughs Wellcome Company. **VFOAT** Ophthalmology; Trends in Ophthalmology. Vol. 1 (Apr. 1979)-. Periodical. English. Wellcome Trends in Ophthalmology, 15 Park Row, New York NY 10038. ***Supersedes in part*** *Clinical Trends in Ophthalmology, Otolaryngology, Allergy, 0529-9675.*

●US/1062-774X
**WORLD MEDICAL REVIEWS IN GLAUCOMA.** [World med. rev. glaucoma]. (1992)-. Periodical. English. qt. $105.00 (institutions). World Medical Reviews Corporation, PO Box 639, Tenafly NJ 07670. **Tel** (201)567-1629. **DD** 616.

CC/1000-4432
**YANKE XUEBAO.** (YEN KO HSUEH PAO.). [Yanke xuebao]. **Added/Corp** Chung-shan Yen Ko Chung Hsin (Canton, China). **VFOAT** Eye Science. (1985)-. Periodical. Chinese (summaries and/or abstracts in English; table of contents in English). qt. $40.00 institution, $28.00 individual. Zhongshan Medical University, Zhongshan Eye Science Institute, Guangzhou Guangdong, People's Republic of China. **NLM** W1; YE466H.
**Ind/Abst** EMBASE [Select. Cov.]; Index Med. (1985-1988).

US/0084-392X
**YEAR BOOK OF OPHTHALMOLOGY, THE.** (1958)-. English. an. $59.95. Mosby Year Book Inc., 11830 Westline Industrial Drive, St Louis MO 63146. **Tel** (800)325-4177, (314)872-8370, FAX (314)432-1380, telex 44-2402. **ED** J Terry Ernest and Thomas A Deustch. **LC** RE6; .Y38. **DD** 617.7058. **NLM** W1 YE285. **Circ:** 5,000. ***Continues in part*** *Yearbook of the Eye, Ear, Nose and Throat.*
**Desc:** Contains abstracts of the most important journal articles in the field of ophthalmology selected from over 650 international journals. Abstracts are accompanied by editorial commentary.

GW/0722-9933
**ZENTRALBLATT OPHTHALMOLOGIE. VFOAT** Ophthalmology. Vol.123, No. 1 (1982)-. German (English; summaries and/or abstracts in English). Thirteen times a year. DM2490.00. Springer-Verlag GmbH & Company KG, Heidelberger Platz 3, D 14197 Berlin Germany. **Tel** 011 49 30 8207223, FAX 011 49 30 8214091, telex 183 319 SPBLN D. **(Subscription address:** Springer Verlag New York Inc. / for North America, 44 Hartz Way, Secaucus NJ 07096.) **ED** W Jaeger, G Meyer-Schwickerath and E Schreck. **NLM** ZWW 100 Z56. **[CCC].** available on microfilm from University Microfilms International (UMI). ***Continues*** *Zentralblatt fur die Gesamte Ophthalmologie und Ihre Grenzgebiete, 0044-4138.*
**Desc:** Contains monographs, essays of general content, handbook texts, convention reports; general and experimental ophthalmology, surgery, histology, allergies and non-operative therapy.

GW/0173-2595
**ZPA. ZEITSCHRIFT FUER PRAKTISCHE AUGENHEILKUNDE.** (ZEITSCHRIFT FUER PRAKTISCHE AUGENHEILKUNDE : ZPA.). [ZPA. Z. prakt. Augenheilkd.]. **VFOAT** ZPA. No. 1 (Feb. 1980)-. Periodical. German. Twelve times a year. DM166.00 Germany; DM170.00 others. Dr. Alfred Huethig Verlag GmbH, Postfach 102869, D 69018 Heidelberg Germany. **Tel** 011 49 6221 489281. **(Subscription address:** Heidelberger Verlagsservice, Postfach 102869, D 69018 Heidelberg Germany.) **ED** R. Kaden. **NLM** W1 ZE55J. **Bk Rev. Ad Acc. Circ:** 3,500 (ctrl).
**Desc:** News and scientific papers concerning the work in ophthalmology.

## ORTHOPEDICS

US/0883-1211
**ABMS DIRECTORY OF CERTIFIED ORTHOPAEDIC SURGEONS.** ***Title Change.*** [ABMS dir. certif. orthop. surg.]. **Added/Corp** American Board of Medical Specialties. American Board of Orthopaedic Surgery. **VFOAT** Directory of Certified Orthopaedic Surgeons. **VAT** American Board of Medical Specialties Directory of Certified Orthopaedic Surgeons. (1985)-(199?). Directory. English. be. American Board of Medical Specialties, 1 Rotary Center, Suite 805, Evanston IL 60201. **Tel** (708)491-9091. **LC** RD724; .A26. **DD** 617/.3/002573. **NLM** WE 22.1; A1523. ***Continued by*** *Official American Board of Medical Specialties (ABMS) Directory of Board Certified Orthopaedic Surgeons, 0000-1597.*

XR/0001-5415
**ACTA CHIRURGIAE ORTHOPAEDICAE ET TRAUMATOLOGIAE CECHOSLOVACA.** [Acta chir. orthop. traumatol. Cech.]. Vol. 17 (1950)-. Academic Scholarly Publication. Czech (table of contents in Russian, English and German). bm. $84.00. Avicenum Medical Press, Malostranske Nam 28, 11802 Prague Czech Republic. **Tel** 011 42 2 530643. **(Subscription address:** Artia Pegas Press Ltd., Palac Metro Narodni Trida 25, 11210 Prague 1 Czech Republic.) **UDC** 617.3-089. **NLM** W1 AC776N. **[CCC].** Index available in last issue of volume--attached. ***Continues*** *Sbornik Pro Chirurgii Pohyboveho Ustroji.*
**Ind/Abst** EMBASE; Index Med.; Saf. Health Work; SportSearch.

BE/0001-6462
**ACTA ORTHOPAEDICA BELGICA.** [Acta orthop. belg.]. **Added/Corp** Societe Belge de Chirurgie Orthopedique et de Traumatologie. Societe Belge d'Orthopedie et de Chirurgie de l'Appareil Moteur. Societe Belge d'Orthopedie, de Traumatologie et de Chirurgie de l'Appareil Moteur. Vol. 12 (1946)-. Academic Scholarly Publication. French (summaries and/or abstracts in Dutch, English, Esperanto, German, Italian and Spanish). Four times a year. 3000F Belgium; 3500F other. Association for the Society of Scientifique Medica Belgique, Avenue Circulaire 138A, B-1180 Brussels Belgium. **Tel** 011 32 2 3745158. **NLM** W1 AC8896. **CODEN** AOBEAF. Index available in last issue of volume--attached. Documents available from BIOSIS Document Express. ***Continues*** *Bulletin de la Societe Belge d'Orthopedie et de Chirurgie de l'Appareil Moteur, 0772-7585.*
**Ind/Abst** Biol. Abstr.; Dev. Med. Child Neurol. (-1990); EMBASE; Health Plan. Adminis.; Index Med.; Life Sci. Collect.; SportSearch (1966-1991).

DK/0001-6470
**ACTA ORTHOPAEDICA SCANDINAVICA.** [Acta orthop. Scand.]. Vol. 1 (1930)-. Academic Scholarly Publication. English. bm (Feb., Apr., June, Aug., Oct., Dec.). kr1050.00, $168.00. Scandinavian University Press, PO Box 2959 Toeyen, N 0608 Oslo 6 Norway. **Tel** 011 47 2 2575400, FAX 011 47 2 2575353, telex 71896 UROR N. **(Subscription address:** Scandinavian University Press, 200 Meacham Ave., Elmont NY 11003.) **ED** Goran H. C. Bauer. **NLM** W1 AC8924. **CODEN** AOSAAK. **[CCC].** Index available. cum. index. **Ad Acc. Pr Rev. Circ:** 4,200. Documents available from The Genuine Article, BIOSIS Document Express, CASDDS.
**Desc:** Publishes original papers on orthopaedic surgery, including traumatology.
**Ind/Abst** Biol. Abstr.; Chem. Abstr.; Curr. Contents Clin. Med.; Curr. Contents Life Sci.; Dev. Med. Child Neurol.; EMBASE; Energy Res. Abstr.; Health Plan. Adminis.; Index Med.; Index Vet.; INIS Atomindex [Micro.]; Life Sci. Collect.; Res. Alert [Full Cov.]; Sci. Cit. Index; SCISEARCH; Soc. Sci. Cit. Index [Select. Cov.]; SportSearch; Vet. Bull.

DK/0300-8827
**ACTA ORTHOPAEDICA SCANDINAVICA. SUPPLEMENTUM.** [Acta orthop. Scand., Suppl.]. (1934)-. Academic Scholarly Publication. English (French and German). Price varies per volume. Scandinavian University Press, PO Box 2959 Toeyen, N 0608 Oslo 6 Norway. **Tel** 011 47 2 2575400, FAX 011 47 2 2575353, telex 71896 UROR N. **(Subscription address:** Scandinavian University Press, 200 Meacham Ave., Elmont NY 11003.) **NLM** W1 AC8925. **CODEN** AOSUAC. Documents available from BIOSIS Document Express, CASDDS.
**Ind/Abst** Biol. Abstr.; Chem. Abstr.; EMBASE; Health Plan. Adminis.; Index Med.; Life Sci. Collect.

US
**ADVANCES IN ORTHOPEDICS.** English. an. $69.95. Mosby Year Book Inc., 11830 Westline Industrial Drive, St Louis MO 63146. **Tel** (800)325-4177, (314)872-8370, FAX (314)432-1380, telex 44-2402.

RU
**AKTUALNYE VOPROSY TRAVMATOLOGII I ORTOPEDII. Added/Corp** Tsentralnyi Institut Travmatologii i Ortopedii. (197?)-. Periodical. Russian. **NLM** W1 AK99RS.

SZ/0378-8504
**AKTUELLE PROBLEME IN CHIRURGIE UND ORTHOPADIE. See** Medical Science and Technology-Surgery.

●US/1078-4519
**AMERICAN JOURNAL OF ORTHOPEDICS, THE.** (1995)-. Periodical. English. mo. $95.00 (institutions), $72.00 (individuals) US; $115.00 (institutions), $98.00 (individuals). Excerpta Medica / US, PO Box 3085, Princeton NJ 08543-3085. **Tel** (908)874-8550, FAX (908)874-5611. **(Subscription address:** American Journal of Orthopedics, PO Box 3000, Denville NJ 07834.) ***Continues*** *Orthopaedic Review, 0094-6591.*

FR
**ANNALES ORTHOPEDIQUES DE L'OUEST. Added/Corp** Societe d'Orthopedie de l'Ouest. No. 1 (1969)-. French. an. 110.00F. Mademoiselle Solange Rive, 3 rue St Leonard, 49044 Angers France. **Tel** 011 33 41 687373. Index available (Free upon request).

US/0090-1393
**ANNUAL BIBLIOGRAPHY OF ORTHOPAEDIC SURGERY.** [Annu. bibliogr. orthop. surg.]. **Added/Corp** National Research Council (U.S.). Subcommittee on Orthopedic Information Services. National Library of Medicine (U.S.). No. 1 (1969)-. English. an. $10.00. Journal of Bone and Joint Surgery, 20 Pickering Street, Needham MA 02192-3157. **Tel** (617)449-9738, FAX (617)449-9742. **NLM** ZWE 168 A615.
**Desc:** Consists of citations retrieved by computer from the MEDLARS data base of the National Library of Medicine.

US/0732-8826
**ANNUAL REPORT / INTERNATIONAL CENTER FOR THE DISABLED. See** Physically Impaired.

UK/0263-2535
**ANNUAL REPORT OF THE OXFORD ORTHOPAEDIC ENGINEERING CENTRE. See** Medical Science and Technology-Biotechnology.

SP/0213-0645
**APARATO LOCOMOTOR.** [Apar. locomot.]. (1984)-. Periodical. Spanish. qt. 5000ptas. Editores Medicos SA, Calle Gabriela Mistral 2, 28035 Madrid Spain. **Tel** 011 34 1 3860033, 34 1 3860366, FAX 34 1 3739907. **UDC** 616.7. ***Continues*** *Cuadernos de Reumatologia, 0210-2986.*

GW/0936-8051
**ARCHIVES OF ORTHOPAEDIC AND TRAUMA SURGERY. See** Medical Science and Technology-Surgery.

IT/0390-7368
**ARCHIVIO DI ORTOPEDIA E REUMATOLOGIA. See** Medical Science and Technology-Musculoskeletal System.

US/0749-8063
**ARTHROSCOPY.** [Arthroscopy]. **Added/Corp** Arthroscopy Association of North America. International Arthroscopy Association. Vol. 1, No. 1 (1985)-. Periodical. English. bm. $170.00 (individuals), $235.00 (institutions) US; $220.00 (individuals), $280.00 (institutions) other. Raven Press, 1185 Avenue of the Americas, 37th Floor, New York NY 10036. **Tel** (212)930-9500, (212)930-9604, FAX (212)869-3495, (212)302-8507, telex 640073. **ED** Gary G. Poehling. **DD** 617. **NLM** W1; AR953YD. **CODEN** ARTHE3. **[CCC].** available on microfilm and microfiche from University Microfilms International (UMI). Documents available from The Genuine Article, BIOSIS Document Express.
**Desc:** The official publication of the Arthroscopy Association of North America focuses on the emerging area of orthopedic surgery. It explores the current trends and latest innovations in both diagnostic and operative arthroscopy.
**Ind/Abst** Biol. Abstr. (1986-); Curr. Contents Clin. Med.; EMBASE; Health Plan. Adminis.; Index Med. (1985-); Res. Alert [Select. Cov.].

GW/0933-7946
**ARTHROSKOPIE. See** Medical Science and Technology-Surgery.

IT
**ATTI E MEMORIE DELLA S.O.T.I.M.I. : UFFICIALE DELLA SOCIETA DI ORTOPEDIA E TRAUMATOLOGIA DELL'ITALIA MERIDIONALE ED INSULARE. VFOAT** Atti e Memorie della SOTIMI; Atti e Memorie della Societa di Ortopedia e Traumatologia dell'Italia Meridionale ed Insulare. Periodical. Italian. Casa Editrice Libr Idelson Gnocchi, Via Alcide de Gasperi 55, 80133 Naples Italy. **Tel** 011 39 81 552-4733. **NLM** W1; AT799.

GW/0068-3388
**BUCHEREI DES ORTHOPADEN.** Vol. 1 (1969)-. Periodical. German. ir. Price varies. Ferdinand Enke Verlag, Ruedigerstrasse 14, D-70469 Stuttgart Germany. **Tel** 011 49 711 8931124, 011 49 711 893123. **(Subscription address:** Georg Thieme Verlag Stuttgart, Postfach 301120, D 70451 Stuttgart Germany.) **ED** P. Otte and K. F. Schlegel.
**Desc:** Deals with practical and clinical relevant subjects from the whole subject of orthopedics. The volumes are a supplement to Zeitschrift fuer Orthopadie.

US/1049-9741
**BULLETIN / AMERICAN ACADEMY OF ORTHOPAEDIC SURGEONS.** [Bull. - Am. Acad. Orthop. Surg.]. **Added/Corp** American Academy of Orthopaedic Surgeons. **VFOAT** AAOS Bulletin. (19??)-. Periodical. English. Twice a year. American Academy of Orthopaedic Surgeons, 6300 North River Road, Rosemont IL 60018. **Tel** (708)823-7186, (800)626-6726. **ED** E. Richard Cantrall. **DD** 617. **Bk Rev. Circ:** 18,000 (ctrl). available on microfilm and microfiche from University Microfilms International (UMI).
**Desc:** Membership publication of the academy. Reports news, current developments and educational programs of the academy, as well as socio-economic items of interest to orthopaedists.

CN/0714-878X
**CANADIAN ORTHO-PROS, THE.** [Can. ortho-pros]. **VFOAT** Ortho-Pros Canadien; Ortho Pros. Periodical. English. sa. $8.00. Canadian Association of Prosthetists and Orthotists, c/o E. Cameron, 827 Glenwood Ave., Burlington Ontario L7T 2J8 Canada. **DD** 617/.307.

IT/0009-4749
**CHIRURGIA DEGLI ORGANI DI MOVIMENTO.** See Medical Science and Technology-Surgery.

PL/0009-479X
**CHIRURGIA NARZADOW RUCHY I ORTOPEDIA POLSKA.** [Chir. narzadow ruchu ortop. pol.]. **Added/Corp** Polskie Towarzystwo Ortopedyczne. Chirurgia Narzadow Ruchy i Ortopedia Polska. Polskie Towarzystwo Ortopedyczne i Traumatologiczne. Chirurgia Narzadow Ruchy i Ortopedia Polska. **VFOAT** Chirurgia Organum Motus et Orthopaedica Polonica; Acta Societatis Orthopaedicae Polonicae. Vol. 1 (1928)-. Academic Scholarly Publication. Polish (summaries and/or abstracts in French, German, English and Russian). bm. $96.00. **(Subscription address:** ARS Polona, PO Box 1001, 00068 Warsaw Poland.**) NLM** W1 CH8263. **CODEN** CNROA4. Documents available from BIOSIS Document Express.
**Ind/Abst** Biol. Abstr.; EMBASE (?-1975); Index Med.; SportSearch.

US/0009-921X
**CLINICAL ORTHOPAEDICS AND RELATED RESEARCH.** [Clin. orthop. relat. res.]. **Added/Corp** Hip Society (U.S.) Knee Society (U.S.) Association of Bone and Joint Surgeons. (1963)-. Academic Scholarly Publication. English. mo. $279.00 (individuals), $429.00 (institutions) US; $389.00 (individuals), $499.00 (institutions) other. J.B. Lippincott Company, 227 East Washington Square, Philadelphia PA 19106-3780. **Tel** (215)238-4200 or 4454, FAX (215)238-4227. **(Subscription address:** J.B. Lippincott, PO Box 350, Hagerstown MD 21740.**) LC** RD701; .C55. **NLM** W1 CL761. **CODEN** CORTBR. **[CCC].** cum. index. **Pr Rev.** available on microfilm and microfiche from University Microfilms International (UMI). Documents available from The Genuine Article, CASDDS. ***Continues*** *Clinical Orthopaedics, 0095-8654.*
**Ind/Abst** Abr. Index Med.; Calcium Calcif. Tissue Abstr.; Chem. Abstr.; CSA Neuro. Abstr. (?-?); Cumul. Index Nurs. Allied Health Lit.; Curr. Contents Clin. Med.; Curr. Contents Life Sci.; Dev. Med. Child Neurol.; EMBASE; Energy Res. Abstr.; Health Devices Alerts; Health Plan. Adminis.; Helminthol. Abstr. (1991-); Index Med.; Index Vet.; INIS Atomindex [Micro.]; Microbiol. Abstr. Sect. B (19??-19??); Nutr. Abstr. Rev., Ser. B, Live Feeds and Feed.; Nutr. Abstr. Rev., Ser. A, Hum. Exp.; Life Sci. Collect.; Physic. Medline Plus; Ref. Upd. Deluxe Ed.; Res. Alert [Full Cov.]; Rev. Med. Vet. Mycology; Rev. Plant Pathol.; Sci. Cit. Index; SCISEARCH; Soc. Sci. Cit. Index [Select. Cov.]; SPORT Discus.

CN/0832-0128
**COA BULLETIN.** [COA bull.]. **VFOAT** Bulletin ACO. **VAT** Canadian Orthopaedic Association Bulletin; Bulletin Association Canadienne d'Orthopedie. No. 1 (Vol. 1, 1983)-. Bulletin. English (French). ir. Free to members. Canadian Orthopaedic Association, 1117 St Catherine West/Suite 223, Montreal Quebec H3B 1H9 Canada. **DD** 617/.3/00971.

US/0887-1736
**COMPLICATIONS IN ORTHOPEDICS.** Vol. 1, No. 1 (1986)-. Periodical. English. Six times a year (Jan., Mar., May, July, Sept., Nov.). $54.13 New York residents (includes 8.25 sales tax); $50.00 others. SCP Communications Inc, 134 West 29th Street, New York NY 10001. **Tel** (212)714-1740, FAX (212)629-3760. **ED** Harry R. Gossling. **DD** 617. **NLM** W1; CO452D. **[CCC].** Index available. cum. index. **Bk Rev. Pr Rev. Circ:** 18,000 (ctrl).
**Desc:** Provides practical reports from the scientific and clinical arenas to help orthopedic surgeons avoid complications.

US/0194-8458
**CONTEMPORARY ORTHOPAEDICS.** Vol. 1 (Feb. 1979)-. Periodical. English. mo. $53.00 US; $63.00 Canada; $80.00 other. Bobit Publishing, 2512 Artesia Boulevard, Redondo Beach CA 90278. **Tel** (310)376-8788, (800)334-8152, FAX (213)376-9043. **(Subscription address:** Bobit Publishing Co., PO Box 469009, Escondido CA 92046.**) NLM** W1 CO769NN.

US/0193-2349
**CONTINUING EDUCATION IN ORTHOPAEDIC SURGERY. SOUND RECORDING.** See Medical Science and Technology.

US/0886-9634
**CRANIO.** See Medical Science and Technology.

US
**CURRENT CONCEPTS IN ORTHOPAEDIC SURGERY.** (1991)-. Monographic series. English. ir. Price varies per volume. Springer-Verlag New York Inc., 175 5th Avenue, New York NY 10010. **Tel** (212)460-1500, telex 232 235 SPB UR. **(Subscription address:** Springer Verlag New York Inc. / for North America, 44 Hartz Way, Secaucus NJ 07096.**) ED** P. Bedeschi.
**Desc:** Each year this series will examine one specific aspect of the locomoter apparatus with particular interest in traumatology, pathology, radiology, and surgery.

UK/0952-7494
**CURRENT MEDICAL LITERATURE ORTHOPAEDICS.** [Curr. med. lit., Orthop.]. (1987)-. Periodical. English. qt. £20.00 UK; $40.00 other. Current Medical Literature Ltd., 40-42 Osnaburgh Street, London NW1 3ND England. **Tel** 011 44 71 4658377, FAX 011 44 71 4658380. **(Subscription address:** Royal Society Medicine Services, 1 Wimpole Street, London W1M 8AE England (telephone 011 44 71 408-2119 Ext. 292)**) DD** 016.6173.

US/1041-9918
**CURRENT OPINION IN ORTHOPAEDICS.** [Curr. opin. orthop.]. **VFOAT** Current Opinion in Orthopedics. Vol. 1, No. 1 (Aug. 1990)-. Periodical. English. Six times a year. $449.95 (institutions), $224.95 (individuals). Current Science, 20 North 3rd Street, Philadelphia PA 19106. **Tel** (215)574-2266, (800)552-5866, FAX (215)574-2270. **ED** William R. J. Rennie, F. Behrens, R. R. Camille, D. S. Drummond, L. L. Fleming, D. L. Hamblen, R. B. Heppenstall, G. E. Johnson, J. C. Y. Leong, P. J. Mulligan, B. E. Nilsson, R. J. Sanders and N. S. Schachar. **DD** 616. **NLM** W1; CU799GGCL. **[CCC]. Ad Acc. Circ:** 500. available on diskette.
**Desc:** Directed toward researchers and practicing orthopedists. Presents review articles from an area of concentration covering an entire year's literature with annotated references. Each issue features a bibliography of the current world literature published during the previous year.
**Ind/Abst** Cumul. Index Nurs. Allied Health Lit.

UK/0268-0890
**CURRENT ORTHOPAEDICS.** Vol. 1, No. 1 (Sept. 1986)-. Periodical. English. qt. £146.00 Europe; £158.68 (air mail), £147.00 Other (institutions). Churchill Livingstone, 1-3 Baxter's Place, Leith Walk, Edinburgh EH1 3AF Scotland. **Tel** 011 44 31 556 2424, FAX 011 44 31 558 1278, telex 727511. **(Subscription address:** Maruzen Company Ltd., PO Box 5050, Import & Export Department, Tokyo 100 31 Japan.**) ED** R A Dickson. **NLM** W1; CU799GJ. **CODEN** CUOREH. **[CCC].** available on microfilm from University Microfilms International (UMI). Documents available from BIOSIS Document Express.
**Desc:** Presents a unique collection of international review articles summarizing the current state of knowledge and research in orthopaedics.
**Ind/Abst** Biol. Abstr. (1986-); EMBASE; Ref. Upd. Deluxe Ed.

US
**DIRECTORY OF DIPLOMATES.** **Main/Corp** The American Board of Orthopaedic Surgery. (1937)-. Directory. English. ir. American Board of Orthopaedic Surgery, 225 South Meramec, Suite 310, St. Louis MO 63105. **Tel** (314)727-5039. **Circ:** 3,000 (ctrl).
**Desc:** Names, addresses, certification and re-certification year for certified orthopaedists. Alphabetical list of deceased diplomates included.

UA/0013-242X
**EGYPTIAN ORTHOPEDIC JOURNAL.** **Added/Corp** Egyptian Orthopaedic Association. Vol. 1 (Dec. 1966)-. Periodical. English (French and Arabic; table of contents in Arabic). qt (4 issues). free to members of The Egyptian Orthopaedic Association. Egyptian Orthopaedic Journal, PO Box 4, Alexandria, Egypt, ET 21111. **ED** Prof. Dr. Amin Rida. **Ad Acc, Adv Mgr Tel** (03)422 5626.
**Desc:** Articles on orthopedic surgery and related disciplines.

GW/0344-5046
**EXTRACTA ORTHOPAEDICA.** Periodical. German. bm. DM45.00. Acron Verlag, Potsdamer Strasse 89, 1000 Berlin 30 Germany. **Tel** 030/262-20-21, FAX 030/262 40 13. **ED** Wolfgang Dorn. Index available. cum. index. **Bk Rev. Ad Acc. Circ:** 3,200 (ctrl).
**Desc:** Practical scientific briefings, book reports, original texts, serving the physician keeping track of recent developments in the international discussion on orthopedics and related domains.

US/0749-0399
**FACIAL ORTHOPEDICS AND TEMPOROMANDIBULAR ARTHROLOGY.** ***Suspended.*** **Added/Corp** Foundation for Advanced Research & Training (Evans, Ga.). Vol. 1, No. 1 (1984)-(19??). Periodical. English. mo. $225.00. Facial Orthopedics, 4771 Bass Drive, Evans GA 30809. **Tel** (404)860-5074. **ED** Eugene H. Williamson. **DD** 617. **NLM** W1; FA1853F. **Bk Rev. Circ:** 1,000 (ctrl).
**Desc:** Devoted to a comprehensive review and digest of the world literature on the scientific basis and clinical practice of the diagnosis, prognosis and treatment of facial orthopedic dysfunction, disorders and diseases.
**Ind/Abst** Index Dent. Lit. (1985-).

UK/0958-2592
**FOOT, THE.** Vol. 1, No. 1 (Apr. 1991)-. Periodical. English. qt. £157.00 Europe; £158.00 Other (Institutions). Churchill Livingstone, 1-3 Baxter's Place, Leith Walk, Edinburgh EH1 3AF Scotland. **Tel** 011 44 31 556 2424, FAX 011 44 31 558 1278, telex 727511. **(Subscription address:** Maruzen Company Ltd., PO Box 5050, Import & Export Department, Tokyo 100 31 Japan.**) NLM** W1; FO5110. **CODEN** FOOTEE. **[CCC].**

US/0198-0211
**FOOT & ANKLE.** ***Title Change.*** (FOOT & ANKLE : THE OFFICIAL JOURNAL OF THE AMERICAN ORTHOPAEDIC FOOT SOCIETY.). [Foot ankle]. **Added/Corp** American Orthopaedic Foot and Ankle Society. American Orthopaedic Foot Society. **VFOAT** Foot and Ankle. Vol. 1, No. 1 (July 1980)-(1993). Periodical. English. mo. Williams & Wilkins Company, 428 East Preston Street, Baltimore MD 21202-3993. **Tel** (410)528-4000, (800)638-6423, FAX (410)528-8596, telex 87669. **(Subscription address:** Williams & Wilkins, PO Box 64380, Baltimore MD 21264.**) ED** Melvin H. Jahss. **LC** RD781; .F57. **DD** 617/.585. **NLM** W1; FO511P. **CODEN** FANKDJ. **[CCC]. Ad Acc. Pr Rev. Circ:** 3,500. available on microfilm. Documents available from , The Genuine Article, BIOSIS Document Express, , Quick Copies. ***Continued by*** *Foot & Ankle International, 1071-1007.*
**Desc:** International articles on new approaches to foot and ankle disorders and surgical treatment, for orthopedic surgeons and podiatrists.
**Ind/Abst** Biol. Abstr. (1986-); Curr. Contents Clin. Med. (?-?); EMBASE (?-?); Health Plan. Adminis. (?-?); Index Med. (?-?); Res. Alert (?-?) [Select. Cov.]; SCISEARCH (?-?); SPORT Discus (?-?); SportSearch (?-?).

GW/0930-8326
**GIATROSERTHOPAEDIE.** [Giatrosorthopaedie]. **VFOAT** Jatrosorthopaedie. (1986)-. Periodical. German. mo. DM150.00. Universimed Verlag GmbH, August-Schanz Strasse 21, W-6000 Frankfurt 50 Germany. **Tel** 011 49 69 5480000, FAX 069/54 80 00-77. **UDC** 617.3. **Bk Rev. Ad Acc. Pr Rev. Circ:** 4,000 (ctrl).

IT/0390-0134
**GIORNALE ITALIANO DI ORTOPEDIA E TRAUMATOLOGIA.** [G. ital. ortop. traumatol.]. **Added/Corp** Societa Italiana di Ortopedia e Traumatologia. (1975)-. Italian. Six times a year (quarterly with two supplements). $200.00. Aulo Gaggi Editore, Via Andrea Costa 131-5, 40134 Bologna Italy. **Tel** 011 39 51 6142067, telex 43 61 19. **NLM** W1 GI814.

US/0749-0712
**HAND CLINICS.** [Hand clin.]. Vol. 1, No. 1 (Feb. 1985)-. Periodical. English. qt. $111.00 (individual), $134.00 (institution) US; $147.00 (individual), $154.00 (institution) other. W.B. Saunders Company, A Subsidiary of Harcourt Brace Jovanovich, Inc., The Curtis Center/Suite 300, Independence Square West, Philadelphia PA 19106-3399. **Tel** (215)238-7800 or, 5587, FAX (215)238-7883, telex 173146. **(Subscription address:** W. B. Saunders Company / North America Subscriptions, c/o Periodicals, 6277 Sea Harbour Drive, 4th Floor, Orlando FL 32887.**) DD** 617. **NLM** W1; HA51D. **[CCC].** Index available. **Pr Rev. Circ:** 2,750. available on microfilm and microfiche from University Microfilms International (UMI). Documents available from The Genuine Article.
**Ind/Abst** Curr. Contents Clin. Med.; EMBASE; Index Med. (Vol. 1, No. 1, 1985-); Res. Alert [Select. Cov.]; Rev. Med. Vet. Entomol.; SCISEARCH; Soc. Sci. Cit. Index [Select. Cov.].

JA/0018-3377
**HOKKAIDO SEIKEI SAIGAI GEKA ZASSHI.** **VFOAT** Hokkaido Journal of Orthopedic & Traumatic Surgery. (1954)-. Periodical. Multiple languages. sa. Hokkaido Orthopedic and Traumatic Surgery Society, North 14-jo, West 5-chome, Kita-ku, Sapporo-shi Japan. **DD** 617.3.
**Ind/Abst** EMBASE.

II/0019-5413
**INDIAN JOURNAL OF ORTHOPAEDICS.** [Indian j. orthop.]. (1967)-. Periodical. English. sa. $20.00.

**(Subscription address:** Prints India, 11 Darya Ganj, New Delhi 110002 India.**)** **NLM** W1 IN223R. **CODEN** INJOAU.

US
**INDIANA HAND CENTER NEWSLETTER.** **See** Medical Science and Technology.

US/0065-6895
**INSTRUCTIONAL COURSE LECTURES.** **See** Medical Science and Technology-Surgery.

UK/0960-2941
**INTERNATIONAL JOURNAL OF ORTHOPAEDIC TRAUMA.** Vol. 1, No. 1 (1991)-. Periodical. English. qt. £60.00 (individuals), £85.00 (institutions) UK; £68.00 (individuals), £94.00 (institutions) other. Castle House Publications Ltd, 28-30 Church Road, Tunbridge Wells Kent, TN1 1JP England. **Tel** 011 44 892 539606, FAX 011 44 892 517005, telex 957565 CBJ AG. **ED** D. Rowley. **NLM** W1; IN771F. Index available. **Ad Acc**, **Adv Mgr:** Wendy Reinders. **Pr Rev.** ctrl circ.
**Desc:** Uses a thematic format and aims to cover the spectrum of orthopaedic trauma over a three-year period. The proposed themes are hand and wrist, knee, upper spine, lower spine and hip.

GW/0341-2695
**INTERNATIONAL ORTHOPAEDICS.** [Int. orthop.]. **Added/Corp** International Society of Orthopaedic Surgery and Traumatology. Vol. 1 (1977)-. Periodical. Multiple languages (English and French). Six times a year. DM580.00. Springer-Verlag GmbH & Company KG, Heidelberger Platz 3, D 14197 Berlin Germany. **Tel** 011 49 30 8207223, FAX 011 49 30 8214091, telex 183 319 SPBLN D. **(Subscription address:** Springer Verlag New York Inc. / for North America, 44 Hartz Way, Secaucus NJ 07096.**)** **ED** A Trias, J Evrard, and F T Horan. **NLM** W1 IN827H. **[CCC]. Pr Rev.** available on microfilm and microfiche from University Microfilms International (UMI). Documents available from The Genuine Article.
**Desc:** Publishes original papers from all over the world dealing with clinical orthopaedic surgery or basic research directly connected with orthopaedic surgery.
**Ind/Abst** Calcium Calcif. Tissue Abstr.; Curr. Contents Clin. Med.; EMBASE; Energy Res. Abstr. (Sept. 1982-); Index Med.; Life Sci. Collect.; Res. Alert [Select. Cov.]; Rev. Med. Vet. Mycology; SCISEARCH; SportSearch.

IT/0390-5489
**ITALIAN JOURNAL OF ORTHOPAEDICS AND TRAUMATOLOGY.** ***Ceased.*** [Ital. j. orthop. traumatol.]. **Added/Corp** Societa Italiana di Ortopedia e Traumatologia. Vol. 1 (Apr. 1975)-(Dec. 1993). Academic Scholarly Publication. English (Italian). qt (Mar., June, Sept., Dec.). Springer-Verlag GmbH & Company KG, Heidelberger Platz 3, D 14197 Berlin Germany. **Tel** 011 49 30 8207223, FAX 011 49 30 8214091, telex 183 319 SPBLN D. **(Subscription address:** Springer Verlag New York Inc. / for North America, 44 Hartz Way, Secaucus NJ 07096.**)** **ED** G. Monticelli. **NLM** W1 IT136. **[CCC].** Index available. **Bk Rev. Circ:** 500 (ctrl). ***Supersedes*** *Orthopaedica Italica.*
**Desc:** Covers current thought, practice and research of orthopaedics in Italy.
**Ind/Abst** EMBASE; Index Med.; SportSearch.

FR/0242-648X
**JOURNAL DE READAPTATION MEDICALE.** (1981)-. Periodical. French. qt. $152.00. Masson Editeur, Box Postale 22, 41353 Vineuil 16 France. **Tel** 011 33 54 438994. **UDC** 615.8. **[CCC].**

US/0021-9355
**JOURNAL OF BONE AND JOINT SURGERY. AMERICAN VOLUME (PRINT ED.).** (JOURNAL OF BONE AND JOINT SURGERY.). [J. bone jt. surg., Am. vol.]. Vol. 30A (Jan. 1948)-. Academic Scholarly Publication. English. mo. $76.00; £88.00 (combined with British volume). Journal of Bone and Joint Surgery, 20 Pickering Street, Needham MA 02192-3157. **Tel** (617)449-9738, FAX (617)449-9742. **ED** Henry R. Cowell. **DD** 617. **NLM** W1 JO57. **CODEN** JBJSA3. cum. index. **Bk Rev. Ad Acc. Pr Rev. Circ:** 40,000. available on microfilm and microfiche from University Microfilms International (UMI). Documents available from The Genuine Article, BIOSIS Document Express, CASDDS. ***Continues in part*** *Journal of Bone and Joint Surgery, 0375-9229.*
**Desc:** An orthopaedic journal covering all aspects of orthopaedic surgery, trauma and rheumatology.
**Ind/Abst** Abr. Index Med.; Abstr. Anthropol.; Biol. Abstr.; Calcium Calcif. Tissue Abstr.; Chem. Abstr.; CSA Neuro. Abstr. (?-?); Cumul. Index Nurs. Allied Health Lit.; Curr. Aware. Biol. Sci., CABS; Curr. Contents Clin. Med.; Curr. Contents Life Sci.; Dev. Med. Child Neurol.; EMBASE; Energy Res. Abstr.; Health Devices Alerts; Health Period. Database; Index Med.; INIS Atomindex [Micro.]; Med. Abstr. Newsl.; Life Sci. Collect.; Physic. Medline Plus; Phys. Med. Biol. (19??-19??); Ref. Upd. Deluxe Ed.; Res. Alert [Full Cov.]; Rev. Med. Vet. Mycology; Sci. Cit. Index; Soc. Sci. Cit. Index [Select. Cov.]; SPORT Discus; SportSearch.

UK/0301-620X
**JOURNAL OF BONE AND JOINT SURGERY. BRITISH VOLUME. See** Medical Science and Technology-Surgery.

●US/1067-2516
**JOURNAL OF FOOT AND ANKLE SURGERY, THE. See** Medical Science and Technology-Surgery.

●US/1066-9817
**JOURNAL OF MANUAL & MANIPULATIVE THERAPY, THE.** [J. man. manip. ther.]. **VFOAT** Journal of Manual and Manipulative Therapy. Vol. 1, No. 1 (Winter 1993)-. Periodical. English. Four times a year (Feb., May, Aug., Nov.). $45.00 (individuals), $150.00 (institutions). Journal of Manual Manipulative Therapy, PO Box 713, Forest Grove OR 97116. **Tel** (503)359-2322, FAX (503)359-3542. **ED** Dr. John M. Medeiros Ph.D. (editor's phone: (503)359-2322). **DD** 615. **NLM** W1; JO748DEV. Index available (Bound in 4th iss. in Nov. ($45.00)). cum. index. **Ad Acc, Adv Mgr:** M. Holton, **Tel** (407)677-5194. **Pr Rev. Circ:** 2,500. available on an online database.
**Desc:** A specialty source for current topics in the field of orthopedics manual therapy.

US/0890-6599
**JOURNAL OF NEUROLOGICAL & ORTHOPAEDIC MEDICINE & SURGERY, THE. See** Medical Science and Technology-Surgery.

US/0190-6011
**JOURNAL OF ORTHOPAEDIC AND SPORTS PHYSICAL THERAPY, THE.** [J. orthop. sports phys. ther.]. **Added/Corp** American Physical Therapy Association (1921- ). Orthopaedic Section. American Physical Therapy Association (1921- ). Sports Medicine Section. **VFOAT** JOSPT. Vol. 1 (Summer 1979)-. Periodical. English. mo. $80.00 (individual), $130.00 (institution) US; $120.00 (individual), $170.00 (institution), other. Williams & Wilkins Company, 428 East Preston Street, Baltimore MD 21202-3993. **Tel** (410)528-4000, (800)638-6423, FAX (410)528-8596, telex 87669. **(Subscription address:** Williams & Wilkins, PO Box 64380, Baltimore MD 21264.**)** **ED** James A. Gould and George J. Davies. **LC** RD701; .J69. **DD** 617/.3/005. **NLM** W1 JO804S. **CODEN** JOSPDV. **[CCC]. Ad Acc. Circ:** 14,500. available on microfilm. Documents available from , The Genuine Article, BIOSIS Document Express, , Quick Copies.
**Desc:** The latest clinical developments in sports medicine for practicing PT's, athletic trainers, and orthopedic surgeons.
**Ind/Abst** Annals Behav. Med.; Biol. Abstr. (1987-); Cumul. Index Nurs. Allied Health Lit.; Curr. Contents Clin. Med.; Electron. Commun. Abstr. J.; EMBASE; Health Saf. Sci. Abstr.; Index Med. (Jan. 1993-); ISMEC Bull.; Life Sci. Collect.; Phys. Educ. Index; Pollut. Abstr. Indexes; Res. Alert [Select. Cov.]; Saf. Sci. Abstr. J.; SPORT Discus; SportSearch.

CN
**JOURNAL OF ORTHOPAEDIC MEDICINE.** English. 35.00Can$. Society of Orthopaedic Medicine, 145 Queenstown Street, Suite 87, St. Catherine's L2R 2Z8 Canada.

US/0736-0266
**JOURNAL OF ORTHOPAEDIC RESEARCH.** (JOURNAL OF ORTHOPAEDIC RESEARCH : OFFICIAL PUBLICATION OF THE ORTHOPAEDIC RESEARCH SOCIETY.). [J. orthop. res.]. **Added/Corp** Bioelectric Repair and Growth Society. Orthopaedic Research Society. Vol. 1, No. 1 (1983)-. Academic Scholarly Publication. English. bm. $231.00 (institutions), $164.00 (individuals) US; $260.00 (institutions), $190.00 (individuals) other. Journal of Bone and Joint Surgery, 20 Pickering Street, Needham MA 02192-3157. **Tel** (617)449-9738, FAX (617)449-9742. **ED** Wayne H. Akeson and Wilson C. Hayes. **DD** 616. **NLM** W1; JO804SF. **CODEN** JOREDR. **[CCC]. Pr Rev.** available on microfilm and microfiche from University Microfilms International (UMI). Documents available from Article Express International, The Genuine Article, CASDDS.
**Desc:** Provides a central forum for the rapid publication of manuscripts and short communications reporting new information on experimental, theoretical, and clinical aspects of the field of orthopaedic research.
**Ind/Abst** Chem. Abstr. (1983-); Curr. Contents Life Sci.; Ei Page One; EMBASE; Eng. Index Annu.; Index Med. (Vol. 1, No. 1, 1983-);(Vol. 1, No. 1, 1983-); Index Vet.; Ref. Upd. Deluxe Ed.; Res. Alert [Full Cov.]; Sci. Cit. Index; SCISEARCH; SportSearch (Vol. 1, No. 1, 1983-); Vet. Bull.

UK/0951-9580
**JOURNAL OF ORTHOPAEDIC RHEUMATOLOGY.** (JOURNAL OF ORTHOPAEDIC RHEUMATOLOGY : JOR.). [J. orthop. rheumatol.]. **VFOAT** JOR. Vol. 1, No. 1 (1988)-. Periodical. English. qt. $275.00 US; £165.00 other. Rapid Communications of Oxford Ltd, The Old Malthouse, Paradise Street, Oxford OX1 1LD England. **Tel** 011 44 0865 790447, FAX 011 44 0865 244012, telex 9403712. **ED** J. H. Moll, Clement Sledge, Matthew Liang. **DD** 616. **NLM** W1; JO804SG. **CODEN** JORHE3. **[CCC]. Bk Rev. Ad Acc. Pr Rev. Circ:** 150.
**Desc:** Covers the common ground between orthopaedics and rheumatology.
**Ind/Abst** Curr. Contents Clin. Med.; EMBASE.

●HK/1022-5536
**JOURNAL OF ORTHOPAEDIC SURGERY. Added/Corp** Western Pacific Orthopaedic Association. Vol. 1, No. 1 (Dec. 1993)-. Periodical. English. Three times a year. $50.00. Western Pacific Orthopaedic Association, 7 Sha Wan Dr, 4F Maclehose Med, Hong Kong Hong Kong. **Tel** 011 852 5 8183761. ***Continues*** *Journal of the Western Pacific Orthopaedic Association, 0043-4019.*

FR
**JOURNAL OF ORTHOPAEDIC SURGERY, THE.** ***Ceased.*** **Added/Corp** Societe Francaise de Chirurgie Orthopedique et Traumatologique. **VFOAT** French Journal of Orthopaedic Surgery. Vol. 6, No. 1 (Mar. 1992)-(1993). Periodical. English. qt. Masson Editeur, Box Postale 22, 41353 Vineuil 16 France. **Tel** 011 33 54 438994. **(Subscription address:** Masson, BP 22, 41353 Vineuil 16 France.**)** ***Continues*** *French Journal of Orthopaedic Surgery, 0981-1974.*

UK/0334-0236
**JOURNAL OF ORTHOPAEDIC SURGICAL TECHNIQUES, THE.** [J. orthop. surg. tech.]. (1985)-. Periodical. English. qt. $120.00 (institutions), $60.00 (individuals). Med Advanced Techniques Publ, 48 Aylestone Avenue, London NW6 7AA England. **NLM** W1; JO804SH. **CODEN** JOSTEA. **Bk Rev. Ad Acc. Circ:** 1,000 (ctrl). Documents available from BIOSIS Document Express.
**Ind/Abst** Biol. Abstr. (1985-); EMBASE.

●US/1056-7437
**JOURNAL OF ORTHOPAEDIC TECHNIQUES.** [J. orthop. tech.]. Vol. 1, No. 1 (1993)-. Periodical. English. qt (4 issues). $85.00 (individual), $126.00 (institution) US. Churchill Livingstone Inc., 650 Avenue of the Americas, New York NY 10011. **Tel** (212)206-5062, FAX (212)727-7808. **(Subscription address:** Churchill Livingstone Inc., 5 South 250 Frontenac Road, Naperville, IL 60563 (telephone: (800)553-5426 or (708)416-3939)**)** **ED** Kennth A. Krackow. **DD** 616. **NLM** W1; JO804SJ. **[CCC].**

US/0890-5339
**JOURNAL OF ORTHOPAEDIC TRAUMA.** Vol. 1, No. 1 (1987)-. Periodical. English. bm (6 issues). $124.00 (individuals), $160.00 (institutions) US; $154.00 (individuals), $198.00 (institutions) other. Raven Press, 1185 Avenue of the Americas, 37th Floor, New York NY 10036. **Tel** (212)930-9500, (212)930-9604, FAX (212)869-3495, (212)302-8507, telex 640073. **ED** Phillip G. Spiegel. **DD** 617. **NLM** W1; JO804sm. **CODEN** JORTE5. **[CCC].** available on microfilm and microfiche from University Microfilms International (UMI).
**Desc:** Devoted to the diagnosis and management of hard and soft tissue trauma, including injuries to bone, muscle, ligament, and tendons and spinal cord injuries.
**Ind/Abst** Index Med.; Physic. Medline Plus.

●UK/1353-3258
**JOURNAL OF ORTHOPAEDICS.** (1994)-. Periodical. English. Four times a year. £128.00 Europe; £129.00 Other (Institutions). Churchill Livingstone, 1-3 Baxter's Place, Leith Walk, Edinburgh EH1 3AF Scotland. **Tel** 011 44 31 556 2424, FAX 011 44 31 558 1278, telex 727511. **(Subscription address:** Maruzen Company Ltd., PO Box 5050, Import & Export Department, Tokyo 100 31 Japan.**)**

US/0271-6798
**JOURNAL OF PEDIATRIC ORTHOPEDICS. See** Medical Science and Technology-Pediatrics.

●US/1060-152X
**JOURNAL OF PEDIATRIC ORTHOPEDICS. PART B.** (JOURNAL OF PEDIATRIC ORTHOPEDICS. PART B / EUROPEAN PAEDIATRIC ORTHOPAEDIC SOCIETY, PEDIATRIC ORTHOPAEDIC SOCIETY OF NORTH AMERICA.). [J. pediatr. orthop., Part B]. **Added/Corp** European Paediatric Orthopaedic Society. Pediatric Orthopaedic Society of North America. Vol. 1, No. 1 (1992)-. Academic Scholarly Publication. English. Twice a year. $89.00 (individuals), $115.00 (institutions) US; $99.00 (individuals), $125.00 (institutions) other. Raven Press, 1185 Avenue of the Americas, 37th Floor, New York NY 10036. **Tel** (212)930-9500, (212)930-9604, FAX (212)869-3495, (212)302-8507, telex 640073. **ED** Henri

Bensahel. **DD** 617. **NLM** W1; JO828FEL. **Pr Rev.** available on microfilm and microfiche from University Microfilms International (UMI). Documents available from The Genuine Article, BIOSIS Document Express.
**Desc:** Highlights important recent developments from the European community. Each issue includes original, peer-reviewed articles; announcements from the European Pediatric Orthopaedic Society; and a section of topic-oriented reviews, guest-edited by a leading pediatric orthopaedist.
**Ind/Abst** Biol. Abstr.; Curr. Contents; EMBASE; Index Med.; Res. Alert [Select. Cov.].

US/0740-0926
**JOURNAL OF THE AMERICAN OSTEOPATHIC ACADEMY ORTHOPEDICS.** ***Suspended.*** [J. Am. Osteopath. Acad. Orthop.]. Vol. 1, No. 1 (1982)-Suspended with 1989-90 issue. English. an. $10.00. American Osteopathic Academy of Orthopedics, 1217 Salem Avenue, Dayton OH 45406. **Tel** (313)422-8400. **ED** Daniel Morrison. **NLM** W1 JO909Z. **Circ:** 600 (ctrl).

US/0884-8424
**JOURNAL OF THE ASSOCIATION OF CHILDREN'S PROSTHETIC-ORTHOTIC CLINICS.** ***Ceased.*** (JOURNAL OF THE ASSOCIATION OF CHILDREN'S PROSTHETIC-ORTHOTIC CLINICS : JACPOC.). [J. Assoc. Child. Prosthet.-Orthot. clin.]. **Added/Corp** Association of Children's Prosthetic-Orthotic Clinics (U.S.). Meeting. Association of Children's Prosthetic-Orthotic Clinics (U.S.). **VFOAT** JACPOC. Vol. 20, No. 3 (Autumn 1985)- Vol. 28 (1993). Periodical. English. qt. Association of Children's Prosthetic Orthotic Clinics, PO Box 94020, Palatine IL 60094. **Tel** (708)698-1694. **ED** Joan Edelstein. **LC** RD701; .I13. **DD** 617.3/07. **NLM** W1; JO912ER. **Bk Rev. Ad Acc. Circ:** 1,100 (ctrl). ***Continues*** *Inter-Clinic Information Bulletin, 0028-7911.*
**Desc:** Prosthetic-orthotic management of orthopedically disabled children, including book reviews and proceedings of annual meetings of the Association of Children's Prosthetic-Orthotic Clinics.

●US/1069-6970
**JOURNAL OF THE CLINICAL ORTHOPAEDIC SOCIETY.** **Added/Corp** Clinical Orthopaedic Society. (1994)-. Periodical. English. Six times a year. $175.00 (US); $235.00 (Canada & Mexico); $257.50 (other). John Wiley & Sons, Inc., 605 Third Avenue, New York NY 10158-0012. **Tel** (212)850-6000, (212)850-6645, FAX (212)850-6088, telex 12-7063. **(Subscription address:** John Wiley & Sons / England, Baffins Lane, Chichester, West Sussex PO19 1UD England.**)** **ED** James P. Ahstrom, Jr., MD.
**Desc:** Publishes original papers on a range of topics of critical interest to orthopedic surgeons practicing in all specialties.

●US/1059-1052
**JOURNAL OF THE SOUTHERN ORTHOPAEDIC ASSOCIATION.** [J. South. Orthop. Assoc.]. **Added/Corp** Southern Orthopaedic Association. **VFOAT** JSOA. Vol. 1, No. 1 (Jan./Feb. 1992)-. Periodical. English. Four times a year (Spring, Summer, Fall and Winter). $30.00 US; $45.00 others. Southern Orthopaedic Association, 35 Lakeshore Drive, PO Box 190088, Birmingham AL 35219-0088. **Tel** (800)423-4992, (205)945-1840, FAX (205)942-0642. **ED** Dr. L. Andrew Koman, MD, (editor's address: PO Box 1114, Winston-Salem, NC, 27157-1114). **DD** 617. **NLM** W1; JO955VK. Index available (Index bound in Jan./Feb.). **Bk Rev. Ad Acc, Adv Mgr:** Wendy Reid. **Pr Rev. Circ:** 3000 (ctrl).
**Desc:** It serves as a forum for exchange of information and the presentation of new techniques and procedures, as well as updates about the ongoing educational activities of interest to all practicing orthopaedists.

HK/0043-4019
**JOURNAL OF THE WESTERN PACIFIC ORTHOPAEDIC ASSOCIATION, THE.** ***Title Change.*** [J. West. Pac. Orthop. Assoc.]. **Added/Corp** Western Pacific Orthopaedic Association. Vol. 1-29 (Mar. 1964)-(1992). Academic Scholarly Publication. English. sa. Western Pacific Orthopaedic Association, 7 Sha Wan Dr, 4F Maclehose Med, Hong Kong Hong Kong. **Tel** 011 852 5 8183761. **ED** S. F. Lam. **NLM** W1 JO963I. **Bk Rev. Ad Acc. Circ:** 1,200 (ctrl). available on microfilm from University Microfilms International (UMI). ***Continued by*** *Journal of Orthopaedic Surgery (Hong Kong), 1022-5536.*
**Desc:** Enables orthopedic surgeons of the Western Pacific region to exchange views and discuss new discoveries and methods of handling orthopedic problems.
**Ind/Abst** EMBASE.

JA/0389-7087
**KANTO SEIKEI SAIGAI GEKA GAKKAI ZASSHI.** [Kanto Seikei Saigaigeka Gakkai zasshi]. **VFOAT** Kanto Journal of Orthopedics and Traumatology. Vol. 12, No. 1 (Feb. 1981)-. Academic Scholarly Publication. Japanese. sa. Department of Orthopaedic Surgery, Faculty of Medicine, Kyushu University, Maedashi 3-1-1, Higashi-ku Fukuoka 812 Japan. **CODEN** KSSZDW. Documents available from CASDDS. ***Continues*** *Kanto Seikei Geka Saigai Gekakai Zasshi, 0388-3442.*
**Ind/Abst** Chem. Abstr.

●US/1068-6991
**LOWER EXTREMITY, THE.** (THE LOWER EXTREMITY : JOURNAL OF THE AMERICAN COLLEGE OF FOOT ORTHOPAEDISTS.). **Added/Corp** American College of Foot Orthopaedists. (1994)-. Periodical. English. qt. $119.00 institution, $79.00 individual. Churchill Livingstone Inc., 650 Avenue of the Americas, New York NY 10011. **Tel** (212)206-5062, FAX (212)727-7808. **(Subscription address:** Churchill Livingstone Inc., 5 South 250 Frontenac Road, Naperville, IL 60563; (telephone: (800)553-5426 or (708)416-3939)**)** **[CCC].**

IT
**MEDICINA ORTOPEDICA.** Ghedini Libraio, V Pezzotti 4, 20141 Milan Italy. **Tel** 011 39 2 76023133.

US/0737-6073
**MEDIGUIDE TO ORTHOPAEDICS.** [Mediguide orthop.]. Vol. 3, Issue 1-. Periodical. English. bm. Dellacorte Publications, 919 3rd Avenue, New York NY 10022. **Tel** (212)751-2806. **NLM** W1 ME787GC. ***Continues*** *Mediguide to Orthopedics, 0737-6073.*

IT
**MINERVA ORTOPEDICA E TRAUMATOLOGICA.** **Added/Corp** Societa Piemontese-Ligure-Lombarda di Ortopedia e Traumatologia. Vol. 37, No. 6 (June 1986)-. Periodical. Italian (summaries and/or abstracts in English). mo. $110.00 (individuals), $150.00 (institutions). Edizioni Minerva Medica, Corso Bramante 83-85, 10126 Turin Italy. **Tel** 011 39 11 678282, FAX 011 39 11 674502. **ED** P Gallinono, F Pipino, and M Pizzehi. **NLM** W1; MI649J. Index available. **Bk Rev. Ad Acc. Circ:** 5,000. ***Continues*** *Minerva Ortopedica, 0026-4911.*
**Desc:** The journal is addressed to specialists in orthopedics and tramuatology.
**Ind/Abst** EMBASE.

US/0077-0159
**MODERN TRENDS IN ORTHOPAEDICS.** 1st-. Periodical. English. sm. **ED** Editors: 1950-56: Sir Harry Platt; 1962-64: John M. P. Clark; 1967- W.D. Graham. **NLM** W1 MO175P.

AU/0177-7955
**NEURO-ORTHOPEDICS.** **See** Medical Science and Technology-Neurology.

JA/0021-5325
**NIPPON SEIKEIGEKAGAKKAI ZASSHI.** (NIPPON SEIKEIGEKA GAKKAI ZASSHI. THE JOURNAL OF THE JAPANESE ORTHOPAEDIC ASSOCIATION. ZEITSCHRIFT DER JAPANISCHEN ORTHOPADISCH-CHIRURGISCHEN GESELLSCHAFT.). [Nippon Seikeigekagakkai zasshi]. **Added/Corp** Nippon Seikeigeka Gakkai. Nippon Seikeigeka Gakkai. Sokai Enzetsu Shoroku. **VFOAT** The Journal of the Japanese Orthopaedic Association; Journal of the Japanese Orthopaedic Surgical Society; Zeitschrift der Japanischen Orthopadisch-Chirurgischen Gesellschaft. Vol. 1 (1926)-. Academic Scholarly Publication. Japanese (English and German; summaries and/or abstracts in English and German). mo. $192.00. **(Subscription address:** Kyowa Book Company Inc., 1-38 Kanda Jinbo-Cho, Chiyoda-Ku Tokyo 101, Japan**)** **NLM** W1 NI932F. **CODEN** NSGZA2. Documents available from BIOSIS Document Express, CASDDS.
**Ind/Abst** Biol. Abstr.; Chem. Abstr.; EMBASE; Index Med.

●US/0000-1597
**OFFICIAL AMERICAN BOARD OF MEDICAL SPECIALTIES (ABMS) DIRECTORY OF BOARD CERTIFIED ORTHOPAEDIC SURGEONS, THE.** [Off. Am. Board Med. Spec. (ABMS) dir. board certif. orthop. surg.]. **Added/Corp** American Board of Medical Specialties. **VFOAT** Directory of Board Certified Orthopaedic Surgeons; Official ABMS Directory of Board Certified Orthopaedic Surgeons. 5th Ed. (1994)-. Directory. English. be. American Board of Medical Specialties, 1 Rotary Center, Suite 805, Evanston IL 60201. **Tel** (708)491-9091. **LC** RD724; .A26. **DD** 617/.3/002573. ***Continues*** *ABMS Directory of Certified Orthopaedic Surgeons, 0883-1211.*

GW/0934-6694
**OPERATIVE ORTHOPADIE UND TRAUMATOLOGIE.** (1989)-. Periodical. German (English). qt. DM332.00 Germany; DM340.00 other. Urban & Vogel, Postfach 152209, D-80052 Munich Germany. **Tel** 011 49 89 53292140, FAX 089/536052, telex 521701. **ED** Prof. W. Blanth, Prof. U. Holz, and Prof. Uhthoff. **UDC** 617.5. Index available. cum. index. **Bk Rev. Ad Acc. Circ:** 2,500.

US/1056-7097
**OPERATIVE ORTHOPAEDICS UPDATES.** [Oper. orthop. updat.]. **VFOAT** Operative Orthopaedics. Vol. 1, No. 1 (July/Sept. 1991)-. Periodical. English. qt. $60.00 (institutions). J.B. Lippincott Company, 227 East Washington Square, Philadelphia PA 19106-3780. **Tel** (215)238-4200 or 4454, FAX (215)238-4227. **DD** 617. **NLM** W1; OP15E.

US/1048-6666
**OPERATIVE TECHNIQUES IN ORTHOPAEDICS.** [Oper. tech. orthop.]. **VFOAT** Operative Techniques in Orthopedics. (1991)-. Periodical. English. qt (Jan., Apr., July, Oct.). $99.00 (individual), $150.00 (institution) US; $173.00 (individual), $190.00 (institution) other. W.B. Saunders Company, A Subsidiary of Harcourt Brace Jovanovich, Inc., The Curtis Center/Suite 300, Independence Square West, Philadelphia PA 19106-3399. **Tel** (215)238-7800 or, 5587, FAX (215)238-7883, telex 173146. **(Subscription address:** W. B. Saunders Company / North America Subscriptions, c/o Periodicals, 6277 Sea Harbour Drive, 4th Floor, Orlando FL 32887.**)** **DD** 616. **NLM** W1; OP15H. **[CCC].** ***Absorbed*** *Seminars in Orthopaedics, 0882-052X.*

GW/0085-4530
**ORTHOPADE, DER.** [Orthopaede]. Vol. 1 (April 1972)-. Academic Scholarly Publication. German. Six times a year. DM424.00. Springer-Verlag GmbH & Company KG, Heidelberger Platz 3, D 14197 Berlin Germany. **Tel** 011 49 30 8207223, FAX 011 49 30 8214091, telex 183 319 SPBLN D. **(Subscription address:** Springer Verlag New York Inc. / for North America, 44 Hartz Way, Secaucus NJ 07096.**)** **ED** R Bauer, N Gschwend, D Hohmann, E Morscher, L Schweiberer, H Tscherne, and H Wagner. **DD** 617.3. **NLM** W1 OR79KN. **CODEN** ORHPBG. **[CCC]. Pr Rev.** Documents available from The Genuine Article.
**Desc:** Each issue is dedicated to one specific subject of orthopedics or related areas and gives a clear review of current knowledge. Special emphasis is on diagnosis, prophylaxis and therapy.
**Ind/Abst** Curr. Contents; Curr. Contents Clin. Med.; EMBASE; Index Med.; Res. Alert [Select. Cov.]; SCISEARCH.

GW/0030-588X
**ORTHOPADISCHE PRAXIS.** [Orthop. Prax.]. **VFOAT** Baden-Badener Reihe feur Arztliche Fortbildung. Vol. 1 (Sept. 1965)-. Periodical. German. Twelve times a year. DM191.00 Germany; DM204.00 other. Medizinisch Literarische Verlag, Postfach 1151 + 1152, W 3110 Uelzen 1 F R Germany. **Tel** 011 49 581 808151, FAX 011 49 581 808158, telex 841 91326. **NLM** W1; OR805. **CODEN** OPBAAS. **[CCC].** Documents available from BIOSIS Document Express.
**Ind/Abst** Biol. Abstr. (1987-); EMBASE.

US/0892-7685
**ORTHOPAEDIC KNOWLEDGE UPDATE ... HOME STUDY SYLLABUS.** [Orthop. knowl. update home study syllabus]. **VFOAT** Home Study Syllabus. 1-. English. American Academy of Orthopaedic Surgeons, 6300 North River Road, Rosemont IL 60018. **Tel** (708)823-7186, (800)626-6726. **LC** RD732; .O76. **DD** 617. **NLM** WE 39; 077.

US/1059-311X
**ORTHOPAEDIC NETWORK NEWS.** [Orthop. netw. news]. (Oct. 1990)-. Periodical. English. qt (4 issues). $250.00. Mendenhall Associates, Inc., 1500 Cedar Boulevard, Ann Arbor MI 48105. **Tel** (313)741-4710, FAX (313)741-7277. **(Subscription address:** Orthopedic Newtwork News, Subscription Office, PO Box 830430, Birmingham AL 35283-0430.**)** **ED** Stan Mendenhall. **DD** 617. **Circ:** 1,000 (ctrl).
**Desc:** Provides up-to-date information to hospital administrators, physicians, manufacturers and distributors concerned with the business side of orthopedics. Each issue contains information on implant and other orthopedic device prices, reimbursement, manufacturer market share and procedure volumes on the US orthopedic market. Also profiles what individual hospitals are doing to reduce their costs and improve the quality of their orthopedic services.

●US/1059-1516
**ORTHOPAEDIC PHYSICAL THERAPY CLINICS OF NORTH AMERICA.** **See** Physical Therapy.

UK/0954-4755
**ORTHOPAEDIC PRODUCT NEWS.** [Orthop. prod. news]. (1987)-. Periodical. English. Five times a year. £12.00 UK; £18.00 Europe; £28.00 others. Orthopaedic Product News, 9 Sibford Road, Hook Norton Oxon OX15 5LA England. **Tel** 011 44 608 737504, FAX 011 44 608 730475. **ED** Michael J. Whitaker. **DD** 617.307. Index available. cum. index. **Bk Rev. Ad Acc. Circ:** 7,500 (ctrl).
**Desc:** Devoted to current developments and new products in the field of orthopaedics.

US/0094-6591
**ORTHOPAEDIC REVIEW.** [Orthop. rev.]. Vol. 1 (July 1972)-. Academic Scholarly Publication. English. mo. $95.00 (institutions), $72.00 (individuals). Excerpta

Medica / US, PO Box 3085, Princeton NJ 08543-3085. **Tel** (908)874-8550, FAX (908)874-5611. **LC** RD701; .O75. **DD** 617/.3/005. **NLM** W1 OR796R. **CODEN** ORTRDG. **[CCC].** Index available. **Bk Rev. Ad Acc. Pr Rev. Circ:** 25,000 (ctrl).
**Desc:** Clinical/surgical journal that meets the needs of the practicing orthopedic surgeon.
**Ind/Abst** EMBASE; Index Med. (Vol. 15, No. 1, 1986-).

US/0162-9379
**ORTHOPAEDIC TRANSACTIONS.** Vol. 1 (May 1977)-. Periodical. English. Three times a year. $32.00. Journal of Bone and Joint Surgery, 20 Pickering Street, Needham MA 02192-3157. **Tel** (617)449-9738, FAX (617)449-9742. **NLM** W1 OR796T. **CODEN** ORTTDM. Index available. cum. index. **Circ:** 7,000. Documents available from BIOSIS Document Express.
**Desc:** Consists of author-prepared abstracts of up to 700 words of papers read on the programs of the participating societies.
**Ind/Abst** Biol. Abstr.

US/0271-132X
**ORTHOPAEDICS (GLENDALE, CALIF.).** (ORTHOPAEDICS. SOUND RECORDING.). [Orthop.]. **Added/Corp** Audio-Digest Foundation. **VFOAT** Audio-Digest. Orthopaedics Sound Recording. (1978)-. Periodical. English. mo. $89.88 US; $101.40 Canada; $123.72 other. Audio-Digest Foundation, 1577 Chevy Chase Drive, Glendale CA 91206. **Tel** (213)245-8505, (800)423-2308, FAX (818)240-7379. **ED** Claron L. Oakley. **DD** 617. **NLM** W1 AU201DT. Index available (Free). ctrl circ.
**Desc:** Interactive system of audio cassette postgraduate medical education, with each one-hour program eligible for two Category I credit hours.

●US
**ORTHOPAEDICS INTERNATIONAL EDITION.** (1993)-. English. bm. $135.00 institution, $120.00 individual (US). Slack Inc., 6900 Grove Road, Thorofare NJ 08086. **Tel** (609)848-1000, (800)257-8290, FAX (609)853-5991, telex 517108 SLACK INC VD.

GW/0340-5591
**ORTHOPAEDIE-TECHNIK. VFOAT** Orthopedie Technique; Orthopedic Technology. (19??)-. Periodical. German. mo. DM195.00. Verlag Orthopaedie Technik, Postfach 100651, Reinoldstr 7-9, D-44135 Dortmund 1 Germany. **Tel** 011 49 231 579321, or 579322. **UDC** 615.477. **CODEN** 617.3.

US/0030-5898
**ORTHOPEDIC CLINICS OF NORTH AMERICA, THE.** [Orthop. clin. North Am.]. Vol. 1 (1970)-. Academic Scholarly Publication. English. qt. $100.00 (individual), $121.00 (institution) US; $134.00 (individual), $141.00 (institution) other. W.B. Saunders Company, A Subsidiary of Harcourt Brace Jovanovich, Inc., The Curtis Center/Suite 300, Independence Square West, Philadelphia PA 19106-3399. **Tel** (215)238-7800 or, 5587, FAX (215)238-7883, telex 173146. **(Subscription address:** W. B. Saunders Company / North America Subscriptions, c/o Periodicals, 6277 Sea Harbour Drive, 4th Floor, Orlando FL 32887.**) ED** Christine Battle. **NLM** W1 OR81K. **CODEN** OCLNAQ. **[CCC].** Index available. **Pr Rev. Circ:** 6,000. available on microfilm and microfiche from University Microfilms International (UMI). Documents available from The Genuine Article, BIOSIS Document Express.
**Desc:** Clinical updates on surgical techniques and management written by experts in the field.
**Ind/Abst** Abr. Index Med.; Biol. Abstr.; Calcium Calcif. Tissue Abstr.; Cumul. Index Nurs. Allied Health Lit.; Curr. Contents Clin. Med.; Dev. Med. Child Neurol.; EMBASE; Energy Res. Abstr. (April 1974-); Index Med.; Life Sci. Collect.; Physic. Medline Plus; Res. Alert [Full Cov.]; Sci. Cit. Index; SCISEARCH; SportSearch.

US/0744-6020
**ORTHOPEDIC NURSING / NATIONAL ASSOCIATION OF ORTHOPEDIC NURSES.** [Orthop. nurs.]. **Added/Corp** National Association of Orthopedic Nurses (U.S.) National Association of Orthopaedic Nurses (U.S.). **VFOAT** Orthopedic Nursing. Vol. 1, No. 1 (Jan./Feb. 1982)-. Periodical. English. bm. $36.00 (institutions), $24.00 (individuals) US; $49.00 (institutions), $37.00 (individuals) other. A.J. Jannetti Inc., East Holly Avenue, Box 56, Pitman NJ 08071-0056. **Tel** (609)256-2300, FAX (609)589-7463. **ED** Ann Butler Maher. **DD** 610. **NLM** W1 OR811H. **[CCC].** cum. index. **Bk Rev. Ad Acc. Pr Rev. Circ:** 10,000 (ctrl).
**Ind/Abst** Cumul. Index Nurs. Allied Health Lit.; Int. Nurs. Index; Physic. Medline Plus; SportSearch.

US/1042-704X
**ORTHOPEDIC PRODUCT NEWS.** ***Ceased.*** [Orthop. prod. news]. (1983)-Ceased June 1991. Periodical. English. mo. J.B. Lippincott Company, 227 East Washington Square, Philadelphia PA 19106-3780. **Tel** (215)238-4200 or 4454, FAX (215)238-4227. **(Subscription address:** Journal Fulfillment Department, Lippincott/Harper, Downsville Pike, Route 3, Box 20-B, Hagerstown, MD 21740; telephone: (800)638-3030**) DD** 610.
**Desc:** Covers products and news for the orthopedic, physical medicine, rehabilitation and sports medicine specialist.

US/1056-4543
**ORTHOPEDIC RESIDENT, THE.** ***Ceased.*** [Orthop. resid.]. (Oct. 1991)-(Feb. 1994). Periodical. English. bm. Slack Inc., 6900 Grove Road, Thorofare NJ 08086. **Tel** (609)848-1000, (800)257-8290, FAX (609)853-5991, telex 517108 SLACK INC VD. **DD** 617.

US/0276-4350
**ORTHOPEDIC SURGEON'S COMPENDIUM OF DRUG THERAPY, THE.** (THE ORTHOPEDIC SURGEON'S COMPENDIUM OF DRUG THERAPY : A PUBLICATION OF BIOMEDICAL INFORMATION CORPORATION.). [Orthop. surg. compend. drug ther.]. **VFOAT** Compendium of Drug Therapy. 1981/1982-. English. an. Biomedical Information Corporation, 800 Second Avenue, New York NY 10017. **Tel** (212)262-9662.

US/0147-7447
**ORTHOPEDICS (THOROFARE).** (ORTHOPEDICS.). [Orthopedics]. Vol. 1 (Jan/Feb 1978)-. Periodical. English. mo. $150.00 institution, $140.00 individual (US). Slack Inc., 6900 Grove Road, Thorofare NJ 08086. **Tel** (609)848-1000, (800)257-8290, FAX (609)853-5991, telex 517108 SLACK INC VD. **ED** Linda L. Jones. **LC** RD701; .O795. **DD** 617/.3/005. **NLM** W1 OR812A. Index available. cum. index. **Bk Rev. Ad Acc. Pr Rev. Circ:** 30,600 (ctrl). available on microfilm and microfiche from University Microfilms International (UMI). Documents available from The Genuine Article.
**Desc:** Original, clinical papers on orthopedic and related subjects involving case presentations, studies and reports.
**Ind/Abst** Calcium Calcif. Tissue Abstr.; Curr. Contents Clin. Med.; Dev. Med. Child Neurol.; EMBASE; Energy Res. Abstr. (Aug. 1982-); Index Med.; Res. Alert [Select. Cov.]; Rev. Med. Vet. Mycology; SCISEARCH; SPORT Discus.

US/0279-5647
**ORTHOPEDICS TODAY.** [Orthop. today]. Vol. 1 No. 1 (Jan/Feb 1981)-. Periodical. English. mo. $170.00 institution, $160.00 individual (US). Slack Inc., 6900 Grove Road, Thorofare NJ 08086. **Tel** (609)848-1000, (800)257-8290, FAX (609)853-5991, telex 517108 SLACK INC VD. **NLM** W1 OR813. **[CCC].**

FR/0940-3264
**ORTHOPEDIE TRAUMATOLOGIE : EUROPEAN JOURNAL OF ORTHOPAEDIC SURGERY & TRAUMATOLOGY : ORGANE OFFICIEL DE LA SOCIETE D'ORTHOPEDIE ET DE TRAUMATOLOGIE DE L'EST DE LA FRANCE (SOTEST) ET DU GROUPE D'ETUDE POUR LA CHIRURGIE OSSEUSE (GECO). Added/Corp** Societe d'Orthopedie et de Traumatologie de l'Est de la France. Groupe d'Etude pour la Chirurgie Osseuse. Vol. 1, No 1 (1991)-. Periodical. French (summaries and/or abstracts in English). qt. 1100.00F. Springer-Verlag France, 26 rue des Carmes, F 75005 Paris France. **Tel** 011 33 1 44411599, FAX 011 33 43250225. **(Subscription address:** Springer Verlag New York Inc. / for North America, 44 Hartz Way, Secaucus NJ 07096.**) NLM** W1; OR815. **[CCC].** available on microfilm and microfiche from University Microfilms International (UMI).

IT/0392-1417
**ORTOPEDIA E TRAUMATOLOGIA OGGI.** Vol. 1, No. 1 (Jan./Mar. 1981)-. Periodical. Italian (summaries and/or abstracts in English). qt. L60000 Italy; $60.00 other. CIC Edizioni Internazionali, Via L Spallanzani 11, 00161 Rome Italy. **Tel** 011 39 6 841-2673, FAX 011 39 6 844-3365, telex 622099 CIC I. **NLM** W1; OR872B. **[CCC].**
**Ind/Abst** EMBASE.

RU/0030-5987
**ORTOPEDIJA, TRAVMATOLOGIJA I PROTEZIROVANIE.** (ORTOPEDIIA, TRAVMATOLOGIIA I PROTEZIROVANIE.). [Ortop., travmatol. protez.]. **Added/Corp** Soviet Union. Ministerstvo Zdravookhraneniia. (Jan./Febr. 1955)-. Academic Scholarly Publication. Russian. Four times a year. $87.00. Izdatelstvo Meditsina / Russian Academy of Medical Sciences, Ulitsa Solyanka 14, 109801 Moscow Russia. **Tel** 011 95 297-05-04. **(Subscription address:** Victor Kamkin, 4956 Boiling Brook Parkway, Rockville, MD 20852**) NLM** W1 OR875. **CODEN** ORTPA7. Documents available from CASDDS. ***Continues*** *Ortopediia i Travmatologiia, 0473-4378.*
**Ind/Abst** Chem. Abstr. (?-1977); EMBASE; Index Med.; SportSearch.

FR/0761-2265
**PASCAL EXPLORE. E79, PATHOLOGIE ET PHYSIOLOGIE OSTEOARTICULAIRES.** ***Title Change.*** **VFOAT** Pathologie et Physiologie Osteoarticulaires; Physiology and Diseases of the Bones and Joints. No. 1 (1984)-(Jan. 1990). Periodical. French. mo. Institut de l'Information Scientique et Technique (INIST), 2 Allee du Parc de Brabois, 54514 Vandoeuvre Nancy Cedex France. **Tel** 011 33 83 504600, FAX 011 33 83 504650. **NLM** ZQ 1; B936SE. ***Continues*** *Bulletin Signaletique 357: Maladies des os et des Articulations. Chirurgie Orthopedique. Traumatologie.* ***Continued by*** *Pathologie et Physiologie Osteoarticulaires.*

US/1045-375X
**PERSPECTIVES IN ORTHOPAEDIC SURGERY.** ***Ceased.*** **See** Medical Science and Technology-Surgery.

US/0888-7357
**PHYSICAL MEDICINE AND REHABILITATION.** [Phys. med. rehabil.]. Vol. 1, No. 1 (Feb. 1987)-. Periodical. English. Three times a year. $72.00 (US & possessions); $82.00 (other). Hanley & Belfus Inc., 210 South 13th Street, Philadelphia PA 19107. **Tel** (215)546-7293, FAX (215)790-9330. **(Subscription address:** PO Box 6467, Duluth, MN 55806-9854; telephone: (800)654-2452**) LC** RD755; .P48. **DD** 617/.307. **NLM** W1; PH706. **[CCC].**

DK/0309-3646
**PROSTHETICS AND ORTHOTICS INTERNATIONAL. See** Physically Impaired.

UK/0308-4914
**RECENT ADVANCES IN ORTHOPAEDICS.** No. 1 (1969)-. Periodical. English. ir. $59.00. Churchill Livingstone, 1-3 Baxter's Place, Leith Walk, Edinburgh EH1 3AF Scotland. **Tel** 011 44 31 556 2424, FAX 011 44 31 558 1278, telex 727511. **(Subscription address:** Churchill Livingstone / US, 5 S 250 Frontenac Road, Naperville IL 60563.**) NLM** W1 RE105W.

US/0164-0526
**REGISTRY OF THE AMERICAN BOARD FOR CERTIFICATION IN ORTHOTICS AND PROSTHETICS, INC.** (REGISTRY OF THE AMERICAN BOARD FOR CERTIFICATION IN ORTHOTICS AND PROSTHETICS.). **Added/Corp** American Board for Certification in Orthotics and Prosthetics. **VFOAT** Registry - American Board for Certification in Orthotics and Prosthetics. (1976)-. Periodical. English. an. $75.00. American Academy of Prosthetics and Orthotics, 1650 King Street, Suite 500, Alexandria VA 22314. **Tel** (703)836-7116, FAX (708)836-0838. **NLM** WE 22 AA1 R27. ***Continues*** *Registry of Accredited Facilities and Certified Individuals in Orthotics and Prosthetics, 0190-5090.*

SP/0482-5985
**REVISTA DE ORTOPEDIA Y TRAUMATOLOGIA.** (1957)-. Periodical. Multiple languages (Portuguese and Spanish). bm. $72.54 Spain; $120.00 Europe; $140.00 other. Societad Espanola Cirugia Orto Trau, C Orense 16 14 A, 28020 Madrid Spain. **Tel** 011 34 1 4551411.
**Ind/Abst** Indice Med. Esp.

FR
**REVUE DE CHIRURGIE ORTHOPEDIQUE ET TRAUMATOLOGIQUE.** French. Nine times a year. $148.00. Masson Editeur, Box Postale 22, 41353 Vineuil 16 France. **Tel** 011 33 54 438994.

IT
**RIVISTA ITALIANA DI ORTOPEDIA E TRAUMATOLOGIA.** Italian. Six times a year. L30000.00 Italy; L60000.00 other. Casa Editrice Maccari, Via Trento 53, 43100 Parma Italy. **Tel** 011 39 521 771268, FAX 011 39 521 771268.

IT
**RIVISTA ITALIANA DI ORTOPEDIA E TRAUMATOLOGIA PEDIATRICA.** Aulo Gaggi Editore, Via Andrea Costa 131-5, 40134 Bologna Italy. **Tel** 011 39 51 6142067, telex 43 61 19.

US/0195-9565
**SAUNDERS MONOGRAPHS IN CLINICAL ORTHOPAEDICS.** ***Ceased.*** Vol. 1-?. Monographic series. English. ir. W.B. Saunders Company, A Subsidiary of Harcourt Brace Jovanovich, Inc., The Curtis Center/Suite 300, Independence Square West, Philadelphia PA 19106-3399. **Tel** (215)238-7800 or, 5587, FAX (215)238-7883, telex 173146. **(Subscription address:** W. B. Saunders Company / North America Subscriptions, c/o Periodicals, 6277 Sea Harbour Drive, 4th Floor, Orlando FL 32887.**) NLM** W1 SA975.

JA
**SEIKEI GEKA MOOK.** 1- 1978-. Monographic series. Japanese. Price varies per volume. Kanehara Shuppan K.K., (Kanehara Shuppan Ltd.), 31-14, Yushima 2 Chome, Bunkyoku, Tokyoto 113-91, Japan. **NLM** W1 SE2516G.

US/0882-052X
**SEMINARS IN ORTHOPAEDICS.** ***Title Change.*** [Sem. orthop.]. Vol. 1, No. 1 (March 1986)-(19??). Periodical. English. qt (4 issues). W.B. Saunders Company, A Subsidiary of Harcourt Brace Jovanovich, Inc., The Curtis Center/Suite 300, Independence Square West, Philadelphia PA 19106-3399. **Tel** (215)238-7800 or, 5587, FAX (215)238-7883, telex 173146. **(Subscription address:** W. B. Saunders Company / North America Subscriptions, c/o Periodicals, 6277 Sea Harbour Drive, 4th Floor, Orlando FL 32887.**) ED** James W Harkess, Sean P F Hughes, and K P Schulitz. **DD** 617. **NLM** W1; SE489EG. **CODEN** SEORED. **[CCC].** Documents available from BIOSIS Document Express. ***Absorbed by*** *Operative Techniques in Orthopaedics.*
**Desc:** Dedicated to the timely dissemination of information regarding the latest advances in orthopedic surgery techniques.
**Ind/Abst** Biol. Abstr.; Dev. Med. Child Neurol.; EMBASE.

UK/1055-6583
**SLIDE ATLAS OF CURRENT ORTHOPAEDICS.** (SLIDES ATLAS OF CURRENT ORTHOPAEDICS [SLIDES].). [Slide atlas curr. orthop.]. Update 1 (Feb. 1991)-. Periodical. English. bm. $375.00. Current Science, 20 North 3rd Street, Philadelphia PA 19106. **Tel** (215)574-2266, (800)552-5866, FAX (215)574-2270.

●US/1072-3730
**SPINE LETTER.** [Spine lett.]. (March 1994)-. Newsletter. English. mo. $95.00 (individuals), $130.00 (institutions) US; $159.95 (individuals), $190.00 (institutions) other. J.B. Lippincott Company, 227 East Washington Square, Philadelphia PA 19106-3780. **Tel** (215)238-4200 or 4454, FAX (215)238-4227. **(Subscription address:** J.B. Lippincott, PO Box 350, Hagerstown MD 21740.**) DD** 617.
**Desc:** Information and literature on the study of the spine. For professionals who diagnose and treat patients with spinal disorders.

US/0891-1800
**SURGICAL ROUNDS FOR ORTHOPAEDICS.** ***Ceased.*** [Surg. rounds orthop.]. Jan. (1987)-Ceased Sept. (1990). Periodical. English. mo. Romaine Pierson Publishing Inc., 80 Shore Road, Port Washington NY 11050. **Tel** (516)883-6350. **DD** 617. **NLM** W1; SU767LK. available on microfilm from University Microfilms International (UMI).

KO
**TAEHAN CHONGHYONG OEKWA HAKHOE CHI.** **VFOAT** The Journal of the Korean Orthopedic Association; Journal of the Korean Orthopedic Association. Periodical. Korean (summaries and/or abstracts in English). bm. Taehan Chonghyong Oekwa Hakhoe, 302-75 Tongbu Ichon-dong Yongsan-ku, Seoul Korea. **LC** RD701; .T33. **NLM** W1; TA392CT. ***Continues*** *Taehan Chonghyong Oekwa Hakhoe Chapchi.*

US/0885-9698
**TECHNIQUES IN ORTHOPAEDICS (ROCKVILLE, MD.).** (TECHNIQUES IN ORTHOPAEDICS : TIO.). [Tech. orthop.]. **Added/Corp** Aspen Systems Corporation. **VFOAT** TIO. Vol. 1, No. 1 (April 1986)-. Periodical. English. qt. $128.00 (individuals), $138.00 (institutions) US; $158.00 (individuals), $166.00 (institutions) other. Raven Press, 1185 Avenue of the Americas, 37th Floor, New York NY 10036. **Tel** (212)930-9500, (212)930-9604, FAX (212)869-3495, (212)302-8507, telex 640073. **ED** Lawrence D. Dorr. **DD** 617. **NLM** W1; TE197CH. **[CCC]. Ad Acc.**
**Desc:** Provides information on the latest orthopaedic procedures as they are devised and used by top orthopaedic surgeons.
**Ind/Abst** EMBASE.

US/0149-6433
**TRANSACTIONS OF THE ANNUAL MEETING OF THE ORTHOPAEDIC RESEARCH SOCIETY.** **Main/Corp** Orthopaedic Research Society. (19??)-. Periodical. English. an. $40.00. Orthopaedic Research Society, 6300 North River Road, Suite 727, Rosemont IL 60018. **Tel** (708)698-1625, FAX (708)823-0536. **ED** Wilson C. Hayes, Ph.D and Joseph A. Buckwalter, M.D. (Editors' telephone: (617)735-2940 and (319)356-2595). **NLM** W1 TR225GF. **Ad Acc, Adv Mgr:** Amber Howard, **Tel** (617)449-9745. **Pr Rev.**

AJ
**TRUDY - BAKINSKII NAUCHNO-ISSLEDOVATEL'SKII INSTITUT TRAVMATOLOGII I ORTOPEDII.** **Added/Corp** Bakinskii Nauchno-Issledovatel'Skii Institut Travmatologii i Ortopedii. (196?)-. Russian. **NLM** W1 TR947T.

US/0276-1092
**YEAR BOOK OF ORTHOPEDICS, THE.** [Year book orthop.]. (1980)-. English. an. $59.95. Mosby Year Book Inc., 11830 Westline Industrial Drive, St Louis MO 63146. **Tel** (800)325-4177, (314)872-8370, FAX (314)432-1380, telex 44-2402. **LC** RD711; .Y4. **DD** 617/.3/005. **NLM** W1 YE287Z. ***Continues*** *Year Book of Orthopedics and Traumatic Surgery, 0084-3938.*

GW/0044-3220
**ZEITSCHRIFT FUER ORTHOPADIE UND IHRE GRENZGEBIETE.** [Z. Orthop. ihre Grenzgeb.]. **Added/Corp** Deutsche Gesellschaft fuer Orthopaedie und Traumatologie. Deutsche Orthopadische Gesellschaft. Vol. 64 (Oct. 1935)-. Academic Scholarly Publication. German. bm. $321.00. Ferdinand Enke Verlag, Ruedigerstrasse 14, D-70469 Stuttgart Germany. **Tel** 011 49 711 8931124, 011 49 711 893123. **(Subscription address:** Thieme Medical Publishers Inc., 381 Park Avenue South, New York NY 10016.**) NLM** W1 ZE529. **CODEN** ZOIGAP. **[CCC]. Pr Rev.** Documents available from The Genuine Article, BIOSIS Document Express, ADONIS. ***Continues*** *Zeitschrift fuer Orthopadische Chirurgie Einschliesslich der Heilgymnastik und Massage.*
**Ind/Abst** ADONIS; Biol. Abstr.; CSA Neuro. Abstr. (?-?); Curr. Contents Clin. Med.; EMBASE; Index Med.; Int. Nurs. Index; Life Sci. Collect.; Res. Alert [Select. Cov.]; Saf. Health Work; Soc. Sci. Cit. Index [Select. Cov.]; SportSearch.

CC/0253-2352
**ZHONGHUA GUKE ZAZHI.** (CHUNG-HUA KU KO TSA CHIH.). [Zhonghua guke zazhi]. **VFOAT** Chinese Journal of Orthopedics. Vol. 1, 1981-. Periodical. Chinese. bm. RMBY10,000. Science Press, 16 Donghuangchenggen North Street, Beijing 100707, People's Republic of China. **Tel** 011 86 1 4019821, 011 86 1 4010642, FAX 011 86 1 4012180, 011 86 1 4019810, telex 210147. **NLM** W1 CH982K. **Ad Acc. Circ:** 25,000.

## OTORHINOLARYNGOLOGY

SP
**A.N.A. AUDIOLOGIA PROTESICA.** ***Ceased.*** (19??)-(199?). Spanish. ir (every four months). Reclamo Tecnico SA, Casanova 212, P 1 2, 08036 Barcelona, Spain. **Tel** 011 34 3 4104372. **Bk Rev. Ad Acc. Pr Rev.**

US/0883-3001
**ABMS DIRECTORY OF CERTIFIED OTOLARYNGOLOGISTS.** ***Title Change.*** [ABMS dir. certif. otolaryngol.]. **Added/Corp** American Board of Medical Specialties. American Board of Otolaryngology. **VFOAT** Directory of Certified Otolaryngologists. **VAT** American Board of Medical Specialties Directory of Certified Otolaryngologists. (1985)-(199?). Directory. English. be. American Board of Medical Specialties, 1 Rotary Center, Suite 805, Evanston IL 60201. **Tel** (708)491-9091. **LC** RF28; .A25. **DD** 617/.51/002573. **NLM** WV 22.1; A1523. ***Continued by*** *Official American Board of Medical Specialties (ABMS) Directory of Board Certified Otolaryngologists, 0000-1600.*

UK/0309-698X
**ACADEMIC AND CLINICAL REPORTS - INSTITUTE OF LARYNGOLOGY AND OTOLOGY ASSOCIATED WITH THE ROYAL NATIONAL THROAT, NOSE AND EAR HOSPITAL.** (ACADEMIC AND CLINICAL REPORTS.). V. 21- 1973/74-. Academic Scholarly Publication. English. **NLM** W1 AC33N. ***Continues*** *Reports - Institute of Laryngology and Otology and Royal National Throat, Nose and Ear Hospital, 0301-3723.*
**Desc:** Includes abstracts of articles from various journals.

SW/0001-6489
**ACTA OTO-LARYNGOLOGICA.** [Acta oto-laryngol.]. Vol. 1 (1918)-. Academic Scholarly Publication. English (French and German). bm. Kr1495.00, $242.00. Scandinavian University Press, PO Box 2959 Toeyen, N 0608 Oslo 6 Norway. **Tel** 011 47 2 2575400, FAX 011 47 2 2575353, telex 71896 UROR N. **(Subscription address:** Scandinavian University Press, 200 Meacham Ave., Elmont NY 11003.**) ED** Prof Borje Drettner. **NLM** W1 AC8941. **CODEN** AOLAAJ. **Pr Rev.** Documents available from The Genuine Article, BIOSIS Document Express, CASDDS. ***Supersedes*** *Nordisk Tidskrift for Oto-Rhino-Laryngologi.*
**Desc:** Accepts review articles, original papers and case reports. Short communications and therapeutic notes are intended as preliminary reports or contributions which are thought to warrant rapid publication.
**Ind/Abst** Biol. Abstr. (1971-1985); Chem. Abstr.; CSA Neuro. Abstr. (?-?); Curr. Aware. Biol. Sci., CABS; Curr. Contents Clin. Med.; Curr. Contents Life Sci.; Dent. Abstr. (-1991); EMBASE; Energy Res. Abstr.; Health Plan. Adminis.; Index Med.; Index Sci. Rev.; Int. Aerosp. Abstr.; Linguist. Lang. Behav. Abstr.; Nutr. Res. Newsl.; Life Sci. Collect.; PESTDOC; Protozoolog. Abstr.; Psychol. Abstr. (1928-); PsycINFO; PsycLit; Ref. Upd. Deluxe Ed.; Res. Alert [Full Cov.]; Risk Abstr.; Saf. Health Work; Sci. Cit. Index; SCISEARCH; Soc. Plann. Policy Dev. Abstr.; Soc. Sci. Cit. Index [Select. Cov.]; Sociol. Abstr.

SW/0365-5237
**ACTA OTO-LARYNGOLOGICA. SUPPLEMENT.** [Acta oto-laryngol. Suppl.]. No. 1 (1920)-. Academic Scholarly Publication. English (French and German). ir. Price varies per volume. Scandinavian University Press, PO Box 2959 Toeyen, N 0608 Oslo 6 Norway. **Tel** 011 47 2 2575400, FAX 011 47 2 2575353, telex 71896 UROR N. **(Subscription address:** Scandinavian University Press, 200 Meacham Ave., Elmont NY 11003.**) NLM** W1 AC8942. **CODEN** AOLSA5. Documents available from BIOSIS Document Express, CASDDS.
**Ind/Abst** Biol. Abstr.; Chem. Abstr.; CSA Neuro. Abstr. (?-?); Curr. Aware. Biol. Sci., CABS; EMBASE; Index Med.; Life Sci. Collect.; SportSearch.

BE/0001-6497
**ACTA OTO-RHINO-LARYNGOLOGICA BELGICA.** [Acta oto-rhino-laryngol. belg.]. **Added/Corp** Societe Belge d'Oto-Rhino-Laryngologie et de Chirurgie Cervico-Faciale. (1947)-. Periodical. French. qt. 3000.00F Belgium; 3200.00F other. Association for the Society of Scientifique Medica Belgique, Avenue Circulaire 138A, B-1180 Brussels Belgium. **Tel** 011 32 2 3745158. **NLM** W1 AC897. **CODEN** AORLAE. Documents available from BIOSIS Document Express, CASDDS. ***Supersedes*** *Societe Belge d' Otologie, de Rhinologie et de Laryngologie. Bulletin.*
**Ind/Abst** Biol. Abstr.; Chem. Abstr.; EMBASE; Health Plan. Adminis.; Index Med.; Linguist. Lang. Behav. Abstr.; Life Sci. Collect.; Soc. Plann. Policy Dev. Abstr.; Sociol. Abstr.

IT/0392-100X
**ACTA OTORHINO-LARYNGOLOGICA ITALICA.** (ACTA OTORHINOLARYNGOLOGICA ITALICA : ORGANO UFFICIALE DELLA SOCIETA ITALIANA DI OTORINOLARINGOLOGIA E CHIRURGIA CERVICO-FACCIALE.). [Acta otorhino-laryngol. ital.]. **Added/Corp** Societa Italiana di Otorinolaringologia e Chirurgia Cervico-Facciale. Vol. 1, No. 1 (July/Aug. 1981)-. Academic Scholarly Publication. Italian (summaries and/or abstracts in English). Six times a year (Jan., Mar., May, July, Sept., Nov.). L75000 Italy; L95000 other. Pacini Editore Srl, Via A Gherardesca 1, 56121 Ospedaletto Pisa Italy. **Tel** 011 39 50 982439. **NLM** W1 AC898N. ***Continues*** *Annali di Laringologia, Otologia, Rinologia, e Faringologia.*
**Desc:** Contains staff development material for non-professional nursing personnel.
**Ind/Abst** EMBASE; Health Plan. Adminis.; Index Med.

SP/0001-6519
**ACTA OTORRINOLARINGOLOGICA ESPANOLA.** [Acta otorrinolaringol. esp.]. **Added/Corp** Sociedad Espanola de Otorrinolaringologia. Vol. 1 (Oct. 1949)-. Academic Scholarly Publication. Spanish. Six times a year. 52.52ptas Spain; $95.00 Europe & others. Editorial Garsi SA, Juan Bravo 46, 28006 Madrid, Spain. **Tel** 011 34 1 4021212, telex 98358 GARSI E. **NLM** W1 AC898L.
**Ind/Abst** EMBASE; Indice Med. Esp.; Life Sci. Collect.

IT/0392-3088
**ACTA PHONIATRICA LATINA.** [Acta phoniatr. lat.]. (1979)-. Periodical. Multiple languages (summaries and/or abstracts in English). qt. L60000..000 Italy; L120000.00 other. La Garangola, Via Montona 4, 35137 Padua Italy. **Tel** 011 39 49 8750550, FAX 011 39 49 8751743. **UDC** 612.78. cum. index. **Bk Rev. Ad Acc, Adv Mgr:** A. Pagamento. **Pr Rev. Circ:** 1000 (ctrl).
**Ind/Abst** Linguist. Lang. Behav. Abstr.; Soc. Plann. Policy Dev. Abstr.; Sociol. Abstr.

SZ/0065-3071
**ADVANCES IN OTO-RHINO-LARYNGOLOGY.** [Adv. oto-rhino-laryngol.]. **VFOAT** Bibliotheca Oto-Rhino-Laryngologica; Fortschritte der Hals-Nasen-Ohren-Heilhunde; Progres en Oto-Rhino-Laryngologie. Vol. 1 (1953)-. Monographic series. English (French, German and Spanish). an. 250.00F (approx. per volume). S. Karger AG, Allschwilerstrasse 10, PO Box - Postfach - Case Postale, CH-4009 Basel Switzerland. **Tel** 011 41 61 306-1111, FAX 011 41 61 306-1234, telex CH 962 652. **ED** W. Arnold, S. Prasansuk, O. Yamashita. **LC** RF16; .A38. **NLM** W1 AD701. **CODEN** ADORB9. **[CCC].** Documents available from BIOSIS Document Express, CASDDS. ***Continues*** *Fortschritte der Hals-Nasen-Ohren-Heilhunde.*
**Desc:** The series reproduces results from research and clinical studies pertaining to the pathophysiology, diagnosis, clinical symptoms, course, prognosis, and therapy of a variety of ear, nose, and throat disorders. The numerous papers correlating basic research findings and clinical applications are of immense value to all specialists engaged in the ongoing efforts to improve management of these disorders. Acting as a voice for its field, the series has also been instrumental in developing subspecialities into established specialities.
**Ind/Abst** Biol. Abstr.; Chem. Abstr. (1970-1984); Health Plan. Adminis.; Index Med.; Index Dent. Lit.; Life Sci. Collect.; Ref. Upd. Deluxe Ed.

US/0196-0709
**AMERICAN JOURNAL OF OTOLARYNGOLOGY.** [Am. j. otolaryngol.]. Vol. 1 (Fall 1979)-. Academic Scholarly Publication. English. bm (6 issues). $91.00 (individuals), $116.00 (institution) US; $156.00 (individuals), $171.00 (institutions) other. W.B. Saunders Company, A Subsidiary of Harcourt Brace Jovanovich, Inc., The Curtis Center/Suite 300, Independence Square West, Philadelphia PA 19106-3399. **Tel** (215)238-7800 or, 5587, FAX (215)238-7883, telex 173146. **(Subscription address:** W. B. Saunders Company / North America Subscriptions, c/o Periodicals, 6277 Sea Harbour Drive, 4th Floor, Orlando FL 32887.**) ED** Michael Bokulich. **LC** RF1. **DD** 616.2/1. **NLM** W1 AM497N. **CODEN** AJOTDP. **[CCC]. Bk Rev. Ad Acc. Pr Rev. Circ:** 1,000. available on microfilm and microfiche from University Microfilms International (UMI). Documents available from The Genuine Article, CASDDS.
**Desc:** Original articles covering clinical findings of interest to otolaryngologists, otologists, allergists, plastic surgeons, maxillofacial surgeons, and speech scientists.
**Ind/Abst** Chem. Abstr.; Cumul. Index Nurs. Allied Health Lit.; Curr. Contents Clin. Med.; EMBASE; Index Med. (Fall 1979-); Index Vet.; Res. Alert [Select. Cov.]; SCISEARCH.

US/0192-9763
**AMERICAN JOURNAL OF OTOLOGY (NEW YORK, N.Y.), THE.** (THE AMERICAN JOURNAL OF OTOLOGY.). [Am. j. otol.]. **Added/Corp** American Otological Society. American Neurotology Society. Vol. 1 (July 1979)-. Periodical. English. bm (6 issues). $98.00 (individuals), $149.00 (institutions) US and Canada; $129.00 (individuals), $180.00 (institutions) other. Decker Periodicals Publishing Inc, PO Box 620, Station A, Hamilton Ontario L8N 3K7 Canada. **Tel** (416)522-7017, (800) 568-7281, FAX (416)522-7839. **ED** C. Gary Jackson. **DD** 617. **NLM** W1 AM497V. **CODEN** AJOTBN. **[CCC]. Bk Rev. Ad Acc. Pr Rev. Circ:** 1,500 (ctrl). available on microfilm and microfiche from University Microfilms International (UMI). Documents available from The Genuine Article, BIOSIS Document Express, ADONIS.
**Desc:** Features original articles and important reviews by leading investigators and clinicians in otology, neurology and audiology. Coverage includes current clinical topics such as tinnitus, Bell's palsy, Meniere's disease, and facial nerve surgery.
**Ind/Abst** ADONIS; Biol. Abstr.; Curr. Contents Clin. Med.; EMBASE; Health Plan. Adminis.; Index Med. (July 1979-); Res. Alert [Full Cov.]; Rev. Med. Vet. Mycology; Sci. Cit. Index; SCISEARCH.

US/1050-6586
**AMERICAN JOURNAL OF RHINOLOGY.** [Am. j. rhinol.]. Vol. 1, No. 1 (Spring 1987)-. Academic Scholarly Publication. English (Spanish). bm (Feb., Apr., June, Aug., Oct., Dec.). $68.00 individuals, $98.00 institutions. Oceanside Publications, 95 Pitman Street, Providence RI 02906. **Tel** (401)331-2510, FAX (401)331-5138. **ED** David W. Kennedy and John T. Connell. **DD** 616. **NLM** W1; AM521NN. **CODEN** AJRHE5. Index available. cum. index. **Ad Acc. Pr Rev. Circ:** 3,000 (ctrl). Documents available from The Genuine Article, CASDDS.
**Desc:** Devoted to the immunology, physiology, biochemistry, and clinical research of the nasopharynx.
**Ind/Abst** Chem. Abstr. (?-1989); Curr. Contents Clin. Med.; EMBASE [Select. Cov.]; Res. Alert [Full Cov.]; Sci. Cit. Index.

SP
**ANALES DE OTORRINOLARINGOLOGIA.** Spanish. qt. $70.00. Sociedad Otorrinolaringologica fac, Med Madrid SN Granada Spain.

SP/0303-8874
**ANALES OTORRINOLARINGOLOGICOS IBERO-AMERICANOS.** [An. otorrinolaringol. Ibero-Am.]. Vol. 1 (1974)-. Periodical. Spanish (summaries and/or abstracts in English, French and German). Six times a year (Jan., Mar., May, July, Sept., Nov.). $144.90 Latin America, $177.00 others; 13983ptas Spain & Portugal. Anales Otorrinolaringologicos, C Balmes Street #24 Pral 1, 08007 Barcelona Spain. **Tel** 011 34 3 3173646, FAX 011 34 3 3173766. **ED** Dr. Enrique Perello Scherdel (editor's address: Balemes 24, 08007 Barcelona Spain). **NLM** W1 AN189D. **CODEN** AOIAA4. Index available. cum. index. **Bk Rev. Ad Acc, Adv Mgr:** Sr. Javier Moqxo Estton. **Pr Rev. Circ:** 1,000 (ctrl). Documents available from BIOSIS Document Express. ***Supersedes*** *Acta Oto-Rhino-Laringologica Ibero-Americana, 0001-6500.*
**Desc:** Study of ear, nose and throat medicine in Latin America
**Ind/Abst** Biol. Abstr.; EMBASE; Index Med.

FR
**ANNALES D'ORL.** (19??)-. French. $255.00. Masson Editeur, Box Postale 22, 41353 Vineuil 16 France. **Tel** 011 33 54 438994.

FR/0003-438X
**ANNALES D'OTO-LARYNGOLOGIE ET DE CHIRURGIE CERVICO FACIALE : BULLETIN DE LA SOCIETE D'OTO-LARYNGOLOGIE DES HOPITAUX DE PARIS.** [Ann. oto-laryngol. chir. cervico-fac.]. **Added/Corp** Societe d'Oto-Laryngologie des Hopitaux de Paris. Vol. 80 (1963)-. Academic Scholarly Publication. French. Eight times a year. 972.00F France; 8040F Belgium; $255.00 other. Masson Editeur, Box Postale 22, 41353 Vineuil 16 France. **Tel** 011 33 54 438994. **(Subscription address:** 7A Boulevard de Perolles, CH-1701 Fribourg Switzerland**) [CCC].** ***Continues*** *Annales d'Oto-Laryngologie et de Chirurgie de la Face.*
**Ind/Abst** Curr. Titl. Dent.; EMBASE; Health Plan. Adminis.; Index Med.

US/0003-4894
**ANNALS OF OTOLOGY, RHINOLOGY & LARYNGOLOGY, THE.** [Ann. otol. rhinol. laryngol.]. **VAT** Annals of Otology, Rhinology and Laryngology. Vol. 6 (Feb. 1897)-. Academic Scholarly Publication. English. mo. $155.00 US; $175.00 other. Annals Publishing Company, 4507 Laclede Avenue, St. Louis MO 63108. **Tel** (314)367-4987. **ED** Brian F. McCabe. **LC** RF1; .A6. **NLM** W1 AN617L. **CODEN** AORHA2. Index available (bound in Dec. issue). **Bk Rev. Ad Acc. Pr Rev. Acid Free. Circ:** 6,002 (ctrl). available on microfilm and microfiche from University Microfilms International (UMI). Documents available from The Genuine Article, BIOSIS Document Express, CASDDS. ***Continues in part*** *Annals of Ophthalmology and Otology.*
**Desc:** Over 90 years of excellence, publishing peer-reviewed clinical and research papers in the field of otolaryngology. Supplements, historical papers, imaging case studies, pathology consultations, book reviews and letters ot the editor are also published.
**Ind/Abst** Abr. Index Med.; Biol. Abstr.; Chem. Abstr.; CSA Neuro. Abstr. (?-?); Curr. Contents Life Sci.; EMBASE; Energy Res. Abstr.; Health Devices Alerts; Health Period. Database; Health Plan. Adminis.; Index Med.; INIS Atomindex [Micro.]; Int. Aerosp. Abstr.; Iowa Drug Inf. Serv. (1968-); Linguist. Lang. Behav. Abstr.; Nutr. Abstr. Rev., Ser. B, Live Feeds and Feed.; Nutr. Abstr. Rev., Ser. A, Hum. Exp.; Life Sci. Collect.; Physic. Medline Plus; Phys. Med. Biol. (19??-19??); Ref. Upd. Deluxe Ed.; Res. Alert [Full Cov.]; Rev. Med. Vet. Mycology; Sci. Cit. Index; SCISEARCH; Soc. Plann. Policy Dev. Abstr.; Soc. Sci. Cit. Index [Select. Cov.]; Sociol. Abstr.

US/0096-8056
**ANNALS OF OTOLOGY, RHINOLOGY & LARYNGOLOGY. SUPPLEMENT, THE.** [Ann. otol. rhinol. laryngol., Suppl.]. (1971)-. Monographic series. English. Included with subscription to "The Annals of Otology, Rhinology & Laryngology". Annals Publishing Company, 4507 Laclede Avenue, St. Louis MO 63108. **Tel** (314)367-4987. **LC** UNC. **NLM** W1 AN617N. **CODEN** AOLSE9.
**Ind/Abst** Health Plan. Adminis.; Index Med.; Physic. Medline Plus.

JA/0564-7630
**ANNUAL BULLETIN / RESEARCH INSTITUTE OF LOGOPEDICS AND PHONIATRICS, FACULTY OF MEDICINE, UNIVERSITY OF TOKYO.** **Added/Corp** Tokyo Daigaku. Onseigo Igaku Kenkyu Shisetsu. (19??)-. Bulletin. English. an. University of Tokyo, Faculty of Medicine, 7-3-1 Hongo, Bunkyo-ku, Tokyo 113 Japan. **LC** QP306; .T62. **NLM** W1; AN748CJ.
**Ind/Abst** Soc. Plann. Policy Dev. Abstr.

US/0886-4470
**ARCHIVES OF OTOLARYNGOLOGY-HEAD & NECK SURGERY.** [Arch. otolaryngol.--head neck surg.]. **Added/Corp** American Medical Association. American Academy of Facial Plastic and Reconstructive Surgery. American Society for Head and Neck Surgery. American Society of Pediatric Otolaryngology. **VFOAT** Archives of Otolaryngology--Head and Neck Surgery; Archives of Otolaryngology, Head & Neck Surgery. Vol. 112, No. 1 (Jan. 1986)-. Academic Scholarly Publication. English. mo. $145.00 (institution), $125.00 (individual) US. American Medical Association, 515 North State Street, Chicago IL 60610. **Tel** (312)464-5000, (800)262-2350, FAX (312)464-5831. **LC** RF1; .A7. **DD** 617/.51. **NLM** W1; AR464P. **CODEN** AONSEJ. **[CCC].** Index available in last issue of volume--attached. **Ad Acc.** available on microfilm and microfiche from University Microfilms International (UMI); available on an online database (file 442/Full-Text) from DIALOG. Documents available from The Genuine Article, BIOSIS Document Express, CASDDS. ***Continues*** *Archives of Otolaryngology (Chicago, Ill. : 1960), 0003-9977.*
**Desc:** Published as an educational service for physicians who treat conditions of the ear, nose, and throat; who treat communicative disorders; and who perform facial plastic and reconstructive surgery. Oriented toward the clinician, it contains articles applicable to everyday practice.
**Ind/Abst** Abr. Index Med.; Abstr. Anthropol.; Biol. Abstr. (1986-); Chem. Abstr. (1986-); Chemorecept. Abstr.; CSA Neuro. Abstr. (?-?); Curr. Contents Clin. Med.; Curr. Contents Life Sci.; EMBASE; Energy Res. Abstr. (1986-); Health Plan. Adminis.; Index Med. (1986-); INIS Atomindex [Micro.]; Int. Aerosp. Abstr. (1986-); Life Sci. Collect. (1986-); Physic. Medline Plus; Ref. Upd. Deluxe Ed.; Res. Alert [Full Cov.]; Rev. Med. Vet. Mycology; Saf. Health Work (1986-); Sci. Cit. Index; SCISEARCH; SportSearch.

PO
**ARQUIVOS PORTUGUESES DE OTORRINOLARINGOLOGIA E DE PATOLOGIA CERVICO-FACIAL.** **VFOAT** Arquivos Portugueses de Orl. Periodical. Portuguese (Portuguese). qt. $35.00. **NLM** W1; AR927E.

US
**ASHA MEMBERSHIP DIRECTORY.** **Main/Corp** American Speech-Language-Hearing Association. **VFOAT** Membership Directory. **VAT** American Speech-Language-Hearing Association Membership Directory. (198?)-. English. be. $63.52. American Speech Language and Hearing Association, 10801 Rockville Pike, Rockville MD 20852. **Tel** (301)897-5700. **LC** RF28; .A7. **DD** 616.85/5/006073. **NLM** WV 22; AA1 A55a. ***Continues*** *American Speech-Language-Hearing Association. ASHA Directory Supplement, 0884-9846.*

US/0569-8553
**ASHA REPORTS.** [ASHA rep.]. **Added/Corp** American Speech and Hearing Association American Speech-Language-Hearing Association. (1965)-. Monographic series. English. ir. Price varies per volume. American Speech Language and Hearing Association, 10801 Rockville Pike, Rockville MD 20852. **Tel** (301)897-5700. **ED** Arnold Small. **NLM** W1 A152E. **CODEN** AREQEN.
**Desc:** Proceedings of conferences on speech, hearing, language, or related topics.
**Ind/Abst** Psychol. Abstr. (1983-); PsycINFO; PsycLit.

IT
**AUDIOLOGIA ITALIANA : ORGANO UFFICIALE DELLA SOCIETA ITALIANA DI AUDIOLOGIA.** **Added/Corp** Societa Italiana di Audiologia. **VFOAT** Italian Audiology. Vol. 1, No. 1 (Jan./March 1984)-. Periodical. English (Italian). qt. L80000. Edizioni Luigi Pozzi Srl, Via Panama 68, 00198 Rome Italy. **Tel** (06)8553548, FAX (06)8554105. **NLM** W1; AU201ES. ***Continues*** *Bollettino Italiano di Audiologia e Foniatria, 0391-075X.*

SZ/0020-6091
**AUDIOLOGY.** (AUDIOLOGY : OFFICIAL ORGAN OF THE INTERNATIONAL SOCIETY OF AUDIOLOGY.). [Audiology]. **Added/Corp** International Society of Audiology. **VFOAT** Audiologie. Vol. 10 (Jan./Feb. 1971)-. Periodical. English (French). bm (6 issues). $266.00. S. Karger AG, Allschwilerstrasse 10, PO Box - Postfach - Case Postale, CH-4009 Basel Switzerland. **Tel** 011 41 61 306-1111, FAX 011 41 61 306-1234, telex CH 962 652. **ED** J. M. Aran, E. Konig, W. D. Ward. **LC** RF290; .A9. **DD** 617.8/005. **NLM** W1 AU201H. **CODEN** AUDLAK. **[CCC].** Index available in last issue of volume--attached. **Ad Acc. Pr Rev.** Documents available from The Genuine Article, BIOSIS Document Express. ***Continues*** *International Audiology.*
**Desc:** Contains original reports from laboratories involved in research on hearing, hearing loss and rehabilitation. Reflecting the interdisciplinary nature of audiological study and practice, papers come from a range of fields, including anatomy, histology, pathology, physiology, otology, acoustics, psychology, psychiatry, social sciences and epidemiology; features new developments in technical, pharmacological and surgical measures, and provides an account of progress in the prevention, diagnosis and treatment of hearing disorders.
**Ind/Abst** Acoust. Abstr.; Biol. Abstr.; CSA Neuro. Abstr. (?-?); Curr. Contents Life Sci.; Dev. Med. Child Neurol.; EMBASE; Energy Res. Abstr. (Feb. 1982-); Health Plan. Adminis.; Index Med.; Life Sci. Collect.; Psychol. Abstr. (1971-); PsycINFO; PsycLit; Ref. Upd. Deluxe Ed.; Res. Alert [Full Cov.]; Sci. Cit. Index; SCISEARCH; Soc. Sci. Cit. Index [Select. Cov.].

JA/0385-8146
**AURIS, NASUS, LARYNX.** [Auris, nasus, larynx]. **Added/Corp** Society for Promotion of International Otorhinolaryngology. Vol. 1 (1974)-. Academic Scholarly Publication. English (French and German). qt. $60.00. Kokusai Jibi Inko Kagaku Shinkokai, (Society for Promotion of International Otorhinolaryngology), Nihon Gakkai Jimu Senta, 4-16, Yayoi, 2 Chome, Bunkyoku, Tokyoto 113 Japan. **(Subscription address:** Kyowa Book Company Inc., 1 38 Kanda Jinbocho Chiyoda-ku, Tokyo 101 Japan.**) NLM** W1 AU215. **CODEN** ANLADF. Documents available from CASDDS.
**Ind/Abst** Chem. Abstr.; EMBASE; Health Plan. Adminis.; Index Med. (1978-).

AT/0157-1532
**AUSTRALIAN JOURNAL OF AUDIOLOGY, THE.** [Aust. j. audiol.]. **Added/Corp** Audiological Society of Australia. Vol. 1 (May 1979)-. Periodical. English. Twice a year (May & Nov.). 30.00Aus$ (individuals), 55.00Aus$ (institutions)

Australia; 45.00Aus$ (individuals), 80.00Aus$ (institutions) others. Australian Academic Press Pty. Ltd., 32 Jeays Street, Bowen Hills Queensland 4006 Australia. **Tel** 011 61 7 2571176, FAX 011 61 7 2525908. **ED** Denis Byrne, (editor's address: National Acoustic Laboratories, 126 Grevue Street, Chatswood New South Wales, 2067 Australia). **NLM** W1; AU554H. **Pr Rev.** Documents available from Ask*IEEE.
**Desc:** News and information on the hearing disorders and hearing.
**Ind/Abst** Acoust. Abstr.; EMBASE; INSPEC (Nov. 1982-).

•AT/1037-2105
**AUSTRALIAN JOURNAL OF OTO-LARYNGOLOGY : THE OFFICIAL JOURNAL OF THE AUSTRALIAN SOCIETY OF OTO-LARYNGOLOGY HEAD AND NECK SURGERY. Added/Corp** Australian Society of Oto-Laryngology, Head and Neck Surgery. **VFOAT** Australian Journal of Otolaryngology. Vol. 1, No. 1 (Jan. 1992)-. Periodical. English. ir. 50.00Aus$. Australian Society Otolaryngology, 33 35 Atchison Street, St. Leonards New South Wales, 2065 Australia. **Tel** 011 61 2 4385141. **NLM** W1; AU613J. ***Continues*** *Journal of the Oto-Laryngological Society of Australia, 0030-6614.*

UK/0300-5364
**BRITISH JOURNAL OF AUDIOLOGY.** [Br. j. audiol.]. **Added/Corp** Royal National Institute for the Deaf. British Society of Audiology. Vol. 7 (Feb. 1973)-. Academic Scholarly Publication. English. Six times a year (Feb., Apr., June, Aug., Oct., Dec.). £109.00 (institutions), £55.00 (individuals). Whurr Publishers Ltd, 19B Compton Terrace, London N1 2UN England. **Tel** 011 44 71 359 5979, FAX 011 44 71 226 5290. **(Subscription address:** Turpin Distribution Services Limited, Blackhorse Road, Letchworth, Hertfordshire SG6 1HN, United Kingdom.**)** **ED** Mark Lutman. **LC** QP460; .B74. **DD** 617.8/9/05. **NLM** W1 BR507. **CODEN** BJAYAC. **[CCC].** Index available. **Bk Rev. Ad Acc.** Full Page (B&W) ú385.00. Half Page (B&W) ú225.00. available on microfilm and microfiche from University Microfilms International (UMI). Documents available from The Genuine Article, BIOSIS Document Express. ***Continues*** *Sound.*
**Desc:** Covers specialist, technological and practical aspects of audiological studies; includes fundamental psychophysical and physiological research into hearing and hearing loss.
**Ind/Abst** Acoust. Abstr.; Appl. Soc. Sci. Index Abstr.; Biol. Abstr. (1985-); Curr. Contents Clin. Med.; Curr. Contents Life Sci.; EMBASE; Health Plan. Adminis.; Index Med. (1977-); Linguist. Lang. Behav. Abstr.; Res. Alert [Select. Cov.]; Sci. Cit. Index; Soc. Plann. Policy Dev. Abstr.; Soc. Sci. Cit. Index [Select. Cov.]; Sociol. Abstr.

US/0731-8359
**BULLETIN - AMERICAN ACADEMY OF OTOLARYNGOLOGY-HEAD AND NECK SURGERY, THE.** (THE BULLETIN / AMERICAN ACADEMY OF OTOLARYNGOLOGY-HEAD AND NECK SURGERY, INC.). [Bull. - Am. Acad. Otolaryngol.-Head Neck Surg.]. **Added/Corp** American Academy of Otolaryngology--Head and Neck Surgery. **VFOAT** AAO-HNS Bulletin; A.A.O.-H.N.S. Bulletin. Vol. 1, No. 1 (Jan. 1982)-. Bulletin. English. mo. $55.00 US; $65.00 other. American Academy Otolaryngology, One Prince Street, Alexandria VA 22314. **Tel** (703)836-4444. ***Continues*** *American Council of Otolaryngology. Newsletter - American Council of Otolaryngology, 0164-9965.*

FR/0395-3971
**CAHIERS D'OTO. RHINO. LARYNGOLOGIE, DE CHIRURGIE CERVICO. FACIALE ET D'AUDIOPHONOLOGIE, LES.** [Cah. oto-rhino-laryngol. chir. cervico-fac. audiophonol.]. **VFOAT** Cahiers d'Oto, Rhino, Laryngologie, de Chirurgie Cervico Faciale et d'Audiophonologie. Vol. 11 No. 1 (Jan. 1976)-. Academic Scholarly Publication. French. Ten times a year. 400.00F (France); 440.00F (other). Editions la Simarre, ZI 2 rue Joseph Cugnot, 37300 Joue-les-Tours France. **Tel** 11 33 47 535366, or 535134. **NLM** W1; CA143H. **CODEN** CCCADH. Documents available from CASDDS. ***Continues*** *Cahiers de' O.R.L. et de Chirurgie Cervico-Faciale, 0395-398X.*
**Ind/Abst** Chem. Abstr.

XR/0009-0603
**CESKOSLOVENSKA OTOLARYNGOLOGIE.** [Cesk. otolaryngol.]. **Added/Corp** Ceskoslovenska Otolaryngologicka Spolecnost. Vol. 1 (1952)-. Academic Scholarly Publication. Czech (summaries and/or abstracts in Russian and English). Six times a year. $81.90. Avicenum Medical Press, Malostranske Nam 28, 11802 Prague Czech Republic. **Tel** 011 42 2 530643. **(Subscription address:** Artia Pegas Press Ltd., Palac Metro Narodni Trida 25, 11210 Prague 1 Czech Republic.**)** **DD** 617. **NLM** W1 CE899. **CODEN** CEOTA9. **[CCC].** Documents available from CASDDS.
**Ind/Abst** Chem. Abstr. (1952-1983); EMBASE; Index Med.; Saf. Health Work.

UK/0307-7772
**CLINICAL OTOLARYNGOLOGY AND ALLIED SCIENCES.** (CLINICAL OTOLARYNGOLOGY.). [Clin. otolaryngol. allied sci.]. **VFOAT** Clinical Otolaryngology & Allied Sciences. Vol. 1 (1976)-. Academic Scholarly Publication. English. bm (6 issues). $418.00 US & Canada; £245.00 Europe; £269.50 other. Blackwell Scientific Publications Ltd, Marston Book Services, PO Box 87, Oxford OX2 ODT UK. **Tel** 011 44 865 791155, FAX 011 44 865 791927, telex 837 515 MARDIS G. **ED** J. Hibbert. **NLM** W1 CL761M. **CODEN** COTSD2. **[CCC]. Bk Rev. Ad Acc. Pr Rev. Circ:** 935 (ctrl). available on microfilm and microfiche from University Microfilms International (UMI). Documents available from The Genuine Article, BIOSIS Document Express.
**Desc:** Research papers dealing with current otorhinolaryngological practice and with audiology, speech pathology, head and neck oncology, head and neck plastic and reconstructive surgery.
**Ind/Abst** Biol. Abstr.; EMBASE; Index Med.; Res. Alert [Full Cov.]; Sci. Cit. Index; SCISEARCH; Soc. Sci. Cit. Index [Select. Cov.].

SP
**CLINICAS OTORRINOLARINGOLOGICAS DE NORTEAMERICA.** Spanish. McGraw Hill, Interamericana de Espana SA, Manuel Ferrero 13, 28036 Madrid Spain.

US/1054-8505
**CLINICS IN COMMUNICATION DISORDERS.** ***Title Change.*** [Clin. commun. disord.]. **VFOAT** Communication Disorders; CCD. Vol. 1, No. 1 (Spring 1991)-(199?). Periodical. English. qt (Mar., Jun., Sep., Dec.). Butterworth Heinemann / Woburn, MA, 225 Wildwood Avenue, Unit B, Woburn MA 01801. **Tel** (800)366-2665, FAX (617)928-2620, telex 880052. **LC** RC423.A1; C58. **DD** 616.85/5/005. **NLM** W1; CL831AH. **[CCC]. *Merged into*** *Journal of Communication Disorders.*

US/0734-0710
**CONJOINT DIRECTORY OF AMERICAN ACADEMY OF OTOLARYNGOLOGY-HEAD AND NECK SURGERY, AND AMERICAN ACADEMY OF FACIAL PLASTIC AND RECONSTRUCTIVE SURGERY, AND AMERICAN NEUROTOLOGY SOCIETY, AND AMERICAN RHINOLOGIC SOCIETY, AND AMERICAN SOCIETY OF OPHTHALMOLOGIC AND OTOLARYNGOLOGIC ALLERGY.** [Conjoint dir. Am. Acad. Otolaryngol.-Head Neck Surg. Am. Acad. Facial Plast. Reconstr. Surg. Am. Neurotol. Soc. Am. Rhinol. Soc. Am. Soc. Ophthalmol. Otolaryngol. Allergy]. **Added/Corp** American Academy of Otolaryngology--Head and Neck Surgery. **VFOAT** Conjoint Directory A.A.O., A.A.F.P.R.S., A.N.S., A.R.S. and A.S.O.O.A.; Conjoint Directory AAO, AAFPRS, ANS, ARS, and ASOOA. (1981)-. Directory. English. an (March). $25.00 (members), $100.00 (nonmembers), $250.00 (commercial). American Academy Otolaryngology, One Prince Street, Alexandria VA 22314. **Tel** (703)836-4444. **LC** RF28; .A52a. **DD** 617/.51/006073. ***Continues*** *Conjoint Directory of American Academy of Otolaryngology and American Academy of Facial Plastic and Reconstructive Surgery and American Society of Ophthalmologic and Otolaryngologic Allergy.*

•US/1068-9508
**CURRENT OPINION IN OTOLARYNGOLOGY & HEAD AND NECK SURGERY.** [Curr. opin. otolaryngol. head neck surg.]. **VFOAT** Current Opinion in Otolaryngology and Head and Neck Surgery. Vol. 1, No. 1 (Oct. 1993)-. Periodical. English. Six times a year. $129.95 (individuals); $259.95 (institutions). Current Science, 20 North 3rd Street, Philadelphia PA 19106. **Tel** (215)574-2266, (800)552-5866, FAX (215)574-2270. **DD** 617. **NLM** W1; CU799GGCR.

DK/0105-7200
**DANSK AUDIOLOGOPDI.** [Dan. audiologop.]. **Added/Corp** diologopdisk Forening. (1976)-. Periodical. Danish. Four times a year (Mar., May, Oct., Dec.). kr265.00. Audiologopaedisk Forening, V Inger Bruun Reinettevej 5, DK 8270 Hojbjerg Denmark. **Tel** 011 45 42803423, FAX 011 45 31385315. **ED** Sonja Hurwitz. **DD** 371.912 371.914. **Bk Rev,** (Qty: 20). **Ad Acc.** ctrl circ. ***Continues*** *Medlemsblad for Talepdagogisk Forening, 0105-7219.*

US
**DIRECTORY - LOUISIANA STATE BOARD OF EXAMINERS FOR SPEECH PATHOLOGY AND AUDIOLOGY. Main/Corp** Louisiana. State Board of Examiners for Speech Pathology and Audiology. Directory. English. Louisiana State Board of Examiners for Speech Pathology and Audiology, 712 Bath Street, Metarie LA 70001. **LC** RC428.5; .L68A. **DD** 616/85/506/025763.

IT/1120-8694
**DISEASES OF THE ESOPHAGUS : OFFICIAL JOURNAL OF THE INTERNATIONAL SOCIETY FOR DISEASES OF THE ESOPHAGUS / I.S.D.E. Added/Corp** International Society for Diseases of the Esophagus. Vol. 1, No. 1 (April 1988)-. Periodical. English. Four times a year. £191.00 Europe; £192.00 Other (Institutions). Churchill Livingstone, 1-3 Baxter's Place, Leith Walk, Edinburgh EH1 3AF Scotland. **Tel** 011 44 31 556 2424, FAX 011 44 31 558 1278, telex 727511. **(Subscription address:** Maruzen Company Ltd., PO Box 5050, Import & Export Department, Tokyo 100 31 Japan.**)** **NLM** W1; DI7558. ***Absorbed*** *Gullet.*
**Ind/Abst** EMBASE.

AU/0173-170X
**DISORDERS OF HUMAN COMMUNICATION.** ***Ceased.*** (1980)-Series complete. Monographic series. English. ir. Springer-Verlag Wien, Sachsenplatz 4 6, PO Box 89, A-1201 Vienna Austria. **Tel** 011 43 1 3302415. **(Subscription address:** Springer Verlag New York Inc. / for North America, 44 Hartz Way, Secaucus NJ 07096.**)** **ED** G.E. Arnold, F. Winckel, B.D. Wyke. **LC** UNC. **NLM** W1 DI762.
**Desc:** Concerned with communication disorder, articulation and surgical care of voice disorders.

US/0179-051X
**DYSPHAGIA.** [Dysphagia]. Vol. 1, No. 1 (1986)-. Periodical. English. Four times a year. $148.00. Springer-Verlag New York Inc., 175 5th Avenue, New York NY 10010. **Tel** (212)460-1500, telex 232 235 SPB UR. **(Subscription address:** Springer Verlag New York Inc. / for North America, 44 Hartz Way, Secaucus NJ 07096.**)** **ED** Bronwyn Jones. **NLM** W1; DY997. **CODEN** DYSPE2. **[CCC].** available on microfilm and microfiche from University Microfilms International (UMI). Documents available from BIOSIS Document Express.
**Desc:** Publishes original articles, case reports, review articles, and technical and instrumental notes. Its scope includes all aspects of normal and dysphagic ingestion involving the mouth, pharynx, and esophagus.
**Ind/Abst** Biol. Abstr.; Curr. Titl. Dent.; EMBASE; Health Plan. Adminis.; Index Med. (1990-); Index Dent. Lit. (1986-); Int. Nurs. Index.

US/0196-0202
**EAR AND HEARING.** [Ear hear.]. **Added/Corp** American Auditory Society. Vol. 1 (Jan./Feb. 1980)-. Periodical. English. bm. $52.00 (individual), $94.00 (institution) US; $72.00 (individual), $114.00 (institution) other. Williams & Wilkins Company, 428 East Preston Street, Baltimore MD 21202-3993. **Tel** (410)528-4000, (800)638-6423, FAX (410)528-8596, telex 87669. **(Subscription address:** Williams & Wilkins, PO Box 64380, Baltimore MD 21264.**)** **ED** Robert W. Keith. **LC** RF286; .E18. **DD** 617.8/005. **NLM** W1 EA59. **CODEN** EAHEDS. **[CCC]. Ad Acc. Pr Rev. Circ:** 3,500. available on microfilm. Documents available from , The Genuine Article, BIOSIS Document Express, Quick Copies. ***Supersedes*** *Journal of the American Auditory Society, 0164-5080.*
**Desc:** The official journal of the American Auditory Society. Original articles focus on assessment, diagnosis, and management of auditory disorders for audiologists.
**Ind/Abst** Acoust. Abstr.; Biol. Abstr. (1986-); Curr. Contents Clin. Med.; EMBASE; Energy Res. Abstr. (Aug. 1982-); Health Plan. Adminis.; Index Med. (Feb. 1980-); MLA Int. Bibl. Books Artic. Mod. Lang. Lit.; Life Sci. Collect.; Res. Alert [Full Cov.]; Sci. Cit. Index; SCISEARCH; Soc. Sci. Cit. Index [Select. Cov.].

US/0739-733X
**EAR CLINICS INTERNATIONAL.** [Ear clin. int.]. Vol. 1 (1981)-. Monographic series. English. ir. Price varies per volume. Williams & Wilkins Company, 428 East Preston Street, Baltimore MD 21202-3993. **Tel** (410)528-4000, (800)638-6423, FAX (410)528-8596, telex 87669. **(Subscription address:** Williams & Wilkins, PO Box 64380, Baltimore, MD 21264**)** **ED** Michael M. Paparella and William L. Meyerhoff. **LC** UNC. **DD** 617.8. **NLM** W3 EA117. **CODEN** ECINE7. Each issue contains an index to its own contents (no volume index)--loose. Documents available from , BIOSIS Document Express, , Quick Copies.
**Ind/Abst** Biol. Abstr. (?-1983);(-1983).

US/0145-5613
**EAR, NOSE & THROAT JOURNAL.** [Ear, nose, throat j.]. **VFOAT** ENT. **VAT** Ear, Nose, and Throat Journal. Vol. 55 No. 7 (July 1976)-. Periodical. English. mo. $100.00 (one year), $180.00 (two year), (individuals), $125.00 (one year), $230.00 (two year) (institutions) US; $120.00 (one year), $220.00 (two year), (individuals), $135.00 (one year), $250.00 (two year) (institutions) Canada and Mexico; $140.00 (one year), $260.00 (two year) (individuals), $160.00 (one year), $300.00 (two year) (institutions) other. Medquest Communications Inc., 629 Euclid Avenue, Suite 500, Cleveland OH 44114. **Tel** (216)522-9700. **(Subscription address:** PO Box 20179, Cleveland, OH 44120**)** **ED** Jack Pulec. **DD** 616. **NLM** W1 EA65. **Pr Rev.** available on microfilm and microfiche from

University Microfilms International (UMI). ***Continues*** *Eye, Ear, Nose & Throat Monthly, 0014-5491.*
**Desc:** Case studies for otorhinolaryngologists in private and hospital practice, and physicians in otology, laryngology, rhinology, head and neck surgery, allergy and immunology.
**Ind/Abst** EMBASE; Energy Res. Abstr. (Aug. 1982-); Health Plan. Adminis.; Index Med.; Life Sci. Collect.

GW/0937-4477
**EUROPEAN ARCHIVES OF OTO-RHINO-LARYNGOLOGY.** (EUROPEAN ARCHIVES OF OTO-RHINO-LARYNGOLOGY : OFFICIAL JOURNAL OF THE EUROPEAN FEDERATION OF OTO-RHINO-LARYNGOLOGICAL SOCIETIES (EUFOS).). [Eur. arch. oto-rhino-laryngol.]. **Added/Corp** European Federation of Oto-Rhino-Laryngological Societies. Deutsche Gesellschaft fuer Hals-Nasen-Ohrenheilkunde, Kopf- und Halschirurgie. **VFOAT** European Archives of Otorhinolaryngology. Vol. 247, No. 1 (Jan. 1990)-. Periodical. English. Eight times a year. DM1298.00. Springer-Verlag GmbH & Company KG, Heidelberger Platz 3, D 14197 Berlin Germany. **Tel** 011 49 30 8207223, FAX 011 49 30 8214091, telex 183 319 SPBLN D. **(Subscription address:** Springer Verlag New York Inc. / for North America, 44 Hartz Way, Secaucus NJ 07096.**)** **NLM** W1; EU612FE. **CODEN** EAOTE7. available on microfilm from University Microfilms International (UMI). Documents available from The Genuine Article, BIOSIS Document Express. ***Continues*** *Archives of Oto-Rhino-Laryngology, 0302-9530.*
**Ind/Abst** Biol. Abstr.; Curr. Contents Clin. Med.; EMBASE; Health Plan. Adminis.; Index Med. (1990-); Res. Alert [Full Cov.]; Rev. Med. Vet. Entomol.; Sci. Cit. Index; SCISEARCH.

●GW/0934-2400
**EUROPEAN ARCHIVES OF OTO-RHINO-LARYNGOLOGY. SUPPLEMENT.** **Added/Corp** European Federation of Oto-Rhino-Laryngological Societies. (1992)-. Monographic series. English. ir. Price varies per volume. Springer-Verlag GmbH & Company KG, Heidelberger Platz 3, D 14197 Berlin Germany. **Tel** 011 49 30 8207223, FAX 011 49 30 8214091, telex 183 319 SPBLN D. **(Subscription address:** Springer Verlag New York Inc. / for North America, 44 Hartz Way, Secaucus NJ 07096.**)** **NLM** W1; EU612FEA. ***Continues*** *Archives of Oto-Rhino-Laryngology. Supplement, 0724-7907.*
**Ind/Abst** Index Med. (1992-).

NE/0014-4150
**EXCERPTA MEDICA. SECTION 11. OTO-, RHINO-, LARYNGOLOGY.** (OTO-, RHINO-, LARYNGOLOGY.). [Excerpta Med., Sect. 11, Oto-rhino-. laryngol.]. **VAT** Excerpta Medica. Section Eleven. Oto-, Rhino-, Laryngology. Vol. 1 (Jan. 1948)-. Academic Scholarly Publication. English. Sixteen times a year (2 vols.). Fl1692.00. Excerpta Medica Publishing Group, PO Box 548, 1000 AM Amsterdam Netherlands. **Tel** 011 31 20 5803243. **(Subscription address:** Excerpta Medica Journals, PO Box 85, Limerick Ireland.**)** **ED** M W Woerdeman. **LC** RF1; .O83. **DD** 616.2005. **NLM** ZW 1 E964. **CODEN** ORLGA8. **[CCC].** available on microfilm from University Microfilms International (UMI); available on CD-ROM. Documents available from CASDDS.
**Desc:** The information is organized on an anatomical basis with separate chapters for each part of the body falling within the otorhinolaryngological area.
**Ind/Abst** Chem. Abstr.

SZ/0015-5705
**FOLIA PHONIATRICA.** ***Title Change.*** [Folia phoniatr.]. Vol. 1, No. 1 (1947)-(199?). Periodical. English (French and German). bm. S. Karger AG, Allschwilerstrasse 10, PO Box - Postfach - Case Postale, CH-4009 Basel Switzerland. **Tel** 011 41 61 306-1111, FAX 011 41 61 306-1234, telex CH 962 652. **ED** E Loebell, K G Butler, S Fex, N Kotby, R Luchsinger, H Oyer and J Perello. **LC** RC423. **UDC** 616.22-008.2; 612.789. **NLM** W1 FO281. **CODEN** FOPHAD. **[CCC]. Ad Acc. Pr Rev.** available on microfilm from University Microfilms International (UMI). Documents available from The Genuine Article, BIOSIS Document Express, CASDDS. ***Continued by*** *Folia PHoniatrica et Logopedica.*
**Desc:** Provides a survey of international research in physiology and pathology of speech and the voice organs. Original papers published in this journal report recent findings in the assessment of vocal functions and in the detection, therapy, and rehabilitation of speech disorders. Contributors present results of experimental investigations important for instruction and further study. Thus this periodical is essential reading for medical and other professionals concerned with education, social work and training of singers and actors.
**Ind/Abst** Arts Humanit. Citation Index [Select. Cov.]; Biol. Abstr.; Chem. Abstr.; Cumul. Index Nurs. Allied Health Lit.; Curr. Contents Soc. Behav. Sci.; EMBASE; Health Plan. Adminis.; Index Med.; Middle East Abstr. Index; MLA Int. Bibl. Books Artic. Mod. Lang. Lit.; Life Sci. Collect.; Psychol. Abstr. (1982-); PsycINFO; PsycLit; Ref. Upd. Deluxe Ed.; Res. Alert [Full Cov.]; Soc. Sci. Cit. Index [Full Cov.].

●SZ/1021-7762
**FOLIA PHONIATRICA ET LOGOPAEDICA : OFFICIAL ORGAN OF THE INTERNATIONAL ASSOCIATION OF LOGOPEDICS AND PHONIATRICS (IALP).** **Added/Corp** International Association of Logopedics and Phoniatrics. (Jan./Feb. 1994)-. Periodical. English (French and German). Six times a year. $208.00. S. Karger AG, Allschwilerstrasse 10, PO Box - Postfach - Case Postale, CH-4009 Basel Switzerland. **Tel** 011 41 61 306-1111, FAX 011 41 61 306-1234, telex CH 962 652. **ED** E. Loebell, K.G. Butler, S. Fex, N. Kotby, H. Oyer, J. Perello. **NLM** W1; FO281M. ***Continues*** *Folia Phoniatrica, 0015-5705.*
**Desc:** Provides a survey of international research in physiology and pathology of speech and the voice organs. Original papers report recent findings in the assessment of vocal functions and in the detection, therapy, and rehabilitation of speech disorders.

HU/0016-237X
**FUL-, ORR-, GEGEGYOGYASZAT.** [Ful-, Orr-, Gegegyogy.]. **Added/Corp** Orvos-Egeszsegugyi Szakszervezet. Ful-, Orr-, Gegesz Szakcsoport. Vol. 1 (1955)-. Academic Scholarly Publication. Hungarian (summaries and/or abstracts in English, German and Russian). qt. $36.00. Ifjusagi Lap -es Konyvkiado Vallalat, Revay u. 16, H-1374, Budapest, 6 Hungary. **(Subscription address:** Kultura, PO Box 149, H 1389 Budapest 62 Hungary.**)** **ED** Dr. T. Szekely. **NLM** W1 FU495. **CODEN** FOGGAX. available with illustrations.
**Ind/Abst** EMBASE.

GW/0930-8318
**GIATROS HNO.** [Giatros HNO]. **VFOAT** Giatros Hals, Nasen, Ohren; Jatros HNO. (1986)-. Periodical. German. mo. DM150.00. Universimed Verlag GmbH, August-Schanz Strasse 21, W-6000 Frankfurt 50 Germany. **Tel** 011 49 69 5480000, FAX 069/54 80 00-77. **UDC** 616.21. **Bk Rev. Ad Acc. Pr Rev. Circ:** 3,000 (ctrl).

US/0092-4466
**HEARING INSTRUMENTS.** [Hear. instrum.]. (1951)-. Periodical. English. mo. $50.00 US and possessions; $75.00 Canada; $120.00 other. Advanstar Communications Inc., 131 West First Street, Duluth MN 55802. **Tel** (218)723-9477, (800)346-0085. **ED** Marjorie D Skafte. **LC** RF310; .H43. **DD** 617.8/9. **NLM** W1 HE6415I. **[CCC]. Bk Rev. Ad Acc. Circ:** 18,622 (ctrl). available on microfilm and microfiche from University Microfilms International (UMI). ***Continues*** *Hearing Dealer, 0017-9205.*
**Desc:** Articles detailing new research and products utilized in hearing health care; also covers marketing methods, news of industry, product reviews, listings of industry events.

US/0745-7472
**HEARING JOURNAL, THE.** [Hear. j.]. Vol. 36, No. 1 (Jan. 1983)-. Periodical. English. mo. $45.00 US; $89.00 other. Williams & Wilkins Company, 428 East Preston Street, Baltimore MD 21202-3993. **Tel** (410)528-4000, (800)638-6423, FAX (410)528-8596, telex 87669. **(Subscription address:** Williams & Wilkins, PO Box 64380, Baltimore MD 21264.**)** **ED** David H. Kirkwood. **DD** 617. **NLM** W1; HE6416. **Bk Rev. Ad Acc. Circ:** 20,000 (ctrl). Documents available from Quick Copies. ***Continues*** *Hearing Aid Journal, 0091-2166.*
**Desc:** Features articles on major issues affecting the hearing impaired, technical investigative reports, and industry news for audiologists, hearing aid specialists, otolaryngologists and other health care specialists.
**Ind/Abst** Psychol. Abstr. (1983-).

NE/0378-5955
**HEARING RESEARCH.** [Hear. res.]. Vol. 1 (1978)-. Academic Scholarly Publication. English. Twenty-two times a year (11 volumes). Fl4444.00. Elsevier Science Publishers BV, PO Box 211, 1000 AE Amsterdam Netherlands. **Tel** 011 31 20 5803642, FAX 011 31 20 5862696, telex 15682. **ED** Aage R Moller. **NLM** W1 HE6419. **CODEN** HERED3. **[CCC]. Pr Rev.** available on microfilm and microfiche from University Microfilms International (UMI). Documents available from The Genuine Article, BIOSIS Document Express, Ask*IEEE, CASDDS.
**Desc:** Provides a forum for papers concerned with basic auditory mechanisms. Emphasis is on experimental studies, but theoretical papers will also be considered.
**Ind/Abst** Acoust. Abstr.; Biol. Abstr.; Chem. Abstr.; CSA Neuro. Abstr.; Curr. Aware. Biol. Sci., CABS; Curr. Contents Life Sci.; EMBASE; Index Med.; Index Vet.; INSPEC (Jan. 1984-); Life Sci. Collect.; Pig News Inf.; Ref. Upd. Deluxe Ed.; Res. Alert [Full Cov.]; Rev. Med. Vet. Entomol.; Sci. Cit. Index; SCISEARCH; Soc. Sci. Cit. Index [Select. Cov.]; Vet. Bull.

GW/0017-6192
**HNO.** (HNO; WEGWEISER FUER DIE FACHRZTLICHE PRAXIS. BEIHEFT ZUR ZEITSCHRIFT FUER HALS-, NASEN-, UND OHRENHEILKUNDE.). [HNO]. **VAT** Hals- Nasen- Ohrenheilkunde. (1947)-. Academic Scholarly Publication. German. Twelve times a year. DM348.00. Springer-Verlag GmbH & Company KG, Heidelberger Platz 3, D 14197 Berlin Germany. **Tel** 011 49 30 8207223, FAX 011 49 30 8214091, telex 183 319 SPBLN D. **(Subscription address:** Springer Verlag New York Inc. / for North America, 44 Hartz Way, Secaucus NJ 07096.**)** **ED** K Albegger, K Fleischer, R Chilla, K Ehrenberger, U Fisch, J Helms, O Kleinsasser, E Lehnhardt, C R Pfaltz, H Rudert, K Terrahe, M E Wigand, and H P Zenner. **NLM** W1 H143. **CODEN** HBZHAS. **[CCC]. Pr Rev.** available on microfilm from University Microfilms International (UMI). Documents available from The Genuine Article, BIOSIS Document Express, CASDDS.
**Desc:** Reports on the newest results from research in the field. Articles aimed primarily at practicing doctors for their continuing education.
**Ind/Abst** Biol. Abstr.; Chem. Abstr.; EMBASE; Energy Res. Abstr.; Health Plan. Adminis.; Index Med.; Protozoolog. Abstr.; Res. Alert [Select. Cov.]; Soc. Sci. Cit. Index [Select. Cov.].

GW/0173-9859
**HNO PRAXIS HEUTE.** **VFOAT** H.N.O. Praxis Heute. 1-. German. an. Springer-Verlag New York Inc., 175 5th Avenue, New York NY 10010. **Tel** (212)460-1500, telex 232 235 SPB UR. **(Subscription address:** Springer Verlag New York Inc. / for North America, 44 Hartz Way, Secaucus NJ 07096.**)** **ED** H Ganz. **UDC** 616.21. **NLM** W1 HN677. ***Continues*** *HNO-Erkrankungen.*

US
**HOUSE EAR INSTITUTE. REVIEW.** (19??)-. English. tq. $5.00. House Ear Institute, 2100 W. Third St. 5th Floor, Los Angeles CA 90057. **Tel** (213)483-4431. **ED** Nancy Miron. **Circ:** 22,000. ***Continues*** *Oto Review, 0197-0674.*

II/0019-5421
**INDIAN JOURNAL OF OTOLARYNGOLOGY.** [Indian j. otolaryngol.]. **Added/Corp** Association of Otolaryngologists of India. (1949)-. Periodical. English. Four times a year (Mar., June, Sept., Dec.). $50.00. Association Otolaryngologists India, Old Dog Race C Block LH Flat 4, Calcutta 700 038 India. **ED** Shyamal Kumar. **LC** RF1. **DD** 616.2/1/05. **NLM** W1 IN224. **CODEN** IJOLBJ. **Bk Rev. Ad Acc. Circ:** 2,500 (ctrl). Documents available from BIOSIS Document Express.
**Desc:** Official publication of Association of Otolaryngologists of India containing scientific papers on ear, nose, and throat from authors of India and abroad.
**Ind/Abst** Biol. Abstr.

●II
**INDIAN JOURNAL OF OTOLARYNGOLOGY, AND HEAD, AND NECK : OFFICIAL PUBLICATION OF THE ASSOCIATION OF OTOLARYNGOLOGISTS OF INDIA.** **Added/Corp** Association of Otolaryngologists of India. Vol. 1, No 1 (Mar. 1992)-. Periodical. English. qt. $50.00. **(Subscription address:** Prints India, 11 Darya Ganj, New Delhi 110002 India.**)** **NLM** W1; IN224AL. ***Continues*** *Indian Journal of Otolaryngology, 0019-5421.*

NE/0165-5876
**INTERNATIONAL JOURNAL OF PEDIATRIC OTORHINOLARYNGOLOGY.** **See** Medical Science and Technology-Pediatrics.

US/0147-3026
**INTERNATIONAL OTORHINOLARYNGOLOGICAL REPORTER.** **VFOAT** Otorhinolaryngological Reporter. Vol. 1, (1977)-. Periodical. English. mo. $31.50. Intercontinental Publications, PO Box 5017, Westport CT 06880. **Tel** (203)226-7463, FAX (203)222-8793.

JA/0032-6313
**JIBI INKOKA RINSHO.** [Jibi inkoka rinsho]. **Added/Corp** Jibi Inkoka Rinsho Kai. **VFOAT** Oto-Rhino and Laryngological Clinic; Practica Otologica Kyoto; Zibi-Inko-Ka Rinsyo. (1908)-. Periodical. Japanese. mo. Society of Practical Otolarygology, 54 Shogoin Kawaharaco, Sakyo-ku, 606, Kyoto, Japan. **NLM** W1 JI264. **CODEN** JIBIAG. Documents available from BIOSIS Document Express.
**Ind/Abst** Biol. Abstr.; EMBASE [Select. Cov.].

JA/0386-9687
**JIBI INKOKA TENBO.** [Jibi inkoka tenbo]. **VFOAT** Oto-Rhino-Laryngology Tokyo. (1958)-. Periodical. Multiple languages. bm. Society of Oto-Rhino-Laryngology Tokyo, 25-8 Nishinbashi 3-chome, Minato-ku, 105, Tokyo, Japan. **DD** _a616.21.
**Ind/Abst** EMBASE [Select. Cov.].

JA/0914-3491
**JIBI INKOKA, TOKEIBU GEKA 1988.** [Jibi inkoka, tokeibu geka 1988]. **VFOAT** Otolaryngology-Head and Neck Surgery, Tokyo. (1988)-. Periodical. Multiple languages. Twelve times a year. $462.50. Igaku Shoin Ltd., 5-24-3 Hongo Bunkyo-ku, Tokyo 113 Japan. **Tel** 011 81 3 817 5670. **(Subscription address:** Japan Publications Trading Company, Ltd., PO Box 5030, Tokyo International, Tokyo 100-31 Japan.**)** **DD** 616.21 617.5. ***Continues*** *Jibi Inkoka, 0386-9679.*
**Ind/Abst** EMBASE.

JA/0447-7227
**JIBI TO RINSHO.** [Jibi to rinsho]. **Added/Corp** Kyushu Daigaku. Igakubu. Jibi Inko Kagaku Kyoshitsunai. **VFOAT** Otologia. Began in 1954. Academic Scholarly Publication. Japanese. qt. $110.50. Kushu Daigaku Igakubu, 1276 Kataksu Fukvoka-shi, Fukvoka Japan. **CODEN** JIRIAS. Documents available from BIOSIS Document Express, CASDDS.
**Ind/Abst** Biol. Abstr.; Chem. Abstr. (1954-1983); EMBASE; Soc. Plann. Policy Dev. Abstr.; Sociol. Abstr. (1954-1983).

FR/0398-9771
**JOURNAL FRANCAIS D'OTO-RHINO-LARYNGOLOGIE.** [J. fr. d'oto-rhino-laryngologie]. Vol. 26 (Jan. 1977)-. Periodical. French (summaries and/or abstracts in English). Six times a year. $200.00 Institutions; $85.00 Individual. Societe d'Edition pour l'Information et la Publicite, 49 rue Servient, 69423 Lyon Cedex 03 France. **Tel** 011 33 78 710055. **UDC** 616.21. **NLM** W1 JO442Z. **Ad Acc.** ctrl circ. ***Continues*** *JFORL. Journal Francais d'Oto-Rhino-Laryngologie, 0398-9763.*
**Ind/Abst** EMBASE; Index Med.

●UK/0963-7133
**JOURNAL OF AUDIOLOGICAL MEDICINE.** **Added/Corp** International Association of Physicians in Audiology. **VFOAT** JAM. (1992)-. Periodical. English. Three times a year. £38.00 (individuals), £5.00 (institutions). Whurr Publishers Ltd, 19B Compton Terrace, London N1 2UN England. **Tel** 011 44 71 359 5979, FAX 011 44 71 226 5290. **(Subscription address:** Turpin Distribution Services Limited, Blackhorse Road, Letchworth, Hertfordshire SG6 1HN, United Kingdom.**)** **ED** L. Luxon, S. D. Stephens and V. Colletti. **NLM** W1; JO546J. **Bk Rev. Ad Acc.** Full Page (B&W) ú250.00. Half Page (B&W) ú150.00. **Acid Free.**
**Desc:** Aims to provide forum for the many diverse aspects of audiological medicine. Papers are submitted primarily by Audiological Physicians, but papers from other medical disciplines related to audiological medicine are encouraged. The journal will include occasional reviews of topical subjects together with brief communications which would not justify publication as a full paper.

UK/0022-2151
**JOURNAL OF LARYNGOLOGY AND OTOLOGY.** [J. laryngol. otol.]. Vol. 36 (1921)-. Academic Scholarly Publication. English. Twelve times a year (also includes supplements). £95.00 institutions. £85.00 individuals. Headley Brothers Ltd., The Invicta Press, Queens Road, Ashford Kent TN24 8HH England. **Tel** 011 44 233 623131. **ED** Neil Weir. **NLM** W1; JO736. **CODEN** JLOTAX. cum. index. **Ad Acc. Pr Rev. Circ:** 2,500. available on microfilm and microfiche from University Microfilms International (UMI). Documents available from The Genuine Article, BIOSIS Document Express, CASDDS. ***Continues*** *Journal of Laryngology, Rhinology, and Otology.*
**Desc:** Contains original scientific articles and clinical records in all fields of otology, rhinology and laryngology.
**Ind/Abst** Abr. Index Med.; Biol. Abstr.; Chem. Abstr.; Curr. Contents Clin. Med.; EMBASE; Health Period. Database; Helminthol. Abstr. (1991-); Index Med.; Int. Aerosp. Abstr.; Microbiol. Abstr. Sect. B (19??-19??); Life Sci. Collect.; Physic. Medline Plus; Protozoolog. Abstr.; Res. Alert [Full Cov.]; Rev. Med. Vet. Entomol.; Rev. Med. Vet. Mycology; Rev. Plant Pathol.; Sci. Cit. Index; SCISEARCH; Soc. Sci. Cit. Index [Select. Cov.].

UK/0144-2945
**JOURNAL OF LARYNGOLOGY AND OTOLOGY. SUPPLEMENT, THE.** [J. laryngol. otol., Suppl.]. No. 1 (Oct. 1978)-. English. ir (comes with The Journal of Laryngology and Otology). Includes journal: £95.00 institutions; £85.00 individuals. Headley Brothers Ltd., The Invicta Press, Queens Road, Ashford Kent TN24 8HH England. **Tel** 011 44 233 623131. **NLM** W1 JO736A.
**Ind/Abst** Index Med.

CN/0381-6605
**JOURNAL OF OTOLARYNGOLOGY, THE.** [J. otolaryngol.]. **Added/Corp** O R L Medical Publications. **VFOAT** Journal d'Otolaryngologie. Vol. 5, (Feb. 1976)-. Periodical. English (French; summaries and/or abstracts in French). bm. 125.00Can$ (institutions), 83.00Can$ (individuals) US & Canada; 135.00Can$ (institutions), 99.00Can$ (individuals) other. Decker Periodicals Publishing Inc, PO Box 620, Station A, Hamilton Ontario L8N 3K7 Canada. **Tel** (416)522-7017, (800) 568-7281, FAX (416)522-7839. **ED** Derek Birt. **DD** 616.2/1/05. **NLM** W1 JO812. **CODEN** JOTODX. Index available. cum. index. **Bk Rev. Ad Acc. Pr Rev. Circ:** 1,300 (ctrl). available on microfilm and microfiche from University Microfilms International (UMI). Documents available from The Genuine Article, BIOSIS Document Express. ***Continues*** *Canadian Journal of Otolaryngology, 0045-5083.*
**Desc:** Manuscripts of original material dealing with clinical and new research aspects of otolaryngology in its broadest sense, including audiology and head and neck surgery are published.
**Ind/Abst** Biol. Abstr.; Curr. Contents Clin. Med.; EMBASE; Index Med.; Life Sci. Collect.; Res. Alert [Select. Cov.]; SCISEARCH.

CN/0707-7270
**JOURNAL OF OTOLARYNGOLOGY. SUPPLEMENT, THE.** [J. otolaryngol., Suppl.]. **VFOAT** Journal d'Oto-Rhino-Laryngologie. Supplement. No. 3 (1977)-. Monographic series. English (summaries and/or abstracts in French). ir. Free to subscribers of The Journal of Otolaryngology. Decker Periodicals Publishing Inc, PO Box 620, Station A, Hamilton Ontario L8N 3K7 Canada. **Tel** (416)522-7017, (800) 568-7281, FAX (416)522-7839. **ED** Derek Birt. **DD** 616.2/1/005. **NLM** W1 JO812A. **Bk Rev. Ad Acc. Circ:** 1,200 (ctrl). ***Continues*** *Canadian Journal of Otolaryngology; Journal Canadien d'Otolaryngologie Supplement.*
**Desc:** Official journal of the Canadian Otolaryngology Society - Head and Neck Surgery.
**Ind/Abst** Index Med. (1977-1986).

US
**JOURNAL OF SPEECH-LANGUAGE-HEARING ASSOCIATION OF VIRGINIA.** **Added/Corp** Speech-Language-Hearing Association of Virginia. **VFOAT** SHAV Journal. Vol. 31, No. 1 (Summer 1990)-. Periodical. English. sa. $20.00. Speech & Hearing Association of Virginia, 1604 Cedar Lane, Richmond VA 23225. **Tel** (804)232-4143. **LC** RC423; .S635. **DD** 616.85/5/005. **Pr Rev.** ***Continues*** *Speech and Hearing Association of Virginia. Journal of the Speech and Hearing Association of Virginia.*

US/0149-8886
**JOURNAL OF THE ACADEMY OF REHABILITATIVE AUDIOLOGY.** **Added/Corp** Academy of Rehabilitative Audiology. Vol. 3 No. 2 (Oct. 1970)-. Periodical. English. an. $17.50 North America; $20.00 (surface mail), $25.00 (airmail) other. JARA Business Manager Department of Communicative Disorders, CAC 229, University of Northern Iowa, Cedar Falls IA 50614. **Tel** (319)273-2542, FAX (319)273-3509. **LC** RF297; .A25a. **DD** 362.4/2/05. **NLM** W1 JO907CH. ctrl circ. ***Continues*** *Newsletter (Academy of Rehabilitative Audiology), 0149-8878.*
**Ind/Abst** Except. Child Educ. Resour.; Psychol. Abstr. (1985-); PsycINFO; PsycLit; Soc. Plann. Policy Dev. Abstr.

II/0377-0524
**JOURNAL OF THE ALL INDIA INSTITUTE OF SPEECH AND HEARING, THE.** [J. All India Inst. Speech Hear.]. **Main/Corp** All India Institute of Speech and Hearing. **Added/Corp** All India Institute of Speech and Hearing. A.I.I.S.H. Journal. **VFOAT** A.I.I.S.H. Journal. (19??)-. English. an. $15.00. All India Institute of Speech & Hearing, Mysore, India. **(Subscription address:** Prints India, 11 Darya Ganj, New Delhi, 110002 India, (Phone: 011 91 11 3268645)**)** **LC** RC423.A1; A49a. **DD** 616.8/55/00954. **NLM** W1; JO907R. **CODEN** JAIHDT.

CN/1050-0545
**JOURNAL OF THE AMERICAN ACADEMY OF AUDIOLOGY.** [J. Am. Acad. Audiol.]. **Added/Corp** American Academy of Audiology. **VFOAT** JAAA. Vol. 1, No. 1 (Jan. 1990)-. Periodical. English. Six times a year. $135.00 (institutions), $98.00 (individuals) US & Canada; $160.00 (institutions), $128.00 (individuals) other. Decker Periodicals Publishing Inc, PO Box 620, Station A, Hamilton Ontario L8N 3K7 Canada. **Tel** (416)522-7017, (800) 568-7281, FAX (416)522-7839. **ED** James Jerger. **LC** RF286; .J68. **DD** 617. **NLM** W1; JO907VK. **CODEN** JAAAE3. **[CCC].**
**Desc:** Devoted exclusively to audiology. Features original contributions, abstracts, research rreports, case studies and a clinical forum.
**Ind/Abst** Index Med. (1990-).

US/0957-4271
**JOURNAL OF VESTIBULAR RESEARCH.** [J. vestib. res.]. Vol. 1, No. 1 (1991)-. Periodical. English. Six times a year. $261.00 The Americas; £175.00 other. Pergamon Press, An Imprint of Elsevier Science Ltd., The Boulevard, Langford Lane, Kidlington, Oxford OX5 1GB United Kingdom. **Tel** 011 44 865 843000, 011 44 865 843699, FAX 011 44 865 843010. **(Subscription address:** Elsevier Science Ltd. Oxford Fulfillment Centre, PO Box 800, Kidlington, Oxford OX5 1DX United Kingdom.**)** **ED** Ralph Jell and Desmond Ireland. **LC** QP471; .J68. **DD** 612.8/58. **NLM** W1; JO97J. **CODEN** JVEREH. **[CCC].** available on microfilm and microfiche from University Microfilms International (UMI). Documents available from The Genuine Article.
**Ind/Abst** Curr. Aware. Biol. Sci., CABS; Res. Alert [Full Cov.]; Soc. Sci. Cit. Index [Select. Cov.].

GW/0935-8943
**LARYNGO- RHINO- OTOLOGIE.** **Added/Corp** Deutsche Gesellschaft fuer Hals-Nasen-Ohrenheilkunde, Kopf- und Halschirurgie. Osterreichische Gesellschaft fuer Hals-, Nasen-, Ohrenheilkunde, Kopf- und Halschirurgie. Vol. 68, No. 1 (Jan. 1989)-. Periodical. German (summaries and/or abstracts in English). mo. $232.00. Georg Thieme Verlag Stuttgart, Postfach 301120, D 70451 Stuttgart Germany. **Tel** 011 49 711 89310, FAX 011 49 711 8931298, telex 7 252 275 GTVD. **(Subscription address:** Thieme Medical Publishers Inc., 381 Park Avenue South, New York NY 10016.**)** **NLM** W1; LA777L. **CODEN** LROTEX. available on microfilm from University Microfilms International (UMI). Documents available from The Genuine Article, BIOSIS Document Express. ***Continues*** *Laryngologie, Rhinologie, Otologie, 0340-1588.*
**Ind/Abst** Biol. Abstr. (1989-); Curr. Contents Clin. Med.; EMBASE; Health Plan. Adminis.; Index Med. (Jan. 1989-); Protozoolog. Abstr.; Res. Alert [Select. Cov.]; Rev. Med. Vet. Mycology; SCISEARCH.

US/0023-852X
**LARYNGOSCOPE, THE.** [Laryngoscope]. **Added/Corp** American Otological Society. American Laryngological, Rhinological, and Otological Society. Vol. 1 (July 1896)-. Academic Scholarly Publication. English. mo. $150.00 (institutions), $110.00 (individuals) US; $175.00 (institutions), $135.00 (individuals) other. Laryngoscope, 10 South Broadway, 14th Floor, Suite 1401, St Louis MO 63102-1741. **Tel** (314)621-6550, FAX (314)621-6688. **ED** J. Gershon Spector. **DD** 616. **NLM** W1; LA78. **CODEN** LARYA8. **[CCC].** Index available. cum. index. **Bk Rev. Ad Acc. Pr Rev. Circ:** 8,031 (ctrl). available on microfilm and microfiche from University Microfilms International (UMI). Documents available from The Genuine Article, CASDDS.
**Desc:** A medical journal for clinical and research contributions in otolaryngology, head and neck medicine and surgery, facial plastic and reconstructive surgery, broncho-esophagology, maxillofacial surgery, communicative disorders, otology and otoneurology.
**Ind/Abst** Chem. Abstr.; CSA Neuro. Abstr. (?-?); Curr. Contents Clin. Med.; EMBASE; Energy Res. Abstr.; For. Prod. Abstr.; Health Period. Database; Index Med.; Int. Aerosp. Abstr.; Med. Abstr. Newsl.; Nucl. Sci. Abstr.; Nutr. Abstr. Rev., Ser. A, Hum. Exp.; Life Sci. Collect.; Physic. Medline Plus; Ref. Upd. Deluxe Ed.; Res. Alert [Full Cov.]; Rev. Med. Vet. Mycology; Sci. Cit. Index; SCISEARCH; Soc. Sci. Cit. Index [Select. Cov.].

US
**LARYNGOSCOPE. SUPPLEMENT, THE.** No. 1 (1974)-. Periodical. English. mo. $90.00 US $110.00 other. The Laryngoscope, Business Office, 9216 Clayton Road, St Louis MO 63124-1561. **Tel** (314)997-5070, FAX (314)997-2890. **ED** Gershon J Spector. **UDC** 616.22-072.1. Index available. cum. index. **Bk Rev. Ad Acc. Circ:** 8,400. available on microfilm.
**Desc:** Clinical and research contributions in otolaryngology, head and neck medicine and surgery.

GW
**LOGOTHERAPIA.** Vol. 1, No. 1 (1983)-. Monographic series. German. Price varies per volume. Carl Marhold Verlag, Postfach 191409, W-1000 Berlin 19 Germany. **NLM** W1; LO1055L.

CN/0845-8995
**MEMBERSHIP DIRECTORY / OSLA.** [Membersh. dir. - Ont. Assoc. Speech-Lang. Pathol. Audiol.]. **Main/Corp** Ontario Association of Speech-Language Pathologists and Audiologists. (1987)-. Directory. English. Ontario Speech and Hearing Association, 22 College Street, Suite 401, Toronto, Ont. M5G 1K2 Canada. **DD** 616.85/5/0025713. ***Continues*** *Membership Directory / OSLA, 0821-4921.*

US/0892-1873
**MONOGRAPHS IN CONTEMPORARY AUDIOLOGY.** [Monogr. contemp. audiol.]. Began with: Vol. 1, No. 1, published in 1978. Periodical. English. qt. $6.00. Instrumentation Associates Inc, Darby PA 19082. **Tel** (215)734-2380. **DD** 617. **UDC** 612.85; 616.28-008.1. **NLM** W1; MO567KS.

NZ/0110-571X
**NEW ZEALAND SPEECH-LANGUAGE THERAPISTS' JOURNAL, THE.** **VFOAT** Speech-Language Therapists' Journal. Vol. 38, No. 1 (May 1983)-. Periodical. English. sa (2 issues). 16.00NZ$. Speech Therapy Clinic, Christchurch East School, Gloucester Street, Christchurch New Zealand. **ED** D. Murray Gordon. **NLM** W1; NE984J. **[CCC]. Bk Rev. Ad Acc. Circ:** 300. ***Continues*** *New Zealand Speech Therapists' Journal.*
**Desc:** Articles related to disorders of human communication, including speech and language therapy.
**Ind/Abst** Annu. Bibliogr. Engl. Lang. Lit.

JA/0030-6622
**NIPPON JIBI INKOKA GAKKAI KAIHO.** (NIPPON JIBIINKOKA GAKKAI KAIHO. JOURNAL OF OTOLARYNGOLOGY OF JAPAN.). [Nippon Jibi Inkoka Gakkai Kaiho]. **Added/Corp** Nippon Jibiinkoka Gakkai. Journal of Otolaryngology of Japan. Nippon Jibiinkoka Gakkai. **VFOAT** Journal of Otolaryngology of Japan. (1947)-. Academic Scholarly Publication. English. mo. $244.00. **(Subscription address:** Kyowa Book Company Inc., 1 38 Kanda Jinbocho Chiyoda-ku, Tokyo 101 Japan.**)** **NLM** W1 NI914. ***Continues*** *Dai Nippon Jibiinkoka Kai Kaiho.*
**Ind/Abst** EMBASE [Select. Cov.]; Index Med.; Soc. Plann. Policy Dev. Abstr.; Sociol. Abstr. (?-?).

DK/0105-1539
**NORDISK TIDSSKRIFT FOR LOGOPEDI OG FONIATRI. SCANDINAVIAN JOURNAL OF LOGOPEDICS AND PHONIATRICS.** **Added/Corp** Nordisk Samafbejdsrad for Logopedi og Foniatri. **VFOAT** Scandinavian Journal of Logopedics and Phoniatrics. Vol. 1 (Jan. 1976)-. Periodical. Danish (English, Norwegian and Swedish). qt. Kr610.00, $105.00. Scandinavian University Press, PO Box 2959 Toeyen, N 0608 Oslo 6 Norway. **Tel** 011 47 2 2575400, FAX 011 47 2 2575353, telex 71896 UROR N. **(Subscription address:** Scandinavian University Press, 200 Meacham Ave., Elmont NY 11003.**)** **ED** Peter Kitzing. **LC** RC423.A1; N64. **Desc:** An international forum for research reports and information in the field of communication disorders. Covers not only logopedics and phoniatrics but also other topics related to speech, language, and voice pathology. The ultimate goal is to help the communicatively disabled.

US
**NSSLHA JOURNAL.** **Added/Corp** National Student Speech Language Hearing Association (U.S.). **VFOAT** Journal of the National Student Speech Language Hearing Association. Vol. 11, No. 1 (Dec. 1983)-. Periodical. English. an. $12.48. National Student Speech Language and Hearing Association, 10801 Rockville Pike, Rockville MD 20852. **Tel** (301)897-5700. **LC** RC423.A1; J67. **DD** 616.85/5/005. ***Continues*** *Journal of the National Student Speech Language Hearing Association, 0736-0312.*

IT/0392-1433
**NUOVA CLINICA OTORINOLARINGOIATRICA, LA.** (LA NUOVA CLINICA OTORINOLARINGOIATRICA : ORGANO UFFICIALE DEL GRUPPO SICILIANO DI O.R.L. E PATOLOGIA CERVICO-FACCIALE, GRUPPO PUGLIESE DI O.R.L. E PATOLOGIA CERVICO-FACCIALE.). [Nuova clin. otorinolaringoiatr.]. **Added/Corp** Gruppo Siciliano di O.R.L. e Patologia Cervico-Facciale. Gruppo Pugliese di O.R.L. e Patologia Cervico-Facciale. Universita di Catania. Clinica O.R.L. **VFOAT** La Nuova Clinica O.R.L. (1978)-. Italian (summaries and/or abstracts in English). tq (3 issues). L40000 Italy; L60000 other. Nuova Clinica Otorinolaringoiatrica, OSP Garibaldi PZA S Maria Gesu, 95124 Catania Italy. **Tel** 011 39 95 316207. **NLM** W1 NU236. ***Continues*** *Clinica Otorinolaringoiatrica.*

SP/0210-7309
**O.R.L.-DIPS.** [ORL. DIPS]. **VFOAT** ORL Dips. (1973)-. Periodical. Spanish. bm. 4500ptas. Editorial Rocas SA, Muntaner 393, Pral 2A Desp 4A, 08021 Barcelona Spain. **Tel** 011 34 3 200-1389. **NLM** W1 OR708.
**Ind/Abst** Indice Med. Esp.

●US/0000-1600
**OFFICIAL AMERICAN BOARD OF MEDICAL SPECIALTIES (ABMS) DIRECTORY OF BOARD CERTIFIED OTOLARYNGOLOGISTS, THE.** [Off. Am. Board Med. Spec. (ABMS) dir. board certif. otolaryngol.]. **Added/Corp** American Board of Medical Specialties. **VFOAT** Directory of Board Certified Otolaryngologists; Official ABMS Directory of Board Certified Otolaryngologists. 5th Ed. (1994)-. Directory. English. be. American Board of Medical Specialties, 1 Rotary Center, Suite 805, Evanston IL 60201. **Tel** (708)491-9091. **LC** RF28; .A25. **DD** 617/.51/002573. ***Continues*** *ABMS Directory of Certified Otolaryngologists, 0883-3001.*

FR/0983-8201
**OPA PRATIQUE.** **VFOAT** ORL, Pneumo, Allergo Pratique. (198?)-. Periodical. French. mo (10 issues). 244.86F France; 250.00F other. Len Medical, 48 Bis Avenue Kleber, F-75116 Paris France. **Tel** 011 33 1 47550606. **UDC** 61.

US/1043-1810
**OPERATIVE TECHNIQUES IN OTOLARYNGOLOGY--HEAD AND NECK SURGERY.** [Oper. tech. otolaryngol.--head neck surg.]. (March 1990)-. Periodical. English. qt (Mar., June, Sept., Dec.). $108.00 (individual), $123.00 (institution) US; $138.00 (individual), $148.00 (institution) other. W.B. Saunders Company, A Subsidiary of Harcourt Brace Jovanovich, Inc., The Curtis Center/Suite 300, Independence Square West, Philadelphia PA 19106-3399. **Tel** (215)238-7800 or, 5587, FAX (215)238-7883, telex 173146. **(Subscription address:** W. B. Saunders Company / North America Subscriptions, c/o Periodicals, 6277 Sea Harbour Drive, 4th Floor, Orlando FL 32887.**)** **DD** 617. **NLM** W1; OP151L. **[CCC].**

FI/0358-4852
**OPHTHALMOLOGICA ET OTO-RHINO-LARYNGOLOGICA (OULU).** **See** Medical Science and Technology-Ophthalmology.

US/1064-3842
**ORL-HEAD AND NECK NURSING.** (ORL-HEAD AND NECK NURSING : OFFICIAL JOURNAL OF THE SOCIETY OF OTORHINOLARYNGOLOGY AND HEAD-NECK NURSES.). [ORL-head neck nurs.]. **Added/Corp** Society of Otorhinolaryngology and Head-Neck Nurses (U.S.). **VFOAT** ORL, Head and Neck Nursing. Vol. 9, No. 4 (Sept. 1991)-. Periodical. English. Four times a year. $30.00. Society of Otorhin and Head-Neck Nurses, 116 Canal Street, Suite A, New Smyrna Beach FL 32168. **Tel** (904)428-1695, FAX (904)423-7566. **ED** Barbara Sigler. **DD** 617. **NLM** W1; OR704. cum. index. **Ad Acc, Adv Mgr:** Sandra Schwartz. **Circ:** 1,000 (ctrl). ***Continues*** *Journal (Society of Otorhinolaryngology and Head-Neck Nurses (U.S.)), 0898-2767.*

SZ/0301-1569
**ORL; JOURNAL FOR OTO-RHINO-LARYNGOLOGY AND ITS BORDERLANDS.** [ORL, J. oto-rhino-laryngol. & borderl.]. Vol. 34 (1972)-. Academic Scholarly Publication. English. bm. $383.00. S. Karger AG, Allschwilerstrasse 10, PO Box - Postfach - Case Postale, CH-4009 Basel Switzerland. **Tel** 011 41 61 306-1111, FAX 0011 41 61 306-1234, telex CH 962 652. **ED** W. Arnold. **NLM** W1 O524. **CODEN** ORLJAH. **[CCC].** **Ad Acc.** **Pr Rev.** available on microfilm from University Microfilms International (UMI). Documents available from The Genuine Article, BIOSIS Document Express, CASDDS. ***Continues*** *Practica Oto-Rhino-Laryngologica.*
**Desc:** Contributions are drawn from the basic sciences and cover new knowledge on the anatomy, pathology, pathophysiology, immunology and tumor biology of the auditory and vestibular system, the salivary glands, paranasal sinuses and of the organs of the upper respiratory and digestive tract.
**Ind/Abst** Biol. Abstr.; Chem. Abstr.; EMBASE; Index Med.; Life Sci. Collect.; Protozoolog. Abstr.; Ref. Upd. Deluxe Ed.; Res. Alert [Select. Cov.]; SCISEARCH; Soc. Sci. Cit. Index [Select. Cov.].

US/0197-0674
**OTO REVIEW.** ***Title Change.*** [Oto rev.]. **Added/Corp** Ear Research Institute. Vol. 1 (1966)-(19??). Periodical. English. tq. House Ear Institute, 2100 W. Third St. 5th Floor, Los Angeles CA 90057. **Tel** (213)483-4431. **NLM** W1 OT483. ***Continued by*** *House Ear Institute. Review.*

SZ/1014-8221
**OTO-RHINO-LARYNGOLOGIA NOVA.** (Jan./Feb. 1991)-. Periodical. German (summaries and/or abstracts in English). bm. $345.00. S. Karger AG, Allschwilerstrasse 10, PO Box - Postfach - Case Postale, CH-4009 Basel Switzerland. **Tel** 011 41 61 306-1111, FAX 011 41 61 306-1234, telex CH 962 652. **ED** W. Arnold, J.J. Manni, R.R. Probst. **NLM** W1; OT583.
**Desc:** This practice-oriented German language journal regularly informs its readers about the advances in the treatment of diseases of the ear, nose and throat.
**Ind/Abst** Ref. Upd. Deluxe Ed.

BU/0473-5609
**OTO-RINO-LARINGOLOGIIA.** [Oto-rino-laringol.]. **Added/Corp** Nauchno Druzhestvo na Oto-Rino-Laringolozite. (1964)-. Academic Scholarly Publication. Bulgarian. Three times a year. 39.00F. **(Subscription address:** Hemus Foreign Trade Organization, 6 Tzar Osvoboditel Boulevard, 1000 Sofia Bulgaria.**)** **NLM** W1 OT72.
**Ind/Abst** EMBASE.

PL/0030-6657
**OTOLARYNGOLOGIA POLSKA.** (OTOLARYNGOLOGIA POLSKA. THE POLISH OTOLARYNGOLOGY.). [Otolaryngol. Pol.]. **Added/Corp** Akademia Lekarska w Gdansku. Polskie Towarzystwo Otolaryngologiczne. **VFOAT** Polish Otolaryngology; Journal of Polish Otolaryngology. Vol. 1 (1947)-. Academic Scholarly Publication. Polish (summaries and/or abstracts in English and Russian; table of contents in English and Russian). bm. Price on Request. **(Subscription address:** ARS Polona, PO Box 1001, 00068 Warsaw Poland.**)** **NLM** W1 OT515. **CODEN** OTPOAW. Documents available from BIOSIS Document Express, CASDDS. ***Continues*** *Polskie Przeglad Otolaryngologiczny.*
**Ind/Abst** Biol. Abstr.; Chem. Abstr. (1947-1983); EMBASE; Index Med.

US/0030-6665
**OTOLARYNGOLOGIC CLINICS OF NORTH AMERICA, THE.** [Otolaryngol. clin. North Am.]. Vol. 1 (June 1968)-. Academic Scholarly Publication. English. bm. $111.00 (individual), $145.00 (institution) US; $163.00 (individual), $173.00 (institution) other. W.B. Saunders Company, A Subsidiary of Harcourt Brace Jovanovich, Inc., The Curtis Center/Suite 300, Independence Square West, Philadelphia PA 19106-3399. **Tel** (215)238-7800 or, 5587, FAX (215)238-7883, telex 173146. **(Subscription address:** W. B. Saunders Company / North America Subscriptions, c/o Periodicals, 6277 Sea Harbour Drive, 4th Floor, Orlando FL 32887.**)** **ED** Barbara Cohen-Kligerman. **LC** RF1. **DD** 616.2/1/005. **UDC** 616.21. **NLM** W1 OT518. **CODEN** OCNAB. **[CCC].** Index available. **Pr Rev.** **Circ:** 4,600. available on microfilm and microfiche from University Microfilms International (UMI). Documents available from The Genuine Article, BIOSIS Document Express.
**Desc:** Practical clinical updates on topics of current interest written by experts in the field.
**Ind/Abst** Biol. Abstr.; Curr. Contents Clin. Med.; EMBASE; Energy Res. Abstr. (May 1977-); Index Med.; Life Sci. Collect.; Physic. Medline Plus; Res. Alert [Full Cov.]; Sci. Cit. Index; SCISEARCH; Soc. Sci. Cit. Index [Select. Cov.].

JA
**OTOLARYNGOLOGY.** (19??)-. Periodical. English. Thirteen times a year. $390.00. **(Subscription address:** Maruzen Company Ltd., PO Box 5050, Import & Export Department, Tokyo 100 31 Japan.**)**

CN/1057-3704
**OTOLARYNGOLOGY, AUDIOLOGY : AN ILLUSTRATED DESK DIARY.** [Otolaryngol. audiol.]. (1991)-. English. $14.45. Decker Periodicals Publishing Inc, PO Box 620, Station A, Hamilton Ontario L8N 3K7 Canada. **Tel** (416)522-7017, (800) 568-7281, FAX (416)522-7839. **DD** 617.

US
**OTOLARYNGOLOGY--HEAD AND NECK SURGERY. SOUND RECORDING.** **Added/Corp** Audio-Digest Foundation. **VFOAT** Otolaryngology; Head and Neck Surgery. Vol. 14, No. 13 (July 16, 1981)-. Periodical. English. sm. $179.76 US; $202.80 Canada; $247.44 other. Audio-Digest Foundation, 1577 Chevy Chase Drive, Glendale CA 91206. **Tel** (213)245-8505, (800)423-2308, FAX (818)240-7379. **NLM** W1 AU201DUC. ***Continues*** *Otorhinolaryngology (Glendale, Calif.), 0271-1354.*

●US/1070-8049
**OTOLARYNGOLOGY JOURNAL CLUB JOURNAL, THE.** [Otolaryngol. j. club j.]. Vol. 1, No. 1 (Feb. 1994)-. Periodical. English. bm (6 issues). $95.00 (individual), $110.00 (institutional) US; $105.00 (individual), $120.00 (institutional) other. Raven Press, 1185 Avenue of the Americas, 37th Floor, New York NY 10036. **Tel** (212)930-9500, (212)930-9604, FAX (212)869-3495, (212)302-8507, telex 640073. **DD** 616.

IT/0392-6621
**OTORINOLARINGOLOGIA.** [Otorinolaringologia]. Vol. 31, No. 1 (Jan./March 1981)-. Periodical. Italian (English). bm. $95.00 (individuals), $145.00 (institutions). Edizioni Minerva Medica, Corso Bramante 83-85, 10126 Turin Italy. **Tel** 011 39 11 678282, FAX 011 39 11 674502. **UDC** 616.21. **NLM** W1 OT573. Index available. **Bk Rev.** **Ad Acc.** ***Formed by the union of*** *Minerva Otorinolaringologica, 0026-4938; Nuovo Archivio Italiano di Otologia, Rinologia e Laringologia, 0301-3693; Bollettino delle Malattie dell'Orecchio, della Gola del Naso, 0392-7024* ***and*** *Oto-Rino-Laringologia Italiana.*
**Ind/Abst** EMBASE [Select. Cov.]; Soc. Plann. Policy Dev. Abstr.

IT/1120-3455
**OTORINOLARINGOLOGIA PEDIATRICA, L'.** (1990)-. Periodical. Italian. qt. $60.00. CIC Edizioni Internazionali, Via L Spallanzani 11, 00161 Rome Italy. **Tel** 011 39 6 841-2673, FAX 011 39 6 844-3365, telex 622099 CIC I. **UDC** 616.21.
**Ind/Abst** EMBASE.

US/1064-0207
**OUR VOICE (NEW YORK, N.Y. 1990).** (OUR VOICE.). [Our voice]. **Added/Corp** National Spasmodic Dysphonia Association. (198?)-. Periodical. English. sa (Spring and Fall). $20.00 (one year), $32.00 (two year). Our Voice, 365 West 25th Street, Suite 13E, New York NY 10001. **Tel** (212)929-4299, FAX (212)929-4099. **ED** Midge Kovacs. **DD** 616. **Pr Rev.** **Circ:** 2,500.

PK/0257-4985
**PAKISTAN JOURNAL OF OTOLARYNGOLOGY.** (PAKISTAN JOURNAL OF OTOLARYNGOLOGY : OFFICIAL PUBLICATION OF PAKISTAN SOCIETY OF OTOLARYNGOLOGY.). [Pak. j. otolaryngol.]. **Added/Corp** Pakistan Society of Otolaryngology. (198?)-. Periodical. English. qt (Jan., Apr., July, Oct.). $40.00. Pakistan Journal of Otolaryngology, Anklesaria Nursing Home, Garden Road, Karachi Pakistan. **Tel** 011 92 21 4971762, 011 92 21 4971763, FAX 011 92 21 4971763. **ED** M.H.A. Beg. **NLM** W1; PA356K. **[CCC].** Index available (Published in October issue). **Bk Rev.** **Ad Acc, Adv Mgr:** Asif Afzal. **Circ:** 1,500 (ctrl). available on CD-ROM from Extra-Med Informania Ltd.

FR/0761-2192
**PASCAL EXPLORE. E72, OTORHINOLARYNGOLOGIE, STOMATOLOGIE, PATHOLOGIE CERVICOFACIALE.** ***Title Change.*** **VFOAT** Otorhinolaryngologie, Stomatologie, Pathologie Cervicofaciale; Otorhinolaryngology, Stomatology, Head and Neck Diseases. No. 1 (1984)-?. Periodical. French. mo. Institut de l'Information Scientifique et Technique Technologie Medecine, 2 Allee du Parc de Brabois, 54514 Vandoeuvre Nancy France. **Tel** 011 33 83 504664. **NLM** ZQ 1; B936RP. ***Continues*** *Bulletin Signaletique. 347: Oto-Rhino-Laryngologie, Stomatologie, Pathologie*

*Cervicofaciale, 0301-3375.* ***Continued by*** *Otorhinolaryngologie, Stomatologie, Pathologie, Cervicofaciale, E72.*

GW/0173-301X
**PATHOLINGUISTICA.** Vol. 1, (1977)-. Monographic series. German. ir. Price varies per volume. **ED** G. Peuser. **LC** UNC. **NLM** W1 PA898C.

US/0197-3657
**PROGRESS REPORT - EAR RESEARCH INSTITUTE.** ***Ceased.*** [Prog. rep. - Ear Res. Inst.]. **Main/Corp** Ear Research Institute. (1973)-(19??). English. an. House Ear Institute, 2100 W. Third St. 5th Floor, Los Angeles CA 90057. **Tel** (213)483-4431. **NLM** W1 EA68. ***Continues*** *Progress Report - Los Angeles Foundation of Otology.*

UK/0143-6813
**RECENT ADVANCES IN OTOLARYNGOLOGY.** [Recent adv. otolaryngol.]. 1st Ed. (1935)-. English. ir (every 3-5 years). $106.00 (latest volume) US and Canada. Churchill Livingstone, 1-3 Baxter's Place, Leith Walk, Edinburgh EH1 3AF Scotland. **Tel** 011 44 31 556 2424, FAX 011 44 31 558 1278, telex 727511. **(Subscription address:** Churchill Livingstone / US, 5 S 250 Frontenac Road, Naperville IL 60563.**)** **ED** J. Ransome. **LC** RF1; .R43. **NLM** WV100 R212r.

BL/0034-7299
**REVISTA BRASILEIRA DE OTO-RINO-LARINGOLOGIA.** [Rev. bras. oto-rino-laringol.]. **Added/Corp** Federacao Brasileira das Sociedades de Otorrinolaringologia e Broncoesofagologia. **VFOAT** Revista Brasileira de Otorinolaringologia. (1939)-. Academic Scholarly Publication. Portuguese. bm. Sociedade Brasileira de Otorrinolaringologia, Rua Visconde de Piraja 330 - Grupo 510, Ipanema 22410, Rio de Janeiro, Brazil. **Tel** (21)287-0893. **NLM** W1 RE3449A. **CODEN** RBORAB. Documents available from BIOSIS Document Express. ***Continues*** *Revista Oto-Laringologica de Sao Paulo.*
**Ind/Abst** Biol. Abstr. (1986-); EMBASE.

RM/0377-7863
**REVISTA DE CHIRURGIE ONCOLOGIE, RADIOLOGIE, O.R.L., OFTALMOLOGIE, STOMATOLOGIE. OTO-RINO-LARINGOLOGIA.** ***Title Change.*** **Added/Corp** SocietÊatea de Oto-rino-laringologie. **VFOAT** Oto-Rino-Laringologia. Vol. 19, No. 4 (July/Sept. 1974)-(19??). Periodical. Romanian (Romanian; summaries and/or abstracts in English, French, German and Russian). bm. Uniunea Societ Stiinte Medical, Str Progresului 8, Bucharest Romania. **(Subscription address:** Rompresfilatelia, PO Box 12 201, Bucharest Romania.**)** **NLM** W1 RE378FL. **CODEN** RCOODC. Documents available from BIOSIS Document Express. ***Continues in part*** *Oto-Rino-Laringologia si Oftalmologia, 0303-5123.* ***Continued by*** *Oftalmologia.*
**Desc:** Contains articles in the speciality, clinical and experimental studies.
**Ind/Abst** Biol. Abstr.; EMBASE; Index Med.

SP
**REVISTA DE LOGOPEDIA, FONIATRIA Y AUDIOLOGIA / ASOCIACION ESPANOLA DE LOGOPEDIA, FONIATRIA Y AUDIOLOGIA.** **Added/Corp** Asociacion Espanola de Logopedia, Foniatria y Audiologia. Vol. 6, No. 1 (1986)-. Periodical. Spanish. qt. $38.73 Spain; $57.00 other Europe; $66.00 other. Asociacion Espanola Logopedia, Foniatria y Audio Provenza 319, Barcelona 9 Spain. **Tel** 011 39 2577818. **NLM** W1; RE417H. ***Continues*** *Revista de Logopedia y Fonoaudiologia, 0211-6146.*

AG/0326-7067
**REVISTA ORL.** (REVISTA ORL / FUNDACION DE OTORRINOLARINGOLOGIA.). [Rev. ORL]. **Added/Corp** Fundacion de Otorrinolaringologia (Buenos Aires, Argentina). **VFOAT** Revista O.R.L. **VAT** Revista Otorhinolaringologia. Vol. 1, No. 1 (June 1982)-. Periodical. Spanish. qt. $30.00. **ED** L.C. Barbon, I.E. Lazaro and S.L. Montes. **NLM** W1 RE711F. **Bk Rev. Ad Acc. Circ:** 1,800 (ctrl).
**Desc:** Concerns the diagnosis, treatment and surgery of otorhinolaryngologic diseases.

FR/0035-1334
**REVUE DE LARYNGOLOGIE, D'OTOLOGIE ET DE RHINOLOGIE.** Vol. 36 No. 32/33 (Aug. 15, 1915)-. Academic Scholarly Publication. French (English). Five times a year. 730.00F (surface mail); 830.00F (airmail) other. Revue de Laryngologie, 114 Avenue d'Ares, 33074 Bordeaux Cedex France. **Tel** 011 33 56 243015, FAX 011 33 56 56961317. **ED** Dr. Jacques Verhulst. **NLM** W1 RE783. Index available in last issue of volume--attached. cum. index. **Bk Rev. Ad Acc, Adv Mgr:** V. Lombard. **Pr Rev. Circ:** 1,970 (ctrl). ***Continues*** *Revue Hebdomaire de Laryngologie, d'Otologie et de Rhinologie.*
**Desc:** Includes occasional supplements on a particular subject.
**Ind/Abst** EMBASE; Index Med.; Soc. Plann. Policy Dev. Abstr.; Sociol. Abstr.

FR/1155-1087
**REVUE OFFICIELLE DE LA SOCIETE FRANCAISE D'ORL ET DE PATHOLOGIE CERVICO-FACIALE.** French. Six times a year. 790.00F (individuals), 685.00F (institutions) France; 1100.00F (institutions) 860.00F (individuals) other. Blackwell Scientific Publishers / Arnette, 2 rue Casimir-Delavigne, 75006 Paris France. **Tel** 011 33 1 44860770, FAX 011 33 1 46336797. cum. index. **Bk Rev. Ad Acc. Circ:** 2,200.
**Desc:** The surgical aspects of ear, nose and throat complications.

NE/0300-0729
**RHINOLOGY.** [Rhinology]. **Added/Corp** International Rhinologic Society. Vol. 8 (1970)-. Periodical. English. Four times a year. 195.00F. Rhinology, University Hospital, PO Box 85500 Otorhinolaryngology, 3508 GA Utrecht Netherlands. **Tel** 011 31 30 2591515. **ED** E. H. Huizing. **NLM** W1; RH43. **CODEN** RNGYA8. cum. index. **Bk Rev. Ad Acc. Circ:** 1,250 (ctrl). Documents available from BIOSIS Document Express. ***Continues*** *International Rhinology, 0300-0737.*
**Desc:** Physiology, diagnostics, pathology, medical therapy and surgery of the nose and paranasal sinuses, including allergology.
**Ind/Abst** Biol. Abstr.; EMBASE; Index Med.

IT/0392-1360
**RIVISTA ITALIANA DI OTORINOLARINGOLOGIA, AUDIOLOGIA E FONIATRIA.** [Riv. ital. otorinolaringol. audiol. foniatr.]. Vol. 1, No. 1 (Jan./March 1981)-. Periodical. Italian (English). qt. L60000 Italy; $42.64 other. CIC Edizioni Internazionali, Via L Spallanzani 11, 00161 Rome Italy. **Tel** 011 39 6 841-2673, FAX 011 39 6 844-3365, telex 622099 CIC I. **ED** T. Marullo, G. Bellussi. **NLM** W1; RI776T. **[CCC]. Bk Rev. Ad Acc.** ctrl circ.
**Ind/Abst** EMBASE [Select. Cov.].

SW/0105-0397
**SCANDINAVIAN AUDIOLOGY.** [Scand. audiol.]. **Added/Corp** Nordisk Audiologisk Selskab. (1972)-. Academic Scholarly Publication. English. qt. Kr765.00, $130.00. Scandinavian University Press, PO Box 2959 Toeyen, N 0608 Oslo 6 Norway. **Tel** 011 47 2 2575400, FAX 011 47 2 2575353, telex 71896 UROR N. **(Subscription address:** Scandinavian University Press, 200 Meacham Ave., Elmont NY 11003.**)** **ED** Einar Laukli. **LC** RF1; .S28. **DD** 617.8/9/05. **NLM** W1 SC146A. **CODEN** SNADAS. **[CCC]. Pr Rev.** Documents available from The Genuine Article, BIOSIS Document Express, Ask*IEEE.
**Desc:** Aims at promoting research and exchange of research information and scientific thinking to professional groups and organizations for hard-of-hearing people. International readership.
**Ind/Abst** Acoust. Abstr.; Biol. Abstr.; Curr. Contents Clin. Med.; Curr. Contents Life Sci.; EMBASE; Index Med.; INSPEC (1979-); Life Sci. Collect.; Psychol. Abstr. (1972-); PsycINFO; PsycLit; Res. Alert [Full Cov.]; Risk Abstr.; Sci. Cit. Index; SCISEARCH; Soc. Plann. Policy Dev. Abstr.; Soc. Sci. Cit. Index [Select. Cov.].

SW/0107-8593
**SCANDINAVIAN AUDIOLOGY. SUPPLEMENTUM.** [Scand. audiol., Suppl.]. **Added/Corp** Audiological Society of Denmark, Finland, Iceland, Norway and Sweden. Nordisk Audiologisk Selskab. **VFOAT** Scandinavian Audiology. Supplement. Vol. 1 (1972)-. Academic Scholarly Publication. English. ir. Comes with subscription to Scandinavian Audiology: $130.00. Scandinavian University Press, PO Box 2959 Toeyen, N 0608 Oslo 6 Norway. **Tel** 011 47 2 2575400, FAX 011 47 2 2575353, telex 71896 UROR N. **(Subscription address:** Scandinavian University Press, 200 Meacham Ave., Elmont NY 11003.**)** **NLM** W1 SC146E. **CODEN** SAUSBF. Documents available from BIOSIS Document Express, Ask*IEEE.
**Ind/Abst** Biol. Abstr.; EMBASE; Index Med.; INSPEC (1979-).

US/0734-0451
**SEMINARS IN HEARING.** [Semin. hear.]. Vol. 4, No. 1 (Feb. 1983)-. Periodical. English. qt (Feb., May, Aug., Nov.). $113.00 (institutions), $65.00 (individuals) US; $138.00'(institutions), $90.00 (individuals) other. Thieme Medical Publishers Inc., 381 Park Avenue South, Suite 1201, New York NY 10016. **Tel** (212)683-5088, (212)683-5089, FAX (212)779-9020, telex 220 862 TSINC UR. **ED** Jerry L Northern. **NLM** W1; SE488T. **CODEN** SEMHE7. **[CCC].** cum. index. **Bk Rev. Ad Acc. Circ:** 1,500 (ctrl). available on microfilm and microfiche from University Microfilms International (UMI). Documents available from BIOSIS Document Express. ***Continues in part*** *Seminars, Speech, Language, Hearing, 0196-108X.*
**Desc:** Topic oriented journal for the practitioner specializing in technical advances in audiology and otology.
**Ind/Abst** Biol. Abstr. (1985-); EMBASE.

CN/1198-7421
**SEMINARS IN OTOLARYNGIC ALLERGY.** **See** Medical Science and Technology-Allergy and Immunology.

US/0738-8837
**TEJAS JOURNAL OF AUDIOLOGY AND SPEECH PATHOLOGY.** (TEJAS JOURNAL OF AUDIOLOGY AND SPEECH PATHOLOGY : AN OFFICIAL PUBLICATION OF THE TEXAS SPEECH-LANGUAGE-HEARING ASSOCIATION (TSHA).). [Tejas j. audiol. speech pathol.]. **Added/Corp** Texas Speech-Language-Hearing Association. **VFOAT** Tejas. (19??)-. Periodical. English. Twice a year. $15.00. Texas Speech Language Hearing Association, PO Box 140046, Austin TX 78714. **Tel** (512)452-4571. **Bk Rev. Ad Acc. Pr Rev.** ctrl circ. ***Continues*** *Tejas.*

US/0096-6851
**TRANSACTIONS OF THE AMERICAN OTOLOGICAL SOCIETY.** [Trans. Am. Otol. Soc.]. **Main/Corp** American Otological Society. (1868)-. English. an. $65.00. American Otological Society, c/o J. Farmer, PO Box 3805, Duke University Medical Center, Durham NC 27710. **Tel** (919)684-6357, FAX (919)684-4611. **ED** Joseph C. Farmer, Jr. M. D. **LC** RF1; .A55. **NLM** W1 TR2248. **CODEN** TAOTAW. **Circ:** 350. Documents available from CASDDS.
**Desc:** Scientific papers dealing with the ear and includes business activities of the American Otological Society.
**Ind/Abst** Chem. Abstr.

IT
**VALSALVA, IL.** Italian. qt. $90.00. Edizioni Luigi Pozzi Srl, Via Panama 68, 00198 Rome Italy. **Tel** (06)8553548, FAX (06)8554105.

RU/0042-4668
**VESTNIK OTORINOLARINGOLOGII.** [Vestn. otorinolaringol.]. Vol. 1, (1936)-. Academic Scholarly Publication. Russian. bm. $52.00. Izdatelstvo Meditsina / Russian Academy of Medical Sciences, Ulitsa Solyanka 14, 109801 Moscow Russia. **Tel** 011 95 297-05-04. **(Subscription address:** Victor Kamkin, 4956 Boiling Brook Parkway, Rockville MD 20852.**)** **NLM** W1 VE843. **CODEN** VORLA7. Index available. **Bk Rev.** Documents available from BIOSIS Document Express. ***Supersedes*** *Vestnik Sovetskoi Otorinolaringologii.*
**Ind/Abst** Biol. Abstr.; EMBASE [Select. Cov.]; Index Med.; Int. Aerosp. Abstr.

●UK/0966-789X
**VOICE LONDON. 1992.** (VOICE.). [Voice Lond. 1992]. (1992)-. Periodical. English. sa. £35.00 (individual), £54.00 (institution). Whurr Publishers Ltd, 19B Compton Terrace, London N1 2UN England. **Tel** 011 44 71 359 5979, FAX 011 44 71 226 5290. **(Subscription address:** Turpin Distribution Services Limited, Blackhorse Road, Letchworth, Hertfordshire SG6 1HN, United Kingdom.**)** **ED** David M. Howard. **DD** 612.78. **Ad Acc.** Full Page (B&W) £150.00. Half Page (B&W) £100.00. **Pr Rev.**
**Desc:** Supports the association in its promotion and encouragement of research into such areas as the early detection and treatment of malignant and non-malignant diseases of the vocal tract presenting as voice disorder, the development of technology to enable the objective assessment assessment function, and the psychology of stress related voice disorder in adults and children.

GW/0340-5214
**ZENTRALBLATT HALS- NASEN-OHRENHEILKUNDE, PLASTISCHE CHIRURGIE AN KOPF UND HALS.** **See** Medical Science and Technology-Surgery.

UN/0044-4650
**ZURNAL USNYH, NOSOVYH I GORLOVYH BOLEZNEJ.** (ZHURNAL USHNYKH, NOSOVYKH I GORLOVYKH BOLEZNEI.). [Z. usn., nos. gorl. bolez.]. **Added/Corp** Soviet Union. Narodnyi Kommissariat Zdravookhraneniia. Soviet Union. Ministerstvo Zdravookhraneniia. **VFOAT** Journal of Otology, Rhinology, and Laryngology. Vol. 1 (1924)-. Academic Scholarly Publication. Russian. bm. $89.95. **(Subscription address:** East View Publications Inc., 3020 Harbor Lane North, Suite 110, Minneapolis MN 55447.**)** **NLM** W1 ZH424. **CODEN** ZUNBA9. Documents available from CASDDS.
**Ind/Abst** Chem. Abstr. (1924-1982); EMBASE [Select. Cov.]; Int. Aerosp. Abstr.; Life Sci. Collect.; Soc. Plann. Policy Dev. Abstr.

## PATHOLOGY

AT
**A I M L S SELF ASSESSMENT PROGRAMMES SERIES.** **VFOAT** Australian Institute of Medical Laboratory Scientists Self Assessment Programmes Series. (19??)-. Monographic series. English. ir. $12.00 to $25.00 each. Australian Institute of Medical Laboratory Scientists, PO Box 450, Toowong Queensland 4006 Australia. **Tel** 61-7-371-3370, FAX 61-7-870-4857. **ED** Brendon Walker. **Pr Rev. Circ:** 2,400 (ctrl).

**Desc:** Series of programs for medical scientists to assess their level of knowledge in various disciplines of medical laboratory science.

US/0883-1203
**ABMS DIRECTORY OF CERTIFIED PATHOLOGISTS.** [ABMS dir. certif. pathol.]. **VFOAT** Directory of Certified Pathologists. **VAT** American Board of Medical Specialties Directory of Certified Pathologists. 1985-. Directory. English. be. $34.95. American Board of Medical Specialties, 1 Rotary Center, Suite 805, Evanston IL 60201. **Tel** (708)491-9091. **LC** RB10. **DD** 616.07/025/73. **UDC** 616-05(060.21)(73). **NLM** QZ 22.1; A1523.

GW/0001-6322
**ACTA NEUROPATHOLOGICA.** [Acta neuropathol.]. **Added/Corp** World Federation of Neurology. Research Group for Neuropathology. World Federation of Neurology. Research Group for Comparative Neuropathology. World Federation of Neurology. Research Group for Neurooncology. Vol. 1 (May 1961)-. Academic Scholarly Publication. Multiple languages (English, French and German; summaries and/or abstracts in English, French and German). Twelve times a year. DM3248.00. Springer-Verlag GmbH & Company KG, Heidelberger Platz 3, D 14197 Berlin Germany. **Tel** 011 49 30 8207223, FAX 011 49 30 8214091, telex 183 319 SPBLN D. **(Subscription address:** Springer Verlag New York Inc. / for North America, 44 Hartz Way, Secaucus NJ 07096.**) ED** K Jellinger, P Kleihues, G W Kreutzberg, J M Schroeder, and H M Wisniewski. **NLM** W1 AC872N. **CODEN** ANPTAL. **[CCC]. Bk Rev. Pr Rev.** available on microfilm and microfiche from University Microfilms International (UMI). Documents available from The Genuine Article, BIOSIS Document Express, CASDDS.
**Desc:** Provides rapid, first-rate information on subjects related to nerve-tissue research based on modern investigative techniques, including histochemistry, electron microscopy, immunology, tissue culture, biophysics, neurochemistry, and experimental neuropathology.
**Ind/Abst** Biol. Abstr.; Chem. Abstr.; CSA Neuro. Abstr.; Curr. Aware. Biol. Sci., CABS; Curr. Contents Life Sci.; EMBASE; Energy Res. Abstr.; Health Plan. Adminis.; Helminthol. Abstr.; Index Med.; Index Vet.; Int. Aerosp. Abstr.; Nutr. Abstr. Rev., Ser. B, Live Feeds and Feed.; Nutr. Abstr. Rev., Ser. A, Hum. Exp.; Oncog. Growth Factors Abstr.; Life Sci. Collect.; Protozoolog. Abstr.; Ref. Upd. Basic Ed.; Ref. Upd. Deluxe Ed.; Res. Alert [Full Cov.]; Sci. Cit. Index; SCISEARCH; Small Anim. Abstr. Bibliogr.; Vet. Bull.

JA/0001-6632
**ACTA PATHOLOGICA JAPONICA.** ***Title Change.*** [Acta pathol. jpn.]. **Added/Corp** Nihon Byori Gakkai. Nippon Byori Gakkai. **VFOAT** APJ. Vol. 1 (1951)-(1993). Academic Scholarly Publication. English (French and German). mo. Nihon Byori Gakkai (Japanese Society of Pathology), c/o Clinical Laboratory Division, National Cancer Center Hospital, 1-1 Tsukiji 5-chome, Chuo-ku Tokyo 104, Japan. **(Subscription address:** Japan Publications Trading Company, Ltd., PO Box 5030, Tokyo International, Tokyo 100-31 Japan.**) NLM** W1 AC9126. **CODEN** APJAAG. **Pr Rev.** available on microfilm and microfiche from University Microfilms International (UMI). Documents available from The Genuine Article, BIOSIS Document Express, CASDDS. ***Continued by*** *Pathology International, 1320-5463.*
**Ind/Abst** Biol. Abstr.; Chem. Abstr.; Curr. Aware. Biol. Sci., CABS; Curr. Contents Life Sci.; EMBASE; Health Plan. Adminis.; Index Med.; Oncog. Growth Factors Abstr.; Life Sci. Collect.; Protozoolog. Abstr.; Res. Alert [Full Cov.]; Sci. Cit. Index; SCISEARCH.

●US/1072-4109
**ADVANCES IN ANATOMIC PATHOLOGY.** (ADVANCES IN ANATOMIC PATHOLOGY : JOURNAL CLUB JOURNAL.). (1994)-. Periodical. English. bm (6 issues). $85.00 (individuals), $118.00 (institutions) US; $95.00 (individuals), $128.00 (institutions) other. Raven Press, 1185 Avenue of the Americas, 37th Floor, New York NY 10036. **Tel** (212)930-9500, (212)930-9604, FAX (212)869-3495, (212)302-8507, telex 640073.

US/0065-2423
**ADVANCES IN CLINICAL CHEMISTRY.** [Adv. clin. chem.]. Vol. 1 (1958)-. Academic Scholarly Publication. English. ir. Price varies per volume. Academic Press, Inc., 6277 Sea Harbor Drive, Orlando FL 32887. **Tel** (800)543-9534, (407)345-4100, FAX (407)363-9661. **LC** RB1; .A2. **DD** 616.0756. **UDC** 616-098. **NLM** W1 AD54. **CODEN** ACLCA9. **[CCC].** cum. index. **Pr Rev.** Documents available from The Genuine Article, CASDDS.
**Desc:** Information on clinical chemistry, biochemistry, pathology and laboratory diagnosis.
**Ind/Abst** Chem. Abstr.; Curr. Aware. Biol. Sci., CABS; Energy Res. Abstr. (Aug. 1982-); Health Plan. Adminis.; Index Med.; Index Sci. Rev. [Full Cov.]; Res. Alert [Full Cov.]; Sci. Cit. Index; SCISEARCH.

US/0099-1147
**ADVANCES IN PATHOBIOLOGY.** **See** Biology.

US/1057-1256
**ADVANCES IN PATHOLOGY AND LABORATORY MEDICINE.** [Adv. pathol. lab. med.]. Vol. 4 (1991)-. English. $59.95 US. Mosby Year Book Inc., 11830 Westline Industrial Drive, St Louis MO 63146. **Tel** (800)325-4177, (314)872-8370, FAX (314)432-1380, telex 44-2402. **DD** 616. **NLM** W1; AD717. ***Continues*** *Advances in Pathology, 0889-3969.*

US/0743-5592
**ADVANCES IN THE BIOLOGY OF DISEASE.** [Adv. biol. dis.]. Vol. 1 (1984)-. English. an. $35.00. Williams & Wilkins Company, 428 East Preston Street, Baltimore MD 21202-3993. **Tel** (410)528-4000, (800)638-6423, FAX (410)528-8596, telex 87669. **(Subscription address:** Williams & Wilkins, PO Box 64380, Baltimore, MD 21264**) ED** Emanuel Rubin and Ivan Damjanov. **LC** RB1; .A22. **DD** 616.07/05. **NLM** W1; AD8792M. **CODEN** ABDIEI. Documents available from BIOSIS Document Express, , Quick Copies.
**Ind/Abst** Biol. Abstr. (-1984).

US/0498-3564
**AFIP LETTER.** **Main/Corp** Armed Forces Institute of Pathology (U.S.). **VAT** Armed Forces Institute of Pathology Letter. Vol. 1 (1951)-. Periodical. English. bm. UAREP - Registry of Comparative Pathology, Armed Forces Institute of Pathology, Washington DC 20306. **Tel** (202)576-2452, FAX (202)576-2164. **NLM** W2 A2 A7A.

SG/0002-0516
**AFRIQUE MEDICALE.** Vol. 1, No. 1 (1962)-. Periodical. French. bm. 240.00CFAF Africa; 290.00CFAF other. Africa, 10 rue Borgix Dr Thez, BP 1826, Dakar Senegal. **Tel** 011 221 210880, 011 221 220776, FAX 22.12.01.22.07.02, telex 1301 AFRICA. **ED** Joel Decupper. **NLM** W1 AF628. **Ad Acc. Circ:** 15,000.
**Desc:** Tropical pathology, distributed throughout the French-speaking worldwide tropical zone, of interest to practitioners.
**Ind/Abst** Nutr. Abstr. Rev., Ser. B, Live Feeds and Feed.; Nutr. Abstr. Rev., Ser. A, Hum. Exp.; Rev. Med. Vet. Entomol.; Trop. Dis. Bull.

AU/0253-5297
**AKTUELLE PROBLEME DER NEUROPATHOLOGIE.** (AKTUELLE PROBLEME DER NEUROPATHOLOGIE : AUSGEWAHLTE BEITRAEGE.). [Aktuelle Probl. Neuropathol.]. **Main/Corp** Osterreichische Arbeitsgemeinschaft fur Neuropathologie. Jahrestagung. **VFOAT** Current Topics in Neuropathology : Selected Papers; Current Topics in Neuropathology. Vol. 3 (April 28, 1976)-. Academic Scholarly Publication. German (English). an. **ED** K. Jellinger and H. Gross. **UDC** 616.8. **NLM** W1; AK9954. **CODEN** APRNDU. Documents available from CASDDS. ***Continues*** *Aktuelle Probleme der Neuropathologie, 0253-5297.*
**Ind/Abst** Chem. Abstr.

US/0002-9173
**AMERICAN JOURNAL OF CLINICAL PATHOLOGY.** [Am. j. clin. pathol.]. **Added/Corp** American Society of Clinical Pathologists. Vol. 1 (Jan. 1931)-. Academic Scholarly Publication. English (summaries and/or abstracts in Interlingua). mo. $165.00 (individuals), $265.00 (institutions) US; $240.00 (individuals), $325.00 (institutions) other. J.B. Lippincott Company, 227 East Washington Square, Philadelphia PA 19106-3780. **Tel** (215)238-4200 or 4454, FAX (215)238-4227. **(Subscription address:** J.B. Lippincott, PO Box 350, Hagerstown MD 21740.**) ED** Myrton F. Beeler. **LC** RB1; .A3. **DD** 616.05. **NLM** W1 AM45L. **CODEN** AJCPAI. **[CCC]. Bk Rev. Ad Acc. Pr Rev. Circ:** 15,200. available on microfilm and microfiche from University Microfilms International (UMI). Documents available from The Genuine Article, BIOSIS Document Express, CASDDS.
**Desc:** Reports on original studies and observations in clinical and anatomic pathology; also articles on laboratory use, management, and information.
**Ind/Abst** Abr. Index Med.; Biol. Abstr.; Chem. Abstr.; Curr. Aware. Biol. Sci., CABS; Curr. Contents Clin. Med.; Curr. Contents Life Sci.; Dairy Sci. Abstr.; Dent. Abstr. (-1991); EMBASE; Energy Res. Abstr.; Health Devices Alerts; Helminthol. Abstr. (19??-19??); Immunol. Abstr.; Index Med.; Index Vet.; Iowa Drug Inf. Serv. (1966-); Microbiol. Abstr. Sect. B; Microbiol. Abstr. Sect. A; Microbiol. Abstr. Sect. C; Nutr. Abstr. Rev., Ser. B, Live Feeds and Feed.; Nutr. Abstr. Rev., Ser. A, Hum. Exp.; Oncog. Growth Factors Abstr.; Life Sci. Collect.; PESTDOC; Physic. Medline Plus; Protozoolog. Abstr.; Ref. Upd. Basic Ed.; Ref. Upd. Deluxe Ed.; Res. Alert [Full Cov.]; Rev. Med. Vet. Entomol.; Rev. Med. Vet. Mycology; Rev. Plant Pathol.; Sci. Cit. Index; SCISEARCH; Soc. Sci. Cit. Index [Select. Cov.]; SportSearch; Stat. Theory Method Abstr. (1959-1963); Vet. Bull.; Trop. Dis. Bull.; Virol. AIDS Abstr.

US/0195-7910
**AMERICAN JOURNAL OF FORENSIC MEDICINE AND PATHOLOGY, THE.** **See** Medical Science and Technology-Forensic Medicine, Medical Jurisprudence.

US/0002-9440
**AMERICAN JOURNAL OF PATHOLOGY, THE.** [Am. j. pathol.]. **Added/Corp** American Association of Pathologists and Bacteriologists. American Society for Experimental Pathology. American Association of Pathologists. American Society for Investigative Pathology. Vol. 1, No. 1 (Jan. 1925)-. Academic Scholarly Publication. English. mo. $230.00 (institution), $160.00 (individual) US; $295.00 (institution), $225.00 (indvidual) other. American Society for Investigative Pathology, 9650 Rockville Pike, Bethesda MD 20814. **Tel** (301)530-7130. **(Subscription address:** Fulco, 30 Broad Street, Denville NJ 07834.**) ED** Vincent T. Marchesi. **LC** RB1; .A4. **DD** 616.07/05. **NLM** W1 AM498. **CODEN** AJPAA4. **[CCC].** Index available. cum. index. **Ad Acc. Pr Rev. Circ:** 5,103. available on microfilm and microfiche from University Microfilms International (UMI). Documents available from The Genuine Article, BIOSIS Document Express, CASDDS. ***Supersedes*** *Journal of Medical Research, 0097-3599.*
**Desc:** Basic research findings on disease pathogenesis using experimental systems and human material. Features cellular, molecular, biochemical and immunological approaches to human disease. Periodic reports on the most promising molecular probes and new animal models.
**Ind/Abst** Abr. Index Med.; AgBiotech News Inf.; Anim. Breed. Abstr.; Biol. Abstr.; Biol. Dig.; Chem. Abstr.; CSA Neuro. Abstr. (?-?); Curr. Aware. Biol. Sci., CABS; Curr. Contents Clin. Med.; Curr. Contents Life Sci.; Curr. Ref. Fish Res.; Dairy Sci. Abstr.; EMBASE; Energy Res. Abstr.; Fish Rev.; Genet. Abstr.; Health Plan. Adminis.; Helminthol. Abstr. (1991-); Immunol. Abstr.; Index Med.; Index Vet.; INIS Atomindex [Micro.]; Microbiol. Abstr. Sect. B; Nutr. Abstr. Rev., Ser. B, Live Feeds and Feed.; Nutr. Abstr. Rev., Ser. A, Hum. Exp.; Oncog. Growth Factors Abstr.; Life Sci. Collect.; PESTDOC; Physic. Medline Plus; Pig News Inf.; Poult. Abstr.; Protozoolog. Abstr.; Ref. Upd. Basic Ed.; Ref. Upd. Deluxe Ed.; Res. Alert [Full Cov.]; Rev. Med. Vet. Mycology; Rev. Plant Pathol.; Sci. Cit. Index; SCISEARCH; SportSearch; Stat. Theory Method Abstr. (1961-1963); Vet. Bull.; Trop. Dis. Bull.; Virol. AIDS Abstr.; Wildl. Rev.

US/0147-5185
**AMERICAN JOURNAL OF SURGICAL PATHOLOGY, THE.** [Am. j. surg. pathol.]. Vol. 1 (March 1977)-. Periodical. English. mo. $175.00 (individuals), $305.00 (institutions) US; $255.00 (individuals), $385.00 (institutions) other. Raven Press, 1185 Avenue of the Americas, 37th Floor, New York NY 10036. **Tel** (212)930-9500, (212)930-9604, FAX (212)869-3495, (212)302-8507, telex 640073. **ED** Stephen S. Sternber. **LC** RD57; .A43. **DD** 617.71/05. **NLM** W1; AM523BJ. **CODEN** AJSPDX. **[CCC]. Pr Rev.** available on microfilm and microfiche from University Microfilms International (UMI). Documents available from The Genuine Article, BIOSIS Document Express.
**Desc:** Geared to residents and clinical pathologists, this journal focuses on practical issues of immediate relevance to diagnostic problems in human surgical pathology.
**Ind/Abst** Biol. Abstr.; Curr. Contents Clin. Med.; Curr. Contents Life Sci.; EMBASE; Energy Res. Abstr. (Sept. 1979-); Index Med.; INIS Atomindex [Micro.]; Life Sci. Collect.; Physic. Medline Plus; Protozoolog. Abstr.; Ref. Upd. Deluxe Ed.; Res. Alert [Full Cov.]; Rev. Med. Vet. Mycology; Sci. Cit. Index; SCISEARCH; SportSearch.

FI/0358-4895
**ANATOMICA, PATHOLOGICA, MICROBIOLOGICA.** **See** Medical Science and Technology-Anatomy.

US
**ANIMAL MODELS OF HUMAN DISEASE.** **Added/Corp** Registry of Comparative Pathology. **VFOAT** Handbook: Animal Models of Human Disease. (1972)-. English. ir. $15.00 (without binder); $21.00 (with binder). UAREP - Registry of Comparative Pathology, Armed Forces Institute of Pathology, Washington DC 20306. **Tel** (202)576-2452, FAX (202)576-2164. **ED** C. Capen, L. K. Johnson and G. Migala. cum. index (With fascicle.). **Pr Rev.**
**Desc:** Research on animals models for testing of human disease.

FR/0003-3898
**ANNALES DE BIOLOGIE CLINIQUE (PARIS).** (ANNALES DE BIOLOGIE CLINIQUE.). [Ann. biol. clin.]. **Added/Corp** Societe Francaise de Biologie Clinique. (1943)-. Academic Scholarly Publication. French (summaries and/or abstracts in English). mo (11 issues). 2350.00F France; 2630.00F other. Editions Scientifique Elsevier, 141 rue de Javel, 75747 Paris Cedex 15 France. **Tel** 011 33 1 47 07 11 22, FAX 011 33 1 43 36 80 93. **(Subscription address:** Editions Scientifiques Elsevier / for North America, PO Box 7247-7576, Philadelphia PA 19170-7576.**) LC** RB1; .S752. **DD** 616.07/05. **NLM** W1 AN327B. **CODEN** ABCLAI. **[CCC].** Index available. **Bk Rev. Ad Acc. Pr Rev. Circ:** 6,000. Documents available from The Genuine Article, BIOSIS Document Express, CASDDS.
**Ind/Abst** Biol. Abstr.; Chem. Abstr.; Curr. Contents Life Sci.; EMBASE; Energy Res. Abstr.; Food Sci. Technol. Abstr.; Health Plan. Adminis.; Index Med.; Nutr. Abstr. Rev., Ser. B, Live Feeds and Feed.; Nutr. Abstr. Rev.,

Ser. A, Hum. Exp.; Life Sci. Collect.; Protozoolog. Abstr.; Res. Alert [Full Cov.]; Rev. Med. Vet. Mycology; Saf. Health Work; Sci. Cit. Index; SCISEARCH.

FR/0242-6498
**ANNALES DE PATHOLOGIE.** [Ann. pathol.]. Vol. 1, No. 1 (1981)-. Academic Scholarly Publication. French (summaries and/or abstracts in English). bm. $278.00. Masson Editeur, Box Postale 22, 41353 Vineuil 16 France. **Tel** 011 33 54 438994. **(Subscription address:** 7A Boulevard de Perolles, CH-1701 Fribourg Switzerland**) NLM** W1 AN374C. **CODEN** ASPAD2. **[CCC]. Pr Rev.** available on microfilm and microfiche from University Microfilms International (UMI). Documents available from The Genuine Article, BIOSIS Document Express, CASDDS. ***Continues*** *Annales d'Anatomie Pathologique, 0003-3871.*
**Ind/Abst** Biol. Abstr.; Chem. Abstr. (1981-1983); Curr. Contents Life Sci.; EMBASE; Health Plan. Adminis.; Helminthol. Abstr. (1991-); Index Med. (1981-); Life Sci. Collect.; Res. Alert [Full Cov.]; Rev. Med. Vet. Entomol.; Rev. Med. Vet. Mycology; Sci. Cit. Index; SCISEARCH.

US/0091-7370
**ANNALS OF CLINICAL AND LABORATORY SCIENCE.** [Ann. clin. lab. sci.]. **Added/Corp** Institute for Clinical Science (Philadelphia, Pa.) Association of Clinical Scientists. **VFOAT** Annals of Clinical & Laboratory Science. Vol. 3, No. 3 (May/June 1973)-. Academic Scholarly Publication. English. bm. $70.00 (individuals), $105.00 (institutions) US; $90.00 (individuals), $110.00 (institutions) Canada and Mexico; $105.00 (individuals), $115.00 (institutions) other. Association of Clinical Scientists, 1833 Delancey Place, Philadelphia PA 19103. **Tel** (215)922-6554. **ED** F. William Sunderman. **LC** RB37.A1; A5. **DD** 616.07/05. **NLM** W1 AN57K. **CODEN** ACLSCP. **[CCC].** Index available. **Bk Rev. Ad Acc. Pr Rev. Circ:** 2,000 (ctrl). Documents available from The Genuine Article, BIOSIS Document Express, CASDDS. ***Continues*** *Annals of Clinical Laboratory Science, 0091-7370.*
**Desc:** Research in clinical studies. Critical reviews of subjects in clinical pathology, clinical chemistry, and physiology.
**Ind/Abst** Biol. Abstr.; Chem. Abstr.; Curr. Contents Clin. Med.; Curr. Contents Life Sci.; EMBASE; Energy Res. Abstr. (Jan. 1976-); Health Plan. Adminis.; Helminthol. Abstr. (1991-); Index Med.; INIS Atomindex [Micro.]; Microbiol. Abstr. Sect. B (19??-19??); Nutr. Abstr. Rev., Ser. B, Live Feeds and Feed.; Nutr. Abstr. Rev., Ser. A, Hum. Exp.; Life Sci. Collect.; Protozoolog. Abstr.; Ref. Upd. Deluxe Ed.; Res. Alert [Full Cov.]; Rev. Med. Vet. Mycology; Sci. Cit. Index; SCISEARCH.

FR/0395-501X
**ARCHIVES D'ANATOMIE ET DE CYTOLOGIE PATHOLOGIQUES. See** Medical Science and Technology-Anatomy.

US/0003-9985
**ARCHIVES OF PATHOLOGY & LABORATORY MEDICINE.** [Arch. pathol. lab. med.]. **Added/Corp** American Medical Association. College of American Pathologists. **VFOAT** Archives of Pathology and Laboratory Medicine. Vol. 100 (Jan. 1976)-. Academic Scholarly Publication. English. mo. $135.00. College of American Pathologists, Q Probes Department, 325 Waukegan Road, Northfield IL 60093. **Tel** (708)446-8800, FAX (708)446-8807. **LC** RB1; .A7. **DD** 616.07/05. **NLM** W1 AR468A. **CODEN** APLMAS. **[CCC].** Index available (bound in last issue). **Bk Rev. Ad Acc. Pr Rev. Circ:** 216,000. available on microfilm and microfiche from University Microfilms International (UMI); available on an online database (file 442/Full-Text) from DIALOG; and MEDIS. Documents available from The Genuine Article, BIOSIS Document Express, CASDDS. ***Continues*** *Archives of Pathology, 0363-0153.*
**Desc:** Published as an educational service for physicians who specialize in pathology, and to physicians of other specialties, interested in pathology, who need to keep abreast of advances in the field.
**Ind/Abst** Abr. Index Med.; AgBiotech News Inf.; Biol. Abstr.; Chem. Abstr.; Coal Abstr.; Cumul. Index Nurs. Allied Health Lit.; Curr. Contents Clin. Med.; Curr. Contents Life Sci.; Dairy Sci. Abstr.; EMBASE; Energy Res. Abstr. (Jan. 1976-); Health Plan. Adminis.; Helminthol. Abstr. (19??-19??); Hospit. Health Admin. Index; Immunol. Abstr.; Index Med.; Index Vet.; Iowa Drug Inf. Serv. (1968-); Med. Abstr. Newsl.; Microbiol. Abstr. Sect. B; Microbiol. Abstr. Sect. A; Microbiol. Abstr. Sect. C; Nutr. Abstr. Rev., Ser. B, Live Feeds and Feed.; Nutr. Abstr. Rev., Ser. A, Hum. Exp.; Life Sci. Collect.; Physic. Medline Plus; Protozoolog. Abstr.; Ref. Upd. Basic Ed.; Ref. Upd. Deluxe Ed.; Res. Alert [Full Cov.]; Rev. Med. Vet. Mycology; Rev. Plant Pathol.; Sci. Cit. Index; SCISEARCH; Soc. Sci. Cit. Index [Select. Cov.]; Vet. Bull.; Trop. Dis. Bull.; Virol. AIDS Abstr.

RU/0004-1955
**ARHIV PATOLOGIJ.** (ARKHIV PATOLOGII.). [Arh. patol.]. **Added/Corp** Vsesoiuznoe Nauchnoe Obshchestvo Patologoanatomov. Vol. 8 (1946)-. Academic Scholarly Publication. Russian (summaries and/or abstracts in English; table of contents in English). Six times a year. $79.95. Izdatelstvo Meditsina / Russian Academy of Medical Sciences, Ulitsa Solyanka 14, 109801 Moscow Russia. **Tel** 011 95 297-05-04. **(Subscription address:** East View Publications Inc., 3020 Harbor Lane North, Suite 110, Minneapolis MN 55447.**) NLM** W1 AR8287. **CODEN** ARPTAF. **[CCC].** Index available in last issue of volume--attached. **Bk Rev. Pr Rev.** Documents available from The Genuine Article, BIOSIS Document Express, CASDDS. ***Continues*** *Arkhiv Patologicheskoi Anatomifi i Patologicheskoi Fiziologii.*
**Ind/Abst** Biol. Abstr.; Chem. Abstr.; CIS Abstr.; Curr. Contents Clin. Med.; EMBASE; Helminthol. Abstr. (1991-); Index Med.; Int. Aerosp. Abstr.; Nutr. Abstr. Rev., Ser. B, Live Feeds and Feed.; Nutr. Abstr. Rev., Ser. A, Hum. Exp.; Life Sci. Collect.; PESTDOC; Protozoolog. Abstr.; Res. Alert [Select. Cov.]; Rev. Med. Vet. Mycology; Saf. Health Work; SCISEARCH.

PO/0004-2714
**ARQUIVIO DE PATOLOGIA.** [Arq. patol.]. Portuguese. ir. Inst Portuges de Oncologia de Francisco, Gentil Palhava, Lisbon Portugal. **UDC** 616. **NLM** W1 AR864. **CODEN** APALA4. Documents available from BIOSIS Document Express, CASDDS.
**Ind/Abst** Biol. Abstr.; Chem. Abstr.; EMBASE; Index Med.

US/1052-7893
**ASCP WASHINGTON REPORT ON NATIONAL AND STATE LABORATORY ISSUES.** [ASCP Wash. rep. natl. state lab. issues]. **Added/Corp** American Society of Clinical Pathologists. **VFOAT** Washington Report on National and State Laboratory Issues; Washington Report; ASCP Washington Report. **VAT** American Society of Clinical Pathologists Washington Report on National and State Laboratory Issues. (1991)-. Periodical. English. bm (6 issues). $96.00 (non-member), $58.00 (members). American Society of Clinical Pathologists, 2100 West Harrison Street, c/o L. Fields, Chicago IL 60612. **Tel** (312)738-1336, (800)621-4142, FAX (312)738-1619. **DD** 610. ***Continues*** *Washington Report (American Society of Clinical Pathologists).*

GW/0722-9674
**BERICHTE PATHOLOGIE. VFOAT** Pathology. Vol. 97, No. 1 (1982)-. Periodical. German (English). Twenty-six times a year. DM3398.00. Springer-Verlag GmbH & Company KG, Heidelberger Platz 3, D 14197 Berlin Germany. **Tel** 011 49 30 8207223, FAX 011 49 30 8214091, telex 183 319 SPBLN D. **(Subscription address:** Springer Verlag New York Inc. / for North America, 44 Hartz Way, Secaucus NJ 07096.**) ED** K Goerttler, G Mall, R Waldherr. **NLM** ZQZ 4 B511. **[CCC]. Bk Rev. *Continues*** *Berichte Uber die Allgemeine Und Spezielle Pathologie.*
**Desc:** Morphology, cytology, neuropathology, digestive diseases, vascular systems, methodology and preparation, symposia reports, and monographs.

US/0163-4984
**BIOLOGICAL TRACE ELEMENT RESEARCH. See** Biology-Biochemistry.

SP/0210-4199
**BIOMETRICA.** [Biometrica]. (1976)-. Periodical. Spanish. qt. Biolecta SA, Paseo de la Castellana 268, 28046 Madrid Spain. **NLM** W1 BI858T.

SZ/1015-6305
**BRAIN PATHOLOGY. See** Medical Science and Technology-Neurology.

UK/0308-2555
**BROADSHEET - ASSOCIATION OF CLINICAL PATHOLOGISTS.** (BROADSHEET.). [Broadsh. - Assoc. Clin. Pathol.]. **Main/Corp** Association of Clinical Pathologists (Great Britain). **Added/Corp** British Medical Society. British Medical Association. **VFOAT** ACP Broadsheet. No. 1 (195?)-. Periodical. English. ir. £6.75. BMJ / British Medical Journal Publishing Group, British Medical Association House, Tavistock Square, London WC1H 9JR England. **Tel** 011 44 71 3874499, FAX 011 44 71 383 6402, telex 290034 HBJ MN.

CN/1187-7758
**BULLETIN - ASSOCIATION DES PATHOLOGISTES DU QUEBEC.** (BULLETIN.). [Bull. - Assoc. pathol. Que.]. **Added/Corp** Association des Pathologistes du Quebec. Vol. 1, No 1 (Dec. 1991)-. Bulletin. French. qt. Free for Members. Association des Pathologistes du Quebec, Bureau 3000, 2 Complexe Desjardins, CP 216, Succurale Desjardins, Montreal Quebec H5B 1G8 Canada. **DD** 610.69.

FR
**BULLETIN DE LA SOCIETE DE PATHOLOGIE EXOTIQUE. Added/Corp** Societe de Pathologie Exotique. (1990)-. Periodical. French (summaries and/or abstracts in English; table of contents in English). Five times a year. $147.00. Masson Editeur, Box Postale 22, 41353 Vineuil 16 France. **Tel** 011 33 54 438994. **NLM** W1; BU5110. ***Continues*** *Bulletin de la Societe de Pathologie Exotique et de ses Filiales, 0037-9085.*
**Ind/Abst** Index Med. (1990-); Rev. Med. Vet. Entomol.

UK/0959-972X
**BULLETIN OF THE ROYAL COLLEGE OF PATHOLOGISTS.** (THE BULLETIN OF THE ROYAL COLLEGE OF PATHOLOGISTS.). [Bull. R. Coll. Pathol.]. **Added/Corp** Royal College of Pathologists. (197?)-. Bulletin. English. qt. **DD** 616.07.
**Ind/Abst** Trop. Dis. Bull.

US/0891-1525
**CAP TODAY.** [CAP today]. **VAT** College of American Pathologists Today. Vol. 1. No. 1 (Jan. 1987)-. Periodical. English. mo. $15.00. College of American Pathologists, Q Probes Department, 325 Waukegan Road, Northfield IL 60093. **Tel** (708)446-8800, FAX (708)446-8807. **ED** Sherrie Rice. **DD** 574. **UDC** 616. **Ad Acc. Circ:** 40,000 (ctrl). ***Formed by the union of*** *Pathologist, 0031-3017; LAP Newsletter; Summing Up; Q-Tips; Perceptions (Skokie, Ill.); Capitol Scan* ***and*** *Counterpoints (Skokie, Ill.), 0740-3275.*
**Desc:** Includes advances in tests and equipment, trends in management and clinical operation, regulatory changes and finance, plus news about the laboratory improvement programs of the College of American Pathologists.
**Ind/Abst** Health Plan. Adminis.; Hospit. Health Admin. Index (Vol. 1, No. 1, 1987-Vol. 1, No. 12, 1987-).

•US/1054-8807
**CARDIOVASCULAR PATHOLOGY. See** Medical Science and Technology-Cardiology.

SP/0211-6553
**CARDIOVASCULAR REVIEWS & REPORTS EDICION ESPANOLA. See** Medical Science and Technology-Cardiology.

US/0737-7983
**CATALOG OF CELL LINES.** [Cat. cell lines]. **Added/Corp** National Institutes of Health (U.S.) National Institute of General Medical Sciences (U.S.) National Institute on Aging. Institute for Medical Research (Camden, N.J.) Coriell Institute for Medical Research (U.S.). (1982)-?. Catalog. English. an. US Department of Health and Human Services National Institutes of Health, 9000 Rockville Pike, Bethesda MD 20892. **Tel** (301)496-9291, FAX (301)496-2443. **LC** RB155; .I527a. **DD** 616/.042. **NLM** QS 26 H918. ***Continues*** *Human Genetic Mutant Cell Repository, 0148-835X.* ***Continued in part by*** *Catalog of Cell Lines (National Institute on Aging).*

US
**CATALOG OF CELL LINES / NATIONAL INSTITUTE ON AGING. Added/Corp** National Institute on Aging. National Institutes of Health (U.S.) Coriell Institute for Medical Research (U.S.). **VFOAT** National Institute on Aging ... Catalog of Cell Lines; NIA Aging Cell Repository. (198?)-. Catalog. English. Cornell Institute for Medical Research, 401 Haddon Avenue, Camden NJ 08103. ***Continues*** *Catalog of Cell Lines, 0737-7983.*

XR/0009-0611
**CESKOSLOVENSKA PATOLOGIE.** [Cesk. patol.]. **Added/Corp** Ceskoslovenska Lekarska Spolecnost J.E. Purkyne. Sekce Soudniho Lekarstvi. Spolecnost Patologickych Anatomu. Vol. 1 (1965)-. Academic Scholarly Publication. Czech (summaries and/or abstracts in English and Russian). Four times a year. $53.50. Avicenum Medical Press, Malostranske Nam 28, 11802 Prague Czech Republic. **Tel** 011 42 2 530643. **(Subscription address:** Artia Pegas Press Ltd., Palac Metro Narodni Trida 25, 11210 Prague 1 Czech Republic.**) NLM** W1 CE902G. **CODEN** CPSLAE. **[CCC].** Documents available from CASDDS.
**Ind/Abst** Chem. Abstr.; EMBASE; Index Med.

CC/0529-5807
**CHUNG-HUA PING LI HSUEH TSA CHIH. VFOAT** Chinese Journal of Pathology. (1955)-. Periodical. Chinese (summaries and/or abstracts in English; table of contents in English). qt. $36.60. **(Subscription address:** China International Book Trading Corporation, PO Box 399, Library Service Department, Beijing 100044 People's Republic of China.**) DD** 616.
**Ind/Abst** Index Med. Vol. 14, No. 1, 1985-.

NE/0009-8981
**CLINICA CHIMICA ACTA. See** Chemistry.

IT/0391-8998
**CLINICA OCULISTICA E PATOLOGIA OCULARE.** [Clin. ocul. patol. ocul.]. (1980)-. Periodical. Italian. qt. $60.00. CIC Edizioni Internazionali, Via L Spallanzani 11, 00161 Rome Italy. **Tel** 011 39 6 841-2673, FAX 011 39 6 844-3365, telex 622099 CIC I. **UDC** 617. **[CCC].**
**Ind/Abst** EMBASE [Select. Cov.].

US/0197-8454
**CLINICAL LAB LETTER.** [Clin. lab lett.]. Vol. 1 (Jan. 1, 1980)-. Periodical. English. sm (published once during January and August). $241.00 US, Canada and Mexico; $275.00 other. Quest Publishing Company, 1351 Titan Way, Brea CA 92621. **Tel** (714)738-6400, FAX (714)525-6258. **ED** Allan F. Pacela. **NLM** W1 CL726. **[CCC].** Index available. **Bk Rev.** Documents available

from UMI Article Clearinghouse.
**Desc:** Written for hospital clinical laboratory personnel.
**Ind/Abst** Pharm. News Index (Dec. 1987-).

GW/0722-5091
**CLINICAL NEUROPATHOLOGY.** [Clin. neuropathol.]. Vol. 1, No. 1 (1st Quarter, 1982)-. Periodical. English. bm (6 issues). $143.00 (individuals), $173.00 (institutions). Dustri-Verlag, Dr Karl Feistle, Postfach 49, D 82032 Deisenhofen Germany. **Tel** 011 49 89 6138610, FAX 011 49 89 6135412. **ED** Wolfgang Schlote. **NLM** W1 CL731S. **CODEN** CLNPDA. **[CCC].** Index available. **Bk Rev. Ad Acc. Pr Rev.** ctrl circ. available on microfiche. Documents available from The Genuine Article, BIOSIS Document Express.
**Desc:** Reports on recent advances in the entire field of clinical neuropathology.
**Ind/Abst** Biol. Abstr. (1986-); Curr. Aware. Biol. Sci., CABS; Curr. Contents Clin. Med.; EMBASE; Health Plan. Adminis.; Index Med. (1982-); Res. Alert [Full Cov.]; Sci. Cit. Index; SCISEARCH; Soc. Sci. Cit. Index [Select. Cov.].

US
**COLLEGE OF AMERICAN PATHOLOGISTS SURVEYS.** (19??)-. English. Four times a year. $444.00. College of American Pathologists, Q Probes Department, 325 Waukegan Road, Northfield IL 60093. **Tel** (708)446-8800, FAX (708)446-8807.

US
**COLLEGE OF AMERICAN PATHOLOGISTS SURVEYS. ASHI. CAP HISTORCOMPATIBILTY.** English. Four times a year. $436.00. College of American Pathologists, Q Probes Department, 325 Waukegan Road, Northfield IL 60093. **Tel** (708)446-8800, FAX (708)446-8807.

US/0161-6935
**COMPARATIVE PATHOBIOLOGY.** [Comp. pathobiol.]. Vol. 1 (1976)-. Academic Scholarly Publication. English. ir. Price varies per volume. Plenum Press, 233 Spring Street, New York NY 10013-1578. **Tel** (212)620-8000, (800)221-9369, FAX (212)463-0742, (212)807-1047, telex 23/421139. **NLM** W1; CO436ME. **CODEN** CPATDJ. Documents available from CASDDS.
**Ind/Abst** AGRICOLA [Select. Cov.]; Chem. Abstr.

US/1041-116X
**COMPARATIVE PATHOLOGY BULLETIN.** [Comp. pathol. bull.]. **Added/Corp** Registry of Comparative Pathology. Vol. 1, (Nov. 1969)-. Bulletin. English. qt. $15.00 (1 year), $25.00 (2 year), $40.00 (3 year). UAREP - Registry of Comparative Pathology, Armed Forces Institute of Pathology, Washington DC 20306. **Tel** (202)576-2452, FAX (202)576-2164. **ED** L. Johnson, C. Kirk., C. Leonard. **DD** 616. **NLM** W1 CO436N. **Circ:** 1,000.
**Desc:** Includes a feature article, two descriptions of animal models of human disease, and announcement of meetings, publications and materials available to human pathologists.
**Ind/Abst** AGRICOLA; Index Vet.; Pig News Inf.; Rev. Med. Vet. Entomol.; Small Anim. Abstr. Bibliogr.; Vet. Bull.

US/1040-8363
**CRITICAL REVIEWS IN CLINICAL LABORATORY SCIENCES.** [Crit. rev. clin. lab. sci.]. **VFOAT** CRC Critical Reviews in Clinical Laboratory Sciences. **VAT** Chemical Rubber Company Critical Reviews in Clinical Laboratory Sciences. Vol. 12, Issue 3 (1980)-. Academic Scholarly Publication. English. bm (6 issues). $420.00 institution. CRC Press Inc., 2000 Corporate Boulevard Northwest, Boca Raton FL 33431. **Tel** (407)994-0555, (800)272-7737, FAX (407)998-9784, telex 568689. **LC** RB37; .C46. **DD** 616.07/5. **NLM** W1; C555B. **CODEN** CRCLBH. **[CCC]. Pr Rev.** Documents available from The Genuine Article, BIOSIS Document Express, CASDDS, ADONIS. ***Continues*** *CRC Critical Reviews in Clinical Laboratory Sciences, 0590-8191.*
**Desc:** Provides a detailed, critical evaluation of new concepts, methods, and data by recognized leaders.
**Ind/Abst** ADONIS; Biol. Abstr.; Chem. Abstr.; Curr. Aware. Biol. Sci., CABS; Curr. Contents Clin. Med.; EMBASE; Energy Res. Abstr.; Health Plan. Adminis.; Index Med. (1980-); Index Sci. Rev. [Full Cov.]; INIS Atomindex [Micro.]; Life Sci. Collect.; Ref. Upd. Deluxe Ed.; Res. Alert [Full Cov.]; Sci. Cit. Index; SCISEARCH.

SP
**CUADERNOS DE SECCION. MEDICINA / SOCIEDAD ES ESTUDIOS VASCOS.**
**Added/Corp** Sociedad de Estudios Vascos (San Sebastian, Spain). **VFOAT** Medicina. (198?)-. Periodical. Spanish. ir. 1590ptas Spain; 2046ptas North America; 1696ptas other. Eusko-Ikaskuntza, Legazpi 10-1o, 20004 San Sebastian Spain. **Tel** 425111, FAX 422250. **NLM** W1; CU138N.

UK/0968-6053
**CURRENT DIAGNOSTIC PATHOLOGY.**
**See** Medical Science and Technology.

GW/0070-2188
**CURRENT TOPICS IN PATHOLOGY.** (CURRENT TOPICS IN PATHOLOGY. ERGEBNISSE DER PATHOLOGIE.). [Curr. top. pathol.]. **VFOAT** Ergebnisse der Pathologie. Vol. 51 (1970)-. Monographic series. English. ir. Price varies per volume. Springer-Verlag GmbH & Company KG, Heidelberger Platz 3, D 14197 Berlin Germany. **Tel** 011 49 30 8207223, FAX 011 49 30 8214091, telex 183 319 SPBLN D. **(Subscription address:** Springer Verlag New York Inc. / for North America, 44 Hartz Way, Secaucus NJ 07096.**) ED** C.L. Berry. **NLM** W1 CU821H. **CODEN** CTPHBG. **[CCC].** Documents available from CASDDS. ***Continues*** *Ergebnisse der Allgemeinen Pathologie und Pathologischen Anatomie.*
**Desc:** Topics include bone and joint disorders, drug-induced pathology, pulmonary diseases, and dermatopathology.
**Ind/Abst** Chem. Abstr.; Health Plan. Adminis.; Index Med.; Index Vet.; Life Sci. Collect.; Vet. Bull.

IT
**DEVELOPMENTAL PHYSIOPATHOLOGY & CLINICS.** English. Four times a year (Mar., June, Sept., Dec.). $90.00. Athena Congress SRL, via Spartaco 36, 20135 Milan Italy. **Tel** 011 39 2 59900918, FAX 011 39 2 5484918. **Pr Rev.**

US/1052-9551
**DIAGNOSTIC MOLECULAR PATHOLOGY.** (DIAGNOSTIC MOLECULAR PATHOLOGY : THE AMERICAN JOURNAL OF SURGICAL PATHOLOGY, PART B.). [Diagn. mol. pathol.]. Vol. 1, No. 1 (Mar. 1992)-. Periodical. English. qt. $88.00 (individuals), $110.00 (institutions) US; $104.00 (individuals), $122.00 (institutions) other. Raven Press, 1185 Avenue of the Americas, 37th Floor, New York NY 10036. **Tel** (212)930-9500, (212)930-9604, FAX (212)869-3495, (212)302-8507, telex 640073. **ED** Ronald A. DeLellis and Hubert J. Wolfe. **DD** 616. **NLM** W1; DI258JG. **CODEN** DMPAES. **[CCC]. Pr Rev.** available on microfilm and microfiche from University Microfilms International (UMI).
**Desc:** Focuses on new molecular diagnostic techniques with applications for surgical pathology. It publishes original, peer reviewed contributions on molecular probes for diagnosis, such as tumor suppressor genes, oncogenes, the polymerase chain reaction, and in-situation hybridization. Articles demonstrate how these highly sensitive techniques can be applied for more accurate diagnosis.
**Ind/Abst** Curr. Aware. Biol. Sci., CABS; Sci. Cit. Index.

CN/0712-1997
**DIRECTORY - CANADIAN ASSOCIATION OF PATHOLOGISTS.** (DIRECTORY / CANADIAN ASSOCIATION OF PATHOLOGISTS, CANADIAN SOCIETY OF CYTOLOGY.). [Dir. - Can. Assoc. Pathol.]. **Main/Corp** Canadian Association of Pathologists. **VFOAT** Annuaire. Directory. English. an. K Pritzker, Mount Sinai Hospital, Department of Laboratories, Toronto Ontario M5G 1X5 Canada. **DD** 616/.07/06071. **UDC** 616(060.21)(71).

US/0095-3725
**DIRECTORY OF CLINICAL LABORATORIES, CLINICAL LABORATORY PERSONNEL.** **VFOAT** California Clinical Laboratory Technology; Laboratory Directory. Directory. English. $2.00. Office of Procurement, Department of General Services, PO Box 20191, Sacramento CA 95820. **LC** RB37.6; .D55. **DD** 616.07/5/025794. **UDC** 615.4-05(058.7)(794).

US
**DIRECTORY OF PATHOLOGY TRAINING PROGRAMS IN THE UNITED STATES AND CANADA.** **Added/Corp** Intersociety Committee on Pathology Information. 21st Ed. (1989/1990)-. Directory. English. an (June). $25.00. Intersociety Committee on Pathology Information, 4733 Bethesda Avenue, Suite 735, Bethesda MD 20814. **Tel** (301)656-2944, FAX (301)656-3179. **ED** Eileen M. Lavine. **NLM** QZ 22; AA1 D5. Index available. **Circ:** 2,400 (ctrl). ***Continues*** *Directory of Pathology Training Programs.*
**Desc:** Listings of pathology residency training programs in the US and Canada, also fellowship programs in subspecialties of pathology.

NE/0014-4096
**EXCERPTA MEDICA. SECTION 5. GENERAL PATHOLOGY AND PATHOLOGICAL ANATOMY.** **See** Medical Science and Technology-Abstracting, Bibliographies and Statistics.

US/0014-4800
**EXPERIMENTAL AND MOLECULAR PATHOLOGY.** [Exp. mol. pathol.]. Vol. 1 (Feb. 1962)-. Academic Scholarly Publication. English. bm (6 issues). $480.00 US and Canada; $565.00 other. Academic Press, Inc., 6277 Sea Harbor Drive, Orlando FL 32887. **Tel** (800)543-9534, (407)345-4100, FAX (407)363-9661. **ED** Frederick Coulston, Wilbur A. Thomas and Sean Moore. **LC** RB1; .E9. **DD** 616.07/05. **NLM** W1 EX47. **CODEN** EXMPA6. **[CCC]. Pr Rev.** Documents available from The Genuine Article, BIOSIS Document Express, CASDDS.
**Desc:** Articles on disease processes in relation to structural and biochemical alterations in mammalian tissues and fluids. Also contains articles on the application of newer techniques of analytical chemistry, histochemistry, pharmacology, toxicology, and electron microscopy to problems of pathology in man and animals.
**Ind/Abst** AGRICOLA; Biol. Abstr.; Chem. Abstr.; Chem. Titles; CSA Neuro. Abstr. (?-?); Curr. Aware. Biol. Sci., CABS; Curr. Contents Life Sci.; Dairy Sci. Abstr.; EMBASE; Energy Res. Abstr.; Health Plan. Adminis.; Helminthol. Abstr.; Index Med.; Index Vet.; INIS Atomindex [Micro.]; Nutr. Abstr. Rev., Ser. B, Live Feeds and Feed.; Nutr. Abstr. Rev., Ser. A, Hum. Exp.; Life Sci. Collect.; Poult. Abstr.; Protozoolog. Abstr.; Ref. Upd. Basic Ed.; Ref. Upd. Deluxe Ed.; Res. Alert [Full Cov.]; Sci. Cit. Index; SCISEARCH; Vet. Bull.

●GW/0940-2993
**EXPERIMENTAL AND TOXICOLOGIC PATHOLOGY : OFFICIAL JOURNAL OF THE GESELLSCHAFT FUR TOXIKOLOGISCHE PATHOLOGIE.** **See** Medical Science and Technology-Toxicology.

GW/0232-1513
**EXPERIMENTAL PATHOLOGY (1981).** ***Title Change.*** (EXPERIMENTAL PATHOLOGY.). [Exp. pathol.]. Vol. 19, No. 1 (1981)-(1992). Academic Scholarly Publication. English. ir (issued every four weeks). Gustav Fischer Verlag Jena, Postfach 100537, D 07705 Jena Germany. **Tel** 011 49 3641 27332, FAX 011 49 3641 626500. **(Subscription address:** 303 NW 12th Avenue, Deerfield Beach FL 33442; telephone: (305)428-5566**) ED** F Bolck. **NLM** W1 EX511T. **CODEN** EXPADD. **[CCC].** Index available. **Bk Rev. Ad Acc. Circ:** 540. Documents available from BIOSIS Document Express, CASDDS. ***Continues*** *Experimentelle Pathologie.* ***Continued by*** *Experimental and Toxicologic Pathology, 0940-2993.*
**Desc:** Covering the whole range of experimental research in pathomorphology, pathophysiology, pathobiochemistry, immunology. Aim: biological bases of medicine, oncology, immunology, therapy, environmental health.
**Ind/Abst** Biol. Abstr.; Chem. Abstr.; Curr. Contents Life Sci.; Dairy Sci. Abstr.; EMBASE; Health Plan. Adminis.; Index Med.; Life Sci. Collect.; Poult. Abstr.; Ref. Upd. Basic Ed.; Ref. Upd. Deluxe Ed.; Weed Abstr.

●US
**GRIPE/ GROUP FOR RESEARCH IN PATHOLOGY EDUCATION.** English. ir. $900.00 US; $925.00 Canada; $950.00 other. USC School of Medicine, 2011 Zonal Avenue, Department of Pathology, Los Angeles CA 90033. **Tel** (213)342-1283, FAX (213)342-3049. **Bk Rev**, (Qty: varies). **Ad Acc**, **Adv Mgr:** M. Libman, **Tel** (213)342-1283. ctrl circ.

US/0886-0238
**HEMATOLOGIC PATHOLOGY.** [Hematol. pathol.]. Vol. 1, No. 1 (1987)-. Periodical. English. qt (four issues per volume). $450.00 US; $464.00 other. Marcel Dekker Inc., 270 Madison Avenue, New York NY 10016. **Tel** (212)696-9000, (800)228-1160, FAX (212)685-4540, telex 421419. **(Subscription address:** Marcel Dekker Inc, PO Box 5017, Monticello NY 12701.**) ED** Sanford A. Stass. **DD** 616. **NLM** W1; HE868H. **CODEN** HEPAEG. **[CCC].** available on microfiche. Documents available from The Genuine Article, BIOSIS Document Express.
**Desc:** Comprehensive in its coverage of hematologic pathology, this authoritative journal focuses attention on new and previously unpublished research in hematopathology and its related disciplines, diagnostic-related information concerning hematologic diseases and prognosis, and data on the application and development of new hematologic procedures. Contains articles on basic and applied investigation, editorials on vital topics, review articles highlighting particularly important areas, letters to the editor, plus a technical section on important laboratory applications.
**Ind/Abst** Biol. Abstr. (1987-); Curr. Contents Clin. Med.; EMBASE; Index Med.; Ref. Upd. Deluxe Ed.; Res. Alert [Select. Cov.]; SCISEARCH.

SP/0213-3911
**HISTOLOGY AND HISTOPATHOLOGY.**
**See** Biology-Cytology and Histology.

UK/0309-0167
**HISTOPATHOLOGY.** [Histopathology]. **Added/Corp** International Academy of Pathology. British Division. Vol. 1 (1977)-. Academic Scholarly Publication. English. mo (12 issues). $442.00 US & Canada; £258.00 Europe; £285.00 other. Blackwell Scientific Publications Ltd, Marston Book Services, PO Box 87, Oxford OX2 ODT UK. **Tel** 011 44 865 791155, FAX 011 44 865 791927, telex 837 515 MARDIS G. **ED** R. N. M. MacSween. **NLM** W1 HI774. **CODEN** HISTDD. **[CCC].** Index available (bound in last issue). **Bk Rev. Ad Acc. Pr Rev. Circ:** 2,320 (ctrl). available on microfilm and microfiche from University Microfilms International (UMI). Documents available from The Genuine Article, BIOSIS Document Express, ADONIS.
**Desc:** Original histopathological material with clinical applications to human disease. Of practical importance to diagnostic histopathologists and workers in clinicopathological research.
**Ind/Abst** ADONIS; Biol. Abstr.; Curr. Contents Clin.

Med.; Curr. Contents Life Sci.; Curr. Titl. Dent.; Dairy Sci. Abstr.; EMBASE; Health Plan. Adminis.; Helminthol. Abstr.; Index Med.; Index Vet.; Life Sci. Collect.; Protozoolog. Abstr.; Ref. Upd. Deluxe Ed.; Res. Alert [Full Cov.]; Sci. Cit. Index; SCISEARCH; Vet. Bull.

US/0046-8177
**HUMAN PATHOLOGY.** (HUMAN PATHOLOGY : A CLINICOPATHOLOGIC QUARTERLY.). [Human pathol.]. Vol. 1 (March 1970)-. Academic Scholarly Publication. English. mo (12 issues). $116.00 (individual), $159.00 (institution) US; $179.00 (individual), $197.00 (institution) other. W.B. Saunders Company, A Subsidiary of Harcourt Brace Jovanovich, Inc., The Curtis Center/Suite 300, Independence Square West, Philadelphia PA 19106-3399. **Tel** (215)238-7800 or, 5587, FAX (215)238-7883, telex 173146. **(Subscription address:** W. B. Saunders Company / North America Subscriptions, c/o Periodicals, 6277 Sea Harbour Drive, 4th Floor, Orlando FL 32887.**) ED** Michael Bokulich. **DD** 616. **NLM** W1; HU46K. **CODEN** HPCQA4. **[CCC].** Index available. **Bk Rev. Ad Acc. Pr Rev. Circ:** 5,000. available on microfilm and microfiche from University Microfilms International (UMI). Documents available from The Genuine Article, BIOSIS Document Express, CASDDS.
**Desc:** Articles are drawn from morphologic and clinical laboratory studies relevant to the understanding of disease in man - including theoretical and experimental pathology and molecular biology.
**Ind/Abst** Biol. Abstr.; Chem. Abstr.; Coal Abstr.; Curr. Aware. Biol. Sci., CABS; Dairy Sci. Abstr.; EMBASE; Energy Res. Abstr. (Feb. 1972-); Health Plan. Adminis.; Helminthol. Abstr.; Immunol. Abstr.; Index Med.; INIS Atomindex [Micro.]; Microbiol. Abstr. Sect. C; Life Sci. Collect.; Physic. Medline Plus; Protozoolog. Abstr.; Ref. Upd. Basic Ed.; Ref. Upd. Deluxe Ed.; Res. Alert [Full Cov.]; Sci. Cit. Index; Virol. AIDS Abstr.

II/0377-4929
**INDIAN JOURNAL OF PATHOLOGY & MICROBIOLOGY.** [Indian j. pathol. microbiol.]. **Added/Corp** Indian Association of Pathologists & Microbiologists. **VFOAT** Indian Journal of Pathology and Microbiology. Vol. 18, No. 1, April 1975-. Academic Scholarly Publication. English. qt. $60.00. The Nizam's Institute of Medical Sciences, c/o J Path, Punjagutta Hyderabad 500-482 India. **Tel** 24811. **(Subscription address:** Prints India, 11 Darya Ganj, New Delhi 110002 India.**) ED** J Path. **NLM** W1 IN224H. **CODEN** IJPMDT. cum. index. **Bk Rev. Ad Acc. Circ:** 2,000 (ctrl). Documents available from BIOSIS Document Express. ***Continues*** *Indian Journal of Pathology & Bacteriology, 0019-5448.*
**Desc:** Covers diagnosis of diseases, laboratory diagnostic methods, cancer, experimental pathology, infectious diseases and blood disorders.
**Ind/Abst** Biol. Abstr.; EMBASE [Select. Cov.]; Index Med.; Index Vet.; Life Sci. Collect.; Rev. Med. Vet. Mycology; Rev. Plant Pathol.; Vet. Bull.

UK/0959-9673
**INTERNATIONAL JOURNAL OF EXPERIMENTAL PATHOLOGY.** [Int. j. exp. pathol.]. **VFOAT** Journal of Experimental Pathology. Vol. 71, No. 4 (Aug. 1990)-. Academic Scholarly Publication. English. bm (6 issues). $300.00 US & Canada; £177.50 Europe; £194.00 other. Blackwell Scientific Publications Ltd, Marston Book Services, PO Box 87, Oxford OX2 ODT UK. **Tel** 011 44 865 791155, FAX 011 44 865 791927, telex 837 515 MARDIS G. **NLM** W1; IN766IP. **CODEN** IJEPEI. **[CCC].** available on microfilm and microfiche from University Microfilms International (UMI). Documents available from The Genuine Article, BIOSIS Document Express, CASDDS, ADONIS. ***Continues*** *Journal of Experimental Pathology (Oxford, England), 0958-4625.*
**Ind/Abst** ADONIS; Biol. Abstr. (1991-); Chem. Abstr.; Curr. Aware. Biol. Sci., CABS; Curr. Contents Life Sci.; EMBASE; Helminthol. Abstr. (1991-); Index Med. (1990-); Index Vet.; PESTDOC; Pig News Inf.; Protozoolog. Abstr.; Ref. Upd. Basic Ed.; Ref. Upd. Deluxe Ed.; Res. Alert [Full Cov.]; Sci. Cit. Index; SCISEARCH; Vet. Bull.; Trop. Dis. Bull.

US/0277-1691
**INTERNATIONAL JOURNAL OF GYNECOLOGICAL PATHOLOGY.** (INTERNATIONAL JOURNAL OF GYNECOLOGICAL PATHOLOGY : OFFICIAL JOURNAL OF THE INTERNATIONAL SOCIETY OF GYNECOLOGICAL PATHOLOGISTS.). [Int. j. gynecol. pathol.]. **Added/Corp** International Society of Gynecological Pathologists. Vol. 1, No. 1 (1982)-. Periodical. English. qt. $172.00 (individuals), $248.00 (institutions) US; $216.00 (individuals), $305.00 (institutions) other. Raven Press, 1185 Avenue of the Americas, 37th Floor, New York NY 10036. **Tel** (212)930-9500, (212)930-9604, FAX (212)869-3495, (212)302-8507, telex 640073. **ED** Henry J. Norris. **NLM** W1 IN766U. **[CCC]. Pr Rev.** available on microfilm and microfiche from University Microfilms International (UMI). Documents available from The Genuine Article.
**Desc:** Dedicated to advances in the understanding and management of gynecological disease. Emphasis is placed on investigations in the field of anatomic pathology.
**Ind/Abst** Curr. Aware. Biol. Sci., CABS; Curr. Contents Clin. Med.; EMBASE; Index Med.; Res. Alert [Full Cov.]; Sci. Cit. Index; SCISEARCH.

●US/1066-8969
**INTERNATIONAL JOURNAL OF SURGICAL PATHOLOGY.** [Int. j. surg. pathol.]. **Added/Corp** International Academy of Pathology. Australasian Division. International Academy of Pathology. Hong Kong Division. Vol. 1, No. 1 (July 1993)-. Periodical. English. qt. $138.00 (Institutions), $104.00 (Individuals). Churchill Livingstone Inc., 650 Avenue of the Americas, New York NY 10011. **Tel** (212)206-5062, FAX (212)727-7808. **(Subscription address:** Churchill Livingstone Inc., 5 South 250 Frontenac Road, Naperville, IL 60563; (telephone: (800)553-5426 or (708)416-3939)**) DD** 616. **NLM** W1; IN791H. **[CCC].**

US/0074-7718
**INTERNATIONAL REVIEW OF EXPERIMENTAL PATHOLOGY.** [Int. rev. exp. pathol.]. Vol. 1 (1962)-. Monographic series. English. ir. Price varies per volume. Academic Press, Inc., 6277 Sea Harbor Drive, Orlando FL 32887. **Tel** (800)543-9534, (407)345-4100, FAX (407)363-9661. **ED** J. B. Cragg. **LC** RB6; .I55. **DD** 616.07. **UDC** 616; 591.2; 619. **NLM** W1 IN832M. **CODEN** IRXPAT. **[CCC].** Documents available from The Genuine Article, BIOSIS Document Express, CASDDS.
**Ind/Abst** Biol. Abstr.; Chem. Abstr.; Curr. Aware. Biol. Sci., CABS; EMBASE; Energy Res. Abstr.; Index Med.; Index Sci. Rev. [Full Cov.]; Index Vet.; Life Sci. Collect.; Res. Alert [Full Cov.]; Sci. Cit. Index; SCISEARCH; Vet. Bull.; Trop. Dis. Bull.

RU/0202-7135
**ITOGI NAUKI I TEKHNIKI. SERIIA PATOLOGICHESKAIA ANATOMIIA.** **Added/Corp** Vsesoiuznyi Institut Nauchnoi i Tekhnicheskoi Informatsii (Soviet Union). **VFOAT** Seriia Patologicheskaia Anatomiia; Patologicheskaia Anatomiia; A.Itogi nauki i tekhniki. P.Patologicheskaîa anatomiîa. Vol. 1 (1978)-. Monographic series. Russian. Price varies per volume. VINITI - Vsesoyuznyi Institut Nauchno-Tekhnicheskoi Informatsii, All-Union Scientific and Technical Information Institute, Baltiiskaia Ulitsa 14, 125219 Moscow Russia. **Tel** 238-46-00, FAX 9430060, telex 411160. **NLM** W1 PA986.

UK/0021-9746
**JOURNAL OF CLINICAL PATHOLOGY.** [J. clin. pathol.]. **Added/Corp** British Medical Association. Association of Clinical Pathologists (Great Britain). Vol. 1 (1947)-. Academic Scholarly Publication. English. mo. £265.00. BMJ / British Medical Journal Publishing Group, British Medical Association House, Tavistock Square, London WC1H 9JR England. **Tel** 011 44 71 3874499, FAX 011 44 71 383 6402, telex 290034 HBJ MN. **ED** John Lilleyman. **DD** 616. **NLM** W1 JO5896. **CODEN** JCPAAK. **[CCC]. Pr Rev.** available on microfilm and microfiche from University Microfilms International (UMI). Documents available from The Genuine Article, BIOSIS Document Express, CASDDS, ADONIS.
**Desc:** Original and specially commissioned articles on each branch of pathology, with prominence given to its clinical application.
**Ind/Abst** Abr. Index Med.; ADONIS; Biol. Abstr.; Calcium Calcif. Tissue Abstr.; Chem. Abstr.; Chem. Hazards Ind.; CSA Neuro. Abstr. (?-?); Cumul. Index Nurs. Allied Health Lit.; Curr. Aware. Biol. Sci., CABS; Curr. Contents Clin. Med.; Curr. Contents Life Sci.; Dairy Sci. Abstr.; EMBASE; Health Devices Alerts; Health Period. Database; Helminthol. Abstr. (1991-); Immunol. Abstr.; Index Med.; Lab. Hazards Bull.; Microbiol. Abstr. Sect. B; Microbiol. Abstr. Sect. A; Microbiol. Abstr. Sect. C; Nutr. Abstr. Rev., Ser. B, Live Feeds and Feed.; Nutr. Abstr. Rev., Ser. A, Hum. Exp.; Oncog. Growth Factors Abstr.; Life Sci. Collect.; PESTDOC; Physic. Medline Plus; Protozoolog. Abstr.; Ref. Upd. Basic Ed.; Ref. Upd. Deluxe Ed.; Res. Alert [Full Cov.]; Rev. Med. Vet. Mycology; Rev. Plant Pathol.; Saf. Health Work; Sci. Cit. Index; SCISEARCH; Soc. Sci. Cit. Index [Select. Cov.]; Trop. Dis. Bull.; Virol. AIDS Abstr.

UK/0144-0349
**JOURNAL OF CLINICAL PATHOLOGY. SUPPLEMENT. (ASSOCIATION OF CLINICAL PATHOLOGISTS).** [J. clin. pathol., Suppl. Assoc. Clin. Pathol. symp.]. **VFOAT** Journal of Clinical Pathology. Vol. 1 (1967)-. Academic Scholarly Publication. English. mo. £265.00. BMJ / British Medical Journal Publishing Group, British Medical Association House, Tavistock Square, London WC1H 9JR England. **Tel** 011 44 71 3874499, FAX 011 44 71 383 6402, telex 290034 HBJ MN. **NLM** W1 JO5896A. **CODEN** JCPPDY. Documents available from CASDDS.
**Ind/Abst** Chem. Abstr. (1967-1978); Index Med. (19??-).

UK/0144-0330
**JOURNAL OF CLINICAL PATHOLOGY. SUPPLEMENT (ROYAL COLLEGE OF PATHOLOGISTS).** [J. clin. pathol. Suppl. R. Coll. Pathol. symp.]. **VFOAT** Journal of Clinical Pathology. Supplement. Royal College of Pathologists Symposia. Began with: No. 4, published in 1970. Academic Scholarly Publication. English. an. Price varies per volume. BMJ / British Medical Journal Publishing Group, British Medical Association House, Tavistock Square, London WC1H 9JR England. **Tel** 011 44 71 3874499, FAX 011 44 71 383 6402, telex 290034 HBJ MN. **UDC** 616. **NLM** W1 JO5896C. **CODEN** JPHSBO. Documents available from CASDDS.
**Ind/Abst** Chem. Abstr.; Index Med.

UK/0021-9975
**JOURNAL OF COMPARATIVE PATHOLOGY.** [J. comp. pathol.]. Vol. 75 (Jan. 1965)-. Academic Scholarly Publication. English. Eight times a year. £218.00 UK and Europe; $392.00 other (institution). Harcourt Brace & Company Ltd., Foots Cray, High Street, Sidcup Kent DA14 5HP England. **Tel** 011 44 81 300 3322, FAX 011 44 81 309 0807. **(Subscription address:** W. B. Saunders Company / North America Subscriptions, c/o Periodicals, 6277 Sea Harbour Drive, 4th Floor, Orlando FL 32887.**) ED** E. J. H. Ford. **UDC** 591.2; 616; 619. **NLM** W1 JO595H. **CODEN** JCVPAR. **[CCC].** Index available (bound in issue). **Pr Rev.** Documents available from The Genuine Article, BIOSIS Document Express, CASDDS. ***Continues*** *Journal of Comparative Pathology and Therapeutics.*
**Desc:** Of interest to workers in veterinary and medical science who investigate diseases of all vertebrate animals, including domesticated, zoo, wild, and marine species as well as man. Publishes articles of original research on all these species when viewed against the general background of vertbrate pathology. An important forum for the field, the journal has a long-established reputation for publishing research findings relevant to the diseases of man and domesticated and other vertebrate animals, with emphasis on developing areas and on the use of modern techniques.
**Ind/Abst** AgBiotech News Inf.; AGRICOLA [Select. Cov.]; Anim. Breed. Abstr.; Biol. Abstr.; Chem. Abstr.; CSA Neuro. Abstr. (?-?); Curr. Contents, Agric. Biol. Environ. Sci.; Curr. Contents Life Sci.; Curr. Ref. Fish Res.; Dairy Sci. Abstr.; EMBASE; Fish Rev.; Grasslands For. Abstr.; Helminthol. Abstr. (19??-19??); Index Med.; Index Vet.; Nutr. Abstr. Rev., Ser. B, Live Feeds and Feed.; Nutr. Abstr. Rev., Ser. A, Hum. Exp.; Life Sci. Collect.; PESTDOC; Pig News Inf.; Poult. Abstr.; Protozoolog. Abstr.; Res. Alert [Full Cov.]; Rev. Med. Vet. Entomol.; Rev. Med. Vet. Mycology; Rev. Plant Pathol.; Sci. Cit. Index; SCISEARCH; Small Anim. Abstr. Bibliogr.; Vet. Bull.; Weed Abstr.; Wildl. Rev.

DK/0303-6987
**JOURNAL OF CUTANEOUS PATHOLOGY.** See Medical Science and Technology-Dermatology.

US/0730-8485
**JOURNAL OF EXPERIMENTAL PATHOLOGY.** ***Ceased.*** [J. exp. pathol.]. Vol. 1, No. 1, (1983)-(1991). Academic Scholarly Publication. English. qt. Mary Ann Liebert Inc., 1651 Third Avenue, New York NY 10128. **Tel** (212)289-2300, (800)M-LIEBERT, FAX (212)289-4697. **DD** 619. **NLM** W1 JO644R. **CODEN** JEPAD3. Documents available from CASDDS.
**Ind/Abst** AgBiotech News Inf.; Chem. Abstr. (1983-); CSA Neuro. Abstr. (Vol. 1 No. 1, 1985-?); Index Med. (Vol. 1, No. 1, 1985-); Index Vet.; Oncog. Growth Factors Abstr.; Life Sci. Collect.; Vet. Bull. (?-?); Virol. AIDS Abstr. (1983-).

US/0022-2011
**JOURNAL OF INVERTEBRATE PATHOLOGY.** See Zoology-Entomology.

IT
**JOURNAL OF PALEOPATHOLOGY.** **Added/Corp** Universita "G. D'Annunzio." Facolta di Medicina e Chirurgia. Vol. I, No. 1 (1987)-. Periodical. English. Three times a year. L120000. Journal of Paleopathology, Museo Arche Naz Villa Comun 3, 66100 Chieti Italy. **Tel** 011 39 871 65704. **LC** R134.8; .J68. **DD** 616.07. **NLM** W1; JO826R.

UK/0022-3417
**JOURNAL OF PATHOLOGY.** (THE JOURNAL OF PATHOLOGY : A JOURNAL OF THE PATHOLOGICAL SOCIETY OF GREAT BRITAIN AND IRELAND.). [J. pathol.]. **Added/Corp** Pathological Society of Great Britain and Ireland. Vol. 97 (1969)-. Academic Scholarly Publication. English. mo. $525.00. John Wiley & Sons Ltd., Baffins Lane, Chichester West Sussex PO19 1UD England. **Tel** 0243 779777, FAX 0243 776128 BTG:JWP001, telex 86290 WIBOOKG. **(Subscription address:** John Wiley / Philadelphia, PO Box 7247, Philadelphia PA 19170.**) ED** D. H. Wright. **DD** 616. **NLM** W1 JO828B. **CODEN** JPTLASJPTCAS. **[CCC]. Bk Rev. Ad Acc. Circ:** 2,500. available on microfilm and microfiche from University Microfilms International (UMI). Documents available from The Genuine Article, BIOSIS Document Express, CASDDS, ADONIS. ***Continues*** *Journal of Pathology and Bacteriology, 0368-3494.* ***Absorbed in part by*** *Diagnostic Histopathology, 0272-7749.*
**Desc:** Publishes papers in the fields of pathology and clinico-pathological correlation. Also, covers the field of experimental pathology, relevant to the understanding of human disease, and includes papers on the use of techniques such as immunology and molecular biology to elucidate disease mechanisms.
**Ind/Abst** ADONIS; AgBiotech News Inf.; AGRICOLA;

Biol. Abstr.; Chem. Abstr.; CSA Neuro. Abstr. (?-?); Curr. Aware. Biol. Sci., CABS; EMBASE; Health Period. Database; Immunol. Abstr.; Index Med.; Life Sci. Collect.; Protozoolog. Abstr.; Ref. Upd. Basic Ed.; Ref. Upd. Deluxe Ed.; Res. Alert [Full Cov.]; Rev. Med. Vet. Mycology; Saf. Health Work; Sci. Cit. Index; SCISEARCH; Small Anim. Abstr. Bibliogr.; Trop. Dis. Bull.; Virol. AIDS Abstr.

JA/0914-9198
**JOURNAL OF TOXICOLOGIC PATHOLOGY.** [J. toxicol. pathol.]. (1988)-. Periodical. Multiple languages. sa. Japanese Society of Toxicologic Pathology, Tokyo Japan. **DD** 615.9. Documents available from CASDDS.
**Ind/Abst** Chem. Abstr.

CN/0828-5942
**K.V.P. MANITOBA NEWS.** [K.V.P. Manit. news]. **VAT** MAMRT News Manitoba Association of Medical Radiation Technologists News. Vol. 20, No. 3 (Sept. 1984)-. Periodical. English. ir (five issues per year). Manitoba Association of Medical Radiation Technologists, Suite 215/819 Sargent Avenue, Winnipeg Manitoba R3E 0B9 Canada. **DD** 616.07/57/0607127. **UDC** 615.849-05(060.21)(712). **Ad Acc. Circ:** 700. ***Continues*** *K V P News, 0022-7439.*

●RU/0869-2084
**KLINICHESKAIA LABORATORNAIA DIAGNOSTIKA.** **Added/Corp** Russia (Federation). Ministerstvo Zdravookhraneniia. Soiuz Nauchnykh Obshchestv Klinicheskoi Laboratornoi Diagnostiki. Russia (Federation). Ministerstvo Zdravookhraneniia i Meditsinskoi Promyshlennosti. (1992)-. Academic Scholarly Publication. Russian (summaries and/or abstracts in English; table of contents in English). Six times a year. $69.95 US & Canada; $79.95 Europe; $94.95 others. **(Subscription address:** East View Publications Inc., 3020 Harbor Lane North, Suite 110, Minneapolis MN 55447.) **LC** RB1; .L3. **NLM** W1; KL186. **CODEN** KLDIES. Documents available from CASDDS. ***Continues*** *Laboratornoe Delo, 0023-6748.*
**Ind/Abst** Chem. Abstr.; Index Med. (1992-).

US/0023-6837
**LABORATORY INVESTIGATION.** [Lab. invest.]. **Added/Corp** International Association of Medical Museums. International Academy of Pathology. United States and Canadian Academy of Pathology. Vol. 1 (Spring 1952)-. Academic Scholarly Publication. English. mo. $147.00 (individual), $249.00 (institution) US; $197.00 (individual), $299.00 (institution) other. Williams & Wilkins Company, 428 East Preston Street, Baltimore MD 21202-3993. **Tel** (410)528-4000, (800)638-6423, FAX (410)528-8596, telex 87669. **(Subscription address:** Williams & Wilkins, PO Box 64380, Baltimore MD 21264.) **ED** Emanuel Rubin. **LC** RB1; .I5. **NLM** W1 LA208. **CODEN** LAINAW. **[CCC].** Index available. **Ad Acc. Pr Rev. Circ:** 6,100 (ctrl). Documents available from The Genuine Article, BIOSIS Document Express, CASDDS, Quick Copies. ***Supersedes*** *Bulletin of the International Association of Medical Museums, 0160-452X.*
**Desc:** Experimental, anatomical, and comparative pathology; cytologic and histologic methods, and tissue culturing for pathologists and laboratory technicians.
**Ind/Abst** AGRICOLA; Anim. Breed. Abstr.; Biol. Abstr.; Chem. Abstr.; CSA Neuro. Abstr. (?-?); Curr. Aware. Biol. Sci., CABS; Curr. Contents Life Sci.; Dairy Sci. Abstr.; EMBASE; Energy Res. Abstr.; Fish Rev.; Helminthol. Abstr. (1991-); Immunol. Abstr.; Index Med.; Int. Aerosp. Abstr.; Nucl. Sci. Abstr.; Nutr. Abstr. Rev., Ser. A, Hum. Exp.; Life Sci. Collect.; Pig News Inf.; Poult. Abstr.; Protozoolog. Abstr.; Ref. Upd. Basic Ed.; Ref. Upd. Deluxe Ed.; Res. Alert [Full Cov.]; Rev. Med. Vet. Mycology; Sci. Cit. Index; SCISEARCH; Small Anim. Abstr. Bibliogr.; Virol. AIDS Abstr.; Wildl. Rev.

US/0076-2881
**MAJOR PROBLEMS IN PATHOLOGY.** [Major probl. pathol.]. (1970)-. Monographic series. English. ir. Price varies per volume. Holt Rinehart and Winston, 6277 Sea Harbor Drive, Orlando FL 32887. **Tel** (407)345-2500, 800 545-2522. **ED** J. L. Bennington. **NLM** W1 MA492X. Each issue contains an index to its own contents (no volume index)--loose.
**Ind/Abst** Energy Res. Abstr. (Aug. 1982-).

MY/0126-8635
**MALAYSIAN JOURNAL OF PATHOLOGY, THE.** [Malays. j. pathol.]. **Added/Corp** Malaysian Society of Pathologists. Vol. 1, (Aug. 1978)-. Periodical. English. Twice a year. $30.00. University of Malaya / Department of Pathology, Faculty of Medicine, 59100 Kuala Lumpur Malaysia. **Tel** 603-7502064, FAX 603-7573661, telex UNIMAL MA 39845. **ED** Professor Lai-Menl Looi. **NLM** W1 MA5247F. (one in three years). cum. index. **Bk Rev. Ad Acc, Adv Mgr:** Dr. PL Chzah, **Tel** 603 7502481. **Pr Rev. Circ:** 500 (ctrl).
**Ind/Abst** Index Med.; Trop. Dis. Bull.

US
**MANUAL FOR LABORATORY WORKLOAD RECORDING METHOD.** (19??)-. English. College of American Pathologists, Q Probes Department, 325 Waukegan Road, Northfield IL 60093. **Tel** (708)446-8800, FAX (708)446-8807. ***Continues*** *Workload Recording Method & Personnel Management Manual.*

US/0733-4265
**MASSON MONOGRAPHS IN DIAGNOSTIC PATHOLOGY.** [Masson monogr. diagn. pathol.]. (1981)-. Academic Scholarly Publication. English. qt. Price varies per volume. Masson Distribution Inc, Box C 762, Brooklyn NY 11205. **ED** Stephen S Sternberg. **NLM** W1 MA9309S. Documents available from CASDDS.
**Ind/Abst** Chem. Abstr.

US/0090-7065
**MEDICAL EXAMINATION REVIEW BOOK. PATHOLOGY SPECIALTY BOARD REVIEW.** **VFOAT** Pathology Specialty Board Review. 1st- Ed. English. ir. Medical Exam Publishing Company, 52 Vanderbilt Avenue Elsevier, New York NY 10017-3808. **Tel** (212)463-1052.
**Desc:** Prepared by three educators, this volume features 703 questions and answers. The explanatory answers are useful in helping students to prepare for course and board examinations.

US/0893-3952
**MODERN PATHOLOGY.** [Mod. path.]. **Added/Corp** United States and Canadian Academy of Pathology. Meeting. Society for Pediatric Pathology (U.S.). Meeting. United States and Canadian Academy of Pathology. Vol. 1, No. 1 (Jan. 1988)-. Periodical. English. bm. $139.00 (individual), $227.00 (institution), US; $184.00 (individual), $272.00 (institution), other. Williams & Wilkins Company, 428 East Preston Street, Baltimore MD 21202-3993. **Tel** (410)528-4000, (800)638-6423, FAX (410)528-8596, telex 87669. **(Subscription address:** Williams & Wilkins, PO Box 64380, Baltimore MD 21264.) **LC** RB37.A1; M63. **DD** 616.07. **NLM** W1; MO167L. **CODEN** MODPEO. **[CCC]. Pr Rev.** Documents available from The Genuine Article, BIOSIS Document Express, Quick Copies.
**Desc:** Provides a forum for the presentation of advances in the understanding of pathological processes. Reviews papers in advancing methodology as they relate to improving the diagnostic capabilities of pathologists.
**Ind/Abst** Biol. Abstr.; Chicano Index; Curr. Contents Clin. Med.; Curr. Contents Life Sci.; Index Med. (1988-); Protozoolog. Abstr.; Res. Alert [Full Cov.]; Sci. Cit. Index; SCISEARCH; Soc. Sci. Cit. Index [Select. Cov.].

US/0077-0922
**MONOGRAPHS IN PATHOLOGY.** [Monogr. pathol.]. **Main/Corp** International Academy of Pathology. **VFOAT** International Academy of Pathology Monograph. No. 1 (1960)-. Monographic series. English. ir. Price varies per volume. Williams & Wilkins Company, 428 East Preston Street, Baltimore MD 21202-3993. **Tel** (410)528-4000, (800)638-6423, FAX (410)528-8596, telex 87669. **(Subscription address:** Riddenhouse Book Distributors, 511 Feheley Drive, King of Prussia PA 19406.) **LC** UNC. **NLM** W1 MO568H. **CODEN** IAPMAV. Documents available from BIOSIS Document Express, CASDDS.
**Ind/Abst** Biol. Abstr.; Chem. Abstr.; Energy Res. Abstr. (Aug. 1982-); Index Med.

UK/0305-1846
**NEUROPATHOLOGY AND APPLIED NEUROBIOLOGY.** [Neuropathol. appl. neurobiol.]. **Added/Corp** British Neuropathological Society. Vol. 1 (Jan. 1975)-. Academic Scholarly Publication. English. bm (6 issues). $682.00 US & Canada; £398.50 Europe; £440.00 other. Blackwell Scientific Publications Ltd, Marston Book Services, PO Box 87, Oxford OX2 ODT UK. **Tel** 011 44 865 791155, FAX 011 44 865 791927, telex 837 515 MARDIS G. **ED** J. B. Cavanagh and R. O. Weller. **NLM** W1 NE337R. **CODEN** NANEDL. **[CCC].** Index available (bound in last issue). **Bk Rev. Ad Acc. Pr Rev. Circ:** 400 (ctrl). available on microfilm and microfiche from University Microfilms International (UMI). Documents available from The Genuine Article, BIOSIS Document Express, CASDDS.
**Desc:** Original clinical and experimental papers on problems and pathological processes in neuropathology and muscle disease.
**Ind/Abst** AgBiotech News Inf.; Biol. Abstr.; Chem. Abstr.; CSA Neuro. Abstr. (?-?); Curr. Contents Life Sci.; Dev. Med. Child Neurol.; EMBASE; Index Med.; Index Vet.; Life Sci. Collect.; Ref. Upd. Basic Ed.; Ref. Upd. Deluxe Ed.; Res. Alert [Full Cov.]; Sci. Cit. Index; SCISEARCH; Small Anim. Abstr. Bibliogr.; Vet. Bull.

BU/0324-1998
**OBSCA I SRAVNITELNA PATOLOGIJA.** (OBSHTA I SRAVNITELNA PATOLOGIIA.). [Obsca sravn. patol.]. **Added/Corp** Bulgarska Akademiia na Naukite. **VFOAT** General and Comparative Pathology. Vol. 1 (1976)-. Academic Scholarly Publication. Bulgarian (summaries and/or abstracts in English and Russian; table of contents in English and Russian). sa. Izdatelstvo na Bulgarskata, Akademiia na Naukite, Institut za Muzikoznanie, Ul Dimitur Poliznov 21, 1504 Sofia Bulgaria. **NLM** W1 OB459. **CODEN** OSPADK. Documents available from CASDDS. ***Continues*** *Izvestiia na Instituta Po Obshta i Sravnitelna Patologiia.*
**Ind/Abst** AGRICOLA; Chem. Abstr.; EMBASE; Index Vet.

CN/0836-4362
**OSLA. ONTARIO ASSOCIATION OF SPEECH-LANGUAGE PATHOLOGISTS AND AUDIOLOGISTS.** (OSLA.). [OSLA, Ont. Assoc. Speech-Lang. Pathol. Audiol.]. **Added/Corp** Ontario Association of Speech-Language Pathologists and Audiologists. **VFOAT** OSLA Newsletter. **VAT** Ontario Association of Speech-Language Pathologists and Audiologists. Vol. 11, No. 4 (Dec. 1986)-. Periodical. English. qt. Limited free distribution. Ontario Speech and Hearing Association, 22 College Street, Suite 401, Toronto, Ont. M5G 1K2 Canada. **DD** 616.85/5/0060713. ***Continues*** *O S H A., 0705-8713.*

NE/0304-3959
**PAIN (AMSTERDAM).** (PAIN.). [Pain]. **Added/Corp** International Association for the Study of Pain. Vol. 1 (Mar. 1975)-. Academic Scholarly Publication. English. mo (4 volumes). Fl1256.00. Elsevier Science Publishers BV, PO Box 211, 1000 AE Amsterdam Netherlands. **Tel** 011 31 20 5803642, FAX 011 31 20 5862696, telex 15682. **ED** P D Wall. **LC** RB127; .P33. **NLM** W1 PA29. **CODEN** PAINDB. **[CCC]. Pr Rev.** available on microfilm and microfiche from University Microfilms International (UMI). Documents available from The Genuine Article, BIOSIS Document Express, CASDDS, ADONIS.
**Desc:** Its intention is to bring together information about the nature, mechanisms and treatment of pain.
**Ind/Abst** ADONIS; Annals Behav. Med.; Biol. Abstr.; Chem. Abstr.; CSA Neuro. Abstr.; Cumul. Index Nurs. Allied Health Lit.; Curr. Contents Clin. Med.; Curr. Contents Life Sci.; EMBASE; Index Med.; Med. Abstr. Newsl.; Life Sci. Collect.; PESTDOC; Psychol. Abstr. (1976-); PsycINFO (1990-); PsycLit; Ref. Upd. Basic Ed.; Ref. Upd. Deluxe Ed.; Res. Alert [Full Cov.]; Sci. Cit. Index; SCISEARCH; Soc. Sci. Cit. Index [Select. Cov.].

SZ/1015-2008
**PATHOBIOLOGY (BASEL).** (PATHOBIOLOGY : JOURNAL OF IMMUNOPATHOLOGY, MOLECULAR AND CELLULAR BIOLOGY.). [Pathobiology]. (Jan./Feb. 1990)-. Periodical. English. bm (6 issues). $489.00. S. Karger AG, Allschwilerstrasse 10, PO Box - Postfach - Case Postale, CH-4009 Basel Switzerland. **Tel** 011 41 61 306-1111, FAX 011 41 61 306-1234, telex CH 962 652. **ED** J. M. Cruse, R. E. Lewis, M. I. Greene, G. V. Sherbet, C. Sorg. **LC** RB125; .P37. **NLM** W1; PA8955. **CODEN** PATHEF. **[CCC].** Documents available from The Genuine Article, BIOSIS Document Express. ***Formed by the union of*** *Experimental Cell Biology, 0304-3568* ***and*** *Pathology and Immunopathology Research, 0257-2761.*
**Desc:** Formulated to reflect the latest in current basic medical research. Original articles and interpretive review papers address timely topics in pathobiology, immunopathology, cellular and molecular biology, and medicine. Investigators from around the world have great freedom in the interpretation and presentation of their own experimental data. A valued feature is special theme issues, published at intervals.
**Ind/Abst** Biol. Abstr.; Curr. Aware. Biol. Sci., CABS; Curr. Contents Life Sci.; EMBASE; Health Plan. Adminis.; Index Med. (1990-); PESTDOC; Ref. Upd. Deluxe Ed.; Res. Alert [Full Cov.]; Sci. Cit. Index; SCISEARCH.

GW/0172-8113
**PATHOLOGE, DER.** [Pathologe]. Vol. 1 (Nov. 1979)-. Periodical. German. Six times a year. DM368.00. Springer-Verlag GmbH & Company KG, Heidelberger Platz 3, D 14197 Berlin Germany. **Tel** 011 49 30 8207223, FAX 011 49 30 8214091, telex 183 319 SPBLN D. **(Subscription address:** Springer Verlag New York Inc. / for North America, 44 Hartz Way, Secaucus NJ 07096.) **ED** R Bassler, V Becker, G Dhom, W Doerr, M Eder, H J Fodisch, A Georgii, F Gloor, Kl Goerttler, E Grundmann, Th Hardmeier, J H Holzner, F K Koessling, J Kracht, W Schachenmayr, G Seifert, M Stolte, and C Thomas. **NLM** W1 PA898D. **[CCC]. Pr Rev.** available on microfilm from University Microfilms International (UMI). Documents available from The Genuine Article.
**Desc:** Combines pathological science with practice. Offers classification problems, new syndromes, tips and diagnostics, as well as symposium reports and career news.
**Ind/Abst** Curr. Contents Life Sci.; EMBASE; Helminthol. Abstr. (1991-); Index Med.; Res. Alert [Full Cov.]; Sci. Cit. Index; SCISEARCH.

IT/0031-2983
**PATHOLOGICA.** [Pathologica]. V. 1- (No. 1- ); 15 Nov. 1908-. Academic Scholarly Publication. English (Italian). mo. L40000 Italy; L50000 other. Pathologica, Via Alessandro Volta 8, Genova Italy. **UDC** 616. **NLM** W1 PA899. **CODEN** PATHAB. Documents available from BIOSIS Document Express, CASDDS.
**Ind/Abst** Biol. Abstr.; Chem. Abstr.; EMBASE [Select. Cov.]; Index Med.; Saf. Health Work.

FR/0369-8114
**PATHOLOGIE ET BIOLOGIE (PARIS).** (PATHOLOGIE BIOLOGIE.). [Pathol. biol.]. Vol. 17 (Jan. 1969)-. Academic Scholarly Publication. French (English). mo (10 times a year). 1300.00F France; 1720.00F other. Semaine de Hopitaux, 31 Boulevard de la

Tour-Maubourg, 75007 Paris, France. **Tel** 011 33 1 40 62 64 00. **NLM** W1 PA95. **CODEN** PTBIAN. **Pr Rev.** Documents available from The Genuine Article, CASDDS. ***Continues*** *Pathologie et Biologie, 0369-8114.*
**Ind/Abst** AGRICOLA; Chem. Abstr.; CIS Abstr.; Curr. Contents Life Sci.; Dairy Sci. Abstr.; EMBASE [Select. Cov.]; Energy Res. Abstr. (May 1981-); Helminthol. Abstr.; Index Med.; Index Vet.; Microbiol. Abstr. Sect. B; Microbiol. Abstr. Sect. A; Nutr. Abstr. Rev., Ser. A, Hum. Exp.; Life Sci. Collect.; Poult. Abstr.; Protozoolog. Abstr.; Res. Alert [Full Cov.]; Rev. Med. Vet. Mycology; Saf. Health Work; Sci. Cit. Index; SCISEARCH; Soyabean Abstr.; Vet. Bull.

FR
**PATHOLOGIE ET PHYSIOLOGIE OSTEOARTICULAIRES.** French. ir. 990.37F France; 1030.00F other. CNRS / Institut d'Information Scientifique et Technique, (Centre National de la Recherche Scientifique), 15 Quai Anatole France, Paris 75700 France. **Tel** 011 33 1 47531515, telex 299 356 F. ***Continues*** *Pascal Explore : E79, Pathologie et Physiologie, Osteoarticulaires.*

AT/0031-3025
**PATHOLOGY.** [Pathology]. **Added/Corp** College of Pathologists of Australia. Royal College of Pathologists of Australia. Royal College of Pathologists of Australasia. Vol. 1 (1969)-. Academic Scholarly Publication. English. Four times a year. 150.00Aus$ Australia; 170.00Aus$ others. Royal College of Pathologists of Australia, Durham Hall, 207 Albion Street, Surry Hills New South Wales 2010 Australia. **Tel** 011 61 2 332-4266, FAX 011 61 2 331-1431. **ED** B. A. Warren. **NLM** W1; PA962G. **CODEN** PTLGAX. **[CCC].** Index available (bound in 4th issue). **Bk Rev. Ad Acc. Pr Rev. Circ:** 1,800. Documents available from The Genuine Article, BIOSIS Document Express, CASDDS.
**Desc:** Original articles on anatomical pathology, hematology, clinical chemistry, immunology, bacteriology, and experimental pathology.
**Ind/Abst** Biol. Abstr.; Chem. Abstr.; Curr. Aware. Biol. Sci., CABS; Curr. Biotechnol.; EMBASE; Index Med.; Microbiol. Abstr. Sect. B (19??-19??); Microbiol. Abstr. Sect. A; Life Sci. Collect.; Res. Alert [Full Cov.]; Rev. Med. Vet. Mycology; Sci. Cit. Index; SCISEARCH.

US/0079-0184
**PATHOLOGY ANNUAL.** [Pathol. annu.]. Vol. 1 (1966)-. English. Twice a year. $75.00. Appleton & Lange, (A Subsidiary of Simon & Schuster), 25 Van Zant Street, East Norwalk CT 06855. **Tel** (203)838-4400, (800)423-1359, FAX (203)854-9486. **ED** Sheldon C. Sommers, Paul Peter Rosen and Robert Fechner. **LC** RB1; .P655. **DD** 616.0705. **NLM** W1 PA962H. **CODEN** PATABP. **[CCC].** Documents available from The Genuine Article, BIOSIS Document Express, CASDDS.
**Desc:** Collection of original articles in the field of pathology.
**Ind/Abst** Biol. Abstr.; Chem. Abstr.; Energy Res. Abstr. (Oct. 1978-); Index Med.; Index Sci. Rev. [Full Cov.]; Res. Alert [Full Cov.]; Sci. Cit. Index; SCISEARCH.

●AT/1320-5463
**PATHOLOGY INTERNATIONAL.**
**Added/Corp** Nihon Byori Gakkai. Vol. 44, Issue 1 (Jan. 1994)-. Academic Scholarly Publication. English. mo. 496.00Aus$ Australia; ¥34700 Japan; $347.00 other. Blackwell Scientific Publications Australia, 54 University Street, PO Box 378, Carlton Victoria 3053 Australia. **Tel** 011 61 3 3470300, FAX 011 61 3 3475001, telex 10716421. **NLM** W1; PA962NL. **CODEN** PITEES. Documents available from CASDDS. ***Continues*** *Acta Pathologica Japonica, 0001-6632.*
**Ind/Abst** Chem. Abstr.; Index Med. (1994-).

US/1050-9194
**PATHOLOGY PATTERNS.** (PATHOLOGY PATTERNS : ASCP COMMENTARY ON THE ENVIRONMENT OF LABORATORY MEDICINE.). [Pathol. patterns]. **Added/Corp** American Society of Clinical Pathologists. (Apr. 1989)-. Periodical. English. sa. **DD** 616.
**Ind/Abst** Trop. Dis. Bull.

●US/1041-3480
**PATHOLOGY (PHILADELPHIA, PA.).** (PATHOLOGY.). [Pathology]. **Added/Corp** California Society of Pathologists. **VFOAT** Pathology, State of the Art Reviews. Vol. 1, No. 1 (1992)-. Periodical. English. Twice a year. $70.00 (US & possessions); $80.00 (other). Hanley & Belfus Inc., 210 South 13th Street, Philadelphia PA 19107. **Tel** (215)546-7293, FAX (215)790-9330. **DD** 616. **[CCC].**

GW/0344-0338
**PATHOLOGY, RESEARCH AND PRACTICE.** [Pathol., res. pract.]. **Added/Corp** European Society of Pathology. Vol. 162, (1978)-. Academic Scholarly Publication. English (French and German). mo. DM1264.00 Germany; DM1288.00 other. Gustav Fischer Verlag Stuttgart, Postfach 720143, Wollgrasweg 49, D 70577 Stuttgart Germany. **Tel** 011 49 711 458030, FAX 0711-4580334, telex 2627-7111488. **(Subscription address:** VCH Publishers Inc., 303 Northwest 12th Avenue, Journals Department, Deerfield FL 33442.**) ED** E Grundmann and Chr Witting. **NLM** W1 PA963D. **CODEN** PARPDS. **[CCC]. Pr Rev.** Documents available from The Genuine Article, BIOSIS Document Express, CASDDS. ***Continues*** *Beitrage zur Pathologie.*
**Desc:** Pursues the essential goal of providing the international foundation for the entire field of pathology. All aspects of the field are represented from pure theory to daily practice.
**Ind/Abst** Biol. Abstr.; Chem. Abstr.; Curr. Aware. Biol. Sci., CABS; Curr. Contents Life Sci.; EMBASE; Energy Res. Abstr. (May 1981-); Index Med.; Oncog. Growth Factors Abstr.; Life Sci. Collect.; Protozoolog. Abstr.; Res. Alert [Full Cov.]; Rev. Med. Vet. Entomol.; Rev. Med. Vet. Mycology; Sci. Cit. Index; SCISEARCH; Virol. AIDS Abstr.

NE/0928-4680
**PATHOPHYSIOLOGY.** Academic Scholarly Publication. English. Four times a year (1 volume). Fl402.00. Elsevier Science Publishers BV, PO Box 211, 1000 AE Amsterdam Netherlands. **Tel** 011 31 20 5803642, FAX 011 31 20 5862696, telex 15682. **[CCC].**

SP
**PATOLOGIA.** Spanish. Sociedad Espanola de Anatomia Patologica, Velazquez 114, 28006 Madrid Spain.
**Ind/Abst** Indice Med. Esp.

PL/0031-3114
**PATOLOGIA POLSKA.** ***Title Change.*** [Patol. pol.]. **Added/Corp** Polskie Towarzystwo Patologow. Vol. 1 (Jan. 1950)-(1993). Academic Scholarly Publication. Polish (Polish; summaries and/or abstracts in Russian, English and French; table of contents in Russian and English). qt. **(Subscription address:** ARS Polona, PO Box 1001, 00068 Warsaw Poland.**) NLM** W1; PA976. **CODEN** PAPOAC. Documents available from BIOSIS Document Express, CASDDS. ***Continued by*** *Polish Journal of Pathology.*
**Ind/Abst** Biol. Abstr. (?-?); Chem. Abstr. (?-?); EMBASE (?-?); Index Med. (?-?).

US/0277-0938
**PEDIATRIC PATHOLOGY.** ***Title Change.*** (PEDIATRIC PATHOLOGY / AFFILIATED WITH THE INTERNATIONAL PAEDIATRIC PATHOLOGY ASSOCIATION.). [Pediatr. pathol.]. **Added/Corp** International Paediatric Pathology Association. Society for Pediatric Pathology (U.S.). Vol. 1, No. 1, (Jan./Mar. 1983)-(1994). Periodical. English. bm (6 issues). Taylor & Francis Ltd., Rankine Road, Basingstoke Hampshire, RG24 8PR United Kingdom. **Tel** 011 44 256 840366, FAX 011 44 256 479438, telex 858540. **(Subscription address:** Taylor & Francis Inc., 1900 Frost Road, Suite 101, Bristol PA 19007-1598.**) ED** Frank Gonzalez-Gussi. **DD** 618. **NLM** W1; PE169R. **CODEN** PPATDQ. **[CCC]. Bk Rev. Ad Acc. Circ:** 800. available on microfilm and microfiche from University Microfilms International (UMI). Documents available from The Genuine Article, BIOSIS Document Express. ***Continued by*** *Pediatric Pathology and Laboratory Medicine, 1077-1042.*
**Desc:** An established international journal for the study of disease in the developing human for those active in the area of human growth and development. Publishes original articles, case reports and reviews which cover a wide range of topics, including placentology, intrauterine development and the pathology of pediatrics, and the pediatric subspecialties.
**Ind/Abst** Biol. Abstr. (1984-); Curr. Contents Clin. Med.; EMBASE; Index Med. (Vol. 1, No. 1, 1983-);; Life Sci. Collect.; Res. Alert [Full Cov.]; Sci. Cit. Index.

●UK/1077-1042
**PEDIATRIC PATHOLOGY AND LABORATORY MEDICINE.** (1995)-. English. bm. £261.00 UK; $430.00 other. Taylor & Francis Ltd., Rankine Road, Basingstoke Hampshire, RG24 8PR United Kingdom. **Tel** 011 44 256 840366, FAX 011 44 256 479438, telex 858540. **(Subscription address:** Taylor & Francis Inc., 1900 Frost Road, Suite 101, Bristol PA 19007-1598.**)** ***Continues*** *Pediatric Pathology, 0277-0938.*

SZ/0091-2921
**PERSPECTIVES IN PEDIATRIC PATHOLOGY.** **See** Medical Science and Technology-Pediatrics.

●PL
**POLISH JOURNAL OF PATHOLOGY : OFFICIAL JOURNAL OF THE POLISH SOCIETY OF PATHOLOGISTS.** [Patol. pol.]. **Added/Corp** Polskie Towarzystwo Patologow. Vol. 45, No. 1 (1994)-. Academic Scholarly Publication. English (Polish; summaries and/or abstracts in Russian, English and French; table of contents in Russian and English). qt. Price on request. **(Subscription address:** ARS Polona, PO Box 1001, 00068 Warsaw Poland.**) NLM** W1; PO23LM. Documents available from BIOSIS Document Express, CASDDS. ***Continues*** *Patologia Polska, 0031-3114.*
**Ind/Abst** Biol. Abstr.; Chem. Abstr.; EMBASE; Index Med.

US/0896-534X
**PRACTICAL REVIEWS IN PATHOLOGY.** (PRACTICAL REVIEWS IN PATHOLOGY [SOUND RECORDING].). [Pract. rev. pathol.]. **Added/Corp** Educational Reviews, Inc. Albert Einstein College of Medicine. Montefiore Medical Center. **VFOAT** Practical Reviews. (197?)-. Periodical. English. mo. $175.00 Physicians/Dentists; $125.00 Residents. Educational Reviews Inc., 6801 Cahaba Valley Road, Birmingham AL 35242. **Tel** (205)991-5188, (800)633-4743, FAX (205)995-1926. **DD** 616.
**Desc:** Summary: Abstract cards of articles found in the journal literature.

US/1042-363X
**PROGRESS IN AIDS PATHOLOGY.** **See** Public Health and Safety.

US
**Q-PROBES ANATOMIC PATHOLOGY MODULE. 3 Q-PROBES.** (19??)-. English. Four times a year. $195.00. College of American Pathologists, Q Probes Department, 325 Waukegan Road, Northfield IL 60093. **Tel** (708)446-8800, FAX (708)446-8807.

US
**Q-PROBES CLINICAL PATHOLOGY MODULE. 6 Q-PROBES.** (19??)-. English. Four times a year (Jan., Apr., July, Oct.,). $390.00 (one year); $585.00 (one year) Comes with Combination ofAnatomic Pathology Module 3 Q-Probes & 9 Q-Probes. College of American Pathologists, Q Probes Department, 325 Waukegan Road, Northfield IL 60093. **Tel** (708)446-8800, FAX (708)446-8807.

RU/0131-1301
**REFERATIVNYI ZHURNAL : OBSHCHIE VOPROSY PATOLOGII.** **Added/Corp** Vsesoiuznyi Institut Nauchnoi i Tekhnicheskoi Informatsii. **VFOAT** Obshchie Voprosy Patologii. (1975)-. Periodical. Russian. mo. Vsesoiuznyi Institut Nauchnoi I Tekhnicheskoi Informatsii, A-219 Baltiiskaia Ulitsa 14, 125219 Moscow Russia. **Tel** 238-46-00, telex 411160. **NLM** ZQZ 4 R33. ***Continues in part*** *Referativnyi Zhurnal: Obshchie Voprosy Patologii. Onkologiia, 0486-2368.* ***Continued in part by*** *Referativnyi Zhurnal. Immunologiia. Allergologiia, 0202-9030;* ***Absorbed in part by*** *Referativnyi Zhurnal. Biologiia, 0202-9030.*

BL/0034-7302
**REVISTA BRASILEIRA DE PATOLOGIA CLINICA.** [Rev. bras. patol. clin.]. **Added/Corp** Sociedade Basileira de Patologia Clinica. (1950)-. Academic Scholarly Publication. Portuguese (English and Spanish). Four times a year (Mar., June, Sept., Dec.). $60.00. Sociedade Brasileira de Patologia Clinica, rua Sampaio Viana 92/Rio Compr, 20261 Rio de Janeiro Brazil. **Tel** 011 55 21 2933848, FAX 011 55 21 2932041. **ED** Jerzy Alfred Sturm. **CODEN** RBPTBN. Index available. **Ad Acc, Adv Mgr:** Cristina Maria Regis Morgado. **Circ:** 3,000 (ctrl). Documents available from CASDDS.
**Desc:** Clinical pathology, laboratory medicine, hematology, immunology, bacteriology, nuclear medicine, toxicology, virology, biochemistry, endocrinology, parasitology, etc.
**Ind/Abst** Chem. Abstr.

SP
**REVISTA DE LA SOCIEDAD ANDALUZA DE PATOLOGIA DIGESTIVA.** Spanish. Ediciones Reuniones y Congresos SA, Parque de la Colina 6, 28027 Madrid Spain.
**Ind/Abst** Indice Med. Esp.

SP
**REVISTA DE SENOLOGIA Y PATOLOGIA MAMARIA.** Spanish. Editorial Garsi SA, Juan Bravo 46, 28006 Madrid, Spain. **Tel** 011 34 1 4021212, telex 98358 GARSI E.
**Ind/Abst** Indice Med. Esp.

SP/1131-9178
**REVISTA GALLEGA DE PATOLOGIA DIGESTIVA.** [Rev. gallega patol. dig.]. (1991)-. Periodical. Spanish. sa. Boletin de la Sociedad Gallega de Patologia Digestiva, Gran Via 8/2 dcha, 36203 Vigo Spain. **UDC** 616.3. ***Continues*** *Boletin de la Sociedad Gallega de Patologia Digestiva, 0212-3673.*

VE/0300-9068
**REVISTA LATINOAMERICANA DE PATOLOGIA.** [Rev. latinoam. patol.]. **Added/Corp** Sociedad Latinoamericana de Patologia. Vol. 9 (March 1970)-. Periodical. Spanish (English). qt. $120,000 Mexico; $50,00 other. Assn Mexicana de Patologos, Apartado Postal 101-14, 04530 Mexico DF Mexico. **Tel** 573-0293. **ED** Eduardo Lopez Corella. Index available. **Bk Rev. Ad Acc. Pr Rev. Circ:** 4,800.

NE/1013-0047
**RHINOLOGY. SUPPLEMENT.** [Rhinol., Suppl.]. Monographic series. English (summaries and/or abstracts in French). qt. Price varies per volume. Rhinology, University Hospital, PO Box 85500 Otorhinolaryngology, 3508 GA Utrecht Netherlands. **Tel** 011 31 30 2591515. **ED** E H Huizing. **NLM** W1; RH43a. **CODEN** RHSUEI. (y). cum. index. **Bk Rev. Pr Rev. Circ:** 1,750.
**Desc:** Contains information dealing with physiology, diagnostics, pathology, medical therapy and surgery of the nose and paranasal sinuses, including allergology.
**Ind/Abst** Health Plan. Adminis.; Index Med. (1987-).

JA/0047-1860
**RINSHO BYORI.** [Rinsho byori]. **Added/Corp** Nihon Rinsho Byori Gakkai. **VFOAT** Japanese Journal of Clinical Pathology. Vol. 1 (1953)-. Academic Scholarly Publication. Japanese (English). Twelve times a year. $336.00. **(Subscription address:** Kyowa Book Company Inc., 1 38 Kanda Jinbocho Chiyoda-ku, Tokyo 101 Japan.**)** **NLM** W1 RI216F. **CODEN** RBYOAI. Documents available from CASDDS.
**Ind/Abst** Chem. Abstr.; Curr. Biotechnol.; Index Med.

IT
**RIS : RIVISTA ITALIANA DE STOMATOLOGIA.** **VFOAT** Rivista Italiana di Stomatologia. (1986)-. Periodical. Italian. Attualita Dentale Srl, P Le G Cesare N 4, 20145 Milan Italy. ***Continues*** *Rivista Italiana di Stomatologia.*

IT/0035-6417
**RIVISTA DI PATOLOGIA E CLINICA.** [Riv. patol. clin.]. (1946)-. Periodical. Italian. Six times a year. L60000.00 Italy; L120000.00 other. Casa Editrice Maccari, Via Trento 53, 43100 Parma Italy. **Tel** 011 39 521 771268, FAX 011 39 521 771268. **NLM** W1 RI602.
**Ind/Abst** Life Sci. Collect.

US/0740-2570
**SEMINARS IN DIAGNOSTIC PATHOLOGY.** [Sem. diagn. pathol.]. Vol. 1 No. 1 (Feb. 1984)-. Periodical. English. qt. $105.00 (individual) $151.00 (institutions) US; $157.00 (individuals) $172.00 (institution) other. W.B. Saunders Company, A Subsidiary of Harcourt Brace Jovanovich, Inc., The Curtis Center/Suite 300, Independence Square West, Philadelphia PA 19106-3399. **Tel** (215)238-7800 or, 5587, FAX (215)238-7883, telex 173146. **(Subscription address:** W. B. Saunders Company / North America Subscriptions, c/o Periodicals, 6277 Sea Harbour Drive, 4th Floor, Orlando FL 32887.**)** **ED** Daniel J Santa Cruz. **DD** 616. **NLM** W1; SE487N. **[CCC]. Pr Rev.** Documents available from The Genuine Article.
**Desc:** Aims to serve as a forum for the dissemination of current information in the field of human pathology. Created to cover specific areas in pathology with emphasis on the diagnostic aspects of human pathology. Contains solicited reviews on topics relevant to diagnostic anatomic pathology.
**Ind/Abst** Curr. Contents Clin. Med.; EMBASE; Index Med. (1984-); Res. Alert [Select. Cov.].

XR
**SOUDNI LEKARSTVI CESKOSLOVENSKA PATOLOGIE.** Czech. JE Purkyne, Prague 1, Sokolska 31, Czech Republic. **ED** J E Purkyne.
**Ind/Abst** Index Med.

SZ/0887-2392
**SOVIET MEDICAL REVIEWS. SECTION B, PHYSICOCHEMICAL ASPECTS OF MEDICINE REVIEWS.** ***Ceased.*** [Sov. med. rev., B Physicochem. asp. med. rev.]. **Added/Corp** Soviet Medical Reviews (Firm : Chur, Switzerland). **VFOAT** Physicochemical Aspects of Medicine Reviews. Vol. 1 (1987)-(1993). Periodical. English. an. Harwood Academic Publishers, PO Box 90, Reading RG1 8JL England. **Tel** 011 44 734 560080. **(Subscription address:** International Publishers Distributor at one of the following addresses: 820 Town Center Drive, Langhorne, PA 19047; or PO Box 90, Reading Berkshire RG1 8JL UK; or Kent Ridge PO Box 1180, Singapore 9111, Republic of Singapore**)** **LC** RB112.5; .S68. **DD** 510/.1/53. **CODEN** SRBRE5. **[CCC].**

GW/0081-3699
**SPEZIELLE PATHOLOGISCHE ANATOMIE.** (SPEZIELLE PATHOLOGISCHE ANATOMIE; EIN LEHR- UND NACHSCHLAGEWERK.). (1966)-. German. ir. Springer-Verlag New York Inc., 175 5th Avenue, New York NY 10010. **Tel** (212)460-1500, telex 232 235 SPB UR. **(Subscription address:** Springer Verlag New York Inc. / for North America, 44 Hartz Way, Secaucus NJ 07096.**)**

US/0344-4325
**SPRINGER SEMINARS IN IMMUNOPATHOLOGY.** **See** Medical Science and Technology-Allergy and Immunology

US/0899-8175
**SURGICAL PATHOLOGY.** (SURGICAL PATHOLOGY / SPONSORED BY INTERNATIONAL ACADEMY OF PATHOLOGY, AUSTRALASIAN DIVISION.). [Surg. pathol.]. **Added/Corp** International Academy of Pathology. Australasian Division. Vol. 1, No. 1 (Jan. 1988)-. Periodical. English. Four times a year. $154.00 US & Canada; $179.00 Europe; $184.00 Latin America & Africa; $189.00 others. Field & Wood, Inc., 4156 Manayunk Avenue, Philadelphia PA 19128. **Tel** (215)828-4010. **(Subscription address:** Field & Wood, PO Box 975, Blue Bell PA 19422.**)** **DD** 617. **NLM** W1; SU767FH.
**Ind/Abst** Ref. Upd. Deluxe Ed.

US/1056-7208
**TECHNIQUES IN DIAGNOSTIC PATHOLOGY (BALTIMORE, MD.).** (TECHNIQUES IN DIAGNOSTIC PATHOLOGY / UNITED STATES AND CANADIAN ACADEMY OF PATHOLOGY, INC.). [Tech. diagn. pathol.]. **Added/Corp** United States and Canadian Academy of Pathology. No. 1 (1991)-. Monographic series. English. ir. Williams & Wilkins Company, 428 East Preston Street, Baltimore MD 21202-3993. **Tel** (410)528-4000, (800)638-6423, FAX (410)528-8596, telex 87669. **(Subscription address:** Williams & Wilkins, PO Box 64380, Baltimore, MD 21264-4380**)** **DD** 616. **NLM** W1; TE197AM. **CODEN** TDPAE5. Documents available from BIOSIS Document Express, , Quick Copies.
**Ind/Abst** Biol. Abstr. (1991-).

US/0192-6233
**TOXICOLOGIC PATHOLOGY.** [Toxicol. pathol.]. **Added/Corp** Society of Toxicologic Pathologists (U.S.) Society of Pharmacological and Environmental Pathologists (U.S.). (1978)-. Academic Scholarly Publication. English. bm (6 issues). $195.00 US, Canada, Mexico and South & Central America; $215.00 other. Society of Toxicologic Pathologists. **(Subscription address:** Toxicologic Pathology, PO Box 1897, Lawrence KS 66044-8897.**)** **ED** Benjamin F. Trump. **LC** RB1; .S755a. **DD** 616.07/05. **NLM** W1 TO892. **CODEN** TOPADD. **[CCC].** Index available. **Bk Rev. Ad Acc. Pr Rev. Acid Free. Circ:** 850 (ctrl). Documents available from The Genuine Article, BIOSIS Document Express, CASDDS. ***Continues*** *Bulletin of the Society of Pharmacological and Environmental Pathologists, 0094-1824.*
**Desc:** Deals with investigative toxicology, pathology and factors. Also covers mechanisms that modify pathological responses, experimental results that address carcinogenesis and clinical pathology studies.
**Ind/Abst** Biol. Abstr.; Chem. Abstr.; Curr. Aware. Biol. Sci., CABS; Curr. Contents Life Sci.; EMBASE; Index Med. (Vol. 12, No. 1, 1984-); Index Vet.; Life Sci. Collect.; Pig News Inf.; Poult. Abstr.; Res. Alert [Select. Cov.]; Rev. Med. Vet. Mycology; Small Anim. Abstr. Bibliogr.; Vet. Bull.

US/0191-3123
**ULTRASTRUCTURAL PATHOLOGY.** [Ultrastruct. pathol.]. Vol. 1 (Jan./Mar. 1980)-. Academic Scholarly Publication. English. bm (6 issues). £309.00 UK; $510.00 other. Taylor & Francis Ltd., Rankine Road, Basingstoke Hampshire, RG24 8PR United Kingdom. **Tel** 011 44 256 840366, FAX 011 44 256 479438, telex 858540. **(Subscription address:** Taylor & Francis Inc., 1900 Frost Road, Suite 101, Bristol PA 19007-1598.**)** **ED** Jan Vincents Johannessen (editor's address: Director of The Norwegian Radium Hospital and Norsk Hydro's Institute for Cancer Research, Oslo 3 Norway) and Victor E. Gould (editor's address: Department of Pathology, Rush-Presbyterian-St. Luke's Medical Center, 1753 West Congress Parkway, Chicago, IL 60612, USA). **LC** RB25; .U46. **DD** 616.07/582. **NLM** W1 UL753. **CODEN** ULPAD3. **[CCC]. Bk Rev. Ad Acc. Pr Rev. Circ:** 1,300. available on microfilm and microfiche from University Microfilms International (UMI). Documents available from The Genuine Article, BIOSIS Document Express, CASDDS, ADONIS.
**Desc:** Highly recommended to all pathologists and to everyone interested in the ultrastructural features of human disease, whether they are newcomers or experienced electron microscopists.
**Ind/Abst** ADONIS; Biol. Abstr.; Chem. Abstr.; Curr. Aware. Biol. Sci., CABS; Curr. Contents Life Sci.; EMBASE; Index Med.; Life Sci. Collect.; Ref. Z.; Ref. Upd. Deluxe Ed.; Res. Alert [Full Cov.]; Rev. Med. Vet. Mycology; Sci. Cit. Index; SCISEARCH.

US/0730-6482
**ULTRASTRUCTURAL PATHOLOGY PUBLICATION SERIES, AN.** ***Ceased.*** [Ultrastruct. pathol. publ. ser.]. **VFOAT** Ultrastructural Pathology Publication. (1985)-(19??). Monographic series. English. ir. Taylor & Francis Ltd., Rankine Road, Basingstoke Hampshire, RG24 8PR United Kingdom. **Tel** 011 44 256 840366, FAX 011 44 256 479438, telex 858540. **(Subscription address:** Taylor & Francis Inc., 1900 Frost Road, Suite 101, Bristol PA 19007-1598.**)** **DD** 616.

GW/0070-4113
**VERHANDLUNGEN DER DEUTSCHEN GESELLSCHAFT FUER PATHOLOGIE.** [Verh. Dtsch. Ges. Pathol.]. **Added/Corp** Deutsche Gesellschaft fur Pathologie. **VFOAT** Verhandlungen Deutscher Pathologen. 32nd Meeting (1948)-. Academic Scholarly Publication. German. an. VCH Gesellschaft GmbH, Postfach 101161, D 69451 Weinheim Germany. **Tel** 011 49 6201 606459, FAX 011 49 6201 606184. **(Subscription address:** VCH Publishers Inc., 303 Northwest 12th Avenue, Journals Department, Deerfield FL 33442.**)** **NLM** W1 VE483T. **CODEN** VDGPAN. **[CCC].** cum. index. Documents available from CASDDS. ***Continues*** *Deutsche Pathologische Gesellschaft. Verhandlungen.*
**Ind/Abst** Chem. Abstr. (19??-); Energy Res. Abstr. (19??-); Index Med. (19??-); Life Sci. Collect. (19??-).

GW/0340-241X
**VEROEFFENTLICHUNGEN AUS DER PATHOLOGIE.** [Veroeff. Pathol.]. **VFOAT** Progress in Pathology. (1974)-. Monographic series. German (summaries and/or abstracts in English). ir. Price varies per volume. Gustav Fischer Verlag Stuttgart, Postfach 720143, Wollgrasweg 49, D 70577 Stuttgart Germany. **Tel** 011 49 711 458030, FAX 0711-4580334, telex 2627-7111488. **ED** W. Buengeler, G. Dhom, M. Eder, R. Fischer, H. Holzner, K. Lennert, G. Peters, W. Sandritter, G. Seifert, W. Thoeness. **NLM** W1 VE783E. **CODEN** VEPADX. **[CCC].** Documents available from BIOSIS Document Express. ***Continues*** *Veroeffentlichungen aus der Morphologischen Pathologie, 0372-6312.*
**Desc:** Series covering pathology.
**Ind/Abst** Biol. Abstr. (1989-); Index Med. (19??-); Index Sci. Rev. (19??-) [Full Cov.].

GW
**VIRCHOWS ARCHIV.** Twelve times a year. DM2250.00. Springer-Verlag GmbH & Company KG, Heidelberger Platz 3, D 14197 Berlin Germany. **Tel** 011 49 30 8207223, FAX 011 49 30 8214091, telex 183 319 SPBLN D. **(Subscription address:** Springer Verlag New York Inc. / for North America, 44 Hartz Way, Secaucus NJ 07096.**)** ***Formed by the union of*** *Virchows Archiv. Section A, Pathological Anatomy and Histopathology* ***and*** *Virchows Archiv. Section B, Cell Pathology.*

GW/0174-7398
**VIRCHOWS ARCHIV. A, PATHOLOGICAL ANATOMY AND HISTOPATHOLOGY.** ***Title Change.*** [Virchows Arch., A, Pathol. anat. histopathol.]. **VFOAT** Pathological Anatomy and Histopathology. Vol. 398, No. 1 (Dec. 1982)-(19??). Academic Scholarly Publication. English. Twelve times a year. Springer-Verlag GmbH & Company KG, Heidelberger Platz 3, D 14197 Berlin Germany. **Tel** 011 49 30 8207223, FAX 011 49 30 8214091, telex 183 319 SPBLN D. **(Subscription address:** Springer Verlag New York Inc. / for North America, 44 Hartz Way, Secaucus NJ 07096.**)** **ED** C L Berry and G Seifert. **LC** RB1. **DD** 616.07. **NLM** W1; VI764AB. **CODEN** VAAHDJ. **[CCC]. Pr Rev.** available on microfilm from University Microfilms International (UMI). Documents available from The Genuine Article, CASDDS. ***Continues*** *Virchows Archiv. A: Pathological Anatomy and Histology, 0340-1227.* ***Continued by*** *Virchows Archiv.*
**Desc:** A medium for the publication of fundamental research on disease in the widest sense and on human pathological anatomy and histology in particular.
**Ind/Abst** Chem. Abstr.; CSA Neuro. Abstr. (?-?); Curr. Aware. Biol. Sci., CABS; Curr. Contents Life Sci.; EMBASE; Helminthol. Abstr. (1991-); Index Med.; Life Sci. Collect.; Protozoolog. Abstr.; Ref. Upd. Basic Ed.; Ref. Upd. Deluxe Ed.; Res. Alert [Full Cov.]; Rev. Med. Vet. Entomol.; Rev. Med. Vet. Mycology; Sci. Cit. Index; SCISEARCH.

GW/0340-6075
**VIRCHOWS ARCHIV. B, CELL PATHOLOGY.** ***Title Change.*** (VIRCHOWS ARCHIV. B, CELL PATHOLOGY INCLUDING MOLECULAR PATHOLOGY.). [Virchows Arch. B]. **VFOAT** Cell Pathology including Molecular Pathology. Vol. 30, No. 1 (1979)-(19??). Academic Scholarly Publication. English. Twelve times a year. Springer-Verlag GmbH & Company KG, Heidelberger Platz 3, D 14197 Berlin Germany. **Tel** 011 49 30 8207223, FAX 011 49 30 8214091, telex 183 319 SPBLN D. **(Subscription address:** Springer Verlag New York Inc. / for North America, 44 Hartz Way, Secaucus NJ 07096.**)** **ED** O Kraupp and H Sinzinger. **UDC** 616-092.18. **NLM** W1; VI764AE. **CODEN** VAAZA2. **[CCC].** available on microfilm from University Microfilms International (UMI). Documents available from The Genuine Article, BIOSIS Document Express, CASDDS. ***Continues*** *Virchows Archiv. B, Cell Pathology, 0042-6431.* ***Continued by*** *Virchows Archiv.*
**Desc:** Devoted to cellular pathology using both classic and modern techniques.
**Ind/Abst** AGRICOLA; Biol. Abstr.; Chem. Abstr.; Curr. Aware. Biol. Sci., CABS; Curr. Contents Life Sci.; EMBASE; Helminthol. Abstr.; Index Med.; Index Vet.; Oncog. Growth Factors Abstr.; Life Sci. Collect.; Protozoolog. Abstr.; Ref. Upd. Basic Ed.; Ref. Upd. Deluxe Ed.; Res. Alert [Full Cov.]; Sci. Cit. Index; SCISEARCH; Small Anim. Abstr. Bibliogr.; Vet. Bull.

US
**WORKLOAD RECORDING METHOD & PERSONNEL MANAGEMENT MANUAL.** ***Title Change.*** **Added/Corp** College of American Pathologists. Workload and Personnel Management Committee. **VFOAT** Workload Recording Method and Personnel Management Manual. (1992)-(19??). English. College of American Pathologists, Q Probes Department, 325 Waukegan Road, Northfield IL 60093. **Tel** (708)446-8800, FAX (708)446-8807. **NLM** QY 39; M294. ***Changed back to*** *Manual for Laboratory Workload Recording Method, 0747-9158.*

US/0084-3946
**YEAR BOOK OF PATHOLOGY AND CLINICAL PATHOLOGY, THE.** [Year b. pathol. clin. pathol.]. **VFOAT** Yearbook of Pathology and Clinical Pathology. (1947)-. English. an. $59.95. Mosby

Year Book Inc., 11830 Westline Industrial Drive, St Louis MO 63146. **Tel** (800)325-4177, (314)872-8370, FAX (314)432-1380, telex 44-2402. **DD** 616. **UDC** 616. **NLM** W1 YE293. ***Continues*** *Year Book of Pathology and Immunology, 0891-3617.*

GW/0863-4106
**ZENTRALBLATT FUER PATHOLOGIE : GENERAL PATHOLOGY/PATHOLOGICAL ANATOMY.** Vol. 137, No. 1, (1991)-. Periodical. German (English). bm. DM380.00 Germany; DM392.00 other. Gustav Fischer Verlag Jena, Postfach 100537, D 07705 Jena Germany. **Tel** 011 49 3641 27332, FAX 011 49 3641 626500. **(Subscription address:** VCH Publishers Inc., 303 Northwest 12th Avenue, Journals Department, Deerfield FL 33442.**) LC** RB1; .Z4. **NLM** W1; ZE783. **CODEN** ZEPAEA. ***Continues*** *Zentralblatt fur Allgemeine Pathologie und Pathologische Anatomie, 0044-4030.*
**Ind/Abst** EMBASE [Select. Cov.]; Health Plan. Adminis.

## PEDIATRICS

US
**AAP PEDIATRIC UPDATE.** English. $170.00 members, $195.00 nonmembers US; $210.00 members, $235.00 nonmembers other. Medical Information Systems, 2 Sealview Blvd., Port Washington NY 11050. **Tel** (516)621-7200.

US/0884-1497
**ABMS DIRECTORY OF CERTIFIED PEDIATRICIANS.** ***Title Change.*** [ABMS dir. certif. pediatr.]. **Added/Corp** American Board of Medical Specialties. **VFOAT** Directory of Certified Pediatricians. **VAT** American Board of Medical Specialties Directory of Certified Pediatricians. (1984)-(199?). Directory. English. be. American Board of Medical Specialties, 1 Rotary Center, Suite 805, Evanston IL 60201. **Tel** (708)491-9091. **LC** RJ29; .A25. **DD** 618.92/00232/02573. **NLM** WS 22.1; A1523. ***Continued by*** *Official American Board of Medical Specialties (ABMS) Directory of Board Certified Pediatricians, 0000-1627.*

FR/0297-8156
**ABSTRACT PEDIATRIE PARIS.** [Abstr. pediatr Paris]. (1986)-. Periodical. French. mo (10 issues). 142.02F France; 200.00F other. Abstract, 25 Bis Av Pierre Grenier, 92100 Boulogne Billanct France. **Tel** 011 33 1 49100606. **UDC** 616-053.2.

HU/0231-441X
**ACTA PAEDIATRICA HUNGARICA.** [Acta paediatr. Hung.]. **Added/Corp** Magyar Tudomanyos Akademia. **VFOAT** Acta Paediatrica. Vol. 24, No. 1 (1983)-. Academic Scholarly Publication. English (French, German and Russian). qt. $92.00. Akademiai Kiado, Publishing House of the Hungarian Academy of Sciences, Prielle Kornelia u. 19-35, H-1117 Budapest Hungary. **Tel** 011 36 1 1811991, FAX 011 36 1 1811991, telex 22-6228 AKNYO H. **ED** Miklos Miltenyi (editor's address: Acta Paediatrica Hungarica, Bokay J u 53, H-1085 Budapest Hungary). **NLM** W1 AC904. **CODEN** APHUDZ. **[CCC].** Index available. **Bk Rev. Ad Acc.** Documents available from CASDDS. ***Continues*** *Acta Paediatrica Academiae Scientiarum Hungaricae, 0001-6527.*
**Desc:** Presents original communications on subjects connected with the theoretical and practical aspects of pediatrics, including the fields of perinatal medicine, clinical genetics, pediatric surgery, pediatric psychology, etc.
**Ind/Abst** Chem. Abstr. (1983-); EMBASE [Select. Cov.]; Index Med.; Life Sci. Collect.; Ref. Upd. Basic Ed.; Ref. Upd. Deluxe Ed.

JA/0374-5600
**ACTA PAEDIATRICA JAPONICA. OVERSEAS EDITION.** [Acta paediatr. Jpn. Overs. ed.]. **Added/Corp** Nihon Shonika Gakkai. (1958)-. Academic Scholarly Publication. English. Six times a year. 278.00Aus$ Australia; ¥19500 Japan; $194.00 other. Blackwell Scientific Publications Australia, 54 University Street, PO Box 378, Carlton Victoria 3053 Australia. **Tel** 011 61 3 3470300, FAX 011 61 3 3475001, telex 10716421. **NLM** W1 AC905E. **CODEN** APDJBE. **[CCC].** Documents available from BIOSIS Document Express, CASDDS, ADONIS.
**Desc:** Includes summary or abstracts of the original articles in English published in Acta Paediatrica.
**Ind/Abst** ADONIS; Biol. Abstr.; Chem. Abstr.; Dairy Sci. Abstr.; EMBASE; Health Plan. Adminis.; Index Med.; Nutr. Res. Newsl.

IT/0365-5504
**ACTA PAEDIATRICA LATINA.** [Acta paediatr. lat.]. (1948)-. Academic Scholarly Publication. Italian. Four times a year (Mar., June, Sept., Dec.). L50000.00 Italy; L80000.00 other. Acta Paediatrica Latina / AGE, Via Casorati 29, 42100 Reggio Emilia Italy. **Tel** 011 39 522 921276. **ED** Silvio Volpato. **NLM** W1 AC905. **Bk Rev. Ad Acc, Adv Mgr:** Luigi Menozzi. **Pr Rev. Circ:** 2500.
**Desc:** Contains original articles about pediatrics and includes notes and news.
**Ind/Abst** EMBASE.

SP/0213-0580
**ACTA PAEDIATRICA SCANDINAVICA ED. ESPANOLA.** ***Ceased.*** [Acta paediatr. Scand.Ed. esp.]. Vol. 54, No. 1 (1965)-(19??). Periodical. Multiple languages. mo (11 issues per year). Editorial Saned SA, Apolonio Morales 6, 28036 Madrid Spain. **Tel** 011 34 1 359-4092, FAX 011 34 1 457-9918. **UDC** 616-053.2. **CODEN** APSVAM.
**Ind/Abst** AgBiotech News Inf.; Anim. Breed. Abstr.; Dairy Sci. Abstr.; Nutr. Abstr. Rev., Ser. A, Hum. Exp.; Nutr. Res. Newsl.; Soyabean Abstr.

SW/0300-8843
**ACTA PAEDIATRICA SCANDINAVICA. SUPPLEMENT.** ***Title Change.*** [Acta pdiatr. Scand., Suppl.]. (1965-199?). Academic Scholarly Publication. English. Scandinavian University Press, PO Box 2959 Toeyen, N 0608 Oslo 6 Norway. **Tel** 011 47 2 2575400, FAX 011 47 2 2575353, telex 71896 UROR N. **(Subscription address:** Scandinavian University Press, 200 Meacham Ave., Elmont NY 11003.**) NLM** W1 AC905K. **CODEN** APSQA7. Documents available from BIOSIS Document Express, CASDDS. ***Continues*** *Acta Pdiatrica. Supplement.* ***Continued by*** *Acta Pdiatrica (Oslo, Norway : 1992). Supplement.*
**Ind/Abst** Biol. Abstr.; Chem. Abstr.; Dairy Sci. Abstr.; EMBASE; Health Plan. Adminis.; Index Med.; Nutr. Abstr. Rev., Ser. A, Hum. Exp.; Life Sci. Collect.

●NO/0803-5253
**ACTA PAEDIATRICA (OSLO).** (ACTA PEDIATRICA.). [Acta paediatr.]. Vol. 81, No.1 Jan. (1992)-. Academic Scholarly Publication. English. mo. Kr1945.00, $316.00. Scandinavian University Press, PO Box 2959 Toeyen, N 0608 Oslo 6 Norway. **Tel** 011 47 2 2575400, FAX 011 47 2 2575353, telex 71896 UROR N. **(Subscription address:** Scandinavian University Press, 200 Meacham Ave., Elmont NY 11003.**) ED** Rolf Zetterstrom. **NLM** W1; AC899. **CODEN** APAEEL. **[CCC].** available on microfilm and microfiche from University Microfilms International (UMI). Documents available from The Genuine Article, BIOSIS Document Express, CASDDS. ***Continues*** *Acta Pdiatrica Scandinavica, 0001-656X.*
**Desc:** Provides papers covering both clinical and experimental research in all fields of paediatrics, including developmental physiology. Also includes psychological, social and third world aspects.
**Ind/Abst** Biol. Abstr. (?-1988, 1992-); Chem. Abstr.; Curr. Contents Clin. Med.; Curr. Contents Life Sci.; EMBASE; Helminthol. Abstr.; Index Med. (1992-); Life Sci. Collect.; Protozoolog. Abstr.; Res. Alert [Full Cov.]; Risk Abstr.; Saf. Health Work; Sci. Cit. Index; SCISEARCH; Soc. Sci. Cit. Index [Select. Cov.].

●NO/0803-5326
**ACTA PAEDIATRICA. SUPPLEMENT.** (199?)-. Periodical. English. ir. $316.00. Scandinavian University Press, PO Box 2959 Toeyen, N 0608 Oslo 6 Norway. **Tel** 011 47 2 2575400, FAX 011 47 2 2575353, telex 71896 UROR N. **(Subscription address:** Scandinavian University Press, 200 Meacham Ave., Elmont NY 11003.**) CODEN** APUPEI. ***Continues*** *Acta Pdiatrica Scandinavica. Supplement, 0300-8843.*
**Ind/Abst** EMBASE.

SZ/0001-6586
**ACTA PAEDOPSYCHIATRICA.** ***Ceased.*** **See** Medical Science and Technology-Psychiatry.

SP
**ACTA PEDIATRICA ESPANOLA.** Vol. 4 (1946)-. Spanish (summaries and/or abstracts in English). mo (except August). 5500.00ptas. Acta Pediatrica Espanola, Apartado de Correos 54284, 28080 Madrid Spain. **Tel** 011 34 1 3735564. **ED** Ignacio Villa Elizaga. Index available. cum. index. **Bk Rev. Ad Acc. Circ:** 8,000 (ctrl). available on microfilm and microfiche from University Microfilms International (UMI). ***Continues*** *Acta Pediatrica.*
**Ind/Abst** Dairy Sci. Abstr.; Indice Med. Esp.; Nutr. Abstr. Rev., Ser. A, Hum. Exp.

US/0932-8610
**ADOLESCENT AND PEDIATRIC GYNECOLOGY.** **See** Medical Science and Technology-Gynecology and Obstetrics.

US/0044-6335
**ADOLESCENT MEDICINE (GLENVIEW).** (ADOLESCENT MEDICINE.). Vol. 1 (1969)-. Periodical. English. Twelve times a year. $69.00 US; $70.00 Canada; $74.00 other. British Trading Company Ltd., 821 Delaware Avenue Southwest, Washington DC 20024. **Tel** (202)488-7533. **ED** Nathaniel Polster, Dorothy Miller, and Sara Gurgen. **Bk Rev.**
**Desc:** Practical advice to physicians, nurses, athletic directors and medical staff on adolescent medicine. Research reports; news affecting adolescent physical and mental care.

US/0160-8231
**ADOLESCENT MEDICINE (NEW YORK).** (ADOLESCENT MEDICINE.). Vol. 1 (1976)-. Periodical. English. ir. Spectrum Publications Inc, 175-20 Wexford Terrace, Jamaica NY 11432. **Tel** (718)658-0888. **ED** R. I. Lopez. **NLM** W1 AD37HC.

US/0065-2008
**ADOLESCENT PSYCHIATRY.** [Adolesc. psych.]. Vol. 1 (1971)-. Monographic series. English. ir. Price varies per volume. University of Chicago Press / Book Department, 11030 South Langley Avenue, Chicago IL 60628. **Tel** (800)621-2736, (312)568-1550, FAX (312)753-0811, telex 23933. **ED** Sherman C. Feinstein. **LC** RJ499.A1; A29. **DD** 618.92/8/9. **NLM** W1 AD37K. cum. index. available on microfilm and microfiche from University Microfilms International (UMI). Documents available from The Genuine Article.
**Desc:** Inaugurated in 1971 to explore adolescence as a distinct stage of psychological, social, and biological development. An essential resource for psychiatrists, psychologists, social and behavioral scientists, and others working with youth. Contents of each volume range from specific clinical and theoretical issues to considerations of social, cultural, and even political themes.
**Ind/Abst** Cumul. Index Nurs. Allied Health Lit.; Health Plan. Adminis.; Index Med. (1978-); Psychol. Abstr. (1974-); PsycINFO; PsycLit; Res. Alert [Full Cov.].

US/0149-4732
**ADVANCES IN CLINICAL CHILD PSYCHOLOGY.** **See** Psychology.

US/0737-7452
**ADVANCES IN DEVELOPMENTAL AND BEHAVIORAL PEDIATRICS.** [Adv. dev. behav. pediatr.]. Vol. 3 (1982)-. Monographic series. English. ir. Prices varies per volume. Jessica Kingsley Publishers, 118 Pentonville Road, London N1 9JN England. **Tel** 011 44 71 833 2307, FAX 011 44 71 837 2917. **(Subscription address:** Taylor & Francis Inc., 1900 Frost Road, Suite 101, Bristol PA 19007-1598.**) ED** Mark Volraich and Donald K Routh. **LC** RJ47.5; .A37. **DD** 618.92/0001/9. **NLM** W1; AD5467. **CODEN** ADBPE9. Documents available from BIOSIS Document Express. ***Continues*** *Advances in Behavioral Pediatrics, 0198-7089.*
**Ind/Abst** Biol. Abstr. (1985-); Psychol. Abstr. (1982-); PsycINFO.

US/0884-9404
**ADVANCES IN PEDIATRIC INFECTIOUS DISEASES.** [Adv. pediatr. infect. dis.]. **VFOAT** Pediatric Infectious Diseases. Vol. 1 (1986)-. English. an. $66.00 (latest volume). Mosby Year Book Inc., 11830 Westline Industrial Drive, St Louis MO 63146. **Tel** (800)325-4177, (314)872-8370, FAX (314)432-1380, telex 44-2402. **DD** 618. **NLM** W1; AD718. **CODEN** APIDEO. **[CCC].** Documents available from BIOSIS Document Express.
**Ind/Abst** Biol. Abstr. (1986-); Health Plan. Adminis.; Index Med.

US/0065-3101
**ADVANCES IN PEDIATRICS.** [Adv. pediatr.]. Vol. 1 (1942)-. English. ir. $72.00 (latest volume). Mosby Year Book Inc., 11830 Westline Industrial Drive, St Louis MO 63146. **Tel** (800)325-4177, (314)872-8370, FAX (314)432-1380, telex 44-2402. **ED** A. G. de Sanctis. **LC** RJ23; .A4. **DD** 618.9. **NLM** W1 AD722. **[CCC].** available on microfilm from University Microfilms International (UMI).
**Ind/Abst** Cumul. Index Nurs. Allied Health Lit.; Energy Res. Abstr. (Jan. 1981-); Health Plan. Adminis.; Index Med.; INIS Atomindex [Micro.].

IT/0002-0958
**AGGIORNAMENTO PEDIATRICO.** [Aggiorn. pediatr.]. (1950)-. Academic Scholarly Publication. Italian. bm (6 issues). L60000 Italy; L120000 other. Verduci Editore, Via Gregorio VII 186, 00165 Rome Italy. **Tel** 011 39 6 39375224. **NLM** W1 AG339. **CODEN** AGPEAT. Documents available from CASDDS.
**Ind/Abst** Chem. Abstr.; EMBASE.

US/0899-7411
**AMERICAN JOURNAL OF ASTHMA & ALLERGY FOR PEDIATRICIANS, THE.** **See** Medical Science and Technology-Respiratory System.

US/0002-922X
**AMERICAN JOURNAL OF DISEASES OF CHILDREN (1960).** ***Title Change.*** (AMERICAN JOURNAL OF DISEASES OF CHILDREN. AMA.). [Am. j. dis. child.]. **Added/Corp** American Medical Association. **VFOAT** AJDC. Vol. 100, No. 1 (July 1960)-Vol. 147, No. 12 (Dec. 1993). Academic Scholarly Publication. English (French). mo. American Medical Association, 515 North State Street, Chicago IL 60610. **Tel** (312)464-5000, (800)262-2350, FAX (312)464-5831. **ED** Vincent A. Fulginiti. **LC** RJ1; .A5. **DD** 618. **NLM** W1; A118. **CODEN** AJDCAI. **[CCC].** Index available. **Bk Rev. Ad Acc. Pr Rev. Circ:** 52,000. available on microfilm and microfiche from University Microfilms International (UMI); available on an online database (file 442/Full-Text) from DIALOG; and MEDIS. Documents available from The Genuine Article, BIOSIS Document Express, CASDDS. ***Continues*** *Journal of Diseases of Children, 0096-6916.* ***Continued by*** *Archives of Pediatrics & Adolescent Medicine, 1072-4710.*

**Desc:** Published as an educational service for physicians who practice pediatrics as a primary specialty, and to physicians of other specialties who treat children. It is oriented toward the clinician. Every issue offers new concepts and methods applicable to everyday practice, and helps readers successfully resolve today's issues.
**Ind/Abst** Abr. Index Med.; Abstr. Anthropol.; Agric. Eng. Abstr. (1991-); Biol. Abstr.; Biol. Dig.; Biotechnol. Res. Abstr.; Calcium Calcif. Tissue Abstr.; Chem. Abstr. (1960-1983); Chicano Index; Comb. Cumul. Index Pediatr.; Cumul. Index Nurs. Allied Health Lit.; Curr. Aware. Biol. Sci., CABS; Curr. Contents Life Sci.; Dairy Sci. Abstr.; Dev. Med. Child Neurol.; EMBASE; Energy Res. Abstr.; Health Index (1989-); Health Period. Database; Health Plan. Adminis.; Health Ref. Cent. (Jan. 1989-) [Full Cov.]; Health Serv. Abstr.; Highw. Res. Abstr.; Immunol. Abstr.; Index Med.; Index Sci. Rev.; Index Vet.; INIS Atomindex [Micro.]; Int. Nurs. Index; Int. Pharm. Abstr.; Iowa Drug Inf. Serv. (1967-); J. Watch (19??-); Med. Abstr. Newsl.; Microbiol. Abstr. Sect. B; Mod. Med.; Nutr. Abstr. Rev., Ser. B, Live Feeds and Feed.; Nutr. Abstr. Rev., Ser. A, Hum. Exp.; Nutr. Res. Newsl.; Life Sci. Collect.; PESTDOC; Physic. Medline Plus; Protozoolog. Abstr.; Psychol. Abstr.; Ref. Upd. Basic Ed.; Ref. Upd. Deluxe Ed.; Res. Alert [Full Cov.]; Rev. Med. Vet. Mycology; Rev. Plant Pathol.; Risk Abstr.; Sci. Cit. Index; SCISEARCH; Small Anim. Abstr. Bibliogr.; Soc. Sci. Cit. Index [Select. Cov.]; Soyabean Abstr.; SPORT Discus; SportSearch; Trop. Dis. Bull.; Virol. AIDS Abstr.

US/0192-8562
**AMERICAN JOURNAL OF PEDIATRIC HEMATOLOGY/ONCOLOGY, THE.** ***Title Change.*** [Am. j. pediatr. hematol./oncol.]. **Added/Corp** American Society of Pediatric Hematology/Oncology. **VAT** American Journal of Pediatric Hematology Oncology. Vol. 1, (Spring 1979)-(19??). Periodical. English. qt. Raven Press, 1185 Avenue of the Americas, 37th Floor, New York NY 10036. **Tel** (212)930-9500, (212)930-9604, FAX (212)869-3495, (212)302-8507, telex 640073. **ED** Carl Pochedly. **LC** RJ411; .A47. **DD** 618.9/215. **NLM** W1 AM498BJ. **CODEN** APHODH. **[CCC]. Pr Rev.** available on microfilm and microfiche from University Microfilms International (UMI). Documents available from The Genuine Article, BIOSIS Document Express. ***Continued by*** *Journal of Pediatric Hematology/Oncology.*
**Desc:** Reports on major advances in the diagnosis and treatment of cancer and blood diseases in children.
**Ind/Abst** Biol. Abstr.; Curr. Aware. Biol. Sci., CABS; Curr. Contents Clin. Med.; EMBASE; Health Plan. Adminis.; Index Med. (Spring 1979-); INIS Atomindex [Micro.]; Life Sci. Collect.; Res. Alert [Full Cov.]; Sci. Cit. Index; SCISEARCH; Soc. Sci. Cit. Index [Select. Cov.].

SP/0302-4342
**ANALES ESPANOLES DE PEDIATRIA.** [An. Esp. Pediatr.]. Academic Scholarly Publication. Spanish. mo. 9400.00ptas doctors; 10900.00ptas institutions Spain; $166.00 institutions; $130.00 institutions Europe; $136.00 doctors; $115.00 doctors Europe. Editorial Garsi SA, Juan Bravo 46, 28006 Madrid, Spain. **Tel** 011 34 1 4021212, telex 98358 GARSI E. **UDC** 616-053.2. **CODEN** AEPEDI. **[CCC]. Bk Rev. Ad Acc. Pr Rev.** ctrl circ. Documents available from CASDDS.
**Ind/Abst** Chem. Abstr.; EMBASE; Index Med.; Indice Med. Esp.; Life Sci. Collect.

SP/0213-9146
**ANALES ESPANOLES DE PEDIATRIA. SUPLEMENTO.** [An. esp. pediatr., Supl.]. **Added/Corp** Asociacion Espanola de Pediatria. (1974)-. Periodical. Multiple languages. ir. Editorial Garsi SA, Juan Bravo 46, 28006 Madrid, Spain. **Tel** 011 34 1 4021212, telex 98358 GARSI E. **UDC** 616-053.2.
**Ind/Abst** EMBASE.

FR/0066-2097
**ANNALES DE PEDIATRIE (PARIS).** (ANNALES DE PEDIATRIE.). [Ann. pediatr.]. (1954)-. Academic Scholarly Publication. French (summaries and/or abstracts in English; table of contents in English). ir (10 issues per year). 1100.00F France; $1450.00 other. Semaine de Hopitaux, 31 Boulevard de la Tour-Maubourg, 75007 Paris, France. **Tel** 011 33 1 40 62 64 00. **UDC** 616-053.2. **NLM** W1 AN374E. **CODEN** APSHAE. **Bk Rev. Ad Acc. Pr Rev. Circ:** 8,700. Documents available from The Genuine Article, BIOSIS Document Express, CASDDS.
**Ind/Abst** Biol. Abstr.; Chem. Abstr.; Curr. Contents Clin. Med.; Dairy Sci. Abstr.; Dev. Med. Child Neurol.; EMBASE; Energy Res. Abstr.; Health Plan. Adminis.; Helminthol. Abstr. (1991-); Index Med.; Nutr. Abstr. Rev., Ser. B, Live Feeds and Feed.; Nutr. Abstr. Rev., Ser. A, Hum. Exp.; Life Sci. Collect.; Protozoolog. Abstr.; Res. Alert [Select. Cov.]; Rev. Med. Vet. Entomol.; SCISEARCH; Soc. Sci. Cit. Index [Select. Cov.].

II
**ANNALS - INSTITUTE OF CHILD HEALTH.** **Main/Corp** Institute of Child Health. V. 1- July 1972-. English. $5.00. Institute of Child Health / Calcutta, 11 Dr Biresh Guha Road, Calcutta 17 India. **LC** RJ1; .I5755A. **DD** 618.9/2/0005. **UDC** 616-053.2.

II/0970-2121
**ANNALS OF PAEDIATRIC SURGERY.** (ANNALS OF PAEDIATRIC SURGERY : OFFICIAL JOURNAL OF THE ASIAN ASSOCIATION OF PAEDIATRIC SURGEONS.). [Ann. paediatr. surg.]. **Added/Corp** Asian Association of Paediatric Surgeons. Vol. 1, No. 1 (Jan. 1984)-. Periodical. English. Four times a year. $22.00. Cosmo Publications, 24-B Ansari Road, Darya Ganj, New Delhi 110002 India. **ED** S. Kapoor. **NLM** W1; AN617NH. **Bk Rev. Ad Acc. Pr Rev.**

US/0066-4030
**ANNUAL PROGRESS IN CHILD PSYCHIATRY AND CHILD DEVELOPMENT.** [Annu. prog. child psych. child dev.]. (1968)-. English. an. $67.45. Brunner Mazel, 19 Union Square West, New York NY 10003. **Tel** (212)924-3344, (800)825-3089. **ED** S. Chess and A. Thomas. **LC** RJ499.A1; A53. **DD** 618.92/89/05. **NLM** W1 AN758P.
**Ind/Abst** Psychol. Abstr. (1976-); PsycINFO; PsycLit.

US/0197-873X
**ANNUAL VOLUME OF PEDIATRICS CLUB BY CONTRIBUTING MEMBERS.** [Annu. vol. Pediatr. Club contrib. memb.]. V. 1- 1979-. Periodical. English. an. Burgress Beckwithn, 7108 OHMS Lane, Minneapolis MN 55435. **ED** R M Ehrlich. **UDC** 616-053.2. **NLM** W1 AN782R.

●FR/0929-693X
**ARCHIVES DE PEDIATRIE : ORGANE OFFICIEL DE LA SOCIETE FRANCAISE DE PEDIATRIE.** **Added/Corp** Societe Francaise de Pediatrie. Vol 1, No 1 (Jan. 1994)-. Academic Scholarly Publication. French. Twelve times a year. 1035.00F France; 1135.00F other. Editions Scientifique Elsevier, 141 rue de Javel, 75747 Paris Cedex 15 France. **Tel** 011 33 1 47 07 11 22, FAX 011 33 1 43 36 80 93. **(Subscription address:** Editions Scientifiques Elsevier / for North America, PO Box 7247-7576, Philadelphia PA 19170-7576.**) NLM** W1; AR342MM. **CODEN** APEDE4. ***Formed by the union of*** *Archives Francaises de Pediatrie, 0003-9764* ***and*** *Pediatrie (Lyons, France : 1948).*

FR/0003-9764
**ARCHIVES FRANCAISES DE PEDIATRIE.** (ARCHIVES FRANCAISES DE PEDIATRIE : ORGANE DE LA SOCIETE DE PEDIATRIE DE PARIS.). [Arch. fr. pediatr.]. **Added/Corp** Societe de Pediatrie de Paris. Association Francaise de Pediatrie. Association des Pediatres de Langue Francaise. Societe Francaise de Pediatrie. Vol. 1 (1942)-. Academic Scholarly Publication. French. mo (ten issues per year). Doin Editeurs, 8 Place de l'Odeon, F 75006 Paris France. **Tel** 011 33 1 46332237. **(Subscription address:** Subscription Office, PO Box 830399, Birmingham, AL 35283-0399; telephone: (800)633-4931 or (205)991-6920 (outside US and Canada); FAX: (205)995-1588**) ED** D. Alagille, D. Dupuis, J. Frezal, J.P. Gallet, J. Laugier, C. Regnier and J. Rey. **NLM** W1 AR381H. **CODEN** AFPEAM. **[CCC].** Index available. **Bk Rev. Ad Acc. Pr Rev. Circ:** 3,100 (ctrl). available on microfilm and microfiche from University Microfilms International (UMI). Documents available from The Genuine Article, BIOSIS Document Express, CASDDS. ***Formed by the union of*** *Archives de Medicine des Enfants; Societe de Pediatrie de Paris. Bulletin.* ***and*** *Revue Francaise de Pediatrie.*
**Desc:** The leading outlet for French research in pediatrics.
**Ind/Abst** Biol. Abstr.; Chem. Abstr.; Curr. Contents Clin. Med.; Dairy Sci. Abstr.; Dev. Med. Child Neurol.; EMBASE; Health Plan. Adminis.; Helminthol. Abstr. (19??-19??); Index Med.; Index Vet.; Nutr. Abstr. Rev., Ser. B, Live Feeds and Feed.; Nutr. Abstr. Rev., Ser. A, Hum. Exp.; Life Sci. Collect.; Protozoolog. Abstr.; Res. Alert [Full Cov.]; Rev. Med. Vet. Entomol.; Rev. Med. Vet. Mycology; Sci. Cit. Index; SCISEARCH; Soc. Sci. Cit. Index [Select. Cov.]; Wheat Barley Trit. Abstr.

II/0044-8710
**ARCHIVES OF CHILD HEALTH.** [Arch. child health]. (19??)-. Academic Scholarly Publication. English. bm. **NLM** W1 AR451P. **CODEN** ACHHA4. Documents available from BIOSIS Document Express.
**Ind/Abst** Biol. Abstr. (-1982); EMBASE; Trop. Dis. Bull.

UK/0003-9888
**ARCHIVES OF DISEASE IN CHILDHOOD.** [Arch. dis. child.]. **Added/Corp** British Paediatric Association. Vol. 1 (Feb. 1926)-. Academic Scholarly Publication. English. Sixteen times a year. £204.00. BMJ / British Medical Journal Publishing Group, British Medical Association House, Tavistock Square, London WC1H 9JR England. **Tel** 011 44 71 3874499, FAX 011 44 71 383 6402, telex 290034 HBJ MN. **ED** Bernard Valman and Malcolm Chiswick. **LC** [RJ1]. **NLM** W1 AR453. **CODEN** ADCHAK. **[CCC]. Pr Rev.** available on microfilm and microfiche from University Microfilms International (UMI). Documents available from The Genuine Article, BIOSIS Document Express, CASDDS, ADONIS. ***Absorbed*** *British Journal of Children's Diseases.*
**Desc:** Devoted to child health and disease, with emphasis on clinical paediatrics.
**Ind/Abst** Abr. Index Med.; ADONIS; Biol. Abstr.; Chem. Abstr.; Cumul. Index Nurs. Allied Health Lit.; Curr. Contents Clin. Med.; Curr. Contents Life Sci.; Dairy Sci. Abstr.; Dev. Med. Child Neurol.; EMBASE; Except. Child Educ. Resour.; Health Period. Database; Health Plan. Adminis.; Health Serv. Abstr.; Helminthol. Abstr. (19??-19??); Index Med.; Iowa Drug Inf. Serv. (1970-); Microbiol. Abstr. Sect. B; Mod. Med.; Nutr. Abstr. Rev., Ser. B, Live Feeds and Feed.; Nutr. Abstr. Rev., Ser. A, Hum. Exp.; Nutr. Res. Newsl.; Life Sci. Collect.; Physic. Medline Plus; Protozoolog. Abstr.; Ref. Upd. Clinical Ed.; Ref. Upd. Deluxe Ed.; Res. Alert [Full Cov.]; Rev. Med. Vet. Mycology; Rev. Plant Pathol.; Sci. Cit. Index; SCISEARCH; Soc. Sci. Cit. Index [Select. Cov.]; Soyabean Abstr.; SportSearch; Trop. Dis. Bull.

●US/1072-4710
**ARCHIVES OF PEDIATRICS & ADOLESCENT MEDICINE.** [Arch. pediatr. adolesc. med.]. **Added/Corp** American Medical Association. **VFOAT** Archives of Pediatrics and Adolescent Medicine. Vol. 148, No. 1 (Jan. 1994)-. Periodical. English. mo. $125.00 (institution), $100.00 (individual) non-member; $50.00 member of AMA. American Medical Association, 515 North State Street, Chicago IL 60610. **Tel** (312)464-5000, (800)262-2350, FAX (312)464-5831. **DD** 618. **NLM** W1; AR471M. **CODEN** APAMEB. Index available (free). **Pr Rev.** available on microfilm from University Microfilms International (UMI). ***Continues*** *American Journal of Diseases of Children (1960), 0002-922X.*

IT/0393-6392
**ARCHIVIO SICILIANO DI MEDICINA E CHIRURGIA. 5, ACTA PEDIATRICA MEDITERRANEA.** [Acta pediatr. mediter.]. **VFOAT** Acta Pediatrica Mediterranea. Vol. 1, No. 1 (1985)-. Periodical. Italian (summaries and/or abstracts in English). bm. L40000.00 Italy; L60000.00 other. Edizioni Carbone Alfonsa, Via G Daita 29, 90139 Palermo Italy. **Tel** 011 39 91 321273, FAX 39 91 322736. **ED** Antonino Pennino. **NLM** W1; AR597TC. **Bk Rev. Ad Acc. Circ:** 4,000. ***Continues in part*** *Archivio Siciliano di Medicina e Chirurgia, 0392-2049.*
**Ind/Abst** Trop. Dis. Bull.

SP/0402-9054
**ARCHIVOS DE PEDIATRIA.** (19??)-. Spanish. Twelve times a year. $56.34 Spain; $80.00 Europe; $90.00 others. Esmon Publishers, Calle Mallorca 272 274, 08037 Barcelona Spain. **Tel** 011 34 3 2153531, FAX 011 34 3 3210565, telex SAEDI E 53132. **(Subscription address:** Editorial Garsi, C Juan Bravo, 28006 Madrid Spain.**)**
**Ind/Abst** Indice Med. Esp.

DR/0004-0606
**ARCHIVOS DOMINICANOS DE PEDIATRIA.** (1965)-. Periodical. Spanish (summaries and/or abstracts in English). tq. **NLM** W1 AR712M.
**Ind/Abst** Trop. Dis. Bull.

US/0749-971X
**BABY TALK (1977).** (BABY TALK.). [Baby talk]. Vol. 42, No. 4 (Apr. 1977)-. Periodical. English. Twelve times a year. $12.95. Robert Cornwell Associates, Baby Talk Magazine, Sub Department, Paramus NJ 07652. **Tel** (212)989-8181. **ED** The Parenting Group, (editor's address: 636 6th Avenue New York City, N. Y. 10011 (212)989-8181),. **DD** 649. cum. index. **Ad Acc, Adv Mgr:** Merrill Sugarman, **Tel** (212)989-8181. **Circ:** 1,050,000 (monthly) (ctrl). ***Continues*** *New Baby Talk, 0364-1554.*
**Desc:** Covers the physical and emotional aspects of pregnancy, newborn care, and the physical and emotional development of young children through the toddler years.

●UK/0906-6714
**BAILLIERE'S CLINICAL PAEDIATRICS.** (1992)-. English. qt (4 issues). £86.00 (institution). Harcourt Brace & Company Ltd., Foots Cray, High Street, Sidcup Kent DA14 5HP England. **Tel** 011 44 81 300 3322, FAX 011 44 81 309 0807. **(Subscription address:** W. B. Saunders Company / North America Subscriptions, c/o Periodicals, 6277 Sea Harbour Drive, 4th Floor, Orlando FL 32887.**)**

BG/0257-3490
**BANGLADESH JOURNAL OF CHILD HEALTH.** [Bangladesh j. child health]. (1984)-. Periodical. English. qt. Bangladesh Journal of Child Health, Shahbagh Avenue, 1000 Dacca Bangladesh. **UDC** 613.95. ***Continues*** *Review - International Council of Sports Science and Physical Education, 0256-4327.*
**Ind/Abst** EMBASE [Select. Cov.].

SZ/0006-3126
**BIOLOGY OF THE NEONATE.** [Biol. neonate]. Vol. 15 (1970)-. Academic Scholarly Publication. English (French and German). mo. $650.00. S. Karger AG, Allschwilerstrasse 10, PO Box - Postfach - Case Postale, CH-4009 Basel Switzerland. **Tel** 011 41 61 306-1111, FAX 011 41 61 306-1234, telex CH 962 652. **ED** J. P. Relier, A. Minkowski, F. C. Battaglia, G. Duc, J. Girard, B. Salle, M. Delivoria-Papadopoulos. **LC** RJ251; .B5. **DD** 612.6/52/05. **NLM** W1 BI852P. **CODEN** BNEOBV. **[CCC].** Index available. **Ad Acc. Pr Rev.** available on microfilm from University Microfilms International (UMI). Documents available from The Genuine Article, BIOSIS Document Express, CASDDS. ***Continues*** *Biologia Neonatorum.*

**Desc:** Information concerning developments in fetal and neonatal research. Original papers present laboratory findings from both human and animal studies covering the physiological and biochemical events taking place during the period leading up to and immediately following birth, whether full-term or premature. In recognition of the growing possibilities for therapeutic intervention, includes carefully selected papers exploring the specific clinical problems of the fetus and newborn. These basic and clinically-oriented investigations are supplemented by a forum for short preliminary reports and observations of particular current interest.
**Ind/Abst** Biol. Abstr.; Chem. Abstr.; Curr. Contents Life Sci.; Dairy Sci. Abstr.; Dev. Med. Child Neurol.; EMBASE; Health Plan. Adminis.; Index Med.; Nutr. Abstr. Rev., Ser. B, Live Feeds and Feed.; Nutr. Abstr. Rev., Ser. A, Hum. Exp.; Life Sci. Collect.; Pig News Inf.; Ref. Upd. Deluxe Ed.; Res. Alert [Full Cov.]; Rev. Med. Vet. Mycology; Sci. Cit. Index; SCISEARCH.

SP/0377-8207
**BOLETIN DE LA CATEDRA DE PEDIATRIA DE MADRID.** Vol. 1 (1958)-. Periodical. Spanish (summaries and/or abstracts in English and French). bm. Hospital Clinico de San Carlos, Spain. **NLM** W1 BO2395.

SP/0211-2051
**BOLETIN DE LA SOCIEDAD ARAGONESA DE PEDIATRIA.** [Bol. Soc. Aragon. Pediatr.]. (1970)-. Periodical. Spanish. bm. Sociedad Aragonesa de Pediatria, Paseo Ruisenores 2, 50006 Zaragoza Spain. **UDC** 616 - 053.2.

SP/0489-3824
**BOLETIN DE LA SOCIEDAD VALENCIANA DE PEDIATRIA.** Vol. 1 (1959)-. Spanish. bm. Sociedad Valenciana de Pediatria, Avda de la Plata 20, 46013 Valencia Spain.

SP/0037-8658
**BOLETIN DE LA SOCIEDAD VASCO-NAVARRA DE PEDIATRIA.** **Added/Corp** Sociedad Vasco-Navarra de Pediatria. Vol. 1 (Jan./June 1966)-. Periodical. Multiple languages (Spanish and French). qt. 2120ptas Spain; $35.00 other. Editorial Garsi SA, Juan Bravo 46, 28006 Madrid, Spain. **Tel** 011 34 1 4021212, telex 98358 GARSI E. **NLM** W1 BO25T. **Ad Acc. Pr Rev. Circ:** 625.

SP/0214-2597
**BOLETIN DE PEDIATRIA.** [Bol. pediatr.]. (1988)-. Periodical. Multiple languages. qt. Publifinanza, Londres 17, 28028 Madrid Spain. **UDC** 616-053.2. ***Continues*** *Boletin de la Sociedad Castellano-Astur-Leonesa de Pediatria, 0037-8429.*
**Ind/Abst** Indice Med. Esp.

MX/0539-6115
**BOLETIN MEDICO DEL HOSPITAL INFANTIL DE MEXICO (SPANISH EDITION).** (BOLETIN MEDICO DEL HOSPITAL INFANTIL DE MEXICO.). [Bol. med. Hosp. Infant. Mex.]. **Added/Corp** Hospital Infantil de Mexico. (1944)-. Academic Scholarly Publication. Spanish (summaries and/or abstracts in English). mo. $90.00. Hospital Infantil de Mexico, Calle del Dr Marquez No 162, Mexico City 7 DF Mexico. **Tel** 011 52 5 7610333. **ED** Luis Valasquez Jones. **NLM** W1 BO425F. **CODEN** BMHIAK. Index available. **Bk Rev. Ad Acc. Circ:** 3,500 (ctrl). Documents available from CASDDS.
**Desc:** Articles on pediatrics and related topics: original articles, clinical cases and reviews.
**Ind/Abst** Chem. Abstr. (1944-1983); Child Dev. Abstr. Bibliogr.; Curr. Aware. Biol. Sci., CABS; EMBASE; Index Med.

GW/0373-3165
**BUCHEREI DES PADIATERS.** No. 67 (1972)-. Monographic series. German. ir. Price varies per volume. Ferdinand Enke Verlag, Ruedigerstrasse 14, D-70469 Stuttgart Germany. **Tel** 011 49 711 8931124, 011 49 711 893123. **(Subscription address:** Georg Thieme Verlag Stuttgart, Postfach 301120, D 70451 Stuttgart Germany.**)** **ED** W. Burmeister, G. Heimann and F. C. Sitzmann. **Ad Acc.** ctrl circ. ***Continues*** *Beihefte zur Archiv fuer Kinderheilkunde, 0066-6378.*
**Desc:** Deals with practical and clinical relevant subjects from the whole subject of pediatrics. The volumes are supplements of the journal "Klinische Padiatrie".
**Ind/Abst** Nutr. Abstr. Rev., Ser. B, Live Feeds and Feed.; Nutr. Abstr. Rev., Ser. A, Hum. Exp.; Soyabean Abstr.

FR/0245-9337
**BULLETIN OF THE INTERNATIONAL PEDIATRIC ASSOCIATION.** ***Suspended.*** [Bull. Int. Pediatr. Assoc.]. **Main/Corp** International Pediatric Association. **VFOAT** Bulletin de l'Association Internationale de Pediatrie; Boletin de la Asociacion Internacional de Pediatria. No. 1 (Jan. 1975)-Suspended. Bulletin. English (French and Spanish). qt. $30.00. Prof Gavin C Arneil, c/o University Department of Child Health, Royal Hospital for Sick Children, Yorkhill Glasgow G3 8SJ Scotland. **Tel** 339-88-88. **ED** Gavin C Arneil. **UDC** 616-053.2. **NLM** W1 BU853NI. **Ad Acc. Circ:** 2,350. ***Continues*** *Bulletin - International Paediatric Association.*
**Desc:** Articles of interest to pediatricians which includes reports of the International Pediatrics Association organized meetings, progress in pediatric specialties, special contributions. Major topics in pediatrics treated.

SP/0210-721X
**BUTLLETI DE LA SOCIETAT CATALANA DE PEDIATRIA.** [Butll. Soc. Catalana Pediatr]. (1977)-. Academic Scholarly Publication. Multiple languages (Catalan, English, French and Spanish); summaries and/or abstracts in English, French and Spanish). bm. Elena Gisbert, Provenza 60 1, 08029 Barcelona Spain. **NLM** W1 BU9749. **CODEN** BSCPDR. Documents available from CASDDS. ***Continues*** *Boletin de la Sociedad Catalana de Pediatria.*
**Ind/Abst** Chem. Abstr. (1977-1983); EMBASE; Indice Med. Esp.

JA
**BYOJAKUJI NO JIREI KENKYU.** Japanese. Kokuritsu Tokushu Kyoiku Sogo Kenkyujo, 5-1-1 Nobi, Yokosuka 239 Japan. **Tel** 011 81 469 48 4121. **LC** LC4564.J3; B9.

US/0882-3421
**CALIFORNIA PEDIATRICIAN.** [Calif. pediatr.]. Vol. 1, No. 1 (Winter 1984/85)-. Periodical. English. Three times a year. Free to members of the American Academy of Pediatrics California District. California Pediatrician, 1295 East Hillsdale Boulevard, Foster City CA 94404. **Tel** (415)574-2774. **ED** Marvin Auerback. **DD** 618. **Ad Acc. Circ:** 5,000 (ctrl).
**Desc:** Contains articles on topics of interest to pediatricians and pediatric nurses. Summarizes activities of the American Academy of Pediatrics within the California district.

CN/1183-3181
**CALYX (TORONTO).** (CALYX.). [Calyx]. **Added/Corp** Hospital for Sick Children. Dept. of Bioethics. Vol. 1, No. 1 (Winter 1991)-. Periodical. English. qt. Free. Hospital for Sick Children, Department of Bioethics, 555 University Avenue, Toronto Ontario M5G 1X8 Canada. **DD** 174.

CN/0843-4263
**CANADIAN JOURNAL OF PEDIATRICS, THE.** [Can. j. pediatr.]. Vol. 1, No. 1 (Winter 1989)-. Periodical. English. Six times a year (Jan., Mar., May, July, Sept., Nov.). $60.00 Canada; $67.00 US; $79.00 other. Contemporary Journals, 19180 Trans Canada, Boie d'Urfe Quebec H9X 3T9 Canada. **Tel** (514)457-2673. **DD** 618.92/0005. **NLM** W1; CA598L. ***Continues*** *Contemporary Pediatrics Canada, 0832-7831.*
**Ind/Abst** Can. Index.

US/1057-9087
**CANCERGRAM. SERIES CT10 PEDIATRIC ONCOLOGY.** ***Ceased.*** **See** Medical Science and Technology-Neoplasma, Neoplastic.

●US
**CAPSULES & COMMENTS IN PEDIATRIC NURSING.** **See** Medical Science and Technology-Nursing.

XR/0069-2328
**CESKOSLOVENSKA PEDIATRIE.** [Cesk. pediatr.]. Vol. 10, Feb. 1955-. Academic Scholarly Publication. Czech. mo. $122.50. **(Subscription address:** Artia Pegas Press Ltd., Palac Metro Narodni Trida 25, 11210 Prague 1 Czech Republic.**)** **NLM** W1 CE902L. **CODEN** CEPEA3. **[CCC].** Documents available from CASDDS. ***Continues*** *Pediatricke Listy.*
**Ind/Abst** Chem. Abstr. (1955-1983); EMBASE [Select. Cov.]; Helminthol. Abstr.; Index Med.; Life Sci. Collect.

US/0160-290X
**CHILD ADVOCACY PROGRAMS.** 1975-. Periodical. English. US Department of Health and Human Services National Institutes of Health, 9000 Rockville Pike, Bethesda MD 20892. **Tel** (301)496-9291, FAX (301)496-2443. **UDC** 616-053.2(794). **NLM** WS 22 AA1 C4.
**Desc:** State, local, and regional child advocacy programs in the United States. Also includes related programs. Geographical arrangement by states. Entries include program, address, and contract.

US/0731-7107
**CHILD & FAMILY BEHAVIOR THERAPY.** **See** Psychology.

CN/0838-9683
**CHILD CARE.** (SANTE INFANTILE : LE BULLETIN DE L'INSTITUT CANADIEN DE LA SANTE INFANTILE.). [Child care]. **Added/Corp** Institut Canadien de La Sante Infantile. **VFOAT** Child Health. Vol. 9, No 4 (Dec. 1987)-. Bulletin. French (English). Four times a year (Mar., June, Sept., Dec.). 20.00Can$ (individuals); 60.00Can$ (institutions). Canadian Institute of Child Health, 885 Meadowlands Drive East, Ottawa Ontario K2C 3N2 Canada. **Tel** (613)224-4141, FAX (613)224-4145. **DD** 613/.0432. **Ad Acc, Adv Mgr:** Carric Kelly. ***Continues*** *Institut Canadien de La Sante Infantile (Bulletin)., 0838-9675.*

UK/0305-1862
**CHILD CARE, HEALTH AND DEVELOPMENT.** [Child care health dev.]. Vol. 1 (Jan./Feb. 1975)-. Academic Scholarly Publication. English. bm (6 issues). $197.00 US & Canada; £115.00 Europe; £127.00 other. Blackwell Scientific Publications Ltd, Marston Book Services, PO Box 87, Oxford OX2 ODT UK. **Tel** 011 44 865 791155, FAX 011 44 865 791927, telex 837 515 MARDIS G. **ED** R. B. Jones. **NLM** W1 CH646D. **CODEN** CCHDDH. **[CCC]. Bk Rev. Ad Acc. Pr Rev. Circ:** 740 (ctrl). available on microfilm and microfiche from University Microfilms International (UMI). Documents available from The Genuine Article, BIOSIS Document Express.
**Desc:** Publishes material on the development of all children, particularly those handicapped by physical, intellectual, emotional and social problems.
**Ind/Abst** AGRICOLA [Select. Cov.]; Appl. Soc. Sci. Index Abstr.; Biol. Abstr.; Br. Educ. Index; Cumul. Index Nurs. Allied Health Lit.; Curr. Contents Clin. Med.; Curr. Contents Soc. Behav. Sci.; Dev. Med. Child Neurol.; EMBASE; Except. Child Educ. Resour.; Health Plan. Adminis.; Index Med.; Nutr. Abstr. Rev., Ser. B, Live Feeds and Feed.; Nutr. Abstr. Rev., Ser. A, Hum. Exp.; Life Sci. Collect.; Physic. Medline Plus; Psychol. Abstr. (1975-); PsycINFO; PsycLit; PsycScan: Develop. Psych.; Res. Alert [Full Cov.]; SCISEARCH; Soc. Sci. Cit. Index [Full Cov.]; Spec. Educ. Needs Abstr.; SportSearch; Trop. Dis. Bull.

US/0009-3939
**CHILD DEVELOPMENT ABSTRACTS AND BIBLIOGRAPHY.** **See** Medical Science and Technology-Abstracting, Bibliographies and Statistics.

HK
**CHILD HEALTH MAGAZINE.** Chinese. mo. $22.00 Asia; $36.00 other. Hygeia Publishing Co. Ltd., Stanhope House, 734 King Road, Room 112-114, North Point Hong Kong. **Tel** 5 648449.

US/0093-2175
**CHILD PERSONALITY AND PSYCHOPATHOLOGY.** (CHILD PERSONALITY & PSYCHOPATHOLOGY : CURRENT TOPICS.). V. 1- 1974-. English. John Wiley & Sons, Inc., 605 Third Avenue, New York NY 10158-0012. **Tel** (212)850-6000, (212)850-6645, FAX (212)850-6088, telex 12-7063. **(Subscription address:** John Wiley & Sons / England, Baffins Lane, Chichester, West Sussex PO19 1UD England.**)** **LC** RJ499.A1; C427. **DD** 618.9/28/9005. **UDC** 616.89-053.2. **NLM** W1 CH668G.

II/0009-3998
**CHILD PSYCHIATRY QUARTERLY.** ***Ceased.*** [Child psychiatr. q.]. Periodical. English. qt. Community Mental Health Center Indira, 7th Road Banjara Hills, Hyderabad 500034 India. **Tel** 35765. **ED** Jaya Naganaja. **UDC** 616.89-053.2. **NLM** W1 CH668P. **CODEN** CPQUDY. Index available. cum. index. **Bk Rev. Ad Acc. Circ:** 1,000. available on diskette; available on videocassette; available on microfilm and microfiche from University Microfilms International (UMI).
**Desc:** Topics include child and adolescent psychiatry, research, and clinical family counseling.
**Ind/Abst** EMBASE; Psychol. Abstr. (1972-); PsycINFO; PsycLit.

FR/0379-2269
**CHILDREN IN THE TROPICS.** **See** Medical Science and Technology-Tropical Medicine.

US/0273-9615
**CHILDREN'S HEALTH CARE.** [Child. health care]. **Added/Corp** Association for the Care of Children's Health. **VFOAT** JACCH. Vol. 9 No. 2 (Fall 1980)-. Periodical. English. qt. $100.00 US & Canada; $125.00 other. Lawrence Erlbaum Associates, 365 Broadway, Suite 102, Hillsdale NJ 07642. **Tel** (201)666-4110, (800)926-6579, FAX (201)666-2394. **ED** Terri Shelton. **LC** RJ242; .A88a. **DD** 362.1/9892. **NLM** W1 CH696. Index available. **Bk Rev. Ad Acc. Pr Rev. Circ:** 4,500 (ctrl). available on microfilm and microfiche from University Microfilms International (UMI). ***Continues*** *Journal of the Association for the Care of Children's Health, 0274-8916.*
**Desc:** Addresses psychosocial aspects of pediatric care. Includes media and book reviews. Special theme issues occasionally.
**Ind/Abst** Cumul. Index Nurs. Allied Health Lit.; Except. Child Educ. Resour.; Health Plan. Adminis.; Hospit. Health Admin. Index; Psychol. Abstr. (1980-); PsycINFO; PsycLit.

US/0899-5869
**CHILDREN'S HOSPITAL QUARTERLY.** (CHILDREN'S HOSPITAL QUARTERLY : A JOURNAL OF THE SCHNEIDER CHILDREN'S HOSPITAL, LONG ISLAND JEWISH MEDICAL CENTER.). [Child. hosp. q.]. **Added/Corp** Schneider Children's Hospital. Vol. 1, No. 1 (Spring 1989)-. Periodical. English. qt. $175.00 US; $205.00 other. Human Sciences Press, PO Box 735, 233 Spring Street, New York NY 10013. **Tel** (212)620-8000, FAX (212)807-1047, telex 23421139. **(Subscription address:** Eurospan Ltd., Journals and Serials Division, 3

Henrietta Street, Covent Garden, London WC2E 8LU England.) **ED** Philip Lanzkowsky, Bernard Gauthier, and Ronald Shenker. **DD** 616. **NLM** W1; CH696F. **CODEN** CHQUED. **[CCC].** available on microfilm and microfiche from University Microfilms International (UMI).
**Desc:** Presents the practicing pediatrician with the latest information available in the various pediatric subspecialties, including basic research, as seen and interpreted by the staff of the Schneider Children's Hospital.
**Ind/Abst** EMBASE.

US/0882-2301
**CHILD'S DOCTOR, THE.** (THE CHILD'S DOCTOR : JOURNAL OF THE CHILDREN'S MEMORIAL HOSPITAL.). [Child's dr.]. **Added/Corp** Children's Memorial Hospital (Chicago, Ill.). Vol. 1, No. 1 (Fall 1983)-. Periodical. English. sa. Children's Memorial Hospital, 2300 Children's Plaza, Chicago IL 60614. **DD** 618. **NLM** W1; CH66E.

GW/0256-7040
**CHILD'S NERVOUS SYSTEM.** (CHILD'S NERVOUS SYSTEM : CHNS : OFFICIAL JOURNAL OF THE INTERNATIONAL SOCIETY FOR PEDIATRIC NEUROSURGERY.). [Child nerv. syst.]. **Added/Corp** International Society for Paediatric Neurosurgery. **VFOAT** ChNS. Vol. 1, No. 1 (Feb. 1985)-. Periodical. English. Twelve times a year. DM1198.00. Springer-Verlag GmbH & Company KG, Heidelberger Platz 3, D 14197 Berlin Germany. **Tel** 011 49 30 8207223, FAX 011 49 30 8214091, telex 183 319 SPBLN D. **(Subscription address:** Springer Verlag New York Inc. / for North America, 44 Hartz Way, Secaucus NJ 07096.) **ED** A J Raimondi. **NLM** W1; CH667H. **CODEN** CNSYE9. **[CCC]. Pr Rev.** available on microfilm from University Microfilms International (UMI). Documents available from The Genuine Article, BIOSIS Document Express. ***Continues** Child's Brain, 0302-2803.*
**Desc:** Encompasses all aspects of the pediatric neurosciences: growth; trauma; degenerative disorders; hereditary diseases; neurophysiology, neurology, and neurosurgery.
**Ind/Abst** Biol. Abstr. (1987-); Curr. Contents Arts Humanit.; Dev. Med. Child Neurol.; EMBASE; Health Plan. Adminis.; Helminthol. Abstr.; Index Med. (Vol. 1, No. 1, 1985-); Res. Alert [Full Cov.]; Sci. Cit. Index; SCISEARCH; Soc. Sci. Cit. Index [Select. Cov.].

US/0882-6390
**CHILDSCOPE.** [Childscope]. Periodical. English. mo. $15.00 US; $20.00 other. Sundrrops Enterprises, Childscope, Box 837, Broken Arrow OK 74013. **ED** Judy A Rollins. **DD** 649. **UDC** 616-053.2. **Bk Rev. Circ:** 250 (ctrl).
**Desc:** Creative resources, programs, activities, news, reviews, events, playthings, people, and other information of interest to child health care professionals. Emphasis is on the hospitalized child.

CC/0578-1310
**CHUNG-HUA ERH KO TSA CHI. / ZHONGHUA ERKE ZAZHI / CHINESE JOURNAL OF PEDIATRICS. VFOAT** Chinese Journal of Pediatrics. July (1950). Periodical. Chinese (English; summaries and/or abstracts in English; table of contents in English). qt. $13.50. **DD** 618.92.

SP
**CIENCIA PEDIATRIKA (MADRID, SPAIN : 1986).** (CIENCIA PEDIATRIKA.). **VFOAT** Pediatrika. Jan. (1986)-. Academic Scholarly Publication. Spanish (English). mo (10 issues per year). 7500ptas, $120.00 (US). Alpe Editores SA, C Pedro Rico 27, Oficinas 11 & 12, 28029 Madrid Spain. **Tel** 011 34 1 7338811, FAX 011 34 1 3159652. **ED** Dr. Juan Casado Flores. Index available. **Bk Rev. Ad Acc, Adv Mgr:** McCarmen Alvarez, **Tel** 733-88-92. Full Page (Color) 150000ptas. **Circ:** 6,500 (ctrl). available with charts; available with illustrations. Documents available from CASDDS, BLDSC. ***Continues** Pediatrika (Madrid, Spain), 0211-3465.*
**Ind/Abst** Chem. Abstr.; EMBASE.

SP
**CIRUGIA PEDIATRICA : ORGANO OFICIAL DE LA SOCIEDAD ESPANOLA DE CIRUGIA PEDIATRICA. Added/Corp** Sociedad Espanola de Cirugia Pediatrica. Vol. 1, No. 1 (Jan. 1988)-. Periodical. Spanish (summaries and/or abstracts in English). qt. $103.00. Editorial Garsi SA, Juan Bravo 46, 28006 Madrid, Spain. **Tel** 011 34 1 4021212, telex 98358 GARSI E. **NLM** W1; CI8785L.

IT/0009-9058
**CLINICA PEDIATRICA. *Suspended.*** [Clin. pediatr.]. Vol. 1 (1919)-Suspended with (April 1986). Periodical. Italian. mo. $20.50. La Clinica Pediatrica, Via Siepelunga 48/2, 40141 Bologna Italy. **Tel** 051 491329. **UDC** 616-053.2. **NLM** W1 CL554.

US/0069-4797
**CLINICAL APPROACHES TO PROBLEMS OF CHILDHOOD.** V. 1- 1965-. Monographic series. English. Price varies per volume. Science and Behavior Books, 599 College Avenue, Palo Alto CA 94306. **UDC** 616-053.2.

US/0733-933X
**CLINICAL DISORDERS ON PEDIATRIC NUTRITION. See** Nutrition and Dietetics.

US/0009-9228
**CLINICAL PEDIATRICS.** [Clin. pediatr.]. Vol. 1 (Oct. 1962)-. Academic Scholarly Publication. English. mo. $78.00 (US), $93.00 (Canada), $98.00 (other) individual; $98.00 (US), $113.00 (Canada), $118.00 (other) institution. Cortlandt Group Inc., 500 Executive Boulevard, Ossining NY 10562. **Tel** (914)762-0647, FAX (914)762-8820. **ED** David M. Cornfeld. **LC** RJ1; .C55. **DD** 618.92/0005. **NLM** W1 CL762. **CODEN** CPEDAM. **Ad Acc. Pr Rev. Circ:** 24,250. available on microfilm and microfiche from University Microfilms International (UMI). Documents available from The Genuine Article, BIOSIS Document Express. ***Formed by the union of** American Practitioner, 0517-4465; Archives of Pediatrics, 0096-6630 **and** Quarterly Review of Pediatrics, 0097-0107.*
**Desc:** Recent advances in pediatrics relating to office practice emphasis on more commonly encountered conditions.
**Ind/Abst** Abr. Index Med.; AGRICOLA [Select. Cov.]; Biol. Abstr.; Chicano Index; Comb. Cumul. Index Pediatr.; Cumul. Index Nurs. Allied Health Lit.; Curr. Contents Clin. Med.; Dairy Sci. Abstr.; Dev. Med. Child Neurol.; EMBASE; Energy Res. Abstr.; Health Plan. Adminis.; Index Med.; INIS Atomindex [Micro.]; Int. Pharm. Abstr.; Iowa Drug Inf. Serv. (1966-); Med. Abstr. Newsl.; Microbiol. Abstr. Sect. B; Mod. Med.; Life Sci. Collect.; Physic. Medline Plus; Protozoolog. Abstr.; Psychol. Abstr. (1982-); PsycINFO; PsycLit; Res. Alert [Full Cov.]; Rev. Med. Vet. Mycology; Risk Abstr.; Sci. Cit. Index; SCISEARCH; Soc. Sci. Cit. Index [Select. Cov.]; SportSearch.

US/0193-9742
**CLINICAL PEDIATRICS, MATERNAL AND CHILD HEALTH.** (19??)-. Monographic series. English. ir. Price varies per volume. John Wiley & Sons, Inc., 605 Third Avenue, New York NY 10158-0012. **Tel** (212)850-6000, (212)850-6645, FAX (212)850-6088, telex 12-7063. **(Subscription address:** John Wiley & Sons Inc / New Jersey, PO Box 2575, Secaucus NJ 07096-2575.)

US/0883-7198
**CLINICAL PEDIATRICS (NEW YORK. 1985).** (CLINICAL PEDIATRICS.). [Clin. pediatr.]. Vol. 1 (1984)-. Academic Scholarly Publication. English. Price varies per volume. Marcel Dekker Inc., 270 Madison Avenue, New York NY 10016. **Tel** (212)696-9000, (800)228-1160, FAX (212)685-4540, telex 421419. **(Subscription address:** Marcel Dekker Inc, PO Box 5017, Monticello NY 12701.) **ED** Fima Lifshitz. **DD** 618. **NLM** W1; CL761Y. **CODEN** CLPEEM. Documents available from BIOSIS Document Express, CASDDS.
**Desc:** Presents information on topics in clinical pediatrics such as congenital metabolic disease and food allergy.
**Ind/Abst** Biol. Abstr. (1988-); Chem. Abstr. (1984-1985); Health Period. Database; Health Ref. Cent. (Jan. 1989-) [Full Cov.]; Ref. Upd. Deluxe Ed.

US/0501-798X
**CLINICAL PROGRAMS FOR MENTALLY RETARDED CHILDREN. Main/Corp** United States. Health Services Administration. Bureau of Community Health Services. English. Recon Publishing, PO Box 14602, Philadelphia PA 19134. **LC** RJ506.M4; U54A. **DD** 362.7/8/302573. **UDC** 616.89-008.454-053.2. **NLM** WS 22 AA1 C6. ***Continues** Clinical Programs for Mentally Retarded Children, A Listing.*

US/0883-0290
**CLINICAL UPDATE IN PEDIATRICS.** [Clin. update pediatr.]. Periodical. English. bw. $295.00. Nassau Publications Inc., 11 Forest Street, New Canaan CT 06840. **DD** 618. **UDC** 616-053.2.

SP
**CLINICAS PEDIATRICAS DE NORTEAMERICA.** Spanish. McGraw Hill, Interamericana de Espana SA, Manuel Ferrero 13, 28036 Madrid Spain.

US/0190-4981
**COMBINED CUMULATIVE INDEX TO PEDIATRICS. See** Medical Science and Technology-Abstracting, Bibliographies and Statistics.

SZ/0251-2068
**CONCEPTS IN PEDIATRIC NEUROSURGERY.** (CONCEPTS IN PEDIATRIC NEUROSURGERY / AMERICAN SOCIETY FOR PEDIATRIC NEUROSURGERY.). [Concepts peddiatr. neurosurg.]. **Added/Corp** American Society for Pediatric Neurosurgery. **VFOAT** Pediatric Neurosurgery. (1981)-. English. an. 150.00F (approx. per volume). S. Karger AG, Allschwilerstrasse 10, PO Box - Postfach - Case Postale, CH-4009 Basel Switzerland. **Tel** 011 41 61 306-1111, FAX 011 41 61 306-1234, telex CH 962 652. **NLM** W1 CO459RM. **CODEN** COPNDZ. **[CCC].** Documents available from BIOSIS Document Express.
**Desc:** Offers access to the most up-to-date thoughts and conclusions of neurosurgeons actively involved in the care of children afflicted with neurologic disease. The series is authored and edited by members of the American Society for Pediatric Neurosurgery, who present their most significant academic work in the hopes that this knowledge will help pediatric neurosurgeons improve the care of children.
**Ind/Abst** Biol. Abstr.; Ref. Upd. Deluxe Ed.

US/0893-8822
**CONTEMPORARY ISSUES IN FETAL AND NEONATAL MEDICINE. See** Medical Science and Technology-Gynecology and Obstetrics.

US/8750-0507
**CONTEMPORARY PEDIATRICS (MONTVALE, N.J.).** (CONTEMPORARY PEDIATRICS.). [Contemp. pediatr.]. (198?)-. Periodical. English. Thirteen times a year (plus 1 special issue). $75.00 US; $87.00 other. Medical Economics Publishing, Five Paragon Drive, Second Floor, Montvale NJ 07645. **Tel** (800)432-4570, (201)358-2210. **(Subscription address:** Fulco Medical Economics, PO Box 3000, Denville NJ 07834.) **DD** 618. **NLM** W1; CO769NP.
**Desc:** Experts in the various pediatric fields describe the latest procedures, concepts and techniques as they apply to patient care. Editorial focus is on the diagnosis and management of clinical problems from neonatology through adolescence.
**Ind/Abst** Comb. Cumul. Index Pediatr.

NE/0376-5040
**CORE JOURNALS IN PEDIATRICS.** [Core j. pediatr.]. (1977)-. Academic Scholarly Publication. English. Eleven times a year (1 volume). Fl549.00. Excerpta Medica Publishing Group, PO Box 548, 1000 AM Amsterdam Netherlands. **Tel** 011 31 20 5803243. **(Subscription address:** Excerpta Medica Journals, PO Box 85, Limerick Ireland.) **NLM** ZWS 100 C797. **CODEN** CJPED7. **[CCC].** available on microfilm from University Microfilms International (UMI). Documents available from CASDDS.
**Desc:** This publication is intended to optimize the busy clinician's time by providing an overview of the most significant clinical studies in his/her field.
**Ind/Abst** Chem. Abstr.

GW/0172-1232
**CURRENT DIAGNOSTIC PEDIATRICS.** Vol. 1 (1977)-. Monographic series. English. ir. Price varies per volume. Springer-Verlag GmbH & Company KG, Heidelberger Platz 3, D 14197 Berlin Germany. **Tel** 011 49 30 8207223, FAX 011 49 30 8214091, telex 183 319 SPBLN D. **(Subscription address:** Springer Verlag New York Inc. / for North America, 44 Hartz Way, Secaucus NJ 07096.) **LC** UNC. **NLM** W1 CU788DP.
**Desc:** Contains articles on pediatric radiology, kidney and urinary tracts, and pediatric traumas.

UK/0951-9610
**CURRENT MEDICAL LITERATURE / PAEDIATRICS.** [Curr. med. lit., Paediatr.]. **VFOAT** Paediatrics (London). (1987)-. Periodical. English. Four times a year. $40.00. Current Medical Literature Ltd., 40-42 Osnaburgh Street, London NW1 3ND England. **Tel** 011 44 71 4658377, FAX 011 44 71 4658380. **(Subscription address:** Royal Society Medicine Services, 1 Wimpole Street, London W1M 8AE England.) **DD** 016.61892.

UK/0951-9610
**CURRENT MEDICAL LITERATURE. PAEDIATRICS / THE ROYAL SOCIETY OF MEDICINE. Added/Corp** Royal Society of Medicine (Great Britain). **VFOAT** Paediatrics; Pediatrics; Current Medical Literature. Pediatrics. (19??)-. Periodical. English. qt. £20.00. Current Medical Literature Ltd., 40-42 Osnaburgh Street, London NW1 3ND England. **Tel** 011 44 71 4658377, FAX 011 44 71 4658380. **(Subscription address:** Royal Society Medicine Services, 1 Wimpole Street, London W1M 8AE England.) **NLM** ZWS 200; C976.

US/1040-8703
**CURRENT OPINION IN PEDIATRICS.** [Curr. opin. pediatr.]. Vol. 1, No. 1 (Oct. 1989)-. Periodical. English. Six times a year. $119.95 (individual); $239.95 (institution). Current Science, 20 North 3rd Street, Philadelphia PA 19106. **Tel** (215)574-2266, (800)552-5866, FAX (215)574-2270. **ED** David G. Nathan. **LC** RJ1; .C87. **DD** 618.92/0005. **NLM** W1; CU799GGD. **CODEN** COPEE9. **[CCC].** available on diskette. Documents available from BIOSIS Document Express.
**Desc:** Directed toward researchers and practicing pediatricians. Presents review articles from an area of concentration covering an entire year's literature with annotated references. Each issue features a bibliography of the current world literature published during the previous year.
**Ind/Abst** Biol. Abstr. (1990-); Cumul. Index Nurs. Allied Health Lit.; Curr. Aware. Biol. Sci., CABS; EMBASE.

UK/0957-5839
**CURRENT PAEDIATRICS. VFOAT** Current Pediatrics. Vol. 1, No. 1 (March 1991)-. Periodical. English. Four times a year. £155.00 Europe; £156.00 Other (Institutions). Churchill Livingstone, 1-3 Baxter's Place, Leith Walk, Edinburgh EH1 3AF Scotland. **Tel** 011

44 31 556 2424, FAX 011 44 31 558 1278, telex 727511. **(Subscription address:** Maruzen Company Ltd., PO Box 5050, Import & Export Department, Tokyo 100 31 Japan.) **NLM** W1; CU799GS. **[CCC].**
**Ind/Abst** Curr. Aware. Biol. Sci., CABS.

US/0093-8556
**CURRENT PEDIATRIC DIAGNOSIS & TREATMENT.** [Curr. pediatr. diagn. treat.]. **VFOAT** Current Pediatric Diagnosis and Treatment. 1st Ed. (1970)-. English. be. $39.95 (latest edition). Appleton Century Crofts, Prentice Hall, 200 Old Tappan Road, Old Tappan NJ 07675. **Tel** (201)767-5188, (800)922-0579. **ED** C. Henry Kempe, Henry K. Silver, Donough O'Brien and Vincent A. Fulginiti. **LC** RJ1; .K45. **DD** 618.9/2/0005. **NLM** W1 CU799H.
**Desc:** Presents the essential principles of clinical diagnosis and treatment of pediatric disorders, including psychiatric disorders, the role of nutrition, and drug therapy.

US/0045-9380
**CURRENT PROBLEMS IN PEDIATRICS (ENGLISH ED.).** (CURRENT PROBLEMS IN PEDIATRICS.). [Curr. probl. pediatr.]. **VFOAT** CPP. Vol. 1 (Nov. 1970)-. Academic Scholarly Publication. English. Ten times a year. $103.00 (institutions), $75.00 (individuals) US; $112.00 (institutions), $84.00 (individuals) other. Mosby Year Book Inc., 11830 Westline Industrial Drive, St Louis MO 63146. **Tel** (800)325-4177, (314)872-8370, FAX (314)432-1380, telex 44-2402. **DD** 618. **NLM** W1 CU804P. **[CCC]. Ad Acc.** available on microfilm and microfiche from University Microfilms International (UMI).
**Desc:** Addressed to the general pediatrician, Each issue is a single topic discussion that includes elements of pathophysiology, diagnosis, drug therapy, surgical management, family factors, and developmental issues.
**Ind/Abst** EMBASE; Energy Res. Abstr. (Aug. 1982-); Health Plan. Adminis.; Index Med.; SportSearch.

UK/0012-1622
**DEVELOPMENTAL MEDICINE & CHILD NEUROLOGY.** **See** Medical Science and Technology-Abstracting, Bibliographies and Statistics.

US/8755-2701
**DIALOGUES IN PEDIATRIC MANAGEMENT.** [Dialogues pediatr. manage.]. Vol. 1, No. 1 (1985)-. Monographic series. English. ir. $55.00 (per copy) latest edition. Appleton Century Crofts, Prentice Hall, 200 Old Tappan Road, Old Tappan NJ 07675. **Tel** (201)767-5188, (800)922-0579. **ED** David Cornfeld and Benjamin K Silverman. **LC** UNC. **DD** 618. **NLM** W1; DI261H.

US/0164-9507
**DIALOGUES IN PEDIATRIC UROLOGY.** (197?)-. Periodical. English. mo. $54.00. William J. Miller Associates Inc., 45 Villa Road, Pearl River NY 10965. **Tel** (914)735-7853, (212)832-6557. **ED** Richard M. Ehrlich. cum. index. **Circ:** 550.
**Desc:** Clinical publication for physicians and other medical personnel interested in the field of pediatric urology.

US/8756-2170
**DIRECTORY OF RESIDENTIAL FACILITIES FOR EMOTIONALLY HANDICAPPED CHILDREN AND YOUTH.** ***Ceased.*** **See** Medical Science and Technology-Psychiatry.

IT/0394-7238
**DOCTOR PEDIATRIA.** ***Suspended.*** [Dr. Pediatr.]. (1987)-Suspended (Apr. 1994). Periodical. Italian. ir. Ariete Edizioni SRL, Via G Stephenson 33, 20157 Milan Italy. **Tel** 011 39 2 332141. **UDC** 616-053.2.

SZ
**DOCUMENTS SCIENTIFIQUES.** **See** Nutrition and Dietetics.

CN/0824-703X
**DRUGS IN PEDIATRICS.** [Drugs pediatr.]. No. 1 (1983)-. Periodical. English. sa. 50.00Can$. STA Communications Inc., 955 St. John Boulevard, Suite 306, Pt Claire, Quebec H9R 5K3 Canada. **Tel** (514)695-7623. **ED** Paul Brand. **DD** 615.5/8/088054. **UDC** 615.2:616-053.2. **Ad Acc. Circ:** 1,500 (ctrl).
**Desc:** Drug reference manuals.

●US/1073-7782
**EMERGENCY AND OFFICE PEDIATRICS.** [Emerg. off. pediatr.]. Vol. 6, No. 6 (Dec. 1993)-. Periodical. English. bm. $76.00. Mary Ann Liebert Inc., 1651 Third Avenue, New York NY 10128. **Tel** (212)289-2300, (800)M-LIEBERT, FAX (212)289-4697. **DD** 618. **NLM** W1; EM661EG. ***Continues*** *Emergency Pediatrics, 1044-3797.*

US/1044-3797
**EMERGENCY PEDIATRICS.** ***Title Change.*** [Emerg. pediatr.]. (1989)-(1993). Periodical. English. bm. Mary Ann Liebert Inc., 1651 Third Avenue, New York NY 10128. **Tel** (212)289-2300, (800)M-LIEBERT, FAX (212)289-4697. **ED** Fred Agre, M.D., Peter S. Liebert, M.D. and Andrew Peter Mezey, M.D. **DD** 618. **NLM** W1; EM664DU. **CODEN** EPEDEE. ***Continues*** *Pediatric Emergency News, 0897-2850.* ***Continued by*** *Emergency and Office Pediatrics, 1073-7782.*
**Desc:** Devoted to physicians and nurses who deliver care to children in emergency rooms and other ambulatory settings. Provides current information on how to manage the acutely and urgently ill pediatric patient. Each issue includes review articles on medical and surgical problems, questions and answers, practical tips, abstracts and commentary.

FR/0399-4988
**ENFANT D'ABORD, L'.** [Enfant d'abord]. (1976)-. Periodical. French. Eleven times a year. 360.00F France; 470.00F other. L Enfant d Abord, 32 rue Basfroi, 75011 Paris France. **Tel** 011 33 1 43712850, FAX 011 33 1 43712949. **UDC** 36. **Bk Rev. Ad Acc.** ctrl circ.

FR/0013-7561
**ENFANT EN MILIEU TROPICAL, L'.** [Enfant milieu trop.]. **Added/Corp** Universite de Dakar. Institut de Pediatrie Sociale. International Children's Centre. No. 1 (1961)-. Periodical. French (English and Spanish). Six times a year. $40.00. Centre International de L Enfrance / International Children's Centre, Chateau des Longchamp Bois de Boulogne, 75016 Paris France. **Tel** 44 30 20 00, FAX 45 25 73 67, telex 648 378 F. **ED** Anne-Marie Masse-Raimbault. **NLM** W1 EN575. **Circ:** 15,000 (ctrl).
**Desc:** Journal furnishes practical information that can be directly applied to health, and information agents for development. Each issue deals with a specific topic.

GW/0071-111X
**ERGEBNISSE DER INNEREN MEDIZIN UND KINDERHEILKUNDE.** **See** Medical Science and Technology-Internal Medicine.

IT/0392-0658
**ETA EVOLUTIVA (FIRENZE).** (ETA EVOLUTIVA.). [Eta evol.]. No. 1 (Nov. 1978)-. Periodical. Italian. Three times a year. L75000 Italy; L85000 other. Giunti Editore, Via Bolognese 165, 50139 Florence Italy. **Tel** 011 39 55 6679267, FAX 011 39 55 268312, telex 571438. **LC** RJ131. **DD** 612/.65/05. **UDC** 612.65. **NLM** W1 ET35.
**Ind/Abst** Psychol. Abstr. (1979-); PsycINFO; PsycLit.

GW/0939-7248
**EUROPEAN JOURNAL OF PEDIATRIC SURGERY : OFFICIAL JOURNAL OF AUSTRIAN ASSOCIATION OF PEDIATRIC SURGERY ... ZEITSCHRIFT FUER KINDERCHIRURGIE.** **See** Medical Science and Technology-Surgery.

GW/0340-6199
**EUROPEAN JOURNAL OF PEDIATRICS.** [Eur. j. pediatr.]. **VFOAT** Zeitschrift fur Kinderheilkunde. Vol. 121 (1975)-. Academic Scholarly Publication. English (German). Twelve times a year. DM2200.00. Springer-Verlag GmbH & Company KG, Heidelberger Platz 3, D 14197 Berlin Germany. **Tel** 011 49 30 8207223, FAX 011 49 30 8214091, telex 183 319 SPBLN D. **(Subscription address:** Springer Verlag New York Inc. / for North America, 44 Hartz Way, Secaucus NJ 07096.) **ED** J Spranger, L Corbeel, and A Fanconi. **NLM** W1 EU72DP. **CODEN** EJPEDT. **[CCC]. Pr Rev.** available on microfilm and microfiche from University Microfilms International (UMI). Documents available from The Genuine Article, BIOSIS Document Express, CASDDS, ADONIS. ***Continues*** *Zeitschrift fur Kinderheilkunde, 0044-2917;* ***Absorbed*** *Acta Paediatrica Belgica, 0001-6535.*
**Desc:** Strives to serve pediatrics and pediatricians as a truly European journal.
**Ind/Abst** ADONIS; Biol. Abstr.; Chem. Abstr.; Curr. Contents Clin. Med.; Curr. Contents Life Sci.; Dairy Sci. Abstr.; EMBASE; Energy Res. Abstr. (Feb. 1980-); Index Med.; Nutr. Abstr. Rev., Ser. B, Live Feeds and Feed.; Nutr. Abstr. Rev., Ser. A, Hum. Exp.; Nutr. Res. Newsl.; Life Sci. Collect.; PESTDOC; Protozoolog. Abstr.; Ref. Upd. Deluxe Ed.; Res. Alert [Full Cov.]; Rev. Med. Vet. Entomol.; Risk Abstr.; Sci. Cit. Index; SCISEARCH; Soc. Sci. Cit. Index [Select. Cov.].

NE/0373-6512
**EXCERPTA MEDICA. SECTION 7. PEDIATRICS AND PEDIATRIC SURGERY.** **See** Medical Science and Technology-Abstracting, Bibliographies and Statistics.

US/1047-0638
**FAMILY PRACTICE PEDIATRICS.** **See** Medical Science and Technology-Family Practice.

US
**FOCUS AND OPINION: PEDIATRICS.** (19??)-. English. bm. $112.50 (institutions), $68.00 (individuals) US; $116.50 (institutions), $72.00 (individuals) Canada; $126.50 (institutions), $82.00 (individuals) other. Mosby Year Book Inc., 11830 Westline Industrial Drive, St Louis MO 63146. **Tel** (800)325-4177, (314)872-8370, FAX (314)432-1380, telex 44-2402.

IT/0390-5845
**GASLINI GENOVA.** [Gaslini Genova]. (1969)-. Periodical. Multiple languages. Three times a year. $90.00 (individuals), $140.00 (institutions). Edizioni Minerva Medica, Corso Bramante 83-85, 10126 Turin Italy. **Tel** 011 39 11 678282, FAX 011 39 11 674502. **UDC** 61. **CODEN** GSLNAG.
**Desc:** Covers pediatrics and pediatric specialties.

UA/0304-484X
**GAZETTE OF THE EGYPTIAN PAEDIATRIC ASSOCIATION.** [Gaz. Egypt. Paediatr. Assoc.]. **Main/Corp** Egyptian Paediatric Association. Academic Scholarly Publication. English. qt. Egyptian Pediatrics Association, PO Box 1441, Cairo Egypt. **UDC** 616-053.2. **NLM** W1 GA777M. **CODEN** GEPAB2. Documents available from CASDDS.
**Ind/Abst** Chem. Abstr. (1952-1976).

●US/1069-2460
**GELLIS & KAGAN'S CURRENT PEDIATRIC THERAPY.** [Gellis & Kagan's curr. pediatr. ther.]. **VFOAT** Current Pediatric Therapy; Gellis and Kagan's Current Pediatric Therapy. (1993)-. English. be. W.B. Saunders Company, A Subsidiary of Harcourt Brace Jovanovich, Inc., The Curtis Center/Suite 300, Independence Square West, Philadelphia PA 19106-3399. **Tel** (215)238-7800 or, 5587, FAX (215)238-7883, telex 173146. **(Subscription address:** W. B. Saunders Company / North America Subscriptions, c/o Periodicals, 6277 Sea Harbour Drive, 4th Floor, Orlando FL 32887.) **LC** RJ52; .C8. **DD** 618.9/2006. ***Continues*** *Current Pediatric Therapy, 0070-2021.*

GW/0177-9095
**GIATROSPAEDIATRIE.** [Giatrospaediatrie]. **VFOAT** Jatrospaediatrie. (1985)-. Periodical. German. mo. DM150.00. Universimed Verlag GmbH, August-Schanz Strasse 21, W-6000 Frankfurt 50 Germany. **Tel** 011 49 69 5480000, FAX 069/54 80 00-77. **UDC** 616-053.2. **Bk Rev. Ad Acc. Pr Rev. Circ:** 5,200 (ctrl).
**Desc:** A scientific seminar paper journal, containing brief summaries of original medical articles. Also congress reports, interviews, and patient information.

IT/1120-0499
**GIORNALE INTERNAZIONALE DI DERMATOLOGIA PEDIATRICA.** **See** Medical Science and Technology-Dermatology.

US/0898-6630
**GROWTH GENETICS & HORMONES.** [Growth genet. horm.]. **VFOAT** Growth, Genetics and Hormones. Vol. 1, No. 1 (March 1985)-. Periodical. English. Four times a year. Free. SynerMed, Route 513 Trimmer Road, PO Box 458, Califon NJ 07830. **Tel** (908)832-2247, FAX (908)832-7098. **ED** Robert Blizzard. **DD** 616. **NLM** W1; GR919CE. Index available. **Bk Rev. Pr Rev. Circ:** 12,000 (ctrl).
**Desc:** Quarterly newsletter reviewing and highlighting human growth, genetics and hormone topics.

HU/0017-5900
**GYERMEKGYOGYASZAT.** [Gyermekgyogyaszat]. **Added/Corp** Magyar Gyermekorvosok Tarsasaga. Orvos-Egeszsegugyi Szakszervezet (Hungary). Gyermekorvos Szakcsoport. Vol. 1 (1950)-. Periodical. Hungarian (summaries and/or abstracts in German and Russian). qt. $38.50. Ifjusagi Lap -es Konyvkiado Vallalat, Revay u. 16, H-1374, Budapest, 6 Hungary. **(Subscription address:** Kultura, PO Box 149, H 1389 Budapest 62 Hungary.) **ED** Dr. A. Brantner. **NLM** W1; GY379. Index Available, published separately, free-automatically sent. **Ad Acc. Circ:** 2,000.
**Ind/Abst** Energy Res. Abstr. (Dec. 1979-).

SZ/0018-0181
**HELVETICA CHIRURGICA ACTA.** ***Ceased.*** [Helv. chir. acta]. **Added/Corp** Schweizerische Gesellschaft fur Chirurgie. Vol. 12 (1945)-(19??). Academic Scholarly Publication. German (French; summaries and/or abstracts in English). Six times a year. Schwabe & Company Ltd., Farnsburgerstrasse 8 PF 254, CH-4132 Muttenz 1 Switzerland. **Tel** 011 41 61 4613001, FAX 01 41 61 4612500. **ED** M Rossetti and A Jost. **NLM** W1 HE851. **CODEN** HCATAE. **[CCC]. Bk Rev. Ad Acc. Pr Rev. Circ:** 1,400 (ctrl). Documents available from The Genuine Article, BIOSIS Document Express, CASDDS. ***Continues*** *Helvetica Medica Acta.*
**Desc:** Original articles on the whole field of pediatrics.
**Ind/Abst** Biol. Abstr.; Chem. Abstr.; Curr. Contents Clin. Med.; EMBASE; Health Plan. Adminis.; Index Med.; Nutr. Abstr. Rev., Ser. A, Hum. Exp.; Life Sci. Collect.; Protozoolog. Abstr.; Res. Alert [Select. Cov.]; SCISEARCH; SportSearch.

SZ/0018-022X
**HELVETICA PAEDIATRICA ACTA.** [Helv. paediatr. acta]. V. 1- Aug. 1945-. Academic Scholarly Publication. German (French; summaries and/or abstracts in French, Italian, English and German). bm. Price varies per volume. Schwabe & Company Ltd., Farnsburgerstrasse 8 PF 254, CH-4132 Muttenz 1 Switzerland. **Tel** 011 41 61 4613001, FAX 01 41 61 4612500. **UDC** 616-053.2. **NLM** W1 HE857. **CODEN** HPAAAE. Index available. cum. index. **Ad Acc.** ctrl circ. Documents available from BIOSIS Document Express,

CASDDS.
**Desc:** The official organ of the Swiss Society of Pediatrics; original articles of the whole field of pediatrics.
**Ind/Abst** Biol. Abstr.; Chem. Abstr.; Dairy Sci. Abstr.; EMBASE; Health Plan. Adminis.; Index Med.; Nutr. Abstr. Rev., Ser. B, Live Feeds and Feed.; Nutr. Abstr. Rev., Ser. A, Hum. Exp.; Life Sci. Collect.; Protozoolog. Abstr.

SZ/0073-1811
**HELVETICA PAEDIATRICA ACTA. SUPPLEMENTUM.** (HELVETICA PAEDIATRICA ACTA. SUPPLEMENT.). [Helv. paediatr. acta. Suppl.]. (1945)-. Academic Scholarly Publication. German. Schwabe & Company Ltd., Farnsburgerstrasse 8 PF 254, CH-4132 Muttenz 1 Switzerland. **Tel** 011 41 61 4613001, FAX 01 41 61 4612500. **NLM** W1 HE8751. **CODEN** HEPSAW. Documents available from BIOSIS Document Express, CASDDS.
**Ind/Abst** Biol. Abstr. (-1989); Chem. Abstr.; Health Plan. Adminis.; Index Med.; Life Sci. Collect.

II/0019-5456
**INDIAN JOURNAL OF PEDIATRICS.** [Indian j. pediatr.]. (1933)-. Academic Scholarly Publication. English. bm. Rs900.00 (institutions), Rs500.00 (individuals), Rs375.00 (students and residents) India; $130.00 (institutions), $60.00 (individuals), $50.00 (students and residents) other. Department of Pediatrics, All-India Institute of Medical Sciences, New Delhi 110 029 India. **Tel** 91 11 661123, FAX 91 11 6886646, 91 11 6862663, telex 31 73042 AIMS IN. **(Subscription address:** Prints India, 11 Darya Ganj, New Delhi 110002 India.**) ED** I C Verma. **NLM** W1 IN224J. **CODEN** IJPEA2. Index available. **Bk Rev. Ad Acc. Circ:** 3,000. available on microfilm and microfiche from University Microfilms International (UMI). Documents available from BIOSIS Document Express, CASDDS.
**Desc:** All aspects of child health.
**Ind/Abst** Biol. Abstr.; Chem. Abstr.; Cumul. Index Nurs. Allied Health Lit.; EMBASE; Helminthol. Abstr.; Index Med.; Nutr. Abstr. Rev., Ser. B, Live Feeds and Feed.; Nutr. Abstr. Rev., Ser. A, Hum. Exp.; Life Sci. Collect.; Rev. Med. Vet. Entomol.

II/0019-6061
**INDIAN PEDIATRICS.** (INDIAN PEDIATRICS : JOURNAL OF THE INDIAN ACADEMY OF PEDIATRICS.). [Indian pediatr.]. Vol. 1, No. 1 (1964)-. Academic Scholarly Publication. English. Twelve times a year. $220.00 (institution); $160.00 (individual). Indian Pediatrics, PO Box 4509, New Delhi India 016 India. **Tel** 011 91 11 3316031, 011 91 1 3316660. **(Subscription address:** Prints India, 11 Darya Ganj, New Delhi, 110002 India, (Phone: 011 91 11 3268645)**) ED** Prof. R.K. Puri. **UDC** 616-053.2. **NLM** W1 IN263F. **CODEN** INPDAR. Index Available, published separately, free-automatically sent. **Bk Rev. Ad Acc. Pr Rev. Circ:** 7,500 (ctrl). Documents available from BIOSIS Document Express, CASDDS. ***Formed by the union of*** *Indian Journal of Child Health* ***and*** *Journal of the Indian Pediatric Society.*
**Desc:** Carries specialized articles on child health.
**Ind/Abst** Biol. Abstr.; Chem. Abstr.; CSA Neuro. Abstr. (?-?); Dairy Sci. Abstr.; EMBASE [Select. Cov.]; Index Med.; Microbiol. Abstr. Sect. B (19??-19??); Nutr. Abstr. Rev., Ser. A, Hum. Exp.; Life Sci. Collect.; Rural Dev. Abstr.; Trop. Dis. Bull.; Virol. AIDS Abstr.

US/0163-9641
**INFANT MENTAL HEALTH JOURNAL. See** Psychology.

US/0886-1315
**INFANT SCREENING.** [Infant screen.]. **Added/Corp** Howard University. Dept. of Pediatrics. **VFOAT** Infant Screening Newsletter. (19??)-. Periodical. English. Four times a year. $15.00 (one year), $40.00 (three year). Infant Screening, 3907 Galacia Drive, Austin TX 78759. **Tel** (512)458-7430. **ED** B.C. Therrell. **DD** 613. **Circ:** 500.

US/1053-5586
**INFANT-TODDLER INTERVENTION.** (INFANT-TODDLER INTERVENTION : THE TRANSDISCIPLINARY JOURNAL.). [Infant-toddler interv.]. **VFOAT** Infant, Toddler Intervention. (1991)- Vol. 3 (Mar. 1993)-. Periodical. English. Four times a year (Mar., June, Sept., Dec.). $58.00 (institutions); $36.00 (individual). Singular Publishing Group, 4284 41st Street, San Diego CA 92105. **Tel** (800)521-8545, (619)521-8000, FAX (619)563-9008. **(Subscription address:** Louis M Rossetti**) ED** Louis Rossetti, Ph. D, Speech & Hearing Clinic, (414)424-2421, University of Wisconsin, Oshkosh, WI 54901. **LC** RG580.D76; I53. **DD** 362. Index available (Bound in the 4th issue, publish in December). **Pr Rev. Circ:** 1,000.
**Desc:** Information for all members of an early intervention team providing services to infants and toddlers, their caregivers, and families in the spirit of P.L.
**Ind/Abst** Except. Child Educ. Resour.

US/0896-3746
**INFANTS AND YOUNG CHILDREN.** [Infants young child.]. Vol. 1, No. 1 (July 1988)-. Periodical. English. qt. $66.00 US. Aspen Publishers Inc., 7201 McKinney Circle, Frederick MD 21701. **Tel** (800)234-1660, (301)698-7100, FAX (301)251-5784, telex 5106014543. **(Subscription address:** Aspen Publishers Inc., PO Box 990, Frederick MD 21701.**) ED** James A. Blackman, MD, MPH. **LC** RJ102; .I54. **DD** 618./92/0005. **NLM** W1; IN402. **CODEN** IYCHEL. **[CCC]. Pr Rev.** available on microfilm and microfiche from University Microfilms International (UMI).
**Desc:** Devoted to clinical management of infants and young children (birth to three years of age) and their families with or at-risk for development disabilities. Combines research and clinical information and offers practical applications for the clinician.
**Ind/Abst** Cumul. Index Nurs. Allied Health Lit.; Except. Child Educ. Resour.; Soc. Plann. Policy Dev. Abstr.

CN/1185-5479
**INTERNATIONAL ABSTRACTS, PEDIATRIC UROLOGY. See** Medical Science and Technology-Urology and Nephrology.

NE
**INTERNATIONAL JOURNAL OF NEONATAL AND LATER SCREENING.** Vol. 1 (1991)-. Academic Scholarly Publication. English. Four times a year. Fl305.00. Elsevier Science Publishers BV, PO Box 211, 1000 AE Amsterdam Netherlands. **Tel** 011 31 20 5803642, FAX 011 31 20 5862696, telex 15682.

UK/0960-7439
**INTERNATIONAL JOURNAL OF PAEDIATRIC DENTISTRY / THE BRITISH PAEDONDONTIC SOCIETY [AND] THE INTERNATIONAL ASSOCIATION OF DENTISTRY FOR CHILDREN. See** Dentistry.

NE/0165-5876
**INTERNATIONAL JOURNAL OF PEDIATRIC OTORHINOLARYNGOLOGY.** [Int. j. pediatr. otorhinolaryngol.]. **VFOAT** Pediatric Otorhinolaryngology. Vol. 1 (July 1979)-. Academic Scholarly Publication. English. Nine times a year (3 vols.). $667.00. Elsevier Science Ireland Ltd., Bay 15, Shannon Industrial Estate, Co Clare Ireland. **Tel** 011 353 61 471944. **ED** R.J. Ruben and G. Pestalozza. **NLM** W1 IN771P. **CODEN** IPOTDJ. **[CCC]. Pr Rev.** available on microfilm and microfiche from University Microfilms International (UMI). Documents available from The Genuine Article, BIOSIS Document Express.
**Desc:** Concentrates and disseminates information concerning prevention, cure and care of otorhinolaryngological disorders in infants and children due to developmental, degenerative, infectious, neoplastic, social, psychiatric, and economic causes.
**Ind/Abst** Biol. Abstr.; Biostatistica (19??-19??); Curr. Aware. Biol. Sci., CABS; Curr. Contents Clin. Med.; EMBASE; Index Med.; Life Sci. Collect.; Ref. Upd. Deluxe Ed.; Res. Alert [Full Cov.]; Sci. Cit. Index; SCISEARCH; Soc. Sci. Cit. Index [Select. Cov.].

US/0885-6265
**INTERNATIONAL PEDIATRICS.** (INTERNATIONAL PEDIATRICS : THE JOURNAL OF THE MIAMI CHILDREN'S HOSPITAL.). [Int. pediatr.]. **Added/Corp** Miami Children's Hospital (Miami, Fla.). Vol. 1, No. 1 (Jan./Mar. 1986)-. Periodical. English. Four times a year (Mar., June, Sept., Dec.). $22.50. MCH Medical Journal Inc / Miami Children's Hospital, 3100 Southwest 62nd Avenue, Miami FL 33155. **Tel** (305)663-6823, FAX (305)663-8446. **(Subscription address:** International Pediatrics, PO Box 5046, Brentwood TN 37024-5046.**) ED** Oscar Papazian MD. **DD** 618. **NLM** W1; IN827JE. Index available. cum. index. **Ad Acc. Circ:** 13,000. ***Continues*** *Journal (Miami Children's Hospital (Miami, Fla.).*

●CN/1188-4525
**INTERNATIONAL SEMINARS IN PAEDIATRIC GASTROENTEROLOGY AND NUTRITION. See** Medical Science and Technology-Gastroenterology.

US/0146-0862
**ISSUES IN COMPREHENSIVE PEDIATRIC NURSING. See** Medical Science and Technology-Nursing.

US
**ISSUES IN PEDIATRIC MENTAL HEALTH.** Monograph No. 2 (1985)-. Monographic series. English. ir. Price varies per volume. Pediatric Projects Inc, PO Box 571555, Tarzana CA 91357. **Tel** (818)705-3660, (800)947-0947. **ED** Pat Azarnoff. **NLM** W1; IS669F. ***Continues*** *Monograph (Pediatric Projects Inc.), 0888-7632.*
**Desc:** Covers current aspects of children's mental health in health care settings.

JA
**JAPANESE JOURNAL OF CHILD AND ADOLESCENT PSYCHIATRY. See** Medical Science and Technology-Psychiatry.

BL/0021-7557
**JORNAL DE PEDIATRIA.** [J. Pediatr.]. (19??)-. Portuguese. Sociedade Brasileira Pediatria, Rua Visconde de Silva 52, Salas 503/504 22.281, Rio de Janeiro, Brazil. **Tel** (21)286-2789. **CODEN** JOPOA. available on microfilm from University Microfilms International (UMI).
**Ind/Abst** EMBASE [Select. Cov.].

FR
**JOURNAL DE PEDIATRIE ET DE PUERICULTURE.** No. 1 (Feb. 1988)-. Academic Scholarly Publication. French. Eight times a year. 475.00F France; 530.00F other. Editions Scientifique Elsevier, 141 rue de Javel, 75747 Paris Cedex 15 France. **Tel** 011 33 1 47 07 11 22, FAX 011 33 1 43 36 80 93. **(Subscription address:** Editions Scientifiques Elsevier / for North America, PO Box 7247-7576, Philadelphia PA 19170-7576.**) NLM** W1; JO326S. ***Continues*** *Jonctions des Professions de Sante et des Professions Sociales.*

UK/0140-1971
**JOURNAL OF ADOLESCENCE (LONDON, ENGLAND).** (JOURNAL OF ADOLESCENCE.). [J. adolesc.]. Vol. 1, Issue 1 (March 1978)-. Academic Scholarly Publication. English. bm (6 issues). $225.00. Academic Press Ltd., A Division of Harcourt Brace & Company Ltd., 24-28 Oval Road, London NW1 7DX England. **Tel** 071 267 4466, FAX 071 482 2293, 071 485 4752, telex 25775 ACPRES G. **(Subscription address:** Harcourt Brace & Company, Ltd., Foots Cray, High Street, Sidcup Kent DA14 5HP England.**) ED** John C. Coleman and Alan Waterman. **LC** RJ499.A1. **DD** 616.89/022/05. **UDC** 616-053.7. **NLM** W1 JO533R. **[CCC]. Pr Rev.** Documents available from The Genuine Article, BIOSIS Document Express, UMI Article Clearinghouse.
**Desc:** Provides a forum for all who are concerned with the nature of adolescence, whether they are teaching, carrying out research, providing a service, or offering treatment, guidance, or counseling. Addresses itself to issues of professional and academic importance.
**Ind/Abst** Acad. Abstr. Full Text Elite (Jan. 1992-); Acad. Abstr. (Jan. 1992-); Acad. Search (July 1993-); AGRICOLA [Select. Cov.]; Am. Hist. Life (1986-); Appl. Soc. Sci. Index Abstr.; Biol. Abstr. (1985-); Br. Educ. Index; Chicano Index; Crim. Justice Abstr.; Curr. Contents Soc. Behav. Sci.; Curr. Index J. Educ. (March 1990); EMBASE; Expand. Acad. Index (1989-); Index Med.; INFO-SOUTH Abstr.; Mag. Search; Newsp. Period. Abstr. (1992-); Psychol. Abstr. (1980-); PsycINFO (1990-); PsycLit; Res. Alert [Full Cov.]; School Organ. Manage. Abstr.; Soc. Plann. Policy Dev. Abstr.; Soc. Sci. Source (Jan. 1992-); Soc. Sci. Cit. Index [Full Cov.]; Soc. Sci. Index; Soc. Sci. Index Fulltext (Sept. 1988-) [Full Txt.]; Soc. Work Abstr. (?-?); SportSearch; Stud. Women Abstr.

US/0883-0738
**JOURNAL OF CHILD NEUROLOGY.** [J. child neurol.]. Vol. 1, No. 1 (Jan. 1986)-. Periodical. English. Six times a year. $170.00 (institutions), $130.00 (individuals) US & Canada; $200.00 (institutions), $160.00 (individuals) other. Decker Periodicals Publishing Inc, PO Box 620, Station A, Hamilton Ontario L8N 3K7 Canada. **Tel** (416)522-7017, (800) 568-7281, FAX (416)522-7839. **ED** Roger A. Brumback (editor's address: University of Rochester Medical Center Rochester, USA). **DD** 618. **NLM** W1; JO583P. **CODEN** JOCNEE. **[CCC]. Bk Rev. Ad Acc. Pr Rev. Circ:** 700. available on microfilm and microfiche from University Microfilms International (UMI). Documents available from The Genuine Article, BIOSIS Document Express.
**Desc:** Covers all aspects of nervous system disorders in children, including medical, surgical, pathological, and psychological perspectives. Features topics of interest to clinical and research pediatric neurologists, pediatricians, pediatric neuropathologists, neuropathologists, neuroradiologists, and behavioral pediatricians.
**Ind/Abst** Biol. Abstr. (1986-); Curr. Aware. Biol. Sci., CABS; Curr. Contents Clin. Med.; Curr. Contents Life Sci.; Dev. Med. Child Neurol.; EMBASE; Index Med. (1986-); INIS Atomindex [Micro.]; Physic. Medline Plus; Psychol. Abstr. (1986-); PsycINFO; PsycLit; Res. Alert [Full Cov.]; Sci. Cit. Index; SCISEARCH; Soc. Sci. Cit. Index [Select. Cov.].

UK/0021-9630
**JOURNAL OF CHILD PSYCHOLOGY AND PSYCHIATRY AND ALLIED DISCIPLINES. See** Psychology.

US/1053-4628
**JOURNAL OF CLINICAL PEDIATRIC DENTISTRY, THE. See** Dentistry.

US/0196-206X
**JOURNAL OF DEVELOPMENTAL AND BEHAVIORAL PEDIATRICS.** (JOURNAL OF DEVELOPMENTAL AND BEHAVIORAL PEDIATRICS : JDBP.). [J. dev. behav. pediatr.]. **Added/Corp** Society for Behavioral Pediatrics (U.S.). **VFOAT** JDBP. Vol. 1, No. 1 (March 1980)-. Academic Scholarly Publication. English. bm. $114.00 (individual), $169.00 (institution) US; $138.00 (individual), $194.00 (institution) other. Williams & Wilkins Company, 428 East Preston Street, Baltimore MD 21202-3993. **Tel** (410)528-4000, (800)638-6423, FAX (410)528-8596, telex 87669. **(Subscription address:** Williams & Wilkins, PO Box 64380, Baltimore MD 21264.**) ED** Stanford Friedman. **LC** RJ1; .J17. **DD** 618.92/0005. **NLM** W1; J0619T. **CODEN** JDBPD5. **[CCC]. Ad Acc. Pr Rev. Circ:** 1,600. available on

microfilm. Documents available from , The Genuine Article, BIOSIS Document Express, , Quick Copies. **Desc:** Official journal of the Society for Behavioral Pediatrics. Articles cover learning disabilities, behavioral reactions of childhood and family dynamics for pediatricians, child psychiatrists, and special educators. **Ind/Abst** Appl. Soc. Sci. Index Abstr.; Biol. Abstr. (1986-); Curr. Contents Clin. Med.; Curr. Contents Soc. Behav. Sci.; Dev. Med. Child Neurol.; EMBASE; Index Med.; Psychol. Abstr. (1980-); PsycINFO; PsycLit; PsycScan: Develop. Psych.; Res. Alert [Full Cov.]; Risk Abstr.; SCISEARCH; Soc. Sci. Cit. Index [Full Cov.].

AT/1034-4810
**JOURNAL OF PAEDIATRICS AND CHILD HEALTH.** [J. paediatr. child health]. **Added/Corp** Australian College of Paediatrics. Paediatric Research Society of Australia. Australian Association of Paediatric Surgeons. **VFOAT** Journal of Pediatrics and Child Health. Vol. 26, No. 1 (Feb. 1990)-. Academic Scholarly Publication. English. Six times a year. 224.00Aus$ Australia; $308.00 other. Blackwell Scientific Publications Australia, 54 University Street, PO Box 378, Carlton Victoria 3053 Australia. **Tel** 011 61 3 3470300, FAX 011 61 3 3475001, telex 10716421. **ED** J.M. Court, F. Oberklaid, and D.R. Roberton. **NLM** W1; JO824P. **CODEN** JPCHE3. **[CCC].** Index available. available on microfilm and microfiche from University Microfilms International (UMI). Documents available from The Genuine Article, BIOSIS Document Express. ***Continues*** *Australian Paediatric Journal, 0004-993X.* **Desc:** Encompasses both the formal aspects of paediatric medicine and surgery and the broader fields of child health. **Ind/Abst** Biol. Abstr.; Curr. Contents Clin. Med.; EMBASE; Health Plan. Adminis.; Index Med. (1990-); Res. Alert [Full Cov.]; Sci. Cit. Index; SCISEARCH; Soc. Sci. Cit. Index [Select. Cov.].

HK/1012-8875
**JOURNAL OF PAEDIATRICS, OBSTETRICS, AND GYNAECOLOGY.** [J. paediatr. obstet. gynaecol.]. (197?)-. Periodical. English. Six times a year. $42.00. MediMedia Pacific Limited, 8 F Pacific Plaza, 410 Dex Voeux Road West, Hong Kong. **Tel** 11 65 5701231, FAX 11 65 5705076, telex 83358 IMSPL HX. **ED** Kristen Fox. **NLM** W1; JO825. Index available. cum. index. **Bk Rev. Circ:** 15,000. **Desc:** Continuing medical education in drugs and therapeutics.

US/8756-6206
**JOURNAL OF PEDIATRIC & PERINATAL NUTRITION.** ***Ceased.*** [J. pediatr. perinat. nutr.]. **VFOAT** Journal of Pediatric and Perinatal Nutrition. Vol. 1, No. 1 (Spring/Summer 1987)-Vol. 3 (199?). Periodical. English. sa. The Haworth Press Inc, 10 Alice Street, Binghamton NY 13904-1580. **Tel** (607)722-5857, (800)3-HAWORTH, FAX (607)722-1424. **ED** Cristine Trahms (editor's address: Rd-20 University of Washington, Seattle, WA 98195). **DD** 613. **NLM** W1; JO828DM. **Bk Rev. Ad Acc. Pr Rev. Acid Free. Circ:** 263. available on microfilm and microfiche from University Microfilms International (UMI). Documents available from Haworth Document Delivery Service. **Desc:** Focuses on the nutrition needs of patients in pediatrics and perinatal care. Deals with both normal and therapeutic needs, and will assist the practitioner in anticipating conditions that require nutritional management. **Ind/Abst** Abstr. Anthropol. (19??-); AGRICOLA [Select. Cov.]; Dairy Sci. Abstr.; EMBASE; Int. Nurs. Index (1987-); Sage Fam. Stud. Abstr. (?-?); Soc. Work Abstr. [Select. Cov.].

UK/0334-018X
**JOURNAL OF PEDIATRIC ENDOCRINOLOGY, THE.** [J. pediatr. endocrinol.]. Vol. 1, No. 1 (Jan./March 1985)-. Academic Scholarly Publication. English. ir. $220.00. Freund Publishing House Ltd, PO Box 35010, 61 Nachmani Street, Tel Aviv 61350 Israel. **Tel** 011 972 3 5662925, FAX 011 972 3 5605335. **(Subscription address:** Freund Publishing House Ltd., Suite 500 Chesham House, 150 Regent Street, London W1R 5FA England.**) ED** H. J. Hirsch. **UDC** 616.4-053.2. **NLM** W1; JO828DR. **CODEN** JPENEV. **Bk Rev. Ad Acc. Pr Rev.** Documents available from BIOSIS Document Express, CASDDS. **Desc:** A coverage of endocrine problems in the neonatal, pediatric and adolescent age groups which will enable endocrinologists, pediatricians, gynecologists, etc., to keep abreast of the latest research and clinical experience in the field. **Ind/Abst** Biol. Abstr. (1985-); Chem. Abstr. (1985-); CSA Neuro. Abstr. (?-?); Curr. Contents Life Sci.; EMBASE; Sci. Cit. Index.

US/0277-2116
**JOURNAL OF PEDIATRIC GASTROENTEROLOGY AND NUTRITION.** [J. pediatr. gastroenterol. nutr.]. **Added/Corp** North American Society for Pediatric Gastroenterology and Nutrition. European Society of Pediatric Gastroenterology and Nutrition. Vol. 1, No. 1 (1982)-. Academic Scholarly Publication. English. Eight times a year. $182.00 (individuals), $342.00 (institutions) US; $198.00 (individuals), $432.00 (institutions) other. Raven Press, 1185 Avenue of the Americas, 37th Floor, New York NY 10036. **Tel** (212)930-9500, (212)930-9604, FAX (212)869-3495, (212)302-8507, telex 640073. **ED** Emanuel Lebenthal. **LC** Discard. **NLM** W1 JO828E. **CODEN** JPGND6. **[CCC]. Pr Rev.** available on microfilm and microfiche from University Microfilms International (UMI). Documents available from The Genuine Article, CASDDS. **Desc:** This journal provides a forum for original papers and reviews dealing with nutrition in normal and abnormal functions of the alimentary tract and its associated organs, including the salivary glands, pancreas, gallbladder, and liver. **Ind/Abst** AGRICOLA [Select. Cov.]; Chem. Abstr.; Comb. Cumul. Index Pediatr.; Curr. Aware. Biol. Sci., CABS; Curr. Contents Clin. Med.; Curr. Contents Life Sci.; Dairy Sci. Abstr.; EMBASE; Index Med.; Int. Nurs. Index; Iowa Drug Inf. Serv. (1985-); Nutr. Abstr. Rev., Ser. B, Live Feeds and Feed.; Nutr. Abstr. Rev., Ser. A, Hum. Exp.; Nutr. Res. Newsl.; Pig News Inf.; Protozoolog. Abstr.; Res. Alert [Full Cov.]; Rice Abstr.; Sci. Cit. Index; SCISEARCH; Soyabean Abstr.

US/0891-5245
**JOURNAL OF PEDIATRIC HEALTH CARE.** (JOURNAL OF PEDIATRIC HEALTH CARE : OFFICIAL PUBLICATION OF NATIONAL ASSOCIATION OF PEDIATRIC NURSE ASSOCIATES & PRACTITIONERS.). [J. pediatr. health care]. **Added/Corp** National Association of Pediatric Nurse Associates and Practitioners. Vol. 1, No. 1 (Jan./Feb. 1987)-. Periodical. English. bm. $81.00 (institutions), $42.00 (individuals) US; $91.00 (institutions), $52.00 (individuals). Mosby Year Book Inc., 11830 Westline Industrial Drive, St Louis MO 63146. **Tel** (800)325-4177, (314)872-8370, FAX (314)432-1380, telex 44-2402. **ED** Bobbie Crew Nelms. **DD** 618. **NLM** W1; JO828EH. **CODEN** JPHCED. **[CCC].** Index available. **Bk Rev. Ad Acc. Pr Rev. Circ:** 3,500. available on microfilm and microfiche from University Microfilms International (UMI). Documents available from BIOSIS Document Express. **Desc:** Serves the pediatric nurse practitioner/associate and other related health care professionals who work in pediatric health care. Presents current information concerning pediatric clinical practice, health care policy, or role issues relevant to the the pediatric nurse practicing in an expanded role. **Ind/Abst** Biol. Abstr. (1987-); Cumul. Index Nurs. Allied Health Lit.; Int. Nurs. Index (May-June 1987-); Nurs. Abstr.

US/0882-5963
**JOURNAL OF PEDIATRIC NURSING.** **See** Medical Science and Technology-Nursing.

US/1043-4542
**JOURNAL OF PEDIATRIC ONCOLOGY NURSING.** **See** Medical Science and Technology-Nursing.

US/0191-3913
**JOURNAL OF PEDIATRIC OPHTHALMOLOGY AND STRABISMUS.** [J. pediatr. ophthalmol. strabismus]. Vol. 15 (Jan/Feb 1978)-. Periodical. English. bm. $120.00 institution, $110.00 individual (US). Slack Inc., 6900 Grove Road, Thorofare NJ 08086. **Tel** (609)848-1000, (800)257-8290, FAX (609)853-5991, telex 517108 SLACK INC VD. **ED** Henry Metz. **UDC** 617.7-053.2; 617.761-053.2. **NLM** W1 JO828FD. **CODEN** JPOSDR. Index available. **Bk Rev. Ad Acc. Pr Rev. Circ:** 1,500 (ctrl). available on microfilm and microfiche from University Microfilms International (UMI). Documents available from The Genuine Article, BIOSIS Document Express. ***Continues*** *Journal of Pediatric Ophthalmology, 0022-345X.* **Desc:** Peer-reviewed articles of clinical interest to pediatric ophthalmologists. Also, articles concerning pediatric and adult strabismus. **Ind/Abst** Biol. Abstr.; Curr. Contents Clin. Med.; EMBASE; Energy Res. Abstr. (Aug. 1982-); Index Med.; INIS Atomindex [Micro.]; Mod. Med.; Life Sci. Collect.; Res. Alert [Select. Cov.]; SCISEARCH.

US/0271-6798
**JOURNAL OF PEDIATRIC ORTHOPEDICS.** [J. pediatr. orthop.]. **VFOAT** Journal of Pediatric Orthopaedics. Vol. 1, No. 1 (1981)-. Periodical. English. bm (6 issues). $142.00 (individuals), $242.00 (institutions) US; $185.00 (individuals), $286.00 (institutions) other. Raven Press, 1185 Avenue of the Americas, 37th Floor, New York NY 10036. **Tel** (212)930-9500, (212)930-9604, FAX (212)869-3495, (212)302-8507, telex 640073. **ED** Lynn T. Staheli and Robert N. Hensinger. **NLM** W1; JO828FE. **CODEN** JPORDO. **[CCC]. Pr Rev.** available on microfilm and microfiche from University Microfilms International (UMI). Documents available from The Genuine Article, BIOSIS Document Express. **Desc:** Publishes high-quality, peer-reviewed papers from around the world on the diagnosis and treatment of pediatric orthopaedic disorders. It cuts across disciplinary as well as national boundaries to provide the broadest possible coverage of the unique problems facing the pediatric orthopaedist. **Ind/Abst** Biol. Abstr.; Dev. Med. Child Neurol.; EMBASE; Index Med.; Int. Nurs. Index; Res. Alert [Select. Cov.]; SCISEARCH; SportSearch.

US/0146-8693
**JOURNAL OF PEDIATRIC PSYCHOLOGY.** **See** Psychology.

US/0022-3468
**JOURNAL OF PEDIATRIC SURGERY.** **See** Medical Science and Technology-Surgery.

US/0022-3476
**JOURNAL OF PEDIATRICS, THE.** [J. pediatr.]. **Added/Corp** American Academy of Pediatrics. Vol. 1, (July 1932)-. Academic Scholarly Publication. English. mo. $211.00 (institutions), $102.00 (individuals) US; $238.00 (institutions), $129.00 (individuals) other. Mosby Year Book Inc., 11830 Westline Industrial Drive, St Louis MO 63146. **Tel** (800)325-4177, (314)872-8370, FAX (314)432-1380, telex 44-2402. **ED** Joseph M. Garfunkel. **LC** RJ1; .A453. **DD** 618.9205. **NLM** W1 JO828H. **CODEN** JOPDAB. **[CCC].** Index available. **Bk Rev. Ad Acc. Pr Rev. Circ:** 25,222. available on microfilm and microfiche from University Microfilms International (UMI). Documents available from The Genuine Article, BIOSIS Document Express, CASDDS, ADONIS. ***Supersedes*** *Transactions - American Academy of Pediatrics.* **Desc:** Serves as a practical guide for the continuing education of physicians who diagnose and treat disorders in infants and children. **Ind/Abst** Abr. Index Med.; ADONIS; AGRICOLA [Select. Cov.]; Annals Behav. Med.; Appl. Soc. Sci. Index Abstr.; Arts Humanit. Citation Index [Select. Cov.]; Biol. Abstr.; Biol. Dig.; Calcium Calcif. Tissue Abstr.; Chem. Abstr.; Comb. Cumul. Index Pediatr.; CSA Neuro. Abstr. (?-?); Cumul. Index Nurs. Allied Health Lit.; Curr. Aware. Biol. Sci., CABS; Curr. Contents Clin. Med.; Curr. Contents Life Sci.; Dairy Sci. Abstr.; Dev. Med. Child Neurol.; EMBASE; Energy Res. Abstr.; Except. Child Educ. Resour.; Genet. Abstr.; Health Saf. Sci. Abstr.; Health Devices Alerts; Health Period. Database; Immunol. Abstr.; Index Med.; INIS Atomindex [Micro.]; Int. Pharm. Abstr.; Iowa Drug Inf. Serv. (1966-); J. Watch; Maize Abstr.; Med. Abstr. Newsl.; Microbiol. Abstr. Sect. B; Mod. Med.; Nutr. Abstr. Rev., Ser. A, Hum. Exp.; Nutr. Res. Newsl.; Life Sci. Collect.; PESTDOC; Physic. Medline Plus; Potato Abstr.; Ref. Upd. Basic Ed.; Ref. Upd. Deluxe Ed.; Res. Alert [Full Cov.]; Rev. Med. Vet. Entomol.; Rev. Med. Vet. Mycology; Rice Abstr.; Saf. Health Work; Sci. Cit. Index; SCISEARCH; Soc. Sci. Cit. Index [Select. Cov.]; Soc. Work Abstr. (?-?); Soyabean Abstr.; SportSearch; Trop. Dis. Bull.; Virol. AIDS Abstr.

●US
**JOURNAL OF SUDDEN INFANT DEATH SYNDROME AND INFANT MORTALITY.** (1994)-. Periodical. English. Four times a year. $150.00 institutions, $48.00 individuals US; $175.00 institutions, $56.00 individuals other. Plenum Press, 233 Spring Street, New York NY 10013-1578. **Tel** (212)620-8000, (800)221-9369, FAX (212)463-0742, (212)807-1047, telex 23/421139.

UK/0142-6338
**JOURNAL OF TROPICAL PEDIATRICS (1980).** (JOURNAL OF TROPICAL PEDIATRICS.). [J. trop. pediatr.]. **Added/Corp** British Postgraduate Medical Foundation. Tropical Child Health Unit. Vol. 26 (Feb. 1980)-. Periodical. English. bm. £99.00 UK and Europe; $180.00 other. Oxford University Press, Walton Street, Oxford OX2 6DP England. **Tel** 011 44 865 56767, FAX 011 44 865 267773, telex 837330 OXPRES G. **(Subscription address:** Oxford University Press / USA, Journals Marketing Department, Oxford University Press, 2001 Evans Road, Cary NC 27513.**) ED** G. J. Ebrahim. **NLM** W1 JO966VC. **CODEN** JTRPAO. **[CCC].** Index available. **Bk Rev. Ad Acc.** available on microfilm from University Microfilms International (UMI). Documents available from The Genuine Article, BIOSIS Document Express. ***Continues*** *Journal of Tropical Pediatrics and Environmental Child Health, 0300-9920.* **Desc:** All aspects of child health and nutrition, including locality and quality of environment. Most of the papers report the results of clinical and community research and considerations of program development. **Ind/Abst** AGRICOLA [Select. Cov.]; Biol. Abstr. (1985-); Curr. Aware. Biol. Sci., CABS; Curr. Contents Clin. Med.; Dairy Sci. Abstr.; EMBASE; Helminthol. Abstr. (1991-); Index Med.; Nutr. Abstr. Rev., Ser. A, Hum. Exp.; Life Sci. Collect.; Protozoolog. Abstr.; Ref. Upd. Deluxe Ed.; Res. Alert [Full Cov.]; Rice Abstr.; Risk Abstr.; Rural Dev. Abstr.; Sci. Cit. Index; SCISEARCH; Soc. Sci. Cit. Index [Select. Cov.]; Soyabean Abstr.; Trop. Dis. Bull.

FR/0399-029X
**JOURNEES PARISIENNES DE PEDIATRIE.** [Journ. paris. pediatr.]. Academic Scholarly Publication. French. an. Flammarion Medecine Sciences, 4 rue Casimir Delavigne, 95006 Paris France. **CODEN** JPPEDO. Documents available from CASDDS. **Ind/Abst** Chem. Abstr. (1966-1981).

CI/0448-0171
**JUGOSLAVENSKA PEDIJATRIJA.** [Jugosl. pedijatr.]. (1958)-. Periodical. Multiple languages. qt.

Urednistvo Jugoslavenska Pedijatrija, Kispaticeva 12, 41000 Zagreb Croatia. **UDC** 616-053.2. **CODEN** JPPIA. **Ind/Abst** EMBASE [Select. Cov.]; Nutr. Abstr. Rev., Ser. A, Hum. Exp.

GW/0023-1495
**KINDERARZTLICHE PRAXIS.** ***Title Change.*** [Kinderarzte. Prax.]. Vol. 1 (Sept. 1930)-(19??). Academic Scholarly Publication. German. Ten times a year. Georg Thieme Verlag Stuttgart, Postfach 301120, D 70451 Stuttgart Germany. **Tel** 011 49 711 89310, FAX 011 49 711 8931298, telex 7 252 275 GTVD. **(Subscription address:** Thieme Medical Publishers Inc., 381 Park Avenue South, New York, NY 10016**)** **UDC** 616-053.2. **NLM** W1 KI623. **[CCC].** ***Merged into*** *Sozialpaediatrie und Kinderaerztliche Praxis.*
**Ind/Abst** Dairy Sci. Abstr.; EMBASE [Select. Cov.]; Index Med.; Nutr. Abstr. Rev., Ser. A, Hum. Exp.; Life Sci. Collect.; Rev. Med. Vet. Mycology; Weed Abstr.

GW/0932-6596
**KINDERHEILKUNDE UND JUGENDMEDIZIN.** [Kinderheilkd. Jugendmed.]. Vol. 1 (1986)-. German. Perimed, Verlag Dr Med D Straube, W-8520 Erlangen Germany. **NLM** W1; KI625H.

GW/0723-2276
**KINDERKRANKENSCHWESTER.** (KINDERKRANKENSCHWESTER : ORGAN DER SEKTION KINDERKRANKENPFLEGE, DEUTSCHE GESELLSCHAFT FUER SOZIALPADIATRIE UND DEUTSCHE GESELLSCHAFT FUER KINDERHEILKUNDE.). [Kinderkrankenschwester]. **Added/Corp** Deutsche Gesellschaft fur Kinderheilkunde. Deutsche Gesellschaft fur Sozialpadiatrie. Sektion Kinderkrankenpflege. (1982)-. Periodical. German. mo. Schmidt Roemhild, Mengstrasse 16 PF 2051, D 23552 Luebeck, Germany. **Tel** 11 49 451 16050. **NLM** W1 KI626.
**Ind/Abst** Health Plan. Adminis.

GW/0300-8630
**KLINISCHE PADIATRIE.** [Klin. Padiat.]. Vol. 184 (1972)-. Academic Scholarly Publication. German (English and German; summaries and/or abstracts in English and German). bm. $231.00. Ferdinand Enke Verlag, Ruedigerstrasse 14, D-70469 Stuttgart Germany. **Tel** 011 49 711 8931124, 011 49 711 893123. **(Subscription address:** Thieme Medical Publishers Inc., 381 Park Avenue South, New York NY 10016.**)** **NLM** W1 KL52. **CODEN** KLPDB2. **[CCC]. Pr Rev.** Documents available from The Genuine Article, BIOSIS Document Express, CASDDS, ADONIS. ***Continues*** *Archiv fuer Kinderheilkunde, 0003-9179.*
**Ind/Abst** ADONIS; Biol. Abstr. (-1983); Chem. Abstr.; Curr. Contents Clin. Med.; Dairy Sci. Abstr.; Dev. Med. Child Neurol.; EMBASE; Energy Res. Abstr. (April 1979-); Index Med.; Nutr. Abstr. Rev., Ser. A, Hum. Exp.; Life Sci. Collect.; PESTDOC; Protozoolog. Abstr.; Res. Alert [Full Cov.]; Sci. Cit. Index; SCISEARCH; SportSearch.

SP
**M.D.P. MONOGRAFIAS DE PEDIATRIA.** Spanish. bm. 3.000ptas Spain; 5.000ptas other. Jarpyo Editores SA, Antonio Lopez Aguados 4, 28029 Madrid, Spain. **Tel** 011 34 1 3144338, 011 34 1 3144458. **(Subscription address:** Antonio Lopez Aguado 1-4, 28029 Madrid Spain**)** **ED** A Nogales Espert. **Ad Acc. Circ:** 3,000 (ctrl).

HU/0303-5042
**MAGYAR PEDIATER.** **Added/Corp** Magyar Gyermekorvosok Tarsasaga. (1967)-. Periodical. Hungarian. qt. $21.00. **(Subscription address:** Kultura, PO Box 149, H 1389 Budapest 62 Hungary**)** **NLM** W1 MA406K. ctrl circ.

US/0736-0088
**MASSON MONOGRAPHS IN PEDIATRIC HEMATOLOGY/ONCOLOGY.** [Masson monogr. pediatr. hematol./oncol.]. **VAT** Masson Monographs in Pediatric Hematology Oncology. (1980)-. Monographic series. English. ir. Price varies per volume. Mosby Year Book Inc., 11830 Westline Industrial Drive, St Louis MO 63146. **Tel** (800)325-4177, (314)872-8370, FAX (314)432-1380, telex 44-2402. **ED** Carl Pochedly and Denis R. Miller. **LC** UNC. **NLM** W1 MA9309T.

RU/0869-2114
**MATERINSTVO I DETSTVO / MINISTERSTVO ZDRAVOOKHRANENIIA ROSSIISKOI FEDERATSII.** ***Title Change.*** **Added/Corp** Russia (Federation). Ministerstvo Zdravookhraneniia. (1992)-(1992). Periodical. Russian (summaries and/or abstracts in English; table of contents in English). bm. Izdatelstvo Meditsina / Russian Academy of Medical Sciences, Ulitsa Solyanka 14, 109801 Moscow Russia. **Tel** 011 95 297-05-04. ***Continues*** *Voprosy Okhrany Materinstva i Detstva, 0042-8825.* ***Continued by*** *Rossiiskii Vestnik Perinatologii i Pediatrii.*

UK/0262-0200
**MATERNAL & CHILD HEALTH (RICHMOND, SURREY).** **See** Medical Science and Technology-Family Practice.

US/0090-0702
**MATERNAL-CHILD NURSING JOURNAL.** **See** Medical Science and Technology-Nursing.

US/0190-0757
**MATERNAL/NEWBORN ADVOCATE.** ***Ceased.*** **See** Medical Science and Technology-Gynecology and Obstetrics.

US/0361-929X
**MCN, THE AMERICAN JOURNAL OF MATERNAL CHILD NURSING.** **See** Medical Science and Technology-Nursing.

FR/0025-6773
**MEDECINE INFANTILE, LA.** ***Ceased.*** [Med. infant.]. (Feb. 1897)-(Jan. 1994). Academic Scholarly Publication. French. mo. Editions Maloine, 27 rue de l'Ecole de Medecine, F-75006 Paris France. **Tel** 011 33 1 43256045, FAX 011 33 1 46340589, telex 203215 F. **NLM** W1 ME143. **CODEN** MINFAW. available on microfilm from University Microfilms International (UMI). Documents available from CASDDS.
**Ind/Abst** Chem. Abstr.; EMBASE [Select. Cov.].

US/0098-1532
**MEDICAL AND PEDIATRIC ONCOLOGY.** [Med. pediatr. oncol.]. Vol. 1 (1975)-. Periodical. English. mo. $648.00 (US); $768.00 (Canada and Mexico); $813.00 (other). John Wiley & Sons, Inc., 605 Third Avenue, New York NY 10158-0012. **Tel** (212)850-6000, (212)850-6645, FAX (212)850-6088, telex 12-7063. **(Subscription address:** John Wiley & Sons / England, Baffins Lane, Chichester, West Sussex PO19 1UD England.**)** **ED** Alvin M. Mauer. **LC** RC261.A1; M4. **DD** 616.9/92/005. **NLM** W1 ME18L. **CODEN** MPONDB. **[CCC]. Pr Rev.** Documents available from The Genuine Article, BIOSIS Document Express, CASDDS.
**Desc:** An international journal, providing broad coverage of significant advances in clinical oncology. Publishes original articles on the pathophysiology, diagnosis, prognosis, and therapy of malignant diseases in adults and children.
**Ind/Abst** Biol. Abstr.; Biostatistica (19??-19??); Chem. Abstr.; Curr. Contents Clin. Med.; EMBASE; Index Med.; INIS Atomindex [Micro.]; Life Sci. Collect.; Res. Alert [Full Cov.]; Sci. Cit. Index; SCISEARCH.

US/0740-8226
**MEDICAL AND PEDIATRIC ONCOLOGY. SUPPLEMENT.** [Med. pediatr. oncol., Suppl.]. 1 (1982)-. Monographic series. English. ir. Price varies per volume. **UDC** 616-006-053.2. **NLM** W1 ME18LA.
**Ind/Abst** Index Med.

US/0090-7030
**MEDICAL EXAMINATION REVIEW BOOK. VOLUME 11. PEDIATRICS.** **VFOAT** Pediatrics. **VAT** Medical Examination Review Book. Volume Eleven. Pediatrics. English. ir. Medical Exam Publishing Company, 52 Vanderbilt Avenue Elsevier, New York NY 10017-3808. **Tel** (212)463-1052. **UDC** 616-053.2.

IT
**MEDICO E BAMBINO.** **Added/Corp** Associazione Culturale Pediatri (Italy). (198?)-. Periodical. Italian. mo (except July and Aug.). L30000. Edifarm, Viale Sabotino 19 2, 20135 Milan Italy. **Tel** 011 39 2 58318401. **NLM** W1; ME753M.

US/0897-9774
**MEDIGUIDE TO PEDIATRICS.** (1990)-. Periodical. English. qt. Dellacorte Publications, 919 3rd Avenue, New York NY 10022-3904. **Tel** (212)751-2806.

IT/0026-4946
**MINERVA PEDIATRICA.** [Min. Ped.]. Vol. 1 (Jan. 1949)-. Academic Scholarly Publication. Italian (summaries and/or abstracts in English). Twelve times a year. $110.00 (individuals), $150.00 (institutions). Edizioni Minerva Medica, Corso Bramante 83-85, 10126 Turin Italy. **Tel** 011 39 11 678282, FAX 011 39 11 674502. **ED** M Migro. **NLM** W1 MI652. **CODEN** MIPEA5. **Bk Rev. Ad Acc.** available on microfilm from University Microfilms International (UMI). Documents available from CASDDS. ***Formed by the union of*** *Policlinico Infantile; Pediatria del Medico Practico; Medicina Italiana* ***and*** *Rivista di Clinica Pediatrica.*
**Desc:** Journal addressed to practitioners and specialists in pediatrics in Italy and abroad. It deals with topics in pediatrics, scientific practice and research.
**Ind/Abst** Chem. Abstr.; Dairy Sci. Abstr.; EMBASE [Select. Cov.]; Index Med.; Nutr. Abstr. Rev., Ser. A, Hum. Exp.; Life Sci. Collect.; Protozoolog. Abstr.

GW/0026-9298
**MONATSSCHRIFT FUER KINDERHEILKUNDE.** (MONATSSCHRIFT KINDERHEILKUNDE : ORGAN DER DEUTSCHEN GESELLSCHAFT FUER KINDERHEILKUNDE.). [Monatschr. Kinderheilk.]. **Added/Corp** Deutsche Gesellschaft fuer Kinderheilkunde. Vol. 128, No. 8 (Aug. 1980)-. Academic Scholarly Publication. German (summaries and/or abstracts in English). Twelve times a year. DM398.00. Springer-Verlag GmbH & Company KG, Heidelberger Platz 3, D 14197 Berlin Germany. **Tel** 011 49 30 8207223, FAX 011 49 30 8214091, telex 183 319 SPBLN D. **(Subscription address:** Springer Verlag New York Inc. / for North America, 44 Hartz Way, Secaucus NJ 07096.**)** **ED** F Blaeker and W Schroeter. **NLM** W1 MO364. **CODEN** MOKIAY. **[CCC]. Pr Rev.** available on microfilm from University Microfilms International (UMI). Documents available from The Genuine Article, CASDDS. ***Continues*** *Monatsschrift fur Kinderheilkunde.*
**Desc:** Journal of the German Association for Pediatrics. Scientific information and continued education for the pediatrician in the hospital or practice. New and important developments, reviews of international works and difficult cases are discussed.
**Ind/Abst** Chem. Abstr.; Curr. Contents Clin. Med.; Dairy Sci. Abstr.; Dev. Med. Child Neurol.; EMBASE; Energy Res. Abstr.; Index Med.; Life Sci. Collect.; Protozoolog. Abstr.; Res. Alert [Select. Cov.]; Rev. Med. Vet. Entomol.; SCISEARCH; Soc. Sci. Cit. Index [Select. Cov.]; Soyabean Abstr.

US/1044-4882
**MONOGRAPHS IN CLINICAL PEDIATRICS.** (1990)-. Monographic series. English. ir. Price varies per volume. Harwood Academic Publishers / New York, PO Box 786, Cooper Station, New York NY 10276. **Tel** (212)206-8900, (201)643-7500. **(Subscription address:** International Publishers Distributor at one of the following addresses: 820 Town Center Drive, Langhorne, PA 19047; or PO Box 90, Reading Berkshire RG1 8JL UK; or Kent Ridge PO Box 1180, Singapore 9111, Republic of Singapore**)**

US/0162-6906
**MONOGRAPHS IN DEVELOPMENTAL PEDIATRICS.** [Monogr. dev. pediatr.]. Vol. 1 (1978)-. Monographic series. English. Price varies per volume. University Park Press, PO Box 4034, New York NY 10163. **LC** UNC. **DD** 618. **NLM** W1 MO567LP. **CODEN** MDPED7. Documents available from BIOSIS Document Express.
**Ind/Abst** Biol. Abstr. (?-1979).

US/0065-6852
**MONOGRAPHS OF THE JOURNAL OF THE AMERICAN ACADEMY OF CHILD PSYCHIATRY.** **Main/Corp** American Academy of Child Psychiatry. **Added/Corp** American Academy of Child Psychiatry. Journal of the American Academy of Child Psychiatry. No. 1 (1966)-. Monographic series. English. qt. Price varies per volume. Yale University Press, PO Box 209040, New Haven CT 06520. **Tel** (203)432-0940, (800)987-7323, FAX (203)432-0948. **LC** UNC. **NLM** W1 MO569QS.

SP/0210-8135
**MTA. PEDIATRIA.** [MTA, Pediatr.]. **VFOAT** Metodos Terapeutico-Diagnosticos de Actualidad. Pediatria; MTA. Metodos Terapeutico-Diagnosticos de Actualidad. Pediatria. (1980)-. Periodical. Spanish. mo. $75.00. Prous Science Publishers, Apartado de Correos 540, 08080 Barcelona Spain. **Tel** 011 34 3 4592220, FAX 011 34 3 4581535. **ED** F Prandi Farras. **UDC** 616-053.2. Index available. **Bk Rev. Ad Acc. Circ:** 2,500 (ctrl).
**Desc:** Original articles and summaries of international literature dealing with topics in the field of pediatrics.

US/1062-2454
**NEONATAL INTENSIVE CARE.** **See** Medical Science and Technology-Gynecology and Obstetrics.

US/0730-0832
**NEONATAL NETWORK.** (NEONATAL NETWORK : NN.). [Neonatal netw.]. **Added/Corp** Neonatal Network. **VFOAT** N.N.; NN. Vol. 1, No. 1 (Oct. 1981)-. Periodical. English. Eight times a year. $44.00 (institutions), $32.00 (individuals). Neonatal Network, 1304 Southpoint Boulevard, Suite 280, Petaluma CA 94954. **Tel** (707)762-2646. **ED** Charles Rait. **LC** Discard. **NLM** W1; NE19W. **CODEN** NEONEE. Index available. **Bk Rev. Ad Acc. Pr Rev. Circ:** 11,500.
**Desc:** Practical and theoretical information for nurses working in level II and level III neonatal intensive care units.
**Ind/Abst** Cumul. Index Nurs. Allied Health Lit.; Int. Nurs. Index (Vol. 3, No. 6, 1985-).

US/1056-8956
**NEONATAL PHARMACOLOGY QUARTERLY.** ***Ceased.*** **See** Pharmacy and Pharmacology.

UY
**NEUROPEDIATRIA LATINOAMERICANA.** Periodical. Spanish. Avenida Italia, 2817 Casilla de Correo No 847, Montevideo Uruguay. **UDC** 616.8-053.2.

GW/0174-304X
**NEUROPEDIATRICS.** **See** Medical Science and Technology-Neurology.

US/0737-4216
**NEW YORK PEDIATRICIAN.** (NEW YORK PEDIATRICIAN : OFFICIAL PUBLICATION OF DISTRICT II, AMERICAN ACADEMY OF PEDIATRICS, STATE OF NEW YORK.). [N.Y. pediatr.]. Vol. 1, No. 1 (Winter 1983)-. Periodical. English. sa. $15.00. Coney Island Hospital, Department of Pediatrics, 2601 Ocean

Parkway, Brooklyn NY 11235. **Tel** (718)615-5378. **ED** Henry A Schaeffer. **UDC** 616-053.2(747). **Ad Acc. Circ:** 3,000 (ctrl).
**Desc:** News and commentaries on matters that affect pediatric practice and practitioners of this region.

US/0093-0237
**NEWSLETTER OF THE A.A.P.S.C.** (NEWSLETTER.). [Newsl. A.A.P.S.C.]. **Main/Corp** American Association of Psychiatric Services for Children. **VFOAT** AAPSC Newsletter. **VAT** Newsletter of the American Association of Psychiatric Services for Children. V. 17- Spring 1970-. Newsletter. English. qt. American Association of Psychiatric Services for Childre, 1701 18th Street NW, Washington DC 20009. **LC** RJ501.A2; A73. **DD** 618.9/28/900973. **UDC** 616.89-053.2. ***Continues*** *American Association of Psychiatric Clinics for Children. Newsletter of the AAPCC.*

US/0741-4684
**NICHD ANNUAL REPORT.** [NICHD annu. rep.]. **Main/Corp** National Institute of Child Health and Human Development (U.S.). **VFOAT** N.I.C.H.D. Annual Report. **VAT** National Institute of Child Health and Human Development Annual Report. English. an. National Institute of Child Health and Human Development, 9000 Rockville Pike, Bethesda MD 20014. **LC** RJ101; .N375A. **DD** 618.92/0005. **UDC** 616-053.2(73). available on microfiche (Vols. for 1980/1981-(1982/1983) distributed to depository libraries).

NR/0302-4660
**NIGERIAN JOURNAL OF PAEDIATRICS.** [Niger. j. paediatr.]. **Added/Corp** Paediatric Association of Nigeria. Vol. 1 (Jan. 1974)-. Academic Scholarly Publication. English. qt. N16.00. Paediatric Association of Nigeria, Dept of Paediatrics Univ College, Ibadan Nigeria. **NLM** W1 NI393G. **CODEN** NJPDAK. Documents available from BIOSIS Document Express.
**Ind/Abst** Biol. Abstr.; EMBASE; Trop. Dis. Bull.

JA/0001-6543
**NIHON SHONIKA GAKKAI ZASSHI.** [Nippon Shonika Gakkai zasshi]. **Added/Corp** Nihon Shonika Gakkai. **VFOAT** Acta Paediatrica Japonica. (1951)-. Academic Scholarly Publication. Japanese. bm. $132.50. Nihon Shonika Gakkai, (Japan Pediatric Soc.), 1-5, Koraku 1 Chome, Bunkyoku, Tokyoto 112, Japan. **(Subscription address:** Japan Publications Trading Company, Ltd., PO Box 5030, Tokyo International, Tokyo 100-31 Japan.**) CODEN** NIPOAC. **[CCC].** Documents available from CASDDS.
**Ind/Abst** Chem. Abstr. (1951-1983); Life Sci. Collect.

●US/0000-1627
**OFFICIAL AMERICAN BOARD OF MEDICAL SPECIALTIES (ABMS) DIRECTORY OF BOARD CERTIFIED PEDIATRICIANS, THE.** [Off. Am. Board Med. Spec. (ABMS) dir. board certif. pediatr.]. **Added/Corp** American Board of Medical Specialties. **VFOAT** Directory of Board Certified Pediatricians; Official ABMS Directory of Board Certified Pediatricians. 5th Ed. (1994)-. English. be. American Board of Medical Specialties, 1 Rotary Center, Suite 805, Evanston IL 60201. **Tel** (708)491-9091. **LC** RJ29; .A25. **DD** 618.92/00232/02573; 618. ***Continues*** *ABMS Directory of Certified Pediatricians, 0884-1497.*

NE/0167-6784
**OPHTHALMIC PAEDIATRICS AND GENETICS.** ***Title Change.*** **See** Biology-Genetics.

US/1071-233X
**ORIGINAL NEWS PEPPER, THE.** (THE ORIGINAL NEWS PEPPER : A "PEDS" PATIENT NEWSLETTER.). [Orig. news pepper]. **VFOAT** News Pepper. Vol. 1, No. 1 (Aug. 1990)-. Newsletter. English. Twelve times a year. $138.00. News Pepper, 477 Congress Street, Suite 400, Portland ME 04101. **Tel** (207)874-9045, FAX (207)874-9046. **ED** Ruth Gordon. **DD** 618. **Pr Rev. Circ:** 75 (ctrl).
**Desc:** Written and designed for children who are in the hospital.

IT/0020-6274
**OSPEDALI ITALIANI-PEDIATRIA (E SPECIALITA CHIRURGICHE).** (1966)-. Italian. bm. Ospedali Italiani - Pediatria, Via Cimarosa 180-A, 80127, Napoli, Italy. **Tel** (81)379280.
**Ind/Abst** EMBASE [Select. Cov.].

GW/0030-932X
**PADIATRIE UND GRENZGEBIETE.** [Paediatr. Grenzgeb.]. Vol. 1 (1962)-. Periodical. German. Six times a year. Price varies. Harwood Academic Publishers, PO Box 90, Reading RG1 8JL England. **Tel** 011 44 734 560080. **(Subscription address:** Gordon & Breach Science Publishers / Singapore, PO Box 1180, Kent Ridge PO, Singapore 9111 Singapore.**) NLM** W1; PA264J. **[CCC].** Index Available, published separately, free-automatically sent.
**Ind/Abst** EMBASE [Select. Cov.]; Index Med.

AU/0030-9338
**PADIATRIE UND PADOLOGIE.** [Padiatr. Padol.]. **Added/Corp** Osterrichische Gesellschaft fuer Kinderheilkunde. Vol. 1 (April 1965)-. Academic Scholarly Publication. German (English, French and German; summaries and/or abstracts in English and German). Six times a year. $236.50. Springer-Verlag Wien, Sachsenplatz 4 6, PO Box 89, A-1201 Vienna Austria. **Tel** 011 43 1 3302415. **(Subscription address:** Springer Verlag New York Inc. / for North America, 44 Hartz Way, Secaucus NJ 07096.**) ED** H. Berger, R. Kurz, and G. Weippl. **NLM** W1 PA264P. **CODEN** PAPAB5. **[CCC].** available on microfilm from University Microfilms International (UMI). Documents available from BIOSIS Document Express, CASDDS. ***Supersedes*** *Neue Osterreichische Zeitschrift fur Kinderheilkunde.*
**Desc:** Covers all areas of pediatrics and other sciences as they relate to the nature and development of the child. Main part consists of original articles, also includes reviews and convention notices.
**Ind/Abst** Biol. Abstr.; Chem. Abstr.; Dev. Med. Child Neurol.; EMBASE [Select. Cov.]; Index Med.

AU/0300-9556
**PADIATRIE UND PADOLOGIE. SUPPLEMENTUM.** [Paediatr. Paedol., Suppl.]. Monographic series. German (summaries and/or abstracts in English). ir. Price varies per volume. Springer-Verlag Wien, Sachsenplatz 4 6, PO Box 89, A-1201 Vienna Austria. **Tel** 011 43 1 3302415. **(Subscription address:** Springer Verlag New York Inc. / for North America, 44 Hartz Way, Secaucus NJ 07096.**) UDC** 616-053.2. **NLM** W1 PA264Q. available on microfilm from University Microfilms International (UMI).
**Ind/Abst** Index Med.

GW/0030-9346
**PADIATRISCHE PRAXIS.** [Padiatr. prax.]. Vol. 1 (1962)-. Academic Scholarly Publication. German. qt. DM268.00. Hans Marseille Verlag GmbH, Buerkleinstrasse 12, D 80538 Munich Germany. **Tel** 011 49 89 227988, FAX 011 49 89 2904643. **NLM** W1 PA265. **[CCC].** cum. index. available on microfilm from University Microfilms International (UMI).
**Ind/Abst** EMBASE.

FR/1155-5645
**PAEDIATRIC ANAESTHESIA.** **VAT** Pediatric Anesthesia. Vol. 1, No. 1 (1991)-. Periodical. English. qt. 680.00F (individuals), 930.00F (institutions) France; $137.00 (individuals), $185.00 (institutions) other. Blackwell Scientific Publishers / Arnette, 2 rue Casimir-Delavigne, 75006 Paris France. **Tel** 011 33 1 44860770, FAX 011 33 1 46336797. **(Subscription address:** Service Abbonements, 1 rue de Lille, 75007 Paris France.**) NLM** W1; PA263H. cum. index. **Bk Rev. Ad Acc. Pr Rev. Circ:** 1,000. available on microfilm and microfiche from University Microfilms International (UMI).
**Desc:** Concerns all aspects of anesthesia in pediatrics.

UK/0269-5022
**PAEDIATRIC AND PERINATAL EPIDEMIOLOGY.** **See** Medical Science and Technology-Epidemiology.

UK/0261-7021
**PAEDIATRIC CARDIOLOGY.** [Paediatr. cardiol.]. Vol. 1 (1977)-. Periodical. English. an. Churchill Livingstone, 1-3 Baxter's Place, Leith Walk, Edinburgh EH1 3AF Scotland. **Tel** 011 44 31 556 2424, FAX 011 44 31 558 1278, telex 727511. **(Subscription address:** US/ Churchill Livingstone, Fulfillment Office, PO Box 11318, Birmingham, AL 35202**) NLM** W1 PA263J.

UK
**PAEDIATRIC NURSING.** **See** Medical Science and Technology-Nursing.

IO/0030-9311
**PAEDIATRICA INDONESIANA.** [Paediatr. Indones.]. **Added/Corp** Indonesian Paediatric Society. Djakarta. Universitas Indonesia. Fakultas Kedokteran. Vol. 1 (1961)-. Academic Scholarly Publication. Indonesian (English). Six times a year. $30.00. Department of Child Health Medical School, University of Indonesia, PO Box 3620, 6 Salemba Jakarta Indonesia. **Tel** (061)-331168. **ED** Bambang Madiyono, Abdul Latief, I Budiman, Maria Abdulsalam, Rulina Suradi, Siti Zuraida Zulkarnain, Sudigdo Sastroasmoro and Titi Sunarwati Sularyo. **NLM** W1 PA263P. **CODEN** PIDOA8. **Bk Rev. Ad Acc. Circ:** 2,000 (ctrl). available on microfilm and microfiche from University Microfilms International (UMI). Documents available from BIOSIS Document Express.
**Desc:** Publishes reports on research programs, clinical studies, case reports and literature reviews.
**Ind/Abst** Biol. Abstr.; EMBASE; Index Med.

SZ/0078-7795
**PAEDIATRISCHE FORTBILDUNGSKURSE FUER DIE PRAXIS.** ***Ceased.*** [Paediatr. Fortbildungsk. Prax.]. Vol. 1 (1962)-Series complete with Volume 62. Periodical. German. Seven times a year. S. Karger AG, Allschwilerstrasse 10, PO Box - Postfach - Case Postale, CH-4009 Basel Switzerland. **Tel** 011 41 61 306-1111, FAX 011 41 61 306-1234, telex CH 962 652. **ED** E Rossi. **NLM** W1 PA2645. **CODEN** PFPXA6. **[CCC].** Documents available from BIOSIS Document Express.
**Desc:** Each issue deals with a different aspect of childhood diseases-prevention, chronic illnesses, handicaps, and infections.
**Ind/Abst** Biol. Abstr.

PK
**PAKISTAN PEDIATRIC JOURNAL.** (19??)-. Periodical. English. qt. Rs10.00. Association of Pediatricians of Pakistan, 111-D 27-7 Nazimabad, Karachi 18 Pakistan. **ED** Abdul Jamil Khan. **Bk Rev. Ad Acc.** available with charts; available with illustrations.

FR/0397-9180
**PEDIATRE, LE.** [Pediatre]. (1967)-. Periodical. French (summaries and/or abstracts in English). bm. 550.00F. Societe le Pediatre Parisien, BP 132, 75821 Paris Cedex 17 France. **Tel** 33 1 42672713. **ED** Dr. Jean Feigedlson (editor's address: 153 rue de Saussure, 75017 Paris France; editor's phone: 33 1 42671215). **UDC** 616-053.2. Index available. cum. index. **Bk Rev**, (Qty: 6). **Ad Acc, Adv Mgr:** same as editor. **Pr Rev.**
**Ind/Abst** EMBASE.

●RM/1220-580X
**PEDIATRIA / ASOCIATIA MEDICALA ROMANA, SOCIETATEA ROMANA DE PEDIATRIE.** **Added/Corp** Societatea Romana de Pediatrie. Vol. 42, No. 1 (Jan./Mar. 1993)-. Periodical. Romanian (summaries and/or abstracts in English; table of contents in English). Four times a year. DM225.00. **(Subscription address:** Kubon & Sagner, ABT Zeitschriftenimport, D 80328 Munich Germany.**) NLM** W1; PE202. ***Continues*** *Pediatrie (Bucharest, Romania).*

PE/1012-8964
**PEDIATRIA (LIMA, PERU).** (PEDIATRIA / UNIVERSIDAD NACIONAL MAYOR DE SAN MARCOS.). [Pediatria]. V. 1, No. 1 (Jan./June 1976)-. Periodical. Spanish (summaries and/or abstracts in English). sa. **UDC** 616-053.2. **NLM** W1 PE135L.

IT/0391-5387
**PEDIATRIA MEDICA E CHIRURGICA, LA.** [Pediatr. med. chir.]. **VFOAT** Medical and Surgical Pediatrics. Vol. 1, No. 1 (Jan./Feb. 1979)-. Academic Scholarly Publication. Italian (English; summaries and/or abstracts in English). bm (6 issues). L70000 Italy; L100000 other. Pediatria Medica Chirurgica, Division of Pediatric Surgery Osp, Via le Dante 49, 36100 Vicenza Italy. **Tel** 011 39 444 993887, 011 39 44 993563, FAX 011 39 444 993809. **ED** Oiampiero Belloli. **NLM** W1 PE1564. **CODEN** PMECD8. Index available. cum. index. **Bk Rev. Ad Acc. Circ:** 1,500. Documents available from CASDDS.
**Ind/Abst** Chem. Abstr.; EMBASE [Select. Cov.]; Index Med.

BL/0031-3920
**PEDIATRIA MODERNA.** [Pediatr. Mod.]. (19??)-. Portuguese. bm (7 issues). $136.00. Moreira Jr Editora Medica Ltda, Rue Henrique Martins 493, 04504 Sao Paulo SP Brazil. **Tel** 011 55 11 8849911, FAX 011 55 11 2800491. **ED** Friederich T. Simon. **CODEN** PEMOA. **Bk Rev. Ad Acc. Circ:** 15,000.

IT/0031-3890
**PEDIATRIA (NAPOLI).** (PEDIATRIA. RIVISTA D'IGIENE MEDICINA E CHIRURGIA DELL'INFANZIA.). [Pediatria]. Periodical. Italian. qt. $24.00. Clinica Pediatrica, S Andrea Delle/Dame 4, 80138 Naples Italy. **UDC** 616-053.2. **NLM** W1 PE137.
**Ind/Abst** Index Med.

IT/0391-898X
**PEDIATRIA OGGI MEDICA E CHIRURGICA.** [Pediatr. oggi med. chir.]. (198?)-. Periodical. Italian (summaries and/or abstracts in English). qt. $70.00. CIC Edizioni Internazionali, Via L Spallanzani 11, 00161 Rome Italy. **Tel** 011 39 6 841-2673, FAX 011 39 6 844-3365, telex 622099 CIC I. **NLM** W1; PE157T. **[CCC].**
**Ind/Abst** EMBASE [Select. Cov.].

PL/0031-3939
**PEDIATRIA POLSKA.** [Pediatr. Pol.]. **Added/Corp** Polskie Towarzystwo Pediatryczne. Instytut Matki i Dziecka (Warsaw, Poland). Vol. 1 (1921)-. Academic Scholarly Publication. Polish. mo. $120.00. **(Subscription address:** ARS Polona, PO Box 1001, 00068 Warsaw Poland.**) NLM** W1 PE159. **CODEN** PEPOA6. Documents available from BIOSIS Document Express, CASDDS. ***Supersedes*** *Przegled Pedyatryczny.*
**Ind/Abst** Biol. Abstr.; Chem. Abstr.; EMBASE [Select. Cov.]; Index Med.; Life Sci. Collect.; SportSearch.

CL/0375-9563
**PEDIATRIA (SANTIAGO).** (PEDIATRIA.). [Pediatria]. (1958)-. Academic Scholarly Publication. Spanish (summaries and/or abstracts in English, German, French and Italian). Four times a year. $20.00. University of Chile Facultad Medicina, Casilla 9183, Santiago Chile. **Tel** 011 56 2 7370081 ext. 5340, FAX 56 2 5510174. **(Subscription address:** University of Chile Facultad Medicina Pediatria, Zanartu 1085, Santigo Chile.**)**
**Ind/Abst** EMBASE [Select. Cov.].

BL/0101-3858
**PEDIATRIA (SAO PAULO).** ***Suspended.*** (PEDIATRIA (S. PAULO) : REVISTA DO CENTRO DE

ESTUDOS PROF. PEDRO DE ALCANTARA, EM CONVENIO COM INSTITUTO DA CRIANCA, HOSPITAL DAS CLINICAS, FMUSP.). [Pediatria (Sao Paulo)]. Vol. 1, No. 1 (March 1979)-?. Periodical. Portuguese. qt. Pediatria, Caixa Postal, 12 927 01000, V Mariana Sao Paulo Brazil. **UDC** 616-053.2. **NLM** W1 PE163E.

US/1045-5418
**PEDIATRIC AIDS AND HIV INFECTION.** **See** Medical Science and Technology-Allergy and Immunology.

IT
**PEDIATRIC ALERT.** ***Ceased.*** (19??)-(19??). Italian. bw. Eurotrend Srl, V Le Regina Giovanna 39, 20129 Milan Italy. **Tel** 011 39 2 29514419.

US/0160-0184
**PEDIATRIC ALERT.** (197?)-. Periodical. English. bw. $65.00 (1 year), $120.00 (2 year), $177.00 (3 year) individuals, $85.00 (1 year), $170.00 (2 year), $235.00 (3 year) institutional, US; $85.00 (1 year), $160.00 (2 year), $237.00 (3 year) individuals, $105.00 (1 year), $210.00 (2 year), $295.00 (3 year) institutional, other. Pediatric Alert, PO Box 338, Newton Highlands MA 02161. **Tel** (617)699-8027.

FR
**PEDIATRIC ANAESTHESIA.** **See** Medical Science and Technology-Anesthesiology.

SZ/0304-4254
**PEDIATRIC AND ADOLESCENT ENDOCRINOLOGY.** [Pediatr. adolesc. endocrinol.]. Vol. 1 (1976)-. Academic Scholarly Publication. English. an. 260.00F (approx. per volume). S. Karger AG, Allschwilerstrasse 10, PO Box - Postfach - Case Postale, CH-4009 Basel Switzerland. **Tel** 011 41 61 306-1111, FAX 011 41 61 306-1234, telex CH 962 652. **ED** Z. Laron. **LC** UNC. **NLM** W1 PE163H. **CODEN** PAENDP. **[CCC].** Documents available from BIOSIS Document Express, CASDDS.
**Desc:** Books in this series collect basic and clinical research designed to improve the understanding and management of pediatric and adolescent diseases and disorders involving the endocrine system. Volumes explore how factors, such as age, size, and maturation of the growing body, can influence the interactions of hormones with bodily functions and dysfunctions. Previous titles have offered information on such topics as sexual differentiation, diabetes, obesity, and the various hormonal interactions between mother and fetus.
**Ind/Abst** Biol. Abstr.; Chem. Abstr.; Ref. Upd. Deluxe Ed.

SZ/1017-5989
**PEDIATRIC AND ADOLESCENT MEDICINE.** [Pediatr. adolesc. med.]. Vol. 1 (1991)-. Monographic series. English. an. 230.00F (approx. per volume). S. Karger AG, Allschwilerstrasse 10, PO Box - Postfach - Case Postale, CH-4009 Basel Switzerland. **Tel** 011 41 61 306-1111, FAX 011 41 61 306-1234, telex CH 962 652. **ED** D. Branski. **NLM** W1; PE163HL. **CODEN** PEAMEV. Index available. cum. index. Documents available from BIOSIS Document Express. ***Formed by the union of*** *Modern Problems in Paediatrics, 0303-884X* ***and*** *Monographs in Paediatrics, 0077-0914.*
**Desc:** Deals with rapidly evolving pediatric subspecialties such as perinatal medicine, pediatric endocrinology, immunology, neurology and cardiology, and all topics which are dictating important new trends in monitoring child development and subsequent adult health. Furthermore, this series will also pay close attention to medical issues relating especially to adolescents.
**Ind/Abst** Biol. Abstr.; Ref. Upd. Deluxe Ed.

US/0090-4481
**PEDIATRIC ANNALS.** [Pediatr. ann.]. Vol. 1 (Oct 1972)-. Academic Scholarly Publication. English. mo. $120.00 institution, $110.00 individual (US). Slack Inc., 6900 Grove Road, Thorofare NJ 08086. **Tel** (609)848-1000, (800)257-8290, FAX (609)853-5991, telex 517108 SLACK INC VD. **ED** Donna Carpenter. **LC** RJ1; .P274. **DD** 618.9/2/0005. **UDC** 616-053.2. **NLM** W1 PE163N. Index available in last issue of volume--attached. **Bk Rev. Ad Acc. Pr Rev. Circ:** 30,000 (ctrl). available on microfilm and microfiche from University Microfilms International (UMI). Documents available from The Genuine Article.
**Desc:** Provides the pediatrician with new information on diagnosis and patient management that will be useful to him in his practice.
**Ind/Abst** AGRICOLA; Comb. Cumul. Index Pediatr.; Cumul. Index Nurs. Allied Health Lit.; Curr. Aware. Biol. Sci., CABS; Curr. Contents Clin. Med.; EMBASE; Energy Res. Abstr. (Aug. 1982-); Index Med.; Life Sci. Collect.; Res. Alert [Select. Cov.]; Rev. Med. Vet. Entomol.; SCISEARCH; Soc. Sci. Cit. Index [Select. Cov.]; SportSearch.

US/0883-1874
**PEDIATRIC ASTHMA, ALLERGY & IMMUNOLOGY.** [Pediatr. asthma allergy immunol.]. **VFOAT** Pediatric Asthma, Allergy, and Immunology. Vol. 1, No. 1 (Winter 1987)-. Periodical. English. qt. $166.95. Mary Ann Liebert Inc., 1651 Third Avenue, New York NY 10128. **Tel** (212)289-2300, (800)M-LIEBERT, FAX (212)289-4697. **ED** Herbert Mansmann, Jr. **DD** 618. **NLM** W1; PE163T. **CODEN** PAAIEP. Documents available from The Genuine Article, BIOSIS Document Express.
**Desc:** Devoted to pediatric asthma, allergy and immunology as a specific area of medical specialization. A forum for papers on the optimal care of the infant, child, and adolescent. Emphasizes the developmental implications of the morphologic, physiologic, pharmacologic and sociologic components of these problems in infants, children, and adolescents, and the impact of disease processes on their families.
**Ind/Abst** Biol. Abstr. (1987-); Curr. Contents Clin. Med.; Res. Alert [Select. Cov.]; SCISEARCH; Soc. Sci. Cit. Index [Select. Cov.].

US/0172-0643
**PEDIATRIC CARDIOLOGY.** [Pediatr. cardiol.]. Vol. 1 (1980)-. Periodical. English. Six times a year. $138.00. Springer-Verlag New York Inc., 175 5th Avenue, New York NY 10010. **Tel** (212)460-1500, telex 232 235 SPB UR. **(Subscription address:** Springer Verlag New York Inc. / for North America, 44 Hartz Way, Secaucus NJ 07096.**)** **ED** I Carr, and J Taylor. **LC** RJ421; .P42. **DD** 618.92/12. **NLM** W1 PE164L. **CODEN** PECAD4. **[CCC]. Pr Rev.** available on microfilm and microfiche from University Microfilms International (UMI). Documents available from The Genuine Article.
**Desc:** Contains technical notes on the latest instruments, unusual electrocardiographic, echocardiographic, and surgical observations in children, letters to the editors, and editorials and reviews on important clinical and scientific issues.
**Ind/Abst** Curr. Contents Clin. Med.; EMBASE; Index Med.; Life Sci. Collect.; Res. Alert [Full Cov.]; Sci. Cit. Index; SCISEARCH.

II/0048-3133
**PEDIATRIC CLINICS OF INDIA.** (1966)-. Periodical. English. qt. $50.00. LTMG Hospital, Sion, Bombay, India. **(Subscription address:** Prints India, 11 Darya Ganj, New Delhi 110002 India.**)**

US/0031-3955
**PEDIATRIC CLINICS OF NORTH AMERICA, THE.** [Pediatr. clin. North Am.]. Vol. 1 (Feb. 1954)-. Academic Scholarly Publication. English. bm. $77.00 (individual), $100.00 (institution) US; $108.00 (individual), $115.00 (institution) other. W.B. Saunders Company, A Subsidiary of Harcourt Brace Jovanovich, Inc., The Curtis Center/Suite 300, Independence Square West, Philadelphia PA 19106-3399. **Tel** (215)238-7800 or, 5587, FAX (215)238-7883, telex 173146. **(Subscription address:** W. B. Saunders Company / North America Subscriptions, c/o Periodicals, 6277 Sea Harbour Drive, 4th Floor, Orlando FL 32887.**)** **ED** Mary K. Smith. **LC** RJ23. **DD** 618.92082. **UDC** 616-053.2. **NLM** W1 PE165. **CODEN** PCNAA8. **[CCC].** Index available. cum. index. **Pr Rev. Circ:** 4,500. available on microfilm and microfiche from University Microfilms International (UMI). Documents available from The Genuine Article, BIOSIS Document Express, CASDDS.
**Desc:** Clinical updates on topics of current interest to pediatricians. Each issue addresses a single topic in patient care.
**Ind/Abst** Abr. Index Med.; Biol. Abstr.; Chem. Abstr.; Comb. Cumul. Index Pediatr.; Cumul. Index Nurs. Allied Health Lit.; Curr. Contents Clin. Med.; Curr. Contents Life Sci.; Dev. Med. Child Neurol.; EMBASE; Energy Res. Abstr.; Index Med.; Int. Pharm. Abstr.; Microbiol. Abstr. Sect. B (19??-19??); Nutr. Abstr. Rev., Ser. A, Hum. Exp.; Life Sci. Collect.; Physic. Medline Plus; Ref. Upd. Deluxe Ed.; Res. Alert [Full Cov.]; Sci. Cit. Index; SCISEARCH; Soc. Sci. Cit. Index [Select. Cov.]; SportSearch.

US/0097-5982
**PEDIATRIC CONFERENCES FROM THE CHILDREN'S HOSPITAL OF NEWARK.** 1970-. Periodical. English. Childrens Hospital of Newark, 15 South 9th Street, Newark NJ 07107. **UDC** 616-053.2. **NLM** W1 PE167. ***Continues*** *Pediatric Conferences from the Babies' Hospital Unit, United Hospitals of Newark, New Jersey, 0031-3963.*

US/1046-2791
**PEDIATRIC DENTISTRY TODAY.** **See** Dentistry.

US/0736-8046
**PEDIATRIC DERMATOLOGY.** [Ped. dermatol.]. Vol. 1, No. 1 (July 1983)-. Academic Scholarly Publication. English. qt. $250.00 (institution), $140.00 (individual) US; $280.00*(institution), $170.00 (individual) other. Blackwell Scientific Publishers, 238 Main Street, Cambridge MA 02142. **Tel** (617)547-7110, (800)835-6770, FAX (617)547-0789. **ED** Nancy Esterley and Lawrence Solomon. **UDC** 616.5-053.2. **NLM** W1; PE167F. **[CCC].** Index available. **Bk Rev. Ad Acc. Pr Rev. Circ:** 1,000. available on microfilm and microfiche from University Microfilms International (UMI). Documents available from The Genuine Article.
**Desc:** Official publication of Society for Pediatric Dermatology. Original articles on research and clinical findings pertaining to genetics, infectious diseases; dysmorphic disorders and diseases of unknown etiology.
**Ind/Abst** Curr. Contents Clin. Med.; EMBASE; Index Med. (Vol. 1, No. 1, 1983-); Index Vet.; Res. Alert [Select. Cov.]; Rev. Med. Vet. Entomol.; Rev. Med. Vet. Mycology; SCISEARCH.

US/1059-0870
**PEDIATRIC EMERGENCY & CRITICAL CARE.** [Pediatr. emerg. crit. care]. **VFOAT** Pediatric Emergency and Critical Care. Vol. 4, No. 10 (Oct. 1991)-. Periodical. English. mo. $85.00 institution, $55.00 individual. Riverpress Inc., PO Box 23, Jersey City NJ 07303. **Tel** (201)434-5073, FAX (201)434-7230. **ED** D. Wagner. **DD** 618. Index available (published in Dec.). **Bk Rev**, (Qty: 2-4). **Pr Rev. Circ:** 2,000. ***Continues*** *Pediatric Trauma & Acute Care, 0894-1122.*
**Desc:** Review of studies and articles on care of the acutely ill or injured child selected for clinical relevance. Invited editorial comments by an expert in each problem provide state-of-the-art perspective. Updates from clinical meetings provide rapid publication of clinical pearls.

US/0749-5161
**PEDIATRIC EMERGENCY CARE.** **See** Medical Science and Technology-Emergency Medicine.

US/0899-8493
**PEDIATRIC EXERCISE SCIENCE.** [Pediatr. exerc. sci.]. **Added/Corp** North American Society of Pediatric Exercise Medicine. Vol. 1, No. 1 (Feb. 1989)-. Periodical. English. qt (Feb., May, Aug., Nov.). $40.00 (individual), $90.00 (institution) US; $44.00 (individual), $94.00 (institution) other. Human Kinetics Publishers Inc, 1607 North Market Street, PO Box 5076, Champaign IL 61825-5076. **Tel** (217)351-5076, FAX (217)351-2674. **ED** Thomas W. Rowland. **DD** 618. **NLM** W1; PE167FK. **[CCC].** Index available (Included in Nov. issue). **Ad Acc.**
**Desc:** Committed to enriching the scientific knowledge of exercise during childhood and adolescence. Seeks to stimulate better understanding and greater awareness of the importance of childhood exercise to scientists, health care providers, and physical educators.
**Ind/Abst** Phys. Educ. Index; Soc. Sci. Cit. Index [Select. Cov.]; SPORT Discus.

US/0731-5902
**PEDIATRIC HABILITATION.** [Pediatr. habilit.]. Vol. 1 (1980)-. Monographic series. English. ir. Price varies per volume. Marcel Dekker Inc., 270 Madison Avenue, New York NY 10016. **Tel** (212)696-9000, (800)228-1160, FAX (212)685-4540, telex 421419. **(Subscription address:** Marcel Dekker Inc, PO Box 5017, Monticello NY 12701.**)** **ED** Alfred Scherzer. **LC** UNC. **DD** 618.92. **NLM** W1 PE167K. **CODEN** PEHAEU. Documents available from BIOSIS Document Express.
**Desc:** Series covering topics in pediatrics such as developmental disabilities and parenting children with disabilities.
**Ind/Abst** Biol. Abstr. (1991-).

US/0888-0018
**PEDIATRIC HEMATOLOGY AND ONCOLOGY.** **See** Medical Science and Technology-Hematology.

US/0891-3668
**PEDIATRIC INFECTIOUS DISEASE JOURNAL, THE.** [Pediatr. infect. dis. j.]. Vol. 6, No. 1 (Jan. 1987)-. Periodical. English. mo. $93.00 (individual), $149.00 (institution) US; $133.00 (individual), $189.00 (institution) other. Williams & Wilkins Company, 428 East Preston Street, Baltimore MD 21202-3993. **Tel** (410)528-4000, (800)638-6423, FAX (410)528-8596, telex 87669. **(Subscription address:** Williams & Wilkins, PO Box 64380, Baltimore MD 21264.**)** **DD** 616. **NLM** W1; PE168FE. **CODEN** PIDJEV. **[CCC]. Pr Rev.** available on CD-ROM. Documents available from The Genuine Article, BIOSIS Document Express, Quick Copies. ***Continues*** *Pediatric Infectious Disease, 0277-9730.*
**Desc:** Articles for pediatricians, family practitioners and infectious disease specialists cover the treatment for viral and bacterial illness in children.
**Ind/Abst** Biol. Abstr. (1987-); Comb. Cumul. Index Pediatr.; Cumul. Index Nurs. Allied Health Lit.; Dairy Sci. Abstr.; Dev. Med. Child Neurol.; EMBASE; Helminthol. Abstr. (19??-19??); Index Med. (Jan. 1987-); Index Vet.; Int. Nurs. Index; Int. Pharm. Abstr.; Microbiol. Abstr. Sect. B (19??-19??); Microbiol. Abstr. Sect. C; Physic. Medline Plus; Protozoolog. Abstr.; Ref. Upd. Deluxe Ed.; Res. Alert [Full Cov.]; Rev. Med. Vet. Entomol.; Rev. Med. Vet. Mycology; Risk Abstr.; Sci. Cit. Index; SCISEARCH; Small Anim. Abstr. Bibliogr.; Trop. Dis. Bull.; Virol. AIDS Abstr.

US/0891-1223
**PEDIATRIC LENGTH OF STAY BY DIAGNOSIS AND OPERATION, UNITED STATES.** [Pediatr. length stay diagn. oper. U. S.]. **Added/Corp** Commission on Professional and Hospital Activities. **VFOAT** Length of Stay by Diagnosis, by Operation, United States, Pediatric; Length of Stay, Pediatric. (1981)-. Periodical. English. an. $171.95. HCIA Inc., 300 E Lombard Street, Baltimore MI 21202. **Tel** 800 568-3282, (410)576-9600. **LC** RJ27.2; .P43. **DD** 362.1/9892/000973021. **NLM** W1; PE168H. available on microfiche; available on magnetic tape; available on diskette. ***Continues*** *Pediatric Length of Stay in PAS Hospitals, by Diagnosis and Operation, United States, 0732-6076.*

US/1051-3272
**PEDIATRIC MANAGEMENT.** ***Suspended.*** [Pediatr. manage.]. (Sept. 1990)-(Apr. 1994). Periodical. English. mo. $60.00 US; $75.00 other. Dowden

Publishing Company, 110 Summit Avenue, Montvale NJ 07645. **Tel** (201)391-9100, FAX (201)391-2778. **ED** Carroll V. Dowden. **DD** 618. ctrl circ.
**Desc:** Editorial emphases specialty, specific practice-management information.

US/0278-4998
**PEDIATRIC MENTAL HEALTH.** [Pediatr. ment. health]. **Added/Corp** Pediatric Projects Inc. Vol. 1, No. 1 (Jan./Feb. 1982)-. Periodical. English. bm (6 issues). $32.00. Pediatric Projects Inc, PO Box 571555, Tarzana CA 91357. **Tel** (818)705-3660, (800)947-0947. **ED** Pat Azarnoff. **NLM** W1; PE168J. Index available. **Bk Rev. Circ:** 1,000.
**Desc:** A professional publication describing theory and practice of psychological preparation, therapeutic play, and supported parenting of children in health care.

US/0097-5257
**PEDIATRIC NEPHROLOGY.** [Pediatr. nephrol.]. (1974)-. Academic Scholarly Publication. English. ir. Price varies per volume. Plenum Press, 233 Spring Street, New York NY 10013-1578. **Tel** (212)620-8000, (800)221-9369, FAX (212)463-0742, (212)807-1047, telex 23/421139. **ED** Jose Strauss. **LC** RJ466; .P36. **DD** 618.9/26/1005. **NLM** W1 PE168K. **CODEN** PENED3. **Circ:** 2,000. Documents available from The Genuine Article, CASDDS.
**Desc:** Current aspects of diagnosis and treatment of urological and renal disorders in pediatrics.
**Ind/Abst** Chem. Abstr. (1974-1979); Curr. Contents Clin. Med.; Nutr. Abstr. Rev., Ser. A, Hum. Exp.; Ref. Upd. Deluxe Ed.; Res. Alert [Select. Cov.].

GW/0931-041X
**PEDIATRIC NEPHROLOGY (BERLIN, WEST).** (PEDIATRIC NEPHROLOGY : JOURNAL OF THE INTERNATIONAL PEDIATRIC NEPHROLOGY ASSOCIATION.). [Pediatr. nephrol.]. **Added/Corp** International Paediatric Nephrology Association. Vol. 1, No. 1 (Jan. 1987)-. Academic Scholarly Publication. English. Six times a year. DM1074.00. Springer-Verlag GmbH & Company KG, Heidelberger Platz 3, D 14197 Berlin Germany. **Tel** 011 49 30 8207223, FAX 011 49 30 8214091, telex 183 319 SPBLN D. **(Subscription address:** Springer Verlag New York Inc. / for North America, 44 Hartz Way, Secaucus NJ 07096.**)** **ED** A M Robson. **NLM** W1; PE1685JD. **CODEN** PEDNEF. **[CCC]. Pr Rev.** available on microfilm and microfiche from University Microfilms International (UMI). Documents available from BIOSIS Document Express, CASDDS.
**Desc:** Publishes original laboratory or clinical research and new or important clinical observations pertaining to any aspect of the wide spectrum of acute and chronic diseases that affect renal function in children as well as on hypertension and fluid and electrolyte metabolism.
**Ind/Abst** Biol. Abstr.; Chem. Abstr. (1987-); EMBASE; Health Plan. Adminis.; Index Med. (Jan. 1987-); SCISEARCH.

US/0742-1605
**PEDIATRIC NETWORK.** [Pediatr. netw.]. Periodical. English. mo. $9.00. Thagard Enterprises, PO Box 8396, Calabasas CA 91302. **Tel** (310)884-0315. **UDC** 616-053.2.

US/0887-8994
**PEDIATRIC NEUROLOGY.** [Pediatr. neurol.]. Vol. 1, No. 1 (Jan./Feb. 1985)-. Academic Scholarly Publication. English. Eight times a year (2 volumes). $175.00 US; $209.00 other. Elsevier Science Publishing Company Inc, Madison Square Station, PO Box 882, New York NY 10159-0882. **Tel** (212)633-3950, FAX (212)633-3990. **ED** Kenneth F. Swaiman. **DD** 616. **NLM** W1; PE168M. Index available. cum. index. **Bk Rev. Ad Acc, Adv Mgr:** Richard Geyer. **Pr Rev. Circ:** 2,000. Documents available from The Genuine Article.
**Desc:** Contains original papers, reviews, case reports, news, and professional announcements which provide the most current, accurate, and useful information on diseases affecting the immature nervous system. Contents are of interest to pediatric and adult neurologists, pediatricians, neurosurgeons, and psychiatrists as well as pediatric nurse clinicians, child psychologists, etc.
**Ind/Abst** Curr. Aware. Biol. Sci., CABS; Curr. Contents Clin. Med.; Curr. Contents Life Sci.; Dev. Med. Child Neurol.; EMBASE; Health Plan. Adminis.; Index Med.; Ref. Upd. Deluxe Ed.; Res. Alert [Full Cov.]; Rev. Med. Vet. Entomol.; Rev. Med. Vet. Mycology; SCISEARCH; Soc. Sci. Cit. Index [Select. Cov.].

SZ/1016-2291
**PEDIATRIC NEUROSURGERY.** **Added/Corp** American Society for Pediatric Neurosurgery. (1991)-. Academic Scholarly Publication. English. mo. $592.00. S. Karger AG, Allschwilerstrasse 10, PO Box - Postfach - Case Postale, CH-4009 Basel Switzerland. **Tel** 011 41 61 306-1111, FAX 011 41 61 306-1234, telex CH 962 652. **ED** F. J. Epstein, D. H. Reigel. **NLM** W1; PE168ML. **CODEN** PDNEEV. Index available. **Bk Rev. Ad Acc. Pr Rev. Circ:** 1,200. available on microfilm and microfiche. Documents available from The Genuine Article, BIOSIS Document Express, CASDDS. ***Continues** Pediatric Neuroscience, 0255-7975.*
**Desc:** Articles published feature new information and observations in pediatric neurosurgery and the allied fields of neurology, neuroradiology, and neuropathology as they relate to the etiology of neurologic diseases and the care of affected patients. In addition to experimental and clinical studies, the journal presents critical reviews which provide the reader with an update on selected topics as well as case histories and reports on advances in methodology and technique. Such focus promotes many studies which are of interest to surgeons, physicians, and investigators concerned with the diseases of the nervous system.
**Ind/Abst** Biol. Abstr.; Chem. Abstr.; Curr. Contents Clin. Med.; EMBASE; Index Med.; Life Sci. Collect.; Ref. Upd. Deluxe Ed.; Res. Alert [Full Cov.]; Sci. Cit. Index; SCISEARCH.

US/0031-398X
**PEDIATRIC NEWS.** [Pediatr. news]. Vol. 1 (Jan. 1967)-. Periodical. English. mo. $60.00 US; $81.00 other. International Medical News Group, 12230 Wilkins Avenue, Rockville MD 20852. **Tel** (301)770-6170. **LC** RJ1; .P275. **DD** 618.92. **NLM** W1 PE168N. available on microfilm from University Microfilms International (UMI).

US/0738-8691
**PEDIATRIC NOTES.** [Pediatr. notes]. Vol. 1 (1977)-. Periodical. English. wk (Friday). $75.00 US & Canada; $85.00 other. Pediatric Notes, PO Box 59, c/o S. Gellis, Newtonville MA 02160. **Tel** FAX (617)965-2451. **ED** Sydney S. Gellis, M.D. Index available. cum. index.
**Desc:** This publication features abstracts of the pediatric literature comments by the editor.

US/0097-9805
**PEDIATRIC NURSING.** **See** Medical Science and Technology-Nursing.

US/0097-9805
**PEDIATRIC NURSING [MICROFORM].** **See** Medical Science and Technology-Nursing.

US/0277-0938
**PEDIATRIC PATHOLOGY.** ***Title Change.*** **See** Medical Science and Technology-Pathology.

US/0898-5669
**PEDIATRIC PHYSICAL THERAPY.** (PEDIATRIC PHYSICAL THERAPY : THE OFFICIAL PUBLICATION OF THE SECTION ON PEDIATRICS OF THE AMERICAN PHYSICAL THERAPY ASSOCIATION.). [Pediatr. phys. ther.]. **Added/Corp** American Physical Therapy Association (1921-). Section on Pediatrics. Vol. 1, No. 1 (Spring 1989)-. Periodical. English. qt. $50.00 (individual), $88.00 (institution) US; $70.00 (individual), $108.00 (institution) other. Williams & Wilkins Company, 428 East Preston Street, Baltimore MD 21202-3993. **Tel** (410)528-4000, (800)638-6423, FAX (410)528-8596, telex 87669. **(Subscription address:** Williams & Wilkins, PO Box 64380, Baltimore MD 21264.**)** **DD** 618. **NLM** W1; PE17HH. **CODEN** PPTHEI. **[CCC]. Pr Rev.** Documents available from Quick Copies.
**Desc:** Devoted entirely to pediatric physical therapy. Each issue delivers practical, authoritative information on the full range of pediatric conditions including developmental, orthopedic and respiratory concerns.
**Ind/Abst** Cumul. Index Nurs. Allied Health Lit.; Dev. Med. Child Neurol.; EMBASE; Except. Child Educ. Resour.

●US/1071-5711
**PEDIATRIC PRIMARY CARE.** (1993)-. Periodical. English. mo. $80.00 institution, $45.00 individual. Riverpress Inc., PO Box 23, Jersey City NJ 07303. **Tel** (201)434-5073, FAX (201)434-7230. Index available (bound in Dec. issue). **Bk Rev**, (Qty: 2-4). **Pr Rev.** ***Continues** Pediatric Therapeutics & Toxicology, 0893-6218.*

US/8755-6863
**PEDIATRIC PULMONOLOGY.** [Pediatr. pulmonol.]. Vol. 1 No. 1 (Jan./Feb. 1985)-. Periodical. English. Twelve times a year. $380.00 US; $600.00 Canada and Mexico; $645.00 other. John Wiley & Sons, Inc., 605 Third Avenue, New York NY 10158-0012. **Tel** (212)850-6000, (212)850-6645, FAX (212)850-6088, telex 12-7063. **(Subscription address:** John Wiley & Sons / England, Baffins Lane, Chichester, West Sussex PO19 1UD England.**)** **ED** George Polgar. **DD** 618. **NLM** W1; PE171R. **CODEN** PEPUES. **[CCC]. Pr Rev.** available on microfilm and microfiche from University Microfilms International (UMI). Documents available from The Genuine Article, BIOSIS Document Express.
**Desc:** Devoted to the study of the respiratory system in health and disease as it develops from interauterine life through adolescence.
**Ind/Abst** Biol. Abstr. (1987-); Curr. Aware. Biol. Sci., CABS; Curr. Contents Clin. Med.; Index Med. (1985-); Protozoolog. Abstr.; Ref. Upd. Deluxe Ed.; Res. Alert [Full Cov.]; Rev. Med. Vet. Mycology; Sci. Cit. Index; SCISEARCH; Virol. AIDS Abstr.

US/1054-187X
**PEDIATRIC PULMONOLOGY. SUPPLEMENT.** [Pediatr. pulmonol., Suppl.]. (1987)-. Monographic series. English. ir. Price varies per volume. Wiley Liss, 605 3rd Avenue, New York NY 10158. **Tel** (212)850-8800, (212)850-6645. **(Subscription address:** John Wiley / Philadelphia, PO Box 7247, Philadelphia PA 19170.**)** **DD** 618. **NLM** W1; PE171Ra.
**Ind/Abst** Health Plan. Adminis.; Index Med. (1987-).

GW/0301-0449
**PEDIATRIC RADIOLOGY.** **See** Medical Science and Technology-Radiology.

US/1065-1284
**PEDIATRIC REPORT'S CHILD HEALTH NEWSLETTER.** ***Ceased.*** [Pediatr. rep. child health newsl.]. **VFOAT** Child Health Newsletter. Vol. 7, No. 8 (Oct. 1990)-Vol. 11, No. 3. Newsletter. English. Eleven times a year (Monthly except July). IGM Enterprises Inc., 71 Hope Street, Box 155, Providence RI 02906. **Tel** (401)434-7390, FAX (401)435-3634. **DD** 618. Index available. available on an online database (file 149/Full-Text) from DIALOG. ***Continues** Parents' Pediatric Report.*
**Ind/Abst** Consum. Health Nutr. Index; Health Index (1990-); Health Period. Database [Full Txt.]; Health Ref. Cent. (Jan. 1989-) [Full Txt.] [Full Cov.].

US/0031-3998
**PEDIATRIC RESEARCH.** [Pediatr. res.]. **Added/Corp** International Pediatric Research Foundation. Vol. 1 (Jan. 1967)-. Academic Scholarly Publication. English (French). mo. $152.00 (individual), $265.00 (institution) US; $197.00 (individual), $310.00 (institution) other. Williams & Wilkins Company, 428 East Preston Street, Baltimore MD 21202-3993. **Tel** (410)528-4000, (800)638-6423, FAX (410)528-8596, telex 87669. **(Subscription address:** Williams & Wilkins, PO Box 64380, Baltimore MD 21264.**)** **ED** Delbert A. Fisher. **LC** RJ1; .P277. **DD** 618. **NLM** W1 PE175. **CODEN** PEREBL. **[CCC]. Ad Acc. Pr Rev. Circ:** 2,965. Documents available from , The Genuine Article, BIOSIS Document Express, CASDDS, Quick Copies. ***Supersedes** Annales Paediatrici.*
**Desc:** Covers advances in the understanding and management of pediatric pulmonary, endocrinological, gastroenterological and nutrition disorders.
**Ind/Abst** Biol. Abstr.; Calcium Calcif. Tissue Abstr.; Chem. Abstr.; Comb. Cumul. Index Pediatr.; CSA Neuro. Abstr.; Curr. Aware. Biol. Sci., CABS; Curr. Contents Life Sci.; Dairy Sci. Abstr.; Dev. Med. Child Neurol.; EMBASE; Energy Res. Abstr.; Immunol. Abstr.; Index Med.; Lang. Lang. Behav. Abstr.; Microbiol. Abstr. Sect. B; Nucl. Sci. Abstr.; Nutr. Abstr. Rev., Ser. B, Live Feeds and Feed.; Nutr. Abstr. Rev., Ser. A, Hum. Exp.; Nutr. Res. Newsl.; Life Sci. Collect.; Pig News Inf.; Ref. Upd. Basic Ed.; Ref. Upd. Deluxe Ed.; Res. Alert [Full Cov.]; Rev. Med. Vet. Entomol.; Rice Abstr.; Risk Abstr.; Sci. Cit. Index; SCISEARCH; Small Anim. Abstr. Bibliogr.; Soc. Sci. Cit. Index [Select. Cov.].

SZ/0882-9225
**PEDIATRIC REVIEWS AND COMMUNICATION.** [Pediatr. rev. commun.]. Vol. 1, No. 1 (Jan. 1987)-. Periodical. English. qt (1 volume). $271.00 (academic institutions), $423.00 (corporate institutions). Harwood Academic Publishers, PO Box 90, Reading RG1 8JL England. **Tel** 011 44 734 560080. **(Subscription address:** International Publishers Distributor at one of the following addresses: 820 Town Center Drive, Langhorne, PA 19047; or PO Box 90, Reading Berkshire RG1 8JL UK; or Kent Ridge PO Box 1180, Singapore 9111, Republic of Singapore**)** **ED** David Burman. **DD** 618. **NLM** W1; PE175E. **CODEN** PRECEA. **[CCC]. Bk Rev. Ad Acc.** available in microform.
**Ind/Abst** EMBASE; Trop. Dis. Bull.

●US/1062-8789
**PEDIATRIC ROUNDS.** (1992)-. Periodical. English. qt. Free. Pediatric Rounds, Route 513 & Trimmer Road, PO Box 458, Califon NJ 07830. **NLM** W1; PE175M.

US/0195-5926
**PEDIATRIC SOCIAL WORK.** [Pediatr. soc. work]. Vol. 1, No. 1 (Jan. 1980)-. Periodical. English. qt. $25.00. Eterna Press, PO Box 157941, Chicago IL 60615. **Tel** (312)969-0318. **NLM** W1 PE175R.
**Ind/Abst** PsycINFO; PsycLit.

GW/0179-0358
**PEDIATRIC SURGERY INTERNATIONAL.** [Pediatr. surg. int.]. **VFOAT** Pediatric Surgery. Vol. 1, No. 1 (March 1986)-. Periodical. English. Eight times a year. DM625.00. Springer-Verlag GmbH & Company KG, Heidelberger Platz 3, D 14197 Berlin Germany. **Tel** 011 49 30 8207223, FAX 011 49 30 8214091, telex 183 319 SPBLN D. **(Subscription address:** Springer Verlag New York Inc. / for North America, 44 Hartz Way, Secaucus NJ 07096.**)** **ED** A F Scharli. **NLM** W1; PE177. **CODEN** PSUIED. **[CCC]. Pr Rev.** available on microfilm and microfiche from University Microfilms International (UMI). Documents available from The Genuine Article, BIOSIS Document Express.
**Desc:** Devoted to the publication of important information from the entire spectrum of pediatric surgery. The major purpose of the journal will be to promote postgraduate training and further education in the surgery of infants and children.
**Ind/Abst** Biol. Abstr. (1989-); Curr. Contents Clin. Med.; EMBASE; Helminthol. Abstr. (1991-); Protozoolog. Abstr.; Res. Alert [Select. Cov.]; Rev. Med. Vet. Mycology; SCISEARCH.

US/0893-6218
**PEDIATRIC THERAPEUTICS AND TOXICOLOGY.** ***Title Change.*** [Pediatr. ther. toxicol.]. **VFOAT** Pediatric Therapeutics and Toxicology. Vol. 1, No. 1 (March 1987)-(1993). Periodical. English. mo. Riverpress Inc., PO Box 23, Jersey City NJ 07303. **Tel** (201)434-5073, FAX (201)434-7230. **ED** Douglas W. E. Wagner. **DD** 618. **NLM** W1; PE178. **[CCC].** Index available (published in Dec. issue). cum. index. **Bk Rev. Pr Rev. Circ:** 1,800. ***Continued by*** *Pediatric Primary Care, 1071-5711.*
**Desc:** PT&T is a monthly digest of articles from a broad literature selected for their practical clinical value in dealing with common problems in general pediatrics. Comments by leading experts put the study finding in perspective and updates from subspecialty meetings offer clinical pearls useful in daily practice.

US
**PEDIATRIC THERAPY.** 1st- Ed.; 1964-. Periodical. English. ir. Mosby Year Book Inc., 11830 Westline Industrial Drive, St Louis MO 63146. **Tel** (800)325-4177, (314)872-8370, FAX (314)432-1380, telex 44-2402. **UDC** 616-053.2-085.

US/0479-785X
**PEDIATRIC WORLD.** [Pediatr. world]. **Added/Corp** Ross Laboratories. Vol. 1 (Jan. 1963)-. Periodical. English. mo. Free. Ross Laboratories, 625 Cleveland Avenue, Columbus OH 43216. **Tel** (614)227-3333. **DD** 618. **NLM** W1 PE179.

SZ/0300-1245
**PEDIATRICIAN.** ***Ceased.*** [Pediatrician]. (Oct. 1985)-Vol. 18, No. 4 (1991). Academic Scholarly Publication. English. qt. S. Karger AG, Allschwilerstrasse 10, PO Box - Postfach - Case Postale, CH-4009 Basel Switzerland. **Tel** 011 41 61 306-1111, FAX 011 41 61 306-1234, telex CH 962 652. **ED** J M Cruse, R E Lewis, M I Greene, G V Sherbet, C Sorg. **UDC** 616-053.2. **NLM** W1; PE179T. **CODEN** PEDIEY. **[CCC].** Documents available from BIOSIS Document Express, CASDDS. ***Continues*** *Paediatrician, 0300-1245.*
**Desc:** Gives pediatricians and family practitioners a unique link to international experience in the management of situations frequently encountered in everyday practice.
**Ind/Abst** Biol. Abstr. (1985-); Chem. Abstr. (1985-); Dev. Med. Child Neurol.; EMBASE; Index Med. (1985-); Life Sci. Collect. (1985-); Psychol. Abstr. (1988-); PsycINFO; PsycLit.

US/0198-6341
**PEDIATRICS DIGEST (1979).** (PEDIATRICS DIGEST.). V. 21, No. 8/9- Aug./Sept. 1979-. English. mo. $27.50. Medical Digest, 444 Frontage Road, PO Box 8021, Northfield IL 60093. **UDC** 616-053.2. **NLM** W1 PE193. ***Continues*** *Journal of Continuing Education in Pediatrics, 0160-7766.*

SP/0210-5721
**PEDIATRICS. EDICION ESPANOLA.** [Pediatrics, Ed. esp.]. (1976)-. Periodical. Spanish. mo. $78.00. Ediciones Doyma SA, Travesera de Gracia 17 21, 08021 Barcelona Spain. **Tel** 011 34 3 2000711, 011 34 3 4145706, FAX 011 34 3 2091136, telex 51964 INK E. **UDC** 616-053.2. **[CCC]. Pr Rev.**

IT/1120-7507
**PEDIATRICS EDIZIONE ITALIANA.** [Pediatrics Ed. ital.]. (1989)-. Periodical. Italian. bm (6 issues). L90000 Italy; L120000 other. Editrice CSH Srl, Casella Postale 10046, 20111 Milan Italy. **Tel** 011 39 2 58103565. **UDC** 616.

US/0031-4005
**PEDIATRICS (EVANSTON).** (PEDIATRICS.). [Pediatrics]. **Added/Corp** American Academy of Pediatrics. Vol. 1 (Jan. 1948)-. Academic Scholarly Publication. English (summaries and/or abstracts in Spanish). mo. $160.00 US, $175.00 other (institutions); $95.00 US, $110.00 other (individuals). American Academy of Pediatrics, 141 Northwest Point Boulevard, Elk Grove Village IL 60009-0927. **Tel** (708)981-7903, FAX (708)228-5088. **ED** Jerold Lucey. **LC** RJ1; .A4533. **DD** 618.9205. **NLM** W1 PE191. **CODEN** PEDIAU. **[CCC].** Index available. **Ad Acc**, **Adv Mgr Tel** (708)981-7902. **Pr Rev. Circ:** 52,000. available on microfilm and microfiche from University Microfilms International (UMI); available on CD-ROM. Documents available from The Genuine Article, BIOSIS Document Express, CASDDS.
**Desc:** Officially from the American Academy of Pediatrics. A professional publication edited for pediatricians and those concerned with child health and development. Each issue contains papers on original research and special features or review articles in the field of pediatrics as broadly defined.
**Ind/Abst** Abr. Index Med.; AGRICOLA [Select. Cov.]; Annals Behav. Med.; Arts Humanit. Citation Index [Select. Cov.]; Biol. Abstr.; Chem. Abstr.; Comb. Cumul. Index Pediatr.; CSA Neuro. Abstr.; Cumul. Index Nurs. Allied Health Lit.; Curr. Aware. Biol. Sci., CABS; Curr. Contents Clin. Med.; Curr. Contents Life Sci.; EMBASE; Energy Res. Abstr.; Except. Child Educ. Resour.; Health Devices Alerts; Health Index (1989-); Health Period. Database; Health Ref. Cent. (Jan. 1989-) [Full Cov.]; Index Med.; Int. Nurs. Index; Int. Pharm. Abstr.; J. Watch (199?-); Med. Abstr. Newsl.; Nutr. Abstr. Rev., Ser. A, Hum. Exp.; Life Sci. Collect.; PESTDOC; Physic. Medline Plus; Protozoolog. Abstr.; Res. Alert [Full Cov.]; Rev. Med. Vet. Entomol.; Sci. Cit. Index; SCISEARCH; Soc. Sci. Cit. Index [Select. Cov.]; Soc. Work Abstr. (?-?); SPORT Discus; SportSearch; Sug. Indus. Abstr.; Trop. Dis. Bull.; Virol. AIDS Abstr.

US/0730-6725
**PEDIATRICS FOR PARENTS.** (PEDIATRICS FOR PARENTS : THE MONTHLY NEWSLETTER FOR CARING PARENTS.). (19??)-. Periodical. English. mo (July/Aug issues combined). $18.00 (one year), $30.00 (two year), $45.00 (three year). Pediatrics for Parents, PO Box 1069, Bangor ME 04402-1069. **Tel** (207)942-7334, FAX (207)947-3134. **ED** Richard J. Sagall, (207)942-6212. Index available. **Bk Rev. Circ:** 1,000. available on an online database (file 149/Full-Text) from DIALOG.
**Desc:** Pediatric and general medical articles for parents and others who care for children.
**Ind/Abst** Acad. Abstr. Full Text Elite (Jan. 1992-); Acad. Abstr. (Jan. 1992-); Acad. Search (Jan. 1992-); Health Index (1989-); Health Period. Database; Health Ref. Cent. (Jan. 1989-) [Full Cov.]; Health Source (Jan. 1992-); INFO-SOUTH Abstr.; Mag. Search.

US/0271-1346
**PEDIATRICS (GLENDALE, CALIF.).** (PEDIATRICS [SOUND RECORDING].). [Pediatri.]. **Added/Corp** Audio-Digest Foundation. **VFOAT** Audio-Digest Pediatrics; Audio Digest Pediatrics. (1955)-. Periodical. English. sm. $179.76 US; $202.80 Canada; $247.44 other (audiocassette). Audio-Digest Foundation, 1577 Chevy Chase Drive, Glendale CA 91206. **Tel** (213)245-8505, (800)423-2308, FAX (818)240-7379. **DD** 618. **NLM** W1 AU201E.

US/0191-9601
**PEDIATRICS IN REVIEW.** (PEDIATRICS IN REVIEW / AMERICAN ACADEMY OF PEDIATRICS.). [Pediatr. rev.]. **Added/Corp** American Academy of Pediatrics. Vol. 1, No. 1 (July 1979)-. Periodical. English. mo. $160.00 (non-members and institutions), $130.00 (AAP fellows), $105.00 (AAP candidate fellows). American Academy of Pediatrics, 141 Northwest Point Boulevard, Elk Grove Village IL 60009-0927. **Tel** (708)981-7903, FAX (708)228-5088. **ED** Robert J. Haggerty. **DD** 618. **NLM** W1 PE193H. cum. index. **Circ:** 24,000. available on microfilm and microfiche from University Microfilms International (UMI).
**Desc:** Contains timely review articles related to the practice of pediatric medicine. Also contains editorials and abstracts.
**Ind/Abst** Comb. Cumul. Index Pediatr.; Index Med. (Vol. 7, No. 7, 1986-); Trop. Dis. Bull.

US/0079-0400
**PEDIATRICS (NEW YORK, N.Y.).** (PEDIATRICS.). [Pediatrics]. (19??)-. Periodical. English. Medical World News, 299 Park Avenue, New York NY 10017. **LC** RJ1; .P29. **DD** 618.9/2/0005.

FR/0031-4021
**PEDIATRIE.** ***Title Change.*** [Pediatrie]. Vol. 1 (1912)-(199?). Academic Scholarly Publication. French (summaries and/or abstracts in English). Twelve times a year (1 volume). Editions Scientifique Elsevier, 141 rue de Javel, 75747 Paris Cedex 15 France. **Tel** 011 33 1 47 07 11 22, FAX 011 33 1 43 36 80 93. **ED** L David and P G Chatelain. **UDC** 616-053.2. **NLM** W1 PE203. **CODEN** PEDRAN. **[CCC].** Index available. cum. index. **Bk Rev. Ad Acc. Circ:** 1,500 (ctrl). available on microfilm and microfiche from University Microfilms International (UMI). Documents available from The Genuine Article, BIOSIS Document Express, CASDDS. ***Merged with*** *Archives Francaises de Pediatrie* ***to form*** *Archives de Pediatrie.*
**Desc:** The major advances which have occurred over the past ten years have emphasized the necessity for a French publication which could complement scientific information and teaching while remaining practical and comprehensive and being concise and clear, a link between research, the hospital and everyday practice.
**Ind/Abst** Biol. Abstr.; Chem. Abstr. (1912-1984); Curr. Contents Clin. Med.; Dairy Sci. Abstr.; Dev. Med. Child Neurol.; EMBASE; Helminthol. Abstr. (1991-); Index Med.; Index Vet.; Protozoolog. Abstr.; Res. Alert [Select. Cov.]; Rev. Med. Vet. Entomol.; SCISEARCH; Small Anim. Abstr. Bibliogr.; Soc. Sci. Cit. Index [Select. Cov.]; SportSearch.

FR/0993-9717
**PEDIATRIE PRATIQUE PARIS.** (PEDIATRIE PRATIQUE.). (1988)-. Periodical. French. mo (10 issues). 244.86F France; 250.00F other. Len Medical, 48 Bis Avenue Kleber, F-75116 Paris France. **Tel** 011 33 1 47550606. **UDC** 616.053.2.

RM/1220-580X
**PEDIATRIE / UNIUNEA SOCIETATILOR DE STIINTE MEDICALE DIN ROMANIA.** ***Title Change.*** **Added/Corp** Uniunea Societatilor de Stiinte Medicale. Societatea de Pediatrie (Romania). **VFOAT** Pediatria. Vol. 39, 2 (Apr.-June 1990)-Vol. 41, No. 4 (Oct.-Dec. 1992). Periodical. Romanian (summaries and/or abstracts in English and Russian; table of contents in English and Russian). qt. **(Subscription address:** Rompresfilatelia, PO Box 12 201, Bucharest Romania.**) NLM** W1; PE202. ***Continues*** *Revista de Pediatrie, Obstetrica si Ginecologie. Pediatria, 0303-8416.* ***Continued by*** *Pediatria (Bucharest, Romania : 1993).*
**Ind/Abst** EMBASE [Select. Cov.].

RU/0031-403X
**PEDIATRIJA.** (PEDIATRIIA.). [Pediatrija]. **Added/Corp** Russian S.F.S.R. Narodnyi Komissariat Zdravookhraneniia. Soviet Union. Narodnyi Komissariat Zdravookhraneniia. Soviet Union. Ministerstvo Zdravookhraneniia. Vsesoiuznoe Nauchnoe Obshchestvo Detskikh Vrachei (Soviet Union). (1937)-. Periodical. Russian (summaries and/or abstracts in English and French). Six times a year. $69.95. Izdatelstvo Meditsina / Russian Academy of Medical Sciences, Ulitsa Solyanka 14, 109801 Moscow Russia. **Tel** 011 95 297-05-04. **(Subscription address:** East View Publications Inc., 3020 Harbor Lane North, Suite 110, Minneapolis MN 55447.**) NLM** W1 PE208. **CODEN** PEDTAT. Documents available from BIOSIS Document Express, CASDDS. ***Continues*** *Sovetskaia Pediatriia, 0301-5424.*
**Ind/Abst** Biol. Abstr.; Chem. Abstr. (1937-1983); EMBASE [Select. Cov.]; Index Med.; Life Sci. Collect.

BU/0479-7876
**PEDIATRIJA (SOFIA).** (PEDIATRIIA / PEDIATRIA.). [Pediatrija]. **Added/Corp** Bulgaria. Ministerstvo no Narodnoto Zdrave i Sotsialnite Grizhi. **VFOAT** Pediatria. Vol. 1 (1962)-. Academic Scholarly Publication. Bulgarian (summaries and/or abstracts in English and Russian). bm (6 issues). 24lv. Izdatelstvo Meditsina i Fizkultura, 11 Pl. Slaveikov, Sofiia Bulgaria. **(Subscription address:** Hemus Foreign Trade Organization, 6 Tzar Osvoboditel Boulevard, 1000 Sofia Bulgaria.**) ED** Sh. Ninjo. **NLM** W1 PE227. **CODEN** PDTAAB. **Circ:** 1,950. Documents available from CASDDS.
**Ind/Abst** Chem. Abstr. (1962-1983); Dev. Med. Child Neurol.; EMBASE [Select. Cov.]; Index Med.; SportSearch.

TU/1016-5142
**PEDIATRIK CERRAHI DERGISI.** **VFOAT** Pediatric Surgery. (1987)-. Turkish. Logos Yayincilik A.S., Altan Erbulak Sok., Birlik Apt. No. 7/6, Mecidiyekoy 80300, Istanbul Turkey.
**Ind/Abst** EMBASE.

SZ/0091-2921
**PERSPECTIVES IN PEDIATRIC PATHOLOGY.** [Perspect. pediatr. pathol.]. Vol. 1 (1973)-. Monographic series. English. an. 230.00F (approx. per volume). S. Karger AG, Allschwilerstrasse 10, PO Box - Postfach - Case Postale, CH-4009 Basel Switzerland. **Tel** 011 41 61 306-1111, FAX 011 41 61 306-1234, telex CH 962 652. **ED** H. S. Rosenberg and J. Bernstein. **LC** RJ49; .P45. **DD** 618.9/2/00705. **NLM** W1 PE871D. **CODEN** PPEPDY. **[CCC].** Documents available from BIOSIS Document Express.
**Desc:** Provides a critical review of current topics in pediatric medicine viewed from the perspective of the pathologist. The contents reflect the general nature of pediatric pathology, emphasizing etiology, pathogenesis, diagnostic criteria, pathologic physiology, and clinical correlations. Individual reports amalgamate information from many disciplines including embryology, anatomy, physiology, immunology, teratology, microbiology, cell biology, and genetics. Focusing on normal and abnormal development and disease in the placenta, embryo, fetus, neonate, infant and child, this series highlights the similarities to and differences from disease in adult life.
**Ind/Abst** Biol. Abstr. (1986-); Energy Res. Abstr. (Aug. 1982-); Index Med.; Ref. Upd. Deluxe Ed.; SportSearch.

US/0194-2638
**PHYSICAL & OCCUPATIONAL THERAPY IN PEDIATRICS.** **See** Physical Therapy.

US/8755-5476
**POCKETBOOK OF PEDIATRIC ANTIMICROBIAL THERAPY.** **See** Pharmacy and Pharmacology.

US
**PRACTICAL PEDIATRICS.** Vol. 1, (1981)-. English. **ED** Richard H. Rapkin. **NLM** ZWS 100 P894.

US/0896-5455
**PRACTICAL REVIEWS IN PEDIATRICS.** (PRACTICAL REVIEWS IN PEDIATRICS [SOUND RECORDING].). [Pract. rev. pediatr.]. **Added/Corp** Educational Reviews, Inc. Albert Einstein College of Medicine. Montefiore Medical Center. **VFOAT** Practical Reviews. (197?)-. Periodical. English. mo. $175.00 Physicians/Dentists; $125.00 Residents. Educational Reviews Inc., 6801 Cahaba Valley Road, Birmingham AL 35242. **Tel** (205)991-5188, (800)633-4743, FAX (205)995-1926. **DD** 618.

UK
**PREVENTIVE PEDIATRICS.** ***Ceased.*** Vol. 1, No. 1 (1988)-(1992). Periodical. English. qt. Freund Publishing House Ltd, PO Box 35010, 61 Nachmani Street, Tel Aviv 61350 Israel. **Tel** 011 972 3 5662925, FAX 011 972 3 5605335. **NLM** W1; PR507WJ. **CODEN** PPEDEX.

FR
**PROCEEDINGS - ASSOCIATION OF EUROPEAN PAEDIATRIC CARDIOLOGISTS.** **Main/Corp** Association of European Paediatric Cardiologists. **VFOAT** Bulletin de

# Medical Science and Technology —Pediatrics

l'Association des Cardiologues Pediatres Europeens. No. 1- 1966?-. Proceedings. English (French). **UDC** 616.11-089-053.2.

SZ/0251-5601
**PROGRES EN NEONATOLOGIE / JOURNEES NATIONALES DE NEONATOLOGIE. Main/Conf** Journees Nationales de Neonatologie. Vol. 1 (1981)-. French (summaries and/or abstracts in English). an. 150.00F (approx. per volume). S. Karger AG, Allschwilerstrasse 10, PO Box - Postfach - Case Postale, CH-4009 Basel Switzerland. **Tel** 011 41 61 306-1111, **FAX** 011 41 61 306-1234, telex CH 962 652. **ED** J. P. Relier. **NLM** W3; JO739. Documents available from BIOSIS Document Express.
**Ind/Abst** Biol. Abstr.

●US/1058-9813
**PROGRESS IN PEDIATRIC CARDIOLOGY. See** Medical Science and Technology-Cardiology.

US/0146-1540
**PROGRESS IN PEDIATRIC HEMATOLOGY/ONCOLOGY. See** Medical Science and Technology-Hematology.

GW/0079-6654
**PROGRESS IN PEDIATRIC SURGERY.** [Progr. pediatr. surg.]. 1- 1970-. English (summaries and/or abstracts in French and German). $117.90. Springer-Verlag GmbH & Company KG, Heidelberger Platz 3, D 14197 Berlin Germany. **Tel** 011 49 30 8207223, **FAX** 011 49 30 8214091, telex 183 319 SPBLN D. **(Subscription address:** Springer Verlag New York Inc. / for North America, 44 Hartz Way, Secaucus NJ 07096.) **UDC** 616-089-053.2. **NLM** W1 PR677KA. **CODEN** PPDSAZ. **[CCC]**. Documents available from BIOSIS Document Express.
**Desc:** Designed to give up-to-date, in-depth information on individual topics from the field of pediatric surgery and its neighboring disciplines.
**Ind/Abst** Biol. Abstr.; Index Med.

IT/0301-3642
**PROSPETTIVE IN PEDIATRIA.** Vol. 1 (Jan./March 1971)-. Periodical. Italian. Four times a year. L72000 Italy; L80000 others. Centro Informazione Sanitaria, Via San Siro 1, 20149 Milan Italy. **Tel** 011 39 2 4694542.

IT
**QUADERNI DI PSICOTERAPIA INFANTILE.** Italian. Twice a year. L60.000 Italy; $90.00 other. Edizioni Borla, Via delle Fornaci 50, 00165 Rome, Italy. **Tel** 011 39 6 39376728.

UK/0308-4906
**RECENT ADVANCES IN PAEDIATRIC SURGERY.** No. 1-. English. Churchill Livingstone, 1-3 Baxter's Place, Leith Walk, Edinburgh EH1 3AF Scotland. **Tel** 011 44 31 556 2424, **FAX** 011 44 31 558 1278, telex 727511. **(Subscription address:** US/ Churchill Livingstone, Fulfillment Office, PO Box 11318, Birmingham, AL 35202) **ED** A W Wilkinson. **UDC** 616-089-053.2. **NLM** W1 RE105X.

UK/0309-0140
**RECENT ADVANCES IN PAEDIATRICS.** [Recent. adv. paediatr.]. (1954)-. English. ir (published every 3 to 5). price varies per volume. Churchill Livingstone, 1-3 Baxter's Place, Leith Walk, Edinburgh EH1 3AF Scotland. **Tel** 011 44 31 556 2424, **FAX** 011 44 31 558 1278, telex 727511. **(Subscription address:** Churchill Livingstone / US, 5 S 250 Frontenac Road, Naperville IL 60563.) **NLM** W1 RE105XF.

US/1050-964X
**REPORT ON PEDIATRIC INFECTIOUS DISEASES, THE. See** Medical Science and Technology-Communicable Diseases.

CL/0370-4106
**REVISTA CHILENA DE PEDIATRIA.** [Rev. Chil. pediatr.]. **Added/Corp** Sociedad Chilena de Pediatria. Vol. 1 (Jan. 1930)-. Academic Scholarly Publication. Spanish (summaries and/or abstracts in Portuguese, English and German). Six times a year (Feb., Apr., June, Aug., Oct., Dec.). $82.00 (one year); $152.00 (two years); $228.00 (three years). Sociedad Chilena de Pediatria, Av Eliodoro Yanez 1984, Department 405, Casilla 16257 Correo 9, Santiago Chile. **Tel** (02) 225 4393, **FAX** (02) 223-2351. **ED** Carlos Toro A. **NLM** W1 RE351E. Index available. cum. index. **Bk Rev. Ad Acc. Pr Rev. Circ:** 1,200 (ctrl). available on microfilm from University Microfilms International (UMI).
**Desc:** Basic sciences, clinical, educational, academic and public health aspects of pediatric medicine and health care. Original publications and reviews.
**Ind/Abst** EMBASE [Select. Cov.]; Index Med.

CU/0034-7531
**REVISTA CUBANA DE PEDIATRIA.** (1946)-. Periodical. Spanish (summaries and/or abstracts in English, French and Russian). bm. Ediciones Cubanas, Obispo 527, Altos ESQ Bernaza, CP 10100 Havana Cuba. **Tel** 011 632980, 631942, **FAX** 011 631011, telex 512337, 6540. **UDC** 613.95.
**Ind/Abst** EMBASE [Select. Cov.]; Trop. Dis. Bull.

IT/0392-4416
**REVISTA DE PEDIATRIA PREVENTIVA E SOCIALE. NIPIOLOGIA.** (RIVISTA DI PEDIATRIA PREVENTIVA E SOCIALE, NIPIOLOGIA : ORGANO UFFICIALE TRIMESTRALE SOCIETA ITALIANA DI PEDIATRIA PREVENTIVA E SOCIALE, NIPIOLOGIA.). [Riv. pediatr. prev. soc., Nipiol.]. **Added/Corp** Societa Italiana di Pediatria Preventiva e Sociale, Nipiologia. **VFOAT** Pediatria Preventiva e Sociale, Nipiologia. Vol. 30, No. 1 (Jan./March 1980)-. Periodical. Italian (summaries and/or abstracts in English). qt. $90.00 (individuals), $140.00 (institutions). Edizioni Minerva Medica, Corso Bramante 83-85, 10126 Turin Italy. **Tel** 011 39 11 678282, **FAX** 011 39 11 674502. **ED** E Memsi. **NLM** W1 RI608P. **Bk Rev. Ad Acc. Continues** Minerva Nipiologica.
**Desc:** Journal addressed to practitioners and specialists in social pediatrics in Italy and abroad. It deals with topics in scientific practice and research.

AG/0521-517X
**REVISTA DEL HOSPITAL DE NINOS (BUENOS AIRES).** [Rev. Hosp. Ninos]. V. 1- (No. 1- ); 1959-. Academic Scholarly Publication. Spanish (Spanish). ir. Free. Hospital del Ninos, Apartado 4087, Zona 5, Panama Republica de Panama. **Tel** 011 507 251 546. **UDC** 616-053.2. **NLM** W1 RE51.
**Ind/Abst** EMBASE.

SP/0034-947X
**REVISTA ESPANOLA DE PEDIATRIA.** [Rev. esp. pediatr.]. (1945)-. Academic Scholarly Publication. Spanish. Six times a year. $37.32 Spaing, $63.00 Europe; $73.00 others. Editorial Garsi SA, Juan Bravo 46, 28006 Madrid, Spain. **Tel** 011 34 1 4021212, telex 98358 GARSI E. **NLM** W1 RE547. **CODEN** REPEAW. **[CCC]**. Documents available from BIOSIS Document Express, CASDDS.
**Ind/Abst** Biol. Abstr.; Chem. Abstr. (1945-1981); Dairy Sci. Abstr.; EMBASE; Indice Med. Esp.; Nutr. Abstr. Rev., Ser. A, Hum. Exp.

MX/0035-0052
**REVISTA MEXICANA DE PEDIATRIA.** (1939)-. Academic Scholarly Publication. Spanish. bm. $50.00. Mundo Medico SA, Ejercicto Nacional 381, 11520 Mexico DF Mexico. **Tel** 011 52 5 2038111. **ED** Ignacio Avila Cisneros. Index available. cum. index. **Bk Rev. Ad Acc. Circ:** 10,000 (ctrl).
**Desc:** Technical articles from Mexican doctors and scientists covering all aspects of pediatrics, including case histories, original research studies, diagnostics and pharmacology. Each number centers on a theme which it studies.
**Ind/Abst** EMBASE [Select. Cov.].

FR
**REVUE DU PEDIATRE.** (1988)-. Periodical. French. Eight times a year. $146.00. Masson Editeur, Box Postale 22, 41353 Vineuil 16 France. **Tel** 011 33 54 438994. **NLM** W1; RE838J.

FR
**REVUE INTERNATIONALE DE PEDIATRIE.** French. mo. 280.00F students, 295.00F other. Galliena Promotion, 58 A rue du Dessous des Berges, 75013 Paris France. **Tel** 011 33 1 45849766.

IT
**RIVISTA DI INFETTIVOLOGIA PEDIATRICA.** (19??)-. Italian. qt. L110000. Congress Studio, V Cappuccio 19, 20123 Milan Italy. **Tel** 011 39 2 8053435.

●RU
**ROSSIISKII VESTNIK PERINATOLOGII I PEDIATRII / MINISTERSTVO ZDRAVOOKHRANENIIA ROSSIISKOI FEDERATSII, MOSKOVSKII NII PEDIATRII I DETSKOI KHIRURGII, MOSKOVSKII OBLASTNOI NII AKUSHERSTVA I GINEKOLOGII.** **Added/Corp** Russia (Federation). Ministerstvo Zdravookhraneniia. Russia (Federation). Ministerstvo Zdravookhraneniia i Meditsinskoi Promyshlennosti. Moskovskii NII Pediatrii i Detskoi Khirurgii. Moskovskii Oblastnoi NII Akusherstva i Ginekologii. (1993)-. Periodical. Russian (table of contents in English). bm. Izdatelstvo Meditsina / Russian Academy of Medical Sciences, Ulitsa Solyanka 14, 109801 Moscow Russia. **Tel** 011 95 297-05-04. **Continues** Materinstvo i Detstvo, 0869-2114.

GW/0933-3525
**SCHRIFTENREIHE DES DEUTSCHEN KINDERHILFSWERKES E.V.** (SCHRIFTENREIHE DES DEUTCHEN KINDERHILFSWERKES E.V. / HERAUSGEBER, DEUTSCHES KINDERHILFSWERK E.V. IN ZUSAMMENARBEIT MIT DEM AKTIONSKOMITEE KIND IM KRANKENHAUS E.V.). [Schr.reihe Dtsch. Kinderhilfsw. e.V.]. **Added/Corp** Deutsches Kinderhilfswerk. Aktionskomitee Kind im Krankenhaus (Germany). (198?)-. Monographic series. German. ir. Price varies per volume. **NLM** W1; SC329FC. **Continues** Schriftenreihe des Kinderhilfswerkes E.V.

●NE/0925-6164
**SCREENING: JOURNAL OF THE INTERNATIONAL SOCIETY OF NEONATAL SCREENING. See** Medical Science and Technology-Gynecology and Obstetrics.

CN/1188-0244
**SEMINARS IN PEDIATRIC GASTROENTEROLOGY AND NUTRITION.** [Semin. pediatr. gastroenterol. nutr.]. **Added/Corp** Harvard Medical School. Combined Program in Pediatric Gastroenterology and Nutrition. Children's Hospital (Boston, Mass.) Massachusetts General Hospital. **VFOAT** Pediatric Gastroenterology and Nutrition. Vol. 1, No. 1 (1990)-. Periodical. English. qt. $78.00 (institutions), $52.00 (individuals) US & Canada; $105.00 (institutions), $79.00 (individuals) other. Decker Periodicals Publishing Inc, PO Box 620, Station A, Hamilton Ontario L8N 3K7 Canada. **Tel** (416)522-7017, (800) 568-7281, **FAX** (416)522-7839. **DD** 618.92. **NLM** W1; SE489EJ.

US/1045-1870
**SEMINARS IN PEDIATRIC INFECTIOUS DISEASES. See** Medical Science and Technology-Communicable Diseases.

●US/1055-8586
**SEMINARS IN PEDIATRIC SURGERY. See** Medical Science and Technology-Surgery.

JA/0385-6313
**SHONI GEKA.** (SHONI GEKA. JAPANESE JOURNAL OF PEDIATRIC SURGERY.). [Shoni geka]. **VFOAT** Japanese Journal of Pediatric Surgery. Vol. 9 (Jan. 1977)-. Periodical. Japanese. Twelve times a year. ¥40200. Tokyo Igaku Sha Company, 35 4 3 Chome Hongo Buwkyo Ku, Tokyo Japan. **Tel** 011 81 3 38114119. **ED** Keijiro Suruga. **NLM** W1 SH52G. **Bk Rev. Ad Acc. Circ:** 5,000 (ctrl). **Continues in part** Shoni Geka, Naika.
**Desc:** Journal on neonatal surgery for junior doctors and nurses.
**Ind/Abst** Energy Res. Abstr. (Sept. 1980-).

JA/0385-6305
**SHONI NAIKA.** (SHONI NAIKA. JAPANESE JOURNAL OF PEDIATRIC MEDICINE.). [Shoni naika]. **VFOAT** Japanese Journal of Pediatric Medicine. Vol. 9 (Jan. 1977)-. Periodical. Japanese. mo. $382.00. Tokyo Igaku Sha Company, 35 4 3 Chome Hongo Buwkyo Ku, Tokyo Japan. **Tel** 011 81 3 38114119. **(Subscription address:** Kyowa Book Company Inc., 1-38 Kanda Jinbo-Cho, Chiyoda-Ku Tokyo 101, Japan) **NLM** W1 SH529. **Continues in part** Shoni Geka, Naika.
**Ind/Abst** Energy Res. Abstr. (Sept. 1980-).

JA/0003-4495
**SHONIKA KIYO.** (SHONIKA KIYO. ANNALS OF PEDIATRICS. ANNALES PAEDIATRICI JAPONICI.). [Shonika kiyo]. **Added/Corp** Kyoto Daigaku. Igakubu. Shonika Kyoshitsu. **VFOAT** Annales Paediatrici Japonici; Annals of Pediatrics. Vol. 1 (1955)-. Periodical. Japanese (summaries and/or abstracts in English; table of contents in English). qt. Shonika Kiyo Kankokai, (Soc. for the Publication of Annales Paediatrici Japondici), c/o Kyoto Daigaku Igakubu Shoni, Kagaku Kyoshitu, 53, Shogoin, Kawaracho, Sakyoku, Kyotoshi, Kyotofu 606, Japan. **NLM** W1 SH5416. **CODEN** SHKIAH. Documents available from CASDDS. **Supersedes** Nyujigaku Zasshi. ( Oriental Journal of Diseases of Infants.).
**Ind/Abst** Chem. Abstr.

US
**SILVER, KEMPE, BRUYN & FULGINITI'S HANDBOOK OF PEDIATRICS. VFOAT** Silver, Kempe, Bruyn, and Fulginiti's Handbook of Pediatrics; Handbook of Pediatrics. 16th Ed. (1991)-. English (Italian, Portuguese and Spanish). ir. $23.95 (latest edition). Appleton Century Crofts, Prentice Hall, 200 Old Tappan Road, Old Tappan NJ 07675. **Tel** (201)767-5188, (800)922-0579. **LC** RJ48; .S64. **NLM** WS 39; S587. **Continues** Handbook of Pediatrics, 0440-1921.

KO
**SOAKWA. VFOAT** Journal of the Korean Pediatric Association. Periodical. Korean (summaries and/or abstracts in English). 28 Yongon-dong, Chongno-ku, Seoul Korea. **LC** RJ1; .S48. **UDC** 616-053.2. **NLM** W1 SO101.

GW/0171-9327
**SOZIALPAEDIATRIE IN PRAXIS UND KLINIK. Title Change. Added/Corp** Deutsche Gesellschaft fuer Sozialpaediatrie. Vol. 1-15. (Sept. 1979)-(19??). Periodical. German (summaries and/or abstracts in English). mo. Verlag Kirchheim & Company GmbH, Postfach 2524, D 55015 Mainz Germany. **Tel** 011 49 6131 960700, **FAX** 011 49 6131 638843. **NLM** W1 SO999Q. **CODEN** SPKLEI. **Merged with** Sozialpaediatrie und Kinderaerztliche Praxis.

## Medical Science and Technology —Pediatrics

**GW**
**SOZIALPAEDIATRIE UND KINDERAERZTLICHE PRAXIS.** (19??)-. English. ir. DM129.18 Germany; DM150.00. Verlag Kirchheim & Company GmbH, Postfach 2524, D 55015 Mainz Germany. **Tel** 011 49 6131 960700, FAX 011 49 6131 638843. *Continues Sozialpaediatries in Praxis und Klinik.*

**US/0735-6897**
**THEORY AND RESEARCH IN BEHAVIORAL PEDIATRICS.** [Theory res. behav. pediatr.]. Vol. 1 (1982)-. Monographic series. English. ir. Price varies per volume. Plenum Press, 233 Spring Street, New York NY 10013-1578. **Tel** (212)620-8000, (800)221-9369, FAX (212)463-0742, (212)807-1047, telex 23/421139. **ED** Hiram E. Fitzgerald, Barry M. Lester, and Michael W. Yogman. **LC** RJ131; .T54. **DD** 618.92/02/9. **NLM** W1 TH123Y (P).

**NE/0376-7442**
**TIJDSCHRIFT VOOR KINDERGENEESKUNDE.** [Tijdschr. kindergeneeskd.]. Vol. 44 (Feb. 1976)-. Academic Scholarly Publication. Dutch (summaries and/or abstracts in English). bm (6 issues). Fl98.00. Bohn Stafleu Van Loghum BV, Postbus 246, 3990 GA Houten Netherlands. **Tel** 011 31 3403 95782. **(Subscription address:** Intermedia BV, Postbus 4, 2400 MA Alphen Rijn Netherlands.) **NLM** W1 TI654N. **CODEN** TIKID4. Documents available from CASDDS. *Continues Maandschrift voor Kindetgeneeskunde.*
  **Ind/Abst** Chem. Abstr.; EMBASE [Select. Cov.]; Index Med.; Life Sci. Collect.

**US/0892-0435**
**TOPICS IN PEDIATRICS. / MINNEAPOLIS CHILDREN'S HEALTH CENTER.** [Top. pediatr.]. **Added/Corp** Minneapolis Children's Health Center. Vol. 1, No. 1 (Spring 1982)-. Periodical. English. Three times a year. Free. Minneapolis Child Medical Center, 2525 Chicago Avenue South, Minneapolis MN 55404. **Tel** (612)863-6611, FAX (612)863-6674. **ED** Liz Simpson. **DD** 618. **NLM** W1; TO54FH. Index available. cum. index. **Circ**: 11,000.
  **Desc:** Articles by pediatric health care professionals that contain practical, clinical information especially useful for primary practitioners.

**TU/0041-4301**
**TURKISH JOURNAL OF PEDIATRICS, THE.** [Turk. j. pediatr.]. **Added/Corp** Cocuk Saglg B S.A. Enstitusu. Hacettepe Cocuk Hastanesi, Ankara. Hacettepe Tp Merkezi, Ankara. Hacettepe Universitesi. Cocuk Saglg Enstitusu. Vol. 1, (1958)-. Academic Scholarly Publication. English. Four times a year (Mar., July, Sept., Dec.). $50.00. Turkish Journal of Pediatrics, P K 66 Samanpazari, 06240 Ankara Turkey. **Tel** 011 90 4 3112253, FAX 011 90 4 3112253, telex 42999. **ED** Dr. Keriman Tinaztepe. **NLM** W1 TU973. Index available (Bound in 4th iss. (Dec)). cum. index. **Bk Rev**. **Pr Rev**. **Circ**: 2,000. available on microfilm and microfiche from University Microfilms International (UMI). Documents available from The Genuine Article.
  **Desc:** General pediatrics-clinical and research.
  **Ind/Abst** Curr. Contents Clin. Med.; EMBASE [Select. Cov.]; Index Med.; Res. Alert [Select. Cov.]; Trop. Dis. Bull.

**US/0160-676X**
**U.S. FACILITIES AND PROGRAMS FOR CHILDREN WITH SEVERE MENTAL ILLNESSES : DIRECTORY.** **VAT** United States Facilities and Programs for Children with Severe Mental Illnesses. Directory. English. US Department of Health & Human Services / Public Health Service, 200 Independence Avenue SW, Room 716G, Washington DC 20201. **Tel** (202)690-6867, FAX (202)690-6274. **LC** RJ111; .U44. **DD** 362.7/8/20973. **UDC** 616-089-053.2(73).

**RU/0137-0162**
**VOPROSY AKUSHERSTVA I PEDIATRII.** Vol. 1 (1956)-. Russian. **NLM** W1 VO6061H.

**US/0892-614X**
**WORLD MEDICAL REVIEWS IN PERINATOLOGY.** [World med. rev. perinatal.]. (198?)-. Periodical. English. Twelve times a year. $60.00 (individuals), $70.00 (physicians), $80.00 (institutons). World Medical Reviews Corporation, PO Box 639, Tenafly NJ 07670. **Tel** (201)567-1629. **ED** Jacqueline Seaver. **DD** 618.
  **Desc:** Brief news summaries of important papers in scientific literature bearing on obstetrics and the neonate.

**US/0084-3954**
**YEAR BOOK OF PEDIATRICS, THE.** [Year b. pediatr.]. **VFOAT** Yearbook of Pediatrics. (1933)-. English (Spanish). an. $59.95. Mosby Year Book Inc., 11830 Westline Industrial Drive, St Louis MO 63146. **Tel** (800)325-4177, (314)872-8370, FAX (314)432-1380, telex 44-2402. **ED** Frank A Oski and James A Stockman. **LC** RJ16; .Y4. **NLM** W1 YE297. **[CCC]**. cum. index. *Continues Pediatrics.*
  **Ind/Abst** Chicano Index; Microbiol. Abstr. Sect. B (19??-19??).

**SP**
**YEARBOOK DE PEDIATRIA.** (19??)-. Spanish. an. 10200.00ptas. Editorial Medical Panamericana Vega, Hilarion Eslava 55 de la Vega, 28015 Madrid Spain. **Tel** 011 34 1 5496101.

**PL/0324-8526**
**ZAGADNIENIA WYCHOWAWCZE A ZDROWIE PSYCHICZNE.** [Zag. wychow. zdr. psych.]. Periodical. Polish (summaries and/or abstracts in English and Russian). bm. **(Subscription address:** ARS Polona, PO Box 1001, 00068 Warsaw Poland.) **LC** RJ499.A1; Z34. **NLM** W1 ZA359BF.

**GW/0722-8953**
**ZENTRALBLATT KINDERHEILKUNDE.** **Added/Corp** Deutsche Gesellschaft fuer Kinderheilkunde. **VFOAT** Paediatrics. Vol. 129, No. 1 (1982)-. Periodical. German (English and German). Thirteen times a year. DM2598.00. Springer-Verlag GmbH & Company KG, Heidelberger Platz 3, D 14197 Berlin Germany. **Tel** 011 49 30 8207223, FAX 011 49 30 8214091, telex 183 319 SPBLN D. **(Subscription address:** Springer Verlag New York Inc. / for North America, 44 Hartz Way, Secaucus NJ 07096.) **ED** O Linderkamp, G Mittermaier, K Scharer, H E Ulmer, and E Willich. **NLM** ZWS 100; Z56. **[CCC]**. *Continues Zentralblatt fur die Gesamte Kinderheilkunde.*
  **Desc:** Covers social and preventive pediatrics, genetics, reonatology and premature birth, vaccination, psychology, nuclear medicine, pharmacology, diagnostics, surgery, statistics and pre-natal medicine.

**US/0736-8038**
**ZERO TO THREE.** [Zero three]. **Added/Corp** National Center for Clinical Infant Programs. (1980)-. Periodical. English. Six times a year (Feb., Apr., June, Aug., Oct., Dec.). $37.00 (one year); $69.00 (two years); $99.00 (three years). National Center for Clinical Infant Programs, PO Box 25494, Richmond VA 23260. **ED** Emily Fenichel. Index available. cum. index. **Bk Rev**. **Circ**: 7,500.
  **Desc:** Articles and issues about the violence, drug abuse and other related topics that is among our society today.
  **Ind/Abst** PsycINFO (?-?).

**CH/0001-6578**
**ZHONGHUA MINGUO XIAOERKE YIXUEHUI ZAZHI.** (CHUNG-HUA MIN KUO HSIAO ERH KO I HSUEH HUI TSA CHIH.). [Zhonghua minguo xiaoerke yixuehui zazhi]. **Added/Corp** Chung-Hua Min Kuo Hsiao Erh Ko I Hsueh Hui. **VFOAT** Acta Paediatrica Sinica. (1960)-. Academic Scholarly Publication. Chinese (English and Multiple languages; summaries and/or abstracts in English). Six times a year (Feb., Apr., June, Aug., Oct., Dec.). $66.00. Chinese Taipei Pediatric Association, 11 Ching Tao West Road 4F 4, Taipei 10022 Taiwan. **Tel** 011 886 2 3970800 ext. 2131, FAX 011 886 2 3142184. **ED** Mei-Hwei Chang M.D. (phone: (02)3970800 Ext. 2131). **CODEN** CHEKAL. Index available (Bound in next iss., Dec.). cum. index (Every 5-10 year). **Bk Rev**, (Qty: 6). **Pr Rev**. **Circ**: 2,500 (ctrl). Documents available from BIOSIS Document Express, CASDDS.
  **Desc:** Original articles on clinical and laboratory researches, brief communications, case reports, and special articles of pediatric subjects and related fields.
  **Ind/Abst** Biol. Abstr.; Chem. Abstr.; EMBASE; Health Plan. Adminis.; Index Med. (1965-1968, 1988-); Trop. Dis. Bull.

## PHYSICIANS AND MEDICAL PERSONNEL

**CN/0384-5915**
**A C P D Q BULLETIN.** See Dentistry.

**US/0883-2994**
**ABMS DIRECTORY OF CERTIFIED ALLERGY AND IMMUNOLOGY PHYSICIANS.** See Medical Science and Technology-Allergy and Immunology.

**US/0883-122X**
**ABMS DIRECTORY OF CERTIFIED ANESTHESIOLOGISTS.** *Title Change.* See Medical Science and Technology-Anesthesiology.

**US/0884-1470**
**ABMS DIRECTORY OF CERTIFIED COLON AND RECTAL SURGEONS.** *Title Change.* See Medical Science and Technology-Surgery.

**US/0884-1489**
**ABMS DIRECTORY OF CERTIFIED DERMATOLOGISTS.** *Title Change.* See Medical Science and Technology-Dermatology.

**US/0884-643X**
**ABMS DIRECTORY OF CERTIFIED FAMILY PHYSICIANS.** See Medical Science and Technology-Family Practice.

**US/0884-6448**
**ABMS DIRECTORY OF CERTIFIED INTERNISTS.** See Medical Science and Technology-Internal Medicine.

**US/0882-2832**
**ABMS DIRECTORY OF CERTIFIED NEUROLOGICAL SURGEONS.** *Title Change.* See Medical Science and Technology-Surgery.

**US/0884-1500**
**ABMS DIRECTORY OF CERTIFIED NEUROLOGISTS.** See Medical Science and Technology-Neurology.

**US/0884-1535**
**ABMS DIRECTORY OF CERTIFIED OBSTETRICIANS AND GYNECOLOGISTS.** See Medical Science and Technology-Gynecology and Obstetrics.

**US/8756-9175**
**ABMS DIRECTORY OF CERTIFIED OPHTHALMOLOGISTS.** *Title Change.* See Medical Science and Technology-Ophthalmology.

**US/0883-1211**
**ABMS DIRECTORY OF CERTIFIED ORTHOPAEDIC SURGEONS.** *Title Change.* See Medical Science and Technology-Orthopedics.

**US/0883-3001**
**ABMS DIRECTORY OF CERTIFIED OTOLARYNGOLOGISTS.** *Title Change.* See Medical Science and Technology-Otorhinolaryngology.

**US/0883-1203**
**ABMS DIRECTORY OF CERTIFIED PATHOLOGISTS.** See Medical Science and Technology-Pathology.

**US/0884-1497**
**ABMS DIRECTORY OF CERTIFIED PEDIATRICIANS.** *Title Change.* See Medical Science and Technology-Pediatrics.

**US/0883-2986**
**ABMS DIRECTORY OF CERTIFIED PHYSICAL MEDICINE AND REHABILITATION PHYSICIANS.** See Medical Science and Technology.

**US/0749-839X**
**ABMS DIRECTORY OF CERTIFIED PLASTIC SURGEONS.** *Title Change.* See Medical Science and Technology-Surgery.

**US/0883-2978**
**ABMS DIRECTORY OF CERTIFIED PREVENTIVE MEDICINE PHYSICIANS.** See Medical Science and Technology.

**US/0884-1519**
**ABMS DIRECTORY OF CERTIFIED PSYCHIATRISTS.** See Medical Science and Technology-Psychiatry.

**US**
**ABMS ... DIRECTORY OF CERTIFIED RADIOLOGISTS AND RADIOLOGICAL PHYSICISTS.** See Medical Science and Technology-Radiology.

**US/0884-1527**
**ABMS DIRECTORY OF CERTIFIED SURGEONS.** *Title Change.* See Medical Science and Technology-Surgery.

**US/0884-1462**
**ABMS DIRECTORY OF CERTIFIED THORACIC SURGEONS.** *Title Change.* See Medical Science and Technology-Surgery.

**US/0742-0374**
**ABMS DIRECTORY OF CERTIFIED UROLOGISTS.** *Title Change.* See Medical Science and Technology-Urology and Nephrology.

●**US**
**ABMS RECORD.** See Medical Science and Technology.

**US**
**ACTION REPORT / MEDICAL BOARD OF CALIFORNIA.** **Main/Corp** Medical Board of California. No. 39 (Feb. 1990)-No.42 (Dec. 1990) ; Vol. 43 (June 1991)-. English. Medical Board of California, 1430 Howe Avenue/Suite 85A, Sacramento CA 95825. **Tel** (916)920-6393. **LC** RA399.A4; C2. *Continues California. Board of Medical Quality Assurance. Action Report.*

## Medical Science and Technology — Physicians and Medical Personnel

CN/0229-9429
**ACTUALITE MEDICALE, L'.** [Actual. med.]. Vol. 1, No. 1 (Nov. 4, 1980)-. Periodical. French. Forty-Four times a year. 65.00Can$ Canada; 131.00Can$ other. MacLean Hunter Ltd. Business Publishers / Canada, Box 9100, Station A, Toronto ONT M5W 1A5 Canada. **Tel** (416)946-8420, (800)567-0444. **(Subscription address:** Indas, 35 Riviera Drive, Building 17, Markham Ontario L3R 8N4 Canada.) **DD** 610/.9714.

CN/0319-5031
**ALBERTA PHYSICIANS AND SURGEONS, PROVINCE OF ALBERTA.** **Title Change.** (1975)-. Periodical. English. College of Physicians and Surgeons of Alberta, 9901-108 Street, Edmonton Alberta T5K 1G9 Canada. **Tel** (403)423-4764. **DD** 610.69/52/0257123. **Supersedes** List of Members of the College of Physicians and Surgeons of Alberta, 0318-157X. **Continued by** Medical Directory, College of Physicians and Surgeons of Alberta, 0702-7826.

US
**AMERICAN MEDICAL DIRECTORY UPDATE / AMERICAN MEDICAL ASSOCIATION.** 1981-. Directory. English.

CN/0035-8800
**ANNALS OF THE ROYAL COLLEGE OF PHYSICIANS AND SURGEONS OF CANADA.** (ANNALS / ROYAL COLLEGE OF PHYSICIANS AND SURGEONS OF CANADA.). [Ann. R. Coll. Phys. Surg. Can.]. **Added/Corp** Royal College of Physicians and Surgeons of Canada. **VFOAT** Annales; Annals RCPSC; Annales CRMCC. Vol. 10, No. 1 (Jan. 1977)-. Academic Scholarly Publication. English (French; summaries and/or abstracts in French). Eight times a year. 40.00Can$ Canada; 50.00Can$ US; 60.00Can$ other. Royal College of Physicians & Surgeons, 774 Promenade Echo Drive, Ottawa Ontario K1S 5N8 Canada. **Tel** (613)730-6200, FAX (613)730-8830. **ED** John Last and Lynne Quon-Mak (associate editor). **DD** 610/.5. Index available in last issue of volume--attached. **Bk Rev**, (Qty: 80). **Ad Acc, Adv Mgr:** Maclean Hunter, **Tel** (416)596-5949. **Circ:** 28,000 (ctrl). **Continues** Royal College of Physicians and Surgeons of Canada. Annals of the Royal College of Physicians and Surgeons of Canada, 0035-8800.
**Desc:** Contains original papers of interest to all medical specialists.
**Ind/Abst** EMBASE.

US/0094-8942
**ANNUAL HEALTH MANPOWER CONFERENCE.** (ANNUAL HEALTH MANPOWER CONFERENCE. PROCEEDINGS.). **Main/Conf** Health Manpower Conference. Proceedings. English. an. **LC** RA410.8.C2; H4A. **DD** 331.7/61/6106909794.

US/1075-6507
**ANNUAL MEMBERSHIP DIRECTORY - NATIONAL ASSOCIATION OF ADVISORS FOR THE HEALTH PROFESSIONS.** (ANNUAL MEMBERSHIP DIRECTORY.). [Annu. membsh. dir. - Natl. Assoc. Advis. Health Prof.]. **Main/Corp** National Association of Advisors for the Health Professions. (199?)-. English. National Association Advisors Health Professionals, PO Box 5017, Station A, Champaign IL 61820. **Tel** (217)333-0090. **ED** Nancy Williams. **LC** R690; .N297a. **DD** 610.69/0973. **Ad Acc. Circ:** 1,200. **Continues** National Association of Advisors for the Health Professions. Directory of the National Association of Advisors for the Health Professions, 1043-6669.
**Desc:** Contains listings with addresses for all member health professions advisors (undergraduate level) and all member health professional schools.

CN/0707-1434
**ANNUAL REPORT - ALBERTA HEALTH AND SOCIAL SERVICES DISCIPLINES COMMITTEE.** [Annu. rep. - Alta. Health Soc. Serv. Discipl. Comm.]. **Main/Corp** Alberta Health and Social Services Disciplines Committee. 1st- 1976/77-. English. an. Free. Alberta Health and Social Services Disciplines Committee, 424 Legislative Building, Edmonton Alberta T5K 2B6 Canada. **Tel** (403)427-6904. **LC** RA410.9.C2; A43A. **DD** 354/.7123/00841. **Circ:** 700.
**Desc:** Contains information on history, mandates, membership, major activities of committee, manpower planning, surveys of personnel, associations, training programs, manpower indicators, and liaison activities of committee.

US/0095-5574
**ANNUAL REPORT - KENTUCKY MANPOWER DEVELOPMENT, INC.** **Main/Corp** Kentucky Manpower Development, Inc. 12th- 1973/74-. English. an. Kentucky Manpower Development Inc., 412 Executive Park, Louisville KY 40207. **LC** RA790.65.K4; K465A. **DD** 331.1/26.

US/0146-1524
**ANNUAL REPORT - NATIONAL BOARD OF MEDICAL EXAMINERS.** **Main/Corp** National Board of Medical Examiners. 1975-. English. an. National Board of Medical Examiners, 3930 Chestnut Street, Philadelphia PA 19104. **Tel** (215)349-6400. **NLM** W1 NA3284N.

US/0734-337X
**ANNUAL REPORT OF BOARD OF MEDICAL EXAMINERS.** (ANNUAL REPORT OF BOARD OF MEDICAL EXAMINERS / BOARD OF MEDICAL EXAMINERS OF MARYLAND.). **Main/Corp** Board of Medical Examiners of Maryland. English. an. Board of Medical Examiners of Maryland, 201 West Preston Street, Baltimore MD 21201. **LC** RA396.A4; M32A. **DD** 353.97520084/1046/05.

US
**ANNUAL REPORT / THE ARIZONA BOARD OF MEDICAL EXAMINERS.** **Main/Corp** Arizona Board of Medical Examiners. English. an. Arizona Board of Medical Examiners, 1990 West Camelback Road 401, Phoenix AZ 85015. **LC** RA396.A4; A62A. **DD** 353.97910084.

US
**ANNUAL REPORT TO THE CALIFORNIA LEGISLATURE - CALIFORNIA. HEALTH MANPOWER POLICY COMMISSION.** **Main/Corp** California. Health Manpower Policy Commission. Began with Vol. for 1974. English. an. Health Manpower Development Section, 714 P Street, Sacramento CA 95814. **LC** RA410.8.C2; C33A. **DD** 331.1/1. **NLM** W2 AC2 H4A.

US
**BALANCE FOR WOMEN PHYSICIANS.** English. bm. Free to women physicians; $24.00 other. Weisner Publishing Company, 7009 South Potomac Street, Englewood CO 80112. **Tel** (303)397-7600.

US/0023-1592
**BULLETIN - KING COUNTY MEDICAL SOCIETY, THE.** Began with V. 1, 1922. Bulletin. English. mo (except Aug.). $12.95. Journal & Bulletin Agency Inc, PO Box 10249, Bainbridge Island WA 98110. **Tel** (206)623-7325. **NLM** W1 BU671M. **Bk Rev. Ad Acc. Circ:** 4,000 (ctrl).
**Desc:** Bulletin and yearly photo roster.

CN/1180-260X
**BUSINESS ROUNDS.** [Bus. rounds]. **Added/Corp** MD Management Limited. Canadian Medical Association. No. 1 (1990)-. Periodical. English. qt. Limited free distribution. MD Management Limited, 1867 Alta Vista Drive, Ottawa, Ontario K1G 3Y6 Canada. **DD** 332.024/61/05.

CN/0068-9203
**CANADIAN MEDICAL DIRECTORY.** [Can. med. dir.]. 1st (1955)-. Directory. English. an. 169.00Can$. Southam Information and Technology Group Inc., 1450 Don Mills Road, Don Mills Ontario M3B 2X7 Canada. **Tel** (416)445-6641, (800)668-2374, FAX (416)442-2261. **DD** 610.69/52/02571. **NLM** W 22 DC2 C22.
**Desc:** Complete source covering Canada's entire medical profession. Contains detailed profile of 45,000 physicians alphabetically and geographically across Canada.

UK/0965-5751
**CLINICIAN IN MANAGEMENT.** (1992)-. Newsletter. English. Six times a year. £71.00 Europe; £72.00 Other (Institutions. Churchill Livingstone, 1-3 Baxter's Place, Leith Walk, Edinburgh EH1 3AF Scotland. **Tel** 011 44 31 556 2424, FAX 011 44 31 558 1278, telex 727511. **(Subscription address:** Maruzen Company Ltd., PO Box 5050, Import & Export Department, Tokyo 100 31 Japan.)
**Desc:** Official Journal of the British Association of Medical Managers.

US
**COLORADO MEDICAL SOCIETY PHYSICIAN'S RESOURCE BOOK.** (19??)-. English. an. $48.00. Colorado Medical Society, PO 17550, Denver CO 80217. **Tel** (303)779-5455. **Continues** Colorado Medicine Physicians's Directory.

US/0743-5037
**COLORADO MEDICINE. DIRECTORY OF PHYSICIANS.** **Title Change. See** Insurance.

US
**CONSORTIUM NEWS / HEALTH SCIENCES CONSORTIUM.** **Added/Corp** Health Sciences Consortium (U.S.). (19??)-. Periodical. English. qt (published within the seasons). Free. Health Sciences Consortium, 201 Silver Cedar Court, Chapel Hill NC 27514. **Tel** (919)942-8731, FAX (919)942-3689. **ED** Jorja Croker. **Ad Acc, Adv Mgr:** Bret Kuner. **Circ:** 3,000 (ctrl).
**Desc:** Covers the activities of the consortium and provides news on instructional programs.

PN/0417-5433
**DIRECTORIO MEDICO PANAMENO.** (1961)-. Periodical. Spanish. be. $10.00. Directorio Medico Panameno, Association Medico Nacional, Apartado Postal 2020, Panama 1 Panama. **Tel** 011 507 64 4894. **DD** 610.

US
**DIRECTORY / AMERICAN HOLISTIC MEDICAL ASSOCIATION AND FOUNDATION.** **Main/Corp** American Holistic Medical Association. **Added/Corp** American Holistic Medical Foundation. **VFOAT** AHMA/F Member Directory. (1989/90)-. Directory. English. American Holistic Medical Association / Washington, 2002 Eastlake Avenue East, Seattle WA 98102-3510. **Tel** (206)322-6842. **NLM** W 22.1; A512d. **Continues** Directory of Members (American Holistic Medical Foundation), 0732-9571.

US/0196-6421
**DIRECTORY OF CERTIFIED PSYCHIATRISTS AND NEUROLOGISTS.** **See** Medical Science and Technology-Psychiatry.

US/0271-9851
**DIRECTORY OF KOREAN PHYSICIANS: DISTRICT OF COLUMBIA, MARYLAND, AND VIRGINIA.** **Added/Corp** Korean Medical Association of District of Columbia, Maryland, and Virginia. (19??)-. Directory. English (Korean). 4412 Powder Mill Road, Suite 200, Beltsville MD 20705. **LC** R712.W3; D57. **DD** 610.69/52/025753.

US
**DIRECTORY OF LICENTIATES, REGULATIONS, AND REGISTRATION LAW / ARKANSAS STATE MEDICAL BOARD.** (1986)-. Directory. English. an. Joe Verser, PO Box 102, Harrisburg AR 72432. **LC** R712.A2; A84. **DD** 610.69/52/025767. **Continues** Directory of Licentiates and Registration Law.

US/0070-5829
**DIRECTORY OF MEDICAL SPECIALISTS.** **Title Change. Added/Corp** American Board of Medical Specialties. 16th-25th ed.; (1974/75)-(1991/92). Directory. English. be. Marquis Who's Who, A Reed Reference Publishing Company, Part of Reed International PLC, 121 Chanlon Road, New Providence NJ 07974. **Tel** (908)464-6800, (800)521-8110, FAX (908)665-6688, telex 138 755. **LC** R712.A1; D5. **DD** 610/.2/573. **NLM** W 22; DA2 D5982. **Continues** Directory of Medical Specialists Holding Certification by American Specialty Boards. **Merged with** ABMS Compendium of Certified Medical Specialists, 0884-1543 **to form** Official American Board of Medical Specialties (ABMS) Directory of Board Certified Medical Specialists, 0000-1406.
**Desc:** Valued by both the medical and reference communities. An essential information source to specialists, hospitals, medical schools libraries, clinics, insurance agencies, and research foundations.

US
**DIRECTORY OF MEMBERS / LOS ANGELES COUNTY MEDICAL ASSOCIATION.** **Main/Corp** Los Angeles County Medical Association. (19??)-. Directory. English. an. $110.00. Los Angeles County Medical Association, PO Box 3465 Terminal Annex, Los Angeles CA 90051-1465. **Tel** (310) 483-1581, FAX (213) 483-4560. **Ad Acc. Circ:** 13,000 (ctrl).
**Desc:** Membership directory of Los Angeles County Medical Association's 10,000 members, including biographic and geographic data.

US
**DIRECTORY OF OFFICIALS AND STAFF / AMERICAN MEDICAL ASSOCIATION.** **See** Encyclopedias and General Reference Books.

●US
**DIRECTORY OF PHYSICIANS IN THE UNITED STATES / AMERICAN MEDICAL ASSOCIATION.** **See** Encyclopedias and General Reference Books.

US
**DIRECTORY OF REGISTERED LICENSEES, BOARD OF MEDICAL EXAMINERS OF THE STATE OF OREGON.** **Main/Corp** Board of Medical Examiners of the State of Oregon. Directory. English. an. **LC** R712.A2; O86. **DD** 610/.25/.795. **Continues** Directory of Board of Medical Examiners of the State of Oregon.

US
**DIRECTORY OF REGISTERED LICENTIATES IN NORTH DAKOTA.** Directory. English. an. North Dakota Board of Nursing, Kirkwood Office Tower 504, Bismarck ND 58501-5881. **LC** R712.A2; N94. **DD** 610.69/52025/784.

US/1043-6669
**DIRECTORY OF THE NATIONAL ASSOCIATION OF ADVISORS FOR THE HEALTH PROFESSIONS.** ***Title Change.*** [Dir. Natl. Assoc. Advis. Health Prof.]. **Main/Corp** National Association of Advisors for the Health Professions. (1988/1989)-(199?). Directory. English. an. National Association Advisors Health Professionals, PO Box 5017, Station A, Champaign IL 61820. **Tel** (217)333-0090. **ED** Nancy Williams. **LC** R690; .N297a. **DD** 610.69/0973. **Ad Acc. Circ:** 1,200. ***Continues*** *National Association of Advisors for the Health Professions. National Directory of Health Professions Advisors, 0737-1616.* ***Continued by*** *National Association of Advisors for the Health Professions. Annual Membership Directory, 1075-6507.*
**Desc:** Contains listings with addresses of all member health professions advisors (undergraduate level) and all member health professional schools.

US/0194-0554
**DIRECTORY - STATE BOARD OF MEDICAL EXAMINERS OF SOUTH CAROLINA.** **Main/Corp** South Carolina. State Board of Medical Examiners. Directory. English. an. $30.00. State Board of Medical Examiners of South Carolina, 1220 Pickens Street, Columbia SC 29201-3428. **Tel** (803)734-8901. **LC** R712.A2; S67. **DD** 610/.25757.
**Desc:** Detailed information on all physicians with South Carolina licenses (name, address, license number, school, etc.).

US/0363-4825
**DIVERSION (TITUSVILLE).** **See** Recreation, Leisure.

US
**DOCTOR'S FINANCIAL REPORT.** **See** Business-Banking and Finance.

US/0733-2262
**DOCTOR'S OFFICE, THE.** Vol. 1, No. 1 (June 1982)-. Periodical. English. mo. $98.00; $84.00 (one year trial subscription); $9.00 (single issue). Wentworth Publishing Company, 1866 Colonial Village Lane, Lancaster PA 17605. **Tel** (800)331-5196, (717)393-1000. **(Subscription address:** Wentworth Publishing Co., PO Box 10488, Lancaster PA 17605.**)** **ED** Ann Ash. **Circ:** 3,000.
**Desc:** Practice management and marketing newsletter for physician's office staffs.

CN/0318-9503
**EDUCATIONAL REQUIREMENTS AND SCHOOLS OF STUDY FOR HEALTH CAREERS.** 1973-. Periodical. English. an. Ontario Hospital Association, 150 Ferrand Drive, Don Mills Ontario M3C 1H6 Canada. **Tel** (905)429-2661 ext. 7736. **DD** 610/.7/11713. ***Supersedes*** *Hospital Careers, 0318-949X.*

US/0098-1524
**EPLB. EMERGENCY PHYSICIAN LEGAL BULLETIN.** **See** Medical Science and Technology-Emergency Medicine.

US/0888-5648
**EXCHANGE (FORT WORTH, TEX.).** (EXCHANGE. THE FEDERATION OF STATE MEDICAL BOARDS OF THE UNITED STATES, INC.). [Exchange]. **Added/Corp** Federation of State Medical Boards of the United States. (1986)-. English. an. $60.00. Federation of State Medical Boards of the United States, 6000 West Place, Suite 707, Ft Worth TX 76107. **Tel** (817)735-8445, FAX (817)738-6629. **ED** Dale G. Breaden. **LC** RA396.A3; E93. **DD** 353.0084/1046. **NLM** W 39; E96e. **[CCC].** ***Continues*** *Legislative and Regulatory Exchange.*
**Desc:** Board operation and structure, and physician discipline.

US
**FEDERAL HOSPITAL PHONE BOOK.** (19??)-. English. ir. $37.50 per copy. Reed Reference Publishing, 121 Chanlon Road, New Providence NJ 07974. **Tel** (908)464-6800, (800)521-8110 Ext. 3387, (800)223-1797, FAX (908)665-3560.

US/1042-4644
**FOLIO'S MEDICAL DIRECTORY OF CONNECTICUT AND RHODE ISLAND.** **Added/Corp** Folio Associates. **VFOAT** MD CT, MD RI; Medical Directory of Connecticut and Rhode Island. 5th Ed. (1989)-. Directory. English. an (March). $46.20 Massachusetts residents; $44.00 other. Folio Associates Inc, 111 Perkins Street, Boston MA 02130. **Tel** (617)522-5200. **ED** Patricia Wirtenberg. **LC** R712.A2; F66. **DD** 610/.25/746. **NLM** W 22; AC8 F6. Index available. available on diskette ((8 inch)); available on labels. ***Continues*** *Folio's Medical Directory of Connecticut, 0741-2428.*

US/0741-241X
**FOLIO'S MEDICAL DIRECTORY OF MASSACHUSETTS.** **VFOAT** Medical Directory of Massachusetts; MDMA; M.D.M.A. (1980)-. English. an (Mar.). $54.60 Massachusetts; $52.00 others. Folio Associates Inc, 111 Perkins Street, Boston MA 02130. **Tel** (617)522-5200. **ED** Patricia Wirtenberg. **LC** R712.A2; M39. **DD** 610/.25/744. Index available. **Circ:** 6,000. available on diskette. ***Continues*** *Datawell's Medical Directory of Massachusetts, 0192-5091.*

NE
**GENEESKUNDIG ADRESBOEK VOOR NEDERLAND.** 1984/85-. Dutch. an. Nijgh Periodieken BV, Postbus 122, 3100 AC Schiedam Netherlands. **Tel** 011 31 10 4274174. **LC** R713.49; .G46. **NLM** W 22; GN4 G29. **Ad Acc.** ***Continues*** *Geneeskundig Adresboek.*

IE/0790-567X
**GENERAL REGISTER OF MEDICAL PRACTITIONERS. PART 1, FULLY REGISTERED MEDICAL PRACTITIONERS AS AT ... / THE MEDICAL COUNCIL.** [Gen. regist. med. pract.]. **VFOAT** Fully Registered Medical Practitioners as at ... . Periodical. English. **NLM** W 22; GI6 M46. ***Continues*** *Medical Register of Ireland.*

NZ/1039-7469
**GP GENERAL PRACTITIONER.** ***Ceased.*** **See** Medical Science and Technology-Family Practice.

FR
**GUIDE ROSENWALD.** French. 430.00F (one volume), 780.00F (two volumes);, 1130.00F (three volumes). IC Publications Ediafric, 10 rue Vineuse, 75116 Paris France. **Tel** 011 33 1 44308100. **LC** R713.43.A6; G8. **DD** 616/.0025/44. ***Continues*** *Guide Medical et Pharmaceutique Rosenwald.*

CN/0833-9457
**HEALTH CAREER PATHS.** [Health career paths]. Nov. 1984-. English. an. Ontario Hospital Association, 150 Ferrand Drive, Don Mills Ontario M3C 1H6 Canada. **Tel** (905)429-2661 ext. 7736. **DD** 610/.7/11713. Index available. ***Continues*** *Health Careers: Educational Requirements and Program Locations, 0381-6435.*

NP/0258-3178
**HEALTH MANPOWER DIRECTORY.** [Health manpow. dir.]. Directory. English (Nepali). **LC** R713.81.N66. **NLM** W 22 JN4 H4.

US/0192-6101
**HEALTH MANPOWER PILOT PROJECTS PROGRAM. ANNUAL REPORT TO THE LEGISLATURE AND THE HEALING ARTS LICENSING BOARDS.** (HEALTH MANPOWER PILOT PROJECTS PROGRAM.). **Main/Corp** California. Office of Statewide Health Planning and Development. English. an. Health & Welfare Agency, Office of Statewide Health Planning & Development, 1600 9th Street/Room 440, Sacramento CA 95814. **LC** RA396.A4; C23A. **DD** 362.1/09794. **Circ:** 250 (ctrl). ***Continues*** *Experimental Health Manpower Pilot Projects, 0190-4825.*

UK
**HEALTH MANPOWER RESOURCES.** **Main/Corp** New Zealand. Dept. of Health. Management Services and Research Unit. English. Workforce Planning and Production, Department of Health, PO Box 5013, Wellington New Zealand. **LC** RA410.9.N42. **DD** 331.1/1.

AT
**HEALTH RESOURCES MEDICAL MANPOWER.** **Added/Corp** Western Australia. Public Health Dept. Statistics Branch. (19??)-. English. an. **LC** RA410.9.A8; H42. **DD** 331.12/9161/09941.

●US
**HEALTHCARE CAREER DIRECTORY. NURSES AND PHYSICIANS.** **VFOAT** Nurses and Physicians; Health Care Career Directory. Nurses and Physicians. 2nd Ed. (1993)-. Directory. English. be. $29.95 (hardcover), $17.95 (softcover). Gale Research Inc., 835 Penobscot Building, Detroit MI 48226. **Tel** (800)877-GALE, (313)961-2242, FAX (313)961-6083, telex TWX 810-221-7086. **LC** R690; .H425. ***Continues in part*** *Healthcare Career Directory, 1062-5976.*
**Desc:** Discusses pediatrics, surgery, oncology nursing, neurology and more.

●US/1060-9253
**HEALTHCARE HUMAN RESOURCES.** [Healthc. hum. resour.]. Vol. 1, No. 1 (Jan. 1992)-. Periodical. English. mo. $128.00 US and Canada; $140.00 other. COR Healthcare Resources, (A Division of COR Research Inc.), PO Box 40959, Santa Barbara CA 93140. **Tel** (805)564-2177, FAX (805)564-2146. **DD** 658. **NLM** W1; HE303R. **[CCC].**
**Ind/Abst** Hospit. Manage. Rev. (199?-).

CN/0227-1842
**INFORM - A P I Q, L'.** **Main/Corp** Association Professionelle des Inhalotherapeutes du Quebec. V. 1-Spring 1980-. Periodical. French. qt. Free to members. Association Professionnelle Des Inhalotherapeutes Du Quebec, Bureau 315, Rue Du Trianon, Montreal Quebec H1M 2S5 Canada. **DD** 331.7/61615836.

US/8755-0229
**JOURNAL OF MEDICAL PRACTICE MANAGEMENT, THE.** (THE JOURNAL OF MEDICAL PRACTICE MANAGEMENT : MPM.). [J. med. pract. manage.]. **VFOAT** MPM; Medical Practice Management. Vol. 1, No. 1 (July 1985)-. Periodical. English. bm. $99.00 (individual), $110.00 (institution) US; $129.00 (individual), $140.00 (institutions) other. Williams & Wilkins Company, 428 East Preston Street, Baltimore MD 21202-3993. **Tel** (410)528-4000, (800)638-6423, FAX (410)528-8596, telex 87669. **(Subscription address:** Williams & Wilkins, PO Box 64380, Baltimore MD 21264.**)** **ED** Marcel Frenkel. **DD** 610. **NLM** W1; JO753W. **[CCC]. Ad Acc. Circ:** 1,800. available on microfilm. Documents available from Quick Copies.
**Desc:** Perspectives on legislation, litigation, office management and other key issues that affect the medical practice of office-based physicians and health care professionals.
**Ind/Abst** EMBASE; Hospit. Health Admin. Index (1985-1989).

US/0098-8421
**JOURNAL OF THE AMERICAN MEDICAL WOMEN'S ASSOCIATION (1972).** **See** Medical Science and Technology.

US/1048-9886
**JOURNAL OF THE ASSOCIATION FOR ACADEMIC MINORITY PHYSICIANS.** (JOURNAL OF THE ASSOCIATION FOR ACADEMIC MINORITY PHYSICIANS : THE OFFICIAL PUBLICATION OF THE ASSOCIATION FOR ACADEMIC MINORITY PHYSICIANS.). [J. Assoc. Acad. Minor. Physicians]. **Added/Corp** Association for Academic Minority Physicians. **VFOAT** Journal for the Association for Academic Minority Physicians; JAAMP. Vol. 1, No. 1 (July-Sept. 1989)-. Periodical. English. qt. $80.00 (institution), $40.00 (individual). Association of the Academy of Minority Physicians, University of Maryland, School of Medicine, Deans Office, Baltimore MD 21201. **Tel** (410)706-4100. **DD** 616. **NLM** W1; JO912B. **CODEN** JAMPE6.
**Ind/Abst** Index Med. (1989-).

JA/0388-6042
**KANAGAWA KENRITSU EISEI TANKI DAIGAKU KIYO.** [Kanagawa Kenritsu Eisei Tanki Daigaku kiyo]. **VFOAT** Bulletin - Kanagawa Prefectural Junior College of Nursing and Medical Technology. (1969)-. Periodical. Japanese. an. Kanagawa Kenritsu Eisei Tanki Daigaku, (Kanagawa Prefectural College of Nursing & Medical Technology), 50-1, Nakocho, Asahiku, Yokohamashi, Kanagawaken 241, Japan. **DD** 060. Documents available from CASDDS.
**Ind/Abst** Chem. Abstr.

FI/0780-1785
**LAAKARIT.** **See** Dentistry.

US/0162-7163
**LACMA PHYSICIAN.** [LACMA physician]. **Main/Corp** Los Angeles County Medical Association. **VAT** Los Angeles County Medical Association Physician. Vol. 108 No. 16 (Aug. 17, 1978)-. Periodical. English. Twenty times a year. $30.00. Los Angeles County Medical Association, PO Box 3465 Terminal Annex, Los Angeles CA 90051-1465. **Tel** (310) 483-1581, FAX (213) 483-4560. **ED** Michael Villaire. **NLM** W1 L1P. **Bk Rev. Ad Acc. Circ:** 10,500. ***Continues*** *Los Angeles County Medical Association Bulletin, 0047-5076.*
**Desc:** Socio-economic, non-clinical journal published by the Association for its membership. Contains healthcare news and information, as well as continuing medical education notices, etc.
**Ind/Abst** Cumul. Index Nurs. Allied Health Lit.

SW/0282-633X
**LAEKARMATRIKELN.** (19??)-. Swedish. an. Scandinavian University Press, PO Box 2959 Toeyen, N 0608 Oslo 6 Norway. **Tel** 011 47 2 2575400, FAX 011 47 2 2575353, telex 71896 UROR N. **(Subscription address:** Scandinavian University Press, 200 Meacham Ave., Elmont NY 11003.**)** **LC** R713.61; .L34.

CN/0823-6909
**LIST OF MEDICAL PRACTITIONERS CURRENTLY LICENSED TO PRACTISE IN THE PROVINCE / THE COLLEGE OF PHYSICIANS AND SURGEONS OF MANITOBA.** [List med. pract. curr. licens. pract. prov.]. **Main/Corp** College of Physicians and Surgeons of Manitoba. Sept. 8th, 1981-. Periodical. English. sa. College of Physicians and Surgeons of Manitoba, 1410-155 Carlton Street, Winnipeg Manitoba R3C 3H8 Canada. **Tel** (204)947-1694. **DD** 610.69/52/0257127. **Circ:** 2,900 (ctrl). ***Continues*** *College of Physicians and Surgeons of Manitoba. List of Medical Practitioners Currently Registered and Entitled to Practise in the Province, 0823-6666.*

## Medical Science and Technology —Physicians and Medical Personnel

US/0276-2250
**LIST OF REGISTERED DOCTORS OF MEDICINE AND SURGERY, DOCTORS OF OSTEOPATHY LICENSED TO PRACTICE MEDICINE AND SURGERY, DOCTORS OF OSTEOPATHY LICENSED TO PRACTICE OSTEOPATHY, DOCTORS OF CHIROPRACTIC, DOCTORS OF PODIATRY.** Mar. 1978-. English. te. **NLM** W 22 AK3 L7; W 22 AK3 L7. *Continues List of Registered Doctors of Medicine and Surgery, Doctors of Osteopathy Licensed to Practice Medicine and Surgery, Doctors to Practice Osteopathy, Doctors of Chiropractic.*

UK/0307-7462
**LIST OF THE MEMBERS OF THE ROYAL COLLEGES OF PHYSICIANS OF THE UNITED KINGDOM.** 1971-. English. te. Royal College of Physicians, 11 St Andrews Place, Regents Park, London NW1 4LE England. **Tel** 011 44 71 935 1174, FAX 011 44 71 487 5218. **LC** R713.29; .L58. **DD** 610/.6/241. **NLM** W 22 FA1 L7.

US/0276-0495
**MALPRACTICE PREVENTION FOR PHYSICIANS.** See Law.

US/0738-1026
**MALPRACTICE REPORTER, THE.** See Law.

●US/1071-3255
**MANAGEMENT & DOCTORS.** (MANAGEMENT & DOCTORS : MD.). [Manag. dr.]. **VFOAT** MD. Vol. 6, No. 1 (Jan. 1993)-. Periodical. English. mo (12 issues). $198.00. The Beckham Company, 1901 East Cumberland Boulevard, Whitefish Bay WI 53211. **Tel** (414)963-8935. **ED** J. Daniel Beckham. **DD** 658. **Circ**: 250. *Continues Marketing to Doctors, 1043-5417.*
**Desc:** Health care's leading newsletter on the hospital-physician partnership.

US
**MANUAL OF CRITERIA FOR MEDICAL AUTHORIZATION /INCLS UPDATES.** English (French). ir. $23.85. State California General Services, PO Box 1015, North Highlands CA 95660. **Tel** (916)973-3700.

US
**MATTERS OF HEALTH.** Periodical. English. wk. $400.00. University Hospital/ V Trainor, 88 East Newton Street, VOSE-205, Boston MA 02118. **Tel** (617)638-8165, FAX (617)638-8924.

US/0047-648X
**MEDICAL DIMENSIONS.** V. 1- Mar. 1972-. Periodical. English. bm. $12.00 US; $14.00 other. MBA Communications, 730 Third Avenue, New York NY 10017. **LC** R707. **DD** 362.1. **NLM** W1 ME2991.

UK/0305-3342
**MEDICAL DIRECTORY.** V. 1- 1845-. Directory. English. an. $62.00. Churchill Livingstone, 1-3 Baxter's Place, Leith Walk, Edinburgh EH1 3AF Scotland. **Tel** 011 44 31 556 2424, FAX 011 44 31 558 1278, telex 727511. (**Subscription address:** US/ Churchill Livingstone, Fulfillment Office, PO Box 11318, Birmingham, AL 35202) **LC** R713.29. **DD** 614.240942. Index available. **Ad Acc.**
**Desc:** The medical directory gives an alphabetical listing of more than 100,000 doctors registered to practice in the UK as well as other health care coverage.

CN/0702-7826
**MEDICAL DIRECTORY - COLLEGE OF PHYSICIANS AND SURGEONS OF ALBERTA.** (MEDICAL DIRECTORY.). **Main/Corp** College of Physicians and Surgeons of Alberta. 1976-. Directory. English. be. Free to registered physicians in Alberta, $10.00 each number others. College of Physicians and Surgeons of Alberta, 9901-108 Street, Edmonton Alberta T5K 1G9 Canada. **Tel** (403)423-4764. **DD** 610.69/52/0257123. *Continues Alberta Physicians and Surgeons, Province of Alberta, 0319-5031.*

AT
**MEDICAL DIRECTORY OF AUSTRALIA.** (19??)-. Directory. English. ir. 260.00Aus$. Australasian Medical Publishing Company, 76 Berry Street Level 1, North Sydney 2059 Australia. **Tel** 011 61 2 9548666, FAX 11 61 02 5023626. **ED** J. Astles and G. Norton. *Continues Medical Directory of Australia, New Zealand, etc.*
**Desc:** Alphabetical list of doctors in Australia, New Zealand and Papua New Guinea. Includes health authorities, gazetteer hospitals, organizations, universities, colleges, societies and research institutes.

CN/0069-5726
**MEDICAL DIRECTORY (VANCOUVER).** (MEDICAL DIRECTORY - COLLEGE OF PHYSICIANS AND SURGEONS OF B.C.). **Main/Corp** College of Physicians and Surgeons of British Columbia. 1956/57-. Directory. English. an. College of Physicians and Surgeons of British Columbia, 1807 West 10th Avenue, Vancouver British Columbia V6J 2A9 Canada. **DD** 610.69/52/025711. **NLM** W 22 DC2.1B8M. *Continues College of Physicians and Surgeons of British Columbia. Council. Directory, 0315-2294.*

US/0145-5583
**MEDICAL DIRECTORY (WATERVILLE).** (MEDICAL DIRECTORY.). Directory. English. Maine Board of Registration in Medicine, 100 College Avenue, Waterville ME 04901. **LC** R712.A2; M26. **DD** 610/.25/741.

US/0199-1272
**MEDICAL LIABILITY ADVISORY SERVICE.** [Med. liabil. advis. serv.]. **Added/Corp** Capitol Publications, inc. (197?)-. Periodical. English. mo. $225.00. Business Publishers Inc., 951 Pershing Drive, Silver Spring MD 20910-4464. **Tel** (301)587-6300, (800)274-0122, FAX (301)585-9075. **LC** KF2905.3.A15; M43. **DD** 346.7303/32; 347.306332. **NLM** W1 ME366H. [CCC].
**Desc:** Brings you full details on legislation and court decisions. Special attention is paid to the "bellwether states" whose legislative reforms tend to be adopted by other states. You'll get practical information on just what triggers a lawsuit - information you can pass on to your staff to "claim-proof" your procedures in key areas.
**Ind/Abst** Health Devices Alerts.

US/0199-1833
**MEDICAL LIABILITY REPORTER.** See Law.

US/0747-8925
**MEDICAL MALPRACTICE LAW & STRATEGY.** See Law.

US/0277-7266
**MEDICAL MALPRACTICE LITIGATION.** See Law.

US/0882-8555
**MEDICAL MALPRACTICE LITIGATION REPORTER.** *Title Change.* See Law.

US/0888-658X
**MEDICAL MALPRACTICE VERDICTS, SETTLEMENTS & EXPERTS.** See Law.

UK
**MEDICAL REGISTER, THE. Added/Corp** General Medical Council (Great Britain). (1858)-. Periodical. English. an. £115.50 UK; £121.90 Australia; £90.00 UK. General Medical Council, 44 Hallam Street, London W1N 6AE England. **Tel** 011 44 71 580 7642. **NLM** W 22 FA1 M48. **Circ**: 1,000. *Continues The Medical Register, Printed and Published under the Direction of the General Council of Medical Education and Registration of the United Kingdom ... Comprising the Names and Addresses of Medical Practitioners... .*
**Desc:** Lists doctors registered in principal list of register on first January in year of publication and gives general information on medical registration.

UK
**MEDICAL SCIENCES INTERNATIONAL WHO'S WHO. Added/Corp** Gale Research Company. 3rd Ed. (1987)-. Directory. English. an (March). $585.00. Longman Group Ltd., Fourth Avenue, Longman House, Harlow Essex CM19 5SR England. **Tel** 011 44 279 429655, FAX 011 44 279 431059, telex 81259. (**Subscription address:** US and Canada: Gale Research Co., 835 Penobscot Building, Detroit, MI 48226) **LC** R134; .I57. **DD** 610/.92/2; B. **NLM** W 22.1; I64. *Continues International Medical Who's Who.*
**Desc:** Provides biographical information on nearly 8,000 senior biomedical scientists and their researchers working in more than 90 countries worldwide. Conveniently arranged by scientist's last name, entries provide complete contact details as well as information on degrees, work experience, present position, employers, directorships held, national appointments and memberships and more.

US
**MEDICAL STAFF BRIEFING.** See Medical Science and Technology-Hospital Administration and Medical Centers.

US/0899-8981
**MEDICAL STAFF COUNSELOR, THE.** *Ceased.* [Med. staff couns.]. Vol. 1, No. 1 (Summer 1987)-(Sept. 1993). Periodical. English. qt. Matthew Bender & Company Inc., 1275 Broadway, Albany NY 12204. **Tel** (800)833-9844, (518)487-3000. **DD** 362. **NLM** W1; ME498KG.
**Ind/Abst** Hospit. Health Admin. Index (Summer 1987-); Hospit. Manage. Rev.

US/0730-1448
**MEDICAL STAFF DIRECTORY.** See Dentistry.

●US/1070-7271
**MEDICAL TECHNOLOGISTS AND TECHNICIANS CAREER DIRECTORY.** **VFOAT** Technologists and Technicians Career Directory. (1993)-. Directory. English. be. $29.95 (hardcover), $17.95 (softcover). Gale Research Inc., 835 Penobscot Building, Detroit MI 48226. **Tel** (800)877-GALE, (313)961-2242, FAX (313)961-6083, telex TWX 810-221-7086. **NLM** W1; ME518W.
**Desc:** Covers careers such as nuclear, medical, surgical or laboratory technicians, radiology specialists and many others.

US/8750-9741
**MEDIGRAM (EAST LANSING, MICH. : 1985).** See Medical Science and Technology.

GW
**MEDIZIN IN WEST-BERLIN, DIE.** German. DM33.00. J. Kugler / Berlin, Schutzallee 45, 1000 Berlin 37 Germany. **Tel** (030)8018096. **ED** Joachim Kugler. **LC** R713.45; .M43. **Ad Acc. Circ**: 4,300.
**Desc:** Directory of health service of Berlin (West) medical practitioners, hospitals, pharmacies, etc. Remedial gymnastics, midwives, and domestic nursing, etc.

US
**MEMBERSHIP DIRECTORY. Main/Corp** American Medical Women's Association. (1978)-. English. mo. $20.00. American Medical Women's Association, 801 North Fairfax Street, Suite 400, Alexandria VA 22314. **Tel** (703)838-0500, FAX (703)549-3864.

●US/1070-7298
**MENTAL HEALTH AND SOCIAL WORK CAREER DIRECTORY. VFOAT** Mental Health Career Directory. (1993)-. Directory. English. be. $29.95 (hardcover), $17.95 (softcover). Gale Research Inc., 835 Penobscot Building, Detroit MI 48226. **Tel** (800)877-GALE, (313)961-2242, FAX (313)961-6083, telex TWX 810-221-7086.
**Desc:** Covers family therapist, substance abuse counselor, developmental psychologist, forensic psychologist and many other related occupations.

US/0196-5247
**MISSOURI HEALTH MANPOWER. Added/Corp** Missouri Center for Health Statistics. (19??)-. English. an. $17.50. Missouri Department of Health, Financial Services, PO Box 570, Jefferson City MO 65102. **Tel** (314)751-6279, (314)751-6400. **LC** RA410.8.M8; M58. **DD** 331.11/9161/09778. **NLM** W2 AM8 B83M. **Circ**: 500.
**Desc:** Provides summary data for instate chiropractors, dental hygienists, dentists, medical doctors, registered nurses, DOs, LPNs, optometrists, pharmacists, podiatrists, physical therapists, veterinarians and psychologists.

GW/0930-4622
**MTA.** (MTA : OFFIZIELLES ORGAN DES DEUTSCHEN VERBANDES TECHNISCHER ASSISTENTEN IN DER MEDIZIN E.V. UND DES BERBANDES DER DIPLOMIERTEN MED.-TECHN. ASSISTENTEN OSTERREICHS.). [MTA]. **Added/Corp** Deutscher Verband Technischer Assistenten in der Medizin. Verband der Diplomierten Med.-Tech. Assistenten Osterreichs. Vol. 1, No. 1 (Jan. 1986)-. Academic Scholarly Publication. German. mo. DM136.80 Germany; DM157.20 other. Umschau Verlag, Postfach 110262, D-60037 Frankfurt Germany. **Tel** 011 49 69 2600692, FAX 011 49 69 2600223, telex 411964. **NLM** W1; M4999. **CODEN** MTAAEX. Documents available from CASDDS. *Formed by the union of MTA-Journal (Frankfurt Am Main, Germany), 0171-8037 and MTA-Praxis.*
**Ind/Abst** Chem. Abstr. (1986-).

US
**NATIONAL OPPORTUNITES FOR ALLIED HEALTH.** (19??)-. Periodical. English. $7.95 US; $12.00 other. Medical Economics Publishing, Five Paragon Drive, Second Floor, Montvale NJ 07645. **Tel** (800)432-4570, (201)358-2210.

US
**NATIONAL SURVEY OF HOSPITAL AND MEDICAL SCHOOL SALARIES.** English. an. University of Texas / Medical Branch, 301 University Boulevard, Galveston TX 77550. **LC** RA410.7; .N39. **DD** 331.2/8161/09764. **NLM** W1; NA759D.

US
**NEBRASKA HEALTH MANPOWER REPORTS. PODIATRISTS, PHYSICAL THERAPISTS, CHIROPRACTORS, SPEECH PATHOLOGISTS, AUDIOLOGISTS, VETERINARIANS. Added/Corp** Nebraska. Division of Health Data Systems. Nebraska. Bureau of Examining Boards. **VFOAT** Podiatrists, Physical Therapists, Chiropractors, Speech Pathologists, Audiologists, Veterinarians. English. Nebraska State Department of Health, PO Box 95007, Lincoln NE 68509. **Tel** (402)471-2133, FAX (402)471-0383. **LC** RA410.8.N2; N45. **DD** 331.11/91362172/09782. *Formed by the union of Nebraska Physical Therapists, 0098-5731; Nebraska Health Manpower Reports. Podiatrists, 0363-7611; Nebraska Health Manpower Reports, Speech Pathologists; Nebraska Health Manpower Reports,*

# Medical Science and Technology — Physicians and Medical Personnel

Audiologists; Nebraska Health Manpower Reports. Chiropractors **and** Nebraska Health Manpower Reports. Veterinarians.

US
**NEED FOR WORKERS IN SELECTED OCCUPATIONS RELATED TO VOCATIONAL & TECHNICAL EDUCATION PROGRAMS. REGION 11.** **Main/Corp** Indiana. Employment Security Division. Research and Statistics Section. **VFOAT** Indiana Labor Market. English. an. Indiana Employment Security Division, Research and Statistics Section, 10 North Senate Avenue, Indianapolis IN 46204. **Tel** (317)232-7187. **LC** HD5725.I6; I53O. **DD** 331.12/3/097722.

AT/0313-2153
**NEW DOCTOR.** (NEW DOCTOR : JOURNAL OF THE DOCTORS' REFORM SOCIETY.). [New dr.]. **Added/Corp** Doctors' Reform Society (New South Wales). (1976)-. Periodical. English. ir (2 or 3 per year). 27.00Aus$ (one year); 50.00Aus$ (two year). Doctors Reform Society of New South Wales, Box 14, 4 Goulburn St, Sydney NSW 2000 Australia. **Tel** 011 61 2 264 9084, FAX 011 61 2 264 9084. **ED** Greg Heron. **Bk Rev**, (Qty: 2). **Ad Acc, Adv Mgr:** C. Zarresh. **Circ:** 2,000 (ctrl). **Ind/Abst** APAIS, Aust. Public Aff. Inf. Ser. (1983-).

NZ
**NEW ZEALAND MEDICAL REGISTER / MEDICAL COUNCIL OF NEW ZEALAND.** **Added/Corp** Medical Council of New Zealand. (19??)-. Periodical. English. an. 23.00NZ$. Medical Council of New Zealand, PO Box 11 649, Wellington New Zealand. **Tel** 011 64 4 3847635. **LC** R713.93; .N45. **DD** 610.69/52/025931. **NLM** W 22 KN4 M4.

US/0112-8868
**NEW ZEALAND MEDICAL WORKFORCE STATISTICS ... .** **See** Medical Science and Technology-Abstracting, Bibliographies and Statistics.

NZ/0300-2217
**NEW ZEALAND REGISTER OF SPECIALISTS.** English. an. 20.00NZ$; (medical register); 6.00 NZ$ (Specialists register). Medical Council of New Zealand, PO Box 11 649, Wellington New Zealand. **Tel** 011 64 4 3847635. **LC** R713.93; .N47. **DD** 616/.0025/931. **NLM** W 22 KN4 N5.
**Desc:** Alpha listing of medical practitioners registered in New Zealand as specialists in each category of specialty.

CN/0078-0316
**NEWFOUNDLAND MEDICAL DIRECTORY.** 1961-. Directory. English. an. Free. Newfoundland Medical Board, 47 Queen's Road, St John's Newfoundland A1C Y2B Canada. **DD** 610.69/52/025718. **NLM** W 22 DC2 N4N. **Continues** Newfoundland Medical Register, 0317-8374.

US/0029-2559
**NORTH CAROLINA MEDICAL JOURNAL (WINSTON-SALEM).** (NORTH CAROLINA MEDICAL JOURNAL.). [N. C. med. j.]. **Added/Corp** Medical Society of the State of North Carolina. North Carolina Medical Society. North Carolina Public Health Association. Proceedings. **VFOAT** North Carolina Medical Journal for Doctors and Their Patients; NCMJ. Vol. 1 (Jan. 1940)-. Periodical. English. mo. $17.00 (US); $18.00 (other). North Carolina Medical Society, PO Box 27167, Raleigh NC 27611. **Tel** (919)833-3836, FAX (919)833-2023. **ED** Francis Neelon, MD, Box 3910, Duke Medical Center, Durham, NC 27710, Tel. (919)286-6410. **LC** R11; .N93. **DD** 610.5. **NLM** W1 NO407. Index available (Dec.). cum. index. **Ad Acc, Adv Mgr:** Don French, Tel (919)467-8515. **Circ:** 8,500. available on microfilm and microfiche from University Microfilms International (UMI).
**Desc:** Includes Transactions of the auxiliary to the Medical society of the State of North Carolina and Proceedings of the North Carolina Public Health Association.
**Ind/Abst** Cumul. Index Nurs. Allied Health Lit.; Index Med.; Life Sci. Collect.; Rev. Med. Vet. Entomol.; Saf. Health Work; SportSearch.

●US/0000-1546
**OFFICIAL AMERICAN BOARD OF MEDICAL SPECIALTIES (ABMS) DIRECTORY OF BOARD CERTIFIED ANESTHESIOLOGISTS, THE. See** Medical Science and Technology-Anesthesiology.

●US/0000-1406
**OFFICIAL AMERICAN BOARD OF MEDICAL SPECIALTIES (ABMS) DIRECTORY OF BOARD CERTIFIED MEDICAL SPECIALISTS, THE. See** Medical Science and Technology.

US/0000-1406
**OFFICIAL AMERICAN BOARD OF MEDICAL SPECIALTIES (ABMS) DIRECTORY OF BOARD CERTIFIED MEDICAL SPECIALISTS, THE.** *Title Change.* **See** Medical Science and Technology.

●US/0000-1457
**OFFICIAL AMERICAN BOARD OF MEDICAL SPECIALTIES (ABMS) DIRECTORY OF BOARD CERTIFIED NUCLEAR MEDICINE SPECIALISTS, THE. See** Medical Science and Technology-Nuclear Medicine.

●US/0000-1600
**OFFICIAL AMERICAN BOARD OF MEDICAL SPECIALTIES (ABMS) DIRECTORY OF BOARD CERTIFIED OTOLARYNGOLOGISTS, THE. See** Medical Science and Technology-Otorhinolaryngology.

●US/0000-1678
**OFFICIAL AMERICAN BOARD OF MEDICAL SPECIALTIES (ABMS) DIRECTORY OF BOARD CERTIFIED SURGEONS, THE. See** Medical Science and Technology-Surgery.

●US/0000-1481
**OFFICIAL AMERICAN BOARD OF MEDICAL SPECIALTIES (ABMS) DIRECTORY OF BOARD CERTIFIED THORACIC SURGEONS, THE. See** Medical Science and Technology-Surgery.

US/0148-3579
**OFFICIAL DIRECTORY OF REGISTERED DOCTORS OF MEDICINE, MEDICAL CORPORATIONS AND DOCTORS OF CHIROPODY-PODIATRY.** [Off. dir. regist. dr. med. med. corp. dr. chirop.-podiatry]. **Added/Corp** West Virginia Medical Licensing Board. (19??)-. English. ir. West Virginia Board of Medicine, 100 Dee Drive/Suite 104, Charleston WV 25311. **Tel** (304)348-2921. **LC** R712.A2; W4. **DD** 610/.25/754. **Continues** Official Directory of Registered Doctors of Medicine.

CN/0712-6689
**ONTARIO MEDICINE.** [Ont. med.]. Vol. 1, No. 1 (Nov. 15, 1982)-. Periodical. English. Twenty-two times a year. 58.00Can$ Canada; 106.00Can$ other. MacLean Hunter Ltd. Business Publishers / Canada, Box 9100, Station A, Toronto ONT M5W 1A5 Canada. **Tel** (416)946-8420, (800)567-0444. **(Subscription address:** Indas, 35 Riviera Drive, Building 17, Markham Ontario L3R 8N4 Canada.) **DD** 610/.9713. available on microfilm and microfiche from University Microfilms International (UMI).

US
**PHYSICIAN.** (19??)-. Periodical. English. mo. Free to physicians. Focus on the Family, Colorado Springs CO 80995. **Tel** (800)232-6459.
**Desc:** A Christian magazine for physicians.

US/0898-2759
**PHYSICIAN EXECUTIVE.** [Physician exec.]. **Added/Corp** American Academy of Medical Directors. Vol. 12, No. 1 (Jan./Feb. 1986)-. Periodical. English. mo. Free (members American College of Physician Executives); $48.00 other. American College of Physician Executives, 4890 West Kennedy Boulevard / Suite 200, Tampa FL 33609. **Tel** (813)287-2000, (800)562-8088, FAX (813)287-8993. **ED** Wesley Curry. **DD** 658. **NLM** W1; PH776D. Index available. **Bk Rev. Ad Acc. Pr Rev. Circ:** 8,000. available on microfilm; available on an online database (file 149/Full-Text) from DIALOG. **Continues** Medical Director.
**Desc:** For physician managers; contains information on health care issues and on career development.
**Ind/Abst** Health Index (1989-); Health Period. Database [Full Txt.]; Health Plan. Adminis.; Health Ref. Cent. (Jan. 1989-) [Full Txt.] [Full Cov.]; Hospit. Health Admin. Index (1986-); Hospit. Manage. Rev.

US
**PHYSICIAN EXECUTIVE REVIEW.** English. qt. $35.00 (members of American College of Physician Executives); $70.00 other. American College of Physician Executives, 4890 West Kennedy Boulevard / Suite 200, Tampa FL 33609. **Tel** (813)287-2000, (800)562-8088, FAX (813)287-8993. **ED** Gwen Zins. **Bk Rev**, (Qty: 2-3).

US/0148-5490
**PHYSICIAN MANPOWER IN OREGON DATA BOOK.** [Physician manpow. Or. data book]. **Main/Corp** Comprehensive Health Planning Association for the Metropolitan Portland Area. English. Westridge Gardens II, Suite 114/5201 Southwest Westgate Drive, Portland OR 97221. **LC** RA410.8.O7; C65A. **DD** 331.1/1.

●US
**PHYSICIAN SALARY SURVEY REPORT, HOSPITAL-BASED AND GROUP PRACTICE. Added/Corp** Hospital Compensation Service. **VFOAT** Physician Salary Survey Report. (1992)-. English. an (March). $250.00. Hospital & Healthcare Compensation Service, PO Box 376, 69 Minnehaha Blvd., Oakland NJ 07436. **Tel** (201)405-0075, FAX (201)405-1258. **LC** R728.5; .C65. **DD** 331.2/816106952. **NLM** W1; PH777E. **Continues** Compensation Report on Hospital-Based and Group Practice Physicians, 1046-9435.
**Desc:** Covers salary and bonus data on thirty-three physician specialties, interns, and residencies according to geographic region, hospital-based, hmo, or group practice status.

US
**PHYSICIAN'S ADVISORY, THE.** English. mo. $220.00. MCA Publications, 140 West Germantown Pike, Suite 200, Plymouth Meeting PA 19462. **Tel** (215)828-3888.
**Ind/Abst** Hospit. Manage. Rev. (19??-).

US
**PHYSICIAN'S DRG WORKING GUIDEBOOK, THE.** (1984)-. English. an. $73.20. St. Anthony's Publishing Co., 500 Montgomery Street /Suite 700, Alexandria VA 22314. **Tel** (800)632-0123 ext. 5746. **(Subscription address:** St. Anthony Publishing Inc., PO Box 14212, Washington DC 20044.) **NLM** WX 39; P578.

US
**PHYSICIANS FEE GUIDE / AS COMPILED BY HEALTHCARE CONSULTANTS, INC.** *Title Change.* **See** Medical Science and Technology-Hospital Administration and Medical Centers.

CN
**PHYSICIAN'S MANAGEMENT MANUAL.** (19??)-. English. 34.00Can$ Canada; 61.00Can$ other. MacLean Hunter Ltd. Business Publishers / Canada, Box 9100, Station A, Toronto ONT M5W 1A5 Canada. **Tel** (416)946-8420, (800)567-0444. **(Subscription address:** Indas, 35 Riviera Drive, Building 17, Markham Ontario L3R 8N4 Canada.)

CN/0705-6311
**PHYSICIAN'S MANAGEMENT MANUALS.** *Ceased.* [Physician's manage. man.]. (Fall 1976)-(Oct. 1994). Periodical. English. Twelve times a year. MacLean Hunter Ltd. Business Publishers / Canada, Box 9100, Station A, Toronto ONT M5W 1A5 Canada. **Tel** (416)946-8420, (800)567-0444. **(Subscription address:** Indas, 35 Riviera Drive, Building 17, Markham Ontario L3R 8N4 Canada.) **ED** Oleu Edur. **DD** 658/.91/610971. **Ad Acc. Circ:** 33,000 (ctrl). available on microfilm from University Microfilms International (UMI).
**Desc:** Written to serve the practice and financial needs of Canadian physicians. Many topics are covered in the areas of taxes, personal finances, retirement, law and real estate.

CN/0848-676X
**PHYSICIAN'S NEWSLETTER (1990).** (PHYSICIAN'S NEWSLETTER.). [Phys. newsl.]. **Added/Corp** British Columbia. Medical Services Commission. Issue No. 14/2 (May 1990)-. Newsletter. English. **DD** 354.7110082/56. **Continues** Teleplan Newsletter., 1180-8756; *Separated from* Practitioner's Newsletter., 0225-5227.

US
**PHYSICIAN'S RELATIONS UPDATE.** (199?)-. English. mo. $219.00. American Health Consultants, 3525 Piedmont Road, Suite 400, Atlanta GA 30305. **Tel** (800)688-2421, (404)262-7436. **(Subscription address:** American Health Consultants, PO Box 95278, Chicago IL 60694.) **Continues** Physician's Relations Advisor.

US/0091-200X
**PHYSICIAN'S WORLD.** Periodical. English. mo. $15.00. Physicians World Inc, 488 Madison Avenue, New York NY 10020. **LC** R11; .P68. **DD** 610/.5. **NLM** W1 PH835.

US/0275-0503
**PROFESSIONAL LIABILITY. See** Law.

US/0741-4749
**PROFESSIONAL REGULATION NEWS.** Began with Aug. 1981 issue. Periodical. English. mo. $65.00 members, $95.00 nonmembers. National Commission for Health Certifying Agencies, 1101 30th Street NW, Suite 108, Washington DC 20007. **LC** KF2905.1 .A15; P76. **DD** 344.73/041; 347.30441.

# Medical Science and Technology —Podiatry

US
**QUADRENNIAL REPORT TO THE PRESIDENT ON THE ADEQUACY OF SPECIAL PAY FOR PHYSICIANS AND DENTISTS IN THE DEPARTMENT OF VETERANS AFFAIRS. Main/Corp** United States. Dept. of Veterans Affairs. **Added/Corp** United States. Congress. House. Committee on Veterans' Affairs. (1989)-. English. ir.

US/0739-2079
**QUARTERLY - PHI LAMBDA KAPPA MEDICAL FRATERNITY.** (QUARTERLY / PHI LAMBDA KAPPA MSAS.). **VFOAT** PLK Mass Quarterly; P.L.K.-M.S.A.S. Quarterly. **VAT** Phi Lambda Kappa Medical Student's Aid Society Quarterly. Vol. 39, No. 1 (March 1964)-. Periodical. English. qt. $10.00. Phi Lambda Kappa Medical Fraternity, Bucks County Office Center, 1200 New Rodgers Road/Suite B4A, Bristol PA 19007. Tel (215)785-2325. **ED** Louis Pelner. **NLM** W1 QU158ML. **Bk Rev. Ad Acc. Circ:** 1,200 (ctrl). **Continues** Phi Lambda Kappa Quarterly, 0733-4400.
**Desc:** General medical information and fraternal news book reviews and also general information to acquaint even lay people with current updates in medicine.

US/1054-1675
**RECORD (SOMERVILLE, MASS.). See** Political Science-Civil Rights.

BL
**RECURSOS HUMANOS. Main/Corp** Santa Catarina, Brazil. Secretaria da Saude. 1974-. Portuguese. **LC** RA410.9.B7; S25A.

US
**REGISTERED PHYSICIANS IN THE STATE OF NEVADA.** English. **LC** R712.A2; N33. **DD** 614.24. **NLM** W 22 AN2 S7R.

US
**RELATIVE VALUES FOR PHYSICIANS.** (19??)-. Periodical. English. qt. $242.50. McGraw Hill Publishing Company, Inc., 1221 Avenue of the Americas, New York NY 10020. **Tel** (212)512-6410, (800)525-5003, FAX (212)512-6111.

CN/0225-901X
**REPORT - DIVISION OF HEALTH SERVICES RESEARCH AND DEVELOPMENT, UNIVERSITY OF BRITISH COLUMBIA.** [Rep. - Div. Health Serv. Res. Dev., Univ. B.C.]. **Main/Corp** University of British Columbia. Division of Health Services Research and Development. Began publication in 197-. Periodical. English. Office of the Coordinator, Division of Health Services Research and Development, Health Sciences Centre, University of British Columbia V6T 1W5 Canada. **Tel** FAX (604)228-2495. **DD** 610.69/09711.

CN/0707-3542
**ROLLCALL.** 1974-. English. be. $5.00. Office of the Coordinator, Division of Health Services Research and Development, Health Sciences Centre, University of British Columbia V6T 1W5 Canada. **Tel** FAX (604)228-2495. **DD** 610.69/09711.

US/0097-9147
**ROSTER OF REGISTERED PRACTITIONERS OF THE HEALING ARTS LICENSED AND REGISTERED IN THE STATE OF VIRGINIA. Main/Corp** Virginia State Board of Medicine. **VFOAT** Roster of Practitioners of the Healing Arts Licensed and Registered in the Commonwealth of Virginia. English. an. Virginia State Board of Medicine, 505 Washington Ave No.200, Portsmouth VA 23704. **LC** R712.A2; V8. **DD** 610/.25/755. **NLM** W 22 AV8 S7R. **Continues** Roster of Registered Practitioners of the Healing Art, in Active Practice in Virginia.

CN/0824-8451
**SASKATCHEWAN HEALTH MANPOWER REPORT.** [Sask. health manpow. rep.]. **VFOAT** Annual Report. 1979/1981-. English. an. Policy Research and Management Services Branch, Saskatchewan Department of Health, 3475 Albert Street, Regina Saskatchewan S4S 6X6 Canada. **LC** RA410.9.C2; S27A. **DD** 331.12/5161/097124. **Continues** Saskatchewan Health Manpower Annual Report, 0702-9330.

CN/1183-580X
**SENS DES AFFAIRES (OTTAWA. PRINTEMPS 1990).** (LE SENS DES AFFAIRES.). [Sens aff.]. **Added/Corp** Compagnie de Gestion MD Limitee. Association Medicale Canadienne. (Spring 1990)-. Periodical. French. qt. Limited free distribution. MD Management Limited, 1867 Alta Vista Drive, Ottawa, Ontario K1G 3Y6 Canada. **DD** 332.024/61/05.

US/0742-2709
**SOCIOECONOMIC CHARACTERISTICS OF MEDICAL PRACTICE.** [Socioecon. charact. med. pract.]. **Added/Corp** Center for Health Policy Research (American Medical Association). (1983)-. English. an. $110.00. American Medical Association, 515 North State Street, Chicago IL 60610. **Tel** (312)464-5000, (800)262-2350, FAX (312)464-5831. **(Subscription address:** American Medical Association, PO Box 109050, Chicago IL 60610.**) LC** R729; .S62. **DD** 338.4/73621/720973. **NLM** W1; SO878L. **Continues in part** SMS Report (Chicago, Ill. : 1987).

BE
**STATISTISCHE GEGEVENS BETREFFENDE HET GENEESHERENKORPS. Main/Corp** Belgium. Ministere de la Sante Publique et de la Famille. Centre de Traitement de l'Information. **VFOAT** Donnees Statistiques Concernant le Corps Medical. Dutch (French). **LC** RA410.9.B4; B44A.

●US/1070-7263
**THERAPISTS AND ALLIED HEALTH PROFESSIONALS CAREER DIRECTORY. VFOAT** Allied Health Career Directory. (1993)-. Directory. English. be. $29.95 (hardcover), $17.95 (softcover). Gale Research Inc., 835 Penobscot Building, Detroit MI 48226. **Tel** (800)877-GALE, (313)961-2242, FAX (313)961-6083, telex TWX 810-221-7086. **NLM** W1; TH666.
**Desc:** Some of the careers covered include chiropractor, dietitian, dental hygienist, pharmacist, occupational therapist and recreational therapist.

US/0098-8413
**U.S. ALPHABETICAL PHYSICIAN REFERENCE LISTING. VAT** United States Alphabetical Physician Reference Listing. English. Fisher-Stevens Inc, 120 Brighton Road, Clifton NJ 07012. **LC** R712.A1; U48. **DD** 610.69/52/02573.

US/0741-6326
**U.S. MEDICAL LICENSURE STATISTICS ... AND LICENSURE REQUIREMENTS ... See** Medical Science and Technology-Abstracting, Bibliographies and Statistics.

US/0191-6246
**U.S. MEDICINE.** [U. S. med.]. **VAT** United States Medicine. (19??)-. Periodical. English. Twelve times a year. $125.00 one year; $250.00 two years; $375.00 three years. US Medicine Inc, 2033 M Street Northwest, Suite 505, Washington DC 20036. **Tel** (202)463-6000. **ED** Nancy Tomich. **NLM** W1 U752. **Bk Rev. Ad Acc. Circ:** 32,000 (ctrl).
**Desc:** Clinical, political and economic stories of interest to physicians employed by government.
**Ind/Abst** Hospit. Health Admin. Index.

US/0098-986X
**U.S. PHYSICIAN REFERENCE LISTING. VAT** United States Physician Reference Listing. 1973-. English. Fisher-Stevens Inc, 120 Brighton Road, Clifton NJ 07012. **LC** R712.A1; U52. **DD** 610/.25/73. **NLM** W 22 AA1 U59. **Continues** AMA Physician Reference Listing, 0360-0998.

US/0161-7176
**WASHINGTON PHYSICIANS DIRECTORY, THE.** (19??)-. English. $10.00. Washington Physicians, PO Box 4436, Silver Spring MD 20904. **Tel** (301)384-1506. **LC** R712.A3; W42. **DD** 610/.25/753. **NLM** W 22 AD6 W3.

US/0743-1333
**WEST VIRGINIA DOCTORS OF MEDICINE.** English. West Virginia Statistics Center, 1800 Washington Street, East Charleston WV 25305. **LC** RA410.8.W4. **DD** 331.12/5161/09754. **NLM** W2; AW4 B9wc.

US/0361-817X
**WISCONSIN PHYSICIANS : DESCRIPTION AND DISTRIBUTION.** English. an. Department of Health & Social Services / Wisconsin, 1 West Wilson Street, PO Box 309, Madison WI 53701. **LC** RA410.8.W6; W6. **DD** 331.1/1.

## PODIATRY

US/8750-2585
**APMA NEWS.** (APMA NEWS : NEWS FROM THE AMERICAN PODIATRIC MEDICAL ASSOCIATION.). [APMA news]. **Added/Corp** American Podiatric Medical Association. **VFOAT** A.P.M.A. News. **VAT** American Podiatric Medical Association News. Vol. 5, No. 9 (Sept. 15, 1984)-. Periodical. English. Twelve times a year. $50.00 US; $60.00 others. American Podiatric Medical Association, 9312 Old Georgetown Road, Bethesda MD 20814. **Tel** (301)571-9200, FAX (301)530-2752. **ED** David J. Zych. **DD** 617. **Bk Rev. Ad Acc. Circ:** 14,000. **Continues** American Podiatry Association. APA Report, 0272-7722.
**Desc:** General news and feature stories concerning podiatric medicine.

US/0092-7651
**ARCHIVES OF PODIATRIC MEDICINE AND FOOT SURGERY.** V. 1- July 1973-. Periodical. English. qt. $20.00. Futura Publishing Company Inc., 135 Bedford Road, PO Box 418, Armonk NY 10504-0418. **Tel** (914)273-1014, (800)877-8761, FAX (914)273-1015, (914)273-1016. **LC** RD563; .A73. **DD** 617/.585/005. **NLM** W1 AR477M.

US/0164-2553
**ARCHIVES OF PODIATRIC MEDICINE AND FOOT SURGERY. SUPPLEMENT.** 1-. Monographic series. English. Price varies per volume. Futura Publishing Company Inc., 135 Bedford Road, PO Box 418, Armonk NY 10504-0418. **Tel** (914)273-1014, (800)877-8761, FAX (914)273-1015, (914)273-1016. **NLM** W1 AR477MA.

AT/0311-3612
**AUSTRALIAN PODIATRIST.** [Aust. podiatr.]. (1974)-. Periodical. English. Four times a year (Mar., June, Sept., Dec). 60.00Aus$ Australia; 70.00Aus$ other. Australian Podiatry Council, 71A Burwood Road, Hawthorn Victoria 3122 Australia. **Tel** 011 61 03 8190755, FAX 011 61 03 8190788. **DD** _a617.5850994. **Bk Rev. Ad Acc, Adv Mgr:** S. Reardon, **Tel** 03 8829666. **Pr Rev. Circ:** 1,300. **Continues** Australian Journal of Chiropody.
**Desc:** Professional information and new articles on podiatry profession.

UK/0955-8160
**BRITISH JOURNAL OF PODIATRIC MEDICINE & SURGERY. Added/Corp** Podiatry Association. Vol. 1, No. 1 (Jan. 1989)-. English. mo. £3.50 (single copy); £34.00 (annual subscription). Society of Chiropodists, 53 Welbeck Street, (Brian Berry), London W1M 7HE England. **Tel** 011 44 71 486-3381, FAX 011 44 71 935-6359. **ED** Brian Berry. **NLM** W1; BR613G. Index available. **Bk Rev. Ad Acc. Pr Rev. Circ:** 7,500. available on microfilm. **Continues** Podiatry Journal.
**Desc:** Chiropodial/Podiatric journal containing articles, surveys, and reports at a learned level.

CN/0820-8212
**CANADIAN PODIATRY ASSOCIATION NEWSLETTER. Ceased.** [Can. podiatry Assoc. newsl.]. (Fall 1981)-Ceased (1988). Newsletter. English. qt. Canadian Podiatric Association East/Suite 801, Toronto Ontario M4P 1P2 Canada. **DD** 617.585/0971. **Continues** Canadian Podiatrist, 0008-4786.

UK/0009-4714
**CHIROPODY REVIEW.** (19??)-. English. Six times a year (Jan., Mar., May, July, Sept., Nov.). £12.00 UK; £15.00 others. Institute of Chiropodists, 27 Wright Street Southport, Merseys PR9 0TL England. **Tel** 011 44 704 546141, FAX 011 44 704 500477. **ED** P.G.F. Basham. **Bk Rev, (Qty: 6)**. **Ad Acc, Adv Mgr:** A.D. Nines. **Circ:** 1,400 (ctrl).

IT/0392-0771
**CHIRURGIA DEL PIEDE.** [Chir. piede]. **VFOAT** Foot Surgery. (1977)-. Periodical. Multiple languages. Six times a year. $95.00 (individuals), $145.00 (institutions). Edizioni Minerva Medica, Corso Bramante 83-85, 10126 Turin Italy. **Tel** 011 39 11 678282, FAX 011 39 11 674502. **UDC** 617-089.
**Desc:** Official journal of the Italian and Swiss Society of Foot Medicine and Surgery.
**Ind/Abst** EMBASE.

US/0191-7870
**CLINICAL BIOMECHANICS.** [Clin. biomech.]. Vol. 1 (1971)-. Monographic series. English. bm. Price varies per volume. Clinical Biomechanics Corporation, PO Box 35185, Los Angeles CA 90035. **NLM** W1 CL668U.
**Ind/Abst** Ergon. Abstr.; Ref. Upd. Deluxe Ed.; SCISEARCH.

US/0891-8422
**CLINICS IN PODIATRIC MEDICINE AND SURGERY.** [Clin. podiatr. med. surg.]. **VFOAT** Podiatric Medicine and Surgery. Vol. 3, No. 1 (Jan. 1986)-. English. qt. $89.00 (individual), $111.00 (institution) US; $125.00 (individual), $132.00 (institution) other. W.B. Saunders Company, A Subsidiary of Harcourt Brace Jovanovich, Inc., The Curtis Center/Suite 300, Independence Square West, Philadelphia PA 19106-3399. **Tel** (215)238-7800 or, 5587, FAX (215)238-7883, telex 173146. **(Subscription address:** W. B. Saunders Company / North America Subscriptions, c/o Periodicals, 6277 Sea Harbour Drive, 4th Floor, Orlando FL 32887.**) ED** Barbara A. Connover. **LC** RD563. **DD** 617/.585/005. **NLM** W1; CL831DE. Index available. **Pr Rev. Circ:** 3,300. available on microfilm and microfiche from University Microfilms International (UMI). **Continues** Clinics in Podiatry, 0742-0668.
**Desc:** Practical updates on medical and surgical procedures and techniques written by experts in the field. Each issue addresses a single topic.
**Ind/Abst** Health Plan. Adminis.; Index Med. (1986-); INIS Atomindex [Micro.].

US
**DESK REFERENCE.** **Main/Corp** American Podiatric Medical Association. (1984)-. English. ir. American Podiatric Medical Association, 9312 Old Georgetown Road, Bethesda MD 20814. **Tel** (301)571-9200, FAX (301)530-2752. **LC** RD563; .A582. **DD** 617/.585/005. **NLM** WE 22; AA1 A55D. ***Continues*** *American Podiatry Association. Desk Reference, 0364-7226.*

US/0364-7226
**DESK REFERENCE - AMERICAN PODIATRY ASSOCIATION.** ***Title Change.*** (DESK REFERENCE.). **Main/Corp** American Podiatry Association. **Added/Corp** American Podiatry Association. Journal. Vol. for (1958)-(198?). English. an. American Podiatric Medical Association, 9312 Old Georgetown Road, Bethesda MD 20814. **Tel** (301)571-9200, FAX (301)530-2752. **LC** RD563; .A582a. **DD** 617/.585/005. **NLM** WE 22 AA1 A55D. ***Continued by*** *American Podiatric Medical Association. Desk Reference.*

●US/1071-1007
**FOOT & ANKLE INTERNATIONAL.** (FOOT & ANKLE INTERNATIONAL AMERICAN ORTHOPAEDIC FOOT AND ANKLE SOCIETY / SWISS FOOT AND ANKLE SOCIETY.). [Foot ankle int.]. **Added/Corp** American Orthopaedic Foot and Ankle Society. Swiss Foot and Ankle Society. **VFOAT** Foot and Ankle International; Foot & Ankle. Vol. 15, No. 1 (Jan. 1994)-. Periodical. English. mo. $95.00 (individual), $110.00 (institutions), US; $125.00 (individual), $140.00 (institution) other. Williams & Wilkins Company, 428 East Preston Street, Baltimore MD 21202-3993. **Tel** (410)528-4000, (800)638-6423, FAX (410)528-8596, telex 87669. **(Subscription address:** Williams & Wilkins, PO Box 64380, Baltimore MD 21264.**)** **DD** 617. **CODEN** FAINE4. **Ad Acc. Pr Rev. Circ:** 3,500. available on microfilm. Documents available from Quick Copies. ***Continues*** *Foot & Ankle, 0198-0211.*
**Desc:** International articles on new approaches to foot and ankle disorders and surgical treatment for orthapedic surgeons and podiatrists.

●US/1068-3100
**FOOT AND ANKLE QUARTERLY.** [Foot ankle q.]. Vol. 6, No. 1 (Spring 1993)-. Periodical. English. qt. $295.00 (institutions). Data Trace Publishing Group, PO Box 1239, Brooklandville MD 21022. **Tel** (410)494-4994, (800)342-0454, FAX (410)494-0515. **(Subscription address:** Data Trace Medical Publishers, Inc., PO Box 1239, Brooklandville MD 21022.**)** **DD** 616. ***Continues*** *Podiatry Tracts, 0894-6116.*

US/0196-4925
**ICPM. SERIES 1.** **VAT** Illinois College of Podiatric Medicine. Series One. No. 1- June 1975-. Monographic series. English. Price varies per volume. **NLM** W1 I216.

UK/0961-6055
**JOURNAL OF BRITISH PODIATRIC MEDICINE LONDON 1991.** [J. Br. podiatr. med.Lond., 1991]. (1991)-. Periodical. English. mo. £40.00 UK; £57.00 other. Society of Chiropodists, 53 Welbeck Street, (Brian Berry), London W1M 7HE England. **Tel** 011 44 71 486-3381, FAX 011 44 71 935-6359. **DD** 617.5850941. ***Continues*** *Chiropodist (London), 0009-4706.*

US/0893-2034
**JOURNAL OF CURRENT PODIATRIC MEDICINE, THE.** ***Ceased.*** [J. curr. podiatr. med.]. Vol. 35, No. 1 (Jan. 1986)-(19??). Periodical. English. mo. Current Podiatry Publications, PO Box 141, Fall River WI 53932. **DD** 617. **NLM** W1; JO612DH. **CODEN** JCPMEQ. Documents available from BIOSIS Document Express. ***Continues*** *Current Podiatric Medicine, 0891-7876.*
**Ind/Abst** Biol. Abstr. (1986-); EMBASE.

US/0449-2544
**JOURNAL OF FOOT SURGERY, THE.** ***Title Change.*** [J. foot surg.]. **Added/Corp** American College of Foot Surgeons. (1967) Vol. 31 (1967)-Nov./Dec. (1992). Periodical. English. bm. Williams & Wilkins Company, 428 East Preston Street, Baltimore MD 21202-3993. **Tel** (410)528-4000, (800)638-6423, FAX (410)528-8596, telex 87669. **(Subscription address:** US/ PO Box 64380, Baltimore, MD 21264-4380; Japan/ Igaku-Shoin MYW Ltd, 1-28-36 Hongo, Bunkyo-ku Tokyo 113 Japan; European/ The Broadway House, 2-6 Fulham Broadway, London SW6 1AA England; telephone: (800)638-6423**)** **ED** Richard Reinherz. **DD** 617. **NLM** W1 JO653. **CODEN** JFSUBF. **Ad Acc. Circ:** 5,400. available on microfilm. Documents available from BIOSIS Document Express, Quick Copies. ***Continues*** *American College of Foot Surgeons Journal, 0517-0591.* ***Continued by*** *Journal of Foot and Ankle Surgery, 1067-2516.*
**Desc:** Clinical advances in foot surgery present for podiatrists and orthopaedic foot surgeons.
**Ind/Abst** Biol. Abstr. (1986-); EMBASE; Energy Res. Abstr. (Aug. 1982-); Index Med.; INIS Atomindex [Micro.]; SportSearch.

US/0093-7339
**JOURNAL OF PODIATRIC MEDICAL EDUCATION.** ***Ceased.*** [J. podiatr. med. educ.]. Vol. 5 (1974)-Vol. 16 (1987). Periodical. English. sa. American Association of Colleges in Podiatric Medicine. **Tel** (301)984-9351. **ED** Suzanne H Howard. **NLM** W1 JO837E. **Circ:** 1,300 (ctrl). ***Continues*** *Journal of Podiatric Education, 0092-4024.*
**Desc:** Dedicated to publishing information and studies pertaining to the field of podiatric medical education.
**Ind/Abst** Curr. Index J. Educ.

US/8750-7315
**JOURNAL OF THE AMERICAN PODIATRIC MEDICAL ASSOCIATION.** [J. Am. Podiatr. Med. Assoc.]. **Added/Corp** American Podiatric Medical Association. National Library of Medicine (U.S.). Vol. 75, No. 1 (Jan. 1985)-. Academic Scholarly Publication. English. Twelve times a year. $75.00 US; $85.00 other. American Podiatric Medical Association, 9312 Old Georgetown Road, Bethesda MD 20814. **Tel** (301)571-9200, FAX (301)530-2752. **LC** RD563.A2; A515. **DD** 617/.585/005. **NLM** W1; JO91G. **CODEN** JAPAEA. Index available. cum. index. **Bk Rev. Ad Acc. Pr Rev. Acid Free. Circ:** 12,000 (ctrl). available on microfilm and microfiche from University Microfilms International (UMI). Documents available from BIOSIS Document Express. ***Continues*** *Journal of the American Podiatry Association, 0003-0538.*
**Desc:** Scientific journal of the Professional Membership Association of Doctors of Podiatric Medicine in the United States.
**Ind/Abst** Biol. Abstr. (1985-); Curr. Contents Clin. Med.; EMBASE; Energy Res. Abstr.; Helminthol. Abstr. (19??-19??); Index Med.; INIS Atomindex [Micro.]; Nutr. Abstr. Rev., Ser. A, Hum. Exp.; Life Sci. Collect.; Rev. Med. Vet. Mycology; SCISEARCH; Soc. Sci. Cit. Index [Select. Cov.].

FR/0759-2280
**MEDECINE ET CHIRURGIE DU PIED.** (MEDECINE ET CHIRURGIE DU PIED / SOCIETE FRANCAISE DE MEDECINE ET CHIRURGIE DU PIED.). [Med. chir. pied]. **Added/Corp** Societe Francaise de Medecine et Chirurgie du Pied. Vol. 1, No. 1 (June 1984)-. Periodical. French (summaries and/or abstracts in English). Four times a year. 1000.00F France; 1100.00F other. Expansion Scientifique Francaise, 31 Boulevard de la Tour-Maubourg, 75007 Paris France. **Tel** 011 33 1 40 62 64 00, 011 33 1 40626439. **NLM** W1; ME139NG. **[CCC].**

US/0890-3972
**PODIATRIC PRODUCTS.** [Podiatr. prod.]. (1986)-. Periodical. English. Six times a year (Jan., Mar., May., July, Sept., Nov.). $12.00. Novicom Inc, 3510 Torrance Boulevard, Suite 315, Torrance CA 90503. **Tel** (310)316-8112. **(Subscription address:** PO Box 698, Redondo Beach CA 90277**)** **ED** Susan Fennell. **DD** 617. Index Bound in First Issue. **Bk Rev. Ad Acc. Circ:** 12,000 (ctrl). ***Continues*** *Podiatry Products Report, 0888-0484.*
**Desc:** Covers product news and articles related to the podiatric medical profession.

US/0744-3528
**PODIATRY MANAGEMENT.** [Podiatry manage.]. Vol. 1, No. 1 (Jan. 1982)-. Periodical. English. Eight times a year. $30.00 (one year); $49.00 (two years). Kane Communications Inc, 7000 Terminal Square, Suite 210, Upper Darby PA 19082. **Tel** (215)734-2420, FAX (215)734-2423. **ED** Barry H. Block. **DD** 617. cum. index. **Bk Rev. Ad Acc.**

US/0894-6116
**PODIATRY TRACTS.** ***Title Change.*** [Podiatry tracts]. Vol. 1, No. 1 (Feb. 1988)-(1992). Periodical. English. bm. Data Trace Publishing Group, PO Box 1239, Brooklandville MD 21022. **Tel** (410)494-4994, (800)342-0454, FAX (410)494-0515. **DD** 616. **[CCC].** ***Continued by*** *Foot and Ankle Quarterly, 1068-3100.*

CN
**RAPPORT ANNUEL - L'ORDRE DES PODIATRES DU QUEBEC.** **Main/Corp** Ordre des Podiatres du Quebec. 1.- 1974/75-. French. an. Casier Postal 275, Succursale Postale Montreal-Nord, Montreal-Nord Quebec H1H 5L4 Canada. **LC** RD563; .O67A. **DD** 617/.585/0062714.

FR/0300-1296
**REVUE DE PODOLOGIE.** ***Title Change.*** **Added/Corp** Federation Nationale des Podologues. Societe de Podologie. Annee 1 No. 1 (1952)-Nouv. Ser., No. 1 (Jan./Fev. 1971)-No. 65 (Janv.-Fevr. 1992). Periodical. French. bm. Federation Nationale Podologue, 163 rue Saint Honore, 75001 Paris France. **Tel** 33 1 42606245. **NLM** W1; RE799T. ***Absorbed*** *Revue du Praticien en Podologie, 0300-130X.* ***Continued by*** *Podologue.*

US/0742-194X
**YEAR BOOK OF PODIATRIC MEDICINE AND SURGERY (CHICAGO, ILL.), THE.** (THE YEAR BOOK OF PODIATRIC MEDICINE AND SURGERY.). [Year book of podiatr. med. surgery]. **Added/Corp** Year Book Medical Publishers. **VFOAT** Yearbook of Podiatric Medicine and Surgery; Podiatric Medicine and Surgery. (1985)-. English. an. $59.95. Mosby Year Book Inc., 11830 Westline Industrial Drive, St Louis MO 63146. **Tel** (800)325-4177, (314)872-8370, FAX (314)432-1380, telex 44-2402. **LC** RD563; .Y38. **DD** 617/.585/005.

US/0276-6744
**YEARBOOK OF PODIATRIC MEDICINE AND SURGERY.** [Yearb. podiatr. med. surg.]. (1981)-. English. an. Futura Publishing Company Inc., 135 Bedford Road, PO Box 418, Armonk NY 10504-0418. **Tel** (914)273-1014, (800)877-8761, FAX (914)273-1015, (914)273-1016. **ED** T. H. Clarke. **LC** RD563; .Y4. **DD** 617/.585/05. **NLM** W1 YE316F. ***Continues*** *Yearbook of Podiatry.*

---

## PSYCHIATRY

---

US/0884-1519
**ABMS DIRECTORY OF CERTIFIED PSYCHIATRISTS.** [ABMS dir. certif. psychiatr.]. **Added/Corp** American Board of Medical Specialties. American Board of Psychiatry and Neurology. **VFOAT** Directory of Certified Psychiatrists. **VAT** American Board of Medical Specialties Directory Psychiatrists. 1st Ed. (1985)-. English. be (every two years). $42.45. American Board of Medical Specialties, 1 Rotary Center, Suite 805, Evanston IL 60201. **Tel** (708)491-9091. **LC** RC335; .A25. **DD** 616.89/0025/73. **NLM** WM 22.1; A1523.

US/1042-9670
**ACADEMIC PSYCHIATRY.** (ACADEMIC PSYCHIATRY : THE JOURNAL OF THE AMERICAN ASSOCIATION OF DIRECTORS OF PSYCHIATRIC RESIDENCY TRAINING AND THE ASSOCIATION FOR ACADEMIC PSYCHIATRY.). [Acad. psychiatry]. **Added/Corp** American Association of Directors of Psychiatric Residency Training. Association for Academic Psychiatry. Vol. 13, No. 1 (Spring 1989)-. Academic Scholarly Publication. English. qt (4 issues). $135.00 US; $150.00 other (institution). American Psychiatric Press Inc., 1400 K Street Northwest, Suite 1101, Washington DC 20005. **Tel** (202)682-6222, FAX (202)789-2648. **LC** RC336; .J68. **DD** 616.89/0071/1. **NLM** W1; AC33NP. **Ad Acc. Pr Rev.** available on microfilm and microfiche from University Microfilms International (UMI). ***Continues*** *Journal of Psychiatric Education, 0363-1907.*
**Desc:** Publishes work describing educational efforts by and for psychiatrists, and articles addressing teaching, research, administrative, clinical, organizational and economic issues relevant to the academic missions of the department of psychiatry. Overview articles present empirical research and critical analyses of important topics in academic psychiatry.
**Ind/Abst** Abstr. Res. Pastor. Care Couns.; Annals Behav. Med.; Contents Pages Educ.; Curr. Contents Soc. Behav. Sci.; EMBASE; Psychol. Abstr. (1977-).

US/0192-1088
**ACADEMY FORUM (NEW YORK), THE.** (THE ACADEMY FORUM.). V. 22- Spring 1978-. Periodical. English. qt. Free to qualified, $15.00 other. Ann Ruth Turkel MD, 350 Central Park West, New York NY 10025. **Tel** (212)679-4105. **(Subscription address:** American Academy of Psychoanalysis, 30 East 40th Street/Suite 206, New York, NY 10016**)** **ED** Ann Ruth Turkel. **LC** RC500; .A23. **DD** 616.89/17/05. **NLM** W1 AC482. **Bk Rev. Ad Acc. Circ:** 4,000 (ctrl). ***Continues*** *Academy, 0197-5781.*
**Desc:** News and opinions on matters of interest of psychoanalysts.

NE
**ACTA NEURO PSYCHIATRICA.** See Medical Science and Technology-Neurology.

SZ/0001-6586
**ACTA PAEDOPSYCHIATRICA.** ***Ceased.*** [Acta paedopsychiatr.]. **Added/Corp** International Association for Child Psychiatry and Allied Professions. European Union for Child Psychiatry. Vol. 20 (1953)-Vol. 56. Periodical. English (French and German). Four times a year. Springer-Verlag GmbH & Company KG, Heidelberger Platz 3, D 14197 Berlin Germany. **Tel** 011 49 30 8207223, FAX 011 49 30 8214091, telex 183 319 SPBLN D. **(Subscription address:** Springer Verlag New York Inc. / for North America, 44 Hartz Way, Secaucus NJ 07096.**)** **ED** H.G. Reinhard and W. Bettschart. **NLM** W1 AC906. **CODEN** ACPDAW. **[CCC].** Documents available from BIOSIS Document Express. ***Continues*** *Zeitschrift fur Kinderpsychiatrie.*
**Desc:** Encompasses all aspects of child psychiatry. Of interest to psychiatrists, physicians, and psychologists playing a positive role in the mental development of today's children and youth.
**Ind/Abst** Biol. Abstr. (-1985); EMBASE; Index Med.; Psychol. Abstr. (1953-).

AG/0001-6896
**ACTA PSIQUIATRICA Y PSICOLOGICA DE AMERICA LATINA.** [Acta psiquiatr. psicol. Am. Lat.]. **Added/Corp** Acta, Fondo Para la Salud Mental. Fundacion Acta, Fondo Para la Salud Mental. **VFOAT** Acta. Vol. 10, No. 1 (March 1964)-. Periodical. Spanish (summaries and/or abstracts in English). qt (4 issues). $70.00. Acta Psiquiatrica Y Psicologica de America Latina, Malabia 2274 13 A, 1425 Buenos Aires Argentina. **Tel** 54 1 711998, FAX 54 1 8545602. **ED** Guillermo Vidal. **NLM** W1 AC93H. **CODEN** APQPAS. **Bk Rev**, (Qty: 40). **Ad Acc, Adv Mgr:** Ms. Perez-Feinandez, **Tel** 54 1 8545602. **Pr Rev. Circ:** 3,200. available on CD-ROM. ***Continues*** *Acta Psiquiatrica y Psicologica Argentina.*
**Desc:** Scientific journal featuring the development of psychiatry, psychology and related sciences in Latin America.
**Ind/Abst** Index Med.; Psychol. Abstr. (1964-); PsycINFO; PsycLit.

BE/0300-8967
**ACTA PSYCHIATRICA BELGICA.** [Acta psychiatr. Belg.]. **Added/Corp** Groupement Belge de Psychopathologie de l'Expression. Societe Royale de Medicine Mentale de Belgique. Vol. 70, (Jan. 1970)-. Academic Scholarly Publication. French (summaries and/or abstracts in English, German, Italian, Spanish and Dutch). Six times a year. 3250.00F Belguim; 3500.00F other. Acta Psychiatrica Belgica, Rue Jean Paquot 6 Mr Charles, 1050 Brussels Belgium. **Tel** 322 648 2110. **NLM** W1 AC93R. **CODEN** APBABB. **Bk Rev. Ad Acc. Circ:** 400. Documents available from BIOSIS Document Express. ***Continues in part*** *Acta Neurologica et Psychiatrica Belgica.*
**Ind/Abst** Biol. Abstr.; EMBASE; Health Plan. Adminis.; Index Med.; Middle East Abstr. Index; Psychol. Abstr. (1970-); PsycINFO; PsycLit.

DK/0001-690X
**ACTA PSYCHIATRICA SCANDINAVICA.** [Acta psychiatr. Scand.]. Vol. 37 (1961)-. Academic Scholarly Publication. German (French and English). mo. kr2660.00 US, Canada and Japan; kr2570.00 other. Munksgaard International Publishers Ltd, PO Box 2148, DK-1016 Copenhagen K Denmark. **Tel** 011 45 33 12 70 30, FAX 011 45 33 12 93 87, telex 19431 MUNKS DK. **ED** Jan-Otto Ottosson. **UDC** 616.89. **NLM** W1 AC9325. **CODEN** APYSA9. **[CCC].** Index available. **Bk Rev. Ad Acc. Pr Rev. Circ:** 1,400 (ctrl). Documents available from The Genuine Article, BIOSIS Document Express, CASDDS, ADONIS. ***Continues in part*** *Acta Psychiatrica et Neurologica Scandinavica.*
**Desc:** Publishes original papers in English on psychiatry and adjacent fields.
**Ind/Abst** ADONIS; Biol. Abstr.; Chem. Abstr.; Crim. Penol. Police Sci. Abstr.; Cumul. Index Nurs. Allied Health Lit.; Curr. Aware. Biol. Sci., CABS; Curr. Contents Clin. Med.; Curr. Contents Life Sci.; Curr. Contents Soc. Behav. Sci.; Dev. Med. Child Neurol.; EMBASE; Energy Res. Abstr.; Health Plan. Adminis.; Index Med.; Index Period. Artic. Relat. Law (19??-19??); INIS Atomindex [Micro.]; Middle East Abstr. Index; Life Sci. Collect.; PESTDOC; Psychol. Abstr. (1961-); PsycINFO; PsycLit; Res. Alert [Full Cov.]; Sci. Cit. Index; SCISEARCH; Soc. Plann. Policy Dev. Abstr.; Soc. Sci. Cit. Index [Full Cov.]; Sociol. Abstr. (?-?).

DK/0065-1591
**ACTA PSYCHIATRICA SCANDINAVICA. SUPPLEMENTUM.** [Acta psychiatr. Scand., Suppl.]. No. 160 (1961)-. Academic Scholarly Publication. English (German and French). kr2660.00 US, Canada & Japan; kr2570.00 other (includes the journal Acta Psychiatrica Scandinavica). Munksgaard International Publishers Ltd, PO Box 2148, DK-1016 Copenhagen K Denmark. **Tel** 011 45 33 12 70 30, FAX 011 45 33 12 93 87, telex 19431 MUNKS DK. **NLM** W1 AC93251. **CODEN** ASSUA6. **[CCC].** Documents available from CASDDS. ***Continues in part*** *Acta Psychiatrica et Neurologica Scandinavica. Supplementum.*
**Ind/Abst** Chem. Abstr.; Curr. Aware. Biol. Sci., CABS; EMBASE; Health Plan. Adminis.; Index Med.; Middle East Abstr. Index; Life Sci. Collect.

SP/0300-5062
**ACTAS LUSO-ESPANOLAS DE NEUROLOGIA, PSIQUIATRIA Y CIENCIAS AFINES.** **See** Medical Science and Technology-Neurology.

FR/0766-3897
**ACTUALITES MEDICALES INTERNATIONALES PSYCHIATRIE.** [Actual. med. int. psychiatr.]. **VFOAT** Psychiatrie Actualites Medicales Internationales; Actualites Medicales Internationales en Psychiatrie. (1984)-. Periodical. French. Twenty times a year. 235.06F France; 450.00F other. Medica Press Intl, 14 rue de Silly, 92000 Boulogne France. **Tel** 011 33 1 48251110. **UDC** 616.89.

FR/0300-8274
**ACTUALITES PSYCHIATRIQUES.** [Actual. psychiatr.]. (1971)-. Periodical. French (summaries and/or abstracts in English). Eight times a year. 400.00F Canada; 195.89F France; 350.00F North Africa & other Europe. Actualites Psychiatriques, 36 Allee Des Haras Richou, 92420 Vaucresson France. **Tel** 011 34 611818. **UDC** 616.89.

US/0065-2008
**ADOLESCENT PSYCHIATRY.** **See** Medical Science and Technology-Pediatrics.

SZ/0378-7354
**ADVANCES IN BIOLOGICAL PSYCHIATRY.** [Adv. biol. psychiatry]. Vol. 1 (1978)-. Academic Scholarly Publication. English. an. 120.00F (approx. per volume). S. Karger AG, Allschwilerstrasse 10, PO Box - Postfach - Case Postale, CH-4009 Basel Switzerland. **Tel** 011 41 61 306-1111, FAX 011 41 61 306-1234, telex CH 962 652. **ED** J. Mendlewicz and H. M. van Praag. **NLM** W1 AD44. **CODEN** ABPSD5. **[CCC].** Documents available from BIOSIS Document Express, CASDDS.
**Desc:** Focused on exploring the biological determinants of behavior and psychopathology, volumes in this series provide clinicians and researchers with references to the most significant international work being conducted on selected topics. The distinct progress made possible through multidisciplinary collaboration is apparent in each publication. The importance of new methodological developments in the biological sciences is also stressed by the editors.
**Ind/Abst** Biol. Abstr.; Chem. Abstr.; Psychol. Abstr. (1980-); PsycINFO; PsycLit; Ref. Upd. Deluxe Ed.

US/1052-0465
**ADVANCES IN EATING DISORDERS.** (ADVANCES IN EATING DISORDERS : A RESEARCH ANNUAL.). [Adv. eat. disord.]. **VFOAT** Eating Disorders. Vol. 1 (1987)-. English. ir. £88.00 (latest volume). Jessica Kinglsey Publishers, 118 Pentonville Road, London N1 9JN England. **Tel** (071)833-2307. **(Subscription address:** Taylor & Francis Inc., 1900 Frost Road, Suite 101, Bristol PA 19007-1598.**) ED** William Johnson. **LC** RC552.E18; A38. **DD** 616.85/2. **NLM** W1; AD549V. **Pr Rev.**

US/0270-9228
**ADVANCES IN FAMILY INTERVENTION, ASSESSMENT AND THEORY.** [Adv. fam. intervent. assess. theory]. Vol. 1 (1980)-. English. ir. Price varies. Jessica Kingsley Publishers, 118 Pentonville Road, London N1 9JN England. **Tel** 011 44 71 833 2307, FAX 011 44 71 837 2917. **(Subscription address:** Taylor & Francis Inc., 1900 Frost Road, Suite 101, Bristol PA 19007-1598.**) ED** John P. Vincent. **LC** RC488.5; .A35. **DD** 616.89/156. **NLM** W1 AD564. **CODEN** AFITE2. Documents available from BIOSIS Document Express.
**Ind/Abst** Biol. Abstr. (1987-); Psychol. Abstr. (1980-); PsycINFO; PsycLit.

US/0887-4298
**ADVANCES IN FAMILY PSYCHIATRY.** [Adv. fam. psychiatry]. Vol. 1 (1979)-. English. an. $50.00. International Universities Press Inc., 59 Boston Post Road, PO Box 1524, Madison CT 06443-1524. **Tel** (203)245-4000, FAX (203)245-0775, telex 282986 IUP BK. **ED** John G. Howells. **LC** RC455.4.F3; A38. **DD** 616.89/156. **NLM** W1 AD566.
**Desc:** Covers aspects of family functioning and dysfunctioning as well as family diagnostic and treatment considerations.
**Ind/Abst** Psychol. Abstr. (1979-).

US/0747-6353
**ADVANCES IN FORENSIC PSYCHOLOGY AND PSYCHIATRY.** **See** Psychology.

UK/0271-9266
**ADVANCES IN MENTAL HANDICAP RESEARCH.** ***Ceased.*** [Adv. ment. handicap res.]. Vol. 1-?. English. John Wiley & Sons Ltd., Baffins Lane, Chichester West Sussex PO19 1UD England. **Tel** 0243 779777, FAX 0243 776128 BTG:JWP001, telex 86290 WIBOOKG. **(Subscription address:** North, South and Central America/ John Wiley & Sons, Inc., PO Box 7247-8491, Philadelphia, PA 19170-8491**) ED** J Hogg and P J Mittler. **LC** RC569.7; .A37. **DD** 616.85/88/005. **UDC** 616.89. **NLM** W1 AD679R.

US/0742-6313
**ADVANCES IN MENTAL RETARDATION AND DEVELOPMENTAL DISABILITIES.** [Adv. ment. retard. dev. disabil.]. Vol. 1 (1983)-. English. ir. Jessica Kingsley Publishers, 118 Pentonville Road, London N1 9JN England. **Tel** 011 44 71 833 2307, FAX 011 44 71 837 2917. **(Subscription address:** Taylor & Francis Inc., 1900 Frost Road, Suite 101, Bristol PA 19007-1598.**) LC** RC569.7; .A38. **DD** 616.85/88/005. **NLM** W1; AD679V.

US
**ADVANCES IN NEUROPSYCHIATRY AND PSYCHOPHARMACOLOGY.** **See** Medical Science and Technology-Neurology.

●UK
**ADVANCES IN PSYCHIATRIC TREATMENT.** (1994)-. English. Eight times a year. $80.00 US; £50.00 UK & Europe; £60.00 other. Royal Society of Medicine Press, 1 Wimpole Street, London W1M 8AE England. **Tel** 011 44 71 2902928.

NE/0922-3061
**ADVANCES IN SUICIDOLOGY.** (1989)-. Monographic series. English. ir. Price varies per volume. E. J. Brill, Postbus 9000, 2300 PA Leiden Netherlands. **Tel** 011 31 71 312624, FAX 011 31 71 317532, telex 39296 BRILL NL. **NLM** W1; AD876D.
**Desc:** Series covering suicide. Volumes have covered topics such as suicide prevention.

NR/0331-0175
**AFRICAN JOURNAL OF PSYCHIATRY, THE.** [Afr. j. psychiatry]. **VFOAT** Le Journal Africain de Psychiatrie. Academic Scholarly Publication. Hebrew (French). qt. Literamed Publications Ltd, Oregun Village PMB 1068, Ikeja Lagos Nigeria Africa. **UDC** 616.89. **NLM** W1 AF542.
**Ind/Abst** EMBASE; Health Plan. Adminis.; Index Med. (Jan. 1981-); Psychol. Abstr. (1978-).

SZ/0082-4917
**AKTUELLE FRAGEN DER PSYCHIATRIE UND NEUROLOGIE.** (AKTUELLE FRAGEN DER PSYCHIATRIE UND NEUROLOGIE. TOPICAL PROBLEMS IN PSYCHIATRY AND NEUROLOGY.). **VFOAT** Topical Problems in Psychiatry and Neurology. Vol. 1 (1964)-. Monographic series. German (English). ir. Price varies per volume. Verlag Hans Huber Ag Bern, Laenggass Strasse 76, CH 3000 Bern 9 Switzerland. **Tel** 011 41 31 3004500. **(Subscription address:** Jugoslovenska Knjiga, PO Box 36, YU 11001 Belgrade Yugoslovia.**) NLM** W1 BI429 Fasc.122 etc.

FR/0299-2507
**ALZHEIMER ACTUALITES.** **See** Medical Science and Technology-Neurology.

US/0734-6026
**AMERICAN ASSOCIATION FOR GERIATRIC PSYCHIATRY NEWSLETTER.** [Am. Assoc. Geriatr. Psychiatr. newsl.]. **Added/Corp** American Association for Geriatric Psychiatry. (19??)-. Periodical. English. Four times a year (Jan., Apr., July, Oct.). $20.00. American Association for Geriatric Psychiatry, PO Box 376 A, Greenbelt MD 20770. **Tel** (301)220-0952.

US/0007-4764
**AMERICAN JOURNAL OF ART THERAPY.** **See** The Arts-Art.

US/0163-1942
**AMERICAN JOURNAL OF FORENSIC PSYCHIATRY, THE.** [Am. J. Forensic Psych.]. **Added/Corp** American College of Forensic Psychiatry. Vol. 1 (May 1978)-. Periodical. English. Four times a year (Jan., Apr., July, Oct.). $65.00 (one year); $110.00 (two years). American College of Forensic Psychiatry, PO Box 5870, Balboa Island CA 92662. **Tel** (714)831-0236, FAX (714)675-1107. **ED** Debra Miller. **LC** RA1151; .A45. **DD** 614/.1/05. **NLM** W1 AM451S. cum. index. **Bk Rev. Ad Acc.** available on microfilm from Williams S Hein & Co.
**Desc:** Professional journal for psychiatrists who testify in civil and criminal cases and for attorneys representing mental disability claimants, and interested in mental disability law.
**Ind/Abst** Psychol. Abstr. (1982-); PsycINFO (?-?); PsycLit.

US/1064-7481
**AMERICAN JOURNAL OF GERIATRIC PSYCHIATRY, THE.** **See** Medical Science and Technology-Geriatrics.

US/0002-9432
**AMERICAN JOURNAL OF ORTHOPSYCHIATRY.** [Am. j. orthopsychiatr.]. **Added/Corp** American Orthopsychiatric Association. American Orthopsychiatric Association. Proceedings. Vol. 1 (Oct. 1930)-. Academic Scholarly Publication. English. qt. $65.00 (institutions), $45.00 (individuals) US; $70.00 (institutions), $55.00 (individuals) other. American Orthopsychiatric Association, 19 West 44th Street, Suite 1616, New York NY 10036. **Tel** (212)564-5930. **(Subscription address:** American Orthopsychiatric Association, 49 Sheridan Avenue, Department M, Albany NY 12210.**) ED** Albert A. Cain. **LC** RA790.A1; A5. **DD** 150.5. **NLM** W1 AM497L. **CODEN** AJORAG. **[CCC].** Index available (bound in last issue). cum. index. **Bk Rev. Ad Acc. Pr Rev.** available on microfilm and microfiche from University Microfilms International (UMI). Documents available from The Genuine Article, UMI Article Clearinghouse.
**Desc:** Promotes an interdisciplinary approach (psychiatry, psychology, social work, education, nursing, etc.) to mental health practice. Publishes research, theoretical, clinical, and administrative articles.
**Ind/Abst** Acad. Abstr. Full Text Elite (Jan. 1991-); Acad. Abstr. (Jan. 1991-); Acad. Ind. [Computer File] (1987-);

Acad. Search (Jan. 1991-); Appl. Soc. Sci. Index Abstr.; Book Rev. Digest; Crim. Justice Abstr.; Crim. Penol. Police Sci. Abstr.; Cumul. Index Nurs. Allied Health Lit.; Curr. Contents Clin. Med.; Curr. Contents Soc. Behav. Sci.; Curr. Lit. Fam. Plan.; Dev. Med. Child Neurol. (-1990); Educ. Index; EMBASE; Except. Child Educ. Resour. (19??-19??); Expand. Acad. Index (1987-); Gen. Sci. Source (Jul. 1990-); Health Plan. Adminis.; Index Med.; Index Period. Artic. Relat. Law (19??-19??); INFO-SOUTH Abstr.; Int. Bibliogr. Sociol.; Linguist. Lang. Behav. Abstr.; Mag. Search; Middle East Abstr. Index; Multicult. Educ. Abstr.; Newsp. Period. Abstr. (1990-); Nutr. Abstr. Rev., Ser. B, Live Feeds and Feed.; Nutr. Abstr. Rev., Ser. A, Hum. Exp.; Peace Res. Abstr. J. (1964-1975); Life Sci. Collect.; Psychol. Abstr. (1930-); PsycINFO; PsycLit; PsycScan: Clin. Psych.; PsycScan: Develop. Psych.; Res. Alert [Full Cov.]; Sage Fam. Stud. Abstr.; Sci. Cit. Index; SCISEARCH; Soc. Plann. Policy Dev. Abstr.; Soc. Sci. Source (Jul. 1990-); Soc. Sci. Cit. Index [Full Cov.]; Soc. Sci. Index; Soc. Sci. Index Fulltext (Oct. 1988-) [Full Txt.]; Soc. Work Abstr. [Full Cov.]; Sociol. Abstr.; Sociol. Educ. Abstr.; Spec. Educ. Needs Abstr.; Stud. Women Abstr.; Women Stud. Abstr.

US/0002-953X

**AMERICAN JOURNAL OF PSYCHIATRY, THE.** [Am. j. psychiatr.]. **Added/Corp** American Psychiatric Association. Vol. 78 (July 1921)-. Academic Scholarly Publication. English. Twelve times a year. $90.00 US; $120.00 other (institution). American Psychiatric Association, 1400 K Street Northwest, Washington DC 20005. **Tel** (202)682-6240, FAX (202)682-6114. **ED** John C. Nemiah. **LC** RC321; .A52. **DD** 616. **NLM** W1 AM513. **CODEN** AJPSAO. **[CCC].** Index available. **Bk Rev. Ad Acc. Pr Rev. Circ:** 44,600. available on microfilm and microfiche from University Microfilms International (UMI). Documents available from The Genuine Article, BIOSIS Document Express, UMI Article Clearinghouse, CASDDS. ***Continues*** *American Journal of Insanity, 1044-4815.*
**Desc:** Indispensable for all psychiatrists and other mental health professionals who need to keep up with developments in the clinical, theoretical and research aspects of psychiatric illness as well as with social, political and ethical issues in psychiatry.
**Ind/Abst** Abr. Index Med.; Abstr. Res. Pastor. Care Couns. (19??-); Acad. Abstr. Full Text Elite (Jan. 1992-); Acad. Abstr. (Jan. 1992-); Acad. Search (Jan. 1992-); Annals Behav. Med.; Appl. Soc. Sci. Index Abstr.; Biol. Abstr.; Chem. Abstr.; Crim. Justice Abstr.; Crim. Penol. Police Sci. Abstr.; Cumul. Index Nurs. Allied Health Lit.; Curr. Contents Clin. Med.; Curr. Contents Life Sci.; Curr. Contents Soc. Behav. Sci.; Dairy Sci. Abstr.; Dev. Med. Child Neurol.; EMBASE; Expand. Acad. Index (1989-); Gen. Sci. Source (Jan. 1992-); Health Period. Database; Health Plan. Adminis.; High. Educ. Abstr. (1965-); Highw. Res. Abstr.; Index Med.; Index Period. Artic. Relat. Law; INFO-SOUTH Abstr.; Int. Aerosp. Abstr.; Int. Nurs. Index; Int. Pharm. Abstr.; Iowa Drug Inf. Serv. (1966-); J. Watch; Linguist. Lang. Behav. Abstr.; Mag. Search; Med. Abstr. Newsl.; Middle East Abstr. Index; Mod. Med.; Newsp. Period. Abstr. (1989-); Nutr. Abstr. Rev., Ser. B, Live Feeds and Feed.; Nutr. Abstr. Rev., Ser. A, Hum. Exp.; Life Sci. Collect.; PESTDOC; Physic. Medline Plus; Psychol. Abstr. (1928-); PsycINFO; PsycLit; PsycScan: Clin. Psych.; Ref. Upd. Deluxe Ed.; Res. Alert [Full Cov.]; Rev. Med. Vet. Mycology; Risk Abstr.; Saf. Health Work; Sci. Cit. Index; SCISEARCH; Soc. Plann. Policy Dev. Abstr.; Soc. Sci. Source (Jan. 1992-); Soc. Sci. Cit. Index [Full Cov.]; Soc. Sci. Index; Soc. Sci. Index Fulltext (Sept. 1988-) [Full Txt.]; Soc. Work Abstr. [Select. Cov.]; Sociol. Abstr.; Women Stud. Abstr.

US/0002-9548

**AMERICAN JOURNAL OF PSYCHOANALYSIS.** [Am. j. psychoanal.]. **Added/Corp** Association for the Advancement of Psychoanalysis. Vol. 1 (1941)-. Academic Scholarly Publication. English. qt. £29.00 (individuals), £110.00 (institutions) UK & Europe; $155.00 US; $180.00 other. Human Sciences Press, PO Box 735, 233 Spring Street, New York NY 10013. **Tel** (212)620-8000, FAX (212)807-1047, telex 23421139. **(Subscription address:** Eurospan Ltd., Journals and Serials Division, 3 Henrietta Street, Covent Garden, London WC2E 8LU England.**) ED** Douglas Ingram. **LC** RC321; .A53. **DD** 616.805. **NLM** W1 AM516. **CODEN** AJPYA8. **[CCC].** cum. index. available on microfilm and microfiche from University Microfilms International (UMI). Documents available from BIOSIS Document Express, UMI Article Clearinghouse.
**Desc:** Contributions to the journal communicate modern concepts of psychoanalytic theory and practice, and related investigations in allied fields. The articles present significant information for everyone interested in the understanding and therapy of emotional problems.
**Ind/Abst** Acad. Search (July 1993-); Biol. Abstr.; Chicano Index; Cumul. Index Nurs. Allied Health Lit.; EMBASE; Expand. Acad. Index (1989-); Health Plan. Adminis.; Index Med.; Index Period. Artic. Relat. Law (19??-19??); INFO-SOUTH Abstr.; Mag. Search; Middle East Abstr. Index; Newsp. Period. Abstr. (1991-); Psychol. Abstr. (1928-); PsycINFO; PsycLit; Soc. Sci. Source (Jul. 1993-); Soc. Sci. Index; Soc. Sci. Index Fulltext (Fall 1988-) [Full Txt.]; Soc. Work Abstr. [Select. Cov.]; Women Stud. Abstr.

US/0002-9564

**AMERICAN JOURNAL OF PSYCHOTHERAPY.** [Am. j. psychother.]. **Added/Corp** Association for the Advancement of Psychotherapy. Vol. 1 (Jan. 1947)-. Academic Scholarly Publication. English. qt. $83.00 US; $89.00 Canada; $94.00 other (institution). Association for the Advancement of Psychotherapy, PO Box 260, Monsey NY 10952. **Tel** (800)524-4723. **ED** Stanley Lesse. **LC** RC321; .A54. **DD** 616.805. **NLM** W1 AM518. **CODEN** AJPTAR. Index available (free). **Pr Rev.** available on microfilm and microfiche from University Microfilms International (UMI). Documents available from The Genuine Article, BIOSIS Document Express, UMI Article Clearinghouse.
**Ind/Abst** Abstr. Res. Pastor. Care Couns. (19??-); Acad. Search (July 1993-); Arts Humanit. Citation Index [Select. Cov.]; Biol. Abstr.; Crim. Penol. Police Sci. Abstr.; Cumul. Index Nurs. Allied Health Lit.; Curr. Contents Soc. Behav. Sci.; EMBASE; Expand. Acad. Index (1989-); Health Period. Database; Health Plan. Adminis.; Index Med.; INFO-SOUTH Abstr.; Linguist. Lang. Behav. Abstr.; Mag. Search; Middle East Abstr. Index; Mod. Med.; Newsp. Period. Abstr. (1989-); Psychol. Abstr. (1947-); PsycINFO; PsycLit; PsycScan: Clin. Psych.; Res. Alert [Full Cov.]; Sci. Cit. Index; SCISEARCH; Soc. Plann. Policy Dev. Abstr.; Soc. Sci. Source (Jul. 1993-); Soc. Sci. Cit. Index [Full Cov.]; Soc. Sci. Index; Soc. Sci. Index Fulltext (Oct. 1988-) [Full Txt.]; Soc. Work Abstr. (?-?); Sociol. Abstr.

US/0277-8173

**AMERICAN JOURNAL OF SOCIAL PSYCHIATRY, THE.** ***Ceased.*** [Am. j. soc. psych.]. Vol. 1, No. 1 (April 1981)-(Dec. 1987). Periodical. English. qt. Brunner Mazel, 19 Union Square West, New York NY 10003. **Tel** (212)924-3344, (800)825-3089. **ED** John L Carleton. **LC** RC455; .A465. **DD** 616.89. **UDC** 301.151:616.89. **NLM** W1 AM522G. Index available. **Bk Rev. Ad Acc. Circ:** 800. available on microfilm and microfiche from University Microfilms International (UMI).
**Desc:** Interdisciplinary coverage of psychiatry in relation to many areas of the human condition.
**Ind/Abst** Psychol. Abstr. (1981-); PsycINFO (?-?).

●US/1055-0496

**AMERICAN JOURNAL ON ADDICTIONS, THE.** **See** Drug Abuse and Alcoholism.

●CN/1193-2805

**AMITIE SP : BULLETIN DE L'ASSOCIATION QUEBECOISE DES AMIS DE LA SCLEROSE EN PLAQUES.** [Amitie SP]. **Added/Corp** Association Quebecoise des Amis de la Sclerose en Plaques. **VFOAT** Amitie Sclerose en Plaques. (Spring 1992)-. Bulletin. French. qt. Free for members. Association Quebecoise des Amis de la Sclerose en Plaques, Bureau 105, 1012 Est Mont-Royal, Montreal Quebec H2J 1X6 Canada. **DD** 616.8/34/005.

SP/0213-0599

**ANALES DE PSIQUIATRIA.** (198?)-. Periodical. Spanish (summaries and/or abstracts in English and Spanish; table of contents in English). Twelve times a year. 125ptas. Aran Ediciones SA, Avda General Peron, 20 5 DCHA, 28020 Madrid Spain. **Tel** 011 34 1 5332525. **NLM** W1; AN375M. **CODEN** APSIEL.
**Ind/Abst** EMBASE; Indice Med. Esp.

SZ/1011-6982

**ANIMAL MODELS OF PSYCHIATRIC DISORDERS.** ***Ceased.*** Vol. 1 (1988)-(19??). Monographic series. English. an. S. Karger AG, Allschwilerstrasse 10, PO Box - Postfach - Case Postale, CH-4009 Basel Switzerland. **Tel** 011 41 61 306-1111, FAX 011 41 61 306-1234, telex CH 962 652. **ED** P Simon, P Soubrie, and D Widlocher. **[CCC].** Index available. available on microfiche; available on microfilm.
**Desc:** Animal models of psychiatric disorders such as schizophrenia, depression, anxiety are important for the understanding of behavioral problems seen by psychiatrists. They are a means to investigate underlying pathophysiological mechanisms, and to predict the efficacy of psychotherapeutic drugs. Individual volumes in this series investigate animal models of human psychopathology in terms of their validation for animal/human comparison. To that end, articles are accompanied by a commentary from a psychiatrist. With this approach, the series intends to generate new hypothese on the pathophysiology of mental disorders and new lines of investigation with laboratory animals.
**Ind/Abst** Ref. Upd. Deluxe Ed.

FR/0768-7559

**ANNALES DE PSYCHIATRIE.** [Ann. psychiatr.]. (1986)-. Periodical. French. qt. 550.00F France; 795.00F other. Semaine de Hopitaux, 31 Boulevard de la Tour-Maubourg, 75007 Paris, France. **Tel** 011 33 1 40 62 64 00. **UDC** 616.89.
**Ind/Abst** EMBASE.

FR/0338-9375

**ANNALES DE PSYCHOTHERAPIE.** [Ann. psychother.]. (1970)-. Periodical. French. ir. Les Editions ESF, 17 rue Viete, 75854 Paris Cedex 17 France. **Tel** 011 33 1 44156200. **UDC** 615.851.

IT

**ANNALI DI NEUROLOGIA E PSICHIATRIA.** (19??)-. Periodical. Italian (English). qt. L40000. USL di Perugia Serv, Tesoreria, 06100 Perugia Italy. **Tel** 011 39 75 5782600. **NLM** W1; AN496. **CODEN** ANEPEQ. ***Continues*** *Annali dell'Ospedale Psichiatrico di Perugia.*

US/1040-1237

**ANNALS OF CLINICAL PSYCHIATRY.** (ANNALS OF CLINICAL PSYCHIATRY : OFFICIAL JOURNAL OF THE AMERICAN ACADEMY OF CLINICAL PSYCHIATRISTS.). [Ann. clin. psychiatry]. **Added/Corp** American Academy of Clinical Psychiatrists. Vol. 1, No. 1 (Mar. 1989)-. Periodical. English. Four times a year. $162.00 institutions, $48.00 individuals US; $190.00 institutions, $56.00 individuals other. Plenum Press, 233 Spring Street, New York NY 10013-1578. **Tel** (212)620-8000, (800)221-9369, FAX (212)463-0742, (212)807-1047, telex 23/421139. **ED** Charles L. Rich. **LC** RC321; .A615. **DD** 616.89/005. **NLM** W1; AN571H. **CODEN** APSYEZ. **[CCC]. Bk Rev. Ad Acc. Pr Rev.** available on microfilm and microfiche from University Microfilms International (UMI).
**Ind/Abst** EMBASE; Psychol. Abstr. (1989-); PsycINFO.

FR

**ANNUAIRE DE LA MEDIATIQUE.** French. an. Com 7, 5 Place du Colonel Fabien, 75491 Paris Cedex 10 France.

US/0092-5055

**ANNUAL OF PSYCHOANALYSIS, THE.** ***Ceased.*** [Annu. psychoanal.]. **Added/Corp** Institute for Psychoanalysis. Vol. 1 (1973)-Ceased ?. English. an. International Universities Press Inc., 59 Boston Post Road, PO Box 1524, Madison CT 06443-1524. **Tel** (203)245-4000, FAX (203)245-0775, telex 282986 IUP BK. **LC** RC500; .A56. **DD** 616.8/917/05. **NLM** W1 AN756P. **CODEN** APSACT. **[CCC]. Bk Rev.** Documents available from BIOSIS Document Express.
**Desc:** Appearance of original articles devoted to the theoretical, clinical, educational, historical, and applied psychoanalysis from the world.
**Ind/Abst** Biol. Abstr.; PsycINFO (?-?); PsycLit.

US/0066-4030

**ANNUAL PROGRESS IN CHILD PSYCHIATRY AND CHILD DEVELOPMENT.** **See** Medical Science and Technology-Pediatrics.

US

**ANNUAL REPORT FOR FISCAL YEAR ... / VERMONT STATE HOSPITAL.** **See** Medical Science and Technology-Hospital Administration and Medical Centers.

CN/1180-5463

**ANNUAL REPORT / FORENSIC PSYCHIATRIC SERVICES COMMISSION OF BRITISH COLUMBIA.** [Annu. rep. - Forensic Psychiatr. Serv. Comm. B.C.]. **Main/Corp** Forensic Psychiatric Services Commission of British Columbia. **Added/Corp** British Columbia. Ministry of Health. (1989/1990)-. English. **DD** 614/.1/09711.

CN/1187-7243

**ANNUAL REPORT - MENTAL HEALTH COMMISSION OF NEW BRUNSWICK. REGION II.** (ANNUAL REPORT.). [Annu. rep. - Ment. Health Comm. N.B., Reg. II]. **Main/Corp** Mental Health Commission of New Brunswick. Region II. (1990/1991)-. English. **DD** 354.715.

US

**ANNUAL REPORT / MICHIGAN DEPARTMENT OF MENTAL HEALTH, RECIPIENT RIGHTS COMMITTEE.** **Main/Corp** Michigan. Dept. of Mental Health. Recipient Rights Committee. English. ***Continues*** *Annual Report.*

US/0747-6531

**ANNUAL REPORT - NATIONAL INSTITUTE OF MENTAL HEALTH (U.S.). DIVISION OF INTRAMURAL RESEARCH PROGRAMS.** (ANNUAL REPORT / DIVISION OF INTRAMURAL RESEARCH PROGRAMS, NATIONAL INSTITUTE OF MENTAL HEALTH.). **Main/Corp** National Institute of Mental Health (U.S.). Division of Intramural Research Programs. **VFOAT** N.I.M.H. D.I.R.P. ... Annual Report; NIMH DIRP ... Annual Report. Oct. 1, 1982-Sept. 30, 1983-. English. an. US Department of Health and Human Services, 200 Independence Avenue Southwest, Washington DC 20201. **LC** RC337; .N326A. **DD** 616.89/0072073. **UDC** 616.89.001.5(047.1)(73). **NLM** W2; A N2051a. ***Continues*** *Annual Report, Mental Health Intramural Research Program--Division of Clinical and Behavioral Research, Division of Biological and Biochemical Research, and Division of Special Mental Health Research.*

US/0198-8034

**ANNUAL REPORT OF THE BOARD OF VISITORS OF THE BUFFALO PSYCHIATRIC CENTER TO THE DEPARTMENT OF MENTAL HYGIENE.** **Main/Corp** Buffalo Psychiatric Center. Board of Visitors. 105th- 1974/75-. English. Buffalo Psychiatric Center,

Board of Visitors, Buffalo NY 14203. **LC** RC445; .N615. **DD** 353.9747/9700842. **UDC** 616.89(047.1)(747). ***Continues*** *Annual Report of the Board of Visitors of the Buffalo State Hospital to the Department of Mental Hygiene, 0197-226X.*

US
**ANNUAL REPORT: STATE HOSPITALS FOR THE MENTALLY DISORDERED.** **See** Medical Science and Technology-Hospital Administration and Medical Centers.

US/0198-9731
**ANNUAL REVIEW OF FAMILY THERAPY.** ***Ceased.*** (ANNUAL REVIEW OF FAMILY THERAPY / GERALD BERENSON, HARVEY WHITE.). [Annu. rev. fam. ther.]. Vol. 1 (1980)-(19??). English. an. Human Sciences Press, PO Box 735, 233 Spring Street, New York NY 10013. **Tel** (212)620-8000, FAX (212)807-1047, telex 23421139. **ED** Gerald Berenson & Harvey White. **LC** RC488.5; .A55. **DD** 616.89/156. **NLM** W1 AN771D.
**Desc:** Covers family psychotherapy.

FR
**APERTURA (PARIS, FRANCE).** (APERTURA.). Vol. 1 (1987)-. Monographic series. French. Price varies per volume. Springer-Verlag France, 26 rue des Carmes, F 75005 Paris France. **Tel** 011 33 1 44411599, FAX 011 33 43250225. **ED** J.R. Freymann, A. Michels. **NLM** W1; AP114.
**Desc:** Collection of psychoanalytic research.
**Ind/Abst** PROMT.

US/1056-9111
**APPELBAUM/GRISSO REPORT ON LAW AND MENTAL HEALTH, THE.** ***Ceased.*** **See** Law.

US/0003-990X
**ARCHIVES OF GENERAL PSYCHIATRY.** [Arch. gen. psychiatry]. **Added/Corp** American Medical Association. Vol. 3 (July 1960)-. Academic Scholarly Publication. English. mo. $110.00 (institution), $95.00 (individual) US. American Medical Association, 515 North State Street, Chicago IL 60610. **Tel** (312)464-5000, (800)262-2350, FAX (312)464-5831. **ED** Daniel X. Freedman. **LC** RC321; .A66. **DD** 616.8905. **NLM** W1 AR455AK. **CODEN** ARGPAQ. **[CCC].** Index available (free). **Ad Acc. Pr Rev. Circ:** 24,000. available on microfilm and microfiche from University Microfilms International (UMI); available on an online database (file 442/Full-Text) from DIALOG; and MEDIS. Documents available from The Genuine Article, BIOSIS Document Express, CASDDS. ***Continues*** *A.M.A. Archives of General Psychiatry, 0375-8532.*
**Desc:** Published as an educational service for physicians who practice psychiatry as a primary specialty, and to physicians of other specialties who treat emotional problems. Noted for its emphasis on psychiatric problems of biological etiology, and oriented toward the clinician, it contains information useful in everyday practice.
**Ind/Abst** Abr. Index Med.; Biol. Abstr.; Chem. Abstr.; Crim. Justice Abstr. (19??-199?); CSA Neuro. Abstr. (?-?); Cumul. Index Nurs. Allied Health Lit.; Curr. Contents Clin. Med.; Curr. Contents Life Sci.; Curr. Contents Soc. Behav. Sci.; Dev. Med. Child Neurol.; EMBASE; Health Plan. Adminis.; Hospit. Health Admin. Index; Index Med.; Index Period. Artic. Relat. Law; Int. Pharm. Abstr.; Iowa Drug Inf. Serv. (1966-); Med. Abstr. Newsl.; Middle East Abstr. Index; Mod. Med.; Nutr. Abstr. Rev., Ser. B, Live Feeds and Feed.; Nutr. Abstr. Rev., Ser. A, Hum. Exp.; Life Sci. Collect.; PESTDOC; Physic. Medline Plus; Psychol. Abstr. (1960-); PsycINFO; PsycLit; Ref. Upd. Deluxe Ed.; Res. Alert [Full Cov.]; Risk Abstr.; Sage Race Relat. Abstr.; Sci. Cit. Index; SCISEARCH; Soc. Sci. Cit. Index [Full Cov.]; Soc. Work Abstr. (?-?).

IT/0004-0150
**ARCHIVIO DI PSICOLOGIA, NEUROLOGIA E PSICHIATRIA.** **See** Psychology.

VE
**ARCHIVOS VENEZOLANOS DE PSIQUIATRIA Y NEUROLOGIA.** Periodical. Spanish. Apdo 3380 Carmelitas, Caracas 1010-A Venezuela. **UDC** 616.8.

BL/0004-282X
**ARQUIVOS DE NEURO-PSIQUIATRIA.** **See** Medical Science and Technology-Neurology.

US/0197-4556
**ARTS IN PSYCHOTHERAPY, THE.** [Arts psychother.]. Vol. 7 (1980)-. Academic Scholarly Publication. English. Five times a year. $276.00 The Americas; £185.00 other. Pergamon Press, An Imprint of Elsevier Science Ltd., The Boulevard, Langford Lane, Kidlington, Oxford OX5 1GB United Kingdom. **Tel** 011 44 865 843000, 011 44 865 843699, FAX 011 44 865 843010. **(Subscription address:** Elsevier Science Ltd. Oxford Fulfillment Centre, PO Box 800, Kidlington, Oxford OX5 1DX United Kingdom.**) ED** Robert Landy. **LC** RC489.A7; A76. **DD** 616.89/165. **NLM** W1 AR959M. **CODEN** APCYAJ. **[CCC]. Bk Rev. Ad Acc.** ctrl circ. available on microfilm and microfiche from University Microfilms International (UMI). Documents available from The Genuine Article, BIOSIS Document Express. ***Continues*** *Art Psychotherapy, 0090-9092.*
**Desc:** Publishes the latest research about the creative arts in therapy by psychotherapists, psychiatrists and psychologists. Also comments on national and international conferences in these disciplines.
**Ind/Abst** ARTbibliogr. Mod.; Arts Humanit. Citation Index [Select. Cov.]; Biol. Abstr.; Curr. Contents Soc. Behav. Sci.; EMBASE; Except. Child Educ. Resour.; Middle East Abstr. Index; Psychol. Abstr. (1980-); PsycINFO; PsycLit; Res. Alert [Full Cov.]; Soc. Sci. Cit. Index [Full Cov.].

AT/0004-8674
**AUSTRALIAN AND NEW ZEALAND JOURNAL OF PSYCHIATRY.** [Aust. N.Z. j. psychiatry]. **Added/Corp** Australian & New Zealand College of Psychiatrists. Vol. 1 (Mar. 1967)-. Academic Scholarly Publication. English. qt. 95.00Aus$ (institutions), 65.00Aus$ (individuals) Australia; 115.00Aus$ (institutions), 75.00Aus$ (individuals) other. Australian and New Zealand Journal of Psychiatry, PO Box 126, Karrinyup WA 6018 Australia. **Tel** 011 61 9 4475312. **ED** Gordon Parker. **LC** RC321; .A86. **NLM** W1 AU498. **CODEN** ANZPBQ. **Bk Rev. Ad Acc. Pr Rev. Circ:** 2,500 (ctrl). Documents available from The Genuine Article, BIOSIS Document Express.
**Desc:** Contains editorial comment, case reports, letters to the editor, original articles, and clinical research issues.
**Ind/Abst** Biol. Abstr.; Curr. Contents Clin. Med.; Curr. Contents Soc. Behav. Sci.; EMBASE; Health Plan. Adminis.; Index Med.; Int. Nurs. Index; Middle East Abstr. Index; Nutr. Abstr. Rev., Ser. B, Live Feeds and Feed.; Nutr. Abstr. Rev., Ser. A, Hum. Exp.; Life Sci. Collect.; Psychol. Abstr. (1969-); PsycINFO; PsycLit; Res. Alert [Full Cov.]; Sci. Cit. Index; SCISEARCH; Soc. Sci. Cit. Index [Full Cov.].

●UK/1074-8806
**BAILLIERE'S CLINICAL PSYCHIATRY.** **VFOAT** Clinical Psychiatry. (1995)-. Periodical. English. qt. £90.00 (institution). Harcourt Brace & Company Ltd., Foots Cray, High Street, Sidcup Kent DA14 5HP England. **Tel** 011 44 81 300 3322, FAX 011 44 81 309 0807. **(Subscription address:** W. B. Saunders Company / North America Subscriptions, c/o Periodicals, 6277 Sea Harbour Drive, 4th Floor, Orlando FL 32887.**)**

●UK/1072-0847
**BEHAVIORAL INTERVENTIONS.** [Behav. interv.]. (1994)-. Academic Scholarly Publication. English. qt. $205.00. John Wiley & Sons, Inc., 605 Third Avenue, New York NY 10158-0012. **Tel** (212)850-6000, (212)850-6645, FAX (212)850-6088, telex 12-7063. **(Subscription address:** John Wiley & Sons / England, Baffins Lane, Chichester, West Sussex PO19 1UD England.**) ED** Frederick J. Fuoco. **DD** 616. **NLM** W1; BE13GG. ***Continues*** *Behavioral Residential Treatment, 0884-5581.*
**Desc:** Publishes reports of research involving the utilization of behavioral techniques in applied settings.
**Ind/Abst** EMBASE; Psychol. Abstr.

US/0884-5581
**BEHAVIORAL RESIDENTIAL TREATMENT.** ***Title Change.*** [Behav. resid. treat.]. Vol. 1, No. 1 (Jan. 1986)-(1992). Periodical. English. qt. John Wiley & Sons, Inc., 605 Third Avenue, New York NY 10158-0012. **Tel** (212)850-6000, (212)850-6645, FAX (212)850-6088, telex 12-7063. **(Subscription address:** John Wiley & Sons / England, Baffins Lane, Chichester, West Sussex PO19 1UD England.**) ED** Frederick J Fuoco. **LC** RJ505.B4.; B45. **DD** 616.89/142. **NLM** W1; BE131H. **[CCC].** available on microfilm and microfiche from University Microfilms International (UMI). ***Continued by*** *Behavioral Interventions.*
**Desc:** Deals specifically with the application of behavioral techniques in residential treatment settings. The journal examines controversial issues, ranging from legal and ethical concerns involving the use of aversive behavior modification techniques, to the continuing questions about the appropriateness of some types of behavioral residential treatment settings.
**Ind/Abst** EMBASE; Psychol. Abstr. (1988-); PsycINFO (1990-); PsycLit.

UK/0005-7967
**BEHAVIOUR RESEARCH AND THERAPY.** [Behav. res. ther.]. Vol. 1 (May 1963)-. Academic Scholarly Publication. English. Eight times a year. $552.00 The Americas; £370.00 other. Pergamon Press, An Imprint of Elsevier Science Ltd., The Boulevard, Langford Lane, Kidlington, Oxford OX5 1GB United Kingdom. **Tel** 011 44 865 843000, 011 44 865 843699, FAX 011 44 865 843010. **(Subscription address:** Elsevier Science Ltd. Oxford Fulfillment Centre, PO Box 800, Kidlington, Oxford OX5 1DX United Kingdom.**) ED** S. Rachman. **LC** RC321; .B4. **DD** 616.89/005. **NLM** W1 BE135. **CODEN** BRTHAA. **[CCC]. Pr Rev.** available on microfilm and microfiche from University Microfilms International (UMI); available on microfiche from the publisher. Documents available from The Genuine Article, BIOSIS Document Express, UMI Article Clearinghouse. ***Continues*** *Behavioral Assessment, 0191-5401.*
**Desc:** Contributions stress equally the application of existing knowledge to psychiatric and social problems, experimental research into fundamental questions arising from these attempts, and learning theory and high level theoretical attempts to lay more secure foundations for experimental and observational studies along these lines.
**Ind/Abst** AGRICOLA (Vol. 31, No. 1, 1993) [Select. Cov.]; Annals Behav. Med.; Biol. Abstr.; Crim. Penol. Police Sci. Abstr.; Cumul. Index Nurs. Allied Health Lit.; Curr. Aware. Biol. Sci., CABS; Curr. Contents Soc. Behav. Sci.; Dev. Med. Child Neurol. (?-1990); EMBASE; Expand. Acad. Index (1989-); Health Plan. Adminis.; High. Educ. Abstr. (1982-); Index Med.; Linguist. Lang. Behav. Abstr.; MLA Int. Bibl. Books Artic. Mod. Lang. Lit.; Newsp. Period. Abstr. (1991-); Life Sci. Collect.; Psychol. Abstr. (1963-); PsycINFO (1990-); PsycLit; PsycScan: Clin. Psych.; Res. Alert [Full Cov.]; Soc. Plann. Policy Dev. Abstr.; Soc. Sci. Cit. Index [Full Cov.]; Soc. Sci. Index; Soc. Sci. Index Fulltext (1988-) [Full Txt.]; Soc. Work Abstr. [Select. Cov.]; Sociol. Abstr.; Women Stud. Abstr.

GW/0138-5097
**BEITRAEGE ZUR KLINISCHEN NEUROLOGIE UND PSYCHIATRIE.** **See** Medical Science and Technology-Neurology.

GW/0067-5210
**BEITRAEGE ZUR SEXUALFORSCHUNG.** [Beitr. sexualforsch.]. Vol. 1 (1952)-. Monographic series. German. ir. Price varies per volume. Ferdinand Enke Verlag, Ruedigerstrasse 14, D-70469 Stuttgart Germany. **Tel** 011 49 711 8931124, 011 49 711 893123. **(Subscription address:** Georg Thieme Verlag Stuttgart, Postfach 301120, D 70451 Stuttgart Germany.**) NLM** W1 BE459. **CODEN** BSXFAV. Documents available from BIOSIS Document Express.
**Ind/Abst** Biol. Abstr. (-1976); Health Plan. Adminis.; Index Med.

SZ/0067-8147
**BIBLIOTHECA PSYCHIATRICA.** [Bibl. psychiatr.]. Vol. 143 (1970)-. German. an. 150.00F (approx. per volume). S. Karger AG, Allschwilerstrasse 10, PO Box - Postfach - Case Postale, CH-4009 Basel Switzerland. **Tel** 011 41 61 306-1111, FAX 011 41 61 306-1234, telex CH 962 652. **ED** B. Saletu. **LC** UNC. **NLM** W1 BI429. **CODEN** BIBPBI. **[CCC].** Documents available from BIOSIS Document Express, CASDDS. ***Continues*** *Bibliotheca Psychiatrica et Neurologica.*
**Desc:** Through the years, individual volumes have functioned to outline the specific problems and controversies which have characterized the growth of psychiatry and the broadened acceptance of its methods and applications. Reflecting this progress, recent volumes have been distinguished by their close concern with practical psychiatry, including concepts of classification and therapy, precision of description and classification, differential diagnosis, and critical evaluation of methodologies.
**Ind/Abst** Biol. Abstr.; Chem. Abstr.; Health Plan. Adminis.; Index Med.; Life Sci. Collect.; Ref. Upd. Deluxe Ed.

UK/0260-1222
**BIMH MENTAL HANDICAP BULLETIN.** [BIMH Ment. Handicap Bull.]. **VFOAT** British Institute of Mental Handicap Mental Handicap Bulletin; Mental Handicap Bulletin. (1979)-. English. qt. £26.00 UK, $59.00 US. Multilingual Matters Ltd., Frankfurt Lodge, Clevedon Hall, Clevedon Avon, BS21 7SJ England. **Tel** 011 44 275 876519, FAX 011 44 275 343096. ***Continues*** *IMS Mental Handicap Bulletin.*

US/0743-4804
**BIOENERGETIC ANALYSIS.** (BIOENERGETIC ANALYSIS : THE CLINICAL JOURNAL OF THE INTERNATIONAL INSTITUTE FOR BIOENERGETIC ANALYSIS.). [Bioenerg. anal.]. **Added/Corp** International Institute for Bioenergetic Analysis (New York, N.Y.). Vol. 1., No. 1 (Spring 1984)-. Periodical. English. sa. $28.00 institutions; $15.00 individuals. Bioenergetic Analysis, Hog Hill Road, Pepperell MA 01463. **Tel** (617)433-9277. **ED** Philip M. Helfaer. **LC** RC489.B5; B56. **DD** 616.89/14. Index available. **Bk Rev. Circ:** 2,000.
**Desc:** Clinical articles on bioenergetic analysis, a holistic, body/mind form of psychotherapy based on the work of Lowen.

US/0363-3586
**BIOFEEDBACK AND SELF-REGULATION.** **See** Psychology.

US/0882-2506
**BIOGRAPHICAL DIRECTORY - AMERICAN PSYCHIATRIC ASSOCIATION.** ***Ceased.*** **See** Biographies.

US/0006-3223
**BIOLOGICAL PSYCHIATRY (1969).** (BIOLOGICAL PSYCHIATRY.). [Biol. psychiatry]. **Added/Corp** Society of Biological Psychiatry. **VFOAT** Biol Psychiatry. Vol. 1 (Jan. 1969)-. Academic Scholarly Publication. English. Twenty-four times a year (2 volumes). $928.00 US; $1034.00 other. Elsevier Science Publishing Company Inc, Madison Square Station, PO Box 882, New York NY 10159-0882. **Tel** (212)633-3950, FAX (212)633-3990. **ED** Joseph Wortis. **LC** RC321; .B55. **DD** 616.89/005. **NLM** W1 BI754L. **CODEN** BIPCBF. **[CCC]. Ad Acc. Pr Rev. Circ:** 1,200. available on microfilm and microfiche from University Microfilms

International (UMI). Documents available from The Genuine Article, BIOSIS Document Express, CASDDS, ADONIS. ***Continues*** *Recent Advances in Biological Psychiatry.*
**Desc:** Contributions accepted from all disciplines and research areas relevant to psychiatry: pathology, physiology, pharmacology, electroencephalography, biochemistry, genetics, and related fields, including clinical, psychological, epidemiological, and normative studies.
**Ind/Abst** ADONIS; Annals Behav. Med.; Biol. Abstr.; Chem. Abstr.; CSA Neuro. Abstr.; Curr. Aware. Biol. Sci., CABS; Curr. Contents Life Sci.; Dairy Sci. Abstr.; EMBASE; Health Plan. Adminis.; Index Med.; Index Vet.; Int. Aerosp. Abstr.; Nutr. Abstr. Rev., Ser. A, Hum. Exp.; Life Sci. Collect.; Pig News Inf.; Psychol. Abstr. (1969-); PsycINFO (1990-); PsycLit; Ref. Upd. Deluxe Ed.; Res. Alert [Full Cov.]; Sci. Cit. Index; SCISEARCH; Small Anim. Abstr. Bibliogr.; Soc. Sci. Cit. Index [Select. Cov.]; Vet. Bull.

UK/0266-2124
**BIOLOGICAL PSYCHIATRY (LONDON, ENGLAND).** (BIOLOGICAL PSYCHIATRY.). [Biol. psychiatr. new prospects]. 1-. Monographic series. English. Price varies per volume. John Libbey & Company Ltd, 13 Smiths Yard, Summerley Street, London SW18 4HR England. **Tel** 01-947 2777, FAX 01-947 2664, telex 94013503 JOHN G. **UDC** 616.89. **NLM** W1; BI754J.

US/1044-422X
**BIOLOGICAL THERAPIES IN PSYCHIATRY NEWSLETTER.** (BIOLOGICAL THERAPIES IN PSYCHIATRY NEWSLETTER / ALAN J. GELENBERG.). [Biol. ther. psychiatry newsl.]. **VFOAT** Biological Therapies in Psychiatry. (198?)-. Newsletter. English. mo. $70.00 (institutions), $52.00 (institutions) US; $77.00 (institutions), $59.00 (individuals) other. Mosby Year Book Inc., 11830 Westline Industrial Drive, St Louis MO 63146. **Tel** (800)325-4177, (314)872-8370, FAX (314)432-1380, telex 44-2402. **DD** 616. **NLM** W1; BI759V. ***Continues*** *Biological Therapies in Psychiatry, 0895-8262.*
**Desc:** Provides updates on the clinical use of psychotropic drugs to practicing psychiatrists, psychiatric house staff, residents, and students. Each issue considers several current drug topics critical to everyday practice, offering practical advice and new insights based upon actual experience.

IT/0393-4853
**BOLLETTINO DI PSICHIATRIA BIOLOGICA.** [Boll. psichiatr. biol.]. (1985)-. Periodical. Multiple languages. tq. Casa Editrice Libraria Idelson Gnocchi, via Alcide De Gasperi 55, 80133 Naples Italy. **Tel** 011 39 81 5524733. **UDC** 159.929.
**Ind/Abst** EMBASE [Select. Cov.].

CN/0715-741X
**BORDURES.** [Bordures]. Vol. 1 (Dec. 1982)-. Periodical. French. ir. 7.00Can$. Bordures, C P 836 Succursale Notre-Dame-de-Grace, Montreal Quebec H4A 3S2 Canada. **DD** 616.89/17/05. **UDC** 616.89.

CN/0825-9178
**BOUSSOLE.** (LA BOUSSOLE : BULLETIN DU REGROUPMENT DES PARENTS ET AMIS DU MALADE MENTAL.). [Boussole (Que.).]. **Added/Corp** Association Canadienne pour la Sante Mentale. Regroupement des Parents et Amis du Malade Mental. (1984)-. Bulletin. French. qt. 10.00Can$. La Boussole, 980 Avenue Holland, Suite 103, Quebec Que G1S 3T1 Canada. **Tel** (418)682-3780. **DD** 362.2/09714.

NE/0924-0314
**BRILL'S STUDIES IN EPISTEMOLOGY, PSYCHOLOGY AND PSYCHIATRY. See** Psychology.

UK/0264-2689
**BRITISH ASSOCIATION FOR PSYCHOPHARMACOLOGY MONOGRAPH.** [Br. Assoc. Psychopharmacol. monogr.]. **Added/Corp** British Association for Psychopharmacology. **VFOAT** Monograph. No. 1 (1979)-. Monographic series. English. ir. Price varies per volume. Oxford University Press, Walton Street, Oxford OX2 6DP England. **Tel** 011 44 865 56767, FAX 011 44 865 267773, telex 837330 OXPRES G. **(Subscription address:** Oxford University Press / USA, Journals Marketing Department, Oxford University Press, 2001 Evans Road, Cary NC 27513.**) LC** UNC. **DD** 615/.78. **NLM** W1 BR343D. **CODEN** BAPMEQ. Documents available from CASDDS.
**Ind/Abst** Chem. Abstr.

CN/0849-9888
**BRITISH COLUMBIA ASSOCIATION FOR COMMUNITY LIVING NEWS.** [B.C. Assoc. Community Living news]. **Added/Corp** British Columbia Association for Community Living. **VFOAT** Community Living News. Vol. 7, No. 3 (Sept./Oct./Nov. 1989)-. Periodical. English. qt. Free. BCACL, #300 30 East 6th Avenue, Vancouver BC V5T 4P4 Canada. **DD** 362.3/06/0711. ***Continues*** *BCMHP News, 0827-2344.*

UK/0951-0192
**BRITISH JOURNAL OF CLINICAL AND SOCIAL PSYCHIATRY.** [Br. j. clin. soc. psychiatry]. (19??)-. Periodical. English. qt (4 issues). £5.00 UK. Social Clinical Psychiatrists, Harrogate Clinic, 23 Rippon Road, Harrogate HG12 2JL England. **Tel** 011 44 423 500599. ***Continues*** *Newsletter of the Society of Clinical Psychiatrists.*

UK/0007-1250
**BRITISH JOURNAL OF PSYCHIATRY, THE.** [Br. j. psychiatry]. **Added/Corp** Royal Medico-Psychological Association. Royal College of Psychiatrists. Vol. 109, No. 458 (March 1963)-. Academic Scholarly Publication. English. mo. $295.00 (institution), $210.00 (individual) US; £148.00 (institution), £130.00 (individual) UK & Europe; £175.00 (institution), £138.00 (individual) other. Royal Society of Medicine Press, 1 Wimpole Street, London W1M 8AE England. **Tel** 011 44 71 2902928. **ED** H L Freeman. **LC** RC321; .J82. **NLM** W1 BR616. **CODEN** BJPYAJ. **[CCC].** Index available. cum. index. **Bk Rev. Ad Acc. Pr Rev. Circ:** 12,000. Documents available from The Genuine Article, BIOSIS Document Express, CASDDS, ADONIS. ***Continues*** *Journal of Mental Science, 0368-315X.*
**Desc:** Contains papers relating to all aspects of psychiatry.
**Ind/Abst** ADONIS; Arts Humanit. Citation Index [Select. Cov.]; Biol. Abstr.; Chem. Abstr.; Crim. Penol. Police Sci. Abstr.; Cumul. Index Nurs. Allied Health Lit.; Curr. Aware. Biol. Sci., CABS; Dev. Med. Child Neurol.; EMBASE; Health Period. Database; Health Plan. Adminis.; Index Med.; Int. Pharm. Abstr.; Med. Abstr. Newsl.; Middle East Abstr. Index; Nutr. Abstr. Rev., Ser. B, Live Feeds and Feed.; Nutr. Abstr. Rev., Ser. A, Hum. Exp.; Life Sci. Collect.; PESTDOC; Protozoolog. Abstr.; Psychol. Abstr. (1963-); PsycINFO; PsycLit; Ref. Upd. Deluxe Ed.; Res. Alert [Full Cov.]; Risk Abstr.; Sci. Cit. Index; SCISEARCH; Soc. Sci. Cit. Index [Full Cov.]; Trop. Dis. Bull.; Women Stud. Abstr.

UK/0960-5371
**BRITISH JOURNAL OF PSYCHIATRY. SUPPLEMENT, THE.** [Br. j. psychiatr., Suppl.]. **Added/Corp** Royal College of Psychiatrists. No. 1 (1988)-. Monographic series. English. ir. Price varies per volume. Royal Society of Medicine Press, 1 Wimpole Street, London W1M 8AE England. **Tel** 011 44 71 2902928. **NLM** W1; BR615R. Documents available from ADONIS.
**Ind/Abst** ADONIS; Health Plan. Adminis.; Index Med. (1988-).

UK/0265-9883
**BRITISH JOURNAL OF PSYCHOTHERAPY.** [Br. j. psychother.]. Vol. 1, No. 1 (Autumn 1984)-. Periodical. English. Four times a year. £23.00 (individuals), £45.00 (institutions) UK; £30.00 (individuals), £52.00 (institutions) other. Artesian Books, 18 Artesian Road, London W2 5AR England. **Tel** 011 44 71 2292855, FAX 011 44 71 7922543. **ED** R. D. Hinshilwood. **NLM** W1; BR619R.
**Desc:** Emphasizes clinically orientated papers which concern the practice of analytical psychotherapy, or that have theoretical implications.
**Ind/Abst** EMBASE; Psychol. Abstr. (1987-); PsycINFO (1990-); PsycLit.

US/0004-542X
**BULLETIN - ASSOCIATION FOR PSYCHOANALYTIC MEDICINE. Main/Corp** Association for Psychoanalytic Medicine. Bulletin. English. ir (two-three issues per year). $10.00 US; $15.00 other. Association of Psychoanalytic Medicine, 4560 Delafield Avenue, Riverdale NY 10471. **Tel** (212)548-6088. **ED** Elizabeth Auchincloss. **LC** RC500; .A87A. **DD** 616.8/914/005. **UDC** 616.89-072.87. **Bk Rev. Circ:** 2,000 (ctrl).

US/0091-634X
**BULLETIN OF THE AMERICAN ACADEMY OF PSYCHIATRY AND THE LAW.** [Bull. Am. Acad. Psych. Law]. **Main/Corp** American Academy of Psychiatry and the Law. Vol. 1 (Autumn 1972)-. Academic Scholarly Publication. English. Four times a year (Mar., June, Sept., Dec.). $75.00 (institutions), $50.00 (individual). American Academy of Psychiatry & The Law, PO Box 30, One Regency Drive, Bloomfield CT 06002. **Tel** (203)242-5450, (800)331-1389, FAX (203)286-0787. **ED** Dr. Seymour L. Halleck MD. **LC** RA1151; .A43a. **DD** 614/.19. **NLM** W1 BU841H. Index available. **Bk Rev. Circ:** 2,000 (ctrl). available on microfilm and microfiche from University Microfilms International (UMI).
**Desc:** Devoted to scholarly articles in the field of forensic psychiatry.
**Ind/Abst** Crim. Justice Abstr.; Crim. Penol. Police Sci. Abstr.; Curr. Law Index (1984-); EMBASE; Index Med.; Leg. Resour. Index (1984-); LegalTrac (1980-); Psychol. Abstr. (1974-); PsycINFO; PsycLit.

UK/0267-3061
**BULLETIN OF THE ANNA FREUD CENTRE. Added/Corp** Anna Freud Centre. Vol. 8, Pt. 1 (1985)-. Periodical. English. Four times a year (Mar., June, Sept., Dec.). £22.00 UK, £50.00 others. Bulletin of the Anna Freud Centre, 21 Maresfield Gardens, London NW3 5SU England. **Tel** 011 44 71 7942313, FAX 011 44 71 7946506. **ED** Clifford Yorke. **NLM** W1; BU84HF. **Bk Rev. Circ:** 500. ***Continues*** *Bulletin of the Hampstead Clinic, 0263-9688.*
**Desc:** Reporting on the work of the Centre for the psychoanalytic study and treatment of children; also of value to diagnosticians, therapists and allied workers.

US/0025-9284
**BULLETIN OF THE MENNINGER CLINIC.** [Bull. Menninger Clin.]. **Main/Corp** Menninger Clinic. **Added/Corp** Menninger Foundation. Vol. 1 (Sept. 1936)-. Academic Scholarly Publication. English. Four times a year (Jan., Apr., July, Oct.). $75.00 (institutions), $50.00 (individuals) US; $85.00 (institutions), $60.00 (individuals) other. Bulletin of the Menninger Clinic, PO Box 829, Topeka KS 66601. **Tel** (913)273-7500 Ext. 5850, FAX (913)273-8625. **ED** Jon G. Allen. **LC** RC321; .M4. **DD** 616.8/9/005. **NLM** W1 BU858. **CODEN** BMCLA4. **[CCC].** Index available. **Bk Rev. Ad Acc. Pr Rev. Acid Free. Circ:** 2,200. available on microfilm and microfiche from University Microfilms International (UMI). Documents available from The Genuine Article, BIOSIS Document Express.
**Desc:** A multidisciplinary journal for mental health professionals. Offers a psychodynamic perspective on the application of theory and research in outpatient psychotherapy, hospital treatment, education, and other areas of mental health. A typical 144 page issue contains theoretical and clinical articles, clinical case reports and literature reviews.
**Ind/Abst** Acad. Search (July 1993-); Arts Humanit. Citation Index [Select. Cov.]; Biol. Abstr.; Crim. Penol. Police Sci. Abstr.; Curr. Contents Soc. Behav. Sci.; EMBASE; Health Plan. Adminis.; Hospit. Health Admin. Index; Index Med.; Index Period. Artic. Relat. Law (19??-19??); INFO-SOUTH Abstr.; Int. Nurs. Index; Linguist. Lang. Behav. Abstr.; Mag. Search; Middle East Abstr. Index; Psychol. Abstr. (1936-); PsycINFO; PsycLit; Res. Alert [Full Cov.]; Soc. Plann. Policy Dev. Abstr.; Soc. Sci. Cit. Index [Full Cov.]; Soc. Work Abstr. (Summer 1987-) [Select. Cov.]; Sociol. Abstr.

US/0547-7115
**BULLETIN OF THE NATIONAL GUILD OF CATHOLIC PSYCHIATRISTS, INC, THE.** ***Suspended.*** [Bull. Natl. Guild Cathol. Psychiatr.]. **Main/Corp** National Guild of Catholic Psychiatrists. Vol. 15, No. 3 (July 1968)-Suspended. Bulletin. English. an. $15.00 US and Canada; $17.00 other. National Guild of Catholic Psychiatrists, Sr Anna Polcino, 1211 Boulevard, Seaside Park NJ 08752. **Tel** (201)830-4078. **ED** Anna Polcino. **LC** RC321; .G8. **DD** 261.8/32/205. **UDC** 616.89. **Bk Rev. Ad Acc. Circ:** 250 (ctrl). ***Continues*** *Bulletin of the Guild of Catholic Psychiatrists, 0275-0775.*
**Desc:** Topics are on the theological reflections on the practice of psychiatry and psychology and/or ethics. It is geared to psychiatrists, psychologists and other mental health professionals.
**Ind/Abst** Abr. Cathol. Period. Lit. Index; Cathol. Period. Lit. Index.

CN/0711-6012
**BULLETIN / (UNIVERSITY OF WESTERN ONTARIO, DEPT. OF PSYCHIATRY).** [Bull. - Univ. West. Ont. Dep. Psychiatr.]. **Added/Corp** University of Western Ontario. Dept. of Psychiatry. No. 8201 (1982)-. Bulletin. English. Price varies per volume. D B Weldon Library, University of Western Ontario, London Ontario N6A 3K7 Canada. **DD** 610.

US
**CALIFORNIA ALLIANCE FOR THE MENTALLY ILL.** (1990)-. Periodical. English. qt. $25.00. California Alliance for the Mentally Ill, 1111 Howe Avenue, Suite 475, Sacramento CA 95825. **Tel** (916)567-0163, FAX (916)567-1757. **ED** Dan E. Weisburd. **Circ:** 14,000.
**Desc:** Devoted to media and mental illness. Contains articles of myths, misconceptions and stereotypes about mental illness. In an effort to educated the public about mental illness the media plays a key role.

US
**CALIFORNIA LAWS FOR PSYCHOTHERAPISTS. See** Law-Family Law.

CN/0823-3594
**CALOTTE, LA.** [Calotte]. Vol. 1, No. 1 (Winter 83)-. Periodical. French. qt. $2.00 Per No. Auto Psy, 835 Brown/404, Quebec Quebec G1S 4S1 Canada. **Tel** (418)529-1978. **DD** 362.2/1/09714.

●CN/1188-7605
**CANADIAN CHILD PSYCHIATRIC BULLETIN, THE.** [Can. child psychiatr. bull.]. **Added/Corp** Canadian Academy of Child Psychiatry. **VFOAT** Bulletin Pedopsychiatrique Canadien. (1992)-. Bulletin. English ( and ). qt. $20.00 per year. Canadian Academy of Child Psychiatry, c/o P Barker, Alberta Children's Hospital, 1820 Richmond Road South West, Calgary Alberta T2T 5C7 Canada. **DD** 616.89. ***Continues*** *Bulletin (Canadian Academy of Child Psychiatry).*

CN/0008-4174
**CANADIAN JOURNAL OF OCCUPATIONAL THERAPY (1939).** (CANADIAN JOURNAL OF OCCUPATIONAL THERAPY.). [Can. j. occup. ther.]. **VFOAT** Revue Canadienne d'Ergotherapie. V. 6, No. 2- Oct. 1939-. Periodical. English (French). Five times a year. 35.00Can$ Canada; 50.00Can$ other. Canadian Association of Occupational Therapy, Box 660, Hudson Heights Quebec J0P 1J0 Canada. **Tel** (416)487-5404. **(Subscription address:** 110 Eglinton Avenue West, 3rd Floor, Toronto Ontario M4R 1A3 Canada**) ED** Geraldine Moore. **UDC** 615.851.35. **NLM** W1 CA597. **Bk Rev. Ad Acc. Circ:** 5,000. available on microfilm and microfiche from University Microfilms International (UMI). ***Continues*** *Canadian Journal of Occupational Therapy and Physiotherapy, 0315-1034.*
**Desc:** Publishes articles and information which contribute to occupational therapy practice, theory, research and education.
**Ind/Abst** Cumul. Index Nurs. Allied Health Lit.; EMBASE; Health Plan. Adminis.; Hospit. Health Admin. Index.

CN/0706-7437
**CANADIAN JOURNAL OF PSYCHIATRY.** (CANADIAN JOURNAL OF PSYCHIATRY. REVUE CANADIENNE DE PSYCHIATRIE.). [Can. j. psychiatry]. **Added/Corp** Canadian Psychiatric Association. **VFOAT** Revue Canadienne de Psychiatrie. Vol. 24 (Feb. 1979)-. Periodical. English (French; summaries and/or abstracts in French). mo. 84.11Can$ Canada; 110.00Can$ other. Canadian Psychiatric Association, 237 Argyle Avenue/ Suite 200, Ottawa Ontario K2P 1B8 Canada. **Tel** (613)234-2815. **LC** RC321; .C3. **DD** 616.8/9/00971. **NLM** W1 CA602V. **CODEN** CPAJAK. **[CCC].** Index available in last issue of volume--attached. cum. index. **Bk Rev. Ad Acc. Pr Rev. Circ:** 3,300 (ctrl). available on microfilm and microfiche from University Microfilms International (UMI). Documents available from The Genuine Article. ***Continues*** *Canadian Psychiatric Association. Canadian Psychiatric Association Journal, 0008-4824.*
**Desc:** Provides a forum for a broad spectrum of peer reviewed, well edited articles in the field of psychiatry.
**Ind/Abst** Appl. Soc. Sci. Index Abstr.; Arts Humanit. Citation Index [Select. Cov.]; Commun. Abstr. (?-?); Crim. Penol. Police Sci. Abstr.; Cumul. Index Nurs. Allied Health Lit.; Curr. Contents Clin. Med.; Curr. Contents Soc. Behav. Sci.; Dev. Med. Child Neurol.; EMBASE; Index Med. (1979-); Int. Nurs. Index; Linguist. Lang. Behav. Abstr.; Middle East Abstr. Index; Mod. Med.; Life Sci. Collect.; Psychol. Abstr. (1979-); PsycINFO; PsycLit; Res. Alert [Full Cov.]; Sage Fam. Stud. Abstr. (?-?); Sci. Cit. Index; SCISEARCH; Soc. Plann. Policy Dev. Abstr.; Soc. Sci. Cit. Index [Full Cov.]; Sociol. Abstr.; Spec. Educ. Needs Abstr.

●US
**CAPSULES AND COMMENTS IN PSYCHIATRIC NURSING.** See Medical Science and Technology-Nursing.

US
**CERVELLO E FARMACI.** (19??)-. Periodical. English. Four times a year. Included with Rivista di Psichiatria: L140000 institutions; L85000 individuals. Il Pensiero Scientifico Editore s.r.l., Via Bradano 3C, 00199 Rome Italy. **Tel** 011 39 6 86207158, 86207159, 86207168, 86207169, FAX 011 39 6 86207160. **Circ:** 1,200.

XR/0069-2336
**CESKOSLOVENSKA PSYCHIATRIE.** [Cesk. psychiatr.]. (1956)-. Periodical. Czech (summaries and/or abstracts in English and Russian). Six times a year. $86.00. **(Subscription address:** Artia Pegas Press Ltd., Palac Metro Narodni Trida 25, 11210 Prague 1 Czech Republic.**) UDC** 616.89. **NLM** W1 CE902P. **CODEN** CEPYAX. [CCC]. ***Supersedes in part*** *Neurologie a Psychiatrie Ceska.*
**Ind/Abst** EMBASE; Index Med.; Psychol. Abstr. (1959-); PsycINFO; PsycLit; Saf. Health Work.

●US/1071-2828
**CHILD AND ADOLESCENT MENTAL HEALTH CARE.** See Psychology.

●US/1056-4993
**CHILD AND ADOLESCENT PSYCHIATRIC CLINICS OF NORTH AMERICA.** (1992)-. Periodical. English. qt. $95.00 (individual), $110.00 (institution) US; $124.00 (individual), $131.00 (institution) other. W.B. Saunders Company, A Subsidiary of Harcourt Brace Jovanovich, Inc., The Curtis Center/Suite 300, Independence Square West, Philadelphia PA 19106-3399. **Tel** (215)238-7800 or, 5587, FAX (215)238-7883, telex 173146. **(Subscription address:** W. B. Saunders Company / North America Subscriptions, c/o Periodicals, 6277 Sea Harbour Drive, 4th Floor, Orlando FL 32887.**) NLM** W1; CH642RS.

CN
**CHILD AND YOUTH PSYCHIATRY, EUROPEAN PERSPECTIVES.** Vol. 1 (1990)-. English. Hogrefe & Huber Publishers, 12 Bruce Park Avenue, Toronto Ontario M4P 2S3 Canada. **Tel** (416)482-6339, FAX (416)484-4200. **NLM** W1; CH643L.

NE/0929-7049
**CHILD NEUROPSYCHOLOGY.** (199?)-. Periodical. English. Three times a year. Fl264.00 (institution). Swets & Zeitlinger BV, Heereweg 347B PO Box 825, 2160 SZ Lisse Holland. **Tel** 011 31 2521 35111, FAX 02521-15888, telex 41325. **(Subscription address:** Swets & Zeitlinger BV, P.O. Box 825, 2160 SZ LISSE, Holland**)**

US/0009-398X
**CHILD PSYCHIATRY AND HUMAN DEVELOPMENT.** [Child psychiatr. hum. dev.]. Vol. 1 (Fall 1970)-. Academic Scholarly Publication. English. qt. £45.00 (individuals), £190.00 (institutions) UK; $235.00 US; $275.00 other. Human Sciences Press, PO Box 735, 233 Spring Street, New York NY 10013. **Tel** (212)620-8000, FAX (212)807-1047, telex 23421139. **(Subscription address:** Eurospan Ltd., Journals and Serials Division, 3 Henrietta Street, Covent Garden, London WC2E 8LU England.**) ED** Jack Westman. **LC** RJ499.A1; C43. **DD** 618.9/28/91405. **NLM** W1 CH668K. **CODEN** CPHDA3. **[CCC].** Index available. **Bk Rev. Ad Acc. Pr Rev.** available on microfilm and microfiche from University Microfilms International (UMI). Documents available from The Genuine Article, BIOSIS Document Express.
**Desc:** Founded to serve allied professional groups of specialists in child psychiatry, social science, pediatrics and psychology, and to define the developing child and adolescent in health and in conflict.
**Ind/Abst** Acad. Search (July 1993-); Appl. Soc. Sci. Index Abstr.; Biol. Abstr.; Child Dev. Abstr. Bibliogr.; Curr. Contents Clin. Med.; Curr. Contents Soc. Behav. Sci.; Curr. Index J. Educ.; Dev. Med. Child Neurol.; Educ. Index; EMBASE; Except. Child Educ. Resour.; Health Plan. Adminis.; Index Med.; INFO-SOUTH Abstr.; Linguist. Lang. Behav. Abstr.; Mag. Search; Life Sci. Collect.; Psychol. Abstr. (1970-); PsycINFO; PsycLit; PsycScan: Develop. Psych.; Res. Alert [Full Cov.]; SCISEARCH; Soc. Plann. Policy Dev. Abstr.; Soc. Sci. Cit. Index [Full Cov.]; Soc. Work Abstr. (Spring, Summer 1987-) [Select. Cov.]; Sociol. Abstr.; Women Stud. Abstr.

II/0009-3998
**CHILD PSYCHIATRY QUARTERLY.** ***Ceased.* See** Medical Science and Technology-Pediatrics.

KO
**CHONGSIN PAKYAK YONGU. Added/Corp** Sina Chaehwalwon (Korea) Hanguk Chongsin Pakyak Yonguso. **VFOAT** Mentally Retarded Research Papers. (1990)-. Periodical. Korean. Hanguk Chongsin Pakyak Yonguso, 251-33 Koyo-dong Songpa-ku, Seoul, Korea. **LC** IN PROCESS.

US/0270-6644
**CLINICAL PSYCHIATRY NEWS.** [Clin. psychiatr. news]. Vol.1 (Nov. 1973)-. Periodical. English. mo. $60.00 US; $81.00 other. International Medical News Group, 12230 Wilkins Avenue, Rockville MD 20852. **Tel** (301)770-6170. **ED** William Rubin. **DD** 616. **NLM** W1 CL768CS. **Bk Rev. Ad Acc. Circ:** 28,000 (ctrl). available on microfilm from University Microfilms International (UMI).
**Desc:** Coverage of clinical meetings, symposia, and conventions to report clinical developments in the fields of psychiatry and neurology.

US/0091-1674
**CLINICAL SOCIAL WORK JOURNAL. See** Sociology-Social Services and Welfare.

●NZ/1172-7047
**CNS DRUGS : THE CLINICAL REVIEW OF DRUGS AND THERAPEUICS IN PSYCHIATRY AND NEUROLOGY. See** Pharmacy and Pharmacology.

UK/0045-7663
**COMMUNICATION LONDON. 1967.** (COMMUNICATION.). [Communication Lond., 1967]. (1967)-. Periodical. English. tq (Spring, Summer, Winter). £10.00 UK; £15.00 other. National Autistic Society, 276 Willesden Lane, London NW2 5RB England. **Tel** 011 44 1 451 3844. **ED** Christine Nickles. **DD** 371.9. **Bk Rev.** ctrl circ.

UK/0265-7007
**COMMUNITY PSYCHIATRIC NURSING JOURNAL.** ***Title Change.* See** Medical Science and Technology-Nursing.

CN
**COMMUNITY PSYCHIATRIC PRACTICE.** English. Four times a year. $36.00 (individuals), $45.00 (institutions) add $8.00 postage US; $39.00 (individuals), $49.00 (institutions) add $8.00 postage Canada. Hogrefe and Huber Publishers, PO Box 2487, Kirkland WA 98083. **Tel** (800)228-3749, (206)820-1500, FAX (206)823-8324.

US/1051-7782
**COMPREHENSIVE MENTAL HEALTH CARE.** ***Title Change.* See** Psychology.

US/0010-440X
**COMPREHENSIVE PSYCHIATRY.** [Compr. psych.]. Vol. 1 (Feb. 1960)-. Academic Scholarly Publication. English. bm (6 issues). $130.00 (individual), $189.00 (institution) US; $184.00 (individual), $213.00 (institution) other. W.B. Saunders Company, A Subsidiary of Harcourt Brace Jovanovich, Inc., The Curtis Center/Suite 300, Independence Square West, Philadelphia PA 19106-3399. **Tel** (215)238-7800 or, 5587, FAX (215)238-7883, telex 173146. **(Subscription address:** W. B. Saunders Company / North America Subscriptions, c/o Periodicals, 6277 Sea Harbour Drive, 4th Floor, Orlando FL 32887.**) ED** Ralph A. O'Connell. **LC** RC321. **DD** 616.8/9/005. **UDC** 616.89. **NLM** W1 CO453. **CODEN** COPYAV. **[CCC]. Pr Rev.** Documents available from The Genuine Article, BIOSIS Document Express.
**Ind/Abst** Biol. Abstr.; Cumul. Index Nurs. Allied Health Lit.; Curr. Contents Clin. Med.; Curr. Contents Soc. Behav. Sci.; EMBASE; Health Plan. Adminis.; Index Med.; Middle East Abstr. Index; Mod. Med.; Psychol. Abstr. (1960-); PsycINFO; PsycLit; Res. Alert [Full Cov.]; Sci. Cit. Index; SCISEARCH; Soc. Sci. Cit. Index [Full Cov.]; Women Stud. Abstr.

US/0275-7222
**COMPREHENSIVE PSYCHOTHERAPY.** (COMPREHENSIVE PSYCHOTHERAPY / EDITED FOR THE NATIONAL INSTITUTE FOR THE PSYCHOTHERAPIES.). [Compr. psycother.]. **Added/Corp** National Institute for the Psychotherapies. Vol. 1 (1980)-. Periodical. English. ir. Price varies. Gordon & Breach Science Publishers, Inc., PO Box 786, Cooper Station, New York NY 10276. **Tel** (212)206-8900, FAX (212)645-2459. **(Subscription address:** International Publishers Distributor at one of the following addresses: 820 Town Center Drive, Langhorne, PA 19047; or PO Box 90, Reading Berkshire RG1 8JL UK; or Kent Ridge PO Box 1180, Singapore 9111, Republic of Singapore**) ED** Paul Olsen. **LC** RC475; .C57. **DD** 616.89/14/05. **NLM** W1 CO453F.
**Ind/Abst** Psychol. Abstr. (1980-).

US/0738-3614
**COMPUTERS IN PSYCHIATRY/PSYCHOLOGY.** [Comput. psychiatr./psychol.]. **VFOAT** CP/P; C.P./P. **VAT** Computers in Psychiatry Psychology. Began with: Vol. 2, No. 1 (June-July 1979)-. Periodical. English. qt. $45.00 (institutions), $40.00 (individuals). CP/P, 26 Trumbull Street, New Haven CT 06511. **NLM** W1; CO4572H. **CODEN** CPSHD5. Documents available from Ask*IEEE. ***Continues*** *Micro-Psych.*
**Ind/Abst** INSPEC (1980-1986).

SP/0210-1424
**COMUNICACION PSIQUIATRICA.** (COMUNICACION PSIQUIATRICA : ANALES DE LA CATEDRA DE PSIQUIATRIA.). [Comun. psiquiatr.]. (1977)-. Spanish (summaries and/or abstracts in French, German and English). an. Free. Hospital Clinico Universitario Catedra de Psiquiatria, Avda Gomez Laguna s/n, 50009 Zaragoza Spain. **Tel** (976)559795. **ED** A Seva. **NLM** W1 CO458N. **CODEN** COPSEH. Index available. **Bk Rev. Pr Rev. Circ:** 1,000. Documents available from BIOSIS Document Express.
**Desc:** A collection of the research studies and doctoral dissertations undertaken each year in the psychiatry department of the University of Zaragoza.
**Ind/Abst** Biol. Abstr. (1987-); Indice Med. Esp.

SP
**CONFRONTACIONES PSIQUIATRICAS.** Spanish. ir. Rhodia Iberica, Apartado 16, 28080 Alorcon (Madrid) Spain.

FR/0153-9329
**CONFRONTATIONS PSYCHIATRIQUES PARIS.** [Confront. psychiatr. Paris]. (1968)-. Periodical. Multiple languages. an. Free on request. Theraplix, 46-52 rue Albert, 75640 Paris Cedex 13 France. **Tel** 011 33 1 40773000. **UDC** 616.89.
**Ind/Abst** EMBASE; PsycINFO (1973-); PsycLit.

US/0277-8041
**CONTEMPORARY PSYCHIATRY (NEW YORK, N.Y.).** ***Ceased.*** (CONTEMPORARY PSYCHIATRY.). [Contemp. psychiatr.]. Vol. 1, No. 1 (Mar. 1982)-Vol 9 (?). Periodical. English. qt. Plenum Press, 233 Spring Street, New York NY 10013-1578. **Tel** (212)620-8000, (800)221-9369, FAX (212)463-0742, (212)807-1047, telex 23/421139. **ED** Seymour L Halleck. **LC** RC321. **DD** 616.89. **UDC** 616.89. **NLM** W1 CO769V. **CODEN** CPCHDR. **[CCC].** Index available. available on microfilm and microfiche from University Microfilms International (UMI).
**Desc:** This journal is devoted solely to the critical evaluation and review of those books of special interest to, and by psychiatric practitioners, psychiatry teachers and residents.

US/0010-7530
**CONTEMPORARY PSYCHOANALYSIS.** [Contemp. psychoanal.]. **Added/Corp** William Alanson White Psychoanalytic Society. William Alanson White Institute. Vol. 1 (Fall 1964)-. Academic Scholarly Publication. English. qt (Jan., Apr., Jul., Aug.). $49.50 (individuals), $72.50 (institutions) US; $61.50 (individuals), $84.50 (institutions) other. Sheridan Press, PO Box 465, Hanover PA 17331. **Tel** (800)352-2210, (717)632-3535, FAX (717)633-8900. **ED** Arthur H. Feiner. **LC** RC500; .C6. **DD** 616.8/917/05. **NLM** W1 CO769W. **CODEN** CPPSBL. **[CCC].** cum. index. **Pr Rev. Circ:**

1,650 (ctrl). available on microfilm and microfiche from University Microfilms International (UMI). Documents available from The Genuine Article.
**Desc:** Presents an informed and scholarly approach to the contemporary psychoanalytic scene. While it officially represents the interpersonal position, all points of view are presented regularly.
**Ind/Abst** Abstr. Res. Pastor. Care Couns. (19??-); Curr. Contents Soc. Behav. Sci.; EMBASE; Linguist. Lang. Behav. Abstr.; Middle East Abstr. Index; Psychol. Abstr. (1968-); PsycINFO; PsycLit; Res. Alert [Full Cov.]; Soc. Plann. Policy Dev. Abstr.; Soc. Sci. Cit. Index [Full Cov.]; Soc. Work Abstr. [Select. Cov.]; Sociol. Abstr.

US/0737-9544
**CONTEMPORARY PSYCHOTHERAPY REVIEW.** (CONTEMPORARY PSYCHOTHERAPY REVIEW : JOURNAL OF THE INSTITUTE FOR CONTEMPORARY PSYCHOTHERAPY AND THE SOCIETY OF THE INSTITUTE FOR CONTEMPORARY PSYCHOTHERAPY.). [Contemp. psychother. rev.]. **Added/Corp** Institute for Contemporary Psychotherapy. Society of the Institute for Contemporary Psychotherapy. Vol. 1 (Fall 1983)-. English. an. $10.00. Contemporary Psychotherapy, One West 91st Street, New York NY 10024. **NLM** W1; CO769WI.
**Ind/Abst** Psychol. Abstr. (1983-); PsycINFO (1990-); PsycLit.

US/0093-1551
**CORRECTIVE AND SOCIAL PSYCHIATRY AND JOURNAL OF BEHAVIOR TECHNOLOGY METHODS AND THERAPY.** [Correct. soc. psychiatr. j. behav. technol. methods ther.]. **Added/Corp** Medical Correctional Association (U.S.) American Association of Mental Health Professionals in Corrections. Martin Psychiatric Research Foundation. **VFOAT** Journal of Behavior Technology Methods and Therapy. Vol. 20 (1974)-. Periodical. English. qt. $35.00. Martin Psychiatric Research, PO Box 3365, Fairfield CA 94533. **Tel** (707)864-0910. **LC** RC321; .J86. **DD** 616.8/9/005. **NLM** W1 CO898R. **CODEN** CPSTDD. available on microfilm and microfiche from University Microfilms International (UMI). ***Continues*** *Corrective and Social Psychiatry and Journal of Applied Behavior Therapy, 0091-2611.*
**Ind/Abst** Crim. Justice Abstr.; Crim. Justice Period. Index (-1989); EMBASE; Psychol. Abstr. (1974-); PsycINFO; PsycLit.

NE/0165-005X
**CULTURE, MEDICINE AND PSYCHIATRY.** [Cult. med. psychiatry]. Vol. 1 (April 1977)-. Periodical. English. qt. $366.00. Kluwer Academic Publishers, Postbus 322, 3300 AH Dordrecht, The Netherlands. **Tel** 011 (31) 78 524400, FAX 011 31 78 183273, telex 20083. **ED** Byron J Good, Mary-Jo Delvecchio-Good. **LC** RC455.4.E8; C85. **DD** 616.8/9/005. **NLM** W1 CU446. **CODEN** CMPSD2. **[CCC]. Bk Rev. Ad Acc. Pr Rev. Acid Free. Circ:** 800. available on microfilm and microfiche from University Microfilms International (UMI). Documents available from The Genuine Article, BIOSIS Document Express.
**Desc:** Serves as an international and interdisciplinary forum for three interrelated fields: medical and psychiatric anthropology; cross-cultural psychiatry; and related cross-societal and clinical and epidemiological studies.
**Ind/Abst** Abstr. Anthropol. (1977-); Acad. Search (July 1993-); Anthropol. Lit.; Biol. Abstr.; Curr. Contents Soc. Behav. Sci.; EMBASE; Health Source (Jul. 1993-); Index Med. (1977-); Int. Bibliogr. Sociol.; Linguist. Lang. Behav. Abstr.; Mag. Search; Middle East Abstr. Index; Prev. Hum. Serv.; Psychol. Abstr. (1977-); PsycINFO; PsycLit; Ref. Z.; Res. Alert [Full Cov.]; Soc. Plann. Policy Dev. Abstr.; Soc. Sci. Cit. Index [Full Cov.]; Sociol. Abstr.; SportSearch (1977-).

GW/0344-8622
**CURARE.** (CURARE / HERAUSGEGEBEN VON DER ARBEITSGEMEINSCHAFT ETHNOMEDIZIN E.V.). [Curare]. **Added/Corp** Arbeitsgemeinschaft Ethnomedizin. Vol. 1 (1978)-. Periodical. German (English and French). Twice a year. DM90.00 Germany; DM94.00 others. VWB Verlag Wissenschaft Building, Postfach 110368, D 10833 Berlin Germany. **Tel** 011 49 30 2510415. **ED** Ekkehard Schroder. **LC** RC455.4.E8; C86. **DD** 616.89/005. **NLM** W1 CU484. **[CCC]. Bk Rev. Ad Acc. Circ:** 820.
**Desc:** Journal for ethnomedicine and psychiatry.
**Ind/Abst** Anthropol. Lit.; Linguist. Lang. Behav. Abstr.; Soc. Plann. Policy Dev. Abstr.; Sociol. Abstr.; Trop. Dis. Bull.

US/0360-7569
**CURRENT CONCEPTS IN PSYCHIATRY.** V. 1- Oct. 1975-. Periodical. English. bm. Professional Communications Associates, 625 North Michigan Avenue, Chicago IL 60611. **LC** RC321; .C86. **DD** 616.8/9/005. **UDC** 616.89. **NLM** W1 CU788AY.

UK/0951-7367
**CURRENT OPINION IN PSYCHIATRY.** [Curr. opin. psychiatr.]. Vol. 1, No. 1 (Jan./Feb. 1988)-. Periodical. English. Six times a year. $119.95 (individual); $239.95 (institution). Current Science / England, Middlesex House, 34-42 Cleveland Street, London W1P 5FB England. **Tel** 011 44 71 580 8393, 011 44 71 323 0323, FAX 011 44 81 580 1938. **(Subscription address:** Current Science, 20 North 3rd Street, Philadelphia PA 19106.**) ED** Hugh L. Freeman and David J. Kupfer. **DD** 616. **NLM** W1; CU799GH. **CODEN** COPPE8. **[CCC]. Circ:** 4,000. available on diskette (and bibliographic literature database).
**Desc:** Directed toward researchers and practicing psychiatrists. Presents review articles from an area of concentration covering an entire year's literature with annotated references. Each issue features a bibliography of the current world literature published during the previous year.
**Ind/Abst** Cumul. Index Nurs. Allied Health Lit.; EMBASE.

US/0144-316X
**CURRENT THEMES IN PSYCHIATRY.** ***Ceased.*** [Curr. themes psychiatr.]. Vol. 1 (1978)-?. English. an. Spectrum Publications Inc, 175-20 Wexford Terrace, Jamaica NY 11432. **Tel** (718)658-0888. **ED** Raghu N Gaind. **LC** RC321; .C88. **DD** 616.89/005. **NLM** W1 CU814.

SZ/0254-6221
**DASEINSANALYSE (BASEL).** (DASEINSANALYSE.). [Daseinsanalyse]. **Added/Corp** Daseinsanalytisches Institut fuer Psychoterapie und Psychosomatik (Medard-Boss-Stiftung). (Oct. 1984)-. Periodical. German. qt. $75.00. S. Karger AG, Allschwilerstrasse 10, PO Box - Postfach - Case Postale, CH-4009 Basel Switzerland. **Tel** 011 41 61 306-1111, FAX 011 41 61 306-1234, telex CH 962 652. **ED** G. Condrau and A. Hicklin. **NLM** W1; DA91. **CODEN** DABAD9. **[CCC].** Documents available from BIOSIS Document Express.
**Desc:** Covers all aspects of this particular psychotherapy which unites the principles of Sigmund Freud's psychoanalysis with those of Martin Heidegger's existential philosophy.
**Ind/Abst** Biol. Abstr. (1987-); Life Sci. Collect.

●US/1066-5056
**DEMENTIA REVIEWS.** [Dement. rev.]. (1992)-. Monographic series. English. ir. Price varies per volume. Marcel Dekker Inc., 270 Madison Avenue, New York NY 10016. **Tel** (212)696-9000, (800)228-1160, FAX (212)685-4540, telex 421419. **(Subscription address:** Marcel Dekker Inc, PO Box 5017, Monticello NY 12701.**) DD** 616. **NLM** W1; DE134D. **CODEN** DMRVEX.

●US/1062-6417
**DEPRESSION (NEW YORK, N.Y.). See** Psychology.

US/0892-8150
**DEVELOPMENTAL CLINICAL PSYCHOLOGY AND PSYCHIATRY. See** Psychology.

NE/0166-2481
**DEVELOPMENTS IN PSYCHIATRY.** [Dev. psychiatry]. Vol. 1 (1979)-. Academic Scholarly Publication. English. ir. Price varies per volume. Elsevier Science Publishers BV, PO Box 211, 1000 AE Amsterdam Netherlands. **Tel** 011 31 20 5803642, FAX 011 31 20 5862696, telex 15682. **(Subscription address:** Elservier Science Inc., New York Books, 655 Avenue of the Americas, New York, NY 10010, telephone: (212)633-3650**) LC** UNC. **NLM** W1 DE998P. **CODEN** DPSYDX. Documents available from CASDDS.
**Ind/Abst** Chem. Abstr.

CN/1181-7720
**DIARY / CANADIANS FOR HEALTH RESEARCH. See** Public Health and Safety.

US/0012-2769
**DIGEST OF NEUROLOGY AND PSYCHIATRY. See** Medical Science and Technology-Neurology.

NE
**DIRECTIEVE THERAPIE.** Dutch. Kluwer BV, Postbus 23, 7400 GA Deventer Netherlands. **Tel** 011 31 5700 33155, 011 31 5700 48999, FAX 011 31 5700 11504, telex 42829.

US/0891-3870
**DIRECTIONS IN PSYCHIATRY.** [Dir. psychiatry]. (1981)-. Periodical. English. bw. $125.00 (US), $145.00 (Pan-American nations), $150.00 (other) library membership; $257.00 (US), $277.00 (Pan-American nations), $282.00 (other) all others. Directions in Psychiatry, 420 East 51 Street, New York NY 10022. **Tel** (800) 367-2550, (355) 0882. **DD** 616. **NLM** W1; DI659B.

US/0733-2920
**DIRECTORY / AMERICAN GROUP PSYCHOTHERAPY ASSOCIATION.** **Main/Corp** American Group Psychotherapy Association. Directory. English. $10.00 members, $20.00 nonmembers. American Group Psychotherapy Association, 25 East 21st Street/16th Floor, New York NY 10010-6207. **LC** RC488; .A663A. **DD** 616.89/152/02573. **UDC** 616.89-085.851(058.7).

US/0272-5940
**DIRECTORY - COUNCIL OF SPECIALISTS IN PSYCHIATRIC AND MENTAL HEALTH NURSING. See** Medical Science and Technology-Nursing.

US/0196-6421
**DIRECTORY OF CERTIFIED PSYCHIATRISTS AND NEUROLOGISTS. Added/Corp** American Board of Medical Specialties. Marquis Academic Media. American Board of Psychiatry and Neurology. (1979)-. English. be. Marquis Who's Who, A Reed Reference Publishing Company, Part of Reed International PLC, 121 Chanlon Road, New Providence NJ 07974. **Tel** (908)464-6800, (800)521-8110, FAX (908)665-6688, telex 138 755. **NLM** WM 22 AA1 D28.
**Desc:** Consists of a directory of physicians certified by the American Board of Psychiatry and Neurology.

US/0147-3921
**DIRECTORY OF INPATIENT FACILITIES FOR THE MENTALLY RETARDED. See** Medical Science and Technology-Hospital Administration and Medical Centers.

US/0740-8250
**DIRECTORY OF PSYCHIATRY RESIDENCY TRAINING PROGRAMS.** (DIRECTORY OF PSYCHIATRY RESIDENCY TRAINING PROGRAMS / AMERICAN ASSOCIATION OF DIRECTORS OF PSYCHIATRIC RESIDENCY TRAINING, AMERICAN MEDICAL STUDENT ASSOCIATION, AMERICAN PSYCHIATRIC ASSOCIATION.). [Dir. psych. resid. train. programs]. **VFOAT** Psychiatry Residency Training Programs. 1st Ed. (1982)-. Directory. English. an. American Psychiatric Press Inc, 1400 K Street Northwest, Suite 1101, Washington DC 20005. **Tel** (202)682-6222. **UDC** 616.89(058.7). **NLM** WM 22 AA1 D52.

US/8756-2170
**DIRECTORY OF RESIDENTIAL FACILITIES FOR EMOTIONALLY HANDICAPPED CHILDREN AND YOUTH.** ***Ceased.*** [Dir. res. facil. emot. handicap. child. youth]. 2nd Ed. (1988)-(19??). Directory. English. Oryx Press, 4041 North Central Avenue, #700, Phoenix AZ 85012-3397. **Tel** (800)279-ORYX, (602)265-2651, FAX (602)265-6250, (800)279-4663, (800)279-6799. ***Continues*** *Directory of Residential Treatment Facilities for Emotionally Disturbed Children.*

FR
**DISCOURS PSYCHANALYTIQUE, LE.** French. qt. 230.00F France; $30.00 other. Masson SA, Avenue Beauregard 12, CH-1701 Fribourg Switzerland. **Tel** 011 41 37 249585, FAX 011 41 37 247559, telex 942658 SEMI CH.

CN/1182-946X
**DISENPLUS (MONTREAL).** (LE DISENPLUS : UNE PUBLICATION DU CENTRE D'ACCUEIL JEAN-OLIVIER CHENIER.). [Disenplus]. **Added/Corp** Centre d'Accueil Jean-Olivier Chenier. **VFOAT** Dis-En-Plus. Vol. 1, No 1 (Spring 1990)-. Periodical. French. qt. 20.00Can$. Centre d'Accueil Jean-Olivier Chenier, 8000 Ouest Rue Notre-Dame, Ville-Saint-Pierre, Montreal, Quebec H8R 1H2 Canada. **DD** 362.3/09714/2805.

US/0162-2315
**DOWNSTATE SERIES OF RESEARCH IN PSYCHIATRY AND PSYCHOLOGY, THE.** (1977)-. Monographic series. English. ir. Price varies per volume. Plenum Press, 233 Spring Street, New York NY 10013-1578. **Tel** (212)620-8000, (800)221-9369, FAX (212)463-0742, (212)807-1047, telex 23/421139. **NLM** W1 DO945.

CN/0824-7102
**DRUGS IN PSYCHIATRY (POINTE-CLAIRE). See** Pharmacy and Pharmacology.

GW/0012-740X
**DYNAMISCHE PSYCHIATRIE.** (DYNAMISCHE PSYCHIATRIE. DYNAMIC PSYCHIATRY.). [Dyn. Psychiatr.]. **Added/Corp** Lehr- und Forschungsinstitut fuer Psychodynamische Psychiatrie und Gruppendynamik. (Apr. 1968)-. Periodical. German (English). bm (Jan., Mar., May, July, Sep., Nov.). DM96.00 Germany; DM102.00 Europe; DM106.00 other. Pinel Verlag fur Human Psychiatrie, Kantstrasse 120 121, D 10625 Berlin Germany. **Tel** 011 49 30 3132698. **ED** Guenter Ammon. **DD** 616.8. **NLM** W1 DY989. **CODEN** DYPSAQ. Index available. **Bk Rev. Ad Acc. Circ:** 1,000. Documents available from The Genuine Article, BIOSIS Document Express.
**Desc:** Presentation of theory and practice of dynamic psychiatry developed by Gunter Ammon, an interdisciplinary holistic approach to mental and psychosomatic illness with international contributions.
**Ind/Abst** Biol. Abstr.; Curr. Contents Soc. Behav. Sci.; EMBASE; Psychol. Abstr. (1968-); PsycINFO; PsycLit; Res. Alert [Full Cov.]; Soc. Sci. Cit. Index [Full Cov.].

●US/1064-0266
**EATING DISORDERS.** See Psychology.

IT
**ECOLOGIA DELLA MENTE.** **VFOAT** Ecology of the Mind. Vol. 1, No. 1 (1986)-. Periodical. Italian (Spanish; summaries and/or abstracts in Spanish and English). Twice a year (June & Dec.). $60.00. Il Pensiero Scientifico Editore s.r.l., Via Bradano 3C, 00199 Rome Italy. **Tel** 011 39 6 86207158, 86207159, 86207168, 86207169, FAX 011 39 6 86207160. **NLM** W1; EC91S.

AG
**EIDON.** **Added/Corp** Centro de Investigacion en Medicina Psicosomatica. Vol. 1 (March 1974)-. Spanish.

US/0743-071X
**EMPIRICAL STUDIES OF PSYCHOANALYTICAL THEORIES.** [Empir. stud. psychoanal. theor.]. Vol. 1 (1983)-. English. ir. Analytic Press, 365 Broadway, Hillsdale NJ 07642. **Tel** (201)666-4110, FAX (201)666-2394. **ED** Joseph Masling. **NLM** W1 EM682. **[CCC].**

FR/0013-7006
**ENCEPHALE.** See Medical Science and Technology-Neurology.

●IT/1121-189X
**EPIDEMIOLOGIA E PSICHIATRIA SOCIALE.** See Medical Science and Technology-Epidemiology.

US/1059-3551
**ERNEST BECKER.** (THE RESHAPING OF PSYCHOANALYSIS FROM FREUD TO ERNEST BECKER.). (1992)-. Periodical. English. ir. Peter Lang Publishing, 62 West 45th Street, 4th Floor, New York NY 10036. **Tel** (212)764-1471, (800)770-5264, telex 6973364 PLNY. **Pr Rev. Circ:** 400-1000.
**Desc:** Works concerned with reshaping and revitalizing psychoanalysis.

●US/1064-8771
**ETHICS & PSYCHOTHERAPY.** See Ethics.

GW/0940-1334
**EUROPEAN ARCHIVES OF PSYCHIATRY AND CLINICAL NEUROSCIENCE.** [Eur. arch. psychiatry clin. neurosci.]. **Added/Corp** Gesamtverband Deutscher Nervenarzte. **VFOAT** Psychiatry and Clinical Neuroscience. Vol. 240, No. 1 (Sept. 1990)-. Periodical. English. bm. DM876.00. Springer-Verlag GmbH & Company KG, Heidelberger Platz 3, D 14197 Berlin Germany. **Tel** 011 49 30 8207223, FAX 011 49 30 8214091, telex 183 319 SPBLN D. **(Subscription address:** Springer Verlag New York Inc. / for North America, 44 Hartz Way, Secaucus NJ 07096.**)** **NLM** W1; EU576U. **CODEN** EAPNES. available on microfilm from University Microfilms International (UMI). Documents available from The Genuine Article, BIOSIS Document Express. ***Continues*** *European Archives of Psychiatry and Neurological Sciences, 0175-758X.*
**Ind/Abst** Biol. Abstr. (1991-); EMBASE; Index Med. (1991-); Psychol. Abstr. (1971-); Res. Alert [Full Cov.]; Sci. Cit. Index; SCISEARCH.

●CN
**EUROPEAN CHILD AND ADOLESCENT PSYCHIATRY.** **Added/Corp** European Society of Child and Adolescent Psychiatry. **VFOAT** European Child and Adolescent Psychiatry. Vol. 1, Issue 1 (Jan. 1992)-. Periodical. English (summaries and/or abstracts in French and German). Four times a year. 92.00F (members), 124.00F (nonmembers). Verlag Hans Huber Ag Bern, Laenggass Strasse 76, CH 3000 Bern 9 Switzerland. **Tel** 011 41 31 3004500. **(Subscription address:** Hogrefe & Huber Publishers, Seattle Office, Box 2487, Kirkland WA 98083.**)** **ED** Christopher Gillberg. **NLM** W1; EU613E. **CODEN** EAPSE9. **Circ:** 1,000.
**Desc:** Promotes the growth of empirically based clinical child and adolescent psychiatry throughout Europe (and elsewhere) by publishing original papers on systematic scientific studies, review articles, annotations, etc.

●CN
**EUROPEAN CHILD & ADOLESCENT PSYCHIATRY. SUPPLEMENT.** **VFOAT** European Child and Adolescent Psychiatry. Supplement. No. 1 (Jan. 1992)-. Periodical. English. Hogrefe & Huber Publishers, 12 Bruce Park Avenue, Toronto Ontario M4P 2S3 Canada. **Tel** (416)482-6339, FAX (416)484-4200. **NLM** W1; EU613F.

SP/0213-6163
**EUROPEAN JOURNAL OF PSYCHIATRY, THE.** [Eur. j. psychiatry]. Vol. 1, No. 1 (Jan./March 1987)-. Periodical. English. qt. $115.00 institutions, $90.00 individuals. Libreria Certeza, Maria Moliner, 4 Sr Zalgiyei, 50007 Zaragoza Spain. **Tel** 011 34 76 272907. **ED** A. Seva. **LC** RC321; .E85. **DD** 616.89/005. **NLM** W1; EU72ECH. **CODEN** EJOPEO. Index available. **Bk Rev. Ad Acc. Pr Rev. Circ:** 5,000 (ctrl). Documents available from The Genuine Article, BIOSIS Document Express.
**Ind/Abst** Abstr. Res. Pastor. Care Couns. (19??-); Biol. Abstr. (1987-); Curr. Contents Soc. Behav. Sci.; EMBASE; Indice Med. Esp.; Psychol. Abstr. (1987-); PsycINFO (?-?); PsycLit; Res. Alert [Full Cov.]; Soc. Plann. Policy Dev. Abstr.; Soc. Sci. Cit. Index [Full Cov.]; Sociol. Abstr.

NE/0924-977X
**EUROPEAN NEUROPSYCHOPHARMACOLOGY : THE JOURNAL OF THE EUROPEAN COLLEGE OF NEUROPSYCHOPHARMACOLOGY.** See Medical Science and Technology-Neurology.

FR/0924-9338
**EUROPEAN PSYCHIATRY.** (EUROPEAN PSYCHIATRY : THE JOURNAL OF THE ASSOCIATION OF EUROPEAN PSYCHIATRISTS.). [Eur. psychiatr.]. **Added/Corp** Association of European Psychiatrists. Vol. 6, No. 1 (1991)-. Academic Scholarly Publication. English. Eight times a year (1 volume). 1780.00F France; 1995.00F other. Editions Scientifique Elsevier, 141 rue de Javel, 75747 Paris Cedex 15 France. **Tel** 011 33 1 47 07 11 22, FAX 011 33 1 43 36 80 93. **(Subscription address:** Editions Scientifiques Elsevier / for North America, PO Box 7247-7576, Philadelphia PA 19170-7576.**)** **NLM** W1; EU722G. **CODEN** EUPSED. **[CCC].** Documents available from BIOSIS Document Express. ***Continues*** *Psychiatrie & Psychobiologie, 0767-399X.*
**Ind/Abst** Biol. Abstr. (1991-); EMBASE; Ref. Upd. Deluxe Ed.

FR/0014-3855
**EVOLUTION PSYCHIATRIQUE, L'.** [Evol. psychiatr.]. (1925)-. Periodical. French. Four times a year. 440.00 France; 680.00F other. Dunod Gauthier Villars, 15 rue Gossin, 92543 Montrouge cedex France. **Tel** 011 33 1 46 56 52 66, FAX 011 33 1 46 57 40 69. **(Subscription address:** Centrale des Revues, 11 rue Gossin, 92543 Montrouge Cedex France.**)** **NLM** W1 EV635. **CODEN** EVPSAG. **[CCC].** cum. index. **Bk Rev. Ad Acc. Circ:** 2,900 (ctrl). Documents available from BIOSIS Document Express.
**Desc:** Original research in psychiatry and clinical psychopathology.
**Ind/Abst** Biol. Abstr. (1986-); EMBASE; Psychol. Abstr. (1929-); PsycINFO; PsycLit; Soc. Plann. Policy Dev. Abstr.; Sociol. Abstr. (?-?).

NE/0014-4363
**EXCERPTA MEDICA. SECTION 32. PSYCHIATRY.** See Medical Science and Technology-Abstracting, Bibliographies and Statistics.

CN/1183-6342
**EXPANDING HORIZONS, PSYCHIATRIC RESEARCH BULLETIN.** [Expand. horiz. psychiatr. res. bull.]. **Added/Corp** Lakehead Psychiatric Hospital. Research & Ethics Committee. Ontario. Ministry of Health. Lakehead Psychiatric Hospital. **VFOAT** Psychiatric Research Bulletin. Vol. 1, No. 1 (1991)-. Bulletin. English. **DD** 616.89. **NLM** W1; EX206.

US/0272-6408
**EXPERIMENTAL AND CLINICAL PSYCHIATRY.** [Exp. clin. psychiatr.]. Vol. 1 (1979)-. Academic Scholarly Publication. English. Price varies per volume. Marcel Dekker Inc., 270 Madison Avenue, New York NY 10016. **Tel** (212)696-9000, (800)228-1160, FAX (212)685-4540, telex 421419. **(Subscription address:** Marcel Dekker Inc, PO Box 5017, Monticello NY 12701.**)** **LC** UNC. **NLM** W1 EX465. **CODEN** ECPSDM. Documents available from CASDDS.
**Desc:** Series covering aspects of psychiatry and mental disorders. Topics include brain mechanisms and abnormal behavior and psychotropic drugs.
**Ind/Abst** Chem. Abstr.; Psychol. Abstr. (1981-).

US/0091-6544
**FAMILY THERAPY.** (FAMILY THERAPY : THE JOURNAL OF THE CALIFORNIA SCHOOL OF FAMILY PSYCHOLOGY.). [Fam. ther.]. **Added/Corp** Family Therapy Institute of Marin. California Graduate School of Marital and Family Therapy. Vol. 1 (Summer 1972)-. Periodical. English. Three times a year. $62.00 (one year), $122.00 (two year) (individuals), $70.00 (one year), $138.00 (two year) (institutions) US; $69.00 (one year), $136.00 (two year) (individuals), $75.00 (one year), $148.00 (two year) (institutions) other. Libra Publishers Inc, 3089C Clairemont Drive, Suite 383, San Diego CA 92117. **Tel** (619)571-1414. **ED** Martin Blinder. **LC** RC488.5.A1; F33. **DD** 616.8/915. **NLM** W1 FA454M. **CODEN** FATHD6. **[CCC]. Circ:** 1,500. available on microfilm and microfiche from University Microfilms International (UMI).
**Desc:** Clinical articles devoted to techniques in the fields of family and marital therapy.
**Ind/Abst** Appl. Soc. Sci. Index Abstr.; Middle East Abstr. Index; Psychol. Abstr. (1972-); PsycINFO (1990-); PsycLit; PsycScan: Develop. Psych.; Sage Fam. Stud. Abstr.; Soc. Work Abstr. (Spring, Summer 1987-) [Select. Cov.]; Spec. Educ. Needs Abstr.

●CN/1192-1412
**FILIGRANE (MONTREAL).** (FILIGRANE.). [Filigrane]. **VFOAT** Ecoutes Psychotherapiques. No. 1 (1992)-. French. an (May). 24.00Can$ (individuals), 28.00Can$ (institutions) two years; 34.00Can$ (individuals), 42.00Can$ (institutions) three years. Centre Sante Mentale Communaute, Case Postale 548 Place d'Armes, Montreal Quebec H2Y 3H3 Canada. **Tel** (514)844-5536, FAX (514)844-4194. **DD** 616.89. ctrl circ.

US
**FIRST AND READMISSIONS TO STATE AND COUNTY PSYCHIATRIC HOSPITALS BY COUNTY, MUNICIPALITY OF RESIDENCE, AND SERVICE AREA.** See Medical Science and Technology-Hospital Administration and Medical Centers.

GW
**FORENSIA JAHRBUCH.** (19??)-. Periodical. German. an. Springer-Verlag GmbH & Company KG, Heidelberger Platz 3, D 14197 Berlin Germany. **Tel** 011 49 30 8207223, FAX 011 49 30 8214091, telex 183 319 SPBLN D. ***Continues*** *Forensia, 0724-844X.*

IT
**FORMAZIONE PSICHIATRICA : PERIODICO TRIMESTRALE A CURA DELLA CLINICA PSICHIATRICA DELL'UNIVERSITA DI CATANIA.** **Added/Corp** Universita di Catania. Clinica Psichiatrica. No. 1 (Jan./March 1980)-. Academic Scholarly Publication. Italian (summaries and/or abstracts in English). Four times a year (Jan., Apr., July, Oct.). L70000 (individual), L100000 (institutions) Italy; L100000 (individuals), L130000 (institutions) other. Formazione Psichiatrica, Via Battista Grassi N 11, 90125 Catania Italy. **Tel** 011 39 95 222442, FAX 011 39 95 222442. **LC** RC321; .F67. **DD** 616.89/005. **NLM** W1; FO627. **Bk Rev. Ad Acc.**
**Ind/Abst** EMBASE; Psychol. Abstr. (1980-).

GW/0720-4299
**FORTSCHRITTE DER NEUROLOGIE, PSYCHIATRIE.** See Medical Science and Technology-Neurology.

SP/0212-100X
**FORTSCHRITTE DER NEUROLOGIE - PSYCHIATRIE EDICION ESPANOLA.** [Fortschr. Neurol. - Psychiatr.Ed. esp.]. (1982)-. Periodical. Spanish. tw. Georg Thieme Verlag Stuttgart, Postfach 301120, D 70451 Stuttgart Germany. **Tel** 011 49 711 89310, FAX 011 49 711 8931298, telex 7 252 275 GTVD. **(Subscription address:** Thieme Medical Publishers Inc., 381 Park Avenue South, New York NY 10016.**)** **UDC** 616.8.

UK/0267-0887
**FREE ASSOCIATIONS.** Vol. 1 (1985)-. Periodical. English. qt. $65.00 US; $80.00 Canada & Mexico (institutions). Free Association Books, 26 Freegrove Road, London N7 9RQ England. **Tel** 011 44 71 6095646. **(Subscription address:** Guilford Publications, Inc., 72 Spring Street, New York NY 10012.**)** **ED** Robert Young. **LC** BF175.4.C84; F73. **NLM** W1; FR596. **[CCC]. Bk Rev. Ad Acc.**
**Desc:** Readers will find articles ranging from the clinical to cultural studies, plus a series of in-depth interviews with major figures in the profession and in related fields.
**Ind/Abst** Altern. Press Index; Appl. Soc. Sci. Index Abstr.; Int. Bibliogr. Sociol.; Left Index; Soc. Plann. Policy Dev. Abstr.

FR/0767-3744
**FRENESIE.** **Added/Corp** Societe Internationale d'Histoire de la Psychiatrie et de la Psychanalyse. No. 1 (1986)-. Periodical. French. sa. 250.00F France; 300.00F other. Editions Frenesie, 119 rue Danremont, 75018 Paris France. **Tel** 011 33 1 42528232. **LC** RC503; .F68. **DD** 616.89/009. **NLM** W1; FR839F.

GW/0931-0428
**FUNDAMENTA PSYCHIATRICA.** Vol. 1, No. 1 (March 1987)-. Periodical. German. qt (Mar., June, Sep., Dec.). DM178.00 Europe; $110.60 other. F K Schattauer Verlagsgesellschaft mbH, Postfach 10 45 45, D 70040 Stuttgart Germany. **Tel** 011 49 711 2298726. **ED** E. Lungershausen and R. Zundler. **NLM** W1; FU537D. **[CCC]. Ad Acc.**

UK
**GENDER DYSPHORIA.** Vol. 1, No. 1 (1991)-. Periodical. English. $60.00. Whiting and Birch Ltd., 90 Dartmouth Road Forest Hill, London SE23 3HL England. **Tel** 011 44 81 2442421. **NLM** W1; GE184L.

US/0163-8343
**GENERAL HOSPITAL PSYCHIATRY.** [Gen. hosp. psych.]. Vol. 1 (Apr. 1979)-. Academic Scholarly Publication. English. Six times a year (1 volume). $284.00 US; $324.00 other. Elsevier Science Publishing Company Inc, Madison Square Station, PO Box 882, New York NY 10159-0882. **Tel** (212)633-3950, FAX (212)633-3990. **ED** Don R Lipsitt. **NLM** W1 GE249H. **CODEN** GHPSDB. **[CCC]. Bk Rev. Ad Acc. Pr Rev.**

**Circ:** 800. available on microfilm and microfiche from University Microfilms International (UMI). Documents available from The Genuine Article.
**Desc:** Explores the linkages and interfaces between psychiatry, medicine and primary care. Emphasizes a biopsychosocial approach to illness and health, and provides a forum for communication among professionals with clinical, academic, and research interests in psychiatry's essential function in 'the mainstream of medicine'.
**Ind/Abst** Abstr. Res. Pastor. Care Couns. (19??-); Annals Behav. Med.; Cumul. Index Nurs. Allied Health Lit.; Curr. Contents Clin. Med.; Curr. Contents Soc. Behav. Sci.; EMBASE; Health Plan. Adminis.; Index Med.; INIS Atomindex [Micro.]; Int. Nurs. Index; Mod. Med.; Life Sci. Collect.; Psychol. Abstr. (1980-); PsycINFO; PsycLit; Res. Alert [Full Cov.]; Sci. Cit. Index; SCISEARCH; Soc. Sci. Cit. Index [Full Cov.]; Soc. Work Abstr. (Summer 1987-) [Select. Cov.].

US/0190-0412
**GESTALT JOURNAL, THE.** **See** Psychology.

UK/0533-3164
**GROUP ANALYSIS.** [Group anal.]. **Added/Corp** Institute of Group Analysis. Group-Analytic Society (London). Vol. 1 (1967)-. Academic Scholarly Publication. English. qt. £99.00. Sage Publications Ltd., 6 Bonhill Street, London EC2A 4PU, UK. **Tel** 071 374 0645, FAX 071 374 8741, telex 296207 SAGE G. **ED** Malcolm Pines (editor's address: 138 Bramley Road, London N14 4HU England). **LC** RC500; .G76. **DD** 616.89/15/05. **NLM** W1 GR81. Index available. cum. index. **Bk Rev**. **Ad Acc**. **Acid Free. Circ:** 1,000.
**Desc:** Fosters the development of feminist theory and practice in the development, implementation and utilization of evaluation studies.
**Ind/Abst** Abstr. Res. Pastor. Care Couns. (19??-); EMBASE; Psychoanal. Abstr.; Psychol. Abstr. (1990-); PsycINFO; PsycLit; PsycScan: Appl. Exp. Eng. Psych.; PsycScan: LD/MR; PsycScan: Neuropsych.

US/0363-714X
**GROUP STUDIES JOURNAL.** V. 1- 1973-. English. Psychiatric Institute Foundation, Center for Group Studies, Michigan Avenue and Franklin Street NW, Washington DC 20017. **LC** RC488.A1; G754. **DD** 616.8/915. **UDC** 615.85; 616.8-085.851. **NLM** W1 GR872.

US/1057-3291
**HABILITATIVE MENTAL HEALTHCARE NEWSLETTER, THE.** [Habilit. ment. healthc. newsl.]. Vol. 9, No. 1 (Jan. 1990)-. Periodical. English. Six times a year. $63.00 (institutions), $49.00 (individuals) US; $74.00 (institutions), $58.00 (individuals) Canada and Mexico; $85.00 (institutions), $66.00 (individuals) other. Psych Media Inc., PO Box 57, Bear Creek NC 27207. **Tel** (919)581-3700, FAX (919)581-3766. **ED** Margaret Zwilling. **DD** 362. **Ad Acc. Circ:** 2,000. ***Continues*** *Psychiatric Aspects of Mental Retardation Reviews.*
**Desc:** Deals with that affecting a developmentally disabled person as well as pharmaceutical issues.

US/1057-5022
**HARVARD MENTAL HEALTH LETTER, THE.** [Harv. ment. health lett.]. **Added/Corp** Harvard Medical School. **VFOAT** Mental Health Letter. Vol. 7, No. 1 (July 1990)-. Periodical. English. mo. $48.00 (one year), $84.00 (two year), $114.00 (three year). The Harvard Medical School, 521 Fifth Avenue, New York NY 10075. **Tel** (212)986-0555. **(Subscription address:** Palm Coast Data, PO Box 420235, Agency Department, Palm Coast FL 32142.**)** **DD** 616. ***Continues*** *Harvard Medical School Mental Health Letter, 0884-3783.*
**Desc:** Features current mental health topics, written for the professional or the interested layperson.
**Ind/Abst** Consum. Health Nutr. Index; Mag. Artic. Summar. Elite (July 1994-).

●US/1067-3229
**HARVARD REVIEW OF PSYCHIATRY.** [Harv. rev. psychiatr.]. **Added/Corp** Harvard Medical School. Dept. of Psychiatry. Vol. 1, No. 1 (May/June 1993)-. Periodical. English. bm. $97.00 (institutions), $72.00 (individuals) US; $117.00 (institutions), $92.00 (individuals) other. Mosby Year Book Inc., 11830 Westline Industrial Drive, St Louis MO 63146. **Tel** (800)325-4177, (314)872-8370, FAX (314)432-1380, telex 44-2402. **DD** 616. **NLM** W1; HA64H. **[CCC].**

US/0193-5216
**HILLSIDE JOURNAL OF CLINICAL PSYCHIATRY, THE.** ***Ceased.*** [Hillside j. clin. psychiatr.]. Vol. 1-Ceased (Dec. 1990). Academic Scholarly Publication. English. sa. Human Sciences Press, PO Box 735, 233 Spring Street, New York NY 10013. **Tel** (212)620-8000, FAX (212)807-1047, telex 23421139. **LC** RC321. **DD** 616.8/9/005. **UDC** 616.89. **NLM** W1 HI406U. **CODEN** HJCPDU. **[CCC].** Documents available from BIOSIS Document Express. ***Continues*** *Journal of the Hillside Hospital.*
**Desc:** The dual thrusts of this journal are: to contribute to the expansion of knowledge and to disseminate new developments in psychiatry and the mental health field. Although the primary focus is on clinical psychiatry and psychopathology, there are also enlightening articles from related fields of biology, biochemistry, sociology and anthropology.
**Ind/Abst** Biol. Abstr.; EMBASE; Health Plan. Adminis.; Index Med.; Psychol. Abstr. (1979-); PsycINFO (?-?); PsycLit.

UK/0957-154X
**HISTORY OF PSYCHIATRY.** Vol. 1, No. 1 (March 1990)-. Periodical. English. Four times a year. £65.00 (institutions), £38.00 (individuals) UK; $135.00 (institutions), $76.00 (individuals) Noth & South America & Japan; £70.00 (institutions), £40.00 (individuals) other. Alpha Academic, Mill Lane, Chalfont St Giles, Buckingham HP8 4NR England. **Tel** 44 494 872509. **NLM** W1; HI85Q.
**Ind/Abst** Am. Hist. Life (1990-).

US/0734-9831
**HISTORY OF PSYCHOANALYSIS MONOGRAPH.** ***Ceased.*** (HISTORY OF PSYCHOANALYSIS.). [Hist. psychoanal.]. **Added/Corp** Institute for Psychoanalysis. **VFOAT** History of Psychoanalysis Monograph Series. Monograph 1 (1984)-(19??). Monographic series. English. ir. International Universities Press Inc., 59 Boston Post Road, PO Box 1524, Madison CT 06443-1524. **Tel** (203)245-4000, FAX (203)245-0775, telex 282986 IUP BK. **LC** UNC. **DD** 616. **NLM** W1; HI85T.
**Desc:** Original contributions reviewing the work and lives of the pioneers of psychology, psychiatry, and psychoanalysis from a variety of scholarly and theoretical viewpoints.
**Ind/Abst** PsycINFO.

US
**HOGG FOUNDATION NEWS.** Periodical. English. qt. Free. PO Box 7998 University Station, Austin TX 78713. **Tel** (512)471-5041. **ED** Charlene Warren. **UDC** 616.89. **Circ:** 7,700 (ctrl).
**Desc:** A newsletter announcing new publications of the Hogg Foundation for Mental Health.

US/0022-1597
**HOSPITAL & COMMUNITY PSYCHIATRY.** (HOSPITAL & COMMUNITY PSYCHIATRY : A JOURNAL OF THE AMERICAN PSYCHIATRIC ASSOCIATION.). **Added/Corp** American Psychiatric Association. **VFOAT** Hospital and Community Psychiatry; H & CP; H and CP. Vol. 17, No. 1 (Jan. 1966)-. Academic Scholarly Publication. English. mo. $60.00 (institutions) US; $80.00 (institutions) other. American Psychiatric Association, 1400 K Street Northwest, Washington DC 20005. **Tel** (202)682-6240, FAX (202)682-6114. **ED** John A. Talbott. **LC** RC443.A1; M4. **DD** 362.2/1/05. **NLM** W1 HO71L. **CODEN** HSCPAM. Index available. **Bk Rev**. **Ad Acc**. **Pr Rev. Circ:** 22,800. available on microfilm and microfiche from University Microfilms International (UMI). Documents available from The Genuine Article, BIOSIS Document Express. ***Continues*** *Mental Hospitals, 0096-5502.*
**Desc:** Takes an interdisciplinary approach to issues related to the delivery of mental health services in organized settings. Features articles, research reports and commentary on topics at the forefront of psychiatry.
**Ind/Abst** Abstr. Clin. Care Guidel.; Abstr. Res. Pastor. Care Couns. (19??-); Biol. Abstr.; Crim. Justice Abstr.; Crim. Penol. Police Sci. Abstr.; Cumul. Index Nurs. Allied Health Lit.; Curr. Contents Clin. Med.; Curr. Contents Soc. Behav. Sci.; EMBASE; Health Plan. Adminis.; Hospit. Health Admin. Index; Index Med.; Index Period. Artic. Relat. Law; Int. Nurs. Index; Med. Rev. Dig.; Mod. Med.; Life Sci. Collect.; Physic. Medline Plus; Psychol. Abstr. (1960-); PsycINFO; PsycLit; Res. Alert [Full Cov.]; Sci. Cit. Index; SCISEARCH; Soc. Sci. Cit. Index [Full Cov.]; Soc. Work Abstr. [Select. Cov.]; SportSearch.

US/0022-1597
**HOSPITAL & COMMUNITY PSYCHIATRY [MICROFILM].** ***Ceased.*** **Added/Corp** American Psychiatric Association. **VAT** Hospital and Community Psychiatry. (19??)-(19??). Periodical. English. mo. Kraus Reprint and Periodicals, 358 Saw Mill River Road, Millwood NY 10546. **Tel** (914)762-2200, (800)223-8323, FAX (914)762-1195, telex 6818112. ***Continues*** *Mental Hospitals, 0096-5502.*

II/0019-5545
**INDIAN JOURNAL OF PSYCHIATRY.** [Indian j. psychiatry]. **Added/Corp** Indian Psychiatric Society. Vol. 1, (1958)-. Periodical. English. qt. $35.00. Indian Psychiatric Society, Poona, India. **(Subscription address:** Prints India, 11 Darya Ganj, New Delhi 110002 India.**)** **NLM** W1 IN227. **CODEN** IJRPAB. Documents available from CASDDS.
**Ind/Abst** Chem. Abstr. (1958-1981); EMBASE; Psychol. Abstr. (1981-); PsycINFO; PsycLit.

II/0253-7176
**INDIAN JOURNAL OF PSYCHOLOGICAL MEDICINE.** [Indian j. psychol. med.]. **Added/Corp** Indian Psychiatric Society. South Zone. (Jan. 1978)-. Periodical. English. sa. $25.00. Panikacheril, Matteethra Colony, YWCA Lane, Kottayam-1, Kerala 686001, India. **(Subscription address:** Prints India, 11 Darya Ganj, New Delhi, 110002 India, (Phone: 011 91 11 3268645)**)** **NLM** W1 IN227H. **CODEN** IJPMEU. Documents available from BIOSIS Document Express.
**Ind/Abst** Biol. Abstr.; Psychol. Abstr. (1985-); PsycLit.

SP/0210-7279
**INFORMACIONES PSIQUIATRICAS.** **Added/Corp** Congregacion de las Hermanas Hospitalarias del Sagrado Corazon de Jesus. Instituto Psiquiatrico Femenino, San Baudilio de Llobregat. No. 1 (1955)-. Periodical. Spanish. qt. 1000ptas Spain; 4000ptas other. Instituto Psiquiatrico, Sra. De los Dolores, Dr Pujadas 21, 08830 Sant Boi de Llobregat, Barcelona Spain. **Tel** 011 34 640-2400, 011 34 640-0062. **ED** Dr. C. Ganoza Garcia. **NLM** W1 IN415JF.
**Ind/Abst** Indice Med. Esp.

UK/0922-7857
**INFORMATION BULLETIN / INTERNATIONAL ASSOCIATION ON THE POLITICAL USE OF PSYCHIATRY (IAPUP).** (19??)-. Bulletin. English. International Association on the Political Use of Psychiatry (IAPUP), 7A Norland Square, c/o Dr C Shaw, London W11 England.
**Ind/Abst** Hum. Rights Intern. Rep.

FR/0020-0204
**INFORMATION PSYCHIATRIQUE.** (1946)-. French (summaries and/or abstracts in Italian, Spanish and English). Ten times a year. 950.00F French Overseas Territories and EEC Except France; 675.00F France; 1250.00F other. PDG Communications, 30 rue D Armaille, F 75017 Paris France. **Tel** 011 33 1 40550595. **ED** P. Noel.
**Ind/Abst** Point Repere (1979-1980); PsycINFO (1990-).

US/1062-7553
**INNOVATIONS & RESEARCH IN CLINICAL SERVICES, COMMUNITY SUPPORT, AND REHABILITATION.** [Innov. res. clin. serv. community support rehabil.]. **Added/Corp** National Alliance for the Mentally Ill (U.S.) Sargent College of Allied Health Professions. Center for Psychiatric Rehabilitation. **VFOAT** Innovations and Research in Clinical Services, Community Support, and Rehabilitation; Innovations and Research; Innovations & Research. Vol. 1, No. 1 (Dec. 1991)-. Periodical. English. Four times a year (Mar., June, Sept., Dec.). $35.00 (individuals); $70.00 (institutions). Boston University/Center Psychosocial Rehabilitation, 730 Commonwealth Avenue, Boston MA 02215. **Tel** (617)353-3549, FAX (617)353-7700. **ED** Dr. LeRoy Spaniol Ph.D. **LC** RC321; .I554. **DD** 362.2/05. **NLM** W1; IN455BF. **CODEN** IRCRE2. **Bk Rev**, (Qty: 12). **Ad Acc**, **Adv Mgr:** LeRoy Spaniol, **Tel** (617)353-3549. **Circ:** 3,500. available on microfilm and microfiche from University Microfilms International (UMI).
**Desc:** Information on new clinical developments, clinical services and community support, in the psychiatric rehabilitation field. Innovations information regarding research findings, demonstration treatment and medication. Approaches other issues such as, policy issues, professional trainings, self-help and advocacy programs.
**Ind/Abst** Soc. Work Abstr. [Select. Cov.].

US/0735-3847
**INTEGRATIVE PSYCHIATRY.** [Integr. psychiatr.]. (1983)-. Periodical. English. qt. $57.00 (individuals), $113.00 (institutions), US; $137.00 other. International Universities Press Inc., 59 Boston Post Road, PO Box 1524, Madison CT 06443-1524. **Tel** (203)245-4000, FAX (203)245-0775, telex 282986 IUP BK. **ED** Alfred M. Freedman. **LC** [RC321; .I557]. **DD** 616.89. **CODEN** IPSYDK. **[CCC]**. **Ad Acc. Circ:** 300. Documents available from BIOSIS Document Express.
**Desc:** Explores how psychiatry, medicine and all the biological and behavioral sciences can be integrated for the advancement of knowledge, for the stimulation of research, and for mutual enrichment.
**Ind/Abst** Biol. Abstr. (1986-);(1986-1988, 1991-); EMBASE; PsycINFO; Soc. Plann. Policy Dev. Abstr.

US/0161-6749
**INTERACTION (WASHINGTON. 1977).** (INTERACTION.). **Added/Corp** Psychiatric Institutes of America. Vol. 1 (Summer 1977)-. Periodical. English. qt. Psychiatric Inst of America, 1010 Wisconsin Street NW, Washington DC 20007. **Tel** (202)337-5600. **NLM** W1 IN654Q.

US/1071-0752
**INTERNATIONAL ANNALS OF ADOLESCENT PSYCHIATRY.** [Int. annals adolesc. psychiatry]. **Added/Corp** International Society for Adolescent Psychiatry. Vol. 1 (1988)-. English. ir. University of Chicago Press / Book Department, 11030 South Langley Avenue, Chicago IL 60628. **Tel** (800)621-2736, (312)568-1550, FAX (312)753-0811, telex 23933. **ED** Aaron H. Esman. **DD** 616. **NLM** W1; IN703J. **Pr Rev.**
**Desc:** Responds to the issues that concern adolescents and the professionals who serve them. Providing a forum for international and interdisciplinary research in adolescent psychiatry. Features papers on a variety of developmental and clinical topics.

US/0020-6571
**INTERNATIONAL DRUG THERAPY NEWSLETTER.** **See** Pharmacy and Pharmacology.

US/0730-6695
**INTERNATIONAL JOURNAL OF BEHAVIORAL GERIATRICS.** See Medical Science and Technology-Geriatrics.

●US/1062-3051
**INTERNATIONAL JOURNAL OF COMMUNICATIVE PSYCHOANALYSIS AND PSYCHOTHERAPY, THE.** [Int. j. commun. psychoanal. psychother.]. **Added/Corp** International Society for Communicative Psychoanalysis and Psychotherapy. Vol. 7, No. 1 (1992)-. Periodical. English. qt. $60.00. International Society for Communicative Psychoanalysis, and Psychotherapy, 1932-1st Avenue #906, Seattle WA 98101-1040. **DD** 616. ***Continues*** *Society for Psychoanalytic Psychotherapy Bulletin, 1052-0724.*

UK/0885-6230
**INTERNATIONAL JOURNAL OF GERIATRIC PSYCHIATRY.** See Medical Science and Technology-Geriatrics.

US/0020-7284
**INTERNATIONAL JOURNAL OF GROUP PSYCHOTHERAPY, THE.** [Int. j. group psychother.]. **Added/Corp** American Group Psychotherapy Association. Vol. 1 (April 1951)-. Academic Scholarly Publication. English. Four times a year. $135.00 (institutions); $155.00 others. Guilford Publications Inc., 72 Spring Street, New York NY 10012. **Tel** (212)431-9800, (800)365-7006, FAX (212)966-6708. **ED** William Piper. **LC** RC488; .A53. **DD** 616.805. **NLM** W1 IN766N. **CODEN** IJGPAO. **[CCC]. Bk Rev. Ad Acc. Pr Rev. Circ:** 2,000. available on microfilm and microfiche from University Microfilms International (UMI). Documents available from The Genuine Article, BIOSIS Document Express.
**Desc:** Devoted to reporting and interpreting the research and practice of group psychotherapy, it reflects the diversity of work being done and promotes appropriate validation.
**Ind/Abst** Abstr. Res. Pastor. Care Couns.; Appl. Soc. Sci. Index Abstr. (1951-); Biol. Abstr. (-1991); Curr. Contents Soc. Behav. Sci.; EMBASE; Hum. Resour. Abstr. (?-?); Index Med.; Middle East Abstr. Index; Psychol. Abstr. (1951-); PsycINFO; PsycLit; Res. Alert [Full Cov.]; Sage Fam. Stud. Abstr. (?-?); Soc. Plann. Policy Dev. Abstr.; Soc. Sci. Cit. Index [Full Cov.]; Soc. Work Abstr. [Select. Cov.]; Sociol. Abstr.; Women Stud. Abstr.

US/0160-2527
**INTERNATIONAL JOURNAL OF LAW AND PSYCHIATRY.** See Law.

US/0020-7411
**INTERNATIONAL JOURNAL OF MENTAL HEALTH.** [Int. j. ment. health]. Vol. 1 (Spring/Summer 1972)-. Academic Scholarly Publication. English. qt. $402.00 US; $442.00 other. M. E. Sharpe Inc., 80 Business Park Drive, Armonk NY 10504. **Tel** (914)273-1800, (800)541-6563, FAX (914)273-2106. **ED** Martin Gittelman. **LC** RA790.A1; I525. **DD** 614.5/8/05. **NLM** W1 IN769W. **CODEN** IJMHBV. **Bk Rev. Ad Acc. Pr Rev. Circ:** 300 (ctrl). available on microfilm from University Microfilms International (UMI). Documents available from The Genuine Article.
**Desc:** This journal bridges the gaps in knowledge globally, conceptually speaking, as well as geographically for mental health scientists.
**Ind/Abst** Abstr. Anthropol.; Appl. Soc. Sci. Index Abstr.; Curr. Contents Soc. Behav. Sci.; EMBASE; Middle East Abstr. Index; Psychol. Abstr. (1972-); PsycINFO; PsycLit; Res. Alert [Full Cov.]; Soc. Sci. Cit. Index [Full Cov.]; Soc. Work Abstr. (Summer 1987-?) [Select. Cov.]; Stud. Women Abstr.

UK/1049-8931
**INTERNATIONAL JOURNAL OF METHODS IN PSYCHIATRIC RESEARCH.** [Int. j. methods psychiatr. res.]. **VFOAT** Methods in Psychiatric Research. (1991)-. Periodical. English. Four times a year (Jan., Apr., July, Oct.). $225.00. John Wiley & Sons Ltd., Baffins Lane, Chichester West Sussex PO19 1UD England. **Tel** 0243 779777, FAX 0243 776128 BTG:JWP001, telex 86290 WIBOOKG. **(Subscription address:** John Wiley / Philadelphia, PO Box 7247, Philadelphia PA 19170.**) ED** Chris Thompson and Lee N .Robins. **LC** RC337; .I58. **DD** 616.89/0072. **NLM** W1; IN769WH. **CODEN** IPSREY. available on microfilm and microfiche from University Microfilms International (UMI).
**Desc:** Publishes work of a high scientific standard pertaining to important issues in the methods of psychiatric research, the measurement of psychiatric phenomena and related biological variables.
**Ind/Abst** Soc. Sci. Cit. Index [Full Cov.].

US/0091-2174
**INTERNATIONAL JOURNAL OF PSYCHIATRY IN MEDICINE, THE.** [Int. j. psychiatry med.]. Vol. 4 (Winter 1973)-. Academic Scholarly Publication. English. qt. $118.00. Baywood Publishing Company Inc., 26 Austin Avenue, PO Box 337, Amityville NY 11701. **Tel** (516)691-1270, (800)638-7819, FAX (516)691-1770. **ED** Daniel Schubert. **LC** RC321; .P96. **DD** 616.8/9/005. **NLM** W1 IN776J. **CODEN** IJMEDO. cum. index. **Pr Rev.** Documents available from The Genuine Article, BIOSIS Document Express. ***Continues*** *Psychiatry in Medicine, 0033-278X.*
**Desc:** Committed to research carried out within the increasingly broad conceptual framework to which the term "psychosomatic" is applicable; publishes articles which apply the methods of psychiatry and psychology to the further understanding of disorders which are not primarily psychiatric, among others.
**Ind/Abst** Abstr. Anthropol. (19??-); Annals Behav. Med.; Biol. Abstr.; Crim. Penol. Police Sci. Abstr.; Curr. Contents Clin. Med.; Curr. Contents Soc. Behav. Sci.; EMBASE; Energy Res. Abstr. (Aug. 1982-); Index Med.; Middle East Abstr. Index; Nutr. Abstr. Rev., Ser. B, Live Feeds and Feed.; Nutr. Abstr. Rev., Ser. A, Hum. Exp.; Life Sci. Collect.; Psychol. Abstr. (1973-); PsycINFO; PsycLit; Res. Alert [Full Cov.]; SCISEARCH; Soc. Sci. Cit. Index [Full Cov.]; Soc. Work Abstr. [Select. Cov.].

UK/0020-7578
**INTERNATIONAL JOURNAL OF PSYCHO-ANALYSIS, THE.** See Psychology.

UK/0020-7640
**INTERNATIONAL JOURNAL OF SOCIAL PSYCHIATRY, THE.** [Int. j. soc. psychiatry]. Vol. 1 (Summer 1955)-. Academic Scholarly Publication. English. Four times a year (Mar., June, Sept., Dec.). £50.00 (institutions), £30.00 (individuals) UK; £155.00 (institutions), £115.00 (individuals) other. Avenue Publishing Company, 55 Woodstock Avenue, London NW11 9RG England. **Tel** 11 44 81 455 2940. **ED** Dr. Frank Holloway, (editor's address: Department of Psychological Medicine, Maudsley Hospital, Denmark Hill, London SE5 8AZ England). **LC** RC321; .I58. **DD** 362.2/05. **NLM** W1 IN7888. **CODEN** IJSPAX. Index available in last issue of volume--attached. cum. index. **Bk Rev**, (Qty: 16-20). **Circ:** 800. available on microfilm from University Microfilms International (UMI). Documents available from UMI Article Clearinghouse.
**Desc:** Directed toward doctors and those associated with working, teaching in hospitals and universities, stressing partnership between the various disciplines.
**Ind/Abst** Abstr. Res. Pastor. Care Couns. (19??-); Acad. Abstr. Full Text Elite (Jan. 1992-); Acad. Abstr. (Jan. 1992-); Acad. Search (Jan. 1992-); Appl. Soc. Sci. Index Abstr.; Cumul. Index Nurs. Allied Health Lit.; EMBASE; Expand. Acad. Index (1992-); Health Serv. Abstr.; High. Educ. Abstr. (1980-19??); Index Med.; INFO-SOUTH Abstr.; Int. Bibliogr. Sociol.; Middle East Abstr. Index; Newsp. Period. Abstr. (1992-); Psychol. Abstr. (1955-); PsycINFO; PsycLit; Sage Race Relat. Abstr.; Soc. Plann. Policy Dev. Abstr.; Soc. Sci. Source (Jan. 1992-); Soc. Sci. Index; Soc. Sci. Index Fulltext (Autumn 1988-) [Full Txt.]; Soc. Welf. Soc. Plan./Policy Soc. Dev.; Sociol. Abstr.

US/1041-6102
**INTERNATIONAL PSYCHOGERIATRICS / IPA.** See Medical Science and Technology-Geriatrics.

US/0020-8477
**INTERNATIONAL REHABILITATION REVIEW.** See Physically Impaired.

US/1048-0021
**INTERNATIONAL REVIEW OF PSYCHIATRY.** [Int. rev. psychiatry]. (1990)-. Periodical. English. bm. $95.00. MedViews Educational Services Inc, 3176 Pullman Street/Suite 104, Costa Mesa CA 92626. **DD** 616.

UK/0954-0261
**INTERNATIONAL REVIEW OF PSYCHIATRY (ABINGDON, ENGLAND).** (INTERNATIONAL REVIEW OF PSYCHIATRY.). Vol. 1, No. 1/2 (1989)-. Periodical. English. qt. £178.00. Carfax Publishing Company, PO Box 25 Abingdon, Oxfordshire OX14 3UE England. **Tel** 011 44 235 555335, FAX (0279)31067, telex 817484. **(Subscription address:** US and Canada/ PO Box 2025, Dunnellon, FL 34430-2025; telephone:(904)489-6996**) ED** Paul E. Bebbington. **NLM** W1; IN834G. **CODEN** IRPSE2. **[CCC].** Index available. available on microfiche. Documents available from BIOSIS Document Express.
**Ind/Abst** Biol. Abstr. (1990-); EMBASE; Psychol. Abstr. (1989-); PsycINFO; PsycLit; Soc. Plann. Policy Dev. Abstr.; Spec. Educ. Needs Abstr.

●US/1066-3657
**INTERNATIONAL REVIEW OF PSYCHIATRY (WASHINGTON, D.C.).** (INTERNATIONAL REVIEW OF PSYCHIATRY.). **Added/Corp** American Psychiatric Press. (1993)-. English. $65.00. American Psychiatric Press Inc., 1400 K Street Northwest, Suite 1101, Washington DC 20005. **Tel** (202)682-6222, FAX (202)789-2648.

US/0074-7750
**INTERNATIONAL REVIEW OF RESEARCH IN MENTAL RETARDATION.** **VFOAT** Research in Mental Retardation. Vol. 1 (1966)-. Monographic series. English. ir. Price varies per volume. Academic Press, Inc., 6277 Sea Harbor Drive, Orlando FL 32887. **Tel** (800)543-9534, (407)345-4100, FAX (407)363-9661. **ED** N. R. Ellis. **LC** RC570; .I5. **DD** 157.808. **NLM** W1 IN834N. **[CCC].** Documents available from The Genuine Article.
**Ind/Abst** Res. Alert [Full Cov.]; Soc. Sci. Cit. Index [Full Cov.].

SZ/0373-3793
**INTERPERSONAL DEVELOPMENT.** ***Suspended.*** [Interpers. dev.]. Vol. 1 (1970)-?. Periodical. English. qt. S. Karger AG, Allschwilerstrasse 10, PO Box - Postfach - Case Postale, CH-4009 Basel Switzerland. **Tel** 011 41 61 306-1111, FAX 011 41 61 306-1234, telex CH 962 652. **LC** RC488.A1; I5. **DD** 616.89/15/05. **UDC** 616.89. **NLM** W1 IN969.
**Ind/Abst** Soc. Plann. Policy Dev. Abstr.; Sociol. Abstr. (?-?).

UK/0309-152X
**IRCS MEDICAL SCIENCE. PSYCHOLOGY AND PSYCHIATRY.** [IRCS med. sci. Psychol. psychiatr.]. **VFOAT** International Research Communications System Medical Science. Psychology and Psychiatry. (1976)-. Academic Scholarly Publication. English. bm (6 issues). Elsevier Science Publishers Ltd, Crown House, Linton Road, Barking Essex IG11 8JU England. **Tel** 011 44 81 5947272, FAX 081-594-5942, telex 896950. ***Formed by the union of*** *IRCS Medical Science. Psychology, 0305-6902* ***and*** *IRCS Medical Science. Psychiatry and Clinical Psychology, 0305-6899.*

IE/0790-1186
**IRISH JOURNAL OF PSYCHIATRY.** [Ir. j. psychiatry]. **Added/Corp** Irish Institute of Psychiatry. Vol. 1, No. 1 (Autumn 1981)-. Periodical. English. Twice a year (Mar. & Sept.). £2.00. Irish Institute of Psychiatry, 73 Lower Baggot Street, Dublin 2 Ireland. **Tel** 01 761176. **NLM** W1; IR433M.
**Ind/Abst** Psychol. Abstr. (1986-); PsycINFO (1990-); PsycLit.

IE/0790-9667
**IRISH JOURNAL OF PSYCHOLOGICAL MEDICINE.** [Ir. j. psychol. med.]. **Added/Corp** Irish Institute of Psychological Medicine. Vol. 5, No. 1 (March 1988)-. Periodical. English. qt. $96.00 US; £43.00 UK & Europe; £53.00 other. Irish Institute of Psychological Medicine, St. Brendans Hospital, PO Box 418, Dublin 7 Ireland. **Tel** 011 353 88 578406, FAX 011 353 1 2800504. **(Subscription address:** Royal Society Medicine Services, 1 Wimpole Street, London W1M 8AE England.**) ED** Dr. Mark Hartman. **NLM** W1; IR433S. **CODEN** IPMEEX. **[CCC].** Index available in last issue of volume--attached. **Bk Rev. Ad Acc. Adv Mgr:** Ray Hurrell. **Pr Rev. Circ:** 3,000. available on microfilm and microfiche from University Microfilms International (UMI); available on CD-ROM from ADONIS B.V. Documents available from The Genuine Article, BIOSIS Document Express. ***Continues*** *Irish Journal of Psychotherapy and Psychosomatic Medicine, 0790-9616.*
**Desc:** Original scientific contributions to psychiatry, and related clinical and basic sciences.
**Ind/Abst** Biol. Abstr. (1989-); Curr. Contents Soc. Behav. Sci.; EMBASE; Psychol. Abstr. (1982-); PsycINFO (1990-); PsycLit; Res. Alert [Full Cov.]; Soc. Plann. Policy Dev. Abstr.; Soc. Sci. Cit. Index [Full Cov.]; Soc. Work Abstr. [Select. Cov.].

IS/0333-7308
**ISRAEL JOURNAL OF PSYCHIATRY AND RELATED SCIENCES, THE.** [Isr. j. psychiatry relat. sci.]. **Added/Corp** Israel Psychiatric Association. Vol. 18, No. 1 (1981)-. Periodical. English. qt (Feb., May, Aug., Nov.). $75.00 (institution) US; $55.00 (individual) US; $85.00 other. Gefen Publishing House, PO Box 6056, Jerusalem 91060 Israel. **Tel** 972 2 536944, FAX 972 2 536723. **ED** David Greenberg. **LC** RC321; .I8. **DD** 616.89/005. **NLM** W1 IS636UD. **CODEN** IPRDAH. **[CCC].** Index available. **Bk Rev. Ad Acc. Circ:** 1,100 (ctrl). available on microfilm and microfiche from University Microfilms International (UMI). Documents available from The Genuine Article. ***Continues*** *Israel Annals of Psychiatry and Related Disciplines.*
**Desc:** Mental health problems of Jewish and Israeli interest. Empirical and theoretical research in general psychiatry and related fields.
**Ind/Abst** Curr. Contents Soc. Behav. Sci.; EMBASE; Index Med.; Middle East Abstr. Index; Psychol. Abstr. (1981-); PsycINFO; PsycLit; Res. Alert [Full Cov.]; Soc. Sci. Cit. Index [Full Cov.]; Soc. Work Abstr. (?-?).

GW/0075-2363
**JAHRBUCH DER PSYCHOANALYSE.** [Jahrb. Psychoanal.]. Vol. 1 (1960)-. German (English). an. DM98.00. Fromman-Holzboog Verlag, Postfach 500460, D 70334 Stuttgart Germany. **Tel** 011 49 711 9559692, telex 7 254 754 FRHO-D. **ED** Gunther Holzboog. **NLM** W1 JA18. **Ad Acc. Circ:** 1,000.
**Desc:** Articles on psychoanalysis by different authors.
**Ind/Abst** Psychol. Abstr. (1981-); PsycINFO; PsycLit.

JA
**JAPANESE JOURNAL OF CHILD AND ADOLESCENT PSYCHIATRY.** **Added/Corp** Nippon Jido Seishin Igakkai. Vol. 20, No. 1 (Dec. 1978/Feb. 1979)-. Periodical. Japanese. qt (5 issues). $275.00. Nihon Jido Seinen Seishin Igakkai, (Japanese Soc. of Child & Adolescent Psychiatry), Kyoto Daigaku

Igakubu Seishin Igaku, Kyoshitsu, 53, Shogoin Kawaracho, Sakyoku, Kyotoshi, Kyotofu 606 Japan. **(Subscription address:** Maruzen Company Ltd., PO Box 5050, Import & Export Department, Tokyo 100 31 Japan.**)** **CODEN** JJCPAF. Documents available from BIOSIS Document Express. ***Continues*** *Japanese Journal of Child Psychiatry.*
**Ind/Abst** Biol. Abstr. (1986-); Psychol. Abstr. (1978-); PsycINFO (1960-); PsycLit.

JA/0912-2036
**JAPANESE JOURNAL OF PSYCHIATRY AND NEUROLOGY, THE.** [Jpn. j. psychiatry neurol.]. Vol. 40, No. 1 (March 1986)-. Academic Scholarly Publication. English. qt. $175.00. Foria Kankokai, (Folia Publishing Society), YMCA Biru, 20-6, Mukogaoka 1 Chome, Bunkyoku, Tokyoto 113 Japan. **(Subscription address:** Kyowa Book Company Inc., 1-38 Kanda Jinbo-Cho, Chiyoda-Ku, Tokyo 101, Japan**)** **NLM** W1; JA971J. **CODEN** JJPNEA. **Pr Rev.** Documents available from The Genuine Article, BIOSIS Document Express, CASDDS. ***Continues*** *Folia Psychiatrica et Neurologica Japonica, 0015-5720.*
**Ind/Abst** Biol. Abstr. (1987-); Chem. Abstr.; Curr. Contents Clin. Med.; EMBASE; Index Med. (1986-); Res. Alert [Full Cov.]; SCISEARCH; Soc. Plann. Policy Dev. Abstr.; Soc. Sci. Cit. Index [Select. Cov.].

US
**JEFFERSON JOURNAL OF PSYCHIATRY, THE.** **Added/Corp** Jefferson Medical College. Dept. of Psychiatry. Residency Training Program. American Psychiatric Association. Committee of Residents. **VFOAT** JJP. Vol. 1, No. 1 (Spring 1983)-. Periodical. English. sa. Jefferson Medical College, Residency Training Program, Department of Psychiatry, 1020 Locust Street, Philadelphia PA 19107. **NLM** W1; JE185K.

BL/0047-2085
**JORNAL BRASILEIRO DE PSIQUIATRIA.** [J. Bras. psiquiatr.]. **Added/Corp** Rio de Janeiro. Universidade do Brasil. Instituto de Psiquiatria. Rio de Janeiro. Universidade Federal. Instituto de Psiquiatria. (1948)-. Academic Scholarly Publication. Portuguese (summaries and/or abstracts in English and French). mo. $100.00. ECN-Editora Cientifica Nacional Ltda., Caixa Postal 590, 20001-Rio de Janeiro RJ Brazil. **Tel** 011 55 21 2622825, 011 55 21 2213235, FAX 011 55 21 2521691. **ED** E. Carvalho Neto. **NLM** W1 JO195. **CODEN** JBPSAX. Index available. **Bk Rev. Ad Acc. Circ:** 3,000 (ctrl). Documents available from BIOSIS Document Express, CASDDS. ***Supersedes*** *Anais do Instituto de Psiquiatria.*
**Desc:** Electric publication dedicated to psychiatry and psychology.
**Ind/Abst** Biol. Abstr.; Chem. Abstr.; EMBASE [Select. Cov.]; Psychol. Abstr. (1964-); PsycINFO; PsycLit.

FR
**JOURNAL DE PSYCHANALYSE DE L'ENFANT.** French. 300.00F France 350.00F other. Editions Centurion, 41 rue Francois Premier, 75008 Paris France. **ED** Picne Geissmann. **Bk Rev.**

US/0091-0627
**JOURNAL OF ABNORMAL CHILD PSYCHOLOGY.** **See** Psychology.

US/0162-3257
**JOURNAL OF AUTISM AND DEVELOPMENTAL DISORDERS.** [J. autism dev. disord.]. Vol. 9 (Mar. 1979)-. Periodical. English. Six times a year. $295.00 institutions, $58.00 individuals US; $345.00 institutions, $68.00 individuals other. Plenum Press, 233 Spring Street, New York NY 10013-1578. **Tel** (212)620-8000, (800)221-9369, FAX (212)463-0742, (212)807-1047, telex 23/421139. **ED** Eric Schopler. **LC** RJ499; .A1J58. **NLM** W1 JO547N. **CODEN** JADDDQ. **[CCC].** Index available. **Pr Rev.** available on microfilm and microfiche from University Microfilms International (UMI). Documents available from The Genuine Article, BIOSIS Document Express. ***Continues*** *Journal of Autism and Childhood Schizophrenia, 0021-9185.*
**Desc:** Devoted to all severe psychopathologies on childhood and is not necessarily limited to autism and childhood schizophrenia.
**Ind/Abst** Acad. Search (July 1993-); Appl. Soc. Sci. Index Abstr.; Biol. Abstr.; Cumul. Index Nurs. Allied Health Lit.; Curr. Contents Soc. Behav. Sci.; Curr. Index J. Educ.; Dev. Med. Child Neurol.; Educ. Index; EMBASE; Except. Child Educ. Resour.; Index Med.; INIS Atomindex [Micro.]; Mag. Search; Middle East Abstr. Index; Psychol. Abstr. (1979-); PsycINFO; PsycLit; PsycScan: Develop. Psych.; Res. Alert [Full Cov.]; Soc. Sci. Cit. Index [Full Cov.]; Soc. Work Abstr. [Select. Cov.].

UK/0005-7916
**JOURNAL OF BEHAVIOR THERAPY AND EXPERIMENTAL PSYCHIATRY.** [J. behav. ther. exp. psychiatry]. **Added/Corp** Behavior Therapy Society. **VFOAT** Behavior Therapy and Experimental Psychiatry. Vol. 1 (Mar. 1970)-. Academic Scholarly Publication. English. qt. $321.00 The Americas; £215.00 other. Pergamon Press, An Imprint of Elsevier Science Ltd., The Boulevard, Langford Lane, Kidlington, Oxford OX5 1GB United Kingdom. **Tel** 011 44 865 843000, 011 44 865 843699, FAX 011 44 865 843010. **(Subscription address:** Elsevier Science Ltd. Oxford Fulfillment Centre, PO Box 800, Kidlington, Oxford OX5 1DX United Kingdom.**)** **ED** Joseph Wolpe and Leo Reyna. **LC** RC489.B4; J65. **DD** 616.89/1. **NLM** W1 JO555. **CODEN** JBTEAB. **[CCC]. Pr Rev.** available on microfilm and microfiche from Microfilms International Marketing Corp. Documents available from The Genuine Article, BIOSIS Document Express.
**Desc:** Publishes material intended to provide training in behavior therapy for psychiatrists. It is the only journal that has a special concern for the practice of behavior therapy in clinical psychiatry.
**Ind/Abst** Annals Behav. Med.; Appl. Soc. Sci. Index Abstr.; Biol. Abstr.; Cumul. Index Nurs. Allied Health Lit.; Curr. Contents Soc. Behav. Sci.; EMBASE; Health Period. Database; High. Educ. Abstr.; Index Med.; Middle East Abstr. Index; Psychol. Abstr. (1970-); PsycINFO; PsycLit; Res. Alert [Full Cov.]; Soc. Plann. Policy Dev. Abstr.; Soc. Sci. Cit. Index [Full Cov.]; Sociol. Abstr.

US/0897-9685
**JOURNAL OF CHILD AND ADOLESCENT PSYCHIATRIC AND MENTAL HEALTH NURSING.** ***Title Change.*** [J. child adolesc. psychiatr. ment. health nurs.]. **VFOAT** Child and Adolescent Psychiatric and Mental Health Nursing Journal. Vol. 1, No. 1 (July/Sept. 1988)-(199?). Periodical. English. qt. NURSECOM Inc., 1211 Locust Street, Philadelphia PA 19107. **Tel** (215)545-7222, (800)242-6757, FAX (215)545-8107. **ED** Elizabeth Poster and Brooke Randell (UCLA Neuropsychiatric Institute ). **DD** 610. **NLM** W1; JO583JH. **CODEN** JCPNEZ. **Bk Rev**, (Qty: 12/yr). **Ad Acc, Adv Mgr:** Joseph Braden, **Tel** (215)545-7222. **Circ:** 1,597. available on microfilm and microfiche from University Microfilms International (UMI). ***Continued by*** *The Journal of Child and Adolescent Psychiatric Nursing.*
**Desc:** A forum for nurses involved in the promotion of mental health for children and adolescents and the care of emotionally disturbed youth and their families. Analysis of trends in the field; youth advocacy issues; innovative prevention or intervention programs; research; research utilization in clinical settings; critical reviews; and educational issues.
**Ind/Abst** Cumul. Index Nurs. Allied Health Lit.; Int. Nurs. Index (1988-).

●US/1073-6077
**JOURNAL OF CHILD AND ADOLESCENT PSYCHIATRIC NURSING.** **See** Medical Science and Technology-Nursing.

US/1044-5463
**JOURNAL OF CHILD AND ADOLESCENT PSYCHOPHARMACOLOGY.** [J. child adolesc. psychopharmacol.]. **VFOAT** JCAP. Vol. 1, No. 1 (Spring 1990)-. Periodical. English. qt. $105.00. Mary Ann Liebert Inc., 1651 Third Avenue, New York NY 10128. **Tel** (212)289-2300, (800)M-LIEBERT, FAX (212)289-4697. **DD** 615. **NLM** W1; JO583JK.
**Desc:** Specializing in biological and biomedical aspects of child and adolescent neuropsychiatry.

UK/0075-417X
**JOURNAL OF CHILD PSYCHOTHERAPY.** [J. child psychother.]. **Added/Corp** Association of Child Psychotherapists. Vol. 1 (Dec. 1963)-. English. Three times a year. $105.00 (US & Canada); £70.00 (UK) £75.00 (other). Routledge, 11 New Fetter Lane, London EC4P 4EE England. **Tel** 071 583 9855, FAX 071 842 2298. **(Subscription address:** Kinokuniya Company Ltd., 38-1 Sakuragaoka 5, chome Setagaya-ku, Tokyo 156 Japan.**)** **NLM** W1 JO584K. **Bk Rev**, (Qty: 6-10). **Ad Acc. Circ:** 1,000 (ctrl).
**Desc:** Articles on psychoanalytic theory and technique as applied to children and young people.
**Ind/Abst** Middle East Abstr. Index; Psychol. Abstr. (1977-); PsycINFO (1990-); PsycLit; Soc. Work Abstr. (?-?).

US/0160-6689
**JOURNAL OF CLINICAL PSYCHIATRY, THE.** [J. clin. psychiatry]. Vol. 39 (Jan. 1978)-. Academic Scholarly Publication. English. mo. $66.00 US; $110.00 other. Physicians Postgraduate Press, PO Box 240008, Memphis TN 38124. **Tel** (901)682-1001, FAX (901)682-6992. **ED** Alan J. Gelenberg. **LC** RC321; .D5. **DD** 616.8/9/005. **NLM** W1 JO59I. **CODEN** JCLPDE. Index available. cum. index. **Bk Rev. Ad Acc. Pr Rev. Circ:** 32,000 (ctrl). available on microfilm and microfiche from University Microfilms International (UMI). Documents available from The Genuine Article, BIOSIS Document Express, CASDDS. ***Continues*** *Diseases of the Nervous System, 0012-3714.*
**Desc:** Clinical material dealing with psychiatric disorders.
**Ind/Abst** Annals Behav. Med.; Appl. Soc. Sci. Index Abstr.; Biol. Abstr.; Chem. Abstr.; CSA Neuro. Abstr. (?-?); Cumul. Index Nurs. Allied Health Lit.; Curr. Contents Clin. Med.; Dairy Sci. Abstr.; EMBASE; Health Saf. Sci. Abstr.; Highw. Res. Abstr.; Index Med.; Int. Nurs. Index; Iowa Drug Inf. Serv. (1969-); Med. Abstr. Newsl.; Mod. Med.; Nutr. Abstr. Rev., Ser. B, Live Feeds and Feed.; Nutr. Abstr. Rev., Ser. A, Hum. Exp.; Life Sci. Collect.; PESTDOC; Physic. Medline Plus; Pollut. Abstr. Indexes; Psychol. Abstr. (1978-); PsycINFO; PsycLit; Res. Alert [Full Cov.]; Risk Abstr.; Sci. Cit. Index; SCISEARCH; Soc. Plann. Policy Dev. Abstr.; Soc. Sci. Cit. Index [Full Cov.]; Sociol. Abstr.

US/1056-2141
**JOURNAL OF CLINICAL PSYCHIATRY ADVANCES IN PSYCHIATRIC TREATMENT MONOGRAPH SERIES, THE.** **VFOAT** Advances in Psychiatric Treatment Monograph Series. Vol. 1, No. 1. (1991)-. Monographic series. English. ir. Price varies per volume. Physicians Postgraduate Press, PO Box 240008, Memphis TN 38124. **Tel** (901)682-1001, FAX (901)682-6992. **DD** 616. ***Continues*** *Journal of Clinical Psychiatry Monograph Series, 0742-1915.*

●US
**JOURNAL OF CLINICAL PSYCHOANALYSIS.** **Added/Corp** New York Psychoanalytic Institute. New York Psychoanalytic Society. Vol. 1, No. 1 (1992)-. Periodical. English. qt. $77.50 (institutions), $51.50 (individuals) US; $116.75 (institutions), $93.50 (individuals) other. International Universities Press Inc., 59 Boston Post Road, PO Box 1524, Madison CT 06443-1524. **Tel** (203)245-4000, FAX (203)245-0775, telex 282986 IUP BK. **ED** Herbert M. Wyman and Stephen M. Rittenberg. **NLM** W1; JO59R. **Bk Rev. Ad Acc, Adv Mgr:** David Loiterstein, **Tel** (203)245-0775. **Pr Rev. Circ:** 1,000 (ctrl).

US/0894-8577
**JOURNAL OF CONTEMPLATIVE PSYCHOTHERAPY.** [J. contempl. psychother.]. **Added/Corp** Naropa Institute. Vol. 4 (1987)-. Periodical. English. ir. $6.94 (latest volume); $11.00 (individuals); $21.00 (institutions). The Naropa Institute, Journal of Psychology, 2130 Arapahoe Avenue, Boulder CO 80302. **Tel** (303)444-0202. **ED** Fred Wegela. **LC** RC489.E93; N37. **DD** 616.89/14. **Bk Rev.** ***Continues*** *NAROPA Institute Journal of Psychology, 0271-7557.*

US
**JOURNAL OF DEPRESSION & STRESS.** English. sa. $45.00 (individuals), $80.00 (institutions) US; $84.00 (individuals), $104.00 (institutions) other. International Universities Press Inc., 59 Boston Post Road, PO Box 1524, Madison CT 06443-1524. **Tel** (203)245-4000, FAX (203)245-0775, telex 282986 IUP BK. **ED** George H. Pollock and Harold M. Visotsky. **Bk Rev. Ad Acc, Adv Mgr:** David Loitorston. **Pr Rev.**

US/0196-206X
**JOURNAL OF DEVELOPMENTAL AND BEHAVIORAL PEDIATRICS.** **See** Medical Science and Technology-Pediatrics.

UK/0163-4445
**JOURNAL OF FAMILY THERAPY.** [J. fam. ther.]. Vol. 1, No. 1 (Feb. 1979)-. Academic Scholarly Publication. English. Four times a year. £75.50 UK and Europe; $129.00 North America; £83.50 other. Basil Blackwell Publishers Ltd, 108 Cowley Road, Oxford 0X4 1JF England. **Tel** 011 44 865 791100, FAX 011 44 865 791347, telex 837022 OXBOOK G. **(Subscription address:** Blackwell Publishers / UK, Marston Book Services, PO Box 87, Oxford OX2 0DT England.**)** **ED** Bryan Lask. **LC** RC488.5; .J68. **DD** 616.89/156. **UDC** 616.89-058.8-085. **NLM** W1 JO6445H. **[CCC]. Pr Rev.** available on microfilm and microfiche from University Microfilms International (UMI). Documents available from The Genuine Article.
**Desc:** A journal committed to areas of families and family therapy.
**Ind/Abst** Appl. Soc. Sci. Index Abstr.; Curr. Contents Soc. Behav. Sci.; Int. Bibliogr. Sociol.; Psychol. Abstr. (1980-); PsycINFO; PsycLit; Res. Alert [Full Cov.]; Soc. Plann. Policy Dev. Abstr.; Soc. Sci. Cit. Index [Full Cov.]; Sociol. Abstr.

UK/0958-5184
**JOURNAL OF FORENSIC PSYCHIATRY, THE.** (199?)-. Periodical. English. Three times a year (Apr., Aug., Sep.). $120.00 (US & Canada); £76.00 (UK); £80.00 (other). Routledge, 11 New Fetter Lane, London EC4P 4EE England. **Tel** 071 583 9855, FAX 071 842 2298. **(Subscription address:** Kinokuniya Company Ltd., 38-1 Sakuragaoka 5, chome Setagaya-ku, Tokyo 156 Japan.**)** **NLM** W1; JO656J. **[CCC].**
**Ind/Abst** Int. Bibliogr. Sociol.

US/0022-1414
**JOURNAL OF GERIATRIC PSYCHIATRY.** [J. geriatr. psychiatry]. **Added/Corp** Boston Society for Gerontologic Psychiatry. **VFOAT** Geriatric Psychiatry. Vol. 1 (Fall 1967)-. Academic Scholarly Publication. English. sa. $73.50 (institutions), $51.50 (individuals) US; $118.50 (institutions), $90.00 (individuals) other. International Universities Press Inc., 59 Boston Post Road, PO Box 1524, Madison CT 06443-1524. **Tel** (203)245-4000, FAX (203)245-0775, telex 282986 IUP BK. **ED** David Blay and Ralph J. Kahana. **LC** RC451.4.A5; J68. **DD** 616. **NLM** W1 JO669N. **CODEN** JGPSBZ. **Ad Acc. Circ:** 1,800 (ctrl). Documents available from The Genuine Article, BIOSIS Document Express.
**Desc:** Presents the latest thinking and recent findings in

the field of geriatric psychiatry.
**Ind/Abst** Abstr. Soc. Gerontol.; Biol. Abstr.; Cumul. Index Nurs. Allied Health Lit.; Curr. Contents Soc. Behav. Sci.; EMBASE; Index Med.; Middle East Abstr. Index; Psychol. Abstr. (1973-); PsycINFO; PsycLit; Res. Alert [Full Cov.]; Soc. Plann. Policy Dev. Abstr.

US/0891-9887
**JOURNAL OF GERIATRIC PSYCHIATRY AND NEUROLOGY.** **See** Medical Science and Technology-Geriatrics.

US/0731-1273
**JOURNAL OF GROUP PSYCHOTHERAPY, PSYCHODRAMA AND SOCIOMETRY.** [J. group psychother. psychodrama sociom.]. **Added/Corp** American Society of Group Psychotherapy and Psychodrama. Vol. 34 (1981)-. Periodical. English. qt. $43.00 (individual), $69.00 (institution). Heldref Publications, 1319 Eighteenth Street Northwest, Washington DC 20036-1802. **Tel** (202)296-6267, (800)365-9753, FAX (202)296-5149. **ED** Adam Blatner, Antonina Garcia, and Thomas W Treadwell. **LC** RC488.A1; G73. **DD** 616.89/15/05. **NLM** W1 JO669QH. **[CCC]. Ad Acc.** available on microfilm and microfiche from University Microfilms International (UMI). ***Continues** Group Psychotherapy, Psychodrama and Sociometry, 0146-6178.*
**Desc:** Features articles on the application of action methods to the fields of psychotherapy, counseling, and education. Action techniques include psychodrama, role playing, and social skill training.
**Ind/Abst** Appl. Soc. Sci. Index Abstr.; Psychol. Abstr. (1981-); PsycINFO; PsycLit; Soc. Plann. Policy Dev. Abstr.

US/0729-8579
**JOURNAL OF INTEGRATIVE AND ECLECTIC PSYCHOTHERAPY.** **VFOAT** JIEP. Vol. 6, No. 1 (Spring 1987)-. Periodical. English. qt. $65.00. International Academy Eclectic, Psychotherapists, APDO 51042, 45080 Guadalajara Jal Mexico. **LC** RC489.E24; I57. **DD** 616.89/14/05. **UDC** 616.8-085.851. **NLM** W1; JO176C. **[CCC]. *Continues** International Journal of Eclectic Psychotherapy, 0729-8579.*
**Ind/Abst** Psychol. Abstr. (1982-); PsycINFO (1990-); PsycLit.

●UK/0963-8237
**JOURNAL OF MENTAL HEALTH.** Vol. 1, No. 1 (Mar. 1992)-. Periodical. English. qt. £118.00 EC; $242.00 US; £142.00 other. Carfax Publishing Company, PO Box 25 Abingdon, Oxfordshire OX14 3UE England. **Tel** 011 44 235 555335, FAX (0279)31067, telex 817484. **(Subscription address:** US and Canada/ PO Box 2025, Dunnellon, FL 34430-2025; telephone:(904)489-6996) **NLM** W1; JO76KJ. **[CCC].** available on microfiche.
**Ind/Abst** PsycLit.

US/0022-3018
**JOURNAL OF NERVOUS AND MENTAL DISEASE, THE.** **See** Medical Science and Technology-Neurology.

UK/0022-3050
**JOURNAL OF NEUROLOGY, NEUROSURGERY AND PSYCHIATRY.** **See** Medical Science and Technology-Neurology.

US/0895-0172
**JOURNAL OF NEUROPSYCHIATRY AND CLINICAL NEUROSCIENCES, THE.** **VFOAT** Supplement to the Journal of Neuropsychiatry and Clinical Neurosciences; Journal of Neuropsychiatry. Vol. 1, No. 1 (Winter 1989)-. Periodical. English. Four times a year. $135.00 US; $150.00 other (institution). American Psychiatric Press Inc., 1400 K Street Northwest, Suite 1101, Washington DC 20005. **Tel** (202)682-6222, FAX (202)789-2648. **LC** RC321; .J8372. **DD** 616.8/005. **NLM** W1; JO795BD. **CODEN** JNCNE7. **Ad Acc. Pr Rev.** available on microfilm and microfiche from University Microfilms International (UMI). Documents available from The Genuine Article.
**Desc:** Original research related to the assessment and treatment of neuropsychiatric disorders.
**Ind/Abst** Curr. Contents Clin. Med.; EMBASE; Index Med. (Winter 1989-); Psychol. Abstr. (1989-); PsycINFO; PsycLit; Res. Alert [Full Cov.]; Sci. Cit. Index; Soc. Sci. Cit. Index [Select. Cov.]; Soc. Work Abstr. [Select. Cov.].

US/0047-2638
**JOURNAL OF OPERATIONAL PSYCHIATRY.** [J. oper. psych.]. Vol. 1 (Jan. 1970)-. Periodical. English. sa (June and Nov.). Free. University of Missouri at Columbia, Medical Center, Columbia MO 65201. **Tel** (314)882-3176. **LC** RC321; .J8375. **DD** 616.8/9/005. **UDC** 616.89-089. **NLM** W1 JO803G. **CODEN** JOPYB7. available on microfilm and microfiche from University Microfilms International (UMI).
**Ind/Abst** Middle East Abstr. Index; Psychol. Abstr. (1974-); PsycINFO; PsycLit; Soc. Plann. Policy Dev. Abstr.; Sociol. Abstr. (?-?).

CN/0834-4825
**JOURNAL OF ORTHOMOLECULAR MEDICINE.** [J. orthomol.med.]. **Added/Corp** Academy of Orthomolecular Medicine. Vol. 1, No. 1 (1st Quarter 1986)-. Periodical. English. qt. $95.00 (institutions), $85.00 (individuals) US and Canada; $110.00 (institutions), $100.00 (individuals) other. Canadian Schizophrenia Foundation / Ontario, 16 Florence Avenue, Toronto Ontario M2N 1E9 Canada. **Tel** (416)733-2117. **ED** A Hoffer. **DD** 616.89/1. **CODEN** JORMEI. **Bk Rev. Ad Acc.** available on microfilm and microfiche from University Microfilms International (UMI). ***Continues** Journal of Orthomolecular Psychiatry, 0317-0209.*
**Ind/Abst** Psychol. Abstr. (1975-); PsycINFO; PsycLit.

US/0737-1195
**JOURNAL OF POLYMORPHOUS PERVERSITY.** **See** Psychology.

US/1049-6343
**JOURNAL OF PREVENTIVE PSYCHIATRY AND ALLIED DISCIPLINES.** ***Ceased.*** (JOURNAL OF PREVENTIVE PSYCHIATRY AND ALLIED DISCIPLINES : OFFICIAL JOURNAL OF THE CENTER FOR PREVENTIVE PSYCHIATRY, INC.). [J. prev. psychiatry allied discipl.]. **Added/Corp** Center for Preventive Psychiatry. Vol. 4, No. 1 (Spring 1990)-Vol.4, No.4 (199?). Periodical. English. qt. Human Sciences Press, PO Box 735, 233 Spring Street, New York NY 10013. **Tel** (212)620-8000, FAX (212)807-1047, telex 23421139. **LC** RA790.A1; J69. **DD** 616.89/05. **NLM** W1; JO844L. **CODEN** JPADEF. ***Continues** Journal of Preventive Psychiatry, 0197-9353.*

UK/1351-0126
**JOURNAL OF PSYCHIATRIC AND MENTAL HEALTH NURSING.** (199?)-. Academic Scholarly Publication. English. Six times a year. $170.00 (institutions), $60.00 (individuals) US & Canada; £100.00 (institutions), £35.00 (individuals) Europe; £110.00 (institutions), £38.50 (individuals) other. Blackwell Scientific Publications Ltd, Marston Book Services, PO Box 87, Oxford OX2 ODT UK. **Tel** 011 44 865 791155, FAX 011 44 865 791927, telex 837 515 MARDIS G.

UK/0022-3956
**JOURNAL OF PSYCHIATRIC RESEARCH.** [J. psychiatr. res.]. Vol. 1 (Oct. 1961)-. Academic Scholarly Publication. English. Six times a year. $403.00 The Americas; £270.00 other. Pergamon Press, An Imprint of Elsevier Science Ltd., The Boulevard, Langford Lane, Kidlington, Oxford OX5 1GB United Kingdom. **Tel** 011 44 865 843000, 011 44 865 843699, FAX 011 44 865 843010. **(Subscription address:** Elsevier Science Ltd. Oxford Fulfillment Centre, PO Box 800, Kidlington, Oxford OX5 1DX United Kingdom.) **ED** Merton Sandler and Joseph Schildkraut. **LC** RC321; .J838. **DD** 616.89005. **NLM** W1 JO854. **CODEN** JPYRA3. **[CCC]. Pr Rev.** available on microfilm and microfiche from University Microfilms International (UMI). Documents available from The Genuine Article, BIOSIS Document Express, CASDDS.
**Desc:** Offers innovative and timely coverage of psychiatric research.
**Ind/Abst** Biol. Abstr.; Chem. Abstr.; CSA Neuro. Abstr. (?-?); Curr. Aware. Biol. Sci., CABS; Curr. Contents Clin. Med.; Curr. Contents Life Sci.; Curr. Contents Soc. Behav. Sci.; EMBASE; Index Med.; Int. Aerosp. Abstr.; Middle East Abstr. Index; Life Sci. Collect.; Psychol. Abstr. (1961-); PsycINFO; PsycLit; Res. Alert [Full Cov.]; Sci. Cit. Index; SCISEARCH; Soc. Plann. Policy Dev. Abstr.; Soc. Sci. Cit. Index [Full Cov.].

US/0093-1853
**JOURNAL OF PSYCHIATRY & LAW, THE.** **See** Law.

CN/1180-4882
**JOURNAL OF PSYCHIATRY & NEUROSCIENCE.** (JOURNAL OF PSYCHIATRY & NEUROSCIENCE : JPN.). [J. psychiatry neurosci.]. **VFOAT** Journal of Psychiatry and Neuroscience; JPN. Vol. 16 No. 1 (Mar. 1991)-. Periodical. English (French). Five times a year (Mar., June, Sept., Oct., Nov.). $75.00 (individuals), $95.00 (institutions) other. Journal of Psychiatry and Neuroscience, c/o Canadian Psychiatric Association, 200-237 Argyle Avenue, Ottawa, Ontario, K2P 1B8 Canada. **Tel** (613)234-2815, FAX (613)234-9857. **LC** RC321; .U49a. **DD** 616.89/005. **NLM** W1; JO856J. **CODEN** JPNEEF. **Bk Rev. Ad Acc, Adv Mgr:** M. Watkins. **Acid Free.** Documents available from The Genuine Article, BIOSIS Document Express. ***Continues** University of Ottawa. Dept. of Psychiatry. Psychiatric Journal of the University of Ottawa, 0702-8466.*
**Desc:** Publishes original research articles and review papers in clinical psychiatry (adult and child) and neuroscience which relate to major psychiatric disorders, particularly schizophrenia, affective disorders and neurodegenerative diseases. The journal provides a forum for original basic and clinical science research which will present its readership with an integrated perspective on current and emerging issues in clinical and biological psychiatry.
**Ind/Abst** Biol. Abstr. (1991-); Curr. Contents Soc. Behav. Sci.; EMBASE [Select. Cov.]; Health Plan. Adminis.; Index Med. (1991-); Psychol. Abstr. (1991-); PsycINFO; Res. Alert [Full Cov.]; Soc. Plann. Policy Dev. Abstr.; Soc. Sci. Cit. Index [Full Cov.].

US/0279-3695
**JOURNAL OF PSYCHOSOCIAL NURSING AND MENTAL HEALTH SERVICES.** **See** Medical Science and Technology-Nursing.

US/1053-0479
**JOURNAL OF PSYCHOTHERAPY INTEGRATION.** **See** Psychology.

●US/1055-050X
**JOURNAL OF PSYCHOTHERAPY PRACTICE AND RESEARCH, THE.** [J. psychother. pract. res.]. **Added/Corp** American Psychiatric Press. **VFOAT** Psychotherapy Practice and Research. Vol. 1, No. 1 (Winter 1992)-. Periodical. English. qt. $135.00 US; $150.00 other (institution). American Psychiatric Press Inc., 1400 K Street Northwest, Suite 1101, Washington DC 20005. **Tel** (202)682-6222, FAX (202)789-2648. **LC** RC475; .J633. **DD** 616.89/14/05. **NLM** W1; JO859FL. **Bk Rev. Ad Acc. Pr Rev.**
**Desc:** Provides a forum for the presentation of relevant, original research and clinical reports related to psychotherapy.

US/0022-4197
**JOURNAL OF RELIGION AND HEALTH.** **See** Religion and Theology.

●US/1045-5876
**JOURNAL OF RELIGION IN PSYCHOTHERAPY.** (1993)-. Periodical. English. qt. $60.00 US; $84.00 other. The Haworth Press Inc, 10 Alice Street, Binghamton NY 13904-1580. **Tel** (607)722-5857, (800)3-HAWORTH, FAX (607)722-1424. **ED** William M. Clements (editor's address: The Medical Center, Department of Family Practice, 710 Center Street, PO Box 951, Columbus, GA 31994-2299). **Bk Rev. Ad Acc. Pr Rev. Acid Free.** available on microfiche. Documents available from Haworth Document Delivery Service. ***Continues** Journal of Pastoral Psychotherapy, 0886-5477.*
**Desc:** For therapists and researchers who are interested in the role and dynamic of religion in the healing process of psychotherapy. Pastoral counselors, psychologists, sociologists, marriage and family therapists, psychiatrists, social workers and other helping professionals will be challenged by the mix of theoretical, clinical and research topic presented in each volume.
**Ind/Abst** Abstr. Res. Pastor. Care Couns. (19??-); Commun. Abstr. (?-?); Psychol. Abstr. (1987-); Soc. Work Abstr. [Select. Cov.].

US/0092-3931
**JOURNAL OF RESEARCH AND TRAINING, THE.** [J. res. train.]. **VFOAT** IDMH Journal of Research & Training. V. 1- Summer 1973-. Periodical. English. qt. Illinois Mental Health Institutes, 1601 West Taylor Street, Chicago IL 60612. **LC** RC321; .J854. **DD** 616.8/9/005.

●US/1061-0413
**JOURNAL OF RUSSIAN AND EAST EUROPEAN PSYCHIATRY.** (JOURNAL OF RUSSIAN AND EAST EUROPEAN PSYCHIATRY : A JOURNAL OF TRANSLATIONS.). [J. Russ. East Eur. psychiatry]. Vol. 25, No. 1 (Spring 1992)-. Periodical. English (translations available in Russian). qt. $421.00 US; $462.00 other. M. E. Sharpe Inc., 80 Business Park Drive, Armonk NY 10504. **Tel** (914)273-1800, (800)541-6563, FAX (914)273-2106. **DD** 616. **NLM** W1; JO871R. **CODEN** JEEPES. Documents available from BIOSIS Document Express. ***Continues** Soviet Neurology & Psychiatry, 0038-559X.*
**Ind/Abst** Biol. Abstr.; Psychol. Abstr.

US/0092-623X
**JOURNAL OF SEX & MARITAL THERAPY.** **See** Sexual Life.

CN/0711-5075
**JOURNAL OF STRATEGIC AND SYSTEMIC THERAPIES, THE.** ***Title Change.*** [J. strateg. syst. ther.]. Vol. 1, No. 1 (Summer 1981)-(19??). Periodical. English. Four times a year. Journal of Strategic and Systemic Therapies, Box 2484 Station A, London Ontario N6A 4G7 Canada. **Tel** (519)433-3101. **ED** Don Efron. **DD** 615.5/05. **[CCC]. Bk Rev. Ad Acc. Circ:** 1,400. ***Continued by** Journal of Systemic Therapies.*
**Desc:** Specialized journal for therapists using strategic-systemic models in individual and family therapy. Example given Haley, Erickson, MRI, Milan. Emphasis on clinical usefulness and therapy. No research.
**Ind/Abst** Psychol. Abstr. (1983-); PsycINFO; PsycLit.

# Medical Science and Technology — Psychiatry

**US/0890-8567**
**JOURNAL OF THE AMERICAN ACADEMY OF CHILD AND ADOLESCENT PSYCHIATRY.** [J. Am. Acad. Child Adolesc. Psych.]. **Added/Corp** American Academy of Child and Adolescent Psychiatry. Vol. 26, No. 1 (Jan. 1987)-. Periodical. English. Nine times a year. $109.00 (individual), $199.00 (institution) US; $74.00 (individual), $144.00 (institutions) other. Williams & Wilkins Company, 428 East Preston Street, Baltimore MD 21202-3993. **Tel** (410)528-4000, (800)638-6423, FAX (410)528-8596, telex 87669. **(Subscription address:** Williams & Wilkins, PO Box 64380, Baltimore MD 21264.) **ED** Melvin Lewis. **LC** RJ499.A1; A4. **DD** 618.92/89. **NLM** W1; JO907VN. **CODEN** JAAPEE. **[CCC]. Ad Acc. Pr Rev. Circ:** 6,200. available on microfilm. Documents available from The Genuine Article, BIOSIS Document Express, UMI Article Clearinghouse, Quick Copies. **Continues** American Academy of Child Psychiatry. Journal of the American Academy of Child Psychiatry, 0002-7138.
**Desc:** Leading journal in child psychiatry publishes high quality original papers in psychiatric research and treatment of the child and adolescent.
**Ind/Abst** Acad. Search (July 1993-); Annals Behav. Med.; Biol. Abstr. (1988-); Comb. Cumul. Index Pediatr.; Cumul. Index Nurs. Allied Health Lit.; Curr. Contents Soc. Behav. Sci.; Dev. Med. Child Neurol.; Educ. Index (?-1992); EMBASE; Except. Child Educ. Resour. (19??-19??); Expand. Acad. Index (1989-); Index Med. (1987-?); INFO-SOUTH Abstr.; Mag. Search; Newsp. Period. Abstr. (1989-); Nutr. Res. Newsl.; Psychol. Abstr.; PsycINFO (1990-); PsycLit; Res. Alert [Full Cov.]; Sci. Cit. Index; SCISEARCH; Soc. Sci. Source (Jul. 1993-); Soc. Sci. Cit. Index [Full Cov.]; Soc. Sci. Index; Soc. Sci. Index Fulltext (July 1988-) [Full Txt.]; Soc. Work Abstr. [Select. Cov.]; Women Stud. Abstr.

**US/0362-4870**
**JOURNAL OF THE AMERICAN ACADEMY OF PSYCHIATRY AND NEUROLOGY.** **Main/Corp** American Academy of Psychiatry and Neurology. **VFOAT** Journal of the AAPN. V. 1- Jan./March 1976-. Periodical. English. qt. $30.00. AAPN, 17 Kingston Road, Scarsdale NY 10583. **LC** RC321; .A475A. **DD** 616.8/005. **UDC** 616.8. **NLM** W1 JO907XG. available on microfilm from University Microfilms International (UMI).

**US/0090-3604**
**JOURNAL OF THE AMERICAN ACADEMY OF PSYCHOANALYSIS, THE.** [J. Am. Acad. Psychoanal.]. **Added/Corp** American Academy of Psychoanalysis. Vol. 1 (1973)-. Academic Scholarly Publication. English. Four times a year. $130.00 (institutions); $150.00 others. Guilford Publications Inc., 72 Spring Street, New York NY 10012. **Tel** (212)431-9800, (800)365-7006, FAX (212)966-6708. **(Subscription address:** Turpin Distribution Services Limited, Blackhorse Road, Letchworth, Hertfordshire SG6 1HN, United Kingdom.) **ED** Jules Bemporad. **LC** RC500; .A47. **DD** 616.8/917/05. **NLM** W1 JO907Y. **CODEN** JAAPCC. **[CCC]. Ad Acc. Pr Rev. Circ:** 1,800. available on microfilm and microfiche from University Microfilms International (UMI).
**Desc:** Provides a forum for inquiry into all areas of human behavior. Offers insights into new biological, cultural and other discoveries related to the human psyche and psychoanalysis. Also amongst topics discussed are group, marital, child and sex therapy.
**Ind/Abst** Curr. Contents Soc. Behav. Sci.; EMBASE; Index Med.; Psychol. Abstr. (1973-); PsycINFO; PsycLit; Sage Race Relat. Abstr.; Soc. Sci. Cit. Index [Full Cov.]; Soc. Work Abstr. [Select. Cov.].

**UK/0307-4765**
**JOURNAL OF THE BALINT SOCIETY.** [J. Balint Soc.]. **Added/Corp** Balint Society. Vol. 1 (June 1971)-. Periodical. English. an. £10.00. Journal of the Balint Society, 149 Altmore Avenue, London E6 2BT England. **Tel** 011 44 81 472 4822. **NLM** W1 JO913C.

**US/0094-1476**
**JOURNAL OF THE PHILADELPHIA ASSOCIATION FOR PSYCHOANALYSIS.** [J. Philadelphia Assoc. Psychoanal.]. **Main/Corp** Philadelphia Association for Psychoanalysis. V. 1- Mar. 1974-. Periodical. English. qt. $7.00. 15 St Asaph's Road, Bala Cynwyd PA 19004. **LC** RC500; .P515. **DD** 616.8/917/05. **UDC** 616.89-072.87; 615.851.13. **NLM** W1 JO946E. **Supersedes** Bulletin of the Philadelphia Association for Psychoanalysis, 0480-2780.
**Ind/Abst** EMBASE.

**US/0894-9867**
**JOURNAL OF TRAUMATIC STRESS.** See Psychology.

**GW/0343-9429**
**KLINISCHE PSYCHOLOGIE UND PSYCHOPATHOLOGIE.** See Psychology.

**NE**
**KNIPSELKRANT PSYCHIATRIE.** (19??)-. Dutch. ir (48 issues). Fl375.00. Media Nieuws, Postbus 40, 8855 ZM Sexbierum, Netherlands. **Tel** 011 31 5179 1663.

**BE**
**KNIPSELKRANT VOOR GEESTELIJKE GEZONDHEIDSZORG.** Dutch. Vlaamse Ver Geestel Gezondhd, Kortrijksesteenweg 369, B-9000 Ghent Belgium.

**JA**
**KOKURITSU MUSASHI RYOYOJO SHINKEI SENTA NENPO.** See Medical Science and Technology-Neurology.

**GW/0937-289X**
**KRANKENHAUSPSYCHIATRIE.** [Krankenhauspsychiatrie]. (1990)-. Periodical. Multiple languages. qt. $90.00. Georg Thieme Verlag Stuttgart, Postfach 301120, D 70451 Stuttgart Germany. **Tel** 011 49 711 89310, FAX 011 49 711 8931298, telex 7 252 275 GTVD. **(Subscription address:** Thieme Medical Publishers Inc., 381 Park Avenue South, New York NY 10016.) **UDC** 61.

**JA/0023-6144**
**KYUSHU SHINKEI SEISHIN IGAKU.** [Kyushu shinkei seishin igaku]. **VFOAT** Kyushu Neuro-Psychiatry. Began in 1949. Academic Scholarly Publication. Japanese (summaries and/or abstracts in English). Three times a year. $33.00. Kyushu Association of Neuro Psychiatry, Department of Neuro Psychiatry, Faculty of Medicine, Kyushu University 60, Fukuoka 812 Japan. **Tel** (092)641-1151. **ED** Nobutada Tashiro. **UDC** 616.89. **NLM** W1 KY9975. **CODEN** KSSIAC. Index available. **Bk Rev. Ad Acc. Circ:** 900. Documents available from CASDDS.
**Desc:** Paper about general psychiatry.
**Ind/Abst** Chem. Abstr.

**UK/0143-7534**
**LEARNING AND MEMORY / ISSUED BY UNIVERSITY OF SHEFFIELD BIOMEDICAL INFORMATION SERVICE.** (19??)-. Bulletin. English. mo. £80.00. SUBIS, Mansion House, 19 Kingfield Road, Sheffield S11 9AS England. **Tel** 011 44 114 255 4433, FAX 011 44 114 255 4626. **Ad Acc.**
**Desc:** Current awareness service for researchers in clinical and life sciences.

**US/0883-0924**
**LEGAL ASPECTS OF PSYCHIATRIC PRACTICE.** See Law.

**FR**
**LETTRE DU PSYCHIATRE, LA.** French. Ten times a year. 254.00F France; $79.00 US; £57.00 other. Masson SA, Avenue Beauregard 12, CH-1701 Fribourg Switzerland. **Tel** 011 41 37 249585, FAX 011 41 37 247559, telex 942658 SEMI CH.

**FR/0223-9434**
**LETTRE DU PSYCHIATRE PARIS, LA.** [Lett. psych. Paris]. (1979)-. Periodical. French. mo (10 issues). $88.00. Masson Editeur, Box Postale 22, 41353 Vineuil 16 France. **Tel** 011 33 54 438994. **UDC** 61. **[CCC].**

**US/1040-2160**
**LONG ISLAND MENTAL HEALTH CLINICIAN : JOURNAL OF CENTRAL NASSAU GUIDANCE & COUNSELING SERVICES, INC.** [Long Isl. ment. health clin.]. Periodical. English. sa. $12.00. Central Nassau Guidance & Counseling Services, 246 Old Country Road, Hicksville NY 11801. **DD** 158.

**GW/0933-3347**
**LUZIFER-AMOR.** See Psychology.

**UK/0076-5465**
**MAUDSLEY MONOGRAPHS.** (1955)-. Monographic series. English. ir. Price varies per volume. Oxford University Press / New York, 200 Madison Avenue, New York NY 10016. **Tel** (212)679-7300, (919)677-0977, (800)451-7556, (800)445-9714, FAX (919)677-1303.

**US/0363-0226**
**MCLEAN HOSPITAL JOURNAL.** [McLean Hosp. j.]. **Main/Corp** McLean Hospital. **Added/Corp** McLean Hospital. Journal. Vol. 1 (Winter 1976)-. Periodical. English. qt. McLean Hospital, c/o Evelyn M Stone, 115 Mill Street, Belmont MA 02178. **Tel** (617)855-2186. **ED** Shervert H Frazier and Evelyn M Stone. **NLM** W1 MA165H. **CODEN** MHJODZ. ctrl circ. Documents available from BIOSIS Document Express.
**Ind/Abst** Biol. Abstr.; EMBASE.

**SP**
**MEDICAL DIGEST. PSIQUIATRIA.** Spanish. Editorial M.C.R. SA, Mallorca 310, 08037 Barcelona Spain.

**US/0894-5098**
**MEDICAL HYPNOANALYSIS JOURNAL.** See Psychology.

**YU/0351-4501**
**MEDITERRANEAN JOURNAL OF SOCIAL PSYCHIATRY / MEDITERRANEAN SOCIOPSYCHIATRIC ASSOCIATION.** Periodical. English. sa. $10.00. **NLM** W1; ME794J.
**Ind/Abst** EMBASE.

**CN/0576-5986**
**MEMBERSHIP DIRECTORY - CANADIAN PSYCHIATRIC ASSOCIATION. REPERTOIRE DES MEMBRES - ASSOCIATION DES PSYCHIATRES DU CANADA.** **Main/Corp** Canadian Psychiatric Association. **Added/Corp** Canadian Psychiatric Association. Repertoire des Membres. **VFOAT** Repertoire des Membres - Association des Psychiatres du Canada. (1967)-. Directory. Multiple languages (English and French). ir. Free to members. $25. per no. Canadian Psychiatric Association, 237 Argyle Avenue/ Suite 200, Ottawa Ontario K2P 1B8 Canada. **Tel** (613)234-2815. **DD** 616.8/9/006271. **NLM** WM 22 DC2 C3M.

**UK/0142-5447**
**MEMBERSHIP LIST - ROYAL COLLEGE OF PSYCHIATRISTS.** [Membsh. list - R. Coll. Psychiatr.]. **Main/Corp** Royal College of Psychiatrists. 1977-. English. an. Royal College of Psychiatrists, 17 Belgrave Square, London SW1X 8PG England. **Tel** 01 235 8857. **UDC** 616.89(060.21)(410). **NLM** WM 22 FA1 R8Y. **Supersedes** Royal Medico-Psychological Association, London. Yearbook.

●**US/1066-937X**
**MENNINGER LETTER, THE.** [Menninger lett.]. **Added/Corp** Menninger Clinic. Vol. 1, No. 1 (Jan. 1993)-. Periodical. English. Twelve times a year. $24.00. Menninger Clinic, Box 829, Topeka KS 66601. **Tel** (913)273-7500. **ED** Mary Ann Clifft. **DD** 362. **Pr Rev. Circ:** 70,000 (ctrl).

**US/0025-9292**
**MENNINGER PERSPECTIVE.** **Added/Corp** Menninger Foundation. Office of Information. Menninger School of Psychiatry. Alumni Association. Vol. 1 (April/May 1970)-. Periodical. English. qt. $25.00 Comes with Menninger Foundation membership. Menninger Foundation, PO Box 829, Topeka KS 66601-0829. **Tel** (913)273-7500. **ED** Emlin E. North Jr. and Judith L. Craig. **LC** RC321; .M42. **DD** 616.89/005. **NLM** W1 ME9199K. **CODEN** MNPVB. **Circ:** 21,000 (ctrl). available on microfilm and microfiche from University Microfilms International (UMI). **Supersedes** Menninger Quarterly.
**Desc:** Articles related to mental health topics such as: psychiatric treatment, research, professional education, public advocacy, and the work of Menninger.

**UK/0952-9608**
**MENTAL HANDICAP RESEARCH.** **Added/Corp** British Institute of Mental Handicap. Vol. 1, No. 1 (Jan. 1988)-. Periodical. English. sa. £62.00 UK; $135.00 other. Multilingual Matters Ltd., Frankfurt Lodge, Clevedon Hall, Clevedon Avon, BS21 7SJ England. **Tel** 011 44 275 876519, FAX 011 44 275 343096. **NLM** W1; ME9229T.
**Ind/Abst** Br. Educ. Index; Spec. Educ. Needs Abstr.

**US**
**MENTAL HEALTH MANUAL.** (19??)-. Periodical. English. ir. $75.00. Joint Commission on Accreditation of Hospitals, 1 Renaissance Boulevard, Headquarters Center, Oakbrook Terrace IL 60181. **Tel** (708)916-5800. **Continues** Consolidated Standards Manual for Child, Adolescent and Adult Psychiatric, Alcoholism, and Drug Abuse Facilities.

●**US**
**MENTAL HEALTH NEWS ALERT.** See Sociology-Social Services and Welfare.

**UK**
**MENTAL HEALTH NURSING.** See Medical Science and Technology-Nursing.

**US/0273-3498**
**MENTAL HEALTH SERVICE SYSTEM REPORTS. SERIES GN, METHODOLOGY / U.S. DEPARTMENT OF HEALTH AND HUMAN SERVICES, PUBLIC HEALTH SERVICE, ALCOHOL, DRUG ABUSE, AND MENTAL HEALTH ADMINISTRATION, NATIONAL INSTITUTE OF MENTAL HEALTH.** **VFOAT** Methodology. No. 1- 1980-. Monographic series. English. Price varies per volume. US Department of Health and Human Services, 200 Independence Avenue Southwest, Washington DC 20201. **UDC** 616.89(73). **NLM** W1 ME928FD.

**US/0361-9311**
**MENTAL HEALTH STATISTICAL NOTE.** See Public Health and Safety.

# Medical Science and Technology —Psychiatry

CN/0821-3305
**MENTAL HEALTH (TORONTO. 1979).**
(SANTE MENTALE: COMMUNIQUE NATIONAL DE ASSOCIATION CANADIENNE.). [Ment. health]. **Added/Corp** Canadian Mental Health Association. **VAT** Sante Hentale (Toronto). Vol. 3 No 1 (Sept. 1979)-. Periodical. French (English). qt. Canadian Mental Health Association, 10050 112th Street, 9th Floor, Edmonton Alberta T5K 2J1 Canada. **Tel** (403)482-6091. **DD** 362.2/06/071. **Continues** Communique National., 0705-811X.

US/1058-1103
**MENTAL HEALTH WEEKLY. See** Psychology.

US/0091-6315
**MENTAL RETARDATION AND DEVELOPMENTAL DISABILITIES. Ceased.**
[Ment. retard. dev. disabil.]. Vol. 5 (1973)-(19??). Academic Scholarly Publication. English. ir. Elsevier Science Publishing Company Inc, Madison Square Station, PO Box 882, New York NY 10159-0882. **Tel** (212)633-3950, FAX (212)633-3990. **ED** J. Wortis. **LC** RC570; .M38. **DD** 618.9/28/58805. **UDC** 616.899. **NLM** W1 ME936JE. **CODEN** MRDDD8. Documents available from BIOSIS Document Express. **Continues** Mental Retardation, 0076-647X.
**Ind/Abst** Biol. Abstr.

IT/0391-1772
**MINERVA PSICHIATRICA.** [Min. psic.]. Vol. 17 (Jan./March 1976)-. Periodical. Italian (summaries and/or abstracts in English). qt. $90.00 (individuals), $140.00 (institutions). Edizioni Minerva Medica, Corso Bramante 83-85, 10126 Turin Italy. **Tel** 011 39 11 678282, FAX 011 39 11 674502. **ED** G Campailla and A Petiziol. **NLM** W1 MI652G. **Bk Rev**. **Ad Acc**. available on microfilm from University Microfilms International (UMI). **Continues** Minerva Psichiatrica E Psicologica.
**Desc**: Addressed to practitioners and specialists in psychiatry and psychology in Italy and abroad; deals with topics in scientific practice and research.
**Ind/Abst** EMBASE [Select. Cov.]; Index Med.; Soc. Plann. Policy Dev. Abstr.; Sociol. Abstr. (?-?).

SZ/0077-0094
**MODERN PROBLEMS OF PHARMACOPSYCHIATRY.** [Mod. probl. pharmacopsychiatry]. **VFOAT** Moderne Probleme der Pharmakopsychiatrie; Problemes Actuels de Pharmacopsychiatrie. Vol. 1 (1968)-. Periodical. English. an. 150.00F (approx. per volume. S. Karger AG, Allschwilerstrasse 10, PO Box - Postfach - Case Postale, CH-4009 Basel Switzerland. **Tel** 011 41 61 306-1111, FAX 011 41 61 306-1234, telex CH 962 652. **ED** H. J. Freyberger, R. D. Stieglitz. **LC** RC483; .M6. **DD** 616.89/18/05. **NLM** W1 MO168P. **CODEN** MPPPBK. **[CCC]**. Documents available from BIOSIS Document Express, CASDDS.
**Desc**: Clinical conditions which may be altered or improved by psychiatric drugs form the focus for volumes in this series, which features findings from studies of new drugs, comparative evaluations of drugs in use, theoretical approaches to understanding mode of action, and biological factors implicated in disorders of mood and behavior.
**Ind/Abst** Biol. Abstr.; Chem. Abstr.; Index Med.; Psychol. Abstr. (1984-); PsycINFO; PsycLit; Ref. Upd. Deluxe Ed.

IT/0394-0101
**MONOGRAFIE DE IL LAVORO NEUROPSICHIATRICO, LE. Ceased.**
[Monograf. "Lav. neuropsichiatr."]. **VFOAT** Lavoro Neuropsichiatrico. Ceased vol. 1, No. 4 (1989). Periodical. Italian. qt. Direzione Radazione Amministra. **UDC** 616.89. **NLM** W1 MO543R.
**Ind/Abst** Psychol. Abstr. (1973-).

CN/0227-8561
**MONOGRAPH - CHILDREN'S PSYCHIATRIC RESEARCH INSTITUTE.**
**Main/Corp** Children's Psychiatric Research Institute. No. 1 (1970)-. Periodical. English. Children's Psychiatric Research Institute, PO Box 2460, London Ontario N6A 4G6 Canada. **DD** 362.2.

US/0742-3187
**MONOGRAPH SERIES / AMERICAN GROUP PSYCHOTHERAPY ASSOCIATION.** [Monogr. ser. - Am. Group Psychother. Assoc.]. **Added/Corp** American Group Psychotherapy Association. **VFOAT** AGPA Monograph Series; A.G.P.A. Monograph Series. Monograph 1 (1983)-. Monographic series. English. ir. Price varies per volume. International Universities Press Inc., 59 Boston Post Road, PO Box 1524, Madison CT 06443-1524. **Tel** (203)245-4000, FAX (203)245-0775, telex 282986 IUP BK. **LC** UNC. **DD** 616.89/152. **NLM** W1 MO559PU.

GW/0077-0671
**MONOGRAPHIEN AUS DEM GESAMTGEBIETE DER PSYCHIATRIE.**
**See** Medical Science and Technology-Neurology.

US/0065-6852
**MONOGRAPHS OF THE JOURNAL OF THE AMERICAN ACADEMY OF CHILD PSYCHIATRY. See** Medical Science and Technology-Pediatrics.

NE/0923-2370
**NEDERLANDS TIJDSCHRIFT VOOR ZWAKZINNIGENZORG.** [Ned. tijdschr. zwakzinnigenzorg]. (1989)-. Periodical. Dutch. qt. Fl49.53 Netherlands; Fl59.53 Europe; Fl64.53 other. Nederlands Tijdschrift voor Zwakzinnigenzorg, Postbus 415, 3500 AK Utrecht Netherlands. **Tel** 011 31 30 333504. **UDC** 364.4.
**Continues** Ruit, 0166-7270.

GW/0028-2804
**NERVENARZT. See** Medical Science and Technology-Neurology.

GW/0722-1541
**NERVENHEILKUNDE. See** Medical Science and Technology-Neurology.

FR/0988-4068
**NERVURE (PARIS).** (NERVURE.). [Nervure Paris]. Periodical. French. Ten times a year. 460.33F (1 year), 714.99F (2 year) France; 660.33F (1 year), 914.99F (2 year) other. Maxmed, 54 BD de la Tour Maubourg, F-75007 Paris France. **Tel** 011 33 1 45502308, FAX 011 33 1 45556080. **UDC** 616.89. Index available. **Bk Rev**. **Ad Acc**. **Pr Rev**.
**Desc**: For psychiatric doctors, neuropsychiatrists, pedopsychiatrists, neurologists, and hospitals.

BL/0028-3800
**NEUROBIOLOGIA (RECIFE). See** Medical Science and Technology-Neurology.

GR/0253-9446
**NEUROLOGIA ET PSYCHIATRIA. See** Medical Science and Technology-Neurology.

IT
**NEUROLOGIA PSICHIATRIA SCIENZE UMANE. Added/Corp** Fondazione Centro Praxis (Italy). **VFOAT** NPS; N.P.S. Vol. 1, No. 1 (April 1981)-. Periodical. Italian (summaries and/or abstracts in English and Italian). bm. L70000.00 institutions; L60000.00 individuals. Centro Praxis, Via Napoli, 81028 S Maria A Vico Italy. **Tel** 011 39 823 808308, FAX 011 39 823 808308. **NLM** W1; NE329N. **Bk Rev**. **Ad Acc**. **Pr Rev**. **Circ**: 7,000.
**Ind/Abst** EMBASE.

IT/0028-3916
**NEUROPSICHIATRIA. See** Medical Science and Technology-Neurology.

US/0723-0931
**NEUROPSYCHIATRIA CLINICA.** Vol. 1, No. 1 (1 Sept. 1982)-. Periodical. English (German; table of contents in English and German). qt. $75.00. VCH Publishers Inc, 220 East 23rd Street, New York NY 10010. **Tel** (212)683-8333, , FAX (212)481-0897. **(Subscription address:** VCH Publishers Inc., 303 Northwest 12th Avenue, Journals Department, Deerfield FL 33442.) **UDC** 616.89. **NLM** W1 NE339G.

GW
**NEUROPSYCHIATRIE.** (19??)-. DM125.00. Dustri-Verlag, Dr Karl Feistle, Postfach 49, D 82032 Deisenhofen Germany. **Tel** 011 49 89 6138610, FAX 011 49 89 6135412.
**Ind/Abst** Soc. Sci. Cit. Index [Select. Cov.].

US/0894-878X
**NEUROPSYCHIATRY, NEUROPSYCHOLOGY, BEHAVIORAL NEUROLOGY. See** Medical Science and Technology-Neurology.

SZ/0302-282X
**NEUROPSYCHOBIOLOGY. See** Medical Science and Technology-Neurology.

NE/0304-3940
**NEUROSCIENCE LETTERS. See** Medical Science and Technology-Neurology.

IE/0168-0102
**NEUROSCIENCE RESEARCH. See** Medical Science and Technology-Neurology.

BU/0548-3794
**NEVROLOGIJA, PSIHIATRIJA I NEVROHIRURGIJA. See** Medical Science and Technology-Neurology.

US/0148-7361
**NEW DIMENSIONS IN PSYCHIATRY.**
(NEW DIMENSIONS IN PSYCHIATRY: A WORLD VIEW.). [New dimens. psychiatr.]. Vol. 1 (1975)-. English. be. John Wiley & Sons, Inc., 605 Third Avenue, New York NY 10158-0012. **Tel** (212)850-6000, (212)850-6645, FAX (212)850-6088, telex 12-7063. **(Subscription address:** John Wiley & Sons / England, Baffins Lane, Chichester, West Sussex PO19 1UD England.) **ED** Silvano Arieti and Gerard Chrzanowski. **LC** RC331; .N445. **DD** 616.8/9/005. **NLM** W1 NE373. **Continues** World Biennial of Psychiatry and Psychotherapy, 0084-1420.

US/8756-260X
**NEW RESEARCH IN MENTAL HEALTH. See** Public Health and Safety.

IT/0393-5310
**NEW TRENDS IN EXPERIMENTAL AND CLINICAL PSYCHIATRY.** Vol. 1, No 1 (July-Sept. 1985)-. Periodical. English. qt. L70.000 Italy; $80.00 other. CIC Edizioni Internazionali, Via L Spallanzani 11, 00161 Rome Italy. **Tel** 011 39 6 841-2673, FAX 011 39 6 844-3365, telex 622099 CIC I. **ED** Giordano Invernizzi (Milan). **NLM** W1; NE513F. **CODEN** NTEPE7.
**Ind/Abst** EMBASE; Psychol. Abstr. (1985-); PsycINFO; PsycLit.

US
**NEW WAYS (EVANSTON, ILL.).** (NEW WAYS.). English. qt. $36.00US; $54.00 other. First Publications, PO Box 5072, Evanston IL 60204. **Tel** (312)869-7210. **ED** Mark Russell. **Bk Rev**. **Ad Acc**.
**Continues** Ways.
**Desc**: For everyone who wants to bring a better life to people with mental retardation.

US/0896-5633
**NEWSLETTER (AMERICAN ACADEMY OF PSYCHIATRY AND THE LAW).**
(NEWSLETTER / AMERICAN ACADEMY OF PSYCHIATRY & THE LAW.). [Newsl. - Am. Acad. Psychiatr. Law]. **Added/Corp** American Academy of Psychiatry and the Law. **VFOAT** AAPL Newsletter. Vol. 6, No. 2 (Aug. 1981)-. Newsletter. English. Three times a year (Apr., Sept., Dec.). $25.00 Comes with Bulletin of the American Academy of Psychiatry and the Law. American Academy of Psychiatry & The Law, PO Box 30, One Regency Drive, Bloomfield CT 06002. **Tel** (203)242-5450, (800)331-1389, FAX (203)286-0787. **ED** Dr. Alan Felthous, (editor's address: Department of Psychology and Behavioral Sciences, University of Texas Medical Branch, Galveston, TX 77550). **LC** KF8922; .N48. **DD** 614/.1. **Bk Rev**, (Qty: varies). **Circ**: 2,000. available on microfilm. **Continues** Newsletter of the American Academy of Psychiatry and the Law.
**Desc**: News and information on the articles of forensic psychiatry and updates on legal cases.
**Ind/Abst** Crim. Penol. Police Sci. Abstr.

US
**NEWSLETTER - MEN'S AWARENESS NETWORK. Main/Corp** Men's Awareness Network. **Added/Corp** Knoxville Men's Resource Collective. **VFOAT** MAN Newsletter. (1975)-. Newsletter. English. Four times a year. Men's Resource Center, 2036 SE Morrison, Portland OR 97214-2824. **Tel** (503)235-3433.

US/0027-8637
**NEWSLETTER (NATIONAL ASSOCIATION OF PRIVATE PSYCHIATRIC HOSPITALS). See** Medical Science and Technology-Hospital Administration and Medical Centers.

US/0093-0237
**NEWSLETTER OF THE A.A.P.S.C. See** Medical Science and Technology-Pediatrics.

CN/0319-6992
**NEWSLETTER - WORLD FEDERATION FOR MENTAL HEALTH. Main/Corp** World Federation for Mental Health. **VAT** President's Newsletter - World Federation for Mental Health. Vol. 1 (Feb. 1975)-. Newsletter. English. qt. Free to members. World Federation of Mental Health, 1021 Prince Street, Alexandria VA 22314. **Tel** (703)684-7722. **ED** Elena Berger. **NLM** W1 NE9985. **Supersedes** Bulletin - World Federation for Mental Health, 0043-8456.

II
**NIMHANS JOURNAL. Added/Corp** NIMHANS (Institute). **VFOAT** N.I.M.H.A.N.S. Journal. **VAT** National Institute of Mental Health and Neuro Sciences Journal. Vol. 1, No. 1 (Jan. 1983)-. English. sa. $30.00. National Institute of Mental Health and Neuro Sciences, c/o Publication Department, PB 2900 Bangalore 560029 India. **Tel** 641256, telex 2186 NIMH. **(Subscription address:** Prints India, 11 Darya Ganj, New Delhi 110002 India.) **ED** S M Channabasavanna. **NLM** W1; NI589. Index available. **Bk Rev**. **Ad Acc**. **Pr Rev**. **Circ**: 700.
**Desc**: Publishes papers in mental health and neuro sciences in its broadest sense, including basic sciences.
**Ind/Abst** Arts Humanit. Citation Index [Select. Cov.]; Psychol. Abstr. (1986-); PsycINFO; PsycLit; Soc. Sci. Cit. Index [Select. Cov.].

NO/0803-9488
**NORDIC JOURNAL OF PSYCHIATRY.**
[Nord. j. psychiatry]. **VFOAT** Nordisk Psykiatrisk Tidsskrift. (1992)-. Periodical. Multiple languages. bm. $110.00. Scandinavian University Press, PO Box 2959 Toeyen, N 0608 Oslo 6 Norway. **Tel** 011 47 2 2575400, FAX 011 47 2 2575353, telex 71896 UROR N. **(Subscription address:** Scandinavian University Press, 200 Meacham Ave., Elmont NY 11003.) **ED** Lars von

# Medical Science and Technology — Psychiatry

Knorring. **DD** 616.8. **Continues** Nordisk Psykiatrisk Tidsskrift, 0029-1455.
 **Desc:** All relevant themes in psychiatry are represented- from psychotherapy to psychopharmacology. The contents cover original articles, review articles, congress and symposium reports, special topic issues, supplements, debate columns, book reviews and a congress diary. English-language articles are given equal consideration to the Scandinavian ones. The journal is distributed to members of the Nordic Psychiatric Associations as well as to all members of the Nordic Associations for Child and Adolescent Psychiatry.

NO/0803-9496
**NORDIC JOURNAL OF PSYCHIATRY. SUPPLEMENT.** [Nord. j. psychiatry, Suppl.]. (1992)-. Monographic series. Multiple languages. ir. Comes with Nordic Journal of Psychiatry. Scandinavian University Press, PO Box 2959 Toeyen, N 0608 Oslo 6 Norway. **Tel** 011 47 2 2575400, FAX 011 47 2 2575353, telex 71896 UROR N. **(Subscription address:** Scandinavian University Press, 200 Meacham Ave., Elmont NY 11003.) **DD** 616.8. **Continues** Nordisk Psykiatrisk Tidsskrift. Supplement (Oslo), 0346-8852.
**Ind/Abst** EMBASE [Select. Cov.].

US/0164-212X
**OCCUPATIONAL THERAPY IN MENTAL HEALTH. See** Industrial Health and Safety.

DK/0105-0621
**ODENSE UNIVERSITY STUDIES IN PSYCHIATRY AND MEDICAL PSYCHOLOGY.** Vol. 1 (1973)-. Monographic series. Danish (summaries and/or abstracts in English). ir. Price varies per volume. Odense University Press, 55 Campusvej, DK-5230 Odense M Denmark. **Tel** 66 15 79 99, FAX 66 15 81 26. **NLM** W1 OD115.
 **Desc:** Series covering psychiatric diseases.

US/1054-075X
**ORGONOMIC FUNCTIONALISM (RANGELEY, ME.).** (ORGONOMIC FUNCTIONALISM.). **Added/Corp** Wilhelm Reich Infant Trust Fund. Vol. 1 (Spring 1990)-. Periodical. English. an. $18.95. Reich Museum, PO Box 687, Rangeley ME 04970. **Tel** (207)864-3443. **DD** 150. Index available. cum. index. ctrl circ.

IT/0048-2285
**OSPEDALE PSICHIATRICO.** [Osp. psichiatr.]. (1933)-. Academic Scholarly Publication. English. Four times a year. USL 42, Via Don Bosco, 80100 Naples Italy. **Tel** 011 39 81 7801811. **CODEN** OSPSA3.
**Ind/Abst** EMBASE.

US/0891-9208
**OUR TIMES.** *Ceased.* Vol. 1, No. 1 (July 1986)-(March 1987). Periodical. English. mo. Our Times / Texas, PO Box 1046, Manchaca TX 78652. **DD** 051.

FR
**PASCAL. 65, PSYCHOLOGIE, PSYCHOPATHOLOGIE, PSYCHIATRIE. See** Psychology.

AU/0253-5254
**PERSONATION AND PSYCHOTHERAPY.** [Person. psychother.]. Vol. 1 (1976)-. Monographic series. English (Italian and German). ir. Price varies per volume. Resch Verlag, Maximilianstr 8, Postfach 8, A-6010 Innsbruck Austria. **NLM** W1 PE864.

●CN/1193-1248
**PERSPECTIVES / ALBERTA ASSOCIATION OF REGISTERED OCCUPATIONAL THERAPISTS.** [Perspect. - Alta. Assoc. Regist. Occup. Ther.]. **Added/Corp** Alberta Association of Registered Occupational Therapists. Vol. 20, No. 9 (Mar. 1992). Periodical. English. mo. Alberta Association of Registered Occupational Therapists, Suite 311, 4245-97 Street, Whitemund Business Park 1, Edmonton Alberta T6E 5Y7 Canada. **DD** 615.8/515/060713. **Continues** AAROT Newsletter., 0831-6061.

US/0031-5990
**PERSPECTIVES IN PSYCHIATRIC CARE. See** Medical Science and Technology-Nursing.

UK
**PERSPECTIVES IN PSYCHIATRY.** Vol. 1 (1991)-. Monographic series. English. Price varies per volume. John Wiley & Sons Ltd., Baffins Lane, Chichester West Sussex PO19 1UD England. **Tel** 0243 779777, FAX 0243 776128 BTG:JWP001, telex 86290 WIBOOKG. **(Subscription address:** North, South and Central America/ John Wiley & Sons, Inc., Subscription Department, 605 Third Avenue, New York, NY 10158-0012, USA; telephone: (212)850-6645; FAX: (212)850-6021) **NLM** W1; PE871F.

FR/0031-6032
**PERSPECTIVES PSYCHIATRIQUES PARIS.** [Perspect. psychiatr. Paris]. (1963)-. Periodical. French. Five times a year. 362.39F France; 440.00F others. Galliena Promotion, 58 A rue du Dessous des Berges, 75013 Paris France. **Tel** 011 33 1 45849766. **UDC** 616.89.

GW/0176-3679
**PHARMACOPSYCHIATRY. See** Pharmacy and Pharmacology.

GW/0936-9589
**PHARMACOPSYCHIATRY SUPPLEMENT. See** Pharmacy and Pharmacology.

US
**PHILOSOPHY, PSYCHIATRY, & PSYCHOLOGY. See** Philosophy.

CN/0710-1457
**PHOENIX RISING (TORONTO, ONT.).** *Ceased.* (PHOENIX RISING.). [Phoenix rising]. Vol. 1 No. 1 (Spring 1980)-Vol. 8 No. 3 (1992). Periodical. English. ir (two to four issues per year). Phoenix Rising / Ontario, PO Box 7251 Station A, Toronto Ontario M5W 1X9 Canada. **Tel** (416)929-2079. **DD** 362.2/1/09713. **NLM** W1; PH419T. Index available. **Bk Rev. Ad Acc. Circ:** 3,000 (ctrl).
 **Desc:** Outspoken advocate of psychiatric inmates' rights and a critic of psychiatric oppression.
**Ind/Abst** Altern. Press Index (-1992).

SZ
**PMS AKTUELL. VAT** Pro Mente Sana Aktuell. Periodical. German (French and Italian). qt. 25.00F. Pro Mente Sana, Freiestr 26, 8570 Weinfelden Switzerland. **LC** RA790.A1; P538. **DD** 362.2/09494/05.

AG
**PORTAVOZ PICHONIANO. See** Psychology.

US/0896-5358
**PRACTICAL REVIEWS IN PSYCHIATRY (BIRMINGHAM, ALA.).** (PRACTICAL REVIEWS IN PSYCHIATRY [SOUND RECORDING].). [Pract. rev. psychiatry]. **Added/Corp** Educational Reviews, Inc. Montefiore Medical Center. **VFOAT** Practical Reviews. Vol. 1, No. 1 (1976)-. Periodical. English. mo. $175.00 Physicians/Dentists; $125.00 Residents. Educational Reviews Inc., 6801 Cahaba Valley Road, Birmingham AL 35242. **Tel** (205)991-5188, (800)633-4743, FAX (205)995-1926. **DD** 616.
 **Desc:** Summary: Abstract cards of articles found in the journal literature.

US/0196-8459
**PRATT INSTITUTE CREATIVE ARTS THERAPY REVIEW.** [Pratt Inst. creat. arts ther. rev.]. **Added/Corp** Pratt Institute. Creative Arts Therapy Dept. Masters of Professional Studies Graduate Program. **VFOAT** Creative Arts Therapy Review. Vol. 1 (1980)-. English. an. $8.00. Pratt Institute, 200 Willoughby Avenue, Brooklyn NY 11205. **Tel** (718)636-3428. **ED** Estelle Peisach. **LC** RC489.A7; P73. **DD** 616.89/1656. **Circ:** 400 (ctrl).
 **Desc:** Contains articles pertaining to issues such as transference, countertransference, the use of creative movement and the role of aggression as applied to the creative arts therapies.
**Ind/Abst** Psychol. Abstr. (1980-); PsycINFO; PsycLit.

GW/0032-7034
**PRAXIS DER KINDERPSYCHOLOGIE UND KINDERPSYCHIATRIE. See** Psychology.

GW
**PRAXIS DER KINDERPSYCHOLOGIE UND KINDERPSYCHIATRIE BEIHEFT. See** Psychology.

GW/0933-842X
**PRAXIS DER KLINISCHEN VERHALTENSMEDIZIN UND REHABILITATION.** 1. Jahrg., Heft 1 (Marz 1988)-. Periodical. German. qt. DM86.00. Verlag Modernes Lernen Dortmund, Hohe Str 39, Postfach 10 05 55, W-4600 Dortmund 1 Germany. **Tel** 0231/128008, FAX 0231/125640. **ED** Manfred Sielke and Zochen Sturm. **NLM** W1; PR319H. Index available. **Bk Rev. Ad Acc. Circ:** 1,260.
 **Desc:** Covers behavioral medicine and rehabilitation.

●UK/1355-2570
**PRIMARY CARE PSYCHIATRY.** (March 1995)-. English. qt. $255.00 US; £150.00 other. Rapid Communications of Oxford Ltd, The Old Malthouse, Paradise Street, Oxford OX1 1LD England. **Tel** 011 44 0865 790447, FAX 011 44 0865 244012, telex 9403712. **ED** Dr. George Beaumont.
 **Desc:** Provides an international medium for material relevant to all aspects of the management of psychiatric illness in the community. Publishes review articles and original research papers, along with literature reviews and debates on controversial issues.

US/0161-8776
**PRIMARY PREVENTION OF PSYCHOPATHOLOGY. Added/Corp** University of Vermont. Vol. 1 (1975)-. Monographic series. English. ir. price varies per volume. SAGE Periodical Press, 2455 Teller Road, Thousand Oaks CA 91320. **Tel** (805)499-0721, FAX (805)499-0871, telex 100799. **ED** G. W. Albee and J. M. Joffe. **LC** RC454; .P683. **NLM** W3 PR945CK. Index available.
 **Desc:** Source of up-to-date information on research and conceptualization in the field of primary prevention of psychopathology.

US/0162-9913
**PRIVATE PSYCHIATRIC HOSPITALS. See** Medical Science and Technology-Hospital Administration and Medical Centers.

●US/1056-7151
**PROGRESS IN EXPERIMENTAL PERSONALITY AND PSYCHOPATHOLOGY RESEARCH.** [Prog. exp. pers. psychopathol. res.]. **Added/Corp** Society for Research in Psychopathology. **VFOAT** Progress in Experimental Personality and Psychopathology Research. (1992)-. Periodical. English. ir. $49.95 (Volume 17). Springer Publishing Company, 536 Broadway, New York NY 10012-3955. **Tel** (212)431-4370, FAX (212)941-7842. **LC** BF698; .P68. **DD** 137.072. **Continues** Progress in Experimental Personality Research, 0079-6255.

UK/0278-5846
**PROGRESS IN NEURO-PSYCHOPHARMACOLOGY & BIOLOGICAL PSYCHIATRY. See** Pharmacy and Pharmacology.

IT/0393-9774
**PSICHIATRIA E PSICOTERAPIA ANALITICA.** [Psichiatr. psicoter. anal.]. **VFOAT** Analytic Psychotherapy and Psychopathology. (1982)-. Periodical. Italian (English). qt. $70.00 US; 50000.00F (individuals), 70000.00F (institutions) other. Giovanni Fioriti, V Trionfale 11224, 00135 Rome Italy. **Tel** 011 39 6 30818097, FAX 011 30 6 30818097. **ED** Nicola Ciarni. **UDC** 616.89. **Bk Rev. Ad Acc. Circ:** 4,000 (ctrl).
 **Desc:** Psychiatry from cultural, human, ethological, and biological points of view.
**Ind/Abst** Psychol. Abstr. (1986-); PsycINFO (1986-); PsycLit.

IT
**PSICHIATRIA E TERRITORIO.** (19??)-. Periodical. Italian. Three times a year. L60000 institution; L40000 individual. Max Maur S.N.C., Via del Molinetto 1, 55022 Bagni di Lucca, Italy. **Tel** 011 39 583 87992.

IT/0555-5299
**PSICHIATRIA GENERALE E DELL'ETA EVOLUTIVA.** [Psichiatr. gen. eta evol.]. (1963)-. Periodical. Italian (summaries and/or abstracts in English). qt. L60000.00 Italy; L120000.00 other. La Garangola, Via Montona 4, 35137 Padua Italy. **Tel** 011 39 49 8750550, FAX 011 39 49 8751743. **UDC** 616.89. cum. index. **Bk Rev. Ad Acc. Adv Mgr:** A. Pagamento. **Pr Rev.** ctrl circ.

IT/0393-6902
**PSICOANALISI CONTRO.** [Psicoanal. contro]. (1985)-. Periodical. Italian (summaries and/or abstracts in English and French). Three times a year. L40000.00 Italy; L50000.00 other. Psicoanalisi Contro, Via Arenula 21, 00186 Rome Italy. **Tel** 011 39 6 6867495, FAX (6)686-7509, telex 6899552. **ED** Sandro Gindro. **UDC** 159.9642. Index available. cum. index. **Bk Rev. Ad Acc.**
 **Desc:** Magazine of psychoanalysis, culture and arts.

SP/0211-5549
**PSICOPATOLOGIA.** (PSICOPATOLOGIA : PS.). [Psicopatologia]. **VFOAT** PS. (1981)-. Periodical. Spanish (summaries and/or abstracts in English; table of contents in English). qt (Jan., Apr., July, Oct.). $73.00 Spain; $63.00 other. Editorial Garsi SA, Juan Bravo 46, 28006 Madrid, Spain. **Tel** 011 34 1 4021212, telex 98358 GARSI E. **NLM** W1; PS166. **CODEN** PSICE3. Documents available from BIOSIS Document Express.
**Ind/Abst** Biol. Abstr.; EMBASE [Select. Cov.]; Indice Med. Esp.

IT
**PSICOTERAPIA E SCIENZE UMANE.** (1967)-. Periodical. Italian. Three times a year. L88000 Italy; L125000 other. Franco Angeli Riviste SRL, Viale Monza 106, 20127 Milan Italy. **Tel** 011 39 2 2827651, 011 39 2 289562. cum. index.

YU/0350-2538
**PSIHIJATRIJA DANAS.** [Psihijatr. danas]. **Added/Corp** Savremena Cdministracija. Zavod Za Mentalno Zdravlje. **VFOAT** Psychiatry Today. (1976)-. Academic Scholarly Publication. Serbo-Croatian (Roman) (summaries and/or abstracts in English and French). qt. $30.00. Instituta Za Mentalno Zdravlje, Palmoticeva 37/IV, Belgrad Yugoslavia. **NLM** W1 PS18F. **CODEN**

AZMZB7. ***Continues*** *Anali Zavoda za Mentalno Zdravlje.*
**Ind/Abst** EMBASE; Psychol. Abstr. (1976-?); PsycINFO (1969-); PsycLit.

SP/0210-8348
**PSIQUIS.** (PSIQUIS.). [Psiquis]. (1979)-. Periodical. Spanish. Ten times a year. 7500ptas Spain; $80.00 Europe; $120.00 others. Alpe Editores SA, C Pedro Rico 27, Oficinas 11 & 12, 28029 Madrid Spain. **Tel** 011 34 1 7338811, FAX 011 34 1 3159652. **NLM** W1 PS182T. **Bk Rev. Ad Acc, Adv Mgr:** Carmen Acuadez. **Circ:** 6,000 (ctrl).
**Desc:** Themes related to psychiatry.
**Ind/Abst** Indice Med. Esp.; Psychol. Abstr. (1981-); PsycINFO (1990-); PsycLit.

FR/0242-9616
**PSYCHANALYSTES.** ***Ceased.*** [Psychanalystes]. (1981)-(June 1994). Periodical. French. qt. College de Psychanalystes, 13 Rue Fallampin, 75015 Paris France. **UDC** 159.964.2-05.
**Ind/Abst** PsycINFO (1986-); PsycLit.

CI/0353-5053
**PSYCHIATRIA DANUBINA.** [Psychiatria Danub.]. (1989)-. Periodical. Multiple languages. qt. University of Zagreb / Sveuciliste u Zagrebu, PO Box 815, TRG Marsala Tita 14, 41000 Zagreb Croatia. **Tel** (041)272-411. **UDC** 616.89.
**Ind/Abst** EMBASE [Select. Cov.].

JA/0033-2658
**PSYCHIATRIA ET NEUROLOGIA JAPONICA.** (SEISHIN SHINKEIGAKU ZASSHI.). [Psychiatr. neurol. Jpn.]. (1935)-. Academic Scholarly Publication. Japanese (summaries and/or abstracts in English). mo. $307.50. Nihon Seishin Shinkei Gakkai, (Japanese Soc. of Psychiatry & Neurology), 38-11, Hongo 3 Chome, Bunkyoku, Tokyoto 113, Japan. **(Subscription address:** Japan Publications Trading Company, Ltd., PO Box 5030, Tokyo International, Tokyo 100-31 Japan.**)** **NLM** W1 SE259. **CODEN** SSHZAS. Documents available from BIOSIS Document Express, CASDDS. ***Continues*** *Neurologia.*
**Ind/Abst** Biol. Abstr.; Chem. Abstr.; EMBASE; Index Med.

IT/0079-7227
**PSYCHIATRIA FENNICA.** [Psychiatr. fenn.]. **VFOAT** Finnish Psychiatry. 1970-. English. Akakeeminen-Kirjakuppa, PO Box 128, 00101 Helsinki Finland. **Tel** 011/358/0/90/12141, FAX +358 0 121 4441, telex 125080 AKAHE SF. **LC** RC321. **DD** 616.89/005. **UDC** 616.89. **NLM** W1 PS239E. **CODEN** PSFNBI.
**Desc:** Yearbook for 1970 includes a history of the Lapinlahte Hospital, the former name of the Psychiatric Clinic.
**Ind/Abst** Cumul. Index Nurs. Allied Health Lit.; EMBASE; Psychol. Abstr. (1972-); PsycINFO; PsycLit.

PL/0033-2674
**PSYCHIATRIA POLSKA.** [Psychiatr. pol.]. **Added/Corp** Polskie Towarzystwo Psychiatryczne. Vol. 1 (Jan./Feb. 1967)-. Academic Scholarly Publication. Polish (table of contents in English and Russian). bm. Price on Request. **(Subscription address:** ARS Polona, PO Box 1001, 00068 Warsaw Poland.**)** **NLM** W1 PS239K. **CODEN** PSPOB3. Index Available, published separately, free-automatically sent. ***Supersedes in part*** *Neurologia, Neurochirurgia I Psychiatria Polska.*
**Ind/Abst** EMBASE; Index Med.; Psychol. Abstr. (1972-); PsycINFO (?-?); PsycLit; SportSearch.

US/1042-041X
**PSYCHIATRIC ABSTRACTS AND COMMENT.** ***Ceased.*** [Psychiatr. abstr. comment]. No. 1 (April 1989)-?. Periodical. English. mo. Churchill Livingstone Inc., 650 Avenue of the Americas, New York NY 10011. **Tel** (212)206-5062, FAX (212)727-7808. **ED** Samuel B Guze. **DD** 616.

US/0048-5713
**PSYCHIATRIC ANNALS.** [Psychiatr. ann.]. Vol. 1 (Sept 1971)-. Academic Scholarly Publication. English. mo. $120.00 institution, $110.00 individual (US). Slack Inc., 6900 Grove Road, Thorofare NJ 08086. **Tel** (609)848-1000, (800)257-8290, FAX (609)853-5991, telex 517108 SLACK INC VD. **ED** John Carter. **LC** RC321; .P892. **DD** 616.89/005. **NLM** W1 PS249. **CODEN** PSANCS. **[CCC]. Bk Rev. Ad Acc. Pr Rev. Circ:** 28,000 (ctrl). available on microfilm and microfiche from University Microfilms International (UMI). Documents available from The Genuine Article.
**Desc:** Features articles on new developments that will affect the practice of psychiatry in the U.S.
**Ind/Abst** Curr. Contents Soc. Behav. Sci.; EMBASE; Middle East Abstr. Index; Psychol. Abstr. (1971-); PsycINFO; PsycLit; Res. Alert [Full Cov.]; Soc. Sci. Cit. Index [Full Cov.].

UK/0955-6036
**PSYCHIATRIC BULLETIN OF THE ROYAL COLLEGE OF PSYCHIATRISTS.** (PSYCHIATRIC BULLETIN.). [Psychiatr. bull. R. Coll. Psychiatr.]. **Added/Corp** Royal College of Psychiatrists. **VFOAT** Psychiatric Bulletin of the Royal College of Psychiatrists. Vol. 12, No. 10 (Oct. 1988)-. Bulletin. English. Twelve times a year. $60.00 US; £40.00 other. Royal Society of Medicine Press, 1 Wimpole Street, London W1M 8AE England. **Tel** 011 44 71 2902928. **ED** Alan Kerr and Greg Wilkinson. **NLM** W1; PS239KB. **Bk Rev. Circ:** 7,000. ***Continues*** *Bulletin of the Royal College of Psychiatrists, 0140-0789.*
**Desc:** Contains articles, correspondence and news of general interest to psychiatrists.

US/0193-953X
**PSYCHIATRIC CLINICS OF NORTH AMERICA, THE.** [Psychiatr. clin. North Am.]. Vol. 1, No. 1 (April 1978)-. Monographic series. English. qt. $94.00 (individual), $117.00 (institution) US; $127.00 (individual), $135.00 (institution) other. W.B. Saunders Company, A Subsidiary of Harcourt Brace Jovanovich, Inc., The Curtis Center/Suite 300, Independence Square West, Philadelphia PA 19106-3399. **Tel** (215)238-7800 or, 5587, FAX (215)238-7883, telex 173146. **(Subscription address:** W. B. Saunders Company / North America Subscriptions, c/o Periodicals, 6277 Sea Harbour Drive, 4th Floor, Orlando FL 32887.**)** **ED** Brenda Frank. **LC** RC321; .P894. **DD** 616.89. **NLM** W1 PS255. **[CCC].** Index available. **Pr Rev. Circ:** 3,500. available on microfilm and microfiche from University Microfilms International (UMI). Documents available from The Genuine Article.
**Desc:** Practical updates for the clinician on the latest advances. Each issue addresses a single topic in patient care.
**Ind/Abst** Cumul. Index Nurs. Allied Health Lit.; Curr. Contents Soc. Behav. Sci.; EMBASE; Index Med.; Physic. Medline Plus; Psychol. Abstr. (1982-); PsycINFO; PsycLit; Res. Alert [Full Cov.]; Soc. Sci. Cit. Index [Full Cov.].

US/0033-2690
**PSYCHIATRIC FORUM, THE.** [Psychiatr. forum]. **Added/Corp** William S. Hall Psychiatric Institute. Vol. 1, No. 1 (Winter 1969)-. Periodical. English. Twice a year (May, Oct.). Free. WS Hall Psychiatric Institute, Box 202, Columbia SC 29202. **Tel** (803)758-7154, (803)734-7154. **ED** Lucius C. Pressley. **LC** RC321; .P896. **NLM** W1 PS256R. **CODEN** PSYFAKPSYAKOPSFYA. **Bk Rev. Circ:** 4,000 (ctrl).
**Desc:** Contents are original articles related to mental health.
**Ind/Abst** Cumul. Index Nurs. Allied Health Lit.; EMBASE; Psychol. Abstr. (1971-); PsycINFO; PsycLit.

UK/0955-8829
**PSYCHIATRIC GENETICS. See** Biology-Genetics.

US/0885-7717
**PSYCHIATRIC HOSPITAL, THE.** ***Ceased.*** **See** Medical Science and Technology-Hospital Administration and Medical Centers.

US/0898-0543
**PSYCHIATRIC LENGTH OF STAY BY DIAGNOSIS, UNITED STATES. See** Medical Science and Technology-Hospital Administration and Medical Centers.

US/0898-0527
**PSYCHIATRIC LENGTH OF STAY BY DIAGNOSIS, UNITED STATES, NORTHEASTERN REGION. See** Medical Science and Technology-Hospital Administration and Medical Centers.

US/0898-0519
**PSYCHIATRIC LENGTH OF STAY BY DIAGNOSIS, UNITED STATES, SOUTHERN REGION. See** Medical Science and Technology-Hospital Administration and Medical Centers.

US/0898-0535
**PSYCHIATRIC LENGTH OF STAY BY DIAGNOSIS. UNITED STATES, WESTERN REGION. See** Medical Science and Technology-Hospital Administration and Medical Centers.

US/0732-0868
**PSYCHIATRIC MEDICINE.** ***Ceased.*** [Psychiatr. med.]. Vol. 1, No. 1 (Jan. 1983)-Vol.10 No.4 (Nov. 1992). Periodical. English. qt. SP Medical & Scientific Books, 200 Park Avenue, New York NY 10003-1503. **Tel** (718)658-0888. **ED** Richard C W Hall. **DD** 616. **UDC** 616.89. **NLM** W1 PS26J. **CODEN** PSMDEQ. **Circ:** 500. Documents available from BIOSIS Document Express.
**Desc:** This journal leads the way for new directions in medical psychiatry.
**Ind/Abst** Biol. Abstr. (1985-); Index Med. (1983-); PsycINFO (?-?).

US/0163-1721
**PSYCHIATRIC MEDICINE UPDATE.** 1979-. Academic Scholarly Publication. English. an. Elsevier Science Publishing Company Inc, Madison Square Station, PO Box 882, New York NY 10159-0882. **Tel** (212)633-3950, FAX (212)633-3990. **LC** RC321; .P897. **DD** 616.89/005. **UDC** 616.89. **NLM** W1 PS26K.

US/0033-2704
**PSYCHIATRIC NEWS.** [Psych. news]. Vol. 1- (Jan. 1966)-. Periodical. English. sm. $60.00 US; $80.00 other (institution). American Psychiatric Association, 1400 K Street Northwest, Washington DC 20005. **Tel** (202)682-6240, FAX (202)682-6114. **ED** Robert J Campbell III. **LC** RC321; .P898. **UDC** 616.89. **NLM** W1 PS26T. **Ad Acc. Circ:** 35,400. available on microfilm and microfiche from University Microfilms International (UMI). ***Continues*** *Newsletter - American Psychiatric Association.*
**Desc:** Delivers up-to-the-minute information on everything from government and legislative activities to the latest developments in the drug and therapy fields. Concise articles provide timely information on grants, meetings, seminars, and on the activities of the APA and other professional societies.
**Ind/Abst** Crim. Penol. Police Sci. Abstr.; Hospit. Health Admin. Index; Index Period. Artic. Relat. Law; Soc. Work Abstr. [Select. Cov.].

US/0091-0422
**PSYCHIATRIC OUTPATIENT PROGRAM. Main/Corp** Hawaii. Mental Health Division. Research & Records Services. English. an. Hawaii Department of Health / Mental Health Division, Honolulu HI 96813. **LC** RC445.H32; H38A. **DD** 362.2/1. **UDC** 351.77:613.865(799). **NLM** W2 AH3 M5PA.

US/0033-2720
**PSYCHIATRIC QUARTERLY.** [Psychiatr. q.]. **Added/Corp** New York (State). Dept. of Mental Hygiene. Vol. 1, No. 1 (Jan. 1927)-. Academic Scholarly Publication. English. qt. $245.00 US; $285.00 other. Human Sciences Press, PO Box 735, 233 Spring Street, New York NY 10013. **Tel** (212)620-8000, FAX (212)807-1047, telex 23421139. **(Subscription address:** Eurospan Ltd., Journals and Serials Division, 3 Henrietta Street, Covent Garden, London WC2E 8LU England.**)** **ED** Stephen Rachlin and Raul Vispo. **DD** 616. **NLM** W1 PS262. **CODEN** PSQUAP. **[CCC].** available on microfilm and microfiche from University Microfilms International (UMI). Documents available from BIOSIS Document Express. ***Continues*** *State Hospitals Quarterly.*
**Desc:** Maintaining the standards of excellence established over a long and distinguished history, this journal has two major objectives: to be an independent voice, openly speaking its mind in the field of mental illness care, and to assist mental health professionals, particularly those in policy making areas, in keeping up with pertinent scientific and delivery system data. It includes articles on the social, clinical, administrative, political and ethical aspects of mental illness care.
**Ind/Abst** Biol. Abstr.; Cumul. Index Nurs. Allied Health Lit.; EMBASE; Index Med.; Index Period. Artic. Relat. Law (19??-19??); Psychol. Abstr. (1977-); PsycINFO; PsycLit; Soc. Plann. Policy Dev. Abstr.

US/1058-1693
**PSYCHIATRIC RESIDENT.** ***Ceased.*** (1991)-(Feb. 1994). Periodical. English. bm. Slack Inc., 6900 Grove Road, Thorofare NJ 08086. **Tel** (609)848-1000, (800)257-8290, FAX (609)853-5991, telex 517108 SLACK INC VD.

US/0893-2905
**PSYCHIATRIC TIMES, THE.** (198?)-. Periodical. English. mo. $120.00 US; $200.00 other. CME Incorporated, 1924 East Deere Avenue, Santa Ana CA 92705. **Tel** (714)250-1008, FAX (714)250-0445. **ED** John L. Schwartz. **DD** 616. **NLM** W1; PS29. **Bk Rev. Ad Acc. Pr Rev. Circ:** 42,000 (ctrl).
**Desc:** Educational service to psychiatrists and psychiatrically-sensitive primary care physicians who require a working knowledge of advances in the treatment of mental illness.

FR/0079-726X
**PSYCHIATRIE DE L'ENFANT, LA.** [Psychiatr. enfant]. Vol. 1 (1958)-. Academic Scholarly Publication. French (summaries and/or abstracts in English and Spanish). sa. 390.00F France; 460.00F other. Presses Universitaires de France, Department des Revues, 14 Avenue du Bois de l'Epine, BP 90, 91003 Evry Cedex France. **Tel** (1)60 77 82 05, FAX (1) 60 79 20 45, telex PUF 600 474 F. **NLM** W1 PS332. **CODEN** PSYEAH. **[CCC]. Pr Rev.** Documents available from The Genuine Article.
**Desc:** Contemporary child psychiatry is explored in articles detailing original research, personal ideas and theory.
**Ind/Abst** Curr. Contents Soc. Behav. Sci.; EMBASE; Index Med.; PsycINFO; PsycLit; Res. Alert [Full Cov.]; Soc. Sci. Cit. Index [Full Cov.].

BE
**PSYCHIATRIE EN VERPLEGING.** French. bm. 300.00F. Psychiatrie en Verpleging, Stropstraat 119, 9000 Gent Belgium. **Tel** 011 32 91 2213309.
**Desc:** Articles about psychiatric nursing and related sciences.

FR
**PSYCHIATRIE : ENCYCLOPEDIE MEDICO CHIRURGICALE.** French. bm. 3294.00F. Editions Techniques, 141 rue de Javel, 75747 Paris Cedex 15 France. **Tel** 011 33 1 45589100.

FR/1147-7970
**PSYCHIATRIE MAGAZINE ROYAN.** (PSYCHIATRIE MAGAZINE.). [Psychiatr. mag. Royan]. (1990)-. Periodical. French. mo (10 issues). 84.32F France; 130.00F other. MPH Editions, 8 Bis Av des

Vagues, BP 521, 17211 Royan Cedex France. **Tel** 011 33 46384267. **UDC** 616.89. ***Continues*** *Psychiatrie Pratique du Medecin (1986), 0992-4280.*

GW
**PSYCHIATRIE, NEUROLOGIE UND MEDIZINISCHE PSYCHOLOGIE. BEIHEFTE.** No. 1/2 (1963)-. Periodical. German. ir. S. Hirzel Verlag Leipzig, Sternwartenstrasse 8, D 04103 Leipzig Germany. **NLM** W1 PS338.
**Ind/Abst** Index Med.

CN/1180-5501
**PSYCHIATRIE, RECHERCHE ET INTERVENTION EN SANTE MENTALE DE L'ENFANT : P.R.I.S.M.E.** [P.R.I.S.M.E., Psychiatr. rech. interv. sante ment. enfant]. **Added/Corp** Hopital Sainte-Justine. Departement de Psychiatrie. **VFOAT** P.R.I.S.M.E; Prisme. (1990)-. Periodical. French. qt. 70.00F (institutions), 38.00F (individuals) Canada; 80.00F (institutions), 50.00F (individuals) other. Hopital Sainte-Justine Cise, 3175 Cote Ste-Catherine, Montreal, Quebec H3T 1C5 Canada. **Tel** (514)731-4931. **DD** 618.92/89/005. **Bk Rev. Ad Acc.**

GW/0303-4259
**PSYCHIATRISCHE PRAXIS.** [Psychiatr. Prax.]. Vol. 1 (March 1974)-. Academic Scholarly Publication. German (summaries and/or abstracts in English). bm. $120.00. Georg Thieme Verlag Stuttgart, Postfach 301120, D 70451 Stuttgart Germany. **Tel** 011 49 711 89310, FAX 011 49 711 8931298, telex 7 252 275 GTVD. **(Subscription address:** Thieme Medical Publishers Inc., 381 Park Avenue South, New York NY 10016.**) NLM** W1 PS348N. **[CCC]. Pr Rev.** available on microfilm from University Microfilms International (UMI). Documents available from The Genuine Article.
**Ind/Abst** Curr. Contents Soc. Behav. Sci.; EMBASE; Index Med.; Int. Nurs. Index; Res. Alert [Full Cov.]; Soc. Sci. Cit. Index [Full Cov.].

US/1050-6489
**PSYCHIATRIST'S CLINICAL UPDATE.** (PSYCHIATRIST'S CLINICAL UPDATE : A MONTHLY DIGEST OF NEW DEVELOPMENTS IN PSYCHIATRY / SPONSORED BY ALBERT EINSTEIN COLLEGE OF MEDICINE/MONTEFIORE MEDICAL CENTER.). [Psychiatr. clin. update]. **Added/Corp** Albert Einstein College of Medicine. Montefiore Medical Center. (1990)-. Periodical. English. mo. $135.00 Physicians, $95.00 Residents US; $150.00 Physicians, $110.00 Residents Other. Educational Reviews Inc., 6801 Cahaba Valley Road, Birmingham AL 35242. **Tel** (205)991-5188, (800)633-4743, FAX (205)995-1926. **DD** 616.

US/0276-4393
**PSYCHIATRIST'S COMPENDIUM OF DRUG THERAPY, THE.** (THE PSYCHIATRIST'S COMPENDIUM OF DRUG THERAPY : A PUBLICATION OF BIOMEDICAL INFORMATION CORPORATION.). [Psychiatr. compend. drug ther.]. **Added/Corp** Biomedical Information Corporation. **VFOAT** Compendium of Drug Therapy. (1982)-. English. an. Biomedical Information Corporation, 800 Second Avenue, New York NY 10017. **Tel** (212)262-9662.

US
**PSYCHIATRY.** (1985)-. English. ir. J.B. Lippincott Company, 227 East Washington Square, Philadelphia PA 19106-3780. **Tel** (215)238-4200 or 4454, FAX (215)238-4227. **ED** Jesse O Cavenar.

US/0363-8952
**PSYCHIATRY AND THE HUMANITIES.** **Added/Corp** Forum on Psychiatry and the Humanities. Vol. 1 (1976)-. Monographic series. English. ir. $20.00. Johns Hopkins University Press, 2715 North Charles Street, Baltimore MD 21218-4319. **Tel** (410)516-6987, FAX (410)516-6968. **LC** RC321; .P943. **DD** 616.8/9/005. **NLM** W1 PS354T.

US/0278-4602
**PSYCHIATRY DIGEST (1979).** (PSYCHIATRY DIGEST.). [Psychiatr. dig.]. Began with Aug./Sept. 1979 issue. Periodical. English. qt. $20.00. Medical Digest, 444 Frontage Road, PO Box 8021, Northfield IL 60093. **LC** RC321; .P95. **DD** 616.89/005. **UDC** 616.89. **NLM** W1 PS356M. available on microfilm and microfiche from University Microfilms International (UMI). ***Continues*** *Journal of Continuing Education in Psychiatry, 0149-0265.*

US/0894-4873
**PSYCHIATRY DRUG ALERTS.** [Psychiatry drug alerts]. (198?)-. Periodical. English. Twelve times a year. $59.00 US; $76.00 Canada; $83.00 other. M. J. Powers and Company Publishers, 374 Millburn Avenue, Millburn NJ 07041. **Tel** (201)467-4556. **DD** 615.

US/0271-1311
**PSYCHIATRY (GLENDALE, CALIF.).** (PSYCHIATRY [SOUND RECORDING].). [Psychiatry]. **Added/Corp** Audio-Digest Foundation. **VFOAT** Audio-Digest Psychiatry; Audio Digest Psychiatry. Vol. 1, No. 1 (July 10, 1972)-. Periodical. English. sm. $179.76 US; $202.80 Canada; $247.44 other. Audio-Digest Foundation, 1577 Chevy Chase Drive, Glendale CA 91206. **Tel** (213)245-8505, (800)423-2308, FAX (818)240-7379. **DD** 616. **NLM** W1 AU201DW.

UK/0262-5377
**PSYCHIATRY IN PRACTICE.** [Psychiatry pract.]. Vol. 1, No. 1 (Sept. 1981)-. Periodical. English. qt. £30.00 UK; £34.00 other. Hayward Medical Communications, 44 Earlham Street Covent Garden, London WC2H 9LA England. **Tel** 011 44 71 240 4493. **(Subscription address:** Hayward Medical Communications, Essex House Cromwell, Park Chipping, Norton Oxon OX7 5SR England.**) ED** George Beaumont. **UDC** 616.89. **NLM** W1 PS357M. **Bk Rev. Ad Acc. Circ:** 20,800 (ctrl).
**Desc:** Articles on management and treatment of psychiatric and neurological disease states, research, book reviews, news for psychiatrists and neurologists.

US/1062-3523
**PSYCHIATRY MALPRACTICE PROTECTOR.** ***Ceased.*** [Psychiatry malpract. prot.]. **Added/Corp** American Health Consultants. Vol. 1, No. 1 (July 1991)-(1992). Periodical. English. mo. American Health Consultants, 3525 Piedmont Road, Suite 400, Atlanta GA 30305. **Tel** (800)688-2421, (404)262-7436. **DD** 346.

US/0897-6317
**PSYCHIATRY (NORWALK, CONN.).** (PSYCHIATRY.). [Psychiatry]. (1989)-. English. ir. Appleton & Lange, (A Subsidiary of Simon & Schuster), 25 Van Zant Street, East Norwalk CT 06855. **Tel** (203)838-4400, (800)423-1359, FAX (203)854-9486. **DD** 616. **NLM** WM 34; P974.

IE/0165-1781
**PSYCHIATRY RESEARCH.** [Psychiatry res.]. **VFOAT** Psychiatry Research. Neuroimaging; Neuroimaging. Vol. 1 (July 1979)-. Academic Scholarly Publication. English. Fifteen times a year (5 vols.). $1063.00; $1126.00 with Neuroimaging Section. Elsevier Science Ireland Ltd., Bay 15, Shannon Industrial Estate, Co Clare Ireland. **Tel** 011 353 61 471944. **ED** Monte S. Buchsbaum, Frederick K. Goodwin, and Sherry Buchsbaum. **NLM** W1 PS358. **CODEN** PSRSDR. **[CCC]. Pr Rev.** available on microfilm and microfiche from University Microfilms International (UMI). Documents available from The Genuine Article, BIOSIS Document Express, CASDDS.
**Desc:** Provides very rapid publication of short but complete research reports in the field of psychiatry.
**Ind/Abst** Biol. Abstr.; Chem. Abstr.; Curr. Aware. Biol. Sci., CABS; Curr. Contents Life Sci.; EMBASE; Index Med.; Life Sci. Collect.; PESTDOC; Psychol. Abstr. (1979-); PsycINFO; PsycLit; Ref. Upd. Deluxe Ed.; Res. Alert [Full Cov.]; Sci. Cit. Index; SCISEARCH; Soc. Sci. Cit. Index [Select. Cov.]; SportSearch.

IE/0925-4927
**PSYCHIATRY RESEARCH : NEUROIMAGING SECTION.** (19??)-. Academic Scholarly Publication. English. Four times a year (1 volume). $170.00. Elsevier Science Ireland Ltd., Bay 15, Shannon Industrial Estate, Co Clare Ireland. **Tel** 011 353 61 471944. **[CCC].** Documents available from The Genuine Article, ADONIS.
**Ind/Abst** ADONIS; Curr. Aware. Biol. Sci., CABS; Curr. Contents Life Sci.; EMBASE; Psychol. Abstr. (1990-); PsycINFO; PsycLit; Ref. Upd. Deluxe Ed.; Res. Alert [Full Cov.]; Sci. Cit. Index; SCISEARCH; Soc. Sci. Cit. Index [Select. Cov.].

US/0033-2747
**PSYCHIATRY (WASHINGTON, D.C.).** (PSYCHIATRY.). [Psychiatry]. **Added/Corp** William Alanson White Psychiatric Foundation. Washington School of Psychiatry. **VFOAT** Psychiatry, Interpersonal and Biological Processes. Vol. 1 (Feb. 1938)-. Academic Scholarly Publication. English. Four times a year. $115.00 (institutions); $135.00 others. Guilford Publications Inc., 72 Spring Street, New York NY 10012. **Tel** (212)431-9800, (800)365-7006, FAX (212)966-6708. **(Subscription address:** Turpin Distribution Services Limited, Blackhorse Road, Letchworth, Hertfordshire SG6 1HN, United Kingdom.**) ED** David Reiss. **LC** RC321; .P93. **DD** 132.05; 159.9705. **NLM** W1 PS352. **CODEN** PSYCAB. **[CCC].** Index available. cum. index. **Bk Rev. Ad Acc. Pr Rev. Circ:** 2,100. available on microfilm and microfiche from University Microfilms International (UMI). Documents available from The Genuine Article, BIOSIS Document Express, UMI Article Clearinghouse, CASDDS.
**Desc:** Interdisciplinary psychiatric journal emphasizing integration of psychological, biological, and social viewpoints. Publishes research, critiques, surveys, reviews and clinical studies.
**Ind/Abst** Acad. Search (July 1993-); Am. Hist. Life (1970-1984); Biol. Abstr.; Chem. Abstr.; Crim. Justice Abstr.; Crim. Penol. Police Sci. Abstr.; Cumul. Index Nurs. Allied Health Lit.; EMBASE; Expand. Acad. Index (1989-); Index Med.; Mag. Search; MLA Int. Bibl. Books Artic. Mod. Lang. Lit.; Newsp. Period. Abstr. (1991-); Peace Res. Abstr. J. (1960-1971); Psychol. Abstr. (1938-); PsycINFO (1990-); PsycLit; Res. Alert [Full Cov.]; Sage Fam. Stud. Abstr.; Sci. Cit. Index; SCISEARCH; Soc. Plann. Policy Dev. Abstr.; Soc. Sci. Cit. Index [Full Cov.]; Soc. Sci. Index; Soc. Sci. Index Fulltext (Aug. 1988-) [Full Txt.]; Soc. Work Abstr. [Select. Cov.]; Sociol. Abstr.; Women Stud. Abstr.

US/1057-5723
**PSYCHOANALYSIS AND PSYCHOTHERAPY.** [Psychoanal. psychother.]. **Added/Corp** Postgraduate Center for Mental Health (New York, N.Y.). Vol. 7, No. 1 (Spring/Summer 1989)-. Periodical. English. sa. $38.50 (individuals), $72.00 (institutions) US; $62.50 (individuals), $96.00 (institutions) other. International Universities Press Inc., 59 Boston Post Road, PO Box 1524, Madison CT 06443-1524. **Tel** (203)245-4000, FAX (203)245-0775, telex 282986 IUP BK. **DD** 616. **NLM** W1; PS396. ***Continues*** *Dynamic Psychotherapy, 0736-508X.*
**Ind/Abst** PsycLit.

US/0735-1690
**PSYCHOANALYTIC INQUIRY.** [Psychoanal. inq.]. Vol. 1, No. 1 (1981)-. Academic Scholarly Publication. English. qt. $130.00 US & Canada; $155.00 other. Lawrence Erlbaum Associates, 365 Broadway, Suite 102, Hillsdale NJ 07642. **Tel** (201)666-4110, (800)926-6579, FAX (201)666-2394. **LC** RC500; .P82. **DD** 616.89/17/05. **NLM** W1 PS427. **[CCC].** available on microfilm and microfiche from University Microfilms International (UMI). Documents available from The Genuine Article.
**Ind/Abst** Curr. Contents Soc. Behav. Sci.; EMBASE; Psychol. Abstr. (1983-); PsycINFO; PsycLit; Res. Alert [Full Cov.]; Soc. Sci. Cit. Index [Full Cov.].

US/0899-9244
**PSYCHOANALYTIC INQUIRY BOOK SERIES.** [Psychoanal. inq. book ser.]. Vol. 1 (1983)-. Monographic series. English. ir. Price varies per volume. Analytic Press, 365 Broadway, Hillsdale NJ 07642. **Tel** (201)666-4110, FAX (201)666-2394. **ED** Joseph D. Lichtenberg. **DD** 616. **NLM** W1; PS427F.
**Desc:** A topical journal for mental health professionals.

UK/0266-8734
**PSYCHOANALYTIC PSYCHOTHERAPY.** **Added/Corp** Association for Psychoanalytic Psychotherapy in the National Health Service. (19??)-. Periodical. English. Three times a year (Jan., May, Sept.). £24.00 (individuals), £30.00 (institutions). Association of Psychoanalytic Psychother, 24 Middleton Road, London E8 4BS England. **Tel** 011 44 71 2413696. **ED** Robin Anderson. **NLM** W1; P5428H.
**Desc:** It is concerned with the clinical application and theoretical aspects of psychoanalytic psychotherapy in the Public Services of Health, Education, Social Work, and others.
**Ind/Abst** Psychol. Abstr. (1985-); PsycINFO (1990-); PsycLit.

US/0079-7294
**PSYCHOANALYTIC STUDY OF SOCIETY.** **See** Social Sciences.

US
**PSYCHODRAMA AND GROUP PSYCHOTHERAPY MONOGRAPHS.** No. 28- 1955-. Monographic series. English. ir. Price varies per volume. Beacon House Inc, PO Box 311, Beacon NY 12508. **Tel** (914)831-2318. **UDC** 615.851.6. ***Continues*** *Psychodrama Monographs.*

XO
**PSYCHOLOGIA A PATOPSYCHOLOGIA DIETATA.** **Added/Corp** Vyskumny Ustav Detskej Psychologie a Patopsychologie. (1966)-. Academic Scholarly Publication. Czech (summaries and/or abstracts in English and Russian). qt. Vydavatef, Sasinkova 5, Bratislava, Slovakia. **LC** RJ499.A1; P84. **NLM** W1 PS528E. **CODEN** PPDIB6.
**Ind/Abst** EMBASE; Psychol. Abstr. (1966-?); PsycINFO (1966-); PsycLit.

SZ/0254-4962
**PSYCHOPATHOLOGY.** [Psychopathology]. Vol. 17, No. 1 (Jan./Feb. 1984)-. Academic Scholarly Publication. English. bm (6 issues). $266.00. S. Karger AG, Allschwilerstrasse 10, PO Box - Postfach - Case Postale, CH-4009 Basel Switzerland. **Tel** 011 41 61 306-1111, FAX 011 41 61 306-1234, telex CH 962 652. **ED** P. Berner, E. Gabriel. **NLM** W1; PS74. **CODEN** PSYHEU. **[CCC].** Index available in last issue of volume--attached. **Ad Acc. Pr Rev.** Documents available from The Genuine Article, BIOSIS Document Express, CASDDS. ***Continues*** *Psychiatria Clinica.*
**Desc:** A record of research centered on the concepts, models and diagnostic categories of clinical psychiatry. The journal publishes studies designed to increase the reliability and precision of explanatory concepts applied in descriptive psychopathology, phenomenology, and clinical diagnostics. Findings relevant to unresolved problems of classification and differential diagnosis are stressed together with papers illustrating the dynamics of psychopathologic phenomena.
**Ind/Abst** Biol. Abstr. (1984-); Chem. Abstr. (1984-); Curr. Contents Clin. Med.; Curr. Contents Soc. Behav. Sci.; EMBASE; Index Med.; Life Sci. Collect.; Psychol. Abstr. (1984-); PsycINFO; PsycLit; Ref. Upd. Deluxe Ed.; Res. Alert [Full Cov.]; Sci. Cit. Index; SCISEARCH; Soc. Sci. Cit. Index [Full Cov.].

US/0147-5622
**PSYCHOSOCIAL REHABILITATION JOURNAL.** [Psychosoc. rehabil. j.]. **Added/Corp** International Association of Psychosocial Rehabilitation Services. Sargent College of Allied Health Professions. Dept. of Rehabilitation Counseling. Psychosocial Rehabilitation Associates. Vol. 1, (Fall 1976)-. Periodical. English. Four times a year (Jan., Apr., July, Oct.). $75.00 (institutions), $39.00 (individuals) US; $95.00 (institutions), $59.00 (individuals) other. Boston University/Center Psychosocial Rehabilitation, 730 Commonwealth Avenue, Boston MA 02215. **Tel** (617)353-3549, FAX (617)353-7700. **ED** LeRoy Spaniol Ph.D. **LC** RC439.5; .P89. **DD** 362.2/05. **NLM** W1 PS81H. **Bk Rev**, (Qty: 24). **Ad Acc, Adv Mgr:** LeRoy Spaniol, **Tel** (617)353-3549. **Pr Rev. Circ:** 2,800 (ctrl). available on microfilm and microfiche from University Microfilms International (UMI).
**Desc:** The purpose of this journal is to provide information relevant to rehabilitation of persons with severe psychiatric disability. It is intended for the professional, consumers, and family members.
**Ind/Abst** Acad. Search (July 1993-); Cumul. Index Nurs. Allied Health Lit.; INFO-SOUTH Abstr.; Mag. Search; Nurs. Abstr.; Psychol. Abstr. (1977-); PsycINFO; PsycLit; Soc. Plann. Policy Dev. Abstr.; Soc. Sci. Source (Jul. 1993-); Sociol. Abstr.

US/0033-3174
**PSYCHOSOMATIC MEDICINE. See** Medical Science and Technology.

SZ/0251-737X
**PSYCHOTHERAPIES (GENEVA, SWITZERLAND).** (PSYCHOTHERAPIES.). [Psychotherapies]. Vol. 1, No. 1 (1981)-. Periodical. French (summaries and/or abstracts in English). qt. 92.00F (individuals); 128.00F (institutions). Medecine et Hygiene, Case Postale 456, CH-1211 Geneve 4 Switzerland. **Tel** 011 41 22 3469355, 011 41 22 3469356. **NLM** W1; PS83H. **CODEN** PSYTEW. **[CCC].**
**Ind/Abst** EMBASE.

SZ/0033-3190
**PSYCHOTHERAPY AND PSYCHOSOMATICS.** [Psychother. psychosom.]. **Added/Corp** International Federation for Medical Psychotherapy. Vol. 13, (1965)-. Academic Scholarly Publication. English. Eight times a year. $380.00. S. Karger AG, Allschwilerstrasse 10, PO Box - Postfach - Case Postale, CH-4009 Basel Switzerland. **Tel** 011 41 61 306-1111, FAX 011 41 61 306-1234, telex CH 962 652. **ED** G. A. Fava, H. Freyberger. **LC** RC49; .A28. **DD** 616.08. **NLM** W1 PS86K. **CODEN** PSPSBF. **[CCC]. Ad Acc. Pr Rev.** available on microfilm from University Microfilms International (UMI). Documents available from The Genuine Article, BIOSIS Document Express. ***Continues*** *Acta Psychotherapeutica et Psychosomatica, 0365-5822.*
**Desc:** The journal features editorials and review articles on current and controversial issues, original investigations of psychotherapy research and on the interface between medicine and behavioral sciences, as well as practical descriptions of psychotherapeutic models and techniques.
**Ind/Abst** Biol. Abstr.; Curr. Contents Clin. Med.; Curr. Contents Soc. Behav. Sci.; EMBASE; Index Med.; Life Sci. Collect.; Psychol. Abstr. (1965-); PsycINFO; PsycLit; Ref. Upd. Deluxe Ed.; Res. Alert [Full Cov.]; Sci. Cit. Index; Soc. Sci. Cit. Index [Full Cov.]; Women Stud. Abstr.

US/0033-3204
**PSYCHOTHERAPY (CHICAGO, ILL.).** (PSYCHOTHERAPY.). [Psychotherapy]. **Added/Corp** American Psychological Association. Division of Psychotherapy. Psychologists Interested in the Advancement of Psychotherapy (U.S.). **VFOAT** Psychotherapy: Theory, Research and Practice. Vol. 1, No. 1 (Aug. 1963)-. Academic Scholarly Publication. English. qt. $20.00 individuals, $30.00 institutions, $13.00 students. American Psychological Association / Division of Psychotherapy, 3875 North 44th Street, Suite 102, Phoenix AZ 85018. **Tel** (602)952-8656. **ED** Donald K Freedheim. **LC** RC475; .P73. **DD** 616.8/914/05. **NLM** W1 PS88. **CODEN** PSYOAD. cum. index. **Bk Rev. Ad Acc. Circ:** 7,500. available on microfilm and microfiche from University Microfilms International (UMI). Documents available from The Genuine Article.
**Desc:** Psychotherapy theory, research and practice training.
**Ind/Abst** Abstr. Res. Pastor. Care Couns. (19??-); Curr. Contents Soc. Behav. Sci.; EMBASE; Psychol. Abstr. (1963-); PsycINFO; PsycLit; PsycScan: Clin. Psych.; Res. Alert [Full Cov.]; Soc. Sci. Cit. Index [Full Cov.]; Women Stud. Abstr.

US/1062-9475
**PSYCHOTHERAPY LETTER, THE. See** Psychology.

US/0738-6176
**PSYCHOTHERAPY PATIENT, THE.** [Psychother. patient]. Vol. 1, No. 1 (Fall 1984)-. Monographic series. English. ir. $135.00 US; $189.00 other. The Haworth Press Inc, 10 Alice Street, Binghamton NY 13904-1580. **Tel** (607)722-5857, (800)3-HAWORTH, FAX (607)722-1424. **ED** E. Mark Stern (editor's address: 215 East 11 Street, New York, NY 10003). **DD** 616. **NLM** W1; PS87. **CODEN** PSPAEW. **Bk Rev. Ad Acc. Pr Rev. Acid Free. Circ:** 199. available on microfiche. Documents available from BIOSIS Document Express, Haworth Document Delivery Service.
**Desc:** Each issue focuses on diagnostic, behavioral or phenomenological groupings of persons in psychotherapy that psychotherapists in clinical practice are increasingly likely to see.
**Ind/Abst** Abstr. Soc. Gerontol.; Biol. Abstr. (1985-); Psychol. Abstr. (1984-); PsycINFO; PsycLit; Soc. Work Abstr. [Select. Cov.].

IT
**QUADERNI ITALIANI DI PSICHIATRIA.** Vol. 1, No. 1 (Oct. 1982)-. Periodical. Italian. bm (6 issues). L105000 Italy. Masson S.P.A, Via Statuto 2/4, 20121 Milan Italy. **Tel** 011 39 2 63671, FAX 011 39 2 6367211. **NLM** W1; QU152.

CN/0822-4048
**R.P.N.A.M. UPDATE. See** Medical Science and Technology-Nursing.

NE/0166-4298
**RAAKPUNT (MAARSSEN). See** Family and Marriage.

IT/0033-9636
**RASSEGNA DI STUDI PSICHIATRICI.** [Rass. studi psichiatr.]. Vol. 1 (1911)-. Periodical. Italian. qt. L80000 Italy; L100000 other. Arti Grafiche Ticci, Loc Pian Dei Mori278, 53018 Sovicille SI Italy. **Tel** 011 39 577 349222. **NLM** W1 RA71. Index available. cum. index. **Circ:** 300 (ctrl).
**Desc:** Journal publishes articles from medical journals concerning psychiatry and scientific notes for professionals in medicine.
**Ind/Abst** EMBASE [Select. Cov.].

BL
**RBM. PSIQUIATRIA. VFOAT** Psiquiatria. Portuguese (summaries and/or abstracts in English). bm. Rua Pinheiros 504, CEP 05422 Sao Paulo SP Brazil. **UDC** 616.89. ***Continues*** *Revista Brasileira de Medicina. Psiquiatria.*

US/0886-3784
**READINGS - AMERICAN ORTHOPSYCHIATRIC ASSOCIATION.** (READINGS.). [Read. - Am. Orthopsychiatr. Assoc.]. **Added/Corp** American Orthopsychiatric Association. Vol. 1, No. 1 (March 1986)-. Periodical. English. qt. $35.00 (institutions), $25.00 (individuals). American Orthopsychiatric Association, 19 West 44th Street, Suite 1616, New York NY 10036. **Tel** (212)564-5930. **(Subscription address:** American Orthopsychiatric Association, 49 Sheridan Avenue, Department M, Albany NY 12210.**) ED** Ernest Herman. **DD** 362. **NLM** ZWM 105; R287r. **Bk Rev. Ad Acc. Circ:** 14,000.
**Desc:** An interdisciplinary mental health journal devoted exclusively to book reviews. Each issue features major essay reviews plus brief reviews of new books for professionals.
**Ind/Abst** Book Rev. Digest.

GW/0724-2247
**RECHT & PSYCHIATRIE. VFOAT** Recht und Psychiatrie; R & P. Recht & Psychiatrie. (1983)-. Periodical. German. ir. Psychiatrie Verlag GmbH, Celsiusstr. 112, 5300 Bonn 1 Germany. **UDC** 616.89.
**Ind/Abst** PsycINFO (1987-); PsycLit.

US/0888-3394
**REPORT - GROUP FOR THE ADVANCEMENT OF PSYCHIATRY (1984).** (REPORT / GROUP FOR THE ADVANCEMENT OF PSYCHIATRY.). [Rep. - Group Adv. Psychiatr.]. **Added/Corp** Group for the Advancement of Psychiatry. **VFOAT** GAP Report. No. 116 (1984)-. Monographic series. English. ir (3 issues per year). Price varies per volume. American Psychiatric Press Inc., 1400 K Street Northwest, Suite 1101, Washington DC 20005. **Tel** (202)682-6222, FAX (202)789-2648. **LC** RC321; .G7. **DD** 616. **NLM** W1; RE209BR. **CODEN** GPSRB9. Documents available from BIOSIS Document Express. ***Continues*** *Publication (Group for the Advancement of Psychiatry), 0149-2640.*
**Ind/Abst** Biol. Abstr. (1985-); Health Plan. Adminis.; Index Med. (No. 116, 1984-).

CN/0711-6926
**RESEARCH BULLETIN - ST. THOMAS PSYCHIATRIC HOSPITAL.** (RESEARCH BULLETIN.). [Res. bull. - St. Thomas Psychiatr. Hosp.]. **VFOAT** St. Thomas Psychiatric Hospital Research Bulletin. Vol. 1, No. 1 (Jan. 1982)-. Bulletin. English. ir. Free. St Thomas Psychiatric Hospital, Ontario N5P 3V9 Canada. **ED** A J Cooper. **DD** 616.89/007/2071335. **UDC** 616.89(047.31)(713). **Circ:** 125.
**Desc:** Publishes reports of research done at St. Thomas Psychiatric Hospital.

US/0362-2428
**RESEARCH COMMUNICATIONS IN PSYCHOLOGY, PSYCHIATRY AND BEHAVIOR. See** Psychology.

US/0091-7443
**RESEARCH PUBLICATIONS - ASSOCIATION FOR RESEARCH IN NERVOUS AND MENTAL DISEASE. See** Medical Science and Technology-Neurology.

US/1041-5882
**REVIEW OF PSYCHIATRY.** [Rev. psychiatry]. **VFOAT** American Psychiatric Press Review of Psychiatry. Vol. 7 (1988)-. English. an. $59.95. American Psychiatric Press Inc., 1400 K Street Northwest, Suite 1101, Washington DC 20005. **Tel** (202)682-6222, FAX (202)789-2648. **LC** RC321; .P936. **DD** 616.89/005. **NLM** W1; RE254J. ***Continues*** *Psychiatry Update, 0736-1866.*

UK/0307-238X
**REVIEWS OF RESEARCH AND PRACTICE OF THE INSTITUTE FOR RESEARCH INTO MENTAL AND MULTIPLE HANDICAP.** [Rev. res. pract. Inst. Res. Ment. Mult. Handicap]. **Main/Corp** Institute for Research into Mental and Multiple Handicap. **VFOAT** IRMMH Reviews of Research and Practice. (1975)-. Academic Scholarly Publication. English. ir. Price varies per volume. Elsevier Science Publishers Ltd, Crown House, Linton Road, Barking Essex IG11 8JU England. **Tel** 011 44 81 5947272, FAX 081-594-5942, telex 896950. **NLM** W3 RE96. **CODEN** RRPHDX. Documents available from CASDDS. ***Continues*** *IRMMH Symposium, 0305-7852.*
**Ind/Abst** Chem. Abstr.

BL/0102-7646
**REVISTA ABP-APAL.** [Rev. ABP-APAL]. **VFOAT** Revista da Associacao Brasileira de Psiquiatria e da Associacao Psiquiatria da America Latina. (1986)-. Periodical. Multiple languages. qt. Associacao Brasileira de Psiquiatria, Rua Borges Lagoa 394, 04038, Sao Paulo, Brazil. **Tel** (11)5496699. **UDC** 61. ***Continues*** *ABP Revista, 0101-5311.*
**Ind/Abst** EMBASE [Select. Cov.]; PsycINFO (1986-).

BL/0100-7343
**REVISTA BRASILEIRA DE MEDICINA. PSIQUIATRIA.** [Rev. Bras. med., Psiquiatr.]. **VFOAT** Psiquiatria. Began in 1979. Portuguese. bm. $82.00. Revista Brasileira de Medicina, rua Pinheiros 504, 05422 Sao Paula SP Brazil. **UDC** 616.89. **NLM** W1 RE343J.

CL/0034-7388
**REVISTA CHILENA DE NEURO-PSIQUIATRIA.** [Rev. chil. neuro-psiquiatr.]. **Added/Corp** Sociedad Chilena de Neurologia, Psiquiatria, y Neurocirugia. Vol. 1 (1962)-. Academic Scholarly Publication. Spanish (summaries and/or abstracts in English). Four times a year (Mar., May, Aug., Nov.). $30.00. Sociedad de Neurologia Psiquiatria y Neurocirurgica, Pres Riesco 6007, Clasifi 1 27, Santiago Chile. **Tel** 011 56 2 2243 175. **NLM** W1 RE349A. ***Supersedes*** *Revista Chilena de Neuro-Psiquiatria.*
**Ind/Abst** EMBASE; Psychol. Abstr. (1981-); PsycINFO (1990-?); PsycLit.

CK/0034-7450
**REVISTA COLOMBIANA DE PSIQUIATRIA.** [Rev. colomb. psiquiatr.]. **Added/Corp** Sociedad Colombiana de Psiquiatria. (1964)-. Periodical. Spanish. Four times a year. $40.00. Sociedad Colombiana de Psiquiatria, Carrera 18 No 84 87 Oficina 203, Bogota de 2 Colombia. **Tel** 011 57 1 2561148. **NLM** W1 RE358P. **CODEN** RCPSBR.
**Ind/Abst** Psychol. Abstr. (1971-).

SP/0211-5735
**REVISTA DE LA ASOCIACION ESPANOLA DE NEUROPSIQUIATRIA.** **Added/Corp** Asociacion Espanola de Neuropsiquiatria. (198?)-. Periodical. Spanish. qt. $100.00 new subscriptions; $95.00 renewals. Aran Ediciones SA, Avda General Peron, 20 5 DCHA, 28020 Madrid Spain. **Tel** 011 34 1 5332525. **ED** T Angosto. **NLM** W1; RE406H. **Bk Rev. Ad Acc. Pr Rev. Circ:** 3,000.
**Desc:** We publish original papers in the field of mental health and psychiatric assistance but we also include reviews, theoretical and historical papers.
**Ind/Abst** Indice Med. Esp.

RM/0377-497X
**REVISTA DE MEDICINA-INTERNA, NEUROLOGIE, PSIHIATRIE, NEUROCHIRURGIE, DERMATO-VENEROLOGIE. NEUROLOGIE, PSIHIATRIE, NEUROCHIRURGIE.** [Rev. med.-interna neurol. psihiatr. neurochir. derm.-venerol., Neurol. psihiat. neurochir.]. **Added/Corp** Societatea de Neurologie. **VFOAT** Neurologie, Psihiatrie, Neurochirurgie. Vol. 19, No. 4 (July/Sept. 1974)-. Academic Scholarly Publication. Romanian (summaries and/or abstracts in English, French, German and Russian). Uniunea Societ Stiinte Medical, Str Progresului 8, Bucharest Romania. **(Subscription address:** Rompresfilatelia, PO Box 12 201, Bucharest Romania.**) NLM** W1 RE427HC. **CODEN**

RMNPDC. Documents available from BIOSIS Document Express, CASDDS. ***Continues*** *Neurologia, Psihiatria, Neurochirurgia, 0028-386X.*
**Desc:** Publishes original articles and studies on subjects in the speciality.
**Ind/Abst** Biol. Abstr. (-1988); Chem. Abstr. (1974-1979); EMBASE [Select. Cov.]; Index Med.; Psychol. Abstr. (1974-).

PE/0034-8597
**REVISTA DE NEURO-PSIQUIATRIA. See** Medical Science and Technology-Neurology.

CL/0716-1220
**REVISTA DE PSIQUIATRIA CLINICA DEL DEPARTAMENTO DE PSIQUIATRIA Y SALUD MENTAL, DIVISION DE CIENCIAS MEDICAS NORTE, FACULTAD DE MEDICINA, UNIVERSIDAD DE CHILE. VFOAT** Revista de Psiquiatria Clinica. (19??)-. Spanish (English). Universidad de Chile /Psiquiatria, Departmento de Psiquiatria y Salud Mental, Division de Ciencias Medicas Norte, Facultad de Medicina, Santiago, Chile. **NLM** W1; RE469DF.
**Ind/Abst** PsycINFO (1981-); PsycLit.

SP/0210-1793
**REVISTA DE PSIQUIATRIA DE LA FACULTAD DE MEDICINA DE BARCELONA. VFOAT** Revista de Psiquiatria, Barcelona. Vol. 14, No. 1 (Jan./Feb. 1987)-. Periodical. Spanish. ir. $100.00. Editorial Rocas SA, Muntaner 393, Pral 2A Desp 4A, 08021 Barcelona Spain. **Tel** 011 34 3 200-1389. **NLM** W1; RE469E. ***Continues*** *Revista del Departamento de Psiquiatria, Facultad de Medicina de Barcelona.*
**Ind/Abst** EMBASE [Select. Cov.]; PsycINFO (1979-); PsycLit.

SP
**REVISTA DE PSIQUIATRIA Y PSICOLOGIA MEDICA DE EUROPA Y AMERICA LATINAS. *Ceased.*** Spanish. qt. Sciencia, Apartado 9118, 08080 Barcelona Spain.

CU/0440-436X
**REVISTA DEL HOSPITAL PSIQUIATRICO DE LA HABANA.** [Rev. Hosp. psiquiatr. La Habana]. **Main/Corp** Hospital Psiquiatrico de la Habana, Mazorra, Cuba. (19??)-. Periodical. Spanish (summaries and/or abstracts in English). Twice a year. 35.93Cub$ North America; 33.36Cub$ South America; 38.30Cub$ others. Ediciones Cubanas, Obispo 527, Altos ESQ Bernaza, CP 10100 Havana Cuba. **Tel** 011 632980, 631942, FAX 011 631011, telex 512337, 6540. **UDC** 616.89. **NLM** W1 RE51T. **Circ:** 50,000 (ctrl).
**Desc:** A publication that offers complete information related to mental health in the Psychiatric Hospital of Havana. It publishes articles by the Cubans and other Latin American specialists on psychiatry, psychology, anthropology, neurophysiology, biochemistry of the nervous system, and psycho-pharmacology.
**Ind/Abst** EMBASE [Select. Cov.]; Psychol. Abstr. (1982-); PsycINFO (?-?); PsycLit.

PR
**REVISTA PUERTORRIQUENA DE PSICOLOGIA. See** Psychology.

FR/0035-161X
**REVUE DE NEUROPSYCHIATRIE DE L'OUEST.** [Rev. neuropsychiatr. Ouest]. (1963)-. Periodical. French. qt. 150.00F. Soc Neuropsychiatrie I Ouest, BP 226, Docteur Kersauze, 35011 Rennes France. **Tel** 011 33 99 333900. **UDC** 616.89.

CN/0847-5733
**REVUE FRANCOPHONE DE LA DEFICIENCE INTELLECTUELLE. See** Medical Science and Technology-Neurology.

FR/1150-6652
**REVUE INTERNATIONALE DE PSYCHOPATHOLOGIE PARIS.** (REVUE INTERNATIONALE DE PSYCHOPATHOLOGIE.). [Rev. int. psychopathol. Paris]. (1990)-. Periodical. French (English). qt. 500.00F France; 560.00F other. Presses Universitaires de France, Department des Revues, 14 Avenue du Bois de l'Epine, BP 90, 91003 Evry Cedex France. **Tel** (1)60 77 82 05, FAX (1) 60 79 20 45, telex PUF 600 474 F. **UDC** 616.89.

RM/1017-5644
**REVUE ROUMAINE DE NEUROLOGIE ET PSYCHIATRIE (1990). See** Medical Science and Technology-Neurology.

IT/0035-6433
**RIVISTA DI PATOLOGIA NERVOSA E MENTALE. *Suspended.*** [Riv. patol. nerv. ment.]. Vol. 1 (Jan. 1896)-Suspended (1984). Academic Scholarly Publication. Italian (summaries and/or abstracts in English, French and German). bm. L75000. Clinica Malattie Nervose e Mentali, Viale Morgagni 85, 1 50134 Firenze Italy. **Tel** 055-416969. **ED** Luigi Amaducci. **UDC** 616.89. **NLM** W1 RI608. **Bk Rev. Ad Acc.** ctrl circ.
**Ind/Abst** EMBASE; Index Med.

IT/0035-6484
**RIVISTA DI PSICHIATRIA.** [Riv. psichiatr.]. (1966)-. Academic Scholarly Publication. Italian (summaries and/or abstracts in English). Six times a year. L85000 (individuals), L140000 (institutions). Il Pensiero Scientifico Editore s.r.l., Via Bradano 3C, 00199 Rome Italy. **Tel** 011 39 6 86207158, 86207159, 86207168, 86207169, FAX 011 39 6 86207160. **ED** Gian Carlo Reda and Paolo Pancheri. **NLM** W1 RI61. **CODEN** RPSID3. Index available. **Ad Acc, Adv Mgr:** Dott Dalla, **Tel** 06-86207165. Full Page (B&W) L1.650.000. **Circ:** 1,200. Documents available from FAXON Xpress.
**Ind/Abst** Biol. Abstr.; EMBASE [Select. Cov.]; Psychol. Abstr. (1966-); PsycINFO (1966-); PsycLit.

IT
**RIVISTA ITALIANA DEL DISTURBO INTELLETTIVO : ORGANO UFFICIALE DEL GRUPPO ITALIANO PER LO STUDIO SCIENTIFICO E TERAPIA DELL'INSUFFICIENZA MENTALE, MONGOLISMO E AUTISMO INFANTILI. VFOAT** Italian Journal of Intellective Impairment. Vol. 1, No. 1 (June 1988)-. Periodical. Italian (English). sa. **NLM** W1; RI759L.
**Ind/Abst** PsycINFO (1988-); PsycLit.

IT/0370-7261
**RIVISTA SPERIMENTALE DI FRENIATRIA E MEDICINA LEGALE DELLE ALIENAZIONI MENTALI.** [Riv. sper. freniatr. med. leg. alien. ment.]. (1875)-. Academic Scholarly Publication. Italian. bmbm. L60000.00 Italy; L80000.00 other. Unita Sanitaria Locale No 9, Via Amendola 2, 42100 Reggio Emilia Italy. **NLM** W1 RI965. **CODEN** RSFMA2. cum. index. **Bk Rev. Ad Acc. Pr Rev. Circ:** 3000. ***Formed by the union of*** *Archivio Italiano per le Malattie Nervose e Mentali, 0365-3277.*
**Ind/Abst** EMBASE [Select. Cov.]; Psychol. Abstr. (1972-).

CN/1187-0400
**RPNABC PROFILE. See** Medical Science and Technology-Nursing.

MX/0185-3325
**SALUD MENTAL (MEXICO).** (SALUD MENTAL.). [Salud ment.]. **Added/Corp** Centro Mexicano de Estudios en Salud Mental. Centro Mexicano de Estudios en Farmacodependencia. Vol. 1, No. 1 (Aug. 1977)-. Periodical. Spanish. Revista Salud Mental, Calz. Mexico-Xochimilco-101, Col. San Lorenzo Huipulco, 14370 Delegacion Tlalpan C.P.,D.F. Mexcio. **NLM** W1; SA3666D. Documents available from The Genuine Article.
**Ind/Abst** Curr. Contents Soc. Behav. Sci.; PsycINFO (1979-); PsycLit; Res. Alert [Full Cov.]; Soc. Sci. Cit. Index [Full Cov.].

CN/0833-8590
**SANTE CULTURE.** (SANTE CULTURE: CULTURE HEALTH.). [Sante cult.]. **Added/Corp** GIRAME. **VFOAT** Culture Health. Vol. 3, No. 1 (1985)-. Periodical. French (English). irtq. $30.00 (individuals), $60.00 (institutions). Universite de Montreal / SOCP, SOCP, CP 6128 Succursale A, Montreal Quebec H3C 3J7 Canada. **Tel** (514)343-6185, FAX (514)343-2270. **DD** 362.1/09714. ***Continues*** *Bulletin d'Information en Anthropologie Medicale et en Psychiatrie Transculturelle., 0715-9358.*

CN/0383-6320
**SANTE MENTALE AU QUEBEC.** [Sante ment. Que.]. Vol. 1, (Sept. 1976)-. Periodical. French. Twice a year. 22.00Can$ (individuals), 32.00Can$ (institutions). Centre Sante Mentale Communaute, Case Postale 548 Place d'Armes, Montreal Quebec H2Y 3H3 Canada. **Tel** (514)844-5536, FAX (514)844-4194. **DD** 614.5/8/09714. **CODEN** SMQUEK. **Bk Rev. Circ:** 1,100 (ctrl).
**Desc:** Research projects and ideas in mental health.
**Ind/Abst** Health Plan. Adminis.; Int. Bibliogr. Sociol.; Point Repere (1983-); Soc. Plann. Policy Dev. Abstr.; Soc. Work Abstr. [Select. Cov.].

US/0586-7614
**SCHIZOPHRENIA BULLETIN.** [Schizophr. bull.]. **Added/Corp** National Institute of Mental Health (U.S.) United States. Alcohol, Drug Abuse, and Mental Health Administration. Center for Studies of Schizophrenia (U.S.) National Clearinghouse for Mental Health Information (U.S.). (Dec. 1969)-. Academic Scholarly Publication. English. qt. $18.00 US; $22.50 other. Superintendent of Documents, US Government Printing Office, Washington DC 20402. **Tel** (202)275-3328, FAX (202)786-2377. **LC** RC514; .S336. **NLM** W1 SC17E. **CODEN** SCZBB3. **Pr Rev.** available on microfilm and microfiche from University Microfilms International (UMI). Documents available from The Genuine Article, BIOSIS Document Express.
**Desc:** Facilitates the dissemination and exchange of information about schizophrenia and provides abstracts of the recent literature on the subject.
**Ind/Abst** Biol. Abstr.; Cumul. Index Nurs. Allied Health Lit.; Curr. Aware. Biol. Sci., CABS; Curr. Contents Life Sci.; Curr. Contents Soc. Behav. Sci.; EMBASE; Index Med.; Psychol. Abstr. (1969-); PsycINFO; PsycLit; Ref. Upd. Deluxe Ed.; Res. Alert [Full Cov.]; Sci. Cit. Index; SCISEARCH; Soc. Sci. Cit. Index [Full Cov.].

NE/0920-9964
**SCHIZOPHRENIA RESEARCH.** [Schizophr. res.]. Vol. 1, No. 1 (Jan./Feb. 1988)-. Academic Scholarly Publication. English. Twelve times a year (4 vols.). Fl2080.00. Elsevier Science Publishers BV, PO Box 211, 1000 AE Amsterdam Netherlands. **Tel** 011 31 20 5803642, FAX 011 31 20 5862696, telex 15682. **NLM** W1; SC17F. **CODEN** SCRSEH. **[CCC]. Pr Rev.** available on microfilm and microfiche from University Microfilms International (UMI). Documents available from The Genuine Article, BIOSIS Document Express.
**Ind/Abst** Biol. Abstr.; Curr. Contents Life Sci.; EMBASE; Health Plan. Adminis.; Index Med. (Jan.-Feb. 1989-); Psychol. Abstr. (1988-); PsycINFO (1991-); PsycLit; Ref. Upd. Deluxe Ed.; Res. Alert [Full Cov.]; Sci. Cit. Index; SCISEARCH; Soc. Sci. Cit. Index [Select. Cov.].

AU/1012-912X
**SCHRIFTENREIHE INFANS CEREBROPATHICUS.** [Schr.reihe infans cerebropath.]. (1983)-. Monographic series. German. ir. Price varies per volume. Akademie-Verlag GmbH, Muehlenstrasse 33 34, D 13162 Berlin Germany. **Tel** 011 49 30 47889300, FAX 011 49 30 47889357. **ED** A. Rett. **NLM** W1; SC34R.

SZ
**SCHWEIZER ARCHIV FUR NEUROLOGIE UND PSYCHIATRIE (ZURICH, SWITZERLAND : 1985). See** Medical Science and Technology-Neurology.

JA
**SEISHIN HOKEN KENKYU. Added/Corp** Kokuritsu Seishin Shinkei Senta (Japan). Seishin Hoken Kenkyujo. **VFOAT** Journal of Mental Health. (1987)-. Periodical. Japanese (summaries and/or abstracts in English). National Institute of Mental Health Japan, 1-7-3 Koonodai, Ichikawa City, Chiba-Ken Japan. **LC** RA790.A1; S38. **NLM** W1; SE2577W. ***Continues*** *Seishin Eisei Kenkyu, 0559-3158.*
**Ind/Abst** PsycINFO (1962-).

US/1044-5633
**SERIES IN PSYCHOSOCIAL EPIDEMIOLOGY.** [Ser. psychosoc. epidemiol.]. Vol. 4 (1985)-. Monographic series. English. ir. Price varies per volume. Rutgers University Press, PO Box 4869, Distribution Center, Baltimore MD 21211. **Tel** (301)338-6947. **DD** 362. **NLM** W1; SE718R. **Bk Rev. Ad Acc.** ctrl circ. ***Continues*** *Monographs in Psychosocial Epidemiology, 0735-0155.*
**Desc:** Studies of psychosocial epidemiological research, findings, methodology, ethics policy, on drug abuse, children, stressful life events, illness behavior, community psychiatric surveys, etc.

SZ/0080-9012
**SERIES PAEDOPSYCHIATRICA.** [Ser. paedopsychiatr.]. (1965)-. Monographic series. French (German; summaries and/or abstracts in English and Spanish). ir. Price varies per volume. Schwabe & Company Ltd., Farnsburgerstrasse 8 PF 254, CH-4132 Muttenz 1 Switzerland. **Tel** 011 41 61 4613001, FAX 01 41 61 4612500. **NLM** W1 SE73. **CODEN** SPPSAQ. **[CCC].** Documents available from BIOSIS Document Express.
**Ind/Abst** Biol. Abstr. (-1985); Health Plan. Adminis.; Index Med.

GW/0933-7954
**SOCIAL PSYCHIATRY AND PSYCHIATRIC EPIDEMIOLOGY.** [Soc. psychiatry psychiatr. epidemiol.]. Vol. 23, No. 1 (1988)-. Periodical. English. Six times a year. DM628.00. Springer-Verlag GmbH & Company KG, Heidelberger Platz 3, D 14197 Berlin Germany. **Tel** 011 49 30 8207223, FAX 011 49 30 8214091, telex 183 319 SPBLN D. **(Subscription address:** Springer Verlag New York Inc. / for North America, 44 Hartz Way, Secaucus NJ 07096.**) ED** P Bebbington, P Bovet, R S Daniels, and H Katschnig. **LC** RC321; .S6. **DD** 616.89/005. **NLM** W1; SO123LH. **CODEN** SPPEEM. **[CCC].** available on microfilm and microfiche from University Microfilms International (UMI). Documents available from The Genuine Article, BIOSIS Document Express. ***Continues*** *Social Psychiatry, 0037-7813.*
**Desc:** Provides a medium for the prompt publication of scientific contributions concerned with the effects of behaviour and the relationship between psychiatric disorder and the social environment.
**Ind/Abst** Abstr. Res. Pastor. Care Couns. (19??-); Biol. Abstr. (1988-); Chicano Index; Curr. Contents Soc. Behav. Sci.; EMBASE; High. Educ. Abstr. (1988-); Index Med. (1988-); Int. Nurs. Index; Psychol. Abstr. (1966-); PsycINFO (1990-); PsycLit; Res. Alert [Full Cov.]; Soc. Sci. Cit. Index [Full Cov.]; Trop. Dis. Bull.

US/0098-1389
**SOCIAL WORK IN HEALTH CARE. See** Sociology-Social Services and Welfare.

CI/0303-7908
**SOCIJALNA PSIHIJATRIJA.** [Soc. psihijatr.]. **Added/Corp** Medicinski Fakultet u Zagrebu. Psihijatrijska Klinika. Vol. 1 (1973)-. Periodical. Multiple languages ( and English; summaries and/or abstracts in English and Serbo-Croatian (Roman)). qt. $75.00. Socijalna Psihijatrija, Kispaticeva 12, 41000 Zagreb Rebro Croatia. **NLM** W1 SO878J. **CODEN** SPSIDE.
**Ind/Abst** Psychol. Abstr. (1973-); PsycINFO (1973-); PsycLit.

FR/0241-6972
**SOINS. PSYCHIATRIE.** [Soins. Psychiatr.]. **Added/Corp** S.F.I.R.E.C. (Society). **VFOAT** Psychiatrie. No. 1 (March 1980)-. Periodical. French. Ten times a year. 145.00F (individuals), 210.00F (institutions) Switzerland;, 230.00F (individuals), 290.00F (institutions) others. Intereditions, 7 rue de L Laromiguiere, 75005 Paris France. **Tel** 011 33 1 46342160. **(Subscription address:** OPI SA, 33 Chemin des Hutins, 1247 Aniere Geneva Switzerland.**)** **NLM** W1 SO8862T. **Bk Rev. Ad Acc.**
**Desc:** Psychiatric care and nursing.
**Ind/Abst** Int. Nurs. Index.

US/0147-5231
**SOMATICS. See** Philosophy.

US/0038-559X
**SOVIET NEUROLOGY & PSYCHIATRY.** ***Title Change.*** **See** Medical Science and Technology-Neurology.

UK
**SPECIAL PUBLICATION (GASKELL (PUBLISHER)).** (SPECIAL PUBLICATION.). Vol. 1 (1981)-. Monographic series. English. Price varies per volume. **NLM** W1 SP295DK.

US/0740-4212
**SPRINGER SERIES ON PSYCHIATRY.** [Springer ser. psych.]. (1982)-. Monographic series. English. ir. Price varies per volume. Springer Publishing Company, 536 Broadway, New York NY 10012-3955. **Tel** (212)431-4370, FAX (212)941-7842. **NLM** W1 SP685SFM.
**Desc:** Covers the spectrum of clinical psychopathology; diagnosis, clinical care and management based on current research and scientific knowledge.

US/0162-2374
**STATE MENTAL HOSPITALS. See** Medical Science and Technology-Hospital Administration and Medical Centers.

CN/0706-7992
**SUBJECT TO CHANGE.** V. 1- Dec. 1978-. Periodical. English. Three times a year. $5.00. Gestalt Institute of Toronto, 395 Markham Street, Toronto Ontario M6G 2K8 Canada. **DD** 616.8/914.

US/0162-7171
**SYNOPSIS OF FAMILY THERAPY PRACTICE. Main/Conf** Maryland/D.C./Virginia Network Symposium Family Therapy Practice. **VFOAT** Synopsis of the Annual Maryland/D.C./Virginia Network Symposium Family Therapy Practice. 1978-. English. an. $7.95. Family Therapy Practice Network, 18114 Hillcrest Avenue, Olney MD 20832. **LC** RC488.5; .M38A. **DD** 616.89/156/05. **UDC** 616.89-058.8.

US/1048-4159
**TASK FORCE REPORT.** [Task force rep. - Am. Psychiatr. Assoc.]. No. 1 (April 1970)-. English. ir. Price varies. American Psychiatric Press Inc., 1400 K Street Northwest, Suite 1101, Washington DC 20005. **Tel** (202)682-6222, FAX (202)789-2648. **DD** 616. **UDC** 616.89. **NLM** W1 TA82.

CN/0831-6570
**TECHNOLOGIE ET THERAPIE DU COMPORTEMENT.** [Technol. ther. comport.]. Vol. 9, No 1 (Spring 1985)-. Periodical. French. tq. 80,00 $ par annee. Technologie et Therapie du Comportement, Bureau 011 6975 Taschereau, Brossard, Quebec, J4Z 1A7 Canada. **DD** 616.89/142/05. ***Continues*** *La Technologie du Comportement., 0705-2707.*
**Ind/Abst** Point Repere (1985).

IT
**TECNICHE : DI PSICOTERAPIA.** (19??)-. Italian. sa. L50000 Italy; L100000 other. Edizioni Riza, Via Luigi Anelli 1, 20122 Milan, Italy. **Tel** 011 39 2 58301022.

AG/0325-4437
**TEMAS DE PSICOLOGIA Y PSIQUIATRIA DE LA NINEZ Y ADOLESCENCIA.** (TEMAS DE PSICOLOGIA Y PSIQUIATRIA DE LA NINEZ Y ADOLESCENCIA.). **Added/Corp** Centro de Estudios y Asistencia Medico-Psicologica de la Ninez y la Adolescencia. (1969)-. Periodical. Spanish (summaries and/or abstracts in English and French). **NLM** W1 TE305K.

●UK
**THERAPEUTIC CARE AND EDUCATION : THE JOURNAL OF THE ASSOCIATION OF WORKERS FOR CHILDREN WITH EMOTIONAL AND BEHAVIOURAL DIFFICULTIES. See** Psychology.

NE/0303-7339
**TIJDSCHRIFT VOOR PSYCHIATRIE.** [Tijdschr. psychiatr.]. **Added/Corp** Nederlandse Vereniging van Psychiaters in Dienstverband. Nederlandse Vereniging voor Psychiatrie. Vereniging van Vlaamse Zenuwartsen. Vol. 16 (Jan. 1974)-. Academic Scholarly Publication. Dutch (summaries and/or abstracts in English). Ten times a year. Fl83.25. Uitgeverij Boom, Postbus 400, 7940 AK Meppel Netherlands. **Tel** 011 31 20 5220 57012, FAX 011 31 20 5220 54452, telex 42829. **ED** P.T. Tongerius. **NLM** W1 TI715P. **CODEN** TPSYB3. **Bk Rev. Ad Acc. Circ:** 3,250. Documents available from BIOSIS Document Express. ***Continues*** *Nederlands Tijdschrift voor Psychiatrie, 0028-2197.*
**Desc:** Official journal of the Dutch Society for Psychiatry and Society of Flemish Psychiatrists (Belgium).
**Ind/Abst** Biol. Abstr. (1986-); Crim. Penol. Police Sci. Abstr.; EMBASE; PsycINFO (1985-); PsycLit.

NE
**TIJDSCHRIFT VOOR PSYCHOTHERAPIE.** bm (6 issues). Fl180.00. Bohn Stafleu Van Loghum BV, Postbus 246, 3990 GA Houten Netherlands. **Tel** 011 31 3403 95782. **(Subscription address:** Intermedia BV, Postbus 4, 2400 MA Alphen Rijn Netherland; telephone: 011 31 1720 66481**)**
**Ind/Abst** EMBASE; PsycLit.

JA/0301-5041
**TOKYO-TO SHINKEI KAGAKU SOGO KENKYUJO NEMPO. See** Medical Science and Technology-Neurology.

CN/0041-1108
**TRANSCULTURAL PSYCHIATRIC RESEARCH REVIEW.** Vol. 6 (April 1969)-. Periodical. English. qt. $32.00 (individuals), $50.00 (institutions). Transcultural Psychiatric Research Review, 1033 Pine Avenue West, Montreal Quebec H3A 1A1 Canada. **Tel** (514)398-7302, FAX (514)398-4370. **ED** Laurence J Kirmayer, MD. **NLM** W1 TR228QB. Index available (bound in last issue). **Bk Rev**, (Qty: 20). **Pr Rev. Circ:** 550. available on microfilm from University Microfilms International (UMI). ***Continues*** *Transcultural Psychiatric Research, 0315-4386.*
**Desc:** Provides a channel of communication for those psychiatrists and social scientists in different parts of the world who are concerned with the relationship between culture, mental health, and mental ill-health. Its purpose is to help coordinate scientific effort by pooling information about current research in many countries. It continues to be the most comprehensive and eclectic journal in the field. Each issue includes an extensive bibliographic review of a key area as well as book reviews and abstracts which are of sufficient scope to provide both a summary of content and critical comment.
**Ind/Abst** Middle East Abstr. Index; Psychol. Abstr. (1987-); PsycINFO; PsycLit.

FR
**TRANSITION : REVUE INTERNATIONALE D'ASEPSI DU CHANGEMENT PSYCHIATRIQUE ET SOCIAL.** (19??)-. French. Four times a year. 300.00F France; 350.00F other. EPSI / Association pour l'Etude et la Promotion des Structures Intermediares, 71 rue Ampere, 75017 Paris France. **Tel** 011 46 22 79 28.

RU/0455-6550
**TRUDY LENINGRADSKOGO NAUCHNO-ISSLEDOVATELSKOGO PSIKHONEVROLOGICHESKOGO INSTITUTA IM. V. M. BEKHTEREVA. See** Medical Science and Technology-Neurology.

GW/0935-3224
**TW NEUROLOGIE, PSYCHIATRIE. See** Medical Science and Technology-Neurology.

FR/0396-8669
**V.S.T.** (VST. VIE SOCIALE ET TRAITEMENTS.). [V.S.T.]. **Added/Corp** Centres d'Entrainement aux Methodes d'Education Active (Paris, France). **VFOAT** Vie Sociale et Traitements. Vol. 20, No. 96 (1974)-. Periodical. French. bm (6 issues). 377.08F France; 385.00F other. CEMEA - Centres d'Entrainement aux Methodes d'Education Actives, 76 Boulevard de la Villette, 75940 Paris Cedex 19 France. **Tel** 011 33 1 42063810, 011 33 1 40404390, FAX 011 33 1 42066650. **NLM** W1 V156. **Bk Rev. *Continues*** *Vie Sociale et Traitements, 0504-1864.*
**Desc:** Covers psychiatric nursing and mental health.

SZ/1016-6262
**VERHALTENSTHERAPIE BASEL.** [Verhaltenstherapie Basel]. (1991)-. Periodical. German. qt. $78.00. S. Karger AG, Allschwilerstrasse 10, PO Box - Postfach - Case Postale, CH-4009 Basel Switzerland. **Tel** 011 41 61 306-1111, FAX 011 41 61 306-1234, telex CH 962 652. **ED** I. Hand and H. U. Wittchen. **UDC** 61.
**Desc:** Concentrates on clinical and experimental aspects of behavioral therapy.

US/0042-8272
**VOICES (AMERICAN ACADEMY OF PSYCHOTHERAPISTS).** (VOICES; THE ART AND SCIENCE OF PSYCHOTHERAPY.). **Added/Corp** American Academy of Psychotherapists. Vol. 1 (Fall 1965)-. Periodical. English. Four times a year. $72.50 US; $87.50 other. Readers Services / Voices, c/o Dr. Monique Savlin, 2752 Ridge Avenue, Evanston IL 60201. **ED** Dr. Monique Savlin. **LC** RC475; .V6. **NLM** W1 VO341. **[CCC]. Bk Rev. Ad Acc. Pr Rev. Circ:** 1,500. available on microfilm and microfiche from University Microfilms International (UMI).
**Desc:** Explores psychotherapy relationship through experimental accounts of the therapeutic process, editorials, interviews, theoretical articles, reviews, peer supervision, humor, and poetry.

US/0196-6537
**WASHINGTON PSYCHIATRIC SOCIETY DIRECTORY, THE. Main/Corp** Washington Psychiatric Society, Washington, DC. 14th- Ed.; 1978/79-. Directory. English. Washington Psychiatric Society, Washington DC 20005. **UDC** 616.89(058.7)(753). **NLM** WM 22 AD6 D5. ***Continues*** *Directory of Members and Clinical Psychiatric Facilities in the Washington Area.*

US/0161-4568
**WEEKLY PSYCHIATRY UPDATE SERIES.** 1- 1976-. Periodical. English. wk. Continuing Professional Education Center, 1101 State Road/Building Q, Princeton NJ 08540. **Tel** (609)924-4500. **UDC** 616.89. **NLM** W1 WE156.

US/0043-860X
**WORLD JOURNAL OF PSYCHOSYNTHESIS. VFOAT** Shijiee Jingshenn Zonghexue Yueekan; Journal Mondiale de Psychosynthese. V. 1- Sept. 1969-. Periodical. English. an. $20.00. World Journal Press, Box 859, East Lansing MI 48823. **Tel** (517)372-4660. **ED** H C Tien. **LC** RC475; .W67. **DD** 616.89/1/05. **UDC** 616.89; 615.851.212. **NLM** W1 WO88H. **Bk Rev. Ad Acc. Circ:** 300 (ctrl). available on microfilm and microfiche from University Microfilms International (UMI).
**Desc:** Topics include psychiatry, psychology, video techniques, family psychiatry, Chinese language and medicine. Covers a wide range of U.S. and international articles.

US/0084-3970
**YEAR BOOK OF PSYCHIATRY AND APPLIED MENTAL HEALTH, THE.** [Year b. psychiatry appl. ment. health]. **VFOAT** Psychiatry and Applied Mental Health. **VAT** Yearbook of Psychiatry and Applied Mental Health. (1970)-. English. an. $59.95. Mosby Year Book Inc., 11830 Westline Industrial Drive, St Louis MO 63146. **Tel** (800)325-4177, (314)872-8370, FAX (314)432-1380, telex 44-2402. **ED** Herbert Weiner, John C Nemiah, Daniel X Freedman, Herbert Y Meltzer, John A Talbott, Reginald S Lourie. **LC** RC329; .Y422. **DD** 616.89/005. **UDC** 616.89(058). **NLM** W1 YE316K. ***Supersedes in part*** *Yearbook of Neurology, Psychiatry and Neurosurgery (Chicago, ILL. : 1953), 0364-5126.*

US/0277-6790
**YEARBOOK OF THE INTERNATIONAL ASSOCIATION FOR CHILD AND ADOLESCENT PSYCHIATRY AND ALLIED PROFESSIONS.** [Yearb. Int. Assoc. Child Adolesc. Psychiatr. Allied Prof.]. Vol. 6-. Monographic series. English. an. Price varies per volume. John Wiley & Sons, Inc., 605 Third Avenue, New York NY 10158-0012. **Tel** (212)850-6000, (212)850-6645, FAX (212)850-6088, telex 12-7063. **(Subscription address:** John Wiley & Sons / England, Baffins Lane, Chichester, West Sussex PO19 1UD England.**)** **ED** E James Anthony. **UDC** 616.89-053.2/.7(058). **NLM** W1 YE42. Index available in last issue of volume--attached. ***Continues*** *Yearbook of the International Association for Child Psychiatry and Allied Professions, 0090-6719.*

PL/0324-8526
**ZAGADNIENIA WYCHOWAWCZE A ZDROWIE PSYCHICZNE. See** Medical Science and Technology-Pediatrics.

SZ/1011-6877
**ZEITSCHRIFT FUER GERONTOPSYCHOLOGIE & -PSYCHIATRIE. See** Medical Science and Technology-Geriatrics.

SZ/0301-6811
**ZEITSCHRIFT FUER KINDER- UND JUGENDPSYCHIATRIE.** [Z. Kinder-Jugendpsychiatr.]. (1973)-. Periodical. German. qt (4 issues). 109.00F. Verlag Hans Huber Ag Bern, Laenggass Strasse 76, CH 3000 Bern 9 Switzerland. **Tel** 011 41 31 3004500. **ED** H. Remschmidt, M. H. Schmidt, P. Strunk. **[CCC]. Pr Rev. Circ:** 1,300. Documents

available from The Genuine Article. ***Continues*** *Jahrbuch fuer Jugendpsychiatrie und Ihre Grenzgebiete., 0448-1534.*
**Ind/Abst** Curr. Contents Soc. Behav. Sci.; EMBASE; Index Med.; PsycINFO (1976-); PsycLit; Res. Alert [Full Cov.]; Soc. Sci. Cit. Index [Full Cov.].

GW/0722-3064
**ZENTRALBLATT NEUROLOGIE, PSYCHIATRIE. See** Medical Science and Technology-Neurology.

NE
**ZET M OP. See** Children and Youth Interests.

RU/0044-4588
**ZURNAL NEVROPATOLOGII I PSIHIATRII IM S.S. KORSAKOVA.** ***Ceased.*** **See** Medical Science and Technology-Neurology.

## RADIOLOGY

●US/0942-8925
**ABDOMINAL IMAGING.** Vol. 18, No. 1 (1993)-. Periodical. English. Six times a year. $224.00. Springer-Verlag New York Inc., 175 5th Avenue, New York NY 10010. **Tel** (212)460-1500, telex 232 235 SPB UR. **(Subscription address:** Springer Verlag New York Inc. / for North America, 44 Hartz Way, Secaucus NJ 07096.**) ED** Morton Meyers, Gary Ghahremani. **NLM** W1; AB145. **CODEN** ABIMEL. ***Formed by the union of*** *Gastrointestinal Radiology, 0364-2356* ***and*** *Urologic Radiology, 0171-1091.*
**Desc:** Devoted to radiological imaging of both the alimentary and genitourinary tracts. Contains a special section devoted to urologic radiology.
**Ind/Abst** Curr. Contents Clin. Med.; Index Med. (1993-); Sci. Cit. Index.

US
**ABMS ... DIRECTORY OF CERTIFIED RADIOLOGISTS AND RADIOLOGICAL PHYSICISTS. Added/Corp** American Board of Medical Specialties. ABMS Research and Education Foundation. American Board of Radiology. **VFOAT** Directory of Certified Radiologists and Radiological Physicists. **VAT** American Board of Medical Specialties Directory of Certified Radiologists and Radiological Physicists. (19??)-. Directory. English. be. American Board of Medical Specialties, 1 Rotary Center, Suite 805, Evanston IL 60201. **Tel** (708)491-9091. **LC** R895.A4; A245. **DD** 616.07/57/02573. **NLM** WN 22; AA1 A152. ***Continues*** *ABMS Directory of Certified Radiologists, 0883-1238.*

US
**ABSTRACTS FOR THE SOCIETY OF MAGNETIC RESONANCE IMAGING.** Abstracting/Indexing Service. English. an. $25.00. Society fro Magnetic Recource Imaging., 213 W Institute Place, Suite 501, Chicago IL 60610. **Tel** (312)751-2590.

US/0098-6070
**ACR BULLETIN.** ***Title Change.*** [ACR bull.]. **Added/Corp** American College of Radiology. Vol. 25 (Jan. 15, 1969)-. Periodical. English. Twelve times a year. American College of Radiology, 1891 Preston White Drive, Reston VA 22091. **Tel** (703)648-8900, FAX (703)648-3240. **ED** Marion M Dinitz. **DD** 616. **NLM** W1; A1138K. Index available. cum. index. **Circ:** 20,000. ***Continues*** *American College of Radiology Bulletin, 0098-6100.* ***Continued by*** *Bulletin (American College of Radiology).*

SW/0284-1851
**ACTA RADIOLOGICA (STOCKHOLM, SWEDEN : 1987).** (ACTA RADIOLOGICA.). [Acta radiol.]. Vol. 28, Issue 1 (Jan./Feb. 1987)-. Academic Scholarly Publication. English. bm. kr1020.00 Europe; kr1100.00 other. Munksgaard International Publishers Ltd, PO Box 2148, DK-1016 Copenhagen K Denmark. **Tel** 011 45 33 12 70 30, FAX 011 45 33 12 93 87, telex 19431 MUNKS DK. **ED** Erik Boijsen. **UDC** 616-073.7. **NLM** W1; AC9411G. **CODEN** ACRAE3. **[CCC].** cum. index. **Bk Rev. Ad Acc. Circ:** 6,000 (ctrl). Documents available from Article Express International, The Genuine Article, BIOSIS Document Express, Ask*IEEE, CASDDS. ***Continues*** *Acta Radiologica. Diagnosis, 0567-8056.*
**Desc:** Six issues each of diagnosis and oncology. In diagnosis: medical imaging and all varieties of clinical and experimental radiology. In oncology: radiotherapy, radiobiology and physics.
**Ind/Abst** Biol. Abstr.; Chem. Abstr.; Curr. Contents Clin. Med.; Curr. Contents Life Sci.; Ei Page One; EMBASE; Eng. Index Annu. [Select. Cov.]; Health Plan. Adminis.; Helminthol. Abstr. (19??-19??); Index Med. (1987-); INSPEC (Jan./Feb. 1987-); PESTDOC; Ref. Upd. Deluxe Ed.; Res. Alert [Full Cov.]; Rev. Med. Vet. Mycology; Sci. Cit. Index; SCISEARCH.

SW/0365-5954
**ACTA RADIOLOGICA. SUPPLEMENTUM.** [Acta radiol., Suppl.]. **VFOAT** Supplementum. Vol. 1 (1921)-. Monographic series. English (French and German). ir. Price varies per volume. Munksgaard International Publishers Ltd, PO Box 2148, DK-1016 Copenhagen K Denmark. **Tel** 011 45 33 12 70 30, FAX 011 45 33 12 93 87, telex 19431 MUNKS DK. **NLM** W1 AC9412. **CODEN** ARASA5. **[CCC]. Circ:** 1,000. Documents available from BIOSIS Document Express.
**Ind/Abst** Biol. Abstr.; EMBASE (-1986); Index Med.

IT/0392-0712
**ACTA THERMOGRAPHICA. SUPPLEMENT.** [Acta thermographica. Suppl.]. **VFOAT** Supplement to Acta Thermographica. 1-. Monographic series. English. Three times a year. Price varies per volume. Department of Radiology, University Hospital, 37100 Verona Italy. **UDC** 772.96. **NLM** W1 AC95UF.

US/0738-6974
**ADMINISTRATIVE RADIOLOGY.** (ADMINISTRATIVE RADIOLOGY : AR.). [Adm. radiol.]. **VFOAT** A.R.; AR. (198?)-. Periodical. English. Twelve times a year. $42.00. Glendale Publishing Corporation, 1305 West Glenoaks Boulevard, Glendale CA 91201. **Tel** (818)500-1872. **ED** Darla Haight. **LC** RA975.5.R3; A35. **NLM** W1; AD346. available on microfilm and microfiche from University Microfilms International (UMI).
**Ind/Abst** Health Plan. Adminis.; Hospit. Health Admin. Index (1986-).

US/0160-1636
**ADVANCED EXERCISES IN DIAGNOSTIC RADIOLOGY.** ***Ceased.*** [Adv. exerc. diagn. radiol.]. (1977)-Completed Series (19??). Monographic series. English. ir. W.B. Saunders Company, A Subsidiary of Harcourt Brace Jovanovich, Inc., The Curtis Center/Suite 300, Independence Square West, Philadelphia PA 19106-3399. **Tel** (215)238-7800 or, 5587, FAX (215)238-7883, telex 173146. **(Subscription address:** W. B. Saunders Company / North America Subscriptions, c/o Periodicals, 6277 Sea Harbour Drive, 4th Floor, Orlando FL 32887.**) LC** RC78; .E89. **DD** 616.07/57/05. **UDC** 616-073.7. **NLM** W1 AD402E. **CODEN** AEDREW. Documents available from BIOSIS Document Express. ***Continues*** *Exercises in Diagnostic Radiology.*
**Ind/Abst** Biol. Abstr. (1987-).

UK/0925-5206
**ADVANCES IN ECHO-CONTRAST. VFOAT** Advances in Echocontrast. (199?)-. Periodical. English. qt. $133.00. Kluwer Academic Publishers, Postbus 322, 3300 AH Dordrecht, The Netherlands. **Tel** 011 (31) 78 524400, FAX 011 31 78 183273, telex 20083. **NLM** W1; AD549VH. **CODEN** ADECEJ. **[CCC].** available on microfilm and microfiche from University Microfilms International (UMI).
**Desc:** Strives to help keep you in touch with the most recent advances in imaging technology, echo-enhancing agents and the clinical impact of these developments. Each issue combines an editorial review of recent advances, based on the latest published evidence, with abstracts of important papers published in journals or presented at specialist meetings.

US
**ADVANCES IN MAGNETIC RESONANCE IMAGING.** (19??)-. English. ir. Price varies per volume. Ablex Publishing Corporation, 355 Chestnut Street, Norwood NJ 07648. **Tel** (201)767-8450, (201)767-8455 (Customer Service), FAX (201)767-6717. **ED** Ephraim Zeig.
**Desc:** Details state-of-the-art research in magnetic resonance imaging.

US/0925-9848
**ADVANCES IN MRI CONTRAST.** English. qt. $121.00. Kluwer Academic Publishers, Postbus 322, 3300 AH Dordrecht, The Netherlands. **Tel** 011 (31) 78 524400, FAX 011 31 78 183273, telex 20083. **ED** Robert Brasch, Allen Elster, and Roland Felix. **Pr Rev. Acid Free.**
**Desc:** Helps keep you in touch with the most recent advances in imaging techniques, contrast-enhancing agents and the clinical impact of these developments.

US/0065-3292
**ADVANCES IN RADIATION BIOLOGY. See** Biology.

US/0376-0308
**ADVANCES IN X-RAY ANALYSIS.** (ADVANCES IN X-RAY ANALYSIS : PROCEEDINGS OF THE ... ANNUAL CONFERENCE ON APPLICATION OF X-RAY ANALYSIS.). [Adv. x-ray anal.]. **Main/Conf** Conference on Application of X-Ray Analysis. **Added/Corp** Denver Research Institute. **VFOAT** Advances in X-Ray Analysis; Proceedings of the ... Annual Conference on Application of X-Ray Analysis. Vol. 1 (Aug. 7-9, 1957)-. Proceedings. English. an. Price varies per volume. Plenum Press, 233 Spring Street, New York NY 10013-1578. **Tel** (212)620-8000, (800)221-9369, FAX (212)463-0742, (212)807-1047, telex 23/421139. **LC** TA417.25; .C65a. **DD** 539.7/222. **NLM** W3 AD25. **CODEN** AXRAAA. Documents available from Article Express International, Ask*IEEE, CASDDS.
**Ind/Abst** Bioeng. Abstr.; Chem. Abstr.; Ei Page One; Energy Res. Abstr.; Eng. Index Annu.; GeoRef; INSPEC; Soils Fert.; World Ceram. Abstr.

NE/0928-1509
**ADVANCES IN X-RAY CONTRAST.** qt. $136.00. Kluwer Academic Publishers, Postbus 322, 3300 AH Dordrecht, The Netherlands. **Tel** 011 (31) 78 524400, FAX 011 31 78 183273, telex 20083.
**Desc:** Each issue combines an expert editorial overview of the state of the art, based on published evidence from clinical research, with abstracts of important papers published in the journals or presented at specialist meetings.

GW/0939-267X
**AKTUELLE RADIOLOGIE.** [Aktuelle Radiol.]. No., 1 (Jan. 1991)-. Periodical. German (summaries and/or abstracts in English). bm (6 issues). $149.00. Georg Thieme Verlag Stuttgart, Postfach 301120, D 70451 Stuttgart Germany. **Tel** 011 49 711 89310, FAX 011 49 711 8931298, telex 7 252 275 GTVD. **(Subscription address:** Thieme Medical Publishers Inc., 381 Park Avenue South, New York NY 10016.**) NLM** W1; AK9955K. **CODEN** AKRAEP. available on microfilm from University Microfilms International (UMI). Documents available from BIOSIS Document Express. ***Continues*** *Rontgen-Blatter, 0300-8592.*
**Ind/Abst** Biol. Abstr. (1991-); EMBASE; Health Plan. Adminis.; Index Med. (1991-).

US/0887-7971
**AMERICAN JOURNAL OF CARDIAC IMAGING. See** Medical Science and Technology-Cardiology.

US/0195-6108
**AMERICAN JOURNAL OF NEURORADIOLOGY. See** Medical Science and Technology-Neurology.

US/0361-803X
**AMERICAN JOURNAL OF ROENTGENOLOGY (1976).** (AJR, AMERICAN JOURNAL OF ROENTGENOLOGY.). [Am. j. roentgenol.]. **Added/Corp** American Roentgen Ray Society. American Radium Society. **VFOAT** AJR; American Journal of Roentgenology. Vol. 126 (Jan. 1976)-. Periodical. English. mo. $125.00 (individual), $135.00 (institution) US; $180.00 (individual), $190.00 (institution), other. American Roentgen Ray Society, 1891 Preston White Drive, Reston VA 22091. **Tel** (703)648-8992, (800)438-2777, FAX (703)264-8863. **(Subscription address:** AJR American Journal of Roentgenology, PO Box 17266, Baltimore MD 21297**) ED** Robert N. Berk. **LC** RM845; .A3. **DD** 616.07/57/05. **NLM** W1 A117GR; W1 AM522. **CODEN** AJROAM. **[CCC].** Index available (Free). **Ad Acc. Pr Rev. Circ:** 21,000. available on microfilm and microfiche from University Microfilms International (UMI). Documents available from The Genuine Article, BIOSIS Document Express. ***Continues*** *American Journal of Roentgenology, Radium Therapy, and Nuclear Medicine, 0002-9580.*
**Desc:** High quality original articles on all aspects of general and diagnostic radiology, covering all current modalities including MRI.
**Ind/Abst** Abr. Index Med.; Biol. Abstr.; Calcium Calcif. Tissue Abstr.; CSA Neuro. Abstr. (?-?); Cumul. Index Nurs. Allied Health Lit.; Curr. Contents Clin. Med.; Curr. Contents Life Sci.; Dairy Sci. Abstr.; Dev. Med. Child Neurol.; EMBASE; Energy Res. Abstr. (March 1980-); Health Devices Alerts; Helminthol. Abstr. (19??-19??); Index Med.; INIS Atomindex [Micro.]; Int. Pharm. Abstr.; Iowa Drug Inf. Serv. (1968-); Mod. Med.; Nutr. Abstr. Rev., Ser. A, Hum. Exp.; Life Sci. Collect.; PESTDOC; Physic. Medline Plus; Protozoolog. Abstr.; Ref. Upd. Basic Ed.; Ref. Upd. Deluxe Ed.; Res. Alert [Full Cov.]; Rev. Med. Vet. Mycology; Rev. Plant Pathol.; Sci. Cit. Index; SCISEARCH; Soc. Sci. Cit. Index [Select. Cov.]; SportSearch; Toxicol. Abstr. (19??-19??); Virol. AIDS Abstr.

FR/0003-4185
**ANNALES DE RADIOLOGIE.** [Ann. radiol.]. Vol. 1 (1958)-. Academic Scholarly Publication. French (summaries and/or abstracts in English). ir (8 issues). 1450.00F France, 2025.00F other. Semaine de Hopitaux, 31 Boulevard de la Tour-Maubourg, 75007 Paris, France. **Tel** 011 33 1 40 62 64 00. **NLM** W1 AN377. **CODEN** ANLRAT. **[CCC].** cum. index. **Bk Rev. Ad Acc. Pr Rev. Circ:** 4,000. Documents available from The Genuine Article, BIOSIS Document Express, CASDDS.
**Ind/Abst** Biol. Abstr.; Chem. Abstr.; CIS Abstr.; Curr. Contents Clin. Med.; EMBASE; Energy Res. Abstr. (May 1981-); Health Plan. Adminis.; Helminthol. Abstr. (1991-); Index Med.; Nucl. Sci. Abstr.; Life Sci. Collect.; Protozoolog. Abstr.; Res. Alert [Select. Cov.]; Saf. Health Work; SCISEARCH; SportSearch.

JA
**ANNALS OF NUCLEAR MEDICINE. Added/Corp** Nihon Kaku Igakkai. Vol. 1, No. 1 (Sept. 1987)-. Periodical. English. Three times a year. $103.50. Nihon Kaku Igakkai, (Japnense Soceity of Nuclear Medicine), Nihon Aisotopu Kyokai,, 28-45 Honkomagome, 2 Chome, Bunkyoku, Tokyoto 113 Japan. **(Subscription address:** Japan Publications Trading Company, Ltd., PO Box 5030, Tokyo International, Tokyo 100-31 Japan.**) NLM** W1; AN6157. Documents available from CASDDS.
**Ind/Abst** Chem. Abstr.; EMBASE; Health Plan. Adminis.

UK/0146-6453
**ANNALS OF THE ICRP.** [Ann. ICRP]. **Added/Corp** International Commission on Radiological Protection. **VAT** Annals of the International Commission on Radiological Protection. Vol. 1, (1977)-. Academic Scholarly Publication. English. qt. $194.00 The Americas; £130.00 other. Pergamon Press, An Imprint of Elsevier Science Ltd., The Boulevard, Langford Lane, Kidlington, Oxford OX5 1GB United Kingdom. **Tel** 011 44 865 843000, 011 44 865 843699, FAX 011 44 865 843010. **(Subscription address:** Elsevier Science Ltd. Oxford Fulfillment Centre, PO Box 800, Kidlington, Oxford OX5 1DX United Kingdom.**)** **ED** H. Smith (editor's address: ICRP, Box No. 35, Didcot, Oxfordshire Ox110RJ United Kingdom). **LC** RA1231.R2; I2 subser. **DD** 614.8/39. **NLM** W1 AN626U. **CODEN** ANICD6. **[CCC].** available on microfilm; available on microfiche. Documents available from Article Express International, BIOSIS Document Express, CASDDS, Documents on Demand.
**Desc:** Provides general guidance on the widespread use of radiation sources.
**Ind/Abst** Bioeng. Abstr.; Biol. Abstr.; Chem. Abstr.; Ei Page One; EMBASE; Energy Inf. Abstr.; Eng. Index Annu.; Environ. Abstr.; Health Plan. Adminis.; Index Med. (1980-); Saf. Health Work (1980-).

US/0193-5224
**ANNUAL PROGRESS REPORT - UNIVERSITY OF CALIFORNIA, LABORATORY OF NUCLEAR MEDICINE AND RADIATION BIOLOGY.** **See** Medical Science and Technology-Nuclear Medicine.

US
**ANNUAL REPORT OF THE DIVISION OF BIOLOGICAL EFFECTS, BUREAU OF RADIOLOGICAL HEALTH / PREPARED BY DIVISION OF BIOLOGICAL EFFECTS STAFF.** **Added/Corp** United States. Bureau of Radiological Health. Division of Biological Effects. WHO Collaborating Center for Training and General Tasks in Radiation Medicine. (1979)-. English. an. Radiological Health Bulletin, Center for Devices & Radiological Health, HFZ 30, 5600 Fishers Lane, Rockville MD 20857. **Tel** (301)443-5807. **LC** Discard. Documents available from CASDDS. ***Continues*** *Quadrennial Report of the Division of Biological Effects.*
**Ind/Abst** Chem. Abstr.

RU/0365-4141
**APPARATURA I METODY RENTGENOVSKOGO ANALIZA.** [Appar. i metod. rentgenovskogo anal.]. (1967)-. Russian. ir. **UDC** 621.386. Documents available from CASDDS.
**Desc:** Information on x-ray apparatus and methods of x-ray analysis.
**Ind/Abst** Chem. Abstr.

US/0160-9963
**APPLIED RADIOLOGY (1976).** (APPLIED RADIOLOGY.). [Appl. radiol.]. Vol. 5 No. 4 (July/Aug. 1976)-. Periodical. English. mo. $55.00 US; $92.00. Romaine Pierson Publishing Inc., 80 Shore Road, Port Washington NY 11050. **Tel** (516)883-6350. **ED** Betsy Schreiber. **LC** RM845; .A65. **DD** 616.07/57/05. **UDC** 616-073.7. **NLM** W1 AP528TE. Index available. **Bk Rev. Ad Acc. Circ:** 27,000 (ctrl). ***Continues*** *Applied Radiology and Nuclear Medicine, 0099-2364.*
**Desc:** Devoted to both radiologists and radiologic technologists in diagnostic radiology, radiation therapy, computed tomography, ultrasound, thermography, MRI and nuclear medicine. Articles cover the entire gamut of professional interests - technical advances, case histories, facilities reports, equipment, supplies, etc.
**Ind/Abst** Cumul. Index Nurs. Allied Health Lit.; EMBASE; Health Devices Alerts; Health Plan. Adminis.; Hospit. Health Admin. Index.

US/0161-3863
**ASRT SCANNER.** [ASRT scan.]. **Main/Corp** American Society of Radiologic Technologists. **VAT** American Society of Radiologic Technologists Scanner. Periodical. English. bm. $25.00. American Society of Radiologic Technologists, 15000 Central Avenue Southeast, Albuquerque NM 87123-3917. **Tel** (505)298-4500, FAX (505)298-5063. **DD** 610. **UDC** 616-073.7-057.86(73). ctrl circ.

AT/0004-8461
**AUSTRALASIAN RADIOLOGY.** [Australas. radiol.]. **Added/Corp** Royal Australasian College of Radiologists. Vol. 10 (1966)-. Academic Scholarly Publication. English. Four times a year. 157.00Aus$ Australia; 224.00Aus$ other. Blackwell Scientific Publications Australia, 54 University Street, PO Box 378, Carlton Victoria 3053 Australia. **Tel** 011 61 3 3470300, FAX 011 61 3 3475001, telex 10716421. **ED** John Palmer. **NLM** W1 AU335N. **CODEN** AURDAW. Index available in last issue of volume--attached. cum. index. **Bk Rev. Ad Acc, Adv Mgr:** Bloxham Chambers. **Circ:** 1,950 (ctrl). Documents available from BIOSIS Document Express, CASDDS. ***Continues*** *College of Radiologists of Australasia. Journal.*
**Desc:** Diagnostic radiology, radiation, oncology and other sciences of direct or indirect importance to these medical specialties.
**Ind/Abst** Biol. Abstr.; Calcium Calcif. Tissue Abstr.; Chem. Abstr.; EMBASE; Energy Res. Abstr.; Health Plan. Adminis.; Index Med.; Life Sci. Collect.

GW/0932-6588
**BILDGEBENDE VERFAHREN IN DER NEURORADIOLOGIE.** **See** Medical Science and Technology-Neurology.

SZ/1012-5655
**BILDGEBUNG (BASEL).** (BILDGEBUNG.). [Bildgebung]. **VFOAT** Imaging. Vol. 56, No. 1 (Nov. 1988)-. Periodical. German (English). Four times a year (one volume per year). $106.00. S. Karger AG, Allschwilerstrasse 10, PO Box - Postfach - Case Postale, CH-4009 Basel Switzerland. **Tel** 011 41 61 306-1111, FAX 011 41 61 306-1234, telex CH 962 652. **ED** W.G. Zoller. **NLM** W1; BI615NH. **CODEN** BILDEZ. Index available. cum. index. **Bk Rev. Ad Acc. Circ:** 5,000 (ctrl). available in microform. Documents available from BIOSIS Document Express. ***Continues*** *Diagnostic Imaging in Clinical Medicine, 0254-881X.*
**Desc:** Provides coverage of the latest technical developments in radiology and other non-invasive means of diagnosis. Describes the various procedures available to the contemporary radiologist as a result of rapid technological advances: endoscopy, ultrasound, Doppler sonography and nuclear resonance imaging.
**Ind/Abst** Biol. Abstr.; EMBASE; Health Plan. Adminis.; Index Med. (Nov. 1988-); Ref. Upd. Deluxe Ed.

UK/0961-2653
**BJR SUPPLEMENT.** [BJR suppl.]. **Added/Corp** British Institute of Radiology. (1989)-. Monographic series. English. Price varies per volume. British Institute of Radiology, 36 Portland Place, London W1N 4AT England. **Tel** 011 44 71 580 4085. **NLM** W1; BI996. ***Continues*** *British Journal of Radiology. Supplement, 0306-8854.*
**Ind/Abst** Health Plan. Adminis.; Index Med. (1989-).

UK/0007-1285
**BRITISH JOURNAL OF RADIOLOGY, THE.** [Br. j. radiol.]. **Added/Corp** British Institute of Radiology. Vol. 1 (Jan. 1928)-. Academic Scholarly Publication. English. mo. £210.00 UK and EEC; £230.00 other. British Institute of Radiology, 36 Portland Place, London W1N 4AT England. **Tel** 011 44 71 580 4085. **(Subscription address:** British Institute of Radiology, PO Box 294, London WC1H 9TB United Kingdom.**)** **ED** J.T. Patton and N.J. McNally. **LC** QC1; .B72. **NLM** W1 BR624R. **CODEN** BJRAAP. Index available. **Bk Rev. Ad Acc. Pr Rev. Circ:** 4,600. available on microfilm and microfiche from University Microfilms International (UMI). Documents available from The Genuine Article, BIOSIS Document Express, Ask*IEEE, CASDDS. ***Formed by the union of*** *British Journal of Radiology. B. I. R. Section* ***and*** *British Journal of Radiology. Roentgen Society Section.*
**Desc:** Covers the clinical aspects of radiology, radiotherapy and oncology, and medical physics, radiobiology and radiation protection.
**Ind/Abst** Abr. Index Med.; Biol. Abstr.; Chem. Abstr.; Curr. Aware. Biol. Sci., CABS; Curr. Contents Clin. Med.; Curr. Contents Life Sci.; Dairy Sci. Abstr.; Ei Page One; EMBASE; Energy Res. Abstr.; Health Plan. Adminis.; Helminthol. Abstr.; Index Med.; INSPEC (1968-); Nutr. Abstr. Rev., Ser. B, Live Feeds and Feed.; Nutr. Abstr. Rev., Ser. A, Hum. Exp.; Peace Res. Abstr. J. (1984-1987); Life Sci. Collect.; PESTDOC; Phys. Med. Biol. (19??-19??); Protozoolog. Abstr.; Ref. Upd. Deluxe Ed.; Res. Alert [Full Cov.]; Rev. Med. Vet. Mycology; Risk Abstr. (19??-19??); Saf. Health Work; Sci. Cit. Index; SCISEARCH.

●US
**BULLETIN / AMERICAN COLLEGE OF RADIOLOGY.** **VFOAT** A.ARC bulletin. Vol. 48, issue 8 (Aug. 1992)-. Periodical. English. mo. $60.00. American College of Radiology, 1891 Preston White Drive, Reston VA 22091. **Tel** (703)648-8900, FAX (703)648-3240. **NLM** W1; BU478HAG. ***Continues*** *ACR Bulletin, 0098-6070.*

US/0194-1399
**BUREAU OF RADIOLOGICAL HEALTH PUBLICATIONS SUBJECT INDEX.** [Bur. Radiol. Health publ. subj. index]. **Main/Corp** United States. Bureau of Radiological Health. Office of Management and Systems. Technical Information Staff. (Aug. 1979)-. English. ir. Radiological Health Bulletin, Center for Devices & Radiological Health, HFZ 30, 5600 Fishers Lane, Rockville MD 20857. **Tel** (301)443-5807. **NLM** ZWN 100 B11B. ***Continues*** *United States. Bureau of Radiological Health. Bureau of Radiological Health Publications Subject Index, 0194-1399.*

CN/0846-5371
**CANADIAN ASSOCIATION OF RADIOLOGISTS JOURNAL.** [Can. Assoc. Radiol. j.]. **Added/Corp** Canadian Association of Radiologists. **VFOAT** Journal l'Association Canadienne des Radiologistes; Journal of the Canadian Association of Radiologists. Vol. 37, No. 1 (March 1986)-. Academic Scholarly Publication. English (summaries and/or abstracts in French). bm (Feb., Apr., June, Aug., Oct., Dec.). 110.00Can$ Canada; $110.00 US. Canadian Association of Radiologists, 5105 Buchan Street, Suite 510, Montreal Quebec H4P 2R9 Canada. **Tel** (514) 738-3111. **(Subscription address:** Canadian Medical Association, CMA House PO Box 8650, Ottawa, Ontario K1G 0G8 Canada**)** **DD** 616.07/57/05. **NLM** W1; CA529. **CODEN** CARJE4. **[CCC]. Bk Rev. Ad Acc.** Documents available from BIOSIS Document Express, CASDDS. ***Continues*** *Canadian Association of Radiologists. Journal of the Canadian Association of Radiologists, 0008-2902.*
**Desc:** The journal reports the most recent advances in the field of radiology, including equipment, technique and procedures. Information appears in the form of review articles, original research articles and case reports, enhanced by appropriate photographs and diagrams.
**Ind/Abst** Biol. Abstr.; Chem. Abstr.; EMBASE; Index Med. (1986-); Sci. Cit. Index.

CN/0820-5930
**CANADIAN JOURNAL OF MEDICAL RADIATION TECHNOLOGY.** [Can. j. med. radiat. technol.]. **Added/Corp** Canadian Association of Medical Radiation Technologists. **VFOAT** Medical Radiation Technology. Vol. 18, No. 1 (March 1987)-. Periodical. Multiple languages (French and English). Four times a year (Mar., May, Aug., Oct.). 26.75Can$ Canada; 30.00Can$ North America; 35.00Can$ other. Canadian Association of Medical Radiation Technologists, 294 Albert Street, Suite 601, Ottawa Ontario K1P 6E6 Canada. **Tel** (613)234-0012, (800)463-9729, FAX (613)234-1097. **ED** Suzette Besner. **DD** 616.07/57/05. Index available (Bound in 4th iss.(Oct.)). **Bk Rev. Ad Acc, Adv Mgr:** S. Besner. **Circ:** 10,000. available on microfilm. ***Continues*** *Canadian Journal of Radiography, Radiotherapy, Nuclear Medicine, 0319-4434;* ***Absorbed*** *Journal Canadien des Tehniques en Radiation Medicale, 0835-7544.*
**Desc:** Featuring topical research submissions, techniques and findings from medical radiation technologists.
**Ind/Abst** Cumul. Index Nurs. Allied Health Lit.; Hospit. Health Admin. Index.

US/1057-9052
**CANCERGRAM. SERIES CT15, CLINICAL TREATMENT OF CANCER. RADIATION THERAPY.** ***Ceased.*** **See** Medical Science and Technology-Neoplasma, Neoplastic.

US/0174-1551
**CARDIOVASCULAR AND INTERVENTIONAL RADIOLOGY.** [Cardiovasc. intervent. radiol.]. **Added/Corp** European College of Angiography. Society of Cardiovascular Radiology. North American Society for Cardiac Radiology. European Society of Cardiovascular and Interventional Radiology. Vol. 3 (Feb. 1980)-. Periodical. English. bm. $180.00. Springer-Verlag New York Inc., 175 5th Avenue, New York NY 10010. **Tel** (212)460-1500, telex 232 235 SPB UR. **(Subscription address:** Springer Verlag New York Inc. / for North America, 44 Hartz Way, Secaucus NJ 07096.**)** **ED** Klemens Barth. **NLM** W1 CA77MI. **CODEN** CAIRDG. **[CCC]. Bk Rev. Pr Rev.** available on microfilm and microfiche from University Microfilms International (UMI). Documents available from The Genuine Article. ***Continues*** *Cardiovascular Radiology, 0342-7196.*
**Desc:** Publishes papers describing recent progress in both imaging and interventional techniques, and presents reviews evaluating the successes, failures, and complications of these innovations.
**Ind/Abst** Curr. Contents Clin. Med.; EMBASE; Health Plan. Adminis.; Helminthol. Abstr. (1991-); Index Med.; INIS Atomindex [Micro.]; Life Sci. Collect.; Res. Alert [Select. Cov.]; SCISEARCH.

XR/0069-2344
**CESKOSLOVENSKA RADIOLOGIE.** [Cesk. radiol.]. Vol. 18- 1964-. Academic Scholarly Publication. Czech (summaries and/or abstracts in English and Russian; table of contents in English and Russian). bm. $71.40. **(Subscription address:** Artia Pegas Press Ltd., Palac Metro Narodni Trida 25, 11210 Prague 1 Czech Republic.**)** **UDC** 616-073.7. **NLM** W1 CE903. **[CCC].** ***Continues*** *Ceskoslovenska Rentgenologie.*
**Ind/Abst** EMBASE; Energy Res. Abstr.; Index Med.; Life Sci. Collect.

CC/0529-5661
**CHUNG-HUA FANG SHE HSUEH TSA CHIH.** (CHUNG-HUA FANG SHE HSUEH TSA CHIH / CHUNG-HUA I HSUEH HUI FANG SHE HSUEH HUI CHU PIEN.). [Chung-hua fang she hsueh tsa chih]. **Added/Corp** Chung-Hua i Hsueh Hui. Fang She Hsueh Hui. **VFOAT** Chinese Journal of Radiology; Zhonghua Fangshexue Zazhi. (1953)-. Academic Scholarly Publication. Chinese (summaries and/or abstracts in English; table of contents in English). bm (6 issues). $97.56. **(Subscription address:** China International Book Trading Corporation, PO Box 399, Library Service Department, Beijing 100044 People's Republic of China.**)** **CODEN** CHFSAG. Documents available from CASDDS.
**Ind/Abst** Chem. Abstr. (1953-1983); Index Med. (1979-1989).

US/0899-7071
**CLINICAL IMAGING.** [Clin. imaging]. Vol. 13, No. 1 (Mar. 1989)-. Academic Scholarly Publication. English. qt (1 volume). $258.00 US; $288.00 other. Elsevier Science Publishing Company Inc, Madison Square

Station, PO Box 882, New York NY 10159-0882. **Tel** (212)633-3950, FAX (212)633-3990. **LC** RC78.7.T6; C64. **DD** 616.07/54/05. **NLM** W1; CL71N. **CODEN** CLIMEB. **[CCC]. Pr Rev.** available on microfilm and microfiche from University Microfilms International (UMI). Documents available from Article Express International, The Genuine Article, BIOSIS Document Express. ***Continues*** *Journal of Computed Tomography, 0149-936X.*
**Ind/Abst** Biol. Abstr. (1989-); Curr. Contents Clin. Med.; EMBASE; Energy Res. Abstr.; Eng. Index Annu.; Health Plan. Adminis.; Index Med. (1989-); Index Vet.; INIS Atomindex [Micro.]; Protozoolog. Abstr.; Ref. Upd. Deluxe Ed.; Res. Alert [Full Cov.]; Sci. Cit. Index; SCISEARCH.

US/0363-9762
**CLINICAL NUCLEAR MEDICINE. See** Medical Science and Technology-Nuclear Medicine.

UK/0009-9260
**CLINICAL RADIOLOGY.** [Clin. radiol.]. **Added/Corp** Royal College of Radiologists (Great Britain). Vol. 11 (Jan. 1960)-. Academic Scholarly Publication. English. mo (12 issues). $251.00 US & Canada; £147.50 Europe; £162.00 other. Blackwell Scientific Publications Ltd, Marston Book Services, PO Box 87, Oxford OX2 ODT UK. **Tel** 011 44 865 791155, FAX 011 44 865 791927, telex 837 515 MARDIS G. **ED** I. H. Kerr. **NLM** W1 CL768GK. **CODEN** CLRAAG. **[CCC]. Bk Rev. Ad Acc. Pr Rev.** available on microfilm and microfiche from University Microfilms International (UMI). Documents available from The Genuine Article, BIOSIS Document Express, CASDDS. ***Continues*** *Faculty of Radiologists. Journal of the Faculty of Radiologists.*
**Desc:** Devoted to radiodiagnosis, radiotherapy, oncology and allied subjects, with emphasis on clinical aspects of radiology. An international forum for exchange of news, research, techniques, and case studies.
**Ind/Abst** Biol. Abstr.; Chem. Abstr.; Curr. Aware. Biol. Sci., CABS; Curr. Contents Clin. Med.; EMBASE; Health Plan. Adminis.; Index Med.; Nutr. Abstr. Rev., Ser. B, Live Feeds and Feed.; Nutr. Abstr. Rev., Ser. A, Hum. Exp.; Life Sci. Collect.; Phys. Med. Biol. (19??-19??); Protozoolog. Abstr.; Ref. Upd. Deluxe Ed.; Res. Alert [Full Cov.]; Saf. Health Work; Sci. Cit. Index; SCISEARCH; Soc. Sci. Cit. Index [Select. Cov.].

US/0172-4843
**COMPREHENSIVE MANUALS IN RADIOLOGY.** (1978)-. Monographic series. English. ir. Price varies per volume. Springer-Verlag New York Inc., 175 5th Avenue, New York NY 10010. **Tel** (212)460-1500, telex 232 235 SPB UR. **(Subscription address:** Springer Verlag New York Inc. / for North America, 44 Hartz Way, Secaucus NJ 07096.**) ED** H.G. Jacobson.
**Desc:** Contains articles on radiology of the heart.

US/0895-6111
**COMPUTERIZED MEDICAL IMAGING AND GRAPHICS.** (COMPUTERIZED MEDICAL IMAGING AND GRAPHICS : THE OFFICIAL JOURNAL OF THE COMPUTERIZED MEDICAL IMAGING SOCIETY.). [Comput. med. imaging graph.]. **Added/Corp** Computerized Medical Imaging Society. Vol. 12, No. 1 (Jan./Feb. 1988)-. Periodical. English. bm. $686.00 The Americas; £460.00 other. Pergamon Press, An Imprint of Elsevier Science Ltd., The Boulevard, Langford Lane, Kidlington, Oxford OX5 1GB United Kingdom. **Tel** 011 44 865 843000, 011 44 865 843699, FAX 011 44 865 843010. **(Subscription address:** Elsevier Science Ltd. Oxford Fulfillment Centre, PO Box 800, Kidlington, Oxford OX5 1DX United Kingdom.**) ED** Robert S. Ledley. **DD** 616. **NLM** W1; CO457LK. **CODEN** CMIGEY. **Pr Rev.** available on microfilm and microfiche from University Microfilms International (UMI). Documents available from Article Express International, The Genuine Article, BIOSIS Document Express. ***Continues*** *Computerized Radiology, 0730-4862.*
**Desc:** Publication for the exchange of information concerning new developments in medical imaging and graphics and the medical application of imaging and graphics to patient care, including diagnosis, prognosis, and treatment.
**Ind/Abst** Biol. Abstr.; Curr. Aware. Biol. Sci., CABS; Curr. Contents Clin. Med.; Ei Page One; EMBASE; Eng. Index Annu.; Health Plan. Adminis.; Index Med. (Jan.-Feb. 1988, Jan.-Feb. 1988-); INIS Atomindex [Micro.]; Res. Alert [Full Cov.]; SCISEARCH.

US/0149-9009
**CONTEMPORARY DIAGNOSTIC RADIOLOGY.** [Contemp. diagn. radiol.]. Vol. 1, No. 1 (1978)-. Periodical. English. bw. $247.00 (institution) US. Williams & Wilkins Company, 428 East Preston Street, Baltimore MD 21202-3993. **Tel** (410)528-4000, (800)638-6423, FAX (410)528-8596, telex 87669. **(Subscription address:** Williams & Wilkins, PO Box 64380, Baltimore MD 21264.**) ED** Robert Campbell. **NLM** W1; CO769MGH. **CODEN** CDRAEW. **[CCC]. Ad Acc. Circ:** 1,700 (ctrl). Documents available from BIOSIS Document Express, Quick Copies. ***Continues*** *Radiologic Science Update.*
**Desc:** Twenty-six lesson series features original articles offering an overview of radiology.
**Ind/Abst** Biol. Abstr. (1988-).

UK
**CONTEMPORARY ISSUES IN COMPUTED TOMOGRAPHY.** Vol. 1 (1983)-. Monographic series. English. ir. Price varies per volume. Churchill Livingstone, 1-3 Baxter's Place, Leith Walk, Edinburgh EH1 3AF Scotland. **Tel** 011 44 31 556 2424, FAX 011 44 31 558 1278, telex 727511. **(Subscription address:** US and Canada/ Churchill Livingstone Inc., 5 South 250 Frontenac Road, Naperville, IL 60563; (telephone: (800)553-5426 or (708)416-3939)**) ED** Elliot K. Fishman. **NLM** W1 CO769MQK.
**Desc:** Information-packed book series focusing on key aspects of one of today's fastest growing, most sophisticated diagnostic techniques. Each volume offers state-of-the-art reviews covering the clinical usefulness and the limitations of computed tomography in the diagnosis of disease in a particular organ, organ system or anatomical region. Features the finest quality tomographic scans and numerous valuable case studies.

US/1040-8371
**CRITICAL REVIEWS IN DIAGNOSTIC IMAGING.** [Crit. rev. diagn. imaging]. **VFOAT** CRC Critical Reviews in Diagnostic Imaging. **VAT** Chemical Rubber Company Critical Reviews in Diagnostic Imaging. Vol. 13, Issue 1 (1980)-. Academic Scholarly Publication. English. bm (6 issues). $420.00 institution. CRC Press Inc., 2000 Corporate Boulevard Northwest, Boca Raton FL 33431. **Tel** (407)994-0555, (800)272-7737, FAX (407)998-9784, telex 568689. **(Subscription address:** CRC Press Inc., PO Box 750, Pearl River NY 10965.**) ED** Yen Wang. **LC** RC78.A1; C44a. **DD** 616.07/57/05. **NLM** W1; C555CI. **CODEN** CRDIDF. **Pr Rev.** Documents available from The Genuine Article, BIOSIS Document Express, CASDDS. ***Continues*** *CRC Critical Reviews in Diagnostic Imaging, 0147-6750.*
**Desc:** Provides a critical evaluation of current research and developments.
**Ind/Abst** Biol. Abstr.; Chem. Abstr.; Curr. Aware. Biol. Sci., CABS; Curr. Contents Clin. Med.; EMBASE; Health Plan. Adminis.; Index Med. (1980-); Index Sci. Rev. [Full Cov.]; Res. Alert [Full Cov.]; Sci. Cit. Index; SCISEARCH.

US/0191-2089
**CSU-FDA COLLABORATIVE RADIOLOGICAL HEALTH LABORATORY ANNUAL REPORT.** (CSU-FDA COLLABORATIVE RADIOLOGICAL HEALTH LABORATORY ANNUAL REPORT / PREPARED BY COLLABORATIVE RADIOLOGICAL HEALTH LABORATORY.). **Added/Corp** Center for Devices and Radiological Health (U.S.) Collaborative Radiological Health Laboratory. Collaborative Radiological Health Laboratory. Annual Report. United States. Bureau of Radiological Health. National Cancer Institute (U.S.). **VFOAT** C.S.U.-F.D.A. Collaborative Radiological Health Laboratory Annual Report; Health Effects of Prenatal and Postnatal Whole-Body Exposure to Ionizing Radiation in the Beagle Dog. **VAT** Colorado State University-Food and Drug Administration Collaborative Radiological Health Laboratory Annual Report. (1975)-. English. an. Radiological Health Bulletin, Center for Devices & Radiological Health, HFZ 30, 5600 Fishers Lane, Rockville MD 20857. **Tel** (301)443-5807. **LC** RA1231.R2; C53a. **DD** 616.9/897. **NLM** W1 C94E. ***Continues*** *CSU-PHS Collaborative Radiological Health Laboratory Annual Report, 0090-368X.*
**Desc:** Contains reports on ongoing investgations being conducted by the Laboratory for its long-term study of the mortality, morbidity, and physiopathology of beagles exposed to a single low dosage of radiology.

US/0149-2454
**CURRENT CONCEPTS IN RADIOLOGY.** V. 1- 1972-. Periodical. English. ir. Mosby Year Book Inc., 11830 Westline Industrial Drive, St Louis MO 63146. **Tel** (800)325-4177, (314)872-8370, FAX (314)432-1380, telex 44-2402. **LC** RC78.A1; C86. **DD** 616.07/57. **NLM** WN 100 C976.

UK/0955-1476
**CURRENT MEDICAL LITERATURE. RADIOLOGY.** [Curr. med. lit., Radiol.]. (1989)-. Periodical. English. qt. £20.00 UK; $40.00 other. Current Medical Literature Ltd., 40-42 Osnaburgh Street, London NW1 3ND England. **Tel** 011 44 71 4658377, FAX 011 44 71 4658380. **(Subscription address:** Royal Society Medicine Services, 1 Wimpole Street, London W1M 8AE England.**) DD** 016.6160757.

US/1040-869X
**CURRENT OPINION IN RADIOLOGY.** ***Ceased.*** [Curr. opin. radiol.]. Vol. 1, No. 1 (June 1989)-(Dec. 1992). Periodical. English. bm. Current Science, 20 North 3rd Street, Philadelphia PA 19106. **Tel** (215)574-2266, (800)552-5866, FAX (215)574-2270. **ED** Alexander R. Margulis. **LC** RC78.A1; C865. **DD** 616.07/57/05. **NLM** W1; CU799GHI. **CODEN** CORAE7. **[CCC]. Circ:** 1,500. available on diskette. Documents available from The Genuine Article, BIOSIS Document Express.
**Desc:** Directed toward researchers and practicing radiologists. Presents review articles from an area of concentration covering an entire year's literature with annotated references. Each issue features a bibliography of the current world literature published during the previous year.

**Ind/Abst** Biol. Abstr. (1990-); Curr. Aware. Biol. Sci., CABS; Curr. Contents Clin. Med.; EMBASE; Health Plan. Adminis.; Res. Alert [Full Cov.]; SCISEARCH.

US/0363-0188
**CURRENT PROBLEMS IN DIAGNOSTIC RADIOLOGY.** [Curr. probl. diagn. radiol.]. **VFOAT** Diagnostic Radiology; CPDR. Vol. 6, (Jan./Feb. 1976)-. Academic Scholarly Publication. English. bm. $95.00 (institutions), $68.00 (individuals) US; $101.00 (institutions), $74.00 (individuals) other. Mosby Year Book Inc., 11830 Westline Industrial Drive, St Louis MO 63146. **Tel** (800)325-4177, (314)872-8370, FAX (314)432-1380, telex 44-2402. **NLM** W1 CU804M. **CODEN** CPDRDS. **[CCC].** available on microfilm and microfiche from University Microfilms International (UMI). Documents available from BIOSIS Document Express. ***Continues*** *Current Problems in Radiology, 0045-9399.*
**Desc:** Addressed to the physician with interests that span the breadth of general radiology. Brings the general radiologist up to date on developments in radiologic subspecialties; however, such issues keep in mind the needs of the generalist rather than of the subspecialist.
**Ind/Abst** Biol. Abstr.; EMBASE; Energy Res. Abstr. (Aug. 1982-); Health Plan. Adminis.; Index Med.

US/0161-7818
**CURRENT RADIOLOGY.** (1978)-. Monographic series. English. ir. Price varies per volume. Mosby Year Book Inc., 11830 Westline Industrial Drive, St Louis MO 63146. **Tel** (800)325-4177, (314)872-8370, FAX (314)432-1380, telex 44-2402. **LC** RC78.A1; C88. **DD** 616.07/57/05. **NLM** W1 CU808.

●US/1068-3879
**CURRENT TECHNIQUES IN INTERVENTIONAL RADIOLOGY.** (1993)-. English. an (June). $101.95 US & Canada; $108.45 others. Current Science, 20 North 3rd Street, Philadelphia PA 19106. **Tel** (215)574-2266, (800)552-5866, FAX (215)574-2270.

UK/0250-832X
**DENTO MAXILLO FACIAL RADIOLOGY. See** Dentistry.

US/0898-2473
**DIAGNOSTIC IMAGING INTERNATIONAL.** [Diagn. imag. int.]. (1985)-. Periodical. English. Seven times a year. $75.00 US. Miller Freeman Inc., 600 Harrison Street, San Francisco CA 94107. **Tel** (415)905-2337, FAX (415)905-2240, telex 278273. **(Subscription address:** Hallmark Data Systems, PO Box 1165, Skokie IL 60076.**) DD** 615.

US/0194-2514
**DIAGNOSTIC IMAGING (SAN FRANCISCO, CALIF.).** (DIAGNOSTIC IMAGING.). [Diagn. imag.]. Vol. 1 (Nov. 1979)-. Periodical. English. mo. $185.00. Miller Freeman Inc., 600 Harrison Street, San Francisco CA 94107. **Tel** (415)905-2337, FAX (415)905-2240, telex 278273. **(Subscription address:** Hallmark, PO Box 1064, Skokie, IL 60076-8067**) ED** Peter Ogle. **LC** RC78.7.D53; D52. **DD** 615. **NLM** W1; DI258ID. **[CCC]. Ad Acc. Circ:** 30,000 (ctrl). available on microfilm and microfiche from University Microfilms International (UMI).
**Desc:** Reports news and developments about the medical imaging specialty: radiology, ultrasound, nuclear medicine, computed tomography and magnetic resonance. Features news and news analysis of state and federal legislation, technology, research, reimbursement, regulations, meetings and symposia, continuing education, literature and books about this specialty.

US
**DIAGNOSTIC IMAGING SCAN.** (19??)-. English. sm. $627.00 (1rst class mail), $140.00 (fax) North America; $677.00 (1rst class mail), $140.00 (fax) other. Miller Freeman Inc., 600 Harrison Street, San Francisco CA 94107. **Tel** (415)905-2337, FAX (415)905-2240, telex 278273. **ED** Roger Lindahl. Index available. **Circ:** 700. available via fax.
**Desc:** Business newsletter for worldwide medical imaging, equipment vendors/service providers for profit.

US/1042-7872
**DIAGNOSTIC RADIOLOGY (1982).** (DIAGNOSTIC RADIOLOGY.). [Diagn. radiol.]. **Added/Corp** University of California, San Francisco. Dept. of Radiology. (1982)-. Academic Scholarly Publication. English. Academic Press, Inc., 6277 Sea Harbor Drive, Orlando FL 32887. **Tel** (800)543-9534, (407)345-4100, FAX (407)363-9661. **LC** RC78.A1; D5. **DD** 616. **NLM** W3; DI619Q. ***Continues*** *Innovations in Diagnostic Radiology, 0732-8931.*

US/0742-8383
**DIAGNOSTIC RADIOLOGY SERIES (NEW YORK, N.Y.).** (DIAGNOSTIC RADIOLOGY SERIES.). [Diagn. radiol. ser.]. Vol. 1 (1983)-. Monographic series. English. ir. Price varies per volume. Marcel Dekker Inc., 270 Madison Avenue, New York NY 10016. **Tel** (212)696-9000, (800)228-1160, FAX (212)685-4540, telex 421419. **(Subscription address:** Marcel Dekker Inc, PO Box 5017, Monticello NY 12701.**) NLM** W1 DI258JR. **CODEN** DRSEDL. Documents

available from BIOSIS Document Express.
**Desc:** This is an ongoing series. Each title has a different subject.
**Ind/Abst** Biol. Abstr. (?-1983);(-1983).

IT
**DIAGNOSTICA PER IMMAGINI.** Vol. 1, No. 1 (Dec. 1981)-. Periodical. Italian (summaries and/or abstracts in English). qt. L30000 Italy; $50.00 US. Diagnostica Per Immagini, Via Petrarca 5, 43100 Parma Italy. **Tel** 0521 206126. **ED** Lucio Rossi. **NLM** W1; DI258P. Index available. cum. index. **Ad Acc. Circ:** 2,000. ***Continues*** *Annali di Radiologia Diagnostica.*

GW/0724-7591
**DIGITALE BILDDIAGNOSTIK.** [Digit. Bilddiagn.]. Vol. 4, No. 1 (March 1984)-. Periodical. German (English; summaries and/or abstracts in English and German; table of contents in English and German). qt. Georg Thieme Verlag Stuttgart, Postfach 301120, D 70451 Stuttgart Germany. **Tel** 011 49 711 89310, FAX 011 49 711 8931298, telex 7 252 275 GTVD. **(Subscription address:** Thieme Medical Publishers Inc., 381 Park Avenue South, New York NY 10016.**) NLM** W1; DI582. **[CCC].** ***Continues*** *Computertomographie, 0720-0501.*
**Ind/Abst** Health Plan. Adminis.; Index Med.; SCISEARCH.

US
**DIRECTORY OF LICENSEES - OREGON STATE BOARD OF RADIOLOGIC TECHNOLOGY. Main/Corp** Oregon State Board of Radiologic Technology. **VFOAT** Radiologic Technologists; Directory of Licensed Radiologic Technologists. Directory. English. an. Oregon State Board of Radiologic Technology, Box 231, Portland OR 97207. **LC** R895.A4; O74A. **DD** 362.1/77.

CN/0820-6295
**ECHO-X.** (ECHO-X : JOURNAL DE L'ORDRE DES TECHNICIENS EN RADIOLOGIE DU QUEBEC.). [Echo-X]. Periodical. French. ir. Free. O T R Q, 654 Est Boulevard Cremazie, Montreal Quebec H2P 1E9 Canada. **Tel** 376-0052. **DD** 616.07/57/060714. **Bk Rev. Ad Acc. Circ:** 3,500.
**Desc:** Information about radiological technology, research, scientific lectures, new products, and about the Association itself.

IT
**EIDO ELECTA : EE : REVISTA MEDITERRANEA DI RADIOLOGIA E DIAGNOSTICA PER IMMAGINI. VFOAT** EE; Eido-Electa. (1991)-. Periodical. English (French and Italian). qt. **NLM** W1; EI44R.

GW/0013-4724
**ELECTROMEDICA.** [Electromedica]. **Added/Corp** Siemens Aktiengesellschaft. Wernerwerk fuer Medizinische Technik. (1967)-. Periodical. English. Twice a year. $18.00. Siemens AG ZWD V Verlag, Naegelsbachstrasse 26, D 91052 Erlangen Germany. **Tel** 011 49 9131 723004, FAX 011 49 9131 725022. **(Subscription address:** VCH Publishers Inc., 303 Northwest 12th Avenue, Journals Department, Deerfield FL 33442.**) NLM** W1 EL331. **CODEN** ELMCBK. **[CCC].** Documents available from BIOSIS Document Express, Ask*IEEE. ***Supersedes*** *SRW News.*
**Ind/Abst** Biol. Abstr.; EMBASE; Energy Res. Abstr. (Jan. 1971-); INSPEC (1973-); Phys. Med. Biol. (19??-19??).

GW/0340-5389
**ELECTROMEDICA. DEUTSCHE AUSGABE.** (1967)-. Periodical. German. Twice a year. $18.00. Siemens AG ZWD V Verlag, Naegelsbachstrasse 26, D 91052 Erlangen Germany. **Tel** 011 49 9131 723004, FAX 011 49 9131 725022. **(Subscription address:** VCH Publishers Inc., 303 Northwest 12th Avenue, Journals Department, Deerfield FL 33442.**) UDC** 616-7 : 621.386. **[CCC].**

US/0275-2204
**ELECTRON MICROSCOPY AND X-RAY APPLICATIONS TO ENVIRONMENTAL AND OCCUPATIONAL HEALTH ANALYSIS.** [Electron microsc. X-ray appl. environ. occup. health anal.]. Vol. 1 (1978)-. Academic Scholarly Publication. English. an. $39.95. Ann Arbor Science Publishers Inc, PO Box 1425, Ann Arbor MA 48106. **LC** RA566.26; .E43. **DD** 628.5/028/7. **NLM** W3 EL31H. **CODEN** EMXADA. Documents available from CASDDS.
**Ind/Abst** Chem. Abstr.

●US/1070-3004
**EMERGENCY RADIOLOGY.** (1994)-. Periodical. English. bm. $84.00 (individual), $119.00 (institution) US; $104.00 (individual), $139.00 (institution) other. Williams & Wilkins Company, 428 East Preston Street, Baltimore MD 21202-3993. **Tel** (410)528-4000, (800)638-6423, FAX (410)528-8596, telex 87669. **(Subscription address:** Williams & Wilkins, PO Box 64380, Baltimore MD 21264.**) NLM** W1; EM664L. Documents available from Quick Copies.
**Desc:** Provides radiologists and emergency medicine physicians with immediate, practical information covering the full range of imaging specialties.

GW/0720-048X
**EUROPEAN JOURNAL OF RADIOLOGY.** [Eur. j. radiol.]. Vol. 1, No. 1 (Mar. 1981)-. Academic Scholarly Publication. English. Six times a year (2 vols.). $434.00. Elsevier Science Ireland Ltd., Bay 15, Shannon Industrial Estate, Co Clare Ireland. **Tel** 011 353 61 471944. **NLM** W1 EU72ED. **CODEN** EJRADR. **Pr Rev.** available on microfilm and microfiche from University Microfilms International (UMI). Documents available from Article Express International, BIOSIS Document Express, CASDDS. ***Continues*** *Journal of Medical Imaging.*
**Ind/Abst** Biol. Abstr.; Chem. Abstr. (1981-1985); Curr. Aware. Biol. Sci., CABS; Curr. Contents Clin. Med.; Ei Page One; EMBASE; Energy Res. Abstr. (Sept. 1982-); Eng. Index Annu.; Health Plan. Adminis.; Helminthol. Abstr. (1991-); Index Med.; Ref. Upd. Deluxe Ed.; Rev. Med. Vet. Mycology; SCISEARCH.

IE/0929-8266
**EUROPEAN JOURNAL OF ULTRASOUND.** (19??)-. Academic Scholarly Publication. English. Four times a year (1 volume). $181.00. Elsevier Science Ireland Ltd., Bay 15, Shannon Industrial Estate, Co Clare Ireland. **Tel** 011 353 61 471944. **ED** J.M. Thijssen. **[CCC]. Ad Acc.**
**Desc:** Serves as a forum for the European scientific and clinical community, working in the fields of ultrasound in medicine and biology. Addresses all aspects of ultrasound research.

GW/0938-7994
**EUROPEAN RADIOLOGY. Added/Corp** European Association of Radiology. Vol. 1, No. 1 (1991)-. Periodical. English. bm. DM444.00. Springer-Verlag GmbH & Company KG, Heidelberger Platz 3, D 14197 Berlin Germany. **Tel** 011 49 30 8207223, FAX 011 49 30 8214091, telex 183 319 SPBLN D. **(Subscription address:** Springer Verlag New York Inc. / for North America, 44 Hartz Way, Secaucus NJ 07096.**) NLM** W1; EU722HL. **[CCC].** available on microfilm and microfiche from University Microfilms International (UMI). ***Absorbed*** *Diagnostic and Interventional Radiology.*
**Desc:** Features original papers and state-of-the-art reviews written by leading radiologists. Aims to continually update the scientific knowledge in radiology.

NE/0014-4185
**EXCERPTA MEDICA. SECTION 14. RADIOLOGY.** **See** Medical Science and Technology-Abstracting, Bibliographies and Statistics.

US
**EXERCISES IN DENTAL RADIOLOGY (MICROFICHE).** **See** Dentistry.

FR/0181-9801
**FEUILLETS DE RADIOLOGIE.** [Feuill. radiol.]. Vol. 18 (Jan./Feb. 1978)-. Academic Scholarly Publication. French. bm. $191.00. Masson Editeur, Box Postale 22, 41353 Vineuil 16 France. **Tel** 011 33 54 438994. **(Subscription address:** 7A Boulevard de Perolles, CH-1701 Fribourg Switzerland**) NLM** W1 FE853. **[CCC].** available on microfilm from University Microfilms International (UMI). ***Continues*** *Feuillets d'Electroradiologie, 0015-0444.*
**Ind/Abst** EMBASE; Energy Res. Abstr. (April 1982-).

CN/0833-8493
**FILTER (BRANTFORD).** (FILTER : THE BULLETIN OF THE ONTARIO ASSOCIATION OF MEDICAL RADIATION TECHNOLOGISTS.). [Filter]. **Added/Corp** Ontario Association of Medical Radiation Technologists. Ontario Society of Radiological Technicians. (196?)-. Periodical. English. Ten times a year (July/Aug. & Mar./Apr. issues combined). $40.00. Ontario Association of Medical Radiation Technologists, PO Box 1054, Brantford Ontario N3T 5S7 Canada. **ED** Robin Hesler (phone: (519)753-6037). **DD** 616.07/57/060713. **Ad Acc. Circ:** 5,000 (ctrl).

GW/0178-4609
**FORTSCHRITTE AUF DEM GEBIETE DER RONTGENSTRAHLEN UND DER NUKLEARMEDIZIN. ERGANZUNGSBAND.** [Fortschr. Geb. Rontgenstrahlen Nukl.med., Erganz.bd.]. **VFOAT** Fortschritte auf dem Gebiete der Rontgenstrahlen und der Nuklearmedizin. Supplement. (1956)-. Monographic series. German. Georg Thieme Verlag Stuttgart, Postfach 301120, D 70451 Stuttgart Germany. **Tel** 011 49 711 89310, FAX 011 49 711 8931298, telex 7 252 275 GTVD. **(Subscription address:** Thieme Medical Publishers Inc., 381 Park Avenue South, New York NY 10016.**) LC** UNC. ***Continues*** *Archiv und Atlas der Normalen und Pathologischen Anatomie in Typischen Rontgenbildern, 0342-6114.*
**Ind/Abst** Health Plan. Adminis.; Index Med.

US/0071-9676
**FRONTIERS OF RADIATION THERAPY AND ONCOLOGY.** **See** Medical Science and Technology-Neoplasma, Neoplastic.

US/0364-2356
**GASTROINTESTINAL RADIOLOGY.** ***Title Change.*** [Gastrointest. radiol.]. V. 1- 1976-. Periodical. English. Four times a year. Springer-Verlag New York Inc., 175 5th Avenue, New York NY 10010. **Tel** (212)460-1500, telex 232 235 SPB UR. **(Subscription address:** Springer Verlag New York Inc. / for North America, 44 Hartz Way, Secaucus NJ 07096.**) ED** M A Meyers and G G Ghahremani. **NLM** W1 GA459R. **CODEN** GARADK. **[CCC]. Pr Rev.** available on microfilm and microfiche from University Microfilms International (UMI). Documents available from The Genuine Article. ***Continued by*** *ABDOMINAL IMAGING.*
**Desc:** Brings together previously disparate information of value to radiologists, internists, and surgeons who work with diagnostic imaging of the alimentary tract. Features original papers, case reports, technical and instrumental notes, and invited review articles.
**Ind/Abst** EMBASE; Energy Res. Abstr. (March 1979-); Helminthol. Abstr. (19??-19??); Index Med.; INIS Atomindex [Micro.]; Life Sci. Collect.; Protozoolog. Abstr.; Res. Alert [Full Cov.]; Sci. Cit. Index (19??-19??); SCISEARCH.

US/0161-2824
**GOLDEN'S DIAGNOSTIC RADIOLOGY.** [Golden's diagn. radiol.]. Sect. 1 (1969)-. Academic Scholarly Publication. English. ir. Price varies per volume. Williams & Wilkins Company, 428 East Preston Street, Baltimore MD 21202-3993. **Tel** (410)528-4000, (800)638-6423, FAX (410)528-8596, telex 87669. **(Subscription address:** Williams & Wilkins, PO Box 64380, Baltimore, MD 21264**) CODEN** GDRAD7. Documents available from CASDDS, Quick Copies.
**Ind/Abst** Chem. Abstr.

US/0748-3333
**HEALTH PHYSICS/RADIATION PROTECTION ENROLLMENTS AND DEGREES.** [Health phys./radiat. prot. enroll. degrees]. **VFOAT** Health Physics, Radiation Protection Enrollments and Degrees. English. an. National Technical Information Service - NTIS, Room 2027S, 5285 Port Royal Road, Springfield VA 22161. **Tel** (703)487-4630, (703)487-4660, (703)487-4650, FAX (703)321-8547, telex 89-9405. **LC** RA569; .H39. **DD** 616.07/57/0289.

UK/0074-2740
**ICRP PUBLICATION.** [ICRP publ.]. **Added/Corp** International Commission on Radiological Protection. No. 1 (1959)-. Academic Scholarly Publication. English. ir. Price varies per volume. Pergamon Press, An Imprint of Elsevier Science Ltd., The Boulevard, Langford Lane, Kidlington, Oxford OX5 1GB United Kingdom. **Tel** 011 44 865 843000, 011 44 865 843699, FAX 011 44 865 843010. **(Subscription address:** Elsevier Science Inc., 660 White Plains Road, Tarrytown NJ 10591**) LC** RA1231.R2; I2. **DD** 614.715. **CODEN** RDPTC4. Documents available from BIOSIS Document Express, CASDDS.
**Ind/Abst** Biol. Abstr.; Chem. Abstr.

US/0579-5435
**ICRU REPORT.** [ICRU rep.]. **Added/Corp** International Commission on Radiation Units and Measurements. **VAT** International Commission on Radiation Units and Measurements report. (19??)-. Monographic series. English. ir. Price varies per volume. ICRU Publications, 7910 Woodmont Avenue, Suite 1016, Bethesda MD 20814. **Tel** (301)657-2652, FAX (301)907-8768. **LC** RA1231.R2; I55. **DD** 612/.01448. **Circ:** 15,000. ***Continues*** *International Commission on Radiation Units and Measurements. Report.*
**Desc:** Scientific publications dealing with radiation units and measurements.

US/0278-0062
**IEEE TRANSACTIONS ON MEDICAL IMAGING.** [IEEE trans. med. imag.]. **Added/Corp** Institute of Electrical and Electronics Engineers. IEEE Acoustics, Speech, and Signal Processing Society. **VFOAT** Medical Imaging; I.E.E.E. Imaging; Transaction on Medical Imaging. **VAT** Institute of Electrical and Electronics Engineers Transactions on Medical Imaging. Vol. MI-1, No. 1 (July 1982)-. Periodical. English. qt. $160.00. IEEE, Institution of Electrical and Electronics Engineers, Inc., 345 East 47th Street, New York NY 10017-2394. **Tel** (908)981-1393, FAX (908)981-9667. **(Subscription address:** IEEE / Institute of Electrical and Electronics Engineers, 445 Hoes Lane, PO Box 1331, Piscataway NJ 08855-1331.**) LC** RC78.A1; I35. **DD** 616.07/57/05. **NLM** W1; I224D. **CODEN** ITMID4. **[CCC]. Pr Rev.** available on microfiche. Documents available from Article Express International, The Genuine Article, Ask*IEEE.
**Desc:** Covers the imaging of body organs, usually in situ, rather than microscopic biological entities; the associated equipment and techniques such as instrumentation systems, transducers, computing hardware and software.
**Ind/Abst** Curr. Aware. Biol. Sci., CABS; Curr. Contents Clin. Med.; Curr. Contents Eng. Tech. Appl. Sci.; Ei Page One; Eng. Index Annu.; Expand. Acad. Index (1992-); Index IEEE Publ.; INSPEC (July 1982-); Life Sci. Collect.; Pollut. Abstr. Indexes; Res. Alert [Full Cov.]; Sci. Cit. Index; SCISEARCH.

US/1055-1476
**IMAGES (RESTON, VA.).** (IMAGES / AMERICAN RADIOLOGICAL NURSES ASSOCIATION.). [Images]. **Added/Corp** American Radiological Nurses Association. (198?)-. Periodical. English. Four times a year. $50.00. American Radiological Nurses Association /

ARNA, 2021 Spring Road, Suite 600, Oak Brook IL 60521. **Tel** (708)571-9072. **ED** Margaret Doherty-Simor RN, BSNE (editor's address: University of California at San Francisco, Department of Radiology, 505 Parnassus Avenue, M-361, San Francisco, CA 94143-0628, phone: (415)476-0839 or (415)476-3131). **DD** 616. Index available. cum. index. **Ad Acc, Adv Mgr Tel** (708)571-9072. **Pr Rev. Circ:** 1,200 (ctrl).
**Desc:** A source of informative articles, patients teaching tools, and patient care plans. Includes a training program for radiologic technologists and strikes and nerve in today's changing health care environment.
**Ind/Abst** Nurs. Allied Health Index.

●UK/0965-6812
**IMAGING : AN INTERNATIONAL JOURNAL OF CLINICO-RADIOLOGICAL PRACTICE.** Vol. 4, No. 1 (Mar. 1992)-. Periodical. English. qt. $230.00 US; £135.00 other. Rapid Communications of Oxford Ltd, The Old Malthouse, Paradise Street, Oxford OX1 1LD England. **Tel** 011 44 0865 790447, FAX 011 44 0865 244012, telex 9403712. **NLM** W1; IM457TK. **CODEN** IAGIEC. **[CCC].** ***Continues** Current Imaging.*
**Ind/Abst** Curr. Aware. Biol. Sci., CABS.

●US/1073-9718
**IMAGING DECISIONS.** [Imaging decis.]. Vol. 1, No. 1 (March/April 1994)-. Periodical. English. qt. $34.00 US; $42.00 Canada; $58.00 other. Physicians World Comm Group, 400 Plaza Drive, Secaucus NJ 07096. **Tel** (201)865-7500. **DD** 616. ***Continues** MRI Decisions, 0896-0704.*

US/1041-0082
**IN SERVICE REVIEWS IN RADIOLOGIC TECHNOLOGY.** (IN SERVICE REVIEWS IN RADIOLOGIC TECHNOLOGY [SOUND RECORDING].). [In serv. rev. radiol. technol.]. **VFOAT** In-Service Reviews in Radiologic Technology. (19??)-. Periodical. English. mo. $175.00. Educational Reviews Inc., 6801 Cahaba Valley Road, Birmingham AL 35242. **Tel** (205)991-5188, (800)633-4743, FAX (205)995-1926. **DD** 616.

GW/0343-3331
**INDEX RADIOLOGIAE.** Periodical. English. Medico-Informationsdienste GmbH, Bremerstr 5, W-1000 Berlin 45 Germany. **NLM** ZWN 100 I38.

II/0970-2016
**INDIAN JOURNAL OF RADIOLOGY & IMAGING, THE.** [Indian j. radiol. imaging]. **Added/Corp** Indian Radiological & Imaging Association. **VFOAT** Indian Journal of Radiology and Imaging. Vol. 38, No. 1 (Feb. 1984)-. Periodical. English. qt. $70.00. Indian Radiological and Imaging Association, Bombay India. **(Subscription address:** Prints India, 11 Darya Ganj, New Delhi, 110002 India, (Phone: 011 91 11 3268645)) **NLM** W1; IN234H. Documents available from BIOSIS Document Express. ***Continues** Indian Journal of Radiology, 0019-560X.*
**Ind/Abst** Biol. Abstr.; EMBASE [Select. Cov.]; Energy Res. Abstr. (1984).

SI/0129-0835
**INTERNATIONAL JOURNAL OF PIXE.** Vol. 1, No. 1 (March 1990)-. Periodical. English. qt. $115.00 individuals, $250.00 institutions. World Scientific Publishing Company, PO Box 128, Farrer Road, Singapore 9128 Singapore. **Tel** 011 65 3825663, FAX 011 65 3825919, telex RS 28561 WSPC. **(Subscription address:** US: World Scientific Publishing Co., Inc., 1060 Main Street, River Edge, NJ 07661 Telephone: (201)487-9655, Fax: (201)487-9656; Europe: World Scientific Publishing Co Ltd, 73 Lynton Mead, Totteridge, London N20 8DH United Kingdom Telephone: 011 44 81 4462461, Fax: 011 44 81 4463356; India: World Scientific Publishing Co Pte Ltd, 4911 9th Floor, High Point IV, 45 Palace Road, Bangalore 560 001 India Telephone: (80) 2205972, Fax: (80) 3344593, Telex: 0845-2900 PCO IN; Hong Kong: World Scientific Publishing (HK) Co, PO Box 72482, Kowloon Central Post Office, Hong Kong Telephone: 852-7718791, Fax: 852-7718155) **LC** QD96.X2; I67. **DD** 543/.08586. **[CCC].**
**Desc:** Covers the latest developments in the various aspects of Particle-Induced X-ray Emission (PIXE), including the fundamentals of this process, its applications and the techniques employed in different kinds of applications.

UK/0955-3002
**INTERNATIONAL JOURNAL OF RADIATION BIOLOGY.** [Int. j. radiat. biol.]. **VFOAT** Radiation Biology. Vol. 54, No. 1 (July 1988)-. Academic Scholarly Publication. English. mo. £564.00 UK; $930.00 other. Taylor & Francis Ltd., Rankine Road, Basingstoke Hampshire, RG24 8PR United Kingdom. **Tel** 011 44 256 840366, FAX 011 44 256 479438, telex 858540. **(Subscription address:** Taylor & Francis Inc., 1900 Frost Road, Suite 101, Bristol PA 19007-1598.) **ED** J. H. Hendry (editor's address: Paterson Institute for Cancer Research, Christie Hospital and Holt Radium Institute, Wilmslow Road, Manchester M20 9BX UK). **LC** QH652; .I55. **NLM** W1; IN778F. **CODEN** IJRBE7. **[CCC]. Pr Rev.** available on microfilm and microfiche from University Microfilms International (UMI). Documents available from The Genuine Article, BIOSIS Document Express, CASDDS, ADONIS. ***Continues** International Journal of Radiation Biology and Related Studies in Physics, Chemistry, and Medicine, 0020-7616.*
**Desc:** Publishes original papers and reviews on the effects of ionizing, UV and visible radiation, accelerated particles, microwaves, ultrasound, heat and related modalities. The focus is on the biological effects of such radiations: from radiation chemistry to the spectrum of responses of living organisms and underlying mechanisms, including genetic changes; cell death; repair phenomena; abnormal growth, differentiation and genotype; neoplasia. Application of basic studies to medical uses of radiation extends the coverage to practical problems such as physical and chemical adjuvants which improve the effectiveness of radiation in cancer therapy, and assessment of the hazards to man of radiation.
**Ind/Abst** ADONIS; Biol. Abstr. (1988-); Chem. Abstr.; Curr. Aware. Biol. Sci., CABS; Curr. Contents Life Sci.; Dairy Sci. Abstr.; Field Crop Abstr.; Genet. Abstr.; Health Saf. Sci. Abstr.; Index Med. (July 1988-); Index Vet.; Nutr. Abstr. Rev., Ser. A, Hum. Exp.; Oncog. Growth Factors Abstr.; Phys. Med. Biol. (19??-19??); Pig News Inf.; Pollut. Abstr. Indexes; Res. Alert [Full Cov.]; Sci. Cit. Index; SCISEARCH; Seed Abstr.; Toxicol. Abstr.

US/0020-9996
**INVESTIGATIVE RADIOLOGY.** [Invest. radiol.]. **Added/Corp** Association of University Radiologists. Vol. 1 (Jan./Feb. 1966)-. Academic Scholarly Publication. English (summaries and/or abstracts in Interlingua). mo. $179.00 (individuals), $254.00 (institutions) US; $239.00 (individuals), $324.00 (institutions) other. J.B. Lippincott Company, 227 East Washington Square, Philadelphia PA 19106-3780. **Tel** (215)238-4200 or 4454, FAX (215)238-4227. **(Subscription address:** J.B. Lippincott, PO Box 350, Hagerstown MD 21740.) **ED** Charles E. Putman. **LC** RC78; .A167. **DD** 616.07/57/05. **NLM** W1 IN995E. **CODEN** INVRAV. **[CCC]. Pr Rev. Circ:** 2,600. available on microfilm and microfiche from University Microfilms International (UMI). Documents available from The Genuine Article, CASDDS.
**Desc:** Official publication of the Association of University Radiologists and the Society of Chairmen of academic radiology departments. Original reports of basic and applied investigations in diagnostic radiology.
**Ind/Abst** Chem. Abstr.; Curr. Aware. Biol. Sci., CABS; Curr. Contents Life Sci.; EMBASE; Energy Res. Abstr.; Index Med.; INIS Atomindex [Micro.]; Int. Aerosp. Abstr.; Life Sci. Collect.; PESTDOC; Ref. Upd. Deluxe Ed.; Res. Alert [Full Cov.]; Sci. Cit. Index; SCISEARCH; Soc. Sci. Cit. Index [Select. Cov.].

IT/0394-1574
**ITALIAN CURRENT RADIOLOGY.** [Ital. curr. radiol.]. (1982)-. Periodical. Multiple languages. qt (Jan., Apr., July, Oct.). L90000. Casa Editrice Libr Idelson Gnocchi, Via Alcide de Gasperi 55, 80133 Naples Italy. **Tel** 011 39 81 552-4733. **UDC** 616-073.7.
**Ind/Abst** EMBASE.

JA
**JAPANESE JOURNAL OF RADIOLOGICAL TECHNOLOGY.** **Added/Corp** Nihon Hoshasen Gijutsu Gakkai. No. 1 (1981)-. English. mo. $358.00. Nihon Hoshasen Gijutsu Gakkai, (Japanese Soc. of Radiological Technology), Nijo Puraza, 88, Nishinokyo, Kitatsubocho, Nakagyoku, Kyotoshi,, Kyotofu 604 Japan. **(Subscription address:** Kyowa Book Company Inc., 1-38 Kanda Jinbo-Cho, Chiyoda-Ku, Tokyo 101, Japan) **NLM** W1 JA975H.

BE/0021-7646
**JOURNAL BELGE DE RADIOLOGIE (1924).** (JOURNAL BELGE DE RADIOLOGIE.). [J. belg. radiol.]. **Added/Corp** Societe Royale Belge de Radiologie. Societe Belge de Radiologie. Association Belge de Radioprotection. **VFOAT** Belgisch Tijdschrift Voor Radiologie. Vol. 13 (1924)-. Periodical. English (French and Dutch). bm. 4602F Belgium; 6000F common market countries; 6500F other. Claude H. Catteau, 10 Avenue des Eglantines, B 1150 Brussels Belgium. **Tel** 011 32 2 7716868. **ED** J. Pringot. **NLM** W1 JO234. **CODEN** JBRAAN. Index available. cum. index. **Bk Rev. Ad Acc. Circ:** 6,000. Documents available from Ask*IEEE. ***Continues** Journal de Radiologie, 0302-7449.*
**Desc:** Articles on diagnostic radiology and related imaging techniques, therapeutic radiology, nuclear medicine and allied sciences.
**Ind/Abst** EMBASE; Energy Res. Abstr.; Index Med.; INSPEC (Jan./Feb. 1973-); Life Sci. Collect.; Protozoolog. Abstr.; Saf. Health Work.

FR/0221-0363
**JOURNAL DE RADIOLOGIE.** [J. radiol.]. **Added/Corp** Societe Francaise de Radiologie Medicale. Vol. 60 (1979)-. Periodical. French (summaries and/or abstracts in English). Ten times a year. $283.00. Masson Editeur, Box Postale 22, 41353 Vineuil 16 France. **Tel** 011 33 54 438994. **(Subscription address:** 7A Boulevard de Perolles, CH-1701 Fribourg Switzerland) **NLM** W1 JO344C. available on microfilm and microfiche from University Microfilms International (UMI). ***Continues** Journal de Radiologie, d'Electrologie, et de Medecine Nucleaire, 0368-3966.*
**Ind/Abst** EMBASE; Energy Res. Abstr. (Sept. 1980-); Index Med.; Life Sci. Collect.

FR/0243-1203
**JOURNAL EUROPEEN DE RADIOTHERAPIE.** ***Ceased.*** [J. eur. radiother.]. **VFOAT** European Journal of Radiation Oncology. ( )-1989. Academic Scholarly Publication. English (French). qt. Masson SA, Avenue Beauregard 12, CH-1701 Fribourg Switzerland. **Tel** 011 41 37 249585, FAX 011 41 37 247559, telex 942658 SEMI CH. **(Subscription address:** 7A Boulevard de Perolles, CH-1701 Fribourg Switzerland) **NLM** W1; JO37705. **CODEN** JEURDB. **[CCC].** Documents available from BIOSIS Document Express.
**Ind/Abst** Biol. Abstr. (1986-); EMBASE; Energy Res. Abstr. (July 1981-); SCISEARCH.

US/0363-8715
**JOURNAL OF COMPUTER ASSISTED TOMOGRAPHY.** [J. comput. assist. tomogr.]. Vol. 1, No. 1 (Jan. 1977)-. Periodical. English. bm (6 issues). $140.00 (individuals), $325.00 (institutions) US; $185.00 (individuals), $370.00 (institutions) other. Raven Press, 1185 Avenue of the Americas, 37th Floor, New York NY 10036. **Tel** (212)930-9500, (212)930-9604, FAX (212)869-3495, (212)302-8507, telex 640073. **ED** Giovanni Di Chiro. **LC** RC78.7.T6; J68. **DD** 616.07/572. **NLM** W1 JO595L. **CODEN** JCATD5. **[CCC]. Pr Rev.** available on microfilm and microfiche from University Microfilms International (UMI). Documents available from The Genuine Article, BIOSIS Document Express, Ask*IEEE.
**Desc:** Forum for basic and clinical aspects of developing technologies in computer assisted imaging, including nuclear magnetic resonance, computed tomography, PET scanning and ultrasound CT.
**Ind/Abst** Biol. Abstr.; Curr. Contents Clin. Med.; Curr. Contents Life Sci.; EMBASE; Energy Res. Abstr. (July 1980-); Helminthol. Abstr. (1991-); Index Med.; INIS Atomindex [Micro.]; INSPEC (July 1980-); Nutr. Abstr. Rev., Ser. B, Live Feeds and Feed.; Nutr. Abstr. Rev., Ser. A, Hum. Exp. (Dec. 1980-); Life Sci. Collect.; Ref. Upd. Deluxe Ed.; Res. Alert [Full Cov.]; Rev. Med. Vet. Mycology; Sci. Cit. Index; SCISEARCH; Soc. Sci. Cit. Index [Select. Cov.].

US/0897-1889
**JOURNAL OF DIGITAL IMAGING.** [J. digit. imaging]. (Nov. 1988)-. Periodical. English. qt (4 issues). $157.00 (individual), 225.00 (institution) US; $240.00 (individual), $269.00 (institution) other. W.B. Saunders Company, A Subsidiary of Harcourt Brace Jovanovich, Inc., The Curtis Center/Suite 300, Independence Square West, Philadelphia PA 19106-3399. **Tel** (215)238-7800 or, 5587, FAX (215)238-7883, telex 173146. **(Subscription address:** W. B. Saunders Company / North America Subscriptions, c/o Periodicals, 6277 Sea Harbour Drive, 4th Floor, Orlando FL 32887.) **DD** 616. **NLM** W1; JO622I. **[CCC].**
**Ind/Abst** Health Plan. Adminis.

UK/0268-0882
**JOURNAL OF INTERVENTIONAL RADIOLOGY.** [J. interv. radiol.]. **Added/Corp** British Society of Interventional Radiology. Vol. 1, No. 1 (Sept. 1986)-. Periodical. English. qt. £136.00 Europe; £137.00 Other (Institutions). Churchill Livingstone, 1-3 Baxter's Place, Leith Walk, Edinburgh EH1 3AF Scotland. **Tel** 011 44 31 556 2424, FAX 011 44 31 558 1278, telex 727511. **(Subscription address:** Maruzen Company Ltd., PO Box 5050, Import & Export Department, Tokyo 100 31 Japan.) **ED** Gordon McLean and Robert A Wilkins. **NLM** W1; JO719E. **CODEN** JIRAE8. **[CCC].** available on microfilm from University Microfilms International (UMI). Documents available from BIOSIS Document Express.
**Desc:** Offers unparalleled coverage of this repidly expanding subspecialty of radiology including medical, scientific, technical and practical aspects of interventional procedures.
**Ind/Abst** Biol. Abstr. (1986-); EMBASE; Ref. Upd. Deluxe Ed.

US/1053-1807
**JOURNAL OF MAGNETIC RESONANCE IMAGING.** (JOURNAL OF MAGNETIC RESONANCE IMAGING : JMRI.). [J. magn. reson. imaging]. **Added/Corp** Society for Magnetic Resonance Imaging. Radiological Society of North America. **VFOAT** JMRI. (1991)-. Periodical. English. bm. $300.00 (institutions), $125.00 (individuals) US; $350.00 (institutions), $145.00 (individuals) Canada and Mexico; $350.00 (institutions), $150.00 (individuals) other. JMRI, 1991 Northampton Street, Easton PA 18042. **Tel** (215) 250-7241, FAX (215) 250-7202. **ED** Gary Fullerton, Ph.D. **DD** 616. **NLM** W1; JO748DEL. (Indexed in Index Medicus). **Ad Acc, Adv Mgr:** Tom Shimala, **Tel** (708) 571-7819. **Pr Rev. Circ:** 1,900. available on microfilm. Documents available from The Genuine Article.
**Desc:** Devoted to the timely publication of basic and clinical research, educational and review articles, and other information related to the diagnostic application of magnetic resonance.
**Ind/Abst** Curr. Contents Clin. Med.; Index Med. (Jan./Feb. 1991-); Res. Alert [Select. Cov.].

FR/0150-9861
**JOURNAL OF NEURORADIOLOGY.** **See** Medical Science and Technology-Neurology.

IT
**JOURNAL OF NUCLEAR BIOLOGY AND MEDICINE : OFFICIAL PUBLICATION OF THE ITALIAN ASSOCIATION OF NUCLEAR MEDICINE (AIMN), THE.** **Added/Corp** Associazione Italiana di Medicina Nucleare. Vol. 35, No. 1 (Jan./Mar. 1991)-. Periodical. English. qt. $90.00 (individuals), $140.00 (institutions). Edizioni Minerva Medica, Corso Bramante 83-85, 10126 Turin Italy. **Tel** 011 39 11 678282, FAX 011 39 11 674502. **LC** R61; .M5. **DD** 616.07/575/05. **NLM** W1; JO795KL. available on microfilm and microfiche from University Microfilms International (UMI). ***Continues*** *Journal of Nuclear Medicine and Allied Sciences, 0392-0208.*
**Ind/Abst** EMBASE; Index Med. (1991-).

US/0091-4916
**JOURNAL OF NUCLEAR MEDICINE TECHNOLOGY.** **See** Medical Science and Technology-Nuclear Medicine.

US/0278-4297
**JOURNAL OF ULTRASOUND IN MEDICINE.** (JOURNAL OF ULTRASOUND IN MEDICINE : OFFICIAL JOURNAL OF THE AMERICAN INSTITUTE OF ULTRASOUND IN MEDICINE.). [J. ultrasound med.]. **Added/Corp** American Institute of Ultrasound in Medicine. Vol. 1, No. 1 (Jan./Feb. 1982)-. Periodical. English. mo. $132.00 US; $166.00 other (institution); Comes also with membership. American Institute of Ultrasound in Medicine, 14750 Sweitzer Lane, Suite 100, Laurel MD 20707-5906. **Tel** (301)498-4100, FAX (301)498-4450. **ED** George R. Leopold, M.D. **LC** Discard. **DD** 616. **NLM** W1 JO968C. **CODEN** JUMEDA. **[CCC]. Bk Rev. Ad Acc. Pr Rev. Acid Free. Circ:** 9,000. Documents available from The Genuine Article, BIOSIS Document Express.
**Desc:** Dedicated to the rapid, accurate publication of original articles dealing with the aspects of diagnostic ultrasound, particularly its direct application to patient care, but also relevant to basic science, advances in instrumentation, and biologic effects.
**Ind/Abst** Acoust. Abstr.; Biol. Abstr. (1987-); Curr. Contents Clin. Med.; EMBASE; Helminthol. Abstr.; Index Med.; Protozoolog. Abstr.; Res. Alert [Full Cov.]; Sci. Cit. Index; SCISEARCH.

US/1051-0443
**JOURNAL OF VASCULAR AND INTERVENTIONAL RADIOLOGY.** (JOURNAL OF VASCULAR AND INTERVENTIONAL RADIOLOGY : JVIR.). [J. vasc. interv. radiol.]. **Added/Corp** Society of Cardiovascular and Interventional Radiology. **VFOAT** JVIR. Vol. 1, No. 1 (Nov. 1990)-. Periodical. English. Six times a year (Jan., Mar., May, July, Sept., Nov.). $60.00 (resident), $125.00 (individual), $150.00 (institutions) US; $75.00 (resident), $150.00 (individuals), $175.00 (institutions) others. Society of Cardiovascular and Interventional Radiology, 10201 Lee Highway Suite 160, Fairfax VA 22030. **Tel** (703)691-1805, FAX (703)691-1855. **ED** Gary Becker and Daniel Picus. **DD** 617. **NLM** W1; JO97BH. **CODEN** JVIRE3. **Bk Rev. Ad Acc. Pr Rev. Circ:** 2,600.
**Desc:** Scientific information on intervention radiology.
**Ind/Abst** Index Med. (Nov. 1990-).

US/0895-3996
**JOURNAL OF X-RAY SCIENCE AND TECHNOLOGY.** [J. X-ray sci. technol.]. **VFOAT** Journal of X Ray Science and Technology. Vol. 1, No. 1 (July 1989)-. Academic Scholarly Publication. English. qt (4 issues). $126.50 US and Canada; $140.00 other. Academic Press, Inc., 6277 Sea Harbor Drive, Orlando FL 32887. **Tel** (800)543-9534, (407)345-4100, FAX (407)363-9661. **ED** Larry Knight, E. Dibble and James M. Thorne. **LC** QC480.8; .J68. **DD** 539.7/222. **NLM** W1; JO974EK. **CODEN** JXSTE5. **[CCC].** Documents available from Ask*IEEE.
**Desc:** Designed to provide scientists and engineers with a single literature source covering new developments in the field of xray imaging and analysis techniques. Reports of original research and timely reviews of the technical and esthetic quality will be published.
**Ind/Abst** Ei Page One; INSPEC (Sept. 1990-).

US/1040-8479
**KEY INTERVENTIONAL RADIOLOGY.** ***Ceased.*** [Key interv. radiol.]. (1989)-(1990). Periodical. English. qt. Mosby Year Book Inc., 11830 Westline Industrial Drive, St Louis MO 63146. **Tel** (800)325-4177, (314)872-8370, FAX (314)432-1380, telex 44-2402. **DD** 615. **Ad Acc.**

GW/0342-443X
**KLINISCH-RADIOLOGISCHES SEMINAR.** [Klin.-radiol. Semin.]. Academic Scholarly Publication. German. Price varies per volume. Georg Thieme Verlag Stuttgart, Postfach 301120, D 70451 Stuttgart Germany. **Tel** 011 49 711 89310, FAX 011 49 711 8931298, telex 7 252 275 GTVD. **(Subscription address:** Thieme Medical Publishers Inc., 381 Park Avenue South, New York NY 10016.**) NLM** W3 KL63. **CODEN** KRSEDU. Documents available from CASDDS.
**Ind/Abst** Chem. Abstr. (1972-1981).

GW/0939-7116
**KLINISCHE NEURORADIOLOGIE.** ***Ceased.*** [Klin. Neuroradiol.]. (1991)-(1993). Periodical. German (English and Multiple languages). Four times a year. Thieme Medical Publishers Inc., 381 Park Avenue South, Suite 1201, New York NY 10016. **Tel** (212)683-5088, (212)683-5089, FAX (212)779-9020, telex 220 862 TSINC UR. **UDC** 61. Documents available from The Genuine Article.
**Ind/Abst** Res. Alert.

CN/0713-7621
**LIEN (ORDRE DES TECHNICIENS EN RADIOLOGIE DU QUEBEC).** (LE LIEN / ORDRE DES TECHNICIENS EN RADIOLOGIE DU QUEBEC.). [Lien - Ordre tech. radiol. Que.]. V. 1, No 1 (Feb. 1980)-. Periodical. French. Free to members. Le Lien, c/o O T R Q, 654 East Boulevard Cremazie, Montreal Quebec H2P 1E9 Canada. **DD** 616.07/57/060714.

US/1059-2156
**LIPPINCOTT'S REVIEWS. RADIOLOGY.** ***Ceased.*** [Lippincott's rev., Radiol.]. **VFOAT** Radiology. Vol. 1, No. 1 (Mar. 1992)-(Oct/Dec 1992). Monographic series. English. qt. J.B. Lippincott Company, 227 East Washington Square, Philadelphia PA 19106-3780. **Tel** (215)238-4200 or 4454, FAX (215)238-4227. **ED** Erich K Lang, MD, FACR; Anton N Hasso, MD, FACR; and John V Crues, III, MD. **DD** 616. **NLM** W1; LI647M. Index available. **Pr Rev. Circ:** 1005. available on microfilm from University Microfilms International (UMI).
**Desc:** Explores a single topic in depth, with original articles by clinical radiologists renowned for their work in a particular subspecialty. Articles discuss clinical problems encountered firsthand by the authors, offer new clinical insights and describe cutting-edge techniques and procedures for diagnosis and treatment.

US/1063-5122
**MAGMA (BLUE BELL, PA.).** ***Title Change.*** (MAGMA : MAGNETIC RESONANCE MATERIALS.). **VFOAT** Magnetic Resonance Materials. (1993)-(19??). Periodical. English. Four times a year. Chapman & Hall, 2-6 Boundary Row, London SE1 8HN England. **Tel** 011 44 71 865 0066, FAX 011 44 71 522 9623, telex 290164 Chapmag. ***Continued by*** *Magnetic Resonance Materials in Physics, Biology and Medicine.*

US/0730-725X
**MAGNETIC RESONANCE IMAGING.** [Magn. reson. imag.]. Vol. 1, No. 1 (1982)-. Academic Scholarly Publication. English. Eight times a year. $611.00 The Americas; £410.00 other. Pergamon Press, An Imprint of Elsevier Science Ltd., The Boulevard, Langford Lane, Kidlington, Oxford OX5 1GB United Kingdom. **Tel** 011 44 865 843000, 011 44 865 843699, FAX 011 44 865 843010. **(Subscription address:** Elsevier Science Ltd. Oxford Fulfillment Centre, PO Box 800, Kidlington, Oxford OX5 1DX United Kingdom.**) ED** John C. Gore and Francis W. Smith. **LC** RC78.7.N83; M33. **DD** 616.07/57. **NLM** W1 MA34H. **CODEN** MRIMDQ. **[CCC]. Pr Rev.** available on microfilm and microfiche from University Microfilms International (UMI). Documents available from The Genuine Article, BIOSIS Document Express, Ask*IEEE, CASDDS. ***Absorbed*** *Reviews of Magnetic Resonance in Medicine, 0883-8291.*
**Desc:** International multidisciplinary journal for both clinicians and basic scientists. Covers clinical, physical and life science investigations relating to the development and use of magnetic resonance methods and instrumentation, including both imaging and spectroscopic techniques and their applications.
**Ind/Abst** Biol. Abstr.; Chem. Abstr.; Curr. Aware. Biol. Sci., CABS; Curr. Contents Clin. Med.; EMBASE; Index Med. (Vol. 1, No. 1, 1983-); INIS Atomindex [Micro.]; INSPEC (1984-); Pollut. Abstr. Indexes; Ref. Upd. Deluxe Ed.; Res. Alert [Select. Cov.]; SCISEARCH.

US/0740-3194
**MAGNETIC RESONANCE IN MEDICINE.** (MAGNETIC RESONANCE IN MEDICINE : OFFICIAL JOURNAL OF THE SOCIETY OF MAGNETIC RESONANCE IN MEDICINE.). [Magn. reson. med.]. **Added/Corp** Society of Magnetic Resonance in Medicine (U.S.). Vol. 1, No. 1 (Feb. 1984)-. Academic Scholarly Publication. English. mo. $394.00 (individual) $527.00 (institution) US; $479.00 (individual), $612.00 (institution) other. Williams & Wilkins Company, 428 East Preston Street, Baltimore MD 21202-3993. **Tel** (410)528-4000, (800)638-6423, FAX (410)528-8596, telex 87669. **(Subscription address:** Williams & Wilkins, PO Box 64380, Baltimore MD 21264.**) ED** Felix W. Wehrli. **LC** RC78.7.N83; M347. **DD** 538/.362. **NLM** W1; MA34IF. **CODEN** MRMEEN. **[CCC]. Pr Rev.** Documents available from The Genuine Article, BIOSIS Document Express, Ask*IEEE, CASDDS, Quick Copies.
**Desc:** Devoted to the publication of original investigations concerned with all aspects of the development and use of nuclear magnetic renosance and electron paramagnetic resonance techniques for medical application.
**Ind/Abst** Biol. Abstr. (1986-); Chem. Abstr. (1984-); Curr. Contents Clin. Med.; EMBASE; Index Med. (Vol. 1, No. 1, 1984-); INSPEC (March 1989-); Ref. Upd. Deluxe Ed.; Res. Alert [Full Cov.]; Sci. Cit. Index; SCISEARCH.

US
**MAGNETIC RESONANCE MATERIALS IN PHYSICS, BIOLOGY AND MEDICINE.** (199?)-. Periodical. English. Four times a year. $200.00 US and Canada; £125.00 Europe; £140.00 Other. Chapman & Hall, 2-6 Boundary Row, London SE1 8HN England. **Tel** 011 44 71 865 0066, FAX 011 44 71 522 9623, telex 290164 Chapmag. **(Subscription address:** Chapman & Hall, Cheriton House, North Way, Andover, Hampshire, SP10 5BE England.**)** ***Continues*** *Magma: Magnetic Resonance Materials, 1063-5122.*

US/0899-9422
**MAGNETIC RESONANCE QUARTERLY.** [Magn. reson. q.]. Vol. 5, No. 1 (Jan. 1989)-. Periodical. English. qt. $110.00 (individuals), $150.00 (institutions) US; $134.00 (individuals), $182.00 (institutions) other. Raven Press, 1185 Avenue of the Americas, 37th Floor, New York NY 10036. **Tel** (212)930-9500, (212)930-9604, FAX (212)869-3495, (212)302-8507, telex 640073. **LC** RC78.7.N83; M348. **DD** 538. **NLM** W1; MA34IP. **CODEN** MRQUEN. **[CCC].** available on microfilm and microfiche from University Microfilms International (UMI). Documents available from BIOSIS Document Express, Ask*IEEE. ***Continues*** *Magnetic Resonance Annual, 8756-9787.*
**Ind/Abst** Biol. Abstr. (1989-); Health Plan. Adminis.; INSPEC (Jan. 1991-); Sci. Cit. Index.

US/0887-5707
**MAGNETS IN YOUR FUTURE.** ***Ceased.*** [Magn. your future]. **VFOAT** Magnets. Vol. 1, No. 1 (Jan. 1986)-(Dec. 1993). Periodical. English. mo. L H Publishing Agency, PO Box 250, Ash Flat AR 72513. **Tel** (501)856-3877, FAX (501)856-3590. **ED** Les Adams. **LC** TK454.4.E5; M33. **DD** 621.34. **Ad Acc. Pr Rev. Circ:** 3,000.
**Desc:** World's only monthly magazine dealing with magnetic information: permanent magnetic materials, magnetic designs, new applications and background information. Information is gathered from around the world with the primary audience being engineers and a strong secondary audience in the academic field.

US
**MEDICAL DOSIMETRY : OFFICIAL JOURNAL OF THE AMERICAN ASSOCIATION OF MEDICAL DOSIMETRISTS.** **Added/Corp** American Association of Medical Dosimetrists. Vol. 12, No. 1 (1987)-. Periodical. English. qt. $168.00 The Americas; £113.00 other. Pergamon Press, An Imprint of Elsevier Science Ltd., The Boulevard, Langford Lane, Kidlington, Oxford OX5 1GB United Kingdom. **Tel** 011 44 865 843000, 011 44 865 843699, FAX 011 44 865 843010. **(Subscription address:** Elsevier Science Ltd. Oxford Fulfillment Centre, PO Box 800, Kidlington, Oxford OX5 1DX United Kingdom.**) ED** Ray Garcia. **NLM** W1; ME306. **CODEN** MEDOEJ. available on microfilm and microfiche from University Microfilms International (UMI). ***Continues*** *Journal (American Association of Medical Dosimetrists), 0739-0211.*
**Ind/Abst** Health Plan. Adminis.; Index Med. (Vol. 13, No. 1, 1988-).

US/0149-6727
**MEDICAL IMAGING.** V. 1- 1976-. Periodical. English. qt. $30.00. Mosby Year Book Inc., 11830 Westline Industrial Drive, St Louis MO 63146. **Tel** (800)325-4177, (314)872-8370, FAX (314)432-1380, telex 44-2402. **NLM** W1 ME341EI.

US/0025-746X
**MEDICAL RADIOGRAPHY AND PHOTOGRAPHY.** ***Ceased.*** [Med. radiogr. photogr.]. Vol. 23 (1947) - Vol. 64 (1988). Academic Scholarly Publication. English. Eastman Kodak Company, 343 State Street, Department 412 L, Rochester NY 14650. **Tel** (716)724-4000, (800)242-2424. **NLM** W1 ME423. **CODEN** MRPHA9. Documents available from BIOSIS Document Express. ***Continues*** *Radiography and Clinical Photography, 0093-2922.*
**Ind/Abst** Biol. Abstr.; EMBASE; Energy Res. Abstr.; Index Med.; Saf. Health Work.

US/0887-0675
**MEDICASSETTE. RADIOLOGY.** ***Ceased.*** (MEDICASSETTE. RADIOLOGY SOUND RECORDING.). **VFOAT** Radiology. Vol. 1, Issue 1, (1986)-(1989). Periodical. English. bm. Mosby Year Book Inc., 11830 Westline Industrial Drive, St Louis MO 63146. **Tel** (800)325-4177, (314)872-8370, FAX (314)432-1380, telex 44-2402. **DD** 616.

RU/0025-8334
**MEDICINSKAJA RADIOLOGIJA.** (MEDITSINSKAIA RADIOLOGIIA.). [Med. radiol.]. **Added/Corp** Soviet Union. Ministerstvo Zdravookhraneniia. Vol. 1, (Jan./Feb. 1956)-. Academic Scholarly Publication. Russian (summaries and/or abstracts in English). mo. $149.95. Izdatelstvo Meditsina / Russian Academy of Medical Sciences, Ulitsa Solyanka 14, 109801 Moscow Russia. **Tel** 011 95 297-05-04. **(Subscription address:** East View Publications Inc., 3020 Harbor Lane North, Suite 110, Minneapolis MN 55447.**) LC** RM845; .M44. **NLM** W1 ME801. **CODEN** MERAA9. Index available. **Bk Rev.** Documents available from Article Express International, BIOSIS Document Express, Ask*IEEE, CASDDS.

**Ind/Abst** Biol. Abstr.; Chem. Abstr.; CSA Neuro. Abstr. (?-?); Ei Page One; EMBASE [Select. Cov.]; Eng. Index Annu.; Index Med.; INSPEC (July 1981-); Life Sci. Collect. (1985-); PESTDOC; Toxicol. Abstr.

HU/0209-732X
**MEDICOR NEWS.** [Medicor news]. No. 3, 1971-. Periodical. English. **CODEN** MENED4. Documents available from Ask*IEEE.
**Ind/Abst** Energy Res. Abstr. (Oct. 1979-); INSPEC (1977-).

US/0361-0497
**MIRD PAMPHLETS.** (NM/MIRD PAMPHLET.). [MIRD pam.]. **Main/Corp** Society of Nuclear Medicine (1953-). Medical Internal Radiation Dose Committee. **VFOAT** MIRD Pamphlets. **VAT** Nuclear Medicine/Medical Internal Radiation Dose Pamphlet; Medical Internal Radiation Dose Pamphlets. (1968)-. Academic Scholarly Publication. English. ir. Price varies per volume. Society of Nuclear Medicine, 136 Madison Avenue/8th Floor, New York NY 10016. **Tel** (212)889-0717, FAX (212)545-0221. **LC** R895.A1; S62a. **CODEN** MIRPDH. Documents available from CASDDS.
**Ind/Abst** Chem. Abstr.

GW
**MITGLIEDERVERZEICHNIS - GESELLSCHAFT FUR NUCLEARMEDIZIN.** **Main/Corp** Society of Nuclear Medicine (1963- ). **VFOAT** Membershiplist - Society of Nuclear Medicine. English (German, French and Spanish). Gesellschaft fur Nuclearmedizin, W-8032 Grafelfing, Germany. **LC** R895.A1; G47A.

GW/0138-2934
**MODERNE RONTGENFOTOGRAPHIE / ORWO.** [Mod. Rontgenfotogr.]. Periodical. German. **NLM** W1; MO183P.

SP
**MONOGRAFIAS DE DIAGNOSTICO POR IMAGEN : MDI.** Spanish. qt. 9000ptas. Somerdisa, C/ Aviacion Espanola 3, 28003 Madrid Spain. **Tel** 31 1 254 8641, 34 1 234 9715.

US/1055-6273
**MR (SAN FRANCISCO, CALIF.).** (MR : THE QUARTERLY MAGAZINE OF MAGNETIC RESONANCE.). **VFOAT** Magnetic Resonance. Vol. 1, No. 1 (Spring 1991)-. Periodical. English. qt. $50.00 US; $70.00 other. Miller Freeman Inc., 600 Harrison Street, San Francisco CA 94107. **Tel** (415)905-2337, FAX (415)905-2240, telex 278273. **(Subscription address:** Magnetic Resonance, 1450 Author Ave., Oak Grove Village IL 60007.**)** **DD** 616. **NLM** W1; MR232.

●US/1064-9689
**MRI CLINICS OF NORTH AMERICA.** (1993)-. Periodical. English. qt. $122.00 (institutions), $101.00 (individuals) US; $135.00 (institutions), $141.00 (individuals) other. W.B. Saunders Company, A Subsidiary of Harcourt Brace Jovanovich, Inc., The Curtis Center/Suite 300, Independence Square West, Philadelphia PA 19106-3399. **Tel** (215)238-7800 or, 5587, FAX (215)238-7883, telex 173146. **(Subscription address:** W. B. Saunders Company / North America Subscriptions, c/o Periodicals, 6277 Sea Harbour Drive, 4th Floor, Orlando FL 32887.**)** **ED** Dr. Jeffrey Weinreb. **NLM** W1; MA34HM.
**Desc:** Articles cover the different aspects of magnetic resonance imaging.

US/0896-0704
**MRI DECISIONS.** ***Title Change.*** [MRI decis.]. **VAT** Magnetic Resonance Imaging Decisions. Vol. 1, No. 1 (Nov./Dec. 1987)-(19??). Periodical. English. qt. Physicians World Comm Group, 400 Plaza Drive, Secaucus NJ 07096. **Tel** (201)865-7500. **DD** 616. **NLM** W1; MR234. ***Continued by*** *Imaging Decisions, 1073-9718.*

US/0195-9557
**MULTIPLE IMAGING PROCEDURES.** (1979)-. Monographic series. English. ir. Price varies per volume. Grune & Stratton Inc., 6277 Sea Harbor Drive, Orlando FL 32887. **Tel** (800)782-4479, (407)345-2567. **ED** L.M. Freeman and J.H. Shapiro. **LC** UNC. **NLM** W1 MU397I.

SZ/1013-204X
**NEUE ASPEKTE RADIOLOGISCHER DIAGNOSTIK UND THERAPIE : JAHRBUCH ... DER SCHWEIZERISCHEN GESELLSCHAFT FUR RADIOLOGIE UND NUKLEARMEDIZIN.** [Neue Asp. radiol. Diagn. Ther.]. Periodical. German (English and French). **NLM** W1; NE293M.

GW/0028-3940
**NEURORADIOLOGY.** **See** Medical Science and Technology-Neurology.

JA/0048-0428
**NIHON IGAKU HOSHASEN GAKKAI ZASSHI.** [Nihon Igaku Hoshasen Gakkai zasshi]. **Main/Corp** Nihon Igaku Hoshasen Gakkai. **VFOAT** Nippon Acta Radiologica. Vol. 1 (1923)-. Academic Scholarly Publication. Japanese (summaries and/or abstracts in English; table of contents in English). mo. $148.00. **(Subscription address:** Kyowa Book Company Inc., 1-38 Kanda Jinbo-Cho, Chiyoda-Ku Tokyo 101, Japan**)** **CODEN** NHGZAR. Documents available from BIOSIS Document Express, CASDDS. ***Formed by the union of*** *Nihon Hoshasen Igakkai Zasshi. Nihon Hoshasen Igakkai.* ***and*** *Nihon Retogen Gakkai Zasshi. Nihon Rentogen Gakkai.*
**Ind/Abst** Biol. Abstr.; Chem. Abstr.; EMBASE; Index Med.; Phys. Med. Biol. (19??-19??).

UK
**NRPB REPORT.** **Added/Corp** Great Britain. National Radiological Protection Board. **VFOAT** National Radiological Protection Board Report. (1987/1989)-. Academic Scholarly Publication. English. National Radiological Protection Board, Information Services, Chilton Oxon OX11 0RQ England. **Tel** 011 44 235 831600. **CODEN** NRBRAE. Documents available from Ask*IEEE, CASDDS.
**Ind/Abst** Chem. Abstr.; INSPEC; Phys. Med. Biol. (19??-19??).

JA/0911-6028
**ORAL RADIOLOGY.** **See** Dentistry.

GW/0301-0449
**PEDIATRIC RADIOLOGY.** [Pediatr. radiol.]. Vol. 1 (Mar. 1973)-. Academic Scholarly Publication. English. Eight times a year. DM732.00. Springer-Verlag GmbH & Company KG, Heidelberger Platz 3, D 14197 Berlin Germany. **Tel** 011 49 30 8207223, FAX 011 49 30 8214091, telex 183 319 SPBLN D. **(Subscription address:** Springer Verlag New York Inc. / for North America, 44 Hartz Way, Secaucus NJ 07096.**)** **ED** W. E. Berdon and P. G. Small. **NLM** W1 PE173. **CODEN** PDRYA5. **[CCC].** Index available in last issue of volume--attached. **Bk Rev.** **Pr Rev.** available on microfilm and microfiche from University Microfilms International (UMI). Documents available from The Genuine Article.
**Desc:** The only journal devoted exclusively to the various aspects of diagnostic imaging in children. Fields of interest are diagnostics, radiology, pediatrics and gynecology.
**Ind/Abst** Curr. Contents Clin. Med.; Dev. Med. Child Neurol.; EMBASE; Energy Res. Abstr. (May 1979-); Index Med.; Nutr. Abstr. Rev., Ser. A, Hum. Exp.; Life Sci. Collect.; Res. Alert [Full Cov.]; Rev. Med. Vet. Mycology; Sci. Cit. Index; SCISEARCH.

US
**PHYSICIANS' DESK REFERENCE FOR RADIOLOGY AND NUCLEAR MEDICINE.** **VFOAT** PDR for Radiology and Nuclear Medicine. 1st Ed. (1971)-. English. an. **LC** RM852; .P58. **DD** 616.07/57. **NLM** QV 772 P577.

PL/0860-1089
**POLSKI PRZEGLAD RADIOLOGII.** **See** Medical Science and Technology-Nuclear Medicine.

US/0273-0278
**POSTGRADUATE RADIOLOGY.** [Postgrad. radiol.]. Vol. 1, No. 1 (Jan. 1981)-. Academic Scholarly Publication. English. qt. $119.00 (institutions), $88.00 (individuals) US; $126.00 (institutions), $95.00 (individuals) other. Mosby Year Book Inc., 11830 Westline Industrial Drive, St Louis MO 63146. **Tel** (800)325-4177, (314)872-8370, FAX (314)432-1380, telex 44-2402. **ED** Herbert L. Abrams. **NLM** W1 PO958F. **CODEN** PORADD. **[CCC].** Index available. **Ad Acc. Circ:** 1,400. available on microfilm from University Microfilms International (UMI). Documents available from BIOSIS Document Express.
**Desc:** Provides an international forum for the publication of original articles encompassing the discipline of radiology. As a journal of continuing education, a multiple-choice self-assessment quiz accompanies each article.
**Ind/Abst** Biol. Abstr. (1986-); EMBASE.

US/0896-5374
**PRACTICAL REVIEWS IN RADIOLOGY.** (PRACTICAL REVIEWS IN RADIOLOGY [SOUND RECORDING].). [Prac. rev. radiol.]. **Added/Corp** Educational Reviews, Inc. Montefiore Medical Center. **VFOAT** Practical Reviews. Vol. 13, No. 7 (Nov. 1987)-. Periodical. English. mo. $195.00 Physicians/Dentists; $140.00 Residents. Educational Reviews Inc., 6801 Cahaba Valley Road, Birmingham AL 35242. **Tel** (205)991-5188, (800)633-4743, FAX (205)995-1926. **DD** 616. ***Continues*** *Radiologist's Journal Outreach, 0896-6060.*

BU
**PROBLEMI NA NUKLEARNATA MEDITSINA, RADIOBIOLOGIIATA I RADIATSIONNATA KHIGIENA / MEDITSINSKA AKADEMIIA.** **Added/Corp** Meditsinska Akademiia (Sofia, Bulgaria). (1989)-. Academic Scholarly Publication. Bulgarian (summaries and/or abstracts in English and Russian). an. **NLM** W1; PR572FG. Documents available from CASDDS. ***Continues*** *Problemi na Rentgenologiiata i Radiobiologiiata, 0205-0420.*
**Ind/Abst** Chem. Abstr.

US
**PROBLEMS IN RADIOLOGY.** English. qt. $99.00 (institutions), $89.00 (individuals) US; $130.00 (institutions), $120.00 (individuals) other. J.B. Lippincott Company, 227 East Washington Square, Philadelphia PA 19106-3780. **Tel** (215)238-4200 or 4454, FAX (215)238-4227.

US/0195-7740
**PROCEEDINGS OF THE ... ANNUAL MEETING OF THE NATIONAL COUNCIL ON RADIATION PROTECTION AND MEASUREMENTS.** [Proc. annu. meet. Natl. Counc. Radiat. Prot. Meas.]. **Main/Corp** National Council on Radiation Protection and Measurements. Meeting. 15th (Mar. 14-15, 1979)-. Academic Scholarly Publication. English. an. National Council on Radiation Protection and Measurements Report, 7910 Woodmont Avenue, Suite 800, Bethesda MD 20814. **Tel** (301)657-2652, (800)229-2652. **ED** W. Roger Ney. **CODEN** PNRME9. **Circ:** 1,000. Documents available from CASDDS.
**Desc:** Presentations on radiation protection and measurement matters at the annual meetings, a wide range of topics, medical, occupational, environmental standards and philosophy.
**Ind/Abst** Chem. Abstr.; GeoRef.

US/0093-8580
**PROFESSIONAL SELF-EVALUATION AND CONTINUING EDUCATION PROGRAM.** **Added/Corp** American College of Radiology. (1972)-. Monographic series. English. ir. price varies per volume. American College of Radiology, 1891 Preston White Drive, Reston VA 22091. **Tel** (703)648-8900, FAX (703)648-3240. **NLM** W1 PR606.

US/0730-2339
**PROGRESS IN MEDICAL RADIATION PHYSICS.** [Prog. med. radiat. phys.]. (1982)-. Academic Scholarly Publication. English. ir. Price varies per volume. Plenum Press, 233 Spring Street, New York NY 10013-1578. **Tel** (212)620-8000, (800)221-9369, FAX (212)463-0742, (212)807-1047, telex 23/421139. **ED** Colin G. Orton (editor's address: Wayne State University, School of Medicine, Detroit, Michigan). **LC** R895.A1; P764. **DD** 616.07/57. **NLM** W1 PR6711D. **CODEN** PMRPDA. Documents available from CASDDS.
**Ind/Abst** Chem. Abstr. (1982-1982).

IT/0048-6086
**QUADERNI DI RADIOLOGIA.** [Quad. radiol.]. Academic Scholarly Publication. Italian. bm. Instituto di Fisiologia Genera Universita, 35100 Padua Italy. **UDC** 616-073.7.
**Ind/Abst** EMBASE; Energy Res. Abstr.

UK/0264-6412
**RAD HARLOW.** (RAD MAGAZINE.). [Rad Harlow]. **VFOAT** Rad Magazine. (1975)-. English. mo. £51.00 UK; £60.00 Europe; £79.20 Post Office Worldwide Zone 1; £96.00 Post Office Worldwide Zone 2. Kingsmoor Publications Ltd, PO Box 3, Harlow Essex CM19 4RF England. **Tel** 011 44 279 429731, FAX 011 44 279 441038, telex 8950511. **ED** D. Messer. **Bk Rev.** **Ad Acc, Adv Mgr:** D. Roberts. **Circ:** 10,000 (ctrl). ***Continues*** *Consultant Radiologist* ***and*** *Radiotherapist.*
**Desc:** Items of scientific and technical interest in diagnostic medical image.

US/0197-8039
**RADIATION CURING BUYER'S GUIDE.** [Radiat. curing buy. guide]. (1980)-. English. an (May). $25.00 US; $30.00 others. Technology Marketing Corporation, One Technology Plaza, Norwalk CT 06854. **Tel** (203)852-6800, FAX (203)853-2845. **ED** Carolyn Kovachik. **LC** TP156.C8; R325. **DD** 660.29/8. **Ad Acc. Circ:** 2,000. ***Continues*** *Buyer's Guide for Radiation Curing and Processing, 0146-5031.*
**Desc:** Vendor selection directory of manufacturers and distributors of chemicals, equipment, printed circuit suppliers, product formulators, and consulting and marketing services.

JA/0288-2043
**RADIATION MEDICINE.** [Radiat. med.]. **Added/Corp** Radiation Medicine Association (Japan). Vol. 1, No. 1 (Jan./March 1983)-. Academic Scholarly Publication. English. bm. $80.00. University of Tokyo, Faculty of Medicine, 7-3-1 Hongo, Bunkyo-ku, Tokyo 113 Japan. **(Subscription address:** Igaku-Shoin Medical Publishers, One Madison Avenue, New York NY 10010.**)** **ED** Masahiro Iio. **NLM** W1; RA162H. **CODEN** RAMEER. Index available. **Bk Rev.** **Ad Acc. Circ:** 1,000. Documents available from CASDDS.
**Desc:** A comprehensive journal dealing with new developments in the field of radiation medicine.
**Ind/Abst** Chem. Abstr. (1984-); EMBASE; Index Med. (Vol. 1, No. 1, 1983-).

AT/0729-7963
**RADIATION PROTECTION IN AUSTRALIA.** **See** Public Health and Safety.

●US
**RADIATION THERAPIST: THE JOURNAL OF THE RADIATION ONCOLOGY SCIENCES.** **Added/Corp** American Society of Radiologic Technologists. Vol. 1, No. 1 (Jan. 1992)-. Periodical. English. sa. $25.00 US; $50.00 other. American Society of Radiologic Technologists, 15000 Central Avenue Southeast, Albuquerque NM 87123-3917. **Tel** (505)298-4500, FAX (505)298-5063. **ED** Nora Tuggle. **NLM** W1; RA171L. **Pr Rev.**

GW/0033-8184
**RADIOBIOLOGIA. RADIOTHERAPIA.** ***Ceased.*** [Radiobiol., Radiother.]. Vol. 1 (April/May 1960)-Ceased (Dec. 1990). Academic Scholarly Publication. German (English, French and Russian). bm. VCH Publishers Inc, 220 East 23rd Street, New York NY 10010. **Tel** (212)683-8333, , FAX (212)481-0897. **(Subscription address:** 303 NW 12th Avenue, Deerfield Beach FL 33442; telephone: (305)428-5566**)** **LC** RM845. **UDC** 615.849. **NLM** W1 RA196. **CODEN** RDBGAT. **[CCC].** Documents available from BIOSIS Document Express, CASDDS.
**Ind/Abst** Biol. Abstr.; Chem. Abstr.; EMBASE; Energy Res. Abstr.; Index Med.; Life Sci. Collect.

RU/0033-8192
**RADIOBIOLOGIIA.** ***Title Change.*** [Radiobiologiia]. **Added/Corp** Akademiia Nauk SSSR. **VFOAT** Radiobiology. Vol. 1 (1961)-(1993). Academic Scholarly Publication. Russian (summaries and/or abstracts in English; table of contents in English). bm. **(Subscription address:** Victor Kamkin, 4956 Boiling Brook Parkway, Rockville MD 20852.**)** **NLM** W1 RA21. **CODEN** RADOA8. **[CCC].** Documents available from Article Express International, BIOSIS Document Express, Ask*IEEE, CASDDS. ***Continued by*** *Radiatsionnaia Biologiia, Radioecologiia.*
**Ind/Abst** AGRICOLA; Biol. Abstr.; Chem. Abstr.; CSA Neuro. Abstr.; EMBASE [Select. Cov.]; Energy Res. Abstr.; Eng. Index Annu.; Index Med.; INSPEC (July-Aug. 1981-); Int. Aerosp. Abstr.; Life Sci. Collect.; Pollut. Abstr. Indexes; Toxicol. Abstr.

US/0271-5333
**RADIOGRAPHICS.** (RADIOGRAPHICS : A REVIEW PUBLICATION OF THE RADIOLOGICAL SOCIETY OF NORTH AMERICA, INC.). [Radiographics]. **Added/Corp** Radiological Society of North America. **VAT** Radio Graphics. Vol. 1, No. 1 (Spring 1981)-. Periodical. English. Six times a year. $90.00 US; $100.00 Canada and Mexico; $105.00 other; comes also with Radiological Society of North America membership. Radiological Society of North America, 1991 Northampton Street, Easton PA 18042. **Tel** (215)250-7277, FAX (215)250-7202. **ED** William Olmstead. **LC** RC78.A1; R32. **DD** 616.07/57/05. **[CCC].** Index available. **Ad Acc. Circ:** 24,500. available on microfilm from University Microfilms International (UMI). Documents available from The Genuine Article.
**Desc:** A pictorial journal based on selected scientific exhibits and refresher courses presented at the annual meeting of the Radiological Society of North America.
**Ind/Abst** Curr. Contents Clin. Med.; Index Med. (Vol. 6, 1986-); Res. Alert [Full Cov.]; Rev. Med. Vet. Mycology; Sci. Cit. Index; SCISEARCH; Soc. Sci. Cit. Index [Select. Cov.].

RU/0033-8311
**RADIOHIMIJA.** (RADIOKHIMIIA.). [Radiohimija]. **Added/Corp** Akademiia Nauk SSSR. Vol. 1, No. 1, (1959)-. Academic Scholarly Publication. Russian (table of contents in English). bm. $188.00. **(Subscription address:** East View Publications Inc., 3020 Harbor Lane North, Suite 110, Minneapolis MN 55447.**)** **NLM** W1 RA265K. **CODEN** RADKAU. Documents available from CASDDS.
**Ind/Abst** Chem. Abstr.; Energy Res. Abstr.

GW
**RADIOLIT.** (1992)-. Periodical. German. an. $72.00. Georg Thieme Verlag Stuttgart, Postfach 301120, D 70451 Stuttgart Germany. **Tel** 011 49 711 89310, FAX 011 49 711 8931298, telex 7 252 275 GTVD. **(Subscription address:** Thieme Medical Publishers Inc., 381 Park Avenue South, New York NY 10016.**)**

GW/0033-832X
**RADIOLOGE, DER.** [Radiologe]. Vol. 1 (April 1961)-. Academic Scholarly Publication. German. Twelve times a year. DM498.00. Springer-Verlag GmbH & Company KG, Heidelberger Platz 3, D 14197 Berlin Germany. **Tel** 011 49 30 8207223, FAX 011 49 30 8214091, telex 183 319 SPBLN D. **(Subscription address:** Springer Verlag New York Inc. / for North America, 44 Hartz Way, Secaucus NJ 07096.**)** **ED** P E Peters, G van Kaick, and W Wenz. **NLM** W1 RA266. **CODEN** RDLGBC. **[CCC].** **Pr Rev.** available on microfilm from University Microfilms International (UMI). Documents available from The Genuine Article, BIOSIS Document Express.
**Desc:** Reports on x-ray diagnostics and therapy, including computer topography, contrast improvement, radionuclear application and combined x-ray and chemotherapy therapy.
**Ind/Abst** Biol. Abstr.; Curr. Contents; Curr. Contents Clin. Med.; EMBASE; Energy Res. Abstr.; Index Med.; Nucl. Sci. Abstr.; Life Sci. Collect.; Protozoolog. Abstr.; Res. Alert [Full Cov.]; Sci. Cit. Index; SCISEARCH.

GW/0033-8354
**RADIOLOGIA DIAGNOSTICA.** ***Ceased.*** (RADIOLOGIA DIAGNOSTICA; INTERNATIONALE ZEITSCHRIFT FUER DAS GEBIET DER ROENTGENDIAGNOSTIK.). [Radiol. diagn.]. Vol. 1 (1960)-(1994). Academic Scholarly Publication. German (English, French, German and Russian; summaries and/or abstracts in English, French, German and Russian). bm. Walter de Gruyter Inc., PO Box 303421, D 10728 Berlin Germany. **Tel** 011 49 30 260050, FAX 011 49 30 26005251. **NLM** W1 RA294. **CODEN** RDGNA7. **[CCC].** Documents available from CASDDS.
**Ind/Abst** Chem. Abstr.; EMBASE; Energy Res. Abstr.; Index Med.

XV/0485-893X
**RADIOLOGIA IUGOSLAVICA.** [Radiol. Iugosl.]. **Added/Corp** Udruzenje za Radiologiju i Nuklearnu Medicinu Jugoslavije. Udruzenje za Nuklearnu Medicinu Jugoslavije. (1964)-. Academic Scholarly Publication. Slovenian (Serbo-Croatian (Roman); summaries and/or abstracts in English). qt. $20.00 (individuals), $40.00 (institutions). Yugoslav Society of Radiology/Nuclear Medicine, Zaloska 2, 61105 Ljubljana Slovenia. **Tel** (61)327-955. **NLM** W1; RA309. **CODEN** RDIUA4. Documents available from CASDDS.
**Ind/Abst** Chem. Abstr.; EMBASE [Select. Cov.]; Phys. Med. Biol.

SP/0033-8338
**RADIOLOGIA MADRID.** [Radiologia Madrid]. (1963)-. Periodical. Spanish. Nine times a year. $64.79 Spain; $104.00 other Europe; $114.00 other. Editorial Garsi SA, Juan Bravo 46, 28006 Madrid, Spain. **Tel** 011 34 1 4021212, telex 98358 GARSI E. **UDC** 615.849. **CODEN** RBSEB. ***Continues*** *Boletin de la Sociedad Espafnola de Radiologia y Electrologia Medica y de Medicina Nuclear, 0210-3613.*
**Ind/Abst** EMBASE [Select. Cov.]; Indice Med. Esp.

IT/0033-8362
**RADIOLOGIA MEDICA.** (RADIOLOGIA MEDICA, RIVISTA MENSILE.). [Radiol. med.]. (1914)-. Academic Scholarly Publication. Italian. mo. $130.00 (individuals), $160.00 (institutions). Edizioni Minerva Medica, Corso Bramante 83-85, 10126 Turin Italy. **Tel** 011 39 11 678282, FAX 011 39 11 674502. **ED** M. DiGuglielmo. **NLM** W1 RA314. **Bk Rev. Ad Acc.** available on microfilm from University Microfilms International (UMI). ***Absorbed*** *Minerva Radiologica, 0026-4962.*
**Desc:** Journal addressed to practitioners and specialists in radiology in Italy and abroad. It deals with topics such as radiology, scientific practice and research.
**Ind/Abst** EMBASE [Select. Cov.]; Energy Res. Abstr.; Index Med.; Life Sci. Collect.

US/0033-8389
**RADIOLOGIC CLINICS OF NORTH AMERICA, THE.** [Radiol. clin. North Am.]. **VFOAT** Radiologic Clinics. Vol. 1, No. 1 (April 1963)-. Academic Scholarly Publication. English. bm. $117.00 (individual), $136.00 (institution) US; $159.00 (individual), $168.00 (institution) other. W.B. Saunders Company, A Subsidiary of Harcourt Brace Jovanovich, Inc., The Curtis Center/Suite 300, Independence Square West, Philadelphia PA 19106-3399. **Tel** (215)238-7800 or 5587, FAX (215)238-7883, telex 173146. **(Subscription address:** W. B. Saunders Company / North America Subscriptions, c/o Periodicals, 6277 Sea Harbour Drive, 4th Floor, Orlando FL 32887.**)** **ED** Barbara Conover. **LC** RM846. **DD** 616.07/57/05. **UDC** 616-073.7. **NLM** W1 RA332. **CODEN** RCNAAU. **[CCC].** cum. index. **Pr Rev. Circ:** 9,500. available on microfilm and microfiche from University Microfilms International (UMI). Documents available from The Genuine Article, BIOSIS Document Express.
**Desc:** Practical updates for the clinician on the latest advances. Each issue addresses a single topic in patient care.
**Ind/Abst** Abr. Index Med.; Biol. Abstr.; Curr. Contents Clin. Med.; Curr. Contents Life Sci.; EMBASE; Energy Res. Abstr.; Index Med.; Physic. Medline Plus; Res. Alert [Full Cov.]; Sci. Cit. Index; SCISEARCH.

US/0033-8397
**RADIOLOGIC TECHNOLOGY.** [Radiol. technol.]. **Added/Corp** American Society of X-Ray Technicians. American Society of Radiologic Technologists. Vol. 35, (July 1963)-. Academic Scholarly Publication. English. Six times a year (Jan., Mar., May, July, Sept., Nov.). $49.00 US; $55.00 other. American Society of Radiologic Technologists, 15000 Central Avenue Southeast, Albuquerque NM 87123-3917. **Tel** (505)298-4500, FAX (505)298-5063. **ED** Paul Young. **NLM** W1; RA332E. **CODEN** RATIB3. Index available. cum. index. **Bk Rev. Ad Acc. Pr Rev. Circ:** 16,000. available on microfilm. Documents available from BIOSIS Document Express. ***Continues*** *X-Ray Technician.*
**Desc:** A scientific journal dedicated to the education and professional advancement of radiologic technologists.
**Ind/Abst** Biol. Abstr.; Cumul. Index Nurs. Allied Health Lit.; EMBASE; Energy Res. Abstr.; Index Med.

FI/0358-4887
**RADIOLOGICA (OULU).** (RADIOLOGICA.). [Radiologica]. No. 1-. Monographic series. English (Finnish). ir. Price varies per volume. Professor Leo Hirvonen, University of Oulu, 90100 Oulu 10 Finland. **Tel** 358-81-332133. **ED** Leo Hirvonen. **UDC** 616-073.7. **NLM** W1 AC954NM. **Ad Acc. Circ:** 450 (ctrl).
**Desc:** Monographs, reviews and dissertations in the field of diagnostic radiology.

US/0888-8086
**RADIOLOGICAL HEALTH BULLETIN.** (RADIOLOGICAL HEALTH BULLETIN / NATIONAL CENTER FOR DEVICES AND RADIOLOGICAL HEALTH.). [Radiol. health bull.]. **Added/Corp** National Center for Devices and Radiological Health (U.S.) Center for Devices and Radiological Health (U.S.). **VFOAT** DRH Radiological Health Bulletin. Vol. 16, No. 10 (Oct. 18, 1982)-. Periodical. English. Twelve times a year. Free. Radiological Health Bulletin, Center for Devices & Radiological Health, HFZ 30, 5600 Fishers Lane, Rockville MD 20857. **Tel** (301)443-5807. **ED** Mickie Kivel. **DD** 363. **NLM** W1; RA332T. Index available. **Circ:** 3,500 (ctrl). ***Continues*** *BRH Bulletin, 0364-1023.*
**Desc:** Contains articles about the programs and activities of the Center for Devices and Radiological Health designed to protect the public from unnecessary exposure to man-made ionizing and nonionizing radiation.
**Ind/Abst** Health Devices Alerts.

GW/0720-3322
**RADIOLOGIE.** ***Ceased.*** (RADIOLOGIE : JOURNAL DU CEPUR / COLLEGE D'ENSIEGNEMENT POST-UNIVERSITAIRE DE RADIOLOGIE.). [Radiologie]. **Added/Corp** College d'Enseignement Post-Universitaire de Radiologie. Vol. 1, No. 1 (March 1981)- ceased publication after Vol. 11, No. 5 (1992). Periodical. French. Six times a year. Springer-Verlag GmbH & Company KG, Heidelberger Platz 3, D 14197 Berlin Germany. **Tel** 011 49 30 8207223, FAX 011 49 30 8214091, telex 183 319 SPBLN D. **(Subscription address:** Springer Verlag New York Inc. / for North America, 44 Hartz Way, Secaucus NJ 07096.**)** **ED** A Wackenheim. **NLM** W1 RA339. **[CCC].** available on microfilm from University Microfilms International (UMI).
**Desc:** Of interest to radiologists, physicians and medical students, goal of this journal is to educate in radiological fields past the university level. Prints courses offered in many European countries concerning diagnostic radiology.
**Ind/Abst** EMBASE.

●US/1069-1286
**RADIOLOGIST (BALTIMORE, MD.), THE.** (THE RADIOLOGIST.). (1994)-. Periodical. English. bm. $89.00 (individual), $134.00 (institution) US; $114.00 (individual), $159.00 (institution) other. Williams & Wilkins Company, 428 East Preston Street, Baltimore MD 21202-3993. **Tel** (410)528-4000, (800)638-6423, FAX (410)528-8596, telex 87669. **(Subscription address:** Williams & Wilkins, PO Box 64380, Baltimore MD 21264.**)** **NLM** W1; RA353. Documents available from Quick Copies.
**Desc:** Streamlines radiology literature, offering condensed reviews to keep radiologists up-to-date on new developments.

US
**RADIOLOGY.** (19??)-. English. mo. $120.00 US and Canada; $151.00 other. Lexington Data Inc., Box 371, Ashland MA 01721. **Tel** (508)881-2576. **ED** James R. Critser. Index available ($45.00). cum. index.
**Ind/Abst** Health Saf. Sci. Abstr.

US/0033-8419
**RADIOLOGY.** [Radiology]. **Added/Corp** Radiological Society of North America. Radiological Society of North America. Scientific Assembly. Vol. 1 (Sept. 1923)-. Academic Scholarly Publication. English. Twelve times a year. $195.00 US; $235.00 Canada and Mexico; $240.00 other (surface mail); comes also with Radiological Society of North America membership. Radiological Society of North America, 1991 Northampton Street, Easton PA 18042. **Tel** (215)250-7277, FAX (215)250-7202. **ED** Stanley Seigelman. **LC** RC78; .A3. **DD** 616.07/57/05. **NLM** W1; RA354. **CODEN** RADLAX. **[CCC].** Index available (mailed as part 2 of Jan. issue; each year contains index for previous 3 years). cum. index. **Bk Rev. Ad Acc. Pr Rev. Circ:** 34,500. available on microfilm and microfiche from University Microfilms International (UMI). Documents available from The Genuine Article, BIOSIS Document Express, Ask*IEEE, CASDDS.
**Ind/Abst** Abr. Index Med.; Biol. Abstr.; Calcium Calcif. Tissue Abstr.; Chem. Abstr.; CSA Neuro. Abstr. (?-?); Cumul. Index Nurs. Allied Health Lit.; Curr. Aware. Biol. Sci., CABS; Curr. Contents Clin. Med.; Curr. Contents Life Sci.; Dev. Med. Child Neurol.; EMBASE; Energy Res. Abstr.; Health Devices Alerts; Health Period. Database; Helminthol. Abstr. (1991-); Index Med.; INSPEC (Feb. 1980-); Int. Aerosp. Abstr.; Int. Nurs. Index; Int. Pharm. Abstr.; Iowa Drug Inf. Serv.; Leadscan; Microbiol. Abstr. Sect. C; Mod. Med.; Life Sci. Collect.; PESTDOC; Physic. Medline Plus; Phys. Med. Biol. (19??-19??); Protozoolog. Abstr.; Ref. Upd. Basic Ed.; Ref. Upd. Deluxe Ed.; Res. Alert [Full Cov.]; Rev. Med. Vet. Mycology; Saf. Health Work; Sci. Cit. Index; SCISEARCH; Soc. Sci. Cit. Index [Select. Cov.].

US/0741-160X
**RADIOLOGY & IMAGING LETTER.** **See** Medical Science and Technology-Nuclear Medicine.

US
**RADIOLOGY ECONOMIC STRATEGIES.** English. Twelve times a year. $397.00. Miller Freeman Inc., 600 Harrison Street, San Francisco CA 94107. **Tel** (415)905-2337, FAX (415)905-2240, telex 278273.

US/0198-7097
**RADIOLOGY MANAGEMENT.** [Radiol. manage.]. **Added/Corp** American Hospital Radiology Administrators. Vol. 1 (Jan. 1979)-. Periodical. English. Four times a year (Feb., Apr., July, Oct.). $36.00 US; $41.00 Canada; $46.00 other; $145.00 Comews with American Healthcare Radiology and Administrators membership. American Healthcare Radiology Administrators, PO Box 334, Sudbury MA 01776. **Tel** (508)443-7591, FAX (508)443-8046. **ED** Susan Carr. **LC** RA975.5.R3; R33. **NLM** W1 RA354F. Index available (bound in winter issue). cum. index. **Bk Rev**, (Qty: 1-2). **Ad Acc, Adv Mgr:** Teresa Cryan. **Pr Rev. Circ:** 4,000.
**Desc:** Covers a full range of management topics, including productivity, cost containment, employee relations, and information relative to current equipment purchases.
**Ind/Abst** Hospit. Health Admin. Index.

US/0896-8748
**RADIOLOGY OUTLOOK.** [Radiol. outlook]. Periodical. English. mo. $165.00 (individuals), $244.00 (institutions) US; $171.00 (individuals), $250.00 (institutions) Canada; $193.00 (individuals), $281.00 (institutions) other. Quality Medical Publishing, 11970 Borman Drive, Suite 222, St. Louis MO 63146. **Tel** (314)878-7808, (800)423-6865, FAX (314)878-9937. **DD** 616. **UDC** 616-073.7.
**Desc:** Designed to keep the busy radiologist up to date with the world literature in an enjoyable and time-saving manner.

US/1063-8563
**RADIOLOGY RESIDENT, THE.** ***Ceased.*** [Radiol. resid.]. (1992)-(199?). Periodical. English. bm. Slack Inc., 6900 Grove Road, Thorofare NJ 08086. **Tel** (609)848-1000, (800)257-8290, FAX (609)853-5991, telex 517108 SLACK INC VD. **NLM** W1; RA354NI.

US/0893-1054
**RADIOLOGY TODAY.** (RADIOLOGY TODAY : A MEDICAL NEWSPAPER FOR RADIOLOGISTS.). [Radiol. today]. (198?)-. Periodical. English. mo. $170.00 institution, $160.00 individual (US). Slack Inc., 6900 Grove Road, Thorofare NJ 08086. **Tel** (609)848-1000, (800)257-8290, FAX (609)853-5991, telex 517108 SLACK INC VD. **DD** 617. **NLM** W1; RA354Y. **[CCC].**

US
**RADIOLOGY. [MICROFICHE].** (19??)-. English. ir. University Microfilms International, 300 North Zeeb Road, Ann Arbor MI 48106-1346. **Tel** (313)761-4700, (800)521-0600 Exts. 2490, 2491, FAX (313)973-1540. available in print.

NE/0167-8140
**RADIOTHERAPY AND ONCOLOGY.** **See** Medical Science and Technology-Neoplasma, Neoplastic.

GS
**RADIOTSIONNYE ISSLEDOVANIIA.** **Added/Corp** Institut Fiziologii (Sakartvelos SSR Mecnierebata Akademia). Nauchnyi Sovet po Radiobiologii. (1974)-. Academic Scholarly Publication. Russian (summaries and/or abstracts in English). Izdatelstvo Metsniereba / Science Publishers, Ulitsa Kutuzova 19, 380060 Tbilisi 60 Georgia (Republic). **LC** QP82.2.I53; R35. **NLM** W1 RA373. **CODEN** RAISDE. Documents available from CASDDS.
**Desc:** Information on ionizing radiation and radiobiology.
**Ind/Abst** Chem. Abstr. (1975-1978).

IT/0390-7740
**RAYS.** [Rays]. Vol. 1 (1976)-. Academic Scholarly Publication. English (Italian). Four times a year. L135000 (institution); L80000 (individual). Il Pensiero Scientifico Editore s.r.l., Via Bradano 3C, 00199 Rome Italy. **Tel** 011 39 6 86207158, 86207159, 86207168, 86207169, FAX 011 39 6 86207160. **ED** Pasquale Marano. **NLM** W1 RA977. **CODEN** RAYSDQ. Index available. **Bk Rev. Ad Acc, Adv Mgr:** Dott Dalla, **Tel** 06-86207165. Full Page (B&W) L1.750.000. **Circ:** 1,500. Documents available from BIOSIS Document Express, CASDDS.
**Ind/Abst** Biol. Abstr.; Chem. Abstr.; EMBASE; Index Med. (1985-); Life Sci. Collect. (1985-).

UK/0143-6961
**RECENT ADVANCES IN RADIOLOGY AND MEDICAL IMAGING.** No. 6-. Periodical. English. Longman Group Ltd., Fourth Avenue, Longman House, Harlow Essex CM19 5SR England. **Tel** 011 44 279 429655, FAX 011 44 279 431059, telex 81259. **(Subscription address:** Fourth Avenue, Harlow Essex CM19 5AA England**)** **ED** Sir T Lodge and R E Steiner. **UDC** 616-073.7. **NLM** W1 RE105YEK. ***Continues*** *Recent Advances in Radiology.*

BU/0486-400X
**RENTGENOLOGIJA I RADIOLOGIJA.** (RENTGENOLOGIIA I RADIOLOGIIA / RENTGENOLOGIJA I RADIOLOGIJA.). [Rentgenol. radiol.]. **Added/Corp** Bulgaria. Ministerstvo na Narodnoto Zdrave. Nauchno Druzhestvo na Rentgenolozite i Radiolozite (Bulgaria). **VFOAT** Rentgenologija i Radiologija. Vol. 1, No. 1 (1962)-. Academic Scholarly Publication. Bulgarian (summaries and/or abstracts in English and Russian). qt. DM67.00. Medicina i Fizkultura, 11 Slaveikov Square, 1000 Sofia Bulgaria. **Tel** 879111. **(Subscription address:** Kubon & Sagner, ABT Zeitschriftenimport, D 80328 Munich Germany.**)** **CODEN** RENRAR. Documents available from CASDDS.
**Ind/Abst** Chem. Abstr.; EMBASE [Select. Cov.]; Energy Res. Abstr.

MX/0370-6486
**REVISTA MEXICANA DE RADIOLOGIA.** [Rev. mex. radiol.]. (1947)-. Periodical. Multiple languages. qt. **DD** 612. Documents available from The Genuine Article.
**Ind/Abst** Helminthol. Abstr. (1991-); Protozoolog. Abstr.; Res. Alert [Full Cov.].

FR/0998-4321
**REVUE D'IMAGERIE MEDICALE.** **Added/Corp** Societe Francaise de Radiologie. Conseil des Enseignants en Radiologie de France. (1989)-. Periodical. French (summaries and/or abstracts in English). Twelve times a year. 2185.00F. Springer-Verlag France, 26 rue des Carmes, F 75005 Paris France. **Tel** 011 33 1 44411599, FAX 011 33 43250225. **(Subscription address:** Springer Verlag New York Inc. / for North America, 44 Hartz Way, Secaucus NJ 07096.**)** **NLM** W1; RE832S. **CODEN** RDIMEI. **[CCC].** available on microfilm and microfiche from University Microfilms International (UMI).

JA/0009-9252
**RINSHO HOSHASEN. JAPANESE JOURNAL OF CLINICAL RADIOLOGY.** [Rinsho hoshasen]. **VFOAT** Japanese Journal of Clinical Radiology. Vol. 1 (1956)-. Academic Scholarly Publication. Japanese ( and English; summaries and/or abstracts in English). Thirteen times a year. $480.00. Kamehara Shuppan Company, 31-34 2 chome Yushima Bunkyoku, Tokyo 113 Japan. **Tel** FAX 03-813-0288. **(Subscription address:** Kyowa Book Company Inc., 1 38 Kanda Jinbocho Chiyoda-ku, Tokyo 101 Japan.**)** **ED** Fumio Kinoshita. **NLM** W1 RI2163K. **CODEN** RHOSAM. **Bk Rev. Circ:** 8,000 (ctrl). Documents available from CASDDS.
**Ind/Abst** Chem. Abstr.; EMBASE; Energy Res. Abstr. (Oct. 1975-); Index Med.

IT
**RIVISTA DI NEURORADIOLOGIA.** **See** Medical Science and Technology-Neurology.

GW/0936-6652
**ROFO. FORTSCHRITTE AUF DEM GEBIETE DER RONTGENSTRAHLEN UND DER NEUEN BILDGEBENDEN VERFAHREN.** **Added/Corp** Deutsche Rontgengesellschaft. Osterreichische Rontgengesellschaft. **VFOAT** Fortschritte Auf dem Gebiete der Rontgenstrahlen und der Neuen Bildgebenden Verfahren. Vol. 151, No. 1 (July 1989)-. Periodical. German (English and French; summaries and/or abstracts in English; table of contents in English). mo. $426.00. Georg Thieme Verlag Stuttgart, Postfach 301120, D 70451 Stuttgart Germany. **Tel** 011 49 711 89310, FAX 011 49 711 8931298, telex 7 252 275 GTVD. **(Subscription address:** Thieme Medical Publishers Inc., 381 Park Avenue South, New York NY 10016.**)** **NLM** W1; RO287R. **CODEN** RFGVEF. available on microfilm from University Microfilms International (UMI). Documents available from The Genuine Article. ***Continues*** *ROFO. Fortschritte Auf dem Gebiete der Rontgenstrahlen und der Nuklearmedizin, 0340-1618.*
**Ind/Abst** Curr. Contents Clin. Med.; EMBASE; Health Plan. Adminis.; Helminthol. Abstr. (1991-); Index Med. (1989-); Res. Alert [Full Cov.]; Sci. Cit. Index.

GW/0302-7813
**RONTGEN-BERICHTE.** [Rontgen-Berichte]. **VFOAT** Rontgen Berichte. V. 1, No. 1 (Oct. 1972)-. Periodical. German. qt. **UDC** 616-073.7. **NLM** W1 RO255W.
**Ind/Abst** Energy Res. Abstr. (June 1977-).

GW/0035-7820
**RONTGENPRAXIS (STUTTGART).** (RONTGENPRAXIS; ZEITSCHRIFT FUER RADIOLOGISCHE TECHNIK.). [Rontgenpraxis]. **VFOAT** Zeitschrift fur Radiologische Technik. Vol. 16 (Jan. 1963)-. Academic Scholarly Publication. German. mo. DM231.00. S. Hirzel Verlag Stuttgart, Postfach 101061, D 70009 Stuttgart Germany. **Tel** 011 49 711 25820, FAX 0711/2582 290, telex 723636 daz d. **ED** Paul Gerhardt. **NLM** W1 RO286T. **CODEN** RGPXB2. **[CCC]. Bk Rev. Ad Acc. Circ:** 2,900 (ctrl). Documents available from Ask*IEEE. ***Continues in part*** *Rontgen- und Laboratoriumspraxis.*
**Desc:** Concerned with x-ray diagnostics, radiotherapy and nuclear medicine.
**Ind/Abst** EMBASE; Energy Res. Abstr.; Index Med.; INSPEC (Dec. 1970-); Phys. Med. Biol. (19??-19??).

US/1041-2182
**RT IMAGE.** (RT IMAGE : AFFILIATED WITH THE AMERICAN SOCIETY OF RADIOLOGIC TECHNOLOGISTS.). [RT image]. **Added/Corp** American Society of Radiologic Technologists. Vol. 1, No. 1 (Aug. 1, 1988)-. Periodical. English. Fifty-two times a year. Free to radiation therapy personnel; $13.00 other. Valley Forge Press, 1288 Valley Forge Road, Box 1135, Valley Forge PA 19482. **Tel** (800)220-4979, (215)935-3301. **DD** 610. **NLM** W1; R123.

US/1048-227X
**RT RECRUITER.** **VAT** Radiologic Technology Recruiter. (1991)-. Periodical. English. bw. Free. RT Recruiter, 3870 La Sierra Avenue/Suite 392, Riverside CA 92505.

US/0277-853X
**SAUNDERS MONOGRAPHS IN CLINICAL RADIOLOGY.** ***Ceased.*** [Saunders monogr. clin. radiol.]. Vol. 1-?. Monographic series. English. ir. W.B. Saunders Company, A Subsidiary of Harcourt Brace Jovanovich, Inc., The Curtis Center/Suite 300, Independence Square West, Philadelphia PA 19106-3399. **Tel** (215)238-7800 or, 5587, FAX (215)238-7883, telex 173146. **(Subscription address:** W. B. Saunders Company / North America Subscriptions, c/o Periodicals, 6277 Sea Harbour Drive, 4th Floor, Orlando FL 32887.**)** **UDC** 616-073.7. **NLM** W1 SA975B.

US/0739-9529
**SEMINARS IN INTERVENTIONAL RADIOLOGY.** [Semin. intervent. radiol.]. Vol. 1, No. 1 (Mar. 1984)-. Periodical. English. qt (Mar., June, Sep., Dec.). $141.00 (institutions), $99.00 (individuals) US; $166.00*(institutions), $124.00 (individuals) other. Thieme Medical Publishers Inc., 381 Park Avenue South, Suite 1201, New York NY 10016. **Tel** (212)683-5088, (212)683-5089, FAX (212)779-9020, telex 220 862 TSINC UR. **ED** P R Mueller. **DD** 616. **NLM** W1; SE489BK. **CODEN** SIRAE5. **[CCC].** cum. index. **Bk Rev. Ad Acc. Pr Rev. Circ:** 1,600 (ctrl). available on microfilm from University Microfilms International (UMI). Documents available from The Genuine Article, BIOSIS Document Express.
**Desc:** Topic-oriented journal for the practitioner specializing in all phases of radiology.
**Ind/Abst** Biol. Abstr. (1985-); Curr. Contents Clin. Med.; EMBASE; Res. Alert [Select. Cov.].

US/1053-4296
**SEMINARS IN RADIATION ONCOLOGY.** **See** Medical Science and Technology-Neoplasma, Neoplastic.

●US/1070-535X
**SEMINARS IN RADIOLOGIC TECHNOLOGY.** [Semin. radiol. technol.]. (1993)-. Periodical. English. qt. $69.00 (individual), $101.00 (institution) US; $110.00 (individual), $125.00 (institution) other. W.B. Saunders Company, A Subsidiary of Harcourt Brace Jovanovich, Inc., The Curtis Center/Suite 300, Independence Square West, Philadelphia PA 19106-3399. **Tel** (215)238-7800 or, 5587, FAX (215)238-7883, telex 173146. **(Subscription address:** W. B. Saunders Company / North America Subscriptions, c/o Periodicals, 6277 Sea Harbour Drive, 4th Floor, Orlando FL 32887.**)** **DD** 616. **NLM** W1; SE489GP. **[CCC].**

US/0037-198X
**SEMINARS IN ROENTGENOLOGY.** [Semin. roentgenol.]. **VFOAT** Roentgenology. Vol. 1 (Jan. 1966)-. Academic Scholarly Publication. English. qt (Jan., Apr., July, Oct.). $98.00 (individual), $146.00 (institution) US; $162.00 (individual), $179.00. W.B. Saunders Company, A Subsidiary of Harcourt Brace Jovanovich, Inc., The Curtis Center/Suite 300, Independence Square West, Philadelphia PA 19106-3399. **Tel** (215)238-7800 or, 5587, FAX (215)238-7883, telex 173146. **(Subscription address:** W. B. Saunders Company / North America Subscriptions, c/o Periodicals, 6277 Sea Harbour Drive, 4th Floor, Orlando FL 32887.**)** **ED** Benjamin Felson. **LC** RC78; .A372. **DD** 616.07/57/05. **NLM** W1 SE489L. **CODEN** SEROAF. **[CCC]. Pr Rev. Circ:** 10,609. Documents available from The Genuine Article, BIOSIS Document Express, CASDDS.
**Desc:** Designed primarily for the practicing radiologist and the resident.
**Ind/Abst** Biol. Abstr.; Chem. Abstr.; Curr. Contents Clin. Med.; Dev. Med. Child Neurol.; EMBASE; Energy Res. Abstr.; Index Med.; Mod. Med.; Life Sci. Collect.; Res. Alert [Full Cov.]; Sci. Cit. Index; SCISEARCH.

US/0887-2171
**SEMINARS IN ULTRASOUND, CT, AND MR.** [Semin. ultrasound CT MR]. **VFOAT** Seminars in Ultrasound, CT, and MRI. Vol. 5, No. 1 (Mar. 1984)-. Periodical. English. bm (6 issues). $104.00 (individual), $139.00 (institution) US; $165.00 (individual), $181.00 (institution) other. W.B. Saunders Company, A Subsidiary of Harcourt Brace Jovanovich, Inc., The Curtis Center/Suite 300, Independence Square West, Philadelphia PA 19106-3399. **Tel** (215)238-7800 or, 5587, FAX (215)238-7883, telex 173146. **(Subscription**

**address:** W. B. Saunders Company / North America Subscriptions, c/o Periodicals, 6277 Sea Harbour Drive, 4th Floor, Orlando FL 32887.) **ED** Howard W. Raymond, William J. Zwiebel and Ric Harnsberger. **DD** 616. **NLM** W1; SE489R. **CODEN** SEULDO. **[CCC]. Pr Rev. Circ:** 3,800. Documents available from The Genuine Article, BIOSIS Document Express. ***Continues*** *Seminars in Ultrasound, 0194-1720.*
**Desc:** Directed to all physicians in the performance and interpretation of ultrasound, computed tomography, and magnetic resonance imaging procedures.
**Ind/Abst** Biol. Abstr. (1984-); Curr. Contents Clin. Med.; EMBASE; Health Plan. Adminis.; Res. Alert [Select. Cov.].

NE/0167-465X
**SERIES IN RADIOLOGY. VFOAT** Radiological Examination of the Gastrointestinal Tract. (1979)-. Monographic series. English. ir. Price varies per volume. Kluwer Academic Publishers, Postbus 322, 3300 AH Dordrecht, The Netherlands. **Tel** 011 (31) 78 524400, FAX 011 31 78 183273, telex 20083. **(Subscription address:** Kluwer Academic Publishers / US Subscriptions, PO Box 253, Accord Station, Hingham MA 02018.) **NLM** W1 SE719.

NZ/1170-9758
**SHADOWS CHRIST CHURCH.** (SHADOWS). [Shadows Christ Ch.]. (19??)-. Periodical. English. Four times a year (Mar., June, Sept., Dec.). 60.00NZ$. New Zealand Institute Medical Radiation Technology, Cashmere Road, Princess Margaret Hospital, ChristChurch New Zealand. **Tel** 011 64 3 3377200, FAX 011 64 3 3377214. **ED** Jan Palmer. **DD** 616.075705 615.84205. **Ad Acc. Circ:** 800.

US/0364-2348
**SKELETAL RADIOLOGY.** [Skelet. radiol.]. **Added/Corp** International Skeletal Society. Vol. 1 (1976)-. Periodical. English. Eight times a year. DM698.00. Springer-Verlag GmbH & Company KG, Heidelberger Platz 3, D 14197 Berlin Germany. **Tel** 011 49 30 8207223, FAX 011 49 30 8214091, telex 183 319 SPBLN D. **(Subscription address:** Springer Verlag New York Inc. / for North America, 44 Hartz Way, Secaucus NJ 07096.) **ED** H G Jacobson, T E Keats and D J Stoker. **NLM** W1 SK582. **[CCC]. Pr Rev.** available on microfilm and microfiche from University Microfilms International (UMI). Documents available from The Genuine Article.
**Desc:** Serves as a forum for the dissemination of current knowledge and information dealing with disorders of the skeleton.
**Ind/Abst** Calcium Calcif. Tissue Abstr.; Curr. Contents Clin. Med.; Dev. Med. Child Neurol.; EMBASE; Energy Res. Abstr. (May 1979-); Helminthol. Abstr. (1991-); Index Med.; Life Sci. Collect.; Ref. Upd. Deluxe Ed.; Res. Alert [Full Cov.]; Sci. Cit. Index; SCISEARCH.

UK/1055-6567
**SLIDE ATLAS OF CURRENT RADIOLOGY.** ***Ceased.*** (SLIDE ATLAS OF CURRENT RADIOLOGY [SLIDES].). [Slide atlas curr. radiol.]. Update 1 (Feb. 1991)-(1993). Periodical. English. bm. Current Science, 20 North 3rd Street, Philadelphia PA 19106. **Tel** (215)574-2266, (800)552-5866, FAX (215)574-2270.

GW/0081-5888
**STRAHLENSCHUTZ IN FORSCHUNG UND PRAXIS.** [Strahlenschutz Forsch. Prax.]. **Added/Corp** Vereinigung Deutscher Strahlenschutzarzte. Vol. 1 (1961)-. Academic Scholarly Publication. German. an. Price varies per volume. Gustav Fischer Verlag Stuttgart, Postfach 720143, Wollgrasweg 49, D 70577 Stuttgart Germany. **Tel** 011 49 711 458030, FAX 0711-4580334, telex 2627-7111488. **ED** E. Dienstl, K. Niklas, W. Boerner, F. Holeczke, O. Messerschmidt. **NLM** W1 ST756. **CODEN** STFPAT. Documents available from CASDDS.
**Desc:** Series providing information on radiology and radiation protection.
**Ind/Abst** Chem. Abstr.; Energy Res. Abstr.; Index Med.

GW/0930-1038
**SURGICAL AND RADIOLOGIC ANATOMY (ENGLISH ED.). See** Medical Science and Technology-Anatomy.

KO/0301-2867
**TAEHAN PANGSASON HAKHOE CHI. Main/Corp** Taehan Panssasfon Hakhoe. **VFOAT** Journal of the Korean Radiological Society. No. 1 - 1964-. Periodical. Korean (summaries and/or abstracts in English). **UDC** 616-073.7. **NLM** W1 TA393P.

US/0892-7340
**TECHNOLOGY FOR IMAGING AND RADIOLOGY.** ***Ceased.*** (TECHNOLOGY FOR IMAGING AND RADIOLOGY / ECRI.). [Technol. imaging radiol.]. **Added/Corp** ECRI (Organization). Vol. 1, No. 1 (May 1987)-(Dec. 1993). Periodical. English. mo. ECRI Emergency Care Research Institute, 5200 Butler Pike, Plymouth Meeting PA 19462. **Tel** (215)825-6000, FAX (215)834-1275, telex 510-660-8023. **DD** 616. **[CCC].**

US
**TEX-RAYS : OFFICIAL JOURNAL TEXAS SOCIETY OF RADIOLOGIC TECHNOLOGISTS, INC. Added/Corp** Texas Society of Radiologic Technologists. (19??)-. Periodical. English. Four times a year. $12.00. Texas Society of Radiologic Technologists, PO Box 1604, Nacogdoches TX 75961. **Tel** (409)569-0895 ext. 465. **ED** Betty Shinn (phone: (409)569-9481). **Bk Rev. Ad Acc. Circ:** 1,200 (ctrl).
**Desc:** State publication for the Texas Society of Radiologic Technologists.

US/0899-3459
**TOPICS IN MAGNETIC RESONANCE IMAGING.** (TOPICS IN MAGNETIC RESONANCE IMAGING : TMRI.). [Top. magn. reson. imaging]. **VFOAT** TMRI. Vol. 1, No. 1 (Dec. 1988)-. Periodical. English. qt. $134.00 (individuals), $145.00 (institutions) US; $162.00 (individuals), $172.00 (institutions) other. Raven Press, 1185 Avenue of the Americas, 37th Floor, New York NY 10036. **Tel** (212)930-9500, (212)930-9604, FAX (212)869-3495, (212)302-8507, telex 640073. **ED** Joseph K. T. Lee. **DD** 616. **NLM** W1; TO539V. **CODEN** TMRIEY. **[CCC].** Index available. **Ad Acc. Circ:** 1,500. available on microfiche.
**Desc:** Provides practicing radiologists with practical, state-of-the-art information regarding clinical application of MRI in the evaluation of the entire body.
**Ind/Abst** EMBASE; Index Med. (1988-).

US/0171-1091
**UROLOGIC RADIOLOGY.** ***Title Change.*** **See** Medical Science and Technology-Urology and Nephrology.

NE/0921-2574
**VANGNET.** (VANGNET : OFFICIEEL TIJDSCHRIFT VAN DE VERENIGING VAN ASSISTENTEN IN DE NUCLEAIRE GENEESKUNDE.). [Vangnet]. (1978)-. Academic Scholarly Publication. Dutch. bm. **CODEN** VNGTD6. Documents available from CASDDS.
**Ind/Abst** Chem. Abstr. (1982-).

RU/0042-4676
**VESTNIK RENTGENOLOGII I RADIOLOGII.** [Vestn. rentgenol. radiol.]. **Added/Corp** Gosudarstvennyi Rentgenologicheskii Radiologicheskii i Rakovyi Institut. Soviet Union. Ministerstvo Zdravookhraneniia. Soviet Union. Narodnyi Komissariat Zdravookhraneniia. Vsesoiuznaia Assotsiatsia Rentgenologov i Radiologov (Soviet Union). **VFOAT** Annales de Roentgenologie et de Radiologie. Vol. 1 (1920)-. Academic Scholarly Publication. Russian (summaries and/or abstracts in English, French and German). bm. $80.00. Izdatelstvo Meditsina / Russian Academy of Medical Sciences, Ulitsa Solyanka 14, 109801 Moscow Russia. **Tel** 011 95 297-05-04. **(Subscription address:** Victor Kamkin, 4956 Boiling Brook Parkway, Rockville, MD 20852) **NLM** W1 VE844. **CODEN** VRRAAT. Documents available from Article Express International, BIOSIS Document Express.
**Desc:** Information on radiology and radiotherapy.
**Ind/Abst** Biol. Abstr.; Ei Page One; EMBASE; Eng. Index Annu.; Index Med.; Life Sci. Collect.

●US/1058-8183
**VETERINARY RADIOLOGY & ULTRASOUND. See** Veterinary Sciences.

US/1052-2182
**VIDEO JOURNAL OF COLOR FLOW IMAGING.** (1991)-. Periodical. English. Four times a year. $250.00 US; $270.00 Canada and (surface mail) other; $295.00 (airmail) other. Dynamedia Inc., 2 Fulham Court, Silver Spring MD 20902. **Tel** (301)649-6886, FAX (301)649-3447. **ED** Chris Merritt and D.E. Strandness. **[CCC].** Index available in last issue of volume--attached. **Ad Acc. Pr Rev. Circ:** 800 (ctrl). available on videocassette. ***Continues*** *Dynamic Cardiovascular Imaging, 0891-9313.*
**Desc:** Articles by leading radiologists and vascular specialists on ultrasound color flow imaging. Consists of tutorials, reviews, original research and case reports.

US/0277-2566
**WILEY SERIES IN DIAGNOSTIC AND THERAPEUTIC RADIOLOGY.** [Wiley ser. diagn. ther. radiol.]. (19??)-. Monographic series. English. ir. Price varies per volume. John Wiley & Sons, Inc., 605 Third Avenue, New York NY 10158-0012. **Tel** (212)850-6000, (212)850-6645, FAX (212)850-6088, telex 12-7063. **(Subscription address:** John Wiley & Sons / England, Baffins Lane, Chichester, West Sussex PO19 1UD England.)

US/0098-1672
**YEAR BOOK OF DIAGNOSTIC RADIOLOGY, THE.** [Year b. diagn. radiol.]. **VFOAT** Yearbook of Diagnostic Radiology. (1975)-. English. an. Price varies. Mosby Year Book Inc., 11830 Westline Industrial Drive, St Louis MO 63146. **Tel** (800)325-4177, (314)872-8370, FAX (314)432-1380, telex 44-2402. **LC** RC78; .Y4. **DD** 616.07/572/05. **NLM** W1 YE122. **CODEN** YBDRE3. Documents available from BIOSIS Document Express. ***Continues*** *Year Book of Radiology, 0084-3989.*
**Ind/Abst** Biol. Abstr. (1985-).

●US/1062-337X
**YEAR BOOK OF NEURORADIOLOGY, THE.** [Year book neuroradiol.]. **VFOAT** Yearbook of Neuroradiology. (1992)-. English. an. $79.95. Mosby Year Book Inc., 11830 Westline Industrial Drive, St Louis MO 63146. **Tel** (800)325-4177, (314)872-8370, FAX (314)432-1380, telex 44-2402. **DD** 616.

US/0084-3903
**YEAR BOOK OF NUCLEAR MEDICINE, THE. See** Medical Science and Technology-Nuclear Medicine.

GW/0722-3072
**ZENTRALBLATT RADIOLOGIE.** [Zentralbl. Radiol.]. **Added/Corp** Deutsche Rontgengesellschaft. **VFOAT** Radiology. Vol. 125, No. 1 (1982)-. Periodical. English (German; summaries and/or abstracts in German). Twenty-six times a year. DM5998.00. Springer-Verlag GmbH & Company KG, Heidelberger Platz 3, D 14197 Berlin Germany. **Tel** 011 49 30 8207223, FAX 011 49 30 8214091, telex 183 319 SPBLN D. **(Subscription address:** Springer Verlag New York Inc. / for North America, 44 Hartz Way, Secaucus NJ 07096.) **ED** B Chone. **NLM** ZWN 100 Z56. **[CCC].** ***Continues*** *Zentralblatt fur die Gesamte Radiologie, 0044-4146.*
**Desc:** Covers x-ray diagnostics, computer tomography, somography, x-ray therapy, isotopes, natural radioactive sources, chemotherapy, convention reports, and oncology.
**Ind/Abst** Energy Res. Abstr. (March 1982-)(Mar. 1982-).

GW/0323-8776
**ZFI-MITTEILUNGEN.** (ZFI-MITTEILUNGEN / AKADEMIE DER WISSENSCHAFTEN DER DDR, ZENTRALINSTITUT FUER ISOTOPEN- UND STRAHLENFORSCHUNG.). [Zfl-MiH.]. **Added/Corp** Zentralinstitut fuer Isotopen- und Strahlenforschung (Akademie der Wissenschaften der DDR). **VFOAT** Zfl Mitteilungen; Z.f.I.-Mitteilungen. **VAT** Zentralinstitut fur Isotopen- und Strahlenforschung Mitteilungen. No. 1 (1975)-. Academic Scholarly Publication. German (English and Russian). ir. Free on request. Akademie der Wissenschaften Zentinst, Permoserstrasse 15, O-7010 Leipzig Germany. **ED** H Huebner. **LC** QD601.A1; Z45. **DD** 541.3/8/05. **CODEN** ZIMIDC. cum. index. **Circ:** 250. available in microform. Documents available from BIOSIS Document Express, CASDDS.
**Desc:** Papers, reports, reviews, bibliographies, etc. concerning isotope and radiation research (including stable isotopes and their applications), radiochemistry and analytical chemistry, and information science.
**Ind/Abst** Anal. Abstr.; Biol. Abstr.; Chem. Abstr.; Ecol. Abstr. (?-?); Energy Res. Abstr. (July 1976-); Food Sci. Technol. Abstr.; Geol. Abstr.; GeoRef; Ref. Z.

CC/0254-5098
**ZHONGHUA FANGSHE YIXUE YU FANGHU ZAZHI.** (CHUNG-HUA FANG SHE I HSUEH YU FANG HU TSA CHIH.). [Zhonghua fangshe yixue yu fanghu zazhi]. **VFOAT** Chinese Journal of Radiological Medicine and Protection. Vol. 1, (1981)-. Academic Scholarly Publication. Chinese. bm. $6.50. Science Press, 16 Donghuangchenggen North Street, Beijing 100707, People's Republic of China. **Tel** 011 86 1 4019821, 011 86 1 4010642, FAX 011 86 1 4012180, 011 86 1 4019810, telex 210147. **ED** Lu-xin Wei. **UDC** 616-073.7; 615.849. **NLM** W1 CH9816. **CODEN** ZFYZDY. **Circ:** 6,000. Documents available from CASDDS. ***Continues*** *Fang Shi I Hsueh Yu Fang Hu.*
**Desc:** Biological effect of ionizing radiation, clinical and experimental studies of radiation injury, radiotoxicology, radiation protection, dosimetry, environmental and personnel monitoring, management of radiation emergency, etc.
**Ind/Abst** Chem. Abstr.; Phys. Med. Biol. (19??-19??).

## RESPIRATORY SYSTEM

US/0893-8520
**AARCTIMES.** [AARC times]. **Added/Corp** American Association for Respiratory Care. **VFOAT** AARC Times. **VAT** American Association for Respiratory Care Times. Vol. 11, Issue 1 (Jan. 1987)-. Periodical. English. mo. $50.00 US and Puerto Rico; $70.00 other. American Association of Respiratory Care, PO Box 29686, 11030 Albes Lane, Dallas TX 75229. **Tel** (214)243-2272. **(Subscription address:** Daedalus Enterprises (address same as publisher)) **ED** Sherry Milligan. **DD** 615. **NLM** W1; AA101F. **CODEN** AATIEN. **Ad Acc. Circ:** 27,000. available on microfilm and microfiche from University Microfilms International (UMI). ***Continues*** *AARTimes, 0195-1777.*
**Desc:** Provides updates on respiratory care trends across the country, legislative news, education topics, management and legal issues. Meetings listed, as well as job opportunities.
**Ind/Abst** Cumul. Index Nurs. Allied Health Lit. (1987-).

US/0164-7075
**ADVANCES IN ASTHMA ALLERGY & PULMONARY DISEASES.** ***Suspended.*** **VFOAT** Asthma Allergy & Pulmonary Diseases. **VAT** Advances in Asthma Allergy and Pulmonary Diseases. V. 4, No. 2- 1977-Suspended. Periodical. English. qt. Fisons Corporation, 2 Prestion Ct, Bedford MA 01730. **Tel** (617)275-1000. **UDC** 616-056.3:616.248. **NLM** W1 AD436BP. ***Continues*** *Advances in Asthma & Allergy.*

US/0163-1578
**ADVANCES IN ASTHMA & ALLERGY.** **VAT** Advances in Asthma and Allergy. Vol. 1 (July 1974)-. Periodical. English. ir. Free. Fisons Corporation, 2 Prestion Ct, Bedford MA 01730. **Tel** (617)275-1000. **NLM** W1 AD436C.

US/0899-7411
**AMERICAN JOURNAL OF ASTHMA & ALLERGY FOR PEDIATRICIANS, THE.** [Am. j. asthma allergy pediatr.]. **VFOAT** American Journal of Asthma and Allergy for Pediatricians; Asthma & Allergy. Vol. 1, No. 1 (Oct. 1987)-. Periodical. English. qt. $111.00 institution; $96.00 individual (US). Slack Inc., 6900 Grove Road, Thorofare NJ 08086. **Tel** (609)848-1000, (800)257-8290, FAX (609)853-5991, telex 517108 SLACK INC VD. **DD** 616. **NLM** W1; AM448AH.

US/1040-0605
**AMERICAN JOURNAL OF PHYSIOLOGY. LUNG CELLULAR AND MOLECULAR PHYSIOLOGY.** [Am. j. physiol., Lung cell. mol. physiol.]. **Added/Corp** American Physiological Society (1887- ). **VFOAT** Lung Cellular and Molecular Physiology; AJP. P.Lung Cellular and Molecular Physiology. Vol. 1, No. 1 (Aug. 1989)-. Periodical. English. mo. $144.00 US; $174.00 Canada and Mexico; $185.00 other (non-member, institution). American Physiological Society, 9650 Rockville Pike, Bethesda MD 20814. **Tel** (301)530-7180, FAX (301)571-1814. **ED** D.J. Massaro. **LC** QP121.A1; A46. **DD** 612.2/05. **CODEN** APLPE7. **Circ:** 500 (ctrl). available on microfilm and microfiche from University Microfilms International (UMI).
**Desc:** Deals with molecular, cellular, and morphological aspects of the normal and abnormal function and response of cells and components of the respiratory system.
**Ind/Abst** Ref. Upd. Basic Ed.; Ref. Upd. Deluxe Ed.

●US/1073-449X
**AMERICAN JOURNAL OF RESPIRATORY AND CRITICAL CARE MEDICINE.** (AMERICAN JOURNAL OF RESPIRATORY AND CRITICAL CARE MEDICINE : AN OFFICIAL JOURNAL OF THE AMERICAN THORACIC SOCIETY, MEDICAL SECTION OF THE AMERICAN LUNG ASSOCIATION.). [Am. j. respir. crit. care med.]. **Added/Corp** American Thoracic Society. American Lung Association. Vol. 149, No. 1 (Jan. 1994)-. Periodical. English. mo. $220.00 US; $260.00 other (institution). American Lung Association, 1740 Broadway, New York NY 10019. **Tel** (212)315-6440. **DD** 616. **NLM** W1; AM521NF. **CODEN** AJCMED. ***Continues*** *American Review of Respiratory Disease, 0003-0805.*

US/1044-1549
**AMERICAN JOURNAL OF RESPIRATORY CELL AND MOLECULAR BIOLOGY.** (AMERICAN JOURNAL OF RESPIRATORY CELL AND MOLECULAR BIOLOGY : AN OFFICIAL JOURNAL OF THE AMERICAN THORACIC SOCIETY, MEDICAL SECTION OF THE AMERICAN LUNG ASSOCIATION.). [Am. j. resir. cell mol. biol.]. **Added/Corp** American Thoracic Society. American Lung Association. **VFOAT** Red Journal; AJRCMB. Vol. 1, No. 1 (July 1989)-. Periodical. English. mo. $95.00 US Canada and Mexico; $115.00 other. American Lung Association, 1740 Broadway, New York NY 10019. **Tel** (212)315-6440. **LC** QP121.A1; A48. **DD** 599/.012/05. **NLM** W1; AM521NG. **CODEN** AJRBEL. **[CCC]. Pr Rev.** available on microfilm and microfiche from University Microfilms International (UMI). Documents available from The Genuine Article, BIOSIS Document Express, CASDDS.
**Ind/Abst** Biol. Abstr. (1991-); Chem. Abstr.; Curr. Aware. Biol. Sci., CABS; Curr. Contents Life Sci.; Index Med. (1989-); Res. Alert [Full Cov.]; Sci. Cit. Index; SCISEARCH.

US/0003-0805
**AMERICAN REVIEW OF RESPIRATORY DISEASE, THE.** ***Title Change.*** [Am. rev. respir. dis.]. **Added/Corp** American Lung Association. American Trudeau Society. American Thoracic Society. National Tuberculosis Association. National Tuberculosis and Respiratory Disease Association. Vol. 80 (July 1959)-(1993). Academic Scholarly Publication. English. mo. American Lung Association, 1740 Broadway, New York NY 10019. **Tel** (212)315-6440. **ED** Robert Klocke. **LC** RC306; .A5. **DD** 616.2/005. **NLM** W1 AM7503. **CODEN** ARDSBL. **[CCC].** Index available. cum. index. **Bk Rev. Ad Acc. Pr Rev. Circ:** 15,500 (ctrl). available on microfilm and microfiche from University Microfilms International (UMI). Documents available from The Genuine Article, BIOSIS Document Express, CASDDS. ***Continues*** *American Review of Tuberculosis and Pulmonary Diseases, 0096-039X.* ***Continued by*** *American Journal of Respiratory and Critical Care Medicine, 1073-449X.*
**Desc:** Features original articles in basic science, clinical problems and comprehensive reviews of the state of the art in respiratory topics.
**Ind/Abst** Abr. Index Med.; Anim. Breed. Abstr.; Annals Behav. Med.; Biol. Abstr.; Biol. Dig.; Chem. Abstr.; Chem. Hazards Ind.; Coal Abstr.; CSA Neuro. Abstr. (?-?); Cumul. Index Nurs. Allied Health Lit.; Curr. Aware. Biol. Sci., CABS; Curr. Contents Clin. Med.; Curr. Contents Life Sci.; Dairy Sci. Abstr.; EMBASE; Energy Res. Abstr. (Aug. 1982-Aug. 1982); For. Abstr.; Health Saf. Sci. Abstr.; Health Devices Alerts; Health Period. Database; Health Plan. Adminis.; Helminthol. Abstr. (19??-19??); Hospit. Health Admin. Index; Immunol. Abstr.; Index Med.; Index Vet.; INIS Atomindex [Micro.]; Iowa Drug Inf. Serv. (1967-); J. Watch (199?-); Lab. Hazards Bull.; Med. Abstr. Newsl.; Microbiol. Abstr. Sect. B; Microbiol. Abstr. Sect. A; Microbiol. Abstr. Sect. C; Nutr. Abstr. Rev., Ser. A, Hum. Exp.; Life Sci. Collect.; PESTDOC; Physic. Medline Plus; Pollut. Abstr. Indexes; Poult. Abstr.; Protozoolog. Abstr.; Ref. Upd. Basic Ed.; Ref. Upd. Clinical Ed.; Ref. Upd. Deluxe Ed.; Res. Alert [Full Cov.]; Rev. Med. Vet. Entomol.; Rev. Med. Vet. Mycology; Rev. Plant Pathol.; Risk Abstr.; Saf. Health Work; Sci. Cit. Index; SCISEARCH; Soc. Sci. Cit. Index [Select. Cov.]; Sug. Indus. Abstr.; Vet. Bull.; Toxicol. Abstr.; Trop. Dis. Bull.; Virol. AIDS Abstr.

AG/0326-5412
**ANALES DE LA CATEDRA DE TISIONEUMONOLOGIA.** [An. catedra Tisioneumonol.]. Vol. 37 (1978)-. Periodical. Spanish. an. Universidad de Buenos Aires / Medicina, Facultad de Medicina, Chorroarin 847 Dto A, 1427 Buenos Aires Argentina. **Tel** 011 54 1 513336. **UDC** 616-002.5. **CODEN** ACTIE3. Documents available from BIOSIS Document Express. ***Continues*** *Anales de la Catedra de Patologia y Clinica de la Tuberculosis, 0301-8911.*
**Ind/Abst** Biol. Abstr. (1986-).

IT
**ANNALI DELL'ISTITUTO CARLO FORLANINI (1981).** (ANNALI DELL'INSTITUTO CARLO FORLANINI / UNITA SANITARIA LOCALE, RM 16.). **Added/Corp** Istituto "Carlo Forlanini". Unita Sanitaria Locale, RM 16. Vol. 1, N. 1 (1981)-. Periodical. Italian (English). qt. L60000 (Italy); $90.00 (other). Edizioni Luigi Pozzi Srl, Via Panama 68, 00198 Rome Italy. **Tel** (06)8553548, FAX (06)8554105. **NLM** W1; AN486A. ***Continues*** *Annali dell'Istituto Carlo Forlanini, 0021-2431.*

CN/0702-9306
**ANNUAL REPORT - DIVISION OF TUBERCULOSIS CONTROL (LEDGERS).** (ANNUAL REPORT / PROVINCE OF BRITISH COLUMBIA, MINISTRY OF HEALTH, PREVENTIVE SERVICES, DIVISION OF TUBERCULOSIS CONTROL.). Began with 1965. English. an. Ministry of Health / Victoria, 1515 Blanshard Street, Victoria British Columbia V8W 3C8 Canada. **Tel** 387-2749. **LC** RA185.B7; B15. **DD** 614.5/42/09711. **UDC** 616-002.5(047.1)(711). ***Continues*** *British Columbia. Division of Tuberculosis Control. Yearly Report of Ledgers.*

KE/1015-0072
**ANNUAL REPORT / KENYA TUBERCULOSIS AND RESPIRATORY DISEASES RESEARCH CENTRE.** ***Title Change.*** [Annu. rep. - Kenya Tuberc. Respir. Dis. Res. Cent.]. **Main/Corp** Kenya Tuberculosis and Respiratory Diseases Research Centre. English. an. Director Kenya Tuberculosis and Respiratory Diseases Research Centre, PO Box 47855, Nairobi Kenya. **Tel** 724262/4/5. **LC** RC306. **DD** 616.2/007206762. **UDC** 616-002.5(047.1)(676.2). **CODEN** ARKCEB. **Ad Acc. Circ:** 200 (ctrl). Documents available from BIOSIS Document Express. ***Continued by*** *Respiratory Diseases Research Center.*
**Desc:** The activities of the research carried on during the year in question.
**Ind/Abst** Biol. Abstr. (-1981).

CN/0078-2505
**ANNUAL REPORT - TUBERCULOSIS CONTROL SERVICES, NOVA SCOTIA.** **Main/Corp** Nova Scotia. Tuberculosis Control Services. 1st- 1957-. Periodical. English. Miller Unit, Kentville Hospital Association, Kentville Nova Scotia Canada. **Tel** (902)678-3251. **UDC** 616-002.5(047.1)(716); 616.24. **NLM** W2 DC2.1 N9T9A.

US/0887-8242
**ANNUAL REVIEW PULMONARY AND CRITICAL CARE MEDICINE.** ***Ceased.*** [Annu. rev. pulm. crit. care med.]. (1986/1987)-(19??). Periodical. English. be. Hanley & Belfus Inc., 210 South 13th Street, Philadelphia PA 19107. **Tel** (215)546-7293, FAX (215)790-9330. **LC** RC756; .P825. **DD** 616.2/4. **NLM** W1; AN7796KF. **CODEN** ARPMEW. Documents available from BIOSIS Document Express. ***Continues*** *Pulmonary Disease Reviews, 0272-7900.*
**Ind/Abst** Biol. Abstr. (1986-19??).

IT/1120-0391
**ARCHIVIO MONALDI PER LE MALATTIE DEL TORACE.** ***Title Change.*** [Arch. Monaldi mal. torace]. Vol. 42, No. 1 (Jan/Feb. 1987)-Vol. 47 in (1992). Periodical. Italian (English). bm. Casa Editrice Libr Idelson Gnocchi, Via Alcide de Gasperi 55, 80133 Naples Italy. **Tel** 011 39 81 552-4733. **NLM** W1; AR596QV. **CODEN** AMMTE3. ***Continues*** *Archivio Monaldi per la Tisiologia e le Malattie dell'Apparato Respiratorio, 0004-0185.* ***Continued by*** *Monaldi Archives for Chest Disease.*
**Ind/Abst** Index Med. (Jan.-Feb. 1987-?), (1987-1992).

SP/0300-2896
**ARCHIVOS DE BRONCONEUMOLOGIA.** (ARCHIVOS DE BRONCONEUMOLOGIA : ORGANO OFICIAL DE LA SOCIEDAD ESPANOLA DE PATOLOGIA RESPIRATORIA, S.E.P.A.R.). [Arch. bronconeumol.]. **Added/Corp** Sociedad Espanola de Patologia Respiratoria. (1964)-. Academic Scholarly Publication. Spanish. Nine times a year. $62.00. Ediciones Doyma SA, Travesera de Gracia 17 21, 08021 Barcelona Spain. **Tel** 011 34 3 2000711, 011 34 3 4145706, FAX 011 34 3 2091136, telex 51964 INK E. **ED** D. Francisco Coll Colome. **CODEN** ARBRDA. Index available. cum. index. **Bk Rev. Ad Acc. Pr Rev. Circ:** 5,000 (ctrl). Documents available from BIOSIS Document Express.
**Desc:** Official organ of the Spanish Society of Respiratory Pathology. Original articles of the most outstanding studies of Spanish specialists.
**Ind/Abst** Biol. Abstr. (1986-); EMBASE; Indice Med. Esp.

UK/0269-1493
**ARI NEWS.** [ARI news]. **VFOAT** Acute Respiratory Infections News. (1985)-. English (Spanish, Chinese and Nepali). Three times a year. £10.00. AHRTAG, 1 London Bridge Street, 3 Castle, London SE1 9SG England. **Tel** 011 44 71 378 1403, FAX 011 44 71 403 6003, telex 912881 TXG. **ED** Felicity Savage and Kathy Altawell. **DD** 616.2005. Index available. **Bk Rev. Pr Rev. Circ:** 90,000.
**Desc:** News and views on acute respiratory infections.
**Ind/Abst** Trop. Dis. Bull.

●US/1050-5253
**ASTHMA MANAGEMENT.** [Asthma manag.]. Vol. 1, No. 1 (Spring 1992)-. Periodical. English. qt. $140.00. Mary Ann Liebert Inc., 1651 Third Avenue, New York NY 10128. **Tel** (212)289-2300, (800)M-LIEBERT, FAX (212)289-4697. **ED** James Allen Pollowitz and Carl Sherter. **DD** 616. **NLM** ZWF 553; A853.
**Desc:** Management techniques for clinicians and other health care professionals who treat patients with asthma. Current therapies, new treatment modalities, and sources for professional and patient information are included.

US/8756-4734
**ASTHMA UPDATE.** (Winter 1985)-. Periodical. English. Four times a year (Jan., Apr., July, Oct.). $12.00 (one year); $20.00 (two years). Asthma Update, 123 Monticello Avenue, Annapolis MD 21401. **Tel** (410)267-8329, . **ED** David C. Jamison, (phone: (410)267-0309). **DD** 616. Index available. **Bk Rev. Circ:** 350.
**Desc:** Newsletter for people with asthma reporting current developments in asthma research and treatment from medical journals.

AT
**ASTHMA WELFARER.** English. Three times a year (Apr., Aug., Dec.). 12.50Aus$. Asthma Foundation of New South Wales, 82-86 Pacific Highway, St. Leonards 2065 Australia. **Tel** 011 61 2 9063233, FAX 011 61 2 9064493. **ED** Clair Isbister. **Bk Rev. Ad Acc, Adv Mgr:** Dorothy Nardi. **Circ:** 5,500 (ctrl).
**Desc:** Journal of the Asthma Foundation of New South Wales - a voluntary organization involved in research, welfare, and education to assist those who suffer from asthma.

GW/0341-3055
**ATEMWEGS- UND LUNGENKRANKHEITEN.** [Atemwegs-Lungenkr.]. Volume 1 (1975)-. Academic Scholarly Publication. German. mo. DM228.00. Dustri-Verlag, Dr Karl Feistle, Postfach 49, D 82032 Deisenhofen Germany. **Tel** 011 49 89 6138610, FAX 011 49 89 6135412. **NLM** W1 AT212C. **CODEN** ATLUDF. **[CCC].** Index available. **Bk Rev. Ad Acc.** ctrl circ. Documents available from CASDDS.
**Ind/Abst** Chem. Abstr.; EMBASE; Life Sci. Collect.; Protozoolog. Abstr.; Sci. Cit. Index (19??-19??); SCISEARCH.

GW/0342-4456
**BUCHEREI DES PNEUMOLOGEN.** Vol. 1-1976-. Monographic series. German. Price varies per volume. Georg Thieme Verlag Stuttgart, Postfach 301120, D 70451 Stuttgart Germany. **Tel** 011 49 711 89310, FAX 011 49 711 8931298, telex 7 252 275 GTVD. **(Subscription address:** Thieme Medical Publishers Inc., 381 Park Avenue South, New York NY 10016.**) UDC** 616.24. **NLM** W1 BU157K. ***Supersedes*** *Tuberkulose-Bucherei, 0344-6239.*

US/0092-5659
**BULLETIN - AMERICAN LUNG ASSOCIATION.** (BULLETIN.). [Bull. - Am. Lung Assoc.]. **Main/Corp** American Lung Association. Vol. 59 No. 5 (June 1973)-. Bulletin. English. bm. **LC** RC756; .A63a. **DD** 616.2/4/005. **NLM** WI AM563. **[CCC].** ***Continues*** *National Tuberculosis and Respiratory Disease Association. Bulletin, 0028-0313.*
**Ind/Abst** Cumul. Index Nurs. Allied Health Lit.; Energy Res. Abstr. (Aug. 1982-); Health Plan. Adminis.; Int. Nurs. Index.

FR/1011-7903
**BULLETIN DE L'UNION INTERNATIONALE CONTRE LA TUBERCULOSE ET LES MALADIES RESPIRATOIRES.** ***Ceased.*** [Bull. Union int. contre tuberc. mal. respir.]. (1986)-(1992). Periodical. French (French and Spanish). qt. Intl Union Vs TB & Lung Disease, 68 Boulevard Saint Michel, 75006 Paris France. **Tel** 011 33 1 46330830, FAX 011 33 1 43299087. **ED** J. Chretien, Prof. Hershfield, Prof. Chaulet, Prof. Murray. **UDC** 61. **Bk Rev. Ad Acc. Pr Rev. Circ:** 5,000 (ctrl). ***Continues*** *Bulletin de l'Union Internationale Contre la Tuberculose, 0373-3041.*
**Desc:** Presents scientific articles on respiratory disease, AIDS & tuberculosis, and community health.

NE/0014-4193
**CHEST DISEASES, THORACIC SURGERY AND TUBERCULOSIS.** **Added/Corp** Excerpta Medica Foundation. (19??)-. English. Sixteen times a year (2 vols.). FI1810.00. Excerpta Medica Publishing Group, PO Box 548, 1000 AM Amsterdam Netherlands. **Tel** 011 31 20 5803243. **(Subscription address:** Excerpta Medica Journals, PO Box 85, Limerick Ireland.**)** **LC** RC306; .T82. **DD** 617/.54/005. **NLM** ZW 1 E968. **[CCC]. Ad Acc. Circ:** 300. available on microfilm from University Microfilms International (UMI). ***Continues*** *Chest Diseases.*
**Desc:** For pathological anatomists and physiologists, respiratory disease specialists, cancer specialists, public health workers, inhalation toxicologists. Covers all aspects on chest diseases and is organized on an etiopathological basis.

US/1044-0690
**CHOICES IN RESPIRATORY MANAGEMENT.** ***Ceased.*** [Choices respir. manage.]. **VFOAT** Respiratory Management. (1989)-Vol. 22. Periodical. English. bm. Choices Publishing Group, 129 Washington Street, Hoboken NJ 07030. **DD** 616. **NLM** W1; CH883M. ***Continues*** *Respiratory Management, 0892-9289.*
**Ind/Abst** Health Devices Alerts; Health Plan. Adminis.; Hospit. Health Admin. Index (1989).

●US/1073-1644
**CLINICAL ADVANCES IN CARDIO-RESPIRATORY CARE.** (CLINICAL ADVANCES IN CARDIO-RESPIRATORY CARE [SOUND RECORDING].). [Clin. adv. cardio-respir. care]. (1994)-. Periodical. English. mo. $175.00. Educational Reviews Inc., 6801 Cahaba Valley Road, Birmingham AL 35242. **Tel** (205)991-5188, (800)633-4743, FAX (205)995-1926. **DD** 615. ***Continues*** *In Service Reviews in Respiratory Therapy, 1041-0058.*

SP/1130-0965
**CORE JOURNALS EN ENFERMEDADES PULMONARES.** [Core j. enferm. pulm.]. (1990)-. Periodical. Spanish. bm. Mayo SA, Muntaner 374-376, 08006 Barcelona Spain. **Tel** 209 02 55, FAX 202 06 43. **ED** Jose Mayoral and Josep Ferrando. **UDC** 616.24(048.3). **Ad Acc. Circ:** 5,000.
**Desc:** Abstracts of world literature about pulmonary disease.

UK/0950-8724
**CURRENT MEDICAL LITERATURE / REVERSIBLE OBSTRUCTIVE AIRWAYS DISEASE.** [Curr. med. lit., Revers. obstr. airw. dis.]. (1987)-. English. qt. £20.00 UK; $40.00 other. Current Medical Literature Ltd., 40-42 Osnaburgh Street, London NW1 3ND England. **Tel** 011 44 71 4658377, FAX 011 44 71 4658380. **(Subscription address:** Royal Society Medicine Services, 1 Wimpole Street, London W1M 8AE England.**)** **DD** 016.61624.

US/0890-1449
**CURRENT TOPICS IN PULMONARY PHARMACOLOGY AND TOXICOLOGY.** **See** Medical Science and Technology-Toxicology.

FR
**ENCYCLOPEDIE MEDICO CHIRURGICALE. MEDECINE GENERALE & SPECIALITES. POUMON PLEVRE.** French. Editions Techniques, 141 rue de Javel, 75747 Paris Cedex 15 France. **Tel** 011 33 1 45589100.

DK/0903-1936
**EUROPEAN RESPIRATORY JOURNAL, THE.** (THE EUROPEAN RESPIRATORY JOURNAL : OFFICIAL JOURNAL OF THE EUROPEAN SOCIETY FOR CLINICAL RESPIRATORY PHYSIOLOGY.). [Eur. respir. j.]. **Added/Corp** European Society for Clinical Respiratory Physiology. Vol. 1, No. 1 (Jan. 1988)-. Periodical. English (summaries and/or abstracts in French). mo. kr2460.00 US, Canada and Japan; kr2365.00 other. Munksgaard International Publishers Ltd, PO Box 2148, DK-1016 Copenhagen K Denmark. **Tel** 011 45 33 12 70 30, FAX 011 45 33 12 93 87, telex 19431 MUNKS DK. **ED** Erik Berglund and J C Yernault. **NLM** W1; EU722K. **CODEN** ERJOEI. **[CCC]. Pr Rev.** Documents available from The Genuine Article, BIOSIS Document Express, CASDDS. ***Formed by the union of*** *Clinical Respiratory Physiology, 0272-7587* ***and*** *European Journal of Respiratory Diseases, 0106-4339.*
**Desc:** Official journal of the European Society for Clinical Respiratory Physiology.
**Ind/Abst** Biol. Abstr. (1988-); Chem. Abstr.; Coal Abstr.; Curr. Aware. Biol. Sci., CABS; Curr. Contents Life Sci.; EMBASE; Health Plan. Adminis.; Helminthol. Abstr. (1991-); Index Med. (Jan. 1988-); PESTDOC; Res. Alert [Full Cov.]; Rev. Med. Vet. Mycology; Sci. Cit. Index; SCISEARCH; Soc. Sci. Cit. Index [Select. Cov.]; Soyabean Abstr.

DK/0904-1850
**EUROPEAN RESPIRATORY JOURNAL. SUPPLEMENT, THE.** [Eur. respir. j., Suppl.]. Vol. 1 (Sept. 1988)-. Monographic series. English. kr2460.00 US, Canada & Japan; kr2365.00 other (comes with subscription to European Respiratory Journal). Munksgaard International Publishers Ltd, PO Box 2148, DK-1016 Copenhagen K Denmark. **Tel** 011 45 33 12 70 30, FAX 011 45 33 12 93 87, telex 19431 MUNKS DK. **NLM** W1; EU722KA. **[CCC].** ***Continues*** *European Journal of Respiratory Diseases. Supplement, 0106-4347.*
**Ind/Abst** EMBASE; Health Plan. Adminis.; Index Med. (1988-).

DK/0905-9180
**EUROPEAN RESPIRATORY REVIEW : AN OFFICIAL JOURNAL OF THE EUROPEAN RESPIRATORY SOCIETY.** **Added/Corp** European Respiratory Society. Vol. 1, Review No. 1 (Mar. 1991)-. Periodical. English (French and German). ir (5-6 issues per year). kr926.00 US, Canada and Japan; kr850.00 other. Munksgaard International Publishers Ltd, PO Box 2148, DK-1016 Copenhagen K Denmark. **Tel** 011 45 33 12 70 30, FAX 011 45 33 12 93 87, telex 19431 MUNKS DK. **ED** Jean Claud Yernault. **NLM** W1; EU728. **CODEN** EREWEH. **[CCC].** Index available. **Bk Rev. Ad Acc. Pr Rev. Circ:** 2,500 (ctrl).
**Desc:** Offers all scientists a digest and opinion of current views, clinical and experimental, of all aspects of respiratory medicine and pathophysiology.
**Ind/Abst** EMBASE.

US/0190-2148
**EXPERIMENTAL LUNG RESEARCH.** [Exp. lung res.]. Vol. 1 (Mar. 1980)-. Academic Scholarly Publication. English. bm. £270.00 UK; $445.00 other. Taylor & Francis Ltd., Rankine Road, Basingstoke Hampshire, RG24 8PR United Kingdom. **Tel** 011 44 256 840366, FAX 011 44 256 479438, telex 858540. **(Subscription address:** Taylor & Francis Inc., 1900 Frost Road, Suite 101, Bristol PA 19007-1598.**)** **ED** Paul Nettesheim (editor's address: Pulmonary Function and Toxicology Laboratory, National Institute of Environmental Health Sciences, Research Triangle Park, NC). **LC** QP121.A1. **DD** 616.2/4. **UDC** 616.24. **NLM** W1 EX504U. **CODEN** EXLRDA. **[CCC].** Index available. **Bk Rev. Ad Acc. Pr Rev. Circ:** 700. available on microfilm and microfiche from University Microfilms International (UMI). Documents available from The Genuine Article, BIOSIS Document Express, CASDDS, ADONIS.
**Desc:** Provides original studies emphasizing mechanisms of pulmonary biology and pathobiology, investigated at the biochemical, subcellular, cellular, and tissue levels. A subscription to this important publication guarantees receipt of key methodological advances, as well as invited reviews of especially timely research topics.
**Ind/Abst** ADONIS; Biol. Abstr.; Chem. Abstr.; CSA Neuro. Abstr. (?-?); Curr. Aware. Biol. Sci., CABS; Curr. Contents Life Sci.; EMBASE; Health Plan. Adminis.; Immunol. Abstr.; Index Med.; Index Vet.; INIS Atomindex [Micro.]; Life Sci. Collect.; Ref. Upd. Deluxe Ed.; Res. Alert [Full Cov.]; Sci. Cit. Index; SCISEARCH; Vet. Bull.

IT/0017-0437
**GIORNALE ITALIANO DELLE MALATTIE DEL TORACE.** ***Ceased.*** [G. Ital. Mal. Torace]. Vol. 20 (Jan./Feb. 1966)-(19??). Academic Scholarly Publication. Italian (English; summaries and/or abstracts in English, French, German and Spanish). bm. Giornale Italiano Delle, Via Luca Comercio 5, 20145 Milan Italy. **Tel** 02/3495026-469648, FAX 33301417. **ED** Bottero Aldo. **NLM** W1 GI761N. **CODEN** GIMTB4GIMTB. Index available. cum. index. **Ad Acc. Circ:** 2,000 (ctrl). available in microform; available on microfilm. Documents available from BIOSIS Document Express, CASDDS. ***Continues*** *Giornale Italiano della Tubercolosi e delle Malattie del Torace.*
**Desc:** Medical news from the world. Seven original works per issue about respiratory, cardiovascular, senological and allergic diseases of the chest; book reviews, notices, advertisements.
**Ind/Abst** Biol. Abstr.; Chem. Abstr.; EMBASE [Select. Cov.].

KO/0378-0066
**GYERHAIG MIC HOHUBGI JIROHAN.** (KYORHAEK MIT HOHUPKI CHIRHWAN.). [Gyerhaig mic hohubgi jirohan]. **VFOAT** Tuberculosis and Respiratory Diseases; Journal of the Korean Academy of Tuberculosis. Academic Scholarly Publication. English (Korean). qt. 121-150 Tangsan-dong, Yongdungpo-ku, Seoul Korea. **LC** RC306. **UDC** 616.24; 616-002.5. **NLM** W1 KY973H. **CODEN** KHCHAM. Documents available from CASDDS.
**Ind/Abst** Chem. Abstr. (1955-1984); EMBASE.

SW/0280-4638
**HJARTA, KARL, LUNGOR.** **Added/Corp** Svenska Nationalforeningen mot Hjart- och Lungsjukdomar. (1982)-. Periodical. Swedish. qt. Kr25.00 Sweden; $5.00 US. Svenska Nationalforeningen mot Hjart-Och Lungsjukdomar, Kungsgatan 54, 111 35 Stockholm Sweden. **Tel** 46-8 11 01 74. **ED** Ake Hanngren. **Circ:** 2,500. Documents available from BIOSIS Document Express. ***Continues*** *Kvartalsskrift (Svenska Nationalforeningen mot Hjart- och Lungsjukdomar), 0373-2665.*
**Desc:** Popular scientific articles on research and treatment of heart and lung diseases.
**Ind/Abst** Biol. Abstr. (1982-1988).

US/1066-534X
**I.V.U.N. NEWS.** (I.V.U.N. NEWS / INTERNATIONAL VENTILATORS USERS NETWORK.). [I.V.U.N. news]. **Added/Corp** International Ventilators Users Network. Gazette International Networking Institute. **VAT** International Ventilators Users Network News. (1987)-. Periodical. English. sa (Apr., Oct.). $20.00 US; $22.00 other. Gazette International Networking Institute, 5100 Oakland Avenue, Number 206, St Louis MO 63110. **Tel** (314)534-0475, FAX (314)534-5070. **DD** 615. **NLM** W1; IV828.

US/1041-0058
**IN SERVICE REVIEWS IN RESPIRATORY THERAPY.** ***Title Change.*** (IN SERVICE REVIEWS IN RESPIRATORY THERAPY [SOUND RECORDING].). [In serv. rev. respir. therapy]. **VFOAT** In-Service Reviews in Respiratory Therapy. Vol. 1, No. 1 (1988)-(1994). Periodical. English. mo. Educational Reviews Inc., 6801 Cahaba Valley Road, Birmingham AL 35242. **Tel** (205)991-5188, (800)633-4743, FAX (205)995-1926. **DD** 615. ***Continued by*** *Clinical Advances in Cardio-Respiratory Care, 1073-1644.*

II/0377-9343
**INDIAN JOURNAL OF CHEST DISEASES & ALLIED SCIENCES, THE.** **See** Medical Science and Technology-Cardiology.

II/0019-5707
**INDIAN JOURNAL OF TUBERCULOSIS.** [Indian j. tuberc.]. **Added/Corp** Tuberculosis Association of India. (19??)-. Academic Scholarly Publication. English. qt. $40.00. Tuberculosis Association of India, 3 Red Cross Road, New Delhi-110001 India. **(Subscription address:** Prints India, 11 Darya Ganj, New Delhi 110002 India.**)** **NLM** W1 IN239. **CODEN** IJTBAD. Documents available from BIOSIS Document Express, CASDDS.
**Ind/Abst** Biol. Abstr. (?-1985); Chem. Abstr.; EMBASE; Trop. Dis. Bull.

JA
**JAPANESE JOURNAL OF THORACIC SURGERY.** (1948)-. Periodical. English. Thirteen times a year. ¥46000.00. Nankodo, (Nankodo Co., Ltd.), 42-6, Hongo 3 Chome, Bunkyoku, Tokyoto 113 Japan. **Bk Rev. Ad Acc. Circ:** 3,300.
**Desc:** Devoted to surgery of the respiratory and cardiac system.
**Ind/Abst** Index Med.

BL/0102-3586
**JORNAL DE PNEUMOLOGIA : PUBLICACAO OFICIAL DA SOCIEDADE BRASILEIRA DE PNEUMOLOGIA E TISIOLOGIA.** **Added/Corp** Sociedade Brasileira de Pneumologia e Tisiologia. (197?)-. Periodical. Portuguese (summaries and/or abstracts in English; table of contents in English). Four times a year. Price varies. Ponto Cardeal Publicacoes Ltd., Rua Sete de Abril 261 CJ, 01043 Sao Paulo, Brazil. **Tel** 011 55 11 2557340. **NLM** W1; JO199H.
**Ind/Abst** EMBASE [Select. Cov.].

US/0894-2684
**JOURNAL OF AEROSOL MEDICINE.** (JOURNAL OF AEROSOL MEDICINE : THE OFFICIAL JOURNAL OF THE INTERNATIONAL SOCIETY FOR AEROSOLS IN MEDICINE.). [J. aerosol med.]. **Added/Corp** International Society for Aerosols in Medicine. Vol. 1, No. 1 (1988)-. Periodical. English. qt. $152.00. Mary Ann Liebert Inc., 1651 Third Avenue, New York NY 10128. **Tel** (212)289-2300, (800)M-LIEBERT, FAX (212)289-4697. **ED** Gerald Smalldone. **DD** 616. **NLM**

W1; JO534AD. **CODEN** JAEMEP. Documents available from The Genuine Article.
**Desc:** Serves as a forum for the publication of studies involving inhalation of particles and gases in the respiratory tract, covering the use of aerosols as tools to study basic physiologic phenomena, their use as selective delivery systems for medication, and the toxic effects of inhaled agents.
**Ind/Abst** Res. Alert [Select. Cov.]; SCISEARCH.

US/0277-0903
**JOURNAL OF ASTHMA, THE.** [J. asthma]. **Added/Corp** Association for the Care of Asthma (U.S.) Asthma Publications Society. Vol. 18, No. 1 (Jan. 1981)-. Academic Scholarly Publication. English. bm. $550.00 US; $571.00 other. Marcel Dekker Inc., 270 Madison Avenue, New York NY 10016. **Tel** (212)696-9000, (800)228-1160, FAX (212)685-4540, telex 421419. **(Subscription address:** Marcel Dekker Inc, PO Box 5017, Monticello NY 12701.**) ED** David G. Tinkelman, Lawrence T. Chiaramonte, Christopher Fanta and Lyndon E. Mansfield. **LC** RC591; .J6. **DD** 616.2/38/005. **NLM** W1 JO544S. **CODEN** JOUADU. **[CCC]. Bk Rev. Ad Acc.** ctrl circ. available on microfiche. Documents available from The Genuine Article, BIOSIS Document Express, CASDDS, ADONIS. ***Continues*** *Journal of Asthma Research, 0021-9134.*
**Desc:** Provides information on new developments in the understanding and management of asthma. Contains valuable guidelines for the basic understanding of asthma cases, emergency as well as long-term care, environmental counseling, preventative measures, patient education and psychological support, and relevant developments in fields ranging from molecular biology to government legislation.
**Ind/Abst** ADONIS; Biol. Abstr.; Chem. Abstr.; Curr. Aware. Biol. Sci., CABS; Curr. Contents Clin. Med.; EMBASE; Index Med.; INIS Atomindex [Micro.]; Med. Abstr. Newsl.; Nutr. Res. Newsl.; Life Sci. Collect.; Psychol. Abstr. (1981-); PsycINFO; PsycLit; Ref. Upd. Deluxe Ed.; Res. Alert [Select. Cov.]; Rev. Med. Vet. Entomol.; SCISEARCH; Soc. Sci. Cit. Index [Select. Cov.]; SportSearch.

●US/1070-8030
**JOURNAL OF BRONCHOLOGY.** (JOURNAL OF BRONCHOLOGY : AN OFFICIAL QUARTERLY PUBLICATION OF AMERICAN ASSOCIATION FOR BRONCHOLOGY, WORLD ASSOCIATION FOR BRONCHOLOGY.). **Added/Corp** American Association for Bronchology. World Association for Bronchology. Vol. 1, No. 1 (Jan. 1994)-. Periodical. English. qt. $89.00 (individuals), $116.00 (institutions) US; $110.00 (individuals), $132.00 (institutions) other. Raven Press, 1185 Avenue of the Americas, 37th Floor, New York NY 10036. **Tel** (212)930-9500, (212)930-9604, FAX (212)869-3495, (212)302-8507, telex 640073. **ED** Udaya B.S. Prakash. **DD** 616.

US/0194-259X
**JOURNAL OF RESPIRATORY DISEASES, THE.** Vol. 1 (Oct. 1979)-. Periodical. English. mo. $70.00 US; $90.00 other. Cliggott Publishing Company, 55 Holly Hill Lane, Box 4010, Greenwich CT 06830. **Tel** (203)661-0600, (212)993-0440. **LC** RC705; .J67. **DD** 616.2/005. **NLM** W1 JO87D. **[CCC].**
**Desc:** Provides practical information about diagnosis and treatment pertaining to the respiratory system, both as the site of primary disease and as a complication of other clinical problems.

JA/0022-9776
**KEKKAKU. VFOAT** Tuberculosis. (1923)-. Academic Scholarly Publication. Japanese (English). mo. ¥15000. Japanese Society for Tuberculosis, c/o Research Institute of Tuberculosis, 3-1-24 Matsuyama, Kiyose-shi, Tokyo Japan204. **Tel** 011 81 3 3269 2131, FAX 011 81 3 3269 8655. **ED** Teruo Aoyagi. Index available. **Ad Acc. Circ:** 3,000 (ctrl).
**Desc:** Publishes original research works on tuberculosis and related diseases.
**Ind/Abst** EMBASE; Immunol. Abstr.; Index Med.; Microbiol. Abstr. Sect. B; Microbiol. Abstr. Sect. A; Rev. Med. Vet. Mycology.

JA/0286-9314
**KOKYU.** [Kokyu]. **VFOAT** Respiration Research. (1982)-. Periodical. Multiple languages. mo. Tokyo Resupireshon Risachi Faundshon, Tokyo Japan. **DD** 616.2. Documents available from CASDDS.
**Ind/Abst** Chem. Abstr.

IT/0368-7546
**LOTTA CONTRO LA TUBERCOLOSI E LE MALATTIE POLMONARI SOCIALI.** [Lotta tuberc. mal. polm. soc.]. **Added/Corp** Federazione Italiana Contro la Tubercolosi e le Malattie Polmonari Sociali. Federazione Italiana Contro la Tubercolosi. Vol. 42 (Jan./March 1972)-. Periodical. Italian (summaries and/or abstracts in English). Four times a year. $80.00. Federazione Italiana Contro la Tubercolosi e le Malattie, Via G da Procida 7 D, 00162 Rome Italy. **Tel** 011 39 6 44240682. **NLM** W1 LO865. **Bk Rev. Ad Acc. Pr Rev.** ***Continues*** *Lotta Contro la Tubercolosi.*
**Desc:** Our review is concerning the problems of respiratory diseases, tuberculosis, chest diseases, and sanitary education.
**Ind/Abst** EMBASE; Trop. Dis. Bull.

GW/0341-2040
**LUNG.** [Lung]. **Added/Corp** Gesellschaft fuer Lungen- und Atmungsforschung. Vol. 154 (1976)-. Academic Scholarly Publication. English (German). Six times a year. $219.00. Springer-Verlag New York Inc., 175 5th Avenue, New York NY 10010. **Tel** (212)460-1500, telex 232 235 SPB UR. **(Subscription address:** Springer Verlag New York Inc. / for North America, 44 Hartz Way, Secaucus NJ 07096.**) ED** T Higenbottam, H Magnussem, P D Pare, and M H Williams Williams Jr. **NLM** W1 LU618. **CODEN** LUNGD9. **[CCC]. Pr Rev.** available on microfilm and microfiche from University Microfilms International (UMI). Documents available from The Genuine Article, BIOSIS Document Express, CASDDS, Documents on Demand, ADONIS. ***Continues*** *Pneumonologie, 0033-4073.*
**Desc:** Publishes a wide range of original scientific articles on all aspects of basic and clinical research dealing with the lungs, airways, and breathing including developmental, environmental and genetic aspects.
**Ind/Abst** ADONIS; Biol. Abstr.; Chem. Abstr.; Curr. Contents; Curr. Contents Clin. Med.; Curr. Contents Life Sci.; EMBASE; Energy Inf. Abstr.; Energy Res. Abstr. (May 1979-); Environ. Abstr.; Index Med.; Index Vet.; Life Sci. Collect.; PESTDOC; Res. Alert [Full Cov.]; Sci. Cit. Index; SCISEARCH; Vet. Bull.

GW/0176-1749
**LUNG & RESPIRATION.** [Lung respir.]. **VFOAT** Lung and Respiration. Vol. 1, No. 1 (May 1984)-. Periodical. English. Four times a year. Free on request. PMI Verlag GmbH, August-Schanz Strasse 21, D 60433 Frankfurt Germany. **Tel** 011 49 69 5480000, FAX 069/548000-77, telex 412952 PMI D. **NLM** W1; LU618E.

US/0362-3181
**LUNG BIOLOGY IN HEALTH AND DISEASE.** [Lung biol. health dis.]. Vol. 1 (1976)-. Academic Scholarly Publication. English. ir. Price varies per volume. Marcel Dekker Inc., 270 Madison Avenue, New York NY 10016. **Tel** (212)696-9000, (800)228-1160, FAX (212)685-4540, telex 421419. **(Subscription address:** Marcel Dekker Inc., PO Box 5017, Monticello, NY 12701-5176; (telephone: (800)228-1160)**) NLM** W1 LU62. **CODEN** LBHDD7. Documents available from CASDDS.
**Desc:** Presents information on the lungs and respiratory system. Topics include respiratory disease, pulmonary development, and more.
**Ind/Abst** Chem. Abstr.

US/1078-2877
**LUNG DISEASE WEEKLY.** (19??)-. English. wk (48 issues). $995.00 US, Canada and Mexico; $1195.00 other. CW Henderson, PO Box 5528, Atlanta GA 30307-0528. **Tel** (404)377-8895, FAX (404)378-5411. **(Subscription address:** CW Henderson, Subscription Office, PO Box 830409, Birmingham AL 35283-0409.**)**
**Desc:** Helps researchers and clinicians keep abreast of current issues and news concerning the world's major lung diseases and their treatments.

II/0970-2113
**LUNG INDIA.** (LUNG INDIA : OFFICIAL ORGAN OF INDIAN CHEST SOCIETY.). [Lung India]. **Added/Corp** Indian Chest Society. Vol. 1, No. 1 (Aug. 15, 1982)-. Periodical. English. qt. $20.00. Indian Chest Society, Bombay, India. **(Subscription address:** Prints India, 11 Darya Ganj, New Delhi 110002 India.**) NLM** W1; LU68.

GW/0720-0706
**LUNGE + ATMUNG. A. VFOAT** Lunge und Atmung. A. (197?)-. Periodical. German. Four times a year. DM40.00. PMI Verlag GmbH, August-Schanz Strasse 21, D 60433 Frankfurt Germany. **Tel** 011 49 69 5480000, FAX 069/548000-77, telex 412952 PMI D. **UDC** 616-23/.25.
**Desc:** Brief summaries of original scientific articles, congress reports, interviews and therapeutic advice.

IT
**MEDICINA TORACICA. Added/Corp** Societa Italiana di Fisiopatologia Respiratoria. (19??)-. Periodical. Italian (English). qt. L85500 Italy. Masson S.P.A, Via Statuto 2/4, 20121 Milan Italy. **Tel** 011 39 2 63671, FAX 011 39 2 6367211. **NLM** W1; ME629JJ.

IT/0026-4954
**MINERVE PNEUMOLOGICA.** [Minerva pneumol.]. (1962)-. Periodical. Italian. qt. $90.00 (individuals), $140.00 (institutions). Edizioni Minerva Medica, Corso Bramante 83-85, 10126 Turin Italy. **Tel** 011 39 11 678282, FAX 011 39 11 674502. **UDC** 612.2+616.2.
**Desc:** Covers the pathophysiology and clinical medicine of the diseases of the respiratory system.
**Ind/Abst** EMBASE [Select. Cov.].

●IT
**MONALDI ARCHIVES FOR CHEST DISEASE. ARCHIVIO MONALDI PER LE MALATTIE DEL TORACE / FONDAZIONE CLINICA DEL LAVORO, IRCCS [AND] ISTITUTO DI CLINICA TISIOLOGICA E MALATTIE APPARATO RESPIRATORIO, UNIVERSITA DI NAPOLI, SECONDO ATENEO. Added/Corp** Fondazione Clinica del Lavoro. Universit·a di Napoli--Secondo Ateneo. Istituto di Clinica Tisiologica e Malattie Apparato Respiratorio. **VFOAT** Archivio Monaldi per le Malattie del Torace. Vol. 48, No. 1 (Feb. 1993)-. Periodical. English. bm. $130.00. PI ME Tipografia Editrice, Viale Sardegna 64, 27100 Pavia Italy. **Tel** 011 39 382 539124. **NLM** W1; MO2036. ***Continues*** *Archivio Monaldi per le Malattie del Torace, 1120-0391.*
**Ind/Abst** Index Med. (1993-).

FR/0983-8201
**OPA PRATIQUE. See** Medical Science and Technology-Otorhinolaryngology.

FR/1146-5581
**PASCAL. E 74, PNEUMOLOGIE. VFOAT** PASCAL. E 74, Pneumology; PASCAL. E Soixante-quatorze, Pneumologie. (1990)-. Periodical. Multiple languages. Eleven times a year. 1085.00F France; 1155.00F other. CNRS / Institut d'Information Scientifique et Technique, (Centre National de la Recherche Scientifique), 15 Quai Anatole France, Paris 75700 France. **Tel** 011 33 1 47531515, telex 299 356 F. **UDC** 011. ***Continues*** *Pascal Explore. E74, Pneumologie, 0761-2214.*

FR/0761-2214
**PASCAL EXPLORE. E74, PNEUMOLOGIE.** ***Title Change.*** **VFOAT** Pneumologie; Pneumology. No. 1 (1984)-?. Periodical. French. mo. Centre National de la Recherche Scientifique, Informascience, 26 rue Boyer, 75971 Paris France. **Tel** 61.41.11.05, telex CNRSDOC 220880 F. **NLM** ZWF 140; P278. ***Continues*** *Bulletin Signaletique. 352, Maladies de l'Appareil Respiratoire, du Coeur et des Vaisseaux.* ***Continued by*** *Pneumologie, E74.*

US/1054-187X
**PEDIATRIC PULMONOLOGY. SUPPLEMENT. See** Medical Science and Technology-Pediatrics.

UK/0738-4688
**PERSPECTIVES IN ASTHMA.** [Perspect. asthma]. (1982)-. Academic Scholarly Publication. English. ir. Price varies per volume. Academic Press Ltd., A Division of Harcourt Brace & Company Ltd., 24-28 Oval Road, London NW1 7DX England. **Tel** 071 267 4466, FAX 071 482 2293, 071 485 4752, telex 25775 ACPRES G. **(Subscription address:** Harcourt Brace Jovanovich Limited, Footscray High Street, Sidcup, Kent DA14 5HP UK, (Phone: 081-300-3322)**) LC** UNC. **DD** 616.2/38/005. **NLM** W1 PE8705L. **CODEN** PEASDE. Documents available from CASDDS.
**Ind/Abst** Chem. Abstr.

GW/0934-8387
**PNEUMOLOGIE. Added/Corp** Deutsche Gesellschaft fuer Pneumologie und Tuberkulose. Vol. 43, No. 1 (Jan. 1989)-. Academic Scholarly Publication. German (summaries and/or abstracts in English). mo. $204.00. Georg Thieme Verlag Stuttgart, Postfach 301120, D 70451 Stuttgart Germany. **Tel** 011 49 711 89310, FAX 011 49 711 8931298, telex 7 252 275 GTVD. **(Subscription address:** Thieme Medical Publishers Inc., 381 Park Avenue South, New York NY 10016.**) NLM** W1; PN285. **CODEN** PNEMEC. available on microfilm from University Microfilms International (UMI). Documents available from CASDDS, ADONIS. ***Continues*** *Praxis und Klinik der Pneumologie, 0342-7498.*
**Ind/Abst** ADONIS; Chem. Abstr.; EMBASE; Helminthol. Abstr. (1991-); Index Med. Jan. 1989-; PESTDOC; Rev. Med. Vet. Mycology.

PL
**PNEUMONOLOGIA I ALERGOLOGIA POLSKA : ORGAN POLSKIEGO TOWARZYSTWA FTYZJOPNEUMONOLOGICZNEGO, POLSKIEGO TOWARZYSTWA ALERGOLOGICZNEGO, I INSTYTUT U GRUZLICY I CHOROB PUC. Added/Corp** Polskie Towarzystwo Ftizjopneumonologiczne. Polskie Towarzystwo Alergologiczne. Instytut Gruzlicy i Chorob Puc. (1991)-. Periodical. Polish (summaries and/or abstracts in English; table of contents in English). mo. **NLM** W1; PN2897. ***Continues*** *Pneumonologia Polska, 0376-4761.*
**Desc:** Medical information on hypersensitivity, lung disease and respiratory hypersensitivity.
**Ind/Abst** Index Med. (1992-).

PL/0376-4761
**PNEUMONOLOGIA POLSKA.** ***Title Change.*** [Pneumonol. pol.]. **Added/Corp** Instytut Gruzlicy w Warszawie. Polskie Towarzystwo Ftizjopneumonologiczne. Instytut Gruzlicy i Chorob Puc. Vol. 44- (1976)-(199?). Academic Scholarly Publication. Polish (English and Russian; summaries and/or abstracts in English and Russian). mo. **(Subscription address:** ARS Polona, PO Box 1001, 00068 Warsaw Poland.**) NLM** W1; PN2991. **CODEN** PNPOD4. Documents available from CASDDS. ***Continues*** *Gruzlica I Choroby Puc.* ***Continued by*** *Pneumonologia i Alergologia Polska.*
**Ind/Abst** Chem. Abstr. (-1990); EMBASE [Select. Cov.]; Index Med.

BU/0324-1491
**PNEVMOLOGIIA I FTIZIATRIIA.** [Pnevmol. ftiziatr.]. **Added/Corp** Nauchno Druzhestvo na Pnevmolozite i Ftiziatrite. **VFOAT** Pneumologia i Ftiziatria; Ftiziatria. (1975)-. Academic Scholarly Publication. Bulgarian (summaries and/or abstracts in English). qt. 22.00F. **(Subscription address:** Hemus Foreign Trade Organization, 6 Tzar Osvoboditel Boulevard, 1000 Sofia Bulgaria.**)** **NLM** W1 PN41. **CODEN** PNFTD3. Documents available from CASDDS. ***Continues*** *Ftiziatrija, 0532-7709.*
**Ind/Abst** Chem. Abstr.; EMBASE [Select. Cov.]; Saf. Health Work.

CN/0318-9236
**POUMONS.** V. 8, No 1- May/July 1974-. Periodical. French. qt. Societe du Timbre de Noel du Quebec, 264 rue Chenier, Quebec Quebec G1K 1R2 Canada. **DD** 616.2/4/05. **UDC** 616.24. ***Continues*** *Observation, Opinion, Orientation, 0029-7674.*

US/0897-9677
**PROBLEMS IN RESPIRATORY CARE.** ***Ceased.*** [Probl. respir. care]. Vol. 1, No. 1 (July-Sept. 1988)-(Dec. 1991). English. qt. J.B. Lippincott Company, 227 East Washington Square, Philadelphia PA 19106-3780. **Tel** (215)238-4200 or 4454, FAX (215)238-4227. **(Subscription address:** Journal Fulfillment Department, Lippincott/Harper, Downsville Pike, Route 3, Box 20-B, Hagerstown, MD 21740; telephone: (800)638-3030**)** **ED** Richard D Branson and Neil McIntyre. **LC** RC731; .P66. **DD** 616.2/005. **NLM** W1; PR573MH. **[CCC].** available on microfilm from University Microfilms International (UMI).
**Desc:** Clinically oriented articles are directed to the problems encountered in daily practice with acute or chronic respiratory conditions.

RU/0032-9533
**PROBLEMY TUBERKULEZA.** (1923)-. Academic Scholarly Publication. Russian. Six times a year. $79.95. Izdatelstvo Meditsina / Russian Academy of Medical Sciences, Ulitsa Solyanka 14, 109801 Moscow Russia. **Tel** 011 95 297-05-04. **(Subscription address:** East View Publications Inc., 3020 Harbor Lane North, Suite 110, Minneapolis MN 55447.**)** **CODEN** PRTUAX. **[CCC].** Index available. **Bk Rev.** Documents available from CASDDS.
**Ind/Abst** Chem. Abstr.; EMBASE [Select. Cov.]; Health Saf. Sci. Abstr.; Immunol. Abstr.; Index Med.; Microbiol. Abstr. Sect. B.

US/0192-9305
**PROGRAM REPORT / NATIONAL HEART, LUNG, AND BLOOD INSTITUTE, DIVISION OF LUNG DISEASES.** **Added/Corp** National Heart, Lung, and Blood Institute. Division of Lung Diseases. (197?)-. English. an. National Institutes of Health / Division of Lung Disease, National Heart Lung and Blood Institute, 533 Westbard Avenue, Bethesda MD 20014. **LC** RC756; .N38b. **DD** 353.0084/1. **NLM** WF 20 P964.

SZ/0079-6751
**PROGRESS IN RESPIRATION RESEARCH.** [Progr. respir. res.]. (19??)-. English. an. 230.00F (approx. per volume). S. Karger AG, Allschwilerstrasse 10, PO Box - Postfach - Case Postale, CH-4009 Basel Switzerland. **Tel** 011 41 61 306-1111, FAX 011 41 61 306-1234, telex CH 962 652. **ED** H. Herzog. **LC** QP121.A1; P7. **NLM** W3 PR948. **CODEN** PGRRB6. **[CCC].** Documents available from BIOSIS Document Express, CASDDS. ***Continues*** *Progress in Research in Emphysema and Chronic Bronchitis.*
**Desc:** Important aspects of the respiratory system, from its role in the alimentation and protection of the organism to its susceptibility to disease, receive attention in the monographs published in this series. Some volumes present debates on topics vital to respiration research. Others represent the unique experiences of a single renowned author and stand as first-time comprehensive treatments of specific issues.
**Ind/Abst** Biol. Abstr.; Chem. Abstr.; Ref. Upd. Deluxe Ed.

US/1047-9708
**PULMONARY PAPER, THE.** [Pulm. pap.]. (Sept. 1989)-. Periodical. English. Eight times a year. $17.95 one year; $31.95 two years. Pulmonary Paper, PO Box 877, Ormond Beach FL 32175. **Tel** (904)673-7501. **ED** Celeste Belyea. **DD** 616. **Bk Rev**, (Qty: varies). **Ad Acc**, **Adv Mgr:** Mary Anne Harvey. **Circ:** 20,000.
**Desc:** Informative newsletter for people suffering from chronic respiratory disorders such as chronic bronchitis and asthma.

UK/0952-0600
**PULMONARY PHARMACOLOGY (EDINBURGH).** (PULMONARY PHARMACOLOGY.). [Pulm. pharmacol.]. Vol. 1, No. 1 (1988)-. Academic Scholarly Publication. English. bm (6 issues). $310.00. Academic Press Ltd., A Division of Harcourt Brace & Company Ltd., 24-28 Oval Road, London NW1 7DX England. **Tel** 071 267 4466, FAX 071 482 2293, 071 485 4752, telex 25775 ACPRES G. **(Subscription address:** Harcourt Brace & Company, Ltd., Foots Cray, High Street, Sidcup Kent DA14 5HP England.**)** **ED** Peter J. Barnes and J. Douglas. **DD** 615. **NLM** W1; PU885G. **CODEN** PUPHEX. **[CCC].** Index available. **Ad Acc. Circ:** 200 (ctrl). available on microfilm from University Microfilms International (UMI). Documents available from The Genuine Article, BIOSIS Document Express, CASDDS.
**Desc:** Publishes international contributions on all aspects of lung pharmacology, both basic and clinical, and includes original research papers on pharmacology related to the lungs, particularly vessels, lung parenchyma and pulmonary diseases.
**Ind/Abst** Biol. Abstr. (1990-); Chem. Abstr.; Curr. Contents Life Sci.; EMBASE; PESTDOC; Res. Alert [Full Cov.]; Sci. Cit. Index; SCISEARCH.

UK/0308-6623
**RECENT ADVANCES IN RESPIRATORY MEDICINE.** [Recent adv. respir. med.]. No. 1 (1976)-. Periodical. English. ir (every 3 to 5 years). Churchill Livingstone, 1-3 Baxter's Place, Leith Walk, Edinburgh EH1 3AF Scotland. **Tel** 011 44 31 556 2424, FAX 011 44 31 558 1278, telex 727511. **(Subscription address:** Churchill Livingstone / US, 5 S 250 Frontenac Road, Naperville IL 60563.**)** **ED** T.B. Stretton. **NLM** W1 RE105YG.

US/0897-103X
**REFERENCE (SAINT LOUIS, MO.).** (REFERENCE.). [Reference]. (19??)-. Periodical. English. mo. $75.00 US; $95.00 other. Hospital Features, PO Box 9452, St Louis MO 63117. **Tel** (314)569-6363. **ED** Paul Reading. **LC** Z6660; .R43. **DD** 610. cum. index. ctrl circ.
**Desc:** A listing of authors, titles, and journals of interest to repiratory care practitioners that is published monthly.

SZ/0025-7931
**RESPIRATION.** [Respiration]. Vol. 25 (1968)-. Academic Scholarly Publication. English (French and German). bm. $394.00. S. Karger AG, Allschwilerstrasse 10, PO Box - Postfach - Case Postale, CH-4009 Basel Switzerland. **Tel** 011 41 61 306-1111, FAX 011 41 61 306-1234, telex CH 962 652. **ED** H. Herzog. **LC** RC705; .M4. **NLM** W1 RE248D. **CODEN** RESPBD. **[CCC].** Index available in last issue of volume--attached. **Ad Acc. Pr Rev.** available on microfilm from University Microfilms International (UMI). Documents available from The Genuine Article, BIOSIS Document Express, CASDDS. ***Continues*** *Medicina Thoracalis.*
**Desc:** Brings together the results of experimental and clinical studies through original papers concerning the physiology, biochemistry, immunology, and morphology of respiration and respiratory organs. The journal communicates basic research on chest and lung diseases and cardio-circulatory conditions connected with respiration bearing directly on modern health problems aggravated by environmental factors.
**Ind/Abst** Biol. Abstr.; Chem. Abstr.; Curr. Contents Clin. Med.; Curr. Contents Life Sci.; EMBASE; Index Med.; Nutr. Abstr. Rev., Ser. A, Hum. Exp.; Life Sci. Collect.; Protozoolog. Abstr.; Ref. Upd. Deluxe Ed.; Res. Alert [Full Cov.]; Saf. Health Work; Sci. Cit. Index; SCISEARCH; SportSearch.

US/0020-1324
**RESPIRATORY CARE.** (RESPIRATORY CARE : THE OFFICIAL JOURNAL OF THE AMERICAN ASSOCIATION FOR RESPIRATORY THERAPY.). [Respir. care]. **Added/Corp** American Association for Respiratory Therapy. American Association for Inhalation Therapy. **VFOAT** RC. Vol. 16 (Jan./Feb. 1971)-. Academic Scholarly Publication. English. mo. $50.00 US and Puerto Rico; $70.00 other. American Association of Respiratory Care, PO Box 29686, 11030 Albes Lane, Dallas TX 75229. **Tel** (214)243-2272. **(Subscription address:** Daedalus Enterprises (address same as publisher)**)** **ED** Phil Kittredge and Pat Brougher. **LC** RM161; .I5. **DD** 615/.64/05. **NLM** W1 RE248J. Index available in last issue of volume--attached. **Bk Rev. Ad Acc. Circ:** 28,000. available on microfilm and microfiche from University Microfilms International (UMI); available in bound issues. ***Continues*** *Inhalation Therapy.*
**Desc:** Published for respiratory therapists, physicians, and other medical professionals involved in the application of respiratory/pulmonary therapy.
**Ind/Abst** Cumul. Index Nurs. Allied Health Lit.; EMBASE; Health Devices Alerts; Health Plan. Adminis.; Hospit. Health Admin. Index; Life Sci. Collect.

●US/1076-6030
**RESPIRATORY CARE MANAGER.** [Respir. care manag.]. **VFOAT** RCM. (19??)-. Periodical. English. mo. $117.00. Medical Records Briefing, PO Box 1168, Marblehead MA 01945. **Tel** (617)639-1872. **(Subscription address:** Respiratory Care Manager, PO Box 1168, Marblehead MA 01945.**)** **DD** 362. **NLM** W1; RE248JC.

UK/0262-7043
**RESPIRATORY DISEASE IN PRACTICE.** [Respir. dis. pract.]. Vol. 1, No. 1 (Sept. 1982)-. Periodical. English. bm. The Medical News Group, Tower House, Southampton Street, London WC2E 7LS England. **Tel** (01)379-6005. **NLM** W1; RE2485D.

KE
**RESPIRATORY DISEASES RESEARCH CENTER.** Free. Department of Kenya Medical Research Institute, PO Box 47855, Nairobi Kenya. **Tel** 254 2 724262 415. **Ad Acc. Circ:** 100 (ctrl).
**Desc:** Report of research in previous calendar year at the centre.

UK/0954-6111
**RESPIRATORY MEDICINE.** [Respir. med.]. Vol. 83, No. 1 (Jan. 1989)-. Periodical. English. Ten times a year (10 issues). £142.00 (institution), £101.00 (individual)*UK/Europe; $256.00 (institution), $186.00*(individual). Harcourt Brace & Company Ltd., Foots Cray, High Street, Sidcup Kent DA14 5HP England. **Tel** 011 44 81 300 3322, FAX 011 44 81 309 0807. **(Subscription address:** W. B. Saunders Company / North America Subscriptions, c/o Periodicals, 6277 Sea Harbour Drive, 4th Floor, Orlando FL 32887.**)** **ED** R. Davies. **NLM** W1; RE248KJ. **CODEN** RMEDEY. **[CCC]. Pr Rev.** available on microfilm and microfiche from University Microfilms International (UMI). Documents available from The Genuine Article, BIOSIS Document Express. ***Continues*** *British Journal of Diseases of the Chest, 0007-0971.*
**Desc:** Provides an international forum for all those involved in the varied disciplines concerned with all aspects of respiratory diseases. Devoted to the rapid publication of original articles of current clinical and research interest on an international basis. Additional features include editorials, topical reviews, and supplements covering important symposia.
**Ind/Abst** Biol. Abstr.; Curr. Aware. Biol. Sci., CABS; Curr. Contents Clin. Med.; Curr. Contents Life Sci.; EMBASE; Helminthol. Abstr. (1991-); Index Med. Jan. 1989-; PESTDOC; Postharvest News Inf.; Protozoolog. Abstr.; Res. Alert [Full Cov.]; Rev. Med. Vet. Entomol.; Rev. Med. Vet. Mycology; Saf. Health Work; Sci. Cit. Index; SCISEARCH; Soc. Sci. Cit. Index [Select. Cov.]; Trop. Dis. Bull.

UK/0149-2950
**RESPIRATORY PHYSIOLOGY.** V.1- 1974-. English. be. Butterworth Heinemann Publishers, Linacre House, Jordan Hill, Oxford OX2 8DP England. **Tel** 011 44 865 310366.
**Ind/Abst** Curr. Ref. Fish Res.

UK/0142-8780
**RESPIRATORY SYSTEM.** [Respir. syst.]. (1975)-. English. mo. £75.00. SUBIS, Mansion House, 19 Kingfield Road, Sheffield S11 9AS England. **Tel** 011 44 114 255 4433, FAX 011 44 114 255 4626. **DD** 016.574. **Ad Acc.**
**Desc:** Current awareness service for researchers and clinicians.

FR/0754-9245
**RESPIRER.** [Respirer]. (1982)-. Periodical. French. qt. 60.00F. CNMRT, 66 BD St Michel, F-75006 Paris France. **Tel** 011 33 1 46345880. **UDC** 616.24. **Circ:** 20,000. ***Continues*** *Bulletin - Comite National et Comites Departementaux Contre la Tuberculose et les Maladies Respiratoires, 0754-9237.*
**Desc:** Studies the relationship between environment and the respiratory system.

CN/0848-7421
**RESPIROLOGIE (POINTE-CLAIRE).** ***Ceased.*** (RESPIROLOGIE.). [Respirologie]. **Added/Corp** STA Communications. (1990)-Vol. 3, No. 4 (Dec. 1992). Periodical. French. qt. STA Communications Inc., 955 St. John Boulevard, Suite 306, Pt Claire, Quebec H9R 5K3 Canada. **Tel** (514)695-7623. **DD** 615.8/36.

IE/0300-9572
**RESUSCITATION.** [Resuscitation]. Vol. 1 (March 1972)-. Academic Scholarly Publication. English. Six times a year (2 vols.). $403.00. Elsevier Science Ireland Ltd., Bay 15, Shannon Industrial Estate, Co Clare Ireland. **Tel** 011 353 61 471944. **ED** John B. McCabe. **NLM** W1 RE2497K. **CODEN** RSUSBS. **[CCC].** Index available. **Ad Acc. Pr Rev.** available on microfilm and microfiche from University Microfilms International (UMI). Documents available from The Genuine Article, BIOSIS Document Express, CASDDS.
**Desc:** An international interdisciplinary medical journal dealing with papers on etiology, pathophysiology, diagnosis and treatment of acute disease.
**Ind/Abst** Biol. Abstr.; Chem. Abstr.; Curr. Contents Clin. Med.; EMBASE; Health Devices Alerts; Index Med.; Life Sci. Collect.; Res. Alert [Select. Cov.]; Soc. Sci. Cit. Index [Select. Cov.].

FR/0761-8417
**REVUE DE PNEUMOLOGIE CLINIQUE : LE POUMON ET LE COEUR.** [Rev. pneumol. clin.]. **VFOAT** Pneumologie Clinique. Vol. 40, No. 1 (Jan./Feb. 1984)-. Academic Scholarly Publication. French (summaries and/or abstracts in English). bm. $194.00. Masson Editeur, Box Postale 22, 41353 Vineuil 16 France. **Tel** 011 33 54 438994. **(Subscription address:** 7A Boulevard de Perolles, CH-1701 Fribourg Switzerland**)** **NLM** W1; RE799LF. **CODEN** RPCLEZ. **[CCC].** available on microfilm and microfiche from University Microfilms International (UMI). Documents available from BIOSIS Document Express, CASDDS. ***Continues*** *Poumon et le Coeur, 0032-5821.*
**Ind/Abst** Biol. Abstr. (1985-); Chem. Abstr. (1984-); EMBASE; Index Med.; Life Sci. Collect.; Saf. Health Work (1984-).

FR/0761-8425
**REVUE DES MALADIES RESPIRATOIRES.** [Rev. mal. respir.]. **Added/Corp** Societe de Pneumologie de Langue Francaise. Vol. 1 (1984)-. Academic Scholarly Publication. French (summaries and/or abstracts in English). bm. $210.00. Masson Editeur, Box Postale 22, 41353 Vineuil 16 France. **Tel** 011 33 54 438994. **(Subscription address:** 7A Boulevard de Perolles, CH-1701 Fribourg Switzerland**) NLM** W1; RE792H. **CODEN** RMREEY. **[CCC]. Pr Rev.** Documents available from The Genuine Article, BIOSIS Document Express, CASDDS. ***Continues*** *Revue Francaise des Maladies Respiratoires, 0301-0279.*
**Ind/Abst** Biol. Abstr. (1984-); Chem. Abstr. (1984-); Curr. Contents Clin. Med.; EMBASE; Index Med. (1984-); Life Sci. Collect. (1984-); Protozoolog. Abstr.; Res. Alert [Select. Cov.]; Saf. Health Work (1984-); Soc. Sci. Cit. Index [Select. Cov.].

IT
**RIVISTA DELLA TUBERCOLOSI E DELLE MALATTIE DELL APPARATO RESPIRATORIO.** Riv Tubercolosi Malattie Respiratorio, c/o L Coppola, V Portuense 332, 00149 Rome Italy.

IT/0302-4717
**RIVISTA DI PATOLOGIA E CLINICA DELLA TUBERCOLOSI E DI PNEUMOLOGIA.** ***Suspended.*** [Riv. patol. clin. tuberc. pneumol.]. **Added/Corp** Federazione Italiana Contro la Tubercolosi e le Malattie Polmonari Sociali. Associazione Emilia-Romagna. (1972)-Suspended (1990). Periodical. Italian. bm. Rivista di Patologia e Clinica della Tubercolosi e di Pneumologia, Via Brugnoli 5, 40122 Bologna Italy. **Tel** 011 39 51 522090. **NLM** W1 RI604. ***Continues*** *Rivista di Patologia e Clinica della Tubercolosi.*
**Ind/Abst** EMBASE.

CN/0831-2478
**RRT.** (RRT : THE CANADIAN JOURNAL OF RESPIRATORY THERAPY : LE JOURNAL CANADIEN DE LA THERAPEUTIQUE RESPIRATOIRE.). [RRT]. **Added/Corp** Canadian Society of Respiratory Therapists. **VAT** Registered Respiratory Therapist. Vol. 21, Issue 4 (1985)-. Periodical. English. Five times a year. 30.00Can$ Canada; $30.00 other. Canadian Medical Association, 1867 Alta Vista Drive, Ottawa Ontario K1G 3Y6 Canada. **Tel** (613)731-9331 ext. 2028, FAX (613)731-4797. **(Subscription address:** Canadian Medical Association, CMA House, PO Box 8650, Ottawa Ontario K1G 0G8 Canada.**) ED** John Unrau. **DD** 615.8/36. **NLM** W1; RR112. **Bk Rev. Ad Acc. Pr Rev. Circ:** 2,500 (ctrl). Documents available from BIOSIS Document Express. ***Continues*** *Respiratory Technology, 0319-1494.*
**Desc:** National journal for Canadian respiratory therapists. Research reports, literature reviews and discussions of issues that concern practising therapists form the core of the journal.
**Ind/Abst** Biol. Abstr.; Cumul. Index Nurs. Allied Health Lit.

US/1040-6050
**RT (LOS ANGELES, CALIF.).** (RT.). [RT]. **VAT** Respiratory Therapist. (1988)-. Periodical. English. bm. $60.00. Curant Communications, 4676 Admiralty Way, Suite 202, Marina Del Ray CA 90292. **Tel** (310)479-1769. **DD** 616. **NLM** W1; RT119. **Circ:** 20,000.
**Desc:** Targeted to 20,000 respiratory care practitioners.

JA/0371-2761
**SCIENCE REPORTS OF THE RESEARCH INSTITUTES. SERIES C, MEDICINE, THE.** **See** Medical Science and Technology-Communicable Diseases.

NE/0166-056X
**SELECTED PAPERS.** [Sel. pap. - R. Neth. Tuberc. Assoc.]. **Main/Corp** Royal Netherlands Tuberculosis Association. **VFOAT** Selected Papers - Royal Netherlands Tuberculosis Association. V. 1- 1961-. Academic Scholarly Publication. English. an. **UDC** 616-002.5; 616.24. **NLM** W1 SE32NP. ***Supersedes*** *Proceedings of the Tuberculosis Research Council.*
**Ind/Abst** EMBASE; Trop. Dis. Bull.

●US/1069-3424
**SEMINARS IN RESPIRATORY AND CRITICAL CARE MEDICINE.** (1994)-. Periodical. English. bm (Jan., Mar., May, July, Sep., Nov.). $145.00 (institutions), $105.00 (individuals) US; $170.00*(institutions), $130.00 (individuals) other. Thieme Medical Publishers Inc., 381 Park Avenue South, Suite 1201, New York NY 10016. **Tel** (212)683-5088, (212)683-5089, FAX (212)779-9020, telex 220 862 TSINC UR. **NLM** W1; SE489D. ***Continues*** *Seminars in Respiratory Medicine, 0192-9755.*

US/0882-0546
**SEMINARS IN RESPIRATORY INFECTIONS.** [Semin. respir. infect.]. Vol. 1, No. 1 (March 1986)-. Periodical. English. qt (Feb., May, Aug., Nov.). $92.00 (individual), $123.00 (institution) US; $152.00 (individual), $138.00 (institution) other. W.B. Saunders Company, A Subsidiary of Harcourt Brace Jovanovich, Inc., The Curtis Center/Suite 300, Independence Square West, Philadelphia PA 19106-3399. **Tel** (215)238-7800 or, 5587, FAX (215)238-7883, telex 173146. **(Subscription address:** W. B. Saunders Company / North America Subscriptions, c/o Periodicals, 6277 Sea Harbour Drive, 4th Floor, Orlando FL 32887.**) ED** George A. Sarosi. **DD** 616. **NLM** W1; SE489HI. **CODEN** SRINES. **[CCC].**
**Desc:** Designed to provide coverage of topics related to respiratory infections. Each issue deals with one specific type of infection relative to pulmonary or chest disorders.
**Ind/Abst** EMBASE; Index Med. (1986-).

US/0192-9755
**SEMINARS IN RESPIRATORY MEDICINE.** ***Title Change.*** [Semin. respir. med.]. **VFOAT** Respiratory Medicine. Vol. 1 (July 1979)-Vol. 14 (Nov. 1993). Periodical. English. bm. Thieme Medical Publishers Inc., 381 Park Avenue South, Suite 1201, New York NY 10016. **Tel** (212)683-5088, (212)683-5089, FAX (212)779-9020, telex 220 862 TSINC UR. **ED** Thomas Petty and Reuben Cherniack. **DD** 616. **NLM** W1 SE489I. **CODEN** SRMEDK. **[CCC].** cum. index. **Bk Rev. Ad Acc. Pr Rev. Circ:** 2,600 (ctrl). available on microfilm and microfiche from University Microfilms International (UMI). Documents available from The Genuine Article, BIOSIS Document Express. ***Continued by*** *Seminars in Respiratory and Critical Care Medicine, 1069-3424.*
**Desc:** Topic-oriented journal designed for practitioners specializing in respiratory medicine and diseases.
**Ind/Abst** Biol. Abstr. (1985-); Curr. Contents Clin. Med.; EMBASE; Helminthol. Abstr. (19??-19??); Protozoolog. Abstr.; Res. Alert [Full Cov.]; Sci. Cit. Index; SCISEARCH; Soc. Sci. Cit. Index [Select. Cov.].

●US/1065-982X
**TB WEEKLY.** **See** Medical Science and Technology-Communicable Diseases.

US/8756-8616
**TECHNOLOGY FOR RESPIRATORY THERAPY.** [Technol. respir. ther.]. **Added/Corp** Emergency Care Research Institute. (1984)-. Periodical. English. mo. $95.00 US; $105.00 Canada; $125.00 other. ECRI Emergency Care Research Institute, 5200 Butler Pike, Plymouth Meeting PA 19462. **Tel** (215)825-6000, FAX (215)834-1275, telex 510-660-8023. **ED** J. Nobel. **DD** 616. **[CCC]. Bk Rev.** ***Continues*** *Health Devices Update. Respiratory Therapy.*
**Desc:** A newsletter for pulmonary specialists and respiratory therapists, summarizing health care technology issues, and reporting recalls, hazards, and problems with medical devices.

UK/0040-6376
**THORAX.** [Thorax]. **Added/Corp** Association for the Study of Diseases of the Chest. Thoracic Society. British Medical Association. Vol. 1 (1946)-. Academic Scholarly Publication. English. mo. £185.00. BMJ / British Medical Journal Publishing Group, British Medical Association House, Tavistock Square, London WC1H 9JR England. **Tel** 011 44 71 3874499, FAX 011 44 71 383 6402, telex 290034 HBJ MN. **ED** S.G. Spiro. **NLM** W1 TH898. **CODEN** THORA7. **[CCC].** cum. index. **Bk Rev. Ad Acc. Pr Rev. Circ:** 4,000. available on microfilm and microfiche from University Microfilms International (UMI). Documents available from The Genuine Article, BIOSIS Document Express, CASDDS, ADONIS.
**Desc:** Original work on the anatomy, physiology and pathology of the chest and heart with relevant anatomical and physiological studies. Also provides coverage of the recent developments in basic biomedical sciences, including cellular biochemistry and molecular biology, enabling the thoracic specialist to remain abreast in advances.
**Ind/Abst** ADONIS; Biol. Abstr.; Chem. Abstr.; Chem. Hazards Ind.; Coal Abstr.; Curr. Aware. Biol. Sci., CABS; Curr. Contents Clin. Med.; Curr. Contents Life Sci.; EMBASE; Health Devices Alerts; Helminthol. Abstr. (1991-); Index Med.; Lab. Hazards Bull.; Life Sci. Collect.; Physic. Medline Plus; Protozoolog. Abstr.; Ref. Upd. Basic Ed.; Ref. Upd. Clinical Ed.; Ref. Upd. Deluxe Ed.; Res. Alert [Full Cov.]; Rev. Med. Vet. Entomol.; Rev. Med. Vet. Mycology; Saf. Health Work; Sci. Cit. Index; SCISEARCH; Soc. Sci. Cit. Index [Select. Cov.]; SportSearch; Wheat Barley Trit. Abstr.

US/1042-2846
**TODAY IN MEDICINE. RESPIRATORY DISEASE.** [Today med., Respir. dis.]. **Added/Corp** Data Centrum Communications, Inc. Schering Corporation. **VFOAT** Respiratory Disease. (198?)-. Periodical. English. Six times a year. $45.00. Data Centrum Communications Inc, The Soho Building, 110 Greene Street, Suite 505, New York NY 10012. **Tel** (212)226-5252. **DD** 616. **Pr Rev.**

US/0891-8295
**TRANSACTIONS - AMERICAN BRONCHO-ESOPHAGOLOGICAL ASSOCIATION. MEETING.** (TRANSACTIONS / AMERICAN BRONCHO-ESOPHAGOLOGICAL ASSOCIATION.). [Trans. - Am. Broncho-Esophagol. Assoc., Meet.]. **Main/Corp** American Broncho-Esophagological Association. Meeting. **VFOAT** Transactions of the American Broncho-Esophagological Association. 60th Edition (1980)-. English. an (May). $40.00. American Broncho Esophagological Association, NEMC 850, 750 Washington, Boston MA 02111. **Tel** (617)956-1688. **ED** Gerald B. Healy. **DD** 616. ***Continues*** *Transactions of the Annual Meeting of the American Broncho-Esophagological Association, 0065-7603.*
**Desc:** Compendium of all papers published at meetings of the Association. It includes obituaries, directory and membership listing.

●UK/0962-8479
**TUBERCLE AND LUNG DISEASE : THE OFFICIAL JOURNAL OF THE INTERNATIONAL UNION AGAINST TUBERCULOSIS AND LUNG DISEASE.** **Added/Corp** International Union Against Tuberculosis and Lung Disease. Vol. 73, No. 1 (Feb. 1992)-. Periodical. English. bm. £190.00 Europe; £191.00 Other (Institutions). Churchill Livingstone, 1-3 Baxter's Place, Leith Walk, Edinburgh EH1 3AF Scotland. **Tel** 011 44 31 556 2424, FAX 011 44 31 558 1278, telex 727511. **(Subscription address:** Maruzen Company Ltd., PO Box 5050, Import & Export Department, Tokyo 100 31 Japan.**) ED** Jacques Chretien. **NLM** W1; TU26. **[CCC].** Documents available from The Genuine Article, ADONIS. ***Formed by the union of*** *Tubercle* ***and*** *Bulletin of the International Union Against Tuberculosis and Lung Disease.*
**Desc:** Covers all aspects of tuberculosis and other respiratory diseases. It will publish original primary articles and commissioned reviews on both research and clinical work in tuberculosis and all other lung diseases, with particular emphasis on community health.
**Ind/Abst** ADONIS; Curr. Contents Clin. Med.; EMBASE; Index Med. (1992-); Microbiol. Abstr. Sect. B; Res. Alert [Full Cov.]; Sci. Cit. Index; SCISEARCH.

FR
**TUBERCULOSE. TUBERCULOSIS.** **Added/Corp** International Union Against Tuberculosis. **VFOAT** Tuberculosis. No. 32, (Mar. 1974)-. Periodical. French (English). qt. ***Continues*** *Tuberculosis.*

US/0095-1129
**TUBERCULOSIS BEDS IN HOSPITALS.** English. Tuberculosis Beds in Hospitals. **LC** RC313; .A12. **DD** 362.1/9/699500973. **UDC** 616-002.5(73). ***Continues*** *Tuberculosis Beds in Hospitals and Sanatoria, 0732-5061.*

US/0092-959X
**TUBERCULOSIS IN INDIANA.** [Tuberc. Indiana]. English. an. Indiana State Board of Health, 1330 West Michigan Street, Indianapolis IN 46206. **Tel** (317)633-0109. **LC** RC313.I6; T83. **DD** 614.5/42/09772. **UDC** 616-002.5(772).

US/0090-9351
**TUBERCULOSIS PROGRAMS.** [Tuberc. prog.]. 1970-. English. an. Centers for Disease Control, 1600 Clifton Road NE, Atlanta GA 30333. **Tel** (404)639-3311, FAX (404)639-3296. **LC** RC306; .T84. **DD** 312/.39/950973. **UDC** 616-002.5.

US/8756-3452
**YEAR BOOK OF PULMONARY DISEASE, THE.** [Year book pulm. dis.]. **Added/Corp** Year Book Medical Publishers. **VFOAT** Yearbook of Pulmonary Disease; Pulmonary Disease. (1986)-. Periodical. English. an. $69.95. Mosby Year Book Inc., 11830 Westline Industrial Drive, St Louis MO 63146. **Tel** (800)325-4177, (314)872-8370, FAX (314)432-1380, telex 44-2402. **LC** RC705; .Y43. **DD** 616.2/4. **NLM** W1; YE322H.

GW/0303-657X
**ZEITSCHRIFT FUER ERKRANKUNGEN DER ATMUNGSORGANE.** ***Ceased.*** [Z. Erkr. Atmungsorg.]. **Added/Corp** Gesellschaft fuer Bronchologie der DDR. Gesellschaft fuer Lungenkrankheiten und Tuberkulose der DDR. International Society for Aerosols in Medicine. Vol. 140 (March 1974)-?. Academic Scholarly Publication. German. Deutscher Judo Verband, Redaktion Ippon Segewaldweg 40, D 12557 Berlin Germany. **Tel** 011 49 711 210770, telex 051 678. **ED** W Schilling. **NLM** W1 ZE321Q. **CODEN** ZEATAM. **Bk Rev. Ad Acc.** ctrl circ. Documents available from BIOSIS Document Express, CASDDS. ***Continues*** *Zeitschrift fur Erkrankungen der Atmungsorgane Mit Folia Bronchologica, 0044-2631;* ***Supersedes in part*** *Monatsschrift fur Lungenkrankheiten und Tuberkulosebekampfung, 0026-931X.*
**Desc:** Publishes new medical literature on all diseases of the respiratory organs for practitioners, research workers and other specialists dealing with diagnostics, treatment, prevention, and control of these diseases.
**Ind/Abst** Biol. Abstr. (?-?); Chem. Abstr. (?-?); EMBASE (?-?) [Select. Cov.]; Index Med. (?-?); Life Sci. Collect. (?-?).

CC/1001-0939
**ZHONGHUA JIEHE HE HUXI ZAZHI.** (CHUNG-HUA CHIEH HO HO HU HSI TSA CHIH.). [Zhonghua jiehe he huxi zazhi]. **Added/Corp** Chung-hua I Hsueh Hui (China : 1949- ). **VFOAT** Zhonghua Jiehe He

Huxi Zazhi; Chinese Journal of Tuberculosis and Respiratory Diseases. (1987)-. Periodical. Chinese (summaries and/or abstracts in Chinese and English). bm. **(Subscription address:** China International Book Trading Corporation, PO Box 399, Library Service Department, Beijing 100044 People's Republic of China.**)** **NLM** W1; CH979F. **CODEN** ZJHZEC. ***Continues*** *Chung-Hua Chieh Ho Ho Hu Hsi Hsi Chi Ping Tsa Chih, 0253-2689.*
**Ind/Abst** Index Med. (1987-); NAPRALERT.

## SPORTS MEDICINE

●US
**ACSM MEMBERSHIP DIRECTORY/ AMERICAN COLLEGE OF SPORTS MEDICINE.** **Main/Corp** American College of Sports Medicine. **VFOAT** Membership Directory. **VAT** American College of Sports Medicine Membership Directory. (1992)-. English. American College of Sports Medicine / Indiana, 401 West Michigan Street, Indianapolis IN 46202-3233. **Tel** (317)637-9200. **LC** RC1200; .A45a. **DD** 617/.1027/06073. ***Continues*** *Membership Directory, 0732-7056.*

FR/0223-2928
**ACTUALITES EN MEDECINE DU SPORT.** (1985)-. Monographic series. French (table of contents in English). Ten times a year. Price varies per volume. MPH Editions, 8 Bis Av des Vagues, BP 521, 17211 Royan Cedex France. **Tel** 011 33 46384267. **NLM** W1; AC991WL.

FR/1151-3195
**ACTUALITES SPORT ET MEDECINE ROYAN.** (ACTUALITES SPORT ET MEDECINE.). (1990)-. Periodical. French. Ten times a year. 120.00F France; 150.00F other. MPH Editions, 8 Bis Av des Vagues, BP 521, 17211 Royan Cedex France. **Tel** 011 33 46384267. **UDC** 61(44).

US
**AMERICAN ACADEMY OF PODIATRIC SPORTS MEDICINE NEWSLETTER.** **Added/Corp** American Academy of Podiatric Sports Medicine. **VFOAT** AAPSM Newsletter. Vol. 1, No. 1 (Nov. 1984)-. Periodical. English. Four times a year. $20.00. American Academy of Podiatric Sports Medicine, 1729 Glastonberry Road, Potomac MD 20854. **Tel** (301)424-7440.
**Ind/Abst** SPORT Discus.

US/0363-5465
**AMERICAN JOURNAL OF SPORTS MEDICINE, THE.** [Am. j. sports med.]. **Added/Corp** American Orthopaedic Society for Sports Medicine. Vol. 4 (Jan./Feb. 1976)-. Academic Scholarly Publication. English. bm (6 issues). $95.00 (institution), $80.00 (individual) US; $99.00 (institution), $95.00 (individual) other. American Orthopaedic Society for Sports Medicine, 230 Calvary Street, Waltham MA 02154. **Tel** (617)736-0707. **(Subscription address:** American Journal of Sports Medicine, Subscription Office, PO Box 830259, Birmingham AL 35283-0259.**)** **ED** Jack C. Hughston. **LC** RC1200; .J66. **DD** 617/.1027. **NLM** W1 AM522M. **CODEN** AJSMDO. **[CCC].** cum. index ($15.00). **Bk Rev. Ad Acc. Pr Rev. Circ:** 10,000. available on microfilm and microfiche from University Microfilms International (UMI). Documents available from The Genuine Article, BIOSIS Document Express. ***Continues*** *Journal of Sports Medicine, 0090-4201.*
**Desc:** Dedicated exclusively to sports medicine, so you get outstanding coverage of the latest literature, innovations and research in this important field. Focus is placed on the causes and effects of disorders that either result from or are caused by various athletic activities.
**Ind/Abst** Acad. Abstr. Full Text Elite (Jan. 1992-); Acad. Abstr. (Jan. 1992-); Acad. Search (Jan. 1992-); Annals Behav. Med.; Biol. Abstr.; Cumul. Index Nurs. Allied Health Lit.; Curr. Contents Clin. Med.; Educ. Index; EMBASE; Gen. Sci. Index; Gen. Sci. Source (Jan. 1992-); Health Index (1989-); Health Period. Database [Full Txt.]; Health Ref. Cent. (Jan. 1989-) [Full Txt.] [Full Cov.]; Health Source (Jan. 1992-); Index Med.; Index Vet.; INFO-SOUTH Abstr.; Mag. Search; Mod. Med.; Nutr. Res. Newsl.; Life Sci. Collect.; Phys. Educ. Index; Physic. Medline Plus; Res. Alert [Select. Cov.]; SCISEARCH; SPORT Discus; SportSearch.

SP/0213-3717
**APUNTS. MEDICINA DE L'ESPORT.** (1985)-. Periodical. Spanish (Catalan). Three times a year. Free. Centre D'Estudis De L' Alt Rendiment Esportiu, Av Paisos Catalans 12, 08950 Esplugues de Llobregat Barcelona Spain. **Tel** 3-3719011, FAX 3-3720184, telex 54845 GCDE. **ED** Jesus Galilea. **UDC** 616-057. cum. index. **Circ:** 2,000 (ctrl).
**Ind/Abst** SPORT Discus; SportSearch (May 1987-).

SP/0212-8799
**ARCHIVOS DE MEDICINA DEL DEPORTE : PUBLICACION DE LA FEDERACION ESPANOLA DE MEDICINA DEL DEPORTE / FEMEDE.** **Added/Corp** Federacion Espanola de Medicina del Deporte. (198?)-. Periodical. Spanish (summaries and/or abstracts in English; table of contents in English). qt (4 issues). 6000ptas. Federacion Espanola de Medicina del Deporte, Apartado 1027, 31080 Pamplona Spain. **Tel** 34 3 2007344, or 2011698. **ED** Juan Jose Gonzalez Iturri. **NLM** W1; AR689H. **Bk Rev. Ad Acc, Adv Mgr:** John Ajuria. **Pr Rev. Circ:** 2,000. available on CD-ROM.
**Desc:** Information on sports medicine, orthopedics and physiology.
**Ind/Abst** Indice Med. Esp.; SportSearch (May 1987-).

●US/1076-5786
**ATHLETIC TRAINING (ST. LOUIS, MO.).** (ATHLETIC TRAINING : SPORTS HEALTH CARE PERSPECTIVES.). (1994)-. Periodical. English. qt. $54.50 (institutions), $39.95 (individual). Mosby Year Book Inc., 11830 Westline Industrial Drive, St Louis MO 63146. **Tel** (800)325-4177, (314)872-8370, FAX (314)432-1380, telex 44-2402.

AT
**AUSTRALIAN JOURNAL OF SCIENCE AND MEDICINE IN SPORT.** **Added/Corp** Australian Sports Medicine Federation. Australian Council for Health, Physical Education and Recreation. **VFOAT** Australian Journal of Science & Medicine in Sport. Vol. 16, No. 1 (June 1984)-. Periodical. English. Four times a year (Mar., June, Sept., Dec.). 25.00Aus$ Australia; 36.00Aus$ other. Australian Sports Medicine Federation, PO Box 897, Belconnen ACT 2616 Australia. **Tel** 011/61/6/251944, FAX 011/61/6/2531489, telex 62400. **ED** Bruce Abernethy. **LC** GV557; .A97. **NLM** W1; AU624K. **Bk Rev. Ad Acc. Pr Rev. Circ:** 2,800 (ctrl). ***Formed by the union of*** *Australian Journal of Sports Medicine and Exercise Sciences, 0811-6377* ***and*** *Australian Journal of Sport Sciences.*
**Ind/Abst** EMBASE; Ergon. Abstr.; Phys. Educ. Index; SPORT Discus; SportSearch.

PL/0860-021X
**BIOLOGY OF SPORT.** (BIOLOGY OF SPORT / INSTITUTE OF SPORT.). [Biol. sport]. **Added/Corp** Instytut Sportu (Warsaw, Poland). Vol. 1, (1984)-. Periodical. English (summaries and/or abstracts in Polish and Russian). qt. $38.00. **(Subscription address:** ARS Polona, PO Box 1001, 00068 Warsaw Poland.**)** **NLM** W1; BI852NH.
**Ind/Abst** SPORT Discus.

UK/0306-3674
**BRITISH JOURNAL OF SPORTS MEDICINE.** [Br. j. sports med.]. **Added/Corp** British Association of Sport and Medicine. Vol. 4 (1969)-. Academic Scholarly Publication. English. Six times a year. $217.00 The Americas; £145.00 other. Butterworth Heinemann Publishers, Linacre House, Jordan Hill, Oxford OX2 8DP England. **Tel** 011 44 865 310366. **(Subscription address:** Elsevier Science Ltd. Oxford Fulfillment Centre, PO Box 800, Kidlington, Oxford OX5 1DX United Kingdom.**)** **ED** Peter N. Sperryn. **NLM** W1 BR637K. **CODEN** BJSMDZ. **[CCC].** Index available. **Bk Rev. Ad Acc. Circ:** 1,700. available on microfilm and microfiche from University Microfilms International (UMI). Documents available from CASDDS. ***Continues*** *Bulletin - British Association of Sport and Medicine, 0306-3690.*
**Desc:** Covers fitness, exercise, physiology, injury prevention and treatment, doping, anthropometry including various ethnic groups. Sports psychology vehicle for communication with our members.
**Ind/Abst** Chem. Abstr. (-1982); Cumul. Index Nurs. Allied Health Lit.; EMBASE; Ergon. Abstr.; Index Med.; Nutr. Res. Newsl.; Phys. Educ. Index; Ref. Upd. Deluxe Ed.; Soc. Sci. Cit. Index [Select. Cov.]; SPORT Discus; SportSearch.

FR/0007-9782
**CAHIERS DE KINESITHERAPIE.** [Cah. kinesither.]. (1962)-. Periodical. French. bm. $134.00. Masson Editeur, Box Postale 22, 41353 Vineuil 16 France. **Tel** 011 33 54 438994. **(Subscription address:** Masson, BP 22, 41353 Vineuil 16 France**)** **UDC** 61.

US/0833-1235
**CANADIAN JOURNAL OF SPORT SCIENCES.** ***Title Change.*** [Can. j. sport sci.]. **Added/Corp** Canadian Academy of Sport Medicine. Canadian Association of Sports Sciences. **VFOAT** Journal Canadien des Sciences du Sport; Revue Canadienne des Sciences du Sport. Vol. 12 No. 1 (Mar. 1987)-Vol. 17 No. 4 (Dec. 1992). Periodical. English (French). qt. Human Kinetics Publishers Inc, 1607 North Market Street, PO Box 5076, Champaign IL 61825-5076. **Tel** (217)351-5076, FAX (217)351-2674. **ED** Roy J. Shephard, MD. **LC** GV557; .C36. **DD** 796/.05. **NLM** W1; CA608. **CODEN** CJSSEV. **[CCC]. Bk Rev. Ad Acc. Pr Rev. Circ:** 1,300 (ctrl). available on microfilm and microfiche from University Microfilms International (UMI). Documents available from The Genuine Article, BIOSIS Document Express. ***Continues*** *Canadian Journal of Applied Sport Sciences, 0700-3978.* ***Continued by*** *Canadian Journal of Applied Physiology, 1066-7814.*

**Desc:** Devoted to the publication of original research in the fields of applied human biomechanics, physiology and motor learning and the sociocultural aspects of sports medicine.
**Ind/Abst** Biol. Abstr. (1987-); Can. Index; Curr. Contents Clin. Med.; Health Plan. Adminis.; Index Med. (1987-); Phys. Educ. Index; PsycINFO (1990-); Res. Alert [Select. Cov.]; SCISEARCH; SPORT Discus.

US/1056-9677
**CERTIFIED NEWS : A NEWSLETTER FOR CERTIFIED CLINICAL AND HEALTH & FITNESS PROFESSIONALS.** [Certif. news]. **Added/Corp** American College of Sports Medicine. Vol. 1, No. 1 (Apr. 1991)-. Newsletter. English. Three times a year. $10.00 (nonmembers), $5.00 (members). American College of Sports Medicine / Indiana, 401 West Michigan Street, Indianapolis IN 46202-3233. **Tel** (317)637-9200. **DD** 617.

US/0889-6976
**CHIROPRACTIC SPORTS MEDICINE.** [Chiropr. sports med.]. **VFOAT** CSM. Vol. 1, No. 1 (Jan. 1987)-. Periodical. English. qt. $95.00 (institution) $65.00 (individual) US; $85.00 (individual), $115.00 (institution) other. Williams & Wilkins Company, 428 East Preston Street, Baltimore MD 21202-3993. **Tel** (410)528-4000, (800)638-6423, FAX (410)528-8596, telex 87669. **(Subscription address:** Williams & Wilkins, PO Box 64380, Baltimore MD 21264.**)** **ED** Robert Hazel. **DD** 617. **NLM** W1; CH8148. **CODEN** CHSMEX. **[CCC]. Circ:** 4,000. Documents available from BIOSIS Document Express, Quick Copies.
**Desc:** Covers chiropractic diagnosis and treatment of sports injuries, as well as physical fitness, athletic training and injury prevention.
**Ind/Abst** Biol. Abstr. (1987-); EMBASE; Phys. Educ. Index; SPORT Discus.

US/1050-642X
**CLINICAL JOURNAL OF SPORT MEDICINE.** (CLINICAL JOURNAL OF SPORT MEDICINE : OFFICIAL JOURNAL OF THE CANADIAN ACADEMY OF SPORT MEDICINE.). [Clin. j. sport med.]. **Added/Corp** Canadian Academy of Sport Medicine. Vol. 1, No. 1 (Jan. 1991)-. Periodical. English. qt. $104.00 (individuals), $142.00 (institutions) US; $115.00 (individuals), $170.00 (institutions) other. Raven Press, 1185 Avenue of the Americas, 37th Floor, New York NY 10036. **Tel** (212)930-9500, (212)930-9604, FAX (212)869-3495, (212)302-8507, telex 640073. **ED** Gordon O. Matheson. **LC** RC1200; .C55. **DD** 617.1/027/05. **NLM** W1; CL724G. **CODEN** CJSMED. **[CCC]. Pr Rev.** available on microfilm and microfiche from University Microfilms International (UMI).
**Desc:** International refereed journal published for clinicians with a primary interest in sports medicine practice. The journal publishes original research and reviews covering diagnostics, therapeutics, and rehabilitation in health and physically challenged individuals of all ages and levels of sport and exercise participation.
**Ind/Abst** Phys. Educ. Index (19??-); SPORT Discus.

UK/0953-9875
**CLINICAL SPORTS MEDICINE.** ***Ceased.*** [Clin. sports med.]. Vol. 1, No. 1 (1989)-(19??). Periodical. English. qt. Chapman & Hall, 2-6 Boundary Row, London SE1 8HN England. **Tel** 011 44 71 865 0066, FAX 011 44 71 522 9623, telex 290164 Chapmag. **NLM** W1; CL786. **Bk Rev. Ad Acc. Circ:** 700.
**Desc:** Clinical articles, papers and reviews on sports medicine.
**Ind/Abst** Phys. Educ. Index.

US/0740-7238
**CLINICAL UPDATE. SPORTS MEDICINE.** ***Ceased.*** [Clin. update, Sports med.]. **VFOAT** Sports Medicine. Vol. 1, No. 1 (Jan./Feb. 1984)-(19??). Periodical. English. bm. Circulation Manager / Atlanta, 615 Peachtree Street NE/Suite 1100, Atlanta GA 30308.

US/0278-5919
**CLINICS IN SPORTS MEDICINE.** [Clin. sports med.]. **VFOAT** Sports Medicine. Vol. 1, No. 1 (March 1982)-. Monographic series. English. qt (4 issues). $95.00 (individual), $116.00 (institution) US; $127.00 (individual), $135.00 (institution) other. W.B. Saunders Company, A Subsidiary of Harcourt Brace Jovanovich, Inc., The Curtis Center/Suite 300, Independence Square West, Philadelphia PA 19106-3399. **Tel** (215)238-7800 or, 5587, FAX (215)238-7883, telex 173146. **(Subscription address:** W. B. Saunders Company / North America Subscriptions, c/o Periodicals, 6277 Sea Harbour Drive, 4th Floor, Orlando FL 32887.**)** **ED** Edward Yeager. **DD** 617/.1027. **NLM** W1; CL831DM. **[CCC]. Pr Rev. Circ:** 4,000. available on microfilm and microfiche from University Microfilms International (UMI). Documents available from The Genuine Article.
**Desc:** Practical updates for the clinician on the latest advances. Each issue addresses a single topic in patient care.
**Ind/Abst** Cumul. Index Nurs. Allied Health Lit.; Curr. Contents Clin. Med.; EMBASE; Health Plan. Adminis.; Index Med.; Physic. Medline Plus; Res. Alert [Select. Cov.]; SCISEARCH; SPORT Discus; SportSearch (May 1987-).

●US/1069-5842
**CURRENT REVIEW OF SPORTS MEDICINE.** (1994)-. Periodical. English. an. £196.95 UK; £194.95 Europe; £192.95 others. Current Science, 20 North 3rd Street, Philadelphia PA 19106. **Tel** (215)574-2266, (800)552-5866, FAX (215)574-2270.

US/0831-8670
**CURRENT THERAPY IN SPORTS MEDICINE.** [Curr. ther. sports med.]. (1985/1986)-. English. be. Mosby Year Book Inc., 11830 Westline Industrial Drive, St Louis MO 63146. **Tel** (800)325-4177, (314)872-8370, FAX (314)432-1380, telex 44-2402. **ED** R. Peter Welsh and Roy J. Shephard. **LC** RC1200; .C8. **DD** 617/.1027/05. **NLM** W1; CU819R.

GW/0344-5925
**DEUTSCHE ZEITSCHRIFT FUER SPORTMEDIZIN.** [Dtsch. Z. Sportmed.]. 29.-Yearly volume; Jan. 1978-. Academic Scholarly Publication. German (summaries and/or abstracts in English). mo. DM72.00. Deutscher Aerzte Verlag GmbH, Postfach 404265, D-50832 Cologne Germany. **Tel** 011 49 2234 7011219. **ED** Hans J Engel. **NLM** W1 DE909. **CODEN** DZSPD8. Index available. **Bk Rev. Ad Acc. Circ:** 11,500. Documents available from BIOSIS Document Express, CASDDS. ***Continues** Sportarzt und Sportmedizin.*
**Desc:** Official organ of the German Association of Doctors of Sports Medicine and of the League of Austrian Sports Doctors. Includes articles on research studies in the field of sports medicine, case histories from doctors in the sports medicine specialties, articles on prevention and rehabilitation.
**Ind/Abst** Biol. Abstr. (1986-); Chem. Abstr.; SportSearch.

IT
**DOCTOR (MILAN, ITALY).** ***Ceased.*** (DOCTOR.). Vol. 1, No. 1 (Jan./Feb. 1983)-Ceased (Nov. 1990). Periodical. Italian. mo. Ariete Edizioni SRL, Via G Stephenson 33, 20157 Milan Italy. **Tel** 011 39 2 332141. **NLM** W1; DO23G.

UK
**ERGOGENIC AIDS IN SPORTS.** (19??)-. English. bm (6 issues). £7.50. National Sports Medicine Institute, c/o Medical College of St. Bartholomew's Hospital, Charterhouse Square, London EC1M 6BQ United Kingdom. **Tel** 011 44 71 251 0583, FAX 011 44 71 251 0774.

AT/0817-4792
**EXCEL.** ***Suspended.*** **Added/Corp** Australian Institute of Sport. Vol. 2, No. 4 (June 1986)-(19??). Academic Scholarly Publication. English. qt. 130.00Aus$ Australasia; $130.00 US; £94.00 UK; 169.00Aus$ other (institutions), 86.00Aus$ Australasia; $86.00 US; £62.00 UK; 86.00Aus$ other (individuals). Blackwell Scientific Publications Australia, 54 University Street, PO Box 378, Carlton Victoria 3053 Australia. **Tel** 011 61 3 3470300, FAX 011 61 3 3475001, telex 10716421. **ED** P Fricker, R Smith and R Telford. **LC** RC1235; .E93. **DD** 617.1/027/05. **NLM** W1; EX195. **[CCC].** available on microfilm and microfiche from University Microfilms International (UMI). ***Continues** Sports Science & Medicine Quarterly.*
**Desc:** Multidisciplinary journal covering sports science and medicine. It also publishes reviews, research articles and information concerning all aspects of sports medicine, physiology and science.
**Ind/Abst** SPORT Discus.

US/0091-6331
**EXERCISE AND SPORT SCIENCES REVIEWS.** [Exerc. sport sci. rev.]. Vol. 1 (1973)-. English. ir. $49.95. Williams & Wilkins Company, 428 East Preston Street, Baltimore MD 21202-3993. **Tel** (410)528-4000, (800)638-6423, FAX (410)528-8596, telex 87669. **(Subscription address:** Williams & Wilkins, PO Box 64380, Baltimore, MD 21264) **LC** RC1200; .E94. **DD** 612/.76/05. **NLM** W1 EX203. **CODEN** ESSRB8. **[CCC].** Documents available from The Genuine Article, BIOSIS Document Express, Quick Copies.
**Ind/Abst** Biol. Abstr. (-1975); Index Med.; Index Sci. Rev. [Full Cov.]; Res. Alert [Full Cov.]; SCISEARCH; SPORT Discus; SportSearch.

US/0748-3155
**EXERCISE PHYSIOLOGY (NEW YORK, N.Y.).** (EXERCISE PHYSIOLOGY : CURRENT SELECTED RESEARCH.). [Exerc. physiol.]. Vol. 1 (1985)-. English. an. $45.00. AMS Press Inc., 56 East 13th Street, New York NY 10003. **Tel** (212)777-4700, FAX (212)995-5413, telex 710 581 2302. **ED** Charles O Dotson and James H Humphrey. **LC** QP301; .E97. **DD** 612/.76. **NLM** W1; EX204. Index available. **Bk Rev.**
**Desc:** Designed to serve professionals in the various disciplines that compose exercise and sports science. Invited contributions deal with aerobics, metabolism, muscular fatigue, thermal regulations, specificity of training, and special populations.

US
**FIRST AIDER.** (19??)-. Periodical. English. Four times a year. Free to US schools and athletic trainers; $4.00 others. Cramer Products Inc., PO Box 1001, Gardner KS 66030. **Tel** (913)884-7511, FAX (913)884-5626. **ED** J. Eric Kelley. **Bk Rev. Circ:** 120,000 (ctrl).
**Desc:** Dedicated to sharing information concerning the care and prevention of athletic injuries; geared to high school/college coaches, athletic trainers and students.
**Ind/Abst** SPORT Discus; SportSearch (May 1987-).

US/1069-7004
**FOCUS ON. SPORTS, SCIENCE AND MEDICINE.** **See** Recreation, Leisure-Sports.

NE/0016-6448
**GENEESKUNDE EN SPORT.** [Geneeskd. sport]. Vol. 1 (1968)-. Dutch (summaries and/or abstracts in English). bm (6 issues). Fl62.50 Netherlands; Fl75.00 other. Uitgeversmij de Tijdstroom, Postbus 14, 7240 Lochem Netherlands. **Tel** 05730-53651, FAX 05730-56724. **CODEN** GESPBS. **Bk Rev. Ad Acc. Circ:** 4,000. Documents available from BIOSIS Document Express.
**Desc:** Covers sports medicine and sport sciences, including psychology, motor skills, mental and physical training.
**Ind/Abst** Biol. Abstr.; SportSearch.

IT/0431-8722
**GINNASTICA MEDICA, LA.** (1953)-. Periodical. Italian. bm (6 issues). L80000.00 Italy; L100000.00 other. Societa Italiana di Ginnastica Medica, Via F Portinari 62, 00151 Rome Italy. **UDC** 796.

JA/0474-795X
**HOKEN TAIIKUGAKU KENKYU KIYO / OSAKA SHIRITSU DAIGAKU.** **See** Education-Physical Education and Training.

US/1070-7778
**HUGHSTON HEALTH ALERT.** [Hughston health alert]. **Added/Corp** Hughston Sports Medicine Foundation. (1989)-. Newsletter. English. Four times a year (Jan., Apr., July, Oct.). Free. Hughston Sports Medicine Foundation Inc., PO Box 9517, 6262 Hamilton Road, Colombus GA 31995. **Tel** (706)576-3322. **ED** Dr. Fred Flandry, (phone: (706)324-6661). **DD** 613. **Bk Rev**, (Qty: 1). **Circ:** 10,000.
**Desc:** Articles are written by orthopaedists and primary care physicians, who are concern with musculoskeletal injuries and illnesses affecting the athletes.

US/1049-9679
**INTERNATIONAL JOURNAL OF SPORT MEDICINE.** (1991)-. Periodical. English. qt. $64.00 (institutions). Human Kinetics Publishers Inc, 1607 North Market Street, PO Box 5076, Champaign IL 61825-5076. **Tel** (217)351-5076, FAX (217)351-2674.

GW/0172-4622
**INTERNATIONAL JOURNAL OF SPORTS MEDICINE.** [Int. j. sports med.]. Vol. 1 (1980)-. Academic Scholarly Publication. English. Eight times a year. $243.00. Georg Thieme Verlag Stuttgart, Postfach 301120, D 70451 Stuttgart Germany. **Tel** 011 49 711 89310, FAX 011 49 711 8931298, telex 7 252 275 GTVD. **(Subscription address:** Thieme Medical Publishers Inc., 381 Park Avenue South, New York NY 10016.) **ED** H J Apell, D Costill, D Dufaux, H Kuipers. **NLM** W1 IN791E. **CODEN** IJSMDA. **[CCC]. Pr Rev. Circ:** 5,000. Documents available from The Genuine Article, CASDDS, ADONIS.
**Desc:** Promotes world-wide communication in sports medicine. Of interest to physiologists, biochemists, biomechanics, internists - in short, to all specialists and to all practitioners interested in problems arising in sports medicine.
**Ind/Abst** ADONIS; Chem. Abstr.; Curr. Aware. Biol. Sci., CABS; Curr. Contents Life Sci.; EMBASE; Index Med.; Nutr. Abstr. Rev., Ser. A, Hum. Exp.; Nutr. Res. Newsl.; Phys. Educ. Index; Ref. Upd. Deluxe Ed.; Res. Alert [Full Cov.]; Sci. Cit. Index; SCISEARCH; Soc. Sci. Cit. Index [Select. Cov.]; SPORT Discus; SportSearch.

US/0160-0559
**INTERNATIONAL SERIES ON SPORT SCIENCES.** ***Ceased.*** [Int. ser. sport sci.]. (1974)-Vol. 21 (19??). Monographic series. English. ir. Human Kinetics Publishers Inc, 1607 North Market Street, PO Box 5076, Champaign IL 61825-5076. **Tel** (217)351-5076, FAX (217)351-2674. **DD** 617. **CODEN** ISSSDN. Documents available from BIOSIS Document Express, CASDDS.
**Ind/Abst** Biol. Abstr.; Chem. Abstr.

US/0190-9541
**INTERNATIONAL SPORT SCIENCES.** (INTERNATIONAL SPORT SCIENCES / BY INFORMATION SERVICES DEPARTMENT, SCIENCE INFORMATION SERVICES ORGANIZATION.). Vol. 1, No. 1 (Apr. 1979)-. Periodical. English. mo. $95.00. Gardiner Caldwell Communications Ltd., The Old Ribbon Mill, Pitt Street, Macclesfield Cheshire, SK11 7PT England. **Tel** 011 44 625 618507, FAX 011 44 625 610260. **LC** RC1200; .I53. **DD** 617/.1027/05. **NLM** ZQT 260 I61. **CODEN** ISSCD9.

IT/0391-4089
**ITALIAN JOURNAL OF SPORTS TRAUMATOLOGY.** [Ital. j. sports traumatol.]. Vol. 1 (Jan./Mar. 1979)-. Academic Scholarly Publication. English (Italian). qt. L80000 Italy; $80.00 surface mail. Editrice Kurtis SRL, Via Luigi Zoja 30, Milan 20153 Italy. **Tel** 011 39 2 48202740, FAX 011 39 2 48201219. **ED** L Perugia. **NLM** W1 IT136M. **CODEN** IJSTDV. **Ad Acc. Circ:** 5,000 (ctrl). Documents available from BIOSIS Document Express.
**Desc:** Original studies on the clinical and experimental research in sports traumatology.
**Ind/Abst** Biol. Abstr. (1984-1990); EMBASE; Phys. Educ. Index; SportSearch (May 1987-).

FR/0762-915X
**JOURNAL DE TRAUMATOLOGIE DU SPORT.** [J. traumatol. sport]. (1984)-. Periodical. French (summaries and/or abstracts in English and French). qt. $124.00. Masson Editeur, Box Postale 22, 41353 Vineuil 16 France. **Tel** 011 33 54 438994. **NLM** W1; JO366G. **[CCC].** available on microfilm and microfiche from University Microfilms International (UMI).
**Ind/Abst** SPORT Discus.

US/0190-6011
**JOURNAL OF ORTHOPAEDIC AND SPORTS PHYSICAL THERAPY, THE.** **See** Medical Science and Technology-Orthopedics.

US/0893-3871
**JOURNAL OF OSTEOPATHIC SPORTS MEDICINE : JOSM.** ***Ceased.*** [J. osteopath. sports med.]. **Added/Corp** American Osteopathic Academy of Sports Medicine. **VFOAT** JOSM. Vol. 1 No. 1 (April 1987)-(19??). Periodical. English. qt. Journal of Osteopathic Sports Medicine, 7034 W North Avenue, Chicago IL 60635. **DD** 615.
**Ind/Abst** SPORT Discus.

●US/1056-6716
**JOURNAL OF SPORT REHABILITATION.** [J. sport rehabil.]. **VFOAT** JSR. Vol. 1, No. 1 (Feb. 1992)-. Periodical. English. qt (Feb., May, Aug., Nov.). $36.00 (individual), $80.00 (institution) US; $40.00 (individual), $84.00 (institution) other. Human Kinetics Publishers Inc, 1607 North Market Street, PO Box 5076, Champaign IL 61825-5076. **Tel** (217)351-5076, FAX (217)351-2674. **ED** David H. Perrin, PhD. **LC** RD97; .J68. **DD** 617.1/03. **NLM** W1; JO903J. **CODEN** JSRHEV. **[CCC].** Index available (Included in Nov. issue).
**Desc:** Information for athletic trainers, team physicians, sport physical therapists, sport podiatrists, sport nutritionists, exercise physiologists, and strength and conditioning coaches.
**Ind/Abst** Acad. Search (July 1993-); Health Source (Jul. 1993-); SPORT Discus.

IT/0022-4707
**JOURNAL OF SPORTS MEDICINE AND PHYSICAL FITNESS.** [J. sports med. phys. fitness]. **Added/Corp** International Federation of Sports Medicine. International Federation of Sports Medicine. FIMS. Vol. 1 (1961)-. Academic Scholarly Publication. English (summaries and/or abstracts in French and Spanish). qt. $90.00 (individuals), $140.00 (institutions). Edizioni Minerva Medica, Corso Bramante 83-85, 10126 Turin Italy. **Tel** 011 39 11 678282, FAX 011 39 11 674502. **ED** Dalmonte C. Tuccimei. **NLM** W1 JO903. **CODEN** JMPFA3. Index available. **Bk Rev. Ad Acc. Pr Rev.** Documents available from The Genuine Article, UMI Article Clearinghouse, CASDDS.
**Desc:** Articles cover medical aspects of sport and physical training for improving and maintaining health, and psychological, physiological, and pathological effects of muscular activity.
**Ind/Abst** Acad. Abstr. Full Text Elite (July 1990-); Acad. Abstr. (July 1990-); Acad. Search (July 1990-); Chem. Abstr.; Cumul. Index Nurs. Allied Health Lit.; Curr. Contents Clin. Med.; EMBASE; Health Source (Jul. 1990-); Index Med.; INFO-SOUTH Abstr.; Int. Aerosp. Abstr.; Mag. Artic. Summar. Elite (July 1990-); Mag. Artic. Summar. Select (July 1990-); Mag. Artic. Summar. CD-ROM (July 1990-); Mag. Search; Mod. Med.; Newsp. Period. Abstr. (1992-); Nutr. Abstr. Rev., Ser. A, Hum. Exp.; Phys. Educ. Index; Res. Alert [Select. Cov.]; SCISEARCH; Soc. Sci. Cit. Index [Select. Cov.]; SPORT Discus; SportSearch; Vocat. Search (July 1990-).

CN/0225-9877
**JOURNAL OF THE CANADIAN ATHLETIC THERAPISTS ASSOCIATION, THE.** ***Suspended.*** [J. Can. Athl. Ther. Assoc.]. **Added/Corp** Canadian Athletic Therapists Association. **VAT** Journal - Canadian Athletic Therapists Association; C.A.T.A. Journal; Canadian Athletic Therapists Association Journal. (1974)-(1992). Periodical. English. qt. 20.00Can$. Canadian Athletic Therapists Association, 1600 James Naismith Drive, Gloucester Ontario K1B 5N4 Canada. **Tel** (613)748-5671. **ED** Brent McKay. **DD** 617/.1027/06071. **Bk Rev. Ad Acc. Circ:** 500 (ctrl).
**Desc:** Publication of the CATA dealing specifically with the prevention and care of athletic injuries in the area of sports medicine.
**Ind/Abst** Phys. Educ. Index; SPORT Discus; SportSearch.

GW/0341-7387
**LEISTUNGSSPORT.** [Leistungssport]. Vol. 1 (1971)-. Periodical. German (summaries and/or abstracts

in English and French). bm. DM48.00 Germany; DM54.00 other. Philippka Verlag, Postfach 6540, D-48034 Muenster Germany. **Tel** 011 49 251 230-0522. **NLM** W1 LE67S.
**Ind/Abst** SportSearch (May 1987-).

FR/0025-6722
**MEDECINE DU SPORT.** [Med. sport]. Vol. 42 (1968)-. Periodical. French (English, German and Spanish). Five times a year. 450.54F France; 530.00F other. Galliena Promotion, 58 A rue du Dessous des Berges, 75013 Paris France. **Tel** 011 33 1 45849766. **ED** Robert J. Lederer. **NLM** W1 ME136F. **CODEN** MNSPBL. **[CCC].** Index available. cum. index. **Bk Rev. Ad Acc. Circ:** 3,000. Documents available from BIOSIS Document Express. ***Continues*** *Medecine, Education Physique et Sport.*
**Desc:** Medicine of sports, surgery, traumatology, physiology, biology, rehabilitation and public health.
**Ind/Abst** Biol. Abstr.; SPORT Discus; SportSearch (May 1987-).

IT
**MEDICINA DELLO SPORT. Added/Corp** Federazione Medico-Sportiva Italiana. Vol. 1 (1938)-. Periodical. Italian. Four times a year. $90.00 (individuals), $140.00 (institutions). Edizioni Minerva Medica, Corso Bramante 83-85, 10126 Turin Italy. **Tel** 011 39 11 678282, FAX 011 39 11 674502. **ED** Lubich C Zeppilli. **Bk Rev. Ad Acc.**
**Desc:** Journal addressed to practitioners and specialists. It deals with topics in sports medicine, scientific practice and research.
**Ind/Abst** Soc. Sci. Cit. Index [Select. Cov.]; SportSearch (May 1987-).

US/0195-9131
**MEDICINE AND SCIENCE IN SPORTS AND EXERCISE.** [Med. sci. sports exerc.]. **Added/Corp** American College of Sports Medicine. Vol. 12 (Spring 1980)-. Academic Scholarly Publication. English. mo. $109.00 (individual), $192.00 (institution) US; $154.00 (individual), $237.00 (institution) other. Williams & Wilkins Company, 428 East Preston Street, Baltimore MD 21202-3993. **Tel** (410)528-4000, (800)638-6423, FAX (410)528-8596, telex 87669. **(Subscription address:** Williams & Wilkins, PO Box 64380, Baltimore MD 21264.**) ED** Elsworth R. Buskirk. **LC** RC1200; .M44. **DD** 617/.1027/05. **NLM** W1 ME649NB. **CODEN** MSPEDA. **[CCC]. Ad Acc. Pr Rev. Circ:** 14,900. available on microfilm and microfiche from University Microfilms International (UMI). Documents available from The Genuine Article, BIOSIS Document Express, CASDDS, Quick Copies. ***Continues*** *Medicine and Science in Sports, 0025-7990.*
**Desc:** Original investigations of sports medicine topics for exercise physiologists, physical therapists and athletic trainers.
**Ind/Abst** Biol. Abstr.; Chem. Abstr.; Cumul. Index Nurs. Allied Health Lit.; Curr. Aware. Biol. Sci., CABS; Curr. Contents Life Sci.; Educ. Index (1992-); Electron. Commun. Abstr. J.; EMBASE; Energy Res. Abstr. (1980-); Index Med.; Index Vet.; Int. Aerosp. Abstr. (1983-); ISMEC Bull.; Mod. Med.; Nucl. Sci. Abstr.; Nutr. Abstr. Rev., Ser. A, Hum. Exp.; Nutr. Res. Newsl.; Life Sci. Collect.; Phys. Educ. Index; Pollut. Abstr. Indexes; Psychol. Abstr. (1983-); PsycINFO; PsycLit; Ref. Upd. Deluxe Ed.; Res. Alert [Full Cov.]; Saf. Sci. Abstr. J.; Sci. Cit. Index; SCISEARCH; Soc. Sci. Cit. Index [Select. Cov.]; SPORT Discus; SportSearch; Women Stud. Abstr.

SZ/0254-5020
**MEDICINE AND SPORT SCIENCE.** [Med. sport sci.]. Vol. 17 (1984)-. Academic Scholarly Publication. English. an. 200.00F (approx. per volume). S. Karger AG, Allschwilerstrasse 10, PO Box - Postfach - Case Postale, CH-4009 Basel Switzerland. **Tel** 011 41 61 306-1111, FAX 011 41 61 306-1234, telex CH 962 652. **ED** M. Hebbelinck and R. J. Shephard. **LC** UNC. **NLM** W1; ME649Q. **[CCC].** Documents available from BIOSIS Document Express, CASDDS. ***Continues*** *Medicine and Sport, 0076-6070.*
**Desc:** This series was inaugurated at a time when the sports sciences were separated from medicine. From the first volume on, the editors have united these two areas in order to give topics in sports medicine the full benefit of current advances being made in clinical medicine. Contributions from biophysics, biochemistry, engineering, and mathematics are also incorporated into this. Individual volumes clarify problems whose outlines have been known for some time and replace assumptions with medical evidence.
**Ind/Abst** Biol. Abstr. (1984-); Chem. Abstr. (1984-); Int. Aerosp. Abstr. (1984-); Ref. Upd. Deluxe Ed.

NZ/0110-6384
**NEW ZEALAND JOURNAL OF SPORTS MEDICINE, THE.** [N.Z. j. sports med.]. **Added/Corp** New Zealand Federation of Sports Medicine. Vol. 1 (Nov. 1969)-. Periodical. English. qt (Mar., June, Sep., Dec.). $40.00. New Zealand Federation of Sports Medicine, PO Box 6398, Dunedin North New Zealand. **Tel** 011 64 34 76389. **ED** N Roydhouse. **NLM** W1 NE974. Index available. **Bk Rev. Ad Acc. Pr Rev. Circ:** 1,300 (ctrl). ***Continues*** *Sports Medicine Bulletin.*
**Desc:** Sports medicine; the study of all the health implications of man in activity, physiology, psychology, illness and injury rehabilitation.
**Ind/Abst** Phys. Educ. Index; SPORT Discus.

CN/0822-7578
**NEWSLETTER - CANADIAN ATHLETIC THERAPISTS ASSOCIATION.** (NEWSLETTER.). [Newsl. - Can. Athl. Ther. Assoc.]. **VAT** CATA Newsletter; Canadian Athletic Therapists Association Newsletter. Newsletter. English (French). qt. Canadian Athletic Therapists Association, 1600 James Naismith Drive, Gloucester Ontario K1B 5N4 Canada. **Tel** (613)748-5671. **ED** Brent A MacKay. **DD** 617/.1027/06071. **Ad Acc. Circ:** 650.

CN/0824-2917
**NEWSLETTER - CANADIAN PHYSIOTHERAPY ASSOCIATION. SPORTS PHYSIOTHERAPY DIVISION.** (NEWSLETTER / SPORTS PHYSIOTHERAPY DIVISION.). [Newsl. - Can. Physiother. Assoc., Sports Physiother. Assoc.]. **VFOAT** Sports Physiotherapy Newsletter. **VAT** Newsletter - Sports Physiotherapy Division. Vol. 7, No. 1 (Nov. 1981)-. Newsletter. English (French). Six times a year. $25.00. Sports Physiotherapy Division, 1600 James Naismith Drive, Gloucester Ontario K1B 5N4 Canada. **Tel** (613)748-5671. **ED** Ha Howley and Susan Moorman. **DD** 617/.1027/05. Index available. **Bk Rev. Ad Acc. Circ:** 1,300 (ctrl). ***Continues*** *Sports Medicine Division Newsletter, 0715-3880.*
**Ind/Abst** SPORT Discus.

●US/1060-1872
**OPERATIVE TECHNIQUES IN SPORTS MEDICINE.** [Oper. tech. sports med.]. Vol. 1, No. 1 (Jan. 1993)-. Periodical. English. qt (Jan., Apr., July, Oct.). $99.00 (individual), $146.00 (institution) US; $140.00 (individual), $187.00 (institutions) other. W.B. Saunders Company, A Subsidiary of Harcourt Brace Jovanovich, Inc., The Curtis Center/Suite 300, Independence Square West, Philadelphia PA 19106-3399. **Tel** (215)238-7800 or, 5587, FAX (215)238-7883, telex 173146. **(Subscription address:** W. B. Saunders Company / North America Subscriptions, c/o Periodicals, 6277 Sea Harbour Drive, 4th Floor, Orlando FL 32887.**) DD** 617. **[CCC].**

AU
**OSTERREICHISCHES JOURNAL FUER SPORTMEDIZIN.** Vol. 1 (1971)-. German. qt. Osterreichisches Institut fur Sportmedizin, Auf der Schmelz 6, A-1150 Vienna Austria.
**Ind/Abst** SportSearch (May 1987-).

●US/1064-2188
**PENNSTATE SPORTS MEDICINE NEWSLETTER.** [PennState sports med. newsl.]. **Added/Corp** Pennsylvania State University. **VFOAT** Sports Medicine Newsletter; Penn State Sports Medicine Newsletter. Vol. 1, No. 1 (Sept. 1992)-. Newsletter. English. mo. $40.00. Sports Medicine Publications, 11 Gorham Road, Scarsdale NY 10583. **Tel** (914)725-3990, FAX (914)725-3993. **DD** 617.

●US/1062-9297
**PHYS ED JOURNAL OF SPORTS MEDICINE, THE. VFOAT** PEJ. (1992)-. Periodical. English. mo. $120.00. Phys Ed Fitness, Ltd, 532 Laguardia Place #709, New York NY 10012.

US/0163-2582
**PHYSICAL FITNESS/SPORTS MEDICINE.** ***Ceased.*** **See** Health and Personal Fitness.

US/0091-3847
**PHYSICIAN AND SPORTSMEDICINE, THE.** [Phys. sportsmed.]. **VFOAT** Sportsmedicine. Vol. 1, (June 1973)-. Academic Scholarly Publication. English. mo. $46.00 US; $49.53 other (except South Africa). McGraw Hill Publishing Company, Inc., 1221 Avenue of the Americas, New York NY 10020. **Tel** (212)512-6410, (800)525-5003, FAX (212)512-6111. **ED** Richard H. Strauss. **LC** RC1200; .P47. **DD** 617/.1027. **NLM** W1 PH773M. **[CCC].** cum. index. **Bk Rev. Ad Acc. Circ:** 104,200 (ctrl). available on microfilm and microfiche from University Microfilms International (UMI); available on an online database (files 149,624,648/Full-Text) from DIALOG. Documents available from The Genuine Article, UMI Article Clearinghouse.
**Desc:** Provides practical information on the medical aspects of sports, exercise and fitness. Categories of articles include clinical/medical, sports/fitness, injury prevention/conditioning, injury treatment/cure, and rehabilitation/maintenance.
**Ind/Abst** Acad. Abstr. Full Text Elite (Jan. 1992); Acad. Abstr. (Jan. 1992-); Acad. Search (Jan. 1992-); Bus. Index (1981-?); Cumul. Index Nurs. Allied Health Lit.; Curr. Contents Clin. Med.; Curr. Index J. Educ.; Educ. Index; EMBASE; Expand. Acad. Index (1984-); Gen. Period. Index (1985-); Gen. Sci. Index; Gen. Sci. Source (Jan. 1992-); Health Index (1989-); Health Period. Database [Full Txt.]; Health Ref. Cent. (Jan. 1989-) [Full Cov.]; Health Source (Jan. 1992-); INFO-SOUTH Abstr.; Mag. Search; Mod. Med.; Newsp. Period. Abstr. (1988-); Nutr. Abstr. Rev., Ser. A, Hum. Exp.; Phys. Educ. Index; Res. Alert [Select. Cov.]; Risk Abstr.; SCISEARCH; Soc. Sci. Cit. Index [Select. Cov.]; SPORT Discus; SportSearch; Trade Ind. Index (1981-?).

UK/0954-0741
**PHYSIOTHERAPY IN SPORT.** [Physiother. sport]. (1978)-. Academic Scholarly Publication. English. Three times a year (Feb., June, Oct.). £4.50 UK; £15.00 other. Association Chartered Physiotherapists in Sports Medicine, 344A Upper Richmond Road West, London SW14 7JT England. **Tel** 011 44 1 789 9352. **ED** Sharon Turl (editor's address: 33 Dagnan Road, London SW12 9LH England). **DD** 615.82. **Bk Rev**, (Qty: 3). **Ad Acc, Adv Mgr:** Joanne Mansfield. **Pr Rev. Circ:** 1,000 (ctrl).
**Ind/Abst** SPORT Discus.

IT
**PROGRESSI IN MEDICINA DELLO SPORT.** Vol. 1 (1982)-. Monographic series. Italian. an. Price varies per volume. Aulo Gaggi Editore, Via Andrea Costa 131-5, 40134 Bologna Italy. **Tel** 011 39 51 6142067, telex 43 61 19. **NLM** W1; PR698S.

US/0033-6297
**QUEST (NATIONAL ASSOCIATION FOR PHYSICAL EDUCATION IN HIGHER EDUCATION).** (QUEST.). [Quest]. **Added/Corp** National Association for Physical Education in Higher Education. National Association for Physical Education of College Women. National College Physical Education Association for Men. Vol. 1 (1963)-. Periodical. English. qt (Feb., May, Aug., Nov.). $36.00 (individual), $80.00 (institution) US; $40.00 (individual), $84.00 (institution) other. Human Kinetics Publishers Inc, 1607 North Market Street, PO Box 5076, Champaign IL 61825-5076. **Tel** (217)351-5076, FAX (217)351-2674. **ED** Amelia Lee. **LC** GV201; .Q43. **DD** 613.7/05. **[CCC].** Index available (Included in Nov. issue). **Bk Rev. Pr Rev. Circ:** 1,400. available on microfilm and microfiche from University Microfilms International (UMI). Documents available from The Genuine Article. ***Absorbed*** *National Association for Physical Education in Higher Education (U.S.). Conference. Proceedings.*
**Desc:** Contains theoretical and applied articles synthesizing recent research development in the sport sciences and other subdisciplines of human movement.
**Ind/Abst** Abstr. Anthropol.; AGRICOLA; Coal Abstr.; Contents Pages Educ.; Curr. Contents Soc. Behav. Sci.; Curr. Index J. Educ.; Educ. Index; Leis. Recreat. Tour. Abstr. (?-?); Phys. Educ. Index; Res. Alert [Full Cov.]; Soc. Sci. Cit. Index [Full Cov.]; SPORT Discus; Women Stud. Abstr.

II
**RESEARCH JOURNAL OF SPORTS MEDICINE AND BIOMECHANICS.** (19??)-. Research of Sports Medicine and Biomechanics, 131 Acharya Jagadish Chandra Bose Road, Calcutta 14 India.

DK/0905-7188
**SCANDINAVIAN JOURNAL OF MEDICINE & SCIENCE IN SPORTS.** **VFOAT** Scandinavian Journal of Medicine and Science in Sports; Medicine & Science in Sports. Vol. 1, No. 1 (Feb. 1991)-. Periodical. English. qt (Feb., May, Aug., and Nov.). kr930.00 US, Canada and Japan; kr890.00 other. Munksgaard International Publishers Ltd, PO Box 2148, DK-1016 Copenhagen K Denmark. **Tel** 011 45 33 12 70 30, FAX 011 45 33 12 93 87, telex 19431 MUNKS DK. **ED** Benyl Salkin (Stockholm). **LC** RC1200; .S28. **NLM** W1; SC151. **CODEN** SMSSEO. **[CCC].** Index available (bound in issue). **Ad Acc, Adv Mgr:** Hanne Staheschmidt, **Tel** 45-33-12-70-30. **Circ:** 3,500 (ctrl). ***Continues*** *Scandinavian Journal of Sports Sciences, 0357-5632.*
**Desc:** Articles on orthopaedic traumatology, physiology, biomedicine, rehabilitation and sociology.
**Ind/Abst** EMBASE; Soc. Plann. Policy Dev. Abstr.; Soc. Sci. Cit. Index [Select. Cov.].

●SZ/1022-6699
**SCHWEIZERISCHE ZEITSCHRIFT FUER MEDIZIN UND TRAUMATOLOGIE.** **Added/Corp** Schweizerische Gesellschaft fuer Sportmedizin. **VFOAT** Revue Suisse pour Medecine et Traumatologie; Schweizerische Zeitschrift fuer Sportmedizin und Sporttraumatologie. (1994)-. Periodical. French (German and Italian; summaries and/or abstracts in English). Four times a year. 30.00F Switzerland; 36.00F Germany; 40.00F other. Verlag Paul Haupt, Falkenplatz 11, CH-3001 Bern Switzerland. **Tel** 011 41 31 3012435, FAX 011 41 30 243023, telex 912 906 HAUP CH. **NLM** W1; SC544. ***Continues*** *Schweizerische Zeitschrift fuer Sportmedizin.*
**Ind/Abst** Index Med. (1994-).

SZ/0036-7885
**SCHWEIZERISCHE ZEITSCHRIFT FUER SPORTMEDIZIN.** ***Title Change.*** (SCHWEIZERISCHE ZEITSCHRIFT FUER SPORTMEDIZIN. REVUE SUISSE DE MEDECINE SPORTIVE. REVISTA SVIZZERA DI MEDICINA SPORTIVA.). [Schweiz. Z. Sportmed.]. **Added/Corp** Schweizerische Gesellschaft fuer Sportmedizin. Schweizerischer Landesverband fuer Leibesubungen.

Sportarztlicher Dienst. **VFOAT** Revue Suisse de Medecine Sportive; Revista Svizzera di Medicina Sportiva. (1953)-(1993). Academic Scholarly Publication. English (French and German). qt. Verlag Paul Haupt, Falkenplatz 11, CH-3001 Bern Switzerland. **Tel** 011 41 31 3012435, FAX 011 41 30 243023, telex 912 906 HAUP CH. **ED** Paul Haupt Bern. **LC** RC1200; .S35. **NLM** W1; SC612. **CODEN** SZSSED. **[CCC]. Bk Rev. Ad Acc.** ctrl circ. ***Continued by*** *Schweizerische Zeitschrift fuer Medizin und Traumatologie.*
**Desc:** Deals with sports-medicine.
**Ind/Abst** EMBASE; Index Med.; SportSearch.

FR/0765-1597
**SCIENCE & SPORTS.** [Sci. sports]. **Added/Corp** Societe Francaise de Medecine du Sport. **VFOAT** Science et Sports. Vol. 1, No. 1 (March 1986)-. Academic Scholarly Publication. French (summaries and/or abstracts in English). qt (1 volume). 825.00F France; 950.00F other. Editions Scientifique Elsevier, 141 rue de Javel, 75747 Paris Cedex 15 France. **Tel** 011 33 1 47 07 11 22, FAX 011 33 1 43 36 80 93. **(Subscription address:** Editions Scientifiques Elsevier / for North America, PO Box 7247-7576, Philadelphia PA 19170-7576.**) NLM** W1; SC686F. **CODEN** SCSPED. **[CCC].** available on microfilm and microfiche from University Microfilms International (UMI). Documents available from BIOSIS Document Express, CASDDS.
**Ind/Abst** Biol. Abstr. (1987-); Chem. Abstr. (1986-); EMBASE; SPORT Discus.

CN/0822-6792
**SCIENCE DU SPORT. See** Education-Physical Education and Training.

FR
**SCIENCE ET MOTRICITE : SM : REVUE SCIENTIFIQUE DE L'A.C.A.P.S., ASSOCIATION DES CHERCHEURS EN ACTIVITES PHYSIQUES ET SPORTIVES. Added/Corp** Association des Chercheurs en Activites Physiques et Sportives. Institut National du Sport et de l'Education Physique (France). **VFOAT** SM. (1987)-. Periodical. French (summaries and/or abstracts in English, German, Italian and Spanish). Three times a year. 209.00F France; 290.00F other. Editions Insep, 11 Avenue du Trembley, 75012 Paris France. **Tel** 011 33 1 43741121. **NLM** W1; SC694.
**Ind/Abst** SPORT Discus.

IT/0392-9647
**SPORT & MEDICINA. VFOAT** Sport e Medicina. (1984)-. Periodical. Italian. bm. L30000.00 Italy. EDI Ermes Srl, Via Enrico Forlanini 65, 20134 Milan Italy. **Tel** 011 39 2 70209911, FAX 02/70209919. **UDC** 61. Index available. **Bk Rev. Ad Acc. Pr Rev. Circ:** 20,000.
**Desc:** Sports medicine, prevention of injuries and training.

AT/0812-8308
**SPORT HEALTH.** (SPORT HEALTH : OFFICIAL GAZETTE OF AUSTRALIAN SPORTS MEDICINE FEDERATION.). [Sport health]. **Added/Corp** Australian Sports Medicine Federation. Vol. 1, No. 1 (May/June 1983)-. Periodical. English. Four times a year (Mar., June, Sept., Dec.). 25.00Aus$ (Australia); 36.00Aus$ (other). Australian Sports Medicine Federation, PO Box 897, Belconnen ACT 2616 Australia. **Tel** 011/61/6/251944, FAX 011/61/6/2531489, telex 62400. **ED** Alexander Grant. **NLM** W1; SP488M. Index available.
**Ind/Abst** SPORT Discus; SportSearch (May 1987-).

CN/0229-1541
**SPORT MEDICINE DIRECTORY.** (SPORT MEDICINE DIRECTORY / SMCC.). [Sport med. dir.]. **VFOAT** Repertoire de la Medecine Sportive. 1980-. Directory. English (French). be. Sport Medicine Council of Canada, 333 River Road, Ottawa Ontario K1L 8H9 Canada. **Tel** (613)748-5671, telex 0533660. **DD** 617/.1027. **Ad Acc. Circ:** 3,000.
**Desc:** Identifies certified athletic therapists, physicians, physiotherapists, and sport scientists in Canada dedicated to the medical and paramedical care of amateur athletes. Also contains a clinic registry, information on provincial and athlete medical plans and a glossary of terms.

CN/0824-4219
**SPORTMEDINFO FROM THE SPORT MEDICINE COUNCIL OF CANADA.** [Sportmedinfo]. **Added/Corp** Sport Medicine Council of Canada. **VFOAT** Sportmedinfo du Conseil Canadien de la Medecine Sportive. Periodical. English (French). qt. $5.00. Sport Medicine Council of Canada, 333 River Road, Ottawa Ontario K1L 8H9 Canada. **Tel** (613)748-5671, telex 0533660. **DD** 617/.1027/05. ***Continues*** *Sportmedinfo du Conseil Canadien de la Medecine Sportive., 0824-4219.*

HU/0209-682X
**SPORTORVOSI SZEMLE.** (SPORTORVOSI SZEMLE. HUNGARIAN REVIEW OF SPORTS MEDICINE.). [Sportorv. szle.]. **Added/Corp** Orszagos Testneveles-es Sportegeszsegugyi Intezet. **VFOAT** Hungarian Review of Sports Medicine. Vol. 21 (1980)-. Academic Scholarly Publication. Hungarian (English; summaries and/or abstracts in Russian). qt. Akademiai Kiado, Publishing House of the Hungarian Academy of Sciences, Prielle Kornelia u. 19-35, H-1117 Budapest Hungary. **Tel** 011 36 1 1811991, FAX 011 36 1 1811991, telex 22-6228 AKNYO H. **NLM** W1 SP509. ***Continues*** *Testneveles- es Sportegeszsegugyi Szemle, 0563-2013.*
**Ind/Abst** SPORT Discus; SportSearch (May 1987-).

CN/0820-6457
**SPORTS (COACHING ASSOCIATION OF CANADA : 1980).** ***Title Change.* See** Education-Physical Education and Training.

●UK/1351-0029
**SPORTS, EXERCISE AND INJURY.** (1994)-. English. Four times a year. £123.00 Europe; £124.00 Other (Institutions). Churchill Livingstone, 1-3 Baxter's Place, Leith Walk, Edinburgh EH1 3AF Scotland. **Tel** 011 44 31 556 2424, FAX 011 44 31 558 1278, telex 727511. **(Subscription address:** Maruzen Company Ltd., PO Box 5050, Import & Export Department, Tokyo 100 31 Japan.**)**

●US/1062-8592
**SPORTS MEDICINE AND ARTHROSCOPY REVIEW.** Vol. 1, No. 1 (Spring 1993)-. Periodical. English. qt. $95.00 (individuals), $122.00 (institutions) US; $115.00 (individuals), $144.00 (institutions) other. Raven Press, 1185 Avenue of the Americas, 37th Floor, New York NY 10036. **Tel** (212)930-9500, (212)930-9604, FAX (212)869-3495, (212)302-8507, telex 640073. **DD** 617. **NLM** W1; SP511CM. **[CCC].**

NZ/0112-1642
**SPORTS MEDICINE (AUCKLAND).** (SPORTS MEDICINE.). [Sports med.]. Vol. 1, No. 1 (Jan./Feb. 1984)-. Periodical. English. mo (12 issues). 570.00F Europe; $345.00 other. ADIS International Ltd, 41 Centorian Drive, Private Bag 65901, Mairangi Bay, Auckland 10 New Zealand. **Tel** 011 64 9 4798100, FAX 011 64 9 4791418. **(Subscription address:** Japan Publications Trading Company, Ltd., PO Box 5030, Tokyo International, Tokyo 100-31 Japan.**) NLM** W1; SP509H. **CODEN** SPMEE7. **[CCC].** Documents available from CASDDS.
**Ind/Abst** Chem. Abstr. (1984-1988); EMBASE; Int. Pharm. Abstr. (199?-); Soc. Sci. Cit. Index [Select. Cov.].

UK/0952-4630
**SPORTS MEDICINE BULLETIN (LONDON, ENGLAND).** (SPORTS MEDICINE BULLETIN.). Vol. 1 (Sept. 1987)-. Bulletin. English. mo. Sports Medicine Institute, Medcial College, St Bartholomews Hospital Library, London EC1M 6BQ England. **Tel** 011 44 71 251-0583. **NLM** ZQT 260; S764.
**Ind/Abst** SportSearch (May 1987-).

US/0731-9770
**SPORTS MEDICINE DIGEST.** Vol. 6, No. 6 (June 1984)-. Newsletter. English. Twelve times a year. $52.00 North America; $78.00 other. Raven Press, 1185 Avenue of the Americas, 37th Floor, New York NY 10036. **Tel** (212)930-9500, (212)930-9604, FAX (212)869-3495, (212)302-8507, telex 640073. Index available. **Bk Rev. Circ:** 4,000. ***Continues*** *Sportsmedicine Digest, 0731-9770.*
**Ind/Abst** SPORT Discus.

US/0271-2857
**SPORTS MEDICINE (MOUNT KISCO).** (SPORTS MEDICINE.). [Sports med.]. 1978-. Periodical. English. an. Futura Publishing Company Inc., 135 Bedford Road, PO Box 418, Armonk NY 10504-0418. **Tel** (914)273-1014, (800)877-8761, FAX (914)273-1015, (914)273-1016. **LC** RD560; .S67. **DD** 617/.585. Documents available from The Genuine Article.
**Ind/Abst** Curr. Contents Clin. Med.; Health Saf. Sci. Abstr.; Nutr. Res. Newsl.; Life Sci. Collect.; Phys. Educ. Index; Res. Alert [Select. Cov.].

US
**SPORTS MEDICINE NEWS.** English. mo. $46.00 North America; $70.00 other. McMahon Publishing Company, 148 West 24th Street, 8th Floor, New York NY 10011. **Tel** (212)620-4600, FAX (212)620-5928. **ED** James Prudden. **Ad Acc. Circ:** 19,000 (ctrl).
**Desc:** Clinical medical newsmonthly for orthopedic surgeons covering arthroscopy, arthroplasty, pain management, and economic issues, with a special focus on orthopedic sports medicine.

US/1041-696X
**SPORTS MEDICINE STANDARDS AND MALPRACTICE REPORTER, THE.** [Sports med. stand. malpract. report.]. **Added/Corp** Professional Reports Corporation. **VFOAT** SMSMR. Vol. 1, No. 1 (Jan. 1989)-. Periodical. English. qt. $39.95 US; $43.95 Canada; $47.95 other. Professional Reports Corporation, 4418 Belden Village Street Northwest, Canton OH 44718. **Tel** (216)492-6063, (800)336-0083, FAX (216)492-6176. **ED** David L. Heubert. **LC** KF2910.S653; A136. **DD** 344.73/041; 347.30441. Index available. cum. index. **Bk Rev. Ad Acc.**
**Desc:** Written to provide accurate and authoritative information relevant to the subject matter presented.

SZ/1057-8315
**SPORTS MEDICINE, TRAINING, AND REHABILITATION.** [Sports med. train. rehabil.]. Vol. 3, No. 1 (Oct. 1991)-. Periodical. English. Four times a year. $373.00 (academic institutions), $582.00 (corporate institutions). Harwood Academic Publishers, PO Box 90, Reading RG1 8JL England. **Tel** 011 44 734 560080. **(Subscription address:** International Publishers Distributor at one of the following addresses: 820 Town Center Drive, Langhorne, PA 19047; or PO Box 90, Reading Berkshire RG1 8JL UK; or Kent Ridge PO Box 1180, Singapore 9111, Republic of Singapore**) DD** 617. **CODEN** SMTJE2. ***Continues*** *Sports Training, Medicine and Rehabilitation, 0893-102X.*

US
**SPORTS MEDICINE UPDATE. Added/Corp** Healthsouth Rehabilitation Corporation. American Sports Medicine Institute. Healthsouth Sports Medicine Network. (198?)-. Periodical. English. Four times a year. $15.00 universities and college libraries; $18.00 other. Healthsouth Medicine Network, PO Box 550039, Birmingham AL 35255. **Tel** (205)324-4500. **LC** RC1200; .S76. **NLM** W1; SP511M.

UK/0967-7755
**SPORTS PHYSIOLOGY & MEDICINE.** (19??)-. English. £75.00. SUBIS, Mansion House, 19 Kingfield Road, Sheffield S11 9AS England. **Tel** 011 44 114 255 4433, FAX 011 44 114 255 4626.

AT/1032-5506
**SPORTS TRAINERS DIGEST : A CONTINUING EDUCATION SERVICE OF THE AUSTRALIAN SPORTS MEDICINE FEDERATION / NATIONAL SPORTS TRAINERS SCHEME. Added/Corp** Australian Sports Medicine Federation. National Sports Trainers Scheme (Australia). (198?)-. Periodical. English. Four times a year (Mar., June, Sept., Dec.). 15.00Aus$ Australia; 22.00Aus$ others. Australian Sports Medicine Federation, PO Box 897, Belconnen ACT 2616 Australia. **Tel** 011/61/6/251944, FAX 011/61/6/2531489, telex 62400. **NLM** W1; SO511H. **Circ:** 8,000.
**Desc:** Provide basic sports medicine including first aid, crisis management and injury prevention to sports participants.

US/0731-9770
**SPORTSMEDICINE DIGEST.** ***Title Change.*** [Sportsmed. dig.]. Vol. 1 (Sept. 1979)-(1984). Periodical. English. mo. PM Inc., PO Box 10172, Van Nuys CA 91409. **Tel** (213)873-4399, FAX (818)997-1316. **ED** Gerald McKee and Lewis Yocum. Index available. **Bk Rev. Circ:** 2,500. ***Continued by*** *Sports Medicine Digest.*
**Desc:** Newsletter for health care professionals. Publication is dedicated to the prevention, treatment and rehabilitation of sports and recreational injuries.

GW/0932-0555
**SPORTVERLETZUNG, SPORTSCHADEN.** (SPORTVERLETZUNG SPORTSCHADEN : ORGAN DER GESELLSCHAFT FUER ORTHOPADISCH-TRAUMATOLOGISCHE SPORTMEDIZIN.). [Sportverletz. Sportschaden]. **Added/Corp** Gesellschaft fuer Orthopadisch-Traumatologische Sportmedizin. **VFOAT** Sportverletzung-Sportschaden. Vol. 1, No. 1 (April 1987)-. Periodical. German (summaries and/or abstracts in English). qt. $108.00. Georg Thieme Verlag Stuttgart, Postfach 301120, D 70451 Stuttgart Germany. **Tel** 011 49 711 89310, FAX 011 49 711 8931298, telex 7 252 275 GTVD. **(Subscription address:** Thieme Medical Publishers Inc., 381 Park Avenue South, New York NY 10016.**) NLM** W1; SP514.
**Ind/Abst** Index Med. (April 1987-)(Apr. 1987-).

HU/0563-2013
**TESTMEVELES- ES SPORTEGESZSEGUGYI SZMELE.** ***Title Change.*** 1960-?. Academic Scholarly Publication. Hungarian (summaries and/or abstracts in English and Russian; table of contents in English and Russian). qt. Akademiai Kiado, Publishing House of the Hungarian Academy of Sciences, Prielle Kornelia u. 19-35, H-1117 Budapest Hungary. **Tel** 011 36 1 1811991, FAX 011 36 1 1811991, telex 22-6228 AKNYO H. **(Subscription address:** Kultura, Hungarian Foreign Trading Company, PO Box 149, H-1389 Budapest Hungary**) NLM** W1 TE631. ***Continued by*** *Sportorvosi Szemle, 0209-682X.*

TU
**TURKISH JOURNAL OF SPORTS MEDICINE.** (19??)-. English (Turkish). qt. $15.00. University of Ege Institute of Sports Medicine, Faculty of Medicine, Bornova Izmir Turkey. **Tel** 011 90 51 181097.
**Ind/Abst** SPORT Discus.

US/0162-0908
**YEAR BOOK OF SPORTS MEDICINE, THE.** [Year book sports med.]. (1979)-. English. an. $72.00. Mosby Year Book Inc., 11830 Westline Industrial Drive, St Louis MO 63146. **Tel** (800)325-4177, (314)872-8370, FAX (314)432-1380, telex 44-2402. **LC** RC1200; .Y4. **DD** 617/.1027/05. **UDC** 798.9:636.596(058)(71). **NLM** W1 YE333M.

CC/1000-6710
**ZHONGGUO YUNDONG YIXUE ZAZHI.** (CHUNG-KUO YUN TUNG I HSUEH TSA CHIH / CHUNG-KUO TI YU KO HSUEH HSUEH HUI YUN TUNG I HSUEH HSUEH HUI.). [Zhongguo yundong yixue zazhi]. **Added/Corp** Chung-kuo ti yu ko Hsueh Hsueh Hui. Yun Tung I Hsueh Hsueh Hui. **VFOAT** Chinese Journal of Sports Medicine. (1982)-. Periodical. Chinese (summaries and/or abstracts in English; table of contents in English). qt. Zhongguo Tiyu Kexue Xuehui, China Sports Science Society, Renmin Tiyu Chubanshe, (People's Sports Publishing House), 8 Tiyuguan Lu, Chongwen Qu, Beijing 100061 People's Republic of China. **Tel** 5112466, FAX 7016129. **ED** Q. Jincheng. **NLM** W1; CH991F.
**Ind/Abst** SPORT Discus.

## SURGERY

US/0884-1470
**ABMS DIRECTORY OF CERTIFIED COLON AND RECTAL SURGEONS.** ***Title Change.*** [ABMS dir. certif. colon rectal surg.]. **Added/Corp** American Board of Medical Specialties. American Board of Colon and Rectal Surgery. **VFOAT** Directory of Certified Colon and Rectal Surgeons. **VAT** American Board of Medical Specialties Directory of Certified Colon and Rectal Surgeons. 1st Ed. (1984)-(19??). Directory. English. be. American Board of Medical Specialties, 1 Rotary Center, Suite 805, Evanston IL 60201. **Tel** (708)491-9091. **LC** RD10.U6; A23. **DD** 617/.5547/002573. **NLM** WI 22.1; A1523. **Circ:** 250 (ctrl). ***Continued by*** *Official American Board of Medical Specialties (ABMS) Directory of Board Certified Colon and Rectal Surgeons, 0000-1414.*
**Desc:** Biographical listing of certified medical specialists.

US/0882-2832
**ABMS DIRECTORY OF CERTIFIED NEUROLOGICAL SURGEONS.** ***Title Change.*** [ABMS dir. certif. neurol. surg.]. **Added/Corp** American Board of Medical Specialties. American Board of Neurological Surgery. **VFOAT** Directory of Certified Neurological Surgeons. 1st Ed. (1984)-(19??). Directory. English. be. American Board of Medical Specialties, 1 Rotary Center, Suite 805, Evanston IL 60201. **Tel** (708)491-9091. **LC** RD592.5; .A25. **DD** 617/.48/002573. **NLM** WL 22.1; A1523. **Bk Rev. Ad Acc.** ***Continued by*** *Official American Board of Medical Specialties (ABMS) Directory of Board Certified Neurological Surgeons, 0000-1449.*

US/0749-839X
**ABMS DIRECTORY OF CERTIFIED PLASTIC SURGEONS.** ***Title Change.*** [ABMS dir. certif. plast. surg.]. **Added/Corp** American Board of Medical Specialties. American Board of Plastic Surgery. **VFOAT** A.B.M.S. Directory of Certified Plastic Surgeons; Directory of Certified Plastic Surgeons. 1st Ed. (1983)-(19??). Directory. English. be. American Board of Medical Specialties, 1 Rotary Center, Suite 805, Evanston IL 60201. **Tel** (708)491-9091. **LC** RD10.U6; A24. **DD** 617/.95/002573; 610. **NLM** WO 22.1; A1523. **Ad Acc. Circ:** 600 (ctrl). ***Continued by*** *Official American Board of Medical Specialties (ABMS) Directory of Board Certified Plastic Surgeons, 0000-1473.*
**Desc:** Biographic listings of certified medical specialists.

US/0884-1527
**ABMS DIRECTORY OF CERTIFIED SURGEONS.** ***Title Change.*** [ABMS dir. certif. surg.]. **Added/Corp** American Board of Medical Specialties. American Board of Surgery. **VFOAT** Directory of Certified Surgeons. **VAT** American Board of Medical Specialties Directory of Certified Surgeons. (1985)-(199?). Directory. English. be. American Board of Medical Specialties, 1 Rotary Center, Suite 805, Evanston IL 60201. **Tel** (708)491-9091. **LC** RD10.U6; A245. **DD** 617/.0025/73. **NLM** WO 22.1; A15235. ***Continued by*** *Official American Board of Medical Specialties (ABMS) Directory of Board Certified Surgeons, 0000-1678.*

US/0884-1462
**ABMS DIRECTORY OF CERTIFIED THORACIC SURGEONS.** ***Title Change.*** [ABMS dir. certif. thorac. surg.]. **Added/Corp** American Board of Medical Specialties. American Board of Thoracic Surgery. **VFOAT** Directory of Certified Thoracic Surgeons. **VAT** American Board of Medical Specialties Directory of Certified Thoracic Surgeons. (1983)-(19??). Directory. English. be. American Board of Medical Specialties, 1 Rotary Center, Suite 805, Evanston IL 60201. **Tel** (708)491-9091. **LC** RD10.U6; A26. **DD** 617/.54059/02573. **NLM** WF 22.1; A116. ***Continued by*** *Official American Board of Medical Specialties (ABMS) Directory of Board Certified Thoracic Surgeons, 0000-1481.*

US/0099-250X
**ABSTRACTS, ANNUAL MEETING - AMERICAN SOCIETY FOR ARTIFICIAL INTERNAL ORGANS.** **Added/Corp** American Society for Artificial Internal Organs. Vol. 1 (1972)-. English. an. $20.00. American Society of Artificial Internal Organs, PO Box C, Boca Raton FL 33429. **Tel** (202)833-9680. **ED** George E. Schreiner. **NLM** W1 AB879H. **Circ:** 1,500.
**Desc:** Artificial internal organs research in the same field.

XR/0001-5423
**ACTA CHIRURGIAE PLASTICAE (ANGLICKA VERZE).** (ACTA CHIRURGIAE PLASTICAE.). [Acta chir. plast.]. **VFOAT** International Journal of Plastic Surgery. (1959)-. Academic Scholarly Publication. English (summaries and/or abstracts in German, French, Spanish and Russian). qt. 185.00F Switzerland; DM226.00 Germany; $114.00 US. Avicenum Medical Press, Malostranske Nam 28, 11802 Prague Czech Republic. **Tel** 011 42 2 530643. **(Subscription address:** Artia Pegas Press Ltd., Palac Metro Narodni Trida 25, 11210 Prague 1 Czech Republic.**) UDC** 616-089.844. **NLM** W1 AC7762. Documents available.
**Ind/Abst** EMBASE; Index Med.; Life Sci. Collect.

AU/0001-544X
**ACTA CHIRURGICA AUSTRIACA.** [Acta Chir. Austriaca]. **Added/Corp** Osterreichische Gesellschaft fuer Chirurgie. Vol. 1 (1969)-. Academic Scholarly Publication. German (English; summaries and/or abstracts in English). bm (6 issues). S2160.00 Austria; S2240.00 other. Blackwell MZV Medizinische Zeitschriftenverlags Gesellschaft, Feldgasse 13, A-1238 Vienna Austria. **Tel** 011 43 1 8893646, FAX 011 43 1 889364724. **ED** F. Helmer, F. Piza, K. Meissner. **NLM** W1 AC7768. **CODEN** ACAUB9. Index available. **Bk Rev. Ad Acc. Circ:** 1,500. available on microfilm from University Microfilms International (UMI). Documents available from BIOSIS Document Express, ADONIS.
**Desc:** Covers Austrian surgery.
**Ind/Abst** ADONIS; Biol. Abstr.; EMBASE; Life Sci. Collect.

BE/0001-5458
**ACTA CHIRURGICA BELGICA.** [Acta chir. belg.]. **Added/Corp** Societe Belge de Chirurgie, Brussels. Vol. 45 (1946)-. Periodical. Multiple languages (French, English and Dutch). bm. 1950F Belgium; 2200F other. Association for the Society of Scientifique Medica Belgique, Avenue Circulaire 138A, B-1180 Brussels Belgium. **Tel** 011 32 2 3745158. **ED** Mendes da Costa. **NLM** W1 AC777. **CODEN** ACBEAX. **Bk Rev. Ad Acc. Pr Rev. Circ:** 1,050 (ctrl). Documents available from The Genuine Article, BIOSIS Document Express, CASDDS. ***Continues*** *Journal de Chirurgie et Annales de la Societe Belge de Chirurgie.*
**Desc:** General surgery periodical. All aspects of different clinical specialities and research accepted with original texts.
**Ind/Abst** Biol. Abstr.; Chem. Abstr.; Curr. Contents Clin. Med.; EMBASE; Health Plan. Adminis.; Hospit. Health Admin. Index; Index Med.; Life Sci. Collect.; Res. Alert [Select. Cov.]; Saf. Health Work; SCISEARCH.

SP/0211-660X
**ACTA CHIRURGICA CATALONIAE.** [Acta chir. Cataloniae]. (1980)-. Periodical. Spanish. qt. 6000ptas. Pulso Ediciones SA, Sant Elies 21 4-Art, 08006 Barcelona Spain. **Tel** 011 34 3 2000877, FAX 011 34 3 2022117. **UDC** 617. Index available. **Bk Rev. Ad Acc.**
**Desc:** Journal of the Catalan Society of Surgery.
**Ind/Abst** Indice Med. Esp.

HU/0231-4614
**ACTA CHIRURGICA HUNGARICA.** [Acta chir. Hung.]. **Added/Corp** Magyar Tudomanyos Akademia. **VFOAT** Acta Chirurgica. Vol. 24, No. 1 (1983)-. Academic Scholarly Publication. English (summaries and/or abstracts in German and Russian). qt. $88.00. Akademiai Kiado, Publishing House of the Hungarian Academy of Sciences, Prielle Kornelia u. 19-35, H-1117 Budapest Hungary. **Tel** 011 36 1 1811991, FAX 011 36 1 1811991, telex 22-6228 AKNYO H. **ED** Antal Babis (editor's address: Acta Chirurgica Hungarica, Istvan Korhaz, Urologia, Nagyvarad ter 1, H-1096 Budapest Hungary). **NLM** W1 AC7773. **[CCC].** ***Continues*** *Acta Chirurgica Academiae Scientiarum Hungaricae, 0001-5431.*
**Desc:** Provides a forum for the publication of papers in the field of surgery, including general surgical aspects of gynecology, urology, otolaryngology, orthopedics, ophthalmology, as well as nerve and brain surgery, pulmonary, oral surgery, heart and blood vessel surgery.
**Ind/Abst** EMBASE [Select. Cov.]; Health Plan. Adminis.; Index Med.

IT/0001-5466
**ACTA CHIRURGICA ITALICA.** [Acta chir. ital.]. Vol. 10 (1954)-. Academic Scholarly Publication. Italian (summaries and/or abstracts in English). bm. L80000.00 Italy; L120000.00 other. La Garangola, Via Montona 4, 35137 Padua Italy. **Tel** 011 39 49 8750550, FAX 011 39 49 8751743. **UDC** 616-089. **NLM** W1 AC7778. **CODEN** ACHIA7. Index available (bound in last issue). **Bk Rev. Ad Acc, Adv Mgr:** A. Pagamento. **Pr Rev. Circ:** 1500 (ctrl). Documents available from BIOSIS Document Express. ***Continues*** *Acta Chirurgica Patavina, 0390-6892.*
**Ind/Abst** Biol. Abstr.; EMBASE [Select. Cov.].

CI/0001-5474
**ACTA CHIRURGICA IUGOSLAVICA.** [Acta chir. jugosl.]. (1954)-. Multiple languages ( and Serbian; summaries and/or abstracts in English, French and German). ir. $65.00 (included with Journal of Wildlife Management). Udruzenje Hirurga Jugoslavije / Association of Yugoslav Surgeons, Univerzitetski Klinicki Centar, Institut za Bdesti Digestivnog Sistema, Ul. Koste Todorivica 6, 11000 Belgrade Yugoslavia. **(Subscription address:** Mladost Export Import, PO Box 1028, Ilica 30, 41000 Zagreb Croatia.**) NLM** W1 AC7775. ***Supersedes*** *Acta Chirurgica.*
**Ind/Abst** Index Med. (June 6, 1963-May 5, 1966).

AU/0001-6268
**ACTA NEUROCHIRURGICA.** [Acta neurochir.]. **Added/Corp** European Association of Neurosurgical Societies. Vol. 1 (Feb. 1950)-. Academic Scholarly Publication. English (French, German, Italian and Spanish; summaries and/or abstracts in French, German, Italian and Spanish). Twenty-four times a year. DM2058.00. Springer-Verlag Wien, Sachsenplatz 4 6, PO Box 89, A-1201 Vienna Austria. **Tel** 011 43 1 3302415. **(Subscription address:** Springer Verlag New York Inc. / for North America, 44 Hartz Way, Secaucus NJ 07096.**) ED** F. Loew. **NLM** W1 AC866. **CODEN** ACNUA5. **[CCC]. Bk Rev. Pr Rev.** available on microfilm and microfiche from University Microfilms International (UMI). Documents available from The Genuine Article, BIOSIS Document Express, CASDDS.
**Desc:** The scientific link between significant European research, innovation and clinical work and an international readership not only among neurosurgeons and neurotraumatologists, but also neurologists and basic neuroscientists.
**Ind/Abst** Arts Humanit. Citation Index [Select. Cov.]; Biol. Abstr.; Chem. Abstr.; Dev. Med. Child Neurol.; EMBASE; Health Plan. Adminis.; Helminthol. Abstr.; Index Med.; INIS Atomindex [Micro.]; Life Sci. Collect.; Res. Alert [Full Cov.]; Sci. Cit. Index; SCISEARCH.

AU/0065-1419
**ACTA NEUROCHIRURGICA : SUPPLEMENTUM.** [Acta neurochir. Suppl.]. (1950)-. Monographic series. English. ir. Price varies per volume. Springer-Verlag Wien, Sachsenplatz 4 6, PO Box 89, A-1201 Vienna Austria. **Tel** 011 43 1 3302415. **(Subscription address:** Springer Verlag New York Inc. / for North America, 44 Hartz Way, Secaucus NJ 07096.**) ED** F. Loew. **UDC** 616.8-089. **NLM** W1 AC8661. **CODEN** ANCSBM. **[CCC].** available on microfilm from University Microfilms International (UMI). Documents available from BIOSIS Document Express.
**Desc:** Series covering neurosurgery.
**Ind/Abst** Biol. Abstr.; Health Plan. Adminis.; Index Med.; INIS Atomindex [Micro.]; Life Sci. Collect.

FR/0376-6276
**ACTUALITES CHIRURGICALES.** **Added/Corp** Association Francaise de Chirurgie. (1971)-. French. ir. 160.00F (latest volume). Scientific & Medical Publishers of France, 100 East 42nd Street, Suite 1002, New York NY 10017-5613. **Tel** (212)983-6278. **ED** C. Olivier. **NLM** W3 AC192. **Circ:** 3,000. ***Formed by the union of*** *Congres Francais de Chirurgie. Rapports, Discussions et Communications Particulieres - Congres Francais de Chirurgie* ***and*** *Congres Francais de Chirurgie. Informations et Rapports -Congres Francais de Chirurgie, 0997-4334.*

US/0095-4829
**ADVANCES AND TECHNICAL STANDARDS IN NEUROSURGERY.** Vol. 1 (1974)-. Monographic series. English. ir. Price varies per volume. Springer-Verlag New York Inc., 175 5th Avenue, New York NY 10010. **Tel** (212)460-1500, telex 232 235 SPB UR. **(Subscription address:** Springer Verlag New York Inc. / for North America, 44 Hartz Way, Secaucus NJ 07096.**) ED** L. Symon, J. Brihaye, L. Calliauw, F. Cohadon, B. Guidetti, J. Lobo Antunes, F. Loew, J.D. Miller, H. Nornes, E. Pasztor, B. Pertuiset, J.D. Pickard, A.J. Strong, M.G. Yasargil. **NLM** W1 AD407. **Circ:** 800.
**Desc:** Publishes contributions from those fields of neurosurgery and related areas in which important recent advances have been made. Part of each volume is dedicated to detailed descriptions of standard operative procedures.
**Ind/Abst** Health Plan. Adminis.; Index Med. (1984-).

US/0889-5074
**ADVANCES IN CARDIAC SURGERY.** [Adv. card. surg.]. Vol. 1 (1990)-. English. an (Sept.). Price varies. Mosby Year Book Inc., 11830 Westline Industrial Drive, St Louis MO 63146. **Tel** (800)325-4177, (314)872-8370, FAX (314)432-1380, telex 44-2402. **LC** RD598; .A34. **DD** 617.4/12/005. **NLM** W1; AD53CL.

GW/0302-2366
**ADVANCES IN NEUROSURGERY.** [Adv. Neurosurg.]. (1973)-. Monographic series. English. ir. Price varies per volume. Springer-Verlag GmbH & Company KG, Heidelberger Platz 3, D 14197 Berlin Germany. **Tel** 011 49 30 8207223, FAX 011 49 30

8214091, telex 183 319 SPBLN D. **(Subscription address:** Springer Verlag New York Inc. / for North America, 44 Hartz Way, Secaucus NJ 07096.**)** **LC** UNC. **NLM** W1 AD684N. **CODEN** AVNSBV. Documents available from CASDDS.
**Desc:** Studies in neurosurgery.
**Ind/Abst** Chem. Abstr.

US/0276-3508
**ADVANCES IN OPHTHALMIC PLASTIC AND RECONSTRUCTIVE SURGERY.** [Adv. ophthalmic plast. reconstr. surg.]. Vol. 1 (1982)-. English. ir. Price varies. McGraw Hill Publishing Company, Inc., 1221 Avenue of the Americas, New York NY 10020. **Tel** (212)512-6410, (800)525-5003, FAX (212)512-6111. **ED** Stephen L. Bosniak (editor's address: 300 Central Park West, New York, NY 10024). **[CCC].** available on microfilm.
**Desc:** Features original articles and reviews on topics such as ptosis, eyelid reconstruction, orbital diagnosis and surgery, lacrimal problems, and eyelid malposition.
**Ind/Abst** Health Plan. Adminis.; Index Med.

US/0738-2278
**ADVANCES IN ORTHOPAEDIC SURGERY.** [Adv. orthop. surg.]. Vol. 7, No. 1 (July/Aug. 1983)-. Academic Scholarly Publication. English. bm (6 issues). $70.00 (individual), $150.00 (institutional) US; $100.00 (individual), $182.00 (institutional) other. Raven Press, 1185 Avenue of the Americas, 37th Floor, New York NY 10036. **Tel** (212)930-9500, (212)930-9604, FAX (212)869-3495, (212)302-8507, telex 640073. **ED** William P. Cooney, III. **LC** RD701; .O79. **DD** 617/.3/005. **NLM** ZWE 168; O77. **CODEN** AOSUEG. **[CCC].** Index available. **Ad Acc. Circ:** 2,500. available on microfilm. Documents available from BIOSIS Document Express. ***Continues*** *Orthopaedic Survey, 0147-6793.*
**Desc:** Condensations with commentary on key articles from the current literature plus review articles.
**Ind/Abst** Biol. Abstr. (1986-)(1986-1989); Curr. Aware. Biol. Sci., CABS; EMBASE.

US/0887-6916
**ADVANCES IN OTOLARYNGOLOGY--HEAD AND NECK SURGERY.** [Adv. otolaryngol.--head neck surg.]. **VFOAT** Advances in Otolaryngology, Head and Neck Surgery; Advances in Otolaryngology; Head and Neck Surgery. Vol. 1 (1987)-. Periodical. English. an. $69.95. Mosby Year Book Inc., 11830 Westline Industrial Drive, St Louis MO 63146. **Tel** (800)325-4177, (314)872-8370, FAX (314)432-1380, telex 44-2402. **LC** RF1; .A33. **DD** 617/.51. **NLM** W1; AD698. **[CCC].**

US/0748-5212
**ADVANCES IN PLASTIC AND RECONSTRUCTIVE SURGERY.** [Adv. plast. reconstr. surg.]. **VFOAT** Plastic and Reconstructive Surgery. Vol. 1 (1984)-. Periodical. English. an. $77.00. Mosby Year Book Inc., 11830 Westline Industrial Drive, St Louis MO 63146. **Tel** (800)325-4177, (314)872-8370, FAX (314)432-1380, telex 44-2402. **LC** RD118.A1; A38. **DD** 617/.95. **NLM** W1; AD78P. **[CCC].**

US/0065-3411
**ADVANCES IN SURGERY (CHICAGO).** (ADVANCES IN SURGERY.). [Adv. surg.]. Vol. 1 (1965)-. English. an. Price varies. Mosby Year Book Inc., 11830 Westline Industrial Drive, St Louis MO 63146. **Tel** (800)325-4177, (314)872-8370, FAX (314)432-1380, telex 44-2402. **ED** Ronald K. Tompkins. **LC** RD1; .A27. **DD** 617.007. **NLM** W1 AD877. **[CCC].** available on microfilm from University Microfilms International (UMI).
**Desc:** Covers all the latest advancements in the field of surgery.
**Ind/Abst** Energy Res. Abstr. (Aug. 1982-); Health Plan. Adminis.; Index Med.

●US/1069-7292
**ADVANCES IN VASCULAR SURGERY.** (1993)-. English. an. $69.95. Mosby Year Book Inc., 11830 Westline Industrial Drive, St Louis MO 63146. **Tel** (800)325-4177, (314)872-8370, FAX (314)432-1380, telex 44-2402.

US/0364-216X
**AESTHETIC PLASTIC SURGERY.** [Aesthet. plast. surg.]. **Added/Corp** International Society of Aesthetic Plastic Surgery. Vol. 1 (1976)-. Periodical. English. Six times a year. $257.00. Springer-Verlag New York Inc., 175 5th Avenue, New York NY 10010. **Tel** (212)460-1500, telex 232 235 SPB UR. **(Subscription address:** Springer Verlag New York Inc. / for North America, 44 Hartz Way, Secaucus NJ 07096.**)** **ED** B O Rogers. **LC** RD119; .A36. **DD** 617/.95/005. **NLM** W1 AE957. **[CCC].** **Pr Rev.** available on microfilm and microfiche from University Microfilms International (UMI). Documents available from The Genuine Article.
**Desc:** Devoted to aesthetic surgery of the entire body surface, including facial surgery, body surgery, and extremity surgery.
**Ind/Abst** Curr. Contents Clin. Med.; EMBASE; Health Plan. Adminis.; Index Med.; INIS Atomindex [Micro.]; Med. Abstr. Newsl.; Life Sci. Collect.; Res. Alert [Select. Cov.]; SCISEARCH.

IT/0393-3873
**AGGIORNAMENTI IN CHIRURGIA GENERALE.** ***Ceased.*** [Aggiorn. chir. gen.]. Periodical. Italian. bm. Soc Edit Universo, Via G B Morgagni 1, Rome 00161 Italy. **UDC** 616-089. **NLM** W1 AG336C.

GW/0001-785X
**AKTUELLE CHIRURGIE.** [Aktuel. chir.]. (1974)-. Academic Scholarly Publication. German. bm (6 issues). $200.00. Georg Thieme Verlag Stuttgart, Postfach 301120, D 70451 Stuttgart Germany. **Tel** 011 49 711 89310, FAX 011 49 711 8931298, telex 7 252 275 GTVD. **(Subscription address:** Thieme Medical Publishers Inc., 381 Park Avenue South, New York NY 10016.**)** **NLM** W1 AK991C. **[CCC].** cum. index. available on microfilm from University Microfilms International (UMI). ***Continues*** *Actuelle Chirurgie.*
**Ind/Abst** EMBASE; Life Sci. Collect.

SZ/0378-8504
**AKTUELLE PROBLEME IN CHIRURGIE UND ORTHOPADIE.** [Aktuelle Probl. Chir. Orthop.]. Vol. 1 (1977)-. Monographic series. German. ir. Price varies per volume. Verlag Hans Huber Ag Bern, Laenggass Strasse 76, CH 3000 Bern 9 Switzerland. **Tel** 011 41 31 3004500. **NLM** W1 AK995R. ***Supersedes*** *Aktuelle Probleme in der Chirurgie, 0065-5589.*
**Ind/Abst** Health Plan. Adminis.; Index Med.

●UK/0966-6532
**AMBULATORY SURGERY.** Vol. 1, No. 1 (1993)-. English. qt. $179.00 The Americas; £120.00 other. Butterworth Heinemann Publishers, Linacre House, Jordan Hill, Oxford OX2 8DP England. **Tel** 011 44 865 310366. **(Subscription address:** Elsevier Science Ltd. Oxford Fulfillment Centre, PO Box 800, Kidlington, Oxford OX5 1DX United Kingdom.**)** **ED** Paul E.M. Jarrett, UK; Bernard Wetchler, US. Index available ((bound in last issue of calendar year)). **Pr Rev.**
**Desc:** Provides an efficient and flexible approach to the provision of many surgical and therapeutic procedures. It will promote and develop this system of patient management by providing a multidisciplinary international forum for all health care professionals involved in day-care surgery.

US/0748-8068
**AMERICAN JOURNAL OF COSMETIC SURGERY, THE.** (THE AMERICAN JOURNAL OF COSMETIC SURGERY : JOURNAL OF THE AMERICAN SOCIETY OF COSMETIC SURGEONS [AND] OFFICIAL PUBLICATION OF THE AMERICAN SOCIETY OF LIPO-SUCTION SURGERY.). [Am. j. cosmet. surg.]. **Added/Corp** American Academy of Cosmetic Surgery. American Society of Lipo-Suction Surgery. American Society of Cosmetic Surgeons. Vol. 1, No. 1 (Winter 1984)-. Periodical. English. qt (4 issues). $75.00 US; $85.00 other; Free to members of The American Academy of Cosmetic Surgery and The American Society of Lipo- Suction Surgery. American Academy of Cosmetic Surgery Inc, 401 North Michigan Avenue, Chicago IL 60611-4267. **Tel** (312)527-6713, FAX (312)321-6869. **ED** Richard Aronsohn. **DD** 617. **NLM** W1; AM45LM. Index available (included free). **Bk Rev. Ad Acc. Circ:** 5,000 (ctrl).
**Desc:** Only medical journal devoted exclusively to cosmetic surgery. In addition to the clinical and scientific articles presented, each issue will include a "Message from the President", a section dealing with the history of cosmetic surgery, announcements, news items and editorial opinions of interest and pertinence to the cosmetic surgery community.

US/0899-7403
**AMERICAN JOURNAL OF KNEE SURGERY, THE.** [Am. j. knee surg.]. **VFOAT** Knee Surgery. Vol. 1 No. 1 (Jan. 1988)-. Periodical. English. qt. 125.00 institution; $110.00 individual (US). Slack Inc., 6900 Grove Road, Thorofare NJ 08086. **Tel** (609)848-1000, (800)257-8290, FAX (609)853-5991, telex 517108 SLACK INC VD. **DD** 617. **NLM** W1; AM473H. available on microfilm from University Microfilms International (UMI).

US/0002-9610
**AMERICAN JOURNAL OF SURGERY, THE.** [Am. j. surg.]. Vol. 18 (April 1905)-. Academic Scholarly Publication. English. mo. $120.00 (institutions), $80.00 (individuals). Excerpta Medica / US, PO Box 3085, Princeton NJ 08543-3085. **Tel** (908)874-8550, FAX (908)874-5611. **(Subscription address:** American Journal of Surgery, PO Box 7724, Riverton NJ 08077-7724.**)** **ED** Gail Bonfante. **LC** RD1; .A37. **DD** 617. **NLM** W1 AM523. **CODEN** AJSUAB. cum. index. **Pr Rev.** available on microfilm and microfiche from University Microfilms International (UMI). Documents available from The Genuine Article, CASDDS. ***Continues*** *American Surgery and Gynecology, 0271-6402.*
**Desc:** Specializes in clinical papers on general surgery. Keeps the busy surgeon up-to-date on the latest operative techniques and procedures.
**Ind/Abst** Abr. Index Med.; Chem. Abstr.; Curr. Aware. Biol. Sci., CABS; Curr. Contents Clin. Med.; Curr. Contents Life Sci.; Dairy Sci. Abstr.; EMBASE; Energy Res. Abstr.; Health Index (1989-); Health Period. Database [Full Txt.]; Health Plan. Adminis.; Helminthol. Abstr. (1991-); Index Med.; INIS Atomindex [Micro.]; Iowa Drug Inf. Serv. (1967-); Med. Abstr. Newsl.; Microbiol. Abstr. Sect. B; Mod. Med.; Nutr. Abstr. Rev., Ser. B, Live Feeds and Feed.; Nutr. Abstr. Rev., Ser. A, Hum. Exp.; Life Sci. Collect.; Physic. Medline Plus; Protozoolog. Abstr.; Ref. Upd. Deluxe Ed.; Res. Alert [Full Cov.]; Rev. Med. Vet. Mycology; Rev. Plant Pathol.; Saf. Health Work; Sci. Cit. Index; SCISEARCH; Soc. Sci. Cit. Index [Select. Cov.].

US/0147-5185
**AMERICAN JOURNAL OF SURGICAL PATHOLOGY, THE.** **See** Medical Science and Technology-Pathology.

US/0003-1348
**AMERICAN SURGEON, THE.** [Am. surgeon]. **Added/Corp** Southeastern Surgical Congress. North Pacific Surgical Association (U.S.) Midwest Surgical Association. American College of Surgeons. Southern California Chapter. Vol. 17 (Jan. 1951)-. Academic Scholarly Publication. English. mo. $155.00 (institution), $95.00 (individual) US; $180.00 (institution), $120.00 (individual) other, except Japan. Southeaster Surgical Congress, 1776 Peachtree Street, Suite 410N, Atlanta GA 30309. **Tel** (404)607-8958. **(Subscription address:** Fulco, 30 Broad Street, Denville NJ 07834.**)** **ED** Arlie R. Mansberger. **LC** RD1; .S77. **NLM** W1 AM816. **CODEN** AMSUAW. **[CCC].** Index available (bound in Dec. issue). **Pr Rev. Circ:** 3,800. available on microfilm and microfiche from University Microfilms International (UMI). Documents available from The Genuine Article, BIOSIS Document Express. ***Continues*** *Southern Surgeon.*
**Desc:** Official publication of the Southeastern Surgical Congress, the Midwest Surgical Association, and the Association of Clinical Anatomists. Clinical articles cover the spectrum of general and thoracic surgery.
**Ind/Abst** Biol. Abstr.; Curr. Contents Clin. Med.; EMBASE; Energy Res. Abstr.; Health Plan. Adminis.; Index Med.; INIS Atomindex [Micro.]; Int. Aerosp. Abstr.; Nutr. Abstr. Rev., Ser. B, Live Feeds and Feed.; Nutr. Abstr. Rev., Ser. A, Hum. Exp.; Life Sci. Collect.; Res. Alert [Full Cov.]; Sci. Cit. Index; SCISEARCH; Soc. Sci. Cit. Index [Select. Cov.].

AG/0066-1465
**ANALES DE CIRUGIA.** V. 1- June 1935-. Periodical. Spanish. an. Calle Paraguay No 40, Rosario Argentina. **UDC** 616-089. **NLM** W1 AN142L.

SP/0210-7058
**ANALES DE LA REAL ACADEMIA DE MEDICINA Y CIRUGIA DE CADIZ.** [An. R. Acad. Med. Cir. Cadiz]. (1967)-. Periodical. Spanish. sa. Real Academia de Medicina y Cirugia de Cadiz, 11071 Cadiz Spain. **UDC** 61.

SP/0210-6523
**ANALES DE LA REAL ACADEMIA DE MEDICINA Y CIRUGIA DE VALLADOLID.** [An. R. Acad. Med. Cir. Valladolid]. (1963)-. Periodical. Spanish. qt. Real Academia de Medicina y Cirugia de Valldolid, J de Miguel, Plaza de Libertad 1, 47002 Valladolid Spain. **UDC** 61.

US/1057-4131
**ANALGESIA COMPUTERFILE.** (ANALGESIA COMPUTERFILE [COMPUTER FILE].). [Analg. computerFile]. **Added/Corp** Dannemiller Memorial Educational Foundation. **VFOAT** Analgesia Computer File. (1991)-. English. mo. $235.00 (5-1/4 in. disk), $245.00 (3-1/2 in. disk) US; $245.00 (5-1/4 in. disk), $255.00 (3-1/2 in. disk) Canada. Dannemiller Memorial Educational Foundation, 12500 Network Boulevard, Suite 101, San Antonio TX 78249-3302. **Tel** (800)328-2308, (512)641-8329. **DD** 617.
**Desc:** System requirements: IBM MS-DOS or compatibles. Available in 3 1/2" or 5 1/4" formats.

US/0747-4679
**ANESTHESIOLOGY NEWS.** [Anesthesiol. news]. (19??)-. Periodical. English. mo. $55.00 US; $79.00 other. McMahon Publishing Company, 148 West 24th Street, 8th Floor, New York NY 10011. **Tel** (212)620-4600, FAX (212)620-5928.
**Ind/Abst** Health Devices Alerts.

FR/0003-3944
**ANNALES DE CHIRURGIE.** [Ann. chir.]. **VFOAT** Annales de Chirurgie Thoracique et Cardiovasculaire. Vol. 3 (1950)-. Academic Scholarly Publication. French (summaries and/or abstracts in English). Ten times a year. 1100.00F France; 1520.00F other. Semaine de Hopitaux, 31 Boulevard de la Tour-Maubourg, 75007 Paris, France. **Tel** 011 33 1 40 62 64 00. **NLM** W1 AN327L. **[CCC].** **Bk Rev. Ad Acc. Pr Rev. Circ:** 3,000. Documents available from The Genuine Article. ***Continues*** *Cahiers et Annales de Chirurgie.*
**Ind/Abst** Curr. Contents Clin. Med.; EMBASE; Health Plan. Adminis.; Helminthol. Abstr. (19??-19??); Index Med.; Nutr. Abstr. Rev., Ser. A, Hum. Exp.; Life Sci. Collect.; Res. Alert [Select. Cov.]; SCISEARCH; Soc. Sci. Cit. Index [Select. Cov.].

FR/1153-2424
**ANNALES DE CHIRURGIE DE LA MAIN ET DU MEMBRE SUPERIEUR.** [Ann. chir. main memb. super.]. **Added/Corp** Belgian Hand Group.

Groupe d'Etude de la Main. Societe Suisse de Chirurgie de la Main. **VFOAT** Annals of Hand and Upper Limb Surgery. (1990)-. Periodical. French (English; summaries and/or abstracts in English, French and Spanish; table of contents in English and French). Five times a year. 1150.00F (individuals), 1560.00F (institutions) France; 1380.00F (individuals), 1940.00F (institutions) other. Semaine de Hopitaux, 31 Boulevard de la Tour-Maubourg, 75007 Paris, France. **Tel** 011 33 1 40 62 64 00. **NLM** W1; AN327LP. **CODEN** AMSPEL. Documents available from BIOSIS Document Express. ***Continues*** *Annales de Chirurgie de la Main, 0753-9053.*
**Ind/Abst** Biol. Abstr. (1991-); EMBASE; Health Plan. Adminis.; Index Med. (1990-).

FR/0003-3960
**ANNALES DE CHIRURGIE PLASTIQUE ET ESTHETIQUE.** [Ann. chir. plast. esthet.]. **Added/Corp** Societe Francaise de Chirurgie Plastique Reconstructrice et Esthetique. Vol. 28, No. 1, (1983)-. Periodical. French (summaries and/or abstracts in English). bm (6 issues). 1400.00F France; $1630.00 other. Semaine de Hopitaux, 31 Boulevard de la Tour-Maubourg, 75007 Paris, France. **Tel** 011 33 1 40 62 64 00. **NLM** W1; AN328D. ***Continues*** *Annales de Chirurgie Plastique, 0003-3960.*
**Ind/Abst** EMBASE; Health Plan. Adminis.; Index Med.; SCISEARCH.

FR/0066-2054
**ANNALES DE CHIRURGIE THORACIQUE ET CARDIOVASCULAIRE.** **Added/Corp** Societe de Chirurgie Thoracique de Langue Francaise. Vol. 1 (April 1962)-. Periodical. French. sa. Expansion Scientifique Francaise, 31 Boulevard de la Tour-Maubourg, 75007 Paris France. **Tel** 011 33 1 40 62 64 00, 011 33 1 40626439. **NLM** W1 AN327L. **CODEN** ACSSBP. Documents available from BIOSIS Document Express.
**Ind/Abst** Biol. Abstr.; Health Plan. Adminis.; Index Med.

FR/0299-2213
**ANNALES DE CHIRURGIE VASCULAIRE.** [Ann. chir. vasc.]. **VFOAT** Annals of Vascular Surgery. (1986)-. Periodical. French. bm. 1011.80F (institutions), 674.54F (individuals) EEC; 1500.00F (institutions), 1000.00F (individuals) other. GRP Hospital Pitie Salp, M. Kieffer Hopital, Chirurgie Vasculaire, Boulevard de l'Hopital, 75651 Paris Cedex 13 France. **Tel** 011 33 1 45702528. **UDC** 617.

IT/0003-469X
**ANNALI ITALIANI DI CHIRURGIA.** [Ann. Ital. chir.]. Vol. 1, (Jan. 1922)-. Academic Scholarly Publication. Italian (English). Six times a year. $100.00. GEM Srl Nuova Cappelli, Via Farini 14, 40124 Bologna Italy. **Tel** 011 39 51 239060. **ED** Nicola Picardi. **NLM** W1 AN541. **CODEN** AICHAL. Index available. cum. index. **Bk Rev**. **Ad Acc. Circ:** 2,000 (ctrl). Documents available from BIOSIS Document Express.
**Desc:** Covers general surgery.
**Ind/Abst** Biol. Abstr.; EMBASE; Index Med.

II/0970-2121
**ANNALS OF PAEDIATRIC SURGERY.**
**See** Medical Science and Technology-Pediatrics.

US/0148-7043
**ANNALS OF PLASTIC SURGERY.** [Ann. plast. surg.]. Vol. 1 (Jan. 1978)-. Periodical. English. mo. $235.00 (institutions), $161.00 (individuals) US; $265.00 (institutions), $186.00 (individuals) Canada; $323.00 (institutions), $245.00 (individuals) other. Little Brown & Company, 34 Beacon Street, Boston MA 02108. **Tel** (617)227-0730, (800)759-0190. **(Subscription address:** Little Brown and Company, PO Box 7671, Riverton NJ 08077-7671.**)** **ED** Lars M. Vistnes. **LC** RD118.AI; A66. **DD** 617/.95/005. **NLM** W1 AN62L. **CODEN** APCSD4. **[CCC]**. **Bk Rev**. **Ad Acc**. **Pr Rev. Circ:** 4,000. available on microfilm and microfiche from University Microfilms International (UMI). Documents available from The Genuine Article, BIOSIS Document Express.
**Desc:** For the worldwide community of plastic surgery and related disciplines. Presents original articles on clinical, plastic and reconstructive surgery.
**Ind/Abst** Biol. Abstr.; Cumul. Index Nurs. Allied Health Lit.; Curr. Contents Clin. Med.; EMBASE; Energy Res. Abstr. (May 1981-); Health Devices Alerts; Health Plan. Adminis.; Index Med. (1978-); INIS Atomindex [Micro.]; Res. Alert [Full Cov.]; Rev. Med. Vet. Entomol.; Sci. Cit. Index; SCISEARCH.

US/0003-4932
**ANNALS OF SURGERY.** [Ann. surg.]. **Added/Corp** American Surgical Association. New York Surgical Society. Philadelphia Academy of Surgery. Southern Surgical Association (U.S.) Central Surgical Association. Vol. 1 (Jan. 1885)-. Academic Scholarly Publication. English. mo. $99.00 (individuals), $183.00 (institutions) US; $164.00 (individuals), $233.00 (institutions) other. J.B. Lippincott Company, 227 East Washington Square, Philadelphia PA 19106-3780. **Tel** (215)238-4200 or 4454, FAX (215)238-4227. **(Subscription address:** J.B. Lippincott, PO Box 350, Hagerstown MD 21740.**)** **ED** Jackie Spargo. **LC** RD1; .A5. **DD** 617/.005. **NLM** W1 AN626. **CODEN** ANSUA5. **[CCC]**. cum. index. **Pr Rev**. available on microfilm and microfiche from University Microfilms International (UMI). Documents available from The Genuine Article, BIOSIS Document Express, CASDDS.
**Desc:** Includes the transactions of the American Surgical Association, New York Surgical Society, Philadelphia Academy of Surgery, Southern Surgical Association, and Central Surgical Association.
**Ind/Abst** Abr. Index Med.; Biol. Abstr.; Chem. Abstr.; Curr. Contents Clin. Med.; Curr. Contents Life Sci.; EMBASE; Energy Res. Abstr.; Health Devices Alerts; Health Period. Database; Health Plan. Adminis.; Index Med.; INIS Atomindex [Micro.]; Int. Aerosp. Abstr.; Iowa Drug Inf. Serv. (1967-); Med. Abstr. Newsl.; Mod. Med.; Nutr. Abstr. Rev., Ser. B, Live Feeds and Feed.; Nutr. Abstr. Rev., Ser. A, Hum. Exp.; Life Sci. Collect.; Physic. Medline Plus; Protozoolog. Abstr.; Ref. Upd. Basic Ed.; Ref. Upd. Deluxe Ed.; Res. Alert [Full Cov.]; Sci. Cit. Index; SCISEARCH; Soc. Sci. Cit. Index [Select. Cov.].

•US/1068-9265
**ANNALS OF SURGICAL ONCOLOGY.** [Ann. surg. oncol.]. **Added/Corp** Society of Surgical Oncology, Inc. Vol. 1, No. 1 (1994)-. Periodical. English. bm. $126.00 (individual), $184.00 (institutional) US; $148.00 (individual), $205.00 (institutional) other. Raven Press, 1185 Avenue of the Americas, 37th Floor, New York NY 10036. **Tel** (212)930-9500, (212)930-9604, FAX (212)869-3495, (212)302-8507, telex 640073. **DD** 616. **NLM** W1; AN626HG.

UK/0035-8843
**ANNALS OF THE ROYAL COLLEGE OF SURGEONS OF ENGLAND.** [Ann. R. Coll. Surg. Engl.]. **Main/Corp** Royal College of Surgeons of England. Vol. 1, (July 1947)-. Periodical. English. Six times a year. $95.00 UK & Ireland; $105.00 other. Headley Brothers Ltd., The Invicta Press, Queens Road, Ashford Kent TN24 8HH England. **Tel** 011 44 233 623131. **ED** R.M. Kirk. **NLM** W1 AN627E. **CODEN** ARCSAF. Index available in last issue of volume--attached. cum. index. **Bk Rev**. **Ad Acc**. **Pr Rev. Circ:** 9,000. available on microfilm from University Microfilms International (UMI). Documents available from The Genuine Article, BIOSIS Document Express.
**Desc:** Reports clinical advances in all forms of surgery and dental surgery.
**Ind/Abst** Biol. Abstr.; Cumul. Index Nurs. Allied Health Lit.; Curr. Contents Clin. Med.; EMBASE; Health Devices Alerts; Health Plan. Adminis.; Helminthol. Abstr. (1991-); Index Med.; Nutr. Abstr. Rev., Ser. B, Live Feeds and Feed.; Nutr. Abstr. Rev., Ser. A, Hum. Exp.; Life Sci. Collect.; Protozoolog. Abstr.; Res. Alert [Full Cov.]; Sci. Cit. Index; SCISEARCH; Soc. Sci. Cit. Index [Select. Cov.].

US/0003-4975
**ANNALS OF THORACIC SURGERY, THE.** [Ann. thorac. surg.]. **Added/Corp** Society of Thoracic Surgeons. Southern Thoracic Surgical Association. Vol. 1 (Jan. 1965)-. Academic Scholarly Publication. English. mo (2 volumes). $240.00 Us; $323.00 Europe; $345.00 Japan; $282.00 (surface*mail) other. Elsevier Science Publishing Company Inc, Madison Square Station, PO Box 882, New York NY 10159-0882. **Tel** (212)633-3950, FAX (212)633-3990. **ED** Thomas B Ferguson. **LC** RD536; .A75. **DD** 617/.374/005. **NLM** W1 AN627H. **CODEN** ATHSAK. **[CCC]**. **Bk Rev**. **Ad Acc**. **Pr Rev. Circ:** 7,600. available on microfilm and microfiche from University Microfilms International (UMI). Documents available from The Genuine Article, BIOSIS Document Express.
**Desc:** Timely articles by outstanding cardiovascular and thoracic surgeons in the U.S. and abroad, including how-to articles on surgical techniques.
**Ind/Abst** Abr. Index Med.; Biol. Abstr.; Cumul. Index Nurs. Allied Health Lit.; Curr. Contents Clin. Med.; Curr. Contents Life Sci.; EMBASE; Energy Res. Abstr.; Health Devices Alerts; Health Period. Database; Health Plan. Adminis.; Helminthol. Abstr. (1991-); Index Med.; INIS Atomindex [Micro.]; Iowa Drug Inf. Serv. (1969-); Med. Abstr. Newsl.; Life Sci. Collect.; Physic. Medline Plus; Protozoolog. Abstr.; Ref. Upd. Basic Ed.; Ref. Upd. Deluxe Ed.; Res. Alert [Full Cov.]; Rev. Med. Vet. Mycology; Rev. Plant Pathol.; Sci. Cit. Index; SCISEARCH.

US/0890-5096
**ANNALS OF VASCULAR SURGERY.** [Ann. vasc. surg.]. **Added/Corp** French Society for Vascular Surgery. German Society for Vascular Surgery. Peripheral Vascular Surgery Society, USA. Association pour la Promotion de la Chirurgie Vasculaire, Paris. Vol. 1, No. 1 (May 1986)-. English (summaries and/or abstracts in French). bm. $135.00 (institutions), $75.00 (individuals) US; $150.00 (institutions), $85.00 (individuals) Canada and Mexico; $175.00 (institutions), $110.00 (individuals) other. Quality Medical Publishing, 11970 Borman Drive, Suite 222, St. Louis MO 63146. **Tel** (314)878-7808, (800)423-6865, FAX (314)878-9937. **(Subscription address:** UK/ Marston Book Services, PO Box 87, Oxford UK; Aus/ 54 University Street, Carlton Victoria 3053 Australia; Germany/ Meinekestrasse 4, D-1000 Berlin 15 Germany; France/ Arnette, 2 rue Casimir Delavigne, 75006 Paris France; Austria/ Blackwell MZV, Medizinische Zeitschriftenverlags Gesellschaft, Feldgasse 13, A-1238 Vienna Austria**)** **DD** 617. **NLM** W1; AN630. **CODEN** AVSUEV. **Ad Acc**. available on microfilm and microfiche from University Microfilms International (UMI).
**Desc:** For vascular surgeons and physicians and health care professionals in allied fields.
**Ind/Abst** EMBASE; Health Plan. Adminis.; Index Med.; Indice Med. Esp.

US
**ANNUAL MEETING OF NORDISK NEUROKIRURGISK FORENING, THE.** **Added/Corp** Scandinavian Neurosurgical Society. (1949)-. Periodical. English. **NLM** W1 AN754Q.

UK/0952-0562
**ANNUAL OF CARDIAC SURGERY.** (1989)-. English. an. $142.45. Current Science / England, Middlesex House, 34-42 Cleveland Street, London W1P 5FB England. **Tel** 011 44 71 580 8393, 011 44 71 323 0323, FAX 011 44 81 580 1938. **(Subscription address:** Current Science, 20 North 3rd Street, Philadelphia PA 19106.**)** **ED** Magdi Yacoub and J. Pepper. **NLM** W1; AN755Q. **Ad Acc**. **Circ:** 3,000 (ctrl).
**Desc:** Targeted toward cardiac surgeons, cardiologists and researchers involved with coronary artery disease. Reviews important papers of each year and presents invited reviews in featured areas such as pediatric and fetal cardiac surgery.

US/0001-2092
**AORN JOURNAL.** **See** Medical Science and Technology-Nursing.

SP/0213-0645
**APARATO LOCOMOTOR.** **See** Medical Science and Technology-Orthopedics.

JA/0003-9152
**ARCHIV FUER JAPANISCHE CHIRURGIE. NIPPON GEKA HOKAN.** [Arch. Jap. Chir.]. **Added/Corp** Kyoto. University. Dept. of Medicine. **VFOAT** Nippon Geka Hokan.; Nihon Geka Hokan. (1924)-. Academic Scholarly Publication. Multiple languages (summaries and/or abstracts in English and German; table of contents in English and German). bm. $124.50. Nihon Geka Ho Kan Henshushitsu, 54 Shogoin Kawaracho, Sakyo-ku, 606 Kyoto Japan. **(Subscription address:** Japan Publications Trading Company, Ltd., PO Box 5030, Tokyo International, Tokyo 100-31 Japan.**)** **NLM** W1 NI898M. **CODEN** NIGHAE. Documents available from BIOSIS Document Express, CASDDS.
**Ind/Abst** Biol. Abstr.; Chem. Abstr.; EMBASE; Health Plan. Adminis.; Index Med.; Life Sci. Collect.

GW/0936-8051
**ARCHIVES OF ORTHOPAEDIC AND TRAUMA SURGERY.** [Arch. orthop. trauma surg.]. **VFOAT** Archives of Orthopedic and Trauma Surgery. Vol. 108, No. 1 (1989)-. Periodical. English. bm. DM778.00. Springer-Verlag GmbH & Company KG, Heidelberger Platz 3, D 14197 Berlin Germany. **Tel** 011 49 30 8207223, FAX 011 49 30 8214091, telex 183 319 SPBLN D. **(Subscription address:** Springer Verlag New York Inc. / for North America, 44 Hartz Way, Secaucus NJ 07096.**)** **ED** H Wagner. **NLM** W1; AR464M. **CODEN** AOTSEF. available on microfilm from University Microfilms International (UMI). Documents available from The Genuine Article, BIOSIS Document Express. ***Continues*** *Archives of Orthopedics and Traumatic Surgery, 0344-8444.*
**Desc:** Gives quick access to some of the most original thinking going on in the field today. The clinically and most relative manuscripts from around the world are included.
**Ind/Abst** Biol. Abstr. (1989-); Calcium Calcif. Tissue Abstr.; Curr. Contents Clin. Med.; EMBASE; Health Plan. Adminis.; Index Med. (1989-); Res. Alert [Full Cov.]; Sci. Cit. Index; SCISEARCH.

US/0004-0010
**ARCHIVES OF SURGERY (CHICAGO. 1960).** (ARCHIVES OF SURGERY.). [Arch. surg.]. **Added/Corp** American Medical Association. Central Surgical Association. Western Surgical Association. International Cardiovascular Society. Vol. 81 (July 1960)-. Academic Scholarly Publication. English. mo. $115.00 (institution), $100.00 (individual) US. American Medical Association, 515 North State Street, Chicago IL 60610. **Tel** (312)464-5000, (800)262-2350, FAX (312)464-5831. **ED** Arthur E. Bave. **NLM** W1 A139. **CODEN** ARSUAX. **[CCC]**. Index available (Free). **Ad Acc**. **Pr Rev. Circ:** 43,000. available on microfilm and microfiche from University Microfilms International (UMI); available on an online database (file 442/Full-Text) from DIALOG; and MEDIS. Documents available from The Genuine Article, BIOSIS Document Express, CASDDS. ***Continues*** *A.M.A. Archives of Surgery, 0096-6908.*
**Desc:** Published as an educational service for physicians who practice surgery as a primary specialty, and for physicians of other specialties who practice surgery to some degree. It focuses on clinical activities and research, emphasizing information that is useful and worthwhile in direct patient care.
**Ind/Abst** Abr. Index Med.; Biol. Abstr.; Chem. Abstr.; Cumul. Index Nurs. Allied Health Lit.; Curr. Contents Clin. Med.; Curr. Contents Life Sci.; EMBASE; Energy Res. Abstr.; Health Devices Alerts; Health Period. Database; Health Plan. Adminis.; Helminthol. Abstr.; Immunol. Abstr.; Index Med.; INIS Atomindex [Micro.]; Int. Nurs. Index; Iowa Drug Inf. Serv. (1969-); Med. Abstr. Newsl.; Microbiol. Abstr. Sect. B; Mod. Med.; Nutr. Abstr. Rev.,

Ser. B, Live Feeds and Feed.; Nutr. Abstr. Rev., Ser. A, Hum. Exp.; Life Sci. Collect.; Physic. Medline Plus; Protozoolog. Abstr.; Ref. Upd. Basic Ed.; Ref. Upd. Deluxe Ed.; Res. Alert [Full Cov.]; Rev. Med. Vet. Mycology; Risk Abstr.; Saf. Health Work; Sci. Cit. Index; SCISEARCH; Soc. Sci. Cit. Index [Select. Cov.].

IT/0004-007X
**ARCHIVIO DI CHIRURGIA TORACICA E CARDIOVASCOLARE.** [Arch. chir. torac. cardiovasc.]. **Added/Corp** Societa Italiana di Chirugia Cardiaca e Vascolare. (1966)-. Periodical. Italian. bm. L100000 (Italy); $120.00 (other). Edizioni Luigi Pozzi Srl, Via Panama 68, 00198 Rome Italy. **Tel** (06)8553548, FAX (06)8554105. **NLM** W1 AR532. **CODEN** ACTOBI. Documents available from BIOSIS Document Express, CASDDS. ***Continues*** *Archivio di Chirurgia del Torace.*
**Ind/Abst** Biol. Abstr.; Chem. Abstr.; Index Med.

IT/0066-670X
**ARCHIVIO PUTTI DI CHIRURGIA DEGLI ORGANI DI MOVIMENTO.** [Arch. "Putti" chir. org. mov.]. Vol. 1 (1951)-. Academic Scholarly Publication. Italian. sa. $80.00. Aulo Gaggi Editore, Via Andrea Costa 131-5, 40134 Bologna Italy. **Tel** 011 39 51 6142067, telex 43 61 19. **ED** L. Barile, L. D'Elia and G.V. Di Muria. **NLM** W1 AR597. Index available. cum. index. **Bk Rev. Ad Acc. Circ:** 3,000 (ctrl).
**Desc:** Surgery on the moving parts of the body.
**Ind/Abst** EMBASE; Index Med.

IT/0393-6384
**ARCHIVIO SICILIANO DE MEDICINA E CHIRURGIA. 4, ACTA MEDICA MEDITERRANEA.** **VFOAT** Acta Medica Mediterranea. Vol. 1, No. 1 (1985)-. Periodical. Italian (summaries and/or abstracts in English). Six times a year. L40000.00 Italy; L60000.00 other. Edizioni Carbone Alfonsa, Via G Daita 29, 90139 Palermo Italy. **Tel** 011 39 91 321273, FAX 39 91 322736. **ED** Antonino Pennino. **NLM** W1; AR597TBA. **Ad Acc. Circ:** 4,000. ***Continues in part*** *Archivio Siciliano di Medicina e Chirurgia, 0392-2049.*
**Desc:** Covers dermatology, forensic medicine, homeopathy, neurology, otorhinolaryngology, and psychiatry.
**Ind/Abst** Trop. Dis. Bull.

IT
**ARCHIVIO SICILIANO DI MEDICINA E CHIRURGIA. 1, ACTA CHIRURGICA MEDITERRANEA.** **VFOAT** Acta Chirurgica Mediterranea. Vol. 1, No. 1 (1985)-. Periodical. Italian (English). bm. L35000 Italy; L55000 other. Edizioni Carbone Alfonsa, Via G Daita 29, 90139 Palermo Italy. **Tel** 011 39 91 321273, FAX 39 91 322736. **ED** Carmelo Pennino. **NLM** W1; AR597S. **Bk Rev. Ad Acc. Circ:** 4,000 (ctrl). ***Continues in part*** *Archivio Siciliano di Medicina e Chirurgia, 0392-2049.*
**Desc:** Review on surgery: anaesthesia, orthopedics, obstetrics, gynaecology, otorhinolaryngology, imaging, odontostomatology, urology, etc.

BL/0102-6720
**ARQUIVOS BRASILEIROS DE CIRURGIA DIGESTIVA ABCD: BRAZILIAN ARCHIVES OF DIGESTIVE SURGERY.** **Added/Corp** Universidade de Sao Paulo. Disciplina de Cirurgia do Aparelho Digestivo. **VFOAT** ABCD; Brazilian Archives of Digestive Surgery. (198?)-. Periodical. English (summaries and/or abstracts in Portuguese). Four times a year. Cr25.00. Arquivos Brasileiros de Cirurgia Digestiva, Av. Dr. Eneas de Carvalho Aguiar,, 255 - 9 andar, 05403 Sao Paulo Brazil. **Tel** 011 282 8832, FAX 011 883 7720. **ED** Bruno Zilberstein. **NLM** W1; AR868C.
**Desc:** Updates and information on articles of surgical techniques medical progress on the digestive system.
**Ind/Abst** Nutr. Abstr. Rev., Ser. A, Hum. Exp.

US
**ARTHROSCOPY: THE JOURNAL OF ARTHROSCOPIC AND RELATED SURGERY.** English. bm. $170.00 (individual), $235.00 (institution) US; $227.00 (individual), $294.00 (institution) other. W.B. Saunders Company, A Subsidiary of Harcourt Brace Jovanovich, Inc., The Curtis Center/Suite 300, Independence Square West, Philadelphia PA 19106-3399. **Tel** (215)238-7800 or, 5587, FAX (215)238-7883, telex 173146. **(Subscription address:** W. B. Saunders Company / North America Subscriptions, c/o Periodicals, 6277 Sea Harbour Drive, 4th Floor, Orlando FL 32887.**)**

GW/0933-7946
**ARTHROSKOPIE.** **Added/Corp** Deutschsprachige Arbeitsgemeinschaft fuer Arthroskopie. Vol. 1, No. 1 (Apr. 1988)-. Periodical. German. Six times a year. DM288.00. Springer-Verlag GmbH & Company KG, Heidelberger Platz 3, D 14197 Berlin Germany. **Tel** 011 49 30 8207223, FAX 011 49 30 8214091, telex 183 319 SPBLN D. **(Subscription address:** Springer Verlag New York Inc. / for North America, 44 Hartz Way, Secaucus NJ 07096.**) ED** W Glinz, H R Henche, H Hofer, and J Kraemer. **NLM** W1; AR953YS. available on microfilm and microfiche from University Microfilms International (UMI).

US/0160-564X
**ARTIFICIAL ORGANS.** [Artif. organs]. Vol. 1- (Aug. 1977)-. Academic Scholarly Publication. English. mo. $495.00 (institution), $325.00 (individual) US;`$535.00 (institution), $365.00 (individual) other. Blackwell Scientific Publishers, 238 Main Street, Cambridge MA 02142. **Tel** (617)547-7110, (800)835-6770, FAX (617)547-0789. **ED** Yukihiko Nose. **LC** RD130. **DD** 617/.95. **UDC** 616-089.28. **NLM** W1 AR956E. **CODEN** ARORD7. **[CCC]. Pr Rev.** Documents available from The Genuine Article, BIOSIS Document Express, CASDDS.
**Desc:** This journal brings together in one multidisciplinary publication reports of basic and applied research and development in this rapidly expanding field.
**Ind/Abst** Biol. Abstr.; Chem. Abstr.; Curr. Contents Clin. Med.; EMBASE; Health Devices Alerts; Index Med.; Life Sci. Collect.; Res. Alert [Full Cov.]; Sci. Cit. Index; SCISEARCH; Soc. Sci. Cit. Index [Select. Cov.].

●US/1058-2916
**ASAIO JOURNAL (1992).** (ASAIO JOURNAL: A PEER-REVIEWED JOURNAL OF THE AMERICAN SOCIETY FOR ARTIFICIAL INTERNAL ORGANS.). [ASAIO j.]. **Added/Corp** American Society for Artificial Internal Organs. **VAT** American Society for Artificial Internal Organs Journal. Vol. 38, No. 1 (Jan.-Mar. 1992)-. Academic Scholarly Publication. English. qt. $180.00 (individuals), $250.00 (institutions) US; $280.00 (individuals), $370.00 (institutions) other. J.B. Lippincott Company, 227 East Washington Square, Philadelphia PA 19106-3780. **Tel** (215)238-4200 or 4454, FAX (215)238-4227. **(Subscription address:** J.B. Lippincott, PO Box 350, Hagerstown MD 21740.**) ED** Eli A. Friedman. **DD** 617. **NLM** W1; AS111CL. **CODEN** AJOUET. Index available. **Ad Acc, Adv Mgr:** Kathleen Phelan, **Tel** (215)238-4492. **Pr Rev. Circ:** 2465. available on an online database, CD-ROM, magnetic tape, and microfilm from University Microfilms International (UMI). Documents available from The Genuine Article, BIOSIS Document Express, CASDDS. ***Continues*** *ASAIO Transactions, 0889-7190.*
**Desc:** Ideas regarding artificial organ research and development; investigations, laboratory and clinical trials, discussions and opinions.
**Ind/Abst** Biol. Abstr.; Chem. Abstr.; Index Med. (1992-); INIS Atomindex [Micro.]; Res. Alert [Full Cov.].

II/0301-0368
**ASIAN ARCHIVES OF ANAESTHESIOLOGY & RESUSCITATION.** [Asian arch. anaesthesiol. resusc.]. **Added/Corp** Anaesthesiology and Resuscitation Forum. Jawaharlal Institute of Post-Graduate Medical Education and Research. Dept. of Anaesthesiology and Resuscitation. **VFOAT** Asian Archives of Anaesthesiology and Resuscitation. Vol. 2 (July/Aug. 1972)-. Academic Scholarly Publication. English. sa. $90.00. Jawaharlal Institute, Department of Anaesthesiology & Resuscitation, Pondicherry, India. **(Subscription address:** Prints India, 11 Darya Ganj, New Delhi 110002 India.**) NLM** W1 AS139E. **CODEN** AAARDM. Documents available from CASDDS. ***Continues*** *Archives of Anaesthesiology & Resuscitation, 0300-5100.*
**Ind/Abst** Chem. Abstr.

HK/1015-9584
**ASIAN JOURNAL OF SURGERY.** (ASIAN JOURNAL OF SURGERY : OFFICIAL PUBLICATION OF THE ASIAN SURGICAL ASSOCIATION.). [Asian j. surg.]. **Added/Corp** Asian Surgical Association. (19??)-. Periodical. English. Four times a year (Jan., Apr., July, Oct.). $70.00. Asian Surgical Association / Department of Surgery, University of Hong Kong, Queen Mary Hospital, Hong Kong. **Tel** 11 852 5 8192235, FAX 011 852 8551897, telex 71919 CEREB HX. **ED** Dr. Edward Cheuk-seen LAI (phone: 011 852 8554080). **CODEN** AJSUEF. **Ad Acc. Circ:** 1,200. Documents available from BIOSIS Document Express. ***Continues*** *Southeast Asian Journal of Surgery, 0258-3186.*
**Ind/Abst** Biol. Abstr.; EMBASE.

●US/1061-3315
**ATLAS OF THE ORAL AND MAXILLOFACIAL SURGERY CLINICS OF NORTH AMERICA.** [Atlas oral maxillofac. surg. clin. N. Am.]. Vol. 1, No. 1 (Mar. 1993)-. Periodical. English. sa (Mar. and Sept.). $94.00 (nonsubscribers), $74.00 (subscribers) US; $119.00 (nonsubscribers), $99.00 (subscribers) other. W.B. Saunders Company, A Subsidiary of Harcourt Brace Jovanovich, Inc., The Curtis Center/Suite 300, Independence Square West, Philadelphia PA 19106-3399. **Tel** (215)238-7800 or, 5587, FAX (215)238-7883, telex 173146. **(Subscription address:** W. B. Saunders Company / North America Subscriptions, c/o Periodicals, 6277 Sea Harbour Drive, 4th Floor, Orlando FL 32887.**) ED** Dr. Leon A. Assnel. **DD** 617.
**Desc:** Includes articles on the different aspects and problems with maxillofacial surgery. Also contains drawings and photographs.

IT/0390-5527
**ATTUALITA IN CHIRURGIA.** ***Ceased.*** Vol. 1 (1976)-?. Periodical. Italian. ir. Edizioni Luigi Pozzi Srl, Via Panama 68, 00198 Rome Italy. **Tel** (06)8553548, FAX (06)8554105. **ED** G F Fegiz, L Gioffre. **UDC** 616-089.8. **NLM** W1 AT8485. Index available. **Ad Acc. Circ:** 1,000.

AT/0004-8682
**AUSTRALIAN AND NEW ZEALAND JOURNAL OF SURGERY.** (THE AUSTRALIAN AND NEW ZEALAND JOURNAL OF SURGERY.). [Aust. N.Z. j. surg.]. **Added/Corp** Royal Australasian College of Surgeons. **VFOAT** Journal of Surgery. (June 1931)-. Academic Scholarly Publication. English. Four times a year. 276.00Aus$ Australia; $392.00 other. Blackwell Scientific Publications Australia, 54 University Street, PO Box 378, Carlton Victoria 3053 Australia. **Tel** 011 61 3 3470300, FAX 011 61 3 3475001, telex 10716421. **(Subscription address:** UK/ Marston Book Services, PO Box 87, Oxford UK; US/ 3 Cambridge Center, Suite 208, Cambridge MA 02142; Germany Meinekestrasse 4, D-1000 Berlin 15 Germany; France/ Arnette, 2 rue Casimir Delavigne, 75006 Paris France; Austria/ Blackwell MZV, Medizinische Zeitschriftenverlgas Gesellschaft, Feldgasse 13, A-1238 Vienna Austria**) ED** G.J.A Clunie and J. Ludbrook. **NLM** W1 AU499. **CODEN** ANZJA7. **[CCC].** Index available. cum. index. **Bk Rev. Ad Acc. Pr Rev. Circ:** 4,800. available on microfilm and microfiche from University Microfilms International (UMI). Documents available from The Genuine Article, BIOSIS Document Express. ***Continues*** *Journal of the College of Surgeons of Australasia.*
**Desc:** Provides a medium for the publication of original contributions related to clinical practice and/or research in all fields of surgery and related disciplines. It also provides a program of continuing education for surgeons at all levels of experience, and records important events related to the continuing activities and growth of the college.
**Ind/Abst** Biol. Abstr.; Curr. Contents Clin. Med.; EMBASE; Health Devices Alerts; Health Plan. Adminis.; Index Med.; Int. Aerosp. Abstr.; Nutr. Abstr. Rev., Ser. B, Live Feeds and Feed.; Nutr. Abstr. Rev., Ser. A, Hum. Exp.; Life Sci. Collect.; Res. Alert [Select. Cov.]; Rev. Med. Vet. Entomol.; Sci. Cit. Index; SCISEARCH; Soc. Sci. Cit. Index [Select. Cov.]; SportSearch.

SP
**AVANCES EN CIRUGIA.** 1-. Periodical. Spanish. Salvat Editores SA, Calle Mallorca 45-49, Barcelona 08029 Spain. **Tel** 011 34 3 2010911, FAX 011 34 3 321-0565, telex SAEDI E 53132. **(Subscription address:** Salvat Publicaciones Cientificas SA, Avda Burgos 19 50 D, Madrid 28036 Spain**) UDC** 616-089.8. **NLM** W1; AD407K.

SP/0304-4475
**BARCELONA QUIRURGICA.** [Barcelona quir.]. (1957)-. Periodical. Spanish. sm (24 issues per year). 4000ptas. Editorial Rocas SA, Muntaner 393, Pral 2A Desp 4A, 08021 Barcelona Spain. **Tel** 011 34 3 200-1389. **UDC** 617. **Ad Acc. Circ:** 3,500 (ctrl).
**Ind/Abst** Indice Med. Esp.

SZ/1013-7459
**BASLER BEITRAEGE ZUR CHIRURGIE.** [Basl. Beitr. Chir.]. Vol. 1 (Oct. 2, 1988)-. Monographic series. German. an. $80.00 (approx. per volume). Schwabe & Company Ltd., Farnsburgerstrasse 8 PF 254, CH-4132 Muttenz 1 Switzerland. **Tel** 011 41 61 4613001, FAX 01 41 61 4612500. **ED** U Laffer. **CODEN** BBCHEL. cum. index. Documents available from BIOSIS Document Express.
**Ind/Abst** Biol. Abstr. (1989-).

JA/0287-1645
**BESSATSU SEIKEI GEKA.** [Bessatsu seikei geka]. **VFOAT** Seikei Geka; Orthopedic Surgery. No. 1 (1982)-. Periodical. Japanese. mo. $470.50. Nankodo, (Nankodo Co., Ltd.), 42-6, Hongo 3 Chome, Bunkyoku, Tokyoto 113 Japan. **(Subscription address:** Japan Publications Trading Company, Ltd., PO Box 5030, Tokyo International, Tokyo 100-31 Japan.**) NLM** W1 BE954F. **CODEN** SEGEAW. **Bk Rev. Ad Acc. Circ:** 9,000. Documents available from BIOSIS Document Express.
**Desc:** The number one Japanese journal on orthopedic surgery.
**Ind/Abst** Biol. Abstr.

US
**BINOCULAR VISION & EYE MUSCLE SURGERY QUARTERLY.** **See** Medical Science and Technology-Ophthalmology.

●US/1065-2523
**BODY CONTOURING SURGERY.** (1993)-. Periodical. English. Three times a year. $195.00. Field & Wood, Inc., 4156 Manayunk Avenue, Philadelphia PA 19128. **Tel** (215)828-4010.

AG
**BOLETINES Y TRABAJOS - ACADEMIA ARGENTINA DE CIRUGIA.** **Added/Corp** Academia Argentina de Cirugia. Vol. 53 (1969)-. Periodical. Spanish. **NLM** W1; BO447. ***Continues*** *Boletines y Trabajos - Sociedad de Cirugia de Buenos Aires.*

IT
**BOLLETTINO DELLA SOCIETA MEDICO CHIRURGICA DELLA PROVINCIA DI CRIMONA. Added/Corp** Societa Medico Chirurgica della Provincia di Cremona. (1983)-. Periodical. Italian (summaries and/or abstracts in English). sa. **NLM** W1; BO489H. ***Continues*** *Bollettino della Societa Medico Chirurgica e Degli Ospedali Provincia di Cremona, 0391-5999.*

IT/0366-1970
**BOLLETTINO E MEMORIE DELLA SOCIETA PIEMONTESE DE CHIRURGIA.** [Boll. Mem. Soc. Piemont. Chir.]. (1931)-. Periodical. Italian. ir. $130.00 (individuals), $160.00 (institutions) Comes with Minerva Chirurgica. Societa Piemontese Chirurgia, CSA A M Dogliotti 14, 10134 Turin Italy. **Tel** 011 39 11 6625523. **CODEN** BOMSALBOMSAL.
**Ind/Abst** EMBASE [Select. Cov.].

UK/0268-8697
**BRITISH JOURNAL OF NEUROSURGERY. See** Medical Science and Technology-Neurology.

UK/0266-4356
**BRITISH JOURNAL OF ORAL & MAXILLOFACIAL SURGERY, THE.** [Br. j. oral maxillofac. surg.]. **Added/Corp** British Association of Oral & Maxillofacial Surgeons. **VFOAT** British Journal of Oral and Maxillofacial Surgery; Oral and Maxillofacial Surgery; Oral & Maxillofacial Surgery. Vol. 22, No. 1 (Feb. 1984)-. Periodical. English. bm. £130.00 Europe; £132.00 Other (Institutions). Churchill Livingstone, 1-3 Baxter's Place, Leith Walk, Edinburgh EH1 3AF Scotland. **Tel** 011 44 31 556 2424, FAX 011 44 31 558 1278, telex 727511. **(Subscription address:** Maruzen Company Ltd., PO Box 5050, Import & Export Department, Tokyo 100 31 Japan.) **ED** M J C Wake. **NLM** W1; BR593. **[CCC]. Pr Rev.** available on microfilm and microfiche from University Microfilms International (UMI). Documents available from The Genuine Article. ***Continues*** *British Journal of Oral Surgery, 0007-117X.*
**Desc:** Presents well-referenced papers on the latest techniques and operative procedures from oral pathologists, plastic and reconstructive surgeons and oral and maxillofacial surgeons throughout the world.
**Ind/Abst** Curr. Contents Clin. Med.; Curr. Titl. Dent.; EMBASE; Index Med.; Life Sci. Collect.; Ref. Upd. Deluxe Ed.; Res. Alert [Full Cov.]; Sci. Cit. Index; SCISEARCH; Soc. Sci. Cit. Index [Select. Cov.]; SportSearch.

UK/0007-1226
**BRITISH JOURNAL OF PLASTIC SURGERY.** [Br. j. plast. surg.]. **Added/Corp** British Association of Plastic Surgeons. Vol. 1 (April 1948)-. Academic Scholarly Publication. English. Eight times a year. £119.00 Europe; £160.44 (air mail), £127.00 (Institutions) Other. Churchill Livingstone, 1-3 Baxter's Place, Leith Walk, Edinburgh EH1 3AF Scotland. **Tel** 011 44 31 556 2424, FAX 011 44 31 558 1278, telex 727511. **(Subscription address:** Maruzen Company Ltd., PO Box 5050, Import & Export Department, Tokyo 100 31 Japan.) **ED** Anthony C H Watson. **NLM** W1 BR613. **CODEN** BJPSAZ. **[CCC]. Bk Rev. Ad Acc. Pr Rev.** available on microfilm and microfiche from University Microfilms International (UMI). Documents available from The Genuine Article, BIOSIS Document Express, CASDDS.
**Desc:** Presents significant findings from international contributors on the latest techniques and procedures, profusely illustrated with useful photographs. Includes a regular book review section to help readers select 'best buys' in the literature of plastic and reconstructive surgery.
**Ind/Abst** Biol. Abstr.; Chem. Abstr.; Curr. Contents Clin. Med.; EMBASE; Health Plan. Adminis.; Helminthol. Abstr.; Index Med.; Life Sci. Collect.; Ref. Upd. Deluxe Ed.; Res. Alert [Full Cov.]; Sci. Cit. Index; SCISEARCH.

UK/0007-1323
**BRITISH JOURNAL OF SURGERY.** [Br. j. surg.]. Vol. 1 (1913)-. Academic Scholarly Publication. English (Spanish). mo (12 issues). $192.00 (institutions), $126.00 (individuals) US & Canada; £110.50 (institutions), £72.00 (individuals) Europe; £192.00 (institutions), £126.00 (individuals) other. Blackwell Scientific Publications Ltd, Marston Book Services, PO Box 87, Oxford OX2 ODT UK. **Tel** 011 44 865 791155, FAX 011 44 865 791927, telex 837 515 MARDIS G. **ED** R. C. G. Russell and D. C. Carter. **NLM** W1 BR638X. **CODEN** BJSUAM. **[CCC].** Index available (bound in last issue). cum. index. **Bk Rev. Ad Acc. Pr Rev. Circ:** 3,000. available on microfilm and microfiche from University Microfilms International (UMI). Documents available from The Genuine Article, BIOSIS Document Express, CASDDS, ADONIS.
**Desc:** International journal of general surgery. Features original and review articles, leading articles, surgical research reports, short notes and case reports. There is a correspondence column, a book review section and a calendar of meetings.
**Ind/Abst** Abr. Index Med.; ADONIS; Biol. Abstr.; Chem. Abstr.; Cumul. Index Nurs. Allied Health Lit.; Curr. Aware. Biol. Sci., CABS; Curr. Contents Clin. Med.; Curr. Contents Life Sci.; EMBASE; Health Period. Database; Health Plan. Adminis.; Helminthol. Abstr. (19??-19??); Hospit. Health Admin. Index; Index Med.; Index Vet.; Microbiol. Abstr. Sect. B (19??-19??); Nutr. Abstr. Rev., Ser. B, Live Feeds and Feed.; Nutr. Abstr. Rev., Ser. A, Hum. Exp.; Life Sci. Collect.; PESTDOC; Physic. Medline Plus; Protozoolog. Abstr.; Ref. Upd. Deluxe Ed.; Res. Alert [Full Cov.]; Rev. Med. Vet. Mycology; Sci. Cit. Index; SCISEARCH; Soc. Sci. Cit. Index [Select. Cov.]; SportSearch; Vet. Bull.

SP
**BRITISH JOURNAL OF SURGERY (SPANISH EDITION), THE.** Spanish. Ediciones Doyma SA, Travesera de Gracia 17 21, 08021 Barcelona Spain. **Tel** 011 34 3 2000711, 011 34 3 4145706, FAX 011 34 3 2091136, telex 51964 INK E.

UK
**BRITISH JOURNAL OF THEATRE NURSING : NATNEWS : THE OFFICIAL JOURNAL OF THE NATIONAL ASSOCIATION OF THEATRE NURSES, THE. See** Medical Science and Technology-Nursing.

FR/0339-9710
**BULLETIN DE L'ACADEMIE NATIONALE DE CHIRURGIE DENTAIRE.** [Bull. Acad. chir. dent.]. **Added/Corp** Academie Nationale de Chirurgie Dentaire (France). (1982/83)-. Bulletin. French. an (Published in November). 200.00F. Academie National Chirurgie Dentaire, 22 rue Emile Menier, 75116 Paris France. **Tel** 011 33 1 47046540, FAX 011 33 1 47043655. **ED** E. Cunin. **NLM** W1; BU524P. **Circ:** 300 (ctrl). ***Continues*** *Bulletin de l'Academie de Chirurgie Dentaire, 0339-9710.*
**Desc:** Report of lectures given at the Academie National de Chirurgie Dentaire and the activities of the ANCD.
**Ind/Abst** Health Plan. Adminis.; Index Dent. Lit. (1983-).

US/0002-8045
**BULLETIN OF THE AMERICAN COLLEGE OF SURGEONS.** [Bull. Am. Coll. Surg.]. **Main/Corp** American College of Surgeons. (1916)-. Bulletin. English. mo. Free on request. American College of Surgeons, 55 East Erie Street, Chicago IL 60611. **Tel** (312)664-4050. **LC** RD1; .A36. **DD** 617.05. **NLM** W1 BU8413. available on microfilm and microfiche from University Microfilms International (UMI).
**Desc:** Includes the college's hospital standardization report.
**Ind/Abst** Health Devices Alerts; Health Plan. Adminis.; Hospit. Health Admin. Index.

BL/0100-0462
**CADERNOS DE CIRURGIA (SAO BERNARDO DO CAMPO).** (CADERNOS DE CIRURGIA.). V. 1- Jan./Mar. 1974-. Periodical. English (Portuguese). **UDC** 616-089.8. **NLM** W1 CA109D.

CN/0008-428X
**CANADIAN JOURNAL OF SURGERY.** [Can. j. surg.]. **Added/Corp** Canadian Medical Association. Royal College of Physicians and Surgeons of Canada. **VFOAT** Journal Canadien de Chirurgie; CJS. Vol. 1 (Oct. 1957)-. Academic Scholarly Publication. English (French; summaries and/or abstracts in English and French). bm (Feb., Apr., June, Aug., Oct., Dec.). 63.00Can$ Canada; $68.00 other. Canadian Medical Association, 1867 Alta Vista Drive, Ottawa Ontario K1G 3Y6 Canada. **Tel** (613)731-9331 ext. 2028, FAX (613)731-4797. **(Subscription address:** Canadian Medical Association, CMA House, PO Box 8650, Ottawa Ontario K1G 0G8 Canada.) **ED** L. D. MacLean and C. B. Mueller. **NLM** W1 CA611. **CODEN** CJSUAX. **[CCC]. Bk Rev. Ad Acc. Pr Rev. Acid Free. Circ:** 9,000. available on microfilm and microfiche from University Microfilms International (UMI). Documents available from The Genuine Article, BIOSIS Document Express, CASDDS.
**Desc:** Contributes to the effective continuing education of surgical specialists and provides Canadian surgeons with an effective vehicle for the dissemination of their observations in research.
**Ind/Abst** Biol. Abstr.; Chem. Abstr.; Curr. Contents Clin. Med.; EMBASE; Health Devices Alerts; Health Plan. Adminis.; Helminthol. Abstr. (1991-); Index Med.; Index Dent. Lit.; Index Sci. Rev.; Mod. Med.; Nutr. Abstr. Rev., Ser. A, Hum. Exp.; Life Sci. Collect.; Protozoolog. Abstr.; Res. Alert [Full Cov.]; Rev. Med. Vet. Entomol.; Sci. Cit. Index; SCISEARCH.

US/0887-9850
**CARDIAC SURGERY. *Ceased.*** [Card. surg.]. Vol. 1, No. 1 (Oct. 1986)-Vol. 7 No. 2 (Dec. 1993). Periodical. English. Three times a year. Mosby Year Book Inc., 11830 Westline Industrial Drive, St Louis MO 63146. **Tel** (800)325-4177, (314)872-8370, FAX (314)432-1380, telex 44-2402. **LC** RD598; .C344. **DD** 617/.412. **NLM** W1; CA764CE. **[CCC].**

US/0163-7029
**CARDIAC/THORACIC SURGERY. VAT** Cardiac Thoracic Surgery. (1979)-. English. Futura Publishing Company Inc., 135 Bedford Road, PO Box 418, Armonk NY 10504-0418. **Tel** (914)273-1014, (800)877-8761, FAX (914)273-1015, (914)273-1016.

US/0893-8725
**CARDIOTHORACIC SURGERY. See** Medical Science and Technology-Cardiology.

US
**CARDIOVASCULAR SURGERY. Added/Corp** Council on Cardiovascular Surgery (American Heart Association) Cardiovascular Surgery. (1962)-. English. ir. $10.00 (per issue). American Heart Association, 7272 Greenville Avenue, Dallas TX 75231-4596. **Tel** (214)706-1310, (214)373-6300, FAX (214)691-6342. **(Subscription address:** American Heart Association, PO Box 843543, Dallas TX 75284-3543.)
**Desc:** Publishes original articles, reviews, short notes and case reports on basic and clinical research on all aspects of cardiovascular disease.

US
**CARE OF THE SURGICAL PATIENT. *Title Change.*** English. ir. Scientific American Medicine, 415 Madison Avenue, New York NY 10017. **Tel** (212)754-0550, (800)333-1199. ***Continued by*** *Scientific American Surgery.*
**Desc:** Designed in conjunction with the American College of Surgeons, a reference on perioperative management techniques.

US/1052-3359
**CHEST SURGERY CLINICS OF NORTH AMERICA.** (1991)-. Periodical. English. qt. $89.00 (individual), $105.00 (institution) US; $119.00 (individual), $127.00 ) institution other. W.B. Saunders Company, A Subsidiary of Harcourt Brace Jovanovich, Inc., The Curtis Center/Suite 300, Independence Square West, Philadelphia PA 19106-3399. **Tel** (215)238-7800 or, 5587, FAX (215)238-7883, telex 173146. **(Subscription address:** W. B. Saunders Company / North America Subscriptions, c/o Periodicals, 6277 Sea Harbour Drive, 4th Floor, Orlando FL 32887.)

GW/0009-4722
**CHIRURG.** (CHIRURG; ZEITSCHRIFT FUER ALLE GEBIETE DER OPERATIVEN MEDIZIN.). [Chirurg]. (1928)-. Academic Scholarly Publication. German. Twelve times a year. DM488.00. Springer-Verlag GmbH & Company KG, Heidelberger Platz 3, D 14197 Berlin Germany. **Tel** 011 49 30 8207223, FAX 011 49 30 8214091, telex 183 319 SPBLN D. **(Subscription address:** Springer Verlag New York Inc. / for North America, 44 Hartz Way, Secaucus NJ 07096.) **ED** Ch Herfarth, G Heberer, and E Kern. **NLM** W1 CH818F. **[CCC]. Pr Rev.** available on microfilm from University Microfilms International (UMI). Documents available from The Genuine Article.
**Desc:** Publishes clear descriptions of general medical as well as surgical discoveries, for the use of practicing doctors. Traces important surgical themes over the course of several years and shows latest developments.
**Ind/Abst** Curr. Contents Clin. Med.; EMBASE; Energy Res. Abstr.; Health Plan. Adminis.; Helminthol. Abstr.; Index Med.; Life Sci. Collect.; PESTDOC; Res. Alert [Full Cov.]; Rev. Med. Vet. Mycology; Sci. Cit. Index; SCISEARCH; Soc. Sci. Cit. Index [Select. Cov.].

IT/0394-9508
**CHIRURGIA.** Periodical. Italian. mo. $130.00 (individuals), $160.00 (institutions). Edizioni Minerva Medica, Corso Bramante 83-85, 10126 Turin Italy. **Tel** 011 39 11 678282, FAX 011 39 11 674502. **ED** Rocco A Marnotti and Piero Zannini. Index available. cum. index. **Bk Rev. Ad Acc. Circ:** 6,000 (ctrl).
**Desc:** Articles on general surgery.
**Ind/Abst** EMBASE.

IT
**CHIRURGIA.** Italian. qt. L40000 Italy; L6000 other. Casa Editrice Ambrosiana, Via G Frua 6, 20146 Milan Italy. **Tel** 011 39 2 463936.

IT/0009-4749
**CHIRURGIA DEGLI ORGANI DI MOVIMENTO.** [Chir. organi mov.]. Vol. 1 (1917)-. Periodical. Italian (summaries and/or abstracts in English). qt. L80000 Italy; $100.00 other. GEM Srl Nuova Cappelli, Via Farini 14, 40124 Bologna Italy. **Tel** 011 39 51 239060. **ED** Mario Campanacci. **NLM** W1 CH818V. **CODEN** CHOMA9. Index available (free). cum. index. **Bk Rev. Ad Acc. Circ:** 3,500 (ctrl). Documents available from BIOSIS Document Express.
**Desc:** Bone and joint surgery.
**Ind/Abst** Biol. Abstr.; Health Plan. Adminis.; Index Med.; SportSearch.

IT
**CHIRURGIA DELLA TESTA E DEL COLLO : QUADERNI A.I.C.M.F., A.S.C.M.F.O.I. Added/Corp** Associazione Italiana Chirurgi Maxillo-Facciali. Associazione Stomatologi e Chirurghi Maxillo-Facciali Ospedalieri Italiani. **VFOAT** Surgery of the Head and Neck. Vol. 1, No. 1 (1984)-. Periodical. Italian (summaries and/or abstracts in English). sa (2 issues). L30000 Italy; L60000 other. La Garangola, Via Montona 4, 35137 Padua Italy. **Tel** 011 39 49 8750550, FAX 011 39 49 8751743. **NLM** W1; CH8183. **CODEN** CHTCE8. Index available (bound in last issue). **Pr Rev. Circ:** 500.
**Desc:** Covers surgery of the head and neck.

IT/0412-264X
**CHIRURGIA E PATOLOGIA SPERIMENTALE. SUPPLEMENTO.** [Chir. patol. sper., Suppl.]. Vol. 1 (1954)-. Monographic series.

Italian. ir. Price varies per volume. Clinica Chirurgica Unicattoic, Via Peneta Sacchetti 526, 0016 Rome Italy. **UDC** 616-089.8. ***Continues*** *Patologia Sperimentale e Chirurgia. Supplemento.*

IT/0393-1471
**CHIRURGIA EPATOBILIARE.** ***Suspended.*** **Added/Corp** Universita Cattolica del Sacro Cuore. Istituto di Patologia Chirurgica. Vol. 1, No. 1 (Jan./March 1982)-. Periodical. English (French and Italian). qt. **NLM** W1; CH81855.

IT/0009-4773
**CHIRURGIA ITALIANA.** [Chir. ital.]. (1947)-. Academic Scholarly Publication. Italian (English). bm. L240000 Italy; L300000 other. BI & GI Editori Verona, Via ca di Cozzi 41, 37124 Verona Italy. **Tel** 011 39 45 8300968, FAX 011 39 45 8300970. **NLM** W1 CH822. **Bk Rev.**
**Ind/Abst** EMBASE; Health Plan. Adminis.; Index Med.

PL/0009-479X
**CHIRURGIA NARZADOW RUCHY I ORTOPEDIA POLSKA.** **See** Medical Science and Technology-Orthopedics.

IT/0393-1463
**CHIRURGIA OGGI : ORGANO UFFICIALE DELLA SOCIETA EMILIANO-ROMAGNOLA DI CHIRURGIA.** (198?)-. Periodical. Italian (summaries and/or abstracts in English and Italian). tq. L25000. Editrice Compositori, Via Stalingrado 97/2, 40128 Bologna Italy. **Tel** 011 39 51 327811. **NLM** W1; CH827B.

IT/0366-6298
**CHIRURGIA TORACICA, LA.** [Chir. torac.]. V. 1- Feb. 1948-. Academic Scholarly Publication. Italian. bm. L90000. Seros, Via Augusto Murri 4, 00161 Rome Italy. **Tel** 6 4958300. **UDC** 616.12/.14-089.8. **NLM** W1 CH829.
**Ind/Abst** EMBASE.

IT/0009-4811
**CHIRURGIA TRIVENETA.** [Chir. Triv.]. **Added/Corp** Ospedale Civile Maggiore, Verona. Societa Triveneta di Chirurgia. Vol. 1 (Jan./June 1961)-. Periodical. Italian (summaries and/or abstracts in French, English and German). qt (4 issues). L100000. Chirurgica Ospedale Civile, Maggiore Piazzale A Stefani 1, 37126 Verona Italy. **Tel** 011 39 45 8072474. **NLM** W1 CH83. Index available (free). **Ad Acc. Circ:** 900 (ctrl).
**Desc:** Publishes original works, case histories of surgical and medical interest and the communications of the meetings of the Society.

FI/0358-4917
**CHIRURGICA (OULU).** (CHIRURGICA.). [Chirurgica]. No. 1- 1972-. Monographic series. English (Finnish). ir. Price varies per volume. Professor Leo Hirvonen, University of Oulu, 90100 Oulu 10 Finland. **Tel** 358-81-332133. **ED** Leo Hirvonen. **UDC** 616-089.8. **NLM** W1 AC954NM no. 15 etc. cum. index. **Ad Acc. Circ:** 450 (ctrl).
**Desc:** Monographs, reviews, and dissertations in the field of surgery.

FR/0001-4001
**CHIRURGIE.** **Added/Corp** Association Francaise de Chirurgie. (1975)-. Periodical. French. Ten times a year. $299.00. Masson Editeur, Box Postale 22, 41353 Vineuil 16 France. **Tel** 011 33 54 438994. **ED** Editor: 1975- J. Patel. **NLM** W3 C155L. **[CCC].**

FR/0001-4001
**CHIRURGIE (PARIS).** (CHIRURGIE.). [Chirurgie]. **Added/Corp** Academie de Chirurgie (France). Vol. 96 (Jan. 1970)-. Academic Scholarly Publication. French. Ten times a year. $299.00 US. Masson Editeur, Box Postale 22, 41353 Vineuil 16 France. **Tel** 011 33 54 438994. **NLM** W1 CH831K. **[CCC].** available on microfilm and microfiche from University Microfilms International (UMI). ***Continues*** *Academie de Chirurgie (France). Memoires de l'Academie de Chirurgie, 0368-8291;* ***Formed by the union of*** *Congres Francais de Chirurgie. Information et Rapports -Congres Francais de Chirurgie, 0997-4334* ***and*** *Congres Francais de Chirurgie. Rapports, Discussions et Communications Particulieres -Congres Francais de Chirurgie.*
**Ind/Abst** EMBASE; Health Plan. Adminis.; Index Med.; Life Sci. Collect.

GW/0177-9990
**CHIRURGISCHE GASTROENTEROLOGIE MIT INTERDISZIPLINAREN GESPRACHEN.** **See** Medical Science and Technology-Gastroenterology.

GW/0009-4846
**CHIRURGISCHE PRAXIS.** [Chir. Prax.]. (1957)-. Academic Scholarly Publication. German. qt. DM300.00. Hans Marseille Verlag GmbH, Buerkleinstrasse 12, D 80538 Munich Germany. **Tel** 011 49 89 227988, FAX 011 49 89 2904643. **NLM** W1 CH835. **CODEN** CHPXBE. **[CCC].** Index Available, published separately, free-automatically sent. cum. index. available on microfilm and microfiche from University Microfilms International (UMI).
**Ind/Abst** EMBASE.

GW/0303-6227
**CHIRURGISCHES FORUM FUER EXPERIMENTELLE UND KLINISCHE FORSCHUNG.** **Added/Corp** Deutsche Gesellschaft fur Chirurgie. (1972)-. Monographic series. German (summaries and/or abstracts in English). ir. Price varies. Springer-Verlag GmbH & Company KG, Heidelberger Platz 3, D 14197 Berlin Germany. **Tel** 011 49 30 8207223, FAX 011 49 30 8214091, telex 183 319 SPBLN D. **(Subscription address:** Springer Verlag New York Inc. / for North America, 44 Hartz Way, Secaucus NJ 07096.) **NLM** W1 CH84. **CODEN** CFEKA7. Documents available from CASDDS.
**Ind/Abst** Chem. Abstr.; Health Plan. Adminis.

CC/0529-5815
**CHUNG-HUA WAI KAO TSA CHIH.** [Chung-hua wai ko tsa chih]. **Added/Corp** Chung-Hua I Hsueh Hui, Peking. Wai Ko Hsueh Hui. **VFOAT** Zhonghua Waike Zazhi; Chinese Journal of Surgery. Vol. 1 (Feb. 1953)-. Periodical. Chinese (summaries and/or abstracts in English; table of contents in English). mo. $3.00. **(Subscription address:** China International Book Trading Corporation, PO Box 399, Library Service Department, Beijing 100044 People's Republic of China.) **DD** 617.6. **NLM** W1 CH985.
**Ind/Abst** Index Med. (1979-); NAPRALERT.

SP/0213-5353
**CIRUGIA DE URGENCIA.** ***Suspended.*** **See** Medical Science and Technology-Emergency Medicine.

UY/0009-7381
**CIRUGIA DEL URUGUAY.** [Cir. Urug.]. **Added/Corp** Sociedad de Cirugia del Uruguay. Vol. 4 (1970)-. Academic Scholarly Publication. Spanish (summaries and/or abstracts in English and French). Four times a year. $37.50. Sociedad de Cirugia del Uruguay, Calle Gral Flores 3440, Montevideo Uruguay. **ED** Gustavo Bocliaccini. **NLM** W1 CI874T. **CODEN** CRGUAT. Index available. cum. index. **Bk Rev. Ad Acc. Pr Rev. Circ:** 500 (ctrl). Documents available from BIOSIS Document Express. ***Continues*** *Revista de Cirugia del Uruguay.*
**Desc:** Covers the total experience and field of Uruguayan surgery. Includes themes of related interest. Also transcribes papers presented at annual surgery conferences in Uruguay.
**Ind/Abst** Biol. Abstr.; EMBASE.

SP/0009-739X
**CIRUGIA ESPANOLA.** [Cir. Esp.]. **Added/Corp** Asociacion Espanola de Cirujanos. (19??)-. Academic Scholarly Publication. Spanish. Twelve times a year. $83.00. Ediciones Doyma SA, Travesera de Gracia 17 21, 08021 Barcelona Spain. **Tel** 011 34 3 2000711, 011 34 3 4145706, FAX 011 34 3 2091136, telex 51964 INK E. **CODEN** CRESAD. Documents available from CASDDS. ***Continues*** *Cirugia, Ginecologia y Urologia.*
**Ind/Abst** Chem. Abstr.; EMBASE; Indice Med. Esp.

SP/0376-7892
**CIRUGIA PLASTICA IBERO-LATINOAMERICANA.** [Cir. plast. iberolatinoam.]. **Added/Corp** Federacion Ibero-Latinoamericana de Cirugia Plastica. Sociedad Espanola de Cirugia Plastica. Vol. 1 (Jan./March 1975)-. Academic Scholarly Publication. Spanish (summaries and/or abstracts in English). Four times a year (Jan., Apr., July, Oct.). $54.00. Cirugia Plastica Ibero-Latinoamericana, Apdo 10059, 28080 Madrid Spain. **Tel** 011 34 1 908603814, FAX 011 34 1 4454934. **NLM** W1 CI8786. **Bk Rev. Ad Acc. Pr Rev. Circ:** 1,000. ***Formed by the union of*** *Revista Latinoamericana de Cirugia Plastica, 0034-9755* ***and*** *Revista Espanola de Cirugia Plastica, 0034-9364.*
**Ind/Abst** EMBASE; Indice Med. Esp.

MX/0009-7411
**CIRUGIA Y CIRUJANOS.** [Cir. & cir.]. **Added/Corp** Academia Mexicana de Cirugia. Vol. 1 (Aug 1933)-. Periodical. Spanish (summaries and/or abstracts in English, French and German). Six times a year (Jan., Mar., May, July, Sept, Nov.). $100.00. Academia Nacional Cirugia, Avenue Ejercito Nacional 617-304, 11560 Mexico DF Mexico. **Tel** 011 52 5 5898909, 011 52 5 2805191, FAX 011 52 5 7612581. **ED** Dr. Humberto Hurtado Andrade. **NLM** W1 CI946. Index available. cum. index. **Ad Acc, Adv Mgr:** Bruno Vanneuville, **Tel** 011 52 5 2600048. **Pr Rev. Circ:** 3,000 (ctrl). available on microfilm from University Microfilms International (UMI).
**Desc:** Original articles, research, reviews, clinical cases and other related topics in the field of surgery.
**Ind/Abst** EMBASE.

US/1055-6656
**CLEFT PALATE-CRANIOFACIAL JOURNAL.** **See** Medical Science and Technology.

IT
**CLINICA CHIRURGICA DEL NORD AMERICA, LA.** Italian. bm (6 issues). $180.00. Piccin Editore, Via Altinate 107, 35121 Padua Italy. **Tel** 011 39 49 655566, FAX 011 39 49 8750693.

NE/0303-8467
**CLINICAL NEUROLOGY AND NEUROSURGERY.** **See** Medical Science and Technology-Neurology.

US/0069-4827
**CLINICAL NEUROSURGERY.** [Clin. neurosurg.]. **Main/Conf** Congress of Neurological Surgeons. Vol. 1 (1953)-. English. an. $85.00. Williams & Wilkins Company, 428 East Preston Street, Baltimore MD 21202-3993. **Tel** (410)528-4000, (800)638-6423, FAX (410)528-8596, telex 87669. **(Subscription address:** Williams & Wilkins, PO Box 64380, Baltimore, MD 21264) **LC** RD593.A1; C63. **DD** 617.48. **NLM** W1 CL732. **CODEN** CLNEA8. **[CCC].** cum. index. Documents available from CASDDS, Quick Copies.
**Ind/Abst** Chem. Abstr. (1953-1980); Energy Res. Abstr. (Oct. 1977-); Health Plan. Adminis.; Index Med.; INIS Atomindex [Micro.].

UK/0263-4422
**CLINICAL SURGERY INTERNATIONAL.** [Clin. surg. int.]. (1981)-. Monographic series. English. ir. Price varies per volume. Churchill Livingstone, 1-3 Baxter's Place, Leith Walk, Edinburgh EH1 3AF Scotland. **Tel** 011 44 31 556 2424, FAX 011 44 31 558 1278, telex 727511. **(Subscription address:** Churchill Livingstone / US, 5 S 250 Frontenac Road, Naperville IL 60563.) **LC** UNC. **DD** 617. **NLM** W1 CL795U.

US/0890-9016
**CLINICAL TRANSPLANTS.** [Clin. transpl.]. **Added/Corp** UCLA Tissue Typing Laboratory. (1986)-. English. an. $90.00. UCLA Tissue Typing Laboratory, 950 Veteran Avenue, Box A, Los Angeles CA 90024. **Tel** (310)825-7651, FAX (310)206-3216. **LC** RD120.7; .C59. **DD** 617/.95. **NLM** W1; CL797KM. ***Continues*** *Clinical Kidney Transplants, 0883-914X.*
**Ind/Abst** Health Plan. Adminis.; Index Med. (1986-).

SP
**CLINICAS QUIRURGICAS DE NORTEAMERICA.** Spanish. McGraw Hill, Interamericana de Espana SA, Manuel Ferrero 13, 28036 Madrid Spain.

US/0094-1298
**CLINICS IN PLASTIC SURGERY.** [Clin. plast. surg.]. **VFOAT** Clinics, Plastic Surgery. Vol. 1 (Jan. 1974)-. Academic Scholarly Publication. English. qt. $129.00 (individual), $156.00 (institution) US; $174.00 (individual), $184.00 (institution) other. W.B. Saunders Company, A Subsidiary of Harcourt Brace Jovanovich, Inc., The Curtis Center/Suite 300, Independence Square West, Philadelphia PA 19106-3399. **Tel** (215)238-7800 or, 5587, FAX (215)238-7883, telex 173146. **(Subscription address:** W. B. Saunders Company / North America Subscriptions, c/o Periodicals, 6277 Sea Harbour Drive, 4th Floor, Orlando FL 32887.) **DD** 617. **NLM** W1 CL831D. **[CCC].** available on microfilm and microfiche from University Microfilms International (UMI). Documents available from The Genuine Article.
**Ind/Abst** Curr. Contents Clin. Med.; EMBASE; Energy Res. Abstr. (Jan. 1981-); Index Med.; INIS Atomindex [Micro.]; Life Sci. Collect.; Res. Alert [Select. Cov.]; SCISEARCH; Soc. Sci. Cit. Index [Select. Cov.].

US/0162-6477
**COLLECTED LETTERS / CORRESPONDENCE SOCIETY OF SURGEONS.** [Collect. lett. - Corresp. Soc. Surg.]. **Main/Corp** Correspondence Society of Surgeons. **Added/Corp** Correspondence Society of Surgeons. **VFOAT** Correspondence Society of Surgeons Collected Letters; Collected Letters of the Correspondence Society of Surgeons; Collected Letters in Surgery. (1977)-. Periodical. English. mo. $97.00. Laux Company Inc, 63 Great Road, Maynard MA 01754. **Tel** (508)897-5552, FAX (508)897-6824. **ED** Terry Brown. **DD** 617. **NLM** W1; CO169CV. **[CCC]. Bk Rev. Circ:** 500.

GW/0174-2450
**COLO-PROCTOLOGY, INTERNATIONAL EDITION.** (COLO-PROCTOLOGY.). [Colo-proctol., Int. ed.]. Vol. 2, No. 4 (July/Aug. 1980)-. Periodical. English (summaries and/or abstracts in French). bm. $95.00 Australia, New Zealand, Polynesia; $90.00 South America, Far East; $98.00 Europe; $85.00 other. Edition Nymphenburg GmbH & Co, Fuerstdobl 9 Editorial Office, D 94127 Neuburg A Inn Germany. **Tel** 011 49 8507 1771. **NLM** W1 CO242. ***Continues*** *Protocology (English Ed.).*

US/0894-8062
**COLON AND RECTAL SURGERY OUTLOOK.** [Colon rectal surg. outlook]. Vol. 1, No. 1 (Jan. 1988)-. Periodical. English. Ten times a year. Comes with QMP Clinical Series in Colon and Rectal Surgery. Quality Medical Publishing, 11970 Borman Drive, Suite 222, St. Louis MO 63146. **Tel** (314)878-7808, (800)423-6865, FAX (314)878-9937. **ED** Theodore R. Schrock. **DD** 617. Index available. **Circ:** 450.
**Desc:** Timely series reflecting current information in the field of colon and rectal surgery. Emphasis on technique rather than clinical research.

US/1056-1943
**COMPASS PATHFINDER.** (COMPASS PATHFINDER : INFORMATION & PERSPECTIVES ON DIRECTIONS IN STEREOTACTIC NEUROSURGERY.). [COMPASS pathfinder]. Issue No. 1 (Apr. 1991)-. Periodical. English. qt. Stereotactic Medical Systems, 1118 7th Street NW, Rochester MN 55901. **DD** 617.

US/1053-749X
**COMPLICATIONS IN SURGERY.** Vol. 10, No. 1 (Jan. 1991)-. Periodical. English. mo. $59.54 New York City (includes sales tax); $55.00 other. SCP Communications Inc, 134 West 29th Street, New York NY 10001. **Tel** (212)714-1740, FAX (212)629-3760. **DD** 617. **NLM** W1; CO452DE. Documents available from The Genuine Article. ***Continues*** *Infections in Surgery, 0277-7746.*
**Ind/Abst** Curr. Contents Clin. Med.; Protozoolog. Abstr.; Res. Alert [Select. Cov.]; Rev. Med. Vet. Mycology; SCISEARCH.

US/0734-0710
**CONJOINT DIRECTORY OF AMERICAN ACADEMY OF OTOLARYNGOLOGY-HEAD AND NECK SURGERY, AND AMERICAN ACADEMY OF FACIAL PLASTIC AND RECONSTRUCTIVE SURGERY, AND AMERICAN NEUROTOLOGY SOCIETY, AND AMERICAN RHINOLOGIC SOCIETY, AND AMERICAN SOCIETY OF OPHTHALMOLOGIC AND OTOLARYNGOLOGIC ALLERGY.** **See** Medical Science and Technology-Otorhinolaryngology.

US/0163-2108
**CONTEMPORARY NEUROSURGERY.** [Contemp. neurosurg.]. (1979)-. Periodical. English. bw. $257.00. Williams & Wilkins Company, 428 East Preston Street, Baltimore MD 21202-3993. **Tel** (410)528-4000, (800)638-6423, FAX (410)528-8596, telex 87669. **(Subscription address:** Williams & Wilkins, PO Box 64380, Baltimore MD 21264.) **ED** George T. Tindall. **NLM** W1 CO769ND. **CODEN** CNEUET. **[CCC]. Ad Acc. Circ:** 1,100. Documents available from , BIOSIS Document Express, Quick Copies.
**Desc:** A twenty-seven lesson series features original articles on current topics in neurosurgery.
**Ind/Abst** Biol. Abstr. (1987-).

US/0045-8341
**CONTEMPORARY SURGERY.** [Contemp. surg.]. Vol. 1 (Jan./Feb. 1972)-. Periodical. English. mo. $53.00 US; $63.00 Canada; $80.00 other. Bobit Publishing, 2512 Artesia Boulevard, Redondo Beach CA 90278. **Tel** (310)376-8788, (800)334-8152, FAX (213)376-9043. **ED** Peggy Plendl. **LC** RD1; .C74. **DD** 617/.005. **NLM** W1 CO769Y. **CODEN** CSGYA. **Circ:** 46,650. available on microfilm and microfiche from University Microfilms International (UMI).
**Ind/Abst** Health Plan. Adminis.

GW/0939-0146
**CRITICAL REVIEWS IN NEUROSURGERY : CR. VFOAT** CR. Vol. 1, No. 1 (Feb. 1991)-. Periodical. English. Six times a year. DM524.00. Springer-Verlag GmbH & Company KG, Heidelberger Platz 3, D 14197 Berlin Germany. **Tel** 011 49 30 8207223, FAX 011 49 30 8214091, telex 183 319 SPBLN D. **(Subscription address:** Springer Verlag New York Inc. / for North America, 44 Hartz Way, Secaucus NJ 07096.) **ED** A J Raimondi. **NLM** W1; CR216ZDL. **CODEN** CRRNEX. available on microfilm and microfiche from University Microfilms International (UMI). Documents available from The Genuine Article.
**Desc:** Communicates the significance of articles published in neurosurgical journals and related specialties. Brings together neurosurgeons and specialists in areas interrelating functionally and regularly with neurosurgery.
**Ind/Abst** Res. Alert [Full Cov.].

IT
**CUORE, IL.** **See** Medical Science and Technology-Cardiology.

UK/0953-7112
**CURRENT ANAESTHESIA AND CRITICAL CARE.** Vol. 1, No. 1 (Sept. 1989)-. Periodical. English. Four times a year. £144.00 Europe; £145.00 Other (Institutions). Churchill Livingstone, 1-3 Baxter's Place, Leith Walk, Edinburgh EH1 3AF Scotland. **Tel** 011 44 31 556 2424, FAX 011 44 31 558 1278, telex 727511. **(Subscription address:** Maruzen Company Ltd., PO Box 5050, Import & Export Department, Tokyo 100 31 Japan.) **ED** B J Pollard. **NLM** W1; CU685. **CODEN** CCCAEI. **[CCC].** available on microfilm and microfiche from University Microfilms International (UMI).
**Desc:** A unique review journal publishing the very latest thinking, research and advances in all branches of anaesthesia and critical care.
**Ind/Abst** EMBASE.

II/0011-3700
**CURRENT MEDICAL PRACTICE.** [Curr. med. pract.]. Vol. 1 (Jan. 1957)-. Periodical. English. mo. $15.00. Current Technical Literature, Malhotra House, Box 1374, Bombay 400001 India. **(Subscription address:** Prints India, 11 Darya Ganj, New Delhi 110002 India.) **NLM** W1 CU789. **CODEN** CMDPAW. Documents available from CASDDS.
**Ind/Abst** Chem. Abstr.

●US/1065-6243
**CURRENT OPINION IN GENERAL SURGERY.** [Curr. opin. gen. surg.]. (1993)-. English. an. $139.95. Current Science / England, Middlesex House, 34-42 Cleveland Street, London W1P 5FB England. **Tel** 011 44 71 580 8393, 011 44 71 323 0323, FAX 011 44 81 580 1938. **(Subscription address:** Current Science, 20 North 3rd Street, Philadelphia PA 19106.) **DD** 617.

●US/1068-9508
**CURRENT OPINION IN OTOLARYNGOLOGY & HEAD AND NECK SURGERY.** **See** Medical Science and Technology-Otorhinolaryngology.

●UK/0969-8868
**CURRENT OPINION IN SURGICAL INFECTIONS.** Vol. 1, No. 1 (1993)-. Periodical. English. Four times a year. $109.95 (individuals); $219.95 (institutions). Current Science / England, Middlesex House, 34-42 Cleveland Street, London W1P 5FB England. **Tel** 011 44 71 580 8393, 011 44 71 323 0323, FAX 011 44 81 580 1938. **(Subscription address:** Current Science, 20 North 3rd Street, Philadelphia PA 19106.) **NLM** W1; CU799GID.

UK/0952-0627
**CURRENT PRACTICE IN SURGERY.** Vol. 1, No. 1 (March 1989)-. Periodical. English. Four times a year. £125.00 Europe; £126.00 Other (Institutions). Churchill Livingstone, 1-3 Baxter's Place, Leith Walk, Edinburgh EH1 3AF Scotland. **Tel** 011 44 31 556 2424, FAX 011 44 31 558 1278, telex 727511. **(Subscription address:** Maruzen Company Ltd., PO Box 5050, Import & Export Department, Tokyo 100 31 Japan.) **ED** W E G Thomas. **NLM** W1; CU803K. **CODEN** CRPSE4. **[CCC].** available on microfilm and microfiche from University Microfilms International (UMI).
**Desc:** An international review journal which systematically and comprehensively covers all the disciplines of general surgery over a three-year period. Each issue contains invited clinical reviews, written by highly regarded international experts on the following subjects: general surgical management of a disorder, minor but common surgical ailments, operative techniques and possible complications, etc.
**Ind/Abst** EMBASE.

US/0147-197X
**CURRENT PROBLEMS IN ANESTHESIA AND CRITICAL CARE MEDICINE.** V. 1- July 1977-. Monographic series. English. mo. Price varies per volume. Mosby Year Book Inc., 11830 Westline Industrial Drive, St Louis MO 63146. **Tel** (800)325-4177, (314)872-8370, FAX (314)432-1380, telex 44-2402. **UDC** 616-089.5. **NLM** W1 CU804E. available on microfilm from University Microfilms International (UMI).

US/0011-3840
**CURRENT PROBLEMS IN SURGERY.** [Curr. probl. surg.]. (Jan. 1964)-. Academic Scholarly Publication. English. mo. $110.00 (institutions), $82.00 (individuals) US; $122.00 (institutions), $94.00 (individuals) other. Mosby Year Book Inc., 11830 Westline Industrial Drive, St Louis MO 63146. **Tel** (800)325-4177, (314)872-8370, FAX (314)432-1380, telex 44-2402. **ED** Mark M. Ravitch. **LC** RD1; .C9. **DD** 617. **NLM** W1 CU804S. **CODEN** CPSUA. **[CCC].** available on microfilm and microfiche from University Microfilms International (UMI). Documents available from The Genuine Article.
**Desc:** Each issue provides a discussion of a clinical problem commonly seen by general surgeons. Issues also focus on topics in surgical research and emerging ideas in surgical subspecialties.
**Ind/Abst** Abr. Index Med.; EMBASE; Energy Res. Abstr. (Aug. 1982-); Health Plan. Adminis.; Index Med.; Index Sci. Rev. [Full Cov.]; Life Sci. Collect.; Physic. Medline Plus; Res. Alert [Full Cov.]; Sci. Cit. Index; SCISEARCH.

US/0896-1182
**CURRENT REVIEWS FOR POST ANESTHESIA CARE NURSES.** **See** Medical Science and Technology-Nursing.

US/0149-7944
**CURRENT SURGERY.** [Curr. surg.]. **Added/Corp** Association of Program Directors in Surgery (U.S.). Vol. 35 (Jan./Feb. 1978)-. Academic Scholarly Publication. English. Nine times a year. $105.00 (institution), $80.00 (individual), US; $145.00 (institution), $120.00 (individual), other. Williams & Wilkins Company, 428 East Preston Street, Baltimore MD 21202-3993. **Tel** (410)528-4000, (800)638-6423, FAX (410)528-8596, telex 87669. **(Subscription address:** Williams & Wilkins, PO Box 64380, Baltimore MD 21264.) **LC** RD1; .C95. **DD** 617/.005. **NLM** ZWO 100 Q2. **CODEN** CUSUDB. **[CCC]. Bk Rev. Ad Acc. Circ:** 2,474. available on microfilm and microfiche from University Microfilms International (UMI). Documents available from CASDDS, Quick Copies. ***Continues*** *Review of Surgery, 0034-6780.*
**Desc:** Provides surgeons with succinct reports prepared by well-known authorities who draw on their own clinical experience to relate new findings to current practice.
**Ind/Abst** Chem. Abstr. (1978-1983); Energy Res. Abstr. (April 1982-); Health Plan. Adminis.; Index Med. (?-Nov./Dec. 1990).

US/0894-2277
**CURRENT SURGICAL DIAGNOSIS & TREATMENT.** [Curr. surg. diagn. treat.]. **VFOAT** Current Surgical Diagnosis and Treatment; Surgical Diagnosis & Treatment. 1st Ed.(1973)-. Monographic series. English. be. $39.95 (latest edition). Appleton Century Crofts, Prentice Hall, 200 Old Tappan Road, Old Tappan NJ 07675. **Tel** (201)767-5188, (800)922-0579. **DD** 617. **NLM** W1 CU812.

UK/0141-3368
**CURRENT SURGICAL PRACTICE.** V. 1- 1976-. Periodical. English. Mosby Year Book Inc., 11830 Westline Industrial Drive, St Louis MO 63146. **Tel** (800)325-4177, (314)872-8370, FAX (314)432-1380, telex 44-2402. **UDC** 616-089.8. **NLM** W1 CU813.

US/0835-3689
**CURRENT SURGICAL THERAPY.** [Curr. surg. ther.]. English. Mosby Year Book Inc., 11830 Westline Industrial Drive, St Louis MO 63146. **Tel** (800)325-4177, (314)872-8370, FAX (314)432-1380, telex 44-2402. **ED** John L Cameron. **LC** RD1; .C96. **DD** 617/.005. **UDC** 616-089.8. **NLM** W1; CU813E.

●US/1068-4107
**CURRENT TECHNIQUES IN ARTHROSCOPY.** (1994)-. English. an. $153.45. Current Science, 20 North 3rd Street, Philadelphia PA 19106. **Tel** (215)574-2266, (800)552-5866, FAX (215)574-2270. **DD** 617.

●US/1065-0717
**CURRENT TECHNIQUES IN SURGERY.** (1992)-. Periodical. English. bm. Free. Medical Publications Inc., 300 Mt. Lebanon Boulevard, Suite 201-A, Pittsburgh PA 15234. **Tel** (412)341-1775, FAX (412)341-2028.

US/1040-1733
**DEBATES IN CLINICAL SURGERY.** [Debates clin. surg.]. English. an. $35.00. Mosby Year Book Inc., 11830 Westline Industrial Drive, St Louis MO 63146. **Tel** (800)325-4177, (314)872-8370, FAX (314)432-1380, telex 44-2402. **NLM** W1; DE101S.

AT/0311-0699
**DENTAL ANAESTHESIA AND SEDATION.** ***Suspended.*** **See** Dentistry.

●US/1076-0512
**DERMATOLOGIC SURGERY.** **See** Medical Science and Technology-Dermatology.

US
**DETAILED DIAGNOSES AND SURGICAL PROCEDURES FOR PATIENTS DISCHARGED FROM SHORT-STAY HOSPITALS, UNITED STATES.** ***Title Change.*** English. an. US Department of Health and Human Services, 200 Independence Avenue Southwest, Washington DC 20201. **UDC** 311:616-089.5(73). **NLM** W2 A N148D. ***Continued by*** *Detailed Diagnoses and procedures for Patients Discharged from Short-Stay Hospitals, United States, 0891-5067.*

GW/0343-3137
**DEUTSCHE ZEITSCHRIFT FUER MUND-, KIEFER- UND GESICHTS- CHIRURGIE.** [Dtsch. Z. Mund- Kiefer- Gesicht-Chir.]. **Added/Corp** Bundesverband der Facharzte fuer Mund- und Kieferchirurgie (Germany) Bundesverband Deutscher Arzte fuer Mund-Kiefer-Gesichtschirurgie. Deutsche Gesellschaft fuer Mund-, Kiefer- und Gesichtschirurgie. (1977)-. Periodical. German (summaries and/or abstracts in English and French; table of contents in English). Six times a year. DM375.00. Carl Hanser Verlag, Postfach 860420, D 81631 Munich Germany. **Tel** 011 49 89 998300, FAX 011 49 89 984809. **ED** R Becker. **NLM** W1; DE903F. **[CCC].** Index available. **Bk Rev. Ad Acc. Circ:** 7,900 (ctrl).
**Desc:** Contains articles on oral pathology and new diagnostic and therapeutic methods, to inform the researcher as well as the clinical physician. Reports on conferences and continuing education.
**Ind/Abst** Curr. Titl. Dent.; Health Plan. Adminis.; Index Dent. Lit. (1977-);(1, 1977-).

SZ/0253-4886
**DIGESTIVE SURGERY.** [Dig. surg.]. Vol. 1 (1984)-. Periodical. English. bm (6 issues). $432.00. S. Karger AG, Allschwilerstrasse 10, PO Box - Postfach - Case Postale, CH-4009 Basel Switzerland. **Tel** 011 41 61 306-1111, FAX 011 41 61 306-1234, telex CH 962 652. **ED** E.H. Farthmann. **NLM** W1; DI575. **[CCC].** Documents available from The Genuine Article, BIOSIS Document Express. ***Continues*** *Surgical Gastroenterology, 0730-2681.*

**Desc:** Answers the complete information needs of surgeons concerned with diseases of the alimentary tract. Interdisciplinary in scope, the journal keeps the specialist aware of advances in all fields contributing to improvements in the diagnosis and treatment of gastrointestinal disease. Particular emphasis is given to articles which report and evaluate recent developments, including results of basic research and technical innovations, such as new endoscopic and laparoscopic procedures. Each contribution is carefully aligned with the needs of digestive surgeons.
**Ind/Abst** Biol. Abstr.; EMBASE; Helminthol. Abstr. (1991-); Life Sci. Collect.; Ref. Upd. Deluxe Ed.; Res. Alert [Select. Cov.]; SCISEARCH.

US
**DIRECTORY OF MEMBERS. Main/Corp** American Society of Anesthesiologists. **VFOAT** ASA Directory of Members. **VAT** American Society of Anesthesiologists Directory of Members. Directory. English. American Society of Anesthesiologists, 520 North Northwest Highway, Park Ridge IL 60068. **Tel** (708)825-5586. **LC** RD83.A1; A5. **UDC** 616-089.5(060.21)(73). **NLM** WO 222 AA1 A5D.

US/0012-3706
**DISEASES OF THE COLON & RECTUM.** **See** Medical Science and Technology-Gastroenterology.

FR
**EMC INSTANTANES CHIRURGICAUX.** French. bm (6 issues). Editions Techniques, 141 rue de Javel, 75747 Paris Cedex 15 France. **Tel** 011 33 1 45589100.

FR
**ENCYCLOPEDIE MEDICO-CHIRURGICALE : KINESITHERAPIE. REEDUCATION FONCTIONNELLE.** (19??)-. French. ir. Editions Techniques, 141 rue de Javel, 75747 Paris Cedex 15 France. **Tel** 011 33 1 45589100.

FR
**ENCYCLOPEDIE MEDICO-CHIRURGICALE : MEDECINE GENERALE ET SPECIALITES. ANESTHESIE ET REANIMATION.** (19??)-. French. Five times a year. Editions Techniques, 141 rue de Javel, 75747 Paris Cedex 15 France. **Tel** 011 33 1 45589100.

FR
**ENCYCLOPEDIE MEDICO-CHIRURGICALE : MEDECINE GENERALE ET SPECIALITES. COEUR VAISSEAUX.** (19??)-. French. ir. Editions Techniques, 141 rue de Javel, 75747 Paris Cedex 15 France. **Tel** 011 33 1 45589100.

FR
**ENCYCLOPEDIE MEDICO-CHIRURGICALE : RADIODIAGNOSTIC I-VI.** (19??)-. French. ir. 2210.00F. Editions Techniques, 141 rue de Javel, 75747 Paris Cedex 15 France. **Tel** 011 33 1 45589100.

GW/0942-6027
**ENDOSCOPIC SURGERY AND ALLIED TECHNOLOGIES.** Six times a year. $217.00. Georg Thieme Verlag Stuttgart, Postfach 301120, D 70451 Stuttgart Germany. **Tel** 011 49 711 89310, FAX 011 49 711 8931298, telex 7 252 275 GTVD. **(Subscription address:** Thieme Medical Publishers Inc., 381 Park Avenue South, New York NY 10016.**)**

IT/1122-8695
**ENDOSURGERY.** (19??)-. English (Italian). tq. $90.00 (individuals), $140.00 (institutions). Edizioni Minerva Medica, Corso Bramante 83-85, 10126 Turin Italy. **Tel** 011 39 11 678282, FAX 011 39 11 674502.
**Desc:** Covers laparoscopy, thoracoscopy, surgical endoscopy and minimally invasive surgery. Official publication of the Italian Society of Endoscopic Surgery.

GW/1010-7940
**EUROPEAN JOURNAL OF CARDIO-THORACIC SURGERY : OFFICIAL JOURNAL OF THE EUROPEAN ASSOCIATION FOR CARDIO-THORACIC SURGERY.** **Added/Corp** European Association for Cardio-Thoracic Surgery. **VFOAT** European Journal of Cardiothoracic Surgery. Vol. 1 No. 1 (July 1987)-. Periodical. English. Twelve times a year. DM398.00. Springer-Verlag GmbH & Company KG, Heidelberger Platz 3, D 14197 Berlin Germany. **Tel** 011 49 30 8207223, FAX 011 49 30 8214091, telex 183 319 SPBLN D. **(Subscription address:** Springer Verlag New York Inc. / for North America, 44 Hartz Way, Secaucus NJ 07096.**) ED** Hans G Borst. **NLM** W1; EU72BF. **[CCC].** available on microfilm and microfiche from University Microfilms International (UMI). Documents available from The Genuine Article.
**Desc:** Primary goal is to provide a medium for the publication of material documenting progress made in cardiac and thoracic surgery. Publishes reports of significant clinical and experimental advances relating to surgery of the heart, the great vessels and the chest.
**Ind/Abst** Health Plan. Adminis.; Index Med. (1988-); Res. Alert [Select. Cov.]; SCISEARCH.

IT/1122-8660
**EUROPEAN JOURNAL OF FOOT AND ANKLE SURGERY.** (19??)-. English (Italian). tq. $100.00 (individuals), $140.00 (institutions). Edizioni Minerva Medica, Corso Bramante 83-85, 10126 Turin Italy. **Tel** 011 39 11 678282, FAX 011 39 11 674502.
**Desc:** Covers orthopedic and reconstructive surgery of the foot and ankle. Official journal of the European Society of Foot and Ankle Surgeons.

GW/0939-7248
**EUROPEAN JOURNAL OF PEDIATRIC SURGERY : OFFICIAL JOURNAL OF AUSTRIAN ASSOCIATION OF PEDIATRIC SURGERY ... ZEITSCHRIFT FUER KINDERCHIRURGIE.** [Eur. j. pediatr. surg.]. **Added/Corp** Osterreichische Gesellschaft fur Kinderchirurgie. **VFOAT** Zeitschrift fur Kinderchirurgie. Vol. 1, No. 1 (Feb. 1991)-. Periodical. English. bm. $309.00. Masson Editeur, Box Postale 22, 41353 Vineuil 16 France. **Tel** 011 33 54 438994. **(Subscription address:** Georg Thieme Verlag Stuttgart, Postfach 301120, D 70451 Stuttgart Germany.**) ED** A M Holschneider, S Juskiewenski. **NLM** W1; EU72DNP. **CODEN** EPSUEX. **[CCC].** Documents available from The Genuine Article, BIOSIS Document Express. ***Formed by the union of** Zeitschrift fur Kinderchirurgie, 0174-3082* ***and** Chirurgie Pediatrique, 0180-5738.*
**Desc:** Aims to integrate and coordinate all endeavors in pediatric surgery and related disciplines in accordance with European standards, to widen the scope and variety of published papers in the specialty, and to provide a European forum for pediatric surgery and specialties.
**Ind/Abst** Biol. Abstr. (1991-); Curr. Contents Clin. Med.; EMBASE; Health Plan. Adminis.; Index Med. (1991-); Res. Alert [Full Cov.]; Sci. Cit. Index (1991-); SCISEARCH.

GW/0930-343X
**EUROPEAN JOURNAL OF PLASTIC SURGERY.** [Eur. j. plast. surg.]. **Added/Corp** Austrian Society for Plastic and Reconstructive Surgery. Vol. 9, No. 1 (1986)-. Periodical. English. Six times a year. DM498.00. Springer-Verlag GmbH & Company KG, Heidelberger Platz 3, D 14197 Berlin Germany. **Tel** 011 49 30 8207223, FAX 011 49 30 8214091, telex 183 319 SPBLN D. **(Subscription address:** Springer Verlag New York Inc. / for North America, 44 Hartz Way, Secaucus NJ 07096.**) ED** I T Jackson and D E Tolhurst. **NLM** W1; EU72EB. **[CCC].** available on microfilm from University Microfilms International (UMI). Documents available from The Genuine Article. ***Continues** Chirurgia Plastica, 0340-5664.*
**Desc:** Creates a focal point for the input of new advances in clinical techniques and in research, and provides information on what is going on elsewhere in the world, and it is also willing to accept contributions from outside of Europe.
**Ind/Abst** Curr. Contents Clin. Med.; EMBASE; Res. Alert [Select. Cov.].

SW/1102-4151
**EUROPEAN JOURNAL OF SURGERY, THE.** (EUROPEAN JOURNAL OF SURGERY.). **VFOAT** Acta Chirurgica. Vol. 157, No 1, January (1991)-. Academic Scholarly Publication. English. mo. Kr1390.00, $230.00. Scandinavian University Press, PO Box 2959 Toeyen, N 0608 Oslo 6 Norway. **Tel** 011 47 2 2575400, FAX 011 47 2 2575353, telex 71896 UROR N. **(Subscription address:** Scandinavian University Press, 200 Meacham Ave., Elmont NY 11003.**) ED** Sten Lennquist. **NLM** W1; EU72HH. **CODEN** ACHIEB. Documents available from The Genuine Article, BIOSIS Document Express, CASDDS. ***Formed by the union of** Acta Chirurgica Scandinavica, 0001-5482* ***and** Netherlands Journal of Surgery, 0167-2487.*
**Desc:** An organ mainly for European surgeons but also publishes original papers, case reports and short communications within the field of general surgery from all other parts of the world. Clinical reviews and book reviews published on invitation from the editors.
**Ind/Abst** Biol. Abstr. (1991-); Chem. Abstr.; Curr. Contents Clin. Med.; EMBASE; Energy Res. Abstr.; Index Med. (1991-); Mod. Med.; Nutr. Abstr. Rev., Ser. B, Live Feeds and Feed.; Nutr. Abstr. Rev., Ser. A, Hum. Exp.; Life Sci. Collect.; Protozoolog. Abstr.; Ref. Upd. Deluxe Ed.; Res. Alert [Full Cov.]; Sci. Cit. Index; SCISEARCH; Soc. Sci. Cit. Index [Select. Cov.]; SportSearch.

SW
**EUROPEAN JOURNAL OF SURGERY. SUPPLEMENT / ACTA CHIRURGICA. SUPPLEMENT, THE.** **VFOAT** Acta Chirurgica. Supplement; European Journal of Surgery. Supplementum. (1991)-. Monographic series. English. ir. Comes with European Journal of Surgery. Scandinavian University Press, PO Box 2959 Toeyen, N 0608 Oslo 6 Norway. **Tel** 011 47 2 2575400, FAX 011 47 2 2575353, telex 71896 UROR N. **(Subscription address:** Scandinavian University Press, 200 Meacham Ave., Elmont NY 11003.**) NLM** W1; EU72HHA. **CODEN** ACTCEJ. ***Continues** Acta Chirurgica Scandinavica. Supplementum, 0301-1860.*
**Ind/Abst** EMBASE; Index Med. (1991-).

UK/0950-821X
**EUROPEAN JOURNAL OF VASCULAR SURGERY.** [Eur. j. vasc. surg.]. Vol. 1, No. 1 (Feb. 1987)-. Periodical. English. bm. £205.00 (institution), £84.00 (individual) UK & Europe; $369.00 (institution), $126.00 (individual) other. Harcourt Brace & Company Ltd., Foots Cray, High Street, Sidcup Kent DA14 5HP England. **Tel** 011 44 81 300 3322, FAX 011 44 81 309 0807. **(Subscription address:** W. B. Saunders Company / North America Subscriptions, c/o Periodicals, 6277 Sea Harbour Drive, 4th Floor, Orlando FL 32887.**) ED** P R F Bell. **NLM** W1; EU72PE. Documents available from The Genuine Article.
**Desc:** Primarily aimed at vascular surgeons dealing with patients with arterial, venous, and lymphatic diseases. Contributions are included on the diagnosis, investigation, and management of vascular disorders. Encourages papers on technical aspects of vascular surgery and includes some invited state-of-the-art review articles from time to time.
**Ind/Abst** Curr. Contents Clin. Med.; EMBASE; Health Plan. Adminis.; Index Med. (Vol. 1, No. 1, 1987-); Res. Alert [Select. Cov.].

●GW/0940-6719
**EUROPEAN SPINE JOURNAL : OFFICIAL PUBLICATION OF THE EUROPEAN SPINE SOCIETY, THE EUROPEAN SPINAL DEFORMITY SOCIETY, AND THE EUROPEAN SECTION OF THE CERVICAL SPINE RESEARCH SOCIETY.** **Added/Corp** European Spine Society. European Spinal Deformities Society. Cervical Spine Research Society. European Section. Vol. 1, No. 1 (1992)-. Periodical. English (summaries and/or abstracts in French). Six times a year. DM428.00. Springer-Verlag GmbH & Company KG, Heidelberger Platz 3, D 14197 Berlin Germany. **Tel** 011 49 30 8207223, FAX 011 49 30 8214091, telex 183 319 SPBLN D. **(Subscription address:** Springer Verlag New York Inc. / for North America, 44 Hartz Way, Secaucus NJ 07096.**) ED** M. Aebi, S. Nazarian. **NLM** W1; EU732T.
**Desc:** Devoted to spine surgery and all the disciplines related to it, like functional and surgical anatomy of the spine, biochemistry and pathophysiology of the spine including basic sciences, diagnostics procedures, and neurology.

SZ/0014-312X
**EUROPEAN SURGICAL RESEARCH.** [Eur. surg. res.]. **Added/Corp** European Society for Experimental Surgery. **VFOAT** Europaische Chirurgische Forschung; Recherches Chirurgicales Europeenes. Vol. 1 (1969)-. Academic Scholarly Publication. English. bm (6 issues). $335.00. S. Karger AG, Allschwilerstrasse 10, PO Box - Postfach - Case Postale, CH-4009 Basel Switzerland. **Tel** 011 41 61 306-1111, FAX 011 41 61 306-1234, telex CH 962 652. **ED** K. Messmer. **NLM** W1 EU733. **CODEN** EUSRBM. **[CCC]. Ad Acc. Pr Rev.** available on microfilm and microfiche from University Microfilms International (UMI). Documents available from The Genuine Article, BIOSIS Document Express, CASDDS.
**Desc:** Features original clinical and experimental papers and short technical notes serving the information needs of investigators in various fields of operative medicine. Coverage includes surgery, surgical pathophysiology, drug usage, and new surgical techniques. Special consideration is given to information on the use of physiological and biological methods as well as biophysical measuring and recording systems. The journal is of particular value for workers interested in new techniques and in how these can be introduced into clinical work or applied when critical decisions are made concerning the use of new procedures or drugs.
**Ind/Abst** Biol. Abstr.; Chem. Abstr.; Contents Recent Econ. J.; Curr. Contents Life Sci.; EMBASE; Health Plan. Adminis.; Index Med.; Index Vet.; Life Sci. Collect.; Ref. Upd. Deluxe Ed.; Res. Alert [Full Cov.]; Sci. Cit. Index; SCISEARCH; Vet. Bull.

NE/0014-4134
**EXCERPTA MEDICA. SECTION 9. SURGERY.** ***Title Change.*** **See** Medical Science and Technology-Abstracting, Bibliographies and Statistics.

US/0736-6825
**FACIAL PLASTIC SURGERY.** (FACIAL PLASTIC SURGERY : FPS.). [Facial plast. surg.]. **VFOAT** FPS. Vol. 1, No. 1 (Fall 1983)-. Monographic series. English. qt (Jan., Apr., July, Oct.). $155.00 (institutions), $105.00 (individuals) US; $180.00˚(institutions), $130.00 (individuals) other. Thieme Medical Publishers Inc., 381 Park Avenue South, Suite 1201, New York NY 10016. **Tel** (212)683-5088, (212)683-5089, FAX (212)779-9020, telex 220 862 TSINC UR. **ED** M E Tardy Jr. and T R Bull. **DD** 617. **NLM** W1; FA1853R. **CODEN** FPSUEA. **[CCC]. Bk Rev. Ad Acc. Circ:** 1,500 (ctrl). available on microfilm from University Microfilms International (UMI). Documents available from BIOSIS Document Express.
**Desc:** Current state-of-the-art review of facial plastic

surgical techniques.
**Ind/Abst** Biol. Abstr. (1984-); EMBASE; Health Plan. Adminis.

●US/1064-7406
**FACIAL PLASTIC SURGERY CLINICS OF NORTH AMERICA.** (1993)-. Periodical. English. qt. $015.00 (individuals), $127.00 (institutions) US; $142.00 (individuals), $153.00 (institutions) other. W.B. Saunders Company, A Subsidiary of Harcourt Brace Jovanovich, Inc., The Curtis Center/Suite 300, Independence Square West, Philadelphia PA 19106-3399. **Tel** (215)238-7800 or, 5587, FAX (215)238-7883, telex 173146. **(Subscription address:** W. B. Saunders Company / North America Subscriptions, c/o Periodicals, 6277 Sea Harbour Drive, 4th Floor, Orlando FL 32887.**)** **ED** Dr. J. Regan Thomas & Dr. Wayne F. Larravee, Jr.
**Desc:** Articles emphasize procedures and techniques involved in facial plastic surgery.

US/0742-9819
**FOCUS ON SURGICAL EDUCATION.** (FOCUS ON SURGICAL EDUCATION: A PUBLICATION OF THE EDUCATIONAL CLEARINGHOUSE OF THE ASSOCIATION FOR SURGICAL EDUCATION.). [Focus surg. educ.]. **Added/Corp** Association for Surgical Education. Educational Clearinghouse. Vol. 1, No. 1 (Dec. 1983)-. Periodical. English. qt (March, June, Sept., Dec.). Free to members, $12.00 (nonmembers). Focus on Surgical Education, PO Box 19230, Southern Illinois University, Springfield IL 62794. **Tel** (217)785-3835, FAX (217)524-1793. **ED** Susan Kepner. **Bk Rev**. **Circ:** 800 (ctrl).
**Desc:** This publication features articles and commentaries on surgical education as well as abstracts of papers presented at the annual meeting.

GW
**FORSCHUNG UND FORTBILDUNG IN DER CHIRURGIE DES BEWEGUNGSAPPARATES.** German. **UDC** 616.7-089.8. **NLM** W1; FO643.

JA/0433-2644
**GEKA CHIRYO.** **VFOAT** Surgical Therapy. Vol. 1 (Aug. 1950)-. Periodical. Japanese. mo. $428.00. Nagai Shoten, (Nagai Shoten Co., Ltd.), 21-15, Fukushima 8 Chome, Fukushimaku, Osakashi,, Osakafu 553 Japan. **(Subscription address:** Kyowa Book Company Inc., 1 38 Kanda Jinbocho Chiyoda-ku, Tokyo 101 Japan.**)**

JA
**GEKA SHINRYO.** [Geka shinryÂo]. **VFOAT** Surgical Diagnosis & Treatment; Surgical Diagnosis and Treatment. (1959)-. Periodical. Japanese. mo. $364.00. **(Subscription address:** Kyowa Book Company, Inc., 1-38 Kanda Jinbo-Cho, Chiyoda-Ku Tokyo 101, Japan**)** **CODEN** GESHB4.

JA/0389-5564
**GEKA TO TAISHA, EIYO.** [Geka to taisha, eiyo]. **VFOAT** The Japanese Journal of Surgical Metabolism and Nutrition; Japanese Journal of Surgical Metabolism and Nutrition; Surgical Metabolism and Nutrition. (1981)-. Academic Scholarly Publication. Japanese (Japanese). qt (with one supplement). ¥2000. Nihon Geka Taisha Eiyo Gakkai, 3-28-6 Mejirodai Bunkyo-ku, Tokyo 112 Japan. **Tel** 03-817-5801. **CODEN** GTEIDA. **Ad Acc.** ctrl circ. Documents available from CASDDS. ***Continues*** *Jutsugo Taisha Kenkyu Kaishi.*
**Ind/Abst** Chem. Abstr.

US
**GENERAL SURGERY AND LAPARASCOPY NEWS.** English. mo. $50.00 US; $74.00 other. McMahon Publishing Company, 148 West 24th Street, 8th Floor, New York NY 10011. **Tel** (212)620-4600, FAX (212)620-5928. ***Continues*** *General Surgery News.*

US/1065-7088
**GENERAL SURGERY & LAPAROSCOPY NEWS.** **VFOAT** General Surgery and Laparoscopy News. Vol. 12, No. 12 (Dec. 1991)-. Periodical. English. mo. $50.00 (US); $74.00 (other). McMahon Publishing Company, 148 West 24th Street, 8th Floor, New York NY 10011. **Tel** (212)620-4600, FAX (212)620-5928. **DD** 617. **NLM** W1; GE272F. ***Continues*** *General Surgery News.*

US/1047-6954
**GENERAL SURGERY (GLENDALE, CALIF.).** (GENERAL SURGERY [SOUND RECORDING].). [Gen. surg.]. **Added/Corp** Audio-Digest Foundation. **VFOAT** Audio Digest General Surgery; Audio Digest Foundation General Surgery; Audio-Digest General Surgery; Audio-Digest Foundation General Surgery. Vol. 37, No. 1 (Jan. 10, 1990)-. English. sm. $179.76 US; $202.80 Canada; $247.44 other. Audio-Digest Foundation, 1577 Chevy Chase Drive, Glendale CA 91206. **Tel** (213)245-8505, (800)423-2308, FAX (818)240-7379. **DD** 617. Index available (Free, published in Feb.). ***Continues*** *Surgery (Glendale, Calif.), 0271-1273.*

US/1040-7898
**GENERAL SURGERY REPORT.** [Surg. rep.]. (1990)-. Periodical. English. Three times a year. $52.50. Mosby Year Book Inc., 11830 Westline Industrial Drive, St Louis MO 63146. **Tel** (800)325-4177, (314)872-8370, FAX (314)432-1380, telex 44-2402. **NLM** W1; SU75K.

IT/0391-9005
**GIORNALE DI CHIRURGIA, IL.** [G. chir.]. Vol. 1, No. 1 (Jan./Feb. 1980)-. Periodical. Italian (summaries and/or abstracts in English and Italian). Ten times a year. L90000, $63.96. CIC Edizioni Internazionali, Via L Spallanzani 11, 00161 Rome Italy. **Tel** 011 39 6 841-2673, FAX 011 39 6 844-3365, telex 622099 CIC I. **NLM** W1; GI503.
**Ind/Abst** Health Plan. Adminis.; Index Med. (1984-).

IT/0017-0453
**GIORNALE ITALIANO DI CHIRURGIA.** [G. ital. chir.]. (1945)-. Academic Scholarly Publication. Italian. tq. L2460000.00. Casa Libreria l'Antologia, via Suarez 5, 80129 Naples Italy. **Tel** 011 39 81 5785065. **NLM** W1 GI772.
**Ind/Abst** EMBASE.

IT/0392-128X
**GIORNALE ITALIANO DI ONCOLOGIA.** **See** Medical Science and Technology-Neoplasma, Neoplastic.

UK
**HANDBOOK LONDON. ROYAL COLLEGE OF SURGEONS OF ENGLAND.** **Main/Corp** London. Royal College of Surgeons of England. (19??)-. English. ir. Lincoln's Inn Fields, London WC2A 3PN England. **LC** R773; .L773. **DD** 610/.7/1142132. **NLM** WO 1; R889ha. ***Continues*** *Royal College of Surgeons of England. Calendar of the Royal College of Surgeons of England.*

GW/0722-1819
**HANDCHIRURGIE, MIKROCHIRURGIE, PLASTISCHE CHIRURGIE.** (HANDCHIRURGIE, MIKROCHIRURGIE, PLASTISCHE CHIRURGIE : ORGAN DER DEUTSCHSPRACHIGEN ARBEITSGEMEINSCHAFT FUER HANDCHIRURGIE : ORGAN DER DEUTSCHSPRACHIGEN ARBEITSGEMEINSCHAFT FUER MIKROCHIRURGIE DER PERIPHEREN NERVEN UND GEFASSE : ORGAN DER VEREINIGUNG DER DEUTSCHEN PLASTISCHEN CHIRURGEN.). [Handchir. Mikrochir. plast. Chir.]. **Added/Corp** Deutschsprachige Arbeitsgemeinschaft fuer Handchirurgie. Deutschsprachige Arbeitsgemeinschaft fuer Mikrochirurgie der Peripheren Nerven und Gefasse. Vereinigung der Deutschen Plastischen Chirurgen. Vol. 1, (1982)-. Academic Scholarly Publication. German (summaries and/or abstracts in English). bm (Jan., Mar., May, July, Sep., Nov.). $206.00. Hippokrates Verlag, Postfach 102263, W 70018 Stuttgart Germany. **Tel** 011 49 711 89310. **(Subscription address:** Thieme Medical Publishers Inc., 381 Park Avenue South, New York NY 10016.**)** **ED** D. Buck Gramcko, H. Millesil, and E. Biemer. **NLM** W1 HA52R. **CODEN** HMPCD9. **[CCC]**. **Bk Rev**. **Ad Acc**. **Circ:** 1,650. Documents available from BIOSIS Document Express. ***Formed by the union of*** *Zeitschrift fur Plastische Chirurgie, 0342-29278* ***and*** *Handchirurgie.*
**Desc:** This journal covers the field of hand surgery, microsurgery and plastic surgery. Its purpose is also addressed to general surgeons and orthopedists as well as to accident and reconstructive surgeons.
**Ind/Abst** Biol. Abstr.; EMBASE; Health Plan. Adminis.; Index Med.

GW/0171-9734
**HANDCHIRURGISCHE TASCHENBUCHER.** V. 1-. Monographic series. German. Price varies per volume. Perimed, Verlag Dr Med D Straube, W-8520 Erlangen Germany. **UDC** 617.576. **NLM** W1 HA52T.

US/1043-3074
**HEAD & NECK.** [Head neck]. **Added/Corp** New York Head and Neck Society. **VFOAT** Head and Neck. Vol. 11, No. 1 (Jan./Feb. 1989)-. Periodical. English. Six times a year (Jan., Mar., May, July, Sept., Nov.). $372.00 (US); $432.00 (Canada and Mexico); $454.50 (other). John Wiley & Sons, Inc., 605 Third Avenue, New York NY 10158-0012. **Tel** (212)850-6000, (212)850-6645, FAX (212)850-6088, telex 12-7063. **(Subscription address:** John Wiley & Sons / England, Baffins Lane, Chichester, West Sussex PO19 1UD England.**)** **ED** Helmuth Goepfert. **LC** RD523; .H4. **DD** 617.5/1/005. **NLM** W1; HE115. **CODEN** HEANEE. available on microfilm and microfiche from University Microfilms International (UMI). Documents available from The Genuine Article, BIOSIS Document Express. ***Continues*** *Head & Neck Surgery, 0148-6403.*
**Desc:** Thoroughly examines the management and prevention of all diseases in the head and neck area, including benign and malignant tumors, congenital deformities, and trauma.
**Ind/Abst** Biol. Abstr. (1990-); Curr. Contents Clin. Med.; EMBASE; Health Plan. Adminis.; Index Med. (1989-); Res. Alert [Full Cov.]; Rev. Med. Vet. Mycology; Sci. Cit. Index; SCISEARCH.

US/0887-1779
**HEAD INJURY UPDATE.** [Head inj. update]. Vol. 1, No. 1 (Jan. 1986)-. Periodical. English. Twelve times a year. $60.00. HDI Publishers, 5626 Weeping Willow, Houston TX 77092. **Tel** (713)682-8700, FAX (713)681-9595. **ED** Dr. L. Don Lehmkuhl (phone: (713)666-9550). **DD** 617. cum. index. **Bk Rev**, (Qty: 12). **Ad Acc**.
**Desc:** An interdisciplinary source of information that summarizes the latest development, research, literature and activities of the entire head injury rehabilitation field. Features concise research abstracts plus articles on new treatment techniques, medico-legal issues, grant opportunities and people in the news.

CN/1180-243X
**HEALTH REPORTS. SUPPLEMENT. SURGICAL PROCEDURES AND TREATMENTS.** (HEALTH REPORTS. SUPPLEMENT. SURGICAL PROCEDURES AND TREATMENTS / STATISTICS CANADA, CANADIAN CENTRE FOR HEALTH INFORMATION.). [Health rep., Suppl., Surg. proced. treat.]. **Added/Corp** Canadian Centre for Health Information. **VFOAT** Surgical Procedures and Treatments; Interventions Chirurgicales et Traitements; Rapports sur la Sante. Interventions Chirurgicales et Traitements. (1985)-. English (French). an. 35.00Can$ Canada; $36.50 other. Statistics Canada, Publications Sales & Services, Main Building Room 1710, Ottawa Ontario K1A 0T6 Canada. **Tel** (613)951-5078, (800)267-6677, FAX (613)951-1584, telex 053-3585. **LC** RA407.5.C2; H426. **DD** 617/.0971/021. ***Continues*** *Surgical Procedures and Treatments, 0317-3720.*

GR
**HELLENIKO PERIODIKO GIA STOMATIKE & GNATHOPROSOPIKE CHEIROURGIKE / EPISEMO ORGANO TES HETAIREIAS STOMATOGNATHOPROSOPIKES CHEIROURGIKES, TO.** **VFOAT** Helleniko Periodiko Gia Stomatike Kai; Gnathoprosopike Cheirourgike; Greek Journal of Oral and Maxillofacial Surgery; Greek Journal of Oral & Maxillofacial Surgery. Vol. 1, No. 1 (March 1986)-. Periodical. Greek, Modern (summaries and/or abstracts in English and Greek, Modern). qt. $30.00. **NLM** W1; HE794H.
**Ind/Abst** Index Dent. Lit. (March 1986-).

US/0743-9202
**HIGHLIGHTS FROM INFECTIONS IN SURGERY.** (HIGHLIGHTS FROM INFECTIONS IN SURGERY : A SERVICE TO THE SURGICAL PROFESSION FROM MSD, MERCK SHARP & DOHME.). [Highlights Infect. surg.]. Vol. 1, No. 1 (June 1984)-. Periodical. English. ir. Infections In Surgery Associates, 256 Fifth Avenue, New York NY 10001. **DD** 617. **UDC** 616.94:616-089.8.

RU/0023-1207
**HIRURGIJA (MOSKVA).** (KHIRURGIIA.). [Hirurgija]. **Added/Corp** Soviet Union. Ministerstvo Zdravookhraneniia. Vsesoiuznoe Nauchnoe Obshchestvo Khirurgov (Soviet Union) Soviet Union. Narodnyi Komissariat Zdravookhraneniia. Vsesoiuznaia Assotsiatsiia Khirurov (Soviet Union). (1937)-. Academic Scholarly Publication. Russian (summaries and/or abstracts in English). mo. Izdatelstvo Nauka / Akademiia Nauk, Publishing House of the Russian Academy of Sciences, Leninskii Porspekt 14, 117901 Moscow Russia. **Tel** 011 95 954-21-53, FAX 011 95 938-21-44, telex 411964. **NLM** W1 KH58. **CODEN** KHIRAE. **[CCC]**. Index available. **Bk Rev**. Documents available from The Genuine Article, CASDDS. ***Continues*** *Sovetskaia Khirurgiia, 0302-6027.*
**Ind/Abst** Chem. Abstr. (-1973); EMBASE; Helminthol. Abstr. (1991-); Index Med.; Protozoolog. Abstr.; Res. Alert [Select. Cov.]; SCISEARCH; Soc. Sci. Cit. Index [Select. Cov.].

BU/0450-2167
**HIRURGIJA (SOFIJA).** (KHIRURGIIA.). [Hirurgija]. **VFOAT** Chirurgia. (1948)-. Periodical. Bulgarian. mo. Izdatelstvo Medicina i Fizkult, PL Slavejkov 11, 1000 Sofia Bulgaria. **(Subscription address:** Victor Kamkin, 4956 Boiling Brook Parkway, Rockville MD 20852.**)** **NLM** W1 KH586. **CODEN** KHIGAF. Documents available from CASDDS.
**Ind/Abst** Chem. Abstr.; EMBASE; Helminthol. Abstr.; Index Med.

JA/0018-3377
**HOKKAIDO SEIKEI SAIGAI GEKA ZASSHI.** **See** Medical Science and Technology-Orthopedics.

SZ/0894-8569
**HPB SURGERY.** (HPB SURGERY : A WORLD JOURNAL OF HEPATIC, PANCREATIC AND BILIARY SURGERY.). [HPB surg.]. **VFOAT** HPB. **VAT** Hepatic, Pancreatic and Biliary Surgery. Vol. 1 No. 1 (Sept. 1988)-. Periodical. English. qt. $288.00 (academic institutions), $449.00 (corporate institutions). Harwood Academic Publishers, PO Box 90, Reading RG1 8JL England. **Tel** 011 44 734 560080. **(Subscription address:** Harwood Academic Publishers, PO Box 786, Cooper Station, New York NY 10276.**)** **ED** Stig Bengmark. **DD** 617. **NLM** W1; HP986. **CODEN** HPBSE9. **[CCC]**.
**Ind/Abst** EMBASE; Health Plan. Adminis.; Index Med. (1988-).

IT/0391-8629
**INCONTRI DE ANESTESIA, RIANIMAZIONE E SCIENZE AFFINI.** [Incontri anest., rianim. sci. affini]. **VFOAT** Incontri. (1977)-. Academic Scholarly Publication. Italian. qt. Edizioni Incontri / Naples, Via Grande Archivio 32, 80138 Naples Italy. **Tel** 011 39 81 5454373, 011 39 81 7472928. **CODEN** IARAD8. Documents available from CASDDS.
**Ind/Abst** Chem. Abstr. (1966-1977).

II/0970-0358
**INDIAN JOURNAL OF PLASTIC SURGERY.** (INDIAN JOURNAL OF PLASTIC SURGERY : OFFICIAL PUBLICATION OF THE ASSOCIATION OF PLASTIC SURGEONS OF INDIA.). [Indian j. plast. surg.]. **Added/Corp** Association of Plastic Surgeons of India. (1968)-. Periodical. English. sa. $30.00. Association Plastic Surgeons of India, Varanasi, India. **(Subscription address:** Prints India, 11 Darya Ganj, New Delhi 110002 India.**)** **UDC** 617. **NLM** W1; IN226R.

II/0019-5650
**INDIAN JOURNAL OF SURGERY.** [Indian j. surg.]. **Added/Corp** Association of Surgeons of India. Vol. 1 (Mar. 1939)-. Academic Scholarly Publication. English. mo. $35.00. Association of Surgeons of India, c/o Madurai Medical College, Madurah India. **(Subscription address:** Prints India, 11 Darya Ganj, New Delhi, 110002 India, (Phone: 011 91 11 3268645)**)** **LC** RD1. **NLM** W1 IN235F. **CODEN** IJSUAV. Documents available from BIOSIS Document Express, CASDDS.
**Ind/Abst** Biol. Abstr.; Chem. Abstr.; EMBASE; Life Sci. Collect.

US/0883-4954
**INNOVATIONS IN SURGERY AT THE LAHEY CLINIC MEDICAL CENTER.** [Innov. surg.]. **VFOAT** Innovations in Surgery; Surgery. Periodical. English. bm. $19.00. Medical Publishers Enterprises, 15 22 Fair Lawn Avenue, Fair Lawn NJ 07410. **Tel** (201)796-6500. **DD** 617. **UDC** 616-089.8.

US/0065-6895
**INSTRUCTIONAL COURSE LECTURES.** [Instr. course lect.]. **Main/Corp** American Academy of Orthopaedic Surgeons. **VFOAT** Instructional Course Lectures of the American Academy of Orthopaedic Surgeons. Vol. 5 (1948)-. English. an (Feb.). $114.00 US and Canada. American Academy of Orthopaedic Surgeons, 6300 North River Road, Rosemont IL 60018. **Tel** (708)823-7186, (800)626-6726. **LC** RD711; .A55. **DD** 617. **NLM** W1 IN627V.
**Ind/Abst** Index Med.

FR/0242-3960
**INTER BLOC.** [Inter bloc]. (Feb. 1980)-. Periodical. French. qt. $26.00. Masson Editeur, Box Postale 22, 41353 Vineuil 16 France. **Tel** 011 33 54 438994. **(Subscription address:** 7A Boulevard de Perolles, CH-1701 Fribourg Switzerland**)** **NLM** W1 IN653V. **[CCC].**

IT/0392-9590
**INTERNATIONAL ANGIOLOGY.** (INTERNATIONAL ANGIOLOGY : A JOURNAL OF THE INTERNATIONAL UNION OF ANGIOLOGY.). [Int. angiol.]. **Added/Corp** International Union of Angiology. Vol. 1, No. 1 (June 1982)-. Periodical. English. qt. $90.00 (individuals), $140.00 (institutions). Edizioni Minerva Medica, Corso Bramante 83-85, 10126 Turin Italy. **Tel** 011 39 11 678282, FAX 011 39 11 674502. **ED** P Balas. **NLM** W1 IN703. **CODEN** INANEK. **Pr Rev.** Documents available from The Genuine Article, BIOSIS Document Express.
**Desc:** Articles cover the broad field of angiology, including rare cases, historical notices, new surgical techniques, and letters to the editor.
**Ind/Abst** Biol. Abstr.; Curr. Contents Clin. Med.; EMBASE; Index Med. (Vol. 4, No. 1, 1985-);(v4n1, 1985-); Res. Alert [Select. Cov.]; SCISEARCH.

JA/0285-6506
**INTERNATIONAL JOURNAL OF AESTHETIC SURGERY / INTERNATIONAL SOCIETY OF AESTHETIC SURGERY.** [Int. j. aesthet. surg.]. Vol. 1, No. 1 (Aug. 1981)-. Periodical. English. Kokusai Biyo Geka Gakkai, (International Soc. of Aesthetic Surgery), 12-15, Shinbashi 1 Chome, Minatoku, Tokyoto 105 Japan. **UDC** 616-089.84; 617-089.844. **NLM** W1; IN7652U.

DK/0901-5027
**INTERNATIONAL JOURNAL OF ORAL AND MAXILLOFACIAL SURGERY.** [Int. j. oral maxillofac. surg.]. **Added/Corp** International Association of Oral and Maxillofacial Surgeons. **VFOAT** Oral and Maxillofacial Surgery. Vol. 15, No. 1 (Feb. 1986)-. Academic Scholarly Publication. English. bm. kr1590.00 US, Canada and Japan; kr1580.00 other. Munksgaard International Publishers Ltd, PO Box 2148, DK-1016 Copenhagen K Denmark. **Tel** 011 45 33 12 70 30, FAX 011 45 33 12 93 87, telex 19431 MUNKS DK. **ED** P J W Stoelinga. **NLM** W1; IN77TP. **CODEN** IJOSE9. **[CCC].** Index available. **Bk Rev. Ad Acc. Circ:** 1,200 (ctrl). Documents available from The Genuine Article, BIOSIS Document Express, CASDDS. ***Continues*** *International Journal of Oral Surgery, 0300-9785.*
**Desc:** Official publication of the International Association of Oral and Maxillofacial Surgeons.
**Ind/Abst** Biol. Abstr. (1986-); Chem. Abstr. (1986-); Curr. Contents Clin. Med.; Curr. Titl. Dent.; EMBASE; Energy Res. Abstr. (1986-); Helminthol. Abstr. (1991-); Index Med. (1986-); Index Dent. Lit. (1986-); Life Sci. Collect. (1986-); Protozoolog. Abstr.; Res. Alert [Full Cov.]; Rev. Med. Vet. Mycology; Sci. Cit. Index; SCISEARCH.

●US/1066-8969
**INTERNATIONAL JOURNAL OF SURGICAL PATHOLOGY.** **See** Medical Science and Technology-Pathology.

IT/1122-8687
**INTERNATIONAL JOURNAL OF SURGICAL SCIENCES.** (19??)-. English (Italian). mo. $130.00 (individuals), $160.00 (institutions). Edizioni Minerva Medica, Corso Bramante 83-85, 10126 Turin Italy. **Tel** 011 39 11 678282, FAX 011 39 11 674502.
**Desc:** Covers clinical and experimental surgery. The official journal of the European Association of Surgical Sciences.

IT/0020-8868
**INTERNATIONAL SURGERY.** [Int. surg.]. **Added/Corp** International College of Surgeons. Vol. 45 (Jan. 1966)-. Academic Scholarly Publication. English (Undetermined). Four times a year. $90.00 (individuals), $140.00 (institutions). Edizioni Minerva Medica, Corso Bramante 83-85, 10126 Turin Italy. **Tel** 011 39 11 678282, FAX 011 39 11 674502. **NLM** W1 IN865. **CODEN** INTSAO. **Ad Acc. Pr Rev. Circ:** 9,000. available on microfilm and microfiche from University Microfilms International (UMI). Documents available from The Genuine Article, BIOSIS Document Express, CASDDS. ***Continues*** *Journal of the International College of Surgeons, 0096-557X;* ***Absorbed*** *International Surgery Bulletin, 0097-5621.*
**Desc:** Original articles from research and clinical practice in the various surgical fields.
**Ind/Abst** Biol. Abstr.; Chem. Abstr.; Cumul. Index Nurs. Allied Health Lit.; Curr. Contents Clin. Med.; EMBASE; Energy Res. Abstr.; Index Med.; Nucl. Sci. Abstr.; Life Sci. Collect.; Res. Alert [Select. Cov.]; SCISEARCH.

US/0891-3382
**INTERNATIONAL TRENDS IN THORACIC SURGERY.** ***Ceased.*** [Int. trends gen. thorac. surg.]. Vol. 1-Ceased Vol. 2 (1987). Monographic series. English. W.B. Saunders Company, A Subsidiary of Harcourt Brace Jovanovich, Inc., The Curtis Center/Suite 300, Independence Square West, Philadelphia PA 19106-3399. **Tel** (215)238-7800 or, 5587, FAX (215)238-7883, telex 173146. **(Subscription address:** W. B. Saunders Company / North America Subscriptions, c/o Periodicals, 6277 Sea Harbour Drive, 4th Floor, Orlando FL 32887.**)** **DD** 617. **UDC** 616.12-089.8. **NLM** W1; IN914.

US/0392-3525
**ITALIAN JOURNAL OF SURGICAL SCIENCES, THE.** ***Ceased.*** [Ital. j. surg. sci.]. (1981)-Ceased (Dec. 1989). Academic Scholarly Publication. English. qt. Masson SA, Avenue Beauregard 12, CH-1701 Fribourg Switzerland. **Tel** 011 41 37 249585, FAX 011 41 37 247559, telex 942658 SEMI CH. **(Subscription address:** 7A Boulevard de Perolles, CH-1701 Fribourg Switzerland**)** **ED** Vincenzo Speranza. **UDC** 616-089.8. **NLM** W1 IT36P. **CODEN** IJSSET. **Bk Rev. Ad Acc. Circ:** 5,000 (ctrl). Documents available from BIOSIS Document Express. ***Continues*** *Surgery in Italy, 0390-5640.*
**Desc:** Official organ of the Societa Italiana di Chirurgia.
**Ind/Abst** Biol. Abstr.; EMBASE; Index Med.

JA/0047-1909
**JAPANESE JOURNAL OF SURGERY.** ***Title Change.*** [Jpn. j. surg.]. **Added/Corp** Nihon Geka Gakkai. Vol. 1 (March 1971)-(Jan. 1992). Academic Scholarly Publication. English. bm. **(Subscription address:** Kyowa Book Company Inc., 1-38 Kanda Jinbo-Cho Chiyoda-Ku, Tokyo 101 Japan**)** **NLM** W1 JA975K. **CODEN** JJSGAY. Documents available from BIOSIS Document Express, CASDDS.
**Ind/Abst** Biol. Abstr.; Chem. Abstr.; EMBASE; Index Med.; Life Sci. Collect.; SCISEARCH.

FR/0021-7697
**JOURNAL DE CHIRURGIE.** [J. chir.]. (1908)-. Academic Scholarly Publication. French. mo (except July and Aug.). $273.00. Masson Editeur, Box Postale 22, 41353 Vineuil 16 France. **Tel** 011 33 54 438994. **(Subscription address:** 7A Boulevard de Perolles, CH-1701 Fribourg Switzerland**)** **NLM** W1 JO301. **CODEN** JOCHAQ. **[CCC].** cum. index. **Pr Rev.** available on microfilm and microfiche from University Microfilms International (UMI). Documents available from The Genuine Article, BIOSIS Document Express.
**Ind/Abst** AGRICOLA; Biol. Abstr.; Curr. Contents Clin. Med.; EMBASE; Helminthol. Abstr. (1991-); Index Med.; Life Sci. Collect.; Protozoolog. Abstr.; Res. Alert [Select. Cov.]; Saf. Health Work; SCISEARCH.

US/0883-5403
**JOURNAL OF ARTHROPLASTY, THE.** [J. arthr.]. Vol. 1, No. 1 (1986)-. Periodical. English. qt. $175.00 institution, $138.00 individual. Churchill Livingstone Inc., 650 Avenue of the Americas, New York NY 10011. **Tel** (212)206-5062, FAX (212)727-7808. **(Subscription address:** Churchill Livingstone Inc., 5 South 250 Frontenac Road, Naperville, IL 60563; (telephone: (800)553-5426 or (708)416-3939)**)** **ED** Davis S. Hungerford. **DD** 617. **NLM** W1; JO544KJ. **CODEN** JOAREG. **[CCC].** Index available (bound in Dec. issue). **Bk Rev.** available on microfilm from University Microfilms International (UMI). Documents available from The Genuine Article, BIOSIS Document Express.
**Desc:** Brings together all the basic scientific and clinical information on joint replacement surgery in one source. Spans the entire range of scientific research that impacts on this dynamic field. Presents highly informative case reports offering unique insights into particular aspects of arthroplasty. Features a section on current contents and letters to the editor. Readership: orthopaedic surgeons.
**Ind/Abst** Biol. Abstr. (1987-); EMBASE; Index Med. (1986-); Ref. Upd. Deluxe Ed.; Res. Alert [Full Cov.].

US/0021-9355
**JOURNAL OF BONE AND JOINT SURGERY. AMERICAN VOLUME (PRINT ED.).** **See** Medical Science and Technology-Orthopedics.

UK/0301-620X
**JOURNAL OF BONE AND JOINT SURGERY. BRITISH VOLUME.** (JOURNAL OF BONE AND JOINT SURGERY.). [J. bone jt. surg., Br. vol.]. Vol. 30-B (Feb. 1948)-. Academic Scholarly Publication. English. Nine times a year (6 issues and 3 supplements). £38.00 British volume; £88.00 (combined with American volume). The Journal of Bone and Joint Surgery, 35-43 Lincoln's Inn Fields, London WC2A 3PN United Kingdom. **Tel** 071 405 7227, FAX 071 405 8865. **(Subscription address:** Journal of Bone and Joint Surgery, 20 Pickering Street, Needham, MA 02192; Telephone: (612)734-2875**)** **NLM** W1 JO57B. **CODEN** JBSUAK. **Pr Rev.** available on microfilm and microfiche from University Microfilms International (UMI). Documents available from The Genuine Article, CASDDS. ***Continues in part*** *Journal of Bone and Joint Surgery, 0375-9229.*
**Ind/Abst** Abr. Index Med.; Calcium Calcif. Tissue Abstr.; Chem. Abstr. (1948-1987); Curr. Aware. Biol. Sci., CABS; Curr. Contents Clin. Med.; Curr. Contents Life Sci.; Dev. Med. Child Neurol.; EMBASE; Health Devices Alerts; Helminthol. Abstr. (1991-); Index Med.; Nutr. Abstr. Rev., Ser. A, Hum. Exp.; Life Sci. Collect.; Physic. Medline Plus; Ref. Upd. Deluxe Ed.; Res. Alert [Full Cov.]; Rev. Med. Vet. Mycology; Sci. Cit. Index; SCISEARCH; Soc. Sci. Cit. Index [Select. Cov.]; SPORT Discus.

US/1058-2436
**JOURNAL OF BONE AND JOINT SURGERY (COMPUTER FILE), THE.** (THE JOURNAL OF BONE AND JOINT SURGERY.). (1991)-. Periodical. English. be. $295.00 members; $375.00 nonmembers; $495.00 institutions;. Journal of Bone and Joint Surgery, 20 Pickering Street, Needham MA 02192-3157. **Tel** (617)449-9738, FAX (617)449-9742.

US
**JOURNAL OF BONE AND JOINT SURGERY. QUINQUENNIAL INDEX.** Vol. 30/34 (1948/52)-. Periodical. English. ir. Price varies per volume. Journal of Bone and Joint Surgery, 20 Pickering Street, Needham MA 02192-3157. **Tel** (617)449-9738, FAX (617)449-9742.

US
**JOURNAL OF BONE AND JOINT SURGERY. SUBJECT BIBLIOGRAPHY.** 1948/57-. Bibliography. English. The Journal of Bone and Joint Surgery, 35-43 Lincoln's Inn Fields, London WC2A 3PN United Kingdom. **Tel** 071 405 7227, FAX 071 405 8865. ***Supersedes*** *Journal of Bone and Joint Surgery. Subject Index.*
**Desc:** Bibliography of articles in both the American and British volumes of the journal.

US/0886-0440
**JOURNAL OF CARDIAC SURGERY.** [J. card. surg.]. Vol. 1, No. 1 (March 1986)-. Periodical. English. bm (6 issues plus supplements). $115.00 US & Canada; $143.00 other. Futura Publishing Company Inc., 135 Bedford Road, PO Box 418, Armonk NY 10504-0418. **Tel** (914)273-1014, (800)877-8761, FAX (914)273-1015, (914)273-1016. **ED** Lawrence H. Cohn. **DD** 616. **NLM** W1; JO574P. Index available. cum. index. **Bk Rev. Ad Acc. Circ:** 2,637. Documents available from The Genuine Article.
**Desc:** Contains technical and review articles on all aspects of cardiac surgery. This journal will publish concise, well-illustrated technical articles by experienced surgeons in both acquired and congenital heart surgery.
**Ind/Abst** Curr. Contents Clin. Med.; EMBASE; Index Med. (Mar. 1986-); Res. Alert [Select. Cov.]; SCISEARCH.

IT/0021-9509
**JOURNAL OF CARDIOVASCULAR SURGERY.** [J. cardiovasc. surg.]. **Added/Corp** International Cardiovascular Society. Vol. 1 (July 1960)-. Academic Scholarly Publication. English. bm. $110.00 (individuals), $150.00 (institutions). Edizioni Minerva Medica, Corso Bramante 83-85, 10126 Turin Italy. **Tel** 011 39 11 678282, FAX 011 39 11 674502. **ED** R. A. Deterling Jr. and S. S. Rose. **NLM** W1 JO577. **CODEN** JCVSA2. **Pr Rev.** Documents available from The Genuine Article, BIOSIS Document Express, CASDDS.
**Desc:** Covers clinical, experimental, and surgical aspects of diseases of the heart and the entire vascular system.
**Ind/Abst** Biol. Abstr.; Chem. Abstr.; Curr. Contents Clin. Med.; EMBASE; Helminthol. Abstr. (1991-); Index Med.; Nucl. Sci. Abstr.; Life Sci. Collect.; Res. Alert [Select. Cov.]; SCISEARCH.

US/1044-5471
**JOURNAL OF CLINICAL LASER MEDICINE & SURGERY.** [J. clin. laser med. surg.]. **Added/Corp** International Society for Laser Surgery and Medicine. **VFOAT** Journal of Clinical Laser Medicine and Surgery; JCLMS. Vol. 8, No. 1 (Feb. 1990)-. Periodical. English. bm. $153.00. Mary Ann Liebert Inc., 1651 Third Avenue, New York NY 10128. **Tel** (212)289-2300, (800)M-LIEBERT, FAX (212)289-4697. **ED** Eugene W. Friedman. **DD** 610. **NLM** W1; JO588N. **CODEN** JCLSEO. **Pr Rev.** ***Continues*** *Laser Medicine & Surgery News, 0736-9417.*
**Desc:** Contains articles of advances and expanded applications and procedures, clinical and basic research, safety programs, and new instrumentation. Feature articles include profiles of laser institutes, companies, and physicians. The official journal of the International Society for Laser Surgery and Medicine.
**Ind/Abst** EMBASE.

GW/1010-5182
**JOURNAL OF CRANIO-MAXILLO-FACIAL SURGERY.** (JOURNAL OF CRANIO-MAXILLO-FACIAL SURGERY / OFFICIAL PUBLICATION OF THE EUROPEAN ASSOCIATION FOR CRANIO-MAXILLO-FACIAL SURGERY.). [J. cranio-maxillo-fac. surg.]. **Added/Corp** European Association for Cranio-Maxillo-Facial Surgery. Vol. 15, No. 1 (Feb. 1987)-. Periodical. English. bm. £105.00 Europe; £123.60 (air mail), £106.00 Other (institution). Churchill Livingstone, 1-3 Baxter's Place, Leith Walk, Edinburgh EH1 3AF Scotland. **Tel** 011 44 31 556 2424, FAX 011 44 31 558 1278, telex 727511. **(Subscription address:** Maruzen Company Ltd., PO Box 5050, Import & Export Department, Tokyo 100 31 Japan.**)** **NLM** W1; JO602WE. **CODEN** JCMSET. **Circ:** 2,200. available on microfilm and microfiche from University Microfilms International (UMI). Documents available from The Genuine Article, BIOSIS Document Express. ***Continues*** *Journal of Maxillofacial Surgery, 0301-0503.*
**Ind/Abst** Biol. Abstr.; Curr. Titl. Dent.; Index Med. (Feb. 1987-); Res. Alert [Full Cov.]; Rev. Med. Vet. Mycology; Sci. Cit. Index (1989-); SCISEARCH.

CN/1049-2275
**JOURNAL OF CRANIOFACIAL SURGERY, THE.** [J. craniofac. surg.]. Vol. 1, No. 1 (Jan. 1990)-. Periodical. English. bm. $335.00 (institutions), $240.00 (individuals) US; $360.00 (institutions), $263.00 (individuals) Canada; $377.00 (institutions), $280.00 (individuals) other. Little Brown & Company, 34 Beacon Street, Boston MA 02108. **Tel** (617)227-0730, (800)759-0190. **(Subscription address:** Little Brown and Company, PO Box 7671, Riverton NJ 08077-7671.**)** **DD** 617. **NLM** W1; JO602U. **CODEN** JSURE8. **[CCC].**
**Ind/Abst** Health Plan. Adminis.

US/0148-0812
**JOURNAL OF DERMATOLOGIC SURGERY AND ONCOLOGY, THE.** ***Title Change.*** [J. dermatol. surg. oncol.]. Vol. 3 (Jan./Feb. 1977)-(1995). Academic Scholarly Publication. English. mo (1 volume). Elsevier Science Publishing Company Inc, Madison Square Station, PO Box 882, New York NY 10159-0882. **Tel** (212)633-3950, FAX (212)633-3990. **ED** C W Hanke. **LC** RD520; .J6. **DD** 617/.477. **NLM** W1 JO619G. **[CCC].** Index available. cum. index. **Bk Rev. Ad Acc. Pr Rev. Circ:** 15,500 (ctrl). available on microfilm. Documents available from The Genuine Article. ***Continues*** *Journal of Dermatologic Surgery, 0097-9716.* ***Continued by*** *Dermatologic Surgery.*
**Desc:** Publishes up-to-date information on new research, methods and instruments used in performing all types of cutaneous surgery. Material relevant to dermatologic surgery and oncology, such as plastic and reconstructive surgery, dentistry, and psychiatry are also sought.
**Ind/Abst** Curr. Contents Clin. Med.; EMBASE; Energy Res. Abstr. (March 1982-); Index Med.; INIS Atomindex [Micro.]; Mod. Med.; Life Sci. Collect.; Protozoolog. Abstr.; Res. Alert [Full Cov.]; Sci. Cit. Index; SCISEARCH.

IT/1120-8708
**JOURNAL OF EMERGENCY SURGERY AND INTENSIVE CARE, THE.** [J. emerg. surg. intensive care]. (1990)-. Periodical. Italian. qt. L83000. Masson S.P.A, Via Statuto 2/4, 20121 Milan Italy. **Tel** 011 39 2 63671, FAX 011 39 2 6367211. **UDC** 617. ***Continues*** *Urgentis Chirurgiae Commentaria, 0392-8101.*

●US/1074-6218
**JOURNAL OF ENDOVASCULAR SURGERY.** (JOURNAL OF ENDOVASCULAR SURGERY : JEVS.). **Added/Corp** International Society for Endovascular Surgery. **VFOAT** JEVS. (1994)-. Periodical. English. qt (4 issues). $70.00 US & Canada; $90.00 other. Futura Publishing Company Inc., 135 Bedford Road, PO Box 418, Armonk NY 10504-0418. **Tel** (914)273-1014, (800)877-8761, FAX (914)273-1015, (914)273-1016.

●US/1067-2516
**JOURNAL OF FOOT AND ANKLE SURGERY, THE.** [J. foot ankle surg.]. **Added/Corp** American College of Foot and Ankle Surgeons. Vol. 32, No. 1 (Jan./Feb. 1993)-. Periodical. English. bm. $109.00 (one year), $139.00 (institution) US; $134.00 (individual), $164.00 (institutions) other. Williams & Wilkins Company, 428 East Preston Street, Baltimore MD 21202-3993. **Tel** (410)528-4000, (800)638-6423, FAX (410)528-8596, telex 87669. **(Subscription address:** Williams & Wilkins, PO Box 64380, Baltimore MD 21264.**)** **DD** 617. **NLM** W1; JO652S. **CODEN** JFSUEI. Documents available from BIOSIS Document Express, Quick Copies. ***Continues*** *Journal of Foot Surgery, 0449-2544.*
**Desc:** Clinical advances in foot surgery presented for podiatrists and orthopedic foot surgeons.
**Ind/Abst** Biol. Abstr.; Energy Res. Abstr.; Index Med. (1993-).

UK/0266-7681
**JOURNAL OF HAND SURGERY, BRITISH VOLUME.** (THE JOURNAL OF HAND SURGERY : JOURNAL OF THE BRITISH SOCIETY FOR SURGERY OF THE HAND.). [J. hand surg., Br. vol.]. **Added/Corp** British Society for Surgery of the Hand. British Vol. 9B, No. 1 (Feb. 1984)--. Periodical. English. Six times a year. £145.00 Europe; £153.00 Other (Institutions). Churchill Livingstone, 1-3 Baxter's Place, Leith Walk, Edinburgh EH1 3AF Scotland. **Tel** 011 44 31 556 2424, FAX 011 44 31 558 1278, telex 727511. **(Subscription address:** Maruzen Company Ltd., PO Box 5050, Import & Export Department, Tokyo 100 31 Japan.**)** **ED** Harold Bolton and H Graham Stack. **NLM** W1; JO669RC. available on microfilm and microfiche from University Microfilms International (UMI). Documents available from The Genuine Article. ***Continues*** *Hand, 0072-978X.*
**Desc:** An international journal which covers all aspects of hand and upper limb surgery.
**Ind/Abst** Curr. Contents Clin. Med.; Dev. Med. Child Neurol.; EMBASE; Energy Res. Abstr. (1984-); Index Med.; Life Sci. Collect.; Physic. Medline Plus; Ref. Upd. Deluxe Ed.; Res. Alert [Select. Cov.]; SCISEARCH; SportSearch.

US/0363-5023
**JOURNAL OF HAND SURGERY (ST. LOUIS, MO.), THE.** (THE JOURNAL OF HAND SURGERY.). [J. hand surg.]. **Added/Corp** American Society for Surgery of the Hand. **VFOAT** Hand Surgery. Vol. 1 (July 1976)-. Periodical. English. bm (6 issues). $149.00 (institution), $85.00 (individual) US. Churchill Livingstone Inc., 650 Avenue of the Americas, New York NY 10011. **Tel** (212)206-5062, FAX (212)727-7808. **(Subscription address:** Churchill Livingstone Inc., 5 South 250 Frontenac Road, Naperville, IL 60563; (telephone: (800)553-5426 or (708)416-3939)**)** **ED** Adrian E. Flatt. **LC** RD559; .J68. **DD** 617/.575/005. **NLM** W1 JO669R. **CODEN** JHSUDV. **[CCC].** Index available (bound in last issue). **Bk Rev. Ad Acc. Pr Rev. Circ:** 7,641. available on microfilm and microfiche from University Microfilms International (UMI). Documents available from The Genuine Article, BIOSIS Document Express.
**Desc:** Devoted to the various aspects of surgery of the hand, including surgical techniques, diagnosis, and evaluation of the loss of function. Edited for hand, orthopaedic, plastic, reconstructive, and general surgeons who seek to restore function of the hand and upper extremity.
**Ind/Abst** Biol. Abstr.; Calcium Calcif. Tissue Abstr.; Curr. Contents Clin. Med.; Dev. Med. Child Neurol.; EMBASE; Index Med.; INIS Atomindex [Micro.]; Physic. Medline Plus; Ref. Upd. Deluxe Ed.; Res. Alert [Select. Cov.]; Risk Abstr.; SCISEARCH; SportSearch.

US/1053-2498
**JOURNAL OF HEART AND LUNG TRANSPLANTATION, THE.** (THE JOURNAL OF HEART AND LUNG TRANSPLANTATION : THE OFFICIAL PUBLICATION OF THE INTERNATIONAL SOCIETY FOR HEART TRANSPLANTATION.). [J. heart lung transplant.]. **Added/Corp** International Society for Heart Transplantation. Vol. 10, No. 1, Pt. 1 (Jan./Feb. 1991)-. Periodical. English. bm (6 issues). $117.00 (institutions), $77.00 (individuals) US; $147.00 (institutions), $107.00 (individuals) other. Mosby Year Book Inc., 11830 Westline Industrial Drive, St Louis MO 63146. **Tel** (800)325-4177, (314)872-8370, FAX (314)432-1380, telex 44-2402. **LC** RD598; .J68. **DD** 617.4/120592/05. **NLM** W1; JO67BS. **CODEN** JHLTES. **[CCC].** available on microfilm from University Microfilms International (UMI). Documents available from The Genuine Article, BIOSIS Document Express. ***Continues*** *Journal of Heart Transplantation, 0887-2570.*
**Desc:** Serves as a worldwide forum for the exchange of information about the field of intrathoracic transplantation and replacement.
**Ind/Abst** Biol. Abstr.; EMBASE; Health Plan. Adminis.; Index Med. (1991-); INIS Atomindex [Micro.]; Res. Alert [Select. Cov.]; SCISEARCH.

GW/0944-1166
**JOURNAL OF HEPATO-BILIARY-PANCREATIC SURGERY.** (19??)-. English. Four times a year. DM260.00. Springer-Verlag GmbH & Company KG, Heidelberger Platz 3, D 14197 Berlin Germany. **Tel** 011 49 30 8207223, FAX 011 49 30 8214091, telex 183 319 SPBLN D. **(Subscription address:** Springer Verlag New York Inc. / for North America, 44 Hartz Way, Secaucus NJ 07096.**)**

US/0894-1939
**JOURNAL OF INVESTIGATIVE SURGERY.** (JOURNAL OF INVESTIGATIVE SURGERY : THE OFFICIAL JOURNAL OF THE ACADEMY OF SURGICAL RESEARCH.). [J. invest. surg.]. **Added/Corp** Academy of Surgical Research (U.S.). Vol. 1, No. 1 (1988)-. Periodical. English. bm. £139.00 UK; $230.00 other. Taylor & Francis Ltd., Rankine Road, Basingstoke Hampshire, RG24 8PR United Kingdom. **Tel** 011 44 256 840366, FAX 011 44 256 479438, telex 858540. **(Subscription address:** Taylor & Francis Inc., 1900 Frost Road, Suite 101, Bristol PA 19007-1598.**)** **ED** Andreas F. Von Recum. **DD** 617. **NLM** W1; JO73D. **CODEN** JISUE5. **[CCC].** Index available. **Bk Rev. Ad Acc. Pr Rev. Circ:** 500. available on microfilm from University Microfilms International (UMI).
**Desc:** Encompasses the individual and collaboratative efforts of scientists of multiple professional backgrounds who are engaged in surgical research. Publishes original scientific and technical contributions and reviews on: development of novel surgical concepts; development of surgical models, devices, and instruments; development of surgical methodologies; evaluation of surgical methodologies and implants; application of surgical research to the evaluation of devices for use in medicine and surgery, etc. on topics and trends.
**Ind/Abst** EMBASE; Health Plan. Adminis.

US/1052-3901
**JOURNAL OF LAPAROENDOSCOPIC SURGERY.** [J. laparoendosc. surg.]. Vol. 1, No. 1 (1990)-. Periodical. English. bm. $183.00. Mary Ann Liebert Inc., 1651 Third Avenue, New York NY 10128. **Tel** (212)289-2300, (800)M-LIEBERT, FAX (212)289-4697. **ED** Warren Grundfest and John White. **DD** 617. **NLM** W1; JO734J. **CODEN** JLSUEQ. **Ad Acc. Pr Rev.**
**Desc:** Forum for disseminating information on the surgical techniques that encompass laparoscopy and endoscopy. Focuses on these techniques in general surgery and in areas of specialization that include gastroenterology, gynecology, ENT, cardiovascular and thoracic surgery. Each issue contains original papers and reviews that are pertinent for practicing surgeons.
**Ind/Abst** EMBASE; Index Med. (1990-).

●UK/0967-7720
**JOURNAL OF MEDICAL BIOGRAPHY.** **Added/Corp** Royal Society of Medicine (Great Britain). Vol. 1, No. 1 (Feb. 1993)-. Periodical. English. qt. $88.00 (institution), $67.00 (individual) US; £47.00 (institution), £36.00 (individual) other. Royal Society of Medicine Press, 1 Wimpole Street, London W1M 8AE England. **Tel** 011 44 71 2902928. **ED** J. M. H. Moll. **NLM** W1; JO749Q.

US/0890-6599
**JOURNAL OF NEUROLOGICAL & ORTHOPAEDIC MEDICINE & SURGERY, THE.** [J. neurol. orthop. med. surg.]. **Added/Corp** American Academy of Neurological and Orthopaedic Surgeons. **VFOAT** Journal of Neurological and Orthopaedic Medicine and Surgery; JONOMAS. Vol. 6, Issue 1 (April 1985)-. Periodical. English. Four times a year. $112.00. Springer-Verlag New York Inc., 175 5th Avenue, New York NY 10010. **Tel** (212)460-1500, telex 232 235 SPB UR. **(Subscription address:** Springer Verlag New York Inc. / for North America, 44 Hartz Way, Secaucus NJ 07096.**)** **ED** Michael R Rask. **LC** RD593; .J68. **DD** 617/.48/005. **NLM** W1; JO7875. Index available. cum. index. **Bk Rev. Ad Acc. Pr Rev.** ctrl circ. available on microfiche; available on microfilm. Documents available from The Genuine Article. ***Continues*** *Journal of Neurological and Orthopaedic Surgery, 0271-1575.*
**Desc:** Publishes original articles, case reports, topical reviews and "how-to" articles in orthopaedic medicine and surgery, with an emphasis on pain and pain management. The official journal of the American Academy of Neurological and Orthopaedic Surgeons.
**Ind/Abst** EMBASE; Res. Alert [Full Cov.]; Soc. Sci. Cit. Index [Select. Cov.].

US/0022-3085
**JOURNAL OF NEUROSURGERY.** See Medical Science and Technology-Neurology.

US/0898-4921
**JOURNAL OF NEUROSURGICAL ANESTHESIOLOGY.** [J. neurosurg. anesthesiol.]. Vol. 1, No. 1 (Mar. 1989)-. Periodical. English. qt. $116.00 (individuals), $184.00 (institutions) US; $172.00 (individuals), $210.00 (institutions) other. Raven Press, 1185 Avenue of the Americas, 37th Floor, New York NY 10036. **Tel** (212)930-9500, (212)930-9604, FAX (212)869-3495, (212)302-8507, telex 640073. **ED** James E. Cottrell. **DD** 617. **NLM** W1; JO795CF. **CODEN** JNANEV. **[CCC]. Pr Rev.** available on microfilm and microfiche from University Microfilms International (UMI). Documents available from The Genuine Article.
**Desc:** Keeps practitioners abreast of advances in neurosurgical anesthesiology that directly impact on current clinical practice or will affect clinical practice in the future. Each issue contains peer-reviewed articles presenting results in major clinical and laboratory research projects and clinical reports detailing the results of preliminary clinical investigations and studies using small numbers of patients.
**Ind/Abst** Curr. Contents Clin. Med.; EMBASE; Index Vet.; Res. Alert [Full Cov.]; SCISEARCH.

IT/0390-5616
**JOURNAL OF NEUROSURGICAL SCIENCES.** [J. neurosurg. sci.]. **Added/Corp** Societa Italiana di Neurochirurgia. **VFOAT** Minerva Neurochirurgica. Vol. 17 (Jan./June 1973)-. Academic Scholarly Publication. English. qt. $90.00 (individuals), $140.00 (institutions). Edizioni Minerva Medica, Corso Bramante 83-85, 10126 Turin Italy. **Tel** 011 39 11 678282, FAX 011 39 11 674502. **ED** P. E. Maspes. **NLM** W1 JO795D. **Ad Acc.** available on microfilm and microfiche from University Microfilms International (UMI). ***Continues in part*** *Minerva Neurochirurgica, 0026-4881.*
**Desc:** Journal addressed to practitioners and specialists in neurosurgery in Italy and abroad. It deals with topics in scientific practice and research.
**Ind/Abst** EMBASE; Index Med.

UK/0963-5386
**JOURNAL OF ONE-DAY SURGERY.** (THE JOURNAL OF DAY SURGERY.). [J. one-day surg.]. (1991)-. English. qt. Free (members British Association of Day Surgery); £12.00 UK; £14.00 other. Newton Mann Limited, Stretton Road, Tansley, Matlock, Derbyshire DE4 5GE England. **Tel** 0629 3941, FAX 0629 580479. **ED** Dr. H.T. Davenport. **DD** 362.197. **Bk Rev. Ad Acc. Pr Rev.**

US/0278-2391
**JOURNAL OF ORAL AND MAXILLOFACIAL SURGERY.** (JOURNAL OF ORAL AND MAXILLOFACIAL SURGERY : OFFICIAL JOURNAL OF THE AMERICAN ASSOCIATION OF ORAL AND MAXILLOFACIAL SURGEONS.). [J. oral maxillofac. surg.]. **Added/Corp** American Association of Oral and Maxillofacial Surgeons. Vol. 40 No. 1 (Jan. 1982)-. Periodical. English. mo. $85.00 (individual), $106.00 (institutions), US; $138.00 (individual), $149.00 (institutions), other. W.B. Saunders Company, A Subsidiary of Harcourt Brace Jovanovich, Inc., The Curtis Center/Suite 300, Independence Square West, Philadelphia PA 19106-3399. **Tel** (215)238-7800 or, 5587, FAX (215)238-7883, telex 173146. **(Subscription address:** W. B. Saunders Company / North America Subscriptions, c/o Periodicals, 6277 Sea Harbour Drive, 4th Floor, Orlando FL 32887.**) ED** Daniel M. Laskin. **LC** RK1; .J78. **DD** 617. **NLM** W1 JO803SM. **CODEN** JOMSDA. **[CCC].** Index available. cum. index. **Bk Rev. Ad Acc. Pr Rev. Circ:** 8,900. available on microfilm and microfiche from University Microfilms International (UMI). Documents available from The Genuine Article, BIOSIS Document Express. ***Continues*** *Journal of Oral Surgery (American Dental Association : 1965), 0022-3255.*
**Desc:** Coverage of new techniques, developments and ideas. Practice-applicable articles to help develop and expand methods used to handle dentoalveolar surgery, facial injuries and deformities, TMJ disorders, oral cancer, jaw reconstruction, anesthesia and analgesia.
**Ind/Abst** Abr. Index Med.; Biol. Abstr. (1986-); Calcium Calcif. Tissue Abstr.; CSA Neuro. Abstr. (?-?); Curr. Contents Clin. Med.; Curr. Titl. Dent.; Dent. Abstr.; EMBASE; Energy Res. Abstr.; Hospit. Health Admin. Index; Index Med.; Index Dent. Lit.; Iowa Drug Inf. Serv. (1968-); Life Sci. Collect.; Physic. Medline Plus; Res. Alert [Full Cov.]; Rev. Med. Vet. Entomol.; Rev. Med. Vet. Mycology; Sci. Cit. Index; SCISEARCH.

●HK/1022-5536
**JOURNAL OF ORTHOPAEDIC SURGERY.** See Medical Science and Technology-Orthopedics.

FR
**JOURNAL OF ORTHOPAEDIC SURGERY, THE.** ***Ceased.*** **See** Medical Science and Technology-Orthopedics.

UK/0334-0236
**JOURNAL OF ORTHOPAEDIC SURGICAL TECHNIQUES, THE. See** Medical Science and Technology-Orthopedics.

US/0022-3468
**JOURNAL OF PEDIATRIC SURGERY.** [J. pediatr. surg.]. Vol. 1 (Feb. 1966)-. Academic Scholarly Publication. English. mo. $189.00 (individual), $259.00 (institution) US; $279.00 (individual), $295.00 (institution) other. W.B. Saunders Company, A Subsidiary of Harcourt Brace Jovanovich, Inc., The Curtis Center/Suite 300, Independence Square West, Philadelphia PA 19106-3399. **Tel** (215)238-7800 or, 5587, FAX (215)238-7883, telex 173146. **(Subscription address:** W. B. Saunders Company / North America Subscriptions, c/o Periodicals, 6277 Sea Harbour Drive, 4th Floor, Orlando FL 32887.**) ED** Stephen L. Gans. **LC** RD137.A1. **DD** 617. **UDC** 616-089-053.2. **NLM** W1 JO828FH. **CODEN** JPDSA3. **[CCC].** Index available (bound in issue). **Pr Rev.** Documents available from The Genuine Article, BIOSIS Document Express.
**Desc:** Presents original contributions together with a complete international abstracts section and other special departments to provide a quick source of the latest information and reference.
**Ind/Abst** Biol. Abstr.; Comb. Cumul. Index Pediatr.; CSA Neuro. Abstr. (?-?); Curr. Contents Clin. Med.; Dev. Med. Child Neurol.; EMBASE; Energy Res. Abstr.; Helminthol. Abstr. (19??-19??); Index Med.; Life Sci. Collect.; Protozoolog. Abstr.; Ref. Upd. Deluxe Ed.; Res. Alert [Full Cov.]; Rev. Med. Vet. Mycology; Sci. Cit. Index; SCISEARCH; Soc. Sci. Cit. Index [Select. Cov.].

US/1077-2847
**JOURNAL OF PELVIC SURGERY.** (19??)-. Periodical. English. bm. $99.00 (individuals), $144.00 (institutions) US; $154.00 (individuals), $184.00 (institutions) other. J.B. Lippincott Company, 227 East Washington Square, Philadelphia PA 19106-3780. **Tel** (215)238-4200 or 4454, FAX (215)238-4227. **(Subscription address:** J.B. Lippincott, PO Box 350, Hagerstown MD 21740.**)**
**Desc:** Covers scientific advances and clinical experience related to pelvic surgery.

US/0743-684X
**JOURNAL OF RECONSTRUCTIVE MICROSURGERY.** [J. reconstr. microsurg.]. Vol. 1, No. 1 (July 1984)-. Periodical. English. bm (Jan., Mar., May, July, Sep., Nov.). $179.00 (institutions), $145.00 (individuals) US; $204.00*(institutions), $170.00 (individuals) other. Thieme Medical Publishers Inc., 381 Park Avenue South, Suite 1201, New York NY 10016. **Tel** (212)683-5088, (212)683-5089, FAX (212)779-9020, telex 220 862 TSINC UR. **ED** Berish Strauch. **DD** 617. **NLM** W1; JO866H. **CODEN** JRMIE2. **[CCC]. Bk Rev. Ad Acc. Pr Rev. Circ:** 1,000 (ctrl). available on microfilm from University Microfilms International (UMI). Documents available from The Genuine Article, BIOSIS Document Express.
**Desc:** Publishes original articles containing clinical information. In addition, special sections will discuss new technologies, innovations, materials, and significant problem cases. Comprehensive reviews of the literature may be invited or submitted without invitation; however, all articles will undergo a process of peer review before being accepted for publication.
**Ind/Abst** Biol. Abstr. (1984-); Curr. Contents Clin. Med.; EMBASE; Helminthol. Abstr. (1991-); Index Med. (Vol. 1, No. 1, 1984-);(1984-);; Res. Alert [Select. Cov.]; SCISEARCH.

●US/1058-2746
**JOURNAL OF SHOULDER AND ELBOW SURGERY.** (JOURNAL OF SHOULDER AND ELBOW SURGERY / AMERICAN SHOULDER AND ELBOW SURGEONS ... [ET AL.].). **Added/Corp** American Shoulder and Elbow Surgeons (Organization). Vol. 1, No. 1 (Jan./Feb. 1992)-. Periodical. English. bm. $105.00 (institutions), $86.00 (individuals) US; $126.00 (institutions), $107.00 (individuals) other. Mosby Year Book Inc., 11830 Westline Industrial Drive, St Louis MO 63146. **Tel** (800)325-4177, (314)872-8370, FAX (314)432-1380, telex 44-2402. **DD** 617. **NLM** W1; JO877FL. **[CCC]. Ad Acc. Pr Rev.**
**Desc:** Focuses on medical/surgical techniques for restoring form and function of the shoulder girdle, arm and elbow. Original articles cover techniques, instruments and materials.

●US/1059-9509
**JOURNAL OF STONE DISEASE, THE.** ***Suspended.*** [J. stone dis.]. Vol. 4, No. 1 (1992)-(Dec. 1993). Periodical. English. qt. $90.00. Futura Publishing Company Inc., 135 Bedford Road, PO Box 418, Armonk NY 10504-0418. **Tel** (914)273-1014, (800)877-8761, FAX (914)273-1015, (914)273-1016. **DD** 616. **NLM** W1; JO904Q. ***Continues*** *Journal of Lithotripsy & Stone Disease, 1040-2152.*

US/0022-4790
**JOURNAL OF SURGICAL ONCOLOGY. See** Medical Science and Technology-Neoplasma, Neoplastic.

US/0022-4804
**JOURNAL OF SURGICAL RESEARCH, THE.** [J. surg. res.]. **Added/Corp** Association for Academic Surgery (U.S.) Association of Veterans Administration Surgeons (U.S.). Vol. 1 (May 1961)-. Academic Scholarly Publication. English. mo. $503.00 US and Canada; $616.00 other. Academic Press, Inc., 6277 Sea Harbor Drive, Orlando FL 32887. **Tel** (800)543-9534, (407)345-4100, FAX (407)363-9661. **ED** Christopher K. Zarins, Bruce L. Gewertz, Dana K. Anderson, Mark K. Ferguson and Ronald V. Maier. **LC** RD1; .J68. **DD** 617. **NLM** W1 JO905Q. **CODEN** JSGRA2. **[CCC]. Pr Rev.** Documents available from The Genuine Article, BIOSIS Document Express, CASDDS.
**Desc:** Publishes original articles concerned with clinical and laboratory investigations relevant to surgical practice and teaching. Emphasizes reports of clinical investigations or fundamental research bearing directly on surgical management that will be of general interest to a broad range of surgeons and surgical researchers. Articles presented need not have been the products of surgeons or of surgical laboratories. Also features review articles and special articles relating to educational, research, or social issues of interest to the academic surgical community.
**Ind/Abst** Biol. Abstr.; Chem. Abstr.; CSA Neuro. Abstr. (?-?); Curr. Contents Life Sci.; EMBASE; Energy Res. Abstr.; Immunol. Abstr.; Index Med.; Life Sci. Collect.; Ref. Upd. Basic Ed.; Ref. Upd. Deluxe Ed.; Res. Alert [Full Cov.]; Sci. Cit. Index; SCISEARCH.

●US/1072-7515
**JOURNAL OF THE AMERICAN COLLEGE OF SURGEONS.** [J. Am. Coll. Surg.]. **Added/Corp** American College of Surgeons. Vol. 178, No. 1 (Jan. 1994)-. Periodical. English. mo. $70.00 (institution), $60.00 (individual) US & Canada. American College of Surgeons, 55 East Erie Street, Chicago IL 60611. **Tel** (312)664-4050. **(Subscription telephone:** (312)787-9282**) DD** 617. **NLM** W1; JO908UM. Index available (bound in issue). ***Continues*** *Surgery, Gynecology & Obstetrics, 0039-6087.*

US/0362-0727
**JOURNAL OF THE HOSPITAL FOR SPECIAL SURGERY, THE.** [J. Hosp. Spec. Surg.]. **Main/Corp** Hospital for Special Surgery. Vol. 1 (Nov. 1975)-. Periodical. English. New York Society for Relief of Ruptured and Crippled, 535 East 70th Street, New York NY 10021. **LC** RD701; .H68a. **DD** 617/.3/005. **NLM** W1 JO929.

US
**JOURNAL OF THE ROYAL COLLEGE OF PHYSICIANS AND SURGEONS OF THE UNITED STATES OF AMERICA : JRCP&S.** **Added/Corp** Royal College of Physicians and Surgeons of the United States of America. **VFOAT** JRCP&S; JRCP and S; JRCPS; JRCPS USA. (1991)-. English. ir (Publishes once in odd years and twice in even years). $95.00 (individuals), $120.00 (institutions). American Academy of Tropical Medicine & Surgery, 16126 East Warren, Detroit MI 48224. **Tel** (313)882-0641, FAX (313)882-5110. **ED** Dr. Ben Alli (editor's address: PO Box 24224, Detroit MI 48224, phone: (313)882-0641). **NLM** W1; JO95T. **Pr Rev. Circ:** 3,000. ***Continues*** *Journal of the American Academy of Tropical Medicine & Surgery, 0891-544X.*
**Desc:** News and information on general and tropical medicines.

UK/0035-8835
**JOURNAL OF THE ROYAL COLLEGE OF SURGEONS OF EDINBURGH.** [J. R. Coll. Surg. Edinb.]. **Added/Corp** Royal College of Surgeons of Edinburgh. Vol. 1 (Sept. 1955)-. Academic Scholarly Publication. English. bm (6 issues). $194.00 US & Canada; £113.00 Europe; £125.00 other. Blackwell Scientific Publications Ltd, Marston Book Services, PO Box 87, Oxford OX2 ODT UK. **Tel** 011 44 865 791155, FAX 011 44 865 791927, telex 837 515 MARDIS G. **ED** Alfred Cuschieri. **NLM** W1 JO95Y. **CODEN** JRCSAC. **[CCC].** Index available. **Bk Rev. Ad Acc.** available on microfilm and microfiche from University Microfilms International (UMI). Documents available from BIOSIS Document Express.
**Desc:** Publishes a wide range of papers of interest to the practicing surgeon, with contributions drawn from members of the Royal College and other surgeons worldwide. Regular features include surgeon's workshop, clinical notes, book reviews and correspondence.
**Ind/Abst** Biol. Abstr.; Cumul. Index Nurs. Allied Health Lit.; EMBASE; Index Med.

US/0022-5223
**JOURNAL OF THORACIC AND CARDIOVASCULAR SURGERY.** [J. thorac. cardiovasc. surg.]. **Added/Corp** American Association for Thoracic Surgery. Vol. 38, (July 1959)-. Academic Scholarly Publication. English. mo. $223.00 (institutions), $130.00 (individuals) US; $253.00 (institutions), $160.00 (individuals) other. Mosby Year Book Inc., 11830 Westline Industrial Drive, St Louis MO 63146. **Tel** (800)325-4177, (314)872-8370, FAX (314)432-1380, telex 44-2402. **ED** John W. Kirklin. **DD** 618. **NLM** W1 JO966I. **CODEN** JTCSAQ. **[CCC].** Index available. cum. index. **Ad Acc. Pr Rev. Circ:** 9,972. available on microfilm and microfiche from University Microfilms International (UMI). Documents available from The Genuine Article, BIOSIS Document Express. ***Continues*** *Journal of Thoracic Surgery, 0096-5588.*
**Desc:** Articles are devoted to conditions of the heart, lungs, chest, and great vessels where surgical intervention is indicated.
**Ind/Abst** Abr. Index Med.; Biol. Abstr.; Curr. Aware. Biol. Sci., CABS; Curr. Contents Clin. Med.; Curr. Contents Life Sci.; EMBASE; Energy Res. Abstr.; Health Devices

Alerts; Health Period. Database; Helminthol. Abstr.; Index Med.; Iowa Drug Inf. Serv. (1970-); Life Sci. Collect.; Physic. Medline Plus; Ref. Upd. Basic Ed.; Ref. Upd. Deluxe Ed.; Res. Alert [Full Cov.]; Saf. Health Work; Sci. Cit. Index; SCISEARCH; Soc. Sci. Cit. Index [Select. Cov.].

US/0022-5282
**JOURNAL OF TRAUMA, THE.** [J. trauma]. **Added/Corp** American Association for the Surgery of Trauma. Vol. 1 (Jan. 1961)-. Academic Scholarly Publication. English. mo. $131.00 (individual), $171.00 (institution) US; $181.00 (individual), $221.00 (institution) other. Williams & Wilkins Company, 428 East Preston Street, Baltimore MD 21202-3993. **Tel** (410)528-4000, (800)638-6423, FAX (410)528-8596, telex 87669. **(Subscription address:** Williams & Wilkins, PO Box 64380, Baltimore MD 21264.**) ED** John H. Davis. **LC** RD92; .J67. **NLM** W1 JO966P. **CODEN** JOTRA5. **[CCC]. Ad Acc. Pr Rev. Circ:** 6,350. available on CD-ROM. Documents available from The Genuine Article, BIOSIS Document Express, CASDDS, Quick Copies.
**Desc:** Diagnosis, management, and recommendations for surgical approaches to traumatic injury for orthopaedic, plastic, and general surgeons.
**Ind/Abst** Abr. Index Med.; Biol. Abstr.; Chem. Abstr.; CIS Abstr.; CSA Neuro. Abstr. (?-?); Cumul. Index Nurs. Allied Health Lit.; Curr. Contents Clin. Med.; EMBASE; Energy Res. Abstr.; Highw. Res. Abstr.; Immunol. Abstr.; Index Med.; Mod. Med.; Nucl. Sci. Abstr.; Nutr. Abstr. Rev., Ser. A, Hum. Exp.; Life Sci. Collect.; Physic. Medline Plus; Res. Alert [Full Cov.]; Risk Abstr.; Saf. Health Work; Sci. Cit. Index; SCISEARCH; Soc. Sci. Cit. Index [Select. Cov.]; SportSearch.

US/0741-5214
**JOURNAL OF VASCULAR SURGERY.** [J. vasc. surg.]. **Added/Corp** Society for Vascular Surgery (U.S.) International Society for Cardiovascular Surgery. North American Chapter. Vol. 1, No. 1 (Jan. 1984)-. Periodical. English. mo. $214.00 (institutions), $114.00 (individuals) US; $242.00 (institutions), $142.00 (individuals) other. Mosby Year Book Inc., 11830 Westline Industrial Drive, St Louis MO 63146. **Tel** (800)325-4177, (314)872-8370, FAX (314)432-1380, telex 44-2402. **ED** D. Emerick Szilagyi. **LC** RD598.5; .J68. **DD** 617/.413/005. **NLM** W1; JO97CH. **[CCC].** Index available. **Bk Rev. Ad Acc. Pr Rev. Circ:** 5,091. available on microfilm and microfiche from University Microfilms International (UMI). Documents available from The Genuine Article.
**Desc:** Serves as a comprehensive forum for presenting the latest knowledge concerning the peripheral vascular system and the practice of vascular surgery.
**Ind/Abst** Abr. Index Med.; Curr. Aware. Biol. Sci., CABS; Curr. Contents Clin. Med.; Curr. Contents Life Sci.; EMBASE; Health Period. Database; Index Med. (Vol. 1, No. 1, 1984-); INIS Atomindex [Micro.]; Mod. Med.; Physic. Medline Plus; Ref. Upd. Basic Ed.; Ref. Upd. Deluxe Ed.; Res. Alert [Full Cov.]; Sci. Cit. Index; SCISEARCH; Soc. Sci. Cit. Index [Select. Cov.].

JA/0021-5228
**KEISEI GEKA.** [Keisei Geka]. **VFOAT** Japanese Journal of Plastic and Reconstructive Surgery. (19??)-. Japanese. Kokuseido Shuppan K.K., (Kokuseido Publishing Co., Ltd.), 23-5-202, Hongo 3 Chome, Bunkyoku, Tokyoto 113 Japan. **CODEN** KEGEA.
**Ind/Abst** EMBASE.

US/0886-8018
**KEY NEUROLOGY AND NEUROSURGERY. See** Medical Science and Technology-Neurology.

RU
**KHIRURGICHESKAIA I ORTOPEDICHESKAIA STOMATOLOGIIA.** Vol. 8 (1978)-. Periodical. Russian. **NLM** W1 KH53. ***Continues*** *Khirurgicheskaia Stomatologiia.*

UN/0023-2130
**KLINICESKAJA HIRURGIJA (KIEV).** (KLINICHESKAIA KHIRURGIIA.). [Klin. hir.]. (May 1962)-. Periodical. Russian. mo. $150.00. Izdatelstvo Zdorovia, Ulitsa Chkalova 65, 252054 Kiev Ukraine. **(Subscription address:** Victor Kamkin, 4956 Boiling Brook Parkway, Rockville, MD 20852**) NLM** W1 KL185. **CODEN** KLKHAM. **[CCC].** Documents available from CASDDS. ***Continues*** *Novyi Khirurgicheskii Archiv.*
**Ind/Abst** Chem. Abstr. (1962-1983); EMBASE; Index Med.

●GW/0942-2056
**KNEE SURGERY, SPORTS TRAUMATOLOGY, ARTHROSCOPY. Added/Corp** European Society of Sports Traumatology, Knee Surgery and Arthroscopy. Vol. 1, No. 1 (Mar. 1993)-. Periodical. English. qt. DM280.00. Springer-Verlag GmbH & Company KG, Heidelberger Platz 3, D 14197 Berlin Germany. **Tel** 011 49 30 8207223, FAX 011 49 30 8214091, telex 183 319 SPBLN D. **(Subscription address:** Springer Verlag New York Inc. / for North America, 44 Hartz Way, Secaucus NJ 07096.**) ED** E. Eriksson. **[CCC].**

GW
**LANGENBECKS ARCHIV FEUR CHIRURGIE. SUPPLEMENT. KONGRESSBAND. Main/Corp** Deutsche Gesellschaft Fur Chirurgie. Kongress. **VFOAT** Kongressband. (1991)-. German (summaries and/or abstracts in English). Springer-Verlag GmbH & Company KG, Heidelberger Platz 3, D 14197 Berlin Germany. **Tel** 011 49 30 8207223, FAX 011 49 30 8214091, telex 183 319 SPBLN D. **(Subscription address:** Springer Verlag New York Inc. / for North America, 44 Hartz Way, Secaucus NJ 07096.**) NLM** W1; LA601A. ***Continues*** *Langenbecks Archiv Fur Chirurgie. Supplement II, Verhandlungen der Deutschen Gesellschaft Fur Chirurgie.*
**Ind/Abst** Index Med. (1991-).

GW/0023-8236
**LANGENBECKS ARCHIV FUER CHIRURGIE.** [Langenbecks Arch. Chir.]. **Added/Corp** Deutsche Gesellschaft fur Chirurgie. Deutsche Gesellschaft fur Chirurgie. Verhandlungen der Tagung. Vol. 324 (1969)-. Academic Scholarly Publication. German (summaries and/or abstracts in English). Six times a year. DM698.00. Springer-Verlag GmbH & Company KG, Heidelberger Platz 3, D 14197 Berlin Germany. **Tel** 011 49 30 8207223, FAX 011 49 30 8214091, telex 183 319 SPBLN D. **(Subscription address:** Springer Verlag New York Inc. / for North America, 44 Hartz Way, Secaucus NJ 07096.**) ED** M Allgower, D Carter, Ch Herfarth, R Pichlmayr, H W Schreiber, R Siewert, M Trede. **NLM** W1 LA601. **CODEN** LAACBS. **[CCC]. Pr Rev.** available on microfilm from University Microfilms International (UMI). Documents available from The Genuine Article, BIOSIS Document Express. ***Continues*** *Langenbecks Archiv fur Klinische Chirurgie;* ***Absorbed*** *Bruns' Beitrage zur Klinischen Chirurgie, 0007-2680.* ***Continued in part by*** *Deutsche Gesellschaft fuer Chirurgie. Kongress. Langenbecks Archiv fuer Chirurgie. Supplement II, Verhandlungen der Deutschen Gesellschaft fuer Chirurgie.*
**Desc:** Original research on animal experiments and clinical observation. Publishes reports of conferences of the German Surgery Society, editorials on current surgical topics, and a discussion forum where specialists world-wide focus on a surgical problem.
**Ind/Abst** Biol. Abstr.; CSA Neuro. Abstr. (?-?); Curr. Contents Clin. Med.; EMBASE; Energy Res. Abstr.; Index Med.; Life Sci. Collect.; Res. Alert [Select. Cov.]; SCISEARCH.

●CN/1188-0252
**LAPAROSCOPIC SURGERY.** [Laparosc. surg.]. (Jan. 1992)-. Periodical. English. tq. $175.00 (institutions), $129.00 (individuals) US & Canada; $200.00 (institutions), $154.00 (individuals) other. Decker Periodicals Publishing Inc, PO Box 620, Station A, Hamilton Ontario L8N 3K7 Canada. **Tel** (416)522-7017, (800) 568-7281, FAX (416)522-7839. **DD** 617.5. **NLM** W1; LA644.

GW/0938-765X
**LASERMEDIZIN : ORGAN DER DEUTSCHEN GESELLSCHAFT FUER LASERMEDIZIN. Added/Corp** Deutsche Gesellschaft fuer Lasermedizin. **VFOAT** Laser Medizin. Vol. 7, No. 1 (May 1991)-. Periodical. German (English). Four times a year. DM256.00 Germany; DM264.00 other. Gustav Fischer Verlag Stuttgart, Postfach 720143, Wollgrasweg 49, D 70577 Stuttgart Germany. **Tel** 011 49 711 458030, FAX 0711-4580334, telex 2627-7111488. **(Subscription address:** VCH Publishers Inc., 303 Northwest 12th Avenue, Journals Department, Deerfield FL 33442.**) NLM** W1; LA782. ***Continues*** *Laser in Medicine and Surgery.*

US/0196-8092
**LASERS IN SURGERY AND MEDICINE.** [Lasers surg. med.]. **Added/Corp** American Society for Laser Medicine and Surgery. International Society for Laser Surgery. Gynecological Laser Society. Vol. 1 (1980)-. Academic Scholarly Publication. English. Nine times a year. $621.00 (US); $711.00 (Canada and Mexico); $744.75 (other). John Wiley & Sons, Inc., 605 Third Avenue, New York NY 10158-0012. **Tel** (212)850-6000, (212)850-6645, FAX (212)850-6088, telex 12-7063. **(Subscription address:** John Wiley & Sons / England, Baffins Lane, Chichester, West Sussex PO19 1UD England.**) ED** Carmen A. Puliafito. **DD** 617. **NLM** W1; LA784. **CODEN** LSMEDI. **[CCC]. Pr Rev.** Documents available from The Genuine Article, CASDDS.
**Desc:** Serves as the preeminent journal in laser biology and medicine, covering all aspects of the biomedical applications of lasers.
**Ind/Abst** Chem. Abstr. (1980-1983); Curr. Contents Clin. Med.; EMBASE; Health Devices Alerts; Index Med.; Res. Alert [Full Cov.]; Risk Abstr.; Sci. Cit. Index; SCISEARCH.

●US/1064-6698
**LIPPINCOTT'S ORAL AND MAXILLOFACIAL SURGERY. VFOAT** Oral and Maxillofacial Surgery. (1993)-. Periodical. English. qt. $95.00. J.B. Lippincott Company, 227 East Washington Square, Philadelphia PA 19106-3780. **Tel** (215)238-4200 or 4454, FAX (215)238-4227.

US/0883-8410
**LITERATURE SCAN. TRANSPLANTATION.** [Lit. scan. Transplant.]. Vol. 1, No. 1 (July 1985)-. Periodical. English. qt. $60.00 US; $80.00 other. World Medical Communications Organizations, 7 Ridgedale Avenue, Cedar Knolls NJ 07927. **Tel** (201)455-1121. **ED** Barry D Kahan. **DD** 617. **NLM** ZWO 660; L776. Index available. **Bk Rev. Ad Acc. Circ:** 12,000 (ctrl).
**Desc:** Contains reviews of the most current literature in organ transplantation and related immunology. Each issue consists of 60 reviews from the International Literature and each are followed by the reviewer's personal assessment of the article.

●US/1074-3022
**LIVER TRANSPLANTATION AND SURGERY.** (1995)-. Periodical. English. bm. $90.00 (individual), $140.00 (institution) US; $110.00 (individual), $160.00 (institution) other. W.B. Saunders Company, A Subsidiary of Harcourt Brace Jovanovich, Inc., The Curtis Center/Suite 300, Independence Square West, Philadelphia PA 19106-3399. **Tel** (215)238-7800 or, 5587, FAX (215)238-7883, telex 173146. **(Subscription address:** W. B. Saunders Company / North America Subscriptions, c/o Periodicals, 6277 Sea Harbour Drive, 4th Floor, Orlando FL 32887.**)**

US/0731-3063
**LOMA LINDA UNIVERSITY SURGEON.** ***Ceased.*** [Loma Linda Univ. surg.]. Vol. 1, No. 1 (Sept. 1982)-?. Periodical. English. sa. Loma Linda University, Medical Center/Room 2563, Loma Linda CA 92534. **Tel** (909)824-4335. **UDC** 616.089. **NLM** W1 LO108J.

SZ/0024-7782
**LYON CHIRURGICAL.** [Lyon chir.]. **Added/Corp** Societe de Chirurgie de Lyon. Union Europeene des Societe Nationales de Chirurgie. (Nov. 1908)-. Academic Scholarly Publication. French (summaries and/or abstracts in English). bm. 450.00F France; 500.00F other. Lyon Chirurgical, Hotel Dieu, 69288 Lyon Cedex 02 France. **Tel** 011 33 78 922081, FAX 011 33 78 370364. **(Subscription address:** 7A Boulevard de Perolles, CH-1701 Fribourg Switzerland**) NLM** W1 LY53. **[CCC]. Pr Rev.** available on microfilm from University Microfilms International (UMI).
**Ind/Abst** EMBASE; Helminthol. Abstr. (19??-19??); SCISEARCH.

HU/0025-0317
**MAGYAR TRAUMATOLOGIA, ORTHOPAEDIA ES HELYREALLIT SEBESZET. Added/Corp** Orszagos Traumatologiai Intezet (Hungary). (Feb. 1960)-. Periodical. Hungarian (Russian, German and English). qt. **(Subscription address:** Kultura, PO Box 149, H 1389 Budapest 62 Hungary**) NLM** W1; MA429. ***Continues*** *Traumatologiai es Orthopaediai Kozlemenyek; Magyar Traumatologia, Ortopedia, Kezsebeszet, Plasztikai Sebeszet.*
**Ind/Abst** Index Med.

US
**MALPRACTICE REPORTER. SURGERY : MPR, THE. See** Law.

FR/0047-6412
**MEDECINE & CHIRURGIE DIGESTIVES.** [Med. chir. dig.]. **Added/Corp** College de Medecine des Hopitaux de Paris. Centre d'Enseignement d'Hepatologie. **VFOAT** MCD. **VAT** Medecine et Chirurgie Digestives; MCD. Vol. 1 (1972)-. Academic Scholarly Publication. French (summaries and/or abstracts in English, French and German). ir. 519.10F France; 580.00F others. BC Diffusion, 116 Ave des Champs Elysees, 75008 Paris France. **Tel** 011 33 1 44218116. **NLM** W1 ME139N. **CODEN** MCDGBC. **[CCC].** available on microfilm from University Microfilms International (UMI). Documents available from BIOSIS Document Express, CASDDS. ***Supersedes*** *Revue Medico-Chirurgicale de Maladies du Foie.*
**Ind/Abst** Biol. Abstr.; Chem. Abstr. (1972-1982); EMBASE; Helminthol. Abstr. (1991-); Index Med.; Life Sci. Collect.

US/0744-4206
**MEDICAL ECONOMICS FOR SURGEONS.** [Med. econ. surg.]. **Added/Corp** Medical Economics Company. Vol. 1, No. 1 (March 1982)-. Periodical. English. mo. $64.00 US; $109.00 other. Medical Economics Publishing, Five Paragon Drive, Second Floor, Montvale NJ 07645. **Tel** (800)432-4570, (201)358-2210. **(Subscription address:** Fulco Medical Economics, PO Box 3000, Denville NJ 07834.**) LC** RD27.42; .M4. **DD** 617/.0068/1. **NLM** W1; ME309J.
**Desc:** Designed to help surgeons with their non-clinical problems. Serves the surgeon's special needs for information on practice management, hospital relationships, and his finances.

US/0278-9779
**MEDICO INTERAMERICANO. See** Medical Science and Technology.

●US
**MEDSURG NURSING : OFFICIAL JOURNAL OF THE ACADEMY OF MEDICAL- SURGICAL NURSES.**
**Added/Corp** Academy of Medical-Surgical Nurses. Vol. 1, No. 1 (Sept. 1992)-. Periodical. English. bm. $32.00 (institutions), $24.00 (individuals). A.J. Jannetti Inc., East Holly Avenue, Box 56, Pitman NJ 08071-0056. **Tel** (609)256-2300, FAX (609)589-7463. **LC** RD99.A1; M4. **NLM** W1; ME862L.
**Ind/Abst** Int. Nurs. Index (Sept. 1992-).

US
**MEMBERSHIP-TEAM DIRECTORY.**
**Main/Corp** American Cleft Palate-Craniofacial Association. 1988-. Directory. English. an. $6.00 (members). American Cleft Palate Association, 1218 Grandview Avenue, Pittsburgh PA 15211. **Tel** (412)481-1376. **NLM** WV 22.1; A512m. **Circ:** 2,000 (ctrl). ***Continues*** *Membership-Team Directory / American Cleft Palate Association, 0733-8120.*
**Desc:** Directory of members of the American Cleft Palat

US/0738-1085
**MICROSURGERY.** [Microsurgery]. Vol. 4, No. 1 (1983)-. Periodical. English. Twelve times a year. $396.00 (US); $516.00 (Canada and Mexico); $561.00 (other). John Wiley & Sons, Inc., 605 Third Avenue, New York NY 10158-0012. **Tel** (212)850-6000, (212)850-6645, FAX (212)850-6088, telex 12-7063. **(Subscription address:** John Wiley & Sons / England, Baffins Lane, Chichester, West Sussex PO19 1UD England.**) ED** John S .Gould. **LC** RD33.6; .M467. **DD** 617/.9. **NLM** W1 MI313L. **[CCC].** Documents available from The Genuine Article. ***Formed by the union of*** *Journal of Microsurgery, 0191-3239* ***and*** *International Journal of Microsurgery, 0222-5069.*
**Desc:** A multidisciplinary publication containing comprehensive investigations regarding the use of the operating microscope in a variety of areas - vascular surgery, pediatric surgery, neurosurgery, plastic surgery, gynecology, ophthalmology, otolaryngology, urology, and general surgery.
**Ind/Abst** Curr. Contents Clin. Med.; EMBASE; Index Med.; Index Vet.; Res. Alert [Select. Cov.]; SCISEARCH; Small Anim. Abstr. Bibliogr.; SportSearch; Vet. Bull.

IT/0026-4733
**MINERVA CHIRURGICA.** [Minerva chir.]. Vol. 1 (March 1946)-. Academic Scholarly Publication. Italian. Twelve times a year. $130.00 (individuals), $160.00 (institutions). Edizioni Minerva Medica, Corso Bramante 83-85, 10126 Turin Italy. **Tel** 011 39 11 678282, FAX 011 39 11 674502. **ED** P A Oludice. **NLM** W1 MI637. **Bk Rev. Ad Acc.** available on microfilm from University Microfilms International (UMI).
**Desc:** Journal addressed to practitioners and specialists in surgery in Italy and abroad; deals with topics in scientific practice and research.
**Ind/Abst** EMBASE; Index Med.

GW
**MINIMALLY INVASIVE NEUROSURGERY.** **See** Medical Science and Technology-Neurology.

●US/1068-5685
**MINIMALLY INVASIVE SURGICAL NURSING.** **See** Medical Science and Technology-Nursing.

UK/0961-625X
**MINIMALLY INVASIVE THERAPY.**
**Added/Corp** Society for Minimally Invasive Therapy. Vol. 1, No. 1 (1991)-. Academic Scholarly Publication. English. bm (6 issues). $259.00 (institutions), $149.00 (individuals) US & Canada; £152.00 (institutions), £88.00 (individuals) Europe; £167.00 (institutions), £96.00 (individuals) other. Blackwell Scientific Publications Ltd, Marston Book Services, PO Box 87, Oxford OX2 ODT UK. **Tel** 011 44 865 791155, FAX 011 44 865 791927, telex 837 515 MARDIS G. **NLM** W1; MI663. **CODEN** MITREY. Documents available from The Genuine Article.
**Ind/Abst** Curr. Contents Clin. Med.; Res. Alert [Select. Cov.].

●US/1058-1650
**MVP VIDEO JOURNAL OF GENERAL SURGERY.** (MVP VIDEO JOURNAL OF GENERAL SURGERY: VIDEORECORDING.). [MVP video j. surg.]. **Added/Corp** Medical Video Productions. **VFOAT** Video Journal of General Surgery; VJGS. **VAT** Medical Video Productions Video Journal of General Surgery. (1992)-. Periodical. English. qt. $189.00 (institutions), $139.00 (individuals) US; $159.00 (individuals) Canada and Mexico; $179.00 (individuals) other. Medical Video Productions, 450 North New Ballas, Suite 266, St. Louis MO 63141. **Tel** (800)822-3100, (314)991-5510. **DD** 617.

UN/0131-6842
**NEJROHIRURGIJA.** (NEIROKHIRURGIIA.). [Nejrohirurgija]. **Added/Corp** Kievskii Nauchno-Iissledovatel'Skii Institut Neirokhirurgii. (1971)-. Russian. **NLM** W1 NE195P. ***Continues*** *Problemy Neirokhirurgii, 0301-1674.*

IT
**NEU.** **See** Medical Science and Technology-Neurology.

FR/0028-3770
**NEURO-CHIRURGIE.** [Neuro-chir.]. **Added/Corp** Societe de Neuro-Chirurgie de Langue Francaise. Vol. 1 (1955)-. Academic Scholarly Publication. French (summaries and/or abstracts in English). Eight times a year. $312.00. Masson Editeur, Box Postale 22, 41353 Vineuil 16 France. **Tel** 011 33 54 438994. **ED** P.M. Hurth. **NLM** W1 NE326. **CODEN** NUREB9. **[CCC].** Index available. **Bk Rev. Ad Acc. Pr Rev.** available on microfilm and microfiche from University Microfilms International (UMI); available with illustrations. Documents available from The Genuine Article, BIOSIS Document Express.
**Ind/Abst** Biol. Abstr.; Dev. Med. Child Neurol.; EMBASE; Index Med.; Life Sci. Collect.; Res. Alert [Full Cov.]; Sci. Cit. Index.

GW/0028-3819
**NEUROCHIRURGIA.** ***Title Change.*** [Neurochirurgia]. **Added/Corp** Deutsche Gesellschaft fuer Neurochirurgie. Vol. 1 (June 1958)-(Sept. 1994). Academic Scholarly Publication. English (French and German; summaries and/or abstracts in Spanish). Four times a year. Georg Thieme Verlag Stuttgart, Postfach 301120, D 70451 Stuttgart Germany. **Tel** 011 49 711 89310, FAX 011 49 711 8931298, telex 7 252 275 GTVD. **(Subscription address:** Thieme Medical Publishers Inc., 381 Park Avenue South, New York, NY 10016**) ED** G Brocklehurst, H Dietz, E Metzel. **NLM** W1 NE324. **CODEN** NURABV. **[CCC]. Pr Rev.** available on microfilm from University Microfilms International (UMI). Documents available from The Genuine Article, BIOSIS Document Express. ***Continued by*** *Minimally Invasive Neurosurgery.*
**Desc:** Of interest to neurosurgeons, neurologists, surgeons in general, traumatologists, anesthesiologists.
**Ind/Abst** Biol. Abstr.; Curr. Contents Clin. Med.; Dev. Med. Child Neurol.; EMBASE; Energy Res. Abstr. (June 1981-); Index Med.; Life Sci. Collect.; Res. Alert [Full Cov.]; Sci. Cit. Index (19??-19??); SCISEARCH.

US/0148-396X
**NEUROSURGERY.** [Neurosurgery]. **Added/Corp** Congress of Neurological Surgeons. Vol. 1 (July/Aug. 1977)-. Periodical. English. mo. $145.00 (individual), $200.00 (institution) US; $205.00 (individual), $260.00 (institution) other. Williams & Wilkins Company, 428 East Preston Street, Baltimore MD 21202-3993. **Tel** (410)528-4000, (800)638-6423, FAX (410)528-8596, telex 87669. **(Subscription address:** Williams & Wilkins, PO Box 64380, Baltimore MD 21264.**) ED** Clark Watts. **LC** RD593; .N416. **NLM** W1 NE343U. **[CCC]. Ad Acc. Pr Rev. Circ:** 7,100. available on microfilm. Documents available from The Genuine Article, BIOSIS Document Express, Quick Copies.
**Desc:** Practical, clinical information on neurosurgical techniques and devices plus pertinent research in neuroscience for the neurosurgeon.
**Ind/Abst** Biol. Abstr.; CSA Neuro. Abstr. (?-?); Curr. Contents Life Sci.; Dev. Med. Child Neurol.; EMBASE; Energy Res. Abstr. (April 1981-);; Health Devices Alerts; Index Med.; Life Sci. Collect.; Physic. Medline Plus; Ref. Upd. Basic Ed.; Ref. Upd. Deluxe Ed.; Res. Alert [Full Cov.]; Rev. Med. Vet. Mycology; Sci. Cit. Index; SCISEARCH; Soc. Sci. Cit. Index [Select. Cov.].

US/1042-3680
**NEUROSURGERY CLINICS OF NORTH AMERICA.** [Neurosurg. clin. N. Am.]. **VFOAT** Neurosurgery Clinics. Vol. 1 No. 1 (Jan. 1990)-. Periodical. English. qt. $107.00 (individuals), $134.00 (institutions) US; $147.00 (individual), $155.00 (institution) other. W.B. Saunders Company, A Subsidiary of Harcourt Brace Jovanovich, Inc., The Curtis Center/Suite 300, Independence Square West, Philadelphia PA 19106-3399. **Tel** (215)238-7800 or, 5587, FAX (215)238-7883, telex 173146. **(Subscription address:** W. B. Saunders Company / North America Subscriptions, c/o Periodicals, 6277 Sea Harbour Drive, 4th Floor, Orlando FL 32887.**) DD** 617. **NLM** W1; NE343S.
**Ind/Abst** Index Med. (1990-).

US/1050-6438
**NEUROSURGERY QUARTERLY.**
[Neurosurg. q.]. **VFOAT** Neurosurgery Reviews. Vol. 1, No. 1 (Mar. 1991)-. Periodical. English. qt. $108.00 (individuals), $140.00 (institutions) US; $140.00 (individuals), $165.00 (institutions) other. Raven Press, 1185 Avenue of the Americas, 37th Floor, New York NY 10036. **Tel** (212)930-9500, (212)930-9604, FAX (212)869-3495, (212)302-8507, telex 640073. **DD** 617. **NLM** W1; NE343UL. **[CCC].** available on microfilm and microfiche from University Microfilms International (UMI). Documents available from The Genuine Article.
**Ind/Abst** EMBASE; Res. Alert [Full Cov.]; SCISEARCH.

US/1051-1490
**NEUROSURGICAL OPERATIVE ATLAS.**
**Added/Corp** American Association of Neurological Surgeons. (1991)-. English. bm. $225.00. Williams & Wilkins Company, 428 East Preston Street, Baltimore MD 21202-3993. **Tel** (410)528-4000, (800)638-6423, FAX (410)528-8596, telex 87669. **(Subscription address:** Williams & Wilkins, PO Box 64380, Baltimore, MD 21264**)** Documents available from Quick Copies.

GW/0344-5607
**NEUROSURGICAL REVIEW.** [Neurosurg. rev.]. **Added/Corp** Deutsche Gesellschaft fuer Neurochirurgie. Vol. 1 (1978)-. Academic Scholarly Publication. English (summaries and/or abstracts in German). qt. $309.00. Walter de Gruyter Inc., PO Box 303421, D 10728 Berlin Germany. **Tel** 011 49 30 260050, FAX 011 49 30 26005251. **ED** H. W. Pia and K. Sano. **NLM** W1 NE344W. **CODEN** NSREDV. **[CCC]. Ad Acc. Pr Rev.** Documents available from The Genuine Article, BIOSIS Document Express.
**Desc:** An international forum in the field of neurosurgery. Presents scientific papers on the most recent developments in techniques and technology.
**Ind/Abst** Biol. Abstr. (1985-); Curr. Contents Clin. Med.; EMBASE; Index Med.; Res. Alert [Full Cov.]; SCISEARCH.

US
**NEW MOBILITY.** (199?)-. English. Nine times a year. $18.00 US; $26.00 Canada; $28.00 other. Miramar Publishing Company, 6133 Bristol Parkway, PO Box 3640, Culver City CA 90231. **Tel** (800)543-4116, (310)337-9717. **(Subscription address:** New Mobility, PO Box 15518, North Hollywood CA 91615.**)** ***Continues*** *Spinal Network's New Mobility, 1065-2124.*

JA/0301-4894
**NIHON GEKA GAKKAI ZASSHI.** [Nihon Geka Gakkai zasshi]. **Main/Corp** Nihon Geka Gakkai. **VFOAT** Verhandlungen der Japanischen Chirurgischen Gesellschaft; Zeitschrift der Japanischen Chirurgischen Gesellschaft; Journal of the Japanese Surgical Society; Nippon Geka Gakkai Zasshi. Vol. 8 (July 1907)-. Academic Scholarly Publication. Japanese (summaries and/or abstracts in English and German; table of contents in German). mo. $134.00. **(Subscription address:** Kyowa Book Company Inc., 1 38 Kanda Jinbocho Chiyoda-ku, Tokyo 101 Japan.**) NLM** W1 NI898. **CODEN** NGGZAK. Documents available from CASDDS. ***Continues*** *Nihon Geka Gakkai Shi, 0301-4886.*
**Ind/Abst** Chem. Abstr.; EMBASE; Index Med.

JA/0389-4703
**NIHON KEISEI GEKA GAKKAI KAISHI.**
**VFOAT** Journal of Japan Society of Plastic and Reconstructive Surgery. (1981)-. Periodical. Japanese. bm. Do Gakkai, Keto Tsushin 19-ban 30-go Mita, 2-chome Minato-ku, Tokyo 108 Japan. **NLM** W1; NI426TK.

JA/0369-4739
**NIHON KYOBU GEKA GAKKAI ZASSHI.**
[Nihon Kyobu Geka Gakkai zasshi]. **Added/Corp** Nihon KyÂobu Geka Gakkai. **VFOAT** Journal of the Japanese Association for Thoracic Surgery; JJATS. **VAT** JJATS. Vol. 1 (1953)-. Academic Scholarly Publication. Japanese (summaries and/or abstracts in English). Thirteen times a year. $192.00. Nihon Kyobu Geka Gakkai, (Japanese Assoc. for Thoracic Surgery), Hakuo biru, 3-10, Koraku 2 Chome, Bunkyoku, Tokyoto 112, Japan. **(Subscription address:** Kyowa Book Company Inc., 1 38 Kanda Jinbocho Chiyoda-ku, Tokyo 101 Japan.**) NLM** W1 NI921K. **CODEN** NKZAAY. Documents available from BIOSIS Document Express.
**Ind/Abst** Biol. Abstr.; EMBASE [Select. Cov.]; Index Med.; SEA Abstr.

JA
**NIPPON KOKU GEKA GAKKAI ZASSHI.**
**VFOAT** Japanese Journal of Oral Surgery. (1967)-. Periodical. Japanese. mo. $299.50. Nippon Koku Geka Gakkai, (Japanese Soc. of Oral & Maxillofacial Surgeons), 3-1, Doshomachi, Higashiku, Osakashi, Osakafu 541, Japan. **(Subscription address:** Japan Publications Trading Company, Ltd., PO Box 5030, Tokyo International, Tokyo 100-31 Japan.**)** ***Continues*** *Koku Geka Gakkai Zasshi.*

IT/0392-3584
**NOTIZIARIO CHIRURGICO.** [Not. chir.]. Vol. 1, No. 1 (Oct.-Dec. 1980)-. Academic Scholarly Publication. Italian. qt. $37.32. Edizioni Minerva Medica, Corso Bramante 83-85, 10126 Turin Italy. **Tel** 011 39 11 678282, FAX 011 39 11 674502. **NLM** W1 NO813I.
**Ind/Abst** EMBASE.

●US
**O.R. PRODUCT DIRECTORY / ASSOCIATION OF OPERATING ROOM NURSES.** **VFOAT** OR Product Directory. (1994)-. English. an (Oct.). $45.00. Association of Operating Room Nurses, Inc., 2170 South Parker Road, Suite 300, Denver CO 80231-5711. **Tel** (303)755-6300, (303)755-6304. **NLM** WO 22; AA1 O11. ***Continues*** *Operating Room Product Directory.*
**Desc:** Contains information on surgical equipment and supplies.

UK/0960-8923
**OBESITY SURGERY.** **Added/Corp** American Society for Bariatric Surgery. Obesity Surgery Society of Australia and New Zealand. Vol. 1, No. 1 (March 1991)-. Periodical. English. qt. $255.00 US; £150.00 other. Rapid Communications of Oxford Ltd, The Old Malthouse, Paradise Street, Oxford OX1 1LD England. **Tel** 011 44 0865 790447, FAX 011 44 0865 244012, telex 9403712. **NLM** W1; OB402KD. **[CCC]. Ad Acc. Acid Free.**

Documents available from The Genuine Article.
**Desc:** Aims to answer the demand for bariatric surgeons for a specific publication on obesity surgery. The primary objective of the journal is to provide a new international and interdisciplinary opportunity for publishing and communicating important research and techniques in bariatric surgery. The scope of the journal covers the complete area of obesity related to surgery. It provides an essential source of new information for everyone working in this field.
**Ind/Abst** Curr. Contents Clin. Med.; EMBASE; Res. Alert [Select. Cov.]; SCISEARCH; Soc. Sci. Cit. Index [Select. Cov.].

US/0748-2892
**OCULAR REVIEW.** [Ocul. rev.]. **Added/Corp** Illinois Eye and Ear Infirmary. (1984)-. English. mo. $32.00 US; $16.00 other. Ocular Review, c/o M Winnike, University of Illinois at Chicago, Eye & Eye Infirmary Library, PO Box 98, Chicago IL 60680. **Tel** (800)902-8527, (312)823-1204 IN ILLINOIS. **LC** Z6669; .O27; RE1. **DD** 016.6177.

US/8750-3085
**OCULAR SURGERY NEWS.** [Ocul. surg. news]. Vol. 2, No. 17 (Sept. 1, 1984)-. Periodical. English. bw. $305.00 institution, $290.00 individual (US). Slack Inc., 6900 Grove Road, Thorofare NJ 08086. **Tel** (609)848-1000, (800)257-8290, FAX (609)853-5991, telex 517108 SLACK INC VD. **ED** Donald R. Sanders. **DD** 617. **Bk Rev. Ad Acc. Circ:** 17,000 (ctrl). ***Continues*** *IOL & Ocular Surgery News, 0745-709X.* ***Continued in part by*** *Ocular Surgery News, 1047-9120.*
**Desc:** News coverage of the latest developments affecting the practice of ophthalmology, together with special features of interest to the ophthalmic surgeon.

US/1047-9120
**OCULAR SURGERY NEWS INTERNATIONAL EDITION.** [Ocul. surg. news]. (1990)-. Periodical. English. mo. $220.00 institution, $205.00 individual (US). Slack Inc., 6900 Grove Road, Thorofare NJ 08086. **Tel** (609)848-1000, (800)257-8290, FAX (609)853-5991, telex 517108 SLACK INC VD. **DD** 617. ***Continues*** *Ocular Surgery News, 8750-3085.*

KO
**OEKWA HAKHOE CHI. Main/Corp** Taehan Oekwa Hakhoe. **VFOAT** Journal of the Korean Surgical Society. Periodical. Korean (summaries and/or abstracts in English). Taehan Oekwa Hakhoe, 1 2-ka Myong-dong, Chung-ku, Seoul South Korea. **LC** RD1; .T33A. **UDC** 616-089.8.

●US/0000-1678
**OFFICIAL AMERICAN BOARD OF MEDICAL SPECIALTIES (ABMS) DIRECTORY OF BOARD CERTIFIED SURGEONS, THE.** (THE OFFICIAL AMERICAN BOARD OF MEDICAL SPECIALTIES (ABMS) DIRECTORY OF BOARD CERTIFIED SURGEONS.). [Off. Am. Board Med. Spec. (ABMS) dir. board certif. surg.]. **Added/Corp** American Board of Medical Specialties. **VFOAT** Directory of Board Certified Surgeons; Official ABMS Directory of Board Certified Surgeons. 5th Ed. (1994)-. Directory. English. be. American Board of Medical Specialties, 1 Rotary Center, Suite 805, Evanston IL 60201. **Tel** (708)491-9091. **LC** RD10.U6; A245. **DD** 617/.0025/73. ***Continues*** *ABMS Directory of Certified Surgeons, 0884-1527.*

●US/0000-1481
**OFFICIAL AMERICAN BOARD OF MEDICAL SPECIALTIES (ABMS) DIRECTORY OF BOARD CERTIFIED THORACIC SURGEONS, THE.** [Off. Am. Board Med. Spec. (ABMS) dir. board certif. thorac. surg.]. **Added/Corp** American Board of Medical Specialties. American Board of Thoracic Surgery. **VFOAT** Directory of Board Certified Thoracic Surgeons; Thoracic Surgeons; Official ... ABMS Directory of Bboard Certified Thoracic Surgeons. 5th Ed. (1992)-. Directory. English. be. $59.95. Marquis Who's Who, A Reed Reference Publishing Company, Part of Reed International PLC, 121 Chanlon Road, New Providence NJ 07974. **Tel** (908)464-6800, (800)521-8110, FAX (908)665-6688, telex 138 755. **DD** 617. ***Continues*** *ABMS Directory of Certified Thoracic Surgeons, 0884-1462.*

●US/1071-0949
**OPERATIVE TECHNIQUES IN PLASTIC AND RECONSTRUCTIVE SURGERY.** (1994)-. Periodical. English. qt (Feb., May, Aug., Nov). $115.00 (individual), $140.00 (institution) US; $131.00 (individual), $157.00 (institution) other. W.B. Saunders Company, A Subsidiary of Harcourt Brace Jovanovich, Inc., The Curtis Center/Suite 300, Independence Square West, Philadelphia PA 19106-3399. **Tel** (215)238-7800 or, 5587, FAX (215)238-7883, telex 173146. **(Subscription address:** W. B. Saunders Company / North America Subscriptions, c/o Periodicals, 6277 Sea Harbour Drive, 4th Floor, Orlando FL 32887.**)**

US/0740-9303
**OPHTHALMIC PLASTIC AND RECONSTRUCTIVE SURGERY. See** Medical Science and Technology-Ophthalmology.

US/0022-023X
**OPHTHALMIC SURGERY.** [Ophthalmic surg.]. (1970)-. Academic Scholarly Publication. English. mo. $72.00 institution, $49.00 individual (US). Slack Inc., 6900 Grove Road, Thorofare NJ 08086. **Tel** (609)848-1000, (800)257-8290, FAX (609)853-5991, telex 517108 SLACK INC VD. **LC** RE80; .O65. **DD** 617/.71. **NLM** W1 OP25. **CODEN** OPSGAT. **Bk Rev. Ad Acc. Pr Rev.** available on microfilm and microfiche from University Microfilms International (UMI). Documents available from The Genuine Article, BIOSIS Document Express. ***Supersedes*** *Journal of Cryosurgery.*
**Ind/Abst** Biol. Abstr.; Curr. Contents Clin. Med.; EMBASE; Energy Res. Abstr. (Sept. 1981-); Index Med.; Life Sci. Collect.; Protozoolog. Abstr.; Res. Alert [Full Cov.]; Sci. Cit. Index; SCISEARCH; Soc. Sci. Cit. Index [Select. Cov.].

US/8756-8047
**OR MANAGER. See** Medical Science and Technology-Nursing.

●US/1065-8173
**OR REPORTS.** [OR rep.]. **VAT** Operating Room Reports. Vol. 1, No. 1 (Sept./Oct. 1992)-. Periodical. English. Six times a year. $88.00 US; $98.00 Canada; $108.00 others. OR Manager Inc, PO Box 17487, Boulder CO 80308-7487. **Tel** (303)442-1661, FAX (303)442-5960. **ED** Judith M. Mathias. **DD** 617. **NLM** W1; OR1015.
**Desc:** Abstracts of scientific research relaxing to the OR (operating room) environment.

US/1042-3699
**ORAL AND MAXILLOFACIAL SURGERY CLINICS OF NORTH AMERICA.** [Oral maxillofac. surg. clin. North Am.]. **VFOAT** Oral and Maxillofacial Surgery. Vol. 1 No. 1 (Sept. 1989)-. Periodical. English. Four times a year (Feb., May, Aug., Nov.). $94.00 (individual), $113.00 (institution) US; $127.00 (individuals), $134.00 (institutions) others. W.B. Saunders Company, A Subsidiary of Harcourt Brace Jovanovich, Inc., The Curtis Center/Suite 300, Independence Square West, Philadelphia PA 19106-3399. **Tel** (215)238-7800 or, 5587, FAX (215)238-7883, telex 173146. **(Subscription address:** W. B. Saunders Company / North America Subscriptions, c/o Periodicals, 6277 Sea Harbour Drive, 4th Floor, Orlando FL 32887.**)** **DD** 617. **NLM** W1; OR98. Index available. **Pr Rev. Circ:** 2,000.
**Desc:** Focuses on oral and maxillofacial subjects in every issue. New procedures and instrumentation is featured.

US/0147-1449
**ORAL AND MAXILLOFACIAL SURGERY DIRECTORY OF THE WORLD. VFOAT** Oral Maxillofacial Surgeons Directory of the World. Directory. English. 761 Osage Road, Pittsburgh PA 15243. **LC** RD523; .O7. **DD** 617/.522/0025. **UDC** 616.31-089.8. ***Continues*** *Oral Surgery Directory of the World.*

US/0030-4220
**ORAL SURGERY, ORAL MEDICINE, ORAL PATHOLOGY.** ***Title Change.* See** Dentistry.

NE/0167-6830
**ORBIT (AMSTERDAM). See** Medical Science and Technology-Ophthalmology.

NE/0014-4371
**ORTHOPEDIC SURGERY. See** Medical Science and Technology-Abstracting, Bibliographies and Statistics.

IT/0030-6266
**OSPEDALI D'ITALIA-CHIRURGIA.** [Osp. Ital.-chir.]. Vol. 1 (Nov. 1959)-. Academic Scholarly Publication. Italian. bm (6 issues). L100000. Mozzon Giuntina SPA, Via Mannelli 29R, 50136 Florence, Italy. **Tel** 011 39 55 2476781, FAX 055/2478568. **ED** Carlo Massimo. **NLM** W1 OS542. **Bk Rev. Ad Acc. Circ:** 1,000.
**Ind/Abst** EMBASE [Select. Cov.]; Life Sci. Collect.

US/0030-6517
**OSTOMY QUARTERLY.** [Ostomy q.]. (1963)-. Periodical. English. qt. $25.00 US; $30.00 other. United Ostomy Association Inc, 36 Executive Park/#120, Irvine CA 92714-6744. **Tel** (714)660-8624, FAX (714)660-9262. **ED** Kathryn L Pape. **NLM** W1 OS96. **Bk Rev. Ad Acc. Circ:** 50,000 (ctrl). available on an online database (file 149/Full-Text) from DIALOG.
**Desc:** Concerned with life following abdominal ostomy surgery, new techniques in ostomy surgery and national association activities. Includes research briefs and rotating departments (seniors, penpals, clinical cases, etc.).
**Ind/Abst** Cumul. Index Nurs. Allied Health Lit.; Health Index (1989-); Health Period. Database [Full Txt.]; Health Ref. Cent. (Jan. 1989-) [Full Cov.].

US/0194-5998
**OTOLARYNGOLOGY AND HEAD AND NECK SURGERY.** (OTOLARYNGOLOGY--HEAD AND NECK SURGERY : OFFICIAL JOURNAL OF AMERICAN ACADEMY OF OTOLARYNGOLOGY--HEAD AND NECK SURGERY.). [Otolaryngol. head neck surg.]. **Added/Corp** American Academy of Otolaryngology--Head and Neck Surgery. American Academy of Otolaryngology--Head and Neck Surgery Foundation. American Academy of Otolaryngology--Head and Neck Surgery. Meeting. Otolaryngology and Head and Neck Surgery American Academy of Otolaryngology--Head and Neck Surgery Foundation. Meeting. Otolaryngology and Head and Neck Surgery. Vol. 89, No. 1 (Jan./Feb. 1981)-. Periodical. English. mo. $196.00 (institutions), $117.00 (individuals) US; $222.00 (institutions), $143.00 (individuals) other. Mosby Year Book Inc., 11830 Westline Industrial Drive, St Louis MO 63146. **Tel** (800)325-4177, (314)872-8370, FAX (314)432-1380, telex 44-2402. **ED** Bruce Pearson. **DD** 617. **NLM** W1; OT52W. **[CCC].** Index available. **Bk Rev. Ad Acc. Pr Rev. Circ:** 8,531. available on microfilm and microfiche from University Microfilms International (UMI). Documents available from The Genuine Article, BIOSIS Document Express. ***Continues*** *Otolaryngology and Head and Neck Surgery, 0194-5998.*
**Desc:** Serves the clinical and continuing education needs of specialists in otolaryngology-head and neck surgery.
**Ind/Abst** Abr. Index Med.; Biol. Abstr.; Curr. Contents Clin. Med.; EMBASE; Index Med. (1981-); Life Sci. Collect.; Protozoolog. Abstr.; Ref. Upd. Basic Ed.; Ref. Upd. Deluxe Ed.; Res. Alert [Full Cov.]; Rev. Med. Vet. Mycology; Sci. Cit. Index; SCISEARCH; Soc. Sci. Cit. Index [Select. Cov.].

US/0885-1166
**OUTPATIENT SURGERY.** ***Ceased.*** (19??)-(19??). Periodical. English. qt. Hanley & Belfus Inc., 210 South 13th Street, Philadelphia PA 19107. **Tel** (215)546-7293, FAX (215)790-9330. **UDC** 616-089.8.

IT/0391-5387
**PEDIATRIA MEDICA E CHIRURGICA, LA. See** Medical Science and Technology-Pediatrics.

IT/0391-898X
**PEDIATRIA OGGI MEDICA E CHIRURGICA. See** Medical Science and Technology-Pediatrics.

GW/0179-0358
**PEDIATRIC SURGERY INTERNATIONAL. See** Medical Science and Technology-Pediatrics.

TU/1016-5142
**PEDIATRIK CERRAHI DERGISI. See** Medical Science and Technology-Pediatrics.

US/0198-5000
**PELVIC SURGEON, THE.** [Pelvic surg.]. V. 1-Apr. 1980-. Periodical. English. mo. $75.00. The Pelvic Surgeon, PO Box 98, Riderwood MD 21139. **Tel** (301)528-4144. **UDC** 616.718.19-089.8. **NLM** W1 PE269.

CN/1187-2934
**PERIODIQUE : PUBLICATION DE L'ORDRE DES DENTUROLOGISTES DU QUEBEC, LE.** [Period. - Ordre denturol. Que.]. **Added/Corp** Ordre des Denturologistes du Quebec. No. 29 (Summer 1991)-. Periodical. French. qt. Limited free distribution. Ordre des Denturologistes du Quebec, Bureau 106, 45 Place Charles-Lemoyne, Longueuil Quebec J4K 5G5 Canada. **DD** 617.6/0233/060714. ***Continues*** *Le Nouveau Periodique., 0842-5310.*

US/0894-8054
**PERSPECTIVES IN COLON AND RECTAL SURGERY.** [Perspect. colon rectal surg.]. Vol. 1, No. 1 (1988)-. Periodical. English. Twice a year. $145.00 (individuals), $224.00 (institutions) US; $151.00 (individuals), $230.00 (institutions) Canada; $194.50 (individuals), $281.50 (institutions) others Comes with QMP Clinical Series in Colon and Rectal Surgery. Quality Medical Publishing, 11970 Borman Drive, Suite 222, St. Louis MO 63146. **Tel** (314)878-7808, (800)423-6865, FAX (314)878-9937. **ED** Theodore R. Schrock. **DD** 617. **NLM** W1; PE871AM. **[CCC].**

US/1045-3741
**PERSPECTIVES IN GENERAL SURGERY.** [Perspect. gen. surg.]. Vol. 1, No. 1 (1990)-. Periodical. English. sa (2 issues). $99.00 (institution) US. Quality Medical Publishing, 11970 Borman Drive, Suite 222, St. Louis MO 63146. **Tel** (314)878-7808, (800)423-6865, FAX (314)878-9937. **ED** Barry A. Levine. **DD** 617. **NLM** W1; PE871ANC. **[CCC].**

US/1045-3733
**PERSPECTIVES IN NEUROLOGICAL SURGERY.** [Perspect. neurol. surg.]. (1990)-. Periodical. English. sa. $85.00 (individuals), $112.25 (institutions) US; $91.00 (individuals), $118.25 (institutions) Canada; $123.50 (individuals), $153.50 (institutions) airmail-other. Quality Medical Publishing,

11970 Borman Drive, Suite 222, St. Louis MO 63146. **Tel** (314)878-7808, (800)423-6865, FAX (314)878-9937. **ED** Daniel L. Barrow. **DD** 617. **NLM** W1; PE871CL.

US/1045-375X
**PERSPECTIVES IN ORTHOPAEDIC SURGERY.** ***Ceased.*** [Perspect. orthop. surg.]. **VFOAT** Perspectives in Orthopedic Surgery. (1990)-Vol. 3, No. 1 (19??). Periodical. English. be. Quality Medical Publishing, 11970 Borman Drive, Suite 222, St. Louis MO 63146. **Tel** (314)878-7808, (800)423-6865, FAX (314)878-9937. **ED** Robert Poss. **DD** 617. **NLM** W1; PE871CP.

US/0892-3957
**PERSPECTIVES IN PLASTIC SURGERY.** [Perspect. plast. surg.]. **VFOAT** Plastic Surgery. Vol. 1, No. 1 (1987)-. Periodical. English. be. $185.00 (individuals), $244.00 (institutions) US; $191.00 (individuals), $250.00 (institutions) Canada; $213.00 (individuals), $281.00 (institutions) other. Quality Medical Publishing, 11970 Borman Drive, Suite 222, St. Louis MO 63146. **Tel** (314)878-7808, (800)423-6865, FAX (314)878-9937. **ED** Fritz E Barton, John Bostwick III, Joel J Feldman, Ian T Jackson, Stephen J Mathes, Thomas D Rees, and Jack H Sheen. **LC** RD118.A1; P47. **DD** 617. **NLM** W1; PE871DK. **CODEN** PPSUEI. **[CCC]. Ad Acc.** Documents available from BIOSIS Document Express. **Ind/Abst** Biol. Abstr. (1987-).

US/0894-8046
**PERSPECTIVES IN VASCULAR SURGERY.** [Perspect. vasc. surg.]. Vol. 1 (1988)-. Periodical. English. sa. $165.00 (individuals), $244.00 (institutions) US; $171.00 (individuals), $250.00 (institutions) Canada; $193.00 (individuals), $281.00 (institutions) other. Quality Medical Publishing, 11970 Borman Drive, Suite 222, St. Louis MO 63146. **Tel** (314)878-7808, (800)423-6865, FAX (314)878-9937. **ED** Jerry Goldstone. **LC** RD598.5; .P48. **NLM** W1; PE871T. **[CCC].**

US
**PLASTIC AND RECONSTRUCTIVE BREAST SURGERY.** (1989)-. English. $295.00. Quality Medical Publishing, 11970 Borman Drive, Suite 222, St. Louis MO 63146. **Tel** (314)878-7808, (800)423-6865, FAX (314)878-9937.
**Desc:** Provides a personal but comprehensive approach to surgery of the breast and gives the reader a particular insight into his approach to evaluating and communicating with the patient, developing treatment plans, selecting the appropriate technique for each patient, performing specific surgical procedures and dealing with complications should they occur.

US/0032-1052
**PLASTIC AND RECONSTRUCTIVE SURGERY (1963).** (PLASTIC AND RECONSTRUCTIVE SURGERY.). [Plast. reconstr. surg.]. **Added/Corp** American Society of Plastic and Reconstructive Surgery, Inc. American Association of Plastic Surgeons. American Society for Aesthetic Plastic Surgery, Inc. American Society of Maxillofacial Surgeons. Vol. 31 (1963)-. Academic Scholarly Publication. English. Fourteen times a year. $193.00 (individual) $226.00 (institution) US; $253.00 (individual), $286.00 (institution) other. Williams & Wilkins Company, 428 East Preston Street, Baltimore MD 21202-3993. **Tel** (410)528-4000, (800)638-6423, FAX (410)528-8596, telex 87669. **(Subscription address:** Williams & Wilkins, PO Box 64380, Baltimore MD 21264.**) ED** Robert M. Goldwyn. **NLM** W1 PL118. **CODEN** PRSUAS. **[CCC]. Ad Acc. Pr Rev. Circ:** 12,000. available on microfilm. Documents available from The Genuine Article, BIOSIS Document Express, CASDDS, Quick Copies. ***Continues*** *Plastic and Reconstructive Surgery and the Transplantation Bulletin, 0096-8501.*
**Desc:** The leading journal in the field for every specialist using plastic and reconstructive surgery techniques.
**Ind/Abst** Abr. Index Med.; Biol. Abstr.; Chem. Abstr.; CIS Abstr.; Curr. Contents Clin. Med.; Curr. Contents Life Sci.; EMBASE; Energy Res. Abstr. (April 1977-);; Health Devices Alerts; Index Med.; Med. Abstr. Newsl.; Nucl. Sci. Abstr.; Life Sci. Collect.; Physic. Medline Plus; Ref. Upd. Deluxe Ed.; Res. Alert [Full Cov.]; Saf. Health Work; Sci. Cit. Index; SCISEARCH; Soc. Sci. Cit. Index [Select. Cov.]; SportSearch.

NE/0014-438X
**PLASTIC SURGERY.** ***Title Change.***
**Added/Corp** Excerpta Medica Foundation. (Jan. 1970)-(19??). English. bm. Elsevier Science Publishers BV, PO Box 211, 1000 AE Amsterdam Netherlands. **Tel** 011 31 20 5803642, FAX 011 31 20 5862696, telex 15682. **LC** RD118.A1; P6. **DD** 617/.95/005. **NLM** ZW 1 E978N. **Ad Acc. Circ:** 250. available on microfilm from University Microfilms International (UMI); available on CD-ROM. ***Merged into*** *Excerpta Medica. Section 9. Surgery, 0014-4134.*
**Desc:** Covers aspects such as transplantation, rehabilitation, psychiatry and social problems, congenital malformations, tumors and traumatology, surgical management (instruments and techniques, grafts, implants, etc.), and corrective surgery.

US/1043-4119
**PLASTIC SURGERY NEWS (ARLINGTON HEIGHTS, ILL.).** (PLASTIC SURGERY NEWS.). [Plast. surg. news]. 1989-. Periodical. English. mo. $35.00 (members), $75.00 (nonmembers). American Society of Plastic and Reconstructive Surgeons, 233 North Michigan Avenue/Suite 900, Chicago IL 60601. **Tel** (312)856-1818. **DD** 617. ***Continues*** *Plastic Surgeon, 0883-7848.*

US/0892-3965
**PLASTIC SURGERY OUTLOOK.** [Plast. surg.]. Vol. 1, No. 1 (Oct. 1987)-. Periodical. English. Ten times a year. Free to subscribers of Perspectives in Plastic Surgery. Quality Medical Publishing, 11970 Borman Drive, Suite 222, St. Louis MO 63146. **Tel** (314)878-7808, (800)423-6865, FAX (314)878-9937. **ED** Fritz E. Barton, John Bostwick III, Joel J. Feldman, Ian T. Jackson, Stephen J. Mathes, Thomas D. Rees, and Jack H. Sheen. **DD** 617.

US/0741-5206
**PLASTIC SURGICAL NURSING. See** Medical Science and Technology-Nursing.

IT/0032-2636
**POLICLINICO, SEZIONE CHIRURGICA.** [Policlin., Sez. Chir.]. (1893)-. Periodical. Italian. bm. Edizione Luigi Pozzi S.r.l., Via Panama 68, 00198, Roma, Italy. **Tel** (6)8553548. **CODEN** PSCHAIPSCHAI.
**Ind/Abst** EMBASE [Select. Cov.].

IT
**POLICLINICO; SEZIONE PRACTICA.** **VFOAT** Policlinico (Supplemento Settimanle 1900-1902). Vol. 7 (Nov. 3, 1900)-. Periodical. Italian (summaries and/or abstracts in French and English). wk. L110000 (Italy); $170.00 (other). Edizioni Luigi Pozzi Srl, Via Panama 68, 00198 Rome Italy. **Tel** (06)8553548, FAX (06)8554105.

PL/0032-373X
**POLSKI PRZEGLAD CHIRURGICZNY.** [Pol. prz. chir.]. **Added/Corp** Towarzystwo Chirurgow Polskich. (1922)-. Periodical. Polish (summaries and/or abstracts in English). mo. Price on Request. **(Subscription address:** ARS Polona, PO Box 1001, 00068 Warsaw Poland.**) NLM** W1 PO284.
**Ind/Abst** Index Med.

US
**PRACTICAL REVIEWS IN GENERAL SURGERY.** (19??)-. English. mo. $265.00 Physicians/Dentists, $185.00 Residents (for audio tapes and quick cards). Educational Reviews Inc., 6801 Cahaba Valley Road, Birmingham AL 35242. **Tel** (205)991-5188, (800)633-4743, FAX (205)995-1926.

US/0896-5447
**PRACTICAL REVIEWS IN ORAL MAXILLOFACIAL SURGERY.** (PRACTICAL REVIEWS IN ORAL MAXILLOFACIAL SURGERY [SOUND RECORDING].). [Pract. rev. oral maxillofac. surg.]. **Added/Corp** Educational Reviews, Inc. Montefiore Medical Center. **VFOAT** Practical Reviews. (198?)-. Periodical. English. mo. $175.00 Physicians/Dentists; $125.00 Residents (members); $190.00 Physicians/Dentists; $125.00 Residents (nonmembers). Educational Reviews Inc., 6801 Cahaba Valley Road, Birmingham AL 35242. **Tel** (205)991-5188, (800)633-4743, FAX (205)995-1926. **DD** 617.

US/0896-5404
**PRACTICAL REVIEWS IN SURGERY.** (PRACTICAL REVIEWS IN SURGERY [SOUND RECORDING].). [Pract. rev. surg.]. **Added/Corp** Educational Reviews, Inc. Montefiore Medical Center. **VFOAT** Practical Reviews. (1987)-. Periodical. English. mo. $275.80 Alabama; $265.00 US. Educational Reviews Inc., 6801 Cahaba Valley Road, Birmingham AL 35242. **Tel** (205)991-5188, (800)633-4743, FAX (205)995-1926. **DD** 617.
**Desc:** Summary: Abstract cards of articles found in the journal literature.

GW/0932-9196
**PRAXIS DER ANASTHESIOLOGIE UND INTENSIVMEDIZIN.** Periodical. German. ir. DM60.00. **ED** Gholam Sehhati Chafai. **NLM** W1; PR3113. **Circ:** 1,000.
**Desc:** Actual developments, methods and materials in anaesthesiology and intensive care.
**Ind/Abst** SCISEARCH.

US/0739-8328
**PROBLEMS IN GENERAL SURGERY.** ***Ceased.*** [Probl. gen. surg.]. Vol. 1, No. 1 (Jan. 1984)-(Oct./Dec. 1994). Periodical. English. qt. J.B. Lippincott Company, 227 East Washington Square, Philadelphia PA 19106-3780. **Tel** (215)238-4200 or 4454, FAX (215)238-4227. **(Subscription address:** J.B. Lippincott, PO Box 350, Hagerstown MD 21740.**) ED** Lloyd M. Nyhus. **LC** RD98; .P76. **DD** 617./01/05. **NLM** W1; PR573M. **[CCC]. Circ:** 2,500. available on microfilm and microfiche from University Microfilms International (UMI).
**Desc:** Features a symposium on a specific topic in general surgery in each issue.
**Ind/Abst** SCISEARCH.

US/1050-0197
**PROBLEMS IN PLASTIC AND RECONSTRUCTIVE SURGERY.** ***Ceased.*** [Probl. plast. reconstr. surg.]. (1991)-(Aug. 1993). Monographic series. English. Three times a year. J.B. Lippincott Company, 227 East Washington Square, Philadelphia PA 19106-3780. **Tel** (215)238-4200 or 4454, FAX (215)238-4227. **(Subscription telephone:** (800)638-3030**) DD** 617. **NLM** W1; PR573MKG.

BE/0772-1404
**PROCEEDINGS - BELGIAN CONGRESS OF ANESTHESIOLOGY.** [Proc. - Bel. Congr. Anesthesiol.]. **Main/Conf** Belgian Congress of Anesthesiology. (1975)-. Proceedings. English (summaries and/or abstracts in Dutch and French). **NLM** W1 AC749 v.26 1975 Suppl. etc.

US
**PROCEEDINGS OF THE FORUM SESSIONS / FORUM ON FUNDAMENTAL SURGICAL PROBLEMS.** (1950)-. Proceedings. English. W.B. Saunders Company, A Subsidiary of Harcourt Brace Jovanovich, Inc., The Curtis Center/Suite 300, Independence Square West, Philadelphia PA 19106-3399. **Tel** (215)238-7800 or, 5587, FAX (215)238-7883, telex 173146. **(Subscription address:** W. B. Saunders Company / North America Subscriptions, c/o Periodicals, 6277 Sea Harbour Drive, 4th Floor, Orlando FL 32887.**) LC** RD11; .F6. **DD** 617.082.

CN/0711-4915
**PROCEEDINGS OF THE RED DEER SURGICAL SOCIETY.** [Proc. Red Deer Surg. Soc.]. **Main/Corp** Red Deer Surgical Society. Proceedings. English. an. Free to physicians and medical libraries. Red Deer Surgical Society, 4914-46 Street, Red Deer Alberta T4N 1N3 Canada. **DD** 610. **UDC** 616-089.8.

SZ
**PROGRESS IN NEUROLOGICAL SURGERY.** Vol. 1 (1967)-. English. an. 190.00F (approx. per volume). S. Karger AG, Allschwilerstrasse 10, PO Box - Postfach - Case Postale, CH-4009 Basel Switzerland. **Tel** 011 41 61 306-1111, FAX 011 41 61 306-1234, telex CH 962 652. **ED** A. M. Landolt. Documents available from BIOSIS Document Express.
**Desc:** Volumes feature contributions from distinguished international surgeons, who review the literature from the perspective of their own personal experience. The result is a series of works providing critical distillations of developments having central importance to the theory and practice of neurological surgery.
**Ind/Abst** Biol. Abstr.; Index Med.; Ref. Upd. Deluxe Ed.

GW/0079-6654
**PROGRESS IN PEDIATRIC SURGERY.** **See** Medical Science and Technology-Pediatrics.

SZ/0079-6824
**PROGRESS IN SURGERY.** [Prog. surg.]. **VFOAT** Progres en Chirurgie; Fortschritte der Chirurgie. Vol. 1, (1961)-. English (French and German; summaries and/or abstracts in French). an. 190.00F (approx. per volume). S. Karger AG, Allschwilerstrasse 10, PO Box - Postfach - Case Postale, CH-4009 Basel Switzerland. **Tel** 011 41 61 306-1111, FAX 011 41 61 306-1234, telex CH 962 652. **ED** E. H. Farthmann. **LC** RD11. **DD** 617.082. **NLM** W1 PR681M. **CODEN** PSURA2. **[CCC].** Documents available from BIOSIS Document Express.
**Desc:** Presents in-depth reviews on topics selected as representing either controversial issues or areas where recent developments have concentrated.
**Ind/Abst** Biol. Abstr.; Index Sci. Rev. [Full Cov.]; Life Sci. Collect.; Ref. Upd. Deluxe Ed.

US/0271-2350
**PROGRESS IN SURGICAL PATHOLOGY.** [Prog. surg. pathol.]. Vol. 1 (1980)-. English. ir. Field & Wood, Inc., 4156 Manayunk Avenue, Philadelphia PA 19128. **Tel** (215)828-4010. **(Subscription address:** Field and Wood, PO Box 975, Blue Bell PA 19422.**) LC** RD57; .P74. **DD** 617/.07. **NLM** W1; PR681R.

IT/0393-764X
**PROGRESSI CLINICI. CHIRUGIA.** Vol. 1, No. 1 (1984)-. Periodical. Italian. Six times a year (Feb., Apr., June, Aug., Oct., Dec.). $114.60 Italy; $180.00 other. Piccin Editore, Via Altinate 107, 35121 Padua Italy. **Tel** 011 39 49 655566, FAX 011 39 49 8750693. **NLM** W1; PR697.

IT/0370-1514
**PROGRESSO MEDICO (ROMA).** (IL PROGRESSO MEDICO.). [Progr. med.]. Vol.1 (Aug. 1944). Periodical. Italian (English). bm. L96.000 Italy. Lembardo Editore, Via Verona 22, 00161 Rome Italy. **Tel** (06)428543. **ED** Mario Condorelli. **UDC** 616-089.8. **NLM** W1 PR706. **CODEN** PRMOAE. **Bk Rev. Ad Acc. Circ:** 7,000.
**Desc:** Editorials, reviews, original articles, case reports

and clinical trials in the fields of internal medicine and surgery.
**Ind/Abst** EMBASE [Select. Cov.].

IT/0393-5930
**QUADERNI DI MEDICINA E CHIRURGIA : QMC.** **VFOAT** QMC. Vol. 1, No. 1 (1985)-. Periodical. Italian (summaries and/or abstracts in English). sa. Comitato Progetto Cultura Medica Q M C, Via M. Stanzione 18, 80129, Napoli, Italy. **Tel** (81)5565285. **NLM** W1; QU132.
**Ind/Abst** EMBASE [Select. Cov.].

II/0033-5657
**QUARTERLY JOURNAL OF SURGICAL SCIENCES.** (1965)-. Periodical. English. Four times a year (Mar., June, Sept., Dec.). $2.00 India; $5.00 others. Banaras Hindu University Surgical Research Lab, College of Medical Science, Varanasi-5 India. **NLM** W1 QU295N. **CODEN** QJSSAB. available on microfilm and microfiche from University Microfilms International (UMI). Documents available from CASDDS.
**Ind/Abst** Chem. Abstr. (1965-1981).

IT
**RADIO COLLEZIONE COMPLETA : ENCYCLOPEDIE MEDIE CHIRURGICALE.** Editions Techniques, 141 rue de Javel, 75747 Paris Cedex 15 France. **Tel** 011 33 1 45589100.

IT/0390-0495
**RASSEGNA ITALIANA DI CHIRURGIA PEDIATRICA.** [Rass. it. chir. ped.]. V. 18- Jan./Mar. 1976-. Periodical. Italian. qt. Casa Editrice Leo S. Olschki, Viuzzo del Pozzetto, Casella Postale 66, 50126 Florence Italy. **Tel** 011 39 55 6530684, FAX 011 39 55 6530214. **UDC** 616-053.2-089.8. **NLM** W1 RA805P. ***Continues*** *Rivista di Chirurgia Pediatrica, 0035-5801.*
**Ind/Abst** EMBASE.

UK/0309-2674
**RECENT ADVANCES IN PLASTIC SURGERY.** No. 1 (1976)-. Periodical. English. ir. £80.00 (latest volume). Churchill Livingstone, 1-3 Baxter's Place, Leith Walk, Edinburgh EH1 3AF Scotland. **Tel** 011 44 31 556 2424, FAX 011 44 31 558 1278, telex 727511. **(Subscription address:** Churchill Livingstone / US, 5 S 250 Frontenac Road, Naperville IL 60563.**) ED** J. Calnan. **NLM** W1 RE105YC.

UK/0143-8395
**RECENT ADVANCES IN SURGERY.** [Recent adv. surg.]. (1928)-. Monographic series. English. ir. Price varies per volume. Longman Group Ltd., Fourth Avenue, Longman House, Harlow Essex CM19 5SR England. **Tel** 011 44 279 429655, FAX 011 44 279 431059, telex 81259. **ED** W.H. Ogilvie. **NLM** W1 RE105YJL. Each issue contains an index to its own contents (no volume index)--loose.

SZ/0080-0260
**RECONSTRUCTION SURGERY AND TRAUMATOLOGY.** [Reconstr. surg. traumatol.]. Vol. 10 (1968)-. Monographic series. English. an. 150.00F (approx. per volume). S. Karger AG, Allschwilerstrasse 10, PO Box - Postfach - Case Postale, CH-4009 Basel Switzerland. **Tel** 011 41 61 306-1111, FAX 011 41 61 306-1234, telex CH 962 652. **ED** R. de Roche, N. J. Luscher. **NLM** W1 RE111I. **[CCC].** Documents available from BIOSIS Document Express. ***Continues*** *Wiederherstellungschirurgie und Traumatologie.*
**Desc:** Books published in this series help familiarize readers with new techniques and procedures as described by the surgeons responsible for their development. Recognizing that rapid introduction of new procedures may improve patient survival and quality of life, the editor concentrates on featuring entirely original work in the detail adequate to facilitate its immediate clinical utility.
**Ind/Abst** Biol. Abstr.; Index Med.; Life Sci. Collect.; Ref. Upd. Deluxe Ed.

US
**RECONSTRUCTIVE SURGERY.** (1989)-. English. $295.00. Quality Medical Publishing, 11970 Borman Drive, Suite 222, St. Louis MO 63146. **Tel** (314)878-7808, (800)423-6865, FAX (314)878-9937. **LC** RD118.R366. **DD** 617.9/5.
**Desc:** Includes all three surgical techniques-microsurgery, tissue expansion and flaps as they apply to the entire body. Emphasizes clinical problem-solving to help the reader decide which reconstructive approach is appropriate for a particular reconstructive problem.

PL
**REPORTS ON SURGERY OF THE HAND.** Monographic series. Multiple languages (English and Polish). Price varies per volume. **UDC** 616.717.7-089.8. **NLM** W1 RE213C. ***Continues*** *Biuletyn Informacyjny Sekcji Chirurgii Reki.*

SP/0214-5987
**RESEARCH IN SURGERY.** **Added/Corp** Hospital General Universitario de Valencia. Centro de Investigacion. Sociedad Espanola de Investigaciones Quirurgicas. (1989)-. Periodical. English. Three times a year. 3000ptas (individuals), 3500ptas (institutions) Spain; $40.00 (individuals), $45.00 (institutions) other. Centro de Investigacion Hospital General de Valencia, Avda Tres Cruces S/N, 46014 Valencia Spain. **NLM** W1; RE227NE. **CODEN** RSURES.
**Ind/Abst** EMBASE; Indice Med. Esp.

SP/0214-5995
**RESEARCH IN SURGERY. SUPLEMENTO.** (1989)-. Periodical. Spanish (Spanish). Centro de Investigacion Hospital General de Valencia, Avda Tres Cruces S/N, 46014 Valencia Spain. **NLM** W1; RE227NEa.
**Ind/Abst** EMBASE; Psychol. Read. Guide.

AG
**REVISTA ARGENTINA DE CIRUGIA.** **Added/Corp** Asociacion Argentina de Cirugia. (19??)-. Periodical. Spanish (English). Eight times a year. $90.00 Argentina; $120.00 other. Asociacion Argentina de Cirugia, Marcelo T Alvear 2419, CP 1122 Buenos Aires Argentina. **Tel** 011 54 1 843180, 011 54 1 8212905, FAX 011 54 1 8253649, telex 821-2905. **ED** Eduardo Arribalzaga. Index available. cum. index. **Bk Rev**, (Qty: 32/yr). **Ad Acc. Circ:** 4,000 (ctrl).

BL/0034-7124
**REVISTA BRASILEIRA DE CIRURGIA.** [Rev. Bras. cir.]. Vol. 1 (1932)-. Periodical. Portuguese. bm. $180.00. Cidade Editora Cientifica Ltda, rue Mexico 90, 2 Andar CEP, 20031 Rio de Janeiro Brazil. **Tel** 011 55 21 2404578, 011 55 21 2404728. **NLM** W1 RE311. **CODEN** RBCHAN. Documents available from BIOSIS Document Express.
**Ind/Abst** Biol. Abstr.

CU/0034-7493
**REVISTA CUBANA DE CIRUGIA.** V. 1- Jan./Feb. 1962-. Periodical. Spanish. bm. Ediciones Cubanas, Obispo 527, Altos ESQ Bernaza, CP 10100 Havana Cuba. **Tel** 011 632980, 631942, FAX 011 631011, telex 512337, 6540.
**Desc:** Contains studies of cases, mainly of Cuban authors. Publishes articles of general surgery and surgical specialties.

BL
**REVISTA DA SOCIEDADE BRASILEIRA DE CIRURGIA PLASTICA.** **Added/Corp** Sociedade Brasileira de Cirurgia Plastica. No. 1 (1986)-. Periodical. Portuguese (English). sa. Redprint Editora Ltda., Rua Domingos de Morais 254, 401-B 04010 Sao Paulo Brazil. **Tel** (11)5724813. **NLM** W1; RE371D. **CODEN** RSBPET.
**Ind/Abst** EMBASE.

VE/0378-1852
**REVISTA DE LA SOCIEDAD MEDICO-QUIRURGICA DEL HOSPITAL DE EMERGENCIA "PEREZ DE LEON.".** **Added/Corp** Sociedad Medico-Quirurgica del Hospital de Emergencia "Perez de Leon.". (196?)-. Periodical. Spanish. Three times a year. Revista de la Sociedad Mexico, Apartado de Correos Altamira 68 557, Caracas 1062-A Venezuela. **Tel** 261 02 07. **NLM** W1 RE414P.

SP/0556-6177
**REVISTA DE MEDICINA DE LA UNIVERSIDAD DE NAVARRA.** [Rev. med. Univ. Navarra]. **Added/Corp** Universidad de Navarra. Vol. 7 (March 1963)-. Academic Scholarly Publication. Spanish (English, French, German and Italian; summaries and/or abstracts in English, French, German and Spanish). qt. $30.00. Servicio de Publicaciones de la Universidad de Navarra SA, Edificio Muga, Campus Universitario, 31008 Pamplona Spain. **Tel** 011 34 48 282700 ext. 2887. **ED** Diego Martinez Caro. **NLM** W1 RE423H. **[CCC]. Bk Rev. Ad Acc. Circ:** 12,000 (ctrl). ***Continues*** *Revista de Medicina de la Universidad de Navarra.*
**Desc:** A means of communication between current university members, graduates, and other professors and hospitals in Spain. Features include research reports, therapeutics, new medicine, resumes of doctoral theses, continued education, and current surgery and oncology.
**Ind/Abst** EMBASE; Index Med.; Indice Med. Esp.; Life Sci. Collect.

AG/0326-3428
**REVISTA DE NEFROLOGIA, DIALISIS Y TRANSPLANTE : PUBLICACION CONJUNTA DE LA ASOCIACION REGIONAL DE DIALISIS Y TRASPLANTES RENALES DE CAPITAL FEDERAL Y PROVINCIA DE BUENOS AIRES Y LA SOCIEDAD ARGENTINA DE NEFROLOGIA.** **See** Medical Science and Technology.

BL/0100-6991
**REVISTA DO COLEGIO BRASILEIRO DE CIRURGIOES.** [Rev. Col. Bras. Cir.]. **Main/Corp** Colegio Brasileiro de Cirurgioes. (1974)-. Periodical. Portuguese (summaries and/or abstracts in English). bm (6 issues). $30.00 Brazil; $45.00 other. Colegio Brasileiro Cirurgioes, rua Visconde de Silva 52 30 An, 22281 Rio de Janeiro RJ Brazil. **Tel** (021)286-2795, FAX (021)286-3795. **ED** Marcos F. Moraes. **NLM** W1 RE519P. cum. index. **Bk Rev. Ad Acc. Pr Rev. Circ:** 7,000 (ctrl).
**Desc:** Surgical journal dedicated to publishing research and clinical papers.

SP/0211-089X
**REVISTA ESPANOLA DE CIRUGIA CARDIACA, TORACICA Y VASCULAR.** ***Ceased.*** [Rev. esp. cir. card., torac. vasc.]. **VFOAT** CTV; CTV. Revisa de Cirugia Cardiaca, Toracica y Vascular; Revista CTV. (1980)-(1993). Periodical. Multiple languages. qt. Revista Espanola de Cirugia Cardiaca, Toracica y Vascular, Paseo Bonanova No 54 50 1A, 08037 Barcelona Spain. **Tel** 011 34 3 2126070. **UDC** 616.1.
**Ind/Abst** Indice Med. Esp.

SP/0210-2323
**REVISTA ESPANOLA DE CIRUGIA DE LA MANO.** (1973)-. Periodical. Spanish. sa. Grupo de Estudio del Aparato Locomotor (GEAL), Avenida de Goya 49, 50006 Zaragoza Spain. **Tel** 011 34 76 557210. **UDC** 616.7.
**Ind/Abst** Indice Med. Esp.

SP
**REVISTA ESPANOLA DE CIRUGIA ORAL Y MAXILOFACIAL.** (198?)-. Spanish. Sociedad Espanola de Cirugia Oral y Maxilofacial, Villanueva 11, 28001 Madrid Spain. **NLM** W1; RE532C. ***Continues*** *Revista Iberoamericana de Cirugia Oral y Maxilofacial : Publicacion Oficial de la Sociedad Espanola de Cirugia Oral y Maxilofacial.*

SP
**REVISTA ESPANOLA DE CIRUGIA OSTEOARTICULAR.** Spanish. Facta, Avellanas 4, 46003 Valencia Spain.
**Ind/Abst** Indice Med. Esp.

SP
**REVISTA ESPANOLA DE CIRURGIA OSTEOARTICULAR.** Spanish. bm. 6900ptas. Libreria Cano, Menendez y Pelayo 5-7, 46010 Valencia Spain. **Tel** 011 34 96 3624460.

RM/0300-8738
**REVISTA MEDICO-CHIRURGICALA A SOCIETATII DE MEDICI SI NATURALISTI DIN IASI.** [Rev. med.-chir. Soc. Med. Nat. Iasi]. **Main/Corp** Societatea de Medici Si Naturalisti Din Iasi. **Added/Corp** Societatea de Medicisi Naturalisti din Iasi. **VFOAT** Medical-Surgical Journal of the Society of Physicians and Naturalists IASI; Revue Medico-Chirurgicale de la Societe des Medecins et de Naturalistes; Zeitschrift fur Medezin und Chirurgie der Gesellschaft der Arzte und Naturforscher in Jassy; Mediko-Khirurgischeski Zhurnal Obshchestva Vrachei i Naturalisto V G Iassy. Vol. 60 (Jan./March 1956)-. Academic Scholarly Publication. Romanian (summaries and/or abstracts in English, French, German and Russian; table of contents in English, French, German and Russian). qt. **(Subscription address:** Rompresfilatelia, PO Box 12 201, Bucharest Romania.**) NLM** W1 RE656. ***Continues*** *Revue Medico-Chirurgicale.*
**Ind/Abst** EMBASE [Select. Cov.]; Index Med.; Trop. Dis. Bull.

FR/0035-1040
**REVUE DE CHIRURGIE ORTHOPEDIQUE ET REPARATRICE DE L'APPAREIL MOTEUR.** [Rev. chir. orthop. repar. appar. mot.]. **Added/Corp** Societe Francaise de Chirurgie Orthopedique et Traumatologique. Societe Francaise d'Orthopedie et de Traumatologie. Vol. 37 (Jan./March 1951)-. Academic Scholarly Publication. French. Nine times a year. $179.00. Masson Editeur, Box Postale 22, 41353 Vineuil 16 France. **Tel** 011 33 54 438994. **NLM** W1 RE777. **[CCC].** Index Available, published separately, free-automatically sent. cum. index. **Pr Rev.** available on microfilm and microfiche from University Microfilms International (UMI). Documents available from The Genuine Article. ***Continues in part*** *Revue d'Orthopedie et de Chirurgie de l'Appareil Moteur.*
**Desc:** Includes the reports of the Society's annual meetings and its symposia.
**Ind/Abst** Curr. Contents Clin. Med.; Dev. Med. Child Neurol.; EMBASE; Index Med.; Nutr. Abstr. Rev., Ser. A, Hum. Exp.; Life Sci. Collect.; Res. Alert [Select. Cov.]; SportSearch.

FR/0035-1768
**REVUE DE STOMATOLOGIE ET DE CHIRURGIE MAXILLO-FACIALE.** [Rev. stomatol. chir. maxillo-fac.]. Vol. 70 (1969)-. Academic Scholarly Publication. French. bm. $300.00. Masson Editeur, Box Postale 22, 41353 Vineuil 16 France. **Tel** 011 33 54 438994. **(Subscription address:** 7A Boulevard de Perolles, CH-1701 Fribourg Switzerland**) NLM** W1 RE805L. **CODEN** RSCMAL. **[CCC].** available on microfilm and microfiche from University Microfilms International (UMI). Documents available from BIOSIS

Document Express. **Continues** *Revue de Stomatologie.* **Ind/Abst** Biol. Abstr.; Curr. Titl. Dent.; EMBASE; Index Med.; Index Dent. Lit.; Life Sci. Collect.

SP
**REVUE IBEROAMERICANA DE CIRUGIA ORAL MAXILOFACIAL.** Spanish. ir. Ediciones Ergon, C Antonio Lopez Aguado No 1, 28029 Madrid Spain. **Tel** 011 34 1 3144157.

IT/0080-3243
**RIVISTA DI CHIRURGIA DELLA MANO.** [Riv. chir. mano]. (1963)-. Periodical. Italian. Three times a year. $125.00. Piccin Editore, Via Altinate 107, 35121 Padua Italy. **Tel** 011 39 49 655566, FAX 011 39 49 8750693. **UDC** 617.57.

IT/0035-6689
**RIVISTA GENERALE ITALIANA DI CHIRURGIA.** [Riv. gen. ital. chir.]. (1960)-. Periodical. Multiple languages. Six times a year. L60000.00 Italy; L120000.00 other. Casa Editrice Maccari, Via Trento 53, 43100 Parma Italy. **Tel** 011 39 521 771268, FAX 011 39 521 771268. **UDC** 617.

IT/1120-7558
**RIVISTA ITALIANA DI CHIRURGIA MAXILLO-FACCIALE.** [Riv. ital. chir. maxillo-facc.]. (1990)-. Periodical. Italian. Three times a year (Mar., July, Oct.). L40000.00. Edizioni Calderini, Casella Postale 2202, 40139 Bologna Italy. **Tel** 39-51-492211, FAX 39-51-493660, telex 1-510336 EDAGRI. **UDC** 617. **Ad Acc, Adv Mgr:** Uff. Starpa Calderini, **Tel** 051 492211. **Pr Rev. Circ:** 2,500.

IT/0391-2221
**RIVISTA ITALIANA DI CHIRURGIA PLASTICA.** [Riv. ital. chir. plast.]. **Added/Corp** Societa Italiana di Chirurgia Plastica. Vol. 1 (Jan./April 1969)-. Periodical. Italian (summaries and/or abstracts in English). Four times a year. L80000 Italy; L150000 others. La Garangola, Via Montona 4, 35137 Padua Italy. **Tel** 011 39 49 8750550, FAX 011 39 49 8751743. **NLM** W1 RI767. Index available. **Bk Rev. Ad Acc. Circ:** 1,500.
**Desc:** Official organ of the Italian Society of Plastic Surgery.
**Ind/Abst** EMBASE.

IT
**RIVISTA ITALIANA DI COLON-PROCTOLOGIA.** Vol. 4, No. 3 (1985)-. Periodical. Italian (summaries and/or abstracts in English). Three times a year. L90000. La Garangola, Via Montona 4, 35137 Padua Italy. **Tel** 011 39 49 8750550, FAX 011 39 49 8751743. **NLM** W1; RI767H. **Continues** *Rivista Italiana di Colo-Proctologia.*
**Ind/Abst** EMBASE [Select. Cov.].

XR/0035-9351
**ROZHLEDY V CHIRURGII.** [Rozhl. chir.]. Vol. 16- 1937/38. Periodical. Czech. mo. $117.60. **(Subscription address:** Artia Pegas Press Ltd., Palac Metro Narodni Trida 25, 11210 Prague 1 Czech Republic.**) UDC** 616-089.8. **NLM** W1 RO981. **[CCC]. Continues** *Rozhledy v Chirurgii a Gynaekologii.*
**Ind/Abst** Index Med.

US/0887-7033
**RUNNING RESEARCH NEWS. See** Recreation, Leisure-Sports.

US/0190-5066
**SAME-DAY SURGERY.** [Same-day surg.]. **VFOAT** SDS. **VAT** Same Day Surgery. Vol. 1 (Apr. 1977)-. Periodical. English. mo. $319.00. American Health Consultants, 3525 Piedmont Road, Suite 400, Atlanta GA 30305. **Tel** (800)688-2421, (404)262-7436. **(Subscription address:** American Health Consultants, PO Box 95278, Chicago IL 60694.**) ED** Jane Benners. **UDC** 616-089.8. **NLM** W1 SA448T. **[CCC]. Circ:** 2,850. available on microfilm and microfiche from University Microfilms International (UMI).
**Ind/Abst** Cumul. Index Nurs. Allied Health Lit.

SW/0284-4311
**SCANDINAVIAN JOURNAL OF PLASTIC AND RECONSTRUCTIVE SURGERY AND HAND SURGERY.** [Scand. j. plast. reconstr. surg. hand surg.]. Vol. 21, No. 1 (1987)-. Periodical. English. qt. Kr855.00, $137.00. Scandinavian University Press, PO Box 2959 Toeyen, N 0608 Oslo 6 Norway. **Tel** 011 47 2 2575400, FAX 011 47 2 2575353, telex 71896 UROR N. **(Subscription address:** Scandinavian University Press, 200 Meacham Ave., Elmont NY 11003.**) ED** Jan Lilja. **NLM** W1; SC152C. **CODEN** SJPSEM. Documents available from The Genuine Article, BIOSIS Document Express. **Continues** *Scandinavian Journal of Plastic and Reconstructive Surgery, 0036-5556.*
**Desc:** Official organ of the Scandinavian Association of Plastic Surgery. Serves as a forum for plastic surgery, hand surgery and related research in Scandinavia. Studies on operative methods, follow-ups, hand surgery, cranio-maxillofacial surgery, microvascular surgery ETC are published.
**Ind/Abst** Biol. Abstr. (1987-); Curr. Contents Clin. Med.; EMBASE; Index Med. (1987-); Life Sci. Collect. (1987-); Ref. Upd. Deluxe Ed.; Res. Alert [Full Cov.]; Sci. Cit. Index; SCISEARCH.

SW/0036-5580
**SCANDINAVIAN JOURNAL OF THORACIC AND CARDIOVASCULAR SURGERY.** [Scand. j. thorac. cardiovasc. surg.]. **Added/Corp** Society for the Publication of Acta Chirurgica Scandinavica. Scandinavian Association of Thoracic and Cardiovascular Surgery. Vol. 1 (1967)-. Academic Scholarly Publication. English. Three times a year. Kr825.00, $132.00. Scandinavian University Press, PO Box 2959 Toeyen, N 0608 Oslo 6 Norway. **Tel** 011 47 2 2575400, FAX 011 47 2 2575353, telex 71896 UROR N. **(Subscription address:** Scandinavian University Press, 200 Meacham Ave., Elmont NY 11003.**) ED** Axel Henze. **LC** RD536; .S35. **DD** 617/.54/005. **NLM** W1 SC154C. **CODEN** SJTCAO. **Pr Rev.** Documents available from The Genuine Article, BIOSIS Document Express.
**Desc:** Presents research and developments in the field of thoracic, cardiac and central vascular surgery, including cardiac transplantation. Now recognized as an international journal although most articles are of Scandinavian origin. All papers published in English. Doctoral theses publishes as supplements.
**Ind/Abst** Biol. Abstr.; Curr. Contents Clin. Med.; EMBASE; Energy Res. Abstr. (April 1977-);; Helminthol. Abstr. (19??-19??); Index Med.; Mod. Med.; Life Sci. Collect.; Ref. Upd. Deluxe Ed.; Res. Alert [Full Cov.]; Rev. Med. Vet. Mycology; Sci. Cit. Index; SCISEARCH.

US/0731-1680
**SCIENCE AND PRACTICE OF SURGERY.** [Sci. pract. surg.]. (1980)-. Academic Scholarly Publication. English. ir. Price varies per volume. Marcel Dekker Inc., 270 Madison Avenue, New York NY 10016. **Tel** (212)696-9000, (800)228-1160, FAX (212)685-4540, telex 421419. **(Subscription address:** Marcel Dekker Inc, PO Box 5017, Monticello NY 12701.**) LC** UNC. **NLM** W1 SC679. **CODEN** SCSUDR. Documents available from BIOSIS Document Express, CASDDS.
**Desc:** Presents topics such as cryosurgery, vascular surgery and more.
**Ind/Abst** Biol. Abstr. (1988-); Chem. Abstr. (1980-1981).

US
**SCIENTIFIC AMERICAN SURGERY.** English. ir. $320.50 (1 year), $486.45 (2 year) (institutions), $258.00 (1 year), $383.60 (2 year) (individuals) US; $335.50 (1 year), $503.45 (2 year) (institutions), $273.00 (1 year), $400.60 (2 year) (individuals) Canada; $370.45 (1 year), $558.50 (2 year) (institutions), $268.00 (1 year), $395.60 (2 year) (individuals) Far East. Scientific American Medicine, 415 Madison Avenue, New York NY 10017. **Tel** (212)754-0550, (800)333-1199. **Continues** *Care of the Surgical Patient.*

US
**SELECTED READINGS IN GENERAL SURGERY.** (1974)-. Periodical. English. Eleven times a year. $169.00. Selected Readings, 5323 Harry Hines Boulevard, Dallas TX 75235. **Tel** (214)688-2756.

US/0739-5523
**SELECTED READINGS IN PLASTIC SURGERY.** (SELECTED READINGS IN PLASTIC SURGERY / THE UNIVERSITY OF TEXAS HEALTH SCIENCE CENTER; BAYLOR UNIVERSITY MEDICAL CENTER.). [Sel. read. plast. surg.]. **Added/Corp** University of Texas Health Science Center at Dallas. Baylor University . Medical Center. **VFOAT** SRPS; S.R.P.S. (19??)-. Monographic series. English. ir. Price varies per volume. Selected Readings in Plastic Surgery, 411 Washington, Suite 6900, Dallas TX 75246. **Tel** (214)824-0154.

US/1045-4527
**SEMINARS IN ARTHROPLASTY.** [Semin. arthroplasty]. (July 1990)-. Periodical. English. qt (Jan., Apr., July, Oct.). $89.00 (individual), $116.00 (institution) US; $147.00 (individual), $157.00 (institution), other. W.B. Saunders Company, A Subsidiary of Harcourt Brace Jovanovich, Inc., The Curtis Center/Suite 300, Independence Square West, Philadelphia PA 19106-3399. **Tel** (215)238-7800 or, 5587, FAX (215)238-7883, telex 173146. **(Subscription address:** W. B. Saunders Company / North America Subscriptions, c/o Periodicals, 6277 Sea Harbour Drive, 4th Floor, Orlando FL 32887.**) DD** 617. **NLM** W1; SE4877. **[CCC].**

US/1043-1489
**SEMINARS IN COLON & RECTAL SURGERY.** [Semin. colon rectal surg.]. **VFOAT** Seminars in Colon and Rectal Surgery. (March 1990)-. Periodical. English. qt (Jan., Apr., July, Oct.). $94.00 (individual), $120.00 (institution) US; $136.00 (individual), $152.00 (institution) other. W.B. Saunders Company, A Subsidiary of Harcourt Brace Jovanovich, Inc., The Curtis Center/Suite 300, Independence Square West, Philadelphia PA 19106-3399. **Tel** (215)238-7800 or, 5587, FAX (215)238-7883, telex 173146. **(Subscription address:** W. B. Saunders Company / North America Subscriptions, c/o Periodicals, 6277 Sea Harbour Drive, 4th Floor, Orlando FL 32887.**) ED** Malcolm C. Veidenheimer. **DD** 617. **NLM** W1; SE487F. **[CCC].** Index available. **Bk Rev. Ad Acc.**
**Desc:** Gives an in-depth review of a particular subject in the colon and rectal surgery field. Work is practically oriented. Allows for up to the minute state of the art review of a particular subject.

●US/1071-5517
**SEMINARS IN LAPAROSCOPIC UURGERY.** [Semin. laparosc. surg.]. **VFOAT** Laparoscopic Surgery. Vol. 1, No. 1 (Mar. 1994)-. Periodical. English. qt. $79.00 (individual), $99.00 (institutions) US; $115.00 (individual), $128.00 (institution) other. W.B. Saunders Company, A Subsidiary of Harcourt Brace Jovanovich, Inc., The Curtis Center/Suite 300, Independence Square West, Philadelphia PA 19106-3399. **Tel** (215)238-7800 or, 5587, FAX (215)238-7883, telex 173146. **(Subscription address:** W. B. Saunders Company / North America Subscriptions, c/o Periodicals, 6277 Sea Harbour Drive, 4th Floor, Orlando FL 32887.**) DD** 617. **NLM** W1; SE489BR.

US/0160-2489
**SEMINARS IN NEUROLOGICAL SURGERY.** [Semin. neurol. surg.]. **VFOAT** Seminars in Neurological Surgery Series. (1978)-. Academic Scholarly Publication. English. ir. Price varies per volume. Raven Press, 1185 Avenue of the Americas, 37th Floor, New York NY 10036. **Tel** (212)930-9500, (212)930-9604, FAX (212)869-3495, (212)302-8507, telex 640073.
**Ind/Abst** EMBASE.

●US/1055-8586
**SEMINARS IN PEDIATRIC SURGERY.** [Semin. pediatr. surg.]. (1992)-. Periodical. English. qt (Mar., June, Sept., Dec.). $105.00 (individual), $129.00 (institution) US; $134.00 (individual), $171.00 (institution) other. W.B. Saunders Company, A Subsidiary of Harcourt Brace Jovanovich, Inc., The Curtis Center/Suite 300, Independence Square West, Philadelphia PA 19106-3399. **Tel** (215)238-7800 or, 5587, FAX (215)238-7883, telex 173146. **(Subscription address:** W. B. Saunders Company / North America Subscriptions, c/o Periodicals, 6277 Sea Harbour Drive, 4th Floor, Orlando FL 32887.**) DD** 617. **NLM** W1; SE489EN. **[CCC].**

●US/1056-8670
**SEMINARS IN PERIOPERATIVE NURSING. See** Medical Science and Technology-Nursing.

US/1040-7383
**SEMINARS IN SPINE SURGERY.** [Semin. spine surg.]. Vol. 1, No. 1 (March 1989)-. Periodical. English. qt (Mar., June, Sept., Dec.). $96.00 (individual), $116.00 (institution) US; $141.00 (individual), $151.00 (institution) other. W.B. Saunders Company, A Subsidiary of Harcourt Brace Jovanovich, Inc., The Curtis Center/Suite 300, Independence Square West, Philadelphia PA 19106-3399. **Tel** (215)238-7800 or, 5587, FAX (215)238-7883, telex 173146. **(Subscription address:** W. B. Saunders Company / North America Subscriptions, c/o Periodicals, 6277 Sea Harbour Drive, 4th Floor, Orlando FL 32887.**) DD** 617. **NLM** W1; SE489LN. **[CCC].**
**Ind/Abst** EMBASE.

US/8756-0437
**SEMINARS IN SURGICAL ONCOLOGY. See** Medical Science and Technology-Neoplasma, Neoplastic.

US/1043-0679
**SEMINARS IN THORACIC AND CARDIOVASCULAR SURGERY.** [Semin. thorac. cardiovasc. surg.]. Vol. 1, No. 1 (July 1989)-. Periodical. English. qt. $104.00 (individual), $131.00 (institution), US; $153.00 (individual), $165.00 (institution) other. W.B. Saunders Company, A Subsidiary of Harcourt Brace Jovanovich, Inc., The Curtis Center/Suite 300, Independence Square West, Philadelphia PA 19106-3399. **Tel** (215)238-7800 or, 5587, FAX (215)238-7883, telex 173146. **(Subscription address:** W. B. Saunders Company / North America Subscriptions, c/o Periodicals, 6277 Sea Harbour Drive, 4th Floor, Orlando FL 32887.**) DD** 617. **NLM** W1; SE489LW.
**Ind/Abst** Health Plan. Adminis.; Index Med. (July 1989-); Int. Nurs. Index.

US/0895-7967
**SEMINARS IN VASCULAR SURGERY.** [Semin. vasc. surg.]. (March 1988)-. Periodical. English. qt (Mar., June, Sept., Dec.). $102.00 (individual), $141.00 (institution) US; $142.00 (individual), $170.00 (institution) other. W.B. Saunders Company, A Subsidiary of Harcourt Brace Jovanovich, Inc., The Curtis Center/Suite 300, Independence Square West, Philadelphia PA 19106-3399. **Tel** (215)238-7800 or, 5587, FAX (215)238-7883, telex 173146. **(Subscription address:** W. B. Saunders Company / North America Subscriptions, c/o Periodicals, 6277 Sea Harbour Drive, 4th Floor, Orlando FL 32887.**) DD** 617. **NLM** W1; SE484RG. **[CCC].**
**Ind/Abst** EMBASE.

JA/0385-6313
**SHONI GEKA. See** Medical Science and Technology-Pediatrics.

US/1052-1453
**SKULL BASE SURGERY.** [Skull base surg.]. Vol. 1, No. 1 (Jan. 1991)-. Periodical. English. qt (Jan., Apr., July, Oct.). $159.00 (institutions), $115.00 (individuals) US; $184.00*(institutions), $140.00 (individuals) other. Thieme Medical Publishers Inc., 381 Park Avenue South, Suite 1201, New York NY 10016. **Tel** (212)683-5088, (212)683-5089, FAX (212)779-9020, telex 220 862 TSINC UR. **ED** U Fisch, D Mattox. **DD** 617. **NLM** W1; SK75. **CODEN** SBSUEL. **Pr Rev.** available on microfilm and microfiche from University Microfilms International (UMI). Documents available from The Genuine Article.
**Desc:** A multidisciplinary, journal that publishes original articles and illustrations containing clinical and experimental information for the practicing skull base surgeon. Draws from the expertise of anatomy, neurosurgery, otolaryngology, head and neck surgery, plastic and reconstructive surgery, oral and maxillofacial surgery, and neuroradiology to bring the most up-to-date information in the field. Covers new technologies, innovations, the latest materials, and significant problem cases. Peer-reviewed articles are taken from all relevant disciplines, and include original contributions, reviews, case reports, and clinical problems relative to the skull base.
**Ind/Abst** Curr. Contents Clin. Med.; Res. Alert [Full Cov.]; SCISEARCH.

●US/1064-5446
**SLIDE ATLAS OF OPHTHALMIC LASER SURGERY.** See Medical Science and Technology-Ophthalmology.

●US/1060-9458
**SLS REPORT, THE.** (THE SLS REPORT/ THE SOCIETY OF LAPAROENDOSCOPIC SURGEONS.). [SLS rep.]. **Added/Corp** Society of Laparoendoscopic Surgeons. **VAT** Society of Laparoendoscopic Surgeons Report. Vol. 1, No.1 Feb. (1992)-. Periodical. English. qt. $80.00 (institutions), 45.00 (individuals). SLS, 7330 Southwest 62nd Place, Suite 410, South Maimi FL 33143. **DD** 617. **NLM** W1; SL66M.

US/0193-3302
**SOCIO-ECONOMIC FACTBOOK FOR SURGERY.** **Added/Corp** American College of Surgeons. Dept. of Surgical Practice. American College of Surgeons. Socioeconomic Affairs Dept. (1977)-. English. an. $5.00. American College of Surgeons, 55 East Erie Street, Chicago IL 60611. **Tel** (312)664-4050. **LC** RD27.42; .S62. **DD** 338.4/7/6170973. **NLM** W1 SO878M.

FR/0249-6429
**SONS, CHIRURGIE (PARIS, FRANCE : 1982).** (SOINS. CHIRURGIE.). [Soins, Chirurg.]. **VFOAT** Chirurgie. (1982)-. Periodical. French. Ten times a year. 518.00F. Soins, 2307 rue Frontenac, Montreal Quebec H2K 2Z8 Canada. **Tel** (514)521-4957. **UDC** 616-089.8. **NLM** W1; SO8862KW. ***Continues*** *Soins. Chirurgie Generale et Specialisee, 0249-6429.*
**Ind/Abst** Int. Nurs. Index (1982-).

SA/0038-2361
**SOUTH AFRICAN JOURNAL OF SURGERY.** (SOUTH AFRICAN JOURNAL OF SURGERY. SUID-AFRIKAANSE TYDSKRIF VIR CHIRURGIE.). [S. Afr. j. surg.]. **Added/Corp** Association of Surgeons of South Africa. **VFOAT** Suid-Afrikaanse Tydskrif vir Chirurgie. Vol. 1 (1963)-. Academic Scholarly Publication. English (Afrikaans). Four times a year. R63.16 South Africa; R110.00 others. Medical Association of South Africa, Private Bag X1, 7430 Pinelands South Africa. **Tel** 011 27 21 5313081, FAX 534126, telex 5-20378 CT. **ED** C. Bremner. **NLM** W1 SO9057. **CODEN** SAJSBS. Index available. **Bk Rev. Ad Acc. Pr Rev. Circ:** 1,000 (ctrl). available on microfilm and microfiche from University Microfilms International (UMI). Documents available from The Genuine Article, BIOSIS Document Express.
**Desc:** Original and review articles on surgical topics. Also case reports, abstracts, letters to the editor and book reviews.
**Ind/Abst** Biol. Abstr.; Curr. Contents Clin. Med.; EMBASE; Index Med.; Index Dent. Lit.; Life Sci. Collect.; Protozoolog. Abstr.; Res. Alert [Select. Cov.]; Rev. Med. Vet. Mycology; Trop. Dis. Bull.

US/0038-4348
**SOUTHERN MEDICAL JOURNAL (BIRMINGHAM).** (SOUTHERN MEDICAL JOURNAL.). [South. med. j.]. **Added/Corp** Southern Medical Association. Vol. 1 (July 1908)-. Academic Scholarly Publication. English. mo. $70.00 US; $95.00 other. Southern Medical Association, PO Box 190088, 35 Lakeshore Drive, Birmingham AL 35219-0088. **Tel** (800)423-4992, (205)945-1840, FAX (205)942-0642. **ED** J. Graham Smith, Jr. M.D. **LC** R11; .S68. **DD** 610. **NLM** W1 S0955. **CODEN** SMJOAV. Index available. **Ad Acc. Pr Rev. Circ:** 40,000. available on microfilm and microfiche from University Microfilms International (UMI). Documents available from The Genuine Article, BIOSIS Document Express, CASDDS. ***Absorbed*** *Gulf States Journal of Medicine and Surgery* ***and*** *Mobile Medical and Surgical Journal.*
**Desc:** Official journal publishing more than 450 original clinical articles annually. All articles are directed to the practicing physician and surgeon.
**Ind/Abst** Abr. Index Med.; Biol. Abstr.; Chem. Abstr.; Chicano Index; Coal Abstr.; Cumul. Index Nurs. Allied Health Lit.; Curr. Contents Clin. Med.; Dairy Sci. Abstr.; EMBASE; Energy Res. Abstr.; Health Devices Alerts; Helminthol. Abstr. (19??-19??); Highw. Res. Abstr.; Index Med.; Int. Nurs. Index; Iowa Drug Inf. Serv. (1970-); Maize Abstr.; Med. Abstr. Newsl.; Microbiol. Abstr. Sect. B; Mod. Med.; Nutr. Abstr. Rev., Ser. A, Hum. Exp.; Nutr. Res. Newsl.; Life Sci. Collect.; PESTDOC; Physic. Medline Plus; Protozoolog. Abstr.; Ref. Upd. Basic Ed.; Ref. Upd. Deluxe Ed.; Res. Alert [Full Cov.]; Rev. Med. Vet. Entomol.; Rev. Med. Vet. Mycology; Rice Abstr.; Saf. Health Work; Sci. Cit. Index; SCISEARCH; Soc. Sci. Cit. Index [Select. Cov.]; SportSearch; Trop. Dis. Bull.

US/1065-2124
**SPINAL NETWORK'S NEW MOBILITY.** ***Title Change.*** [Spinal netw. new mobil.]. **VFOAT** New Mobility. (Summer 1992)-(199?). Periodical. English. bm. Spinal Network's New Mobility, 1911-11th Street, Suite 301, Boulder CO 80302. **LC** RD594.3.S69 1987 Suppl. **DD** 362.4/3. **NLM** W1; SP467. ***Continues*** *Spinal Network EXTRA, 1058-3483.* ***Continued by*** *New Mobility.*

US/0887-9869
**SPINE (PHILADELPHIA, PA. 1986).** (SPINE.). [Spine]. Vol. 1, No. 1 (Sept. 1986)-. Periodical. English. Three times a year. $93.00 (US & possessions); $103.00 (other). Hanley & Belfus Inc., 210 South 13th Street, Philadelphia PA 19107. **Tel** (215)546-7293, FAX (215)790-9330. **LC** RD768; .S68. **DD** 617/.375/005. **NLM** W1; SP474. **[CCC].**
**Ind/Abst** Curr. Contents Clin. Med.

SZ/1011-6125
**STEREOTACTIC AND FUNCTIONAL NEUROSURGERY.** [Stereotact. funct. neurosurg.]. **Added/Corp** World Society for Stereotactic and Functional Neurosurgery. American Society for Stereotactic and Functional Neurosurgery. Vol. 52, No. 1 (1989)-. Periodical. English. Eight times a year. $320.00. S. Karger AG, Allschwilerstrasse 10, PO Box - Postfach - Case Postale, CH-4009 Basel Switzerland. **Tel** 011 41 61 306-1111, FAX 011 41 61 306-1234, telex CH 962 652. **ED** Ph L. Gildenberg and Patricia O. Franklin. **NLM** W1; ST445K. **CODEN** SFUNE4. **[CCC]. Pr Rev.** Documents available from The Genuine Article, BIOSIS Document Express. ***Continues*** *Applied Neurophysiology, 0302-2773.*
**Desc:** Reflects the continuing growth and development in this highly specialized area of surgery and the new emphasis on state-of-the-art clinical and technical developments. Issues feature advances in the use of imaging-guided techniques in stereotactic biopsy, the impact of AIDS on the rapidly increasing use of stereotactic techniques, the role of stereotactically implanted radiotherapeutics in the treatment of malignancies, as well as the background and development of neural transplantation for the treatment of various CNS disorders.
**Ind/Abst** Biol. Abstr.; EMBASE; Index Med.; Psychol. Abstr. (1979-); PsycINFO (1990-); PsycLit; Ref. Upd. Deluxe Ed.; Res. Alert [Full Cov.]; Sci. Cit. Index (19??-19??); SCISEARCH.

US/0039-6060
**SURGERY.** [Surgery]. **Added/Corp** Society of University Surgeons. Society for Vascular Surgery (U.S.) Central Surgical Association. Vol. 1 (Jan. 1937)-. Academic Scholarly Publication. English. mo. $211.00 (institutions), $104.00 (individuals) US; $234.00 (institutions), $127.00 (individuals) other. Mosby Year Book Inc., 11830 Westline Industrial Drive, St Louis MO 63146. **Tel** (800)325-4177, (314)872-8370, FAX (314)432-1380, telex 44-2402. **ED** Walter F. Ballinger and George D. Zuidema. **LC** RD1; .S78. **DD** 617.05. **NLM** W1 SU746. **CODEN** SURGAZ. **[CCC].** Index available. **Ad Acc. Pr Rev. Circ:** 9,526. available on microfilm and microfiche from University Microfilms International (UMI). Documents available from The Genuine Article, BIOSIS Document Express, CASDDS, ADONIS.
**Desc:** Provides original articles for the leadership segment of surgeons, including the university-affiliated surgeon and the practicing general surgeon who has a need to keep abreast of developments in clinical and experimental surgery. Clinical papers are featured on topics such as trauma, gastrointestinal, vascular, and transplantation surgery.
**Ind/Abst** Abr. Index Med.; ADONIS; Biol. Abstr.; Calcium Calcif. Tissue Abstr.; Chem. Abstr.; Curr. Aware. Biol. Sci., CABS; Curr. Contents Clin. Med.; Curr. Contents Life Sci.; EMBASE; Energy Res. Abstr.; Health Devices Alerts; Index Med.; Maize Abstr.; Med. Abstr. Newsl.; Microbiol. Abstr. Sect. B; Mod. Med.; Nutr. Abstr. Rev., Ser. A, Hum. Exp.; Life Sci. Collect.; Physic. Medline Plus; Ref. Upd. Basic Ed.; Ref. Upd. Deluxe Ed.; Res. Alert [Full Cov.]; Sci. Cit. Index; SCISEARCH; Soc. Sci. Cit. Index [Select. Cov.].

US/0748-1942
**SURGERY ALERT.** ***Ceased.*** [Surg. alert]. Vol. 1, No. 1 (July 1984)-(May 1994). Periodical. English. mo. American Health Consultants, 3525 Piedmont Road, Suite 400, Atlanta GA 30305. **Tel** (800)688-2421, (404)262-7436. **ED** William Silen and Michael Steer. **DD** 617. **UDC** 616-089.8. Index available. **Ad Acc. Circ:** 2,500.
**Desc:** Abstracts and reviews of the medical literature specific surgery.

IT
**SURGERY AND IMMUNITY.** Vol. 1, 1 (June 1988)-. Periodical. English (Italian). sa. Edizioni Minerva Medica, Corso Bramante 83-85, 10126 Turin Italy. **Tel** 011 39 11 678282, FAX 011 39 11 674502. **NLM** W1; SU746E.
**Ind/Abst** EMBASE.

US/0081-9638
**SURGERY ANNUAL.** [Surg. annu.]. Vol. 1 (1969)-. English. an. $75.00. Appleton & Lange, (A Subsidiary of Simon & Schuster), 25 Van Zant Street, East Norwalk CT 06855. **Tel** (203)838-4400, (800)423-1359, FAX (203)854-9486. **ED** Lloyd Nyhus. **LC** RD9; .S8. **DD** 617/.005. **NLM** W1 SU747. **CODEN** SURABI. **[CCC].** Documents available from BIOSIS Document Express, CASDDS.
**Desc:** Collection of timely articles for the practicing surgeon.
**Ind/Abst** Biol. Abstr.; Chem. Abstr.; Energy Res. Abstr. (April 1981-); Index Med.

NO
**SURGERY COMBINED.** Twenty-four times a year ((20 issues per year)). Kr2520.00, $400.00. Scandinavian University Press, PO Box 2959 Toeyen, N 0608 Oslo 6 Norway. **Tel** 011 47 2 2575400, FAX 011 47 2 2575353, telex 71896 UROR N. **(Subscription address:** Scandinavian University Press, 200 Meacham Ave., Elmont NY 11003.**)**
**Desc:** European Journal of Surgery included combined subscription to Scandinavian Journal of Plastic and Reconstructive Surgery and Hand Surgery, Scandinavian Journal of Thoracic and Cardiovascular Surgery, Scandinavian Journal of Urology and Nephrology and supplements to all four journals.

US/0039-6087
**SURGERY, GYNECOLOGY & OBSTETRICS.** ***Title Change.*** [Surg. gynecol. obstet.]. **Added/Corp** Franklin H. Martin Memorial Foundation. American College of Surgeons. **VFOAT** SGO. **VAT** Surgery, Gynecology and Obstetrics. Vol. 1 (July 1905)-(1993). Academic Scholarly Publication. English. mo. Franklin H Martin Memorial Foundation, 54 East Erie Street, Chicago IL 60611. **Tel** (312)787-9282, FAX (312)440-7026. **ED** G Tom Shires. **LC** RD1; .S8. **DD** 617/.005. **NLM** W1 SU748. **CODEN** SGOBA9. **[CCC].** Index available. **Bk Rev. Ad Acc. Pr Rev. Circ:** 20,000. available on microfilm and microfiche from University Microfilms International (UMI). Documents available from The Genuine Article, BIOSIS Document Express, CASDDS. ***Continued by*** *Journal of the American College of Surgeons, 1072-7515.*
**Desc:** A general surgical journal edited by practicing surgeons. Material published is of interest to general surgeons, surgical specialists and other doctors who do surgery.
**Ind/Abst** Biol. Abstr.; Chem. Abstr.; Curr. Aware. Biol. Sci., CABS; Curr. Contents Clin. Med.; Curr. Contents Life Sci.; EMBASE; Energy Res. Abstr.; Health Devices Alerts; Helminthol. Abstr. (1991-); Index Med.; Iowa Drug Inf. Serv. (1969-); Life Sci. Collect.; Physic. Medline Plus; Ref. Upd. Basic Ed.; Ref. Upd. Deluxe Ed.; Res. Alert [Full Cov.]; Sci. Cit. Index; SCISEARCH; SportSearch.

UK/0263-9319
**SURGERY (OXFORD).** (SURGERY.). [Surgery]. Vol. 1, No. 1 (June 1983)-. Periodical. English. Twelve times a year. £68.40 UK; £72.00 other. Medicine Group (Journals) Ltd., Publishing House / United Kingdom, 62 Stert Street, Abingdon Oxon OX14 3UQ England. **Tel** 011 44 235 555770, FAX 011 44 235 554691, telex 85183147. **ED** J. S. P. Lumley and J. L. Craven. **NLM** W1; SU745. Index available. **Bk Rev. Ad Acc.** ctrl circ.
**Desc:** Comprehensive text of modern surgical practice, including all aspects of general surgery and most specialties, surgical techniques and principles.

SA/0254-6361
**SURGERY (SOUTHERN AFRICAN ED.).** [Surgery S. Afr. ed.]. (1983)-. Periodical. English. mo. R112.28 South Africa; R158.00 other. Medicine International, PO Box 1930, Randburg 2125 South Africa. **Tel** 011 27 11 7894010. **UDC** 617.

GW/0941-1291
**SURGERY TODAY.** (1992)-. mo. DM810.00. Springer-Verlag GmbH & Company KG, Heidelberger Platz 3, D 14197 Berlin Germany. **Tel** 011 49 30 8207223, FAX 011 49 30 8214091, telex 183 319 SPBLN D. **(Subscription address:** Springer Verlag New York Inc. / for North America, 44 Hartz Way, Secaucus NJ 07096.**)** Documents available from The Genuine Article. ***Continues*** *Japanese Journal of Surgery, 0047-1909.*
**Ind/Abst** Curr. Contents Clin. Med.; Res. Alert [Select. Cov.]; SCISEARCH; Soc. Sci. Cit. Index [Select. Cov.].

GW/0930-1038
**SURGICAL AND RADIOLOGIC ANATOMY (ENGLISH ED.).** See Medical Science and Technology-Anatomy.

US/0039-6109
**SURGICAL CLINICS OF NORTH AMERICA, THE.** [Surg. clin. North Am.]. Vol. 1, No. 1 (Feb. 1921)-. Academic Scholarly Publication. English. bm. $100.00 (individual), $123.00 (institution) US; $135.00 (individual), $141.00 (institution), other. W.B. Saunders Company, A Subsidiary of Harcourt Brace Jovanovich, Inc., The Curtis Center/Suite 300, Independence Square West, Philadelphia PA 19106-3399. **Tel** (215)238-7800 or, 5587, FAX (215)238-7883, telex 173146. **(Subscription address:** W. B. Saunders Company / North America Subscriptions, c/o Periodicals, 6277 Sea Harbour Drive, 4th Floor, Orlando FL 32887.**) ED** Livia Berardi. **LC** RD34; .S85. **DD** 617/.005. **NLM** W1 SU764L. **CODEN** SCNAA7. **[CCC].** Index available. cum. index. **Pr Rev. Circ:** 12,000. available on microfilm and microfiche from University Microfilms International (UMI). Documents available from The Genuine Article, BIOSIS Document Express, CASDDS. ***Continues** Surgical Clinics of Chicago, 0748-6650.*
**Desc:** Clinical updates on topics of current interest, including techniques and guidelines used by experts in the field.
**Ind/Abst** Abr. Index Med.; Biol. Abstr.; Chem. Abstr. (1921-1983); Curr. Contents Clin. Med.; Curr. Contents Life Sci.; EMBASE; Energy Res. Abstr.; Hospit. Health Admin. Index; Index Med.; Life Sci. Collect.; Physic. Medline Plus; Res. Alert [Full Cov.]; Sci. Cit. Index; SCISEARCH.

GW/0930-2794
**SURGICAL ENDOSCOPY.** [Surg. endosc.]. Vol. 1, No. 1 (April 1987)-. Periodical. English. Twelve times a year. $236.00. Springer-Verlag New York Inc., 175 5th Avenue, New York NY 10010. **Tel** (212)460-1500, telex 232 235 SPB UR. **(Subscription address:** Springer Verlag New York Inc. / for North America, 44 Hartz Way, Secaucus NJ 07096.**) ED** K. A. Forde, A. Cuschieri. **NLM** W1; SU764TU. **CODEN** SUREEX. **[CCC].** available on microfilm and microfiche from University Microfilms International (UMI). Documents available from The Genuine Article, BIOSIS Document Express.
**Desc:** Represents the surgical aspects of interventional endoscopy, ultrasound and other techniques, in the fields of gastroenterology, obstetrics, gynecology and urology as well as gastroenterologic, thoracic, traumatic, orthopedic and pediatric surgery.
**Ind/Abst** Biol. Abstr.; Curr. Contents Clin. Med.; Index Med. (Vol. 1, No. 1, 1987-); Res. Alert [Select. Cov.].

US/0071-8041
**SURGICAL FORUM.** [Surg. forum]. **Main/Corp** American College of Surgeons. **VFOAT** Postgraduate Medicine and Surgery. Vol. 1 (1950)-. Academic Scholarly Publication. English. an (Nov.). $20.00. American College of Surgeons, 55 East Erie Street, Chicago IL 60611. **Tel** (312)664-4050. **ED** Maxine Gere. **DD** 617. **NLM** W1 SU765F. **CODEN** SUFOAX. **Circ:** 3,000. available on microfilm and microfiche from University Microfilms International (UMI). Documents available from BIOSIS Document Express, CASDDS.
**Desc:** Contains research papers originally presented at the Forum of Fundamental Surgical Problems during ACS Clinical Congress.
**Ind/Abst** Biol. Abstr.; Chem. Abstr.; EMBASE; Energy Res. Abstr.; Index Med.; Life Sci. Collect.

US/0147-4154
**SURGICAL FORUM (BIRMINGHAM).** (SURGICAL FORUM.). **Added/Corp** Baptist Medical Center-Princeton. Surgical Forum. (Summer 1975)-. Periodical. English. Four times a year. Free on request. Baptist Medical Center - Princeton, 701 Princeton Avenue SW, Birmingham AL 35211. **Tel** (205)783-3078. **NLM** W1 SU765G.

US/1051-7200
**SURGICAL LAPAROSCOPY AND ENDOSCOPY.** [Surg. laparosc. endosc.]. **VFOAT** Surgical Laparoscopy and Endoscopy. Vol. 1, No. 1 (Mar. 1991)-. Periodical. English. bm (6 issues). $110.00 (individuals), $168.00 (institutions) US; $132.00 (individuals), $168.00 (institutions) other. Raven Press, 1185 Avenue of the Americas, 37th Floor, New York NY 10036. **Tel** (212)930-9500, (212)930-9604, FAX (212)869-3495, (212)302-8507, telex 640073. **ED** Karl Zucker. **DD** 617. **NLM** W1; SU766P. **CODEN** SLENEY. **[CCC]. Pr Rev.** available on microfilm and microfiche from University Microfilms International (UMI).
**Desc:** It provides peer-reviewed articles on techniques and equipment, surgical indications, and complications; objective product reviews; in-depth review articles by renowned experts; and superb, full-color illustrations.
**Ind/Abst** EMBASE; Sci. Cit. Index.

US/0090-3019
**SURGICAL NEUROLOGY.** [Surg. neurol.]. Vol. 1 (Jan. 1973)-. Academic Scholarly Publication. English. mo (2 volumes). $335.00 US; $430.00 Europe; $450.00 Japan; $402.00 (surface mail) other. Elsevier Science Publishing Company Inc, Madison Square Station, PO Box 882, New York NY 10159-0882. **Tel** (212)633-3950, FAX (212)633-3990. **ED** Eben Alexander Jr and Robert J White. **LC** RD593; .S87. **DD** 617/.48/005. **NLM** W1 SU767F. **CODEN** SGNRAI. **[CCC]. Bk Rev. Ad Acc. Pr Rev. Circ:** 4,400. available on microfilm and microfiche from University Microfilms International (UMI). Documents available from The Genuine Article, BIOSIS Document Express.
**Desc:** Presents full-length research and clinical papers and review articles in the field of neurosurgery, including studies relating to both humans and animals.
**Ind/Abst** Biol. Abstr.; Curr. Contents Clin. Med.; Dev. Med. Child Neurol.; EMBASE; Energy Res. Abstr. (Jan. 1976-); Helminthol. Abstr. (1991-); Index Med.; Res. Alert [Full Cov.]; Rev. Med. Vet. Mycology; Sci. Cit. Index; SCISEARCH.

●UK/0960-7404
**SURGICAL ONCOLOGY.** **See** Medical Science and Technology-Neoplasma, Neoplastic.

US/0899-8175
**SURGICAL PATHOLOGY.** **See** Medical Science and Technology-Pathology.

US/1062-4732
**SURGICAL PRODUCTS.** [Surg. prod.]. (19??)-. Periodical. English. mo (9 issues). $18.00 US, Canada & Mexico; $26.00 (surface mail), $60.00 (airmail) other. Cahners Publishing Company, 249 West 17th Street, New York NY 10011. **Tel** (212)645-0067, FAX (212)242-6987. **(Subscription address:** Gordon Publications, Inc., Paid Circulation Department, 301 Gibralter Drive, Box 650, Morris Plains NJ 07950-0650.**) DD** 617. ***Continues** Surgical Product News, 0279-4829.*
**Desc:** Focus is on hospital, surgicenters and emergicenters engaged in surgical procedures.

SZ/0882-9233
**SURGICAL RESEARCH COMMUNICATIONS.** [Surg. res. commun.]. Vol. 1, No. 1 (1987)-. Periodical. English. Four times a year. $328.00 (academic institutions), $511.00 (corporate institutions). Harwood Academic Publishers, PO Box 90, Reading RG1 8JL England. **Tel** 011 44 734 560080. **(Subscription address:** International Publishers Distributor at one of the following addresses: 820 Town Center Drive, Langhorne, PA 19047; or PO Box 90, Reading Berkshire RG1 8JL UK; or Kent Ridge PO Box 1180, Singapore 9111, Republic of Singapore**) ED** D. J. Leaper. **DD** 617. **NLM** W1; SU767KJ. **CODEN** SRCOEZ. **[CCC].**
**Ind/Abst** EMBASE.

US/1063-8547
**SURGICAL RESIDENT, THE.** ***Ceased.*** [Surg. resid.]. (1992)-(199?). Periodical. English. bm. Slack Inc., 6900 Grove Road, Thorofare NJ 08086. **Tel** (609)848-1000, (800)257-8290, FAX (609)853-5991, telex 517108 SLACK INC VD. **DD** 617. **NLM** W1; SU767KM.

US/0161-1372
**SURGICAL ROUNDS.** [Surg. rounds]. Vol. 1 (Jan. 1978)-. Periodical. English. Twelve times a year. $50.00 US; $92.00 others. Romaine Pierson Publishing Inc., 80 Shore Road, Port Washington NY 11050. **Tel** (516)883-6350. **LC** RD1; .S84. **DD** 617/.005. **NLM** W1 SU767LH. available on microfilm and microfiche from University Microfilms International (UMI).
**Ind/Abst** Cumul. Index Nurs. Allied Health Lit.

US/0164-4238
**SURGICAL TECHNOLOGIST, THE.** **See** Medical Science and Technology.

US/8756-8624
**TECHNOLOGY FOR SURGERY.** ***Ceased.*** [Technol. surg.]. Vol. 5, No. 7 (Jan. 1985)-Ceased January (1993). Periodical. English. mo. ECRI Emergency Care Research Institute, 5200 Butler Pike, Plymouth Meeting PA 19462. **Tel** (215)825-6000, FAX (215)834-1275, telex 510-660-8023. **ED** J Nobel. **DD** 617. **UDC** 616-089.8. **[CCC]. Bk Rev.** ***Continues** Health Devices Update. Surgery.*
**Desc:** A newsletter for surgeons and operating room supervisors, summarizing health care technology issues and reporting on product recalls, hazards, and problems.

TH/0125-6068
**THAI JOURNAL OF SURGERY.** (THAI JOURNAL OF SURGERY : OFFICIAL PUBLICATION OF THE ROYAL COLLEGE OF SURGEONS OF THAILAND.). [Thai j. surg.]. Vol. 1, No. 1 (Jan./March 1980)-. Periodical. English. qt (March, June, September, and December). 100.00B Thailand; $16.00 (surface mail), $56.00 (airmail) other. Thongdee Shaipanich, The Thai Journal of Surgery, c/o Bangkok Medical Publisher, 3/3 Sukumvit 49 Sukumvit Road, Bangkok 10110 Thailand. **Tel** 258-7954. **ED** Thongdee Shaipanich. **UDC** 616-089.8. **NLM** W1 TH116. **CODEN** TJSUDJ. Index available. **Ad Acc. Circ:** 1,200 (ctrl). Documents available from BIOSIS Document Express.
**Desc:** Original articles in the field of clinical and experimental surgery as well as surgical foundation.
**Ind/Abst** Biol. Abstr.

GW/0179-8669
**THEORETICAL SURGERY.** ***Ceased.*** [Theor. surg.]. Vol. 1, No. 1 (Apr. 1986)-Vol. 9 (1994). Periodical. English. qt. Springer-Verlag GmbH & Company KG, Heidelberger Platz 3, D 14197 Berlin Germany. **Tel** 011 49 30 8207223, FAX 011 49 30 8214091, telex 183 319 SPBLN D. **(Subscription address:** Springer Verlag New York Inc. / for North America, 44 Hartz Way, Secaucus NJ 07096.**) ED** J H Baron and W Lorenz, and M McPeek. **NLM** W1; TH12KD. **CODEN** THSUE6. **[CCC].** available on microfilm and microfiche from University Microfilms International (UMI). Documents available from The Genuine Article, BIOSIS Document Express.
**Desc:** Publishes contributions on all non-operative aspects of the care of the surgical patient, including anaesthesia and intensive care.
**Ind/Abst** Biol. Abstr.; Curr. Contents Clin. Med.; EMBASE; Res. Alert [Select. Cov.].

SZ/0040-5930
**THERAPEUTISCHE UMSCHAU.** [Ther. Umsch.]. **VFOAT** TU; Revue Therapeutique. Vol. 17, No. 12 (Dec. 1960)-. Academic Scholarly Publication. German (French). mo. 105.00F. Verlag Hans Huber Ag Bern, Laenggass Strasse 76, CH 3000 Bern 9 Switzerland. **Tel** 011 41 31 3004500. **(Subscription address:** Hogrefe International Inc., 12 14 Bruce Park Avenue, Toronto Ontario M4P 2S3 Canada.**) ED** T. Gordonoff. **NLM** W1 TH549H. **[CCC]. Bk Rev. Ad Acc. Pr Rev. Circ:** 6,000. Documents available from The Genuine Article. ***Continues** Therapeutische Umschau und Medizinizche Bibliographie.*
**Desc:** Concerned with the subjects of medicine and surgery.
**Ind/Abst** EMBASE [Select. Cov.]; Helminthol. Abstr. (1991-); Index Med.; Nutr. Abstr. Rev., Ser. A, Hum. Exp.; Life Sci. Collect.; Protozoolog. Abstr.; Res. Alert [Select. Cov.]; Rev. Med. Vet. Entomol.; RILM Abstr.; Saf. Health Work.

GW/0171-6425
**THORACIC AND CARDIOVASCULAR SURGEON, THE.** [Thorac. cardiovasc. surg.]. **Added/Corp** Deutsche Gesellschaft fur Thorax-, Herz- und Gefasschirurgie. Vol. 27 (Feb. 1979)-. Academic Scholarly Publication. English. bm. $209.00. Georg Thieme Verlag Stuttgart, Postfach 301120, D 70451 Stuttgart Germany. **Tel** 011 49 711 89310, FAX 011 49 711 8931298, telex 7 252 275 GTVD. **(Subscription address:** Thieme Medical Publishers Inc., 381 Park Avenue South, New York NY 10016.**) ED** K Stapenhorst. **NLM** W1 TH895. **CODEN** TCSUD4. **[CCC]. Pr Rev. Circ:** 1,600. available on microfilm from University Microfilms International (UMI). Documents available from The Genuine Article, CASDDS. ***Continues** Thoraxchirurgie; Vaskulare Chirurgie, 0040-6384.*
**Desc:** Contains proceedings of the Society's meeting and editorials which are made up of internationally respected surgeons who select original manuscripts from authors all over the world.
**Ind/Abst** Chem. Abstr. (1979-1982); Curr. Contents Clin. Med.; EMBASE; Helminthol. Abstr. (19??-19??); Index Med.; Life Sci. Collect.; Res. Alert [Full Cov.]; Sci. Cit. Index; SCISEARCH.

US/0194-5181
**TODAY'S OR NURSE.** **See** Medical Science and Technology-Nursing.

UK/0264-3014
**TOPICAL REVIEWS IN VASCULAR SURGERY.** [Top. rev. vasc. surg.]. **VFOAT** Vascular Surgery. Vol. 1-. English. ir. **ED** J G Pollock and A J McKay. **UDC** 616.14-089.8. **NLM** W1 TO533F.

US/0066-0833
**TRANSACTIONS OF THE MEETING OF THE AMERICAN SURGICAL ASSOCIATION.** [Trans. meet. Am. Surg. Assoc.]. **Main/Corp** American Surgical Association. **VFOAT** Transactions of the American Surgical Association. (1935)-. Periodical. English. an. $30.00. J.B. Lippincott Company, 227 East Washington Square, Philadelphia PA 19106-3780. **Tel** (215)238-4200 or 4454, FAX (215)238-4227. **(Subscription address:** J.B. Lippincott, PO Box 350, Hagerstown MD 21740.**) DD** 617. **NLM** W1 TR226M. cum. index. available on microfilm from University Microfilms International (UMI). ***Continues** Transactions of the American Surgical Association, 1059-5538.*

GW/0934-0874
**TRANSPLANT INTERNATIONAL.** (TRANSPLANT INTERNATIONAL : OFFICIAL JOURNAL OF THE EUROPEAN SOCIETY FOR ORGAN TRANSPLANTATION.). [Transpl. int.]. **Added/Corp** European Society for Organ Transplantation. Vol. 1, No. 1 (April 1988)-. Periodical. English. Six times a year. DM748.00. Springer-Verlag GmbH & Company KG, Heidelberger Platz 3, D 14197 Berlin Germany. **Tel** 011 49 30 8207223, FAX 011 49 30 8214091, telex 183 319 SPBLN D. **(Subscription address:** Springer Verlag New York Inc. / for North America, 44 Hartz Way, Secaucus NJ 07096.**) ED** G Kootstra. **LC** RD120.7; .T65. **DD** 617.9/5. **NLM** W1; TR233G. **[CCC]. Pr Rev.** available on microfilm and microfiche from University Microfilms International (UMI). Documents available from The Genuine Article.
**Desc:** Primary aim is to publish high quality papers in all fields of transplantation.
**Ind/Abst** Curr. Contents Clin. Med.; EMBASE; Health Plan. Adminis.; Index Med. (Vol. 1, No. 1 1988-); Res. Alert [Select. Cov.]; Soc. Sci. Cit. Index [Select. Cov.].

US/0748-1861
**TRANSPLANTATION AND IMMUNOLOGY LETTER.** [Transplant. immunol. lett.]. **VFOAT** Transplantation & Immunology Letter. Vol. 1, No. 1 (Sept. 1984)-. Periodical. English. qt. Free to related physicians and transcript specialists; $40.00 other. World Medical Communications Organizations, 7 Ridgedale Avenue, Cedar Knolls NJ 07927. **Tel** (201)455-1121. **ED** Barry D. Kahan. **DD** 616. **NLM** W1; TR234ST. Index available. **Bk Rev. Ad Acc. Circ:** 12,000 (ctrl).
**Desc:** Up-to-date information on developments and techniques in the fields of transplantation and immunology, written by leaders in these fields, with tele-lecture presentation.

CN/0849-1070
**TRANSPLANTATION, IMPLANTATION TODAY.** ***Ceased.*** **See** Biology-Cytology and Histology.

US/0041-1345
**TRANSPLANTATION PROCEEDINGS.** [Transplant. proc.]. **Added/Corp** Transplantation Society. Vol. 1 (Mar. 1969)-. Academic Scholarly Publication. English. bm. $305.00 institution, $180.00 individual. Appleton & Lange, (A Subsidiary of Simon & Schuster), 25 Van Zant Street, East Norwalk CT 06855. **Tel** (203)838-4400, (800)423-1359, FAX (203)854-9486. **(Subscription address:** Transplantation Proceedings, PO Box 3000, Department TP, Denville NJ 07834.) **ED** Felix T. Rapaport. **LC** RD120.7; .T68. **DD** 617/.95/005. **NLM** W1 TR235K. **CODEN** TRPPA8. **[CCC]. Ad Acc. Pr Rev. Acid Free. Circ:** 3,630. available on microfilm and microfiche from University Microfilms International (UMI). Documents available from The Genuine Article, BIOSIS Document Express, CASDDS.
**Desc:** Brings you the latest reports on transplantation biology and medicine. Each issue includes the latest research reports, descriptions of new techniques, original articles, biology and medicine.
**Ind/Abst** AgBiotech News Inf.; Anim. Breed. Abstr.; Biol. Abstr.; Chem. Abstr.; Cumul. Index Nurs. Allied Health Lit.; Curr. Aware. Biol. Sci., CABS; Curr. Contents Life Sci.; EMBASE; Energy Res. Abstr. (Aug. 1982-); Immunol. Abstr.; Index Med.; Int. Nurs. Index; Life Sci. Collect.; Pig News Inf.; Protozoolog. Abstr.; Ref. Upd. Basic Ed.; Ref. Upd. Deluxe Ed.; Res. Alert [Full Cov.]; Rev. Med. Vet. Mycology; Sci. Cit. Index; SCISEARCH; Soc. Sci. Cit. Index [Select. Cov.].

US/0955-470X
**TRANSPLANTATION REVIEWS (ORLANDO, FLA.).** (TRANSPLANTATION REVIEWS.). [Transplant. rev.]. Vol. 1 (1987)-. Periodical. English. qt (Jan., Apr., July, Oct.). $119.00 (individual), $150.00 (institutios), US; $163.00 (individual), $175.00 (institutions) other. W.B. Saunders Company, A Subsidiary of Harcourt Brace Jovanovich, Inc., The Curtis Center/Suite 300, Independence Square West, Philadelphia PA 19106-3399. **Tel** (215)238-7800 or, 5587, FAX (215)238-7883, telex 173146. **(Subscription address:** W. B. Saunders Company / North America Subscriptions, c/o Periodicals, 6277 Sea Harbour Drive, 4th Floor, Orlando FL 32887.) **LC** RD120.7; .P76. **DD** 617.9/5/005. **NLM** W1; TR235NT. **[CCC].** ***Continues*** *Progress in Transplantation, 0266-4852.*
**Ind/Abst** Index Med. (Vol. 1, 1987-).

US/0091-2719
**TRANSPLANTATION TODAY.** ***Ceased.*** **Main/Corp** Transplantation Society. V. 1-Ceased with Vol. 9, (1987). Periodical. English. ir. Grune & Stratton Inc., 6277 Sea Harbor Drive, Orlando FL 32887. **Tel** (800)782-4479, (407)345-2567. **LC** RD120.7; .T72A. **DD** 617/.95. **UDC** 616-089.843. **NLM** W3 TR826N.

SP/0214-820X
**TRASPLANTE OF ORGANS AND TISSUES.** [Trasplant. organs tissues]. **Added/Corp** Spanish Transplantation Society Sociedad Espaƒnola de Trasplante. (1989)-. Periodical. English. qt. Editorial Saned SA, Apolonio Morales 6, 28036 Madrid Spain. **Tel** 011 34 1 359-4092, FAX 011 34 1 457-9918. **UDC** 617.5-089.843.
**Ind/Abst** EMBASE.

US/0883-0304
**TRAUMA (PRINCETON, N.J.).** (TRAUMA.). [Trauma]. Periodical. English. bw. $305.00. Nassau Publications Inc., 11 Forest Street, New Canaan CT 06840. **DD** 617. **UDC** 616.001.

US/0743-6637
**TRAUMA QUARTERLY.** ***Ceased.*** [Trauma q.]. **VFOAT** Trauma. Vol. 1, No. 1 (Nov. 1984)-(1993). Academic Scholarly Publication. English. qt. Raven Press, 1185 Avenue of the Americas, 37th Floor, New York NY 10036. **Tel** (212)930-9500, (212)930-9604, FAX (212)869-3495, (212)302-8507, telex 640073. **DD** 617. **NLM** W1; TR258. **CODEN** TRAUEK. **[CCC].** available on microfilm and microfiche from University Microfilms International (UMI). Documents available from BIOSIS Document Express, CASDDS.
**Ind/Abst** Biol. Abstr. (1986-); Chem. Abstr. (1986-); Cumul. Index Nurs. Allied Health Lit.

RU/0302-8402
**TRUDY INSTITUTA - NAUCNO-ISSLEDOVATELSKIJ INSTITUT KLINICESKOJ I EKSPERIMENTALNOJ HIRURGII M.Z. S.S.S.R.** (TRUDY INSTITUTA - NAUCHNO-ISSLEDOVATELSKII INSTITUT KLINICHESKOI I EKSPERIMENTALNOI KHIRURGII MZ SSSR.). **Main/Corp** Nauchno-Issledovatelskii Institut Klinicheskoi i Eksperimentalnoi Khirurgii. **VFOAT** Trudy Nauchnogo-Issledovatelskogo Instituta Klinicheskoi i Eksperimentalnoi Khirurgii MZ SSSR. (196?)-. Periodical. Russian. **NLM** W1 TR958P.

GW/0340-2649
**UNFALLCHIRURGIE.** (UNFALLCHIRURGIE. ACCIDENT SURGERY.). [Unfallchirurgie]. **VFOAT** Accident Surgery. Vol. 1 (1975)-. Periodical. English (German). Six times a year. DM265.90 Germany; DM277.00 others. Urban & Vogel, Postfach 152209, D-80052 Munich Germany. **Tel** 011 49 89 53292140, FAX 089/536052, telex 521701. **(Subscription address:** Verlegerdienst Muenchen, Postfach 1280, D 82197 Gilching Germany.) **NLM** W1 UN1033. **[CCC].**
**Ind/Abst** EMBASE; Index Med.; SportSearch.

US/0193-8568
**UROLOGIC SURGERY (MT. KISCO).** (UROLOGIC SURGERY.). [Urol. surg.]. English. sa. Futura Publishing Company Inc., 135 Bedford Road, PO Box 418, Armonk NY 10504-0418. **Tel** (914)273-1014, (800)877-8761, FAX (914)273-1015, (914)273-1016. **UDC** 616.62-089.8.

US/0748-8971
**VASCULAR REPORTS.** ***Suspended.*** [Vasc. rep.]. Vol. 1, No. 1 (July-Aug. 1984)-?. Periodical. English. qt. $82.50. Appleton Davies Inc, 32 South Raymond Avenue/Suite 4, Pasadena CA 91105-9990. **Tel** (818)792-3046. **ED** Wiley F Barker. **DD** 617. **UDC** 616.14. **NLM** W1; VA921. **Bk Rev. Ad Acc. Circ:** 1,500.
**Desc:** Articles, case reports, and patient problems in diagnosis and treatment of vascular disease. Includes educational reviews and self-assessment exams, book reviews and announcements.

US/0042-2835
**VASCULAR SURGERY.** [Vasc. surg.]. **Added/Corp** American College of Angiology. Angiology Research Foundation. International College of Angiology. Vol. 1 (April 1967)-. Academic Scholarly Publication. English. bm. $120.00 (individual), $150.00 (institution) US; $130.00 (individual), $160.00 (institution) other. Westminster Publications Inc., 708 Glen Cove Avenue, Glen Head NY 11545. **Tel** (516)759-0025. **LC** RD598; .V37. **NLM** W1 VA922. **CODEN** VASUA9. **[CCC].** Index available in last issue of volume--attached. cum. index. **Ad Acc. Pr Rev. Circ:** 2,000 (ctrl). Documents available from The Genuine Article, BIOSIS Document Express.
**Ind/Abst** Biol. Abstr.; Curr. Contents Clin. Med.; EMBASE; Energy Res. Abstr. (Aug. 1976-); Life Sci. Collect.; Res. Alert [Select. Cov.].

US/0894-8038
**VASCULAR SURGERY OUTLOOK.** Vol. 1, No. 1 (Jan. 1989)-. Periodical. English. Ten times a year. $165.00 (individuals), $244.00 (institutions) US; $171.00 (individuals), $250.00 (institutions) Canada; $216.50 (individuals), $303.50 (institutions) airmail-other. Quality Medical Publishing, 11970 Borman Drive, Suite 222, St. Louis MO 63146. **Tel** (314)878-7808, (800)423-6865, FAX (314)878-9937. **ED** Jerry Goldstone. **DD** 617. Index available. **Circ:** 900.
**Desc:** Timely series reflecting current information in the field of vascular surgery. Emphasis on technique rather than clinical research.

SP
**VIDEO : REVISTA DE CIRURGIA.** English (Spanish, French and Italian). bm. 20.000ptas Spain; $400.00 US; 1.700F France. Video Medica SA, Badal 102 Bis Local 1, 08014 Barcelona Spain. **Tel** 3 7319666, FAX 3 4219942. Index available. cum. index. **Ad Acc. Pr Rev. Circ:** 5,000 (ctrl). available on videocassette.
**Desc:** Different publications about general surgery.

US/1058-7357
**VIDEOSCOPIC SURGERY.** ***Ceased.*** (VIDEOSCOPIC SURGERY : A BIWEEKLY REVIEW OF PROGRESS IN LAPAROSCOPY AND THORACOSCOPY.). Vol. 1, Issue 1 (Mar. 1993)-Vol. 1, No. 8. Periodical. English. bw (26 issues). Williams & Wilkins Company, 428 East Preston Street, Baltimore MD 21202-3993. **Tel** (410)528-4000, (800)638-6423, FAX (410)528-8596, telex 87669. **(Subscription address:** Williams & Wilkins, PO Box 64380, Baltimore, MD 21264-4380) **DD** 617. **NLM** W1; VI198L. Documents available from Quick Copies. ***Continues*** *Consultations in Laporascopic Surgery.*
**Desc:** A fully illustrated series on techniques, instruments, and case management- every advance in video-controlled surgery for the general surgeon.

IT/0394-6134
**VISCOCHIRURGIA.** [Viscochirurgia]. (1985)-. Periodical. Italian. qt. L50000 Italy; L70000 other. Ghedini Libraio, V Pezzotti 4, 20141 Milan Italy. **Tel** 011 39 2 76023133. **UDC** 617.7.

RU/0042-8817
**VOPROSY NEJROHIRURGII.** (ZHURNAL VOPROSY NEIROKHIRURGII IMENI N. N. BURDENKO.). **Added/Corp** Vsesoiuznoe Nauchnoe Obshchestvo Neirokhirurgov. Vol. 1 (Jan. 1977)-. Academic Scholarly Publication. Russian (summaries and/or abstracts in English). Four times a year. $62.00. Izdatelstvo Meditsina / Russian Academy of Medical Sciences, Ulitsa Solyanka 14, 109801 Moscow Russia. **Tel** 011 95 297-05-04. **(Subscription address:** Victor Kamkin, 4956 Boiling Brook Parkway, Rockville MD 20852.) **NLM** W1 ZH4243. **CODEN** ZVNBDJ. Documents available from CASDDS. ***Continues*** *Voprosy Neiirokhirurgii, 0042-8817.*
**Ind/Abst** Chem. Abstr.; EMBASE; Index Med.

NR/0331-054X
**WEST AFRICAN JOURNAL OF SURGERY.** V. 1- Feb. 1976-. Periodical. English. Three times a year. N25.50 Nigeria; $100.00 US. Professor J O Sodipo, DSC FFARCS, Box 2601 Surulere, Lagos Nigeria. **Tel** (01)837818. **ED** Paul Omo-Dare, Joseph Sodipo. **UDC** 616-089.8. **NLM** W1 WE329S. **Bk Rev. Ad Acc. Circ:** 2,000 (ctrl).
**Desc:** Devoted to the publication on information on surgical practice and science in West African region.

US/0276-5306
**WORLD DIRECTORY OF NEUROLOGICAL SURGEONS. PART 1, UNITED STATES OF AMERICA AND CANADA.** [World dir. neurol. surg., Part 1, U. S. A. Can.]. **VFOAT** Directory of Neurological Surgeons in the United States of America and Canada. **VAT** World Directory of Neurological Surgeons. Part One, United States of America and Canada. Directory. English. be. Free. World Directory Committee, 324-10th Avenue/Suite 140, Salt Lake City UT 84103. **LC** RD592.5; .W67. **DD** 617/.48/0025. **UDC** 616.8-089.8(058.7)(71+73). **NLM** WL 22.1; W9265. ctrl circ.

US/0364-2313
**WORLD JOURNAL OF SURGERY.** [World j. surg.]. **Added/Corp** International Society of Surgery. Vol. 1 (Jan. 1977)-. Academic Scholarly Publication. English (summaries and/or abstracts in French). Six times a year. $233.00. Springer-Verlag New York Inc., 175 5th Avenue, New York NY 10010. **Tel** (212)460-1500, telex 232 235 SPB UR. **(Subscription address:** Springer Verlag New York Inc. / for North America, 44 Hartz Way, Secaucus NJ 07096.) **ED** Ronald K. Tompkins. **NLM** W1 WO88K. **CODEN** WJSUDI. **[CCC]. Bk Rev. Pr Rev.** available on microfilm and microfiche from University Microfilms International (UMI). Documents available from The Genuine Article, CASDDS. ***Supersedes*** *Bulletin de la Societe Internationale de Chirurgie.*
**Desc:** Provides the reader with in-depth coverage of recent surgical developments. Each issue contains a feature focusing on a single topic of current interest to surgeons.
**Ind/Abst** Chem. Abstr.; Curr. Contents Clin. Med.; EMBASE; Energy Res. Abstr. (Aug. 1982-); Helminthol. Abstr. (1991-); Index Med.; Life Sci. Collect.; Protozoolog. Abstr.; Ref. Upd. Deluxe Ed.; Res. Alert [Full Cov.]; Rev. Med. Vet. Mycology; Sci. Cit. Index; SCISEARCH; Soc. Sci. Cit. Index [Select. Cov.].

US/0739-5949
**YEAR BOOK OF HAND SURGERY, THE.** [Year book hand surg.]. **VFOAT** Yearbook of Hand Surgery; Hand Surgery. (1985)-. English. an. $59.95. Mosby Year Book Inc., 11830 Westline Industrial Drive, St Louis MO 63146. **Tel** (800)325-4177, (314)872-8370, FAX (314)432-1380, telex 44-2402. **LC** RD559; .Y36. **DD** 617/.575059. **NLM** ZWE 830; Y39. **CODEN** YBHSEQ. Documents available from BIOSIS Document Express.
**Ind/Abst** Biol. Abstr. (1985-).

US/1041-892X
**YEAR BOOK OF OTOLARYNGOLOGY. HEAD AND NECK SURGERY, THE.** [Year b. otolaryngol.--head neck surg.]. **VFOAT** Yearbook of Otolaryngology--Head and Neck Surgery; Year Book of Otolaryngology, Head and Neck Surgery. (1985)-. English. an. $64.95. Mosby Year Book Inc., 11830 Westline Industrial Drive, St Louis MO 63146. **Tel** (800)325-4177, (314)872-8370, FAX (314)432-1380, telex 44-2402. **DD** 617. **NLM** W1; YE292. ***Continues*** *Year Book of Otolaryngology, 0146-7247.*

US/1040-175X
**YEAR BOOK OF PLASTIC, RECONSTRUCTIVE, AND AESTHETIC SURGERY.** [Year b. plast. reconstr. aesthet. surg.]. **VFOAT** Plastic, Reconstructive, and Aesthetic Surgery. (1989)-. English. an. Price varies. Mosby Year Book Inc., 11830 Westline Industrial Drive, St Louis MO 63146. **Tel** (800)325-4177, (314)872-8370, FAX (314)432-1380, telex 44-2402. **LC** RD118.A1; Y4. **NLM** W1; YE199W. ***Continues*** *Year Book of Plastic and Reconstructive Surgery, 0084-3962.*

US/0090-3671
**YEAR BOOK OF SURGERY, THE.** [Year book surg.]. **VFOAT** Yearbook of Surgery. (1971)-. English. an. $59.95. Mosby Year Book Inc., 11830 Westline Industrial Drive, St Louis MO 63146. **Tel**

(800)325-4177, (314)872-8370, FAX (314)432-1380, telex 44-2402. **LC** RD9; .Y4. **DD** 617/.005. **UDC** 616-089.8(058). **NLM** W1 YE182. ***Continues*** *Year Book of General Surgery, 0084-3776.*

●US/1060-2968
**YEAR BOOK OF TRANSPLANTATION.** **VFOAT** Yearbook of Transplantation. (1992)-. English. $59.95. Mosby Year Book Inc., 11830 Westline Industrial Drive, St Louis MO 63146. **Tel** (800)325-4177, (314)872-8370, FAX (314)432-1380, telex 44-2402.

US/0749-4041
**YEAR BOOK OF VASCULAR SURGERY, THE.** [Year book vasc. surg.]. **VFOAT** Yearbook of Vascular Surgery. (1986)-. English. an. $59.95. Mosby Year Book Inc., 11830 Westline Industrial Drive, St Louis MO 63146. **Tel** (800)325-4177, (314)872-8370, FAX (314)432-1380, telex 44-2402. **LC** RD598.5; .Y43. **DD** 617/.413. **NLM** W1; YE42J.
**Ind/Abst** Ref. Upd. Deluxe Ed.

GW/0930-9225
**ZEITSCHRIFT FUER HERZ THORAX UND GEFAESSCHIRURGIE.** **VFOAT** Herz-, Thorax- und Gefasschirurgie; HTG. Vol. 1, No. 1 (Feb. 1987)-. Periodical. German (summaries and/or abstracts in English; table of contents in English). bm. DM218.00. Dr Dietrich Steinkopff Verlag, PO Box 111442, D 64229 Darmstadt Germany. **Tel** 011 49 6151 17450. **(Subscription address:** Springer Verlag New York Inc. / for North America, 44 Hartz Way, Secaucus NJ 07096.**)** **ED** R. Hetzer, B.J. Messmer, W. Sandmann, and I. Voigt-Moykopf. **NLM** W1; ZE363G. **[CCC].** Index available. cum. index. **Ad Acc. Pr Rev.**
**Desc:** Covers heart-, vessel-, and thoracic surgery.

GW/0044-409X
**ZENTRALBLATT FUER CHIRURGIE.** [Zentralbl. Chir.]. Vol. 30 (Jan. 3, 1903)-. Academic Scholarly Publication. German. Twenty-four times a year. DM306.00. Johann Ambrosius Barth, Prager Strasse 16 B, D 04103 Leipzig Germany. **Tel** 011 49 341 7137570. **(Subscription address:** Huethig Publishing Inc., 29 Macintosh Drive, Oxford CT 06478.**)** **ED** W. Schmitt. **NLM** W1 ZE777H. **CODEN** ZECHAU. **Bk Rev. Ad Acc. Pr Rev.** ctrl circ. available on microfilm from University Microfilms International (UMI). Documents available from The Genuine Article, CASDDS. ***Continues*** *Centralblatt fuer Chirurgie.*
**Desc:** Deals with errors and risks in surgery.
**Ind/Abst** Chem. Abstr.; Curr. Contents Clin. Med.; EMBASE; Index Med.; Life Sci. Collect.; Protozoolog. Abstr.; Res. Alert [Select. Cov.]; Rev. Med. Vet. Mycology.

GW/0044-409X
**ZENTRALBLATT FUER CHIRURGIE. SONDERBAND.** (19??)-. German (summaries and/or abstracts in English). bm. LKG Leipziger Kommissions & Grossbuchhandel, Leninstrasse 16, Postfach 520, D 04005 Leipzig, Germany. **Tel** 011 49 341 71370. **ED** H. Wolff. **Bk Rev. Ad Acc.**
**Desc:** Readers are given current, versatile and concise information about practice, clinic, research and postgraduate training.

GW/0044-4251
**ZENTRALBLATT FUER NEUROCHIRURGIE.** [Zentralbl. Neurochir.]. Vol. 1 (Aug. 1936)-. Academic Scholarly Publication. German (German, Russian, English and French; summaries and/or abstracts in English, French, German and Russian). Four times a year. DM265.00. Johann Ambrosius Barth, Prager Strasse 16 B, D 04103 Leipzig Germany. **Tel** 011 49 341 7137570. **(Subscription address:** Huethig Publishing Inc., 29 Macintosh Drive, Oxford CT 06478.**)** **ED** H.G. Neibeling. **NLM** W1 ZE78. **Bk Rev. Ad Acc.** ctrl circ. Documents available from The Genuine Article.
**Desc:** Publishes treatises from the entire field of neurosurgery.
**Ind/Abst** EMBASE; Index Med.; Life Sci. Collect.; Res. Alert [Full Cov.].

GW/0340-5214
**ZENTRALBLATT HALS- NASEN- OHRENHEILKUNDE, PLASTISCHE CHIRURGIE AN KOPF UND HALS.** [Zentralbl. Hals- Nasen- Ohrenheild., plast. chir. Kopf Hals]. **Added/Corp** Deutsche Gesellschaft fuer Hals-Nasen-Ohrenheilkunde, Kopf- und Halschirurgie. **VFOAT** Zentralblatt Hals-Nasen-Ohrenheilkunde, Plastische Chirurgie an Kopf und Hals; Oto-Rhino-Laryngology, Plastic Surgery of Head and Neck; Zentralblatt Hals-, Nasen- und Ohrenheilkunde, Plastische Chirurgie an Kopf und Hals. Vol. 128, No. 1 (1982)-. German (English; summaries and/or abstracts in English). Thirteen times a year. DM2298.00. Springer-Verlag GmbH & Company KG, Heidelberger Platz 3, D 14197 Berlin Germany. **Tel** 011 49 30 8207223, FAX 011 49 30 8214091, telex 183 319 SPBLN D. **(Subscription address:** Springer Verlag New York Inc. / for North America, 44 Hartz Way, Secaucus NJ 07096.**)** **ED** H.J. Denecke, R. Link, O. Novotny and L. Ruedi. **NLM** ZWV 100 Z56. **[CCC].** ***Continues*** *Zentralblatt fuer Hals- Nasen- und Ohrenheilkunde, Plastische Chirurgie an Kopf und Hals, 0340-5214.*
**Desc:** Plastic surgery of head and neck, anesthesia, instruments, radiology, genetics, allergies, immunology, skull, head and facial structure, special problems of neck and and nose and chemotherapy.

GW/0722-6985
**ZENTRALORGAN CHIRURGIE. Added/Corp** Deutsche Gesellschaft fur Chirurgie. **VFOAT** Surgery. Vol. 226, No. 1 (1982)-. Periodical. German (English and German). Twenty-six times a year. DM3698.00. Springer-Verlag GmbH & Company KG, Heidelberger Platz 3, D 14197 Berlin Germany. **Tel** 011 49 30 8207223, FAX 011 49 30 8214091, telex 183 319 SPBLN D. **(Subscription address:** Springer Verlag New York Inc. / for North America, 44 Hartz Way, Secaucus NJ 07096.**)** **ED** G Herberer, F Linder and W Wachsmuth. **NLM** ZWO 100 Z56. **[CCC].** ***Continues*** *Zentralorgan fur die Gesamte Chirurgie und Ihre Grenzgebiete.*
**Desc:** Covers surgical pathophysiology, intensive care, shock, experimental surgery, organ transplants, plastic surgery, physical therapy and radiology, instruments and techniques, pre- and post-op.

CH/1011-6788
**ZHONGHUA MINGUO WAIKE YIXUE HUI ZAZHI.** **VFOAT** Journal of Surgical Association Republic of China; Journal of Surgical Association R.O.C. (1968)-. Periodical. Multiple languages. Six times a year. Surgical Association / Taiwan, No. 31, 3F Nanjing East Road, Sec. 5 10571, Taipei Taiwan. **Tel** 011 886 2 7656630.
**Ind/Abst** EMBASE.

CC/1000-7806
**ZHONGHUA ZHENGXING SHAOSHANG WAIKE ZAZHI.** (CHUNG-HUA CHENG HSING SHAO SHANG WAI KO TSA CHIH.). [Zhonghua zhengxing shaoshang waike zazhi]. **Added/Corp** Chung-kuo i Hsueh ko Hsueh Yuan. Cheng Hsing Wai ko i Yuan. **VFOAT** Zhonghua Zheng Xing Shao Shang Waike Zazhi; Zhonghua Zheng Xing Shao Shang Waikf Zazhi; Chinese Journal of Plastic Surgery and Burns. Vol. 1, No. 1 (1985)-. Periodical. Chinese (summaries and/or abstracts in English; table of contents in English). qt. $22.48. **(Subscription address:** China International Book Trading Corporation, PO Box 399, Library Service Department, Beijing 100044 People's Republic of China.**)** **NLM** W1; CH9771C.
**Ind/Abst** Index Med. (Vol. 1, No. 1, 1985-).

## TOXICOLOGY

IT/0393-635X
**ACTA TOXICOLOGICA ET THERAPEUTICA.** [Acta toxicol. ther.]. (1980)-. Academic Scholarly Publication. Italian (English). Four times a year. L60000.00 Italy; L120000.00 other. Casa Editrice Maccari, Via Trento 53, 43100 Parma Italy. **Tel** 011 39 521 771268, FAX 011 39 521 771268. **NLM** W1; AC95W. **CODEN** ATTHEH. Documents available from BIOSIS Document Express, CASDDS.
**Ind/Abst** Biol. Abstr.; Chem. Abstr. (1986-); EMBASE; Index Med.

US/8755-4259
**ACTIVITIES / CHEMICAL INDUSTRY INSTITUTE OF TOXICOLOGY.** [Act. - Chem. Ind. Inst. Toxicol.]. **Main/Corp** Chemical Industry Institute of Toxicology. **VFOAT** CIIT Activities. Vol. 1, No. 1 (June 1981)-. English. Twelve times a year. Free. Chemical Industry Institute of Toxicology, PO Box 12137, 6 Davis Drive, Research Triangle Park NC 27709. **Tel** (919)558-1215, FAX (919)558-1300. **ED** Willamia Griffin (phone: (919)558-1310). **LC** RA1190; .C47a. **DD** 615.9/005. Index available. cum. index. **Circ:** 5,000 (ctrl).
**Desc:** This newsletter reports on the research, testing, and training activities of CIIT, a not-for-profit toxicology laboratory engaged in the study of chemical safety.

US/1044-2049
**ACUTE TOXICITY DATA.** ***Ceased.*** [Acute toxic. data]. (1990)-(199?). Periodical. English. bm. Mary Ann Liebert Inc., 1651 Third Avenue, New York NY 10128. **Tel** (212)289-2300, (800)M-LIEBERT, FAX (212)289-4697. **LC** RA1190; .A34. **DD** 615.9/07/05. **NLM** W1; JO908VB. **CODEN** ATDAEI.

US/0749-7431
**ADVANCES IN ANALYTICAL TOXICOLOGY.** ***Ceased.*** [Adv. anal. toxicol.]. Vol. 1 (1984)-(19??). Academic Scholarly Publication. English. Biomedical Publications, PO Box 8209, Foster City CA 94404. **ED** Randall Ca Baselt. **LC** RA1221; .A3. **DD** 615.9/07/05. **NLM** W1; AD433F. **CODEN** AATOE7. Documents available from CASDDS.
**Ind/Abst** Chem. Abstr. (1984-).

US/0276-5063
**ADVANCES IN MODERN ENVIRONMENTAL TOXICOLOGY.** **See** Industrial Health and Safety.

UK/0044-6394
**ADVERSE DRUG REACTION BULLETIN.** [Adverse drug react. bull.]. **Added/Corp** Shotley Bridge General Hospital. Adverse Drug Reaction Research Unit. (1966)-. Academic Scholarly Publication. English (Italian and Spanish). bm. $30.00 US & Canada; £15.00 Europe; £18.00 other. Chapman & Hall, 2-6 Boundary Row, London SE1 8HN England. **Tel** 011 44 71 865 0066, FAX 011 44 71 522 9623, telex 290164 Chapmag. **(Subscription address:** Chapman & Hall, Cheriton House, North Way, Andover, Hampshire, SP10 5BE England.**)** **ED** D.M. Davies. **NLM** W1 AD93. **CODEN** ADRBBA. **[CCC].** Index available. **Circ:** 100,000. available on microfilm and microfiche from University Microfilms International (UMI). Documents available from BIOSIS Document Express.
**Desc:** Includes brief reviews on adverse drug reactions.
**Ind/Abst** BioBusiness; Biol. Abstr.; EMBASE; Int. Pharm. Abstr.; Iowa Drug Inf. Serv. (1973-); Life Sci. Collect.; Toxicol. Abstr.; Trop. Dis. Bull.

UK/0964-198X
**ADVERSE DRUG REACTIONS AND TOXICOLOGICAL REVIEWS.** [Adverse drug react. toxicol. rev.]. **VFOAT** Adverse Drug Reactions and Toxicology Reviews. Vol. 10, No. 1 (Spring 1991)-. Academic Scholarly Publication. English. qt. £95.00 UK and Europe; $180.00 other. Oxford University Press, Walton Street, Oxford OX2 6DP England. **Tel** 011 44 865 56767, FAX 011 44 865 267773, telex 837330 OXPRES G. **(Subscription address:** Oxford University Press / USA, Journals Marketing Department, Oxford University Press, 2001 Evans Road, Cary NC 27513.**)** **LC** RM302.5; .A38. **DD** 615/.704. **NLM** W1; AD92L. **CODEN** ADRRER. **[CCC].** available on microfilm and microfiche from University Microfilms International (UMI). Documents available from The Genuine Article, BIOSIS Document Express, CASDDS, ADONIS. ***Continues*** *Adverse Drug Reactions and Acute Poisoning Reviews, 0260-647X.*
**Ind/Abst** ADONIS; Biol. Abstr.; Chem. Abstr.; Curr. Aware. Biol. Sci., CABS; Curr. Contents Clin. Med.; EMBASE; Health Plan. Adminis.; Index Med.; Res. Alert [Full Cov.]; Sci. Cit. Index; SCISEARCH.

SZ/0379-0363
**AGENTS AND ACTIONS. SUPPLEMENTS.** [Agents actions suppl.]. **VFOAT** Agents and Actions Supplements. Vol. 1 (1977)-. Academic Scholarly Publication. English. ir. Price varies per volume. Birkhaeuser Verlag Ag, Klosterberg 23, PO Box 133, CH-4010 Basel Switzerland. **Tel** 011 41 61 2717400, FAX 011 41 0 61 2717666, telex 963475 birk ch. **(Subscription address:** Birkhaueuser Boston Inc., PO Box 19429, Newark NJ 07195.**)** **ED** K. Brune, R. Hess, A. Lewis, W. Lorenz, P. May, O. Otterness, M. Parnham and B. Vergaftig. **LC** UNC. **NLM** W1 AG33A. **CODEN** AASUDJ. **[CCC].** Documents available from CASDDS.
**Desc:** Provides for a rapid publication of the proceedings of symposia on topics of current interest in inflammation, allergy and thrombosis.
**Ind/Abst** Chem. Abstr.; Index Med.; Life Sci. Collect.

IT
**AGGIORNAMENTI SULLE TOSSICODIPENDENZE.** (19??)-. Italian. qt. Free to members; L50000 (membership). Associazione Italiana Contro la Diffusione della Droga, Via Andrea Doria 17, 20124 Milan Italy. **Tel** 011 39 2 6690741.

US/0737-402X
**ALTERNATIVE METHODS IN TOXICOLOGY.** [Altern. methods toxicol.]. **VFOAT** Alternative Methods in Toxicology Series. Vol. 1 (1983)-. Academic Scholarly Publication. English. ir. $195.95. Mary Ann Liebert Inc., 1651 Third Avenue, New York NY 10128. **Tel** (212)289-2300, (800)M-LIEBERT, FAX (212)289-4697. **ED** Alan M. Goldberg. **LC** RA1199; .A49. **DD** 363.1/964. **NLM** W1; AL987F. **CODEN** AMTOEN. **Circ:** 75. Documents available from BIOSIS Document Express, CASDDS.
**Desc:** Covers in vitro toxicology, which produces a reduction in animals used in testing, while more effective methodologies evolve to evaluate safety. Seeks to develop scientific knowledge that can lead to innovative methods for evaluation.
**Ind/Abst** AGRICOLA [Full Cov.]; Biol. Abstr. (1986-); Chem. Abstr. (1983-).

FR/0242-6110
**ANNALES DES FALSIFICATIONS, DE L'EXPERTISE CHIMIQUE ET TOXICOLOGIQUE.** (ANNALES DES FALSIFICATIONS, DE L'EXPERTISE CHIMIQUE ET TOXICOLOGIQUE / PUBLIEES PAR LA SOCIETE DES EXPERTS-CHIMISTES DE FRANCE.). [Ann. falsif., expert. chim. toxicol.]. **Added/Corp** Societe des Experts-Chimistes de France. Vol. 72 No. 780 (Nov. 1979)-. Academic Scholarly Publication. French. Eleven times a year (July/Aug. issues combined). 606.00F France; 727.00F other. Societe des Experts Chimistes de France, 39 Bis rue de Dantzig, 75015 Paris France. **Tel** 011 33 1 45311480. **LC** TX501; .A6. **NLM** W1 AN397AB. **CODEN** AFETDF. Documents available from CASDDS. ***Continues*** *Annales des Falsifications et de l'Expertise Chimique, 0003-4274.*
**Ind/Abst** Chem. Abstr.; Food Sci. Technol. Abstr.

US
**ANNUAL PLAN FOR FISCAL YEAR ... / NATIONAL TOXICOLOGY PROGRAM.** **Main/Corp** National Toxicology Program (U.S.). **VFOAT** Annual Plan; National Toxicology Program Annual Plan. 1980-. English. an. Public Information Office / North Carolina, National Toxicology Program, PO Box 12233, Research Triangle Park NC 27709. **LC** RA1199; .N38A. **DD** 353.0084/1. **NLM** W2 A N42A. available on microfiche (Vols. for 1985- distributed to depository libraries). ***Continues*** *National Toxicology Program (U.S.). Annual Plan, 0270-8213.*

US/0149-4392
**ANNUAL REPORT OF THE INHALATION TOXICOLOGY RESEARCH INSTITUTE.** **Main/Corp** Inhalation Toxicology Research Institute. **Added/Corp** United States. Energy Research and Development Administration. Division of Biomedical and Environmental Research. United States. Dept. of Energy. Office of Health and Environmental Research. **VFOAT** Inhalation Toxicology Research Institute Annual Report. 1972/73-. English. an. $10.60. National Technical Information Service - NTIS, Room 2027S, 5285 Port Royal Road, Springfield VA 22161. **Tel** (703)487-4630, (703)487-4660, (703)487-4650, FAX (703)321-8547, telex 89-9405. **LC** RA1245; .I53a. **DD** 615.9/1. **NLM** W1; AN76P. ***Continues*** *Lovelace Foundation for Medical Education and Research. Fission Product Inhalation Program.* ***Continued in part by*** *Annual Rreport on Long-Term Dose-Response Studies of Inhaled or Injected Radionuclides.*

US/0362-1642
**ANNUAL REVIEW OF PHARMACOLOGY AND TOXICOLOGY.** **See** Pharmacy and Pharmacology.

UK/0959-4973
**ANTI-CANCER DRUGS.** [Anti-cancer drugs]. **VFOAT** Anticancer Drugs. Vol. 1, No. 1 (Oct. 1990)-. Periodical. English. bm. $499.00 US; £295.00 other. Rapid Communications of Oxford Ltd, The Old Malthouse, Paradise Street, Oxford OX1 1LD England. **Tel** 011 44 0865 790447, FAX 011 44 0865 244012, telex 9403712. **ED** M Sluyser. **NLM** W1; AN859L. **CODEN** ANTDEV. **[CCC].** Index available. cum. index. **Bk Rev. Ad Acc. Pr Rev. Acid Free.** Documents available from The Genuine Article, BIOSIS Document Express, CASDDS.
**Desc:** Focuses on clinical and experimental effects of toxic and non-toxic cancer agents, particularly breakthroughs in cancer treatment.
**Ind/Abst** Biol. Abstr.; Chem. Abstr.; Curr. Aware. Biol. Sci., CABS; Curr. Contents Life Sci.; Res. Alert [Full Cov.]; Sci. Cit. Index; SCISEARCH.

US
**API TOXICOLOGICAL REVIEWS.** **Added/Corp** American Petroleum Institute. (19??)-. English. ir. American Petroleum Institute, 275 Seventh Avenue, New York NY 10001. **Tel** (212)366-4040, FAX (212)366-4298. **(Subscription address:** 1970 Chain Bridge Road, McLean, VA 22109-6000**)**

NE/0166-445X
**AQUATIC TOXICOLOGY (AMSTERDAM, NETHERLANDS).** (AQUATIC TOXICOLOGY.). [Aquat. toxicol.]. Vol. 1, No. 1 (April 1981)-. Academic Scholarly Publication. English. mo (3 vols.). Fl1419.00. Elsevier Science Publishers BV, PO Box 211, 1000 AE Amsterdam Netherlands. **Tel** 011 31 20 5803642, FAX 011 31 20 5862696, telex 15682. **ED** D C Malins and A Jensen. **LC** QH545.W3; A66. **DD** 574.5/263. **NLM** W1; AQ926. **CODEN** AQTODG. **[CCC]. Pr Rev.** available on microfilm and microfiche from University Microfilms International (UMI). Documents available from Article Express International, The Genuine Article, BIOSIS Document Express, CASDDS, Documents on Demand.
**Desc:** Provides a forum for the publication of original scientific papers dealing with: environmental toxicologists, marine biologists, ecotoxicologists, biochemical toxicologists, environmental monitoring and conservationists.
**Ind/Abst** AQUAREF; Aquat. Sci. Fish. Abstr. (Computer File); Bioeng. Abstr.; Biol. Abstr.; Chem. Abstr.; Chem. Titles; CSA Neuro. Abstr. (?-?); Curr. Aware. Biol. Sci., CABS; Curr. Contents, Agric. Biol. Environ. Sci.; Curr. Ref. Fish Res.; Ecol. Abstr.; Ecology Abstr.; Ei Page One; EMBASE; Energy Inf. Abstr.; Eng. Index Annu.; Environ. Abstr. (Nov. 29, 1990-); Fish Rev.; Food Sci. Technol. Abstr.; Helminthol. Abstr. (1991-); Index Vet.; Mar. Sci. Contents Tables; Microbiol. Abstr. Sect. C; Nutr. Abstr. Rev., Ser. B, Live Feeds and Feed.; Ocean. Abstr.; Life Sci. Collect.; PESTDOC; Pollut. Abstr. Indexes; Res. Alert [Full Cov.]; Rev. Med. Vet. Entomol.; Risk Abstr. (19??-19??); Sci. Cit. Index; SCISEARCH; Toxicol. Abstr.; Weed Abstr.; Wildl. Rev.

US/0734-1687
**AQUATIC TOXICOLOGY SERIES.** **See** Environmental Issues-Ecology.

US/0090-4341
**ARCHIVES OF ENVIRONMENTAL CONTAMINATION AND TOXICOLOGY.** **See** Environmental Issues.

GW/0340-5761
**ARCHIVES OF TOXICOLOGY.** [Arch. toxicol.]. **Added/Corp** Deutsche Pharmakologische Gesellschaft. Deutsche Gesellschaft fuer Rechtsmedizin. European Society of Toxicology. **VFOAT** Archiv fur Toxicologie. Vol. 32, No. 1 (1974)-. Academic Scholarly Publication. English (German; summaries and/or abstracts in German). Ten times a year. DM1650.00. Springer-Verlag GmbH & Company KG, Heidelberger Platz 3, D 14197 Berlin Germany. **Tel** 011 49 30 8207223, FAX 011 49 30 8214091, telex 183 319 SPBLN D. **(Subscription address:** Springer Verlag New York Inc. / for North America, 44 Hartz Way, Secaucus NJ 07096.**) ED** H M Bolt. **NLM** W1 AR49G. **CODEN** ARTODN. **[CCC]. Bk Rev.** available on microfilm and microfiche from University Microfilms International (UMI). Documents available from The Genuine Article, BIOSIS Document Express, CASDDS, Documents on Demand, ADONIS. ***Continues*** *Archiv fur Toxikologie, 0003-9446.*
**Desc:** Publishes review articles, original investigations, short communications and letters to the editors; acceptable papers should provide some advance in the science of toxicology by studies from any relevant discipline.
**Ind/Abst** ADONIS; AgBiotech News Inf.; AGRICOLA [Select. Cov.]; Biol. Abstr.; Chem. Abstr.; Chem. Hazards Ind.; Chem. Titles; CSA Neuro. Abstr. (?-?); Curr. Aware. Biol. Sci., CABS; Curr. Contents Life Sci.; Curr. Ref. Fish Res.; Dairy Sci. Abstr.; EMBASE; Energy Inf. Abstr.; Energy Res. Abstr. (Oct. 1979-); Environ. Abstr.; Fish Rev.; Health Period. Database; Index Med.; Index Vet.; Lab. Hazards Bull.; Microbiol. Abstr. Sect. C; NAPRALERT; Nutr. Abstr. Rev., Ser. B, Live Feeds and Feed.; Nutr. Abstr. Rev., Ser. A, Hum. Exp.; Nutr. Res. Newsl.; Life Sci. Collect.; PESTDOC; Pig News Inf.; Pollut. Abstr. Indexes; Poult. Abstr.; Protozoolog. Abstr.; Ref. Upd. Deluxe Ed.; Res. Alert [Full Cov.]; Rev. Agric. Entomol.; Rev. Med. Vet. Entomol.; Rev. Med. Vet. Mycology; Risk Abstr.; Saf. Health Work; Sci. Cit. Index; SCISEARCH; Vet. Bull.; Toxicol. Abstr.; Weed Abstr.

GW/0171-9750
**ARCHIVES OF TOXICOLOGY. SUPPLEMENT.** [Arch. toxicol., Suppl.]. **VFOAT** Archiv fur Toxikologie. Supplement. (1978)-. Academic Scholarly Publication. English. ir. Price varies per volume. Springer-Verlag GmbH & Company KG, Heidelberger Platz 3, D 14197 Berlin Germany. **Tel** 011 49 30 8207223, FAX 011 49 30 8214091, telex 183 319 SPBLN D. **(Subscription address:** Springer Verlag New York Inc. / for North America, 44 Hartz Way, Secaucus NJ 07096.**) LC** RA1190; .E8 Suppl. **DD** 615.9. **NLM** W1 AR49GA. **CODEN** ATSUDG. **[CCC].** Documents available from CASDDS, ADONIS.
**Ind/Abst** ADONIS; Chem. Abstr.; Index Med.; NAPRALERT; Nutr. Abstr. Rev., Ser. B, Live Feeds and Feed.; Nutr. Abstr. Rev., Ser. A, Hum. Exp.

SP/0304-8616
**ARCHIVOS DE FARMACOLOGIA Y TOXICOLOGIA.** ***Ceased.*** **See** Pharmacy and Pharmacology.

UK/0261-1929
**ATLA : ALTERNATIVES TO LABORATORY ANIMALS.** [ATLA, Altern. lab. anim.]. **Added/Corp** Fund for the Replacement of Animals in Medical Experiments. **VFOAT** Alternatives to Laboratory Animals. Vol. 11 No. 1 (Sept. 1983)-. Academic Scholarly Publication. English. bm. £65.00. FRAME, Eastgate House, 34 Stoney Street, Nottingham NG1 1NB England. **Tel** 011 44 602 584740, FAX (0602)503570. **ED** Gilly Griffin. **[CCC].** Index available. **Bk Rev**, (Qty: 20). **Ad Acc. Pr Rev. Circ:** 850. Documents available from BLDSC, The Genuine Article. ***Continues*** *Alternatives to Laboratory Animals : ATLA.*
**Desc:** All aspects of the development, validation, introduction and use of alternatives to laboratory animals in biomedical research and toxicity testing.
**Ind/Abst** Curr. Aware. Biol. Sci., CABS; Index Vet.; Life Sci. Collect. (1985-); Res. Alert [Full Cov.]; Soc. Sci. Cit. Index [Select. Cov.].

US/0740-5197
**BASH MAGAZINE, THE.** ***Ceased.*** **Added/Corp** BASH (Group). **VFOAT** Bash Magazine. Vol. 7, No. 6 (June 1988)-Vol. 11, No.7 (July 1992). Periodical. English. mo. BASH Inc, 522 North Ballas Road/Suite 206, St Louis MO 63141. **NLM** W1; BA807. ***Continues*** *B.A.S.H., Inc.*

US/0739-4012
**BENCHMARK PAPERS IN TOXICOLOGY.** Vol. 1 (1983)-. Monographic series. English. ir. Price varies per volume. Princeton Scientific Publishing Company Inc., PO Box 2155, Princeton NJ 08543. **Tel** (609)683-4750, FAX (609)683-0838. **ED** M. Mehlman. **NLM** W1; BE517T. **Circ:** 1,000.
**Desc:** Gives in-depth treatments of controversial areas of toxicology (use of alternate species). Focuses on new methodologies such as computer modeling.

UK/0268-2222
**BIBRA BULLETIN.** [BIBRA bull.]. Bulletin. English. mo. **NLM** W1; BI520.
**Ind/Abst** Index Vet.; Vet. Bull.

US/0149-0923
**BIORESEARCH TODAY. INDUSTRIAL HEALTH & TOXICOLOGY.** ***Ceased.*** **See** Industrial Health and Safety.

US/0894-4024
**BOSTON BULLETIN ON CHEMICALS AND DISEASE.** **See** Pharmacy and Pharmacology.

PL/0365-9445
**BROMATOLOGIA I CHEMIA TOKSYKOLOGICZNA.** [Bromatol. chem. toksykol.]. **Added/Corp** Polskie Towarzystwo Farmaceutyczne. (1971)-. Periodical. Polish (summaries and/or abstracts in English and Russian; table of contents in English and Russian). qt. Price on Request. **(Subscription address:** ARS Polona, PO Box 1001, 00068 Warsaw Poland.**) LC** RA1258; .B76. **NLM** W1 BR784. **CODEN** BCTKAG. Documents available from CASDDS. ***Continues*** *Zeszyty Naukowe Bromatologii i Chemii Toksykologicznej.*
**Ind/Abst** Chem. Abstr.; Dairy Sci. Abstr.; EMBASE; Field Crop Abstr.; Food Sci. Technol. Abstr.; Hortic. Abstr.; Index Vet.; Maize Abstr.; Nutr. Abstr. Rev., Ser. B, Live Feeds and Feed.; Nutr. Abstr. Rev., Ser. A, Hum. Exp.; Life Sci. Collect.; Postharvest News Inf.; Potato Abstr.; Soils Fert.; Sug. Indus. Abstr.; Vet. Bull.; Toxicol. Abstr. (19??-); Wheat Barley Trit. Abstr.

CN/0829-5557
**BULLETIN D'INFORMATION TOXICOLOGIQUE.** [Bull. inf. toxicol.]. **Added/Corp** Centre de Toxicologie du Quebec. Vol. 2, No. 1 (Jan. 1986)-. Periodical. French. Four times a year. 15.00Can$. Centre Toxicologie Quebec, Chul 2705 Boul Laurier, Ste-Foy Quebec G1V 4G2 Canada. **Tel** (418)654-2254. **DD** 615.9/005.
**Desc:** Information on clinical, industrial and environmental toxicology. Contents case reports, literature and book reviews. Articles are on different aspects of toxicology and human poisoning.

US/0007-4861
**BULLETIN OF ENVIRONMENTAL CONTAMINATION AND TOXICOLOGY.** [Bull. environ. contam. toxicol.]. Vol. 1 (Jan./Feb. 1966)-. Academic Scholarly Publication. English. Twelve times a year. $371.00. Springer-Verlag New York Inc., 175 5th Avenue, New York NY 10010. **Tel** (212)460-1500, telex 232 235 SPB UR. **(Subscription address:** Springer Verlag New York Inc. / for North America, 44 Hartz Way, Secaucus NJ 07096.**) ED** H Nigg. **LC** RA565.A1; B8. **DD** 613.1. **NLM** W1 BU761C. **CODEN** BECTA6. **[CCC]. Pr Rev.** available on microfilm and microfiche from University Microfilms International (UMI). Documents available from Article Express International, The Genuine Article, BIOSIS Document Express, Petroleum Abstracts Document Delivery Service, CASDDS, Documents on Demand.
**Desc:** Disseminates advances and discoveries in the areas of air, soil, water and food contamination and pollution. Provides a meeting ground for researchers to share in new discoveries as soon as they are made.
**Ind/Abst** Abstr. Bull. Inst. Pap. Sci. Tech.; AgBiotech News Inf.; AGRICOLA [Select. Cov.]; Anal. Abstr.; AQUAREF; Aquat. Sci. Fish. Abstr. (Computer File); BioBusiness; Biocont. News Inf. (1991-); Biodeter. Abstr. (19??-19??); Bioeng. Abstr.; Biol. Agric. Index; Biol. Abstr.; Chem. Abstr.; Chem. Hazards Ind.; Chem. Titles; Coal Abstr.; Crop Physiol. Abstr.; Curr. Aware. Biol. Sci., CABS; Curr. Contents, Agric. Biol. Environ. Sci.; Curr. Contents Life Sci.; Curr. Ref. Fish Res.; Dairy Sci. Abstr.; Ecol. Abstr.; Ecology Abstr.; Ei Page One; EMBASE; Energy Inf. Abstr.; Energy Res. Abstr.; Eng. Index Annu.; Entomol. Abstr.; Environ. Abstr.; Environ. Period. Bibliogr. (?-?); Field Crop Abstr.; Fish Rev.; Food Sci. Technol. Abstr.; For. Prod. Abstr. (1991-); For. Abstr.; Geogr. Abstr. Phys. Geogr.; Geogr. Abstr. Human Geogr.; Geol. Abstr.; Grasslands For. Abstr.; Health Saf. Sci. Abstr.; Health Plan. Adminis.; Helminthol. Abstr. (1991-); Hortic. Abstr.; Index Med.; Index Vet.; INIS Atomindex [Micro.]; Int. Aerosp. Abstr.; Irr. Drain. Abstr.; Lab. Hazards Bull.; Leadscan; Maize Abstr.; Mass Spect. Bull.; Microbiol. Abstr. Sect. B; Microbiol. Abstr. Sect. A; Microbiol. Abstr. Sect. C; Nematol. Abstr.; Nutr. Abstr. Rev., Ser. B, Live Feeds and Feed.; Nutr. Abstr. Rev., Ser. A, Hum. Exp.; Nutr. Res. Newsl.; Ornamental Hort.; Life Sci. Collect.; PESTDOC; Pet. Abstr.; Plant Breed. Abstr.; Pollut. Abstr. Indexes; Potato Abstr.; Poult. Abstr.; Res. Alert [Full Cov.]; Rev. Agric. Entomol.; Rev. Med. Vet. Entomol.; Rev. Med. Vet. Mycology; Rev. Plant Pathol.; Rice Abstr.; Risk Abstr.; Sci. Cit. Index; SCISEARCH; Soc. Sci. Cit. Index [Select. Cov.]; Soils Fert.; Vet. Bull.; Toxicol. Abstr.; Vitis Vitic. Enol. Abstr.; Weed Abstr.; Wheat Barley Trit. Abstr.; Wildl. Rev.

NE/0742-2091
**CELL BIOLOGY AND TOXICOLOGY (PRINCETON SCIENTIFIC PUBLISHERS).** **See** Biology-Cytology and Histology.

US/0893-228X
**CHEMICAL RESEARCH IN TOXICOLOGY.** [Chem. res. toxicol.]. **Added/Corp** American Chemical Society. Vol. 1, No. 1 (Jan./Feb. 1988)-. Academic Scholarly Publication. English. Eight

times a year. $375.00 (institution) US. American Chemical Society, 1155 Sixteenth Street Northwest, Washington DC 20036. **Tel** (800)333-9511, (800)227-5558, (614)447-3776, FAX (202)833-7736. **(Subscription address:** American Chemical Society / Ohio, Department L 0011, Columbus OH 43268-0011.**)** **ED** Lawrence J. Marnett. **LC** RA1190; .C475. **DD** 615.9/005. **NLM** W1; CH262. **CODEN** CRTOEC. **[CCC].** **Ad Acc, Adv Mgr:** Centcom, **Tel** (203)256-8211. **Pr Rev. Acid Free.** available on microfilm and microfiche from University Microfilms International (UMI). Documents available from The Genuine Article, BIOSIS Document Express, CASDDS, Documents on Demand.
**Desc:** A comprehensive journal on all aspects of toxicology. Includes structural elucidation of novel toxic agents, chemical and physical studies, experimental and theoretical investigations and much more.
**Ind/Abst** Biol. Abstr. (1988-); Chem. Abstr. (1988-); Chem. Ind. Notes (Jan.-Feb. 1988-); Chem. Titles (1988-); Curr. Aware. Biol. Sci., CABS; Curr. Contents Life Sci.; EMBASE; Environ. Abstr.; Index Med. (Jan.-Feb. 1988-); Nutr. Abstr. Rev., Ser. A, Hum. Exp.; Ref. Upd. Deluxe Ed.; Res. Alert [Full Cov.]; Rev. Agric. Entomol.; Rev. Med. Vet. Entomol.; Rev. Med. Vet. Mycology; Sci. Cit. Index; SCISEARCH; Toxicol. Abstr. (19??-).

UK/0886-5140
**COMMENTS ON TOXICOLOGY.**
(COMMENTS ON MODERN BIOLOGY. PART B, COMMENTS ON TOXICOLOGY.). [Comments toxicol.]. **VFOAT** Comments on Toxicology; Comments Toxicology. Vol. 1, No. 1 (July 1986)-. Academic Scholarly Publication. English. bm (1 volume). $407.00 (academic institutions), $635.00 (corporate institutions). Gordon & Breach Science Publishers, PO Box 90, Reading RG1 8JL England. **Tel** 011 44 734 560080, FAX 011 44 734 568211. **DD** 615. **NLM** W1; CO375N. **CODEN** COTXEI. **[CCC].** available in microform. Documents available from CASDDS.
**Ind/Abst** Chem. Abstr. (1988-); Toxicol. Abstr. (19??-19??).

UK/0742-8413
**COMPARATIVE BIOCHEMISTRY AND PHYSIOLOGY. C, COMPARATIVE PHARMACOLOGY AND TOXICOLOGY.**
***Title Change.*** **See** Pharmacy and Pharmacology.

US/1040-8444
**CRITICAL REVIEWS IN TOXICOLOGY.**
[Crit. rev. toxicol.]. **VFOAT** CRC Critical Reviews in Toxicology. **VAT** Chemical Rubber Company Critical Reviews in Toxicology. Vol. 7, Issue 1 (1980)-. Academic Scholarly Publication. English. Six times a year. $420.00 institution. CRC Press Inc., 2000 Corporate Boulevard Northwest, Boca Raton FL 33431. **Tel** (407)994-0555, (800)272-7737, FAX (407)998-9784, telex 568689. **ED** Roger O. McClellan. **LC** RA1190; .C48. **DD** 615.9/005. **NLM** W1; C555N. **CODEN** CRTXB2CRTYB. **[CCC].** Documents available from The Genuine Article, BIOSIS Document Express, CASDDS, Documents on Demand, ADONIS. ***Continues** CRC Critical Reviews in Toxicology, 0045-6446.*
**Desc:** Provides up-to-date, objective analyses of important topics in toxicology.
**Ind/Abst** ADONIS; AGRICOLA [Select. Cov.]; Biol. Abstr.; Chem. Abstr.; Curr. Aware. Biol. Sci., CABS; Curr. Contents Life Sci.; EMBASE; Energy Res. Abstr. (Feb. 1974-); Environ. Abstr.; Environ. Period. Bibliogr.; Fish Rev.; Food Sci. Technol. Abstr.; Index Med.; Index Sci. Rev. [Full Cov.]; Index Vet.; INIS Atomindex [Micro.]; NAPRALERT; Life Sci. Collect.; Ref. Upd. Basic Ed.; Ref. Upd. Deluxe Ed.; Res. Alert [Full Cov.]; Saf. Health Work; Sci. Cit. Index; SCISEARCH; Vet. Bull.; Toxicol. Abstr.; Wildl. Rev.

●UK/0965-0512
**CURRENT ADVANCES IN TOXICOLOGY.** **See** Medical Science and Technology-Abstracting, Bibliographies and Statistics.

UK/0951-9602
**CURRENT MEDICAL LITERATURE-INFECTIOUS DISEASES.**
English. qt. £20.00 UK; $40.00 US; £20.00 other. Current Medical Literature Ltd., 40-42 Osnaburgh Street, London NW1 3ND England. **Tel** 011 44 71 4658377, FAX 011 44 71 4658380. **(Subscription address:** Royal Society Medicine Services, 1 Wimpole Street, London W1M 8AE England.**)** **Pr Rev.** ctrl circ.
**Desc:** Reviews of current articles published in the field of infectious diseases.

US/0890-1449
**CURRENT TOPICS IN PULMONARY PHARMACOLOGY AND TOXICOLOGY.**
[Curr. top. pulm. pharmacol. toxicol.]. **VFOAT** Pulmonary Pharmacology and Toxicology. Vol. 1, (1986)-. Academic Scholarly Publication. English. ir. Price varies per volume. Elsevier Science Publishing Company Inc, Madison Square Station, PO Box 882, New York NY 10159-0882. **Tel** (212)633-3950, FAX (212)633-3990. **LC** RM388; .C87. **DD** 616.2/4061/05. **NLM** W1; CU821HH. **CODEN** CTPTEL. Documents available from CASDDS.
**Ind/Abst** Chem. Abstr. (1986-).

US/1069-4587
**CURRENT TOXICOLOGY.** [Curr. toxicol.]. (1993)-. Periodical. English. Four times a year. $295.00. Nova Science Publishers Inc., 6080 Jericho Turnpike, Suite 207, Commack NY 11725-2808. **Tel** (516)499-3103, (516)499-3106, FAX (516)499-3146. **NLM** W1; CU822F.

IT
**CURRENTS IN TOXICOLOGY AND THERAPY.** L50000.00 Italy; L100000.00 other. Casa Editrice Maccari, Via Trento 53, 43100 Parma Italy. **Tel** 011 39 521 771268, FAX 011 39 521 771268.

NE/0165-2214
**DEVELOPMENTS IN TOXICOLOGY AND ENVIRONMENTAL SCIENCE.** [Dev. toxicol. environ. sci.]. Academic Scholarly Publication. English. ir. Price varies per volume. Elsevier Science Publishers BV, PO Box 211, 1000 AE Amsterdam Netherlands. **Tel** 011 31 20 5803642, FAX 011 31 20 5862696, telex 15682. **NLM** W1 DE998T. **CODEN** DTESD7. Documents available from CASDDS.
**Ind/Abst** Chem. Abstr.; Health Plan. Adminis.; Index Med. (1981-).

US/0892-1881
**DIRECTORY OF TOXICOLOGY TESTING INSTITUTIONS IN THE UNITED STATES.**
***Ceased.*** [Dir. toxicol. test. inst. U. S.]. 1st Ed. (1983)-Ceased. Directory. English. an. Texas Research Institute, PO Box 20165, Houston TX 77225. **Tel** (713)790-9835. **DD** 615. **NLM** QV 605; AA1 D49.

US/0148-0545
**DRUG AND CHEMICAL TOXICOLOGY (NEW YORK, N.Y. 1978).** (DRUG AND CHEMICAL TOXICOLOGY.). [Drug chem. toxicol.]. Vol. 1 (1977/78)-. Academic Scholarly Publication. English. qt. $450.00 US; $464.00 other. Marcel Dekker Inc., 270 Madison Avenue, New York NY 10016. **Tel** (212)696-9000, (800)228-1160, FAX (212)685-4540, telex 421419. **(Subscription address:** Marcel Dekker Inc, PO Box 5017, Monticello NY 12701.**)** **ED** Gerald L. Fisher, Michael A. Gallo and William M. Kluwe. **LC** RA1190; .D78. **DD** 615.9/005. **NLM** W1 DR513G. **CODEN** DCTODJ. **[CCC].** **Bk Rev. Ad Acc. Pr Rev.** ctrl circ. available on microfiche. Documents available from The Genuine Article, BIOSIS Document Express, CASDDS, Documents on Demand, ADONIS.
**Desc:** Featuring full-length research papers, review articles, and short notes, this outstanding journal presents the most up-to-date findings on a broad range of topics related to the safety evaluation of drugs, chemicals, and medical products. 'Drug and Chemical Toxicology' is essential reading for all those concerned with the safety evaluation of drugs and chemicals. Designed especially to provide rapid communication, the vital contributions to this important journal encompass animal toxicology, teratology, mutagenesis, and carcinogenesis.
**Ind/Abst** ADONIS; Art Archaeol. Tech. Abstr.; BioBusiness; Biol. Abstr.; Chem. Abstr.; Curr. Aware. Biol. Sci., CABS; Curr. Contents Life Sci.; EMBASE; Environ. Abstr.; Environ. Period. Bibliogr.; Health Plan. Adminis.; Index Med. (1977/78-); Index Vet.; Int. Pharm. Abstr.; NAPRALERT; Nutr. Abstr. Rev., Ser. B, Live Feeds and Feed.; PESTDOC; Pollut. Abstr. Indexes; Ref. Upd. Deluxe Ed.; Res. Alert [Full Cov.]; Rev. Agric. Entomol.; Rev. Med. Vet. Mycology; Sci. Cit. Index; SCISEARCH; Vet. Bull.; Toxicol. Abstr.

US/0888-8337
**DRUG AND CHEMICAL TOXICOLOGY (NEW YORK, N.Y. 1984).** (DRUG AND CHEMICAL TOXICOLOGY.). [Drug chem. toxicol.]. Vol. 1 (1984)-. Monographic series. English. ir. Price varies per volume. Marcel Dekker Inc., 270 Madison Avenue, New York NY 10016. **Tel** (212)696-9000, (800)228-1160, FAX (212)685-4540, telex 421419. **(Subscription address:** Marcel Dekker Inc, PO Box 5017, Monticello NY 12701.**)** **DD** 615. **NLM** W1; DR513F. **CODEN** DCTOEK.
**Desc:** Series covering such topics as neurotoxicology, and chemically induced birth defects.

NZ/0114-5916
**DRUG SAFETY.** **See** Pharmacy and Pharmacology.

JA
**EISHI JOHO.** **VFOAT** NIHS Information. No. 1 (1981)-. Periodical. Japanese (Japanese). Kokuritsu Eisei Shikenjo, 18-1 Kami Yoga 1-chome, Setagaya-ku 158, Tokyo Japan. **Tel** 03 3700 1141 454, FAX 03 3700 7592. **LC** RA1190; .E38.

US/1053-4725
**ENVIRONMENTAL TOXICOLOGY AND WATER QUALITY.** [Environ. toxicol. water qual.]. Vol. 6, No. 1 (Feb. 1991)-. Academic Scholarly Publication. English. qt. $224.00 US; $264.00 Canada and Mexico; $279.00 other. John Wiley & Sons, Inc., 605 Third Avenue, New York NY 10158-0012. **Tel** (212)850-6000, (212)850-6645, FAX (212)850-6088, telex 12-7063. **(Subscription address:** John Wiley & Sons / England, Baffins Lane, Chichester, West Sussex PO19 1UD England.**)** **ED** Dickson Liu and Bernard Dutka. **LC** QH90.57.B5; T69. **DD** 628.1/61. **CODEN** ETWQEZ. available on microfilm and microfiche from University Microfilms International (UMI). Documents available from The Genuine Article, BIOSIS Document Express, CASDDS. ***Continues** Toxicity Assessment, 0884-8181.*
**Desc:** Journal includes original research papers on all aspects of environmental toxicology and water quality research, monitoring, criteria/standards and policies.
**Ind/Abst** AGRICOLA [Select. Cov.]; Biol. Abstr.; Chem. Abstr. (1991-); Curr. Aware. Biol. Sci., CABS; Curr. Contents, Agric. Biol. Environ. Sci.; EMBASE; Environ. Period. Bibliogr.; Res. Alert (1991-) [Select. Cov.]; SCISEARCH (1991-); Weed Abstr.

NE/0167-8353
**EXCERPTA MEDICA. SECTION 52. TOXICOLOGY.** **See** Medical Science and Technology-Abstracting, Bibliographies and Statistics.

●GW/0940-2993
**EXPERIMENTAL AND TOXICOLOGIC PATHOLOGY : OFFICIAL JOURNAL OF THE GESELLSCHAFT FUR TOXIKOLOGISCHE PATHOLOGIE.**
**Added/Corp** Gesellschaft Fur Toxikologische Pathologie. Vol. 44, No. 1 (Mar. 1992)-. Academic Scholarly Publication. English. Six times a year. DM660.00 Germany; DM672.00 other. Gustav Fischer Verlag Jena, Postfach 100537, D 07705 Jena Germany. **Tel** 011 49 3641 27332, FAX 011 49 3641 626500. **(Subscription address:** VCH Publishers Inc., 303 Northwest 12th Avenue, Journals Department, Deerfield FL 33442.**)** **NLM** W1; EX47H. **CODEN** ETPAEK. **[CCC].** Documents available from The Genuine Article, CASDDS. ***Continues** Experimental Pathology, 0232-1513.*
**Ind/Abst** Chem. Abstr.; Curr. Aware. Biol. Sci., CABS; Curr. Contents Life Sci.; EMBASE; Index Med. (1992-); Res. Alert [Full Cov.]; Sci. Cit. Index.

UK/0278-6915
**FOOD AND CHEMICAL TOXICOLOGY.**
(FOOD AND CHEMICAL TOXICOLOGY : AN INTERNATIONAL JOURNAL PUBLISHED FOR THE BRITISH INDUSTRIAL BIOLOGICAL RESEARCH ASSOCIATION.). [Food chem. toxicol.]. **Added/Corp** British Industrial Biological Research Association. Vol. 20, No. 1 (Feb. 1982)-. Academic Scholarly Publication. English. mo. $924.00 The Americas; £620.00 other. Pergamon Press, An Imprint of Elsevier Science Ltd., The Boulevard, Langford Lane, Kidlington, Oxford OX5 1GB United Kingdom. **Tel** 011 44 865 843000, 011 44 865 843699, FAX 011 44 865 843010. **(Subscription address:** Elsevier Science Ltd. Oxford Fulfillment Centre, PO Box 800, Kidlington, Oxford OX5 1DX United Kingdom.**)** **ED** Robert A. Neal and Gordon C. Hard. **LC** RA1190; .B715. **DD** 615.9/005. **NLM** W1 FO403. **CODEN** FCTOD7. **[CCC].** **Bk Rev. Ad Acc.** available on microfilm and microfiche from University Microfilms International (UMI). Documents available from The Genuine Article, BIOSIS Document Express, CASDDS, ADONIS. ***Continues** Food and Cosmetics Toxicology, 0015-6264.*
**Desc:** Publishes original research reports and occasional interpretative reviews on the toxic effects, in animals or humans, of natural or synthetic chemicals occurring in the human environment.
**Ind/Abst** ADONIS; AgBiotech News Inf.; AGRICOLA [Select. Cov.]; Anal. Abstr.; Aqualine Abstr.; BioBusiness; Biodeter. Abstr. (1991-); Biol. Abstr.; Chem. Abstr.; Chem. Hazards Ind.; Chem. Titles; CSA Neuro. Abstr. (?-?); Curr. Aware. Biol. Sci., CABS; Curr. Contents Life Sci.; Dairy Sci. Abstr.; EMBASE; Food Sci. Technol. Abstr.; Foods Adlibra; Health Saf. Sci. Abstr.; Health Plan. Adminis.; Helminthol. Abstr. (19??-19??); Index Med.; Index Vet.; Lab. Hazards Bull.; Maize Abstr.; Mass Spect. Bull.; Microbiol. Abstr. Sect. A; Microbiol. Abstr. Sect. C; NAPRALERT; Nutr. Abstr. Rev., Ser. B, Live Feeds and Feed.; Nutr. Abstr. Rev., Ser. A, Hum. Exp.; Nutr. Res. Newsl.; Life Sci. Collect.; PESTDOC; Pig News Inf.; Pollut. Abstr. Indexes; Postharvest News Inf.; Potato Abstr.; Protozoolog. Abstr.; Ref. Upd. Deluxe Ed.; Res. Alert [Full Cov.]; Rev. Med. Vet. Mycology; Risk Abstr.; Sci. Cit. Index; SCISEARCH; Soc. Sci. Cit. Index [Select. Cov.]; Sug. Indus. Abstr.; Vet. Bull.; Toxicol. Abstr.; Weed Abstr.; World Surf. Coat. Abstr.

US/1048-8731
**FORENSIC DRUG ABUSE ADVISOR, THE.** **See** Drug Abuse and Alcoholism.

US/0272-0590
**FUNDAMENTAL AND APPLIED TOXICOLOGY.** (FUNDAMENTAL AND APPLIED TOXICOLOGY : OFFICIAL JOURNAL OF THE SOCIETY OF TOXICOLOGY.). [Fundam. appl. toxicol.]. **Added/Corp** Society of Toxicology. Vol. 1, No. 1 (Jan./Feb. 1981)-. Academic Scholarly Publication. English. Ten times a year. $440.00 US and Canada. Academic Press, Inc., 6277 Sea Harbor Drive, Orlando FL 32887. **Tel** (800)543-9534, (407)345-4100, FAX (407)363-9661. **ED** Henry D. Heck. **LC** RA1190; .F86. **DD** 615.9/005. **NLM** W1 FU538M. **CODEN** FAATDF. **[CCC].** **Bk Rev. Pr Rev.** Documents available from The Genuine Article, CASDDS.
**Desc:** Presents current articles and reports relating to broad aspects of toxicology relevant to assessing the risk of exposure of toxic agents (chemicals, including drugs and natural products or forms of energy) to human and

other animal health.
**Ind/Abst** AGRICOLA [Select. Cov.]; Anal. Abstr.; Chem. Abstr.; Chem. Hazards Ind.; Chem. Titles; Coal Abstr.; CSA Neuro. Abstr. (?-?); Curr. Aware. Biol. Sci., CABS; Curr. Contents Life Sci.; EMBASE; Fish Rev.; Foods Adlibra; Health Saf. Sci. Abstr.; Health Plan. Adminis.; Immunol. Abstr.; Index Med.; Index Period. Artic. Relat. Law (19??-19??); Index Vet.; Ind. Hyg. Dig.; INIS Atomindex [Micro.]; Lab. Hazards Bull.; Nematol. Abstr.; Nutr. Abstr. Rev., Ser. B, Live Feeds and Feed.; Nutr. Res. Newsl.; Life Sci. Collect.; PESTDOC; Pig News Inf.; Pollut. Abstr. Indexes; Protozoolog. Abstr.; Ref. Upd. Deluxe Ed.; Res. Alert [Full Cov.]; Rev. Agric. Entomol.; Rev. Med. Vet. Entomol.; Rev. Med. Vet. Mycology; Risk Abstr.; Sci. Cit. Index; SCISEARCH; Small Anim. Abstr. Bibliogr.; Vet. Bull.; Toxicol. Abstr.; Weed Abstr.; Wildl. Rev.

US/0163-9099
**HAZARDOUS AND TOXIC SUBSTANCES.** **See** Environmental Issues-Pollution and Waste Management.

UK/0960-3271
**HUMAN & EXPERIMENTAL TOXICOLOGY.** [Hum. exp. toxicol.]. **Added/Corp** British Toxicology Society. **VFOAT** Human and Experimental Toxicology. Vol. 9, No. 1 (Jan. 1990)-. Periodical. English. bm. £280.00 UK and EEC; £290.00 (surface mail), £348.00 (airmail) other. Macmillan Magazines Ltd., Houndmills, Basingstoke, Hampshire RG21 2XS England. **Tel** 011 44 256 29242, FAX 011 44 256 812358, telex 858493. **ED** Paul Turner. **LC** RA1190; .H83. **NLM** W1; HU44N. **CODEN** HETOEA. available on microfilm and microfiche from University Microfilms International (UMI). Documents available from The Genuine Article, BIOSIS Document Express, CASDDS. ***Continues** Human Toxicology, 0144-5952.*
**Desc:** An international journal in an area of increasing scientific importance. Each issue features: original research papers in both experimental and human toxicology, expert editorial comment on matters of current concern and interest, correspondence from readers and a calendar of forthcoming meetings.
**Ind/Abst** Biol. Abstr.; Chem. Abstr.; Curr. Aware. Biol. Sci., CABS; Curr. Contents Life Sci.; EMBASE; Health Saf. Sci. Abstr.; Index Med. (1990-); Index Vet.; Nutr. Abstr. Rev., Ser. A, Hum. Exp.; Pollut. Abstr. Indexes; Res. Alert [Full Cov.]; Rev. Med. Vet. Entomol.; Rev. Med. Vet. Mycology; Sci. Cit. Index; SCISEARCH; Small Anim. Abstr. Bibliogr.; Weed Abstr.

US
**IDENTIDEX. CD-ROM.** English. qt. $500.00. Micromedex Inc, 600 Grant Street, Denver CO 80203. **Tel** (303)831-1400, FAX (303)837-1717. **ED** D G Spoerke and B H Rumack. **Circ:** 2,500. available on microfiche.
**Desc:** Identification of pharmaceutical tablets and capsules by manufacturers imprint code; manufacturer logo and telephone number; index of drug-related slang terms.

US/0892-3973
**IMMUNOPHARMACOLOGY AND IMMUNOTOXICOLOGY.** **See** Medical Science and Technology-Allergy and Immunology.

US/0888-319X
**IN VITRO TOXICOLOGY.** [In vitro toxicol.]. Vol. 1, No. 1 (Fall 1986/1987)-. Academic Scholarly Publication. English. qt. $155.00. Mary Ann Liebert Inc., 1651 Third Avenue, New York NY 10128. **Tel** (212)289-2300, (800)M-LIEBERT, FAX (212)289-4697. **ED** David Brusick. **DD** 615. **NLM** W1; IN106DK. **CODEN** IVTOE4. Documents available from BIOSIS Document Express, CASDDS.
**Desc:** Offers a range of current investigative work about the molecular and cellular basis and expression of diverse toxic phenomena. Topics include methods, developments, and validation of in vitro toxicology tests; the impact of in vitro methodology on product safety testing; and methods for in vitro to in vivo extrapolation.
**Ind/Abst** AGRICOLA [Select. Cov.]; Biol. Abstr. (1987-); Chem. Abstr. (1986-1987); Environ. Period. Bibliogr.; Ref. Upd. Deluxe Ed.; Toxicol. Abstr. (19??-).

UK/0895-8378
**INHALATION TOXICOLOGY.** [Inhal. toxicol.]. Vol. 1, No. 1 (Winter 1989)-. Periodical. English. Nine times a year. £200.00 UK; $330.00 other. Taylor & Francis Ltd., Rankine Road, Basingstoke Hampshire, RG24 8PR United Kingdom. **Tel** 011 44 256 840366, FAX 011 44 256 479438, telex 858540. **(Subscription address:** Taylor & Francis Inc., 1900 Frost Road, Suite 101, Bristol PA 19007-1598.**)** **DD** 616. **NLM** W1; IN4495F. **CODEN** INHTE5. **[CCC].** available on microfilm and microfiche from University Microfilms International (UMI). Documents available from CASDDS, Documents on Demand.
**Desc:** Provides the latest advances in all aspects of inhalation toxicology, to improve the understanding of the respiratory system in disease and health - for both humans and animals. Includes in its scope state-of-the-art concepts in the pathogenesis and mechanism of lung disease, extrapolation of animal data to humans, effects of inhaled chemicals on extrapulmonary organs, etc. Moreover, epidemiological and clinical toxicology findings identify significant health effects from inhalation of environmental and occupational agents.
**Ind/Abst** Chem. Abstr.; Curr. Aware. Biol. Sci., CABS; Environ. Abstr.; Pollut. Abstr. Indexes; Sci. Cit. Index; Toxicol. Abstr.

GW/0174-4879
**INTERNATIONAL JOURNAL OF CLINICAL PHARMACOLOGY, THERAPY AND TOXICOLOGY (1980).** ***Title Change.* See** Pharmacy and Pharmacology.

US/1053-9557
**INTERNATIONAL JOURNAL OF OCCUPATIONAL HEALTH AND TOXICOLOGY.** **See** Industrial Health and Safety.

●II
**INTERNATIONAL JOURNAL OF TOXICOLOGY, OCCUPATIONAL, AND ENVIRONMENTAL HEALTH.** **VFOAT** Toxicology, Occupational, and Environmental Health. Vol. 1, No. 1 (Nov. 1991)-. Periodical. English. Three times a year. $120.00. John Wiley & Sons Ltd., Baffins Lane, Chichester West Sussex PO19 1UD England. **Tel** 0243 779777, FAX 0243 776128 BTG:JWP001, telex 86290 WIBOOKG. **(Subscription address:** Prints India, 11 Darya Ganj, New Delhi 110002 India.**)** **LC** RA1190; .I68. **DD** 615.9/02. **CODEN** IJTHEZ.

UK/0266-0512
**INTERNATIONAL MONOGRAPHS ON RISK.** [Int. monogr. risk]. (1984)-. Monographic series. English. ir. Price varies per volume. John Libbey & Company Ltd, 13 Smiths Yard, Summerley Street, London SW18 4HR England. **Tel** 01-947 2777, FAX 01-947 2664, telex 94013503 JOHN G. **ED** A J Jouhar. **NLM** W1; IN8254.

US/0740-8242
**ISSUES AND REVIEWS IN TERATOLOGY.** **See** Biology-Physiology.

●US/1061-3439
**ISSX PROCEEDINGS.** **See** Pharmacy and Pharmacology.

FR/0753-2830
**JOURNAL DE TOXICOLOGIE CLINIQUE ET EXPERIMENTALE.** ***Ceased.*** [J. toxicol. clin. exp.]. Vol. 5, No. 1 (Jan./Feb. 1985)-Ceased with Vol. 12, No. 3 (199?). Academic Scholarly Publication. French (English). bm. Masson SA, Avenue Beauregard 12, CH-1701 Fribourg Switzerland. **Tel** 011 41 37 249585, FAX 011 41 37 247559, telex 942658 SEMI CH. **(Subscription address:** 7A Boulevard de Perolles, CH-1701 Fribourg Switzerland**)** **NLM** W1; JO3653D. **CODEN** JTCEEM. **[CCC].** **Pr Rev.** Documents available from The Genuine Article, CASDDS. ***Continues** Journal de Toxicologie Medicale, 0249-6216.*
**Ind/Abst** Chem. Abstr. (1985-199?); Curr. Contents Clin. Med. (?-?); EMBASE (?-?); Fish Rev. (?-?); Index Med. (Vol. 5, No. 1, 1985-199?); Nutr. Res. Newsl. (?-?); Life Sci. Collect. (?-?); Res. Alert [Select. Cov.]; Rev. Med. Vet. Mycology (?-?); SCISEARCH; Weed Abstr.; Wildl. Rev. (?-?).

US/0146-4760
**JOURNAL OF ANALYTICAL TOXICOLOGY.** [J. anal. toxicol.]. **VFOAT** JAT. Vol. 1 (Jan./Feb. 1977)-. Academic Scholarly Publication. English. Seven times a year. $230.00 US; $245.00 other. Preston Publications Inc., 7800 Merrimac Avenue, PO Box 48312, Niles IL 60714. **Tel** (708)965-0566, FAX (708)965-7639, telex 910-223-1780 PRESTON NILE. **ED** Randall C. Baselt. **LC** RA1221; .J68. **DD** 615.9/07/05. **NLM** W1 JO536CK. **CODEN** JATOD3. **[CCC].** Index available. cum. index. **Bk Rev.** **Ad Acc.** **Pr Rev. Circ:** 1,500. available on microfilm; available on microfiche. Documents available from The Genuine Article, BIOSIS Document Express, CASDDS.
**Desc:** International journal publishing scientific communications relating to the isolation, identification and quantitation of potentially toxic substances and their biotransformation.
**Ind/Abst** Anal. Abstr.; Biol. Abstr.; Chem. Abstr.; Chem. Titles; Coal Abstr.; CSA Neuro. Abstr. (?-?); Curr. Contents Life Sci.; Dairy Sci. Abstr.; EMBASE; Energy Res. Abstr. (March 1979-); Food Sci. Technol. Abstr.; Highw. Res. Abstr.; Index Med.; Index Vet.; INIS Atomindex [Micro.]; Mass Spect. Bull.; Life Sci. Collect.; Protozoolog. Abstr.; Res. Alert [Full Cov.]; Rev. Agric. Entomol.; Rev. Med. Vet. Entomol.; Rev. Plant Pathol.; Sci. Cit. Index; SCISEARCH; SPORT Discus; Vet. Bull.; Toxicol. Abstr.; Weed Abstr.

UK/0260-437X
**JOURNAL OF APPLIED TOXICOLOGY.** (JOURNAL OF APPLIED TOXICOLOGY : JAT.). [J. appl. toxicol.]. **Added/Corp** Genetic Toxicology Association. **VFOAT** JAT; J.A.T. Vol. 1, No. 1 (Feb. 1981)-. Academic Scholarly Publication. English. Six times a year (Feb., Apr., June, Aug., Oct., Dec.). $565.00. John Wiley & Sons Ltd., Baffins Lane, Chichester West Sussex PO19 1UD England. **Tel** 0243 779777, FAX 0243 776128 BTG:JWP001, telex 86290 WIBOOKG. **(Subscription address:** John Wiley / Philadelphia, PO Box 7247, Philadelphia PA 19170.**)** **ED** Harry Salem, Laszlo Magos, Richard A. Parent, David Clegg, and Michael R. Greenwood. **LC** RA1190; .J65. **DD** 615.9/005. **NLM** W1 JO544KC. **CODEN** JJATDK. **[CCC].** **Pr Rev. Circ:** 800. available on microfilm and microfiche from University Microfilms International (UMI). Documents available from The Genuine Article, BIOSIS Document Express, CASDDS, Documents on Demand, ADONIS.
**Desc:** Devoted to high quality original papers which relate to the field of applied toxicology. This includes the study of toxic effects of chemicals and materials in the field of teratology, reproduction, mutagenesis, carcinogenesis, health, the environment, pathology, pharmacokinetics and biochemical mechanisms.
**Ind/Abst** ADONIS; AGRICOLA [Select. Cov.]; Biol. Abstr.; Chem. Abstr.; Chem. Hazards Ind.; Chem. Titles; Coal Abstr.; CSA Neuro. Abstr. (?-?); Curr. Aware. Biol. Sci., CABS; Curr. Contents Life Sci.; EMBASE; Energy Inf. Abstr.; Environ. Abstr.; Environ. Period. Bibliogr.; Fish Rev. (Jan. 1989-July 1992); Grasslands For. Abstr.; Health Saf. Sci. Abstr.; Index Med.; Index Vet.; Ind. Hyg. Dig.; Lab. Hazards Bull.; NAPRALERT; Nutr. Abstr. Rev., Ser. B, Live Feeds and Feed.; Nutr. Abstr. Rev., Ser. A, Hum. Exp.; Nutr. Res. Newsl.; Life Sci. Collect.; Pollut. Abstr. Indexes; Poult. Abstr.; Ref. Upd. Deluxe Ed.; Res. Alert [Full Cov.]; Rev. Agric. Entomol.; Rev. Med. Vet. Entomol.; Rev. Med. Vet. Mycology; Sci. Cit. Index; SCISEARCH; Vet. Bull.; Toxicol. Abstr.; Wheat Barley Trit. Abstr.; Wildl. Rev. (Jan. 1989-July 1992); World Surf. Coat. Abstr.

US/0887-2082
**JOURNAL OF BIOCHEMICAL TOXICOLOGY.** [J. biochem. toxicol.]. Vol. 1, No. 1 (March 1986)-. Academic Scholarly Publication. English. Six times a year. $270.00. VCH Publishers Inc, 220 East 23rd Street, New York NY 10010. **Tel** (212)683-8333, , FAX (212)481-0897. **(Subscription address:** VCH Publishers Inc., 303 Northwest 12th Avenue, Journals Department, Deerfield FL 33442.**)** **DD** 615. **NLM** W1; JO563C. **CODEN** JBTOEB. **[CCC].** **Pr Rev.** Documents available from The Genuine Article, BIOSIS Document Express, CASDDS.
**Desc:** Aim of the journal is to increase understanding at the molecular level of the biochemical and physiological processes that can alter and/or be altered by toxic agents. Emphasizes the mechanisms and toxicological effects of agricultural and industrial chemicals, natural products, food additives, hormones and drugs on enzymes, receptors, genes, and biomolecules at all stages of the life cycle.
**Ind/Abst** Biol. Abstr. (1986-); Chem. Abstr. (1986-); Curr. Contents Life Sci.; Index Med. (Vol. 1 No. 1, 1986-); Res. Alert [Full Cov.]; Rev. Agric. Entomol.; Rev. Med. Vet. Mycology; Sci. Cit. Index; SCISEARCH.

US/0360-1234
**JOURNAL OF ENVIRONMENTAL SCIENCE AND HEALTH. PART B, PESTICIDES, FOOD CONTAMINANTS, AND AGRICULTURAL WASTES.** **See** Environmental Issues.

US/1052-1070
**JOURNAL OF GENETIC AND DEVELOPMENTAL TOXICOLOGY.** (1991)-. Periodical. English. qt. $115.00. Princeton Scientific Publishing Company Inc., PO Box 2155, Princeton NJ 08543. **Tel** (609)683-4750, FAX (609)683-0838.

●US/1058-8108
**JOURNAL OF NATURAL TOXINS.** (1992)-. English. Six times a year. $195.00 US; $270.00 other. John Wiley & Sons, Inc., 605 Third Avenue, New York NY 10158-0012. **Tel** (212)850-6000, (212)850-6645, FAX (212)850-6088, telex 12-7063. **(Subscription address:** John Wiley & Sons / England, Baffins Lane, Chichester, West Sussex PO19 1UD England.**)**

●US/1054-044X
**JOURNAL OF OCCUPATIONAL MEDICINE AND TOXICOLOGY.** [J. occup. med. toxicol.]. **Added/Corp** International Society of Occupational Medicine and Toxicology. **VFOAT** International Journal of Occupational Medicine and Toxicology. Vol. 1, No. 1 (Jan. 1992)-. Periodical. English. Four times a year. $140.00. Princeton Scientific Publishing Company Inc., PO Box 2155, Princeton NJ 08543. **Tel** (609)683-4750, FAX (609)683-0838. **ED** Nachman Brautbar, MD. **DD** 616. **Bk Rev.** **Ad Acc, Adv Mgr:** M A Mehlman. **Pr Rev. Circ:** 250.

●US/1056-8719
**JOURNAL OF PHARMACOLOGICAL AND TOXICOLOGICAL METHODS.** **See** Pharmacy and Pharmacology.

UK/0959-2431
**JOURNAL OF SMOKING-RELATED DISORDERS, THE.** (199?)-. Periodical. English. ir (2 or 3 times a year). £70.00. Gardiner Caldwell Communications Ltd., The Old Ribbon Mill, Pitt Street, Macclesfield Cheshire, SK11 7PT England. **Tel** 011 44

625 618507, FAX 011 44 625 610260. **NLM** W1; JO877HP. **CODEN** JSRDEJ. **Bk Rev. Ad Acc, Adv Mgr:** Kathryn Wilkinson, **Tel** 44 625 618507.

US/0730-0913
**JOURNAL OF THE AMERICAN COLLEGE OF TOXICOLOGY.** [J. Amer. Coll. Toxicol.]. **Added/Corp** American College of Toxicology. **VFOAT** Acute Toxicity Data. Vol. 1, No. 1 (1982)-. Academic Scholarly Publication. English. bm (6 issues). $175.00 (individuals), $206.00 (institutions) US; $192.00 (individuals), $228.00 (institutions) other. Raven Press, 1185 Avenue of the Americas, 37th Floor, New York NY 10036. **Tel** (212)930-9500, (212)930-9604, FAX (212)869-3495, (212)302-8507, telex 640073. **ED** Robert Diener. **LC** RA1190; .J668. **DD** 615.9/005. **NLM** W1; JO908V. **CODEN** JACTDZ. **Bk Rev. Ad Acc. Pr Rev.** Documents available from The Genuine Article, CASDDS, Documents on Demand. ***Absorbed*** *Journal of the American College of Toxicology. Part B, Acute Toxicity Data, 1044-2049.*
**Desc:** Provides original peer-reviewed research papers as well as reports of issues and events that influence the field. The journal covers the following: general toxicology; safety evaluation and risk assessment; developmental and reproductive toxicology; epidemiology and clinical toxicology; carcinogenesis; genetic toxicology; mechanisms of toxicity; development of non-animal testing techniques; forensic toxicology; immunotoxicology; quality assurance; and veterinary toxicology. The journal also publishes reports of the Cosmetic Ingredient Review Expert Panel as special additional issues.
**Ind/Abst** Chem. Abstr.; Chem. Hazards Ind.; CSA Neuro. Abstr. (?-?); Curr. Contents Life Sci.; Electron. Commun. Abstr. J.; EMBASE; Environ. Abstr.; Health Saf. Sci. Abstr.; Index Vet.; ISMEC Bull.; Lab. Hazards Bull.; NAPRALERT; Nutr. Res. Newsl.; Life Sci. Collect.; Pollut. Abstr. Indexes; Res. Alert [Full Cov.]; Risk Abstr.; Saf. Sci. Abstr. J.; Sci. Cit. Index; SCISEARCH; Toxicol. Abstr.

JA/0388-1350
**JOURNAL OF TOXICOLOGICAL SCIENCES, THE.** [J. toxicol. sci.]. **Added/Corp** Doku Sayo Kenkyukai. Vol. 1 (Jan. 1976)-. Academic Scholarly Publication. English (Japanese). qt. ¥7000.00. Japanese Society of Toxicological Sciences, 2 4 16 Yayoi Bunkyo Ku, Tokyo 113 Japan. **Tel** 011 81 3 38123093. **ED** Morio Kanno and Jun-ichi Sudo. **NLM** W1 JO966J. **CODEN** JTSCDR. **Ad Acc.** ctrl circ. Documents available from BIOSIS Document Express, CASDDS.
**Ind/Abst** Biol. Abstr.; Chem. Abstr.; EMBASE; Index Med.; Index Vet.; Small Anim. Abstr. Bibliogr.; Vet. Bull.; Trop. Dis. Bull.

US/0098-4108
**JOURNAL OF TOXICOLOGY AND ENVIRONMENTAL HEALTH.** [J. toxicol. environ. health]. Vol. 1 (Sept. 1975)-. Academic Scholarly Publication. English. mo. £482.00 UK; $795.00 other. Taylor & Francis Ltd., Rankine Road, Basingstoke Hampshire, RG24 8PR United Kingdom. **Tel** 011 44 256 840366, FAX 011 44 256 479438, telex 858540. **(Subscription address:** Taylor & Francis Inc., 1900 Frost Road, Suite 101, Bristol PA 19007-1598.**) ED** Sam Kacew. **LC** RA1190; .J67. **DD** 615.9/005. **NLM** W1 JO966K. **CODEN** JTEHD6. **[CCC]. Bk Rev. Ad Acc. Pr Rev. Circ:** 1,100. available on microfilm and microfiche from University Microfilms International (UMI). Documents available from The Genuine Article, BIOSIS Document Express, CASDDS, Documents on Demand, ADONIS.
**Desc:** This highly acclaimed and authoritative periodical publishes strictly refereed papers about original research concerning special interest fields such as carcinogenesis, mutagenesis, teratology, neurotoxicity, environmental factors affecting health, and other toxicological phenomena. Emphasis is on toxicological effect of natural and anthropogenic environmental pollutants and their action on intact organisms as well as in vitro systems. An important added new feature is to publish refereed critical reviews in scientific areas of current toxicological interest.
**Ind/Abst** ADONIS; AGRICOLA [Select. Cov.]; AQUAREF; Aquat. Sci. Fish. Abstr. (Computer File); Biol. Abstr.; Biol. Dig.; Can. Environ.; Chem. Abstr.; Chem. Hazards Ind.; Chem. Titles; Coal Abstr.; CSA Neuro. Abstr. (?-?); Curr. Ref. Fish Res.; Dairy Sci. Abstr.; EMBASE; Energy Inf. Abstr.; Energy Res. Abstr. (Oct. 1975-); Environ. Abstr.; Environ. Period. Bibliogr.; Fish Rev. (Jan. 1989-July 1992); Health Saf. Sci. Abstr.; Index Med.; Index Vet.; Ind. Hyg. Dig. (19??-); Key Word Index Wildl. Res.; Lab. Hazards Bull.; Leadscan; NAPRALERT; Nutr. Abstr. Rev., Ser. A, Hum. Exp.; Nutr. Res. Newsl.; Life Sci. Collect.; PESTDOC; Pollut. Abstr. Indexes; Ref. Upd. Deluxe Ed.; Res. Alert [Full Cov.]; Rev. Agric. Entomol.; Rev. Med. Vet. Entomol.; Rev. Med. Vet. Mycology; Risk Abstr.; Sci. Cit. Index; SCISEARCH; Small Anim. Abstr. Bibliogr.; Soc. Sci. Cit. Index [Select. Cov.]; Vet. Bull.; Toxicol. Abstr.; Trop. Dis. Bull.; Weed Abstr.; Wildl. Rev. (Jan. 1989-July 1992).

US/0731-3810
**JOURNAL OF TOXICOLOGY. CLINICAL TOXICOLOGY.** [J. toxicol., Clin. toxicol.]. **VFOAT** Clinical Toxicology. Vol. 19, No. 1 (Mar 1982)-. Academic Scholarly Publication. English. Six times a year. $875.00 US; $896.00 other. Marcel Dekker Inc., 270 Madison Avenue, New York NY 10016. **Tel** (212)696-9000, (800)228-1160, FAX (212)685-4540, telex 421419. **(Subscription address:** Marcel Dekker Inc, PO Box 5017, Monticello NY 12701.**) ED** Carol R. Angle. **LC** RA1190; .C56. **DD** 615.9/005. **NLM** W1 JO966KC. **CODEN** JTCTDWJTCDW. **[CCC]. Bk Rev. Ad Acc. Pr Rev.** available on microfiche. Documents available from The Genuine Article, BIOSIS Document Express, CASDDS, Documents on Demand, ADONIS. ***Continues*** *Clinical Toxicology, 0009-9309.*
**Desc:** Providing an authoritative international resource for all facets of medical toxicology, this journal integrates the varied disciplines that deal directly with, and contribute to, the practical aspects of poison management. In critical articles, notes, case histories, and reviews, the journal examines such vital topics as specific poisons; pharmacologic mechanisms; selected mammalian toxicities; and the epidemiology of regional, national, and international overdoses by utilizing data from such sources as accidents, suicides, homicides, and drug abuse. Additionally, selected symposia investigating current toxicologic problems are featured during the year.
**Ind/Abst** Abr. Index Med.; ADONIS; AGRICOLA [Select. Cov.]; Biol. Abstr.; Biol. Dig.; Chem. Abstr.; Chem. Hazards Ind.; Curr. Aware. Biol. Sci., CABS; Curr. Contents Life Sci.; Dairy Sci. Abstr.; EMBASE; Energy Res. Abstr. (Feb. 1983-); Environ. Abstr.; Environ. Period. Bibliogr.; Fish Rev.; Health Period. Database [Full Txt.]; Hortic. Abstr.; Index Med.; INIS Atomindex [Micro.]; Int. Pharm. Abstr.; Iowa Drug Inf. Serv. (1982-); Lab. Hazards Bull.; Mod. Med.; NAPRALERT; Nutr. Res. Newsl.; Life Sci. Collect.; Pollut. Abstr. Indexes; Protozoolog. Abstr.; Psychol. Abstr.; Ref. Upd. Deluxe Ed.; Res. Alert [Full Cov.]; Rev. Agric. Entomol.; Rev. Med. Vet. Mycology; Saf. Health Work; Sci. Cit. Index; SCISEARCH; Toxicol. Abstr.; Trop. Dis. Bull.; Weed Abstr.

US
**JOURNAL OF TOXICOLOGY. CUTANEOUS AND OCULAR TOXICOLOGY.** [J. toxicol., Cutan. ocul. toxicol.]. **VFOAT** Cutaneous and Ocular Toxicology. Vol. 1, No. 1 (1982)-. Academic Scholarly Publication. English. qt. $595.00 US; $609.00 other. Marcel Dekker Inc., 270 Madison Avenue, New York NY 10016. **Tel** (212)696-9000, (800)228-1160, FAX (212)685-4540, telex 421419. **(Subscription address:** Marcel Dekker Inc, PO Box 5017, Monticello NY 12701.**) ED** Edward M. Jackson, Paul Lazar, F. T. Fraunfelder, Joseph F. Borzelleca. **NLM** W1; JO966KCH. **CODEN** JTOTDO. **Bk Rev. Ad Acc. Pr Rev.** ctrl circ. available on microfiche. Documents available from The Genuine Article, CASDDS, Documents on Demand. ***Continues*** *Lens and Eye Toxicity Research.*
**Desc:** Each issue of this vital journal contains significant reviews and original research articles by some of the most innovative and active researchers in their respective fields. Responding to the need for comprehensive coverage of developments in a wide range of interrelated fields, 'Cutaneous and Ocular Toxicology' focuses on dermatological, toxicological, and ophthalmological studies to broaden the understanding of such phenomena as sensitization, irritation, phototoxicity, and photoallergenicity to drugs, cosmetics, soaps, fragrances, textiles, preservatives, adhesives, and both environmental and occupational exposures.
**Ind/Abst** Chem. Abstr.; Curr. Aware. Biol. Sci., CABS; EMBASE; Environ. Abstr.; Environ. Period. Bibliogr.; Int. Pharm. Abstr.; Nutr. Res. Newsl.; Life Sci. Collect.; Ref. Upd. Deluxe Ed.; Res. Alert [Full Cov.]; Sci. Cit. Index; SCISEARCH; Weed Abstr.

US/0731-3837
**JOURNAL OF TOXICOLOGY. TOXIN REVIEWS.** [J. toxicol., toxin rev.]. **VFOAT** Toxin Reviews. Vol. 1, No. 1 (1982)-. Academic Scholarly Publication. English. Four times a year. $575.00 US; $589.00 other. Marcel Dekker Inc., 270 Madison Avenue, New York NY 10016. **Tel** (212)696-9000, (800)228-1160, FAX (212)685-4540, telex 421419. **(Subscription address:** Marcel Dekker Inc, PO Box 5017, Monticello NY 12701.**) ED** W. T. Shier and A. T. Tu. **LC** RA1190; .J669. **DD** 615.9/005. **NLM** W1 JO966KD. **CODEN** JTTRD9. **[CCC]. Bk Rev. Ad Acc. Pr Rev.** ctrl circ. available on microfiche. Documents available from The Genuine Article, CASDDS, Documents on Demand.
**Desc:** Gathers the latest interdisciplinary findings on toxins and toxin mechanisms into one convenient, extraordinarily valuable compendium. Featuring a dual emphasis on classifying toxins by their mechanisms of action, and on new, underutilized substances, this outstanding journal brings scientists exactly the right combination of up-to-date, easily absorbed and applied information and bold new ideas in lively brief notices and reviews.
**Ind/Abst** Biodeter. Abstr. (1991-); Chem. Abstr.; CSA Neuro. Abstr. (?-?); Curr. Aware. Biol. Sci., CABS; Dairy Sci. Abstr.; EMBASE; Environ. Abstr.; Fish Rev.; Index Vet.; NAPRALERT; Nutr. Abstr. Rev., Ser. B, Live Feeds and Feed.; Nutr. Abstr. Rev., Ser. A, Hum. Exp.; Nutr. Res. Newsl.; Life Sci. Collect.; Pig News Inf.; Postharvest News Inf.; Poult. Abstr.; Ref. Upd. Deluxe Ed.; Res. Alert [Full Cov.]; Rev. Med. Vet. Entomol.; Rev. Med. Vet. Mycology; Rev. Plant Pathol.; Rice Abstr.; Sci. Cit. Index; SCISEARCH; Vet. Bull.; Toxicol. Abstr.; Wheat Barley Trit. Abstr.

KO/0258-2368
**KOREAN JOURNAL OF TOXICOLOGY, THE.** [Korean j. toxicol.]. (1985)-. Periodical. Multiple languages. Korean Society of Toxicology, Seoul Korea. **UDC** 615.9. Documents available from CASDDS.
**Ind/Abst** Chem. Abstr.

GW
**MAXIMUM CONCENTRATIONS AT THE WORKPLACE AND BIOLOGICAL TOLERANCE VALUES FOR WORKING MATERIALS.** ***Title Change.*** **Added/Corp** Deutsche Forschungsgemeinschaft. Kommission zur Prufung Gesundheitsschadlicher Arbeitsstoffe. **VFOAT** List of MAK and BAT Values. **VAT** List of Maximale Arbeitsplatzkonzentrationen and Biologische Arbeitsstofftoleranzwerte. (198?)-(199?). English (German). an. VCH Gesellschaft GmbH, Postfach 101161, D 69451 Weinheim Germany. **Tel** 011 49 6201 606459, FAX 011 49 6201 606184. **(Subscription address:** VCH Publishers Inc., 303 NW 12th Avenue, Journals Department, Deerfield Beach, FL 33442 (800-442-8824)**) LC** RA1229.5; .M39. **DD** 615.9/02. ***Continues*** *Maximum Concentrations at the Workplace.* ***Continued by*** *MAK-and BAT-Values.*

●US
**MEDICAL TOXICOLOGY.** (1993)-. Monographic series. English. ir. Price varies per volume. Marcel Dekker Inc., 270 Madison Avenue, New York NY 10016. **Tel** (212)696-9000, (800)228-1160, FAX (212)685-4540, telex 421419. **(Subscription address:** Marcel Dekker Inc, PO Box 5017, Monticello NY 12701.**)**

GW/0934-4640
**MITTEILUNGEN - DEUTSCHE GESELLSCHAFT FUR PHARMAKOLOGIE UND TOXIKOLOGIE.** **See** Pharmacy and Pharmacology.

US/0098-6925
**MODERN PHARMACOLOGY-TOXICOLOGY.** **See** Pharmacy and Pharmacology.

UK/0273-2939
**MONOGRAPHS IN TOXICOLOGY : ENVIRONMENTAL AND SAFETY ASPECTS.** [Monogr. toxicol.: environ. saf. asp.]. Monographic series. English. Price varies per volume. John Wiley & Sons Ltd., Baffins Lane, Chichester West Sussex PO19 1UD England. **Tel** 0243 779777, FAX 0243 776128 BTG:JWP001, telex 86290 WIBOOKG. **(Subscription address:** North, South and Central America/ John Wiley & Sons, Inc., Subscription Department, 605 Third Avenue, New York, NY 10158-0012, USA; telephone: (212)850-6645; FAX: (212)850-6021**)**

NE
**MUTATION RESEARCH. GENETIC TOXICOLOGY.** **See** Biology-Genetics.

NE
**MUTATION RESEARCH. GENETIC TOXICOLOGY TESTING AND BIOMONITORING OF ENVIRONMENTAL OR OCCUPATIONAL EXPOSURE.** ***Title Change.*** **VFOAT** Genetic Toxicology Testing and Biomonitoring of Environmental or Occupational Exposure; Genetic Toxicology Testing. Vol. 204, No. 1 (Jan. 1988)-(19??). Academic Scholarly Publication. English. Sixteen times a year (4 volumes). Elsevier Science Publishers BV, PO Box 211, 1000 AE Amsterdam Netherlands. **Tel** 011 31 20 5803642, FAX 011 31 20 5862696, telex 15682. **CODEN** MUREAV. ***Continues*** *Mutation Research. Genetic Toxicology Testing, 0165-1218.* ***Continued by*** *Mutation Research / Genetic Toxicology.*
**Ind/Abst** Curr. Aware. Biol. Sci., CABS; Protozoolog. Abstr.; Rev. Med. Vet. Mycology.

NE/0165-1110
**MUTATION RESEARCH. REVIEWS IN GENETIC TOXICOLOGY.** [Mutat. res., Rev. genet. toxicol.]. **VFOAT** Reviews in Genetic Toxicology. Vol. 32, No. 1 (Mar. 1975)-. Academic Scholarly Publication. English. Six times a year (2 vols.). Fl884.00; Fl9499.00 combined subscription with Mutation Research/DNAging, Mutation Research/DNA Repair, Mutation Research/Environmental Mutagenesis and Related Subjects Including Methodology, Mutation Research/Genetic Toxicology Testing, and Mutation Research Letters. Elsevier Science Publishers BV, PO Box 211, 1000 AE Amsterdam Netherlands. **Tel** 011 31 20 5803642, FAX 011 31 20 5862696, telex 15682. **NLM** W1 MU973. **CODEN** MRRTEP. **[CCC].** available on microfilm from University Microfilms International (UMI). Documents available from ADONIS. ***Continues*** *Mutation Research, 0027-5107.*
**Ind/Abst** ADONIS; Curr. Aware. Biol. Sci., CABS; EMBASE; Helminthol. Abstr. (1991-); Index Med.; Plant Breed. Abstr.; Ref. Upd. Basic Ed.; Ref. Upd. Deluxe Ed.

US/0027-9269
**NATIONAL FLUORIDATION NEWS.** ***Suspended.*** [Natl. fluorid. news]. **Added/Corp** Association for the Protection of Our Water Supply. Pure Water Association of America. California Committee. Vol. 1 (Jan. 1955)-(Jan. 1991). Periodical. English. qt. $4.00 U.S. and other. The National Fluoridation News, PO Box 1611, San Anselmo CA 94960. **Tel** (415)453-0158. **ED** Shirley Graves. **DD** 617. **Bk Rev. Circ:** 4,500.
**Desc:** Articles on research as reported in medical and scientific journals on the toxicity of fluorides and fluoridation. Statements by professionals, legislation and accident update, and news items.

US/0888-8051
**NATIONAL TOXICOLOGY PROGRAM TECHNICAL REPORT SERIES.** (TECHNICAL REPORT SERIES / NATIONAL TOXICOLOGY PROGRAM.). [Natl. Toxicol. Program tech. rep. ser.]. **Added/Corp** National Toxicology Program (U.S.) National Institutes of Health (U.S.). **VFOAT** NTP Technical Report. No. 201 (1980)-. Academic Scholarly Publication. English. ir. Free on request. National Toxicology Program, PO Box 12233, Research Triangle NC 27709. **Tel** (919)541-3991. **LC** RA1199; .T42. **DD** 615.9/07/05. **NLM** W1; NA766. Documents available from CASDDS. ***Continues*** *National Cancer Institute Carcinogenesis Technical Report Series, 0163-7185.*
**Ind/Abst** Chem. Abstr.

●US/1056-9014
**NATURAL TOXINS.** [Nat. toxins]. **VFOAT** Journal of Natural Toxins. Vol. 1, No. 1 (1992)-. Academic Scholarly Publication. English. bm. $240.00 US; $300.00 Canada and Mexico; $322.50 other. John Wiley & Sons, Inc., 605 Third Avenue, New York NY 10158-0012. **Tel** (212)850-6000, (212)850-6645, FAX (212)850-6088, telex 12-7063. **(Subscription address:** John Wiley & Sons / England, Baffins Lane, Chichester, West Sussex PO19 1UD England.**) ED** John W. ApSimon and J. David Miller. **LC** QP631; .N37. **DD** 615.9/005. **NLM** W1; NA806P. **CODEN** NATOEE. Documents available from CASDDS, Documents on Demand.
**Desc:** Provides a forum for original research on the occurrence, isolation, identification, and characterization of natural products with toxic activities.
**Ind/Abst** Chem. Abstr.; Curr. Aware. Biol. Sci., CABS; Environ. Abstr.

US/0161-813X
**NEUROTOXICOLOGY (PARK FOREST SOUTH).** See Medical Science and Technology-Neurology.

JA/0300-8533
**OYO YAKURI.** See Pharmacy and Pharmacology.

FR/1146-5514
**PASCAL. E 63, TOXICOLOGIE.** **VFOAT** PASCAL. E 63, Toxicology; PASCAL. E Soixante-Trois, Toxicologie. (1990)-. Periodical. Multiple languages. Ten times a year. 935.00F France; 990.00F other. CNRS / Institut d'Information Scientifique et Technique, (Centre National de la Recherche Scientifique), 15 Quai Anatole France, Paris 75700 France. **Tel** 011 33 1 47531515, telex 299 356 F. **(Subscription address:** Institut de l'Information Scientifique et Technique, 2 Allee du Parc de Brabois, 54514 Vandoeuvre Nancy France**) UDC** 011. ***Continues*** *Pascal Explore. E63, Toxicologie, 0761-215X.*

FR/0761-215X
**PASCAL EXPLORE. E63, TOXICOLOGIE.** ***Title Change.*** **VFOAT** Toxicologie; Toxicology. (1984)-?. Periodical. French (English). mo. Institut de l'Information Scientique et Technique (INIST), 2 Allee du Parc de Brabois, 54514 Vandoeuvre Nancy Cedex France. **Tel** 011 33 83 504600, FAX 011 33 83 504650. **NLM** ZQ 1; P2778. ***Continues in part*** *Bulletin Signaletique 330: Sciences Pharmacologiques, Toxicologie, 0007-5442.* ***Continued by*** *Toxicologie. E63.*

UK
**PESTDOC.** See Pest Control-Abstracting, Bibliographies and Statistics.

DK/0901-9928
**PHARMACOLOGY & TOXICOLOGY.** See Pharmacy and Pharmacology.

DK/0901-9936
**PHARMACOLOGY & TOXICOLOGY. SUPPLEMENT.** See Pharmacy and Pharmacology.

●US/1063-8946
**PHARMACOLOGY, TOXICOLOGY & THERAPEUTICS.** See Pharmacy and Pharmacology.

US
**POLTOX [COMPUTER FILE].** See Environmental Issues-Pollution and Waste Management.

US/0083-8969
**PROCEEDINGS OF THE WESTERN PHARMACOLOGY SOCIETY.** See Pharmacy and Pharmacology.

●US/1076-2833
**QUINTESSENCE (CHICAGO, ILL.).** See Medical Science and Technology-Abstracting, Bibliographies and Statistics.

US/0361-2546
**REGISTRY OF TOXIC EFFECTS OF CHEMICAL SUBSTANCES [MICROFORM].** [Regist. toxic eff. chem. subst.]. **Added/Corp** National Institute for Occupational Safety and Health. Tracor Jitco, Inc. Advanced Engineering & Planning Corp. **VFOAT** RTECS Microfiche Quarterly Complete File; RTECS Quarterly Microfiche. (Oct 1977)-No longer available in microfiche. Government Publication. English. qt. $62.00 domestic; $77.50 other. Superintendent of Documents, US Government Printing Office, Washington DC 20402. **Tel** (202)275-3328, FAX (202)786-2377. **DD** 615. available on CD-ROM.

US/0273-2300
**REGULATORY TOXICOLOGY AND PHARMACOLOGY.** See Pharmacy and Pharmacology.

US/0888-2681
**REPORT OF THE INTERAGENCY TOXIC SUBSTANCES DATA COMMITTEE.** [Rep. Interag. Toxic Subst. Data Comm.]. 1st (Nov. 1980)-. English. Environmental Protection Administration, Office of Pesticides and Toxic Substances, Office of Toxics Integration TS-777, Office of Network Administration, 401 M Street SW, Washington DC 20460. **DD** 363. **NLM** W1; RE209SV.

US/0890-6238
**REPRODUCTIVE TOXICOLOGY (ELMSFORD, N.Y.).** (REPRODUCTIVE TOXICOLOGY.). **Added/Corp** Reproductive Toxicology Center (Washington, D.C.). Vol. 1, No. 1 (1987)-. Periodical. English. Six times a year. $537.00 The Americas; £360.00 other. Pergamon Press, An Imprint of Elsevier Science Ltd., The Boulevard, Langford Lane, Kidlington, Oxford OX5 1GB United Kingdom. **Tel** 011 44 865 843000, 011 44 865 843699, FAX 011 44 865 843010. **(Subscription address:** Elsevier Science Ltd. Oxford Fulfillment Centre, PO Box 800, Kidlington, Oxford OX5 1DX United Kingdom.**) ED** Anthony Scialli. **DD** 616. **NLM** W1; RE213PG. **CODEN** REPTED. **[CCC].** available on microfilm and microfiche from University Microfilms International (UMI). Documents available from The Genuine Article, BIOSIS Document Express, CASDDS. ***Continues*** *Reproductive Toxicology, 0736-5098.*
**Desc:** Publishes original research on the influence of chemical and physical agents on reproduction. Written by and for obstetricians, embryologists, teratologists, geneticists, toxicologists, andrologists, pediatricians and others interested in detecting potential reproductive hazards. The journal is a forum for communication among researchers and practitioners.
**Ind/Abst** Biol. Abstr.; Chem. Abstr.; Curr. Aware. Biol. Sci., CABS; Curr. Contents Life Sci.; Index Med. (1987-); Int. Pharm. Abstr. (199?-); Nutr. Abstr. Rev., Ser. A, Hum. Exp.; Pollut. Abstr. Indexes; Res. Alert [Full Cov.]; Risk Abstr.; Sci. Cit. Index; SCISEARCH; Soc. Sci. Cit. Index [Select. Cov.]; Toxicol. Abstr.

US/0737-0547
**REVIEW OF CURRENT DHHS, DOE, AND EPA RESEARCH RELATED TO TOXICOLOGY.** (REVIEW OF CURRENT DHHS, DOE, AND EPA RESEARCH RELATED TO TOXICOLOGY / NATIONAL TOXICOLOGY PROGRAM.). [Rev. curr. DHHS, DOE, EPA res. relat. toxicol.]. **VFOAT** Review of Current D.H.H.S., D.O.E., AND E.P.A. Research Related to Toxicology; N.T.P. Review of Current DHHS, DOE & EPA Research Related; NTP Review of Current DHEW Research Related to Toxicology. English. an. Public Information Office / North Carolina, National Toxicology Program, PO Box 12233, Research Triangle Park NC 27709. **LC** RA1199; .R48. **DD** 615.9/0072073. available on microfiche (Vols. for (1982-) distributed to depository libraries). ***Continues*** *Review of Current DHEW Research Related to Toxicology, 0270-0573.*

US/0163-7673
**REVIEWS IN BIOCHEMICAL TOXICOLOGY.** [Rev. biochem. toxicol.]. (1979)-. Academic Scholarly Publication. English. ir. Price varies per volume. Elsevier Science Publishing Company Inc, Madison Square Station, PO Box 882, New York NY 10159-0882. **Tel** (212)633-3950, FAX (212)633-3990. **(Subscription address:** Elsevier Science Inc. / New York Books, 655 Avenue of the Americas, New York NY 10010.**) LC** RA1190; .R48. **DD** 615.9/005. **NLM** W1 RE257CEC. **CODEN** RBTODU. **[CCC]. Pr Rev.** Documents available from BIOSIS Document Express, CASDDS.
**Ind/Abst** AGRICOLA [Select. Cov.]; Biol. Abstr.; Chem. Abstr.; Index Sci. Rev. [Full Cov.].

SP/0212-7113
**REVISTA DE TOXICOLOGIA.** **Added/Corp** Asociacion Espanola de Toxicologia. Vol. 1, No. 1 (1984)-. Periodical. Spanish (summaries and/or abstracts in English; table of contents in English). tq. 8600.00ptas. Springer Verlag Iberica SA, Avinguda Diagonal 468 4 C, 08006 Barcelona Spain. **Tel** 011 34 3 4157620, 011 34 3 4157621. **(Subscription address:** Springer Verlag New York Inc. / for North America, 44 Hartz Way, Secaucus NJ 07096.**) NLM** W1; RE5049. **CODEN** REVTE9.
**Ind/Abst** EMBASE; Indice Med. Esp.

●FR/1240-2494
**REVUE DOCUMENTAIRE - TOXIBASE LYON.** (REVUE DOCUMENTAIRE.). **VFOAT** Toxibase (Lyon). (1992)-. Periodical. French. Eight times a year. 350.00F France; 450.00F other with Bulletin Bibliographique. Toxibase, 14 Avenue Berthelot, F-69007 Lyon France. **Tel** 011 33 78 724745. **ED** Thomas Rouault. **UDC** 615.9. **Circ:** 300. ***Continues*** *Revue Bibliographique - Toxibase (Lyon), 0996-8393.*

IT/0390-6019
**RIVISTA DI TOSSICOLOGIA : SPERIMENTALE E CLINICA.** [Riv. tossicol. sper. clin.]. **Added/Corp** Centro Nazionale Contro le Intossicazioni. Societa Italiana di Tossicologia. Associazione Europea dei Centri Antiveleni. Vol. 5 (1975)-. Academic Scholarly Publication. Multiple languages (English, French and Italian). Three times a year. L66000 Italy; L132000 other. Societa Editrice Universo, Via GB Morgagni 1, 00161 Rome Italy. **Tel** 011 39 6 44231171. **NLM** W1 RI656D. **CODEN** RTSCDD. Documents available from CASDDS. ***Continues*** *Rivista de Clinica Tossicologica, 0390-6027.*
**Ind/Abst** Chem. Abstr.; EMBASE.

UK/0036-0325
**RUSSIAN PHARMACOLOGY AND TOXICOLOGY.** See Pharmacy and Pharmacology.

US
**THRESHOLD LIMIT VALUES AND BIOLOGICAL EXPOSURE INDICES FOR ... .** See Industrial Health and Safety.

JA/0287-8712
**TOKISHIKOROJI FORAMU.** [Tokishikoroji foramu]. **VFOAT** Toxicology Forum. Vol. 6, No. 1 (Jan. 1983)-. Academic Scholarly Publication. Japanese. bm. $160.00. **(Subscription address:** Maruzen Company Ltd., PO Box 5050, Import & Export Department, Tokyo 100 31 Japan.**) CODEN** TOFOD5. Documents available from CASDDS. ***Continues*** *Henigen to Dokusei, 0387-9712.*
**Ind/Abst** Chem. Abstr.; Curr. Biotechnol.

US/0276-2242
**TOXIC CONTROL.** Vol. 4-. Monographic series. English. Price varies per volume. Office of State Examiner / Baton Rouge, Municipal Fire and Police Civil Service, 150 Riverside Mall, Baton Rouge LA 70801. **DD** 363.1/79. **NLM** W3 TO7375. ***Continues*** *Toxic Substances Control, 0275-5432.*

●UK/1076-9188
**TOXIC SUBSTANCE MECHANISMS.** (1995)-. English. qt. £102.00 UK; $169.00 other. Taylor & Francis Ltd., Rankine Road, Basingstoke Hampshire, RG24 8PR United Kingdom. **Tel** 011 44 256 840366, FAX 011 44 256 479438, telex 858540. **(Subscription address:** Taylor & Francis Inc., 1900 Frost Road, Suite 101, Bristol PA 19007-1598.**)** ***Continues*** *Toxic Substances Journal, 0199-3178.*

UK/0953-7414
**TOXIC SUBSTANCES BULLETIN.** [Toxic subst. bull.]. **VFOAT** TSB. (1984)-. Periodical. English. Three times a year (April, August, December). £8.50. Health & Safety Executive, Room 414 St Hughs House Stanley, Btle Merseyside L20 3QY England. **Tel** 011 44 51 951 4000, FAX 011 44 51 922 5394, telex 628235. **(Subscription address:** HSE Books, PO Box 1999, Sudbury Suffolk CO10 6FS England.**) Bk Rev**, (Qty: 6). **Circ:** 2,000.
**Desc:** Includes details of the occupational exposure limits which are adopted and any changes which the Health and Safety Executive intend to adopt. Contains information on the guidance notes, toxicity reviews, codes of practice, regulations, consultative documents and European directives in the field of toxic substances.

US/0199-3178
**TOXIC SUBSTANCES JOURNAL.** ***Title Change.*** [Toxic subst. j.]. Vol. 1 (Summer 1979)-(1994). Academic Scholarly Publication. English. qt (4 issues). Taylor & Francis Ltd., Rankine Road, Basingstoke Hampshire, RG24 8PR United Kingdom. **Tel** 011 44 256 840366, FAX 011 44 256 479438, telex 858540. **(Subscription address:** Taylor & Francis Inc., 1900 Frost Road, Suite 101, Bristol PA 19007-1598.**) ED** George S. Dominguez. **LC** RA1190; .T67. **DD** 615.9/005. **CODEN** TSUJDP. **[CCC].** Index available. **Bk Rev. Ad Acc. Circ:** 500. available on microfilm and microfiche from University Microfilms International (UMI). Documents available from CASDDS, Documents on Demand. ***Continued by*** *Toxic Substance Mechanisms, 1076-9188.*
**Desc:** Provides a forum for examining all aspects of toxic

substances, with an emphasis on public policy considerations. The scope also encompasses the global perspective of toxic issues as well as govenment, public, and private sectors.
**Ind/Abst** Acad. Search (Jan. 1994-); AGRICOLA; Bus. Index (1985-?); Chem. Abstr.; Curr. Aware. Biol. Sci., CABS; Curr. Biotechnol.; EMBASE; Energy Inf. Abstr.; Environ. Abstr.; Environ. Period. Bibliogr.; Gen. BusinessFile (1985-?); Gen. Period. Index (1985-?); INFO-SOUTH Abstr.; Mag. Search; Manage. Contents (1979-?); Pollut. Abstr. Indexes; Risk Abstr.; Toxicol. Abstr. (19??-19??); Trade Ind. Index.

US/0192-6233
**TOXICOLOGIC PATHOLOGY.** See Medical Science and Technology-Pathology.

UK/0277-2248
**TOXICOLOGICAL AND ENVIRONMENTAL CHEMISTRY.** [Toxicol. environ. chem.]. Vol. 3, No. 3/4 (March 1981)-. Academic Scholarly Publication. English. ir. $847.00 (academic institutions), $1321.00 (corporate institutions). Gordon & Breach Science Publishers, PO Box 90, Reading RG1 8JL England. **Tel** 011 44 734 560080, FAX 011 44 734 568211. **ED** Otto Hutzinger and Roland W. Frei. **LC** RA1190; .T68. **NLM** W1 TO892Z. **CODEN** TECSDY. **[CCC].** Index available. **Bk Rev. Ad Acc. Pr Rev.** Documents available from Article Express International, The Genuine Article, BIOSIS Document Express, CASDDS. ***Continues*** *Toxicological and Environmental Chemistry Reviews, 0092-9867.*
**Desc:** An international journal devoted to the fundamental aspects of analysis, metabolism and general chemistry and biology of xenobiotic compounds and natural toxins as related to the environment and human health.
**Ind/Abst** AgBiotech News Inf.; Aquat. Sci. Fish. Abstr. (Computer File); Biodeter. Abstr. (1991-); Biol. Abstr. (-1984); Chem. Abstr.; Chem. Titles; Civ. Struct. Eng. Abstr.; Curr. Aware. Biol. Sci., CABS; Ei Page One; Elect. Comm. Abstr.; EMBASE; Eng. Index Annu.; Environ. Eng. Abstr.; Environ. Period. Bibliogr.; Food Sci. Technol. Abstr.; For. Abstr.; Helminthol. Abstr.; Index Vet.; Maize Abstr.; Mater. Sci. Eng. Abstr.; Nematol. Abstr.; Nutr. Abstr. Rev., Ser. A, Hum. Exp.; Life Sci. Collect.; Res. Alert; Rev. Agric. Entomol.; Rev. Med. Vet. Entomol.; Sci. Cit. Index; SCISEARCH; Small Anim. Abstr. Bibliogr.; Solid State Supercond. Abstr.; Weed Abstr.

FR/0249-6402
**TOXICOLOGICAL EUROPEAN RESEARCH.** (TOXICOLOGICAL EUROPEAN RESEARCH. RECHERCHE EUROPEENE EN TOXICOLOGIE.). [Toxicol. Eur. res.]. **Added/Corp** Societe Francaise de Toxicologie. **VFOAT** Recherche Europeene en Toxicologie. Vol.1 (Jan 1978)-. Academic Scholarly Publication. French (English). bm. **NLM** W1 TO894. **CODEN** TOERD9. Documents available from BIOSIS Document Express, CASDDS. ***Continues*** *European Journal of Toxicology and Environmental Hygiene, 0397-4693.*
**Ind/Abst** Biol. Abstr.; Chem. Abstr. (1978-1983); EMBASE; Index Med.; PESTDOC.

US
**TOXICOLOGICAL EVALUATIONS.** (1991)-. English. an. $39.00. Springer-Verlag New York Inc., 175 5th Avenue, New York NY 10010. **Tel** (212)460-1500, telex 232 235 SPB UR. **(Subscription address:** Springer Verlag New York Inc. / for North America, 44 Hartz Way, Secaucus NJ 07096.**)**
**Desc:** A study of hazards caused by industrial work substances.

US/0731-9193
**TOXICOLOGIST, THE.** (THE TOXICOLOGIST: AN OFFICIAL PUBLICATION OF THE SOCIETY OF TOXICOLOGY.). [Toxicologist]. **Added/Corp** Society of Toxicology. Vol. 1, No. 1 (Mar. 1981)-. Periodical. English. an (Dec.). $38.00 (includes postage). Society of Toxicology, 1101 14th Street Northwest, Suite 1100 A, Washington DC 20005. **Tel** (202)371-1393, FAX (202)371-1090. **ED** Shawn Lopez (editor's telephone: (703)438-3115). **LC** RA1190; .S626. **DD** 615.9/005. **[CCC]. Pr Rev. Circ:** 4,500 (ctrl).
**Desc:** Abstracts of papers presented during the Society of Toxicology annual meeting.

US/0140-5365
**TOXICOLOGY ABSTRACTS.** See Medical Science and Technology-Abstracting, Bibliographies and Statistics.

IE/0300-483X
**TOXICOLOGY (AMSTERDAM).** (TOXICOLOGY.). [Toxicology]. Vol. 1 (March 1973)-. Academic Scholarly Publication. English. Twenty-four times a year (8 vols.). $1635.00. Elsevier Science Ireland Ltd., Bay 15, Shannon Industrial Estate, Co Clare Ireland. **Tel** 011 353 61 471944. **ED** H.P. Witschi and K.J. Netter. **LC** RA1190; .T69. **DD** 615.9/005. **NLM** W1 TO896. **CODEN** TXCYAC. **[CCC]. Pr Rev.** available on microfilm and microfiche from University Microfilms International (UMI). Documents available from The Genuine Article, BIOSIS Document Express, CASDDS, ADONIS.
**Desc:** Original scientific papers on the biological effects arising from the administration of chemical compounds, principally to animals, tissues, or cells, but also to man.
**Ind/Abst** ADONIS; AgBiotech News Inf.; Biol. Abstr.; Calcium Calcif. Tissue Abstr.; Chem. Abstr.; Chem. Hazards Ind.; CSA Neuro. Abstr. (?-?); Curr. Contents Life Sci.; Curr. Ref. Fish Res.; EMBASE; Environ. Period. Bibliogr.; Fish Rev.; Food Sci. Technol. Abstr.; Geogr. Abstr. Human Geogr.; Health Saf. Sci. Abstr.; Helminthol. Abstr. (1991-); Index Med.; Lab. Hazards Bull.; NAPRALERT; Life Sci. Collect.; PESTDOC; Pig News Inf.; Pollut. Abstr. Indexes; Protozoolog. Abstr.; Ref. Upd. Basic Ed.; Ref. Upd. Deluxe Ed.; Res. Alert [Full Cov.]; Rev. Agric. Entomol.; Rev. Med. Vet. Mycology; Sci. Cit. Index; SCISEARCH; Toxicol. Abstr.; Weed Abstr.; Wildl. Rev.

US/0041-008X
**TOXICOLOGY AND APPLIED PHARMACOLOGY.** [Toxicol. appl. pharmacol.]. **Added/Corp** Society of Toxicology. Vol. 1 (Jan. 1959)-. Academic Scholarly Publication. English. mo. $999.00 US and Canada. Academic Press, Inc., 6277 Sea Harbor Drive, Orlando FL 32887. **Tel** (800)543-9534, (407)345-4100, FAX (407)363-9661. **ED** I. Glenn Sipes. **LC** RA1190; .S627. **DD** 615/.05. **NLM** W1 TO95. **CODEN** TXAPA9. **[CCC]. Pr Rev.** Documents available from The Genuine Article, BIOSIS Document Express, CASDDS.
**Desc:** Publishes original scientific research pertaining to action on tissue structure or function resulting from administration of chemicals, drugs, or natural products to animals or human. Articles address mechanistic approaches to physiological, biochemical, cellular, or molecular understanding of toxicologic/pathologic lesions and to methods used to describe these responses.
**Ind/Abst** AGRICOLA [Select. Cov.]; Biol. Abstr.; Calcium Calcif. Tissue Abstr.; Chem. Abstr.; Chem. Hazards Ind.; Chem. Titles; CSA Neuro. Abstr.; Curr. Aware. Biol. Sci., CABS; Curr. Contents Life Sci.; Dairy Sci. Abstr.; EMBASE; Energy Res. Abstr.; Fish Rev. (Jan. 1989-July 1992); Foods Adlibra; Health Saf. Sci. Abstr.; Helminthol. Abstr.; Index Med.; Ind. Hyg. Dig. (19??-); Int. Aerosp. Abstr.; Int. Pharm. Abstr.; Iowa Drug Inf. Serv. (1966-); Lab. Hazards Bull.; Med. Abstr. Newsl.; Microbiol. Abstr. Sect. C; NAPRALERT; Nutr. Abstr. Rev., Ser. A, Hum. Exp.; Nutr. Res. Newsl.; Life Sci. Collect.; PESTDOC; Pig News Inf.; Pollut. Abstr. Indexes; Protozoolog. Abstr.; Ref. Upd. Basic Ed.; Ref. Upd. Deluxe Ed.; Res. Alert [Full Cov.]; Rev. Agric. Entomol.; Rev. Med. Vet. Entomol.; Rev. Med. Vet. Mycology; Saf. Health Work; Sci. Cit. Index; SCISEARCH; Toxicol. Abstr.; Trop. Dis. Bull.; Weed Abstr.; Wildl. Rev. (Jan. 1989-July 1992).

●UK/1350-4592
**TOXICOLOGY AND ECOTOXICOLOGY NEWS.** (1993)-. English. qt (4 issues). £115.00 UK; $193.00 other. Taylor & Francis Ltd., Rankine Road, Basingstoke Hampshire, RG24 8PR United Kingdom. **Tel** 011 44 256 840366, FAX 011 44 256 479438, telex 858540. **(Subscription address:** Taylor & Francis Inc., 1900 Frost Road, Suite 101, Bristol PA 19007-1598.**)**

US/0748-2337
**TOXICOLOGY AND INDUSTRIAL HEALTH.** [Toxicol. ind. health]. Vol. 1, No. 1 (Sept. 1985)-. Academic Scholarly Publication. English. Six times a year. $148.00 US; $168.00 other. Princeton Scientific Publishing Company Inc., PO Box 2155, Princeton NJ 08543. **Tel** (609)683-4750, FAX (609)683-0838. **ED** James Withey and M A Mehlman. **LC** RA1199; .T686. **DD** 615.9. **NLM** W1; T095B. **CODEN** TIHEEC. **[CCC].** Index available. cum. index. **Bk Rev. Ad Acc, Adv Mgr:** M A Mehlman. **Pr Rev. Acid Free. Circ:** 700 (ctrl). Documents available from The Genuine Article, BIOSIS Document Express, CASDDS.
**Desc:** Publishes scientific data dealing with basic and applied research in the fields of toxicology, biochemical toxicology, genetic toxicology, pathology, and risk assessment associated with hazardous waste and ground water.
**Ind/Abst** Biol. Abstr. (1985-); Chem. Abstr. (1985-); Chem. Hazards Ind.; Curr. Aware. Biol. Sci., CABS; Curr. Contents Life Sci.; EMBASE; Index Med. (Vol. 1, No. 1, 1985-); Lab. Hazards Bull.; Nematol. Abstr.; Nutr. Res. Newsl.; Res. Alert [Full Cov.]; Rev. Agric. Entomol.; Rev. Med. Vet. Entomol.; Rev. Med. Vet. Mycology; Sci. Cit. Index; SCISEARCH; Soc. Sci. Cit. Index [Select. Cov.].

UK/0887-2333
**TOXICOLOGY IN VITRO.** (TOXICOLOGY IN VITRO : AN INTERNATIONAL JOURNAL PUBLISHED IN ASSOCIATION WITH BIBRA.). [Toxicol. in vitro]. **Added/Corp** British Industrial Biological Research Association. Vol. 1, No. 1 (1987)-. Academic Scholarly Publication. English. Six times a year. $425.00 The Americas; £285.00 other. Pergamon Press, An Imprint of Elsevier Science Ltd., The Boulevard, Langford Lane, Kidlington, Oxford OX5 1GB United Kingdom. **Tel** 011 44 865 843000, 011 44 865 843699, FAX 011 44 865 843010. **(Subscription address:** Elsevier Science Ltd. Oxford Fulfillment Centre, PO Box 800, Kidlington, Oxford OX5 1DX United Kingdom.**) ED** D. Acosta, Ian Purchase, and Sharat Gangolli. **DD** 615. **NLM** W1; TO95BH. **CODEN** TIVIEQ. **[CCC]. Bk Rev. Ad Acc. Pr Rev.** available on microfilm and microfiche from University Microfilms International (UMI). Documents available from The Genuine Article, BIOSIS Document Express, CASDDS, ADONIS.
**Desc:** Journal for the benefit of academic, government and industrial laboratories. It stimulates and promotes an approach to toxic substance testing that reduces the use of live animals, bringing the twin advantages of cost effectiveness and avoidance of ethical problems.
**Ind/Abst** ADONIS; Biol. Abstr. (1988-); Chem. Abstr. (1987-); CSA Neuro. Abstr. (?-?); Curr. Aware. Biol. Sci., CABS; Curr. Contents Life Sci.; EMBASE; Health Saf. Sci. Abstr.; Index Vet.; Nutr. Abstr. Rev., Ser. B, Live Feeds and Feed.; Pollut. Abstr. Indexes; Poult. Abstr.; Res. Alert [Full Cov.]; Rev. Agric. Entomol.; Rev. Med. Vet. Entomol.; Rev. Med. Vet. Mycology; Risk Abstr.; Sci. Cit. Index; SCISEARCH; Vet. Bull.; Toxicol. Abstr.

NE/0378-4274
**TOXICOLOGY LETTERS.** [Toxicol. lett.]. Vol. 1 (July 1977)-. Academic Scholarly Publication. English. Eighteen times a year (6 vols.). $1293.00. Elsevier Science Ireland Ltd., Bay 15, Shannon Industrial Estate, Co Clare Ireland. **Tel** 011 353 61 471944. **ED** H. Kappus and D.B. Menzel. **NLM** W1 TO95BL. **CODEN** TOLED5. **[CCC]. Pr Rev.** available on microfilm and microfiche from University Microfilms International (UMI). Documents available from The Genuine Article, BIOSIS Document Express, CASDDS, Documents on Demand, ADONIS.
**Desc:** A forum for research results in all areas of mammalian toxicology of sufficient novelty, importance and breadth of interest to warrant rapid publication.
**Ind/Abst** ADONIS; AGRICOLA [Select. Cov.]; Biol. Abstr.; Chem. Abstr.; Chem. Hazards Ind.; Chem. Titles; CSA Neuro. Abstr.; Curr. Contents Life Sci.; Curr. Ref. Fish Res.; EMBASE; Energy Inf. Abstr.; Environ. Abstr.; Food Sci. Technol. Abstr.; Health Saf. Sci. Abstr.; Index Med.; Index Vet.; Int. Nurs. Index; Int. Pharm. Abstr.; Lab. Hazards Bull.; Microbiol. Abstr. Sect. C; NAPRALERT; Nutr. Abstr. Rev., Ser. B, Live Feeds and Feed.; Nutr. Abstr. Rev., Ser. A, Hum. Exp.; Nutr. Res. Newsl.; Life Sci. Collect.; PESTDOC; Pollut. Abstr. Indexes; Protozoolog. Abstr.; Ref. Upd. Deluxe Ed.; Res. Alert [Full Cov.]; Rev. Agric. Entomol.; Rev. Med. Vet. Entomol.; Rev. Med. Vet. Mycology; Sci. Cit. Index; SCISEARCH; Soc. Sci. Cit. Index [Select. Cov.]; Vet. Bull.; Toxicol. Abstr.; Weed Abstr.; Wildl. Rev.

US/1051-7235
**TOXICOLOGY METHODS.** [Toxicol. methods]. Vol. 1, No. 1 (Mar. 1991)-. Academic Scholarly Publication. English. qt. $94.00 (individuals), $298.00 (institutions) US; $110.00 (individuals), $340.00 (institutions) other. Raven Press, 1185 Avenue of the Americas, 37th Floor, New York NY 10036. **Tel** (212)930-9500, (212)930-9604, FAX (212)869-3495, (212)302-8507, telex 640073. **LC** RA1221; .T69. **DD** 615.9/07/05. **NLM** W1; TO95BF. **CODEN** TOMEEB. **[CCC].** available on microfilm and microfiche from University Microfilms International (UMI). Documents available from CASDDS.
**Ind/Abst** Chem. Abstr.; Curr. Aware. Biol. Sci., CABS; Sci. Cit. Index.

UK/0041-0101
**TOXICON (OXFORD).** See Pharmacy and Pharmacology.

US/0145-6296
**VETERINARY AND HUMAN TOXICOLOGY.** See Veterinary Sciences.

UK/0049-8254
**XENOBIOTICA.** [Xenobiotica]. Vol. 1 (Jan. 1971)-. Academic Scholarly Publication. English (French and German). mo. £530.00 UK; $875.00 other. Taylor & Francis Ltd., Rankine Road, Basingstoke Hampshire, RG24 8PR United Kingdom. **Tel** 011 44 256 840366, FAX 011 44 256 479438, telex 858540. **(Subscription address:** Taylor & Francis Inc., 1900 Frost Road, Suite 101, Bristol PA 19007-1598.**) ED** G. G. Gibson. **NLM** W1 XE17. **CODEN** XENOBH. **[CCC]. Pr Rev.** available on microfilm and microfiche from University Microfilms International (UMI). Documents available from The Genuine Article, BIOSIS Document Express, CASDDS, ADONIS.
**Desc:** Covers three main areas: general xenobiochemistry, including the metabolism and disposition of drugs and environmental chemicals in animals, plants and micro-organisms, and the related methodology; molecular toxicology, publishing papers on mechanisms of toxicity and methodology directed to the study of toxicology at the molecular level; and clinical pharmacokinetics and metabolism.
**Ind/Abst** ADONIS; AGRICOLA [Select. Cov.]; Anal. Abstr.; Biol. Abstr.; Chem. Abstr.; Chem. Hazards Ind.; Chem. Titles; Curr. Aware. Biol. Sci., CABS; Curr. Biotechnol.; Curr. Contents Life Sci.; EMBASE; Environ. Period. Bibliogr.; Helminthol. Abstr.; Index Med.; Index Vet.; Lab. Hazards Bull.; Mass Spect. Bull.; NAPRALERT; Nutr. Abstr. Rev., Ser. A, Hum. Exp.; Life Sci. Collect.; PESTDOC; Pollut. Abstr. Indexes; Poult. Abstr.; Ref. Upd. Deluxe Ed.; Res. Alert [Full Cov.]; Rev. Agric. Entomol.; Rev. Med. Vet. Entomol.; Rev. Med. Vet. Mycology; Sci. Cit. Index; SCISEARCH; Vet. Bull.; Toxicol. Abstr.; Weed Abstr.

CC/1000-3002
**ZHONGGUO YAOLIXUE YU DULIXUE ZAZHI.** (CHUNG-KUO YAO LI HSUEH YU TU LI HSUEH TSA CHIH.). [Zhongguo yaolixue yu dulixue zazhi]. **Added/Corp** Chung-kuo Yao Li Hsueh Hui. **VFOAT** Chinese Journal of Pharmacology and Toxicology. (198?)-. Academic Scholarly Publication. Chinese. qt. $22.16. Chinese Journal of Pharmacology and Toxicology, 27 Tai-ping Road, 100850 Beijing, People's Republic of China. **(Subscription address:** China National Publishers / Industry & Trade, PO Box 782, Beijing, China.) **CODEN** ZYYZEW. Documents available from BIOSIS Document Express, CASDDS.
**Ind/Abst** Biol. Abstr. (1988-); Chem. Abstr.; EMBASE.

## TROPICAL MEDICINE

IT/0392-9515
**ACTA MEDITERRANEA DI PATOLOGIA INFETTIVA E TROPICALE.** (ARCHIVIO SICILIANO DI MEDICINA E CHIRURGIA. 2, ACTA MEDITERRANEA DI PATOLOGIA INFETTIVA E TROPICALE.). [Acta mediterr. patol. infett. trop.]. **VFOAT** Acta Mediterranea di Patologia Infettiva e Tropicale. Vol. 1, No. 1 (1982)-. Periodical. Italian (summaries and/or abstracts in English). Three times a year. L40000.00 Italy; L60000.00 other. Edizioni Carbone Alfonsa, Via G Daita 29, 90139 Palermo Italy. **Tel** 011 39 91 321273, FAX 39 91 322736. **ED** Serafino Mansueto. **NLM** W1; AR597T. ***Separated from*** *Archivio Siciliano di Medicina e Chirurgia, 0392-2049.*
**Desc:** Publishes original papers concerning epidemiological and clinic effects of infectious and tropical diseases, immunology, microbiology, and preventive medicine. Review of clinical case, description of the treatment, results, and casuistry of hospitalized patients.
**Ind/Abst** Trop. Dis. Bull.

SZ/0001-706X
**ACTA TROPICA.** [Acta trop.]. Vol. 1 (1944)-. Academic Scholarly Publication. English (German; summaries and/or abstracts in French). mo (3 volumes). Fl1443.00. Elsevier Science Publishers BV, PO Box 211, 1000 AE Amsterdam Netherlands. **Tel** 011 31 20 5803642, FAX 011 31 20 5862696, telex 15682. **ED** R. Geigy, R. Gigon, F. Speiser, and R. Tschudi. **LC** Q3; .A25. **DD** 505. **NLM** W1 AC951. **CODEN** ACTRAQ. **[CCC]. Bk Rev. Ad Acc. Pr Rev.** available on microfilm and microfiche from University Microfilms International (UMI). Documents available from The Genuine Article, BIOSIS Document Express, CASDDS.
**Desc:** International journal of biomedical sciences which gives attention to every aspect of this field relevant to human health, including veterinary medicine and biology in the tropics.
**Ind/Abst** AgBiotech News Inf.; AGRICOLA [Select. Cov.]; Biocont. News Inf. (1991-); Biol. Abstr.; Chem. Abstr.; Curr. Contents Life Sci.; EMBASE; Entomol. Abstr.; Fish Rev. (Jan. 1989-July 1992); Health Plan. Adminis.; Helminthol. Abstr. (19??-19??); Immunol. Abstr.; Index Med.; Index Vet.; Microbiol. Abstr. Sect. C; Nutr. Abstr. Rev., Ser. B, Live Feeds and Feed.; Nutr. Abstr. Rev., Ser. A, Hum. Exp.; Life Sci. Collect.; PESTDOC; Plant Breed. Abstr.; Protozoolog. Abstr.; Ref. Upd. Deluxe Ed.; Res. Alert [Full Cov.]; Rev. Med. Vet. Entomol.; Sci. Cit. Index; SCISEARCH; Small Anim. Abstr. Bibliogr.; Soc. Sci. Cit. Index [Select. Cov.]; Soils Fert.; Vet. Bull.; Trop. Dis. Bull.; Wildl. Rev. (Jan. 1989-July 1992).

SZ/0365-1541
**ACTA TROPICA. SUPPLEMENTUM.** (1945)-. Monographic series. English (French and German). Elsevier Science Publishers BV, PO Box 211, 1000 AE Amsterdam Netherlands. **Tel** 011 31 20 5803642, FAX 011 31 20 5862696, telex 15682. **LC** UNC. **NLM** W1 AC9511. **CODEN** ACTSBU.
**Ind/Abst** Health Plan. Adminis.; Index Med. (1966-1987).

SA/0253-052X
**AFRICAN JOURNAL OF CLINICAL AND EXPERIMENTAL IMMUNOLOGY.** ***Ceased.*** [Afr. j. clin. exp. immunol.]. Vol. 1 (Jan. 1980)-Ceased (July 1982). Academic Scholarly Publication. English. qt. Editor-in-Chief Fac Med UOFS, PO Box 339, G1 ZA-9300 Bloemfontein Republic of South Africa. **NLM** W1 AF518. **CODEN** AJCIDY. Documents available from BIOSIS Document Express, CASDDS.
**Ind/Abst** Biol. Abstr.; Chem. Abstr.; Life Sci. Collect.; Protozoolog. Abstr.

US/0002-9637
**AMERICAN JOURNAL OF TROPICAL MEDICINE AND HYGIENE, THE.** [Am. j. trop. med. hyg.]. **Added/Corp** American Society of Tropical Medicine and Hygiene. **VFOAT** Tropical Medicine and Hygiene. Vol. 1 (Jan. 1952)-. Academic Scholarly Publication. English. mo. $115.00 US; $170.00 other. Allen Press Inc., 810 East 10th Street, PO Box 1897, Lawrence KS 66044-8897. **Tel** (913)843-1221, (800)627-0629, FAX (913)843-1274. **ED** W. D. Tigertt. **LC** RC960; .A53. **DD** 616.9/88/305. **NLM** W1 AM527. **CODEN** AJTHAB. **[CCC]. Bk Rev. Pr Rev. Acid Free. Circ:** 3,800 (ctrl). Documents available from The Genuine Article, BIOSIS Document Express, CASDDS. ***Formed by the union of*** *American Journal of Tropical Medicine, 0096-6746* ***and*** *Journal of the National Malaria Society, 0096-7017.*
**Desc:** Publishes original research papers, reviews, book reviews, etc., which contribute to the advancement of knowledge of tropical medicine and hygiene.
**Ind/Abst** Abr. Index Med.; Abstr. Anthropol.; AgBiotech News Inf.; AGRICOLA [Select. Cov.]; Biocont. News Inf. (1991-); Biol. Abstr.; Chem. Abstr.; CSA Neuro. Abstr. (?-?); Curr. Aware. Biol. Sci., CABS; Curr. Contents Clin. Med.; Curr. Contents Life Sci.; Dairy Sci. Abstr.; EMBASE; Entomol. Abstr.; Health Plan. Adminis.; Helminthol. Abstr. (19??-19??); Immunol. Abstr.; Index Med.; INIS Atomindex [Micro.]; Irr. Drain. Abstr.; Microbiol. Abstr. Sect. B; Microbiol. Abstr. Sect. C; NAPRALERT; Nematol. Abstr.; Nutr. Abstr. Rev., Ser. B, Live Feeds and Feed.; Nutr. Abstr. Rev., Ser. A, Hum. Exp.; Life Sci. Collect.; PESTDOC; Pig News Inf.; Protozoolog. Abstr.; Ref. Upd. Deluxe Ed.; Res. Alert [Full Cov.]; Rev. Med. Vet. Entomol.; Rev. Med. Vet. Mycology; Rev. Plant Pathol.; Rural Dev. Abstr.; Sci. Cit. Index; SCISEARCH; Soc. Sci. Cit. Index [Select. Cov.]; Stat. Theory Method Abstr. (1961-1963); Trop. Dis. Bull.; Virol. AIDS Abstr.; Wildl. Rev.

BE/0365-6527
**ANNALES DE LA SOCIETE BELGE DE MEDECINE TROPICALE.** [Ann. soc. belge med. trop.]. **VFOAT** Annales van de Belgische Vereniging voor Tropische Geneeskunde. Vol. 52 (1972)-. Academic Scholarly Publication. Multiple languages (English, French and Dutch; summaries and/or abstracts in French, Dutch and English). Four times a year. 2800F. Association for the Society of Scientifique Medica Belgique, Avenue Circulaire 138A, B-1180 Brussels Belgium. **Tel** 011 32 2 3745158. **NLM** W1 AN341T. **CODEN** ASBMAX. **Pr Rev.** Documents available from The Genuine Article, BIOSIS Document Express, CASDDS. ***Continues*** *Annales des Societes Belges de Medecine Tropicale, de Parasitologie, et de Mycologie.*
**Ind/Abst** Biol. Abstr.; Chem. Abstr.; Curr. Contents Clin. Med.; EMBASE; Helminthol. Abstr. (1991-); Index Med.; Nutr. Abstr. Rev., Ser. B, Live Feeds and Feed.; Nutr. Abstr. Rev., Ser. A, Hum. Exp.; Life Sci. Collect.; Pig News Inf.; Protozoolog. Abstr.; Res. Alert [Full Cov.]; Rev. Med. Vet. Entomol.; Rev. Med. Vet. Mycology; Rev. Plant Pathol.; Sci. Cit. Index; SCISEARCH; Small Anim. Abstr. Bibliogr.; Soc. Sci. Cit. Index [Select. Cov.]; Trop. Dis. Bull.

UK/0003-4983
**ANNALS OF TROPICAL MEDICINE AND PARASITOLOGY.** [Ann. trop. med. parasitol.]. Vol. 1 (Feb. 1907)-. Academic Scholarly Publication. English. bm (6 issues). £167.00 UK and Europe; $300.00 other (institution). Harcourt Brace & Company Ltd., Foots Cray, High Street, Sidcup Kent DA14 5HP England. **Tel** 011 44 81 300 3322, FAX 011 44 81 309 0807. **(Subscription address:** W. B. Saunders Company / North America Subscriptions, c/o Periodicals, 6277 Sea Harbour Drive, 4th Floor, Orlando FL 32887.) **ED** W. Crewe. **LC** RC960. **NLM** W1 AN627P. **CODEN** ATMPA2. **[CCC]. Pr Rev.** available on microfilm from University Microfilms International (UMI). Documents available from The Genuine Article, BIOSIS Document Express, CASDDS. ***Supersedes*** *Liverpool School of Medicine. Memoir.*
**Desc:** A key international journal for research workers dealing with tropical diseases and with medical and veterinary parasitology and entomology in their broadest aspects.
**Ind/Abst** Anim. Breed. Abstr.; Biocont. News Inf. (1991-); Biol. Abstr.; Chem. Abstr.; Chemorecept. Abstr.; Curr. Aware. Biol. Sci., CABS; Curr. Contents Clin. Med.; Curr. Contents Life Sci.; Dairy Sci. Abstr.; EMBASE; Entomol. Abstr.; Fish Rev.; Health Plan. Adminis.; Helminthol. Abstr. (19??-19??); Immunol. Abstr.; Index Med.; Index Vet.; Microbiol. Abstr. Sect. B (19??-19??); Microbiol. Abstr. Sect. C; Nutr. Abstr. Rev., Ser. B, Live Feeds and Feed.; Nutr. Abstr. Rev., Ser. A, Hum. Exp.; Life Sci. Collect.; PESTDOC; Protozoolog. Abstr.; Res. Alert [Full Cov.]; Rev. Med. Vet. Entomol.; Rev. Med. Vet. Mycology; Rev. Plant Pathol.; Sci. Cit. Index; SCISEARCH; Small Anim. Abstr. Bibliogr.; Soc. Sci. Cit. Index [Select. Cov.]; Soils Fert.; Vet. Bull.; Trop. Dis. Bull.; Wildl. Rev.

UK/0272-4936
**ANNALS OF TROPICAL PAEDIATRICS.** [Ann. trop. paediatr.]. **Added/Corp** Liverpool School of Tropical Medicine. Vol. 1, No. 1 (March 1981)-. Periodical. English. qt (Mar., Jun., Sep. and Dec.). £138.00. Carfax Publishing Company, PO Box 25 Abingdon, Oxfordshire OX14 3UE England. **Tel** 011 44 235 555335, FAX (0279)31067, telex 817484. **(Subscription address:** US and Canada/ PO Box 2025, Dunnellon, FL 34430-2025; telephone:(904)489-6996) **ED** R. G. Hendrickse. **NLM** W1 AN627U. **CODEN** ATPAD9. **[CCC].** Index available. **Ad Acc. Pr Rev.** available on microfiche. Documents available from The Genuine Article, BIOSIS Document Express.
**Desc:** Provides an international forum for problems and achievements in child health and pediatrics in the tropics and sub-tropics, presenting papers on the full spectrum of diseases in childhood and the social and cultural background in which they appear.
**Ind/Abst** Biol. Abstr. (1984-); Cumul. Index Nurs. Allied Health Lit.; Curr. Aware. Biol. Sci., CABS; Curr. Contents Clin. Med.; Dairy Sci. Abstr.; EMBASE; Health Plan. Adminis.; Helminthol. Abstr. (19??-19??); Index Med.; Nutr. Abstr. Rev., Ser. A, Hum. Exp.; Protozoolog. Abstr.; Res. Alert [Select. Cov.]; Rev. Med. Vet. Mycology; Rural Dev. Abstr.; SCISEARCH; Soc. Sci. Cit. Index [Select. Cov.]; Soyabean Abstr.; Trop. Dis. Bull.

GW/0301-567X
**BEITRAEGE ZUR TROPISCHEN LANDWIRTSCHAFT UND VETERINARMEDIZIN.** [Beitr. trop. Landwirtsch. Veterinarmed.]. V. 11- 1973-. Academic Scholarly Publication. German (summaries and/or abstracts in English, French, Russian and Spanish; table of contents in English, French, Russian and Spanish). qt. 26.80F Switzerland; 28.40F other. Deutscher Judo Verband, Redaktion Ippon Segewaldweg 40, D 12557 Berlin Germany. **Tel** 011 49 711 210770, telex 051 678. **NLM** W1 BE461L. **CODEN** BTLVBR. Documents available from CASDDS. ***Continues*** *Beitrage zur Tropischen und Subtropischen Landwirtschaft und Tropenveterinarmedizin, 0005-8203.*
**Ind/Abst** AgBiotech News Inf.; Agric. Eng. Abstr. (1991-); Agrofor. Abstr. (19??-19??); Biodeter. Abstr.; Chem. Abstr.; Crop Physiol. Abstr.; Dairy Sci. Abstr.; EMBASE; Field Crop Abstr.; Food Sci. Technol. Abstr.; GeoRef; Grasslands For. Abstr.; Health Plan. Adminis.; Hortic. Abstr.; Index Med.; Index Vet.; Int. Dev. Abstr. (?-?); Irr. Drain. Abstr.; Nematol. Abstr.; Nutr. Abstr. Rev., Ser. B, Live Feeds and Feed.; Life Sci. Collect.; Pig News Inf.; Plant Breed. Abstr.; Plant Grow. Reg. Abstr.; Postharvest News Inf.; Protozoolog. Abstr.; Rev. Agric. Entomol.; Rev. Med. Vet. Mycology; Rev. Plant Pathol.; Rice Abstr.; Rural Dev. Abstr.; Seed Abstr.; Soils Fert.; Sorghum Mill. Abstr.; Soyabean Abstr.; Vet. Bull.; Weed Abstr.; World Agric. Econ.

FR
**BULLETIN DE LA SOCIETE DE PATHOLOGIE EXOTIQUE.** **See** Medical Science and Technology-Pathology.

II/0068-5372
**BULLETIN OF THE CALCUTTA SCHOOL OF TROPICAL MEDICINE.** **Added/Corp** Calcutta School of Tropical Medicine. Vol. 1 (July 1953)-. Bulletin. English. qt. **NLM** W1 BU844R.
**Ind/Abst** Index Med. (Apr. 1965-1973); Trop. Dis. Bull.

PL/0324-8542
**BULLETIN OF THE INSTITUTE OF MARITIME AND TROPICAL MEDICINE IN GDYNIA.** [Bull. Inst. Marit. Trop. Med. Gdyn.]. **Added/Corp** Instytut Medycyny Morskiej i Tropikalnej w Gdyni. **VFOAT** Biuletyn Instytutu Medycyny Morskiej i Tropiaklnej w Gdyni; Biulleten Instituta Morskoi i Tropicheskoi Meditsiny v Gdanske. Vol. 26, No. 1 (1975)-. Academic Scholarly Publication. English (summaries and/or abstracts in Polish and Russian). Twice a year. $30.00. Institute of Maritime and Tropical Medicine, Powstania Styczniowego 9B, 81519 Gdynia Poland. **Tel** 223011, FAX 233354, telex 0048-58. **ED** S. Tomaszunas. **NLM** W1 BU852U. **CODEN** BIMGDE. cum. index. **Bk Rev. Ad Acc. Pr Rev. Circ:** 600. Documents available from CASDDS. ***Continues*** *Biuletyn Instytutu Medycyny Morskiej w Gdansku, 0020-4463.*
**Ind/Abst** Chem. Abstr. (?-1990); EMBASE; Helminthol. Abstr. (1991-); Index Med.; Protozoolog. Abstr.; Rev. Med. Vet. Entomol.; Trop. Dis. Bull.

IV/0253-5580
**CARDIOLOGIE TROPICALE.** (CARDIOLOGIE TROPICALE / TROPICAL CARDIOLOGY.). [Cardiol. trop.]. **VFOAT** Tropical Cardiology. (1970)-. Periodical. English (French). Four times a year. 160.00F France & Africa; 200.00F others. Tropical Cardiology, PR Bertrand Hospital Nord, 13326 Marseille Cedex 15 France. **Tel** 011 33 91 968711. **NLM** W1 CA7698.
**Ind/Abst** Trop. Dis. Bull.

FR/0379-2269
**CHILDREN IN THE TROPICS.** (CHILDREN IN THE TROPICS / EDITED BY THE INSTITUT DE PEDIATRIE SOCIALE, UNIVERSITY OF DAKAR AND THE INTERNATIONAL CHILDREN'S CENTRE, PARIS.). [Child. trop.]. **Added/Corp** International Children's Centre. Universite de Dakar. Institut de Pediatre Sociale. Institut National de Sante Publique--Abidjan (Ivory Coast). No. 52 (1968)-. Newsletter. English (Spanish and French). Six times a year. $40.00. Centre International de L Enfrance / International Children's Centre, Chateau des Longchamp Bois de Boulogne, 75016 Paris France. **Tel** 44 30 20 00, FAX 45 25 73 67, telex 648 378 F. **ED** A. M. Masse-Raimbault. **LC** RJ103.T76; C47. **DD** 613/.0432/091305. **NLM** W1 CH694R. **Acid Free. Circ:** 15,000 (ctrl).
**Desc:** Articles aimed at providing practical and immediately usable information to members of the health team, teaching staff, and development workers working in developing countries.
**Ind/Abst** Trop. Dis. Bull.

US/0737-609X
**CRITICAL REVIEWS IN TROPICAL MEDICINE.** [Crit. rev. trop. med.]. (1982)-. Monographic series. English. ir. Price varies per volume. Plenum Press, 233 Spring Street, New York NY 10013-1578. **Tel** (212)620-8000, (800)221-9369, FAX

(212)463-0742, (212)807-1047, telex 23/421139. **ED** R.K. Chandra. **LC** RC960; .C74. **DD** 616.9/88/3. **NLM** W1 CR216Y.

FR/0013-7561
**ENFANT EN MILIEU TROPICAL, L'.** **See** Medical Science and Technology-Pediatrics.

US/0011-9059
**INTERNATIONAL JOURNAL OF DERMATOLOGY.** **See** Medical Science and Technology-Dermatology.

BL/0103-054X
**JORNAL SUL-TROPICAL DE MEDICINA / SOUTH TROPICAL JOURNAL OF MEDICINE.** **VFOAT** South Tropical Journal of Medicine. (Jan. 1988)-. Periodical. English (Portuguese). an (Jan.). $35.00. Norma Editora Ltda, Av Rio Branco 185 1711, 20040 Rio de Janeiro Brazil. **Tel** 31 857-691 0001-78. **NLM** W1; JO208M.
**Ind/Abst** Trop. Dis. Bull.

US
**JOURNAL OF THE ROYAL COLLEGE OF PHYSICIANS AND SURGEONS OF THE UNITED STATES OF AMERICA : JRCP&S.** **See** Medical Science and Technology-Surgery.

UK/0963-0880
**JOURNAL OF TROPICAL & GEOGRAPHICAL NEUROLOGY : THE OFFICIAL JOURNAL OF THE RESEARCH GROUP ON TROPICAL NEUROLOGY OF THE WORLD FEDERATION OF NEUROLOGY.** ***Ceased.*** **See** Medical Science and Technology-Neurology.

UK/0022-5304
**JOURNAL OF TROPICAL MEDICINE AND HYGIENE.** [J. trop. med. hyg.]. **Added/Corp** London School of Hygiene and Tropical Medicine. Vol. 10 (1907)-. Academic Scholarly Publication. English. bm (6 issues). $294.00 US & Canada; £172.50 Europe; £189.50 other. Blackwell Scientific Publications Ltd, Marston Book Services, PO Box 87, Oxford OX2 ODT UK. **Tel** 011 44 865 791155, FAX 011 44 865 791927, telex 837 515 MARDIS G. **ED** D. J. Bradley. **NLM** W1 JO966U. **CODEN** JTMHA9. **[CCC]**. Index available. **Bk Rev. Ad Acc. Pr Rev. Circ:** 870 (ctrl). available on microfilm and microfiche from University Microfilms International (UMI). Documents available from The Genuine Article, CASDDS. ***Continues*** *Journal of Tropical Medicine, 0301-5459.*
**Ind/Abst** Biocont. News Inf.; Chem. Abstr.; Curr. Aware. Biol. Sci., CABS; Curr. Contents Clin. Med.; Dairy Sci. Abstr.; EMBASE; Entomol. Abstr.; Helminthol. Abstr. (19??-19??); Hospit. Health Admin. Index; Index Med.; Index Vet.; Int. Dev. Abstr.; Microbiol. Abstr. Sect. B; Microbiol. Abstr. Sect. C; NAPRALERT; Nutr. Abstr. Rev., Ser. A, Hum. Exp.; Pig News Inf.; Protozoolog. Abstr.; Ref. Upd. Deluxe Ed.; Res. Alert [Full Cov.]; Rev. Med. Vet. Entomol.; Rev. Med. Vet. Mycology; Rural Dev. Abstr.; Sci. Cit. Index; SCISEARCH; Soc. Sci. Cit. Index [Select. Cov.]; Vet. Bull.; Trop. Dis. Bull.; Virol. AIDS Abstr.

UK/0142-6338
**JOURNAL OF TROPICAL PEDIATRICS (1980).** **See** Medical Science and Technology-Pediatrics.

FR/0025-682X
**MEDECINE TROPICALE.** (MEDECINE TROPICALE : REVUE DU CORPS DE SANTE COLONIAL.). [Med. trop.]. **Added/Corp** Corps de Sante Colonial (France) Ecole d'Application du Service de Sante des Troupes Coloniales (France) France. Service de Sante des Troupes d'Outre-mer. France. Service de Sante des Troupes de Marine. France. Service de Sante des Troupes Coloniales. Ecole d'Application et Centre d'Instruction et de Recherche. France. Service de Sante des Troupes d'Outre-mer. Ecole d'Application et Centre d'Instruction et de Recherche. France. Service de Sante des Troupes de Marine. Ecole d'Application et Centre d'Instruction et de Recherche. Vol. 1 (1941)-. Academic Scholarly Publication. French (summaries and/or abstracts in English). Four times a year. 250.00F. Institut de Medecine Tropicale, Parc du Pharo BP 46, 13998 Marseille Armees France. **Tel** 011 33 91 523568 ext 135. **ED** J. J. Pico. **NLM** W1; ME149. **CODEN** METRA2. Index available. **Bk Rev**, (Qty: 4/yr). **Ad Acc. Pr Rev. Circ:** 1,500 (ctrl). Documents available from BIOSIS Document Express, CASDDS. ***Continues*** *Annales de Medecine et de Pharmacie Coloniales.*
**Desc:** Original works in tropical medicine, epidemiology and public health.
**Ind/Abst** Biocont. News Inf.; Biol. Abstr.; Chem. Abstr.; EMBASE; Helminthol. Abstr. (19??-19??); Index Med.; Life Sci. Collect.; Protozoolog. Abstr.; Rev. Med. Vet. Entomol.; Rev. Med. Vet. Mycology; Small Anim. Abstr. Bibliogr.; Trop. Dis. Bull.

RU/0025-8326
**MEDICINSKAJA PARAZITOLOGIJA I PARAZITARNYE BOLEZNI.** (MEDITSINSKAIA PARAZITOLOGIIA I PARAZITARNYE BOLEZNI.). [Med. parazitol. parazit. bolezni]. **Added/Corp** Soviet Union. Ministerstvo Zdravookhraneniia. Soviet Union. Narodnyi Komissariat Zdravookhraneniia. **VFOAT** Medical Parasitology and Parasitic Diseases. Vol. 1, (1932)-. Academic Scholarly Publication. Russian (summaries and/or abstracts in English). Four times a year. $89.95. Izdatelstvo Meditsina / Russian Academy of Medical Sciences, Ulitsa Solyanka 14, 109801 Moscow Russia. **Tel** 011 95 297-05-04. **(Subscription address:** East View Publications Inc., 3020 Harbor Lane North, Suite 110, Minneapolis MN 55447.**)** **LC** RC960; .M4. **NLM** W1 ME796. **CODEN** MPPBAB. Index available. Documents available from BIOSIS Document Express, CASDDS. ***Supersedes*** *Tropicheskaia Meditsina i Veterinariia.*
**Ind/Abst** Biocont. News Inf.; Biol. Abstr.; Chem. Abstr.; EMBASE; Helminthol. Abstr. (1991-); Index Med.; Life Sci. Collect.; PESTDOC; Protozoolog. Abstr.; Rev. Med. Vet. Entomol.; Sel. Water Resour. Abstr.; Small Anim. Abstr. Bibliogr.

JA/0385-5643
**NETTAI IGAKU.** (NETTAI IGAKU. TROPICAL MEDICINE.). [Nettai igaku]. **Added/Corp** Nagasaki Daigaku. Nettai Igaku Kenkyusho. Nagasaki Daigaku. Fudobyo Kenkyusho. **VFOAT** Tropical Medicine. (1967)-. Periodical. Japanese (English). qt. Institute of Tropical Medicine, 12-4 Sakamoto-machi, 852 Nagasaki Japan. **NLM** W1 NE2342V. **CODEN** NETTAJ. Documents available from BIOSIS Document Express. ***Continues*** *Nagasaki Daigaku Fudobyo Kiyo.*
**Ind/Abst** Biol. Abstr.; EMBASE; Helminthol. Abstr. (1991-); Life Sci. Collect.; Protozoolog. Abstr.; Trop. Dis. Bull.

LB/0189-0964
**NIGERIAN MEDICAL PRACTITIONER, THE.** Vol. 1, No. 1 (Mar. 1981)-. Periodical. English. mo. **NLM** W1 NI41H.
**Ind/Abst** Trop. Dis. Bull.

JA/0304-2146
**NIPPON NETTAI IGAKKAI ZASSHI.** **VFOAT** Japanese Journal of Tropical Medicine and Hygiene. (1973)-. Periodical. Multiple languages (Japanese and English). qt. $55.00. Japanese Society of Tropical Medicine, 12 4 Sakamonto Machi, Nagasakiken 852 Japan. **Tel** 011 81 0958472111. **NLM** W1 NI924. ***Supersedes*** *Japanese Journal of Tropical Medicine, 0303-836X.*
**Ind/Abst** Biocont. News Inf.; Helminthol. Abstr. (1991-); Index Vet.; Protozoolog. Abstr.; Trop. Dis. Bull.

FR/0758-6868
**POPULATION ET SANTE TROPICALES.** [Popul. sante trop.]. (1983)-. Periodical. French. bm. **UDC** a61(6).
**Ind/Abst** Trop. Dis. Bull.

US/0895-5727
**PSYCHOTROPICS (RENO, NEV.).** (PSYCHOTROPICS.). [Psychotropics]. **Added/Corp** Truckee Meadows Hospital. (198?)-. Periodical. English. Four times a year (Jan., Apr., July, Oct.). $18.00 (regular) one year; $34.00 (regular) two years; $22.00 (library) one years; $42.00 (library) two years. Publicare, PO Box 6510, Reno NV 89513. **Tel** (702)852-7792. **ED** Ken Bender, Dr. Tom Alcins Ph.D., and Dr. Mike Irwin M.D. **DD** 615. **NLM** W1; PS78J. **[CCC]**. cum. index (Iss. #4, (Fall), annual.). **Bk Rev**, (Qty: 2). **Pr Rev. Circ:** 7,000.
**Desc:** Bulletin of psychopharmotropic developments by the multidisciplinary editorial board for mental health professionals.

US/0192-6640
**QUARTERLY BIBLIOGRAPHY OF MAJOR TROPICAL DISEASES.** Began with Vol. 1, No. 1 (4th Quarter, 1978)-. Bibliography. English. qt. Free. Special Programme for Research and Training in Tropical Diseases, World Health Organization, 1211 Geneva 27 Switzerland. **Tel** 92.38.09. **NLM** ZWC 680 Q1. **Circ:** 9,000 (ctrl).
**Desc:** Bibliographic listing of papers on tropical disease research appearing in world literature.
**Ind/Abst** Trop. Dis. Bull.

UK/0266-3775
**RECENT ADVANCES IN TROPICAL MEDICINE.** [Recent adv. trop. med.]. No. 1 (1985)-. English. ir. Longman Group Ltd., Fourth Avenue, Longman House, Harlow Essex CM19 5SR England. **Tel** 011 44 279 429655, FAX 011 44 279 431059, telex 81259. **ED** H.W. Gilles. **LC** RC960; .R36. **DD** 616.9/88/3. **NLM** W1; RE105YL.

CU/0375-0760
**REVISTA CUBANA DE MEDICINA TROPICAL.** [Rev. cuba. med. trop.]. V. 18, No. 1 (August 1966)-. Periodical. Spanish. Three times a year. $21.00 North America; $23.00 South America; $28.00 other. Ediciones Cubanas, Obispo 527, Altos ESQ Bernaza, CP 10100 Havana Cuba. **Tel** 011 632980, 631942, FAX 011 631011, telex 512337, 6540. **NLM** W1 RE362L. **CODEN** RCMTBF. **Circ:** 20,000 (ctrl). Documents available from BIOSIS Document Express, CASDDS. ***Continues*** *Revista Kuba de Medicina.*
**Desc:** A magazine specializing in tropical medicine, specifically parasitology. It also publishes papers on epidemiology, microbiology, and other related specialties.
**Ind/Abst** Biol. Abstr.; Chem. Abstr.; Helminthol. Abstr. (19??-19??); Index Med.; Index Vet.; Nematol. Abstr.; Protozoolog. Abstr.; Rev. Med. Vet. Entomol.; Rev. Med. Vet. Mycology; Rural Dev. Abstr.; Trop. Dis. Bull.

BL/0037-8682
**REVISTA DA SOCIEDADE BRASILEIRA DE MEDICINA TROPICAL.** **Added/Corp** Sociedade Brasileira de Medicina Tropical. Brazil. Superintendencia de Campanhas de Saude Publica. (19??)-. Periodical. Portuguese (English). Four times a year. $60.00. Faculdad Med Triangulo Mineiro, Caixa Postal 118, 38001 970 Uberaba MG Brazil. **Tel** 011 55 34 3127722 ext. 1255, FAX 011 55 34 3126640, telex 3206. **(Subscription address:** AV Rio Branco, 109 703 20 040, Rio de Janeiro, Brazil.**)** **ED** Prof. Aluizio Prata. Index available (bound in 4th issue). **Bk Rev. Ad Acc.** ctrl circ.
**Ind/Abst** EMBASE [Select. Cov.]; Helminthol. Abstr. (1991-); Index Med.; Index Vet.; Poult. Abstr.; Protozoolog. Abstr.; Rev. Med. Vet. Entomol.; Rev. Med. Vet. Mycology; Trop. Dis. Bull.

CR/0034-7744
**REVISTA DE BIOLOGIA TROPICAL.** [Rev. biol. trop.]. **Added/Corp** Universidad de Costa Rica. Vol. 1 (July 1953)-. Periodical. Spanish (English and Spanish). ir (Publishes two or three issues per year). $30.00. Universidad de Costa Rica / Editorial, Apartado 75, 2060 Ciudad Universitaria, San Jose Costa Rica. **Tel** 011 506 2247051, 2253133. **ED** Julian Monge-Najera. **LC** RC960; .R4. **DD** 616.9/88/305. **NLM** W1 RE377. **CODEN** RBTCAP. Index available (1953-1987). cum. index. **Bk Rev. Pr Rev. Circ:** 1,500 (ctrl). available on microfilm and microfiche from University Microfilms International (UMI). Documents available from The Genuine Article, BIOSIS Document Express, CASDDS.
**Desc:** Original research originating in the neotropics on general biology, ecology, botany, zoology (vertebrates and invertebrates).
**Ind/Abst** AGRICOLA; Agrofor. Abstr. (1991-); Biocont. News Inf. (1991-); Biodeter. Abstr. (1991-); Biol. Abstr.; Chem. Abstr.; Curr. Contents, Agric. Biol. Environ. Sci.; Ecol. Abstr. (?-?); Fish Rev.; For. Prod. Abstr. (1991-); For. Abstr.; Geogr. Abstr. Phys. Geogr. (?-?); Geol. Abstr.; Grasslands For. Abstr.; Helminthol. Abstr. (1991-); Hortic. Abstr.; Index Med.; Int. Dev. Abstr. (?-?); Irr. Drain. Abstr.; Nutr. Abstr. Rev., Ser. B, Live Feeds and Feed.; Life Sci. Collect.; Protozoolog. Abstr.; Res. Alert [Select. Cov.]; Rev. Agric. Entomol.; Rev. Med. Vet. Entomol.; Rice Abstr.; Seed Abstr.; Soils Fert.; Sug. Indus. Abstr.; Trop. Dis. Bull.; Wildl. Rev.

BL/0301-0406
**REVISTA DE PATOLOGIA TROPICAL.** (REVISTA DE PATOLOGIA TROPICAL : ORGAO OFICIAL DO INSTITUTO DE PATOLOGIA TROPICAL DA UNIVERSIDADE FEDERAL DO GOIAS.). [Rev. patol. trop.]. **Added/Corp** Universidade Federal de Goias. Instituto de Patologia Tropical. Vol. 1 (Jan./March 1972)-. Periodical. Portuguese (English). sa (2 issues). $50.00. Revista de Patologia Tropical, Caixa Postal 131, Goiania Goias 74000 Brazil. **Tel** 011 55 2510190. **ED** Sydney Schmidt.
**Desc:** Contains information on tropical medicine.
**Ind/Abst** Helminthol. Abstr. (1991-); Protozoolog. Abstr.; Rev. Med. Vet. Entomol.; Trop. Dis. Bull.

BL/0036-4665
**REVISTA DO INSTITUTO DE MEDICINA TROPICAL DE SAO PAULO.** [Rev. Inst. Med. Trop. Sao Paulo]. **Main/Corp** Instituto de Medicina Tropical de Sao Paulo. **Added/Corp** Universidade de Sao Paulo. Instituto de Medicina Tropical de Sao Paulo. (1959)-. Academic Scholarly Publication. Portuguese (English). bm. $200.00. Universidade de Sao Paulo / Medicina Tropical, Av Dr Eneas Carvalh Aguiar 470, 05403-000 Paulo Brazil. **Tel** (011)852 2174, FAX (011)852-3622. **ED** Thales de Brito. **NLM** W1 RE521H. **CODEN** RMTSAE. Index available. **Ad Acc. Pr Rev. Circ:** 1,300. available on microfilm from University Microfilms International (UMI). Documents available from The Genuine Article, CASDDS.
**Ind/Abst** Chem. Abstr. (1959-1983); Curr. Contents Life Sci.; EMBASE [Select. Cov.]; Helminthol. Abstr. (1991-); Index Med.; Nutr. Abstr. Rev., Ser. A, Hum. Exp.; Life Sci. Collect.; Protozoolog. Abstr.; Res. Alert [Full Cov.]; Rev. Med. Vet. Mycology; Sci. Cit. Index; SCISEARCH; Small Anim. Abstr. Bibliogr.; Trop. Dis. Bull.

EC/0048-7775
**REVISTA ECUATORIANA DE HIGIENE Y MEDICINA TROPICAL.** **Added/Corp** Guayaquil. Instituto Nacional de Higiene "Leopoldo Izquieta Perez". Vol. 1 (1944)-. Periodical. Spanish. Twice a year. Free on request. Instituto Nacional de Higiene, Casilla de Correos No 3961, Guayaquil Ecuador. **Tel** 593 4 281540, FAX 394189, telex 04-3334. **ED** Dr. Telmo Fernandez. **NLM** W1 RE524. **CODEN** REHMAG.

**Circ:** 3,500 (ctrl). Documents available from BIOSIS Document Express.
**Ind/Abst** Biol. Abstr. (?-1979)(-1979).

PL/0066-1945
**ROCZNIKI POMORSKIEJ AKADEMII MEDYCZNEJ IM. GEN. KAROLA SWIERCZEWSKIEGO W SZCZECINIE.** (ANNALES ACADEMIAE MEDICAE STETINENSIS.). [Rocz. Pomor. Akad. Med. im. gen. Karola Swierczewskiego Szczec.]. **Added/Corp** Pomorska Akademia Medyczna im. Generaa Karola Swierczewskiego w Szczecinie. **VFOAT** Roczniki Pomorskiej Akademii Medycznej Im. Gen. Karola Swierczewskiego w Szczecinie. Vol. 9 (1963)-. Academic Scholarly Publication. Polish (summaries and/or abstracts in Russian and English). an. Panstwowy Zakad Wydawnictw Lekarskich, Ul Duga 38/40, 00-238 Warszawa Poland. **(Subscription address:** ARS Polona, PO Box 1001, 00068 Warsaw Poland.**) NLM** W1 AN307F. **CODEN** RPMKAA. Documents available from CASDDS.
**Ind/Abst** Chem. Abstr.; EMBASE [Select. Cov.]; Index Med.

SZ
**TDR NEWS. Added/Corp** Special Programme for Research and Training in Tropical Diseases. Periodical. English (French and Portuguese). qt. **NLM** W1; TD15. ***Continues*** *Newsletter (Special Programme for Research and Training in Tropical Diseases).*
**Ind/Abst** Trop. Dis. Bull.

UK/0035-9203
**TRANSACTIONS OF THE ROYAL SOCIETY OF TROPICAL MEDICINE AND HYGIENE.** [Trans. R. Soc. trop. med. hyg.]. **Main/Corp** Royal Society of Tropical Medicine and Hygiene. Vol. 14 (May 1920)-. Academic Scholarly Publication. English. bm (6 issues). £50.00 (members), £105.00 (nonmembers). Royal Society of Tropical Medicine & Hygiene, Manson House, 26 Portland Place, London W1N 4EY England. **Tel** 011 44 71 580-2127, FAX 011 44 71 436-1389. **ED** J.R. Bakor. **NLM** W1 TR227M. **CODEN** TRSTAZ. Index available. **Bk Rev. Ad Acc. Pr Rev. Circ:** 4,000 (ctrl). Documents available from The Genuine Article, CASDDS. ***Continues*** *Transactions of the Society of Tropical Medicine and Hygiene.*
**Desc:** Articles on research and treatment of diseases in man and other animals in warm climates.
**Ind/Abst** AgBiotech News Inf.; AGRICOLA [Select. Cov.]; Biodeter. Abstr. (1991-); Chem. Abstr.; Curr. Aware. Biol. Sci., CABS; Curr. Contents Life Sci.; Dairy Sci. Abstr.; EMBASE; Entomol. Abstr.; Helminthol. Abstr. (19??-19??); Immunol. Abstr.; Index Med.; Index Vet.; Irr. Drain. Abstr.; Microbiol. Abstr. Sect. B; Microbiol. Abstr. Sect. A; Microbiol. Abstr. Sect. C; NAPRALERT; Nutr. Abstr. Rev., Ser. A, Hum. Exp.; Pig News Inf.; Poult. Abstr.; Protozoolog. Abstr.; Ref. Upd. Basic Ed.; Ref. Upd. Clinical Ed.; Ref. Upd. Deluxe Ed.; Res. Alert [Full Cov.]; Rev. Med. Vet. Entomol.; Rev. Med. Vet. Mycology; Rice Abstr.; Rural Dev. Abstr.; Sci. Cit. Index; SCISEARCH; Small Anim. Abstr. Bibliogr.; Soc. Sci. Cit. Index [Select. Cov.]; Soils Fert.; Vet. Bull.; Trop. Dis. Bull.; Virol. AIDS Abstr.; Weed Abstr.; Wildl. Rev.

NE/0041-3232
**TROPICAL AND GEOGRAPHICAL MEDICINE.** [Trop. geogr. med.]. Vol. 10 (1958)-. Academic Scholarly Publication. English (summaries and/or abstracts in Spanish). qt. £88.00 (institutions), £55.65 (individuals). Foris Publications, PO Box 509, 3300 AM Dordrecht Netherlands. **Tel** 011 31 78 510454. **ED** A de Geus. **NLM** W1 TR878M. **Bk Rev. Ad Acc. Pr Rev. Circ:** 1,100. available on microfilm and microfiche from University Microfilms International (UMI). Documents available from The Genuine Article. ***Continues*** *Documenta de Medicine Geographica et Tropica.*
**Desc:** Tropical diseases and disease in the tropics; tropical public health and geographical pathology; pathology and parasitology in the tropics and medical care in developing countries.
**Ind/Abst** AGRICOLA; Curr. Contents Life Sci.; Dairy Sci. Abstr.; EMBASE; Helminthol. Abstr. (19??-19??); Index Med.; Life Sci. Collect.; Protozoolog. Abstr.; Ref. Upd. Deluxe Ed.; Res. Alert [Full Cov.]; Rev. Med. Vet. Entomol.; Rev. Med. Vet. Mycology; Sci. Cit. Index; SCISEARCH; Soc. Sci. Cit. Index [Select. Cov.]; SportSearch; Trop. Dis. Bull.; Weed Abstr.

MY/0127-5720
**TROPICAL BIOMEDICINE.** [Trop. biomed.]. **Added/Corp** Malaysian Society of Parasitology and Tropical Medicine. Vol. 1, No. 1 (June 1984)-. Periodical. English. Twice a year (June & Dec.). $30.00 (institutions), $15.00 (individuals). Ibs Buku Sdn Bhd, B3 06 P J Industrial Park, Selangor Malaysia. **Tel** 011 60 03 7579283, 011 60 03 7579470. **NLM** W1; TR88E. **CODEN** TRBIEN. Documents available from BIOSIS Document Express.
**Ind/Abst** Biocont. News Inf. (1991-); Biol. Abstr. (1985-); Helminthol. Abstr. (1991-); Index Vet.; Nutr. Abstr. Rev., Ser. A, Hum. Exp.; Protozoolog. Abstr.; Rev. Med. Vet. Entomol.; Vet. Bull.; Trop. Dis. Bull.

UK/0041-3240
**TROPICAL DISEASES BULLETIN. See** Medical Science and Technology-Abstracting, Bibliographies and Statistics.

UK/0049-4755
**TROPICAL DOCTOR.** [Trop. doct.]. **Added/Corp** Royal Society of Medicine (Great Britain). Vol. 1 (Jan. 1971)-. Academic Scholarly Publication. English. qt. $70.00 US; £32.00 UK & Europe; £36.00 other. Royal Society of Medicine Press, 1 Wimpole Street, London W1M 8AE England. **Tel** 011 44 71 2902928. **ED** M. E. Molyngux. **LC** RC960; .T67. **DD** 616.9/88/305. **NLM** W1 TR88G. **CODEN** TPDCAV. **[CCC].** Index available. cum. index. **Bk Rev. Pr Rev. Circ:** 1,500. available on microfilm and microfiche from University Microfilms International (UMI). Documents available from The Genuine Article, BIOSIS Document Express, ADONIS.
**Desc:** Contains contributions on prevention, management and treatment of prevalent diseases in tropical countries. Also provides information on primary health care and community medicine.
**Ind/Abst** ADONIS; Biol. Abstr.; Cumul. Index Nurs. Allied Health Lit.; Curr. Contents Clin. Med.; Dairy Sci. Abstr.; EMBASE; Helminthol. Abstr. (19??-19??); Index Med.; Nutr. Abstr. Rev., Ser. A, Hum. Exp.; Life Sci. Collect.; Protozoolog. Abstr.; Res. Alert [Select. Cov.]; Rev. Med. Vet. Entomol.; Soc. Sci. Cit. Index [Select. Cov.]; Trop. Dis. Bull.

II/0250-636X
**TROPICAL GASTROENTEROLOGY.** (TROPICAL GASTROENTEROLOGY : OFFICIAL JOURNAL OF THE DIGESTIVE DISEASES FOUNDATION.). [Trop. gastroenterol.]. **Added/Corp** Digestive Diseases Foundation (India). Vol. 1, No. 1 (Jan.-Mar. 1980)-. Periodical. English. qt. $35.00. Digestive Diseases Foundation, New Delhi, India. **(Subscription address:** Prints India, 11 Darya Ganj, New Delhi 110002 India.**) NLM** W1 TR88L.
**Ind/Abst** Index Med.

US/0041-3275
**TROPICAL MEDICINE AND HYGIENE NEWS.** [Trop. med. hyg. news]. **Added/Corp** American Society of Tropical Medicine and Hygiene. (Feb. 1952)-. English. bm. (Non-members free on request on exchange basis only). American Society of Tropical Medicine & Hygiene, 6436 31st Street NW, Washington DC 20015. **Tel** (301)496-6721. **LC** RC960; .A5318. **DD** 616.9/88/3. **NLM** W1 TR881. **CODEN** TMHNAT. Documents available from BIOSIS Document Express. ***Supersedes*** *Tropical Medicine News.*
**Ind/Abst** Biol. Abstr. (19??-); Trop. Dis. Bull. (19??-).

GW/0177-2392
**TROPICAL MEDICINE AND PARASITOLOGY.** [Trop. med. parasitol.]. **Added/Corp** Deutsche Tropenmedizinische Gesellschaft. Deutsche Gesellschaft fuer Technische Zusammenarbeit. Vol. 36, No. 1 (March 1985)-. Academic Scholarly Publication. English. qt. $211.00. Georg Thieme Verlag Stuttgart, Postfach 301120, D 70451 Stuttgart Germany. **Tel** 011 49 711 89310, FAX 011 49 711 8931298, telex 7 252 275 GTVD. **(Subscription address:** Thieme Medical Publishers Inc., 381 Park Avenue South, New York NY 10016.**) ED** D W Buttner, R Garms, R Korte, D Mehlitz. **NLM** W1; TR882. **CODEN** TMPAEY. **[CCC]. Pr Rev.** available on microfilm from University Microfilms International (UMI). Documents available from The Genuine Article, CASDDS, ADONIS. ***Continues*** *Tropenmedizin und Parasitologie, 0303-4208.*
**Desc:** Of interest to physicians engaged in institutes of tropical diseases, physicians in human and in veterinary medicine, research laboratories of the pharmaceutical industry, hospital physicians and residents in the tropics and subtropics, missionary doctors, doctors engaged in development aid work, bacteriologists (especially virologists), immunologists, hematologists.
**Ind/Abst** ADONIS; AgBiotech News Inf.; AGRICOLA; Chem. Abstr. (1985-); Curr. Aware. Biol. Sci., CABS; Curr. Contents Life Sci.; EMBASE; Helminthol. Abstr. (19??-19??); Immunol. Abstr.; Index Med. Vol. 36, No. 1, 1985- (V36N1, 1985-); Index Vet.; Microbiol. Abstr. Sect. A; Microbiol. Abstr. Sect. C; PESTDOC; Pig News Inf.; Protozoolog. Abstr.; Res. Alert [Full Cov.]; Rev. Med. Vet. Entomol.; Rural Dev. Abstr.; Sci. Cit. Index; SCISEARCH; Soc. Sci. Cit. Index [Select. Cov.]; Vet. Bull.; Trop. Dis. Bull.

NR/0253-4851
**TROPICAL VETERINARIAN.** [Trop. vet.]. **Added/Corp** University of Ibadan. Faculty of Veterinary Medicine. (Aug. 1983)-. Periodical. English. sa. $50.00 (personal subscription), $80.00 (institution), $12.00 (airmail postage). University of Ibadan Department of Veterinary Pathology, Ibadan Nigeria. **Tel** 011 234 61 390880, telex 62652. **ED** Dr B E Olufemi, Telephone: 022 400550 Ext 2078. **NLM** W1; TR888. **CODEN** TRVTDJ. Index available. **Bk Rev,** (Qty: 5). **Ad Acc, Adv Mgr:** Dr S A Agbede, **Tel** 022 400550 Ext 1538. **Pr Rev. Circ:** 200. Documents available from BIOSIS Document Express.
**Desc:** International journal devoted to all aspects of health and disease of animals in the tropics.
**Ind/Abst** AGRICOLA [Full Cov.]; Biol. Abstr. (1988-); Fish Rev. (Jan. 1989-July 1992); Helminthol. Abstr. (19??-19??); Index Vet.; Nutr. Abstr. Rev., Ser. B, Live Feeds and Feed.; Life Sci. Collect. (1985-); Poult. Abstr.; Protozoolog. Abstr.; Wildl. Rev. (Jan. 1989-July 1992).

NR/0794-4845
**TROPICAL VETERINARIAN IBADAN.** ***Ceased.*** [Trop. Vet.blb.]. (19??)-(19??). Periodical. English. sa. University of Ibadan Department of Veterinary Pathology, Ibadan Nigeria. **Tel** 011 234 61 390880, telex 62652. **DD** 636.089'05.

TH/0858-0375
**TROPMED NEWSLETTER. Added/Corp** SEAMEO Regional Tropical Medicine and Public Health. **VFOAT** Newsletter. Vol. 1 No.1 (Mar. 1990)-. Newsletter. English. qt.
**Ind/Abst** Helminthol. Abstr. (1991-); Nutr. Abstr. Rev., Ser. A, Hum. Exp.; Protozoolog. Abstr.

UK/0080-4711
**YEAR BOOK - ROYAL SOCIETY OF TROPICAL MEDICINE AND HYGIENE.** [Year book, R. Soc. Trop. Med. Hyg.]. **Added/Corp** Royal Society of Tropical Medicine and Hygiene. (1920)-. Periodical. English. an. £15.00. Royal Society of Tropical Medicine & Hygiene, Manson House, 26 Portland Place, London W1N 4EY England. **Tel** 011 44 71 580-2127, FAX 011 44 71 436-1389. **NLM** W1 YE375. **Ad Acc. Circ:** 3,500 (ctrl). ***Continues*** *Year Book - Society of Tropical Medicine and Hygiene, London.*
**Desc:** Covers laws of the society, and contains a list of members, alphabetically and by country.

KO/0375-5207
**YONSEI REPORTS ON TROPICAL MEDICINE.** [Yonsei rep. trop. med.]. V. 1- 1970-. Periodical. English. an. Yonsei University, Institute of Tropical Medicine, Seoul Korea. **NLM** W1 YO683. **CODEN** YRTMA6. Documents available from CASDDS.
**Ind/Abst** Chem. Abstr.; EMBASE; Life Sci. Collect.

## UROLOGY AND NEPHROLOGY

US/1046-1051
**A.U.A. TODAY.** [A.U.A. today]. **Added/Corp** American Urological Association. **VFOAT** AUA Today. **VAT** American Urological Association Today. (Jan. 1988)-. Periodical. English. mo. $109.00 (individual), $129.00 (institution) US; $144.00 (individual), $164.00 (institution). Williams & Wilkins Company, 428 East Preston Street, Baltimore MD 21202-3993. **Tel** (410)528-4000, (800)638-6423, FAX (410)528-8596, telex 87669. **(Subscription address:** Williams & Wilkins, PO Box 64380, Baltimore MD 21264.**) DD** 616. **[CCC].** Documents available from Quick Copies.
**Desc:** Source for news and developments in urology.

US/0742-0374
**ABMS DIRECTORY OF CERTIFIED UROLOGISTS.** ***Title Change.*** [ABMS dir. certif. urol.]. **Added/Corp** American Board of Medical Specialties. American Board of Urology. **VFOAT** A.B.M.S. Directory of Certified Urologists. 1st Ed. (1983)-(19??). Directory. English. be. American Board of Medical Specialties, 1 Rotary Center, Suite 805, Evanston IL 60201. **Tel** (708)491-9091. **LC** RC870; .A25. **DD** 616.6/0025/73. **NLM** WJ 22; AA1 A1. **Bk Rev. Ad Acc. Circ:** 1,250 (ctrl). ***Continued by*** *Official American Board of Medical Specialties (ABMS) Directory of Board Certified Urologists, 0000-149X.*
**Desc:** Biographical listing of certified medical specialists.

BE/0001-7183
**ACTA UROLOGICA BELGICA.** [Acta urol. Belg.]. **Main/Corp** Societe Belge d'Urologie. Vol. 23 (1955)-. Academic Scholarly Publication. French (English, Spanish, German and Italian; summaries and/or abstracts in English). Four times a year. 2800F Belgium; 3800F other. Association des Societes Scientifiques Medicales Belges, Avenue Circulaire 138A, B 1180 Brussels Belgium. **Tel** 011 32 2 3745158. **ED** Christian Bouffioux. **NLM** W1 AC95524K. **CODEN** AUBEAN. Index available in last issue of volume--attached. **Bk Rev. Ad Acc. Circ:** 600. Documents available from BIOSIS Document Express, CASDDS. ***Continues*** *Journal Belge d'Urologie.*
**Desc:** Covers clinical and investigative papers in urology.
**Ind/Abst** Biol. Abstr.; Chem. Abstr.; EMBASE [Select. Cov.]; Health Plan. Adminis.; Index Med.; Life Sci. Collect.

IT/0394-2511
**ACTA UROLOGICA ITALICA.** (ACTA UROLOGICA ITALICA : ORGANO UFFICIALE DELLA SOCIETA ITALIANA DI UROLOGIA.). [Acta urol. ital.]. **Added/Corp** Societa Italiana di Urologia. Societa Italiana di Urologia. Congresso Nazionale. Vol. 1, No. 1 (Jan./Feb. 1987)-. Periodical. Italian (English). Six times a year. L105000. Societa Italian Urologia, DIP URO Barcci, Un Sapienza Policlin, Umberto 1, 00161 Rome Italy. **Tel** 011 39 6 490853. **NLM** W1; AC95524P. **CODEN** AUITE5.
**Ind/Abst** EMBASE.

SP/0213-2885
**ACTAS DE LA FUNDACION PUIGVERT : UROLOGIA, NEFROLOGIA, ANDROLOGIA / INSTITUTO DE UROLOGIA, NEFROLOGIA, ANDROLOGIA, HOSPITAL DE LA SANTA CRUZ Y SAN PABLO.** **Added/Corp** Fundacion Puigvert. Instituto de Urologia, Nefrologia, y Andrologia. Vol. 1, No. 1 (1982)-. Periodical. Spanish (summaries and/or abstracts in English). Four times a year. 6000ptas Spain; 9000ptas other. Pulso Ediciones SA, Sant Elies 21 4-Art, 08006 Barcelona Spain. **Tel** 011 34 3 2000877, FAX 011 34 3 2022117. **NLM** W1; AC959G. Index available. **Ad Acc.** ***Continues*** *Anales de la Fundacion Puigvert, 0303-4690.*
**Desc:** Official journal of Fundacion Puigvert.
**Ind/Abst** Indice Med. Esp.

SP/0210-4806
**ACTAS UROLOGICAS ESPANOLAS.** [Actas urol. esp.]. **Added/Corp** Asociacion Espanola de Urologia. Vol. 1 (Jan./Feb. 1977)-. Periodical. Spanish (summaries and/or abstracts in English and French). Ten times a year. $140.00. Ene Ediciones SL, Paseo de la Habana 204 Local 1, 28016 Madrid Spain. **Tel** 011 34 1 3459819, 011 34 1 3459820. **NLM** W1 AC967H.
**Ind/Abst** EMBASE; Index Med.; Indice Med. Esp.

FR/0567-8811
**ACTUALITES NEPHROLOGIQUES DE L'HOPITAL NECKER.** [Actual. nephrol. Hop. Necker]. **Added/Corp** Hopital Necker, Paris. Clinique des Maladies Metaboliques. (1960)-. Academic Scholarly Publication. French. an. 693.52F France; 729.75F EEC countries; 778.40F others. UD Union Distributor, 106 rue du Petit LeRoy, F 94550 Chevilly LaRue France. **Tel** 011 33 1 41802020. **NLM** W1 AC9953. **CODEN** ANQNA8. Documents available from CASDDS.
**Desc:** Lectures from the hospital's clinic of metabolics.
**Ind/Abst** Chem. Abstr.; EMBASE.

US/0084-5957
**ADVANCES IN NEPHROLOGY FROM THE NECKER HOSPITAL.** [Adv. nephrol. Necker Hosp.]. **Added/Corp** Hopital Necker Enfants-Malades (Paris, France). Vol. 1, (1971)-. Academic Scholarly Publication. English. ir. Price varies per volume. Mosby Year Book Inc., 11830 Westline Industrial Drive, St Louis MO 63146. **Tel** (800)325-4177, (314)872-8370, FAX (314)432-1380, telex 44-2402. **LC** RC902.A1; A36. **DD** 616.6/1/005. **NLM** W1 AD684. **CODEN** ANGYBQ. **[CCC].** available on microfilm from University Microfilms International (UMI). Documents available from CASDDS.
**Ind/Abst** Chem. Abstr.; Health Plan. Adminis.; Index Med.

●US/1073-4449
**ADVANCES IN RENAL REPLACEMENT THERAPY.** (A.ADVANCES IN RENAL REPLACEMENT THERAPY : A JOURNAL OF THE NATIONAL KIDNEY FOUNDATION.). [Adv. renal replace. ther.]. **Added/Corp** National Kidney Foundation. Vol. 1, No. 1 (Apr. 1994)-. Periodical. English. qt. $90.00 (individual), $109.00 (institutions) US; $106.00 (individual), $125.00 (institution) other. W.B. Saunders Company, A Subsidiary of Harcourt Brace Jovanovich, Inc., The Curtis Center/Suite 300, Independence Square West, Philadelphia PA 19106-3399. **Tel** (215)238-7800 or, 5587, FAX (215)238-7883, telex 173146. **(Subscription address:** W. B. Saunders Company / North America Subscriptions, c/o Periodicals, 6277 Sea Harbour Drive, 4th Floor, Orlando FL 32887.**)** **DD** 616. **NLM** W1; AD83P.

US/0894-4385
**ADVANCES IN UROLOGY.** [Adv. urol.]. Vol. 1 (1988)-. Periodical. English. an. $75.00. Mosby Year Book Inc., 11830 Westline Industrial Drive, St Louis MO 63146. **Tel** (800)325-4177, (314)872-8370, FAX (314)432-1380, telex 44-2402. **LC** RC870; .A38. **DD** 616.6/005. **NLM** W1; AD884. **[CCC].**

GW/0001-7868
**AKTUELLE UROLOGIE.** [Aktuel. urol.]. (1974)-. Academic Scholarly Publication. German (summaries and/or abstracts in English). bm (6 issues). $227.00. Georg Thieme Verlag Stuttgart, Postfach 301120, D 70451 Stuttgart Germany. **Tel** 011 49 711 89310, FAX 011 49 711 8931298, telex 7 252 275 GTVD. **(Subscription address:** Thieme Medical Publishers Inc., 381 Park Avenue South, New York NY 10016.**)** **NLM** W1 AK996K. **[CCC].** available on microfilm from University Microfilms International (UMI). Documents available from The Genuine Article. ***Continues*** *Actuelle Urologie;* ***Absorbed*** *Zeitschrift feur Urologie und Nephrologie, 0044-3611.*
**Ind/Abst** Curr. Contents Clin. Med.; EMBASE; Energy Res. Abstr.; Life Sci. Collect. (1977-); Res. Alert [Select. Cov.]; SCISEARCH.

US/0272-6386
**AMERICAN JOURNAL OF KIDNEY DISEASES.** (AMERICAN JOURNAL OF KIDNEY DISEASES : THE OFFICIAL JOURNAL OF THE NATIONAL KIDNEY FOUNDATION.). [Am. j. kidney dis.]. **Added/Corp** National Kidney Foundation. **VFOAT** AJKD. Vol. 1, No. 1 (July 1981)-. Academic Scholarly Publication. English. mo. $186.00 (individuals), $317.00 (institutions), US; $329.00 (individuals), $347.00 (institutions) other. W.B. Saunders Company, A Subsidiary of Harcourt Brace Jovanovich, Inc., The Curtis Center/Suite 300, Independence Square West, Philadelphia PA 19106-3399. **Tel** (215)238-7800 or, 5587, FAX (215)238-7883, telex 173146. **(Subscription address:** W. B. Saunders Company / North America Subscriptions, c/o Periodicals, 6277 Sea Harbour Drive, 4th Floor, Orlando FL 32887.**)** **ED** Robert G. Luke. **LC** Discard. **DD** 616. **NLM** W1 AM473. **[CCC].** **Pr Rev.** Documents available from The Genuine Article, CASDDS.
**Ind/Abst** Chem. Abstr.; Curr. Contents Clin. Med.; EMBASE; Health Plan. Adminis.; Index Med.; Int. Pharm. Abstr.; Mod. Med.; Ref. Upd. Clinical Ed.; Ref. Upd. Deluxe Ed.; Res. Alert [Full Cov.]; Rev. Med. Vet. Mycology; Sci. Cit. Index; SCISEARCH; Soc. Sci. Cit. Index [Select. Cov.].

SZ/0250-8095
**AMERICAN JOURNAL OF NEPHROLOGY.** [Am. j. nephrol.]. (April 1981)-. Academic Scholarly Publication. English. bm (6 issues). $423.00. S. Karger AG, Allschwilerstrasse 10, PO Box - Postfach - Case Postale, CH-4009 Basel Switzerland. **Tel** 011 41 61 306-1111, FAX 011 41 61 306-1234, telex CH 962 652. **ED** S. G. Massry, V. M. Campese, M. Benson. **NLM** W1 AM494M. **CODEN** AJNED9. **[CCC].** Index available. **Ad Acc.** **Pr Rev.** available on microfilm and microfiche. Documents available from The Genuine Article, BIOSIS Document Express, CASDDS.
**Desc:** Aims to improve the clinical care of adult and pediatric nephrology patients. Editorial scope ranges from studies on the biochemistry and immunology of kidney diseases to new knowledge on such established clinical problems as dialysis, transplantation, and hypertension. Presents information in a readable way with illustrations in order to encourage its immediate integration into practice. In addition to invited reviews and original papers, there are several additional features, including panel evaluations of challenging cases, briefing on legal and political developments, and a quiz to be solved by readers with a referenced discussion of the correct answer.
**Ind/Abst** Biol. Abstr.; Chem. Abstr.; Curr. Contents Clin. Med.; EMBASE; Health Plan. Adminis.; Index Med. (1981-); Life Sci. Collect.; Ref. Upd. Deluxe Ed.; Res. Alert [Full Cov.]; Sci. Cit. Index; SCISEARCH; Soc. Sci. Cit. Index [Select. Cov.].

SP/0303-4690
**ANALES DE LA FUNDACION PUIGVERT.** [An. Fund. Puigvert]. (1971)-. Periodical. Spanish. San Elias 21 4 2A, 08006 Barcelona Spain. **NLM** W1 AN149P.
**Ind/Abst** EMBASE.

US/8750-0779
**ANNA JOURNAL.** **See** Medical Science and Technology-Nursing.

FR/0003-4401
**ANNALES D'UROLOGIE.** [Ann. urol.]. Vol. 1 (Feb. 1967)-. Academic Scholarly Publication. French (summaries and/or abstracts in English, German and Spanish). ir (7 issues). 1345.00F France; 1900.00F other. Semaine de Hopitaux, 31 Boulevard de la Tour-Maubourg, 75007 Paris, France. **Tel** 011 33 1 40 62 64 00. **NLM** W1 AN407. **CODEN** AUROAV. **[CCC].** **Bk Rev.** **Ad Acc.** **Pr Rev.** **Circ:** 3,900. Documents available from The Genuine Article, BIOSIS Document Express, CASDDS. ***Continues in part*** *Annales de Chirurgie, 0003-3944.*
**Ind/Abst** Biol. Abstr.; Chem. Abstr. (1985); Curr. Contents Clin. Med.; EMBASE; Health Plan. Adminis.; Index Med.; Protozoolog. Abstr.; Res. Alert [Select. Cov.]; SCISEARCH.

US
**ANNUAL CONTRACTORS' CONFERENCE : PROGRAM.** **Added/Corp** National Institute of Arthritis, Metabolism, and Digestive Diseases. Artificial Kidney-Chronic Uremia Program. 6th (1973)-. English. an. US Department of Health and Human Services National Institutes of Health, 9000 Rockville Pike, Bethesda MD 20892. **Tel** (301)496-9291, FAX (301)496-2443. ***Continues*** *Contractors' Conference of Conference the Artificial Kidney Program of the National Institute of Arthritis and Metabolic Diseases. Annual Contractors' Conference.*

IT
**ARCHIVIO ITALIANO DI UROLOGIA ANDROLOGIA.** (19??)-. English. Five times a year. L87000 Italy. Masson S.P.A, Via Statuto 2/4, 20121 Milan Italy. **Tel** 011 39 2 63671, FAX 011 39 2 6367211. ***Continues*** *Archivio Urologia Nefrologia.*

IT
**ARCHIVIO UROLOGIA NEFROLOGIA.** ***Title Change.*** English. Five times a year. Masson S.P.A, Via Statuto 2/4, 20121 Milan Italy. **Tel** 011 39 2 63671, FAX 011 39 2 6367211. ***Continues*** *Archivio Italiano di Urologia Nefrologia Andrologia.* ***Continued by*** *Archivio Italiano di Urologia Andrologia.*

SP/0004-0614
**ARCHIVOS ESPANOLES DE UROLOGIA.** [Arch. esp. urol.]. (1944)-. Periodical. Spanish (English). Ten times a year. 12000ptas (individual), 115500ptas (institution) Spain; £140.00 Europe, £160.00 other. Bok SA, San Gregorio 8 3 PTA 4, 28004 Madrid Spain. **Tel** 011 34 1 3196001, FAX 011 34 1 3197768. **ED** Dr. E. Perez Castro. **NLM** W1 AR718N. **[CCC].** Index available. cum. index. **Bk Rev.** **Ad Acc,** **Adv Mgr Tel** 34 1 319 6001. **Pr Rev.** **Circ:** 2,500 (ctrl).
**Ind/Abst** EMBASE; Health Plan. Adminis.; Index Med. (June 1963-May 1966); Indice Med. Esp.

●US/1063-5777
**ATLAS OF THE UROLOGIC CLINICS OF NORTH AMERICA.** [Atlas urol. clin. N. Am.]. Vol. 1, No. 1 (Apr. 1993)-. Periodical. English. sa (April and October). $94.00 (nonsubscribers); $74.00 (subscribers) US; $119.00 (ninsubscribers), $99.00 (subscribers) other. W.B. Saunders Company, A Subsidiary of Harcourt Brace Jovanovich, Inc., The Curtis Center/Suite 300, Independence Square West, Philadelphia PA 19106-3399. **Tel** (215)238-7800 or, 5587, FAX (215)238-7883, telex 173146. **(Subscription address:** W. B. Saunders Company / North America Subscriptions, c/o Periodicals, 6277 Sea Harbour Drive, 4th Floor, Orlando FL 32887.**)** **ED** Dr. Martin I. Resnik. **DD** 616. **NLM** W1; AT56R.
**Desc:** Articles cover the techniques and problems involved in urologic surgery. Also includes drawings and photographs.

US/0740-7386
**AUA UPDATE SERIES.** [AUA updat. ser.]. **Added/Corp** American Urological Association. Office of Education. **VFOAT** Update Series. **VAT** American Urological Association Update Series. Vol. 1, Lesson 1 (1981)-. English. Forty times a year. $295.00. AUA Office of Education, 6750 West Loop South, Suite 900, Bellaire TX 77401. **Tel** (713)665-7500. **ED** Thomas P Ball Jr, 118 Paseo Encinal, San Antonio, TX 78212. **LC** Discard. **NLM** W1 AU14D. Index available. cum. index. **Circ:** 3,500.
**Desc:** Series of 40 original articles describing most recent techniques and changes in urology. Self-study program can be used for continuing medical education credits.

BG/1015-0889
**BANGLADESH RENAL JOURNAL.** (BANGLADESH RENAL JOURNAL : OFFICIAL ORGAN OF RENAL ASSOCIATION, BANGLADESH.). [Bangladesh renal j.]. **Added/Corp** Bangladesh Renal Association. (198?)-. Periodical. English. sa. $7.50 Bangladesh; $10.00 other. Bangdalesh Renal Association, Department of Neurology, Institute of Postgraduate Medicine and Research, 100 Dhaka Bangdalesh. **NLM** W1; BA644R. **CODEN** BRJOEJ.
**Ind/Abst** EMBASE.

SZ/0250-3212
**BEITRAEGE ZUR UROLOGIE.** [Beitr. Urol.]. Vol. 1 (1979)-. Monographic series. German. an. 100.00F (approx. per volume). S. Karger AG, Allschwilerstrasse 10, PO Box - Postfach - Case Postale, CH-4009 Basel Switzerland. **Tel** 011 41 61 306-1111, FAX 011 41 61 306-1234, telex CH 962 652. **ED** H. Melchior. **NLM** W1 BE461P. **CODEN** BEURDP. **[CCC].** Documents available from BIOSIS Document Express.
**Desc:** Covers experimental and applied urology. Monographic issues covering all aspects of urology, diagnosis and therapy of prostate cancer, and solving of kidney stones; for urologists, nephrologists, and oncologists.
**Ind/Abst** Biol. Abstr.

UK/0007-1331
**BRITISH JOURNAL OF UROLOGY.** (BRITISH JOURNAL OF UROLOGY : OFFICIAL JOURNAL OF THE BRITISH ASSOCIATION OF UROLOGICAL SURGEONS.). [Br. j. urol.]. **Added/Corp** British Association of Urological Surgeons. Vol. 1 (March 1929)-. Academic Scholarly Publication. English. mo (12 issues). $268.00 US & Canada; £156.00 Europe; £173.00 other. Blackwell Scientific Publications Ltd, Marston Book Services, PO Box 87, Oxford OX2 ODT UK. **Tel** 011 44 865 791155, FAX 011 44 865 791927, telex 837 515 MARDIS G. **NLM** W1 BR646. **CODEN** BJURAN. **[CCC].** cum. index. **Bk Rev.** **Ad Acc.** **Pr Rev.** available on microfilm and microfiche from University Microfilms International (UMI). Documents available from The Genuine Article, BIOSIS Document Express, CASDDS, ADONIS.
**Desc:** Features original articles on urological subjects, including nephrology, from all over the world. Profusely illustrated with x-ray reproductions, diagrams and drawings.
**Ind/Abst** ADONIS; Biol. Abstr.; Calcium Calcif. Tissue Abstr.; Chem. Abstr.; Curr. Aware. Biol. Sci., CABS; Curr. Contents Clin. Med.; EMBASE; Health Plan. Adminis.; Helminthol. Abstr. (19??-19??); Index Med.; Index Vet.; Microbiol. Abstr. Sect. B (19??-19??); Mod. Med.; Nutr. Res. Newsl.; Life Sci. Collect.; Ref. Upd. Deluxe Ed.; Res. Alert [Full Cov.]; Rev. Med. Vet. Entomol.; Rev. Med. Vet. Mycology; Sci. Cit. Index; SCISEARCH; Soc. Sci. Cit. Index [Select. Cov.].

UK/0260-0196
**BUTTERWORTHS INTERNATIONAL MEDICAL REVIEWS. UROLOGY.**
[Butterworths int. med. rev. Urol.]. **VFOAT** Urology. 1-. Monographic series. English. Price varies per volume. Butterworth Heinemann Publishers, Linacre House, Jordan Hill, Oxford OX2 8DP England. **Tel** 011 44 865 310366. **UDC** 616.6. **NLM** W1; BU99U.

SZ/1012-6694
**CHILD NEPHROLOGY AND UROLOGY.**
***Ceased.*** [Child nephrol. urol.]. (1989)-Vol. 12, (1992). Periodical. English. Four times a year (one volume per year). S. Karger AG, Allschwilerstrasse 10, PO Box - Postfach - Case Postale, CH-4009 Basel Switzerland. **Tel** 011 41 61 306-1111, FAX 011 41 61 306-1234, telex CH 962 652. **ED** C Giordano, B H Broecker, N G De Santo, J W Duckett, R D Jeffs, J W Kaplan, F Santos, R J Schottmeijer. **NLM** W1; CH667R. **CODEN** CNUREW. **[CCC].** Index available. cum. index. **Ad Acc. Pr Rev. Circ:** 1,200 (ctrl). available in microform. Documents available from The Genuine Article, BIOSIS Document Express. ***Continues*** *International Journal of Pediatric Nephrology, 0391-6510.*
**Desc:** This journal, already well established in its field, has now extended it remit to cover all aspects of pediatric nephrology and urology. It presents the reader with original papers derived from international clinical and basic research into these specialities of growing interest and importance. Articles are published in two main sections; the one containing detailed findings from recent clinical investigation, the other a regular series of informative case reports. 'Child Nephrology and Urology' constitutes an indispensable source for all those concerned with and active in, pediatric nephrology and urology and their associated disciplines.
**Ind/Abst** Biol. Abstr.; Curr. Contents Clin. Med.; EMBASE; Health Plan. Adminis.; Index Med. (1989-); Ref. Upd. Deluxe Ed.; Res. Alert [Full Cov.]; Sci. Cit. Index (19??-19??); SCISEARCH.

GW/0301-0430
**CLINICAL NEPHROLOGY.** [Clin. nephrol.]. Vol. 1 (Jan./Feb. 1973)-. Academic Scholarly Publication. English. mo. $172.00 (individuals), $207.00 (institutions). Dustri-Verlag, Dr Karl Feistle, Postfach 49, D 82032 Deisenhofen Germany. **Tel** 011 49 89 6138610, FAX 011 49 89 6135412. **ED** Reinhold Kluthe. **NLM** W1 CL731N. **CODEN** CLNHBI. **[CCC].** Index available. **Bk Rev. Ad Acc. Pr Rev.** ctrl circ. Documents available from The Genuine Article, BIOSIS Document Express, CASDDS.
**Desc:** Information on the latest developments in clinical nephrology.
**Ind/Abst** Biol. Abstr.; Chem. Abstr.; CSA Neuro. Abstr. (?-?); Curr. Aware. Biol. Sci., CABS; Curr. Contents Life Sci.; EMBASE; Energy Res. Abstr. (Oct. 1977-); Health Plan. Adminis.; Index Med.; Nutr. Abstr. Rev., Ser. B, Live Feeds and Feed.; Nutr. Abstr. Rev., Ser. A, Hum. Exp.; Life Sc. Collect.; Protozoolog. Abstr.; Ref. Upd. Deluxe Ed.; Res. Alert [Full Cov.]; Rev. Med. Vet. Mycology; Rev. Plant Pathol.; Sci. Cit. Index; SCISEARCH.

US/0091-1682
**CLINICAL TRENDS IN UROLOGY.** ***Ceased.*** **Added/Corp** Burroughs Wellcome and Company. Vol. 1 (May 1972)-Ceased (19??). Periodical. English. bm. Science & Medicine Publishing Company, 909 3rd Avenue, New York NY 10022. **NLM** W1 CL798N.

US/0164-7032
**CNSW NEWSLETTER.** **Main/Corp** National Kidney Foundation. Council of Nephrology Social Workers. **VAT** Council of Nephrology Social Workers Newsletter. (19??)-. Periodical. English. qt. Free to members. National Kidney Foundation, 30 East 33rd Street, Suite 1100, New York NY 10016. **Tel** (212)889-2210, (800)622-9010, FAX (212)689-9261. **ED** Mary Strope. **Circ:** 1,000 (ctrl).
**Desc:** Covers the field of nephrology social work and activities of the CNSW. Geared toward CNSW membership.

US/0899-837X
**CONTEMPORARY DIALYSIS & NEPHROLOGY.** [Contemp. dial. nephrol.]. **VFOAT** Contemporary Dialysis and Nephrology; CD&N; CD and N. Vol. 8, No. 1 (Jan. 1987)-. Periodical. English. mo. $42.00 US; $47.00 Canada & Mexico; $67.00 other. Contemporary Dialysis Inc, 6300 Variel Avenue, Suite I, Woodland Hills CA 91367. **Tel** (818)704-5555, FAX (818)704-6500. DD 616. **NLM** W1; CO769MH. **[CCC].** ***Continues*** *Contemporary Dialysis & Nephrology Magazine, 0885-9108.*

US/0161-9934
**CONTEMPORARY ISSUES IN NEPHROLOGY.** [Contemp. issues nephrol.]. Vol. 1 (1978)-. Academic Scholarly Publication. English. ir. Price varies per volume. Churchill Livingstone, 1-3 Baxter's Place, Leith Walk, Edinburgh EH1 3AF Scotland. **Tel** 011 44 31 556 2424, FAX 011 44 31 558 1278, telex 727511. **(Subscription address:** US and Canada/ Churchill Livingstone Inc., 5 South 250 Frontenac Road, Naperville, IL 60563; (telephone: (800)553-5426 or (708)416-3939)) **ED** B. M. Brenner and J. H. Stein. **DD** 616. **NLM** W1 CO769MR. **CODEN** CISND8. Documents available from CASDDS.
**Desc:** Monograph series containing up-to-date, comprehensive, concise and practical reviews of the pathogenesis, clinical significance and management of key areas within the domain of nephrology.
**Ind/Abst** Chem. Abstr.

US/0278-1700
**CONTEMPORARY NEPHROLOGY.**
[Contemp. nephrol.]. (1981)-. Academic Scholarly Publication. English. ir. Price varies per volume. Plenum Press, 233 Spring Street, New York NY 10013-1578. **Tel** (212)620-8000, (800)221-9369, FAX (212)463-0742, (212)807-1047, telex 23/421139. **ED** Saulo Klahr and Shaul G. Massry. **LC** Discard. **NLM** W1 CO769MX. **CODEN** CONHD7. **[CCC].** Documents available from CASDDS.
**Ind/Abst** Chem. Abstr. (1981-1983).

US/1042-2250
**CONTEMPORARY UROLOGY.** [Contemp. urol.]. **Added/Corp** Medical Economics Company. (1989)-. Periodical. English. mo. $89.00 US; $109.00 other. Medical Economics Publishing, Five Paragon Drive, Second Floor, Montvale NJ 07645. **Tel** (800)432-4570, (201)358-2210. **(Subscription address:** Fulco Medical Economics, PO Box 3000, Denville NJ 07834.) **ED** James E. Swan. **DD** 616. **NLM** W1; CO77N. **Circ:** 9,000.
**Desc:** Provides information on the disorders and clinical problems related to urology.

CN/1185-2526
**CONTEMPORARY UROLOGY (MISSISSAUGA).** (CONTEMPORARY UROLOGY.). [Contemporary urology]. **Added/Corp** Thomson Healthcare Communications. (July/Aug. 1990)-. Periodical. English. qt. Limited free distribution. Thomson Healthcare, 1120 Birchmount Road, Suite 200, Scarborough Ontario M1K 5G4 Canada. **Tel** (905)750-8900. **DD** 616.6/005.

SZ/0302-5144
**CONTRIBUTIONS TO NEPHROLOGY.**
[Contrib. nephrol.]. Vol. 1 (1975)-. Monographic series. English. ir. 200.00F (approx. per volume). S. Karger AG, Allschwilerstrasse 10, PO Box - Postfach - Case Postale, CH-4009 Basel Switzerland. **Tel** 011 41 61 306-1111, FAX 011 41 61 306-1234, telex CH 962 652. **ED** G. M. Berlyne and S. Giovannetti. **LC** UNC. **NLM** W1 CO778UN. **CODEN** CNEPDD. **[CCC].** Documents available from BIOSIS Document Express, CASDDS.
**Desc:** The speed of developments in nephrology has been fueled by the promise that new findings may improve the care of patients suffering from renal disease. Participating in these rapid advances, this series has released a number of volumes that explore problems of immediate importance for clinical nephrology. Focus ranges from discussion of innovative treatment strategies to critical evaluations of investigative methodology.
**Ind/Abst** Biol. Abstr.; Chem. Abstr.; Cumul. Index Nurs. Allied Health Lit.; Energy Res. Abstr. (Dec. 1981-); Index Med.; Nutr. Abstr. Rev., Ser. A, Hum. Exp.; Ref. Upd. Deluxe Ed.

CN/0383-0330
**COURIER (MONTREAL).** (COURIER.). **VFOAT** Le Courrier. V. 1- Oct. 1969-. Periodical. English (French). qt. Kidney Foundation of Canada, Suite 200, 5780 Decelles Avenue, Montreal Quebec H3S 2C7 Canada. **DD** 616.6/1/006271. **UDC** 616.61.

US/0743-8036
**CURRENT LITERATURE IN NEPHROLOGY.** ***Ceased.*** [Curr. lit. nephrol.]. (198?)-(19??). English. mo. Current Literature Publications, 1513 E Street, Bellingham WA 98225-3007. **Tel** (202)671-6664, telex 551152 CURLIT BELL. **ED** Jon C Ransom. **DD** 616. **Circ:** 1,200.
**Desc:** Bibliography of articles on clinical nephrology.

UK/0951-9629
**CURRENT MEDICAL LITERATURE / NEPHROLOGY AND UROLOGY.** [Curr. med. lit., Nephrol. urol.]. **VFOAT** Nephrology and Urology. (1987)-. Periodical. English. qt. £20.00 UK; 40.00 US; £20.00 other. Current Medical Literature Ltd., 40-42 Osnaburgh Street, London NW1 3ND England. **Tel** 011 44 71 4658377, FAX 011 44 71 4658380. **(Subscription address:** Royal Society Medicine Services, 1 Wimpole Street, London W1M 8AE England.) **DD** 016.6166. **Pr Rev.** ctrl circ.
**Desc:** Reviews of current articles published in the field of nephrology and urology.

US/0148-4265
**CURRENT NEPHROLOGY.** (1977)-. Academic Scholarly Publication. English. an. $81.95. Mosby Year Book Inc., 11830 Westline Industrial Drive, St Louis MO 63146. **Tel** (800)325-4177, (314)872-8370, FAX (314)432-1380, telex 44-2402. **LC** RC902.A1; C86. **DD** 616.6/1. **NLM** W1 CU799E. **CODEN** CUNED6. **[CCC].** Documents available from CASDDS.
**Ind/Abst** Chem. Abstr.

●US/1062-4821
**CURRENT OPINION IN NEPHROLOGY AND HYPERTENSION.** [Curr. opin. nephrol. hypertens.]. **VFOAT** Current Opinion in Nephrology & Hypertension. Vol. 1, No. 1 (Oct. 1992)-. Periodical. English. Six times a year. $169.95 (individual); $345.50 (institution). Current Science, 20 North 3rd Street, Philadelphia PA 19106. **Tel** (215)574-2266, (800)552-5866, FAX (215)574-2270. **DD** 616. **NLM** W1; CU799GFN. **[CCC].**

UK/0963-0643
**CURRENT OPINION IN UROLOGY.** Vol. 1, No. 1 (Oct. 1991)-. Periodical. English. Six times a year. $169.95 (individual); $345.50 (institution). Current Science / England, Middlesex House, 34-42 Cleveland Street, London W1P 5FB England. **Tel** 011 44 71 580 8393, 011 44 71 323 0323, FAX 011 44 81 580 1938. **(Subscription address:** Current Science, 20 North 3rd Street, Philadelphia PA 19106.) **NLM** W1; CU799GII. **CODEN** CUOUEQ. **[CCC].** Documents available from BIOSIS Document Express.
**Ind/Abst** Biol. Abstr.; Curr. Aware. Biol. Sci., CABS.

US/1046-5111
**CURRENT PROBLEMS IN UROLOGY.**
***Ceased.*** (1991)-(Nov. 1992). Periodical. English. bm. Mosby Year Book Inc., 11830 Westline Industrial Drive, St Louis MO 63146. **Tel** (800)325-4177, (314)872-8370, FAX (314)432-1380, telex 44-2402.
**Desc:** Each issue presents an in-depth treatise on a single urologic topic. To provide coverage of the encompassing diseases and disorders seen in urologic practice, a "core curriculum" of 24 to 30 topics in areas of oncology, pediatrics, infection and stones, and infertility and impotence will be rotated over a four or five year period.

US/1052-4010
**CURRENT PROBLEMS IN UROLOGY.**
***Ceased.*** [Curr. prob. urol.]. Vol. 1, No. 1 (Mar. 1991)-(1992). Periodical. English. bm. Mosby Year Book Inc., 11830 Westline Industrial Drive, St Louis MO 63146. **Tel** (800)325-4177, (314)872-8370, FAX (314)432-1380, telex 44-2402. **DD** 616. **NLM** W1; CU804U.

US/0731-5910
**CURRENT TRENDS IN UROLOGY.**
***Ceased.*** [Curr. trends urol.]. Vol. 1 (1981)-(19??). English. ir. Williams & Wilkins Company, 428 East Preston Street, Baltimore MD 21202-3993. **Tel** (410)528-4000, (800)638-6423, FAX (410)528-8596, telex 87669. **(Subscription address:** US/ PO Box 64380, Baltimore, MD 21264-4380; Japan/ Igaku- Shoin MYW Ltd, 1-28-36 Hongo, Bunkyo-Ku Tokyo 113 Japan; European/ The Broadway House, 2-6 Fulham Broadway, London SW6 1AA England; telephone: (800)638-6423) **ED** Martin I Resnick. **UDC** 616.6. **NLM** W1 CU822T. Documents available from Quick Copies.

US/0167-8205
**DEVELOPMENTS IN NEPHROLOGY.**
[Dev. nephrol.]. Vol. 1 (1981)-. Academic Scholarly Publication. English. ir. Price varies per volume. Kluwer Academic Publishers / Massachusetts, PO Box 358, Accord Station, Hingham MA 02018. **Tel** (617)871-6600. **(Subscription address:** Kluwer Academic Publishers / Netherlands, PO Box 322, 3300 AH Dordrecht Netherlands.) **LC** UNC. **DD** 616.6/1/005. **NLM** W1; DE998EB. **CODEN** DNEPDO. Documents available from BIOSIS Document Express, CASDDS.
**Ind/Abst** Biol. Abstr.; Chem. Abstr.

US/0164-9507
**DIALOGUES IN PEDIATRIC UROLOGY.**
**See** Medical Science and Technology-Pediatrics.

FR
**ENCYCLOPEDIE MEDICO CHIRURGICALE / TECHNIQUES CHIRURGICALES. UROLOGIE.** French. Editions Techniques, 141 rue de Javel, 75747 Paris Cedex 15 France. **Tel** 011 33 1 45589100.

US/0275-2298
**END-STAGE RENAL DISEASE ANNUAL REPORT TO CONGRESS.** [End-stage renal dis. annu. rep. Congr.]. **Main/Corp** U. S. Health Care Financing Administration. Office of Special Programs. 2d-1979/80-. English. an. Health Care Financing Administration, 6325 Security Boulevard, Room 700, Baltimore MD 21207. **Tel** (410)966-3000, FAX (410)966-5267. **UDC** 616.61(047.1)(73). **NLM** W2 A H615E. ***Continues*** *End-Stage Renal Disease Program, Annual Report to Congress.*

SZ/0302-2838
**EUROPEAN UROLOGY.** [Eur. urol.]. **Added/Corp** European Association of Urology. Vol. 1 (1975)-. Academic Scholarly Publication. English. Eight times a year. $614.00. S. Karger AG, Allschwilerstrasse 10, PO Box - Postfach - Case Postale, CH-4009 Basel Switzerland. **Tel** 011 41 61 306-1111, FAX 011 41 61 306-1234, telex CH 962 652. **ED** C. C. Schulman. **NLM** W1 EU735. **CODEN** EUURAV. **[CCC].** Index available. **Ad Acc. Pr Rev.** available on microfilm; available on microfiche. Documents available from The Genuine Article, BIOSIS Document Express, CASDDS.
**Desc:** Contains original articles on a wide range of urological problems. Carefully selected articles offer useful information on such topics as oncology, impotence, infertility, pediatrics, lithiasis and infections. Recent advances in techniques, instrumentation, surgery and pediatric urology are supported by topical reviews and

papers on applied research to provide readers with a complete guide to international developments in urology. The journal's value as a practical reference for all urologists is further enhanced by clear illustrations and the convenient organization of contributions under separate section headings.
**Ind/Abst** Biol. Abstr.; Calcium Calcif. Tissue Abstr.; Chem. Abstr.; Curr. Contents Clin. Med.; EMBASE; Health Plan. Adminis.; Helminthol. Abstr.; Index Med.; Mod. Med.; Nutr. Res. Newsl.; Life Sci. Collect.; Protozoolog. Abstr.; Ref. Upd. Deluxe Ed.; Res. Alert [Full Cov.]; Sci. Cit. Index; SCISEARCH.

UK/0968-7645
**EUROPEAN UROLOGY UPDATE SERIES.** [Eur. urol. update ser.]. (1992)-. Periodical. English. bm. $185.00. European Board of Urology Education Committee, PO Box 25285, 3001 HG Rotterdam Netherlands. **Tel** 011 31 10 4366665, FAX 011 31 10 4366669. **ED** H.N. Whitfield. **DD** 616.6. ctrl circ.

NE/0014-4320
**EXCERPTA MEDICA. SECTION 28. UROLOGY AND NEPHROLOGY. See** Medical Science and Technology-Abstracting, Bibliographies and Statistics.

SZ/1018-7782
**EXPERIMENTAL NEPHROLOGY.** (1993)-. Periodical. English. bm. $423.00. S. Karger AG, Allschwilerstrasse 10, PO Box - Postfach - Case Postale, CH-4009 Basel Switzerland. **Tel** 011 41 61 306-1111, FAX 011 41 61 306-1234, telex CH 962 652. **ED** L. G. Fine. **UDC** 611.6. **Pr Rev.**
**Desc:** Devoted to the biology of the kidney and to the scientific basis of renal diseases. Included are clinical studies on the mechanisms of diseases and their responses to treatment. Its high-quality papers aim at not only documenting but defining mechanisms of biomedical phenomena.
**Ind/Abst** Ref. Upd. Deluxe Ed.

GW/0344-5038
**EXTRACTA UROLOGICA.** Vol. 1, (1978)-. Periodical. German. bm. DM45.00. Acron Verlag, Potsdamer Strasse 89, 1000 Berlin 30 Germany. **Tel** 030/262-20-21, FAX 030/262 40 13. **ED** Jurgen Bodeker. **NLM** W1 EX752M. cum. index. **Bk Rev. Ad Acc. Circ:** 2,400 (ctrl).
**Desc:** Practical scientific briefings, book reports, and original texts, serving the physician keeping track of recent developments in the international discussion of urology and related issues.

US/0892-1245
**GENERAL UROLOGY.** [Gen. urol.]. 1st Ed. (1957)-. English. ir (every three years). $29.95 (latest edition). Appleton Century Crofts, Prentice Hall, 200 Old Tappan Road, Old Tappan NJ 07675. **Tel** (201)767-5188, (800)922-0579. **DD** 616.

NE/0924-8455
**GERIATRIC NEPHROLOGY AND UROLOGY.** Vol. 1, No. 1 (1991)-. Periodical. English. Three times a year. $242.00. Kluwer Academic Publishers, Postbus 322, 3300 AH Dordrecht, The Netherlands. **Tel** 011 (31) 78 524400, FAX 011 31 78 183273, telex 20083. **ED** Dimitros Oreopoulos and Michael Michelis. **NLM** W1; GE457BT. **CODEN** GNURE8. **[CCC]. Pr Rev. Acid Free.** available on microfilm and microfiche from University Microfilms International (UMI).
**Desc:** Devoted to the dissemination of information concerning the diagnosis and therapy of nephrologic and urologic disorders in elderly patients.

GW/0178-7527
**GIATROSUROLOGIE.** [Giatrosurologie]. **VFOAT** Jatrosurologie. (1985)-. Periodical. German. mo. DM150.00. Universimed Verlag GmbH, August-Schanz Strasse 21, W-6000 Frankfurt 50 Germany. **Tel** 011 49 69 5480000, FAX 069/54 80 00-77. **UDC** 616.61/.65. **Bk Rev. Ad Acc. Pr Rev. Circ:** 2,700 (ctrl).
**Desc:** A seminar paper journal containing brief summaries of original scientific articles . Also congress reports, interviews and patient information.

IT/0394-9362
**GIORNALE DI TECNICHE NEFROLOGICHE & DIALITICHE.** [G. tec. nefrol. dial.]. **VFOAT** Giornale di Tecniche Nefrologiche e Dialitiche. (1989)-. Periodical. Italian. qt. L90000 (Italy). Wichtig Editore, Via Friuli 72 74, 20135 Milan Italy. **Tel** 011 39 2 55195443. **UDC** 616.61.

IT/0393-5590
**GIORNALE ITALIANO DI NEFROLOGIA.** [G. ital. nefrol.]. (1984)-. Periodical. Italian. bm. L140000 (Italy). Wichtig Editore, Via Friuli 72 74, 20135 Milan Italy. **Tel** 011 39 2 55195443. **UDC** 616.61.
**Ind/Abst** EMBASE.

US/0164-4912
**GU, THE JOURNAL OF GENITOURINARY MEDICINE. VFOAT** Journal of Genitourinary Medicine. V. 1- Jan. 1979-. Periodical. English. mo. $35.00 US; $40.00 other. Office Center, Princeton Building 1000, Plainsboro NJ 08536. **Tel** (609)275-1900. **LC** RC870; .G18. **DD** 616.6/005. **UDC** 616.6; 611.6.

JA/0018-1994
**HINYOKIKA KIYO.** (HINYOKIKA KIYO. ACTA UROLOGICA JAPONICA.). [Hinyokika kiyo]. **Added/Corp** Kyoto Daigaku. Igakubu. Hinyokikagaku Kyoshitsu. **VFOAT** Acta Urologica Japonica. (1955)-. Academic Scholarly Publication. Japanese (summaries and/or abstracts in English). mo. $190.00. Kyoto Daigaku Igakubu Hinyokikagaku Kyoshitsu, (Dept. of Urology Faculty of Medicine, Kyoto University), 54, Kawaracho, Shogoin, Sakyoku, Kyotoshi, Kyotofu 606 Japan. **(Subscription address:** Kyowa Book Company Inc., 1 38 Kanda Jinbocho Chiyoda-ku, Tokyo 101 Japan.**) NLM** W1 HI409. **CODEN** HIKYAJ. Documents available from BIOSIS Document Express, CASDDS.
**Ind/Abst** Biol. Abstr.; Chem. Abstr.; EMBASE; Health Plan. Adminis.; Index Med.

II/0970-1591
**INDIAN JOURNAL OF UROLOGY.** (INDIAN JOURNAL OF UROLOGY : IJU : JOURNAL OF THE UROLOGICAL SOCIETY OF INDIA.). [Indian j. urol.]. **Added/Corp** Urological Society of India. **VFOAT** IJU. Vol. 1, No. 1 (Sept. 1984)-. Periodical. English. sa. $35.00. Sanjay Gandhi Postgraduate Institute of Medical Science, PO Box 375, Raebareli Road, 226 001 U.P., Lucknow India. **Tel** 51643. **(Subscription address:** Prints India, 11 Darya Ganj, New Delhi 110002 India.**) NLM** W1; IN239T.
**Ind/Abst** EMBASE.

US/0740-3615
**INFECTION CONTROL & UROLOGICAL CARE.** ***Ceased.*** [Infect. control urol. care]. **VAT** Infection Control and Urological Care. Vol. 2 (Jan./Feb. 1977)-Ceased ?. Periodical. English. qt. SPRINGHOUSE, 103 North Second Street/Suite 200, Dundee IL 60118. **Tel** (708)426-6100, (800)621-4432. **UDC** 616.6. **NLM** W1 IN406E. ***Continues*** *Infection Control in Urological Care, 0740-3615.*
**Ind/Abst** Cumul. Index Nurs. Allied Health Lit.

US/0896-9647
**INFECTIONS IN UROLOGY.** [Infect. urol.]. Vol. 1, No. 1 (Jan./Feb. 1988)-. Periodical. English. bm. $54.13 New York City (includes sales tax); $50.00 other. SCP Communications Inc, 134 West 29th Street, New York NY 10001. **Tel** (212)714-1740, FAX (212)629-3760. **DD** 616. **NLM** W1; IN406HKE. **[CCC].**
**Ind/Abst** Ref. Upd. Deluxe Ed.

US/0883-4962
**INNOVATIONS IN UROLOGY.** [Innov. urol.]. **VFOAT** Urology; Innovations in Urology, University of California School of Medicine. Periodical. English. bm. $19.00. Medical Publishers Enterprises, 15 22 Fair Lawn Avenue, Fair Lawn NJ 07410. **Tel** (201)796-6500. **DD** 616. **UDC** 616.6.

US/1058-0166
**INNOVATIONS IN UROLOGY NURSING. See** Medical Science and Technology-Nursing.

CN/1185-5479
**INTERNATIONAL ABSTRACTS, PEDIATRIC UROLOGY.** [Int. abstr. pediatr. urol.]. **VFOAT** Pediatric Urology; International Abstracts, Pediatrics Urology; International Abstracts in Pediatric Urology. (Apr. 22nd, 1991)-. Periodical. English. qt. Doer Press, Suite 302, 640 St. Paul Street West, Montreal Quebec H3C 1L9 Canada. **DD** 618.92/6.

JA/0919-8172
**INTERNATIONAL JOURNAL OF UROLOGY.** (19??)-. Four times a year. £132.00 Europe; £143.00 Other (International). Churchill Livingstone, 1-3 Baxter's Place, Leith Walk, Edinburgh EH1 3AF Scotland. **Tel** 011 44 31 556 2424, FAX 011 44 31 558 1278, telex 727511. **(Subscription address:** Maruzen Company Ltd., PO Box 5050, Import & Export Department, Tokyo 100 31 Japan.**)**
**Desc:** Official Journal of the Japanese Urological Association.

US/0276-2315
**INTERNATIONAL PERSPECTIVES IN UROLOGY.** [Int. perspect. urol.]. **VFOAT** I.P.U.; IPU. Vol. 1 (1981)-. Monographic series. English. ir. Price varies per volume. Williams & Wilkins Company, 428 East Preston Street, Baltimore MD 21202-3993. **Tel** (410)528-4000, (800)638-6423, FAX (410)528-8596, telex 87669. **(Subscription address:** Williams & Wilkins, PO Box 64380, Baltimore, MD 21264-4380**) LC** UNC. **NLM** W1 IN827K. **CODEN** IPUREA. Documents available from BIOSIS Document Express, Quick Copies.
**Ind/Abst** Biol. Abstr. (?-1984).

HU/0301-1623
**INTERNATIONAL UROLOGY AND NEPHROLOGY.** [Int. urol. nephrol.]. **Added/Corp** Magyar Tudomanyos Akademia. Vol. 2 (1970)-. Academic Scholarly Publication. English. bm. DM520.00. VSP International Science Publishers, Godfried van Seystlaan 47, 3703 BR Zeist Netherlands. **Tel** 011 31 3404 25790, FAX 011 31 3404 32081, telex 40217 USP NL. **(Subscription address:** VSP International Science Publishers, PO Box 346, 3700 AH Zeist Netherlands.**) ED** J. Kondas. **NLM** W1 IN928G. **CODEN** IURNAE. **[CCC]. Bk Rev. Ad Acc. Circ:** 600. Documents available from BIOSIS Document Express, CASDDS. ***Continues*** *Urology and Nephrology.*
**Desc:** Publishes original papers, preliminary reports and reviews which contribute to progress in all fields related to urological surgery, nephrology and andrology.
**Ind/Abst** Biol. Abstr.; Chem. Abstr.; EMBASE; Helminthol. Abstr. (1991-); Index Med.; Life Sci. Collect.

US/0921-9862
**INTERNATIONAL YEARBOOK OF NEPHROLOGY.** [Int. yearb. nephrol.]. **VFOAT** International Yearbooks of Nephrology. (1989)-. Periodical. English. an. Springer Verlag New York Inc., PO Box 19386 Books, Newark NJ 07195. **Tel** (201)348-4033. **LC** RC902.A1; I59. **DD** 616.6/1/005. **NLM** W1; IN931C. **Pr Rev.** Documents available from The Genuine Article.
**Ind/Abst** Res. Alert [Full Cov.]; Sci. Cit. Index (19??-19??); SCISEARCH.

JA/0914-9635
**JAPANESE JOURNAL OF ENDOUROLOGY AND ESWL. Added/Corp** Japanese Society of Endourology and ESWL. Vol. 1, No. 1 (1988)-. Periodical. English. sa. $100.00. **(Subscription address:** Maruzen Company Ltd., PO Box 5050, Import & Export Department, Tokyo 100 31 Japan.**) NLM** W1; JA951L. **CODEN** JJEEEU.
**Desc:** Provides progress change of treatment of upper urinary tract stone with appearance of perautaneous procedure and transarethral endoscopic treatment.
**Ind/Abst** EMBASE.

JA/0385-2385
**JAPANESE JOURNAL OF NEPHROLOGY, THE.** [Nihon Jinzo Gakkaishi]. **VFOAT** Nihon Jinzo Gakkai Shi. (1968)-. Academic Scholarly Publication. Japanese (Japanese). mo. $73.22. Japanese Journal of Nephrology Nihon University, School of Medicine, Oyaguchi Ku Tokyo Japan. **CODEN** NJGKAU. Documents available from BIOSIS Document Express, CASDDS.
**Ind/Abst** Biol. Abstr. (1985-); Chem. Abstr.; EMBASE [Select. Cov.]; Index Med.

●IT/1121-8428
**JN. JOURNAL OF NEPHROLOGY.** (1992)-. English. bm. $160.00. Wichtig Editore, Via Friuli 72 74, 20135 Milan Italy. **Tel** 011 39 2 55195443. **(Subscription address:** Wichtig Editore, Subscription Office, PO Box 830350, Birmingham AL 35283-0350.**) *Continues*** *Journal of Nephrology, 1120-3625.*

BL/0100-0519
**JORNAL BRASILEIRO DE UROLOGIA.** [J. bras. urol.]. **Added/Corp** Sociedade Brasileira de Urologia. Vol. 1, (Jan./March 1975)-. Portuguese (English; summaries and/or abstracts in English). Four times a year (Mar., June, Sept., Dec.). $68.75. Moreira Jr Editora Medica Ltda, Rue Henrique Martins 493, 04504 Sao Paulo SP Brazil. **Tel** 011 55 11 8849911, FAX 011 55 11 2800491. **ED** Nelson Rodrigues Netto. **NLM** W1 JO195H. Index available. **Bk Rev. Ad Acc. Circ:** 4,000.
**Desc:** Prints original research studies, instructional, texts, and articles on anatomical function and case histories.
**Ind/Abst** EMBASE; Index Med.

CN
**JOURNAL CANNT, LE. Added/Corp** Canadian Association of Nephrology Nurses and Technicians. **VFOAT** CANNT Journal; CANNT. (Spring 1990)-. Periodical. English (French). Four times a year. 30.00Can$. Pappin Communications, 73 Pembroke Street West, Pembroke Ontario K8A 5M5 Canada. **Tel** (613)735-0952. **(Subscription address:** CANNT, 2175 Sheppard Avenue East, Suite 110, Willowdale Ontario M2J 1W8 Canada.**) NLM** W1; JO235M.
**Ind/Abst** Cumul. Index Nurs. Allied Health Lit.

FR/0248-0018
**JOURNAL D'UROLOGIE.** [J. urol.]. **Added/Corp** Societe Francaise d'Urologie. (1980)-. Academic Scholarly Publication. French (summaries and/or abstracts in English and French). bm. $229.00. Masson Editeur, Box Postale 22, 41353 Vineuil 16 France. **Tel** 011 33 54 438994. **NLM** W1 JO375M. **CODEN** JOURDD. **[CCC]. Pr Rev.** available on microfilm and microfiche from University Microfilms International (UMI). Documents available from The Genuine Article, BIOSIS Document Express, CASDDS. ***Continues in part*** *Journal d'Urologie et de Nephrologie, 0021-8200.*
**Desc:** Includes reports of meetings held by the French Society of Urology and related organizations.
**Ind/Abst** Biol. Abstr.; Chem. Abstr.; Curr. Contents Clin. Med.; EMBASE; Index Med.; Life Sci. Collect.; Res. Alert [Select. Cov.]; SCISEARCH.

US/0892-7790
**JOURNAL OF ENDOUROLOGY.** (JOURNAL OF ENDOUROLOGY / ENDOUROLOGICAL SOCIETY.). [J. endourol.]. **Added/Corp** Endourological Society. Vol. 1, No. 1 (Spring 1987)-. Periodical. English. bm. $174.00. Mary Ann Liebert Inc., 1651 Third Avenue, New York NY 10128. **Tel** (212)289-2300, (800)M-LIEBERT, FAX (212)289-4697. **ED** Ralph Clayman and Arthur Smith. **DD**

616. **NLM** W1; JO643H. **CODEN** JENDE3. **Pr Rev.** Documents available from The Genuine Article, BIOSIS Document Express.
**Desc:** Devoted to the closed, controlled manipulation of the urinary tract. Publishes papers on procedures that include percutaneous renal and ureteral procedures, including extraction of calculi, dilation of strictures, and diagnosis and treatment of urinary tract tumors, ureteroscopy for diagnostic and therapeutic indications, laparoscopic urological procedures, endoscopic use of lasers, and extracorporeal lithotripsy of renal and uteteral stones.
**Ind/Abst** Biol. Abstr. (1987-); Curr. Contents Clin. Med.; Index Med. (Feb. 1993-); Res. Alert [Full Cov.]; Sci. Cit. Index; SCISEARCH.

IT
**JOURNAL OF NEPHROLOGY.** ***Title Change.*** **Added/Corp** Societa Italiana di Nefrologia. (198?)-(1992). Periodical. English. qt. Wichtig Editore, Via Friuli 72 74, 20135 Milan Italy. **Tel** 011 39 2 55195443. **(Subscription address:** Wichtig Editore, Subscription Office, PO Box 830350, Birmingham AL 35283-0350.**)** **NLM** W1; JO777TL. **CODEN** JLNEEL. ***Continued by*** *JN. Journal of Nephrology, 1121-8428.*
**Ind/Abst** EMBASE.

US/1051-2276
**JOURNAL OF RENAL NUTRITION.** (JOURNAL OF RENAL NUTRITION : THE OFFICIAL JOURNAL OF THE COUNCIL ON RENAL NUTRITION OF THE NATIONAL KIDNEY FOUNDATION.). [J. renal nutr.]. **Added/Corp** National Kidney Foundation. Council on Renal Nutrition. Vol. 1, No. 1 (Jan. 1991)-. Periodical. English. qt (Jan., Apr., July, Oct.). $65.00 (individual), $88.00 (institution) US; $90.00 (individiual), $105.00 (istitution) other. W.B. Saunders Company, A Subsidiary of Harcourt Brace Jovanovich, Inc., The Curtis Center/Suite 300, Independence Square West, Philadelphia PA 19106-3399. **Tel** (215)238-7800 or, 5587, FAX (215)238-7883, telex 173146. **(Subscription address:** W. B. Saunders Company / North America Subscriptions, c/o Periodicals, 6277 Sea Harbour Drive, 4th Floor, Orlando FL 32887.**)** **DD** 616. **NLM** W1; JO868F. **[CCC].**

US/1046-6673
**JOURNAL OF THE AMERICAN SOCIETY OF NEPHROLOGY.** (JOURNAL OF THE AMERICAN SOCIETY OF NEPHROLOGY : JASN.). [J. Am. Soc. Nephrol.]. **Added/Corp** American Society of Nephrology. **VFOAT** JASN. Vol. 1, No. 1 (July 1990)-. Academic Scholarly Publication. English. mo. $130.00 (individual), $185.00 (institution), US; $175.00 (individual), $230.00 (institution) other. Williams & Wilkins Company, 428 East Preston Street, Baltimore MD 21202-3993. **Tel** (410)528-4000, (800)638-6423, FAX (410)528-8596, telex 87669. **(Subscription address:** Williams & Wilkins, PO Box 64380, Baltimore MD 21264.**)** **DD** 616. **NLM** W1; JO911BB. **CODEN** JASNEU. **[CCC]. Pr Rev.** Documents available from The Genuine Article, BIOSIS Document Express, CASDDS, Quick Copies.
**Desc:** Encourages dynamic interaction between basic and clinical sciences and facilitates rapid communication between nephrologists and other specialists in related disciplines.
**Ind/Abst** Biol. Abstr. (1991-); Chem. Abstr.; Curr. Contents Clin. Med.; Curr. Contents Life Sci.; Health Plan. Adminis.; Index Med. (July 1990-); Res. Alert [Full Cov.]; Sci. Cit. Index; SCISEARCH; Soc. Sci. Cit. Index [Select. Cov.].

US/1054-8734
**JOURNAL OF UROGENITAL PATHOLOGY.** Vol. 1, No. 1 (1991)-. Periodical. English. qt. $115.00 (institutions). Field & Wood, Inc., 4156 Manayunk Avenue, Philadelphia PA 19128. **Tel** (215)828-4010. **DD** 616. **NLM** W1; JO968G.

●US/1067-1919
**JOURNAL OF UROLOGIC PATHOLOGY.** (JOURNAL OF UROLOGIC PATHOLOGY : THE OFFICIAL JOURNAL OF THE INTERNATIONAL SOCIETY OF UROLOGIC PATHOLOGY.). [J. urol. pathol.]. **Added/Corp** International Society of Urologic Pathology. Vol. 1, No. 1 (Spring 1993)-. Periodical. English. qt. $200.00 US; $240.00 other. Humana Press Inc., 999 Riverview Drive, Suite 208, Totawa NJ 07512. **Tel** (201)256-1699, FAX (201)256-8341. **ED** David G. Bostwick, M.D. **DD** 616. **NLM** W1; JO968GL. **[CCC].**

US/0738-7350
**JOURNAL OF UROLOGICAL NURSING.** [J. urol. nurs.]. **Added/Corp** International Urological Sciences, Inc. **VFOAT** JUN. (198?)-. Periodical. English. Four times a year. $40.00 US; $47.00 other. International Urological Sciences Inc, PO Box 408, Long Valley NJ 07853. **Tel** (908)852-8789, FAX (908)584-9620. **ED** Ellen Shipes, (editor's address: 791 Rhonda Ave, Nashville, TN 37205, phone: (615)356-8543). **NLM** W1; JO906P. Index available (Each iss.). cum. index. **Bk Rev**, (Qty: 1-4 per year). **Ad Acc. Pr Rev. Circ:** 8,500 (ctrl). ***Continues*** *Urology Nurse Journal.*
**Desc:** Strives to assist the health care professionals in learning usable skills that will enable them to add continuously to their knowledge base and to improve competence in working with urological patients.
**Ind/Abst** Cumul. Index Nurs. Allied Health Lit.

US/0022-5347
**JOURNAL OF UROLOGY, THE.** (THE JOURNAL OF UROLOGY : OFFICIAL JOURNAL OF THE AMERICAN UROLOGICAL ASSOCIATION, INC.). [J. urol.]. **Added/Corp** American Urological Association. Vol. 1 (Feb. 1917)-. Academic Scholarly Publication. English. mo. $229.00 (individual), $255.00 (institution), US; $304.00 (individual), $330.00 (institution) other. Williams & Wilkins Company, 428 East Preston Street, Baltimore MD 21202-3993. **Tel** (410)528-4000, (800)638-6423, FAX (410)528-8596, telex 87669. **(Subscription address:** Williams & Wilkins, PO Box 64380, Baltimore MD 21264.**)** **ED** John T. Grayhack. **LC** RC870; .J6. **DD** 616.605. **NLM** W1 JO968H. **CODEN** JOURAA. **[CCC].** cum. index. **Ad Acc. Pr Rev. Circ:** 17,500. available on microfilm. Documents available from The Genuine Article, BIOSIS Document Express, CASDDS, ADONIS, Quick Copies. ***Absorbed*** *Investigative Urology, 0021-0005* ***and*** *Urological Survey, 0042-1146;* ***Continues*** *American Urological Association. Transactions of the American Urological Association, 0894-0398.*
**Desc:** The premier journal in the field presents clinical papers, abstracts, commentary, research and innovative techniques for the urologist.
**Ind/Abst** Abr. Index Med.; ADONIS; Art Archaeol. Tech. Abstr.; Biol. Abstr.; Calcium Calcif. Tissue Abstr.; Chem. Abstr.; CIS Abstr.; CSA Neuro. Abstr. (?-?); Curr. Aware. Biol. Sci., CABS; Curr. Contents Clin. Med.; Curr. Contents Life Sci.; EMBASE; Energy Res. Abstr.; Health Devices Alerts; Helminthol. Abstr. (19??-19??); Immunol. Abstr.; Index Med.; Iowa Drug Inf. Serv. (1966-); Med. Abstr. Newsl.; Microbiol. Abstr. Sect. B; Mod. Med.; Nucl. Sci. Abstr.; Nutr. Abstr. Rev., Ser. A, Hum. Exp.; Nutr. Res. Newsl.; Life Sci. Collect.; PESTDOC; Physic. Medline Plus; Protozoolog. Abstr.; Ref. Upd. Basic Ed.; Ref. Upd. Deluxe Ed.; Res. Alert [Full Cov.]; Rev. Med. Vet. Mycology; Saf. Health Work; Sci. Cit. Index; SCISEARCH; Soc. Sci. Cit. Index [Select. Cov.]; Virol. AIDS Abstr.

US/0023-1304
**KIDNEY, THE.** ***Suspended.*** [Kidney]. **Added/Corp** National Kidney Foundation. **VFOAT** KF, The Kidney. Vol. 1, No. 1 (Sept. 1967)-Suspended. Academic Scholarly Publication. English. bm (6 issues). $25.00. National Kidney Foundation, 30 East 33rd Street, Suite 1100, New York NY 10016. **Tel** (212)889-2210, (800)622-9010, FAX (212)689-9261. **NLM** W1 KI586N. **CODEN** KIDNA. Documents available from BIOSIS Document Express.
**Desc:** 600 summaries in each volume of the most important and clinically relevant articles from world literature; critical appraisal in the form of commentaries, editorials, and reviews.
**Ind/Abst** Biol. Abstr.; EMBASE.

●US/0940-7936
**KIDNEY: A CURRENT SURVEY OF WORLD LITERATURE.** Vol. 1, No. 1 (1992)-. Periodical. English. bm. $99.00. Springer-Verlag New York Inc., 175 5th Avenue, New York NY 10010. **Tel** (212)460-1500, telex 232 235 SPB UR. **(Subscription address:** Springer Verlag New York Inc. / for North America, 44 Hartz Way, Secaucus NJ 07096.**)** **ED** George Dunea, Jose Arruda. **NLM** ZWJ 300; K46.
**Desc:** A complete overview of the world literature available to clinicians and specialists in nephrology and its related fields. Each volume contains 600 summaries of important and clinically relevant articles from the world literature.

US/0270-062X
**KIDNEY DISEASE.** [Kidney dis.]. Vol. 1 (1979)-. Academic Scholarly Publication. English. ir. Price varies per volume. Marcel Dekker Inc., 270 Madison Avenue, New York NY 10016. **Tel** (212)696-9000, (800)228-1160, FAX (212)685-4540, telex 421419. **(Subscription address:** Marcel Dekker Inc, PO Box 5017, Monticello NY 12701.**)** **LC** UNC. **NLM** W1 KI586R. **CODEN** KIDID6. Documents available from BIOSIS Document Express, CASDDS.
**Desc:** Each title covers a different topic in nephrology and kidney disease. Topics include kidney transplant failure and hepatorenal disorders.
**Ind/Abst** Biol. Abstr.; Chem. Abstr.

US/0085-2538
**KIDNEY INTERNATIONAL.** [Kidney int.]. **Added/Corp** International Society of Nephrology. Vol. 1, (Jan. 1972)-. Academic Scholarly Publication. English (French; summaries and/or abstracts in French). Twelve times a year. $660.00 (institutions), $400.00 (individuals). Blackwell Scientific Publishers, 238 Main Street, Cambridge MA 02142. **Tel** (617)547-7110, (800)835-6770, FAX (617)547-0789. **ED** T. E. Andreoli. **LC** RC902.A1; K53. **DD** 616.6/1/005. **NLM** W1 KI586S. **CODEN** KDYIA5. **[CCC]. Pr Rev.** available on microfilm and microfiche from University Microfilms International (UMI). Documents available from The Genuine Article, BIOSIS Document Express, CASDDS.
**Desc:** Each issue of the journal covers recent laboratory and clinical research data on renal physiology, biochemistry, pathology, immunology, and morphology.
**Ind/Abst** Biol. Abstr.; Calcium Calcif. Tissue Abstr.; Chem. Abstr.; CSA Neuro. Abstr. (?-?); Curr. Aware. Biol. Sci., CABS; Curr. Contents Clin. Med.; Curr. Contents Life Sci.; EMBASE; Helminthol. Abstr.; Index Med.; Nutr. Abstr. Rev., Ser. A, Hum. Exp.; Life Sci. Collect.; Physic. Medline Plus; Protozoolog. Abstr.; Ref. Upd. Basic Ed.; Ref. Upd. Clinical Ed.; Ref. Upd. Deluxe Ed.; Res. Alert [Full Cov.]; Sci. Cit. Index; SCISEARCH; Virol. AIDS Abstr.

US/0098-6577
**KIDNEY INTERNATIONAL. SUPPLEMENT.** [Kidney inter., Suppl.]. **Added/Corp** International Society of Nephrology. (1974)-. Monographic series. English. ir. Price varies per volume. Blackwell Scientific Publishers, 238 Main Street, Cambridge MA 02142. **Tel** (617)547-7110, (800)835-6770, FAX (617)547-0789. **LC** UNC. **DD** 616. **NLM** W1 KI586SA. **CODEN** KISUDF. Documents available from BIOSIS Document Express, CASDDS.
**Ind/Abst** Biol. Abstr.; Chem. Abstr.; Curr. Aware. Biol. Sci., CABS; Index Med.; Nutr. Abstr. Rev., Ser. A, Hum. Exp.; Life Sci. Collect.

US
**KIDNEY, UROLOGY, AND HEMATOLOGY.** ***Ceased.*** **Added/Corp** National Institute of Arthritis, Diabetes, and Digestive and Kidney Diseases (U.S.) National Institutes of Health (U.S.). **VFOAT** NIADDK Research Advances; NIADDK. (197?)-(19??). English. National Institute of Arthritis Metabolism and Digestive Diseases, National Institutes of Health, 9000 Rockville Pike, Bethesda MD 20014. **NLM** W1; KI586U. ***Continues*** *Kidney & Urinary Tract Diseases and Treatment.*

GW/0174-2752
**KLINISCHE UND EXPERIMENTELLE UROLOGIE.** V. 1-. Academic Scholarly Publication. German. Price varies per volume. **UDC** 616.6. **NLM** W1 KL575J. **CODEN** KEURDM. Documents available from CASDDS.
**Ind/Abst** Chem. Abstr.

HU/0864-8921
**MAGYAR UROLOGIA.** [Magy. urol.]. (1989)-. Periodical. Hungarian. Four times a year. $64.00. Society of Hungarian Urological Surgeons, PO Box 29, H-4012, Debrecen, Hungary. **(Subscription address:** Kultura, PO Box 149, H 1389 Budapest 62 Hungary.**)** **UDC** 616.6. ***Continues*** *Urologiai es Nephrologiai Szemle, 0133-3127.*
**Ind/Abst** EMBASE.

SP
**MEDICAL DIGEST. UROLOGIA.** Spanish. Editorial M.C.R. SA, Mallorca 310, 08037 Barcelona Spain.

IT/0393-2249
**MINERVA UROLOGICA E NEFROLOGICA.** [Minerva urol. nefrol.]. **VFOAT** Italian Journal of Urology and Nephrology. Vol. 36, No. 1 (Jan./March 1984)-. Academic Scholarly Publication. Italian (summaries and/or abstracts in English). qt. $90.00 (individuals), $140.00 (institutions). Edizioni Minerva Medica, Corso Bramante 83-85, 10126 Turin Italy. **Tel** 011 39 11 678282, FAX 011 39 11 674502. **ED** P Stratta. **NLM** W1; MI655. **Bk Rev. Ad Acc.** available on microfilm from University Microfilms International (UMI). Documents available from CASDDS. ***Formed by the union of*** *Minerva Urologica* ***and*** *Minerva Nefrologica, 0026-4873.*
**Desc:** Journal addressed to specialists in urology and nephrology in Italy and abroad. It deals with topics in scientific practice and research.
**Ind/Abst** Chem. Abstr. (1984-); EMBASE [Select. Cov.]; Index Med. (Vol. 36, No. 1, 1984-);(V36N1, 1984-).

US/0198-7577
**MONOGRAPHS IN UROLOGY.** ***Ceased.*** [Monogr. urol.]. **Added/Corp** Burroughs Wellcome Company. Vol. 1, No. 1 (Apr./May 1980)-Ceased (Dec. 1987). Monographic series. English. bm. Burroughts Wellcome Company, 3030 Cornwallis Drive, Research Triangle Park NC 27709. **Tel** (609)737-2250. **DD** 616.6. **NLM** W1 MO569M. ***Continues*** *Urology Digest, 0197-7709.*

SP/0211-6995
**NEFROLOGIA.** (NEFROLOGIA : PUBLICACION OFICIAL DE LA SOCIEDAD ESPANOLA DE NEFROLOGIA.). [Nefrologia]. **Added/Corp** Sociedad Espanola de Nefrologia. (1981)-. Periodical. Spanish (summaries and/or abstracts in English). bm. 6500ptas Spain; 5000ptas other. Grupo Aula Medica, Isabel Colbrand S N Alfa 3, 28050 Madrid Spain. **Tel** 011 34 1 3588657. **NLM** W1 NE193P. **Pr Rev.** Documents available from The Genuine Article.
**Ind/Abst** Curr. Contents Clin. Med.; EMBASE; Indice Med. Esp.; Nutr. Abstr. Rev., Ser. A, Hum. Exp.; Res. Alert [Select. Cov.]; SCISEARCH; Soc. Sci. Cit. Index [Select. Cov.].

SZ/0250-4960
**NEPHROLOGIE.** (NEPHROLOGIE : JOURNAL TRIMESTRIEL PUBLIE PAR LA SOCIETE DE NEPHROLOGIE.). [Nephrologie]. **Added/Corp** Societe de Nephrologie (Switzerland). Vol. 1, No 1 (1980)-. Academic Scholarly Publication. French (summaries and/or abstracts in English). Six times a year. 108.00F (individuals), 158.00F (institutions). Medecine et Hygiene, Case Postale 456, CH-1211 Geneve 4 Switzerland. **Tel** 011 41 22 3469355, 011 41 22 3469356. **NLM** W1 NE204D. **CODEN** NEPHDY. **[CCC]. Pr Rev.** Documents

available from The Genuine Article, BIOSIS Document Express, CASDDS.
**Ind/Abst** Biol. Abstr.; Chem. Abstr.; Curr. Contents Clin. Med.; EMBASE; Index Med.; Res. Alert [Select. Cov.]; SCISEARCH.

AT/1320-5358
**NEPHROLOGY.** (19??)-. Academic Scholarly Publication. English. Six times a year. 357.00Aus$ Australia; ¥25000 Japan; $250.00 other. Blackwell Scientific Publications Australia, 54 University Street, PO Box 378, Carlton Victoria 3053 Australia. **Tel** 011 61 3 3470300, FAX 011 61 3 3475001, telex 10716421.

UK/0931-0509
**NEPHROLOGY, DIALYSIS, TRANSPLANTATION.** (NEPHROLOGY, DIALYSIS, TRANSPLANTATION : OFFICIAL PUBLICATION OF THE EUROPEAN DIALYSIS AND TRANSPLANT ASSOCIATION - EUROPEAN RENAL ASSOCIATION.). [Nephrol. dial. transplant.]. **Added/Corp** European Dialysis and Transplant Association - European Renal Association. Vol. 1, No. 1 (1986)-. Periodical. English. mo. £240.00 UK and Europe; $450.00 other. Oxford University Press, Walton Street, Oxford OX2 6DP England. **Tel** 011 44 865 56767, FAX 011 44 865 267773, telex 837330 OXPRES G. **(Subscription address:** Oxford University Press / USA, Journals Marketing Department, Oxford University Press, 2001 Evans Road, Cary NC 27513.**) NLM** W1; NE204FH. **CODEN** NDTREA. **[CCC]. Pr Rev.** available on microfilm and microfiche from University Microfilms International (UMI). Documents available from The Genuine Article, BIOSIS Document Express. ***Continues** European Dialysis and Transplant Association - European Renal Association. Congress. Proceedings of the European Dialysis and Transplant Association - European Renal Association.*
**Desc:** Publishes papers relating to clinical or laboratory investigation of relevance to nephrology, dialysis or transplantation.
**Ind/Abst** Biol. Abstr. (1986-); Curr. Aware. Biol. Sci., CABS; Curr. Contents Clin. Med.; EMBASE; Index Med. (1986-); Nutr. Abstr. Rev., Ser. A, Hum. Exp.; Res. Alert [Full Cov.]; Sci. Cit. Index; SCISEARCH.

US/1054-1810
**NEPHROLOGY EXCHANGE, THE.** [Nephrol. exch.]. Vol. 1, No. 1 (Jan. 1991)-. Periodical. English. sa. Free. Abbott Laboratories, Professional Liason Group, D-975, AP-30, Abbott Park IL 60064-3500. **DD** 616.

US/0896-1263
**NEPHROLOGY NEWS & ISSUES.** [Nephrol. news issues]. **VFOAT** Nephrology News and Issues; NN&I. Vol. 1, No. 1 (Feb. 1987)-. Periodical. English. mo. $50.00 US; $85.00 other. Nephrology News & Issues Inc, 15150 North Hayden Road, Suite 101, Scottsdale AZ 85260. **Tel** (602)443-4635, FAX (602)443-4528, telex 3303120 MCI UW. **ED** Mark E. Neumann and Cynthia Knapp Lefton. **DD** 616. **NLM** W1; NE204FJ. **CODEN** NNISES. **Ad Acc, Adv Mgr:** Lawrence Coutts. **Pr Rev. Circ:** 16,000 (ctrl).
**Desc:** Covers the issues and problems affecting the management of end-stage kidney disease.
**Ind/Abst** Int. Nurs. Index (Feb. 1987-).

SZ/0028-2766
**NEPHRON.** [Nephron]. **Added/Corp** International Society of Nephrology. Vol. 1 (1964)-. Academic Scholarly Publication. English (French). mo. $741.00. S. Karger AG, Allschwilerstrasse 10, PO Box - Postfach - Case Postale, CH-4009 Basel Switzerland. **Tel** 011 41 61 306-1111, FAX 011 41 61 306-1234, telex CH 962 652. **ED** G. M. Berlyne, S. Giovannetti. **NLM** W1 NE204G. **CODEN** NPRNAY. **[CCC]. Pr Rev.** available on microfilm from University Microfilms International (UMI). Documents available from The Genuine Article, BIOSIS Document Express, CASDDS.
**Desc:** Gives extensive coverage to the most important developments concerning the structure, functions and diseases of kidneys. Each issue contains practice-oriented findings drawn from a wide range of fields, including anatomy, pathophysiology, biochemistry, microbiology, endocrinology, immunology and pharmacology. New diagnostic and therapeutic techniques are also featured, particularly advances in transplantation, dialysis and hemofiltration. Frequently cited papers are supported by editorials, reviews, 'Grand Rounds in Nephrology', 'Controversies in Nephrology', short communications and case reports to provide a complete and practical guide to current progress in all aspects of nephrology, including renal disease and hypertension.
**Ind/Abst** Biol. Abstr.; Calcium Calcif. Tissue Abstr.; Chem. Abstr.; Curr. Aware. Biol. Sci., CABS; Curr. Contents Clin. Med.; Curr. Contents Life Sci.; EMBASE; Index Med.; Int. Aerosp. Abstr.; Nutr. Abstr. Rev., Ser. B, Live Feeds and Feed.; Nutr. Abstr. Rev., Ser. A, Hum. Exp.; Life Sci. Collect.; Pig News Inf.; Protozoolog. Abstr.; Ref. Upd. Basic Ed.; Ref. Upd. Deluxe Ed.; Res. Alert [Full Cov.]; Rev. Med. Vet. Mycology; Sci. Cit. Index; SCISEARCH; Soc. Sci. Cit. Index [Select. Cov.].

US/0733-2467
**NEUROUROL. URODYN. See** Medical Science and Technology-Neurology.

NE
**NEW CLINICAL APPLICATIONS. NEPHROLOGY. VFOAT** Nephrology. (1990)-. Monographic series. English. ir. Price varies per volume. Kluwer Academic Publishers, Postbus 322, 3300 AH Dordrecht, The Netherlands. **Tel** 011 (31) 78 524400, FAX 011 31 78 183273, telex 20083. **NLM** W1; NE372E.

JA/0021-5287
**NIPPON HINYOKIKA GAKKAI ZASSHI.** (JAPANESE JOURNAL OF UROLOGY.). [Nippon Hinyokika Gakkai zasshi]. **Added/Corp** Japanese Urological Association. **VFOAT** Nippon Hinyokika Gakkai Zasshi. (19??)-. Academic Scholarly Publication. Japanese. mo. $192.00. **(Subscription address:** Kyowa Book Company Inc., 1 38 Kanda Jinbocho Chiyoda-ku, Tokyo 101 Japan.**) NLM** W1 NI903R. **CODEN** NGKZA6. available on microfilm from University Microfilms International (UMI). Documents available from CASDDS. ***Continues** Nippon Hinyo-Kibyo Gakkai Zasshi.*
**Ind/Abst** Chem. Abstr.; EMBASE; Index Med.

JA/0029-0726
**NISHI NIHON HINYOKIKA. VFOAT** Nishi Nihon Journal of Urology. (1969)-. Periodical. Japanese. bm. $176.00. Nishinihon Section of Japan, 1-1 Maidashi 3-chome, Higashi-ku 812 Fukuoka, Japan. **(Subscription address:** Kyowa Book Company Inc., 1 38 Kanda Jinbocho Chiyoda-ku, Tokyo 101 Japan.**) DD** 616.6. **UDC** 616.6. ***Continues** Hifu to Hinyo, 0011-9091. **Continued in part by** Hifu to Hinyo, 0011-9091.*
**Ind/Abst** EMBASE.

IT/0392-4629
**NUA : INTERNATIONAL JOURNAL OF NEPHROLOGY, UROLOGY, ANDROLOGY.** [NUA]. **VFOAT** International Journal of Nephrology, Urology, Andrology; N.U.A.; Nephrology, Urology, Andrology. Began in 1980. Academic Scholarly Publication. English. bm. **UDC** 616.6. **NLM** W1 NU106T. **CODEN** NIJADB. Documents available from BIOSIS Document Express.
**Ind/Abst** Biol. Abstr. (-1982); EMBASE.

FR/1146-5611
**PASCAL. E 77, NEPHROLOGIE, VOIES URINAIRES. VFOAT** PASCAL. E 77, Nephrology, Urinary Tract; PASCAL. E Soixante-dix-sept, Nephrology, Voies Urinaires. (1990)-. Periodical. Multiple languages. Eleven times a year. 1070.00F France; 1135.00F other. CNRS / Institut d'Information Scientifique et Technique, (Centre National de la Recherche Scientifique), 15 Quai Anatole France, Paris 75700 France. **Tel** 011 33 1 47531515, telex 299 356 F. **UDC** 011. ***Continues** Pascal Explore. E77, Nephrologie, Voies Urinaires, 0761-2249.*

US/0097-5257
**PEDIATRIC NEPHROLOGY. See** Medical Science and Technology-Pediatrics.

GW/0931-041X
**PEDIATRIC NEPHROLOGY (BERLIN, WEST). See** Medical Science and Technology-Pediatrics.

US/0896-5420
**PRACTICAL REVIEWS IN UROLOGY.** (PRACTICAL REVIEWS IN UROLOGY [SOUND RECORDING].). [Pract. rev. urol.]. **Added/Corp** Educational Reviews, Inc. Montefiore Medical Center. **VFOAT** Practical Reviews. (198?)-. Periodical. English. mo. $175.00 Physicians/Dentists; $125.00 Residents (members); $190.00 Physicians/Dentists; $125.00 Residents (nonmembers). Educational Reviews Inc., 6801 Cahaba Valley Road, Birmingham AL 35242. **Tel** (205)991-5188, (800)633-4743, FAX (205)995-1926. **DD** 616.

US/0889-471X
**PROBLEMS IN UROLOGY. *Ceased.*** [Probl. urol.]. Vol. 1, No. 1 (Jan./March 1987)-(Oct./Dec. 1994). Periodical. English. qt. J.B. Lippincott Company, 227 East Washington Square, Philadelphia PA 19106-3780. **Tel** (215)238-4200 or 4454, FAX (215)238-4227. **(Subscription address:** J.B. Lippincott, PO Box 350, Hagerstown MD 21740.**) LC** RC870; .P68. **DD** 616.6. **NLM** W1; PR573MN. **CODEN** PRUREX. **[CCC].** cum. index. available on microfilm from University Microfilms International (UMI).
**Ind/Abst** EMBASE.

US/0094-6044
**PROCEEDINGS OF THE CLINICAL DIALYSIS AND TRANSPLANT FORUM.** [Proc. Clin. Dial. Transplant Forum]. Vol. 1 (1971)-. Proceedings. English. an. ASAIO, PO Box 5028, Alexandria VA 22305. **UDC** 616.61-78; 612.6.02. **NLM** W1 PR585A. **CODEN** PCDFDA. Documents available from CASDDS.
**Ind/Abst** Chem. Abstr.; Energy Res. Abstr. (May 1977-).

US
**PROCEEDINGS OF THE U.S. PUBLIC HEALTH SERVICE COOPERATIVE STUDIES (RENAL DISEASE AND HYPERTENSION). See** Medical Science and Technology-Cardiology.

FR
**PROGRES EN UROLOGIE : JOURNAL DE L'ASSOCIATION FRANCAISE D'UROLOGIE ET DE LA SOCIETE FRANCAISE D'UROLOGIE. Added/Corp** Association Francaise d'Urologie. Societe Francaise d'Urologie. Association des Urologues du Quebec. (1991)-. Periodical. French (summaries and/or abstracts in English, German, Italian and Spanish; table of contents in English). bm. 700.00F. Progres en Urologie, 7-9 Boulevard Flandrin, 75116 Paris France. **Tel** 011 33 1 45033196, 011 33 1 45049165, FAX 011 33 1 45047289. **ED** B. Gattegno. **NLM** W1; PR64R.

FR
**PROGRESS IN UROLOGY : JOURNAL OF THE FRENCH UROLOGICAL ASSOCIATION AND OF THE FRENCH SOCIETY OF UROLOGY. Added/Corp** Association Francaise d'Urologie. Societe Francaise d'Urologie. Vol. 1, No. 1 (Feb. 1991)-. Periodical. English. bm. $90.00. **NLM** W1; PR684L.

US/1050-5881
**PROSTATE. SUPPLEMENT, THE.** [Prostate, Suppl.]. (1981)-. Monographic series. English. bm. Wiley Liss, 605 3rd Avenue, New York NY 10158. **Tel** (212)850-8800, (212)850-6645. **NLM** W1; PR77Va.
**Ind/Abst** Health Plan. Adminis.; Index Med. (1981-).

US/0731-5899
**PSYCHONEPHROLOGY. *Ceased.*** [Psychonephrology]. (1981)-Series complete with Vol. 2. Monographic series. English. ir. Plenum Press, 233 Spring Street, New York NY 10013-1578. **Tel** (212)620-8000, (800)221-9369, FAX (212)463-0742, (212)807-1047, telex 23/421139. **ED** N.B. Levy. **NLM** W1 PS748F.

CN/1184-0161
**RAPPORT ... INSUFFISANCE RENALE AU CANADA.** (RAPPORT ... INSUFFISANCE RENALE AU CANADA / LE REGISTRE CANADIEN DES INSUFFISANCE ET DES TRANSPLANTATIONS D'ORGANES.). [Rapp. insuffis. renale Can.]. **Main/Corp** Registre Canadien des Insuffisances et des Transplantations d'Organes. **Added/Corp** Hospital Medical Records Institute. **VFOAT** Rapport, Insuffisance Renale au Canada. (1987)-. French. Hospital Medical Records Institute, 250, Promenade Ferrand, CP 3900, Don Mills, Ontario M3C 2T9 Canada. **DD** 616.6/14/00971021. ***Continues** Rapport de ... / Registre de l'Insuffisance Renale, 0821-7831; **Supersedes in part** Report of the Canadian Renal Failure Registry, 0821-7823; **Continues** Report of the Canadian Renal Failure Registry., 0821-7823.*

IT/0033-992X
**RASSEGNA DI UROLOGIA E NEFROLOGIA.** [Rass. urol. nefrol.]. (1965)-. Periodical. Italian. Six times a year. L30000.00 Italy; L60000.00 other. Casa Editrice Maccari, Via Trento 53, 43100 Parma Italy. **Tel** 011 39 521 771268, FAX 011 39 521 771268. **UDC** 616.6. ***Continues** Rassegna Urologica, 0392-7172.*

UK/0264-3081
**RECENT ADVANCES IN RENAL MEDICINE. *Ceased.*** [Recent adv. renal med.]. No. 2 (1982)-?. Monographic series. English. Churchill Livingstone, 1-3 Baxter's Place, Leith Walk, Edinburgh EH1 3AF Scotland. **Tel** 011 44 31 556 2424, FAX 011 44 31 558 1278, telex 727511. **ED** Norman F Jones and D K Peters. **UDC** 616.61. **NLM** W1 RE105YFC. ***Continues** Recent Advances in Renal Disease, 0309-2429.*

UK/0261-8788
**RECENT ADVANCES IN UROLOGY/ANDROLOGY.** [Recent adv. urol. androl.]. No. 3 (1981)-. English. ir. Price varies per volume. Churchill Livingstone, 1-3 Baxter's Place, Leith Walk, Edinburgh EH1 3AF Scotland. **Tel** 011 44 31 556 2424, FAX 011 44 31 558 1278, telex 727511. **ED** W. F. Hendry. **NLM** W1 RE105YP.

AT/0816-990X
**RENAL EDUCATOR.** [Ren. educ.]. (1986)-. Periodical. English. Four times a year (Mar., June, Sept., Dec.). 40.00Aus$ Australia; 60.00Aus$ others. Renal Educator, PO Box 41, Little Bay NSW 2036 Australia. **Tel** 011 61 3 494907. **ED** P. Humphreys. **DD** 616.614005. **Bk Rev. Ad Acc. Circ:** 1,000 (ctrl). ***Continues** Dialysis, 0726-2744.*

US/0886-022X
**RENAL FAILURE.** [Ren. fail.]. Vol. 10, No. 1 (1987)-. Academic Scholarly Publication. English. Six times a year. $525.00 US; $546.00 other. Marcel Dekker Inc., 270 Madison Avenue, New York NY 10016. **Tel** (212)696-9000, (800)228-1160, FAX (212)685-4540, telex 421419. **(Subscription address:** Marcel Dekker Inc, PO Box 5017, Monticello NY 12701.**) ED** William F. Finn. **LC** RC918.R4; R46. **DD** 616. **NLM** W1; RE198B. **CODEN** REFAE8. **[CCC]. Bk Rev. Ad Acc. Pr Rev.** available on microfiche. Documents available from The Genuine Article, BIOSIS Document Express, CASDDS.

***Continues*** *Uremia Investigation, 0740-1353.*
**Desc:** Concentrates on acute renal injury and its consequence. Also addresses advances in the fields of chronic renal failure, hypertension, and renal transplantation. Bringing together both clinical and experimental aspects of renal failure, this publication presents timely, practical information on pathology and pathophysiology of acute renal failure; nephrotoxicity of drugs and other substances; prevention, treatment, and therapy of renal failure; renal failure in association with transplantation; hypertension; and diabetes mellitus.
**Ind/Abst** Biol. Abstr. (1987-); Chem. Abstr. (1987-); Curr. Contents Clin. Med.; EMBASE; Index Med. (1987-); Life Sci. Collect. (1987-); Protozoolog. Abstr.; Ref. Upd. Deluxe Ed.; Res. Alert [Select. Cov.]; Rev. Med. Vet. Mycology; Soc. Sci. Cit. Index [Select. Cov.].

CN/0714-8879
**RENAL FAMILY.** ***Ceased.*** (THE RENAL FAMILY.). [Ren. fam.]. (1979)-(19??). Periodical. English. Five times a year. Multimed Publications Inc., 1120 Finch Avenue West Suite 601, Toronto Ontario M3J 3H7 Canada. **Tel** (416)650-0610, FAX (416)650-0639. **DD** 616.6/1/005. **NLM** W1 RE198D.

CN/0820-7283
**RENAL FAMILY (ED. FRANCAISE).** (THE RENAL FAMILY.). **Added/Corp** Fondation Canadienne des Malacies du Rein. Vol. 4 (March 1982)-. Periodical. French. qt. **DD** 616.6/1/005.

UK/0300-3434
**RENAL PHYSIOLOGY.** **Added/Corp** University of Sheffield. Biomedical Information Project. (1970)-. English. Twenty-four times a year. £110.00. SUBIS, Mansion House, 19 Kingfield Road, Sheffield S11 9AS England. **Tel** 011 44 114 255 4433, FAX 011 44 114 255 4626. **[CCC].** **Bk Rev.** available on diskette. Documents available from CASDDS.
**Desc:** Contains references on the physiology, biochemistry and pharmacology of the renal system. Also details of forthcoming events.
**Ind/Abst** Chem. Abstr.; Sci. Cit. Index (19??-19??); SCISEARCH.

SZ/1011-6524
**RENAL PHYSIOLOGY AND BIOCHEMISTRY.** [Renal physiol. biochem.]. (Jan./Feb. 1988)-. Academic Scholarly Publication. English. Six times a year. $296.00. S. Karger AG, Allschwilerstrasse 10, PO Box - Postfach - Case Postale, CH-4009 Basel Switzerland. **Tel** 011 41 61 306-1111, FAX 011 41 61 306-1234, telex CH 962 652. **ED** G. M. Berlyne, F. Lang. **NLM** W1; RE198G. **CODEN** RPBIEL. **[CCC].** Index available. cum. index. **Ad Acc.** **Pr Rev. Circ:** 600 (ctrl). available on microfilm and microfiche. Documents available from The Genuine Article, BIOSIS Document Express, CASDDS. ***Continues*** *Renal Physiology (Basel, Switzerland), 0378-5858.*
**Desc:** Original papers and editorials, contributed by leading investigators throughout the world, provide in-depth information on the anatomy, physiology, pathophysiology, biochemistry and pharmacology of the kidneys. The editors have added a special section, Rapid Communications, to provide accelerated publication of new findings of particular importance.
**Ind/Abst** Biol. Abstr.; Chem. Abstr. (1988-); Curr. Contents Life Sci.; EMBASE; Index Med. (1988-); Ref. Upd. Deluxe Ed.; Res. Alert [Full Cov.]; Sci. Cit. Index.

US/1052-3987
**REPORT ON UROLOGIC TECHNIQUES, THE.** ***Suspended.*** [Rep. urol. tech.]. Vol. 1, No. 1 (July/Aug. 1991)-Suspended. Periodical. English. Ten times a year. $49.00 (one year), $98.00 (two years), $147.00 (three years) Individuals; $69.00 (one year), $138.00 (two years), $207.00 (three years) Institutions. Churchill Livingstone, 1-3 Baxter's Place, Leith Walk, Edinburgh EH1 3AF Scotland. **Tel** 011 44 31 556 2424, FAX 011 44 31 558 1278, telex 727511. **ED** R Lawrence Kroovand. **DD** 616. **NLM** W1; RE212GL.

SP
**REUNIONES REGIONALES DE UROLOGIA.** Spanish. Reycosa, Orense 39/ 1-C, 28020 Madrid Spain.

SP
**REVISTA DE LA ASOCIACION ESPANOLA DE A.T.S. EN UROLOGIA.** Spanish. Asociacion Espanola de ATS en Urologia, Travesera del Arenal 1/ 3-8, 28013 Madrid Spain.

JA/0385-2393
**RINSHUO HINYUOKIKA.** [Rinshuo hinyuokika]. **VFOAT** Japanese Journal of Clinical Urology. (1967)-. Periodical. Japanese. mo. Igaku Shoin Ltd., 5-24-3 Hongo Bunkyo-ku, Tokyo 113 Japan. **Tel** 011 81 3 817 5670. **DD** 616.6. ***Continues*** *Rinshuo Hifu Hinyuokika.*
**Ind/Abst** EMBASE [Select. Cov.].

SW/0036-5599
**SCANDINAVIAN JOURNAL OF UROLOGY AND NEPHROLOGY.** [Scand. j. urol. nephrol.]. **Added/Corp** Scandinavian Association of Urology. Scandinavian Association of Nephrology. Society for the Publication of Acta Chirurgica Scandinavica. Vol. 1 (1967)-. Academic Scholarly Publication. English. qt. Kr955.00, $147.00. Scandinavian University Press, PO Box 2959 Toeyen, N 0608 Oslo 6 Norway. **Tel** 011 47 2 2575400, FAX 011 47 2 2575353, telex 71896 UROR N. **(Subscription address:** Scandinavian University Press, 200 Meacham Ave., Elmont NY 11003.**)** **ED** Stig Colleen. **NLM** W1 SC154E. **CODEN** SJUNAS. Index available in last issue of volume--attached. **Bk Rev.** **Ad Acc.** **Pr Rev. Circ:** 4,000. Documents available from The Genuine Article, BIOSIS Document Express, CASDDS.
**Desc:** Organ of the Scandinavian Associations of Urology and Nephrology. Presents papers on urological and nephrological topics preferentially from the Nordic countries.
**Ind/Abst** Biol. Abstr.; Chem. Abstr.; Curr. Contents Clin. Med.; EMBASE; Index Med.; Mod. Med.; Life Sci. Collect.; PESTDOC; Ref. Upd. Deluxe Ed.; Res. Alert [Full Cov.]; Rev. Med. Vet. Mycology; Sci. Cit. Index; SCISEARCH; Soc. Sci. Cit. Index [Select. Cov.].

SW/0300-8886
**SCANDINAVIAN JOURNAL OF UROLOGY AND NEPHROLOGY. SUPPLEMENT.** [Scand. j. urol. nephrol., Suppl.]. (1968)-. English. ir. Comes with Scandinavian Journal of Urology and Nephrology: $147.00. Scandinavian University Press, PO Box 2959 Toeyen, N 0608 Oslo 6 Norway. **Tel** 011 47 2 2575400, FAX 011 47 2 2575353, telex 71896 UROR N. **(Subscription address:** Scandinavian University Press, 200 Meacham Ave., Elmont NY 11003.**)** **NLM** W1 SC154F. **CODEN** SJUNBT. Documents available from CASDDS.
**Ind/Abst** Chem. Abstr. (1968-1983); Curr. Contents Clin. Med.; Index Med.; Life Sci. Collect.

US/0270-9295
**SEMINARS IN NEPHROLOGY.** [Semin. nephrol.]. Vol. 1, No. 1 (Mar. 1981)-. Academic Scholarly Publication. English. bm. $125.00 (individual), $174.00 (institution) US; $188.00 (individual), $207.00 (institution) other. W.B. Saunders Company, A Subsidiary of Harcourt Brace Jovanovich, Inc., The Curtis Center/Suite 300, Independence Square West, Philadelphia PA 19106-3399. **Tel** (215)238-7800 or, 5587, FAX (215)238-7883, telex 173146. **(Subscription address:** W. B. Saunders Company / North America Subscriptions, c/o Periodicals, 6277 Sea Harbour Drive, 4th Floor, Orlando FL 32887.**)** **ED** Neil A. Kurtzman. **UDC** 616.6. **NLM** W1 SE489CM. **CODEN** SNEPDJ. **[CCC].** **Pr Rev. Circ:** 3,142. Documents available from The Genuine Article, CASDDS.
**Desc:** Intended as a timely source for the publication of new concepts and research findings directly applicable to day-to-day clinical practice.
**Ind/Abst** Chem. Abstr.; Curr. Contents Clin. Med.; EMBASE; Index Med. (1985-); Nutr. Abstr. Rev., Ser. A, Hum. Exp.; Res. Alert [Full Cov.]; Sci. Cit. Index; SCISEARCH.

US/0730-9147
**SEMINARS IN UROLOGY.** [Semin. urol.]. Vol. 1, No. 1 (Feb. 1983)-. Periodical. English. qt (Feb., May, Aug., Nov.). $85.00 (individual), $111.00 (institution); $122.00 (individual), $137.00 (institution) other. W.B. Saunders Company, A Subsidiary of Harcourt Brace Jovanovich, Inc., The Curtis Center/Suite 300, Independence Square West, Philadelphia PA 19106-3399. **Tel** (215)238-7800 or, 5587, FAX (215)238-7883, telex 173146. **(Subscription address:** W. B. Saunders Company / North America Subscriptions, c/o Periodicals, 6277 Sea Harbour Drive, 4th Floor, Orlando FL 32887.**)** **ED** E. Darracott Vaughan, Jr. **NLM** W1; SE489R. **[CCC].** **Circ:** 3,713.
**Desc:** Provides the urologist with a review of important topics in the field. Each issue is devoted to an area of particular importance in which invited experts discuss a wealth of clinical experience.
**Ind/Abst** EMBASE; Index Med.; Nutr. Res. Newsl.; Physic. Medline Plus.

KO
**TAEHAN PINYOGIKWA HAKHOE CHI.** **VFOAT** The Korean Journal of Urology; Korean Journal of Urology; Taehan Pinyohoe Chi. Periodical. Korean (summaries and/or abstracts in English). Taehan Pinyogikwa Hakhoe, c/o Department of Urology, Catholic Medical College, Seoul Korea. **LC** RC870; .T335. **UDC** 616.6.

US
**TECHNIQUES IN UROLOGY.** Vol. 1 (1995)-. Periodical. English. qt. $85.00 (individuals), $115.00 (institutions) US; $95.00 (individuals), $130.00 (institutions) other. Raven Press, 1185 Avenue of the Americas, 37th Floor, New York NY 10036. **Tel** (212)930-9500, (212)930-9604, FAX (212)869-3495, (212)302-8507, telex 640073.

GW/0936-2002
**TW-UROLOGIE, NEPHROLOGIE.** [TW-Urol. Nephrol.]. **VFOAT** Therapie-Woche-Urologie, Nephrologie. (1989)-. Periodical. German. bm. G Braun Verlag, Postfach 1709, D 76006 Karlsruhe Germany. **Tel** 011 49 721 165392. **UDC** 61.
**Ind/Abst** EMBASE [Select. Cov.].

GW/0340-2592
**UROLOGE. AUSGABE. A, DER.** [Urol. Ausg. A]. Vol. 9 (Jan. 1970)-. Academic Scholarly Publication. German. bm. DM488.00. Springer-Verlag GmbH & Company KG, Heidelberger Platz 3, D 14197 Berlin Germany. **Tel** 011 49 30 8207223, FAX 011 49 30 8214091, telex 183 319 SPBLN D. **(Subscription address:** Springer Verlag New York Inc. / for North America, 44 Hartz Way, Secaucus NJ 07096.**)** **ED** R Hautmann, C Chaussy, and J Soekeland. **NLM** W1 UR624Q. **CODEN** URGABW. **[CCC].** **Pr Rev.** available on microfilm from University Microfilms International (UMI). Documents available from The Genuine Article, BIOSIS Document Express. ***Continues*** *Der Urologe.*
**Desc:** Goal is to further the education of the urologist and doctors in related fields through presentation of current problems in clinic and practice.
**Ind/Abst** Biol. Abstr.; Curr. Contents Clin. Med.; EMBASE; Energy Res. Abstr. (Jan. 1971-); Index Med.; Life Sci. Collect.; Res. Alert [Full Cov.]; Sci. Cit. Index; SCISEARCH.

GW/0042-1111
**UROLOGE. AUSGABE B.** (UROLOGE. B : ORGAN DES BERUFSVERBANDES DER DEUTSCHEN UROLOGEN.). [Urologe, Ausg. B]. (1970)-. Academic Scholarly Publication. German. bm. DM518.00. Springer-Verlag GmbH & Company KG, Heidelberger Platz 3, D 14197 Berlin Germany. **Tel** 011 49 30 8207223, FAX 011 49 30 8214091, telex 183 319 SPBLN D. **(Subscription address:** Springer Verlag New York Inc. / for North America, 44 Hartz Way, Secaucus NJ 07096.**)** **ED** W Knipper, J Soekeland, P May, M Richter-Reichhelm, K Schalkhaeuser, and M Ziegler. **NLM** W1 UR624R. **[CCC].** available on microfilm from University Microfilms International (UMI). ***Supersedes in part*** *Der Urologe.*
**Desc:** Covers continued education for urologists including new experiences and research results in anesthesia, bacteriology, biomedical technology, surgery, dermato-venerology, gynecology and obstetrics, internal medicine and pediatrics.
**Ind/Abst** EMBASE; Life Sci. Collect.

IT/0391-5603
**UROLOGIA.** [Urologia]. **Added/Corp** Societa Italiana di Urologia. Vol. 1, (Mar. 1934)-. Academic Scholarly Publication. Italian (English, French, German, Italian and Spanish; summaries and/or abstracts in English and Italian). Six times a year. L150000.00 Italy; $170.00 other. Canova, CP 252, 31100 Treviso Italy. **Tel** 011 39 422 382383. **NLM** W1 UR627. Index available. cum. index. **Bk Rev,** (Qty: 20-25). **Ad Acc.** **Pr Rev. Circ:** 1,000 (ctrl).
**Desc:** A scientific journal and official organ of the North Italian Society of Urology.
**Ind/Abst** EMBASE.

SZ/0042-1138
**UROLOGIA INTERNATIONALIS.** [Urol. int.]. **Added/Corp** International Continence Society. (1955)-. Academic Scholarly Publication. English. Eight times a year. $650.00. S. Karger AG, Allschwilerstrasse 10, PO Box - Postfach - Case Postale, CH-4009 Basel Switzerland. **Tel** 011 41 61 306-1111, FAX 011 41 61 306-1234, telex CH 962 652. **ED** D. Hauri, R. Ackermann, Y. Aso, G. Bartsch, F. M. J. Debruyne, P. Graber, F. Schroder. **NLM** W1 UR632. **CODEN** URINAC. **[CCC].** **Ad Acc.** **Pr Rev.** available on microfilm from University Microfilms International (UMI). Documents available from The Genuine Article, BIOSIS Document Express, CASDDS.
**Desc:** Brief but fully substantiated reports of practice-oriented research into the etiology, pathophysiology and management of diseases of the urinary and urogenital tract form the nucleus of original papers in this journal. Essential issues receiving regular coverage include the experimental introduction of new techniques and instrumentation, clinical evidence for the evaluation of function tests, and diagnostic tools. Special attention is also given to advances in chemotherapy and experimental surgical techniques. Apart from offering new data on such problems as infectious diseases, infertility and lithiasis, high priority is placed on improvements in the diagnosis and treatment of cancer through progress in tumor staging and marking.
**Ind/Abst** Biol. Abstr.; Chem. Abstr.; CSA Neuro. Abstr. (?-?); Curr. Contents Clin. Med.; EMBASE; Helminthol. Abstr. (1991-); Index Med.; Index Vet.; Pig News Inf.; Ref. Upd. Deluxe Ed.; Res. Alert [Select. Cov.]; Soc. Sci. Cit. Index [Select. Cov.].

PL/0500-7208
**UROLOGIA POLSKA.** (UROLOGIA POLSKA : ORGAN POLSKIEGO TOWARZYSTWA UROLOGICZNEGO.). [Urol. Pol.]. **Added/Corp** Polskie Towarzystwo Urologicznie. (1951)-. Periodical. Polish (summaries and/or abstracts in English and Russian). qt. Price on Request. **(Subscription address:** ARS Polona, PO Box 1001, 00068 Warsaw Poland.**)** **CODEN** URPOAG. Documents available from CASDDS.
**Ind/Abst** Chem. Abstr. (1951-1978).

US/0094-0143
**UROLOGIC CLINICS OF NORTH AMERICA, THE.** [Urol. clin. North Am.]. Vol. 1 (Feb. 1974)-. Academic Scholarly Publication. English. qt. $100.00 (individual), $130.00 (institution) US; $142.00 (individual), $149.00 (institution) other. W.B. Saunders Company, A Subsidiary of Harcourt Brace Jovanovich, Inc., The Curtis Center/Suite 300, Independence Square West, Philadelphia PA 19106-3399. **Tel** (215)238-7800 or, 5587, FAX (215)238-7883, telex 173146.

**(Subscription address:** W. B. Saunders Company / North America Subscriptions, c/o Periodicals, 6277 Sea Harbour Drive, 4th Floor, Orlando FL 32887.) **ED** Livia Berardi. **UDC** 725.51:616.6(73). **NLM** W1 UR638. **CODEN** UCNADW. **[CCC]. Pr Rev. Circ:** 6,000. available on microfilm and microfiche from University Microfilms International (UMI). Documents available from The Genuine Article, BIOSIS Document Express.
**Desc:** Practical updates for the clinician on the latest advances. Each issue addresses a single topic in patient care.
**Ind/Abst** Abr. Index Med.; Biol. Abstr.; Curr. Contents Clin. Med.; EMBASE; Energy Res. Abstr. (July 1982-); Index Med.; Life Sci. Collect.; Physic. Medline Plus; Res. Alert [Full Cov.]; Sci. Cit. Index; SCISEARCH; Soc. Sci. Cit. Index [Select. Cov.]; SportSearch.

US/1053-816X
**UROLOGIC NURSING. See** Medical Science and Technology-Nursing.

US/0171-1091
**UROLOGIC RADIOLOGY.** ***Title Change.*** [Urol. radiol.]. Vol. 1-14 No. 4 (1979)-(1992). Periodical. English. qt. Springer-Verlag New York Inc., 175 5th Avenue, New York NY 10010. **Tel** (212)460-1500, telex 232 235 SPB UR. **(Subscription address:** Springer Verlag New York Inc. / for North America, 44 Hartz Way, Secaucus NJ 07096.) **ED** J Becker, M A Bosniak, and L Dalla Palma. **NLM** W1 UR638R. **[CCC]. Pr Rev.** available on microfilm and microfiche from University Microfilms International (UMI). Documents available from The Genuine Article. ***Merged with*** *Gastrointestinal Radiology, 0364-2356* ***to form*** *Abdominal Imaging, 0942-8925.*
**Desc:** Focuses on the study of the urinary tract utilizing radiography, angiography, ultrasonography, nuclear medicine, computed tomography, invasive techniques and associated modalities.
**Ind/Abst** Curr. Contents Clin. Med.; EMBASE; Index Med.; Life Sci. Collect.; Res. Alert [Full Cov.]; Sci. Cit. Index; SCISEARCH.

GW/0300-5623
**UROLOGICAL RESEARCH.** [Urol. res.]. Vol. 1 (Jan. 1973)-. Academic Scholarly Publication. English. bm. DM648.00. Springer-Verlag GmbH & Company KG, Heidelberger Platz 3, D 14197 Berlin Germany. **Tel** 011 49 30 8207223, FAX 011 49 30 8214091, telex 183 319 SPBLN D. **(Subscription address:** Springer Verlag New York Inc. / for North America, 44 Hartz Way, Secaucus NJ 07096.) **ED** L Andersson, G D Chisholm, J Frick, H Hisazumi, G Rutishauser, F H Schroeder, R Ackermann, F M J Debruyne, M J Droller, and R Hartung. **DD** 616.6. **NLM** W1 UR639. **CODEN** URLRA5. **[CCC]. Pr Rev.** available on microfilm and microfiche from University Microfilms International (UMI). Documents available from The Genuine Article, CASDDS.
**Desc:** Publishes original articles on research in the fields of clinical medicine, animal experimentation and laboratory techniques. Contents are designed to increse the reader's understanding of the functions of the genitourinary system in normal and diseases states.
**Ind/Abst** Calcium Calcif. Tissue Abstr.; Chem. Abstr.; Curr. Contents Clin. Med.; Curr. Contents Life Sci.; EMBASE; Index Med.; Life Sci. Collect.; Res. Alert [Full Cov.]; Sci. Cit. Index; SCISEARCH.

RU/0042-1154
**UROLOGIJA I NEFROLOGIJA.** (UROLOGIIA I NEFROLOGIIA.). [Urol. nefrol.]. **Added/Corp** Soviet Union. Ministerstvo Zdravookhraneniia. Vsesoiuznoe Nauchnoe Obshchestvo Urologov (Soviet Union). Vol. 30, (Jan./Feb. 1965)-. Academic Scholarly Publication. Russian (summaries and/or abstracts in English). bm. $69.95. Izdatelstvo Meditsina / Russian Academy of Medical Sciences, Ulitsa Solyanka 14, 109801 Moscow Russia. **Tel** 011 95 297-05-04. **(Subscription address:** East View Publications Inc., 3020 Harbor Lane North, Suite 110, Minneapolis MN 55447.) **NLM** W1 UR679A. **CODEN** URNEAA. **Bk Rev.** Documents available from BIOSIS Document Express, CASDDS. ***Continues*** *Urologiia.*
**Ind/Abst** Biol. Abstr.; Chem. Abstr. (1965-1983); EMBASE; Index Med.

US/0889-6283
**UROLOGY ANNUAL.** [Urol. annu.]. (1987)-. English. an (Dec.). $85.00. Maxwell Macmillan Professional Business Division, 910 Sylvan Avenue, Englewood Cliffs NJ 07632-3310. **Tel** (800)431-9025. **(Subscription address:** Maxwell Macmillan, PO Box 41264, Philadelphia PA 19162.) **ED** Stephen N. Rous. **LC** RC870; .U774. **DD** 616.6/005. **NLM** W1; UR68C. **[CCC].**

US/0271-1338
**UROLOGY (GLENDALE, CALIF.).** (UROLOGY. SOUND RECORDING.). [Urol.]. **Added/Corp** Audio-Digest Foundation. **VFOAT** Audio-Digest. Urology Sound Recording. (1978)-. Periodical. English. mo. $89.88 US; $101.40 Canada; $123.72 other. Audio-Digest Foundation, 1577 Chevy Chase Drive, Glendale CA 91206. **Tel** (213)245-8505, (800)423-2308, FAX (818)240-7379. **ED** Claron L. Oakley. **DD** 616. **NLM** W1 AU201EG. Index available. ctrl circ.
**Desc:** Interactive system of audio cassette postgraduate medical programs, eligible for two Category I credit hours.

●UK/1352-9544
**UROLOGY INTERNATIONAL.** (1994)-. Periodical. English. qt. Complete Medical Communications, CMC House, Jordangate, Macclesfield Cheshire SK10 1EW, United Kingdom. **Tel** 011 44 625 619855, FAX 011 44 625 619812. **ED** Mark Soloway.
**Desc:** Strives to meet the informational, educational and practical needs of urologists from around the world. Also offers special features that address practical issues affecting worldwide urological treatment such as patient management, clinical trials and case studies.

US/0090-4295
**UROLOGY (RIDGEWOOD, N.J.).** (UROLOGY.). [Urology]. Vol. 1 (Jan. 1973)-. Periodical. English. mo. $85.00 (individuals), $135.00 (institutions). Excerpta Medica / US, PO Box 3085, Princeton NJ 08543-3085. **Tel** (908)874-8550, FAX (908)874-5611. **(Subscription address:** Urology, PO Box 7725, Riverton NJ 08077.) **ED** Pablo Morales. **LC** RC870; .U77. **DD** 616.6. **NLM** W1 UR679P. **CODEN** URGYA. cum. index. **Ad Acc. Pr Rev.** available on microfilm and microfiche from University Microfilms International (UMI). Documents available from The Genuine Article, BIOSIS Document Express.
**Desc:** Contains practical case studies on important research findings and new clinical applications on sterility/fertility, pediatric urology, uropathology, uroradiology, endourology, urochemotherapy and more.
**Ind/Abst** Biol. Abstr.; Curr. Contents Clin. Med.; EMBASE; Energy Res. Abstr. (Aug. 1974-); Index Med.; Med. Abstr. Newsl.; Nutr. Res. Newsl.; Life Sci. Collect.; Physic. Medline Plus; Res. Alert [Full Cov.]; Rev. Med. Vet. Mycology; Sci. Cit. Index; SCISEARCH; Soc. Sci. Cit. Index [Select. Cov.]; SportSearch.

US/0093-9722
**UROLOGY TIMES.** [Urol. times]. (1973)-. Periodical. English. mo. $95.00 US and possessions; $140.00 Canada; $185.00 other. Advanstar Communications Inc., 131 West First Street, Duluth MN 55802. **Tel** (218)723-9477, (800)346-0085. **ED** Dean Celia. **DD** 616. **NLM** W1 UR68T. **[CCC]. Circ:** 8,619. available on an online database (file 16/Full-Text) from DIALOG.
**Desc:** A scientific tabloid providing news of urology.
**Ind/Abst** F&S Index Plus Text, Int. [Full Txt.] [Select. Cov.]; PROMT [Full Txt.].

GW/0070-413X
**VERHANDLUNGSBERICHT DER DEUTSCHEN GESELLSCHAFT FUER UROLOGIE.** [Verhandlungsber. Dtsch. Ges. Urol.]. **Added/Corp** Deutsche Gesellschaft fuer Urologie. (1949)-. Monographic series. German. ir. Price varies per volume. Springer-Verlag GmbH & Company KG, Heidelberger Platz 3, D 14197 Berlin Germany. **Tel** 011 49 30 8207223, FAX 011 49 30 8214091, telex 183 319 SPBLN D. **(Subscription address:** Springer Verlag New York Inc. / for North America, 44 Hartz Way, Secaucus NJ 07096.) **NLM** W1 VE4871D. ***Continues*** *Verhandlungsbericht der Urologentagung, 0372-8595.*
**Desc:** Contains articles about urology.

RU/0042-4625
**VESTNIK HIRURGII IM. I.I. GREKOVA.** (VESTNIK KHIRURGII IM. I.I. GREKOVA.). [Vestn. hir. im. I.I. Grekova]. **Added/Corp** Soviet Union. Ministerstvo Zdravookhraneniia. Soviet Union. Narodnyi Komissariat Zdravookhraneniia. Vsesoiuznoe Nauchnoe Obshchestvo Khirurgov (Soviet Union) Khirurgicheskoe Obshchestvo Pirogova. (1935)-. Periodical. Russian (summaries and/or abstracts in English). mo. $119.95. **(Subscription address:** East View Publications Inc., 3020 Harbor Lane North, Suite 110, Minneapolis MN 55447.) **NLM** W1 VE836. **Pr Rev.** Documents available from The Genuine Article. ***Continues*** *Vestnik Khirurgii i Porganichnykh Oblastei.*
**Ind/Abst** Dairy Sci. Abstr.; EMBASE [Select. Cov.]; Helminthol. Abstr. (1991-); Index Med.; Nutr. Abstr. Rev., Ser. A, Hum. Exp.; Res. Alert [Select. Cov.]; SportSearch.

US/1048-2547
**WELLCOME TRENDS IN UROLOGY/NEPHROLOGY.** [Wellcome trends urol./nephrol.]. **Added/Corp** Burroughs Wellcome Company. **VFOAT** Trends in Urology/Nephrology; Urology/Nephrology. Vol. 6, No. 3 (June 1984)-. Periodical. English. bm. Wellcome Trends in Urology/Nephrology, 15 Park Row, New York NY 10038. **DD** 616. ***Continues*** *Wellcome Trends in Urology.*

GW/0724-4983
**WORLD JOURNAL OF UROLOGY.** [World j. urol.]. **Added/Corp** Urological Research Society. Vol. 1, No. 1 (Apr. 1983)-. Periodical. English. Six times a year. DM448.00. Springer-Verlag GmbH & Company KG, Heidelberger Platz 3, D 14197 Berlin Germany. **Tel** 011 49 30 8207223, FAX 011 49 30 8214091, telex 183 319 SPBLN D. **(Subscription address:** Springer Verlag New York Inc. / for North America, 44 Hartz Way, Secaucus NJ 07096.) **ED** U Jonas and R J Krane. **NLM** W1; WO88KD. **[CCC]. Ad Acc. Pr Rev. Circ:** 668. available on microfilm and microfiche from University Microfilms International (UMI). Documents available from The Genuine Article.
**Desc:** Conveys regularly, the essential results of urological research and their practical and clinical relevance to a broad audience of urologists in research and clinical practice.
**Ind/Abst** Curr. Contents Clin. Med.; EMBASE; Index Med. (1993-); Nutr. Res. Newsl.; Res. Alert [Full Cov.]; Sci. Cit. Index; SCISEARCH.

●US/1046-6266
**YEAR BOOK OF NEPHROLOGY, THE.** [Year book nephrol.]. **VFOAT** Yearbook of Nephrology. (1992)-. English. an. $64.95. Mosby Year Book Inc., 11830 Westline Industrial Drive, St Louis MO 63146. **Tel** (800)325-4177, (314)872-8370, FAX (314)432-1380, telex 44-2402. **LC** IN PROCESS. **DD** 616. **NLM** W1; YE199K.

US/0084-4071
**YEAR BOOK OF UROLOGY, THE.** [Year book urol.]. **VFOAT** Yearbook of Urology. (1933)-. English. an. $59.95. Mosby Year Book Inc., 11830 Westline Industrial Drive, St Louis MO 63146. **Tel** (800)325-4177, (314)872-8370, FAX (314)432-1380, telex 44-2402. **DD** 616. **UDC** 616.6(058). **NLM** W1 YE346. ***Continues*** *Urology.*

## MEN'S INTERESTS

US/1070-6836
**ALADDIN'S WINDOW.** [Aladdin's window]. (Nov. 1991)-. Periodical. English. qt. $12.00. Afterglow Publications, 28936 Shingle Creek Lane, Shingletown CA 96088-9658. **Tel** (916)474-1385. **ED** J.R. Molloy. **DD** 305. **Bk Rev. Ad Acc.** available on magnetic tape.
**Desc:** Articles deal with the psychological aspects of evolution and awareness as they pertain to a variety of men's issues.

US/1058-5826
**ALBERTSEN'S SINGLES DIRECTORY.** [Albertsen's singles dir.]. **VFOAT** Singles Directory. (1991)-. Directory. English. sa. $9.00. Albertsen's, Box 339, Nevada City CA 95959. **Tel** (916)292-3655, FAX (916)477-0915. **DD** 646.

US/1059-4701
**AMERICAN SINGLES MAGAZINE.** (1991)-. Periodical. English. mo. $24.00. American Publishing Group, PO Box 10189, Salinas CA 93912-7189.

JA
**BRUTUS MAGAZINE.** English. sm. $141.00. Magazine House, 3-13-20 Ginza, Chuo-ku, Tokyo 104 Japan. **Tel** 03-3545-7100. **(Subscription address:** Japan Publications Trading Company, Ltd., PO Box 5030, Tokyo International, Tokyo 100-31 Japan.)

CN/1183-7675
**CELIBATAIRES MAGAZINE.** [Celibat. mag.]. Vol. 1, No 1 (Jul. 1991)-. Periodical. French. ir. 1.00Can$ per issue. Jass, Inc., 8578 Rue Rene-LaBelle, Montreal Quebec H2M 2L7 Canada. **DD** 305.9/0652/097142805.

US
**CHANGING MEN.** Periodical. English. mo. Men's Resource Center, 2036 SE Morrison, Portland OR 97214-2824. **Tel** (503)235-3433.

US/0889-7174
**CHANGING MEN (MADISON, WIS.).** (CHANGING MEN.). [Chang. men]. **Added/Corp** University YMCA Community Center (Madison, Wis.). No. 14 (Spring 1985)-. Periodical. English. Twice a year (July and Nov.). $35.00. Feminist Men's Publication Inc., 306 North Brooks Street, Madison WI 53715. **Tel** (608)256-2565. **ED** Michael Biernbaum and Rick Cole. **LC** HQ1090.3; .M23. **DD** 305.3/1/0973. **Bk Rev**, (Qty: 28). **Ad Acc, Adv Mgr:** Peter Bresnick. **Circ:** 5,000. ***Continues*** *M (Madison, Wis.), 0885-4386.*
**Desc:** Examines traditional masculinity and provides alternative viewpoints on male socialization, sexuality and sex roles and looks at gender relationships, parenthood and topical issues in the nineties. Includes fiction, art, poetry, sports, history, and humor.
**Ind/Abst** Altern. Press Index.

BE/1016-9660
**CINE & MEDIA. See** Communication.

US/0747-0819
**CLUB INTERNATIONAL (NEWTOWN, CONN.).** (CLUB INTERNATIONAL.). Periodical. English. mo. $39.00 North America; $46.00 other. Fiona Press Inc, 308 East Hitt Street, Mt Morris IL 61054. **Tel** (203)775-1065. **(Subscription address:** PO Box 143, Mt Morris, IL 61054) **ED** Simon Belter. **Ad Acc. Circ:** 295,000 (ctrl).
**Desc:** Beauties from around the world adorn this top adult title with steaming full-color photographic sets, and coverage of unusual and daring sexual happenings, plus exciting editorial features, outrageous columns and a selection of reader's photographic entries.

US/0011-4707
**D.A.C. NEWS. See** Recreation, Leisure-Sports.

US
**DAD.** See Family and Marriage.

US/0740-4921
**DETAILS (NEW YORK, N.Y.).** (DETAILS.). [Details]. **VFOAT** Details for Men. Vol. 1, No. 2 (June 1982)-. Periodical. English. mo. $15.00. Conde Nast Publications / New York, 350 Madison Avenue, New York NY 10017. **Tel** (212)880-8800, (800)777-0700. **(Subscription address:** Neodata / Colorado, PO Box 2606, Boulder Boulder CO 80322.**) LC** NX504; .D47. **DD** 700/.5. **Bk Rev**. **Ad Acc.** available on microfilm from University Microfilms International (UMI).
**Desc:** Men's magazine emphasizing style, fashion, grooming, adventure and music.
**Ind/Abst** Access (1991-).

US/1058-4188
**DIRECTIONS FOR PENNSYLVANIA SINGLES!.** See Women's Interests.

US/0277-9625
**DIRECTORY OF MEN'S & BOYS' WEAR SPECIALTY STORES.** See Clothing Industry and Fashion.

●US/1061-8481
**DIRT (NEW YORK, N.Y.).** (DIRT.). [Dirt]. Vol. 1, No. 1, Spring (1992)-. Periodical. English. qt. Available on newsstands only. Lang Communications, 230 Park Avenue, New York NY 10169. **Tel** (212)551-9500, FAX (212)599-4597. **ED** Mark Lewman. **DD** 051. **Ad Acc, Adv Mgr:** Andrew Crossfield, **Tel** (212)551-9333. **Circ:** 150,000.
**Desc:** Lifestyle magazine for young men covering sports, music, girls, fashion and celebrities.

US/0884-4879
**EBONY MAN.** (EBONY MAN : EM.). [Ebony man]. **VFOAT** EM. Vol. 1, No. 1 (Nov. 1985)-. Periodical. English. mo. $16.00 (one year), $28.00 (two year), $40.00 (three year). Johnson Publishing Company / Illinois, 820 South Michigan Avenue, Chicago IL 60605. **Tel** (312)322-9200, (800)272-6602. **LC** IN PROCESS. **DD** 646. **Ad Acc.**
**Desc:** Contains articles on fashion, grooming, fitness, health care, sports, career advancement, personal finances, male-female relationships, interior design, entertainment, autos, electronics, and travel. Celebrity and achiever interviews. Annual swimsuit issue in January.
**Ind/Abst** Acad. Abstr. Full Text Elite (Jul. 1993-) [Full Txt.]; Acad. Abstr. (July 1993-); Acad. Search (July 1993-); Mag. Artic. Summar. Elite (July 1993-) [Full Txt.]; Mag. Artic. Summar. CD-ROM (July 1993-); Mid. Search (Aug. 1993-) [Full Txt.].

UK
**FOR HIM.** English. bm. £11.00 UK; £18.00 other. Tayvale, 9211 Curtain Road, London EC2A 3LT England. **Tel** 011 44 71 2475447.

US/1041-9470
**FOX (NEW YORK, N.Y. 1984).** (FOX.). (1984)-. Periodical. English. Thirteen times a year (Extra iss. in Oct./Nov.). $25.00 US; $39.00 other. Montcalm Publishing Corporation, 401 Park Avenue South, New York NY 10016. **Tel** (212)779-8900, FAX (212)725-7215. **ED** Barry Janoff. **Bk Rev**. **Ad Acc. Circ:** 150,000.

US/1055-2367
**FULL-TIME DADS.** See Family and Marriage.

US/0195-072X
**GALLERY (NEW YORK, N.Y.).** (GALLERY.). [Gallery]. (197?)-. Periodical. English. Thirteen times a year. $25.00 US; $39.00 other. Gallery Magazine, PO Box 254, Mt. Morris IL 61054. **Tel** (212)779-8900, (800)435-0715. **ED** Barry Janoff. **DD** 051. **Bk Rev**. **Ad Acc, Adv Mgr:** T. Martoran.

UK/0953-5233
**GENDER & HISTORY.** See Women's Interests.

US/0016-6979
**GQ.** [GQ]. **VFOAT** G.Q.; Gentlemen's Quarterly. Vol. 53, No. 6 (June 1983)-. Periodical. English. mo. $20.00. Conde Nast Publications / New York, 350 Madison Avenue, New York NY 10017. **Tel** (212)880-8800, (800)777-0700. **(Subscription address:** Neodata / Colorado, PO Box 2606, Boulder Boulder CO 80322.**) ED** Arthur Cooper. **LC** TT570; .A6. **DD** 646/.32/05. **Bk Rev**. **Ad Acc.** available on microfilm and microfiche from University Microfilms International (UMI). Documents available from UMI Article Clearinghouse. ***Continues*** *Gentlemen's Quarterly, 0016-6979.*
**Desc:** Provides authoritative and helpful guidance in men's fashion, grooming and fitness. Also features travel, recreation, food, entertainment, humor, home, technology and career information.
**Ind/Abst** Acad. Abstr. Full Text Elite (July 1989-); Acad. Abstr. (July 1989-); Access (1986-1988); Gen. Period. Index (1989-); Mag. Artic. Summar. Elite (July 1989-); Mag. Artic. Summar. Select (July 1989-); Mag. Artic. Summar. CD-ROM (July 1989-); Mag. Index Plus (1989-); Mag. Index. Sel. (1986-); Mag. Search; Newsp. Period. Abstr. (1988-); Read. Guide Abstr. Select Ed.; Read. Guide Period. Lit.; Mag. Index (1989-); Vocat. Search (July 1989-).

UK/0954-8750
**GQ (UK EDITION).** (GQ : GENTLEMEN'S QUARTERLY (UK EDITION).). **VFOAT** Gentlemen's Quarterly. (1989)-. Consumer Publication. English. mo. $73.50. Conde Nast Publications Ltd, Perrymount Road, Haywards Heath, West Sussex RH16 3DH England. **Tel** 011 44 444 440421, FAX 011 44 444 440619. **ED** Micheal Ver Meulen. **Bk Rev**, (Qty: 48). **Ad Acc, Adv Mgr:** Tony Long, **Tel** 011 44 71 499 9080. **Acid Free. Circ:** 100,424.

●US/1056-4551
**GROOM'S GUIDE, THE.** **VFOAT** Piedmont Triad Groom's Guide. (1992)-. English. Free. Joy Productions, PO Box 38632, Greensboro NC 27438-8632.

US
**HAWK.** English. ir. $36.00 (subscription), $4.95 (cover price). Killer Joe Productions Inc., 801 Second Avenue, New York NY 10017. **Tel** (212)661-7878. **ED** Bob Johnson. **Circ:** 250,000.
**Desc:** Targeted to men in their 20's and 30's, with some editorial on fashion, fitness and music.

US
**HEARTBOUND.** (Winter 1990)-. English. $24.95. CM Productions Inc, PO Box 18851, West Palm Beach FL 33416-8851. **Tel** (407)683-3757, (407)641-4775.
**Desc:** Exciting, upscale magazine with photos and profiles of single ladies who want to correspond with single men around the United States.

●US/1064-8976
**HOMBRE INTERNACIONAL.** [Hombre int.]. **VFOAT** Hombre. Vol. 17, No. 3 (Apr. [i.e., Mar.] 1992)-. Periodical. Spanish. mo (12 issues). $25.50. Editorial America SA, 6355 Northwest 36th Street, Miami FL 33166. **Tel** (305)871-6400. **(Subscription address:** CDS, SIFD Agency Control, 1901 Bell Avenue, Demoine, IA 50315 (Phone: (515)246-6812)**) LC** AP63; .H715. **DD** 056/.1. ***Continues*** *Hombre de Mundo.*
**Desc:** In-depth articles on the economy, the business world, politics, travel, fashion, the arts and sports. Also includes interviews and profiles on leading personalities and celebrities from around the world.

●US/1066-4181
**HOT ROD SWIMSUIT SPECIAL.** (1993)-. English. $3.95. Petersen Publishing Company, 6420 Wilshire Bouldevard, Los Angeles CA 90048. **Tel** (213)782-2485.

US/0149-4635
**HUSTLER (COLUMBUS).** (HUSTLER.). (July 1974)-. Periodical. English. Twelve times a year. LFP Inc., 9171 Wilshire Boulevard/Suite 300, Beverly Hills CA 90210. **Tel** (310)858-7100, FAX (310)274-7985. **ED** Doug Oliver. **LC** AP2; .H967. **DD** 051. **Bk Rev**. **Ad Acc. Circ:** 1,000,000.
**Desc:** Male entertainment features.
**Ind/Abst** Index Period. Artic. Relat. Law.

US/0199-5405
**HUSTLER HUMOR.** (19??)-. Periodical. English. Nine times a year. LFP Inc., 9171 Wilshire Boulevard/Suite 300, Beverly Hills CA 90210. **Tel** (310)858-7100, FAX (310)274-7985. **(Subscription address:** LFP Inc., PO Box 16958, North Hollywood CA 91615.**)**

AT
**INSIDE EDGE.** (19??)-. Periodical. English. Nine times a year. 45.00Aus$ Australia; 66.00Aus$ New Zealand; 83.70Aus$ other. Australian Consolidated Press Ltd, GPO Box 5252, Sydney New South Wales 2001 Australia. **Tel** 011 61 2 2600000.

●US/1064-7597
**INSIDE EDGE FOR MEN.** [Inside edge men]. **VFOAT** Inside Edge. Vol. 1, No. 1 (1993)-. Periodical. English. Ten times a year. $19.95. SH Eliot Publishers Group Inc., 50 Church Street, PO Box 712, Cambridge MA 02138. **Tel** (617)497-5621. **DD** 051.

US/0893-4460
**JOE WEIDER'S MEN'S FITNESS.** See Health and Personal Fitness.

US/1062-6751
**JOURNAL OF GENDER STUDIES (SOUTH PORTLAND, ME.).** (THE JOURNAL OF GENDER STUDIES.). [J. gend. stud.]. **Added/Corp** Human Outreach and Achievement Institute. Vol. 13, No. 1 (Spring 1991)-. Periodical. English. sa. $16.00. Human Outreach and Achievement Institute, 405 Western Avenue, Suite 345, South Portland ME 04106. **DD** 305. ***Continues*** *Outreach Beacon.*

●US/1060-8265
**JOURNAL OF MEN'S STUDIES, THE.** [J. men's stud.]. Vol. 1, No. 1 (Aug. 1992)-. Academic Scholarly Publication. English. Four times a year (Feb., May, Aug., Nov.). $45.00 North America; $50.00 other. Men's Studies Press, PO Box 32, Harriman TN 37748. **Tel** (615)369-3442, FAX (615)882-4562. **ED** James A. Doyle. **LC** HQ1088; .J68. **DD** 155.3/32. Index available (bound in fourth issue). cum. index. **Bk Rev**, (Qty: 20-30). **Ad Acc. Pr Rev. Circ:** 500.
**Desc:** Presents original multi-disciplinary and multi-cultural articles by men's studies scholars drawn from various perspectives (cultural, historical, political and social) and various disciplines (anthropology, history, law, literature, psychology and sociology). Presents men's experiences as primarily social constructions.

US/1061-8538
**JOURNEYMEN (CANDIA, N.H.).** (JOURNEYMEN.). [Journeymen]. (1991)-. Periodical. English. qt. $18.00 (US); $24.00 (other). Journeymen, 513 Chester Turnpike, Candia NH 03034. **Tel** (603) 483-8029. **ED** Paul Boynton. **DD** 305. **Bk Rev**, (Qty: 12 /yr). **Ad Acc. Circ:** 1,000.

NE
**KARWEI.** See Interior Design.

●US/1058-6652
**KEEN ON NEW YORK SURVEY OF TOP-RATED SERVICES, THE.** (1991)-. English. $9.95. Keen on New York, 360 East 72nd Street, New York NY 10021.

US/0734-4295
**LEG SHOW.** (19??)-. Periodical. English. mo. $44.95. Modernismo Publications, 462 Broadway, New York NY 10013. **Tel** (212)966-8400.

US/1040-3760
**LIBERATOR (1988), THE.** See Sociology.

FR/0750-3520
**LUI PARIS.** ***Ceased.*** [Lui Paris]. (1963)-(May 1994). Periodical. French. Six times a year. Publications Filipacchi, 63-65 Champs Elysees, 75008 Paris France. **Tel** 011 33 1 40747000, telex 651-294. **UDC** 088.
**Desc:** European men's lifestyle magazine.

GW/0177-7246
**MAENNER-VOGUE.** [Manner-Vogue]. (1984)-. Periodical. German. mo. $130.00 US; $145.00 other. Conde Nast Verlag, Leopoldstr 44, D 80802 Munich Germany. **Tel** 011 49 89 381040, FAX 011 49 89 38104230, telex 528188. **(Subscription address:** International Subscriptions, 30 Montgomery Street 7th Floor, Jersey City, NJ 07302**) UDC** 05.

US/1056-5175
**MAN! (AUSTIN, TEX.).** ***Ceased.*** (MAN! : MEN'S ISSUES, RELATIONSHIPS AND RECOVERY.). [MAN!]. **Added/Corp** Austin Men's Center (Austin, Tex.). (1990)-No. 17 (19??). Periodical. English. qt. MAN!, 1611 West 6th, Austin TX 78703. **Tel** (512)477-9595. **ED** Lyman Grant. **DD** 155. **Bk Rev**. **Ad Acc, Adv Mgr:** Judi Roberts, **Tel** (512)474-6401. **Circ:** 10,000. ***Continues*** *Austin Men's Center Newsletter.*
**Desc:** Essays, poems, and articles concerning men in our modern culture. Topics include male roles, family relationships, recovery from abuse and addiction, issues of men and women's relationships, and mythological studies.

CN/0825-3498
**MAN TO MAN (OTTAWA).** See Sociology.

●US/1072-8538
**MASCULINITIES : OFFICIAL PUBLICATION OF THE MEN'S STUDIES ASSOCIATION, NATIONAL ORGANIZATION FOR MEN AGAINST SEXISM.** **Added/Corp** Men's Studies Association (U.S.). Vol. 1, No. 1 & 2 (Winter 1993)-. Periodical. English. Four times a year. $65.00 (institutions); $80.00 others. Guilford Publications Inc., 72 Spring Street, New York NY 10012. **Tel** (212)431-9800, (800)365-7006, FAX (212)966-6708. **ED** Michael Kimmel. ***Continues*** *Men's Studies Review, 0890-9741.*

UK/0025-6161
**MAYFAIR LONDON.** (MAYFAIR.). [Mayfair Lond.]. (1946)-. Periodical. English. Twelve times a year. £33.00 UK; £39.00 other. MRM Promotional Services Ltd., Premier House, Farndon Road, Market Hrbr. LEI LE16 9NR England. **Tel** 011 44 858 410510. **DD** 070.48346.

●US/1066-5706
**MEN'S CONFIDENTIAL.** [Men's confid.]. **VFOAT** Men's Confidential Newsletter; MC. Vol. 9, No. 1 (Jan. 1993)-. Periodical. English. mo. $48.00 US; 456.00 all except Canada. Rodale Press Inc., 400 South 10th Street, Emmaus PA 18098. **Tel** (215)967-5171, (800)666-2503. **DD** 613. available on microfilm and microfiche from University Microfilms International (UMI). ***Continues*** *Men's Health (Newsletter), 0747-8461.*
**Desc:** A newsletter that pays particular attention to topics such as vasectomy, hernia, drugs, sexual dysfunction, male stress syndrome, and prostate cancer.
**Ind/Abst** Acad. Abstr. Full Text Elite; Acad. Abstr.; Consum. Health Nutr. Index; Foods Adlibra; Gen. Period. Index; Health Source; INFO-SOUTH Abstr.; Mag. Artic. Summar. Select; Mag. Artic. Summar. CD-ROM; Mag. Search; Mag. Index; Vocat. Search.

US/1054-4836
**MEN'S HEALTH (MAGAZINE).** See Health and Personal Fitness.

## Men's Interests

●US/1063-4657
**MEN'S JOURNAL (NEW YORK, N.Y.).**
(MEN'S JOURNAL.). [Men's j.]. Vol. 1, No. 1 (May/June 1992)-. Periodical. English. Ten times a year. $14.97. Wenner Media Inc., 1290 Avenue of the Americas, 2nd Floor, New York NY 10104. **Tel** (212)484-1616, FAX (212)759-2966. **(Subscription address:** Neodata / Colorado, PO Box 2606, Boulder Boulder CO 80322.**) LC** GV191.2; .M46. **DD** 051.
**Ind/Abst** Access (1992-).

US/0748-5913
**MEN'S NEWS MAGAZINE.** [Men's news mag.]. **VFOAT** Men's Newsmagazine; Men's Magazine. Vol. 9, No. 1 (Jan.-Feb. 1983)-. Periodical. English. bm. $25.00. Men International, 1816 Florida Avenue, Palm Harbor FL 34683-4931. *Continues* Men's.

US/1058-3041
**MEN'S WORKOUT.** [Men's Workout]. (1990)-. Periodical. English. bm. $14.97. Harris Publications, 1115 Broadway/8th Floor, New York NY 10010. **Tel** (212)807-7100. **ED** Michael Cataravas. **DD** 613.

US/0883-296X
**MODERN BLACK MEN.** *Ceased.* (MODERN BLACK MEN : MBM.). [Mod. black men]. Vol. 1, No. 1 (July 1985)-(1987). Periodical. English. mo. NJGP Inc., 475 Park Avenue South, New York NY 10016. **ED** George C Pryce. **DD** 051.
**Desc:** Articles of interest to the upwardly, mobile black man.

IT/0393-8085
**MONDO UOMO.** [Mondo uomo]. (1981)-. Periodical. Italian. Six times a year. $115.00 US; L43200 Italy; L85000 other. Rusconi Editore Spa, Servicio Abbonements, V Le Sarca 235, 20126 Milan Italy. **Tel** 011 39 2 66192634. **UDC** 391.1.

●US/1065-8327
**OFFICIAL STRIP JOINT GUIDE : THE O.S.J.G, THE.** [Off. strip joint guide]. **VFOAT** O.S.J.G. Vol. 1, No. 1 (1992)-. Periodical. English. sa. $34.00. O. S. J. G., PO Box 568, Quincy IL 62306-0568. **DD** 647.

CN/0827-8725
**ON YOUR OWN, A DIRECTORY FOR YOUNG MEN.** See Sociology-Social Services and Welfare.

US/1055-1522
**OUR MEN.** (1991)-. Periodical. English. mo. $3.25. FFI Fashion Flair, PO Box 2137, Manhattan NY 10027-2137.

JA
**PASSION MENS.** (19??)-. English. sa. $55.00. **(Subscription address:** Image Media International Inc., 4054 Del Rey Avenue, Suite 203, Marina Del Rey CA 90292.**)**
**Desc:** Reviews of men's hair fashion.

US/1043-0210
**PENTHOUSE FORUM (1988).** (PENTHOUSE FORUM.). [Penthouse forum]. **VFOAT** Forum. (198?)-. Periodical. English. Thirteen times a year. $30.00. General Media Publishing Company, 1965 Broadway, New York NY 10023. **Tel** (212)496-6100. **(Subscription address:** CDS Agency Hard Copy, PO Box 4966, Des Moines IA 50340.**) LC** HQ1; .F65. **DD** 306.77/05. available on microfilm and microfiche from University Microfilms International (UMI). *Continues* Forum, 0160-2195.
**Desc:** Male entertainment features.

US/0898-1086
**PENTHOUSE HOT TALK.** [Penthouse hot talk]. (1984)-. Periodical. English. Ten times a year. $4.95 per issue. General Media Publishing Company, 1965 Broadway, New York NY 10023. **Tel** (212)496-6100. **DD** 051.
**Desc:** Male entertainment features.

US/0883-8798
**PENTHOUSE LETTERS.** (198?)-. Periodical. English. mo. $28.00. General Media Publishing Company, 1965 Broadway, New York NY 10023. **Tel** (212)496-6100. **(Subscription address:** CDS Agency Hard Copy, PO Box 4966, Des Moines IA 50340.**) DD** 176. *Continues* Best of Penthouse Letters.
**Desc:** Male entertainment features.

US/0090-2020
**PENTHOUSE (NEW YORK).** (PENTHOUSE.). [Penthouse]. Vol. 1, No. 1 (Sept. 1969)-. Periodical. English. mo. $36.00. General Media Publishing Company, 1965 Broadway, New York NY 10023. **Tel** (212)496-6100. **(Subscription address:** CDS Agency Hard Copy, PO Box 4966, Des Moines IA 50340.**) LC** AP2; .P413. **DD** 051. available on microfilm and microfiche from University Microfilms International (UMI).
**Desc:** Male entertainment features.
**Ind/Abst** Access (1975-); Film Lit. Index (1973-1986); Gen. Period. Index (Jan. 1985-Dec. 1985); Index Period. Artic. Relat. Law (1977-); Mag. Index (1978-Dec. 1985).

US/0274-5143
**PENTHOUSE VARIATIONS. VFOAT** Variations. (19??)-. Periodical. English. mo. $27.00. General Media Publishing Company, 1965 Broadway, New York NY 10023. **Tel** (212)496-6100. **(Subscription address:** CDS Agency Hard Copy, PO Box 4966, Des Moines IA 50340.**)**
**Desc:** Male entertainment features.

US/0032-1478
**PLAYBOY (CHICAGO).** (PLAYBOY.). [Playb]. Vol. 1 (Dec. 1953)-. Periodical. English (French and Italian). mo (12 issues). $29.97 US; $45.00 other. Playboy Magazine, 747 Third Avenue, New York NY 10017. **Tel** (212)688-3030. **(Subscription address:** CDS Agency Hard Copy, PO Box 4966, Des Moines IA 50340.**) LC** AP2; .P692. **DD** 051. cum. index. **Bk Rev. Ad Acc.** available on microfilm and microfiche from University Microfilms International (UMI); available on an online database (file 647/Full-Text) from DIALOG. Documents available from UMI Article Clearinghouse.
**Desc:** For men's entertainment. Contains humor, cartoons and party jokes. Revealing interviews with celebrated personalities, special insights into the world of sports, politics, business, and the arts, tips on fashion, lifestyle, movies, books, and music, and photos of the world's most beautiful women.
**Ind/Abst** Access (1975-); Annu. Bibliogr. Engl. Lang. Lit.; Film Lit. Index; Gen. Period. Index (1985-); Index Am. Period. Verse; Index Period. Artic. Relat. Law; Mag. Index Plus (1989-); Mag. Index. Sel. (1986-); Med. Rev. Dig.; Newsp. Period. Abstr. (1988-); Pop. Period. Index; Mag. Index (1977-).

CN/0228-7226
**PLAYBOY COLLECTORS GUIDE & PRICE LIST, THE.** [Playb. collect. guide price list]. **VAT** Playboy Collectors Guide & Pricelist. 5Th Ed. (1982/1983)-. English. be. $10.95 per vol. Budget Enterprises, PO Box 592 Snowdon Station, Montreal Quebec H3X 3T7. **DD** 051. *Continues* Collector's Guide and Price List of Playboy Back Issues, 0315-3177.

US
**PLAYBOY INDEX, THE.** Vol. 1/15 (Dec. 1953-Dec.1968)-. English. ir. Price varies. Playboy Enterprises Inc., 919 North Michigan Avenue, Chicago IL 60611. **Tel** (312)751-8000. Index available. ctrl circ.
**Ind/Abst** Mag. Index (?-?).

●US/1062-2284
**PLAYBOY PRESENTS INTERNATIONAL PLAYMATES.** [Playboy presents int. playmates]. **VFOAT** International Playmates. (Feb. 1992)-. English. Playboy Enterprises Inc., 919 North Michigan Avenue, Chicago IL 60611. **Tel** (312)751-8000. **DD** 051.
**Desc:** Male entertainment features.

●US/1063-9608
**PLAYBOY'S BEAUTY QUEENS. VFOAT** Beauty Queens. (1993)-. Periodical. English. $5.95. Playboy Enterprises Inc., 919 North Michigan Avenue, Chicago IL 60611. **Tel** (312)751-8000.

●US/1063-9616
**PLAYBOY'S CALENDER GIRLS. VFOAT** Calender Girls. (1992)-. Periodical. English. $5.95. Playboy Enterprises Inc., 919 North Michigan Avenue, Chicago IL 60611. **Tel** (312)751-8000.

●US/1061-9070
**PLAYBOY'S CAREER GIRLS. VFOAT** Career Girls. (1992)-. Periodical. English. $4.95.

●US/1061-9089
**PLAYBOY'S GIRLS OF THE WORLD. VFOAT** Girls of the World. (1992)-. Periodical. English. $4.95. Playboy Enterprises Inc., 919 North Michigan Avenue, Chicago IL 60611. **Tel** (312)751-8000.

●US/1066-5110
**PLAYBOY'S TWINS. VFOAT** Twins. (1993)-. English. $5.95. Playboy Enterprises Inc., 919 North Michigan Avenue, Chicago IL 60611. **Tel** (312)751-8000.

US/0149-466X
**PLAYERS.** Vol. 1 (Nov. 1973)-. Periodical. English. mo. $36.00 (one year), $66.00 (two year) US; $46.00 (one year), $86.00 (two year) other. Players International, 8060 Melrose Avenue, Los Angeles CA 90046. **Tel** (310)653-8060. **ED** H L Sorrell. **LC** AP2; .P6925. **Bk Rev. Ad Acc. Circ:** 175,000.
**Desc:** Men's entertainment magazine; fashions, articles, pictorials, etc. Directed to the black male reader, ages 18-45.

US/0733-5695
**PLAYGUY.** Periodical. English. mo. $32.00 US; $41.00 other. Playguy, 155 Avenue of the Americas, New York NY 10013.

US/1061-124X
**ROMANCE OF LIFE.** See Women's Interests.

PO
**SEMANARIO.** (19??)-. Periodical. Portuguese. wk. Semanario, Av 24 de Julho No. 6, 1200 Lisbon, Portugal. **Tel** 011 351 1 604 003.
**Ind/Abst** Infomat Int. Bus.

US
**SINGLE GENTLEMEN & WOMEN.** (May 1992)-. Periodical. English. bm. $19.95. Mail Sort, Inc., 3880 Best Mill Road, Winston-Salem NC 27103. **Tel** (919)659-1100. **ED** Jill Hester. **Ad Acc. Circ:** 40,000 (ctrl).
**Desc:** Consists of profiles and color photographs submitted by single men and women.

US/1058-0638
**SINGLES CHOICE.** [Singles choice]. (July 1991)-. Periodical. English. mo. $12.00. Singles Choice, PO Box 454, Milwaukee WI 53201-0454. **DD** 646.

US/1057-2015
**SINGLES SOLUTIONS.** (Nov./Dec. 1990)-. Periodical. English. qt. $12.00 US. Singles Solutions, Subscription Coordinator, PO Box 402, Afton MN 55001.

US/0748-7355
**TODAY'S SINGLE.** See Women's Interests.

IT/1121-5496
**UOMO HARPER'S BAZAAR.** See Clothing Industry and Fashion.

IT
**UOMO MANAGER.** *Suspended.* (19??)-(April 1991). Italian. Editrice Renoma Srl, Via Ippolito Nievo 33, 20145 Milan Italy. *Continues* L'Ufficio Moderno.

IT
**UOMO VOGUE, L'.** See Clothing Industry and Fashion.

US/0274-8010
**VELVET TALKS.** (197?)-. Periodical. English. mo. Eton Publishing Company Inc., 475 Park Avenue South, New York NY 10016. **Tel** (212)213-8620, FAX (212)532-1309.

---

## METALS AND METALLURGY

US/0149-1210
**33 METAL PRODUCING.** [33 met. prod.]. **VFOAT** Metal Producing. **VAT** Thirty-Three Metal Producing. (Jan. 1977)-. Periodical. English. Twelve times a year. $50.00 US; $65.00 Canada; $75.00 Mexico; $85.00 other. Penton Publishing, 1100 Superior Avenue, Cleveland OH 44114-2543. **Tel** (216)696-7000, FAX (216)696-0836. **LC** TS300; .T47. **DD** 669/.005. **CODEN** THMMAG. **[CCC]. Ad Acc.** ctrl circ. available on microfilm and microfiche from University Microfilms International (UMI). *Continues* 33, 0040-6155.
**Desc:** Completely devoted to metal producing; covers iron, steel, aluminum, brass, copper, lead, magnesium, zinc and everything else in a foundry. Answers informational needs of executives, operating managers and engineers who must keep abreast of new production methods, mill and foundry design, equipment, etc.
**Ind/Abst** Alum. Ind. Abstr.; Met. Abstr.; World Ceram. Abstr.

IT/0515-2291
**ACCIAIO INOSSIDABILE, L'.** [Acciaio inossid.]. **Added/Corp** Societa Italiana Acciai Inossidabili Lerici. Vol. 1 (Feb. 1933)-. Academic Scholarly Publication. Italian. Four times a year. Free on request. Avesta Sheffield Spa, Via Lancetti 36, 20158 Milan Italy. **Tel** 11 39 2 69651. **LC** TA479.S7; A25. **CODEN** ACCIAG. cum. index. **Bk Rev. Circ:** 2,000 (ctrl). Documents available from CASDDS.
**Ind/Abst** Alum. Ind. Abstr.; Chem. Abstr.; Met. Abstr.

SP/0001-4850
**ACERO Y ENERGIA.** [Acero energ.]. Vol. 1; 1944-. Academic Scholarly Publication. Spanish. ir. Jose Antonio Primo de Riviera, 134 138 Esplugas de Llobregat, Barcelona Spain. **CODEN** ACEBA5. Documents available from CASDDS.
**Ind/Abst** Chem. Abstr.; Surf. Treat. Technol. Abstr.

US/0956-7151
**ACTA METALLURGICA ET MATERIALIA.** [Acta metall. mater.]. **Added/Corp** ASM International. American Institute of Mining, Metallurgical, and Petroleum Engineers. Vol. 38, No. 1 (Jan. 1990)-. Academic Scholarly Publication. English (French and German). mo. $995.00 The Americas; £668.00 other. Pergamon Press, An Imprint of Elsevier Science Ltd., The Boulevard, Langford Lane, Kidlington, Oxford OX5 1GB United Kingdom. **Tel** 011 44 865 843000, 011 44 865 843699, FAX 011 44 865 843010. **(Subscription address:** Elsevier Science Ltd. Oxford Fulfillment Centre, PO Box 800, Kidlington, Oxford OX5 1DX United Kingdom.**) ED** Michael Ashby. **LC** IN PROCESS; TN1.A1; A25. **CODEN** AMATEB. **[CCC].** available on microfilm from Microfilms International

# Metals and Metallurgy

Marketing Corp. Documents available from Article Express International, The Genuine Article, Ask*IEEE, CASDDS. **Continues** Acta Metallurgica, 0001-6160.
**Desc:** Publishes original papers and occasional critical reviews which advance the understanding of properties of materials.
**Ind/Abst** Alum. Ind. Abstr.; Appl. Mech. Rev.; Bioeng. Abstr.; Ceram. Abstr. (199?-); Chem. Abstr. (1990-); Civ. Struct. Eng. Abstr.; Comput. Inf. Syst. Abstr. J. [Full Cov.]; Ei Page One; Elect. Comm. Abstr.; Energy Res. Abstr.; Eng. Index Annu.; GeoRef; INIS Atomindex [Micro.]; INSPEC (Jan. 1990-); Int. Aerosp. Abstr. (1991-); Leadscan; Manuf. Process Eng. Abstr.; Mater. Sci. Eng. Abstr.; Met. Abstr.; MINPROC; Mintec, Min. Technol. Abstr.; Res. Alert [Full Cov.]; Sci. Cit. Index; SCISEARCH.

CC/1000-9442
## ACTA METALLURGICA SINICA. SERIES A, PHYSICAL METALLURGY & MATERIALS SCIENCE. Ceased. Added/Corp
Chung-Kuo Chin Shu Hseh Hui. **VFOAT** Physical Metallurgy & Materials Science; Chin Shu Hsueh Pao. Vol. 1A, No. 1 (July 1988)-(19??). Periodical. English. bm. Allerton Press, Inc., 150 Fifth Avenue, New York NY 10011. **Tel** (212)924-3950, FAX (212)463-9684, telex 427441 ALPRES. **LC** TN689; .A25. **DD** 669/.9/05. **CODEN** AMMSEY. **[CCC].** Documents available from Article Express International.
**Ind/Abst** Ei Page One; Eng. Index Annu.

CC/1000-9450
## ACTA METALLURGICA SINICA. SERIES B, PROCESS METALLURGY & MISCELLANEOUS. Ceased. Added/Corp
Chung-Kuo Chin Shu Hseh Hui. **VFOAT** Process Metallurgy & Miscellaneous; Chin Shu Hsueh Pao. (1988)-(19??). Periodical. English. bm. Allerton Press, Inc., 150 Fifth Avenue, New York NY 10011. **Tel** (212)924-3950, FAX (212)463-9684, telex 427441 ALPRES. **LC** TN600; .A25. **DD** 669/.05. **CODEN** ASBME3. **[CCC].** Documents available from Article Express International.
**Ind/Abst** Ei Page One; Eng. Index Annu.

FI/0781-2698
## ACTA POLYTECHNICA SCANDINAVICA. CHEMICAL TECHNOLOGY AND METALLURGY SERIES. See
Engineering-Chemical Engineering.

UK
## ADHESIVES & SEALANTS YEARBOOK AND DIRECTORY /BASA, BRITISH ADHESIVES AND SEALANTS ASSOCIATION. Main/Corp
British Adhesives and Sealants Association. **VFOAT** Adhesives and Sealants Yearbook and Directory. (198?)-. Directory. English. an. £66.50 UK; $113.00 other. Argus Press Group, Queensway House, 2 Queensway Redhill, Surrey RH1 1QS England. **Tel** 011 44 737 768611, 011 44 737 761685, FAX 011 44 737 760510, telex 948669 TOPJNL G. **Continues** British Adhesives and Sealants Association. Yearbook & Directory, 0950-3072.

UK
## ADVANCE DATA SERVICE / INTERNATIONAL LEAD AND ZINC STUDY GROUP.
(19??)-. Periodical. English. mo. £40.00 UK; $75.00 US. International Lead and Zinc Study Group, Metro House, 58 St. James Street, London SW1A 1LD England. **Tel** 011 44 71 4999373, FAX 011 44 71 4933725, telex 299819 ILZSG G. plt circ.
**Desc:** Provides early each month by fax the key data on concentrate and metal production, metal consumption and stocks in major countries and the world totals.

UK/0957-9729
## ADVANCED METALS TECHNOLOGY. Ceased.
(19??)-(June 1992). Academic Scholarly Publication. English. mo. Elsevier Science Publishers Ltd, Crown House, Linton Road, Barking Essex IG11 8JU England. **Tel** 011 44 81 5947272, FAX 081-594-5942, telex 896950. **[CCC].** available on an online database (file 636/Full-Text) from DIALOG.
**Ind/Abst** PTS Newsl. Database [Full Txt.].

UK
## ADVANCES IN EXTRACTIVE METALLURGY.
**VFOAT** Advances in Extractive Metallurgy and Refining. 1968-. English. Institution of Mining and Metallurgy, 44 Portland Place, London W1N 4BR England. **Tel** 011 44 71 580-3802, FAX 011 44 71 436-5388, telex 261410.

●US/1065-5824
## ADVANCES IN POWDER METALLURGY & PARTICULATE MATERIALS.
[Adv. powder metall. part. mat.]. **Added/Corp** Metal Powder Industries Federation. **VFOAT** Advances in Powder Metallurgy and Particulate Materials. (1992)-. Academic Scholarly Publication. English. an. Metal Powder Industries Federation, 105 College Road East, Princeton NJ 08540. **Tel** (609)452-7700, FAX (609)987-8523, telex 510 685 2516. **LC** TN695; .P653a. **DD** 671.3/7/05. **CODEN** APMME3. Documents available from CASDDS.

**Continues** Powder Metallurgy Conference & Exhibition., 1042-8860; Advances in Powder Metallurgy.
**Ind/Abst** Chem. Abstr.

UK/0267-4009
## ADVANCES IN SPECIAL ELECTROMETALLURGY. Added/Corp
Instytut Electrozvariuvannia im. IE.O. Patona. Vol. 1, No. 1 (1985)-. Periodical. English (translations available in Russian). Four times a year. £159.00. Riecansky Science Publishing Company, 7 Meadow Walk, Great Abington, Cambridge CB1 6AZ England. **Tel** 011 44 223 893295, FAX 011 44 462 480947, telex 825372 TURPIN G. **LC** TN681; .P75. **DD** 669/.028/4.

PL/0075-7012
## AKADEMIA GORNICZP-HUTNICZA IM. STANISLAWA STASZICA. ZESZYTY NAUKOWE: CERAMIKA. VFOAT
Scientific Bulletins of the Stanisaw Staszic University of Mining and Metallurgy. Ceramics. (1967)-. Academic Scholarly Publication. Polish. Documents available from CASDDS.
**Ind/Abst** Chem. Abstr.; Int. Aerosp. Abstr.

SJ/0253-9659
## AL-SULB AL-ARABI. See
Economics-Industry and Production.

US/0149-1997
## ALLEGHENY LUDLUM HORIZONS.
**Main/Corp** Allegheny Ludlum Industries. A L Metals Group. Vol. 39, No. 3 (1977)-. Periodical. English. qt. Allegheny Ludlum Industries, 20th Floor/Oliver Building, Pittsburgh PA 15222. **LC** TS300; .S744. **DD** 672/.0973. **Continues** Steel Horizons.

US/0002-614X
## ALLOY DIGEST.
(Sept. 1952)-. Periodical. English. Twelve times a year. $150.00. Alloy Digest Inc, 27 Canfield Street, Orange NJ 07050. **Tel** (201)677-9161. **ED** Robert Raudebaugh (phone: (201)677-9161). Index available. cum. index. **Circ:** 1,000.
**Desc:** Provides detailed information on commercially available metals and alloys. Covers a wide range of metals and alloys (from platinum to cast irons) and nonmetallic engineering materials. Designed for use by anyone who produces, sells, buys or uses metals, alloys, plastics, composites and ceramics in a wide range of activities such as sales, technical service, purchasing, designing, engineering, teaching, etc.
**Ind/Abst** Alum. Ind. Abstr.; Met. Abstr.

US/0094-8233
## ALLOYS INDEX. Added/Corp
American Society for Metals. Metals Society. (Jan. 1974)-. Periodical. English. mo. $410.00 North America; $475.00 other. American Society for Metals International, c/o Deborah Barthelmes, Materials Park OH 44073-0002. **Tel** (216)338-5151, FAX (216)338-4634, telex 980-619. **(Subscription address:** ASM International, Materials Information, Materials Park OH 44073.**) ED** H. David Chafe. **LC** Z6679.A4; A43. **DD** 016.669. **[CCC].** cum. index. available on CD-ROM from DIALOG.
**Desc:** Provides immediate, easy access to worldwide literature on specific alloys, metallurgical systems and intermetallic compounds.

IT
## ALLUMINIO E LEGHE.
Italian. mo (11 issues - July/August issue combined). L120000 Italy; L170000 other. Edimet, Via Corfu 102, 25124 Brescia Italy. **Tel** 011 39 30 2421043, FAX 011 39 30 223802. Index available. cum. index. **Bk Rev. Ad Acc. Circ:** 5,500 (ctrl).

DK
## ALUMINIUM.
March 1972-. Periodical. Danish. ir. kr48.00. Aluminium Branches Oplysingrad Forlags, Fredericiagade 16, 1310 Kbenhavn K Denmark. **LC** TA690; .A38.

GW/0002-6689
## ALUMINIUM (DUSSELDORF).
(ALUMINIUM.). [Aluminium]. **Added/Corp** Aluminium-Zentrale. (1919)-. Academic Scholarly Publication. German (English and German). Twelve times a year. DM419.00 Europe; DM276.00 others. Aluminium Verlag GmbH, Koenigsallee 30, D 40212 Dusseldorf 1 Germany. **Tel** 011 49 211 137427, FAX 011 49 211 132567, telex 8587407. **ED** P. Johne, Antonie Pastoors and Evelyn Grunewald. **CODEN** ALUMAB. **[CCC].** Index available. **Bk Rev. Ad Acc. Circ:** 3,100. Documents available from Article Express International, CASDDS.
**Continued in part by** Aluminium English, 0343-7442.
**Desc:** International journal for industry, research and application.
**Ind/Abst** Alum. Ind. Abstr.; Bioeng. Abstr.; Chem. Abstr.; Ei Page One; EMBASE; Energy Res. Abstr.; Eng. Mater. Abstr.; Eng. Index Annu.; F&S Index Plus Text, Int. [Select. Cov.]; Fluid Abstr., Civil Eng.; Fluid Abstr. Proc. Eng.; FLUIDEX; GeoRef; Int. Aerosp. Abstr.; Met. Abstr.; PROMT; Surf. Treat. Technol. Abstr.

GW/0343-7442
## ALUMINIUM ENGLISH.
[Alum., Suppl. engl.]. **VFOAT** Aluminium. Vol. 59, No. 7 (July 1983)-. Periodical. English. mo. Aluminium Verlag GmbH, Koenigsallee 30, D 40212 Dusseldorf 1 Germany. **Tel** 011 49 211 137427, FAX 011 49 211 132567, telex 8587407. **CODEN**

ALUMAB. Index Available in last issue of each volume--loose separately paged. **Separated from** Aluminium News, 0002-6689.

UK/0268-5280
## ALUMINIUM INDUSTRY.
[Alum. ind.]. **VFOAT** ALI Aluminium Industry; Aluminum Industry. (1982)-. Periodical. English. bm. $289.00. MCB University Press, 60 62 Toller Lane, Bradford West Yorkshire BD8 9BX England. **Tel** 011 44 274 499821, FAX 011 44 274 547143, telex 51317 MCBUNI G. **(Subscription address:** MCB University Press / US and Canada Subscriptions, PO Box 10812, Birmingham AL 35201-0812.**) DD** 338.47669722. **[CCC]. Bk Rev. Ad Acc. Circ:** 5,000 (ctrl). available on microfilm.
**Desc:** The leading English language aluminium materials journal. The journal has acquired a reputation of satisfying the requirements of users of aluminium in industry as well as the aluminium industry itself.

●US/1066-0623
## ALUMINIUM INDUSTRY ABSTRACTS. See
Metals and Metallurgy-Abstracting, Bibliographies and Statistics.

UK/0955-8209
## ALUMINIUM TODAY. See
Engineering-Materials Engineering and Mechanics.

AT/0810-8056
## AMDEL NEWS. Ceased.
[Amdel news]. **Added/Corp** AMDEL. (19??)-(19??). English. ir. Australian Mineral Development Laboratories, Flemington Street, Frewville SA 5063 Australia. **DD** 549.05.
**Ind/Abst** AESIS Q.

US
## AMERICAN IRON & STEEL INSTITUTE BASIC STEEL OPERATION STATISTICS. AIS 7, 10 & 16. See
Metals and Metallurgy-Abstracting, Bibliographies and Statistics.

US
## AMERICAN IRON & STEEL INSTITUTE FOREIGN TRADE STATISTICS. APPARENT STEEL SUPPLY REPORT. See
Metals and Metallurgy-Abstracting, Bibliographies and Statistics.

US
## AMERICAN IRON & STEEL INSTITUTE FOREIGN TRADE STATISTICS. IMPORTS 3 & IMPORTS 4. See
Metals and Metallurgy-Abstracting, Bibliographies and Statistics.

US
## AMERICAN IRON & STEEL INSTITUTE FOREIGN TRADE STATISTICS. INDIVIDUAL IMPORT & EXPORT REPORTS. See
Metals and Metallurgy-Abstracting, Bibliographies and Statistics.

US
## AMERICAN IRON & STEEL INSTITUTE MONTHLY PACKAGE.
English. Twelve times a year. $100.00. American Iron & Steel Institute, 1101 17th Street Northwest, Suite 1300, Washington DC 20036. **Tel** (202)452-7100 or 7151.

US
## AMERICAN IRON & STEEL INSTITUTE QUARTERLY AIS PACKAGE.
English. Four times a year. $100.00. American Iron & Steel Institute, 1101 17th Street Northwest, Suite 1300, Washington DC 20036. **Tel** (202)452-7100 or 7151.

US/1041-7958
## AMERICAN MACHINIST (1988). See
Engineering-Mechanical Engineering and Machinery.

US/0731-5368
## AMERICAN MACHINIST MANUFACTURING COST ESTIMATING GUIDE. See
Manufacturing.

US
## AMERICAN METAL MARKET. VFOAT
American Metal Market. Metalworking News Edition; AMM. Vol. 33, No. 1 (Jan. 2, 1926)-. Periodical. English. ir (252 issues) $560.00 US, Canada & Mexico; $1000.00 Europe, Central & South America; $1170.00 other. Chilton, 825 7th Avenue, New York NY 10019. **Tel** (212)887-8560. **LC** HD9506.U6; A4. **Continues** American Metal Market and Daily Iron and Steel Report; **Absorbed** Metalworking News, 0026-1025. **Continued in part by** Metalworking News (New York, N.Y. : 1987), 0891-4036.
**Ind/Abst** Bus. ASAP (1990-) [Full Txt.]; F&S Index Plus Text, Int. [Full Txt.] [Select. Cov.]; Gen. Period. Index (1985-).

US/0192-5709
## AMERICAN TOOL, DIE & STAMPING NEWS. See
Manufacturing.

# Metals and Metallurgy

RM
**ANALELE UNIVERSITABII DIN GALATI. FASCICULA IX, METALURGIE SI COCSERIE.** Added/Corp Universitatea din Galati. VFOAT Metalurgie si Cocserie. (1983)-. Periodical. Romanian. an. Price varies. Redactia Analelor, 6200 Galati, Str Domneasca Nr. 47 Romania. Tel 40 93 413602, FAX 40 93 412328. CODEN AUGCEC. Documents available from CASDDS. *Continues in part Buletinul Universitatii din Galati. Fascicula V, Tehnologii in Constructii [sic] de Masini, Metalurgie, 0254-5543.*
Ind/Abst Chem. Abstr.

US/0079-6719
**ANNUAL POWDER METALLURGY CONFERENCE PROCEEDINGS.** Main/Conf Powder Metallurgy Conference. 1983-. Proceedings. English. an. $120.00 (members), $150.00 (nonmembers). Metal Powder Industries Federation, 105 College Road East, Princeton NJ 08540. Tel (609)452-7700, FAX (609)987-8523, telex 510 685 2516. LC TN695; .N323A. DD 671.3/7/05. UDC 621.762(063). [CCC]. Index available. *Continues National Powder Metallurgy Conference Proceedings, 0162-6299.*
Desc: Conference proceedings of the latest powder metallurgy developments. State of the art technology, research in progress, and includes selected special workshop papers on varied topics.

AT/0155-3437
**ANNUAL REPORT - AMDEL.** (AMDEL ANNUAL REPORT.). [Annual rep. - AMDEL]. Main/Corp Australian Mineral Development Laboratories. VAT Annual Report - Australian Mineral Development Laboratories. (19??)-. English. Australian Mineral Development Laboratories, Flemington Street, Frewville SA 5063 Australia.
Ind/Abst AESIS Q.

UK/0074-9125
**ANNUAL REPORT - INTERNATIONAL TIN COUNCIL. Ceased.** Main/Corp International Tin Council. 1st- (1956/57)-Ceased ?. English (French). an. International Tin Council, Haymarket House, 1 Oxendon Street, London SW1Y 4EQ England. Tel 011 44 71 930 0451, telex 918939. LC HD9539.T5; I356. UDC 669.6(047.1). Circ: 750.
Desc: Reviews July and June financial year of council; synopsis of council sessions, standing subsidiary bodies and committees. Financial appendixes on buffer stock and administrative accounts.

RH
**ANNUAL REPORT / THE ROASTING PLANT.** Main/Corp Roasting Plant (Zimbabwe). English. Roasting Plant, PO Box 118, Kwekwe Zimbabwe. LC HD9536.Z553; K857a. DD 338.7/6223422/09689105.

US/0736-2455
**ANNUAL SILVER REVIEW AND OUTLOOK.** [Annu. silver rev. outlook]. English. an. J Aron & Company, 160 Water Street, New York NY 10038. LC HD9536.A1; A56. DD 338.2/7421/05. UDC 338.3:669.22.

US
**ANNUAL STATISTICAL REPORT - AMERICAN IRON AND STEEL INSTITUTE. See** Metals and Metallurgy-Abstracting, Bibliographies and Statistics.

IT
**ANNUARIO SEAT. VOL. A, SIDERURGIA E MECCANICA.** VFOAT Siderurgia e Meccanica; Annuario S.E.A.T. Vol. A, Siderurgia e Meccanica. Italian. an. L35000. Casella Postale N 512, 10100 Torino Centro Italy. Tel 011-33301, FAX 4472953, telex 212248 I. LC TS203; .A58. DD 671/.025/45. UDC 669.1. Index available. Ad Acc. Circ: 28,300 (ctrl).
Desc: Yearbook of Italian companies operating in metallurgy of iron and mechanics. Additional information on specific situations in Italy are available.

US/0271-8286
**ANODIC BEHAVIOR OF METALS AND SEMICONDUCTOR SERIES, THE.** [Anodic behav. met. semicond. ser.]. (1972)-. Monographic series. English. ir. Price varies per volume. Marcel Dekker Inc., 270 Madison Avenue, New York NY 10016. Tel (212)696-9000, (800)228-1160, FAX (212)685-4540, telex 421419. (Subscription address: Marcel Dekker Inc, PO Box 5017, Monticello NY 12701.) CODEN ABMSDO.

SP/0066-510X
**ANUARIO DE LA RELOJERIA Y ARTE EN METAL PARA ESPANA E HISPANOAMERICA.** (ANUARIO DE LA RELOJERIA Y ARTE EN METAL.). [Anu. reloj. arte met. Esp. Hispanoam.]. VFOAT Anuario de la Relojeria para Espana e Hispanoamerica; Anuario de la Relojeria en Espana. (1955)-. Spanish. be. Ediciones Cedel, Mallorca 257, 1#, 08008 Barcelona Spain. UDC 681.11.

BL
**ANUARIO ESTATISTICO / CONSIDER, CONSELHO DE NAO-FERROSOS E DE SIDERURGIA / STATISTICAL YEARBOOK / THE IRON, STEEL, AND NONFERROUS METALS COUNCIL. See** Metals and Metallurgy-Abstracting, Bibliographies and Statistics.

US/0889-177X
**ANVIL'S RING, THE.** [Anvil's ring]. Began with V. 1, No. 1 (Spring, 1973). Periodical. English. qt. $25.00. Artist-Blacksmiths Association of North America, PO Box 1181, Nashville TN 47448. Tel (812)988-6919. ED Robert Owings and Kathleen Owings. DD 682. UDC 682; 621.73. Index available. Bk Rev. Ad Acc. Circ: 3,000.
Desc: A journal for the field of blacksmithing. A showcase of art produced media in iron. Includes tip/techniques, feature articles, calendar of events, business forum, shoptalk, classifieds.

US/1051-0303
**APERIODICITY AND ORDER.** [Aperiod. order]. (1988)-. Monographic series. English. ir. Price varies per volume. Academic Press, Inc., 6277 Sea Harbor Drive, Orlando FL 32887. Tel (800)543-9534, (407)345-4100, FAX (407)363-9661. DD 530.
Ind/Abst Math. Rev.

PL/0004-0770
**ARCHIWUM HUTNICTWA.** (ARCHIWUM HUTNICTWA / POLSKA AKADEMIA NAUK, KOMITET HUTNICTWA.). [Arch. hut.]. Added/Corp Polska Akademia Nauk. Komitet Hutnictwa. Polska Akademia Nauk. Komitet Metalurgii. Polska Akademia Nauk. Komitet Nauki o Materiaach. VFOAT Archives of Metallurgy. Vol. 1, Part. 1 (1956)-. Academic Scholarly Publication. Polish (English; summaries and/or abstracts in Russian; table of contents in Russian). qt. $60.00. (Subscription address: ARS Polona, PO Box 1001, 00068 Warsaw Poland.) LC TN4.P57; A3. CODEN AHUTA4. Documents available from Article Express International, Ask*IEEE, CASDDS. *Continues in part Archiwum Gornictwa I Hutnictwa.*
Ind/Abst Alum. Ind. Abstr.; Bioeng. Abstr. (1968-); Ceram. Abstr.; Chem. Abstr.; Ei Page One (1968-); Eng. Mater. Abstr.; Eng. Index Annu.; INSPEC (1968-); Met. Abstr.

CL
**AREA METALURGIA.** VFOAT Metalurgia. Periodical. Spanish (summaries and/or abstracts in English). Direccion de Investigaciones Cientificas y Tecnologicas de la Universidad Tecnica del Estado etc, Avda Ecuador 3469, Santiago Chile. LC TN600; .A75. UDC 669.

FR/0220-3332
**ARGUS DES METAUX PARIS.** [Argus met. Paris]. (1977)-. Periodical. French. da. 5093.05F France; 5400.00F other. Bureau d'Info Professionnelles, 142 rue Montmartre, 75073 Paris Cedex 02 France. Tel 011 33 1 40268321, FAX 011 33 1 40399752, telex 220528 BIP. UDC 65 + 38. *Continues Argus Quotidien d'Informations Professionnelles, 0398-7493.*

US/0044-7889
**ASM NEWS (METALS PARK, OHIO). Title Change.** (ASM NEWS.). [ASM news]. Main/Corp ASM International. VAT American Society for Metals News. Vol. 17, No. 11 (Nov. 1986)-(19??). Periodical. English. Twelve times a year. American Society for Metals International, c/o Deborah Barthelmes, Materials Park OH 44073-0002. Tel (216)338-5151, FAX (216)338-4634, telex 980-619. DD 669. *Continues ASM News, 0044-7889. Merged into Advanced Materials & Processes, 0882-7958.*

US
**ASM SERIES IN METAL PROCESSING.** VFOAT A.S.M. Series in Metal Processing; Series in Metal Processing. (1983)-. Monographic series. English. Price varies per volume. American Technical Publ Ltd, 27-29 Knowl Piece Wilbury Way, Hitchin Herts SG4 0SX England.

BE/0001-2696
**ATB METALLURGIE (BRUSSELS, BELGIUM).** (ATB METALLURGIE : ACTA TECHNICA BELGICA.). Added/Corp Benelux M,etallurgie. VFOAT Acta Technica Belgica; A.T.B. Metallurgie; Revue ATB Metallurgie. Vol. 1 (1956)-. Periodical. English (French). qt. $70.00. Benelux Metallurgie, Rue Ravenstein 3, B-1000 Brussels Belgium. Tel 011 32 2 6492993. available on microfilm from University Microfilms International (UMI). Documents available from CASDDS. *Continues Metallurgie, 0543-5757.*
Ind/Abst Chem. Abstr.; Ei Page One.

AT/0817-654X
**AUSTRALIAN GOLD, GEM AND TREASURE MAGAZINE.** [Aust. gold gem treasure mag.]. (1986)-. Periodical. English. mo. 39.00Aus$ Australia; 54.00Aus$ other. Express Publications Pty. Ltd., 2 Stauley Street, North Auburn 2144 Australia. Tel 011 61 2 7480599. DD 622.10994. *Continues Australian Gem & Treasure Hunter, 0159-6322.*
Ind/Abst AESIS Q.

AT/1030-7915
**AUSTRALIAN NUGGET JOURNAL.** [Aust. nugget j.]. (1987)-. Trade Publication. English (Chinese). qt. Free (trade on application). Goldcorp Australia, 310 Hay Street, East Perth Western Australia 6004 Australia. Tel (09)421-7222, FAX (09)221-3812, telex 197171. (Subscription address: Goldcorp Australia, GPO Box 7924, Perth Western Australia 6001) ED Ron Barry. DD 332.4520994. Pr Rev. Circ: 4,000 (ctrl).
Desc: Information on precious metals, investments, coins and numismatics.

●US/1071-3220
**AUTOMOTIVE INTELLIGENCE REPORTS' METALWORKING.** [Automot. intell. rep. metalwork.]. (1992)-. Periodical. English. sm. $350.00. Automotive Intelligence Report, 93 Kercheval, Suite 1, Grosse Pointe Farms MI 48236. Tel (313)884-3539, FAX (313)884-1612. ED Paul Lienert. DD 629.

US/1058-9376
**AUTOMOTIVE RECYCLING. See** Transportation-Automobiles.

RU/0320-0825
**AVTOMATIZACIJA METALLURGICESKOGO PROIZVODSTVA.** (AVTOMATIZATSIIA METALLURGICHESKOGO PROIZVODSTVA.). [Avtom. metall. proizvod.]. Added/Corp Russia (1923-U.S.S.R.). Ministerstvo Chernoi Metallurgii. Vsesoiuznyi Nauchno-Issledovatelskii Institut Avtomatizatsii Chernoi Metallurgii. (1973)-. Academic Scholarly Publication. Russian. 1.49rub single issue. Izdatelstvo Metallurgiia, 2-i Obydenskii Per.14, G-34, Moscow Russia. LC TN675.5; .A94. CODEN AMPRDB. Documents available from CASDDS.
Ind/Abst Chem. Abstr. (?-1977).

UK/0953-9794
**BASE METAL CONCENTRATES.** [Base met. conc.]. (1988)-. Periodical. English. bm. £650.00. Metals & Minerals Research Service Ltd, 24 Henry Street, Bath Avon, BA1 1JT England. Tel 011 44 225 481585. DD 338.47669.

UK/0964-7686
**BASE METALS MONTHLY.** (1991)-. Trade Publication. English. mo. £600.00 UK: $1,020.00. Metal Bulletin PLC, PO Box 28E, Worcester Park, Surrey KT4 7HX England. Tel 011 44 71 827 9977, FAX 011 44 81 337 8943. ED Neil Buxton.

NE/0168-3020
**BASIS-METAALINDUSTRIE / CENTRAAL BUREAU VOOR DE STATISTIEK, HOOFDAFDELING STATISTIEKEN VAN INDUSTRIE EN BOUWNIJVERHEID.** VFOAT Basis Metaalindustrie; Basic Metal Industry. Dutch (summaries and/or abstracts in English). an. Fl13.70. Centraal Bureau voor de Statistiek, AFD ALG Zaken, Postbus 959, 2270 AZ Voorburg Netherlands. Tel 011 31 70 3373800, FAX 011 31 038 7429, telex 32692 CBS NL. LC HD9525.N4; N47A. UDC 311:669(492). *Continues Netherlands. Centraal Bureau Voor de Statistiek. Produktiestatistieken: Basis-Metaalindustrie.*

GW
**BAYERNMETALL.** Added/Corp Fachverband Metall Bayern fuer das Schlosser-, Schmiede-, Maschinenbauer-, Werkzeugmacher- und Formenbauer-, Dreher-, Metallformer- und Metallgiesser-Handwerk. (19??)-. Trade Publication. German. mo. $20.00. Wirtschaftsgesellschaft des Fachverbandes Metall Bayern mbH, Erhardtstr. 6, D 80469 Munich Germany. Tel 089/201 49 36, FAX 089/201 00 23. LC TS200; .B34. Index available. Bk Rev. Ad Acc. Circ: 5,000 (ctrl).

UK/0268-3393
**BCIRA ABSTRACTS OF INTERNATIONAL LITERATURE ON METAL CASTINGS PRODUCTION.** Added/Corp British Cast Iron Research Association. VFOAT Abstracts of International Literature on Metal Castings Production. (Jan. 1986)-. Periodical. English. bm (Jan., Mar., May, Jul., Sep., Nov.). £95.00 (nonmember); Free to members. British Cast Iron Research Association, Alvechurch, Birmingham B48 7QB England. Tel 44 527 66414, FAX 44 527 585070, telex 337125. LC Z7914.F7; B74a; TS228.99. DD 671.2/05. Pr Rev. *Continues BCIRA Abstracts of International Foundry Literature.*
Desc: Each issue contains 200-300 abstracts of important articles, patents and conference papers on iron, steel and non-ferrous castings production technology. Indispensable to foundrymen, metallurgists and establishments of higher education offering related courses.

DK
**BERETNING OM VIRKSOMHEDEN I ... .** **Main/Corp** Statens Kontrol Med Dle Metaller (Denmark). Danish. **LC** HD9536.D4; S73A.

AU/0067-5768
**BERG- UND HUTTENMANNISCHE MONATSCHEFTE. SUPPLEMENTUM.** ***Ceased.* See** Earth Sciences-Mineralogy.

AT/0313-5942
**BHP JOURNAL.** ***Ceased.*** [BHP j.]. **VFOAT** Brocken Hill Proprietary Journal. (1969)-(19??). Periodical. English. sa. BHP Steelworks, PO Box 196 B, Newcastle NSW 2300 Australia. **DD** _a338.476691. **Ind/Abst** AESIS Q.

US/0045-1983
**BIG BOOK OF METALWORKING MACHINERY.** (1970)-. English. ir. $58.00. Zulch & Zulch, Inc., 16255 Ventura Boulevard, Encino CA 91436. **ED** William C. Zulch. **LC** TS215; .B53. **DD** 338.4/7/671. Index available. cum. index. **Ad Acc.** available with charts; available with illustrations.

GW/0006-4688
**BLECH, ROHRE, PROFILE.** [Blech, Rohre, Profile]. Vol. 17 (1970)-. Academic Scholarly Publication. German. mo. DM158.00 Germany; DM174.00 other. Meisenbach GmbH, Postfach 2069, D 96011 Bamberg Germany. **Tel** 011 49 951 861135. **UDC** 621.774. **CODEN** BRPFBJ. Documents available from Article Express International, CASDDS. ***Continues*** *Blech.* **Ind/Abst** Alum. Ind. Abstr.; Bioeng. Abstr.; Chem. Abstr.; Ei Page One; EMBASE; Energy Res. Abstr. (March 1976-); Eng. Mater. Abstr.; Eng. Index Annu.; Met. Abstr.

AG
**BOLETIN ESTADISTICO.** **Main/Corp** Centro de Industriales Siderurgicos (Buenos Aires, Argentina). (19??)-. Spanish. an. Centro de Industriales Siderurgicos, Buenos Aires Argentina. **LC** HD9524.A9; C364.

UK
**BRITISH NON-FERROUS METALS DIRECTORY, THE.** **Added/Corp** Metal Information Bureau (London, England). (19??)-. Directory. English.

UK/0007-182X
**BRITISH STEEL. See** Economics-Industry and Production.

RM/0254-5543
**BULETINUL UNIVERSITATII DIN GALATI. FASCICULA V, TEHNOLOGII IN CONSTRUCTII SIC DE MASINI, METALURGIE.** [Bul. Univ. Galati, Fasc. V, tehnol.]. **Added/Corp** Universitatea din Galati. Vol. 1 (1978)-. Academic Scholarly Publication. English (French and German; summaries and/or abstracts in Romanian). an. Redactia Buletinului, 6200 Galati Str, Republicii Nr 47 Romania. **LC** TJ4; .B85. **DD** 669/.005. **CODEN** BUGMDI. Documents available from CASDDS. **Ind/Abst** Alum. Ind. Abstr.; Chem. Abstr. (1978-1982); Eng. Mater. Abstr.; Met. Abstr.

BE/0379-0401
**BULLETIN - BISMUTH INSTITUTE.** **Main/Corp** Bismuth Institute. Vol. 1 (1973)-. Academic Scholarly Publication. English. ir (3-4 per year). Free on request. Bismuth Institute, Information Centre, 301 Borgstraat, B 1850 Grimbergen Belgium. **Tel** 011 32 2 2524747, FAX 011 32 2 2522775. **CODEN** BBIBDW. Index available. cum. index. **Bk Rev. Circ:** 2,000. Documents available from CASDDS. **Ind/Abst** Alum. Ind. Abstr.; Ceram. Abstr. (19??-); Chem. Abstr. (1973-1980); Energy Inf. Abstr.; Met. Abstr.

FR
**BULLETIN DE LA CHAMBRE SYNDICALE DE LA SIDERURGIE FRANCAISE. SERIE ROUGE. See** Economics-Industry and Production.

FR
**BULLETIN DE LA CHAMBRE SYNDICALE DE LA SIDERURGIE FRANCAISE. SERIE VERTE, STATISTIQUES MENSUELLES. See** Economics-Industry and Production.

FR
**BULLETIN DE LA CHAMBRE SYNDICALE DE LA SIDERURGIE FRANCAISE. [SERIE BLEUE]. See** Economics-Industry and Production.

FR/0366-4104
**BULLETIN DU CERCLE D'ETUDES DES METAUX.** [Bull. Cercle etud. met.]. **Added/Corp** Cercle d'Etudes des m'Etaux. (1935)-. Bulletin. French (English). sa. 900.00F institutions; 500.00F individuals. Cercle d'Etudes des Metaux, 158 Cours Fauriel, 42023 St Etienne Cedex France. **Tel** 011 33 77 420123. **Circ:** 1,000. ***Continues in part*** *Etudes et Documentation Metallurgiques, 0421-5923.* **Ind/Abst** Alum. Ind. Abstr.; Met. Abstr.

FR
**BULLETIN SIGNALETIQUE 221: GISEMENTS METALLIQUES ET NON METALLIQUES, ECONOMIE MINIERE.** ***Title Change.*** **Added/Corp** France. Centre National de la Recherche Scientifique. Centre de Documentation. France. Bureau de Recherches Geologiques et Minieres. Vol. 37 (1976)-(19??). Bulletin. French. ir. Editions du CNRS, 22 rue Saint Armand, F 75015 Paris France. **Tel** 011 33 1 45075050. ***Continues*** *Bulletin Signaletique 221: Gitologie, Economie Miniere.* ***Continued by*** *Pascal Folio F41 Gisements Metalliques et non Metalliques, 1146-5182.*

FR/0007-5655
**BULLETIN SIGNALETIQUE. 740, METAUX, METALLURGIE.** **Added/Corp** Centre National de la Recherche Scientifique (France). Centre de Documentation. **VFOAT** Metaux, Metallurgie. Vol. 30 (1969)-. Bulletin. French. mo. Centre National de la Recherche Scientifique, Informascience, 26 rue Boyer, 75971 Paris France. **Tel** 61.41.11.05, telex CNRSDOC 220880 F. **LC** Z6678; .B84. **DD** 016.669. ***Supersedes in part*** *Bulletin Signaletique. 8, Chimie II: Chimie Appliquee, Metallurgie.*

US/0737-626X
**BUREAU OF MINES RESEARCH. See** Engineering-Mines and Mining Engineering.

US/1049-1384
**C2C ABSTRACTS JAPAN. METALS. See** Metals and Metallurgy-Abstracting, Bibliographies and Statistics.

●US/1066-1174
**CA SELECTS: STRESS CORROSION - METALS. See** Chemistry-Abstracting, Bibliographies and Statistics.

US
**CAB, CURRENT AWARENESS BULLETIN.** **Added/Corp** Battelle Memorial Institute, Columbus, Ohio. Metals and Ceramic Information Center. **VFOAT** Current Awareness Bulletin. No. 1 (Jan. 1977)-. Bulletin. English. mo. Free to subscribers approved by the Metals and Ceramics Information Center. Battelle Columbus Lab, 505 King Avenue, Columbus OH 43201-2693. **Tel** (614)424-6384. **ED** Gerald O. Davis. **Circ:** 4,200 (ctrl). ***Supersedes in part*** *MCIC Reviews of Metal Technology; MCIC Ceramics Review* ***and*** *MCIC Newsletter.* **Desc:** Reviews of current literature within the scope of the Metals and Ceramics Information Center by expert technologists plus news about the Center's operation. **Ind/Abst** Print. Abstr.

UK/0309-1139
**CADMIUM ABSTRACTS.** ***Title Change.*** [Cadmium abstr.]. Vol. 1 (Jan. 1977) - (Oct. 1986). Periodical. English. qt. Cadmium Association, 34 Berkeley Square, London W1X 6AG England. **Tel** 01-499 6636. **UDC** 546.48(048.3); 669.73(048.3). **CODEN** CAABDU. ***Continued by*** *CADSCAN, 0950-1576.* **Ind/Abst** World Surf. Coat. Abstr.

UK
**CADSCAN.** Vol. 1, No. 1 (Oct. 1986)-. English. qt. $52.82 Australia; $121.42 UK and Europe; $126.85 other. SCAN Journals, 42 Weymouth Street, London W1N 3LQ England. **Tel** 071-499-8425, FAX 071-4931555, telex 261286. **ED** Clive Larson. **Bk Rev. Ad Acc. Circ:** 250. available on microfilm and microfiche from University Microfilms International (UMI); available on CD-ROM. ***Continues*** *Cadmium Abstracts.* **Ind/Abst** Corros. Abstr. (199?-); World Ceram. Abstr.

US
**CAN SHIPMENTS REPORT. See** Manufacturing.

CN/0008-3291
**CANADIAN COPPER.** (CANADIAN COPPER. : CUIVRE CANADIEN.). [Can. copp.]. **Added/Corp** Canadian Copper & Brass Development Association. **VFOAT** Cuivre Canadien. (Winter 1968)-. Periodical. English (French). qt. Free. Canadian Copper and Brass, 10 Gateway Boulevard, Suite 375, Don Mills ONT M3C 3A1 Canada. **Tel** (416)421-0788, FAX (416)421-8092. **ED** R.J. Catterall. **Circ:** 15,000 (ctrl). ***Continues*** *Canadian Coppermetals., 0319-5503.* **Desc:** New developments and applications for copper, brass, and bronze. **Ind/Abst** Met. Abstr.

US/0008-4433
**CANADIAN METALLURGICAL QUARTERLY.** (CANADIAN METALLURGICAL QUARTERLY [MICROFORM].). [Can. metall. q.]. **Added/Corp** Canada. Mines Branch. Canadian Institute of Mining and Metallurgy. Metallurgical Society of CIM. Vol. 1 (1962)-. English (summaries and/or abstracts in French). Microforms International, Fairview Park, Elmsford NY 10523. **DD** 669/.005. **[CCC].**

CN/0008-4433
**CANADIAN METALLURGICAL QUARTERLY.** [Can. metall. q.]. **Added/Corp** Canada. Mines Branch. Canadian Institute of Mining and Metallurgy. Metallurgical Society of CIM. **VFOAT** Metallurgical Society of CIM Annual Volume. Vol. 1 (July/Sept. 1962)-. Academic Scholarly Publication. English. qt (1 volume). $425.00 The Americas; £285.00 other. Pergamon Press, An Imprint of Elsevier Science Ltd., The Boulevard, Langford Lane, Kidlington, Oxford OX5 1GB United Kingdom. **Tel** 011 44 865 843000, 011 44 865 843699, FAX 011 44 865 843010. **(Subscription address:** Elsevier Science Ltd. Oxford Fulfillment Centre, PO Box 800, Kidlington, Oxford OX5 1DX United Kingdom.**) ED** H. Henein. **DD** 669/.005. **CODEN** CAMQAUCAMGAU. **[CCC].** Index available. cum. index. **Ad Acc. Pr Rev.** available on microfilm and microfiche from University Microfilms International (UMI). Documents available from Article Express International, The Genuine Article, Ask*IEEE, CASDDS. **Desc:** Devoted to the science, practice and technology of metallurgy. Provides a forum for the discussion and presentation of both basic and applied research developments in the areas of metallurgy and materials. **Ind/Abst** Alum. Ind. Abstr.; Ceram. Abstr.; Chem. Abstr.; Curr. Biotechnol.; Curr. Contents Eng. Tech. Appl. Sci.; Ei Page One; Eng. Mater. Abstr.; Eng. Index Annu.; GeoRef; INSPEC (July/Sept. 1969-1976, 1985-); Leadscan; Met. Abstr.; Res. Alert [Full Cov.]; Sci. Cit. Index; SCISEARCH.

CN/0705-5196
**CANMET REPORT. See** Earth Sciences-Mineralogy.

UK
**CANNING HANDBOOK, THE.** 23rd Ed. (1982)-. English. ir. **LC** TS653.A1; C36. **DD** 671.7/05. **UDC** 621.357.7; 672.4. ***Continues*** *Canning Handbook on Electroplating.*

UK
**CAPACITY CHANGES IN LEAD AND ZINC IN THE 1980'S.** (Sept. 1990)-. Periodical. English. £25.00 UK; $40.00 US. International Lead and Zinc Study Group, Metro House, 58 St. James Street, London SW1A 1LD England. **Tel** 011 44 71 4999373, FAX 011 44 71 4933725, telex 299819 ILZSG G. ctrl circ. **Desc:** Reviews the capacity changes in lead and zinc mines and metallurgical works during the 1980's, a period which first witnessed a steep decline in consumption followed by a strengthening of demand in recent years. Capacity figures are compared with actual production, giving an indication of capacity utilisation rates. The changing pattern of types of plants and their regional distribution are also illustrated.

UK/0953-4962
**CAST METALS.** [Cast met.]. (1988)-. Periodical. English. qt (Mar., June, Sept., Dec.). £212.00. Cast Metal Development Limited, Alve Church, Birmingham B48 7QB England. **Tel** 011 44 052766414, FAX 011 44 0527585070. **ED** R.M.B. Smith. **DD** 671.25. **Bk Rev,** (Qty: 12). **Ad Acc. Circ:** 250. **Desc:** The journal provides an international vehicle for the dissemination of knowledge relating to all aspects of cast-metal science and technology. The emphasis is on original work carried out in universities, research and development establishments, and within the industry.

US
**CASTEEL.** ***Ceased.*** 1, (Fall 1966)-Ceased ?. Periodical. English. Three times a year. Steel Founders Society of American, 455 State Street, Des Plaines IL 60016. **Tel** (708)299-9160. **UDC** 669-14. **Ind/Abst** Alum. Ind. Abstr.; Met. Abstr.

US/1051-1237
**CASTING DESIGN & APPLICATION.** [Cast. des. appl.]. **VFOAT** Casting Design and Application. Vol. 1, No. 1 (Fall 1989)-. Periodical. English. an. $25.00 US and Canada; $30.00 other. Penton Publishing, 1100 Superior Avenue, Cleveland OH 44114-2543. **Tel** (216)696-7000, FAX (216)696-0836. **(Subscription address:** Penton Publishing, PO Box 96732, Chicago IL 60693.**) DD** 671. available on microfilm and microfiche from University Microfilms International (UMI). **Desc:** This publication covers metals used in castings, casting processes, special considerations in designing components as castings, converting fabrications to castings, and computer aided designs.

US/0887-9060
**CASTING WORLD.** ***Suspended.*** [Cast. world]. Vol. 18, No. 1 (Winter 85/86)-Suspended. Periodical. English. qt. $20.00 US; $24.00 other. Continental Communications Inc, PO Box 1919, Bridgeport CT 06604. **Tel** (203)377-5566. **ED** William H Moore and W W Troland. **LC** TS200; .C263. **DD** 671.2/05. **UDC** 669-14. **Bk Rev. Ad Acc. Circ:** 70,000 (ctrl). ***Continues*** *Casting Engineering & Foundry World, 0273-9607.* **Desc:** For producers and users of metal castings; of special interest to design engineers, foundry management and casting buyers. **Ind/Abst** Ei Page One; Eng. Mater. Abstr.; Leadscan.

AT/0008-7521
**CASTINGS.** [Castings]. V. 1- 1955-. Periodical. English. mo. 22.60Aus$. FW Publishers, GPO Box 2457, Sydney New South Wales 2001 Australia. **Tel**

(02)2671187. **ED** Berry Smith. **LC** TS200; .C27. **UDC** 669-14. **Bk Rev. Ad Acc. Circ:** 1,350. available on microfilm from University Microfilms International (UMI).
**Desc:** Foundry casting industry, technical and up-to-date information.
**Ind/Abst** Alum. Ind. Abstr.; Eng. Mater. Abstr.; Met. Abstr.; Saf. Health Work.

SP
**CENIMM; CENTRO NACIONAL DE INVESTIGACIONES METALURGICAS.** Spanish. bm. 6.500ptas Spain; 9.500ptas other. Centro Nacional de Investigaciones Metal, Avd Gregorio del Ano 8, 28040 Madrid Spain. **Tel** 34-1-5538900, FAX 34-1-5347425, telex 42182 CSICE E. **ED** J M Sistiaga. Index available. cum. index. **Bk Rev. Ad Acc. Pr Rev. Circ:** 2,500.

RM/0524-8140
**CERCETARI METALURGICE. INSTITUL DE CERCETARI METALURGICE (BUCURESTI).** (CERCETARI METALURGICE.). [Cercet. met. Inst. Cercet. Metal.]. **Added/Corp** Institutul de Cercetari Metalurgice. (1962)-. Academic Scholarly Publication. Romanian (summaries and/or abstracts in English, French, German and Russian). **LC** TN4; .B74. **CODEN** CERMB4. Documents available from CASDDS. ***Continues*** *Cercetari Metalurgice si Mineere.*
**Ind/Abst** Ceram. Abstr. (19??-); Chem. Abstr.; Coal Abstr.

●FR/1146-1497
**CFE INDUSTRIE. See** Engineering-Electricity, Electrical Engineering, Electronics.

US/0569-5910
**CHARTING STEEL'S PROGRESS. See** Economics-Industry and Production.

CC/0412-1961
**CHIN SHU HSUEH PAO.** [Chin shu hsueh pao]. **Added/Corp** Chung-kuo Chin Shu Hsueh Hui. **VFOAT** Acta Metallurgica and Sinica; Jin shu Xuebao. (Mar. 1956)-. Academic Scholarly Publication. Chinese (summaries and/or abstracts in English and Russian). mo. $136.80. Science Press, 16 Donghuangchenggen North Street, Beijing 100707, People's Republic of China. **Tel** 011 86 1 4019821, 011 86 1 4010642, FAX 011 86 1 4012180, 011 86 1 4019810, telex 210147. **ED** S. Changxu. **LC** TN4; .C458. **DD** 669/.005. **CODEN** CHSPA4. **Circ:** 5,000. available on microfilm from University Microfilms International (UMI). Documents available from Article Express International, CASDDS, BLDSC, Ask*IEEE, CASDDS.
**Desc:** The majority of papers describes the results of research studies. Series A deals with metallic material science and metal physics. Series B reflects production metallurgy and miscellaneous.
**Ind/Abst** AESIS Q.; Alum. Ind. Abstr.; Bioeng. Abstr.; Ceram. Abstr.; Chem. Abstr.; Ei Page One; Eng. Index Annu.; GeoRef; INSPEC (1974-); Int. Aerosp. Abstr. (1991-); Met. Abstr.

JA/0577-9391
**CHITANIUMU, JIRUKONIUMU.** [Chitaniumu, jirukoniumu]. **Added/Corp** Chitaniumu Konwakai (Japan) Chitaniumu Kyokai (Japan). **VFOAT** Titanium & Zirconium; Titanium and Zirconium. (1962)-. Academic Scholarly Publication. Japanese. qt. $82.00. Chitanyumu Kyokai, (Japan Titanium Society), 2-9, Kanda Nishikicho, Chiyodaku, Tokyoto 101 Japan. **(Subscription address:** Maruzen Company Ltd., PO Box 5050, Import & Export Department, Tokyo 100 31 Japan. **LC** TA480.T54; C46. **CODEN** CHJIA6. Documents available from CASDDS. ***Continues*** *Chitaniumu.*
**Ind/Abst** Chem. Abstr.

KO
**CHOLGANG TONGGYE. See** Economics-Industry and Production.

KO
**CHOLGANG TONGGYE YONBO. See** Economics-Industry and Production.

SA/0256-0038
**CHROMIUM REVIEW.** [Chromium rev.]. No. 1 (April 1983)-. Periodical. English. Three times a year. Free. International Chromium Development Association, PO Box 72398, Parkview 2122 South Africa. **Tel** 27 11 484-3685, FAX 27 11 484-3320. **ED** W K Armitage and L M Thatcher. **UDC** 669.26. **Bk Rev. Circ:** 5,500 (ctrl).
**Desc:** Promotes the usage and selling of chromium, and the transfer of technology relating to chromium.
**Ind/Abst** AESIS Q.; Alum. Ind. Abstr.; Ei Page One; GeoRef; Met. Abstr.

JA
**CHUKEN HOKOKU.** [Chuken hokoku]. **Main/Corp** Waseda Daigaku, Tokyo Imono Kenkyujo. **VFOAT** Transactions of the Castings Research Laboratory, Waseda University. **VAT** Waseda Daigaku Imono Kenkyujo Hokoku. No. 1- ; 1942-. Academic Scholarly Publication. Japanese (English). 8-26 Nishi Waseda 2, Shinjuku-ku, Tokyo 160 Japan. **LC** TS236; .W36A. **UDC** 669-14. **CODEN** CHHCDH. Documents available from CASDDS.
**Ind/Abst** Chem. Abstr.

JA/0387-0502
**CHUTANZO TO NETSUSHORI.** [Chutanzo to netsushori]. **Added/Corp** Shinnihon Chutanzo Kyokai. **VFOAT** Casting, Forging and Heat Treatment; Casting, Forging & Heat Treatment. (1978)-. Periodical. Japanese. mo. $132.00. Shinnihon Chutanzo Kyokai, Kyobashi 3-13, Higashi-ku, Osaka 540 Japan. **(Subscription address:** Kyowa Book Co., Inc., 1 38 Kanda Jinbocho Chiyoda Ku, Tokyo 101 Japan, Tel. 81 3 3293 0727) **CODEN** CTONDV. Documents available from CASDDS. ***Continues*** *Chutanzo.*
**Ind/Abst** Chem. Abstr.

BL/0103-0078
**CIS DOCUMENTACAO / CENTRO DE INFORMACOES SIDERURGICAS.** [CIS doc.]. **VFOAT** C.I.S. Documentacao. Periodical. Portuguese. mo. **LC** Z6332; .C57; TN705. **UDC** 669.
**Ind/Abst** Alum. Ind. Abstr.; Met. Abstr.

US/0747-3362
**CNC WEST. See** Manufacturing.

SP/0010-0544
**COLADA.** [Colada]. **Added/Corp** Asociacion Tecnica y de Investigacion de Fundicion. (1970)-. Academic Scholarly Publication. Spanish. mo (11 issues). $50.00. Asociacion Tecnica y de Investigacion, Rosario Pino 6 9 B, Madrid 20 Spain. **CODEN** CLDADH. **Bk Rev. Ad Acc. Circ:** 22,500. Documents available from CASDDS.
**Ind/Abst** Chem. Abstr. (-1983); Met. Abstr.; World Alum. Abstr.

FR/0069-5807
**COLLOQUE DE METALLURGIE.** [Colloq. metall.]. **Added/Corp** Centre d'Etudes Nucleaires de Saclay. (19??)-. French (summaries and/or abstracts in English). an. **CODEN** CQMTAF. Documents available from CASDDS.
**Ind/Abst** Chem. Abstr.

US/1071-250X
**COMMODITIES (WASHINGTON, D.C.).** (COMMODITIES.). [Commodities]. **Added/Corp** Institute of Scrap Recycling Industries. (195?)-. Periodical. English. bw. $145.00. ISRI Institute of the Scrap Recycling Industries Inc, 1325 G Street Northwest, Washington DC 20005. **Tel** (202)737-1770, FAX (202)626-0900. **DD** 628.
**Desc:** Explores scrap commodity market fundamentals.

AT/0728-7178
**CONFERENCE SERIES - AUSTRALASIAN INSTITUTE OF MINING AND METALLURGY. See** Engineering-Mines and Mining Engineering.

AT/1030-2581
**CONSTRUCT IN STEEL. See** Building and Construction.

FR/0045-8198
**CONSTRUCTION METALLIQUE.** [Constr. met.]. **Added/Corp** Centre Technique Industriel de la Construction Metallique (Puteaux, France). (1964)-. Periodical. French. Four times a year (Jan., Apr., July, Oct.). 617.04F France; 850.00F other. Centre Technique Industrial de la Construction Metallique, Domain de Saint Paul, 78470 St Remy Chevreuse France. **Tel** 011 33 1 30852000. **DD** 691. **CODEN** COMQAQ. Documents available from Article Express International.
**Ind/Abst** Bioeng. Abstr.; Ei Page One; Eng. Index Annu.; Int. Civil Eng. Abstr.; Soft. Abstr. Eng.

UK
**COPPER AND COPPER ALLOY MILL PRODUCTS.** (19??)-. English. bm (6 issues). £565.00. Commodities Research Unit Ltd, 31 Mount Pleasant, London WC1X 0AD England. **Tel** 011 44 71 278 0414, FAX 011 44 71 837 0976, telex 264008 CRULDN G. ***Continues*** *Brass Mill Products.*

UK
**COPPER & COPPER ALLOYS COMPUTER FILE / COPPER DEVELOPMENT ASSOCIATION.** **Added/Corp** Copper Development Association. **VFOAT** Copper and Copper Alloys. (1990)-. Monographic series. English. £5.00. Copper Development Association, Orchard House Mutton Lane, Potters Bar EN6 3AP England. **Tel** (0707) 650711, FAX (0707) 642769.

YU/0350-6142
**COPPER (BOR, SERBIA).** (COPPER.). [Copper]. Academic Scholarly Publication. English (summaries and/or abstracts in Serbo-Croatian (Roman)). qt. Copper Publications, 192 10 Bor Ure Akovica 14, PO Box 13, Yugoslavia. **LC** TN445.Y8; C6. **DD** 669/.3. **UDC** 669.3. **CODEN** COPPD7. Documents available from CASDDS.
**Ind/Abst** Chem. Abstr.

US
**COPPER INDUSTRY ANNUAL SUPPLEMENT / U.S. DEPARTMENT OF THE INTERIOR, BUREAU OF MINES. See** Engineering-Abstracting, Bibliographies and Statistics.

UK
**COPPER METAL SERVICE.** (19??)-. English. $7000.00. Brook Hunt & Associates Ltd, Woburn House, 45 High Street, Addlestone Surrey KT1S 1TV England. **Tel** 011 44 932 855198, FAX 011 44 932 846914. **ED** Simon Hunt.

UK
**COPPER-NICKEL ALLOYS / COMPUTER FILE NICKEL DEVELOPMENT INSTITUTE. ALUMINIUM BRONZE ALLOYS / THE ALUMINIUM BRONZE ADVISORY SERVICE.** **Added/Corp** Nickel Development Institute (Great Britain) Aluminium Bronze Advisory Service. **VFOAT** Aluminium Bronze Alloys. (1991)-. English. Copper Development Association, Orchard House Mutton Lane, Potters Bar EN6 3AP England. **Tel** (0707) 650711, FAX (0707) 642769.

US/0091-2204
**COPPER STUDIES.** [Copp. stud.]. (1973)-. English. mo. £900.00. Commodities Research Unit Ltd, 31 Mount Pleasant, London WC1X 0AD England. **Tel** 011 44 71 278 0414, FAX 011 44 71 837 0976, telex 264008 CRULDN G. **ED** R. H. Lesemann. **LC** HD9539.C5; C65. **DD** 338.4/7/67330973. Index available. cum. index. **Pr Rev. Circ:** 300.
**Desc:** Articles on various aspects of the copper industry.
**Ind/Abst** Alum. Ind. Abstr.; Met. Abstr.

GW/0177-1469
**CP + T INTERNATIONAL CASTING PLANT AND TECHNOLOGY.** [CPT, Cast. plant technol.]. **VFOAT** Casting Plant and Technology. (1985)-. Periodical. English. qt. DM133.00. Giesserei Verlag GmbH, Postfach 102532, D 4000 Duesseldorf Germany. **Tel** 011 49 211 6707. **UDC** 621.74.

UK
**CRU METAL MONITOR.** English. mo. Commodities Research Unit Ltd, 31 Mount Pleasant, London WC1X 0AD England. **Tel** 011 44 71 278 0414, FAX 011 44 71 837 0976, telex 264008 CRULDN G. ctrl circ.

US
**CURRENT INDUSTRIAL REPORTS. MA33E, NONFERROUS CASTINGS / U.S. DEPARTMENT OF COMMERCE, BUREAU OF THE CENSUS. See** Economics-Industry and Production.

US/0011-4189
**CUTTING TOOL ENGINEERING.** [Cutt. tool eng.]. (Jan. 1961)-. Periodical. English. Nine times a year. $40.00 US. CTE Publications Inc, 464 Central Avenue, Northfield IL 60093. **Tel** (708)441-7520, FAX (708)441-8740. **ED** Don Nelson, James Schaible and Phillip Craig. **DD** 621. **CODEN** CTEGAP. **[CCC]. Bk Rev. Ad Acc. Circ:** 38,000 (ctrl). available on microfilm and microfiche from University Microfilms International (UMI). Documents available from Article Express International. ***Continues*** *Carbide Engineering, 0096-1590;* ***Absorbed*** *Carbide & Tool Journal, 0192-8333.*
**Desc:** Written and edited for decision makers in the metalworking and materials field who use cutting tools, abrasives and accessories.
**Ind/Abst** Alum. Ind. Abstr.; Bioeng. Abstr.; Ceram. Abstr. (19??-); Ei Page One; Eng. Mater. Abstr.; Eng. Index Annu.; Met. Abstr.; Pollut. Abstr. Indexes.

KO/0253-3847
**DAIHAN GUMSOG HAGHOI JI.** (TAEHAN KUMSOK HAKHOE CHI.). [Daihan gumsog haghoi ji]. **Main/Corp** Taehan Kumsok Hakhoe. **VFOAT** Journal of the Korean Institute of Metals. Academic Scholarly Publication. Korean (English). mo. Free to members. The Korean Institute of Metals. **Tel** 02-734-0595, (02)734-0596. **ED** Y S Kim, I G Moon, J Y Lee and S R Yoon. **LC** TN4; .T3A. **UDC** 669. **CODEN** TKHCDJ. **Ad Acc. Circ:** 2,500 (ctrl). Documents available from Ask*IEEE, CASDDS.
**Desc:** Original papers and technical reviews in materials and metals.
**Ind/Abst** Alum. Ind. Abstr.; Chem. Abstr.; Coal Abstr.; INSPEC (June 1971-); Int. Aerosp. Abstr.; Met. Abstr.

SP/0210-685X
**DEFORMACION METALICA.** [Deform. met.]. (1974)-. Periodical. Spanish. Seven times a year. $160.00. Elsevier Prensa SA, Avenida Paral Lel 180, 08015 Barcelona Spain. **Tel** 011 34 3 3255350, FAX 011 34 3 4252880. **UDC** 621.7. **Ad Acc.** Full Page (B&W) 140000ptas. Half Page (B&W) 110000ptas. Full Page (Color) 165000ptas. Half Page (Color) 135000ptas. **Circ:** 4,000.
**Desc:** Covers manufacturing techniques finishings and transformation of strip-iron, tin-plates, tubes and pipes and wire.

US/0731-3640
**DEMONSTRATED RESERVE BASE OF COAL IN THE UNITED STATES ON JANUARY 1, ... .** [Demonstr. reserve base coal U.S.]. 1979-. Government Publication. English. an. $4.75. US Department of Energy, 1000 Independence Avenue

SW, Washington DC 20585. **Tel** (202)586-5000, FAX (202)586-4073. **LC** TN805.A3; D44. **DD** 553.2/4/0973. **UDC** 553.94(73).

JA/0011-8389
**DENKI-SEIKO.** (DENKI-SEIKO. ELECTRIC FURNACE STEEL.). [Denki-seiko]. **VFOAT** Electric Furnace Steel. (1925)-. Academic Scholarly Publication. Japanese. Four times a year. $50.00. Dnki Seiko Kenkyukai, (Electric Furnace Steel Research Association), Daido Seiko K.K., Kenkyu Kaihatsu Honbu, 2-30, Daidocho, Minamiku, Nagoyashi, Aichiken 457 Japan. **(Subscription address:** Maruzen Company Ltd., PO Box 5050, Import & Export Department, Tokyo 100 31 Japan.) **CODEN** DESEAT. ctrl circ. Documents available from CASDDS.
**Ind/Abst** Alum. Ind. Abstr.; Chem. Abstr.; Eng. Mater. Abstr.; Met. Abstr.

US/0418-7679
**DESIGN IN STEEL.** [Des. steel]. 1963-. English. be. American Iron & Steel Institute, 1101 17th Street Northwest, Suite 1300, Washington DC 20036. **Tel** (202)452-7100 or 7151. **LC** TA684; .D43. **DD** 672. **UDC** 672.

NE/0925-9635
**DIAMOND AND RELATED MATERIALS.** Vol. 1, No. 1 (Aug. 15, 1991)-. Academic Scholarly Publication. English. mo (1 volume). 1250.00F. Elsevier Sequoia SA, PO Box 564, CH-1001 Lausanne 1 Switzerland. **Tel** 011 41 21 3207381. **ED** R. Messier. **[CCC].** Documents available from Article Express International, The Genuine Article, Ask*IEEE, CASDDS.
**Desc:** Publishes articles covering both basic and applied research on diamond materials, as well as related materials, including cubic boron nitride and materials with characteristics and properties approaching or possibly exceeding those of diamond.
**Ind/Abst** Chem. Abstr.; Eng. Mater. Abstr.; Eng. Index Annu.; Fluid Abstr., Civil Eng.; Fluid Abstr. Proc. Eng.; FLUIDEX; GeoRef; INSPEC (Aug. 1991-); Met. Abstr.; Res. Alert [Full Cov.]; Sci. Cit. Index; Surf. Treat. Technol. Abstr.

JA/0917-4540
**DIAMOND FILMS AND TECHNOLOGY.** Vol. 1, No. 1 (1991)-. Periodical. English. qt. $250.00. Diamond Films and Technology, 2-32-3 Sendagi, Bunkyo-ku, Tokyo 113 Japan. **(Subscription address:** Maruzen Company Ltd., PO Box 5050, Import & Export Department, Tokyo 100 31 Japan.) **CODEN** DFTEEB. Documents available from The Genuine Article.
**Ind/Abst** Res. Alert.

AT
**DIRECTORS' REPORT - AUSTRALIAN MINES AND METALS ASSOCIATION.** **See** Engineering-Mines and Mining Engineering.

UK
**DIRECTORY - EUROPEAN COIL COATING ASSOCIATION.** **Main/Corp** European Coil Coating Association. **VFOAT** European Coil Coating Directory. Directory. Multiple languages (English, French and German). Fl2.25. John Adam House, John Adam Street, London WC2N 6JN England. **LC** TS203; .E85A. **DD** 671.7/3.

UK
**DIRECTORY OF OWNERSHIP LINKS IN THE LEAD AND ZINC INDUSTRY.** (19??)-. English. £120.00 UK; $220.00 US. International Lead and Zinc Study Group, Metro House, 58 St. James Street, London SW1A 1LD England. **Tel** 011 44 71 4999373, FAX 011 44 71 4933725, telex 299819 ILZSG G.

US
**DIRECTORY OF THE IRON AND STEEL WORKS OF THE UNITED STATES AND CANADA / AMERICAN IRON AND STEEL INSTITUTE.** **Added/Corp** American Iron and Steel Institute. 18th Ed. (1916)-. Directory. English. an (Pulbished every 3 or 4 years). $30.00. Association of Iron and Steel Engineers, Three Gateway Centre, Suite 2350, Pittsburgh PA 15222. **Tel** (412)281-6323, FAX (412)281-4657. **LC** TS301; .A6. ***Continues*** *Directory of the Iron and Steel Works of the United States and Canada.*

US/0092-6418
**DIRECTORY OF THE LEADING FIRMS IN THE JOB PLATING AND ENAMELING INDUSTRY.** (DIRECTORY OF THE LEADING FIRMS IN THE JOB PLATING AND ENAMELING INDUSTRY WHO ARE MEMBERS OF THE NATIONAL ASSOCIATION OF METAL FINISHERS, INC.). **Main/Corp** National Association of Metal Finishers. **VFOAT** N.A.M.F. Directory of Electro Plating and Enameling Firms. (19??)-. English. Directory of the Leading Firms in the Job Plating and Enameling Industry, Dime Building, Detroit MI 48226. **LC** TS670.A1; N38a. **DD** 671.7/06/273.

AT
**DIRECTORY / THE AUSTRALASIAN INSTITUTE OF MINING AND METALLURGY.** **Main/Corp** Australasian Institute of Mining and Metallurgy. (June 1985)-. Directory. English. Australasian Institute of Mining and Metallurgy, PO Box 122, Parkville Victoria 3052 Australia. **Tel** 011 61 3 3473166, FAX 011 61 3 3478525, telex 33552.
**Ind/Abst** AESIS Q.

US/0360-2001
**DISTRIBUTION OF STEEL CASTINGS SALES BY END USE OF PRODUCT.** **See** Business-Marketing.

GW/0012-5911
**DRAHT.** [Draht]. (1950)-. Academic Scholarly Publication. English. mo. DM158.00 Germany; DM174.00 other. Meisenbach GmbH, Postfach 2069, D 96011 Bamberg Germany. **Tel** 011 49 951 861135. **ED** Klaus Ohlwein. **LC** Discard. **CODEN** DRAHA5. **Ad Acc. Circ:** 4,855 (ctrl). Documents available from Article Express International, CASDDS.
**Desc:** Technical journal covering all aspects of wire and bar production and treatment.
**Ind/Abst** Bioeng. Abstr.; Chem. Abstr.; Coal Abstr.; Ei Page One; EMBASE; Energy Res. Abstr. (Jan. 1972-); Eng. Index Annu.; Leadscan; Surf. Treat. Technol. Abstr.

GW/0012-592X
**DRAHT-WELT.** **VFOAT** Drahtwelt International; Drahtwelt (1951); Drahtwelt (Wurzburg). (1951)-. Multiple languages. bm (6 issues). DM95.00 Germany; DM110.00 other. Vogel Verlag, Postfach 6740, D-97064 Wuerzburg Germany. **Tel** 011 49 931 4182145, 011 49 931 4182483, FAX 011 49 931 4182670, telex 841 680131. **UDC** 621.778. **[CCC].**

US
**DUCTILE IRON PIPE NEWS.** **Added/Corp** Cast Iron Pipe Research Association. (Winter 1975/1976)-. Periodical. English. Twice a year. Free. Ductile Iron Pipe Research Association, 245 Riverchase Parkway East, Suite O, Birmingham AL 35244. **Tel** (205)988-9870. ctrl circ. ***Continues*** *Cast Iron Pipe News.*

US/0278-8799
**DUN'S INDUSTRIAL GUIDE, THE METALWORKING DIRECTORY.** [Dun's ind. guide, metalwork. dir.]. **Added/Corp** Dun and Bradstreet, Inc. **VFOAT** Metalworking Directory. (1981)-. English. an. $795.00. Dun & Bradstreet Information Services, 3 Sylvan Way, Parsippany NJ 07054. **Tel** (201)605-6000, (800)526-0651. **LC** TS203; .D8. **DD** 671/029/473. **Bk Rev.** ***Continues*** *Dun & Bradstreet Metalworking Directory.*
**Desc:** Source that identifies the products, processes and purchases of more than 65,000 plants and distributors throughout the US. A comprehensive source to the multi-billion dollar metalworking industry.

II/0012-8856
**EASTERN METALS REVIEW, THE.** (19??)-. Periodical. English. wk. **LC** HD9506.I4; M4.
**Ind/Abst** Ceram. Abstr. (19??-).

UK
**ECONOMIC GROWTH AND LEAD AND ZINC CONSUMPTION.** (June 1990)-. Periodical. English. £45.00 UK; $70.00 US. International Lead and Zinc Study Group, Metro House, 58 St. James Street, London SW1A 1LD England. **Tel** 011 44 71 4999373, FAX 011 44 71 4933725, telex 299819 ILZSG G. ctrl circ.
**Desc:** Investigates for the first time the relationship between the consumption of lead and zinc, industrial production or gross national product, metal and energy prices in 16 major consuming countries over 1960 to 1988.

US/0361-2686
**ELECTROCHEMICAL INDUSTRY.** ***Title Change.*** **See** Chemistry-Electrochemistry.

US/0099-0043
**ENGRAVERS JOURNAL, THE.** **See** Printing Industry.

FR
**ENQUETE ANNUELLE D'ENTREPRISE : TRAVAIL DES METAUX.** **Main/Corp** Centre d'Enquetes Statistiques de Caen. French. Documentation Francaise, 29 Quai Voltaire, 75344 Paris Cedex 7 France. **Tel** 011 33 1 40157000, FAX 011 33 1 40157230, telex 204 826 DOCFRAN. **LC** HD9506.F7; C45A. **DD** 338.4/7671/0944. **UDC** 311:672/673(44).

GW/0044-2658
**ERZMETALL.** (ERZMETALL.). [Erzmetall]. **Added/Corp** Gesellschaft Deutscher Metallhutten- und Bergleute. Vol. 22, No. 1 (Jan. 1969)-. Academic Scholarly Publication. German. mo. DM522.00 Germany; DM568.00 The Americas; DM544.00 other. VKT Verlag F Kunst & Touristik, Wettiner Strasse 8, D 04105 Leipzig Germany. **Tel** 011 49 341 290111, FAX 011 49 341 275218. **LC** TN3; .Z42. **CODEN** ERZMAK. **[CCC].** Documents available from Article Express International, CASDDS. ***Continues*** *Zeitschrift fur Erzbergbau und Metallhuttenwesen, 0372-848X.*

**Ind/Abst** Alum. Ind. Abstr.; Art Archaeol. Tech. Abstr.; Bioeng. Abstr.; Chem. Abstr.; CIS Abstr.; Coal Abstr.; Ei Page One; EMBASE; Energy Res. Abstr. (June 1971-); Eng. Index Annu.; GeoRef; Leadscan; Met. Abstr.; MINPROC; Mintec, Min. Technol. Abstr.; Saf. Health Work; World Alum. Abstr.

GW
**EUROPEAN METALWORKING MANUAL.** (19??)-. English. an. $60.00. Sprechsaal Publishing Group, PO Box 2962, D-96418 Coburg Germany. **Tel** 011 49 9561 742810, FAX 011 49 9561 90009, telex 179561817.

FR
**EUROPEAN REFINING ACTIVITY.** English. mo. 15000.00F. WEFA / France, 25 Rue de Ponthieu, 75008 Paris France. **Tel** 011 33 1 45631910.

UK
**EUROPEAN STEEL REVIEW.** (19??)-. English. mo. £700.00 UK; £720.00 other. MEPS (Europe) Ltd, 263 Glossop Road, Sheffield S10 2GZ, England. **Tel** 011 44 742 750570, FAX 011 44 742 759808, telex 547938 EXPERT G. **ED** P. Fish. **Ad Acc.**
**Desc:** Covers all key aspects of the European steel industry; market prices for main steel producers in six countries in the EEC; commentary on price movements and trends in user markets; details of major developments in the indutry and important industry data.

CN/0835-0124
**FABRICATED METAL PRODUCTS INDUSTRIES.** (FABRICATED METAL PRODUCTS INDUSTRIES / STATISTICS CANADA, INDUSTRY DIVISION, CENSUS OF MANUFACTURES SECTION.). [Fabr. met. prod. ind.]. **Added/Corp** Statistics Canada. Industry Division. Statistics Canada. Census of Manufactures Section. **VFOAT** Industries de la Fabrication des Produits Metalliques. (1985)-. English (French). an. 38.00Can$ Canada; $46.00 US; $54.00 other. Statistics Canada, Publications Sales & Services, Main Building Room 1710, Ottawa Ontario K1A 0T6 Canada. **Tel** (613)951-5078, (800)267-6677, FAX (613)951-1584, telex 053-3585. **LC** HD9506.C2; F32. **DD** 338.4/7671/0971021. ***Formed by the union of*** *Hardware, Tool, and Cutlery Industries, 0828-9905; Wire and Wire Products Industries, 0828-9913; Ornamental and Architectural Metal Products Industry, 0828-9921; Heating Equipment Industry, 0828-993X; Stamped, Pressed, and Coated Metal Products Industries, 0828-9794; Other Metal Fabricating Industries, 0828-9948; Power Boilers, Heat Exchanger, and Fabricated Structural Metal Products Industries, 0828-9956* ***and*** *Machine Shop Industry, 0828-9816.*
**Desc:** Annual census of manufacturers.

GW/0340-8043
**FACHBERICHTE HUTTENPRAXIS METALLWEITERVERARBEITUNG.** ***Title Change.*** [Fachber. Huttenprax. Metallweiterverarb.]. **VFOAT** Neue Fachberichte. Vol. 3 (Oct. 1975)-(19??). Academic Scholarly Publication. German (English). Twelve times a year. Sprechsaal Publishing Group, PO Box 2962, D-96418 Coburg Germany. **Tel** 011 49 9561 742810, FAX 011 49 9561 90009, telex 179561817. **(Subscription address:** Domhardt Pressevertrieb, Naegleinsgasse 2, D 96450 Coburg Germany.) **ED** Klaus Hoffmann. **CODEN** FACHDN. **Bk Rev. Ad Acc. Circ:** 8,300 (ctrl). Documents available from CASDDS. ***Continues*** *Fachberichte fuer Oberflachentechnik.* ***Continued by*** *Steel & Materials Technology Now Recycling Praxis.*
**Desc:** International magazine dealing with iron and steel technologies, procedures and equipment raw material preparation, iron and steelmaking, refractories, continuous casting, rolling and finishing.
**Ind/Abst** Alum. Ind. Abstr.; Chem. Abstr.; Coal Abstr.; EMBASE; Energy Res. Abstr. (March 1978-); Eng. Mater. Abstr.; Met. Abstr.

US/0163-3899
**FACTS (WASHINGTON).** ***Ceased.*** (FACTS.). **Main/Corp** Institute of Scrap Iron and Steel. (19??)-(1992). English. an. Institute of Scrap Iron and Steel, 1627 K Street Northwest, Washington DC 20006. **Tel** (202)466-4050. **ED** Debra Levin and Terry Ann Hamilton. **LC** TS200; .I64. **DD** 338.4/7/6691. **Circ:** 3,000. ***Continues*** *Institute of Scrap Iron & Steel Yearbook, 0073-9685.*
**Desc:** Statistical data on ferrous, non-ferrous and paper stock industries. Ten year historical data also included. Domestic and export tonnage by grade of scrap, and scrap composite prices.

GW/0934-7054
**FBM FERTIGUNGS-TECHNOLOGIE.** **VFOAT** Fertigungs-Technologie. **VAT** Fachberichte fuer Metallbearbeitung Fertigungs-Technologie; FBM Fertigungs Technologie. Vol. 65 No. 1 (1988)-. Academic Scholarly Publication. German. bm. DM360.00 other. Sprechsaal Publishing Group, PO Box 2962, D-96418 Coburg Germany. **Tel** 011 49 9561 742810, FAX 011 49 9561 90009, telex 179561817. **LC** TS200; .F33. **DD** 671/.05. **CODEN** FBMFE7. Documents available from CASDDS. ***Continues*** *Fachberichte fuer Metallbearbeitung, 0173-6922.*
**Ind/Abst** Appl. Sci. Technol. Index (1991-199?); Chem. Abstr. (?-1990).

UK/0266-3198
**FERRO-ALLOY DIRECTORY.** (1984)-. Directory. English. ir. Metal Bulletin PLC, PO Box 28E, Worcester Park, Surrey KT4 7HX England. **Tel** 011 44 71 827 9977, FAX 011 44 81 337 8943. **[CCC].**

UK/0266-3198
**FERRO-ALLOY DIRECTORY & DATABOOK.** (1984)-. Directory. English. ir. $139.00. Metal Bulletin PLC, PO Box 28E, Worcester Park, Surrey KT4 7HX England. **Tel** 011 44 71 827 9977, FAX 011 44 81 337 8943. **[CCC]. Ad Acc. Circ:** 5,000.
**Desc:** Directory of international ferro-alloys producers and traders.

UK
**FERRO ALLOYS MONTHLY.** (19??)-. Trade Publication. English. mo. £725.00 UK; $1,235.00 US, Canada & South America. Metal Bulletin PLC, PO Box 28E, Worcester Park, Surrey KT4 7HX England. **Tel** 011 44 71 827 9977, FAX 011 44 81 337 8943.

US
**FERROALLOYS. See** Metals and Metallurgy-Abstracting, Bibliographies and Statistics.

GW
**FEUERVERZINKEN. Added/Corp** Verband Deutscher Feuerverzinkereien. Stichting Doelmatig Verzinken. (19??)-. Periodical. German (Dutch). qt. DM26.00 plus postage. Institut Feuerverzinken GmbH, Sohnstrasse 70, D 40237 Dusseldorf Germany. **Tel** 0211/670004, FAX 0211/689599. **ED** H Bucholz. **LC** TS660; .V47. **Bk Rev. Circ:** 33,000 German, 5,000 Dutch. ***Continues*** *Verzinken.*
**Desc:** Information on hot dip galvanizing and galvanization.

GW/0430-4578
**FILO METALLICO, IL.** [Filo. met.]. (1954)-. Academic Scholarly Publication. Italian (German; translations available in German). qt. DM77.00. Meisenbach GmbH, Postfach 2069, D 96011 Bamberg Germany. **Tel** 011 49 951 861135. **CODEN** FIMEBG. Documents available from CASDDS.
**Ind/Abst** Chem. Abstr.

US/0015-2358
**FINISHERS' MANAGEMENT. See** Business-General Management.

RU/0136-3638
**FIZICESKIE SVOJSTVA METALLOV I SPLAVOV.** (FIZICHESKIE SVOISTVA METALLOV I SPLAVOV / MINISTERSTVO VYSSHEGO I SREDNEGO SPETSIALNOGO OBRAZOVANIIA RSFSR, URALSKII ORDENA TRUDOVOGO KRASNOGO ZNAMENI POLITEKHNICHESKII INSTITUT IM. S.M. KIROVA.). [Fiz. svojstva met. splavov]. **Added/Corp** Uralskii Politekhnicheskii Institut im. S.M. Kirova. (1976)-. Periodical. Russian. **CODEN** FSMSDS. Documents available from CASDDS.
**Ind/Abst** Chem. Abstr.

RU/0015-3230
**FIZIKA METALLOV I METALLOVEDENIE.** [Fiz. met. metalloved.]. **Added/Corp** Akademiia Nauk SSSR. Akademiia Nauk SSSR. Ural'Skii Filial, Sverdlosk. (1955)-. Academic Scholarly Publication. Russian. mo. $273.00. Izdatelstvo Nauka / Akademiia Nauk, Publishing House of the Russian Academy of Sciences, Leninskii Porspekt 14, 117901 Moscow Russia. **Tel** 011 95 954-21-53, FAX 011 95 938-21-44, telex 411964. **(Subscription address:** East View Publications Inc., 3020 Harbor Lane North, Suite 110, Minneapolis MN 55447.**) LC** TN690; .F53. **CODEN** FMMTAK. **[CCC].** Documents available from Article Express International, The Genuine Article, Ask*IEEE, CASDDS.
**Ind/Abst** Alum. Ind. Abstr.; Chem. Abstr.; Chem. Titles; Curr. Contents Eng. Tech. Appl. Sci.; Curr. Contents Phys. Chem. Earth Sci.; Ei Page One; Energy Res. Abstr.; Eng. Mater. Abstr.; Eng. Index Annu.; GeoRef; INSPEC (1968-); Int. Aerosp. Abstr.; Leadscan; Met. Abstr.; Res. Alert [Full Cov.]; Sci. Cit. Index; SCISEARCH; Surf. Treat. Technol. Abstr.

RU
**FIZIKO-KHIMICHESKIE ISSLEDOVANIIA METALLURGICHESKIKH PROTSESSOV. Added/Corp** Sverdlovsk, Russia. Uralskii Politekhnicheskii Institut. (1973)-. Russian. **LC** TN600; .F58. **CODEN** FKIPDB. Documents available from CASDDS.
**Ind/Abst** Chem. Abstr.

UK/0967-9618
**FOCUS ON TIN.** [Focus tin]. (1992)-. Periodical. English. International Tin Research Institute, Kingston Lane, Uxbridge UB8 3PJ England. **Tel** 011 44 0895 72406. **DD** 669.605. ***Continues*** *Tin and Its Uses.*

IT/0015-6078
**FONDERIA. Added/Corp** Associazione Italiana Modellisti Fonderia. (19??)-. Academic Scholarly Publication. Italian. bm (6 issues). L70000 Italy; L90000 other. Editoriale Tecnica Macchine, Via Ugo Lenzi 1, 40122 Bologna Italy. **Tel** 011 39 51 523183. **LC** TS200; .A796. **DD** 671.2/05. **CODEN** FNDAAR. Documents available from CASDDS. ***Continues*** *Fonderia Italiana.*
**Ind/Abst** Chem. Abstr.; Eng. Mater. Abstr.

FR/0249-3136
**FONDERIE, FONDEUR D'AUJOURD'HUI.** [Fonderie fondeur aujourd'hui]. New Series, 1 (Jan. 1981)-. Academic Scholarly Publication. French (summaries and/or abstracts in English and German). mo. $75.83. Editions Techniques Industries, 44 Avenue de la Division Leclerc, 92310 Sevres Cedex France. **Tel** 011 33 1 45342754. **LC** TS200; .F6953. **DD** 671.2/05. **UDC** 621.74. **CODEN** FFAUDJ. **Bk Rev. Ad Acc. Circ:** 3,500 (ctrl). Documents available from Ask*IEEE, CASDDS. ***Formed by the union of*** *Fonderie, 0015-6094* ***and*** *Fondeur d'Aujourd'hui.*
**Desc:** Science technology and information for foundries. Metallurgy (steel, cast-iron, non-ferrous alloys) moulding, risering, gating, coremaking, finishing equipment, health and safety inspection.
**Ind/Abst** Alum. Ind. Abstr.; Art Archaeol. Tech. Abstr.; Chem. Abstr.; Ei Page One; Energy Res. Abstr. (Dec. 1982-); Eng. Mater. Abstr.; INSPEC (Feb. 1981-1985); Leadscan; Met. Abstr.

IT
**FORMAZIONE INDICATIVA DEL COSTA DI PRODUZIONE DEI GETTI DI GHISA.** ASsn Nazionale Fonderie, Via Copernico 54, 20090 Trezzano S Nav Mi Italy.

US/0533-005X
**FOUNDRY CATALOG FILE.** ***Ceased.*** **VFOAT** Catalog File. (19??)-(19??). Catalog. English. an. Penton Publishing, 1100 Superior Avenue, Cleveland OH 44114-2543. **Tel** (216)696-7000, FAX (216)696-0836. **ED** Robert Rodgers, Wallace Huskonen, and Hans Heine. **LC** WMLC L 83/3459.

US/0360-8999
**FOUNDRY MANAGEMENT & TECHNOLOGY.** [Foundry manage. technol.]. **VFOAT** Foundry Management and Technology; Foundry M&T. **VAT** Foundry Management and Technology. Vol. 102, No. 5, (May 1974)-. Periodical. English. Twelve times a year. $45.00 US; $60.00 Canada; $75.00 Mexico; $90.00 other. Penton Publishing, 1100 Superior Avenue, Cleveland OH 44114-2543. **Tel** (216)696-7000, FAX (216)696-0836. **(Subscription address:** Penton Publishing, PO Box 96732, Chicago IL 60693.**) LC** TS200; .F7. **DD** 671.2/05. **CODEN** FNMTBS. **[CCC].** Index available. **Circ:** 23,000. available on microfilm and microfiche from University Microfilms International (UMI); available on an online database (file 648/Full-Text) from DIALOG. Documents available from Article Express International, CASDDS. ***Continues*** *Foundry, 0015-9034.*
**Desc:** Serves management and technical needs of foundry personnel in metal casting plants in the U.S. and Canada.
**Ind/Abst** Alum. Ind. Abstr.; Appl. Sci. Technol. Index; Bioeng. Abstr.; Bus. ASAP (1990-) [Full Txt.]; Bus. Index (1985-); Ceram. Abstr.; Chem. Abstr.; Coal Abstr.; Ei Page One; EMBASE; Eng. Mater. Abstr.; Eng. Index Annu. [Select. Cov.]; Ergon. Abstr. (?-?); Gen. BusinessFile (1985-); Gen. Period. Index (1985-); Mag. Search; Met. Abstr.; Stat. Ref. Index; Trade Ind. ASAP [Full Txt.]; Trade Ind. Index (1981-) [Full Txt.]; Vocat. Search (July 1993-).

US/0147-8796
**FOUNDRY OPERATIONS PLANBOOK.** English. $5.00 single issue. McGraw Hill Publishing Company, Inc., 1221 Avenue of the Americas, New York NY 10020. **Tel** (212)512-6410, (800)525-5003, FAX (212)512-6111. **LC** TS228.99; .F67. **DD** 671.2/05. **UDC** 621.74.

UK/0015-9042
**FOUNDRY TRADE JOURNAL, THE.** [Foundry trade j.]. **Added/Corp** Institute of British Foundrymen. Welsh Engineers' and Founders' Association. Foundry Trades' Equipment & Supplies Association. (1902)-. Academic Scholarly Publication. English. mo. £122.45 UK; £163.60, $253.60 other. Argus Press Group, Queensway House, 2 Queensway Redhill, Surrey RH1 1QS England. **Tel** 011 44 737 768611, 011 44 737 761685, FAX 011 44 737 760510, telex 948669 TOPJNL G. **LC** TS200; .F8. **CODEN** FUTJAD. available on microfilm and microfiche from University Microfilms International (UMI). Documents available from Article Express International, CASDDS. ***Absorbed*** *Iron and Steel Trades Journal;* ***Continues*** *Foundry Trade Journal and Pattern Maker.*
**Desc:** Leading UK foundry industry publication.
**Ind/Abst** Alum. Ind. Abstr.; Art Archaeol. Tech. Abstr.; Bioeng. Abstr.; Chem. Abstr. (1902-1983); Coal Abstr.; Curr. Technol. Index; Ei Page One; EMBASE; Eng. Mater. Abstr.; Eng. Index Annu.; Ergon. Abstr.; Leadscan; Met. Abstr.; Saf. Health Work; Surf. Treat. Technol. Abstr.

UK/0143-6902
**FOUNDRY TRADE JOURNAL INTERNATIONAL.** [Foundry trade j. int.]. (1978)-. Periodical. English (summaries and/or abstracts in French, German, Italian and Spanish; table of contents in French, German, Italian and Spanish). qt. £88.95 UK; £107.00, $165.80 other. Argus Press Group, Queensway House, 2 Queensway Redhill, Surrey RH1 1QS England. **Tel** 011 44 737 768611, 011 44 737 761685, FAX 011 44 737 760510, telex 948669 TOPJNL G. **ED** Cyril McCombe. **CODEN** FTJIDO. **Ad Acc.** ctrl circ. Documents available from Article Express International.
**Desc:** Encompasses the whole range of foundry technology: traditional sand-based foundry practices, investment casting, die-casting, etc.
**Ind/Abst** Alum. Ind. Abstr.; Bioeng. Abstr.; Ei Page One; Eng. Mater. Abstr.; Eng. Index Annu. [Select. Cov.]; Met. Abstr.

UK/0264-5319
**FOUNDRY YEAR BOOK.** (1972)-. English. an. £98.50 UK; $164.00 other. Argus Press Group, Queensway House, 2 Queensway Redhill, Surrey RH1 1QS England. **Tel** 011 44 737 768611, 011 44 737 761685, FAX 011 44 737 760510, telex 948669 TOPJNL G. **LC** TS229; .F66. **DD** 671.2/0941.

UK/0007-0718
**FOUNDRYMAN, THE. Added/Corp** Institute of British Foundrymen. Vol. 80, Pt. 7 (Aug./Sept. 1987)-. Periodical. English. Ten times a year. £68.00 UK; £82.00 other. TG Scott Subscriber Services, 6 Bourne Enterprise Center, Wrotham Road, Borough Green, Kent TN15 8DG England. **Tel** 011 44 01 732 884023, FAX 011 44 01 732 884034. **ED** Lynn Postle. **LC** TS200; .F82. **DD** 671.2. Index available. cum. index. **Bk Rev**, (Qty: 15). **Ad Acc, Adv Mgr:** Les Rivers, **Tel** 0432 350448. **Pr Rev. Circ:** 2,421. available on microfilm from University Microfilms International (UMI). Documents available from UMI Article Clearinghouse, Article Express International. ***Continues*** *British Foundryman.*
**Desc:** Deals with the cast metals industry in Great Britain. Contains informative technical papers written by experts, as well as up-to-date information on news and developments taking place within the industry, along with company profiles of foundries in the UK and overseas.
**Ind/Abst** Ei Page One; Eng. Index Annu. [Select. Cov.]; Ergon. Abstr.

GW/0071-9420
**FREIBERGER FORSCHUNGSHEFTE. REIHE B.** (FREIBERGER FORSCHUNGSHEFTE. [REIHE] B. [METALLURGIE]). [Freib. Forsch.heft. B]. **Added/Corp** Bergakademie Freiberg. (1951)-. Monographic series. German. ir. Price varies per volume. Deutscher Verlag Grundstoffind, Karl Heine Strasse 27, D 04211 Leipzig Germany. **Tel** 011 49 341 4081011. **LC** TN607; .F7. **CODEN** FFRBAA. Documents available from CASDDS.
**Ind/Abst** Chem. Abstr.

JA/0532-8799
**FUNTAI OYOBI FUMMATSU YAKIN.** [Funtai oyobi fummatsu yakin]. **Added/Corp** Funmatsu Yakin Gijutsu Kyokai. Funtai Funmatsu Yakin Kyokai. **VFOAT** Journal of the Japan Society of Powder and Powder Metallurgy; Science of Powder. (1947)-. Academic Scholarly Publication. Japanese (summaries and/or abstracts in English). Nine times a year. $550.00. Funtai Funmatsu Yakin Kyokai, (Japan Society of Powder & Powder Metallurgy), Seisan Kaihatsu Kagaku Kenkyujo, 15, Shimogamo Morimotocho, Sakyoku, Kyotoshi, Kyotofu 606 Japan. **(Subscription address:** Kyowa Book Company Inc., 1-38 Kanda Jinbo-Cho, Chiyoda-Ku Tokyo 101, Japan**) CODEN** FOFUA2. Documents available from Article Express International, Ask*IEEE, CASDDS.
**Ind/Abst** Alum. Ind. Abstr.; Bioeng. Abstr.; Ceram. Abstr.; Chem. Abstr.; Ei Page One; Eng. Index Annu.; INSPEC (Jan. 1990-); Met. Abstr.

US
**GALLIUM IN ... . See** Metals and Metallurgy-Abstracting, Bibliographies and Statistics.

FR/0302-6477
**GALVANO-ORGANO. VFOAT** Galvano-Organo-Traitements de Surface. **VAT** Galvano Organo. (198?)-. Periodical. French. Ten times a year (Monthly with June/July combined, no issue in Aug.). 480.00F France; 540.00F other. Galvano-Organo-Traitements de Surface, 22 24 rue President Wilson, F-92300 Levals Perret France. **Tel** 011 33 1 47393481, FAX 011 33 1 47393479. **LC** TS200; .G3. **DD** 671.7. Documents available from CASDDS. ***Continues*** *Galvano-Organo-Traitements de Surface.*
**Ind/Abst** Chem. Abstr.

CC/0449-749X
**GANGTIE.** (KANG TIEH.). [Gangtie]. **Added/Corp** Chung-kuo Chin Shu Hsueh Hui. **VFOAT** Iron and Steel. (1954)-. Periodical. Chinese. mo. Yejin Gongye Chubanshe / Metallurgical Industry Publishers, 39 Songzhuyuan Beixiang, Shatan, Beijing 100009, People's Republic of China. **Tel** 4015782. **ED** L. Da. **LC** TS300; .K34. **DD** 669/.1/05. **CODEN** KATIAR. Documents available from Article Express International, CASDDS, BLDSC, CASDDS.
**Ind/Abst** Alum. Ind. Abstr.; Bioeng. Abstr.; Chem. Abstr.; Coal Abstr.; Ei Page One; Eng. Index Annu.; Met. Abstr.

BL/0100-4921
**GEOLOGIA E METALURGIA.** (GEOLOGIA E METALURGIA; BOLETIM.). [Geol. metal.]. Began with

No. 1, Oct. 1945. Bulletin. Portuguese. **LC** TN239.B8; G4. **UDC** 553; 669. **CODEN** GMTBAC.
**Ind/Abst** GeoRef.

GW/0016-9765
**GIESSEREI.** (GIESSEREI : ZEITSCHRIFT FUER DAS GESAMTE GIESSEREWIESEN.). [Giesserei]. **Added/Corp** Verein Deutscher Giessereifachleute. Vol. 1, No. 1 (Jan. 11, 1951)-. Academic Scholarly Publication. German (table of contents in English and French). Twenty-four times a year. DM213.00 Germany; DM311.00 other. Giesserei Verlag GmbH, Postfach 102532, D 4000 Duesseldorf Germany. **Tel** 011 49 211 6707. **LC** TS200; .N48. **[CCC].** Index available. **Bk Rev. Ad Acc.** ctrl circ. Documents available from CASDDS. ***Continues** Neue Giesserei, 0369-3848; **Absorbed** Giesserei-Technik, 0016-9803.*
**Ind/Abst** Chem. Abstr.; EMBASE; Energy Res. Abstr.; Eng. Mater. Abstr.; F&S Index Plus Text, Int. [Select. Cov.]; Numis. Lit.; PROMT; Saf. Health Work.

AU/0016-979X
**GIESSEREI RUNDSCHAU.**
[Giesserei-Rundsch.]. **Added/Corp** Verein Osterreichischer Giessereifachleute. Osterreichisches Giesserei-Institut. Fachverband der Giessereiindustrie (Austria). **VFOAT** Giesserei-Rundschau. (1954)-. Academic Scholarly Publication. German. Six times a year. S528.00. Verlag Lorenz, Ebendorferstrasse 10, A-1010 Vienna Austria. **Tel** 011 43 222 426695, FAX 011 43 222 438693. **CODEN** GIERBQ. Documents available from CASDDS.
**Ind/Abst** Chem. Abstr.; Energy Res. Abstr. (March 1982-).

GW/0046-5933
**GIESSEREIFORSCHUNG.**
[Giessereiforschung]. Vol. 19 (1967)-. Academic Scholarly Publication. German (English). Four times a year. DM292.00 Europe; DM321.00 other. Giesserei Verlag GmbH, Postfach 102532, D 4000 Duesseldorf Germany. **Tel** 011 49 211 6707. **CODEN** GSFGBY. **[CCC].** Index available. **Ad Acc. Circ:** 500. Documents available from Article Express International, CASDDS. ***Continues** Die Giesserei. Technisch-Wissenschaftliche Beihefte. Metalkunde und Giessereiwesen.*
**Desc:** Foundry research.
**Ind/Abst** Alum. Ind. Abstr.; Bioeng. Abstr.; Chem. Abstr.; Ei Page One. Energy Res. Abstr. (May 1973-); Eng. Mater. Abstr.; Eng. Index Annu.

JA
**GIJUTSU RENKAN CHOSA KENKYU HOKOKUSHO. Main/Corp** Chusho Kigyo Shinko Jigyodan. **Added/Corp** Chusho Kigyo Joho Senta. (1974)-. Periodical. Japanese. Chusho Kigyo Jigyodan Chusho Kigyo Joho Senta, (Small Business Information Center,, Japan Small Business Corporation), Toranomon 37, Mori Building 5-1 Toranomon 3-chome, Minatoku Tokyoto 105 Japan. **LC** TS200; .C49a.

SW/0017-0682
**GJUTERIET.** [Gjuteriet]. (1915)-. Academic Scholarly Publication. English. Twelve times a year. Kr450.00. AB Gjuteriinformation i Jonkoping, Box 2033, S-550 02 Jonkoping Sweden. **Tel** 011 46 36 30 12 12, FAX 011 4636 16 68 66. **CODEN** GJUTAG. Documents available from Article Express International, CASDDS.
**Ind/Abst** Alum. Ind. Abstr.; Chem. Abstr.; Ei Page One; Eng. Mater. Abstr.; Eng. Index Annu.; Met. Abstr.

US/0196-3546
**GOLD & SILVER SURVEY.** ***Suspended.*** **Added/Corp** International Currency Review Research Unit. **VAT** Gold and Silver Survey. Vol. 1 (Feb. 1980)-(19??). Periodical. English. mo (ten issues per year). £215.00 Uk and Ireland; $525.00 other. World Reports Ltd., 108 Horse Ferry Road, Westminster, London SW1P 2EF United Kingdom. **Tel** 011 44 71 222 3836, FAX 11 44 71 233 0185.
**Desc:** Intended for investors who understand the potential importance of gold in their portfolios, yet also recognize the dangers inherent in the volatile precious metals markets.

AT/0816-455X
**GOLD GAZETTE.** [Gold gaz.]. (1985)-. Periodical. English. sm. 140.00Aus$ Australia; 200.00Aus$ New Zealand and Papua New Guinea; 225.00Aus$ other. Resource Information Unit, 100 Ahy Street Suite 8 10, R Louthean, Subiaco WA 6008 Australia. **Tel** 011 61 9 3823955. **DD** 622.34220994.
**Ind/Abst** AESIS Q.

FR/0301-8539
**GUIDE DU TRAVAIL DES METAUX.**
French. 65.00. Compagnie Francaise d'Editions. **LC** TS203; .G83. **DD** 338.4/7/6817. **UDC** 621.7.

KO/0253-3081
**GUMSOG PYOMYEN CERI.** (KUMSOK PYOMYON CHORI.). [Gumsog pyomyen ceri]. **VFOAT** Journal of the Metal Finishing Society of Korea; Journal of the Metal Finishing Society of Korea. Academic Scholarly Publication. Korean (Korean). Hanguk Kumsok Pyonyon Konghakhoe, 72-1 Sangsu-dong, Mapo-ku, Seoul South Korea. **LC** TS653.A1; K85. **UDC** 672. **CODEN** KPCHDD. Documents available from CASDDS.
**Ind/Abst** Chem. Abstr.

UK
**HANDBOOK AND ... LIST OF MEMBERS - INSTITUTE OF METALS. Main/Corp** Institute of Metals. **VFOAT** List of Members; Institute of Metals Handbook and ... List of Members. 1986-. Periodical. English. The Institute of Materials, 1 Carlton House Terrace, London SW1Y 5DB England. **Tel** 011 44 71 839 4071, FAX (071)839 2078.

KO
**HANGUK KUMHYONG KONGOP CHONGNAM.** ***Title Change.*** **Added/Corp** Hanguk Kumhyong Kisul Chongbo Sento. **VFOAT** Korea Mould Industrial Directory. (19??)-(19??). Korean. Hanguk Kumhyong Kisul Chongbo Sento, 54-34 Munnae-dong 3-ka Yongdungpo-ku, Seoul Korea. **LC** TS229; .H36. ***Continued by** Hanguk Kumhyong Sanop Chongnam.*

US/0017-9345
**HEAT TREATING.** ***Title Change.*** [Heat treat.]. (19??)-(1994). Academic Scholarly Publication. English. mo. Diversified Publishing, 825 7th Avenue, 6th Floor, New York NY 10019. **Tel** (212)887-8565, FAX (212)887-8493. **LC** TN672; .H34. **DD** 671.3/6/05. **CODEN** HETRDI. **[CCC].** available on microfilm and microfiche from University Microfilms International (UMI). Documents available from CASDDS. ***Continued by** Metal Heat Treating.*
**Ind/Abst** Alum. Ind. Abstr.; Chem. Abstr. (1969-1980); Eng. Mater. Abstr.; Met. Abstr.

UK/0305-4829
**HEAT TREATMENT OF METALS.** [Heat treat. met.]. **Added/Corp** Wolfson Heat Treatment Centre. Vol. 1 (1974)-. Academic Scholarly Publication. English. qt. $161.00. Wolfson Heat Treatment Centre, Aston University/Aston Triangle, Birmingham B4 7ET England. **Tel** 011 44 21 3593611 ext. 5212, FAX (021)359 6470, telex 336997 UNIAST G. **ED** Alan J. Hick. **LC** TN672; .H374. **DD** 671.3/6/05. **CODEN** HTRMBS. Index available. cum. index. **Bk Rev. Ad Acc. Pr Rev. Circ:** 1,000 (ctrl). Documents available from Article Express International, The Genuine Article, Ask*IEEE, CASDDS.
**Desc:** Devoted to heat treatment practice and innovation.
**Ind/Abst** Alum. Ind. Abstr.; Bioeng. Abstr.; Chem. Abstr.; Curr. Contents Eng. Tech. Appl. Sci.; Ei Page One; Eng. Mater. Abstr.; Eng. Index Annu.; Fluid Abstr., Civil Eng.; Fluid Abstr. Proc. Eng.; FLUIDEX; INSPEC (1981-); Leadscan; Manuf. Process Eng. Abstr.; Met. Abstr.; Res. Alert [Full Cov.]; SCISEARCH.

UK/0142-3304
**HISTORICAL METALLURGY.** [Hist. metall.]. **Added/Corp** Historical Metallurgy Society. **VFOAT** Journal of the Historical Metallurgy Society. Vol. 8 (1974)-. Academic Scholarly Publication. English. sa. £31.00 UK; £35.65 other. The Institute of Materials, 1 Carlton House Terrace, London SW1Y 5DB England. **Tel** 011 44 71 839 4071, FAX (071)839 2078. **ED** R.F. Tylecote. **CODEN** HIMED6. **Bk Rev. Ad Acc. Circ:** 800. Documents available from CASDDS. ***Continues** Bulletin of the Historical Metallurgy Group.*
**Desc:** Contains research papers, reviews, papers presented at the Historical Metallurgy Society's Annual Conference, book reviews, news and notes, and abstracts.
**Ind/Abst** Art Archaeol. Tech. Abstr.; Br. Archaeol. Bibliogr.; Chem. Abstr.; Ei Page One; Numis. Lit. (?-?).

JA/0916-0930
**HITACHI KINZOKU GIHO. VFOAT** Hitachi Metals Technical Review. (1985)-. Periodical. Multiple languages. an. Hitachi Kinzoku K.K., (Hitachi Metals Ltd.), 102, Marunouchi 2 Chome, Chiyodaku, Tokyoto 100 Japan. **DD** 669. **CODEN** HIKGE3. Documents available from CASDDS.
**Ind/Abst** Chem. Abstr.

CH/1001-2052
**HUAGONG YEJIN. See** Engineering-Chemical Engineering.

XR/0018-8069
**HUTNICKE LISTY.** [Hut. listy]. **Added/Corp** Ceskolovensk Hute. Czechoslovakia. Ministerstvo Hutniho Prumysiu a Rudnych Dolu. (1946)-. Academic Scholarly Publication. English (Czech). mo. $105.70. **(Subscription address:** Artia Pegas Press Ltd., Palac Metro Narodni Trida 25, 11210 Prague 1 Czech Republic.) **LC** TN4; .H8. **CODEN** HUTLA7. Documents available from Article Express International, CASDDS.
**Ind/Abst** Alum. Ind. Abstr.; Anal. Abstr.; Art Archaeol. Tech. Abstr.; Bioeng. Abstr.; Chem. Abstr.; Coal Abstr.; Ei Page One; Eng. Mater. Abstr.; Eng. Index Annu.; Leadscan; Met. Abstr.; Saf. Health Work; Surf. Treat. Technol. Abstr.

PL/0018-8077
**HUTNIK (KATOWICE).** (NUTNIK; MIESIECZNIK ORGANIZCYJ HUTNICZYCH.). [Hutnik]. **Added/Corp** Zwiazek Polskich Hut Zelaznych, Warsaw. Vol. 1 (July 20, 1929)-. Academic Scholarly Publication. Polish. mo. $120.00. **(Subscription address:** ARS Polona, PO Box 1001, 00068 Warsaw Poland.) **LC** TS200; .H95. **DD** 672.05. **CODEN** HUTNAD. Documents available from Article Express International, CASDDS.
**Ind/Abst** Alum. Ind. Abstr.; Bioeng. Abstr.; Ceram. Abstr.; Chem. Abstr.; Coal Abstr.; Ei Page One; Eng. Mater. Abstr.; Eng. Index Annu.; Met. Abstr.

PL/1230-3534
**HUTNIK, WIADOMOSCI HUTNICZE.** [Hut. Wiad. Hut.]. **Added/Corp** Association of Engineers and Technicians of Metallurgical Industry. (1992)-. Periodical. Multiple languages. mo. **UDC** 669. ***Formed by the union of** Hutnik (Warszawa), 0018-8077 **and** Wiadomosci Hutnicze, 0043-5139.*

US
**HVAC DUCT CONSTRUCTION STANDARDS. (METAL & FLEXIBLE).**
English. ir. $87.00 (US); $89.00 (Canada); $92.00 (other). SMACNA / Sheet Metal and Air Conditioning Contractors National Association, 4201 LaFayette Center Drive, Chantilly VA 22021. **Tel** (703) 803-2980.
**Desc:** Prescribes construction detail alternatives for uncoated steel, galvanized steel, aluminum, and stainless steel ductwork consisting of straight sections, transitions, elbows and united and divided flow fittings, plus accessory items such as access doors, volume dampers, belt guards, hangers, casings, louvers, and vibration isolation.

NE/0304-386X
**HYDROMETALLURGY.** [Hydrometallurgy]. Vol. 1 (Sept. 1975)-. Academic Scholarly Publication. English. Nine times a year (3 volumes). Fl1470.00. Elsevier Science Publishers BV, PO Box 211, 1000 AE Amsterdam Netherlands. **Tel** 011 31 20 5803642, FAX 011 31 20 5862696, telex 15682. **ED** G M Ritcey and M J Slater. **LC** TN688; .H89. **DD** 669/.0283/05. **CODEN** HYDRDA. **[CCC]. Bk Rev. Ad Acc. Pr Rev.** available on microfilm and microfiche from University Microfilms International (UMI). Documents available from Article Express International, The Genuine Article, CASDDS.
**Desc:** Aims to bring together studies on novel processes, process design, chemistry, modelling, control economics and interfaces between unit operations. Provides forum for discussions on case histories and operational difficulties.
**Ind/Abst** AESIS Q.; Alum. Ind. Abstr.; Bioeng. Abstr.; Chem. Abstr.; Chem. Titles; Coal Abstr.; Curr. Contents Eng. Tech. Appl. Sci.; Curr. Titles Electrochem.; Ei Page One; Energy Res. Abstr. (Oct. 1977-); Eng. Index Annu.; GeoRef; Leadscan; Met. Abstr.; MINPROC; Proc. Chem. Eng.; Res. Alert [Full Cov.]; Sci. Cit. Index; SCISEARCH; Theoret. Chem. Eng.

JM
**IBA REVIEW. Added/Corp** International Bauxite Association. **VFOAT** IBA Quarterly Review. (19??)-. Periodical. English (French). Four times a year. $50.00. International Bauxite Association, PO Box 551, Kingston 5 Jamaica. **Tel** 011 80 9264536. **ED** Shirley Davis. **LC** TN490.A5; I18. **DD** 669/.722. **Circ:** 300.
**Desc:** Covers developments in bauxite, alumina, the aluminum industry and markets.
**Ind/Abst** Alum. Ind. Abstr.

SZ
**IMF NEWS. Added/Corp** International Metalworkers' Federation. (19??)-. Periodical. English. sm. Free. International Metalworkers Federation, Route des Acacias 54 Bis, CH-1227 Geneva Switzerland. **ED** Denis MacShane.

UK/0019-0020
**IMM ABSTRACTS.** [IMM abstr.]. **Main/Corp** Institution of Mining and Metallurgy (Great Britain). Vol. 1 (July 1950)-. Periodical. English. bm (6 issues). £208.00. Institution of Mining and Metallurgy, 44 Portland Place, London W1N 4BR England. **Tel** 011 44 71 580-3802, FAX 011 44 71 436-5388, telex 261410. **ED** Michael McGarr. **[CCC]. Bk Rev. Ad Acc.**
**Desc:** Economic geology, mining and extraction technology, and developments in the non-ferrous metals and industrial minerals fields.
**Ind/Abst** AESIS Q.; MINPROC; Mintec, Min. Technol. Abstr.

US/1045-5779
**INCAST (DALLAS, TEX.).** (INCAST : INTERNATIONAL NEWS MAGAZINE OF THE INVESTMENT CASTING INDUSTRY.). [INCAST]. **Added/Corp** Investment Casting Institute. (198?)-. Periodical. English. Eleven times a year. $60.00 US; $90.00 other. Investment Casting Institute, 8350 North Central Expressway, Suite M1110, Dallas TX 75206. **Tel** (214)368-8896, FAX (214)368-8852, telex 3792 373 ICIIN. **ED** Leland D Martin. **DD** 671. **Ad Acc. Pr Rev. Circ:** 2,000 (ctrl).
**Desc:** News, trends and technology for international investment casting industry.

II/0379-5446
**INDIAN FOUNDRY JOURNAL.** [Indian foundry j.]. **Added/Corp** Institute of Indian Foundrymen. (1955)-. Academic Scholarly Publication. English. mo. $150.00. Institute of Indian Foundrymen, Calcutta, 700 071 India. **(Subscription address:** Prints India, 11 Darya Ganj, New Delhi 110002 India.) **CODEN** IFOJAI. Documents available from CASDDS.
**Ind/Abst** Alum. Ind. Abstr.; Art Archaeol. Tech. Abstr.; Ceram. Abstr.; Chem. Abstr.; Leadscan; Met. Abstr.

IT/0391-1586
**INDUSTRIA MINERARIA (ROMA. 1957). See** Earth Sciences-Geology.

CN/0820-6759
**INDUSTRIAL PRODUCT IDEAS!. See** Manufacturing.

FR
**INDUSTRIE SIDERURGIQUE. IRON AND STEEL INDUSTRY, L'. Main/Corp** Organization for Economic Cooperation and Development. **VFOAT** Iron and Steel Industry. (1975)-. Periodical. French (English). an. $34.00. OECD Publications and Information Center, 2 rue Andre-Pascal, 75775 Paris Cedex 16 France. **Tel** 011 33 1 45248167, US:(202)785-6323, FAX 011 33 1 45248500 OR 45248176, telex 620 160 OCDE. **(Subscription address:** OECD Publications Center, 2001 L Street, Suite 700, Washington DC 20036.**)** ***Continues*** *Organization for Economic Cooperation and Developmnt. Industrie Siderurgique et Tendances.*
**Ind/Abst** F&S Index Plus Text, Int. [Select. Cov.]; Predicasts Forecasts; World Ceram. Abstr.

FR
**INDUSTRIE SIDERURGIQUE. THE IRON AND STEEL INDUSTRY, L'. See** Economics-Industry and Production.

US/0039-0895
**INDUSTRY WEEK.** [Ind. week]. Vol. 166 (Jan. 5, 1970)-. Periodical. English. Twenty-four times a year. $60.00 US; $80.00 Canada; $90.00 Mexico; $100.00 other. Penton Publishing, 1100 Superior Avenue, Cleveland OH 44114-2543. **Tel** (216)696-7000, FAX (216)696-0836. **(Subscription address:** Penton Publishing, PO Box 96732, Chicago IL 60693.**) LC** TS300; .I745. **DD** 658/.96/9105. **CODEN** IWEEA4. **[CCC].** available on microfilm and microfiche from University Microfilms International (UMI). Documents available from UMI Article Clearinghouse, Documents on Demand. ***Continues*** *Steel.*
**Ind/Abst** Acad. Search (July 1993-); Bus. ASAP (1990-) [Full Txt.]; Bus. Source (Jul. 1993-); Comput. Lit. Index; Ei Page One; Environ. Abstr.; F&S Index Plus Text, Int. [Select. Cov.]; Gen. Period. Index (1985-); INFO-SOUTH Abstr.; Mag. ASAP Plus [Full Txt.]; Mag. Index Plus (1989-); Mag. Search; Newsp. Period. Abstr. (1988-); Stat. Ref. Index; Mag. Index (1977-); TOM Gen. Index (1992-) [Full Txt.]; UMI ABI/Inform--Bus. Period. Ondisc (Nov. 1987-) [Full Txt.].

GW/0170-9526
**INFORMATIONSDIENST - VEREIN DEUTSCHER INGENIEURE. BLECHBEARBEITUNG.** [Inf.dienst - Ver. Dtsch. Ing., Blechbearb.]. (1978)-. German. bm. DM297.00 Germany; DM315.00 other. VDI Verlag GmbH, Postfach 101054, D 40001 Dusseldorf Germany. **Tel** 011 49 211 6188313, FAX 011 49 211 6188133. **UDC** 621.98 (048.1). **[CCC].** ***Continues*** *VDI-Informationsdienst. Blechbearbeitung, 0341-1613.*

BL
**INFORME ESTATISTICO ANUAL, SETOR METALURGICO. See** Metals and Metallurgy-Abstracting, Bibliographies and Statistics.

BL
**INFORME ESTATISTICO, SETOR METALURGICO. See** Economics-Industry and Production.

US/0020-1685
**INORGANIC MATERIALS. See** Chemistry-Inorganic Chemistry.

UK/0073-9464
**INSTITUTE OF METALS MONOGRAPH AND REPORT SERIES. Added/Corp** Institute of Metals. **VFOAT** Monograph and Report Series. (1947)-. Monographic series. English. ir. Price varies per volume. The Institute of Materials, 1 Carlton House Terrace, London SW1Y 5DB England. **Tel** 011 44 71 839 4071, FAX (071)839 2078.
**Desc:** These books cover a broad spectrum of subjects from fundamental physical principles to process metallurgy and applications.

UK/0371-9553
**INSTITUTION OF MINING AND METALLURGY. TRANSACTIONS. SECTION C : MINERAL PROCESSING AND EXTRACTIVE METALLURGY.** (TRANSACTIONS. SECTION C, MINERAL PROCESSING & EXTRACTIVE METALLURGY.). [Inst. Min. Metall., Trans. C]. **Added/Corp** Institution of Mining and Metallurgy (Great Britain). **VFOAT** Transactions of the Institution of Mining and Metallurgy. Section C, Mineral Processing and Extractive Metallurgy; Mineral Processing & Extractive Metallurgy; Mineral Processing and Extractive Metallurgy. Vol. 75 (March 1966)-. Periodical. English. Three times a year (Feb., June, & Oct.). £65.00. Institution of Mining and Metallurgy, 44 Portland Place, London W1N 4BR England. **Tel** 011 44 71 580-3802, FAX 011 44 71 436-5388, telex 261410. **LC** TN496; .T73. **DD** 622/.7/05. **CODEN** TMEMAB. **[CCC]. Bk Rev. Circ:** 3,200. Documents available from Article Express International, The Genuine Article, CASDDS. ***Continues in part*** *Transactions of the Institution of Mining and Metallurgy, 0371-7836.* ***Continued in part by*** *IMM Bulletin, 0308-9789.*
**Desc:** Contains technical papers, review papers and technical notes.
**Ind/Abst** AESIS Q.; Alum. Ind. Abstr.; Bioeng. Abstr.; Ceram. Abstr. (19??-); Chem. Abstr.; Coal Abstr.; Curr. Contents Eng. Tech. Appl. Sci.; Curr. Technol. Index; Curr. Titles Electrochem.; Ei Page One; Energy Inf. Abstr.; Energy Res. Abstr. (Aug. 1973-); Eng. Index Annu.; GeoRef; Leadscan; Manuf. Process Eng. Abstr.; Mater. Sci. Eng. Abstr.; Met. Abstr.; MINPROC; Proc. Chem. Eng.; Res. Alert [Full Cov.]; Solid State Supercond. Abstr.; Theoret. Chem. Eng.

RU
**INSTRUMENTALNYE I PODSHIPNIKOVYE STALI. Added/Corp** Soviet Union. Ministerstvo Chernoi Metallurgii. No. 1 (1973)-. Academic Scholarly Publication. Russian. 0.64rub single issue. Izdatelstvo Metallurgiia, 2-i Obydenskii Per.14, G-34, Moscow Russia. **LC** TS320; .I45. **CODEN** IPSTD5. Documents available from CASDDS.
**Ind/Abst** Chem. Abstr. (?-1975);(-1975).

US/0278-9337
**INSULATED WIRE AND CABLE. See** Economics-Industry and Production.

●UK/0966-9795
**INTERMETALLICS.** Vol. 1, No. 1 (1993)-. Academic Scholarly Publication. English. Six times a year. $433.00 The Americas; £290.00 other. Elsevier Applied Science, An Imprint of Elsevier Science Ltd., The Boulevard, Langford Lane, Kidlington, Oxford OX5 1GB United Kingdom. **Tel** 011 44 865 843000, 011 44 865 843699, FAX 011 44 865 843010. **(Subscription address:** Elsevier Science Ltd. Oxford Fulfillment Centre, PO Box 800, Kidlington, Oxford OX5 1DX United Kingdom.**) ED** R. W. Cahn, C. T. Liu, M. Yamaguchi, G. Sauthoff. **LC** TN689; .I54. **DD** 669. **CODEN** IERME5. **[CCC].**
**Desc:** Concerned with all aspects of ordered chemical compounds between two or more metals, notably with their applications.

UK/0309-2216
**INTERNATIONAL COPPER INFORMATION BULLETIN. *Ceased.* See** Metals and Metallurgy-Abstracting, Bibliographies and Statistics.

US/0147-300X
**INTERNATIONAL GLASS/METAL CATALOG. See** Glass and Ceramics.

US/0888-7462
**INTERNATIONAL JOURNAL OF POWDER METALLURGY (PRINCETON, N.J.).** (INTERNATIONAL JOURNAL OF POWDER METALLURGY.). [Int. j. powder metall.]. **Added/Corp** American Powder Metallurgy Institute. **VFOAT** Journal of Powder Metallurgy; Powder Metallurgy. Vol. 22, (Jan. 1986)-. Academic Scholarly Publication. English. Four times a year (Jan., Apr., July, Oct.). $145.00 US & Canada & Mexico; $165.00 other. American Powder Metallurgy Institute, 105 College Road East, Princeton NJ 08540. **Tel** (609)452-7700, FAX (609)987-8523. **LC** TN695; .I57. **DD** 671.3/7/05. **CODEN** IPMTEA. **[CCC]. Ad Acc. Pr Rev.** available on microfilm and microfiche from University Microfilms International (UMI). Documents available from Article Express International, The Genuine Article, Ask*IEEE, CASDDS. ***Continues*** *International Journal of Powder Metallurgy & Powder Technology, 0361-3488.*
**Desc:** Aimed at powder metallurgists, materials engineers, scientists, educators and technical managers, which offers current information about basic and applied developments in all aspects of P/M technology.
**Ind/Abst** Appl. Sci. Technol. Index; Chem. Abstr. (1986-); Ei Page One; Eng. Index Annu.; INSPEC (Jan. 1986-); Leadscan; Res. Alert [Full Cov.]; Sci. Cit. Index; SCISEARCH.

UK/0265-0916
**INTERNATIONAL JOURNAL OF RAPID SOLIDIFICATION.** [Int. j. rapid solidif.]. Vol. 1, No. 1 (1984)-. Academic Scholarly Publication. English. ir. Price varies. AB Academic Publishers, PO Box 42 Bicester, OXON OX6 7NW England. **Tel** 011 44 869 320949. **CODEN** IJRSEO. **Pr Rev.** Documents available from Article Express International, The Genuine Article, Ask*IEEE, CASDDS.
**Ind/Abst** Chem. Abstr. (1984-); Civ. Struct. Eng. Abstr.; Curr. Contents Eng. Tech. Appl. Sci.; Ei Page One; Eng. Index Annu.; INSPEC (1985-); Manuf. Process Eng. Abstr.; Mater. Sci. Eng. Abstr.; Res. Alert [Full Cov.]; Sci. Cit. Index; SCISEARCH; Solid State Supercond. Abstr.

UK/0263-4368
**INTERNATIONAL JOURNAL OF REFRACTORY METALS & HARD MATERIALS.** [Int. j. refract. metals hard mater.]. **Added/Corp** International Plansee Society. International Tungsten Industry Association. **VFOAT** Refractory Metals & Hard Materials; Refractory Metals and Hard Materials; RM and HM; RM & HM. **VAT** International Journal of Refractory Metals and Hard Materials. Vol. 8, No. 1, March (1989)-. Academic Scholarly Publication. English. Six times a year. $306.00 The Americas; £205.00 other. Elsevier Applied Science, An Imprint of Elsevier Science Ltd., The Boulevard, Langford Lane, Kidlington, Oxford OX5 1GB United Kingdom. **Tel** 011 44 865 843000, 011 44 865 843699, FAX 011 44 865 843010. **(Subscription address:** Elsevier Science Ltd. Oxford Fulfillment Centre, PO Box 800, Kidlington, Oxford OX5 1DX United Kingdom.**) ED** B. Lux. **DD** 620. **CODEN** IRMME3. **[CCC]. Bk Rev. Ad Acc. Circ:** 1,100. Documents available from Article Express International, CASDDS. ***Continues*** *International Journal of Refractory & Hard Metals, 0263-4368.*
**Desc:** Contains technical papers covering production and properties of refractory metals and hard materials, plus news and reviews.
**Ind/Abst** Chem. Abstr.; Ei Page One; Eng. Index Annu.

UK/0950-6608
**INTERNATIONAL MATERIALS REVIEWS.** [Int. mater. rev.]. **Added/Corp** Institute of Metals. ASM International. Vol. 32 No. 1-2 (1987)-. Periodical. English. bm. $490.00 (nonmembers); $221.00 (members). American Society for Metals International, c/o Deborah Barthelmes, Materials Park OH 44073-0002. **Tel** (216)338-5151, FAX (216)338-4634, telex 980-619. **ED** John Woodruff. **LC** TN1; .M513. **DD** 669/.05. **CODEN** INMREOINMRED. **[CCC].** Documents available from Article Express International, The Genuine Article, Ask*IEEE, CASDDS. ***Continues*** *International Metals Reviews, 0308-4590.*
**Desc:** Treatment of specific topics from theory and practice of extraction, production, fabrication, properties and behavior of metals, to actual usage.
**Ind/Abst** Chem. Abstr.; Civ. Struct. Eng. Abstr.; Curr. Contents Eng. Tech. Appl. Sci.; Curr. Technol. Index; Ei Page One; Eng. Index Annu.; Index Sci. Rev. [Full Cov.]; INSPEC (1987-); Int. Aerosp. Abstr.; Manuf. Process Eng. Abstr.; Mater. Sci. Eng. Abstr.; Mech. Eng. Abstr.; Res. Alert [Full Cov.]; Sci. Cit. Index; SCISEARCH; Solid State Supercond. Abstr.

US/0074-8218
**INTERNATIONAL SERIES OF MONOGRAPHS ON METAL PHYSICS AND PHYSICAL METALLURGY.** (19??)-. Monographic series. English. ir. Price varies per volume. Pergamon Press, An Imprint of Elsevier Science Ltd., The Boulevard, Langford Lane, Kidlington, Oxford OX5 1GB United Kingdom. **Tel** 011 44 865 843000, 011 44 865 843699, FAX 011 44 865 843010.

UK/0952-6803
**INTERNATIONAL STEEL STATISTICS : SUMMARY TABLES. See** Metals and Metallurgy-Abstracting, Bibliographies and Statistics.

UK/0307-7608
**INTERNATIONAL STEEL STATISTICS, UNITED KINGDOM. See** Metals and Metallurgy-Abstracting, Bibliographies and Statistics.

UK
**INTERNATIONAL TIN STATISTICS.** English. ir. Intl Trade Centre UNCTAD/GATT, Palais des Nations, 1211 Geneva 10 Switzerland. **Tel** 011 41 22 7300111. ***Continues*** *Tin Statistics.*

US/0897-4365
**IRON AGE (NEW YORK, N.Y. 1987). *Title Change.*** (IRON AGE : THE MANAGEMENT MAGAZINE FOR METAL PRODUCERS.). [Iron age]. Vol. 3, No. 12 (Dec. 1987)-Vol. 9, No. 9 (Sept. 1993). Periodical. English. Twelve times a year. Hitchcock Publishing Company, 191 South Gary Avenue, Carol Stream IL 60188. **Tel** (708)665-1000. **(Subscription address:** ABC Capital Cities, Inc., 825 7th Avenue, 7th Floor, New York NY 10019.**) LC** HD9506.U6; C48. **DD** 672/.05. **[CCC].** available on microfilm and microfiche from University Microfilms International (UMI). ***Continues*** *Iron Age. Metals Producer, 0893-9616.* ***Continued by*** *New Steel, 1074-1690.*
**Ind/Abst** Acad. Search (Jan. 1993-Sept. 1993); Appl. Sci. Technol. Index; Bus. ASAP (1990-) [Full Txt.]; Bus. Period. Index; INFO-SOUTH Abstr.; Mag. Search; Stat. Ref. Index; Vocat. Search (Jan. 1993-); Wilson Bus. Abstr.

US/0021-1559
**IRON AND STEEL ENGINEER.** [Iron steel eng.]. **Added/Corp** Association of Iron and Steel Engineers. Association of Iron and Steel Electrical Engineers (U.S.) Association of Iron and Steel Engineers. Proceedings. Vol. 1 (1924)-. Academic Scholarly Publication. English. Twelve times a year. $50.00 US & Mexico, $53.50 Canada, $72.00 other (surface mail); $127.00 (airmail). Association of Iron and Steel Engineers, Three Gateway Centre, Suite 2350, Pittsburgh PA 15222. **Tel** (412)281-6323, FAX (412)281-4657. **ED** Dennis Fuga. **LC** TS300; .I63. **DD** 672.05. **CODEN** IRSEA5. Index available. **Bk Rev. Ad Acc, Adv Mgr:** S. Seem. **Circ:** 12,000 (ctrl). available on microfilm and microfiche from University Microfilms International (UMI). Documents available from Article Express International, Ask*IEEE, CASDDS. ***Supersedes*** *Association of Iron and Steel Electrical Engineers (U.S.) Bulletin.*
**Desc:** Information relating to the design, construction,

operation and maintenance of iron and steel producing facilities and related equipment.
**Ind/Abst** Alum. Ind. Abstr.; Appl. Sci. Technol. Index; Bioeng. Abstr.; Ceram. Abstr. (19??-); Chem. Abstr.; Coal Abstr.; Ei Page One; EMBASE; Eng. Index Annu.; INSPEC (Dec. 1968-); Leadscan; Met. Abstr.; Surf. Treat. Technol. Abstr.; World Ceram. Abstr.

US/0732-8621
**IRON AND STEEL FOUNDRIES AND STEEL INGOT PRODUCERS.** (CURRENT INDUSTRIAL REPORTS. M33A, IRON AND STEEL FOUNDRIES AND STEEL INGOT PRODUCERS / U.S. DEPARTMENT OF COMMERCE, BUREAU OF THE CENSUS.). [Iron steel foundries steel ingot prod.]. **Added/Corp** United States. Bureau of the Census. **VFOAT** Iron and Steel Foundries and Steel Ingot Producers. (19??)-. Government Publication. English. US Department of Commerce, 14th Street & Constitution Avenue NW, Washington DC 20230. **Tel** (202)482-2000, FAX (202)482-3772. **LC** HD9511; .C87. **DD** 338.4/7672/0973.

UK/0952-5505
**IRON AND STEEL INDUSTRY ANNUAL STATISTICS FOR THE UNITED KINGDOM.** **See** Metals and Metallurgy-Abstracting, Bibliographies and Statistics.

UK
**IRON & STEEL INTERNATIONAL.** (19??)-. English. an. £71.70 UK; $122.00 other. Argus Press Group, Queensway House, 2 Queensway Redhill, Surrey RH1 1QS England. **Tel** 011 44 737 768611, 011 44 737 761685, FAX 011 44 737 760510, telex 948669 TOPJNL G.

LU/0378-7559
**IRON AND STEEL (LUXEMBOURG, LUXEMBOURG : 1986).** (IRON AND STEEL.). **Added/Corp** Statistical Office of the European Communities. **VFOAT** Siderurgie. Vol. 1 (1986)-. English (French, German and Italian). mo. $110.00. Office for Official Publications of the European Communities, 2 Rue Mercier, 2985 Luxembourg Luxembourg. **Tel** 011 352 499281, FAX 011 352 488573. **(Subscription address:** Unipub, 4611 F Assembly Drive, Lanham, MD 20706 (800-274-4888)) **LC** HD9525.A2; S725b. ***Continues*** *Eisen und Stahl, 0378-7559.*

LU
**IRON AND STEEL. MONTHLY STATISTICS.** Multiple languages. mo. £51.90 UK; 56.30p Ireland. Office for Official Publications of the European Communities, 2 Rue Mercier, 2985 Luxembourg Luxembourg. **Tel** 011 352 499281, FAX 011 352 488573.

II/0578-7661
**IRON & STEEL REVIEW.** Vol.1 (June 1957)-. Periodical. English. mo. $114.00. Commercial Publication, Calcutta, India. **(Subscription address:** Prints India, 11 Darya Ganj, New Delhi 110002 India.) **LC** HD9526.I6; I7.

US
**IRON AND STEEL SCRAP IN ... / U.S. DEPARTMENT OF THE INTERIOR, BUREAU OF MINES.** **See** Economics-Industry and Production.

UK
**IRON AND STEEL WORKS OF THE WORLD.** (1952)-. Directory. English. ir. Metal Bulletin PLC, PO Box 28E, Worcester Park, Surrey KT4 7HX England. **Tel** 011 44 71 827 9977, FAX 011 44 81 337 8943. **ED** Board. **Ad Acc. Circ:** 6,700.
**Desc:** Detailed information on the world's major iron and steel producers. Over 1,900 entries given, where possible. head office address, capacity, work details, products, subsidiaries and management.

US/0275-8687
**IRON & STEELMAKER.** (IRON & STEELMAKER : A PUBLICATION OF THE IRON AND STEEL SOCIETY.). [Iron steelmak.]. **Added/Corp** Iron and Steel Society of AIME. **VFOAT** Iron and Steelmaker; I and SM; I & SM. **VAT** Iron and Steelmaker. Vol. 7, No. 5 (May 1980)-. Academic Scholarly Publication. English. mo. $35.00 US; $41.00 other. Iron and Steel Society Inc., 410 Commonwealth Drive, Warrendale PA 15086. **Tel** (412)776-9460, FAX (412)776-0430, telex 6503113570. **ED** Lawrence G Kuhn, Thomas P McAloon and William A Tony. **LC** TS300; .I14. **DD** 669/.1/05. **CODEN** IRSTDJ. Index available. cum. index. **Bk Rev. Ad Acc. Circ:** 700 (ctrl). Documents available from Article Express International, CASDDS. ***Continues*** *I & SM, 0097-8388.*
**Desc:** The only magazine in North America that is published exclusively for primary iron and steelmakers. Editorial contributions are international in scope.
**Ind/Abst** Alum. Ind. Abstr.; Bioeng. Abstr.; Ceram. Abstr.; Chem. Abstr.; Ei Page One; Eng. Mater. Abstr.; Eng. Index Annu.; Met. Abstr.

US/0075-0883
**IRON ORE (CLEVELAND, OHIO).** (IRON ORE.). [Iron ore]. **Added/Corp** American Iron Ore Association. (1957)-. English. an. American Iron Ore Association, Bulkley Building, Cleveland OH 44803. **LC** HD9512; .I7. **DD** 338.2/73/05. **CODEN** IRORDR.
**Ind/Abst** GeoRef.

JA
**IRON ORE MANUAL.** (197?)-. Periodical. English (Japanese). an (Jan.). $205.00 North America & Australia; $200.00 Southeast & Asia; $210.00 others. The Tex Report Ltd, 11-7-2 chome Kanda Nishikicho, Chiyoda ku Tokyo 101 Japan. **Tel** 011 81 3 32330811. **ED** H. Sano. **Ad Acc.** ctrl circ.
**Desc:** Emphases put on analysis of iron ore markets in Japan and Europe. Physical distribution of ore, trade relation country-by-country, seaborne trade.

UK/0301-9233
**IRONMAKING & STEELMAKING.** [Ironmaking steelmaking]. **Added/Corp** Metals Society. American Society for Metals. Vol. 1 (1974)-. Periodical. English (summaries and/or abstracts in French and German). bm. £203.00 EEC countries; £233.45 other. The Institute of Materials, 1 Carlton House Terrace, London SW1Y 5DB England. **Tel** 011 44 71 839 4071, FAX (071)839 2078. **ED** Trevor Hughes. **LC** TS300; .I749. **DD** 669/.14/05. **CODEN** IMKSB7. **[CCC]. Bk Rev. Ad Acc. Pr Rev. Circ:** 1,200. available on microfilm and microfiche from University Microfilms International (UMI). Documents available from Article Express International, The Genuine Article, CASDDS. ***Supersedes*** *Iron and Steel Institute. Journal.*
**Desc:** Monitors technological advances in the industry, with an input of engineering and product related material. Company and academic research profiles, and analytical reports on conferences. Includes regional reports on industrial developments worldwide. Contains refereed papers covering all aspects of iron- and steelmaking, including the rolling and application of ferrous products.
**Ind/Abst** Alum. Ind. Abstr.; Art Archaeol. Tech. Abstr.; Bioeng. Abstr.; Ceram. Abstr.; Chem. Abstr.; Coal Abstr.; Curr. Contents Eng. Tech. Appl. Sci.; Curr. Technol. Index; Ei Page One; Eng. Mater. Abstr.; Eng. Index Annu.; Leadscan; Met. Abstr.; Res. Alert [Full Cov.]; Sci. Cit. Index; SCISEARCH; Soc. Sci. Cit. Index [Select. Cov.].

JA/0915-1559
**ISIJ INTERNATIONAL / IRON AND STEEL INSTITUTE OF JAPAN.** **See** Economics-Industry and Production.

RU
**ITOGI NAUKI I TEKHNIKI: DIAGRAMMY SOSTOIANIIA NEMETALLICHESKIKH SISTEM. OKISNYE SISTEMY.** **Added/Corp** Vsesoiuznyi Institut Nauchnoi i Tekhnicheskoi Informattsii. **VFOAT** Diagrammy Sostoianiia Nemetallicheskikh Sistem. Okisnye Sistemy; Itogi Nauki I Tekhniki: Seriia Diagrammy Sostoianiia Nemetallicheskikh Sistem. Okisnye Sistemy. (1974)-. Academic Scholarly Publication. Russian. 0.60rub single issue. VINITI - Vsesoiuznyi Institut Nauchno-Tekhnicheskoi Informatsii, All-Union Scientific and Technical Information Institute, Baltiiskaia Ulitsa 14, 125219 Moscow Russia. **Tel** 238-46-00, FAX 9430060, telex 411160. **LC** TN690; .I847. **CODEN** IDSNA2. Documents available from CASDDS.
**Ind/Abst** Chem. Abstr. (?-1976).

RU/0202-7690
**ITOGI NAUKI I TEKHNIKI: TEKHNOLOGIIA I OBORUDOVANIE KUZNECHNO-SHTAMPOVOCHNOGO PROIZVODSTVA.** **Added/Corp** Vsesoiuznyi Institut Nauchnoi i Tekhnicheskoi Informatsii (Soviet Union). **VFOAT** Tekhnologiia I Oborudovanie Kuznechno-Shtampovochnogo Proizvodstva; Itogi Nauki i Tekhniki: Seriia Tekhnologiia i Oborudovanie Kuznechno-Shtampovochnogo Proizvodstva. Vol. 1 (1975)-. Monographic series. Russian. wk. Price varies per volume. VINITI - Vsesoiuznyi Institut Nauchno-Tekhnicheskoi Informatsii, All-Union Scientific and Technical Information Institute, Baltiiskaia Ulitsa 14, 125219 Moscow Russia. **Tel** 238-46-00, FAX 9430060, telex 411160. **(Subscription address:** Victor Kamkin, 4956 Boiling Brook Parkway, Rockville MD 20852.) **LC** TS225; .I86.

UK/0144-3143
**ITRI PUBLICATION.** [ITRI publ.]. **VFOAT** International Tin Research Institute Publication. (1977)-. Monographic series. English. ir. International Tin Research Institute, Kingston Lane, Uxbridge UB8 3PJ England. **Tel** 011 44 0895 72406. Documents available from CASDDS. ***Continues*** *Publication - Tin Research Institute, Greenford, 0372-1140.*
**Ind/Abst** Chem. Abstr.

RU
**IZVESTIIA VYSSHIKH UCHEBNYKH ZAVEDENII. CHERNAIA METALLURGIIA.** **Added/Corp** Soviet Union. Ministerstvo Vysshego Obrazovaniia. Soviet Union. Ministerstvo Vysshego i Srednego Spetsialnogo Obrazovaniia. Sibirskii Metallurgicheskii Institut. Moskovskii Institut Stali. Moskovskii Institut Stali i Splavov. **VFOAT** Chernaia Metallurgiia. (1958)-. Academic Scholarly Publication. Russian. mo. $199.95. **(Subscription address:** East View Publications Inc., 3020 Harbor Lane North, Suite 110, Minneapolis MN 55447.) **CODEN** IVUMAX. Documents available from Article Express International, CASDDS. ***Absorbed in part*** *Soviet Union. Ministerstvo Vysshego Obrazovaniia. Nauchnye Doklady Vysshei Shkoly. Metallurgiia.*
**Ind/Abst** Alum. Ind. Abstr.; Bioeng. Abstr.; Chem. Abstr.; Ei Page One; Eng. Index Annu.; Met. Abstr.

RU/0021-3438
**IZVESTIJA VYSSIKH UCEBNYH ZAVEDENIJ. CVETNAJA METALLURGIJA.** (IZVESTIIA VYSSHIKH UCHEBNYKH ZAVEDENII. TSVETNAIA METALLURGIIA.). [Izv. vyss. ucebn. zaved., Cvet. metall.]. **Added/Corp** Severo-Kavkazskii Gorno-Metallurgicheskii Institut. **VFOAT** Tsvetnaia Metallurgiia. (1958)-. Periodical. Russian. bm. **(Subscription address:** Victor Kamkin, 4956 Boiling Brook Parkway, Rockville MD 20852.) **LC** TN758; .I98. **CODEN** IVUTAK. **[CCC].** Documents available from CASDDS.
**Ind/Abst** Chem. Abstr.

GW/0075-2819
**JAHRBUCH OBERFLACHENTECHNIK.** **Added/Corp** MSV. Zeitschrift fur Metall- und Schmuckwaren-Fabrikation sowie Verchromung. (1939)-. German. an. DM185.00. Metall Verlag Gmbh, Hubertusallee 18, 14193 Berlin. **Tel** 011 49 30 8919055, FAX 011 49 30 8922112. **LC** TS670; .A45. **CODEN** JBOFAN. **Circ:** 4,500. Documents available from Article Express International, CASDDS.
**Ind/Abst** Bioeng. Abstr.; Chem. Abstr.; Ei Page One; Eng. Index Annu.; Leadscan.

GW
**JAHRESBEZUGSNACHWEIS FUER DEN GESAMTEN METALLSEKTOR.** ***Ceased.*** (19??)-(19??). German. Carl Hanser Verlag, Postfach 860420, D 81631 Munich Germany. **Tel** 011 49 89 998300, FAX 011 49 89 984809. **LC** WMLC L 83/7959.

JA
**JAKUTO NYUSU / JACT NEWS. CHUZO GIJUTSU FUKKYU KYOKAI.** [JACT news]. **Added/Corp** Chuzo Gijutsu Fukkyu Kyokai (Japan). **VFOAT** JACT News; J.A.C.T. News. **VAT** Japanese Association of Casting Technology News. (1972)-. Periodical. Japanese. mo. Chuzo Gijutsu Fukkyu Kyogai, Ginza 5-9-13, Chuo-ku, Tokyo 104 Japan. **CODEN** JACNDH. Documents available from CASDDS.
**Ind/Abst** Chem. Abstr.

US/0894-1149
**JAPAN MATERIALS NEWS (METALS PARK, OHIO).** ***Ceased.*** (JAPAN MATERIALS NEWS.). [Jpn. mater. news]. Vol. 1, No. 1 (June 1987)-Ceased 1989. Periodical. English. mo. American Society for Metals International, c/o Deborah Barthelmes, Materials Park OH 44073-0002. **Tel** (216)338-5151, FAX (216)338-4634, telex 980-619. **DD** 620. **[CCC].**

JA/0021-4523
**JAPAN METAL BULLETIN. AIR MAIL ED.** (JAPAN METAL BULLETIN.). [Jpn. met. bull., Air mail ed.]. (1953)-. Bulletin. English. Fifty-two times a year. $570.00 North and Central America, Oceania and Middle East; $580.00 Europe, South America and Africa; $560.00 Asia. Nalk Corporation, 4 9 18 Shibaura #615 Grand Place, Minato Ku Tokyo 108 Japan. **Tel** 11 81 3 34564416, FAX 11 81 3 34564417. **ED** Isao Nakada; Telephone: 11 81 3 34565205. **DD** 669. **Circ:** 700.

JA
**JAPAN STEEL JOURNAL.** ***Ceased.*** (19??)-(19??). Japanese. da. Japan Steel Struct Journal Co, 4-8-1 Hatcho-Bori Chuo-Ku, Tokyo 104 Japan. **Tel** 011 81 3 35536961.

JA/0075-3475
**JAPAN'S IRON & STEEL INDUSTRY.** **See** Economics-Industry and Production.

CC/0254-6051
**JINSHU RECHULI.** (CHIN SHU JE CHU LI.). [Jinshu Rechuli]. **Added/Corp** Chi Hsieh Kung Yeh Pu Chi Tien Yen Chiu So (China) Chung-Kuo Chi Hsieh Kung Cheng Hsueh Hui (Peking, China). Je Chu Li Hsueh Hui. Pei-Ching Chi Tien Yen Chiu So. **VFOAT** Jinshu Rechuli; Heat Treatment of Metals. (1958)-. Periodical. Chinese (summaries and/or abstracts in English and Chinese). mo. $60.00 US. Beijing Jidian Yanjiusuo / Beijing Research Institute of Mechanical & Electrical Technology, 18 Xueqing lu, PO Box 907, Beijing 100083, People's Republic of China. **Tel** 2017761, FAX 2017108. **(Subscription address:** China International Book Trading Corporation, PO Box 399, Library Service Department, Beijing 100044 People's Republic of China.) **ED** C. Minda. **LC** TN672; .C479. **DD** 671.3/6/05. **CODEN** JRECDB. **Circ:** 20,150. available in microform. Documents available from Article Express International, CASDDS, CASDDS.
**Desc:** Contains information from the field of mechanical engineering and heat treating of metals.
**Ind/Abst** Chem. Abstr.; Ei Page One; Eng. Index Annu.

CC/0254-587X
**JINSHU RECHULI XUEBAO.** (CHIN CHU JE CHU LI HSUEH PAO / CHUNG-KUO CHI HSIEH KUNG CHENG HSUEH HUI, JE CHU LI HSUEH HUI.). [Jinshu rechuli xuebao]. **Added/Corp** Chung-Kuo Chi Hsieh Kung Cheng Hsueh Hui. Je Chu Li Hsueh Hui. **VFOAT** Transactions of Metal Heat Treatment. (1980)-. Periodical. Chinese (summaries and/or abstracts in English). sa. Kai Hsueh Hui, Pei-ching, People's Republic of China. **CODEN** JRXUDO. Documents available from CASDDS.
**Ind/Abst** Chem. Abstr.

CH/0254-5888
**JISHU YU XUNLIAN.** (CHI SHU YU HSUN LIEN / CHUNG-KUO KANG TIEH KU FEN YU HSIEN KUNG SSU.). [Jishu yu xunlian]. **Added/Corp** Chung-kuo Kang Tieh ku fen yu Hsien Kung Ssu. (1976)-. Periodical. Chinese. mo. **LC** TS300; .C47. **DD** 669/.142/05. **CODEN** CSYLDY. Documents available from CASDDS.
**Ind/Abst** Chem. Abstr.

US/1047-4838
**JOM (1989).** (JOM : THE JOURNAL OF MINERALS, METALS & MATERIALS SOCIETY.). [JOM]. **Added/Corp** Minerals, Metals and Materials Society. **VAT** Journal of Metals. Vol. 41, No. 1 (Jan. 1989)-. Academic Scholarly Publication. English. mo. $110.00 (institutions), $56.00 (individuals) US; $125.00 (institutions), $71.00 (individuals) other. Minerals, Metals and Materials Society, 420 Commonwealth Drive, Warrendale PA 15086-7514. **Tel** (412)776-9000 ext. 236, (800)759-4867, FAX (412)776-3770. **LC** TN1; .A513. **DD** 669/.05. **CODEN** JOMMER. **[CCC].** Documents available from Article Express International, The Genuine Article, Ask*IEEE, CASDDS. ***Continues*** *Journal of Metals (1977), 0148-6608.*
**Desc:** Facilitating the dissemination of original research and the presentation of comprehensive technology reviews on the many aspects of materials science and engineering. Expands the application of state-of-the-art processing, fabrication and design technologies.
**Ind/Abst** Alum. Ind. Abstr.; Appl. Sci. Technol. Index; Bioeng. Abstr.; Ceram. Abstr. (19??-); Chem. Abstr.; Civ. Struct. Eng. Abstr.; Coal Abstr.; Comput. Inf. Syst. Abstr. J. [Full Cov.]; Corros. Abstr. (199?-); Curr. Contents Eng. Tech. Appl. Sci.; Ei Page One; EMBASE; Energy Inf. Abstr.; Eng. Index Annu.; Environ. Eng. Abstr.; F&S Index Plus Text, Int. [Select. Cov.]; INSPEC (Feb. 1989-); Int. Aerosp. Abstr.; Leadscan; Manuf. Process Eng. Abstr.; Mater. Sci. Eng. Abstr.; Mech. Eng. Abstr.; Met. Abstr.; MINPROC; Mintec, Min. Technol. Abstr.; Life Sci. Collect.; PROMT; Res. Alert [Full Cov.]; Sci. Cit. Index; SCISEARCH; Soc. Sci. Cit. Index [Select. Cov.]; Solid State Supercond. Abstr.

JA
**JOURNAL - MINING AND METALLURGICAL INSTITUTE OF JAPAN.** **Main/Corp** Mining and Metallurgical Institute of Japan. (1???)-. Periodical. Japanese (summaries and/or abstracts in English; table of contents in English). mo. $284.00. **(Subscription address:** Kyowa Book Company Inc., 1-38 Kanda Jinbo-Cho, Chiyoda-Ku Tokyo 101, Japan**)** **ED** Ryo Suda. **Ad Acc. Circ:** 10,000 (ctrl).
**Desc:** Research and commentary of scientific techniques concerned with mining.
**Ind/Abst** Alum. Ind. Abstr.; Met. Abstr.

SZ/0925-8388
**JOURNAL OF ALLOYS AND COMPOUNDS.** [J. alloys compd.]. Vol. 176, No. 1 (Oct. 21, 1991)-. Academic Scholarly Publication. English (French and German). Thirty-two times a year (16 vols.). 6880.00F. Elsevier Sequoia SA, PO Box 564, CH-1001 Lausanne 1 Switzerland. **Tel** 011 41 21 3207381. **ED** K.H.J. Buschow. **LC** TN1; .J7. **DD** 669/.05. **CODEN** JALCEU. **[CCC]. Ad Acc, Adv Mgr:** Ms. W van Cattenburch (Amsterdam). available on microfilm and microfiche from University Microfilms International (UMI). Documents available from Article Express International, The Genuine Article, Ask*IEEE, CASDDS. ***Continues*** *Journal of the Less-Common Metals, 0022-5088.*
**Desc:** Serves as an international medium for the publication of work on the physical sciences of usually called less-common metals, their compounds and their alloys.
**Ind/Abst** Chem Inform; Chem. Abstr.; Curr. Contents Phys. Chem. Earth Sci.; Ei Page One; Eng. Index Annu.; INSPEC (Oct. 1991-); Leadscan; Met. Abstr.; Phys. Briefs; Res. Alert [Full Cov.]; Sci. Cit. Index; SCISEARCH; World Ceram. Abstr.

US/0190-9177
**JOURNAL OF HEAT TREATING.** ***Title Change.*** [J. heat treat.]. **Added/Corp** American Society for Metals. (1979-1992). Academic Scholarly Publication. English. sa. American Society for Metals International, c/o Deborah Barthelmes, Materials Park OH 44073-0002. **Tel** (216)338-5151, FAX (216)338-4634, telex 980-619. **ED** Jon L Dossett. **LC** TN672; .J68. **DD** 671.3/6/05. **CODEN** JHTRDR. **[CCC]. Bk Rev. Circ:** 1,200. available on microfilm and microfiche from University Microfilms International (UMI). Documents available from Article Express International, CASDDS. ***Merged with*** *Journal of Materials Shaping Technology, 0931-704X* ***and*** *Journal of Materials Engineering, 0931-7058* ***to form*** *Journal of Materials Engineering and Performance, 1059-9495.*
**Desc:** Latest developments in heat treating technology. Peer reviewed.
**Ind/Abst** Alum. Ind. Abstr.; Bioeng. Abstr.; Chem. Abstr.; Ei Page One; Eng. Mater. Abstr.; Eng. Index Annu.; Met. Abstr.

JA
**JOURNAL OF JAPAN FOUNDRYMAN'S SOCIETY.** Japanese. mo. $248.00. Nihon Imono Kyokai, (Japan Foundrymen's Soceity), Toyokawa Biru,, 12-13, Ginza 8 Chome, Chuoku, Tokyoto 104 Japan. **(Subscription address:** Kyowa Book Company Inc., 1-38 Kanda Jinbo-Cho, Chiyoda-Ku, Tokyo 101, Japan (Phone: 03-3293-0727)**)**

UK/0022-2461
**JOURNAL OF MATERIALS SCIENCE.** [J. mater. sci.]. Vol. 1 (Feb. 1966)-. Academic Scholarly Publication. English. Sixty-six times a year. $3395.00 (includes Journal of Materials Science Letters) US and Canada; £1995.00 (includes Journal of Materials Science Letters) European Community; £2150.00 (includes Journal of Materials Science Letters) other. Chapman & Hall, 2-6 Boundary Row, London SE1 8HN England. **Tel** 011 44 71 865 0066, FAX 011 44 71 522 9623, telex 290164 Chapmag. **(Subscription address:** Chapman & Hall, Cheriton House, North Way, Andover, Hampshire, SP10 5BE England.**)** **ED** W Bonfield. **LC** TA401; .J68. **DD** 620.1/1/05. **CODEN** JMTSAS. **[CCC]. Ad Acc.** available on microfilm and microfiche from University Microfilms International (UMI); available on CD-ROM. Documents available from Article Express International, The Genuine Article, Ask*IEEE, CASDDS. ***Continued in part by*** *Continued in part by Journal of Materials Science Letters, 0261-8028.*
**Desc:** Leading source of primary communications on the structure and properties of engineering materials.
**Ind/Abst** Acoust. Abstr.; Alum. Ind. Abstr.; Appl. Sci. Technol. Index; Art Archaeol. Tech. Abstr.; Ceram. Abstr.; Chem. Abstr.; Chem. Titles; Coal Abstr.; Curr. Biotechnol.; Curr. Contents Eng. Tech. Appl. Sci.; Curr. Contents Phys. Chem. Earth Sci.; Curr. Technol. Index; Curr. Titles Electrochem.; Ei Page One; EMBASE; Eng. Mater. Abstr.; Eng. Index Annu.; GeoRef; INSPEC (Sept. 1968-Dec. 1981); Int. Aerosp. Abstr.; Leadscan; Met. Abstr.; Pollut. Abstr. Indexes; Polymer Contents; Res. Alert [Full Cov.]; Sci. Cit. Index; SCISEARCH; World Ceram. Abstr.; World Surf. Coat. Abstr.

US/1054-9714
**JOURNAL OF PHASE EQUILIBRIA.** **Added/Corp** ASM International. Vol. 12, No. 1 (Feb. 1991)-. Academic Scholarly Publication. English. bm. $658.00 (nonmember), $98.00 (ASM member). American Society for Metals International, c/o Deborah Barthelmes, Materials Park OH 44073-0002. **Tel** (216)338-5151, FAX (216)338-4634, telex 980-619. **(Subscription address:** ASM International, Materials Information, Materials Park OH 44073.**)** **ED** Professor J. F. Smith. **LC** TN689; .J68. **DD** 669/.94/05. **CODEN** JPEQE6. **[CCC].** Index available (Bound in Dec. issue). cum. index. **Pr Rev. Circ:** 520. available on microfilm and microfiche from University Microfilms International (UMI). Documents available from Article Express International, CASDDS. ***Formed by the union of*** *Bulletin of Alloy Phase Diagrams, 0197-0216* ***and*** *Journal of Alloy Phase Diagrams, 0970-1478.*
**Desc:** Contains basic and applied research results, evaluated phase diagrams, updates of published systems, and comments and other material pertinent to the previous three areas. The aim is to provide a broad spectrum of information concerning phase equilibrium for the materials community.
**Ind/Abst** Chem. Abstr.; Ei Page One; Eng. Index Annu. [Select. Cov.].

●US/1063-4576
**JOURNAL OF SUPERHARD MATERIALS.** (JOURNAL OF SUPERHARD MATERIALS : SHM.). **VFOAT** SHM. Vol. 14, No. 1 (1992)-. Periodical. English (translations available in Russian). Six times a year. $820.00. Allerton Press, Inc., 150 Fifth Avenue, New York NY 10011. **Tel** (212)924-3950, FAX (212)463-9684, telex 427441 ALPRES. **LC** TA418.45; .S9. **DD** 620.1/1. **[CCC].** ***Continues*** *Soviet Journal of Superhard Metals, 0739-8425.*

SA/0038-223X
**JOURNAL OF THE SOUTH AFRICAN INSTITUTE OF MINING & METALLURGY.** **See** Engineering-Mines and Mining Engineering.

●US/1059-9630
**JOURNAL OF THERMAL SPRAY TECHNOLOGY.** [J. therm. spray technol.]. **Added/Corp** ASM International. **VFOAT** Thermal Spray Technology. Vol. 1, No. 1 (Mar. 1992)-. Periodical. English. qt (4 issues). $425.00. American Society for Metals International, c/o Deborah Barthelmes, Materials Park OH 44073-0002. **Tel** (216)338-5151, FAX (216)338-4634, telex 980-619. **(Subscription address:** ASM International, Materials Information, Materials Park OH 44073.**)** **LC** TS653; .J68. **DD** 671.7/34/05. **CODEN** JTTEE5. **Pr Rev.** Documents available from The Genuine Article.
**Desc:** Information on metal and plasma spraying.
**Ind/Abst** Int. Aerosp. Abstr.; Res. Alert [Full Cov.].

UK
**JOURNAL SILVER SOCIETY.** English. (Comes with Silver Society membership). Silver Society, 14A St Cross Street, Dunstan House, London EC1N 8XD England. **Tel** 44 071 8316741.
**Ind/Abst** BHA : Biblio. Hist. Art.

HU/0302-8720
**K.G.M.T.I. KOZLEMENYEI.** **See** Engineering.

JA/0368-7236
**KAWASAKI SEITETSU GIHO.** [Kawasaki Seitetsu giho]. **Added/Corp** Kawasaki Seitetsu Kabushiki Kaisha. **VFOAT** Kawasaki Steel Giho. (1969)-. Periodical. Japanese. qt. Kawasaki Seitetsu Kabushiki Kaisha, Chiyoda-ku, Yurakucho 2-2-3, Hibiya Kokusai Biru, Tokyo 100 Japan. **CODEN** KWSGBZ. Documents available from CASDDS.
**Ind/Abst** Chem. Abstr.

JA/0388-9475
**KAWASAKI STEEL TECHNICAL REPORT (TOKYO. 1980).** (KAWASAKI STEEL TECHNICAL REPORT.). [Kawasaki steel tech. rep.]. **Added/Corp** Kawasaki Seitetsu Kabushiki Kaisha. Technical Information Section. (1980)-. Academic Scholarly Publication. English. Twice a year (May & Nov.). Free. Kawasaki Steel Corporation Research, 2 3 3 Uchisaiwaicho Chiyodaku, Tokyo 100 Japan. **Tel** 011 81 3 359 74341. **LC** TS300; .K38. **CODEN** KSTRDD. Documents available from Article Express International, CASDDS. ***Continues*** *Kawasaki Steel Technical Bulletin, 0387-8104.*
**Ind/Abst** Alum. Ind. Abstr.; Bioeng. Abstr.; Chem. Abstr.; Civ. Struct. Eng. Abstr.; Coal Abstr.; Comput. Inf. Syst. Abstr. J. [Full Cov.]; Corros. Abstr. (199?-); Ei Page One; Eng. Index Annu.; Environ. Eng. Abstr.; Manuf. Process Eng. Abstr.; Mater. Sci. Eng. Abstr.; Mech. Eng. Abstr.; Met. Abstr.; SEA Abstr.; Solid State Supercond. Abstr.

JA/0451-5994
**KEIKINZOKU.** [Keikinzoku]. **Added/Corp** Keikinzoku Kenkyukai. Keikinzoku Gakkai (Japan). **VFOAT** Light Metals; Journal of Japan Institute of Light Metals. (1951)-. Periodical. Japanese (summaries and/or abstracts in English). mo. $173.50. Keikinzoku Gakkai, (Japan Inst. of Light Metals), 1-3, Nihonbashi 2 Chome, Chuoku, Tokyoto 103, Japan. **(Subscription address:** Japan Publications Trading Company, Ltd., PO Box 5030, Tokyo International, Tokyo 100-31 Japan.**)** **CODEN** KEIKA6. Documents available from Article Express International, Ask*IEEE, CASDDS.
**Ind/Abst** Alum. Ind. Abstr.; Bioeng. Abstr.; Chem. Abstr.; Civ. Struct. Eng. Abstr.; Ei Page One; Elect. Comm. Abstr.; Eng. Index Annu.; INSPEC; Int. Aerosp. Abstr.; Manuf. Process Eng. Abstr.; Mater. Sci. Eng. Abstr.; Mech. Eng. Abstr.; Met. Abstr.; Solid State Supercond. Abstr.

JA/0285-6689
**KINKI ARUMINIUMU HYOMEN SHORI KENKYUKAI KAISHI.** (KINKI ARUMINIUMU HYOMEN SHORI KENKYUKAI KAISHI / ALUMINUM FINISHING SOCIETY OF KINKI.). [Kinki Aruminiumu Hyomen Shori Kenkyukai kaishi]. **Added/Corp** Kinki Aruminiumu Hyomen Shori Kenkyukai. (19??)-. Japanese. Kinki Aruminyumu Hyomen Shori Kenkyukai, (Aluminum Finishing Soc. of Kinki), c/o Kinki Daigaku Rikogakubu, Oyo Kagakuka Yoshimura, Kenkyushitsu, 4-1, Kowakae 3 Chome, Higashiosakashi, Osakafu 577 Japan. **CODEN** KAHKA7. Documents available from CASDDS.
**Ind/Abst** Chem. Abstr.

JA/0368-6337
**KINZOKU.** [Kinzoku]. **VFOAT** Metals and Technology; Metals. (1945)-. Academic Scholarly Publication. Japanese. mo. $342.50. Agune, (Agne Publishing Inc.), 31-9, Nishiwaseda 3 Chome, Shinjukuku, Tokyoto 160, Japan. **(Subscription address:** Japan Publications Trading Company, Ltd., PO Box 5030, Tokyo International, Tokyo 100-31 Japan.**)** **CODEN** KNZKAI. Documents available from CASDDS. ***Continues*** *Koku Kinzoku.*
**Ind/Abst** Alum. Ind. Abstr.; Chem. Abstr.; Coal Abstr.; Met. Abstr.

JA/0285-8452
**KINZOKU HAKUBUTSUKAN KIYO.** [Kinzoku Hakubutsukan kiyo]. **Added/Corp** Kinzoku Hakubutsukan. Nihon Kinzoku Gakkai. **VFOAT** Kiyo / Kinzoku Hakubutsukan; Bulletin of the Metals Museum. Vol. 1 (1976)-. Periodical. Japanese (English; table of contents in English and Japanese). an. Nihon Kinzoku Gakkai Fuzoku Kinzoku Hakubutsukan, (Metals Museum, Japan Inst. of Metals), Aoba, Aramaki, Sendaishi, Miyagiken 980 Japan. **CODEN** KIHKEX. Documents available from CASDDS.
**Ind/Abst** Chem. Abstr.

JA
**KINZOKU ZAIRYO GIJUTSU KENKYUJO NEMPO.** **Main/Corp** Kinzoku Zairyo Gijutsu Kenkyujo (Japan). (1978)-. Japanese. an. Kagaku Gijutsucho Kinzoku Zairyo Gijutsu Kenkyujo, 3-ban 12-go Naka Meguro 2-chome Meguro-ku, Tokyo 153 Japan. **LC** TN207; .K56B.

US/0882-7362
**KIT GUNS & HOBBY GUNSMITHING. See** Hobbies.

US/0277-0725
**KNIVES.** 1st Ed. (81)-. English. an. $11.95. DBI Books Inc, 4092 Commercial Avenue, Northbrook IL 60062. **Tel** (312)272-6310. **ED** Ken Warner. **LC** TS380; .K578. **DD** 621.9/32/05.

JA/0368-654X
**KOGYO REAMETARU.** (KOGYO REA METARU.). [Kogyo reametaru]. **VFOAT** Kogyo Reametaru; Industrial Rare Metals. (195?)-. Periodical. Japanese. qt. Arumu Shuppansha, 2-5-5 Hongo, Bunkyo-ku, Tokyo 113 Japan. **CODEN** KORMAP. Documents available from CASDDS.
**Ind/Abst** Chem. Abstr.

HU/0231-0708
**KOHASZATI ES ONTESZETI SZAKIRODALMI TAJEKOZTATO.** (1983)-. Periodical. Hungarian. mo. 8.700ft. Orszagos Muszaki Informacios Kozpont es Konyvtar (O.M.I.K.K.), National Technical Information Centre and Library Museum, u 17, PO Box 12, 1428 Budapest, Hungary. **Tel** (361)118-1994, FAX (361)138-2414, telex 22-4944 OMIKK H. **(Subscription address:** OMIKK Budapest, POB 12, H-1428 Hungary**) ED** Gabor Libertiny. **UDC** 016. **Circ:** 260.
**Desc:** Information on metals, metallurgy and foundry.

RU/0203-8722
**KOMPLEKSNYE METALLOORGANICESKIE KATALIZATORY POLIMERIZACII OLEFINOV.** [Kompleksn. metalloorg. katal. polim. olefin.]. (1976)-. Russian. ir. **UDC** 541.64. Documents available from CASDDS.
**Ind/Abst** Chem. Abstr.

JA/0387-1096
**KOON GAKKAISHI.** (KOON GAKKAI SHI.). [Koon Gakkaishi]. **Added/Corp** Koon Gakkai (Japan). **VFOAT** Journal of High Temperature Society; Koon Gakkaishi. (1975)-. Periodical. Japanese. bm. Koon Gakkai, (High Temperature Soc. of Japan), Osaka Daigaku Kogakubu Yosetsu, Kogaku Kenkyujo, 11-1, Mihogaoka, Ibarakishi, Osakafu 567, Japan. **CODEN** KGAKDH. Documents available from CASDDS.
**Ind/Abst** Chem. Abstr.

NO
**KORROSJONS-NYTT.** Periodical. Norwegian. bm. Korrosjons-Nytt, Postbnoks 1041, 5001 Bergen Norway.

HU/0133-2546
**KORROZIOS FIGYELO.** (KORROZIOS FIGYELO / NIM MUSZAKI DOKUMENTACIOS ES FORDITO IRODA.). [Korroz. figy.]. **Added/Corp** Hungary. Muszaki Dokumentacios es Fordito. (1961)-. Academic Scholarly Publication. Hungarian. **(Subscription address:** Kultura, PO Box 149, H 1389 Budapest 62 Hungary**) CODEN** KOFIDO. Documents available from CASDDS.
**Ind/Abst** Alum. Ind. Abstr.; Chem. Abstr.; Corros. Abstr. (199?-); Curr. Titles Electrochem.; Met. Abstr.

XO/0023-432X
**KOVOVE MATERIALY.** [Kovove mater.]. (1963)-. Academic Scholarly Publication. Czech (Slovak, English, German and Russian). bm. $99.00. Kovove Materialy, PO Box 95, 803 Bratislava Slovakia. **Tel** 011 42 7 372909. **ED** Matej Bily. **CODEN** KOMAAW. **Bk Rev. Ad Acc. Pr Rev. Circ:** 700. Documents available from Article Express International, The Genuine Article, Ask*IEEE, CASDDS. ***Supersedes** Zvaraesty Sbornik.*
**Desc:** Fundamental research in material science, physical metallurgy and fracture mechanics, including experimental, theoretical and computational methods.
**Ind/Abst** Alum. Ind. Abstr.; Bioeng. Abstr.; Chem. Abstr.; Curr. Contents Eng. Tech. Appl. Sci.; Ei Page One; Eng. Mater. Abstr.; Eng. Index Annu.; INSPEC (1973-); Int. Aerosp. Abstr. (19??-19??); Leadscan; Met. Abstr.; Res. Alert [Full Cov.]; SCISEARCH; Stat. Theory Method Abstr. (1968-1970, 1973, 1980-1981).

PL/0208-9386
**KRZEPNIECIE METALI I STOPOW.** (KRZEPNIECIE METALI I STOPOW / POLSKA AKADEMIA NAUK, ODDZIA W KATOWICACH, KOMISJA ODLEWNICTWA.). [Krzepniecie met. stopow]. Began in 1979. Academic Scholarly Publication. Polish. ir. Z30.00. Zakad Narodowy Im Ossolinskich We Wrocawiu, Krakowskie Przedmiescie 7, 00 068 Warsaw Poland. **LC** TS228.9; .K78. **CODEN** KMSTD6. Documents available from CASDDS.
**Ind/Abst** Chem. Abstr.

RU/0201-7296
**KUZNECNO-STAMPOVOCNOE PROIZVODSTVO (1959).** (KUZNECHNO-SHTAMPOVOCHNOE PROIZVODSTVO.). [Kuzn.-stamp. proizv.]. **Added/Corp** Soviet Union. Ministerstvo Stankostroitelnoi i Instrumentalnoi Promyshlennosti. Nauchno-Tekhnicheskoe Obshchestvo Mashinostroitelnoi Promyshlennosti. (1959)-. Academic Scholarly Publication. Russian. mo. $129.95. **(Subscription address:** East View Publications Inc., 3020 Harbor Lane North, Suite 110, Minneapolis MN 55447.**) CODEN** KSPRAO. Index available in last issue of volume--attached. Documents available from Article Express International, CASDDS.
**Ind/Abst** Alum. Ind. Abstr.; Chem. Abstr.; Ei Page One; Eng. Index Annu.; Met. Abstr.

GW/0937-6186
**KW HEUTE.** (KLOCKNER - WERKE HEUTE.). **VFOAT** Klockner-Werke Heute. (1987)-. Periodical. German (English). qt. Kloeckner Presse und Information GmbH, Kloecknerstrasse 29, POB 100 853, W-4100 Duisburg Germany. **UDC** 669.1. **Circ:** 35,000.
**Desc:** Magazine for shareholders, employees and business associates.

IT/0391-5891
**LAMIERA.** [Lamiera]. Academic Scholarly Publication. Italian. mo. L9000 (single issue); L80000 (one year), L140000 (two year) Italy; L145000 Europe; L200000 other. Tecniche Nuove SPA, Via Ciro Menotti 14, 20129 Milan Italy. **Tel** 011 39 2 75701, FAX 011 39 2 7610351, telex 334647 TECHS I. **CODEN** LAMID6. **Bk Rev. Ad Acc. Circ:** 5,273. Documents available from CASDDS.
**Ind/Abst** Chem. Abstr.

UK
**LEAD AND ZINC IN THE 1990'S - WORLD AND LATIN AMERICA.** (Feb. 1991)-. English. £60.00 UK; $110.00 US. International Lead and Zinc Study Group, Metro House, 58 St. James Street, London SW1A 1LD England. **Tel** 011 44 71 4999373, FAX 011 44 71 4933725, telex 299819 ILZSG G.
**Desc:** Report contains the proceedings of the Special Conference organised by the Study Group in Sao Paulo, Brazil, Feb. 1991.

US/0570-9369
**LEAD AND ZINC INDUSTRY.** (LEAD AND ZINC INDUSTRY; ARIZONA, THE UNITED STATES AND THE WORLD: STATISTICS.). **Main/Corp** Arizona. Dept. of Mineral Resources. (1960)-. English. Arizona Department of Mineral Resources, Mineral Building Fairgrounds, Phoenix AZ 85007. **Tel** (602)255-3791. **LC** HD9539.L38; A75. **DD** 338.4.

UK/0023-9577
**LEAD AND ZINC STATISTICS. See** Metals and Metallurgy-Abstracting, Bibliographies and Statistics.

US
**LEAD / U.S. DEPARTMENT OF THE INTERIOR, BUREAU OF MINES.** **Added/Corp** United States. Bureau of Mines. **VFOAT** Annual Report. Lead. (1990)-. English. ***Continues** Minerals Yearbook. Lead.*
**Desc:** Information on the lead industry and trade as well as mines and mining.

UK/0950-1584
**LEADSCAN. See** Metals and Metallurgy-Abstracting, Bibliographies and Statistics.

AT/0729-5898
**LEMEL. See** Jewelry.

FR/0181-1223
**LETTRE D'INFORMATION METAUX DE LA REVUE LA RECUPERATION.** (1963)-. Periodical. French. Fifty-two times a year. 999.02F France; 1000.00F others. Bureau d'Info Professionnelles, 142 rue Montmartre, 75073 Paris Cedex 02 France. **Tel** 011 33 1 40268321, FAX 011 33 1 40399752, telex 220528 BIP. **UDC** 621.

CC/1001-4020
**LI HUA JIANYAN. HUAXUE FENCE.** (LI HUA CHIEN YEN. HUA HSUEH FEN TSE.). [Li hua jianyan, Huaxue fence]. **Added/Corp** Chung-Kuo Chi Hsieh Kung Cheng Hsueh Hui (Peking, China). Li Hua Chien Yen Hsueh Hui. Shang-Hai Tsai Liao Yen Chiu So. **VFOAT** Hua Hsueh Fen Tse; Chemical Analysis; Physical Testing and Chemical Analysis. Chemical Analysis. (19??)-. Periodical. Chinese (summaries and/or abstracts in English). bm. **LC** QD132; .L5. **CODEN** LJHFE2. Documents available from CASDDS.
**Ind/Abst** Chem. Abstr.

US/0024-3345
**LIGHT METAL AGE.** [Light met. age]. Vol. 1 (May 1943)-. Periodical. English. bm (6 issues). $35.00 (one year), $50.00 (two year), $65.00 (three year). Light Metal Age, 170 South Spruce Avenue, Suite 120, South San Francisco CA 94080. **Tel** (415)588-8832, FAX (415)588-0901. **ED** Roy Fellom. **LC** TN1; .L495. **DD** 669.7. **CODEN** LMAGAL. Index available ($1.50 per year). **Ad Acc. Circ:** 5,800 (ctrl). Documents available from Article Express International, CASDDS.
**Desc:** International coverage of aluminum, magnesium, titanium, beryllium and associated non-ferrous industries. Circulation is to primary plants, production reduction plants and smelters, semi-fabrication plants, rolling mills, extrusion plants, etc.
**Ind/Abst** Alum. Ind. Abstr.; Appl. Sci. Technol. Index; Bioeng. Abstr.; Ceram. Abstr.; Chem. Abstr.; Coal Abstr.; Ei Page One; Eng. Mater. Abstr.; Eng. Index Annu.; F&S Index Plus Text, Int. [Select. Cov.]; Met. Abstr.; PROMT; Surf. Treat. Technol. Abstr.

US/0147-0809
**LIGHT METALS (NEW YORK).** (LIGHT METALS.). [Light met.]. **Main/Corp** American Institute of Mining, Metallurgical, and Petroleum Engineers. **Added/Corp** Metallurgical Society of AIME. Light Metals Committee. (19??)-. English. an (Feb.). $114.00 (individuals members); $168.00 (non-members). Minerals, Metals and Materials Society, 420 Commonwealth Drive, Warrendale PA 15086-7514. **Tel** (412)776-9000 ext. 236, (800)759-4867, FAX (412)776-3770. **ED** H. O. Bohner. **LC** TN773; .A43. **DD** 669/.72. **CODEN** LMPMDF. **[CCC].** Index available. **Bk Rev.** Documents available from Article Express International, CASDDS.
**Ind/Abst** Bioeng. Abstr.; Chem. Abstr.; Ei Page One; Eng. Index Annu.; Surf. Treat. Technol. Abstr.

US/0547-0684
**LIMESTONE (WASHINGTON).** (NLI LIMESTONE.). **Main/Corp** National Limestone Institute (U.S.). **VFOAT** Limestone. **VAT** National Limestone Institute Limestone. Vol. 1 (July 1964)-. Periodical. English. qt. National Limestone Institute, 1840 Wilson Boulevard/Suite 230, Arlington VA 22201. **Tel** (703)273-8517. **LC** TN967; .N3.

RU/0302-9069
**LITEINCE PROIZVODSTVO, METALLOVEDENIE I OBRABOTKA METALLOV DAVLENIEM. Main/Corp** Krasnoyarsk, Siberia. Institut Tsvetnykh Metallov. (19??)-. Russian. 0.47rub single issue. Krasniarskoe Knizhnoe Izdatelstvo, Pro Mira 89, Krasnoiarsk Russia. **LC** TS200; .K73a.

UN/0024-449X
**LITEJNOE PROIZVODSTVO.** (LITEINOE PROIZVODSTVO.). [Litejnoe proizvod.]. **Main/Corp** Kharkivskyi Politekhnichnyi Instytut Imeni V. I. Lenina. (19??)-. Periodical. Russian. mo. $79.95. **(Subscription address:** East View Publications Inc., 3020 Harbor Lane North, Suite 110, Minneapolis MN 55447.**) LC** T4; .K46 subser; TS228.99. **CODEN** LIPRAX. **[CCC].** Documents available from Article Express International, CASDDS.
**Ind/Abst** Alum. Ind. Abstr.; Chem. Abstr.; Ei Page One; Eng. Index Annu.; Met. Abstr.

US/0731-8065
**LITHIUM RESEARCH REVIEW SERIES.** (19??)-. Periodical. English. ir. Human Sciences Press, PO Box 735, 233 Spring Street, New York NY 10013. **Tel** (212)620-8000, FAX (212)807-1047, telex 23421139.

CN/0383-090X
**M P & P, METAL-WORKING PRODUCTION & PURCHASING. VFOAT** Metal-Working Production & Purchasing. Vol. 1 (Oct. 1974)-. Periodical. English. Six times a year. 35.00Can$ (1 year), 65.00Can$ (2 year) Canada; $55.00 (1 year), $105.00 (2 yera) surface mail other; $105.00 airmail other. Action Communications Inc, 135 Spy Ct, Markham Ontario L3R 5H6 Canada. **Tel** (416)477-3222. **ED** Maurice Holtham. **DD** 671. **Ad Acc. Circ:** 24,225 (ctrl).

US/0740-2929
**MACRAE'S INDUSTRIAL DIRECTORY. MARYLAND, D.C., DELAWARE.** ***Title Change.*** **See** Manufacturing.

US/0740-2929
**MACRAE'S STATE INDUSTRIAL DIRECTORY. MARYLAND, DISTRICT OF COLUMBIA, DELAWARE. See** Manufacturing.

PL/0239-3611
**MAGAZYN HUTNICZY.** [Mag. Hut.]. (1972)-. Periodical. Polish. wk. Price on Request. **(Subscription address:** ARS Polona, PO Box 1001, 00068 Warsaw Poland.**) UDC** 669.

US
**MAGNESIUM AND MAGNESIUM COMPOUNDS.** English. qt. US Department of the Interior / Bureau of Mines, Publications Department, PO Box 18070, Cochrans Mill Road, Pittsburgh PA 15236. **Tel** (412)892-6400.
**Desc:** Timely statistical and economic data on magnesium.

GW/0172-908X
**MAGNESIUM-BULLETIN.** (MAGNESIUM-BULLETIN / GESELLSCHAFT FUER MAGNESIUM-FORSCHUNG.). [Magnesium-Bull.]. **Added/Corp** Gesellschaft fuer Magnesiumforschung (Germany). **VAT** Magnesium Bulletin. Vol. 1, No. 1 (1979)-. Periodical. English (German). Four times a year (Mar., June, Sept., Dec.). DM78.00 Germany; DM82.00 others. Verlag fuer Medizin VFM, Postfach 105767, Fritz Frey Str 21, W6900 Heidelberg 1 Germany. **Tel** 011 49 06221/406248, FAX 011 49 06221/400727, telex 461 683

HVVFMD. **LC** Discard. **NLM** W1 MA335. **CODEN** MABUDW. **[CCC].** Documents available from The Genuine Article, CASDDS.
**Ind/Abst** Chem. Abstr.; Res. Alert [Full Cov.]; Sci. Cit. Index; SCISEARCH.

HU/0025-0058
**MAGYAR ALUMINUM.** ***Ceased.*** [M. alum.]. Ceased (Jan. 1991). Academic Scholarly Publication. Hungarian (English). mo. Lapkiado Vallalat, Lenin Korut 9-11, 1073 Budapest 7, Hungary. **Tel** 222-408. **ED** A Domony and I Varga. **LC** HD9539.A63; H855. **CODEN** MAGABT. Index available. **Bk Rev**. **Ad Acc**. **Circ:** 1,100. Documents available from CASDDS.
**Desc:** Technical journal for the aluminum industry of the world, with coverage of the processing, application and use of aluminum. Main articles published in English and Hungarian.
**Ind/Abst** Alum. Ind. Abstr.; Chem. Abstr.; Coal Abstr.; Eng. Mater. Abstr.; Met. Abstr.

UK/0334-7575
**MAIN GROUP METAL CHEMISTRY.** **VFOAT** MGMC. Vol. 10, No. 1 (1987)-. Periodical. English. ir. $380.00. Freund Publishing House Ltd, PO Box 35010, 61 Nachmani Street, Tel Aviv 61350 Israel. **Tel** 011 972 3 5662925, FAX 011 972 3 5605335. **(Subscription address:** Freund Publishing House Ltd., Suite 500 Chesham House, 150 Regent Street, London W1R 5FA England.**) ED** M. Gielen. **LC** QD410; .R48. **DD** 547/.05. Index available. **Bk Rev**. **Ad Acc**. **Circ:** 200. Documents available from CASDDS. ***Continues*** *Silicon, Germanium, Tin and Lead Compounds, 0334-7575.*
**Desc:** Information on organometallic compounds and metals.
**Ind/Abst** Chem. Abstr.

SP/0214-4344
**MANTENIMIENTO BARCELONA.** [Mantenimiento Barc.]. (1983)-. Periodical. Multiple languages. Ten times a year. 7475.00ptas Spain; 9000.00ptas Europe; 10000.00ptas other. Puntex SA, Via Laietana 30 4 F, 08003 Barcelona Spain. **Tel** 011 34 3 2680444. **UDC** 62-7. **Circ:** 5,000. ***Continues*** *Boletin Informativo - Asociacion Espanola de Mantenimiento, 0214-4336.*

NZ
**MANUFACTURING SERIES C. DEPARTMENT OF STATISTICS. NO. 4, MANUFACTURE OF PAPER AND PAPER PRODUCTS, PRINTING, AND PUBLISHING.** **See** Economics-Industry and Production.

UK
**MARKET SITUATION FOR LEAD, THE.** (Jan. 1986)-. English. £30.00 UK; $40.00 US. International Lead and Zinc Study Group, Metro House, 58 St. James Street, London SW1A 1LD England. **Tel** 011 44 71 4999373, FAX 011 44 71 4933725, telex 299819 ILZSG G.
**Desc:** Trends in the market situation for lead since 1979 and issues of concern to the industry are reviewed in a comprehensive report.

UK
**MARKET SITUATION FOR ZINC, THE.** English. £65.00 UK; $90.00 US. International Lead and Zinc Study Group, Metro House, 58 St. James Street, London SW1A 1LD England. **Tel** 011 44 71 4999373, FAX 011 44 71 4933725, telex 299819 ILZSG G.
**Desc:** Main trends in supply and demand for zinc since 1975 are reviewed, together with a more detailed assessment of the market situation during 1985-86.

BU/0204-7535
**MATERIALOZNANIE I TEKNOLOGIYA.** (MATERIALOZNANIE I TEKHNOLOGIIA.). [Materialoznanie teknol.]. **Added/Corp** Institut po Metaloznanie i Tekhnologiia na Metalite (Bulgarska Akademiia na Naukite). **VFOAT** Materials Science and Technology. (1973)-. Academic Scholarly Publication. Bulgarian (summaries and/or abstracts in English and Russian). ir. 1.20lv per issue. Bulgarska Akademiia na Naukite, 7 Noemvri 1, Sofia Bulgaria. **LC** TA401; .M33. **CODEN** MTEKDE. **Circ:** 470. Documents available from CASDDS.
**Ind/Abst** Chem. Abstr.

AT/1037-7107
**MATERIALS AUSTRALIA.** (MATERIALS AUSTRALIA : THE MAGAZINE OF ENGINEERING MATERIALS TECHNOLOGY.). [Mater. Aust.]. **Added/Corp** Institute of Metals and Materials Australasia. Vol. 23, No. 10 (Nov./Dec. 1991)-. Academic Scholarly Publication. English. Ten times a year. 95.00Aus$ Australia; 143.00Aus$ others. Institute of Metals Materials Australia, PO Box 19, 191 Royal Parade, Parksville Victoria 3052 Australia. **Tel** 011 61 3 3472544, FAX 011 61 3 3481208, telex 10718391. **LC** TA401; .M38. **CODEN** MAUSEK. **Bk Rev**, (Qty: 4). **Ad Acc**. **Circ:** 2,500 (ctrl). Documents available from Ask*IEEE, CASDDS. ***Continues*** *Materials Australasia, 0818-3597.*
**Ind/Abst** Chem. Abstr.; INSPEC.

US/1044-5803
**MATERIALS CHARACTERIZATION.** [Mater. charact.]. **Added/Corp** International Metallographic Society. Vol. 24 No. 1 (Jan. 1990)-. Academic Scholarly Publication. English. Eight times a year (2 volumes). $430.00 US; $475.00 other. Elsevier Science Publishing Company Inc, Madison Square Station, PO Box 882, New York NY 10159-0882. **Tel** (212)633-3950, FAX (212)633-3990. **ED** Chris Bagnall. **LC** TN690; .M39. **DD** 669/.95/05. **CODEN** MACHEX. **[CCC].** available on microfilm and microfiche from University Microfilms International (UMI). Documents available from Article Express International, The Genuine Article, UMI Article Clearinghouse, Ask*IEEE, CASDDS. ***Continues*** *Metallography, 0026-0800.*
**Desc:** Features full length papers and short communications on theoretical and practical aspects of materials structure and behavior.
**Ind/Abst** ABI/INFORM Glob. Ed.; Alum. Ind. Abstr.; Appl. Mech. Rev.; Art Archaeol. Tech. Abstr.; Bioeng. Abstr.; Chem. Abstr. (1990-); Curr. Contents Eng. Tech. Appl. Sci.; Ei Page One; Energy Res. Abstr.; Eng. Index Annu.; Eng. Index Energy Abstr.; INSPEC (1990-); Met. Abstr.; Nucl. Sci. Abstr.; Res. Alert [Full Cov.]; Sci. Cit. Index; SCISEARCH.

UK/0952-5211
**MATERIALS EDGE.** [Mater. edge]. No. 1 (Sept. 1987)-. Periodical. English. mo. $490.00 US, Canada, South America and Europe. Metal Bulletin PLC, PO Box 28E, Worcester Park, Surrey KT4 7HX England. **Tel** 011 44 71 827 9977, FAX 011 44 81 337 8943. **ED** John Mack and Matt Bacon. **LC** TA401; .M36. **CODEN** MAEDEV. **Bk Rev**. **Ad Acc**. Documents available from Ask*IEEE.
**Desc:** New materials and their application in industry.
**Ind/Abst** Ceram. Abstr.; Chem. Bus. Bull.; Chem. Bus. NewsBase (1987-); Chem. Bus. Update; Infomat Int. Bus.; INSPEC (Jan./Feb. 1990-).

UK/0267-0836
**MATERIALS SCIENCE AND TECHNOLOGY.** **See** Engineering-Materials Engineering and Mechanics.

JA/0916-1821
**MATERIALS TRANSACTIONS, JIM.** [Mater. trans., JIM]. **Added/Corp** Nihon Kinzoku Gakkai. **VAT** Materials Transactions, Japan Institute of Metals. Vol. 30, No. 1 (Jan. 1989)-. Periodical. English. mo. $297.00. **(Subscription address:** Kyowa Book Company Inc., 1-38 Kanda Jinbo-Cho, Chiyoda-Ku Tokyo 101, Japan**) LC** TN4; .N5. **DD** 669/.005. **CODEN** TJIMAA. **[CCC].** Documents available from Article Express International, The Genuine Article, Ask*IEEE, CASDDS. ***Continues*** *Nihon Kinzoku Gakkai. Transactions of the Japan Institute of Metals, 0021-4434.*
**Ind/Abst** Chem. Abstr.; Civ. Struct. Eng. Abstr.; Comput. Inf. Syst. Abstr. J. [Full Cov.]; Corros. Abstr. (-199?); Curr. Contents Eng. Tech. Appl. Sci.; Ei Page One; Elect. Comm. Abstr.; Eng. Index Annu.; INSPEC (Jan. 1989-); Int. Aerosp. Abstr.; Manuf. Process Eng. Abstr.; Mater. Sci. Eng. Abstr.; Mech. Eng. Abstr.; Res. Alert [Full Cov.]; Sci. Cit. Index; SCISEARCH; Solid State Supercond. Abstr.

CN/0227-5503
**MCMASTER SYMPOSIUM ON IRON AND STEELMAKING.** [McMaster Symp. Iron Steelmaking.]. **VAT** Proceedings of the McMaster Symposium on Iron and Steelmaking. (1973)-. English. **CODEN** MSIPD8. Documents available from Article Express International, CASDDS.
**Ind/Abst** Bioeng. Abstr.; Chem. Abstr.; Ei Page One; Eng. Index Annu.

US/0147-7781
**MECHANICAL WORKING & STEEL PROCESSING.** (MECHANICAL WORKING AND STEEL PROCESSING : PROCEEDINGS OF THE ... MECHANICAL WORKING AND STEEL PROCESSING CONFERENCE AND SYMPOSIUM ON NEW METAL FORMING PROCESSES.). [Mech. work. steel process.]. **Main/Conf** Mechanical Working & Steel Processing Conference. **Added/Corp** Metallurgical Society of AIME. Mechanical Working and Steel Processing Committee. Metallurgical Society of AIME. Shaping and Forming Committee. Symposium on New Metal Forming Processes. Iron and Steel Society of AIME. Mechanical Working and Steel Processing Division. Vol. 4 (19??)-. Academic Scholarly Publication. English. an (published in Apr.). $80.00 (surface mail). Iron and Steel Society Inc., 410 Commonwealth Drive, Warrendale PA 15086. **Tel** (412)776-9460, FAX (412)776-0430, telex 6503113570. **ED** Lawrence Kuhn. **LC** TS320; .M49. **DD** 672. **CODEN** MWSPDI. Documents available from Article Express International, CASDDS. ***Continues*** *Mechanical Working of Steel.*
**Desc:** Proceedings of the society's annual metalworking and steel rolling conference.
**Ind/Abst** Bioeng. Abstr.; Chem. Abstr. (1963-1985); Ei Page One; Eng. Index Annu.

FR/0245-8292
**MEMOIRES ET ETUDES SCIENTIFIQUES DE LA REVUE DE METALLURGIE.** ***Title Change.*** (REVUE DE METALLURGIE. MEMOIRES ET ETUDES SCIENTIFIQUES.). [Mem. etud. sci. Rev. metall.]. (May 1980)-(19??). Academic Scholarly Publication. French (summaries and/or abstracts in English, German and Spanish). mo. La Revue de Metallurgie, 1 rue Paul Cezanne, F 75008 Paris France. **Tel** 11 33 1 49537226, FAX (33)1 47 67 85 77, telex 611 672 F. **ED** J L Gatelais. **LC** TN2; .M36. **DD** 669/.005. **CODEN** MESMDJ. **[CCC]. Pr Rev. Circ:** 2,400 (ctrl). available on microfilm and microfiche from University Microfilms International (UMI). Documents available from Article Express International, The Genuine Article, Ask*IEEE, CASDDS. ***Continues*** *Memoires Scientifiques de la Revue de Metallurgie.* ***Merged into*** *Cahiers d'Information Techniques de la Revue de Metallurgie.*
**Desc:** Studies and scientific articles on ferrous and non-ferrous metallurgy.
**Ind/Abst** Alum. Ind. Abstr.; Bioeng. Abstr.; Ceram. Abstr.; Chem. Abstr.; Civ. Struct. Eng. Abstr.; Curr. Contents Eng. Tech. Appl. Sci.; Ei Page One; EMBASE; Energy Res. Abstr. (April 1982-); Eng. Mater. Abstr.; Eng. Index Annu.; Environ. Eng. Abstr.; INSPEC (May 1980-); Int. Aerosp. Abstr.; Leadscan; Manuf. Process Eng. Abstr.; Mater. Sci. Eng. Abstr.; Mech. Eng. Abstr.; Met. Abstr.; Res. Alert [Full Cov.]; Sci. Cit. Index; SCISEARCH; Solid State Supercond. Abstr.

CL
**MEMORIA ANUAL / COMISION CHILENA DEL COBRE.** **Main/Corp** Comision Chilena del Cobre. (19??)-. Spanish (English). an. Free. Agustinas, 1161 40 Piso, Casilla 9493 Santiago Chile. **Tel** 726219, telex 645458 CUCOM CT. **LC** HD9539.C7; C34a. **DD** 354.830082/382. **Circ:** 700.

BO
**MEMORIA - EMPRESA NACIONAL DE FUNDICIONES.** **Main/Corp** Empresa Nacional de Fundiciones (Bolivia). Periodical. Spanish. Empresa Nacional de Fundiciones, Av Villazon 1966, 7 Po S Piso Casilla 4301, La Paz Bolivia.

CL/0589-2813
**MEMORIA TECNICA - CONGRESO LATINAMERICANO DE SIDERURGIA.** [Mem. tec. - ILAFA, Congr. Latinoam. Sider.]. **Main/Conf** Congreso Latinoamericano de Siderurgia. **VFOAT** Technical Proceedings - Latin American Iron and Steel Congress. Began in 1961. Academic Scholarly Publication. Spanish. an. Instituto Latinoamericano del Fierro el Acero, Dario Urzua 1994, Santiago 9 Chile. **Tel** 011 56 2 2047764, FAX 011 56 2 2253111, telex 340.348 ILAFA CK. **LC** HD9524.L3; C65A. **CODEN** CLSMBO. Documents available from CASDDS.
**Ind/Abst** Chem. Abstr. (1961-1979).

VE
**MEMORIA Y CUENTA DE LA ASOCIACION DE INDUSTRIALES METALURGICOS Y DE MINERIA DE VENEZUELA.** **Main/Corp** Asociacion de Industriales Metalurgicos y de Mineria de Venezuela. Spanish. Edificio Camara de Industriales, Piso 9 - Esquina Puente Anauco, Caracas Venezuela. **LC** HD9506.V4; A76A.

IT
**MERCATO METALSIDERURGICO.** (19??)-. Italian. sm (one issue in August). L35000.00 Italy; L50000.00 other. Assofermet, C So Venezia 47-49, 20121 Milan Italy. **Tel** 011 39 2 76008807, FAX 011 39 2 781027, telex 333420. **Ad Acc**.
**Desc:** Contains information for steel stockholders, traders, ironmongers, scrap steel and metal facories and merchants , as well as, industries and customers operating in these fields.

US/0364-7919
**MERCURY (UNITED STATES. BUREAU OF MINES).** **See** Metals and Metallurgy-Abstracting, Bibliographies and Statistics.

NE/0026-0460
**METAAL & KUNSTSTOF.** **VFOAT** MK. (1963)-. Periodical. Dutch. ir (25 issues). Fl220.00. Misset Uitgeverij BV, Postbus 9000, 6800 DA Arnhem Netherlands. **Tel** 011 31 85 209911. **UDC** 669. ***Absorbed*** *Toeleveren & Uitbesteden, 0924-7424.* ***Continued in part by*** *Technische Revue, 0165-3202.*

NE
**METAAL EN TECHNIEK.** (19??)-. Dutch. mo. Fl179.50 Netherlands; Fl300.00 other. Misset Uitgeverij BV, Postbus 9000, 6800 DA Arnhem Netherlands. **Tel** 011 31 85 209911.

NE/0168-6429
**METAALPRODUKTENINDUSTRIE, EXCL. MACHINES EN TRANSPORTMIDDELEN / CENTRAAL BUREAU VOOR DE STATISTIEK, HOOFDAFDELING STATISTIEKEN VAN INDUSTRIE EN BOUWNIJVERHEIDI.** **VFOAT** Metaalproduktenindustrie, Exclusief Machines en Transportmiddelen; Metal Products Industry, Excluding Machineries and Vehicles. Dutch (summaries and/or abstracts in English). Fl12.45. Centraal Bureau voor de Statistiek, AFD ALG Zaken, Postbus 959, 2270 AZ

Voorburg Netherlands. **Tel** 011 31 70 3373800, FAX 011 31 038 7429, telex 32692 CBS NL. **LC** HD9506.N2; M47. **UDC** 311:672(492).

MX/0539-4457
**METAL. Added/Corp** International Metalworkers' Federation. Vol. 1 (Jan. 1961)-. Periodical. Spanish. ir. Federal International Trabajador Ind Metal, Plaza Ferrocarriles 11 32, Mexico 1 DF Mexico.

●UK/0793-0291
**METAL-BASED DRUGS. See** Chemistry.

UK/0026-0533
**METAL BULLETIN, THE.** [Met. bull.]. Vol. 1 (1913)-. Bulletin. English. sw. $949.00 US, Canada & South America. Metal Bulletin PLC, PO Box 28E, Worcester Park, Surrey KT4 7HX England. **Tel** 011 44 71 827 9977, FAX 011 44 81 337 8943. **ED** J E Bailey and D S Gilbertson. **LC** TN1; .M38. **UDC** 338.51:669. **CODEN** MTBLAX. **[CCC]. Ad Acc. Circ:** 9,865. Documents available from CASDDS. ***Continued in part by*** *Metal Bulletin Monthly, 0373-4064.*
**Desc:** Provides international news, views, market trends and almost 800 metal steel and scrap prices in each Tuesday and Friday issues.
**Ind/Abst** Chem. Abstr.; Chem. Ind. Notes; Coal Abstr.; F&S Index Plus Text, Int. [Select. Cov.]; GeoRef; Infomat Int. Bus.; Leadscan; PROMT.

UK/0373-4064
**METAL BULLETIN MONTHLY.** [Met. bull. mon.]. **VFOAT** M B Monthly; MBM Metal Bulletin Monthly. No. 1 (Jan. 1971)-. Bulletin. English. mo. $345.00 US, Canada & South America. Metal Bulletin PLC, PO Box 28E, Worcester Park, Surrey KT4 7HX England. **Tel** 011 44 71 827 9977, FAX 011 44 81 337 8943. **ED** Richard Serjeantson. **DD** 669/.005. **[CCC]. Ad Acc. Circ:** 9,958. ***Separated from*** *Metal Bulletin, 0026-0533.*
**Desc:** Deals with all aspects of the steel, metals and scrap industries through global features and integrated supplements. Highlighting developments in processing equipment and machinery.
**Ind/Abst** Alum. Ind. Abstr.; EMBASE; F&S Index Plus Text, Int. [Select. Cov.]; GeoRef; Infomat Int. Bus.; Leadscan Met. Abstr.; PROMT.

UK/0955-6540
**METAL BULLETIN'S INTERNATIONAL SCRAP DIRECTORY.** [Met. bull. int. scrap dir.]. **VFOAT** International Scrap Directory. (1989)-. English. ir (every four years). $153.00. Metal Bulletin PLC, PO Box 28E, Worcester Park, Surrey KT4 7HX England. **Tel** 011 44 71 827 9977, FAX 011 44 81 337 8943. **ED** John Bailey. **LC** IN PROCESS. **Ad Acc.** ***Continues*** *European & North American Scrap Directory, 0261-426X.*
**Desc:** A reference source for scrap traders and professors active worldwide and major national operators, handling secondary ferrous and nonferrous metals.

US/0539-4511
**METAL CENTER NEWS.** Vol. 1 (May 1961)-. Periodical. English. mo. $55.00 US; $70.00 Canada & Mexico; $159.00 other. Diversified Publishing, 825 7th Avenue, 6th Floor, New York NY 10019. **Tel** (212)887-8565, FAX (212)887-8493. **[CCC].** available on microfilm from University Microfilms International (UMI).
**Ind/Abst** F&S Index Plus Text, Int. [Full Txt.] [Select. Cov.]; PROMT [Full Txt.]; Met. Abstr.; World Alum. Abstr.

US/8756-2014
**METAL CONSTRUCTION NEWS. See** Building and Construction.

US/0098-2210
**METAL DISTRIBUTION.** (1975)-. English. an. $40.00. Metal Center News, 191 South Gary Avenue, Carol Stream IL 60188. **Tel** (708)462-2288. **LC** HD9506.U6; M45. **DD** 381/.45/6710973.

US/0026-055X
**METAL FABRICATING NEWS. See** Manufacturing.

US/0026-0568
**METAL FABRICATOR, THE.** ***Ceased.*** Periodical. English. qt. Walter B Frost and Company, 97 Columbia Street, Peace Dale RI 02883. **UDC** 669; 621.7.

US/0026-0576
**METAL FINISHING.** (METAL FINISHING; PREPARATION, ELECTROPLATING, COATING.). [Met. finish.]. Vol. 38, No. 6 (June 1940)-. Academic Scholarly Publication. English. mo (1 volume). $45.00 US; $67.00 Canada & Mexico; $116.00 (surface mail) other. Elsevier Science Publishing Company Inc, Madison Square Station, PO Box 882, New York NY 10159-0882. **Tel** (212)633-3950, FAX (212)633-3990. **ED** Michael Murphy. **CODEN** MEFIA7. **[CCC]. Bk Rev. Ad Acc. Circ:** 8,000. available on microfilm and microfiche from University Microfilms International (UMI). Documents available from Article Express International, Ask*IEEE, CASDDS. ***Continues*** *Metal Industry, 0360-5159;* ***Absorbed*** *Organic Finishing, 0096-2112.*
**Desc:** Strives to keep readers informed on the practical and technical aspects of finishing metal and plastic products, including waste treatment and pollution control.
**Ind/Abst** Alum. Ind. Abstr.; Appl. Sci. Technol. Index; Aqualine Abstr.; Art Archaeol. Tech. Abstr.; Bioeng. Abstr.; Ceram. Abstr. (19??-); Chem. Abstr.; Curr. Titles Electrochem.; Ei Page One; EMBASE; Eng. Index Annu.; F&S Index Plus Text, Int. [Select. Cov.]; INSPEC (Jan. 1985-Dec. 1989); Int. Aerosp. Abstr.; Int. Packag. Abstr.; Leadscan; Met. Abstr.; PROMT; Surf. Treat. Technol. Abstr.; World Surf. Coat. Abstr.

●US/1075-5594
**METAL HEAT TREATING.** [Met. heat treat.]. Vol. 1, No. 1 (Jan./Feb. 1994)-. Periodical. English. Six times a year. $30.00 US; $35.00 Canada; $45.00 Mexico; $50.00 other. Penton Publishing, 1100 Superior Avenue, Cleveland OH 44114-2543. **Tel** (216)696-7000, FAX (216)696-0836. **(Subscription address:** Penton Publishing, PO Box 96732, Chicago IL 60693.**) DD** 671. ***Continues*** *Heat Treating, 0017-9345.*

UK/0026-0657
**METAL POWDER REPORT.** [Met. powder rep.]. **Added/Corp** Powder Metallurgy Ltd. Vol. 1 (Sept. 1946)-. Periodical. English. Twelve times a year. $167.00 The Americas; £112.00 other. Elsevier Advanced Technology, An Imprint of Elsevier Science Ltd., The Boulevard, Langford Lane, Kidlington, Oxford OX5 1GB United Kingdom. **Tel** 011 44 865 843000, 011 44 865 843699, FAX 011 44 865 843010. **(Subscription address:** Elsevier Science Ltd. Oxford Fulfillment Centre, PO Box 800, Kidlington, Oxford OX5 1DX United Kingdom.**) ED** A. Weaver. **LC** TN695; .M43. **[CCC]. Bk Rev. Ad Acc. Circ:** 1,400. available on microfilm and microfiche from University Microfilms International (UMI). Documents available from Article Express International.
**Desc:** Journal for the powder metallurgy () industry providing topical, practical and independent news of the international scene. Topics include company profiles, advanced materials, new production technology, conference achievements, literature reviews and powder prices.
**Ind/Abst** Ei Page One; Eng. Mater. Abstr.; Eng. Index Annu.; Leadscan; World Ceram. Abstr.

US/0047-6870
**METALETTER. VAT** Metal Letter. Periodical. English. mo. American Federation of Labor and Congress of Industrial Organizations, 815 16th Street Northwest, Washington DC 20006. **Tel** (202)637-5000. **UDC** 331.105.443:669(73). ***Supersedes*** *American Federation of Labor and Congress of Industrial Organizations. Metal Trades Dept. Bulletin.*

GW/0026-0746
**METALL (BERLIN).** (METALL.). [Metall]. Vol. 1 (Sept. 1947)-. Academic Scholarly Publication. German (English). mo. $268.00. Dr. Alfred Huethig Verlag GmbH, Postfach 102869, D 69018 Heidelberg Germany. **Tel** 011 49 6221 489281. **(Subscription address:** Huethig Publishing Inc., 29 Macintosh Drive, Oxford CT 06478.**) ED** Gerhard Elbing, Helmut Winkler, Dieter Kamphauser, Gustav Salffner, G Berging. **LC** TN3; .M35. **DD** 338.2/74/05. **CODEN** MTLLAF. **[CCC]. Bk Rev. Ad Acc. Pr Rev. Circ:** 6,000. Documents available from Article Express International, The Genuine Article, CASDDS.
**Desc:** Internationally journal for the metal producing and processing industries and for metal dealers.
**Ind/Abst** Alum. Ind. Abstr.; Art Archaeol. Tech. Abstr.; Bioeng. Abstr.; Chem. Abstr.; Curr. Contents Eng. Tech. Appl. Sci.; Ei Page One; EMBASE; Energy Res. Abstr. (Oct. 1976-); Eng. Index Annu.; F&S Index Plus Text, Int. [Select. Cov.]; GeoRef; Infomat Int. Bus.; Int. Aerosp. Abstr.; Manuf. Process Eng. Abstr.; Mater. Sci. Eng. Abstr.; Mech. Eng. Abstr.; Met. Abstr.; PROMT; Res. Alert [Full Cov.]; SCISEARCH; Soc. Sci. Cit. Index [Select. Cov.]; Solid State Supercond. Abstr.

GW
**METALL. DAS MAGAZIN DER IG METALL. Added/Corp** Industriegewerkschaft Metall. **VFOAT** IGM Metall. (Oct. 10, 1949)-. Periodical. German. Twelve times a year. DM24.00. Industriegewerkschaft Metall, Wilhelm-Leuscher Strasse 79-85, Postfach 3304, 6000 Frankfurt/Main 1 Germany. **ED** Wehrhart Otto. **LC** HD6698.M5; I59. Index available. cum. index. **Acid Free. Circ:** 2,500,000.

NE
**METALLBEWERKING.** Began in 1934. Academic Scholarly Publication. Dutch. mo. Fl195.00 Netherlands; Fl215.00 other. Tech Uitgeverij de Veij Mestdagh, Markt 51, 4331 LK Middelburg Netherlands. **Tel** 01180-81240, FAX 01180-81215. **ED** Ir D J de Korte. **LC** TS200; .M323. **CODEN** MBMEDC. Index available. **Bk Rev. Ad Acc. Circ:** 3,500 (ctrl). Documents available from CASDDS.
**Desc:** Flexible automation and metalworking.
**Ind/Abst** Chem. Abstr. (1978-1984); EMBASE; Saf. Health Work.

GW
**METALLE.** Periodical. German. Haus der Metalle, Tersteegenstrasse 28, Postfach 87, 4 Dusseldorf 1 Germany. **LC** HD9506.G2; N4. **UDC** 669. ***Continues*** *NE-Metalle.*

IT
**METALLI.** Italian. mo (11 issues - August/Sept. combined). L100000 Italy; L140000 other. Edimet, Via Corfu 102, 25124 Brescia Italy. **Tel** 011 39 30 2421043, FAX 011 39 30 223802. **Bk Rev. Ad Acc. Circ:** 5,000 (ctrl).
**Desc:** Economic and statistical data about production, import/export figures for all metals raw or semi-finished; the latest quotations, general business problems, maintain direct contacts with producers.

UK/0264-7303
**METALLIC MATERIALS. VFOAT** Kovove Materialy. (19??)-. Periodical. English (translations available in Czech). bm. $210.00. Riecansky Science Publishing Company, 7 Meadow Walk, Great Abington, Cambridge CB1 6AZ England. **Tel** 011 44 223 893295, FAX 011 44 462 480947, telex 825372 TURPIN G. Documents available from Ask*IEEE.
**Ind/Abst** Elect. Comm. Abstr.; Environ. Eng. Abstr.; INSPEC (1983-); Manuf. Process Eng. Abstr.; Mater. Sci. Eng. Abstr.; Mech. Eng. Abstr.; Solid State Supercond. Abstr.

UK
**METALLICA 2000.** (199?)-. English. Four times a year. $7150.00 US and Canada; £3750.00 other. Mining Journal Ltd., 60 Worship Street, London EC2A 2HD England. **Tel** 011 44 071 377 2020, FAX 071 247 4100, telex 8952809 MINING G. **(Subscription address:** Mining Journal Ltd., PO Box 10 Edenbridge, Kent TN8 5NE England.**)** ***Continues*** *Mining Database.*

FI/0785-0530
**METALLITEOLLISUUS. VFOAT** Metallindustri. Finnish (Swedish). an. Tilastokeskus, PL 504, Annankatu 44, 00101 Helsinki Finland. **Tel** 358-0-17341, FAX 358-0-17342474, telex 1002111 TILASTO SF. **LC** HD9506.F5; M48.

GW/0026-0797
**METALLOBERFLACHE.** [Metalloberflache]. (1947)-. Periodical. German. mo. DM144.00. Carl Hanser Verlag, Postfach 860420, D 81631 Munich Germany. **Tel** 011 49 89 998300, FAX 011 49 89 984809. **ED** W. Jantsch. **LC** TS200; .M464. **DD** 671. **CODEN** MOFEAV. **[CCC].** Index available. **Bk Rev. Ad Acc. Circ:** 4,000 (ctrl). Documents available from Article Express International, CASDDS.
**Desc:** Technical journal on metal surfaces engineering in decorative and functional applications. Special attention is paid to non-corrosive surfaces. Reports on new developments from industry and research concerning organic and manufactured surface processes are presented.
**Ind/Abst** Alum. Ind. Abstr.; Bioeng. Abstr.; Chem. Abstr.; Comput. Inf. Syst. Abstr. J. [Full Cov.]; Curr. Titles Electrochem.; Ei Page One; EMBASE; Energy Res. Abstr.; Eng. Mater. Abstr.; Eng. Index Annu.; Leadscan; Manuf. Process Eng. Abstr.; Mater. Sci. Eng. Abstr.; Mech. Eng. Abstr.; Met. Abstr.; Solid State Supercond. Abstr.; Surf. Treat. Technol. Abstr.; World Alum. Abstr.

UN/0204-3580
**METALLOFIZIKA (KIEV).** (METALLOFIZIKA.). [Metallofiz.]. **Added/Corp** Akademiia Nauk Ukrainskaii RSR. Viddil Fizyky. (1979)-. Academic Scholarly Publication. Russian (summaries and/or abstracts in English). Twelve times a year. $149.95. Izdatelstvo Naukova Dumka / Ukrainian Academy of Sciences, Vladimirskaia Ulitsa 54, 252601 Kiev Ukraine. **Tel** 225-63-66, telex 131376. **(Subscription address:** East View Publications Inc., 3020 Harbor Lane North, Suite 110, Minneapolis MN 55447.**) ED** V. N. Gridnev. **LC** TN689; .M465. **DD** 669/.9/05. **CODEN** MANFDD. Index available. cum. index. **Bk Rev. Ad Acc. Circ:** 1,000 (ctrl). Documents available from Ask*IEEE, CASDDS. ***Supersedes*** *Metallofizika.*
**Ind/Abst** Alum. Ind. Abstr.; Chem. Abstr.; Eng. Mater. Abstr.; INSPEC (1971-); Int. Aerosp. Abstr.; Met. Abstr.; World Alum. Abstr.

US/0090-2098
**METALLOGRAPHIC REVIEW, THE.** [Metallogr. rev.]. V. 1- Sept. 1972-. Periodical. English. qt. $20.00. International Microstructural Analysis Society, PO Box 2329, LaJolla CA 92037. **LC** TN689; .M47. **DD** 669/.95/05. **UDC** 620.18. **CODEN** MTGRB9. Documents available from Article Express International.
**Ind/Abst** Ei Page One; Eng. Index Annu.

RU/0026-0819
**METALLOVEDENIE I TERMICESKAJA OBRABOTKA (KALININ).** (METALLOVEDENIE I TERMICHESKAIA OBRABOTKA.). [Metalloved. term. obrab.]. **Added/Corp** Kalininskii Politekhnicheskii Institut. Kafedra Tekhnologii Metallov. Vol. 1 (1973)-. Academic Scholarly Publication. Russian. mo. $129.95. **(Subscription address:** East View Publications Inc.,

3020 Harbor Lane North, Suite 110, Minneapolis MN 55447.) **CODEN** MTOBD3. **[CCC].** Index available. **Bk Rev.** Documents available from Article Express International, Ask*IEEE, CASDDS.
**Ind/Abst** Chem. Abstr.; Ei Page One; Energy Res. Abstr.; Eng. Index Annu.; INSPEC (1971-).

US/0026-0673
**METALLOVEDENIE I TERMICHESKAYA OBRABOTKA METALLOV.** (METAL SCIENCE AND HEAT TREATMENT.). [Met. sci. heat treat.]. **Added/Corp** Consultants Bureau. Vol. 5, No. 1 and 2 (Jan.-Feb. 1963)-. Periodical. English (Russian). mo. $1215.00 US; $1425.00 other. Consultants Bureau, A Division of Plenum Publishing Corporation, 233 Spring Street, New York NY 10013. **Tel** (212)620-8000, (212)620-8466, FAX (212)463-0742, telex 23/421139. **ED** A. P. Gulyaev. **LC** TN4; .M3213. **DD** 669/.94/05. **CODEN** MHTRAN. **[CCC]. Pr Rev.** available on microfilm and microfiche from University Microfilms International (UMI). Documents available from Article Express International, The Genuine Article, Ask*IEEE, CASDDS. ***Continues*** *Metallovedenie i Termicheskaya Obrabotka Metallov. English. Metal Science and Heat Treatment of Metals.*
**Desc:** This journal is devoted to theoretical and practical aspects of metallurgy. The search for new alloys and the improvement of mechanical and other properties of alloys.
**Ind/Abst** Alum. Ind. Abstr.; Bioeng. Abstr.; Chem. Abstr.; Curr. Contents Eng. Tech. Appl. Sci.; Ei Page One; Eng. Mater. Abstr.; Eng. Index Annu.; INSPEC (Jan./Feb. 1972-); Int. Aerosp. Abstr.; Leadscan; Met. Abstr.; Pollut. Abstr. Indexes; Res. Alert [Full Cov.]; Sci. Cit. Index; SCISEARCH.

GW/0076-6682
**METALLSTATISTIK.** (METALLSTATISTIK / METALLGESELLSCHAFT AKTIENGESELLSCHAFT.). [Metallstatistik]. **Added/Corp** Metallgesellschaft Aktiengesellschaft. Vol. 57 (1969)-. German (English). an. DM100.00 Germany; $60.00 US. Metallgesellschaft AG, Volkswirtschafte L ABT, Postfach 101501, W-6000 Frankfurt AM 1 Germany. **Tel** 69.159 23 90, FAX 69/159 23 90, telex 04 1225-0 MGF D. **ED** Willy Bauer. **LC** HD9539.A1; M43. ***Continues*** *Statistische Zusammenstellungen uber Aluminium, Blei, Kupfer, Zink, Zinn, Kadmium, Magnesium, Nickel, Quecksilber und Silber.*

RU/0026-0827
**METALLURG.** [Metallurg]. **Added/Corp** Russia (1923- U.S.S.R.) Gosudarstvennyi Nauchno-Tekhnicheskii Komitet. Professionalnyi Soiuz Rabochikh Metallicheskikh Izdelii. Tsentralnyi Komitet. Vol. 1, (1956)-. Periodical. Russian. mo. $149.95. **(Subscription address:** East View Publications Inc., 3020 Harbor Lane North, Suite 110, Minneapolis MN 55447.) **LC** TS300; .M4. **CODEN** METGA3. **[CCC].** Index available. **Bk Rev.** Documents available from Article Express International, CASDDS.
**Ind/Abst** Alum. Ind. Abstr.; Chem. Abstr.; Ei Page One; Eng. Mater. Abstr.; Eng. Index Annu.; Met. Abstr.; World Alum. Abstr.

UK/0141-8602
**METALLURGIA (1978).** (METALLURGIA.). [Metallurgia]. **Added/Corp** Institute of Sheet Metal Engineering. Cold Forging Committee. Society of Industrial Furnace Engineers. National Association of Drop Forgers and Stampers. Drop Forging Research Association. Vol. 45 (Jan. 1978)-. Academic Scholarly Publication. English. mo. £99.55 UK; £118.40, $183.50 other. Argus Press Group, Queensway House, 2 Queensway Redhill, Surrey RH1 1QS England. **Tel** 011 44 737 768611, 011 44 737 761685, FAX 011 44 737 760510, telex 948669 TOPJNL G. **LC** TN1; .M426. **DD** 669/.005. **CODEN** MEMFAX. available on microfilm and microfiche from University Microfilms International (UMI). Documents available from Article Express International, CASDDS. ***Continues*** *Metallurgia and Metal Forming.*
**Desc:** Covers metal technology, metal forming, and thermal processing.
**Ind/Abst** Alum. Ind. Abstr.; Appl. Sci. Technol. Index; Bioeng. Abstr.; Chem. Abstr.; Curr. Technol. Index; Ei Page One; EMBASE; Eng. Mater. Abstr.; Eng. Index Annu.; F&S Index Plus Text, Int. [Full Txt.] [Select. Cov.]; Fluid Abstr., Civil Eng.; Fluid Abstr. Proc. Eng.; FLUIDEX; Leadscan; Met. Abstr.; PROMT [Full Txt.]; Trade Ind. ASAP [Full Txt.]; Trade Ind. Index [Full Txt.]; World Ceram. Abstr.

IT/0026-0843
**METALLURGIA ITALIANA, LA.** [Metall. ital.]. **Added/Corp** Associazione Iitaliana di Metallurgia. Associazione Fra Gli Industriali Metallurgici Italiani. Vol. 1 (Nov. 1909)-. Academic Scholarly Publication. Italian. Twelve times a year. L132000 Italy; L170000 other. Franco Angeli Riviste SRL, Viale Monza 106, 20127 Milan Italy. **Tel** 011 39 2 2827651, 011 39 2 289562. **LC** TN4; .M35. **CODEN** MITLAC. **[CCC].** Documents available from Article Express International, CASDDS.
**Ind/Abst** Alum. Ind. Abstr.; Bioeng. Abstr.; Ceram. Abstr.; Chem. Abstr.; Ei Page One; Eng. Mater. Abstr.; Eng. Index Annu. [Select. Cov.]; Met. Abstr.; Pollut. Abstr. Indexes; Surf. Treat. Technol. Abstr.

●US/1073-5615
**METALLURGICAL AND MATERIALS TRANSACTIONS. B, PROCESS METALLURGY AND MATERIALS PROCESSING SCIENCE.** [Metall. mater. trans., B, Proc. metall. mater. proc. sci.]. **Added/Corp** Minerals, Metals and Materials Society. ASM International. Vol. 25B, No. 1 (Feb. 1994)-. Periodical. English. bm. $540.00 (nonmember and institutional member), $36.00 (individual member). American Society for Metals International, c/o Deborah Barthelmes, Materials Park OH 44073-0002. **Tel** (216)338-5151, FAX (216)338-4634, telex 980-619. **(Subscription address:** ASM International, Materials Information, Materials Park OH 44073.) **LC** TN689; .M48. **DD** 669. **CODEN** MTTBCR. Index available (bound in Dec. issue). ***Continues*** *Metallurgical Transactions. B, Process Metallurgy, 0360-2141.*

●US/1073-5623
**METALLURGICAL AND MATERIALS TRANSACTIONS. PHYSICAL METALLURGY AND MATERIALS SCIENCE.** [Metall. mater. trans., A Phys. metall. mater. sci.]. **Added/Corp** Minerals, Metals and Materials Society. ASM International. **VFOAT** Physical Metallurgy and Materials Science. 25A, No. 1 (Jan. 1994)-. Periodical. English. mo. $752.00 (nonmember and institutional member), $50.00 (individual member). American Society for Metals International, c/o Deborah Barthelmes, Materials Park OH 44073-0002. **Tel** (216)338-5151, FAX (216)338-4634, telex 980-619. **(Subscription address:** ASM International, Materials Information, Materials Park OH 44073.) **DD** 669. Index available (bound in Dec. issue). **Pr Rev. *Continues*** *Metallurgical Transactions. A, Physical Metallurgy and Materials Science, 0360-2133.*
**Desc:** Covers physical metallurgy and materials.

UK/0951-0869
**METALLURGICAL JOURNAL.** **VFOAT** Hutnicke Listy. Periodical. English. mo. £120.00 EC; $200.00 other. Riecansky Science Publishing Company, 7 Meadow Walk, Great Abington, Cambridge CB1 6AZ England. **Tel** 011 44 223 893295, FAX 011 44 462 480947, telex 825372 TURPIN G.

GW/0935-7254
**METALLURGICAL PLANT AND TECHNOLOGY INTERNATIONAL : MPT.** **Added/Corp** Verein Deutscher Eisenhuttenleute. **VFOAT** MPT; MPT International; Metallurgical Plant and Technology. Vol. 12 (Jan. 1989)-. Periodical. English. bm (Feb., Apr., June, Aug., Oct., Dec.). DM216.00. Verlag Stahleisen mbH, Postfach 105164, D 40042 Duesseldorf Germany. **Tel** 011 49 211 67070. **LC** TN600; .M454. **DD** 669. Documents available from Article Express International. ***Continues*** *Metallurgical Plant and Technology, 0171-4511.*
**Ind/Abst** Ei Page One; Eng. Index Annu.

GW/0171-4511
**METALLURGICAL PLANT AND TECHNOLOGY : MPT.** ***Title Change.*** [MPT, Metall. plant technol.]. **Added/Corp** Verein Deutscher Eisenhuttenleute. **VFOAT** MPT. (1978)-(198?). Academic Scholarly Publication. English. Six times a year. Verlag Stahleisen mbH, Postfach 105164, D 40042 Duesseldorf Germany. **Tel** 011 49 211 67070. **LC** TN600; .M454. **DD** 669. **CODEN** MMPTDD. **Ad Acc.** ctrl circ. Documents available from Article Express International, CASDDS. ***Continued by*** *Metallurgical Plant and Technology International, 0935-7254.*
**Desc:** An internationally circulated English language technical journal for iron and steel technology.
**Ind/Abst** AESIS Q.; Alum. Ind. Abstr.; Bioeng. Abstr.; Chem. Abstr.; Ei Page One; Eng. Index Annu.; Met. Abstr.

JA/0289-6214
**METALLURGICAL REVIEW OF MMIJ.** [Metall. rev. MMIJ]. **VFOAT** Metallurgical Review of Mining and Metallurgical Institute of Japan. (1984)-. Periodical. English. Twice a year (May, Nov.). $20.00. Mining & Materials Processing, Nogizaka Bldg 9-6-41 Akasaka, Minato-ku Tokyo 107 Japan. **Tel** 03 3402 0541, FAX 03 3403 1776. **DD** 622. Documents available from CASDDS.
**Ind/Abst** Chem. Abstr.

IT
**METALLURGICAL SCIENCE AND TECHNOLOGY.** No. 1 (June 1983)-. Academic Scholarly Publication. English. Three times a year. Teksid SPA, Via Piemonte 123, 10151 Turin Italy. **LC** TN600; .M456. **DD** 669/.05. **CODEN** MESTE7. Documents available from CASDDS.
**Ind/Abst** Alum. Ind. Abstr.; Chem. Abstr.; Met. Abstr.

US/0360-2133
**METALLURGICAL TRANSACTIONS. A. PHYSICAL METALLURGY AND MATERIALS SCIENCE.** ***Title Change.*** [Metall. trans., A, Phys. metall. mater. sci.]. **Added/Corp** Metallurgical Society of AIME. American Society for Metals. **VFOAT** Physical Metallurgy and Materials Science. Vol. 6A, No. 1 (Jan. 1975)-(1994). Periodical. English. mo. American Society for Metals International, c/o Deborah Barthelmes, Materials Park OH 44073-0002. **Tel** (216)338-5151, FAX (216)338-4634, telex 980-619. **ED** David Laughlin. **DD** 669. **CODEN** MTTABN. **[CCC].** Index available. **Ad Acc. Pr Rev. Circ:** 3,000. available on microfilm and microfiche from University Microfilms International (UMI). Documents available from Article Express International, The Genuine Article, Ask*IEEE, CASDDS. ***Continues in part*** *Metallurgical Transactions, 0026-086X.* ***Continued by*** *Metallurgical and Materials Transactions.*
**Desc:** Physical metallurgy-mechanical behavior, alloy phases/structure, transformations, environmental interactions, physical chemistry, transport phenomena; written to transfer basic research from lab to shop.
**Ind/Abst** Alum. Ind. Abstr.; Bioeng. Abstr.; Chem. Abstr.; Chem. Titles; Coal Abstr.; Curr. Contents Eng. Tech. Appl. Sci.; Curr. Contents Phys. Chem. Earth Sci.; Curr. Titles Electrochem.; Ei Page One; Energy Res. Abstr. (June 1975-); Eng. Index Annu.; HTFS Dig.; INIS Atomindex [Micro.]; INSPEC (Jan. 1975-); Int. Aerosp. Abstr.; Leadscan; Mass Spect. Bull.; Met. Abstr.; MINPROC; Res. Alert [Full Cov.]; Sci. Cit. Index; SCISEARCH; World Ceram. Abstr.

US/0360-2141
**METALLURGICAL TRANSACTIONS. B, PROCESS METALLURGY.** ***Title Change.*** [Metall. trans., B, Process metall.]. **Added/Corp** Metallurgical Society of AIME. Metallurgical Society (U.S.) Minerals, Metals and Materials Society. American Society for Metals. ASM International. Iron and Steel Society of AIME. Iron and Steel Society. **VFOAT** Process Metallurgy. Vol. 6B, No. 1 (March 1975)-(1993). Periodical. English. bm. American Society for Metals International, c/o Deborah Barthelmes, Materials Park OH 44073-0002. **Tel** (216)338-5151, FAX (216)338-4634, telex 980-619. **ED** David E. Laughlin. **DD** 669. **CODEN** MTTBCR. **[CCC].** Index available. **Bk Rev. Ad Acc. Pr Rev. Circ:** 1,000. available on microfilm and microfiche from University Microfilms International (UMI). Documents available from Article Express International, The Genuine Article, Ask*IEEE, CASDDS. ***Continues in part*** *Metallurgical Transactions, 0026-086X.* ***Continued by*** *Metallurgical and Materials Transactions. B, Process Metallurgy and Materials Processing Science, 1073-5615.*
**Desc:** Covers extractive and process metallurgy - mineral preparation, pyrometallurgy, hydrometallurgy, electrometallurgy, transport phenomena, process control, physical chemistry, solidification, mechanical working, solid state reactions, beneficiation, welding and joining, and surface treatments.
**Ind/Abst** AESIS Q.; Alum. Ind. Abstr.; Bioeng. Abstr.; Chem. Abstr.; Chem. Titles; Curr. Contents Eng. Tech. Appl. Sci.; Curr. Titles Electrochem.; Ei Page One; Energy Res. Abstr. (Oct. 1975-); Eng. Index Annu.; INIS Atomindex [Micro.]; INSPEC (Dec. 1975-); Int. Aerosp. Abstr.; Leadscan; Mass Spect. Bull.; Met. Abstr.; MINPROC; Res. Alert [Full Cov.]; Sci. Cit. Index; SCISEARCH.

RU/0130-2884
**METALLURGICESKAJA TEPLOTEHNIKA.** (METALLURGICHESKAIA TEPLOTEKHNIKA.). [Metall. teploteh.]. **Added/Corp** Vsesoiuznyi Nauchno-Issledovatelskii Institut Metallurgicheskoi Teplotekhniki (Soviet Union) Soviet Union. Ministerstvo Chernoi Metallurgii. (1972)-. Periodical. Russian. Twelve times a year. $67.00. Izdatelstvo Metallurgiia, 2-i Obydenskii Per.14, G-34, Moscow Russia. **(Subscription address:** Victor Kamkin, 4956 Boiling Brook Parkway, Rockville MD 20852.) **LC** TN600; .M46. **CODEN** METEDY.
**Desc:** Information on metallurgy and heat engineering.
**Ind/Abst** Energy Res. Abstr. (Feb. 1983-).

UN/0543-5749
**METALLURGICSKAJA I GORNORUDNAJA PROMYSLENNOST.** (METALLURGICHESKAIA I GORNORUDNAIA PROMYSHLENNOST.). [Metall. gornorudn. prom.]. (1960)-. Periodical. Russian. qt. $89.95. **(Subscription address:** East View Publications Inc., 3020 Harbor Lane North, Suite 110, Minneapolis MN 55447.) Documents available from CASDDS.
**Ind/Abst** Chem. Abstr.

FR/0154-036X
**METALLURGIE. LEXIQUE.** English (French). mo. 465.00F. Centre National de la Recherche Scientifique, Informascience, 26 rue Boyer, 75971 Paris France. **Tel** 61.41.11.05, telex CNRSDOC 220880 F. **LC** Z695.1.M55; M47. **DD** 025.4/9669. **UDC** 030.8:669.

BE/0543-5757
**METALLURGIE (MONS).** ***Title Change.*** (METALLURGIE.). [Metallurgie]. Periodical. French. qt. Universite Libre de Bruxelles, 50 Avenue F D Roosevelt CP 188, 1050 Brussels Belgium. **Tel** 011 32 2 6423611. **LC** TN2; .M365. **UDC** 669. **CODEN** MTLGAY. Documents available from Article Express International. ***Continues*** *ATB Metallurgie.* ***Continued by*** *ATB Metallurgie.*
**Ind/Abst** Bioeng. Abstr.; Ei Page One; Eng. Index Annu.

US/0026-0894
**METALLURGIST (NEW YORK).**
(METALLURGIST. METALLURG.). [Metallurgist]. **Added/Corp** Consultants Bureau. Consultants Bureau Enterprises. **VFOAT** Metallurg. (Jan. 1957)-. Periodical. English (Russian). mo. $1150.00 US; $1345.00 other. Consultants Bureau, A Division of Plenum Publishing Corporation, 233 Spring Street, New York NY 10013. **Tel** (212)620-8000, (212)620-8466, FAX (212)463-0742, telex 23/421139. **ED** A. G. Belikov. **LC** TS300; .M413. **DD** 669/.05. **CODEN** MTLUA8. **[CCC]. Pr Rev.** available on microfilm and microfiche from University Microfilms International (UMI). Documents available from Article Express International, The Genuine Article, CASDDS.
**Desc:** This journal reviews new techniques developed in international plants for improving the quantity and quality of production in the iron and steel industries.
**Ind/Abst** Alum. Ind. Abstr.; Chem. Abstr.; Coal Abstr.; Curr. Contents Eng. Tech. Appl. Sci.; Ei Page One; EMBASE; Eng. Mater. Abstr.; Eng. Index Annu.; Leadscan; Met. Abstr.; Res. Alert [Full Cov.]; SCISEARCH; Soc. Sci. Cit. Index [Select. Cov.].

US/0094-5447
**METALLURGY/MATERIALS EDUCATION YEARBOOK. Added/Corp** American Society for Metals. **VFOAT** Materials Education Yearbook. (19??)-. English. an (Apr.). $15.00 (members); $35.00 (non-members). American Society for Metals International, c/o Deborah Barthelmes, Materials Park OH 44073-0002. **Tel** (216)338-5151, FAX (216)338-4634, telex 980-619. **(Subscription address:** ASM International, Materials Information, Materials Park OH 44073.**) ED** Kali Mukherjee. **LC** TN675.3; .M46. **DD** 669/.007/1173. Index available. **Circ:** 2,000 (ctrl).
**Desc:** Directory of schools in USA, Canada and Mexico with metallurgy materials science faculties. Also schools with faculties of ceramics and polymer science as well as international schools.

GW/0026-0908
**METALLVERARBEITUNG.**
[Metallverarbeitung]. (1947)-. Periodical. German. bm. Veb Verlag Technik, Literarisches Buro des veb Carl Zeiss Jena, 69 Jena, Carl-Zeiss-Strasse 1 Germany. **CODEN** MLVBAD. Documents available from CASDDS.
**Ind/Abst** Chem. Abstr.

RU
**METALLY / AKADEMIIA NAUK SSSR.**
**Added/Corp** Akademiia Nauk SSSR. (1991)-. Academic Scholarly Publication. Russian (table of contents in English). Six times a year. $168.00. Izdatelstvo Nauka / Akademiia Nauk, Publishing House of the Russian Academy of Sciences, Leninskii Porspekt 14, 117901 Moscow Russia. **Tel** 011 95 954-21-53, FAX 011 95 938-21-44, telex 411964. **(Subscription address:** East View Publications Inc., 3020 Harbor Lane North, Suite 110, Minneapolis MN 55447.**) LC** TN4; .A33462. ***Continues** Izvestiia Akademii Nauk SSSR. Metally, 0568-5303.*

PL/0860-7583
**METALOZNAWSTWO, OBROBKA CIEPLNA, INZYNIERIA POWIERZCHNI.**
**Added/Corp** Instytut Mechaniki Precyzyjnej (Warsaw, Poland). (1987)-. Periodical. Polish (summaries and/or abstracts in English, German and Russian). bm. Price on Request. **(Subscription address:** ARS Polona, PO Box 1001, 00068 Warsaw Poland.**) CODEN** MOCPEJ. Documents available from CASDDS. ***Continues** Metaloznawstwo i Obrobka Cieplna, 0137-3854.*
**Ind/Abst** Chem. Abstr.

UK/0026-0924
**METALS ABSTRACTS. See** Metals and Metallurgy-Abstracting, Bibliographies and Statistics.

UK/0026-0932
**METALS ABSTRACTS INDEX. See** Metals and Metallurgy-Abstracting, Bibliographies and Statistics.

UK/0143-0637
**METALS ANALYSIS AND OUTLOOK.**
[Met. anal. outlook]. **VFOAT** Metals. No. 1 (Jan./Feb. 1976)-. Periodical. English. qt. £450.00. Metals & Minerals Research Service Ltd, 24 Henry Street, Bath Avon, BA1 1JT England. **Tel** 011 44 225 481585. **ED** Graham Deller and Stephen Briggs.
**Desc:** A concise presentation of the forecast near-term prospects for the nine exchange-traded metals which focuses on relationships between metal markets and the economy as a whole.
**Ind/Abst** GeoRef.

US
**METALS AND CERAMICS DIVISION ANNUAL PROGRESS REPORT. Main/Corp** Oak Ridge National Laboratory. Metals and Ceramics Division. (197?)-. English. an. Free on request. Oak Ridge National Laboratory / Tennessee, Box X, Building 4508, Room 203, Oak Ridge TN 37831. **Tel** (615)574-6755.

UK/0266-7185
**METALS AND MATERIALS (BURY ST. EDMONDS).** ***Title Change.*** (METALS AND MATERIALS : THE JOURNAL OF THE INSTITUTE OF METALS.). [Met. mater.]. **Added/Corp** Institute of Metals. Vol. 1 No. 1 (Jan. 1985)-Vol. 8 No. 12 (Dec. 1992). Academic Scholarly Publication. English. mo. The Institute of Materials, 1 Carlton House Terrace, London SW1Y 5DB England. **Tel** 011 44 71 839 4071, FAX (071)839 2078. **LC** TN1; .M51543. **DD** 669/.005. **CODEN** MMIMEQ. available on microfilm from University Microfilms International (UMI). Documents available from Article Express International, The Genuine Article, CASDDS. ***Formed by the union of** Metallurgist and Materials Technologist, 0306-526X **and** Metals Society World, 0265-2722. **Merged with** Plastics and Rubber International, 0309-4561 **and** British Ceramic, Transactions and Journal, 0266-7606 **to form** Materials World, 0967-8638.*
**Desc:** Encompasses every aspect of the science, manufacturing technology, and use of all engineering materials including metals, ceramics, polymers and composites. Contains authoritative technical articles describing developments in metallic and non-metallic materials, their manufacture and applications. Also includes industrial and research news, updates on new products and equipment, conference and exhibition events and institute news.
**Ind/Abst** Art Archaeol. Tech. Abstr.; Chem. Abstr. (1985-); Curr. Technol. Index; Curr. Titles Electrochem.; Ei Page One; Eng. Index Annu.; Res. Alert [Full Cov.].

UK
**METALS & MINERALS ANNUAL REVIEW. See** Engineering-Mines and Mining Engineering.

II/0026-0959
**METALS AND MINERALS REVIEW.** [Met. miner. rev.]. (1962)-. Academic Scholarly Publication. English. Twelve times a year. $30.00. Pandeya Publications, Block F 105C New Alipore, Calcutta 700053 India. **LC** TN600; .M47. **DD** 669/.005. **CODEN** MEMRAZ. Documents available from CASDDS.
**Ind/Abst** Chem. Abstr. (1962-1979); Coal Abstr.; Energy Res. Abstr. (Sept. 1974-); GeoRef.

UK
**METALS FINANCE.** (19??)-. Trade Publication. English. mo. £500.00 UK; $850.00 US. Metal Bulletin PLC, PO Box 28E, Worcester Park, Surrey KT4 7HX England. **Tel** 011 44 71 827 9977, FAX 011 44 81 337 8943.

UK/0265-8321
**METALS INDUSTRY NEWS.** Vol. 1, No. 1 (Sept. 1984)-. Periodical. English. qt. £35.00 UK; £48.00, $86.50 other. Argus Press Group, Queensway House, 2 Queensway Redhill, Surrey RH1 1QS England. **Tel** 011 44 737 768611, 011 44 737 761685, FAX 011 44 737 760510, telex 948669 TOPJNL G. available on an online database (file 648/Full-Text) from DIALOG.
**Ind/Abst** Curr. Technol. Index; Trade Ind. ASAP [Full Txt.]; Trade Ind. Index [Full Txt.].

II/0970-423X
**METALS MATERIALS AND PROCESSES. See** Engineering-Materials Engineering and Mechanics.

US/0026-0975
**METALS WEEK.** ***Title Change.*** [Metals week]. (1967)-(1993). Periodical. English. wk. McGraw Hill Publishing Company, Inc., 1221 Avenue of the Americas, New York NY 10020. **Tel** (212)512-6410, (800)525-5003, FAX (212)512-6111. **LC** HD9506.A1; E2. **DD** 338. available on microfilm and microfiche from University Microfilms International (UMI); available on an online database (file 624/Full-Text) from DIALOG. ***Continues** E and M J Metal and Mineral Markets. **Continued by** Platt's Metals Week, 1076-3937.*
**Ind/Abst** GeoRef (?-199?); Leadscan (?-?); NEXIS (Jan. 5, 1981-?); Trade Ind. Index (?-?).

US/0363-1702
**METALS WEEK PRICE HANDBOOK.**
(19??)-. English (French, German and Italian). an. $210.00. Standard & Poor's Corporation, 25 Broadway, New York NY 10004. **Tel** (212)208-8775. **(Subscription address:** McGraw Hill, 1221 Avenue of the Americas, 41st Floor, New York NY 10020.**) LC** HD9506.U6; M453. **DD** 338.4/3671/0973. available on microfilm from University Microfilms International (UMI).

●BL
**METALURGIA & MATERIAIS / ABM.**
**Added/Corp** Associacao Brasileira de Metalurgia e Materiais. **VFOAT** Metalurgia e Materiais. Vol. 48, No. 405 (May 1992)-. Academic Scholarly Publication. Portuguese (summaries and/or abstracts in English). Twelve times a year. $65.00. Association Brasileira de Metais, rua Antonio Compartado 218, 04605 Sao Paulo SP Brazil. **Tel** 011531 5333. **LC** TN4; .M358. **DD** 669/.05. **CODEN** MEATEJMEMTEB. Documents available from CASDDS. ***Continues** Metalurgia, 0026-0983.*
**Ind/Abst** Alum. Ind. Abstr.; Art Archaeol. Tech. Abstr.; Bioeng. Abstr.; Chem. Abstr.; Coal Abstr.; Met. Abstr.

RM/0461-9579
**METALURGIA (BUCURESTI).**
(METALURGIA.). [Metalurgia]. **Added/Corp** Romania. Ministerul Metalurgiei si Constructiilor de Masini. Consiliul National al Inginerilor si Tehnicienilor din R.P.R. Romania. Ministerul Industriei Metalurgice. Consiliul National al Inginerilor si Tehnicienilor din Republica SocialistEa Romania. Vol. 15, No. 4 (Apr. 1963)-. Periodical. Romanian (summaries and/or abstracts in English, French, German and Russian). mo. $122.00. **(Subscription address:** Orion Press SRL, SPL Independentei 202-A, Bucharest 6 Romania.**) LC** TN4; .M3722. **CODEN** MTURAA. Documents available from Article Express International, CASDDS. ***Continues in part** Metalurgia si Constructia de Masini.*
**Ind/Abst** Bioeng. Abstr.; Ceram. Abstr. (19??-); Chem. Abstr. (19??-1989); Coal Abstr.; Ei Page One; Eng. Index Annu. [Select. Cov.]; Saf. Health Work.

PE
**METALURGIA (LIMA, PERU).** (METALURGIA / AIMP, ASOCIACION DE INGENIEROS METALURGISTAS DEL PERU.). Vol. 1, No. 1 (1980)-. Spanish. **LC** Discard.

BL/0026-0983
**METALURGIA (SAO PAULO).** ***Title Change.*** (METALURGIA.). [Metalurgia]. **Added/Corp** Associacao Brasileira de Metais. Vol. 21 No. 86-Vol. 48 No. 404 (Jan. 1965-April 1992). Academic Scholarly Publication. Portuguese (English). mo. Associagao Brasileira de Metais, rua Antonio Comparato 218, 04605 Sao Paulo SP Brazil. **Tel** (011)531-5333, FAX (011)240-4273, telex (011)57116. **ED** Maria Da Luz and N P Calegari. **LC** TN4; .M358. **CODEN** MABMA5. Index available. **Bk Rev. Ad Acc.** ctrl circ. available on microfilm and microfiche from University Microfilms International (UMI). Documents available from Article Express International, CASDDS. ***Formed by the union of** A.B.M. Boletim **and** A.B.M. Noticiario. **Continued by** Metalurgia & Materiais.*
**Desc:** Studies in the field of ferrous and nonferrous metallurgy.
**Ind/Abst** Alum. Ind. Abstr.; Art Archaeol. Tech. Abstr.; Bioeng. Abstr.; Chem. Abstr.; Coal Abstr.; Ei Page One; Eng. Mater. Abstr. (19??-19??); Eng. Index Annu.; Met. Abstr.

SP/0026-0991
**METALURGIA Y ELECTRICIDAD.** [Metal. electr.]. (1937)-. Academic Scholarly Publication. Spanish. Eleven times a year (monthly with July/Aug. issue combined). 9775ptas (one year), 17250ptas (two years) Spain & Portugal; 15500ptas (one year), 29000ptas (two years) other. Metalurgia Y Electricidad SL, C A Gonzalez Porras 35-37 2DO, 28019 Madrid Spain. **Tel** 011 34 1 4690420 0561, FAX 011 34 1 4690304. **LC** T4; .M4. **DD** 669.05. **CODEN** MYELAF. **Bk Rev. Ad Acc, Adv Mgr:** Antonio Recio Cuevas. **Pr Rev. Circ:** 5,000 (ctrl). Documents available from Ask*IEEE, CASDDS.
**Desc:** Technical journal of metallurgy, equipment, electricity, electronics, instrumentation and control.
**Ind/Abst** Alum. Ind. Abstr.; Chem. Abstr. (1937-1983); Eng. Mater. Abstr.; INSPEC (Sept. 1968-); Met. Abstr.

YU/0543-5846
**METALURGIJA : CASOPIS FAKULTETA, INSTITUTA I ZELJEZARE SISAK.**
**Added/Corp** Tehnoloski Fakultet u Zagrebu. Institut za Metalurgiju i Zeljezare Sisak. (196?)-. Serbo-Croatian (Roman). qt. **LC** WMLC L 83/5416. Documents available from CASDDS.
**Ind/Abst** Chem. Abstr.

AT
**METALWORKING AUSTRALIA.** (19??)-. English. bm (6 issues). 33.00Aus$ Australia; 48.00Aus$ New Zealand, Papua New Guinea; 51.00Aus$ Malaysia, Indonesia, Fiji; 54.00Aus$ Japan, India, Hong Kong; 61.00Aus$ US, Canada, Lebanon; 67.00Aus$ Europe, Africa, former USSR. Thomson Publications / Australia, 47 Chippen Street, Chippendale New South Wales, 2008 Australia. **Tel** 011 61 2 6992411, FAX 011 61 2 698 3920, telex 122226. **(Subscription address:** Thomson Publications Australia, PO Box 815, Strawberry Hills, New South Wales, 2012 Australia.**)** ***Continues** Sheet Metal Australia.*

US/0026-1009
**METALWORKING DIGEST.** [Metalw. dig.]. (19??)-. Periodical. English. mo. $48.00 US; $54.00 Canada and Mexico; $72.00 (surface mail), $112.00 (airmail) other. Cahners Publishing Company, 249 West 17th Street, New York NY 10011. **Tel** (212)645-0067, FAX (212)242-6987. **(Subscription address:** Gordon Publications, Inc., Paid Circulation Department, 301 Gibralter Drive, Box 650, Morris Plains NJ 07950-0650.**) DD** 671. **[CCC].** ***Continues** Industrial Digest.*
**Desc:** Focuses on metalworking plants manufacturing end-products by means of cutting and/or forming-type machine tools and allied equipment.

US/1051-1407
**METALWORKING DISTRIBUTOR, THE.**
***Ceased.*** [Metalwork. distrib.]. **VFOAT** Metal Working Distributor. Vol. 2, No. 1 (Winter 1990)-(19??). Periodical. English. mo. Penton Publishing, 1100 Superior Avenue, Cleveland OH 44114-2543. **Tel** (216)696-7000, FAX (216)696-0836. **LC** HD9506.U6; M454. **DD** 658. ***Continues in part** American Machinist (Cleveland, Ohio), 1041-7958.*

JA/0911-9647
**METALWORKING, ENGINEERING AND MARKETING.** [Metalwork. eng. mark.]. (1979)-. Periodical. English. Four times a yearFour times a year. $25.00 (surface mail); $50.00 (airmail). New Digest Publishing Company Ltd., 3-5-3 Uchiyama, Chikusa ku Nagoya 464 Japan. **Tel** 052-732-2455, FAX 052-732-2459. **ED** Shigeru Kobayashi. **DD** 621.9. ctrl circ.

JA
**METALWORKING ENGINEERING AND MARKETING.** Vol. 1, No. 1 (July 1979)-. Periodical. English. qt. $25.00. News Digest Publishing Company Ltd., 3-5-3 Uchiyama, Chikusa-ku Nagoya 464 Japan. **Tel** 052 732 2455, telex J5954 NEWSDIGT. **(Subscription address:** Maruzen Company Ltd., PO Box 5050, Import & Export Department, Tokyo 100 31 Japan.**) LC** TS200; .M4745. **DD** 671/.05. **Ad Acc. Circ:** 48,000.
**Ind/Abst** Eng. Mater. Abstr.; Pollut. Abstr. Indexes; Robotics Abstr.

US/0885-3827
**METALWORKING MACHINERY.** ***Title Change.*** (CURRENT INDUSTRIAL REPORTS. MQ-35W, METALWORKING MACHINERY / U.S. DEPARTMENT OF COMMERCE, BUREAU OF THE CENSUS.). [Metalwork. mach.]. **Added/Corp** United States. Bureau of the Census. United States. Bureau of Domestic Commerce. **VFOAT** Metalworking Machinery. (19??)-(1992). English. qt. Superintendent of Documents, US Government Printing Office, Washington DC 20402. **Tel** (202)275-3328, FAX (202)786-2377. **LC** HD9506.U6; C87. **DD** 380.1/456817671/0973021. Documents available from Documents on Demand. ***Continued by*** *Current Industrial Reports. MQ35W, Metalworking Machinery (Computer File).*
**Desc:** Presents tables and statistics based on a survey of manufacturers on the total production, value, shipment, and consumption of various products manufactured by industries in the United States-Metalworking Machinery.
**Ind/Abst** Am. Stat. Index (19??-19??).

US/0885-3827
**METALWORKING MACHINERY.** (CURRENT INDUSTRIAL REPORTS. MQ-35W, METALWORKING MACHINERY / U.S. DEPARTMENT OF COMMERCE, BUREAU OF THE CENSUS. [COMPUTER FILE.]). [Metalwork. mach.]. **Added/Corp** United States. Bureau of the Census. United States. Bureau of Domestic Commerce. **VFOAT** Metalworking Machinery. (1992)-. English. qt. $7.00 domestic; $8.75 other. Superintendent of Documents, US Government Printing Office, Washington DC 20402. **Tel** (202)275-3328, FAX (202)786-2377. **LC** HD9506.U6; C87. **DD** 380.1/456817671/0973021.
**Desc:** Presents tables and statistics based on a survey of manufacturers on the total production, value, shipment, and consumption of various products manufactured by industries in the United States-Metalworking Machinery.

US
**METALWORKING MACHINERY / U.S. DEPARTMENT OF COMMERCE, BUREAU OF THE CENSUS. See** Engineering-Mechanical Engineering and Machinery.

UK/0026-1033
**METALWORKING PRODUCTION.** [Metalwork. prod.]. (1955)-. English. mo. £72.00 UK and Northern Ireland; $175.00 other. Morgan Grampian, 40 Beresford Street Woolwich, London SE18 6BQ England. **Tel** 011 44 81 855 7777, FAX 011 44 81 855 5548, telex 896238. **[CCC].** available on microfilm and microfiche from University Microfilms International (UMI). Documents available from Article Express International, Ask*IEEE. ***Continues*** *Machinist.*
**Ind/Abst** Ei Page One; Eng. Index Annu. [Select. Cov.]; INSPEC (June 1968-July 1989); World Text. Abstr.

US/0275-6943
**METALWORKING SALES LEADS.** (METALWORKING SALES LEADS: MSL.). **VFOAT** MSL. No. 43 (Mar. 26, 1981)-. Periodical. English. Twenty-four times a year. $597.00. McGraw Hill Publishing Company, Inc., 1221 Avenue of the Americas, New York NY 10020. **Tel** (212)512-6410, (800)525-5003, FAX (212)512-6111. **ED** Dale H. Kroll. **Circ:** 100. ***Continues*** *Industry Mart's Metalworking Construction Report/MCR, 0193-3132.*
**Desc:** Newsletter reporting new construction and expansions of metalworking plants throughout the United States.

FR/0026-1084
**METAUX. CORROSION INDUSTRIE.** (METAUX.). [Met., Corros. ind.]. Vol. 26, No. 305; Jan. 1951-. Periodical. French. 360.00F. Editions Metaux, 32 rue du Marechal Joffre, 78100 St Germn en Laye France. **Tel** 33 3 451 6211. **LC** TA462; .M43. **DD** 620.1/1223. **UDC** 620.19. **CODEN** MTUXAS. Documents available from Article Express International, CASDDS. ***Formed by the union of*** *Metaux et Industries* ***and*** *Metaux & Corrosion.*
**Ind/Abst** Alum. Ind. Abstr.; Bioeng. Abstr.; Chem. Abstr.; Ei Page One; Eng. Mater. Abstr.; Eng. Index Annu.; Met. Abstr.; Surf. Treat. Technol. Abstr.

US/0026-1297
**METLFAX. VFOAT** Metlfax Magazine. (19??)-. Periodical. English. mo. $45.00 US; $65.00 Canada and Mexico; $95.00 other. Huebcore Communications Inc., 1355 Mendiota Heights, Suite 210, Mendiota Heights MN 55120. **Tel** (612)686-0303. **(Subscription address:** Huebcore Communications Inc., 29100 Aurora Road, Suite 200, Solon OH 44139.**) ED** Thomas H. Dreher. **[CCC]. Bk Rev. Ad Acc. Circ:** 107,000 (ctrl).
**Desc:** Product news for the metalworking field.

CN/0705-2081
**METRIC STEEL. BULLETIN.** (ACIER METRIQUE.). **VFOAT** Metric Steel. **VAT** Bulletin. Acier Metrique. V. 1- Feb. 1974-. Periodical. English (French). Free. Task Force for Metric Conversion in the Canadian Iron and Steel Industry, PO Box 4248 Station D, Hamilton Ontario L8V 4L6 Canada. **DD** 672.8. **UDC** 672.8. ctrl circ.

NE/0168-342X
**METTALBEWERKINGSMACHINE - INDUSTRIE EN MACHINEGEREEDSCHAPPENFABRIEK EN / CENTRAAL BUREAU VOOR DE STATISTIED, HOOFDAFDELING STATISTIEKEN VAN INDUSTRIE EN BOUWNIFVERHEID. See** Engineering-Mechanical Engineering and Machinery.

US/0361-1213
**MICROSTRUCTURAL SCIENCE.** [Microstruct. sci.]. **Main/Corp** International Metallographic Society. **Added/Corp** International Metallographic Society. American Society for Metals. ASM International. Vol. 1 (1972)-. Academic Scholarly Publication. English. ir. Price varies per volume. International Mettalographic Society, PO Box 2489, Columbus OH 43216. **Tel** (614)276-0248. **LC** TN689.2; .I552a. **DD** 669/.95/05. **CODEN** MSSCDJ. **[CCC].** Documents available from Article Express International, CASDDS. ***Continues*** *International Microstructural Analysis Society. Proceedings: Annual Technical Meeting.*
**Ind/Abst** Bioeng. Abstr.; Chem. Abstr.; Coal Abstr.; Ei Page One; Eng. Index Annu.

BL/0100-6908
**MINERACAO METALURGIA (1968).** (MINERACAO METALURGIA.). [Min. metal.]. Vol. 47, No. 281 (May 1968)-. Academic Scholarly Publication. Portuguese. mo. $100.00. Editora Scorpia Ltda, Rua do Catete 202 Grupo 301, CP 22220 Rio de Janeiro Brazil. **ED** Wilson Costa. **CODEN** MINMAJ. **Bk Rev. Ad Acc. Circ:** 15,000. Documents available from CASDDS. ***Continues*** *Engenharia, Mineracao, Metalurgia.*
**Desc:** Unpublished matters with technical subjects by well-known authors and professionals in the mining and metallurgical industry.
**Ind/Abst** Alum. Ind. Abstr.; Chem. Abstr.; Coal Abstr.; Eng. Mater. Abstr.; GeoRef; Met. Abstr.

AT/0818-4968
**MINERAL POLICY ISSUES OCCASIONAL PAPER.** [Miner. policy issues occas. pap.]. **Added/Corp** Australia. Dept. of Resources and Energy. (1986)-. Monographic series. English. ir. Price varies per volume. Australian Bureau of Statistics, PO Box 10, Belconnen Australian Capital Territory, 2616 Australia. **Tel** 011 61 6 2527911, FAX 011 61 6 2516009. **DD** 354.94008238.
**Ind/Abst** AESIS Q.

UK/0882-7508
**MINERAL PROCESSING AND EXTRACTIVE METALLURGY REVIEW. See** Engineering-Mines and Mining Engineering.

UK
**MINERAL SANDS REPORT.** (19??)-. Trade Publication. English. bm. £180.00 UK; $299.00 US, Canada & South America. Metal Bulletin PLC, PO Box 28E, Worcester Park, Surrey KT4 7HX England. **Tel** 011 44 71 827 9977, FAX 011 44 81 337 8943.

US/0747-9182
**MINERALS & METALLURGICAL PROCESSING.** [Miner. metall. process.]. **Added/Corp** Society of Mining Engineers of AIME. **VFOAT** Minerals and Metallurgical Processing. Vol. 1, No. 1 (May 1984)-. Academic Scholarly Publication. English. Four times a year (Feb., May, Aug., Oct.). $90.00 (surface mail), $115.00 (airmail). Society for Mining, Metallurgy and Exploration Inc, 8307 Shaffer Parkway, Littleton CO 80162. **Tel** (303)973-9550, FAX (303)973-3845, telex 881988. **(Subscription address:** Society Mining Metallurgy & Exploration, PO Box 625002, Littleton CO 80162.**) ED** Roshan B. Bhappu. **DD** 669. **CODEN** MMPRE8. Index available. **Bk Rev. Ad Acc. Circ:** 685. available on microfilm from University Microfilms International (UMI). Documents available from Article Express International, CASDDS.
**Desc:** Technical journal documents and disseminates new technological information dealing with the various methods for processing all types of minerals, metals and energy materials.
**Ind/Abst** AESIS Q.; Chem. Abstr. (1984-); Coal Abstr.; Ei Page One; Eng. Index Annu.; MINPROC; Soils Fert.

AT/0727-3800
**MINERALS INDUSTRY SURVEY.** [Miner. ind. surv.]. (1978)-. English. an. **DD** 338.0994.
**Ind/Abst** AESIS Q.

UK
**MINING DATABASE.** ***Title Change.*** **See** Engineering-Mines and Mining Engineering.

SA
**MINTEK RESEARCH DIGEST. Added/Corp** Council for Mineral Technology (South Africa). **VFOAT** Mintek Research Digest. No. 1 (Jan. 1982)-. Periodical. English. bm (6 issues). Free on request. Mintek, Private Bag X3015, Randburg 2125 South Africa. **Tel** 011 27 11 7933511, FAX 011 27 11 7932413, telex 4-24867. **ED** H. W. Glen. **Circ:** 1,000 (ctrl). ***Continues*** *NIM Research Digest.*
**Ind/Abst** AESIS Q.

GW/0722-7736
**MITTEILUNGEN AUS DEM AUSSCHUSS FUER PULVERMETALLURGIE.** [Mitt. Ausschuss Pulvermetall.]. **Added/Corp** Ausschuss fuer Pulvermetallurgie (Germany : West). Nr. 1 (Feb. 1982)-. Academic Scholarly Publication. German. qt. Verlag Schmid Journals GmbH, Postfach 6609, Hofackerstr 92, D 79042 Freiburg 1 Germany. **Tel** 011 49 761 82057, FAX 011 49 761 84863, telex 761 403 CARNEWS D. **CODEN** MAPUDY. Documents available from CASDDS.
**Ind/Abst** Chem. Abstr.

II/0378-6366
**MMR, MINERALS & METALS REVIEW.** [MMR, Miner. met. rev.]. **Added/Corp** Asian Industry & Information Services. **VFOAT** Minerals & Metals Review. **VAT** MMR. Minerals and Metals Review. Vol. 1 (July 1975)-. Academic Scholarly Publication. English. mo. $50.00. Minerals & Metals Review, 28/30 Anantwadi, PO Box 2749, Bombay 400002 India. **Tel** 314003. **(Subscription address:** Prints India, 11 Darya Ganj, New Delhi, 110002 India, (Phone: 011 91 11 3268645)**) ED** Kumar Subramanian. **LC** TN1; .M17. **DD** 338.4/7669/00954. **CODEN** MMREDC. **Bk Rev. Ad Acc. Circ:** 3,000. Documents available from CASDDS. ***Supersedes*** *Eastern Metals Review.*
**Ind/Abst** Alum. Ind. Abstr.; Ceram. Abstr.; Chem. Abstr.; Met. Abstr.

II/0377-1482
**MMTC NEWS. See** Economics-Industry and Production.

US/0277-9951
**MODERN APPLICATIONS NEWS.** (MODERN APPLICATIONS NEWS : MAN / FOUNDED BY THE AMERICAN SOCIETY FOR METALS.). [Mod. appl. news]. **Added/Corp** American Society for Metals. **VFOAT** MAN. Vol. 13 No. 5 (Oct. 1979)-. Periodical. English. Twelve times a year. $93.00 US; $104.00 Canada; $110.00 other; $85.00 (airmail) Brazil, Bulgaria, England, Czechoslovakia, Finland, France, Holland, Italy, Norway, Spain, Switzerland, Germany, North Africa, Caribbean, South America; $105.00 (airmail) Australia, India, Israel, Japan, Korea, Singapore, Taiwan, former USSR, Hong Kong, New Zealand, South Africa, Middle East. Nelson Publishing, 2504 North Tamiami Trail, Nokomis FL 34275. **Tel** (813)966-9521, FAX (813)966-2590. **ED** A. Verner Nelson. **DD** 669. **[CCC]. Bk Rev. Ad Acc. Circ:** 60,000 (ctrl). ***Continues*** *Modern Applications News for Design and Manufacturing, 0026-7473.*
**Desc:** Serves companies that design, develop and manufacture products in the metalworking field. SICs covered included 3300, 3400, 3500, 3600, 3700, 3800, 3900, 7300 and other SICs allied to the field.

US/0026-7562
**MODERN CASTING.** [Mod. cast.]. **Added/Corp** American Foundrymen's Society. Vol. 50, No. 1 (July 1966)-. Academic Scholarly Publication. English. mo. $40.00 US, Canada & Mexico, $50.00 others (surface mail); $75.00 (airmail) other. American Foundrymen's Society, 505 State Street, Des Plaines IL 60016-2277. **Tel** (708)824-0181, (800)537-4237, FAX (708)824-7848. **ED** David P. Kanicki. **LC** TS200; .A7527. **CODEN** MOCAB5. **[CCC].** Index available. **Bk Rev. Ad Acc. Circ:** 24,000 (ctrl). available on microfilm and microfiche from University Microfilms International (UMI); available on an online database (file 648/Full-Text) from DIALOG. Documents available from Article Express International, CASDDS. ***Continues*** *Metalcaster, 0894-0843.*
**Desc:** Published for producers of metal castings. Covers all technical management, marketing and operating aspects of foundry production. Special emphasis on latest technologies.
**Ind/Abst** AESIS Q.; Alum. Ind. Abstr.; Appl. Sci. Technol. Index; Bioeng. Abstr.; Ceram. Abstr.; Chem. Abstr.; Ei Page One; EMBASE; Eng. Mater. Abstr.; Eng. Index Annu.; F&S Index Plus Text, Int. [Select. Cov.]; Met. Abstr.; PROMT; Surf. Treat. Technol. Abstr.; Trade Ind. ASAP [Full Txt.]; Trade Ind. Index [Full Txt.].

CN/0380-2299
**MODERN FINISHING METHODS.** 1st- Ed.; 1966-. English. Canadian Paint and Finishing, 481 University Avenue, Toronto Ontario M5W 1A7 Canada. **Tel** (416)596-5714. **ED** Nick Hancock. **DD** 667/.9/05.

UDC 621.7. **Ad Acc. Circ:** 15,500 (ctrl).
**Desc:** Covers machinery, machine tools, fabricating, foundries, stamping, mold-making, tool-and-die, CADICAM, metalworking in general, industrial surface finishing, and welding.

US/0026-8127
**MODERN METALS.** [Mod. met.]. (1945)-. Academic Scholarly Publication. English. mo. $70.00. Trend Publishing Inc, 625 North Michigan Avenue, Suite 2500, Chicago IL 60611-3109. **Tel** (312)654-2300, FAX (312)654-2323. **LC** TS200; .M63. **DD** 671. **CODEN** MOMLAJ. available on microfilm and microfiche from University Microfilms International (UMI). Documents available from Article Express International, CASDDS.
**Ind/Abst** Alum. Ind. Abstr.; Appl. Sci. Technol. Index; Bioeng. Abstr.; Chem. Abstr.; Ei Page One; EMBASE; Eng. Mater. Abstr.; Eng. Index Annu.; Int. Packag. Abstr.; Met. Abstr.; Surf. Treat. Technol. Abstr.

US/0163-1888
**MOLYBDENUM MOSAIC.** [Molybdenum mosaic]. **Added/Corp** Climax Molybdenum Company. Vol. 1, No. 3 (Spring 1976)-. Academic Scholarly Publication. English. Twice a year. Amax Metals Group / Amax Materials Research Center, PO Box 1568, Ann Arbor MI 48105. **Tel** (203)629-6400. **LC** WMLC L 83/9254. **DD** 669. **CODEN** MMOSD5. Documents available from Article Express International, CASDDS. ***Continues** Mosaic, 0364-0639.*
**Ind/Abst** Alum. Ind. Abstr.; Bioeng. Abstr.; Chem. Abstr. (1976-1983); Ei Page One; Eng. Index Annu.; Met. Abstr.

FR/0544-8379
**MONOGRAPHIES TECHNIQUES SUR L'UTILISATION DES ACIERS SPECIAUX.** **VFOAT** Aciers Speciaux; Aciers Speciaux, Monographies Techniques. Academic Scholarly Publication. French. ir. Price varies per volume. Editions S E M A S, 1 rue Paul Cezanne, BP 710-08, 75360 Paris Cedex 08 France. **Tel** (1)45 63 17 10, FAX (1)45 61 02 91, telex 280172 FRASI A. **UDC** 669.18. **CODEN** MTUAAR. Documents available from CASDDS.
**Ind/Abst** Chem. Abstr. (1963-1981).

●US/1061-6071
**MONOGRAPHS IN P/M SERIES.** **Added/Corp** Metal Powder Industries Federation. **VFOAT** Monographs in P M Series. (1992)-. Monographic series. English. ir. Price varies per monograph. Metal Powder Industries Federation, 105 College Road East, Princeton NJ 08540. **Tel** (609)452-7700, FAX (609)987-8523, telex 510 685 2516. Index available ((bound in each monograph)). **Pr Rev. Circ:** 1,000.
**Desc:** This series is targeted to supply a detailed tutorial of the technologies of powder metallurgy, emphasizing both scientific principles and commercial applications. Each monograph provides a concise, yet thorough detailed treatment of a particular subject area.

JA/0497-1140
**MONTHLY REPORT OF THE IRON & STEEL STATISTICS.** **See** Metals and Metallurgy-Abstracting, Bibliographies and Statistics.

SA
**N I M RESEARCH DIGEST.** **Main/Corp** National Institute for Metallurgy. (1973)-. Periodical. English. bm. Council for Mineral Technology, Private Bag X3015, Randburg 2125 South Africa. **Tel** 011 27 11 7933511.

CC/1001-1935
**NAIHUO CAILIAO.** **VFOAT** Refractories. (1971)-. Periodical. Chinese. bm. $90.00. Yejin Bu / Luoyang Naihuo Cailiao Yanjiusuo, No. 43, Xiyuan lu, Jianxi-qu, Lucyang, Henan 471039, People's Republic of China. **Tel** 86 379 413501, FAX 86 379 413630. **ED** L. Jiehua. **DD** 666.72. **Circ:** 8,500. Documents available from CASDDS.
**Desc:** Covers refractory business in China.
**Ind/Abst** Ceram. Abstr. (199?-).

US/0363-1737
**NATIONAL METAL WORKING BLUE BOOK.** **VFOAT** Metal Working Blue Book. English. National Blue Books Inc, 20929-3 Roscoe Boulevard, Canoga Park CA 91304. **LC** TS203; .N36. **DD** 338.4/7/671302573. **UDC** 338.3:672(73).

RU/0579-8620
**NAUCHNYE TRUDY.** **Main/Corp** Gosudarstvennyi Nauchno-Issledovatelskii i Proektnyi Institut Redkometallicheskoi Promyshlennosti. (1961)-. Academic Scholarly Publication. Russian. Documents available from CASDDS. ***Continues** Gosudarstvennyi Nauchno-Issledovatelskii i Proektnyi Institut Redkometallicheskoi Promyshlennosti. Sbornik Nauchnykh Trudov.*
**Ind/Abst** Chem. Abstr.

RU/0131-5145
**NAUCHNYE TRUDY (MOSKOVSKII INSTITUT STALI I SPLAVOV).** (NAUCHNYE TRUDY - MOSKOVSKII INSTITUT STALI I SPLAVOV.). [Naucn. tr. - Mosk. inst. stali splavov]. **Added/Corp** Moskovskii Institut Stali i Splavov. No. 74 (1972)-. Academic Scholarly Publication. Russian. 0.85rub (single issue). Izdatelstvo Metallurgiia, 2-i Obydenskii Per.14, G-34, Moscow Russia. **LC** TN730; .M62. **CODEN** NTMSDL. Documents available from CASDDS. ***Continues** Moskovskii Institut Stali I Splavov. Sbornik.*
**Ind/Abst** Chem. Abstr. (?-1983).

RU/0028-2448
**NEFTJANOE HOZJAJSTVO.** (NEFTIANOE KHOZIAISTVO.). [Neftjano hoz.]. **Added/Corp** Soviet Union. Ministerstvo Neftianoi Promyshlennosti Vostochnykh Raionov. Soviet Union. Ministerstvo Neftianoi Promyshlennosti Iuzhnykh i Zapadnykh Raionov. Soviet Union. Ministerstvo Neftianoi Promyshlennosti. Nauchno-Tekhnicheskoe Obshchestvo Neftianoi i Gazovoi Promyshlennosti Imeni I.M. Gubkina. Tsentralnoe Pravlenie. (1945)-. Academic Scholarly Publication. Russian (summaries and/or abstracts in English). mo. $109.95. Izdatelstvo Nedra, 3 Pl Belorusskogo Vakzala, 125047 Moscow Russia. **Tel** 250-52-55. **(Subscription address:** East View Publications Inc., 3020 Harbor Lane North, Suite 110, Minneapolis MN 55447.**) LC** TN860; .N465. **CODEN** NEKHA6. **[CCC].** available on microfilm from University Microfilms International (UMI). Documents available from Article Express International, The Genuine Article, CASDDS. ***Continues** Neftianaia Promyshlennost SSSR.*
**Ind/Abst** Bioeng. Abstr.; Chem. Abstr.; Ei Page One; Energy Res. Abstr.; Eng. Index Annu.; GeoRef; Res. Alert [Select. Cov.]; SCISEARCH; Soc. Sci. Cit. Index [Select. Cov.].

JA/0288-0490
**NETSU SHORI.** [Netsu shori]. **Added/Corp** Nihon Netsu Shori Gijutsu Kyokai. (1960)-. Academic Scholarly Publication. Japanese. bm. $120.00. Japan Society for Heat Treatment, Shinsen Building, 8-2 Shinsen-cho, Shibuya-ku, Tokyo 150 Japan. **(Subscription address:** Kyowa Book Company Inc., 1-38 Kanda Jinbo-cho, Chiyoda-Ku Tokyo 101, Japan**) CODEN** NESHDF. Documents available from CASDDS.
**Ind/Abst** Chem. Abstr.

GW/0028-3207
**NEUE HUTTE.** ***Ceased.*** [Neue hutte]. Vol. 1, (Oct. 1955)-(1992). Academic Scholarly Publication. German. mo. DVG, Karl-Heine-Strasse 27, 0-7031 Leipzig Germany. **Tel** 0711 8931-128, FAX 0711 8931-298, telex 7 252 275 gtvd. **LC** TN3; .N4. **UDC** 669. **CODEN** NEUHAM. **Pr Rev.** Documents available from Article Express International, The Genuine Article, CASDDS. ***Supersedes** Metallurgie.*
**Ind/Abst** Alum. Ind. Abstr.; Bioeng. Abstr.; Ceram. Abstr. (19??-); Chem. Abstr.; Coal Abstr.; Curr. Contents Eng. Tech. Appl. Sci.; Ei Page One; Eng. Mater. Abstr.; Eng. Index Annu.; Leadscan; Met. Abstr.; Pollut. Abstr. Indexes; Res. Alert [Full Cov.]; Saf. Health Work; SCISEARCH.

●US/1074-1690
**NEW STEEL.** (IRON AGE NEW STEEL.). [New steel]. Vol. 1, No. 1 (Oct. 1993)-. Periodical. English. mo. $75.00 US; $90.00 Canada & Mexico; $150.00 other. Hitchcock Publishing Company, 191 South Gary Avenue, Carol Stream IL 60188. **Tel** (708)665-1000. **(Subscription address:** ABC Capital Cities, Inc., 825 7th Avenue, 7th Floor, New York NY 10019.**) LC** HD9510.1; .N4. **DD** 672. ***Continues** Iron Age (New York, N.Y. : 1987), 0897-4365.*
**Ind/Abst** Acad. Search (Oct. 1993-).

US/0730-7764
**NICKEL TOPICS (1966).** (NICKEL TOPICS.). [Nickel top.]. Vol. 19, No. 1-. Periodical. English. qt. Nickel Topics, International Nickel Company Inc, One New York Plaza, New York NY 10004. **LC** TN757.N5; I5. **DD** 673.7332/05. **UDC** 669.24. ***Continues** INCO Nickel Topics.*
**Ind/Abst** Fluid Abstr., Civil Eng.; Fluid Abstr. Proc. Eng.; FLUIDEX (1973-).

CN/0829-8351
**NICKEL (TORONTO).** (NICKEL.). [Nickel]. **Added/Corp** Nickel Development Institute (Canada). Vol. 1, No. 1 (Sept. 1985)-. Periodical. English (summaries and/or abstracts in French, German, Spanish and Japanese). qt (Mar., June, Sept., Dec.). Free upon request. Nickel Development Institute, 214 King Street West, Suite 510, Toronto, Ontario M5H 3S6 Canada. **Tel** (416)591-7999, FAX (416)591-7987. **ED** James S. Borland. **DD** 669/.7332/05. Index Available Received separately--bound from publisher. cum. index. **Circ:** 33,000.
**Ind/Abst** AESIS Q.

JA/0369-4747
**NIHON KINZOKU GAKKAI KAIHO.** [Nihon Kinzoku Gakkai kaiho]. **Added/Corp** Nihon Kinzoku Gakkai. **VFOAT** Bulletin of the Japan Institute of Metals. (1962)-. Academic Scholarly Publication. Japanese. mo. $310.00. Nihon Kinzoku Gakkai, (Japan Inst. of Metals), Aoba, Aramaki, Sendaishi, Miyagiken 980 Japan. **(Subscription address:** Maruzen Company Ltd., PO Box 5050, Import & Export Department, Tokyo 100 31 Japan.**) CODEN** NKZKAU. Documents available from CASDDS.
**Ind/Abst** Chem. Abstr.

JA/0021-4876
**NIPPON KINZOKU GAKKAISHI.** [Nippon Kinzoku Gakkaishi]. **Main/Corp** Nihon Kinzoku Gakkai. **Added/Corp** Nihon Kinzoku Gakkai. Journal of the Japan Institute of Metals. **VFOAT** Journal of the Japan Institute of Metals. Vol. 1 (May 1937)-. Academic Scholarly Publication. Japanese (summaries and/or abstracts in English). mo. $222.00. **(Subscription address:** Maruzen Company Ltd., PO Box 5050, Import & Export Department, Tokyo 100 31 Japan.**) CODEN** NIKGAV. **[CCC].** Documents available from Article Express International, The Genuine Article, Ask*IEEE, CASDDS. ***Continues** Nippon Kinzoku Gakkaishi. Series A, 0369-4607; Nippon Kinzoku Gakkaishi. Series B, 0369-4615.*
**Ind/Abst** Alum. Ind. Abstr.; Bioeng. Abstr.; Chem. Abstr.; Ei Page One; Eng. Index Annu.; INSPEC (Aug. 1971-); Int. Aerosp. Abstr.; Leadscan; Met. Abstr.; Res. Alert [Full Cov.]; Sci. Cit. Index; SCISEARCH.

JA/0546-1731
**NIPPON KOKAN TECHNICAL REPORT. OVERSEAS.** (TECHNICAL REPORT : OVERSEAS.). [Nippon Kokan Tech. rep. Overseas]. **Main/Corp** Nippon Kokan Kabushiki Kaisha. No. 1- June 1963-. Academic Scholarly Publication. English. an. Patent and License Department, Nippon Kokan K K 1-2, 1-chome Marunoucht Chiyoda-ku, Tokyo 100 Japan. **LC** TS300; .N56. **CODEN** NKTRAL. Documents available from Article Express International, CASDDS.
**Ind/Abst** Alum. Ind. Abstr.; Bioeng. Abstr.; Chem. Abstr.; Ei Page One; Eng. Mater. Abstr.; Eng. Index Annu.; Int. Aerosp. Abstr.; Met. Abstr.

JA/0048-0452
**NIPPON STEEL NEWS.** **Added/Corp** Shin Nihon Seitetsu Kabushiki Kaisha. No. 1 (1970)-. Periodical. English. mo. Free on request. Nippon Steel Corp, 630 Temachi Chiyoda-ku, Tokyo 100 Japan. **Tel** 011 81 3 3242 4111.
**Ind/Abst** Alum. Ind. Abstr.; Met. Abstr.; World Ceram. Abstr.

JA
**NIPPON STEEL TECHNICAL REPORT.** **Added/Corp** Shin Nihon Seitetsu Kabushiki Kaisha. **VFOAT** NSTR. No. 11 (1978)-. Periodical. English (Japanese). sa. Free on request. Nippon Steel Corp, 630 Temachi Chiyoda-ku, Tokyo 100 Japan. **Tel** 011 81 3 3242 4111. **CODEN** NSTTDI. Documents available from Article Express International. ***Continues** Nippon Steel Technical Report. Overseas.*
**Ind/Abst** Alum. Ind. Abstr.; Bioeng. Abstr.; Ceram. Abstr. (19??-); Corros. Abstr. (199?-); Ei Page One; Eng. Index Annu.; Environ. Eng. Abstr.; J. Ferrocement; Manuf. Process Eng. Abstr.; Mater. Sci. Eng. Abstr.; Mech. Eng. Abstr.; Met. Abstr.; Solid State Supercond. Abstr.; World Ceram. Abstr.

JA/0387-2327
**NISSHIN SEIKO GIHO.** [Nisshin Seiko giho]. **Added/Corp** Nisshin Seiko Kabushiki Kaisha. **VFOAT** Nisshin Steel Technical Report. (1959)-. Academic Scholarly Publication. Japanese (summaries and/or abstracts in English). sa. Nisshin Seiko K.K., (Nisshin Steel Co., Ltd.), 4-1, Marunouchi 3 Chome, Chiyodaku, Tokyoto 100, Japan. **CODEN** NISGA3. Documents available from CASDDS.
**Ind/Abst** Alum. Ind. Abstr.; Chem. Abstr.; Met. Abstr.

II/0027-6839
**NML TECHNICAL JOURNAL.** [NML tech. j.]. **Main/Corp** National Metallurgical Laboratory (India). **Added/Corp** National Metallurgical Laboratory (India). Technical Journal. **VAT** National Metallurgical Laboratory Technical Journal. Vol. 1 (Feb. 1959)-. Academic Scholarly Publication. English. qt. $20.00. National Metallurgical Laboratory, PO Burmamines, Jamshedpur 831 007, Bihar, India. **Tel** 26091, FAX 0657-27356, telex 0626-210. **(Subscription address:** Prints India, 11 Darya Ganj, New Delhi, 110002 India, (Phone: 011 91 11 3268645)**) ED** O N Mohanty. **LC** TN1; .N2. **DD** 669/.005. **CODEN** NLMJA3. **Bk Rev. Circ:** 300. Documents available from Article Express International, CASDDS.
**Desc:** Topics on research development work pertaining to metallurgy and allied areas are published in this journal.
**Ind/Abst** Alum. Ind. Abstr.; Bioeng. Abstr.; Ceram. Abstr.; Chem. Abstr.; Ei Page One; Eng. Mater. Abstr.; Eng. Index Annu.; Met. Abstr.; SEA Abstr.

FR
**NOMENCLATURE DE LA TECHNIQUE DES METAUX.** (19??)-. French. ir. 626.84F France; 690.00F others. Enterprises et Techniques, 5 bis rue Fontaine au Roi, 75011 Paris France. **Tel** 011 48 05 25 70, FAX 011 68 301 051 967.

US/0360-9553
**NON-FERROUS METAL DATA.** [Non-ferr. met. data]. **Added/Corp** American Bureau of Metal Statistics. (1974)-. English. an. $370.00. American Bureau of Metal Statistics, 400 Plaza Drive, PO Box 1405, Secaucus NJ 07094. **Tel** (201)863-6900. **LC** HD9506.U6; A37. **DD** 338.2/0973. **Circ:** 3,000. ***Continues** Year Book of the American Bureau of Metal Statistics.*
**Desc:** Contains data for five comparative years and over 180 statistical tables for mine, smelter, and refined production, consumption, inventories, imports, exports, published prices, and other essential metal statistics.
**Ind/Abst** Stat. Ref. Index.

UK/0078-0987
**NON-FERROUS METAL WORKS OF THE WORLD.** **VFOAT** Nonferrous Metal Works of the World. (1967)-. Directory. English. ir. price varies per volume. Metal Bulletin PLC, PO Box 28E, Worcester Park, Surrey KT4 7HX England. **Tel** 011 44 71 827 9977, FAX 011 44 81 337 8943. **ED** Richard Serjeantson. **LC** HD9539.A1; W62. **Ad Acc.** ***Continues** World's Non-Ferrous Smelters and Refineries.*
**Desc:** Detailed information on non-ferrous metal smelters, refiners, semi-fabricators and secondary info makers including head office address, management, ownership, processes, products, and raw materials used.

US
**NONFERROUS METALS ALERT.** Vol. 7 (Jan. 1991)-. Periodical. English. mo. $200.00 (subscribers of Metals Abstracts), $315.00 (nonsubscribers of Metals Abstracts) North America. American Society for Metals International, c/o Deborah Barthelmes, Materials Park OH 44073-0002. **Tel** (216)338-5151, FAX (216)338-4634, telex 980-619. **(Subscription address:** ASM International, Materials Information, Materials Park OH 44073.**)** ***Continues** Non Ferrous Alert.*

US/1062-0702
**NORTH AMERICAN STEEL MARKET OUTLOOK.** [N. Am. steel mark. outlook]. **Added/Corp** WEFA Group. (1991)-. English. qt. WEFA Group, 401 City Avenue, Suite 300, Bala Cynwyd PA 19004. **DD** 338. ***Continues** Steel Market Quarterly, 1056-022X.*

UK/0535-3378
**NOTES ON TIN.** ***Suspended.*** **Main/Corp** International Tin Council. No. 1, Mar. 1957-?. Periodical. English. mo. £18.00 UK; $27.58 US. International Tin Council, Haymarket House, 1 Oxendon Street, London SW1Y 4EQ England. **Tel** 011 44 71 930 0451, telex 918939. **UDC** 669.6. Index available. **Bk Rev. Circ:** 400. ***Supersedes** International Tin Study Group. Notes on Tin.*
**Desc:** World's press digest on tin prospecting, mining, smelting, recycling, trade, prices, market, government legislation, tinplate and other tin-using industries.

JA
**NRIM CREEP DATA SHEET.** [NRIM creep data sheet]. **VFOAT** Kinzoku Zairyo Gijutsu Kenkyujo Kuripu Deta Shito; N.R.I.M. Creep Data Sheet. **VAT** National Research Institute for Metals Creep Data Sheet. Began in 1972. Academic Scholarly Publication. English. ir. Price varies per volume. National Research Institute for Metals, 2-3-12 Nakameguro Meguro-ku, Tokyo 153 Japan. **CODEN** NCDSDR. Documents available from CASDDS.
**Ind/Abst** Alum. Ind. Abstr.; Chem. Abstr. (1972-1983); Eng. Mater. Abstr.; Met. Abstr.

GW/0029-7488
**OBERFLACHE.** (OBERFLACHE + I.E. UND JOT.). [Oberflache]. **VAT** Oberflache und Journal fur Oberflachen Technik. V. 17, No. 7- July 1977-. Academic Scholarly Publication. German. DM72.00. Bertelsmann Fachzeitschriften GmbH, Carl-Bertelsmann Strasse 270, D-33311 Frankfurt Germany. **Tel** 011 49 5241 802199. **LC** TS653.A1; O23. **UDC** 621.793/.795. **CODEN** OBJTDU. Documents available from CASDDS. ***Formed by the union of** Oberflache **and** Jot.*
**Ind/Abst** Alum. Ind. Abstr.; Art Archaeol. Tech. Abstr.; Chem. Abstr.; EMBASE; Energy Res. Abstr. (March 1982-); Met. Abstr.; Surf. Treat. Technol. Abstr.; World Surf. Coat. Abstr.

SZ/0048-1270
**OBERFLACHE - SURFACE.** ***Title Change.*** (OBERFLACHE.). [Oberfl. - Surf.]. **VFOAT** Surface. Issue 1 (Jan. 1968)-(19??). Academic Scholarly Publication. French (German). mo. SHZ Forster Fachverlag AG, Seestrasse 37, CH-8027 Zurich, Switzerland. **Tel** 011 41 1 202-2046, FAX 011 44 1 910-5155, telex 815 517. **ED** Jurgen Leudolph. **CODEN** OBSUA7. **Bk Rev. Ad Acc. Circ:** 4,150. Documents available from CASDDS. ***Continues** Galvanotechnik + Oberflachenschutz.* ***Continued by** Oberflaechen Werkstoffe.*
**Desc:** Covers electroplating and metals.
**Ind/Abst** Alum. Ind. Abstr.; Chem. Abstr.; EMBASE; Eng. Mater. Abstr.; Met. Abstr.; Surf. Treat. Technol. Abstr.

PL/0472-4313
**OBROBKA PLASTYCZNA.** [Obrob. plast.]. Vol. 1- 1959-. Academic Scholarly Publication. Polish (English; table of contents in Multiple languages). qt. **LC** TS200; .O36. **CODEN** OBPLAX. Documents available from CASDDS.
**Ind/Abst** Alum. Ind. Abstr.; Chem. Abstr.; Eng. Mater. Abstr.; Met. Abstr.

UK
**OCCASIONAL PAPERS OF THE INSTITUTION OF MINING AND METALLURGY.** **See** Engineering-Mines and Mining Engineering.

●US
**OCCUPATIONAL COMPENSATION SURVEY--PAY ONLY. NEW YORK, NEW YORK, METROPOLITAN AREA.** **Added/Corp** United States. Bureau of Labor Statistics. **VFOAT** New York, New York, Metropolitan Area. Apr. (1992)-. English. ***Continues** Area Wage Survey. New York, New York, Metropolitan Area (Washington, D.C. : 1989).*
**Desc:** Statistical survey of employee wages in the New York metropolitan area.

RU
**OCHISTKA VODNOGO I VOZDUSHNOGO BASSEINOV NA PREDORIIATIIAKH CHERNOI METALLURGII.** **Added/Corp** Vsesoiuznyi Nauchno-Issledovatelskii i Proektnyi Institut po Ochistke Tekhnologicheskikh Gazov, Stochnykh Vod i Ispolzovaniiu Vtorichnykh Aenergoresursov Predpriiatii Chernoi Metallurgii. (19??)-. Academic Scholarly Publication. Russian. 1.12rub (single issue). Izdatelstvo Metallurgiia, 2-i Obydenskii Per.14, G-34, Moscow Russia. **LC** TD899.M43; O24. **CODEN** OVVBA3. Documents available from CASDDS.
**Ind/Abst** Chem. Abstr. (1973-1981);(1972-1981).

US/0743-9784
**OFFICIAL PRICE GUIDE TO AMERICAN SILVER AND SILVER PLATE, THE.** **VFOAT** American Silver and Silver Plate; Silver. (19??)-. English. ir. $15.85 ($2.90 Shipping & Handling charges). Random House Inc., 400 Hahn Road, Westminster MD 21157. **Tel** (800)726-0600, (800)733-3000, FAX (800)659-2436. **LC** NK7112; .O38. **DD** 739.2/3773/0750973.

US/0748-1152
**OFFICIAL PRICE GUIDE TO POCKET KNIVES, THE.** **VFOAT** Pocket Knives; Knives. 1st Ed. (1984)-. English. an. $2.95. Random House Inc., 400 Hahn Road, Westminster MD 21157. **Tel** (800)726-0600, (800)733-3000, FAX (800)659-2436. **LC** TS380; .O35. **DD** 621.9/32. **UDC** 338.5:672.71(73).

RU/0369-7290
**OGNEUPORY.** [Ogneupory]. **Added/Corp** Soviet Union. Ministerstvo Chernoi Metallurgii. Nauchno-Tekhnicheskoe Obshchestvo Chernoi Metallurgii. Tsentralnoe Pravlenie. (1933)-. Academic Scholarly Publication. Russian. mo. $149.95. Izdatelstvo Metallurgiia, 2-i Obydenskii Per.14, G-34, Moscow Russia. **(Subscription address:** East View Publications Inc., 3020 Harbor Lane North, Suite 110, Minneapolis MN 55447.**)** **LC** TN677.A1; O4. **CODEN** OGNPA2. Index available. available in microform. Documents available from Article Express International, Ask*IEEE, CASDDS.
**Ind/Abst** Alum. Ind. Abstr.; Ceram. Abstr.; Chem. Abstr.; Coal Abstr.; Ei Page One; Eng. Mater. Abstr.; Eng. Index Annu.; GeoRef; INSPEC (1969-); Met. Abstr.; World Alum. Abstr.

US/0191-5940
**ORNAMENTAL/MISCELLANEOUS METAL FABRICATOR.** [Ornam./misc. met. fabr.]. **Added/Corp** National Ornamental & Miscellaneous Metals Association. **VFOAT** Ornamental Miscellaneous Metal Fabricator; Ornamental & Miscellaneous Metal Fabricator; A.Ornamental and miscellaneous metal fabricator. (19??)-. Periodical. English. bm (Jan., Mar., May, July, Sept., Nov.). $15.00 (one year), $27.00 (two year). National Ornamental & Miscellaneous Metals Association (NOMMA), 804-10 Main Street, Suite E, Forest Park GA 30050. **Tel** (404)363-4009, FAX (404)366-1852. **ED** Todd Daniel. **DD** 739. Index available. cum. index. **Bk Rev**, (Qty: 6). **Ad Acc.**
**Ind/Abst** Constr. Index.

FI
**OUTUKUMPU NEWS.** (19??)-. Periodical. English. ir. Free. Outokumpu Oy, PO Box 280, FIN-02101 Espoo Finland. **Tel** 011 358 0 4211, FAX 011 358 0 421 2429, telex 124441 OKHI SF. **ED** Johanna Lemola and Katarina Lybeck. **Circ:** 15,000 (ctrl).
**Desc:** The mining and metal producers as having extensive vertical integration in base metals production, product diversity and a long record of technolgical innovations.

US/0030-770X
**OXIDATION OF METALS.** [Oxid. met.]. Vol. 1 (Autumn 1969)-. Periodical. English. Twelve times a year. $705.00 US; $825.00 other. Plenum Press, 233 Spring Street, New York NY 10013-1578. **Tel** (212)620-8000, (800)221-9369, FAX (212)463-0742, (212)807-1047, telex 23/421139. **ED** D.L. Douglass. **LC** QD171; .O93. **DD** 541/.39. **CODEN** OXMEAF. **[CCC].** Index available. **Pr Rev.** available on microfilm and microfiche from University Microfilms International (UMI). Documents available from Article Express International, The Genuine Article, Ask*IEEE, CASDDS, Documents on Demand.
**Desc:** Provides a single forum for scientific contributions dealing with all aspects of gas-solid relations. It includes results of experimental and theoretical work.
**Ind/Abst** Alum. Ind. Abstr.; Bioeng. Abstr.; Chem. Abstr.; Chem. Titles; Coal Abstr.; Corros. Abstr.; Curr. Contents Eng. Tech. Appl. Sci.; Ei Page One; Energy Inf. Abstr.; Energy Res. Abstr.; Eng. Mater. Abstr.; Eng. Index Annu.; Environ. Abstr.; GeoRef; INSPEC (June 1976-); Int. Aerosp. Abstr. (19??-19??); Met. Abstr.; Pollut. Abstr. Indexes; Res. Alert [Full Cov.]; Sci. Cit. Index; SCISEARCH.

US/0097-7241
**P/M LITERATURE REFERENCE GUIDE.** **VAT** Powder Metallurgy Literature Reference Guide. 1st-Ed.; 1974/75-. English. American Powder Metallurgy Institute, 105 College Road East, Princeton NJ 08540. **Tel** (609)452-7700, FAX (609)987-8523. **LC** Z6679.P75; P2; TS245. **DD** 016.6713/7. **UDC** 621.762.

US/0734-4805
**P/M TECHNOLOGY NEWSLETTER.** (P/M TECHNOLOGY NEWSLETTER / APMI.). [P/M technol. newsl.]. **Added/Corp** American Powder Metallurgy Institute. **VAT** Powder Metallurgy Technology Newsletter. Vol. 11, No. 1 (Jan. 1982)-. Newsletter. English. Ten times a year. $145.00 US, Canada and Mexico; $165.00 other. American Powder Metallurgy Institute, 105 College Road East, Princeton NJ 08540. **Tel** (609)452-7700, FAX (609)987-8523. **ED** Peter K. Johnson. **Circ:** 2,400. ***Continues** P/M Technology, 0146-972X.*
**Desc:** Covers news of international powder metallurgy industry and technology; marketing, business, technical and personnel.

UK/0959-9983
**PAPERS PRESENTED AT THE ... INDUSTRIAL MINERALS INTERNATIONAL CONGRESS.** [Pap. present. Ind. Miner. Int. Congr.]. **Main/Conf** Industrial Minerals International Congress. **Added/Corp** Metal Bulletin Group (Worcester Park, Surrey). **VFOAT** Industrial Minerals. (May 21-24, 1984)-. Academic Scholarly Publication. English. be. Metal Bulletin PLC, PO Box 28E, Worcester Park, Surrey KT4 7HX England. **Tel** 011 44 71 827 9977, FAX 011 44 81 337 8943. Documents available from Article Express International, CASDDS. ***Continues** Proceedings of the ... Industrial Minerals International Congress, 0265-0770.*
**Ind/Abst** Bioeng. Abstr.; Chem. Abstr. (1984-); Ei Page One; Eng. Index Annu.; GeoRef (1984-).

FR/1146-5182
**PASCAL. F 41, GISEMENTS METALLIQUES ET NON METALLIQUES.** **VFOAT** PASCAL. F 41, Metallic and Non-Metallic Deposits; PASCAL. F Quarante-et-Un, Gisements Metalliques et Non Metalliques. (1990)-. Periodical. Multiple languages. Ten times a year. 1380.00F France; 1465.00F other. CNRS / Institut d'Information Scientifique et Technique, (Centre National de la Recherche Scientifique), 15 Quai Anatole France, Paris 75700 France. **Tel** 011 33 1 47531515, telex 299 356 F. **(Subscription address:** Institut de l'Information Scientifique et Technique, 2 Allee du Parc de Brabois, 54514 Vandoeuvre Nancy France**)** **UDC** 011. ***Continues** Pascal Folio. F41: Gisements Metalliques et Non-Metalliques.*

CH/1001-053X
**PEI-CHING KO CHI TA HSUEH HSUEH PAO.** **Added/Corp** Pei-Ching Ko Chi Ta Hsueh. **VFOAT** Journal of University of Science and Technology, Beijing; Beijing Keji Daxue Xuebao. (Jan. 1989)-. Periodical. Chinese (summaries and/or abstracts in English). bm. **LC** TS300; .P43. Documents available from CASDDS. ***Continues** Pei-Ching Kang Tieh Hsueh Yuan Hsueh Pao, 1000-5609.*
**Ind/Abst** Chem. Abstr.

US/0743-8508
**PENNY MINING STOCK REPORT.** **See** Business-Investments.

US/0275-9144
**PHYSICS OF METALS.** [Phys. metals]. **VFOAT** Metallofizika. Vol. 3, No. 1 (Nov. 1981)-. Periodical. English (Russian). bm. $2543.00 (academic institutions), $3967.00 (corporate institutions). Gordon & Breach Science Publishers, Inc., PO Box 786, Cooper Station, New York NY 10276. **Tel** (212)206-8900, FAX (212)645-2459. **(Subscription address:** International Publishers Distributor at one of the following addresses: 820 Town Center Drive, Langhorne, PA 19047; or PO Box 90, Reading Berkshire RG1 8JL UK; or Kent Ridge PO Box 1180, Singapore 9111, Republic of Singapore**)** **ED** V. N. Gridnev. **LC** TN689; .M466. **DD** 669/.9/05. **CODEN** PMTSDT. **[CCC]. Bk Rev. Ad Acc.** Documents available from Ask*IEEE.
**Ind/Abst** Alum. Ind. Abstr. (1981-1984); INSPEC (1981-1984); Met. Abstr. (1981-1984).

UK/0031-918X
**PHYSICS OF METALS AND METALLOGRAPHY, THE.** ***Ceased.*** [Phys. met. metallogr.]. **Added/Corp** Pergamon Institute. Vol. 4 (1957)-(199?). Periodical. English (Russian). Twelve times a year. Pergamon Press, An Imprint of Elsevier Science Ltd., The Boulevard, Langford Lane, Kidlington, Oxford OX5 1GB United Kingdom. **Tel** 011 44 865 843000, 011 44 865 843699, FAX 011 44 865 843010. **ED** J. W. Christian. **LC** TN690; .F533. **DD** 669.905. **CODEN** PHMMA6. **[CCC].** available on microfilm and microfiche from University Microfilms International (UMI). Documents available from Article Express International,

Ask*IEEE, CASDDS.
**Desc:** Describes theoretical problems and experimental investigation into the physical properties of metals and alloys, and contains studies of phenomena occurring during all phases of manufacture and in the metals in actual use in various applications.
**Ind/Abst** Alum. Ind. Abstr.; Bioeng. Abstr.; Chem. Abstr.; Ei Page One; Eng. Mater. Abstr.; Eng. Index Annu.; INSPEC (1968-); Int. Aerosp. Abstr.; Met. Abstr.; Pollut. Abstr. Indexes.

RU
**PHYSICS OF METALS AND METALLOGRAPHY, THE.** (199?)-. English (translations available in Russian). mo. $1550.00 US and Canada; $1692.00 other. MAIK Nauka / Interperiodica, Ulitsa Profsoyuznaya 90, Moscow 117864 Russia. **(Subscription address:** Interperiodica Publishing, Subscription Office, PO Box 1831, Birmingham AL 35201-1831.**)** Index available (free).
**Desc:** Describes theoretical problems and experimental investigation into the physical properties of metals and alloys, and contains studies of phenomena occurring during all phases of manufacture and in the metals in actual use in various applications.

US
**PLATINUM-GROUP METALS IN ... . See** Metals and Metallurgy-Abstracting, Bibliographies and Statistics.

UK/0032-1400
**PLATINUM METALS REVIEW.** [Platin. met. rev.]. **Added/Corp** Johnson, Matthey and Company, Ltd. Vol. 1 (Jan. 1957)-. Academic Scholarly Publication. English. Four times a year. Free on request. Johnson Matthey, 43 Hatton Garden, London EC1N 8EE England. **Tel** 451 44 71 269 8000, FAX 011 44 71 269 8399, telex 926648. **ED** Susan Ashton. **LC** TN799.P7; P55. **DD** 669.2405. **CODEN** PTMRA3. Index available. **Bk Rev**, (Qty: 3-3). **Circ:** 9,000 (ctrl). Documents available from Article Express International, CASDDS.
**Desc:** Survey of research on the platinum metals and of developments in their application in industry.
**Ind/Abst** Alum. Ind. Abstr.; Bibliogr. Mission.; Bioeng. Abstr.; Ceram. Abstr. (19??-); Chem. Abstr.; Curr. Titles Electrochem.; Ei Page One; EMBASE; Energy Inf. Abstr.; Eng. Index Annu.; Met. Abstr.; Surf. Treat. Technol. Abstr.; World Ceram. Abstr.; World Text. Abstr.

●US/1076-3937
**PLATT'S METALS WEEK.** [Platt's metals week]. **VFOAT** Metals Week. Vol. 64, No. 25 (June 21, 1993)-. Periodical. English. wk. $870.00 US, Canada, and Mexico; $1010.00 other. McGraw Hill Publishing Company, Inc., 1221 Avenue of the Americas, New York NY 10020. **Tel** (212)512-6410, (800)525-5003, FAX (212)512-6111. **LC** HD9506.A1; E2. **DD** 338. ***Continues*** *Metals Week, 0026-0975.*
**Ind/Abst** NEXIS.

US/0079-2357
**PLENUM PRESS HANDBOOKS OF HIGH-TEMPERATURE MATERIALS.** **VFOAT** Handbooks of High-Temperature Materials. (1964)-. Monographic series. English. ir. Price varies per volume. Plenum Press, 233 Spring Street, New York NY 10013-1578. **Tel** (212)620-8000, (800)221-9369, FAX (212)463-0742, (212)807-1047, telex 23/421139. **LC** TN677.A1; P55. **DD** 666.72.

GW/0048-5012
**PMI. POWDER METALLURGY INTERNATIONAL.** ***Ceased.*** (POWDER METALLURGY INTERNATIONAL.). [PMI. Powder metall. int.]. **VFOAT** PMI, Powder Metallurgy International. Vol. 1 (Sept 1969)-(Jan. 1994). Periodical. English (summaries and/or abstracts in French and German). bm. Verlag Schmid Journals GmbH, Postfach 6609, Hofackerstr 92, D 79042 Freiburg 1 Germany. **Tel** 011 49 761 82057, FAX 011 49 761 84863, telex 761 403 CARNEWS D. **ED** H Reh. **CODEN** PWMIBW. Index available. cum. index. **Bk Rev**. **Ad Acc**. **Pr Rev. Circ:** 5,000. Documents available from Article Express International, The Genuine Article, Ask*IEEE, CASDDS.
**Desc:** Sintered metals. Advanced ceramics. Composites.
**Ind/Abst** Alum. Ind. Abstr.; Bioeng. Abstr.; Ceram. Abstr. (19??-); Chem. Abstr.; Curr. Contents Eng. Tech. Appl. Sci.; Ei Page One; Energy Res. Abstr. (Jan. 1971-); Eng. Index Annu.; INSPEC (Nov. 1975-); Int. Aerosp. Abstr.; Leadscan; Met. Abstr.; Pollut. Abstr. Indexes; Res. Alert [Full Cov.]; Sci. Cit. Index; SCISEARCH; World Ceram. Abstr.

US/0038-5735
**POROSHKOVAIA METALLURGIIA.** ***Title Change.*** (SOVIET POWDER METALLURGY AND METAL CERAMICS.). [Sov. powder metall. met. ceram.]. No. 2 (1962)-(1993). Academic Scholarly Publication. English (translations available in Russian). mo. Consultants Bureau, A Division of Plenum Publishing Corporation, 233 Spring Street, New York NY 10013. **Tel** (212)620-8000, (212)620-8466, FAX (212)463-0742, telex 23/421139. **LC** TN695; .P613. **DD** 669. **CODEN** SPMCAV. **[CCC]**. Index available. **Pr Rev.** available on microfilm and microfiche from University Microfilms International (UMI). Documents available from Article Express International, The Genuine Article, Ask*IEEE, CASDDS. ***Continues*** *Poroshkovaia Metallurgiia (Kiev, Ukraine). English. Soviet Powder Metallurgy.* ***Continued by*** *Powder Metallurgy and Metal Ceramics, 1068-1302.*
**Desc:** This journal systematically presents theoretically and applied research in powder metallurgy and describes its application to various branches of industry.
**Ind/Abst** Alum. Ind. Abstr.; Appl. Mech. Rev.; Bioeng. Abstr.; Ceram. Abstr.; Chem. Abstr.; Curr. Contents Eng. Tech. Appl. Sci.; Ei Page One; Eng. Index Annu.; Fluid Abstr., Civil Eng.; Fluid Abstr. Proc. Eng.; FLUIDEX; INSPEC (Jan. 1972-); Int. Aerosp. Abstr.; Met. Abstr.; MINPROC; Pollut. Abstr. Indexes; Res. Alert [Full Cov.].

ER
**POROSHKOVAIA METALLURGIIA / TALLINSKII POLITEKHNICHESKII INSTITUT.** **Added/Corp** Tallinna Polutehniline Instituut. (1976)-. Periodical. Russian (summaries and/or abstracts in English and German). mo. $52.50. **(Subscription address:** Victor Kamkin, 4956 Boiling Brook Parkway, Rockville MD 20852.**)** **LC** TN695; .P61913.
**Desc:** Information on powder metallurgy.

UN/0032-4795
**POROSKOVAJA METALLURGIJA (KIEV).** (POROSHKOVAIA METALLURGIIA.). [Porosk. metall.]. **Added/Corp** Instytut Metalokeramiky i Spetsialnykh Splaviv (Akademiia Nauk Ukrainskoi RSR) Instytut Problem Materialoznavstva (Akademiia Nauk Ukrainskoi RSR). (1961)-. Academic Scholarly Publication. Russian (summaries and/or abstracts in English). mo. $109.95. Izdatelstvo Naukova Dumka / Ukrainian Academy of Sciences, Vladimirskaia Ulitsa 54, 252601 Kiev Ukraine. **Tel** 225-63-66, telex 131376. **(Subscription address:** East View Publications Inc., 3020 Harbor Lane North, Suite 110, Minneapolis MN 55447.**)** **LC** TN695; .P6. **CODEN** PMANAI. **[CCC]**. Documents available from Article Express International, Ask*IEEE, CASDDS.
**Ind/Abst** Alum. Ind. Abstr.; Chem. Abstr.; Eng. Index Annu.; INSPEC (1970-); Int. Aerosp. Abstr. (19??-19??); Met. Abstr.

US/0092-0479
**POWDER COATING CONFERENCE.** **Added/Corp** Society of Manufacturing Engineers. (19??)-. English. ir. Society of Manufacturing Engineers, One SME Drive, PO Box 930, Member's Records Dept., Dearborn MI 48121-0930. **Tel** (313)271-1500, FAX (313)271-2861, telex 297742 SME UR (VIA RCA). **LC** TS653.A1; P68a. **DD** 671.7/3/08 S.

US/0885-7156
**POWDER DIFFRACTION.** [Powder diffr.]. **Added/Corp** JCPDS--International Centre for Diffraction Data. Vol. 1, No. 1 (March 1986)-. Academic Scholarly Publication. English. qt. $95.00. American Institute of Physics, 500 Sunnyside Boulevard, Woodbury NY 11797-2999. **Tel** (516)576-2200, FAX (516)349-7669, telex 960983. **DD** 620. **CODEN** PODIE2PODIEZ. **[CCC]**. **Ad Acc. Circ:** 1,150. Documents available from CASDDS.
**Desc:** An international journal of materials characterization.
**Ind/Abst** Chem. Abstr. (1986-); Curr. Titl. Dent.; Eng. Mater. Abstr.; Geol. Abstr.; GeoRef.

UK/0032-5899
**POWDER METALLURGY.** [Powder metall.]. **Added/Corp** Metals Society. Powder Metallurgy Joint Group of the Iron and Steel Institute and the Institute of Metals. (1958)-. Periodical. English. qt. £168.00 EEC; £193.20 other. The Institute of Materials, 1 Carlton House Terrace, London SW1Y 5DB England. **Tel** 011 44 71 839 4071, FAX (071)839 2078. **LC** TN695; .P63. **CODEN** PWMTAU. **Pr Rev.** available on microfilm from University Microfilms International (UMI). Documents available from Article Express International, The Genuine Article, Ask*IEEE, CASDDS.
**Desc:** Provides coverage of aspects of the science and practice of powder metallurgy, including the plant and equipment involved. Industrial news and feature articles monitoring technical and commercial developments in the powder metallurgy industry worldwide are included.
**Ind/Abst** Alum. Ind. Abstr.; Bioeng. Abstr.; Ceram. Abstr.; Chem. Abstr.; Curr. Contents Eng. Tech. Appl. Sci.; Curr. Technol. Index; Ei Page One; Eng. Mater. Abstr.; Eng. Index Annu.; INSPEC (Spring 1973-); Leadscan; Met. Abstr.; MINPROC; Res. Alert [Full Cov.]; Sci. Cit. Index; SCISEARCH; World Ceram. Abstr.

●US/1068-1302
**POWDER METALLURGY AND METAL CERAMICS.** **VFOAT** Poroshkovaia Metallurgiia; Poroshkovaya Metallurgiya. (1993)-. Academic Scholarly Publication. English (translations available in Russian). mo. $1295.00 US; $1515.00 other. Consultants Bureau, A Division of Plenum Publishing Corporation, 233 Spring Street, New York NY 10013. **Tel** (212)620-8000, (212)620-8466, FAX (212)463-0742, telex 23/421139. **DD** 669. **[CCC]**. Documents available from CASDDS. ***Continues*** *Poroshkovaia Metallurgiia (Kiev, Ukraine). English. Soviet Powder Metallurgy and Metal Ceramics, 0038-5735.*
**Ind/Abst** Alum. Ind. Abstr.; Bioeng. Abstr.; Chem. Abstr.; FLUIDEX (1973-); Int. Aerosp. Abstr.; Met. Abstr.; MINPROC; Pollut. Abstr. Indexes.

US/0048-5020
**POWDER METALLURGY SCIENCE & TECHNOLOGY.** [Powder metall. sci. tech.]. **Added/Corp** Peters Technology Transfer. Franklin Institute (Philadelphia, Pa.). Science Information Service. **VFOAT** Powder Metallurgy Science and Technology; P.M.S. & T.; PMS&T. (1968)-. English. qt. $50.00. Powder Metallurgy Development Center, P-26 Laxminagar Saidabad, Hyderabad 500 659 India. **Tel** 011 91 040 875951, 011 91 040 877001, 011 91 040 875926, FAX 011 91 040 237912, telex 4252184 PSL IN. **LC** TS245; .P66. **DD** 671.3/7/05. **CODEN** PWMSB.

II/0971-0728
**POWDER METALLURGY SCIENCE AND TECHNOLOGY.** [Powder Metall. Sci. Technol.]. (1989)-. Periodical. English. Four times a year (Jan., Apr., July, Oct.). $50.00. Powder Metallurgy Development Center, P-26 Laxminagar Saidabad, Hyderabad 500 659 India. **Tel** 011 91 040 875951, 011 91 040 877001, 011 91 040 875926, FAX 011 91 040 237912, telex 4252184 PSL IN. **(Subscription address:** Prints India, 11 Darya Ganj, New Delhi 110002 India.**)** **ED** N. T. George. **UDC** 621.762. **Circ:** 600 (ctrl).

PL/0137-9941
**PRACE INSTYTUTU METALURGII ZELAZA IM, ST. STASZICA.** (PRACE INSTYTUTU METALURGII ZELAZA.). [Pr. Inst. Metal. Zel. St. Staszica]. **Main/Corp** Instytut Metalurgii Zelaza (Gliwice, Poland). V. 28, No. 2-. Academic Scholarly Publication. Polish (summaries and/or abstracts in English and Russian). **(Subscription address:** ARS Polona, PO Box 1001, 00068 Warsaw Poland.**)** **LC** TN4; .P67. **UDC** 669. **CODEN** PIMZDL. Documents available from Article Express International, CASDDS. ***Continues*** *Prace Intytutow Hutniczych.*
**Ind/Abst** Alum. Ind. Abstr.; Chem. Abstr.; Eng. Index Annu. [Select. Cov.]; Met. Abstr.

PL/0450-8955
**PRACE INSTYTUTU ODLEWNICTWA.** (PRACE INSTYTUTU ODLEWNICTWA / MINISTERSTWO PRZEMYSU MASZYNOWEGO.). [Pr. Inst. Odlew.]. **Added/Corp** Instytut Odlewnictwa (Krakow, Poland). **VFOAT** Transactions of the Foundry Research Institute. (1952)-. Academic Scholarly Publication. Polish (Polish; summaries and/or abstracts in English, French, German and Russian; table of contents in English, French, German and Russian). qt. Price on Request. **(Subscription address:** ARS Polona, PO Box 1001, 00068 Warsaw Poland.**)** **LC** TS200; .K7. **CODEN** PIODAU. Documents available from CASDDS. ***Continues*** *Prace Gownego Instytutu Odlewnictwa.*
**Ind/Abst** Alum. Ind. Abstr.; Chem. Abstr.; Met. Abstr.

PL
**PRACE - KRAKOW. AKADEMIA GORNICZO-HUTNICZA. INSTYTUT PODSTAW BUDOWY MASZY. See** Engineering-Mines and Mining Engineering.

GW/0032-678X
**PRAKTISCHE METALLOGRAPHIE.** [Prakt. Metallogr.]. **Added/Corp** Deutsche Gesellschaft fuer Metallkunde. **VFOAT** Practical Metallography. Vol. 1 (1964)-. Periodical. English (German). mo. DM188.40. Carl Hanser Verlag, Postfach 860420, D 81631 Munich Germany. **Tel** 011 49 89 998300, FAX 011 49 89 984809. **ED** G. Petzow. **LC** TN690; .P65. **CODEN** PMTLA5. **Circ:** 2,000 (ctrl). Documents available from Article Express International, Ask*IEEE, CASDDS.
**Desc:** Covers materials science.
**Ind/Abst** Alum. Ind. Abstr.; Art Archaeol. Tech. Abstr.; Bioeng. Abstr.; Ceram. Abstr.; Chem. Abstr.; Coal Abstr.; Ei Page One; Energy Res. Abstr.; Eng. Mater. Abstr.; Eng. Index Annu.; INSPEC (Oct. 1971-); Met. Abstr.; Nucl. Sci. Abstr.; World Alum. Abstr.

US/0730-1901
**PRECIOUS METALS (BROOKLYN, N.Y.).** (PRECIOUS METALS : A PUBLICATION OF THE INTERNATIONAL PRECIOUS METALS INSTITUTE.). [Precious met.]. **Added/Corp** International Precious Metals Institute. (19??)-. Periodical. English. mo. $24.00. International Precious Metals Institute, 4905 Tilghman Street, Suite 160, Allentown PA 18104. **Tel** (215)395-9700, FAX (215)395-5855.

SA
**PRECIOUS METALS BULLETIN.** Bulletin. Mintek, Private Bag X3015, Randburg 2125 South Africa. **Tel** 011 27 11 7933511, FAX 011 27 11 7932413, telex 4-24867.

US/0735-4770
**PRECIOUS METALS MONTHLY REVIEW.** Vol. 1, No. 1 (Oct. 1982)-. Periodical. English. mo. $36.00. Precious Metals Monthly Review, PO Box 4754, Chicago IL 60680. **Tel** (312)566-4411.

CN/8756-0917
**PRECIOUS METALS (TORONTO, ONT.).** (PRECIOUS METALS.). [Precious met.]. **Main/Corp** International Precious Metals Institute. Conference. (19??)-. English. an. Pergamon Press, An Imprint of Elsevier Science Ltd., The Boulevard, Langford Lane,

Kidlington, Oxford OX5 1GB United Kingdom. **Tel** 011 44 865 843000, 011 44 865 843699, FAX 011 44 865 843010. **LC** TN759; .I58a. **DD** 669/.2. **CODEN** PRCMEU.

US
**PRESTON PIPE REPORT.** (19??)-. English. mo. $600.00 US, Canada & Mexico; $700.00 other. Preston Publishing Company, 6613 East 106th Street, Tulsa OK 74133-7131. **Tel** (918)299-3877, FAX (918)299-4795. **ED** Douglass Yadon.
**Desc:** Covers steel pipe, all commodities. Gives supply and demand analysis.

CN/0380-7851
**PRIMARY IRON AND STEEL.** ***Title Change.*** [Prim. iron steel]. **Main/Corp** Canada. Statistique Canada. Division des Industries Manufacturieres et Primaires. **VFOAT** Fer et Acier Primaire. V. 27- Jan. 1972-. Periodical. Multiple languages (English and French). mo. Statistics Canada, Publications Sales & Services, Main Building Room 1710, Ottawa Ontario K1A 0T6 Canada. **Tel** (613)951-5078, (800)267-6677, FAX (613)951-1584, telex 053-3585. **DD** 338.4/7672/0971. **UDC** 311:669.1(71). ***Continues*** *Primary Iron and Steel.* ***Continued by*** *Production and Shipments of Steel Pipe, Tubing and Fittings, 0703-007X.*
**Desc:** Furnace charges, production and shipments of pig iron and ferro-alloy, steel ingots and castings; production and disposition of rolled steel products.

CN/0835-0116
**PRIMARY METAL INDUSTRIES (1985).** (PRIMARY METAL INDUSTRIES / STATISTICS CANADA, INDUSTRY DIVISION, CENSUS OF MANUFACTURES SECTION.). [Prim. met. ind.]. **Added/Corp** Statistics Canada. Census of Manufactures Section. Statistics Canada. Industry Division. Statistics Canada. Annual Survey of Manufactures Section. **VFOAT** Industries de Premiere Transformation des Metaux. 1st Issue (1985)-. English (French). an. 38.00Can$ Canada; $46.00 US; $54.00 other. Statistics Canada, Publications Sales & Services, Main Building Room 1710, Ottawa Ontario K1A 0T6 Canada. **Tel** (613)951-5078, (800)267-6677, FAX (613)951-1584, telex 053-3585. **LC** HD9539.A3; C37. **DD** 338.4/7671/0971021. ***Formed by the union of*** *Non-Ferrous Metal Smelting and Refining Industries, 0828-9786; Non-Ferrous Metal Rolling, Casting and Extruding Industries, 0828-9964* ***and*** *Primary Steel, Steel Pipe and Tube Industries and Iron Founderies I.E., 0828-9808.*

UK
**PRINCIPAL USES OF LEAD AND ZINC.** **Main/Corp** International Lead and Zinc Study Group. (19??)-. English. ir. £95.00, $175.00. International Lead and Zinc Study Group, Metro House, 58 St. James Street, London SW1A 1LD England. **Tel** 011 44 71 4999373, FAX 011 44 71 4933725, telex 299819 ILZSG G.
**Desc:** A review of trends in the main uses of lead and zinc during 1984-1989 in 23 countries and groups of countries representing 90% of Western World consumption.

UK
**PRINCIPAL USES OF LEAD AND ZINC.** (19??)-. English. £50.00 UK; $85.00 US. International Lead and Zinc Study Group, Metro House, 58 St. James Street, London SW1A 1LD England. **Tel** 011 44 71 4999373, FAX 011 44 71 4933725, telex 299819 ILZSG G.

GW
**PRO METAL.** Began in 1948. French (German). Assoc Metallurgique SA, Postfach 3000, Bern 6 Switzerland. **LC** TS620; .P7.

UN/0235-4233
**PROBLEMY METALLURGICESKOGO PROIZVODSTVA.** [Probl. metall. proizv.]. (1989)-. Periodical. Russian. ir. **UDC** 669. ***Continues*** *Metallurgia i Koksohimia (Kiev), 0543-5765.*

PL/0239-2089
**PROBLEMY PROJEKTOWE.** Vol. 31, No. 1 (Jan./Mar. 1984)-. Periodical. Polish. qt. $110.00. RSW Prasa-Kriazka-Ruch, Centrala Kolportazu Prasy i Wydawnictw, Towarowa 28, 00-958 Warsaw Poland. **LC** TN4; .P75. ***Continues*** *Problemy Projektowe Hutnictwa I Przemysu Maszynowego.*
**Ind/Abst** Eng. Mater. Abstr.

UN/0131-1611
**PROBLEMY SPECIALNOJ ELEKTROMETALLURGII.** (PROBLEMY SPETSIALNOI ELEKTROMETALLURGII / AKADEMIIA NAUK UKRAINSKOI SSR, INSTITUT ELEKTROSVARKI IM. E.O. PATONA.). [Probl. spec. elektrometallurgii]. **Added/Corp** Instytut Elektrozvariuvannia im. IE.O. Patona. (1975)-. Academic Scholarly Publication. Russian. sa. 1.20rub. **LC** TN681; .R33. **DD** 669/.028/405. **CODEN** PSELD9. Documents available from CASDDS. ***Continues*** *Rafiniruiushchie Pereplavy.*
**Ind/Abst** Alum. Ind. Abstr.; Chem. Abstr. (1975-1984); Met. Abstr.

US/0734-9629
**PROCEEDINGS - ABRASIVE ENGINEERING SOCIETY (U.S). CONFERENCE/EXHIBITION.** (PROCEEDINGS.). [Proc. - Abras. Eng. Soc. (U.S.), Conf./Exhib.]. **Main/Corp** Abrasive Engineering Society (U.S.). Conference/Exhibition. (1977)-. English. an (May). $35.00. Meadowlark Technical Services, 108 Elliot Drive, Butler PA 16001. **Tel** (412)282-6210. **LC** TJ1280; .A62. **DD** 621.9/2. Index available. **Ad Acc.** ***Continues*** *Abrasive Engineering Society (U.S.). International Technical Conference & Exhibition. Proceedings, 0363-8065.*
**Desc:** Collection of technical papers on advances in application of industrial abrasives.

UK/0700-5741
**PROCEEDINGS - COMMONWEALTH MINING AND METALLURGICAL CONGRESS.** **See** Engineering-Mines and Mining Engineering.

US/0096-0128
**PROCEEDINGS / ELECTRIC FURNACE CONFERENCE.** [Proc. Elec. Furnace Conf.]. **Main/Conf** Electric Furnace Conference. **Added/Corp** Metallurgical Society of AIME. Electric Furnace Committee. Iron and Steel Society of AIME. Electric Furnace Division. **VFOAT** Electric Furnace Seel Proceedings. Vol. 16 (1958)-. Proceedings. English. an. $40.00 (members); $80.00 (nonmembers). Iron and Steel Society Inc., 410 Commonwealth Drive, Warrendale PA 15086. **Tel** (412)776-9460, FAX (412)776-0430, telex 6503113570. **ED** Lawrence Kuhn. **LC** TN750; .E4. **CODEN** EFCPAY. **Circ:** 700. Documents available from Article Express International, CASDDS. ***Continues*** *Electric Furnace Steel Conference. Proceedings, 0096-0136.*
**Desc:** Proceedings of the Society's annual electric furnace steelmaking conference.
**Ind/Abst** Bioeng. Abstr.; Chem. Abstr.; Ei Page One; Energy Res. Abstr. (Dec. 1976-); Eng. Index Annu.

US/0099-6874
**PROCEEDINGS - IRONMAKING CONFERENCE.** [Proc. Ironmaking Conf.]. **Main/Conf** Ironmaking Conference. **VFOAT** Ironmaking Proceedings. (1963)-. Proceedings. English. an. $80.00. Iron and Steel Society Inc., 410 Commonwealth Drive, Warrendale PA 15086. **Tel** (412)776-9460, FAX (412)776-0430, telex 6503113570. **ED** Lawrence Kuhn. **UDC** 669.1(063). **CODEN** PIRCB9. **Circ:** 700. available on microfilm. Documents available from Article Express International, CASDDS. ***Continues*** *Proceedings - Blast Furnace, Coke Oven, and Raw Materials Committee of the Iron and Steel Division, the Metallurgical Society of the American Institute of Mining, Metallurgical and Petroleum Engineers, 0096-5138.*
**Desc:** Information on all aspects of ironmaking technology.
**Ind/Abst** Bioeng. Abstr.; Ceram. Abstr. (19??-); Chem. Abstr.; Ei Page One; Eng. Index Annu.

US
**PROCEEDINGS OF ALUMINUM EXTRUSION TECHNOLOGICAL SEMINAR.** Proceedings. English. ir. Aluminum Association, 900 19th Street Northwest, Suite 300, Washington DC 20006. **Tel** (202)862-5100, FAX (202)862-5164.

UK
**PROCEEDINGS OF METAL BULLETIN'S INTERNATIONAL FERRO-ALLOYS CONFERENCE.** **Main/Conf** International Ferro-Alloy Conference. **Added/Corp** Metal Bulletin Ltd. (1977)-. Proceedings. English. £33.00 UK; $35.00 (surface mail), $39.00 (airmail) US. Metal Bulletin PLC, PO Box 28E, Worcester Park, Surrey KT4 7HX England. **Tel** 011 44 71 827 9977, FAX 011 44 81 337 8943. **ED** B. L. Nolk. **Circ:** 225.
**Desc:** The proceedings of the 4th international Ferro-Alloys Conference.

US
**PROCEEDINGS OF THE ALUMINIUM EXTRUSION TECHNOLOGICAL SEMINAR.** (19??)-. Proceedings. English. ir. Price varies per volume. Aluminum Association, 900 19th Street Northwest, Suite 300, Washington DC 20006. **Tel** (202)862-5100, FAX (202)862-5164. **(Subscription address:** Aluminium Association, PO Box 753, Waldorf, MD 20604**)**

US/0731-4191
**PROCEEDINGS OF THE ... ANNUAL CONVENTION OF THE WIRE ASSOCIATION INTERNATIONAL, INC.** [Proc. Annu. Conv. Wire Assoc., Int., Inc.]. **Main/Conf** Wire Association International. Convention. **VFOAT** Conference Proceedings ... Annual Convention. Academic Scholarly Publication. English. an. Wire Association International, 1570 Boston Post Road, PO Box H, Guilford CT 06437. **Tel** (203)453-2777, FAX (203)453-8384. **ED** Ralph Edwards. **LC** TS270.A1; C66A. **DD** 671.8/42/05. **UDC** 621.778(063). **CODEN** PCWIDC. Index available. Documents available from Article Express International, CASDDS.
**Ind/Abst** Chem. Abstr.; Eng. Index Annu.

CN/0318-417X
**PROCEEDINGS OF THE ANNUAL MEETING OF THE CANADIAN HYDROMETALLURGISTS.** **Main/Corp** Canadian Hydrometallurgists. 1st- 1971-. Proceedings. English. **DD** 669/.0283.

CN/0590-5850
**PROCEEDINGS OF THE ANNUAL MEETING OF THE CANADIAN MINERAL PROCESSORS.** [Proc. annu. meet. Can. Miner. Process.]. **Main/Corp** Canadian Mineral Processors. 1st, (1969)-. Proceedings. English. an (Jan.). 37.38Can$. Canadian Mineral Processors, 555 Booth Room 126, Ottawa Ontario K1A 0G1 Canada. **Tel** (613)996-2283, FAX (613)996-9673. Index available. **Circ:** 500. ***Supersedes*** *Proceedings of the Annual Meeting of the Canadian Gold Metallurgists, 0384-5931.*
**Desc:** A useful reference for updating existing flowsheets, eliminating the in-plant losses or lowering the recovery cost in the mineral industry in Canada.
**Ind/Abst** AESIS Q.; MINPROC.

US/0895-9900
**PROCEEDINGS OF THE ... STEELMAKING CONFERENCE.** [Proc. Steelmak. Conf.]. **Main/Conf** Steelmaking Conference. **VFOAT** Steelmaking Proceedings. Vol. 67 (April 1-4, 1984)-. Academic Scholarly Publication. English. an. $80.00. Iron and Steel Society of AIME, 410 Commonwealth Drive, Warrendale PA 15086. **Tel** (412)776-9460, FAX (412)776-0430, telex 6503113507. **ED** Lawrence Kuhn. **LC** TN701.5; .S73A. **DD** 669/.142. **UDC** 669.18(063). **Circ:** 800. available on microfilm. Documents available from CASDDS. ***Continues*** *Steelmaking Conference Proceedings, 0896-0429.*
**Desc:** Information available on all aspects of steelmaking technology.
**Ind/Abst** Chem. Abstr. (1984-).

US/0161-5769
**PROCEEDINGS - WORLD MAGNESIUM CONFERENCE.** (PROCEEDINGS / ANNUAL WORLD MAGNESIUM CONFERENCE.). [Proc. - World Magnes. Conf.]. **Added/Corp** International Magnesium Association. (1983)-. Proceedings. English. an. $80.00. International Magnesium Association, 1303 Vincent Place, Suite One, Mclean VA 22101. **Tel** (703)442-8888. **LC** TN799.M2; W67a. **DD** 669/.723. ***Continues*** *World Magnesium Conference & Exposition. Proceedings.*

UK/0032-9762
**PRODUCT FINISHING (LONDON).** (PRODUCT FINISHING.). [Prod. finish.]. Vol. 1 (1948)-. Academic Scholarly Publication. English. Twelve times a year. $199.00. MCB University Press, 60 62 Toller Lane, Bradford West Yorkshire BD8 9BX England. **Tel** 011 44 274 499821, FAX 011 44 274 547143, telex 51317 MCBUNI G. **(Subscription address:** MCB University Press / US and Canada Subscriptions, PO Box 10812, Birmingham AL 35201-0812.**)** **LC** TS200; .P72. **DD** 671.7/05. **CODEN** PRFIAT. Documents available from Article Express International, CASDDS.
**Ind/Abst** Alum. Ind. Abstr.; Bioeng. Abstr.; Chem. Abstr.; Ei Page One; EMBASE; Eng. Index Annu.; Infomat Int. Bus.; Int. Packag. Abstr.; Leadscan; Met. Abstr.; World Surf. Coat. Abstr.

CN/0835-5797
**PRODUCTION AND SHIPMENTS OF STEEL PIPE AND TUBING.** [Prod. shipm. steel pipe tubing]. **Added/Corp** Statistics Canada. Industry Division. **VFOAT** Production et Livraisons de Tuyaux et Tubes en Acier. Vol. 11, No. 1 (Jan. 1987)-. English (French). mo. 60.00Can$ Canada; $72.00 US; $84.00 other. Statistics Canada, Publications Sales & Services, Main Building Room 1710, Ottawa Ontario K1A 0T6 Canada. **Tel** (613)951-5078, (800)267-6677, FAX (613)951-1584, telex 053-3585. **DD** 338.4/7672/0971. ***Continues*** *Production and Shipments of Steel Pipe, Tubing and Fittings, 0703-007X.*
**Desc:** Provides current data on the Canadian iron and steel industry. Includes monthly production and shipment statistics in metric tons for pig iron, steel primary forms and steel castings at the Canadian level.

US/0478-4251
**PRODUCTS FINISHING DIRECTORY.** (1956)-. Directory. English. an. $15.00. Gardner Publications Inc, 6600 Clough Pike, Cincinnati OH 45244. **Tel** (513)231-8020, (513)231-2818, telex 214132. **ED** Gerard H. Poll Jr. **Bk Rev. Ad Acc. Circ:** 25,000 (ctrl).
**Desc:** Electroplating, painting and other finishing operations. Also articles on pollution control, etc.
**Ind/Abst** Ceram. Abstr.

US/0091-6145
**PROGRESS IN EXTRACTIVE METALLURGY.** Vol. 1 (1973)-. English. ir. Gordon & Breach Science Publishers, Inc., PO Box 786, Cooper Station, New York NY 10276. **Tel** (212)206-8900, FAX (212)645-2459. **(Subscription address:** International Publishers Distributor at one of the following addresses: 820 Town Center Drive, Langhorne, PA 19047; or PO Box 90, Reading Berkshire RG1 8JL UK; or Kent Ridge PO Box 1180, Singapore 9111, Republic of Singapore**)** **LC** TN600; .P76. **DD** 669/.05.

# Metals and Metallurgy

RU
**PROIZVODSTVO CHUGUNA / MINISTERSTVO VYSSHEGO I SREDNEGO SPETSIALNOGO OBRAOZOVANIIA RSFSR, MAGNITOGORSKII GORNO-METALLURGICHESKII INSTITUT IM. G.I. NOSOVA.** [Proizvod. cuguna]. **Added/Corp** Magnitogorskii Gorno-Metallurgicheskii Institut Im. G.I. Nosova. (1975)-. Academic Scholarly Publication. Russian. mo. $181.00. **(Subscription address:** Victor Kamkin, 4956 Boiling Brook Parkway, Rockville MD 20852.**) CODEN** PRCHEF. Documents available from CASDDS.
**Ind/Abst** Chem. Abstr. (1975-1982).

RU/0132-5183
**PROIZVODSTVO OGNEUPOROV.** (PROIZVODSTVO OGNEUPOROV / MINISTERSTVO CHERNOI METALLURGII SSSR.). [Proizv. ogneup.]. **Added/Corp** Soviet Union. Ministerstvo Chernoi Metallurgii. (1972)-. Periodical. Russian. **CODEN** OTPOBX. Documents available from CASDDS.
**Ind/Abst** Ceram. Abstr. (19??-); Chem. Abstr. (1972-1981).

RU/0321-4966
**PROIZVODSTVO SPECIALNYH OGNEUPOROV.** (PROIZVODSTVO SPETSIALNYKH OGNEUPOROV.). [Proizvod. spec. ogneuporov]. (1974)-. Periodical. Russian. Izdatelstvo Metallurgiia, 2-i Obydenskii Per.14, G-34, Moscow Russia. **CODEN** PSOGDA. Documents available from CASDDS.
**Ind/Abst** Ceram. Abstr. (19??-); Chem. Abstr. (1974-1981).

RU/0201-873X
**PROIZVODSTVO STALI V KISLORODNO-KONVERTORNYH I MARTENOVSKIH CEHAH.** (PROIZVODSTVO STALI V KISLORODNO-KONVERTORNYKH I MARTENOVSKIKH TSEKHAKH.). [Proizvod. stali kislorodno-konvert. cehah]. **Added/Corp** Soviet Union. Ministerstvo Chernoi Metallurgii. (1976)-. Academic Scholarly Publication. Russian. ir. Izdatelstvo Metallurgiia, 2-i Obydenskii Per.14, G-34, Moscow Russia. **CODEN** PSKTDT. Documents available from CASDDS.
**Ind/Abst** Chem. Abstr. (1976-1978).

US/0897-070X
**PROJECTS IN METAL.** [Proj. met.]. Vol. 1, No. 1 (1988)-. Periodical. English. bm. $21.00 US; $25.23 Canada; $25.00 other. Village Press, 2779 Aero Park Drive, Traverse City MI 49684. **Tel** (800)447-7367, (616)946-3712. **(Subscription address:** Projects in Metal, PO Box 1810, Traverse City MI 49685.**) DD** 684.

UK
**PROMOTIONAL ACTIVITIES IN THE LEAD AND ZINC INDUSTRIES.** (June 1990)-. Periodical. English. £35.00 UK; $60.00 US. International Lead and Zinc Study Group, Metro House, 58 St. James Street, London SW1A 1LD England. **Tel** 011 44 71 4999373, FAX 011 44 71 4933725, telex 299819 ILZSG G.
**Desc:** Contains the results of a survey on "Research, Development and Promotional Activities in the Zinc Industry" carried out by the Study Group plus 17 case histories of promotional activities for lead and zinc in Europe, India, Japan and the United States of America. It concludes with a comprehensive overview on lead and zinc market development associations worldwide.

CN/0843-6819
**PROSPECT (VANCOUVER). See** Engineering-Mines and Mining Engineering.

US/0033-1732
**PROTECTION OF METALS.** [Prot. met.]. **Added/Corp** Consultants Bureau. Consultants Bureau Enterprises. Vol. 1 (Jan./Feb. 1965)-. Academic Scholarly Publication. English (Russian). bm. $1245.00 US; $1455.00 other. MAIK Nauka / Interperiodica, Ulitsa Profsoyuznaya 90, Moscow 117864 Russia. **ED** Ya M. Kolotyrkin. **LC** TA462; .P76. **CODEN** PTNMAR. **[CCC].** Index available on. **Pr Rev.** available on microfilm and microfiche from University Microfilms International (UMI). Documents available from Article Express International, The Genuine Article, Ask*IEEE, CASDDS.
**Desc:** Covers theoretical and practical problems involved in thermodynamics, kinetics and mechanisms of metal detonation in corrosive environments.
**Ind/Abst** Alum. Ind. Abstr.; Art Archaeol. Tech. Abstr.; Bioeng. Abstr.; Chem. Abstr.; Curr. Contents Eng. Tech. Appl. Sci.; Ei Page One; EMBASE; Eng. Mater. Abstr.; Eng. Index Annu.; INSPEC (Jan./Feb. 1988-); Int. Aerosp. Abstr.; Met. Abstr.; Life Sci. Collect.; Pollut. Abstr. Indexes; Res. Alert [Full Cov.].

US/0079-7030
**PROTECTIVE COATINGS ON METALS.** **VFOAT** Zashchitnye Pokrytiia Na Metallakh.; Zashchitnye Pokrytiia Na Metallakh. Vol. 1 (1969)-. English. ir. Plenum Press, 233 Spring Street, New York NY 10013-1578. **Tel** (212)620-8000, (800)221-9369, FAX (212)463-0742, (212)807-1047, telex 23/421139. **LC** TN752.S8; Z3513. **DD** 671; 67L.7/3.

PL/0033-2275
**PRZEGLAD ODLEWNICTWA.** [Prz. odlew.]. **Added/Corp** Stowarzyszenie Naukowo-Techniczne Odlewnikow Polskich. (1951)-. Academic Scholarly Publication. Polish (table of contents in Russian and English). bm. Price on Request. **(Subscription address:** ARS Polona, PO Box 1001, 00068 Warsaw Poland.**) LC** TS200; .P77. **CODEN** PRZOAB. Documents available from CASDDS.
**Ind/Abst** Alum. Ind. Abstr.; Art Archaeol. Tech. Abstr.; Ceram. Abstr.; Chem. Abstr.; Coal Abstr.; Eng. Mater. Abstr.; Met. Abstr.; Saf. Health Work; Surf. Treat. Technol. Abstr.

HU/0324-4679
**PUBLICATIONS OF THE TECHNICAL UNIVERSITY FOR HEAVY INDUSTRY. SERIES B: METALLURGY.** [Publ. Tech. Univ. Heavy Ind. Ser. B. Metal.]. **Main/Corp** Nehezipari Muszaki Egyetem (Hungary). (1975)-. Academic Scholarly Publication. English (German and Russian). **LC** TN600; .M57a. **DD** 669/.05. **CODEN** PTUBDW. Documents available from CASDDS. **Supersedes in part** Nehezipari Muszaki Egyetem Idegennyelvu Kozlemenyei, 0369-4852.
**Ind/Abst** Chem. Abstr.

US/1060-054X
**PURCHASING PERFORMANCE BENCHMARKS FOR THE CARBON STEEL INDUSTRY / CAPS, CENTER FOR ADVANCED PURCHASING STUDIES.** [Purch. perform. benchmarks carbon steel ind.]. **Added/Corp** Center for Advanced Purchasing Studies (Tempe, Ariz.). **VFOAT** Purchasing Performance Benchmarks. (1991)-. Periodical. English. Free. Center for Advanced Purchasing Studies, PO Box 22160, Tempe AZ 85285. **Tel** (602)752-2277. **DD** 658.

US
**QUARTERLY REPORT ON THE STATUS OF THE STEEL INDUSTRY : REPORT TO THE COMMITTEE ON WAYS AND MEANS ON INVESTIGATION NO. 332-226 UNDER SECTION 332 OF THE TARIFF ACT OF 1930. Added/Corp** United States. Congress. House. Committee on Ways and Means. Subcommittee on Trade. United States International Trade Commission. (Mar 1991)-. Periodical. English. qt. United States International Trade Commission, 500 E Street Southwest, Washington DC 20436. **Tel** (202)205-1806. **LC** HD9511; .M66. **DD** 382./423/0973021. Documents available from Documents on Demand. **Continues** Monthly Report on the Status of the Steel Industry.
**Ind/Abst** Am. Stat. Index (1991-).

CN/1186-9275
**QUARTERLY STEEL COMMENT.** [Q. steel comment]. **Added/Corp** RBC Dominion Securities Inc. (July 2, 1991)-. Periodical. English. qt. Limited free distribution. RBC Dominion Securities, PO Box 21, Commerce Ct. South, Toronto Ontario M5L 1A7 Canada. **DD** 332.63.

US
**RAW STEEL PRODUCTION IN 11 PRODUCING DISTRICTS.** English. Fifty-two times a year. $40.00. American Iron & Steel Institute, 1101 17th Street Northwest, Suite 1300, Washington DC 20036. **Tel** (202)452-7100 or 7151.

PE/1010-0962
**RE METALLICA, DE.** (DE RE METALLICA DE LA MINERIA Y LOS METALES : REVISTA DEL INSTITUTO GEOLOGICO, MINERO Y METALURGICO.). [De re met.]. **Added/Corp** Instituto Geologico, Minero y Metalurgico (Peru). **VFOAT** De la Mineria y los Metales. No. 1 (May/June 1984)-. Academic Scholarly Publication. Spanish. bm. Apartado de Correo Nro 1302, Lima 100 Peru. **LC** TN52; .D38. **DD** 622/.0985. **CODEN** DRMMEG. Documents available from CASDDS.
**Ind/Abst** Chem. Abstr. (1984-); Coal Abstr.; GeoRef.

UK
**RECYCLING LEAD AND ZINC: THE CHALLENGE OF THE 1990'S.** (19??)-. English. £65.00 UK; $120.00 US. International Lead and Zinc Study Group, Metro House, 58 St. James Street, London SW1A 1LD England. **Tel** 011 44 71 4999373, FAX 011 44 71 4933725, telex 299819 ILZSG G.

UK
**RECYCLING OF METALLIFEROUS MATERIALS.** English. Institutions of Ming and Metallurgy, 44 Portland Place, London W1N 4BR England. **Tel** 01-580 3802, FAX 01-436 5388, telex 261410 IMM G.

RU/0034-2491
**REFERATIVNYI ZHURNAL : METALLURGIIA. Added/Corp** Akademiia Nauk SSSR. Institut Nauchnoi Informatsii. (1956)-. Abstracting/Indexing Service. Russian. mo. $599.95. VINITI - Vsesoyuznyi Institut Nauchno-Tekhnicheskoi Informatsii, All-Union Scientific and Technical Information Institute, Baltiiskaia Ulitsa 14, 125219 Moscow Russia. **Tel** 238-46-00, FAX 9430060, telex 411160. **(Subscription address:** East View Publications Inc., 3020 Harbor Lane North, Suite 110, Minneapolis MN 55447.**) CODEN** RZMTA5. Documents available from CASDDS.
**Ind/Abst** Alum. Ind. Abstr.; Chem. Abstr.; Eng. Mater. Abstr.; Met. Abstr.; Surf. Treat. Technol. Abstr.

RU/0131-3533
**REFERATIVNYJ ZURNAL - VSESOJUZNYJ INSTITUT NAUCNOJ I TEHNICESKOJ INFORMACII. 66, KORROZIJA I ZASCITA OT KORROZII.** (REFERATIVNYJ ZHURNAL. 66, KORROZIIA I ZASHCHITA OT KORROZII / GOSUDARSTVENNYI KOMITET SOVETA MINISTROV SSSR PO NAUKE I TEKHNIKE, AKADEMIIA NAUK SOIUZA SOVETSKIKH SOTSIALI STICHESKIKH RESPUBLIK, VSESOIUZNYI INSTITUT NAUCHNOI I TEKHNICHESKOI INFORMATSII.). [Ref. z. - Vses. inst. naucn. teh. inf., 66, Korroz. zasc. korroz.]. **Added/Corp** Vsesoiuznyi Institut Nauchnoi i Tekhnicheskoi Informatsii (Soviet Union). **VFOAT** Korroziia i Zashchita ot Korrozii. (1968)-. Abstracting/Indexing Service. Russian. mo. 1.34rub single issue. VINITI - Vsesoyuznyi Institut Nauchno-Tekhnicheskoi Informatsii, All-Union Scientific and Technical Information Institute, Baltiiskaia Ulitsa 14, 125219 Moscow Russia. **Tel** 238-46-00, FAX 9430060, telex 411160. **(Subscription address:** V/O Mezhdunarodnaya Kniga, 113095 Dimitrova Ul 39, Moscow USSR) **LC** Z6679.C7; R43; TA418.74. **CODEN** RKZAK6. **Circ:** 700 (ctrl). Documents available from CASDDS.
**Ind/Abst** Alum. Ind. Abstr.; Chem. Abstr.; Met. Abstr.

US/0034-3102
**REFRACTORIES (NEW YORK).** (REFRACTORIES.). [Refractories.]. **Added/Corp** Consultants Bureau. Consultants Bureau Enterprises. Scripta Technica, Inc. Vol. 1 (Jan./Feb. 1960)-. Academic Scholarly Publication. English (Russian). $1115.00 US; $1350.00 other. Consultants Bureau, A Division of Plenum Publishing Corporation, 233 Spring Street, New York NY 10013. **Tel** (212)620-8000, (212)620-8466, FAX (212)463-0742, telex 23/421139. **ED** Yu D. Sagalevich. **LC** TN677.A1; O412. **CODEN** REFRAL. **[CCC].** available on microfilm and microfiche from University Microfilms International (UMI). Documents available from Article Express International, Ask*IEEE, CASDDS.
**Ind/Abst** Bioeng. Abstr.; Ceram. Abstr. (19??-); Chem. Abstr.; Coal Abstr.; Ei Page One; EMBASE; Eng. Index Annu.; GeoRef; INSPEC (1968-); SEA Abstr.

UK
**REGULATIONS IN THE AREAS OF TRANSPORT, LABELLING, CLASSIFICATION AND STORAGE, AFFECTING THE RECYCLING OF LEAD.** (June 1989)-. English. £10.00 UK; $20.00 US. International Lead and Zinc Study Group, Metro House, 58 St. James Street, London SW1A 1LD England. **Tel** 011 44 71 4999373, FAX 011 44 71 4933725, telex 299819 ILZSG G.
**Desc:** Review of the present situation concerning existing and proposed regulations relating to transporting, labelling, classification and storage which affect the recycling of lead.

BL
**RELATORIO - CONSELHO DE NAO-FERROSOS E DE SIDERURGIA. See** Economics-Industry and Production.

CL
**REPERTORIO SIDERURGICO LATINOAMERICANO. See** Economics-Industry and Production.

SA/0254-1815
**REPORT (COUNCIL FOR MINERAL TECHNOLOGY (SOUTH AFRICA)). See** Earth Sciences-Mineralogy.

US/1066-5552
**REPORT OF INVESTIGATIONS - UNITED STATES. BUREAU OF MINES. See** Engineering-Mines and Mining Engineering.

AT/0158-5088
**REPORT - URANIUM ADVISORY COUNCIL.** [Rep. - Uranium Advis. Counc.]. (1979)-. English. an. **DD** 354.94093.
**Ind/Abst** AESIS Q.

PE
**REPORTE ANUAL / SOUTHERN PERU COPPER CORPORATION, SUCURSAL DEL PERU.** **Main/Corp** Southern Peru Copper Corporation. Sucursal del Peru. Spanish. Avenue Caminos del Inco #171, Chacarilla del Estanque, Santiago de Surco Lima 33 Peru.

US
**RESEARCH REPORT (STEEL FOUNDERS' SOCIETY OF AMERICA).** (RESEARCH REPORT - STEEL FOUNDERS' SOCIETY OF AMERICA.). English. Steel Founders' Society of America, 455 State Street, Cast Metal Fed Bl, Des Plaines IL 60016. **Tel** (708)299-9160. **LC** TS200; .S76. **DD** 627/.2/08. ***Continues*** *Steel Founders' Society of America. Technical Research Committee. Research Report.*

UK/0379-0002
**REVIEWS ON POWDER METALLURGY AND PHYSICAL CERAMICS.** ***Ceased.*** [Rev. powder metall. phys. ceram.]. Vol. 1 (1979)-Vol. 6 (1993). Academic Scholarly Publication. English. Four times a year (1 volume). Elsevier Science Publishers Ltd, Crown House, Linton Road, Barking Essex IG11 8JU England. **Tel** 011 44 81 5947272, FAX 081-594-5942, telex 896950. **ED** M B Waldrond. **UDC** 621.762. **CODEN** RMPCDH. **[CCC].** Documents available from Article Express International, CASDDS.
**Desc:** An international review journal reporting on overall research and development in powder metallurgy and physical ceramics, on topics of interest to the community of scientists, researchers and engineers.
**Ind/Abst** Alum. Ind. Abstr.; Chem. Abstr.; Eng. Mater. Abstr.; Eng. Index Annu.; Met. Abstr.; World Ceram. Abstr.

SP/0034-8570
**REVISTA DE METALURGIA (MADRID).** (REVISTA DE METALURGIA.). [Rev. metal.]. **Added/Corp** Centro Nacional de Investigaciones Metalurgicas (Spain). (Feb. 1965)-. Periodical. Spanish (English). bm (6 issues). 7500ptas Spain & Latin America; 11000ptas other. Centro Nacional de Investigaciones Metalurgicas, Avenida de Gregorio del Amo 8, 28040 Madrid Spain. **Tel** 011 34 1 2020440. **ED** L Froufe Carlos. **LC** TN600; .R48. **CODEN** RMTGAC. Index available. cum. index. **Bk Rev. Ad Acc. Pr Rev. Circ:** 2,000. Documents available from Article Express International, CASDDS.
**Desc:** Covers physical metallurgy corrosion, protection foundry mechanics, non ferrous metals, metallography, extractive metallurgy, minerals and preparation.
**Ind/Abst** Alum. Ind. Abstr.; Anal. Abstr.; Bioeng. Abstr.; Chem. Abstr.; Ei Page One; Eng. Index Annu.; GeoRef; Leadscan; Met. Abstr.; Proc. Chem. Eng.; Theoret. Chem. Eng.

FR
**REVUE DE METALLURGIE. CAHIERS & MEMOIRES.** French. Twenty-two times a year. 2250.00F France; 2835.00F other. La Revue de Metallurgie, 1 rue Paul Cezanne, F 75008 Paris France. **Tel** 11 33 1 49537226, FAX (33)1 47 67 85 77, telex 611 672 F.

FR/0035-1563
**REVUE DE METALLURGIE (PARIS).** (REVUE DE METALLURGIE. CAHIERS D'INFORMATIONS TECHNIQUES.). [Rev. metall.]. **VFOAT** Revue de Metallurgie - C.I.T.; Revue de Metallurgie - CIT; Cahiers d'Informations Techniques - Revue de Metallurgie. Vol. 77, No. 1 (Jan. 1980)-. Academic Scholarly Publication. French (summaries and/or abstracts in English). Eleven times a year. 2200.00F (France); 2650.00F (other). La Revue de Metallurgie, 1 rue Paul Cezanne, F 75008 Paris France. **Tel** 11 33 1 49537226, FAX (33)1 47 67 85 77, telex 611 672 F. **LC** TN2; .R5. **DD** 669/.005. **UDC** 669. **CODEN** CITMDA. **[CCC]. Bk Rev. Ad Acc. Pr Rev. Circ:** 2,400 (ctrl). Documents available from Article Express International, The Genuine Article, CASDDS. ***Continues*** *Revue de Metallurgie, 0035-1563; Memoires et Etudes Scientifiques de la Revue de Metallurgie.*
**Desc:** Covers iron and steel making, products and general metallurgy.
**Ind/Abst** Alum. Ind. Abstr.; Bioeng. Abstr.; Ceram. Abstr. (19??-); Chem. Abstr.; Coal Abstr.; Curr. Contents Eng. Tech. Appl. Sci.; Ei Page One; EMBASE; Energy Res. Abstr. (May 1983-); Eng. Index Annu. [Select. Cov.]; GeoRef; Met. Abstr.; Res. Alert [Full Cov.].

FR/0988-629X
**RFM REVUE FRANCAISE DES METALLURGISTES.** (RFM.). **VFOAT** RFM (Paris. 1987). (1987)-. Periodical. French. Ten times a year. 434.00F France; 875.00F other. Revue Francaise des Metallurgistes, 32 rue Saint Marc, 75002 Paris France. **Tel** 011 31 1 42603151, FAX 011 31 1 42603842. **UDC** 669. ***Continues*** *R.P.M. Revue Pratique des Metallurgistes, 0760-1735.*

GW
**RHEINSTAHL TECHNIK.** **Main/Corp** Rheinstahl Aktiengesellschaft. (19??)-. German. ir. Thyssen Industrie AG, 43 Essen AM Rheinstahlahus 1, Postfach 6980, Essen Germany. **Tel** (0203)5224147, telex 855 401 THY D. **LC** TS300; .R5a. **DD** 672/.094355.

IT
**RILEVAZIONE DEI PREZZI ALL INGROSSO : ASSOMET.** (19??)-. Italian. wk (48 issues). L230000 Italy; L275000 other. Assomet Servizi Srl, Via de Togni 18, 20123 Milan Italy. **Tel** 011 39 2 86455302, FAX 011 39 2 86455332, telex 312031. **Ad Acc.** ctrl circ.
**Desc:** Weekly prices of metals in Italy.

UK/0143-4861
**RLJ. ROSKILL'S LETTER FROM JAPAN.** [RLJ. Roskill's lett. Jpn.]. **VFOAT** Roskill's Letter from Japan. (1976)-. English. mo. £140.00 UK; $250.00 US. Roskill Information Services, 2 Clapham Road, London SW9 0JA England. **Tel** 011 44 71 5825155, FAX 011 44 71 7930008, telex 917867.

XV/0035-9645
**RUDARSKO-METALURSKI ZBORNIK.** [Rud.-metal. zb.]. **VFOAT** Revue des Mines et de Metallurgie; Berg- und Huttenmannische Mitteilungen; Zhurnal Gornogo dela i Metallurgii; Mining and Metallurgy Quarterly. 1952-. Periodical. Slovak (summaries and/or abstracts in English and German; table of contents in English and German). qt. Department of Mining and Metallurgy, Faculty of Natural Science and Technology, Ljubljana Slovenia. **LC** TN4; .R843. **UDC** 6669. **CODEN** RMZBAR. Index available in last issue of volume--attached. available on microfilm from University Microfilms International (UMI). Documents available from CASDDS.
**Ind/Abst** Alum. Ind. Abstr.; Chem. Abstr.; Coal Abstr.; Ei Page One; Eng. Mater. Abstr.; Geogr. Abstr. Phys. Geogr. (?-?); Geol. Abstr.; GeoRef; Met. Abstr.; MINPROC; Mintec, Min. Technol. Abstr.

●US/1068-3690
**RUSSIAN CASTINGS TECHNOLOGY.** **Main/Corp** Kharkivskyi Politekhnichnyi Instytut Imeni V. I. Lenina. (1993)-. Periodical. English (translations available in Russian). Twelve times a year. $690.00. Allerton Press, Inc., 150 Fifth Avenue, New York NY 10011. **Tel** (212)924-3950, FAX (212)463-9684, telex 427441 ALPRES. **[CCC].** ***Continues*** *Soviet Castings Technology, 0891-0316.*

●US/1067-8212
**RUSSIAN JOURNAL OF NON-FERROUS METALS.** (1993)-. Periodical. English. Twelve times a year. $425.00. Allerton Press, Inc., 150 Fifth Avenue, New York NY 10011. **Tel** (212)924-3950, FAX (212)463-9684, telex 427441 ALPRES. **[CCC].**

UK/0036-0295
**RUSSIAN METALLURGY.** **Added/Corp** Scientific Information Consultants. (Jan./Feb. 1962)-. Periodical. English (Russian). Six times a year. $1070.00. Allerton Press, Inc., 150 Fifth Avenue, New York NY 10011. **Tel** (212)924-3950, FAX (212)463-9684, telex 427441 ALPRES. **LC** TN4; .A334623. **[CCC].** Documents available from The Genuine Article, Ask*IEEE.
**Ind/Abst** Ceram. Abstr. (19??-); Curr. Contents Eng. Tech. Appl. Sci.; INSPEC (1984-); Leadscan; Res. Alert [Full Cov.]; Sci. Cit. Index; SCISEARCH.

RU/0320-0132
**SBORNIK NAUCNYH TRUDOV - MAGNITOGORSKIJ GORNOMETALLURGICESKIJ INSTITUT IM. G. J. NOSOVA.** (SBORNIK NAUCHNYKH TRUDOV - MAGNITOGORSKII GORNO-METALLURGICHESKII INSTITUT.). [Sb. naucn. tr. - Magnitogorsk. gornometall. inst. im. G.J. Nosova]. **Main/Corp** Magnitogorskii Gorno-Metallurgicheskii Institut Im. G.I. Nosova. (1973)-. Academic Scholarly Publication. Russian. **(Subscription address:** Victor Kamkin, 4956 Boiling Brook Parkway, Rockville MD 20852.**) CODEN** TMGIDC. Documents available from CASDDS.
**Ind/Abst** Chem. Abstr. (?-1975).

RU
**SBORNIK TRUDOV CHELIABINSKOGO ELEKTROMETALLURICHESKOGO KOMBINATA.** **Main/Corp** Cheliabinskii Elektrometllurgicheskii Kombinat. **Added/Corp** Russia (1923-U.S.S.R.) Glavspetsstal. (19??)-. Academic Scholarly Publication. Russian. 1.13rub single issue. Izdatelstvo Metallurgiia, 2-i Obydenskii Per.14, G-34, Moscow Russia. **LC** TN681; .C44a. **CODEN** of SCEKAQ. Documents available from CASDDS.
**Ind/Abst** Chem. Abstr. (?-1975);(-1975).

XR/0474-8484
**SBORNIK VEDECKYCH PRACI. RADA HUTNICKA. DOKLADY. SERIIA METALLURGICHESKAIA. TRANSACTIONS. METALLURGICAL SERIES.** **Main/Corp** Vysoka Skola Banska v Ostrave. **VFOAT** Doklady. Seriia Metallurgicheskaia; Transactions. Metallurgical Series. (1966)-. Czech (English, German and Russian). **LC** TN4; .O67. **CODEN** SRAHAY. Documents available from CASDDS. ***Continues in part*** *Sbornik Vedeckych Praci.*
**Ind/Abst** Chem. Abstr.

SW/0371-0459
**SCANDINAVIAN JOURNAL OF METALLURGY.** [Scand. j. metall.]. **VFOAT** SJM. (1972)-. Periodical. English. bm. kr1450.00 US, Canada and Japan; kr1410.00 other. Munksgaard International Publishers Ltd, PO Box 2148, DK-1016 Copenhagen K Denmark. **Tel** 011 45 33 12 70 30, FAX 011 45 33 12 93 87, telex 19431 MUNKS DK. **ED** J O Edstrom. **LC** TN1; .S25. **CODEN** SJMLAG. **[CCC].** Index available. **Bk Rev. Ad Acc. Pr Rev. Circ:** 1,100. Documents available from Article Express International, The Genuine Article, Ask*IEEE, CASDDS.
**Desc:** Mining and metallurgy.
**Ind/Abst** Alum. Ind. Abstr.; Bioeng. Abstr.; Ceram. Abstr.; Chem. Abstr.; Coal Abstr.; Curr. Contents Eng. Tech. Appl. Sci.; Ei Page One; Energy Res. Abstr. (April 1973-); Eng. Mater. Abstr.; Eng. Index Annu.; INSPEC (1981-); Met. Abstr.; MINPROC; Res. Alert [Full Cov.]; Sci. Cit. Index; SCISEARCH.

GW/0720-1877
**SCHRIFTENREIHE DER GDMB GESELLSCHAFT DEUTSCHER METALLHUTTEN- UND BERGLEUTE.** **Added/Corp** Gesellschaft Deutscher Metallhutten- und Bergleute. (197?)-. Monographic series. German. Bezirksverwaltung Clausthal-Zellerfeld der Bergbau-Berufsgenossenschaft, Berliner Strasse 2, 3392 Clausthal-Zellerfeld Germany. **CODEN** SGGBD6. Documents available from CASDDS. ***Continues*** *Schriften der GDMB, Gesellschaft Deutscher Metallhutten- und Bergleute, 0342-1376.*
**Ind/Abst** Chem. Abstr.

SZ/0036-7257
**SCHWEIZER ALUMINIUM RUNDSCHAU.** ***Ceased.*** [Schweiz. alum. rundsch.]. **VFOAT** Revue Suisse de l'Aluminium; Swiss Aluminium Review. Vol. 14, No. 1 (Jan. 1964)-(1989). Academic Scholarly Publication. German (French). bm. Schweizer Aluminium Rundschau, PO Box 978, 8034 Zurich Switzerland. **Tel** 01-47 24 10. **ED** Roland Hauert and Rudolf Vogtlin. **UDC** 669.71. **CODEN** SALRAY. **Bk Rev. Ad Acc. Circ:** 6,000. Documents available from Article Express International, CASDDS. ***Continues*** *Aluminium Suisse.*
**Desc:** Covers aluminum and its applications.
**Ind/Abst** Alum. Ind. Abstr.; Bioeng. Abstr.; Chem. Abstr. (1964-1983); Ei Page One; EMBASE; Eng. Mater. Abstr.; Eng. Index Annu.; Int. Packag. Abstr.; Met. Abstr.

YU/0350-820X
**SCIENCE OF SINTERING.** [Sci. sintering]. **Added/Corp** International Institute for the Science of Sintering. Vol. 6, (May 1974)-. Periodical. English (summaries and/or abstracts in Russian). Three times a year (Jan., May, Sept.). $70.00. **(Subscription address:** Jugoslovenska Knjiga, PO Box 36, YU 11001 Belgrade Yugoslovia.**) LC** TN695; .P44. **DD** 671.3/7. **CODEN** SCSNB4. Index available. Documents available from Article Express International, Ask*IEEE, CASDDS. ***Continues*** *Physics of Sintering, 0031-9198.*
**Desc:** Provides a suitable medium for the publication of papers on theoretical and experimental studies which can contribute to the better understanding of the behavior of powders and similar materials during consolidation processes.
**Ind/Abst** Alum. Ind. Abstr.; Bioeng. Abstr.; Ceram. Abstr.; Chem. Abstr.; Ei Page One; Eng. Mater. Abstr.; Eng. Index Annu.; INSPEC (May 1974-); Met. Abstr.; World Ceram. Abstr.

US/0898-0756
**SCRAP PROCESSING AND RECYCLING.** [Scrap process. recycl.]. **Added/Corp** Institute of Scrap Recycling Industries. **VFOAT** Scrap; Processing and Recycling. Vol. 1, No. 1 (Jan./Feb. 1988)-. Periodical. English. Six times a year. $26.00 US; $30.00 Canada and Mexico; $90.00 other. Institute of Scrap Recycling Industries, 1325 G Street NW Suite 1000, Washington DC 20005. **Tel** (202)737-1770. **ED** Elise Browne. **LC** WMLC 93/3334. **DD** 338. Index available. **Bk Rev. Ad Acc. Circ:** 6,000. Documents available from Documents on Demand. ***Continues*** *Scrap Age, 0036-9527.*
**Desc:** Provides current information on running scrap and recycling businesses, federal and state legislation, profiles of top plants and industry news.
**Ind/Abst** Abstr. Bull. Inst. Pap. Sci. Tech.; Alum. Ind. Abstr.; Environ. Abstr.; Met. Abstr.

US/0956-716X
**SCRIPTA METALLURGICA ET MATERIALIA.** [Scr. metall. mater.]. Vol. 24, No. 1 (Jan. 1990)-. Periodical. English. Twenty-four times a year. $655.00 The Americas; £440.00 other. Pergamon Press, An Imprint of Elsevier Science Ltd., The Boulevard, Langford Lane, Kidlington, Oxford OX5 1GB United Kingdom. **Tel** 011 44 865 843000, 011 44 865 843699, FAX 011 44 865 843010. **(Subscription address:** Elsevier Science Ltd. Oxford Fulfillment Centre, PO Box 800, Kidlington, Oxford OX5 1DX United Kingdom.**) ED** J.P. Hirth. **LC** TN1; .S36. **DD** 669/.05.

CODEN SCRMEX. **[CCC].** available on microfilm and microfiche from University Microfilms International (UMI). Documents available from Article Express International, The Genuine Article, BIOSIS Document Express, Ask*IEEE, CASDDS. ***Continues*** *Scripta Metallurgica, 0036-9748.*
**Desc:** International journal on the science of materials.
**Ind/Abst** Alum. Ind. Abstr.; Biol. Abstr.; Chem. Abstr. (1990-); Curr. Contents Eng. Tech. Appl. Sci.; Curr. Contents Phys. Chem. Earth Sci.; Energy Res. Abstr.; Eng. Index Annu.; INSPEC (Jan. 1990-); Int. Aerosp. Abstr.; Leadscan; Met. Abstr.; Res. Alert [Full Cov.]; Sci. Cit. Index; SCISEARCH.

MY
**SEAISI DIRECTORY. Main/Corp** South East Asia Iron and Steel Institute. **VFOAT** S.E.A.I.S.I. Directory. (19??)-. Directory. English. an. $100.00. South East Asia Iron and Steel Institute / Malaysia, PO Box 7094, 40702 Selangor Malaysia. **Tel** 011 60 3 5591102, FAX 011 60 3 5591159, telex 66396. **ED** Takeshi Okada. **LC** TS301; .S65a. **DD** 669/.142/02559. **Ad Acc. Circ:** 1,200 (ctrl).
**Desc:** Lists iron and steel producers, rollers, foundries, pipemakers, wire drawers of nine SEAISI member countries including SEAISI members. Larger plants, some capacity and product details are included.

SI/0129-5721
**SEAISI QUARTERLY.** [SEAISI q.]. **Main/Corp** South East Asia Iron and Steel Institute. Vol. 1 (Jan. 1972)-. Periodical. English. Four times a year. $80.00. South East Asia Iron and Steel Institute / Malaysia, PO Box 7094, 40702 Selangor Malaysia. **Tel** 011 60 3 5591102, FAX 011 60 3 5591159, telex 66396. **ED** Richard Johns and Sung-Ki Kim. **LC** TS300; .S56. **DD** 669/.142/05. **CODEN** SEQUDV. **Ad Acc. Circ:** 1,300 (ctrl). Documents available from Article Express International, CASDDS.
**Ind/Abst** Alum. Ind. Abstr.; Bioeng. Abstr.; Ceram. Abstr. (19??-); Chem. Abstr.; Coal Abstr.; Ei Page One; Eng. Mater. Abstr.; Eng. Index Annu.; Met. Abstr.; SEA Abstr.

GW
**SECONDARY ALUMINIUM, EUROPE, JAPAN, USA. Added/Corp** Organisation of European Aluminium-Smelters. English. **LC** HD9539.A6S43. **DD** 338.4/7/673722/05.

UK/0037-3435
**SHEET METAL INDUSTRIES.** [Sheet met. ind.]. (April 1927)-. Periodical. English (summaries and/or abstracts in French, German and Spanish). mo. £102.00 UK; £130.00, $239.00 other. Argus Press Group, Queensway House, 2 Queensway Redhill, Surrey RH1 1QS England. **Tel** 011 44 737 768611, 011 44 737 761685, FAX 011 44 737 760510, telex 948669 TOPJNL G. **ED** Rick Pendrous. **LC** TS250; .S453. **CODEN** SHMIAR. **Bk Rev. Ad Acc.** available on microfilm and microfiche from University Microfilms International (UMI). Documents available from Article Express International, CASDDS. ***Absorbed*** *Metal Finishing; Press Tool Engineering.*
**Desc:** Covers complete range of sheet forming operations: including rolling, pressworking, forming fabrication and finishing. Details equipment and technological developments. Official organ for several trade bodies.
**Ind/Abst** Alum. Ind. Abstr.; Bioeng. Abstr.; Chem. Abstr.; Curr. Technol. Index; Ei Page One; EMBASE; Eng. Index Annu. [Select. Cov.]; Met. Abstr.; Pollut. Abstr. Indexes; Saf. Health Work; Surf. Treat. Technol. Abstr.; World Surf. Coat. Abstr.

UK/0305-7798
**SHEET METAL INDUSTRIES YEARBOOK.** (19??)-. English. an. £69.00 UK; £80.00, $113.00 other. Argus Press Group, Queensway House, 2 Queensway Redhill, Surrey RH1 1QS England. **Tel** 011 44 737 768611, 011 44 737 761685, FAX 011 44 737 760510, telex 948669 TOPJNL G. **LC** TS250; .S454. **DD** 671.8/23/05.

US/0037-3451
**SHEET METAL WORKERS JOURNAL.** [Sheet met. work. j.]. **Added/Corp** Sheet Metal Workers' International Association. Vol. 29, No. 9 (Sept. 15, 1924)-. Periodical. English. mo. $7.50 North America; $15.90 Australia. Sheet Metal Workers International Association, 1750 New York Avenue NW, Washington DC 20006. **Tel** (202)783-5880, FAX (202)783-0318. **DD** 331. ***Continues*** *Amalgamated Sheet Metal Workers Journal.*

JA/0916-1740
**SHIGEN TO SOZAI. See** Engineering-Mines and Mining Engineering.

JA
**SHIGEN TOKEI NEMPO. YEARBOOK OF MINING, NON-FERROUS METALS, AND PRODUCTS STATISTICS. See** Metals and Metallurgy-Abstracting, Bibliographies and Statistics.

JA/0583-0419
**SHIN KINZOKU KOGYO.** [Shin kinzoku kogyo]. **Added/Corp** Shin Kinzoku Kyokai (Japan). **VFOAT** Newer Metals Industry. (1967)-. Academic Scholarly Publication. Japanese. mo. Shin Kinzoku Kyokai, Shinbashi 1-1-13, Minato-ku, Tokyo-to 105 Japan. **CODEN** SKKOAM. Documents available from CASDDS.
**Ind/Abst** Chem. Abstr.

JA/0370-985X
**SHINDO GIJUTSU KENKYUKAI-SHI.** (SHINDO GIJUTSU KENKYUKAI SHI.). [Shindo Gijutsu Kenkyukai-shi]. **Main/Corp** Shido Gijutsu Kenkyukai (Japan). **Added/Corp** Nihon Shindo Kyokai. **VFOAT** Journal of the Japan Copper and Brass Research Association; Shindo Gijutsu Kenkyu Kaishi. (1962)-. Academic Scholarly Publication. Japanese (summaries and/or abstracts in English). an. ¥5200. Nihon Shingo Kyokai, 12-22 Tsukiji 1 Chuo-ku, Tokyo-t Japan. **LC** PAR. **CODEN** SGKEBX. Documents available from CASDDS.
**Ind/Abst** Chem. Abstr.

US
**SHIPMENTS OF STEEL PRODUCTS: ALL GRADES INCLUDING CARBON, ALLOY AND STAINLESS. Main/Corp** American Iron and Steel Institute. (1971)-. Periodical. English. Twelve times a year. $40.00. American Iron & Steel Institute, 1101 17th Street Northwest, Suite 1300, Washington DC 20036. **Tel** (202)452-7100 or 7151.

AG/0325-0520
**SIDERURGIA (BUENOS AIRES).** (SIDERURGIA.). [Siderurgia]. **Added/Corp** Instituto Argentino de Siderurgia. (Aug./Oct. 1974)-. Periodical. Spanish. qt. Instituto Argentino de Siderurgia, Bernardo de Irigoyen 308 9. Piso, Buenos Aires Argentina. **LC** TS300; .S53. **CODEN** SIDEDE. Documents available from Ask*IEEE, CASDDS.
**Ind/Abst** Alum. Ind. Abstr.; Chem. Abstr. (1974-1983); INSPEC (Jan./March 1975-); Met. Abstr.

CL/0379-7759
**SIDERURGIA LATINOAMERICANA.** [Sider. latinoam.]. No. 189 (1976)-. Academic Scholarly Publication. Spanish. mo. $60.00 (members), $90.00 (nonmembers) Latin America; $70.00 (members), $110.00 (nonmembers) other. Instituto Latinoamericano del Fierro el Acero, Dario Urzua 1994, Santiago 9 Chile. **Tel** 011 56 2 2047764, FAX 011 56 2 2253111, telex 340.348 ILAFA CK. **LC** TS300; .R46. **UDC** 669.1. **CODEN** SILAD8. available on microfilm from University Microfilms International (UMI). Documents available from CASDDS. ***Continues*** *Revista Latinoamericana de Siderurgia.*
**Ind/Abst** Alum. Ind. Abstr.; Chem. Abstr. (1976-1983); Coal Abstr.; Met. Abstr.

CL
**SIDERURGIA LATINOAMERICANA EN ... Y SUS PERSPECTIVAS, LA.** Periodical. Spanish. an. **LC** HD9524.L3; I58A. **DD** 338.4/76691/098. **UDC** 311:669.1(8). ***Continues*** *Instituto Latinoamericano del Fierro y el Acero. Siderurgia en America Latina.*

US
**SILICON IN ... - U.S. DEPARTMENT OF THE INTERIOR, BUREAU OF MINES. See** Metals and Metallurgy-Abstracting, Bibliographies and Statistics.

US/0195-8054
**SILVER & GOLD REPORT. See** Business-Investments.

US/0730-8132
**SILVER INSTITUTE LETTER. Main/Corp** Silver Institute. (19??)-. Periodical. English (Spanish). bm (6 issues). $20.00. The Silver Institute, 1112 16th Street Northwest, Suite 240, Washington DC 20036. **Tel** (202)835-0185, FAX (202)835-0155, telex 904233.
**Desc:** News on silver with interesting stories on new developments, coins, and silver statistics.
**Ind/Abst** Eng. Mater. Abstr.; Stat. Ref. Index.

US/0899-6105
**SILVER (WHITTIER, CALIF.).** (SILVER.). **VFOAT** Silver Magazine. (19??)-. Periodical. English. Six times a year (Jan., Mar., May, July, Sept., Nov.). $35.00. Silver Magazine Inc., PO Box 9690, Rancho Santa Fe CA 92067. **Tel** (619)756-1054. **ED** Connie McNally. **LC** NK7100; .S5. **DD** 739.2/3/075. Index available. cum. index. **Bk Rev,** (Qty: 6). **Ad Acc. Circ:** 2,500 (ctrl). ***Continues*** *Silver Magazine, 0747-4482.*
**Desc:** Articles by noted authors on early american coin and sterling silver, silverplate: flatware, holloware and souvenirs. Auction results, and questions and answers.
**Ind/Abst** BHA : Biblio. Hist. Art.

XR/0037-6825
**SLEVARENSTVI.** [Slevarenstvi]. Began in 1953. Academic Scholarly Publication. Czech (summaries and/or abstracts in English, French, Russian and German; table of contents in English, French, German and Russian). mo. **(Subscription address:** Artia Pegas Press Ltd., Palac Metro Narodni Trida 25, 11210 Prague 1 Czech Republic.**) CODEN** SLEVAK. Documents available from CASDDS.
**Ind/Abst** Alum. Ind. Abstr.; Art Archaeol. Tech. Abstr.; Chem. Abstr.; Eng. Mater. Abstr.; Met. Abstr.; Saf. Health Work; Stat. Theory Method Abstr. (1967).

KO
**SOETMUL.** Periodical. Korean. mo. Pohang Chonghap Chechol, Chusik Hoesa 5, Tongchon-dong Pohang-si Korea. **LC** TS304.K6; S65.

SP/1130-0280
**SOLDADURA Y TECNOLOGIAS DE UNION.** [Sold. tecnol. union]. (1990)-. Periodical. Spanish. Six times a year. $140.00. Elsevier Prensa SA, Avenida Paral Lel 180, 08015 Barcelona Spain. **Tel** 011 34 3 3255350, FAX 011 34 3 4252880. **UDC** 621.79. **Ad Acc.** Full Page (B&W) 135000ptas. Half Page (B&W) 100000ptas. Full Page (Color) 165000ptas. Half Page (Color) 125000ptas. **Circ:** 3,500.
**Desc:** Contains information on soldering and welding techniques, equipment and installation.

UK/0954-0911
**SOLDERING & SURFACE MOUNT TECHNOLOGY : JOURNAL OF THE SMART (SURFACE MOUNT & RELATED TECHNOLOGIES) GROUP. Added/Corp** SMART Group. **VFOAT** Soldering and Surface Mount Technology. (Feb. 1989)-. Academic Scholarly Publication. English. Three times a year. £98.00. Wela Publications Ltd, Asahi House, 10 Church Road, Port Erin, Isle of Man., British Isles. **Tel** 011 44 0 624 836044, FAX 011 44 0 624 835400. **LC** TS610; .S64. **CODEN** SSMOEO. **[CCC]. Bk Rev. Ad Acc.** Documents available from Article Express International, CASDDS. ***Continues*** *Brazing & Soldering, 0263-0060.*
**Desc:** Technical papers by leading members of surface mount industry.
**Ind/Abst** Chem. Abstr.; Ei Page One; Eng. Index Annu.

UK/0968-1043
**SOURCE JOURNALS IN METALS & MATERIALS.** [Source journals metals mater.]. **VFOAT** Source Journals in Metals and Materials. (197?)-. English. ir. $80.00 North America; £50.00 EC countries; $90.00 other. The Institute of Materials, 1 Carlton House Terrace, London SW1Y 5DB England. **Tel** 011 44 71 839 4071, FAX (071)839 2078. **DD** 016.62011.
**Desc:** List of journals abstracted by Materials Information. Provides publishers' addresses and subject categorization.

US/1068-9397
**SOURCE JOURNALS IN METALS & MATERIALS.** [Source j. met. mater.]. **Added/Corp** Metals Information (Information Service) Materials Information (Information Service). **VFOAT** Source Journals in Metals and Materials. (1986)-. English. ir (every 2-3 years). $97.00 North America; $107.00 other. American Society for Metals International, c/o Deborah Barthelmes, Materials Park OH 44073-0002. **Tel** (216)338-5151, FAX (216)338-4634, telex 980-619. **(Subscription address:** ASM International, Materials Information, Materials Park OH 44073.**) LC** Z6678; .S63; TN600. **DD** 016.669/.005. ***Continues*** *Source Journals in Metallurgy, 0278-4181.*

US/0363-5090
**SOUTH CAROLINA METALWORKING DIRECTORY.** Directory. English. an. Free. South Carolina State Development Board, PO Box 927, Columbia SC 29202. **Tel** (803)737-0400, FAX (803)737-0418. **LC** TS203; .S63. **DD** 338.9/7/671025757. **UDC** 672(058.7)(757). **Circ:** 2,000.
**Desc:** Listing of metalworking job shops in South Carolina including a complete equipment breakdown.

US/0891-0316
**SOVIET CASTINGS TECHNOLOGY.** ***Title Change.*** [Sov. cast. technol.]. No. 1 (1986)-(1993). Periodical. English (translations available in Russian). mo. Allerton Press, Inc., 150 Fifth Avenue, New York NY 10011. **Tel** (212)924-3950, FAX (212)463-9684, telex 427441 ALPRES. **LC** TS200; .L563. **DD** 671.2/0947. **UDC** 669-14. **[CCC].** ***Continues*** *Russian Castings Production.* ***Continued by*** *Russian Castings Technology.*
**Ind/Abst** Eng. Mater. Abstr.

US/0888-689X
**SOVIET MATERIALS SCIENCE REVIEWS.** ***Ceased.*** **See** Engineering-Mechanical Engineering and Machinery.

US/0038-5735
**SOVIET POWDER METALLURGY AND METAL CERAMICS.** ***Title Change.*** **Added/Corp** Consultants Bureau. Akademiia Nauk Ukrainskoi RSR. (1962)-(199?). Academic Scholarly Publication. English (Russian). mo. Plenum Press, 233 Spring Street, New York NY 10013-1578. **Tel** (212)620-8000, (800)221-9369, FAX (212)463-0742, (212)807-1047, telex 23/421139. **CODEN** SPMCAV. **[CCC].** available in print. Documents available from Article Express International, CASDDS. ***Continues*** *Soviet Powder Metallurgy.* ***Continued by*** *Powder Metallurgy and Metal Ceramics.*
**Ind/Abst** Appl. Mech. Rev.; Chem. Abstr.; Curr. Contents Eng. Tech. Appl. Sci.; Ei Page One; Eng. Index Annu.

US
**SPECTOR REPORT ALUMINUM INDUSTRY SERVICE.** English. Twelve times a year. $2,200.00. Spector Report Inc., PO Box 467, Hewlett NY 11557. **Tel** (212)309-8310, FAX (516)374-2363.

GW/0340-4803
**STAHL UND EISEN.** [Stahl Eisen]. **Added/Corp** Verein Deutscher Eisenhuttenleute. Verein Deutscher Eisen- und Stahl-Industrieller. Nordwestliche Gruppe. Verband Oberer Angestellter der Eisen- und Stahlindustrie. (Jan./July 1881)-. Periodical. German. mo. DM287.00 Germany; DM391.00 other. Verlag Stahleisen mbH, Postfach 105164, D 40042 Duesseldorf Germany. **Tel** 011 49 211 67070. **LC** TS300; .S7. **DD** 669/.1/05. **CODEN** STEIA3. **[CCC].** Index available (bound in 2nd issue). cum. index. **Bk Rev. Ad Acc. Pr Rev.** ctrl circ. Documents available from Article Express International, The Genuine Article, Ask*IEEE, CASDDS, Documents on Demand. ***Absorbed*** *Klepzig Fachberichte fur die Fuhrungskrafte aus Maschinenbau und Huttenwesen, 0023-2092.*
**Desc:** Iron and steel technology.
**Ind/Abst** Alum. Ind. Abstr.; Arts Humanit. Citation Index [Select. Cov.]; Bioeng. Abstr.; Ceram. Abstr. (19??-); Chem. Abstr.; Coal Abstr.; Corros. Abstr. (199?-); Curr. Contents Eng. Tech. Appl. Sci.; Ei Page One; Energy Inf. Abstr.; Energy Res. Abstr.; Eng. Index Annu.; Environ. Abstr.; F&S Index Plus Text, Int. [Select. Cov.]; INSPEC (Jan. 1984-Dec. 1986); Int. Civil Eng. Abstr.; Met. Abstr.; PROMT; Res. Alert [Full Cov.]; Saf. Health Work; Sci. Cit. Index; SCISEARCH; Soc. Sci. Cit. Index [Select. Cov.]; Soft. Abstr. Eng.

GW/0138-1679
**STAHLBERATUNG.** [Stahlberatung]. **Added/Corp** Deutsche Demokratische Republik. Stahlberatungsstelle des Ministeriums fuer Erzbergbau, Metallurgie und Kali. (1974)-. Academic Scholarly Publication. German. **CODEN** STAHDH. Documents available from CASDDS.
**Ind/Abst** Chem. Abstr.

JA
**STAINLESS.** Japanese. mo. $118.00. Sutenresu Kyokai, (Japan Stainless Steel Assoc.), Tekko Kaikan, 2-10, Nihonbashi, Kayabacho 3 Chome, Chuoku, Tokyoto 103, Japan. **(Subscription address:** Kyowa Book Company Inc., 1-38 Kanda Jinbo-Cho, Chiyoda-Ku, Tokyo 101, Japan (Phone: 03-3293-0727))

US/0195-8747
**STAINLESS STEEL AND ALLOY TOOL STEEL: U.S. IMPORTERS' PRICES, UNSHIPPED ORDERS, AND INVENTORIES, ANNUAL SURVEY.** (STAINLESS STEEL AND ALLOY TOOL STEEL. U.S. IMPORTERS' PRICES, UNSHIPPED ORDERS, AND INVENTORIES, ANNUAL SURVEY : REPORT TO THE PRESIDENT ON INVESTIGATION NO. 332-94 UNDER SECTION 332 OF THE TARIFF ACT OF 1930.). 1978-. English. an. Office of the Secretary, United States International Trade Commission, Washington DC 20436. **Tel** (202)523-0235. **LC** HD9529.S623; U548A. **DD** 338.4/3672/0973. **UDC** 338:669.14.018.8(73). available on microfiche (Vols. for 1978- distributed to depository libraries).

UK
**STAINLESS STEEL DATABOOK.** (1957)-. Directory. English. ir. $144.00. Metal Bulletin PLC, PO Box 28E, Worcester Park, Surrey KT4 7HX England. **Tel** 011 44 71 827 9977, FAX 011 44 81 337 8943. **ED** Henry Cooke and Richard Serjeantson. **Ad Acc. Circ:** 3,000.
**Desc:** Directory of stainless steel producers, processors and traders.

UK/0306-2988
**STAINLESS STEEL INDUSTRY. See** Economics-Industry and Production.

US/0730-8140
**STAINLESS STEELS DIGEST.** [Stainl. steels dig.]. **Added/Corp** American Society for Metals. Technical Divisions and Activities. (19??)-. Periodical. English. mo. $175.00 (nonmembers), $145.00 (members) North America. American Society for Metals International, c/o Deborah Barthelmes, Materials Park OH 44073-0002. **Tel** (216)338-5151, FAX (216)338-4634, telex 980-619. **(Subscription address:** ASM International, Materials Information, Materials Park OH 44073.) **Bk Rev.**
**Desc:** Reproduces complete, subject-relevant abstracts as published in metals abstracts.
**Ind/Abst** Abstr. Bull. Inst. Pap. Sci. Tech.

UK/1355-5634
**STAINLESS STEELS MONTHLY.** (19??)-. Trade Publication. English. mo. £675.00 UK; $1,150.00 US. Metal Bulletin PLC, PO Box 28E, Worcester Park, Surrey KT4 7HX England. **Tel** 011 44 71 827 9977, FAX 011 44 81 337 8943.

RU/0038-920X
**STAL.** [Stal]. **Added/Corp** Soviet Union. Ministerstvo Chernoi Metallurgii. Soviet Union. Narodnyi Komissariat Chernoi Metallurgii. Vol. 1, (1941)-. Periodical. Russian. mo. $189.95. **(Subscription address:** East View Publications Inc., 3020 Harbor Lane North, Suite 110, Minneapolis MN 55447.) **LC** TS300; .S72. **CODEN** STALAQ. **[CCC].** Index available. **Bk Rev. Ad Acc.** available on microfilm from University Microfilms International (UMI). Documents available from Article Express International, CASDDS. ***Absorbed*** *Metallurg; Rabochii Metallurg; Stal (Kharkov, R.S.S.F.R); Teoriia Praktika Metallurgii; Uralskaia Metallurgiia.*
**Ind/Abst** Alum. Ind. Abstr.; Chem. Abstr.; Coal Abstr.; Ei Page One; Eng. Index Annu.; Met. Abstr.; Surf. Treat. Technol. Abstr.; World Alum. Abstr.

US/1043-5093
**STAMPING QUARTERLY.** [Stamp. q.]. Vol. 1, No. 1 (Spring 1989)-. Periodical. English. qt. Free (trade), $15.00 (nontrade) US; $25.00 Canada & Mexico; $45.00 other. Croydon Group Ltd., 833 Featherstone Road, Rockford IL 61107. **Tel** (815)399-8700, FAX (815)399-7279. **ED** Theresa Olmsted. **DD** 671. Index available. cum. index. **Ad Acc, Adv Mgr:** Penni Korte. **Circ:** 35,000 (ctrl).
**Desc:** Covers stamping and pressworking technology.

FR/0254-2552
**STATISTICAL BULLETIN - CIPEC DOCUMENTATION CENTRE. See** Economics-Industry and Production.

US
**STATISTICS OF WORLD TRADE IN STEEL (NEW YORK N.Y. : 1976). See** Economics-Industry and Production.

GW/0941-388X
**STEEL & MATERIALS TECHNOLOGY.** [Steel mater. technol.]. **VFOAT** Steel and Materials Technology; Fachberichte Metallurgie & Werkstofftechnik, Umwelt-Verfahrenstechnik. (1990)-. Periodical. Multiple languages. mo. **UDC** 66/68. ***Continues*** *International Steel & Metals Magazine, 0934-5965.*

US/0039-0925
**STEEL HORIZONS.** ***Title Change.*** 1939-?. Periodical. English. qt. Allegheny Ludlow Steel, 20th Floor/Oliver Building, Pittsburgh PA 15222. ***Superseded by*** *Allegheny Ludlum Horizons, 0149-1997.*

●US/0967-0912
**STEEL IN TRANSLATION. Added/Corp** Institute of Materials (London, England) British Library. Document Supply Centre. Vol. 22, No. 1 (Jan. 1992)-. Periodical. English (translations available in Russian). Twelve times a year. $675.00 UK; $905.00 other. Allerton Press, Inc., 150 Fifth Avenue, New York NY 10011. **Tel** (212)924-3950, FAX (212)463-9684, telex 427441 ALPRES. **LC** TS300; .S745. **DD** 669/.142/05. **CODEN** STETE6. ***Continues*** *Steel in the USSR, 0038-9218.*
**Ind/Abst** Sci. Cit. Index; Soc. Sci. Cit. Index [Select. Cov.].

II/0970-1311
**STEEL INDIA.** [Steel India]. **Added/Corp** Research & Development Centre for Iron & Steel (Ranchi, India). (1978)-. Academic Scholarly Publication. English. sa. $25.00. Research and Development Centre for Iron and Steel, Steel Authority of India, Ranchi, India 834002. **(Subscription address:** Prints India, 11 Darya Ganj, New Delhi, 110002 India, (Phone: 011 91 11 3268645)) **CODEN** STINE8. Documents available from CASDDS.
**Ind/Abst** Ceram. Abstr. (19??-); Chem. Abstr.

JA
**STEEL INDUSTRY OF JAPAN, THE. See** Economics-Industry and Production.

US/0163-206X
**STEEL INDUSTRY REVIEW. See** Economics-Industry and Production.

US/1063-4339
**STEEL INDUSTRY UPDATE.** [Steel ind. upd.]. (1986)-. Newsletter. English. Ten times a year. $295.00 (one year), $550.00 (two year). Locker Associates, 225 Broadway, Suite 2625, New York NY 10007. **Tel** (212)962-2980. **DD** 672. **Bk Rev,** (Qty: 2).
**Desc:** Summarizes the trade press and charts statistical data, and keeps up with the trends and changes in the world steel economy.

FR
**STEEL MARKET IN ... AND THE OUTLOOK FOR ... , THE. Added/Corp** Organisation for Economic Co-Operation and Development. (1978)-. Government Publication. English. an (July). $29.00. OECD Publications and Information Center, 2 rue Andre-Pascal, 75775 Paris Cedex 16 France. **Tel** 011 33 1 45248167, US:(202)785-6323, FAX 011 33 1 45248500 OR 45248176, telex 620 160 OCDE. **(Subscription address:** OECD Publications Center, 2001 L Street, Suite 700, Washington DC 20036.) **LC** HD9510.1; .S73. **DD** 338.4/7669142/05.
**Desc:** An analysis that includes statistics on production, consumption, trade, capacity, and manpower as well as information on the impact of non-OECD countries on the steel market.

UK
**STEEL MARKET PRICE DATA ON TELEFAX.** English. available only to subscribers of "European Steel Review", £100.00 Europe; £120.00 other. MEPS (Europe) Ltd, 263 Glossop Road, Sheffield S10 2GZ, England. **Tel** 011 44 742 750570, FAX 011 44 742 759808, telex 547938 EXPERT G.
**Desc:** Provides price information on flat rolled and long products.

UK/0964-7694
**STEEL MARKETS MONTHLY.** [Steel mark. mon.]. (1991)-. Trade Publication. English. mo. £725.00 UK; $1,235.00 US. Metal Bulletin PLC, PO Box 28E, Worcester Park, Surrey KT4 7HX England. **Tel** 011 44 71 827 9977, FAX 011 44 81 337 8943. **ED** Tony Murray. **DD** 338.47669.

SA
**STEEL METALS MONITOR.** Mintek, Private Bag X3015, Randburg 2125 South Africa. **Tel** 011 27 11 7933511, FAX 011 27 11 7932413, telex 4-24867.

US/0148-2807
**STEEL MILL PRODUCTS (LEXINGTON). See** Economics-Industry and Production.

US/0275-6862
**STEEL MILL PRODUCTS (WASHINGTON, D.C.).** ***Ceased.*** (CURRENT INDUSTRIAL REPORTS. MA-33B, STEEL MILL PRODUCTS / U.S. DEPARTMENT OF COMMERCE, BUREAU OF THE CENSUS.). [Steel mill prod.]. **Added/Corp** United States. Bureau of the Census. **VFOAT** Steel Mill Products. (19??)-(19??). Government Publication. English. an. Superintendent of Documents, US Government Printing Office, Washington DC 20402. **Tel** (202)275-3328, FAX (202)786-2377. **(Subscription address:** US Government Bookstore / O'Neil Building, 2023 3rd Avenue North, Birmingham AL 35203.) **LC** HD9514; .S674a. **DD** 338.4/7672/0973.
**Desc:** Presents timely data on the production, inventories, and orders of approximately 5,000 products, which represents 40 percent of all US manufacturing.

UK
**STEEL OUTLOOK.** (19??)-. Periodical. English. qt. £800.00. MEPS (Europe) Ltd, 263 Glossop Road, Sheffield S10 2GZ, England. **Tel** 011 44 742 750570, FAX 011 44 742 759808, telex 547938 EXPERT G.
**Desc:** Provides comprehensive steel industry analysis with emphasis on Western Europe. Includes regular reports on the European steel scene, comparisons with other major steel consuming and producing areas and steel industry data, with informed comment, to assist executives in making decisions. Contains an analysis of trends to help companies in steel and related industries prepare plans for the future.

US/0275-2239
**STEEL PRODUCTS MANUAL. Added/Corp** American Iron and Steel Institute. (19??)-. Periodical. English. ir. American Iron & Steel Institute, 1101 17th Street Northwest, Suite 1300, Washington DC 20036. **Tel** (202)452-7100 or 7151. **CODEN** SPMAAP.

AT/0726-0865
**STEEL PROFILE.** [Steel profile]. (1981)-. Periodical. English. qt. BHP Steelworks, PO Box 196 B, Newcastle NSW 2300 Australia. **DD** 338.476691420994.
**Ind/Abst** AESIS Q.

GW/0177-4832
**STEEL RESEARCH.** [Steel res.]. **Added/Corp** Verein Deutscher Eisenhuttenleute. Max-Planck-Institut fuer Eisenforschung. **VFOAT** Archiv fur das Eisenhuttenwesen. Vol. 56, No. 1 (1985)-. Academic Scholarly Publication. English (German). mo. DM407.00 Germany; DM478.00 other. Verlag Stahleisen mbH, Postfach 105164, D 40042 Duesseldorf Germany. **Tel** 011 49 211 67070. **LC** TS300; .A85. **DD** 672/.05. **CODEN** STRSEY. **[CCC].** Index Available in first issue of next volume--attached. **Ad Acc. Pr Rev.** Documents available from Article Express International, The Genuine Article, Ask*IEEE, CASDDS. ***Continues*** *Archiv fur das Eisenhuttenwesen, 0003-8962.*
**Ind/Abst** Alum. Ind. Abstr.; Bibliogr. Mission.; Bioeng. Abstr.; Ceram. Abstr.; Chem. Abstr. (1985-); Coal Abstr.; Curr. Contents Eng. Tech. Appl. Sci.; Ei Page One; Elect. Comm. Abstr.; EMBASE; Energy Res. Abstr.; Eng. Index Annu.; Environ. Eng. Abstr.; GeoRef; INSPEC (1985-); Int. Aerosp. Abstr.; Manuf. Process Eng. Abstr.; Mater. Sci. Eng. Abstr.; Mech. Eng. Abstr.; Met. Abstr.; Res. Alert [Full Cov.]; Sci. Cit. Index; SCISEARCH; Solid State Supercond. Abstr.

UK/0953-2412
**STEEL TECHNOLOGY INTERNATIONAL.** (1988)-. Periodical. English. Sterling Publications Ltd., PO Box 799, Brunel House, London W2 1XR England. **Tel** 011 44 71 2580066, FAX 011 44 71 4026441, telex 295819 ESPEEL G. **LC** TS300; .S79. **DD** 672/.05.
**Ind/Abst** Ceram. Abstr. (19??-).

UK/0039-095X
**STEEL TIMES.** [Steel times]. Vol. 188 (Jan. 1964)-. Academic Scholarly Publication. English. mo. £100.15

UK; £137.00, $212.50 other. Argus Press Group, Queensway House, 2 Queensway Redhill, Surrey RH1 1QS England. **Tel** 011 44 737 768611, 011 44 737 761685, FAX 011 44 737 760510, telex 948669 TOPJNL G. **LC** TN1; .I7. **CODEN** STLTA3. available on microfilm and microfiche from University Microfilms International (UMI). Documents available from Article Express International, CASDDS. ***Continues** Steel & Coal.*
**Desc:** Provides expert, modern coverage on European iron and steel making.
**Ind/Abst** Alum. Ind. Abstr.; Art Archaeol. Tech. Abstr.; Bioeng. Abstr.; Ceram. Abstr.; Chem. Abstr.; Coal Abstr.; Curr. Technol. Index (-1988); Ei Page One; EMBASE; Eng. Mater. Abstr.; Eng. Index Annu. [Select. Cov.]; Met. Abstr.; Saf. Health Work; World Ceram. Abstr.

UK/0143-7798
**STEEL TIMES INTERNATIONAL.** [Steel times int.]. (1977)-. Academic Scholarly Publication. English. bm. £84.15 UK; £108.10, $167.60 other. Argus Press Group, Queensway House, 2 Queensway Redhill, Surrey RH1 1QS England. **Tel** 011 44 737 768611, 011 44 737 761685, FAX 011 44 737 760510, telex 948669 TOPJNL G. **LC** TN730; .S692. **DD** 669/.142. **CODEN** STTIDD. Documents available from CASDDS. ***Absorbed** Iron and Steel International, 0308-9142.*
**Desc:** Covers every aspect of the industry from iron ore to the semi finished product.
**Ind/Abst** Alum. Ind. Abstr.; Ceram. Abstr. (19??-19??); Chem. Abstr.; Coal Abstr. (-1988); Ei Page One; Leadscan; Met. Abstr.

JA/0388-0923
**STEEL TODAY & TOMORROW (SEMIANNUAL EDITION).** (STEEL TODAY & TOMORROW : A PUBLICATION OF JAPAN IRON & STEEL EXPORTERS' ASSOCIATION.). [Steel today tomorrow]. **Added/Corp** Japan Iron & Steel Exporters' Association. (19??)-. Periodical. English. sa. Free upon request. Japan Iron & Steel Exporters, 3-2-10 Nihonbashi-Kayabacho, Chuo-ku Tokyo Japan. **Tel** 011 03 669 4811. **Circ:** 15,500 (ctrl).
**Desc:** It has been providing in-depth reporting of significant developments in the Japanese steel industry and furnishing extensive information about iron and steel products.
**Ind/Abst** Alum. Ind. Abstr.; Eng. Mater. Abstr.; Met. Abstr.

US/0730-8388
**STEEL (WASHINGTON, D.C. : 1976).** (STEEL.). [Steel]. Vol. 1; 1976-. Periodical. English. bm. American Iron & Steel Institute, 1101 17th Street Northwest, Suite 1300, Washington DC 20036. **Tel** (202)452-7100 or 7151. available on microfilm from University Microfilms International (UMI). ***Continues in part** Steel Facts, 0039-0917.*

US/0883-3141
**STEELABOR.** **See** Economics-Labor.

US/1048-0307
**STEELS ALERT.** [Steels alert]. **Added/Corp** Institute of Metals. American Society for Metals. Vol. 3, No. 1 (Jan. 1985)-. Periodical. English. mo. $315.00 (nonsubscribers to Metals Abstracts), $200.00 (subscribers to Metals Abstracts) North America. American Society for Metals International, c/o Deborah Barthelmes, Materials Park OH 44073-0002. **Tel** (216)338-5151, FAX (216)338-4634, telex 980-619. **DD** 672. available on CD-ROM from DIALOG. ***Continues** Steels Supplement to Metals Abstracts.*
**Desc:** Keeps abreast of developments all over the world to maintain your company's competitive position in this area.

GW
**STEELS & MATERIAL TECHNOLOGY NOW RECYCLING PRAXIS.** (19??)-. German. ir. Sprechsaal Publishing Group, PO Box 2962, D-96418 Coburg Germany. **Tel** 011 49 9561 742810, FAX 011 49 9561 90009, telex 179561817. **(Subscription address:** Domhardt Pressevertrieb, Naegleinsgasse 2, D 96450 Coburg Germany.**)** ***Continues** Fachberichte Huttenpraxis Metallweiterverarbeitung, 0340-8043.*

JA/0371-408X
**SUIYOKAI SHI.** **See** Engineering-Mines and Mining Engineering.

JA/0039-4963
**SUMITOMO KEIKINZOKU GIHO.** (SUMITOMO KEIKINZOKU GIHO / SUMITOMO LIGHT METAL TECHNICAL REPORTS.). [Sumitomo Keikinzoku giho]. **Added/Corp** Sumitomo Keikinzoku Kogyo Kabushiki Kaisha. Gijutsu Kenkyujo. **VFOAT** Sumitomo Light Metal Technical Reports. (1970)-. Academic Scholarly Publication. Japanese (Japanese; summaries and/or abstracts in English). Four times a year. Y5000.00 US & Canada; Y6000.00 Pan American & Europe; Y8000.00 Japan. Sumitomo Light Metal Industries Ltd., 3-1-12 Chitose Technical Research Laboratory, Minato ke Nagoya 455 Japan. **CODEN** SKEGA2. available on microfilm from University Microfilms International (UMI). Documents available from Article Express International, CASDDS.
**Ind/Abst** Alum. Ind. Abstr.; Bioeng. Abstr.; Chem. Abstr.; Ei Page One; Eng. Index Annu.; Met. Abstr.

JA/0371-411X
**SUMITOMO KINZOKU.** [Sumitomo kinzoku]. **Added/Corp** Sumitomo Kinzoku Kogyo Kabushiki Kaisha. **VFOAT** Sumitomo Metals. (1952)-. Academic Scholarly Publication. Japanese (summaries and/or abstracts in English). qt. Sumitomo Light Metal Industries Ltd., 3-1-12 Chitose Technical Research Laboratory, Minato ke Nagoya 455 Japan. **CODEN** SUKIA6. Documents available from Article Express International, CASDDS. ***Continues** Fuso Kinzoku.*
**Ind/Abst** Alum. Ind. Abstr.; Bioeng. Abstr.; Chem. Abstr.; Coal Abstr.; Ei Page One; Eng. Index Annu.; Met. Abstr.

JA/0585-9131
**SUMITOMO SEARCH, THE.** [Sumitomo search]. **Added/Corp** Sumitomo Kinzoku Kogyo Kabushiki Kaisha. (May 1969)-. Periodical. English. Twice a year. Free on request. Sumitomo Metal America Inc., 420 Lexington Avenue, New York NY 10017. **Tel** (212)949-4760. **LC** TS300.S8. **DD** 669/.142/05. **CODEN** SUSEAY. Documents available from Article Express International, Ask*IEEE, CASDDS.
**Ind/Abst** Alum. Ind. Abstr.; Bioeng. Abstr.; Chem. Abstr.; Coal Abstr.; Corros. Abstr.; Ei Page One; Eng. Mater. Abstr.; Eng. Index Annu.; INSPEC (Nov. 1973-); Met. Abstr.

JA
**SUMITOMO TOKUSHU KINZOKU GIHO.** [Sumitomo tokushu kinzoku giho]. **Added/Corp** Sumitomo Tokushu Kinzoku Kabushiki Kaisha. **VFOAT** Technical Report of Sumitomo Special Metals. (1973)-. Academic Scholarly Publication. Japanese (summaries and/or abstracts in English). Sumitomo Tokushu Kinzoku KK, Kitahama 2-11, Higashi-ku, Osaka 541 Japan. **CODEN** STKGDU. Documents available from CASDDS.
**Ind/Abst** Chem. Abstr.

UK
**SURFACE TREATMENT TECHNOLOGY ABSTRACTS.** **See** Metals and Metallurgy-Abstracting, Bibliographies and Statistics.

FR/0585-9840
**SURFACES.** [Surfaces]. (Nov. 1962)-. Academic Scholarly Publication. French (summaries and/or abstracts in English, German and Italian). Eight times a year. 391.77F France; 560.00F other. Group Cepp Editions Ampere, 25 rue Dagorno, 75012 Paris France. **Tel** 011 33 1 43473020, FAX 011 33 1 43473080. **ED** Claude Chapelon. **LC** TS653.A1; S83. **CODEN** SUFPA2. **[CCC]. Ad Acc. Circ:** 6,373 (ctrl). Documents available from CASDDS.
**Desc:** Metal finishing treatments electroplating - paints.
**Ind/Abst** Alum. Ind. Abstr. (19??-); Chem. Abstr. (19??-); Eng. Mater. Abstr. (19??-); Met. Abstr. (19??-); World Surf. Coat. Abstr. (19??-).

SZ/0379-6779
**SYNTHETIC METALS.** [Synth. met.]. Vol. 1 (Oct. 1979)-. Academic Scholarly Publication. English. Twenty-four times a year (8 vols.). 3200.00F. Elsevier Sequoia SA, PO Box 564, CH-1001 Lausanne 1 Switzerland. **Tel** 011 41 21 3207381. **ED** Alan J. Heeger. **LC** TN693.T7; S96. **DD** 669/.7. **CODEN** SYMEDZ. **[CCC]. Ad Acc, Adv Mgr:** Ms. W van Cattenburch (Amsterdam). **Pr Rev.** available on microfilm and microfiche from University Microfilms International (UMI). Documents available from Article Express International, The Genuine Article, Ask*IEEE, CASDDS.
**Desc:** Integrates research and applications on intercalation compounds of graphite, transition metal compounds and quasi one-dimensional conductors.
**Ind/Abst** Alum. Ind. Abstr.; Bioeng. Abstr.; Chem Inform; Chem. Abstr.; Chem. Titles; Curr. Contents Phys. Chem. Earth Sci.; Curr. Titles Electrochem.; Ei Page One; Elect. Comm. Abstr.; Energy Res. Abstr. (Aug. 1981-); Eng. Mater. Abstr.; Eng. Index Annu.; INSPEC (Oct. 1979-); Mater. Sci. Eng. Abstr.; Met. Abstr.; Pollut. Abstr. Indexes; Polymer Contents; Res. Alert [Full Cov.]; Sci. Cit. Index; SCISEARCH; Solid State Supercond. Abstr.

JA/0039-8993
**TAIKABUTSU.** (TAIKABUTSU. REFRACTORIES.). [Taikabutsu]. **Main/Corp** Taikabutsu Gijutsu Kyokai (Japan). **VFOAT** Refractories; Taikabutsu Kogyo. Vol. 1, No. 1 (June 1949)-. Academic Scholarly Publication. Japanese (summaries and/or abstracts in English and Japanese). mo. $232.00. Taikabutsu Gijutsu Kyokai, (Technical Assoc. of Refractories, Japan), 3-13, Ginza 7 Chome, Chuoku, Tokyoto 104, Japan. **(Subscription address:** Kyowa Book Company Inc., 1-38 Kanda Jinbo-Cho, Chiyoda-Ku Tokyo 101, Japan**) CODEN** TAKOAV. **Ad Acc. Circ:** 2,100 (ctrl). Documents available from CASDDS.
**Ind/Abst** Ceram. Abstr.; Chem. Abstr.; Coal Abstr.; Eng. Mater. Abstr.; World Ceram. Abstr.

US/0270-9554
**TAILING DISPOSAL TODAY.** [Tailing dispos. today]. Vol. 1 (1973)-. English. MFP, 500 Howard Street, San Francisco CA 94105.
**Ind/Abst** GeoRef.

FR/0399-4139
**TECHNIQUES DE L'INGENIEUR. METALLURGIE.** [Tech. ing., Metall.]. **VFOAT** Metallurgie. (1956)-. Academic Scholarly Publication. French. qt. 1695.00F. Editions Techniques, 141 rue de Javel, 75747 Paris Cedex 15 France. **Tel** 011 33 1 45589100. **CODEN** TIMED2. Documents available from CASDDS.
**Ind/Abst** Chem. Abstr.

FR
**TECHNIQUES DE L'INGENIEUR / METAUX & ALLIAGES MAB.** French. Editions Techniques, 141 rue de Javel, 75747 Paris Cedex 15 France. **Tel** 011 33 1 45589100.

US/0082-2558
**TECHNIQUES OF METALS RESEARCH.** [Tech. met. res.]. V. 1, Pt. 1-. Monographic series. English. Price varies per volume. Interscience Publishers, 605 3rd Avenue, New York NY 10016. **ED** R F Bunshah. **DD** 669. **UDC** 669.

GW/0340-5060
**TECHNISCHE BERICHTE - THYSSEN.** ***Ceased.*** (THYSSEN TECHNISCHE BERICHTE.). [Tech. Ber. - Thyssen]. **Main/Corp** August Thyssen-Hutte. Vol. 6 (1974)-(1993. Periodical. German. ir. Free. Thyssen Industrie AG, 43 Essen AM Rheinstahlahus 1, Postfach 6980, Essen Germany. **Tel** (0203)5224147, telex 855 401 THY D. **ED** Alfred Altgeld and Rolf Umbach. **LC** TN690; .T53. **UDC** 669.18; 672. **CODEN** TBTHDV. cum. index. **Circ:** 8,000. Documents available from Article Express International, CASDDS. ***Continues** Thyssenforschung; **Absorbed** Rheinstahl-Technik.*
**Desc:** Production, properties, further processing and utilization of steel; components and finished products made by manufacturing industry.
**Ind/Abst** Alum. Ind. Abstr.; Bioeng. Abstr.; Chem. Abstr.; Coal Abstr.; Ei Page One; EMBASE; Energy Res. Abstr. (July 1976-); Eng. Index Annu. [Select. Cov.]; Int. Aerosp. Abstr.; Met. Abstr.

SZ
**TECHNISCHE MITTEILUNGEN.** **VFOAT** Technische Mitteilungen PTT; PTT Technische Mitteilungen. Vol. 39, No. 2 (Feb. 1961)-. Academic Scholarly Publication. German. mo. Generaldirektion PTT, Viktoriastrassee 21, CH-3000 Bern 33 Switzerland. Documents available from CASDDS.
**Ind/Abst** Chem. Abstr.

GW/0930-9284
**TECHNISCHE MITTEILUNGEN KRUPP (ENGLISH ED.).** (TECHNISCHE MITTEILUNGEN KRUPP.). [Tech. Mitt. Krupp]. No. 1 (June 1986)-. Academic Scholarly Publication. English. Krupp Gemeinschaftsbetriebe, Postfach 917, W-4300 Essen 1 Germany. Documents available from Article Express International, Ask*IEEE, CASDDS. ***Formed by the union of** Technische Mitteilungen Krupp. Forschungsberichte, 0494-9382 **and** Technische Mitteilungen Krupp. Werksberichte, 0494-9390.*
**Ind/Abst** Chem. Abstr. (1986); Ei Page One; Eng. Index Annu.; INSPEC (1986-).

SP/0371-9537
**TECNICA METALURGICA (BARCELONA).** (TECNICA METALURGICA.). [Tec. metal.]. Academic Scholarly Publication. Spanish. mo. **LC** TN4; .T37. **UDC** 669. **CODEN** TMEBAC. Documents available from CASDDS.
**Ind/Abst** Alum. Ind. Abstr.; Chem. Abstr.; Eng. Mater. Abstr.; Met. Abstr.; Surf. Treat. Technol. Abstr.

JA/0021-1575
**TETSU TO HAGANE.** [Tetsu to hagane]. **Added/Corp** Nihon Tekko Kyokai. **VFOAT** Journal of the Iron and Steel Institute of Japan. Vol. 1 (1915)-. Academic Scholarly Publication. Japanese (summaries and/or abstracts in English). mo. $480.00. Nippon Tekko Kyokai, (Iron & Steel Institute of Japan), 9-4, Otemach 1 Chome, Chiyodaku, Tokyoto 100, Japan. **(Subscription address:** Kyowa Book Company Inc., 1-38 Kanda Jinbo-Cho, Chiyoda-Ku Tokyo 101, Japan**) CODEN** TEHAA2. **[CCC]. Pr Rev.** Documents available from Article Express International, The Genuine Article, Ask*IEEE, CASDDS.
**Ind/Abst** Alum. Ind. Abstr.; Bioeng. Abstr.; Ceram. Abstr.; Chem. Abstr.; Coal Abstr.; Curr. Contents Eng. Tech. Appl. Sci.; Ei Page One; Energy Res. Abstr. (June 1980-); Eng. Index Annu.; INSPEC (1968-Nov. 1973); Met. Abstr.; Res. Alert [Full Cov.]; Sci. Cit. Index; SCISEARCH; World Ceram. Abstr.

US/1052-7877
**THESAURUS OF METALLURGICAL TERMS.** (THESAURUS OF METALLURGICAL TERMS / PREPARED BY METALS INFORMATION STAFF, AMERICAN SOCIETY FOR METALS.). [Thesaurus metall. terms]. **Added/Corp** Metals Information (Information Service) ASM International. Institute of Metals. **VFOAT** Materials Information Thesaurus of Metallurgical Terms. 1st Ed. (Jan. 1968)-. English. an. $90.00 North America; £60.00 E.C. countries; $100.00 other. American Society for Metals International, c/o Deborah Barthelmes, Materials Park OH 44073-0002. **Tel** (216)338-5151, FAX (216)338-4634, telex 980-619. **(Subscription address:** ASM International, Materials Information, Materials Park OH 44073.**) LC** Z695.1.M55; T52. **DD** 025.4/9669.

GW/0724-7265
**THYSSEN EDELSTAHL TECHNISCHE BERICHTE.** [Tech. Ber. - Thyssen-Edelstahl]. **Added/Corp** Thyssen Edelstahlwerke AG. Technische Berichte. Bd. 3, Heft 2 (1977)-. Periodical. German. Thyssen Industrie AG, 43 Essen AM Rheinstahlahus 1, Postfach 6980, Essen Germany. **Tel** (0203)5224147, telex 855 401 THY D. **CODEN** TETBDY. Documents available from Article Express International, CASDDS. ***Continues*** *TEW Technische Berichte, 0340-5125.*
**Ind/Abst** Alum. Ind. Abstr.; Bioeng. Abstr.; Chem. Abstr.; Ei Page One; Eng. Index Annu.; Int. Aerosp. Abstr. (1983-); Met. Abstr.

NE
**TIJDSCHRIFTERN VOOR OPPERVLAKTETECHNIEKEN EN CORROSIEBERSTRIJDING.** POB 9943, 1006 AP Amsterdam Netherlands.

UK/0040-7941
**TIN AND ITS USES.** ***Title Change.*** [Tin its uses]. **Added/Corp** International Tin Research Institute. International Tin Research and Development Council. Tin Research Institute. No. 1 (Apr. 1939)-(?). Periodical. English (German, French, Japanese and Spanish). qt. International Tin Research Institute, Kingston Lane, Uxbridge UB8 3PJ England. **Tel** 011 44 0895 72406. **ED** C J Evans. **LC** TN793.A1; T4. **DD** 669.6072. **CODEN** TIUSAD. **Bk Rev. Circ:** 20,000. Documents available from CASDDS. ***Continued by*** *Focus on Tin.*
**Desc:** Features technical and topical stories of tin containing materials and lists publications available from parent organization.
**Ind/Abst** Abstr. Bull. Inst. Pap. Sci. Tech.; Abstr. Graphic Arts Tech. Found. (1979-); AESIS Q.; Alum. Ind. Abstr.; Art Archaeol. Tech. Abstr.; BMT Abstr. (?-199?); Ceram. Abstr.; Chem. Abstr.; Chem. Bus. Bull.; Chem. Bus. NewsBase (1984-); Chem. Bus. Update; Curr. Technol. Index; Curr. Titles Electrochem.; Eng. Mater. Abstr.; Fluid Abstr., Civil Eng.; Fluid Abstr. Proc. Eng.; FLUIDEX (1973-1988); GeoRef; Int. Packag. Abstr. (1973-); Met. Abstr.; Pollut. Abstr. Indexes; Surf. Treat. Technol. Abstr.; World Ceram. Abstr.; World Surf. Coat. Abstr.

US/0040-7968
**TIN NEWS.** ***Ceased.*** [Tin news]. Periodical. English. mo. The Malaysian Tin Bureau, 1625 I Street NW/Room 913, Washington DC 20006. **Tel** (202)331-7550. **ED** Muhamad Nor Muhamad. **LC** HD9539.T5; T5. **UDC** 669.6. **Ad Acc. Circ:** 4,000 (ctrl).
**Desc:** News and information including data on the world tin industry and matters related thereto.
**Ind/Abst** Alum. Ind. Abstr.; Met. Abstr.

UK
**TIN STATISTICS.** ***Title Change.*** **See** Metals and Metallurgy-Abstracting, Bibliographies and Statistics.

US
**TIN TYPE.** Vol. 1, No. 1 (May 1971)-. Periodical. English. mo. $15.00. Tin Container Collectors Association, PO Box 440101, Aurora CO 88044-0101. **LC** TS195.2; .T56. **DD** 739/.532. **UDC** 739.532.

US/0364-7935
**TIN (UNITED STATES. BUREAU OF MINES).** (TIN.). [Tin]. **VFOAT** Tin in ...; Tin Industry. Academic Scholarly Publication. English. mo. US Department of the Interior / Bureau of Mines, Publications Department, PO Box 18070, Cochrans Mill Road, Pittsburgh PA 15236. **Tel** (412)892-6400. **DD** 338. **CODEN** MITID6. available on microfiche (Vols. for (1988-) distributed to depository libraries). Documents available from CASDDS, Documents on Demand.
**Ind/Abst** Am. Stat. Index; Chem. Abstr.

US/0197-1689
**TMS PAPER SELECTION.** [TMS pap. sel.]. **Main/Corp** Metallurgical Society of AIME. **VAT** The Metallurgical Society Paper Selection. Academic Scholarly Publication. English. an. Price varies per volume. Metallurgical Society, 420 Commonwealth Drive, Warrendale PA 15086. **Tel** (412)776-9080, FAX (412)776-3770, telex 910 380 9397. **UDC** 669. **CODEN** TMPSAG. Index available. cum. index. available in microform from University Microfilms International (UMI). Documents available from CASDDS.
**Ind/Abst** Chem. Abstr.; Coal Abstr.; Ei Page One.

JA/0495-7644
**TOKUSHUKO.** [Tokushuko]. **Added/Corp** Tokushu Kurabu (Japan). **VFOAT** Special Steel. (1952)-. Periodical. Japanese. mo. $216.00. Tokushuko Kurabu, (Special Steel Assoc. of Japan), 2-10, Nihonbashi Kayabacho, 3 Chome, Chuoku, Tokyoto 103 Japan. **(Subscription address:** Kyowa Book Company Inc., 1-38 Kanda Jinbo-Cho, Chiyoda-Ku Tokyo 101, Japan**) CODEN** TOKSA5. Documents available from CASDDS.
**Ind/Abst** Chem. Abstr.; Coal Abstr.

FR/0985-5637
**TOLERIE PONTAULT-COMBAULT.** (TOLERIE.). (1987)-. Periodical. French. Nine times a year. 695.48F France; 905.00F other. Marlau Editions, 16 Allee de la Source, 77340 Pontault Combault France. **Tel** 011 33 1 60280533. **UDC** 669. **Ad Acc.**
**Desc:** Sheet metal working publication.

FR/0041-0950
**TRAITEMENT THERMIQUE.** [Trait. therm.]. (19??)-. Academic Scholarly Publication. French. Nine times a year. 690.00F (France); 960.00F (other). PYC Edition, 5 Avenue de Verdun, BP 105, 94208 Ivry S Seine Cedex France. **Tel** 011 33 1 49608636. **LC** TN672; .T7. **CODEN** TRTHA4. **[CCC].** Documents available from CASDDS.
**Ind/Abst** Alum. Ind. Abstr.; Chem. Abstr.; Energy Res. Abstr.; Eng. Mater. Abstr.; Fluid Abstr., Civil Eng.; Fluid Abstr. Proc. Eng.; FLUIDEX (-19??); Met. Abstr.

IT/0041-1027
**TRANCIATURA STAMPAGGIO.** [Tranc. stamp.]. Began in 1964. Periodical. Italian. bm. Editoriale Tecnica Macchine, Via Ugo Lenzi 1, 40122 Bologna Italy. **Tel** 011 39 51 523183. **LC** TS200; .T7. **DD** 671.3/3/05. **UDC** 671.
**Ind/Abst** Alum. Ind. Abstr.; Eng. Mater. Abstr.; Met. Abstr.

JA/0387-4508
**TRANSACTIONS OF JWRI.** [Trans. J.W.R.I.]. **Main/Corp** Osaka Daigaku. Yosetsu Kogaku Kenkyujo. **VAT** Transactions of the Welding Research Institute of Osaka University. Vol. 1 (Sept. 1972)-. English. Osaka Daigaku Yosetsu Kogaku Kenkyujo, Welding Research Inst. of Osaka University), 11-1, Mihogaoka, Ibarakishi, Osakafu 567, Japan. **LC** TS227.A1; O8. **DD** 671.5/2/05. **CODEN** TRJWD2. Documents available from Article Express International, CASDDS.
**Ind/Abst** Alum. Ind. Abstr.; Ceram. Abstr. (19??-); Chem. Abstr.; Ei Page One; Eng. Index Annu.; Met. Abstr.

II/0377-9416
**TRANSACTIONS OF POWDER METALLURGY ASSOCIATION OF INDIA.** [Trans. Powder Metall. Assoc. India]. **Added/Corp** Powder Metallurgy Association of India. **VFOAT** Transactions of the P.M.A.I.; Transactions of the PMAI. (19??)-. Academic Scholarly Publication. English. an. Powder Metallurgy Association of India, DMRL Kanchanbagh, Hyderabad 500258 India. **(Subscription address:** Prints India, 11 Darya Ganj, New Delhi 110002 India.**) LC** TN695; .T75. **DD** 671.3/7/05. **CODEN** TPMIDT. Documents available from Article Express International, CASDDS.
**Ind/Abst** Alum. Ind. Abstr.; Chem. Abstr.; Ei Page One; Eng. Index Annu.; Met. Abstr.

US/0065-8375
**TRANSACTIONS OF THE AMERICAN FOUNDRYMEN'S SOCIETY (ANNUAL).** (TRANSACTIONS / AMERICAN FOUNDRYMEN'S SOCIETY.). **Main/Corp** American Foundrymen's Society. **Added/Corp** American Foundrymen's Society. Journal. American Foundrymen's Society. Transactions. (18??)-. English. an. $150.00. American Foundrymen's Society, 505 State Street, Des Plaines IL 60016-2277. **Tel** (708)824-0181, (800)537-4237, FAX (708)824-7848. **ED** Darcie Sanders. **CODEN** TAFOA6. **[CCC].** Index available. cum. index. **Circ:** 1,000. Documents available from Article Express International, CASDDS.
**Desc:** Scientific, industrial and technical papers from over one hundred international authors in the field of metallurgy and metal casting.
**Ind/Abst** Chem. Abstr.; Ei Page One; Eng. Index Annu.; Surf. Treat. Technol. Abstr.

II/0019-493X
**TRANSACTIONS OF THE INDIAN INSTITUTE OF METALS.** [Trans. Indian Inst. Met.]. **Main/Corp** Indian Institute of Metals. **Added/Corp** Indian Institute of Metals. Technical Papers. Vol. 1 (1948)-. Periodical. English. bm. $100.00. Indian Institute of Metals, 2 Sambhunath Pandit Street, Calcutta 20 India. **(Subscription address:** Prints India, 11 Darya Ganj, New Delhi 110002 India.**) LC** TN4; .I542. **DD** 669/.005. **CODEN** TIIMA3. cum. index. available on microfilm from University Microfilms International (UMI). Documents available from Article Express International, The Genuine Article, Ask*IEEE, CASDDS.
**Ind/Abst** Alum. Ind. Abstr.; Bioeng. Abstr.; Ceram. Abstr.; Chem. Abstr.; Curr. Contents Eng. Tech. Appl. Sci.; Curr. Titles Electrochem.; Ei Page One; Eng. Mater. Abstr.; Eng. Index Annu.; INSPEC (Oct. 1981-); Met. Abstr.; Res. Alert [Full Cov.]; Surf. Treat. Technol. Abstr.

UK/0020-2967
**TRANSACTIONS OF THE INSTITUTE OF METAL FINISHING.** [Trans. Inst. Met. Finish.]. **Main/Corp** Institute of Metal Finishing. Vol. 29, (1953)-. English. Four times a year (Feb., May, Aug., Nov.). £108.00. Institute of Metal Finishing, Exeter House, 48 Holloway Head, Birmingham B1 1N1 England. **Tel** 011 44 21 622 6316, FAX 011 44 21 666 6316. **ED** S. Wernick. **CODEN** TIMFA2. ***Continues*** *Electrodepositors' Technical Society. Journal of the Electrodepositors' Technical Society.*

JA/0021-1583
**TRANSACTIONS OF THE IRON AND STEEL INSTITUTE OF JAPAN.** ***Title Change.*** **Main/Corp** Nippon Tekko Kyokai. Vol. 1 (June 1961)-(Jan. 1989). English. mo. Nippon Tekko Kyokai, (Iron & Steel Institute of Japan), 9-4, Otemach 1 Chome, Chiyodaku, Tokyoto 100, Japan. **(Subscription address:** Maruzen Company Ltd., PO Box 5050, Import & Export Department, Tokyo 100 31 Japan.**) [CCC].** cum. index. **Circ:** 5,500 (ctrl). Documents available from CASDDS. ***Supersedes*** *Tetsu-to-Hagane Abstracts.* ***Continued by*** *ISIJ International, 0915-1559.*
**Desc:** Informing the technique of iron and steel of Japan abroad.
**Ind/Abst** Ceram. Abstr. (19??-19??); Chem. Abstr.; Coal Abstr.; Corros. Abstr. (-1989); Eng. Mater. Abstr.; SEA Abstr.

US/1051-0508
**TRANSACTIONS OF THE IRON & STEEL SOCIETY.** [Trans. Iron Steel Soc.]. **Added/Corp** Iron and Steel Society. ISS Foundation. **VFOAT** Transactions of the Iron and Steel Society of AIME; ISS Transactions. **VAT** Iron and Steel Society Transactions. Vol. 5 (1984)-. English. an. $52.00. Iron and Steel Society of AIME, 410 Commonwealth Drive, Warrendale PA 15086. **Tel** (412)776-9460, FAX (412)776-0430, telex 6503113507. **LC** TS300; .T7. **DD** 669. (author index only). **Pr Rev. Circ:** 150. available on microfilm. Documents available from CASDDS. ***Continues*** *Transactions of the Iron & Steel Society of AIME, 0737-0059.*
**Desc:** Covers all aspects of ironmaking and steelmaking technology.
**Ind/Abst** Chem. Abstr.

JA/0287-041X
**TRANSACTIONS OF THE JAPAN FOUNDRYMEN'S SOCIETY.** [Trans. Jpn. Foundrym. Soc.]. **Added/Corp** Nihon Imono Kyokai. Vol. 1 (May 1982)-. Academic Scholarly Publication. English (translations available in Japanese). an. $70.00. Nihon Imono Kyokai, (Japan Foundrymen's Soceity), Toyokawa Biru,, 12-13, Ginza 8 Chome, Chuoku, Tokyoto 104 Japan. **(Subscription address:** Maruzen Company Ltd., PO Box 5050, Import & Export Department, Tokyo 100 31 Japan.**) LC** WMLC 93/4304. **CODEN** TJFSEH. Documents available from CASDDS.
**Ind/Abst** Chem. Abstr. (1986).

UK/0340-4285
**TRANSITION METAL CHEMISTRY.** [Transit. met. chem.]. Vol. 1 (1975)-. Academic Scholarly Publication. English. bm. $695.00 US and Canada; £410.00 Europe; £440.00 other. Chapman & Hall, 2-6 Boundary Row, London SE1 8HN England. **Tel** 011 44 71 865 0066, FAX 011 44 71 522 9623, telex 290164 Chapmag. **(Subscription address:** Chapman & Hall, Cheriton House, North Way, Andover, Hampshire, SP10 5BE England.**) ED** D. Walton. **CODEN** TMCHDN. **[CCC].** Index available. **Ad Acc. Pr Rev. Circ:** 300. available on microfilm from University Microfilms International (UMI). Documents available from Article Express International, CASDDS.
**Desc:** Covers all aspects of the chemistry of the transition metals.
**Ind/Abst** Bioeng. Abstr.; Chem. Abstr.; Curr. Biotechnol.; Ei Page One; Energy Res. Abstr. (April 1978); Eng. Index Annu.; Sci. Cit. Index.

US/0278-4238
**TRANSLATIONS INDEX (AMERICAN SOCIETY FOR METALS).** ***Ceased.*** (TRANSLATIONS INDEX.). [Transl. index]. **Added/Corp** American Society for Metals. Vol. 5, No. 1 (Feb. 1981)-Vol. 17, No. 2. English. qt. American Society for Metals International, c/o Deborah Barthelmes, Materials Park OH 44073-0002. **Tel** (216)338-5151, FAX (216)338-4634, telex 980-619. **LC** Z6678; .A55a; TA459. **DD** 016.669. cum. index. ***Continues*** *ASM Translations Index, 0163-1659.*
**Desc:** Each issue supplies the complete, computer-generated source and author indexes to all translations currently available from the major translation sources and including Materials Information.
**Ind/Abst** Abstr. Bull. Inst. Pap. Sci. Tech.

IT/0041-1833
**TRATTAMENTI E FINITURA.** [Tratt. finit.]. (1961)-. Periodical. Italian. Nine times a year. L90000.00 Italy; L120000.00 other. Editoriale Tecnica Macchine, Via Ugo Lenzi 1, 40122 Bologna Italy. **Tel** 011 39 51 523183. **UDC** 669. **CODEN** TRFI-A. **Bk Rev. Ad Acc. Pr Rev.**
**Desc:** Technical review concerning treatment, processing, protection and finishing of metals. Processes for treating the metal surface, finishing, protection and paintings.

GW/0374-2261
**TREFILE, LE.** [Trefile]. (19??)-. Academic Scholarly Publication. French. Four times a year (Feb., May, Aug., Nov.). DM77.00. Meisenbach GmbH, Postfach 2069, D 96011 Bamberg Germany. **Tel** 011 49 951 861135.

CODEN TREFDS. Index available. **Bk Rev.** **Ad Acc.** ctrl circ. Documents available from CASDDS.
**Ind/Abst** Alum. Ind. Abstr.; Chem. Abstr.; Met. Abstr.

US/0038-5484
**TSVETNYE METALLY (ENGLISH TRANSLATION ED.).** ***Title Change.*** (THE SOVIET JOURNAL OF NON-FERROUS METALS.). [Tsvet. met.]. **VFOAT** Soviet Journal of Non-Ferrous Metals; Soviet Journal of Non Ferrous Metals; Non-Ferrous Metals; Non Ferrous Metals. Vol. 1, No. 1 (Jan. 1960)-Vol. 33 (1992)-. Periodical. English (translations available in Russian). mo. **(Subscription address:** East View Publications Inc., 3020 Harbor Lane North, Suite 110, Minneapolis MN 55447.**)** **LC** TN758; .T7293. **DD** 669. **[CCC].** Documents available from CASDDS. ***Continued by*** *Russian Journal of Non-Ferrous Metals, 1067-8212.*
**Ind/Abst** Alum. Ind. Abstr.; Chem. Abstr.; Met. Abstr.

US/1051-4120
**TUBE & PIPE QUARTERLY, THE.** (THE TUBE & PIPE QUARTERLY : TPQ.). [Tube pipe q.]. **Added/Corp** Fabricators & Manufacturers Association, International. American Tube Association. American Tube & Pipe Producers Association. Tube & Pipe Fabricators Association, Intl. **VFOAT** Tube and Pipe Quarterly; TPQ. Vol. 1, No. 1 (Summer 1990)-. Periodical. English. qt. Free (trade), $15.00 (nontrade) US; $25.00 Canada & Mexico; $45.00 other. Croydon Group Ltd., 833 Featherstone Road, Rockford IL 61107. **Tel** (815)399-8700, FAX (815)399-7279. **ED** Theresa Olmsted. **LC** TS280; .T785. **DD** 621.8/672. Index available. cum. index. **Ad Acc, Adv Mgr:** Mike Lacny. **Circ:** 30,000 (ctrl).
**Desc:** Technical and management information for tube and pipe producers and fabricators.

UK/0953-2366
**TUBE & PIPE TECHNOLOGY.** (TUBE & PIPE TECHNOLOGY : OFFICIAL JOURNAL OF THE INTERNATIONAL TUBE ASSOCIATION.). [Tube pipe technol.]. **VFOAT** Tube and Pipe Technology; TPT. (1988)-. Periodical. English. bm (6 issues). £92.50. Intras Publications, 46 Holly Walk Leamington Spa, Warwickshire CV32 4HY England. **Tel** 011 44 926 334137, US: (203)790-9330, FAX 011 44 926 314755, (203)743-4810, telex 312589. **DD** 621.8672. Index available. cum. index. **Bk Rev.** **Ad Acc, Adv Mgr:** Caroline Page. Full Page (B&W) $1325.00. Half Page (B&W) $785.00.
**Desc:** Covers metal tube production and processing.

UK/0263-6794
**TUBE INTERNATIONAL.** [Tube int.]. Vol. 1, No. 1 (Sept. 1982)-. Periodical. English. bm (6 issues). Free to manufacturers or distributors of tube or pipe and manufacturers of tubular products; £31.00 UK and North Ireland; £40.00 (airmail) Europe; £44.00 (airmail) other. Publex International Ltd., 110 Station Road East, Oxted Surrey RH8 0QA England. **Tel** 011 44 883 717755, FAX 011 44 883 714554, telex 95359 PUBLEX G. Index available (included in Nov. issue).
**Desc:** The leading publication for metal tube and pipe manufacturers and users throughout the world.
**Ind/Abst** Alum. Ind. Abstr.; Met. Abstr.

US/0049-481X
**TUNGSTEN NEWS.** Periodical. English. Amax Metals Group / Amax Materials Research Center, PO Box 1568, Ann Arbor MI 48105. **Tel** (203)629-6400.
**Ind/Abst** Alum. Ind. Abstr.; Met. Abstr.

GW/0170-9577
**TZ FUER METALLBEARBEITUNG.** ***Ceased.*** [TZ Metallbearb.]. (1977)-(1989). Academic Scholarly Publication. German (summaries and/or abstracts in English). mo. Konradin Verlagsgruppe, Postfach 100252, Ernst Mey Str 8, W-7022 Leinfelden Echterdingen 1 Germany. **Tel** (0711)75940, telex 7 255 421. **ED** Konrad Kohlhammer. **LC** TS200; .T18. **CODEN** TZMEDJ. **[CCC].** **Bk Rev.** **Ad Acc.** **Circ:** 10,100 (ctrl). Documents available from Article Express International, CASDDS. ***Continues*** *TZ fur Praktische Metallbearbeitung.*
**Desc:** Publication for metal working, manufacturing processes, machine tools, measuring and control systems, automation, numerics.
**Ind/Abst** Bioeng. Abstr.; Chem. Abstr.; Ei Page One; Eng. Mater. Abstr.; Eng. Index Annu.

US
**U.S. AND WORLD STEEL EXECUTIVE REPORT.** **Added/Corp** WEFA Group. **VFOAT** United States and World Steel Executive Report; US and World Steel Executive Report; U.S. & World Steel Executive Report. (1991)-. English. WEFA Group, 401 City Avenue, Suite 300, Bala Cynwyd PA 19004. **LC** HD9511; .U17.

SZ
**UHREN UND SCHMUCK.** Periodical. German. bm. Deutscher Judo Verband, Redaktion Ippon Segewaldweg 40, D 12557 Berlin Germany. **Tel** 011 49 711 210770, telex 051 678. **LC** TS720; .U5.

US
**USSR SCIENTIFIC ABSTRACTS: MATERIALS SCIENCE AND METALLURGY.** **Added/Corp** United States. Joint Publications Research Service. No. 1- July 1966-. Periodical. English. **(Subscription address:** National Technical Information Service, Springfield, VA**)** ***Continues*** *USSR and Eastern Europe Scientific Abstracts. Materials Science and Metallurgy, 0734-6271.*

VE
**VENEZUELA METALURGICA Y MINERA.** Spanish. Asociacion de Industriales Metalurgicos Y de Mineria, Av Principal Colinas de Bello Monte Ofic H, Caracas Venezuela. **LC** HD9506.V4; V45. **DD** 338.2/0987.

GW
**VERWALTUNGSBERICHT DES BEZIRKS CLAUSTHAL-ZELLERFELD DER BERGBAU-BERUFSGENOSSENSCHAFT.** **See** Engineering-Mines and Mining Engineering.

JA
**WAGA KUNI NO KOGOGYO: TEKKO HEN.** **Main/Corp** Japan. Tsusho Sangyosho. Daijin Kambo. Chosa Tokeibu. (19??)-. Periodical. Japanese. Daijin Kanbo, 8-9, Ginza 2-chome, Chuo-ku Tokyo 104 Japan. **LC** HD9516.J3; J28a.

GW/0043-2822
**WERKSTOFFE UND KORROSION.** (WERKSTOFFE UND KORROSION. MATERIALS AND CORROSION.). [Werkst. Korros.]. **Added/Corp** Arbeitsgemeinschaft Korrosion. Dechema. Beratungsstelle fuer Werkstoff-Fragen. **VFOAT** Materials and Corrosion. Vol. 1 (Jan. 1950)-. Periodical. German. mo. $660.00. VCH Gesellschaft GmbH, Postfach 101161, D 69451 Weinheim Germany. **Tel** 011 49 6201 606459, FAX 011 49 6201 606184. **(Subscription address:** VCH Publishers Inc., 303 Northwest 12th Avenue, Journals Department, Deerfield FL 33442.**)** **LC** TA401; .W45. **DD** 620.1/1223/05. **CODEN** WSKRAT. **[CCC].** **Pr Rev.** Documents available from Article Express International, The Genuine Article, Ask*IEEE, Petroleum Abstracts Document Delivery Service, CASDDS. ***Supersedes*** *Archiv fur Metallkunde.*
**Ind/Abst** Art Archaeol. Tech. Abstr.; Biodeter. Abstr. (1991-); Bioeng. Abstr.; BMT Abstr.; Chem. Abstr.; Chem. Titles; Civ. Struct. Eng. Abstr.; Coal Abstr.; Corros. Abstr.; Curr. Contents Eng. Tech. Appl. Sci.; Curr. Titles Electrochem.; Ei Page One; EMBASE; Energy Res. Abstr.; Eng. Mater. Abstr.; Eng. Index Annu.; HTFS Dig.; INSPEC (Aug. 1983-); Lit. Pat. Abstr., Oilfield Chem. (1969-); Lit. Abstr., Catal. Catal.; Lit. Abstr., Health Environ.; Lit. Abstr., Pet. Refin. Petrochem.; Lit. Abstr., Pet. Substit.; Lit. Abstr., Transp. Storage; Manuf. Process Eng. Abstr.; Mater. Sci. Eng. Abstr.; Life Sci. Collect.; Pet. Abstr.; Res. Alert [Full Cov.]; Sci. Cit. Index; SCISEARCH; Solid State Supercond. Abstr.; World Surf. Coat. Abstr.

GW/0173-6396
**WERKZEUG MACHINEN FUER DIE METALLBEARBEITUNG, HANDBUCH.** **VFOAT** Werkzeugmachinen fur die Metallbearbeitung. German. an. DM45.00. Vereinigte Fachverlage, Postfach 4068, D 55030 Mainz Germany. **Tel** 011 49 6131 992150. **LC** TJ1180; .W46. **DD** 621.9/02/05.

US
**WESTERN METALWORKING DIRECTORY.** Directory. English. an. $55.00. De Roche Publications, 777 West 19th Street, Suite W, Costa Mesa CA 92627. **Tel** (714)642-9978. **LC** TS203; .W47. **DD** 671/.025/78. **Ad Acc.** **Pr Rev.** **Circ:** 12,000 (ctrl).
**Desc:** Where to buy machine tools and equipment in the West.

●CN/1191-9833
**WHAT'S NEW IN WELDING.** [What's new weld.]. (Feb. 1992)-. Periodical. English. qt. Maclean Hunter Canada / Montreal, 1001 bvd. de Maisonneuve W., Montreal, Quebec H3A 3E1 Canada. **Tel** 514-845-5141, FAX 514-845-4302, telex 055-60604. **DD** 621.9. ***Continues*** *Welding Quarterly., 0845-812X.*

US/0511-9049
**WHO'S WHO IN STEEL AND METALS.** **See** Biographies.

PL/0043-5139
**WIADOMOSCI HUTNICZE.** ***Title Change.*** (WIADOMOSCI HUTNICZYCH : [ORGAN STOWARZYSZENIA INZYNIEROW I TECHNIKOW PRZEMYSU HUTNICZEGO W POLSCE].). [Wiad. hut.]. **Added/Corp** Stowarzyszenia Inzynierow i Technikow Przemysu Hutniczego w Polsce. (1945)-(19??). Academic Scholarly Publication. Polish (summaries and/or abstracts in English and Russian). mo. **CODEN** WIHUAL. Documents available from CASDDS. ***Merged with*** *Hutnik (Warszawa), 0018-8077* ***to form*** *Hutnik, Wiadomosci Hutnicze.*
**Ind/Abst** Alum. Ind. Abstr.; Chem. Abstr. (?-1991); Met. Abstr.

GW/0043-5996
**WIRE.** [Wire]. (1951)-. English. bm (Jan., Mar., May, July, Sep. Nov.). DM114.00. Meisenbach GmbH, Postfach 2069, D 96011 Bamberg Germany. **Tel** 011 49 951 861135. **[CCC].** available on microfilm from University Microfilms International (UMI). Documents available from Article Express International.
**Desc:** Technical journal covering all aspects of wire and bar production and treatment including all related subject.
**Ind/Abst** Alum. Ind. Abstr.; Ei Page One; Eng. Index Annu.; Met. Abstr.

CN/0384-4781
**WIRE AND WIRE PRODUCTS MANUFACTURERS (PRELIMINARY ED.).** ***Title Change. Suspended.*** (WIRE AND WIRE PRODUCTS MANUFACTURERS.). [Wire wire prod. manuf.]. **Main/Corp** Statistics Canada. Manufacturing and Primary Industries Division. **VFOAT** Industrie du Fil Metallique et de Ses Produits. Periodical. English (French). an. Statistics Canada, Publications Sales & Services, Main Building Room 1710, Ottawa Ontario K1A 0T6 Canada. **Tel** (613)951-5078, (800)267-6677, FAX (613)951-1584, telex 053-3585. ***Continued by*** *Suspended (1984).*

UK/0084-0424
**WIRE INDUSTRY YEARBOOK.** [Wire Ind. Yearb.]. (1966)-. English. an. £60.00 UK and Ireland; £62.00 other. Publex International Ltd., 110 Station Road East, Oxted Surrey RH8 0QA England. **Tel** 011 44 883 717755, FAX 011 44 883 714554, telex 95359 PUBLEX G. ***Continues*** *Wire Industry Handbook.*

US/0091-3162
**WIRE JOURNAL DIRECTORY/CATALOG.** **Added/Corp** Wire Association. (19??)-. English. an (Apr.). $75.00 Comes with Wire Association International membership. Wire Association International, 1570 Boston Post Road, PO Box H, Guilford CT 06437. **Tel** (203)453-2777, FAX (203)453-8384. **LC** TS270.A1; W574. **DD** 338.4/7/67184.

US/0277-4275
**WIRE JOURNAL INTERNATIONAL.** [Wire j. int.]. **Added/Corp** Wire Association International. Vol. 14, No. 4 (Apr. 1981)-. Academic Scholarly Publication. English. mo. $60.00 US; $70.00 Canada & Mexico; $80.00 other. Wire Association International, 1570 Boston Post Road, PO Box H, Guilford CT 06437. **Tel** (203)453-2777, FAX (203)453-8384. **ED** Robert F Dixon and Cliff D Addetta. **LC** TS270.A1; W57. **DD** 671.8/42. **CODEN** WJINDF. **[CCC].** Index available. cum. index. **Ad Acc.** **Circ:** 10,994 (ctrl). available on microfilm from University Microfilms International (UMI). Documents available from Article Express International, Ask*IEEE, CASDDS. ***Continues*** *Wire Journal, 0043-602X.*
**Desc:** Covers technical and business aspects of the manufacture and marketing of steel wire and wire products and nonferrous wire, cables, power cables, fiber optic cables, magnet wires, etc.
**Ind/Abst** Alum. Ind. Abstr.; Appl. Sci. Technol. Index; Bioeng. Abstr.; Chem. Abstr.; Ei Page One; EMBASE; Eng. Mater. Abstr.; Eng. Index Annu.; INSPEC (Sept. 1981-); Met. Abstr.

US/0145-2886
**WIRE TECHNOLOGY BUYER'S GUIDE.** English. $10.00. R J Callahan, PO Box 480, Stamford CT 06904. **LC** TS270.A1; W63. **DD** 338.4/7/6718402573.

US/0898-9850
**WIRE TECHNOLOGY INTERNATIONAL.** [Wire technol. int.]. **VFOAT** Wire Technology. Vol. 15, No. 4 (July/August 1987)-. Periodical. English. bm (beginning in January). $35.00 US and Canada; $68.00 other. Initial Publications, 3869 Darrow Road, Suite 101, Stow OH 44224. **Tel** (216)686-9544, FAX (216)686-9563. **ED** Thomas H. Dreher. **LC** TS270.A1; W6. **DD** 671.8/42/05. **CODEN** WTINEI. **Ad Acc.** **Circ:** 10,500 (ctrl). Documents available from Ask*IEEE. ***Continues*** *Wire Tech, 0745-7510.*
**Ind/Abst** Alum. Ind. Abstr. July/Aug. 1987-; INSPEC (July/Aug. 1987-); Met. Abstr. (July/Aug. 1987-).

UK/0951-2233
**WORLD ALUMINIUM DATABOOK.** (19??)-. English. te. $171.60. Metal Bulletin PLC, PO Box 28E, Worcester Park, Surrey KT4 7HX England. **Tel** 011 44 71 827 9977, FAX 011 44 81 337 8943. **ED** Richard Serjeantson. **Ad Acc.**
**Desc:** An extensive reference work on the aluminum industry, providing information to and about all levels of aluminum producers and traders.

UK
**WORLD CALENDAR.** **Added/Corp** Metals Information. **VFOAT** World Calendar of Forthcoming Meetings : Metallurgical and Related Fields. Vol. 6, No. 1 (Jan. 1981)-. English. Four times a year. $160.00. American Society for Metals International, c/o Deborah Barthelmes, Materials Park OH 44073-0002. **Tel** (216)338-5151, FAX (216)338-4634, telex 980-619. **(Subscription address:** ASM International, Materials Information, Materials Park OH 44073.**)** ***Continues*** *World Calendar of Forthcoming Meetings.*

**Desc:** Gives details of forthcoming conferences, exhibitions and courses covering metals and other engineered materials throughout the world.

UK/0950-2262
**WORLD COPPER DATABOOK.** (1974)-. Directory. English. ir. £63.50. Metal Bulletin PLC, PO Box 28E, Worcester Park, Surrey KT4 7HX England. **Tel** 011 44 71 827 9977, FAX 011 44 81 337 8943. **ED** Richard Serjeantson. **Ad Acc. Circ:** 3,000. ***Continues** Metal Bulletin Surveys : Copper Edition.*
**Desc:** Directory of international copper producers, processors and traders.

UK
**WORLD DIRECTORY : LEAD & ZINC MINES & PRIMARY METALLURGICAL WORKS.** (19??)-. Directory. English. £95.00 UK; $145.00 US. International Lead and Zinc Study Group, Metro House, 58 St. James Street, London SW1A 1LD England. **Tel** 011 44 71 4999373, FAX 011 44 71 4933725, telex 299819 ILZSG G.
**Desc:** A comprehensive directory of all principal lead and zinc mines and primary metallurgical plants indicating typical annual mine production rates for lead, zinc, copper, silver and annual smelter and refinery capacities.

UK
**WORLD DIRECTORY: SECONDARY LEAD PLANTS. Main/Corp** International Lead and Zinc Study Group. (Jan. 1989)-. Periodical. English. £90.00 UK; $155.00 US. International Lead and Zinc Study Group, Metro House, 58 St. James Street, London SW1A 1LD England. **Tel** 011 44 71 4999373, FAX 011 44 71 4933725, telex 299819 ILZSG G. ctrl circ.
**Desc:** Full listing of lead smelters and refineries in over 40 countries processing secondary materials showing types of plant operated and current capacities.

UK
**WORLD DIRECTORY: SECONDARY ZINC PLANTS.** (Feb. 1988)-. Periodical. English. £50.00 UK; $90.00 US. International Lead and Zinc Study Group, Metro House, 58 St. James Street, London SW1A 1LD England. **Tel** 011 44 71 4999373, FAX 011 44 71 4933725, telex 299819 ILZSG G. ctrl circ.
**Desc:** Listing of zinc plants producing zinc metal and alloys from secondary materials showing processes used and current capacities.

US/0091-8407
**WORLD MANUFACTURING.** V. 1- Aug. 1973-. Periodical. English. qt. $7.50. McGraw Hill Publishing Company, Inc., 1221 Avenue of the Americas, New York NY 10020. **Tel** (212)512-6410, (800)525-5003, FAX (212)512-6111. **LC** TS200; .W67. **DD** 671/.05. available on microfilm from University Microfilms International (UMI).

UK/0043-8758
**WORLD METAL STATISTICS. See** Metals and Metallurgy-Abstracting, Bibliographies and Statistics.

UK
**WORLD METAL STATISTICS.** (19??)-. Trade Publication. English. mo. £150.00 UK; $1,885.00 US, Canada & South America. Metal Bulletin PLC, PO Box 28E, Worcester Park, Surrey KT4 7HX England. **Tel** 011 44 71 827 9977, FAX 011 44 81 337 8943.

UK/0266-7355
**WORLD METAL STATISTICS YEARBOOK. Added/Corp** World Bureau of Metal Statistics. (1984)-. English. an. £200.00 EC countries; $400.00 other. World Bureau of Metal Statistics, 27A High Street, Ware Herts SG12 9BA England. **Tel** 011 44 0920461274, FAX 011 44 0920464258, telex 817746. **LC** HD9539.A1; W59. **DD** 338.2/74/021.
**Desc:** Documents production, consumption, international trade and stocks for the non-ferrous industry worldwide.

US/1044-7482
**WORLD MINE PRODUCTION OF SILVER.** (WORLD MINE PRODUCTION OF SILVER IN ... WITH PROJECTIONS FOR ...). [World mine prod. silver]. **Added/Corp** Silver Institute. (19??)-. English. ir. $40.00. Silver Institute, 1112 16th Street NW, Suite 240, Washington DC 20036. **Tel** (202)835-0185, FAX (202)783-2127, telex 904233 DAV INC WSH. **LC** HD9536.A1; W68. **DD** 338.2/7421/0712.

UK/0965-0830
**WORLD NICKEL STATISTICS.** [World nickel stat.]. (1991)-. Trade Publication. English. mo. £150.00 UK; $330.00 US, Canada & South America. Metal Bulletin PLC, PO Box 28E, Worcester Park, Surrey KT4 7HX England. **Tel** 011 44 71 827 9977, FAX 011 44 81 337 8943. **DD** 338.476697330212.

NE
**WORLD NICKEL STATISTICS MONTHLY BULLETIN. See** Metals and Metallurgy-Abstracting, Bibliographies and Statistics.

GW
**WORLD STEEL.** English. Four times a year. $60.00. Sprechsaal Publishing Group, PO Box 2962, D-96418 Coburg Germany. **Tel** 011 49 9561 742810, FAX 011 49 9561 90009, telex 179561817.

UK
**WORLD STEEL EXPORTS : QUANTITY. See** Economics-Industry and Production.

UK/0965-0822
**WORLD TIN STATISTICS.** (1988)-. Trade Publication. English. mo. £150.00 UK; $330.00 US, Canada & South America. Metal Bulletin PLC, PO Box 28E, Worcester Park, Surrey KT4 7HX England. **Tel** 011 44 71 827 9977, FAX 011 44 81 337 8943.
**Desc:** International tin industry data from the World Bureau of Metal Statistics, includes mine and refined production, consumption, trade, stocks and prices, collated from diverse sources.

UK
**WORLD TRADE IN LEAD AND ZINC.** (June 1985)-. English. £50.00 UK; $70.00 US. International Lead and Zinc Study Group, Metro House, 58 St. James Street, London SW1A 1LD England. **Tel** 011 44 71 4999373, FAX 011 44 71 4933725, telex 299819 ILZSG G.
**Desc:** Statistical review of the international trade in lead and zinc concentrates, lead bullion and refined lead and zinc covering the period 1973-1983.

UK/0266-7347
**WORLD WROUGHT COPPER STATISTICS.** [World wrought copp. stat.]. (1985)-. English. an. £175.00 EC countries; $350.00 other. World Bureau of Metal Statistics, 27A High Street, Ware Herts SG12 9BA England. **Tel** 011 44 0920461274, FAX 011 44 0920464258, telex 817746. **DD** 338.47669305.
**Desc:** Documents production, consumption, supply and demand of copper and copper alloy semi-manufacturers.

CC/0258-7076
**XIYOU JINSHU.** (HSI YU CHIN SHU.). [Xiyou jinshu]. **Added/Corp** Chung-kuo Chin Shu Hsueh Hui. **VFOAT** Rare Metals. (19??)-. Academic Scholarly Publication. Chinese (summaries and/or abstracts in English). qt. $60.00. Zhongguo Youse Jinshu Xuehui / Chinese Society of Nonferrous Metals, 2 Xinjiekouwai Dajie, Room 603, Beijing 100088, People's Republic of China. **Tel** 2014488, FAX 2015019. **ED** W. Qun. **LC** TN758; .H68 . **DD** 673. **CODEN** XIJID9. **Ad Acc. Circ:** 350. Documents available from CASDDS.
**Desc:** Contains information on theoretical and experimental developments in metal science.
**Ind/Abst** Alum. Ind. Abstr.; Chem. Abstr.; Met. Abstr.

CC
**YEH CHIN FEN HSI. VFOAT** Metallurgical Analysis. (19??)-. Academic Scholarly Publication. Chinese. bm. RMBY0.50. Hsin Hua Shu Tien / Beijing, Pei-Ching Fa Hsing So, Beijing, People's Republic of China. **Tel** 657331-565. **LC** TN565; .Y43 . **DD** 669/.9/05. **CODEN** YEFEET. Documents available from CASDDS.
**Ind/Abst** Chem. Abstr.

CC/1000-7571
**YEJIN FENXI. VFOAT** Metallurgical Analysis. (1981)-. Periodical. Chinese. bm. **DD** 669.9. Documents available from CASDDS.
**Ind/Abst** Chem. Abstr.

CC/0513-3424
**YOUSE JINSHU.** (YU SE CHIN SHU.). [Youse jinshu]. **VFOAT** Nonferrous Metals. Academic Scholarly Publication. Chinese (table of contents in English). qt. $5.40. Science Press, 16 Donghuangchenggen North Street, Beijing 100707, People's Republic of China. **Tel** 011 86 1 4019821, 011 86 1 4010642, FAX 011 86 1 4012180, 011 86 1 4019810, telex 210147. **CODEN** YSCSAE. Documents available from Article Express International, CASDDS.
**Ind/Abst** Alum. Ind. Abstr.; Bioeng. Abstr.; Chem. Abstr.; Ei Page One; Eng. Index Annu.; GeoRef; Met. Abstr.

RU/0044-1856
**ZASCITA METALLOV.** (ZASHCHITA METALLOV.). [Zasc. met.]. **Added/Corp** Soviet Union. Gosudarstvennyi Komitet po Koordinatsii Nauchno-Issledovatelskikh Rabot. Soviet Union. Gosudarstvennyi Komitet po Nauke i Tekhnike. **VFOAT** Metal's Protection; Protection of Metals. Vol. 1 (Jan./Feb. 1965)-. Academic Scholarly Publication. Russian. bm. $101.00. Izdatelstvo Nauka / Akademiia Nauk, Publishing House of the Russian Academy of Sciences, Leninskii Porspekt 14, 117901 Moscow Russia. **Tel** 011 95 954-21-53, FAX 011 95 938-21-44, telex 411964. **(Subscription address:** Victor Kamkin, 4956 Boiling Brook Parkway, Rockville, MD 20852**) LC** TA467; .Z33. **CODEN** ZAMEA9. Documents available from Article Express International, Ask*IEEE, CASDDS.
**Desc:** Information on protective coatings, corrosion, and anti-corrosives.
**Ind/Abst** Alum. Ind. Abstr.; Chem. Abstr.; Curr. Titles Electrochem.; Ei Page One; Energy Res. Abstr.; Eng. Mater. Abstr.; Eng. Index Annu.; INSPEC (1988-1991); Int. Aerosp. Abstr.; Met. Abstr.; World Surf. Coat. Abstr.

UN/0514-5864
**ZASHCHITNYE POKRYTIIA NA METALLAKH / AKADEMIIA NAUK UKRAINSKOI SSR, INSTITUT PROBLEM MATERIALOVEDENIIA. Added/Corp** Instytut Problem Materialoznavstva (Akademiia Nauk Ukrainskoi RSR). (1967)-. Periodical. Russian. Izdatelstvo Naukova Dumka / Ukrainian Academy of Sciences, Vladimirskaia Ulitsa 54, 252601 Kiev Ukraine. **Tel** 225-63-66, telex 131376. **CODEN** ZPMEAC. Documents available from CASDDS.
**Ind/Abst** Chem. Abstr.

GW/0044-3093
**ZEITSCHRIFT FUER METALLKUNDE (STUTTGART, GERMANY).** (ZEITSCHRIFT FUER METALLKUNDE.). [Z. Metallkd.]. **Added/Corp** Deutsche Gesellschaft fuer Metallkunde. Vol. 39, No. 1 (Jan. 1948)-. Periodical. German (German). mo. DM432.00. Carl Hanser Verlag, Postfach 860420, D 81631 Munich Germany. **Tel** 011 49 89 998300, FAX 011 49 89 984809. **ED** G. Petzow. **CODEN** ZEMTAE. **[CCC].** cum. index. **Pr Rev. Circ:** 2,000 (ctrl). available on microfilm from University Microfilms International (UMI). Documents available from Article Express International, The Genuine Article, Ask*IEEE, CASDDS. ***Continues** Metallforschung.*
**Desc:** Journal of development for new materials and progress in materials sciences.
**Ind/Abst** Alum. Ind. Abstr.; Bibliogr. Mission.; Bioeng. Abstr.; Ceram. Abstr. (19??-); Chem Inform; Chem. Abstr.; Curr. Contents, Agric. Biol. Environ. Sci.; Curr. Contents Eng. Tech. Appl. Sci.; Ei Page One; Energy Res. Abstr.; Eng. Index Annu.; GeoRef; INSPEC (1968-); Int. Aerosp. Abstr.; Met. Abstr.; MINPROC; Res. Alert [Full Cov.]; Sci. Cit. Index; SCISEARCH.

PL/0239-5320
**ZESZYTY NAUKOWE AKADEMII GORNICZO-HUTNICZEJ IM. STANISAWA STASZICA. MECHANIKA. VFOAT** Mechanika; Mechanics; Scientific Bulletins of Stanisaw Staszic Academy of Mining and Metallurgy. Mechanics. Monographic series. Polish. ir. Price varies per volume. Akademia Gorniczo-Hutnicza w Krakowie, Instytut Mechaniki i Wibroakustyki, Al Mickiewicza 30, Krakow Poland. **LC** TA349; .Z47. ***Continues** Mechanika (Akademia Gorniczo-Hutniczej Im. S. Staszica w Krakowie), 0239-5282.*

PL/0372-9443
**ZESZYTY NAUKOWE AKADEMII GORNICZO-HUTNICZEJ IM. STANISAWA STASZICA. METALURGIA I ODLEWNICTWO.** [Zesz. nauk. Akad. Gor.-Hut., Stanisawa Staszica. Metal. odlew.]. **VFOAT** Metalurgia I Odlewnictwo. Vol. 1 (1975)-. English (Polish). qt. $28.00. **(Subscription address:** ARS Polona, PO Box 1001, 00068 Warsaw Poland.**) LC** TN600; .M48. **UDC** 669. **CODEN** MEODD6. Documents available from CASDDS.
**Ind/Abst** Alum. Ind. Abstr.; Chem. Abstr.; Met. Abstr.

CC/1000-4343
**ZHONGGUO XITU XUEBAO.** (CHUNG-KUO HSI TU HSUEH PAO = JOURNAL OF THE CHINESE RARE EARTH SOCIETY / CHUNG-KUO HSI TU HSUEH HUI.). [Zhongguo xitu xuebao]. **Added/Corp** Chung-Kuo Hsi Tu Hsueh Hui. **VFOAT** Journal of the Chinese Rare Earth Society. (19??)-. Academic Scholarly Publication. Chinese (summaries and/or abstracts in English). Four times a year (mar., June, Sept., Dec.). $150.70. China National Publishing Import & Export Corporation, 16 Gongti E Rd., Chaoyang Dist., Beijing 100704, People's Republic of China. **Tel** 011 8601 50630169, 5066688, FAX 011 8601 5063101, 5063010, telex 22313. **LC** QD172.R2; C47. **DD** 546/.4. **CODEN** ZXXUE5. **Circ:** 400. Documents available from CASDDS.
**Ind/Abst** Chem. Abstr. (1983-).

CH/0253-4347
**ZHONGNAN KUANGYE XUEYUAN XUEBAO. See** Engineering-Mines and Mining Engineering.

CC/1001-4977
**ZHUZAO.** (CHU TSAO / CHU TSAO HSUEH HUI.). [Zhuzao]. **Added/Corp** Chung-Kuo Chi Hsieh Kung Cheng Hsueh Hui (Peking, China). Chu Tsao Chuan Yeh Hsueh Hui. Shen-Yang Chu Tsao Yen Chiu So. **VFOAT** Foundry. (19??)-. Academic Scholarly Publication. Chinese (summaries and/or abstracts in English). bm. **LC** TS228.99; .C46. **DD** 671.2/05. **CODEN** ZHUZET. Documents available from CASDDS.
**Ind/Abst** Chem. Abstr. (1984-).

CC/1000-8365
**ZHUZAO JISHU. VFOAT** Foundry Technology. (1981)-. Academic Scholarly Publication. Chinese. bm. **DD** 671.2. Documents available from CASDDS.
**Ind/Abst** Chem. Abstr.

CN/0319-6631
**ZINC.** No. 1- 1975-. Multiple languages (English and French). Zinc Institute Inc, 8 King Street East, Toronto Ontario M5C 1B5. **DD** 669/.5. **UDC** 669.5.

●US
**ZINC IN ... / PREPARED IN THE BRANCH OF METALS AND BRANCH OF DATA COLLECTION AND COORDINATION.** **Added/Corp** United States. Bureau of Mines. Branch of Metals. United States. Bureau of Mines. Branch of Data Collection and Coordination. **VFOAT** Zinc, Monthly. (1992)-. Periodical. English. mo. US Department of the Interior / Bureau of Mines, Publications Department, PO Box 18070, Cochrans Mill Road, Pittsburgh PA 15236. **Tel** (412)892-6400. ***Continues** Zinc Industry in ... .*
**Desc:** Provides information and news for the zinc industry and trade.
**Ind/Abst** Am. Stat. Index; Chem. Abstr.; Predicasts.

US
**ZINC INDUSTRY IN ... / U.S. DEPARTMENT OF THE INTERIOR, BUREAU OF MINES.** ***Title Change.*** **Added/Corp** United States. Bureau of Mines. Branch of Nonferrous Metals. United States. Bureau of Mines. Branch of Data Collection and Coordination. United States. Bureau of Mines. Branch of Metals. (1987)-(199?). Academic Scholarly Publication. English. mo. US Department of the Interior / Bureau of Mines, Publications Department, PO Box 18070, Cochrans Mill Road, Pittsburgh PA 15236. **Tel** (412)892-6400. available on microfiche (Vols. for (1987-) distributed to depository libraries). Documents available from CASDDS, Documents on Demand. ***Continues** Zinc Industry in ... and Smelter Production in ... . **Continued by** Zinc in ... (Monthly).*
**Ind/Abst** Am. Stat. Index; Chem. Abstr.

UK/0950-1592
**ZINCSCAN.** Vol. 1 (Dec. 1986)-. Periodical. English. Four times a year (Mar., June, Sept., Dec.). £74.00 UK and Europe; £77.00 other. Scan Journals, Octagon Court, High Wycombe Suite 2 1st Floor, Bucks HP11 2AS England. **Tel** 011 44 494 459339, 011 44 494 713857. **Bk Rev. Ad Acc. Circ:** 900. available on microfilm from University Microfilms International (UMI). ***Continues** Zinc Abstracts, 0044-4731.*
**Desc:** Metallurgy of zinc, its chemistry, compounds and uses with environmental aspects. Includes the health and safety regulations and new markets information.

## ABSTRACTING, BIBLIOGRAPHIES AND STATISTICS

●US/1066-0623
**ALUMINIUM INDUSTRY ABSTRACTS.** [Alum. ind. abstr.]. **Added/Corp** Materials Information (Information Service) ASM International. Institute of Materials (London, England) European Aluminum Association. Keikinzoku Kyokai (Japan). Vol. 1, No. 1 (Jan. 1992)-. Abstracting/Indexing Service. English. mo. $575.00. American Society for Metals International, c/o Deborah Barthelmes, Materials Park OH 44073-0002. **Tel** (216)338-5151, FAX (216)338-4634, telex 980-619. **(Subscription address:** ASM International, Materials Information, Materials Park OH 44073.**) LC** Z6679.A47; W67; TN775. **DD** 016.669/722. Index available (free). **Circ:** 1,110. ***Continues** World Aluminum Abstracts, 0002-6697.*
**Desc:** Information on aluminium and its alloys abstracted from international business and technical literature.

US/0065-6666
**ALUMINUM STATISTICAL REVIEW.** Statistical Publication. English. an. $50.00. Aluminum Association, 900 19th Street Northwest, Suite 300, Washington DC 20006. **Tel** (202)862-5100, FAX (202)862-5164. **LC** HD9539.A6. **DD** 338.2/7/492. **Circ:** 10,000.
**Desc:** Statistical data on aluminum industry, including shipments, markets, supply, foreign trade and per capita consumption in many countries of the world.
**Ind/Abst** Predicasts Forecasts; Stat. Ref. Index.

US
**AMERICAN IRON & STEEL INSTITUTE BASIC STEEL OPERATION STATISTICS. AIS 7, 10 & 16.** English. Twelve times a year. $60.00 (one year); $120.00 (one year) Comes with AIS 7 10 16 and Imports 3. American Iron & Steel Institute, 1101 17th Street Northwest, Suite 1300, Washington DC 20036. **Tel** (202)452-7100 or 7151.

US
**AMERICAN IRON & STEEL INSTITUTE FOREIGN TRADE STATISTICS. APPARENT STEEL SUPPLY REPORT.** English. Twelve times a year. $40.00. American Iron & Steel Institute, 1101 17th Street Northwest, Suite 1300, Washington DC 20036. **Tel** (202)452-7100 or 7151.

US
**AMERICAN IRON & STEEL INSTITUTE FOREIGN TRADE STATISTICS. IMPORTS 3 & IMPORTS 4.** English. Twelve times a year. $100.00. American Iron & Steel Institute, 1101 17th Street Northwest, Suite 1300, Washington DC 20036. **Tel** (202)452-7100 or 7151.

US
**AMERICAN IRON & STEEL INSTITUTE FOREIGN TRADE STATISTICS. INDIVIDUAL IMPORT & EXPORT REPORTS.** English. Twelve times a year. $60.00. American Iron & Steel Institute, 1101 17th Street Northwest, Suite 1300, Washington DC 20036. **Tel** (202)452-7100 or 7151.

US
**ANNUAL BULLETIN OF STEEL STATISTICS FOR EUROPE.** (ANNUAL BULLETIN OF STEEL STATISTICS FOR EUROPE. BULLETIN ANNUEL DE STATISTIQUES DE L'ACIER POUR L'EUROPE. EZHEGODNYI BIULLETIN EVROPEISKOI STATISTIKI CHERNOI METALLURGII.). **Main/Corp** United Nations. Economic Commission for Europe. **Added/Corp** United Nations. Economic Commission for Europe. Bulletin Annuel de Statistiques de l'acier pour l'Europe. United Nations. Economic Commission for Europe. EzhegodnyÊi Biulletin Evropeiskoi Statistiki Chernoi Metallurgii. **VFOAT** Bulletin Annuel de Statistiques de l'Acier pour l'Europe; Ezhegodnyi Biulletin Evropeiskoi Statistiki Chernoi; Allurgii. Vol. 1 (1973)-. Government Publication. English (French and Russian). an. $25.00. United Nations Publications, 2 United Nations Plaza, Room DC2 0853, Department 007C, New York NY 10017. **Tel** (212)963-8303, (800)253-9646. **LC** HD9525.E75; U54a. **DD** 338.4/7/672094.
**Desc:** Provides basic data on the development of steel production and trade, consumption and trade of raw materials, movements of scrap, consumptions of energy in the steel industry, and steel deliveries to consuming industries in Europe, Canada, US, and Japan.

US
**ANNUAL STATISTICAL REPORT - AMERICAN IRON AND STEEL INSTITUTE.** **Main/Corp** American Iron and Steel Institute. **Added/Corp** American Iron and Steel Institute. American Iron and Steel Institute. Bureau of Statistics. **VFOAT** Annual Statistical Report. (1913)-. Statistical Publication. English. an (July). $35.00. American Iron & Steel Institute, 1101 17th Street Northwest, Suite 1300, Washington DC 20036. **Tel** (202)452-7100 or 7151. ***Continues** Statistics of the American and Foreign Iron Trades.*
**Ind/Abst** Predicasts Forecasts.

BL
**ANUARIO ESTATISTICO / CONSIDER, CONSELHO DE NAO-FERROSOS E DE SIDERURGIA / STATISTICAL YEARBOOK / THE IRON, STEEL, AND NONFERROUS METALS COUNCIL.** **Added/Corp** Conselho de Nao-Ferrosos e de Siderurgia (Brazil). **VFOAT** Statistical Yearbook. (19??)-. Statistical Publication. English (Portuguese). an. Free. Esplanada dos Ministerios, Bloco 6 - 5 Andar, CEP 70053, Brasilia DF Brazil. **Tel** 011 55 61 2257479, telex 011 55 61 1012 MNIC-BR. **LC** HD9506.B7; A66. **DD** 338.4/7669/00981021. **Circ:** 3,000.
**Desc:** Presents data on the last ten years, in a historical series covering the period 1975 to 1984.

FR/0249-4418
**BULLETIN BIBLIOGRAPHIQUE FONDERIE.** [Bull. bibliogr. fonderie]. (1981)-. Periodical. French. Four times a year. 881.52F France; 930.00F other. Editions Techniques Industries, 44 Avenue de la Division Leclerc, 92310 Sevres Cedex France. **Tel** 011 33 1 45342754. **UDC** 669.

US/1049-1384
**C2C ABSTRACTS JAPAN. METALS.** [C2C abstr. Jap., Metals]. **VFOAT** Metals. Vol. 1, No. 1 (Feb. 1990)-. English. mo. $200.00. SCAN C2C Inc, Attn Carol G Heffernan Marketing Director, 500 E Street Southwest, Suite 800, 8th Floor, Washington DC 20024. **Tel** (202)863-3850, (800)525-3865, FAX (202)863-3855. **DD** 669. Index available. cum. index. available on CD-ROM from DIALOG; available on an online database from ORBIT; DATA-STAR; and DIALOG.
**Desc:** English abstracts of over 500 Japanese science, technical and business journals in the field of metals.

US
**FERROALLOYS.** (FERROALLOYS IN ...). English. an. US Department of the Interior / Bureau of Mines, Publications Department, PO Box 18070, Cochrans Mill Road, Pittsburgh PA 15236. **Tel** (412)892-6400. **UDC** 669.15-198.
**Desc:** Statistical and economic data on ferroalloys.

US
**GALLIUM IN ... .** English. an. US Department of the Interior / Bureau of Mines, Publications Department, PO Box 18070, Cochrans Mill Road, Pittsburgh PA 15236. **Tel** (412)892-6400. **UDC** 311:669.871; 338.3:669.871.
**Desc:** Statistical and economic data on gallium.

BL
**INFORME ESTATISTICO ANUAL, SETOR METALURGICO.** Portuguese. an. Conselho de Nao-Ferrosos e de Siderurgia, Secretaria Executiva Esplanada dos Ministerios, Bloco 6 50 Andar, CEP 70 053 Brasilia DF Brazil. **LC** HD9506.B7; B66A. **DD** 338.2/74/0981. **UDC** 311:669(81). ***Continues** Informe Estatistico, Produtos Metalurgicos (Annual).*

UK/0309-2216
**INTERNATIONAL COPPER INFORMATION BULLETIN.** ***Ceased.*** [Int. copper inf. bull.]. **Added/Corp** Copper Development Association. (1976)-(May 1993). Abstracting/Indexing Service. English. Three times a year. Copper Development Association, Orchard House Mutton Lane, Potters Bar EN6 3AP England. **Tel** (0707) 650711, FAX (0707) 642769. **ED** G Greetham. **LC** TN780; .I56. **DD** 669.3/05. Index available. **Circ:** 2,000. ***Formed by the union of** Selected Abstracts of Recent Literature on Copper and Copper Alloys **and** Kupfer-Mitteilungen.*
**Desc:** Abstracts of recent reports, publications, books, conferences and standards including production, consumption, marketing and statistics on copper and copper alloys.
**Ind/Abst** Alum. Ind. Abstr.; Leadscan; Met. Abstr.

UK/0952-6803
**INTERNATIONAL STEEL STATISTICS : SUMMARY TABLES.** **Added/Corp** United Kingdom Iron and Steel Statistics Bureau. (1977)-. English. an. £100.00 UK & Europe; £103.00 other. United Kingdom Iron & Steel Statistics Bureau, Canterbury House, 2 Sydenham Road, Croydon CR9 2LZ England. **Tel** 081 686 9050, FAX 081 680 8616, telex 932575. Index available. ctrl circ. ***Continues** International Steel Statistics: World Tables.*
**Desc:** Sets out summary tables for all the countries covered in the series.

UK/0307-7608
**INTERNATIONAL STEEL STATISTICS, UNITED KINGDOM.** **Main/Corp** British Steel Corporation Statistical Services. English. British Steel Corporation, 151 Gower Street, London WCIE 6BB England. **LC** HD9521.4; .B74A. **DD** 338.4/7/6691. **UDC** 311.669.18(410).

UK/0952-5505
**IRON AND STEEL INDUSTRY ANNUAL STATISTICS FOR THE UNITED KINGDOM.** [Iron steel ind. annu. stat. U.K.]. **VFOAT** Iron and Steel Industry Annual Statistics. (?970)-. English. Eight times a year. £75.00 UK & Europe; £78.00 others. United Kingdom Iron & Steel Statistics Bureau, Canterbury House, 2 Sydenham Road, Croydon CR9 2LZ England. **Tel** 081 686 9050, FAX 081 680 8616, telex 932575. ***Continues** Iron and Steel Annual Statistics for the United Kingdom, 0075-0867.*
**Desc:** Forty seven statistical tables relating to the UK with historical comparisons and detailed trade information.

JA
**KEIKINZOKU KOGYO TOKEI NEMPO.** **Added/Corp** Keikinzoku Kyokai. **VFOAT** Light Metal Statistics in Japan. (1950)-. Trade Publication. Multiple languages (English and Japanese). an. ¥15000. Japan Aluminium Federation, Nihonbashi Asahi, Seimei Building, 1-3 Nihonbashi 2-chome, Chuo-ku, Tokyo 103, Japan. **Tel** FAX (03)274-3179. **ED** K. Nagakubo. **LC** HD9539.A3; J348. **Bk Rev. Ad Acc. Circ:** 1,200.

UK/0023-9577
**LEAD AND ZINC STATISTICS.** [Lead zinc stat.]. **Added/Corp** International Lead and Zinc Study Group. **VFOAT** Statistiques du Plomb et du Zinc. Vol. 4 (1964)-. Periodical. English (French). mo. $220.00 US; £135.00 other. International Lead and Zinc Study Group, Metro House, 58 St. James Street, London SW1A 1LD England. **Tel** 011 44 71 4999373, FAX 011 44 71 4933725, telex 299819 ILZSG G. **Circ:** 650 (ctrl). available on an online database. ***Continues** International Lead and Zinc Study Group. Monthly Bulletin of Statistics.*
**Desc:** Tables and graphs on world supply and demand; detailed figures on mine production, metal production, metal consumption, principal imports and exports of concentrates and refined metal, secondary recovery, prices, plus detailed country profiles.
**Ind/Abst** Predicasts F&S Index, U. S. Annu. Ed.

UK/0950-1584
**LEADSCAN.** **Added/Corp** Lead Development Association. Vol. 1, No. 1 (Nov. 1986)-. Abstracting/Indexing Service. English. qt. £74.00 (UK & Europe); 80.00Aus$ (Australia); £77.00 (other). Scan Journals, Octagon Court, High Wycombe Suite 2 1st Floor, Bucks HP11 2AS England. **Tel** 011 44 494 459339, 011 44 494 713857. **Circ:** 1,300. available on microfilm and microfiche from University Microfilms International

(UMI). ***Continues*** *Lead Abstracts (London, England : 1962).*
**Ind/Abst** Corros. Abstr. (-19??); Leadscan; World Ceram. Abstr.; World Surf. Coat. Abstr.

US/0364-7919
**MERCURY (UNITED STATES. BUREAU OF MINES).** (MERCURY.). [Mercury]. **VFOAT** Mercury in ... . Academic Scholarly Publication. English. qt. US Department of the Interior / Bureau of Mines, Publications Department, PO Box 18070, Cochrans Mill Road, Pittsburgh PA 15236. **Tel** (412)892-6400. **DD** 338. **CODEN** MISMDD. ctrl circ. Documents available from CASDDS, Documents on Demand.
**Desc:** Timely statistical and economic data on mercury.
**Ind/Abst** Am. Stat. Index; Chem. Abstr. (-1984).

GW/0170-9933
**METAL STATISTICS (FRANKFURT).** ***Title Change.*** (METAL STATISTICS.). 54th- Ed.; 1957/66-. English (German). an. Metallgesellschaft AG, Volkswirtschafte L ABT, Postfach 101501, W-6000 Frankfurt AM 1 Germany. **Tel** 69.159 23 90, FAX 69/159 23 90, telex 04 1225-0 MGF D. **ED** Willy Bauer. **LC** HD9539.A1. **UDC** 311:669. ***Continues*** *Statistical Tables on Aluminum, Lead, Copper, Zinc, Tin, Cadmium, Nickel, Mercury, and Silver.* ***Continued by*** *Metallstatistik, 0076-6682.*
**Ind/Abst** Predicasts Forecasts.

US/0076-6658
**METAL STATISTICS (NEW YORK, N.Y.).** (METAL STATISTICS; THE PURCHASING GUIDE OF THE METAL INDUSTRIES.). [Met. stat.]. **Added/Corp** American Metal Market Company. (1908)-. English. an. $98.00 (hardcover), $63.00 (softcover). Diversified Publishing, 825 7th Avenue, 6th Floor, New York NY 10019. **Tel** (212)887-8565, FAX (212)887-8493. **LC** HD9506.U6; A5. **DD** 671; 669.

UK/0026-0924
**METALS ABSTRACTS.** [Met. abstr.]. **Added/Corp** Institute of Metals. American Society for Metals. Metals Society. Vol. 1 (Jan. 1968)-. Abstracting/Indexing Service. English. mo. $2115.00 North America; £1345.00 EC countries; $2360.00 other. American Society for Metals International, c/o Deborah Barthelmes, Materials Park OH 44073-0002. **Tel** (216)338-5151, FAX (216)338-4634, telex 980-619. **(Subscription address:** ASM International, Materials Information, Materials Park OH 44073.**) ED** H. David Chafe. **LC** TN1; .M5153. **DD** 669/.008. Index available. cum. index. **Circ:** 1,500. available on CD-ROM; available on diskette; available on an online database. ***Formed by the union of*** *Metallurgical Abstracts, 0428-3171* ***and*** *Review of Metal Literature, 0096-4808.*
**Desc:** Contains nearly 42,000 abstracts a year, plus numerous patents, books and reports. Abstracts are divided into 33 broad subject categories, and includes author and corporate author indexes.

UK/0026-0932
**METALS ABSTRACTS INDEX. Added/Corp** Metals Abstracts Trust. American Society for Metals. Metals Society. Vol. 1 (1968)-. Abstracting/Indexing Service. English. mo. $925.00 North America; £595.00 E.C. countries; $1035.00 other. American Society for Metals International, c/o Deborah Barthelmes, Materials Park OH 44073-0002. **Tel** (216)338-5151, FAX (216)338-4634, telex 980-619. **(Subscription address:** ASM International, Metals Information, Materials Park OH 44073.**) ED** H. David Chafe. ***Formed by the union of*** *Metallurgical Abstracts* ***and*** *Review of Metal Literature, 0096-4808.*
**Desc:** Metals Abstracts companion publication containing detailed subject and corporate author indexes. Utilizes materials information's thesaurus of metallurgical terms as vocabulary authority.

JA/0497-1140
**MONTHLY REPORT OF THE IRON & STEEL STATISTICS. Added/Corp** Nihon Tekko Remmei. **VFOAT** Tekko Gekkan Tokei. (Jan. 1958)-. Periodical. English. mo. ¥6000.00. Japan Iron & Steel Federation, 9 4 1 Chome Keidanren Kaikan, Tokyo 100 Japan. **Tel** 011 81 3 3279 3611, FAX 011 81 3 3245 0144, telex 224210.
**Desc:** Provides statistics on production, supply & demand, exports, imports, raw materials and labor.
**Ind/Abst** AESIS Q.

US
**PLATINUM-GROUP METALS IN ... .** English. qt. US Department of the Interior / Bureau of Mines, Publications Department, PO Box 18070, Cochrans Mill Road, Pittsburgh PA 15236. **Tel** (412)892-6400. **UDC** 311:669.23.
**Desc:** Timely statistical and economic data on the platinum group metals.

JA
**SHIGEN TOKEI NEMPO. YEARBOOK OF MINING, NON-FERROUS METALS, AND PRODUCTS STATISTICS. Added/Corp** Japan. Tsusho Sangyosho. Chosa Tokeibu. **VFOAT** Yearbooks of Mining, Non-Ferrous Metals, and Products Statistics. (1975)-. Japanese. Tsusan Tokei Kyokai, (International Trade & Industry Statistics Assoc.), 8-9, Ginza 2 Chome, Chuoku, Tokyoto 104, Japan. **LC** HD9506.J3; S52. ***Supersedes*** *Hitetsu Kindoku Seihin Tokei Nempo* ***and*** *Hitetsu Kinzoku To Jukyu Tokei Nempo;* ***Supersedes in part*** *Hompo Kogyo No Susei.*

US
**SILICON IN ... - U.S. DEPARTMENT OF THE INTERIOR, BUREAU OF MINES.** English. mo. US Department of the Interior / Bureau of Mines, Publications Department, PO Box 18070, Cochrans Mill Road, Pittsburgh PA 15236. **Tel** (412)892-6400. **UDC** 311:669.782(73). ***Continues*** *Ferrosilicon.*
**Desc:** Timely statistical and economic data on silicon.

UK
**SURFACE TREATMENT TECHNOLOGY ABSTRACTS.** Vol. 28, No. 1 (1986)-. Abstracting/Indexing Service. English. bm (6 issues). $803.00. Finishing Publishing Ltd, PO Box 70, 105 Whitney Drive, Stevenage Herts SG1 4DF England. **Tel** 011 44 438 745115, FAX 011 44 438 364536. **ED** R. Pinner. Index available. **Ad Acc. Circ:** 1,000. ***Continues*** *Metal Finishing Abstracts.*
**Desc:** Abstracts journals, patents, reports, standards, etc. from most industrial countries on the subject of surface treatment and finishing of metals, non-metals and composite materials.
**Ind/Abst** Corros. Abstr.; World Surf. Coat. Abstr.

UK
**TIN STATISTICS.** ***Title Change.*** (1963/73)-?. English (French, Spanish and Russian). an. International Tin Council, Haymarket House, 1 Oxendon Street, London SW1Y 4EQ England. **Tel** 011 44 71 930 0451, telex 918939. **LC** HD9539.T5; I36. **DD** 338.4/7/6736. **UDC** 311:669.6. **Circ:** 600. ***Continues*** *Statistical Year Book. Tin, Tinplate, Canning, 0074-9117.* ***Continued by*** *International Tin Statistics.*
**Desc:** Mine and shelter production of tin, tin consumption, stocks and trade. Production, apparent consumption and trade in tinplate, tin prices and turnover.

UK/0952-0287
**WELDING ABSTRACTS / WELDING INSTITUTE. Added/Corp** Welding Institute. (198?)-. English. mo. $663.00 US; £390.00 other. Weldasearch Services, Abington Hall, Abington, Cambridge CB1 6AL England. **Tel** 011 44 223 891162, FAX 011 44 223 892588, telex 81183 WELDEX G. **ED** Peter Adams. **LC** TS227.A1; W417. **DD** 671.5/2. **Ad Acc. Circ:** 700. available on microfilm and microfiche from University Microfilms International (UMI).
**Desc:** The world's most comprehensive abstracts journal in the field of welding technology. Provides fast, exhaustive coverage of all aspects of welding and allied processes, including brazing, thermal cutting, etc.

UK/0043-8758
**WORLD METAL STATISTICS.** [World met. stat.]. **Added/Corp** World Bureau of Metal Statistics. Vol. 20, No. 6 (June 1967)-. Periodical. English. Twelve times a year. £885.00 UK; £935.00 Europe; £985.00 other. World Bureau of Metal Statistics, 27A High Street, Ware Herts SG12 9BA England. **Tel** 011 44 0920461274, FAX 011 44 0920464258, telex 817746. **LC** HD9539.A1; B722. **[CCC]. Circ:** 350. available on microfilm. ***Continues*** *World Non-Ferrous Metal Statistics.*
**Desc:** Statistics of production, consumption, international trade and stocks for aluminium, antimony, cadmium, copper, lead, molybdenum, nickel, silver and tin.

NE
**WORLD NICKEL STATISTICS MONTHLY BULLETIN.** Bulletin. English. Twelve times a year. F600.00. International Nickel Study Group, Scheveningseweg 62, 2517 KX The Hague Netherlands. **Tel** 011 31 70 3543326, FAX 011 31 70 3584612, telex 30256.
**Desc:** Global statistics on nickel production, consumption, stocks and trade.

UK
**WORLD STAINLESS STEEL STATISTICS. Added/Corp** Inco Europe Limited. Market Research. (19??)-. English. an. $452.00 Europe; $456.00 other. Metal Bulletin PLC, PO Box 28E, Worcester Park, Surrey KT4 7HX England. **Tel** 011 44 71 827 9977, FAX 011 44 81 337 8943. **(Subscription address:** Metal Bulletin Inc., 220 Fifth Avenue, 19th Floor, New York NY 10001-7781.**) LC** HD9529.S62; W67. **DD** 338.4/7/762. **Bk Rev. Circ:** 300.
**Desc:** World stainless steel production and consumption statistics.

UK/0952-5742
**WORLD TRADE STAINLESS, HIGH SPEED AND OTHER ALLOY STEEL.** [World trade stainl. high speed other alloy steel]. (?979)-. English. Four times a year. £300.00 UK & Europe; £320.00 others. United Kingdom Iron & Steel Statistics Bureau, Canterbury House, 2 Sydenham Road, Croydon CR9 2LZ England. **Tel** 081 686 9050, FAX 081 680 8616, telex 932575. **DD** 382.45669142.
**Desc:** Details the export trade of major steel producing countries in selected alloy products.

## WELDING

RU/0136-1732
**ADGEZIA RASPLAVOV I PAJHA MATERIALOV.** (ADGEZIIA RASPLAVOV I PAIKA MATERIALOV.). [Adgez. rasplavov pajha mater.]. **Added/Corp** Instytut Problem Materialoznavstva Akademiia Nauk Ukrainskoi RSR). Vol. 1, (1976)-. Academic Scholarly Publication. Russian. Izdatelstvo Naukova Dumka / Ukrainian Academy of Sciences, Vladimirskaia Ulitsa 54, 252601 Kiev Ukraine. **Tel** 225-63-66, telex 131376. **LC** TA401; .A27. **CODEN** ARPMDV. Documents available from CASDDS.
**Ind/Abst** Chem. Abstr.; Int. Aerosp. Abstr.

RM
**ANALELE UNIVERSITATII DIN GALATI. FASCICULA XII.** Bulletin. Romanian (English and French). an. Price varies. Redactia Analelor, 6200 Galati, Str Domneasca Nr. 47 Romania. **Tel** 40 93 413602, FAX 40 93 412328.

US/0148-9380
**APPROVED WELDING ELECTRODE WIRE-FLUX AND WIRE-GAS COMBINATIONS. Main/Corp** American Bureau of Shipping. (19??)-. English. an. $50.00. American Bureau of Shipping, 2 World Trade Center, 106th Floor, New York NY 10048. **Tel** (212)839-5000, FAX (201)368-0255, telex RCA 232099. **LC** TK4660; .A48a. **DD** 338.4/7/67152025. **Circ:** 3,000.
**Desc:** Lists filler metals by country and manufacturer according to the welding process employed; contains requirements and test schedules for approval; includes an equivalency chart of AWS classifications to ABS grades.

AT
**AUSTRALASIAN WELDING JOURNAL.** English. Four times a year. 45.00Aus$ Australia; 53.00Aus$ New Zealand & Papua New Guinea; 60.00Aus$ other. Welding Technology Institute of Australia, PO Box 28, Lidcombe NSW 2141 Australia. **Tel** 011 61 2 748443, FAX 011 61 2 7482858. ***Continues*** *Australian Welding Journal.*

AT/0005-0431
**AUSTRALIAN WELDING JOURNAL.** ***Title Change.*** [Aust. weld. j.]. Vol. 10, No. 3 (Jan. 1967)-(19??). Academic Scholarly Publication. English. qt. Welding Technology Institute of Australia, PO Box 28, Lidcombe NSW 2141 Australia. **Tel** 011 61 2 748443, FAX 011 61 2 7482858. **ED** Philip Wells. **UDC** 621.791. **CODEN** AUWJA7. **Bk Rev. Ad Acc. Circ:** 20,000 (ctrl). Documents available from CASDDS. ***Continues*** *Welding Fabrication and Design.* ***Continued by*** *Australasian Welding Journal.*
**Desc:** Original technical editorials written by industry authorities.
**Ind/Abst** Alum. Ind. Abstr.; Chem. Abstr.; EMBASE; Eng. Mater. Abstr.; Met. Abstr.; Risk Abstr.

AT/0045-0960
**AUSTRALIAN WELDING RESEARCH.** [Aust. weld. res.]. **Added/Corp** Australian Welding Research Association. **VFOAT** AWRA Report. Vol. 1 (1969)-. Academic Scholarly Publication. English. ir. 30.00Aus$. Welding Technology Institute of Australia, PO Box 28, Lidcombe NSW 2141 Australia. **Tel** 011 61 2 748443, FAX 011 61 2 7482858. **CODEN** AWRSAN. cum. index. **Bk Rev. Ad Acc.** Documents available from CASDDS.
**Ind/Abst** Chem. Abstr.; Ei Page One; Highw. Res. Abstr.

AT
**AWRA TECHNICAL NOTE. VFOAT** AWRA-AWI Technical Note; AWRA-AISC-AWI Technical Note. Monographic series. English. ir. Price varies per volume. Australian Welding Research Association, 118 Alfred Street, Milsons Point New South Wales 2061 Australia. **Tel** (02)922 3711.

US/0043-2326
**BULLETIN - WELDING RESEARCH COUNCIL (U.S.).** (BULLETIN / WELDING RESEARCH COUNCIL.). [Bull. - Weld. Res. Counc. (U. S.)]. **Added/Corp** Welding Research Council (U.S.). **VFOAT** WRC Bulletin Series; WRC Bulletin. No. 70 (July 1961)-. Academic Scholarly Publication. English. mo. Comes with welding research council membership. Welding Research Council, 345 East 47th Street, 13th Floor, New York NY 10017. **Tel** (212)705-7956. **LC** TS227; .A1673. **DD** 671.5/2/05. **CODEN** WRCBA2. Documents available from Article Express International, CASDDS. ***Continues*** *Welding Research Council Bulletin Series.*
**Ind/Abst** Bioeng. Abstr.; Chem. Abstr. (1949-1983); Coal Abstr.; Ei Page One; Eng. Index Annu.; Int. Aerosp. Abstr.; Met. Abstr.

CN
**CANADIAN WELDER AND FABRICATOR. DIRECTORY AND BUYERS' GUIDE.** Began with 1961 issue. Consumer Publication. English. an. Sanford Evans

Communications Ltd., Box 6900, 1700 Church Avenue, Winnipeg Manitoba R3C 3B1 Canada. **Tel** (204)632-2768, FAX (204)694-2347. **DD** 338.4/7/67152028. **UDC** 338:621.791.(71).
**Desc:** Provides a comprehensive listing of products and supplies available for all welding and fabrications operations. Includes complete lists of names and addresses for manufacturers and distributors.

GW/0418-9639
**DVS-BERICHTE.** [DVS Ber.]. **Added/Corp** Deutscher Verband fur Schweisstechnik. **VFOAT** DVS Berichte. **VAT** Deutscher Verband fur Schweisstechnik Berichte. (1967)-. Monographic series. German. Deutscher Verlag fur Schweisstechnik GmbH, Aachener Strasse 172, Postfach 2725, W-4000 Dusseldorf 1 Germany. **Tel** 211/157590, FAX 211/1575950, telex 8582583. **LC** TS227; .A16714. **CODEN** DVSBA3. Documents available from CASDDS.
**Ind/Abst** Chem. Abstr.

UK/0043-2245
**FAB GUIDE.** **VFOAT** Welding and Metal Fabrication Fab Guide. (1975)-. English. £51.00 UK; £60.00, $102.00 other. Argus Press Group, Queensway House, 2 Queensway Redhill, Surrey RH1 1QS England. **Tel** 011 44 737 768611, 011 44 737 761685, FAX 011 44 737 760510, telex 948669 TOPJNL G. ***Continues*** *Fabrication & Equipment Guide.*

SA/0015-9026
**FWP JOURNAL.** ***Title Change.*** [FWP j.]. **VFOAT** Founding, Welding, Production Engineering. **VAT** Founding, Welding, Production Journal. (1962)-(19??). Academic Scholarly Publication. English (Afrikaans). mo. FWP Journal, Box 31548, Braamfontein 2017, South Africa. **Tel** (011)339-6678, FAX (011)403-3798. **ED** Tina Sole. **CODEN** FWPJA7. Index available. **Bk Rev. Ad Acc. Circ:** 4,000. available in microform from Xerox; available on microfilm from University Microfilms International (UMI). Documents available from Article Express International, CASDDS. ***Continued by*** *FWP.*
**Desc:** Covers the broad spectrum of metalworking, metallurgical and production engineering industries.
**Ind/Abst** Alum. Ind. Abstr.; Bioeng. Abstr.; Chem. Abstr.; Ei Page One; EMBASE; Eng. Mater. Abstr.; Eng. Index Annu.; Met. Abstr.; Pollut. Abstr. Indexes.

US
**GASES AND WELDING DISTRIBUTOR, THE.** (19??)-. Periodical. English. Six times a year. $40.00 US; $45.00 Canada; $55.00 Mexico; $60.00 other. Penton Publishing, 1100 Superior Avenue, Cleveland OH 44114-2543. **Tel** (216)696-7000, FAX (216)696-0836. **(Subscription address:** Penton Publishing, PO Box 96732, Chicago IL 60693.**)** ***Continues*** *The Welding Distributor.*

CC/0253-360X
**HANJIE XUEBAO.** (HAN CHIEN HSUEH PAO.). [Hanjie xuebao]. **Added/Corp** Chung-kuo Chi Hsieh Kung Cheng Hsueh Hui (Peking, China). Han Chieh Hsueh Hui. **VFOAT** Hanjie Xuebao; Transactions of the China Welding Institution. (1980)-. Academic Scholarly Publication. Chinese (table of contents in English). qt. $20.00. Harbin Hanjie Yanjiusuo / Harbin Research Institute of Welding, 111 Hexing lu, Harbin, Heilongjiang, 150080 People's Republic of China. **Tel** 6336695. **(Subscription address:** China International Book Trading Corporation, PO Box 399, Library Service Department, Beijing 100044 People's Republic of China.**)** **ED** Li Zhao Shan. **LC** TS227.A1; H36. **DD** 671.5/2/05. **CODEN** HHPAD2. **Ad Acc. Circ:** 15,000. Documents available from CASDDS, BLDSC, CASDDS.
**Desc:** Reports new achievements in research and development concerning welding technology, welding consumables, welding equipment, strength of welded structure and thermal cutting techniques.
**Ind/Abst** Alum. Ind. Abstr.; Chem. Abstr.; Ei Page One; Eng. Mater. Abstr.; Met. Abstr.

AT/1033-7423
**HOT METAL.** [Hot metal]. (1989)-. Periodical. English. Twelve times a year. 40.00Aus$ Australia; 65.00Aus$ New Zealand & PNG Fiji & Indonesia & Malaysia; 75.00Aus$ UK & Europe & US & Israel; 80.00Aus$ others. Futura Pty Ltd., 140 William Street, LVL 6 Olivetti, Sydney NSW 2000 Australia. **Tel** 011 61 2 3573300, FAX 011 61 2 3577661. **DD** 784.5405.

JA/0021-4396
**IMONO.** **See** Chemistry.

II/0046-9092
**INDIAN WELDING JOURNAL.** (INDIAN WELDING JOURNAL : OFICIAL JOURNAL OF THE INDIAN INSTITUTE OF WELDING.). [Indian weld. j.]. **Added/Corp** Indian Institute of Welding. (19??)-. Periodical. English. qt. $20.00. Indian Institute of Welding, 3A Loudon Street, Calcutta 700 017 India. **Tel** 91-33-401350. **(Subscription address:** Prints India, 11 Darya Ganj, New Delhi 110002 India.**)** **CODEN** IWLJAK.

II/0377-7391
**INDUSTRIAL WELDER.** Periodical. English. Zita Villa, 212 Kalina Santa Cruz East, Bombay India. **LC** TS227.A1; I53. **DD** 671.5/2/05.

JA/0368-5306
**KEIKINZOKU YOSETSU.** (KEIKINZOKU YOSETSU : KEIKINZOKU YOSETSU KOZO KYOKAISHI.). [Keikinzoku yosetsu]. **Added/Corp** Keikinzoku Yosetsu Kozo Kyokai (Japan). **VFOAT** Journal of Light Metal Welding & Construction; Journal of Light Metal Welding and Construction. (1963)-. Periodical. Japanese (summaries and/or abstracts in English). Twelve times a year. $168.00. Keikinzoku Yosetsu Kozo Kyokai, (Japan Light Metal Welding & Construction Assoc.), 37-23, Kanda Sakumacho 3 Chome, Chiyodaku, Tokyoto 101 Japan. **(Subscription address:** Maruzen Company Ltd., PO Box 5050, Import & Export Department, Tokyo 100 31 Japan.**)** **CODEN** KEYOBV. Documents available from Article Express International, CASDDS.
**Ind/Abst** Alum. Ind. Abstr.; Bioeng. Abstr.; Chem. Abstr.; Ei Page One; Eng. Index Annu.; Met. Abstr.

NE/0023-8694
**LASTECHNIEK.** [Lastechniek]. Academic Scholarly Publication. Dutch (summaries and/or abstracts in English). mo. Ned Inst Voor Lasterhniek, Laan Van Meerdervoort 2B, 2517 AJ Den Haag Netherlands. **CODEN** LASTAW. Documents available from CASDDS.
**Ind/Abst** Alum. Ind. Abstr.; Chem. Abstr.; EMBASE; Met. Abstr.; Saf. Health Work.

CN/0822-742X
**LIST OF ELECTRODES CERTIFIED TO CSA W48 SERIES OF STANDARDS AND APPLICABLE AWS A5. SPECIFICATIONS.** (LIST OF ELECTRODES CERTIFIED TO CSA W48 SERIES OF STANDARDS AND APPLICABLE AWS A5. SPECIFICATIONS / CANADIAN WELDING BUREAU.). English. an. Canadian Welding Bureau, 254 Merton Street, Toronto Ontario M4S 1A9 Canada. **DD** 671.5/212/028.

US/1040-967X
**METAL STAMPING.** [Metal form.]. **Added/Corp** Precision Metalforming Association (U.S.). Vol. 22, No. 6 (June 1988)-. Academic Scholarly Publication. English. mo. $25.00 U.S. & Canada; $75.00. PMA Services, 27027 Chardon Road, Richmond Heights OH 44143. **Tel** (216)585-8800. **ED** Richard Green. **LC** TS200; .M373. **DD** 671; 671.3/05. **Ad Acc, Adv Mgr:** Kathy Delollis. ***Continues*** *Metal Stamping, 0026-069X.*
**Desc:** PMA provides metalforming companies services, information and materials they can use to operate more effectively, productively, safely and profitably.
**Ind/Abst** Alum. Ind. Abstr.; EMBASE; Met. Abstr.

•CN/1188-9004
**MINERAL INDUSTRY QUARTERLY REPORT.** **See** Earth Sciences-Mineralogy.

UK/0957-798X
**PATON WELDING JOURNAL, THE.** [Paton weld. j.]. (1989)-. Periodical. English. mo. $805.00. Riecansky Science Publishing Company, 7 Meadow Walk, Great Abington, Cambridge CB1 6AZ England. **Tel** 011 44 223 893295, FAX 011 44 462 480947, telex 825372 TURPIN G. **DD** 671.52. ***Continues in part*** *Welding International, 0950-7116.*

NE
**PHILIPS WELDING REPORTER.** **VFOAT** Welding Reporter. 1965/1-. Periodical. English. ir. Philips Industries, Welding Department, Building III-2, Eindhoven The Netherlands. **UDC** 621.791. **CODEN** WEREDW. Documents available from Article Express International. ***Supersedes*** *Welding News.*
**Ind/Abst** Bioeng. Abstr.; Ei Page One; Eng. Index Annu.

BE
**PRATIQUE DU SOUDAGE, LA.** **Added/Corp** Institut Belge de la Soudure. (19??)-. Periodical. French. qt. 1875F. Institut Belge de la Soudure, rue des Drapiers 21, 1050 Bruxelles Belgium. **Tel** 011 32 5 5122892. **LC** TS227.A1; P7. Index available. **Bk Rev. Ad Acc. Circ:** 800. available with charts; available with illustrations. Documents available from BLDSC, CASDDS.

US/0743-1651
**PROGRESS REPORTS (WELDING RESEARCH COUNCIL (US)).** (PROGRESS REPORTS / WELDING RESEARCH COUNCIL.). [Prog. rep. - Weld. Res. Counc. (U.S.)]. **Added/Corp** Welding Research Council (U.S.). (Jan. 1977)-. English. Six times a year. $1,250.00 Comes with Welding Research Council membership. Welding Research Council, 345 East 47th Street, 13th Floor, New York NY 10017. **Tel** (212)705-7956. **LC** TS227.6; .P76. **DD** 671.5/2/05. **CODEN** WCPRDD. ***Continues*** *Reports of Progress of the Welding Research Council, 0161-1437.*
**Desc:** Presents the progress of research being conducted.
**Ind/Abst** Alum. Ind. Abstr.; Met. Abstr.

GW/0340-4749
**REFERATEORGAN SCHWEISSEN UND VERWANDTE VERFAHREN.** [Referateorg. Schweissen verw. Verfahr.]. **VFOAT** Welding and Allied Processes; Schweissen und Verwandte Verfahren. **VAT** Abstract Journal : Welding and Allied Processes. (1972)-. German (English). bm. DM285.00. Deutscher Verlag Schweisstechnk GmbH, Postfach 101965, W 40010 Duesseldorf Germany. **Tel** 011 49 211 15910. **UDC** 621.79(01). Index available. **Bk Rev. Circ:** 400.
**Desc:** Welding and allied processes, materials, testing and applications.

SP/0048-7759
**REVISTA DE SOLDADURA.** [Rev. sold.]. (1971)-. Periodical. Spanish (English). qt. 5000ptas Spain & Latin America; 8000ptas other. Centro Nacional de Investigaciones Metalurgicas, Avenida de Gregorio del Amo 8, 28040 Madrid Spain. **Tel** 011 34 1 2020440. **ED** J Fernandez-Ballesteros. **UDC** 621.7. Index available. cum. index. **Bk Rev. Ad Acc. Pr Rev. Circ:** 2,200. Documents available from CASDDS. ***Continues*** *Revista de Metalurgia (Madrid), 0034-8570.*
**Ind/Abst** Chem. Abstr.

BE/0035-127X
**REVUE DE LA SOUDURE (BRUXELLES).** (REVUE DE LA SOUDURE. LASTIJDSCHRIFT.). [Rev. soudure]. **Added/Corp** Institut Belge de la Soudure. **VFOAT** Lastijdschrift. Vol. 1 (1945)-. Academic Scholarly Publication. French (Dutch and English). Four times a year (Mar., June, Sept., Dec.). 2500F. Institut Belge de la Soudure, rue des Drapiers 21, 1050 Bruxelles Belgium. **Tel** 011 32 5 5122892. **ED** A. Dhooge. **LC** TS227; .A2125. **CODEN** RSOUA3. **Bk Rev. Ad Acc. Circ:** 700. Documents available from Article Express International, CASDDS.
**Ind/Abst** Alum. Ind. Abstr.; Bioeng. Abstr.; Chem. Abstr. (1945-1983); Ei Page One; Energy Res. Abstr.; Eng. Index Annu.; Met. Abstr.

IT/0035-6794
**RIVISTA ITALIANA DELLA SALDATURA.** [Riv. ital. saldatura]. Began with Oct. 1949 issue. Academic Scholarly Publication. Italian (English). bm. L71250 Italy; $145.00 (surface mail), $168.00 (airmail) other. Instituto Italiano Della Saldatura, Lungobisagno Istria 15, I 16141 Genova Italy. **Tel** (010)853111-853049, FAX (010)867780, telex 283054 SALDIS I. **LC** TS227; .A184. **UDC** 621.791. **CODEN** RISAAT. Index available. cum. index. **Bk Rev. Ad Acc. Circ:** 3,000. Documents available from Article Express International, CASDDS.
**Desc:** Official journal of "Istituto Italiano Della Saldatura" (Italian Institute of Welding) Content: technical articles; sections: institute' work, information, book reviews, world welding papers classified.
**Ind/Abst** Alum. Ind. Abstr.; Bioeng. Abstr.; Chem. Abstr. (1949-1983); Ei Page One; Energy Res. Abstr.; Eng. Mater. Abstr.; Eng. Index Annu.; Met. Abstr.

GW/0036-7184
**SCHWEISSEN UND SCHNEIDEN.** [Schweissen + Schneiden]. **Added/Corp** Deutscher Verband fuer Schweisstechnik. Vol. 1 (Jan. 1949)-. Academic Scholarly Publication. English (English). mo. DM254.00 Austria and Switzerland; DM250.00 Germany; DM359.00 other. Deutscher Verlag Schweisstechnk GmbH, Postfach 101965, W 40010 Duesseldorf Germany. **Tel** 011 49 211 15910. **ED** D Flemming. **LC** TS227; .A225. **CODEN** SCSCA4. **[CCC].** Index available. **Bk Rev. Ad Acc. Circ:** 10,000 (ctrl). Documents available from Article Express International, CASDDS. ***Absorbed*** *Schweisstechnik, 0036-7192.*
**Desc:** Technical and scientific journal. Reports on welding, cutting, spraying, soldering, brazing, adhesive bonding, heat treatment, testing of materials, control and regulation.
**Ind/Abst** Alum. Ind. Abstr.; Bioeng. Abstr.; BMT Abstr.; Chem. Abstr.; Civ. Struct. Eng. Abstr.; Coal Abstr.; Ei Page One; Elect. Comm. Abstr.; EMBASE; Energy Res. Abstr.; Eng. Mater. Abstr.; Eng. Index Annu.; Int. Civil Eng. Abstr.; Manuf. Process Eng. Abstr.; Mater. Sci. Eng. Abstr.; Mech. Eng. Abstr.; Met. Abstr.; Saf. Health Work; Soft. Abstr. Eng.; Solid State Supercond. Abstr.

FR/0038-173X
**SOUDAGE ET TECHNIQUES CONNEXES.** [Soudage & tech. connexes]. Vol. 9 (1955)-. Academic Scholarly Publication. French (summaries and/or abstracts in English, German and Spanish). bm (6 issues). 450.54F France; 605.00F other. Publications Soudate et des ses Applications, BP 50-362, 95942 Roissy Charl Gaul France. **Tel** 011 33 1 49903600, FAX 011 33 1 49903650, telex 210335. **LC** TS227; .A238. **CODEN** SOTCAP. Index available. cum. index. **Bk Rev,** (Qty: 6/yr). **Ad Acc. Pr Rev.** ctrl circ. Documents available from Article Express International, Ask*IEEE, CASDDS. ***Continues*** *Soudure et Techniques Connexes.*
**Desc:** Presents information on welding techniques.
**Ind/Abst** Alum. Ind. Abstr.; Bioeng. Abstr.; Chem. Abstr.; Ei Page One; EMBASE; Energy Res. Abstr.; Eng. Mater. Abstr.; Eng. Index Annu.; INSPEC; Met. Abstr.

FR/0246-1900
**SOUDER.** [Souder]. (19??)-. Academic Scholarly Publication. French. bm (6 issues). 393.00. Publications Soudate et des ses Applications, BP 50-362, 95942 Roissy Charl Gaul France. **Tel** 011 33 1 49903600, FAX 011 33 1 49903650, telex 210335. **(Subscription address:** Institut Soudage Canada, 353 Boulevard Sir Wilfried Laurier, Mont Hilaire QC J3H 3P1 Canada**)** **CODEN** SOUDAX. Documents available from Ask*IEEE, CASDDS.
**Ind/Abst** Chem. Abstr.; INSPEC (1968-1985); Saf. Health Work.

SZ/1040-7073
**SOVIET TECHNOLOGY REVIEWS. SECTION C, WELDING AND SURFACING REVIEWS.** [Sov. technol. rev., C Weld. surf. rev.]. **VFOAT** Welding and Surfacing Reviews. Vol. 1, Pt. 1 (1989)-. Monographic series. English (translations available in Russian). an. $441.00 (academic institutions), $688.00 (corporate institutions). Harwood Academic Publishers, PO Box 90, Reading RG1 8JL England. **Tel** 011 44 734 560080. **(Subscription address:** International Publishers Distributor at one of the following addresses: 820 Town Center Drive, Langhorne, PA 19047; or PO Box 90, Reading Berkshire RG1 8JL UK; or Kent Ridge PO Box 1180, Singapore 9111, Republic of Singapore**) LC** TS227.A1; S66. **DD** 671.5/2/05. **CODEN** STCREO. **[CCC].**

RU/0491-6441
**SVAROCNOE PROIZVODSTVO.** (SVAROCHNOE PROIZVODSTVO.). [Svar. proizvod.]. **Added/Corp** Soviet Union. Gosudarstvennyi Komitet po Koordinatsii Nauchno-Issledovatelskikh Rabot. (1955)-. Academic Scholarly Publication. Russian (summaries and/or abstracts in English and German). mo. $109.95. **(Subscription address:** East View Publications Inc., 3020 Harbor Lane North, Suite 110, Minneapolis MN 55447.**) CODEN** SVAPAI. Documents available from Ask*IEEE, CASDDS. ***Continues** Avtogennoe Delo.*
**Ind/Abst** Acoust. Abstr.; Alum. Ind. Abstr.; Chem. Abstr.; Energy Res. Abstr.; Eng. Mater. Abstr.; INSPEC (Feb. 1968-); Int. Aerosp. Abstr.; Met. Abstr.

SW/0346-8577
**SVETSAREN.** [Svetsaren]. V. 5, No. 1/2 (1969)-. Academic Scholarly Publication. English. sa. Free. Esabfack Herkulesgatan 72, 40270 Goteborg Sweden. **Tel** +46-31509000, FAX +46-31509390. **ED** Lennart B Lundberg. **LC** TS227.A1; S9. **UDC** 621.791. **CODEN** SVSEB8. **Circ:** 25,000 (ctrl). Documents available from Article Express International, Ask*IEEE, CASDDS. ***Continues** ESAB's Svetsaren in English.*
**Desc:** Articles on new processes, new applications and R & D in welding and thermal cutting.
**Ind/Abst** Alum. Ind. Abstr.; Bioeng. Abstr.; Chem. Abstr. (1965-1983); Ei Page One; Eng. Mater. Abstr.; Eng. Index Annu.; INSPEC (1970-); Met. Abstr.

SW/0039-7091
**SVETSEN.** [Svetsen]. **Added/Corp** Svetstekniska Foreningen. (1942)-. Academic Scholarly Publication. Swedish (summaries and/or abstracts in English). bm. Kr150.00. Svetstekniska Foreningen Iva, Box 5073, Stockholm 5 Sweden. **Tel** 08 22 07 60. **ED** Gunnar B. Tornguist. **CODEN** SVTNA5. **Bk Rev**. **Ad Acc**. **Circ:** 4,000 (ctrl). Documents available from Article Express International, CASDDS.
**Desc:** Welding technology, metallurgy.
**Ind/Abst** Alum. Ind. Abstr.; Bioeng. Abstr.; Chem. Abstr.; Ei Page One; Energy Res. Abstr. (Sept. 1973-); Eng. Mater. Abstr.; Eng. Index Annu.; Met. Abstr.

JA/0385-9282
**TRANSACTIONS OF THE JAPAN WELDING SOCIETY.** ***Title Change.*** [Trans. Jpn. Weld. Soc.]. **Main/Corp** Yosetsu Gakkai. (1970)-(19??). Academic Scholarly Publication. English. sa. Yosetsu Gakkai, (Japan Welding Society), 1-11, Kanda Sakumacho, Chiyodaku, Tokyoto 101, Japan. **(Subscription address:** Maruzen Company Ltd., PO Box 5050, Import & Export Department, Tokyo 100 31 Japan.**) ED** Keiji Tachiki. **UDC** 621.791. **CODEN** TJWSAU. **[CCC]. Circ:** 600 (ctrl). Documents available from Article Express International, CASDDS. ***Merged into** Journal of the Japan Welding Society.*
**Desc:** Introduces studies results of welding technology in Japan. Serves as an international forum for academic and technological discussions.
**Ind/Abst** Acoust. Abstr.; Alum. Ind. Abstr.; Bioeng. Abstr.; Chem. Abstr.; Ei Page One; Eng. Mater. Abstr.; Eng. Index Annu.; Met. Abstr.

●UK/0963-6927
**TWI JOURNAL.** [TWI j.]. (1992)-. Periodical. English. qt. $270.00 US; £160.00 Europe; £170.00 other. Abington Publishing, Distribution Center Blackhorse Road, Letchworth SG6 1HN England. **Tel** 011 44 462 672555. **DD** 620.1105. **Ad Acc**.
**Desc:** Contains reports from TWI's R & D program.

GW
**VWD-STAHL.** German. da. DM3033.60 Germany; DM3416.40 Europe; DM3668.40 other. Vereinigte Wirtschaftsdienste, Postfach 6105, D 65735 Eschborn Germany. **Tel** 011 49 6196 405208.

UK
**WELDALERT.** ***Title Change.*** (1992)-(199?). English. mo. Weldasearch Services, Abington Hall, Abington, Cambridge CB1 6AL England. **Tel** 011 44 223 891162, FAX 011 44 223 892588, telex 81183 WELDEX G. ***Continued by** Weldasearch Select.*
**Desc:** An SDI service for the welding industry. Provides a personalized selection of abstracts from databases relevant to your particular interest. Experts at TWI, the world centre for materials joining technology based in Cambridge, UK generate the lists once a month from their comprehensive database.

UK
**WELDASEARCH SELECT.** (19??)-. English. mo. £200.00. Weldasearch Services, Abington Hall, Abington, Cambridge CB1 6AL England. **Tel** 011 44 223 891162, FAX 011 44 223 892588, telex 81183 WELDEX G.
**Desc:** Current awareness service designed to help you keep abreast of new technical developments in welding and allied processes.

UK/0952-0287
**WELDING ABSTRACTS / WELDING INSTITUTE. See** Metals and Metallurgy-Abstracting, Bibliographies and Statistics.

US/0278-7067
**WELDING & FABRICATING DATA BOOK.** [Weld. fabr. data book]. **VFOAT** Welding and Fabricating Data Book. (1980/81)-. English. be (every two years). $45.00 US and Canada; $50.00 Mexico; $55.00 other. Penton Publishing, 1100 Superior Avenue, Cleveland OH 44114-2543. **Tel** (216)696-7000, FAX (216)696-0836. **(Subscription address:** Penton Publishing, PO Box 96732, Chicago IL 60693.**) LC** TS227; .A268. **DD** 671.5/2. available on microfilm from University Microfilms International (UMI). ***Continues** Welding Data Book.*

UK/0043-2245
**WELDING AND METAL FABRICATION.** [Weld. met. fabr.]. **VFOAT** Welding & Metal Fabrication. Vol. 19 (Jan. 1951)-. Academic Scholarly Publication. English. Ten times a year. £109.00 UK; £125.00, $230.00 other. Argus Press Group, Queensway House, 2 Queensway Redhill, Surrey RH1 1QS England. **Tel** 011 44 737 768611, 011 44 737 761685, FAX 011 44 737 760510, telex 948669 TOPJNL G. **ED** Rodney Pitt. **CODEN** WLMFAM. **Bk Rev**. **Ad Acc**. Documents available from Article Express International, Ask*IEEE, CASDDS.
**Desc:** Over 50 years service to the industry, this is the major journal for all those involved with, or interested in the UK welding industry.
**Ind/Abst** Alum. Ind. Abstr.; Bioeng. Abstr.; BMT Abstr.; Chem. Abstr.; Curr. Technol. Index; Ei Page One; Eng. Mater. Abstr.; Eng. Index Annu.; INSPEC (1968-); Met. Abstr.; Saf. Health Work.

US/1050-3013
**WELDING-BRAZING-SOLDERING DIGEST.** [Weld.-brazing-solder. dig.]. **Added/Corp** Materials Information (Information Service). **VAT** Welding, Brazing, Soldering Digest. Vol. 14, No. 1 (Jan. 1987)-. English. mo. $175.00 (nonmember), $145.00 (member) North America. American Society for Metals International, c/o Deborah Barthelmes, Materials Park OH 44073-0002. **Tel** (216)338-5151, FAX (216)338-4634, telex 980-619. **(Subscription address:** ASM International, Materials Information, Materials Park OH 44073.**) LC** TS227.A1; W416. **DD** 671.5/2. ***Continues** Welding & Joining Digest, 0361-3747.*

US/0511-4365
**WELDING DATA BOOK.** ***Title Change.*** 1959-?. English. be. Penton Publishing, 1100 Superior Avenue, Cleveland OH 44114-2543. **Tel** (216)696-7000, FAX (216)696-0836. **ED** Rosalie Brosilow. **LC** TS227; .A268. **UDC** 621.791. **Bk Rev**. **Ad Acc**. **Circ:** 24,000 (ctrl). ***Continued by** Welding and Fabricating Data Book, 0278-7067.*
**Desc:** Informs readers of new developments in design and manufacturing of welded products. Includes manufacturing techniques and equipment, up-to-date professional and management skills relating to welding engineering.

US/0043-2253
**WELDING DESIGN & FABRICATION.** [Weld. des. fabr.]. **VFOAT** Welding Design and Fabrication. Vol. 32, No. 7 (July 1959)-. Periodical. English. Twelve times a year. $50.00 US; $70.00 Canada; $75.00 Mexico; $80.00 other. Penton Publishing, 1100 Superior Avenue, Cleveland OH 44114-2543. **Tel** (216)696-7000, FAX (216)696-0836. **(Subscription address:** Penton Publishing, PO Box 96732, Chicago IL 60693.**) ED** Rosalie Brosilow. **LC** TS227; .A168. **CODEN** WDEFAS. **[CCC]. Bk Rev**. **Ad Acc**. **Circ:** 42,000 (ctrl). available on microfilm from University Microfilms International (UMI). Documents available from Ask*IEEE. ***Continues** Industry & Welding, 0096-2589; **Absorbed** Welding Engineer, 0043-227X.*
**Desc:** Information on new developments in design manufacturing, welded metal products, manufacturing techniques and equipment. New materials joining, forming, cutting processes inspection, testing, and quality control.
**Ind/Abst** Alum. Ind. Abstr.; Appl. Sci. Technol. Index (Jan. 1975-); Bioeng. Abstr.; Coal Abstr. (Jan. 1975-); Ei Page One; EMBASE; Eng. Mater. Abstr.; INSPEC (Jan. 1975-); Met. Abstr.; Pollut. Abstr. Indexes; Robotics Abstr.

US/0192-7671
**WELDING DISTRIBUTOR (1966).** ***Title Change.*** (WELDING DISTRIBUTOR.). (Jan./Feb. 1966)-(19??). Periodical. English. bm. Penton Publishing, 1100 Superior Avenue, Cleveland OH 44114-2543. **Tel** (216)696-7000, FAX (216)696-0836. **ED** Chuck Berka. **LC** TS227; .A255116. **DD** 338.4/76715/20973. **[CCC]. Bk Rev**. **Ad Acc. Circ:** 8,000 (ctrl). available on microfilm from University Microfilms International (UMI). ***Continues** Welding Distributor and Safety Supplier. **Continued by** The Gases and Welding Distributor.*
**Desc:** A merchandising magazine for distributors of welding and cutting equipment, supplies, accessories, metal-working, tools and related safety items.

UK/0043-2288
**WELDING IN THE WORLD.** (WELDING IN THE WORLD. SOUDAGE DANS LE MONDE.). [Weld. world]. **Added/Corp** International Institute of Welding. **VFOAT** Soudage dans le Monde. Vol. 1 (1963)-. Academic Scholarly Publication. English. Seven times a year. $254.00 The Americas; £170.00 other. Pergamon Press, An Imprint of Elsevier Science Ltd., The Boulevard, Langford Lane, Kidlington, Oxford OX5 1GB United Kingdom. **Tel** 011 44 865 843000, 011 44 865 843699, FAX 011 44 865 843010. **(Subscription address:** Elsevier Science Ltd. Oxford Fulfillment Centre, PO Box 800, Kidlington, Oxford OX5 1DX United Kingdom.**) ED** J. Hicks and M. Bramat. **LC** TS227; .A183. **CODEN** WDWRAI. **[CCC].** available on microfilm and microfiche from University Microfilms International (UMI). Documents available from Article Express International, CASDDS.
**Desc:** The journal publishes technical reports on all aspects of welding technology. Topics covered include authoritative reports on: processes, welding equipment and consumables; arc and resistance welding; testing, measurement and control of welds and more.
**Ind/Abst** Alum. Ind. Abstr.; Bioeng. Abstr.; Chem. Abstr.; Curr. Technol. Index; Ei Page One; EMBASE; Eng. Mater. Abstr.; Eng. Index Annu.; Met. Abstr.; Pollut. Abstr. Indexes; Saf. Health Work.

UK/0950-7116
**WELDING INTERNATIONAL.** [Weld. int.]. **Added/Corp** Welding Institute. British Library. Document Supply Centre. Vol. 1, No. 1 (1987)-. Periodical. English (translations available in Russian). mo. $1185.00 North and South America; £695.00 Europe; £715.00 other. Abington Publishing, Distribution Center Blackhorse Road, Letchworth SG6 1HN England. **Tel** 011 44 462 672555. **(Subscription address:** Turpin Distribution Services Limited, Blackhorse Road, Letchworth, Hertfordshire SG6 1HN, United Kingdom.**) ED** Richard Smith. **LC** TS227.A1; W429. **DD** 671.5/2. **CODEN** WEINEF. Index available. **Ad Acc. Circ:** 250. Documents available from Ask*IEEE. ***Formed by the union of** Welding Production **and** Automatic Welding.*
**Desc:** Translations of complete articles from leading soviet, japanese, chinese, east european and italian welding journals.
**Ind/Abst** INSPEC (1988-).

US/0043-2296
**WELDING JOURNAL. Added/Corp** American Welding Society. American Welding Society. Proceedings. American Welding Society. Journal. **VFOAT** Welding Journal. (1922)-. Academic Scholarly Publication. English. mo. $90.00; Comes also with American Welding Society membership. American Welding Society, 550 Northwest LeJeune Road, Miami FL 33135. **Tel** (800)443-9353. **(Subscription address:** American Welding Society, PO Box 351040, Miami, FL 33135**) ED** Jeff Weber, Andrew Cullison and Renee Kennedy. **LC** TS227; .A15. **CODEN** WEJUA3. **[CCC].** Index available (bound in Dec. issue). **Bk Rev**. **Ad Acc**. **Pr Rev. Circ:** 39,000. available on microfilm and microfiche from University Microfilms International (UMI). Documents available from The Genuine Article, CASDDS.
**Desc:** Serves the welding-related metal-working market. Readers are heavily involved in the purchase, selection and specification of welding and metalworking products. Job functions include corporate management, engineering, purchasing, training, educating, research, design and production.
**Ind/Abst** Appl. Sci. Technol. Index; Biogr. Index; BMT Abstr. (?-199?); Ceram. Abstr.; Chem. Abstr.; Curr. Contents Eng. Tech. Appl. Sci.; Ei Page One; Eng. Mater. Abstr.; Ergon. Abstr. (?-?); Int. Aerosp. Abstr.; Res. Alert [Full Cov.]; Sci. Cit. Index; SCISEARCH; Soc. Sci. Cit. Index [Select. Cov.]; Surf. Treat. Technol. Abstr.

US/0043-2318
**WELDING RESEARCH ABROAD.** [Weld. res. abroad]. **Added/Corp** Welding Research Council (U.S.). Vol. 1 (Jan. 1955)-. Periodical. English. ir. comes with membership. Welding Research Council, 345 East 47th Street, 13th Floor, New York NY 10017. **Tel** (212)705-7956. **LC** TS227; .A282. **DD** 671. cum. index.
**Ind/Abst** Alum. Ind. Abstr.; Eng. Mater. Abstr.; Met. Abstr.

US/0096-7629
**WELDING RESEARCH (MIAMI).** (WELDING RESEARCH.). **Added/Corp** Welding Research Council (U.S.) American Welding Society. **VFOAT** Welding Research Supplement. (1936)-. Academic Scholarly Publication. English. mo. Welding Research Council, 345 East 47th Street, 13th Floor, New York NY 10017. **Tel** (212)705-7956. **LC** TS227; .A1675. **CODEN** WERSA3. Documents available from CASDDS. ***Continues** Welding Research Council (U.S.). Reprint of Monthly Report.*
**Ind/Abst** Chem. Abstr.

US/0511-4381
**WELDING RESEARCH NEWS.** [Weld. res. news]. **Added/Corp** Welding Research Council (U.S.). (1967)-. Periodical. English. qt. Comes with Welding Research council membership. Welding Research Council, 345 East 47th Street, 13th Floor, New York NY 10017. **Tel** (212)705-7956. **CODEN** WERNA.
**Ind/Abst** Alum. Ind. Abstr.; Eng. Mater. Abstr.; Met. Abstr.

UK/0262-642X
**WELDING REVIEW INTERNATIONAL.** Academic Scholarly Publication. English. qt. £73.00 UK; £96.00, $178.00 other. Argus Press Group, Queensway House, 2 Queensway Redhill, Surrey RH1 1QS England. **Tel** 011 44 737 768611, 011 44 737 761685, FAX 011 44 737 760510, telex 948669 TOPJNL G. **ED** Richard Southgate. available on an online database (file 16/Full-Text) from DIALOG. Documents available from CASDDS. ***Continues*** *Welding Review, 0262-642X.*
**Ind/Abst** Chem. Abstr.; PROMT [Full Txt.].

JA/0288-4771
**YOSETSU GAKKAI RONBUNSHU.** **Added/Corp** Yosetsu Gakkai (Japan). **VFOAT** Quarterly Journal of the Japan Welding Society. (1983)-. Periodical. Japanese (summaries and/or abstracts in English). qt. Japan Welding Society, 1-11 Kanda Sakumacho, Chiyoda-ku, Tokyo 101 Japan. **LC** TS227.A1; Y66. **CODEN** YGRODU. Documents available from Article Express International, CASDDS.
**Ind/Abst** Chem. Abstr. (1983-); Civ. Struct. Eng. Abstr.; Ei Page One; Elect. Comm. Abstr.; Eng. Index Annu.; Manuf. Process Eng. Abstr.; Mater. Sci. Eng. Abstr.; Mech. Eng. Abstr.; Solid State Supercond. Abstr.

JA
**YOSETSU GIJUTSU. WELDING TECHNIQUE.** Japanese. mo. $228.00. Sanpo Shuppan K.K., (Sanpo Publications, Inc.), 2, Kanda Hirakawacho, Chiyodaku, Tokyoto 101, Japan. **(Subscription address:** Kyowa Book Company Inc., 1-38 Kanda Jinbo-Cho, Chiyoda-Ku, Tokyo 101, Japan (Phone: 03-3293-0727)**)**

XO/0322-9785
**ZVARACSKE SPRAVY.** (ZVARACSKE SPRAVY / VUZ.). [Zvaracske spr.]. **Added/Corp** Vyskumny Ustav Zvaracsky v Bratislave. **VFOAT** Welding News. (1951)-. Academic Scholarly Publication. English (Slovak). **CODEN** ZVSPDI. Documents available from CASDDS.
**Ind/Abst** Alum. Ind. Abstr.; Chem. Abstr.; Met. Abstr.

# METROLOGY AND STANDARDIZATION

SW
**ACIDIFICATION RESEARCH IN SWEDEN.** ***Ceased.*** [Acidif. res. Swed.]. **Added/Corp** Sweden. Statens Naturvardsverk. Information Section. (1984)-(19??). Periodical. English (summaries and/or abstracts in English and Swedish). Twice a year. Swedish National Environmental Protection Board, PO Box 1302, Information Section, Solna S17125 Sweden. **Tel** (468)799-1000, FAX (468)984513, telex 11131 ENVIRONS. **ED** Peter Hanneberg.
**Desc:** Gives scientists and others a lead as to what is being done in Sweden, and to stimulate exchanges of experience and knowledge.

JO
**AL-TAQYIS : NASHRAT AL-MUNAZZAMAH AL-ARABIYAH LIL-MUWASAFAT WA-AL-MAQAYIS.** **VFOAT** Standardization. Periodical. Arabic (English and French). mo. Almunazzamah Al-Arabiyah Lil-Muwasafat Wa-Al-Maqayis, Amman Al-Urdun, SB 926161, Amman Jordan. **LC** T59.A1; T36.

US/0094-3096
**AMERICAN METRIC JOURNAL.** ***Ceased.*** [Am. metr. j.]. **VFOAT** AMJ SI Metricpac. Vol. 1, No. 1 (Sept. 1973)-?. English. bm. AMJ Publishing Company, PO Box 3251, Carmarillo CA 93010. **Tel** (805)484-5787. **ED** R A Hopkins and V A Call. **LC** QC92.U54; A44. **DD** 389/.152. **Circ:** 10,200. available on microfiche; available on microfilm.
**Desc:** Metric training and education for schools, colleges and industry.
**Ind/Abst** Appl. Sci. Technol. Index; Curr. Index J. Educ.

US/1075-6809
**AMERICAN NATIONAL STANDARDS CATALOG.** (AMERICAN NATIONAL STANDARDS ... CATALOG / ANSI.). [Am. natl. stand. cat.]. **Added/Corp** American National Standards Institute. **VFOAT** Catalog; Catalog of American National Standards. (1993)-. Catalog. English. an. $24.00. American National Standards Institute, 11 West 42nd Stret, New York NY 10036. **Tel** (212)642-4900. **DD** 620. ***Continues*** *Catalog of American National Standards, 1043-7002.*

US/0883-2862
**ANNUAL REPORT - CENTER FOR MATERIALS SCIENCE (NATIONAL MEASUREMENT LABORATORY).** (ANNUAL REPORT / NATIONAL MEASUREMENT LABORATORY, CENTER FOR MATERIALS SCIENCE.). [Annu. rep. - Cent. Mater. Sci. (Natl. Meas. Lab.)]. **Main/Corp** Center for Materials Science (National Measurement Laboratory). Began with 1979. English. an. Center for Materials Science, National Bureau of Standards, Washington DC 20234. **LC** TA404.2; .C46A. **DD** 620.1/1/05. available on microfiche (Vols. for (1982-) distributed to depository libraries).

TZ
**ANNUAL REPORT / TANZANIA BUREAU OF STANDARDS.** **Main/Corp** Tanzania Bureau of Standards. English. an. Tanzania Bureau of Standards, PO Box 9524 S L P, Dar es Salaam Tanzania. **LC** QC100.T34; T36A. **DD** 354.6780082/1. ***Continues*** *Director's Annual Report / Tanzania Bureau of Standards.*

US
**ANNUAL REPORT / WEIGHTS AND MEASURES BUREAU.** **Main/Corp** Virginia. Weights and Measures Bureau. English. an. 1 North 14th Street, Room 032, Richmond VA 23219. **LC** HF5714; .V57A. **DD** 353.97550082/1. ***Continues*** *Annual Report - Weights and Measures Section.*

US/0038-9676
**ANSI REPORTER.** **Main/Corp** American National Standards Institute. **Added/Corp** American National Standards Institute. **VAT** American National Standards Institute Reporter. Vol. 4, No. 14 (July 3, 1970)-. Periodical. English. Twelve times a year. $200.00. American National Standards Institute, 11 West 42nd Stret, New York NY 10036. **Tel** (212)642-4900. **LC** IN PROCESS. available on microfilm and microfiche from University Microfilms International (UMI). ***Continues*** *Standards Institute Reporter.*

DK
**ARSBERETNING / DANTEST.** **Main/Corp** Dansk Institut for Prvning Og Justering. (1980)-. Periodical. Danish (summaries and/or abstracts in English). an. Free. Dansk Institut for Prvning Og Justering, Amager Boulevard 115, 2300 Kbenhavn S Denmark. **Tel** +45-31 54 0830, FAX +45-31 95 4700, telex 3 12 46 GOVERN DK. **LC** TA416; .D36a. ctrl circ.

DK
**ARSBERETNING - JUSTERVSENET.** **Main/Corp** Denmark. Justervsenet. (1976/77)-. Danish. Justervsenet, Amager Boulevard 115, 2300 Copenhagen S Denmark. **Tel** 45-1-540830. **ED** Axel Vollertzen. **LC** QC100.D4; .D46A. **Circ:** 1,000 (ctrl).
**Desc:** Technical testing within the fields of: (1) fire technology, (2) chemical technology, (3) civil engineering, (4) mechanical engineering and (5) metrology - legal and applied.

UK/0005-3309
**B.S.I. NEWS.** [BSI news]. **Main/Corp** British Standards Institution. **Added/Corp** British Standards Institution. News. **VAT** British Standards Institution News. (Nov. 1956)-. Periodical. English. mo. (only comes with British Standards Institution Membership). British Standards Institute, Linford Wood, Milton Keynes MK14 6LL England. **Tel** 011 44 908 220908, FAX 011 44 908 320856, telex 825777 BSIMK G. **(Subscription address:** CN/ Standards Council of Canada, 45 O'Connor Street, Suite 1200, Ottawa, Ontario K1P 6N7 Canada**)** **LC** T59; .B7. **DD** 606.242. **CODEN** BSINAE. ***Continues*** *B.S.I. Information Sheet.*
**Ind/Abst** Alum. Ind. Abstr.; BMT Abstr. (1973-199?); Fluid Abstr., Civil Eng.; Fluid Abstr. Proc. Eng.; FLUIDEX (1973-); Libr. Inf. Sci. Abstr.; Met. Abstr.; Pap. Board Abstr.; Print. Abstr.; World Ceram. Abstr.; World Publ. Monit.; World Surf. Coat. Abstr.; World Text. Abstr.

●GW
**BECKMAN FOCUS.** (1994)-. Newsletter. German (English and French). Four times a year. Free on request. Beckman Instruments GmbH, Abteilung Offentlichkeitsarbeit Frankfurter Ring 115, D 80807 Munchen 40 Germany. **Tel** 089/3887270, FAX 089/3887490, telex 52395261. **Acid Free. Circ:** 11,000 (ctrl).

GW/0005-755X
**BECKMAN REPORT.** ***Ceased.*** [Beckman-Rep.]. **Added/Corp** Beckman Instruments GmbH. (1959)-(1994). Academic Scholarly Publication. German. sa. Beckman Instruments GmbH, Abteilung Offentlichkeitsarbeit Frankfurter Ring 115, D 80807 Munchen 40 Germany. **Tel** 089/3887270, FAX 089/3887490, telex 52395261. **CODEN** BECRBZ. **Circ:** 11,000 (ctrl). Documents available from CASDDS.
**Ind/Abst** Chem. Abstr.; Energy Res. Abstr. (Feb. 1982-).

PL/0324-8496
**BIULETYN POLSKIEGO KOMITETU NORMALIZACJI I MIAR.** **Main/Corp** Komitet Normalizacji I Miar. (July 1972)-. Periodical. Polish. mo. Price on Request. **(Subscription address:** ARS Polona, PO Box 1001, 00068 Warsaw Poland.**)** **LC** T59.2.P7; A3. ***Continues*** *Poland. Polski Komitet Normalizacyjny. Biuletyn.*

UK
**BRITISH STANDARD.** **Main/Corp** British Standards Institution. **VFOAT** B.S.; British Standard Specification. (1931)-. Periodical. English. British Standards Institute, Linford Wood, Milton Keynes MK14 6LL England. **Tel** 011 44 908 220908, FAX 011 44 908 320856, telex 825777 BSIMK G. ***Continues*** *British Engineering Standards Association. British Standard Specification.*
**Ind/Abst** Agric. Eng. Abstr. (1991-); Biodeter. Abstr. (1991-); Dairy Sci. Abstr.; Food Sci. Technol. Abstr.; For. Prod. Abstr. (19??-19??); Maize Abstr.; Nutr. Abstr. Rev., Ser. A, Hum. Exp.; Pig News Inf.; Postharvest News Inf.; Rev. Agric. Entomol.; Rice Abstr.; Seed Abstr.; Soils Fert.; Sug. Indus. Abstr.; Weed Abstr.; Wheat Barley Trit. Abstr.

UK
**BSI BUYERS GUIDE.** **Added/Corp** British Standards Institution. **VFOAT** Buyers Guide. (1980)-. Consumer Publication. English. an. £95.00 Europe; £110.00 other. British Standards Institute, Linford Wood, Milton Keynes MK14 6LL England. **Tel** 011 44 908 220908, FAX 011 44 908 320856, telex 825777 BSIMK G.

UK/0005-3309
**BSI NEWS.** **Main/Corp** British Standards Institution. **Added/Corp** British Standards Institution. BSI Information Sheet. British Standards Institution. Monthly Information Sheet. (19??)-. Periodical. English. mo. British Standards Institute, Linford Wood, Milton Keynes MK14 6LL England. **Tel** 011 44 908 220908, FAX 011 44 908 320856, telex 825777 BSIMK G.
**Ind/Abst** Archit. Period. Index (Mar. 1978-Apr. 1982); Chem. Hazards Ind.; Ergon. Abstr.; HILITES; Lab. Hazards Bull.; Leadscan.

UK
**BSI STANDARDS CATALOGUE.** **Added/Corp** British Standards Institution. **VFOAT** B.S.I. Standards Catalogue. **VAT** British Standards Institution Standards Catalogue. (1987)-. English. British Standards Institute, Linford Wood, Milton Keynes MK14 6LL England. **Tel** 011 44 908 220908, FAX 011 44 908 320856, telex 825777 BSIMK G. ***Continues*** *BSI Catalogue.*

CN/0228-2690
**BULLETIN, CONVERSION AU SYSTEME METRIQUE.** V. 1- Mar. 1978-. Bulletin. French. Free. Institut Canadien de la Construction en Acier, Bureau 300/201 rue Consumer, Willowdale Ontario M2J 4G8 Canada. **DD** 338.4/76691/0212. **UDC** 389.1.

FR/0473-2812
**BULLETIN DE L'ORGANISATION INTERNATIONALE DE METROLOGIE LEGALE.** [Bull. Organ. Int. Metrol. Leg.]. (1963)-. French. qt. 400.00F Europe; 450.00F other. Organisation Intl de Metrologie Legale, 11 rue Turgot, 75009 Paris France. **Tel** 011 33 1 48781282, 42852711.

BE
**BULLETIN DE METROLOGIE (BELGIUM).** **Main/Corp** Belgium. Administration du Commerce. Bulletin. French. 100. Administration du Commerce, Compte-Postale 191.69, GIE Service de la Metrologie, Bruxelles Belgium. **LC** QC89.B4; B44A. **UDC** 389(493).

FR/0982-2232
**BULLETIN DU BUREAU NATIONAL DE METROLOGIE.** **Added/Corp** France. Bureau National de Metrologie. Bulletin. French. qt. **LC** QC100.F7; F7a. **DD** 354.440082/1. ***Continues*** *Bulletin d'Information / France. Bureau National de Metrologie.*

BE/0029-7682
**BULLETIN MENSUEL. OBSERVATIONS CLIMATOLOGIQUES / INSTITUT ROYAL METEOROLOGIQUE DE BELGIQUE / MAANDBERICHT. KLIMATOLOGISCHE WAARNEMINGEN / KONINKLIJK METEOROLOGISCH INSTITUUT VAN BELGIEE.** **Added/Corp** Institut Royal Meteorologique de Belgique. **VFOAT** Observations Climatologiques Klimatologische Waarnemingen Maandbericht. (19??)-. Periodical. Dutch (French). Twelve times a year. 1200F Belgium; 1500F others. Institut Royal Meteorologique de Belgique, Avenue Circulaire 3, B 1180 Bruxelles Belgium. **Tel** 32-2-3730502, FAX 32-2-3751259. **LC** QC989.B8; B85.

JA/0368-6051
**BULLETIN OF NRLM.** **Added/Corp** Kogyo Gijutsuin Keiryo Kenkyujo (Japan). Vol. 30, No. 1 (1981)-.

Bulletin. Japanese (English; summaries and/or abstracts in English). qt. National Research Laboratory of Metrology, Tokyo Japan. **LC** WMLC L 83/4003. **CODEN** KKYHAH. ***Formed by the union of*** *Kogyo Gijutsuin Keiryo Kenkyujo. Bulletin of the National Research Laboratory of Metrology* ***and*** *Keiryo Kenkyujo Hokoku, 0368-6051.*

US/1043-7002
**CATALOG OF AMERICAN NATIONAL STANDARDS.** ***Title Change.*** (CATALOG OF AMERICAN NATIONAL STANDARDS / AMERICAN NATIONAL STANDARDS INSTITUTE.). [Cat. Am. natl. stand.]. **Main/Corp** American National Standards Institute. **Added/Corp** American National Standards Institute. **VFOAT** Catalog for American National Standards. (1977)-(1992). Catalog. English. an. American National Standards Institute, 11 West 42nd Stret, New York NY 10036. **Tel** (212)642-4900. **LC** Z7914.A22; A43. **DD** 620. ***Continues*** *Catalog (American National Standards Institute).* ***Continued by*** *American National Standards ... Catalog, 1075-6809.*

FR/0750-7046
**CATALOGUE AFNOR.** **Added/Corp** Association Francaise de Normalisation. **VAT** Catalogue Association Francaise de Normalisation. 37th Ed. (1981)-. French. an. 295.00F. Afnor Norex, Tour Europe Cedex 7, 92049 Paris la Defense France. **Tel** 011 33 1 42915555, FAX 011 33 1 42915656. **LC** TA368; .A78. **DD** 602/.18. available on CD-ROM. ***Continues*** *Catalogue des Normes Francaises.*

BE
**CEN CENELEC ETSI BULLETIN.** (19??)-. English. Twelve times a year. 8400F. CEN Comite European Normalis, rue de Stassart 36, B 1050 Brussels Belgium. **Tel** 011 32 2 5196811. ***Continues*** *Ongoing Activities in European Standards.*

BE
**CEN GENERAL TECHNICAL REPORT.** (19??)-. English. an. 2900F. European Committee Standardization, 2 rue Brederode Boite 5, B-1000 Brussels Belgium. **Tel** 011 32 2 519 6811.

FR/0255-3147
**COMITE CONSULTATIF POUR LES ETALONS DE MESURE DES RAYONNEMENTS IONISANTS : RAPPORT.** **Main/Corp** Comite International des Poids et Mesures. Comite Consultatif pour les Etalons de Mesure des Rayonnements Ionisants. **VFOAT** Rapport du Comite Consultatif pour les Etalons de Mesure des Rayonnements Ionisants ... au Comite International des Poids et Mesures. Began with: 3 (1961) issue. French (English). ir. 30.00F. Bureau International des Poids et Mesures, Pavillon de Breteuil, 12 Bis Gde. Rue, 92312 Sevres France. **Tel** 011 33 1 45077070, FAX 011 33 1 65342121, telex 531351 BIPM F. **LC** QC81; .I4. **DD** 539.7/2. **Circ:** 700.

FR
**COMITE INTERNATIONAL DES POIDS ET MESURES, COMITE CONSULTATIF D'ELECTRICITE. RAPPORT.** **Main/Corp** Comite International des Poids et Mesures. Comite Consultatif d'Electricite. **VFOAT** Rapport au Comite International des Poids et Mesures, Comite Consultatif d'Electricite. French (English). ir. 120.00F. Bureau International des Poids et Mesures, Pavillon de Breteuil, 12 Bis Gde. Rue, 92312 Sevres France. **Tel** 011 33 1 45077070, FAX 011 33 1 65342121, telex 531351 BIPM F. **LC** QC81; .C5913. **DD** 537. **UDC** 389.1(047.1). **Bk Rev. Ad Acc. Circ:** 350.
**Desc:** Contains the proceedings of the meetings of the relevant committee, whose attendees are representatives of national laboratories engaged in standardization and related researches.

FR
**COMITE INTERNATIONAL DES POIDS ET MESURES, COMITE CONSULTATIF DES UNITES. RAPPORT.** **Main/Corp** Comite International des Poids et Mesures. Comite Consultatif des Unites. 1- Session; 1967-. French (English). ir. 31.00F. Bureau International des Poids et Mesures, Pavillon de Breteuil, 12 Bis Gde. Rue, 92312 Sevres France. **Tel** 011 33 1 45077070, FAX 011 33 1 65342121, telex 531351 BIPM F. **LC** QC81; .C5918A. **DD** 389/.1. **UDC** 389.1(047.1). **Circ:** 350.
**Desc:** Contains the proceedings of the meetings of the relevant committee, whose attendees are representatives of national laboratories engaged in standardization and related researches.

CN/0380-1314
**CONSENSUS (OTTAWA).** (CONSENSUS.). **Added/Corp** Standards Council of Canada. Vol. 1 (Jan. 1974)-. Periodical. English (French). qt. 12.00Can$. Standards Council of Canada, 45 O'Conner Street, Suite 1200, Ottawa Ontario K1P 6N7 Canada. **Tel** (613)238-3222, (800)267-8220, FAX (613)995-4564, telex 053-4403. **ED** Steven Brasier. **Circ:** 16,000 (ctrl).
**Desc:** Intended especially for industry, government, education and professional communities; contains articles related to standards and standardization at the national and international levels.

GW/0723-7685
**DIN-ANZEIGER FUER TECHNISCHE REGELN.** [DIN-Anz. tech. Regeln]. **VFOAT** Deutsches Institut fuer Normung Anzeiger fuer Technische Regeln; Anzeiger fuer Technische Regeln; Deutsches Institut fuer Normung : DIN-Anzeiger fuer Technische Regeln. (1981)-. Multiple languages. an. DM340.00 Members; DM400.00 other. Beuth Verlag GmbH, Burggrafenstrasse 6, D-10787 Berlin Germany. **Tel** 011 49 30 260112573. **UDC** 006. ***Continues*** *DIN-Normen-Anzeiger, 0723-7693.*

GW
**DIN : CATALOG OF THE GERMAN INSTITUTE OF STANDARDS.** (19??)-. Catalog. English. an. $69.00. American National Standards Institute, 11 West 42nd Stret, New York NY 10036. **Tel** (212)642-4900.

GW/0722-2912
**DIN-MITTEILUNGEN + ELEKTRONORM.** **VFOAT** Deutsches Institut fuer Normung Mitteilungen + Elektronorm; DIN-Mitteilungen und Elektronorm. (1977)-. Periodical. German. mo. DM611.01. Beuth Verlag GmbH, Burggrafenstrasse 6, D-10787 Berlin Germany. **Tel** 011 49 30 260112573. **UDC** 006.3.01. ***Continues*** *DIN-Mitteilungen, 0011-4952.*

CN
**DIRECTORY AND INDEX OF STANDARDS.** **VFOAT** Repertoire des Normes. Directory. English (French). an. 49.95Can$. Standards Council of Canada, 45 O'Conner Street, Suite 1200, Ottawa Ontario K1P 6N7 Canada. **Tel** (613)238-3222, (800)267-8220, FAX (613)995-4564, telex 053-4403. **LC** TA368; .D54. **DD** 602/.18. **UDC** 006.35. **Circ:** 650. available on an online database.
**Desc:** A computer-produced listing of more than 6,500 standards published by the five standards-writing organizations accredited to the National Standards System. It's a valuable reference tool for standard users, libraries, universities and government departments.

SZ
**DIRECTORY OF INTERNATIONAL STANDARDIZING BODIES / REPERTOIRE DES ORGANISMES INTERNATIONAUX A ACTIVITES NORMATIVES.** **Added/Corp** International Organization for Standardization. International Electrotechnical Commission. **VFOAT** Repertoire des Organismes Internationaux a Activites Normatives; ISO Directory; ISB Directory. 1st Ed. (1977)-. English (French). an. 63.00Can$. ISO Central Secretatiat, 1 rue de Varembe, CP 56, CH-1211 Geneva 20 Switzerland. **Tel** 011 41 22 7490111. **(Subscription address:** Standards Council of Canada, 350 Sparks Street, Suite 1200, Ottawa, Ontario K1P 6N7 Canada.) **LC** T59.A1; D57. **DD** 602/.18.

US
**DIRECTORY OF STANDARDS LABORATORIES.** **Added/Corp** National Conference of Standards Laboratories. (19??)-. Directory. English. an. $100.00 (two years). National Conference of Standard Laboratories, 1800 30th Street, Suite 305B, Boulder CO 80301. **Tel** (303)440-3339. ***Continues*** *Directory of Standards Laboratories in the United States.*

GW/0416-5551
**DM.** [DM]. **VFOAT** Deutsche Mark; DM. Deutsche Mark. (1961)-. Periodical. German. mo. DM88.00 includes DM Aktuell. Handelsblatt GmbH, Postfach 102716, D-40018 Duesseldorf Germany. **Tel** 011 49 211 8871730. **(Subscription address:** DM Vertriebsservice, Postfach 3753 Handelsblatt, D 90018 Nuernberg Germany.) **UDC** 658.62/.64 :659.23. **[CCC].**

GW/0936-0530
**ENGLISH TRANSLATIONS OF GERMAN STANDARDS CATALOGUE / ISSUED BY DIN DEUTSCHES INSTITUT FUER NORMUNG E.V.** **Added/Corp** DIN Deutsches Institut fuer Normung. **VFOAT** Catalogue of English Translations of German Standards. (198?)-. English (German). an. DM57.94. Beuth Verlag GmbH, Burggrafenstrasse 6, D-10787 Berlin Germany. **Tel** 011 49 30 260112573. **Ad Acc.** ***Continues*** *Catalogue, English Translations of German Standards.*

FR/0223-4866
**ENJEUX.** [Enjeux]. No. 1; March 1980-. Academic Scholarly Publication. French. mo. 720.00F France, Germany, UK, Benelux, Greece, Spain, Portugal, Denmark, Italy, Ireland; 1,015F other. Afnor Norex, Tour Europe Cedex 7, 92049 Paris la Defense France. **Tel** 011 33 1 42915555, FAX 011 33 1 42915656. ***Formed by the union of*** *Bulletin Mensuel de la Normalisation Francaise* ***and*** *Courrier de la Normalisation.*
**Ind/Abst** Coal Abstr.; EMBASE.

CN/0831-4888
**FOCUS - CANADIAN STANDARDS ASSOCIATION.** (FOCUS.). [Focus - Can. Stand. Assoc.]. **Added/Corp** Canadian Standards Association. Vol. 1, No. 1 (Feb. 1986)-. Periodical. English. bm. Free. Canadian Standards Association, 178 Rexdale Boulevard, Rexdale Ontario M9W 1R3 Canada. **Tel** (416)747-4000, (416)747-4044, telex 06-989344. **DD** 389/.6/06071. ***Continues*** *Standards Forum. English, 0829-3082* ***and*** *Standards Forumupdate. English, 0824-4340.*

RU/0134-8752
**GOSUDARSTVENNYE STANDARTY SSSR : UKAZATEL / GOSUDARSTVENNYI KOMITET STANDARTOV SOVETA MINISTROV SSSR.** **Added/Corp** Soviet Union. Gosudarstvennyi Komitet Standartov. Gosudarstvennyi Komitet SSSR po Standartam. (19??)-. Russian. mo. $119.95. **(Subscription address:** East View Publications Inc., 3020 Harbor Lane North, Suite 110, Minneapolis MN 55447.)
**Ind/Abst** Agric. Eng. Abstr.; Seed Abstr.

GW/0017-4645
**GROSSWETTERLAGEN EUROPAS, DIE.** **Added/Corp** Deutscher Wetterdienst. Zentralamt. (1966)-. Periodical. German. mo. DM22.73. Deutscher Wetterdienst, Frankfurter Strasse 135, D-63067 Offenbach Germany. **Tel** 011 49 69 80622272, FAX 011 49 69 80622484. **ED** Deutscher Wetterdienst. **LC** QC880.4.A8; G76. ***Continues*** *Grosswetterlagen Mitteleuropas.*
**Desc:** Report on the weather situation in Europe.

NE/0921-5956
**INDUSTRIAL METROLOGY.** ***Title Change.*** [Ind. metrol.]. Vol. 1, No. 1 (March 1990)-(199?). Academic Scholarly Publication. English. qt (1 volume). Elsevier Science Publishers BV, PO Box 211, 1000 AE Amsterdam Netherlands. **Tel** 011 31 20 5803642, FAX 011 31 20 5862696, telex 15682. **[CCC]. Bk Rev. Ad Acc.** available on microfilm and microfiche from University Microfilms International (UMI). Documents available from Article Express International, Ask*IEEE, Documents on Demand. ***Continued by*** *Measurement, 0263-2241.*
**Desc:** International journal of automated measurements and control.
**Ind/Abst** Ei Page One; Eng. Index Annu.; Environ. Abstr. (Oct. 31, 1990-); INSPEC (March 1990-).

US
**INDUSTRY STANDARDS AND ENGINEERING DATA.** **Added/Corp** Information Handling Services. American Society for Testing and Materials. Issue 89-06 (Dec. 1989-Jan. 1990)-. Periodical. English. bm. Information Handling Services, 15 Inverness Way East, Englewood CO 80150. **Tel** (800)525-7052, (303)790-0600, FAX (303)397-2599, telex 4322083. ***Continues*** *Industry Standards (Information Handling Services).*

US
**INTERNATIONAL AND NON-U.S. NATIONAL STANDARDS NUMERIC INDEX TO ... .** **Added/Corp** Information Handling Services. **VFOAT** International and Non-U.S. National Standards Microfilm and Microfiche Numeric index; VSMF International and Non-U.S. National Standards Numeric Index. Issue 89-04 (Aug./Sept. 1989)-. Periodical. English. ir. Information Handling Services, 15 Inverness Way East, Englewood CO 80150. **Tel** (800)525-7052, (303)790-0600, FAX (303)397-2599, telex 4322083. ***Continues*** *International and Foreign National Standards. Index.*

US
**INTERNATIONAL STANDARDS INDEX.** English. Six times a year (Feb., Apr., June, Aug., Oct., Dec.). $230.00. Information Handling Services, 15 Inverness Way East, Englewood CO 80150. **Tel** (800)525-7052, (303)790-0600, FAX (303)397-2599, telex 4322083. cum. index. **Circ:** 200.

SZ/0303-805X
**ISO BULLETIN.** [ISO bull.]. Jan. 1970-. Bulletin. English (French and English). mo. ISO Central Secretatiat, 1 rue de Varembe, CP 56, CH-1211 Geneva 20 Switzerland. **Tel** 011 41 22 7490111. **LC** T59.A1; I5613A. **DD** 389/.6/05.
**Ind/Abst** Leadscan.

SZ/0303-3309
**ISO CATALOGUE.** **Main/Corp** International Organization for Standardization. (19??)-. English (French). an. $66.00. ISO Central Secretatiat, 1 rue de Varembe, CP 56, CH-1211 Geneva 20 Switzerland. **Tel** 011 41 22 7490111. **LC** Z7914.A22; I61.

US/0536-2067
**ISO MEMENTO.** **Main/Corp** International Organization for Standardization. **VFOAT** International Organization for Standardization Memento. 1961-. English (French and Russian). American National Standards Inst, 1430 Broadway, New York NY 10018. **Tel** (212)354-3300.

RU/0368-1025
**IZMERITELNAJA TEHNIKA.** (IZMERITELNAIA TEKHNIKA.). [Izmer. teh.]. **Added/Corp** Soviet Union. Komitet po Delam mer i

Izmeritelnykh Priborov. Soviet Union. Komitet Standartov, mer i Izmeritelnykh Priborov. Gosudarstvennyi Komitet Standartov, mer i Izmeritelnykh Priborov SSSR. Soviet Union. Gosudarstvennyi Komitet Standartov. Gosudarstvennyi Komitet SSSR po Standartam. (1940)-. Periodical. Russian. mo. $119.95. Izdatelstvo Standartov, D-22 Novoprensenskii Per 3, Moscow Russia. **(Subscription address:** East View Publications Inc., 3020 Harbor Lane North, Suite 110, Minneapolis MN 55447.) **CODEN** IZTEAW. Documents available from CASDDS. ***Continues*** *Metrologiia i Poverochnoe Delo.* **Ind/Abst** Chem. Abstr.

US/1044-677X
**JOURNAL OF RESEARCH OF THE NATIONAL INSTITUTE OF STANDARDS AND TECHNOLOGY.** [J. res. Natl. Inst. Stand. Technol.]. **Added/Corp** National Institute of Standards and Technology (U.S.). Vol. 93, No. 6 (Nov.-Dec. 1988)-. Academic Scholarly Publication. English. bm. $27.00 domestic; $33.75 other. Superintendent of Documents, US Government Printing Office, Washington DC 20402. **Tel** (202)275-3328, FAX (202)786-2377. **LC** QC100.U6; U55a. **DD** 681/.2. **NLM** W1; JO87H. **CODEN** JRITEF. available on microfilm and microfiche from University Microfilms International (UMI). Documents available from Article Express International, The Genuine Article, Ask*IEEE, CASDDS. ***Continues*** *Journal of Research of the National Bureau of Standards (Washington, D.C. : 1977), 0160-1741.*
**Desc:** Physics, chemistry, engineering, mathematics, and computer sciences.
**Ind/Abst** Abstr. Bull. Inst. Pap. Sci. Tech.; Appl. Sci. Technol. Index (1988-); Chem. Abstr. (1988-); Curr. Contents Eng. Tech. Appl. Sci.; Curr. Contents Phys. Chem. Earth Sci.; Ei Page One (1988-); Energy Res. Abstr.; Eng. Index Annu.; Fluid Abstr., Civil Eng.; Fluid Abstr. Proc. Eng.; FLUIDEX (19??-); INSPEC (1988-); Int. Aerosp. Abstr.; Res. Alert [Full Cov.]; Sci. Cit. Index; SCISEARCH; World Ceram. Abstr.; World Surf. Coat. Abstr.; World Text. Abstr.; Zentralbl. Math. Ihre Grenzgeb.

US/1064-3761
**JOURNAL OF THE QUALITY ASSURANCE INSTITUTE, THE.** [J. Qual. Assur. Inst.]. **Added/Corp** Quality Assurance Institute. Vol. 5, No. 1 (Jan. 1991)-. Periodical. English. qt (Jan., Apr., Jul., Oct.). $43.00 (QUI members), $50.00 (non-members) US; $75.00 other. Quality Assurance Institute, 7575 Dr Phillips Boulevard, Orlando FL 32819. **Tel** (407)363-1111, FAX (407)363-1112. **DD** 620. **CODEN** JQAIE3. ***Continues*** *Quality Data Processing.*

KO
**KS PYOSI SANGPUM MONGNOK.** **Added/Corp** Hanguk Kongop Pyojun Hyophoe. (1985)-. Korean. W30,000. Hanguk Kongop Pyojun Hyophoe, 105-153 Kongduk-dong, Mapo-ku Seoul Korea. **LC** T59.2.K6; K7. ***Continues*** *KS Chongnam.*

BE
**LISTE DES MEMBRES - INSTITUT BELGE DE NORMALISATION.** **Main/Corp** Institut Belge de Normalisation. **VFOAT** Ledenlijst. Multiple languages (Dutch and French). Av de la Brabanconne 29, Bruxelles 1040 Belgium. **LC** T59.2.B4; I58A. **DD** 389/.6/061493. **UDC** 006.35(060.93)(493).

US
**MALCOLM BALDRIGE NATIONAL QUALITY AWARD NEWSLETTER.** Newsletter. English. qt. $395.00. Quality Assurance Institute, 7575 Dr Phillips Boulevard, Orlando FL 32819. **Tel** (407)363-1111, FAX (407)363-1112.

US/0194-1461
**MEASUREMENT & CONTROL NEWS.** [Meas. control news]. **VFOAT** M & C News. **VAT** Measurement and Control News. (1977)-. Periodical. English. Six times a year. $22.00 (surface mail), $95.00 (airmail) Comes with Measurement and Control Journals. Measurement & Data Corporation, 2994 West Liberty Avenue, Pittsburgh PA 15216. **Tel** (412)343-9666, FAX (412)343-9685. **DD** 389. ***Continues*** *Measurement & Data News.*

UK/0263-2241
**MEASUREMENT : JOURNAL OF THE INTERNATIONAL MEASUREMENT CONFEDERATION.** **Added/Corp** International Measurement Confederation. Institute of Measurement and Control. Vol. 1, No. 1 (Jan./March 1983)-. Academic Scholarly Publication. English. Twelve times a year (3 volumes). Fl915.00. Elsevier Science Publishers BV, PO Box 211, 1000 AE Amsterdam Netherlands. **Tel** 011 31 20 5803642, FAX 011 31 20 5862696, telex 15682. **[CCC].** Documents available from Ask*IEEE.
**Ind/Abst** INSPEC (Jan./March 1985-).

NE
**MEET- EN REGELAPPARATEN- EN OVERIGE INSTRUMENTENINDUSTRIE / CENTRAAL BUREAU VOOR DE STATISTIEK, HOOFDAFDELING STATISTIEKEN VAN INDUSTRIE EN BOUWNIJVERHEID.** **VFOAT** Manufacture of Measuring and Controlling Units. 1980-1981-. Dutch (summaries and/or abstracts in English). be. Fl9.25. Centraal Bureau voor de Statistiek, AFD ALG Zaken, Postbus 959, 2270 AZ Voorburg Netherlands. **Tel** 011 31 70 3373800, FAX 011 31 038 7429, telex 32692 CBS NL. **LC** HD9706.2.N4; M43. **UDC** 531.7.

HU/0025-9993
**MERES ES AUTOMATIKA.** [Meres autom.]. **Added/Corp** Merestechnikai es Automatizalasi Tudomanyos Egyesulet (Hungary). (1953)-. Academic Scholarly Publication. Hungarian (Hungarian; summaries and/or abstracts in English, German and Russian). Six times a year. $36.00. **(Subscription address:** Kultura, PO Box 149, H 1389 Budapest 62 Hungary, (phone: 011 36 1 359370)) **CODEN** MEAUAI. Documents available from Article Express International, Ask*IEEE, CASDDS.
**Ind/Abst** Alum. Ind. Abstr.; Bioeng. Abstr.; Chem. Abstr.; Ei Page One; Eng. Index Annu.; Fluid Abstr., Civil Eng.; Fluid Abstr. Proc. Eng.; FLUIDEX (1973-); INSPEC (1968-); Met. Abstr.

CN/0383-9184
**METRIC FACT SHEET.** No. 1- Apr. 1975-. Periodical. English. ir. $5.00 (includes 30 back issues). Canadian Metric Association, PO Box 35, Fonthill Ontario L0S 1E0 Canada. **Tel** (416)960-3288. **ED** Albert J Mettler, Jan van den Andel, and Joseph B Reid. **DD** 389/.152/0971. **UDC** 389.15(71). **Circ:** 1,000.
**Desc:** Educational six-page brochures on various aspects of the Metric System and practical applications.

CN/0700-2408
**METRIC MONITOR.** **VFOAT** Moniteur Metrique. V. 1, No. 1- March 1974-. Periodical. English (French). mo. Metric Commission of Canada, PO Box 4000, Ottawa Ontario K1S 5G8 Canada. **UDC** 389.15.

US/0093-3708
**METRIC NEWS.** Periodical. English. bm. $5.00. Swani Publishing Company, PO Box 248, Roscoe IL 61073. **LC** QC90.8; .M47. **DD** 389/.152/05. **UDC** 389.15.

US/1050-5628
**METRIC TODAY.** [Metr. today]. **Added/Corp** U.S. Metric Association. Vol. 25, No. 2 (Mar./Apr. 1990)-. Periodical. English. bm. $20.00 US; $25.00 Canada and Mexico; $100.00 per year (companies and agencies, with 6 issues of journal). U.S. Metric Association, 10245 Andasol Avenue, Northridge CA 91325. **Tel** (818)368-7443, FAX (818)368-7443. **ED** Valerie Antoine (Editor's Phone: (818)363-5606) 10245 Andasol Avenue, Northridge CA 91325-1504. **DD** 389. **Bk Rev**, (Qty: (6 per year)). **Ad Acc, Adv Mgr:** V. Antoine, **Tel** (818)363-5606. **Circ:** 2.500. ***Continues*** *USMA Newsletter, 0271-2555.*
**Desc:** Updates on the U.S. government's transition to metric system usage, as mandated by congress, plus reports on various industries that are converting and guidelines on obtaining metric conversion supplies and guidance.

GW/0026-1394
**METROLOGIA.** [Metrologia]. Vol. 1 (Jan. 1965)-. Periodical. English (French, German and Spanish). Six times a year (4 regular issue, 1 conference issue, & 1 review issue). $298.00 US & Canada; 1925.00F North Africa & Europe & France; 1950.00F Near East; 1990.00F other. Bureau International des Poids et Mesures, Pavillon de Breteuil, 12 Bis Gde. Rue, 92312 Sevres France. **Tel** 011 33 1 45077070, FAX 011 33 1 65342121, telex 531351 BIPM F. **(Subscription address:** North America/ Journal Fulfillment Services, 44 Hartz Way, Secaucus, NJ 07094; telephone: (201)348-4033) **ED** D. A. Blackburn. **LC** QC81; .M45. **UDC** 389. **CODEN** MTRGAU. **[CCC].** **Bk Rev.** **Pr Rev.** available on microfilm and microfiche from University Microfilms International (UMI). Documents available from Article Express International, The Genuine Article, Ask*IEEE, CASDDS.
**Desc:** Aims at disseminating new and fundamental knowledge in all aspects of scientific metrology. The leading international journal in the field and its articles are written by, and constitute an important exchange of information among, the world's experts in the science of measurement.
**Ind/Abst** Bioeng. Abstr.; Chem. Abstr.; Curr. Contents Eng. Tech. Appl. Sci.; Curr. Contents Phys. Chem. Earth Sci.; Ei Page One; Energy Res. Abstr.; Eng. Index Annu.; INSPEC (1968-); Int. Aerosp. Abstr.; Res. Alert [Full Cov.]; Sci. Cit. Index; SCISEARCH.

RM/0377-8134
**METROLOGIA APLICATA (1975).** (METROLOGIA APLICATA.). [Metrol. apl.]. (1975)-. Periodical. Romany. qt. $50.00. **(Subscription address:** Ilexim Press Department, PO Box 1, 136-1-137, Bucharest, Romania.) **CODEN** MAPBA8. Documents available from Ask*IEEE. ***Continues*** *Calitatea Productiei si Metrologie, 0377-8126.*
**Desc:** Documentary periodical dealing with applied metrology.
**Ind/Abst** INSPEC (1977-).

FR/1161-4951
**METROLOGIE PRATIQUE ET LEGALE.** **VFOAT** Metrologie; Revue de Metrologie. (1991)-. Periodical. French. Twelve times a year. 783.55F France. Editions de Genie Moderne, 102 rue de la Tour, Paris 75016 France. **Tel** 011 33 1 45048011. **LC** QC81; .R4. ***Continues*** *Revue de Metrologie Pratique et Legale, 0035-158X.*

RU/0132-4713
**METROLOGIIA / GOSUDARSTVENNYI KOMITET SSSR PO STANDARTAM.** **Added/Corp** Gosudarstvennyi Komitet SSSR po Standartam. (1969)-. Periodical. Russian. mo. $189.95. Izdatelstvo Standartov, D-22 Novoprensenskii Per 3, Moscow Russia. **(Subscription address:** East View Publications Inc., 3020 Harbor Lane North, Suite 110, Minneapolis MN 55447.)

GW/0232-3915
**METROLOGISCHE ABHANDLUNGEN.** Periodical. German. Four times a year. Free. Amt fur Standardisierung Mebwesen und Warenprufung, Furstenwalder Damm 388, Berlin O-1162 Germany. **Tel** 6441457, telex 011-2630. **LC** T50; .M415. **DD** 530.8/05. **UDC** 531.7; 389. Index available. cum. index. **Circ:** 400 (ctrl).
**Desc:** Length, angle surface measure technology, thermodynamics, acoustics, chemical composition measurements, ionizing radiation, density and viscosity.
**Ind/Abst** Energy Res. Abstr. (March 1982-).

SZ/0026-2854
**MICROTECNIC.** [Microtecnic]. **VFOAT** Micro-News. (Feb. 1947)-. Academic Scholarly Publication. English (German and French). Four times a year. 178.00F Switzerland; 167.00F other. AGIFA Verlag AG, Bruggacherstrasse 26, CH 8117 Faellanden Switzerland. **Tel** 011 41 1 8256464. **LC** QC81; .M55. **DD** 530.78. **CODEN** MITCAJ. Index available. cum. index. **Bk Rev.** **Ad Acc.** **Circ:** 7,000 (ctrl). available on microfilm and microfiche from University Microfilms International (UMI). Documents available from Article Express International, Ask*IEEE, CASDDS.
**Ind/Abst** Acoust. Abstr.; Bioeng. Abstr.; Chem. Abstr.; Ei Page One; Energy Res. Abstr.; Eng. Index Annu.; Fluid Abstr., Civil Eng.; Fluid Abstr. Proc. Eng.; FLUIDEX (1973-); INSPEC (1968-); Saf. Health Work; Shock Vibr. Dig.; Surf. Treat. Technol. Abstr.

TI/0330-8596
**MUWASAFAT / AL-MAHAD AL-QAWMI LIL-MUWASAFAT WA-AL-MILKIYAH AL-SINAIYAH.** **VFOAT** Muwassafat. No. 1 (Nov. 1983)-. Arabic (French). mo (eleven no. a year). $40.00 (plus postage). 10 Bis rue Ibn El Jazzar, 1002 Tunis Belvedere Tunisia. **LC** T59.A1; M87.

US/0083-1840
**NATIONAL STANDARD REFERENCE DATA SERIES.** **Main/Corp** United States. National Bureau of Standards. NSRDS-NBS 1 (1964)-. Monographic series. English. Price varies per volume. US Department of Commerce / National Bureau of Standards / Maryland, Gaithersburg MD 20899. **LC** QC100; .U573. **DD** 602/.1. **CODEN** NSRDAP. cum. index. Documents available from Article Express International, Ask*IEEE.
**Desc:** Quantitative data on physical and chemical properties of materials, compiled from the world's literature and critically evaluated.
**Ind/Abst** Bioeng. Abstr.; Ceram. Abstr.; Ei Page One; Eng. Index Annu.; INSPEC.

US
**NBS HANDBOOK.** **Added/Corp** United States. National Bureau of Standards. **VFOAT** NBS Hand Book. **VAT** National Bureau of Standards Handbook. (19??)-. Monographic series. English. ir. Price varies per volume. Superintendent of Documents, US Government Printing Office, Washington DC 20402. **Tel** (202)275-3328, FAX (202)786-2377. **LC** QC100; .U565. ***Continues*** *National Bureau of Standards Handbook, 0083-1824.*
**Ind/Abst** Ceram. Abstr. (19??-).

US/0194-5149
**NCSL NEWSLETTER.** [NCSL newsl.]. **Main/Corp** National Conference of Standards Laboratories. **VAT** National Conference of Standards Laboratories Newsletter. (19??)-. Newsletter. English. Four times a year (Mar., June, Sept., Dec.). $15.00 (one year); $175.00 (one year membership). National Conference of Standards Laboratories, 1800 30th Street, Suite 305B, Boulder CO 80301. **Tel** (303)440-3339.

US
**NIST CALIBRATION SERVICES USERS GUIDE. FEE SCHEDULE.** **VFOAT** Calibration Services Users Guide. **VAT** National Institute of Standards and Technology Calibration Services Users Guide. Fee Schedule. (March 1989)-. English. ir. Office of Physical Measurement Services, National Institute of Standards and Technology, Physics Building B362, Gaithersburg MD 20899-0001. ***Continues*** *NBS Calibration Services Users Guide. Fee Schedule.*

US/1054-013X
**NIST TECHNICAL NOTE.** [NIST tech. note]. **Added/Corp** National Institute of Standards and Technology (U.S.). **VAT** National Institute of Standards and Technology Technical Note. (198?)-. Academic Scholarly Publication. English. ir. Price varies per volume. National Institute Standards Technology, Building 220, Room 306, Gaithersburg MD 20899. **Tel** (301)975-2316.

LC QC100; .U5753. DD 602/.18. CODEN NTNOEF. Documents available from Ask*IEEE, CASDDS. *Continues NBS Technical Note, 0083-1913.*
**Ind/Abst** Chem. Abstr.; GeoRef; INSPEC.

US
**NIST UPDATE.** **Added/Corp** National Institute of Standards and Technology (U.S.). **VAT** National Institute of Standards and Technology Update. (1988)-. Periodical. English. bw. National Institute Standards Technology, Building 220, Room 306, Gaithersburg MD 20899. **Tel** (301)975-2316. ***Continues** NBS Update.*
**Ind/Abst** F&S Index Plus Text, Int. [Select. Cov.]; PROMT.

NE/0921-8211
**NORMALISATIE MAGAZINE.** ***Title Change.*** [Norm. mag.]. (1979)-(1993). Periodical. Dutch. mo. Kluwer BV, Postbus 23, 7400 GA Deventer Netherlands. **Tel** 011 31 5700 33155, 011 31 5700 48999, FAX 011 31 5700 11504, telex 42829. **UDC** 006. ***Continues** Normalisatie, 0376-6780.* ***Continued by** Normalisatie-Nieuws (Delft), 0929-2985.*

●NE/0929-2985
**NORMALISATIE-NIEUWS (DELFT).** (NORMALISATIE-NIEUWS.). (1993)-. Periodical. Dutch. Ten times a year. Fl60.00. Nederlands Normalisatie Instituut, Postbus 5059, 2600 GB Delft The Netherlands. **Tel** 011 31 15 690390. Index available. **Bk Rev. Ad Acc. Circ:** 5,000. available with illustrations. ***Continues** Normalisatie Magazine, 0921-8211.*

UK
**O'KEEFE'S THE LAWS OF WEIGHTS & MEASURES.** English. £195.00. Butterworth & Co. Ltd. / Kent, England, Borough Green, Sevenoaks Kent TN15 8PH England. **Tel** 011 44 732-884567, FAX 011 44 732-885996. **ED** Anthony A. Painter.
**Desc:** Reference source on the complex field of weights and measures law and practice.

BE
**ONDE METRIQUE ET DECIMETRIQUE.** an (bimonthly supplements). 600.00F. Union Eur Radiodiffusion, Avenue Albert Lancaster 32, 1180 Brussels Belgium. **Tel** 011 32 2 3755990.

BE
**ONGOING ACTIVITIES IN EUROPEAN STANDARDS.** ***Title Change.*** (19??)-(Spring 1992). English. mo. CEN Comite European Normalis, rue de Stassart 36, B 1050 Brussels Belgium. **Tel** 011 32 2 5196811. ***Continued by** CEN Cenelec ETSI Bulletin.*

CH
**PIAO CHUN HUA.** **VFOAT** Standardization; Piao Chun Hua Chi Kan. Vol. 1 (March 1983)-. Periodical. Chinese. qt. NT$50.00. Chung-Hua Min Kuo Piao Chun, Hsieh Hui Box 540077, Taipei Taiwan. **LC** T59.2.T28; P53. **DD** 389.6/0951/249. **UDC** 389(51); 006(51).

CC
**PIAO CHUN HUA TUNG HSUN / BIAOZHUNHUA TONGXUN.** **Added/Corp** Chung-kuo Piao Chun Hua Hsieh Hui. **VFOAT** Biaozhunhua Tongxun; Standarization Journal. (19??)-. Periodical. Chinese. mo. RMBY0.26. Piao Chun Hua Tung Hsun, Post Office, Beijing, People's Republic of China. **LC** T59.A1; P3 . **DD** 389/.6/05.

FR/1162-1982
**QUALITE EN MOUVEMENT PARIS LA DEFENSE.** (QUALITE EN MOUVEMENT.). (1991)-. Periodical. French. Five times a year. 609.50F France; 700.00F other. Afnor Norex, Tour Europe Cedex 7, 92049 Paris la Defense France. **Tel** 011 33 1 42915555, FAX 011 33 1 42915656. **UDC** 658.3(44). ***Continues** Qualite Magazine (Saint-Etienne), 0768-858X.*

UK/0959-3268
**QUALITY FORUM (LONDON).** ***Title Change.*** (QUALITY FORUM.). [Qual. forum]. **Added/Corp** Institute of Quality Assurance. Vol. 16, No. 1 (March 1990)-(1993). Periodical. English. qt. Institute of Quality Assurance, PO Box 712, 61 Southwark Street, London SE1 1SB England. **Tel** 011 44 71 401 7227, FAX 011 44 71 401 2725. **ED** Teresa Harris. **LC** TS156.A1; Q328. **DD** 658.5/62/05. **CODEN** QUFOEF. **Circ:** 12,000. available on microfilm and microfiche from University Microfilms International (UMI). Documents available from Article Express International, Ask*IEEE. ***Continues** Quality Assurance, 0306-2856.* ***Continued by** Quality World. Technical Supplement.*
**Desc:** Papers on all aspects of quality assurance including audits and assessments, inspection, metrology, statistical process control, and standardization.
**Ind/Abst** Eng. Index Annu. [Select. Cov.]; INSPEC (Sept. 1990-19??).

●UK
**QUALITY WORLD. TECHNICAL SUPPLEMENT.** **Added/Corp** Institute of Quality Assurance. **VFOAT** Technical Supplement; QW TS. (Mar. 1994)-. Periodical. English. sa (March and Sept.). £15.00. Institute of Quality Assurance, PO Box 712, 61 Southwark Street, London SE1 1SB England. **Tel** 011 44 71 401 7227, FAX 011 44 71 401 2725. **ED** Teresa Harris. **LC** IN PROCESS. **CODEN** QWTSE9. Documents available from Article Express International, Ask*IEEE. ***Continues** Quality Forum, 0959-3268.*
**Desc:** Papers on all aspects of quality assurance including audits and assessments, inspection, metrology, statistical process control, and standardization.
**Ind/Abst** Eng. Index Annu.; INSPEC.

FR
**RAPPORT AU COMITE INTERNATIONAL DES POIDS ET MESURES.** **Main/Corp** Comite International des Poids et Mesures. Comite Consultatif de Photometrie et Radiometrie. 8.- Session. French. Bureau International des Poids et Mesures, Pavillon de Breteuil, 12 Bis Gde. Rue, 92312 Sevres France. **Tel** 011 33 1 45077070, FAX 011 33 1 65342121, telex 531351 BIPM F. **LC** QC81; .C5916. **DD** 535/.22. **UDC** 389.1. **Circ:** 350. ***Continues** Rapport au Comite International des Poids et Mesures.*
**Desc:** Contains the proceedings of the meetings of the relevant committee whose attendees are representatives of national laboratories engaged in standardization and related researches.

FR/0750-7313
**RAPPORT D'ACTIVITE / BUREAU NATIONAL DE METROLOGIE (FRANCE).** **Main/Corp** France. Bureau National de Metrologie. French. an. 21 rue Casimir Perier, 75007 Paris France. **LC** QC100.F7; F7B. **DD** 354.440082/1. **UDC** 389(047.1)(44).

RU/0034-2505
**REFERATIVNYI ZHURNAL: METROLOGIIA I IZMERITELNAIA TEKHNIKA.** **Added/Corp** Vsesoiuznyi Institut Nauchnoi i Tekhnicheskoi Informatsii (Soviet Union) Akademiia Nauk SSSR. Institut Nauchnoi Informatsii. **VFOAT** Metrologiia i Izmertelnaia Tekhnika. (Jan. 1963)-. Periodical. Russian. mo. VINITI - Vsesoyuznyi Institut Nauchno-Tekhnicheskoi Informatsii, All-Union Scientific and Technical Information Institute, Baltiiskaia Ulitsa 14, 125219 Moscow Russia. **Tel** 238-46-00, FAX 9430060, telex 411160. **(Subscription address:** Victor Kamkin, 4956 Boiling Brook Parkway, Rockville MD 20852.) ***Continues** Referativnyi Zhurnal: Izmeritelnaia Tekhnika.*

UK
**REPORT OF THE CHIEF INSPECTOR OF WEIGHTS & MEASURES, CITY OF BIRMINGHAM.** **Main/Corp** Birmingham, Eng. Weights and Measures Dept. English. an. **LC** QC100.G7; B57A. **DD** 352/.94/210942496.

US/0098-1443
**REPORT TO THE NATION ON THE MANAGEMENT OF METRIC IMPLEMENTATION, A.** **Main/Corp** American National Metric Council. English. $2.00 single issue. American National Metric Council, 1010 Vermont Avenue NW/320, Washington DC 20005. **Tel** (202)628-5757. **LC** QC92.U54; A45A. **DD** 389/.152. **UDC** 389.15(73).

FR/0379-5659
**REUNION - COMITE INTERNATIONAL DES POIDS ET MESURES, COMITE CONSULTATIF POUR LES ETALONS DE MESURE DES RAYONNEMENTS IONISANTS, SECTION III.** [Com. int. poids mes., Com. consult. etal. mes. rayonnem. ionis., Sect. 3 : mes. neutron.]. **Main/Corp** Comite International des Poids et Mesures. Comite Consultatif pour les Etalons de Mesure des Rayonnements Ionisants. Section III. 1.- 1972-. French (English). ir. Bureau International des Poids et Mesures, Pavillon de Breteuil, 12 Bis Gde. Rue, 92312 Sevres France. **Tel** 011 33 1 45077070, FAX 011 33 1 65342121, telex 531351 BIPM F. **LC** QC795.42; .C64C. **DD** 539.7/7. **CODEN** CIMNBA. **Circ:** 700.
**Desc:** Contains the proceedings to the meetings of the relevant committee whose attendees are representatives of national laboratories engaged in standardization and related researches.

FR
**SESSION / COMITE INTERNATIONAL DES POIDS ET MESURES, COMITE CONSULTATIF DE THERMOMETRIE.** **Added/Corp** Comite International des Poids et Mesures. Comite Consultatif de Thermometrie. (1962)-. Academic Scholarly Publication. French (English). ir. Bureau International des Poids et Mesures, Pavillon de Breteuil, 12 Bis Gde. Rue, 92312 Sevres France. **Tel** 011 33 1 45077070, FAX 011 33 1 65342121, telex 531351 BIPM F. **CODEN** CCTMCZ. **Ad Acc. Circ:** 500. Documents available from CASDDS.
**Desc:** Contains the proceedings of the meetings of the relevant committee whose attendees are representatives of national laboratories engaged in standardization and related researches.
**Ind/Abst** Chem. Abstr. (1962-1982).

SI/0129-6256
**SINGAPORE STANDARDS YEARBOOK.** English. be. Free. Singapore Institute of Standards and Industrial Research, 1 Science Park Drive, Singapore Science Park, Singapore 0511 Singapore. **Tel** 011 65 778-7777, FAX 011 65 778-0086, telex RS 28499 SISIR. **LC** TA368; .S42. **DD** 389/.6/095957. **UDC** 006.35(595.7). Index available. **Circ:** 1,500.
**Desc:** Lists and gives brief descriptions of all Singapore standards at time of publication.

GW
**STANDARDISIERUNG UND QUALITAT.** Periodical. German. mo. $12.28. Deutscher Judo Verband, Redaktion Ippon Segewaldweg 40, D 12557 Berlin Germany. **Tel** 011 49 711 210770, telex 051 678. **LC** T59; .S67. **UDC** 006.35(430.2). ***Continues** Standardisierung.*

RM
**STANDARDIZAREA ROMANA.** **Added/Corp** Institutul Roman de Standardizare. (19??)-. Periodical. Romanian. mo. DM327.00. **(Subscription address:** Kubon & Sagner, ABT Zeitschriftenimport, D 80328 Munich Germany.) **LC** TA368; .S67. ***Continues** Standardizarea.*

US/0090-1210
**STANDARDIZATION NEWS : SN.** **Added/Corp** American Society for Testing and Materials. **VFOAT** SN. Vol. 13 No. 1 (Jan. 1985)-. Periodical. English. mo. $18.00 North America; $22.00 other. American Society for Testing and Materials, 1916 Race Street, Philadelphia PA 19103. **Tel** (215)299-5585, FAX (215)299-9679, telex 710 670 1037. **[CCC].** available on microfilm and microfiche from University Microfilms International (UMI). ***Continues** American Society for Testing and Materials. ASTM Standardization News, 0090-1210.*
**Ind/Abst** Abstr. Bull. Inst. Pap. Sci. Tech.; BMT Abstr. (?-199?); Concr. Abstr.; Constr. Index; GeoRef; Int. Aerosp. Abstr.; Surf. Treat. Technol. Abstr.; World Surf. Coat. Abstr.

US/0038-9633
**STANDARDS ACTION.** V. 1- 1970-. Periodical. English. bw. ANSI, 1430 Broadway, New York NY 10018. **UDC** 006.35(73). available on microfilm from University Microfilms International (UMI). ***Continues** Magazine of Standards, 0097-2959.*

US/0038-9668
**STANDARDS ENGINEERING.** [Stand. eng.]. **Added/Corp** Standards Engineering Society. (1949)-. Periodical. English. Six times a year (Jan., Mar., May, July, Sept., Nov.). $40.00 US & Canada; $60.00 others. Standards Engineering Society, 1706 Darst Avenue, Dayton OH 45403-3104. **Tel** (513)258-1955, FAX (513)256-9919. **LC** T59; .S72. **DD** 620. Index available. **Ad Acc. Circ:** 1,000 (ctrl).
**Desc:** Contains articles directly or indirectly relating to the field of standardization but specializing in company, national, and international standards.

II/0970-2628
**STANDARDS INDIA.** **Added/Corp** Bureau of Indian Standards. **VFOAT** Std Ind. Vol. 1, No. 1 (Apr. 1987)-. Periodical. English. Twelve times a year. $35.00. Bureau of Indian Standards, 9 Bahadur Shah Zafar Marg, New Delhi 110002 India. **Tel** 3310131, telex 031-65870. **(Subscription address:** Prints India, 11 Darya Ganj, New Delhi, 110002 India, telephone: 011 91 11 3268645) **LC** T59.2.I4; S7. **DD** 602/.18/0954. **CODEN** STNDE3. ***Continues** ISI Bulletin, 0019-0632.*
**Ind/Abst** Curr. Lit. Sci. Sci.; Food Sci. Technol. Abstr.

BE
**STANDARDS MANUAL : EUROPEAN TYRE AND RIM TECHNICAL ORGANIZATION.** (19??)-. English (French and German). an. 2380F per copy. European Tyre & Rim Technical Organization, Avenue Brugmann 32 Boite 2, B-1060 Brussels Belgium. **Tel** 011 32 2 3444059, FAX 011 32 2 3441234.

RU
**STANDARTY SEV I REKOMENDATSII SEV PO STANDARTIZATSII: UKAZATEL.** **Main/Corp** Council for Mutual Economic Assistance. **Added/Corp** Soviet Union. Gosudarstvennyi Komitet Standartov. Vsesoiuznyi Nauchno-Issledovatelskii Institut Tekhnicheskoi Informatsii, Klassifikatsii i Kodirovaniia (Soviet Union) Vsesoiuznyi Informatsionnyi Fond Standartov i Tekhnicheskikh Uslovii (Soviet Union). **VAT** Standarty Soveta Ekonomicheskoi Vzaimopomoshchi i Rekomendatsii Soveta Ekonomicheskoi Vzaimopomoshchi pe Standartizaisii: Ukazatel. (19??)-. Russian. 2.60rub. Izdatelstvo Standartov, D-22 Novoprensenskii Per 3, Moscow Russia. **LC** T59.2.E8; S62 a.

HU/0237-5265
**SZABVANY ES VILAG.** **Added/Corp** Magyar Szabvanyugyi Hivatal. (1986)-. Periodical. Hungarian. mo. Magyar Szabvanyugyi Hivatal, Budapest VIII, Ulloi Ut 24 Budapest Hungary. **LC** T59; .S9. ***Continues** Szabvanyositas.*

US/0271-969X
**TECHNICAL HIGHLIGHTS - NATIONAL MEASUREMENT LABORATORY.** [Tech. highlights - Natl. Meas. Lab.]. **Main/Corp** National Measurement Laboratory (U.S.). (1979)-. Government

Publication. English. ir. US Department of Commerce, 14th Street & Constitution Avenue NW, Washington DC 20230. **Tel** (202)482-2000, FAX (202)482-3772. **LC** QC100; .U57 subser; QC39. **DD** 602/.18 S; 530.8.

GW/0171-8096
**TECHNISCHES MESSE : TM.** [TM. Tech. Mess.]. **Added/Corp** Normenarbeitsgemeinschaft fuer Mess- und Regeltechnik in der Chemischen Industrie. **VFOAT** TM; T.M. Vol. 46, No. 1 Course 514 (Jan. 1979)-. Academic Scholarly Publication. German (summaries and/or abstracts in English). mo. DM238.00. R Oldenbourg Verlag, Postfach 801360, D 81613 Munich Germany. **Tel** 011 49 89 450190, FAX 011 49 89 45019305. **LC** TA165; .A12. **DD** 681/.2. **CODEN** TMTMDL. **[CCC]**. Index available. **Bk Rev. Ad Acc. Pr Rev. Circ:** 4,000 (ctrl). Documents available from Article Express International, The Genuine Article, Ask*IEEE, CASDDS. **Continues** Technisches Messen Atm.
**Desc:** Covers all aspects of measurement technology in production and operation through detailed articles on automation, quality, flow control and energy and chemical technology. Also provides product information meeting notices.
**Ind/Abst** Alum. Ind. Abstr.; Bioeng. Abstr.; Chem. Abstr.; Civ. Struct. Eng. Abstr.; Comput. Inf. Syst. Abstr. J. [Full Cov.]; Curr. Contents Eng. Tech. Appl. Sci.; Ei Page One; Elect. Comm. Abstr.; EMBASE; Energy Res. Abstr. (July 1982-); Eng. Index Annu.; Environ. Eng. Abstr.; INSPEC (Jan. 1979-); Met. Abstr.; Res. Alert [Select. Cov.]; Shock Vibr. Dig.; Solid State Supercond. Abstr.

US/0270-0123
**TMO UPDATE.** **Main/Corp** Marley Organization. **VAT** The Marley Organization Update. (1977)-. Periodical. English. mo. $90.00. The Marley Organization Inc, 11 Todds Road, Resources Information Service, Ridgefield CT 06877-9990. **Tel** (203)438-3801, FAX (203)438-3801. **ED** Charles W Hyer. **Bk Rev. Circ:** 500.
**Desc:** Reporting of news and opinions concerning current issues in technical standardization and related product certification as they influence laboratory accreditation systems, both US and international.

UK
**TRADING STANDARDS REVIEW: THE MONTHLY JOURNAL OF THE INSTITUTE OF TRADING STANDARDS ADMINISTRATION, THE.** **Added/Corp** Institute of Trading Standards Administration (Great Britain). Vol. 1, No. 1 (Jan. 1988)-. Periodical. English. mo. £36.00. Institute of Trading Standards Administration, 351 London Road, 4-5 Business Center, Hadleigh Essex S57 2BT England. **Tel** 011 44 702 559922. **LC** T59.A1; T73. **Continues** Fairtrader.

CN/0700-9623
**U L C NEWS (EDITION FRANCAISE).** (U L C NEWS.). **Main/Corp** Underwriters' Laboratories of Canada. No. 2- April 1974-. Periodical. French. Free. Underwriters Laboratories of Canada, 7 Crouse Road, Scarborough Ontario M1R 3A9 Canada. **DD** 389.6/05.

US/0270-4838
**U.S. METRIC BOARD ANNUAL REPORT.** **Main/Corp** United States Metric Board. Began with 1979. English. an. US Metric Board, 1600 Wilson Blvd., Arlington VA 22209. **LC** QC92.U54; U56A. **DD** 353.0082/1.

SP
**UNE.** **VFOAT** Boletin de la Normalizacion Espanola. Periodical. Spanish. mo. 5500ptas. AENOR Asociacion Espanola de Normalizacion y Certificacion, Fernandez de la Hoz 52, 28010 Madrid Spain. **Tel** 011 34 1 4104851, 011 34 1 4104855, FAX 410 49 76, telex 46545. **LC** T59.2.S646; I57A. **DD** 602/.18. **Circ:** 1,500. **Continues** Boletin de la normalizacion espnola UNE.

US/0095-537X
**WEIGHING & MEASUREMENT.** **VFOAT** W & M. **VAT** Weighing and Measurement. Vol. 58, (Jan. 1974)-. Periodical. English. Six times a year (Feb., Apr., June, aug., Oct., Dec.). Free (qualified), $30.00 (non-qualified) US; $10.00 (qualified), $40.00 (non-qualified), Canada & Mexico; $45.00 others. Key Markets Publishing Company, PO Box 5867, Rockford IL 61125. **Tel** (815)229-1818. **ED** David M. Mathieu. **LC** TS410; .S25. **DD** 681/.753. **Bk Rev. Ad Acc. Circ:** 14,000 (ctrl). **Continues** Scale Journal.
**Desc:** Application and technical articles pertaining to scales and the weighing industry.

ZA
**ZABS REVIEW : A PUBLICATION OF THE ZAMBIA BUREAU OF STANDARDS.** **Added/Corp** Zambia Bureau of Standards. Vol. 1, No. 1 (June 1988)-. Periodical. English. qt. $15.00. Zambia Bureau of Standards, PO Box RW 50259, Lusaka Zambia. **Tel** 213918. **ED** George Simasiku. **LC** T59.2.Z33; Z33. **DD** 389/.6/096894. **Ad Acc. Circ:** 500 (ctrl). **Continues** Zambian Standards Reporter.
**Desc:** Reviews the Zambia Bureau of Standards activities in metrology and standardization.

---

## ABSTRACTING, BIBLIOGRAPHIES AND STATISTICS

US/0093-9196
**BIBLIOGRAPHY ON ATOMIC TRANSITION PROBABILITIES.** **Added/Corp** United States. National Bureau of Standards. (Jan. 1916/June 1969)-. Government Publication. English. ir. $0.95. Superintendent of Documents, US Government Printing Office, Washington DC 20402. **Tel** (202)275-3328, FAX (202)786-2377. **LC** QC100; .U57 subser. **DD** 389/.08.

---

## MILITARY AND DEFENSE

US/0884-1314
**500 CONTRACTORS RECEIVING THE LARGEST DOLLAR VOLUME OF PRIME CONTRACT AWARDS FOR RESEARCH, DEVELOPMENT, TEST, AND EVALUATION.** (500 CONTRACTORS RECEIVING THE LARGEST DOLLAR VOLUME OF PRIME CONTRACT AWARDS FOR RESEARCH, DEVELOPMENT, TEST, AND EVALUATION / ISSUED ANNUALLY BY DEPARTMENT OF DEFENSE, WASHINGTON HEADQUARTERS SERVICES, DIRECTORATE FOR INFORMATION OPERATIONS AND REPORTS.). [500 contract. receiv. largest dollar vol. prime contract awards res. dev. test eval.]. **Added/Corp** United States. Dept. of Defense. Washington Headquarters Services. Directorate for Information Operations and Reports. Five Hundred Contractors Receiving the Largest Dollar Volume of Prime Contract Awards for Research, Development, Test, and Evaluation. (1981)-. Government Publication. English. an. $2.25. Superintendent of Documents, US Government Printing Office, Washington DC 20402. **Tel** (202)275-3328, FAX (202)786-2377. **LC** UC267; .A15. **DD** 355.6/211/0973. **Continues** 500 Contractors, 0277-7517.

UK
**AAS MILAVNEWS.** **Ceased.** **Main/Corp** Aviation Advisory Services, Ltd. **VAT** Aviation Advisory Services Milavnews. (19??)-(19??). Periodical. English. mo. Aviation Advisory Services, Stapleford Airfield, Abridge Essex England. **LC** UG622; .I57. **DD** 358.4/03/05. **UDC** 358.4. **Continues** International Air Forces & Military Aircraft Directory. Monthly Newsletter Supplement.

US
**ABOVEGROUND STORAGE TANK GUIDE SERVICE.** (19??)-. English. ir. $397.00. Thompson Publishing Group, 7711 Anderson Road, Tampa FL 33634. **Tel** (800)677-3789, (813)282-8607. **Continues** Aboveground Tank Update.

US/1059-6615
**ABOVEGROUND TANK UPDATE.** **Title Change.** [Aboveground tank update]. **VFOAT** Above Ground Tank Update. (1990)-(19??). Periodical. English. Twelve times a year. Thompson Publishing Group, 7711 Anderson Road, Tampa FL 33634. **Tel** (800)677-3789, (813)282-8607. **DD** 343. **[CCC]**. **Merged with** Aboveground Storage Tank Guide Service.

US
**ABSTRACTS OF MASTER OF MILITARY ART AND SCIENCE (MMAS) THESES AND SPECIAL STUDIES / U.S. ARMY COMMAND AND GENERAL STAFF COLLEGE.** **Title Change.** **Added/Corp** United States Army Command and General Staff College. (1977)-(19??). English. an. U S Army Command and General Staff College, Fort Leavenworth KS 66027. **Continued by** Abstracts of Theses/Special Studies.

AG
**ABSTRACTS OF MILITARY BIBLIOGRAPHY.** **Ceased.** **See** Military and Defense-Abstracting, Bibliographies and Statistics.

CR
**ACAFADE / ASOCIACION CENTROAMERICANA DE FAMILIARES DE DETENIDOS-DESAPARECIDOS.** **Added/Corp** Asociacion Centroamericana de Familiares de Detenidos Desaparecidos. (19??)-. Periodical. Spanish. bm.
**Ind/Abst** Hum. Rights Intern. Rep.

NQ
**ACCION CIVICA.** Periodical. Spanish. mo. Guardia Nacional de Nicaragua, Apartado de Correos 546, Primer Batallon Blindado Presidential, Managua Nicaragua. **LC** UA608.N54; A25. **UDC** 356.1(728.5).

AG
**ADMINISTRACION MILITAR Y LOGISTICA.** **Added/Corp** Mutualidad del Personal de Intendencias Militares. **VFOAT** Revista Administracion Militar y Logistica. (196?)-. Periodical. Spanish. mo. **LC** WMLC L 83/4431. **Continues** Revista de los Servicios del Ejercito.
**Ind/Abst** Am. Hist. Life (1970-1971,1973-1974).

US/0884-9471
**ADVANCED MILITARY COMPUTING.** **Title Change.** **See** Computers-Artificial Intelligence.

US/0276-6760
**AERO ARMOR-SERIES.** [Aero armor-ser.]. **VFOAT** Aero Armor Series. English. ir. Tab Books, PO Box 40, Blue Ridge Summit PA 17214. **Tel** (717)794-2191, FAX (717)794-2080. **LC** UG446.5; .A33. **DD** 623.74/75/0943. **UDC** 623.74.

US/1051-9793
**AEROSPACE & DEFENSE SCIENCE.** **Ceased.** **See** Aeronautics, Astronautics.

US
**AEROSPACE NEWS AND REVIEW.** **See** Aeronautics, Astronautics.

PH
**AFP ANNUAL REPORT.** **Main/Corp** Philippines. Armed Forces. **VFOAT** A.F.P. Annual Report. English (Tagalog). an. Civil Relations service, AFP Camp General Emilio, Aguinaldo Quezon City Philippines. **LC** UA853.P6; P46A. **DD** 355/.009599. **UDC** 355.1(599). ctrl circ.
**Desc:** Contains facts and figures on the accomplishments of the Armed Forces of the Philippines for the year covered.

FR/0002-2152
**AIR ACTUALITES PARIS.** [Air actual. Paris]. (1967)-. Periodical. French. Ten times a year. 137.12F France; 180.00F other. OGP Air Actualites, 175 Avenue Jean Jaures, 75019 Paris France. **Tel** 011 33 1 42413010. **UDC** 358.4.

US/0740-803X
**AIR DEFENSE ARTILLERY.** **Title Change.** [Air def. artill.]. **Added/Corp** U.S. Army Air Defense Artillery School. (Winter 1983)-(19??). Periodical. English. bm. Image Southwest, 517 Main Street, Texarkana TX 75501. **Tel** (903)793-5528, FAX (903)794-0080. **LC** UG730; .A36. **DD** 358.4/145/0973. **Continues** Air Defense Magazine, 0192-964X. **Continued by** ADA (Fort Bliss, Tex.).
**Desc:** Presents information on the latest tactical, doctrinal and technical developments in air defense worldwide.
**Ind/Abst** Air Univ. Libr. Index Mil. Period.

FR/0223-0038
**AIR FAN.** (1978)-. Periodical. French. mo. 342.80F France; 420.00F other. Air Fan Societe Edimat, 48 Boulevard des Batignolles, 75017 Paris France. **Tel** 011 33 1 42936724. **UDC** 623.74. **Bk Rev. Ad Acc. Pr Rev. Circ:** 16,000 (ctrl).
**Desc:** Dedicated to the international military aircraft including five pages for aircraft modelers.

US/0002-2365
**AIR FORCE COMPTROLLER, THE.** [Air Force comptrol.]. **Added/Corp** United States. Air Force. Office of Comptroller. United States. Air Force. Financial Management and Comptroller. Vol. 1, No. 1 (Oct. 1967)-. Government Publication. English. qt. $7.00 US; $8.75 other. Superintendent of Documents, US Government Printing Office, Washington DC 20402. **Tel** (202)275-3328, FAX (202)786-2377. **LC** UG633; .U48a. **CODEN** AFCTB3. available on microfilm and microfiche from University Microfilms International (UMI). Documents available from UMI Article Clearinghouse, Documents on Demand.
**Desc:** Provides information to Air Force comptroller personnel relating to mission accomplishment; to assist them in solving problems and improving efficiency of operation; to communicate new developments and techniques; and to stimulate professional thought and development.
**Ind/Abst** ABI/INFORM Glob. Ed.; Air Univ. Libr. Index Mil. Period.; Am. Stat. Index; Bus. Index (1979-?).

US/0270-403X
**AIR FORCE JOURNAL OF LOGISTICS.** [Air Force j. logist.]. **Added/Corp** Air Force Logistics Management Center. Vol. 4, No. 1 (Winter 1980)-. Government Publication. English. qt. $7.50 US; $9.40 other. Superintendent of Documents, US Government Printing Office, Washington DC 20402. **Tel** (202)275-3328, FAX (202)786-2377. **LC** UG1123; .A36. **DD** 358.4/16212/0973. **Continues** Pipeline (Gunter Air Force Station (Ala.)), 0747-7651.
**Desc:** A non-directive periodical published to provide an open forum for presentation of research, ideas, issues

and information of concern to Air Force logisticians and other interested personnel.
**Ind/Abst** Air Univ. Libr. Index Mil. Period.; Health Devices Alerts.

US/0730-6784
**AIR FORCE MAGAZINE.** [Air Force mag.]. **Added/Corp** Air Force Association. Vol. 54, No. 2 (Feb. 1971)-. Periodical. English. mo. $25.00 US (including Alaska and Hawaii); $33.00 Canada and Mexico; $50.00 other. Air Force Association, 1501 Lee Highway, Arlington VA 22209. **Tel** (703)247-5822, (800)727-3337. **ED** John T. Correll. **LC** UG633; .A65. **DD** 358.4/00973. **Bk Rev. Ad Acc. Circ:** 245,000. available on microfilm and microfiche from University Microfilms International (UMI). ***Continues** Air Force and Space Digest, 0002-2349.*
**Desc:** Covers U.S. Air Force life and operations, technical developments, doctrine, policy, Air Force history, and military aspects of space.
**Ind/Abst** Air Univ. Libr. Index Mil. Period.; Am. Hist. Life (1966-1977); Am. Bibliogr. Slavic East Europ. Stud.; Aviat. Tradescan [Full Cov.]; Int. Aerosp. Abstr.

US/0739-635X
**AIR FORCE OFFICER'S GUIDE, THE.** [Air Force off. guide]. 23rd Ed. (19??)-. English. ir. price varies per volume. Stackpole Magazines, 500 Vaughn Street, Harrisburg PA 17110. **Tel** (717)234-5041, (800)732-3669, FAX (717)234-1359. **LC** UG633.A1; A49. **DD** 358.4/00973. ***Continues** Air Officer's Guide.*
**Desc:** We publish military guides and books on hunting, fishing, outdoor skills, and space.

US/0273-4370
**AIR FORCE REPORT.** (AIR FORCE REPORT TO THE ... CONGRESS OF THE UNITED STATES OF AMERICA.). **Main/Corp** United States. Dept. of the Air Force. English. an. **LC** UG633; .U53D. **DD** 358.4/00973. **UDC** 358.4(73).

US/0002-2403
**AIR FORCE TIMES.** [Air Force times]. (1940)-. Periodical. English. wk (52 issues). $48.00 (one year), $88.00 (two year). Army Times Publishing Company, 6883 Commercial Drive, Springfield VA 22159. **Tel** (800)368-5718, (703)750-8099. **ED** Lee Ewing. **DD** 355. **[CCC]. Bk Rev. Ad Acc. Pr Rev. Circ:** 93,000. available on microfilm and microfiche from University Microfilms International (UMI). ***Continues** Air Force Edition. Army Times.*
**Desc:** An independent weekly journal serving career Air Force personnel.
**Ind/Abst** Air Univ. Libr. Index Mil. Period.

UK
**AIR INTERNATIONAL (BOUND VOLUMES).** **See** Aeronautics, Astronautics.

UK
**AIR MAIL.** **Added/Corp** Royal Air Forces Association. **VFOAT** RAFA Journal. **VAT** Royal Air Forces Association Journal. (May 1944)-. Periodical. English. Three times a year. £5.00. RAFA ADS Ltd., 43 Grove Park Road Chiswick, London W4 3RX England. **Tel** 011 44 81 9948504. **LC** UG635.G7; A12. **DD** 358.4.

US/0886-3857
**AIR PROGRESS MILITARY AIRPOWER.** ***Ceased.*** **VFOAT** Military Air Power; Air Progress Military Airpower Review; Military Airpower. ( )-Ceased (Aug./Sept. 1988). Periodical. English. qt. Challenge Publications Inc., 7950 Deering Avenue, Canoga Park CA 91304. **Tel** (818)887-0550. **LC** UG622; .A39. **DD** 358.4/005.

US/0885-2502
**AIR PROGRESS WARBIRDS INTERNATIONAL.** **See** Aeronautics, Astronautics.

US/0002-2586
**AIR UNIVERSITY LIBRARY INDEX TO MILITARY PERIODICALS.** **See** Military and Defense-Abstracting, Bibliographies and Statistics.

US
**AIRBORNE ELECTRONICS FORECAST.** (19??)-. English. Twelve times a year. $1390.00. Forecast International / DMS Inc., 22 Commerce Road, Newtown CT 06470. **Tel** (203)426-0800, FAX (203)426-1964, telex 467615. available on CD-ROM ($1595.00).

US
**AIRBORNE RETROFIT & MODERNIZATION SYSTEMS FORECAST.** (AIRBORNE R&M SYSTEMS FORECAST.). (19??)-. English. Twelve times a year. $1390.00. Forecast International / DMS Inc., 22 Commerce Road, Newtown CT 06470. **Tel** (203)426-0800, FAX (203)426-1964, telex 467615. available on CD-ROM ($1595.00).

US/0002-2756
**AIRMAN, THE.** (AIRMAN.). **Added/Corp** United States. Air Force. Air Force Service Information and News Center (U.S.) Air Force News Center (U.S.) Air Force News Agency (U.S.). (Aug. 1957)-. Government Publication. English. mo. $19.00 US; $23.75 other. Superintendent of Documents, US Government Printing Office, Washington DC 20402. **Tel** (202)275-3328, FAX (202)786-2377. **LC** UG 633.A1; A528. **DD** 358.405. available on microfilm and microfiche from University Microfilms International (UMI).
**Desc:** Official organ of the United States Air Force published for the enlightenment and building of morale of all Air Force personnel. Offers the reader a vivid portrayal of the Air Force story.
**Ind/Abst** Air Univ. Libr. Index Mil. Period. (199?-).

US/0897-0823
**AIRPOWER JOURNAL.** **Added/Corp** Air University (U.S.). Press. United States. Dept. of the Air Force. **VFOAT** Air Power Journal. (Summer 1987)-. Government Publication. English (Spanish and Portuguese). qt. $13.00 US; $16.25 other. Superintendent of Documents, US Government Printing Office, Washington DC 20402. **Tel** (202)275-3328, FAX (202)786-2377. **ED** Keith W. Geiger. **LC** UG633; .A69. **DD** 358.4/03/0973. Index available. cum. index. **Bk Rev. Circ:** 20,000 (ctrl). ***Continues** Air University Review (United States Ed.), 0002-2594.*
**Desc:** A professional journal of the United States Air Force. Focuses on the operational level of war including all factors which contribute to the development, employment and sustaining of combat power with a primary emphasis on air power. Published to stimulate professional thought concerning aerospace doctrines, strategy, tactics and related techniques.
**Ind/Abst** Air Univ. Libr. Index Mil. Period.; Am. Bibliogr. Slavic East Europ. Stud. (1987-); Curr. Mil. Pol. Lit.

IO
**AKABRI.** **VAT** Akademi Angkatan Bersenjata Republik Indonesia. No. 1-. Indonesian. Dinas Penerangan Akabri, Jl Gondangdia Lama No 1 B, Jakarta Indonesia. **LC** U660.I5; A63. **UDC** 355.1(594).

BA
**AL-BAYRAQ.** No. 1- May 1974-. Periodical. Arabic. 3000. Qiyadat Quwat Dofa Al-Bahrayn, PO Box 245, Al-Bahrayn Bahrain. **LC** UA853.B34.

UK
**AL-DIFA AL-ARABI. ARAB DEFENCE JOURNAL.** **VFOAT** Arab Defence Journal. (19??)-. Periodical. Arabic (Arabic). Twelve times a year. £L150.00. Dar Assayad International, 3 Park Place, 12 Lawn Lane, London WS8 1UA England. **Tel** 011 44 71 5822220. **LC** U4; .D55.

LE
**AL-FIKR AL-ISTIRATIJI AL-ARABI.** **VFOAT** Majallat Al-Inma Al-Arabi; Arab Strategic Thought. V. 1, No. 1 (July 1981)-. Periodical. Arabic. £L40.00. Mahad Al-Inma Al-Arabi, Bayrut Al-Ramlah Al-Bayda, 77 Shari Alis Farid Al-Naggash, SB 14/5300, Beirut Lebanon. **Tel** 831026, telex 22234 L E EMARAB. **LC** UA853.A6; F54. **UDC** 355.4(=927).

BA
**AL-QUWAH.** **Added/Corp** Bahrein. Qiyadah al-Ammah li-Quwat Difa al-Bahrayn. (19??)-. Periodical. Arabic. mo. Al-Qiyadah Al-Ammah Li-Quwat Difa Al-Bahrayn Shubat Al-Alaqat Al-Ammah Wa-Al-Thaqafah, PO Box 245, Al-Manamah Bahrain. **LC** UA853.B34; Q8.

US/0741-076X
**ALA ... WORLDWIDE DIRECTORY & FACT BOOK.** [ALA worldw. dir. fact book]. **Main/Corp** American Logistics Association. **VFOAT** ALA ... Worldwide Directory and Fact Book; A.L.A. ... Worldwide Directory & Fact Book. Directory. English. American Logistics Association, 1133 15th Street Northwest, Suite 640, Washington DC 20005. **Tel** (202)466-2520. **ED** Alan Goldstein. **LC** UC263; .A72A. **DD** 355.4/11/06073. **Ad Acc. Circ:** 2,500.
**Desc:** A guidebook to doing business with military retail outlets, including commissaries, exchanges, clubs, and subsistence food service activities. Includes names, addresses, sales data, and charts.
**Ind/Abst** Stat. Ref. Index.

SZ
**ALLGEMEINE SCHWEIZERISCHE MILITARZEITSCHRIFT.** **Added/Corp** Schweizerische Offiziersgesellschaft. **VFOAT** ASMZ. Vol. 114, No. 1 (Jan. 1948)-. Periodical. German. Eleven times a year. 65.00F Switzerland; 85.00F others. Huber & Co Ag, Postfach, CH-8501 Frauenfeld Switzerland. **Tel** 011 41 54 271111. **LC** U3; .A43. **DD** 355/.005. **Bk Rev. Ad Acc. Circ:** 31,539 (ctrl). ***Continues** Allgemeine Schweizerische Militarzeitung; **Absorbed** Schweizerische Monatschrift feur Offiziere Aller Waffen.*
**Desc:** Official publication of the Swiss Officers Company.

US/8755-6952
**ALUMNI DIRECTORY / NEW YORK MILITARY ACADEMY.** **See** College and School Publications-Alumni.

US/0882-1038
**AMERICAN DEFENSE ANNUAL.** [Am. def. annu.]. **Added/Corp** Mershon Center for Education in National Security. **VFOAT** American Defense. (1985/1986)-. English. an (Apr.). $24.95 (softcover); $49.95 (hardcover). Macmillan Publishing Company, 100 Front Street, Box 500, Riverside NJ 08075-7500. **Tel** (800)257-5755, (609)461-6500, FAX (609)461-7070. **LC** UA23.A1; A47. **DD** 355/.033073.
**Ind/Abst** Am. Bibliogr. Slavic East Europ. Stud.; Int. Polit. Sci. Abstr.

US/0883-072X
**AMERICAN INTELLIGENCE JOURNAL.** [Am. intell. j.]. **Added/Corp** National Military Intelligence Association (U.S.). Vol. 1, No. 1 (Fall 1977)-. Periodical. English. qt. $31.25 (US); $$43.25 (Canada); $56.25 (other). National Military Intelligence Association Inc, Pentagon Station, PO Box 46583, Washington DC 20050. **Tel** (301) 840-6642. **LC** NOT IN LC. **DD** 355.
**Desc:** Information on intelligence service.

US/0886-1234
**AMERICAN LEGION, THE.** [Am. Legion]. **Added/Corp** American Legion. Vol. 111, No. 1 (July 1981)-. Periodical. English. Six times a year. $12.00 (one year), $24.00 (two year), $36.00 (three year), $15.75 (one year), $36.00 (two year), $54.00 (three year) Canada; $18.00 (one year), $36.00 (two year) other. American Legion, PO Box 1055, Indianapolis IN 46206. **Tel** (317)630-1200. **ED** Joe Studeville. **DD** 369. **Ad Acc. Circ:** 2,600,000 (ctrl). available on microfilm and microfiche from University Microfilms International (UMI). Documents available from UMI Article Clearinghouse. ***Continues** American Legion. American Legion Magazine, 0002-9734.*
**Desc:** General interest, focusing on national security, foreign relations, and topics of contemporary interest.
**Ind/Abst** Newsp. Period. Abstr. (1988-); Mag. Index (1981-).

US/0272-4480
**AMERICAN MILITARY INSTITUTE DIRECTORY OF MEMBERS.** [Am. Mil. Inst. dir. memb.]. **Main/Corp** American Military Institute. Directory. English. Editor of Military Affairs, Eisenhower Hall, Kansas State University, Manhattan KS 66506. **LC** U1; .A4513. **DD** 355/.007/1173. **UDC** 355(060.21)(73).

US/0886-344X
**AMPHIBIOUS WARFARE REVIEW.** [Amphib. warf. rev.]. **Added/Corp** Marine Corps League (U.S.). Capital Marine Detachment. **VFOAT** AWR. Vol. 1, No. 1 (July 1983)-. Periodical. English. Twice a year. $8.00. Amphibious Warfare Review, 25 South Quaker Lane/Suite 20, Alexandria VA 22314. **Tel** (703)823-5208, FAX (703)823-1340. **ED** Cyril L. Kammeier and Carlton P. White. **DD** 359. **Ad Acc, Adv Mgr:** Carl White. **Circ:** 35,000.

IE
**AN COSANTOIR .** **Added/Corp** Ireland. Army. Ireland. Army. Southern Command. Vol. 1, No. 1 (Dec. 27, 1940)-. Periodical. English. mo. 13p Ireland and UK; 26p other. An Cosantoir, Infirmary Road Parkgate, Dublin 8 Ireland. **Tel** 011 353 1 379911 ext. 2145. **ED** Patrick B. Brennan. **LC** U1; .C8. **DD** 355/.009417. Index available (bound in Dec. issue). cum. index. **Bk Rev. Ad Acc. Circ:** 5,000 (ctrl).
**Desc:** Aims to provide a topical readable magazine on both internal and international military developments.

FR/0298-895X
**ANNUAIRE EUROPEEN DE DEFENSE.** **Added/Corp** Universite de Paris X: Nanterre. Institut de Politique Internationale et Europeenne. French. Universite de Paris, Institut de Politique Internationale et Europeenne, 92001 Nanterre Cedex France.

US
**ANNUAL BULLETIN - UNITED STATES AIR FORCE ACADEMY.** **Main/Corp** United States Air Force Academy. **VFOAT** Bulletin - United States Air Force Academy. Bulletin. English. an. United States Air Force Academy, Colorado Springs CO 80840. **UDC** 358.4(73).

US/0092-7422
**ANNUAL DIRECTORY AND REPORT - AMERICAN DEFENSE PREPAREDNESS ASSOCIATION.** (ANNUAL DIRECTORY AND REPORT.). [Annu. dir. rep. - Am. Def. Prep. Assoc.]. **Main/Corp** American Defense Preparedness Association. (1974)-. Directory. English. an. American Defense Preparedness Association, Two Colonial Place/Suite 400, 2101 Wilson Boulevard, Arlington VA 22201. **Tel** (703)522-1820, FAX (703)522-1885. **LC** UF1; .A542. **DD** 623/.06/273. ***Continues** American Ordnance Association. Directory.*

US/0094-596X
**ANNUAL REPORT AND PROCEEDINGS OF THE ANNUAL ENCAMPMENT (LANSING).** (ANNUAL REPORT AND PROCEEDINGS OF THE ENCAMPMENT.). **Main/Corp** United Spanish War Veterans. Dept. of Michigan. **Added/Corp** United Spanish War Veterans. Dept. of Michigan. Auxiliary. Reports, Proceedings and General Orders of the Annual Encampment. (19??)-. Proceedings. English. an. 122 South Grand Avenue, Lansing MI 48913. **LC** E714.3; .U64. **DD** 369/.181/05. ***Continues** United Spanish War Veterans. Dept. of Michigan. Proceedings ... Annual Encampment.*

AT
**ANNUAL REPORT / AUSTRALIAN DEFENCE FORCE ACADEMY. Main/Corp** Australian Defence Force Academy. (19??)-. English. an. **LC** WMLC L 83/6277.

US
**ANNUAL REPORT / COMMONWEALTH OF VIRGINIA, DEPARTMENT OF MILITARY AFFAIRS. Main/Corp** Virginia. Dept. of Military Affairs. Began with 1970. English. an. 401 East Main Street, Richmond VA 23219. **LC** UA43.V8; V57A. **DD** 355.3/7/09755. **UDC** 355.3(047.3)(755).

CN/0317-4077
**ANNUAL REPORT - DEFENCE CONSTRUCTION (1951) LIMITED. Main/Corp** Defence Construction (1951) Limited. **VFOAT** Rapport Annuel. 1968/69-. English (French). an. Free. Defence Construction, Kenson Building, 225 Metcalfe Street, Ottawa K1A 0K3. **LC** UG460. **DD** 338.7/62/30470971. ***Supersedes*** *Annual Report to the Minister of National Defence, 0317-4077.*

AT
**ANNUAL REPORT / DEPARTMENT OF DEFENCE, DEFENCE SCIENCE AND TECHNOLOGY ORGANISATION, WEAPONS SYSTEMS RESERCH LABORATORY. Main/Corp** Weapons Systems Research Laboratory (Australia). (1979)-. English. an. Weapons Systems Research Laboratory, Defence Research Centre, Salisbury, Box 2151 GPO, Adelaide South Australia 5001. **LC** U395.A8; W4a. **DD** 623.4/072094.

US
**ANNUAL REPORT / DEPARTMENT OF VETERANS AFFAIRS, ALABAMA. Main/Corp** Alabama. Dept. of Veterans Affairs. English. an. Department of Veterans Affairs / Alabama, PO Box 1509, Montgomery AL 35192. **LC** UB358.A2; A44A. **DD** 353.97610081/2. **UDC** 355.292(047.3)(761).

US
**ANNUAL REPORT - DIVISION OF VETERAN'S AFFAIRS (FLORIDA). Main/Corp** Florida. Division of Veterans Affairs. 1975/76-. English. an. Division of Veterans Affairs / Florida, PO Box 1437, St Petersburg FL 33731. **LC** UB358.F6; F63B. **DD** 353.9/759/00848. **UDC** 355.292(047.3)(759). ***Continues*** *Florida. Division of Veterans Affairs. Report of the Department of Community Affairs, Division of Veterans Affairs to the Governor.*

US
**ANNUAL REPORT - MICHIGAN VETERANS TRUST FUND. BOARD OF TRUSTEES. Main/Corp** Michigan Veterans Trust Fund. Board of Trustees. 16th (1946/1962)-. English. an. Michigan Veterans Trust Fund, Board of Trustees, Ottawa St Building, Corner of Ottawa & Pine, PO Box 30026, Lansing MI 48909. **LC** UB358.M5; M53A. **DD** 355.1/151/09774. ***Continues*** *Michigan Veterans Trust Fund. Board of Trustees. Annual Report to the Governor for the Fiscal Year Ended June 30 ... .*

US/0882-2417
**ANNUAL REPORT - NAVY PERSONNEL RESEARCH AND DEVELOPMENT CENTER (U.S.).** (ANNUAL REPORT / NAVY PERSONNEL RESEARCH & DEVELOPMENT CENTER.). [Annu. rep. - Navy Pers. Res. Dev. Cent. (U.S.)]. **Main/Corp** Navy Personnel Research and Development Center (U.S.). (19??)-. English. NPRDC, Public Affairs Office, San Diego CA 92152-6800. **LC** VB258; .N368a. **DD** 359.6/1/072073.
**Ind/Abst** Psychol. Abstr. (1972-).

US
**ANNUAL REPORT / NEW YORK STATE ASSEMBLY, COMMITTEE ON VETERANS' AFFAIRS. Main/Corp** New York (State). Legislature Assembly. Standing Committee on Veterans' Affairs. **VFOAT** Annual Report of the Assembly Standing Committee on Veterans' Affairs. (1983)-. English. an. Assembly - New York Veterans Affairs, State of New York, Standing Committee on Veterans Affairs, Albany NY 12248. **LC** UB358.N7; N48a. **DD** 328.747/07658. ***Continues*** *New York (State). Legislature. Assembly. Standing Committee on Governmental Operations. Subcommittee on Veterans' Affairs. Annual Report of the New York State Assembly Subcommittee on Veterans' Affairs.*
**Desc:** Veteran information.

US/0730-8914
**ANNUAL REPORT OF ACTIVITIES.** (ANNUAL REPORT OF ACTIVITIES FOR CALENDAR YEAR ... / VETERANS ADMINISTRATION MEDICAL RESEARCH SERVICE MERIT REVIEW BOARDS.). **Main/Corp** United States. Veterans Administration. Merit Review Boards. English. an. US Veterans Administration / Washington DC, 810 Vermont Avenue Southwest, Washington DC 20420. **Tel** (202)393-2124. **LC** R853.R46; U54A. **DD** 353.0084/1.

US/0362-6229
**ANNUAL REPORT OF SOUTH CAROLINA DEPARTMENT OF VETERANS AFFAIRS. Main/Corp** South Carolina. Dept. of Veterans Affairs. English. an. Department of Veterans Affairs / South Carolina, 1205 Pendleton Street, Columbia SC 29201. **LC** UB358.S6; S67A. **DD** 353.9/757/00848.

US/0091-0368
**ANNUAL REPORT OF THE DEPARTMENT OF MILITARY AFFAIRS TO THE GOVERNOR OF MONTANA.** (ANNUAL REPORT.). **Main/Corp** Montana. Dept. of Military Affairs. 1971/72-. English. an. Department of Military Affairs / Montana, 1100 North Main Street, Helena MT 59601. **LC** UA300; .M65A. **DD** 353.9/786/00895.

SA
**ANNUAL REPORT - SOUTH AFRICAN NATIONAL MUSEUM OF MILITARY HISTORY.** **See** Museums and Galleries.

US/0747-6795
**ANNUAL REPORT TO CONGRESS ON THE POST-VIETNAM ERA VETERANS' EDUCATIONAL ASSISTANCE PROGRAM.** [Ann. rep. Congr. Post-Vietnam Era Veterans' Educ. Assist. program]. 6th (Feb. 24, 1984)-. English. an. **LC** UB357; .A754. **DD** 355.1/152/0973. available on microfiche (Vols. for 1984- distributed to some depository libraries). ***Continues*** *Implementation of the Post-Vietnam Era Veterans' Educational Assistance Act of 1977 (House Committee Print).*

US
**ANNUAL REPORT TO THE CONGRESS OF THE UNITED STATES FROM THE DIRECTORY OF THE SELECTIVE SERVICE SYSTEM. Main/Corp** United States. Selective Service System. Directory. English. Selective Service System, National Headquarters, Washington DC 20435. **Tel** (202)724-0424. ***Continues*** *Semiannual Report of the Director of Selective Service.*

US
**ANNUAL REPORT TO THE GOVERNOR AND LEGISLATURE - STATE BOARD OF INDIGENTS' DEFENSE SERVICES (KANSAS). Main/Corp** Kansas. State Board of Indigents' Defense Services. 1st-. English. an. Indigents Defense, 900 Southwest Jackson Street/#506, Topeka KS 66612-1255. **LC** KFK578; .A843. **DD** 345.781/01; 347.81051. ctrl circ.

US/0192-4559
**ANNUAL REVIEW / CHIEF, NATIONAL GUARD BUREAU. Main/Corp** United States. National Guard Bureau. **VFOAT** Annual Review of the Chief, National Guard Bureau; Annual Review, CNGB. Began with 1975/76. English. an. National Guard Bureau / Falls Church, c/o NGB-PAH, 5600 Columbia Pike, Falls Church VA 22041. **Tel** (703)756-1980. **ED** Leonid Kondrativk and Renee Hylton-Greene. **LC** UA42; .A15. **DD** 355.3/7/0973. **Circ:** 3,000 (ctrl). available on microfiche (Vols. for (1985-) distributed to depository libraries). ***Continues*** *United States. National Guard Bureau. Annual Report, 0192-4761.*
**Desc:** Official report to the secretaries of the Army and Air Force concerning the National Guard Bureau, Army and Air National Guard.

US/0741-9090
**ANNUAL REVIEW OF MILITARY RESEARCH AND DEVELOPMENT.** [Annu. rev. mil. res. dev.]. 1982-. English. an. Praeger, Publishing Division of Greenwood Press, PO Box 5007, Westport CT 06881. **Tel** (203)226-3571. **LC** U393; .A72. **DD** 355/.07/0973.

US
**ANTI-SUBMARINE WARFARE FORECAST.** (19??)-. English. Twelve times a year. $1390.00. Forecast International / DMS Inc., 22 Commerce Road, Newtown CT 06470. **Tel** (203)426-0800, FAX (203)426-1964, telex 467615. available on CD-ROM ($1595.00).

GW
**AR. VFOAT** A.R. Periodical. German. mo. Militarverlag der DDR Veb, Storkower Str 158 Postfach 46551, DDR-1055 Berlin Germany. **LC** U3; .A73. ***Continues*** *Armee-Rundschau.*

GW
**AR; ARMEE RUNDSCHAU. MICROFORM. VFOAT** Armee Rundschau. German. Deutscher Judo Verband, Redaktion Ippon Segewaldweg 40, D 12557 Berlin Germany. **Tel** 011 49 711 210770, telex 051 678.

GW/0723-5100
**ARAB MEDICO.** **See** Medical Science and Technology.

AT
**ARFFAS VIEWPOINT.** (19??)-. English. Four times a year. 10.00Aus$. Armed Forces Federation of Australia, PO Box 4986, Kingston ACT 2604 Australia. **Tel** 011 61 6 2397322, FAX 011 61 6 2397323. **ED** Jean Bruce. **Ad Acc. Circ:** 5,000 (ctrl).

SZ/0252-9793
**ARMADA INTERNATIONAL.** [Armada int.]. Vol. 1, (Feb. 1977)-. Periodical. English (French and German). Six times a year (Feb., Apr., June, Aug., Oct., Dec.). 106.00F US & Europe: 108.00F others. Armada International, PO Box 139, Ch 8035 Zurich Switzerland. **Tel** 011 41 1 3631126, 011 41 1 3631171, FAX 011 41 1 3619502, telex 815132. **ED** Eric H. Biass, (phone: 011 41 22 7969613). **LC** HD9743.A1; A75. **DD** 338.4/76234/05. **Ad Acc. Circ:** 30,000 (ctrl). available on an online database (file 648/Full-Text) from DIALOG.
**Desc:** A defense publication reporting on ground, naval and airborne equipment and systems.
**Ind/Abst** Air Univ. Libr. Index Mil. Period.; BMT Abstr.; Curr. Mil. Pol. Lit.; Eng. Mater. Abstr.; F&S Index Plus Text, Int. [Select. Cov.]; PROMT.

US/0195-8232
**ARMAMENT & DEFENSE SURVEY. VAT** Armament and Defense Survey. Periodical. English. wk. $275.00. Government Business Worldwide Reports, PO Box 5997, Washington DC 20016. **Tel** (202)244-7050, FAX (202)244-5410. ***Supersedes in part*** *Defense Survey & Directory, 0099-166X.*

SA
**ARMED FORCES.** (Jan. 1976)-. Periodical. English. Eleven times a year (monthly with Dec./Jan. issue combined). R40.00. Military Publications Party, PO Box 23022, Joubert Park, 2044 Johannesburg, South Africa. **Tel** (011 27 011)725-2701, FAX (011 27 011)725-2703. **ED** S J McIntosh. **LC** U1; .A55. **DD** 355/.00968. **Bk Rev. Ad Acc. Circ:** 9,000.
**Desc:** Covers defense matters and strategy.
**Ind/Abst** Air Univ. Libr. Index Mil. Period. (-19??).

US/0095-327X
**ARMED FORCES AND SOCIETY.** [Armed forces soc.]. **VFOAT** Armed Forces & Society. Vol. 1 (Fall 1974)-. Periodical. English. Four times a year. Fl186.00 (individual), Fl316.00 (institution). Transaction Publishers / Rutgers State University, New Brunswick NJ 08903. **Tel** (908)932-2280 Ext. 105, FAX (908)932-3138. **ED** J Stanley. **LC** U21.5; .A74. **DD** 301.5/93/05. **[CCC].** Index available. cum. index. **Bk Rev. Ad Acc. Pr Rev. Circ:** 2,200. available on microfilm and microfiche from University Microfilms International (UMI); available on labels. Documents available from The Genuine Article, UMI Article Clearinghouse.
**Desc:** Interdisciplinary publication devoted to the military establishment and civil-military relations in all parts of the world. The journal provides an international forum for a wide range of topics, including war, revolution, recruitment and conscription policies, arms control, peacekeeping, military history, economics of defense and strategic issues. The official journal of the Inter-University Seminar on Armed Forces and Society.
**Ind/Abst** ABC POL SCI; Acad. Abstr. Full Text Elite (Jan. 1992-); Acad. Abstr. (Jan. 1992-); Acad. Search (Jan. 1992-); Air Univ. Libr. Index Mil. Period.; Am. Hist. Life (1975-); Am. Bibliogr. Slavic East Europ. Stud.; Book Rev. Index; Curr. Contents Soc. Behav. Sci.; Curr. Mil. Pol. Lit.; Expand. Acad. Index (1989-); INFO-SOUTH Abstr.; Int. Bibliogr. Sociol.; Int. Dev. Abstr.; Linguist. Lang. Behav. Abstr.; Mag. Search; Middle East Abstr. Index; Newsp. Period. Abstr. (1990-); PAIS Int. Print (1991-); Res. Alert [Full Cov.]; Soc. Plann. Policy Dev. Abstr.; Soc. Sci. Source (Jan. 1992-); Soc. Sci. Cit. Index [Full Cov.]; Soc. Sci. Index; Soc. Sci. Index Fulltext (Fall 1988-) [Full Txt.]; Sociol. Abstr.; U.S. Polit. Sci. Doc.

US/0004-2188
**ARMED FORCES COMPTROLLER, THE.** [Armed Forces comptrol.]. **Added/Corp** American Society of Military Comptrollers. Vol. 1 (July 1956)-. Periodical. English. Four times a year (Jan., Apr., Aug., Nov.). $10.00. American Society of Military Comptrollers, 225 Reinekers Lane, Suite 250, Alexandria VA 22314. **Tel** (703)549-0360. **ED** James F. McCall. **LC** UC20; .A75. **DD** 355. Index available. cum. index. **Ad Acc, Adv Mgr:** C. Meek, **Tel** (703)998-4000. **Circ:** 20,000. available on microfilm and microfiche from University Microfilms International (UMI).
**Ind/Abst** Acad. Search (July 1993-); Account. Tax Datab. (1974-) [Full Txt.]; Air Univ. Libr. Index Mil. Period.; Bus. Index (1985-); Fed. Tax Artic.; Gen. BusinessFile (1985-); Gen. Period. Index (Jan. 1985-Dec. 1985); INFO-SOUTH Abstr.; Mag. Search.

US/0196-3597
**ARMED FORCES JOURNAL INTERNATIONAL.** [Armed Forces j. int.]. Vol. 110, No. 6 (Feb. 1973)-. Periodical. English. mo. $35.00 US and Canada; $95.00 other. Armed Forces Journal Internationa, 2000 L Street Northwest, Suite 520, Washington DC 20036. **Tel** (202)296-0450. **(Subscription address:** Armed Forces Journal International, PO Box 109, Winchester, MA 01890; (telephone: (617)729-4200)) **ED** Benjamin F. Schemmer. **LC** U1; .A66. **DD** 355/.00973. **CODEN** AFJIE8. Index available (free). **Circ:** 30,773. available on microfilm and microfiche from University Microfilms International (UMI). ***Continues*** *Armed Forces Journal, 0004-220X.*
**Desc:** A magazine for the worldwide professional

defense community -- military, industrial and political leaders and other influencials who are crafting tomorrow's global security relationships.
**Ind/Abst** Air Univ. Libr. Index Mil. Period.; Curr. Mil. Pol. Lit.; Middle East Abstr. Index.

II
**ARMED FORCES PERSONNEL AND CIVILIANS IN DEFENCE ESTABLISHMENT BOOK ON SERVICE CONDITIONS.** **Main/Corp** India. Ministry of Defence. English. an. Government of India / Ministry of Defence, New Delhi India. **LC** UB325.I4; I52A. **DD** 355.6/1/0954.

FR/0004-2242
**ARMEE ET DEFENSE.** Periodical. French. bm. Armee et Defense, 12 Rue Marie Laurencin, F 75012 Paris France. **Tel** 011 33 1 43474016. ***Continues*** *Officier de Reserve.*

FR
**ARMEE RUNDSCHAU.** German. Militaerverlag der DDR, VEB, Storkower Strasse 158, O-1055 Berlin Germany.

FR
**ARMEES D'AUJOURD'HUI.** **Added/Corp** France. Service d'Information et de Relations Publiques des Armees. No. 1 (July 1975)-. Periodical. French. ir. 270.00F (France); 210.00F (other). Addim, 6 rue Saint Charles, 75015 Paris France. **Tel** 011 33 1 45770376. **LC** U2; .A75. **DD** 355/.005. **Bk Rev. Ad Acc. Circ:** 150,000 (ctrl).
**Desc:** General reviews of defense, military, air force, navy and army in France.

FR
**ARMEES ET DEFENSE.** French. mo. 280.00F. EDAF Madame Chevalier, 125 rue du FBG Poissonniere, F 75009 Paris France. **Tel** 011 33 1 49959347. **(Subscription address:** SEPG sprl, Av. Maric-Jose 172, B - 1200 Brussels**)**
**Desc:** All about technology and military and defense. Aeronautics, Naval and ground.

FR
**ARMEMENT.** French. Five times a year. 300.00F. Addim, 6 rue Saint Charles, 75015 Paris France. **Tel** 011 33 1 45770376. **Bk Rev. Ad Acc. Circ:** 10,000.
**Desc:** Publication of french delegation for Armement (defense systems).

FR
**ARMEMENT : REVUE DE LA DELEGATION GENERALE POUR L'ARMEMENT, L'.** **Added/Corp** France. Delegation Generale pour l'Armement. (198?)-. Periodical. French. qt. 310.00F France; 350.00F other. Addim, 6 rue Saint Charles, 75015 Paris France. **Tel** 011 33 1 45770376. **LC** UA700; .A73. **DD** 355/.033044. **CODEN** ARMTE4.
**Ind/Abst** PAIS Int. Print.

RU
**ARMIIA.** ***Ceased.*** **Added/Corp** Soviet Union. Ministerstvo Oborony. (1991)-(July 1994). Periodical. Russian. Twenty-four times a year. **(Subscription address:** East View Publications Inc., 3020 Harbor Lane North, Suite 110, Minneapolis MN 55447.**)** **LC** U717.R9; A27. **CODEN** ARMYEJ. ***Continues*** *Kommunist Vooruzhennykh Sil, 0134-9228.*
**Desc:** Focuses on soldiers.

US/0004-2420
**ARMOR.** [Armor]. **Added/Corp** United States Armor Association. US Army Armor School. US Army Armor Center. Vol. 59, No. 4 (July/Aug. 1950)-. Periodical. English. Six times a year. $16.00 (members), $20.00 (non-members) US; $33.00 (non-members) others. US Armor Association, Post Office Box 607, Ft Knox KY 40121. **Tel** (504)942-8624. **ED** Patrick J. Cooney. **LC** UE1; .C33. Index available. **Bk Rev. Circ:** 16,000. available on microfilm and microfiche from University Microfilms International (UMI). ***Continues*** *Armored Cavalry Journal, 0097-3688.*
**Ind/Abst** Air Univ. Libr. Index Mil. Period.; Curr. Mil. Pol. Lit.

US/0093-6014
**ARMS AND ARMOR ANNUAL.** V. 1- 1973-. English. an. $9.95. R J Hussey Publishing, 1 West Main Street, PO Box 157, Webster NY 14580. **LC** U799; .A75. **DD** 355.8/2.

US
**ARMS CONTROL AND DISARMAMENT AGREEMENTS.** (1959)-. English. ir. US Arms Control and Disarmament Agency, Washington DC 20402.

US/0899-6547
**ARMS CONTROL, DISARMAMENT AND INTERNATIONAL SECURITY.** [Arms control disarm. int. secur.]. **Added/Corp** California State University, Los Angeles. Center for the Study of Armament and Disarmament. Arms Control Association (Washington, D.C.). **VFOAT** Arms Control, Disarmament & International Security. (1987)-. English. be. Regina Books, PO Box 280, Claremont CA 91711. **Tel** (714)624-8466. **ED** Richard Dean Burns. **LC** Z6464.D6; A76; JX1974. **DD** 016.3271/74. Index available. **Ad Acc. Circ:** 1,000.

●US/1065-6383
**ARMS CONTROL DISCUSSION PAPERS.** **Added/Corp** University of Maryland, College Park. Center for International Security Studies at Maryland. (1992)-. Periodical. English. mo. Free. CISSM, University of Maryland, College Park MD 20742.

UK/0144-0381
**ARMS CONTROL (LONDON, ENGLAND).** ***Title Change.*** (ARMS CONTROL.). [Arms control]. Vol. 1, No. 1 (May 1980)-(19??). Periodical. English. Three times a year (Apr., Aug., Dec.). Frank Cass & Company Ltd, Newbury House, 890-900 Eastern Avenue, Newbury Park, Ilford, Essex IG2 7HH United Kingdom. **Tel** 011 44 81 599 8866, FAX 011 44 81 599 0984, telex 897719. **ED** Ian Bellany and Coit D. Blacker. **LC** JX1974; .A76883. **DD** 327.1/74/05. **Bk Rev. Ad Acc, Adv Mgr:** Anne Kidson. ctrl circ. available on microfilm and microfiche from University Microfilms International (UMI). ***Continued by*** *Contemporary Security Policy.*
**Desc:** Of interest to those whose study and research enables them to make a contribution to arms control and disarmament studies.
**Ind/Abst** ABC POL SCI (1988-?); Am. Hist. Life (1983-?); Br. Humanit. Index; Curr. Mil. Pol. Lit.; Int. Polit. Sci. Abstr.; Linguist. Lang. Behav. Abstr.; PAIS Int. Print (1991-?); Soc. Plann. Policy Dev. Abstr.; Sociol. Abstr.

US/0197-2863
**ARMS GAZETTE.** [Arms gaz.]. Periodical. English. mo. $15.00. Bienfeld Publishing Company, 12767 Saticoy Street, North Hollywood CA 91605.

UK/0004-2463
**ARMY, AIR FORCE AND NAVAL AIR STATISTICAL RECORD.** (19??)-. Statistical Publication. English. Ten times a year. $760.00. Aviation Studies, Sussex House Parkside, London SW19 5NB England. **Tel** 011 44 81 946 5082. available on diskette.

US/0004-248X
**ARMY AVIATION.** **See** Aeronautics, Astronautics.

US
**ARMY BATTLEFIELD ENVIRONMENT / US ARMY CORPS OF ENGINEERS.** **Added/Corp** United States. Army. Corps of Engineers. U.S. Army Engineer Topographic Laboratories. U.S. Army Topographic Engineering Center. Vol. 9, No. 3 (Summer 1991)-. Periodical. English. qt. US Army Engineer Topographic Laboratories, Editor, Army Battlefield Environment, Fort Belvoir VA 22060-5546. **LC** UC263; .A76. **DD** 355.8/0973. ***Continues*** *Army Environmental Sciences.*

●US
**ARMY CHAPLAINCY : PROFESSIONAL BULLETIN OF THE UNIT MINISTRY TEAM, THE.** **Added/Corp** United States. Army. Chaplain Corps. (Winter 1993)-. Periodical. English. qt. US Army Chaplain Board, Meyer Hall Building 1207, Fort Monmouth NJ 07703. ***Continues*** *Military Chaplains' Review, 0360-9693.*

US/0270-9848
**ARMY CLUB SYSTEM ANNUAL REPORT, FISCAL YEAR ... .** **Main/Corp** United States. Adjutant-General's Office. Club and Community Activities Management Directorate. 1980-. English. an. Club and Community Activities Management Directorate, Office of the Adjutant General, Headquarters Department of the Army, Washington DC 20402. **LC** U56; .U54A. **DD** 355.3/41. ***Continues*** *Army Club System Annual Report, 0270-9848.*

US/0362-5745
**ARMY COMMUNICATOR, THE.** [Army commun.]. **Added/Corp** U.S. Army Signal School. US Army Signal Center and Fort Gordon. (Winter 1976)-. Government Publication. English. Four times a year. $8.00 US; $10.00. Superintendent of Documents, US Government Printing Office, Washington DC 20402. **Tel** (202)275-3328, FAX (202)786-2377. **ED** Richard Davis Jr. **LC** UA943; .A75. **DD** 358/.24/0973. Index available. cum. index. **Bk Rev. Circ:** 12,000 (ctrl). available on microfilm and microfiche from University Microfilms International (UMI).
**Desc:** Published to promote the professional development of Army communicators through the dissemination of doctrinal and technical information and the presentation of new ideas and concepts relating to communications and electronics.
**Ind/Abst** Curr. Mil. Pol. Lit.

US
**ARMY HISTORY.** No. 13 (Fall 1989)-. Periodical. English. qt. US Army Center of Military History, Southeast Federal Center, 3rd & M Street SE, Building #159, Washington DC 20374-5088. **ED** Arnold G Fisch Jr. **LC** UA25; .A79. **DD** 355/.00973. **Bk Rev. Circ:** 6,000 (ctrl). ***Continues*** *Army Historian, 0748-2299.*
**Desc:** Professional bulletin of short articles, and professional notes for army history professionals and leader development of army officers.

US/0004-2528
**ARMY LOGISTICIAN.** [Army logist.]. **Added/Corp** United States. Army Logistics Management Center. U.S. Army Logistics Management College. United States. Army Materiel Command. **VFOAT** ALOG. Vol. 1, No. 1 (Sept./Oct. 1969)-. Government Publication. English. bm. $9.50 domestic; $11.90 other. Superintendent of Documents, US Government Printing Office, Washington DC 20402. **Tel** (202)275-3328, FAX (202)786-2377. **ED** Terry R. Speights. **LC** U168; .A74. **DD** 355. Index available. **Bk Rev. Circ:** 438,348 (ctrl). available on microfilm and microfiche from University Microfilms International (UMI).
**Desc:** Provides timely and authoritative information on United States Army logistics plans, policies, doctrine, procedures, operations, and developments to the Active Army, Army National Guard, and United States Army Reserve.
**Ind/Abst** Air Univ. Libr. Index Mil. Period.; Curr. Mil. Pol. Lit.

UK
**ARMY MEDICAL SERVICES MAGAZINE.** **See** Medical Science and Technology.

US/0742-728X
**ARMY MORALE, WELFARE, AND RECREATION.** **Main/Corp** United States. Adjutant-General's Office. Nonappropriated Fund Financial Management Directorate. Fiscal Year 1982-. English. an. Nonappropriated Fund Financial Management Directorate, Office of the Adjutant General Headquarters, Department of the Army, Alexandria VA 22331. **LC** UH810; .U54A. **DD** 355.3/46. ***Continues*** *United States. Adjutant-General's Office. Club and Community Activities Management Directorate. Army Morale Support Fund Annual Report.*

US/0195-5632
**ARMY MOTORS.** [Army mot.]. **Added/Corp** Military Vehicle Collectors Club. Military Vehicle Preservation Association. (19??)-. Periodical. English. Four times a year (Jan., Apr., July, Oct.). $35.00 Comes with Military Vehicle Preservation Association Club membership. Military Vehicle Preservation Association, PO Box 520378, Independence MO 64052. **Tel** (816)737-5111, FAX (816)737-5423. **ED** Reginald Hodgson. **DD** 355. Index available. cum. index. **Bk Rev** (Qty: 4-8). **Ad Acc, Adv Mgr:** Kay, **Tel** (816)737-5111. **Circ:** 6,000.
**Desc:** Technical and historical articles as well as information of general Military Vehicle Preservation Association membership interest.

US/0148-6799
**ARMY OFFICER'S GUIDE, THE.** 39th Ed. (1977)-. Monographic series. English. ir (every two years). Price varies per volume. Stackpole Magazines, 500 Vaughn Street, Harrisburg PA 17110. **Tel** (717)234-5041, (800)732-3669, FAX (717)234-1359. **LC** U133.A6; O3. **DD** 355/.00973. ***Continues*** *Officer's Guide.*

UK/0004-2552
**ARMY QUARTERLY AND DEFENCE JOURNAL, THE.** [Army q. def. j.]. Vol. 75, No. 2 (Jan. 1958)-. Periodical. English. qt. £48.00 (one year), £125.00 (three year) UK; $108.00 airmail, $88.00 (one year), $210.00 (two year) surface mail other. Army Quarterly & Defence Journal, 1 West Street, Tavistock PL19 8DS England. **Tel** 011 44 822 613577. **ED** T D Bridge. **LC** U1; .A85. **DD** 355/.005. **Bk Rev. Ad Acc. Circ:** 20,000 (ctrl). available on microfilm. ***Continues*** *Army Quarterly.*
**Desc:** International military journal covering defense policy and strategy, weapons and equipment development, accounts of past battles and campaigns, international defense reports, defense diary, recent appointments, contracts and book reviews.
**Ind/Abst** Air Univ. Libr. Index Mil. Period. (19??-); Am. Hist. Life (1963-); PAIS Int. Print.

US/0892-8657
**ARMY RD & A BULLETIN.** (ARMY R,D & A BULLETIN.). [Army RD A bull.]. **Added/Corp** United States. Army Materiel Command (1984-) United States. Army Acquisition Executive Support Agency. United States. Army Acquisition Corps Proponency Office. **VFOAT** Army R D & A Bulletin; Army R D and A Bulletin; Army Research, Development, & Acquisition Bulletin; Army Research, Development, and Acquisition Bulletin; Army RD & A; Army RD&A Bulletin. **VAT** Army research, development, and acquisition bulletin. (May/June 1987)-. Government Publication. English. bm. $9.50 domestic; $11.90 other. Superintendent of Documents, US Government Printing Office, Washington DC 20402. **Tel** (202)275-3328, FAX (202)786-2377. **LC** U393; .A8. **DD** 355/.07/0973. available on microfilm and microfiche from University Microfilms International (UMI). ***Continues*** *Army RD & A Magazine, 0895-111X.*
**Desc:** Reports on Army research, development, and acquisition.

US/0094-9736
**ARMY RECREATION AND TRAVEL GUIDE.** English. US Department of Defense Department of the Army, The Pentagon, SAPA-CR, Room 3E718, Washington DC 20310. **Tel** (703)695-0363, FAX (703)693-5737. **LC** UH810; .A73. **DD** 355.3/46/02573.

US/0004-2579
**ARMY RESERVE MAGAZINE.** [Army reserve mag.]. **Added/Corp** United States. Office of the Chief, Army Reserve. Nov. (1954)-. Government Publication. English. qt. $5.00 domestic; $6.25 other. Superintendent of Documents, US Government Printing Office, Washington DC 20402. **Tel** (202)275-3328, FAX (202)786-2377. **ED** B. R. Devlim. **DD** 355. **Bk Rev. Circ:** 600,000. available on microfilm and microfiche from University Microfilms International (UMI). ***Continues*** *Army Reservist.*
**Ind/Abst** Index U.S. Gov. Period.

US/0004-2595
**ARMY TIMES.** [Army times]. (1940)-. Periodical. English. wk (52 issues). $48.00 (one year), $88.00 (two year). Army Times Publishing Company, 6883 Commercial Drive, Springfield VA 22159. **Tel** (800)368-5718, (703)750-8099. **ED** Tom Donnelly. **DD** 355. **[CCC]. Bk Rev. Ad Acc. Pr Rev. Circ:** 124,000. available on microfilm and microfiche from University Microfilms International (UMI).
**Desc:** An independent weekly journal serving career Army personnel.

US/0731-3144
**ARMY TRAINER.** [Army train.]. **Added/Corp** United States. Army Training and Doctrine Command. U.S. Army Training Support Center. Vol. 1, No. 1 (Fall 1981)-. Government Publication. English. qt. $9.00 domestic; $11.25 other. Superintendent of Documents, US Government Printing Office, Washington DC 20402. **Tel** (202)275-3328, FAX (202)786-2377. **LC** U408.3; .A73. **DD** 355.5/0973.
**Desc:** Provides information on training plans, policies, and developments, and promotes an exchange of firsthand knowledge and experiences among Active and Reserve components, as well as Department of the Army civilians who are responsible for training.

US/0004-2455
**ARMY (WASHINGTON. 1956).** (ARMY.). [Army]. **Added/Corp** Association of the United States Army. Vol. 6, No. 7 (Feb. 1956)-. Periodical. English. Twelve times a year. $25.00 (one year), $68.00 (three year) surface mail; $55.00 (first class airmail) Canada and Mexico; $105.00 (first class airmail) other. Association of the United States Army, 2425 Wilson Boulevard, Arlington VA 22201. **Tel** (703)841-4300. **ED** L. James Binder. **LC** U1; .A893. available on microfilm and microfiche from University Microfilms International (UMI). ***Continues*** *Army Combat Forces Journal, 0271-7336.* ***Continued in part by*** *Field Artillery Journal (Fort Sill, Okla.), 0191-975X.*
**Desc:** Professional journal for the advancement of the military arts and sciences representing the interest of the entire Army. Publishes articles on strategy, tactics, logistics, operations, management and administration, weapons, leadership and history.
**Ind/Abst** Air Univ. Libr. Index Mil. Period. (19??-); Am. Bibliogr. Slavic East Europ. Stud.

DK/0902-0608
**ARSBERETNING. Main/Corp** Denmark. Sikkerheds- Og Nedrustningspolitiske Udvalg. 1985-. Danish. an. **LC** JX1974; .D433A. ***Continues in part*** *Sikkerhed Og Nedrustning, 0108-7266.*

SW
**ARTILLERI TIDSKRIFT.** (1872)-. Swedish. qt. Artilleri-Tidskrift, S 115 88 Stockholm Sweden.

US/0884-4747
**ARTILLERYMAN, THE.** [Artilleryman]. Vol. 6, No. 3 (Summer 1985)-. Periodical. English. qt (Mar., June, Sept., Dec.). $18.00. The Artilleryman, RR 1 Box 36, Tunbridge VT 05077. **Tel** (802)889-3500, FAX (802)889-5627. **ED** C. Peter Jorgensen. **DD** 358. **Bk Rev. Ad Acc. Circ:** 2,200. ***Continues*** *Muzzleloading Artilleryman, 0195-038X.*
**Desc:** A magazine for collectors an shooters of canon and mortar, including, history, safety, places to visit, shoot reports.

US/1057-9419
**ASA NEWSLETTER - APPLIED SCIENCE AND ANALYSIS, INC, THE.** (THE ASA NEWSLETTER / APPLIED SCIENCE AND ANALYSIS, ASA, INC.). [ASA newsl. - Appl. Sci. Anal. Inc.]. **Added/Corp** Applied Science and Analysis, Inc. **VAT** Applied Science and Analysis, Inc. Newsletter. (198?)-. Periodical. English. Six times a year (Feb., Apr., June, Aug., Oct., Dec.). $180.00 (one year); $325.00 (two years). Applied Science and Analysis Incorporated, PO Box 17532, Portland ME 04101. **Tel** (207)829-6376, FAX (207)829-3040. **ED** Colonel Richard M. Price. **DD** 358. Index available. cum. index. **Bk Rev.** (Qty: 24). **Ad Acc. Pr Rev. Circ:** 1,000 (ctrl).
**Desc:** For the professional in government and industry with an interest in nuclear, biological and chemical defense, disarmament and verification.

AT
**ASIA-PACIFIC DEFENCE REPORTER. VFOAT** Asia Pacific Defence Reporter; Asia-Pacific Defence Reporter. Annual Reference Ed. Vol. 16, No. 12 (June 1990)-. Periodical. English. Six times a year. 60.00Aus$ Australia; 75.00Aus$ Pacific Region; 82.00Aus$ other. Peter Isaacson Publications, 46-50 Porter Street, Prahran Victoria, 3181 Australia. **Tel** 011 61 3 2457777, FAX 011 61 3 2457605. **LC** UA870; .P33. **DD** 355/.033094. Index available.
**Ind/Abst** Air Univ. Libr. Index Mil. Period. (19??-).

AT/1037-1435
**ASIA-PACIFIC DEFENCE REPORTER ANNUAL REFERENCE EDITION.** [Asia-Pac. def. rep. Annu. ref. ed.]. (1991)-. English. an. 34.95Aus$ Australia; 36.95Aus$ Pacific Region; 39.95Aus$ other. Peter Isaacson Publications, 46-50 Porter Street, Prahran Victoria, 3181 Australia. **Tel** 011 61 3 2457777, FAX 011 61 3 2457605. **DD** 355.03359. ***Continues*** *Pacific Defence Reporter (Annual Reference Edition), 0813-5452.*

MY/0126-6403
**ASIAN DEFENCE JOURNAL.** [Asian def. j.]. **VFOAT** Asian Defence. (1973)-. Periodical. English. Twelve times a year. 150.00Mal$ one year; 250.00Mal$ two year; 380.00Mal$ three year, for Malaysia surface mail; $200.00 Americans; $180.00 Europe, Africa & Middle East; $150.00 Australia, New Zealand, India, Pakistan, Japan, South Korea, China & Taiwan; $120.00 Indonesia Philippines, Thailand and Hong Kong. Syed Hussain Publishers Sdn Bhd, PO Box 10836, 50726 Kuala Lumpur Malaysia. **Tel** 11 60 3 4235852, 011 60 3 4238585, FAX 011 60 3 4427840, telex 31147. **ED** Syed Hussain B. Syed Abdul Karim and Mohammad Shuhud Saaid. **LC** UA830; .A8. **DD** 355.03/3059. **Bk Rev. Ad Acc. Circ:** 11,500 (ctrl). available on microfilm and microfiche from University Microfilms International (UMI).
**Desc:** The only journal in southeast Asian and Pacific region to focus on latest defense systems and weapon technology. Geo-political in the defense industry.
**Ind/Abst** Air Univ. Libr. Index Mil. Period.; Curr. Mil. Pol. Lit.

CD
**ASKAR.** Year 1- (No. 1- ); 1971-. French (French). Service d'Information des Forces Armees Tchadiennes etc, BP 171, Ndjamena Chad. **LC** UA859.3; .A74. **DD** 355/.00967/43.

●US/1059-5708
**ASSAULT RIFLES.** (1992)-. Periodical. English. $3.95. Petersen Publishing Company, 6420 Wilshire Bouldevard, Los Angeles CA 90048. **Tel** (213)782-2485.

US/0190-4280
**AT EASE.** **See** Religion and Theology.

US/1053-2404
**ATLANTIC TRADE REPORT & GLOBAL DEFENSE INDUSTRY.** [Atl. trade rep. glob. def. ind.]. **VFOAT** Atlantic Trade Report and Global Defense Industry. Vol. 2, No. 17 (Aug. 1990)-. Periodical. English. bw. $495.00. Bergerac International, Route 1 Box 309, Gainesville VA 22065. **DD** 382. available on an online database (file 636/Full-Text) from DIALOG. ***Formed by the union of*** *Atlantic Trade Report, 1047-0824* ***and*** *Global Military Industrialization, 1049-4448.*
**Ind/Abst** PTS Newsl. Database [Full Txt.].

US
**ATLAS/DATA ABSTRACT FOR THE UNITED STATES AND SELECTED AREAS. Added/Corp** United States. Dept. of Defense. Washington Headquarters Services. Directorate for Information Operations and Reports. **VFOAT** Department of Defense Atlas/Data Abstract for the United States and Selected Areas. **VAT** Atlas, Data Abstract for the United States and Selected Areas. (1986)-. English. Information Operations and Reports, Washington Headquarters Services, Room IC535/The Pentagon, Washington DC 20301. **LC** UC267; .D46. ***Continues*** *Atlas/State Data Abstract for the United States.*

US/0736-9255
**ATOMIC VETERANS' NEWSLETTER.** [At. veterans' newsl.]. Newsletter. English. bm. National Assn Atomic Veterans, 1109 Franklin Street, Burlington IA 52601.

US/0148-3447
**AUDIT REPORT, DEPARTMENT OF MILITARY - TENNESSEE DIVISION OF STATE AUDIT.** ***Title Change.*** **Main/Corp** Tennessee. Division of State Audit. English. be. Tennessee Comptroller of the Treasury, Nashville TN 37219. **LC** UA461; .D58A. **DD** 353.9/768/007232. ***Continued by*** *Audit Report, Military Department of Tennessee, Nashville, Tennessee For the Year Ended June 30.*

US
**AUDIT REPORT MILITARY DEPARTMENT OF TENNESSEE NASHVILLE TENNESSEE FOR THE YEAR ENDED JUNE 30. Main/Corp** Tennessee. Military Dept. **VFOAT** Audit Report. English. an. **LC** UA461; .D58A. ***Continues*** *Audit Report, Department of Military, 0148-3447.*

CN/0821-5499
**AURORA (GREENWOOD).** (THE AURORA / CANADIAN FORCES BASE GREENWOOD = BASE DES FORCES CANADIENNES GREENWOOD.). [Aurora]. **Added/Corp** Canada. Canadian Forces Base (Greenwood, N.S.). Vol. 1, No. 1 (Nov. 19, 1980)-. Periodical. English. VP International, Canadian Forces Base, Greenwood Nova Scotia B0P 1N0 Canada. **Tel** (902)765-3391. **DD** 355.1/09716/34. ***Continues*** *Argus (Canada. Canadian Forces Base (Greenwood, N.S.)), 0821-5480.*

AT/1030-9667
**AUSTRALIAN DEFENCE 2000.** ***Ceased.*** **VFOAT** Australian Defence Two Thousand. Vol. 3, Issue 6 (Dec. 1987)-Vol. 5 (?). Periodical. English. mo. Australian Defence 2000, PO Box 33 12 Allambie Court, MT Eliza Vic 3930 Australia. **Tel** 011 61 3 787 2657. ***Continues*** *Defence 2000, 0816-6080.*

AT/0314-1039
**AUSTRALIAN DEFENCE FORCE JOURNAL : JOURNAL OF THE AUSTRALIAN PROFESSION OF ARMS. Added/Corp** Australia. Dept. of Defence. **VFOAT** Australian Defense Force Journal. No. 86 (Jan./Feb. 1991)-. Periodical. English. bm. Defence Force Journal, Managing Editor, Building B 4-26, Russell Offices, Canberra ACT 2600 Australia. **Tel** 011 06 265 2999, FAX 011 06 265 1099. **LC** U1; .D26. **DD** 355/.00994. Index available (In each Nov./Dec. issue). **Bk Rev. Ad Acc, Adv Mgr:** Irene Coombes, **Tel** 011 06 265 1193. Full Page (B&W) 1,950Aus$. Half Page (B&W) 1,150Aus$. Full Page (Color) 2,500Aus$. Half Page (Color) 1,500Aus$. **Circ:** 20,000. ***Continues*** *Defence Force Journal, 0314-1039.*
**Desc:** The journal of the Profession of Arms serving the Department of defence, the Royal Australian Navy, the Australian Army, and the Royal Australian Air Force.
**Ind/Abst** APAIS, Aust. Public Aff. Inf. Ser. (1991-).

●CN/1191-8004
**AVIATION, AEROSPACE & DEFENCE UPDATE.** **See** Aeronautics, Astronautics.

UK
**BAND INTERNATIONAL : THE JOURNAL OF THE INTERNATIONAL MILITARY MUSIC SOCIETY.** **See** Music.

US/0273-2874
**BARRY FAIN'S PRIVATE BLUE BOOK OF GUN VALUES. VFOAT** Blue Book of Gun Values. Vol. 1, No. 1 (1981)-. English. an. $29.95. Collector Arms Dealers Association, One Appletree Square, Minneapolis MN 55425. **Tel** (800)368-2232, (612)854-3781. **LC** TS532.4; .F34. **DD** 683.4/0075.

●UK/0966-9175
**BASIC REPORTS.** [BASIC rep.]. **VFOAT** British American Security Information Council Reports. (1992)-. English. ir. $50.00. British American Security Information Council, 1601 Connecticut Avenue Northwest, # 302, Washington DC 20015. **Tel** (202)745-2457. ***Continues*** *BASIC Reports on European Arms Control, 0966-3266.*

UK/0005-8645
**BELLONA. KWARTALNIK WOJSKOWO-HISTORYCZNY.** [Bellona]. Began publication with Jan. 1918 Issue. Periodical. Polish (summaries and/or abstracts in English and French). ir. Polish Institut & Sikorski Mus, England. **LC** U4; .B4. cum. index.
**Ind/Abst** Am. Hist. Life (1954-1964).

SZ/0378-7869
**BIBLIOGRAPHIE INTERNATIONALE D'HISTOIRE MILITAIRE / COMITE INTERNATIONAL DES SCIENCES HISTORIQUES, COMMISSION INTERNATIONALE D'HISTOIRE MILITAIRE COMPAREE, COMITE DE BIBLIOGRAPHIE. Added/Corp** International Commission of Military History. Committee of Bibliography. Vol. 2 (1977)-. French (Multiple languages). an (Sept.). 25.00F. Comite Bibliographie de Cihm, rue de l Eglise Br Langenber, CH-1122 Romanel Switzerland. **Tel** 011 41 21 8699368. **LC** Z6724.H6; B84; D25. **DD** 016.355/009. ***Continues*** *Bulletin de Bibliographie (Bern, Switzerland).*

US
**BIENNIAL REPORT - ADJUTANT GENERAL'S DEPARTMENT, STATE OF NORTH DAKOTA. Main/Corp** North Dakota. Adjutant General's Dept. English. be. Adjutant General's Department / North Dakota, Box 1817, Bismarck ND 58505. **LC** UA43; .N9. **DD** 355.3/7.09784. ***Continues*** *North Dakota. Adjutant General's Office. Report.*

US
**BIENNIAL REPORT - STATE OF MINNESOTA, DEPARTMENT OF MILITARY AFFAIRS. Main/Corp** Minnesota. Dept. of Military Affairs. English. be. Department of

Military Affairs / Minnesota, Veterans Service Building, State Capitol, St Paul MN 55101. **LC** UA271; .D46A. **DD** 355.3/7/09776.

US
**BIENNIAL REPORT - STATE OF MINNESOTA, DEPARTMENT OF VETERANS AFFAIRS.** **Main/Corp** Minnesota. Dept. of Veterans' Affairs. 1976/78-. English. be. Minnesota Department of Veterans Affairs, St Paul MN 55101. **LC** UB358.M6; A32. **DD** 353.9/776/00848. ***Continues*** *Annual Report - Department of Veterans Affairs, State of Minnesota.*

US
**BIENNIAL REPORT - STATE OF WISCONSIN, DEPARTMENT OF VETERANS AFFAIRS.** **Main/Corp** Wisconsin. Dept. of Veterans Affairs. 1975/77-. English. be. Department of Veteran Affairs, State of Wisconsin, 77 North Dickinson Street, Madison WI 53702. **LC** UB358.W6; W57A. **DD** 353.9/775/00848.

CC/1000-1093
**BINGGONG XUEBAO.** (PING KUNG HSUEH PAO.). [Binggong xuebao]. **Added/Corp** Chung-kuo Ping Kung Hsueh Hui. **VFOAT** Binggong Xuebao; Acta Armamentarii. (1979)-. Academic Scholarly Publication. Chinese (summaries and/or abstracts in English). qt. $25.44. China Ordnance Society, PO Box 2431, Beijing, People's Republic of China. **Tel** 89.2576. **(Subscription address:** China International Book Trading Corporation, PO Box 399, Library Service Department, Beijing 100044 People's Republic of China.**)** **ED** Li Hong. **LC** UA10; .P53. **DD** 623.4/05. **CODEN** BIXUD9. **Ad Acc. Circ:** 6,000. Documents available from CASDDS.
**Desc:** Covers armoured vehicles, tanks, artillery, small arms, guides missiles, rocketry, ammunitions, propellants, explosives, military optics, and electronics, as well as relevant basic and applied sciences.
**Ind/Abst** Chem. Abstr. (1986-1988); Ei Page One; Int. Aerosp. Abstr. (1991-).

CC/1000-4912
**BINGQI ZHISHI.** (PING CHI CHIH SHIH.). [Bingqi zhishi]. **VFOAT** Bingqi Zhishi; Ordnance Knowledge. (1979)-. Periodical. Chinese. bm. $7.60. **(Subscription address:** China International Book Trading Corporation, PO Box 399, Library Service Department, Beijing 100044 People's Republic of China.**)** **LC** U799; .P56. **DD** 355.8/2/05.

US
**BLACK VET.** (1991)-. Periodical. English. ir (1-2 issues per year). Free on request. Black Veterans for Social Justice, 686 Fulton Street, Brooklyn NY 11217. **Tel** (718)935-1116.

●US/1069-8175
**BMD MONITOR.** [BMD monit.]. Vol. 8, No. 10 (May 21, 1993)-. Periodical. English. bw. $787.00 US; $802.00 other. Pasha Publications Inc., 1616 North Fort Myer Drive, Suite 1000, Arlington VA 22209. **Tel** (800)424-2908, (703)528-1244, FAX (703)528-3742, (703)528-1253. **DD** 355. ***Continues*** *SDI Monitor, 0886-7607.*

JA
**BOEI HANDOBUKKU.** (1975)-. Periodical. Japanese. ¥450. Boei Gakkai, Daini-Matsuda Building, 7-8-7 Roppongi Minato-ku, Tokyo 106 Japan. **Tel** 81 3 3713 2469, FAX 81 3 3713 6149. **LC** UA845; .B63.

PO/0870-4619
**BOLETIM DO ARQUIVO HISTORICO MILITAR.** [Bol. Arq. Hist. Mil.]. **Main/Corp** Portugal. Aquivo Historico Militar. V. 1- 1930-. Bulletin. Portuguese. an. **LC** DP547; .A3. **DD** 946.9.
**Ind/Abst** Am. Hist. Life (1963-).

SP
**BOLETIN OFICIAL DEL MINISTERIO DE DEFENSA.** **Main/Corp** Spain. Ministerio de Defensa. **VFOAT** BOD. Vol. 1, No. 1 (1985)-. Spanish. da. Ministerio de Defensa, C Paseo de la Castellana 109, 28071 Madrid Spain. **Tel** 011 34 1 5350477, FAX 011 34 1 5973540. **LC** UA780; .S6A. **DD** 355.6/0946. ***Formed by the union of*** *Boletin Oficial del Ministerio de Defensa: Diario Oficial del Ejercito; Boletin Oficial del Ministerio de Defensa: Diario Oficial del Ejercito* ***and*** *Del Aire;* ***Continues*** *Boletin Oficial del Ministerio de Defensa: Diario Oficial de Marina.*

IT/0391-7088
**BOLLETTINO DEL'ISTITUTO STORICO E DI CULTURA DELL'ARMA DEL GENIO.** (BOLLETTINO.). [Boll. Ist. stor. cult. arma genio]. **Main/Corp** Istituto Storico e di Cultura dell'Arma del Genio (Rome, Italy). (1935)-. Periodical. Italian. qt. **LC** UG1; .R7.
**Ind/Abst** Am. Hist. Life (1955-1958, 1962-); BHA : Biblio. Hist. Art.

●UK
**BRASSEY'S DEFENCE YEARBOOK / EDITED BY THE CENTRE FOR DEFENCE STUDIES.** **Added/Corp** University of London. Centre for Defence Studies. **VFOAT** Brassey's Defence Year Book. 103rd (1993)-. English. an. $65.00. Brasseys UK Ltd., 33 John Street, London WC1N 2AT England. **Tel** 011 44 71 753 7777, FAX 011 44 71 753 7794. **LC** V10; .N3. **DD** 355/.055. ***Continues*** *Royal United Services Institute for Defence Studies. R.U.S.I. and Brassey's Defence Yearbook, 0097-4803.*

US
**BREAKTHROUGHS.** **Added/Corp** Massachusetts Institute of Technology. Defense and Arms Control Studies Program. Vol. 1, No. 1 (Fall 1990)-. Periodical. English. qt.

UK/0262-3781
**BRIEFING PAPER ON SOUTHERN AFRICA / INTERNATIONAL DEFENCE & AID FUND.** **Added/Corp** International Defence and Aid Fund. No. 1 (Mar. 1981)-. Periodical. English. bm. **LC** PAR.
**Ind/Abst** Hum. Rights Intern. Rep.

UK/0272-4782
**BRITISH DEFENCE DIRECTORY.** [Br. def. dir.]. Vol. 1, No. 1 (Mar. 1982)-. English. qt. £267.00 UK; $507.00 other (institutions); £180.00 (DMA members). Brasseys UK Ltd., 33 John Street, London WC1N 2AT England. **Tel** 011 44 71 753 7777, FAX 011 44 71 753 7794. **(Subscription address:** Turpin Distribution Services Limited, Blackhorse Road, Letchworth, Hertfordshire SG6 1HN, United Kingdom.**)** **ED** Major D.C. Lycett-Gregson. **LC** UA647; .B847. **DD** 354.41066/025. **[CCC].** available on microfilm and microfiche from University Microfilms International (UMI). ***Absorbed*** *Defence Attache, 0265-7910.*
**Desc:** Contains detailed information on the defense establishment; it is frequently updated. Aimed at defense equipment manufacturers, military professionals, diplomatic staff.

UK
**BRITISH DEFENCE EQUIPMENT CATALOGUE.** **VFOAT** B.D.E.C.; BDEC. English. ir. Combined Service Publications, PO Box 4, Farnborough Hampshire GU14 7LR England. **LC** UC460; .B75. **DD** 355.8/029/441.

FR
**BUDGET DE PROGRAMMES / SECRETARIAT GENERAL POUR L'ADMINISTRATION, ACTION SOCIALE DES ARMEES.** **Main/Corp** France. Service Central de l'Action Sociale des Armees. French. an. Action Sociale des Armees, 5 rue de Chazelles, 75017 Paris France. **LC** UH725.F7; F73A. **DD** 355.3/4.

US
**BULLETIN.** **Added/Corp** Idaho. Division of Veterans Services. (198?)-. English. mo. Division of Veterans Affairs / Idaho, PO Box 7765, Boise ID 83707. **LC** UB358.I2; I33a. ***Continues*** *Idaho. Division of Veterans Affairs. Bulletin - State of Idaho, Division of Veterans Affairs, 0364-0310.*

FR
**BULLETIN DES MARCHES DELEGATION GENERALE POUR L'ARMEMENT.** Bulletin. French. mo. 1100.00F. GIP Union, Dept Mission Defense, 5 7 Place d'Alleray, F-75015 Paris France. **Tel** 011 33 1 45315625.

UK/0026-4008
**BULLETIN - MILITARY HISTORICAL SOCIETY.** (BULLETIN.). [Bull. - Mil. Hist. Soc.]. **Main/Corp** Military Historical Society (Great Britain). (19??)-. Bulletin. English. Four times a year. £12.00 UK; £15.00 others. Military Historical Society, c/o E. Dickinson, 83 Loughborough Road, West Bridgeford Nottingham NG2 7JX England. **LC** DA49; .M55. cum. index.
**Desc:** Articles and photographs on various aspects of military history submitted by members.
**Ind/Abst** Am. Hist. Life (1955-1962).

FR
**BULLETIN OFFICIEL DES ARMEES.** Bulletin. French. Fifty-six times a year. Librairie Lavauzelle, BP 8, 87350 Panazoil France. **Tel** 16 55 31 26 26.

FR
**BULLETIN OFFICIEL DES DECORATIONS, MEDAILLES ET RECOMPENSES / REPUBLIQUE FRANCAISE.** **Main/Corp** France. (19??)-. French. ir. 47.00F France; 85.00F other. Direction des Journaux Officiels, 26 rue Desaix, 75727 Paris Cedex 15 France. **Tel** 011 33 1 40587500. **LC** CR4529.F8; F7a.

GW
**BUNDESVERSORGUNGSBLATT.** Periodical. German. W Kohlhammer Verlag GmbH, Postfach 800430, D 70549 Stuttgart Germany. **Tel** 011 49 711 78631, FAX 011 49 711 7863263, telex 7-255820. **LC** UB359.G3; B8. ***Continues*** *Bundesversongungsblatt im Bundesarbeitsblatt.*

US/0749-4408
**CP3SI NEWS.** [Cp3sl news]. **VFOAT** C Three I News. **VAT** Command, Control, Communications Intelligence News. Vol. 1, No. 1 (June 1984)-. Periodical. English. mo. $195.00 (one year), $350.00 (two year), $500.00 (three year). Washington Crime News Services, 3918 Prosperity Avenue, Suite 318, Fairfax VA 22031-3334. **Tel** (703)573-1600, (800)422-9267, FAX (703)573-1604. **DD** 355.
**Desc:** Report on military command control and communication and intelligence systems. Reports latest development funding and opportunities.

US
**C3I FORECAST.** (19??)-. English. Twelve times a year. $1390.00. Forecast International / DMS Inc., 22 Commerce Road, Newtown CT 06470. **Tel** (203)426-0800, FAX (203)426-1964, telex 467615. available on CD-ROM ($1595.00).

US/0889-4728
**C3I REPORT.** ***Title Change.*** [Cp3sl rep.]. Periodical. English. bw. Pasha Publications Inc., 1616 North Fort Myer Drive, Suite 1000, Arlington VA 22209. **Tel** (800)424-2908, (703)528-1244, FAX (703)528-3742, (703)528-1253. **DD** 355. **[CCC].** available on an online database (file 636/Full-Text) from DIALOG. ***Continued by*** *C P4 SI Report, 1050-2483.*
**Desc:** Covers command, control, communication and intelligence programs for Army, Navy and Air Force research and development and procurement; includes contract opportunities, funding politics, electronic warfare, battle management, competitors, tempest and more.

UK
**CADET JOURNAL & GAZETTE.** English. qt (Jan., Apr., Jul., Oct.). £7.00. Army Cadet Force Association, Cheltenham Terrace, London SW3 4RR England. **Tel** 011 44 71 730 9733.

FR/1169-0402
**CAHIERS DE MARS, LES.** (CAHIERS DE MARS BULLETIN DE L'ASSOCIATION DES AMIS DE L'ECOLE SUPERIEURE DE GUERRE.). [Cah. Mars]. **Added/Corp** Association des Amis de l'Ecole Superieure de Guerre (Paris). **VFOAT** Bulletin Trimestriel - Association des Amis de l'Ecole Superieure de Guerre (1988). (1988)-. Bulletin. French. Four times a year. 180.00F. Ecole Superieure de Guerre, 1 Place Joffre Bibliotheque, 75007 Paris France. **Tel** 011 33 1 45553011 ext. 5198. **UDC** 355.23(44). ***Continues*** *Bulletin Trimestriel de l'Association des Amis de l'Ecole Superieure de Guerre, 0750-2222.*

US
**CALIFORNIA MILITARY MONITOR.** **Added/Corp** Pacific Studies Center. No. 1 (Mar. 1988)-. Periodical. English. bm. Pacific Studies Center, 222 B View Street, Mountain View CA 94041.
**Ind/Abst** Hum. Rights Intern. Rep.

CN/0315-3495
**CANADIAN DEFENCE QUARTERLY (TORONTO).** (CANADIAN DEFENCE QUARTERLY.). [Can. def. q.]. **VFOAT** Revue Canadienne de Defense. Vol. 1 No. 1 (Summer 1971)-. Periodical. English (French). Four times a year (Mar., June, Sept., Dec.). 45.00Can$ (one year); 65.00Can$ (three year). Baxter Publishing Company, 310 Dupont Street, Toronto Ontario M5R 1V9 Canada. **Tel** (416)968-7252, FAX (416)968-2377. **ED** John Marteinson. **LC** UA600; .C299. **DD** 355/.033071. **Bk Rev. Ad Acc. Circ:** 10,000 (ctrl). available on microfiche from Micromedia Limited.
**Desc:** The foremost professional military journal, providing highly informed coverage of defence policy and strategic issues, as well as military technology operational concepts, tactics and military history.
**Ind/Abst** Air Univ. Libr. Index Mil. Period.; Am. Hist. Life (1987-); Am. Bibliogr. Slavic East Europ. Stud.; Can. Index; Curr. Mil. Pol. Lit.

CN/0068-8843
**CANADIAN GUNNER (SHILO. 1965).** (THE CANADIAN GUNNER. L'ARTILLEUR CANADIEN). **Added/Corp** Canada. Army. Royal Regiment of Canadian Artillery. **VFOAT** Artilleur Canadien. (1965)-. English (French). an (May). 9.25Can$. Royal Canadian Artillery, Canadian Forces Base Shilo, Shilo Manitoba R0K 2A0 Canada. **Tel** (204)765-3534. **DD** 358/.1/0971. **Ad Acc. Circ:** 3,000. ***Supersedes*** *Gunner Bulletin, 0318-6350.*
**Desc:** A summary of annual activity of Royal Regiment of Canada Artillery.

●CN/1195-8472
**CANADIAN MILITARY HISTORY.** [Can. mil. hist.]. **Added/Corp** Laurier Centre for Military, Strategic and Disarmament Studies. Vol. 1, No. 1/2 (Autumn 1992)-. Periodical. English. Twice a year (spring and autumn). 15.00Can$ (one year), 28.00Can$ (two years) Canada; £13.00 UK; $19.00 other. Wilfrid Laurier University / History Department, Waterloo Ontario N2L 3C5 Canada. **Tel** (519)884-1970 Ext. 2328, FAX (519)886-9351, telex 067-7569. **DD** 355/.00971/05.
**Desc:** Presents articles and features on all aspects of Canada's military past, including all branches of the Canadian Forces. Narratives, anecdotes, and reports from the past are featured in each issue.

CN/0008-4468
**CANADIAN MILITARY JOURNAL.** ***Ceased.*** Vol. 11 (1944)-Ceased ?. Periodical. English (French). qt. Canadian Military Journal, 3450 Durocher/Suite 8, Montreal Quebec H2X 2E1 Canada. ***Continues*** *Salute, 0382-7526.*

US/0196-7886
**CANADIAN STRATEGIC REPORT.** [Can. strateg. rep.]. V. 1- Jan. 1980-. Periodical. English. sm. $37.00. Strategic Publications Inc, 1777 T Street NW, Washington DC 20009.

IT
**CASTELLUM.** **See** Architecture.

US
**CATALOG.** **Main/Corp** Defense Systems Management College. **VFOAT** D.S.M.C. ... Catalog; DSMC ... Catalog. Catalog. English. an. Defense Systems Management College, Fort Belvoir VA 22060. available on microfiche (Vols. for (1987-) distributed to depository libraries).

US/0008-5952
**CCCO NEWS NOTES.** **Main/Corp** Central Committee for Conscientious Objectors, Philadelphia. **VAT** Central Committee for Conscientious Objectors News Notes. (1970)-. Periodical. English. Five times a year. $5.00. CCCO, 2208 South Street, Philadelphia PA 19146. **Tel** (215)545-4626. **ED** Robert A Seeley. **LC** UB342.U5; C45a. **DD** 355.2/24/0973. **Bk Rev.** available on microfilm and microfiche from University Microfilms International (UMI). ***Continues*** *Central Committee for Conscientious Objectors. News Notes.*
**Desc:** Covers war, peace and conscience issues.

CN/0828-8046
**CFB GANDER GAZETTE.** [CFB Gander gaz.]. **VAT** Canadian Forces Base Gander Gazette. Vol. 3, No. 6 (April 1984)-. Periodical. English. mo. CFB Gander Gazette, PO Box 6000, Gander Newfoundland A1V 1X1 Canada. **DD** 355.1/09718. ***Continues*** *CFS Gander Gazette, 0823-7824.*

FR/1017-7566
**CHAILLOT PAPERS.** **Added/Corp** Western European Union. Institute for Security Studies. (Mar. 1991)-. Periodical. English.

CN/1188-2603
**CHAPELHOW CHRONICLE AND COMMUNITY NEWS.** [Chapelhow chron. community news]. **Added/Corp** Royal Canadian Legion. Chapelhow Branch, No. 284. **VFOAT** Chapelhow Chronicle. Vol. 1, No. 1 (Summer 1991)-. Periodical. English. qt. Limited free distribution. Chapelhow Branch Number 284 Royal Canadian Legion, 606-38th Avenue NE, Calgary Alberta T2E 8J9 Canada. **DD** 355.3.

US/1060-8095
**CHEMICAL WEAPONS CONVENTION BULLETIN.** (CHEMICAL WEAPONS CONVENTION BULLETIN : QUARTERLY JOURNAL OF THE HARVARD-SUSSEX PROGRAM ON CBW ARMAMENT AND ARMS LIMITATION.). [Chem. weapons conv. bull.]. **Added/Corp** Harvard-Sussex Program on CBW Armament and Arms Limitation. **VFOAT** CWCB. (19??)-. Periodical. English. Four times a year. $35.00. University of Sussex / SPRU, Harvard Sussex Program Falmer, Brighton BN1 9RF England. **Tel** 0273 686758. **(Subscription address:** Committee for National Security, 1601 Connecticut Avenue Northwest, Washington DC 20009.**)** **DD** 358.

CH/1017-8716
**CHINA'S MILITARY : THE PLA IN ... .** [China's milit. : PLA]. **Added/Corp** Sun Yat-Sen Center for Policy Studies. **VFOAT** SCPS Yearbook; PLA Yearbook. (1991)-. English. be. $49.85. Westview Press Inc, 5500 Central Avenue, Boulder CO 80301. **Tel** (303)444-3541, FAX (303)449-3356. ***Continues*** *SCPS Yearbook on PLA Affairs.*

CH
**CHUNG-HUA CHAN LUEH HSUEH KAN.** Periodical. Chinese. qt. $10.00. Chung-Hua Chan Lueh Hsueh Hui, 170 Hsin Sheng N Road, 3 Section, Taipei Shih Taiwan. **LC** U162; .C534. **DD** 355.4/3/005.

US/0887-9680
**CITIZEN AIRMAN.** (CITIZEN AIRMAN : THE OFFICIAL MAGAZINE OF THE AIR NATIONAL GUARD AND AIR FORCE RESERVE.). **Added/Corp** United States. National Guard Bureau. United States. Air Force Reserve. United States. Air Force. Vol. 37, No. 5 (Winter 1985/1986)-. Government Publication. English. bm. $8.00 domestic; $10.00 other. Superintendent of Documents, US Government Printing Office, Washington DC 20402. **Tel** (202)275-3328, FAX (202)786-2377. **LC** UG633; .A66. **DD** 359.9/7/0973. available on microfilm and microfiche from University Microfilms International (UMI). ***Continues*** *Air Reservist, 0002-2535.*
**Desc:** An official publication of Hq. Complete and up-to-date information of interest to the Air Reserve Forces.
**Ind/Abst** Air Univ. Libr. Index Mil. Period.

SW
**CIVIL.** **See** Psychology.

US/0886-6015
**CIVILIAN-BASED DEFENSE.** (CIVILIAN-BASED DEFENSE. NEWS AND OPINION.). [Civ.-based def.]. **Added/Corp** Association for Transarmament Studies. **VFOAT** Civilian Based Defense. (198?)-. Periodical. English. Six times a year (Jan., Mar., May, July, Sept., Nov.). $15.00. Civilian-Based Defense Association, 154 Auburn Street, Cambridge MA 02139. **ED** Paul Anders, (phone: (617)868-6058). **DD** 327. **Bk Rev**, (Qty: 2). **Ad Acc. Circ:** 1,000.
**Desc:** Civilian-based Defense B published by the Civilian-based Defense Association to provide information about Civilian-Based Defense as an alternative policy for national defense and to make available international news, opinion and research about CBO.

US/0882-8857
**CIVILIAN MANPOWER STATISTICS.** **See** Military and Defense-Abstracting, Bibliographies and Statistics.

US/0899-7047
**CML ARMY CHEMICAL REVIEW.** [CML Army chem. rev.]. **Added/Corp** United States. Army. Chemical Corps. US Army Chemical School. **VFOAT** Army Chemical Review; CML. (June 1987)-. Government Publication. English. sa. $5.00 domestic; $6.25 other. Superintendent of Documents, US Government Printing Office, Washington DC 20402. **Tel** (202)275-3328, FAX (202)786-2377. **DD** 358. ***Continues*** *Army Chemical Journal, 0888-3858.*
**Ind/Abst** Index U.S. Gov. Period.

US/0883-2803
**CODE NAME DIRECTORY. INTERNATIONAL.** ***Suspended.*** [Code name dir., Int.]. **VFOAT** International Code Name Directory; DMS Code Name Directory. International. 3rd Ed. (1984)-?. Directory. English. an. $150.00. DMS Inc, 100 Northfield Street, PO Box 4585, Greenwich CT 06830. **Tel** (203)661-7800. **LC** U26; .C568. **DD** 355/.001/48. ***Continues*** *International Code Name Handbook : Aerospace, Defense, Technology.*

US/0882-7621
**CODE NAME DIRECTORY. US.** ***Suspended.*** [Code name dir., U. S.]. **Added/Corp** Defense Marketing Services, Inc. **VFOAT** US Code Name Directory; DMS Code Name Directory. US. 12th Ed. (1984)-Suspended. Directory. English. an. $150.00. Forecast International / DMS Inc., 22 Commerce Road, Newtown CT 06470. **Tel** (203)426-0800, FAX (203)426-1964, telex 467615. **LC** U26; .C57. **DD** 355/.00148. ***Continues*** *Code Name Handbook : Aerospace, Defense, Technology.*
**Desc:** Covers code names and acronyms used by the US Department of Defense and the aerospace/defense industry.

SP/0213-3156
**COLLECCION LEGISLATIVA DEL MINISTERIO DE DEFENSA. ANO 1988.** Secretaria General Tecnic, Centro De Publicaciones, Paseo de la Castellana 109, 28046 Madrid Spain.

UK/0955-9841
**COMBAT AND SURVIVAL MAGAZINE.** [Combat surviv. mag.]. (1987)-. Periodical. English. Twelve times a year. £20.00 UK; £27.50 Europe; £37.50 others. TG Scott Subscriber Services, 6 Bourne Enterprise Center, Wrotham Road, Borough Green, Kent TN15 8DG England. **Tel** 011 44 01 732 884023, FAX 011 44 01 732 884034.
**Desc:** For the soldiers and military enthusiasts providing detailed reviews of all military equipment, in depth profiles of guns, combat tactics, and step-by-step explanations of survival skills.

US/0010-213X
**COMBAT CREW / STRATEGIC AIR COMMAND.** ***Title Change.*** [Combat crew]. **Added/Corp** United States. Air Force. Strategic Air Command. (1950-1992). Government Publication. English. mo. Superintendent of Documents, US Government Printing Office, Washington DC 20402. **Tel** (202)275-3328, FAX (202)786-2377. **LC** UG633; .A15. **DD** 358.42. available on microfiche (Vols. for (1986-) distributed to depository libraries). ***Continues*** *Professional Pilot.* ***Merged with*** *TAC Attack, 0494-3880* ***to form*** *Combat Edge, 1063-8970.*
**Desc:** A publication of the Strategic Air Command containing articles for the purpose of promoting safety.
**Ind/Abst** Air Univ. Libr. Index Mil. Period.

US/0098-7956
**COMBAT DATA SUBSCRIPTION SERVICE.** **Main/Corp** Historical Evaluation and Research Organization. V. 1- Winter 1975-. Periodical. English. qt. Historical Evaluation and Research Organization, PO Box 157, Dunn Loring VA 22027. **LC** U719; .H56A. **DD** 355.4/05.

●US/1063-8970
**COMBAT EDGE, THE.** **See** Aeronautics, Astronautics.

US/1043-7584
**COMBAT HANDGUNS.** [Combat handguns]. (19??)-. Periodical. English. bm. $15.47 (one year), $26.50 (two year), $37.00 (three year). Harris Publications, 1115 Broadway/8th Floor, New York NY 10010. **Tel** (212)807-7100. **LC** IN PROCESS. **DD** 799.

US/0887-2546
**COMBAT WEAPONS.** ***Ceased.*** [Combat weapons]. (1986)-(1986). Periodical. English. qt. Omega Group Ltd., PO Box 693, Boulder CO 80306. **Tel** (303)449-3750, FAX (303)444-5617, telex 450 129. **DD** 355. ***Continues*** *SOF's Combat Weapons.*

US/0010-2474
**COMMAND (DENVER, COLO.).** (COMMAND.). [Command]. **Added/Corp** Officers' Christian Union. Officers' Christian Fellowship. Vol. 1 (1956)-. Periodical. English. Four times a year. Free for US Military affiliates; $15.00 US; $21.00 other. Officers Christian Fellowship, PO Box 1177, Englewood CO 80150. **Tel** (303)761-1984, FAX (303)761-6226. **ED** Col. Don Martin, Jr. **Bk Rev**, (Qty: 4-8). **Ad Acc, Adv Mgr:** Ted Shadid. ***Continues*** *Officers' Christian Union. Officers' Christian Union Bulletin, 0471-1505.*
**Desc:** Aimed at helping Christians in the US Armed Forces live in accordance with their faith.

US/1059-5651
**COMMAND MAGAZINE (SAN LUIS OBISPO, CALIF.).** (COMMAND MAGAZINE.). Issue #1 (Nov.-Dec. 1989)-. English. bm (Jan., Mar., May, Jul., Sep., Nov.). $25.95 without Game US; $43.95 without Game other; $60.00 with Game US; $78.00 with Game other. XRT Corporation, PO Box 4017, San Luis Obispo CA 93403. **Tel** (805)546-9596, FAX (805)546-0570. **ED** Ty Bomba (editor's address: 3547-D South Higuera, San Luis Obispo, CA 93401). **LC** WMLC L 83/8807. **DD** 793. **Ad Acc, Adv Mgr:** Chris. **Circ:** 16,000.
**Desc:** Military history, covering all periods and wars. Emphasizes force composition and strategies used.

US/0736-1807
**COMMERCIAL ACTIVITIES INVENTORY REPORT AND FIVE-YEAR REVIEW SCHEDULE / DEPARTMENT OF DEFENSE.** **Main/Corp** United States. Dept. of Defense. Fiscal Year 1981-. English. an. US Department of Defense, The Pentagon, Washington DC 20301. **Tel** (703)545-6700. **LC** UC263; .U534B. **DD** 355.3/41/0973. ***Continues*** *Commercial and Industrial-Type Activities Inventory Report and 5-Year Review Schedule.*

US/0145-353X
**COMMUNITY ACTIVITIES (SALEM).** (COMMUNITY ACTIVITIES - OREGON NATIONAL GUARD.). **Main/Corp** Oregon. National Guard. (19??)-. English. an. Community Activities, 2150 Fairgrounds Road Northeast, Salem OR 97303. **LC** UH723; .O73a. **DD** 361/.9795.

US/1057-9222
**COMPANIES PARTICIPATING IN THE DEPARTMENT OF DEFENSE SUBCONTRACTING PROGRAM.** [Co. particip. Dep. Def. subcontract. program]. **Added/Corp** United States. Dept. of Defense. Washington Headquarters Services. Directorate for Information Operations and Reports. (19??)-. Government Publication. English. qt. $23.00 US; $28.75 other. Superintendent of Documents, US Government Printing Office, Washington DC 20402. **Tel** (202)275-3328, FAX (202)786-2377. **DD** 355. available on microfiche (Vols. for 1986- distributed to depository libraries). Documents available from Documents on Demand.
**Desc:** Summarizes information submitted by Department of Defense prime contractors required to submit reports on subcontracting to small and small disadvantaged businesses. An average of 900 companies listed alphabetically shows their location, date of latest Government subcontracting surveillance review, net value of subcontract awards, and amount and percent of awards. Has a section for each of the Military Department and the Defense Logistics Agency. The same data are also shown for the comparable quarter of the previous fiscal year, the current fiscal year to date, and the comparable period of the prior fiscal year.
**Ind/Abst** Am. Stat. Index.

●US/1059-5783
**COMPLETE GUIDE TO 9MM.** **See** Recreation, Leisure-Outdoor Life.

UK
**COMPUTERS IN DEFENSE.** ***Ceased.*** **See** Computers.

US
**CONFERENCE RECORD / IEEE MILITARY COMMUNICATIONS CONFERENCE.** **Added/Corp** Institute of Electrical and Electronics Engineers. IEEE Communications Society. United States. Dept. of Defense. Armed Forces Communications and Electronics Association (U.S.). **VFOAT** Milcom. (1984)-. English. IEEE, Institution of Electrical and Electronics Engineers, Inc., 345 East 47th

# Military and Defense

Street, New York NY 10017-2394. **Tel** (908)981-1393, FAX (908)981-9667. **Continues** *IEEE Military Communications Conference. Proceedings.*
**Ind/Abst** Manuf. Process Eng. Abstr.; Mech. Eng. Abstr.; Solid State Supercond. Abstr.

US/0740-3461
### CONSENSUS (CHICAGO, ILL.).
(CONSENSUS.). [Consensus]. Vol. 1, No. 1 (Winter 1983)-. Periodical. English. qt. Consensus / Illinois, 1451 East 55th Street, #1038, Chicago IL 60615. **LC** UA23; .C672. **DD** 355/.033073.

US
### CONSOLIDATED INDEX OF ARMY PUBLICATIONS AND BLANK FORMS [COMPUTER FILE]. Added/Corp United States.
Dept. of the Army. (19??)-. English. $260.00 US; $520.00 other. US Department of Defense Department of the Army, The Pentagon, SAPA-CR, Room 3E718, Washington DC 20310. **Tel** (703)695-0363, FAX (703)693-5737. **(Subscription address:** National Technical Information Service, 5285 Port Royal Road, Springfield, VA 22161**)**

US
### CONSOLIDATED INDEX OF ARMY PUBLICATIONS AND BLANK FORMS [MICROFORM]. Added/Corp United States. Dept.
of the Army. (April 1982)-. English. qt. $55.00 US; $110.00 other. US Department of Defense Department of the Army, The Pentagon, SAPA-CR, Room 3E718, Washington DC 20310. **Tel** (703)695-0363, FAX (703)693-5737. **(Subscription address:** National Technical Information Service, 5285 Port Royal Road, Springfield, VA 22161**)** available on CD-ROM. *Formed by the union of* Index of Administrative Publications; Index of Blank Forms; Index of Doctrinal Training Organizational Publications *and* Index of Technical Publications; *Continues* Index of Supply Catalogs and Supply Manuals, excluding Types 7, 8, and 9.

US
### CONTRACT AUDIT MANUAL. Title Change.
**Main/Corp** United States. Defense Contract Audit Agency. (1979)-?. English. US Department of Defense / Alexandria, Cameron Station, Alexandria VA 22304. **Continues** *Defense Contract Audit Manual.* **Continued by** *DCAA Contract Audit Manual.*

US/0883-6884
### CONTRIBUTIONS IN MILITARY STUDIES.
[Contrib. mil. stud.]. (19??)-. Monographic series. English. an. Price varies per volume. Greenwood Press Inc., PO Box 5007, Westport CT 06881-5007. **Tel** (203)226-3571, FAX (203)222-1502. **LC** UNC. **DD** 355. **Bk Rev**. **Ad Acc**. **Continues** *Contributions in Military History, 0084-9251.*
**Desc:** The history of the air, sea, and ground forces of the world is the focus of this monograph series.

US/0194-0511
### COUNTY VETERAN POPULATION.
**Main/Corp** United States. Veterans Administration. Reports and Statistics Service. English. US Veterans Administration / Washington DC, 810 Vermont Avenue Southwest, Washington DC 20420. **Tel** (202)393-2124. **LC** UB357; .A5655 subser. **DD** 353.008/48 S; 355.1/15/0973.

UK
### CROSS & COCKADE GREAT BRITAIN JOURNAL. Added/Corp British Society of World War
I Aero Historians. **VFOAT** Cross and Cockade Journal: Great Britain; Cross & Cockade Journal: Great Britain. **VAT** Cross and Cockade Great Britain Journal. (19??)-. Periodical. English. Four times a year (Feb., May, Aug., Nov.). $30.00 Comes with Cross & Cockade Great Britian membership. Cross & Cockade International, Glenside Church Road, West Yorkshire OL14 8H2 England. **Tel** 011 44 1 706812059.

FR/1157-996X
### CULTURES ET CONFLITS. See Political
Science-International Relations.

UK/0954-3589
### CURRENT MILITARY & POLITICAL LITERATURE. Ceased. See Military and
Defense-Abstracting, Bibliographies and Statistics.

US
### CURRENT NEWS. SUPPLEMENT.
**Added/Corp** United States. Dept. of the Air Force. Current News Analysis & Research Service. United States. Dept. of Defense. Current News Analysis & Research Service. (198?)-. Periodical. English. da. Current News Analysis and Research Service, Washington DC 20301-1000. **Continues** *Current News (Washington, D.C.). Supplemental.*

US/1050-4850
### CURRENT WORLD AFFAIRS. [Curr. world
aff.]. Vol. 14, No. 1 (Spring 1990)-. Bibliography. English.

qt. $170.00 US, Canada, and Mexico; $180.00 other. Dupuy Institute, PO Box 617, Great Falls VA 22066. **Tel** (703)759-2085, FAX (703)759-6291. **ED** George A. Daoust. **LC** Z1361.D4; Q37; Z6725.U5; UA23.A1. **DD** 353. **Bk Rev**, (Qty: 100). **Continues** *Quarterly Strategic Bibliography, 0198-9006.*
**Desc:** Articles, editorials, books and government documents pertaining to current international affairs. Information on worldwide arms control, defense and foreign policies, human rights, nuclear weapons, peacekeeping, science and technology.

US
### CUTTER RADAR PROJECT NEWSLETTER. Newsletter. English. bm.
Commandant (G-EEE-1/63), Attn: Radar Project, Washington DC 20590.

US/0730-9058
### CW/PS SPECIAL STUDY. [CW/PS special
study]. **VFOAT** CWPS Special Study. Periodical. English. ir. $20.00. Center for War/Peace Studies, 218 East 18th Street, New York NY 10003.

DK
### DAN MIL. 1971-. Periodical. Danish (summaries
and/or abstracts in English). **LC** UG635.D4; D28.

US/0882-9837
### DATA ON VIETNAM ERA VETERANS.
**See** Military and Defense-Abstracting, Bibliographies and Statistics.

US/1058-076X
### DCAA CONTRACT AUDIT MANUAL.
[DCAA contract audit man.]. **Main/Corp** United States. Defense Contract Audit Agency. **VAT** Defense Contract Audit Agency Contract Audit Manual. (19??)-. Government Publication. English. sa. $31.00 domestic; $38.75 other. Superintendent of Documents, US Government Printing Office, Washington DC 20402. **Tel** (202)275-3328, FAX (202)786-2377. **DD** 355. **CODEN** DCAEEV. **Continues** *Contract Audit Manual.*
**Desc:** Prescribes auditing policies and procedures and furnishes guidance in auditing techniques for personnel engaged in the performance of the DCAA mission.

US/0148-3293
### DCAS MANAGEMENT SYNOPSIS EXECUTIVE SUMMARY. Main/Corp United
States. Defense Supply Agency. **VAT** Defense Contract Administration Services Management Synopsis. Executive Summary. English. an. Plans and Analysis Division, DCAS-JT Defense Supply Agency, Cameron Station, Alexandria VA 22314. **LC** UC267; .U597A. **DD** 355.6/211/0973.

SZ/1043-0717
### DEFENCE ECONOMICS. (DEFENCE
ECONOMICS : THE POLITICAL ECONOMY OF DEFENCE, DISARMAMENT, AND PEACE.). [Def. econ.]. Vol. 1, No. 1 (1990)-. Periodical. English. qt. $360.00. Gordon & Breach Science Publishers, PO Box 90, Reading RG1 8JL England. **Tel** 011 44 734 560080, FAX 011 44 734 568211. **(Subscription address:** Gordon & Breach Science Publishers / US, 820 Town Center Drive, Langhorne PA 19047.**) LC** HC79.D4; D43. **DD** 338. **CODEN** DEECEP. **[CCC].** Documents available from The Genuine Article.
**Ind/Abst** Curr. Contents Soc. Behav. Sci.; Econ. Lit. Index; Res. Alert [Full Cov.]; Soc. Sci. Cit. Index [Full Cov.].

UK/0142-6184
### DEFENCE (ETON). Title Change. (DEFENCE.).
[Defence]. **VFOAT** Defence Digest. Vol. 1 (July 1970)-(Aug. 1993). Periodical. English. mo. Argus Press Group, Queensway House, 2 Queensway Redhill, Surrey RH1 1QS England. **Tel** 011 44 737 768611, 011 44 737 761685, FAX 011 44 737 760510, telex 948669 TOPJNL G. **ED** Chris Jenkins. **LC** UF500; .D43. **DD** 355.8/2/05. Index available. cum. index. **Bk Rev**. **Ad Acc**. **Circ:** 30,185 (ctrl). *Absorbed* Defense Latin America. Spanish. Defensa Latino Americana *and* Defense Africa & Middle East. *Merged into* Defense Electronics, 0278-3479.
**Ind/Abst** Leadscan; PAIS Int. Print (1991-?).

UK/0963-116X
### DEFENCE HELICOPTER. See Aeronautics,
Astronautics.

UK/0263-5062
### DEFENCE HELICOPTER WORLD. Title
Change. **See** Aeronautics, Astronautics.

AT/1033-2898
### DEFENCE INDUSTRY AND AEROSPACE REPORT. [Def. ind. aerosp. rep.].
(1989)-. Periodical. English. Twenty-one times a year (Publishes on Wed. & with one special issue). 299.00Aus$ Australia; 364.00Aus$ New Zealand and Papua New Guinea; 374.00Aus$ Indonesia and Malaysia; 384.00Aus$ Japan, India, and China; 405.00Aus$ US, Israel, and Canada; 414.00Aus$ other. Business Communications Group, PO Box 250, Mawson ACT 2607 Australia. **Tel** 011 61 6 2864605, FAX 011 61 6 2863441. **ED** Trevor J. Thomas. **DD** 355.00994. Index available.

cum. index. **Bk Rev**, (Qty: 1-2). **Ad Acc**. **Circ:** 6,000. available on diskette. **Continues** *Defence Industry, 0811-9449.*

UK/0260-408X
### DEFENCE INDUSTRY DIGEST. English. mo.
£163.00 UK; $290.64 US and Canada; $168.00 other. Longman Group Ltd., Fourth Avenue, Longman House, Harlow Essex CM19 5SR England. **Tel** 011 44 279 429655, FAX 011 44 279 431059, telex 81259. **(Subscription address:** PO Box 11318, Birmingham AL 35202**)**

PK
### DEFENCE JOURNAL. Vol. 1 (Feb. 1975)-.
Periodical. English. Ten times a year. $30.00. Defence Journal, 16 B Central Street, Defence House Society, 46 Karachi Pakistan. **Tel** 011 92 21 541991, 544969. **ED** Brigadier A. R. Siddiqi. **LC** UA11; .D38. **DD** 355/.005. Index available. **Bk Rev**. **Ad Acc**. **Circ:** 3,000.
**Desc:** A mirror and digest of geostrategic affairs.

CN/0383-4638
### DEFENCE (OTTAWA. 1971). (DEFENCE.).
[Defence]. **Main/Corp** Canada. Dept. of National Defence. **VFOAT** Defence; Defence Canada; Defense Canada. 1971-. Periodical. English (French). an. $1.20. Department of National Defense, National Defence Headquarters, Ottawa Ontario K1A OK2 Canada. **LC** UA600; .C26B. **DD** 355.3/0971.

NZ
### DEFENCE REVIEW. Main/Corp New Zealand.
English. Government Printing Office / New Zealand, 10 Mulgrave Street, Wellington New Zealand. **Tel** 011 64 4 4737211, FAX 011 64 4 734943, telex GOVPRINT NZ 31320. **LC** UA874.3; .N48A. **DD** 355/.0330931.

UK
### DEFENCE SYSTEMS INTERNATIONAL : THE INTERNATIONAL REVIEW OF LAND SYSTEMS. (1988)-. English. an. £60.00.
Sterling Publications Ltd., PO Box 799, Brunel House, London W2 1XR England. **Tel** 011 44 71 2580066, FAX 011 44 71 4026441, telex 295819 ESPEEL G.

UK/0953-4970
### DEFENCE SYSTEMS MODERNISATION. [Def. syst. mod.]. (1988)-.
Periodical. English. bm. £34.00 Europe; £45.00 other. Granville Publications Ltd, 30 Queens Terrace, Southampton Hampshire, SO1 1BQ England. **Tel** 011 44 703 220189, 011 44 703 231775, FAX 011 44 703 333641. **ED** Stuart Cassy, Telephone: 44 703 220189. **DD** 623. **Ad Acc**, **Adv Mgr:** David Holmes, **Tel** 44 703 220189. **Circ:** 5200 (ctrl).
**Desc:** Covers modernisation, retrofitting, upgrading of equipment for armies, navies and air forces. Distributed by name to Government and military personnel in 126 countries and manufacturers with defense connections worldwide.

FR
### DEFENSE. (19??)-. French. qt. Free. Assn des
Auditeurs, 21 Place Joffre, 75700 Paris France. **Tel** 011 33 1 45553011.

US
### DEFENSE ACQUISITION CIRCULAR.
**Main/Corp** United States. Dept. of Defense. Began with No. 76-15, (June 1978)-. Government Publication. English. mo. Superintendent of Documents, US Government Printing Office, Washington DC 20402. **Tel** (202)275-3328, FAX (202)786-2377. **Continues** *Defense Procurement Circular, 0364-6734.*

●US/1072-2386
### DEFENSE ACQUISITION REPORT. [Def.
acquis. rep.]. No. 1 (Aug. 1, 1993)-. Periodical. English. sm. $190.00 US; $200.00 other. Callahan Publications, PO Box 1173, McLean VA 22101. **Tel** (703)356-1925, FAX (703)356-9614. **ED** Vincent F. Callahan. **DD** 355. **Bk Rev**, (Qty: 6). *Formed by the union of* Military Research Letter, 0026-413X *and* Missile/Ordnance Letter.
**Desc:** Covers contracting opportunities and legislative initiatives for military procurement, acquisition, and research, development, test and evaluation.

FR
### DEFENSE ACTIVE. Ceased. (19??)-(19??).
French. mo. Defense Active, 161 rue du President Roosevelt, 78100 St Germain Laye France. **ED** Etichle Copel.
**Desc:** Independent view on geopolitical and defense matters.

UK/0743-0175
### DEFENSE ANALYSIS. Vol. 1, No. 1 (March
1985)-. Periodical. English. Three times a year. £85.50 Europe and other; $158.00 North and South America (institution). Brasseys UK Ltd., 33 John Street, London WC1N 2AT England. **Tel** 011 44 71 753 7777, FAX 011

44 71 753 7794. **(Subscription address:** Brasseys UK Ltd., Distribution Center, Blackhorse Road, Letchworth SG6 1HN England.) **ED** Martin Edmonds. **LC** UA11; .D384. **DD** 355/.03/05. **[CCC].** available on microfilm and microfiche from University Microfilms International (UMI).
**Desc:** Provides a forum for interdisciplinary studies and for the publication of articles concerned with defense policy issues, on issues that bear defense policy written from the perspective of different disciplines.
**Ind/Abst** Int. Polit. Sci. Abstr.

US
**DEFENSE & AEROSPACE AGENCIES BRIEFING.** See Aeronautics, Astronautics.

US
**DEFENSE & AEROSPACE COMPANIES.** (19??)-. English. Twelve times a year. $1390.00. Forecast International / DMS Inc., 22 Commerce Road, Newtown CT 06470. **Tel** (203)426-0800, FAX (203)426-1964, telex 467615. available on CD-ROM ($1595.00).

US
**DEFENSE & AEROSPACE COMPANIES BRIEFING.** See Aeronautics, Astronautics.

US/1056-747X
**DEFENSE & AEROSPACE ELECTRONICS.** See Engineering-Electricity, Electrical Engineering, Electronics.

FR
**DEFENSE & ARMEMENT HERACLES.** ***Ceased.*** **VFOAT** Defense et Armement; International Defense & Armement; Defense & Armement Heracles International. (June 1986)-(July 1992). Periodical. French (French). bm. Editions Lariviere Naryse Menn, 15 17 Quai de l Oise Sec. Abonn., 75166 Paris Cedex 19 France. **Tel** 011 33 1 40342207, FAX 33 1 40358441, telex 211678. **LC** UF500; .D45. **DD** 355.8/2/05. ***Formed by the union of*** *Heracles.*

US/0277-4933
**DEFENSE & FOREIGN AFFAIRS.** [Def. foreign aff.]. **VFOAT** Defense and Foreign Affairs. Vol. 7, No. 10 (1979)-. Periodical. English. mo (10 issues). $120.00 (1 year), $220.00 (2 year). International Media Corp Ltd, Empire House, 175 Piccadilly, Suite 1A, London W1V 9DB England. **Tel** 011 44 71 4912044. **LC** UA10; .D428. **DD** 355/.03/05. ***Continues*** *Defense & Foreign Affairs Digest, 0740-2724.*
**Ind/Abst** Air Univ. Libr. Index Mil. Period.; Curr. Mil. Pol. Lit.; NEXIS (Jan. 1981-).

US/0160-5836
**DEFENSE & FOREIGN AFFAIRS HANDBOOK.** [Def. for. aff. handb.]. **VAT** Defense and Foreign Affairs Handbook. (1976/1977)-. English. an. $235.00 US & EEC Countries; $270.00 other. International Media Corp Ltd, Empire House, 175 Piccadilly, Suite 1A, London W1V 9DB England. **Tel** 011 44 71 4912044. **ED** Gregory R. Copley. **LC** UA10; .D43. **DD** 355.03/3004/7. **Ad Acc.**
**Desc:** An encyclopedia of every country and territory with complete political and defense structures, governmental and military organization, defense industries, and defense capabilities, battle order, economic data, etc.

US/0884-4054
**DEFENSE & FOREIGN AFFAIRS WEEKLY.** ***Ceased.*** [Def. foreign aff. wkly.]. **VFOAT** Defense and Foreign Affairs Weekly. Vol. 8, No. 35 (Sept. 6-12, 1982)-?. Periodical. English. wk. International Media Corp, 110 North Royal Street/Suite 307, Alexandria VA 22314. **Tel** (703)684-8455, FAX (703)684-2207. **ED** Gregory R Copley. **DD** 355. **Ad Acc. Circ:** 1,050. ***Continues*** *Strategy Week, 0277-4011.*
**Ind/Abst** NEXIS (Sept. 1982-).

US/0893-8199
**DEFENSE & INDUSTRY WORLD REPORT.** [Def. ind. world rep.]. **VFOAT** Defense and Industry World Report. Issue No. 1045 (May 4, 1987)-. Periodical. English. wk. $360.00. Government Business Worldwide Reports, PO Box 5997, Washington DC 20016. **Tel** (202)244-7050, FAX (202)244-5410. **DD** 355. ***Continues in part*** *Defense & Economy World Report.*

FR/1155-3480
**DEFENSE & TECHNOLOGIE INTERNATIONAL PARIS.** (DEFENSE & TECHNOLOGIE INTERNATIONAL.). **VFOAT** Defense et Technologie International (Paris). (1990)-. Periodical. French (English). qt. 195.00F. Siege Social / Wagram, 58 Avenue de Wagram, 75017 Paris France. **Tel** 33-1-45 30 22 28, FAX 33-1-45 30 22 69. **UDC** 356. **Ad Acc.**

US/0737-1217
**DEFENSE (ARLINGTON, VA.).** (DEFENSE.). [Defense]. **Added/Corp** United States. American Forces Information Service. (Jan. 1980)-. Government Publication. English. bm. $9.50 US; $11.90 other. Superintendent of Documents, US Government Printing Office, Washington DC 20402. **Tel** (202)275-3328, FAX (202)786-2377. **LC** UA23.A1; C64. **DD** 355/.005. available on microfilm and microfiche from University Microfilms International (UMI). ***Continues*** *Command Policy, 0270-9015.*
**Desc:** Provides official and professional information on Defense policies, programs, and interests for commanders and key personell to promote better understanding and teamwork within the Department of Defense.
**Ind/Abst** Air Univ. Libr. Index Mil. Period.

US/0273-2491
**DEFENSE (BOCA RATON).** (DEFENSE.). V. 1, Article 1-. Periodical. English. an. Social Issues Resources Series Inc, PO Box 2348, Boca Raton FL 33427. **Tel** (800)327-0513, (407)994-0079. **ED** Elecor C Goldstein. **LC** UA10; .D424. **DD** 355/.03.
**Desc:** Interdisciplinary resource material consisting of reprinted articles from popular and professional journals, newspapers, magazines and government documents.

US/0364-9008
**DEFENSE BUSINESS.** Began with issue for Jan. 10, 1977. English. wk. $240.00. Government Business Worldwide Reports, PO Box 5997, Washington DC 20016. **Tel** (202)244-7050, FAX (202)244-5410. **LC** UF530; .I57. ***Continues*** *International Defense Business, 0360-8417.*

US
**DEFENSE BUSINESS BRIEFING.** English. wk. $595.00. Teal Group, 3900 University Drive, Suite 220, Fairfax VA 22030. **Tel** (703)385-1992.

US/1052-0635
**DEFENSE CLEANUP.** See Environmental Issues-Pollution and Waste Management.

US/0741-3602
**DEFENSE COMMUNICATION STUDY, THE.** [Def. commun. study]. **Added/Corp** Corporate Communication Studies, Inc. (1984/85)-. English. an. Corporate Communication Studies Inc., PO Box 9538, Daytona Beach FL 32020. **LC** U1; .D32. **DD** 355/.005.

US
**DEFENSE CONTRACT AUDIT MANUAL.** **Main/Corp** United States. Dept. of Defense. July 1977-. Government Publication. English. sa. $27.00 US; $33.75 other. Superintendent of Documents, US Government Printing Office, Washington DC 20402. **Tel** (202)275-3328, FAX (202)786-2377.
**Desc:** Prescribes auditing policies and procedures and furnishes guidance in auditing techniques for personnel engaged in the performance of the Defense Contract Audit Agency mission.

●US/1062-0613
**DEFENSE CONTRACT AWARDS.** (DEFENSE CONTRACT AWARDS: DCA.). **VFOAT** DCA. (1992)-. Periodical. English. sm. $510.00. Dr. Murray Felsher, PO Box 47036, Pentagon Station, Washington DC 20050-7036.

US
**DEFENSE CONTRACTING AGENCY AUDIT MANUAL / DISKETTE.** English. Four times a year (Jan., Apr., July, Oct.). $99.00. EZ - Far Systems, 360 Wire Road, York PA 17402. **Tel** 1-800-388-1415, FAX (717)975-2813. **ED** TSA Inc. 2 Market Plaza Way Mechanicsburg, PA 17055 (717)691-5691. **Ad Acc.** ctrl circ. available on CD-ROM.

●US/1065-8653
**DEFENSE CONVERSION.** [Def. convers.]. **Added/Corp** Pasha Publications (Firm). (1992)-. Periodical. English. bw (25 issues). $397.00 US; $412.00 other. Pasha Publications Inc., 1616 North Fort Myer Drive, Suite 1000, Arlington VA 22209. **Tel** (800)424-2908, (703)528-1244, FAX (703)528-3742, (703)528-1253. **DD** 355.

US/0889-0404
**DEFENSE DAILY.** [Def. dly.]. (19??)-. Periodical. English. da (five times a week). $1495.00 US; $1640.00 other. Phillips Business Information, Inc., 1201 Seven Locks Road, Potomac MD 20854. **Tel** (301)424-3338, (800)777-5006, FAX (301)309-3847. **LC** UA23; .D4165. **DD** 355.6/22/0973. **[CCC].** available on an online database (files 16,80,636,648/Full-Text) from DIALOG. ***Absorbed*** *Aerospace Financial News.*
**Ind/Abst** PROMT [Full Txt.]; PTS Newsl. Database [Full Txt.]; Trade Ind. ASAP [Full Txt.]; Trade Ind. Index [Full Txt.].

US/0278-3479
**DEFENSE ELECTRONICS.** See Engineering-Electricity, Electrical Engineering, Electronics.

US
**DEFENSE INTEGRATED DATA SYSTEMS DIDS PROCEDURES MANUAL. VOL. 4, ITEM IDENTIFICATION.** **VFOAT** DIDS Procedures Manual. Vol. 4, Item Identification; D.I.D.S. Procedures Manual. Vol. 4, Item Identification; Item Identification. English. Defense Logistics Agency / Battle Creek, Defense Logistics Services Center, Federal Center, 74 North Washington, Battle Creek MI 49017-3084.

●US/1061-6845
**DEFENSE INTELLIGENCE JOURNAL.** [Def. intell. j.]. **Added/Corp** Defense Intelligence College Foundation. Vol. 1, No. 1 (Spring 1992)-. Periodical. English. Twice a year (May, Nov.). $25.00 (individuals); $45.00 (institutions). Defense Intelligence College Foundation, 1750 30th Street, Suite 441, Boulder CO 80301. **Tel** (303)444-6684. **LC** UB251.U5; D44. **DD** 355.3/432/05.

●UK
**DEFENSE / INTERNATIONAL DEFENSE REVIEW.** **Added/Corp** Defense and Aerospace Publishing Services. **VFOAT** International Defense Review. Defense. (1992)-. Periodical. English. ir. Jane's Information Group, Sentinel House, 163 Brighton Road, Coulsdon Surrey CR3 2NX England. **Tel** 011 44 81 763 1030, FAX 011 44 81 763 1006. **LC** UG1; .I53. **DD** 338.4/76233/05.

US
**DEFENSE ISSUES.** **Added/Corp** United States. American Forces Information Service. (198?)-. English. American Forces Information Service, 601 North Fairfax Street/#310, Alexandria VA 22314-2007.
**Ind/Abst** Air Univ. Libr. Index Mil. Period. (199?-).

UK/0261-233X
**DEFENSE LATIN AMERICA.** [Def. Latin Am.]. Periodical. English. bm. Granville House, St Peter Street, Winchester England. **Tel** 0628-30313. **ED** Gregor Ferguson. **LC** UF535.L29; D43. **DD** 355.8/2/098. **Bk Rev. Ad Acc.**
**Desc:** Defense equipment, tactics and strategy, political-military affairs, defense economics, news and information.

BE
**DEFENSE MAGAZINE.** Periodical. French. $3.00. Interconair Eurafrique SA, 96 Avenue de Tervueren, 1040 Bruxelles Belgium. **LC** U2; .D43. **DD** 355/.005. ***Continues*** *Defense.*

US/1044-3975
**DEFENSE MARKETING INTERNATIONAL.** ***Title Change.*** [Def. mark. int.]. (July 1989)-(July 1994). Periodical. English. bw (25 issues). Phillips Business Information, Inc., 1201 Seven Locks Road, Potomac MD 20854. **Tel** (301)424-3338, (800)777-5006, FAX (301)309-3847. **DD** 355. **[CCC].** available on an online database (file 636/Full-Text) from DIALOG. ***Absorbed*** *Pac-Rim Defense Marketing.* ***Merged into*** *Technology Transfer Week.*
**Ind/Abst** PTS Newsl. Database [Full Txt.].

US/0893-0619
**DEFENSE MEDIA REVIEW.** [Def. media rev.]. Vol. 1, No. 1 (April 13, 1987)-. Periodical. English. Twelve times a year. $48.00. Center for Defense Journalism, 67 Bay State Road, Boston MA 02215. **Tel** (617)353-3488, FAX (617)353-8707. **ED** Heinz A. J. Kern. **DD** 355. **Bk Rev.**
**Desc:** An analytical survey of key issues in the national security field with a special focus on how the media cover those issues.

US/0195-6450
**DEFENSE MONITOR, THE.** **Added/Corp** Center for Defense Information (Washington, D.C.). Vol. 1 (May 1972)-. Periodical. English. ir. $35.00. Center Defense Information, 1500 Massachusetts Avenue NW, Washington DC 20005. **Tel** (202)862-0700, telex 904059 WSH (CDI). **LC** UA23.A1; D42. **DD** 355.03/073/3. **Bk Rev. Circ:** 90,000 (ctrl). available on microfiche.
**Desc:** Each issue focuses on an important aspect of the United States military, with emphasis on nuclear programs and military spending.
**Ind/Abst** Air Univ. Libr. Index Mil. Period.; Hum. Rights Intern. Rep.; Peace Res. Abstr. J. (1974).

FR/0336-1489
**DEFENSE NATIONALE.** [Def. nat.]. (Jan. 1973)-. Periodical. French. mo (except Aug./Sept. combined). 410.00F France; 620.00F other. Defense Nationale, 1 Place Joffre, 75700 Paris France. **Tel** 011 33 1 45553823, FAX 011 33 1 45553189. **LC** D410; .R45. Index available. cum. index. **Bk Rev. Ad Acc. Circ:** 9,000. ***Continues*** *Revue de Defense Nationale, 0035-1075.*
**Desc:** A review for studies of world military, technological, economical and political problems.
**Ind/Abst** Am. Hist. Life (1955-56,1959-)(1973-); Curr. Mil. Pol. Lit.; Energy Res. Abstr. (Aug. 1976-); Int. Polit. Sci. Abstr.; PAIS Int. Print (1991-).

US/0884-139X
**DEFENSE NEWS (SPRINGFIELD, VA.).** (DEFENSE NEWS.). [Def. news]. Vol. 1, No. 1 (Jan. 20, 1986)-. Periodical. English. wk. $89.00 US; $130.00 Canada; $155.00 other. Army Times Publishing Company, 6883 Commercial Drive, Springfield VA 22159. **Tel** (800)368-5718, (703)750-8099. **ED** Sharon Denny. **DD** 355. **[CCC].** Index available. cum. index. **Bk Rev. Ad Acc. Pr Rev. Circ:** 35,000 (ctrl). available on microfilm and microfiche from University Microfilms International (UMI).
**Desc:** A weekly tabloid that covers the politics and

# Military and Defense

business of the defense industry.
**Ind/Abst** F&S Index Plus Text, Int. [Select. Cov.]; Infomat Int. Bus.; PROMT; Trade Ind. Index.

US/1064-7147
## DEFENSE ORGANIZATION SERVICE.
[Defense organ. serv.]. (Oct. 1991)-. English. ir (updated every 6 weeks). $1,010.00. Carroll Publishing Company, 1058 Thomas Jefferson Street Northwest, Washington DC 20007-3832. **Tel** (202)333-8620, FAX (202)337-7020. **LC** UA23.3; .D44. **DD** 353.6/025. *Continues in part* Federal Organization Service, 0741-5109.
**Desc:** Provides more than 180 uniform fold-out organization charts that clearly spell out the complex structure of the military side of government.

US
## DEFENSE RDT & E/O & M BUDGETS.
**VFOAT** Defense RDT and E/O and M Budgets. **VAT** Defense Research, Development, Test and Evaluation, Operations and Maintenance Budgets. English. an. Defense Marketing Services / Connecticut, 100 Northfield Street, POB 4585, Greenwich CT 06830. **LC** U393.5; .D43A. *Continues* Defense RDT&E Budget, 0149-9947.

II/0011-748X
## DEFENSE SCIENCE JOURNAL. [Def. sci. j.].
**Added/Corp** India. Ministry of Defence. Research and Development Organisation. Defence Science Laboratory (India) Defence Scientific and Documentation Centre (India). (1951)-. English. Four times a year. Director of Research and Development Organisation, Defence Scientific Information and Documentation Centre (DESIDOC), Metcalfe House, New Delhi-110054 India. **Tel** 237362, FAX 031-2919151, telex 031-78030. **(Subscription address:** Prints India, 11 Darya Ganj, New Delhi 110002 India.**) ED** S. S. Murthy. **LC** U395.I5; D4. **DD** 600. **CODEN** DSJOAA. Index available. **Pr Rev. Circ:** 500. Documents available from Article Express International, Ask*IEEE, CASDDS.
**Desc:** Multi-disciplinary journal publishes research and review papers on electronics, food science, physics, chemistry, mathematics, computer science, marine sciences, physiology and papers of applied sciences with an orientation toward defense needs.
**Ind/Abst** Bioeng. Abstr.; Ceram. Abstr.; Chem. Abstr.; Comput. Inf. Syst. Abstr. J. [Full Cov.]; Curr. Mil. Pol. Lit.; Ei Page One; Eng. Index Annu.; Environ. Eng. Abstr.; INSPEC (1968-); Int. Aerosp. Abstr.; Mater. Sci. Eng. Abstr.; Math. Rev.; Mech. Eng. Abstr.; Pollut. Abstr. Indexes; Solid State Supercond. Abstr.; Stat. Theory Method Abstr. (1959-1963); Zentralbl. Math. Ihre Grenzgeb.

US
## DEFENSE STANDARDIZATION AND SPECIFICATION PROGRAM, POLICIES, PROCEDURES, AND INSTRUCTIONS.
**Main/Corp** United States. Office of the Under Secretary of Defense for Research and Engineering. **VFOAT** Defense Standardization Manual. (1978)-. English. ir. $16.00. US Department of Defense, The Pentagon, Washington DC 20301. **Tel** (703)545-6700. *Supersedes* Standardization, Policies, Procedures and Instructions.

US/0099-166X
## DEFENSE SURVEY & DIRECTORY. *Title Change.* [Def. surv. dir.]. **VFOAT** Defense Survey and Directory. Sept. (1975)-?. Directory. English. mo. Government Business Worldwide Reports, PO Box 5997, Washington DC 20016. **Tel** (202)244-7050, FAX (202)244-5410. **LC** UA10; .D433. **DD** 355/.005. *Superseded by* Armament & Defense Survey, 0195-8232.

US/1048-4612
## DEFENSE TECHNOLOGY BUSINESS.
*Title Change.* [Def. technol. bus.]. Vol. 2, No. 4 (Feb. 20, 1990)-(199?). Periodical. English. bw. Pasha Publications Inc., 1616 North Fort Myer Drive, Suite 1000, Arlington VA 22209. **Tel** (800)424-2908, (703)528-1244, FAX (703)528-3742, (703)528-1253. **DD** 338. available on an online database (file 636/Full-Text) from DIALOG.
*Continues* Defense Technology News, 1047-353X; *Absorbed* Aerospace Electronics Business; Evans and Novak Defense Letter. *Merged into* Defense & Aerospace Electronics.
**Ind/Abst** PTS Newsl. Database [Full Txt.]; Trade Ind. Index.

US/0011-7625
## DEFENSE TRANSPORTATION JOURNAL. [Def. transp. j.]. Vol. 23 No. 5 (Sept./Oct. 1967)-. Periodical. English. bm. $35.00 US; $45.00 for. National Defense Transportation Association, 50 South Pickett Street/#220, Alexandria VA 22304. **Tel** (703)751-5011, FAX (703)823-8761. **ED** Denny Edwards. **LC** U1; .A88. **Bk Rev,** (Qty: 15-20). **Ad Acc, Adv Mgr:** Ms. Scofield, **Tel** (804) 979-4913. **Circ:** 8,000 (ctrl). available on microfilm and microfiche from University Microfilms International (UMI). *Continues* National Defense Transportation Journal, 0193-8851.
**Desc:** Aims to advance knowledge and science in defense transportation (partnership between the commercial transportation industry and the government transporter).
**Ind/Abst** Air Univ. Libr. Index Mil. Period.

US/0273-3188
## DEFENSE WEEK. [Def. week]. (1980)-. Periodical. English. wk (50 issues). $1099.00. King Publishing Group, 627 National Press Building, Washington DC 20045. **Tel** (202)638-4260, FAX (202)662-9744. **ED** Paul Bedard. [**CCC**]. **Bk Rev.** available on an online database (file 636/Full-Text) from DIALOG.
**Desc:** Covering defense policy and strategic affairs, domestic and international. Includes coverage of industry, Congress, DOD, White House, and weapons development and acquisition.
**Ind/Abst** PROMT [Full Txt.]; PTS Newsl. Database [Full Txt.].

BL
## DEFESA NACIONAL, A. Vol. 1 No. 1 (1913)-.
Periodical. Portuguese. Four times a year. $50.00. Defesa Nacional, Praca Duque de Caixas 25, Rio de Janeiro 20455 Brazil. **Tel** 011 55 21 2534628. **LC** U4; .D454.

GR
## DELTION. Main/Corp Greece. Stratos. Geographike Hyperesia. No. 1 (1935)-. Periodical. Greek, Modern. sa. **LC** UG470.

US/1049-8672
## DEPARTMENT OF DEFENSE FACT BOOK. (DEPARTMENT OF DEFENSE ... FACT BOOK.). [Dept. Def. fact book]. **Added/Corp** U.S. Organization Chart Service. **VFOAT** Department of Defense Fact Book. (19??)-. English. an. $185.00. US Organization Chart Service, PO Box 1335, La Jolla CA 92038. **Tel** (619)454-3711, FAX (619)443-3873. **LC** UA23.6; .D46. **DD** 353.6/05.

US
## DEPARTMENT OF DEFENSE SUPPLEMENT / DISKETTE. English. Four times a year (Jan., Apr., July, Oct.). $99.00. Weiser Signal American, PO Box 709, Weiser ID 83672. **Tel** (208)549-1717, FAX (208)549-1718. **ED** TSA Inc. 2 Market Plaza Way Mechanicsburg, PA 17055 (717)691-5691. **Ad Acc.** ctrl circ.

US/0092-7880
## DEPARTMENT OF THE ARMY HISTORICAL SUMMARY (WASHINGTON). (DEPARTMENT OF THE ARMY HISTORICAL SUMMARY.). **Main/Corp** Center of Military History. **Added/Corp** United States. Dept. of the Army. Historical Summary. **VFOAT** Historical Summary. (1968/1969)-. English. an. US Department of Defense Department of the Army, The Pentagon, SAPA-CR, Room 3E718, Washington DC 20310. **Tel** (703)695-0363, FAX (703)693-5737. **LC** UA23.A1; V47b. **DD** 353.6/2. *Continues in part* United States. Dept. of Defense. Annual Report for Fiscal Year ... Including the Reports of the Secretary of Defense, Secretary of the Army, Secretary of the Navy, Secretary of the Air Force.

US
## DEPARTMENT OF THE NAVY SUPPLEMENT / DISKETTE. See Naval Science, Navigation.

US
## DEPARTMENT OF VETERANS AFFAIRS PUBLICATIONS INDEX.
**Main/Corp** United States. Dept. of Veterans Affairs. Publications Service. **VFOAT** Index to Department of Veterans Affairs Publications. March 1989-. English. an. Department of Veterans Affairs, Office of Administration, Publications Service, 810 Vermont Avenue Northwest, Washington DC 20420. **Tel** (202)535-8300, FAX (202)233-2807. **LC** Z1223; .V42A; UB357. *Continues* Veterans Administration Publications Index, 8756-0151.

●US/1064-2153
## DEPOT MILITAIRE. (DEPOT MILITAIRE : THE EQUIPMENT EXCHANGE NEWSLETTER FOR MILITARY REENACTORS.). (1992)-. Newsletter. English. qt. $18.00. Cheshire Press, PO Box 1032, Lynnfield MA 01940-3032.

PO
## DESENVOLVIMENTO DO ORCAMENTO DA DESPESA FIXADA PARA O ANO ECONOMICO. Main/Corp Portugal. Ministerio do Exercito. Portuguese. Imprensa Nacional, Av Antonie Jose de al Eida, 1078 Lisbon Codex Portugal. **LC** UA762; .P67A. **DD** 354/.469/066.

UK/0046-0079
## DESPATCH. Added/Corp New South Wales Military Historical Society. (19??)-. Periodical. English. Six times a year. 30.00Aus$. New South Wales Military Historical Society Inc., 397 Willarong Road, Caringbah NSW 2229 Australia. **Tel** 011 61 2 5245095. **ED** Ralph Sutton (editor's address: 67 Beach Street, Coogee, NSW 2034 Australia; phone: 011 61 2 6652869; FAX: 011 61 2 6641207). **Ad Acc.**

US
## DETAILED LISTING OF REAL PROPERTY OWNED BY THE UNITED STATES AND USED BY THE DEPARTMENT OF DEFENSE FOR MILITARY FUNCTIONS THROUGHOUT THE WORLD AS OF SEPTEMBER 30 ... .
English. an. **LC** UC403; .D47. **DD** 355.7/025/73.

IO
## DHARMASENA. Added/Corp Indonesia.
Departemen Pertahanan-Keamanan. (Dec. 1973)-. Periodical. Indonesian. mo. Pusat Penerangan Hankam, Jln Merdeka Barat 13 - 14, Jakarta Indonesia. **LC** UA853.I5; D45.

US/0734-1008
## DICTIONARY OF THE DEFENSE INDUSTRY. [Dict. def. ind.]. **Added/Corp** U.S. Organization Chart Service. **VFOAT** Directory of Aerospace and Military and Technology Abbreviations and Definitions. (1981)-. English (Russian). an. $225.00. US Organization Chart Service, PO Box 1335, La Jolla CA 92038. **Tel** (619)454-3711, FAX (619)443-3873. **LC** U26; .D5. **DD** 355/.00148. *Continues* Directory of Aerospace and Military and Technology Abbreviations.
**Desc:** Exhaustive listing of virtually every abbreviation and definition used within the US and world defense, military, and technology industry, updated.

SA/0250-0280
## DIENSPLIG. VFOAT National Service. Periodical.
Afrikaans (English). an. Gordon Publishing, Postbus 78444, Sandton 2146 South Africa. **LC** UB345.S7; D53. **DD** 355.2/2363/0968.

IT/1120-1657
## DIFESA OGGI. [Dif. oggi]. **VFOAT** D.O. Difesa Oggi. (1977)-. Periodical. Italian (summaries and/or abstracts in English). Nine times a year. $108.00. Publi & Consult Spa, Via Tagliamento 29 2, 00198 Rome Italy. **Tel** 011 39 6 8546754. **UDC** 355.

US/0734-1008
## DIRECTIONARY OF THE DEFENSE INDUSTRY INCLUDING NATO AND WARSAW PACT COUNTRIES. [Dict. def. ind.]. **Added/Corp** U.S. Organization Chart Service. **VFOAT** Directory of Aerospace and Military and Technology Abbreviations and Definitions. English. US Organization Chart Service, PO Box 1335, La Jolla CA 92038. **Tel** (619)454-3711, FAX (619)443-3873. **LC** U26; .D52. *Continues* Dictionary of the Defense Industry, 0734-1008.

US
## DIRECTORY OF DEFENSE ELECTRONIC PRODUCTS AND SERVICES : UNITED STATES SUPPLIERS, THE. 1975-. Directory. English. an. $20.00. Information Clearing House Inc, 500 Fifth Avenue, New York NY 10036. **Tel** (212)354-2424. **LC** UG485; .D57. **DD** 623/.043/02573.

US
## DIRECTORY OF DEPARTMENT OF VETERANS AFFAIRS FACILITIES.
**Main/Corp** United States. Dept. of Veterans Affairs. **Added/Corp** United States. Dept. of Veterans Affairs. Office of the Assistant Secretary for Policy and Planning. **VFOAT** Veterans Affairs Facilities. (Aug 1991)-. Directory. English. be. Department of Veterans Affairs, Office of Administration, Publications Service, 810 Vermont Avenue Northwest, Washington DC 20420. **Tel** (202)535-8300, FAX (202)233-2807. **LC** UB369; .D57. *Continues* Directory of Veterans Administration Facilities, 0741-6032.

US/1055-579X
## DIRECTORY OF NORTH AMERICAN MILITARY AVIATION COMMUNICATIONS, VHF/UHF. CENTRAL. See Aeronautics, Astronautics.

US/1055-582X
## DIRECTORY OF NORTH AMERICAN MILITARY AVIATION COMMUNICATIONS, VHF/UHF. NORTHEASTERN. See Aeronautics, Astronautics.

US/1055-5803
## DIRECTORY OF NORTH AMERICAN MILITARY AVIATION COMMUNICATIONS, VHF/UHF. SOUTHEASTERN. See Aeronautics, Astronautics.

US/1055-5811
## DIRECTORY OF NORTH AMERICAN MILITARY AVIATION COMMUNICATIONS, VHF/UHF. WESTERN. See Aeronautics, Astronautics.

# Military and Defense

US/0096-9990
**DIRECTORY OF U.S.S.R. MINISTRY OF DEFENSE AND ARMED FORCES OFFICIALS.** (DIRECTORY OF USSR MINISTRY OF DEFENSE AND ARMED FORCES OFFICIALS / NATIONAL FOREIGN ASSESSMENT CENTER.). Directory. English. Documents Expediting Project, Exchange and Gift Division, Library of Congress, Washington DC 20540. **Tel** (202)707-9527. **LC** UA770; .D55. **DD** 355.3/0947. available on microfiche (Vols. for (April 1980-) distributed to depository libraries).

NE
**DISARMAMENT CAMPAIGNS.** (1980?)-. Periodical. English. mo. Peace Press International, 22 rue de Toulouse, 1040 Brussels Belgium. **Tel** 011 32 2 2301621.

US
**DISARMAMENT. STUDY SERIES.** **Added/Corp** United Nations Centre for Disarmament. **VFOAT** Study Series. Vol. 1 (1981)-. Monographic series. English. ir. Price varies per volume. United Nations Publications, 2 United Nations Plaza, Room DC2 0853, Department 007C, New York NY 10017. **Tel** (212)963-8303, (800)253-9646. **LC** UNC.

US/0259-3629
**DISARMAMENT TIMES.** [Disarm. times]. **Added/Corp** NGO Committee on Disarmament. (Mar. 1978)-. Periodical. English. Six times a year. $15.00 North America; $20.00 other. Disarmament Times, 777 United Nations Plaza, New York NY 10017. **Tel** (212)687-5340. **LC** JX1974; .D553. **DD** 327.1/74/05.

UK
**DISPATCH (GLASGOW, SCOTLAND).** (DISPATCH.). **Added/Corp** Scottish Military Collectors Society. (19??)-. Periodical. English. Three times a year. £9.00 UK; £12.20 others. Scottish Military Historical Society, 17/14 St. Andrews Crescent Poll, Glasgow G41 5SH Scotland. **Tel** 011 44 41 429 6440. **LC** U799; .D57. **DD** 355.8/2/075. **Circ:** 350.
**Desc:** Historical articles and information of the Scottish military.

AE/0419-4799
**DJEICH : REVUE DE L'ARMEE NATIONALE POPULAIRE, EL. Added/Corp** Algeria. Jaysh al-Watani al-Shabi. Muhafazah al-Siyasiyah. IdĀarah al-Markaziyah. **VFOAT** Revue de l'Armee Nationale Populaire. (1963)-. French. mo. $11.75. El Djeich, 3 Chemin de Gascogne, Algiers Algeria.

US/8756-5447
**DM & S ADP PLAN. See** Medical Science and Technology.

US/0095-0742
**DMAAC TECHNICAL TRANSLATIONS LIST. Main/Corp** Defense Mapping Agency. Aerospace Center. Technical Translation Branch. English. Defense Mapping Agency / St Louis, Aerospace Center, St Louis Air Force Station, St Louis MO 63118. **LC** Z6000; .D43A. **DD** 016.526.

US/1047-8760
**DMS WORLD MISSILES FORECAST.** [DMS world missiles forecast]. **Added/Corp** Defense Marketing Services, Inc. Jane's Information Group. **VFOAT** World Missiles Forecast. **VAT** Defense Marketing Services World Missiles Forecast. English. DMS Inc, 100 Northfield Street, PO Box 4585, Greenwich CT 06830. **Tel** (203)661-7800. **LC** UG1310; .W65. **DD** 623. *Continues World Missiles Forecast, 1040-2918.*

US/0082-8785
**DOCUMENTS ON DISARMAMENT.** [Doc. disarm.]. **Added/Corp** United States. Arms Control and Disarmament Agency. United States. Dept. of State. Historical Office. (1959)-. Government Publication. English. an. $40.00. Superintendent of Documents, US Government Printing Office, Washington DC 20402. **Tel** (202)275-3328, **FAX** (202)786-2377. **(Subscription address:** US Government Bookstore / O'Neil Building, 2023 3rd Avenue North, Birmingham AL 35203.)

US/0095-4349
**DOD DIRECTORY OF CONTRACT ADMINISTRATION SERVICES COMPONENTS. VFOAT** D.O.D. Directory of Contract Administration Services Components. **VAT** Department of Defense Directory of Contract Administration Services Components. Directory. English. sa. Defense Logistics Agency / Alexandria, Attn DLA-XPD, Cameron Station, Alexandria VA 22314. **LC** UC263; .D63. **DD** 355.6/211/02573.

US
**DOD STATISTICAL REPORT ON THE MILITARY RETIREMENT SYSTEM / OFFICE OF ACTUARY, DEFENSE MANPOWER DATA CENTER. See** Military and Defense-Abstracting, Bibliographies and Statistics.

US/0192-1150
**DOMESTIC BASE FACTORS REPORT. Main/Corp** United States. Office of the Assistant Secretary of Defense (Manpower, Reserve Affairs, and Logistics). **VFOAT** Report on Domestic Base Factors. English. an. Office of the Assistant Secretary of Defense, Manpower Reserve Affairs & Logistics, Washington DC 20037. **LC** UA26; .A37A. **DD** 355.7/0973.

US/0420-0942
**DRAFT FACTS FOR GRADUATES AND GRADUATE STUDENTS. Main/Corp** Scientific Manpower Commission. English. $1.00. Scientific Manpower Commission. **LC** UB343; .S36A. **DD** 355.2/23/0973.

US/0883-0606
**DRIS CATALOG OF SUPPORT SERVICES.** [DRIS cat. support serv.]. **Added/Corp** Defense Logistics Services Center (U.S.). **VFOAT** Catalog of Support Services. **VAT** Defense Retail Interservice Support Catalog of Support Services. (19??)-. Catalog. English. an. Defense Logistics Agency / Battle Creek, Defense Logistics Services Center, Federal Center, 74 North Washington, Battle Creek MI 49017-3084. **LC** UC263; .D74. **DD** 355.6/21/0973.

●US
**EAGLE : INFORMATION FOR CALIFORNIA VETERANS FROM THE CALIFORNIA EMPLOYMENT DEVELOPMENT DEPARTMENT, THE. Added/Corp** California. Employment Development Dept. Vol. 1, No. 1 (Apr. 1992)-. English. qt. **LC** UB358.C2; E24.

JA
**EAWARUDO. VFOAT** Air World. (19??)-. Periodical. Japanese. mo. $205.00. Air World Inc, Nichijukin Roppongi Bldg 8F, 4-12-8 Roppongi Minatoku, Tokyo 106 Japan. **Tel** 03(479)3665, **FAX** J/03(478)0269, telex 02427589SKKCO J. **(Subscription address:** Maruzen Company Ltd., PO Box 5050, Import & Export Department, Tokyo 100 31 Japan.) **ED** Motohiko Aso. **LC** UG622; .E23. Index available. **Bk Rev. Ad Acc. Circ:** 55,000 (ctrl).

US/0147-5339
**EEO YEARBOOK. VAT** Equal Employment Opportunity Yearbook. English. an. US Department of Defense / Alexandria, Cameron Station, Alexandria VA 22304. **LC** UC263; .E15.

SP
**EJERCITO.** Ejercito de Tierra, Cuartel General del Ejercito de Tierra, Prim 6, 28004 Madrid Spain.

EC
**EJERCITO, EL. Added/Corp** Ecuador. Ejercito. Estado Mayor General. No. 1 (Oct. 1971)-. Periodical. Spanish. mo. cum. index.
**Ind/Abst** Am. Hist. Life (1964).

SP/0013-2918
**EJERCITO MADRID.** (REVISTA EJERCITO.). [Ejercito Madr.]. (1940)-. Periodical. Spanish. mo (except Aug.). 2678.00ptas Spain; 5974.00ptas other. Ministerio de Defensa, C Paseo de la Castellana 109, 28071 Madrid Spain. **Tel** 011 34 1 5350477, **FAX** 011 34 1 5973540. **UDC** 355.

US/0884-4828
**ELECTRONIC WARFARE DIGEST.** (ELECTRONIC WARFARE DIGEST : THE AUTHORITATIVE WASHINGTON REPORT FOR THE DEFENSE ELECTRONICS INDUSTRY.). [Electron. warf. dig.]. **VFOAT** Defense Electronics Industry. (1978)-. Periodical. English. mo. $195.00 (one year), $350.00 (two year), $500.00. Washington Crime News Services, 3918 Prosperity Avenue, Suite 318, Fairfax VA 22031-3334. **Tel** (703)573-1600, (800)422-9267, **FAX** (703)573-1604. **LC** Current issues only. **DD** 623.

US
**ELECTRONIC WARFARE FORECAST.** (19??)-. English. Twelve times a year. $1390.00. Forecast International / DMS Inc., 22 Commerce Road, Newtown CT 06470. **Tel** (203)426-0800, **FAX** (203)426-1964, telex 467615. available on CD-ROM ($1595.00).

US/1040-2802
**EMERGING TECHNOLOGIES (ALEXANDRIA, VA.).** (EMERGING TECHNOLOGIES.). [Emerg. technol.]. **Added/Corp** Defense Marketing Services, Inc. **VFOAT** Emerging Technologies Market Study. Vol. 2 (1989)-. English. an. $875.00. Forecast International / DMS Inc., 22 Commerce Road, Newtown CT 06470. **Tel** (203)426-0800, **FAX** (203)426-1964, telex 467615. **LC** IN PROCESS. **DD** 623. *Continues Emerging Technologies Market Study, 1042-1017.*

US/0046-1989
**ENGINEER (FORT BELVOIR), THE. See** Engineering.

UK/0951-2721
**ENIGMA VARIATIONS NEWS.** *Suspended.* [Enigma var. news]. (1987)-(19??). Periodical. English. qt. Osprey Media Ptnrs, 33A Church Road, Watford Herts WD1 3PY England. **Tel** 011 44 923 818921. **DD** 004.

US
**EQUIPMENT FORECAST, AN.** (19??)-. English. Twelve times a year. $1390.00. Forecast International / DMS Inc., 22 Commerce Road, Newtown CT 06470. **Tel** (203)426-0800, **FAX** (203)426-1964, telex 467615. available on CD-ROM ($1595.00).

CN/1194-2266
**ESPRIT DE CORPS, CANADIAN MILITARY THEN & NOW.** [Esprit corps Can. mil. then now]. **VFOAT** Esprit de Corps; Canadian Military Then & Now; Canadian Military Then and Now. (May 1991)-. Periodical. English. mo. 39.95Can$. Canadian Military, 702 Albert Street, Ottawa Ontario K1R 6L4 Canada. **Tel** (613)233-0655, (613)238-7186, **FAX** (613)231-5242. **ED** James G. Scott. **DD** 355/.00971/05. **Bk Rev.** (Qty: 24-30). **Ad Acc, Adv Mgr:** S.R. Taylor. **Pr Rev. Circ:** 10,000.
**Desc:** Covers defense-related issues pertinent to Canada, including current deployments, procurements, and defense policy.

CN
**ESTIMATES. PART III, NATIONAL DEFENCE. Main/Corp** Canada. **VFOAT** Budget des Depenses. Partie III, Defense Nationale. (19??)-. English (French). $9.00 Canada; $10.80 other. Canada Communication Group Publishers, Order Processing, Ottawa Ontario K1A 0S9 Canada. **Tel** (819)956-4800, (819)956-4802. **LC** UA640; .C25a. **DD** 355.6/22/0971.

CN
**ESTIMATES. PART III, VETERANS AFFAIRS CANADA. Main/Corp** Canada. **VFOAT** Budget des Depenses. Partie III, Affaires des Anciens Combattants Canada. (19??)-. English (French). $12.00 Canada; $14.40 other. Canada Communication Group Publishers, Order Processing, Ottawa Ontario K1A 0S9 Canada. **Tel** (819)956-4800, (819)956-4802. **LC** UB359.C2; C32a. **DD** 354.710081/2.

AG/0046-2578
**ESTRATEGIA. Added/Corp** Instituto Argentino de Estudios Estrategicos y de las Relaciones Internacionales. Ano. 1, No. 1 (Mayo/Jun. 1969)-. Periodical. Spanish. bm.
**Ind/Abst** HAPI Hisp. Am. Period. Index (19??-).

GW
**EUROPAEISCHE SICHERHEIT. KAMPFTRUPPEN EDITION.** (19??)-. German. mo. DM114.00 Germany; DM144.50 other. Verlag Europaeische Wehrkunde, Steintorwall 17, D 32052 Herford Germany. **Tel** 011 49 5221 59910. **(Subscription address:** Maximilian Verlagsgruppe, Postfatch 2352, D 32045 Herford Germany.) *Continues Europaeische Wehrkunde. Ausgabe A.*

GW/0940-4171
**EUROPAISCHE SICHERHEIT. Added/Corp** Gesellschaft fur Wehr- und Sicherheitspolitik. No. 1 (Jan. 1991)-. Periodical. German (summaries and/or abstracts in English; table of contents in English). mo. Verlag Europaeische Wehrkunde, Steintorwall 17, D 32052 Herford Germany. **Tel** 011 49 5221 59910. *Continues Europaische Wehrkunde, Wehrwissenschaftliche Rundschau, 0723-9432.*

UK
**EUROPEAN SECURITY STUDIES. Added/Corp** Institute for European Defence & Strategic Studies. (1984)-. Monographic series. English. Eight times a year. £6.00 UK; $10.00 other. Institute for European Defense & Strategic Studies, St. Georges House, 14017 Wells Street, London W1P 3FP England. **Tel** 071-637-2152, **FAX** 071-637-2155. **ED** A.J. McHallam. **Bk Rev. Ad Acc, Adv Mgr Tel** same as editor. **Pr Rev.** Documents available from FAXON Xpress, BLDSC.

BE
**EUROSTRATEGIE.** *Title Change.* (198?)-(1992). Periodical. French. mo. Euredit sprl, 69 rue de Stassart, 1050 Bruxelles Belgium. **LC** UA646; .E945. **DD** 355/.03304. *Merged with De Defensa to form De Defensa et Eurostrategie.*

US/1069-708X
**EW DESIGN ENGINEERS' HANDBOOK & MANUFACTURERS DIRECTORY.** *Title Change.* [EW des. eng. handb. manuf. dir.]. **VFOAT** EW Design Engineers' Handbook and Manufacturers Directory; Design Engineers' Handbook & Manufacturers Directory. (19??)-(1993). Directory. English. Horizon House, 685 Canton Street, Norwood MA 02062. **Tel** (617)365-4595. **LC** UG485; .J68. **DD** 623/.043/05. *Continues EW Design Engineers' Handbook, 0895-7541. Continued by EW Reference & Source Guide.*
**Desc:** Information concerning electronics for military use and the military electronics industry.

# Military and Defense

●US
**EW REFERENCE & SOURCE GUIDE.** **VFOAT** Journal of Electronic Defense EW Reference & Source Guide; EW Reference and Source Guide; Journal of Electronic Defense EW Reference and Source Guide. (1994)-. Periodical. English. Horizon House, 685 Canton Street, Norwood MA 02062. **Tel** (617)365-4595. **LC** UG485; .E9. *Continues EW Design Engineers' Handbook & Manufacturers Directory, 1069-708X.*

US/0014-388X
**EX-CBI ROUNDUP.** See History(General)-History of North, South, and Central America.

US/0014-4452
**EXCHANGE & COMMISSARY NEWS.** [Exch. commis. news]. **VFOAT** Exchange Commissary News; Exchange Commissary; E & C News. **VAT** Exchange and Commissary News; E and C news. (19??)-. Periodical. English. mo. $85.00 (one year), $130.00 (two year). Executive Business Media, PO Box 1500, Westbury NY 11590. **Tel** (516)334-3030. **ED** Robert Moran. **DD** 330. **Ad Acc.** ctrl circ. available on microfilm from University Microfilms International (UMI).

US/0738-4203
**F.Y.E.O.** (F.Y.E.O.: FOR YOUR EYES ONLY.). [F.Y.E.O.]. **VFOAT** FYEO. (19??)-. Periodical. English. Twenty-six times a year (Every two weeks). $65.00 one year. Tiger Publications, PO Box 8759, Amarillo TX 79114. **Tel** (806)655-2009, Leanna Cole. **ED** Stephen V. Cole. [**CCC**]. Index available (Free). **Bk Rev. Circ:** 1,000.
**Desc:** An open newsletter about the intelligence summary of current military affairs.

US/0883-3370
**FEDERAL BENEFITS FOR VETERANS AND DEPENDENTS.** (FEDERAL BENEFITS FOR VETERANS AND DEPENDENTS / VETERANS ADMINISTRATION.). [Fed. benefits veterans depend.]. **Added/Corp** United States. Veterans Administration. Central Office. United States. Veterans Administration. United States. Dept. of Veterans Affairs. (19??)-. Government Publication. English. an. $12.75. Superintendent of Documents, US Government Printing Office, Washington DC 20402. **Tel** (202)275-3328, FAX (202)786-2377. (**Subscription address:** Subscription Office, PO Box 1943, Birmingham, AL 35201) **LC** UB357; .F43. **DD** 355.1/15/0973.

US/0192-2211
**FEDERAL MEDICAL CENTERS, HOSPITALS, AND MEDICAL CLINICS WITH REPORTED MORBIDITY DATA.** See Medical Science and Technology-Hospital Administration and Medical Centers.

US/0899-2525
**FIELD ARTILLERY.** [Field artill.]. **Added/Corp** Field Artillery Association (U.S.) Field Artillery School (Fort Sill, Okla.). **VFOAT** Field Artillery Bulletin. (Aug. 1987)-. Periodical. English. Six times a year. $18.00 (1 year), $35.00 (2 year), $52.00 (3 year) US and APO addresses; $30.00 (1 year), $59.00 (2 year), $88.00 (3 year) surface mail, $56.00 (1 year), $111.00 (2 year), $166.00 (3 year) air mail other. US Field Artillery Association, PO Box 33027, Fort Sill OK 73503-0027. **Tel** (405)355-4677, (405)355-8745. **LC** UF1; .F62. **DD** 358.1/2/0973. available on microfilm and microfiche from University Microfilms International (UMI). *Continues Field Artillery Journal (Fort Sill, Okla.), 0191-975X.*
**Desc:** A two-color professional periodical published by the Training and Doctrine Command and distributed to private sector individuals and agencies.
**Ind/Abst** Air Univ. Libr. Index Mil. Period. (199?-).

US/0896-7792
**FINANCIAL AID FOR VETERANS, MILITARY PERSONNEL, AND THEIR DEPENDENTS.** See Sociology-Social Services and Welfare.

US/0146-7328
**FINANCIAL PLANNING GUIDE FOR MILITARY PERSONNEL.** English. $1.95. AFTAC Enterprises, PO Box 34000, San Antonio TX 78265. **LC** U113; .M37. **DD** 332./02/4.

US
**FINANCIAL REPORT / ADJUTANT-GENERAL'S DEPARTMENT (TEXAS).** **Main/Corp** Texas. Adjutant-General's Dept. English. an. Adjutant General's Department / Texas, PO Box 5218, Austin TX 78763. **LC** UA43.T4; T49A. **DD** 353.97640072/31.

IT/0015-2242
**FINANZIERE.** [Finanziere]. (1887)-. Periodical. Italian. mo. L35000. Commando Gen Guardia Finanza Finanziere, Via Sicilia 178, 00187 Rome Italy. **Tel** 011 39 6 44223548. **UDC** 336.

RW
**FORCES ARMEES RWANDAISES, LES.** No. 41 (Nov.-Dec. 1979)-. Periodical. French (Ruanda). bm. Ministere de la Defense, Nationale Service de Documentation, B P 23, Kigali Rwanda. **LC** UA869.R95; F67. **DD** 355/.00967/571. *Continues Forces de Securite au Service de la Nation.*

●US
**FOREIGN MILITARY MARKETS, ASIA & PACIFIC RIM.** (1994)-. English. Twelve times a year. $1390.00. Forecast International / DMS Inc., 22 Commerce Road, Newtown CT 06470. **Tel** (203)426-0800, FAX (203)426-1964, telex 467615. available on CD-ROM ($1595.00).

●US
**FOREIGN MILITARY MARKETS, LATIN AMERICA & CARIBBEAN BASIN.** (1994)-. English. Twelve times a year. $1390.00. Forecast International / DMS Inc., 22 Commerce Road, Newtown CT 06470. **Tel** (203)426-0800, FAX (203)426-1964, telex 467615. available on CD-ROM ($1595.00).

US
**FOREIGN MILITARY MARKETS, MIDDLE EAST & AFRICA.** (19??)-. English. Twelve times a year. $1390.00. Forecast International / DMS Inc., 22 Commerce Road, Newtown CT 06470. **Tel** (203)426-0800, FAX (203)426-1964, telex 467615. available on CD-ROM ($1595.00).

US
**FOREIGN MILITARY MARKETS, NATO & EUROPE.** (19??)-. English. Twelve times a year. $1390.00. Forecast International / DMS Inc., 22 Commerce Road, Newtown CT 06470. **Tel** (203)426-0800, FAX (203)426-1964, telex 467615. available on CD-ROM ($1595.00).

US/8756-5536
**FOREIGN MILITARY SALES, FOREIGN MILITARY CONSTRUCTION SALES AND MILITARY ASSISTANCE FACTS AS OF ....** [Foreign mil. sales foreign mil. constr. sales mil. assist. facts]. Sept. 1981-. Periodical. an. US Department of Defense, The Pentagon, Washington DC 20301. **Tel** (703)545-6700. **LC** UA12; .U4613. **DD** 355/.032/0973. available on microfiche (Vols. for (Sep. 1984-) distributed to depository libraries). *Continues Foreign Military Sales and Military Assistance Facts, 0362-577X.*

UK/0261-586X
**FORT.** [Fort]. **Added/Corp** Fortress Study Group. (Spring 1977)-. Periodical. English. an (Oct.). £15.00 Europe; £20.00 others Comes with Fortress Study Group membership. Fortress Study Group, Blackwater Forge House, Blackwater, Newport, Isle of Wight PO30 3BJ England. **Tel** 011 44 0983 526207. available on microfiche. *Continues Newsletter (Fortress Study Group).*
**Ind/Abst** Archit. Period. Index (1977-); Avery Index Archit. Period. Suppl. Colum. Univ. (1990-); BHA : Biblio. Hist. Art; Br. Archaeol. Bibliogr.

CN/0848-8886
**FORUM / CONFERENCE OF DEFENCE ASSOCIATIONS.** [Forum - Conf. Def. Associations]. **Added/Corp** Conference of Defence Associations. Vol. 1, No. 1 (Jan. 1985)-. Periodical. English. bm. 95.00Can$ (1 year), 180.00Can$ (2 year), 260.00Can$ (3 year). Synergistic Enterprises Inc, 132 Adrian Circle, Markham Ontario L3P 7B3 Canada. **Tel** (416)472-2801, FAX (416)472-3091. **ED** Laurie M Watson. **DD** 355/.033071. cum. index. **Bk Rev** (Qty: 18). **Ad Acc, Adv Mgr:** P.Fogg, **Tel** (416)472-2801. **Circ:** 12,000.
**Desc:** Covers issues and events concerning Canada's defense community.

US/0071-9641
**FRONTIER MILITARY SERIES.** Vol. 1 (1951)-. Monographic series. English. ir. Price varies per volume. Arthur H. Clark Company, PO Box 14707, Spokane WA 99214. **Tel** (509)928-9540, (800)842-9286. **ED** Robert A. Clark. cum. index. **Circ:** 1,000 (ctrl).
**Desc:** An ongoing series of books dealing with the military and their role on the American frontier.

CL
**FUERZA AEREA (SANTIAGO, CHILE).** (FUERZA AEREA.). **VFOAT** Revista de la Fuerza Aerea de Chile; Revista Fuerza Aerea de Chile. (19??)-. Periodical. Spanish. qt. $60.00. Editorial Fuerza Aerea, Av B O'Higgins 1316 of 63, Santiago Chile. **LC** UG635.C5; A32. **DD** 358.4/00983. **Ad Acc. Circ:** 15,000. *Continues Fuerza Aerea de Chile.*

CK/0016-2485
**FUERZAS ARMADAS.** Vol. 1 (1965)-. Periodical. Spanish. mo. Oficina de Relaciones Publicas. **DD** 359.

VE
**FUERZAS ARMADAS DE VENEZUELA (VENEZUELA. MINISTERIO DE LA DEFENSA : 1971).** (FUERZAS ARMADAS DE VENEZUELA : ORGANO DEL MINISTERIO DE LA DEFENSA). No. 251 (1971)-. Periodical. Spanish. ir. Ministerio de la Defensa, El Ministerio, Caracas Venezuela. **LC** U4; .V373. **DD** 355. *Continues Revista de la Fuerzas Armadas de Venezuela; Revista de las Fuerzas Armadas de Venezuela.*
**Ind/Abst** Am. Hist. Life (1965, 1968-1982).

US/0092-5322
**FUSILIER (LA PUENTE).** (FUSILIER.). V. 1- Autumn 1973-. Periodical. English. qt. $4.50. Baron Publishing Company, PO Box 293, LaPuente CA 91747. **LC** U790; .F87. **DD** 355/.0075.

CN/0713-391X
**GAZETTE - CANADIAN FORCES BASE GAGETOWN (1981).** (GAZETTE.). [Gaz. - Can. Forces Base Gagetown]. **Added/Corp** Canada. Canadian Forces Base (Gagetown, N.B.). **VFOAT** Base Gagetown Gazette; Gagetown Gazette; Gagetown Gazette. **VAT** Base Gagetown Gazette (1981); Gagetown Gazette (1981). Vol. 21, No. 36 (Sept. 23, 1981)-. Periodical. English (summaries and/or abstracts in French). wk. Free. Gagetown Gazette, Building H-10/Room 212, CFB Gagetown, Oromocto New Brunswick E0G 2P0 Canada. **Tel** (506)422-2136. **ED** R.B. Wagstaff and R.J. Felder. **DD** 355.1/09715/43. **Bk Rev. Ad Acc. Circ:** 6,000 (ctrl). *Continues Base Gagetown Gazette (1980), 0712-919X.*
**Desc:** Services the military and civilian community of the Combat Training Centre, Canadian Forces Base Gagetown, and Oromocto, and New Brunswick.

JA
**GEKKAN ASAGUMO.** **VFOAT** Asagumo. (19??)-. Periodical. Japanese. ¥3300. Asagumo Shimbun Sha, c/o Korin Kaikan, 3-6-23 Shiba Koen Minato-ku, Tokyo 105 Japan. **LC** UA847; .G44.

US/0741-0611
**GEOGRAPHIC DISTRIBUTION OF VA EXPENDITURES.** (GEOGRAPHIC DISTRIBUTION OF VA EXPENDITURES / VETERANS ADMINISTRATION.). **VFOAT** Geographic Distribution of V.A. Expenditures. **VAT** Geographic Distribution of Veterans Administration Expenditures. English. an. US Veterans Administration / Washington DC, 810 Vermont Avenue Southwest, Washington DC 20420. **Tel** (202)393-2124. **LC** UB357; .G46. **DD** 353.0081/2. **NLM** W2; A V59g.

SP/0436-029X
**GLADIUS.** V. 1- 1961-. English (English, French and Spanish). Instit Estud Sobre Armas Antigua 4, Jarandilla Caceres Spain. **Tel** 927 46 00. **LC** U800.A1; G55.
**Ind/Abst** BHA : Biblio. Hist. Art; Br. Archaeol. Bibliogr.; Numis. Lit.

UK/0017-1204
**GLOBE AND LAUREL.** [Globe laurel]. (1892)-. Periodical. English. Six times a year (Feb., June, Aug., Oct., Dec.). £8.40 UK; £11.40 (surface mail), £16.80 (airmail). Royal Marines, HMS Excellent, Whale Island, Portsmouth, Hants PO2 8ER England. **Tel** 0705 651305, FAX 0705 547207. **ED** A. G. Newing. Index available. cum. index. **Bk Rev. Ad Acc.** ctrl circ.

CI/0352-664X
**GODISNJAK VOJNOMEDICINSKE AKADEMIJE.** See Medical Science and Technology.

US/0892-466X
**GORGET ET SASH : JOURNAL OF THE EARLY MODERN WARFARE SOCIETY.** (198?)-. Periodical. English. qt. $14.00 U.S.; 18.00 other. Gorget and Sash, 5218 Landgrave Lane, Springfield VA 22151. **Tel** (703)321-9072. **ED** Curt Johnson. **DD** 355. Index available. cum. index. **Bk Rev. Ad Acc. Circ:** 400.
**Desc:** Military history of the period 1400-1800. Well-researched and written accounts of uniforms, tactics, organizations, events, personalities and weapons. Includes rules and advice for wargamers.

●US/1071-670X
**GREAT BATTLES.** See History(General).

SP
**GUARDIA CIVIL. REVISTA OFICIAL Y PROFESIONAL DEL CUERPO.** Secretaria General Tecnica Centro de Publicaciones, Amador de los Rios 7, 28071 Madrid Spain. **Tel** 318 39 00.

IT
**GUARDIA COSTIERA.** Guardia Costiera, Via Bronzino 11, 20123 Milan Italy.

UK
**GUARDS MAGAZINE, THE.** (Summer 1968)-. Periodical. English. qt. £9.00. Horse Guards, Whitehall, London SWIA 2AX England. **Tel** 01 930 4466 ext. 2499. *Continues Household Brigade Magazine.*

GT
**GUATEMALA : REVISTA CULTURAL DEL EJERCITO.** **VFOAT** Revista Cultural del Ejercito. Yearly V. 1, V. 1, June 30, 1975)-. Periodical. Spanish. sa. Edificio del Instituto de Prevision Militar, 5A Avenida y Sexta Calle de la Zona 1 Ciudad de Guatemala, Guatemala. **LC** F1461; .G864.

FR
**GUERRES ET CONFLITS D'AUJOURD'HUI.** (198?)-. Periodical. French. Twelve times a year. 300.00F France; 384.62F others. International Moritmer Publishers / I M P, 341 rue des Iselles, 78670 Villennes France. **Tel** 011 33 1 39753158. **LC** U42; .G83.

FR
**GUERRES MONDIALES ET CONFLITS CONTEMPORAINS.** **Added/Corp** Institut d'Histoire des Conflits Contemporains (France). **VFOAT** Guerres et Conflits. Vol. 37, No. 145 (Jan. 1987)-. Periodical. French. qt. 525.00F France; 590.00F other. Presses Universitaires de France, Department des Revues, 14 Avenue du Bois de l'Epine, BP 90, 91003 Evry Cedex France. **Tel** (1)60 77 82 05, FAX (1) 60 79 20 45, telex PUF 600 474 F. **ED** Guy Pedroncini. **LC** D731; .R49. **DD** 909.82/05. **Bk Rev**. ctrl circ. Documents available from The Genuine Article. ***Continues** Revue d'Histoire de la Deuxieme Guerre Mondiale et des Conflits Contemporains, 0755-1584.*
**Ind/Abst** Am. Hist. Life (1954-); Arts Humanit. Citation Index (19??-19??) [Full Cov.]; Curr. Contents Arts Humanit.; Res. Alert [Full Cov.]; Soc. Sci. Cit. Index [Select. Cov.].

US
**GUIDE TO MILITARY INSTALLATIONS IN THE U.S.** (198?)-. English. an. $2.00 subscribers to Air Force Times, Army Times or Navy Times; $4.00 nonsubscribers. Army Times Publishing Company, 6883 Commercial Drive, Springfield VA 22159. **Tel** (800)368-5718, (703)750-8099. **LC** UA26.A2; G84. ***Continues** Times Magazine Guide to Military Installations in the U.S.*

US/0732-3034
**GUIDE TO THE EVALUATION OF EDUCATIONAL EXPERIENCES IN THE ARMED SERVICES.** **See** Education-Higher Education.

US/1042-6450
**GUN TESTS.** [Gun tests]. Vol. 1, No. 1 (Apr. 1989)-. Periodical. English. mo. $72.00 US and Canada; $84.00 other. Belvoir Publications Inc., 75 Holly Hill Lane, Greenwich CT 06836. **Tel** (203)661-6111, FAX (203)661-4802. **ED** Dave Tinker. **DD** 799.
**Desc:** Evaluations, ratings and tests of all kinds of firearms and related accessories.

UK
**GUNNER.** Newsletter. English. mo. £8.00 UK; £14.00 other. Gunner Magazine, Government House, New Road Woolwich, London SE18 6XR England. **Tel** 011 44 81 854 2242, 011 44 81 781 3705. **ED** J.D. Braisby. Index Bound in First Issue. **Bk Rev**, (Qty: 30). **Ad Acc. Circ:** 7,800 (ctrl).
**Desc:** Gunner magazine only issued to serving ex-members of the royal regiment of artillery plus a few local and overseas individual organizations approved by the Ministry of Defence UK.

CC/1001-2486
**GUOFANG KE-JI DAXUE XUEBAO.** **VFOAT** Journal of National University of Defense Technology. (1980)-. Periodical. Chinese. qt. **DD** 623.
**Ind/Abst** Int. Aerosp. Abstr.

UK/0260-8693
**HANDGUNNER.** **See** Recreation, Leisure-Sports.

US/1054-4135
**HANDGUNS FOR SPORT & DEFENSE.** ***Title Change.*** **See** Recreation, Leisure-Sports.

SW
**HANDLINGAR OCH TIDSKRIFT.** **Main/Corp** Kungl. Krigsvetenskapsakademien (Sweden). (19??)-. Swedish. Seven times a year. Kr50.00. Kungliga Krigsvetenskapsakademiens, Handlingar Och Tidskrift, 5 100 45 Stockholm 90 Sweden. **LC** U4; .K85.

US/0073-0394
**HARMON MEMORIAL LECTURES IN MILITARY HISTORY, THE.** [Harmon mem. lect. mil. hist.]. Began with No. 1, published in 1959. Monographic series. English. ir. Price varies per volume. US Air Force Academy / Colorado Springs, Colorado Springs CO 80840. **DD** 900.
**Ind/Abst** Am. Hist. Life (1959-).

US
**HEADQUARTERS HELIOGRAM (COUNCIL ON AMERICA'S MILITARY PAST).** (HEADQUARTERS HELIOGRAM.). **Added/Corp** Council on America's Military Past. No. 139 (Nov. 1981)-. Periodical. English. mo. comes with Council on America's Military Past membership. Council on America's Military Past, 518 West Why Worry Lane, Phoenix AZ 85021. **Tel** (602)943-3552, 800 398-4693. **ED** Herbert M. Hart. Index available. **Ad Acc. Circ:** 1,600. ***Continues** Headquarters Heliogram (Council on Abandoned Military Posts), 0010-9967.*
**Desc:** A tabloid-size newspaper (8 to 12 pages), with time-sensitive articles on historic preservation and military history.

US/0740-1701
**HEALTH MANPOWER STATISTICS.** **See** Military and Defense-Abstracting, Bibliographies and Statistics.

GW/0941-2808
**HEER MELSUNGEN.** [HeerMels.]. (1991)-. Periodical. German. mo. A Bernecker GmbH & Company KG, Postfach 140, D-34212 Melsungen Germany. **Tel** 011 49 5661 7310, FAX 011 49 5661 73189, telex (17)566 1813. **UDC** 355.1. ***Formed by the union of** Heer (Ausg. Regionalredaktion Sud), 0941-2778; Heer (Ausg. Regionalredaktion Nord), 0941-2786 **and** Heer (Ausg. Regionalredaktion Mitte), 0941-2794.*

FR/0248-1626
**HERACLES (ENGLISH EDITION).** ***Ceased.*** (HERACLES.). [Heracles]. (19??)-(1992). Periodical. English. Six times a year. Publi Pyrenees, 127 rue de la Faisanderie, 75116 Paris France. **Tel** 1 504 18 24. **ED** Bernard Jean-Jean. **LC** UF500; .H47. **DD** 355.8/2/05. **Bk Rev. Ad Acc. Circ:** 15,800 (ctrl).
**Ind/Abst** Predicasts.

US/0892-5674
**HIGH FRONTIER NEWSWATCH.** **Added/Corp** High Frontier (Organization). **VFOAT** High Frontier; High Frontier Newsletter; Newswatch. (198?)-. Periodical. English. mo. Free on request. Space Transportation Association and High Frontier, 2800 Shirlington Road, Suite 405A, Arlington VA 22206. **Tel** (703)671-4111, FAX (703)931-6432. **ED** Aleta Jackson. **DD** 355. **Bk Rev**, (Qty: 4). **Circ:** 29,000 (ctrl). ***Continues** High Frontier Newsletter.*
**Desc:** Concentrates on strategic defense initiative and space defense.

US/0091-2271
**HISTORY; ANNUAL SUPPLEMENT.** **Main/Corp** United States Army Infantry Center. English. an. United States Army Infantry Center, Ft Benning GA 31905. **LC** UA28; .U55A. **DD** 356/.1/0710758476.

KO
**HOGUK.** Periodical. Korean. mo. Kukkun Hongbo Kwalliso San, 2 Yongsan-dong Yongsan-ku, Seoul Korea. **LC** UA853.K6; H63.

HK
**HSIEN TAI CHUN SHIH.** **VFOAT** Conmilit. (19??)-. Periodical. Chinese. mo. $43.00 surface mail; $51.00 (air mail) Asia; $59.00 (air mail) other. Conmilit Press Ltd, 11/F Kwong Ah Bldg., 114 Thomson, PO Box 23250, Wanchai, Hong Kong. **Tel** 011-852-838-7608, FAX 011-852-834-2156. **LC** UF530; .H75. **DD** 355/.005.

II
**IDSA JOURNAL.** ***Suspended.*** **VFOAT** I.D.S.A. Journal. **VAT** Institute for Defense Studies and Analyses Journal. Vol. 9, No. 1 (July/Sept. 1976)-?. Periodical. English. qt. Rs40.00 India; Rs40.00 (surface mail), Rs110.00 (airmail) other. Institute for Defence Studies and Analyses, Sapru House, Barakhamba Road, New Delhi 110001 India. **Tel** 011 91 11 3314951. **LC** UA840; .I55. **DD** 355/.033054. **Circ:** 3,000. ***Continues** Institute for Defence Studies and Analyses Journal, 0020-2606.*
**Desc:** Presents in-depth views on issues related to Indian and global security.
**Ind/Abst** Int. Polit. Sci. Abstr.

II
**IDSA NEWS REVIEW ON NORTH AMERICA, EUROPE.** **Added/Corp** Institute for Defence Studies and Analyses. **VFOAT** News Review On North America, Europe. **VAT** Institute for Defence Studies and Analyses News Review on North America, Europe. Vol. 15, No. 1 (Jan. 1984)-?. Periodical. English. mo. Rs12.00. Institute of Defense Studies and Analysis, Sapru House, Barakhamba Road, New Delhi 110 001 India. **Tel** 3314951. **LC** D839; .I455a. **DD** 909.82. Index available. **Circ:** 170. ***Continues** News Review on North America & Europe. **Continued in part by** News Review on USSR/Europe.*
**Desc:** Highly recommended for students of political science, defense studies and for all those interested in strategic developments, in particular regions and security issues, national and international.

II
**IDSA NEWS REVIEW ON SOUTH ASIA/INDIAN OCEAN.** **Added/Corp** Institute for Defence Studies and Analyses. **VFOAT** News Review on South Asia/Indian Ocean. **VAT** Institute for Defence Studies and Analyses News Review on South Asia/Indian Ocean. Vol. 17 No. 1 (Jan. 1984)-. Periodical. English. mo. Institute for Defence Studies and Analyses, Sapru House, Barakhamba Road, New Delhi 110001 India. **Tel** 011 91 11 3314951. **LC** DS331; .I5. **DD** 954/.005. ***Continues** News Review on South Asia and Indian Ocean.*

US
**IFR-- SUPPLEMENT, UNITED STATES.** **VFOAT** DOD Flight Information Publication (Enroute). **VAT** Instrument Flight Rules Supplement, United States. Periodical. English. bm. Defense Mapping Agency / St Louis, Aerospace Center, St Louis Air Force Station, St Louis MO 63118.
**Desc:** Contains an aerodrome/facility directory, special notices and procedures required to support the enroute and area charts.

US/0740-3445
**IMPACT (GREAT FALLS, MONT.).** (IMPACT / UNITED STATES CIVIL DEFENSE COUNCIL.). [Impact]. **Added/Corp** United States Civil Defense Council. Vol. 1, No. 1 (Fall 1982)-. Periodical. English. qt. $12.00. United States Civl Defense Council, Box 6457, Great Falls MT 59406. **LC** UA927; .I48. **DD** 363.3/5/0973.

US/0738-1166
**IMPLEMENTATION OF THE POST-VIETNAM ERA VETERANS' EDUCATIONAL ASSISTANCE ACT OF 1977.** (IMPLEMENTATION OF THE POST-VIETNAM ERA VETERANS' EDUCATIONAL ASSISTANCE ACT OF 1977: AN ANNUAL JOINT REPORT PREPARED BY THE VETERANS ADMINISTRATION AND THE DEPARTMENT OF DEFENSE... SUBMITTED TO THE COMMITTEE ON VETERANS AFFAIRS, UNITED STATES SENATE.). [Implement. Post-Vietnam Era Veterans' Educ. Assist. Act 1977]. English. an. Iowa Department of Corrections, 523 East 12th Street, Capitol Annex, Des Moines IA 50319. **Tel** (515)281-4811, FAX (515)281-7345. **LC** UB357; .U54C. **DD** 355.7/152/0973. ***Continues** Plans for the Implementation of the Post-Vietnam Era Veterans' Educational Assistance Act of 1977, 0190-4930.*

US/1053-7864
**IN PERSPECTIVE OF THE BLACK AMERICAN VETERAN.** [In perspect. black Am. veteran]. **VFOAT** Black American Veteran. Vol. 1, No. 1 (Apr. 1991)-. Periodical. English. Four times a year. $23.80. Elramco Enterprises, Inc., 257 Osborne Road, Albany NY 12211. **Tel** (518)482-1030. **LC** IN PROCESS. **DD** 305.

US/0098-1729
**INCOME TAX GUIDE FOR MILITARY PERSONNEL.** **See** Business-Accounting.

US
**INDEX OF AIR FORCE-NAVY AERONAUTICAL (AN), AIR FORCE-NAVY AERONAUTICAL DESIGN (AND) AND MILITARY (MS) STANDARDS.** **Main/Corp** National Standards Association. (19??)-. Periodical. English. Twelve times a year. $975.00 (latest edition). Global Engineering Documents Services, 15 Inverness Way East, Englewood CO 80112. **Tel** (800)624-3974. **ED** Kitty Stover. Index available.
**Desc:** Paper index to the Air Force navy standards.

US
**INDEX OF BLANK FORMS - UNITED STATES. DEPT. OF THE ARMY.** **Main/Corp** United States. Dept. of the Army. **VFOAT** Military Publications. English. an. US Department of Defense Department of the Army, The Pentagon, SAPA-CR, Room 3E718, Washington DC 20310. **Tel** (703)695-0363, FAX (703)693-5737.

US
**INDEX OF DCAA MEMORANDUMS FOR REGIONAL DIRECTORS (MRDS).** **Main/Corp** United States. Defense Contract Audit Agency. **VFOAT** Index to Defense Contract Audit Agency Memorandums for Regional Directors. (19??)-. Periodical. English. Defense Contract Audit Agency, Cameron Station, Alexandria VA 22314. ***Continues in part** United States. Defense Contract Audit Agency.; Index of DCAA Numbered Publications and Memorandums.*

US/0739-5892
**INDEX OF SOVIET AND CHINESE MILITARY AFFAIRS IN ANNUAL US DEFENSE DEPARTMENT REPORTS.** [Index Sov. Chin. mil. aff. annu. U.S. Def. Dep. rep.]. 1969-1983-. English. an. $24.00. Institute for Defense and Disarmament Studies, 675 Massachusetts Avenue, 8th Floor, Cambridge MA 02139. **Tel** (617)354-4337, FAX (617)354-1450, telex 403618. **ED** Barton Wright. **LC** UF505.S65; I45. **DD** 355.8/2/0947.
**Desc:** Gives the page numbers in three key reports (published from 1959 to 1983) where Soviet and Chinese weapons are discussed.

US/0363-8464
**INDEX OF SPECIFICATIONS AND STANDARDS.** (INDEX OF SPECIFICATIONS AND STANDARDS / DEPARTMENT OF DEFENSE.). **Main/Corp** United States. Dept. of Defense. **Added/Corp** United States. Armed Forces Supply Support Center. Standardization Division. United States. Dept. of Defense.

United States. Armed Forces Supply Support Center. United States. Defense Supply Agency. (Nov. 1960)-. Government Publication. English. ir. $126.00 US; $157.50 other (Part 1 & 2); $57.00 US; $71.25 other (Part 3). Superintendent of Documents, US Government Printing Office, Washington DC 20402. **Tel** (202)275-3328, FAX (202)786-2377. **LC** UC263; .A37326. available on microfiche. ***Formed by the union of*** *United States. Dept. of the Army. Index of Specifications and Standards Used by Department of the Army* ***and*** *United States. Navy Dept. Index of Specifications and Standards Used by Department of the Navy United States. Wright Air Development Division. Index of Specifications and Related Publications Used by U. S. Air Force;* ***Absorbed*** *Federal Supply Classification Listing of DOD Standardization Documents, 0565-2669.* ***Continued in part by*** *Federal Supply Classification Listing of DOD Standardization Documents, 0565-2669.*
**Desc:** Lists the unclassified Federal and military specifications, standards, and related standardization documents, and those non-government documents adopted for DoD use.

US
**INDEX OF STORAGE AND OUTLOADING DRAWINGS FOR AMMUNITION COMMODITIES. Main/Corp** United States. Dept. of the Army. English. Department of the Army, US Army AG Publ Ctr, 2800 East Boulevard, Baltimore MD 21220.

US/0019-9532
**INFANTRY.** [Infantry]. Vol. 47, No. 2 (April 1957)-. Periodical. English. bm. $12.00 (one year), $23.00 (two year). Infantry Magazine, Business Office, PO Box 2005, Ft Benning GA 31905-0605. **Tel** (404)545-2350, (404)687-2841. **ED** Russell A. Eno. **LC** UD1; .I56. Index available (Free on request). cum. index. **Bk Rev. Pr Rev. Circ:** 15,360 (ctrl). available on microfilm and microfiche from University Microfilms International (UMI). ***Continues*** *Infantry School Quarterly.*
**Desc:** Current information on infantry organization, weapons, equipment, tactics and techniques. Serves as a forum for professional ideas.
**Ind/Abst** Air Univ. Libr. Index Mil. Period.; Curr. Mil. Pol. Lit.

US/0270-8906
**INSCOM JOURNAL.** [INSCOM j.]. **Added/Corp** United States. Army. Army Intelligence & Security Command. **VAT** Intelligence and Security Command Journal. Vol. 3, No. 2 (Apr. 1980)-. Periodical. English. ir. Headquarters of United States Army Intelligence and Security Command, Arlington Hall Station, Arlington VA 22212. **Tel** (202)692-5346. **LC** UB251.U5; U5a. **DD** 355.3/432/0973. ***Continues*** *Journal of the U.S. Army Intelligence & Security Command, 0194-9527.*

US
**INSIDE DEFENSE ELECTRONICS WEEKLY REPORT.** (1990)-. English. wk. $485.00 US and Canada; $535.00 other. Inside Washington Publishers, PO Box 7167, Benjamin Franklin Station, Washington DC 20044. **Tel** (703)416-8500, (800)424-9068. ***Continues*** *Electronic Combat Report.*

US
**INSIDE THE ARMY.** English. mo. $425.00 US and Canada; $475.00 other. Inside Washington Publishers, PO Box 7167, Benjamin Franklin Station, Washington DC 20044. **Tel** (703)416-8500, (800)424-9068.

US
**INSIDE THE PENTAGON.** (19??)-. Periodical. English. wk. $745.00. Inside Washington Publishers, PO Box 7167, Benjamin Franklin Station, Washington DC 20044. **Tel** (703)416-8500, (800)424-9068.
**Desc:** Industry report on DOD acquistions/procurement, contract management, and legislative/regulatory policies.

US
**INSIDE THE PENTAGON'S INSIDE THE NAVY. VFOAT** Inside the Navy. (19??)-. Periodical. English. wk. $590.00 US and Canada; $640.00 other. Inside Washington Publishers, PO Box 7167, Benjamin Franklin Station, Washington DC 20044. **Tel** (703)416-8500, (800)424-9068.

US
**INSTRUCTION AND CODE TABLE BOOKLET / VA HEALTH PROFESSIONAL SCHOLARSHIP PROGRAM. Main/Corp** United States. Veterans Administration. Health Professional Scholarship Program. English. ir. Publications Secret Order Department, PO Box 1015, North Highlands CA 95660. **Tel** (916)924-4800. **NLM** WY 18.5; A6521.

FR
**INTELLIGENCE NEWSLETTER.**
**Added/Corp** Association Pour le Droit a l'Information. No. 106 (Oct. 4, 1988)-. Newsletter. English. bw. ***Continues*** *Intelligence/ para Politics (Full Edition), 0762-8374.*

IT
**INTERARMA.** (19??)-. Italian. Twenty-two times a year. L260000.00 Italy; L370000.00 Europe; L410000.00 other. Editoriale Aeronautica, V Due Macelli 23 Scala F Int7, 00817 Rome Italy. **Tel** 011 39 6 6990056.

US/0090-4813
**INTERNATIONAL ARMAMENTS MONTHLY.** No. 1- Oct. 1972-. Periodical. English. mo. $20.00. International Armaments Press, PO Box 40, Kailua HI 96734. **LC** UF520; .I57. **DD** 355.8/2/05.

US
**INTERNATIONAL CONTRACTORS. See** Aeronautics, Astronautics.

US/0145-2584
**INTERNATIONAL COUNTERMEASURES HANDBOOK, THE.** ***Title Change.*** 1st Ed. (1975/76)-. English. an. Cardiff Publishing Company, 6300 South Syracuse Way, Suite 650, Englewood CO 80111. **Tel** (303)220-0600, telex 450726. **(Subscription address:** 5615 Cermak Road, Cicero IL 60650) **ED** Floyd Painter. **LC** UG485; .I53. **DD** 623/.37. **Ad Acc. Circ:** 8,000. available on microfilm. ***Absorbed by*** *International Defense Electronics Systems Handbook.*

GW
**INTERNATIONAL DEFENCE EQUIPMENT CATALOG : IDEC.** (19??)-. Catalog. English. ir (Every 3 years). DM280.00. Moench Publishing Group, Heilsbachstrasse 26, Postfach 140 261, 5300 Bonn 1 Germany. **Tel** 011 49 228 64830, FAX 011 49 228 6483109. **Ad Acc. Circ:** 10,000 (ctrl).
**Desc:** Devoted to military specifications and regulations, to help the user familiarise himself with the requirements of procurement agencies. Contains over 5,000 entries that will prove of great use for anyone working in the defence community.

US/0161-0813
**INTERNATIONAL DEFENSE BUSINESS: DEFENSE SURVEY.** No. 419 (Jan. 1974)-. Periodical. English. wk. Government Business Worldwide Reports, PO Box 5997, Washington DC 20016. **Tel** (202)244-7050, FAX (202)244-5410. **LC** UF530; .I577. **DD** 355/.005. ***Continues*** *International Defense Business. Survey, 0160-9777.*

US/0161-0805
**INTERNATIONAL DEFENSE BUSINESS : REPORT.** Periodical. English. wk. Business Worldwide Reports, PO Box 4875, Washington DC 20008. **LC** UF530; .I576. **DD** 338.4/7/355.

UK/0256-7822
**INTERNATIONAL DEFENSE DIRECTORY. Added/Corp** Interavia Publishing Group. **VFOAT** IDD. (1985)-. Directory. English. an. $410.00 US & Mexico; $502.25 Central & South America. Jane's Information Group, Sentinel House, 163 Brighton Road, Coulsdon Surrey CR3 2NX England. **Tel** 011 44 81 763 1030, FAX 011 44 81 763 1006. **(Subscription address:** Jane's Information Group / US Subscriptions, 1340 Braddock Place, Suite 300, Alexandria VA 22314.) **LC** UC260; .I57. **DD** 355.6/212/025. available on CD-ROM.

US/1041-746X
**INTERNATIONAL DEFENSE INTELLIGENCE.** [Int. def. intell.]. Periodical. English. wk. $300.00. Jane's Information Group, Sentinel House, 163 Brighton Road, Coulsdon Surrey CR3 2NX England. **Tel** 011 44 81 763 1030, FAX 011 44 81 763 1006. **DD** 353. available on an online database (file 587/Full-Text) from DIALOG. ***Continues*** *International Defense DMS Intelligence, 0275-2956.*

SZ/0020-6512
**INTERNATIONAL DEFENSE REVIEW.** [Int. def. rev.]. V. 1- 1968-. Periodical. English. mo. $180.00 US; 277.00Can$ Canada; £104.00 UK; DM519.00 Germany; 1,747F France; 449.00F Switzerland; £144.00 other Europe; £155.00 other. Jane's Information Group, Sentinel House, 163 Brighton Road, Coulsdon Surrey CR3 2NX England. **Tel** 011 44 81 763 1030, FAX 011 44 81 763 1006. **ED** Rupert Pengelly. **LC** U1; .I48. **CODEN** IDRVAL. **[CCC]. Ad Acc. Circ:** 33,000. available on an online database (file 587/Full-text) from DIALOG. Documents available from Ask*IEEE.
**Desc:** Devoted to in-depth reporting on international defense matters.
**Ind/Abst** Air Univ. Libr. Index Mil. Period. (1987-); BMT Abstr.; Curr. Mil. Pol. Lit. (1987-); EMBASE; Infomat Int. Bus.; INSPEC (Jan. 1992-); NEXIS (1984-).

SZ
**INTERNATIONAL DEFENSE REVIEW. SPECIAL SERIES. VFOAT** Special Series International Defense Review. Began in 1976. Periodical. English. ir. Interavia, PO Box 162, CH-1216 Geneva Switzerland. **Tel** 011 41 22 980505.

US/0885-0607
**INTERNATIONAL JOURNAL OF INTELLIGENCE AND COUNTER INTELLIGENCE.** [Int. j. intell. count. intell.]. Vol. 1, No. 1 (Spring 1986)-. Periodical. English. qt. $75.00 (per volume), (add $10.00 for mail charges outside US). In-Tel Publishing Group, PO Box 188, Stroudsburg PA 18360. **Tel** (717)629-3422. **LC** UB250; .I577. **DD** 327.1/2/05.
**Ind/Abst** PAIS Int. Print (1991-).

SZ/1017-5547
**INTERNATIONALES WAFFEN-MAGAZIN.** [Int. Waffen-Mag.]. (1990)-. Periodical. German (summaries and/or abstracts in English). mo (11 issues per year). 67.00F. Edition Habegger SA, Gutenbergstrasse 1, CH 4552 Derendingen, Switzerland. **Tel** 011 41 65 411151. **UDC** 623.9. ***Formed by the union of*** *Schweizer Waffen-Magazin, 0253-4878* ***and*** *Internationaler Waffen-Spiegel, 0723-2942.*
**Desc:** Modern and antique firearms and other weapons, shooting sports, and self defense.

US/0734-3264
**INTERSERVICE JOURNAL OF MILITARY & POLICE SCIENCE AND THE INTELLIGENCE PROFESSION, THE.** [Interserv. j. mil. police sci. intell. prof.]. **VFOAT** Interservice Journal of Military and Police Science and the Intelligence Profession; Interservice Journal. Vol. 1, No. 1 (Jan. 1982)-. Periodical. English. qt. $34.95. Interservice Publishing Company Inc, PO Box 5437, San Francisco CA 94101. **Tel** (415)221-9258. **LC** UB250; .I58. **DD** 355.3/43/05.

UK/0952-116X
**ISLAMIC DEFENCE REVIEW.** [Islam. def. rev.]. Periodical. English. qt. £10.00 airmail. The Islamic Institute of Defence Technology, 16 Grosvenor Crescent, London SW1 England. **LC** UA830; .I74. **DD** 355/.033017/671.

LE
**ISTRATIJYA. VFOAT** Strategia. Periodical. Arabic (Arabic). mo. $200.00. Al-Richeh Shams Building, PO Box 14-5158, Beirut Lebanon. **LC** UF530; .I77.

GW/0075-2428
**JAHRBUCH DER WEHRTECHNIK.** Series 1 (1966)-. German. an. Wehr und Wissen Verlagsges GmbH, Postfach 140261, D 53057 Bonn Germany. **Tel** 011 49 228 64830. **LC** UF530; .J3.

UK
**JANE'S A F V SYSTEMS.** English. £85.00 UK; $145.00 other. Jane's Information Group, Sentinel House, 163 Brighton Road, Coulsdon Surrey CR3 2NX England. **Tel** 011 44 81 763 1030, FAX 011 44 81 763 1006. **ED** Cristopher Foss. Index available. **Bk Rev. Ad Acc.** ctrl circ. available on diskette; available on CD-FOM.
**Desc:** A technical detailed description of all AFV systems available for installation in new and rebuilt vehicles.

UK/0954-3848
**JANE'S AIR LAUNCHED WEAPONS.** [Jane's Air Launched Weapons]. (1989)-. English. tq. $440.00 US and Mexico; $539.00 other. Jane's Information Group, Sentinel House, 163 Brighton Road, Coulsdon Surrey CR3 2NX England. **Tel** 011 44 81 763 1030, FAX 011 44 81 763 1006.

UK/0075-3017
**JANE'S ALL THE WORLD'S AIRCRAFT (LONDON, ENGLAND).** (JANE'S ALL THE WORLD'S AIRCRAFT.). **VFOAT** All the World's Aircraft. (1930)-. English. an. $245.00 US & Mexico;$267.05 Canada; $300.13 Central & South America. Jane's Information Group, Sentinel House, 163 Brighton Road, Coulsdon Surrey CR3 2NX England. **Tel** 011 44 81 763 1030, FAX 011 44 81 763 1006. **(Subscription address:** Jane's Information Group / US Subscriptions, 1340 Braddock Place, Suite 300, Alexandria VA 22314.) **[CCC].** Index available. cum. index. **Bk Rev. Ad Acc. Circ:** 10,000. available in microform; available on CD-ROM. ***Continues*** *All the World's Aircraft.*
**Desc:** Full technical details on the Brazilian-Italian AMX joint light strike aircraft programme.

UK/0143-9952
**JANE'S ARMOUR AND ARTILLERY.** [Jane's armour artill.]. (1980)-. English. an. $245.00 US & Mexico; $267.05 Canada; $300.13 Central & South America. Jane's Information Group, Sentinel House, 163 Brighton Road, Coulsdon Surrey CR3 2NX England. **Tel** 011 44 81 763 1030, FAX 011 44 81 763 1006. **(Subscription address:** Jane's Information Group / US Subscriptions, 1340 Braddock Place, Suite 300, Alexandria VA 22314.) **ED** Christopher F. Foss. **LC** UG446.5; .J28. **DD** 358/.18/05. **[CCC]. Ad Acc.**
**Desc:** Reference guide to armoured fighting vehicles and crewed guns in current service and production worldwide, including development, specifications, and deployment.

UK
**JANE'S ARMOURED FIGHTING VEHICLE RETROFIT SYSTEMS. VFOAT** Armoured Fighting Vehicle Retrofit Systems; AFV Retrofit

Systems; Jane's AFV Retrofit Systems. 3rd Ed. (1991)-. English. an. $255.00 US & Mexico; $312.38 others. Jane's Information Group, Sentinel House, 163 Brighton Road, Coulsdon Surrey CR3 2NX England. **Tel** 011 44 81 763 1030, FAX 011 44 81 763 1006. **(Subscription address:** Jane's Information Group / US Subscriptions, 1340 Braddock Place, Suite 300, Alexandria VA 22314.**) ED** Chris Foss. **LC** UG446.5; .J29. **DD** 358/.18/05. Index available. **Bk Rev. Ad Acc. Pr Rev.** available on CD-ROM. ***Continues*** *Jane's Armoured Fighting Vehicle Systems.*
**Desc:** Comparative product data on AFV systems, product profiles according to system type, country of origin and manufacturers.

UK
**JANE'S AVIONICS.** 1st Ed. (1983)-. English. an. $255.00 US and Canada; $312.38 Central and South America. Jane's Information Group, Sentinel House, 163 Brighton Road, Coulsdon Surrey CR3 2NX England. **Tel** 011 44 81 763 1030, FAX 011 44 81 763 1006. **(Subscription address:** Jane's Information Group / US Subscriptions, 1340 Braddock Place, Suite 300, Alexandria VA 22314.**) ED** Stephen R. Broadbent. **LC** UG1420; .J36. **DD** 623/.043. **Ad Acc.** available on CD-ROM.
**Desc:** Technical and commercial information on current airborne electronics worldwide.

UK
**JANE'S BATTLEFIELD SURVEILLANCE SYSTEMS. Added/Corp** Jane's Information Group. **VFOAT** Battlefield Surveillance Systems. 1st Ed. (1990)-. English. an. $255.00 US and Canada; $312.38 Central and South America. Jane's Information Group, Sentinel House, 163 Brighton Road, Coulsdon Surrey CR3 2NX England. **Tel** 011 44 81 763 1030, FAX 011 44 81 763 1006. **(Subscription address:** Jane's Information Group / US Subscriptions, 1340 Braddock Place, Suite 300, Alexandria VA 22314.**) LC** UG475; .J36. available on CD-ROM. ***Continues in part*** *Jane's Weapon Systems (London, England).*

UK
**JANE'S C31 SYSTEMS.** (19??)-. English. an. $255.00 US; £160.00 other. Jane's Information Group, Sentinel House, 163 Brighton Road, Coulsdon Surrey CR3 2NX England. **Tel** 011 44 81 763 1030, FAX 011 44 81 763 1006. **(Subscription address:** Jane's Information Group / US Subscriptions, 1340 Braddock Place, Suite 300, Alexandria VA 22314.**)**
**Desc:** Guide to C 31 systems in existence.

UK/0265-3818
**JANE'S DEFENCE WEEKLY.** [Jane's def. wkly.]. **VFOAT** Defence Weekly. Vol. 1, No. 1 (Jan. 14, 1984)-. Periodical. English. wk. $197.00 (one year), $374.00 (two year), $531.00 (three year) US; £127.00 (one year), £241.00 (two year), £343.00 (three year), DM469.00 (one year), DM892.00 (two year), DM1,267.00 (three year) Germany; 1,574.00F (one year), 2,990.00F (two year), 4,249.00F (three year); 404.00F (one year), 768.00F (two year), 1,091F (three year) Switzerland; 277.00CAn$ (one year), 527.00Can$ (two year), 749.00Can$ (three year) Canada; £144.00 rest of Europe; £175 other. Jane's Information Group, Sentinel House, 163 Brighton Road, Coulsdon Surrey CR3 2NX England. **Tel** 011 44 81 763 1030, FAX 011 44 81 763 1006. **ED** Derek Wood. **LC** UF530; .J35. **DD** 355.8/2/05. **[CCC].** Index available. **Bk Rev. Ad Acc. Circ:** 25,000 (ctrl). available on an online database from DIALOG. ***Continues*** *Jane's Defence Review, 0144-0470.*
**Desc:** Covers worldwide defense and military developments and world affairs.
**Ind/Abst** Air Univ. Libr. Index Mil. Period. (19??-); BMT Abstr. (-199?); Curr. Mil. Pol. Lit.; F&S Index Plus Text, Int. [Select. Cov.]; Infomat Int. Bus.; Predicasts Forecasts; Trade Ind. Index.

UK
**JANE'S DEFENSE SYSTEMS MODERNISATION.** (19??)-. English. bm. $145.00 (one year), $275.00 (two year), $391.00 (three year), US; £85.00 (one year), £162.00 (two year), £230.00 (three year), UK; DM271.00 (one year), DM515 (two year), 732.00 (three year) Germany; 888.00F (one year), 1,688F (two year), 2,398 (three year), France; 234.00F (one year), 444.00 (two year), 631.00F (three year) Switzerland; 180.00Can$ (one year), 341.00Can$ (two year), 485.00 (three year), Canada £98 other. Jane's Information Group, Sentinel House, 163 Brighton Road, Coulsdon Surrey CR3 2NX England. **Tel** 011 44 81 763 1030, FAX 011 44 81 763 1006.

UK/0075-3025
**JANE'S FIGHTING SHIPS.** **See** Naval Science, Navigation.

UK/0960-7994
**JANE'S HIGH-SPEED MARINE CRAFT.** [Jane's high-speed mar. craft]. **VFOAT** Jane's High Speed Marine Craft; High-Speed Marine Craft; High Speed Marine Craft. 23rd Ed. (1990)-. English. an. $285.00 US and Canada; $349.13 Central and South America. Jane's Information Group, Sentinel House, 163 Brighton Road, Coulsdon Surrey CR3 2NX England. **Tel** 011 44 81 763 1030, FAX 011 44 81 763 1006. **(Subscription address:** Jane's Information Group / US Subscriptions, 1340 Braddock Place, Suite 300, Alexandria VA 22314.**) ED** R.L. Trillo. **LC** IN PROCESS. available on CD-ROM. ***Continues*** *Jane's High-Speed Marine Craft and Air Cushion Vehicles, 0951-3124.*

UK
**JANE'S INFANTRY WEAPONS.** (1975)-. English. an (June). $255.00 US and Mexico; $312.38 other. Jane's Information Group, Sentinel House, 163 Brighton Road, Coulsdon Surrey CR3 2NX England. **Tel** 011 44 81 763 1030, FAX 011 44 81 763 1006. **(Subscription address:** Jane's Information Group / US Subscriptions, 1340 Braddock Place, Suite 300, Alexandria VA 22314.**) ED** Ian V. Hogg. **LC** UD380; .J36. **DD** 623.4. Index available. **Ad Acc. Circ:** 2,700. available on microfiche; available on CD-ROM.
**Desc:** Reference guide to all portable weapons used worldwide. Includes weapon's development, operation, specifications and deployment.

UK/1350-6226
**JANE'S INTELLIGENCE REVIEW. Added/Corp** Jane's Information Group. **VFOAT** Intelligence Review. Vol. 3, No. 6 (June 1991)-. Periodical. English. mo. $250.00 (one year), $476.00 (two year), $676.00 (three year), US; £149.00 (one year), £283.00 (two year), £402.00 (three year), UK; DM519.00 (one year), DM987.00 (two year), DM1,403 (three year), Germany; 1,747.00F (one year), $3,320.00F (two year), 4,718.00F (three year) France; 449.00F (one year), 854.00F (two year), 1,214.00F (three year), Switzerland; 343.00Can$ (one year), 652.00Can$ (two year), 926.00 (three year) Canada; £152.00 rest of Europe; £155.00 other. Jane's Information Group, Sentinel House, 163 Brighton Road, Coulsdon Surrey CR3 2NX England. **Tel** 011 44 81 763 1030, FAX 011 44 81 763 1006. **LC** UA15; .J35. **DD** 355/.005. **CODEN** JINRE5. available on an online database (file 587/Full-Text) from DIALOG. ***Absorbed*** *Jane's Soviet Intelligence Review, 0955-1247.*
**Ind/Abst** Air Univ. Libr. Index Mil. Period. (199?-); Predicasts Forecasts.

UK
**JANE'S LAND-BASED AIR DEFENCE. Added/Corp** Jane's Information Group. **VFOAT** Jane's Land Based Air Defence. (19??)-. Periodical. English. an. $255.00 US & Mexico; $267.05 Canada; $312.38 Central & South America. Jane's Information Group, Sentinel House, 163 Brighton Road, Coulsdon Surrey CR3 2NX England. **Tel** 011 44 81 763 1030, FAX 011 44 81 763 1006. **(Subscription address:** Jane's Information Group / US Subscriptions, 1340 Braddock Place, Suite 300, Alexandria VA 22314.**) ED** Chris Foss. **LC** UG730; .J36. **DD** 358.4/145. **Ad Acc.** available on CD-ROM. ***Continues*** *Jane's Battlefield Air Defense.*
**Desc:** A guide to gun and missle air defense systems in the world.

UK/0144-0004
**JANE'S MILITARY COMMUNICATIONS.** [Jane's mil. communications]. (1980)-. English. an. $255.00 US & Mexico; $312.38 Central & South America. Jane's Information Group, Sentinel House, 163 Brighton Road, Coulsdon Surrey CR3 2NX England. **Tel** 011 44 81 763 1030, FAX 011 44 81 763 1006. **(Subscription address:** Jane's Information Group / US Subscriptions, 1340 Braddock Place, Suite 300, Alexandria VA 22314.**) ED** R. J. Raggett. **LC** UG590; .J35. **DD** 355.8/5. **[CCC]. Ad Acc.** available on CD-ROM.
**Desc:** Guide to communications equipment in service with naval, military and air forces worldwide, from satellite to underwater systems, major networks and handheld items.

UK
**JANE'S MILITARY TRAINING SYSTEMS. Added/Corp** Jane's Information Group. **VFOAT** Military Training Systems. 1st Ed. (1988)-. English. an. $255.00 US & Mexico; $312.38 Central & South America. Jane's Information Group, Sentinel House, 163 Brighton Road, Coulsdon Surrey CR3 2NX England. **Tel** 011 44 81 763 1030, FAX 011 44 81 763 1006. **(Subscription address:** Jane's Information Group / US Subscriptions, 1340 Braddock Place, Suite 300, Alexandria VA 22314.**) LC** U405; .J36. **DD** 355.5/028. **Ad Acc.** available on CD-ROM.
**Desc:** Technical profiles of land, sea and air military training equipment manufactured worldwide.

●UK
**JANE'S MILITARY VEHICLES AND LOGISTICS. Added/Corp** Jane's Information Group. **VFOAT** Military Vehicles and Logistics. 12th Ed. (1992)-. English. an. $255.00 US & Mexico; $312.38 others. Jane's Information Group, Sentinel House, 163 Brighton Road, Coulsdon Surrey CR3 2NX England. **Tel** 011 44 81 763 1030, FAX 011 44 81 763 1006. **(Subscription address:** Jane's Information Group / US Subscriptions, 1340 Braddock Place, Suite 300, Alexandria VA 22314.**) LC** UG615; .J35. **DD** 355.8/3. available on CD-ROM. ***Continues*** *Jane's Military Logistics, 0954-4941.*

UK/0958-126X
**JANE'S NATO HANDBOOK.** ***Ceased.*** [Jane's NATO handb.]. **VAT** Jane's North Atlantic Treaty Organization Handbook. 1st Ed. (1988-89)-Ceased with 1991-1992 Edition. English. Jane's Information Group, Sentinel House, 163 Brighton Road, Coulsdon Surrey CR3 2NX England. **Tel** 011 44 81 763 1030, FAX 011 44 81 763 1006. **LC** UA646.3; .J36. **DD** 355/031/091821.

UK
**JANE'S NAVAL WEAPON SYSTEMS. Added/Corp** Jane's Information Group. **VFOAT** Naval Weapon Systems. (1989)-. English. an. $440.00 US & Mexico; $539.00 Central and South America. Jane's Information Group, Sentinel House, 163 Brighton Road, Coulsdon Surrey CR3 2NX England. **Tel** 011 44 81 763 1030, FAX 011 44 81 763 1006. **(Subscription address:** Jane's Information Group / US Subscriptions, 1340 Braddock Place, Suite 300, Alexandria VA 22314.**)** available on CD-ROM. ***Continues in part*** *Jane's Weapon Systems (London, England).*

UK
**JANE'S NBC PROTECTION EQUIPMENT. Added/Corp** Jane's Information Group. **VFOAT** NBC Protection Equipment. 1st Ed. (1989)-. English. an (Aug.). $255.00 US & Mexico; $267.05 Canada; $312.38 other. Jane's Information Group, Sentinel House, 163 Brighton Road, Coulsdon Surrey CR3 2NX England. **Tel** 011 44 81 763 1030, FAX 011 44 81 763 1006. **(Subscription address:** Jane's Information Group / US Subscriptions, 1340 Braddock Place, Suite 300, Alexandria VA 22314.**) LC** UG447; .J36. **DD** 358/.3/0289. **Ad Acc.** available on CD-ROM.
**Desc:** Covers all types of nuclear, biological and chemical protection equipment.

US
**JANE'S RADAR AND ELECTRONIC WARFARE SYSTEMS. VFOAT** Radar and Electronic Warfare Systems; Jane's Radar and EW Systems. 1st Ed. (1990)-. English. an. $255.00 US and Mexico; $312.38 Central and South America. Jane's Information Group, Sentinel House, 163 Brighton Road, Coulsdon Surrey CR3 2NX England. **Tel** 011 44 81 763 1030, FAX 011 44 81 763 1006. **(Subscription address:** Jane's Information Group / US Subscriptions, 1340 Braddock Place, Suite 300, Alexandria VA 22314.**) LC** UG485; .J36. **DD** 623/.043/05. **Bk Rev. Ad Acc. Circ:** 10,000. available on CD-ROM. ***Continues in part*** *Jane's Weapon Systems (London, England).*

UK
**JANE'S SECURITY AND CO-IN EQUIPMENT. Added/Corp** Jane's Information Group. **VFOAT** Security and Co-In Equipment. **VAT** Jane's Security and Counter-Insurgency Equipment. 2nd Ed. (1990)-. English. an. $245.00 US & Mexico; $267.05 Canada; $300.13 others. Jane's Information Group, Sentinel House, 163 Brighton Road, Coulsdon Surrey CR3 2NX England. **Tel** 011 44 81 763 1030, FAX 011 44 81 763 1006. **(Subscription address:** Jane's Information Group / US Subscriptions, 1340 Braddock Place, Suite 300, Alexandria VA 22314.**) LC** U241; .J36. **DD** 355.02/18/028. available on CD-ROM. ***Continues*** *Jane's Security and CO-IN.*

UK
**JANE'S STRATEGIC WEAPON SYSTEMS.** English. an. £225.00 UK; $395.00 other. Jane's Information Group, Sentinel House, 163 Brighton Road, Coulsdon Surrey CR3 2NX England. **Tel** 011 44 81 763 1030, FAX 011 44 81 763 1006. **ED** Duncan Lennox.
**Desc:** A complete guide to the world's guided missiles, including those carrying nuclear, biological and chemical warheads.

UK
**JANE'S UNDERWATER WARFARE SYSTEMS. Added/Corp** Jane's Information Group. **VFOAT** Underwater Warfare Systems. 1st Ed. (1990)-. English. an. $255.00 US & Mexico; $267.05 Canada; $312.38 Central & South America. Jane's Information Group, Sentinel House, 163 Brighton Road, Coulsdon Surrey CR3 2NX England. **Tel** 011 44 81 763 1030, FAX 011 44 81 763 1006. **(Subscription address:** Jane's Information Group / US Subscriptions, 1340 Braddock Place, Suite 300, Alexandria VA 22314.**) LC** V214; .J36. **DD** 359.9/3/05. available on CD-ROM. ***Continues in part*** *Jane's Weapon Systems (London, England).*

US
**JING BAO JOURNAL.** English. bm. Flying Tigers of the 14th Air Force Association, Box 185, Selden NY 11784. **Tel** (305)973-0277 OR (516)698-1782. **ED** Milt Miller. **Bk Rev. Circ:** 4,000 (ctrl).
**Desc:** Material of interest to war veterans who served in China.

US/1070-0692
**JOINT FORCE QUARTERLY.** (JOINT FORCE QUARTERLY : JFQ.). [Joint force q.]. **Added/Corp** National Defense University. Institute for National Strategic Studies. **VFOAT** JFQ. No. 1 (summer 1993)-. Government Publication. English. qt. $19.00 US; $23.75 other. Superintendent of Documents, US Government Printing Office, Washington DC 20402. **Tel** (202)275-3328, FAX (202)786-2377. **LC** IN PROCESS; U260; .J65. **DD** 355.
**Desc:** Published for officers of the Armed Forces to promote understanding of the integrated employment of land, sea, air, space and special operations forces. Focuses on joint doctrine, coalition warfare, contingency planning, operations conducted by the unified commands, and joint force development.

US/0274-595X
**JOINT PERSPECTIVES.** [Jt. perspect.]. Vol. 1, No. 1 (Summer 1980)-. Periodical. English. qt. Public Affairs Officer, Armed Forces Staff College, Norfolk VA 23511. **LC** U1; .J57. **DD** 355/.005.

US
**JOINT TRAVEL REGULATIONS. VOLUME 1. MEMBERS OF UNIFORMED SERVICES: ARMY, NAVY, MARINE CORPS, AIR FORCE, COAST GUARD, NATIONAL OCEANIC AND ATMOSPHERIC ADMINISTRATION CORPS, PUBLIC HEALTH SERVICE.** **Main/Corp** United States. Dept. of Defense. **VFOAT** Members of Uniformed Services. (19??)-. Government Publication. English. an (January and supplements). $123.00 domestic; $153.75 other. Superintendent of Documents, US Government Printing Office, Washington DC 20402. **Tel** (202)275-3328, FAX (202)786-2377.
**Desc:** Contains basic statutory regulations concerning travel and transportation allowances for members of the uniformed services, including all regular and reserve components.

PO
**JORNAL DE EXERCITO.** Vol. 1; Jan. 1960-. Periodical. Portuguese. Jornal de Exercito, Largo da Graca 94, 1100 Lisbon Portugal. **LC** U4; .J6.

II/0379-5470
**JOURNAL OF ARMAMENT STUDIES.** (JOURNAL OF ARMAMENT STUDIES / INSTITUTE OF ARMAMENT TECHNOLOGY.). [J. armament stud.]. **Added/Corp** Institute of Armament Studies (Poona, India). (19??)-. Periodical. English. **CODEN** JASTDD. Documents available from CASDDS.
**Ind/Abst** Chem. Abstr.

US/0192-429X
**JOURNAL OF ELECTRONIC DEFENSE.** (JOURNAL OF ELECTRONIC DEFENSE : OFFICIAL PUBLICATION OF THE ASSOCIATION OF OLD CROWS.). [J. electron. def.]. **Added/Corp** Association of Old Crows. Vol. 1, No. 1 (July/Aug. 1978)-. Periodical. English. mo. $67.00 (one year), $110.00 (two year) US; $120.00 (one year), $230.00 (two year) other. Horizon House, 685 Canton Street, Norwood MA 02062. **Tel** (617)365-4595. **(Subscription address:** Journal of Electronic Defense, PO Box 9098, Braintree MA 02184.**)** **ED** Hal Gershanoff. **LC** UG485; .J68. **DD** 623/.043/05. **CODEN** JELDER. **[CCC]. Bk Rev. Ad Acc. Circ:** 26,000 (ctrl). available on an online database (file 648/Full-Text) from DIALOG. Documents available from Ask*IEEE.
**Desc:** Presents articles, editorials, product and industry news and columns on military electronics and electronic warfare systems operation. Planning, technology and procurement for US/NATO forces and more are covered.
**Ind/Abst** Air Univ. Libr. Index Mil. Period.; Curr. Mil. Pol. Lit.; F&S Index Plus Text, Int. [Select. Cov.]; INSPEC (Aug. 1989-); Predicasts; PROMT; Trade Ind. ASAP [Full Txt.]; Trade Ind. Index [Full Txt.].

●US/1057-8307
**JOURNAL OF MILITARY AVIATION. See** Aeronautics, Astronautics.

US/0899-3718
**JOURNAL OF MILITARY HISTORY, THE.** [J. mil. hist.]. **Added/Corp** Virginia Military Institute. George C. Marshall Foundation. American Military Institute. Vol. 53, No. 1 (Jan. 1989)-. Periodical. English. qt (4 issues). $45.00 US, Canada & Mexico; $53.00 other. Journal of Military History, George C. Marshall Library, The Virginia Military Institute, Lexington VA 24450. **Tel** (703)464-7468, FAX (703)464-5229. **ED** Henry S. Bausum. **LC** E181; .M55. **DD** 973/.05. Index available. cum. index. **Bk Rev**, (Qty: 120). **Ad Acc, Adv Mgr:** F. Richards. **Pr Rev. Circ:** 3,000. available on microfilm and microfiche from University Microfilms International (UMI). Documents available from The Genuine Article, UMI Article Clearinghouse. ***Continues** Military Affairs, 0026-3931.*
**Desc:** A journal of military history dealing with all periods and geographical areas.
**Ind/Abst** Acad. Search (July 1993-); Am. Hist. Life; Am. Bibliogr. Slavic East Europ. Stud.; Arts Humanit. Citation Index [Full Cov.]; Curr. Contents Arts Humanit.; Expand. Acad. Index (1989-); Hist. Source (July 1993-); Humanit. Index; Humanit. Source (Jul. 1993-); INFO-SOUTH Abstr.; Mag. Search; Newsp. Period. Abstr. (1991-); Res. Alert [Full Cov.]; Soc. Sci. Cit. Index [Select. Cov.].

●UK
**JOURNAL OF SLAVIC MILITARY STUDIES, THE.** Vol. 6, No. 1 (Mar. 1993)-. Periodical. English. qt. $185.00. Frank Cass & Company Ltd, Newbury House, 890-900 Eastern Avenue, Newbury Park, Ilford, Essex IG2 7HH United Kingdom. **Tel** 011 44 81 599 8866, FAX 011 44 81 599 0984, telex 897719. **LC** UA770; .J68. **CODEN** JSMTE8. **Ad Acc, Adv Mgr:** Anne Kidson. ***Continues** Journal of Soviet Military Studies.*

UK/0954-254X
**JOURNAL OF SOVIET MILITARY STUDIES, THE.** ***Title Change.*** Vol. 1, No. 1 (Apr. 1988)-Vol. 5, No. 4 (Dec. 1992). Periodical. English. qt. Frank Cass & Company Ltd, Newbury House, 890-900 Eastern Avenue, Newbury Park, Ilford, Essex IG2 7HH United Kingdom. **Tel** 011 44 81 599 8866, FAX 011 44 81 599 0984, telex 897719. **ED** David M Glawtz and Christopher Donnelly. **LC** UA770; .J68. **CODEN** JSMSE5. Index available. cum. index. **Bk Rev. Ad Acc.** ***Continued by** Journal of Slavic Military Studies.*
**Desc:** Investigates every aspect of evolution of Soviet military art, doctrine and technique used in tactical combat.
**Ind/Abst** Air Univ. Libr. Index Mil. Period.; Am. Hist. Life (1988-).

UK/0140-2390
**JOURNAL OF STRATEGIC STUDIES, THE.** [J. strateg. stud.]. Vol. 1, (May 1978)-. Periodical. English. qt. $185.00. Frank Cass & Company Ltd, Newbury House, 890-900 Eastern Avenue, Newbury Park, Ilford, Essex IG2 7HH United Kingdom. **Tel** 011 44 81 599 8866, FAX 011 44 81 599 0984, telex 897719. **ED** Amos Perlmutter and John Gooch. **LC** U162; .J68. **DD** 355/.005. **Bk Rev. Ad Acc, Adv Mgr:** Anne Kidson. **Circ:** 500. available on microfilm and microfiche from University Microfilms International (UMI). Documents available from The Genuine Article.
**Desc:** The journal exists to bring the subject of strategy into sharp focuses and concentrate the abundant material that has hitherto been dispersed under other headings, and is open to all related areas of strategy and also devotes issues to specific topics.
**Ind/Abst** Am. Hist. Life (1979-); Br. Humanit. Index; Curr. Contents Soc. Behav. Sci.; Curr. Mil. Pol. Lit. (1979-); Int. Polit. Sci. Abstr. (1979-); Res. Alert [Full Cov.]; Soc. Plann. Policy Dev. Abstr.; Soc. Sci. Cit. Index [Full Cov.].

UK/0004-2439
**JOURNAL OF THE ARMS & ARMOUR SOCIETY, THE.** [J. Arms Armour Soc.]. **Added/Corp** Arms and Armour Society. **VFOAT** Journal of the Arms and Armour Society. (1953)-. Periodical. English. Twice a year (Mar. & Sept.). £10.00 (surface mail), £15.00 (airmail). Arms & Armour Society, 135 Peterborough Road, Leyton, London E10 6EL England. **LC** U799; .J68. **DD** 739.7/05.
**Ind/Abst** Am. Hist. Life (1956-1963); BHA : Biblio. Hist. Art.

AT/0729-6274
**JOURNAL OF THE AUSTRALIAN WAR MEMORIAL.** [J. Aust. War Meml.]. **Added/Corp** Australian War Memorial. No. 1 (Oct. 1982)-. Periodical. English. Twice a year (Apr., Nov.). 25.00Aus$ (one year), 45.00Aus$ (two years). Australian War Memorial, PO Box 345, Canberra Australian Capital Territory 2601 Australia. **Tel** 011 61 62 434211, FAX 011 61 62 434325. **[CCC]. Bk Rev. Ad Acc. Pr Rev. Circ:** 800 (ctrl).
**Ind/Abst** APAIS, Aust. Public Aff. Inf. Ser. (1984-).

●CN/1188-164X
**JOURNAL OF THE MILITARY HISTORY SOCIETY OF MANITOBA.** [J. Mil. Hist. Soc. Manit.]. **Added/Corp** Military History Society of Manitoba. (1992)-. English. an. Free to members, $10.00 per vol., others. Military Historical Society of Manitoba, Box 131, Winnipeg Manitoba R3C 2G1 Canada. **Tel** (204)452-7117. **DD** 355/.0097127.

UK/0035-8665
**JOURNAL OF THE ROYAL ARMY MEDICAL CORPS. See** Medical Science and Technology.

UK
**JOURNAL OF THE ROYAL ARTILLERY, THE.** **Added/Corp** Royal Artillery Institution. Vol. 32, No. 4 (July 1905)-. Periodical. English. sa. £4.00. Royal Artillery Institution, Old Royal Military Academy, Woolwich London SE184DN England. **Tel** 011 44 81 8542242 ext. 5620. cum. index. **Bk Rev. Ad Acc. Circ:** 3,500 (ctrl). ***Continues** Royal Artillery Institution. Proceedings of the Royal Artillery Institution.*
**Desc:** Covers artillery matters.

AT/0728-1188
**JOURNAL OF THE ROYAL UNITED SERVICES INSTITUTE OF AUSTRALIA.** [J. Royal United Serv. Inst. Aust.]. **Added/Corp** Royal United Services Institute of Australia. Vol. 3, No. 2 (Nov. 1980)-. Periodical. English. an. 16.00Aus$ Australia; 21.00Aus$ other. Rust Australia Inc., PO Box 590, Canberra Australian Capital Territory 2601 Australia. **Tel** 011 61 62 652590. **ED** John Donovan. Index available. **Ad Acc, Adv Mgr:** N. Wainwright, **Tel** (6)248-6866. **Circ:** 4,500 (ctrl). ***Continues** Australian Journal of Defence Studies.*
**Desc:** The aim of the journal is to advance the study of strategy, national defence and related matters (including military affairs in general).
**Ind/Abst** APAIS, Aust. Public Aff. Inf. Ser. (1980-).

UK/0037-9700
**JOURNAL OF THE SOCIETY FOR ARMY HISTORICAL RESEARCH.** [J. Soc. Army Hist. Res.]. **Main/Corp** Society for Army Historical Research (London, England). Vol. 1 No. 1 (1921)-. Periodical. English. Four times a year. £18.00 UK; $32.00 (surface mail), $46.00 (airmail) US; 43.00Can$ (surface mail), 62.00Can$ (airmail) Canada. Society for Army Historical Research, National Army Museum, Royal Hospital Road, London SW3 4HT England. **ED** Alan Harfield (editor's address: Plum Tree Cottage, Royston Place, Barton-on-Sea Hants BH25 7AJ England; editor's phone: 44 425 621950). **LC** DA49; .S6. **DD** 942.0062. Index available. cum. index. **Bk Rev**, (Qty: 16). **Ad Acc. Circ:** 1,200 (ctrl).
**Ind/Abst** Am. Hist. Life (1955-); Br. Humanit. Index; Ref. Sources; Writ. Am. Hist.

II/0041-770X
**JOURNAL OF THE UNITED SERVICE INSTITUTION OF INDIA, THE.** [J. United Serv. Inst. India]. **Added/Corp** United Service Institution of India. **VFOAT** U.S.I. Journal. (1871)-. Periodical. English. Four times a year. $26.00 sea mail; $33.00 airmail. United Service Institution of India, Kashmir House, Majaji Marg, New Delhi 110011 India. **Tel** 11 91 11 3793012. Index available. **Bk Rev. Ad Acc. Circ:** 5,800 (ctrl). ***Continues** United Service Institution of India. Proceedings.*
**Ind/Abst** Am. Hist. Life (1955-1966, 1971-).

US
**JOURNAL OF THE US ARMY MEDICAL DEPARTMENT, THE. See** Medical Science and Technology.

●US
**JPRS REPORT. CENTRAL EURASIA. MILITARY AFFAIRS / FOREIGN BROADCAST INFORMATION SERVICE.** **Added/Corp** United States. Joint Publications Research Service. United States. Foreign Broadcast Information Service. **VFOAT** Joint Publications Research Service Report. Military Affairs; Central Eurasia. Military Affairs; Military Affairs. (Jan. 10, 1992)-. English. **LC** UA770; .J89. ***Continues** JPRS Report. Soviet Union. Military Policy.*

MK
**JUND UMAN.** Periodical. Arabic. PO Box 113, Masqat Muscat. **LC** UA853.O5; J86.

AU
**KALENDER / OSTERREICHISCHER KAMERADSCHAFTSBUND.** **Added/Corp** Osterreichischer Kameradschaftsbund. (1984)-. German. an. Osterreichischer Kameradschaftsbund, Wahringerstrasse 26/3, 1090 Vienna Austria. **LC** U10.A8; O3. ***Continues** Osterreichischer Soldatenkalendar.*

FR
**KEPI BLANC.** Began publication Apr. 30, 1947. Periodical. French. M le Chef du S I H L E, BP 78, 13673 Aubagne France. **LC** UA703.L5.

IO/0303-4992
**KETAHANAN NASIONAL.** Periodical. Indonesian. qt. Lembaga Pertahanan Nasional, Jalan Kebon Sirih 28, Jakarta Indonesia. **LC** UA853.I5; A3. ***Continues** Madjalah Ketahanan Nasional.*

JA
**KOKUBO MONDAI KENKYUKAI KOENROKUSHU.** Japanese. Kokubungaku Kenkyu Shiryokan, 16-10 Yutakamachi 1-chome, Shinagawa-ku 142, Tokyo Japan. **Tel** (03)785-7131. **LC** UA845; .K624.

KO
**KOREAN JOURNAL OF DEFENSE ANALYSIS.** **Added/Corp** Korea Institute for Defense Analysis. Vol. 1, No.1 (Summer 1989)-. Periodical. English. Twice a year. Free. Korea Inst Defense Analyses, Chang Ryang, PO Box 250, Tong-gu Seoul 130-650, Korea. **Tel** 011 82 2 9611 779, 962 0801.

RU
**KRASNAIA ZVEZDA.** **Added/Corp** Soviet Union. Narodnyi Komissariat Oborony. Soviet Union. Ministerstvo Oborony. (1925)-. Periodical. Russian. ir (260 issues per year). $229.95. **(Subscription address:** East View Publications Inc., 3020 Harbor Lane North, Suite 110, Minneapolis MN 55447.**)** available on microfilm from University Microfilms International (UMI).
**Ind/Abst** Curr. Dig. Post Sov. Press.

US/1050-7310
**LANGUAGE OF DEFENSE : HANDBOOK OF ACRONYMS AND TERMINOLOGY.** ***Ceased.*** (1991)-(199?). English. an. Carrol Publishing Company, 1058 Thomas Jefferson Street NW, Washington DC 20007.

US/0364-6793
**LATEST EDITIONS OF U.S. AIR FORCE AERONAUTICAL CHARTS.** **Main/Corp** National Ocean Survey. **VAT** Latest Editions of United States Air Force Aeronautical Charts. (19??)-. Periodical. English. mo. US Department of Commerce / National Oceanic & Atmospheric Administration NOAA, 6010 Executive Boulevard, Washington Science Center, Building 5, Rockville MD 20852. **Tel** (202)482-6090, FAX (202)482-3154.

US/0023-981X
**LEATHERNECK.** **Added/Corp** Leatherneck Association. Marine Corps Institute (U.S.). Special Programs Dept. (1917)-. Periodical. English. mo. $18.75 (surface), $72.24 (airmail). Marine Corps Association Inc, Box 1775, Quantico VA 22134. **Tel** (703)640-6161, (800)336-0291, FAX (703)640-0823. **ED** William V. H. White, Tom Bartlett, Nancy L. White, Cheryl Adams North, K. V. Stark, Ron Lunn. **LC** D501; .L4. **DD** 359.9/6/0973. Index available. cum. index. **Bk Rev**. **Ad Acc**. **Circ:** 107,115. available on microfilm and microfiche from University Microfilms International (UMI); available on CD-ROM. ***Continues** Quantico Leatherneck.*
**Desc:** Magazine for Marines of all ranks, focusing on history, traditions, schools, training, personalities, physical fitness, weapons and equipment.

CN/0024-0435
**LEGION.** **Added/Corp** Royal Canadian Legion. National Magazine Executive Committee. Vol. 43, No. 8 (Jan. 1969)-. Periodical. English. Ten times a year. 10.00Can$ Canada; 15.00Can$ other. Canvet Publication Ltd, 359 Kent Street, Suite 504, Ottawa Ontario K2P 0R6 Canada. **Tel** (613)235-8741. **ED** Mac Johnston. **Bk Rev**. **Ad Acc**. **Circ:** 534,768. available on microfilm and microfiche from University Microfilms International (UMI). ***Continues** Legionary., 0380-4348.*
**Desc:** General and special interest reading for veterans, their families, plus serving forces RCMP & general public. Topics include military history, veterans affairs, defense, humour health & recreation, seniors' issues, current affairs. Focus on activities of the Royal Canadian Legion.

US/0364-4200
**LEGISLATIVE CALENDAR / UNITED STATES HOUSE OF REPRESENTATIVES, COMMITTEE ON VETERAN AFFAIRS.** **See** Public Administration.

PO
**LIBER 25.** **VFOAT** Liber Viginti Quinque. No. 1 (Mar.-April 1981)-. Periodical. Portuguese (Portuguese). bm. **LC** UA760; .L5. **DD** 355/.009469.

US/0094-4092
**LIST OF LOCAL BOARDS OF THE SELECTIVE SERVICE SYSTEM.** **Main/Corp** United States. Selective Service System. (19??)-. Government Publication. English. ir. Superintendent of Documents, US Government Printing Office, Washington DC 20402. **Tel** (202)275-3328, FAX (202)786-2377. **LC** UB343; .U55a. **DD** 355.2/236.

UK/0306-8390
**LIST OF MEMBERS - INTERNATIONAL INSTITUTE FOR STRATEGIC STUDIES.** **Main/Corp** International Institute for Strategic Studies. English. an. DM392.00 (one year), DM744.80 (two year) includes the journals Adelphi Papers, The Military Balance, Strategic Survey and Survival Germany; $210.00 (one year), $399.00 (two year) includes the journals Adelphi Papers, The Military Balance, Strategic Survey and Survival other. International Institution of Strategic Studies, 18 Adam Street, London WC2 England. **Tel** (0865)794141, FAX (0865)750643, telex 83177. **(Subscription address:** US/ Maxwell House, Fairview Park, Elmsford, NY 10523; Can/ 150 Consumers Road/Suite 104, Willowdale Ontario M2J 1p9; Aus-NZ/ POB 544, Potts Point NSW 2011**)** **LC** U1; .I4914. **DD** 355.03/06/01.

GW
**LISTE DER AUSLANDISCHEN MILITARATTACHES.** German. **LC** UB260; .L57. **DD** 355.3/432.

GW
**LITERATURZUSAMMENSTELLUNGEN ... DER TECHNISCHEN INFORMATIONS- UND DOKUMENTATIONSSTELLE DES BWB.** German. **LC** U3; .L57. **DD** 355/.005.

SW/0024-5372
**LIVRUSTKAMMAREN.** **Added/Corp** Livrustkammaren (Sweden). **VFOAT** Journal of the Royal Armoury; Liv Rust Kammaren. Vol.1, No.1 (1937)-. Periodical. Swedish (English and German). cum. index.
**Ind/Abst** BHA : Biblio. Hist. Art.

UK/0961-8422
**LONDON DEFENCE STUDIES.** **Added/Corp** University of London. Centre for Defence Studies. **VFOAT** London Defense Studies. (1990)-. Monographic series. English. ir (6-8 issues a year). £70.00 Europe and other; $133.00 North & South America (institution). Brasseys UK Ltd., 33 John Street, London WC1N 2AT England. **Tel** 011 44 71 753 7777, FAX 011 44 71 753 7794. **(Subscription address:** Brasseys UK Ltd., Distribution Center, Blackhorse Road, Letchworth SG6 1HN England.**)** **ED** Michael Clarke. **LC** U1; .L66. **DD** 355/.005. **Pr Rev.**
**Desc:** Publishes the results of research on issues of contemporary defense and security.

GW/0343-0103
**LOYAL.** (LOYAL : DAS DEUTSCHE WEHRMAGAZIN.). (1969)-. Periodical. German. mo. DM36.00 Germany; DM42.00 other. Special Publication Service, Karl Mand Str 2, D 56070 Koblenz Germany. **Tel** 011 49 261 807060. **UDC** 355.02. **CODEN** 327.

GW
**LUFTFAHRT INTERNATIONAL.** ***Title Change.*** Periodical. German. mo. Maximilian Verlagsgruppe, Postfach 2352, Steintorwall 17, D 32052 Herford Germany. **Tel** 011 49 5221 599142, 011 49 5221 599161. **LC** UG1240; .L84. **DD** 623.74/6/05. ***Continued by** Pilot and Flugzeug.*

UK
**LYLE OFFICIAL ARMS AND ARMOUR REVIEW, THE.** **VFOAT** Arms and Armour. Began with 1976 Vol. English. an. $16.95. The Putnam Publishing Group, 390 Murray Hill Parkway East, Rutherford NJ 07073. **Tel** (800)631-8571. **LC** U800; .L93. **DD** 739.7/029/4.

US
**MAC FORUM: THE JOURNAL OF THE MILITARY AIRLIFT COMMAND, THE.** ***Title Change.*** **Added/Corp** United States. Air Force. Military Airlift Command. Director of Safety. Vol. 1, No. 1 (Jan. 1992)-Vol. 1, No. 3 (May/June 1992). Government Publication. English. bm. Superintendent of Documents, US Government Printing Office, Washington DC 20402. **Tel** (202)275-3328, FAX (202)786-2377. **LC** UC333; .M33. available in microform from University Microfilms International (UMI). ***Formed by the union of** MAC Flyer, 0024-788X **and** Airlift (Scott Air Force Base, Ill.), 0897-957X. **Continued by** Mobility Forum.*
**Ind/Abst** Air Univ. Libr. Index Mil. Period. (1992).

US/0364-5169
**MAGAZINE FOR EVERY US VETERAN, THE.** **VFOAT** U.S. Veteran. **VAT** The Magazine for Every United States Veteran. Periodical. English. mo. $9.00. 115 Plaza Drive, Sunnyvale CA 94086. **LC** UB357; .M34. **DD** 355.1/15/0973.

TI
**MAJALLAH AL-ASKARIYAH AL-FILASTINIYAH (TUNIS, TUNISIA).** (AL-MAJALLAH AL-ASKARIYAH AL-FILASTINIYAH.). **VFOAT** Revue Militaire Palestinienne. V. 1, No. 1, (Jan. 1, 1984)-. Periodical. Arabic. mo. $80.00. 57, rue Mouaouia Ibn Abi Soufian, El Menzah Vi Tunis Tunisie.

MR
**MAJALLAT AL-QUWAT AL-MUSALLAHAH AL-MALAKIYAH.** **Main/Corp** Morocco. Al-Quwat Al-Musallahah Al-Malakiyah. **VFOAT** Revue des Forces Armees Royales. Periodical. Multiple languages (Arabic and French). 2.00 single issue. 45 Ave Moulay Ismail, Al-Rabat Morocco. **LC** U7; .M67A. ***Continues** Majallat Al-Quwat Al-Musallahah Al-Malakiyah.*

SU
**MAJALLAT KULLIYAT AL-MALIK KHALID AL-ASKARIYAH.** **VFOAT** King Khalid Military Academy Quarterly. Periodical. Arabic (English). qt. 20 Riyals Individuals, 50 Riyals Institutions. PO Box 22140, Riyadh Saudi Arabia. **LC** U4; .M36.

US/0191-3522
**MAN AT ARMS.** [Man at arms]. **Added/Corp** National Rifle Association of America. **VFOAT** Man at Arms Magazine. Vol. 1, No. 1 (Jan./Feb. 1979)-. Periodical. English. Six times a year. $24.00 US and Canada; $32.00 other. Man at Arms Magazine, PO Box 460, Lincoln RI 02865. **Tel** (401)726-8011. **ED** Andrew Mowbray. **LC** NK6900; .M36. **DD** 355.8/24/075. Index available in last issue of volume--attached. cum. index. **Bk Rev**, (Qty: 6/yr). **Ad Acc**. **Circ:** 6,000.
**Desc:** Colorful magazine on firearms, swords, military, security, and field news, including a stolen arms alert, preservation information, show calendar, history, and a question column.

IT
**MARINA ITALIANA.** Silvio Basile, Via Lungo Bisagno Istria 34/C, 16141 Genoa Italy. **Tel** 011 39 10 852151.

US/0025-3170
**MARINE CORPS GAZETTE.** (THE MARINE CORPS GAZETTE.). [Mar. Corps gaz.]. **Added/Corp** Marine Corps Association. Vol. 1 (March 1916)-. Periodical. English. mo. $18.75. Marine Corps Association Inc, Box 1775, Quantico VA 22134. **Tel** (703)640-6161, (800)336-0291, FAX (703)640-0823. **ED** J. E. Greenwood, Joseph D. Dodd, M. M. Roberts and Matthew T. Robinson. **LC** VE7; .M4. **DD** 359.9/6/05. Index available. cum. index. **Bk Rev**. **Ad Acc**. **Circ:** 38,036. available on microfilm and microfiche from University Microfilms International (UMI); available on CD-ROM.
**Desc:** Professional journal of the US Marines covering all aspects of Marine Corps activity. Articles on research and development of military equipment; new weapons systems; theories and concepts on land, sea (amphibious), and aviation (outer space) military operations; foreign military formations, national security issues; current wars of insurgency; terrorism; history on Marine Corps, etc.
**Ind/Abst** Air Univ. Libr. Index Mil. Period.; Am. Hist. Life (1955-); Curr. Mil. Pol. Lit.

US/1075-9069
**MARINE OFFICER.** (1991)-. Periodical. English. mo. District 1 / Pacific Coast Division, MEBA-NMU, 444 North Capitol Street Northwest, Washington DC 20001. **Tel** (202)347-8585. ***Formed by the union of** American Marine Engineer, 0002-9866 **and** Marine Journal (Washington, D.C.), 0887-6738.*
**Ind/Abst** Work Relat. Abstr.

●US/1060-2607
**MARINE SOCIETY VIEWS.** [Mar. Soc. views]. **Added/Corp** Once a Marine, Always a Marine Society. Vol. 1, No. 1, 1st quarter (1992)-. Periodical. English. qt. Once a Marine, Always a Marine Society, PO box 488, College Park MD 27040. **DD** 355.

US/1056-9073
**MARINES (WASHINGTON, D.C.).** (MARINES.). [Marines]. **Added/Corp** United States. Marine Corps. Media Branch. Vol. 12 No. 7 (July 1983)-. Government Publication. English. mo. $18.00 domestic; $22.50 other. Superintendent of Documents, US Government Printing Office, Washington DC 20402. **Tel** (202)275-3328, FAX (202)786-2377. **LC** WMLC L 83/6654. **DD** 359. ***Continues** HQMC Hotline.*
**Desc:** Presents information about current Marine Corps plans, policies, programs, and activities.

UK/0958-4986
**MEDAL NEWS HINDHEAD. 1989.** **See** Hobbies-Numismatics.

US/0737-6529
**MEDALS YEARBOOK.** [Medals yearb.]. **VFOAT** Medals Year Book. Began in 1979/80. English. ir. DF Collins, Contract Station 22, 9297 Federal Building, Box 327, Denver CO 80221. **ED** J Brant. **LC** UB430; .M4. **DD** 355.1/352/0294. **Ad Acc**. **Circ:** 6,000.
**Desc:** Photographic, illustrated price guide on British and Colonial military medals. Over 450 photographs with over 2,300 price valuations.

FR/0300-4937
**MEDECINE ET ARMEES.** [Med. armees]. Vol. 1 (Jan. 1973)-. Periodical. French. Eight times a year. 220.00F (France); 290.00F (other). Addim, 6 rue Saint Charles, 75015 Paris France. **Tel** 011 33 1 45770376. **NLM** W1 ME139G. **CODEN** MDARC4. **Bk Rev**. **Ad Acc**. **Pr Rev**. **Circ:** 6,000 (ctrl). Documents available from The Genuine Article. ***Supersedes** Revue des Corps de Sante des Armees Terre, Mer, Air.*
**Desc:** Review of military physicians and of military hospitals.
**Ind/Abst** EMBASE; Helminthol. Abstr. (1991-); Index Vet.; Nutr. Abstr. Rev., Ser. A, Hum. Exp.; Protozoolog. Abstr.; Res. Alert [Select. Cov.]; Rev. Med. Vet. Entomol.; Rev. Med. Vet. Mycology; Saf. Health Work; SCISEARCH; Small Anim. Abstr. Bibliogr.

GW/0179-1826
**MEDICAL CORPS INTERNATIONAL.** ***Ceased.*** **See** Medical Science and Technology.

II/0377-1237
**MEDICAL JOURNAL, ARMED FORCES INDIA.** **See** Medical Science and Technology.

VE
**MEMORIA Y CUENTA ... QUE EL MINISTRO DE LA DEFENSA PRESENTA AL CONGRESO NACIONAL / REPUBLICA DE VENEZUELA, MINISTERIO DE LA DEFENSA.** **Main/Corp** Venezuela. Ministerio de la Defensa. **VFOAT** Memoria y Cuenta. (19??)-. Spanish. Ministerio Defensa Nacional, Caracas Republica Venezuela. ***Continues** Venezuela. Ministerio de la Defensa Nacional.; Memoria y Cuenta que el Ministerio de la Defensa de la Republica de Venezuela Presenta al Congreso Nacional.*

US/1040-5992
**MHQ (NEW YORK, N.Y.).** (MHQ : THE QUARTERLY JOURNAL OF MILITARY HISTORY.). [MHQ]. **VFOAT** Quarterly Journal of Military History. **VAT** Military History Quarterly. Vol. 1, No. 1 (Autumn 1988)-. Periodical. English. qt (4 issues). $60.00 (without index), $75.00 (with index). MHQ, 29 West 38th Street, New York NY 10018. **Tel** (212)398-1550. **ED** Robert Cowley. **LC** D25; .M44. **DD** 904/.7/05. Index available.
**Desc:** Lavishly illustrated hardcover magazine devoted to the history of warfare and the development of tactics, strategy and weaponry.
**Ind/Abst** Am. Hist. Life (1955-).

IS
**MIDDLE EAST MILITARY BALANCE / JAFFEE CENTER FOR STRATEGIC STUDIES, THE.** **Added/Corp** Merkaz Le-Mehkarim Estrategiyim al Shem Yafeh. Universitat Tel-Aviv. (1983)-. English. an. $69.50. Jerusalem Post, PO Box 81, Jerusalem 91000 Israel. **Tel** 011 972 2 551616. **LC** UA832; .M5. **DD** 355/.033056. **Bk Rev**, (Qty: 30/yr). **Circ:** 1,500.
**Desc:** This review provides a detailed data base available on military forces and the military capacity of each state in the region as well as the PLO.

DK
**MILITAERT TIDSSKRIFT.** Dutch. ir. $14.00. Krigsvidenskabelige Selskab, Postbok 214 Frederiksberg Slot, DK 2000 Frederiksberg Denmark.
**Ind/Abst** Am. Hist. Life (1987-1990).

NE
**MILITAIRE SPECTATOR, DE.** Vol. 1 (1832)-. Periodical. Dutch. Twelve times a year. Fl30.00 Netherlands; Fl40.00 others. ADM Militaire Spectator, Karel Doormanlaan 274, 2283 BB Rijswidjk Netherlands. **ED** J. C. van Rijneveld. **LC** U4; .M6. **Bk Rev**. **Ad Acc**. ctrl circ.

UK
**MILITANT.** English. wk. £33.00 UK; £44.00 Europe; £56.00 other. Militant, 3-13 Hepscott Road, London E9 5HB England. **Tel** 011 44 01 5333311.

UK
**MILITANT INTERNATIONAL REVIEW.** No. 1 (Autumn 1969)-. Periodical. English. qt. £5.00 UK; £6.00 other. Militant, 3-13 Hepscott Road, London E9 5HB England. **Tel** 011 44 01 5333311.

GW
**MILITAR UND SOZIALWISSENSCHAFTEN.** **See** Sociology.

GW
**MILITARGESCHICHTE.** **Added/Corp** Germany (West). Militargeschichtliches Forschungsamt. **VFOAT** Militar Geschichte. (1991)-. Periodical. German. qt. ***Continues*** *Militargeschichtliches Beiheft zur Europaischen Wehrkunde, Wehrwissenschaftliche Rundschau, 0932-0458.*
**Ind/Abst** Am. Hist. Life (1966-1990).

GW/0932-0458
**MI'.ITARGESCHICHTLICHES BEIHEFT ZUR EUROPAISCHEN WEHRKUNDE WIHRWISSENSCHAFTLICHE RUNDSCHAU.** ***Title Change.*** **VFOAT** Europaische Wehrkunde, Wehrwissenschaftliche Rundschau; MGB/EWK/WWR. (Dec. 1986)-?. Periodical. German. bm. Heiko Teegen, Wiesbadener Strasse 59B, D 61462 Koenigstein Germany. **Tel** 011 49 6174 5302, telex 934801. ***Continued by*** *Militargeschichte.*

SW/0023-5369
**MILITARHISTORISK TIDSKRIFT.** **Added/Corp** Kungl. Militarhogskolan (Sweden). Militarhistoriska avd. Kungl. Krigsvetenskapsakademien (Sweden). (1979)-. Swedish (Danish, English, Norwegian and Swedish). an. **LC** U43.D4; M54. ***Continues*** *Aktuellt och Historiskt, 0065-5619.*
**Ind/Abst** Am. Hist. Life (1955-).

BE
**MILITARIA BELGICA.** **Added/Corp** Musee Royal de l'Armee et d'Histoire Militaire. Societe Royale des Amis. (Jan. 1977)-. Academic Scholarly Publication. French (Dutch and French). an. 400F. Musee Royal Armee et Histoire, Militaire Parc Cinquantenaire, B 1040 Brussels Belgium. **Tel** 32 2 7334493, FAX 32 2 7345421. **ED** P. De Gryse. **LC** UC465.B4; M54. **DD** 355.8/1/09493. **Circ:** 800.
**Ind/Abst** BHA : Biblio. Hist. Art.

GW/0171-9033
**MILITARPOLITIK.** (MILITARPOLITIK DOKUMENTATION.). [Militarpolitik]. (1976)-. Monographic series. German. qt. Price varies per volume. Haag + Herchen Verlag GmbH, Fichardstr. 30, 6000 Frankfurt/Main 1 Germany. **LC** UNC.
**Ind/Abst** PAIS Int. Print.

US
**MILITARY AIRCRAFT FORECAST.** (19??)-. English. Twelve times a year. $1390.00. Forecast International / DMS Inc., 22 Commerce Road, Newtown CT 06470. **Tel** (203)426-0800, FAX (203)426-1964, telex 467615. available on CD-ROM ($1595.00).

US/1046-9079
**MILITARY & AEROSPACE ELECTRONICS.** [Mil. aerosp. electron.]. **VFOAT** Military and Aerospace Electronics. Vol. 1, No. 1 (Jan. 1990)-. Periodical. English. mo (includes Product Intelligence Review and Buying Guide). $88.00 US; $170.00 other. PennWell Publishing Company, 1421 South Sheridan, PO Box 1260, Tulsa OK 74101. **Tel** (918)835-3161, (800)331-4463, FAX (918)831-9497. **(Subscription address:** Military & Aerospace Electronics, Publishing Services, PO Box 2847, Tulsa OK 74101.**)** **ED** Tobias Naegele. **LC** UG485; .M484. **DD** 623/.043/05. **[CCC].**
**Desc:** Written for designers, developers, researchers and buyers of military and aerospace electronic components, subsystems and software.

US/0278-3029
**MILITARY ASSISTANCE PROGRAM ADDRESS DIRECTORY.** [Mil. assist. program address dir.]. Directory. English. mo. US Department of Defense, The Pentagon, Washington DC 20301. **Tel** (703)545-6700.

UK/0459-7222
**MILITARY BALANCE, THE.** [Mil. balance]. **Added/Corp** Institute for Strategic Studies (London, England) International Institute for Strategic Studies. (1963/64)-. English. an (October). £37.00 UK and Europe; $59.00 other. Oxford University Press, Walton Street, Oxford OX2 6DP England. **Tel** 011 44 865 56767, FAX 011 44 865 267773, telex 837330 OXPRES G. **LC** UA15; .L652. **DD** 355.03/32/05. available on microfilm and microfiche from University Microfilms International (UMI). ***Continues*** *Communist Bloc and the Western Alliances.*
**Desc:** Provides a timely, quantitative assessment of the military forces and defence expenditures of over 140 countries.

US/0883-3427
**MILITARY BUSINESS REVIEW.** ***Ceased.*** **See** Business-Purchasing.

US/0026-3958
**MILITARY CHAPLAIN, THE.** **Added/Corp** Military Chaplains Association. **VFOAT** Military Chaplain Newsletter; Military Chaplains Association Newsletter. Vol. 19 (July/Aug. 1948)-. Periodical. English. bm. $10.00 (1 year), $25.00 (3 year) US; $12.00 (1 year), $31.00 (3 year), other. Military Chaplains Association USA, PO Box 42660, Washington DC 20015. **Tel** (202)574-2423. **ED** G. William Dando. **Bk Rev**. **Ad Acc**. **Circ:** 1,900. ***Continues*** *Army and Navy Chaplain.*
**Desc:** Newsletter-magazine of the Military Chaplains Association of the United States; covers organization and local chapter news, plus current topics of interest to clergy with military service and/or assignments.

US/0360-9693
**MILITARY CHAPLAINS' REVIEW.** ***Title Change.*** **Added/Corp** United States. Dept. of the Army. United States. Army Chaplain Board. US Army Chaplaincy Services Support Agency. United States. Army. Chaplain Corps. (Jan. 1972)-(Summer 1992). Periodical. English. qt. US Army Chaplain Board, Meyer Hall Building 1207, Fort Monmouth NJ 07703. **ED** Granville E. Tyson. **LC** UH23; .M47. **DD** 355.3/47/0973. Index available. cum. index. **Bk Rev**. **Circ:** 7,000 (ctrl). ***Continued by*** *Army Chaplaincy.*
**Desc:** Designed as a medium in which those interested in the military chaplaincy can share with chaplains the product of their experience and research.
**Ind/Abst** Index Book Rev. Relig. (?-?); Relig. Index One Period. (?-?).

US/0886-8832
**MILITARY CLUB & HOSPITALITY.** **See** Food and Food Industry.

US/0192-2718
**MILITARY CLUBS & RECREATION.** **Added/Corp** International Military Club Executives Association. **VFOAT** Military Clubs and Recreation. Vol. 1, No. 1 (Jan. 1979)-. Periodical. English. mo. $10.00. Clubs & Recreation, PO Box 7088, Alexandria VA 22307. **Tel** (703)765-3388. **Ad Acc**. **Circ:** 7,000 (ctrl). ***Continues*** *Club Executive, 0009-9554.*

US/0026-3966
**MILITARY COLLECTOR & HISTORIAN.** [Mil. collect. hist.]. **VAT** Military Collector and Historian. V. 1- Jan. 1949-. Periodical. English. qt. $30.00. Company of Military Historians CT 06498. **Tel** (203)399-9460. **LC** UC463; .M54. **DD** 355/.00973. cum. index. available on microfilm and microfiche from University Microfilms International (UMI).
**Ind/Abst** Am. Hist. Life (1963-).

US/1051-6069
**MILITARY COST HANDBOOK.** [Mil. cost handb.]. **Added/Corp** Data Search Associates. (1979)-. Periodical. English. an (May). $25.00 US; $26.94 non-tax; $30.00 others. Data Search Associates, PO Box 8361, Fountain Valley CA 92728. **Tel** (714)540-9386, FAX (714)540-9386. **LC** UF533; .M545. **DD** 355.8/2/0973.

US
**MILITARY DEALERS AND COLLECTORS DIRECTORY AND HANDBOOK.** Directory. English. an. HAAS Publications, PO Box 775, Worthington OH 43085. **LC** UC480; .M62. **DD** 355.8/075.

US
**MILITARY ELECTRONICS BRIEFING.** English. mo. $995.00. Teal Group, 3900 University Drive, Suite 220, Fairfax VA 22030. **Tel** (703)385-1992.

US/0026-3982
**MILITARY ENGINEER, THE.** **See** Engineering.

UK/0964-9700
**MILITARY FIREFIGHTER.** **See** Fire Prevention.

●US
**MILITARY FORCE STRUCTURES OF THE WORLD.** (1994)-. English. Four times a year. $2495.00. Forecast International / DMS Inc., 22 Commerce Road, Newtown CT 06470. **Tel** (203)426-0800, FAX (203)426-1964, telex 467615.

US/1058-8620
**MILITARY GROCER.** (1991)-. Periodical. English. bm. $40.00. Downey Communications Inc, Circulation Department, 4800 Montgomery Lane, Suite 710, Bethesda MD 20814. **Tel** (301)718-7600, FAX (301)718-7652.

US/0889-7328
**MILITARY HISTORY (HERNDON, VA.).** (MILITARY HISTORY.). (Aug. 1984)-. Periodical. English. Six times a year (Feb., Apr., June, Aug., Oct., Dec.). $19.95. Cowles Magazines, PO Box 8200, Harrisburg PA 17105. **Tel** (717)657-9555, (800)435-9610. **(Subscription address:** Kable Publishers Aide, 308 East Hitt Street, Subscriptions Department, Mt. Morris, IL 61054**)** **LC** WMLC 93/1472. available on microfilm and microfiche from University Microfilms International (UMI).
**Desc:** News and information on the military history.
**Ind/Abst** Air Univ. Libr. Index Mil. Period. (199?-); Am. Hist. Life (1990-).

SA/0026-4016
**MILITARY HISTORY JOURNAL.** **Added/Corp** South African National Museum of Military History. South African Military History Society. South African National War Museum, Johannesburg. **VFOAT** Krygshistoriese Tydskrif. Vol. 1, (Dec. 1967)-. Periodical. English (Afrikaans). Twice a year (July, Dec.). R30.00 South Africa; R70.00 others. South African National Museum, PO Box 52090, Saxonwold 2132, Transvaal South Africa. **Tel** 011 27 11 6465513. **ED** J. L. Keene. **LC** DT769; .M5. **DD** 968/.005. Index available. cum. index. **Bk Rev**. **Ad Acc**. **Circ:** 700.
**Desc:** Articles on military history, particularly that of South Africa. Includes philosophical aspect of the military.
**Ind/Abst** Curr. Mil. Pol. Lit.

US/0898-8064
**MILITARY HISTORY OF THE SOUTHWEST.** ***Title Change.*** (MILITARY HISTORY OF THE SOUTHWEST : MHS.). [Mil. hist. Southwest]. **Added/Corp** University of North Texas. Center for Studies in Military History. National Guard Association of Texas. **VFOAT** Military History of the South West; MHS. Vol. 19, No. 1 (Spring 1989)-Vol. 22, No. 2 (1992). Periodical. English. sa. University of North Texas Press, PO Box 13856, Denton TX 76203. **Tel** (817)565-2124, FAX (817)369-8770. **ED** Richard Lowe (editor's address: P.O.Box 13735, Denton TX 76205-3735). **LC** F381; .T343. **DD** 976/.005. Index available. **Bk Rev**, (Qty: 40/yr). **Ad Acc**, **Adv Mgr:** Jane Tanner, **Tel** (817)565-2124. **Circ:** 500. ***Continues*** *Military History of Texas and the Southwest, 0047-7389.* ***Continued by*** *Military History of the West, 1071-2011.*
**Desc:** Articles on the military history of Texas and the American Southwest, including campaigns, battles, biography, equipment, weapons, organization, training and operations from the Spanish conquest and occupation to present times.
**Ind/Abst** Am. Hist. Life (1977-19??).

●US/1071-2011
**MILITARY HISTORY OF THE WEST.** [Mil. hist. West]. **Added/Corp** University of North Texas. University of North Texas. Dept. of History. National Guard Association of Texas. Vol. 23, No. 1 (Spring 1993)-. Periodical. English. sa. $12.00 (institutions), $8.00 (individuals) US; $20.00 other. University of North Texas Press, PO Box 13856, Denton TX 76203. **Tel** (817)565-2124, FAX (817)369-8770. **ED** Richard G. Lowe. **LC** F381; .T343. Index available. **Bk Rev**, (Qty: 50). **Ad Acc**, **Adv Mgr:** Jane Tanner. **Pr Rev. Circ:** 500. ***Continues*** *Military History of the Southwest, 0898-8064.*
**Ind/Abst** Am. Hist. Life.

UK/0268-8328
**MILITARY ILLUSTRATED : PAST & PRESENT.** [Mil. illus. past present]. No. 1 (June/July 1986)-. Periodical. English. mo (12 issues). $100.00 (optional binder $11.00). Military Illustrated Ltd, 43 Museum Street, London WC1A 1LY England. **(Subscription address:** Lowtherbond Ltd., 17 Bushby Avenue Rustington, W Sussex BN16 2BY England.**)** Index available.
**Desc:** Covers military history, art, and science.

US/1040-4961
**MILITARY IMAGES.** [Mil. images]. (19??)-. Periodical. English. bm (6 issues). $20.00 (one year), $36.00 (two year). Military Images Magazine, Road 1 Box 99A, Lesoine Drive, Henryville PA 18332. **Tel** (717)476-1388. **DD** 355. ***Continues*** *Military Images Magazine, 0193-9866.*
**Ind/Abst** Am. Hist. Life (1986-).

US/0026-4024
**MILITARY INTELLIGENCE.** [Mil. intell.]. **Added/Corp** United States Army Intelligence Center & School. US Army Intelligence Center. Fort Huachuca (Ariz.). (Jan./March 1977)-. Government Publication. English. qt (Mar., June, Sept., Dec.). $8.50 US; $10.65 other. Superintendent of Documents, US Government Printing Office, Washington DC 20402. **Tel** (202)275-3328, FAX (202)786-2377. **LC** UB250; .M54. **DD** 355. available on microfilm and microfiche from University Microfilms International (UMI). ***Continues** MI Magazine (Ft. Huachuca, Ariz.).*
**Desc:** Provides a forum for the exchange of ideas; attempts to inform, motivate and promote the professional development of all members of the intelligence community.
**Ind/Abst** Air Univ. Libr. Index Mil. Period. (199?-).

US/0885-8403
**MILITARY LIFESTYLE (UNITED STATES EDITION).** (MILITARY LIFESTYLE.). [Mil. lifestyle]. (198?)-. Periodical. English. Twelve times a year. $18.00. Downey Communications Inc, Circulation Department, 4800 Montgomery Lane, Suite 710, Bethesda MD 20814. **Tel** (301)718-7600, FAX (301)718-7652. **ED** Hope Daniels. **LC** AP2; .L23. **DD** 613.7. **Bk Rev**, (Qty: 1). **Ad Acc, Adv Mgr:** Mike Jennings, **Tel** (914)997-6440. **Circ:** 100,000. ***Continues** Ladycom, 0023-7183.*
**Desc:** Editorial centers on the many facets of life experienced by military families. Topics include marriage and child raising, careers, relocation, family help resources and problem solving.

US/0740-5065
**MILITARY LIVING.** Vol. 9 No. 5 (May 1977)-. Periodical. English. mo (12 issues). $11.00. Military Living Publications, PO Box 2347, Falls Church VA 22042. **Tel** (703)237-0203, FAX (703)237-2233. **ED** Ann Crawford. **[CCC].** Index available. cum. index. **Bk Rev. Ad Acc. Circ:** 30,000 (ctrl). ***Continues** Military Living and Consumer Guide.*
**Desc:** Military shopping and recreation facilities guide for military families in Washington, DC area and those on order there.

US/0740-5073
**MILITARY LIVING'S R & R REPORT.** **VFOAT** Military Living's R and R Report; Military Living R and R; Military Living R & R; Military Living's R&R Report. (19??)-. Periodical. English. Six times a year (Jan., Mar., May, July, Sept., Nov.). $14.00 (one year), $22.00 (two year), $30.00 (three year). Military Living Publications, PO Box 2347, Falls Church VA 22042. **Tel** (703)237-0203, FAX (703)237-2233. **ED** Lela Ann Crawford. **[CCC].** Index available. cum. index. **Bk Rev. Ad Acc. Circ:** 10,000 (ctrl).
**Desc:** Recreational publication for military families.

US/0741-1340
**MILITARY MANPOWER STATISTICS.** **See** Military and Defense-Abstracting, Bibliographies and Statistics.

US/0026-4067
**MILITARY MARKET.** **Added/Corp** Army Times Publishing Company. (19??)-. Periodical. English. mo. $84.00 (one year), $144.00 (two years). Army Times Publishing Company, 6883 Commercial Drive, Springfield VA 22159. **Tel** (800)368-5718, (703)750-8099. **ED** Nancy M. Tucker. **Ad Acc. Circ:** 11,000 (ctrl).
**Desc:** Business publication for managers of military post exchanges and commissaries. News, features, new products, interviews, etc.

US/0026-4075
**MILITARY MEDICINE.** **See** Medical Science and Technology.

UK
**MILITARY MICROWAVES ANNUAL CONFERENCE PROCEEDINGS.** (19??)-. Proceedings. English. £70.00. Microwave Exhibitions & Publ, 90 Calverley Road, Tunbridge Wells TN1 2UN England. **Tel** 011 44 892 44027, FAX 011 44 892 541023, telex 95604. **Bk Rev.**
**Desc:** Strives to provide an international forum in the UK for the exchange of ideas and research on microwave projects having a military application.

US/0195-1467
**MILITARY MODELER.** ***Title Change.*** [Mil. model.]. (19??)-(19??). Periodical. English. mo. Challenge Publications Inc., 7950 Deering Avenue, Canoga Park CA 91304. **Tel** (818)887-0550. **LC** U311; .M53. ***Merged into** Scale Modeler.*

US/0275-5823
**MILITARY OPERATIONS RESEARCH.** (MILITARY OPERATIONS RESEARCH : A SERIES OF MONOGRAPHS AND TEXTS SPONSORED BY THE MILITARY OPERATIONS RESEARCH SOCIETY, INC.). [Mil. oper. res.]. **Added/Corp** Military Operations Research Society. Vol. 1 (1981)-. Monographic series. English. ir. Price varies per volume. Gordon & Breach Science Publishers, Inc., PO Box 786, Cooper Station, New York NY 10276. **Tel** (212)206-8900, FAX (212)645-2459. **(Subscription address:** Gordon & Breach Science Publishers / US, 820 Town Center Drive, Langhorne PA 19047.**)**

US/0363-8359
**MILITARY PERSONNEL AND DEPENDENTS IN HAWAII.** **See** Military and Defense-Abstracting, Bibliographies and Statistics.

US/0899-5605
**MILITARY PSYCHOLOGY.** (MILITARY PSYCHOLOGY : THE OFFICIAL JOURNAL OF THE DIVISION OF MILITARY PSYCHOLOGY, AMERICAN PSYCHOLOGICAL ASSOCIATION.). [Mil. psychol.]. **Added/Corp** American Psychological Association. Division of Military Psychology. Vol. 1, No. 1 (1989)-. Periodical. English. qt. $195.00 US & Canada; $220.00 other. Lawrence Erlbaum Associates, 365 Broadway, Suite 102, Hillsdale NJ 07642. **Tel** (201)666-4110, (800)926-6579, FAX (201)666-2394. **ED** Martin F Wiskoff. **LC** U22.3; .M488. **DD** 355/.001/9. **NLM** W1; MI491D.
**Desc:** Focuses on psychological research and practice within a military environment. Facilitates communication between researchers and practitioners. Provides for the timely publication of original empirical research that furthers scientific knowledge in the field.
**Ind/Abst** Ergon. Abstr.; Psychol. Abstr. (1989-); PsycINFO (1990-); PsycLit.

US/0026-4148
**MILITARY REVIEW.** [Mil. rev.]. **Added/Corp** U.S. Army Command and General Staff College. (1939)-. Periodical. English (Spanish and Portuguese). mo. $24.00 US; $32.00 (surface mail), $84.00 (air mail) other. Military Review, Funston Hall, Building 314, Fort Leavenworth KS 66027-6910. **Tel** (913)684-5642, (913)684-5130, FAX (913)684-2448. **ED** Phillip W. Childress. Index available. **Bk Rev. Circ:** 23,000 (ctrl). available on microfilm and microfiche from University Microfilms International (UMI). ***Continues** Quarterly Review of Military Literature.*
**Desc:** Original articles on military related subjects contributing to the development of the military professional. Features are on warfighting and reviews of military books.
**Ind/Abst** Air Univ. Libr. Index Mil. Period.; Am. Hist. Life (1963-); Am. Bibliogr. Slavic East Europ. Stud. (19??-19??); Int. Polit. Sci. Abstr.; PAIS Int. Print (1991-); Peace Res. Abstr. J. (1964-1967).

US/0896-0348
**MILITARY ROBOTICS.** **See** Computers-Artificial Intelligence.

US/1046-2511
**MILITARY (SACRAMENTO, CALIF.).** (MILITARY.). [Military]. Vol. 2, No. 1 (June 1985)-. Periodical. English. mo. $14.00. MHR Publishing Corporated, 2122 28th Street, Sacramento CA 95818. **Tel** (916)457-8990 (800)366-9192. **ED** Michael Mark. **LC** E840.4; .M55. **DD** 322/.5/0973. **Bk Rev**, (Qty: 30-50). **Ad Acc, Adv Mgr:** Rosalie Hernandez, **Tel** (800)4-info-ad. **Circ:** 14,000. ***Continues** Military History Review.*
**Desc:** Military history.

US/0743-7897
**MILITARY SPACE.** **See** Aeronautics, Astronautics.

US
**MILITARY SPACE-A AIR OPPORTUNITIES AROUND THE WORLD.** (19??)-. English. an. $15.95. Military Living Publications, PO Box 2347, Falls Church VA 22042. **Tel** (703)237-0203, FAX (703)237-2233.

GW/0722-3226
**MILITARY TECHNOLOGY.** **VFOAT** MILTECH; Military Technology-MILTECH. No. 82/1 (Feb. 1982)-. Periodical. English. Twelve times a year. $85.00. Moench Publishing Group, Heilsbachstrasse 26, Postfach 140 261, 5300 Bonn 1 Germany. **Tel** 011 49 228 64830, FAX 011 49 228 6483109. **(Subscription address:** Nautical & Aviation Publishing Company, 8 West Madison Street, Baltimore MD 21201.**)** **LC** U1; .M63. ***Continues** Military Technology and Economics, 0344-6352.*
**Ind/Abst** Air Univ. Libr. Index Mil. Period. (199?-).

US/1041-6129
**MILITARY TOWN AND INSTALLATION.** **VFOAT** Military Town & Installation; MTI. (1991)-. Periodical. English. bm. $16.95. PO Box 815, Biloxi MS 39533.

US/0893-3863
**MILITARY VEHICLES.** [Mil. veh.]. Vol. 1, No. 1 (Apr./May 1987)-. Periodical. English. Six times a year (Feb., Apr., June, Aug., Oct., Dec.). $15.00 one year; $25.00 two years. Eagle Press, PO Box 1748, Union NJ 07083. **Tel** (201)688-6015. **DD** 629. **Bk Rev. Ad Acc. Circ:** 10,000.
**Desc:** Covers exclusive tips on military vehicles care and maintenance. Includes a comprehensive calendar of military vehicles rallies and flea markets.

US
**MILITARY VEHICLES FORECAST.** (19??)-. English. Twelve times a year. $1390.00. Forecast International / DMS Inc., 22 Commerce Road, Newtown CT 06470. **Tel** (203)426-0800, FAX (203)426-1964, telex 467615. available on CD-ROM ($1595.00).

II/0076-8782
**MILITARY YEAR-BOOK.** ***Title Change.*** **VFOAT** Military Year Book; Military Yearbook. (1965)-(1992). English. an. Guide Publications, 60/20 Prabhat Road Karol Bagh, New Delhi 110 005 India. **Tel** 572-5793. **(Subscription address:** Prints India, 11 Darya Ganj, New Delhi 110002 India.**)** **ED** S. P. Baranwal. **LC** U10.I5; M5. **Ad Acc. Circ:** 5,800 (ctrl). ***Continued by** SP's Military Yearbook.*
**Desc:** Discusses the organization, administration and function of army, navy, air force and para-military forces in India. Most comprehensive instrument on Indian defense topics; international security environment focused.

DK/0026-3850
**MILITRT TIDSSKRIFT.** [Mil. tidsskr.]. (1871)-. Periodical. Danish. ir (Monthly with combined issues). kr120.00. Krigsvidenskabelige Selskab, Postbook 214 Frederiksberg Slot, DK 2000 Frederiksberg Denmark. **DD** 355. **CODEN** 35.5.

US
**MILSTRIP : MILITARY STANDARD REQUISITIONING & ISSUE PROCEDURES.** **VFOAT** Military Standard Requisitioning & Issue Procedures. **VAT** Military Standard Requisitioning and Issue Procedures. English. US Department of Defense / Alexandria, Cameron Station, Alexandria VA 22304.

US
**MILSTRIP. SUPPLEMENT NO. 1 : ROUTING IDENTIFIER CODES.** **VFOAT** Routing Identifier Codes. **VAT** Military Standard Requisitioning and Issue Procedures. Periodical. English. US Department of Defense, The Pentagon, Washington DC 20301. **Tel** (703)545-6700.

UK/0144-5243
**MILTRONICS.** ***Ceased.*** [Miltronics]. Vol. 1 (Sept. 1980)-Ceased Vol. 11, No. 3. Periodical. English. bm. Argus Press Group, Queensway House, 2 Queensway Redhill, Surrey RH1 1QS England. **Tel** 011 44 737 768611, 011 44 737 761685, FAX 011 44 737 760510, telex 948669 TOPJNL G. **CODEN** MLTREL.

US/0736-718X
**MINERVA (ARLINGTON, VA.).** (MINERVA.). [Minerva]. Vol. 1, No. 1 (Spring 1983)-. Periodical. English. qt (Mar., June, Sept., Dec.). $25.00 students & cadets; $50.00 individuals; $75.00 institutions. Minerva Center Publications, The Minerva Center, 20 Granada Road, Pasadena MD 21122. **Tel** (410)437-5379. **ED** Linda Grant De Pauw. **LC** UB418.W65; M55. **DD** 355/.0088/042. cum. index. **Bk Rev. Circ:** 800.
**Desc:** The only periodical dealing exclusively and extensively with women and the military including service women, military wives, and women veterans.. Carries news, reviews, and commentary. Editorial policy emphasizes diversity.
**Ind/Abst** Am. Hist. Life.

US/0897-6104
**MINERVA'S BULLETIN BOARD.** [Minerva's bull. board]. Vol. 1, No. 1 (Spring 1988)-. Bulletin. English. qt (Mar., June, Sept., Dec.). $12.50 students & cadets; $25.00 individuals; $50.00 institutions. Minerva Center Publications, The Minerva Center, 20 Granada Road, Pasadena MD 21122. **Tel** (410)437-5379. **ED** Linda Grant DePauw. **LC** UB418.W65; M55. **DD** 355. **Ad Acc. Circ:** 1,000. ***Continues** Minerva, 0736-718X.*
**Desc:** News briefs on military women of all nations, women veterans and military wives.

UK
**MINIATURE WARFARE & MODEL SOLDIERS.** Periodical. English. mo. $10.50. Formstan Ltd, Stanhope House, Fairbridge Road, London N19 3HZ England. **LC** U310; .M55. **DD** 355. ***Continues** Miniature Warfare.*

US
**MISSILE FORECAST.** (19??)-. English. mo. $1390.00. Forecast International / DMS Inc., 22 Commerce Road, Newtown CT 06470. **Tel** (203)426-0800, FAX (203)426-1964, telex 467615. available on CD-ROM ($1595.00). ***Absorbed** World Missile Forecast, 0279-5094.*

US/1060-8273
**MISSILE MONITOR.** [Missile monit.]. **Added/Corp** Monterey Institute of International Studies. International Missile Proliferation Project. No. 1 (Fall 1991)-. Periodical. English. qt. Monterey Institute of International Studies, 425 Van Buren Street, Monterey CA 93940. **DD** 358.

●US
**MOBILITY FORUM : THE JOURNAL OF THE AIR MOBILITY COMMAND, THE.** **See** Aeronautics, Astronautics.

UK/0269-0365
**MOD CONTRACTS BULLETIN.** **See** Business.

FR/0997-7139
**MONDE DU RENSEIGNEMENT 1988, LE.** (LE MONDE DU RENSEIGNEMENT.). **Added/Corp**

Association Pour le Droit a l'Information (France). (1988)-. Periodical. French. Twenty-four times a year. 3350.00F. Indigo Publications, 10 rue du Sentier, 75002 Paris France. **Tel** 011 33 1 45081480, FAX 011 33 1 45085983, telex 215405. **ED** Olivier Schmidt. **UDC** 327.84. Index available. cum. index. **Pr Rev. Circ:** 24. ***Continues*** *Le Monde du Renseignement, Parapolitique. Edition Complete, 0765-9776.*
**Desc:** Life of intelligence services.

US
**MONTANA DAV NEWS.** **Added/Corp** Disabled American Veterans. Department of Montana. **VAT** Montana Disabled American Veterans News. (19??)-. Periodical. English. mo. $2.00. Montana Disabled American, Box 7, Kalispell MT 59901.

CN/0319-5562
**MOUNTAINEER (VEDDER CROSSING).** (THE MOUNTAINEER.). V. 1- April 2, 1975-. English. bw. $3.00. The Mountaineer, CFB Chilliwack, Vedder Crossing British Columbia V0X 1Z0 Canada. **DD** 355.1/09711/33.

UK/0937-6348
**MS & T : MILITARY SIMULATION & TRAINING.** **VFOAT** Military Simulation & Training; Military Simulation and Training. (19??)-. Periodical. English. bm (6 issues). DM60.00. Wehr und Wissen Verlagsges GmbH, Postfach 140261, D 53057 Bonn Germany. **Tel** 011 49 228 64830.

BE
**MUSEE D'ARMES : [BULLETIN], LE.** **Added/Corp** Musee d'Armes de Liege. Musee d'Armes de Liege. Amis. Vol. 1, No. 1 (Jan. 1973)-. French. qt. 100F (200F for double issues). Les Amis du Musee d'Armes de Liege, Quai de Maestricht 8, 4000 Liege Belgium. **Tel** 041 21 94 16, 041 21 94 17, FAX 041 21 94 01. **LC** U13.B342; L535. **DD** 355/.0074493/46. Index available. **Acid Free. Circ:** 500.
**Desc:** Illustrated booklet publishing articles primarily about the history, technology and decoration of small arms and armor worldwide; stresses the Belgian connection.

US/0498-1367
**MUTUAL SECURITY PROGRAM FOR FISCAL YEAR 1952-, THE.** **Main/Corp** United States. **Added/Corp** United States. Congress. House. Committee on Foreign Affairs. United States. Congress. Senate. Committee on Foreign Relations. (19??)-. Government Publication. English. ir. Superintendent of Documents, US Government Printing Office, Washington DC 20402. **Tel** (202)275-3328, FAX (202)786-2377. **LC** UA12; .U464. **DD** 355.

YU/0027-7908
**NARODNA ARMIJA.** ***Title Change.*** **Added/Corp** Yugoslavia. Ministarstvo Narodne Odbrane. Vojnoizdavacki I Novinski Centar (Beograd, Serbia). God. 1, Br. 1 (2 Oct. 1945)-(1992). Periodical. Serbo-Croatian (Cyrillic) (Serbo-Croatian (Roman), Macedonian and Slovenian). wk. **(Subscription address:** Jugoslovenska Knjiga, PO Box 36, YU 11001 Belgrade Yugoslovia.**)** **LC** U4; .N34. ***Continued by*** *Vojska, 0354-2750.*

US/0198-6120
**NATIONAL DEFENSE EXECUTIVE RESERVE ANNUAL REPORT TO THE PRESIDENT, THE.** (NATIONAL DEFENSE EXECUTIVE RESERVE ... ANNUAL REPORT TO THE PRESIDENT / FEDERAL EMERGENCY MANAGEMENT AGENCY, OFFICE OF PLANS AND PREPAREDNESS.). [Natl. Def. Exec. Reserv. annu. rep. Pres.]. **VFOAT** Annual Report to the President. English. an. Federal Emergency Management Agency, PO Box 70274, Washington DC 20024. **Tel** (202)646-3989. **LC** UA18.U5; U53A. **DD** 355.2/3.

US/0092-1491
**NATIONAL DEFENSE (WASHINGTON).** (NATIONAL DEFENSE.). [Natl. def.]. **Added/Corp** American Defense Preparedness Association. V. 58, No. 320 (Sept./Oct. 1973)-. Periodical. English. Ten times a year (Monthly with May/June and July/Aug. issues combined). $70.00 (1 year), $105.00 (2 year), $140.00 (3 year) air mail; $35.00 (1 year), $65.00 (2 year), $95.00 (3 year) (surface mail) US; $40.00 (1 year), $75.00 (2 year), $110.00 (3 year) other. American Defense Preparedness Association, Two Colonial Place/Suite 400, 2101 Wilson Boulevard, Arlington VA 22201. **Tel** (703)522-1820, FAX (703)522-1885. **ED** D Ballou. **LC** UF1; .O67. **DD** 355.8/2/05. **CODEN** NTDFA2. Index available. cum. index. **Bk Rev**. **Ad Acc. Circ:** 45,000 (ctrl). available on microfilm and microfiche from University Microfilms International (UMI). Documents available from Ask*IEEE. ***Continues*** *Ordnance, 0030-4557;* ***Formed by the union of*** *Common Defence.*
**Desc:** A source of respected and accurate information on defense systems, new defense opinion, emphasizing the importance of a strong industrial base to ensure national security.
**Ind/Abst** Air Univ. Libr. Index Mil. Period.; Curr. Mil. Pol. Lit.; INSPEC (Feb. 1989-); Shock Vibr. Dig.

US/0363-8618
**NATIONAL GUARD ALMANAC.** (1977)-. English. an (published in February). $5.95. Uniformed Services Almanac, PO Box 4144, Falls Church VA 22044. **Tel** (703)532-1631, FAX (703)532-1635. **ED** Sol Gordon. **LC** U9; .N38. **DD** 355.3/7/0973. **Bk Rev**. **Ad Acc. Circ:** 50,000. ***Continues*** *Uniformed Services Almanac. National Guard Edition, 0363-8588.*
**Desc:** Reference volume on pay and allowances for Guardsmen including state and federal benefits, organization, taxes, and other important subjects of interest to members of the Army and Air National Guard.

US/0163-3945
**NATIONAL GUARD (WASHINGTON. 1978).** (NATIONAL GUARD.). **Added/Corp** National Guard Association of the United States. **VFOAT** National Guard Magazine. Vol. 32, No. 10 (Nov. 1978)-. Periodical. English. mo. $20.00. National Guard / Washington DC, 1 Massachusetts Avenue NW, Washington DC 20001. **Tel** (202)789-0031. **ED** Major Reid K. Beveridge. **LC** UA42; .N24. **DD** 355.3/7/0973. **Ad Acc. Circ:** 65,000. available on microfilm and microfiche from University Microfilms International (UMI). ***Continues*** *Guardsman, 0163-3953.*
**Desc:** Contains articles related to the United States military.
**Ind/Abst** Air Univ. Libr. Index Mil. Period.

CN/1181-8107
**NATIONAL NETWORK NEWS.** (NATIONAL NETWORK NEWS / THE DEFENCE ASSOCIATIONS.). [Natl. netw. news]. **Added/Corp** Defence Associations National Network. Vol. 1, No. 6 (Oct. 27, 1989)-. Periodical. English (French). Four times a year (Jan., Apr., July, Oct.). 20.00Can$ Canada; 23.76Can$ US; 24.70Can$ other. Defence Association National Network News, PO Box 17 STN B, Ottawa ONT K1P 6C3 Canada. **Tel** (613)727-0199, FAX (613)727-5141. **ED** D. N. Mainguy. **DD** 355/.033/071. **Bk Rev**, (Qty: varies). **Circ:** 2,000. ***Continues*** *Network News (Defence Associations National Network).*
**Desc:** Contains proceedings of the Association and its branches as well as timely articles of national interest.

CN/0713-0511
**NATIONAL NEWS LETTER - FEDERATION OF MILITARY AND UNITED SERVICES INSTITUTES OF CANADA.** (NATIONAL NEWS LETTER.). [Natl. news lett. - Fed. Mil. United Serv. Inst. Can.]. **Main/Corp** Federation of Military and United Services Institutes of Canada. Vol. 1, No. 1 (Jan. 31,1974)-. Periodical. English. ir. Free. FMUSIC, 223 Sayward Building, 1207 Douglas Street, Victoria British Columbia V8W 2E7 Canada. **DD** 369/.271.

US/0146-244X
**NATIONAL SECURITY AFFAIRS FORUM, THE.** Periodical. English. Three times a year. National War College, Washington DC 20319. **LC** UA11; .F64. **DD** 355.03/3073. ***Continues*** *Forum (Washington, D.C.).*

US
**NATIONAL SECURITY MANAGEMENT PROGRAMS. ADMINISTRATIVE PROCEDURES.** **Main/Corp** National Defense University. English. US Department of the Defense National Defense University, 4th & P Streets SW, Fort McNair Building 62, Washington DC 20319. **Tel** (202)475-1966, FAX (202)287-9388.
**Desc:** Includes list of testing offices.

PH
**NATIONAL SECURITY REVIEW, THE.** V. 1- Mar. 1973-. Periodical. English. qt. National Defense College of the Philippines (The President), Fort Bonifacio Rizal, Attn National Security Review, Manila Philippines. **LC** HC451; .N34. **DD** 355.03/30599.
**Ind/Abst** Index Philip. Period.

US
**NATIONAL VIETNAM VETERANS REVIEW.** Periodical. English. mo. $15.00. National Vietnam Veterans, 1422 Maggie Street, Fayetteville NC 28303. **Tel** (919)488-1366.

US
**NATO MUTUAL SUPPORT ACT, AS AMENDED (ACQUISITION AND CROSS SERVICING AGREEMENTS WITH NATO ALLIES AND OTHER COUNTRIES); REPORT OF AGREEMENTS AND TRANSACTIONS / DEPARTMENT OF DEFENSE.** **Main/Corp** United States. Dept. of Defense. Washington Headquarters Services. Directorate for Information Operations and Reports. (19??)-. English. Twenty-four times a year. $190.00. Callahan Publications, PO Box 1173, McLean VA 22101. **Tel** (703)356-1925, FAX (703)356-9614. **ED** Vincent Callahan. **LC** UA646.5.U5; U527a. **DD** 355/.031/091821. **Bk Rev**, (Qty: 4).

NE/0169-1821
**NATO'S SIXTEEN NATIONS.** [NATO's sixt. nations]. **Added/Corp** North Atlantic Treaty Organization. Vol. 1, No. 1 (Feb./March 1983)-. Periodical. English. Six times a year. $48.00 one year; $91.00 two years. Jules Perel's Publishing Company, PO Box 237, NL 1420 AE Uithorn Netherlands. **Tel** 011 31 2975 32918, telex 18118. **ED** Frederick Bonnart. **LC** UA646; .F5. **DD** 355/.03304. **Ad Acc.** available on microfilm and microfiche from University Microfilms International (UMI). ***Continues*** *NATO'S Fifteen Nations, 0027-6065.*
**Desc:** An independent review of military, political and economic affairs.
**Ind/Abst** Air Univ. Libr. Index Mil. Period.; PAIS Int. Print; Predicasts.

US/0028-1697
**NAVY TIMES.** **See** Naval Science, Navigation.

US/1040-9270
**NBC BRIEF.** (NBC BRIEF / LEPRECHAUN SYSTEMS-DEFENSE CONSULTANTS.). [NBC brief]. **Added/Corp** Leprechaun Systems-Defense Consultants. **VAT** Nuclear, Biological and Chemical Brief. (19??)-. Periodical. English. Four times a year. Leprechaun Systems Defense Consultants, Box 4594, Ann Arbor MI 48106. **Tel** (313)668-6037. **DD** 355.

US/1058-9058
**NCO JOURNAL, THE.** [NCO j.]. **Added/Corp** US Army Sergeants Major Academy. **VAT** Noncommissioned Officers Journal. Vol. 1, No. 1 (Spring 1991)-. Periodical. English. qt. $13.00 US; $16.25 other. US Army Publications Center, 2800 Eastern Boulevard, Baltimore MD 21220. **LC** WMLC 90/1035; UB408.5; .N36. **DD** 355.

US/0747-0150
**NCOA JOURNAL (SAN ANTONIO, TEX.).** (NCOA JOURNAL / NON-COMMISSIONED OFFICERS ASSOCIATION OF THE UNITED STATES.). [NCAA j.]. **Added/Corp** Non-commissioned Officers Association. **VFOAT** N.C.O.A. Journal. **VAT** Noncommissioned Officers Association of the United States of America Journal. (19??)-. Periodical. English. Twenty-six times a year. $20.00 Comes with Non-Commissioned Officers Association membership. Non-Commissioned Officers Association of the United States, International Headquarters, PO Box 33610, San Antonio TX 78298. **Tel** (512)675-0131, FAX (512)656-6225. **ED** William L. Noonan. **Ad Acc. Circ:** 160,000 (ctrl).
**Desc:** News of armed forces, veterans and retirees. News of worldwide members and chapters.

●US/1063-3588
**NDT UPDATE.** [NDT update]. **VAT** Nondestructive Testing Update. Vol. 1, No. 1 (May 1992)-. Periodical. English. mo. $375.00. NDT Update, PO Box 6273, FDR Station, New York NY 10150. **Tel** (718)706-1007. **DD** 620. available on an online database (file 636/Full-Text) from DIALOG.

US
**NEW ABOLITIONIST : NEWSLETTER OF NUCLEAR FREE AMERICA, THE.** **Added/Corp** Nuclear Free America (Organization). **VFOAT** Newsletter of Nuclear Free America. (198?)-. Periodical. English. Four times a year. $15.00. Nuclear Free America, 325 East 25th Street, Baltimore MD 21218. **Tel** (410)235-3575.

US/0098-3314
**NEW PATRIOT, THE.** [New patriot]. **Added/Corp** Enlisted Association of the National Guard of the United States. Vol. 1 (Feb. 1974)-. Periodical. English. qt. $6.00. Johnny Appleseed Patriotic Publishing, Box 50390, Chicago IL 60650. **LC** UA42.A6; N46. **DD** 355.3/7/0973. available on microfilm from University Microfilms International (UMI).

US
**NEWSLETTER / ARMSTRONG LABORATORY HUMAN RESOURCES DIRECTORATE, HUMAN SYSTEMS DIVISION (AFSC).** **Main/Corp** Armstrong Laboratory (U.S.). Human Resources Directorate. (Jan. 1991)-. Newsletter. English. qt. Department of the Air Force / Armstrong Laboratory, Det 5, Human Resources Directorate, Brooks AFB TX 78235-5601. ***Continues*** *AFHRL Newsletter.*

CN/1181-9413
**NEWSLETTER - CANADIAN WAR MUSEUM. FRIENDS OF THE CANADIAN WAR MUSEUM.** (NEWSLETTER / FRIENDS OF THE CANADIAN WAR MUSEUM.). [Newsl. - Can. War Mus., Friends Can. War Mus.]. **Added/Corp** Canadian War Museum. Friends of the Canadian War Museum. **VFOAT** Communique; Friends of the Canadian War Museum Newsletter. **VAT** Communique - Musee Canadien de la Guerre. Amis du Musee Canadien de la Guerre. (Aug. 1990)-. Periodical. English (French). qt. Free to members. Friends of the Canadian War Museum, 330 Sussex Drive, Ottawa, Ontario K1A 0M8 Canada. **DD** 355/.0074/71. ***Continues*** *Friends of the Canadian War Museum (Bulletin)., 1184-7018.*

JA
**NIKKAN KOKUBO KEIZAI TSUSHIN. THE KOKUBO KEIZAI TSUSHIN.** **VFOAT** The Kokubo Keizai Tsushin. (19??)-. Japanese. ir. ¥90000. Korin Kaikan, Shiba Koen 3-6-23 Linikon Tsushinsha, Minato-ku Tokyo Japan. **Tel** 03-433-4878. **ED** S. Chikada. **LC** UA845; .N577. **Ad Acc.**

DK
**NOD & CONVERSION.** **Added/Corp** Kbenhavns Universitet. Centre of Peace and Conflict Research. **VFOAT** NOD and Conversion; Non-Offensive Defence and Conversion; International Research Newsletter. No. 19 (Aug. 1991)-. Periodical. English. ***Continues*** *Non-Offensive Defense, 0901-8751.*

NO
**NORSK ARTILLERI TIDSSKRIFT.** Norwegian. ir (three to four issues per year). Kr60.00 Norway; Kr90.00 other. Norsk Artilleri Tidsskrift, FO/HST/Artinsp Oslo Mil/Huseby. **Tel** 47-2 498605, FAX 47-2 498312. **ED** Eirik Davidsen. **Ad Acc.** ctrl circ.
**Desc:** Technical and tactical articles on school reports management, leadership and obituaries.

NO/0029-2028
**NORSK MILITRT TIDSSKRIFT.** [Nor. mil. tidsskr.]. (1838)-. Periodical. Norwegian. mo. Kr200.00 Norway; Kr225.00 other. Norsk Militaert Tidskkrift, c/o M Halvorsen, Tollbugt 10, 0152 Oslo 1 Norway. **Tel** 47 3 336233. **ED** Tonne Huitfeldt (editor's phone: 47 22 403854). **LC** U4; .N8. **Bk Rev**, (Qty: 12-15). **Ad Acc. Circ:** 3,000. ***Continues*** *Militrt Tidsscrift.*
**Ind/Abst** Am. Hist. Life (1966-1977);(1966-).

US
**NORTHERN SUN.** **Added/Corp** Northern Sun Alliance (Minneapolis, Minn.). Vol. 8, no. 1 (Jan./Feb. 1985)-. Periodical. English. mo. Northern Sun Alliance, 1519 East Franklin, Minneapolis MN 55404. **Tel** (612)874-1540. ***Continues*** *Northern Sun News.*

US
**NTIS ALERT. ORDNANCE.** **Added/Corp** United States. National Technical Information Service. (19??)-. Periodical. English. Twenty-four times a year. $140.00 US; $195.00 other. National Technical Information Service - NTIS, Room 2027S, 5285 Port Royal Road, Springfield VA 22161. **Tel** (703)487-4630, (703)487-4660, (703)487-4650, FAX (703)321-8547, telex 89-9405.

US/0888-5729
**NUCLEUS (CAMBRIDGE, MASS.).** (NUCLEUS.). [Nucleus]. **Added/Corp** Union of Concerned Scientists. (197?)-. Periodical. English. qt. $15.00. Union of Concerned Scientists, 26 Church Street, Cambridge MA 02238. **Tel** (617)546-5552, FAX (617)864-9405. **ED** Janet S Wager. **DD** 363. **Circ:** 100,000.
**Ind/Abst** Soc. Sci. Cit. Index [Select. Cov.].

US
**OCCASIONAL BULLETIN / PACIFIC & ASIAN AMERICAN CENTER FOR THEOLOGY & STRATEGIES.** **Added/Corp** Pacific & Asian American Center for Theology & Strategies. **VFOAT** PACTS Occasional Bulletin. (19??)-. Bulletin. English. qt. 1798 Scenis Avenue, Berkeley CA 94709.

AU/0048-1440
**OESTERREICHISCHE MILITAERISCHE ZEITSCHRIFT.** Vol. 1 (Jan. 1963)-. Periodical. German. Six times a year. S210.00 Austria; S350.00 other. Oesterreichische Militaerische Zeitschrift, Mariahilferstrasse 22 24 1 3 9, A 1070 Vienna Austria. **LC** U3; .O34. ***Supersedes*** *Fuer den Kommandanten; Reserveoffizier* ***and*** *Landesverteidigung.*
**Ind/Abst** Am. Hist. Life (1988-); Curr. Mil. Pol. Lit.

US/0030-0268
**OFFICER, THE.** **Added/Corp** Reserve Officers Association of the United States. Vol. 1, (Jan. 1924)-. Periodical. English. mo. $12.00 (US); $48.00 (other) outside US. Reserve Officer Association, 1 Constitution Avenue Northeast, Washington DC 20002-5624. **Tel** (202)479-2200, FAX (202)479-0416. **ED** Norman S. Burzynski and Carol T. Wilson. **LC** UA23.A1; R4. **DD** 355.3/32/05. **Ad Acc. Circ:** 125,000. available on microfilm and microfiche from University Microfilms International (UMI).
**Desc:** For those in the military services, both reserve and regular, with emphasis upon legislation and policy affecting the regular and Reserve Forces. Magazine also reports substance of association activities.
**Ind/Abst** Air Univ. Libr. Index Mil. Period.; Urban Aff. Abstr.

US/0732-7587
**OFFICER AND WARRANT OFFICER DIRECTORY.** (OFFICER AND WARRANT OFFICER DIRECTORY / CORPS OF ENGINEERS.). **Main/Corp** United States. Army. Corps of Engineers. **VFOAT** Directory, Corps of Engineers Officers and Warrant Officers; Engineer Officer Directory. Began with 1982. Directory. English. Adjutant General Headquarters, Department of the Army, Washington DC 20310. **LC** UG23; .U46B. **DD** 358/.2/02573. available on microfiche (Vols. for (1986-) distributed to depository libraries). ***Continues*** *United States. Army. Corps of Engineers. Officer Directory.*

US/0736-7317
**OFFICER REVIEW.** (OFFICER REVIEW / THE MILITARY ORDER OF WORLD WARS.). [Off. rev.]. Vol. 12, No. 4 (Jan./Feb. 1974)-. Periodical. English. mo (Except Feb. and Aug.). $10.00 North America; $20.00 other. Military Order of the World Wars, 435 North Lee Street, Alexander VA 22314. **LC** U56; .M54. **DD** 369/.186/0973. **Bk Rev. Ad Acc. Circ:** 15,000 (ctrl). ***Continues*** *World Wars Officer Review, 0512-381X.*

SW
**OFFICERSFORBUNDSBLADET.** **Added/Corp** Svenska Officersforbundet. (1932)-. Periodical. Swedish. mo (ten issues per year). Kr125.00 (Scandinavia); Kr155.00 (other). Svenska Officersforbundet, Sturegatan 8 3 Tr, S 114 35 Stockholm Sweden. **Tel** 08-24 17 22, FAX 46 8 203965. **ED** Carl Sjostrand. **LC** U4; .O35. Index available. **Bk Rev**, (Qty: 5-10). **Ad Acc, Adv Mgr:** Monica Wistedt. **Circ:** 13,000.
**Desc:** Magazine for the members of the Swedish Association of Military Officers; contains reports from army, navy and air force units, debate, military history and union information.

US/0193-6557
**OFFICIAL ARMY NATIONAL GUARD REGISTER.** **Main/Corp** United States. National Guard Bureau. **VFOAT** Army National Guard Register. Began with 1957. English. an. National Guard Bureau / Washington DC, The Pentagon, Washington DC 20310. ***Continues*** *United States. National Guard Register. Official National Guard Register.*

US/0278-6559
**OFFICIAL DIRECTORY / U.S. ARMY CORPS OF ENGINEERS.** **Main/Corp** United States. Army. Corps of Engineers. Directory. English. Image Southwest, 517 Main Street, Texarkana TX 75501. **Tel** (903)793-5528, FAX (903)794-0080. **LC** UG23; .U46A. **DD** 358/.2/02573. ***Continues*** *Directory of Regular Army Officers.*

US/0743-9776
**OFFICIAL PRICE GUIDE TO ANTIQUE & MODERN FIREARMS, THE.** **VFOAT** Antique & Modern Firearms. (1981)-. English. ir. Random House Inc., 400 Hahn Road, Westminster MD 21157. **Tel** (800)726-0600, (800)733-3000, FAX (800)659-2436. **LC** TS532.4; .O37. **DD** 683.4/075.

US/0748-8726
**OFFICIAL PRICE GUIDE TO COLLECTIBLES OF THE THIRD REICH, THE.** **VFOAT** Military. 1st Ed. (1985)-. English. an. $9.95. Random House Inc., 400 Hahn Road, Westminster MD 21157. **Tel** (800)726-0600, (800)733-3000, FAX (800)659-2436. **ED** T E Hudgeons III. **LC** UC465.G3; O33. **DD** 355.8/1/0943.

US/0747-5691
**OFFICIAL PRICE GUIDE TO MILITARY COLLECTIBLES, THE.** **See** Hobbies.

US/1064-007X
**ON GUARD (NEW YORK, N.Y.).** (ON GUARD.). [On guard]. **Added/Corp** Citizen Soldier. (198?)-. Periodical. English. Four times a year. $10.00. Citizen Soldier, 175 Fifth Avenue, Suite 808, New York NY 10010. **Tel** (212)777-3470. **ED** Tod Ensign and Ken Cunningham. **DD** 355. **Bk Rev**, (Qty: 1-2). **Circ:** 15,000. available on microfiche from University Microfilms International (UMI).
**Ind/Abst** Altern. Press Index (199?-).

US/0030-4387
**ORBIS (PHILADELPHIA).** **See** Political Science.

US/0895-822X
**ORDNANCE (ABERDEEN PROVING GROUND, MD.).** ***Ceased.*** (ORDNANCE.). [Ordnance]. **Added/Corp** US Army Ordnance Center and School. **VFOAT** Ordnance Bulletin. (Aug. 1987)-(Mar. 1994). Periodical. English. qt. The Ordnance Magazine, US Army Ordnance Center and School, Aberdeen Proving Ground MD 21005. **Tel** (410)278-5305. **(Subscription address:** Superintendent of Documents, US Government Printing Office, Washington DC 20402.**)** **DD** 355. available on microfilm from University Microfilms International (UMI). ***Continues*** *Ordnance Magazine, 0746-2972.*
**Ind/Abst** Air Univ. Libr. Index Mil. Period. (199?-).

US
**ORDNANCE & MUNITIONS FORECAST.** (19??)-. English. Twelve times a year. $1390.00. Forecast International / DMS Inc., 22 Commerce Road, Newtown CT 06470. **Tel** (203)426-0800, FAX (203)426-1964, telex 467615. available on CD-ROM ($1595.00).

US
**PACIFIC BULLETIN.** **Added/Corp** Pacific Concerns Resource Center. Vol. 2, No. 5 (Oct. 1982)-. Bulletin. English. bm. $10.00. Pacific Concerns Resource Center / Honolulu, PO Box 27692, Honolulu HI 96827. ***Continues*** *Pacific Concerns Resource Center Bulletin.*
**Ind/Abst** Hum. Rights Intern. Rep.

MY
**PAHLAWAN DALAM KENANGAN.** Began with Vol. for 1967. Malay. $1.00. Persatuan Bekas Perajurit Malaysia, Bilek 309/Bangunam Sing Hoe Motor 179 Jalan Ipoh, Kuala Lumpur Malaysia. **LC** UB359.M3; P34.

NE
**PALLAS.** Periodical. Dutch (French). Fl250.00. Association des Officers en Service Actif, Avenue Milcamps 77, 1040 Bruxelles Belgium. **LC** UA11; .P28.

IT/0394-3429
**PANORAMA DIFESA.** [Panor. dif.]. (1982)-. Periodical. Italian. mo (except Feb. & Aug.). L70000 Italy; L85000 other. Ed Ai Srl, Via Guinicelli 4, 50133 Florence Italy. **Tel** 011 39 55 574774, FAX 011 39 55 570103, telex 580217. **UDC** 355.1.

US/0745-9688
**PARAGLIDE.** Periodical. English. qt. $3.50 US; $11.00 other. Eighty-Second Airborne Division Association Inc, 2670 West Stansifer Court, Bloomington IN 47401. **Tel** (812)824-2934. **ED** Jerry J Hladik. **LC** UA27.5 82D; .P37. **Bk Rev. Ad Acc. Circ:** 15,000 (ctrl).
**Desc:** A magazine for and about paratroopers and chapters and members of the Association.

US/0031-1723
**PARAMETERS (CARLISLE, PA.).** (PARAMETERS : JOURNAL OF THE US ARMY WAR COLLEGE.). [Parameters]. **Added/Corp** Army War College (U.S.). (1971)-. Government Publication. English. qt. $10.00 US; 12.50 other. Superintendent of Documents, US Government Printing Office, Washington DC 20402. **Tel** (202)275-3328, FAX (202)786-2377. **ED** Lloyd J. Matthews. **LC** U1; .P32. **DD** 355/.005. **Bk Rev.** available on microfilm and microfiche from University Microfilms International (UMI).
**Desc:** A forum expressing professional thought on the art and science of welfare, national and international security, military history, strategy, leadership, and management.
**Ind/Abst** ABC POL SCI; Air Univ. Libr. Index Mil. Period.; Am. Hist. Life (1980-); Am. Bibliogr. Slavic East Europ. Stud.; Book Rev. Digest; Book Rev. Index; Middle East Abstr. Index; PAIS Int. Print (1991-).

CN/0384-0417
**PARAPET, THE.** **VFOAT** Parapet. V. 1- Jan. 14, 1971-. Periodical. French (English). mo. Free. Canadian Forces Base Montreal, St Hubert Quebec J3Y 5T4 Canada. **Tel** (514)443-7409. **Circ:** 3,000.
**Desc:** Community newspaper published for military members, their dependents and employees of Department of National defence. Topics include articles of interest in the community.

SA
**PARATUS.** **Added/Corp** South Africa. Army. (19??)-. Periodical. Afrikaans (English). Twelve times a year. R40.35 South Africa; $80.00 others. South Africa Department of Defense, Private Bag X158, Pretoria 0001 South Africa. **Tel** 011 27 12 4284227. **ED** A. C. J. Collocott. **LC** U1; .K6. **Bk Rev. Ad Acc. Circ:** 47,000 (ctrl). ***Continues*** *Kommando.*
**Desc:** Military articles and news relating to the South African defence force.

US
**PASS IN REVIEW.** **See** Publishing-Books and Bookmaking.

CN/0316-5418
**PATRICIA NEWS BULLETIN.** Began with Dec. 1963 issue. Bulletin. English. ir. $1.00 per issue, Free (PPCLI veterans of World War I and libraries). Patricia Club News Service, PO Box 782 Station B, Ottawa Ontario K1P 5P8 Canada. **DD** 356.11.
**Desc:** A Patricia Club News Service for Patricias of World War I.

CN/0316-4942
**PATRICIAN, THE.** Began with 1948 issue?. Periodical. English. an. $7.50. The Patrician, Editor, Princess Patricia's Canadian Light Infantry, c/o Regimental Adjutant, Currie Barracks, Calgary Alberta T3E 1T8 Canada. **Tel** 9403)240-7525. **ED** G Manning. **DD** 356/.11/0971. Index available. **Ad Acc.** ctrl circ.

BU
**PATRIOT.** **Added/Corp** TSentralen Suvet na Organizatsiiata za Voennotekhnicheska Podotovka na Naselenieto (Bulgaria). (19??)-. Periodical. Bulgarian. mo. 4.201lv. G Dimitrov, Bul Khristo Botev 48, Sofia 1000 Bulgaria. **LC** U4; .P38.

UK/0031-4080
**PEGASUS.** (19??)-. English. sa (Jun. and Dec.). £7.00 UK. Pegasus Journal, Browning Barracks, Aldersht Hamp GU11 2BS England. **Tel** 0252-24431. **Bk Rev**, (Qty: 12-20). **Ad Acc. Circ:** 6,000.
**Desc:** Information concerning recent events and activities within British Airborne forces, including Associations (Veterans).
**Ind/Abst** Annu. Bibliogr. Engl. Lang. Lit.

US
**PERIODICAL (COUNCIL ON AMERICA'S MILITARY PAST).** (PERIODICAL.). Vol. 11, No. 4 (Nov. 1981)- = No. 45 (Nov. 1981)-. Academic Scholarly Publication. English. qt. $35.00. Council on America's Military Past, 518 West Why Worry Lane, Phoenix AZ 85021. **Tel** (602)943-3552, 800 398-4693. **ED** Dan L Thrapp. Index available. **Bk Rev. Ad Acc. Circ:** 1,600. ***Continues*** *Periodical (Council on Abandoned Military Posts (U.S.)).*
**Desc:** A scholarly journal with detailed discussions of military history topics.

CN/0712-9173
**PETAWAWA POST.** [Petawawa post]. Vol. 30, No. 15 Feb. 11, 1981. Periodical. English (French). wk. $10.00 Per Year. Petawawa Post, c/o Donald F Runge Ltd, 243 Pembroke Street West, Pembroke Ontario K8A 5N4 Canada. **DD** 355.1/09713/81. ***Continues*** *Petawana Base Post, 0316-4462.*

US/0195-1920
**PHALANX (ALEXANDRIA). See** Engineering-Materials Engineering and Mechanics.

US/1056-3334
**POLITICAL WARFARE.** ***Ceased.*** **See** Political Science-International Relations.

US
**POST-SOVIET WEAPONS COMPLEX MONITOR.** (19??)-. Periodical. English. bw. $895.00 US and Canada; $915.00 other. Exchange Publications, 2014 P Street NW, Washington DC 20036. **Tel** (202)296-2814, FAX (202)362-5437. **(Subscription address:** Exchange Publications, PO Box 5757, Washington DC 20016.**)**

CN/1183-8892
**PRESS FOR CONVERSION.** [Press convers.]. **Added/Corp** Coalition to Oppose the Arms Trade. **VFOAT** Newsletter of the Coalition to Oppose the Arms Trade. (Winter 1989/1990)-. Periodical. English. Four times a year (Jan., Apr., July, Oct.). 20.00Can$ Canada; 25.00Can$ others. Coalition Oppose Arms Trade, C/O 489 Metcalfe Street, Ottawa ONT K1S 3N7 Canada. **Tel** (613)231-3076, FAX (613)231-2614. **ED** Richard Sanders. **DD** 327.1/74/05. **Bk Rev**, (Qty: 40). **Ad Acc, Adv Mgr:** Sylvis, **Tel** (613)749-3147. **Circ:** 1,250.
**Desc:** Each of these issues contains news and information from around the world on the practical and theoretical dimensions of converting military industries and bases.

US
**PRIME CONTRACT AWARDS BY REGION AND STATE.** **Main/Corp** United States. Dept. of Defense. Washington Headquarters Services. Directorate for Information Operations and Reports. **VFOAT** Department of Defense Prime Contract Awards by Region and State. English. an. Information Operations and Reports, Washington Headquarters Services, Room IC535/The Pentagon, Washington DC 20301. **LC** UC267; .U598A. **DD** 355.6/211/0973. available on microfiche (Vols. for 1981, 1982 and 1983, distributed to depository libraries). ***Continues*** *Military Prime Contract Awards by Region and State.*

US
**PRIME CONTRACT AWARDS BY SERVICE CATEGORY AND FEDERAL SUPPLY CLASSIFICATION.** **Main/Corp** United States. Dept. of Defense. **Added/Corp** United States. Dept. of Defense. Washington Headquarters Services. Directorate for Information Operations and Reports. (197?)-. Government Publication. English. sa. $9.50 US; $11.90 other. Superintendent of Documents, US Government Printing Office, Washington DC 20402. **Tel** (202)275-3328, FAX (202)786-2377. **LC** UC267; .U598c. **DD** 355.6/211/0973. available on microfiche (Vols. for (Fiscal Years 1980, 1981, 1982, 1983-) distributed to depository libraries). ***Continues*** *Military Prime Contract Awards by Service Category and Federal Supply Classification.*
**Desc:** Presents, in both tables and charts, a variety of current and historical data on the net value of DoD prime contract awards.

US/1058-014X
**PRIME CONTRACT AWARDS IN LABOR SURPLUS AREAS.** ***Ceased.*** (PRIME CONTRACT AWARDS IN LABOR SURPLUS AREAS / DEPARTMENT OF DEFENSE.). [Prime contract awards labor surpl. areas]. **Main/Corp** United States. Dept. of Defense. **Added/Corp** United States. Dept. of Defense. Washington Headquarters Services. Directorate for Information Operations and Reports. (1979)-(19??). Government Publication. English. sa. Superintendent of Documents, US Government Printing Office, Washington DC 20402. **Tel** (202)275-3328, FAX (202)786-2377. **LC** UC267; .U598b. **DD** 355.6/211/0973. available on microfiche (Vols. for 1979- distributed to depository libraries). ***Continues*** *Department of Defense Prime Contract Awards in Areas of Substantial Unemployment.*

US
**PRIME CONTRACT AWARDS OVER $25,000 OUTSIDE THE UNITED STATES.** **VFOAT** Prime Contract Awards over Twenty-Five Thousand Dollars Outside the United States. English. Information Operations and Reports, Washington Headquarters Services, Room IC535/The Pentagon, Washington DC 20301. **LC** UC267; .P78. **DD** 355.6/211.

US
**PROCEEDINGS OF ... NATIONAL CONVENTION OF THE AMERICAN LEGION.** **Main/Corp** American Legion. National Convention. **VFOAT** National Convention of the American Legion. 72nd (Aug. 28-30, 1990)-. Proceedings. English. ***Continues*** *American Legion. National Convention. Proceedings of the ... Annual National Convention.*

CN/0840-1705
**PROCEEDINGS OF THE SPECIAL COMMITTEE OF THE SENATE ON NATIONAL DEFENCE.** (PROCEEDINGS OF THE SPECIAL COMMITTEE OF THE SENATE ON NATIONAL DEFENCE.). [Proc. Spec. Comm. Senate Natl. Def.]. **Main/Corp** Canada. Parliament. Senate. Special Committee on National Defence. **VFOAT** National Defence; Defense Nationale; Deliberations du Comite Special du Senat sur la Defense Nationale; Proceedings of the Standing Senate Committee on National Defence. 32nd Parliament, 2nd Session, Issue No. 1 (Jan. 1984)-. English (French). ir. Canada Communication Group Publishers, Order Processing, Ottawa Ontario K1A 0S9 Canada. **Tel** (819)956-4800, (819)956-4802. **LC** UA600; .C29g. **DD** 355/.0335/71. ***Continues*** *Canada. Parliament. Senate. Subcommittee on National Defence. Proceedings of the Subcommittee on National Defence, 0229-8198.*

CN
**PROCEEDINGS OF THE SUBCOMMITTEE ON NATIONAL DEFENCE.** **Main/Corp** Canada. Parliament. Senate. Subcommittee on National Defence. **VFOAT** Deliberations du Sous-Comite sur la Defense Nationale; National Defence. (19??)-. English (French). Canada Communication Group Publishers, Order Processing, Ottawa Ontario K1A 0S9 Canada. **Tel** (819)956-4800, (819)956-4802. **LC** UA600; .C29e. **DD** 355/.033071.

●CN/1193-1612
**PROCEEDINGS OF THE SUBCOMMITTEE ON SECURITY AND NATIONAL DEFENCE.** [Proc. Subcomm. Secur. Natl. Def.]. **Main/Corp** Canada. Parliament. Senate. Subcommittee on Security and National Defence. **VFOAT** Security and National Defence; Deliberations du Sous-Comite sur la Securite et Defense Nationale. (1992)-. Proceedings. English (French). **DD** 355/.00971/05.

●CN/1193-1612
**PROCEEDINGS OF THE SUBCOMMITTEE ON SECURITY AND NATIONAL DEFENCE (FRENCH EDITION).** [Proc. Subcomm. Secur. Natl. Def.]. **Main/Corp** Canada. Parlement. Senat. Sous-Comite sur la Securite et Defense Nationale. **VFOAT** Securite et Defense Nationale; Deliberations du Sous-Comite sur la Securite et Defense Nationale. (1992)-. Proceedings. French (English). **DD** 355/.00971/05.

US/0145-112X
**PROFILE (NORFOLK, VA.).** (PROFILE.). [Profile]. **Added/Corp** United States. Dept. of Defense. High School News Service. Vol. 20 (Oct. 1976)-. Periodical. English. ir. US Department of Defense High School News Service, Building X-18 Naval Station, Norfolk VA 23511. **LC** UA23.A1; U43a. **DD** 355/.00973. ***Continues*** *United States. Dept. of Defense. High School News Service. Report - High School News Service.* **Ind/Abst** Index Free Period.

BL
**PROJET DE BUDGET DE PROGRAMMES.** **Main/Corp** France. Service Central de l'Action Sociale des Armees. French. Action Sociale des Armees, 5 rue de Chazelles, 75017 Paris France. **LC** UH769.F8; F7A. **DD** 354/.44/066.

US/1071-2194
**PROTOCOL DIGEST.** ***Ceased.*** [Protoc. dig.]. (Dec. 1991)-(Feb. 1994). Periodical. English. bm. Protocol Digest, PO Box 282, Garrison MN 56450. **Tel** (612)692-4138, FAX (612)692-4203. **ED** Jim Peterson. **DD** 399. **Ad Acc. Circ:** 100.

US/0475-2953
**PS (WASHINGTON, D.C.).** (PS.). [PS]. **Added/Corp** United States. Dept. of the Army. **VFOAT** Preventive Maintenance Monthly; PS, the Preventive Maintenance Monthly; PS Magazine. (19??)-. Government Publication. English. mo. $19.00 domestic; $23.75 other. Superintendent of Documents, US Government Printing Office, Washington DC 20402. **Tel** (202)275-3328, FAX (202)786-2377. **LC** UG503; .A35. **DD** 623.
**Desc:** Published for soldiers assigned to combat support units, and soldiers with organizational maintenance and supply duties, this periodical uses cartoons to illustrate maintenance of trucks, military vehicles, and military equipment.

CN/0706-8808
**QUAD (PAISLEY).** (QUAD.). 1- 1977-. Periodical. English. bm. 0.75Can$ each number. Bishops University Students Association, Lennoxville Quebec J1M 1Z7 Canada. **DD** 355.1/0971.

IT
**QUADRANTE.** **Added/Corp** Italy. Ministero della Difesa. Vol. 1 (1966)-. Periodical. Italian. mo (12 issues). L15000 Italy; L2000 other. Ministero Della Difesa Gab Min Serv Pubb, Via XX Settembre 8, 00187 Rome Italy. **Tel** 011 39 6 4827826. **LC** UA740; .Q3. **DD** 355/.000945.

US/0882-6935
**QUADRENNIAL REVIEW OF MILITARY COMPENSATION.** [Quadrenn. rev. mil. compens.]. **Main/Corp** United States. Dept. of Defense. **VFOAT** QRMC. English. ir. US Department of Defense, The Pentagon, Washington DC 20301. **Tel** (703)545-6700. **LC** UC74; .A36A. **DD** 355.6/4/0973.

US
**QUARTERLY SUPPLEMENT TO THE ... ANNUAL DEPARTMENT OF DEFENSE BIBLIOGRAPHY OF LOGISTICS STUDIES AND RELATED DOCUMENTS / DEFENSE LOGISTICS STUDIES INFORMATION EXCHANGE.** **Main/Corp** United States. Defense Logistics Studies Information Exchange. **VFOAT** Bibliography of Logistics Studies and Related Documents. 1st (April 1981)-. Bibliography. English. Three times a year (April, July, and Oct.). Defense Logistics Agency / Alexandria, Attn DLA-XPD, Cameron Station, Alexandria VA 22314. available on microfiche (Vols. for (1986-) distributed to depository libraries).

●US/1055-2081
**R & R MILITARY RETIREE: RETIREMENT & RELOCATION MILITARY RETIREE.** **VFOAT** Retirement & Relocation Military Retiree; Retirement and Relocation Military Retiree; R and R Military Retiree. **VAT** Retirement & Relocation Military Retiree. (1992)-. Periodical. English. qt. $9.00. R & R Military Retiree, POB 179, Belleville IL 62221.

UK
**R.U.S.I. AND BRASSEY'S DEFENCE YEARBOOK.** **Main/Corp** Royal United Services Institute for Defence Studies. **VFOAT** Brassey's Defence Yearbook; Defence Yearbook. **VAT** Royal United Services Institute and Brassey's Defence Yearbook. 85th (1974)-. English. an. $65.00. Brasseys UK Ltd., 33 John Street, London WC1N 2AT England. **Tel** 011 44 71 753 7777, FAX 011 44 71 753 7794. **(Subscription address:** Macmillan Publishing, Front and Brown Street, Riverside NJ 08075.**)** ***Continues*** *Brassey's Annual.*

UK/0097-4803
**R.U.S.I. AND BRASSEY'S DEFENCE YEARBOOK.** ***Title Change.*** **Main/Corp** Royal United Services Institute for Defence Studies. **VFOAT** RUSI and Brassey's Defence Yearbook; Brassey's Defence Yearbook; Defence Yearbook. **VAT** Royal United Services Institute and Brassey's Defence Yearbook. (1974)-(1992). English. an. Pergamon Press, An Imprint of Elsevier Science Ltd., The Boulevard, Langford Lane, Kidlington, Oxford OX5 1GB United Kingdom. **Tel** 011 44 865 843000, 011 44 865 843699, FAX 011 44 865 843010. **LC** V10; .N3. **DD** 355/.055. ***Continues*** *Brassey's Annual, 0068-0702.* ***Continued by*** *Brassey's Defence Yearbook.*

US
**RADAR FORECAST.** (19??)-. English. Twelve times a year. $1390.00. Forecast International / DMS Inc., 22 Commerce Road, Newtown CT 06470. **Tel** (203)426-0800, FAX (203)426-1964, telex 467615. available on CD-ROM ($1595.00).

CN/0714-7805
**RAPPORT ANNUEL / BUREAU DE LA PROTECTION CIVILE DU QUEBEC.** [Rapp. annu. - Bur. prot. civ. Que.]. **Main/Corp** Bureau de la Protection Civile du Quebec. 1980-81-. French. an. Editeur Officiel du Quebec, 1283 Boul Charest Ouest, Quebec Quebec G1N 2C9 Canada. **LC** UA929.Q3; B87A. **DD** 354.7140075/4. ***Continues*** *Protection Civile du Quebec. Rapport d'Activities, 0229-849X.*

SP/0484-1379
**RECONQUISTA.** ***Ceased.*** (RECONQUISTA : REVISTA DE PENSAMIENTO MILITAR.). [Reconquista]. (1950)-(1993). Periodical. Spanish. mo. Editora Adiac, Nuncio 13, 28005 Madrid Spain.

US/0747-573X
**RECRUITER JOURNAL.** [Recruit. j.]. **Added/Corp** United States. Army Recruiting Command. United States. Army Recruiting Command. Public Affairs Office. **VFOAT** USAREC Recruiter Journal. Vol. 36, No. 12 (April 1984)-. Government Publication. English. mo. $22.00 US; $27.50 other. Superintendent of Documents, US Government Printing Office, Washington DC 20402. **Tel** (202)275-3328, FAX (202)786-2377. **LC** UB323; .R4. **DD** 355.2/2362/0973. ***Continues*** *All Volunteer, 0192-6071.*
**Ind/Abst** Index U.S. Gov. Period.

US/0743-1449
**REGISTER OF FORMER CADETS. SUPPLEMENT.** Periodical. English. ir. VMI Alumni Association, Virginia Military Institute, PO Box 932, Lexington VA 24450.

US/0090-2357
**REGISTER OF GRADUATES AND FORMER CADETS OF THE UNITED STATES MILITARY ACADEMY.** [Regist. grad. former cadets U. S. Mil. Acad.]. **Added/Corp** United States Military Academy. Association of Graduates. (1972)-. English. an (Nov.). $40.00 (hardcover US APO & FPO addresses), $46.00 (hardcover other), $35.00 (softcover US APO & FPO addresses), $41.00 (softcover other) nonmembers; $19.00 (hardcover US APO & FPO addresses), $25.00 (hardcover other), $16.00 (softcover US APO & FPO addresses), $22.00 (softcover other) members; $65.00 (nonmember hardcover APO & FPO addresses), $71.00 (nonmember hardcover other), $60.00 (nonmember softcover APO & FPO addresses), $66.00 (nonmember softcover other), $35.00 (members hardcover APO & FPO addresses), $41.00 (members hardcover other), $32.00 (members softcover APO & FPO addresses), $38.00 (members softcover other) combined with Assembly. Association of Graduates, United States Military Academy, West Point NY 10996. **Tel** (914)446-5800, FAX (914)446-6988. **ED** Leslie Rose. **LC** U410; .H35. **DD** 355/.007/1174731. **Ad Acc. Circ:** 15,000. ***Continues*** *West Point Alumni Foundation. Register of Graduates and Former Cadets of the United States Military Academy.*
**Desc:** Provides a listing of all USMA graduates from 1910-1988, with a short biographical section in each; a number of other lists of special interest to USMA graduates.

US/0094-1905
**REGISTER PLANNED EMERGENCY PRODUCERS.** (REGISTER OF PLANNED EMERGENCY PRODUCERS / OFFICE OF THE UNDER SECRETARY OF DEFENSE (RESEARCH AND ENGINEERING).). Began with 1975. English. an. Defense Logistics Agency / Alexandria, Attn DLA-XPD, Cameron Station, Alexandria VA 22314. **LC** UA18.U5; U48A. **DD** 355.2/6/02573. ***Continues*** *Register Planned Emergency Producers, 0094-1905.*

US
**REPLICA WRAP-UP, THE. See** The Arts-Crafts and Decorative Arts.

US
**REPORT, BASIC FACTS ABOUT MILITARY SERVICE. Main/Corp** United States. Dept. of Defense. High School News Service. **VFOAT** Basic Facts about Military Service. English. an. Department of Defense, High School News Service, Service Building X18 Naval Station, Norfolk VA 23511. **LC** UB147; .U474A. **DD** 355/.00973. ***Supersedes in part*** *Report - High School News Service.*

US
**REPORT - MASSACHUSETTS. COMMISSIONER OF VETERANS' SERVICES. Main/Corp** Massachusetts. Commissioner of Veterans' Services. English. an. **LC** J87; .M4 DATE P subser. **DD** 355.115.

US
**REPORT - MISSISSIPPI. STATE VETERANS AFFAIRS BOARD. *Title Change.*** **Main/Corp** Mississippi. State Veterans Affairs Board. **Added/Corp** Mississippi. State Veterans Affairs Commission. **VFOAT** Biennial Report. (19??)-(1969). English. be. **LC** UB358.M7; A33. ***Continued by*** *Annual Report.*

US/0094-7326
**REPORT OF THE NEW MEXICO VETERANS' SERVICE COMMISSION. See** Public Administration.

US/1043-268X
**REPORT ON DEFENSE PLANT WASTES.** [Rep. def. plant wastes]. **VFOAT** Defense Plant Wastes. (1989)-. Periodical. English. bw (26 issues). $507.00. Business Publishers Inc., 951 Pershing Drive, Silver Spring MD 20910-4464. **Tel** (301)587-6300, (800)274-0122, FAX (301)585-9075. **DD** 623. **[CCC].** available on an online database (file 636/Full-Text) from DIALOG.
**Desc:** Devoted to environmental laws, regulations, cleanups, contracting and court action affecting US defense, weapons production and other government facilities. This journal provides concise, clear updates in areas such as contracts, regulations/legislation, technology, and cleanups. Also covers disposal of government hospitals' radioactive waste.
**Ind/Abst** PTS Newsl. Database [Full Txt.].

US
**REPORT ON DEPARTMENT OF VETERANS' AFFAIRS FOR THE FISCAL YEARS ENDED JUNE 30. Main/Corp** Connecticut. Auditors of Public Accounts. **Added/Corp** Connecticut. Dept. of Veterans' Affairs. (1989/1990)-. English. **LC** WMLC 91/2240. ***Continues in part*** *Connecticut. Auditors of Public Accounts. Report on Veterans' Home and Hospital Commission for the Fiscal Years Ended June 30... and Department of Veterans' Affairs for the Fiscal Years Ended June 30.*

US
**REPORT ON THE FEDERAL CATALOGING PROGRAM. Main/Corp** United States. Dept. of Defense. English. an. US Department of Defense, The Pentagon, Washington DC 20301. **Tel** (703)545-6700. **LC** UC263; .A374. **DD** 355.6/21/0973. ***Continues*** *Report, Department of Defense Cataloging and Standardization Programs.*

US/0034-4796
**REPORTER FOR CONSCIENCE' SAKE, THE. Added/Corp** National Interreligious Service Board for Conscientious Objectors. (1944)-. Periodical. English. Four times a year (Jan., Apr., July, Oct.). $20.00. National Interreligious Service Board for Conscientious Objectors, 1601 Connecticut Avenue Northwest, Suite 750, Washington DC 20009. **Tel** (202)483-4510, FAX (202)265-8022. **ED** L. Nilcian Yocton. **LC** UB342.U5; R4. **DD** 355.2/24/0973. Index available (Bound in Feburary issue). **Bk Rev. Circ:** 3,000. available on microfilm and microfiche from University Microfilms International (UMI). ***Continues*** *Reporter.*

US/0163-0202
**RESEARCH AND DEVELOPMENT PROGRAMS GUIDE. *Ceased.*** (DEPARTMENT OF DEFENSE RESEARCH AND DEVELOPMENT PROGRAMS GUIDE.). [Res. dev. programs guide]. **Main/Corp** Information Group Inc. ?. English. an. The Information Group, Box 39013, Washington DC 20016. **Tel** (301)681-5544. **ED** Robert H Todd. **LC** U393; .I54a. **DD** 355.8/2/0973. Index available. **Bk Rev. Circ:** 250.
**Desc:** Guide to defense R&D programs including future plans, current contractors, program manager, and funding for total program and subprojects.

US
**RESEARCH MONOGRAPH - CONNECTICUT OFFICE OF VETERANS AFFAIRS FOR EDUCATION. Main/Corp** Connecticut. Office of Veterans Affairs for Education. No. 1, (1977)-. Monographic series. English. ir. Price varies per volume. Board of Education, PO Box 2219, Hartford CT 06101. **LC** UB358.C8; C57b. **DD** 312/.9.

US/0363-860X
**RESERVE FORCES ALMANAC.** 3rd Ed. (1977)-. English. an (published in February). $5.95. Uniformed Services Almanac, PO Box 4144, Falls Church VA 22044. **Tel** (703)532-1631, FAX (703)532-1635. **ED** Sol Gordon. **LC** U9; .R47. **DD** 355.3/7/0973. **Bk Rev. Ad Acc. Circ:** 50,000. ***Continues*** *Uniformed Services Almanac. Reserve Forces Edition, 0363-8596.*
**Desc:** Accurate comprehensive guide to Reserve Forces compensation and benefits. Deals with drill pay, organizations, promotions, retirement, taxes, and many more subjects to all Military Reserve Forces.

US/0193-1008
**RESERVE FORCES MANPOWER CHARTS. Added/Corp** United States. Office, Deputy Assistant Secretary of Defense (Reserve Affairs). (19??)-. English. Deputy Assistant Secretary of Defense, 1777 T Street NW, Washington DC 20007. **LC** UA42; .A5974a. **DD** 355.2/2.

US/0034-5547
**RESERVE MARINE, THE.** Periodical. English. mo. Commandant of Marine Corps, Headquarters of Marine Corps, Washington DC 20380.

DK
**RESERVEOFFICEREN. Main/Corp** Reserveofficersforeningen i Danmark. Danish. **LC** UA697; .R45a. ***Continues*** *Meddelelser.*

US/0893-1828
**RESOURCE MANAGEMENT.** [Resour. manage.]. **Added/Corp** United States. Office of the Assistant Secretary of the Army (Financial Management) U.S. Army Finance and Accounting Center. United States. Defense Finance and Accounting Service--Indianapolis Center. Vol. 8, No. 1 (May 1987)-. Periodical. English. ir. must orer direct. Resource Management Journal, Department of the Army DACA-RP, Comptroller of Army, Washington DC 20310. **LC** UA25; .R47. **DD** 355. ***Continues*** *Resource Management Journal, 0274-5968.*

US/0149-7197
**RETIRED MILITARY ALMANAC.** (1978)-. English. an (published in March). $5.95. Uniformed Services Almanac, PO Box 4144, Falls Church VA 22044. **Tel** (703)532-1631, FAX (703)532-1635. **ED** Sol Gordon. **LC** UB357; .R47. **DD** 355.1/14. **Bk Rev. Ad Acc. Circ:** 50,000.
**Desc:** Vital information for retired military personnel including listings of military installations, health care, benefits, entitlements, restrictions, survivor benefits and many other interesting and important subjects.

US/0034-6160
**RETIRED OFFICER (ALEXANDRIA, VA.), THE.** (THE RETIRED OFFICER.). **Added/Corp** Retired Officers Association (U.S.). Vol. 35, No. 1 (Jan. 1979)-. Periodical. English. Twelve times a year. $20.00. Retired Officers Association, 201 North Washington Street, Department 05B, Alexandria VA 22314. **Tel** (703)838-8135. **ED** Charles D. Cooper. **LC** UB413; .R4. **DD** 355.3/7/05. **Bk Rev. Ad Acc. Circ:** 358,000. available on microfilm and microfiche from University Microfilms International (UMI). ***Continues*** *Retired Officer Magazine, 0737-724X.*
**Desc:** Edited for the officers of the seven uniformed services, their families and survivors. Reports on current defense issues, legislative affairs and developments on military retirement matters.

US/1061-3102
**RETIRED OFFICER MAGAZINE (ALEXANDRIA, VA.), THE.** (THE RETIRED OFFICER MAGAZINE.). [Retired off. mag.]. **Added/Corp** Retired Officers Association (U.S.). (19??)-. Periodical. English. Twelve times a year. $20.00. Retired Officers Association, 201 North Washington Street, Department 05B, Alexandria VA 22314. **Tel** (703)838-8135. **ED** Col. Charles D. Cooper U.S.A.F. **DD** 355. **Bk Rev**, (Qty: 50). **Ad Acc**, **Adv Mgr:** Hacker. **Circ:** 386,000 (ctrl). available on microfilm and microfiche from University of Michigan. ***Continues*** *Retired Officer (Alexandria, Va.), 0034-6160.*
**Desc:** For the officers of the 7 uniformed services of the USA. It reports on current events, news of legislation and other developments in defense and military retirement matters.

AT
**REVEILLE. Added/Corp** Returned Sailors, Soldiers and Airmen's Imperial League of Australia. New South Wales Branch. 3n. Vol. 1 (19??)-. Periodical. English. bm. 6.00Aus$. Returned Services League, 365 Kent Street / Anzac House, Sydney New South Wales 2000 Australia. **Tel** 011 61 02 292671.

BO
**REVISTA AERONAUTICA.** Spanish. Editorial Aeronautica Fab, Av Montes 734, La Paz Bolivia. **LC** UG635.B5; R48.

AG/0326-6427
**REVISTA ARGENTINA DE ESTUDIOS ESTRATEGICOS : R.A.E.E. *Suspended.*** **VFOAT** R.A.E.E. No. 1 (July/Aug./Sept 1984)-Suspended. Periodical. Spanish. qt. Vaimonte 494 30 Piso of 11, 1053 CF Buenos Aires Argentina. **LC** U4; .R424. **DD** 355/.005.
**Ind/Abst** HAPI Hisp. Am. Period. Index.

SP/0482-5748
**REVISTA DE HISTORIA MILITAR.** [Rev. hist. mil.]. Vol. 1 (1957)-. Periodical. Spanish. sa. **LC** D25; .R395. cum. index.
**Ind/Abst** Am. Hist. Life (1958-).

CL/0034-8511
**REVISTA DE MARINA.** (REVISTA DE MARINA / CIRCULO NAVAL.). [Rev. mar.]. **Added/Corp** Circulo Naval (Chile) Chile. Armada. Estado Mayor General. Vol. 1, No. 1 (July 10, 1885)-. Periodical. Spanish. Six times a year. $70.00. Revista de Marina, Armada Chile, Casilla 220, Correo Central, Valparaiso Chile. **Tel** 011 56 32 259645. **LC** V5; .R33. Each issue contains an index to its own contents (no volume index)--loose. **Bk Rev**, (Qty: 6). **Circ:** 3,200 (ctrl).
**Ind/Abst** Am. Hist. Life (1957-1967, 1980-).

SP
**REVISTA DE SANIDAD MILITAR. See** Medical Science and Technology.

SP
**REVISTA ESPANOLA DE DEFENSA. Added/Corp** Spain. Ministerio de Defensa. **VFOAT** Revista de Defensa. (198?)-. Periodical. Spanish. Eleven times a year. 4200ptas (one year); 7800ptas (two years). Ministerio de Defensa, C Paseo de la Castellana 109, 28071 Madrid Spain. **Tel** 011 34 1 5350477, FAX 011 34 1 5973540. **LC** IN PROCESS.

PO
**REVISTA MILITAR.** Began in Jan. 1849. Periodical. Portuguese. mo. $12.00. Empressa de Revista Militar, Largo da Anunciada 9, Lisbon Portugal. **LC** U4; .R475. ***Formed by the union of*** *Revista Militar; Revista do Exercito e da Armada; Revista da Administracao Militar* ***and*** *Portugal Militar.*
**Ind/Abst** Int. Polit. Sci. Abstr.

PO
**REVISTA TRIMESTRAL - SERVICO DE ADMINISTRACAO MILITAR.** **Main/Corp** Portugal. Servico de Administracao Militar. Portuguese. Servico de Adminstracao Militar, rua Rodrigo da Fonseca No 180, Lisbon Portugal. **LC** UB83; .P65A. **DD** 354/.469/06. ***Continues*** *Revista Bimestral - Servico de Administracao Militar.*

BE/0035-0877
**REVUE BELGE D'HISTOIRE MILITAIRE.** [Rev. belge hist. mil.]. **VFOAT** Belgisch Tijdschrift voor Miltaire Geschiedenis. (1965)-. Periodical. Multiple languages. qt. ***Continues*** *Carnet de la Fourragere, 0774-1820.*
**Ind/Abst** Am. Hist. Life (1987-).

FR/0758-881X
**REVUE DE LA SOCIETE DES AMIS DU MUSEE DE L'ARMEE.** (19??)-. Periodical. French. sa. **UDC** 069.02:93. **CODEN** 355.
**Ind/Abst** BHA : Biblio. Hist. Art.

FR
**REVUE / GENDARMERIE NATIONALE, LA.** **Added/Corp** France. Gendarmerie Nationale. **VFOAT** Revue de la Gendarmerie; Revue d'Etudes et d'Informations de la Gendarmerie Nationale. No 155 (April 1988)-. Periodical. French. Eleven times a year. 89000F. Association pour le Developpement et la Diffusion de l'Information Militaire, 6 rue Saint-Charles, 75015 Paris France. **LC** UB825.F8; A45. ***Continues*** *Revue d'Etudes et d'Informations (France. Gendarmerie Nationale).*

FR/0035-3299
**REVUE HISTORIQUE DES ARMEES.** [Rev. hist. armee]. **Added/Corp** France. Ministere des Armees. (1974)-. Periodical. French. qt. 290.00F France; 510.00F other. Revue Historique de Armees, Chateau de Vincennes, PB 108 00481 Armees France. **Tel** 011 33 1 49573292. **LC** UA700; .R38. **DD** 355/.00944. Index available. **Bk Rev. Ad Acc. Circ:** 5,000. ***Supersedes*** *Revue Historique de l'Armee.*
**Desc:** Articles on military history, a column on military tradition and symbolism, bibliography of periodicals, research, symposia, etc. Illustrated (maps, photos, black and white and color engravings).
**Ind/Abst** Am. Hist. Life (1954-)(1974-); BHA : Biblio. Hist. Art.

BE/0259-8582
**REVUE INTERNATIONALE DES SERVICES DE SANTE DES FORCES ARMEES : ORGANE DU COMITE INTERNATIONAL DE MEDECINE ETUDE PHARMACIE MILITAIRES.** **See** Medical Science and Technology.

SZ
**REVUE MILITAIRE SUISSE.** (18??)-. French. Twelve times a year. 296.75F. Dawson France SA, BP 40, 91121 Palaiseau Cedex France. **Tel** 011 33 1 69104700, telex 220064F. **LC** U2; .R5.
**Ind/Abst** Curr. Mil. Pol. Lit.

FR/0994-1541
**REVUE SCIENTIFIQUE ET TECHNIQUE DE LA DEFENSE.** No. 1 (Oct. 1988)-. Periodical. French (summaries and/or abstracts in English). Four times a year. 400.00F France; 600.00F other. Dunod Gauthier Villars, 15 rue Gossin, 92543 Montrouge cedex France. **Tel** 011 33 1 46 56 52 66, FAX 011 33 1 46 57 40 69. **(Subscription address:** Centrale des Revues, 11 rue Gossin, 92543 Montrouge Cedex France.) **LC** UG1; .R42. ***Continues*** *Sciences et Techniques de l'Armement.*
**Ind/Abst** Int. Aerosp. Abstr.

IT
**RID RIVISTA ITALIANA DIFESA.** (19??)-. Italian. ir. L70000 Italy; L95000 others. Coop Giornalistica Riviera, Via Martiri Liberazione 79/3, 16043 Chiavari Italy. **Tel** 011 39 185 308606, 309171, FAX 011 39 185 309063, telex 270630. **Bk Rev.**

IT
**RIVISTA AERONAUTICA.** **See** Aeronautics, Astronautics.

IT/0035-595X
**RIVISTA DELLA GUARDIA DI FINANZA.** [Riv. guardia finanza]. (1952)-. Periodical. Italian. bm. L8000 Italy; L14000 other. Rivista Guardia Finanza, Piazza Campidano 5, 00162 Rome Italy. **Tel** 011 39 6 47372204, FAX 011 39 6 47372214. **UDC** 336. **Ad Acc.**
**Ind/Abst** PAIS Int. Print.

IT
**RIVISTA DI POLIZIA.** Italian. ir. L70000 Italy; L140000 other. Ed Tipografia Progresso, Via Mazzocchi 175, 81055 S Maria CV Italy.

IT/0035-6980
**RIVISTA MILITARE.** [Riv. mil.]. **Added/Corp** Italy. Ministero Della Difesa. Esercito. Italy. Esercito. Corpo di Stato Maggiore. Italy. Esercito. Corpo di Stato Maggiore. Sezione Amministrativa. (1945)-. Periodical. Italian. Six times a year. L22000.00 Italy; L40000.00 other. SME-Rivista Militare, Via di S Marco 8, 00186 Rome Italy. **Tel** 011 39 6 784639007, FAX 011 39 6 4735371. **LC** U4; .R565. **Bk Rev**, (Qty: 6). **Ad Acc. Circ:** 25,000 (ctrl). ***Continues*** *Rivista Militare Italiana.*
**Desc:** Aim is to function as a vehicle for the dissemination of military thinking and as a forum of study and debate. Also serves as a means of informing the general public about the army.
**Ind/Abst** Am. Hist. Life (1954-1979, 1982-);(1954-).

RM
**ROMANIAN REVIEW OF MILITARY HISTORY.** **Added/Corp** Comisia Romana de Istorie Militara. (19??)-. Periodical. English (table of contents in French, German and Russian). Romanian Commission of Military History, Bucharest 5-7 Drumul Taberei Str. **LC** U4; .R83. **DD** 355.

UK
**ROYAL AIR FORCE NEWS.** English. Portsmouth Publ & Printing Ltd, News Centre, Hilsea Portsmouth, Hampshire PO2 9SX England.

UK
**ROYAL AIR FORCE RETIRED LIST, THE.** **Main/Corp** Great Britain. Royal Air Force. **VFOAT** RAF Retired List. English. an. £1.65. Royal Air Force, Adastral House/Room 610, Theobalds Road, London WC1X 8RU England. **LC** UB415.G7; G7A. **DD** 358.4/11/1502541.

CN/0315-6451
**ROYAL CANADIAN MILITARY INSTITUTE YEARBOOK.** (YEAR BOOK - ROYAL CANADIAN MILITARY INSTITUTE.). **Main/Corp** Royal Canadian Military Institute. Began publication in 1947. Periodical. English. an. Free to members only. Royal Canadian Military Institute, 426 University Avenue, Toronto Ontario M5G 1S9 Canada. **Tel** 597-0286. **ED** David E C Hugigns. **DD** 369/.2/71. **Circ:** 7,000.
**Desc:** Items on military with Canadian emphasis. The purpose is to stimulate and educate serving and retired officers in military matters.

UK/0035-8878
**ROYAL ENGINEERS JOURNAL, THE.** **See** Engineering.

UK
**RUSI JOURNAL / ROYAL UNITED SERVICES INSTITUTE FOR DEFENCE STUDIES, THE.** **Added/Corp** Royal United Services Institute for Defence Studies. Vol. 133, No. 1 (Spring 1988)-. Periodical. English. Six times a year. $80.00. Royal United Services Institute for Defense Studies, Whitehall, London SW1A 2ET England. **Tel** 011 44 71 9305854, FAX 011 44 71 3210943. **ED** Helen Macdonald, Jane Allford and Alexandra Citron. **LC** U1; .R8. **DD** 355/.005. Index available. cum. index. **Bk Rev. Ad Acc. Circ:** 7,000. ***Continues*** *Royal United Services Institute for Defence Studies. RUSI, 0307-1847.*
**Desc:** Promotes military science, military history, technology, industry and development, and international security issues.
**Ind/Abst** Air Univ. Libr. Index Mil. Period.; Am. Hist. Life (1955-); Curr. Mil. Pol. Lit.

GW/0080-4800
**RUSTUNGSBESCHRANKUNG UND SICHERHEIT.** Vol. 1 (1961)-. German. ir. DM28.00. Europa Union Verlag GmbH, Bachstrasse 32, Postfach 1529, D 53115 Bonn Germany. **Tel** 011 49 228 7290010, FAX 011 49 228 7290018, telex 8-86822. **Circ:** 3,000 (ctrl).
**Desc:** Problems of European security regarding East-West confrontation and possibilities of international arms-control and reduction.

AT/0486-8013
**SABRETACHE.** **Added/Corp** Military Historical Society of Australia. (June 1958)-. Periodical. English. qt (4 issues). 26.00Aus$. Military Historical Society of Australia, PO Box 30, Garran ACT 2605 Australia. **Tel** 011 61 6 2896640. **ED** Barry Clissold. **Bk Rev. Ad Acc. Pr Rev. Circ:** 400 (ctrl).
**Desc:** Covers Australian military history from 1788 to the present.
**Ind/Abst** APAIS, Aust. Public Aff. Inf. Ser. (1986-).

US/0197-2790
**SAGAMORE ARMY MATERIALS RESEARCH CONFERENCE PROCEEDINGS.** [Sagamore Army Mater. Res. Conf. proc.]. **Main/Conf** Sagamore Army Materials Research Conference. 21st (1974)-. Academic Scholarly Publication. English. ir. Price varies per volume. Plenum Press, 233 Spring Street, New York NY 10013-1578. **Tel** (212)620-8000, (800)221-9369, FAX (212)463-0742, (212)807-1047, telex 23/421139. **DD** 355. **CODEN** SAMPD2. **[CCC].** Documents available from Ask*IEEE, CASDDS. ***Continues*** *Sagamore Army Materials Research Conference. Proceedings of the ... Sagamore Army Materials Research Conference, 0080-5335.*
**Ind/Abst** Chem. Abstr.; INSPEC.

II/0036-2743
**SAINIK SAMACHAR.** **Added/Corp** India. Ministry of Defence. Vol. 1 (April 4, 1954)-. Periodical. English (English). mo. $15.00. Ministry of Defence, Government of India, M Block Church Road, New Delhi 110001 India. **(Subscription address:** Prints India, 11 Darya Ganj, New Delhi 110002 India.) **LC** U4; .F372. ***Supersedes*** *Fauji Akhbar.*

AT/0811-2711
**SANA UPDATE NEWSLETTER.** [SANA update, Newsl.]. **VFOAT** Scientists Against Nuclear Arms Update. Newsletter. (1982)-. Newsletter. English. Six times a year (Feb., Apr., June, Aug., Oct., Dec.). 25.00Aus$ (associate members), 35.00Aus$ (full members & institutions) Australia; 35.00Aus$ others. Scientists Against Nuclear Arms, PO Box 370, Lane Cove 2066 Australia. **Tel** 011 61 2 427 2547. **ED** Dr. R. D. Haynes (phone: (02)697-2298). **DD** 327.17405. Index available. **Bk Rev. Circ:** 250.

US/0036-4304
**SANEFREEZE NEWS / CAMPAIGN FOR GLOBAL SECURITY.** ***Title Change.*** **Added/Corp** SANE/FREEZE: Campaign for Global Security. **VFOAT** Sane Freeze News; Sane/Freeze News. Vol. 28, No. 2 (Summer 1989)-Vol. 31, No. 4 (Winter 1992/93). Periodical. English. qt. SANE, 711 G Street SE, Washington DC 20003. **Tel** (202)546-7100. **LC** JX1953.A2; S223. ***Continues*** *SANE World/FREEZE Focus.* ***Continued by*** *Peace Action (Washington, D.C. : 1993).*

US/0036-5408
**SCABBARD AND BLADE JOURNAL.** **Added/Corp** National Society of Scabbard and Blade. (19??)-. Periodical. English. ir. $3.00 (one year), $30.00 (lifetime subscription). National Society of Scabbard and Blade, 205 Thatcher Hall, c/o Army ROTC, Stillwater OK 74078. **DD** 322. ***Continues*** *Scabbard and Blade.*

SZ
**SCHWEIZER SOLDAT + MFD.** **VFOAT** Schweizer Soldat mit MFD; MFD; MFD-Zeitung. Periodical. German. mo. 50.00F. Zeitschriften Verlag Stafa, 8712 Stafa AM Zurichsee, Zurich Switzerland. **Tel** 01/928 11 01. **LC** UA800; .S37. ***Continues*** *Schweizer Soldat.*

SZ/0253-4878
**SCHWEIZER WAFFEN-MAGAZIN.** ***Title Change.*** [Schweiz. Waffen-Mag.]. (1982)-(19??). Periodical. German (summaries and/or abstracts in English). mo. Orell Fuessli Zeitschriften, Dietzingerstrasse 3, PF 8036, CH 8036 Zurich Switzerland. **Tel** 044 41 1 4667711. **(Subscription address:** Orell Fussli Graphische Betriebe AG, CH-8036 Zurich Switzerland) **ED** P E Grimm. Index available. **Bk Rev. Ad Acc. Pr Rev.** ***Continued by*** *Internationales Waffen Magazin, 1017-5547.*
**Desc:** Modern and antique firearms and other weapons, shooting sports, and self defense.

US/0892-9882
**SCIENCE & GLOBAL SECURITY.** **See** Political Science-International Relations.

US
**SCREAMING EAGLE, THE.** English. bm. $20.00 North America; $30.00 other. 101st Airborne Division Association, 101 East Morris Street, PO Box 586, Sweetwater TN 37874. **Tel** (615)337-4103. **ED** Ivan E Worrell. **Bk Rev. Ad Acc. Circ:** 5,400 (ctrl).

US/0886-7607
**SDI MONITOR.** ***Title Change.*** [SDI monitor]. Vol. 1, No. 1 (Mar. 1986)-(19??). Periodical. English. sm. Pasha Publications Inc., 1616 North Fort Myer Drive, Suite 1000, Arlington VA 22209. **Tel** (800)424-2908, (703)528-1244, FAX (703)528-3742, (703)528-1253. **DD** 355. **[CCC].** available on an online database (files 636,648/Full-Text) from DIALOG. ***Continued by*** *BMD Monitor, 1069-8175.*
**Ind/Abst** F&S Index Plus Text, Int. [Select. Cov.]; PROMT; PTS Newsl. Database [Full Txt.].

US
**SECURITY INTELLIGENCE.** (199?)-. Periodical. English. bw. $390.00 (one year), $750.00 (two year), $950.00 (three year). Interests Ltd, 8512 Cedar Street, Silver Spring MD 20910-4347. **Tel** (301)588-7916, FAX (301)588-2085, telex 6501701421. **LC** HV6432; .C67. **DD** 363.3/2/05. ***Continues*** *Security Intelligence Report, 1055-8144.*

US/0501-9427
**SELECTED MANPOWER STATISTICS.** **See** Military and Defense-Abstracting, Bibliographies and Statistics.

US/0361-2716
**SELECTIVE SERVICE NEWS.** V. 1- Aug. 1951-. Periodical. English. mo. Selective Service System, National Headquarters, Washington DC 20435. **Tel** (202)724-0424.

CN/0037-2315
**SENTINEL (OTTAWA. 1973).** ***Ceased.*** (SENTINEL.). **Added/Corp** Canada. Dept. of National Defence. Directorate of Information Services. Vol. 5 (1973)-(May 1994). Periodical. English. bm. Statistics Canada, Publications Sales & Services, Main Building Room 1710, Ottawa Ontario K1A 0T6 Canada. **Tel**

(613)951-5078, (800)267-6677, FAX (613)951-1584, telex 053-3585. ***Continues*** *Canadian Forces Sentinel, 0008-3615.*
**Ind/Abst** Am. Hist. Life.

US/0360-7364
**SERGEANTS.** [Sergeants]. **Added/Corp** Air Force Sergeants Association. (19??)-. Periodical. English. ir. $22.00 Comes with Air Force Sergeants Association membership. Air Force Sergeants Association, 5211 Auth Road, Suitland MD 20746. **Tel** (301)899-3500. **LC** UG633; .S39. **DD** 358.4/005.
**Ind/Abst** Air Univ. Libr. Index Mil. Period.

US/0732-104X
**SERVICEMEN'S AND VETERAN'S GROUP LIFE INSURANCE PROGRAMS, ANNUAL REPORT.** (SERVICEMEN'S AND VETERANS GROUP LIFE INSURANCE PROGRAMS, ANNUAL REPORT / VETERAN'S ADMINISTRATION.). English. an. VA Center, Philadelphia PA 19101. **LC** UB373; .A42777. **DD** 368.3/64. available on microfiche (Vols. for (1983-) distributed to depository libraries). ***Continues*** *Annual Report, Servicemen's and Veterans Group Life Insurance Program, 0161-3529.*

JA
**SHIN BOEI RONSHU. Added/Corp** Boei Gakkai. **VFOAT** Journal of National Defense. Vol. 1 (June 1973)-. Academic Scholarly Publication. Japanese (English; summaries and/or abstracts in English). qt. ¥3200. Boei Gakkai, Daini-Matsuda Building, 7-8-7 Roppongi Minato-ku, Tokyo 106 Japan. **Tel** 81 3 3713 2469, FAX 81 3 3713 6149. **ED** Yasuto Fukushima. **LC** UA845; .S53. **Bk Rev. Circ:** 2,200.

US/0080-9292
**SHIPS AND AIRCRAFT OF THE UNITED STATES FLEET, THE.** (1939)-. English. ir. price varies per volume. U. S. Naval Institute, 2062 Generals Highway, Annapolis MD 21402. **Tel** (301)268-6110, (800)233-8764. **LC** VA61; .S472. **DD** 359.8/3/0973.

JA
**SHUKAN BOEI TOKUSHIN.** (19??)-. Periodical. Japanese. OMI Building, 1-18 Misakicho 3-chome Chiyoda-ku, Tokyo 101 Japan. **LC** UA845; .S55.

UK/0732-3662
**SICILIAN DEFENCE, THE.** [Sicil. def.]. 1981-. English. an. Imprint Editions Inc, Menu, Pittsburgh PA 15241-0577.

US/0037-4938
**SIGNAL (1950).** (SIGNALS / ARMED FORCES COMMUNICATIONS ASSOCIATION.). [Signal]. **Added/Corp** Armed Forces Communications Association. Armed Forces Communications and Electronics Association (U.S.). **VFOAT** Signal. Vol. 4, No. 4 (March/April 1950)-. Periodical. English. Twelve times a year. $44.00 nonmembers; $20.00 members. Armed Forces Communications and Electronics Association, 4400 Fair Lakes Court, Fairfax VA 22033. **Tel** (703)631-6191, (703)631-6178, FAX (703)631-4693, telex 901114 AFCEA FFX. **ED** Carolyn N. Frazier. **LC** UG1; .M65. **DD** 358/.24. **CODEN** SGNAAZ. **[CCC]. Bk Rev. Ad Acc. Adv Mgr Tel** (703)631-6187. **Circ:** 39,853. available on microfilm and microfiche from University Microfilms International (UMI). Documents available from Ask*IEEE. ***Continues*** *Military Signals.*
**Desc:** Recognized source of news and commentary for command, control, communications, computing and intelligence and information resources professionals. Each month authoritative experts in their fields contribute exploring scientific research, advanced technologies, new operational concepts and information systems. Respected worldwide for its comprehensive coverage.
**Ind/Abst** Air Univ. Libr. Index Mil. Period; INSPEC (Summer 1988-).

SW/0347-2205
**SIPRI YEARBOOK : WORLD ARMAMENTS AND DISARMAMENT.** ***Title Change.*** **Added/Corp** Stockholm International Peace Research Institute. **VFOAT** World Armaments and Disarmament. (1972)-(19??). English. an. SIPRI, Pipers Vag 28, S-171 73 Solna Sweden. **Tel** (08)55 97 00. **LC** UA10; .S69a. **DD** 355/.033/0047. cum. index. **Circ:** 5,000. available in microform (out-of-print volumes only). ***Continues*** *SIPRI Yearbook of World Armaments and Disarmament, 0579-5508.* ***Continued by*** *SIPRI Yearbook.*
**Desc:** Armament and disarmament analyses of and statistics on negotiations. New weapons, technologies, arms trade, military expenditure, etc., and their implications.

CN/0316-5620
**SITREP. VFOAT** SITRAP. V. 30, No. 8- Sept. 1973-. Periodical. English. mo. Free to members. Royal Canadian Military Institute, 426 University Avenue, Toronto Ontario M5G 1S9 Canada. **Tel** 597-0286. **ED** Sidney Allinson. **DD** 369/.2/71. **Bk Rev. Ad Acc. Circ:** 3,000 (ctrl). ***Continues*** *Royal Canadian Military Institute. Newsletter, 0316-5612.*

US/0090-2276
**SMALL ARMS IN PROFILE (GARDEN CITY, N.Y.).** (SMALL ARMS IN PROFILE.). V. 1- 1973-. English. Doubleday & Company Inc, 501 Franklin Avenue, Garden City NY 11530. **LC** UD380; .S56. **DD** 623.4/42.

UK/0959-2318
**SMALL WARS AND INSURGENCIES.** **VFOAT** Small Wars and Insurgencies. (1990)-. Periodical. English. Three times a year. $145.00. Frank Cass & Company Ltd, Newbury House, 890-900 Eastern Avenue, Newbury Park, Ilford, Essex IG2 7HH United Kingdom. **Tel** 011 44 81 599 8866, FAX 011 44 81 599 0984, telex 897719. **ED** Ian Beckett and Alan Ned Sabrosky. **LC** JC328.5; .S63. Index available. **Bk Rev. Ad Acc, Adv Mgr:** Anne Kidson. **Pr Rev.**
**Desc:** Directed at providing a forum for the discussion of the historical, political, social, economic and psychological aspects of insurgencies, limited wars, peace-keeping operations and shows of force. Its aim is to provide an outlet for academics and policy-makers to discuss and debate the theoretical and practical issues related to this important area of both international and domestic relations.
**Ind/Abst** PAIS Int. Print; Soc. Plann. Policy Dev. Abstr.

NR
**SOJA : A NEWS BULLETIN OF THE NIGERIAN ARMY. Added/Corp** Nigeria. Nigerian Army. (19??)-. Periodical. English. mo. Army Public Relations Department, Bonny Camp, Victoria Island Lagos Nigeria. **LC** UA861.3; .S66. **DD** 355/.009669.

GW/0038-0989
**SOLDAT UND TECHNIK.** [Soldat Tech.]. Vol. 1 (Jan. 1958)-. Periodical. German. mo. $43.26. Umschau Verlag, Postfach 110262, D-60037 Frankfurt Germany. **Tel** 011 49 69 2600692, FAX 011 49 69 2600223, telex 411964. **ED** K H Meude. **LC** U3; .S58. **DD** 355/.005. **[CCC]. Bk Rev. Ad Acc. Circ:** 31,000 (ctrl).
**Desc:** Up-to-date aspects of the use of modern weapons systems in the armed forces of Germany and other world forces, particularly those of the Warsaw Pact.
**Ind/Abst** Bibliogr. Carto.; Curr. Mil. Pol. Lit.; Peace Res. Abstr. J. (1963-1964).

RU
**SOLDATSKAIA SLAVA.** (1963)-. Russian. **LC** DK268.A1; S58.

UK
**SOLDIER. Added/Corp** Great Britain. WWar Office. Vol.1 (Mar. 19, 1945)-. Periodical. English. bw. £23.00 UK; £32.20 other. Soldier, Ordnance Road Aldershot, Hants GU11 2DU England. **Tel** 0252-24431. **ED** Roland Thick. **LC** U1; .S67. **Bk Rev. Ad Acc. Circ:** 24,000 (ctrl).
**Desc:** Magazine of the British army, containing news and features on military matters past and present.

US/0145-6784
**SOLDIER OF FORTUNE.** [Soldier fortune]. **VFOAT** SOF. (Summer 1975)-. Periodical. English. Twelve times a year. $26.95 US; $36.95 Canada; $47.95 other. Omega Group Ltd., PO Box 693, Boulder CO 80306. **Tel** (303)449-3750, FAX (303)444-5617, telex 450 129. **(Subscription address:** Soldier of Fortune, PO Box 348, Mt. Morris IL 61054.**) ED** Robert K. Brown. **LC** G539; .S64. **DD** 355/.005. **Bk Rev. Ad Acc, Adv Mgr:** Facets Advertising, **Tel** (303)494-1177. **Circ:** 151,945.
**Desc:** Military information including national defense, defense budget, US foreign policy, combat reporting worldwide, weapons reviews, and topical military issues.
**Ind/Abst** PAIS Int. Print.

US
**SOLDIER OF FORTUNE PRESENTS FIGHTING FIREARMS.** ***Title Change.*** **VFOAT** Fighting Firearms. Spring (1992)-(199?). English. Omega Group Ltd., PO Box 693, Boulder CO 80306. **Tel** (303)449-3750, FAX (303)444-5617, telex 450 129. **LC** WMLC 91/3313. ***Continued by*** *Soldier of Fortune's Fighting Firearms, 1075-4784.*

●US/1059-194X
**SOLDIERS TODAY.** (1992)-. Periodical. English. qt. $29.99. Publishing & Business Consultants, PO Box 75392, Los Angeles CA 90075. **Tel** (213)732-3477, FAX (213)732-9123. **ED** Andeson Napoleon Atia. **Ad Acc.** Full Page (B&W) $5750.00. Half Page (B&W) $3575.00. Full Page (Color) $8750.00 (2 color). Half Page (Color) $5500.00 (2 color). **Circ:** 153,000 total.
**Desc:** Of interest to those fascinated with the social lifestyle of the military. Features articles on outdoor life, health and travel.

US/0093-8440
**SOLDIERS (WASHINGTON).** (SOLDIERS.). [Soldiers]. Vol. 26, No. 6 (June 1971)-. Government Publication. English. mo. $19.00 domestic; $23.75 other. Superintendent of Documents, US Government Printing Office, Washington DC 20402. **Tel** (202)275-3328, FAX (202)786-2377. **LC** UA23.A1. **DD** 355/.00973. ***Continues*** *Army Digest, 0004-2498.*
**Desc:** Provides timely and authoritative information on the policies, plans, operations and technical developments of the Department of the Army and reserve components.
**Ind/Abst** Air Univ. Libr. Index Mil. Period.

FI/0357-816X
**SOTAHISTORIALLINEN AIKAKAUSKIRJA.** (1980)-. Periodical. Finnish. an. Sotahistoriallinen Seura / Society for Military History, Maurinkatu 1,, 00170 Helsinki 17 Finland. **Tel** 011 358 90 161 6389. **UDC** 355. **Circ:** 1,000.
**Ind/Abst** Am. Hist. Life (1980-).

FI
**SOTILASAVUSTUS. VFOAT** Militarunderstod. 1980-. Finnish (Swedish). an. Sosiaalihallitus, Suunnittelu Ja Tilastotoimisto, Valtion Painatuskeskus, Pl 516, 00101 Helsinki 10 Finland. **LC** UB365.F3; F56A. ***Continues*** *Sotilasavustus ja Kotiuttamisraha.*

RU/0134-8140
**SOVETSKII VOIN.** ***Ceased.*** **Added/Corp** Glavnoe Politicheskoe Upravlenie Sovetskoi Armii i Voenno-Morskogo Flota (Soviet Union). (1919)-(1993). Periodical. Russian. Twelve times a year. **(Subscription address:** East View Publications Inc., 3020 Harbor Lane North, Suite 110, Minneapolis MN 55447.**)** ***Absorbed*** *Sovetskoe Voennoe Obozrenie, 0201-7741.*

US/0148-0928
**SOVIET ARMED FORCES REVIEW ANNUAL. VFOAT** SAFRA. Vol. 1 (1977)-. English. an. $71.00 (standing orders), $91.00 (separate volumes). Academic International Press, Box 1111, Gulf Breeze FL 32561. **ED** David R Jones. **LC** UA770; .S657. **DD** 355/.00947. **Bk Rev.** ctrl circ.
**Desc:** Assembles and organizes into one format all relevant public information on Soviet military affairs. To this data is added analytical topical discussion, documentation, bibliography and historical background. All articles are prepared by experts.
**Ind/Abst** Am. Bibliogr. Slavic East Europ. Stud.

IS/0334-5734
**SOVIET ARMY : A DIGEST FROM THE SOVIET PRESS, THE.** No. 1- 1984-. Periodical. English. mo. $24.00. International Research Center on Contemporary Society, PO Box 687, Jerusalem 91006 Israel.

US
**SPACE SYSTEMS FORECAST.** (19??)-. English. Twelve times a year. $1390.00. Forecast International / DMS Inc., 22 Commerce Road, Newtown CT 06470. **Tel** (203)426-0800, FAX (203)426-1964, telex 467615. available on CD-ROM ($1595.00).

US/0147-3441
**SPARTAN, THE.** **See** Recreation, Leisure-Games and Amusements.

US
**SPECIAL REPORT ON VETERANS.** **Main/Corp** Virginia Employment Commission. Labor Market Information Unit. 1978-. English. an. Virginia Employment Commission, 703 East Main Street, PO Box 1358, Richmond VA 23211. **LC** UB358.V8; V47A. **DD** 355.1/15/09755.

US/1058-0123
**SPECIAL WARFARE : THE PROFESSIONAL BULLETIN OF THE JOHN F. KENNEDY SPECIAL WARFARE CENTER AND SCHOOL.** Bulletin. English. qt. $5.00; $2.25 (single issues) US; $6.25; $2.81 (single issues) other. Special Warfare, USAJFKSWCS, Fort Bragg NC 28307-5000.
**Ind/Abst** Air Univ. Libr. Index Mil. Period.

US/1060-1368
**SPEEDNEWS DEFENSE BIWEEKLY.** **See** Aeronautics, Astronautics.

US/0894-8542
**STARS AND STRIPES, THE NATIONAL TRIBUNE, THE. VFOAT** Stars and Stripes, National Tribune. (Feb. 7, 1963)-. Newspaper. English. wk. $19.00 (1 year), $35.00 (2 year), $50.00 (3 year) US; $31.00 (1 year), $59.00 (2 year), $86.00 (3 year) other. Stars and Stripes National Tribune, Box 1803, Washington DC 20013. **Tel** (202)829-3225. **ED** John Carroll. **LC** Newspaper. **DD** 071. **Bk Rev**, (Qty: 75). **Ad Acc. Circ:** 8,000. available on microfilm. ***Continues*** *National Tribune, the Stars and Stripes.*
**Desc:** Prints news directly related to veterans.

US
**STATE OF NEVADA, DEPARTMENT OF THE MILITARY, AUDIT REPORT.** **Main/Corp** Nevada. Legislature. Legislative Auditor.

(19??)-. English. an. Legislative Auditor, Legislative Building, Capitol Complex, Carson City NV 89710. **LC** UA321; .L43a. **DD** 355.3/7/09793.

●CN/1191-4653
**STATEMENT ON NATIONAL SECURITY / BY THE SOLICITOR GENERAL OF CANADA.** [Statement natl. secur.]. **Added/Corp** Canada. Solicitor General Canada. **VFOAT** Declaration sur la Securite Nationale. (Mar. 19, 1992)-. English (French). **DD** 327.1.

FR/0291-851X
**STATISTIQUE MEDICALE DANS LES ARMEES.** **See** Military and Defense-Abstracting, Bibliographies and Statistics.

II/0970-0161
**STRATEGIC ANALYSIS.** [Strateg. anal.]. **Added/Corp** Institute for Defence Studies and Analyses. Vol. 1 (April 1977)-. Periodical. English. Twelve times a year. $50.00. Institute for Defence Studies and Analyses, Sapru House, Barakhamba Road, New Delhi 110001 India. **Tel** 011 91 11 3314951. **LC** UA11; .S84. **DD** 355.03/30047. **UDC** 355.43. Index available. **Circ:** 3,500.
**Desc:** Deals with international affairs, techno-strategic and security issues.
**Ind/Abst** Curr. Mil. Pol. Lit.; Int. Polit. Sci. Abstr.

US/0890-7331
**STRATEGIC DEFENSE.** ***Ceased.*** [Strateg. def.]. Oct. 1986-?. Periodical. English. wk. Phillips Business Information, Inc., 1201 Seven Locks Road, Potomac MD 20854. **Tel** (301)424-3338, (800)777-5006, FAX (301)309-3847. **ED** Norman Baker. **LC** UG743; .S744. **DD** 358/.1754. **[CCC].** available on an online database (file 636/Full-Text) from DIALOG.
**Desc:** Covers surveillance, anti-satellite operations, laser weapons and military operations in space.

II/0970-017X
**STRATEGIC DIGEST.** [Strateg. dig.]. **Added/Corp** Institute for Defence Studies and Analyses. (1971)-. Periodical. English. mo. $35.00. Institute for Defence Studies and Analyses, Sapru House, Barakhamba Road, New Delhi 110001 India. **Tel** 011 91 11 3314951. **(Subscription address:** Prints India, 11 Darya Ganj, New Delhi 110002 India.**) LC** UA840; .S69. **DD** 355.03/32/54. **UDC** 355.43. **Circ:** 3,500.
**Desc:** Serves as a vehicle to disseminate information on nulcear war doctrines and high technology developments related to war. This also includes Defense and Disarmament Review dealing with nuclear, space, oceanographic and defense technologies.

PK
**STRATEGIC PERSPECTIVES.** **Added/Corp** Institute of Strategic Studies (Islamabad, Pakistan). Vol. 1, No. 1 (Summer 1991)-. Periodical. English. qt (Feb., May, Aug., Nov.). $20.00. Institute of Strategic Studies Pakistan, PO Box 1173, Islamabad, Pakistan. **Tel** 011 92 51 824658 or 821340. **LC** U162; .S767. **DD** 355.03/305. ***Continues*** *Strategic Studies.*

US/0091-6846
**STRATEGIC REVIEW.** [Strateg. rev.]. **Added/Corp** United States Strategic Institute. Vol. 1 (Spring 1973)-. Periodical. English. qt. $25.00 (one year), $70.00 (three year), US; $37.00 (one year), $105.00 (three year), other. US Strategic Institute, Kenmore Station, PO Box 15618, Boston MA 02215. **Tel** (617)353-8707. **ED** MacKubin T. Owens. **LC** U162; .S76. **DD** 355.03/3004/7. **Bk Rev. Circ:** 3,500.
**Desc:** Forum for foward-looking ideas on U.S. national security policy in the new strategic environment of the 1990's. Authors assess current political, economic, social and military factors to define defense priorities and develop creative new policies consistent with new national security requirements and reduced defense budgets.
**Ind/Abst** ABC POL SCI; Air Univ. Libr. Index Mil. Period.; Am. Hist. Life (1987-); Am. Bibliogr. Slavic East Europ. Stud.; Curr. Mil. Pol. Lit.; Index Islam. Lit.; Int. Polit. Sci. Abstr.; Middle East Abstr. Index; PAIS Int. Print.

UK/0459-7230
**STRATEGIC SURVEY.** (STRATEGIC SURVEY / THE INSTITUTE FOR STRATEGIC STUDIES.). [Strateg. surv.]. **Added/Corp** Institute for Strategic Studies (London, England) International Institute for Strategic Studies. (1966)-. English. an (May). £19.50 UK and Europe; $30.00 other. Oxford University Press, Walton Street, Oxford OX2 6DP England. **Tel** 011 44 865 56767, FAX 011 44 865 267773, telex 837330 OXPRES G. **(Subscription address:** Oxford University Press / USA, Journals Marketing Department, Oxford University Press, 2001 Evans Road, Cary NC 27513.**) LC** U162; .S77. **DD** 355.4/3. available on microfilm and microfiche from University Microfilms International (UMI).
**Desc:** The reliable and penetrating annual analysis of global strategic developments.
**Ind/Abst** Int. Polit. Sci. Abstr.

FR
**STRATEGIE ET DEFENSE.** **Added/Corp** Association pour les Recherches et les Etudes de Defense, Paris, France. (19??)-. Periodical. French. ir. 60.00F. Assn Recherche Etudes Defense, 9 Villa Daumesnil, Paris 75012 France. **LC** U2; .S87. **DD** 355.4/3/005.

FR/0224-0424
**STRATEGIQUE.** ***Ceased.*** [Strategique]. No. 1 (1979)-No. 4 (1992). Periodical. French. Librairie Armand Colin, BP 22, 41354 Vineuil Cedex France. **Tel** 011 33 54 438994. **LC** U162; .S8. **DD** 355/.02/05. Index available. **Circ:** 1,200.
**Desc:** Deals with strategical research and studies.
**Ind/Abst** Int. Polit. Sci. Abstr.; PAIS Int. Print.

IE/0307-4420
**STRATEGY & DEFENCE.** **VFOAT** Strategy and Defence. Periodical. English. mo. **LC** UF500; .S87. **DD** 355/.005. ***Formed by the union of*** *Aviation & Marine International; Ground Defence International* ***and*** *Asia & Africa Military Review.*

US/1040-886X
**STRATEGY & TACTICS (CAMBRIA, CALIF.).** (STRATEGY & TACTICS.). [Strategy tactics]. **VFOAT** Strategy and Tactics. Issue 118 (April 1988)-. Periodical. English. Eight times a year. $40.00. 3W Inc, PO Box F, Cambria CA 93428. **Tel** (805)927-5439, FAX (805)927-1852. **ED** Jim Dunnigan. **DD** 355. **Bk Rev. Ad Acc. Circ:** 10,000. ***Continues*** *Strategy & Tactics Magazine, 0736-6531.*
**Desc:** Military History magazine with simulation game in each issue.
**Ind/Abst** Am. Hist. Life (1988-).

US/0736-654X
**STRATEGY & TACTICS MAGAZINE (SPECIAL ED.).** (STRATEGY & TACTICS MAGAZINE.). [Strategy tactics mag.]. **VFOAT** Strategy and Tactics Magazine. Vol. 1, No. 1 (Spring 1983)-. Periodical. English. Six times a year. $59.00 (one year); $109.00 (two years). Decision Games, PO Box 4049, Lancaster CA 93539. **Tel** (805)723-1072. **LC** U310; .S88. **DD** 355.4/8/05. **Circ:** 9,000.

PL/0239-832X
**STUDIA DO DZIEJOW DAWNEGO UZBROJENIA I UNIFORMU WOJSKOWEGO.** **See** History(General).

AU
**STUDIENMATERIAL - INSTITUT FUER MILITAERISCHE GRUNDLAGENFORSCHUNG.** **Main/Corp** Landesverteidigungsakademie (Austria). Institut fuer Militaerische Grundlagenforschung. (19??)-. German. Institut fur Militarische Grundlagenforschung, Stiftgasse 2A Stift-Kaserne, Vienna 1070 Austria. **LC** U3; .L353a.

US/1062-8916
**STUDIES ON DEFENCE ECONOMICS.** **See** Economics.

CN/0713-7508
**SUB-COMMITTEE OF THE STANDING COMMITTEE ON EXTERNAL AFFAIRS AND NATIONAL DEFENCE ON ARMED FORCES RESERVES.** (SUB-COMMITTEE OF THE STANDING COMMITTEE ON EXTERNAL AFFAIRS AND NATIONAL DEFENCE ON ARMED FORCES RESERVES : MINUTES OF PROCEEDINGS AND EVIDENCE.). [Sub-comm. Standing Comm. Extern. Aff. Natl. Def. Armed Forces Reserves]. **Main/Corp** Canada. Parliament. House of Commons. Sub-Committee of the Standing Committee on External Affairs and National Defense on Armed Forces Reserves. **VFOAT** Sous-Comite du Comite Permanent des Affairs Exterieures et de la Defense Nationale Charge d'Etudier les Forces Armees de Reserve; Armed Forces Reserves. Issue No. 1 (May 14, 1981/June 16, 1981)-. Proceedings. English (French). **DD** 355.2/2/0971.

US
**SUMMARIES OF CONCLUSIONS AND RECOMMENDATIONS ON DEPARTMENT OF DEFENSE OPERATIONS : REPORT TO THE HOUSE AND SENATE COMMITTEES ON APPROPRIATIONS BY THE COMPTROLLER GENERAL OF THE UNITED STATES.** **Main/Corp** United States. General Accounting Office. English. an. US General Accounting Office / District of Columbia, 441 G Street NW, Room 4528, Washington DC 20548. **Tel** (202)275-2812. **LC** UA23.2; .G45B. **DD** 353.6/05. available on microfiche (Vols. for (1985-) distributed to depository libraries).

UK
**SUPERBASE.** (1988)-. Monographic series. English. Price varies per volume. Osprey Media Ptnrs, 33A Church Road, Watford Herts WD1 3PY England. **Tel** 011 44 923 818921.

US/8750-0124
**SUPPLY LINE.** (SUPPLY LINE : THE MVCC NEWSLETTER.). **Added/Corp** Military Vehicle Collectors Club. (198?)-. Periodical. English. Six times a year (Jan., Mar., May, July, Sept., Nov.). $35.00 Comes with Military Vehicle Preservation Association Club membership. Military Vehicle Preservation Association, PO Box 520378, Independence MO 64052. **Tel** (816)737-5111, FAX (816)737-5423. **ED** Jerry Cleveland. **Bk Rev**, (Qty: 4-8). **Ad Acc, Adv Mgr:** Kay, **Tel** (816)737-5111. **Circ:** 6,000 (ctrl).
**Desc:** Display and classified ads, club news, and brief articles of general Military Vehicle Preservation Association membership interest.

US/1051-0923
**SURVEILLANT (WASHINGTON, D.C.).** (SURVEILLANT.). [Surveillant]. **Added/Corp** National Intelligence Book Center (U.S.). Vol. 1, No. 1 (July/Aug. 1990)-. Periodical. English. Six times a year (Jan., Mar., May, July, Sept., Nov.). $96.00 US; $104.00 Canada; $114.00 others. National Intelligence Book Center - NIBC, 2020 Pennsylvania Avenue Northwest, Suite 165, Washington DC 20006. **Tel** (202)797-1234, FAX (202)331-7456. **ED** Elizabeth Bancroft, H. Keith Melton, Thomas F. Troy, Samuel Halpern, and Walter L. Pforzheimer. **DD** 327. **[CCC].** Index available. cum. index. **Bk Rev. Ad Acc, Adv Mgr:** Bagley Fordyce, **Tel** (202)797-1234. **Circ:** 7,000.
**Desc:** Covers many topics such as, military intelligence, espionage, psychological warfare, disinformation, deception, narcotics, money laundering, terrorism, computer security, science, histories or accounts of FBI, CIA, NSA, KGB, and other intelligence agencies. Its lists conference, and course announcement, as well as intelligence community news.

US/0193-9327
**SURVEY OF CONTRACTING STATISTICS.** **See** Military and Defense-Abstracting, Bibliographies and Statistics.

UK/0039-6338
**SURVIVAL (LONDON).** (SURVIVAL.). [Survival]. **Added/Corp** International Institute for Strategic Studies. Institute for Strategic Studies (London, England). Vol. 1, (March/April 1959)-. Periodical. English. Four times a year. £37.00 UK and Europe; $54.00 other. Oxford University Press, Walton Street, Oxford OX2 6DP England. **Tel** 011 44 865 56767, FAX 011 44 865 267773, telex 837330 OXPRES G. **(Subscription address:** Oxford University Press / USA, Journals Marketing Department, Oxford University Press, 2001 Evans Road, Cary NC 27513.**) ED** Hans Binnendijk. **LC** U162; .S9. **[CCC]. Bk Rev. Ad Acc. Circ:** 6,500. available on microfilm and microfiche from University Microfilms International (UMI).
**Desc:** Forum for debate and digest of important documents on whole range of strategic issues including East-West relations, military strategy, arms control and regional security issues.
**Ind/Abst** Air Univ. Libr. Index Mil. Period.; Am. Hist. Life (1973-); Curr. Mil. Pol. Lit.; Index Period. Artic. Relat. Law; Int. Polit. Sci. Abstr.; PAIS Int. Print.

US/0494-3880
**TAC ATTACK.** ***Title Change.*** **Added/Corp** United States. Air Force. Tactical Air Command. **VFOAT** Tactical Air Command Attack. **VAT** Tactical Air Command Attack. (19??)-Vol. 32, Issue 5 (May 1992). Government Publication. English. mo. Superintendent of Documents, US Government Printing Office, Washington DC 20402. **Tel** (202)275-3328, FAX (202)786-2377. **DD** 358. available on microfiche (Vols. for (1986-) distributed to depository libraries). ***Merged with*** *Combat Crew* ***to form*** *Combat Edge.*
**Desc:** Safety magazine, written for aviators, maintenance mechanics, munitions handlers, and support workers. Contains articles on safety in flight and on the ground. Also features "Fleagle," a copyright cartoon character who gives lessons in safety, usually by showing the wrong way to do things.
**Ind/Abst** Air Univ. Libr. Index Mil. Period.

US
**TACTICAL NOTEBOOK.** (19??)-. English. qt. $50.00 (one year), $85.00 (two year), $115.00 (three year). Institute of Tactical Education Inc., PO Box 125, Quantico VA 22134. **Tel** (703)640-0304, FAX (703)640-0304. **ED** Bruce Gudmundsson. Index available. cum. index. **Bk Rev**, (Qty: 50). **Circ:** 1,000.
**Desc:** Quarterly journal of military history and ideas. Emphasis is placed on the 19th and 20th centuries.

UK/0039-9418
**TANK.** (19??)-. English. Four times a year (Feb., May, Aug., Nov.). £12.00 UK & BFPO; £13.00 (surface mail), £18.00 (airmail) others. RHQ Royal Tank Regiment Publications Ltd., Stanley Barracks, Bovington Dorset BH20 6JB England. **Tel** 011 44 929 403444, FAX 11 44 929 403488. **ED** Lieutenant Colonel G. Forty. **Bk Rev. Ad Acc, Adv Mgr:** J. Cutler. **Circ:** 2,200 (ctrl).
**Desc:** General articles on armed warfare, its technology and tactics plus regimented news of the Royal Tank Regiment.

US/0099-8508
**TECHNICAL REPORT AFML-TR.** **Main/Corp** United States. Air Force Materials Laboratory, Dayton, Ohio. **VFOAT** AFML-TR. **VAT** Technical Report Air Force Materials Laboratory Technical Report. Academic Scholarly Publication. English. Price varies per

volume. Air Force Materials Laboratory Wright-Patterson Air Force Base OH 45433. **CODEN** XAMFAO. Documents available from CASDDS.
**Ind/Abst** Chem. Abstr. (1979).

US/0886-9324
**TECHNICAL REPORT - U. S. ARMY RESEARCH INSTITUTE FOR THE BEHAVIORAL AND SOCIAL SCIENCES.** (TECHNICAL REPORT.). [Tech. rep. - U. S. Army Res. Inst. Behav. Soc. Sci.]. **Added/Corp** U. S. Army Research Institute for the Behavioral and Social Sciences. (197?)-. Monographic series. English. Price varies per volume. US Army Research Institute for the Behavioral and Social Sciences, c/o Peri-Pot, 5001 Eisenhower Avenue, Alexandria VA 22333. **DD** 300.
**Ind/Abst** Psychol. Abstr. (1974-).

SZ
**TECHNISCHE MITTEILUNGEN FUER SAPPEURE, PONTONIERE, UND MINEURE.** **See** Engineering-Civil Engineering.

●US
**TECHNOLOGY TRANSFER WEEK.** (1994)-. Periodical. English. Fifty-two times a year. $595.00. Phillips Business Information, Inc., 1201 Seven Locks Road, Potomac MD 20854. **Tel** (301)424-3338, (800)777-5006, FAX (301)309-3847. ***Absorbed** Defense Marketing International.*

BL
**TECNOLOGIA & DEFESA.** **VFOAT** Tecnologia e Defesa. (19??)-. Periodical. Portuguese (summaries and/or abstracts in English). mo. Praca Santo Eduardo, 165-2 Andar Vila Maria, Cep 02113 Sao Paulo Brazil. **Tel** 11-264-6914. **LC** UF500; .T44. **DD** 355.8/2/05.

GW/0722-2904
**TECNOLOGIA MILITAR.** Began in 1959. Periodical. Spanish. ir. $40.00. Monch Media Inc, 1701 K Street/#900, Washington DC 20006-1503. **Tel** (703)790-5252. **ED** Marvin Leibstone. **LC** UA10; .T42. **DD** 355.8/2/05. **Ad Acc. Circ:** 31,500 (ctrl).
**Desc:** Importance of Spanish and Latin America countries as strategic and economic entities is emphasized.
**Ind/Abst** Curr. Mil. Pol. Lit.

RU/0201-7490
**TEKHNIKA I VOORUZHENIE : ORGAN NACHALNIKA VOORUZHENII RKKA.** ***Ceased.*** **Added/Corp** Soviet Union. Ministerstvo Oborony. Soviet Union. Narodnyi Komissariat Oborony. **VFOAT** TIV. (1932)-(July 1994). Periodical. Russian. Twelve times a year. **(Subscription address:** East View Publications Inc., 3020 Harbor Lane North, Suite 110, Minneapolis MN 55447.**) LC** U4; .T4.
**Ind/Abst** Curr. Mil. Pol. Lit.

US/0363-6844
**TELEPHONE DIRECTORY - DEPARTMENT OF DEFENSE.** (TELEPHONE DIRECTORY / DEPARTMENT OF DEFENSE.). [Teleph. dir. - Dep. Def.]. **Main/Corp** United States. Department of Defense. **VFOAT** Department of Defense Telephone Directory. (19??)-. Government Publication. English. te. $24.00 US; $30.00 other. Superintendent of Documents, US Government Printing Office, Washington DC 20402. **Tel** (202)275-3328, FAX (202)786-2377. **LC** UA23.2; .A343. **DD** 353.6. available on microfiche (Vols. for (1986-) distributed to depository libraries).
**Desc:** Includes an alphabetical directory of personnel of the Department of Defense, including the Departments of the Army, Navy, and Air Force, and a classified section by agency, for the Washington, DC metropolitan area.

US
**TEMPORARY MILITARY LODGING AROUND THE WORLD.** English. ir (Published every 2 or 3 years). $12.95. Military Living Publications, PO Box 2347, Falls Church VA 22042. **Tel** (703)237-0203, FAX (703)237-2233.

●US/1064-9352
**TERRORISM, SECOND SERIES.** (TERRORISM, SECOND SERIES : DOCUMENTS OF INTERNATIONAL AND LOCAL CONTROL.). (1992)-. Monographic series. English. Price varies per volume. Oceana Publications, Inc., 75 Main Street, Dobbs Ferry NY 10522. **Tel** (914)693-1320, FAX (914)693-0402.

US
**THANG-TIEN.** **Main/Corp** Wisconsin. Resettlement Assistance Office. **VFOAT** Wisconsin Ways. V. 1, No. 1 Dec. 1975-. Periodical. English. mo. Department of Local Affairs and Development, Division of Emergency Government, 4802 Sheboygan Avenue/Room 99-A, Madison WI 53702.

SW/0040-6937
**TIDSKRIFT I FORTIFIKATION.** **Added/Corp** Fortifikationsklubben (Sweden). (18??)- Vol. 20 (Mar. 1993)-. Periodical. Swedish. qt. Kr100.00. Fortifikations Klubben, Tvarvagen 2, % B Fredholm, 17130 Solna Sweden. **LC** UG1; .T54. **Bk Rev**, (Qty: 4). **Ad Acc.** ctrl circ.

US/8750-376X
**TIG BRIEF : THE INSPECTOR GENERAL.** [TIG brief]. **VFOAT** Inspector General; T.I.G. Brief. **VAT** The Inspector General Brief. Vol. 34, No. 1 (Jan. 8, 1982)-. Periodical. English. bm. TIG Brief Magazine, HQ AFISC/CSM, Norton AFB CA 92409-7001. **DD** 358.
**Ind/Abst** Air Univ. Libr. Index Mil. Period.

US
**TITLE 38, UNITED STATES CODE, VETERANS' BENEFITS.** **Main/Corp** United States. **Added/Corp** United States. Congress. Senate. Committee on Veterans' Affairs. **VFOAT** Veterans' Benefits. (1960)-. Government Publication. English. ir (manual and one change per Congress). $25.00. Superintendent of Documents, US Government Printing Office, Washington DC 20402. **Tel** (202)275-3328, FAX (202)786-2377.
**Desc:** Contains the exact text of laws in the field of veterans' affairs which come within the jurisdiction of the House Committee on Veterans' Affairs.

US/1043-7665
**TRADING POST (COLUMBIA, MD.).** (TRADING POST.). [Trading post]. **Added/Corp** American Society of Military Insignia Collectors. (19??)-. Periodical. English. Four times a year (Jan., Apr., July, Oct.). $20.00 US; $25.00 others Comes with American Society of Military Insignia Collectors membership. American Society Military Insignia Collectors, 526 LaFayette Avenue, Palmerton PA 18071. **LC** UC533; .T7. **DD** 790. **Pr Rev.**

US/0041-1639
**TRANSLOG (WASHINGTON, D.C.).** (TRANSLOG : DEFENSE TRANSPORTATION SYSTEM BULLETIN.). [Translog]. **Added/Corp** United States. Military Traffic Management Command. **VFOAT** Defense Transportation System Bulletin. Vol. 1, No. 1, April (1987)-. Periodical. English. qt. $5.50 US; $6.90 other. Military Traffic Management Command, 5611 Columbia Pike, Falls Church VA 22041-5050. **Tel** (703)756-1242, FAX (703)756-2040. **ED** Mona Goss. **LC** UC273; .T73. **DD** 355.8/3. **Circ:** 10,000 (ctrl). ***Continues** Translog, 0041-1639.*
**Desc:** Provides information on policies, plans, operations, and technical developments in the defense transportation field.
**Ind/Abst** Air Univ. Libr. Index Mil. Period.

US/0740-1027
**TRENDS DATA.** (TREND DATA / VETERANS ADMINISTRATION.). [Trend data]. English. an. Veterans Administration Office of Reports and Statistics, 810 Vermont Avenue NW, Washington DC 20420. **LC** UB357; .T73. **DD** 355.1/15/0973. available on microfiche (Vols. for (1957-1981-) distributed to depository libraries).

CN/0025-3413
**TRIDENT (HALIFAX).** (TRIDENT.). **VFOAT** Marine Command Trident. V. 1- 19 Dec. 1966-. Periodical. English. sm. Ford Publishing Company Ltd., PO Box 3358, Halifax N.S.

GW
**TRUPPENPRAXIS.** **Added/Corp** Germany (West). Bundesministerium der Veteidigung. (Jan. 1957)-. Periodical. German. Six times a year. DM64.50 Germany; DM76.50 other. Maximilian Verlagsgruppe, Postfach 2352, Steintorwall 17, D 32052 Herford Germany. **Tel** 011 49 5221 599142, 011 49 5221 599161. **LC** U3; .T7. **Bk Rev. Ad Acc. Circ:** 32,400 (ctrl).
**Desc:** Journal for all problems that officers are concerned with, especially education and military.

TU
**TURKISH DEFENCE & AEROSPACE UPDATE.** English. $200.00. Monch Media Ltd., Ahmet Mithat Efendi SK 20 2, 06550 Cankaya Ankara Turkey.

US
**U.S. ARMS CONTROL AND DISARMAMENT AGENCY ANNUAL REPORT.** **Main/Corp** United States. Arms Control and Disarmament Agency. 1st (1961)-. English. an.

US
**U.S. DEFENSE BUDGET FORECAST.** (19??)-. English. ir (up to 7 per year). $1590.00. Forecast International / DMS Inc., 22 Commerce Road, Newtown CT 06470. **Tel** (203)426-0800, FAX (203)426-1964, telex 467615. available on CD-ROM ($1695.00).

US/0360-7801
**U.S. MISSILE DATA BOOK.** **Added/Corp** Data Search Associates. **VAT** United States Missile Data Book. (1976)-. English. an. $375.00 one year. Data Search Associates, PO Box 8361, Fountain Valley CA 92728. **Tel** (714)540-9386, FAX (714)540-9386. **LC** UG1313; .U54. **DD** 338.4/7/6234519.

US/1064-1467
**U.S. WEAPON SYSTEMS COSTS.** [U.S. weapon syst. costs]. **Added/Corp** Data Search Associates. **VFOAT** US Weapon Systems Costs. (19??)-. English. an. $375.00 one year. Data Search Associates, PO Box 8361, Fountain Valley CA 92728. **Tel** (714)540-9386, FAX (714)540-9386. **LC** UF503; .U17. **DD** 338.43/35582/0973.

SZ/1012-4934
**UNIDIR NEWSLETTER / UNITED NATIONS INSTITUTE FOR DISARMAMENT RESEARCH.** **Added/Corp** United Nations Institute for Disarmament Research. **VFOAT** Lettre de l'UNIDIR. Vol. 1, No. 1 (March 1988)-. Government Publication. English (French). qt. $25.00. United Nations Publications, 2 United Nations Plaza, Room DC2 0853, Department 007C, New York NY 10017. **Tel** (212)963-8303, (800)253-9646. **(Subscription address:** United Nations Publications, Subscription Office, PO Box 361, Birmingham AL 35201-0361.**) LC** JX1974; .U34. **DD** 327.1/74/05.
**Desc:** Focuses on security and disarmament issues, with experts contributing articles. Includes summaries of the latest developments in the disarmament field, and information on upcoming conferences.
**Ind/Abst** PAIS Int. Print.

US/0503-1982
**UNIFORMED SERVICES ALMANAC.** (1959)-. English. an (published in January). $5.95. Uniformed Services Almanac, PO Box 4144, Falls Church VA 22044. **Tel** (703)532-1631, FAX (703)532-1635. **ED** Sol Gordon. **LC** U9; .U5. **DD** 355/.00973. **Bk Rev. Ad Acc. Circ:** 50,000.
**Desc:** Comprehensive volume on military pay, allowances, entitlements and benefits including information on military retirement, health care, taxes and many other subjects of vital interest to active duty members and their families.

SP
**UNIFORMES MILITARES ESPANOLES.** Spanish. ir. 1250.00ptas. Jose M Bueno, Paseo de Miramar 16, Malaga Spain.

US/0731-2865
**UNITED STATES AIR FORCE ACADEMY JOURNAL OF PROFESSIONAL MILITARY ETHICS.** [U. S. Air Force Acad. j. prof. mil. ethics]. **Added/Corp** United States Air Force Academy. **VFOAT** U.S.A.F. Academy Journal of Professional Military Ethics; USAF Academy Journal of Professional Military Ethics. Vol. 1, No. 1 (Apr. 1980)-. English. sa. Department of the Air Force Headquarters, United States Air Force Academy USAF Academy, Colorado Springs CO 80840. **Tel** (303)472-4070. **ED** Charles W Hudlin. **LC** U22; .U53. **DD** 174/.9355. **Bk Rev. Circ:** 1,000 (ctrl).
**Desc:** Articles on professional military ethics, morality and war, nuclear deterrence.
**Ind/Abst** Air Univ. Libr. Index Mil. Period. (-19??).

US
**UNITED STATES AIR FORCE STATISTICAL DIGEST (ABRIDGED) FISCAL YEAR ... ESTIMATE / PREPARED BY DEPUTY ASSISTANT SECRETARY (COST AND ECONOMICS), ASSISTANT SECRETARY OF THE AIR FORCE (FINANCIAL MANAGEMENT AND COMPTROLLER OF THE AIR FORCE).** **Main/Corp** United States. Air Force. Office of the Deputy for Cost and Economics. **VFOAT** United States Air Force Statistical Digest Fiscal Year ... Estimate. **VAT** USAF Statistical Digest (Abridged) Fiscal Year ... Estimate. (1991)-. Statistical Publication. English. ***Formed by the union of** United States Air Force Summary; Air Force Budget **and** United States Air Force budget book in brief.*

UK/0956-2828
**UNITED STATES AIR FORCE YEARBOOK.** English. an. Royal Air Force Benevolent Fund, International Air Tattoo, Building 1108, RAF Fairford Glos GL7 4DL England. **Tel** (0285)713300, FAX (0285)713268, telex 43511 IATFFDG. **ED** Peter R March. **Ad Acc. Circ:** 50,000.
**Desc:** Provides interesting and informative articles on the role of the United States Air Force.

US
**UNITED STATES ARMY AVIATION DIGEST.** **See** Aeronautics, Astronautics.

US/0363-3209
**UNITED STATES COAST PILOT. 1, ATLANTIC COAST. EASTPORT TO CAPE COD.** **See** Naval Science, Navigation.

II
**UNIVERSAL MILITARY ABSTRACTS.** **VFOAT** Military Abstracts; UMA. Vol. 1, No. 1 (Jan./Feb. 1987)-. Periodical. English. bm. $45.00. Sukh Dev & Sons, 10 A Astley Hall, Dehra Dun 248 001 India. **Tel** (1035)25845, FAX (0135)22727, telex 0585-580-DDBC IN. **(Subscription address:** Prints India, 11 Darya Ganj, New Delhi 110002 India.**) ED** Sudhir K. Arora. Index available (published in March issue). cum. index. **Bk Rev**, (Qty: 4-8). **Ad Acc, Adv Mgr:** R. K. Arora. **Circ:**

400.
**Desc:** Abstracts/reprints of military articles from military journals worldwide.

US
**UNMANNED VEHICLE FORECAST.** (19??)-. English. Four times a year. $1025.00. Forecast International / DMS Inc., 22 Commerce Road, Newtown CT 06470. **Tel** (203)426-0800, FAX (203)426-1964, telex 467615. available on CD-ROM ($1595.00).

GW
**UNTERRICHTSBLATTER FUER DIE BUNDESWEHRVERWALTUNG.** (19??)-. Periodical. German. mo. DM102.00. Dr. Alfred Huethig Verlag GmbH, Postfach 102869, D 69018 Heidelberg Germany. **Tel** 011 49 6221 489281. **(Subscription address:** Huethig Publishing Inc., 29 Macintosh Drive, Oxford CT 06478.**)** **LC** UA710; .U65.

US/8756-5064
**US AIR FORCE PLAN FOR DEFENSE RESEARCH SCIENCES.** ***Title Change.*** (FY ... US AIR FORCE PLAN FOR DEFENSE RESEARCH SCIENCES / AIR FORCE OFFICE OF SCIENTIFIC RESEARCH.). **Added/Corp** United States. Air Force. Office of Scientific Research. **VFOAT** F.Y. ... U.S. Air Force Plan for Defense Research Sciences; Research Program. **VAT** Fiscal Year ... United States Air Force Plan for Defense Research Sciences. (19?)-(198?). English. Air Force Office of Scientific Research, Bolling Air Force Base, Washington DC 20332. **LC** UG643; .F9. **DD** 358.4/07/0973. available on microfiche (Vols. for (1987-) distributed to depository libraries). ***Continued by*** *FY ... US Air Force Research Technology Area Plan.*

US/0362-4587
**US MAGAZINE.** English. W.B. Bradbury Company, 6 East 43rd Street, New York NY 10017. **LC** U766; .U8. **DD** 355.1/29.

US
**USA WARS: KOREA. CD-ROM.** English. $74.95. Quanta Press, Inc., 1313 Fifth Street Southeast, Suite 208C, Minneapolis MN 55414. **Tel** (612)379-3956, FAX (612)623-4570.
**Desc:** Covers U.S. involvement in the Korean conflict of the 1950's. Major sections of the disc include biographies, chronology, campaigns, glossaries, and U.N. forces. Available in DOS and MAC formats.

US
**USA WARS: VIETNAM. CD-ROM.** English. $74.95. Quanta Press, Inc., 1313 Fifth Street Southeast, Suite 208C, Minneapolis MN 55414. **Tel** (612)379-3956, FAX (612)623-4570.
**Desc:** Covers U.S. involvement in South East Asia from 1946 to 1976. Major sections of the disc include biographies, statistics, order of battle, equipment, missions, bibliography, chronologies, glossaries, and The WALL. Available in MAC and DOS formats.

US/0274-6824
**USAF FIGHTER WEAPONS REVIEW.** ***Title Change.*** [USAF fight. weapons rev.]. **Added/Corp** USAF Fighter Weapons School. **VAT** United States Air Force Fighter Weapons Review. (Spring 1971)-(19??). Periodical. English. qt. USAF Fighter Weapons School, 57th Fighter Weapons Wing, Nellis AFB NV 89191-5000. **DD** 358. cum. index. available on microfiche (Vols. for (1986) distributed to depository libraries). ***Continues*** *USAF Fighter Weapons Newsletter, 1043-6529.* ***Continued by*** *USAF Weapons Review.*
**Ind/Abst** Air Univ. Libr. Index Mil. Period.

US
**USAF WEAPONS REVIEW.** **See** Aeronautics, Astronautics.

US
**V DNI ZELENYKH SVIAT.** **VFOAT** On Memorial Day. Vol. 1- 1955-. Ukrainian (Ukrainian). ir. **LC** UB365.R8; V12.

SW/0042-2800
**VART FORSVAR, TIDSKRIFT UTG. AF ALLMANNA FORSVARSFORENINGEN OCH FORENINGEN FOR NORRLANDS FASTA FORSVAR.** **Added/Corp** Foreningen for Norrlands Fasta Forsvar. Allmanna Forsvarsforeningen. (19??)-. Swedish. ir. Kr75.00 Sweden; $11.04 US. Allmanna Forsvarsforeningen, Ridd G 13, S 114 51 Stockholm Sweden. **Tel** 011 08 667 22 53. **LC** U4; .V3. **Ad Acc. Circ:** 6,000.
**Desc:** Debate concerning security policy and defence problems in Northern Europe.

XR/0862-7584
**VECKO : B.V.** **Added/Corp** Czechoslovakia. Federalni Ministerstvo Vnitra. **VFOAT** V. (19??)-. Periodical. Czech. mo. Magnet-Press s.p., Vlasislavova 26 116 66, Prague Czech Republic. **Tel** (2)260651-9. **LC** AP52; .V43. ***Continues*** *Cesloslovensky Vojak, 0009-0751.*

CU/0506-6913
**VERDE OLVO.** ***Suspended.*** [Verde olivo]. Vol. 1 (1960)-. Periodical. Spanish. wk. $22.58 North America; $29.02 South America; $32.24 Europe; $44.42 other. Ediciones Cubanas, Obispo 527, Altos ESQ Bernaza, CP 10100 Havana Cuba. **Tel** 011 632980, 631942, FAX 011 631011, telex 512337, 6540. **LC** AP63; .V435. **UDC** 355.1(729.1). **Circ:** 50,000 (ctrl).
**Desc:** Articles, interviews, and photo features on current national and international events including information on the military, cultural, sporting and recreational activities of the armed forces.

SW
**VERKSAMHETSBERATTELSE - CENTRALFORBUNDET FOR BEFALSUTBILDNING.** ***Title Change.*** **Main/Corp** Centralforbundet for Befalsutbildning. Swedish. Centralforbundet for Befalsutbildning, Box 5034, 102 41 5 Stockholm Sweden. **LC** U4; .C3827. **UDC** 355.2(485). ***Continued by*** *Verksamhet (Centralforbundet for Befalsutbildning).*

YU/0067-5660
**VESNIK / VOJNI MUZEJ, BEOGRAD.** **Added/Corp** Vojni Muzej, Beograd. **VFOAT** Vesnik Vojnog Muzeja u Beogradu; Voennyi Muzei v Belgrade; Military Museum in Belgrade; Bulletin du Musee Militaire en Belgrade. (19??)-. Serbo-Croatian (Roman) (summaries and/or abstracts in English and Russian). an. **LC** U4.B37; A2. ***Continues*** *Vesnik (Vojni Muzej Jugoslovenske Narodne Armije (Belgrade, Serbia)).*
**Ind/Abst** Am. Hist. Life (1955-1963,1971-).

US/0893-8547
**VETERAN (WASHINGTON, D.C.).** ***Title Change.*** (VETERAN / VIETNAM VETERANS OF AMERICA.). [Veteran]. **Added/Corp** Vietnam Veterans of America, Inc. (198?)-(199?). Periodical. English. bm. Vietnam Veterans of America, 2001 South Street NW/Suite 700, Washington DC 20009. **LC** DS559.73.U6; V9. **DD** 959.704/3373/05. ***Continues*** *VVA Veteran, 8750-359X.* ***Continued by*** *VVA Veteran (Washington, D.C. : 1993), 1069-0220.*

US/0278-7156
**VETERANOTES.** V. 1- Aug. 1948-. Periodical. English. bm. Mainzer Verlagsanstalt und Druckerie Will und Rothe GmbH & Company KG, Pressehaus Gross E Bleiche 44-50, POB 3120, W-6500 Mainz Germany. **Tel** 06131/144220, telex 4187753. **LC** UB358.M5; V45. **DD** 355.1/15/0973. **UDC** 355.292(73).

US
**VETERANS IN NEBRASKA.** English. an. Nebraska Department of Labor, Box 94600, Statehouse Station, Lincoln NE 68509. **Tel** (402)475-8451. **LC** UB358.N2; V47. **DD** 355.1/15/09782. **UDC** 355.292(782).

US
**VETERANS ORGANIZATIONS ... DIRECTORY.** **Added/Corp** United States. Dept. of Veterans Affairs. Office of the Deputy Assistant Secretary for Veterans Liaison. **VFOAT** Directory of Veterans Organizations. (1989)-. English. an. Deputy Assistant Secretary for Veterans Liaison, Department of Veterans Affairs, 810 Vermont Avenue NW/Room 1018, Washington DC 20420. **LC** UB357; .D54. **DD** 362.86/06/073. ***Continues*** *Directory of Veterans Service Organizations.*

US/0161-8598
**VFW, VETERANS OF FOREIGN WARS MAGAZINE.** **Main/Corp** Veterans of Foreign Wars of the United States. **Added/Corp** Veterans of Foreign Wars of the United States. Veterans of Foreign Wars Magazine. Veterans of Foreign Wars of the United States. VFW Magazine. **VFOAT** Veterans of Foreign Wars Magazine; VFW Magazine. (19??)-. Periodical. English. mo (except July). $10.00. Veterans Foreign Wars, 406 West 34th Street, Kansas City MO 64111. **Tel** (816)756-3390. **ED** Richard Kolb. **Bk Rev. Ad Acc. Circ:** 1,960,000 (ctrl). available on microfilm and microfiche from University Microfilms International (UMI). Documents available from UMI Article Clearinghouse. ***Continues*** *VFW Magazine.*
**Desc:** A veteran's magazine including legislation, services, and, stories.
**Ind/Abst** Newsp. Period. Abstr. (1988-).

RM/0042-5044
**VIATA ARMATEI : REVISTA ILUSTRATA DE LITERATURA SI ARTA EDITATA DE MINISTERUL APARARII NATIONALE.** **Added/Corp** Romania. Ministerul Apararii Nationale. (Jan. 1990)-. Periodical. Romanian. mo. DM158.00. Editura Ministerului, PO Box 12-201, Bucuresti Romania. **(Subscription address:** Kubon & Sagner, ABT Zeitschriftenimport, D 80328 Munich Germany.**)** **LC** U4; .V5. **CODEN** VIARE4. ***Continues*** *Viata Militara, 0042-5044.*

US/0743-2496
**VIETNAM WAR NEWSLETTER.** [Vietnam War newsl.]. Vol. 3, No. 25 (Mar. 1981)-. Periodical. English. Twelve times a year. $24.95. Vietnam War Newsletter, PO Box 122, Collinsville CT 06022. **Tel** (203)585-7122. **ED** Thomas W. Hebert. **LC** DS557; .V56. **DD** 959.704/33/7305. **Bk Rev. Ad Acc. Circ:** 2,500 (ctrl). ***Continues*** *Vietnam Book Report Newsletter.*
**Desc:** Contains current information of interest to Vietnam Veterans and others interested in the Vietnam War.

II
**VIKRANT.** V. 1- Oct. 1970-. Periodical. English. Rs25.00. 1 Todarmal Road, New Delhi 1 India. **LC** UA840; .V45. **DD** 355/.00954. **UDC** 355.1(540).

US
**VIOLENCE AND TERRORISM.** (1991)-. English. an. Dushkin Publishing Group Inc., Sluice Dock, Guilford CT 06437. **Tel** (203)453-4351, (800)243-6532, FAX (203)453-6000. **LC** HV6431; .V55. **DD** 303.6/25/05.

US/0360-5876
**VIRGINIA GUARDPOST.** Periodical. English. qt. Commonwealth of Virginia National Guard, 401 East Main Street, Richmond VA 23219. **LC** UA500; .V54. **DD** 355.3/7/09755. **UDC** 355.3(755).

RU
**VOENNAIA MYSL.** **Added/Corp** Soviet Union. Narodnyi Komissariat Oborony. Soviet Union. Ministerstvo Oborony. (1937)-. Periodical. Russian. mo. $99.95. **(Subscription address:** East View Publications Inc., 3020 Harbor Lane North, Suite 110, Minneapolis MN 55447.**)** **LC** U4; .V82.
**Desc:** Information on military art and science.

BU/0204-4080
**VOENNO-ISTORICHESKI SBORNIK.** **Added/Corp** Voenno-Istoricheska Komisiia pri Shtaba na Armiiata. Bulgaria. Ministerstvo na Narodnata Otbrana. Institut za Voenna Istoriia. **VFOAT** Voenno Istoricheski Sbornik; Voenno-Istoricheski Sbornik. (April/May 1927)-. Periodical. Bulgarian (table of contents in English, French, German and Russian). Six times a year. **(Subscription address:** Hemus Foreign Trade Organization, 6 Tzar Osvoboditel Boulevard, 1000 Sofia Bulgaria.**)** **LC** WMLC 005/94. **Bk Rev.**
**Ind/Abst** Am. Hist. Life (1988-).

RU
**VOENNO-ISTORICHESKII ZHURNAL : ORGAN MINISTERSTVA OBORONY SOIUZA SSR.** **Added/Corp** Soviet Union. Ministerstvo Oborony. (Jan. 1959)-. Periodical. Russian. mo. $74.00. Voenizdat, Bolshoi Kiselnii per., 14 Moscow Russia. **(Subscription address:** Victor Kamkin, 4956 Boiling Brook Parkway, Rockville, MD 20852**)** **LC** DK50; .A3. **DD** 355; 900.
**Ind/Abst** Am. Hist. Life (1964-); Numis. Lit.

RU
**VOENNYE ZNANIIA.** **See** Civil Defense.

RU/0320-0752
**VOENNYJ VESTNIK.** ***Ceased.*** (VOENNYI VESTNIK : ORGAN MINISTERSTVA OBORONY SOIUZA SSR.). [Voen. vestn.]. **Added/Corp** Soviet Union. Narodnyi Komissariat Oborony. Soviet Union. Ministerstvo Oborony. (1921)-(July 1994). Periodical. Russian. mo. **(Subscription address:** East View Publications Inc., 3020 Harbor Lane North, Suite 110, Minneapolis MN 55447.**)** ***Absorbed*** *Krasnaia Armiia / Shkola; Sputnik Politrabotnika; Vystrel.*

YU/0042-8442
**VOJNO-ISTORISKI GLASNIK.** **Added/Corp** Vojnoistorijski Institut (Belgrade, Serbia). **VFOAT** Vojnoistoriski Glasnik; Vojni Istoriski Glasnik; Vojnoistorijski Glasnik. (Apr. 1950)-. Periodical. Serbo-Croatian (Cyrillic) (Serbo-Croatian (Roman); summaries and/or abstracts in English, French and Russian). tq.
**Ind/Abst** Am. Hist. Life (1963-).

YU/0042-8450
**VOJNOSANITETSKI PREGLED.** **See** Medical Science and Technology.

GW/0344-3086
**WAR AND SOCIETY NEWSLETTER.** [War soc. newsl.]. **Added/Corp** Germany (West). Militargeschichtliches Forschungsamt. (1975)-. English (German). sa. DM18.00. University of North Carolina at Chapel Hill / War & Society, CB 3200, 401 Hamilton Hall, Chapel Hill NC 27599. **Tel** (919)962-3093. **LC** Z6724.H6; W36; U27. **DD** 016.355.
**Ind/Abst** Am. Hist. Life.

UK
**WAR ANNUAL.** **Added/Corp** Brassey's Defence Publishers. **VFOAT** Brassey's War Annual. (1986)-. English. **LC** U42; .W35. **DD** 355/.009/04.
**Ind/Abst** Am. Bibliogr. Slavic East Europ. Stud.

US/1058-823X
**WAR RESEARCH INFO SERVICE.** [War res. info serv.]. **Added/Corp** WRIS/University Conversion Project. **VFOAT** War Research Information Service. (1991)-. Periodical. English. qt. $35.00 (institution), $25.00 (individual). War Research Information Service, PO Box 748, Cambridge MA 02142. **Tel** (617)354-9363. **ED** Rich Cowan. **LC** U393; .W37. **DD** 355/.07/0973. **Bk Rev. Ad Acc. Circ:** 800 (ctrl).

CN/0707-8056
**WARRIOR (SHEARWATER. 1978).** (THE WARRIOR.). (July 1978)-. Periodical. English (French). bw. 20.00Can$. The Shearwater Warrior, PO Box 190, Shearwater Nova Scotia B0J 3A0 Canada. **Tel** FAX

463-5111. **ED** William J. Clair. **DD** 355.1/09716/22. **Bk Rev. Ad Acc. Circ:** 6,000. available on CD-ROM. ***Continues*** *Shearwater Warrior, 0705-1980.*
**Desc:** Covers subjects of military interest provided from local and national DND sources, plus articles of community interest to the DND, and civilian communities where the paper is circulated.

US
**WARSHIPS FORECAST.** (19??)-. English. Twelve times a year. $1390.00. Forecast International / DMS Inc., 22 Commerce Road, Newtown CT 06470. **Tel** (203)426-0800, FAX (203)426-1964, telex 467615. available on CD-ROM ($1595.00).

US/1047-8957
**WEAPONS COMPLEX MONITOR.** (WEAPONS COMPLEX MONITOR : WASTE MANAGEMENT & CLEAN UP, COMPREHENSIVE COVERAGE OF HAZARDOUS, MIXED & NUCLEAR DEFENSE WASTE ACTIVITIES.). [Weapons complex monit.]. Vol. 1, No. 1 (June 5, 1989)-. Periodical. English. bw (26 issues). $995.00 US and Canada; $1015.00 other. Exchange Publications, 2014 P Street NW, Washington DC 20036. **Tel** (202)296-2814, FAX (202)362-5437. **(Subscription address:** Exchange Publications, PO Box 5757, Washington DC 20016.**) DD** 363.

GW/0178-3084
**WEHRAUSBILDUNG. Added/Corp** Germany (West). Bundesministerium der Verteidigung. (19??)-. Periodical. German. bm. DM64.40 Germany; DM75.95 other. Verlag Offene Worte, Bonngasse 3, Postfach 2009, W-5300 Bonn 1 Germany. **Tel** 05221/50001. **(Subscription address:** Maximilian Verlagsgruppe, Steintorwall 17, D 32052 Herford, Germany (011 49 5221 599142 or 599161)**) LC** U570; .W38. **DD** 355.3/38. **Bk Rev. Ad Acc. Circ:** 55,400 (ctrl). ***Continues*** *Wehrausbildung in Wort und Bild.*
**Desc:** Journal for all problems that NCO's are concerned with, especially military training.

GW/0043-2172
**WEHRTECHNIK.** [Wehrtechnik]. **Added/Corp** Deutsche Gesellschaft fEur Wehrtechnik. (Jan. 1969)-. Periodical. German. mo. DM105.00, $76.00 Germany; DM115.00, $83.23 other. Wehr und Wissen Verlagsges GmbH, Postfach 140261, D 53057 Bonn Germany. **Tel** 011 49 228 64830. **(Subscription address:** BDK Buecherdienst GmBh, Postfach 900120, D 51111 Cologne Germany.**) LC** U3; .W446. **DD** 355/.005. **CODEN** WHTCAK. Index available. **Bk Rev. Ad Acc. Circ:** 33,300 (ctrl). Documents available from Article Express International. ***Supersedes*** *Wehrtechnische Monatshefte, 0341-9991;* ***Absorbed*** *Wehr und Wirtschaft, 0043-2113.*
**Desc:** An up-to-date highly respected journal on defence economics and the military.
**Ind/Abst** Curr. Mil. Pol. Lit. (19??-); Ei Page One (19??-); EMBASE (19??-); Energy Res. Abstr. (Sept. 1977-); Eng. Index Annu. (19??-); Int. Aerosp. Abstr. (19??-).

US
**WEST'S VETERANS APPEALS REPORTER. Added/Corp** West Publishing Company. United States. Supreme Court. United States. Court of Veterans Appeals. United States. Court of Appeals (Federal Circuit). **VFOAT** Veterans Appeals Reporter. Vol. 1, No. 1 (Oct. 1991)-. Periodical. English. mo. West Publishing Company, 610 Opperman Drive, PO Box 64526, Eagan MN 55123-1308. **Tel** (612)687-5618, (800)328-9352, FAX (612)687-5388, (800)562-2329.

US/0083-9108
**WHAT EVERY VETERAN SHOULD KNOW.** (1937)-. English. an (Mar.). $10.00 (book only): $22.00 (supplements only); $30.00 (including supplements). Veterans Information Service, PO Box 111, East Moline IL 61244. **Tel** (309)797-1868. **ED** Patrick L. Murphy.

PL/0209-0031
**WIEDZA OBRONNA : DWUMIESIECZNIK TOWARZYSTWA WIEDZY OBRONNEJ.** Periodical. Polish. bm. Z1,320. Biuro Zarzadu Gownego Two, SKR Pocztowa 32, 00-911 Warszawa 62 Poland. **Tel** 28-98-92. **(Subscription address:** RSW Prasa-Ksiazka-Ruch, Centralny Kolportaz Prasy I, Wydawnictw, Ul Towarowa 28, 00-958 Warszawa Poland**) ED** Jan Kaliszek. **LC** U4; .W53. cum. index. **Bk Rev. Circ:** 11,000.

PL
**WOJSKO I WYCHOWANIE : PISMO ZONIERZY ZAWODOWYCH WP. Added/Corp** Poland. Wojsko Polskie. Departament Wychowania. (19??)-. Periodical. Polish. mo. $21.00. **(Subscription address:** ARS Polona, PO Box 1001, 00068 Warsaw Poland.**) LC** U717.P7; W65.

US
**WORLD AEROSPACE & DEFENSE INTELLIGENCE. See** Aeronautics, Astronautics.

GW
**WORLD DEFENCE ALMANAC : THE BALANCE OF MILITARY POWER. VFOAT** Military Technology; Military Technology-Miltech. (1986/87)-. English. an. $6.00. Monch Media Inc, 1701 K Street/#900, Washington DC 20006-1503. **Tel** (703)790-5252. **LC** U1; .W67. **DD** 355/.005.
**Desc:** Information on military art and science, the armed forces, and the balance of power.

US/0891-4850
**WORLD DEFENSE FORCES.** ***Suspended.*** [World def. forces]. No. 1 (1987)-(19??). English. $28.50. ABC Clio Press, PO Box 1911, 130 Cremona, Santa Barbara CA 93117. **Tel** (805)968-1911, (800)422-2546, FAX (805)685-9685. **LC** UA15; .W685. **DD** 355/.005.

US
**WORLD MILITARY & CIVIL AIRCRAFT BRIEFING. See** Aeronautics, Astronautics.

US/0363-4795
**WORLD MILITARY AND SOCIAL EXPENDITURES. See** Military and Defense-Abstracting, Bibliographies and Statistics.

US/0897-4667
**WORLD MILITARY EXPENDITURES AND ARMS TRANSFERS.** (WORLD MILITARY EXPENDITURES AND ARMS TRANSFERS / U.S. ARMS CONTROL AND DISARMAMENT AGENCY.). [World mil. expend. arms transf.]. **Added/Corp** United States. Arms Control and Disarmament Agency. (1965-1974)-. Government Publication. English. an. Price varies per volume. Superintendent of Documents, US Government Printing Office, Washington DC 20402. **Tel** (202)275-3328, FAX (202)786-2377. **LC** JX1974.A1; U52 subser. **DD** 338.4/7/355005. ***Continues*** *World Military Expenditures and Arms Trade.*

US
**WORLD MISSLES BRIEFING.** English. mo. $995.00 US and Canada; $1,150.00 other. Teal Group, 3900 University Drive, Suite 220, Fairfax VA 22030. **Tel** (703)385-1992.

US/1058-0328
**WORLDWIDE MANPOWER DISTRIBUTION BY GEOGRAPHICAL AREA. See** Military and Defense-Abstracting, Bibliographies and Statistics.

US
**WORLDWIDE U.S. ACTIVE DUTY MILITARY PERSONNEL CASUALTIES / DEPARTMENT OF DEFENSE. Added/Corp** United States. Dept. of Defense. Washington Headquarters Services. Directorate for Information Operations and Reports. **VFOAT** Worldwide US Active Duty Military Personnel Casualties. **VAT** Worldwide United States Active Duty Military Personnel Casualties. (19??)-. Government Publication. English. qt. $7.50 US; $9.40 other. Superintendent of Documents, US Government Printing Office, Washington DC 20402. **Tel** (202)275-3328, FAX (202)786-2377. **LC** UA23.2; .W67. **DD** 355/.00973/021. Documents available from Documents on Demand.
**Desc:** Provides information on active duty military personell deaths.
**Ind/Abst** Am. Stat. Index.

US/0748-2086
**YEAR IN BRIEF, THE.** (THE YEAR IN BRIEF, THE VA IN ... / VETERANS ADMINISTRATION.). English. an. US Veterans Administration / Washington DC, 810 Vermont Avenue Southwest, Washington DC 20420. **Tel** (202)393-2124. **LC** UB357; .Y37. **DD** 353.0081/2. **UDC** 355.292(73).

US
**YEAR IN REVIEW / AIR FORCE SYSTEMS COMMAND, THE. Main/Corp** United States. Air Force. Systems Command. English. Air Force Systems Command, The Pentagon, Washington DC 20330. **LC** WMLC 91/1155. ***Continues*** *Air Force Systems Command.*

RU
**ZARUBEZHNOE VOENNOE OBOZRENIE. Added/Corp** Soviet Union. Ministerstvo Oborony. (19??)-. Periodical. Russian. mo. $119.95. **(Subscription address:** East View Publications Inc., 3020 Harbor Lane North, Suite 110, Minneapolis MN 55447.**) LC** U4; .Z37.
**Ind/Abst** Curr. Mil. Pol. Lit.

GW/0044-2852
**ZEITSCHRIFT FUER HEERESKUNDE.** [Z. Heereskd.]. (1960)-. Periodical. German. bm. $24.35. Bouvier GMBH & Company KG ABT Verlag, Am HOF 28, D53113 Bonn Germany. **Tel** 011 49 228 7290141. **UDC** 355. cum. index. ***Continues*** *Zeitschrift fuer Heeres- und Uniformkunde.*
**Ind/Abst** Am. Hist. Life (1970-1972, 1976-).

RU
**ZNAMENOSETS.** ***Ceased.*** Vol. 14.- (No. 160- ); Jan. 1974-Ceased Jan. 1990. Periodical. Russian. mo. **(Subscription address:** Victor Kamkin, 4956 Boiling Brook Parkway, Rockville MD 20852.**) LC** U4; .S69. ***Continues*** *Starshina-Serzhant.*

PL/0044-4979
**ZONIERZ POLSKI.** [Zo. Pol.]. (1945)-. Periodical. Polish. mo. $30.00. **(Subscription address:** ARS Polona, PO Box 1001, 00068 Warsaw Poland.**) UDC** 355.1(438).

---

## ABSTRACTING, BIBLIOGRAPHIES AND STATISTICS

---

AG
**ABSTRACTS OF MILITARY BIBLIOGRAPHY.** ***Ceased.*** Vol. 10, No. 2 (April/June 1976)-(19??). Abstracting/Indexing Service. English. qt. Abstracts of Military Bibliography, MAIPU 262, 1084 Buenos Aires Argentina. **LC** U17; .R47. **DD** 355/.005. ***Continues*** *Resumenes Analiticos Sobre Defensa y Seguridad Nacional, 0034-5873.*

US/0002-2586
**AIR UNIVERSITY LIBRARY INDEX TO MILITARY PERIODICALS. Added/Corp** Air University (U.S.). Library. Vol. 14, No. 1 (Jan./Mar. 1963)-. Abstracting/Indexing Service. English. qt (with annual cumulations). Air University Library/LSP, Maxwell Air Force Base, Montgomery AL 36112-5564. **ED** Martha M. Stewart. **NLM** Z 5063 A298. **Circ:** 1,600 (ctrl). available on an online database from Joint Electronic Library. ***Continues*** *Air University Periodical Index.*
**Desc:** Subject index to articles and book reviews appearing in over 81 English language military and aeronautical journals.
**Ind/Abst** Int. Aerosp. Abstr. (1991-).

SW/0004-3788
**ARTILLERI-TIDSKRIFT.** [Artilleri-tidskr.]. (1872)-. Periodical. Swedish. qt. Kr100.00 Sweden; Kr140.00 other. Artilleri-Tidskrift, S 115 88 Stockholm Sweden. **UDC** 355.

US/1056-7410
**BIBLIOGRAPHIES OF BATTLES AND LEADERS.** (1991)-. Periodical. English. Greenwood Publishing Group, PO Box 5007, Westport CT 06881-9990. ***Continues*** *Meckler's Bibliographies of Battles and Leaders.*

US
**CINFAC BIBLIOGRAPHIC REVIEW. SUPPLEMENT. Main/Corp** American University, Washington, D.C. Center for Research in Social Systems. No. 10- June 1966-. Periodical. English. ir. National Technical Information Service - NTIS, Room 2027S, 5285 Port Royal Road, Springfield VA 22161. **Tel** (703)487-4630, (703)487-4660, (703)487-4650, FAX (703)321-8547, telex 89-9405. **LC** Z6724.G7; A632. ***Continues*** *Bibliography on Counterinsurgency, Unconventional Warfare, and Psychological Operations. Supplement.*

US/0882-8857
**CIVILIAN MANPOWER STATISTICS.** (CIVILIAN MANPOWER STATISTICS / DEPARTMENT OF DEFENSE.). [Civ. manpow. stat.]. **Added/Corp** United States. Dept. of Defense. United States. Dept. of Defense. Washington Headquarters Services. Directorate for Information Operations and Reports. (Aug 1980)-. Government Publication. English. qt. $12.00 domestic; $15.00 other. Superintendent of Documents, US Government Printing Office, Washington DC 20402. **Tel** (202)275-3328, FAX (202)786-2377. **LC** UA23.2; .C58. **DD** 355.6/1/0973. available on microfiche (Vols. for (198-) distributed to depository libraries). Documents available from Documents on Demand. ***Continues in part*** *Department of Defense Civilian and Military Personnel, OSD-JCS and Other Defense Activities.*
**Desc:** Comprised of tables containing official summary data on DoD civilian employment levels. Data are broken down by major Defense component, employment category, and location. Also includes selected data on trends in civilian employment, and accession and separation rates.
**Ind/Abst** Am. Stat. Index.

UK/0954-3589
**CURRENT MILITARY & POLITICAL LITERATURE.** ***Ceased.*** **VFOAT** Current Military and Political Literature; CMPL. Vol. 5, No. 1 (1989)-(1993). Abstracting/Indexing Service. English. bm. Taylor & Francis Ltd., Rankine Road, Basingstoke Hampshire, RG24 8PR United Kingdom. **Tel** 011 44 256 840366, FAX 011 44 256 479438, telex 858540. **(Subscription address:** Taylor & Francis Inc., 1900 Frost Road, Suite 101, Bristol PA 19007-1598.**) ED** Simon King and Lt. Col. William A. Burhans, Associate Editor. **LC** Z6725.G7; C87; U43. **DD** 016.355/00941. available on microfilm and microfiche from University Microfilms International (UMI). ***Continues*** *Current Military Literature, 0264-1674.*
**Desc:** Provides subject-classified abstracts and citations of articles from international journals and occasional papers in the areas of international relations, strategic studies, military-political science and history, military organizations, operations and tactics, administration and

logistics, arms industries and procurement, psychological warfare, peace studies and conflict research. Contains author, source and geographical indexes.

US/0882-9837
**DATA ON VIETNAM ERA VETERANS.** [Data Vietnam era veteran]. English. an. US Veterans Administration / Washington DC, 810 Vermont Avenue Southwest, Washington DC 20420. **Tel** (202)393-2124. **LC** UB357; .D34. **DD** 355.1/15/0973.

US
**DOD STATISTICAL REPORT ON THE MILITARY RETIREMENT SYSTEM / OFFICE OF ACTUARY, DEFENSE MANPOWER DATA CENTER.** **Added/Corp** Defense Manpower Data Center (U.S.). Office of Actuary. **VFOAT** D.O.D. Statistical Report on the Military Retirement System; FY ... DOD Statistical Report on the Military Retirement System; FY ... Statistical Report on Military Retirement; Statistical Report on Military Retirement. **VAT** Department of Defense Statistical Report on the Military Retirement System. (19??)-. Statistical Publication. English. an. Office of the Actuary, Defense Manpower Data Center, 1600 North Wilson Boulevard/4th Floor, Arlington VA 22209. **Tel** (202)696-5865. **LC** UB443; .D63. **DD** 355.1/14/0973. **Circ:** 1,500.
**Desc:** Presents military retirement statistics. Categories include type of retirement; retired age; current age; years of service; service; annuity; and geographic location.

US/0740-1701
**HEALTH MANPOWER STATISTICS.** (HEALTH MANPOWER STATISTICS / DEPARTMENT OF DEFENSE.). [Health manpow. stat.]. Began with Vol. for 1981. English. an. US Department of Defense, The Pentagon, Washington DC 20301. **Tel** (703)545-6700. **LC** UH223; .A43. **DD** 355.3/45/0973. **NLM** W2; A D15h. available on microfiche (Vols. for (1985-) distributed to depository libraries).

GW
**MILITARWISSENSCHAFTLICHE QUELLENKUNDE.** **Main/Corp** Zentralbibliothek der Bundeswehr. V. 1- (No. 1- ); Jan./Feb. 1963-. Periodical. German. bm. **LC** Z6726; .Z4.

US/0741-1340
**MILITARY MANPOWER STATISTICS.** (MILITARY MANPOWER STATISTICS / DEPARTMENT OF DEFENSE.). [Mil. manpow. stat.]. **Added/Corp** United States. Dept. of Defense. United States. Dept. of Defense. Washington Headquarters Service. Directorate for Information Operations and Reports. (Apr. 1979)-. Government Publication. English. qt. $19.00 domestic; $23.75 other. Superintendent of Documents, US Government Printing Office, Washington DC 20402. **Tel** (202)275-3328, FAX (202)786-2377. **LC** UB23; .M5. **DD** 355.2/2/0973. available on microfiche (Vols. for (1981-) distributed to depository libraries). Documents available from Documents on Demand.
**Desc:** Consists of statistical tables which contain data pertaining to military personnel on active duty. In addition to summary data, detailed information are included by the Military Departments and Defense components regarding the type of personnel, grade, and location. Selected tables also provide data on active duty women in the military.
**Ind/Abst** Am. Stat. Index.

US/0363-8359
**MILITARY PERSONNEL AND DEPENDENTS IN HAWAII.** **Main/Corp** Hawaii. Dept. of Planning and Economic Development. English. Hawaii Department of Business and Economic Development, PO Box 2359, Honolulu HI 96804. **Tel** (808)586-2423. **LC** HA329.1; .A25 subser; UA26.H38. **DD** 319.69 S; 355.3/38/09969.

US
**NATO MUTUAL SUPPORT ACT, AS AMENDED (ACQUISITION AND CROSS SERVICING AGREEMENTS WITH NATO ALLIES AND OTHER COUNTRIES); REPORT OF AGREEMENTS AND TRANSACTIONS / DEPARTMENT OF DEFENSE.** **See** Military and Defense.

US/0501-9427
**SELECTED MANPOWER STATISTICS.** [Sel. manpow. stat.]. **Added/Corp** United States. Dept. of Defense. Washington Headquarters Services. Directorate for Information Operations and Reports. United States. Dept. of Defense. Directorate for Statistical Services. United States. Assistant Secretary of Defense (Comptroller). Directorate for Information Operations. United States. Assistant Secretary of Defense (Comptroller). Directorate for Information Operations and Control. United States. Assistant Secretary of Defense (Comptroller). Directorate for Management Information, Operations, and Control. (19??)-. English. Twelve times a year. $25.00 US; $28.75 other. Superintendent of Documents, US Government Printing Office, Washington DC 20402. **Tel** (202)275-3328, FAX (202)786-2377. **LC** UA17.5.U5; U5414a. **DD** 355.2/2/0973. available on microfiche (Vols. for (1980-) distributed to depository libraries).

US/0884-1152
**SELECTED MEDICAL CARE STATISTICS.** (SELECTED MEDICAL CARE STATISTICS / DEPARTMENT OF DEFENSE.). [Sel. med. care stat.]. **Added/Corp** United States. Dept. of Defense. United States. Dept. of Defense. Washington Headquarters Services. Directorate for Information Operations and Reports. (19??)-. Periodical. English. qt (4 issues). $14.00 US; $17.50 other. US Department of Defense, The Pentagon, Washington DC 20301. **Tel** (703)545-6700. **(Subscription address:** Superintendent of Documents, US Government Printing Office, Washington DC 20402.**)** **LC** UH223; .A47. **DD** 355.3/45/0973. **NLM** W2; A D15s. available on microfiche. Documents available from Documents on Demand.
**Desc:** Selected utilization statistics of medical care provided at fixed military medical facilities are shown for operating beds, beds occupied on a daily average, operating bassinets, admissions, outpatient visits, and live births according to defense components.
**Ind/Abst** Am. Stat. Index.

FR/0291-851X
**STATISTIQUE MEDICALE DANS LES ARMEES.** **Added/Corp** France. Service de Sante des Armees. Bureau Epidemiologie. Centre de Traitement de l'Information Medicale des Armees (France). **VFOAT** Statistique Medicale des Armees. (1986)-. Statistical Publication. French. an. Centre de Traitement de l'Information Medicale des Armees, 69 Avenue de Paris, 94160-Saint-Mande France. **LC** UH271; .S67. **DD** 355.3/45/0944. Index available. **Circ:** 260 (ctrl).

US/0193-9327
**SURVEY OF CONTRACTING STATISTICS.** Began with Dec. 1978. English. an. US Department of Defense Department of the Navy, Pentagon, Room 4E686, Washington DC 20350. **Tel** (703)695-0911. **LC** VC267.U6; U56A. **DD** 355.6/211.0973. ***Continues*** *Survey of Procurement Statistics, 0565-8497.*

US/0363-4795
**WORLD MILITARY AND SOCIAL EXPENDITURES.** (19??)-. English (Spanish and Swedish). ir. $8.00 North America; $10.50 other. World Priorities Inc., PO Box 25140, Washington DC 20007. **Tel** (202)965-1661. **LC** HJ7469; .S58. **DD** 336.3/9. **Circ:** 75,000.
**Desc:** Military and social statistics for 142 countries showing the detrimental effects of rising military budgets on social needs.
**Ind/Abst** Stat. Ref. Index.

US/1058-0328
**WORLDWIDE MANPOWER DISTRIBUTION BY GEOGRAPHICAL AREA.** [Worldw. manpow. distrib. geogr. area]. **Added/Corp** United States. Dept. of Defense. United States. Dept. of Defense. Washington Headquarters Services. Directorate for Information Operations and Reports. (19??)-. Government Publication. English. qt. $24.00 US; $30.00 other. Superintendent of Documents, US Government Printing Office, Washington DC 20402. **Tel** (202)275-3328, FAX (202)786-2377. **LC** UA17.5.U5; W67. **DD** 355.2/2/0973. Documents available from Documents on Demand.
**Desc:** A report on the distribution of Department of Defense active duty military and civilian personnel, as well as their dependents, showing total figures for the 48 contiguous States, Alaska, Hawaii, the United States territories, and selected locations. Also includes data for personnel located in foreign countries. Data on active military personnel are shown by location, according to military service, and civilian data by regional area and country, which is divided by United States citizen direct hires and foreign direct and indirect hires. The types and numbers of both personnel dependents are shown by location, according to Defense component.
**Ind/Abst** Am. Stat. Index.

# MOTION PICTURE

CN/0820-9545
**16 MM FILM CATALOGUE - RED RIVER COMMUNITY COLLEGE, LEARNING RESOURCES CENTRE.** (16 MM FILM CATALOGUE.). [16 mm film cat. - Red River Community Coll. Learn. Res. Cent.]. **Main/Corp** Red River Community College. Learning Resources Centre. **VFOAT** Film Catalogue. (1982)-. Periodical. English. Red River Community College, 2055 Notre Dame, Winnipeg Manitoba. **DD** 017/.537. ***Continues*** *Red River Community College. Learning Resources Centre. 16 MM Films, 0228-9881.*

CN/0821-1116
**16MM FILM ADDENDUM - MIDWESTERN REGIONAL LIBRARY SYSTEM.** (16 MM FILM ADDENDUM.). [16mm film ad. - Midwest. Reg. Libr. Syst.]. **Main/Corp** Midwestern Regional Library System (Ont.). 1981-. English. Free. Midwestern Regional Library System, 637 Victoria Street North, Kitchener Ontario N2H 5G4 Canada. **DD** 018/.137. **UDC** 017:771.531.3(713). ctrl circ.

CN/0315-7326
**16MM FILMS AVAILABLE FROM THE PUBLIC LIBRARIES OF METROPOLITAN TORONTO.** **Added/Corp** Metropolitan Toronto Library Board. (1970)-. Periodical. English. qt. 80.00Can$ (catalog), $50.00 (supplement). Metropolitan Toronto Library Board, 789 Yonge Street, Toronto Ontario M4W 2G8 Canada. **Tel** (416)393-7134, telex 06-22232. **DD** 018/.1. ***Supersedes*** *16MM Sound Films Available from the Public Libraries of Metropolitan Toronto, 0315-7326.*

CN/0707-9389
**24 IMAGES.** [24 images]. **VAT** Vingt-Quatre Images. No. 1 (Feb. 1979)-. Periodical. French. qt. 29.50Can$ (institutions), 22.00Can$ (individuals) Canada; 35.00Can$ other. 24 Images, 3781 Rue Laval, Montreal, Quebec H2W 2H8 Canada. **Tel** (514)286-1688. **DD** 791.43/05. **Bk Rev. Ad Acc. Circ:** 1,500.
**Desc:** Interviews, films analysis, cinematographic theory, books, reviews, information about films and actuality (especially about Quebec production).
**Ind/Abst** Can. Period. Index (19??-); Film Lit. Index (No. 53, Jan./Feb. 1991-); Point Repere (1981-).

UK
**35/70: JOURNAL OF THE FEATURE FILM INDUSTRY.** **VFOAT** Journal of the Feature Film Industry. Periodical. English. **LC** PN1993.5.G7; T48. **DD** 384/.8/0941. ***Continues*** *Wide-Screen.*

UK/0001-0413
**ABC FILM REVIEW.** English. mo. Assoc Brit Cinemas, Film Review, 92 Queensway, Bletchley, Milton Keynes MK2 2QV England.

US
**ACADEMY PLAYERS DIRECTORY.** **See** Motion Picture-Abstracting, Bibliographies and Statistics.

FR/0397-8435
**ACTIVITE CINEMATOGRAPHIQUE FRANCAISE . / CNC, CENTRE NATIONAL DE LA CINEMATOGRAPHIE, L'.** **Added/Corp** Centre National de la Cinematographie (France). (19??)-. Periodical. French. Six times a year. 180.00F. Centre National Cinematographie, 12 rue de Lubeck, 75784 Paris Cedex 16 France. **Tel** 011 33 1 45051440, FAX 011 33 1 47550491, telex 650306. **ED** D. Wallon. **LC** PN1993.5.F7; A648. **DD** 384/.8/0944. Index available. **Bk Rev. Circ:** 10,000.

US
**ADAM FILM WORLD GUIDE. ADAM FILM WORLD DIRECTORY OF ADULT FILMS.** [Adam film world guide. Adam film world dir. adult films]. **VFOAT** Adam Film World Directory of Adult Films; Film World Guide; Directory of Adult Films. (1984)-. Directory. English. mo. $45.00 (one year), $80.00 (two year). Knight Publishing Corporation, 8060 Melrose Avenue, Los Angeles CA 90046. **Tel** (310)653-8060, FAX (213)655-9452. **ED** Carl Esser. **Ad Acc.**
**Desc:** Six issues devoted to articles and reviews of adult screen and video entertainment; six issues to pictorial and guidebooks, plus annual directory.

US/0277-2914
**ADULT CINEMA REVIEW.** **VFOAT** Adult Cinema. Vol. 1, No. 1 (July 1981)-. Periodical. English. mo. $33.00 US; $39.00 other. Adult Review Magazine, Subscription Department, 300 West 43rd Street, New York NY 10036. **UDC** 791.43-052-053.8.

UK/0261-4472
**AFTERIMAGE (LONDON, ENGLAND).** (AFTERIMAGE.). (1970)-. Periodical. English. $20.00. Afterimage Publishing, 1 Birham Road, London N4 England. **LC** PN1993; .A52. **DD** 791.43/05.

US
**AFVA BULLETIN / AMERICAN FILM AND VIDEO ASSOCIATION.** **Added/Corp** American Film and Video Association. Vol. 11, No. 1 (1988)-. English. bm. Free to members of the American Film and Video Associaton. American Film and Video Association, 85 Van Reypen Street, Jersey City NJ 07306. **ED** Jeanne Sullivan. **LC** LB1044; .E34. **Circ:** 900 (ctrl). ***Continues*** *EFLA Bulletin (1977).*

US/1051-5925
**AFVA EVALUATIONS.** ***Ceased.*** (AFVA EVALUATIONS / AMERICAN FILM & VIDEO ASSOCIATION.). [AFVA eval.]. **Added/Corp** American Film and Video Association. **VFOAT** A.F.V.A. Evaluations. **VAT** American Film and Video Association Evaluations. (1988)-(Dec. 1993). English. an. Highsmith

Press, W 5527 Highway 106, Ft. Akinson WI 53538. **Tel** (800)558-2110, FAX (414)563-7395. **LC** LB1044; .E33. **DD** 011/.37. Index available. **Circ:** 1,000 (ctrl). available on microfilm and microfiche from University Microfilms International (UMI). ***Continues*** *EFLA Evaluations, 0146-3152.*
**Desc:** Summary and evaluation of over 1200 films and videos entered in the American Film and Video Association Film Festival including subject, distributor and director indexes.
**Ind/Abst** Med. Rev. Dig.

UA
**AL-SINIMA AL-ARABIYAH.** Periodical. Arabic. qt. 0.50. Al-Sinima Al-Arabiyah, 218 Shari Al-Jaysh, Al-Qahirah Egypt. **LC** PN1993.5.A65; S55. **UDC** 791.43=927.

UA
**AL-SINIMA WA-AL-MASRAH. Added/Corp** Hayat al-Sinima wa-al-Masrah wa-al-Musiqa. No. 1 (Jan. 1974)-. Periodical. Arabic. mo. 1.00. 9 Orabi Street, Al-Qahirah United Arab Republic Egypt. **LC** PN1993; .S577.

UA
**AL-SINIMA WA-AL-NAS. VFOAT** El Cinema Wal Nas. Vol. 1 (Jan. 1979)-. Periodical. Arabic. £E5.00. Majallat Al-Sinima Wa-Al-Nas Rais Al-Tahrir, PO Box 2742, Cairo Egypt. **LC** PN1993.5.A65; S56. **UDC** 791.43=927.

AG
**AMANTE : CINE, EL. VFOAT** Cine. Vol. 1, No. 1 (Dec. 1991)-. Periodical. Spanish. Twelve times a year. $198.00. Ediciones Tatanka SA, Esmeralda 779 6 A, 1007 Buenos Aires Argentina. **Tel** 011 54 1 3227518.

US
**AMAZING CINEMA.** No. 1 (May 1981)-. Periodical. English. Cinema Enterprises, 12 Moray Court, Baltimore MD 21236. **UDC** 791.43.

US/0002-7928
**AMERICAN CINEMATOGRAPHER.** [Am. cinematogr.]. Vol. 1 (1920)-. Periodical. English. mo. $27.00 US; $42.00 Mexico and Canada; $54.00 other. American Society of Cinematographers, Box 2230, Hollywood CA 90028. **Tel** (213)969-4333. **ED** George Turner. **LC** TR845; .A55. Index available. **Ad Acc. Circ:** 35,000. available on microfilm and microfiche from University Microfilms International (UMI).
**Desc:** Covers film and video production techniques.
**Ind/Abst** Art Index; Film Lit. Index.

US/0361-4751
**AMERICAN FILM.** ***Ceased.*** [Am. film]. Vol. 1 (Oct. 1975)-(1992). Periodical. English. Ten times a year. Billboard Publications Inc., 1515 Broadway Billboard, New York NY 10036. **Tel** (212)764-7300, FAX (305)755-7048, telex WU TWX 710-581-6279. **LC** PN1993. **DD** 791.43/05. **UDC** 791.43(73). **[CCC]. Bk Rev. Ad Acc. Circ:** 140,000. available on microfilm and microfiche from University Microfilms International (UMI). Documents available from UMI Article Clearinghouse, Magazine Collection. ***Absorbed in part*** *Hollywood Reporter.*
**Ind/Abst** Abr. Read. Guide Period. Lit.; Acad. Abstr. Full Text Elite (Jan. 1984-Jan. 1992); Acad. Abstr. (Jan. 1984-Jan. 1992); Acad. Ind. [Computer File] (1984-); Acad. Search (Jan. 1984-Jan. 1992); Access (1976-1988); Art Index; Arts Humanit. Citation Index (19??-19??) [Full Cov.]; Book Rev. Index; Expand. Acad. Index (1985-); Film Lit. Index (1975-1992); Gen. Period. Index (1985-); Humanit. Index (?-?); Humanit. Source (Jan. 1988-Jan. 1992); INFO-SOUTH Abstr.; Mag. Artic. Summar. Elite (Jan. 1984-Jan. 1992); Mag. Artic. Summar. Select (Jan. 1984-Jan. 1992); Mag. Artic. Summar. CD-ROM (Jan. 1984-Jan. 1992); Mag. Express (1986-1992) [Full Txt.]; Mag. Index Plus (1989-); Mag. Index. Sel. (1986-); Mag. Search; Med. Rev. Dig.; Newsp. Period. Abstr. (1986-1992); Read. Guide Abstr. Select Ed.; Read. Guide Period. Lit.; Resource/One Ondisc; Mag. Index (1977-); Vocat. Search (Jan. 1984-Jan. 1992).

US
**AMERICAN FILM INSTITUTE MONOGRAPH SERIES. Added/Corp** American Film Institute. Vol. 1 (1983)-. Monographic series. English. ir. Price varies per volume. Greenwood Press Inc., PO Box 5007, Westport CT 06881-5007. **Tel** (203)226-3571, FAX (203)222-1502.
**Ind/Abst** MLA Int. Bibl. Books Artic. Mod. Lang. Lit.

US
**AMERICAN FILM INSTITUTE VIDEO FESTIVAL : CATALOG. Main/Conf** American Film Institute Video Festival. **Added/Corp** American Film Institute. **VFOAT** AFI Video Festival. (19??)-. Catalog. English. an. American Film Institute / Ohio, PO Box 2046, Marion OH 43305.

US/0279-0041
**AMERICAN PREMIERE. VFOAT** Premiere; American Premiere Magazine. Vol. 2, Issue 6 (May 20, 1981)-. Periodical. English. Four times a year. $16.00 (one year); $30.00 (two years). American Premiere, 8421 Wilshire Boulevard Penthouse, Beverly Hills CA 90211. **Tel** (310)852-0434. **ED** Susan Royal. **LC** PN1993.5.U6; A877. **DD** 384/.8/0973. **Bk Rev. Ad Acc. Circ:** 17,500 (ctrl). ***Continues*** *Premiere, 0274-7766.*
**Desc:** Business magazine for film industry. Includes articles about film production, distribution, exhibition and finance with interviews with major filmmakers and industry leaders.
**Ind/Abst** Film Lit. Index.

●US/1075-6477
**AMIA NEWSLETTER.** (AMIA NEWSLETTER : THE NEWSLETTER OF THE ASSOCIATION OF MOVING IMAGE ARCHIVISTS.). [AMIA newsl.]. **Added/Corp** Association of Moving Image Archivists. American Film Institute. National Center for Film and Video Preservation. **VAT** Association of Moving Image Archivists Newsletter. (1992)-. Newsletter. English. mo. Comes with Association of Moving Image Archivists membership; $150.00 non-profit organizations, $300.00 profit organizations, $50.00 individual. The American Film Institute, Edcational Services, 2021 North Western Avenue, Los Angeles CA 90027. **Tel** (310)856-7725, (310)856-7633. **DD** 778.

BE/0773-5855
**ANDERE SINEMA.** [And. sine.]. **VFOAT** Sinema. Periodical. Dutch. bm. 550F. De Ander Film V.Z.W., Gratiekapelstraat 7, 2000 Antwerpen Belgium. **UDC** 791.43.04:008.
**Ind/Abst** Film Lit. Index.

●US/1061-0308
**ANIMATION JOURNAL.** [Animat. j.]. **VFOAT** Animation. Vol. 1, Issue 1 (Fall 1992)-. Periodical. English. Twice a year (Feb., Sept.). $20.00 (individuals), $40.00 (institutions) US; $25.00 (individuals), $45.00 (institutions) Canada & Mexico; $30.00 (individuals), $50.00 (institutions) others. AJ Press, 2011 Kingsboro Circle, Tustin CA 92680-6733. **Tel** (714)544-6255, FAX (714)544-6255. **ED** Maureen Furniss. **LC** NC1765; .A54. **DD** 791.43/3. Index available. cum. index. **Bk Rev**, (Qty: 4). **Pr Rev. Circ:** 1,000.
**Desc:** Devoted to animation, with research representing the diversity of its production techniques and national origins.

US/1041-617X
**ANIMATION MAGAZINE.** [Animat. mag.]. **VFOAT** Animation. Vol. 1, Issue 1 (Aug. 1987)-. Periodical. English. bm. $21.00 (1 year), $36.00 (2 year) US; $30.00 (1 year), 51.00 (2 year) Canada; $39.00 (1 year), $66.00 (2 year) other. Animation Magazine, 5889 Kanan Road, Suite 317, Agoura Hills CA 91301. **Tel** (818)991-2884, FAX (818)991-3773. **ED** Rita Street. **LC** NC1766.U5; A48. **DD** 741.5/8/05. cum. index. **Bk Rev**, (Qty: 5). **Ad Acc. Circ:** 25,000 (ctrl). ***Continues*** *Animation News.*
**Desc:** Industry and trade magazine for the animation industry. Covers all areas of animation.

US/1042-539X
**ANIMATO! (CAMBRIDGE, MASS.).** (ANIMATO!.). [Animato]. (1983)-. Periodical. English. Four times a year (Jan., Mar., June, Oct.). $14.00. Animato, 17 Spruce Street, Springfield MA 01105. **Tel** (413)731-7928. **ED** G. Michael Dobbs. **DD** 741. **Bk Rev**, (Qty: 5-10). **Ad Acc. Circ:** 4,500.

UK/0964-5586
**ANIMATOR ST. ALBANS.** (ANIMATOR.). [Animator St. Albans]. (1984)-. Periodical. English. an. £8.00 UK. Filmcraft, 13 Ringway Road, Park Street, St Albans Herts AL2 2RE England. **Tel** 011 44 727 72607. **ED** David Jefferson. **Bk Rev. Ad Acc. Circ:** 1,500. ***Continues*** *Animator's Newsletter.*
**Desc:** A guide to professional, student and hobby animation. Looks at how it is done, who is doing it and what they are doing. Includes reports on animation festivals and new equipment.

US/1069-2088
**ANIMATRIX (LOS ANGELES, CALIF.).** (ANIMATRIX : A JOURNAL OF THE UCLA ANIMATION WORKSHOP.). [Animatrix]. **Added/Corp** UCLA Animation Workshop. Vol. 1, No. 1 (Dec. 1984)-. English. an. $7.50. Animatrix, UCLA, Department of Theater Film and TV, Los Angeles CA 90024. **Tel** (310)825-5829. **DD** 791.
**Ind/Abst** Film Lit. Index (19??-).

CN/0849-5726
**ANNUAIRE DU CINEMA QUEBECOIS.** [Annu. cine. que.]. (1988)-. French. an (current year edition published in August of the following year). 20.00Can$. La Cinematheque Quebecoise, 335 Boulevard de Maisonneuve Est, Montreal Quebec H2X 1K1 Canada. **Tel** (514)842-9763, FAX (514)866-4688. **DD** 016.79143/09714. **Bk Rev. Ad Acc.**

US/0163-5123
**ANNUAL INDEX TO MOTION PICTURE CREDITS.** (1978)-. English. an. $68.00 North America; $77.00 other. Academy of Motion Picture Arts and Sciences, 8949 Wilshire Boulevard, Beverly Hills CA 90211-1972. **Tel** (310)247-3000, FAX (310)859-9619, telex 698-614. **ED** Byerly Woodward. **LC** PN1993; .A48A. **DD** 791.43/05. **UDC** 791.43. **Circ:** 400. ***Continues*** *Screen Achievement Records Bulletin, 0147-2313.*
**Desc:** Indexes film credits: alphabetically by title with production data and credits, by major crafts, by distributor, finally, by persons listed alphabetically with credits. Includes ongoing cumulative listing of film titles and dates since 1976.

CN/0837-2446
**ANNUAL REPORT / TELEFILM CANADA.** [Annu. rep. - Telefilm Can.]. **Main/Corp** Telefilm Canada. **VFOAT** Rapport Annuel. (1983/84)-. English (French). Canadian Film Development Corporation, 800 Place Victoria, Montreal Quebec Canada. **DD** 354.710085/4. ***Continues*** *Annual Report / Canadian Film Development Corporation, 0382-2273.*

US
**ANNUAL REPORT / TENNESSEE FILM, TAPE, AND MUSIC COMMISSION. Main/Corp** Tennessee. Film, Tape, and Music Commission. (Sept. 1980-Dec. 1981)-. English. an. Tennessee Film Tape and Music Commission, James K Polk Building/16th Floor, Nashville TN 37219. **LC** PN1993.5.U778; T46a. **DD** 353.97680085/4.

AG
**ANUARIO DEL CINE.** 1977-. Spanish. an. Ediciones Corregidor, Corriente 1585, Buenos Aires C 1042 Argentina. **LC** PN1993; .C37. **DD** 791.43/05. **UDC** 791.43(058).

CK
**ARCADIA VA AL CINE.** Vol. 1, No. 1 (March/April 1982)-. Periodical. Spanish. bm. Augusto Bernal y Co, Transversal 14 No 117 65, Bogota 10 Colombia. **ED** E Acevedo, G Bello and A Bernal. **UDC** 791.43.

FR/0985-2395
**ARCHIVES PERPIGNAN.** (ARCHIVES.). [Archives Perpignan]. (1986)-. Periodical. French. bm. Institut Jean Vigo, 21 rue Mailly, 66000 Perpignan France. **Tel** 011 33 68 663000, 663033. **UDC** 791.43.
**Ind/Abst** Film Lit. Index (19??-).

US
**ART MURPHY'S ... BOXOFFICE REGISTER. VFOAT** Art Murphy's Box Office Register. (198?)-. English. an. $70.00 US & Canada; $80.00 other. Art Murphy's Boxoffice Register, PO Box 14832, San Luis Obispo CA 93406. **Tel** (805)543-6515, FAX (805)543-3567. **ED** Art Murphy. **LC** PN1993; .A74. **DD** 384/.83/05.
**Desc:** Provides information on domestic theatrical film boxoffice grosses.

AU/0391-9064
**ARTIBUS ET HISTORIAE.** [Artibus hist.]. **Added/Corp** IRSA (Organization). No. 1 (1980)-. Periodical. English (French, German and Italian). sa. $139.00. IRSA Verlag GES MBH, Ruedengasse 6, A 1030 Vienna Austria. **Tel** 011-43-222-7130136, FAX 011-43-222-7130130, telex 5704661. **ED** Jozef Grabski, 0222-713-01-36 (phone). **LC** NX1.A1; A77. **DD** 705. **Ad Acc. Circ:** 1,000.
**Desc:** Articles on topics in art history by international scholars; coverage of the current trends in the field.
**Ind/Abst** Am. Hist. Life (1989-); ARTbibliogr. Mod. (1985-); Avery Index Archit. Period. Suppl. Colum. Univ. (19??-199?); BHA : Biblio. Hist. Art.

US
**ARTSAMERICA FINE ART FILM & VIDEO SOURCE BOOK.** ***Ceased.*** **VFOAT** Arts America Fine Art Film & Video Source Book. (1987)-(1987). English. an. Artsamerica Inc, 12 Havemeyer Place, Greenwich CT 06830. **Tel** (203)869-4693. **ED** Dorothy Tucker and Bronwyn Runne. **LC** N369.A74; A78. **DD** 016.7. **UDC** 791.43(036)(73). Index available. ctrl circ.
**Desc:** A reference book which lists over 750 films and video tapes about the visual arts. Indexed by artist, title and distributer, it describes subject matter, awards, format and how to rent or buy.

FR/0986-1351
**AS. ACTUALITE DE LA SCENOGRAPHIE.** (AS.). [AS Actual. scenographie]. **VFOAT** Actualite de la Scenographie (Bruxelles); Actualite de la Scenographie (Paris). (1977)-. Periodical. French. Five times a year. 342.80F France; 425.00F other. Les Editions AS, 58 rue Servan, 75011 Paris France. **Tel** 011 33 1 47001952. **UDC** 792.

US/1059-440X
**ASIAN CINEMA.** (ASIAN CINEMA : A PUBLICATION OF THE ASIAN CINEMA STUDIES SOCIETY.). [Asian cine.]. **Added/Corp** Asian Cinema Studies Society. Vol. 3, No. 2 (1988)-. Newsletter. English. sa. comes with membership. Asian Cinema Studies Society, Brooklyn College Film Department, Brooklyn NY 11210. **Tel** (518)672-7275. **LC** PN1993.5.A75; N4. **DD** 778. ***Continues*** *Newsletter (Asian Cinema Studies Society).*
**Ind/Abst** Film Lit. Index (19??-).

CN/0828-7511
**ASIFA. ASSOCIATION INTERNATIONALE DU FILM D'ANIMATION, CANADA.** (ASIFA : BULLETIN DE L'ASSOCIATION INTERNATIONALE DU FILM

D'ANIMATION, CANADA.). [ASIFA, Assoc. int. film anim. Can.]. **VAT** Association Internationale du Film d'Animation, Canada. Bulletin. French (English). Three times a year. Free to members. ASIFA-Canada, Bureau 3/10707 rue Grande-Allee, Montreal Quebec H3L 2M8 Canada. **Tel** (514)842-9763. **DD** 778.5/347. **UDC** 788.534.6. **Circ:** 300 (ctrl).

IT
**ATTUALITA CINEMATOGRAFICHE.** (1963)-. Italian. an. L38000. Letture, Piazza San Fedele 4, 20121 Milan Italy. **Tel** 011 39 2 722711, FAX 011 39 2 72023481. **LC** PN1993.3; .A87. Index available. cum. index. **Ad Acc. Circ:** 1,500 (ctrl).
**Desc:** Collection of reviews of the principal films of the year which have been previously published in the journal "Letture".

IT/0004-7627
**AUDIOVISIVI.** ***Suspended.*** (19??)-(19??). Italian. Five times a year. Audiovisivi e Periodici Srl, Via Taranto 21, 00182 Rome Italy. **Tel** 011 39 763 86290.

●AT/1035-8005
**AUSTRALIAN AND NEW ZEALAND CATALOGUE OF NEW FILMS AND VIDEOS, THE.** (1991)-. English. an (Sept.). 60.00Aus$ Australia; 75.00Aus$ other. Australian Catalogue, PO Box 204, Albert Park Victoria 3206 Australia. **Tel** 011 61 3 5255302, FAX 011 61 3 5372325. **ED** Peter Tapp. **Ad Acc.** available on CD-ROM. ***Continues*** *The Australian Catalogue of New Films and Videos, 1033-7741.*
**Desc:** Listing of new films and videos available in Australia.

AT/1031-5462
**AUSTRALIAN FILM DATA. Added/Corp** Australian Film Commission. (July 1988)-. English. an. Australian Film Commission, Canberra ACT Australia.

AT/0045-0448
**AUSTRALIAN FILMS.** ***Ceased.*** (1959)-?. Periodical. English. an. National Film Sound Archives, McCoy Circuit, Action Australian Capital Territory Australia. **Tel** (062)671711, FAX (062)474651, telex AA61930. **LC** PN1998. **UDC** 791.43(94). Index available. **Circ:** 1,000.
**Desc:** Lists more than 600 feature, documentary, experimental and animated films, and significant television programs produced in Australia or of Australian association produced overseas and released during the year of given volume; comprehensive index included.

FR/0045-1150
**AVANT-SCENE DU CINEMA, L'.** [Avant-scene. Cine.]. **VFOAT** Cinema, l'Avant-Scene. No. 1, (Feb. 15, 1961)-. Periodical. French. Eleven times a year. 570.03F France; 726.00F other. L'Avant Scene, 6 rue Git le Couer, 75006 Paris France. **Tel** 011 33 1 46342820, FAX 011 33 1 43545014. **LC** PN1993; .A93. cum. index. **Bk Rev. Ad Acc.**
**Desc:** Covers French scripts and photos, critics, etc.
**Ind/Abst** Film Lit. Index; Point Repere (1983-).

NE/0923-7054
**AVPROF AMSTERDAM. See** Sound Recordings and Systems.

US/0005-3635
**BACK STAGE.** [Back stage]. (Dec. 1960)-. Periodical. English. wk. $450.00 (airmail) Korea. Back Stage Publications Inc, 330 West 42nd Street, New York NY 10036. **Tel** (212)947-0020. **ED** Steve Elish. **Bk Rev. Ad Acc.** ctrl circ. available on microfilm and microfiche from University Microfilms International (UMI); available on an online database (file 648/Full-Text) from DIALOG. ***Continued in part by*** *Back Stage Shoot, 1055-9825.*
**Ind/Abst** Bus. ASAP (1990-) [Full Txt.]; Bus. Index (1985-); Gen. BusinessFile (1985-); Gen. Period. Index (1985-); Mag. Search; Trade Ind. ASAP [Full Txt.]; Trade Ind. Index [Full Txt.]; Vocat. Search (July 1993-).

UK
**BBC CHARTER REVIEW SERIES, THE.** (19??)-. Monographic series. English. ir. £6.50 each. British Film Institute, 21 Stephen Street, London W1P 1PL England. **Tel** 11 44 71 2551444, FAX 11 44 71 4367950, telex 27624 BFILDNG.
**Desc:** Presents analyses from the key program-makers, academics, business people and political thinkers in the debate about the future of the BBC in an increasingly competitive and fast-moving broadcasting environment.

UK
**BBC VIDEO WORLD. VIDEORECORDING.** English. bw. BBC Video World, 39-40 Skylines Limeharbor, London E14 9TS England. **Tel** (800)247-8979.

GW
**BEITRAGE ZUR FILM- UND FERNSEHWISSENSCHAFT : SCHRIFTENREIHE DER HOCHSCHULE FUR FILM UND FERNSEHEN DER DDR.** **VFOAT** Schriftenreihe der Hochschule fur Film und Fernsehen der DDR. 82/1-. Periodical. German. bm. Hochschule fuer Film und Fernsehen der DDR, Dokumentation/Publikation, 1502 Potsdam-Babelsberg, Rosa Luxemburg Str 24 Berlin Germany. **LC** PN1993; .F665. **DD** 791.43/05. ***Continues*** *Filmwissenschaftliche Beitrage.*

UK
**BFI FILM AND TELEVISION HANDBOOK. Added/Corp** British Film Institute. **VFOAT** Film and Television Handbook; British Film Institute Film and Television Handbook. (1993)-. Periodical. English. an. $28.95. British Film Institute, 21 Stephen Street, London W1P 1PL England. **Tel** 11 44 71 2551444, FAX 11 44 71 4367950, telex 27624 BFILDNG. **LC** PN1993.3; .F418. **DD** 384/.8/02541. ***Continues*** *Film and Television Handbook, 0956-8409.*

US/1056-6104
**BIB TELEVISION PROGRAMMING SOURCE BOOKS. See** Communication-Broadcasting.

US/0744-723X
**BIG REEL, THE.** (1974)-. Periodical. English. mo. $25.00 US, $35.00 other. Empire Publishing Inc, Route 3 Box 83, Madison NC 27025. **Tel** (919)427-5850, FAX (919)427-7372. **ED** Carol Wood (editor's address: PO Box 4333, Charlottesville, VA 22905). Index available. **Bk Rev**, (Qty: 6). **Ad Acc. Circ:** 7,000.
**Desc:** Monthly tabloid for persons that collect, buy, trade and sell movie memorabilia from the hobby aspect.

GW/0006-2383
**BILD UND TON (BERLIN, DDR).** ***Ceased.*** (BILD UND TON.). [Bild Ton]. (1948)-(19??). Periodical. English. mo. Deutscher Judo Verband, Redaktion Ippon Segewaldweg 40, D 12557 Berlin Germany. **Tel** 011 49 711 210770, telex 051 678. **LC** TR845; .B5. Documents available from Ask*IEEE.
**Ind/Abst** INSPEC (Sept. 1988-).

US
**BILLBOARD'S MUSIC & VIDEO YEARBOOK. See** Music-Abstracting, Bibliographies and Statistics.

US
**BLACK CAMERA : THE NEWSLETTER OF THE BLACK FILM CENTER / ARCHIVES. Added/Corp** Indiana University, Bloomington. Dept. of Afro-American Studies. Indiana University, Bloomington. Black Film Center / Archives. Vol. 1, No. 1 (Summer 1985)-. Periodical. English. Twice a year. Free on request. Indiana University / Department of Afro-American Studies, Memorial Hall E. #32, Bloomington IN 47405. **Tel** (812)855-6041.

UK
**BLACK FILM BULLETIN.** (19??)-. English. qt. £10.00 UK; £12.50 other. British Film Institute, 21 Stephen Street, London W1P 1PL England. **Tel** 11 44 71 2551444, FAX 11 44 71 4367950, telex 27624 BFILDNG.
**Desc:** Provides a forum for the exchange of news and information and a noticeboard for the work of Asian-Caribbean and Asian cinemas locally and internationally.

US/0887-5723
**BLACK FILM REVIEW.** [Black film rev.]. **Added/Corp** Sojourner Productions, Inc. University of the District of Columbia. Black Film Institute. **VFOAT** BFR. No. 1 (1985)-. Periodical. English. Four times a year (Seasonally). $12.00 (individuals), $24.00 (institutions). Black Film Review, 2025 I Street Northwest, Suite 213, Washington DC 20006. **Tel** (202)466-2753. **ED** David Nicholson. **LC** PN1995.9.N4; B48. **DD** 791.43/09/093520396073. **Bk Rev. Ad Acc. Circ:** 5,000.
**Desc:** Film reviews, interviews with black independent and Hollywood film makers, news, and critiques.
**Ind/Abst** Acad. Abstr. (Jan. 1992-); Acad. Search (Jan. 1992-); Film Lit. Index; Mag. Artic. Summar. Elite (Jan. 1994-); Mag. Artic. Summar. CD-ROM (Jan. 1992-).

US/0882-7532
**BLACK VIDEO GUIDE, THE.** [Black video guide]. **Added/Corp** Video Publications Ltd. (Saint Louis, Mo.). **VFOAT** BVG; B V G. (1985/86)-. English. sa. $20.00. Video Publication Limited, PO Box 78335, St Louis MO 63178. **Tel** (314)534-8555. **ED** William Dorsey. **LC** PN1995.9.N4; B52. **DD** 016.79143/09/093520396073; 791. **Ad Acc. Circ:** 100,000.
**Desc:** Home reference directory to blacks appearing in films that are available on video, whether informational, educational, or entertainment, since the year 1900.

AU
**BLIMP.** (1985)-. Periodical. German (summaries and/or abstracts in English). Four times a year (Mar., July, Oct., Dec.). $39.00. Blimp Film Magazine, Muchargasse 12/III/10, 8010 Graz, Austria. **Tel** 011 43 316 679950, FAX 011 43 316 679960. **ED** Bogdan Grbic, Susanne Rieser, and Reinhard Puntigam. **LC** PN1993; .B53. **DD** 791.43/05. Index available. **Bk Rev. Ad Acc. Circ:** 5,000.
**Desc:** Features articles by critics, practitioners and theoreticians from a wide range of professional backgrounds. Our main guideline is to discuss film, video and media art as forms of cultural practices relevant for academic and nonacademic audiences.
**Ind/Abst** Film Lit. Index (19??).

US
**BLU-BOOK ... DIRECTORY. VFOAT** Bluebook ... Directory; Hollywood Reporter ... Bluebook Directory; Hollywood Reporter ... Blu-Book Directory. **VAT** Blu Book ... Directory. (1989)-. English. an. $59.50 US; $75.00 other. Hollywood Reporter, 5055 Wilshire Boulevard, 6th Floor, Los Angeles CA 90036. **Tel** (213)525-2000. **LC** PN1998.A1; H6. ***Continues*** *Hollywood Reporter Studio Blu-Book ... Directory, 0278-419X.*

BL
**BOLETIM INFORMATIVO SIP. Main/Corp** Instituto Nacional do Cinema. Setor do Ingresso Padronizado. **Added/Corp** Instituto do Cinema. Setor do Ingresso Padronizado. Informativo SIP. **VFOAT** Informativo SIP. **VAT** Boletim Informativo Setor do Ingresso Padronizado. (19??)-. Bulletin. Portuguese. Instituto Nacional do Cinema, rua Mayrink Veiga 28-70 Andar, Rio de Janeiro Brazil. **LC** PN1993.5.B6; I58a.

US/0006-8527
**BOXOFFICE.** [Boxoffice]. **VAT** Box Office. Periodical. English. mo. $40.00 (surface mail), $45.00 (airmail) Canada and Mexico; $60.00 other. Boxoffice, 1800 North Highland Avenue/Suite 710, Hollywood CA 90028. **Tel** (310)465-1186, FAX (213)465-5049. **(Subscription address:** Boxoffice Data Center, 1020 South Wabash, Chicago, IL 60605**) ED** Harley W Lond. **LC** PN1993; .B6. **DD** 791. **Bk Rev. Ad Acc. Circ:** 9,500. available on an online database. ***Absorbed*** *Boxoffice.*
**Desc:** Covers the motion picture industry.
**Ind/Abst** Film Lit. Index; Infobank (1979-); Mark. Advert. Ref. Serv.

GW/0406-9595
**BRAVO MUNCHEN.** [Bravo Munchen]. (1956)-. Periodical. German. wk (52 issues). $120.00 US. Heinrich Bauer Verlag, Burchardstr 11, D-20095 Hamburg Germany. **Tel** 011 49 40 30190. **(Subscription address:** US/ German Language Publ. Inc., 153 South Deanstreet, Englewood, NJ 07631; telephone: (201)871-1010**) UDC** 379.8.

US/0193-2314
**BROOKS' STANDARD RATE BOOK, THE. See** Economics-Labor.

BU/0204-8884
**BULGARIAN FILMS.** ***Ceased.*** [Bulg. film]. **Added/Corp** Razprostranenie na Filmi, DP (Bulgaria) Filmbulgare. (1960)-(19??). Periodical. English. Eight times a year. **(Subscription address:** Hemus Foreign Trade Organization, 14 Benkovsky Street, 1000 Sofia Bulgaria**) DD** 791. **Ad Acc.**
**Desc:** Reviews, interviews, news and stills from current Bulgarian films.
**Ind/Abst** Film Lit. Index.

IO/0216-3411
**BULLETIN KFT : MEDIA KARYAWAN FILM DAN TELEVISI INDONESIA. See** Communication-Broadcasting.

UK
**BUSINESS OF FILM, THE.** (1980)-. Trade Publication. English. mo. $200.00 US and Canada; £100.00 UK and Europe; £155.00 other. Business of Film, 24 Charlotte Street, London W1P 1HJ England. **Tel** 010 71 580 0141, FAX 010 71 255 1264. **ED** Michael Goodridge. **Ad Acc, Adv Mgr:** E. Tavares, **Tel** 0101 310 657 2336. **Circ:** 6,000.
**Desc:** International business publication for the film and television industries; covering finance, production, distribution, and marketing worldwide.

FR/0764-8499
**CAHIERS DE LA CINEMATHEQUE, LES.** [Cah. cinematheque]. No. 1-. French. Four times a year. $21.95. Les Cahiers de la Cinematheque, 21 rue Mailly, 66000 Perpignan France. cum. index. **Bk Rev. Ad Acc.** ctrl circ.
**Ind/Abst** Film Lit. Index.

FR/0008-011X
**CAHIERS DU CINEMA.** [Cah. cine.]. No. 1 (Apr. 1951)-. French. mo. 333.01F France; 440.00F other. Dawson France SA, BP 40, 91121 Palaiseau Cedex France. **Tel** 011 33 1 69104700, telex 220064F. **ED** Serge Touviana. **LC** PN1993; .C25. **DD** 791.43/05. Index available. cum. index. **Bk Rev. Ad Acc. Circ:** 40,000 (ctrl). Documents available from The Genuine Article.
**Ind/Abst** Art Index; Arts Humanit. Citation Index (19??-19??) [Full Cov.]; Curr. Contents Arts Humanit.; Film Lit. Index; Point Repere; Res. Alert [Full Cov.].

BE/0775-9479
**CAHIERS DU SCENARIO BRUXELLES, LES.** (1986)-. French. Institut de Sociologie de l'Universite Libre de Bruxelles, Avenue Jeanne 44, 1050 Brussels Belgium. **Tel** 011 32 2 6503359, 011 32 2 6503457, FAX 011 32 2 6503521, telex UNILIB 23069 B.
**Ind/Abst** Film Lit. Index (19??-).

US
**CALL SHEET / SCREEN ACTORS GUILD.** **Added/Corp** Screen Actors Guild. **VFOAT** Screen Actors Guild Call Sheet; Screen Actors Guild Hollywood Call Sheet. (199?)-. Periodical. English. qt. Screen Actors Guild, 7065 Hollywood Boulevard, Hollywood CA 90028. **Tel** (213)465-4600. **ED** Mark Locher. cum. index. **Bk Rev**. **Circ:** 75,000 (ctrl). ***Continues*** *Screen Actor Hollywood, 0890-5266.*
**Desc:** Covers craft and conditions of professional motion picture performing arts, including film, TV and commercials.
**Ind/Abst** Film Lit. Index.

US/0270-5346
**CAMERA OBSCURA (BERKELEY).** (CAMERA OBSCURA.). [Camera obscura]. No. 1 (Fall 1976)-. Periodical. English. Three times a year (January, May, September). $45.00. Indiana University Press, 601 North Morton Street, Bloomington IN 47404. **Tel** (812)855-3830, (800)842-6796. **ED** Janet Bergstrom, Constance Penley and Elisabeth Lyon. **LC** PN1995.9.W6; C28. **DD** 791.43/088042. **Bk Rev**. **Ad Acc**. **Circ:** 3,000 (ctrl). available on microfilm and microfiche from University Microfilms International (UMI). Documents available from The Genuine Article.
**Desc:** Focuses on feminism and film theory; perspectives on the national and international film scene. The thematic issues appeal to scholars, feminists, critics, filmmakers, and artists and cover topics ranging from the avant-garde in filmmaking to popular culture and the mass media.
**Ind/Abst** Altern. Press Index; ARTbibliogr. Mod.; Arts Humanit. Citation Index (19??-19??) [Full Cov.]; Curr. Contents Arts Humanit.; Film Lit. Index; Int. Index Film Period.; MLA Int. Bibl. Books Artic. Mod. Lang. Lit.; Res. Alert [Full Cov.]; Soc. Sci. Cit. Index [Select. Cov.]; Stud. Women Abstr.

FR/0248-8868
**CAMERA STYLO.** (1981)-. French. Camera Stylo, 18 Rue des Fosses-Saint-Jacques, 75005 Paris, France.
**Ind/Abst** Film Lit. Index (19??-).

CN/0315-2715
**CANADIAN FILM-MAKERS DISTRIBUTION CENTRE CATALOGUE.** (CATALOGUE - CANADIAN FILM-MAKERS DISTRIBUTION CENTRE.). **Main/Corp** Canadian Film-Makers Distribution Centre. 1972-. English (French). an. Free. Canadian Filmmakers' Distribution Center, Suite 430, 144 Front Street West, Toronto Ontario M5J 1G2. **DD** 011.

AT/0158-4154
**CANTRILL'S FILMNOTES.** **VFOAT** Filmnotes. No. 1 (March 1971)-. Periodical. English. Four times a year. 25.00Aus$ Australia; 26.00Aus$ New Zealand, Papua, New Guinea; 33.00Aus$ other. Arthur and Corinne Cantrill, PO Box 1295, L GPO, Melbourne Victoria, 3001 Australia. **Tel** 11 61 3 3806416, FAX 011 66 3 3806416. **ED** Arthur and Corinne Cantrill. **LC** PN1993; .C333. **DD** 791.43/05. Index available. cum. index. **Bk Rev**, (Qty: 20). **Circ:** 1,000 (ctrl).
**Ind/Abst** Film Lit. Index.

IT
**CASTORO CINEMA, IL.** ***Ceased.*** (1974)-(19??). Periodical. Italian. bm. La Nuova Italia Editrice Spa, Via Ernesto Codignola, 50018 Scandicci Florence Italy. **Tel** 011 39 55 75901, FAX 011 39 55 7590208. **ED** Fernaldo Di Giammatteo.
**Ind/Abst** Film Lit. Index (19??-).

US
**CATALOG OF BRITANNICA FILMS.** **Main/Corp** Encyclopaedia Britannica Educational Corporation. Catalog. English. Britannica Home Library Service, 310 South Michigan Avenue, Chicago IL 60604. **Tel** (800)323-1229. **LC** LB1044.Z9; E48A. **DD** 011.

US
**CATALOG OF CAPTIONED FILMS/VIDEOS FOR THE DEAF.** **See** Physically Impaired.

US/0163-7320
**CATALOG OF COPYRIGHT ENTRIES, FOURTH SERIES. PART 4, MOTION PICTURES & FILMSTRIPS MICROFORM.** **Main/Corp** Library of Congress. Copyright Office. **Added/Corp** Library of Congress. Copyright Office. Motion Pictures & Filmstrips. **VFOAT** Motion Pictures & Filmstrips; Motion Pictures and Filmstrips. Vol. 2, No. 1 (Jan./June 1979)-. Catalog. English. sa. $5.00 domestic; $6.25 other. Superintendent of Documents, US Government Printing Office, Washington DC 20402. **Tel** (202)275-3328, FAX (202)786-2377. **LC** Microfiche (o) 93/6008; PN1998; Z663.8. **DD** 011/.37. ***Continues*** *Catalog of Copyright Entries, Fourth Series. Part 4, Motion Pictures & Filmstrips. Paper, 0163-7320.*
**Desc:** Lists the material registered during the period covered by each issue-Motion Pictures.

FR/0224-7518
**CATALOGUE DE LA PRODUCTION CINEMATOGRAPHIQUE FRANCAISE.** 1975-. French. an. Centre National de la Cinematographie, Services des Archives du Film, 78390 Bois D'Arcy France. **Tel** 34.60.20.50, FAX 34.60.52.25. **LC** PN1998; .C332. **DD** 016.79143/75/0944. Index available. **Bk Rev**.

CN
**CATALOGUE DES DOCUMENTS AUDIOVISUELS.** **Main/Corp** Quebec (Province). Cinematheque. French. Ministere des Communications, PO Box 1005, Quebec Quebec G1K 7B5 Canada. **Tel** (418)643-5150. **LC** PN1998; .Q417A. **DD** 016.79143.

CN/0826-2861
**CATALOGUE - FUNNEL.** (CATALOGUE - FUNNEL EXPERIMENTAL FILM THEATRE.). [Cat. - Funnel]. **Main/Corp** Funnel Experimental Film Theatre. 1984-. English. an. $3.00. Funnel, 507 King Street East, Toronto Ontario M5A 1M3 Canada. **Tel** (416)364-7003. **DD** 018/.137. **Bk Rev**. **Ad Acc**. **Circ:** 2,000 (ctrl).

AT
**CATALOGUE OF 16 MM. FILMS.** **Main/Corp** National Library of Australia. **Added/Corp** National Library of Australia Film Catalogue. **VFOAT** Film Catalogue. (19??)-. English. National Library of Australia, Parkes Place, Canberra ACT, 2600 Australia. **Tel** 011 61 6 2621374, FAX 011 61 6 2731084. **LC** PN1998.A1; C33. **DD** 371.335230838.

PO/0008-8781
**CELULOIDE.** [Celuloide]. (1958)-. Periodical. Portuguese. mo.
**Ind/Abst** Film Lit. Index.

II
**CFS REVIEW, THE.** **VFOAT** C.F.S. Review. English. an. Chennai Film Society, 6 Madley Road, Madras-17 India. **LC** PN1993.5.I8; C42. **DD** 791.43/0954.

SW/0045-6349
**CHAPLIN.** (CHAPLIN.). [Chaplin]. **Added/Corp** Svenska Filminstitutet. (April 1959)-. Periodical. Swedish. Six times a year (Feb., Apr., June, Sept., Oct. Dec.). Kr225.00 Scandinavia; Kr300.00 Europe; Kr360.00 other. Svenska Filminstitutet, Box 27126, S 102 52 Stockholm Sweden. **Tel** 011 46 8 6651203, FAX 011 46 8 6638009, telex 23326 Filmins S. Index available. **Bk Rev**. **Ad Acc**. **Circ:** 5,400 (ctrl).
**Ind/Abst** Film Lit. Index.

CH
**CHIA HO TIEN YING.** **VFOAT** Golden Movie News. Periodical. Chinese. $32.00. SSU Hai Chu Pan Shih Yeh Yu Hsien King SSU, 122B Argyle Street 1/F, Chiu-Lung China. **LC** PN1993; .C44.

US
**CHICAGO PRODUCTION BIBLE.** English. Forty-eight times a year. $70.00 (one year), $112.00 (two years), $126.00 (three years), $30.00 (25 issues) new subscribers only. Screen Enterprises Inc, 720 North Wabash Avenue/7th Floor, Chicago IL 60611. **Tel** (312)664-5236, FAX (312)664-8425. **ED** Ruth Ratny - Phone: (312)664-5236. Index available ($70.00 per year). **Ad Acc, Adv Mgr:** Maureen Cany, **Tel** (312)664-5236. **Circ:** 7,500. ***Continues*** *Chicago Video Resource.*
**Desc:** Information on the production of television commercials, business TV, multi-image and sales meetings, documentaries and non-profit projects; feature films and television shows, station production, such as talent casting, sound recording, music scoring, editing, equipment rentals, duplication distribution.

US/0883-6922
**CHILDREN'S VIDEO REPORT.** **See** Children and Youth Interests.

US/0895-2094
**CHILDREN'S VIDEO REVIEW NEWSLETTER.** [Child. video rev. newsl.]. **VFOAT** Children's Video Review; CVR. Vol. 1, No. 1 (Apr./May 1987)-. Newsletter. English. Six times a year. $36.00 US; $39.00 (includes postage) Canada; $39.60 (includes postage) other. Children's Video Review Newsletter, 16765 Lena Court, Grass Valley CA 95949. **Tel** (916)273-7471, FAX (916)273-6542. **ED** Eveline Carsman. **DD** 791. cum. index. ctrl circ.
**Desc:** Reviews of 15-20 newly released videocassettes for pre-school to middle-school children. Videos are selected for educational, literary and recreational use. Videos comply with public and school library standards.

II
**CHITRABIKSHAN.** **Added/Corp** Cine Central. Vol. 1 (1975)-. English (English). $4.00. **LC** PN1993; .C47. **DD** 791.43/05.

CC/0577-893X
**CHUNG-JUO YIN MU.** ***Ceased.*** (CHINA'S SCREEN.). [China's screen]. **VFOAT** China Screen; Chung-kuo Yin Mu. (196?)-Issue 4 (1994). Periodical. English. qt. **(Subscription address:** China International Book Trading Corporation, PO Box 399, Library Service Department, Beijing 100044 People's Republic of China.**)** **LC** PN1993.5.C4; C45. **DD** 791.43/0951/05.
**Ind/Abst** Film Lit. Index.

CC
**CHUNG-KUO TIEN YING NIEN CHIEN / CHUNG-KUO TIEN YING CHIA HSIEH HUI PIEN TSUAN.** 1981-. Chinese. an. RMBY20,000.00. Hsin Hua Shu Tien, Beijing, People's Republic of China. **Tel** 551253. **ED** Gao Zhen-he and Cao Hong-xiang. **LC** PN1993.5.C4; .C537. **DD** 791.43/0951. **Ad Acc**. **Circ:** 50,000.
**Desc:** Publishes discussions on Chinese and foreign films with articles on movie production and script writing.

IT
**CIAK SI GIRA.** Vol. 1, No. 1 (May 1985)-. Periodical. Italian (Italian). mo. L64800 Italy; L108600. Arnoldo Mondadori Editore, UFF Cont Abbonamenti, 20090 Segrate MI Italy. **Tel** 011 39 2 75422015, telex 320457 MONDMI I.

GW
**CICIM : REVUE POUR LE CINEMA FRANCAISE.** French. Institut Francaise de Munich, Centre d'Information Cinematographique, Kaulbachstr. 13, 8000 Munchen 22 Germany.
**Ind/Abst** Film Lit. Index (19??-).

IT
**CIEMME.** Italian. qt. L24000 Italy; L30000 other. Cinit Cineforum Italiano, Casella Post 289, 30170 Venice Mestre Italy. **Tel** 011 39 41 988745.

VE/0009-692X
**CINE AL DIA.** [Cine dia]. **Added/Corp** Sociedad Civil Cine al Dia. (19??)-. Periodical. Spanish. Four times a year. Cine Al Dia, Apartado 50446, Sabana Grande, Caracas Venezuela.
**Ind/Abst** Film Lit. Index (1975-1979).

AG
**CINE ARGENTINO.** Spanish. an. Ediciones Corregidor, Corriente 1585, Buenos Aires C 1042 Argentina. **LC** PN1993.5.A7; A24. **DD** 791.43/0982.

CN/0820-8921
**CINE BULLES.** [Cine bulles]. **Added/Corp** Association des Cinemas Paralleles du Quebec. (1982)-. Periodical. French. Four times a year (Mar., June, Sept., Dec.). 12.00Can$ Canada; $15.00 others. Association des Cinemas Paralleles du Quebec, 4545 Pierre de Coubertin CP 1000 Succursale M, Montreal Quebec H1V 3R2 Canada. **Tel** (514)252-3021, FAX (514)251-8038, telex 95-829647. **DD** 791.43/09714. **Bk Rev**, (Qty: 20). **Ad Acc, Adv Mgr:** Martine Mauroy. **Circ:** 1,500 (ctrl). available on CD-ROM. ***Continues*** *Bulletin d'Information de l'A.C.P.Q.*
**Desc:** Quebec and international cinema, documentary, film and book critics.
**Ind/Abst** Film Lit. Index (19??-); Point Repere.

CU/0009-6946
**CINE CUBANO.** ***Suspended.*** [Cine cub.]. (July 1960)-?. Periodical. Spanish. mo. $12.79 North America; $14.91 South America; $21.30 other. Ediciones Cubanas, Obispo 527, Altos ESQ Bernaza, CP 10100 Havana Cuba. **Tel** 011 632980, 631942, FAX 011 631011, telex 512337, 6540. **Bk Rev**. **Ad Acc**. **Circ:** 20,000.
**Desc:** Theoretical and informational organ of Cuban film, reflecting its ideological and aesthetic position as part of the new Latin American cinema; includes interviews, features and articles by outstanding Cuban and other Latin American film makers and commentaries on the movies produced in the world.
**Ind/Abst** Film Lit. Index.

BE/0773-2279
**CINE-FICHES DE GRAND ANGLE, LES.** (1984)-. Periodical. French. Eleven times a year. 900F Belgium; 1300F other. Grand Angle, Rue d'Arschot 29, 5660 Mariembourg Belgium. **Tel** 011 32 60 312168. **ED** Jacques Noel. Index available. cum. index. **Bk Rev**. **Ad Acc**. **Circ:** 3,500.
**Desc:** Information about new films, festivals, books, and records pertaining to the cinema.
**Ind/Abst** Film Lit. Index (19??-).

FR
**CINE TELE REVUE.** **VFOAT** Cine-Tele-Revue; Cine Revue. Vol. 64, No. 44 (Nov. 1, 1984)-. Periodical. French. wk. Cine Tele Revue, Ave Reine Marie Henriette 101, 1190 Brussels Belgium. **Tel** 02 345 99 68. ***Continues*** *Cine-Revue.*

SP
**CINE Y MAS.** Spanish. Cine y Mas, Ballester 54, 08023 Barcelona Spain. **Tel** 011 34 3 4176859.

CN/0826-9866
**CINEACTION!.** **VFOAT** Cine Action. No. 1 (Spring 1985)-. Periodical. English. qt. 35.00Can$ (one year), 60.00Can$ (two year) institutions Canada & US; 18.00Can$ (one year), 30.00Can$ (two year) individuals Canada & US; 50.00Can$ (one year), 90.00Can$ institutions other; 33.00Can$ (one year), 60.00Can$ (two year) individuals other. Cineaction!, 40 Alexander Street/#705, Toronto Ontario M4Y 1B5 Canada. **Tel** (416)964-3534. **LC** PN1993; .C55. **DD** 791.43/05. **[CCC]**. **Circ:** 2,.000.
**Desc:** Film journal dedicated to the publication of politically committed criticism and theory. Articles, which

draw on diverse areas of world cinema, from mainstream to alternative, reflect the various political positions (socialism, feminism, gay liberation) of the magazine's editors and contributors.
**Ind/Abst** Film Lit. Index.

US/0009-7004
**CINEASTE (NEW YORK, N.Y.).** (CINEASTE.). [Cineaste]. Vol. 1 (Summer 1967)-. Periodical. English. qt. $33.00 (institutions), $16.00 (individuals) US; $40.00 (institutions), $26.00 (individuals) other. Cineaste Publishers Inc., 200 Park Avenue South, Room 1601, New York NY 10003. **Tel** (212)982-1241. **ED** Gary Crowdus, Dan Georgakas, Karen Jaehne and Leonard Quart. **LC** PN1993; .C5177. **DD** 791. Index available. **Bk Rev**. **Ad Acc. Circ:** 6,000 (ctrl). available on microfilm and microfiche from University Microfilms International (UMI). Documents available from The Genuine Article, UMI Article Clearinghouse.
**Desc:** America's leading magazine on the art and politics of the cinema including Hollywood, American independent cinema, European films, and emerging cinemas of the third world.
**Ind/Abst** Altern. Press Index; Art Index; Arts Humanit. Citation Index [Full Cov.]; Curr. Contents Arts Humanit.; Expand. Acad. Index (1992-); Film Lit. Index; Left Index; Linguist. Lang. Behav. Abstr.; Mag. Artic. Summar. Elite (July 1994-); Med. Rev. Dig.; MLA Int. Bibl. Books Artic. Mod. Lang. Lit.; Newsp. Period. Abstr. (1992-); Res. Alert [Full Cov.]; Soc. Plann. Policy Dev. Abstr.; Soc. Sci. Cit. Index [Select. Cov.]; Sociol. Abstr.

IT
**CINECRITICA : PERIODICO DI CULTURA CINEMATOGRAFICA A CURA DEL SNCCI.** **Added/Corp** Sindicato Nazionale Critici Cinematografici Italiani. (1977)-. Periodical. Italian. Four times a year. L40000 Italy; L43000 other. Sindacato Nazionale Critici Cinematografici, Via di Monti Brianzo 91, 00186 Rome Italy. **Tel** 011 39 6 68802631.

AT/0813-1600
**CINEDOSSIER.** [Cinedossier]. **Added/Corp** Australian Film Institute. (1982)-. Periodical. English. Fifty times a year. 425.00Aus$ Australia; 450.00Aus$ others. Australian Film Institute, 49 Eastern Road, South Melbourne Victoria 3205 Australia. **Tel** 11 61 03 6961844, FAX 11 61 03 6967972. **ED** Carol Abbott. **DD** 384.80994. Index available. cum. index.

US/0095-1447
**CINEFAN.** No. 1- July 1974-. Periodical. English. ir. $3.50 each, $7.50 three issues. Fandom Unlimited Enterprises, 3378 Valley Forge Way, San Jose CA 95117. **Tel** (415)960-1151. **ED** Randall D Larson. **LC** PN1995.9.F36; C55. **DD** 791.43/0909/15. Index available. **Bk Rev**. **Circ:** 1,500 (ctrl).
**Desc:** In-depth analysis and review of fantasy, horror and science fiction films, emphasizing independent, obscure and international films.

US/0145-6032
**CINEFANTASTIQUE.** [Cinefantastique]. **VFOAT** Cinefantastique Magazine. (19??)-. Periodical. English. Six times a year (Feb., Apr., June, Aug., Oct., Dec.). $27.00 one year; $48.00 two years. Cinefantastique, PO Box 270, Oak Park IL 60303. **Tel** (708)366-5566. **ED** Frederick S. Clarke. **LC** PN1995.9.H6; C48. **DD** 791. Index available. **Ad Acc. Circ:** 30,000.
**Desc:** The review of science fiction, fantasy and horror films. Interviews with directors, producers, effects artists, in-depth articles and behind the scenes insights.
**Ind/Abst** Film Lit. Index; Med. Rev. Dig.

US/0198-1056
**CINEFEX.** [Cinefex]. No. 1 (March 1980)-. Periodical. English (French). qt. $24.00 (one year), $39.00 (two year), $56.00 (three year) US; $32.00 (one year), $56.00 (two year), $82.00 (three year) (surface mail), $40.00 (one year), $70.00 (two year), $100.00 (three year) (air mail) other. Cinefex, PO Box 20027, Riverside CA 92516. **Tel** (909)781-1917, FAX (909)686-6556. **ED** Don Shay. **LC** TR858; .C45. **DD** 778.5/345/05. **Bk Rev**. **Ad Acc. Circ:** 15,000 (ctrl).
**Desc:** Illustrated journal on motion picture special effects, including optical, physical, computer-generated and makeup.
**Ind/Abst** Film Lit. Index; Int. Index Film Period.

US/1059-0900
**CINEFOCUS.** [Cinefocus]. **Added/Corp** Indiana University, Bloomington. College of Arts and Sciences. Film Studies Division. **VFOAT** Cinefocus On .... Vol. 1, No. 1 (Jan. 1990)-. Periodical. English. an. $12.00 (institutions), $5.00 (individuals). Film Studies Division, Indiana University, BH 306, Bloomington IN 47405. **Tel** (812)773-1072. **ED** Katrina Byrd (editor's phone (812)855-7070. **LC** PN1993; .C56. **DD** 791. **Bk Rev**, (Qty: 3). ***Absorbed*** *Flashback, Incorporating Film Notes & Queries, 1056-2753.*
**Ind/Abst** Film Lit. Index (19??-).

IT/0009-7039
**CINEFORUM.** [Cineforum]. **Added/Corp** Federazione Italiana Cineforum. No. 1 (1960)-. Periodical. Italian. mo (10 issues). L80000 Italy; L100000 other. Cineforum, Via Pascoli 3, 24121 Bergamo Italy. **Tel** 011 39 35 244703. **LC** PN1993; .C457. **DD** 791.43/05. Index available. cum. index. Documents available from The Genuine Article.
**Ind/Abst** Arts Humanit. Citation Index [Full Cov.]; Curr. Contents Arts Humanit.; Film Lit. Index; Res. Alert [Full Cov.].

US/0145-3483
**CINEGRAM.** **VFOAT** Cinegram Magazine. V. 1- March/April 1976. Periodical. English. qt. $4.00. Cinegram Magazine, 512 South Main Street, Ann Arbor MI 48103. **LC** PN1993; .C5178. **DD** 791.43/05.

FR/0045-6926
**CINEMA.** [Cinema]. Vol. 1 (Nov. 1954)-. Periodical. French. Twenty-two times a year. 186.09F France; 258.00F other. Cinema, BP 544, 75667 Paris Cedex 14 France. **Tel** 011 33 1 40444929. **LC** PN1993; .C575.
**Ind/Abst** Film Lit. Index; Point Repere (1983).

FR
**CINEMA 19.** French. $25.00 France; $29.00 other. Editions TC Cinema 19, 49 rue du Faubourg Poisonniere, 74009 Paris France.

CN/0225-3151
**CINEMA AU QUEBEC, REPERTOIRE, LE.** [Cine. Que., repert.]. 1979-. French. an. $15.00. Editions Cinema/Quebec, PO Box 309 Outremont Station, Montreal Quebec H2V 4N1 Canada. **DD** 791.43/09714. ***Continues*** *Cinema au Quebec, 0317-2333.*

IT/0392-9981
**CINEMA D'OGGI.** [Cine. oggi]. (1967)-. Periodical. Italian. Twenty-six times a year. L30000 Italy; L50000 other. Attivita Cinematografiche Italia, Viale Regina Mergherita 286, 00198 Rome Italy. **Tel** 011 39 6 44231480. **UDC** 791.4. **Bk Rev**. **Ad Acc**.
**Desc:** Contains informatin on films and movies.

IT
**CINEMA E CINEMA.** ***Ceased.*** **VFOAT** Cinema & Cinema. Year 1 (Oct./Dec. 1974)-(Sept./Dec. 1993). Periodical. Italian. tq. Clueb Coop Libraria Univ Edi, Bologna Via Marsala 24, 40126 Bologna Italy. **Tel** 011 39 51 220736, 224780, FAX 011 39 51 237758. **ED** Guido Fink and Leonardo Quaresima. **LC** PN1995; .C487. **DD** 809.2/3. Index available. cum. index. **Bk Rev**. **Ad Acc. Circ:** 30,000.
**Desc:** Essays on authors, trends, theory, and on the relationships of cinema/literature.
**Ind/Abst** Film Lit. Index (19??-).

II
**CINEMA IN INDIA.** ***Ceased.*** **Added/Corp** National Film Development Corporation of India. Vol. 1, No. 1 (Jan. 1987)-(19??). Periodical. English. qt. National Film Development Corporation Ltd, Discovery India Building Nehru Ctr7, Bombay 400 018 India. **Tel** 011 91 22 4949856. **(Subscription address:** Prints India, 11 Darya Ganj, New Delhi 110002 India.**) ED** Mangala Chandran. **LC** PN1993.5.I8; C52. **DD** 791.43/0954. Index available. **Bk Rev**. **Ad Acc. Circ:** 5,000 (ctrl).
**Ind/Abst** Film Lit. Index (19??-).

US/0009-7101
**CINEMA JOURNAL.** [Cine. j.]. **Added/Corp** Society for Cinema Studies. Society of Cinematologists. (1967)-. Periodical. English. qt. $40.00 (institutions), $25.00 (individuals) US; add $6.00 postage other. University of Texas Press, PO Box 7819, Austin TX 78713. **Tel** (512)471-4531, FAX (512)320-0668, telex 776453 UTEXPRES AUS. **ED** Virginia Wright Wexman. **LC** PN1993; .S62. **DD** 791.43/05. **Ad Acc. Circ:** 1,050. available on microfilm and microfiche from University Microfilms International (UMI). Documents available from The Genuine Article. ***Continues*** *Society of Cinematologists. Journal.*
**Desc:** Articles on film, movie history, television, film criticism, acting, production and film writing.
**Ind/Abst** Art Index; Arts Humanit. Citation Index [Full Cov.]; Curr. Contents Arts Humanit.; Film Lit. Index; Int. Index Film Period.; Middle East Abstr. Index; MLA Int. Bibl. Books Artic. Mod. Lang. Lit.; Res. Alert [Full Cov.].

IT/0009-711X
**CINEMA NUOVO.** [Cine. nuovo]. Vol. 1, No. 1 (Dec. 15, 1952)-. Periodical. Italian. Six times a year. L40000 Italy; L60000 other. Edizioni Dedalo Spa, Casella Postale 362, Bari 70100 Italy. **Tel** 011 39 080 5311400, FAX 011 39 080 5311414. **DD** 791. Index available. **Bk Rev**, (Qty: 10/yr). **Ad Acc, Adv Mgr:** R. Coga. ctrl circ. available on microfilm from University Microfilms International (UMI).
**Ind/Abst** Film Lit. Index.

UK/0578-2988
**CINEMA ONE.** **Added/Corp** British Film Institute. Education Dept. (1967)-. Periodical. English. qt. Secker & Warburg, Michelin House, 81 Fulham Road, London SW3 6RB United Kingdom. **Tel** 011 44 71 581 9393, FAX 011 44 71 589 8421, telex 920191. **DD** 791.

AT/0311-3639
**CINEMA PAPERS.** [Cine. pap.]. (Jan. 1974)-. Periodical. English. Six times a year (Every second month with slight variations). 28.00Aus$ Australia; 37.00Aus$ US & Canada & Middle East; 36.00Aus$ New Zealand & Niugini & Malaysia Fiji & Singapore & China & Hong Kong & India & Philippines & Japan; 37.00Aus$ other. MTV Publishing Ltd., 43 Charles Street, Abbotsford Victoria 3067 Australia. **Tel** (03)429 5511, FAX (03)427 9255. **ED** Scott Murray. **LC** PN1993.5.A8; C56. **DD** 791.43/05. **Bk Rev**, (Qty: 6). **Ad Acc. Circ:** 15,000 (ctrl). ***Absorbed in part by*** *Filmviews, 0158-3778.*
**Desc:** Magazine containing film and book reviews. Also interviews with leading influential people within the motion picture industry. A reference to what is going on in the industry.
**Ind/Abst** APAIS, Aust. Public Aff. Inf. Ser. (1974-); Film Lit. Index; Med. Rev. Dig.

PO
**CINEMA (PORTO, PORTUGAL).** (CINEMA.). No. 1 (Sept. 82-). Periodical. Portuguese. qt. 2$00 Portugal; $6.00 US. Federacao Portuguesa de Cineclubes, rua de Camoes 777-4O DTO, 4000 Porto Portugal. **Tel** 35-2-496002. **LC** PN1993; .F3413. **DD** 791.43/05. **Ad Acc. Circ:** 1,500 (ctrl).
**Desc:** Publication about movies and film societies dealing cinema in a cultural way. It also gives useful information to film societies.

IT
**CINEMA SESSANTA.** (19??)-. Italian. Six times a year. L55000 Italy; L75000 other. Nuova Arnica Editrice, via Dei Reti 19A, 00185 Rome Italy. **Tel** 011 39 6 4441611. **Bk Rev**. **Ad Acc. Circ:** 5,000.

IT/0009-7152
**CINEMA SOCIETA.** No. 1- June 1966-. Periodical. Italian. qt. $12.00. Cinema Societa, Via Porta Maggiore 81, 00185 Rome Italy. **Tel** (06)7314313. **Circ:** 2,000.
**Desc:** Social effect of mass communication, visual art, psychology, and criminology.

IT
**CINEMA STUDIO.** **VFOAT** Cinema/Studio. No. 1 (Mar. 1991)-. Periodical. Italian. qt. Bulzoni Editore Srl, Via dei Liburni 14, 00185 Rome Italy. **Tel** 011 39 6 445-5207, FAX 011 39 6 445-0355.

IT
**CINEMA SUD.** Italian. Cinema Sud, Via Degli Imbimbi 45, 83100 Avellino Italy.
**Ind/Abst** Film Lit. Index (19??-).

UK
**CINEMA TECHNOLOGY.** **Added/Corp** British Kinematograph Sound and Television Society. (1987)-. Periodical. English. qt. British Kinematograph Sound and Television Society, M6-14 Victoria House, Vernon Place, London WC1B 4DF England. **Tel** 011 44 712 428400, FAX 011 44 714 053560. **ED** John Gainsborough. **LC** TR845; .C54. **DD** 778.5/3/05. Index available. **Bk Rev**, (Qty: 3-4). **Ad Acc, Adv Mgr:** Jackson Rudd, **Tel** 071-613-0717. **Circ:** 4,500 (ctrl).
**Desc:** Technical journal dealing with multiplex and cinema design and all aspects of cinema technology.
**Ind/Abst** Film Lit. Index (19??-).

PK
**CINEMA THE WORLD OVER.** V. 1- July 1975-. Periodical. English. mo. Rs20.00. K S Hosain, 204-205 Hotel Metropole, Karachi Pakistan. **LC** PN1993; .C535. **DD** 791.43/05.

UK
**CINEMA TV TODAY.** Nov. 13, 1971-. Periodical. English. wk. 142 Wardour Street, London WIV 4BR England. ***Continues*** *Today's Cinema.*

SZ/1010-3627
**CINEMA (ZURICH, SWITZERLAND).** (CINEMA.). [Cinema]. Periodical. German (German). an. 24.00F. Arbeitsgemeinschaft CINEMA, Postfach 79, CH-4007 Basel Switzerland. **Tel** 061/692 41 80, FAX 061/691 24 06. **ED** Janis Osolin, Mikles Gimes, Jorg Huber, Alfred Messerli. **LC** PN1993; .C5193. **Bk Rev**. **Ad Acc. Circ:** 2,500.
**Ind/Abst** Film Lit. Index.

US/0363-9665
**CINEMABOOK.** V. 1- Spring 1976-. Periodical. English. qt. $3.25. Cinemabook, 344 East 50th Street, New York NY 10022. **LC** PN1993; .C542. **DD** 791.43/05.

US/0198-1064
**CINEMACABRE.** ***Ceased.*** [Cinemacabre]. No. 1- Winter/Spring (1978/79)-?. Periodical. English. ir. George M Stover Jr, PO Box 10005, Baltimore MD 21285-0005. **Tel** (410)828-0286. **ED** George Stover. **Bk Rev**. **Ad Acc. Circ:** 3,000 (ctrl). ***Supersedes*** *Black Oracle, 0045-2246.*
**Desc:** Feature articles, celebrity interviews, plus movie, book, and soundtrack reviews pertaining to the cinema of the fantastic.
**Ind/Abst** Film Lit. Index; Med. Rev. Dig.

FR/0243-4504
**CINEMACTION.** **VFOAT** Cinema Action. (1978)-. Periodical. French. qt. 440.74F France; 460.00F other. Cinemaction, 106 Boulevard St Denis, 92400 Courbevoie France. **Tel** 011 33 1 43337034. **(Subscription address:** Gestion Informatique Stocks, BP 5 Les Allaux, 14410 Vassy France.**) ED** Guy Hennebelle. **Ad Acc. Circ:** 3,000.
**Desc:** Thematic review about cinema and television authors, foreign cinemas, subjects, etc.
**Ind/Abst** Film Lit. Index (19??-).

CN/0709-5635
**CINEMAG.** ***Title Change.*** [CineMag]. No. 11 (Oct. 1978)-?. Periodical. English. mo. Cinema Canada, Box 398 Outremont Station, Montreal Quebec H2V 9Z9 Canada. **Tel** (514)272-5354, FAX (514)270-5068. **DD** 338.4/7/791430971. ***Continues*** *Trade News North, 0705-8799.* ***Continued by*** *Cinema Canada.*
**Ind/Abst** Film Lit. Index (1978-1981).

US/0090-3000
**CINEMAGIC (NEW YORK, N.Y.).** ***Ceased.*** (CINEMAGIC.). [Cinemagic]. Vol. 1, No. 1 ( )-?. Periodical. English. qt. Starlog Press Inc., 475 Park Avenue South, New York NY 10016. **Tel** (212)689-2830, FAX (212)889-7933. **ED** David Hutchison. **LC** TR858; .C462. **DD** 778.5/345. **Bk Rev. Ad Acc. Circ:** 18,000.
**Desc:** Guide to filmmaking.
**Ind/Abst** Film Lit. Index.

UK
**CINEMAS.** **Added/Corp** Great Britain. Business Statistics Office. (19??)-. English. Librarian / England, Business Statistics Office, Cardiff Road, Newport Gwent NPT 1XG England. **LC** PN1993.5.G7; C54. **DD** 384/8/0941.

CN/1181-6945
**CINEMAS (MONTREAL).** (CINEMAS : REVUE D'ETUDES CINEMATOGRAPHIQUES.). [Cinemas]. Vol. 1, Nos 1/2 (Autumn 1990)-. Periodical. French (summaries and/or abstracts in English). Three times a year. 30.00Can$ (institutions), 25.00Can$ (individuals) Canada; 35.00Can$ (institutions), 30.00Can$ (individuals) other. University of Montreal Department of Histoire l'Art, CP 6128, Montreal Quebec H3C 3J7 Canada. **Tel** (514)343-6111 ext 3682, FAX (514)343-2393. **ED** Michel Larouche. **DD** 791.43/75/05. cum. index. **Bk Rev**, (Qty: 10). **Ad Acc. Circ:** 650.

●FR
**CINEMATHEQUE : REVUE SEMESTRIELLE D'ESTHETIQUE ET D'HISTOIRE DU CINEMA.** **Added/Corp** Cinematheque Francaise. **VFOAT** Revue Cinematheque. (May 1992)-. Periodical. French (summaries and/or abstracts in English). sa. **LC** PN1993.5.A1; C57.

CN/1188-3162
**CINEMATOGRAPHE, LE.** [Cinematographe]. **Added/Corp** Universite Laval. Vol. 1, No 1 (1991)-. Periodical. French. qt. Limited free distribution. Le Cinematographie, A/S G. Carigan, Local 3, 960 Raymond-Casgrain, Quebec Quebec G1S 2C9 Canada. **DD** 792.43/05.

II
**CINEMAYA.** (Autumn 1988)-. Periodical. English. qt. $55.00. **(Subscription address:** Prints India, 11 Darya Ganj, New Delhi 110002 India.**)**

US/0162-0126
**CINEMONKEY.** [Cinemonkey]. (1978)-. Periodical. English. qt. $7.00 US; $9.50 other. Cinemonkey, PO Box 8502, Portland OR 97207. **LC** PN1993; .C546. **DD** 791.43/05. ***Continues*** *Scintillation, 0147-5789.*
**Ind/Abst** Film Lit. Index (1978-1979).

US/0895-805X
**CINEVUE.** **See** Photography and Video.

IO
**CITRA FILM.** Periodical. Indonesian. mo. Rp750. Yayasan Pengembangan Perfilman Nasional, Menteng Raya No 62, Jakarta Indonesia. **LC** PN1993; .C588.

US/0275-8423
**CLASSIC IMAGES.** [Class. images]. (19??)-. Periodical. English. mo. $27.50 US; $38.00 other. Classic Images, PO Box 809, Muscatine IA 52761. **Tel** (319)263-2331, FAX (319)262-8042. **ED** Bob King. **LC** PN1995.9.C54; C55. **DD** 791.43/05. Index available (Bound in Aug issue). **Bk Rev**, (Qty: 100-150). **Ad Acc, Adv Mgr:** Bob King. **Circ:** 4,000. available on microfilm from University Microfilms International (UMI). ***Continues*** *Classic Film/Video Images, 0164-5560.*
**Desc:** Complete coverage: classic film, field-film and video market, availability, evaluation, historical articles. Biographies, interviews, movie and book reviews, and animation.
**Ind/Abst** Film Lit. Index; Med. Rev. Dig.

FR
**CNC INFO.** **Added/Corp** Centre National de la Cinematographie (France). **VAT** Centre National de la Cinematographie Info. Periodical. French. bm. Centre National Cinematographie, 12 rue de Lubeck, 75784 Paris Cedex 16 France. **Tel** 011 33 1 45051440, FAX 011 33 1 47550491, telex 650306. ***Continues*** *Informations CNC.*

FR
**CNC STATISTIQUES / CENTRE NATIONAL DE LA CINEMATOGRAPHIE.** **See** Motion Picture-Abstracting, Bibliographies and Statistics.

US
**COLUMBIA FILM VIEW.** **Added/Corp** Columbia University. Film Division. **VFOAT** Film View. (19??)-. Periodical. English. antq. Columbia University School of Arts, 513 Dodge Hall, Film Division, New York NY 10027. **Tel** (212)854-2815.
**Ind/Abst** Film Lit. Index (19??-).

CN/0709-678X
**COMMERCIAL PRICE LIST - N.F.B. PHOTOTHEQUE.** ***Title Change.*** (COMMERCIAL PRICE LIST.). [Commer. price list - N.F.B. Phototheque]. **Main/Corp** National Film Board of Canada. Phototheque. **VFOAT** Tarif Commercial. **VAT** Commercial Price List - National Film Board Phototheque; Tarif Commercial - O.N.F. Phototheque; Tarif Commercial - Office National du Film. Phototheque. Periodical. English (French). National Film Board of Canada, PO Box 6100 Station A, Montreal Quebec H3C 3H5 Canada. **Tel** (514)283-9427, FAX (514)283-7564. ***Supersedes*** *Canada. Information Canada. Phototheque. Commercial Price List, 0706-1684.* ***Continued by*** *Photos Canada: Price List, 0709-6798.*

●US/0899-9902
**COMPARATIVE LITERATURE AND FILM STUDIES.** **See** Literature.

UK
**CONTINENTAL FILM & VIDEO REVIEW.** **VFOAT** Continental Film and Video Review. Vol. 27, No. 10 (Aug. 1980)-. Periodical. English. mo. $28.00. ***Continues*** *Continental Film Review.*

AT/1030-4312
**CONTINUUM (MT. LAWLEY, W.A.).** (CONTINUUM.). **Added/Corp** Western Australian College of Advanced Education. Dept. of Media Studies. Australian Film Commission. Murdoch University. Western Australian College of Advanced Education. Vol. 1, No. 1 (1987)-. English. Twice a year. $25.00 (individual), $45.00 (institution). Continuum / Australia, School of Humanities, Murdoch University, Murdoch WA 6150 Australia. **Tel** 011 61 9 3602734, FAX 011 61 9 3106285. **LC** PN1993; .C675. **DD** 791.43/0994/05.

SP
**CONTRACAMPO.** Yearly V. 1, No. 1, (April 1979)-. Periodical. Spanish. ir. 3000ptas. Contracampo, Apartado 17.048, Madrid Spain. **LC** PN1993; .C68. **DD** 791.43/05.

FR
**CORTO CIRCUITO.** ***Ceased.*** **VFOAT** Court Circuit; Circuito. No. 1 (Oct. 1987)-Number 22 (June 1993). Periodical. Spanish (French and Portuguese). qt. Corto Circuito, 14 Boulevard Argo, F-75013 Paris France.

IT/0393-9162
**COSA VISTA, LA.** **Added/Corp** Universita Degli Studi di Trieste. Centro Universitario Cinematografico. No. 1 (1985)-. Periodical. Italian (summaries and/or abstracts in English). Three times a year. Centro Universitario Cinematografico, Dipartimento di Scienze Politiche, Universita Degli Studi di Trieste, Piazzale Europa 1, 34127 Trieste Italy. **LC** PN1993; .C75. **DD** 791.43/05.
**Ind/Abst** Film Lit. Index (19??-).

UK/0090-9831
**CRITIC (NEW YORK).** ***Suspended.*** (CRITIC.). **Added/Corp** American Federation of Film Societies. **VFOAT** Film Critic. Vol. 1 (Sept./Oct. 1972)-(19??). Periodical. English. wk. £17.45. Film & Television Press Guild, 9 Compayne Gardens, London NW6 United Kingdom. **LC** PN1993; .C78. **DD** 791.43/05. available on microfilm from University Microfilms International (UMI). ***Supersedes*** *Film Society Review.*
**Ind/Abst** Book Rev. Digest.

CN/0821-5561
**CRITIQUE (CLANDEBOYE).** (CRITIQUE.). [Critique]. Autumn 1982-. Periodical. English. qt. $10.00. Critique Publishing, 300 Summergrove Street, Clandeboye Manitoba R0C 0P0 Canada. **DD** 791.43/75/05.

US/0007-9219
**CTVD, CINEMA, TV DIGEST.** **See** Communication.

US/0888-9015
**CUE SHEET, THE.** **See** Music.

US/0748-8580
**CURRENT RESEARCH IN FILM.** ***Ceased.*** [Curr. res. film]. Vol. 1 (1985)-Vol. 5 (?). English. an. Ablex Publishing Corporation, 355 Chestnut Street, Norwood NJ 07648. **Tel** (201)767-8450, (201)767-8455 (Customer Service), FAX (201)767-6717. **ED** Bruce Austin. **LC** PN1993; .C93. **DD** 384/.8/05.
**Desc:** Broadens scope of film scholarship in these areas: the film audience, motion picture economics and legal concerns.
**Ind/Abst** Film Lit. Index.

●GW
**CVA NEWSLETTER / COMMISSION ON VISUAL ANTHROPOLOGY.** **See** Anthropology.

CN/0846-8648
**CVA REVIEW.** [CVA rev.]. **Added/Corp** Commission on Visual Anthropology. International Union of Anthropological and Ethnological Sciences. **VFOAT** CVA Newsletter; Bulletin de la Commission d'Anthropologie Visuelle; Bulletin d'Information; Revue de la Commission d'Anthropologie Visuelle. **VAT** Commission on Visual Anthropology Review; Bulletin d'Information - Commission d'Anthropologie Visuelle. (Fall 1989)-. Periodical. English (French and Spanish). sa. Distributed free of charge; donations accepted. Commission on Visual Anthropology / Montreal, University of Montreal, Anthropology Department, CP 6128, Station A, Montreal, Quebec H3C 3J7 Canada. **DD** 306/.0208. ***Continues*** *CVA Newsletter, 0839-3605.*
**Ind/Abst** Film Lit. Index (19??-).

XR/0011-4588
**CZECHOSLOVAK FILM, THE.** ***Ceased.*** [Czech. film]. **Added/Corp** Ceskoslovensky Statni Film. Ceskoslovensky Filmexport. **VFOAT** Ceskoslovensky Film. Vol. 1 (June 1948)-(19??). Periodical. English. qt. **(Subscription address:** Artia Pegas Press Ltd., Palac Metro Narodni Trida 25, 11210 Prague 1 Czech Republic.**)** **LC** PN1993.5.C9; C9.
**Ind/Abst** Film Lit. Index.

US/0011-5509
**DAILY VARIETY.** **VFOAT** Variety. (1933)-. Periodical. English. da (5 days a week). $157.00 US; $179.00 Canada (surface); $269.00 other. Cahners Publishing Company, 249 West 17th Street, New York NY 10011. **Tel** (212)645-0067, FAX (212)242-6987. **(Subscription address:** Daily Variety, Subscription Department, PO Box 7550, Torrance CA 90504.**)** **ED** Peter Bart. **LC** PN1993; .D3. **[CCC]. Circ:** 22,395.
**Desc:** Hollywood newspaper covering the entire scope of the entertainment business, including film, legitimate theater, music, cable and home video.
**Ind/Abst** Infobank; Mag. Index (?-?).

UA
**DALIL AL-SINIMA AL-ARABIYAH.** **VFOAT** Arab Cinema Guide. Arabic (English). an. £E1.00. 218 Shari Al-Jaysh, Al-Qahirah Misr Egypt. **ED** S Farid. **LC** PN1993.5.A65; D34.

DK
**DANISH FILMS.** English. an. Free. Danish Film Institute, Store Sndervoldstraede, DK-1419 Copenhagen Denmark. **Tel** 45-31-576500, FAX 45-31-576700, telex 31465 D FILM-DK. **ED** Helge Strunk. **LC** PN1993.3; .D33. **Circ:** 4,000 (ctrl).
**Desc:** Survey of the previous year's feature film production plus facts on Danish film situation.

II
**DEEP FOCUS : A FILM QUARTERLY.** Vol. 1, No. 1 (Dec. 1987)-. Periodical. English. qt. $10.00. Deep Focus, Bangalore, India. **(Subscription address:** Prints India, 11 Darya Ganj, New Delhi 110002 India.**)** **LC** PN1993.5.I8; D4. **DD** 791.43/0954/05.

US/1075-6116
**DGA NEWS.** [DGA news]. **Added/Corp** Directors Guild of America. **VFOAT** Directors Guild of America News. **VAT** Directors Guild of America News. Vol. 16, No. 1 (March-April 1991)-. Periodical. English. bm. $24.00 US; $50.00 other. Directors Guild of America, 7920 Sunset Boulevard, Hollywood CA 90046-0907. **Tel** (310)289-2035, FAX (310)289-5340. **ED** Tomm Carroll. **DD** 791. **Bk Rev**, (Qty: 15-20). **Ad Acc, Adv Mgr:** Scott Burnell. **Circ:** 14,000. ***Continues*** *DGA Newsletter.*

MX
**DICINE.** **Added/Corp** Difusion e Investigacion Cinematograficas, A.C. Vol. 1, No. 1 (August 1983)-. Periodical. Spanish. bm. $26.00. Dicine, Leonardo Da Vinci 161A, 03700 Mexico DF Mexico. **Tel** 011 52 5 5986086. **LC** PN1993.5.M4; D54. **DD** 791.43/0972/05.
**Ind/Abst** Film Lit. Index (19??-).

US
**DIGEST.** **Main/Corp** University Film Association. (19??)-. English. Four times a year. $4.50. Southern Illinois University / Carbondale - Cinema & Photography, Department of Cinema and Photography, Carbondale IL 62901. **Tel** (618)453-2365. **LC** PN1993; .U617a. **DD** 791.43/06/2773994. ***Continues*** *UFPA Digest.*

US/0364-8788
**DIRECTORY FOR MEMBERS - SOCIETY OF MOTION PICTURE AND TELEVISION ENGINEERS, INC.** **Main/Corp** Society of Motion Picture and Television Engineers. **Added/Corp** Society of Motion Picture and Television Engineers. SMPTE Directory for Members. **VFOAT** SMPTE Directory for Members. **VAT** Directory For Members - Society of Motion Picture and Television Engineers, Incorporated. (19??)-. Directory. English. ir. $50.00 (individuals), $75.00 (institutions) Comes with Society of Motion Picture & Television Engineers membership. Society of Motion Picture and Television Engineers, 595 West Hartsdale Avenue, White Plains NY 10607. **Tel** (914)761-1100, FAX (914)761-3115, telex 4995348. **LC** TR847.5; .S6a. **DD** 621.36.

US/0277-1500
**DIRECTORY OF BLACK FILM/TV TECHNICIANS & ARTISTS, WEST COAST.** **VFOAT** Directory of Black Film/TV Technicians and Artists, West Coast. **VAT** Directory of Black Film/Television Technicians and Artists, West Coast. Directory. English. $16.00. Togetherness Productions, Box 75796 Sanford Station, Los Angeles CA 90075. **LC** PN1995.9.N4; D57. **DD** 384/.8/08996073.

US
**DIRECTORY OF FILM LIBRARIES IN NORTH AMERICA.** 1971-. Directory. English. be. Film Library Information Council, Box 348, Radio City Station NY 10019. **Tel** (212)270-1207. **LC** PN1998.A1. **DD** 026/.79143/02957.

UK/0268-5256
**DIRECTORY OF INTERNATIONAL FILM AND VIDEO FESTIVALS.** (DIRECTORY OF INTERNATIONAL FILM AND VIDEO FESTIVALS / BFI.). [Dir. int. film video festiv.]. **Added/Corp** British Film Institute. British Council. (1986)-. Directory. English. be. £11.35 UK; £15.25 other. British Film Institute, 21 Stephen Street, London W1P 1PL England. **Tel** 11 44 71 2551444, FAX 11 44 71 4367950, telex 27624 BFILDNG. **LC** IN PROCESS. ***Continues*** *International Film Festivals Directory, 0265-2676.*

US/0419-2052
**DIRECTORY OF MEMBERS - DIRECTORS GUILD OF AMERICA.** **Main/Corp** Directors Guild of America. **VAT** Distilled Spirits Council of the United States News Letter. 1st ed. (1968)-. Directory. English. an. $24.90 US; $33.98 other. Directors Guild of America, 7920 Sunset Boulevard, Hollywood CA 90046-0907. **Tel** (310)289-2035, FAX (310)289-5340. **ED** Adele Field. **LC** PN1998.A1; D52. **DD** 791.43/0922. Index available. **Ad Acc, Adv Mgr:** Adele Field. **Circ:** 12,000. ***Continues*** *Licensed Beverage Industries, Incorporated. Newsletter.*
**Desc:** A roster of members and their credits.

UK
**DIRECTORY OF MEMBERS / DIRECTORS GUILD OF GREAT BRITAIN.** **Main/Corp** Directors Guild of Great Britain. (1984)-. Directory. English. an. $20.00. The Directors Guild of Great Britain, 125 Tottenham Court Road, London W1P 9HN England. **Tel** 011 44 71 387 7131.

BE
**DOCUMENTAIRE EN EUROPE, LE.** (19??)-. French. 500F Belgium & Luxembourg; 160F France; 1000F other. Edimedia ASBL, rue de la Constitution 22, 1030 Brussels Belgium. **Tel** 011 32 2 2180031. **Bk Rev. Ad Acc.**

GW/0724-7117
**DOKUMENTATION. WETTBEWERB, PANORAMA, KINDERFILMFEST / INTERNATIONALE FILMFESTSPIELE BERLIN.** **Main/Corp** Internationale Filmfestspiele Berlin. **VFOAT** Wettbewerb, Panorama, Kinderfilmfest; Competition, Panorama, Children's Film Fest. (19??)-. German (English and French). an.

NE
**DUTCH FILM.** English. ir. Government Printing Office / Netherlands, The Hague Netherlands. **LC** PN1993.3; .D83. **DD** 791.43/09492.

US/0891-6780
**EAST-WEST FILM JOURNAL.** ***Ceased.*** [East West film j.]. Vol. 1, No. 1 (Dec. 1986)-Vol. 8, No. 2. Academic Scholarly Publication. English. sa (January and July). University of Hawaii Press, 2840 Kolowalu Street, Honolulu HI 96822. **Tel** (808)956-8833, (808)948-8697, FAX (808)988-6052. **ED** Wimal Dissanayake, Paul Clark, and Michael Macmillan. **LC** PN1993; .E25. **DD** 791.43/05. Documents available from The Genuine Article.
**Desc:** A response to the recognition that film can uniquely enrich understanding between peoples and cultures at both the popular and scholarly levels. Provides a new forum in which Asian cinemas can be introduced to other Asian and Western audiences and where links can be forged among filmmakers, students and scholars in the countries of East and West.
**Ind/Abst** Arts Humanit. Citation Index [Full Cov.]; Curr. Contents Arts Humanit.; Film Lit. Index; MLA Int. Bibl. Books Artic. Mod. Lang. Lit.; Res. Alert [Full Cov.]; Soc. Sci. Cit. Index [Select. Cov.].

FR
**ECRAN FANTASTIQUE, L'.** (19??)-. Periodical. French. Twelve times a year. I-Media, 69 rue de la Tombe Issoire, 75014 Paris France. **Tel** 011 33 1 43275278.

CN/0822-6350
**ECRITS SUR LE CINEMA (SUPPLEMENT).** (ECRITS SUR LE CINEMA.). [Ecrits cine.]. **Added/Corp** Cinematheque Quebecoise. (1982)-. French. an. La Cinematheque Quebecoise, 335 Boulevard de Maisonneuve Est, Montreal Quebec H2X 1K1 Canada. **Tel** (514)842-9763, FAX (514)866-4688. **ED** Pierre Veronneau. **DD** 016.79143/09714. Index available. **Bk Rev. Ad Acc. Circ:** 1,000 (ctrl).
**Desc:** A bibliography of publications on Quebec cinema from 1911 to 1981.

US/0000-135X
**EDUCATIONAL FILM & VIDEO LOCATOR OF THE CONSORTIUM OF COLLEGE AND UNIVERSITY MEDIA CENTERS AND R. R. BOWKER.** [Educ. film video locator Consort. Coll. Univ. Media Cent. R. R. Bowker]. **Added/Corp** Consortium of College and University Media Centers. R.R. Bowker Company. **VFOAT** Educational Film and Video Locator of the Consortium of College and University Media Centers and R.R. Bowker; Educational Film & Video Locator. 4th Ed. (1991)-. English. ir. $175.00. R R Bowker, A Reed Reference Publishing Company, Part of Reed International PLC, PO Box 31, 121 Chanlon Drive, New Providence NJ 07974. **Tel** (908)464-6800, (800)521-8110, FAX (908)665-6688, telex 138-755. **LC** LB1044.Z9; E37. **DD** 011/.37. ***Continues*** *Educational Film/Video Locator of the Consortium of University Film Centers and R.R. Bowker, 0000-0973.*
**Desc:** The definitive union listing of videos and films. Indexes some 52,000 videos and films available for rental from the 46 Consortium media centers.

JA
**EIGA MOKUROKU.** Japanese. Tokyo Toritsu Hibiya Toshokan, 1-ban 1-go Hibiya Koen, Chiyoda-ku 100, Tokyo-to Japan. **LC** Z5784.M9; E38; PN1993.5.J3.

JA
**EIZO NENKAN.** (19??)-. Japanese. Michi Shuppansha, 8-10 Sarugakucho 2 Chiyoda-ku, Tokyo 101 Japan. **LC** PN1995.9.D6; E38.

RU/0868-9024
**EKRAN.** **Added/Corp** Soiuz Kinematografistov SSSR. Soviet Union. Gosudarstvennyi Komitet po Kinematografii. (1991)-. Periodical. Russian. Twelve times a year. $77.00. **(Subscription address:** Victor Kamkin, 4956 Boiling Brook Parkway, Rockville MD 20852.**) LC** PN1993; .S64. ***Continues*** *Sovetskii Ekran, 0132-0742.*
**Ind/Abst** Film Lit. Index (199?-).

RU
**EKRAN I STSENA.** Vol. 1 (1990)-. Periodical. Russian. wk. $19.95. Izdatelstvo Pressa, Myasnitskaia 24, 101877 Moscow Russia. **Tel** 011 95 923 2122, FAX 011 95 200 2259. **(Subscription address:** East View Publications Inc., 3020 Harbor Lane North, Suite 110, Minneapolis MN 55447.**)**

FI/0785-9015
**ELAVAN KUVAN VUOSIKIRJA.** (1988)-. Finnish. an. Valtion Painatuskeskus, PO Box 516, SF 00101 Helsinki Finland. **Tel** 011 358 0 5660266. ***Continues*** *Studio (Helsinki, Finland).*

AT
**ENCORE DIRECTORY, THE.** (19??)-. Directory. English. an. 65.00Aus$ Australia; 85.00Aus$ Papua New Guinea, New Zealand, and Southeast Asia; 100.00Aus$ other. Reed Business Publishing Pty Ltd. / Australia, 1 5 Railway Street, Level 12 North Tower, Chatswood W 2067 NSW Australia. **Tel** 011 61 2 3725222, FAX 011 61 2 4197533. **LC** IN PROCESS.

AT/0815-2063
**ENCORE MANLY.** [Encore Manly]. (1984)-. Periodical. English. sm (except once in Jan. and Dec.). 99.00Aus$ Australia; 159.00Aus$ Papua New Guinea, New Zealand and Southeast Asia; 199.00Aus$ other. Reed Business Publishing Pty Ltd. / Australia, 1 5 Railway Street, Level 12 North Tower, Chatswood W 2067 NSW Australia. **Tel** 011 61 2 3725222, FAX 011 61 2 4197533. **DD** 790.20994. ***Continues*** *Encore Australia, 0813-6688; Australian Film Review, 0811-384X.*

JA
**ENGEKIGAKU / HENSHU WASEDA DAIGKU ENGEKI GAKKAI.** **See** Theater.

GW
**EPD FILM.** **VFOAT** E.P.D. Film. Vol. 1 (Jan. 1984)-. Periodical. German. mo. DM79.20. Gemeinschaftswerk Evangelisch Publizistik, Westerbacher Str 33 35, W-6000 Frankfurt 90 Germany. **Tel** 011 49 69 71570. ***Formed by the union of*** *EPD Kirche und Film* ***and*** *Filmbeobachter.*
**Ind/Abst** Film Lit. Index (19??-).

CN
**ESTIMATES. PART III, NATIONAL FILM BOARD.** **Main/Corp** Canada. **VFOAT** Budget des Depenses. Partie III, Office National du Film. (19??)-. English (French). $6.00 Canada; $7.20 other. Canada Communication Group Publishers, Order Processing, Ottawa Ontario K1A 0S9 Canada. **Tel** (819)956-4800, (819)956-4802. **LC** PN1999.N26; C3a. **DD** 791.43/06/071.

FR/0014-1992
**ETUDES CINEMATOGRAPHIQUES.** Vol. 1 No 1/2 (Spring 1960)-. Periodical. French. ir. $19.96. Lettres Modernes Minard, 45 rue de Saint Andre, 14123 Fleury Surrey Orne France. **Tel** 011 33 31 844706. Documents available from The Genuine Article.
**Ind/Abst** Arts Humanit. Citation Index (19??-19??) [Full Cov.]; Curr. Contents Arts Humanit.; Point Repere (1979); Res. Alert [Full Cov.].

UK
**EUROPEAN FILMFILE.** English. Three times a year. £395.00 UK; £219.00 Eastern Europe including Albania, Bulgaria, Czechoslovakia, Hungary, Poland, Romania, Yugoslavia, Russia and the former Soviet Republics; £415.00 other. European Filmfile, 30-31 Great Sutton Street, 2nd Floor, London EC1V 0DX England. **Tel** 011 44 71 4908994, FAX 011 44 71 4901686. **ED** Lloyd Shepherd. **Ad Acc, Adv Mgr:** L Martin. **Circ:** 8,000.
**Desc:** Gives a brief profile of every production company and financial details of every film, such as budgets, backers, and their investments. Names producers, directors, writers and leading cast members and gives story lines, locations, delivery dates and the state of progress of each film.

US/0736-3745
**FACETS FEATURES.** **Added/Corp** Facets Multimedia (Chicago, Ill.). (19??)-. Periodical. English. Six times a year. $14.95. Facets Multimedia, 1517 West Fullerton Avenue, Chicago IL 60614. **Tel** (312)281-9075, (800)331-6197. **ED** Milos Stehlik. **Bk Rev. Ad Acc, Adv Mgr:** M. Reyes. **Circ:** 21,000.

US/0278-4203
**FAMOUS MONSTERS.** Periodical. English. mo (except Feb. and Dec.). $17.00 US; $21.00 Canada. Warren Publishing Company / Indiana, 2240 Galahad Drive, Indianapolis IN 46208. **LC** PN1995.9.H6; F27. **DD** 791.43/09/0916. ***Continues*** *Monster World.*

US/0164-2111
**FANGORIA.** [Fangoria]. (1979)-. Periodical. English. Ten times a year. $34.47. Starlog Press Inc., 475 Park Avenue South, New York NY 10016. **Tel** (212)689-2830, FAX (212)889-7933. **(Subscription address:** Kable Publishers Aide, 308 East Hitt Street, Subscription Department, Mt. Morris IL 61054-1473.**) ED** Anthony Timpone and J. Peter Orr. **Bk Rev. Ad Acc.**
**Desc:** A journal about horror movies.

US/0891-074X
**FAVORITE WESTERNS, SERIAL WORLD.** [Favor. west. ser. world]. **VFOAT** Favorite Westerns; Serial World; Favorite Westerns and Serial World; Favorite Westerns and Serial Plus; Favorite Westerns & Serial World; Favorite Westerns & Serial Plus. Issue #24, (1986)-. Periodical. English. qt. $16.00 (one year); $26.00 (two year); $36.00 (three year) US; $20.00 (one year); $34.00 (two year); $48.00 (three year) other. Norman Kietzer, Route 1 Box 103, Vernon Center MN 56090. **Tel** (507)549-3677. **LC** PN1995.9.W4; F36. **DD** 791.43/09/093278. ***Continues*** *Favorite Westerns & Serials Plus, 8750-3166.*
**Desc:** Covers the cowboys of the silver screen and the motion picture artists of the chapter plays.

US
**FEATURE FILMS : A DIRECTORY OF FEATURE FILMS ON 16MM AND VIDEOTAPE AVAILABLE FOR RENTAL, SALE, AND LEASE.** ***Ceased.*** Vol. 1 (1985)-8th Ed. (1993). Directory. English. be. R R Bowker, A Reed Reference Publishing Company, Part of Reed International PLC, PO Box 31, 121 Chanlon Drive, New Providence NJ 07974. **Tel** (908)464-6800, (800)521-8110, FAX (908)665-6688, telex 138-755. **LC** PN1998; .F39. **DD** 016.791437/5. ***Continues*** *Feature Films on 8mm, 16mm, and Videotape, 0273-4907.*
**Desc:** A directory of feature films on 16mm and videotape available for rental, sale or lease.

GW/0015-0142
**FERNSEH- UND KINOTECHNIK.** (FERNSEH- UND KINO-TECHNIK.). [Fernseh-Kinotech.]. **Added/Corp** Deutsche Kinotechnische Gesellschaft fuer Film und Fernsehen. Deutscher Normenausschuss. Fachnormenausschuss Kinotechnik fuer Film und Fernsehen. Verband Technischer Betriebe fuer Film und Fernsehen. Fernseh- und Kinotechnische Gesellschaft (Germany). DIN Deutsches Institut fuer Norming. Normenausschuss Kinotechnik fuer Film und Fernsehen. DIN Deutsches Institut fuer Norming. Normenausschuss Bild und Film. Bereich Kinotechnik. **VFOAT** Fernseh- und Kinotechnik; Fernseh + Kino Technik; Fernseh & Kino Technik; Fernseh und Kino Technik; FKT. (1969)-. Trade Publication. German. Eleven times a year. $117.00 North America. Dr. Alfred Huethig Verlag GmbH, Postfach 102869, D 69018 Heidelberg Germany. **Tel** 011 49 6221 489281. **(Subscription address:** Huethig Publishing Inc., 29 Macintosh Drive, Oxford CT 06478.**) ED** Norbert Bolewski. **CODEN** FNKTAH. **[CCC]. Bk Rev. Ad Acc. Circ:** 33,000 (ctrl). Documents available from Ask*IEEE. ***Continues*** *Kino-Technik;* ***Absorbed*** *Fernseh + Filmtechnikum.*
**Desc:** Trade journal for professional film and television technology, video and audio technology, new media.
**Ind/Abst** Film Lit. Index; INSPEC (Jan. 1971-).

GW
**FERNSEHSPIEL IM ZDF / HERAUSGEGEBEN VOM ZWEITEN DEUTSCHEN FERNSEHEN, INFORMATION UND PRESSE/OFFENTLICHKEITSARBEIT, DAS.** ***Title Change.*** **See** Communication-Broadcasting.

CN/0712-9548
**FESTIVAL DES FILMS DU MONDE.** (FESTIVAL DES FILMS DU MONDE : PROGRAMME.). [Festiv. films monde]. **VFOAT** World Film Festival : Program. 1978-. English (French). an. $4.00 per no. World Film Festival, 1456 Maisonneuve Boulevard West, Montreal Quebec H3G 1M8 Canada. **DD** 791.43/079. ***Continues*** *Festival Canadien des Films du Monde (Program), 0712-953X.*

CN/0703-9824
**FESTIVAL INTERNATIONAL DU FILM DE LA CRITIQUE QUEBECOISE. Main/Corp** Festival International du Film de la Critique Quebecoise. 1977-. Periodical. French. $2.00 per number. 1855 rue du Havre, Montreal Quebec H2K 2K4 Canada. **DD** 010.

FR/0336-9331
**FICHES DU CINEMA.** (1978)-. Periodical. French. Forty-eight times a year. F333.00 France; F490.00 other. Cdi Cinema, 12 rue Mgr Gibier, 78000 Versailles France. **Tel** 011 33 1 39670398. ***Continues*** *Analyse des Films.*

UK
**FIGHT DIRECTOR, THE. See** Theater.

PL
**FILM.** Vol. 1 (1973)-. Periodical. Polish. wk. $143.00. **(Subscription address:** ARS Polona, PO Box 1001, 00068 Warsaw Poland.**)**

US/1055-0836
**FILM ACTORS GUIDE.** [Film actors guide]. **VFOAT** Film Actors. 1st Ed. (1991)-. English. $29.95. Lone Eagle Publishing Inc., 2337 Roscomare Road, Suite 9, Los Angeles CA 90077. **Tel** (310)471-8066, FAX (310)471-4969. **LC** PN1998.A1; F475. **DD** 791.43/028/025.

GW/0934-0378
**FILM & FAKTEN : EIN MAGAZIN DER FSK. Added/Corp** Freiwillige Selbstkontrolle der Filmwirtschaft (Association : Germany). **VFOAT** Film und Fakten. No. 1 (Feb. 1987)-. Periodical. German.
**Ind/Abst** Film Lit. Index (19??-).

US/0360-3695
**FILM & HISTORY (NEWARK, N.J.).** (FILM & HISTORY.). [Film hist.]. **Added/Corp** Historians Film Committee (Newark, N.J.). **VFOAT** Film and History. **VAT** Film and History. (1971)-. Academic Scholarly Publication. English. qt (Feb., May, Sept., Dec.). $15.00 (individuals), $25.00 (institutions) US; $25.00 (individuals), $35.00 (institutions) other. University of Miami History Department, Greg Bush, PO Box 248107, Coral Gables FL 33124. **Tel** (305)284-3660, FAX (305)284-3558. **ED** Gregory Bush. **LC** PN1995.2; .F54. **DD** 791.43/09/09358. cum. index. **Bk Rev**, (Qty: 10). **Ad Acc. Pr Rev. Circ:** 400. ***Continues*** *Historians Film Committee. Newsletter - Historians Film Committee.*
**Desc:** Study of film and television by historians and social scientists for their research, teaching, and scholarly output.
**Ind/Abst** Am. Hist. Life (1972-); Am. Bibliogr. Slavic East Europ. Stud.; Film Lit. Index.

NO/0015-1351
**FILM & KINO.** [Film kino]. **Added/Corp** Kommunale Kinematografers Landsforbund. **VFOAT** Kino. (1965)-. Periodical. Norwegian.
**Ind/Abst** Film Lit. Index.

UK/0956-8409
**FILM AND TELEVISION HANDBOOK / BRITISH FILM INSTITUTE.** ***Title Change.*** **Added/Corp** British Film Institute. **VFOAT** Film and Television Handbook; British Film Institute Film and Television Handbook. (1990)-(1992). English. an. British Film Institute, 21 Stephen Street, London W1P 1PL England. **Tel** 11 44 71 2551444, FAX 11 44 71 4367950, telex 27624 BFILDNG. **LC** PN1993.3; .F418. **DD** 384/.8/02541. ***Continues*** *BFI Film and Television Yearbook.* ***Continued by*** *BFI Film and Television Handbook.*

UK
**FILM AND TELEVISION TECHNICIAN. Added/Corp** Association of Cinematograph, Television and Allied Technicians. (1961)-. Periodical. English. Eleven times a year. Free to members; £15.00 (nonmembers). Association of Cinema Television and Technicians, 111 Wardour Street, London W1V 4AY England. **Tel** 011 44 71 4378506. **ED** Peter Avis. **Bk Rev. Ad Acc. Circ:** 25,000. ***Continues*** *Film and TV Technician.*
**Desc:** A trade union journal.

US/0898-1582
**FILM & VIDEO FINDER.** [Film video finder]. **Added/Corp** National Information Center for Educational Media. **VFOAT** Film and Video Finder; NICEM Film and Video Finder; NICEM Film & Video Finder. 1st Ed. (1987)-. English. an. Price varies per volume. Plexus Publishing Inc., 143 Old Marlton Pike, Medford NJ 08055. **Tel** (609)654-6500, FAX (609)654-4309. **ED** J. C. Johnstone, Patricia Smith and Camille Fullington. **LC** LB1044.Z9; F58. **DD** 011. **NLM** LB 1044; F487. **Bk Rev. Circ:** 2,000 (ctrl). available on CD-ROM from SilverPlatter (US). ***Formed by the union of*** *Index to Educational Videotapes, 0734-6921* ***and*** *Index to 16mm Educational Films, 0734-5488.*
**Desc:** Indexes 16mm films and video cassettes of an educational, informational or documentary nature. Gives current information on name and address of producer and distributor. Lists 90,000 films or videotapes.

US/1041-1933
**FILM & VIDEO (LOS ANGELES, CALIF.).** (FILM & VIDEO.). [Film video]. **VFOAT** Film and Video. Vol. 5, Issue 11 (Nov. 1988)-. Periodical. English. mo. $55.00 US; $80.00 Canada, Mexico, and Central America; $95.00 other. Optic Music Subscriptions, 8455 Beverly Boulevard, Suite 508, Los Angeles CA 90048. **Tel** (213)653-8053, FAX (213)653-8190. **ED** David Swartz. **DD** 791. **Ad Acc. Circ:** 19,000 (ctrl). ***Continues*** *Opticmusic's Film & Video Production, 0894-4423.*
**Desc:** Covers the production of television, commercials, music videos and motion pictures behind the scenes.

US/0270-3289
**FILM AND VIDEO MAKERS DIRECTORY, THE.** [Film video mak. dir.]. Directory. English. be. $5.00. Carnegie Museum of Natural History, 4400 Forbes Avenue, Pittsburgh PA 15213. **Tel** (412)622-3315, FAX (412)622-8837. **ED** Lisa Mertz. **LC** PN1993.5.U6; F48. **DD** 384/.8/025. **Ad Acc. Circ:** 2,000.
**Desc:** Lists screening and lecture tours of independent filmmakers and other information relevant to independents and their exhibitors in the United States and abroad.

CN/1181-6708
**FILM AND VIDEO (OTTAWA). See** Motion Picture-Abstracting, Bibliographies and Statistics.

●US/1061-4214
**FILM ANNUAL.** (1992)-. English. $14.95. Film Annual, 27813 Glenhurst, #115, Aliso Viejo CA 92656.

AT
**FILM AUSTRALIA EDUCATION CATALOGUE.** English. an. Film Australia Pty Ltd, Eton Road, Lindfield New South Wales 2070 Australia. **Tel** 02 413 8777, FAX 02 416 5672, telex 22734. **Circ:** 18,000 (ctrl).

US/0015-1165
**FILM BULLETIN.** [Film bull.]. V. 1- 1933-. Bulletin. English. bm. Wax Publications, 1239 Vine Street, Philadelphia PA 19107. **LC** PN1993; .F435. **DD** 792.9305.
**Ind/Abst** Film Lit. Index; Med. Rev. Dig.

US/0015-119X
**FILM COMMENT.** [Film comment]. **Added/Corp** Film Society of Lincoln Center. Vol. 1, No. 3 (1962)-. Periodical. English. bm. $24.95 (1 year), $42.95 (2 year), $59.95 (3 year) US; $32.00 (1 year), $57.00 (2 year), $80.00 (3 year) Canada and Mexico; $50.00 (1 year), $90.00 (2 year), $130.00 (3 year) other. Film Society of Lincoln Center, 70 Lincoln Center Plaza, New York NY 10023. **Tel** (212)875-5610. **ED** Richard T Jameson. **LC** PN1993; .F438. Index available. **Bk Rev. Ad Acc. Circ:** 47,000 (ctrl). available on microfilm and microfiche from University Microfilms International (UMI). Documents available from The Genuine Article, UMI Article Clearinghouse, Magazine Collection. ***Continues*** *Vision (New York, N.Y.).*
**Desc:** Film journal containing articles directly related to the cinema.
**Ind/Abst** Acad. Abstr. Full Text Elite (Feb. 1984-); Acad. Abstr. (Feb. 1984-); Acad. Ind. [Computer File] (1984-); Acad. Search (Feb. 1984-); Art Index; Arts Humanit. Citation Index [Full Cov.]; Book Rev. Index (1975-); Curr. Contents Arts Humanit.; Expand. Acad. Index (1984-); Film Lit. Index; Gen. Period. Index (1985-); Humanit. Index; Humanit. Source (Jan. 1988-); INFO-SOUTH Abstr.; Mag. Artic. Summar. Elite (Feb. 1984-); Mag. Artic. Summar. Select (Feb. 1984-); Mag. Artic. Summar. CD-ROM (Feb. 1984-); Mag. Express (1986-) [Full Txt.]; Mag. Index Plus (1989-); Mag. Index. Sel. (1986-); Mag. Search; Med. Rev. Dig.; Newsp. Period. Abstr. (1986-); Read. Guide Abstr. Select Ed.; Read. Guide Period. Lit.; Res. Alert [Full Cov.]; Resource/One Ondisc; Mag. Index (1977-); Vocat. Search (Feb. 1984-).

US/1055-081X
**FILM COMPOSERS GUIDE.** [Film compos. guide]. **VFOAT** Film Composers. 1st Ed. (1990)-. English. an. $45.00 US; $55.00 Canada; $60.00 other. Lone Eagle Publishing Inc., 2337 Roscomare Road, Suite 9, Los Angeles CA 90077. **Tel** (310)471-8066, FAX (310)471-4969. **LC** ML128.M7; F54. **DD** 781.5/42/0922.

US/0163-5069
**FILM CRITICISM.** [Film crit.]. Vol. 1 (Spring 1976)-. Academic Scholarly Publication. English. Three times a year. $15.00 (individuals), $18.00 (institutions) US; $18.00 (individuals), $21.00 (institutions) other. Film Criticism, Allegheny College, Meadville PA 16335. **Tel** (814)332-4343, (814)332-4333. **ED** Lloyd Michaels. **LC** PN1993; .F4183. **DD** 791.43/75/05. cum. index. **Bk Rev**, (Qty: 10). **Pr Rev. Circ:** 600. Documents available from The Genuine Article.
**Desc:** Scholarly writing on film.
**Ind/Abst** Arts Humanit. Citation Index [Full Cov.]; Book Rev. Index (1983-); Curr. Contents Arts Humanit.; Film Lit. Index; Lit. Crit. Regist.; MLA Int. Bibl. Books Artic. Mod. Lang. Lit.; Res. Alert [Full Cov.]; Soc. Sci. Cit. Index [Select. Cov.].

US/0015-1211
**FILM CULTURE.** [Film cult.]. No. 1 (Jan. 1955)-. Periodical. English. ir. $20.00 US; $26.00 other. Film Culture, 32 Second Avenue, New York NY 10003. **Tel** (212)505-5181, FAX (212)477-2714. **ED** David Koh. **LC** PN1993; .F44. **DD** 791.4305. Index available. **Bk Rev. Ad Acc. Circ:** 2,000. available on microfilm and microfiche from University Microfilms International (UMI). Documents available from UMI Article Clearinghouse.
**Desc:** A journal devoted to Avant-garde Independent cinema. Writings by film-makers, interviews with film-makers and critical writing by scholars.
**Ind/Abst** Acad. Ind. [Computer File] (1987-); Acad. Search (July 1993-); Art Index; Expand. Acad. Index (1987-); Film Lit. Index; Gen. Period. Index (1987-); Humanit. Source (Jul. 1993-); INFO-SOUTH Abstr.; Mag. Search; Med. Rev. Dig.; Newsp. Period. Abstr. (1992-).

US/0740-1566
**FILM (DENVER, COLO.).** ***Suspended.*** (FILM.). [Film]. (1983)-Suspended with Vol. 2. English. ir. Arden Press, PO Box 418, Denver CO 80201. **Tel** (303)239-6155. **ED** Frederick Ramey. **LC** PN1995.9.E96; F48. **DD** 791.43/75/0973. Index available. **Circ:** 2,000.
**Desc:** Each volume treats the work of 15-20 independent and experimental filmmakers informatively and critically. Each volume has a different author.

IE
**FILM DIRECTIONS.** V. 1-. Periodical. English. qt. £4.50. Arts Council of Northern Ireland, 181A Stranmills Road, Belfast 9 Ireland. **Tel** (0232)667687. **ED** Michael Open. **LC** PN1993.5.I85; F54. **DD** 791.43/05. **Bk Rev. Ad Acc. Circ:** 3,000.
**Desc:** Film reviews, general articles on cinema, video and other related matters.
**Ind/Abst** Film Lit. Index.

UK/0305-1706
**FILM DOPE.** [Film dope]. No. 1 (Dec. 1972)-. Periodical. English. ir (subscriptions cover 4 issues). $24.20. Film Dope, c/o Derek Owen, 74 Julian Road, Nottingham NG2 5AN England. **ED** Bob Baker and Derek Owen. Index available. **Bk Rev. Ad Acc. Circ:** 2,500.
**Desc:** Complete and correct filmographies of the world's major film artists (directors, actors, photographers, composers, art directors, animators, etc.). Many stills.
**Ind/Abst** Film Lit. Index.

FR/0181-4141
**FILM ECHANGE.** [Film echange]. (1978)-. Periodical. French. qt. Societe Auxiliaire pour le Cinema et la Television, 50 Avenue Marceau, 75008 Paris France.
**Ind/Abst** Film Lit. Index (19??-).

BE
**FILM EN TELEVISIE EN VIDEO.** (19??)-. Bulletin. Dutch. mo (10 issues per year). 1100F Belgium; 1450F other. Katholieke Filmliga VZW, Haachtsesteenweg 35, B-1030 Brussels Belgium. **Tel** 011 32 2 2170096, FAX 011 32 2 2170233. Index available. **Bk Rev**, (Qty: 10). **Ad Acc, Adv Mgr:** Ronnie Pede. Full Page (B&W) 735F. Half Page (B&W) 440F. **Pr Rev. Circ:** 10,000.
**Desc:** Extensive reviews of major new film and video releases, profiles and interviews, and festival news.
**Ind/Abst** Film Lit. Index (19??-).

US/0731-5716
**FILM FILE ... , THE.** ***Suspended.*** (1982)-Suspended (19??). Periodical. English. an. Media Referral Service, 15508 McKenzie Boulevard, Minnetonka MN 55345. **Tel** (612)933-2819. **ED** Elizabeth L. Burnam. **LC** PN1998; .F53. **DD** 011/.37. **Circ:** 5,000.
**Desc:** Films and videocassettes available from 150 distributors.

US/1056-6945
**... FILM FINANCIAL RECORD, THE.** [Film financ. rec.]. **Added/Corp** Paul Kagan Associates. (19??)-. English. Twelve times a year. $250.00. Kagan World Media Inc., 126 Clock Tower Place, Carmel CA 93923-8734. **Tel** (408)624-1536, FAX (408)625-3225. **LC** PN1993.5.U6; F49. **DD** 384/.8/0973021.

FR
**FILM FRANCAIS, LE.** ***Title Change.*** No. 1 (1944)-(19??). Periodical. French. wk. Le Film Francais, 90 rue de Flandre, 75943 Paris Cedex 19 France. **Tel** 200

35 00. **LC** PN1993; .F487. ***Merged with*** *Cinematographie Francaise* ***to form*** *Film Francais-La Cinematographie Francaise.*

FR/0759-0385
**FILM FRANCAIS 1983, LE.** (CINEMA DE FRANCE FILM FRANCAIS.). [Film fr.1983]. **VFOAT** Cinema de France. Le Film Francais; Film Francais. Cinema de France. (1983)-. Periodical. Multiple languages. Fifty-two times a year. 1939.28F France; 2490.00F Africa & Europe; 2740.00F other. Film Francais, 103 Boulevard Saint-Michel, 75005 Paris France. **Tel** 011 33 1 43294090. **(Subscription address:** Cinema de France Film Francais, 90 rue de Flandre, 75947 Paris Cedex 19 France.**)** **UDC** 778. ***Continues*** *TLe Nouveau Film Francais (Neuilly-sur-Seine), 0181-3528.*

BO
**FILM/HISTORIA.** V. 1- May 1978-. Periodical. Spanish. $20.00. A G Dragon Film/Historia, Casilla 5828, La Paz Bolivia. **LC** PN1993.5.L3; F55. **DD** 791.43/098.

FI
**FILM IN FINLAND (HELSINKI, FINLAND).** (FILM IN FINLAND.). **Added/Corp** Suomen Elokuvasaatio. (19??)-. Periodical. English.

AT/0015-1289
**FILM INDEX.** (19??)-. English. Four times a year (Feb., May, Aug., Nov.). 160.00Aus$. Rastar PTY Ltd, 26 Casey Drive, Wyong NSW 2259 Australia. **Tel** 011-61-43-532521. **ED** John H. Reid. **LC** PN1993; .F59. **DD** 791.43/05. Index available. cum. index. **Bk Rev**, (Qty: varies). **Ad Acc**, **Adv Mgr:** J. Reid, **Tel** 532 2521. **Circ:** 5,000 (ctrl).
**Desc:** Detailed cast and credit information, background data, and reviews of "Golden Age" motion pictures.

US/0742-6739
**FILM INDUSTRY GAZETTE.** [Film ind. gaz.]. **VFOAT** FIG; F.I.G. Vol. 1, No. 1 (Oct. 1983)-. Periodical. English. mo. $25.00. Film Industry Gazette, 10611 Ayres Avenue, Los Angeles CA 90064.

US/0046-3787
**FILM JOURNAL (HOLLINS), THE.** ***Suspended.*** (THE FILM JOURNAL.). Vol. 1 Issue 1 (Spring 1971)-(19??). Periodical. English. mo. $25.00 (one year), $45.00 (two year). Pubsun Corporation, 244 West 49th Street, Suite 305, New York NY 10019. **Tel** (212)246-6460, FAX (212)265-6428. **ED** Robert H. Sunshine and Kevin Lally. **LC** PN1993; .F613. **DD** 791.43/05. **Bk Rev**. **Ad Acc**. **Circ:** 9,500 (ctrl). available on microfilm from University Microfilms International (UMI).
**Desc:** Coverage of the motion picture industry and ancillary markets, including video, concessions, equipment, film reviews and interviews.
**Ind/Abst** Film Lit. Index; Int. Index Film Period.

US/0199-7300
**FILM JOURNAL (NEW YORK), THE.** (THE FILM JOURNAL.). [Film j.]. Vol. 82, No. 12 (1979)-. Periodical. English. mo. $40.00. Pubsun Corporation, 244 West 49th Street, Suite 305, New York NY 10019. **Tel** (212)246-6460, FAX (212)265-6428. ***Continues*** *Independent Film Journal, 0019-3712.*
**Ind/Abst** Film Lit. Index.

US/0093-6758
**FILM LITERATURE INDEX.** **See** Motion Picture-Abstracting, Bibliographies and Statistics.

UK/0015-1025
**FILM (LONDON, ENGLAND : 1954).** (FILM.). [Film]. **Added/Corp** British Federation of Film Societies. Federation of Film Societies (Great Britain). (Oct. 1954)-; Series 2 (April 1973)-. Periodical. English. bm. £22.00 UK; £20.00 other. Film Graphica, PO Box 1DR, London W1A 1DR England. **Tel** 011 44 71 7349300. **ED** Peter Cargin. **Ad Acc**. **Circ:** 3,000 (ctrl).
**Desc:** Covers film news, books, festival reports, and general information on all aspects of non-commercial cinema.
**Ind/Abst** Film Lit. Index; Med. Rev. Dig.

PL/0137-4877
**FILM NA SWIECIE 1974.** [Film na Swiecie 1974]. (1974)-. Periodical. Polish. bm (6 issues). Price on Request. **(Subscription address:** ARS Polona, PO Box 1001, 00068 Warsaw Poland.**)** **UDC** 791.43. ***Continues*** *Kultura Filmowa, 0137-3951.*

IO
**FILM NEWS.** **Main/Corp** Indonesia. Direktorat Film. No. 1/4-. Indonesian (Indonesian). Mereka Barat 9, Jakarta Indonesia. **LC** PN1993; .I622A. ***Supersedes*** *Film News.*

US/0741-0492
**FILM NEWS INTERNATIONAL.** [Film news int.]. **VFOAT** Film News-International; Film News. (1983)-. Periodical. English. mo. $120.00. Film News International, 1800 Avenue of the Stars, Los Angeles CA 90067. ***Continues*** *VPI International News.*

NO
**FILM OG KINO / KOMMUNALE KINEMATOGRAFERS LANDSFORBUND.** **Added/Corp** Kommunale Kinematographers Landsforbund (Norway). (1938)-. Norwegian. an. **LC** PN1993.3; .F467. **DD** 791.43/05.

US/1058-2630
**FILM PRODUCERS, STUDIOS, AGENTS, AND CASTING DIRECTORS GUIDE.** [Film prod. stud. agents casting dir. guide]. 2nd Ed. (1990)-. English. an. $45.00 US; $55.00 Canada; $60.00 other. Lone Eagle Publishing Inc., 2337 Roscomare Road, Suite 9, Los Angeles CA 90077. **Tel** (310)471-8066, FAX (310)471-4969. **LC** PN1998.A1; F484. **DD** 791.43/0232/02573. ***Continues*** *Film Producers, Studios & Agents Guide, 0894-8666.*

US/0015-1386
**FILM QUARTERLY.** [Film q.]. **Added/Corp** University of California, Berkeley. Vol. 12, No. 1, (1958)-. Periodical. English. qt (Mar., June, Sept., Dec.). $23.00 (individuals), $47.00 (institutions). University of California Press, 2120 Berkeley Way, Berkeley CA 94720. **Tel** (510)642-4191, (510)642-3907, FAX (510)642-9917. **ED** Ann Martin. **LC** PN1993; .H457. **[CCC]**. Index available. **Bk Rev**. **Ad Acc**. **Pr Rev**. **Circ:** 6,900 (ctrl). available on microfilm and microfiche from University Microfilms International (UMI). Documents available from The Genuine Article, UMI Article Clearinghouse, Magazine Collection. ***Continues*** *Quarterly of Film, Radio and Television.*
**Desc:** Articles on commercial and experimental developments in film theory and criticism.
**Ind/Abst** Acad. Abstr. Full Text Elite (July 1990-); Acad. Abstr. (July 1990-); Acad. Ind. [Computer File] (1984-); Acad. Search (July 1990-); Access (1978-?); Am. Bibliogr. Slavic East Europ. Stud.; Art Index; Arts Humanit. Citation Index [Full Cov.]; Biogr. Index; Book Rev. Digest; Book Rev. Index; Curr. Contents Arts Humanit.; Expand. Acad. Index (1984-); Film Lit. Index; Gen. Period. Index (1985-); Humanit. Index; Humanit. Source (Jul. 1990-); INFO-SOUTH Abstr.; Mag. Index Plus (1989-); Mag. Search; Med. Rev. Dig.; Middle East Abstr. Index; MLA Int. Bibl. Books Artic. Mod. Lang. Lit.; Newsp. Period. Abstr. (1986-); Pop. Period. Index; Read. Guide Period. Lit.; Res. Alert [Full Cov.]; Mag. Index (1977-).

US
**FILM REVIEW.** Began publication in 1944?. English. an. W H Allen and Company Ltd, 44 Hill Street, London W1 England. **ED** F M Speed. **LC** PN1993. **DD** 791.4058.

UK
**FILM REVIEW.** **VFOAT** Film Review Now Incorporating Films and Filming. (1951)-. Periodical. English. mo. Plus Publications Ltd, 248 High Street, Croydon Surrey, CR0 1NF England. **Tel** (01)681-7817/8. **LC** PN1993; .F6243. **DD** 791.43/05. ***Absorbed*** *Films and Filming, 0015-167X.*

US/0737-9080
**FILM REVIEW ANNUAL.** [Film rev. annu.]. (1981)-. English. an. $130.00. Jerome S. Ozer Publishing, 340 Tenafly Road, Englewood NJ 07631. **Tel** (201)567-7040, FAX (201)641-8062. **ED** Jerome S. Ozer. **LC** PN1995; .F465. **DD** 791.43/75/0973. Index available. **Pr Rev**. **Circ:** 850. ***Continues*** *Film Review Digest Annual, 0146-1656.*
**Desc:** An annual compilation of film reviews from a variety of sources of feature-length films opening in the US.

US/0098-0471
**FILM REVIEW DIGEST (MILLWOOD).** (FILM REVIEW DIGEST.). [Film rev. dig.]. V. 1 (Fall 1975)-. English. $45.00. Kraus-Thomson Organization, Route 100, Millwood NY 10546. **LC** PN1995; .F46. **DD** 791.43/7.

UK
**FILM REVIEW (ENGLAND).** English. Twelve times a year (along with four special issues). £25.00 UK; $65.00 US; £28.00 Europe; £28.00 other (surface mail), £50.00 (airmail) other. Visual Imagination, I Blades Court Deodar Road, London SW15 2NU United Kingdom. **Tel** 011 44 181 8751520. **ED** Nick Briggs. Index available (bound in Yearbook issue). **Bk Rev**, (Qty: 120). **Ad Acc**, **Adv Mgr Tel** 081-878-5486. **Circ:** 23,500.
**Desc:** Includes film reviews, interviews with stars and directors.

US/0524-1324
**FILM STUDIES.** **Main/Corp** Boston University. School of Public Relations and Communications. Communications Arts Division. **VFOAT** Boston University Film Studies. No. 1- 1964-. Periodical. English. Boston University / Brookline, MA, 745 Commonwealth Avenue, Room 435, Boston MA 02215. **Tel** (617)353-6480.

US/0896-6389
**FILM THREAT.** [Film threat]. Issue 1 (Nov. 1991)-. Periodical. English. bm (6 issues). $11.85. LFP Inc., 9171 Wilshire Boulevard/Suite 300, Beverly Hills CA 90210. **Tel** (310)858-7100, FAX (310)274-7985. **(Subscription address:** Kable Publishers Aide, 308 East Hitt Street, Subscription Department, Mt. Morris IL 61054-1473.**)** **DD** 791. ***Continues*** *Film Threat, 0896-6389.*

US/0896-6389
**FILM THREAT.** ***Title Change.*** [Film threat]. (Feb. 1985)-(19??). Periodical. English. bm. LFP Inc., 9171 Wilshire Boulevard/Suite 300, Beverly Hills CA 90210. **Tel** (310)858-7100, FAX (310)274-7985. **DD** 791. ***Continued by*** *Film Threat (Beverly Hills, Calif. : 1991), 0896-6389.*
**Ind/Abst** Film Lit. Index (19??-).

IT
**FILM : TUTTI I FILM DELLA STAGIONE.** **Added/Corp** Centro Studi Cinematografici (Rome, Italy). (198?)-. Periodical. Italian. bm. $50.00. Centro Studi Cinematografici, Via Gregorio VII 6, 00165 Rome Italy. **Tel** 011 39 6 6382605. **LC** PN1998; .F49. **DD** 016.79143/75. Index available. cum. index. **Ad Acc**. ctrl circ.
**Ind/Abst** Film Lit. Index (19??-).

GW/0934-0378
**FILM UND FARBE.** **Main/Corp** Deutsche Kinotechnische Gesellschaft. German. DM36.00. Spitzenorganisation der Filmwirtschaft, Langenbeckstr 9, Postfach 5129, W-6200 Wiesbaden Germany. **Tel** 06121 17270, FAX 1727 39. **ED** Joachim Grassmann. Index available. cum. index. **Bk Rev**. **Ad Acc**. **Circ:** 3,000.

GW/0323-3227
**FILM UND FERNSEHEN.** [Film Ferns.]. **Added/Corp** Verband der Film- und Fernsehschaffenden der Deutschen Demokratishen Republik. (1955)-. German (table of contents in English and Russian). mo.
**Ind/Abst** Film Lit. Index.

GW/0343-5571
**FILM- UND TV-KAMERAMANN.** [Film-TV-Kameramann]. **VFOAT** Film- und Television-Kameramann; Kameramann; Film- & TV-Kameramann. (1977)-. Periodical. German. mo. DM79.80. Verlag I Weber KG, Postfach 3060, D 89020 Ulm Germany. **Tel** 011 49 731 152056. **UDC** 778.5. ***Continues*** *Der Deutsche Kameramann, 0012-0340.*
**Ind/Abst** Film Lit. Index (19??-).

CN/0836-1002
**FILM/VIDEO CANADIANA.** [Film/video Can.]. **VFOAT** Film/Video Canadiana. 1985/1986-. English (French). 35.00Can$ Canada; $40.00 US. National Film Board of Canada, PO Box 6100 Station A, Montreal Quebec H3C 3H5 Canada. **Tel** (514)283-9427, FAX (514)283-7564. **ED** Jana Vosikovska. **LC** PN1993.5.C2; F55. **DD** 015.71/037. Index available. **Bk Rev**. **Circ:** 1,000. available on an online database. ***Continues*** *Film Canadiana, 0015-1173.*

US/0894-864X
**FILM WRITERS GUIDE.** [Film writ. guide]. **VFOAT** Film Writers. 1st Ed. (1988)-. English. an. $45.00 US; $55.00 Canada; $60.00 other. Lone Eagle Publishing Inc., 2337 Roscomare Road, Suite 9, Los Angeles CA 90077. **Tel** (310)471-8066, FAX (310)471-4969. **LC** PN1996; .F447. **DD** 808/.066791.

IT
**FILMCRITICA.** (1950)-. Periodical. Italian. ir (10 issues per year). L65000 Italy; L90000 other. Editori del Grifo, Via Gracciano Nel Corso 64, 53045 Montepulciano SI Italy. **Tel** 011 39 578 717090. ***Absorbed*** *Spettatore Critico.*
**Ind/Abst** Film Lit. Index.

GW
**FILMECHO, FILMWOCHE, FILMBLAETTER.** (19??)-. German. wk (published on Fri.). DM470.00. Verlag Horst Axtmann GmbH, Wilhelmstrasse 42, D-65183 Wiesbaden Germany. **Tel** 011 49 611 360980.

GW
**FILMFAUST.** Periodical. German. Six times a year. DM116.40. Filmfaust Verlag, Schumanstrasse 64, W-6000 Frankfurt Am Main 1 Germany. **Tel** 069-74.83.05, FAX 069-72.40.823. **ED** Bion Steinborn and Christine von Ecihel-Streiber. **LC** PN1993; .F474. Index available. cum. index. **Bk Rev**. **Ad Acc**. **Circ:** 13,000 (ctrl).
**Ind/Abst** Film Lit. Index.

US/0895-0393
**FILMFAX.** [Filmfax]. **VFOAT** Film Fax. No. 1 (Jan./Feb. 1986)-. Periodical. English. Six times a year. Filmfax, PO Box 1900, Evanston IL 60202. **Tel** (708)866-7155. **ED** Michael Stein and Sharon Williams. **Bk Rev**. **Ad Acc**. **Circ:** 15,000.
**Desc:** Focuses on "unusual film and television" from early 1930's to late 1970's; classics to low-budget "B's," including film noir, horror, exploitation, science fiction, comedy and adventure.
**Ind/Abst** Film Lit. Index.

SZ
**FILMFORDERUNG ... STATISTIK, FILMEINFUHR, STATISTIK / EIDGENOSSISCHES AMT FUER KULTURELLE ANGELEGENHEITEN, SEKTION FILM.** **See** Motion Picture-Abstracting, Bibliographies and Statistics.

# Motion Picture

SW/0345-3057
**FILMHAFTET : TIDSKRIFT OM FILM OCH TV.** (1973)-. Swedish. qt (Jan., Mar., Sept., Dec.). Kr140.00. Filmhaftet, PO Box 16046, Storgatan 15, S75331 Uppsala Sweden. **Tel** 011 46 18 123503.
**Ind/Abst** Film Lit. Index (19??-).

FI
**FILMIHULLU.** [Filmihullu]. (1968)-. Periodical. Finnish.
**Ind/Abst** Film Lit. Index (19??-).

HU/0015-1580
**FILMKULTURA.** [Filmkultura]. **Added/Corp** Magyar Filmtudomanyi Intezet es Filmarchivum. **VFOAT** Film Kultura. (Jan. 1960)-. Periodical. Hungarian (table of contents in English). mo. $32.00. **(Subscription address:** Kultura, PO Box 149, H 1389 Budapest 62 Hungary.**)** available on microfilm from University Microfilms International (UMI).
**Ind/Abst** Film Lit. Index.

AU/0015-1599
**FILMKUNST.** [Filmkunst]. **Added/Corp** Osterreichische Gesellschaft fur Filmwissenschaft, Kommunikations- und Medienforschung. Austria. Bundesministerium fur Unterricht und Kunst. No. 1 (1949/50)-. Periodical. German. qt. S250.00 Austria; S340.00 other. Filmkunst, Postfach 253, Rauhensteingasse5, A1015 Vienna 1 Austria. **Tel** (0222)5129936, FAX 513 53 30. **ED** Ludwig Gesek. **Bk Rev. Ad Acc. Circ:** 1,000.
**Desc:** Motion picture and television as object of scientific research.
**Ind/Abst** Film Lit. Index.

AU
**FILMLOGBUCH.** German. bm. S180.00 Austria; S350.00 other. Erwin Schwaiger Verlag Gesellschaft GmbH, Seilers 13 25, A-1010 Vienna Austria. **Tel** 5133246.

●US/1063-8954
**FILMMAKER (LOS ANGELES, CALIF.).** (FILMMAKER.). [Filmmaker]. **Added/Corp** Independent Feature Project. Independent Feature Project/West. **VFOAT** Film Maker. Vol. 1, No. 1 (Fall 1992)-. Periodical. English. qt. $35.00 (institutions), $14.00 (individual, US), $25.00 (individual, Canada). Filmmaker, 5550 Wilshire Boulevard, Suite 204, Los Angeles CA 90036. **LC** PN1993; .F55663. **DD** 791. **Formed by the union of** Off-Hollywood Report, 1045-1706.

AT/1036-8701
**FILMNEWS.** English. mo. 20.00Aus$ Australia; 35.00Aus$ other. FN Publishing, Paddington Town Hall, PO Box 299, Paddington, New South Wales, 2021 Australia. **Tel** 011 61 2 3607313.
**Ind/Abst** Film Lit. Index (19??-).

US/0195-7546
**FILMROW.** [FilmRow]. **VFOAT** Film Row; Filmrow Motion Picture Marketing Blackbook; Motion Picture Marketing Blackbook. 1981-82-. English. an. Filmrow Communications Group, 8272 Sunset Blvd. West, Hollywood CA 90046. **LC** PN1998.A1; F53. **DD** 384/.8/02573.

SW/0015-1661
**FILMRUTAN.** [Filmrutan]. Vol. 1 (1958)-. Periodical. Swedish. Four times a year (Mar., June. Sept., Dec.). Kr80.00. Filmrutan, Box 82, 2 851 02 Sundsvall Sweden. **Tel** 011 46 60 158740.
**Ind/Abst** Film Lit. Index (1974-1977).

US
**FILMS / A CATALOG OF THE FILM COLLECTION. Main/Corp** New York. Public Library. (19??)-. Catalog. English. ir. Films / A Catalog of the Film Collection, Fifth Avenue & 42nd Street, New York NY 10018. **LC** PN1995.9.D6; N4. **DD** 791.438.

CN/0046-3825
**FILMS A L'ECRAN. Added/Corp** Office des Communications Sociales. (1???)-. Periodical. French. Twenty-one times a year. 25.00Can$ Canada; 35.00Can$ other. Office Des Communications Sociales, 1340 Boulevard St. Joseph EST, Montreal QUE H2J 1M3 Canada. **Tel** (514)524-8223, FAX (514)524-8522. **DD** 791.43/7/05. **Circ:** 850.
**Desc:** Index for the evaluation of new films.

US/0361-4581
**FILMS BY AND/OR ABOUT WOMEN.**
**Ceased. Added/Corp** Women's History Research Center. Women's History Library. ?. English. ir. Womens History Research, 2325 Oak Street, Berkeley CA 94708. **Tel** (510)548-1770.

US/0015-1688
**FILMS IN REVIEW.** [Films rev.]. **Added/Corp** National Board of Review of Motion Pictures (U.S.). Vol. 1 (Feb. 1950)-. Periodical. English. Six times a year. $18.00 US; $22.00 other. National Board of Review of Motion Pictures, PO Box 589, New York NY 10021. **Tel** (212)628-1594. **ED** Robin Little. **LC** PN1993; .F6473. **DD** 791.43/7. cum. index. **Bk Rev. Ad Acc. Circ:** 25,000. available on microfilm and microfiche from University Microfilms International (UMI). Documents available from UMI Article Clearinghouse. **Supersedes** New Movies.
**Desc:** Oldest film magazine published. Articles on actor-actresses, directors, cinematographers. Columns on films, video, TV, film music, film books, film books, rediscovery of "lost" films, complete filmographies. Used by university film departments, film industry, and film buffs.
**Ind/Abst** Acad. Search (July 1993-); Art Index; Book Rev. Index; Expand. Acad. Index (1992-); Film Lit. Index; Humanit. Source (Jul. 1993-); Index Book Rev. Humanit.; INFO-SOUTH Abstr.; Mag. Search; Med. Rev. Dig.; Middle East Abstr. Index; Newsp. Period. Abstr. (1992-); Ref. Sources.

UK
**FILMS ON OFFER ... / COMPILED BY NIGEL ALGAR AND STEPHEN JENKINS.** (19??)-. English. an. £14.95. British Film Institute, 21 Stephen Street, London W1P 1PL England. **Tel** 11 44 71 2551444, FAX 11 44 71 4367950, telex 27624 BFILDNG. **ED** Nigel Algar and Stephen Jenkins. **LC** PN1998; .F58. **DD** 011/.37. **Ad Acc. Circ:** 2,500.
**Desc:** An A-Z listing of all feature films available for non-theatrical hire in Britain.

SZ
**FILMSPIEGEL.** Periodical. German. bw. Deutscher Judo Verband, Redaktion Ippon Segewaldweg 40, D 12557 Berlin Germany. **Tel** 011 49 711 210770, telex 051 678.

DK/0107-1033
**FILMSSONEN, DANSK FILMFORTEGNELSE / UDGIVIT AF BIBLIOTEKSCENTRALEN OG DET DANSKE FILMMUSEUM. VFOAT** Dansk Filmfortegnelse. 79-80-. Periodical. Danish. an. Dansk Bibliotekscenter AS, Tempovej 7 11, DK-2750 Ballerup Denmark. **Tel** 011 45 42 974000. **LC** PN1997.8; .F56.

GW
**FILMVIDEO-JOURNAL.** German (German). an. DM6.80. GFW-Verlag, Poststrasse 21, Postfach 200 340, W-4000 Dusseldorf 1 Germany. **LC** TR845; .F58. **DD** 778.5/05.

HU
**FILMVILAG. VFOAT** Film Vilag. (1958)-. Hungarian (table of contents in English). mo. $31.00 Austria, Croatia, Czech & Slovak Republics, Yugoslavia, Slovenia, & Ukraine; $39.00 other. **(Subscription address:** Kultura, PO Box 149, H 1389 Budapest 62 Hungary)
**Ind/Abst** Film Lit. Index (19??-).

US
**FLORIDA BLUE SHEET.** [Fla. blue sheet]. (1990)-. English. sm (once in Dec. and Jan.). $39.00 U.S.; $49.00 Canada; $65.00 other. Flroida Blue Sheet, 7238 Hiawassee Oak Drive, Orlando FL 32818. **Tel** (407)292-7458. **ED** Karen Kuzsel (editor's phone: (404)774-8778). **DD** 338. **Ad Acc. Circ:** 20,000 (ctrl).

●CN/1189-5012
**FOCAL POINT.** [Focal point]. **Added/Corp** British Columbia Film Commission. (May/June, 1992)-. Periodical. English. **DD** 384/.8/09711.

US/0362-0905
**FOCUS : CHICAGO.** English. mo. $10.00. Facets Multimedia, 1517 West Fullerton Avenue, Chicago IL 60614. **Tel** (312)281-9075, (800)331-6197. **ED** Milos Stehlik. **LC** PN1993.F26; F6. **DD** 791.43/05. **Bk Rev. Ad Acc. Circ:** 25,000.
**Desc:** Art films and video, foreign, independent U.S., classic.

US
**FOCUS MAGAZINE. Added/Corp** University of California, Santa Barbara. Film Studies Program. **VFOAT** Focus. (Winter 1981)-. Periodical. English. Focus Magazine, c/o Film Studies Program, University of California, Santa Barbara CA 93106.
**Ind/Abst** Film Lit. Index (19??-).

US/0145-3556
**FOREMOST FILM OF ... .** 1st Ed. (June 1975). English. $250.00. Gordon Press, PO Box 459 Bowling Green Station, New York NY 10004. **ED** R Gordon. **LC** PN1993.3; .F652. **DD** 791.43/0973.
**Desc:** Yearbook of motion pictures.

CN/0711-3315
**FORMAT CINEMA.** [Format cine.]. No. 1 (June 1981)-. Periodical. French. bw. $25.00 per issue. Format Cinema, PO Box 397, Succ Outremont, Outremont Quebec H2V 4N3 Canada. **Tel** (514)744-4989. **DD** 338.4/779143/09714.

PN
**FORMATO 16. Added/Corp** Grupo Experimental de Cine Universitario. **VFOAT** Formato Dieciseis; Revista Formato 16. (1977)-. Periodical. Spanish. sa. Formato 16, Apartado 60-1775, Estafeta El Dorado, Panama R.P.
**Ind/Abst** Film Lit. Index (19??-).

US/0895-6030
**FRAME/WORK (LOS ANGELES, CALIF.).**
**See** Photography and Video.

UK/0306-7661
**FRAMEWORK. Suspended.** [Framework]. **Added/Corp** University of East Anglia. School of English and American Studies. University of Warwick Arts Federation. Issue No. 1 (1975)-1992. English. Three times a year. $6.00 UK; $16.00 US. Framework Sankofa Film Video, Unit K, 32-34 Gordon House Road, London NW5 1LP United Kingdom. **LC** PN1993; .F75. **DD** 791.43/05.
**Ind/Abst** Film Lit. Index; Med. Rev. Dig.

GW
**FRAUEN UND FILM.** No. 1 (1974)-. Periodical. German. Twice a year. DM40.00. Stroemfeld Roter Stern, Postfach 180147, W-6000 Frankfurt F R Germany. **Tel** 011 49 69 599999, FAX 011 49 69 559336. **ED** Heide Schlupmann and Gertrud Koch. **LC** PN1995.9.W6; F69. **DD** 791.43/088042. cum. index. **Bk Rev. Ad Acc. Circ:** 5,000.
**Desc:** European feminist film journal, including film reviews, feature articles on women film productions, and related question of media reception.
**Ind/Abst** Film Lit. Index.

US/0093-0881
**FREE LOAN FILMS. Main/Corp** Association-Sterling Films. **VFOAT** Free Loan 16 MM. Sound Motion Pictures. (19??)-. English. ir. Association-Sterling Films, 866 Third Avenue, New York NY 10022. **LC** PN1998; .A7. **DD** 011. **Continues** 16 MM. Sound Free Loan Films, Sales and Rental Subjects.

US/0436-1377
**GOLDEN EAGLE FILM AWARDS.**
**Added/Corp** Council on International Non-theatrical Events. (1957)-. Periodical. English. an. Golden Eagle Film Awards, 1201 16th Street NW, Washington DC 20036. **LC** PN1999.4; .G64.

US/0533-2508
**GREEN SHEET.** Periodical. English. mo. Motion Picture, 1133 Sixth Avenue, New York NY 10036-6709. **DD** 791.

IT/0393-3857
**GRIFFITHIANA. Added/Corp** Cineteca D.W. Griffith. Vol. 1, No. 1 (Nov. 1978)-. Periodical. Italian. Twice a year. $52.00 US; $57.00 Canada and Mexico; $62.00 other. La Cineteca del Friuli, Via Osoppo 26, 33014 Gemona Udine Italy. **Tel** 011 39 432 980458. **(Subscription address:** John Hopkins University Press, Journals Publishing Division, PO Box 19966, Baltimore MD 21211.**) LC** PN1993; .G74. **DD** 791.43/05.
**Ind/Abst** Film Lit. Index (19??-).

FR
**GUIDE DE L'AUDIOVISUEL EUROPEEN, LE.** (1989)-. French. an. 3200F Belgium & Luxembourg; 730F France; 4350F other. Edimedia ASBL, rue de la Constitution 22, 1030 Brussels Belgium. **Tel** 011 32 2 2180031. **LC** PN1993; .G8. **Bk Rev. Ad Acc.**

US/0072-8462
**GUIDE TO GOVERNMENT-LOAN FILMS.** 1st Ed.; 1969/70-. English. Serina Press, 70 Kennedy Street, Alexandria VA 22305. **LC** PN1998. **DD** 791.43/8.

US/0148-8538
**GUIDE TO LOCATION INFORMATION.**
**Added/Corp** Association of Motion Picture and Television Producers (U.S.). Public Relations Dept. (19??)-. English. an. $15.00. Guide to Location Info, 14144 Ventura Blvd, Sherman Oaks CA 91423. **Tel** (818)995-3600. **LC** PN1998.A1; G85. **DD** 791.43/0973.

PE/0046-6700
**HABLEMOS DE CINE. Suspended.** [Hablemos cine]. (19??)-Vol. 77. Periodical. Spanish. $15.00. Hablemos de Cine, Libertadores 199 San Isidro, Lima 27 Peru.
**Ind/Abst** Film Lit. Index (1978-1983).

KO
**HAN'GUK YONGHWA YON'GAM.** 1977- Yondopan. Korean. Yonghwe-Chinhung Kongsa, 34-5 Namsan-dong 3-ka, Chung-ku, Seoul South Korea. **LC** PN1993.5.K6; H29.

US/1050-8996
**HBO'S GUIDE TO MOVIES ON VIDEOCASSETTE AND CABLE TV. See** Photography and Video.

AG
**HERALDO DEL CINE.** (1967)-. Periodical. Spanish. wk. Heraldo Del Cine, Moreno 1215 1 Piso 1091, Buenos Aires Argentina. **Continues** Heraldo Del Cinematografista.

FR/0247-7769
**HIFI VIDEO MAGAZINE.** [Hifi Video mag.]. (1979)-. Periodical. French. mo. **Continues** Hifi Magazine, 0397-6424.
**Ind/Abst** Point Repere (1979-1980).

UK/0143-9685
**HISTORICAL JOURNAL OF FILM, RADIO, AND TELEVISION.** [Hist. j. film radio telev.]. **Added/Corp** International Association for Audio-Visual Media in Historical Research and Education. Vol. 1, No. 1 (Mar. 1981)-. Periodical. English. qt (Mar., June, Aug., Oct.). £154.00. Carfax Publishing Company, PO Box 25 Abingdon, Oxfordshire OX14 3UE England. **Tel** 011 44 235 555335, FAX (0279)31067, telex 817484. **(Subscription address:** US and Canada/ PO Box 2025, Dunnellon, FL 34430-2025; telephone:(904)489-6996**)** **ED** David Culbert. **LC** PN1993.5.A1; H54. **DD** 791.4/05. **[CCC]. Bk Rev. Ad Acc.** available on microfiche. Documents available from The Genuine Article, UMI Article Clearinghouse.
**Desc:** An interdisciplinary journal concerned with the media. Evidence produced for historians on the impact of mass communications on the 20th century.
**Ind/Abst** Acad. Search (July 1993-); Am. Hist. Life (1981-); Arts Humanit. Citation Index [Full Cov.]; Curr. Contents Arts Humanit.; Expand. Acad. Index (1992-); Film Lit. Index; Hist. Source (July 1993-); Humanit. Source (Jul. 1993-); INFO-SOUTH Abstr.; Int. Index Film Period.; Mag. Search; Med. Rev. Dig.; Multicult. Educ. Abstr.; Newsp. Period. Abstr. (1992-); Res. Alert [Full Cov.]; Soc. Sci. Cit. Index [Select. Cov.]; Sociol. Educ. Abstr.; Tech. Educ. Train. Abstr.

DK
**HITCH.** Danish (Danish). 6.00 single issue. **LC** PN1993; .H4.

●US/1062-5518
**HITCHCOCK ANNUAL.** [Hitchcock annu.]. **Added/Corp** Hitchcock Annual Association. **VFOAT** Hitchcock. (1992)-. English. an. $10.00 (institution), $7.00 (individual). Hitchcock Annual Association, PO Box 540, Gambier OH 43022. **ED** Christopher Brookhouse, (614)427-3156. **LC** PN1998.3.H58; H55. **DD** 791.43/0233/092. **Bk Rev. Ad Acc.**
**Desc:** Publishes articles of any length on Hitchcock and his films. Encourages a variety of approaches. Also publishes book reviews of film studies in general.

US/1075-6531
**HOLLYWOOD AGENTS/MANAGERS DIRECTORY.** [Hollywood agent/manag. dir.]. **VFOAT** Hollywood Agents and Managers Directory; Hollywood Agents & Managers Directory; A.Hollywood agents/managers direct. (199?)-. English. be. $81.00 US; $87.00 Canada; $99.00 other. Hollywood Creative Directory, 3000 Olympic Boulevard, Santa Monica CA 90404. **Tel** (310)315-4815, FAX (310)315-4816. **LC** PN2277.L59; H65. **DD** 790.2/025794/94. ***Continues*** *Hollywood Agents Directory.*

US/0018-3660
**HOLLYWOOD REPORTER, THE.** [Hollywood report.]. **VFOAT** Hollywood Reporter Magazine. Vol. 1 (1930)-. Periodical. English. da. $165.00 US; $485.00 Canada, Mexico, Central & South America; $985.00 other. Hollywood Reporter, 5055 Wilshire Boulevard, 6th Floor, Los Angeles CA 90036. **Tel** (213)525-2000. **ED** Tichi Wilkerson. **LC** PN1993; .H5. **DD** 384/.8/05. **[CCC]. Circ:** 21,120. available on an online database (files 16,570/Full-Text) from DIALOG. ***Absorbed in part by*** *American Film.*
**Desc:** For those in the entertainment industry; contains information on motion pictures, TV, cable, home video, music and theatre. Regular features include box office grosses, films and TV shows in development and production and celebrity interviews.

US/0195-7481
**HOLLYWOOD REPORTER TV SPECIAL, THE. VFOAT** TV Special. **VAT** Hollywood Reporter. Television Special. (1979)-. Periodical. English. qt. Free to subscribers of Hollywood Reporter. Hollywood Reporter, 5055 Wilshire Boulevard, 6th Floor, Los Angeles CA 90036. **Tel** (213)525-2000. **LC** PN1992; .H65. **DD** 791.45/0973. ***Continues*** *Televisions, 0163-5646.*

US/0894-2188
**HOLLYWOOD STUDIO MAGAZINE.** ***Ceased.*** [Hollywood stud. mag.]. **VFOAT** Hollywood Then and Now; Hollywood Studio Magazine, Then and Now. (1957)-(Oct. 1992). Periodical. English. Ten times a year. R B Productions, 3960 Laurel Canyon Boulevard/Suite 450, Studio City CA 91604-3791. **LC** PN1993; .H54. **DD** 791.43/0973.
**Desc:** Includes stories and rare photos from private collectors that have been assembled over 29 years of publication.
**Ind/Abst** Film Lit. Index.

FR/0755-0863
**HORS CADRE.** (Spring 1983)-. French (Italian). an. 85.00F. Michele Lagny, 152 Boulevard Magenta, 75010 Paris France. **Tel** 45 26 41 35. **LC** PN1993; .H63. **DD** 791.43/75. **Bk Rev. Ad Acc. Circ:** 800 (ctrl).
**Desc:** Each issue is a monograph on a particular theme from the field of motion pictures. This is an interdisciplinary journal that attempts to shift the basis of cinematographical analysis to other perspectives than film itself.

HU
**HUNGARIAN CINEMA.** (1989)-. Periodical. English. ir (three to four issues per year). $2.50, free to professional people. Hungarian Cinema, V Bathori U 10, Budapest PF 39 Hungary 1363. **Tel** 36 1 112-5425. **Ad Acc. Circ:** 2,500 (ctrl). ***Continues in part*** *Hungarofilm Bulletin, 0018-7798.*
**Desc:** Information on particular films (full-length and short films), directors, and other collaborators.

US/0099-1090
**IFPA COMMUNICATOR. Main/Corp** Information Film Producers of America. **VAT** Information Film Producers of America Communicator. Jan. 1973-. English. Information Film Producers of America, PO Box 1470, Hollywood CA 90028. **LC** PN1993.I624; A23. **DD** 791.43. ***Continues*** *IFPA Newsletter.*

NZ/0112-9341
**ILLUSIONS.** [Illusions]. **Added/Corp** Victoria University of Wellington. Drama Studies. No. 1 (Summer 1986)-. Periodical. English. Three times a year. $50.00 (institutions), $25.00 (individuals). Illusions, PO Box 6476 Te Aro, Wellington, New Zealand. **Tel** 011 64 4 8016466.
**Desc:** New Zealand's only magazine devoted to critical writing on the visual media (film, video, television, photography) and the performance arts (theatre, music). Aims to document and critically assess important work (mainly N.Z.) in its chosen areas of coverage, utilising perspectives from contemporary critical theory.
**Ind/Abst** Annu. Bibliogr. Engl. Lang. Lit.; Film Lit. Index (19??-).

PL/0209-3537
**ILUZJON WARSZAWA.** (ILUZJON.). [Iluzjon Warsz.]. (1981)-. Periodical. Polish. qt. $17.00. **(Subscription address:** ARS Polona, PO Box 1001, 00068 Warsaw Poland.**) UDC** 791.45.

UK/0950-2114
**IMAGE TECHNOLOGY (LONDON).** (IMAGE TECHNOLOGY : JOURNAL OF THE BKSTS.). [Image technol.]. **Added/Corp** British Kinematograph Sound and Television Society. Vol. 68, No. 7 (July 1986)-. Periodical. English. Twelve times a year. £65.00. British Kinematograph Sound and Television Society, M6-14 Victoria House, Vernon Place, London WC1B 4DF England. **Tel** 011 44 712 428400, FAX 011 44 714 053560. **ED** John Gainsborough. **LC** TR845; .B75. **DD** 778.5/05. **CODEN** IMATEV. Index available. **Bk Rev. Ad Acc. Circ:** 3,000. available on microfilm from University Microfilms International (UMI). Documents available from Ask*IEEE. ***Continues*** *British Kinematograph Sound and Television Society. BKSTS Journal.*
**Desc:** Technologies of motion picture film, television and sound.
**Ind/Abst** Curr. Technol. Index; Film Lit. Index (19??-); INSPEC (1986-).

PR
**IMAGENES.** ***Ceased.*** Vol. 1, No. 1 (1985)-?. Periodical. Spanish. sa. University of Interameric Puerto Rico, PO Box 1293 Decan Estudiantes, Hato Rey, Puerto Rico 00919.
**Ind/Abst** Film Lit. Index (1987-1988); MLA Int. Bibl. Books Artic. Mod. Lang. Lit.

IT
**IMMAGINE. Added/Corp** Associazione Italiana per le Ricerche di Storia del Cinema. (198?)-. Periodical. Italian. qt. L12000.00. **LC** PN1993; .I58. **DD** 791.43/05.
**Ind/Abst** Film Lit. Index (19??-).

US/0889-6208
**IN MOTION FILM & VIDEO PRODUCTION MAGAZINE.** **See** Photography and Video.

US/0731-5198
**INDEPENDENT (NEW YORK, N.Y. : 1978).** (THE INDEPENDENT.). [Independent]. **Added/Corp** Foundation for Independent Video and Film (U.S.). (1978)-. Periodical. English. Ten times a year (Jan./Feb. & Aug./Sept. issues combined). $45.00 (individuals), $75.00 (libraries), $100.00 (non-profit organization); $150.00 (business & industries), Comes with Association for Independent Video & Filmmakers membership. Association of Independent Video and Filmmakers - AIVF-FIVF, 625 Broadway, 9th Floor, New York NY 10012. **Tel** (212)473-3400, FAX (212)475-0964. **ED** Patricia Thomson. **LC** PN1993; .I617. **DD** 791.43/0973. **Bk Rev**, (Qty: 1-2). **Ad Acc, Adv Mgr:** Laura Davis, **Tel** (212)473-3400. **Circ:** 30,000.
**Desc:** A magazine of practical information for producers of independent film and video, with focus on low-budget, art, and documentary work for non-profit sector.
**Ind/Abst** Altern. Press Index (199?-); Film Lit. Index (19??-).

IT
**INDIAN FILM CULTURE. VFOAT** I.F.C.; IFC. Periodical. English. qt. $5.00 single issue. Federation of Film Societies of India, C-7 Bharat Bhawan 3 Chittaranjan Avenue, Calcutta 700072 India. **LC** PN1993.5.I8; I498. **DD** 791.43/0954.

II/0377-7359
**INDIAN FILMS (POONA).** (INDIAN FILMS.). 1972-. English. an. Rs100.00. B V Dharap, Alaka Talkies, Poona-30 India. **Tel** 443038. **ED** B V Dharap. **LC** PN1998; .I45. **DD** 015/.54. **Circ:** 2,000.
**Desc:** Publication on Indian cinema giving full details about production, distribution, exhibition, foreign markets, government role and screen organizations.

II
**INDIAN MOTION PICTURE ALMANAC.** English. an. 40.00. Shot Publications, 3-B Madan Street, Calcutta 700013 India. **LC** PN1993.3; .I48. **DD** 791.43/0954.

CN/0834-3187
**INFOCUS.** [Infocus]. **Added/Corp** Academy of Canadian Cinema & Television. Vol. 5, No. 4 (Nov. 1986)-. Newsletter. English (French). qt. Free to members. Academy of Canadian Cinema & Television, 2nd Floor 653 Yonge Street, Toronto Ontario M4Y 1Z9 Canada. **Tel** (416)967-0315, telex 06524428 CANAWARDS. **ED** Andra Sheffer and Marily Preston. **DD** 791.43/06/0971. **Circ:** 1,800. ***Continues*** *Newsletter (Academy of Canadian Cinema & Television), 0834-3179.*
**Desc:** A newsletter informing about Academy and Academy members' activities across Canada: Genie, Gemini and Gemeaux Awards, educational programs, publications, services and resources, etc.

BL
**INFORMACOES SOBRE A INDUSTRIA CINEMATOGRAFICA BRASILEIRA.** Portuguese. Empresa Brasileira de Filmes, Departamento de Ingressos Padronizados, rua Mayrink Veiga No 28 70 Andar, Rio de Janeiro Brazil. **LC** PN1993.3; .I52.

FR/0397-8435
**INFORMATIONS CNC.** ***Title Change.*** **Main/Corp** Centre National de la Cinematographie (France). **VFOAT** Bulletin d'Information du Centre National de la Cinematographie. **VAT** Informations Centre National de la Cinematographie. Periodical. French. qt (five no. a year). Centre National Cinematographie, 12 rue de Lubeck, 75784 Paris Cedex 16 France. **Tel** 011 33 1 45051440, FAX 011 33 1 47550491, telex 650306. **LC** PN1993.5.F7; A3. **DD** 338.4/7/791430944. ***Continues*** *Centre National de la Cinematographie (France). Bulletin d'Information.* ***Continued by*** *CNC Info.*

US/1057-1604
**INSTANT HITS.** (INSTANT HITS : YOUR COMPLETE CATALOG OF MOVIES AND EVENTS ON WARNER HOME THEATRE.). [Instant hits]. Vol. 1, Issue 1 (Jan., Feb. 1991)-. Catalog. English. bm. Free with service, $2.00 (single issue). W.C.C.I., 11252 Cornell Park Drive, Cincinnati OH 45242. **DD** 791.

NE
**INTERFILM REPORTS. Main/Corp** Interfilm. English. PO Box 515, Hilversum Netherlands. **LC** PN1993.3; .I537A. **DD** 791.43/05.

US
**INTERNATIONAL DICTIONARY OF FILMS AND FILMMAKERS, THE.** English. $95.00. International Dictionary of Art and Artists, 233 East Ontario Street, Suite 600, Chicago IL 60611. **Tel** (800)345-0392. **ED** James Vinson.
**Desc:** Brings together clearly presented, in-depth information on the world's most significant films and filmmakers from the earliest days of the cinema to the present.

US
**INTERNATIONAL DIRECTORY OF FILMS AND FILMMAKERS.** (1990)-. Directory. English. $495.00. St. James Press, PO Box 33477, Detroit MI 48232-5477. **Tel** (800)345-0392.
**Desc:** Scholarship and criticism on important films, directors, actors, and actresses, writers and production artists.

US/0742-5333
**INTERNATIONAL DOCUMENTARY.** (INTERNATIONAL DOCUMENTARY: THE NEWSLETTER OF THE INTERNATIONAL DOCUMENTARY ASSOCIATION.). [Int. doc.]. **Added/Corp** International Documentary Association. (198?)-. Periodical. English. Ten times a year. $30.00 US; $35.00 others. International Documentary Association, 1551 South Robertson Boulevard, Suite 201, Los Angeles CA 90035. **Tel** (213)284-8422, FAX (213)785-9485. **ED** Diana Rico (editor's phone: (310)284-8426). **LC** PN1995.9.D6; I58. **Bk Rev**, (Qty: 5-10). **Ad Acc, Adv Mgr:** Turnas, **Tel** (213)962-1396. **Circ:** 5,000 (ctrl).
**Ind/Abst** Film Lit. Index (19??-).

US/0361-4131
**INTERNATIONAL FILM BUFF.** [Int. film buff]. **VFOAT** Film Buff. V. 1- Dec. 1975-. Periodical. English. mo. $9.00. Film Buff Inc., 2309 Van Ness Avenue, San Francisco CA. **LC** PN1993; .I6426. **DD** 791.43/05.

UK
**INTERNATIONAL FILMARCHIVE CD-ROM. / FIAF. Added/Corp** International Federation of Film Archives. **VFOAT** International Film

Archive CD-ROM. (19??)-. Periodical. English. sa. $600.00. FIAF / International Federation of Film Archives, 6 Nottingham Street, London W1M 3RB England. **Tel** 011 44 71 2240991. **LC** Z5784.M9; I48.

US/0000-0388
**INTERNATIONAL INDEX TO FILM PERIODICALS.** **See** Motion Picture-Abstracting, Bibliographies and Statistics.

US/0074-7084
**INTERNATIONAL MOTION PICTURE ALMANAC (1956).** (INTERNATIONAL MOTION PICTURE ALMANAC.). [Int. motion pict. alm.]. **VFOAT** Motion Picture Almanac. (1956)-. English. an. price varies per volume. Quigley Publications, 159 West 53rd Street, New York NY 10019. **Tel** (212)247-3100. **ED** Jane Klain. **LC** PN1993.3; .I55. **DD** 791.43/05. **Ad Acc.** available in microform. ***Continues*** *Motion Picture and Television Almanac, 1043-8106.*
**Desc:** Comprehensive reference book on film industry. Includes who's who, producers, distributors, theatres, circuits, independents, drive-ins, equipment, films since 1970, awards, polls, statistics, press, world market.

CN/0847-3994
**INTERNATIONAL VIDEOVUE.** (INTERNATIONAL VIDEOVUE MAGAZINE.). [Int. videovue]. **VFOAT** Videovue. Vol. 1, No. 1 (Oct. 1989)-. Periodical. English. mo. 22.00Can$. Thunder International Corporation, 238 Davenport Road, Suite 265, Toronto Ontario M5R 1J6 Canada. **ED** David Rusk. **DD** 791.43/75/05. **Circ:** 250,000 (ctrl).
**Desc:** Contains video reviews, new releases, past releases, profiles, interviews, etc.

NP
**IPN CINE / DIRECCION DE DIFUSION CULTURAL, DIRECCION DE PUBLICACIONES.** **VFOAT** Cine. **VAT** Instituto Politecnico Nacional Cine. Periodical. Spanish. bm. Barranca del Muerto, 208-304 San Jose Insurgentes, Mexico 19 DF Mexico.

US/0751-7033
**IRIS.** Vol. 1, No. 1 (1983)-. Periodical. English (French). sa. $30.00 (institutions); $18.00 (individuals). Institute for Cinema & Culture, University of Iowa, 162A Communication Studies Building, Iowa City IA 52242. **Tel** (319)335-1348. **LC** PN1995; .I75. **DD** 791.43/05.
**Ind/Abst** Film Lit. Index (19??-).

IE/0791-105X
**IRISH STAGE & SCREEN.** **See** Theater.

RU/0130-6405
**ISKUSSTVO KINO.** [Iskusstvo kino]. **Added/Corp** Gosudarstvennyi Komitet Soveta Ministrov SSSR po Kinematografii. Soiuz Kinematografistov SSSR. (1936)-. Periodical. Russian. mo. $99.95. **(Subscription address:** East View Publications Inc., 3020 Harbor Lane North, Suite 110, Minneapolis MN 55447.**)** available on microfilm from University Microfilms International (UMI). ***Continues*** *Sovetskoe Kino.*
**Ind/Abst** Film Lit. Index.

JA/0448-8830
**JAPANESE FILMS.** **Added/Corp** Nihon Eiga Kaigai FukyÂu KyÂokai. **VFOAT** Japanese Film. (1958)-. English. an. Unijapan Film Association for the Diffusion of Japanese Films Abroad Inc, 9-13 Ginza 5 Chuo-ku, Tokyo 104 Japan. **LC** PN1993.5.J3; J28. **DD** 791.430952. **Circ:** 5,000 (ctrl).
**Desc:** Introduction of Japanese feature films.

FR
**JEUNE CINEMA.** No. 1- Sept./Oct. 1964-. Periodical. French. Eight times a year. 120.00F France; $22.60 US; 200.00F other. Fedn Jean Vigo Cine Clubs, 8 rue Lamarck, Paris 18 France. **Tel** (1)42 54 04 57. Index available. cum. index. **Ad Acc. Circ:** 4,500.
**Ind/Abst** Film Lit. Index.

CN/0705-5188
**JOURNAL DU JEUNE CINEMA QUEBECOIS, LE.** V. 1- 7 June 1978-. Periodical. French. ir. $5.00. Journal du Jeune Cinema Quebecois, Bureau3011, 1600 Berri, Montreal Quebec H2L 4E4. **DD** 791.43/09714.

US/0742-4671
**JOURNAL OF FILM AND VIDEO.** [J. film video]. **Added/Corp** University Film and Video Association. Vol. 36, No. 1 (Winter 1984)-. Periodical. English. Four times a year (Mar., June, Sept., Dec.). $15.00 (institutions). Journal Film and Video, Georgia State University, Department of Communication, Atlanta GA 30303. **Tel** (404)651-3200, FAX (404)651-1409. **ED** Dr. Frank P. Tomasulo. **LC** PN1993; .U63. **DD** 791. Index available (Bound in 4th iss., in (Dec.)). **Bk Rev**, (Qty: 4-6). **Ad Acc. Circ:** 3,000. available on magnetic tape, an online database, and CD-ROM; available on microfilm and microfiche from University Microfilms International (UMI). Documents available from The Genuine Article, UMI Article Clearinghouse. ***Continues*** *Journal of the University Film and Video Association, 0734-919X.*
**Desc:** Academic journal on film and video-television and pedagogy.
**Ind/Abst** Arts Humanit. Citation Index [Full Cov.]; Commun. Abstr.; Curr. Contents Arts Humanit.; Curr. Index J. Educ.; Educ. Technol. Abstr.; Film Lit. Index; Int. Index Film Period.; Newsp. Period. Abstr. (1989-); Res. Alert [Full Cov.].

US/0195-6051
**JOURNAL OF POPULAR FILM AND TELEVISION, THE.** (THE JOURNAL OF POPULAR FILM AND TELEVISION : JPF&T.). [J. pop. film telev.]. **VFOAT** JPF&T; JPF and T. Vol. 7 (1978)-. Periodical. English. qt. $34.00 (individuals), $66.00 (institutions), add $12.00 (foreign postage). Heldref Publications, 1319 Eighteenth Street Northwest, Washington DC 20036-1802. **Tel** (202)296-6267, (800)365-9753, FAX (202)296-5149. **ED** Michael T Marsden and John G Nachbar. **LC** PN1993; .J66. **DD** 791.43/05. **[CCC]**. Index Available in first issue of next volume--attached. **Ad Acc. Circ:** 800. available on microfilm and microfiche from University Microfilms International (UMI). Documents available from The Genuine Article, UMI Article Clearinghouse. ***Continues*** *Journal of Popular Film, 0047-2719.*
**Desc:** Reflecting interest in popular culture studies, this journal has thoughtful articles on stars, directors, producers, studios, networks and the audience.
**Ind/Abst** Acad. Abstr. Full Text Elite (July 1990-) [Full Txt.]; Acad. Abstr. (July 1990-); Acad. Ind. [Computer File] (1987-); Acad. Search (July 1990-); Am. Hist. Life (1973-); Am. Bibliogr. Slavic East Europ. Stud.; Art Index; Arts Humanit. Citation Index [Full Cov.]; Book Rev. Index; Commun. Abstr. (?-?); Curr. Contents Arts Humanit.; Expand. Acad. Index (1987-); Film Lit. Index; Humanit. Index; Humanit. Source (Jul. 1990-) [Full Txt.]; INFO-SOUTH Abstr.; Mag. Artic. Summar. Elite (July 1990-) [Full Txt.]; Mag. Artic. Summar. Select (July 1990-); Mag. Artic. Summar. CD-ROM (July 1990-); Mag. Search; Med. Rev. Dig.; MLA Int. Bibl. Books Artic. Mod. Lang. Lit.; Newsp. Period. Abstr. (1986-); Res. Alert [Full Cov.]; Soc. Sci. Cit. Index [Select. Cov.]; Vocat. Search (July 1990-) [Full Txt.]; West. Hist. Q.

UK
**KEMPS INTERNATIONAL FILM & TELEVISION YEAR BOOK.** ***Title Change.*** **VFOAT** Kemps International Film and Television Year Book; International Film & Television Year Book; International Film and Television Year Book. **VAT** Kemps International Film and Television Year Book. (1978/79)-(19??). English. an. R R Bowker, A Reed Reference Publishing Company, Part of Reed International PLC, PO Box 31, 121 Chanlon Drive, New Providence NJ 07974. **Tel** (908)464-6800, (800)521-8110, FAX (908)665-6688, telex 138-755. **LC** PN1998.A1; K39. ***Continues*** *Kemp's Film and Television Yearbook (International).* ***Continued by*** *Kemps Film, TV & Video Yearbook.*
**Desc:** Yearbook/directory for international film and TV industries.

JA
**KINEMA JUMPO. / KINEJUN: MOTION PICTURE TIMES.** **VFOAT** Kinejun: Motion Picture Times; Kinejun; Motion Picture Times. (19??)-. Periodical. Japanese. Kinema Jumpo Sha, c/o Park Building, 3 Shiba Sakaecho 9, Minato-ku 105, Tokyo Japan. **LC** PN1993; .K45.

GW/0936-3777
**KINEMATOGRAPH FRANKFURT.** (KINEMATOGRAPH.). (1984)-. German. Deutsches Filmmuseum, Schaumainkai 41, Frankfurt au Main 70 Germany.
**Ind/Abst** Film Lit. Index (19??-).

CK/0121-3776
**KINETOSCOPIO, EL.** **Added/Corp** Centro Colombo-Americano De Medellin. (January 1990)-. Periodical. Spanish. bm. $35.00 (six months), $60.00 (twelve months) US; 15.000Col$ (six months) Latin America. Centro Colombo Americano, Apartado Aereo 8734, Medellin Columbia. **Tel** (574)513-4444, FAX (574)513-2666. **ED** Paul Bardwell. **LC** PN1993; .K46. **DD** 791.43/05. Index available (Published in first number of each year for previous year). **Ad Acc, Adv Mgr:** Ana Ramos. **Circ:** 3,500.
**Desc:** Covers international cinema in general with a specific focus on Colombian cinema as well as complete documentation on all films being screened in the country during the time period covered by the current issue.

PL/0023-1673
**KINO.** [Kino]. (1960)-. Polish. mo. $45.00. **(Subscription address:** ARS Polona, PO Box 1001, 00068 Warsaw Poland.**) LC** PN1993; .K475.
**Ind/Abst** Film Lit. Index.

BU/0861-4393
**KINO.** **Added/Corp** Bulgaria. Ministerstvo na Kulturata. Suiuz na Bulgarskite Filmovi Deitsi. (1991)-. Periodical. Bulgarian. bm (6 issues). DM127.00. **(Subscription address:** Kubon & Sagner, ABT Zeitschriftenimport, D 80328 Munich Germany.**)** ***Continues*** *Kinoizkustvo, 0323-9993.*

GW
**KINO.** **Added/Corp** Export-Union des Deutschen Films. (19??)-. German (English, French and Spanish). Export-Union des Deutschen Films, Turkenstrasse 93, D-8000 Munchen 40 Germany. **LC** PN1993.5.G3; K53. **DD** 016.79143/75/0943.
**Ind/Abst** Film Lit. Index (19??-).

GW
**KINO : GERMAN FILM.** German. Dorothea & Ronald Holloway, Helgolander Ufer 6, D-1000 Berlin 21 Germany.
**Ind/Abst** Film Lit. Index (19??-).

RU
**KINO I VREMIA.** **Added/Corp** Nauchno-Isledovatelskii Istitut Torii i Itorii Kino. Vol. 1 (1977)-. Periodical. Russian. 1.40rub single issue. Izdatelstvo Iskusstvo, Vorotnikovskii Pereulok 11, 103009 Moscow Russia. **LC** PN1993; .K477.

XR
**KINO; OBRAZKOVY FILMOVY CRTNACTIDENIK.** (19??)-. Periodical. Czech. bw. **(Subscription address:** Artia Pegas Press Ltd., Palac Metro Narodni Trida 25, 11210 Prague 1 Czech Republic.**) LC** PN1993; .K48.

GW
**KINOBUCH.** 1974/75-. German. 10.00. Vertrieb, Stiftung Deutsche Kinemathek, Pommernalle 1, 19 Berlin 1 Germany. **LC** PN1993; .K49.

RU
**KINOPANORAMA.** Vol. 1 (1975)-. Periodical. Russian. 2.10rub. Izdatelstvo Iskusstvo, Vorotnikovskii Pereulok 11, 103009 Moscow Russia. **LC** PN1993.5.R9; K54.

AU
**KINOSCHRIFTEN : JAHRBUCH DER GESELLSCHAFT FUER FILMTHEORIE.** **Added/Corp** Gesellschaft fuer Filmtheorie. Verband der Wissenschaftlichen Gesellschaften Osterreichs. **VFOAT** Jahrbuch der Gesellschaft fuer Filmtheorie. (1988)-. German. an. Verband der Wissenschaftlichen Gesellschaften Osterreichs, Lindengasse 37, A-1070 Vienna Austria. **Tel** 011 43 1 932166, 011 43 1 934756, telex 847/134981. **LC** PN1993; .K547. **DD** 791.43/05.

UK
**KNOWLEDGE.** English. an. £60.00 UK, (add £10.00 postage) other. PA Publishing Company, Unit 3, Grand Union Center, W Row, London W10 5AS England. **Tel** 011 44 81 969-5777.
**Desc:** Film production trade directory is considered the handbook for anyone involved in any aspect of film-making and program production.

DK/0023-4222
**KOSMORAMA.** [Kosmorama]. **Added/Corp** Danske Filmmuseum. Vol. 1 No. 1 (Oct. 1954)-. Periodical. Danish. qt. kr190.00 Europe; kr210.00 other. Det Danske Filmmuseum, Store Sondervoldstraede, 1419 Copenhagen Denmark. **Tel** 011 41 31 576500, FAX 011 41 31 541312, telex 31465. **ED** Maren Pust. **LC** PN1993; .K63. Index available (published separately). **Bk Rev. Ad Acc. Circ:** 2,000. available on microfilm from World Microfilm Publications Ltd; available on an online database. Documents available from The Genuine Article.
**Desc:** Film periodical with articles and reviews of Danish and international cinema.
**Ind/Abst** Arts Humanit. Citation Index [Full Cov.]; Curr. Contents Arts Humanit.; Film Lit. Index; Res. Alert [Full Cov.].

US/1062-6603
**L.A. 411.** [LA 411]. **VFOAT** LA 411; LA Four One One; LA Four Hundred Eleven. (1979)-. English. an (January). $55.00. LA 411, PO Box 480495, Los Angeles CA 90048. **Tel** (213)460-6304, FAX (231)934-0226. **LC** PN1993.5.U65; L22. **DD** 790. **Ad Acc, Adv Mgr:** C VanDecaslede. **Circ:** 10,000 (ctrl).
**Desc:** Resource directory for television commercial and music video production.

US/1050-2041
**LANDERS FILM & VIDEO REVIEWS.** ***Ceased.*** [Landers film video rev.]. **VFOAT** Landers Film and Video Reviews. Vol. 34, No. 1 (Fall 1989)- Ceased with Vol. 37, No. 2 (199?). Periodical. English. qt. Landers Associates, PO Box 300309, Escondido CA 92030-0309. **Tel** (619)746-8923. **ED** Bertha Landers and Steve Redding. **LC** PN1995; .L27. **DD** 070.1/8. ***Continues*** *Landers Film Reviews, 0023-785X.*

FR
**LAVANT - SCENE DU THEATRE.** No. 1 (March 1949)-. Periodical. French. sm. 680.00F French; 791.00F other. 16 rue des Quatre Vents, 75006 Paris France. **Tel** (16-1)46 34 28 20, FAX (33) 1 46 42 53 88. ***Absorbed*** *Femina Theatre.*
**Desc:** Prints the complete libretto of selected operas in the original language and in French. Includes critical discography, literary and musical analysis.

DK/0108-5697
**LEVENDE BILLEDER.** [Levende bill.]. **VFOAT** LB, Levende Billeder. (1975)-. Periodical. Danish. mo. kr280.00 Denmark; kr380.00 other. Forlaget Sankt Peder af 1985 ApS, Meinungsgade 8D, 3 Sal, DK 2200

Copenhagen N, Denmark. **Tel** 011 45 31 397390, FAX 011 45 35 378976.
**Ind/Abst** Film Lit. Index.

US/0191-541X
**LIGHTING DIMENSIONS.** [Light. dimens.]. Vol. 1 (Jan. 1977)-. Periodical. English. Ten times a year. $40.00 one year; $72.00 two years; $96.00 three years. Lighting Dimensions Association, 32 West 18 Street, New York NY 10011. **Tel** (212)677-5997, FAX (212)677-3857. **(Subscription address:** Lighting Dimensions, PO Box 425, Mt. Morris IL 61054.**)** **ED** Ann Daly. **LC** PN2091.E4; L54. **DD** 792/.025/05. **Bk Rev. Ad Acc. Circ:** 13,500 (ctrl). available on microfilm and microfiche from University Microfilms International (UMI).
**Desc:** Examines the entire spectrum of lighting design, from architecture and interior design to stage and studio.
**Ind/Abst** Foods Adlibra.

CN/0713-3529
**LISTE DES FILMS VISES PAR CATEGORIES DE SPECTATEURS.** ***Title Change.*** [Liste films vises categ. spect.]. **Added/Corp** Quebec (Province). Bureau de Surveillance du Cinema. **VFOAT** Cahier des Films Vises par Categories de Spectateurs. (197?)-(1992). Periodical. French. mo. Gouvernement du Quebec, 600 St Amable 4E Etage, Quebec Quebec G1R 4Z1 Canada. **DD** 791.43/75/05. ***Split into*** *Liste des Films Vises par Categories de Spectateurs, Diffusion Publique, 1191-7415* ***and*** *Liste des Films Vises par Categories de Spectateurs, Diffusion Privee, 1191-7423.*

●CN/1191-7423
**LISTE DES FILMS VISES PAR CATEGORIES DE SPECTATEURS, DIFFUSION PRIVEE.** (LISTE DES FILMS VISES PAR CATEGORIES DE SPECTATEURS, DIFFUSION PRIVEE.). [Liste films vises categ. spect. diffus. privee]. **Added/Corp** Quebec (Province). Regie du Cinema. (1992)-. Periodical. French. **DD** 791.43. ***Continues in part*** *Liste des Films Vises par Categories de Spectateurs., 0713-3529.*

US/0090-4260
**LITERATURE FILM QUARTERLY.** [Lit. film q.]. **Added/Corp** Salisbury State College. **VFOAT** Literature/Film Quarterly. Vol. 1 (Winter 1973)-. Periodical. English. qt (Jan., Apr., Jul., Oct.). $32.00 (institutions), $16.00 (individuals) US, Canada, and Mexico; $36.00 other. Salisbury State College, English Department, 1101 Cander Avenue, Salisbury MD 21801. **Tel** (301)543-6446, FAX (301)543-6068. **ED** James M Welsh. **LC** PN1995.3; .L57. **DD** 791.43/05. Index available. **Bk Rev**, (Qty: 4). **Ad Acc. Circ:** 700. available on microfilm and microfiche from University Microfilms International (UMI). Documents available from The Genuine Article, UMI Article Clearinghouse.
**Desc:** Literature film adaptions, book reviews, and interviews with directors, screenwriters, and critics.
**Ind/Abst** Abstr. Engl. Stud.; Acad. Search (July 1993-); Annu. Bibliogr. Engl. Lang. Lit.; Arts Humanit. Citation Index [Full Cov.]; Curr. Contents Arts Humanit.; Expand. Acad. Index (1989-); Film Lit. Index; Humanit. Index; Humanit. Source (Jul. 1993-); INFO-SOUTH Abstr.; Int. Index Film Period.; Lit. Crit. Regist.; Mag. Search; Med. Rev. Dig.; MLA Int. Bibl. Books Artic. Mod. Lang. Lit.; Newsp. Period. Abstr. (1991-); Res. Alert [Full Cov.]; Soc. Sci. Cit. Index [Select. Cov.].

US/1058-3238
**LOCATION UPDATE.** [Locat. update]. (19??)-. Periodical. English. mo. $14.95 US; $29.95 Canada and Pan-American nations; $34.95 other. Location Update, 6922 Hollywood Boulevard, Suite 612, Hollywood CA 90028. **Tel** (213)461-8887, FAX (213)469-3711. **ED** Manley Witten. **DD** 791. **Ad Acc, Adv Mgr:** L. Burns. **Circ:** 27,000 (ctrl).
**Desc:** Serves the fields of film, television, and video production, specializing in location information.

CN/0835-4790
**LUMIERES (MONTREAL).** ***Ceased.*** (LUMIERES / A.R.R.F.Q., ASSOCIATION DES REALISATEURS ET REALISATRICES DE FILMS DU QUEBEC.). [Lumieres]. **Added/Corp** Association des Realisateurs et Realisatrices de Films du Quebec. Vol. 2, No. 7 (May/June 1987)-(1993). Periodical. French. bm. Revue Lumieres, 1600 de Lorimier Bur 122, Montreal Quebec H2K 3W5 Canada. **Tel** (514)527-2197, FAX (514)521-7081. **DD** 791.43/09714. ***Continues*** *Manivelle (Montreal, Quebec), 0831-7534.*

II
**MAADHYAM : BIMONTHLY ABOUT FILMS, FILMMAKERS & FILM SOCIETIES.** Periodical. English (English). bm. Rs5.00. Maadhyam Publications, PB No 522, Dakar Bombay 400 014 India. **LC** PN1993; .M216. **DD** 791.43/05.

US/0739-2141
**MAGILL'S CINEMA ANNUAL.** 1982-. Periodical. English. an. $54.00. Salem Press Inc, 580 Sylvan Avenue, Englewood Cliffs NJ 07632. **Tel** (201)871-3700, (800)221-1592, FAX (201)871-8668, telex 138881. **ED** F N Magill. **LC** PN1993.3; .M34. **DD** 791.43/75/05. cum. index. available on an online database.
**Desc:** Reviews of films released during the previous calendar year, plus interviews, obituaries, and a listing of major awards.

●US/1065-6553
**MAGILL'S SURVEY OF CINEMA.** (MAGILL'S SURVEY OF CINEMA [COMPUTER FILE] : EBSCO CD-ROM.). **Added/Corp** EBSCO Publishing (Firm). **VFOAT** EBSCO CD-ROM. (1992)-. Periodical. English. an. $99.00. EBSCO Publishing / Boston, 83 Pine Street, Peabody MA 01960. **Tel** (800)653-2726 North America, (508)535-8500, FAX (508)535-8545. **(Subscription address:** EBSCO Publishing - Boston, 83 Pine Street, Peabody, MA 01960**)** Index available. **Pr Rev.** available on an online database (file 299/Full-Text) from DIALOG.
**Desc:** Offers reference information for nearly 15,000 classic and contemporary films.

US/0884-6944
**MALCOLM HULKE STUDIES IN CINEMA AND TELEVISION.** (1990)-. Monographic series. English. ir. Price varies per volume. Borgo Press, PO Box 2845, San Bernardino CA 92406. **Tel** (714)884-5813, (714)885-1161.

US/1073-8924
**MARKEE (SANFORD, FLA.).** (MARKEE.). (198?)-. English. mo. Free. HJK Publications Inc, 655 Fulton Street, Suite 9, Sanford FL 32771. **Tel** (407)324-1733. **ED** Janet Karcher. **Ad Acc. Circ:** 15,000 (ctrl).

CN/0700-5008
**MARQUEE (TORONTO).** (MARQUEE.). (Apr./May 1976)-. Periodical. English. Nine times a year. 19.26Can$ Canada; $27.00 US; 27.00Can$ other. Marquee Communications Inc., 77 Mowat Avenue Suite 621, Toronto Ontario M6K 3E3 Canada. **Tel** (416)538-1000, FAX (416)538-0201. **ED** David Haslam. **LC** PN1993; .M2534. **DD** 791.43/05. Index available (free on request). **Ad Acc. Circ:** 400,000 (ctrl).
**Desc:** Previews motion pictures four to six weeks prior to release.

PL
**MAY ROCZNIK FILMOWY. Added/Corp** Centrala Wynajmu Filmow (Poland). **VFOAT** Filmowy Serwis Prasowy. (19??)-. Periodical. Polish. Twelve times a year. $27.00. **(Subscription address:** ARS Polona, PO Box 1001, 00068 Warsaw Poland.**)**
**Ind/Abst** Film Lit. Index (19??-).

US/0273-3803
**MEANS COLORADO DIRECTORY, THE.** Directory. English. $15.00. The Means Ltd, 521 South Washington, Denver CO 80209. **LC** PN1993.U72; M4. **DD** 791.43/025/788.

BE
**MEDIA FILM.** ir. Acco Academische Cooperatief, Tiensestraat 134-136, 3000 Leuven Belgium. **Tel** 011 32 16 233520.

IO
**MEDIA FILM INDONESIA.** Periodical. Indonesian. Pusat Perfilman H Usmar, Ismail Jl Raya H R Rasuna, Said-Kuningan, Jakarta Indonesia. **LC** PN1993.5.I84; M43.

US/0363-7778
**MEDIA REVIEW DIGEST. See** Motion Picture-Abstracting, Bibliographies and Statistics.

SP
**MEDIOS AUDIO-VISUALES. Added/Corp** Medios Publicitarios Mexicanos. **VFOAT** Directorio MPM : Informacion y Tarifas de Medios Audio-Visuales. (March/May 1978)-. Periodical. Spanish. Ten times a year. $50.00. Movinter Press, Orense 33, 28020 Madrid Spain. **Tel** 011 31 1 5565962. **ED** Antonio Morales. **Bk Rev. Ad Acc. Circ:** 5,000 (ctrl).
**Desc:** Audiovisual world: sound, image, video education and communication.

●FR/1242-0492
**MENSUEL DU CINEMA, LE.** No. 1 (Nov.-Dec. 1992)-. Periodical. French. ir. 250.00F France; 320.00F other. Mensuel du Cinema, 17 rue Sorgentino, 06300 Nice France. ***Continues*** *Revue du Cinema, 0019-2635.*
**Desc:** News concerning the motion picture industry of France.

AT/0312-2654
**METRO (MELBOURNE).** (METRO : MEDIA & EDUCATION MAGAZINE.). [Metro]. **Added/Corp** Association of Teachers of Film and Video. (1974)-. Periodical. English. Four times a year. 50.00Aus$ (individuals), 80.00Aus$ (institutions) Australia; 60.00Aus$ (individuals), 80.00Aus$ (institutions) others. Australian Teachers of Media, PO Box 222, Carlton, South Victoria 3053 Australia. **Tel** 011 61 3 482 2393. ***Continues*** *Film Appreciation Newsletter, 0312-2662.*
**Ind/Abst** Aust. Educ. Index; Film Lit. Index.

US
**MICHAEL SINGER'S FILM DIRECTORS : A COMPLETE GUIDE / COMPILED AND EDITED BY MICHAEL SINGER. VFOAT** Film Directors. (198?)-. English. an. $50.00 US; $60.00 Canada; $65.00 other. Lone Eagle Publishing Inc., 2337 Roscomare Road, Suite 9, Los Angeles CA 90077. **Tel** (310)471-8066, FAX (310)471-4969. **LC** PN1998.A2; D568. ***Continues*** *Film Directors, 0740-2872.*

IT
**MILLECANALI.** (19??)-. Italian. Eleven times a year. L98000 Italy; L196000 other. Gruppo Editoriale JCE SRL, Via Ferri 6, 20092 Cinisello B Milan Italy. **Tel** 011 39 2 660251, FAX 011 39 2 66025343.

US/1064-5586
**MILLENNIUM FILM JOURNAL.** [Millenn. film j.]. Vol. 1 (1977/1978)-. Periodical. English. Twice a year. $20.00 (institutions), $14.00 (individuals). Millennium Film Journal, 66 East 4th Street, New York NY 10003. **Tel** (212)673-0090. **ED** Howard Guttenplan. **DD** 791. Index available. cum. index. **Bk Rev**, (Qty: 2). **Ad Acc.** ctrl circ. Documents available from The Genuine Article.
**Ind/Abst** Arts Humanit. Citation Index (19??-19??) [Full Cov.]; Curr. Contents Arts Humanit.; Film Lit. Index (19??-); Middle East Abstr. Index; Res. Alert [Full Cov.].

US/0164-9655
**MILLIMETER.** [Millimeter]. (1973)-. Periodical. English. Twelve times a year. $60.00 US; $90.00 Canada; $95.00 Mexico; $100.00 other. Penton Publishing, 1100 Superior Avenue, Cleveland OH 44114-2543. **Tel** (216)696-7000, FAX (216)696-0836. **(Subscription address:** Penton Publishing, PO Box 96732, Chicago IL 60693.**)** **ED** Schwartz, Dan Ochiva. **LC** TR845; .M54. **DD** 778.5/05. **[CCC]. Ad Acc. Circ:** 27,400. available on microfilm from University Microfilms International (UMI).
**Desc:** Edited for television and motion picture production professionals. Feature articles cover: technologies, techniques, talent, economics and commerce.
**Ind/Abst** Film Lit. Index; Med. Rev. Dig.

BE/0771-0461
**MINUTES / OCIC. Main/Corp** International Catholic Organization for Cinema and Audiovisual. General Assembly. (198?)-. Bulletin. French (English and Spanish). bm. OCIC, rue de l'Orme 8, B-1040 Brussels Belgium. **Tel** 02/73442 94, FAX 02/73432 07. **ED** Robert Molhant. **LC** PN1993; .I6413a. **DD** 261.5/2/06. **Bk Rev**, (Qty: 20-40). **Ad Acc, Adv Mgr:** Guido Convents. **Circ:** 15,000 (ctrl). Documents available from FAXON Xpress.
**Desc:** Publishes articles and information on quality films and audiovisuals, and the development of media infrastructures which serve the promotion of humans and understanding between peoples.

IO
**MMPI. VFOAT** M.M.P.I. Periodical. Indonesian. ir. Pusat Perfilman H Usmar, Ismail Jl Raya H R Rasuna, Said-Kuningan, Jakarta Indonesia. **LC** PN1993.5.I84; M55. ***Continues*** *Bulletin MMPI.*

US
**MODERN TIMES.** No. 1 (June 1989)-. English. mo. Modern Times, 1931 Scott Avenue, Los Angeles CA 90026.

BE/0771-4874
**MONITEUR DU FILM EN BELGIQUE, LE.** [Moniteur film Belg.]. (1981)-. Periodical. French. mo. $34.00. Le Moniteur du Film en Belgique, Rue du Framboisier 35, 1180 Brussels Belgium. **Tel** 02 374 77 18. **UDC** 791.43. ***Continues*** *Press and Film Service, 0771-4823.*
**Ind/Abst** Film Lit. Index (19??-).

US
**MOTION PICTURE ANNUAL, THE.** (1988)-. English. an. $19.95. CineBooks, 990 Grove Street, Evanston IL 60201. **LC** PN1998; .M65. **DD** 011/.37/05.
**Desc:** Includes information and reviews for 331 films from 1989.

US
**MOTION PICTURE GUIDE, THE.** (1983)-. English. an. $159.95. R R Bowker, A Reed Reference Publishing Company, Part of Reed International PLC, PO Box 31, 121 Chanlon Drive, New Providence NJ 07974. **Tel** (908)464-6800, (800)521-8110, FAX (908)665-6688, telex 138-755. **ED** William Leahy and Jeffrey W Wallenfeldt. **LC** PN1993; .M4334. **DD** 791.43/75/05.
**Desc:** Thorough and detailed, this illustrated resource brings you in-depth entries, reviews, and lively anecdotes about hundreds and hundreds of domestic and foreign features released in the US.

US/0742-8839
**MOTION PICTURE INVESTOR. See** Business-Investments.

CN/0380-6294
**MOTION PICTURE THEATRES AND FILM DISTRIBUTORS. See** Motion Picture-Abstracting, Bibliographies and Statistics.

## Motion Picture

II
**MOVIE (BOMBAY, INDIA).** (MOVIE.). (19??)-. Periodical. English. Twelve times a year. Rs600.00. India Book House Private Ltd, Eruchshaw BLD 3rd Floor, 249 DN Road, Bombay 4000 001 India. **Tel** 011 91 22 26 43 64 5.

US/8750-5401
**MOVIE COLLECTOR'S WORLD. See** Hobbies.

US/1057-0276
**MOVIE GUIDE (CHICAGO, ILL.).** (MOVIE GUIDE : CHICAGO'S NEWSLETTER OF FILM CRITICISM.). [Movie guide]. Vol. 1, No. 1 (June 15th, 1991)-. Newsletter. English. sa. $30.00. American Metal Press, 833 West Buena, #1604, Chicago IL 60613. **DD** 791.

UK/0027-268X
**MOVIE (LONDON).** (MOVIE.). [Movie]. No. 1 (June 1962)-. Periodical. English. ir. Movie, PO Box 1, Moffat, Dumfriesshire DG10 9SU England. **Tel** 011 44 683 20808, FAX 011 44 683 20012, , telex 01-226 5352. **ED** Ian Cameron, Charles Barr, Andrew Britton, Jim Hillier, V.F. Perkins, Douglas Pye, Mark Shivas, Michael Walker, and Robin Wood. **LC** PN1993; .M74516. **Bk Rev.** available on microfilm from University Microfilms International (UMI).
  **Desc:** Film magazine that concentrates on articles dealing with criticism and film theory.
  **Ind/Abst** Film Lit. Index.

US/1049-3859
**MOVIE MAKER.** (1991)-. Periodical. English. qt. $15.00. Sanford B Kennedy, 10753 Magnolia Boulevard, North Hollywood CA 91601.

US/1051-5488
**MOVIE MARKETPLACE. See** Photography and Video.

US/0027-271X
**MOVIE MIRROR.** [Movie mirror]. Periodical. English. bm. no longer available on subscription. Sterling Macfadden, 233 Park Avenue South, New York NY 10003. **Tel** (212)979-4800. **Continues in part** Photoplay combined with Movie Mirror, 0733-2734.

JA
**MOVIE/TV MARKETING. See** Business-Marketing.

CN/0705-9175
**MOVIE WORKS WEEKLY, THE.** Began publication in 1977. Periodical. English. wk. Movie Works Weekly, 112 1 2 McGill Avenue, Toronto Ontario M5B 1H6 Canada. **Tel** (416)368-3022. **DD** 338.4/7/791430971.

US/0090-2039
**MOVIE X.** [Movie X]. Periodical. English. qt. $1.00 single issue. Magnum-Royal Publications, 1560 Broadway, New York NY 10036. **LC** PN1995.9.S45; M68. **DD** 791.43/52.

US/1055-0917
**MOVIELINE (LOS ANGELES, CALIF.).** (MOVIELINE.). [Movieline]. **VFOAT** Movie Line. Vol. 1, No. 1 (Sept. 1989)-. Periodical. English. Twelve times a year. $15.00. Movieline Inc., 1141 South Beverly Drive, Los Angeles CA 90035. **Tel** (310)282-0711, FAX (310)282-0859. **LC** IN PROCESS. **Bk Rev**, (Qty: 11 per year). **Ad Acc**. **Circ:** 1,200.
  **Ind/Abst** Access (1992-); Film Lit. Index (19??-).

US/0742-4116
**MOVIES (NEW YORK, N.Y.), THE. Suspended.** (THE MOVIES.). Vol. 1, No. 1 (July 1983)-Suspended 1983. Periodical. English. mo. $18.00 US; $23.00 other. The Movies, PO Box 2724, Boulder CO 80322. **LC** PN1993; .M7525. **DD** 791.43/05.

US/1044-1336
**MOVIES USA. Ceased.** [Movies U. S. A.]. **Added/Corp** Movietime Network. **VFOAT** Movies. Vol. 2, Issue 5 (1989)-(1992). Periodical. English. mo. Movies USA Inc., 1100 Northmeadow Pkwy 110, Roswell GA 30076. **ED** Noe Goldwasser. **DD** 791. **Ad Acc. Circ:** 1,000,000 (ctrl).

US/0897-0769
**MOVING IMAGE REVIEW.** (MOVING IMAGE REVIEW / NORTHEAST HISTORIC FILM). [Mov. image rev.]. **Added/Corp** Northeast Historic Film (Organization). (Winter 1988)-. Periodical. English. sa. $35.00. Northeast Historic Film, PO Box 900, Bucksport ME 04416. **Tel** (207)469-0924. **ED** Karan Sheldon. **DD** 791. **Bk Rev**. **Circ:** 2,000.
  **Desc:** Dedicated to the preservation of Northern New England motion pictures.

RU
**NA EKRANAKH MIRA.** Vol. 1, (1966)-. Russian. 1.18rub single issue. Izdatelstvo Iskusstvo, Vorotnikovskii Pereulok 11, 103009 Moscow Russia. **LC** PN1993; .N28.

US/0887-9451
**NEW VIDEO. Ceased.** [New video]. **VFOAT** New Video Magazine. (198?)-(19??). Periodical. English. qt. New Video, 276 3rd Avenue, New York NY 10010. **Tel** (212)473-6000. **DD** 791.

US/0884-2744
**NEW YORK FILM ANNEX. Title Change.** (NEW YORK FILM ANNEX : CATALOG.). [N.Y. Film Annex]. **Main/Corp** New York Film Annex. Catalog. English. an. New York Film Annex, 163 Joralemon Street, Brooklyn Heights NY 11201. **LC** PN1998; .N7315A. **DD** 016.79143/75. **Continued by** Obscure Cinema.

US/1054-0652
**NEW YORK NEWSREEL. VFOAT** Newsreel. (June 1978)-. Periodical. English. be. New York Screen Actors Guild, 1515 Broadway, 44th Floor, New York NY 10036. available on microfilm from The State Historical Society of Wisconsin.

US
**NEW YORK TIMES DIRECTORY OF THE FILM, THE. VFOAT** Directory of the Film. 1971-. Directory. English. an. Arno Press, 3 Park Avenue, New York NY 10016. **Tel** (212)725-2050. **LC** PN1995. **DD** 791.43.

US/0362-3688
**NEW YORK TIMES FILM REVIEWS, THE.** 1913/68-. Periodical. English. be. Times Books, 201 East 50th Street, New York NY 10022-7703. **Tel** (212)620-5900. **LC** PN1995; .N4. **DD** 791.43/7.

US
**NEW YORK WOMEN IN FILM.** English. ir (published Sept. through June). $20.00. New York Women in Film., 274 Madison Avenue, Suite 1202, New York NY 10016. **Tel** (212)679-0870, FAX (212)678-0899. **Circ:** 3,000.

YU
**NEWS.** Periodical. English. Jugoslavija Film, Knez Mihailova 19 Cables, Belgrad Yugoslavia. **LC** PN1993; .N47.

CN/0820-3431
**NEWS (CANADIAN SOCIETY OF CINEMATOGRAPHERS).** (NEWS : THE CANADIAN SOCIETY OF CINEMATOGRAPHERS NEWSLETTER.). [News - Can. Soc. Cinematogr.]. **Added/Corp** Canadian Society of Cinematographers. **VFOAT** Canadian Society of Cinematographers Newsletter. (1986)-. Newsletter. English. mo. 75.00Can$ Canada; 90.00Can$ US. Canadian Society of Cinematographers, 89 Pinewood Trail, Port Credit Ontario L5G 2L2 Canada. **DD** 778.5/06/071. **Continues** Newsletter / Canadian Society of Cinematographers, 0229-5989.

CN/0227-5015
**NEWSLETTER - FILM STUDIES ASSOCIATION OF CANADA.** (NEWSLETTER / FILM STUDIES ASSOCIATION OF CANADA = ASSOCIATION CANADIENNE DES ETUDES CINEMATOGRAPHIQUES.). [Newsl. - Film Studies Assoc. Can.]. **Main/Corp** Film Studies Association of Canada. (1977)-. Newsletter. English. qt. FSAC Newsletter, c/o Film Studies Association of Canada, R Hockey Sheridan College, 1430 Trafalgar Road, Oakville Ontario L6H 2L1 Canada. **DD** 791.43/06/071.

NE
**NFI MAGAZINE : NEDERLANDS FILM INSTITUUT. Ceased.** (19??)-(19??). English. an. NFI, Postbus 515, 1200 MA Hilversum Netherlands. **Tel** 011 31 35 217645.

NE/0926-3411
**NFM-THEMAREEKS AMSTERDAM.** (NFM-THEMAREEKS.). [NFM-themareeks Amst.]. **VFOAT** Nederlands FilmMuseum-Themareeks (Amsterdam). (1991)-. Monographic series. Dutch. Nine times a year. Fl50.00. Stichting Nederlands Filmmuseum, Vondelpark 3, 1071 AA Amsterdam Netherlands. **Tel** 31-20-5891400, FAX 31 20. **UDC** 791 :069. Index available. cum. index. **Ad Acc. Circ:** 1,500 (ctrl).
  **Desc:** Specialized articles about film directors, film countries, and film genres.

CN
**NIGHTINGALE REPORT.** English. ir. 149.00Can$. Nightingale & Associates, 45 Barclay Road, Toronto, Ontario, M3H 3E2 Canada. **Tel** (416)638-5423, FAX (416)398-2872. **ED** Trudy Rudolph. **Ad Acc. Circ:** 1,000 (ctrl).
  **Desc:** Contains stories relevant to the film and television industry in Canada. Includes production listings and event and workshop listings.

JA
**NIHON NO YUSHU EIGA. Added/Corp** Nihon Eiga Kaigai Fukyu Kyokai. **VFOAT** Outstanding Japanese Films; Selected Japanese Feature Films. (19??)-. Periodical. English (Japanese). Nihon Eiga Kaigai Fukyu Kyokai, 9-13 Ginza 5 Chuo-ku 104, Tokyo Japan. **LC** PN1993.5.J3; N55.

RM
**NOUL CINEMA.** Vol. 29, No. 12-1 (1990)-. Periodical. Romanian. mo. DM170.00. **(Subscription address:** Kubon & Sagner, ABT Zeitschriftenimport, D 80328 Munich Germany.) **LC** PN1993; .N86. **Continues** Cinema (Bucharest, Romania), 0578-2910.

US/1045-1706
**OFF-HOLLYWOOD REPORT, THE. Title Change.** [Off-Hollywood rep.]. **Added/Corp** Independent Feature Project. **VAT** Off Hollywood Report. (19??)-(19??). Periodical. English. mo. Independent Feature Project, 5550 Willshire Boulevard, Suite 204, Los Angeles CA 90036. **Tel** (213)937-4379. **LC** PN1993; .038. **DD** 791.43/023/05. **Continued by** Filmmaker, 1063-8954.
  **Ind/Abst** Film Lit. Index (19??-19??).

US/0020-5885
**OFFICIAL BULLETIN OF THE THEATRICAL STAGE EMPLOYEES AND MOVING PICTURE MACHINE OPERATORS OF THE UNITED STATES AND CANADA. See** Theater.

US/0748-7606
**OFFICIAL PRICE GUIDE TO RADIO, TV & MOVIE MEMORABILIA, THE. See** Communication-Broadcasting.

NZ/0112-2789
**ON FILM. VFOAT** Onfilm. Vol. 1, No. 1 (Dec. 1983)-. Periodical. English. Eleven times a year (Except Jan.). 90.00NZ$ New Zealand and Australia; 100.00NZ$ other. Onfilm Magazine Ltd., PO Box 37 193, Parnell, Auckland New Zealand. **Tel** 011 64 9 3602009.
  **Ind/Abst** Film Lit. Index (19??-).

US/0161-1585
**ON FILM (SANTA BARBARA). Suspended.** (ON FILM.). Periodical. English. qt. $7.50 individuals, $15.00 institutions. College of Fine Arts, University of California, 405 Hilgard Avenue, Los Angeles CA 90024. **Tel** (310)661-0944.

US/0149-7014
**ON LOCATION. Ceased.** [On locat.]. (1977)-?. Periodical. English. mo. On Location Publishing Inc, PO Box 2180, Hollywood CA 90028. **Tel** (213)467-1268. **ED** Steven Bernard. **LC** PN1993.5.U6; O5. **DD** 791.43/0973. **Bk Rev**. **Ad Acc. Circ:** 24,000 (ctrl).
  **Desc:** Covers all aspects of film, video, commercials, special effects, post-production, audio, music, video and location production. Also covers equipment, facilities, mobile and new technologies used in production of all aspects of the entertainment industry.

US/0740-1159
**ON LOCATION, THE NATIONAL FILM & VIDEOTAPE PRODUCTION DIRECTORY. Ceased.** [On locat., natl. film videotape prod. dir.]. **VFOAT** On Location National Film & Videotape Production Directory; On Location. Vol. 2-1978/79-?. Directory. English. an. On Location Publishing Inc, PO Box 2180, Hollywood CA 90028. **Tel** (213)467-1268. **LC** PN1998.A1; O5. **DD** 338.4/7/0002573. **Continues** On Location Film and Videotape Production Directory, 0160-5933.

●US/1067-6120
**ON PRODUCTION AND POST-PRODUCTION.** [ON prod. post-prod.]. **VFOAT** On Production. Vol. 1, No. 1 (Mar./Apr. 1992)-. Periodical. English. Nine times a year. $36.00 (1 year), $60.00 (2 year) US; $58.00 (1 year), $98.00 (2 year) other. ON Production Inc., 17337 Ventura Boulevard, Suite 226, Encino CA 91316. **Tel** (818)907-6682. **ED** Howard Kunin. **LC** PN1995.9.P7; O5. **DD** 791.43/0232/05. cum. index. **Ad Acc. Circ:** 28,000 (ctrl).
  **Desc:** Covers production and post-production of feature films, television, commercials, corporate communication, and graphics.
  **Ind/Abst** Film Lit. Index (199?-).

AU
**OPER UND BALLETT IM FILM. See** Music.

US/1042-1149
**ORBIT VIDEO. Ceased.** [Orbit video]. Vol. 1, No. 1; Jan. 1989-Ceased April 1990. Periodical. English. mo. Orbit Video, PO Box 607, Vienna VA 22180. **Tel** (703)827-0511. **ED** Phillip Swann. **DD** 791. **Ad Acc**.
  **Desc:** Designed to help the renters and buyers make their purchasing decisions. Reviews of videos are featured, along with a reference card that the video user can take along to the video store to have pertinent information at hand when buying.

CN/1180-5137
**P.O.V. : A NEWSLETTER FOR MANITOBA ACTORS. See** Theater.

US/0731-2059
**PACIFIC COAST STUDIO DIRECTORY.** (PACIFIC COAST STUDIO DIRECTORY : SD.). **VFOAT** SD. (19??)-. Directory. English. qt. $27.00. Pacific Coast

Studio Directory, PO Box V, Pine Mountain CA 93222. **Tel** (805)242-2722. **ED** Harry C Reitz. **Ad Acc. Circ:** 25,000 (ctrl).

XR
**PANORAMA.** Periodical. Czech (summaries and/or abstracts in English, French and Russian). ir. 32.00. Ons-Ued Odd Vyvozu Tisku Jindrisska 14, 125 05 Prague Czech Republic. **LC** PN1993; .P24.

IT
**PATALOGO. CINEMA + TELEVISIONE + VIDEO, IL.** **VFOAT** Patalogo. Cinema + Televisione + Video; Cinema e Televisione e Video; Cinema & Televisione; Cinema e Televisione Patalogo. Vol. 10 (1987)-. Italian. an (Nov. or Dec.). Price varies. Ubulibri, Via Ramazzini 8, 20129 Milan Italy. **Tel** 011 39 2 29404372. **LC** PN1993; .P315. **DD** 791.43/05. ***Continues*** *Patalogo. Cinema e Televisione.*

●US/1064-7236
**PAUL KAGAN'S BOX OFFICE CHAMPIONS. ACTORS/ACTRESSES.** **See** The Arts-Performing Arts.

●US/1063-2573
**PAUL KAGAN'S BOX OFFICE CHAMPIONS. DIRECTORS.** [Paul Kagan's box off. champions, Dir.]. **Added/Corp** Paul Kagan Associates. **VFOAT** Directors; Box Office Champions; Box Office Champions. Directors. 1st Ed. (May 1992)-. English. $95.00. Kagan World Media Inc., 126 Clock Tower Place, Carmel CA 93923-8734. **Tel** (408)624-1536, FAX (408)625-3225. **LC** IN PROCESS. **DD** 791.

●US/1064-7228
**PAUL KAGAN'S BOX OFFICE CHAMPIONS. PRODUCERS.** **See** The Arts-Performing Arts.

●US/1064-7244
**PAUL KAGAN'S BOX OFFICE CHAMPIONS. SCREENWRITERS.** **See** The Arts-Performing Arts.

CN/0715-9862
**PERFORATIONS.** [Perforations]. **Main/Corp** National Film Board of Canada. Technical and Production Services Branch. Vol. 1, No. 1 (Jan. 1981)-. Periodical. English (French). Six times a year. National Film Board of Canada, PO Box 6100 Station A, Montreal Quebec H3C 3H5 Canada. **Tel** (514)283-9427, FAX (514)283-7564. **DD** 791.43/02.

US
**PERSISTENCE OF VISION.** **Added/Corp** City University of New York. Film Faculty. No. 1 (Summer 1984)-. Periodical. English. an. $15.00 (individuals), $20.00 (institutions) North America; $20.00 other (all subscriptions are three year). Persistence of Vision, 53-24 63rd Street, c/o T Pipolo, Maspeth NY 11378. **Tel** (718)779-3936. **ED** Tony Pipolo. **Bk Rev**, (Qty: 1-2). **Ad Acc. Circ:** 1,000.
**Ind/Abst** Film Lit. Index.

US/0196-3007
**PERSPECTIVES ON FILM.** **Added/Corp** Pennsylvania State University. Audio-Visual Services. (19??)-. Periodical. English. sa. Pennsylvania State University / 208 Special Services Building, University Park PA 16802. **LC** PN1995.9.D6; P47. **DD** 791.43/05.

CN/0834-227X
**PHOTOVIDEO.** ***Title Change.*** **See** Photography and Video.

UK/0263-7553
**PICTURE HOUSE.** (1982)-. English.
**Ind/Abst** Archit. Period. Index (Autumn 1985-); Film Lit. Index (19??-).

UK
**PICTURE SHOW ANNUAL.** (1929)-. Periodical. English. an. Amalgamated Press, 110 Peckham Rd, London SE 15 England. **LC** AP4; .P577. **DD** 791.4.

CN/0836-2114
**PLAYBACK (TORONTO).** **See** Communication-Broadcasting.

US/0896-6680
**POCKET GUIDE FOR THE MOVIES ON VIDEO.** [Pocket guide movies video]. **VFOAT** Movies on Video. 1988/89-. English. an. Video Press, 631 Goldsborough Drive, Rockville MD 20850. **DD** 791.

PL
**POLISH ANIMATED FILMS CATALOGUE.** **Main/Corp** Film Polski. 1973-. English (French and German). Film Polski, 6/8 Mazowiecka, 00-048 Warsaw Poland. **Tel** 260849, FAX 27-57-84, telex 813640. **LC** NC1766.P6; F54. **DD** 791.43/7. ***Continues*** *Polish Animated Films.*

PL
**POLISH DOCUMENTARY AND EDUCATIONAL FILMS.** **VFOAT** Filmy Dokumentalne I Oswiatowe; Documentary and Educational Films. Periodical. English (French, German and Polish). an. Free. Film Polski, 6/8 Mazowiecka, 00-048 Warsaw Poland. **Tel** 260849, FAX 27-57-84, telex 813640. **LC** PN1995.9.D6; P64. **DD** 791.43/53. **Circ:** 2,000.

PL
**POLISH FEATURE FILMS.** 1970-. English. an. Free. Film Polski, 6/8 Mazowiecka, 00-048 Warsaw Poland. **Tel** 260849, FAX 27-57-84, telex 813640. **LC** PN1993.5.P55; P58. **DD** 791.43/75/09438. Index available. **Circ:** 1,000. ***Continues*** *Catalogue of Polish Feature Films.*

FR/0048-4911
**POSITIF.** [Positif]. **VFOAT** Revue de Cinema. (May 1952)-. Periodical. French. Eleven times a year (Monthly with double issue in July/Aug.). 370.00F France; 485.00F (surface mail) 615.00F (air mail) other. POL, 8 Villa d'Alesia, 75014 Paris France. **Tel** 011 33 1 45627721. **LC** PN1993; .P67. **DD** 791.43/05. Index available. cum. index. **Bk Rev. Ad Acc. Circ:** 15,000. Documents available from The Genuine Article.
**Desc:** Includes interviews, film reviews, articles on style, writers, producers and actors.
**Ind/Abst** Arts Humanit. Citation Index [Full Cov.]; Curr. Contents Arts Humanit.; Film Lit. Index; Point Repere (1983-); Res. Alert [Full Cov.]; Soc. Sci. Cit. Index [Select. Cov.].

US/0277-9897
**POST SCRIPT (JACKSONVILLE, FLA.).** (POST SCRIPT.). [Post scr.]. Vol. 1, No. 1 (Fall 1981)-. Periodical. English. Three times a year (Mar., Aug., Nov.). $20.00 (institutions), $12.00 (individuals) US; $25.00 other. East Texas State University / Literature, c/o Gerald Duchovnay, Department of Literature and Languages, Commerce TX 75429. **Tel** (903)886-5260, FAX (903)886-5980. **ED** Gerald Duchovnay. **LC** PN1995; .P682. **DD** 791.43/75/05. **Bk Rev**, (Qty: 3-5). **Pr Rev. Circ:** 600 (ctrl).
**Desc:** Film studies, directors, genres, cultural influences. Film and other art and humanities. Essays, interviews, book reviews, film studies bibliography.
**Ind/Abst** Book Rev. Index; Film Lit. Index; Int. Index Film Period.; MLA Int. Bibl. Books Artic. Mod. Lang. Lit.

US
**PRATFALL : THE "WAY OUT WEST" PERIODICAL TRIBUTE TO STAN AND OLLIE.** **Added/Corp** Sons of the Desert. Way out West Tent. (196?)-. Periodical. English. ir. $2.75 (includes postage) single issue (US, Canada & Mexico); $3.00 (sea mail), $3.50 (airmail) single issue (other). Sons of the Desert, Box 8341-B, Universal City CA 91608. **ED** Lori S Jones. **LC** WMLC L 83/3616. **Circ:** 2500 (ctrl).
**Desc:** Deals with the life and times of Laurel and Hardy.
**Ind/Abst** Film Lit. Index (19??-).

PL/0867-2288
**PREMIERA KATOWICE.** (PREMIERA.). [Premiera Katow.]. (1990)-. Periodical. Polish. mo. Price on Request. **(Subscription address:** ARS Polona, PO Box 1001, 00068 Warsaw Poland.**)** **UDC** 791.43.

CN/0701-077X
**PREMIERE, EN.** 23 Sept. 1976-. Periodical. French. En Premiere, CP 309 Succursale Outremont, Montreal Quebec H2V Canada. **DD** 791.43/09714.

CN/0831-9782
**PREMIERE (MISSISSAUGA).** (PREMIERE.). [Premiere]. Vol. 1, No. 3 (1985)-. Periodical. English. mo. 20.00Can$ Canada; 25.00Can$ US; 30.00Can$ other. Premiere / Ontario, 1314 Britannia Road East, Mississauga Ontario L4W 1C8 Canada. **Tel** (905)564-1033. **DD** 778.59/9/0688. ***Separated from*** *Videomania, 0711-7914.*

US/0894-9263
**PREMIERE (NEW YORK, N.Y. 1987).** (PREMIERE.). [Premiere]. Vol. 1, No. 1 (July/Aug. 1987)-. Periodical. English. mo. $20.00. K 3 Magazine Corporation, 200 Madison Avenue 8th Floor, New York NY 10016. **Tel** (212)447-4700, (212)447-4732. **(Subscription address:** Neodata / Colorado, PO Box 2606, Boulder Boulder CO 80322.**)** **ED** C. Van Tune (editor's address: 9171 Wilshire Boulevard/Suite 300, Beverly Hills CA 90210). **LC** PN1993; .P72. **DD** 791.43/05. **Ad Acc.** available on microfilm and microfiche from University Microfilms International (UMI). Documents available from UMI Article Clearinghouse.
**Desc:** Consumer movie magazine.
**Ind/Abst** Abr. Read. Guide Period. Lit.; Acad. Abstr. Full Text Elite (Jan. 1992-); Acad. Abstr. (Jan. 1992-); Access (1988-?); Film Lit. Index; Gen. Period. Index (1989-); Mag. Artic. Summar. Elite (Jan. 1992-); Mag. Artic. Summar. Select (Jan. 1992-); Mag. Artic. Summar. CD-ROM (Jan. 1992-); Mag. Index Plus (1989-); Mag. Index. Sel. (1989-); Mag. Search; Newsp. Period. Abstr. (1989-); Read. Guide Period. Lit.; Mag. Index (1989-); TOM Gen. Index (1989-) [Full Txt.].

US/0194-3847
**PREVIEW (WASHINGTON).** (PREVIEW.). [Preview]. V. 1- May 1979-. Periodical. English. bm. American Film Institute, JFK Center for Performing Arts, Washington DC 20566. **Tel** (202)828-4000. **LC** PN1993; .P74. **DD** 791.43/05. **Circ:** 25,000.
**Desc:** Contains commentary on approximately 105 films.

CN/0714-5551
**PRIX GENIE (1982).** (PRIX GENIE = GENIE AWARDS.). [Genie awards]. **Added/Corp** Academy of Canadian Cinema. **VFOAT** Genie Awards. (1982)-. English (French). an. Genie Awards, c/o Academy of Canadian Cinema, 653 Yonge Street, Toronto Ontario M4Y 1Z9 Canada. **DD** 791.43/0971. ***Continues*** *Genie Awards, 0714-5543.*

US/0361-9559
**PRO MUSICA SANA.** **See** Music.

US/0732-6653
**PRODUCER'S MASTERGUIDE, THE.** **See** Communication-Broadcasting.

GW/0932-0393
**PROFESSIONAL PRODUCTION.** [Prof. prod.]. (1987)-. Periodical. German. mo. DM104.00. Verlag Gerhard Spiehs, Baeckergasse 10, D 82288 Kottgeisering Germany. **Tel** 011 49 8144 1541. **UDC** 778.5.

IT/0393-8379
**QUADERNI DI CINEMA.** Vol. 1, No. 1 (Apr. 1981)-. Periodical. Italian. Six times a year (Feb., Apr., July, Aug., Oct., Dec.). L51750 Italy; L63250 Europe; L86250 US, Asia, Central & South America; L97750 Oceania; L74750 others. Quaderni di Cinema, Via Benedetto Varchi 57, 50132 Florence Italy. **Tel** 011 39 55 243144. **LC** IN PROCESS.
**Ind/Abst** Film Lit. Index.

IT
**QUADERNI DI DOCUMENTAZIONE DELLA CINETECA NAZIONALE.** Monographic series. Italian. ir. Price varies per volume. Edizioni dell'Ateno, Casella Postale 7216, 00100 Rome Italy. **Tel** 759-3456.

SZ/1050-9208
**QUARTERLY REVIEW OF FILM AND VIDEO.** (QUARTERLY REVIEW OF FILM AND VIDEO : QRFV.). [Q. rev. film video]. **VFOAT** Review of Film and Video; QRFV. Vol. 11, No. 1 (May 1989)-. Periodical. English. qt. $215.00 (academic institutions), $335.00 (corporate institutions). Gordon & Breach Science Publishers, PO Box 90, Reading RG1 8JL England. **Tel** 011 44 734 560080, FAX 011 44 734 568211. **(Subscription address:** International Publishers Distributor at one of the following addresses: 820 Town Center Drive, Langhorne, PA 19047; or PO Box 90, Reading Berkshire RG1 8JL UK; or Kent Ridge PO Box 1180, Singapore 9111, Republic of Singapore**)** **ED** Michael Renov. **LC** PN1994; .Q34. **DD** 791.43/05. **CODEN** QRFVEF. **[CCC].** available on microfilm from University Microfilms International (UMI). Documents available from The Genuine Article, UMI Article Clearinghouse. ***Continues*** *Quarterly Review of Film Studies, 0146-0013.*
**Desc:** Publishes critical, theoretical and historical essays and extended book reviews that explore these media in their technological, institutional and cultural contexts.
**Ind/Abst** Acad. Search (Jan. 1994-); Art Index; Arts Humanit. Citation Index [Full Cov.]; Book Rev. Index (?-Nov. 1989); Curr. Contents Arts Humanit.; Expand. Acad. Index (1989-); Film Lit. Index; Humanit. Index; Humanit. Source (Jul. 1993-); INFO-SOUTH Abstr.; Mag. Search; MLA Int. Bibl. Books Artic. Mod. Lang. Lit.; Newsp. Period. Abstr. (1991-); Res. Alert [Full Cov.]; Soc. Sci. Cit. Index [Select. Cov.].

US
**QUARTERLY UPDATE (NATIONAL AUDIOVISUAL CENTER).** ***Title Change.*** (QUARTERLY UPDATE : A COMPREHENSIVE LISTING OF NEW AUDIOVISUAL MATERIALS AND SERVICES OFFERED BY THE NATIONAL AUDIOVISUAL CENTER.). **Added/Corp** National Audiovisual Center. (June 1980)-(1993). Periodical. English. qt. National Audiovisual Center, 8700 Edgeworth Drive, Capitol Heights MD 20743. **Tel** (301)763-1896, (800)788-6282. **LC** LB1043; .Q35. ***Continued by*** *Quarterly Update (United States. National Archives and Records Administration).*

CN/0225-316X
**QUEBEC FILM INDUSTRY HANDBOOK.** [Que. film ind. handb.]. (1979)-. Periodical. English. an. $15.00. Editions Cinema/Quebec, PO Box 309 Outremont Station, Montreal Quebec H2V 4N1 Canada. **DD** 791.43/09714.

CN/0085-543X
**RECUEIL DES FILMS (MONTREAL).** (RECUEIL DES FILMS.). [Recl. films]. **Added/Corp** Centre Diocesain du Cinema, de la Radio et de la Television de Montreal. Centre Catholique National du Cinema, de la Radio et de la Television. Office Catholique National des Techniques de Diffusion. Office des

Communications Sociales. **VFOAT** Index des Films; Recueil des Films. Index des Films. (1956)-. Periodical. French. an. 15.00Can$. Office Des Communications Sociales, 1340 Boulevard St. Joseph EST, Montreal QUE H2J 1M3 Canada. **Tel** (514)524-8223, FAX (514)524-8522. **DD** 010. **Ad Acc. Circ:** 1,500.

US/8755-786X
**REEL DIRECTORY, THE.** [Reel dir.]. Began with Vol. 1, 1979. Directory. English. an. $15.00. The Reel Directory, PO Box 866, Cotati CA 94928. **Tel** (707)795-9367. **ED** Bonnie Carrol. **LC** PN1993.5.U718; R43. **DD** 384/.8/025794. **Ad Acc. Circ:** 4,000.
**Desc:** Guide to production resources for film, video, multi-image in Northern California. Content: approximately 2500 listings, 125 categories. Listing format: name, address, phone, 35 word description.

CN/0821-7947
**REEL WEST DIGEST.** [Reel west dig.]. Vol. 3, No. 1 (1983)-. English. an (Jan.). 23.36Can$. Reel West Productions Inc, 1106 Boundary Road, Burnaby BC V5K 4T5 Canada. **Tel** (604)294-4122. **ED** Sandy Flanagan. **DD** 991.43/02/99. **Ad Acc. Circ:** 8,000. ***Continues*** *Reel West Film and Video Digest, 0821-7939.*
**Desc:** Directory of individuals and companies working within and/or providing a service to the motion picture industry of Western Canada.

US/0890-5231
**RELEASE PRINT.** (RELEASE PRINT : NEWSLETTER OF FILM ARTS FOUNDATION, THE BAY AREA ORGANIZATION OF INDEPENDENT FILM AND VIDEOMAKERS / FAF, FILM ARTS FOUNDATION.). [Release print]. **Added/Corp** Film Arts Foundation (San Francisco, Calif.). (19??)-. Periodical. English. ir. $35.00 (includes membership). Film Arts Foundation, 346 Ninth Street, 2nd floor, San Francisco CA 94103. **Tel** (415)552-8760. **DD** 791. **Ad Acc. Circ:** 3,800 (ctrl).

BE/0774-0115
**REVUE BELGE DU CINEMA.** [Rev. belge cine.]. No. 1 (1982)-. Periodical. French. Three times a year. 1500F. Revue Belge du Cinema, 73 Ave des Coccinelles, 1170 Brussels Belgium. **Tel** 011 32 2 5385791, FAX 011 32 2 5376170. **ED** Olsie de Bacher. Index Available Received separately--bound from publisher. **Bk Rev**, (Qty: 2-3). ***Continues*** *Revue Belge du Cinema, 0774-0115.*

CN/0847-5911
**REVUE CANADIENNE D'ETUDES CINEMATOGRAPHIQUES.** (REVUE CANADIENNE D'ETUDES CINEMATOGRAPHIQUES / CANADIAN JOURNAL OF FILM STUDIES.). [Rev. can. etud. cinematogr.]. **Added/Corp** Film Studies Association of Canada. **VFOAT** Canadian Journal of Film Studies / Revue Canadienne d'Etudes cin,ematographiques.; Canadian Journal of Film Studies; CFS/RCDC. Vol. 1, No. 1 (1990)-. Periodical. English (summaries and/or abstracts in French). Twice a year. 25.00Can$. School for Studies in Art and Culture, Film Studies, Carleton University, 1125 Colonel By Drive, Ottawa, Ontario K1S 5B6 Canada. **Tel** (613)788-2600 ext. 6693, FAX (613)788-3575. **ED** Zuzana M. Pick. **LC** PN1993.5.A1; R43. **DD** 791.43/05. **Bk Rev**, (Qty: 5-6). **Circ:** 500.

CN/0843-6827
**REVUE DE LA CINEMATHEQUE, LA.** [Rev. cinemath.]. **Added/Corp** Cinematheque Quebecoise. **VFOAT** Cinematheque. Vol. 1 (May/June 1989)-. Periodical. French. Five times a year (10 iss. in two years). 20.00Can$ Canada; 25.00 Can$ other. La Cinematheque Quebecoise, 335 Boulevard de Maisonneuve Est, Montreal Quebec H2X 1K1 Canada. **Tel** (514)842-9763, FAX (514)866-4688. **ED** Pierre Jutras and Pierre Veronneali. **Ad Acc. Circ:** 35,000 (ctrl). ***Continues*** *Copie Zero, 0709-0471.*
**Ind/Abst** Film Lit. Index; Int. Index Film Period.; Point Repere.

FR/0019-2635
**REVUE DU CINEMA (PARIS. 1969).** ***Title Change.*** (LA REVUE DU CINEMA.). [Rev. cine.]. **Added/Corp** Ligue Francaise de l'Enseignement et de l'Education Permanente. (19??) No. 485-(Sept. 1992). Periodical. French. mo. 3 rue Recamier, 75341 Paris Cedex 07 France. **LC** PN1993; .L5215. **DD** 791.43/05. available on microfilm and microfiche from University Microfilms International (UMI). Documents available from The Genuine Article. ***Continues*** *Image et Son;* ***Absorbed*** *Ecran (Paris, France).* ***Continued by*** *Mensuel du Cinema.*
**Ind/Abst** Arts Humanit. Citation Index (19??-19??) [Full Cov.]; Curr. Contents Arts Humanit.; Film Lit. Index; Point Repere (1983-); Res. Alert [Full Cov.].

IT/0035-5879
**RIVISTA DEL CINEMATOGRAFO.** [Riv. cinematogr.]. **VFOAT** Rivista del Cinematografo e della Comunicazione Sociale. Periodical. Italian. mo. L60.000 Italy; L170.000 other. Ente dello Spettacolo, Via Giuseppe Palombini 6, 00165 Rome Italy.
**Ind/Abst** Film Lit. Index.

US/0274-7960
**ROB TUCKER'S MEMORY LANE. VFOAT** Memory Lane. (19??)-. Periodical. English. Twelve times a year. $10.00. Memory Lane / Texas, PO Box 1627, Lubbock TX 79408.

US
**ROGER EBERT'S MOVIE HOME COMPANION / BY ROGER EBERT.** ***Title Change.*** **VFOAT** Movie Home Companion. (1985)-(199?). English. an. Andrews McMeel & Parker Inc., 4900 Main Street, Kansas City MO 64112. **Tel** (816)932-6600, (800)826-4216. **LC** PN1995; .E318. **DD** 791.43/75/05. ***Continued by*** *Ebert, Roger. Roger Ebert's Video Companion, 1072-561X.*
**Desc:** Full-length reviews of movies and assessments of films from critic Roger Ebert.

●US/1072-561X
**ROGER EBERT'S VIDEO COMPANION.** [Roger Ebert's video companion]. **VFOAT** Video Companion. (1994)-. English. an. $14.95. Andrews McMeel & Parker Inc., 4900 Main Street, Kansas City MO 64112. **Tel** (816)932-6600, (800)826-4216. **LC** PN1995; .E318. **DD** 791.43/75/05. ***Continues*** *Ebert, Roger. Roger Ebert's Movie Home Companion.*
**Desc:** Full-length reviews of movies and assessments of films from critic Roger Ebert.

RM/0557-2630
**ROMANIAN FILM, THE.** [Rom. film]. **Added/Corp** Romania Films. Foreign Press and Publicity Dept. (1965)-. Periodical. English. ir. Romaniafilm, 25 Juliu Fucik Street, Bucharest Romania. **LC** PN1993; .R65. **DD** 791.43/09498.
**Ind/Abst** Film Lit. Index.

SA
**S A F T T A NEWSLETTER.** Newsletter. South African Film and Television Technicians Association, Craighall 2024 South Africa.

FR
**SCIENCE FILM.** **See** Science and Technology.

UK/0036-9543
**SCREEN. Added/Corp** Society for Education in Film and Television. Vol. 1 (1959)-. Periodical. English. qt. £50.00 UK and Europe; $94.00 other. Oxford University Press, Walton Street, Oxford OX2 6DP England. **Tel** 011 44 865 56767, FAX 011 44 865 267773, telex 837330 OXPRES G. **(Subscription address:** Oxford University Press / USA, Journals Marketing Department, Oxford University Press, 2001 Evans Road, Cary NC 27513.**) ED** John Caughie, Alan Durant, Simon Frith, Norman King and Annette Kuhn. **[CCC]. Bk Rev. Ad Acc.** available on microfilm and microfiche from University Microfilms International (UMI). Documents available from The Genuine Article. ***Continues*** *Film Teacher.*
**Desc:** Contributions by leading critics, practicing writers and film makers. Covers major developments in film and film theory from the pop video to film noir.
**Ind/Abst** Art Index; Arts Humanit. Citation Index [Full Cov.]; Curr. Contents Arts Humanit.; Film Lit. Index (19??-); Res. Alert [Full Cov.]; Soc. Sci. Cit. Index [Select. Cov.]; Stud. Women Abstr.

US/0036-956X
**SCREEN ACTOR.** [Screen actor]. **Added/Corp** Screen Actors Guild. Vol. 1 (Aug. 1959)-. Periodical. English. qt. $7.00. Screen Actors Guild, 7065 Hollywood Boulevard, Hollywood CA 90028. **Tel** (213)465-4600. **LC** PN1993; .S2383. **DD** 791.43/0973.
**Ind/Abst** Film Lit. Index (19??-).

US/0890-5266
**SCREEN ACTOR HOLLYWOOD.** ***Title Change.*** [Screen actor Hollywood]. **Added/Corp** Screen Actors Guild. **VFOAT** Screen Actor; Hollywood. Vol. 7, No. 2 (Summer 1986)-(199?). Periodical. English. qt. Screen Actors Guild, 7065 Hollywood Boulevard, Hollywood CA 90028. **Tel** (213)465-4600. **ED** Mark Locher. **LC** PN1993.5.U65; S37. cum. index. **Bk Rev. Circ:** 75,000 (ctrl). ***Continues*** *Screen Actor News. Hollywood.* ***Continued by*** *Call Sheet.*
**Desc:** Screen Actors Guild official national publication; covers craft and conditions of professional motion picture performing arts, including film, TV and commercials.
**Ind/Abst** Film Lit. Index (19??-).

●US/1070-7573
**SCREEN (CHICAGO, ILL.).** (SCREEN.). [Screen]. Vol. 15, No. 23 (June 21, 1993)-. Periodical. English. wk. $70.00 (1 year), $112.00 (2 year), $126.00 (3 year) US; 80.00 (1 year), $122.00 (2 year), $136.00 (3 year) Canada. Screen Enterprises Inc, 720 North Wabash Avenue/7th Floor, Chicago IL 60611. **Tel** (312)664-5236, FAX (312)664-8425. **ED** Ruth L. Ratny. **LC** PN1995.9.P7; R88. **DD** 791.43/023/0977311. **Ad Acc. Circ:** 15,000 (ctrl). ***Continues*** *Ruth L Ratny's Screen, 0276-153X.*
**Desc:** Film and video production magazine with feature stories and close-up profiles.

UK
**SCREEN DIGEST.** **See** Communication-Broadcasting.

UK/0965-9587
**SCREEN FINANCE.** [Screen financ.]. **VFOAT** Financial Times Screen Finance. (1988)-. Periodical. English. Twenty-four times a year. £495.00. Financial Times England, 8 16 Great New Street, London EC4A 3BN England. **Tel** 011 44 71 353 0305, 353 1040, FAX 011 44 353 0846. **ED** Neil McCartney. available on microfiche; available on an online database from DIALOG.
**Desc:** All aspects of international film financing.
**Ind/Abst** PROMT [Full Txt.]; PTS Newsl. Database [Full Txt.].

UK/0307-4617
**SCREEN INTERNATIONAL.** [Screen int.]. (19??)-. Periodical. English. Fifty-one times per year. $195.00. EMAP Media, 33 39 Bowling Green Lane, London EC1R 0DA England. **Tel** 011 44 71 8371212. **(Subscription address:** Readerlink Subscription Services, 196 High Street, Tonbridge Kent TN9 1EF England.**) LC** PN1993.5.G7; C5. **DD** 338.4/7/791430941. **[CCC].** ***Continues*** *Screen International & Cinema TV Today.*

UK
**SCREEN INTERNATIONAL FILM AND TV YEAR BOOK.** ***Title Change.*** **VFOAT** Screen International Film and Television Year Book. 38th Year (1983/1984)-Vol. (1992/1993). English. an. International Thomson Business Publications, 42 Bedford Square, London WC1B 3SC England. **Tel** 011 44 71 323 6986. **LC** PN1993.3; .B7. **DD** 791.43/025. ***Continues*** *International Film and TV Year Book.* ***Continued by*** *Screen International. International Film & Television Directory.*

●UK
**SCREEN INTERNATIONAL. THE INTERNATIONAL FILM & TELEVISION DIRECTORY. VFOAT** International Film & Television Directory; International Film and Television Directory; Film & Television Directory; Film and Television Directory; Screen International Film and Television Directory; Screen International Film & Television Directory. (1993)-. Directory. English. an. $130.00. Screen International, 7 Swallow Place, 249 259 Regent Street, London W1R 7AA England. **Tel** 011 44 71 491 9484. **LC** PN1993.3; B7. ***Continues*** *Screen International Film and TV Year Book.*

II
**SCREEN WORLD. Added/Corp** Screen World Publication. **VFOAT** Screen World Annual. (19??)-. English. $35.00. Screen World Publications, Bombay, India. **(Subscription address:** Prints India, 11 Darya Ganj, New Delhi 110002 India.**) LC** PN1993.5.I8; S378. **DD** 384/.8/02554.

US
**SCREEN WORLD. VFOAT** John Willis Screen World; Film Annual. Vol. 33 (1982)-. English. an. $45.00. Applause Theater & Book Publs, 212 West 71st Street, New York NY 10023. **Tel** (212)595-4735, FAX (212)721-2856. ***Continues*** *John Willis' Screen World.*

FR/0993-2097
**SCRIPT (PARIS, 1988).** (SCRIPT.). (1988)-. Periodical. French. qt. 100.00F France; 110.00F other. Editions de May, 50 Avenue Marceau, 75008 Paris France. **Tel** 011 33 16 93940777. **UDC** 778.5. **Bk Rev**, (Qty: 500-1000). **Ad Acc, Adv Mgr:** Rene Thevenet, **Tel** 16 1 47 23 70 30.
**Desc:** Contains articles on every new French-speaking publication dealing with cinema and TV (essays, reports, legal or technical studies, biographies, novels, periodical publications). Also presents information on a large number of other publications (in English, German, Italian, Spanish, and Dutch). It presents reports on initiatives in favor of protection of the historical patrimony of cinema.
**Ind/Abst** Film Lit. Index (19??-).

US/0748-6456
**SCRIPTWRITERS MARKET.** [Scr.writ. mark.]. 1983-. English. an. $28.95. Scriptwriters-Filmmakers Publishing, 8033 Sunset Boulevard/Suite 306, West Hollywood CA 90046. **Tel** (818)769-2811. **ED** Gates and Buffum. **LC** PN1993.5.U718; S28. **DD** 791.4/02573. **Bk Rev. Ad Acc. Circ:** 10,000 (ctrl). ***Continues*** *Screenplay Sales Directory, 0734-8592.*
**Desc:** How and where to sell what you write for TV and film, and how to get an agent.

IT/0393-3865
**SEGNOCINEMA. VFOAT** Segno Cinema. Vol. 1, No. 1 (Autumn 1981)-. Periodical. Italian. Six times a year. L35000.00 Italy; L60000.00 other. SegnoCinema, Via Prati 34, 36100 Vicenza Italy. **Tel** 011 39 444 923856. **LC** PN1993; .S36. **DD** 791.43/05.
**Ind/Abst** Film Lit. Index (19??-).

JA
**SELECTED JAPANESE FEATURE FILMS. VFOAT** Nihon No Gekieiga. English (Japanese). Unijapan Film Association for the Diffusion of Japanese Films Abroad Inc, 9-13 Ginza 5 Chuo-ku, Tokyo 104 Japan. **LC** PN1993.5.J3; N55. **DD** 791.43/75/0952. ***Continues*** *Nihon No Yushu Eiga.*

CN/0037-2412
**SEQUENCES (MONTREAL).** (SEQUENCES.). [Sequences]. **Added/Corp** Centre Catholique du Cinema de Montreal. Commission des Cine-Clubs. Office Diocesian des Techniques de Diffusion de Montreal. Service d'Education Cinematographique. No. 1 (1955)-. Periodical. French. bm. $42.00 (institutions), $34.00 (individuals) Canada; $52.00 other. Sequences / Canada, 1340 Boul St. Joseph Est, Montreal H2J 1M2, Canada. **Tel** (514)524-8223. Index available. cum. index. **Ad Acc. Circ:** 3,500.
**Desc:** Magazine devoted to cinema articles, interviews, critics and chronicles.
**Ind/Abst** Can. Period. Index (19??-); Film Lit. Index; Point Repere (1983-).

UK/0037-4806
**SIGHT AND SOUND (LONDON).** (SIGHT AND SOUND.). [Sight sound]. **Added/Corp** British Film Institute. British Institute of Adult Education. **VFOAT** Sight & Sound. Vol. 1 (Spring 1932)-. Academic Scholarly Publication. English. Twelve times a year. £29.50 UK; £36.00 (air mail) Europe; £36.00 (air mail) US and Canada; £36.00 (surface mail), £61.00 (air mail) other. British Film Institute, 21 Stephen Street, London W1P 1PL England. **Tel** 11 44 71 2551444, FAX 11 44 71 4367950, telex 27624 BFILDNG. **ED** Philip Dodd (editor's phone: 11 44 71 9578923). **LC** PN1993; .S56. **DD** 791.43/05. **[CCC].** Index available (free with subscription). cum. index. **Bk Rev**, (Qty: 144). **Ad Acc, Adv Mgr:** Hucksters, **Tel** 11 44 89 2784804. **Circ:** 30,000. available on microfilm from World Microfilm Publications Ltd. Documents available from UMI Article Clearinghouse. ***Absorbed*** *Monthly Film Bulletin.*
**Desc:** Carries full credits and extensive synopsis of all films reviewed. Also includes scholarly and critical features on cinema, past and present.
**Ind/Abst** Acad. Abstr. Full Text Elite (May 1991-); Acad. Abstr. (May 1991-); Acad. Ind. [Computer File] (1987-); Acad. Search (May 1991-); Art Index; Book Rev. Index; Br. Humanit. Index; Curr. Contents Arts Humanit.; Expand. Acad. Index (1987-); Film Lit. Index; Humanit. Index; INFO-SOUTH Abstr.; Mag. Search; Med. Rev. Dig.; Middle East Abstr. Index; Newsp. Period. Abstr. (1990-); Soc. Sci. Cit. Index [Select. Cov.].

CN/0703-1408
**SIGHT & SOUND (MISSISSAUGA).** (SIGHT & SOUND.). Ed. 1- Jan. 1976-. Periodical. English. Braun Electrical Canada Ltd, Motion Picture Division, 3269 American Drive, Mississauga Ontario L4V 1B9 Canada. **DD** 778.5/028. Documents available from The Genuine Article. ***Formed by the union of*** *Sound & Light, 0703-1386* ***and*** *Sound & Light, 0703-1394.*
**Ind/Abst** Arts Humanit. Citation Index [Full Cov.]; Book Rev. Digest; Res. Alert [Full Cov.].

US/0037-4830
**SIGHTLINES (NEW YORK, N.Y.).** ***Ceased.*** (SIGHTLINES.). [Sightlines]. **Added/Corp** Educational Film Library Association. Vol. 1 (Sept./Oct. 1967)-(Dec. 1993). Periodical. English. qt. American Film and Video Association, 85 Van Reypen Street, Jersey City NJ 07306. **ED** Ray Rolff. **LC** LB1044.Z9; S54. **Ad Acc. Circ:** 2,000. available on microfilm and microfiche from University Microfilms International (UMI). ***Formed by the union of*** *Filmlist; Film Review Digest* ***and*** *EFLA Bulletin;* ***Absorbed*** *FLQ, Film Library Quarterly, 0015-1327.* ***Continued in part by*** *EFLA Bulletin (1977).*
**Desc:** Articles focusing on the production, programming, and distribution of nontheatrical film and video. With special subject filmographies, interviews with film and video makers, library management column, film lists, new publications, etc.
**Ind/Abst** Film Lit. Index; Libr. Lit.; Med. Rev. Dig.

US/0037-5209
**SILENT PICTURE, THE.** [Silent pict.]. No. 1- Winter 1968/69-. Periodical. English. qt. $4.00. First Media Press, 6 East 39th Street, New York NY 10016. **LC** PN1993; .S567. **DD** 791.43. available on microfilm from University Microfilms International (UMI).
**Ind/Abst** Am. Hist. Life.

IT
**SIPARIO.** **See** Theater.

NE
**SKOOP.** ***Ceased.*** (19??)-(Jan. 1993). Periodical. Dutch. mo. BV Skoop, Postbus 871, NL 2300 Leiden Netherlands.
**Ind/Abst** Film Lit. Index (19??-).

NE
**SKRIEN.** (19??)-. Periodical. Dutch. bm.
**Ind/Abst** Film Lit. Index (19??-).

US/0036-1682
**SMPTE JOURNAL (1976).** (SMPTE JOURNAL : PUBLICATION OF THE SOCIETY OF MOTION PICTURE AND TELEVISION ENGINEERS.). [SMPTE j.]. **Added/Corp** Society of Motion Picture and Television Engineers. **VFOAT** S.M.P.T.E. Journal. **VAT** Society of Motion Picture and Television Engineers Journal. (Jan. 1976)-. Periodical. English. mo. $75.00 (surface mail); Also comes with membership to SMPTE. Society of Motion Picture and Television Engineers, 595 West Hartsdale Avenue, White Plains NY 10607. **Tel** (914)761-1100, FAX (914)761-3115, telex 4995348. **LC** TR845; .S6. **DD** 778.5/05. **CODEN** SMPJDF. (bound in Dec. issue). cum. index. **Bk Rev**, (Qty: 1/yr). **Ad Acc.** available on microfilm and microfiche from University Microfilms International (UMI). Documents available from Article Express International, The Genuine Article, Ask*IEEE, CASDDS. ***Continues*** *Journal of the SMPTE, 0361-4573.*
**Ind/Abst** Acoust. Abstr.; Appl. Sci. Technol. Index; Bioeng. Abstr.; Chem. Abstr. (1976-1980); Curr. Contents Eng. Tech. Appl. Sci.; Ei Page One; EMBASE; Eng. Index Annu.; Film Lit. Index; Graph. Arts Bull. Inst. Pap. Sci. Technol. (Sept. 1989); INSPEC (Jan. 1976-); Int. Aerosp. Abstr.; Res. Alert [Full Cov.]; Sci. Cit. Index; SCISEARCH.

US/1050-2777
**SOUND & IMAGE.** **See** Music.

BE
**SOUNDTRACK!.** **VFOAT** Sound Track. No. 1 (Mar. 1982)-. Periodical. English. Four times a year (Mar., June, Sept., Dec.). $18.00. Roger Feigelson, 145 North El Camino Real, Suite 210, San Mateo CA 94401. **Tel** (415)343-0495. **Bk Rev. Ad Acc. Circ:** 3,000. ***Continues*** *Soundtrack!.*

RU
**SOVETSKIE KHUDOZHNIKI TEATRA I KINO.** **See** Theater.

RU/0201-8373
**SOVIET FILM.** ***Ceased.*** [Sov. film]. June 1, (1957)-(19??). Periodical. English (French, Spanish, German, Arabic and Russian). mo. **(Subscription address:** Victor Kamkin, 4956 Boiling Brook Parkway, Rockville MD 20852.**) LC** PN1993.5.R9; S543. **DD** 791.43/0947.
**Desc:** Illustrated magazine devoted to Soviet and foreign cinematography, covering the art of film-making, new films, film stars, prominent film directors and other figures in cinema art.
**Ind/Abst** Film Lit. Index (1974-1990).

US/1045-8751
**SPECIAL EFFECTS.** ***Suspended.*** [Spec. eff. mag.]. **VFOAT** Special Effects Magazine. (1989)-?. Periodical. English. qt. $15.00. Sanford B Kennedy, 10753 Magnolia Boulevard, North Hollywood CA 91601. **LC** TR858; .S66. **DD** 778.5/2345/05. ***Continues*** *Special Effects Business, 0898-3186.*
**Desc:** Covers the most exciting aspects of the field of special effects and the growth of the worldwide market for special effects in films, television and commercials.

US/1045-0750
**SPECIAL EFFECTS & STUNTS GUIDE.** [Spec. eff. stunts guide]. **VFOAT** Special Effects and Stunts Guide; Special Effects and Stunts Directory. (1989)-. English. an. $45.95. Lone Eagle Publishing Inc., 2337 Roscomare Road, Suite 9, Los Angeles CA 90077. **Tel** (310)471-8066, FAX (310)471-4969. **LC** TR847.5; .S65. **DD** 791.43/024/02573.

US/1051-0230
**SPECTATOR (LOS ANGELES, CALIF.).** (THE SPECTATOR / DIVISION OF CRITICAL STUDIES OF THE SCHOOL OF CINEMA-TELEVISION, UNIVERITY OF SOUTHERN CALIFORNIA.). [Spectator]. **Added/Corp** University of Southern California. School of Cinema-Television. Division of Critical Studies. Vol. 8, No. 1 (Winter 1987)-. Periodical. English. Twice a year. $10.00 (indiviudals); $20.00 (institutions). University of Southern California Cinema Television Department, University Park, Los Angeles CA 90089. **Tel** (213)740-3334. **ED** Harry Benshoff and Tassilo Schneider. **LC** PN1993; .S677. **DD** 791.43/05. **Circ:** 170. ***Continues*** *USC Spectator.*
**Ind/Abst** Film Lit. Index (19??-); Mag. Search.

DK
**SPOTLIGHT.** Periodical. Danish (Danish). ir. 16.00. Rnnegarden 4, Nissum Seminarieby, 7620 Lemnig Denmark. **LC** PN1993; .S68.
**Desc:** Current in-depth articles, reports, and features on what's really happening in the field. Covers hot topics, trends, and legal issues.

UK
**"SPOTLIGHT" CASTING DIRECTORY, THE.** (19??)-. Directory. English. an. £66.00. Spotlight / London, 7 Leicester Place, London WC2H 7BP England. **Tel** 011 44 1 437 7631, FAX 011 44 1 437 5881. **Ad Acc.** ctrl circ.

US/1057-8234
**SPOTLIGHT CASTING MAGAZINE.** [Spotlight cast. mag.]. **VFOAT** Spotlight. (198?)-. Periodical. English. Fifty-two times a year (Wed.). $55.00. Spotlight Casting Magazine, 1605 North Cahuenga Boulevard, Suite 207, Los Angeles CA 90028. **Tel** (213)462-6775, (213)871-8007. **DD** 791.
**Desc:** For aspiring actors and actresses who want to progress in their acting careers.

US/0883-3125
**STAR TREK III.** [Star trek III]. **VFOAT** Star Trek 3; Star Trek Three. Periodical. English. bm. Star Trek III : The Official Fan Club, 603 Ouray Way, Aurora CO 80011.

US/0191-4626
**STARLOG.** **VFOAT** Star Log. No. 1 (Aug. 1976)-. Periodical. English. Twelve times a year. $39.97 US; $48.97 other. Starlog Press Inc., 475 Park Avenue South, New York NY 10016. **Tel** (212)689-2830, FAX (212)889-7933. **(Subscription address:** Kable Publishers Aide, 308 East Hitt Street, Subscription Department, Mt. Morris IL 61054-1473.**) LC** WMLC 93/1680.
**Desc:** Covers science fiction in film and television.
**Ind/Abst** Sci. Fict. Fantasy Book Rev. Index.

US/0883-6094
**STEVEN SPIELBERG FILM SOCIETY NEWSLETTER, THE.** [Steven Spielberg Film Soc. newsl.]. **VFOAT** Newsletter. Newsletter. English. $10.00. Spielberg Film Society, 4126 East 32nd Street, Tucson AZ 85711. **ED** Judy Hubbard and Don Archer. **DD** 791. **Circ:** 60.
**Desc:** News and articles on the films of Steven Spielberg and others plus music of films in general and music of John Williams in particular.

KO
**SUKURIN (SEOUL, KOREA : 1984).** (SUKURIN / SCREEN.). **VFOAT** Screen. Vol. 1 (1984)-. Periodical. Korean (Korean). mo. $112.00. Wolgan Sukurin, 188 Naesu-Song, Chongo-ku Seoul Korea. **(Subscription address:** Seoul Books and Records, 3450 West Peterson Avenue, Chicago IL 60659.**) LC** PN1993; .S867.

SW
**SWEDISH FILMS. FILMS SUEDOIS.** **Added/Corp** Svenska Filminstitutet. **VFOAT** Films Suedois. (1973)-. English (French). an. Free. Swedish Film Institute, PO Box 27126, S-102 52 Stockholm Sweden. **Tel** 011 46 866 51100. ***Continues*** *Cinema en Suede.*

FR
**TECHNICIEN DU FILM ET DE LA VIDEO, LA TECHNIQUE, L'EXPLOITATION CINEMAGRAPHIQUE, LE.** **VFOAT** Technicien Film & Video; Technicien Film et Video; TFV; Technicien du Film,. Vol. 25, No. 266 (Jan./Feb. 1979)-. Periodical. French. Eleven times a year (except Aug.). 381.98F France; 500.00F other. IF Diffusion, 33 Champs Elysees, F 75008 Paris France. **Tel** 011 33 1 43592484, FAX 011 33 1 42255997. **ED** H. Dujarric and J. F. Mantoux. **LC** PN1993; .T22. **Bk Rev. Ad Acc. Circ:** 25,000. ***Continues*** *Technicien du Film.*
**Desc:** All technical reports about films, equipment for movies and videos, cables, and satellite TV.

US/0149-7359
**TELEVISION NETWORK MOVIES.** ***Ceased.*** Periodical. English. ir. Television Index Inc, 40/29 27th Street/2nd Floor, Long Island City NY 11101. **Tel** (718)937-3990. **ED** Jonathan Miller. **LC** PN1992; .T44. **DD** 791.43/7.
**Desc:** Annual directory of theatrical movies, TV movies and dramas for TV, 90 minutes or longer, non-series, that were on TV during a current season.

SP
**TERROR FANTASTIC.** **VFOAT** T.F. Yearly V. 1- (No. 1- Oct. 1971)-. Periodical. Spanish (Spanish). 50. PJE Pla 11-13, 10-B Barcelona Spain. **LC** PN1995.9.H6; T45. **DD** 791.43/0909/16.

FR
**TEXTES DU CINEMA FRANCAIS.** **Added/Corp** Centre National de la Cinematographie (France). Sous-Direction des Affaires Generales. (19??)-. French. ir. 150.00F. Centre Nationale Cinematographie, Gen Dir, 12 rue de Lubeck, 75784 Paris Cedex 16 France. **Tel** 505 14 40. **LC** LAW. **DD** 343.44/07879143; 344.4037879143. ***Continues*** *Textes Reglementaires du Cinema Francais.*

US
**THEATER FINANCIAL RECORD, THE.** **Added/Corp** Paul Kagan Associates. (19??)-. English. an. $295.00. Kagan World Media Inc., 126 Clock Tower Place, Carmel CA 93923-8734. **Tel** (408)624-1536, FAX (408)625-3225. **LC** PN1993; .T45. **DD** 384/.83/0973.

CH
**TIEN YING TSO PIN.** **VFOAT** Dian Ying Zuo Pin. Periodical. Chinese. bm. NT$0.45. Cheng-Tu Shih Yu Cheng Chu, Cheng-tu, People's Republic of China. **LC** PN1993.5.C4; T48. **DD** 791.43/0951.

II/0040-7836
**TIME & TIDE.** (19??)-. Periodical. English. Twelve times a year. $52.00 (one year); $145.00 (three years). Time & Tide Publications, 1 Ansari Road Darya Ganj, New Delhi 110002 India. **Tel** 011 91 11 3272046, 011 91 11 5592383, FAX 011 91 11 941111. **ED** Devendra Kumar (editor's address: BB-39F Janakpuri, New Delhi 110058 India). **LC** PN1993; .T55. **DD** 791.43/05. Index available. cum. index. **Bk Rev**, (Qty: 24-30). **Ad Acc. Circ:** 55,000. available on microfilm from University Microfilms International (UMI).
**Desc:** The visual scene including cinema, TV and video

Motion Picture

in relationship with society as well as a potential trade. A potential medium of communication dealing in various modes and aspects.

US/0092-9263
**TLF QUARTERLY.** **Main/Corp** Time-Life Films. April/June 1973-. English. qt. Time-Life Films, Room 33/43 Time-Life Building, New York NY 10020. **LC** PN1992.8.F5; T54. **DD** 791.45/7.

US/0193-6085
**TODAY'S FILM MAKER.** **VFOAT** Film Maker. V. 1- Aug. 1971-. Periodical. English. qt. $6.00 US; $8.00 other. American Film Makers Magazine, Inc., 250 Fulton Avenue, Hempstead NY 11550. **LC** TR845; .T63. **DD** 778.5/3/05. available on microfilm from University Microfilms International (UMI).

IT
**TOP VIDEO.** (19??)-. Italian. mo. L49500 Italy; L75000 other. Casa Editrice Universo, Via Margherita de Vizzi 35/39, 20092 Cinisello Balsamo Italy. **Tel** 011 39 2 66030285.

CN/0704-5816
**TORONTO FILMMAKERS' CO-OP.** **Main/Corp** Toronto Filmakers' Co-Operative. (Sept. 1976)-. Periodical. English. Toronto Filmmakers Co-Operative, 67 Portland Street, Toronto Ontario M5V 2M9 Canada. **DD** 791.43/07/152.
**Desc:** Informational booklet on workshops offered, etc.

FR
**TOUS LES FILMS.** Periodical. French. an. Centurion / France, 17 rue de Babylone, 75007 Paris France. **LC** PN1997.8; .T68. **DD** 791.43/05.

CN/0826-1210
**TRIBUTE GOES TO THE MOVIES.** Vol. 1, Issue 1 (Feb. 1, 1984)-. Periodical. English. bm. $12.00. Tribute Publication, 184 Laird Drive, Toronto Ontario M4G 3V7. **DD** 791.43/05.

CN/0823-678X
**TRIBUTE MAGAZINE.** [Tribut. mag.]. **VFOAT** Tribute. Vol. 1, Issue 1 (Winter 1981)-. Periodical. English. ir. $26.00 Canada; $45.00 US; $55.00 other. Tribute Publication, 184 Laird Drive, Toronto Ontario M4G 3V7. **DD** 791.43/05.

UK
**UK FILM INITIATIVES.** (19??)-. Monographic series. English. ir. £6.50. British Film Institute, 21 Stephen Street, London W1P 1PL England. **Tel** 11 44 71 2551444, FAX 11 44 71 4367950, telex 27624 BFILDNG.

US/0279-6244
**UNDER WESTERN SKIES.** (Jan., 1978)-. Periodical. English. ir. $13.00 US; $19.00 other. The World of Yesterday, Rt 3 Box 263-H, Waynesville NC 28786. **Tel** (704)648-5647. **ED** Linda S. Downey. **LC** WMLC L 83/5626. **Bk Rev. Ad Acc. Circ:** 1,000.
**Desc:** Magazine devoted to the western movies of the past and westerns on radio and TV.

US/0042-2738
**VARIETY.** [Variety]. Vol. 1, No. 1 (Dec. 16, 1905)-. Periodical. English. wk (Monday). $167.00 US; $175.00 (includes GST) Canada; $270.00 (airmail) Europe; $470.00 (airmail) Asia/Pacific; $370.00 (airmail) other. Cahners Publishing Company, 249 West 17th Street, New York NY 10011. **Tel** (212)645-0067, FAX (212)242-6987. **(Subscription address:** Variety, Subscription Department, PO Box 6400, Torrance CA 90504-0400.**)** **ED** Peter Bart. **LC** PN2000; .V3. **DD** 790.2/05. **[CCC]. Bk Rev. Ad Acc. Circ:** 33,000 (ctrl). available in microform from Kraus Microform. Documents available from UMI Article Clearinghouse.
**Desc:** Covers all of the entertainment business: film, cable, homevideo, legitimate theater, music and personal appearance. Readers are the top executives in each of these industries: actors, directors, agents and producers, writers, the financial community, ad agency personnel, and students and teachers of film, television, theater and journalism.
**Ind/Abst** Bus. Index (1985-); Chicano Index; Curr. Lit. Fam. Plan. (19??-199?); Expand. Acad. Index (1992-); Film Lit. Index; Gen. BusinessFile (1985-); Gen. Period. Index (1985-); Infobank (Jan. 1969-); Infomat Int. Bus.; Mag. Index Plus (1989-); Mag. Search; Mark. Advert. Ref. Serv.; Med. Rev. Dig.; Music Index; Newsp. Period. Abstr. (1988-); SportSearch; Stat. Ref. Index; Mag. Index (1977-); Topicator.

UK
**VARIETY INTERNATIONAL FILM GUIDE.** **VFOAT** International Film Guide. (1990)-. Periodical. English. an. £15.50 UK; $26.69 US. Variety, c/o Peter Cowie, 34 35 Newman Street, London W1P 3PD England. ***Continues*** *International Film Guide, 0074-6053.*
**Desc:** Long-established international yearbook focusing on trends and personalities in world cinema, providing reference material and film statistics.

US/0149-1830
**VELVET LIGHT TRAP, THE.** [Velv. light trap]. No. 1 (June 1971)-. Periodical. English. sa (Mar. & Sept.). $35.00 (institutions), $18.00 (individuals) US; add $4.00 postage other. University of Texas Press, PO Box 7819, Austin TX 78713. **Tel** (512)471-4531, FAX (512)320-0668, telex 776453 UTEXPRES AUS. **ED** Janet Staiger. **LC** PN1993; .V44. **DD** 791.43/05. **CODEN** VLTREI. Index available. cum. index. **Ad Acc. Circ:** 600 (ctrl). available on microfilm and microfiche from University Microfilms International (UMI).
**Desc:** Offers issues in film studies while expanding its commitment to television as well as film research. Each issue provokes debate about critical, theoretical, and historical topics relating to a particular theme.
**Ind/Abst** Am. Hist. Life (1989-); Am. Humanit. Index (199?-); Film Lit. Index; MLA Int. Bibl. Books Artic. Mod. Lang. Lit.; Soc. Plann. Policy Dev. Abstr.

NE/0168-2121
**VERSUS.** ***Ceased.*** (VERSUS KWARTAALSCHRIFT VOOR FILM EN OPVOERINGSKUNSTEN.). (1982)-(1993). Periodical. Dutch. Three times a year. Uitgeverij Sun, PO Box 1609, 6501 BP Nijmegen Netherlands. **Tel** 011 31 80 221700. **UDC** 791. **Circ:** 180.
**Desc:** Provides a theoretical review of film.

FR/0985-1402
**VERTIGO (PARIS, FRANCE).** (VERTIGO.). (19??)-. French. ir. 250.00F France; $51.47 other. Vertigo, 99 rue Notre-Dame des Champs, 75006 Paris France. **Tel** 011 33 46340541.

UK
**VETERANS NEWSLETTER (CINEMA & TELEVISION VETERANS).** (THE VETERANS NEWSLETTER.). Newsletter. English. **ED** Gordon Coombes.

CN
**VIDEO AND FILM CATALOGUE.** English (French). ir. 9.00Can$. National Film Board of Canada, PO Box 6100 Station A, Montreal Quebec H3C 3H5 Canada. **Tel** (514)283-9427, FAX (514)283-7564. **Circ:** 30,000. available on CD-ROM from Optim Corporation.
**Desc:** Catalogue of films and videos distributed and / or produced by the National Film Board of Canada.

US/0896-2871
**VIDEO CHOICE.** [Video choice]. Vol. 1, No. 1 (March 1988)-. Periodical. English. mo. $24.95 US; $31.75 other. Video Choice, 331 Jaffrey Road, Peterborough NH 03458. **Tel** (603)924-7271. **ED** Deborah Navas. **DD** 384. **Ad Acc.**
**Desc:** A family-oriented home video magazine, reviews and rates at least 80 new videos each month and provides updates on new video equipment.

US/1045-2885
**VIDEO EVENT.** [Video event]. Vol. 1, No. 1 (May 1989)-. Periodical. English. mo. Free. Connell Communications Inc, 331 Jaffrey Road, Peterborough NH 03458. **DD** 791.

US/1046-0837
**VIDEO INSIDER.** **See** Communication-Broadcasting.

US/1046-6045
**VIDEO INVESTOR, THE.** **See** Communication-Telecommunications.

UK/0268-0750
**VIDEO MAKER.** ***Ceased.*** (Oct. 1989)-?. Periodical. English. mo. Subscriptions International Ltd, Unit 4, Durham Road, Borahamwood, Hertsordshira WD6 1LW England. **LC** TR845; .M33. **DD** 778.59/05. ***Continues*** *Making Better Movies, 0268-0750.*

US/1047-7713
**VIDEO MANAGEMENT.** ***Ceased.*** **See** Business-General Management.

US
**VIDEO MOVIE GUIDE.** (1986)-. English. an. $10.89 (includes shipping/handling). Random House Inc., 400 Hahn Road, Westminster MD 21157. **Tel** (800)726-0600, (800)733-3000, FAX (800)659-2436. **LC** PN1992.93; .V53. **DD** 791.43/75/05.

US/0271-5953
**VIDEO PRODUCT NEWS.** ***Title Change.*** Vol. 1 (Oct./Dec. 1980)-(1985). Periodical. English. bm. Steve Tolin, PO Box 2772, Palm Springs CA 92263. **Tel** (310)874-4331. ***Continued by*** *Satellite Directory and Buyers Guide, 0742-7077.*

UK
**VIDEO PRODUCTION TECHNIQUES.** English. £12.00 (No. 26). Longman Group Ltd., Fourth Avenue, Longman House, Harlow Essex CM19 5SR England. **Tel** 011 44 279 429655, FAX 011 44 279 431059, telex 81259. **(Subscription address:** Fourth Avenue, Harlow Essex CM19 5AA England**)**

US/1045-3393
**VIDEO RATING GUIDE FOR LIBRARIES.** **See** Library and Information Sciences.

US/0276-0835
**VIDEO (SAN FRANCISCO, CALIF.).** (VIDEO.). Vol. 1 No. 1 (1980)-. Periodical. English. sa. San Francisco Video Festival, PO Box 11320, San Francisco CA 94101-7320.
**Ind/Abst** Abr. Read. Guide Period. Lit. (19??-); Read. Guide Period. Lit. (19??-).

CN/0838-9586
**VIDEO SCENE.** [Video scene (1987)]. Vol. 7, No. 3 (Dec. 1987)-. Periodical. English. bm. $2.00 (per number), $10.00 (per year). Video Science, 5th Floor/6 Adelaide Street East, Toronto Ontario M5C 1H6 Canada. **DD** 778.59/9/05. ***Continues*** *Video Scene & Electronics, 0834-373X.*

UK
**VIDEO THE MAGAZINE.** (19??)-. English. mo. £20.00 UK; £26.00 other. Selwood Press Ltd, Unit #1 Roaans Road, Amersham Bucks, HP6 6LX England. **Tel** 011 44 494 432433. ***Continues*** *Best of Film & Video, 0958-9147.*

UK
**VIDEO TODAY.** ***Ceased.*** (19??)-(1994). English. Argus Specialist Publications, Queensway House, 2 Queensway Redhill, Surrey RH1 1QS England. **Tel** 0737 768611, FAX 0737 773993, telex 948669 TOPJNL G.

US/1070-9991
**VIDEO WATCHDOG.** [Video watchdog]. No. 1 (1990)-. Periodical. English. Six times a year. $24.00 US; $33.00 other. Video Watchdog, PO Box 5283, Cinncinnati OH 45205-0283. **Tel** (513)471-8989. **ED** Tim Lucas. **DD** 791. **Bk Rev**, (Qty: 6-12 per year). **Circ:** 10,000.
**Desc:** Contains information on film, videotapes, and discs. Provides a global report of what has been added to, and taken out of new and old releases. Coverage is complemented with essays, interviews, photos, and exerpts from major works in progress.

US
**VIDEOHOUND'S GOLDEN MOVIE RETRIEVER.** **VFOAT** Video Hound's Golden Movie Retriever; Golden Movie Retriever. (1991)-. English. $17.95. Gale Research Inc., 835 Penobscot Building, Detroit MI 48226. **Tel** (800)877-GALE, (313)961-2242, FAX (313)961-6083, telex TWX 810-221-7086. **LC** PN1992.95; .V554. **DD** 791.43/75/05.
**Desc:** Presents an array of indexes and over 22,000 videos.

US/0746-7699
**VIDEOLOG.** (VIDEOLOG : ALL IN ONE VIDEO REPORTER.). (19??)-. Periodical. English. wk (52 issues). $322.00 US; $354.00 Canada. Trade Service Corporation, PO Box 85007, San Diego CA 92138. **Tel** (619)457-5920, (800)854-1527, FAX (619)457-1320. **ED** Bonnie Dudley. Index available. **Ad Acc. Circ:** 5,000 (ctrl). available on diskette.
**Desc:** Contains over 26,000 current listings of movies in 12 categories and indexed by title, star and director.

UK/0142-8543
**VISION.** **See** Communication-Broadcasting.

CN/0840-4313
**VISUAL MEDIA.** [Vis. media]. **Added/Corp** Ontario Film Association. **VFOAT** Medias Visuels. Vol. 1, No. 1 (Sept./Oct. 1988)-. Periodical. French (English). ir. 45.00Can$ Canada; 50.00Can$ US; 65.00Can$. Ontario Film Association Inc, 3 1750 Queensway Suite 1341, Etobicoke Ontario M9C 5H5 Canada. **Tel** (416)925-5931. **DD** 791.43/75/05. Index available (Bound in issue).
**Ind/Abst** Can. Index (19??-).

●CN
**VPM MAGAZINE.** (1993)-. English. Ten times a year. 36.00Can$. VPM Publishing Ltd., 1385 Bonhill Road, Unit 2, Mississauga ONT L5T 1M1 Canada. **Tel** (905)564-1515, FAX (905)564-8484. **ED** Ray Lockhart. **Circ:** 6,000.

IT/0394-2384
**VR VIDEOREGISTRARE.** **VFOAT** Videoregistrare. (1985)-. Periodical. Italian. mo (11 issues). L60000.00. Medialite Sas, Via Olanda 6, 20083 Gaggiano Mi Italy. **Tel** 011 39 2 90841673. **UDC** 67. **Ad Acc.** ctrl circ.
**Desc:** Information on video recording.

US/0160-872X
**WAFL BOOK, THE.** **Main/Corp** Washington Area Filmmakers League. **VAT** Washington Area Filmmakers League Book. 1976-. English. $5.45 single issue. Washington Area Filmmakers League, PO Box 6475, Washington DC 20009. **LC** PN1993.5.U79; W38A. **DD** 384.8/025/753.

US/0884-3791
**WARREN'S MOVIE POSTER PRICE GUIDE.** **VFOAT** Movie Poster Price Guide. 1st Ed.-. Periodical. English. an. $12.95. Overstreet Publications Inc, 780 Hunt Cliff Drive NW, Cleveland TN 37311. **Tel** (615)472-4135. **ED** J Warren. **Ad Acc.**
**Desc:** Over 11,000 feature films listed from 1930-1959. Hundreds of rare posters illustrated, prices given for all types of movie paper, major stars index.

UK/0260-7530
**WHAT VIDEO? LONDON. 1980.** (WHAT VIDEO?.). [What video? Lond. 1980]. (1980)-. Periodical. English. mo. £24.00 UK; £40.00 EIRE Europe; £65.00 other. WV Publications, 57-59 Rochester Place, London NW1 9JU England. **Tel** 011 44 71 485-0011. **DD** 778.599.

US/0278-6516
**WHO'S WHO IN THE MOTION PICTURE INDUSTRY.** See Biographies.

US/0160-6840
**WIDE ANGLE.** [Wide angle]. **Added/Corp** Ohio University. School of Film. Athens Center for Film and Video. Athens International Film Festival. Ohio University. Film Dept. **VFOAT** Wide Angles. Vol. 1 (1976)-. Periodical. English. Four times a year (January, April, July, October). $58.00 US; $62.00 Canada & Mexico; $66.80 other. Johns Hopkins University Press, 2715 North Charles Street, Baltimore MD 21218-4319. **Tel** (410)516-6987, FAX (410)516-6968. **(Subscription address:** John Hopkins University Press, Journals Publishing Division, PO Box 19966, Baltimore MD 21211.**) ED** Jeanne Hall. **LC** PN1993; .W48. **DD** 791.43/05. **[CCC]. Bk Rev. Ad Acc. Circ:** 800. available on microfilm and microfiche from University Microfilms International (UMI). Documents available from The Genuine Article.
**Desc:** Presents scholarship in film studies and examines a range of topics from international cinema to the history and aesthetics of film. Each issue concentrates on a single topic and offers articles, interviews with filmmakers, and reviews of recent books in the field.
**Ind/Abst** Arts Humanit. Citation Index [Full Cov.]; Curr. Contents Arts Humanit.; Film Lit. Index; Int. Index Film Period.; Med. Rev. Dig.; MLA Int. Bibl. Books Artic. Mod. Lang. Lit.; Res. Alert [Full Cov.].

US/0740-770X
**WOMEN & PERFORMANCE.** See Theater.

●US/1072-6144
**WORLD GUIDE TO TELEVISION & FILM.** See Communication-Broadcasting.

US
**WRITING AWARDS : REMINDER LIST OF ELIGIBLE RELEASES.** **Main/Corp** Academy of Motion Picture Arts and Sciences. **VFOAT** Annual Academy Awards for Achievements. Periodical. English. an. ***Continues in part*** *Reminder List of Eligible Achievements.*

CH
**YIN MU CHU TSO.** Periodical. Chinese. bm. NT$0.50. Chuan Kuo Ko Ti Yu Chu, Lan-Chou, People's Republic of China. **Tel** 66117, 66293. **LC** PN1993.5.C4; 54. **DD** 791.43/0951.

CC
**YING SHIH CHUN CHIU.** Periodical. Chinese. RMBY0.44. Hsin Hua Shu Tian, Shan-Tung Shen, People's Republic of China. **LC** PN1993.5.C4; Y55. **DD** 791.43/0951.

NO/0800-1464
**Z (OSLO, NORWAY).** (Z.). **Added/Corp** Norsk Filmklubbforbund. (19??)-. Periodical. Norwegian. qt. Kr160.00. Norsk Filmklubbforbund, Pilestredet 30 B, N-0164 Oslo 1 Norway. **Tel** 02 11 42 17, FAX 02 20 79 81. **ED** Jon Iversen. **LC** PN1993; .Z2.
**Desc:** Film analysis, film history. Specialty is Norwegian film.
**Ind/Abst** Film Lit. Index (19??-).

GW/0724-7656
**ZELLULOID.** [Zelluloid]. (1977)-. Periodical. German. qt. Zelluloid Medienzeitschrift Filmhaus, Luxemberg Str 72, W 5000 Cologne 1 Germany. **Tel** 49 221 417568. **UDC** 791.43. Index available.
**Ind/Abst** Film Lit. Index (19??-).

CN/1186-9240
**ZOOM IN : NEW FILMS AND VIDEOS FROM THE NATIONAL FILM BOARD OF CANADA.** [Zoom]. **Main/Corp** National Film Board of Canada. Spring (1991)-. Periodical. English. sa. National Film Board of Canada, PO Box 6100 Station A, Montreal Quebec H3C 3H5 Canada. **Tel** (514)283-9427, FAX (514)283-7564. **DD** 015.71.

CN/0848-7138
**ZOOM ON THE NFB.** [Zoom NFB]. **Main/Corp** National Film Board of Canada. **VFOAT** Zoom sur l'ONF. **VAT** Zoom on the National Film Board of Canada. Vol. 1, No. 1 (Oct. 1990)-. Periodical. English (French). qt. National Film Board of Canada, PO Box 6100 Station A, Montreal Quebec H3C 3H5 Canada. **Tel** (514)283-9427, FAX (514)283-7564. **DD** 791.43/3/06071.

GW/0177-6762
**ZUM : ZEITSCHRIFT FUER URHEBER- UND MEDIENRECHT/FILM UND RECHT.** **VFOAT** Zeitschrift fur Urheber- und Medienrecht/Film und Recht. Vol. 4 (1985)-. Periodical. German. Twelve times a year. DM318.20 Germany; DM325.40 others. Nomos Verlagsgesellschaft, Postfach 610, D-76484 Baden Baden Germany. **Tel** 011 49 7221 21040. **LC** KK6946.A13; Z86. **[CCC].** ***Continues*** *Film und Recht.*

## ABSTRACTING, BIBLIOGRAPHIES AND STATISTICS

US
**ACADEMY PLAYERS DIRECTORY.** **Added/Corp** Academy of Motion Picture Arts and Sciences. **VFOAT** Players Directory. (1943)-. Directory. English. Three times a year (Jan., May, Sept.). $210.00 California; $240.00 Alaska & Hawaii; $225.00 others states; $285.00 Canada; $465.00 others. Academy of Motion Picture Arts and Sciences, 8949 Wilshire Boulevard, Beverly Hills CA 90211-1972. **Tel** (310)247-3000, FAX (310)859-9619, telex 698-614. **LC** PN1998.A1; A3. ***Continues*** *Players Directory Bulletin.*
**Desc:** News and information on each edition of leading women/ingenues, leading men/younger leading men, character comediennes/character comedians, and children/master index.

CN/0074-5944
**BIBLIOGRAPHY : F I A F MEMBERS PUBLICATIONS.** **Main/Corp** International Federation of Film Archives. **VFOAT** Bibliographie : Publications des Membres de la F I A F. Began with 1967 issue?. Bibliography. English (French). an. **LC** Z5784.M9; I482A; PN1993.5. **DD** 016.79143.

FR
**CNC STATISTIQUES / CENTRE NATIONAL DE LA CINEMATOGRAPHIE.** **Added/Corp** Centre National de la Cinematographie (France). **VFOAT** C.N.C. Statistiques; Statistiques. Vol. 21 (1974)-. French. an. 150.00F France; $20.00 US. Centre National Cinematographie, 12 rue de Lubeck, 75784 Paris Cedex 16 France. **Tel** 011 33 1 45051440, FAX 011 33 1 47550491, telex 650306. **LC** PN1993.5.F7; C59. **DD** 384/.8/0944. ***Continues*** *Statistiques du Cinema Francais.*

CN/1181-6708
**FILM AND VIDEO (OTTAWA).** (FILM AND VIDEO : CULTURE STATISTICS, EDUCATION, CULTURE AND TOURISM DIVISION.). [Film video]. **Added/Corp** Statistics Canada. Education, Culture and Tourism Division. **VFOAT** Film et la Video. (1989)-. English (French). an. 20.00Can$ Canada; $29.00 US; $34.00 other. Statistics Canada, Publications Sales & Services, Main Building Room 1710, Ottawa Ontario K1A 0T6 Canada. **Tel** (613)951-5078, (800)267-6677, FAX (613)951-1584, telex 053-3585. **ED** Marie Lavallee-Farah. **DD** 338.4/779143/0971021. **Circ:** 365. ***Continues*** *Film and Video in Canada., 0847-124X.*
**Desc:** Highlights and statistical tables from the annual surveys of the film and video production, distribution and post-production in industries and the survey of motion picture theatres.

US/0093-6758
**FILM LITERATURE INDEX.** [Film lit. index]. Vol. 1 (1973)-. Abstracting/Indexing Service. English. Three times a year (plus an annual cumulation). $325.00 US & Canada; $350.00 other; $125.00 (US & Canada), $135.00 (other) annual cumulation only. Film & Television Documentation Center, Richardson 390C SUNYA, 1400 Washington Avenue, Albany NY 12222. **Tel** (518)442-5745, FAX (518)442-5232, telex (710)441-8257. **ED** Deborah Jamison and Linda Provinzano. **LC** Z5784.M9; F45. **DD** 791.43/01/6. **Circ:** 500 (ctrl).
**Desc:** Author subject index to 150 film/TV journals from 35 countries and 340 selectively indexed journals.

SZ
**FILMFORDERUNG ... STATISTIK, FILMEINFUHR, STATISTIK / EIDGENOSSISCHES AMT FUER KULTURELLE ANGELEGENHEITEN, SEKTION FILM.** **VFOAT** Encouragement du Cinema ..., Statistique, Importation de Films ..., Statistique. French (German). an. Bundesamt fur Kulturpflege, Sektion Film, 3000 Bern 6 Switzerland. **LC** PN1993.5.S9; E37A. **DD** 384/.8/09494. ***Continues*** *Filmforderung, Statistik.*

US/0000-0388
**INTERNATIONAL INDEX TO FILM PERIODICALS.** [Int. index film period.]. **Added/Corp** International Federation of Film Archives. (1972)-. Abstracting/Indexing Service. English. an. £70.00 (Vol. 20) North America; $90.00 other. FIAF / International Federation of Film Archives, 6 Nottingham Street, London W1M 3RB England. **Tel** 011 44 71 2240991. **LC** Z5784.M9; I49. **DD** 016.79143. Index available. cum. index. available on microfiche from the publisher.
**Desc:** Guide to the contents of all major film periodicals, indexed by experts in over 20 countries, with annotations in English.

US/0363-7778
**MEDIA REVIEW DIGEST.** [Media rev. dig.]. **VFOAT** MRD. (1974)-. Abstracting/Indexing Service. English. an. $245.00 (hardcover). Pierian Press, PO Box 1808, Ann Arbor MI 48106. **Tel** (313)434-5530, (800)678-2435, FAX (313)434-6409. **LC** LB1043.Z9; M4. **DD** 011. **NLM** Z 5814.V8 M961. **Circ:** 1,500. ***Continues*** *Multi Media Reviews Index, 0091-5858.*
**Desc:** Comprehensive guide to evaluative reviews of educational and feature films and video topics filmstrips, recordings, and miscellaneous media.

CN/0380-6294
**MOTION PICTURE THEATRES AND FILM DISTRIBUTORS.** [Motion pict. theatres film distrib.]. **Added/Corp** Canada. Bureau Federal de la Statistique. Division de l'Industrie et du Commerce. Canada. Bureau Federal de la Statistique. Division du Commerce et des Services. Statistique Canada. Division du Commerce et des Services. Statistique Canada. Section du Commerce de Service. **VFOAT** Cinemas et Distributeurs de Films. (1957)-. French (English). an. 20.00Can$ Canada; $21.00 other. Statistics Canada, Publications Sales & Services, Main Building Room 1710, Ottawa Ontario K1A 0T6 Canada. **Tel** (613)951-5078, (800)267-6677, FAX (613)951-1584, telex 053-3585. **DD** 384/.83/0971. ***Continues*** *Motion Picture Theatres, Exhibitors and Distributors (1950), 0825-4133.*
**Desc:** Statistics on admissions, number of features shown, prices, etc.

US/0734-7669
**NUC. AUDIOVISUAL MATERIALS.** (NUC. AUDIOVISUAL MATERIALS [MICROFORM] / LIBRARY OF CONGRESS.). [NUC, Audiov. mater.]. **Added/Corp** Library of Congress. **VFOAT** Audiovisual Materials. **VAT** National Union Catalog. Audiovisual Materials. (Jan./March 1983)-. Bibliography. English (Multiple languages). qt. $110.00 US; $125.00 other. Library of Congress / Cataloging Distribution Service, Washington DC 20541-5017. **Tel** (800)255-3666, (202)707-6100, FAX (202)707-1334. Index available. cum. index. ***Continues*** *Audiovisual Materials, 0190-9827.*
**Desc:** Contains bibliographic records for motion pictures, filmstrips, transparency and slide sets, videorecordings, and kits currently cataloged by the Library of Congress.

# MOTORCYCLES

US/0277-9358
**AMERICAN MOTORCYCLIST.** (AMERICAN MOTORCYCLIST : THE MONTHLY JOURNAL OF THE AMERICAN MOTORCYCLIST ASSOCIATION.). [Am. motorcycl.]. **Added/Corp** American Motorcyclist Association. **VFOAT** AM. Vol. 31, No. 8 (Sept. 1977)-. Periodical. English. mo. $13.00. American Motorcyclist Association, PO Box 6114, Westerville OH 43081-6114. **Tel** (614)891-2425, FAX (614)891-5012, telex 245392. **ED** Greg Harrison. **Ad Acc. Circ:** 143,740 (ctrl). ***Continues*** *AMA News, 0003-0074.*
**Desc:** Information for motorcycle enthusiasts who are AMA Members. It has reports on MC legislation, touring articles and competition information.

SP
**ANO DE LOMATO, EL.** **VFOAT** Annee Moto; Moto Year. 1- 1975/76-. Spanish (Spanish). ISAAC, Peral 12, Madrid Spain. **LC** GV1060; . A56.

US/0364-6963
**ANTIQUE MOTORCYCLE, THE.** Periodical. English. qt. $8.50. 714 East Harwood Street, Apt 4, Orlando FL 32803. **LC** TL440; .A58. **DD** 629.22/75/075. ***Continues*** *Antique Motorcycle Club of America. Quarterly Bulletin.*

US/0744-7809
**ATV NEWS.** ***Ceased.*** **VAT** All Terrain Vehicle News. ( )-(Dec. 1988). Periodical. English. bw. Cycle News Inc, PO Box 498, Long Beach CA 90801. **Tel** (213)427-7433. **ED** Mike Larson. **Bk Rev. Ad Acc. Circ:** 50,000 (ctrl).
**Desc:** Edited exclusively for all terrain vehicle enthusiasts, covering all aspects of ATV recreation and utility.

US/1058-7926
**BIKER (AGOURA HILLS, CALIF.).** (BIKER.). [Biker]. (19??)-. Periodical. English. bm. $14.95 US; $26.95 other. Paisano Publications, 28210 Dorothy Drive, Agoura Hills CA 91301-2693. **Tel** (818)889-8740, FAX (818)889-4726. **DD** 796. ***Continues*** *Easyriders Presents Biker, 1046-1604.*

US/8750-765X
**BMW OWNERS NEWS.** (BMW OWNERS NEWS : MAGAZINE OF THE BMW MOTORCYCLE OWNERS OF AMERICA.). Periodical. English. mo. $20.00 (membership). BMW Motorcycle Owners of America Publications, 1295 State Road, Wellington NV 98444. **LC** TL448.B18; B2. **DD** 629.2/275. ***Continues*** *BMW News.*

US
**BRANHAM'S MOTORCYCLE AND SNOWMOBILE REFERENCE.** English. an. Branham Publ Co, PO Box 1948, Santa Monica CA 90406. **Tel** (310)394-8585.

CN/0820-8344
**CANADIAN BIKER MAGAZINE, THE.** [Can. biker mag.]. Vol. 1, No. 15 (July 1982)-. Periodical. English. Eight times a year (eight issues per year). 35.00Can$ US; 27.00Can$ Canada; 40.00Can$ other. Canadian Biker Publication Ltd., Box 4122, Victoria British Columbia, V8X 3X4 Canada. **Tel** (604)384-0333, FAX (604)384-1832. **ED** W. L. Creed. **DD** 796.7/5/0971. **Ad Acc. Circ:** 20,000 (ctrl). ***Continues*** *Western Biker Magazine., 0229-6896.*
**Desc:** Caters to all breeds of motorcycles and motorcyclists, from road racing to touring, from custom riding to motocross, and much more. Produced by people who ride motorcycles themselves, and editorial content is written by people who ride.

CN/0710-0590
**CANADIAN MOTORCYCLE RIDER.** [Can. motorcycle rider]. **VAT** CMR. Canadian Motorcycle Rider. No. 1, (1981)-. Periodical. English. $1.25 per no. BW Hodgson Publishing, 2066 Queen Street East, Toronto Ontario M4E 1C9 Canada. **DD** 796.7/5/0971.

US/1050-0251
**CHILTON'S MOTORCYCLE AND ATV REPAIR MANUAL.** [Chilton's motorcycle ATV repair man.]. **Added/Corp** Chilton Book Company. **VFOAT** Motorcycle and ATV Repair Manual. **VAT** Chilton's Motorcycle and All-Terrain Vehicle Repair Manual. (19??)-. English. ir. Chilton Book Company, 1 Chilton Way, Radnor PA 19089. **Tel** (215)964-4000, (800)695-1214, FAX (215)964-4273, telex 6851035 CHILTON UW. **LC** TL444; .C494. **DD** 629.28/775/05. ***Continues*** *Chilton's Motorcycle Repair Manual, 0741-3246.*

UK
**CLASSIC & MOTORCYCLE MECHANICS.** (19??)-. English. mo. £35.00. Bob Berry Publishing Services, Deene House C Market Square Corby, Northants NN17 1PB England. **Tel** 011 44 536 203003. **(Subscription address:** World-Wide Subscription Services, Unit 4, Gibbs Reed Farm Pashley Road, Ticehurst TN5 7HE England.**)**

US/1061-6519
**CROSSWORDS (WALNUT CREEK, CALIF.).** (CROSSWORDS : THE JOURNAL OF MULTI-PURPOSE, MULTI-TERRAIN BICYCLES.). [Crosswords]. **VFOAT** Cross Words. (1991)-. Periodical. English. qt. $3.00. Crosswords, PO Box 3207, Walnut Creek CA 94598. **DD** 388.

US/0745-0567
**CUSTOM BIKE CHOPPERS.** Periodical. English. mo. Touring Bike Publishing Company, 4247 East Lapalma Avenue, Annaheim CA 92807. **Tel** (714)996-5111. ***Continues*** *Choppers, 0195-069X; Custom Bike, 0363-8138.*

CN/0319-2822
**CYCLE CANADA.** [Cycle Can.]. Vol. 1 (Apr. 1971)-. Periodical. English. mo (10 issues). 27.99Can$ Canada; 37.99Can$ other. Turbopress Inc., 5000 Rue Buchan Bureau 600A, Montreal QUE H4P 1T2 Canada. **Tel** (514)738-9439. **ED** John Cooper. **Ad Acc. Circ:** 42,000.
**Desc:** Designed for the motorcycle enthusiast, features detailed road tests, comparisons, touring stories, product evaluations and technical specifications. Timely, meaningful motorcycle reading all year round.
**Ind/Abst** Can. Index; Can. Period. Index (19??-).

US/0590-4641
**CYCLE GUIDE ROAD TEST ANNUAL.** English. an. $1.25. Quinn Publications Etc, 1440 West Walnut Street, Compton CA 90220. **LC** TL440; .C962. **DD** 629.22/75/05.

US/0090-4775
**CYCLE GUIDE'S MOTORCYCLE ACCESSORIES GUIDE.** [Cycle guide's motorcycle accessories guide]. **VFOAT** Motorcycle Accessories. English. an. $1.00. Cycle Guide Publications, 1440 West Walnut Street, Compton CA 90220. **LC** TL440; .C963. **DD** 629.22/75/05.

US/0272-8923
**CYCLE STREET AND TOURING GUIDE.** **VFOAT** Street and Touring Guide. (19??)-. Periodical. English. an. $4.95. Hachette Magazines Inc., 1633 Broadway, New York NY 10019. **Tel** (212)767-6000. **LC** TL440; .C977. **DD** 629.2/275/05.

US/0011-4286
**CYCLE WORLD.** [Cycle world]. Vol. 1 (Jan. 1962)-. Periodical. English. mo. $20.00. Hachette Magazines Inc., 1633 Broadway, New York NY 10019. **Tel** (212)767-6000. **(Subscription address:** Neodata / Colorado, PO Box 2606, Boulder Boulder CO 80322.**)** **LC** TL440; .C9. **DD** 629. available on microfilm and microfiche from University Microfilms International (UMI). Documents available from UMI Article Clearinghouse, Magazine Collection. ***Absorbed*** *Cycle.*
**Desc:** Blends information and entertainment about motorcycles and the various types of riding. Each issue mixes technical articles with coverage of the world of motocycling.
**Ind/Abst** Acad. Abstr. Full Text Elite (Nov. 1991-); Acad. Abstr. (Nov. 1991-); Gen. Period. Index (1985-); Mag. Artic. Summar. Elite (Nov. 1991-); Mag. Artic. Summar. Select (Nov. 1991-); Mag. Artic. Summar. CD-ROM (Nov. 1991-); Mag. Index Plus (1989-); Mag. Index. Sel. (1992-); Mag. Search; Mid. Search (Nov. 1991-); Newsp. Period. Abstr. (1988-); Prim. Search (Nov. 1991-); Read. Guide Abstr. Select Ed.; Read. Guide Period. Lit.; Mag. Index (1977-); TOM Gen. Index (1992-) [Full Txt.].

US/0270-2746
**CYCLE WORLD TEST ANNUAL & BUYER'S GUIDE.** [Cycle world test annu. & buy. guide]. **VFOAT** Test Annual & Buyer's Guide. **VAT** Cycle World Test Annual and Buyer's Guide. English. an. $2.95. CBS Publications, 1515 Broadway, New York NY 10036. **Tel** (212)503-5064. **LC** TL440; .C984. **DD** 629.2/275/05.

US/0893-2522
**DEALERNEWS (1987).** (DEALERNEWS.). [Dealernews]. **VFOAT** Dealer News. Vol. 23, No. 3 (March 1987)-. Periodical. English. mo (13 issues). $36.00 US and possessions; $48.00 Canada; $75.00 other. Advanstar Communications Inc., 131 West First Street, Duluth MN 55802. **Tel** (218)723-9477, (800)346-0085. **LC** TL440; .M13. **DD** 338.4/7629227/50973. ***Continues*** *Motorcycle Dealernews (Irvine, Calif. : 1986), 0888-4234.*
**Ind/Abst** Bus. Index (1987-); Gen. BusinessFile (1987-); Trade Ind. Index.

US/0364-1546
**DIRT BIKE.** Vol. 1 (June 1971)-. Periodical. English. mo. $18.98 (one year), $35.95 (two year). Hi-Torque Publications, PO Box 9502, Mission Hills CA 91395. **Tel** (805)295-1910. **ED** Ed Arnet. **LC** TL440; .D55. **DD** 796.7. **Ad Acc. Circ:** 150,000. Documents available from UMI Article Clearinghouse.
**Desc:** Directed to off-road motorcyclists of all ages, with equal emphasis on recreational and competitive cycling, plus do-it-yourself maintenance and riding tips.
**Ind/Abst** Mag. Artic. Summar. Elite (July 1989-); Mag. Artic. Summar. Select (July 1989-); Mag. Artic. Summar. CD-ROM (July 1989-); Mag. Search; Mid. Search (Jul. 1989-); Newsp. Period. Abstr. (1992-); Prim. Search (Jul. 1989-); SportSearch (May 1987-).

UK/0262-5628
**DIRT BIKE RIDER.** [Dirt bike rid.]. (1981)-. Periodical. English. Twelve times a year. £39.00 Far East New Zealand & Australia; £37.00 others. Key Publishing Ltd, PO Box 100, Stamford Lincolnshire PE9 1XQ England. **Tel** 011 44 780 55131, FAX 011 44 780 57261, telex 9312134113. **DD** 796.75.

UK/0969-1650
**DIRT BIKE RIDER. GRAND PRIX SPECIAL.** (199?)-. English. mo. £22.50 UK; £31.00 Europe; £27.00 other. Key Publishing Ltd, PO Box 100, Stamford Lincolnshire PE9 1XQ England. **Tel** 011 44 780 55131, FAX 011 44 780 57261, telex 9312134113.

US/0735-4355
**DIRT RIDER.** [Dirt rider]. Issue 1 (Dec. 1982)-. Periodical. English. mo. $19.94 US; $29.90 Canada; $30.94 other. Petersen Publishing Company, 6420 Wilshire Bouldevard, Los Angeles CA 90048. **Tel** (213)782-2485. **(Subscription address:** Neodata / Colorado, PO Box 2606, Boulder Boulder CO 80322.**)** **ED** Charles Morey. **Bk Rev. Ad Acc. Circ:** 150,000. available on microfilm from University Microfilms International (UMI).
**Desc:** Covers the sport of off-road motorcycle riding and racing. Readers will find how-to-ride tips, demanding dirt bike tests and comparisons, equipment evaluations, advice on customizing, an up-close look at the motocross racing scene, and much more.

US
**DUAL SPORTER.** (19??)-. English. bm (6 issues). $20.00. Team Dual Dogs of Southern California, Inc., 8535 Amestoy Avenue, Northridge CA 91325-3403. **Tel** (818)701-1913, FAX (818)886-5260. **ED** Anne Van Beveren. **Ad Acc, Adv Mgr:** Jean P. Offers.
**Desc:** Dedicated to the exciting world of the fastest growing sport in motorcycling. Reaches enthusiasts and their events nationwide.

US/0046-0990
**EASYRIDERS.** (June 1970)-. Periodical. English. mo. Paisano Publications, 28210 Dorothy Drive, Agoura Hills CA 91301-2693. **Tel** (818)889-8740, FAX (818)889-4726. **LC** GV1059.5; .E2. **DD** 796.7/5/05. **Circ:** 2,500,000.
**Desc:** Information on motorcycling, new products and accessories.

US/0092-6272
**ENDURO (COMPTON).** (ENDURO.). English. $1.25. Cycle Guide Publications, 1440 West Walnut Street, Compton CA 90220. **LC** GV1060; .E53. **DD** 796.7/5/05.

CN/0228-6831
**FREEWHEELIN'.** (FREEWHEELIN' : THE MAGAZINE FOR MOTORCYCLE PEOPLE.). [FreeWheelin']. **VAT** Free Wheelin'. Vol. 1, No. 1 (Feb./Mar. 1980) -. Periodical. English. bm. $5.95. PO Box 938, Burlington Ontario L7R 3Y7 Canada. **DD** 629.2/275/0971.

CN/0823-8499
**GUIDE DE LA MOTO (MONTREAL, 1984).** (LE GUIDE DE LA MOTO ...). [Guide moto]. 84-. French. an. $12.95 Per No. Guide de la Moto, a/s Agence de Distribution Populaire, 955 rue Amherst, Montreal Quebec H2L 3K4 Canada. **DD** 629.2/275.

US/1055-033X
**HACK'D (WOODBRIDGE, VA.).** (HACK'D.). (198?)-. Periodical. English. Four times a year (Jan., Apr., June, Sept.). $15.00 U.S.; $22.00 Canada & Mexico; $24.00 other. J. C. Enterprises, Rural Route 5 Box 533A, Buckhannon WV 26201. **Tel** (304)472-6142. **ED** Jim & Chris Dodson (phone: (304)472-6146). **DD** 796. **Bk Rev. Ad Acc. Circ:** 3,500 (ctrl).
**Desc:** The magazine for and about sidecarists.

US/0199-7521
**HOME & AWAY (CHICAGO, ILL.).** (HOME & AWAY.). **Added/Corp** AAA-Chicago Motor Club. **VAT** Home and Away. (19??)-. Periodical. English. bm. $3.00. Chicago Motor Club, 999 E Touhy, Des Plaines IL 60018. **Tel** (312)390-9000, FAX (312)390-9112. **ED** Jonathan Lehrer and Carole Hofmann. ***Continues*** *Motor News, 0194-8520.*

US/8750-3212
**HOT BIKE.** (198?)-. Periodical. English. Twelve times a year. $20.95. McMullen Publishing Inc, 2145 West La Palma Avenue, PO Box 70015, Anaheim CA 92801-1785. **Tel** (714)572-2255, FAX (714)572-1864. **ED** Paul Garson. **Circ:** 74,200. ***Continues*** *Street Chopper, Hot Bike Magazine, 0746-2948.*

US/1059-759X
**IN THE WIND (ANGOURA HILLS, CALIF.).** (IN THE WIND.). **VFOAT** Easyriders in the Wind. (199?)-. Periodical. English. bm. $14.95. Paisano Publications, 28210 Dorothy Drive, Agoura Hills CA 91301-2693. **Tel** (818)889-8740, FAX (818)889-4726. **DD** 796. **Circ:** 105,676. ***Continues*** *Easyriders in the Wind, 0884-5131.*
**Desc:** A pictorial magazine which grew from its popularity as a feature section of "Easyriders." It features the motorcycle enthusiasts doing what they do best - riding and enjoying motorcycles.

●US/1066-419X
**INSIDE MOTOCROSS MAGAZINE.** **VFOAT** Inside Motocross. (1993)-. Periodical. English. qt. $28.00. Inside Motocross Magazine, 24950 Anza Drive, Valencia CA 91355.

UK/0306-5898
**INTERNATIONAL MOTOR-CYCLE RACING BOOK.** English. Souvenir Press, 95 Mortimer Street, London W 1 England. **LC** GV1060; .I57. **DD** 796.7/5.

US/0147-9652
**JAMMER'S HANDBOOK.** Vol. 1 (1973)-. English. Four times a year (Feb., May, Aug., Nov.). $8.00. Jammer Cycle Products Inc, 801 South Main Street, Burbank CA 91506. **Tel** (800)432-2633. **LC** TL440; .J46. **DD** 629.22/75/05.

FR
**LIVRE D'OR DE LA MOTO, LE.** 1976-. French. an. Solar, 8 rue Garanciere, 75006 Paris France. **LC** GV1060.12; .L58. **DD** 796.7/5/05.

CN/0705-2030
**M D T, MOTORCYCLE DEALER & TRADE.** **VFOAT** Motorcycle Dealer & Trade. 1st Issue (April 1978)-. Periodical. English. mo. Free. Brave Beaver Pressworks Ltd, 411 Richmond Street East/Suite 102, Toronto Ontario M5A 3S5 Canada. **Tel** (416)362-7966. **ED** John Cooper. **DD** 338.4/7/62922750971. **Ad Acc. Circ:** 2,500 (ctrl).
**Desc:** Trade publication for the motorcycle industry. Tells what's happening and how it will affect the new products, rules and regulation, changes, and industry statistics.

US/0160-1806
**MOPED BIKING.** Periodical. English. bm. $8.00. Moped Publications, 370 Lexington Avenue, New York NY 10017.

US/0161-4320
**MOPED DEALER.** V. 1- June/July 1978-. Periodical. English. bm. $9.00. Moped Publications, 370 Lexington Avenue, New York NY 10017. **LC** HD9710.6.U5; M66. **DD** 658.89/6292272.

CN/0319-2865
**MOTO JOURNAL.** Vol. 1, (Spring 1972)-. Periodical. French. Ten times a year. 27.99Can$ Canada; 37.99Can$ other. Turbopress Inc., 5000 Rue Buchan Bureau 600A, Montreal QUE H4P 1T2 Canada. **Tel** (514)738-9439. **ED** Jean Pierre Belmonte. **Ad Acc. Circ:** 18,000.
**Desc:** Designed for the motorcycle enthusiast, each

issue features detailed road tests, comparisons, touring stories, product evaluations and technical specifications. A certain element of humor is always present.

FR
**MOTO REVUE. See** Bicycles and Bicycling.

IT/0027-1961
**MOTOCICLISMO.** (19??)-. Italian. mo. 7150000L Italy; 1200000L other. Edisport Editoriale, V Gradisca 11, 20151 Milan Italy. **Tel** 011 39 2 380851.

US/0146-3292
**MOTOCROSS ACTION MAGAZINE.** Vol. 1 (July 1973)-. Periodical. English. mo. $19.98 (one year), $36.95 (two year). Hi-Torque Publications, PO Box 9502, Mission Hills CA 91395. **Tel** (805)295-1910. **ED** Jody Weisel. **LC** GV1060; .M695. **DD** 796.7/5. **Ad Acc. Circ:** 95,000.
**Desc:** A magazine written by and for the motocross racing enthusiast, with articles of interest to the competitive rider and the spectator enthusiast.
**Ind/Abst** SportSearch (May 1987-).

CN/0832-1132
**MOTOCYCLISTE (MONTREAL).**
***Suspended.*** (MOTOCYCLISTE.). [Motocycliste]. **VAT** Motocycliste Motoplan; Motocycliste Magazine. (Mar. 1986)-(19??). Periodical. French. ir. Gevco Publishing Inc., 2021 Union Street, Suite 1150, Montreal Quebec H3A 2S9 Canada. **Tel** (514)284-1732. **DD** 796.7/5.

NE
**MOTOR.** Dutch. Fifty-one times per year. Fl120.00 Netherlands; Fl220.00 North America Fl220.00other. Weekly Motor, PO Box 9943, Attn Dinga van Driel, Amsterdam 1006AP Netherlands. **Tel** (020)5182828, FAX (020)6157013. **ED** Edwin Venema. Index available. **Bk Rev. Ad Acc. Pr Rev. Circ:** 45,000.
**Desc:** Up-to-date information for active and passive motorbike lovers. Besides extensive tests and technical reports attention is being payed to news and backgrounds in the competitive sport.

US/0194-8520
**MOTOR NEWS (CHICAGO).** (MOTOR NEWS.). Periodical. English. mo. Chicago Motor Club, 999 E Touhy, Des Plaines IL 60018. **Tel** (312)390-9000, FAX (312)390-9112.

US/0091-3774
**MOTORCYCLE BLUE BOOK. Added/Corp** Jones, Hap. (19??)-. Periodical. English. sa. $18.00. Hap Jones Distributing Company, PO Box 32368, San Jose CA 95152. **Tel** (408)432-1918, FAX (408)432-1926, telex 3507244. **ED** Hap Jones (editor's address: 1040 Rock Avenue, San Jose, CA 95131). **LC** HD9710.5.U5; M68. **DD** 380.1/45/629227502573.
**Desc:** Current new and used values of motorcycles.

●US/1073-9408
**MOTORCYCLE CONSUMER NEWS.**
[Motorcycle consum. news]. **VFOAT** RR/MCN; MCN. Vol. 24, No. 11 (Nov. 1993)-. Periodical. English. mo. $21.97. Fancy Publications, PO Box 6050, Mission Viejo CA 92690. **Tel** (714)855-8822, (800)426-2516, FAX (714)855-3045. **(Subscription address:** Palm Coast Data, PO Box 420235, Agency Department, Palm Coast FL 32142.**) LC** TL440.5; .R6. **DD** 796.7. ***Continues*** *Road Rider's Motorcycle Consumer News, 1067-8697.*

US/8755-4720
**MOTORCYCLE DEALERNEWS MERCHANDISER. VFOAT** MDN Merchandiser; M.D.N. Merchandiser; Motorcycle Dealer News Merchandiser; Dealernews Merchandiser. Periodical. English. mo. Hester Communications, 1700 East Dryer Road/Suite 250, Santa Ana CA 92705. **Tel** (714)250-8060. **LC** TL440; .M6973. **DD** 629.2/275/0688. ***Continues in part*** *Motorcycle Dealernews, 0192-0219.*

US/0883-7228
**MOTORCYCLE DRAG RACING.** [Motorcycle drag racing]. **Added/Corp** International Drag Bike Association. (198?)-. Periodical. English. mo. $12.00 US; $22.00 other. Lenk Associates, 3936 Raceway Park Road, Mt Olive AL 35117. **Tel** (205)849-6838, FAX (205)841-0553. **ED** Nina Henderson. **DD** 796. **Bk Rev**, (Qty: 2). **Ad Acc. Circ:** 10,500 (ctrl). ***Continues*** *Motorcycle Drag Racing Newspaper, 0199-8544.*
**Desc:** National event coverage and schedules, technical information, rider interviews, what's happening, features, gossip of who is doing what on the national circuit.

US/0731-3470
**MOTORCYCLE INDUSTRY BUSINESS JOURNAL, THE.** ***Ceased.*** [Motorcycle ind. bus. j.]. Vol. 1, No. 1 (Apr./May 1982)-(19??). Periodical. English. ir. Hancock Brown Corporation, 3187 Airway Drive/Suite A 2, Costa Mesa CA 92626. **Tel** (714)957-1809.

US/0884-626X
**MOTORCYCLE INDUSTRY MAGAZINE : MI. VFOAT** Motorcycle Industry; MI. Vol. 6, No. 1 (May 1985)-. Periodical. English. mo. Motorcycle Industry Magazine, PO Box 2087 CVS, Thousand Oaks CA 91360. **Tel** (805)496-1979, FAX (805)494-3211. **ED** Rick Campbell. **Bk Rev. Ad Acc. Circ:** 13,000 (ctrl). ***Continues*** *Motorcycle Industry Shopper, 0274-5437.*

UK/0268-7151
**MOTORCYCLE INTERNATIONAL.**
[Motorcycle Int.]. (1985)-. Periodical. English. Twelve times a year. £14.40 UK; £22.00 others. Advanced Publishing Ltd., 32 Paul Street, London EC2 AHJ England. **Tel** 011 441-729-3922. ***Continues*** *Which Bike.*
**Ind/Abst** Curr. Technol. Index.

US
**MOTORCYCLE, MOPED & ALL TERRAIN VEHICLE TRADE-IN GUIDE.**
**Added/Corp** Intertec Publishing Corporation. Technical Publications Division. **VFOAT** Motorcycle, Moped and All Terrain Vehicle Trade-In Guide; Trade-In Guide, Motorcycle, Moped and All Terrain Vehicles; Trade-In Guide, Motorcycle, Moped & All Terrain Vehicles. (19??)-. Periodical. English. an. $21.70. Intertec Publishing Corporation, 9800 Metcalf, Overland Park KS 66212. **Tel** (913)341-1300. **(Subscription address:** Intertec Publishing Corporation, PO Box 2901, Overland Park KS 66282.**) LC** HD9710.5.A1; M67. **DD** 629.2/275/029473.

US/0164-8349
**MOTORCYCLE PRODUCT NEWS.**
[Motorcycle prod. news]. (19??)-. Trade Publication. English. mo. $35.00 (one year), $62.00 (two year) US; $50.00 (one year), $90.00 (two year) Canada; $125.00 (one year), $225.00 (two year) other. MacLean Hunter Publishing Corporation / Chicago, IL, 29 North Wacker Drive, Chicago IL 60606-3298. **Tel** (312)726-2802, FAX (312)726-3091. **ED** Phil Kunde. **DD** 629. **Ad Acc. Circ:** 14,000 (ctrl).
**Desc:** Product and information magazine edited for the wholesale motorcycle trade and motorcycle dealers. Information, industry news and special features.

US/0736-6116
**MOTORCYCLE RED BOOK.** (MOTORCYCLE RED BOOK / NATIONAL MARKET REPORTS, INC.). [Motorcycle red book]. **Added/Corp** National Market Reports, Inc. **VFOAT** Red Book; Motor Cycle Red Book. Vol. 1, No. 1 (Oct. 1, 1982)-. Periodical. English. Twice a year. $56.50. MacLean Hunter Publishing Corporation / Chicago, IL, 29 North Wacker Drive, Chicago IL 60606-3298. **Tel** (312)726-2802, FAX (312)726-3091. **(Subscription address:** Maclean Hunter Market Reports, 29 North Wacker Drive, Chicago IL 60606.**)**

US/0092-3095
**MOTORCYCLE RIDER'S GUIDE.** Periodical. English. qt. $7.50. Hi-Torque Publications, PO Box 9502, Mission Hills CA 91395. **Tel** (805)295-1910. **LC** TL440; .C465. **DD** 629.22/75/05. ***Continues*** *Chopper Guide.*

US/1056-1455
**MOTORCYCLE ROAD RACER ILLUSTRATED.** [Motocycl. road racer illus.]. **VFOAT** Road Racer; Motorcycle Road Racer Illustrated Yearbook. (July 1988)-. Periodical. English. an. Must order direct. Road Racer, PO Box 498, Long Beach CA 90801. **Tel** (213)427-7433. **ED** Paul Carruthers. **LC** WMLC 91/4981. **DD** 796. **Ad Acc. Circ:** 123,800.
**Desc:** A year in review look back at the season in national and international motorcycle road racing.

US/0149-3027
**MOTORCYCLE STATISTICAL ANNUAL.**
**See** Motorcycles-Abstracting, Bibliographies and Statistics.

US/1041-5734
**MOTORCYCLE TOURING. See** Travel and Tourism.

US/0027-2205
**MOTORCYCLIST (LOS ANGELES, CALIF. 1912).** (THE MOTORCYCLIST.). [Motorcyclist]. **Added/Corp** American Motorcycle Association. American Motorcyclist Association. (July 1912)-. Periodical. English. mo. $19.94 US; $28.83 Canada; $29.94 other. Petersen Publishing Company, 6420 Wilshire Bouldevard, Los Angeles CA 90048. **Tel** (213)782-2485. **(Subscription address:** Neodata / Colorado, PO Box 2606, Boulder Boulder CO 80322.**) ED** Art Friedman. **LC** TL1; .M973. **DD** 629.227505. **Circ:** 207,257. available on microfilm and microfiche from University Microfilms International (UMI).
**Desc:** The all-street motorcycling magazine that addresses tourers, commuters and performance enthusiasts. Monthly features include road tests, how-to's, product evaluations and maintenance tips.
**Ind/Abst** Consum. Index Prod. Eval. Inf. Source.

GW
**MOTORRAD, DAS.** (Aug. 1949)-. Periodical. German. bw. 192.00F. Vereinigte Motor Verlag GmbH, Motor Presse, POB 106036, D 70049 Stuttgart Germany. **Tel** 011 49 711 1821506, 011 49 711 1821545. **(Subscription address:** Deutscher Pressevertrieb Buch, POB 101602 Hansa GMBH, D 20010 Hamburg Germany.**) LC** TL440; .M75.

IT
**MOTOSPRINT.** Conti Editore, Via del Lavoro 7, 40068 S Lazzaro Savena Italy. **Tel** 011 39 51 6227111, FAX 011 39 51 6258112, telex 510283.

US/0197-1980
**N. A. D. A. MOTORCYCLE & MOPED APPRAISAL GUIDE. Main/Corp** National Automobile Dealers Association. **Added/Corp** National Automobile Dealers Association. Motorcycle & Moped Appraisal Guide. **VAT** National Automobile Dealers Association Motorcycle and Moped Appraisal Guide. (19??)-. English. Three times a year. $45.00. NADA Appraisal Guides, PO Box 7800, Costa Mesa CA 92628. **Tel** (714)556-8511, (800)966-6232, FAX (714)556-8715. **ED** Don Christy and Lenny Sims. **LC** HD9710.5.A1; N37b. **DD** 381/.456292275/0973. ***Continues*** *N.A.D.A. Motorcycle Appraisal Guide, 0095-6953.*
**Desc:** Contains used values for all motorcycles, ATV's and mopeds.

US/0746-7893
**NORTHEAST RIDING.** [Northeast rid.]. (1984)-. Periodical. English. mo. $1.50. 225 Palisado Avenue, Windsor CT 06095-2032. **Tel** (203)236-6604. **ED** P Fahy. **DD** 796. ***Continues*** *Connecticut Riding, 0740-3402.*
**Desc:** For the touring motorcycle rider, in regional public northeast Hartford area.

US
**OFF ROAD CYCLING. VFOAT** Cycle Guide's Off Road Cycling. English. $1.25 each issue. Cycle Guide Publications, 1440 West Walnut Street, Compton CA 90220. **LC** GV1059.5; .O35. **DD** 796.7/5.

●FR/1240-8751
**OFFICIEL DU CYCLE ET DE LA MOTO PARIS, L'.** (L'OFFICIEL DU CYCLE ET DE LA MOTO.). (1992)-. Periodical. French. sm. 597.45F France; 770.00F others. EDI 7, 6 rue Ancelle, 92525 Neuilly Sur Seine, Cedex France. **Tel** 011 33 1 40886000. **UDC** 796.61(44). **CODEN** 621(44). ***Continues*** *Official du Cycle et du Motorcycle, 0751-994X.*

FR/0751-994X
**OFFICIEL DU CYCLE ET DU MOTOCYCLE, L'.** ***Title Change.*** (1982)-(1992). Periodical. French. sm. EDI 7, 6 rue Ancelle, 92525 Neuilly Sur Seine, Cedex France. **Tel** 011 33 1 40886000. **UDC** 796.7. ***Continues*** *L'officiel du Cycle, du Motocycle et de la Motoculture, 0030-0519.* ***Continued by*** *L'Officiel du Cycle et de la Moto (Paris), 1240-8751.*

US
**OREGON TRAFFIC ACCIDENTS. FOCUS ON MOTORCYCLES. See** Transportation-Roads and Traffic.

US/0885-2030
**OUTLAW BIKER MAGAZINE.** English. mo. $29.95 US; $39.95. Outlaw Biker Enterprises, 450 7th AveSte 2305, New York NY 10001. **Tel** (212)564-0112, FAX (212)465-8350.

GW
**RADMARKT.** English (German and French). mo. DM165.00. Bielefelder Verlagsanstalt KG, Niederwall 53, D 33602 Bielefeld Germany. **Tel** 011 49 521 595520.

AT
**REVS.** (19??)-. Periodical. English. Twelve times a year. 42.60Aus$ Australia; 102.00Aus$ US & Canada; 78.00Aus$ New Zealand & Papua New Guinea; 109.00Aus$ Europe & Africa; 84.00Aus$ Singapore, Malaysia, Indonesia; 93.00Aus$ other. Federal Publishing Co Pty Ltd, PO Box 199, 180 Bourke Road, Alexandria New South Wales, 2015 Australia. **Tel** 011 61 2 693 6666, FAX 011 61 2 693 9935. **(Subscription address:** Federal Publishing Co. Pty Ltd., PO Box 199, Alexandria NSW 2015 Australia.**)**

US/0095-1625
**RIDER.** Vol. 1, (Summer 1974)-. Periodical. English. Twelve times a year. $16.00. TL Enterprises, Inc., 29901 Agoura Road, Agoura CA 91301. **Tel** (800)234-3450, (805)389-0300. **(Subscription address:** Neodata / Colorado, PO Box 2606, Boulder Boulder CO 80322.**) ED** Tash Matsuoka. **LC** GV1059.5; .R5. **DD** 796.7/5/05. Index available. **Ad Acc. Circ:** 100,000.
**Desc:** Devoted to the road, touring, and sport touring motorcycle market. Dramatic photography visually captures the touring experience.

US/0278-596X
**RIDERANNUAL.** (1981)-. English. an. $3.00. TL Enterprises, 29901 Agoura Road, Agoura CA 91301. **Tel** (800)234-3450, (805)389-0300. **LC** TL440; .R49. **DD** 629.2/275.

US/0035-7243
**ROAD RIDER.** ***Title Change.*** [Road rider]. Vol. 1 No. 3 (Dec. 1969/Jan. 1970)-(1992). Periodical. English. mo. Road Rider, 5509 Santa Monica Boulevard, Los Angeles CA 90038. **Tel** (310)385-2222. **ED** Bob

Carpenter. **LC** TL440.5; .R6. **DD** 796.7. **Circ:** 52,000. **Continues** Road Rider News, 0161-4509. **Continued by** Road Rider's Motorcycle Consumer News, 1067-8697.

CN/0828-5993
**ROLLING EAST.** [Roll. east]. Vol. 1, No. 4 (July 1984)-. Periodical. English. $1.25 per no. Rolling Thunder Publications Rolling Thunder Publications, PO Box 213, Porter's Lake NS B0J 2S0 Canada, Porter's Lake NS B0J 2S0 Canada,. **Tel** , , **FAX** , , **telex** , . **DD** 629.2/275/09715. **Continues** Rolling Thunder (Porter's Lake, N.S.), 0828-5985.

CN/0705-1840
**SANFORD EVANS GOLD BOOK OF MOTORCYCLE DATA AND USED PRICES.** **See** Motorcycles-Abstracting, Bibliographies and Statistics.

CN/0820-7224
**STREET & DIRT.** [Str. dirt]. **VAT** Street and Dirt. Vol. 1, No. 1 (Feb./March 1983)-. Periodical. English. bm. $7.50. Street & Dirt, 23 Stafford Street, Toronto Ontario M5V 2S2 Canada. **DD** 629.2/275/0971.

AT/1034-9294
**STREETBIKE.** [Streetbike]. (1990)-. Periodical. English. bm (6 issues). 26.00Aus$ Australia; 44.70Aus$ New Zealand & Papua New Guinea; 56.00Aus$ US & Canada; 59.00Aus$ Europe & Africa; 46.00Aus$ Singapore, Malaysia, Indonesia; 51.00Aus$ Hong Kong, China, Japan, India. Federal Publishing Co Pty Ltd, PO Box 199, 180 Bourke Road, Alexandria New South Wales, 2015 Australia. **Tel** 011 61 2 693 6666, **FAX** 011 61 2 693 9935. **(Subscription address:** Federal Publishing Co. Pty Ltd., PO Box 199, Alexandria NSW 2015 Australia.**) DD** 629.2275.

●US/1065-9234
**SUPERCROSS.** [Supercross]. **Added/Corp** American Motorcyclist Association. (1992)-. Periodical. English. $39.95. Champs Marketing Inc., 6401 Davis Industrial Parkway, Solon OH 44139. **DD** 796.

US/0162-3923
**SUPERCYCLE (HUNTINGTON BEACH).** (SUPERCYCLE.). [Supercycle]. (19??)-. Periodical. English. mo. $27.95. LPF Inc., 9171 Wilshire Blvd/Suite 300, Beverly Hills CA 90210. **(Subscription address:** Kable Publishers Aide, 308 East Hitt Street, Subscription Department, Mt. Morris IL 61054-1473.**) LC** TL440; .S86. **DD** 796.7.

AT/0041-4700
**TWO WHEELS.** (1968)-. Periodical. English. mo. 53.00Aus$ Australia; 88.00Aus$ New Zealand & Papua New Guinea; 112.00Aus$ US & Canada; 119.00Aus$ Europe & Africa; 94.00Aus$ Singapore, Malaysia, Indonesia; 103.00Aus$ other. Federal Publishing Co Pty Ltd, PO Box 199, 180 Bourke Road, Alexandria New South Wales, 2015 Australia. **Tel** 011 61 2 693 6666, FAX 011 61 2 693 9935. **(Subscription address:** Federal Publishing Co. Pty Ltd., PO Box 199, Alexandria NSW 2015 Australia.**)**

US/0745-273X
**WING WORLD.** Vol. 6, Issue 12 (Dec. 1982)-. Periodical. English. mo. $24.00. Gold Wing Road Riders Association, 3662 West Lawrence Lane, Phoenix AZ 85021. **ED** Glenn Fischel. **Ad Acc. Circ:** 23,000 (ctrl). **Continues** Wing News.
**Desc:** Everything regarding Goldwing motorcycles, their owners, after-market accessories, and activities within the association's environment.

## ABSTRACTING, BIBLIOGRAPHIES AND STATISTICS

US/0149-3027
**MOTORCYCLE STATISTICAL ANNUAL.** **Added/Corp** Motorcycle Industry Council. (1977)-. Statistical Publication. English. an. $25.00. Motorcycle Industry Council Inc, 2 Jenner Street/Suite 150, Irvine CA 92718. **Tel** (714)727-4211. **LC** HD9710.5.U5; M69. **DD** 380.1/45/62922750973.
**Ind/Abst** Predicasts Forecasts.

CN/0705-1840
**SANFORD EVANS GOLD BOOK OF MOTORCYCLE DATA AND USED PRICES.** **VFOAT** Gold Book of Motorcycle Data and Used Prices. (1???)-. English. an (Mar.). 16.50Can$. Sanford Evans Communications Ltd., Box 6900, 1700 Church Avenue, Winnipeg Manitoba R3C 3B1 Canada. **Tel** (204)632-2768, **FAX** (204)694-2347. **ED** Gary Henry. **DD** 338.4/3/62922750971.
**Desc:** Basic motorcycle data on 1978-1991 models. Includes current retail value and original factory prices.

# MUSEUMS AND GALLERIES

ER
**AASTARAAMAT.** **See** Anthropology.

GW
**ABHANDLUNGEN AUS DEM LANDESMUSEUM FUR NATURKUNDE ZU MUNSTER IN WESTFALEN.** [Abh. Landesmus. Naturkd. Munster Westfalen]. **Main/Corp** Munster. Landesmuseum fur Naturkunde. Vol. 1- ; 1930-. German. ir. Abhandlungen aus dem Himmelreichallee, 50 Westfalen Germany. **Supersedes** Jahresbericht des Westfalischen Provinzial-Vereins fur Wissenschaft und Kunst.

GW/0070-7295
**ABHANDLUNGEN UND BERICHTE DES STAATLICHEN MUSEUMS FUER VOLKERKUNDE, DRESDEN.** **Main/Corp** Dresden. Staatliches Museum fuer Volkerkunde. Vol. 21 (1962)-. German (Russian; table of contents in English and Russian). ir. Price varies. Akademie-Verlag GmbH, Muehlenstrasse 33 34, D 13162 Berlin Germany. **Tel** 011 49 30 47889300, FAX 011 49 30 47889357. **(Subscription address:** VCH Publishers Inc., 303 Northwest 12th Avenue, Journals Department, Deerfield FL 33442.**) DD** 572. **Supersedes in part** Dresden. Staatliches Museum fuer Tierkunde und Volkerkunde. Abhandlungen und Berichte.
**Ind/Abst** Anthropol. Index; Anthropol. Lit.; Ethnoarts Index.

CN/0710-0132
**ACCESS (LONDON, ONT.).** **See** Library and Information Sciences.

SA
**ADLER MUSEUM BULLETIN.** **Added/Corp** Adler Museum of the History of Medicine. Vol. 5 (Apr. 1979)-. English. Three times a year (Mar., June, Nov.). R12.00. Adler Museum History of Medicine, PO Box 1038, Johannesburg 2000 South Africa. **Tel** 011 27 012 3241680. **ED** Rose Melzer. **NLM** W1 AD305. **Bk Rev**. **Circ:** 1,500 (ctrl). **Continues** Bulletin of The Adler Museum of the History of Medicine.
**Desc:** All aspects of the history of medicine and the allied sciences as well as biographies and assessments of the great men and women of medicine and surgery.

UK/0142-887X
**AIM.** [AIM]. **VFOAT** Association of Independent Museums; AIM Bulletin. (1978)-. Periodical. English. bm. **Ind/Abst** Museum Abstr.

CN/0380-3279
**ALBERTA MUSEUMS REVIEW.** **Added/Corp** Alberta Museums Association. (Mar. 1974)-. Periodical. English. Twice a year. 30.00Can$. Alberta Museums Association, 9912 106th Street, Suite 40, Edmonton ALTA T5K 1C5 Canada. **Tel** (403)424-2626. **DD** 069/.097123.

US/0191-1945
**ALI-ABA COURSE OF STUDY : LEGAL ASPECTS OF MUSEUM OPERATIONS : MATERIALS.** **See** Law.

US/0191-3069
**ALI-ABA COURSE OF STUDY : LEGAL PROBLEMS OF MUSEUM ADMINISTRATION : MATERIALS.** **See** Law.

CN/0849-5858
**AMM NEWSLETTER.** [AMM newsl.]. **Added/Corp** Association of Manitoba Museums. **VFOAT** Association of Manitoba Museums Newsletter. (November 1988)-. Newsletter. English. bm. Association of Manitoba Museums, 422-167 Lombard Avenue, Winnipeg Manitoba R3B 0T6 Canada. **Tel** (204)947-1782. **DD** 069/.097127. **Continues** Newsletter (Association of Manitoba Museums)., 0834-0757.

UK/0143-361X
**AMSSEE NEWS.** [AMSSEE news]. **VFOAT** Area Museums Service for South Eastern England News. (1979)-. Periodical. English. qt. **Continues** Something Else, 0140-3648.
**Ind/Abst** Museum Abstr.

AT
**ANG NEWS / AUSTRALIAN NATIONAL GALLERY.** **VFOAT** A.N.G. News. Vol. 1, No. 1 (Winter 1981)-. English. Six times a year. Australian National Gallery, Parkes Place, Canberra Australian Capital Territory 2600 Australia. **Tel** (062)712411, FAX (062)712529, telex AA 61500. **ED** Judy Thorne. **Circ:** 12,000 (ctrl).
**Desc:** Contains articles on the programs and collections of the Australian National Gallery.

●AT
**ANH / THE AUSTRALIAN MUSEUM TRUST.** **Added/Corp** Australian Museum. Trust. **VAT** Australian Natural History. (1992)-. Periodical. English. qt. **Continues** Australian Natural History, 0004-9840.

SA
**ANNALS OF THE CAPE PROVINCIAL MUSEUMS. HUMAN SCIENCES.** **VFOAT** Human Sciences. V. 1, Pt. 1 (March 20, 1979)-. Periodical. English. ir. Albany Museum, Somerset Street, Grahamstown 6140 South Africa. **LC** GN1; .A614. **Continues in part** Annals of the Cape Provincial Museums.

SA/0303-2515
**ANNALS OF THE SOUTH AFRICAN MUSEUM.** [Ann. S. Afr. Mus.]. **Main/Corp** South African Museum. **Added/Corp** South African Museum. Annale van die Suid-Afrikaanse Museum. **VFOAT** Annale van die Suid-Afrikaanse Museum. Vol. 1 (June 1898)-. Monographic series. English. ir. Price varies per volume. South African Museum, PO Box 61, Cape Town 8000 South Africa. **Tel** 27 21 243330, , **FAX** 27 21 246716. **ED** E Louw. **LC** QH1; .S67. **CODEN** ASAMAS. Index available. **Pr Rev. Circ:** 350. Documents available from BIOSIS Document Express, CASDDS.
**Desc:** Scientific journal covering ethnography, archaeology, palaeontology, geology, marine biology, invertebrates, herpetology, ornithology and mammalogy.
**Ind/Abst** Abstr. Anthropol.; Biol. Abstr.; Chem. Abstr.; Fish Rev.; GeoRef; Ocean. Abstr.; Life Sci. Collect.; Wildl. Rev.

BE
**ANNUAIRE DES MUSEES ROYAUX DES BEAUX-ARTS DE BELGIQUE.** *Title Change.* **Main/Corp** Brussels. Musees Royaux des Beaux-Arts de Belgique. **VFOAT** Jaarboek der Koninkl. Museums voor Schoone Kunsten van Belge. 1 (1938)-?. Periodical. French (German, English, Dutch and Flemish). Musees Royaux des Beaux-Arts de Belgique, 9 rue du Musee, B-1000 Bruxelles Belgium. **ED** Leo Van Puyvelde. **LC** N6961; .B7. **DD** 708.9493. **Continued by** Bulletin - Musees Royaux des Beaux-Arts de Belgique, 0027-3856.

US/0067-3080
**ANNUAL - BALTIMORE MUSEUM OF ART.** (ANNUAL / THE BALTIMORE MUSEUM OF ART.). [Annu. - Baltimore Mus. Art]. **Main/Corp** Baltimore Museum of Art. (1966)-. English. an. Baltimore Museum of Art, Baltimore MD 21218. **LC** N515; .A18. **DD** 705.

BB
**ANNUAL REPORT.** **Main/Corp** Barbados Museum and Historical Society. **VFOAT** Report of the Council for the Year ... (1987-1988)-. English. Barbados Museum and Historical Society, St. Anns Garrison Barbados. **LC** F2041; .B27a. **DD** 972.981/006/072981. **Continues** Report of the Council for the Year ... .

AT/0314-9919
**ANNUAL REPORT / AUSTRALIAN NATIONAL GALLERY.** **Main/Corp** Australian National Gallery. English. an. Australian National Gallery, Parkes Place, Canberra Australian Capital Territory 2600 Australia. **Tel** (062)712411, FAX (062)712529, telex AA 61500. **LC** N3916; .A18A. **DD** 708.9947/1/05.

VI
**ANNUAL REPORT FOR FISCAL YEAR ... / BUREAU OF LIBRARIES, MUSEUMS, AND ARCHAEOLOGICAL SERVICES.** **See** Library and Information Sciences.

US/0363-3306
**ANNUAL REPORT - HUNTINGTON LIBRARY, ART GALLERY, BOTANICAL GARDENS.** **See** Library and Information Sciences.

US/0091-7222
**ANNUAL REPORT - NATIONAL GALLERY OF ART (U.S.).** **See** The Arts-Art.

CN/1187-3728
**ANNUAL REPORT - NATIONAL MUSEUM OF SCIENCE AND TECHNOLOGY (OTTAWA).** (ANNUAL REPORT.). [Annu. rep. - Natl. Mus. Sci. Technol.]. **Main/Corp** National Museum of Science and Technology (Canada). (1991)-. English. **DD** 507/.4/71. **Continues in part** National Museums of Canada. Annual Report., 0704-1616.

# Museums and Galleries

US/8755-1411
**ANNUAL REPORT - NEWARK MUSEUM.**
(ANNUAL REPORT.). **Main/Corp** Newark Museum. 1982-. English. an. The Newark Museum, 49 Washington Street, PO Box 540, Newark NJ 07101-0540. **Tel** (201)596-6550, FAX (201)642-0459. **ED** Toni Jones and Jane Rappaport. **Circ:** 5,500. *Separated from Newark Museum Quarterly.*
**Desc:** A compilation of lists of acquisitions, donors and members as well as a record of events of the past year.

UK
**ANNUAL REPORT OF THE MUSEUMS ASSOCIATION FOR THE YEAR. Main/Corp** Museums Association. **VFOAT** Annual Report. English. an. *Continues* Annual Report of the Council.

CN/0082-5115
**ANNUAL REPORT - ROYAL ONTARIO MUSEUM. Title Change. Main/Corp** Royal Ontario Museum. No. 1 39th (1949/50)-(July 1988/June 1989). English. an. 100 Queen's Park, Toronto Ontario M5S 2C6 Canada. **Tel** (416)586-5582, FAX (416)586-5863. **ED** Barbara Ibronyi. **LC** AM101; .T624. **DD** 069.0871. ctrl circ. *Continued by* Year in Review.

CN/0082-5115
**ANNUAL REPORT / ROYAL ONTARIO MUSEUM. Main/Corp** Royal Ontario Museum. **VFOAT** Rapport Annuel. 41st (July 1990-June 1991)-. English (French). Royal Ontario Museum Publications Service, 100 Queens Park, Toronto Ontario M5S 2C6 Canada. **Tel** (416)586-5581. *Continues* Year in Review.

SA
**ANNUAL REPORT - SOUTH AFRICAN NATIONAL MUSEUM OF MILITARY HISTORY. Main/Corp** South African National Museum of Military History. **VFOAT** Jaarverslag - Suid-Afrikaanse Nasionale Museum Vir Krygsgeskiedenis. 1974/75-. Multiple languages (Afrikaans and English). South African National Museum of Military History, Erlswold Way Saxonwold, Johannesburg South Africa. **LC** D733; .S6. **DD** 355/.0074/096822. *Continues* South African National War Museum, Johannesburg. Report.

AT
**ANNUAL REPORT / THE NATIONAL MUSEUM OF AUSTRALIA. Main/Corp** National Museum of Australia. (198?)-. English. an. Australian Government Public Service, National Museum of Australia, Canberra ACT Australia. **LC** WMLC L 83/6526.

UK
**ANNUAL REPORTS OF THE SYNDICATE AND OF THE FRIENDS OF THE FITZWILLIAM FOR THE YEAR ENDING ..., THE. Main/Corp** Fitzwilliam Museum. **Added/Corp** Fitzwilliam Museum. Syndicate. Fitzwilliam Museum. Friends. Fitzwilliam Museum. Trust. **VFOAT** Fitzwilliam Museum Report. (1973)-. English. £5.00 UK; $10.00 (airmail) US. University of Cambridge / Fitzwilliam Museum, Fitzwilliam Museum, Trumpington Street, Cambridge CB2 1RB England. **Tel** (0223)332900, FAX (0223)332923, telex 4738. **ED** S.S. Jervis. **LC** AM101.C157; A15. **DD** 069/.09744/4. **Circ:** 4,000. *Continues* Annual Reports of the Fitzwilliam Museum Syndicate and the Friends of the Fitzwilliam Cambridge for the year Ending ... .
**Desc:** Records the activities of the museum, by calendar year, including acquisitions and exhibitions, of the Hamilton Kerr Institute and of the Friends of the Fitzwilliam and of the Fitzwilliam Museum Trust.

FR
**ANTIQUITES NATIONALES.** (1969)-. French. an. 100.00F. Mus des Antiquites Nationales, Chateau de St Germain, F-78103 St Germin en Laye France. **Tel** 33 1 34515365. *Continues* Antiquite et Histoire (Saint-Germain-en-Laye), 0066-4898.
**Ind/Abst** Anthropol. Lit.; BHA : Biblio. Hist. Art.

GE/0402-7817
**ARBEITS- UND FORSCHUNGSBERICHTE ZUR SACHSISCHEN BODENDENKMALPFLEGE. Added/Corp** Dresden. Landesmuseum fur Vorgeschichte. Vol. 1 (1950)-. Periodical. German. ir. World Amateur Boxing Magazine Editor's Office, P.O.Box 0141, 10321 Berlin/GERMANY. **Tel** (049.30)423 5932, (049.30)423 6766, (049.30)423 5943.
**Ind/Abst** Anthropol. Index; Anthropol. Lit.; BHA : Biblio. Hist. Art.

XV/0570-8869
**ARGO / NARODNI MUZEJ V LJUBLJANI. Added/Corp** Narodni Muzej v Ljubljani. Skupnost Muzejev Slovenije. (1962)-. Periodical. Slovenian. qt.
**Ind/Abst** BHA : Biblio. Hist. Art; Numis. Lit.

BL/0365-4508
**ARQUIVOS DO MUSEU NACIONAL.** [Arq. Mus. Nac.]. **Main/Corp** Museu Nacional (Brazil). Vol. 29-. Periodical. Portuguese (English, French and German). ir. Biblioteca, Museu Nacional UFRJ, Av Gal Herculno Gomes s/n, Horto Botanico, Quinta da Boa Vista, Sao Cristovao, 20941 Rio de Janeiro Brasil. **LC** Q33. **DD** 508/.81. **CODEN** AMNJA8. ctrl circ. Documents available from BIOSIS Document Express. *Continues* Archivos de Museu Nacional do Rio de Janeiro.
**Ind/Abst** Biol. Abstr.; GeoRef; Zool. Rec.

NO/0332-7647
**ARSBERETNING / TROMS MUSEUM. Main/Corp** Troms Museum. **Added/Corp** Universitetet i Troms. Instituttt for Museumsvirksomhet. **VFOAT** Arsberetning for ... . (1954)-. Norwegian. ir (1-2 issues per year). Universitet i Tromso, Univ Biblio, Av Tromso Museum, Folkepark, N-9000 Tromso Norway. **LC** AM101; .T8. *Continues* Troms Museum. Beretning for Arene ... .

NO
**ARSBERETNING / UNIVERSITETET I TRONDHEIM, VITENSKAPSMUSEET. See** Natural History.

DK/0109-2731
**ARSSKRIFT - LOLLAND-FALSTERS STIFTSMUSEUM 1983.** (ARSSKRIFT.). **VFOAT** Arsskrift - Lolland-Falsters Kunstmuseum (Maribo. 1983). (1983)-. Danish. UDC 069.094 893. *Continued in part by* Lolland-Falsters Stiftsmuseums Arsskrift, 0542-6820.
**Ind/Abst** BHA : Biblio. Hist. Art.

US
**ART INSTITUTE OF CHICAGO NEWS & EVENTS, THE. See** The Arts-Art.

US/0736-1483
**ART/NOW CALIFORNIA GALLERY GUIDE. See** The Arts-Art.

US/1059-7689
**ART NOW GALLERY GUIDE. INTERNATIONAL. See** The Arts-Art.

US
**ART NOW/NEW YORK GALLERY GUIDE. See** The Arts-Art.

US/1053-4156
**ARTISTS RESOURCE GUIDE TO NEW ENGLAND, THE. See** The Arts-Art.

US/0740-9214
**ARTS QUARTERLY (NEW ORLEANS, LA. 1978). See** The Arts-Art.

US/0733-4869
**ARTSCENE (LOS ANGELES, CALIF.). See** The Arts-Art.

JA
**ASAHI GYARARI NENKAN. VFOAT** Asahi Gallery Annual. 1978-. Periodical. Japanese (Japanese). ¥3000. Kabushiki Kaisha Sampo Janaru, 10-17 Hamamatsucho 1 Minato-ku, Tokyo 105 Japan. **LC** N7358; .A85. *Continues* Asahi Geijutsu Nenkan.

UK
**ASHMOLEAN, THE. Added/Corp** Ashmolean Museum. No. 1 (Christmas 1982-Easter 1983)-. Bulletin. English. sa. £3.60. Ashmolean Museum Publications, Ashmoleum Museum, at Beaumont Street, Oxford OX1 2PH England. **Tel** 0865 278009/10, FAX 0865 278018. **(Subscription address):** UK / Gazelle Book Services, Falcon House, Queen Square, Lancaster LA1 1RN UK (Phone: 0524 68765); North America / Arthur Schwartz & Co. Inc.; 234 Meads Mountain Road, Woodstock, NY 12498, USA, (Phone: (800)669-9080)) **ED** Christopher White and Ian Charlton. **Bk Rev**, (Qty: 2-3). **Circ:** 2,000 (ctrl).
**Desc:** Contains 24 pages, illustrated with monotone line and halftones. It is the "house" magazine of Oxford University's Ashmolean Museum and includes articles on all aspects of the museum's permanent collections and new acquisitions in the field of European and Oriental fine and applied art; European archaeology and numismatics. It includes details and reviews of new museum publications, of "Friends" activities and a detailed calendar of exhibitions and events both in the Ashmolean and in other museums and galleries around Oxford.
**Ind/Abst** ARTbibliogr. Mod.; Numis. Lit.

CN/0822-417X
**AT THE DUNLOP.** [At Dunlop]. April/May/June 1981-. Periodical. English. qt. Free. Dunlop Art Gallery, Regina Public Library, 2311 12th Avenue, Regina Saskatchewan S4P 0N3 Canada. **DD** 708.11/244. *Continues* At the Galleries, 0822-4161.

FI/0789-9343
**ATENEUM HELSINKI. See** The Arts-Art.

GR/1011-1557
**ATHENA (ATHENI). See** College and School Publications.

CN/0824-4251
**ATRIA.** [Atria]. **Main/Corp** Royal Ontario Museum. Nov./Dec. 1982-. English. bm. Royal Ontario Museum Publications Service, 100 Queens Park, Toronto Ontario M5S 2C6 Canada. **Tel** (416)586-5581. **DD** 069.1/09713/541. *Continues* Royal Ontario Museum. What's on at the ROM, 0824-4243.

IT
**ATTI DEI CIVICI MUSEI DI STORIA ED ARTE. Main/Corp** Civici Musei di Storia ed Arte di Trieste. Vol. 1 (1968)-. Monographic series. Italian. **LC** AM55.T74; C59a.
**Ind/Abst** BHA : Biblio. Hist. Art.

CN/0711-7086
**AU FIL DES COLLECTIONS.** (AU FIL DES COLLECTIONS / MUSEE DES BEAUX-ARTS DE MONTREAL.). [Fil collect.]. **Added/Corp** Musee des Beaux-Arts de Montreal. (Aug.14/Nov.14 1982)-. Periodical. French. qt. Free. Musee des Beaux-Arts de Montreal, 3400 Av du Musee, Montreal Quebec H3G 1K3 Canada. **DD** 069/.97/0009714281. ctrl circ.

US/0093-1586
**AUDIT REPORT - STATE OF NEVADA. NEVADA STATE MUSEUM.** (NEVADA STATE MUSEUM AUDIT REPORT.). **Main/Corp** Nevada. Legislature. Legislative Council Bureau. English. an. Legislative Counsel Bureau, Legislative Building, Capitol Complex, Carson City NV 89710. **LC** AM101; .N4635. **DD** 069/.09793/57.

US/0739-7747
**AVISO (WASHINGTON, D.C.).** (AVISO : A MONTHLY DISPATCH FROM THE AAM.). [Aviso]. **Added/Corp** American Association of Museums. (Sept. 1975)-. Periodical. English. mo (12 issues). American Association of Museums, 1225 Eye Street Northwest, Suite 200, Washington DC 20005. **Tel** (202)289-1818. [CCC]. *Continues* Bulletin (American Association of Museums), 0739-7755.

UK/0144-588X
**BCG NEWSLETTER BOLTON.** [BCG newsl.Bolton]. **VFOAT** Biology Curators Group Newsletter. (1975)-. Periodical. English. Three times a year. Biology Curators Group, Leicester Museum, 96 New Walk, Leicester LE1 6TD England. **Tel** 011 44 533 554100. **(Subscription address):** BCG, Membership Secretary, The Natural History Museum, London) **ED** M A Taylor, 0738-32488. Index available. **Bk Rev. Ad Acc. Circ:** 300 (ctrl).
**Desc:** News, views and information of interest to biology curators.
**Ind/Abst** Museum Abstr.

GW
**BELSER KUNSTQUARTAL. VFOAT** Belser Kunst Quartal. (1967)-. Bulletin. German. qt. DM42.00. Belser Verlag, Postfach 100561, D 70004 Stuttgart Germany. **Tel** 011 49 711 21910. **ED** Reiner Brouwer. **Ad Acc. Circ:** 33,000 (ctrl).

US
**BIENNIAL REPORT. Main/Corp** Thomas Burke Memorial Washington State Museum. (1984-86)-. English. be. Washington State Museum, Seattle WA 98121. **LC** AM101.S28; A34. **DD** 508/.074. *Continues* Annual Report, 0093-5670.

US
**BIENNIAL REPORT / SANTA BARBARA MUSEUM OF ART. Main/Corp** Santa Barbara Museum of Art. (1990)-. English. ir (published annually if funds are available). Free with membership: $40.00 general membership; $60.00 associate membership. Santa Barbara Museum of Art, 1130 State Street, Santa Barbara CA 93101. **Tel** (805)963-4364, FAX (805)966-6840. *Continues* Santa Barbara Museum of Art. Triennial Report.

GW/0522-9790
**BILDERHEFTE. Main/Corp** Berlin. Staatliche Museen (West Berlin). No. 1 (1967)-. Monographic series. German. ir. Price varies per volume. Gebruder Mann Verlag, Lindenstrasse 76, D-10969 Berlin Germany. **Tel** 011 49 30 25913589, telex 183723. **Ad Acc. Circ:** 1,000.

# Museums and Galleries

**Desc:** Reports on partial holdings of the different departments of the National Museum sometimes due to special exhibits.

CN/0712-9319
## BIOME (ENGLISH ED.).
(BIOME / NATIONAL MUSEUM OF NATURAL SCIENCES.). [Biome]. Vol. 1:1-. Periodical. English. Three times a year (February, June, October). Free. Information Centre, National Museum of Natural Sciences, PO Box 3443 Station D, Ottawa Ontario K1P 6P4 Canada. **Tel** (613)996-3102. **ED** Nick Belanger. **DD** 505.
**Desc:** A four page tabloid containing topics primarily, but not exclusively, pertaining to National Museum of Natural Sciences research activities.

AT/0814-2262
## BOARD OF THE SOUTH AUSTRALIAN MUSEUM ANNUAL REPORT.
[Board. S. Aust. Mus. annu. rep.]. (1982)-. Periodical. English. an. **DD** 069'.099423'1. *Continues* South Australia Report of the Museum Board, 0375-1619.
**Ind/Abst** AESIS Q.

NO
## BODOBOKA.
**Added/Corp** Nordland Fylkesmuseum. Nordlandsmuseet. **VFOAT** Nordland Fylkesmuseums Arbok. (1984)-. Norwegian. Kr110.00 Norway; Kr150.00 North America; Kr120.00 other. Nordlandsmuseet, Prinsensgt 116, 8000 Bodo Norway. **Tel** 081-21640. **ED** Anne-Marie Forde. **LC** AM101.B537; A14. **Ad Acc.** ctrl circ. *Continues* Arbok (Nordland Fylkesmuseum), 0333-3132.

SP/0210-8143
## BOLETIN DEL MUSEO DEL PRADO.
[Bol. Mus. Prado]. **Main/Corp** Museo del Prado. Vol. 1, No. 1 (Jan./Apr. 1980)-. Bulletin. Spanish. an. Museo del Prado Publicaciones, Paseo del Prado S N, 28014 Madrid Spain. **Tel** 011 34 1 4202836. **LC** AM101.M238; A2. **DD** 069/.0946/41. Documents available from The Genuine Article.
**Ind/Abst** Art Archaeol. Tech. Abstr.; ARTbibliogr. Mod.; Arts Humanit. Citation Index (19??-19??) [Full Cov.]; BHA : Biblio. Hist. Art; Curr. Contents Arts Humanit.; Res. Alert [Full Cov.].

SP/0212-548X
## BOLETIN / MUSEO DE ZARAGOZA.
**Added/Corp** Museo de Zaragoza. No. 1 (1982)-. Spanish. Apartado 848, Zaragoza Brazil. **LC** AM1; .B64. **DD** 069/.0946/553. *Continues* Academia Aragonesa de Nobles y Bellas Artes de San Luis. Boletin de la Academia Aragonesa de Nobles y Bellas Artes de San Luis y del Museo Provincial de Bellas Artes de Zaragoza.
**Ind/Abst** BHA : Biblio. Hist. Art.

IT/0394-1027
## BOLLETTINO (CIVICI MUSEI VENEZIANI D'ARTE E DI STORIA).
(BOLLETTINO - CIVICI MUSEI VENEZIANI D'ARTE E DI STORIA.). **Added/Corp** Civici musei veneziani d'arte e di storia. **VFOAT** Bollettino C. Musei Veneziani. (1980)-. Italian. an. L25000. Civici Musei Venez Arte Storia, San Marco 52, 30124 Venice Italy. **Tel** 011 39 41 5225625. **LC** DG670; .B64. **DD** 708.5/31/05. Index available. ctrl circ. *Continues* Bollettino Dei Musei Civici Veneziani, 0027-3864.

IT/0523-9346
## BOLLETTINO DEI MUSEI COMUNALI DI ROMA.
(BOLLETTINO DEI MUSEI COMUNALI DI ROMA / A CURA DEGLI AMICI DEI MUSEI DI ROMA.). [Boll. Mus. comunali Roma]. **Added/Corp** Amici dei Musei di Roma (Italy). Vol. 1, No.. 1/2 (1954)-. Periodical. Italian. an. **LC** AM55.R6; B6.
**Ind/Abst** BHA : Biblio. Hist. Art.

IT/0393-0750
## BOLLETTINO DEL MUSEO CIVICO DI PADOVA ... .
**Main/Corp** Padua. Museo civico. (1899)-. Italian. an. **ED** Andrea Moschetti. **LC** AS221; .P3.
**Ind/Abst** Avery Index Archit. Period. Suppl. Colum. Univ. (1984-); BHA : Biblio. Hist. Art.

IT/0392-0062
## BOLLETTINO DEL MUSEO CIVICO DI STORIA NATURALE DI VERONA.
[Boll. Mus. Civ. Stor. Nat. Verona]. **Main/Corp** Museo Civico di Storia Naturale di Verona. Vol. 1 (1974)-. Multiple languages (English, French, German and Italian). an. L40000.00. Museo Civico di Storia Naturale, Lungadige Porta Vittoria 9, 37129 Verona Italy. **LC** QH7; .V58a. **CODEN** BMCVD3. Documents available from BIOSIS Document Express.
**Ind/Abst** Anthropol. Index; Biol. Abstr.; GeoRef; Life Sci. Collect.

VC/1018-4317
## BOLLETTINO - MONUMENTI, MUSEI E GALLERIE PONTIFICIE.
**See** The Arts-Art.

PO
## BRASILIA.
V. 1- 1942-. Portuguese. Universidade de Coimbra, 3049 Coimbra Codex Portugal. **LC** AS80. **DD** 068.81.

UK/0965-8297
## BRITISH MUSEUM MAGAZINE.
[Br. Mus. mag.]. (1990)-. Bulletin. English. qt. £12.00 UK; £16.00 other. British Museum Society, c/o The British Museum, London WC1B 3DG England. **Tel** 011 44 071 3238605, FAX 011 44 071 3238614. **ED** Victoria Neumark. **DD** 069.0941. **Bk Rev**, (Qty: 10). **Ad Acc. Circ:** 10,000 (ctrl). Documents available from FAXON Xpress.
*Continues* British Museum Society Bulletin, 0525-5260.
**Desc:** News and information, activities, and exhibitions related to the British Museum.

UK
## BRITISH MUSEUM MAGAZINE : JOURNAL OF THE BRITISH MUSEUM SOCIETY.
**Added/Corp** British Museum. Society. No. 3 (Sept. 1990)-. Bulletin. English. Four times a year. £12.00; £16.00 other. British Museum Society, c/o The British Museum, London WC1B 3DG England. **Tel** 011 44 071 3238605, FAX 011 44 071 3238614. **ED** Victoria Neumark. **LC** AM101.B87; B88. **DD** 069./09421/42. **Bk Rev**, (Qty: 10/year). **Ad Acc. Circ:** 10,000 (ctrl). Documents available from FAXON Xpress.
*Continues* BM Magazine.
**Desc:** News and information, activities, and exhibitions relating to the British Museum.

GW
## BRUCKE-ARCHIVE.
No. 1- 1967-. Periodical. German. an. Bruecke Museum, Bussardsteig 9, 1000 Berlin 33 Germany. **Tel** 030-831 2029. **ED** M M Moeller.

BX
## BRUNEI MUSEUM JOURNAL.
**Main/Corp** Muzium Brunei. V. 1- 1969-. Multiple languages (English and Malay). bm. Brunei Museum, Bandar Seri Begawan, Brunei. **LC** DS646.35; .B76A. **DD** 959.5/5/005.

FR/0339-0195
## BULLETIN DE LA SOCIETE DES AMIS DU CHATEAU DE PAU.
**See** History(General)-History of Europe.

FR/0988-1875
## BULLETIN DE LA SOCIETE DES AMIS DU VIEUX CHINON.
**See** History(General)-History of Europe.

FR/0037-9190
## BULLETIN DE LA SOCIETE DES ANTIQUAIRES DE L'OUEST ET DES MUSEES DE POITIERS.
**Added/Corp** Societe des Antiquaires de l'Ouest (Poitiers, France). (1???)-. Bulletin. French. qt.
**Ind/Abst** BHA : Biblio. Hist. Art.

FR/0521-7032
## BULLETIN DES MUSEES ET MONUMENTS LYONNAIS.
**Added/Corp** Association des Amis du Musee de Lyon. Vol. 1 (1952)-. Bulletin. French. qt. 175.00F. Musee des Beaux-Arts, 20 Place des Terreaux, 69001 Lyon France. **Tel** 78-28-07-66, FAX 78-28-12-45. **ED** Philippe Durey.
**Desc:** Articles on the collections in museums of Lyon and monuments in the city.
**Ind/Abst** ARTbibliogr. Mod.; BHA : Biblio. Hist. Art.

BE
## BULLETIN DES MUSEES ROYAUX D'ART ET D'HISTOIRE.
**Main/Corp** Musees Royaux d'Art et d'Histoire (Belgium). **Added/Corp** Societe des Amis des Musees Royaux de l'Etat, Brussels. **VFOAT** Bulletin van de Koninklijke Musea voor Kunst en Geschiedenis. Vol. 1 (Oct. 1901)-. Multiple languages (French and Flemish). ir. 1000F. Patrimoine Musees Royaux d'Art et d'Histoire, Parc du Cinquantenaire 10, 1040 Bruxelles Belgium. **Tel** 011 32 2 7417211. **(Subscription address:** Editions Peeters SA, Bondgenotenlaan 153, 3000 Leuven Belgium.) **LC** N1835; .A3. **DD** 708.9493. cum. index.
**Ind/Abst** Art Archaeol. Tech. Abstr.; ARTbibliogr. Mod.; BHA : Biblio. Hist. Art; Br. Archaeol. Bibliogr. -?.

FR/1148-8395
## BULLETIN DU MUSEE BASQUE.
(1924)-. Periodical. French. sa (2 issues). 150.00F France; 180.00F other. Societe des Amis Musee Basque, 1 rue Marengo, 64100 Bayonne France. **Tel** 011 33 59 590898. **UDC** 908(466).
**Ind/Abst** BHA : Biblio. Hist. Art.

FR/0399-0060
## BULLETIN DU MUSEE DE BEYROUTH.
**Added/Corp** Mathaf Bayrut. (1937)-. Bulletin. French. an. Maisonneuve Adrien, 11 Rue Saint Sulpice, 75006 Paris France. **Tel** 33 1 43268635. **LC** DS99.L4; A125. cum. index.
**Ind/Abst** BHA : Biblio. Hist. Art.

HU
## BULLETIN DU MUSEE HONGROIS DES BEAUX-ARTS.
**Main/Corp** Szepmuveszeti Muzeum (Hungary). **Added/Corp** Szepmuveszeti Muzeum (Hungary). **VFOAT** Szepmuveszeti Muzeum Kozlemenyei. Vol. 1 1947-. Bulletin. Hungarian (French). sa. Musee Hongrois des Beaux-Arts, Hungary. **Tel** 1-429-759, FAX 36-1-122-82-98. **LC** AM101.B927; A3. **Circ:** 1,400 (ctrl).
**Desc:** Classic archaeology, European art history, egyptology, chiefly thirteenth to the twentieth century.
**Ind/Abst** ARTbibliogr. Mod. (1984-); BHA : Biblio. Hist. Art.

FR/0540-7575
## BULLETIN DU MUSEE INGRES.
**Added/Corp** Societe des Amis du Musee Ingres. (1956)-. Periodical. French. an (Jan.). 160.00F. Societe Amis du Musee Ingres, 7 Rue E Pouirllon, 82000 Montauban France. **Tel** 011 33 63 662688.
**Desc:** The life and works of painter Dominique Ingres and E. A. Bourdelle and their students.
**Ind/Abst** BHA : Biblio. Hist. Art.

PL/0027-3791
## BULLETIN DU MUSEE NATIONAL DE VARSOVIE.
**Main/Corp** Muzeum Narodowe W Warszawie. **Added/Corp** Muzeum Narodowe w Warszawie. Vol. 1 (1960)-. Bulletin. French (English). qt. Price on Request. **(Subscription address:** ARS Polona, PO Box 1001, 00068 Warsaw Poland.) **LC** N3160; .A2.
**Ind/Abst** ARTbibliogr. Mod.; BHA : Biblio. Hist. Art.

US/0147-1902
## BULLETIN - GEORGIA MUSEUM OF ART, THE UNIVERSITY OF GEORGIA.
*Ceased.* (BULLETIN - GEORGIA MUSEUM OF ART.). [Bull.- Georgia Mus. Art, Univ. Georgia]. **Main/Corp** Georgia Museum of Art. **VFOAT** Georgia Museum of Art Bulletin. Vol. 1 (1974)-?. Bulletin. English. an. Georgia Museum of Art, The University of Georgia, Athens GA 30602. **Tel** (404)542-3255. **ED** William U Eiland. **LC** N514.A8; A23A. **DD** 708/.158/18. **Circ:** 1,200.
**Desc:** Scholarly essay with illustrations.
**Ind/Abst** ARTbibliogr. Mod.; BHA : Biblio. Hist. Art.

II/0019-5987
## BULLETIN - INDIAN MUSEUM.
**Main/Corp** Indian Museum, Calcutta. Vol. 1 (Jan. 1966)-. Bulletin. English. an. Rs30.00 India; $10.00 US; £5.00 other. Indian Museum Bulletin, 27 Jawaharlal Nehru Road, Calcutta 13 India. **Tel** 299914, FAX 299902. **ED** R C Sharma. **LC** AM101; .I454. Index available. cum. index. **Circ:** 500 (ctrl).
**Desc:** Provides authoritative information on the collections of the Indian Museum and contains results of study on subjects in humanities and sciences.
**Ind/Abst** Numis. Lit. (?-?).

US/0026-1521
## BULLETIN - METROPOLITAN MUSEUM OF ART.
[Bull.- Metrop. Mus. Art]. **Main/Corp** Metropolitan Museum of Art (New York, N.Y.). **Added/Corp** Metropolitan Museum of Art (New York, N.Y.). Recent Acquisitions. **VFOAT** Metropolitan Museum of Art Bulletin. (1905)-. Bulletin. English. qt. $40.00 (Comes with membership in The Metropolitan Museum of Art). Metropolitan Museum of Art, 1000 5th Avenue & 82nd Street, New York NY 10028. **Tel** (212)879-5500 ext. 2937, telex 4676. **ED** Joan Holt. **LC** N610; .A4. **DD** 708. cum. index. available on microfilm and microfiche from University Microfilms International (UMI). Documents available from The Genuine Article. *Absorbed* Metropolitan Museum of Art (New York, N.Y.). Recent Acquisitions, 0889-6585.
**Desc:** Presents illustrated articles about objects in the collections and about the museum's activities.
**Ind/Abst** Acad. Search (Jan. 1994-); Am. Hist. Life (1963-1972); Art Index; ARTbibliogr. Mod.; Arts Humanit. Citation Index [Full Cov.]; Avery Index Archit. Period. Suppl. Colum. Univ. (19??-19??); BHA : Biblio. Hist. Art; Curr. Contents Arts Humanit.; INFO-SOUTH Abstr.; Mag. Search; Middle East Abstr. Index; Res. Alert [Full Cov.].

SW/0081-5691
## BULLETIN - MUSEUM OF FAR EASTERN ANTIQUITIES.
**See** Archaeology.

CN/0709-2628
## BULLETIN - MUSEUM OF INDIAN ARCHAEOLOGY. UNIVERSITY OF WESTERN ONTARIO.
(BULLETIN - MUSEUM OF INDIAN ARCHAEOLOGY.). Bulletin. English. an. Price varies per volume. London Museum of Archaeology, 1600 Attawandaron Road, London Ontario N6A 3M6 Canada. **Tel** (519)473-1360. **ED** William D Finlayson. **DD** 971.3/01.
**Desc:** Contributors are staff members and associates of the Museum discussing museum collections, field work, and results of research in various archaeological fields.

II/0418-5730
**BULLETIN - NATIONAL MUSEUM, NEW DELHI.** **Main/Corp** Delhi. National Museum of India. No. 1 (1966)-. Bulletin. English. ir. Rs11.00 (Part 2); Rs12.00 (Part 3). Ministry of Information and Broadcasting, Government of India, Patiala House, New Delhi 110 001 India. **Tel** 387983. **LC** DS401; .D44. **DD** 913.34/031/05.

US/0278-3355
**BULLETIN - NEW YORK STATE MUSEUM (1976).** (BULLETIN - NEW YORK STATE MUSEUM.). [Bull. - N. Y. State Mus.]. **Main/Corp** New York State Museum. **Added/Corp** New York State Museum. No. 425 (Feb. 1976)-. Monographic series. English. ir. Price varies per volume. New York State Library, Documents Gift & Exchange Section, Empire State Plaza, Albany NY 12230. **Tel** (518)474-5953. **(Subscription address:** New York State Museum Publications, 3090 Cultural Education Center, Albany NY 12230.**)** **LC** UNC. **DD** 507. ***Continues*** *Bulletin (New York State Museum and Science Service), 0097-028X.*
**Desc:** Contains popular and scholarly guides to the natural history of New York State.
**Ind/Abst** GeoRef.

US/0029-2567
**BULLETIN - NORTH CAROLINA MUSEUM OF ART.** ***Suspended.*** [Bull. - N. C. Mus. Art]. **Main/Corp** North Carolina. Museum of Art, Raleigh. Vol. 1 (Spring 1957)-Suspended. Bulletin. English. ir. Gay M Hertzman, 2110 Blue Ridge Boulevard, Raleigh NC 27607. **Tel** (919)833-1935, ext 139. **LC** N715.R2; A25.
**Ind/Abst** ARTbibliogr. Mod.; BHA : Biblio. Hist. Art.

US/0097-3211
**BULLETIN OF THE ALLYN MUSEUM.** [Bull. Allyn Mus.]. **Added/Corp** Allyn Museum of Entomology. Florida State Museum. Florida Museum of Natural History. No. 1 (1971)-. Monographic series. English. ir. free on request. Allyn Museum of Entomology, 3621 Bay Shore Road, Sarasota FL 34234. **Tel** (813)355-8475. **ED** Lee D. Miller and Jacqueline Y. Miller. **LC** QL461; .B88. **DD** 595.7/005. **CODEN** BLAMBP. Index available. **Pr Rev. Circ:** 415. Documents available from BIOSIS Document Express.
**Desc:** A reviewed journal devoted to the study of lepidoptera, especially rhopalocera. Publications to date include studies on life history, taxonomy, systematics, morphology, and ecology.
**Ind/Abst** AGRICOLA [Full Cov.]; Biol. Abstr.

JA
**BULLETIN OF THE ANCIENT ORIENT MUSEUM.** **VFOAT** Kodai Oriento Hakubutsukan Kiyo. Vol. 1 (1979)-. Bulletin. English (Japanese). an. Ancient Orient Museum, 1-4 Higashi Ikebukuro 3-chome Toshima-ku, Tokyo 170 Japan. **Tel** 03-989-3491, FAX 03-590-3266. **LC** DS56; .B85. **DD** 935/.005.
**Ind/Abst** Anthropol. Lit.

US/0009-8841
**BULLETIN OF THE CLEVELAND MUSEUM OF ART, THE.** ***Ceased.*** **See** The Arts-Art.

FJ
**BULLETIN OF THE FIJI MUSEUM.** **Added/Corp** Fiji Museum. No. 1 (1973)-. Monographic series. English. ir. Price varies per volume. Fiji Museum, PO Box 2023, Suva Fiji Islands. **Tel** 011 679 315043, 011 679 315944.

US/1052-3669
**BULLETIN OF THE FLORIDA MUSEUM OF NATURAL HISTORY. BIOLOGICAL SCIENCES.** **See** Natural History.

II/0523-9702
**BULLETIN OF THE PRINCE OF WALES MUSEUM OF WESTERN INDIA.** **Main/Corp** Bombay. Prince of Wales Museum of Western India. No. 1- 1950/51-. Bulletin. English. ir. Hindustan Book Agency, 17 UB Jawahar Nagar, Delhi 7 India.

US/0093-6812
**BULLETIN OF THE UNIVERSITY OF NEBRASKA STATE MUSEUM.** **See** Natural History.

US/0031-7314
**BULLETIN - PHILADELPHIA MUSEUM OF ART.** **See** The Arts-Art.

US
**BULLETIN SERIES. MUSEUM OF NORTH ARIZONA.** (19??)-. Monographic series. English. ir. Price varies per volume. Museum of Northern Arizona, Route 4 Box 720, Flagstaff AZ 86001. **Tel** (602)774-5213.

US/0009-7691
**BULLETIN - THE ST. LOUIS ART MUSEUM.** [Bull. - St. Louis Art Mus.]. **Added/Corp** St. Louis Art Museum. **VFOAT** Bulletin of the St. Louis Art Museum. **VAT** Bulletin - Saint Louis Art Museum. Vol. 7, No. 5 (Jan./Feb. 1972)-. Bulletin. English. sa. $10.00. Saint Louis Art Museum, #1 Fine Arts Drive, St Louis MO 63110. **Tel** (314)721-0072, FAX (314)721-6172. **ED** Mary Ann Steiner. **LC** N729; .A33. **DD** 708/.178/66. **Circ:** 18,000 (ctrl). ***Continues*** *Bulletin (City Art Museum of St. Louis), 0364-8141.*
**Desc:** Complete information of the various collections of the St. Louis Art Museum; detailed descriptions.
**Ind/Abst** Art Index; ARTbibliogr. Mod.; BHA : Biblio. Hist. Art; RILA, Int. Rep. Lit. Art.

US/0077-8583
**BULLETIN - THE UNIVERSITY OF NEW MEXICO ART MUSEUM.** [Bull. - Univ. N. M., Art Mus.]. **Main/Corp** New Mexico. University. Art Museum. No. 1- Winter 1965/66-. Bulletin. English. an. $5.00. University of New Mexico Art Museum, College of Fine Arts 1017, Albuquerque NM 87131. **Tel** (505)277-4001. **ED** Peter Walch. **LC** N512.A5; A3. **DD** 708.189/61. **Circ:** 1,200.
**Ind/Abst** ARTbibliogr. Mod.; BHA : Biblio. Hist. Art.

US/0076-8391
**BULLETIN - UNIVERSITY OF MICHIGAN. MUSEUM OF ART.** (BULLETIN / MUSEUMS OF ART AND ARCHAEOLOGY, THE UNIVERSITY OF MICHIGAN.). [Bull. - Univ. Mich., Mus. Art]. **Added/Corp** University of Michigan. Museum of Art. Kelsey Museum of Archaeology. University of Michigan. Dept. of the History of Art. Vol. 1 (1978)-. Bulletin. English. sa. $8.00. University of Michigan Museum of Art, 525 South State Street, Ann Arbor MI 48109-1354. **Tel** (313)764-0395. **ED** Marvin Eisenberg and Graham Smith. **LC** N513; .A2. **DD** 708.174/35. **Circ:** 1,000. ***Continues*** *Bulletin (University of Michigan. Museum of Art : 1966), 0076-8391.*
**Desc:** Research on works of art in museums' collections.
**Ind/Abst** Avery Index Archit. Period. Suppl. Colum. Univ. (19??-199?); BHA : Biblio. Hist. Art.

NE/0165-9510
**BULLETIN VAN HET RYKSMUSEUM.** (BULLETIN VAN HET RIJKSMUSEUM.). [Bull. Ryksmus.]. **Main/Corp** Rijksmuseum (Netherlands). (1953)-. Bulletin. Dutch (summaries and/or abstracts in English). qt. Fl32.25 Netherlands; Fl41.50 other. Rijksmuseum, PB 50673, Amsterdam Netherlands. **ED** W Halsema Kubes and J F Heisbroek. **LC** N2460; .A3. **Bk Rev. Circ:** 4,000.
**Desc:** Articles on objects the museum owns: paintings, sculpture, applied arts, graphic arts and also articles on objects illustrating the history of the Netherlands.
**Ind/Abst** Art Index; ARTbibliogr. Mod.; Avery Index Archit. Period. Suppl. Colum. Univ. (19??-199?); BHA : Biblio. Hist. Art.

US/0363-3519
**BULLETIN - VIRGINIA MUSEUM OF FINE ARTS.** (BULLETIN / VIRGINIA MUSEUM OF FINE ARTS.). [Bull. - Va. Mus. Fine Arts]. **Main/Corp** Virginia Museum of Fine Arts. **VFOAT** Virginia Museum Bulletin; Virginia Museum of Fine Arts Bulletin. Vol. 46, No. 1 (Sept./Oct. 1985)-. Bulletin. English. Six times a year. $5.00 US and Canada; $6.00 other. Virginia Museum of Fine Arts, 2800 Grove Avenue, Richmond VA 23221-2466. **Tel** (804)367-0589, FAX (804)367-9393. **ED** Jill Melichar, (804)367-1659. **LC** N716.V45; A18. **DD** 708. **Circ:** 16,000 (ctrl). ***Continues*** *Virginia Museum of Fine Arts. Virginia Museum Bulletin.*
**Desc:** News of current and upcoming events, exhibitions and other special programs of the Virginia museum and its 27 affiliate arts organizations throughout Virginia.
**Ind/Abst** ARTbibliogr. Mod.

●UK
**BULLETIN / WAMP, WEST AFRICAN MUSEUMS PROGRAMME.** **Added/Corp** West African Museums Programme. International African Institute. **VFOAT** West African Museums Programme bulletin; WAMP Bulletin; Bulletin du WAMP. (1993)-. English (French). International African Institute, 210 High Holborn, London WC1V 7BW England. **LC** WMLC 91/5956. ***Continues*** *Bulletin (West African Museums Project, Dakar).*

UK
**BULLETIN / WEST AFRICAN MUSEUMS PROJECT, DAKAR.** ***Title Change.*** **Added/Corp** West African Museums Project, Dakar. International African Institute. **VFOAT** Bulletin du WAMP; WAMP Bulletin. No. 1 (1990)-(1992). Bulletin. English (French). International African Institute, 210 High Holborn, London WC1V 7BW England. **LC** WMLC 91/5956. ***Continued by*** *Bulletin (West African Museums Programme).*
**Ind/Abst** Museum Abstr. (?-?).

JA
**BUNKAZAI NO HOZON.** **See** History(General)-History of Asia.

NO/0084-8212
**BY OG BYGD.** [By bygd]. **Added/Corp** Norsk Folkemuseum. Norsk Folkemuseum. Arsmelding. (1943)-. Periodical. Norwegian. **LC** AM101; .O614. **DD** 069.
**Ind/Abst** Am. Hist. Life (1962-); Anthropol. Index; BHA : Biblio. Hist. Art.

BE/0776-1317
**CAHIERS DE MARIEMONT, LES.** (1970)-. Bulletin. French. an. 200F. Musee Royal de Mariemont, B 7140 Morlanwelz-Mariemont, Belgium. **Tel** 011 32 64212193, FAX 011 32 64262924. **UDC** 069.41. **CODEN** 069.7.
**Desc:** Bulletin of the Royal Museum of Mariemont.
**Ind/Abst** BHA : Biblio. Hist. Art.

CN/0701-0281
**CAIRN, THE.** **Added/Corp** Peter Whyte Foundation. (Fall 1976)-. Periodical. English. Three times a year. Membership: 50.00Can$ (supporting), 100.00Can$ (associate). Whyte Museum of the Canadian Rockies, PO Box 160, Banff Alberta T0L 0C0 Canada. **Tel** (403)762-2291, FAX (403)762-8919. **ED** Patricia Lee. **DD** 708/.1123/3. **Circ:** 3,000 (ctrl).
**Desc:** Museum members information, acquisitions, and gallery shows; all aspects of the museum and museums work.

US/0890-8850
**CALENDAR / UNIVERSITY ART MUSEUM BERKELEY.** [Calendar - Univ. Calif. Berkeley, Univ. Art Mus.]. **Main/Corp** University of California, Berkeley. University Art Museum. **VFOAT** University Art Museum Berkeley; University Art Museum Calendar. Began in 1978?. Periodical. English. mo. $10.00. University Art Museum, 2625 Durant Avenue, Berkeley CA 94720. **Tel** (510)642-1207. **ED** Ronald Egherman and Barbara Berman Webb. **DD** 700. **Circ:** 35,000.
**Desc:** Exhibition listings for the University Art Museum, Berkeley, both art exhibits and films.

US
**CAM NEWSLETTER.** Newsletter. English. Four times a year. $15.00. California Association of Museums, 900 Exposition Boulevard, Los Angeles CA 90007. **Tel** (213)744-3343.

XR/0521-2359
**CASOPIS MORAVSKEHO MUZEA. VEDY PRIRODNI.** (CASOPIS MORAVSKEHO MUSEA V BRNE. 1, VEDY PRIRODNI.). [Cas. Morav. muz. Vedy prir.]. **Added/Corp** Moravske Muzeum V Brne. **VFOAT** Acta Musei Moraviae; Vedy Prirodni. (1951)-. Czech (summaries and/or abstracts in English, German and Russian). an. $29.40. **(Subscription address:** Artia Pegas Press Ltd., Palac Metro Narodni Trida 25, 11210 Prague 1 Czech Republic.**)** **DD** 500. **CODEN** CAMMAI. ***Continues*** *Casopis Moravskeho Musea V Brne. 1, Prirodoveda;* ***Absorbed*** *Folia Mendeliana, 0085-0748.*
**Ind/Abst** GeoRef.

XR/0323-0678
**CASOPIS SLEZSKEHO MUZEA. SERIE B, VEDY HISTORIKE.** **VFOAT** Acta Musei Silesiae. Serie B, Vedy Historicke; Vedy Historicke. 13, 1-. Periodical. Czech (summaries and/or abstracts in German and Russian). Three times a year. **(Subscription address:** Artia Pegas Press Ltd., Palac Metro Narodni Trida 25, 11210 Prague 1 Czech Republic.**)** **LC** AM101; .O493. ***Continues*** *Casopis Slezskeho Musea. Vedy Historicke.*
**Ind/Abst** BHA : Biblio. Hist. Art.

RM
**CERCETARI DE CONSERVARE SI RESTAURARE A PATRIMONIULUI MUZEAL / MUZEUL NATIONAL DE ISTORIE.** **Added/Corp** Muzeul de Istorie al Republicii Socialiste Romania. (1981)-. Periodical. Romanian (summaries and/or abstracts in French). Editura Academia Republicii Socialiste Romania, Calea Victoriei Nr 125, R-79717 Bucuresti Romania. **Tel** telex 10376 PRSFI R. **LC** AM141; .C47.

RM
**CERCETARI ISTORICE / MUZEUL DE ISTORIE A MOLDOVEI.** **See** History(General)-History of Europe.

US/1046-6185
**CHICAGO GALLERY NEWS.** [Chic. gallery news]. (198?)-. Periodical. English. Three times a year (Jan., Apr., and Sept.). $10.00. Chicago Gallery News, 107-A West Deleware Place, Chicago IL 60610. **Tel** (312)649-0064, FAX (312)649-0255. **ED** Natalie von Straaton. **DD** 708. Index available. **Ad Acc. Circ:** 14,000.
**Desc:** Guide to Chicago Art Galleries and art-related services.

US/0270-7926
**CHRYSLER MUSEUM, THE.** **Main/Corp** Chrysler Museum. Vol. 8, No. 10 (Nov. 1979)-. Periodical. English. mo. Chrysler Museum, Olney Road and Mowbray Arch, Norfolk VA 23510. **Tel** (804)622-1211. **ED** Robin Maurice. **LC** N626.5; .A2. **DD** 708.155/521. ***Continues*** *Chrysler Museum at Norfolk.*

CN/1189-461X
**CIMI NEWS.** (CIMI NEWS / COMPUTER INTERCHANGE OF MUSEUM INFORMATION COMMITTEE.). [CIMI news]. **Added/Corp** Computer Interchange of Museum Information Committee. **VFOAT** Computer Interchange of Museum Information News;

Computer Interchange of Museum Information Committee News. No. 1 (Jan. 1991)-. Periodical. English. sa.
**Ind/Abst** Museum Abstr.

CK
**CLAROSCURO. Added/Corp** Museo de Antioquia. Oficina de Publicaciones. (19??)-. Periodical. Spanish. Oficina de Comunicaciones, Museo de Antioquia, A Aereo 51698, Medel Colombia.

CN
**COLLAGE. Added/Corp** Musee des Beaux-Arts de Montreal. (Nov. 1976)-. Periodical. English (French). bm (6 issues). Free to members of the Montreal Museum of Fine Arts. Montreal Museum of Fine Arts, 1379 Sherbrooke Street West, Montreal 109 Quebec Canada. **Tel** (514)285-1600. **DD** 708.11/4281/05.

US/1046-2252
**COLLECTIONS (COLUMBIA, S.C.).** (COLLECTIONS : THE MAGAZINE OF THE COLUMBIA MUSEUM OF ART AND THE GIBBES PLANETARIUM.). [Collections]. **Added/Corp** Columbia Museum of Art and the Gibbes Planetarium. Vol. 1, No. 1 (Fall 1988)-. Periodical. English. qt. Columbia Museum of Art, 1112 Bull Street, Columbia SC 29201. **Tel** (803)799-2810, FAX (803)343-2150. **ED** Salvatore G Ciella. **DD** 708. **Bk Rev. Ad Acc. Pr Rev. Circ:** 3,500 (ctrl). ***Continues** Columbia Museum of Art Magazine.*
**Desc:** Feature articles on conservation, artists and art media.
**Ind/Abst** BHA : Biblio. Hist. Art.

US/0093-1047
**COLLECTORS' AUCTION (BALTIMORE).** (COLLECTORS' AUCTION.). **Main/Corp** Harris Auction Galleries. English. ir. $25.00. Harris Auction Galleries, 873-875 North Howard Street, Baltimore MD 21201. **Tel** (410)728-7040. **ED** Christopher Bready. **LC** Z999; .H322A. **DD** 016.9173/03. **Circ:** 1,000 (ctrl).
**Desc:** Listings include 19th and 20th century photographica, rare books, fine art, graphics and Civil War material.

UY/0077-1244
**COMUNICACIONES ANTROPOLOGICAS DEL MUSEO DE HISTORIA NATURAL DE MONTEVIDEO. Main/Corp** Museo de Historia Natural (Uruguay). No. 1-1956-. Spanish. Museo de Historia Natural, Casilla de Correo 399, 11000 Montevideo Uruguay. **Tel** 011 598 2 960908. **LC** WMLC L 83/771.

PO/0871-178X
**COMUNICACOES DO INSTITUTO DE INVESTIGACAO CIENTIFICA TROPICAL, SERIE DE CIENCIAS ETNOLOGICAS E ETNOMUSEOLOGICAS. See** Ethnic Interests.

US
**CONSERVATION ASSESSMENT PROGRAM, GRANT APPLICATION AND INFORMATION. Added/Corp** Institute of Museum Services. **VFOAT** IMS Conservation Assessment Program. (1991)-. English.

UK/0953-8674
**CONSERVATION BULLETIN.** [Conserv. bull.]. (1987)-. Periodical. English. tq.
**Ind/Abst** Museum Abstr.

UK/0309-2224
**CONSERVATION NEWS (LONDON).** (CONSERVATION NEWS.). [Conserv. news]. **Main/Corp** United Kingdom Institute for Conservation of Historic and Artistic Works. No. 10 (Nov. 1979)-. English. Three times a year. Free to members of the UK Institute for Conservation. UK Institute for Conservation / Westminster, Bridge Road, 6 Whitehorse Mews, London SE1 7QD England. **Tel** 011 44 71 6203371. ***Continues** International Institute for Conservation of Historic and Artistic Works. United Kingdom Group. Conservation News.*
**Ind/Abst** Museum Abstr.

FR/1157-688X
**CONSERVATION RESTAURATION DES BIENS CULTURELS PARIS. See** The Arts-Art.

US/1059-8472
**CORCORAN (WASHINGTON, D.C.). See** The Arts-Art.

IT
**CORPUS VASORUM ANTIQUORUM. ITALIA. Added/Corp** International Union of Academies. Vol. 1 (1925)-. Monographic series. Latin. ir. Price varies per volume. L'Erma di Bretschneider SPA, Via Cassiodoro 19, 00193 Rome Italy. **Tel** 011 39 6 6874127, 011 39 6 6874129, FAX 011 39 6 6874129. **LC** NK4640.C6; I7. **Circ:** 600.
**Desc:** This publication is a corpus of all existing vases in different museums of Italy.

US/0011-3069
**CURATOR (NEW YORK, N.Y.).** (CURATOR.). [Curator]. **Added/Corp** American Museum of Natural History. Vol. 1 (Jan. 1958)-. Periodical. English. qt. $55.00 institution, $30.00 individual. American Museum Natural History, Central Park West at 79th Street, New York NY 10024. **Tel** (212)769-5530, (800)234-5252. **(Subscription address:** Curator Subscriptions, PO Box 3000, Department HHH, Denville NJ 07834.**) ED** T. D. Nicholson. **LC** QH70; .C8. **DD** 574.074. **CODEN** CRTRAH. Index available (bound in last issue). **Pr Rev. Circ:** 1,200. available on microfilm and microfiche from University Microfilms International (UMI). Documents available from BIOSIS Document Express. ***Continued in part by** Recent Publications in Natural History, 0738-0925.*
**Desc:** Provides a forum for curators, conservators, exhibitors and educators from institutions around the world. Its authoritative articles and reviews are written by museum professionals for museum professionals.
**Ind/Abst** Am. Hist. Life (1963-1982, 1985-); Art Archaeol. Tech. Abstr.; Art Index; Biodeter. Abstr.; Biol. Abstr.; Br. Archaeol. Bibliogr. (?-?); GeoRef; Museum Abstr.

CN/0384-9627
**CURRENTLY (TORONTO).** (CURRENTLY.). Vol. 1 (Sept. 1977)-. Periodical. English. bm. 20.00Can$. Ontario Museum Association, George Brown House, 50 Baldwin Street, Toronto Ontario M5T 1L4 Canada. **Tel** (416)367-3677. **ED** Jan Schroer. **DD** 069/.09713. **Bk Rev. Ad Acc. Circ:** 800. available on microfilm from Micromedia Limited.
**Desc:** Newspaper in tabloid-format about museums and museum workers in Ontario and feature articles and current issues.
**Ind/Abst** Museum Abstr.

CN/0703-6507
**DAWSON AND HIND.** [Dawson Hind]. **Added/Corp** Association of Manitoba Museums. Manitoba Museum of Man and Nature. Museums Advisory Service. Vol. 5 (Winter 1975)-. Periodical. English. Three times a year. Free to members of the Association of Manitoba Museums. Association of Manitoba Museums, 422-167 Lombard Avenue, Winnipeg Manitoba R3B 0T6 Canada. **Tel** (204)947-1782. **ED** Marilyn de von Flindt. **DD** 069/.097127. Index available. cum. index. **Bk Rev. Circ:** 300 (ctrl). ***Continues** Grande New Dawson & Hind Quarterly Epistle, 0703-6515.*
**Desc:** Summary of articles, propaganda written by the editor.
**Ind/Abst** Art Archaeol. Tech. Abstr.

HU/0418-4513
**DEBRECENI DERI MUZEUM EVKONYVE, A. Added/Corp** Deri Muzeum. **VFOAT** Annales Musei Debreceniensis de Friderico Deri Nominati. (1???)-. Hungarian (English, German and Hungarian). an. **LC** AM101; .D382.
**Ind/Abst** BHA : Biblio. Hist. Art.

CN/0714-2188
**DIRECTORY OF CANADIAN MUSEUMS AND RELATED INSTITUTIONS.** [Dir. Can. mus. relat. inst.]. **VFOAT** Repertoire des Musees Canadiens et Institutions Connexes. **VAT** Directory of Canadian Museums (1978); Repertoire des Musees Canadiens (1978). 1978-. Directory. French (English). $30.00 per volume. Capital Library Wholesale, 1427 Ogilvie Road, Ottawa Ontario K1J 8M7 Canada. **DD** 069/.025/71. ***Continues** Directory of Canadian Museums, 0714-2161.*

US/1048-3438
**DIRECTORY OF GALLERIES FOR THE FINE ARTIST.** [Dir. galleries fine artist]. **VFOAT** Galleries for the Fine Artist. 1st Ed. (1990)-. Directory. English. $39.95. ArtNetwork, PO Box 369, Renaissance CA 95962. **Tel** (916)692-1355, FAX (916)692-1370. **ED** Constance Franklin. **LC** N510; .D58. **DD** 380.1/457/025.
**Desc:** Designed to be a working reference source for artists wishing to expand their sales and contacts in the art world, both nationally and regionally.

US/1045-456X
**DIRECTORY OF HISTORICAL ORGANIZATIONS IN THE UNITED STATES AND CANADA.** [Dir. hist. organ. U. S. Can.]. **Added/Corp** American Association for State and Local History. **VFOAT** Historical Organizations in the United States and Canada. 14th Ed. (1990)-. Directory. English. be. $79.95 per volume. American Association for State and Local History, 530 Church Street, Suite 600, Nashville TN 37219. **Tel** (615)255-2971, FAX (615)255-2979. **LC** E172; .D5. **DD** 973/.025. **NLM** E 172; D597. ***Continues** Directory, Historical Agencies in North America.*

CN
**DIRECTORY OF ONTARIO MUSEUMS. Added/Corp** Ontario Museum Association. (1982)-. English. Ontario Museum Association, George Brown House, 50 Baldwin Street, Toronto Ontario M5T 1L4 Canada. **Tel** (416)367-3677. **LC** AM21.O6; D57. **DD** 069/.025/713. ***Continues** Directory of Ontario Museums and Related Institutions.*

US/0012-3625
**DISCOVERY (NEW HAVEN, CONN.).** (DISCOVERY.). [Discovery]. **Added/Corp** Peabody Museum of Natural History. Vol. 1 (Fall 1965)-. Periodical. English. sa. $12.00 US; $16.00 (surface mail), $30.00 (air mail) other. Peabody Museum of Natural History, Yale University, 170 Whitney Avenue, PO Box 666, New Haven CT 06511-8161. **Tel** (203)432-3786, FAX (203)432-9816. **ED** Zelda Edelson. **LC** QH1; .D5. **DD** 574. **CODEN** DISCAH. **Circ:** 1,000 (ctrl). Documents available from BIOSIS Document Express.
**Desc:** Magazine of the Yale Peabody Museum. Features authoritative, and well-illustrated articles for the general reader on dinosaurs, human origins, raccoons and other scientific subjects.
**Ind/Abst** Biol. Abstr. (-1988); Biol. Dig.; Can. Index (?-?); Fish Rev. (Jan. 1989-July 1992); GeoRef; Wildl. Rev. (Jan. 1989-July 1992).

CN/0822-5796
**DISCOVERY (VICTORIA).** (DISCOVERY : FRIENDS OF THE BRITISH COLUMBIA PROVINCIAL MUSEUM QUARTERLY REVIEW.). [Discovery]. **VFOAT** Friends of the British Columbia Provincial Museum Quarterly Review. Periodical. English. qt. Free to members, membership 15.00Can$ per year. Friends of the British Columbia Provincial Museum, 675 Belleville Street, Victoria British Columbia V8V 1X4 Canada. **Tel** (604)388-7355, FAX (604)388-9348, telex 049-7347 VIC. **ED** Kay Lines. **DD** 069/.09711. **Bk Rev. Circ:** 5,000. ***Continues** Newsletter (Friends of the British Columbia Provincial Museum).*
**Desc:** Mainly British Columbia research in museum disciplines.

GW/0933-0321
**DOKUMENTATIONEN DES STADTARCHIVS NEUSS. Added/Corp** Stadtarchiv Neuss. 1988-. Monographic series. German. Price varies per volume.

FJ
**DOMODOMO : FIJI MUSEUM QUARTERLY. *Suspended.*** 1 (Mar. 1983)-Suspended (1987). Periodical. English. qt. $10.00 US. Fiji Museum, PO Box 2023, Suva Fiji Islands. **Tel** 011 679 315043, 011 679 315944. **ED** Fergus Clunie. **Ad Acc. Circ:** 1,000 (ctrl).
**Desc:** Factual, well-illustrated articles on Fijian history, culture and natural history.
**Ind/Abst** Anthropol. Lit.

US/0273-5717
**ENCOUNTERS (ST. PAUL, MINN.).** ***Ceased.* See** Science and Technology.

GW
**ERWERBUNGEN, GESCHENKE UND LEIHGABEN. Main/Corp** Germanisches Nationalmuseum Nurnberg. German. an. Germanisches Nationalmuseum, Postfach 9580, Kartausergasse 1, 8500 Nuernberg 1 Germany. **Tel** 0911/203971. **LC** N2350; .A36.

CN
**ESTIMATES. PART III, NATIONAL MUSEUMS OF CANADA. Main/Corp** Canada. **VFOAT** Budget des Depenses. Partie III, Musees Nationaux du Canada. (19??)-. English (French). $9.00 Canada; $10.80 other. Canada Communication Group Publishers, Order Processing, Ottawa Ontario K1A 0S9 Canada. **Tel** (819)956-4800, (819)956-4802. **LC** AM122; .C36a. **DD** 069/.9971.

FR/0248-3351
**ETUDES DE LA REVUE DU LOUVRE ET DES MUSEES DE FRANCE.** (1980)-. Monographic series. French. Price varies per volume. **UDC** 73. **CODEN** 75.
**Ind/Abst** BHA : Biblio. Hist. Art.

US/0889-8197
**EXPLORATORIUM QUARTERLY. *Title Change.* Added/Corp** Exploratorium (Organization). Vol. 10, Issue 1 (Spring 1986)-(1993). Periodical. English. Four times a year (Jan., Apr., July, Oct.). Explorator Magazine, 3601 Lyon Street, San Francisco CA 94123. **Tel** (415)561-0393 or 561-0390. **ED** Pat Murphy. **DD** 069. cum. index. **Circ:** 15,000. ***Continues** Exploratorium. **Continued by** Exploring Magazine.*
**Desc:** An educational extension of the museum, communicating ideas that exhibits can't readily demonstrate. Each issue concentrates on a different subject, examining it from a variety of viewpoints.

●US
**EXPLORING MAGAZINE.** (1993)-. English. Four times a year (Jan., Apr., July, Oct.). $18.00 (individuals); $24.00 (institutions). Explorator Magazine, 3601 Lyon Street, San Francisco CA 94123. **Tel** (415)561-0393 or 561-0390.

IT
**EXPORRE.** Italian (English). Four times a year. L20000.00 Italy; L32000.00 other. Lybra Immagine, P Za Virgilio 4, 20123 Milan Italy. **Tel** 011 39 2 48000818, FAX 011 39 2 48012748. **Circ:** 10,000.

MY/0126-561X
**FEDERATION MUSEUMS JOURNAL.** [Fed. mus. j.]. **Added/Corp** Malaya (Federation) Museums Dept. Malaysia. Jabatan Muzium. Muzium

# Museums and Galleries

Negara (Malaysia). V. 1/2 (1954/1955)-. Periodical. English. an. Jabatan Muzium, Kenua Kerani Ketua Pengagarah, Kuala Lumpur Malaysia. **LC** AM101; .M2444. *Supersedes Journal of the Federated Malay States Museums.*

CN/0384-7225
**FELLOWS LECTURE. VFOAT** Conference des Fellows. 1976-. English (French). an. \$9.00 (each audiocassette). Canadian Museums Association, 280 Metcalfe Street, Suite 400, Ottawa Ontario K2P 1R7 Canada. **Tel** (613)567-0099, FAX (613)233-5438. **DD** 069/.0971.

US
**FINGER PRINTS. See** Children and Youth Interests.

GW/0067-6004
**FORSCHUNGEN UND BERICHTE - STAATLICHE MUSEEN BERLIN.** (FORSCHUNGEN UND BERICHTE.). [Forsch. Ber. - Staatl. Mus. Berl.]. **Main/Corp** Staatliche Museen Zu Berlin (Germany : East). Vol. 1 (1957)-. Monographic series. German. ir. Price varies per volume. Deutscher Kunstverlag, Postfach 190354, D 80603 Munich Germany. **Tel** 011 49 89 1215160. **(Subscription address:** Deutscher Kunstverlag Kno, PF 800620, Koch Neff & Oetinger, D 70506 Stuttgart Germany) **LC** AM101; .B389. cum. index.
**Desc:** Covers the care and preservation of monuments.
**Ind/Abst** Art Archaeol. Tech. Abstr.; BHA : Biblio. Hist. Art; Numis. Lit.

IT/0393-0041
**FORUM IULII. See** Archaeology.

DK/0107-4849
**FRA BORNHOLMS MUSEUM. Added/Corp** Bornholms Museum. (19??)-. Danish. an.
**Ind/Abst** BHA : Biblio. Hist. Art.

US
**FRIENDS' QUARTERLY.** English. qt. free to members and libraries (families), \$10.00 (students). Museum at Lower Shaker Village, 2 LSV, Enfield NH 03748. **Tel** (603)632-4346. **ED** Carolyn Smith and Elaine Loft. **Circ:** 600 (ctrl).
**Desc:** Contains articles of historical interest and information pertaining to museum activities.

JA
**GAKUSO - KYOTO KOKURITSU HAKUBUTSUKAN. Main/Corp** Kyoto Kokuritsu Hakubutsukan. (GAKUSO.). [Kyoto National Museum Bulletin. 1st Ed.- 1979-. Japanese (summaries and/or abstracts in English). Kyoto Kokuritsu Hakubutsukan, 527 Chayacho, Higashiyama-ku, Kyoto Japan. **LC** AM101.K946; A2.

UK/0265-7511
**GALLERIES.** [Galleries]. (1983)-. Periodical. English. Twelve times a year. Barrington Publications, 54 Uxbridge Road, London W12 8LP England. **Tel** 011 44 1 740 7020. **ED** Andrew J. Aitken. **DD** 708.009421. **Bk Rev. Ad Acc. Circ:** 18,000 (ctrl).

US/0739-0475
**GALLERIES (WASHINGTON, D.C.).** (GALLERIES.). Vol. 1, No. 1 (Apr. 1974)-. Periodical. English. Ten times a year. \$16.00. Galleries, PO Box 3705, Washington DC 20007. **Tel** (202)667-1966. **ED** Reid Baro. **Ad Acc. Circ:** 6,000 (ctrl).
**Desc:** A listing of art exhibits showing in the approximately 160 private and public art galleries in the Washington D.C. and Baltimore area.

UK
**GENERAL CATALOGUE OF PRINTED BOOKS / BRITISH MUSEUM. Main/Corp** British Museum. Dept. of Printed Books. (1959)-. English. ir. British Museum Publications, 6 Bedford Square, London WC1B 3RA England. **Tel** 011 44 71 2321234.

UK/0144-5294
**GEOLOGICAL CURATOR / GCG, THE. Added/Corp** Geological Curators' Group. Vol. 2, No. 8 (Sec. Issue 1980)-. Periodical. English. Three times a year Tri-quarterly. £7.00 (individual), £10.00 (institution) UK; £10.00 (individual), £12.00 (institution) other. Geological Curators Group, Department of Archaeology, University of Newcastle U.T., Newcastle U. T. NE1 7RU England. **Tel** 011 44 222 397951 Ext 265. **Continues** *Newsletter of the Geological Curators Group.*
**Ind/Abst** Museum Abstr.

GW/0178-9775
**GESAMTKATALOG DER DUSSELDORFER KULTURINSTITUTE (GDK) [MICROFORM] / BIBLIOTHEKSSTELLE DER DUSSELDORFER KULTURINSTITUTE.** See The Arts-Art.

US/0730-5036
**GILCREASE MAGAZINE OF AMERICAN HISTORY AND ART, THE. Title Change.** (THE GILCREASE MAGAZINE OF AMERICAN HISTORY AND ART / [PRODUCED BY THE THOMAS GILCREASE MUSEUM ASSOCIATION FOR THE SUPPORT OF THE THOMAS GILCREASE INSTITUTE OF AMERICAN HISTORY AND ART].). [Gilcrease mag. Am. hist. art].
**Added/Corp** Thomas Gilcrease Museum Association. Thomas Gilcrease Institute of American History and Art. (1979)-Vol. 14, No. 2 (Fall 1992). Periodical. English. qt. Thomas Gilcrease Museum Association, 1400 Gilcrease Museum Road, Tulsa OK 74127. **Tel** (918)596-2700, FAX (918)592-2248. **ED** Paula Hall. **LC** E151; .G54. **DD** 704.9/49978. **Bk Rev. Circ:** 4,300 (ctrl). **Continues** *American Scene, 0003-0929.* **Continued by** *Gilcrease Journal, 1070-7808.*
**Desc:** Articles on art, American history and the anthropology of the New World as related to paintings, sculpture, books, documents and artifacts in the Gilcrease collection.
**Ind/Abst** Am. Hist. Life.

CN/0710-3697
**GLENBOW (EXHIBITIONS AND EVENTS).** (GLENBOW.). [Glenbow]. **Main/Corp** Glenbow Museum. **Added/Corp** Glenbow-Alberta Institute. (March/April 1981)-. Periodical. English. qt (Mar., June, Sept., Dec.). 15.00Can\$ Canada except Calgary; 21.40Can\$ other (Calagary residents must order membership). Glenbow, 130-9th Avenue Southeast, Calgary Alberta T2G 0P3 Canada. **Tel** (403)268-4100, FAX (403)265-9769. **ED** Donna Livingstone. **DD** 708.11/233. **Ad Acc. Pr Rev. Circ:** 8,000 (ctrl).
**Desc:** Calendar listing of museum exhibitions and events; features on western art and history.

YU/0436-1105
**GODISNJAK GRADA BEOGRADA. Added/Corp** Belgrad. Musej Grada. **VFOAT** Annuaire de la Ville de Beograd; Annuaire du Musee de la Ville de Beograd. (1954)-. Serbian (Serbo-Croatian (Cyrillic); summaries and/or abstracts in French and English). an.
**Ind/Abst** BHA : Biblio. Hist. Art.

US
**GRANTS / ARKANSAS MUSEUM SERVICES. Main/Corp** Arkansas Museum Services. 1983/1985-. English. Arkansas Museum Services, Department of Parks & Tourism, One Capital Mall, Little Rock AR 72201. **LC** AM122; .A75A. **DD** 069/.068/1. **Continues** *Arkansas Museum Services. Grants-in-Aid.*

JA
**GUMMA KENRITSU HAKUBUTSUKAN HO. Main/Corp** Gumma Kenritsu Hakubutsukan. Japanese. Gumma Kenritsu Hakubutsukan, 1353 Ichinomiya 370-24, Tomioka Japan. **LC** AM101.T594; A2.

US
**HAGLEY MUSEUM AND LIBRARY NEWSLETTER. VFOAT** Newsletter. Vol. 13, No. 1 (Spring 1984)-. Newsletter. English. qt. Free on request. Eleutherian Mills Hagley Foundation, Box 3630 Greenville, Wilmington DE 19807. **Tel** (302)658-2400. **Continues** *Newsletter / Eleutherian Mills-Hagley Foundation.*
**Desc:** Contains information regarding Hagley Museum and Library.

JA
**HAKUBUTSUKAN KENKYU. VFOAT** Museum Studies. Japanese (Japanese). \$120.00. Nihon Hakubutsukan Kyokai, Shoyu-Kaikan 3-3-1, Kasumigaseki Chiyoda-ku, Tokyo 100 Japan. **Tel** 03 3591 7190. **LC** AM77.A1; H653.

JA
**HAKUBUTSUKAN NYUSU. Added/Corp** Nihon Hakubutsukan Kyokai. (1966)-. Periodical. Japanese. mo. ¥150. Nihon Hakubutsukan Kyokai, Shoyu-Kaikan 3-3-1, Kasumigaseki Chiyoda-ku, Tokyo 100 Japan. **Tel** 03 3591 7190. **LC** AM77.A1; H67.

US
**HAND TO HAND.** English. qt. \$75.00 (individuals), \$100.00 (museum associates), \$150.00 (full membership with budgets over \$500000.00), \$300.00 (museum sponser). Association of Youth Museums, 70 P Street, Salt Lake City UT 84103. **Tel** (801)359-4350.

CN/0068-1628
**HANDBOOK - BRITISH COLUMBIA PROVINCIAL MUSEUM.** [Handb. - B.C. Prov. Mus.]. **Added/Corp** British Columbia Provincial Museum. No. 1 (1942)-. Monographic series. English. ir. Price varies per volume. Minister of Finance / Victoria British Columbia, 543 Superior Street, Victoria British Columbia V8V 1X4 Canada. **Tel** (604)387-1502.

US/0445-3387
**HANDBOOK OF COLLECTIONS. Main/Corp** Illinois State Museum. No. 1-. Monographic series. English. ir. Price varies per volume. Illinois State Museum, Spring and Edwards Street, Springfield IL 62706. **Tel** (217)782-7386, FAX (217)782-1254. **LC** AM101; .I373. **DD** 069/.09773/56.
**Desc:** Descriptive accounts based on museum collections.

●US/1065-819X
**HARVARD UNIVERSITY ART MUSEUMS REVIEW.** [Harv. Univ. Art Mus. rev.]. **Main/Corp** Harvard University. Art Museums. **VFOAT** A.Review. Vol. 1, No. 1 (Winter 1992)-. Periodical. English. Twice a year. free. Fogg Art Museum, Harvard University, Cambridge MA 02138. **Tel** (617)495-9400, FAX (617)495-9936. **ED** Evelyn Rosenthal. **LC** N526; .H37c. **DD** 708.144/4/05. **Circ:** 5,000. **Continues** *News From the Harvard University Art Museums, 1046-350X.*

JA
**HEIAN HAKUBUTSUKAN KENKYU KIYO. Main/Corp** Heian Hakubutsukan. **VFOAT** Proceedings of the Heian Museum of Ancient History. Japanese (summaries and/or abstracts in English). ¥2000. Sanjo Oji Kita - Takakura, Koji Nishi Chukyo-ku Japan. **LC** DS822; .H43A.

SI
**HERITAGE. Added/Corp** Singapore (City). National Museum. No. 1 (1977)-. Periodical. English. an. National Museum / Singapore, Stamford Road, Singapore 0617 Republic of Singapore. **ED** Lee Chor Lin. **LC** AM1; .H47. **DD** 069/.7/095957. **Circ:** 1,000.
**Desc:** Devoted to studies on the history and culture of Singapore and its surrounding area, in particular, as reflected through the collections of the National Museum.

CN/0841-923X
**HERITAGE HEARTH.** (THE HERITAGE HEARTH : THE NEWSLETTER OF HALTON REGION MUSEUM.). [Herit. hearth]. **Added/Corp** Halton Region Museum. (1984)-. Periodical. English. tq. 5.00Can\$ (one year), 8.00Can\$ (two year). Halton Region Museum, RR #3 Keldo Conservation Area, Milton, Ontario L9T 2X7 Canada. **Tel** (905)875-2200, FAX (905)876-4322. **ED** Linda Twitchell. **DD** 069/.99713/533. **Ad Acc. Circ:** 4,000 (ctrl).

CN/0847-0146
**HERITAGE INSTITUTIONS.** (HERITAGE INSTITUTIONS / STATISTICS CANADA, EDUCATION, CULTURE AND TOURISM DIVISION / LES ETABLISSEMENTS DU PATRIMOINE / STATISTIQUE CANADA, DIVISION DE L'EDUCATION, DE LA CULTURE ET DU TOURISME.). [Herit. inst.]. **Added/Corp** Statistics Canada. Education, Culture and Tourism Division. **VFOAT** Etablissements du Patrimoine; Statistiques de la Culture, les Etablissements du Patrimoine, Statistiques pr,eliminaires; Culture Statistics, Heritage Institutions, Preliminary Statistics. (1985/1986)-. English (French). an. 30.00Can\$ Canada; \$36.00 US; \$42.00 other. Statistics Canada, Publications Sales & Services, Main Building Room 1710, Ottawa Ontario K1A 0T6 Canada. **Tel** (613)951-5078, (800)267-6677, FAX (613)951-1584, telex 053-3585. **LC** AM21.A1; C85. **DD** 069/.0971. **Continues** *Culture Statistics, Heritage Institutions, Museums, Parks, Historic Sites, Archives, Other Related Institutions (e.g. zoos, botanical gardens, exhibition centres-- )., 0833-0344.*
**Desc:** This publication presents survey data highlights and statistical tabulations on non-profit heritage institutions.

HU/0544-4225
**HERMAN OTTO MUZEUM EVKONYVE, A.** [Herman Otto Muz. evkv.]. **VFOAT** Annales de Musee Herman Otto, Miskolc; Annales Musei Miskolciensis de Herman Otto Nominati; Annaly Muzea im. Otto Hermana, Miskol'c; Jahrbuch des Herman Otto Museums, Miskolc; Miskolci Herman Otto Muzeum Evkonyve; Yearbook of the Herman Otto Museum, Miskolc. (1957)-. Multiple languages. ir. **UDC** 069.
**Ind/Abst** BHA : Biblio. Hist. Art.

US/0737-5867
**HIGH TIDINGS.** (HIGH TIDINGS / THE CAPE COD MUSEUM OF NATURAL HISTORY.). **Added/Corp** Cape Cod Museum of Natural History. Vol. 18, Issue 3 (July-Aug. 1983)-. Periodical. English. Six times a year. \$20.00. Cape Cod Museum of Natural History, Drawer R, Brewster MA 02631. **Tel** (508)896-3867. **ED** Kathleen Baker. **Circ:** 3,500 (ctrl). **Continues** *Newsletter (Cape Cod Museum of Natural History).*
**Desc:** Information on the internal workings of the museum.

CN/0711-7078
**HIGHLIGHTS OF THE COLLECTIONS / THE MONTREAL MUSEUM OF FINE ARTS.** [Highlights collect.]. Aug.14/Nov.14 1982-. Periodical. English. qt. Free. Montreal Museum of Fine Arts, 1379 Sherbrooke Street West, Montreal 109 Quebec Canada. **Tel** (514)285-1600. **DD** 069/.97/0009714281. ctrl circ.

SZ
**HISTORISCHES MUSEUM SCHLOSS THUN. See** History(General)-History of Europe.

JA
**HOKKAIDO KAITAKU KINENKAN CHOSA HOKOKU. See** History(General)-History of Asia.

## Museums and Galleries

CN/0823-2393
**HORIZONS (SAINT JOHN. 1982).**
(HORIZONS / ASSOCIATION MUSEUMS NEW BRUNSWICK / ASSOCIATION MUSEES NOUVEAU-BRUNSWICK.). [Horizons]. **Added/Corp** Association Museums New Brunswick. **VFOAT** Horizons. **VAT** Horizons (Saint-Jean, N.B. 1982). (July 1982)-. Periodical. English (French). be. Free to members, $15.00 (individuals), $25.00 (institutions) US. Association Museums of New Brunswick, 503 Queen Street, PO Box 4503, Fredericton New Brunswick E3B 1B8 Canada. **Tel** (506)452-2908. **ED** Charles Allain. **DD** 069/.09715. **Ad Acc. Circ:** 300. *Continues Alerte (Association Museums New Brunswick : 1981). English & French, 0711-5393. Continued in part by Horizons (Saint John, N.B.). French.*

US
**I A S M H F NEWSLETTER.** Newsletter. bm. $20.00 US and North America; $25.00 other. International Association of Sports Museums and Halls of Fame, 101 West Sutton Place, Wilmington DE 19810-4115. **Tel** (302)475-7068. **ED** Al Cartwright. **Ad Acc. Acid Free. Circ:** 200.
**Desc:** Coverage of membership activities.

FR/0018-8999
**I C O M NEWS.** [ICOM news]. **Main/Corp** International Council of Museums. **VFOAT** Nouvelles de l'I C O M. Vol. 1 (Oct. 1, 1948)-. Periodical. French (English and Spanish). Four times a year (Jan., Apr., July, Oct.). International Council of Museums, 1 rue Miollis, 75732 Paris Cedex 15 France. **Tel** 011 33 1 47 340500. **ED** Sabine de Valence. **Bk Rev. Ad Acc. Circ:** 10,000 (ctrl).
**Ind/Abst** Art Archaeol. Tech. Abstr.; Museum Abstr.

US/0883-1343
**ICMM NEWS.** (ICMM NEWS / INTERNATIONAL CONGRESS OF MARITIME MUSEUMS.). [ICMM news]. **Added/Corp** International Congress of Maritime Museums. **VAT** International Congress of Maritime Museums News. (19??)-. Periodical. English. Twice a year (Mar. & Aug.). $8.00. Vancouver Maritime Museum, 1905 Ogden Avenue, Vancouver British Columbia V6J 1A3 Canada. **Tel** (604)737-2211. **ED** Robin Inglis. **DD** 387. **Bk Rev. Circ:** 500 (ctrl).
**Desc:** News and opinions concerning maritime museums worldwide.

FR
**ICOM EDUCATION.** **Added/Corp** International Council of Museums. International Council of Museums. Committee for Education and Cultural Action. **VAT** I C O M Education. No. 7 (1975/1976)-. Periodical. English (French). International Council of Museums, 1 rue Miollis, 75732 Paris Cedex 15 France. **Tel** 011 33 1 47 340500. *Continues Museums' Annual.*
**Ind/Abst** Museum Abstr.

CN/0843-6657
**IICCG BULLETIN.** See The Arts.

IT
**ILLUSTRAZIONE ITALIANA (MILAN, ITALY : 1974).** (L'ILLUSTRAZIONE ITALIANA.). (1974)-. Periodical. Italian. Six times a year. Media Presse, Via Nino Bixio 30, 20129 Milan Italy. **Tel** 011 39 2 2043941. **LC** N6911; .I36. **DD** 708.5.

US/1043-3023
**ILVS REVIEW.** (ILVS REVIEW : SEMIANNUAL PUBLICATION OF THE INTERNATIONAL LABORATORY FOR VISITOR STUDIES.). [ILVS rev.]. **Added/Corp** University of Wisconsin--Milwaukee. International Laboratory for Visitor Studies. **VAT** International Laboratory for Visitor Studies Review. Vol. 1, No. 1 (Fall 1988)-. Periodical. English. sa. $49.50 (individual); $93.50 (library). Exhibit Communications Research Inc, PO Box 11827, Shorewood WI 53211. **Tel** (414)964-8217, FAX (414)964-7211. **ED** Chandler G. Screven (editor's address: 5617 South Dorchester, Unit 4N, Chicago, IL 60615; (312)752-5615). **LC** AM151; .I48. **DD** 069.5. **Ad Acc, Adv Mgr:** P. Hinske, **Tel** (414)238-1916. **Pr Rev. Circ:** 500.
**Desc:** A journal which includes the latest and most reliable information to date on visitor behavior.
**Ind/Abst** Leis. Recreat. Tour. Abstr.

US/1046-6614
**IMAGE FILE.** [Image file]. **Added/Corp** Curt Teich Postcard Collection (Lake County Museum). (1989)-. Periodical. English. qt. $30.00 institutions; $20.00 individuals. Curt Teich Postcard Archives--Lake County Museum, 27277 Forest Preserve Drive, Wauconda IL 60084. **Tel** (708)526-8638, FAX (708)526-1545. **ED** Christine Pyle. **DD** 769. Index available. cum. index. **Bk Rev**, (Qty: 2). **Circ:** 1,300 (ctrl). *Continues Postcard Journal, 0743-7617.*

US/1051-4546
**IN THE FIELD (CHICAGO, ILL.).** (IN THE FIELD : THE BULLETIN OF THE FIELD MUSEUM OF NATURAL HISTORY.). [In field]. **Added/Corp** Field Museum of Natural History. Vol. 61, No. 4 (July/Aug. 1990)-. Periodical. English. Six times a year. $6.00 (institutions); $3.00 (individuals); $12.00 others. Field Museum of Natural History, Roosevelt Road at Lake Shore Drive, Chicago IL 60605-2496. **Tel** (312)922-9410 ext. 402, FAX (312)922-0671. **ED** Ron Dorfman. **LC** AM101.C58; A17. **DD** 508. **Circ:** 26,000. *Continues in part Field Museum of Natural History Bulletin, 0741-2967. Continued in part by Field Museum of Natural History.; Field Museum of Natural History ... Biennial Report.*
**Desc:** Popular science articles by the Field Museum's curators and researchers, plus news of interest to members of the Museum.

CN/0846-6327
**INDEX TO MUSEOLOGICAL LITERATURE.** (INDEX TO MUSEOLOGICAL LITERATURE / LIBRARY SERVICES, MUSEOLOGICAL RESOURCE CENTRE.). [Index museol. lit.]. **Main/Corp** Canadian Conservation Institute. Museological Resource Centre. **VFOAT** Repertoire des Documents Museologiques. (Sept. 1988/May 1989)-. Periodical. English (French). **DD** 016.069.
**Ind/Abst** Museum Abstr.

US/0161-1003
**INDIANA UNIVERSITY ART MUSEUM BULLETIN.** [Indiana Univ. Art Mus. bull.]. **Main/Corp** Indiana University, Bloomington. Art Museum. Vol. 1 (Fall 1977)-. Bulletin. English. sa. $3.50. Indiana University Art Museum, Bloomington IN 47401. **LC** N518.B4; A28. **DD** 708/.172/255.
**Ind/Abst** BHA : Biblio. Hist. Art.

XN/0350-2325
**INFORMATICA MUSEOLOGICA.** (1974)-. Periodical. Serbo-Croatian (Roman). mo. **UDC** 069.
**Ind/Abst** Museum Abstr.

SZ/1016-2690
**INFORMATION - VMS.** [Inf. - VMS]. **VFOAT** Information - Verband der Museen der Schweiz; Information - AMS; Information - Association des Musees Suisses. (1967)-. Periodical. Multiple languages. sa. **UDC** 069.
**Ind/Abst** BHA : Biblio. Hist. Art.

GW
**INFORMATIONEN FUER DIE MUSEEN DER DDR.** Periodical. German. ir. Muggelseedamm 200, 1162 Berlin Germany. **LC** AM49.A1; I53.

US/0195-833X
**INSIDE SEMC.** **Main/Corp** Southeastern Museums Conference. **VAT** Inside Southeastern Museums Conference. No. 1- June 1966-. Periodical. English. bm. $10.00 membership. Southeastern Museums Conference Inc, c/o William Bradshaw/Treasurer, Cumberland Museum and Science Center, 800 Ridley Avenue, Nashville TN 37203.

FR/0768-2050
**INSTITUT / INSTITUT DE FRANCE.** **Added/Corp** Institut de France. (19??)-. Monographic series. French. **LC** AC20; .I49. **DD** 084/.1.
**Ind/Abst** BHA : Biblio. Hist. Art.

US/0095-2893
**INVENTORY OF THE COLLECTIONS.** **Added/Corp** Illinois State Museum. (1969; No. 1, Part 6 1986)-. Monographic series. English. ir. Price varies per volume. Illinois State Museum, Spring and Edwards Street, Springfield IL 62706. **Tel** (217)782-7386, FAX (217)782-1254. **LC** UNC; Q105.U52; S67. **Pr Rev.**
**Desc:** Listings of particular groups of specimens in the museum's collections, for scientific and educational institutions.

IS/0333-7499
**ISRAEL MUSEUM JOURNAL, THE.** [Isr. Mus. j.]. **Main/Corp** Muzeon Yisrael (Jerusalem). Vol. 1 (Spring 1982)-. English. ir. Israel Museum, PO Box 1299, Jerusalem Israel. **LC** N3750.J5; M89. **DD** 708.95694/4. *Continues in part Muzeon Yisrael (Jerusalem). Israel Museum News, 0021-927X.*
**Ind/Abst** Avery Index Archit. Period. Suppl. Colum. Univ.; BHA : Biblio. Hist. Art.

UK/0960-0892
**ISSUE DESIGN MUSEUM.** (ISSUE.). [Issue Design Mus.]. (1989)-. Periodical. English. qt. **DD** 745.44.
**Ind/Abst** Archit. Period. Index.

BU/0324-0533
**IZVESTIA NA NARODNIA MUZEJ-VARNA.** **VFOAT** Bulletin du Musee National de Varna. (1908)-. Periodical. Bulgarian. ir. **UDC** 941.
**Ind/Abst** BHA : Biblio. Hist. Art.

US/0362-1979
**J. PAUL GETTY MUSEUM JOURNAL, THE.** [J. Paul Getty Mus. j.]. **Main/Corp** J. Paul Getty Museum. (1974)-. English. an. $70.00. J. Paul Getty Museum, PO Box 2112, Santa Monica CA 90406. **Tel** (310)459-7611. **LC** N582.M25; A25. **DD** 708/.194/93. Index available.
**Ind/Abst** ARTbibliogr. Mod.; BHA : Biblio. Hist. Art; Numis. Lit.

NE/0922-775X
**JAARBOEK / ORANJE-NASSAU MUSEUM.** **Added/Corp** Oranje-Nassau Museum (Society). (1???)-. Dutch (English). an.
**Ind/Abst** BHA : Biblio. Hist. Art.

BE/0771-839X
**JAARBOEK / STAD BRUGGE, STEDELIJKE MUSEA.** **Added/Corp** Stedelijke Musea Brugge. **VFOAT** Jaarboek ... Stad Brugge Stedelijke Musea; Brugge/Musea; Jaarboek ... Brugge Stedelijke Musea. (1982)-. Dutch (summaries and/or abstracts in English, French and German). be.
**Ind/Abst** BHA : Biblio. Hist. Art.

GW/0440-1417
**JAHRBUCH - ALTONAER MUSEUM IN HAMBURG.** (JAHRBUCH.). [Jahrb. - Altonaer Mus. Hambg.]. **Main/Corp** Altonaer Museum in Hamburg. (1963)-. German (summaries and/or abstracts in English). Dr. Ernst Hauswedell & Co. Verlag, Rosenbergstrasse 113, D 70193 Stuttgart Germany. **Tel** 011 49 711 638265. **LC** AM101; .H214.
**Ind/Abst** BHA : Biblio. Hist. Art.

AU/0376-2556
**JAHRBUCH DES OBEROSTERREICHISCHEN MUSEALVEREINES. ABHANDLUNGEN.** [Jahrb. Oberosterr. Musealver., Abh.]. **VFOAT** Jahrbuch des Oberosterreichischen Musealvereines Gesellschaft fur Landeskunde. I, Abhandlungen. (1926)-. Periodical. German. an. **CODEN** JOOMAX. *Continues Jahresbericht des Oberosterreichischen Musealvereins.*
**Ind/Abst** BHA : Biblio. Hist. Art.

GW/0342-0124
**JAHRBUCH PREUSSISCHER KULTURBESITZ.** (JAHRBUCH PREUSSISCHER KULTURBESITZ / HERAUSGEGEBEN IM AUFTRAG DES STIFTUNGSRATS VOM PRAESIDENTEN DER STIFTUNG PREUSSISCHER KULTURBESITZ.). [Jahrb. Preuss. Kulturbes.]. **Added/Corp** Stiftung Preussischer Kulturbesitz. (1967)-. German. an. DM42.00. Gebrueder Mann Verlag, Lindenstrasse 76, D-10969 Berlin Germany. **Tel** 011 49 30 25913589, telex 183723. (**Subscription address:** Gebrueder Mann Verlag / KNO, Postfach 800620, Koch, Neff & Oetinger, D-70506 Stuttgart Germany.) **LC** AM51.B4; S83. **DD** 069/.0943. Index available. **Circ:** 600. *Continues Jahrbuch der Stiftung Preussischer Kulturbesitz.*
**Desc:** Of interest to all who find culture and its advancement important. Covers Prussian history, culture and philosophy. Articles by archaeologists, ethnologists, archivists, scientists and teachers.
**Ind/Abst** Art Archaeol. Tech. Abstr.; ARTbibliogr. Mod.; Avery Index Archit. Period. Suppl. Colum. Univ. (19??-199?); BHA : Biblio. Hist. Art.

GW/0441-5590
**JAHRESBERICHT / KESTNER-MUSEUM.** **Main/Corp** Kestner-Museum. (19??)-. German. **LC** WMLC L 83/1420.
**Ind/Abst** BHA : Biblio. Hist. Art.

AU/0378-6862
**JAHRESBERICHT - LANDESMUSEUM JOANNEUM GRAZ.** [Jahresber. - Landesmus. Joanneum Graz]. (1929)-. German. an.
**Ind/Abst** BHA : Biblio. Hist. Art.

SZ/1015-3470
**JAHRESBERICHT - SCHWEIZERISCHES LANDESMUSEUM ZURICH.** **Main/Corp** Zurich. Schweizerisches Landesmuseum. **Added/Corp** Switzerland. Eidgenossische Kommission fur das Schweizerische Landesmuseum. (1892)-. German. an.
**Ind/Abst** BHA : Biblio. Hist. Art.

SZ/1013-6959
**JAHRESBERICHTE / HISTORISCHES MUSEUM BASEL.** **Main/Corp** Historisches Museum Basel. **Added/Corp** Verein fur das Historische Museum Basel. (?)-. German. an.
**Ind/Abst** BHA : Biblio. Hist. Art.

AU/0558-3438
**JAHRESSCHRIFT / SALZBURGER MUSEUM CAROLINO AUGUSTEUM.** **Added/Corp** Salzburger Museum Carolino Augusteum. **VFOAT** JSM. (1955)-. Bibliography. German. an (or every two years). S200.00-S400.00. Salzburger Museum, A-5020 Salzburg, Museumplatz 6, Germany. **LC** AM101; .S23. **DD** 936.3. cum. index. **Bk Rev**, (Qty: 2-4). **Circ:** 1,200 (ctrl).
**Ind/Abst** BHA : Biblio. Hist. Art.

HU/0553-4429
**JANUS PANNONIUS MUZEUM EVKONYVE, A.** **VFOAT** Yearbook of the Janus Pannonius Museum ; Annales Musei de Iano Pannonio Nominati; Ezegodnik Muzeja im. Janusa Pannoniusa. (1956)-. Multiple languages. an. **UDC** 058.
**Ind/Abst** BHA : Biblio. Hist. Art.

# Museums and Galleries

CN/0839-105X
**JIB GEMS.** [Jib gems]. **Added/Corp** Marine Museum of the Great Lakes at Kingston. Vol. 1, No. 1 (Spring 1986)-. Periodical. English. Four times a year. 20.00Can$ Comes with Freshwater membership. Marine Museum of the Great Lakes at Kingston, 55 Ontario Street, Kingston Ontario K7L 2Y2 Canada. **Tel** (613)542-2261. **ED** Michele Dale. **DD** 069/.93872/0971372. **Bk Rev. Ad Acc. Circ:** 500 (ctrl). **Continues** Newsletter (Marine Museum of the Great Lakes at Kingston), 0823-5317.
  **Desc:** Marine museum newsletter featuring museum events, marine news and articles about museum's collection.

●CN/1191-9868
**JOURNAL - ART GALLERY OF ONTARIO.** (JOURNAL / ART GALLERY OF ONTARIO / MUSEE DES BEAUX-ARTS DE L'ONTARIO.). [J. - Art Gallery Ont.]. **Added/Corp** Art Gallery of Ontario. **VAT** Journal - Musee des Beaux-Arts de l'Ontario. Vol. 1, No. 1 (Jan./Feb. 1993)-. Periodical. English. ir. 28.04Can$ Toronto; 42.06Can$ others (Comes with AGO News Membership). Art Gallery of Ontario, 317 Dundas Street West, Toronto Ontario M5T 1G4 Canada. **Tel** (416)977-0414. **DD** 708.11/3541. **Continues** AGO News., 0829-4437.

UK/0958-7608
**JOURNAL OF BIOLOGICAL CURATION.** **Added/Corp** Biology Curators' Group (Great Britain). Vol. 1, No. 1 (1989)-. Periodical. English. an. Biology Curators Group, Leicester Museum, 96 New Walk, Leicester LE1 6TD England. **Tel** 011 44 533 554100. **ED** C. W. Pettitt. **CODEN** JBCUEC. **Bk Rev. Ad Acc. Pr Rev. Circ:** 300 (ctrl).
  **Desc:** Articles on the collection, presentation, storage and maintenance of biological material; display; history of collecting and collections; descriptions of museum collections and museum and natural history services.
  **Ind/Abst** Museum Abstr.

UK
**JOURNAL OF EDUCATION IN MUSEUMS.** English. an. Free to members of the Group for Education in Museums. Group for Education in Museums, Fleet Air Arm Museum, Rnas Yeov, D6 Somerset BA22 8HT England.
  **Ind/Abst** Museum Abstr.

US/1059-8650
**JOURNAL OF MUSEUM EDUCATION, THE.** [J. mus. educ.]. **Added/Corp** Museum Education Roundtable. **VFOAT** Roundtable Reports. Vol. 10, No. 1, Winter (1985)-. Periodical. English. Three times a year. $30.00 US; $52.00 other (individual); $45.00 US; $52.00 other (institution). Museum Education Roundtable, PO Box 23664, Washington DC 20026-3664. **Tel** (202)296-2294, FAX (202)223-9533. **DD** 069. **Continues** Roundtable Reports, 0739-4365.
  **Desc:** This journal is devoted to the theory and practice of museum education. The articles explore such relevant topics as learning theory; visitor evaluation; teaching strategies of art, science and history museums; and the responsibilities of museums as public institutions.
  **Ind/Abst** Museum Abstr.

UK/0954-7169
**JOURNAL OF MUSEUM ETHNOGRAPHY / MUSEUM ETHNOGRAPHERS' GROUP. See** Anthropology.

US/0882-8504
**JOURNAL OF THE ARTISTS' CHOICE MUSEUM, THE.** (THE JOURNAL OF THE ARTISTS' CHOICE MUSEUM : ACM). [J. Artists' Choice Mus.]. **VFOAT** ACM; ACM Journal. Periodical. English. sa. $10.00. The Artists Choice Museum, PO Box 8008 JAF, New York NY 10116-8008. **DD** 704. **Continues** ACM Newsletter.

BB/0005-5891
**JOURNAL OF THE BARBADOS MUSEUM AND HISTORICAL SOCIETY, THE.** [J. Barbados Mus. Hist. Soc.]. **Main/Corp** Barbados Museum and Historical Society. **Added/Corp** Barbados Museum and Historical Society. Vol. 1, No. 1 (Nov. 1933)-. English. an. $25.00. Barbados Museum and Historical Society, St. Anns Garrison Barbados. **ED** P. F. Campbell. **LC** F2041; .B217.
  **Ind/Abst** Am. Hist. Life.

UK/0954-6650
**JOURNAL OF THE HISTORY OF COLLECTIONS.** Vol. 1, No. 1 (1989)-. Periodical. English. sa. £54.00 UK and Europe; $99.00 other. Oxford University Press, Walton Street, Oxford OX2 6DP England. **Tel** 011 44 865 56767, FAX 011 44 865 267773, telex 837330 OXPRES G. **(Subscription address:** Oxford University Press / USA, Journals Marketing Department, Oxford University Press, 2001 Evans Road, Cary NC 27513.) **LC** AM221; .J68. **DD** 069/.5. **CODEN** JHCOE2. **[CCC].** available on microfilm and microfiche from University Microfilms International (UMI).
  **Ind/Abst** Am. Hist. Life (1989-); BHA : Biblio. Hist. Art; Museum Abstr.

US/1041-2433
**JOURNAL OF THE MUSEUM OF FINE ARTS, BOSTON.** [J. Mus. Fine Arts Boston]. **Added/Corp** Museum of Fine Arts, Boston. Vol. 1 (1989)-. English. an (Spring). $27.00 members; $30.00 non-members. Northeastern University Press, 360 Huntington Avenue, Suite 272 HN, Boston MA 02115. **Tel** (617)373-5480, FAX (617)437-5483. **(Subscription address:** Northeastern University Press, PO Box 116, Boston MA 02117) **LC** N520; .A25. **DD** 708.144/61.
  **Ind/Abst** Am. Hist. Life; BHA : Biblio. Hist. Art.

CN/0703-0606
**JOURNAL OF THE NEW BRUNSWICK MUSEUM.** [J. N.B. Mus.]. **Main/Corp** New Brunswick Museum. 1977-. English. an. Free to members, $3.00 per no. others. The Association Museums of New Brunswick, PO Box 9, Doaktown New Brunswick E0C 1G0 Canada. **Tel** (506)365-7919. **LC** F1042; .M87. **DD** 971.5/005. **Continues** Museum Memo / New Brunswick Museum, 0027-4062.
  **Ind/Abst** Am. Hist. Life (1980-); GeoRef.

US/0083-7156
**JOURNAL OF THE WALTERS ART GALLERY.** [J. Walters Art Gallery]. **Main/Corp** Walters Art Gallery (Baltimore, Md.). Vol.1 (1938)-. English. an. $42.00 US; $43.00 other. Walters Art Gallery, 600 North Charles Street, Baltimore MD 21201. **Tel** (410)547-9000 ext. 278. **ED** William Johnson, Hiram Woodward. **LC** N5220; .W437. **DD** 708.1. **Circ:** 1400 (ctrl).
  **Desc:** Publishes articles on art history and scholarship from international authorities and scholars.
  **Ind/Abst** Art Index; ARTbibliogr. Mod.; BHA : Biblio. Hist. Art.

UK/0962-7871
**JOURNAL - SOCIAL HISTORY CURATORS GROUP.** (JOURNAL.). [Journal - Soc. Hist. Curators Group]. (197?)-. English. an. **DD** 941.
  **Ind/Abst** Museum Abstr.

CN/0848-0893
**KALEIDOSCOPE REGINA. See** Science and Technology.

AT/0047-312X
**KALORI; JOURNAL OF THE MUSEUMS ASSOCIATION OF AUSTRALIA.** **Added/Corp** Art Galleries and Museums Association, Sydney. Museums Association of Australia. (Oct. 17, 1952)-. Periodical. English. Six times a year. 10.00Aus$. Royal South Australian Society of Arts Inc., Corner North Terrace and Kintore Avenue, Adelaide SA 5000Australia. **Tel** 011 61 8 2234704. **ED** Adam Dutkiewicz. **Bk Rev. Ad Acc.**

GW/0022-7587
**KARNTNER MUSEUMSSCHRIFTEN.** **Added/Corp** Klagenfurt, Austria. Landesmuseum fuer Karnten. Vol. 1 (1954)-. Monographic series. German. ir. Price varies per volume. Dr. Rudolf Habelt GmbH, Postfach 150104, D 53040 Bonn Germany. **Tel** 011 49 228 232015. **LC** AM101; .K246.

GW/0588-344X
**KLEINE SCHRIFTEN. Main/Corp** Cologne. Wallraf-Richartz Museum. 1- 1964-. Periodical. German. J. B. Metzlersche Verlagsbuchhandlung, Kernerstrasse 10 32 41, D-70028 Stuttgart Germany. **Tel** 011 49 711 22902-14, FAX 011 49 711 22902-90.

JA/0286-7400
**KOKURITSU REKISHI MINZOKU HAKUBUTSUKAN KENKYU HOKOKU.** **VFOAT** Bulletin of the National Museum of Japanese History. No. 1-. Japanese (summaries and/or abstracts in English). Kokuritsu Rekishi Minzoku, Hakubutsukan 117 Jonai-Machi Sakura-shi, Chiba-ken 285 Japan. **LC** DS801; .K68.
  **Ind/Abst** Art Archaeol. Tech. Abstr.

GW/0933-257X
**KOLNER MUSEUMS-BULLETIN. VFOAT** Berichte und Forschungen aus den Museen der Stadt Koln. Vol. 1 (1987)-. Bulletin. German. qt. DM30.00. Museen der Stadt Koln, Marspfortengasse 6, 5000 Koln 1 Germany. **Tel** 0049-2214169. **LC** AM51.C64; M87. **DD** 069/.97094355. **Ad Acc. Circ:** 3,000 (ctrl). **Continues** Bulletin (Museen der Stadt Koln), 0178-4218.
  **Ind/Abst** BHA : Biblio. Hist. Art.

PL/0137-5261
**KOSZALINSKIE ZESZYTY MUZEALNE.** (1971)-. Periodical. Polish. an. **UDC** 943.8.
  **Ind/Abst** BHA : Biblio. Hist. Art.

US/0887-9222
**KRESGE ART MUSEUM BULLETIN. See** The Arts-Art.

CH
**KU KUNG HSUEH SHU CHI KAN / KUO LI KU KUNG PO WU YUN PIEN CHI.** **Added/Corp** Kuo Li Ku Kung Po Wu Yuan. **VFOAT** National Palace Museum Research Quarterly; National Palace Museum Quarterly, Second Series. Vol. 1 (Autumn 1983)-. Periodical. Chinese. qt. $45.00. National Palace Museum, Wai-Shuang-Hsi Shih-Lin, Taipei Taiwan. **Tel** 011 886 2 8821230, FAX 011 886 2 8821440. **ED** Fung Ming-chu. **LC** N7340; .K814. **DD** 700/.951. Index available. **Circ:** 1,000. **Continues** Ku Kung Chi Kan.

CC
**KU KUNG PO WU YUAN YUAN KAN.** **Added/Corp** Ku Kung Po Wu Yuan (China). **VFOAT** Palace Museum Journal; Gugong Bowuyuan Yuankan. (19??)-. Periodical. Chinese. qt. $12.40. Chung-Kuo Kuo Chi Shu Tien, PO Box 2820, Beijing, China. **(Subscription address:** China International Book Trading Corporation, PO Box 399, Library Service Department, Beijing 100044 People's Republic of China.) **LC** DS715; .K775.

GW/0344-5690
**KULTUR & TECHNIK.** [Kult. Tech.]. **Added/Corp** Deutsches Museum (Germany). **VFOAT** Kultur und Technik. Issue 1 (Sept. 1977)-. Periodical. German. qt. DM16.00 Germany; DM20.00 other. CH Beck Verlagsbuchhandlung, D 80791 Munich Germany. **Tel** 011 49 89 381891. **LC** T14.7; .K85. **CODEN** KUTEEN. cum. index.
  **Ind/Abst** Am. Hist. Life (1988-); ARTbibliogr. Mod.; Coal Abstr.

DK/0454-6520
**KUNST OG MUSEUM. See** The Arts-Art.

YU/0459-1070
**LESKOVACKI ZBORNIK. See** History(General)-History of Europe.

FR/0993-9067
**LETTRE DES MUSEES ET DES EXPOSITIONS.** French. Eleven times a year. 650.00F Europe; 850.00F other. Provenciales, 33 rue Fbg St Antoine, 75011 Paris France. **Tel** 011 33 1 43468644, FAX 011 33 1 43416719. Index available. cum. index. **Ad Acc. Circ:** 6,000.
  **Desc:** International information about exhibitions, new museums, projects, technologies, and publishing in the museum field.
  **Ind/Abst** Museum Abstr.

CN/0384-8159
**LIFE SCIENCES CONTRIBUTIONS / ROYAL ONTARIO MUSEUM.** [Life sci. contrib., R. Ont. Mus.]. **Added/Corp** Royal Ontario Museum. No. 74 (1969)-. Monographic series. English. ir. Price varies per volume. Royal Ontario Museum Publications Service, 100 Queens Park, Toronto Ontario M5S 2C6 Canada. **Tel** (416)586-5581. **LC** QL1; .T65. **DD** 590/.5. **CODEN** ROMCAD. Documents available from BIOSIS Document Express. **Continues** Contribution (Royal Ontario Museum. Life Sciences Division), 0082-5085.
  **Ind/Abst** Biol. Abstr.; Fish Rev. (199?-); GeoRef; Wildl. Rev. (199?-).

US/0024-5283
**LIVING MUSEUM, THE.** [Living mus.]. **Added/Corp** Illinois State Museum. Vol. 1 (May 1939)-. Periodical. English. ir. Illinois State Museum, Spring and Edwards Street, Springfield IL 62706. **Tel** (217)782-7386, FAX (217)782-1254. **ED** Nancy M. Wells. **LC** QH1; .L925. **DD** 069.09773. **CODEN** LIMUAR. cum. index. **Bk Rev. Circ:** 15,000. Documents available from BIOSIS Document Express.
  **Desc:** Publication providing educational articles about natural history, anthropology and art as these topics relate to the Illinois State Museum.
  **Ind/Abst** Biol. Abstr.; Biol. Dig.; Fish Rev.

US/0276-475X
**LORE (MILWAUKEE, WIS.).** (LORE.). [Lore]. **Added/Corp** Milwaukee Public Museum. Friends of the Museum. Vol. 1, No. 1 (Winter Issue, Dec. 21, 1950)-. Periodical. English. ir. Milwaukee Public Museum, 800 West Wells Street, Milwaukee WI 53233. **Tel** (414)278-2702. **ED** Mary Garity. **LC** WMLC L 83/4620. **Bk Rev. Circ:** 5,500 (ctrl).
  **Desc:** Magazine published for friends of the museum. Articles on human and natural history; book and film/video reviews.

US/0197-5021
**LOS ANGELES COUNTY MUSEUM OF ART REPORT.** [Los Angeles Cty. Mus. Art rep.]. **Main/Corp** Los Angeles County Museum of Art. 1973/75-. English. be. Los Angeles Museum of Art, 5905 Wilshire Boulevard, Los Angeles CA 90036. **Tel** (213)937-4250. **LC** N582.L7; A32. **DD** 708.194/94.

CN/0318-6784
**LYMAN ENTOMOLOGICAL MUSEUM AND RESEARCH LABORATORY MEMOIR.** [Lyman Entomol. Mus. Res. Lab. mem.]. **Main/Corp** Lyman Entomological Museum and Research Laboratory. Began publication in Oct. 1974. Monographic series. English. ir. Price varies per volume. Lyman Entomological Museum & Research Laboratory, MacDonald College, 21111 Lakeshore Road, Sainte

# Museums and Galleries

Anne de Bellevue Province of Quebec H9X 1C0 Canada. **Tel** (514)398-7915. **DD** 595.7/008. **Pr Rev. Circ:** 300.
**Desc:** Scientific entomological works.

UK/0309-6653
**M D A INFORMATION.** *Ceased.* [M D A inf.].
**Main/Corp** Museums Documentation Association (Great Britain). **VFOAT** Museum Documentation Association Information. Vol. 1, No. 1 (1977)- (1992). English. Four times a year. Museum Documentation Association, Building O, 347 Cherry Hinton Road, Cambridge CB1 4HD England. **Tel** 011 44 223 242848.
**Ind/Abst** Museum Abstr.

AT/0819-9000
**M.O.C.A. BULLETIN.** See The Arts-Art.

RU/0202-6538
**MATERIALY I ISSLEDOVANIA - GOSUDARSTVENNYE MUZEI MOSKOVSKOGO KREMLA.** [Mater. issled. - Gos. muz. Mosk. Kremla]. (1973)-. Russian. ir. **UDC** 7.
**Ind/Abst** BHA : Biblio. Hist. Art.

PL/0137-320X
**MATERIAY MUZEUM BUDOWNICTWA LUDOWEGO W SANOKU.** (1966)-. Multiple languages. ir. **UDC** 72.031.4.
**Ind/Abst** BHA : Biblio. Hist. Art.

US/0195-105X
**MEMBERS CALENDAR - MUSEUM OF MODERN ART.** **Main/Corp** Museum of Modern Art (New York, N.Y.). Vol. 1 (March 1980)-. Periodical. English. mo (12 issues). $45.00. Museum of Modern Art, 11 West 53rd Street, New York NY 10019. **Tel** (212)708-9888, **FAX** (212)708-9889. **Circ:** 53,000 (ctrl). *Supersedes* Members Calendar - Museum of Modern Art, 0195-105X.

AT
**MEMOIRS OF THE MUSEUM OF VICTORIA.** **Added/Corp** Museum of Victoria. **VFOAT** Memoirs of the National Museum of Victoria. Memoir 45, No. 1 & 2 (July/Dec. 1983-Jan./June 1984)-. English. an. 15.35Aus$. Museum of Victoria, 285 Russell Street, Melbourne Victoria 3000 Australia. **Tel** (03)669-9888, **FAX** (03)663-3669. **LC** Q93; .V7. **DD** 591.994. **Circ:** 700 (ctrl). *Continues* Memoirs of the National Museum of Victoria, Melbourne, 0083-5986.
**Ind/Abst** Fish Rev.; Wildl. Rev.

AT/1035-4247
**MEMOIRS OF THE MUSEUM OF VICTORIA. ANTHROPOLOGY AND HISTORY.** [Mem. Mus. Vic., Anthropol. hist.]. **VFOAT** Anthropology and History. (1990)-. English. an. 28.00Aus$ Australia; 30.00aus$ other. Museum of Victoria, 285 Russell Street, Melbourne Victoria 3000 Australia. **Tel** (03)669-9888, **FAX** (03)663-3669. **DD** 306.0899915. **Pr Rev. Circ:** 700 (ctrl).
**Desc:** Describes ethnographic collection of G A Robinson historical interpretation and Robinson's unabridged report of his 1841 expedition.

US
**MEMOIRS OF THE PEABODY MUSEUM OF ARCHAEOLOGY AND ETHNOLOGY, HARVARD UNIVERSITY.** See Archaeology.

SP
**MEMORIAS DE LOS MUSEOS ARQUEOLOGICOS PROVINCIALES. (EXTRACTOS).** **Main/Corp** Spain. Inspeccion General de Museos Arqueologicos. (19??)-. Spanish.
**Ind/Abst** Am. Hist. Life (1954-1961).

US
**MESA VERDE RESEARCH SERIES.** Paper No. 1-. Monographic series. English. ir. Price varies per volume. Mesa Verde Museum Association Inc, Mesa Verde National Park CO 81330.

US/0077-8958
**METROPOLITAN MUSEUM JOURNAL.** [Metrop. Mus. j.]. **Main/Corp** Metropolitan Museum of Art (New York, N.Y.). **Added/Corp** Metropolitan Museum of Art (New York, N.Y.). Journal. Vol. 1 (1968)-. English. an. $60.00. University of Chicago Press / Journals Division, PO Box 37005, 5720 South Woodlawn, Chicago IL 60637. **Tel** (312)753-3347, **FAX** (312)753-0811. **ED** Barbara Burn. **LC** N610; .A725. **DD** 708.1471. Index available. cum. index. **Circ:** 1,000. Documents available from The Genuine Article.
**Desc:** Publishes original scholarly research focusing on the Metropolitan Museum's collections.
**Ind/Abst** Art Index; ARTbibliogr. Mod.; Arts Humanit. Citation Index [Full Cov.]; Avery Index Archit. Period. Suppl. Colum. Univ. (1990-); BHA : Biblio. Hist. Art; Curr. Contents Arts Humanit.; Res. Alert [Full Cov.].

US
**MIDWEST MUSEUMS CONFERENCE NEWS BRIEF.** English. Five times a year. $21.00. Midwest Museums Conference, c/o Labor Museum and Learning Center of Michigan, 711 N Saginaw, Flint MI 48503-1729. **Tel** (313)762-0251, **FAX** (313)762-0204. **(Subscription address:** Sloan Museum, 1221 E Kearsley Street, Flint, MI 48503) **ED** Carl R Hansen. **Circ:** 550 (ctrl).
**Desc:** Newsletter on museum field in Midwest and nationally.

RU/0869-8171
**MIR MUZEIA.** **Added/Corp** Russia (Federation). Ministerstvo Kultury. **VFOAT** World of Museum. (199?)-. Periodical. Russian. bm. $69.95. Izdatelstvo Iskusstvo, Vorotnikovskii Pereulok 11, 103009 Moscow Russia. **(Subscription address:** East View Publications Inc., 3020 Harbor Lane North, Suite 110, Minneapolis MN 55447.) **LC** AM1; .S6. *Continues* Sovetskii Muzei (1984), 0208-2403.

US/0082-3082
**MISCELLANEOUS PAPERS - TEXAS MEMORIAL MUSEUM.** [Misc. pap., Texas Mem. Mus.]. **Added/Corp** Texas Memorial Museum. Texas Antiquities Committee. No. 1 (1966)-. Monographic series. English. ir. Price varies per volume. Texas Memorial Museum, 24th & Trinity Street, Austin TX 78705. **LC** UNC. **CODEN** TMMMBI. Documents available from BIOSIS Document Express.
**Ind/Abst** Biol. Abstr. (-1977); GeoRef.

HU/0540-3391
**MISKOLCI HERMAN OTTO MUZEUM KOZLEMENYEI, A.** **Added/Corp** Herman Otto Muzeum. (19??)-. Hungarian. an. **LC** WMLC L 83/5315.
**Ind/Abst** BHA : Biblio. Hist. Art.

US/1052-3030
**MISSION INN MUSUEM JOURNAL.** **Added/Corp** Mission Inn Musuem. (1991)-. Periodical. English. sa. $10.00 (institutions) US and Canada, $8.00 (Mission Inn members). Mission Inn Foundation, 3739 Sixth Street, Riverside CA 92501.

GW/0935-2422
**MITTEILUNGEN - MUSEUM FOLKWANG ESSEN.** (MITTEILUNGEN.). [Mitt. - Mus. Folkwang Essen]. (1968)-. German. ir. **UDC** 069.41 :73/77.
**Ind/Abst** BHA : Biblio. Hist. Art.

GW
**MITTEILUNGEN - MUSEUM FUER VOLKERKUNDE ZU LEIPZIG.** **Main/Corp** Leipzig. Museum fuer Volkerkunde. (1960)-. German.
**Ind/Abst** Anthropol. Lit.; Ethnoarts Index.

GW/0931-4857
**MITTEILUNGSBLATT - MUSEUMSVERBAND FUER NIEDERSACHSEN UND BREMEN E.V.** [Mitt.bl. - Mus.verb. Niedersachs. Brem. e.V.]. (1975)-. Periodical. German. ir. Museumsverband fuer Niedersachsen und Bremen, Staatliches Naturhistorisches Museum, Pockelsstrasse 10a, W-3300 Braunschweig Germany. **UDC** 069.1.

DK/0107-9328
**MIV: MUSEERNE I VIBORG AMT.** See History(General)-History of Europe.

US/0893-0279
**MOMA (NEW YORK, N.Y.).** See The Arts-Art.

HU/0563-0525
**MORA FERENC MUZEUM EVKONYVE, A.** **Added/Corp** Mora Ferenc Muzeum (Szeged, Hungary). **VFOAT** MFM,E; Jahrbuch des Mora Ferenc Museums, Szeged, Ungarn; Almanach of Mora Ferenc Museum, Szeged, Hungary. (1956)-. Hungarian (summaries and/or abstracts in English, French and German; table of contents in English, French, German and Russian). an. **LC** DB901; .S93. *Continues* Szegedi Muzeumi Kiadvanyok.
**Ind/Abst** BHA : Biblio. Hist. Art.

US/0149-4902
**MOTA.** **Main/Corp** Museum of Temporary Art. **VFOAT** Museum of Temporary Art Magazine. Periodical. English. ir. Mota Press, 1206 G Street NW, Washington DC 20005.

US/0077-2194
**MUSE (COLUMBIA).** (MUSE.). [Muse]. **Added/Corp** University of Missouri. Museum of Art and Archaeology. No. 1 (1967)-. English. an. $10.00. Museum of Art & Archaeology, 1 Pickard Hall, University of Missouri, Columbia MO 65211. **Tel** (314)882-3591, **FAX** (314)884-4039. **ED** Morteza Sajadian. **LC** N584.M5; A3. **DD** 708.178/29. Index available ($10.00). cum. index. **Circ:** 2,000 (ctrl).
**Desc:** Report of University of Missouri Museum of Art and Archaeology; articles on museum objects and museum sponsored archaeological excavations.
**Ind/Abst** ARTbibliogr. Mod.; BHA : Biblio. Hist. Art; Can. Index; Numis. Lit.

CN/0820-0165
**MUSE (OTTAWA).** (MUSE / CANADIAN MUSEUMS ASSOCIATIONS.). [Muse]. **Added/Corp** Association des Musees Canadiens. Vol. 1, No. 1 (Spring 1983)-. Periodical. French (English). Four times a year (Winter, Spring, Summer, Fall). 25.00Can$ Canada; 32.00Can$ US; 40.00Can$ other. Canadian Museums Association, 280 Metcalfe Street, Suite 400, Ottawa Ontario K2P 1R7 Canada. **Tel** (613)567-0099, **FAX** (613)233-5438. **DD** 069/.0971. *Continues* Association des Musees Canadiens. Gazette, 0317-6045.
**Desc:** The journal of the Canadian Museums Association.
**Ind/Abst** Am. Hist. Life; Can. Period. Index (19??-); Museum Abstr.

CN/0820-0165
**MUSE (OTTAWA).** (MUSE / CANADIAN MUSEUMS ASSOCIATION.). [Muse]. **Added/Corp** Canadian Museums Association. Vol. 1, No. 1 (Spring 1983)-. Periodical. English (French). Four times a year. 25.00Can$ Canada; 32.00Can$ US; 40.00Can$ other. Canadian Museums Association, 280 Metcalfe Street, Suite 400, Ottawa Ontario K2P 1R7 Canada. **Tel** (613)567-0099, **FAX** (613)233-5438. **ED** Nancy Hall and Jeanne Thibaultz. **DD** 069/.0971. Index available. cum. index. **Bk Rev. Ad Acc.** *Continues* Canadian Museums Association. Gazette, 0317-6045.
**Desc:** The journal of the Canadian Museums Association.
**Ind/Abst** Am. Hist. Life; BHA : Biblio. Hist. Art; Can. Period. Index (19??-).

FR/0767-7243
**MUSEE CONDE.** [Mus. Conde]. (1971)-. Periodical. French. sa. **UDC** 069.
**Ind/Abst** BHA : Biblio. Hist. Art.

GW
**MUSEEN IN BAYERN.** **VFOAT** Bayerische Museen. Monographic series. German. Price varies per volume. Verlag Schnell & Steiner GmbH und Company, Paganistr, W-8000 Munchen 60 Germany.

CN/0706-098X
**MUSEES.** [Musees]. **Added/Corp** Societe des Musees Quebecois. Vol. 1, (Apr. 1978)-. Periodical. French. Three times a year. 42.50Can$ Canada; 49.00Can$ US; 54.00Can$ others. Societe des Musees Quebecois, CP 8888, Succursale A, Montreal Quebec H3C 3P8 Canada. **Tel** (514)282-3390, 987-3264, **FAX** (514)987-3379. **DD** 069/.09714. **Bk Rev,** (Qty: 24). **Ad Acc.** ctrl circ.
**Ind/Abst** Point Repere.

SZ/0027-3821
**MUSEES DE GENEVE.** [Mus. Geneve]. Yearly Vol. 1-16-. Periodical. French. mo. **LC** AM68.G4; M8. **DD** 069/.09494/5. **CODEN** MSGVAD.
**Ind/Abst** Am. Hist. Life (1963-); ARTbibliogr. Mod.; BHA : Biblio. Hist. Art; GeoRef.

FR/0027-383X
**MUSEES ET COLLETIONS PUBLIQUES DE FRANCE.** **Added/Corp** Association Generale des Conservateurs des Collections Publiques de France. No.1 (Oct./Dec. 1954)-. Periodical. French. Four times a year. 400.00F France, 440.00F other. Association des Conservateurs des Coll, Palais du Louvre, 75041 Paris Cedex 01 France. **Tel** 33 1 40153649, **FAX** 33 1 40153640. **ED** J M Humbert and M A Sonrier. **Bk Rev,** (Qty: 4). **Ad Acc, Adv Mgr:** M A Sonrier. *Supersedes* Association Generale des Conservateurs des Collections Publiques de France. Bulletin.
**Ind/Abst** BHA : Biblio. Hist. Art.

FR/0987-0210
**MUSEES STRASBOURG.** (MUSEES.). (198?)-. Periodical. French. **UDC** 06 (443.83). *Continues* Musees a Strasbourg., 0221-9255.

CN/0835-3220
**MUSELETTER (ST. ALBERT, ALTA.).** (MUSELETTER.). [MuseLetter]. Vol. 1, Issue 1 (July 1984)-. Periodical. English (French). qt. free. Heritage Museum, 5 Anne Street, St Albert Alberta T8N 3Z9 Canada. **DD** 069/.0971233.

SP/0211-450X
**MUSEO CANARIO, EL.** [Mus. Canar.]. 1- 19 -. Spanish. an. El Museo Canario, Dr Chile 25, Las Palmas de Gran Canary Isle. **LC** DP302.C36; M8.
**Ind/Abst** Am. Hist. Life (1954-); BHA : Biblio. Hist. Art.

FI/0781-0032
**MUSEO HELSINKI.** [Museo Hels.]. (1984)-. Periodical. Finnish. ir. **UDC** 069. *Continues* Suomen Museoliitto Tiedottaa, 0355-175X.
**Ind/Abst** Museum Abstr.

CN/0380-4623
**MUSEOGRAMME.** **Added/Corp** Canadian Museums Association. **VFOAT** Museogramme. Vol 1 (April 1973)-. Newsletter. English (French). bm. 25.00Can$ Canada; 32.00Can$ US; 40.00Can$ other. Canadian Museums Association, 280 Metcalfe Street, Suite 400, Ottawa Ontario K2P 1R7 Canada. **Tel** (613)567-0099, **FAX** (613)233-5438. **ED** Nancy Hall and Jeanne Thibault. **Ad Acc. Circ:** 2,300.
**Desc:** Newsletter of the Canadian Museums Association.
**Ind/Abst** BHA : Biblio. Hist. Art.

IT/0392-5528
**MUSEOLOGIA.** [Museologia]. **Added/Corp** Centro di Studi per la Museologia. (1972)-. Italian. L43.000. Centro du Studi per la Museologia, Via delle Forbici 24/26, 50133 Florence Italy. **Tel** 575372. **ED** Carlo L Ragghianti. **LC** AM1; .M58. **DD** 069/.05. **Ad Acc.** **Ind/Abst** Avery Index Archit. Period. Suppl. Colum. Univ. (19??-199?); BHA : Biblio. Hist. Art.

IT
**MUSEOLOGIA SCIENTIFICA.** (19??)-. Italian. sa. L100000.00. Assn Natl Musei Scientifica, Via Lapira 4, 50121 Florence Italy. **Tel** 011 39 55 293493.

US/0196-0237
**MUSEOLOGY / TEXAS TECH UNIVERSITY.** Began with No. 1 (Nov. 21, 1975). Monographic series. English. ir. Price varies per volume. Museum Shop, The Museum, Texas Tech University, Lubbock TX 79409.

IT
**MUSEOSCIENZA.** Museo Nazionale del Scienza e della Tecn, Via San Vittore 19, 20123 Milan Italy.

JA
**MUSEUM.** Japanese. mo. $105.50. **(Subscription address:** Kyowa Book Company, Inc., 1-38 Kanda Jinbo-Cho, Chiyoda-Ku, Tokyo 101, Japan (Phone: 03-3293-0727)**)**

UK/0267-8594
**MUSEUM ABSTRACTS.** **See** Museums and Galleries-Abstracting, Bibliographies and Statistics.

UK/0960-0183
**MUSEUM ABSTRACTS INTERNATIONAL.** ***Ceased.*** (1990)- Ceased with Vol. 3 (April, 1993). English. an. Scottish Museums Council, 20 22 Torphichen St County Hse, Edinburgh EH3 8JB Scotland. **Tel** 44 31 2297465, FAX 44 31 2292728.

NR
**MUSEUM AFRICUM.** **Added/Corp** West African Classical Association. University of Ibadan. Dept. of Classics. Vol. 1 (1972)-. English (Latin and Greek, Modern). an (Dec.). N14.00. University of Ibadan Department of Classics, Oya State, Ibadan Nigeria. **LC** DE1; .M79. **DD** 913/.03/05. ***Supersedes** Nigeria and the Classics.*

GW/0341-8634
**MUSEUM (BRAUNSCHWEIG).** ***Ceased.*** (MUSEUM.). [Museum]. (1976)-(1993). Monographic series. German. mo. Georg Westermann Verlag GmbH, GeorgWestermann Allee 66, D 38 04 Braunschweig, Germany. **Tel** 0531 708373, FAX 0531 708127. **ED** Andrea Kastens. **LC** AM49; .M82. **Bk Rev.** **Ad Acc.** Full Page (B&W) DM2400.00. Full Page (Color) DM3000.00. **Circ:** 20,000.

US/0580-6976
**MUSEUM BRIEFS.** **Added/Corp** University of Missouri. Museum of Anthropology. No. 1 (1969)-. Monographic series. English. ir. Price varies per volume. University of Missouri Columbia Museum Anthropology, 104 Swallow Hall, Columbia MO 65211. **Tel** (314)882-3764. **LC** E151; .M87.

IT
**MUSEUM CRITICUM.** ***Ceased.*** **Added/Corp** Universita di Bologna. Istituto di Filologia Classica. **VFOAT** Quaderni dell'Istituto di Filologia Classica dell'Universita di Bologna. Vol. 4, (1969)-(19??). Italian. an. Giardini Editori Stampatori, Via Santa Bibbiana 28, 56127 Pisa Italy. **Tel** 011 39 50 934242. **ED** Benedetto Marzullo. **Ad Acc.** ***Continues** Quaderni dell'Istituto di Filologia Greca.*
**Desc:** The study of Greek and Latin philology.

UK/0268-9855
**MUSEUM DESIGN.** [Mus. des.]. (1985)-. Periodical. English. Three times a year. £15.00 UK (includes membership). Museum Design Group, Manchester Museum, Millwood, Manchester M13 9PL England. **Tel** 011 44 61 2752634. ***Continues** News - Group Designers / Interpreters in Museums.*
**Ind/Abst** Museum Abstr.

UK/0958-1758
**MUSEUM DEVELOPMENT.** English. mo. £95.00 UK; £135.00 other. Museum Development, Studio Five Mill Lane Woolstone, Milton Keynes MK15 OAJ England. **Tel** 011 44 908 672168, FAX 011 44 908 233121.

FR/0304-3002
**MUSEUM ED. FRANCAISE.** ***Title Change.*** [MuseumEd. fr.]. (1947)-(19??). Periodical. French. qt. UNESCO / France, 31 rue Francois Bonvin, 75732 Paris Cedex 15 France. **Tel** 011 33 1 45684564, 011 33 1 45684565, FAX 011 33 1 42733007, telex 204461 Paris. **UDC** 069. **CODEN** NU053. ***Continues** Museum (Bilingual Ed.), 1012-4225.* ***Continued by** Museum International.*
**Ind/Abst** BHA : Biblio. Hist. Art.

UK/0027-3996
**MUSEUM (ENGLISH ED.).** ***Title Change.*** (MUSEUM.). [Museum]. **Added/Corp** Unesco. Vol. 1 (July 1948)-Vol. 44, No. 4 (1992). Academic Scholarly Publication. English (French). Four times a year. Basil Blackwell Publishers Ltd, 108 Cowley Road, Oxford 0X4 1JF England. **Tel** 011 44 865 791100, FAX 011 44 865 791347, telex 837022 OXBOOK G. **(Subscription address:** Marston Book Services, PO Box 87, Oxford OX2 0DT England**)** **LC** AM1; .M63. **DD** 069.05. available on microfilm and microfiche from University Microfilms International (UMI). Documents available from The Genuine Article. ***Continues** Mouseion (Paris, France).* ***Continued by** Museum International.*
**Desc:** Serves as a survey of activities and a means of research in the field of museography; contributors are generally distinguished museologists, educators and research specialists. Covers all kinds of museums: ethnographic, science, craft, industrial and archaeological, in all parts of the world.
**Ind/Abst** Archit. Period. Index (1948-); Art Archaeol. Tech. Abstr.; Art Index; ARTbibliogr. Mod. (1984-); Arts Humanit. Citation Index (19??-199?) [Full Cov.]; Museum Abstr.; Res. Alert [Full Cov.].

●UK/1350-0775
**MUSEUM INTERNATIONAL.** **Added/Corp** Unesco. Vol. 45, No. 1 (1993)-. Academic Scholarly Publication. English. qt. $79.50 North America; £79.50 other. Basil Blackwell Publishers Ltd, 108 Cowley Road, Oxford 0X4 1JF England. **Tel** 011 44 865 791100, FAX 011 44 865 791347, telex 837022 OXBOOK G. **(Subscription address:** Blackwell Publishers / UK, Marston Book Services, PO Box 87, Oxford OX2 0DT England.**)** ***Continues** Museum, 0027-3996.*
**Ind/Abst** Arts Humanit. Citation Index [Full Cov.].

US/0580-261X
**MUSEUM JOURNAL (LUBBOCK), THE.** (THE MUSEUM JOURNAL.). **Added/Corp** West Texas Museum Association. Texas Technological College, Lubbock. West Texas Museum. Report. (1957)-. Monographic series. English. ir. Price varies per volume. West Texas Museum Association, PO Box 4499, Lubbock TX 79409. **Tel** (806)742-2443. **ED** Gale Richardson. **LC** AM1; .W42. **DD** 069/.09764/847.
**Desc:** Primarily for the members of the West Texas Museum Association. Topics deal with history, art, and archaeology.

UK/0964-7775
**MUSEUM MANAGEMENT AND CURATORSHIP (1990).** (MUSEUM MANAGAMENT AND CURATORSHIP.). [Mus. manag. curator.]. Vol. 9, No. 1 (March 1990)-. Periodical. English. qt. $239.00 The Americas; £160.00 other. Butterworth Heinemann Publishers, Linacre House, Jordan Hill, Oxford OX2 8DP England. **Tel** 011 44 865 310366. **(Subscription address:** Elsevier Science Ltd. Oxford Fulfillment Centre, PO Box 800, Kidlington, Oxford OX5 1DX United Kingdom.**)** **LC** AM121; .I57. ***Continues** International Journal of Museum Management and Curatorship, 0260-4779.*
**Ind/Abst** Archit. Period. Index (Mar. 1990-); Art Index.

AT/1320-2677
**MUSEUM MATTERS.** (19??)-. English. Four times a year. 25.00Aus$ Comes with Museum Association of Australia membership (New South Wales Branch). Museum of Applied Arts and Sciences, PO Box K346, Haymarket, New South Wales, 2000 Australia. **Tel** 03 6699973.
**Desc:** Information about conferences, occasional articles, technical information inserts and a list of who's gone where in the museum world.

●AT
**MUSEUM NATIONAL.** [Mus. natl.]. (1992)-. English. Four times a year (Mar., June, Sept., Dec.). 25.00Aus$ Comes with Museum Association of Australia membership (New South Wales Branch). Museum of Applied Arts and Sciences, PO Box K346, Haymarket, New South Wales, 2000 Australia. **Tel** 03 6699973. ***Formed by the union of** Muse News, 0728-8948 **and** AMAA News, 0810-1027.*
**Ind/Abst** Museum Abstr.

UK/0955-2057
**MUSEUM NEWS LONDON.** (MUSEUM NEWS.). [Mus. news Lond.]. (1972)-. English. tq.
**Ind/Abst** Archit. Period. Index (Autumn/Winter 1977-1978); Museum Abstr.

CN/0710-1228
**MUSEUM NEWS - UKRAINIAN MUSEUM OF CANADA.** (MUSEUM NEWS.). [Mus. news - Ukr. Mus. Can.]. **VFOAT** Muzeini Visti. **VAT** Muzejni Visti - Ukrajinskyj Muzej Kanada. Vol. 1, No. 1 (Spring 1979)-. Periodical. English. Three times a year. $10.00. Museum News, Ukrainian Museum of Canada, 910 Spadina Crescent East, Saskatoon Saskatchewan S7K 3G9 Canada. **Tel** (306)244-3800, FAX (306)652-7620. **ED** Albert Kachkowski. **DD** 305.8/91791/071074011242. **Circ:** 3,000 (ctrl).
**Desc:** Includes museum activities and programs, member activities, artifact and exhibits information.

US/0027-4089
**MUSEUM NEWS (WASHINGTON).** (MUSEUM NEWS.). [Mus. news]. **Added/Corp** American Association of Museums. Vol. 1 (Jan. 1, 1924)-. Periodical. English. bm. $34.00 members. American Association of Museums, 1225 Eye Street Northwest, Suite 200, Washington DC 20005. **Tel** (202)289-1818. **ED** James G. Truloue, Susan Waterman, Donald Garfield. **LC** AM1; .A55. **DD** 069/.0973. **NLM** W1 MU969. **CODEN** MUNSAJ. **[CCC]**. Index available. cum. index. **Bk Rev.** **Ad Acc.** **Circ:** 10,000 (ctrl). Documents available from The Genuine Article.
**Desc:** Serves as a forum for contemporary issues and a resource for practical information.
**Ind/Abst** Art Archaeol. Tech. Abstr.; Art Index; ARTbibliogr. Mod.; Arts Humanit. Citation Index [Full Cov.]; Avery Index Archit. Period. Suppl. Colum. Univ. (19??-199?); BHA : Biblio. Hist. Art; Book Rev. Index (1965-1986); Br. Archaeol. Bibliogr.; Ceram. Abstr.; Curr. Contents Arts Humanit.; Museum Abstr.; Res. Alert [Full Cov.]; Soc. Sci. Cit. Index [Select. Cov.].

CN/0709-2725
**MUSEUM NOTES (LONDON).** (MUSEUM NOTES.). [Museum notes]. No. 1-. Periodical. English. London Museum of Archaeology, 1600 Attawandaron Road, London Ontario N6A 3M6 Canada. **Tel** (519)473-1360. **DD** 971.3/201.

CN/0228-2364
**MUSEUM NOTES (VANCOUVER).** (MUSEUM NOTES.). [Mus. notes]. **Added/Corp** University of British Columbia. Museum of Anthropology. (1???)-. Periodical. English. ir. Price varies per no. University of British Columbia NW Marine Drive, Vancouver British Columbia V6T 1W5 Canada. **Tel** (604)228-5087, FAX (604)228-2974. **DD** 732/.2/0971132074011133.

US
**MUSEUM OF CALIFORNIA, THE.** **Added/Corp** Oakland Museum. Public Information Office. (1977)-. Periodical. English. qt. Free (members), $12.00 (nonmembers). Oakland Museum, 1000 Oak Street, Oakland CA 94607. **Tel** (415)273-3401. **ED** Abby Wasserman. **Bk Rev**, (Qty: 4). **Circ:** 15,000 (ctrl).

US/0198-7763
**MUSEUM OF THE GREAT PLAINS NEWSLETTER.** **Main/Corp** Museum of the Great Plains. **Added/Corp** Institute of the Great Plains. Museum of the Great Plains. Newsletter. No. 1 (Spring 1977)-. English. ir. $7.50. Museum of the Great Plains, PO Box 68, Lawton OK 73502. **Tel** (405)581-3460. **ED** Steve Wilson.

US/0090-9890
**MUSEUM PROGRAM GUIDELINES.** **Main/Corp** National Council of the Arts. English. National Endowment for the Arts, 1100 Pennsylvania Avenue Northwest, Washington DC 20506. **Tel** (202)682-5400, (202)682-5435. **LC** AM11; .N35. **DD** 069/.0973.

UK/0954-0423
**MUSEUM REPORTER.** [Mus. report.]. (1988)-. Periodical. English. bm. National Museums of Scotland, Chambers Street, Edinburgh EH1 1JF Scotland. **Tel** 031 225 7534. **DD** 069.
**Ind/Abst** Museum Abstr.

CN/0045-3005
**MUSEUM ROUND-UP.** **Added/Corp** British Columbia Museums Association. No. 1 (Jan. 1961)-. Periodical. English. Six times a year. 47.00Can$ (one year); $36.00 (individuals), $70.00 (institutions) Comes with British Columbia Museums Association membership. British Columbia Museum Association, 514 Government Street, Victoria British Columbia V8V 4X4 Canada. **Tel** (604)387-3315, FAX (604)356-8197. **ED** David and Linda Tanaka. **Ad Acc.** **Circ:** 500 (ctrl).
**Desc:** Articles and news relevant to British Columbia museum and art gallery community.

US
**MUSEUM SOURCE MARKETPLACE.** (19??)-. Periodical. English. qt. Museumedia, 557 North 68th Street, Milwaukee WI 53213. **Tel** (414)778-1998.

US/1040-6999
**MUSEUM STORE.** [Mus. store]. **Added/Corp** Museum Store Association (U.S.). **VFOAT** Museum Store Magazine. (19??)-. Periodical. English. qt. $30.00 US; $50.00 other. Museum Store Association Incorporated, 501 South Cherry Street, Suite 460, Denver CO 80222. **Tel** (303)329-6968. **ED** Dixie Griffen. **DD** 338. Index available. **Ad Acc.** **Circ:** 3,500 (ctrl). ***Continues** MUST.*

UK
**MUSEUM TRAINING INSTITUTE NEWS.** **Main/Corp** Museum Training Institute. **VFOAT** News. No. 1 (Spring 1990)-. Periodical. English. qt.
**Ind/Abst** Museum Abstr.

US/0740-0403
**MUSEUM YEAR, THE.** (THE MUSEUM YEAR : ANNUAL REPORT OF THE MUSEUM OF FINE ARTS, BOSTON.). [Mus. year]. **Main/Corp** Museum of Fine Arts, Boston. 90th (1965)-. English. an. $5.00. Museum of Fine Arts / Boston, 465 Huntington Avenue, Boston MA 02115.

# Museums and Galleries

Tel (617)267-9300. **LC** N520; .A3. **Circ:** 27,000. *Continues* Annual Report of the Museum of Fine Arts Boston.

US/1055-8624
**MUSEUMEDIA (MILWAUKEE, WISC.).** *Title Change.* (MUSEUMEDIA : MM.). [Museumedia]. **VFOAT** MM; Museum Media. Vol. 1, No. 1 (Mar./Apr. 1991)-(19??). Periodical. English. bm. Museumedia, 557 North 68th Street, Milwaukee WI 53213. **Tel** (414)778-1998. **DD** 027. *Merged into* Museum Source Marketplace.

BE
**MUSEUMLEVEN / NEDERLANDTALIGE AFDELING VAN DE BELGISCHE MUSEUMVERENIGING.** No. 1 (1974)-. Dutch (summaries and/or abstracts in English). an. **LC** AM56.A2; M87.

●CN/1191-0925
**MUSEUMNEWS (HALIFAX).** (MUSEUMNEWS / NOVA SCOTIA MUSEUM COMPLEX.). [Museumnews]. **Main/Corp** Nova Scotia Museum. **VFOAT** Museum News. (Jan./Apr. 1992)-. Periodical. English. qt. **DD** 069/.1/0971605. *Continues* Museum News & Views from the Nova Scotia Museum Complex., 0828-2773.

UK/0141-6723
**MUSEUMS AND ART GALLERIES IN GREAT BRITAIN AND IRELAND. VFOAT** Museums & Galleries in Great Britain & Ireland. (1975)-. Periodical. English. an. $15.95 (one year). Hunter Publishing Inc, 300 Raritan Center Parkway, Edison NJ 08818. **Tel** (908) 225-1900, FAX (908) 225-0812. **ED** Sheila Alcock. **LC** N1020; .M82. **DD** 069/.025/41. Index available. **Bk Rev. Ad Acc. Circ:** 30,000 (ctrl). *Continues* Museums and Galleries in Great Britain and Ireland.
**Desc:** Includes over 1,200 museums and galleries in Great Britain and Ireland. These range from the small country to the large national collection, many subjects and topics of interest.

UK
**MUSEUMS AND GALLERIES COMISSION ANNUAL REPORTS.** English. an. Museums & Galleries Commission, 16 Queen Annes Gate, London SW1H 9AA England. **Tel** 011 44 071 2334200.

II
**MUSEUMS IN INDIA. Added/Corp** Museums Association of India. 4th ed. (1985)-. English. Honorary Secretary / Museums Association of India, c/o National Museum of Natural History, Barakhamba Road, New Delhi 110 001 India. **ED** Usha Agrawal. **LC** AM73.A2; B74. *Continues* Brief Directory of Museums in India.

CN/0225-5235
**MUSEUMS IN NOVA SCOTIA.** 1975-. English. an. Nova Scotia Museum, 1747 Summer Street, Halifax Nova Scotia B3H 3A6 Canada. **Tel** (902)429-4610, FAX (902)424-0560. **LC** AM21.N6; M87. **DD** 061/.16.
**Desc:** A catalogue of museums in Nova Scotia.

UK/0027-416X
**MUSEUMS JOURNAL.** [Mus. j.]. **Added/Corp** Museums Association. Vol. 1 (July 1901)-. Periodical. English. Twelve times a year. £60.00 (institutions), £40.00 (individuals) UK; £75.00 (institutions), £55.00 (individuals) other. The Museums Association, 42 Clerkenwell Close, London EC1R 0PA England. **Tel** 44 71 6082933, FAX 44 71 2501929. **ED** Maurice Davies. **LC** AM1; .M7. **DD** 069/.05. **Bk Rev. Ad Acc. Circ:** 4,500. *Supersedes* Museums Association. Report of Proceedings.
**Desc:** Articles and book reviews on museums; relevant developments, achievements, discussions etc.
**Ind/Abst** Anthropol. Index; Archit. Period. Index (1934-); Art Archaeol. Tech. Abstr.; Art Index; ARTbibliogr. Mod.; BHA : Biblio. Hist. Art; Br. Archaeol. Bibliogr.; Br. Humanit. Index; MLA Int. Bibl. Books Artic. Mod. Lang. Lit.; Museum Abstr.

US/0737-7665
**MUSEUMS / NATIONAL ENDOWMENT FOR THE ARTS.** [Mus. - Natl. Endow. Arts]. **Added/Corp** National Endowment for the Arts. **VFOAT** Museum. (19??)-. English. an. Free. National Endowment for the Arts, 1100 Pennsylvania Avenue Northwest, Washington DC 20506. **Tel** (202)682-5400, (202)682-5435. **LC** N8837; .M87. **DD** 700/.79. **Circ:** 2,000.

UK/0307-7675
**MUSEUMS YEARBOOK. Added/Corp** Museums Association. (1976)-. English. mo (Mar.). £40.00 (individual), £60.00 (institution). The Museums Association, 42 Clerkenwell Close, London EC1R 0PA England. **Tel** 44 71 6082933, FAX 44 71 2501929. **ED** Rhonda Oliver. **LC** AM1; .M6734. **DD** 069/.0941. **Ad Acc. Circ:** 1,500. *Continues* Museums Association. Museums Calendar, 0580-2652.
**Desc:** Directory of museums, their administering authorities, members of the Museums Association, for the UK, and other useful addresses and information.

GW/0027-4178
**MUSEUMSKUNDE.** [Museumskunde]. **Added/Corp** Deutscher Museumsbund. Vol. 1 (1905)-. Periodical. German. Three times a year. DM45.00. Rheinland Verlag & Betriebsges, PF 2140 Abtei Brauweiler, D 50250 Pulheim Germany. **Tel** 011 49 2234 8051. **ED** Christoph B. Ruger. **Bk Rev. Ad Acc. Circ:** 1,900.
**Desc:** Discusses conceptions of museums and exhibitions, educational problems and other problems concerning the museum's work.
**Ind/Abst** ARTbibliogr. Mod. (1984-); BHA : Biblio. Hist. Art; Museum Abstr.

NO/0027-4186
**MUSEUMSNYTT. Added/Corp** Norske Kunst- og Kulturhistoriske Museer. Norske Naturhistoriske Museers Landsforbund. Vol. 1 (1951)-. Periodical. Norwegian. qt. Kr120.00. Museumsnytt NKKM NNML, Ullevalsv 11, 0165 Oslo 1 Norway. **Tel** 011 47 2 201402.

BE/0774-1286
**MUSEUMSTRIP.** (1973)-. Periodical. Dutch. bm. **UDC** 069.7.
**Ind/Abst** BHA : Biblio. Hist. Art.

NE/0166-2074
**MUSEUMVISIE.** [Museumvisie]. (1977)-. Periodical. Dutch. qt. **UDC** 069.
**Ind/Abst** Museum Abstr.

SP
**MUSEUS, DE. Added/Corp** Catalonia (Spain). Departament de Cultura. No. 1 (1988)-. Periodical. Catalan. Generalitat de Catalunya, Casa dels Canon C del Bisbe 9, 08002 Barcelona Spain. **Tel** 011 34 1 4121014. **LC** AM65.A3; C3736.
**Ind/Abst** Museum Abstr.

SW
**MUWOP : MUSEOLOGICAL WORKING PAPERS. VFOAT** Museological Working Papers; DOTRAM; Documents de Travail sur la Museologie. No. 1 (1980)-. Periodical. English (French). Statens Historika Museum, Box 5405, S-114 84 Stockholm Sweden. **LC** AM1; .M84. **DD** 069.5.

PL/0464-1086
**MUZEALNICTWO.** [Muzealnictwo]. (1952)-. Polish. ir. **UDC** 069.
**Ind/Abst** BHA : Biblio. Hist. Art.

BU/0324-1793
**MUZEI I PAMETNITSI NA KULTURATA / KOMITET ZA KULTURA. Ceased. Added/Corp** Bulgaria. Komitet za kultura. **VFOAT** MPK; Musees et Monuments. (1961)-Ceased (1989). Periodical. Bulgarian. qt. **(Subscription address:** Hemus Foreign Trade Organization, 1 B Raiko Daskalov Square, 1000 Sofia Bulgaria**)**
**Ind/Abst** BHA : Biblio. Hist. Art (?-?); Numis. Lit.

RU
**MUZEINOE DELO V SSSR. Added/Corp** Soviet Union. Ministerstvo Kultury. Tsentralnyi Muzei Revoliutsii SSSR. (1970)-. Russian. **LC** AM60.A1; M89.

RU/0258-8064
**MUZEJ.** [Muzej]. (1980)-. Periodical. Russian. an. **UDC** 069.
**Ind/Abst** BHA : Biblio. Hist. Art.

XR
**MUZEJNI A VLASTIVEDNA PRACE.** Vol. 1. Periodical. Czech (summaries and/or abstracts in English and Russian). qt. **(Subscription address:** Artia Pegas Press Ltd., Palac Metro Narodni Trida 25, 11210 Prague 1 Czech Republic.**) LC** DB191. *Continues* Casopis Spolecnosti Pratel Starozitnosti.
**Ind/Abst** BHA : Biblio. Hist. Art; Numis. Lit.

XO/0027-5263
**MUZEUM BRATISLAVA.** [Muzeum Bratisl.]. (1954)-. Periodical. Multiple languages. be. **UDC** 069.
**Ind/Abst** Museum Abstr.

HU/0133-4921
**MUZEUMI KOZLEMENYEK - MUVELODESI MINISZTERIUM MUZEUMI OSZTALY.** (MUZEUMI KOZLEMENYEK.). [Muz. kozl. - MM Muz. Oszt.]. **VFOAT** Muzeumi Kozlemenyek - Orszagos Muzeumi Tanacs. (1962)-. Hungarian. ir. **UDC** 069. *Continues* Muzeumi Hrado - Muzeumok es Muemlekek Orszagos Kozpontja, 0200-1969.
**Ind/Abst** BHA : Biblio. Hist. Art.

HU/0133-2392
**MUZSAK.** [Muzsak]. (1970)-. Periodical. Hungarian. qt. **UDC** 069.1.
**Ind/Abst** BHA : Biblio. Hist. Art.

JA
**NARA KOKURITSU HAKUBUTSUKAN NEMPO. VFOAT** Annual Report of Nara National Museum. Japanese (Japanese). 50 Noboriojicho, Nara Japan. **LC** AM101.N26; A25.

UK
**NATIONAL GALLERIES OF SCOTLAND BULLETIN.** Bulletin. National Galleries of Scotland, Information Department, Belford Road, Edinburgh EH4 3DR Scotland.

UK/0953-024X
**NATIONAL GALLERIES OF SCOTLAND EDINBURGH. 1987.** (1987)-. English. National Galleries of Scotland, Information Department, Belford Road, Edinburgh EH4 3DR Scotland.

US
**NATIONAL MUSEUM ACT; GUIDELINES FOR GRANT PROGRAMS. Main/Corp** Smithsonian Institution. English. an. Smithsonian Institute, 1000 Jefferson Drive SW, Washington DC 20560. **Tel** (202)357-1300.

NZ/0110-1447
**NATIONAL MUSEUM OF NEW ZEALAND MISCELLANEOUS SERIES.** (MISCELLANEOUS SERIES / NATIONAL MUSEUM OF NEW ZEALAND.). [Natl. Mus. N. Z. misc. ser.]. (1976)-. Monographic series. English. Price varies per volume. National Museum of New Zealand, New Zealand. **CODEN** MSNZDT. Documents available from BIOSIS Document Express.
**Ind/Abst** Biol. Abstr.

UK/0953-7007
**NATIONAL MUSEUMS OF SCOTLAND ... REPORT.** [Natl. Mus. Scotl. rep.]. **Main/Corp** National Museums of Scotland. **VFOAT** Report. 1st (Oct. 1985-Mar. 1987)-. Periodical. English. an. National Museums of Scotland, Chambers Street, Edinburgh EH1 1JF Scotland. **Tel** 031 225 7534. *Formed by the union of* Annual Report / National Museum of Antiquities of Scotland, 0955-4580 *and* Royal Museum of Scotland Triennial Report, 0144-2961.

CH/0027-9846
**NATIONAL PALACE MUSEUM BULLETIN. Added/Corp** Kuo li ku kung po wu yuan. **VFOAT** Ku Kung Tung Hsun; Bulletin. (Mar. 1966)-. Periodical. English. bm (Jan., Mar., May, July, Sept., Nov.). $23.00 Hong Kong; $25.00 other. National Palace Museum, Wai-Shuang-Hsi Shih-Lin, Taipei Taiwan. **Tel** 011 886 2 8821230, FAX 011 886 2 8821440. **ED** Lin Po-ting (phone: 001 886 2 8818657). **LC** N3750.T32; A16. **Bk Rev. Circ:** 1,000 (ctrl).

RU
**NAUCHNYI REFERATIVNYI SBORNIK: MUZEEVEDENIE I OKHRANA PAMIATNIKOV. Added/Corp** Moscow. Publichnaia Biblioteka. Informatsionnyi Tsentr po Problemam Kultury i Iskusstva. Russia (1923- U.S.S.R.). Ministerstvo Kultury. **VFOAT** Muzeevedenie I Okhrana Pamiatnikovov. (19??)-. Periodical. Russian. sa. $7.50.

SA/0067-9208
**NAVORSINGE VAN DIE NASIONALE MUSEUM. See** Anthropology.

MW
**NDIWULA : THE ANNUAL NEWSLETTER OF THE MUSEUMS OF MALAWI. Main/Corp** Museums of Malawi. No. 1 (Aug. 1988)-. Newsletter. English. The Museum, PO Box 30360, Chichiri, Blantyre 3 Malawi. **LC** AM91.M3; M87b. **DD** 069/.096897. *Continues* Annual Report and Bulletin (Museum of Malawi).
**Ind/Abst** Museum Abstr.

US
**NEMA NEWS. Main/Corp** New England Museum Association. **VFOAT** New England Museum Association News. Vol. 2, No. 3 (Dec. 1978)-. Periodical. English. qt. $75.00 (institutions), $30.00 (individuals). New England Museum Association Historical Park, Charlestown Navy Yard, Boston MA 02129. **Tel** (617)720-1573, FAX (617)241-5797. **ED** Hilary Robbins. **Bk Rev. Ad Acc. Circ:** 1,000 (ctrl). *Continues* NEC News.
**Desc:** Association newsletter.

UK/0267-2618
**NEMS NEWS.** [NEMS news]. **VFOAT** North of England Museums Service News. (1983)-. Periodical. English. qt.
**Ind/Abst** Museum Abstr.

FR
**NEO RESTAURATION.** French. mo. 380.00F France; $535.00 other. CEP Communications Groupe LSA, 6 rue Marius Aufan, 92300 Levallois Perret France. **Tel** 011 33 1 47 582000, FAX 011 33 1 47 586070. **UDC** 68. *Continues* Neo-Restauration Collectivites Hotellerie.

GW/0028-3282
**NEUE MUSEUMSKUNDE. Ceased.** [Neue Museumskd.]. Vol. 1 (1958)-Vol. 34 (1991). Periodical. German. qt. Deutscher Judo Verband, Redaktion Ippon Segewaldweg 40, D 12557 Berlin Germany. **Tel** 011 49

## Museums and Galleries

711 210770, telex 051 678. **LC** AM49; .N46. **Desc:** Supplements accompany some issues. **Ind/Abst** Art Archaeol. Tech. Abstr. (?-?).

AU/0258-8382
**NEUES AUS ALT-VILLACH.** [Neues Alt-Villach]. (1964)-. Periodical. German. an. **UDC** 069.7. **Ind/Abst** BHA : Biblio. Hist. Art.

US
**NEWS & INFO / FRIENDS FOR LONG ISLAND'S HERITAGE.** See Natural History.

UK/0266-0946
**NEWS - MUSEUM PROFESSIONALS GROUP.** [News - Mus. Prof. Group]. **VFOAT** MPG News. (1980)-. English. qt. **DD** 069.6306041. *Continues Newsletter - Museum Assistants' Group.* **Ind/Abst** Museum Abstr.

US/0028-9256
**NEWS NOTES - NEWARK MUSEUM.** (NEWS NOTES - THE NEWARK MUSEUM.). **Main/Corp** Newark Museum Association. Vol. 1 (Feb. 1944)-. Periodical. English. mo. Newark Museum, 43-49 Washington Street, Newark NJ 07101. **Tel** (201)733-6600. **ED** Mary Chris Rospond. **Circ:** 10,000. **Desc:** Lists exhibitions, talks, tours, workshops for children and adults, programs and new books published.

IT
**NEWSLETTER.** **Main/Corp** International Committee for Mosaics Conservation. **VFOAT** Chronique. (19??)-. Newsletter. French. ICCROM, Via Di San Michele 13, 00153 Rome Italy. **Ind/Abst** Museum Abstr.

CH/1011-9086
**NEWSLETTER & GALLERY GUIDE / NATIONAL PALACE MUSEUM.** **Main/Corp** Kuo Li Ku Kung Po Wu Yuan. **VFOAT** Newsletter and Gallery Guide; Ku Kung Chan Lan Tung Hsun; Chan Lan Tung Hsun. Vol. 16, No. 5 (July 1984)-. Periodical. English (Chinese). Four times a year. Free on request. National Palace Museum, Wai-Shuang-Hsi Shih-Lin, Taipei Taiwan. **Tel** 011 886 2 8821230, FAX 011 886 2 8821440. **LC** N3750.T32; A18. **DD** 708/.951/249. *Continues Kuo Li Ku Kung Po Wu Yuan. Newsletter - National Palace Museum, 0027-9854.*

US/0147-7889
**NEWSLETTER - ASSOCIATION OF SYSTEMATICS COLLECTIONS.** **Main/Corp** Association of Systematics Collections. **VFOAT** ASC Newsletter. Vol. 1, Summer (1973)-. Newsletter. English. Six times a year (Feb., Apr., June, Aug., Oct., Dec.). $21.00 (individuals); $35.00 (two years). Association of Systematics Collections, 730 11th Street Northwest, 2nd Floor, Washington DC 20001. **Tel** (202)347-2850, FAX (202)347-0072. **ED** M. Schauff. **Bk Rev**. **Ad Acc**. **Circ:** 1,700. **Desc:** Covers needs of biological collections including grants, computerization, book reviews, awards, positions available, curatorial methods, pest control, collection research and management.

US
**NEWSLETTER - DIXON GALLERY AND GARDENS.** **Main/Corp** Dixon Gallery and Gardens. (197?)-. Newsletter. English. bm. Free on request. Dixon Gallery and Gardens, 4339 Park Avenue, Memphis TN 38117. **Tel** (901)454-0808. **Circ:** 5,000.

IE/0332-284X
**NEWSLETTER - IRISH MUSEUMS ASSOCIATION.** [Newsl. - Ir. Mus. Assoc.]. (1978)-. Periodical. English. tw. **DD** 069. **Ind/Abst** Museum Abstr.

CN/0823-8324
**NEWSLETTER / PRINCE EDWARD ISLAND MUSEUM AND HERITAGE FOUNDATION.** [Newsl. - P.E.I. Mus. Herit. Found.]. **Added/Corp** Prince Edward Island Museum and Heritage Foundation. (1983)-. Newsletter. English. qt. Free to members. Prince Edward Island Museum and Heritage Foundation, 2 Kent Street, Charlottetown C1A 1M6 Canada. **Tel** (902)892-9127, FAX (902)892-3420. **ED** Karen Kearney. **DD** 971.7/005. **Circ:** 1,200 (ctrl). *Continues Newsletter (Prince Edward Island Heritage Foundation), 0823-8316.* **Desc:** Contains information about the activities of the museum and foundation and about current museum and heritage issues.

US/1064-2730
**NEWSLETTER / RENTON HISTORICAL SOCIETY AND MUSEUM.** [Newsl. - (Renton Hist. Soc. Mus.)]. **Added/Corp** Renton Historical Society and Museum. (19??)-. Newsletter. English. qt. $6.00. Renton Historical Society, 235 Mill Avenue South, Renton WA 98055. **Tel** (206)255-3624. **DD** 973. *Continues Newsletter (Renton Historical Society).*

US/1052-0066
**NEWSLETTER - WESTERN ASSOCIATION FOR ART CONSERVATION.** See The Arts.

UK/0968-6266
**NEWSLETTER - WOMEN HERITAGE AND MUSEUMS.** (NEWSLETTER.). [Newsl. - Women Herit. Mus.]. **VFOAT** Newsletter - WHAM!. (1985)-. Newsletter. English. tq. £10.00 (individuals), £15.00 (institutions) UK; £15.00 (individuals), £20.00 (institutions) other. Imperial War Museum, Lambeth Road, London SE1 6HZ England. **Tel** 011 44 71 4165363. **Ind/Abst** Museum Abstr.

JA
**NIHON NO HAKUBUTSUKAN SORAN.** **Added/Corp** Nihon Hakubutsukan Kyokai. (1970)-. Japanese. ¥900. Tokyo Kokuritsu Habubutsukan, Nihon Hakubutsukan Kyokai, 13.9 Ueno Koen Taito-ku, Tokyo 110 Japan. **LC** AM77.A1; N54.

RU
**NOVAIA SOVETSKAIA LITERATURA PO KULTURE I ISKUSSTVU: MUZEEVEDENIE I OKHRANA PAMIATNIKOV.** **Added/Corp** Informtsentr po Problemam Kultury i Iskusstva (Soviet Union). (Nov./Dec. 1974)-. Multiple languages (Russian and Multiple languages). mo. Gosudarstvennaia Biblioteka, Informatsionnyi Tsentr, Imeni V. I. Lenina, Prospekt Kalinina 3, 121019 Moscow Russia. **LC** Z5052; .N68; AM5.

RU
**OBZORNAIA INFORMATSIIA: RESTAVRATSIIA, ISSLEDOVANIE I KHRANENIE MUZEINYKH KHUDOZHESTVENNYKH TSENNOSTEI.** **Added/Corp** Moscow. Publichnaia Biblioteka. Informatsionnyi Tsentr po Problemam Kultury i Iskusstva. Russia (1923-U.S.S.R.). Ministerstvo Kultury. **VFOAT** Restavratsiia, Isslecovanie I Khranenie Muzeinykh Khudozhestvennykh Tsennostei. (19??)-. Periodical. Russian. sa. $4.80. (**Subscription address:** Victor Kamkin, 4956 Boiling Brook Parkway, Rockville MD 20852.)

CN/0704-5824
**OCCASIONAL - NOVA SCOTIA MUSEUM.** (THE OCCASIONAL.). Vol. 1; Spring/Summer 1973-. Periodical. English. sa. Free. Nova Scotia Museum, 1747 Summer Street, Halifax Nova Scotia B3H 3A6 Canada. **Tel** (902)429-4610, FAX (902)424-0560. **ED** Barbara R Robertson. Index available. cum. index. **Bk Rev**. **Circ:** 600 (ctrl). **Desc:** Articles about objects or natural history specimens to help in understanding museum collections and man in his environment. News, book reviews, information exchange and editorials.

US/0893-0589
**OCCASIONAL PAPERS - BOWDOIN COLLEGE. MUSEUM OF ART.** [Occas. pap. - Bowdoin Coll., Mus. Art]. **Main/Corp** Bowdoin College. Museum of Art. No. 1 (1972)-. Monographic series. English. ir. price varies per volume. Bowdoin College, Museum of Art, Brunswick ME 04011. **Tel** (207)725-3275. **DD** 708. **Bk Rev**. **Desc:** Short, scholarly publications on various aspects of the collections of the Bowdoin College Museum of Art. **Ind/Abst** BHA : Biblio. Hist. Art.

US/0077-7919
**OCCASIONAL PAPERS - NEVADA STATE MUSEUM.** [Occas. pap. - Nev. State Mus.]. **Main/Corp** Nevada. State Museum. **VFOAT** Nevada State Museum Occasional Papers. No. 1 (1968)-. Monographic series. English. Price varies per volume. Nevada State Museum, Capitol Complex, Carson City NV 89710. **Tel** (702)885-4810. **LC** UNC.

US/0196-7703
**OCCASIONAL PAPERS OF THE IDAHO MUSEUM OF NATURAL HISTORY.** [Occas. pap. Idaho Mus. of Nat. Hist.]. **Main/Corp** Monographic series. English. Price varies per volume. Idaho Museum of Natural History, Campus Box 8096, Idaho State University, Pocatello ID 83209. **Tel** (208)236-3410, FAX (208)236-4000. **LC** E78.I18; I4. **DD** 970 S. **Circ:** 2,000. *Continues Occasional Papers of the Idaho State University Museum, 0073-4551.* **Desc:** A series of papers dealing with aspects of archaeological research in the intermountain west.

UK/0306-7343
**OCCASIONAL PAPERS ON TECHNOLOGY.** [Occas. pap. tech.]. **Main/Corp** Pitt Rivers Museum. (1944)-. English. ir. Price varies per volume. Pitt Rivers Museum, University of Oxford, South Parks Road, Oxford OX1 3PP England. **Tel** 0865 270927. **CODEN** PRMPAH.

**Desc:** Occasional series on technology (including arts and crafts) with bias towards the museum's collections. **Ind/Abst** GeoRef.

US/0149-175X
**OCCASIONAL PAPERS - THE MUSEUM, TEXAS TECH UNIVERSITY.** [Occas. pap., Mus., Tex. Tech Univ.]. **Added/Corp** Texas Tech University. Museum. **VFOAT** Occasional Papers Museum Texas Tech University. No. 1 (1972)-. Monographic series. English. ir. Price varies per volume. Texas Tech University Press, Administrative Education Room 43, West Basement, Lubbock TX 79409-1037. **Tel** (800)832-4042, (806)742-2982. **LC** QL1; .O213. **DD** 590/.5. **CODEN** OPTMDL. Index available. **Desc:** Timely dissemination of the results of primary research in museum-related sciences; they are self-covered, numbered serially, and paged separately. **Ind/Abst** Fish Rev.; GeoRef; Wildl. Rev.

US/0148-0960
**OCCASIONAL PAPERS - UNIVERSITY OF ARKANSAS MUSEUM.** [Occas. pap., Univ. Arkansas Mus.]. **Main/Corp** University of Arkansas Museum. Academic Scholarly Publication. English. ir. University of Arkansas Museum, Fayetteville AR 72701. **CODEN** UAMOAI. Documents available from CASDDS. **Ind/Abst** Chem. Abstr.

AU/0029-9626
**OESTERREICHISCHE ZEITSCHRIFT FUER KUNST UND DENKMALPFLEGE.** See The Arts-Art.

CN/0829-0474
**OFFICIAL DIRECTORY OF CANADIAN MUSEUMS AND RELATED INSTITUTIONS, THE.** [Off. dir. Can. mus. relat. inst.]. **VFOAT** Repertoire Officiel des Musees Canadiens et Institutions Connexes; Canadian Museums and Related Institutions, Directory; Official Directory of Canadian Museums; Repertoire Officiel des Musees Canadiens. 1984-85-. Directory. English. te. 44.95Can$. Canadian Museums Association, 280 Metcalfe Street, Suite 400, Ottawa Ontario K2P 1R7 Canada. **Tel** (613)567-0099, FAX (613)233-5438. **ED** Raymond Beudall. **LC** AM21.A1; O37. **DD** 069/.025/71. **Ad Acc**. **Circ:** 1,500. available on a computer list (of sub-sets); available on labels. *Continues Directory of Canadian Museums and Related Institutions, 0714-2188.* **Desc:** Address, personnel, collection information, activities information, etc., about 1,893 museums and related institutions in Canada.

US/0090-6700
**OFFICIAL MUSEUM DIRECTORY, THE.** [Off. mus. dir.]. **Added/Corp** American Association of Museums. (1971)-. Directory. English. an (Nov.). $203.25. R R Bowker, A Reed Reference Publishing Company, Part of Reed International PLC, PO Box 31, 121 Chanlon Drive, New Providence NJ 07974. **Tel** (908)464-6800, (800)521-8110, FAX (908)665-6688, telex 138-755. **LC** AM10.A2; O4. **DD** 069/.025/7. **NLM** AM 10 M986. *Continues Museums Directory of the United States and Canada, 0090-6697.* **Desc:** Lists over 7,000 institutions in categories, showing where they are, what they exhibit and who manages them.

US/0276-637X
**OFFICIAL MUSEUM PRODUCTS AND SERVICES DIRECTORY, THE.** **VFOAT** Products and Services. 1981-. Directory. English. bm. $34.00. American Association of Museums, 1225 Eye Street Northwest, Suite 200, Washington DC 20005. **Tel** (202)289-1818. **ED** Ligeia Z Fontaine, Tracey Linton Craig. **LC** AM127; .O36. **DD** 069/.3/02573. **Bk Rev**. **Ad Acc**. **Circ:** 11,000. **Desc:** Devoted to the interests of the museum professional directors, curators, conservators, registrars, museum educators and others. Publishes articles on developments in museum disciplines, keeping the profession up to date. Includes art museums, history museums, science and technology, industry, zoos, arboretums, children's museums, museums devoted to specialized subjects, etc.

JA
**OKINAWA KENRITSU HAKUBUTSUKAN DAYORI.** **Main/Corp** Okinawa Kenritsu Hakubutsukan. No. 1 (1977)-. Periodical. Japanese. an. Okinawa Kenritsu Hakubutsukan, 1-1 Shuri Onakacho, Naha 903 Japan. **Tel** 0988-84-2243. **LC** AM101.N256; A3. **Circ:** 500.

JA
**OKINAWA KENRITSU HAKUBUTSUKAN NEMPO.** **Main/Corp** Okinawa Kenritsu Hakubutsukan. No. 8- 1975-. Japanese. an. Free. Okinawa Kenritsu Hakubutsukan, 1-1 Shuri Onakacho, Naha 903 Japan. **Tel** 0988-84-2243. **LC** AM101.N256; A32. **Circ:** 800. *Supersedes in part Okinawa Kenritsu Hakubutsukan Kampo.* **Desc:** Report of operation of the Okinawa Prefectural Museum.

# Museums and Galleries

US/0744-3781
**OLD STURBRIDGE VISITOR.** Vol. 22, No. 1 (Spring 1982)-. Periodical. English. qt. $25.00. Old Sturbridge Village, 1 Old Sturbridge Village Road, Sturbridge MA 01566. **Tel** (617)347-3362. **ED** Caroline Sloat. **Circ:** 12,000 (ctrl). *Continues Rural Visitor, 0485-6724.*
  **Desc:** Articles relating to early 19th Century New England life as portrayed in the leading outdoor history museum, politics, domestic arts, music, social and economic life.
  **Ind/Abst** Am. Hist. Life.

●CN/1188-9578
**ONTARIO MUSEUM ANNUAL.** [Ont. mus. annu.]. **Main/Corp** Ontario Museum Association. **VFOAT** Annual; Annuaire; Annuaire des Musees de l'Ontario. (1992)-. English (summaries and/or abstracts in French). Free (members), $10.00 (non-members), $15.00 (institutional). Ontario Museum Association, George Brown House, 50 Baldwin Street, Toronto Ontario M5T 1L4 Canada. **Tel** (416)367-3677. **DD** 069/.05. *Continues Museum Quarterly (Toronto, Ont.), 0822-5931.*
  **Ind/Abst** Museum Abstr.

PL/0474-2885
**OPOLSKI ROCZNIK MUZEALNY.** See History(General)-History of Europe.

PL/0239-9989
**OPUSCULA MUSEALIA.** **Added/Corp** Uniwersytet Jagiellonski. Zesz. 1 (1986)-. Polish (summaries and/or abstracts in English and German; table of contents in English and German).
  **Ind/Abst** Numis. Lit. (199?-).

CI/0473-4882
**OSJECKI ZBORNIK.** **Added/Corp** Muzej Slavonije (Osijek, Croatia). (1942)-. Serbo-Croatian (Roman) (German; summaries and/or abstracts in English, French and German; table of contents in German).
  **Ind/Abst** BHA : Biblio. Hist. Art.

●PE
**PACHACAMAC : REVISTA DEL MUSEO DE LA NACION.** **Added/Corp** Museo de la Nacion (Peru). Vol. 1, No. 1 (Agosto 1992)-. Periodical. Spanish. sa. Museo de la Nacion Apdo., Postal 6150, Lima 100 Peru. **ED** Carlos Guerrero Zevallos.

IT
**PADUA MUSEO CIVICO BOLLETTINO.** (19??)-. Italian. sa. Museo Civico, Piazza del Santo, 35123 Padua Italy.

SP/1130-9865
**PANORAMA ENGLISH ED.** [Panorama Engl. ed.]. **VFOAT** Panorama Monthly Journal. (1991)-. Periodical. English. mo. UDC 061.22. *Continues Informatiu - Fundacio Caixa de Pensions (English Ed.), 1130-7854.*
  **Ind/Abst** Museum Abstr.

CN/0703-7058
**PAPERS AND RECORDS - THUNDER BAY HISTORICAL MUSEUM SOCIETY.** **Main/Corp** Thunder Bay Historical Museum Society. Vol. 1, (1973)-. Academic Scholarly Publication. English. an (Nov./Dec.). 6.50Can$ Canada; $7.10 US. Thunder Bay Historical Museum Society, 219 South May Street, Thunder Bay Ontario P7E 1B5 Canada. **Tel** (807)623-0801, FAX (807)622-6880. **ED** Dr. David Kemp (phone: (807)343-8430). Index available. cum. index. **Pr Rev. Circ:** 750 (ctrl). *Supersedes Thunder Bay Historical Society. Annual Reports.*
  **Desc:** Devoted exclusively to the history of the Thunder Bay region. Contains scholarly and popular articles and photo essays.

US/1074-0457
**PEABODY ESSEX MUSEUM COLLECTIONS.** See History(General)-History of North, South, and Central America.

US
**PICKER ART GALLERY JOURNAL / THE PICKER ART GALLERY, COLGATE UNIVERSITY, THE.** See The Arts-Art.

US/0149-9653
**POLISH MUSEUM OF AMERICA QUARTERLY, THE.** Suspended. **Main/Corp** Chicago. Polish Museum of America. (1972)-Suspended (19??). Periodical. English. qt. Polish Museum of America, 984 North Milwaukee Avenue, Chicago IL 60622. **ED** Dorothy A. Michno. **LC** E184.P7; C48a. **DD** 973/.04/9185.

US/0077-7927
**POPULAR SERIES (CARSON CITY, NEV.).** (POPULAR SERIES / NEVADA STATE MUSEUM.). [Pop. ser. - Nev. State Mus.]. No. 1 (Jan. 1965)-. Monographic series. English. ir. Price varies per volume. Nevada State Museum, Capitol Complex, Carson City NV 89710. **Tel** (702)885-4810. **LC** AM101; .N464. **DD** 069/.0979357.
  **Desc:** Anthropology, ethnology, and archaeology reports.

GW/0032-6542
**PRAPARATOR.** (DER PRAPARATOR.). [Praparator]. **Added/Corp** Gemeinnutzigen Vereinigung der Praparatoren und Dermoplastiker Deutschlands. Arbeitsgemeinschaft des Technischen Museumspersonals. Vol. 1 (Jan. 1955)-. Periodical. German. qt. $14.21. Verband Deutscher Praparatoren, Bochum 1 Germany. **Tel** 02 34/700 - 48 19. **LC** AM1; .P7. **NLM** W1 PR201. **CODEN** PPTRAA. **Bk Rev. Ad Acc. Circ:** 2,000 (ctrl).
  **Desc:** Preparation, techniques on biology, geology, paleontology, mineralogy, medicine and museum education and teaching materials.
  **Ind/Abst** BHA : Biblio. Hist. Art; GeoRef.

FR
**PROSOPOPEES : PUBLICATION ERRATIQUE DE L'ACADEMIE DE MUSEOLOGIE EVOCATOIRE.** French. ir. 200.00F (3 issues). Academie Museologie Evocatoire Vatois, 76190 Yvetot France. **Tel** 35 950868.

CN/0826-1164
**PROVENANCE (LONDON).** (PROVENANCE : NEWSLETTER OF THE LONDON HISTORICAL MUSEUMS AND LONDON HISTORICAL MUSEUMS ASSOCIATION.). [Provenance]. **Added/Corp** London Historical Museums (Ont.). London Historical Museums Association (Ont.). Vol. 1, No. 1 (Sept./Oct. 1983)-. Newsletter. English. bm. Free. Provenance, c/o London Historical Museums, 1017 Western Road, London Ontario N6G 1G5 Canada. **DD** 069/.9971326.

GT
**PUBLICACIONES DEL MUSEO MUNICIPAL DE CIENCIAS NATURALES LORENZO SCAGLIA.** **Main/Corp** Museo Municipal de Ciencias Naturales de Mar del Plata Lorenzo Scaglia. V. 2, No. 3, August 1976-. Periodical. Spanish (English). CC 1207 Correo Central, 7600 Mar del Plata Argentina. **CODEN** MPMMBU. *Continues Publicaciones del Museo Municipal de Ciencias Naturales de Mar del Plata.*
  **Ind/Abst** GeoRef.

US
**PUBLICATIONS - VIRGINIA MUSEUM OF FINE ARTS, RICHMOND.** **Main/Corp** Virginia Museum of Fine Arts. Vol. 1 (1936/38)-. English. Virginia Museum of Fine Arts, 2800 Grove Avenue, Richmond VA 23221-2466. **Tel** (804)367-0589, FAX (804)367-9393. **LC** N716.V45; A2. **DD** 708.1.

US/0557-3645
**QUARTERLY BULLETIN / ROSWELL MUSEUM AND ART CENTER.** [Q. bull. - Roswell Mus. Art Cent.]. **Main/Corp** Roswell Museum and Art Center. Began with V. 5, No. 4 in 1957. Bulletin. English. Three times a year. $15.00. Roswell Museum & Art Center, 11th and Main Streets, Roswell NM 88201. **Tel** (505)624-6744. **LC** AM101.R68; A17. **DD** 069/.09789/43. **Circ:** 1,300 (ctrl). *Continues Roswell Museum. Bulletin, 0483-3945.*
  **Desc:** Museum catalog of past and future exhibits and museum activities.

US/0027-4135
**QUARTERLY - MUSEUM OF THE FUR TRADE.** See History(General)-History of North, South, and Central America.

US/0195-864X
**QUARTERLY / SAN BERNARDINO COUNTY MUSEUM ASSOCIATION.** [Q. San Bernard. Cty. Mus. Assoc.]. **Added/Corp** San Bernardino County Museum Association. **VFOAT** San Bernardino County Museum Association Quarterly; Quarterly of San Bernardino County Museum Association; San Bernardino County Museum Association. (1953)-. Monographic series. English. qt. $40.00. San Bernardino County Museum Association, 2024 Orange Tree Lane, Redlands CA 92374. **Tel** (714)798-8570. **LC** E78.C15; S2. **DD** 979.
  **Ind/Abst** GeoRef.

YU/0550-2209
**RAD VOJVOANSKIH MUZEJA.** **Added/Corp** Vojvoanski Muzej. **VFOAT** Travaux des Musees de Voivodine. (1952)-. Serbo-Croatian (Cyrillic) (summaries and/or abstracts in German, French, English and Multiple languages; table of contents in French and German) **LC** DR381.V6; R2.
  **Ind/Abst** Anthropol. Lit.; BHA : Biblio. Hist. Art.

US/0032-843X
**RECORD OF THE ART MUSEUM, PRINCETON UNIVERSITY.** **Main/Corp** Princeton University. Art Museum. V. 1- Spring 1942-. Academic Scholarly Publication. English. sa. $9.00. Princeton University Art Museum, Princeton NJ 08544-1018. **Tel** (609)258-4341. **ED** Jill Guthrie. [CCC]. Index available. **Circ:** 2,000 (ctrl). available on microfilm and microfiche from University Microfilms International (UMI).
  **Desc:** Contains scholarly articles about art objects in the museum's collection. Includes annual listing of new acquisitions of the museum; illustrated.
  **Ind/Abst** Art Index; ARTbibliogr. Mod.; BHA : Biblio. Hist. Art.

NZ/0110-943X
**RECORDS - NATIONAL MUSEUM OF NEW ZEALAND.** [Rec. - Natl. Mus. N.Z.]. **Main/Corp** National Museum of New Zealand. Vol. 1 (Sept. 22, 1975)-. Periodical. English. National Museum of New Zealand, New Zealand. **LC** AM101.W4715; A3. **DD** 069/.09931. **CODEN** RNMZDA. Documents available from BIOSIS Document Express. *Supersedes Records of the Dominion Museum, 0373-7233.*
  **Ind/Abst** Biol. Abstr.

AT/0376-2750
**RECORDS OF THE SOUTH AUSTRALIAN MUSEUM.** [Rec. South Aust. Mus.]. **Main/Corp** South Australian Museum, Adelaide. **Added/Corp** Public Library, Museum, and Art Gallery of South Australia. South Australian Museum. Vol. 1 (May 1918)-. Monographic series. English. sa. 35.00Aus$. South Australian Museum, North Terrace, Adelaide South Australia 5000 Australia. **Tel** 011 61 8 2238823, FAX 011 61 8 2321714. **ED** E. Matthews, P. Jones, P. Horton. **LC** QL1; .S869. **CODEN** RAMUA3. Index available. **Bk Rev. Pr Rev. Circ:** 400. Documents available from BIOSIS Document Express.
  **Desc:** Publishes original papers in zoology, anthropology and earth sciences, with a taxonomic orientation.
  **Ind/Abst** AESIS Q.; Biol. Abstr.; Entomol. Abstr.; Ethnoarts Index; Life Sci. Collect.; Zool. Rec.

US/0733-866X
**REGISTER OF THE SPENCER MUSEUM OF ART, THE.** [Regist. Spencer Mus. Art]. **Main/Corp** Helen Foresman Spencer Museum of Art. Vol. 5, No 5 (1978)-. Periodical. English. ir. University of Kansas Spencer Museum Bookstore, Lawrence KS 66045. **Tel** (913)864-4710. **ED** Carol Shankel. **LC** N582.L25; A35. **DD** 708.181/65. **Bk Rev. Ad Acc. Circ:** 1,000 (ctrl). *Continues University of Kansas. Museum of Art. Register of the Museum of Art, 0041-9672.*
  **Desc:** Articles on art objects in the Spencer Museum collection, and a museum report.
  **Ind/Abst** ARTbibliogr. Mod.; BHA : Biblio. Hist. Art.

US
**REPORT.** **Main/Corp** Brooklyn Museum. English.

UK/0524-6474
**REPORT ON THE BRITISH MUSEUM (NATURAL HISTORY).** See Natural History.

ZA
**RESEARCH NOTES (LIVINGSTONE MUSEUM).** (RESEARCH NOTES / THE LIVINGSTONE MUSEUM.). No. 1 (Oct. 1979)-. English. ir. K20.00. Livingstone Museum, PO Box 60498, Livingstone Zambia. **Tel** 321204 OR 321205. **ED** F B Musonda. **LC** AM101.L5975; A35. **DD** 069/.096894. **Bk Rev. Ad Acc. Circ:** 1,000.
  **Desc:** Welcomes research articles for publication on any subject of relevance to the scholarship of Zambia and adjacent countries.

SP/0034-771X
**REVISTA DE ARCHIVOS BIBLIOTECAS Y MUSEOS (MADRID, SPAIN : 1897).** Suspended. See Library and Information Sciences.

SP
**REVISTA DE LA BIBLIOTECA, ARCHIVO Y MUSEO DEL AYUNTAMIENTO DE MADRID.** See Library and Information Sciences.

AG/0372-4638
**REVISTA DEL MUSEO DE LA PLATA. SECCION ZOOLOGIA.** [Rev. Mus. La Plata, Secc. Zool.]. V. 1-. Periodical. Spanish. **LC** QL1; .L3. **DD** 590/.5. **CODEN** LURZAF. *Continues Notas del Museo de la Plata. Zoologia, 0372-4549; Continues in part Revista del Museo de la Plata, 0375-1147.*
  **Ind/Abst** GeoRef.

PE
**REVISTA DEL MUSEO HISTORICO REGIONAL.** **Main/Corp** Museo Historico Regional. Yearly volume 5- (No. 3/4/5- );Feb. 1970-. Periodical. Spanish. Casa de la Cultura del Peru, Cana Inca Garcilaso, Calle Heladeros, Cuzco Peru. *Continues Revista del Museo Virreynal.*

RM
**REVISTA MUZEELOR.** **Added/Corp** Romania. Ministerul Culturii. Vol. 27, No. 1 (1990)-. Periodical. Romanian (summaries and/or abstracts in French). Ten times a year. DM232.00. (Subscription address: Kubon & Sagner, ABT Zeitschriftenimport, D 80328 Munich Germany.) **LC** AM69.R8; R43. **DD** 069/09498. **CODEN** REMUEZ. *Continues Revista Muzeelor si Monumentelor. Muzee, 0035-0206.*
  **Ind/Abst** BHA : Biblio. Hist. Art.

FR/0758-881X
**REVUE DE LA SOCIETE DES AMIS DU MUSEE DE L'ARMEE.** See Military and Defense.

FR/0035-2608
**REVUE DU LOUVRE ET DES MUSEES DE FRANCE, LA.** [Rev. Louvre mus. Fr.]. Vol. 11 No. 1 (1961)-. Periodical. French. bm. 500.00F (France); 600.00F (other). Centre Distribution Reunion Mus Nat, 1 31 Allee Du 12 Fev 1934, 77186 Noisiel France. **Tel** 11 33 1 60060314. Documents available from The Genuine Article. ***Continues** Revue des Arts. Musees de France.*
**Ind/Abst** Art Archaeol. Tech. Abstr.; Art Index; ARTbibliogr. Mod.; Arts Humanit. Citation Index [Full Cov.]; Avery Index Archit. Period. Suppl. Colum. Univ. (1989-); BHA : Biblio. Hist. Art; Curr. Contents Arts Humanit.; Res. Alert [Full Cov.]; Romant. Move.

GW/0524-0344
**RHEINISCHE LANDESMUSEUM BONN, DAS.** [Rhein. Landesmus. Bonn]. (1966)-. Periodical. German. bm. **UDC** 7:069 (430.1-2.442).
**Ind/Abst** BHA : Biblio. Hist. Art.

PL/0137-2866
**ROCZNIK MUZEUM NARODOWEGO W KIELCACH.** **Main/Corp** Muzeum Narodowe w Kielcach. (1977)-. Polish. **LC** AM101; .K514. ***Continues** Muzeum Swietokrzyskie w Kielcach. Rocznik.*
**Ind/Abst** BHA : Biblio. Hist. Art.

PL/0509-6936
**ROCZNIK MUZEUM NARODOWEGO W WARSZAWIE.** [Rocz. Muz. Nar. Warsz.]. **Added/Corp** Muzeum Narodowe w Warszawie. **VFOAT** Annuaire du Musee National de Varsovie. (1938)-. Polish (summaries and/or abstracts in French and Russian). an. **LC** AM101; .W3674.
**Ind/Abst** BHA : Biblio. Hist. Art.

PL/0495-923X
**ROCZNIK MUZEUM W TORUNIU.** **VFOAT** Annuaire de Musee de Torun. (1962)-. Polish. ir. **UDC** 943.8.
**Ind/Abst** BHA : Biblio. Hist. Art.

CN/0035-8495
**ROTUNDA (TORONTO).** (ROTUNDA.). **Added/Corp** Royal Ontario Museum. Vol. 1 (Winter 1968)-. Periodical. English. qt. 16.95Can$ Canada; 20.95Can$ other. Royal Ontario Museum Publications Service, 100 Queens Park, Toronto Ontario M5S 2C6 Canada. **Tel** (416)586-5581. **ED** Sandra Shaul. **LC** AM101; .T6252. **DD** 069/.0719/541. cum. index. **Ad Acc, Adv Mgr:** John Jory, **Tel** (416)447-7999. **Pr Rev. Circ:** 25,000.
**Desc:** Canadian magazine with an international focus; reflects the worldwide research of specialists at the Royal Ontario Museum and of many other experts around the globe. Reports the latest information on the endeavours of humankind and the ways of nature, both past and present. Full-color photography presents the artifacts and specimens, the people involved and the places visited.
**Ind/Abst** Am. Hist. Life (1987-); Can. Index; Can. Period. Index (19??-).

SP
**RS (CENTRO DE ARTE REINA SOFIA).** See The Arts-Art.

UK/0953-1130
**RUSKIN NEWSLETTER, THE.** [Ruskin newsl.]. **Added/Corp** Ruskin Association. No. 1 (Autumn 1969)-. Newsletter. English. sa. Ruskin Association, Ruskin Galleries, J S Dearden, Bembridge SCH Isle of Wight England. **ED** J.S. Dearden.
**Ind/Abst** MLA Int. Bibl. Books Artic. Mod. Lang. Lit.

CN/0715-5034
**S & L MUSEUM NEWSLETTER.** [S L Mus. newsl.]. **Main/Corp** Sydney & Louisburg Railway Historical Society. **VAT** Sydney and Louisburg Railway Historical Society Museum Newsletter. Newsletter. English. qt. $5.00 (membership), free to members. Sydney & Louisburg Railway Historical Society, Membership Committee, PO Box 225, Louisbourg Nova Scotia B0A 1M0 Canada. **Tel** (902)733-2720, FAX (902)733-2767. **DD** 385/.06/07169. Index available. **Bk Rev. Circ:** 350 (ctrl).
**Desc:** News and information about the society and railway history in general, particularly C.B. railroad history.

JA
**SAGA KENRITSU HAKUBUTSUKAN NEMPO.** **Main/Corp** Saga Kenritsu Hakubutsukan. (1970)-. Japanese. 15-23 Jonai 1-chome, Saga Japan. **LC** AM101.S138; A3.

SA/0370-8314
**SAMAB.** ***Suspended.*** [SAMAB]. **Added/Corp** SAMA. **VFOAT** Bulletin; Bulletin of the Southern African Museums Association; Bulletin van die Suider-Afrikaanse Museumvereniging. Vol. 1 (Sept. 1936)-Suspended (19??). Periodical. English (Afrikaans). qt. R15.00 South Africa; $35.00 US. South African Museums Association, PO Box 29294, Sunnyside 0132 South Africa. **Tel** 011 27 12 341 1320. **ED** M.A. Raath. **LC** AM89.A1; S25. **DD** 069/.0968. Index available. **Bk Rev. Ad Acc. Circ:** 600.
**Desc:** All matters relating to the study of museums, the activities of museums and the Museums Association of Southern Africa.

US
**SANTA BARBARA MUSEUM OF ART NEWSLETTER.** Newsletter. English. Six times a year. Free with membership: $40.00 general membership; $60.00 associate membership. Santa Barbara Museum of Art, 1130 State Street, Santa Barbara CA 93101. **Tel** (805)963-4364, FAX (805)966-6840. **ED** Cathy Pollock (editor's phone: (805)963-4364 Ext. 317). **Circ:** 5,000 (ctrl).

MY/0581-7897
**SARAWAK MUSEUM JOURNAL, THE.** [Sarawak Mus. J.]. **Main/Corp** Sarawak Museum, Kuching. Vol. 1-4, No. 1-15 (1911)-. English. an. Government of Malaysia Sarawak, Sarawak Museum, 93566 Kuching Sarawak Malaysia. **Tel** 011 60 24232. **LC** AM101; .S2613. **CODEN** SWMJAX. Documents available from BIOSIS Document Express.
**Ind/Abst** Anthropol. Lit.; Biodeter. Abstr. (1991-); Biol. Abstr. (-1988); Geogr. Abstr. Human Geogr.; Int. Bibliogr. Sociol.; Int. Dev. Abstr.; Leis. Recreat. Tour. Abstr.; Rice Abstr.; Rural Dev. Abstr.; World Agric. Econ.

RM/1013-4255
**SARGETIA.** [Sargetia]. (1937)-. Periodical. Romanian. ir.
**Ind/Abst** BHA : Biblio. Hist. Art.

GW
**SCHRIFTEN DES LIMESMUSEUMS AALEN.** **Added/Corp** Limesmuseum Aalen. 1984-. Monographic series. German. Price varies per volume. ***Continues** Kleine Schriften zur Kenntnis der Romischen Besetzungsgeschichte Sudwestdeutschlands.*

GW
**SCHULE UND MUSEUM.** Periodical. German. Three times a year. Moritz Diesterweg, Postfach 630180, D-60351 Frankfurt Germany. **Tel** 11 49 69 420810, FAX 11 49 69 42081100.

FR
**SCIENCE ET TECHNOLOGIE DE LA CONSERVATION ET DE LA RESTAURATION DES OEUVRES D'ART ET DU PATRIMOINE.** **VFOAT** STCR; Science et Technologie de la Conservation et de la Restauration; S.T.C.R. No. 1 (Juin 1988)-. Periodical. French. sa. 260.00F France; 280.00F other. Etudes et Realisations Couleur, 68 rue Jean Jaures F, 92800 Puteaux France. **Tel** 011 33 1 47730123.

US
**SEATTLE ART MUSEUM.** **Main/Corp** Seattle Art Museum. (Nov. 1978)-. Periodical. English. mo. Seattle Art Museum, Volunteer Park, Seattle WA 98112. ***Continues** Seattle Art Museum Newsletter, 0197-5242.*

US/0197-5242
**SEATTLE ART MUSEUM NEWSLETTER.** **Main/Corp** Seattle Art Museum. **Added/Corp** Seattle Art Museum. Newsletter. (1976)-. Newsletter. English. ***Continues** Newsletter - Seattle Art Museum.*

US
**SEMC JOURNAL.** **Main/Corp** Southeastern Museums Conference, Inc. (197?)-. Periodical. English. ir. $20.00 Professional; $25.00 (individuals); $30.00 (institutions-budgets below $100,000.00);$55.00 trustee or contributing; $85.00 (institutions-budgets of $100,001.00 - 250,000.00); $175.00 (institutions-budgets over $250,000.00) Comes with Southeastern Museum Conference membership. Southeastern Museum Conference / SEMC Inc., PO Box 3494, Baton Rouge LA 70821. **Tel** (504)383-5042, FAX (504)383-5042. **ED** Pamela Meister.

BL
**SEMINARIOS DO MUSEU DA CASA BRASILEIRA: BOLETIM.** **Main/Corp** Museu da Casa Brasileira. No. 1, (1974)-. Bulletin. Portuguese. Av Brigadeiro Farria, Lima 774 Peru. **LC** F2631; .M9a.

US
**SEROLOGICAL MUSEUM BULLETIN, THE.** ***Ceased.*** **Added/Corp** Rutgers University. Bureau of Biological Research. No. 1 (Oct. 1948)-?. Bulletin. English. sa. Serological Museum, Rutgers University, Bureau of Biological Research, New Brunswick NJ 08903.

CN/0821-2287
**SLATE (TORONTO).** (SLATE : TORONTO GALLERY GUIDE.). [Slate]. **VFOAT** Toronto Gallery Guide. Vol. 3, No. 1 (Jan. 1982)-. Periodical. English. Ten times a year (Except Jan. & Aug.). 22.00Can$ Canada; 33.00Can$ others. Slate Gallery Guide, PO Box 1175, Kingston Ontario K7L 4Y8 Canada. **Tel** (613)542-3717. **DD** 709.713/541/025. ***Continues** Slate Gallery Guide, 0821-2279.*

US/0277-4887
**SONORENSIS.** **VFOAT** ASDM Sonorensis. Vol. 1 (Summer/Fall 1978)-. Periodical. English. qt. Arizona-Sonora Desert Museum, 2021 N Kinney Road, Tucson AZ 85743. **Tel** (602)883-1380. **ED** Lauray Yule. **Circ:** 18,600 (ctrl). ***Supersedes** ASDM Newsletter.*
**Desc:** Sonorensis is a membership newsletter featuring articles by museum curators on the flora and fauna of the Sonoran Desert region.
**Ind/Abst** Fish Rev.; Wildl. Rev.

US/0885-9140
**SOUTH DAKOTA MUSEUM, THE.** [S. D. Mus.]. V. 1, No. 1-. Periodical. English. sa. W H Over Dakota Museum, University of South Dakota, Vermillion SD 57069. **DD** 069. ***Supersedes** W.H. Over North Dakota Museum. Museum News.*
**Ind/Abst** Am. Hist. Life.

UK
**SOUTH YORKSHIRE.** 1- 1974-. English. Doncaster Museum and Art Gallery, Curator, Doncaster England. **LC** DA670.Y59; S65. **DD** 914.27/4/008.

US/0076-0994
**SOUTHWEST MUSEUM PAPERS.** **VFOAT** Papers / Southwest Museum. No. 1 (Apr. 1928)-. English. ir. Southwest Museum, PO Box 128, Los Angeles CA 90042. **Tel** (310)221-2164. **ED** Steven A LeBlanc. **Bk Rev. Ad Acc.**
**Desc:** These occasional papers focus on the anthropology and archaeology of the Americas.

RU/0208-2403
**SOVETSKII MUZEI (1984).** ***Title Change.*** (SOVETSKII MUZEI.). **Added/Corp** Soviet Union. Ministerstvo Kultury. Akademiia Nauk SSSR. **VFOAT** Soviet Museum; Musee Sovietique. (Jan./Feb. 1984)-(1992). Periodical. Russian (table of contents in English, French and Russian). bm. Izdatelstvo Iskusstvo, Vorotnikovskii Pereulok 11, 103009 Moscow Russia. **LC** AM1; .S6. ***Continues** Sovetskii Muzei (1931).* ***Continued by** Mir Muzeia, 0869-8171.*

US/0067-6179
**SPECIAL PUBLICATIONS.** **Main/Corp** Bernice Pauahi Bishop Museum. (1892)-. Monographic series. English. ir. Price varies per volume. Bishop Museum Press, PO Box 19000-A, Honolulu HI 96817. **Tel** (808)847-3511. **ED** Henry Bennett. **Bk Rev. Ad Acc.**

US/0149-1768
**SPECIAL PUBLICATIONS - THE MUSEUM, TEXAS TECH UNIVERSITY.** [Spec. publ. Mus., Tex. Tech. Univ.]. **Main/Corp** Texas Tech University. Museum. **Added/Corp** International Center for Arid and Semi-Arid Land Studies. No. 1 (Dec. 1972)-. Monographic series. English. ir. Price varies per volume. Tech Press, Admin/Educ Building, W Wing Basement/Room 43, Lubbock TX 79409-1037. **Tel** (806)742-2982. **DD** 500; 600.
**Desc:** There purpose is the timely dissemination of the results of primary research in museum- related sciences. Issues range from 48 to 500 printed pages in length. Appropriate numbers are published in split editions (both softcover and hardbound). All manuscripts are subjected to review by the Museum Publications Committee, outside reviewers, and the Managing Editor.
**Ind/Abst** Fish Rev. (Jan. 1989-July 1992); GeoRef; Wildl. Rev. (Jan. 1989-July 1992).

US/1042-3729
**SPECTRA (SYRACUSE, N.Y.).** (SPECTRA : A PUBLICATION OF THE MUSEUM COMPUTER NETWORK, INC.). [Spectra]. **Added/Corp** Museum Computer Network, Inc. Vol. 1 (1974)-. Periodical. English. qt (Mar., June, Sept., Dec.). $60.00. Museum Computer Network, 8720 Georgia Avenue, Suite 501, Silver Spring MD 20912. **Tel** (301)585-4413, FAX (301)495-0810, telex (301)585-4413. **DD** 069.
**Ind/Abst** Museum Abstr.

US
**SPECTRUM.** **Added/Corp** Science Museum of Virginia, Richmond. Vol. 1 (May/June 1978)-. Periodical. English. qt. Free. Science Museum of Virginia, 2500 West Broad Street, Richmond VA 23220. **Tel** (804)257-0037. ***Continues** Newsletter - Science Museum of Virginia.*

US/0899-4730
**ST. LOUIS ART MUSEUM ANNUAL REPORT, THE.** See The Arts-Art.

US/0081-542X
**STEAM PASSENGER SERVICE DIRECTORY.** See Transportation-Railroads.

HU/0133-3046
**STUDIA COMITATENSIA BUDAPEST.** **VFOAT** Naucnye Trudy Muzeev Komitata Pest; Studien aus den Museen des Komitats Pest; Tanulmanyok Pest Megye Uzeumaibol; Studies Published by the Museums of Pest County; Etudes Publiees par les Musees du Comitat Pest. (1972)-. Monographic series. Hungarian. ir. Price varies per volume. **UDC** 39. **CODEN** 99.
**Ind/Abst** Anthropol. Index; BHA : Biblio. Hist. Art.

# Museums and Galleries

PL/0585-5276
**STUDIA I MATERIAY LUBELSKIE / MUZEUM OKREGOWE W LUBLINIE.** **Added/Corp** Muzeum Okregowe w Lublinie. (196?)-. Polish (summaries and/or abstracts in English and Russian). **LC** WMLC L 83/5306.
**Ind/Abst** BHA : Biblio. Hist. Art.

PL/0137-5318
**STUDIA MUZEALNE.** [Stud. Muzealne]. **VFOAT** Etudes. Annuaire du Musee National de Poznan. (1953)-. Multiple languages. **UDC** 069.
**Ind/Abst** BHA : Biblio. Hist. Art.

II/0081-8259
**STUDIES IN MUSEOLOGY.** V. 1- 1965-. English. ir. Indian Books and Periodicals, 2429 Tilak Street, Pahar Ganj, New Delhi 110005 India. **LC** AM1; .S84.

PL
**STUTTHOF / MUZEUM STUTTHOF W SZTUTOWIE.** **VFOAT** Zeszyty Muzeum, Stutthof. (1976)-. Periodical. Polish (summaries and/or abstracts in English, German and Russian). 50.00. **LC** D805.P7; S78.
**Ind/Abst** Am. Hist. Life (1981-).

CN/0704-576X
**SYLLOGEUS - NATIONAL MUSEUM OF NATURAL SCIENCES.** [Syllogeus - Natl. Mus. Nat. Sci.]. **VAT** Syllogeus - Musee National des Sciences Naturelles. Monographic series. English (French). ir. Price varies per volume. McClelland and Stewart Ltd, 25 Hollinger Road, Toronto Ontario M4B 3G2 Canada. **DD** 509.71. **CODEN** SYLGBY. Documents available from BIOSIS Document Express.
**Ind/Abst** ASTIS Curr. Aware. Bull. (1978-); AQUAREF; ASTIS Bibliogr. (1978-); Biol. Abstr.; GeoRef.

US/0889-7425
**SYMBOLS.** See Anthropology.

HU/0138-9947
**SZOLNOK MEGYEI MUZEUMI EVKONYV.** [Szolnok m. muz. evkv.]. **Added/Corp** Szolnok Megyei Muzeumok Igazgatosaga. **VFOAT** Jahrbuch der Museen des Komitates Szolnok; Annual of the Szolnok County Museums. (1973)-. Hungarian. an. **LC** AS205.A1; S95.
**Ind/Abst** BHA : Biblio. Hist. Art.

CN/0713-3901
**TALES OF THE TWELVE.** (TALES OF THE TWELVE : NEWSLETTER OF THE ST. CATHARINES HISTORICAL MUSEUM.). [Tales Twelve]. **VFOAT** Newsletter. Vol. 1, Issue 1 (Spring 1982)-. Newsletter. English. Three times a year. 7.00Can$ Canada; 4.00Can$ other. St Catharines Historical Museum, 343 Merritt Street, St Catharines Ontario L2T 1K7 Canada. **Tel** (416)227-2962. **DD** 069/.9971351. **Bk Rev. Circ:** 650 (ctrl). **Continues** St. Catharines Historical Museum. Newsletter, 0706-7461.
**Desc:** Articles about the activities, programmes, and events of the St. Catharines Historical Museum.

FR
**TECHNICAL HANDBOOKS FOR MUSEUMS AND MONUMENTS.** 1-. Monographic series. English. Price varies per volume. UNESCO / United Nations Educational Scientific and Cultural Organization, 7 Place de Fontenoy, 75700 Paris France. **Tel** 011 33 1 456610000. **DD** 069.5/3.

US/0196-8297
**TECHNICAL REPORTS (UNIVERSITY OF MICHIGAN. MUSEUM OF ANTHROPOLOGY).** (TECHNICAL REPORTS - MUSEUM OF ANTHROPOLOGY, UNIVERSITY OF MICHIGAN.). [Tech. rep. - Mus. Anthropol., Univ. Mich.]. **Added/Corp** University of Michigan. Museum of Anthropology. (1971)-. Monographic series. English. ir. Price varies. Museum of Anthropology / Michigan, University of Michigan, 4009 Museums, Ann Arbor MI 48109. **Tel** (313)764-0485. **LC** UNC.

US/0083-7407
**TEXTILE MUSEUM JOURNAL.** [Tex. Mus. j.]. **Main/Corp** Textile Museum (Washington, D.C.). **Added/Corp** Textile Museum (Washington, D.C.) Journal. Vol. 1 (Nov. 1962)-. Periodical. English. an. $20.00 (one year); $45.00 US, Canada and Mexico; $50.00 others Comes with Textile Museum membership. Textile Museum, 2320 South Street Northwest, Washington DC 20008. **Tel** (202)483-0983, FAX (202)483-0994. **ED** Eileen Martin. **LC** NK8802.W3; A3. **DD** 069/.9746. **Circ:** 3,500 (ctrl). **Supersedes** Textile Museum (Washington, D.C.) Workshop Notes.
**Desc:** Traditional motif evaluation/symbolism; ethnographic relationship between design, weaving and raw materials; new insights as a result of current scholarship and research.
**Ind/Abst** Acad. Search (July 1993-); Anthropol. Lit. ; Art Archaeol. Tech. Abstr.; Art Index; ARTbibliogr. Mod.; BHA : Biblio. Hist. Art; INFO-SOUTH Abstr.; Mag. Search; Text. Technol. Dig.; World Text. Abstr.

CN/1184-6216
**THUNDER BAY MUSEUM NEWSLETTER.** [Thunder Bay Mus. newsl.]. **Added/Corp** Thunder Bay Historical Museum. Thunder Bay Historical Museum Society. (Winter 1990/91)-. Newsletter. English. qt. Free to members. Thunder Bay Historical Museum Society, 219 South May Street, Thunder Bay Ontario P7E 1B5 Canada. **Tel** (807)623-0801, FAX (807)622-6880. **DD** 971.3/12/0074.

JA
**TOKYO DAIGAKU SOGO KENKYU SHIRYOKAN YORAN.** **Main/Corp** Tokyo Daigaku. Sogo Kenkyu Shiryokan. Japanese. 3-1 Hongo 7-chome Bunkyo-ku, Tokyo 113 Japan. **LC** AM101.T555; A3.

NO/0332-6195
**TROMURA. NATURVITENSKAP.** (TROMURA. NATURVITENSKAP : TROMS MUSEUMS RAPPORTSERIE TROMURA.). [Tromura, Naturvitensk.]. **Added/Corp** Universitetet I Troms. Institutt for Museumsvirksomhet. Troms Museum. **VFOAT** Naturvitenskap. No. 1 (1978)-. Monographic series. Norwegian (English). ir (2 to 7 issues per year). Price varies per volume. Universitetet i Troms, Univ. Biblio Tromso Mus Folkepark, N 9000 Tromso, Norway. **LC** UNC.
**Ind/Abst** GeoRef.

UK/0957-0578
**UKIC GRAPEVINE.** [UKIC grapevine]. **VFOAT** United Kingdom Institute for Conservation Grapevine; Grapevine (London. 1989). (1989)-. Periodical. English. bm. **DD** 069.53.
**Ind/Abst** Museum Abstr.

JA
**UNIVERSITY MUSEUM, THE UNIVERSITY OF TOKYO, THE.** **Main/Corp** Tokyo Daigaku. Sogo Kenkyu Shiryokan. (19??)-. English. University of Tokyo Press, 7 3 1 Hongo Bunkyo-ku, Tokyo 113 Japan. **Tel** 011 81 3 3811 0964. **LC** AM101.T555; A32. **DD** 069/.0952/135.

US/0272-0345
**UPDATE (SMITHSONIAN INSTITUTION. TRAVELING EXHIBITION SERVICE).** (UPDATE.). [Update]. **Main/Corp** Smithsonian Institution. Traveling Exhibition Service. English. an. Free. Smithsonian Institution / Traveling Exhibition Service, Traveling Exhibition Service, Washington DC 20560. **Tel** (202)357-3168, FAX (202)357-4324. **ED** Dale E Alward. **LC** Q11; .S79A. **DD** 069.5/09753. Index available. **Circ:** 8,000 (ctrl). **Continues** Smithsonian Institution. Traveling Exhibition Service. Catalogue.
**Desc:** Catalog of traveling exhibitions from the Smithsonian. More than 100 different topics covered. Rental fee charged to exhibitors as low as $2,000 for four weeks.

CN/0821-5235
**UPDATE (UKRAINIAN MUSEUM OF CANADA (SASKATOON, SASK.)).** (UPDATE / UKRAINIAN MUSEUM OF CANADA.). [Update - Ukr. Mus. Can.]. **VFOAT** Novynky; Novynky-Ukrainskyi Muzei Kanady. Vol. 1, No. 1 (Fall 1979)-. Periodical. English (Ukrainian). ir. Free. Update Ukrainian Museum of Canada, 910 Spadina Cresc East 3H5 Canada. **Tel** (306)244-3800. **ED** Albert Kachkowski. **DD** 305.8/91791/071074011242. ctrl circ.
**Desc:** Includes information on museum activities, programs and exhibits.

UK/0967-2273
**V & A CONSERVATION JOURNAL.** [V & A conserv. j.]. **VFOAT** Conservation Journal. (1991)-. Periodical. English. qt.
**Ind/Abst** Museum Abstr.

GW/0931-6280
**VEROFFENTLICHUNGEN DER URGESCHICHTLICHEN SAMMLUNGEN DES LANDESMUSEUMS ZU HANNOVER.** [Veroff. Urgesch. Samml. Landesmus. Hann.]. **VFOAT** Veroffentlichungen der Urgeschichtlichen Abteilung des Provinzial-Museums zu Hannover. (1928)-. Monographic series. German. ir. Price varies per volume. **UDC** 903.
**Ind/Abst** Anthropol. Lit.

NE
**VERSLAG VAN DE HOOFDCONSULENT VOOR DE MUSEA.** **Main/Corp** Netherlands. Ministerie van Cultuur, Recreatie en Maatschappelijk Werk. (19??)-. Dutch. an. **LC** AM57; .N47a.

CI/0042-6083
**VIJESTI MUZEALACA I KONZERVATORA HRVATSKE.** **Added/Corp** Drustvo Drustvo Konzervatora Jugoslavije. Podruznica za Hrvatsku. (1959)-. Serbo-Croatian (Roman) (summaries and/or abstracts in German). bm. **LC** AM69.Y8; V53. **Continues** Drustvo Muzejsko-Konzervatorskih Radnika NR Hrvatske.

Vijesti Drustva Muzejsko-Konzervatorskih Radnika NR Hrvatske.
**Ind/Abst** BHA : Biblio. Hist. Art.

NE
**VITRINE.** SDU Uitgeverij, Postbus 20014, Christoffel Plan, 2500 EA Den Haag Netherlands. **Tel** 011 31 70 3789911.

JA
**WAKAYAMA KENRITSU HAKUBUTSUKAN NEMPO.** **Main/Corp** Wakayama Kenritsu Hakubutsukan. Japanese. an. Wakayama Kenritsu Hakubutsukan, 1 Ichibancho, Wakayama-shi Japan. **LC** AM101.W1937; A37.

US/0511-8824
**WHITNEY REVIEW.** 1960/61-. English. an. Whitney Museum of American Art, 945 Madison Avenue at 75th, New York NY 10021. **Tel** (212)794-0600. **LC** N618; .W45. **DD** 708/.147/1.

US/0049-7657
**WIND ROSE, THE.** Periodical. English. bm. $15.00 membership. Mystic Seaport Museum, 50 Greenmanville Avenue, Mystic CT 06355. **Tel** (203)572-0711. available on microfilm from University Microfilms International (UMI).

US/0000-0698
**WORLD MUSEUM PUBLICATIONS.** (WORLD MUSEUM PUBLICATIONS : A DIRECTORY OF ART AND CULTURAL MUSEUMS, THEIR PUBLICATIONS AND AUDIO-VISUAL MATERIALS.). [World mus. publ.]. (1982)-. Directory. English. ir. $127.00. R R Bowker, A Reed Reference Publishing Company, Part of Reed International PLC, PO Box 31, 121 Chanlon Drive, New Providence NJ 07974. **Tel** (908)464-6800, (800)521-8110, FAX (908)665-6688, telex 138-755. **LC** AM1; .W67. **DD** 069/.025. **NLM** Z 5931 W919.

HU/0865-5464
**WOSINSKY MOR MUZEUM EVKONYVE, A.** [Wosinsky Mor Muz. evkv.]. **VFOAT** Jahrbuch des Wosinsky-Mor-Museums, Szekszard. (1990)-. Multiple languages. be. **UDC** 069.7. **Continues** A Beri Balogh Adam Muzeum Evkonyve, 0236-9354.
**Ind/Abst** BHA : Biblio. Hist. Art.

UK
**YEAR BOOK - ULSTER FOLK AND TRANSPORT MUSEUM.** **Main/Corp** Ulster Folk and Transport Museum. **Added/Corp** Ulster Folk and Transport Museum. Annual Report. Ulster Folk and Transport Museum. Accounts and Balance Sheet. (1973)-. Corporate Report. English. an. £2.50 Ireland; £3.00 other. Ulster Folk & Transport Museum, Cultra Manor, Holywood Co Down, Northern Ireland. **Circ:** 500. **Continues** Ulster Folk Museum. Yearbook.
**Desc:** Annual report of the museum's work, including staff changes, major events, exhibitions, etc. Also contains a summary of the museum's financial accounts for the previous year.

US/1060-5037
**YEAR IN REVIEW - CRANBROOK INSTITUTE OF SCIENCE.** (YEAR IN REVIEW.). [Year rev. - Cranbrook Inst. Sci.]. **Main/Corp** Cranbrook Institute of Science. (1989-1990)-. English. Cranbrook Institute of Science, 500 Lone Pine Road, Bloomfield Hills MI 48013. **Tel** (313)645-3203, FAX (313)645-6545. **DD** 069. **Continues** Annual Report - Cranbrook Institute of Science, 0197-0534.

JA/0386-4286
**YOKOSUKA-SHI HAKUBUTSUKAN SHIRYOSHU.** [Yokosuka-shi Hakubutsukan shiryoshu]. **Main/Corp** Yokosuka-shi Hakubutsukan. **VFOAT** Miscellaneous Report of the Yokosuka City Museum. Vol. 1- ; 1978-. Japanese (summaries and/or abstracts in English). Yokosuka-shi Hakubutsukan, Yokosuka 238 Japan. **LC** AM101.Y58; A34.

ZA
**ZAMBIA MUSEUMS JOURNAL.** Vol. 1; 1970-. English. an. National Museums of Zambia, PO Box 60498, Livingstone Zambia. **LC** DT963.A2; Z37. **DD** 968.9/4/005.
**Ind/Abst** Anthropol. Lit.

XO/0524-2223
**ZBORNIK SLOVENSKEHO NARODNEHO MUZEA.** **Main/Corp** Slovenske Narodne Muzeum. **VFOAT** Zbornik Slovenske Narodne Muzeum; Acta Musei Tyrnaviensis; Acta Rerum Naturalium Museorum Slovaci Bratislava. Vol. 1 (1955)-. Czech (table of contents in Russian and German). an. **CODEN** ZSNMAS. Documents available from BIOSIS Document Express.
**Ind/Abst** Biol. Abstr.; Numis. Lit.; Rev. Med. Vet. Entomol.

## ABSTRACTING, BIBLIOGRAPHIES AND STATISTICS

UK
**BIBLIOGRAPHY OF MUSEUM AND ART GALLERY PUBLICATIONS AND AUDIO-VISUAL AIDS IN GREAT BRITAIN AND IRELAND, THE. VFOAT** Bibliography of Museum Publications. 1977-. Bibliography. English. be. 417 Maitland Avenue, Teaneck NJ 07666. **LC** Z2001; .B54. **DD** 013/.096/0941.

UK/0267-8594
**MUSEUM ABSTRACTS.** Vol. 3 (1987)-. Abstracting/Indexing Service. English. mo. £50.00 UK; £100.00 other; £35.00 Scottish Museums Council members. Scottish Museums Council, 20 22 Torphichen St County Hse, Edinburgh EH3 8JB Scotland. **Tel** 44 31 2297465, FAX 44 31 2292728. **ED** Wilma Alexander. **[CCC].**
**Desc:** Covers all aspects of museums and museum management.

## MUSIC

US/8756-7717
**1/1 (SAN FRANCISCO, CALIF.).** (1/1 : THE QUARTERLY JOURNAL OF THE JUST INTONATION NETWORK.). [1/1]. **Added/Corp** Just Intonation Network (San Francisco, Calif.). **VFOAT** One/One; One One; 1 1. Vol. 1, No. 1 (Winter 1985)-. Periodical. English. ir (Jan. Binder). $25.00. Just Intonation Network, 535 Stevenson Street, San Francisco CA 94103. **Tel** (415)864-8123, FAX (415)864-8726. **ED** David B. Doty. **LC** ML3809; .A12. **DD** 781/.22. Index available. cum. index. **Bk Rev. Ad Acc. Circ:** 300.
**Desc:** Serves composers, musicians, instrument designers, and theorists working with tuning in just intonation. Covers compositional techniques, analysis, historical background, instrument design/construction/modification, programming techniques, notation, scale/chord construction. Include composer interviews, book, record, and software reviews, tutorials, editorials opinions, occasional invective, and obscure humor.
**Ind/Abst** Music Artic. Guide; Music Index; RILM Abstr.

●US/1054-6022
**17TH CENTURY MUSIC.** [17th century music]. **Added/Corp** American Heinrich Schutz Society. **VFOAT** Seventeenth Century Music. Vol. 1, No. 1 (Fall 1991)-. Periodical. English. Twice a year (Spring & Fall). $10.00 Comes with Society for Seventeenth Century Music Membership. Society for 17th Century Music, C 550 Harris Arts Center, Department of Music, Provo UT 84602. **Tel** (314)935-5000. **DD** 780. ***Continues*** *Schutz Society Reports.*

US/0148-2076
**19TH CENTURY MUSIC.** [19th century music]. **VFOAT** Nineteenth Century Music. **VAT** Nineteenth Century Music. Vol. 1 (July 1977)-. Periodical. English. Three times a year (Mar., July, Nov.). $31.00 (individuals), $64.00 (institutions). University of California Press, 2120 Berkeley Way, Berkeley CA 94720. **Tel** (510)642-4191, (510)642-3907, FAX (510)642-9917. **ED** Walter Frisch and James Hepokoski. **LC** ML1; .N77. **DD** 780/.903/4. **[CCC]. Bk Rev. Ad Acc. Pr Rev. Circ:** 1,350 (ctrl). available on microfilm and microfiche from University Microfilms International (UMI). Documents available from The Genuine Article, UMI Article Clearinghouse.
**Desc:** Interdisciplinary studies, history and research on 19th century music.
**Ind/Abst** Acad. Search (Jan. 1993-); Am. Hist. Life (1987-); Am. Bibliogr. Slavic East Europ. Stud.; Arts Humanit. Citation Index [Full Cov.]; Humanit. Index; Humanit. Source (Jul. 1993-); INFO-SOUTH Abstr.; Mag. Search; Music Artic. Guide; Music Index; Newsp. Period. Abstr. (1991-); Res. Alert [Full Cov.]; RILM Abstr.

US/0093-0288
**1810 OVERTURE. Added/Corp** Northwestern University, Evanston, Ill. Music Library. **VAT** Eighteen Hundred and Ten Overture. (19??)-. Periodical. English. Musicians Union, Local 47 AF Of M / 817 Vine St., Los Angeles CA 90038. **Tel** (213)462-2161 ext. 260. **LC** [ML1; .E5]. **DD** 016.78.

US/0360-7178
**AAMOA REPORTS. Main/Corp** Afro-American Music Opportunities Association, Inc. (19??)-. Periodical. English. bm. Afro-American Music Opportunities Association, 2809 Wayzata Boulevard, Minneapolis MN 55405.

GW/0567-4999
**ABHANDLUNGEN ZUR KUNST-, MUSIK- UND LITERATURWISSENSCHAFT.** **See** The Arts.

UK/0001-3242
**ABOUT THE HOUSE.** ***Ceased.*** [About house]. **Added/Corp** Friends of Covent Garden. (Nov. 1962)-Vol. 8 (1992). Periodical. English. Three times a year. Friends of Covent Garden Limited, Royal Opera House, Covent Garden, London WC2E 9DD England. **Tel** 011 44 71 2401200 Ext. 268. **(Subscription address:** Wells House, 15 Elmfield Road, Bromley Kent BR1 1NW England) **ED** Phyllida Ritter. **LC** ML5; .A22. **DD** 782.1/05. Index available. **Ad Acc. Circ:** 21,000 (ctrl). available on microfilm and microfiche from University Microfilms International (UMI). Documents available from The Genuine Article.
**Desc:** Magazine of The Friends of Covent Garden.
**Ind/Abst** Arts Humanit. Citation Index (19??-19??) [Full Cov.]; Curr. Contents Arts Humanit.; Music Index; Res. Alert [Full Cov.]; RILM Abstr.

US/0893-1305
**ABSTRACTS OF PAPERS READ AT THE ... ANNUAL MEETING OF THE AMERICAN MUSICOLOGICAL SOCIETY.** [Abstr. pap. read Annu. Meet. Am. Musicol. Soc.]. **Main/Corp** American Musicological Society. Meeting. (19??)-. English. an (Nov.). $2.50. American Musicological Society, 201 South 34th Street, Philadelphia PA 19104. **Tel** (215)898-8698. **LC** ML1; .A69. **DD** 780. **Circ:** 1,500.
**Desc:** Abstracts of papers read at the annual meeting.

CN/0711-3471
**ACADEMY NEWS!.** [Acad. news]. **Main/Corp** Vancouver Academy of Music. Vol. 1, No. 1 (Dec. 1980)-. Periodical. English. Vancouver Academy of Music, 1270 Chestnut Street, Vancouver British Columbia V6J 4R9 Canada. **DD** 780/.7/2971133.

US/0730-8906
**ACCENT ON MUSIC.** [Accent music]. **VFOAT** Accent. (198?)-. Periodical. English. bm. $5.50 US; $6.25 other. Accent Publications, 12100 West 6th Avenue, Box 15337, Denver CO 80215. **Tel** (303)988-5300. **LC** ML1; .A112. **DD** 780/.5. ***Continues*** *Accent (Evanston, Ill.), 0362-6059.*

CN/0710-6335
**ACCENTS (NEW BRUNSWICK TEACHERS' ASSOCIATION. MUSIC EDUCATION COUNCIL).** (ACCENTS : THE NEWSLETTER OF THE MUSIC EDUCATION COUNCIL OF THE NEW BRUNSWICK TEACHERS' ASSOCIATION.). [Accents (N.B. Teach. Assoc., Music Educ. Counc.)]. **Added/Corp** New Brunswick Teachers' Association. Music Education Council. Vol. 1, No. 1 (Feb. 1975)-. Newsletter. English. ir. Music Education Council of the New Brunswick Teachers' Association, PO Box 752, Fredericton New Brunswick E3B 5R6 Canada. **DD** 780/.7.

US
**ACCORD.** (19??)-. Periodical. English. Ernest Deffner Publishing Inc., PO Box 608, Department S, Mineola NY 11501. **LC** ML990.A4; A2. **DD** 786.9/7.
**Desc:** Accordian journal.

US/1049-9261
**ACOUSTIC GUITAR.** [Acoust. guitar]. Vol. 1, No. 1 (July/Aug. 1990)-. Periodical. English. Six times a year (Jan., Mar., May, July, Sept., Nov.). $36.00. String Letter Press Publishers, 412 Red Hill Avenue 15, San Anselmo CA 94960. **Tel** (415)485-6946, (800)827-6837. **ED** Jeffrey Pepper Rodgers. **LC** ML1015.G9; A35. **DD** 787.87/05. **Ad Acc.**
**Desc:** Written by and for the musicians. Covers a variety of musical styles and includes transcriptions from recordings and solo pieces for guitar.

US/1054-0717
**ACOUSTIC PERFORMER.** ***Ceased.*** [Acoust. perform.]. (Oct. 1989)-Ceased Jan. 1992. Periodical. English. bm. Acoustic Musician, PO Box 231, Delmar CA 92014. **DD** 784.

CN/0226-2541
**ACQUISITIONS - METROPOLITAN TORONTO LIBRARY, MUSIC DEPARTMENT.** (ACQUISITIONS / METROPOLITAN TORONTO LIBRARY, MUSIC DEPARTMENT.). [Acquis. - Metrop. Toronto Libr., Music Dep.]. **Main/Corp** Metropolitan Toronto Library. Music Dept. Vol. 1, No. 1 (Mar. 1980)-. Periodical. English. Metropolitan Toronto Library Board, 789 Yonge Street, Toronto Ontario M4W 2G8 Canada. **Tel** (416)393-7134, telex 06-22232. **DD** 016.78. ***Continues*** *Metropolitan Toronto Library. Music Dept. Selected List of Acquisitions, 0227-7492.*

GW/0001-6233
**ACTA MOZARTIANA.** [Acta Mozart.]. **Added/Corp** Deutsche Mozart-Gesellschaft. (1954)-. Periodical. German. qt. DM 60.00 Comes with German Mozart Society Membership. Deutsche Mozart Gesellschaft, Karlstrasse 6, D 86150 Augsburg Germany. **Tel** 011 49 821 518588. **ED** V. Augsburg. **Bk Rev. Ad Acc.** ctrl circ. Documents available from The Genuine Article.
**Desc:** Publication of the German Mozart Society.
**Ind/Abst** Arts Humanit. Citation Index [Full Cov.]; Curr. Contents Arts Humanit.; Music Index; Res. Alert [Full Cov.]; RILM Abstr.

GW/0001-6241
**ACTA MUSICOLOGICA.** [Acta musicol.]. **Added/Corp** International Musicological Society. Vol. 3 (1931)-. Periodical. English (French, German and Italian). Twice a year. DM110.00. Baerenreiter Verlag Basel, Neuweilerstrasse 15, CH 4015 Basel Switzerland. **Tel** 011 44 61 3025899, FAX 011 44 61 3025804. **(Subscription address:** Foregin Music Distributors, 13 Elkay Drive, Chester NY 10918.) **LC** ML5; .I6. **[CCC].** Index available. cum. index. **Bk Rev. Ad Acc. Circ:** 7,600 (ctrl). ***Continues*** *Mitteilungen der Internationalen Gesellschaft fur Musikwissenschaft.*
**Desc:** The periodical furthers the aims of the IMS: it encompasses music researchers from all nations, administrations, international projects and various reciprocal research.
**Ind/Abst** Curr. Contents Arts Humanit.; Music Index; RILM Abstr.

GW/0567-7874
**ACTA ORGANOLOGICA.** [Acta organol.]. **Added/Corp** Gesellschaft der Orgelfreunde. Vol. 1 (1967)-. German. ir. DM54.00. Verlag Merseburger Berlin GmbH, POB 103880, D 34038 Kassel Germany. **Tel** 011 49 561 772002. **LC** ML5; .A253. **DD** 786.5/05.
**Ind/Abst** RILM Abstr.

GW/0001-6942
**ACTA SAGITTARIANA.** (ACTA SAGITTARIANA : MITTEILUNGEN DER INTERNATIONALEN HEINRICH SCHUETZ-GESELLSCHAFT.). [Acta sagittar.]. **Added/Corp** Internationale Heinrich Schuetz-Gesellschaft. **VFOAT** Mitteilungen der Internationalen Heinrich Schuetz-Gesellschaft. (1955)-. Periodical. German (English and French). International Heinrich Schuetz GES, Heinrich Schuetz Allee, D 34131 Kassel Germany. **LC** WMLC 91/6605.
**Ind/Abst** Music Index (-19??); RILM Abstr.

BE/0001-8171
**ADEM.** [Adem]. **Added/Corp** Madrigaal (Organization : The Netherlands). (19??)-. Periodical. Dutch (summaries and/or abstracts in English and French). Four times a year. $19.15 North America; 800F Belgium; $29.15 other. Adem, Herestraat 53, B-3000 Louvain Belgium. **Tel** 016 233967, FAX 016 222477. **ED** P. Schollaert. Index available in last issue of volume--attached. **Bk Rev. Ad Acc.**
**Desc:** Covers church music, choirs, organs, music education, instrumental and vocal music education as well as the history of music. Contains an anthology of about 120 music reviews, a discography, and a bibliography.
**Ind/Abst** Music Index; RILM Abstr.

US/1063-7494
**ADULT CONTEMPORARY MUSIC RESEARCH LETTER, THE.** [Adult contemp. music res. lett.]. **Added/Corp** Consolidated Communications Consultants. **VFOAT** Adult Contemporary Music Letter; Adult Contemporary Music Research. (1984)-. Periodical. English. Forty-eight times a year. $320.00. Adult Contemporary Music Research Letter, 1837 S E Harold Street, Portland OR 97202-4932. **Tel** (503)232-9787, FAX (503)232-9787. **ED** Eric Norberg. **DD** 384. **Circ:** 75.
**Desc:** Publishes explicit test results of new and current popular music, for appeal to the "core audience" of "adult contemporary" music radio stations.

UK
**AFRICA MUSIC.** (198?)-. Periodical. English. Six times a year. $12.00. Tony Amadi International Ltd., 30B Tabley Road, London N7 ONQ England.

SA/0065-4019
**AFRICAN MUSIC.** [Afr. music]. **Added/Corp** African Music Society (South Africa) International Library of African Music. Vol. 1, No. 1 (1954)-. English (French). ir. International Library of African Music, ISER Rhodes University, PO Box 184, Grahamstown 6140 South Africa. **Tel** 011 46 12 22023 Ext. 557. **ED** Andrew Tracey. **LC** ML5; .A26. **DD** 780.96. **Bk Rev. Ad Acc. Circ:** 100. ***Continues*** *African Music Society Newsletter.*
**Desc:** Articles on African music and related topics.
**Ind/Abst** Anthropol. Index; Anthropol. Lit.; Ethnoarts Index; Music Index; RILM Abstr.

KE
**AFRICAN MUSICOLOGY / INSTITUTE OF AFRICAN STUDIES, UNIVERSITY OF NAIROBI.** ***Suspended.*** **Added/Corp** University of Nairobi. Institute of African Studies. Vol. 1, No. 1 (Sept. 1983)-(1991). Periodical. English (French). an. Institute of African Studies / Kenya, PO Box 30197, University of Nairobi, Nairobi Kenya. **Tel** 011 254 2 742080 78. **LC** ML5; .A28. **DD** 781.7/296.
**Ind/Abst** MLA Int. Bibl. Books Artic. Mod. Lang. Lit.

US
**AGMAZINE.** **Main/Corp** American Guild of Musical Artists. (19??)-. Periodical. English. American Guild of Musical Artists, 1841 Broadway, New York NY 10023. **LC** ML27.U5; A2.
**Ind/Abst** Music Artic. Guide (?-?).

US/0362-5907
**AGO TIMES, THE.** **Main/Corp** American Guild of Organists. New York City Chapter. **Added/Corp** American Guild of Organists. New York City Chapter. Times. **VAT** American Guild of Organists Times. (19??)-. Periodical. English. qt. American Guild of Organists, 475 Riverside Drive, Suite 1260, New York NY 10115. **Tel** (212)870-2310, FAX (212)870-2163. **LC** ML1; .A375. **DD** 786.5/05.

SP
**AIXA : REVISTA ANUAL DE LA GABELLA, MUSEU ETNOLOGIC DEL MONTSENY.** **Added/Corp** Gabella (Museum). (1987)-. Periodical. Catalan. an. **LC** DP302; .M59.

UA
**AL-MAJALLAH AL-MUSIQIYAH.** (1936)-. Periodical. Arabic. mo. £E0.10. Al-Tawzi Dar Al-Ahram, 9 Harat Imad Aldin, Al-Qahirah UA Egypt. **LC** ML5; .M1525.

US
**ALBUM DE ORO.** **See** Biographies.

US/0739-1641
**ALBUM NETWORK, THE.** [Album netw.]. (19??)-. Periodical. English. wk. $300.00. Network Magazine Group, 120 North Victory Boulevard, Burbank CA 91502. **Tel** (818)955-4000, (800)222-4382, FAX (818)955-8048. **ED** Stephen R. Smith. **Bk Rev**. **Ad Acc. Circ:** 5,000 (ctrl).
**Desc:** Source for contemporary music research services.

CN/0825-1754
**ALLA BREVE.** **Added/Corp** Institut Kodaly du Canada. Filiale de Montreal. Vol. 1, No. 1 (May 1984)-. Periodical. French. Twice a year (Mar., Nov.). $10.00Can$ subscription; $15.00 library & others. Kodaly Institute of Canada Kodaly Institute of Canada, Margery Littley Registrar, 1411 Powell Street, Victoria British Columbia, V8V 2J3 Canada, Margery Littley Registrar, 1411 Powell Street, Victoria British Columbia, V8V 2J3 Canada,. **Tel** (604)385-4036, (604)385-4036, FAX , , telex , . **ED** Heather Morris and Jeanette Panagapka. **DD** 780/.7.

US/0002-5704
**ALLEGRO (NEW YORK, N.Y.).** (ALLEGRO.). **Added/Corp** Associated Musicians of Greater New York. (1921)-. Periodical. English. Eleven times a year (Monthly with July/Aug. issue combined). $23.00 US; $28.00 other. Association of Musicians of Greater New York, 322 West 48th Street, Allegro Department, New York NY 10036. **Tel** (212)239-4802. **ED** Tim Ledwith. **LC** ML1; .A195. **DD** 331.881178. **Bk Rev**. **Ad Acc. Circ:** 20,000 (ctrl).

IT
**ALMANACCO MUSICA.** (19??)-. Periodical. Italian. sa. Edizioni Il Formichiere, Via Del Lauro 3, 20121 Milan Italy. **LC** ML3469; .A45. **DD** 780/.42/05.

US/1065-1667
**ALTERNATIVE PRESS (CLEVELAND, OHIO).** (ALTERNATIVE PRESS : AP.). [Altern. press]. **VFOAT** AP. (19??)-. Periodical. English. Twelve times a year. $18.00 (one year); $30.00 (two years). Alternative Press, 1451 West 112th Street, Suite One, Cleveland OH 44102. **Tel** (216)631-1212. **DD** 781.

US
**ALUMNI DIRECTORY / SCHOOL OF MUSIC, UNIVERSITY OF SOUTHERN CALIFORNIA.** **See** College and School Publications-Alumni.

US/0896-9345
**ALWAYS JUKIN'.** [Always jukin']. **Added/Corp** Silver Age Jukebox Club. **VFOAT** Always Juking. (198?)-. Periodical. English. Twelve times a year. $30.00 (one year); $55.00 (two years). Silver Age Juke Box Club, 221 Yesler Way, Seattle WA 98104. **Tel** (206)233-9460, FAX (206)233-9871. **ED** M. Baute. **Bk Rev**, (Qty: 6). **Ad Acc, Adv Mgr:** Rick. **Circ:** 3,000 (ctrl).
**Desc:** News and information on jukeboxes and records.

IT
**AMADEUS : IL MENSILE DELLA GRANDE MUSICA.** Vol. 1, No. 1 (Dec. 1989)-. Periodical. Italian. mo. L174900.00. RCS Rizzoli Periodici, Via A Rizzoli 2, 20132 Milan Italy. **Tel** 011 39 2 27200720. **LC** ML5; .A5. **DD** 780/.5.

CN/0227-4310
**AMATEUR MUSICIEN (1980).** (LE MUSICIEN AMATEUR : JOURNAL DE CAMMAC.). **VFOAT** Amateur Musician. (1991)-. English (French). Cammac Office, PO Box 353, Westmount Quebec H3Z 2T5 Canada.

CN/0227-4310
**AMATEUR MUSICIEN (1980).** (LE MUSICIEN AMATEUR : JOURNAL DE CAMMAC.). **VFOAT** Amateur Musician. (1991)-. French (English). Cammac Office, PO Box 353, Westmount Quebec H3Z 2T5 Canada.

US
**AMC NEWSLETTER.** ***Suspended.*** V. 19- Sept. 1976-Suspended with Vol. 32, No. 2. Newsletter. English. sa. $15.00. American Music Center Inc, 250 West 54th Street/Room 300, New York NY 10019. **Tel** (212)247-3121. **ED** Heidi Waleson. **Ad Acc. Circ:** 1,800 (ctrl). ***Continues*** *American Music Center Newsletter.*
**Desc:** Information on contemporary American music: first performances, new recordings, publications, and news in the new music field.
**Ind/Abst** Music Artic. Guide.

FR/0294-4782
**AME ET LA CORDE, L'.** Vol. 1, (Mar./April 1982)-. Periodical. French. L'Ame et la Corde, 121 Bd de Magenta, 75010 Paris France. **LC** ML749.5; .A45. **DD** 787/.01/05.

US/0748-5905
**AMERICAN FOLK MUSIC AND FOLKLORE RECORDINGS.** (AMERICAN FOLK MUSIC AND FOLKLORE RECORDINGS : A SELECTED LIST.). [Am. folk music folk. rec.]. **Added/Corp** American Folklife Center. (1983)-. English. an. Free on request. American Folklife Center, Library of Congress, Washington DC 20540. **Tel** (202)707-6590, FAX (202)707-2076. **ED** Jennifer Cutting. **LC** ML156.4.F5; A4. **DD** 016.7899/121773. **Circ:** 8,000. available on an online database; available on microfiche.
**Desc:** Describes approximately thirty recordings released during a calendar year which are selected by a panel of specialists in American traditional music.

US/1056-7380
**AMERICAN GOSPEL MAGAZINE.** ***Suspended.*** [Am. gospel mag.]. Vol. 1, No. 1 (May/June 1991)-(Aug. 1992). Periodical. English. bm. $12.00. American Gospel, PO Box 40985, Nashville TN 37204-0985. **DD** 782.

US/1050-7493
**AMERICAN HARMONICA ASSOCIATES NEWSLETTER.** [Am. harmonica assoc. newsl.]. **VFOAT** American Harmonica Newsletter; AHN. (1988)-. Periodical. English. Twelve times a year. $21.00. American Harmonica Newsletter, 2362 West Territorial Road, Battle Creek MI 49015. **Tel** (616)962-2989. **ED** Alan W. Eichler and Phillip W. Lloyd (editor's address: 1595 Welling Drive, Troy, MI 48098-5020; phone: (810)689-3934). **DD** 788. **Bk Rev**, (Qty: 4). **Ad Acc, Adv Mgr:** Alan Eichler, **Tel** (616)962-2989. **Circ:** 1,000.
**Desc:** Focuses on the harmonica musical instrument as an art form; contains news, articles, player profiles, forum opinion, sections covering diatonic and chromatic models and tuning, sourcing for instructional, repair and accessories, and coverage of festivals and conventions events.

US/0002-869X
**AMERICAN HARP JOURNAL, THE.** [Am. harp j.]. **Added/Corp** American Harp Society. Vol. 1, No. 1 (Spring 1967)-. Periodical. English. Twice a year (June, Dec.). $15.00. American Harp Journal, 187 West Palisade Avenue, Englewood NJ 07631. **Tel** (201)569-4674. **ED** Jane B. Weidensaul. **LC** ML1; .A377. **DD** 787. **Bk Rev**. **Ad Acc. Circ:** 3,400 (ctrl). ***Continues*** *Harp News.*
**Desc:** Chronicle of the harp and its history. Articles on the distinguished harpists past, present and bibliographies of their music.
**Ind/Abst** Music Artic. Guide; Music Index; RILM Abstr.

●US/1062-4031
**AMERICAN LISZT SOCIETY STUDIES SERIES.** [Am. Liszt Soc. stud. ser.]. **Added/Corp** American Liszt Society. No. 1 (1991)-. Monographic series. English. ir. Price varies per volume. Pendragon Press, RR 1 Box 159, Stuyvesant NY 12173-9720. **Tel** (518)828-3008. **DD** 780.

US/1041-7176
**AMERICAN LUTHERIE.** (AMERICAN LUTHERIE : THE QUARTERLY JOURNAL OF THE GUILD OF AMERICAN LUTHIERS.). **Added/Corp** Guild of American Luthiers. No. 1 (March 1985)-. Periodical. English. Four times a year (Seasonally). $36.00 Includes Guild of American Luthiers Membership. Guild of American Luthiers, 8222 South Park Avenue, Tacoma WA 98408. **Tel** (206)472-7853. **ED** Timothy L. Olsen. **LC** ML755; .A5. **DD** 787/.19/05. Index available. **Bk Rev**. **Ad Acc. Circ:** 2,000 (ctrl). ***Formed by the union of*** *Guild of American Luthiers. Quarterly - [The Guild of American Luthiers], 0273-4389* ***and*** *Data Sheet.*
**Desc:** Information on all aspects of the craft of making and repairing stringed musical instruments.

US/0734-4392
**AMERICAN MUSIC (CHAMPAIGN, ILL.).** (AMERICAN MUSIC.). [Am. music]. **Added/Corp** Sonneck Society. Vol. 1, No. 1 (Spring 1983)-. Periodical. English. Four times a year (Mar., Jun., Sept., Dec.). $45.00 (one year), $81.00 (two year) institutions; $30.00 (one year), $54.00 (two year) individuals. University of Illinois Press, 1325 South Oak Street, Champaign IL 61820. **Tel** (217)333-0950, FAX (217)244-8082. **ED** John Graziano. **LC** ML1; .A497. **DD** 781.773/05. **[CCC]**. **Bk Rev**. **Ad Acc. Circ:** 1,300. available on microfilm and microfiche from University Microfilms International (UMI). Documents available from The Genuine Article, UMI Article Clearinghouse.
**Desc:** Articles on all aspects of American music and music in America, on composers, performers, publishers, and the music industry.
**Ind/Abst** Acad. Ind. [Computer File] (1992-); Acad. Search (July 1993-); Arts Humanit. Citation Index [Full Cov.]; Curr. Contents Arts Humanit.; Expand. Acad. Index (1989-); Humanit. Index; Humanit. Source (Jul. 1993-); INFO-SOUTH Abstr.; Mag. Search; Music Artic. Guide; Music Index; Newsp. Period. Abstr. (1990-); Res. Alert [Full Cov.].

●US/1058-3572
**AMERICAN MUSIC RESEARCH CENTER JOURNAL, THE.** [Am. Music Res. Cent. j.]. **Added/Corp** American Music Research Center. Vol. 1, (1991)-. English. an (Dec.). $8.00. American Music Research Center, College of Music, Campus Box 301, University of Colorado, Boulder CO 80309. **Tel** (303)492-7540. **ED** Thomas L. Riis. **LC** ML200; .A64. **DD** 780/.973/05. **Pr Rev. Circ:** 500.
**Desc:** Articles of general interest on american music, particularly in subject areas, relevant to its collections.
**Ind/Abst** Music Artic. Guide.

US/0003-0112
**AMERICAN MUSIC TEACHER, THE.** [Am. music teach.]. **Added/Corp** Music Teachers' National Association. Vol. 1, (Sept./Oct. 1951)-. Periodical. English. Six times a year (Feb., Apr., June, Aug., Oct., Dec.). $22.00 (one year), $40.00 (two year) US; $28.00 (one year), $50.00 (two year) Other. Music Teachers National Association, 441 Vine Street, Suite 505 Carew Tower, Cincinnati OH 45202-2434. **Tel** (513)421-1420, FAX (513)421-2503. **ED** Michael Oxley. **LC** ML1; .A5. **DD** 780.7. Index available. cum. index (Article index published in June/July issue). **Bk Rev**. **Ad Acc, Adv Mgr:** Diane DeVillez. **Circ:** 25,000 (ctrl). available on microfilm and microfiche from University Microfilms International (UMI). Documents available from UMI Article Clearinghouse. ***Continues*** *Bulletin of the Music Teachers National Association.*
**Desc:** Features articles on keyboard, major instruments, theory and history which are geared to assist private, studio, secondary and college or university teachers.
**Ind/Abst** Acad. Ind. [Computer File] (1992-); Book Rev. Index; Educ. Index; Expand. Acad. Index (1992-); Music Artic. Guide; Music Index; Newsp. Period. Abstr. (1989-).

US/0003-0228
**AMERICAN OLD TIME FIDDLERS' NEWS.** **Added/Corp** American Old Time Fiddlers' Association. (1964)-. Periodical. English. qt. $3.50. American Old Time Fiddlers' News, 6141 Morrill Avenue, Lincoln NE 68507. **LC** ML1; .A712. **DD** 787/.1/05.

US/0164-3150
**AMERICAN ORGANIST (1979), THE.** (THE AMERICAN ORGANIST.). [Am. organist]. **Added/Corp** American Guild of Organists. Royal Canadian College of Organists. Associated Pipe Organ Builders of America. Vol. 13 (Jan. 1979)-. Periodical. English. Twelve times a year. $42.00. American Guild of Organists, 475 Riverside Drive, Suite 1260, New York NY 10115. **Tel** (212)870-2310, FAX (212)870-2163. **ED** Anthony Baglivi. **LC** ML1; .M327. **DD** 786.5/05. Index available in last issue of volume--attached. cum. index (10 years). **Bk Rev**. **Ad Acc. Circ:** 25,000 (ctrl). available on microfilm and microfiche from University Microfilms International (UMI). ***Continues*** *Music, 0027-4208.*
**Desc:** Written by musicians who cover organbuilding, sacred music, reviews of books, music and recording, and news items.
**Ind/Abst** Music Artic. Guide; Music Index; Ref. Sources.

US/0003-0716
**AMERICAN RECORD GUIDE.** **See** Sound Recordings and Systems.

US/0003-0724
**AMERICAN RECORDER, THE.** [Am. rec.]. **Added/Corp** American Recorder Society. Vol. 1 (Winter 1960)-. Periodical. English. qt. $24.00 US; $28.00 other. American Recorder Society, PO Box 1067, Jackson NJ 08527. **Tel** (908)363-5656. **DD** 788. Index available. cum. index. **Bk Rev**. **Ad Acc. Circ:** 4,500. available on microfilm from University Microfilms International (UMI).
**Desc:** Articles, book and music reviews and reports on events for both the avocational and professional recorder player or early music enthusiast.
**Ind/Abst** Music Artic. Guide; Music Index; RILM Abstr.

US/0896-8993
**AMERICAN SONGWRITER.** (198?)-. Periodical. English. Six times a year (Jan., Mar., May, July, Sept., Nov.). $16.95 (one years); $29.95 (two years). American Songwriter, 121 17th Avenue South, Nashville TN 37203. **Tel** (615)244-6065, FAX (615)742-1123. **ED** Vernell Hackett. **Bk Rev**, (Qty: 12). **Ad Acc, Adv Mgr:** Rick Hogan, **Tel** (615)244-6065. **Circ:** 6,000.
**Desc:** For anyone who hopes to write a popular tune and

offers features and articles covering all aspects of pop music. Columnists give practical advice on how to write and, most importantly, how to sell music.

US/0003-1313
**AMERICAN STRING TEACHER.** [Am. string teach.]. **Added/Corp** American String Teachers Association. Vol. 1 (Jan. 1951)-. Periodical. English. Four times a year (Jan., Apr., July, Oct.). $39.00 schools & libraries; $35.00 (active); $95.00 (business); $200.00 (contributing) Comes with American String Teachers Association membership. American String Teachers Association, 1806 Robert Fulton Road, Suite 300, Reston VA 22091. **Tel** (703)476-1316, FAX (703)476-1317. **ED** Jody Atwood. **LC** ML27.U5; A8356. **DD** 787.07. Index available. cum. index. **Bk Rev. Ad Acc. Circ:** 10,000 (ctrl).
**Desc:** Articles on string pedagogy, pedagogues, events - forums on violin, viola, cello, bass, harp, classical guitar, public and private school teaching, and chamber music. New music reviewed, new publications listed, academic appointments and awards noted. Invaluable to researchers, administrators and teachers/performers involved with stringed instruments, orchestras and string ensembles.
**Ind/Abst** Music Artic. Guide; Music Index.

US/0193-5372
**AMERICAN SUZUKI JOURNAL.** [Am. Suzuki j.]. **Added/Corp** Suzuki Association of the Americas. Vol. 1 (Winter 1973)-. Periodical. English. Four times a year. $35.00 (active members); $17.50 (subscribing members). Suzuki Association of the Americas, PO Box 17310, Boulder CO 80308. **Tel** (303)444-0948, FAX (303)444-0984. **DD** 787. **[CCC]. Bk Rev**, (Qty: 1-4). **Ad Acc. Circ:** 6,200 (ctrl).
**Desc:** Official publication of the Suzuki Association of the Americas, a non-profit, professional association of teachers, parents & supporters in the Americas dedicated to meeting the needs of all those interested in Talent Education, or the "mother tongue" approach to music education.
**Ind/Abst** Music Artic. Guide.

US/1043-5379
**AMICA NEWS BULLETIN, THE.** (THE AMICA NEWS BULLETIN / AUTOMATIC MUSICAL INSTRUMENT COLLECTORS' ASSOCIATION.). [AMICA news bull.]. **Added/Corp** Automatic Musical Instrument Collectors' Association. **VFOAT** AMICA International News Bulletin. **VAT** Automatic Musical Instrument Collectors' Association News Bulletin. (198?)-. Bulletin. English. bm. Automatic Musical Instrument Collectors' Association, 515 Scott Street, Sandusky OH 44870-3736. **Tel** (416)626-1903. **ED** Robin D. Pratt. **LC** ML1050; .A43. **DD** 786.6/19/05. **Bk Rev. Ad Acc.** ctrl circ. ***Continues*** *News Bulletin of the Automatic Musical Instrument Collectors' Association, 0884-0644.*

CN/0826-7464
**ANACRUSIS.** (ANACRUSIS / ASSOCIATION OF CANADIAN CHORAL CONDUCTORS). [Anacursis]. **Added/Corp** Association of Canadian Choral Conductors. Vol. 3, No. 2 (Winter 1983)-. Periodical. English. qt. 20.00Can$. Association of Canadian Choral Conductors, c/o Timothy G Cooper, UNB Bag Service 45333, Fredericton New Brunswick E3B 6E3 Canada. **Tel** (506)453-3503. **ED** Timothy G. Cooper. **DD** 784.9/63/06071. **Bk Rev. Ad Acc. Circ:** 600 (ctrl). ***Continues*** *ACCC, 0711-0448.*
**Desc:** Contains relevant articles, special features, interviews, music and audio reviews, notes on national and international choral events.

GW/0569-9827
**ANALECTA MUSICOLOGICA.** [Analecta musicol.]. **Added/Corp** Deutsches Historisches Institut in Rom. Musikgeschichtliche Abteilung. Deutsches Historisches Institut, Rome. Musikabteilung. Vol. 1, (1963)-. Monographic series. German (English and Italian). ir. Price varies per volume. Laaber Verlag, Regensburger Strasse 19, W 93164 Laaber Germany. **Tel** 011-49-9498-2307. **ED** Friedrich Lippmann. **Circ:** 450.
**Desc:** Research in Italian music history and its relations to the music of other countries.
**Ind/Abst** RILM Abstr.

US/0097-6482
**ANALOG SOUNDS.** [Analog sounds]. No. 1 (Oct. 1974)-. Periodical. English. qt. $16.00. Analog Sounds, 12 West 17th Street, New York NY 10011. **LC** ML1; .A767. **DD** 789.9.
**Ind/Abst** RILM Abstr.

FR/0295-3722
**ANALYSE MUSICALE.** ***Suspended.***
**Added/Corp** Association pour le Developpement de L'Analyse Musicale. Societe Francaise D'Analyse Musicale. Vol. 1. (Nov. 1985)-Issue 33 (Nov. 1993). Periodical. French (French). Four times a year (Jan., Apr., June, Oct.). Analyse Musicale, 83 Bd De Sebastopol, 75002 Paris France. **Tel** 011 33 1 40284572. **LC** ML5; .A54. **DD** 780/.5.

US/0091-7176
**ANCIENT TIMES.** (THE ANCIENT TIMES.). [Anc. times]. **Added/Corp** Company of Fifers & Drummers. (March 1973)-. Periodical. English. qt. $1.00. Fifers and Drummers Inc., 14 Winter Avenue, Deep River CT. **ED** Maurice A. Schoos. **LC** ML1; .A77. **DD** 785/.06/71. **Circ:** 1,000.

FR/0583-8363
**ANNALES MUSICOLOGIQUES, MOYEN-AGE ET RENAISSANCE.**
**Main/Corp** Societe de Musique d'Autrefois. **Added/Corp** France. Centre National de la Recherche Scientifique. (1953)-. French (English). **LC** ML5; .S5774.

SZ
**ANNALES PADEREWSKI.** **Added/Corp** Societe Paderewski. No. 1 (Oct. 1979)-. Periodical. French. an. Free. Societe Paderewski, Hotel de Ville, 1110 Morges Switzerland. **LC** ML410.P114; A8. **DD** 786.1/092/4; B. **Bk Rev. Circ:** 1,000.

US
**ANNALS OF ITALIAN OPERA.** **See** The Arts-Performing Arts.

FR
**ANNEE DU ROCK, L'.** (1982/83)-. Periodical. French. ir. Editions Calmann Levy, 3 Rue Auber, 75009 Paris France. **Tel** 011 33 1 4743833. **LC** ML3533.8; .A55.

US/1051-287X
**ANNOUNCED ... THIS MONTH IN CLASSICAL RECORDINGS.** [Announc. month class. rec.]. **VFOAT** Announced. Vol. 1, No. 1 (June 1988)-. Periodical. English. Twelve times a year. $28.00 North America; $52.00 others. Bushnell Corporation, 880 West Williams Road, Bloomington IN 47404. **Tel** (812)339-2258. **ED** Vinson Bushnell. **LC** ML156.2; .A47. **DD** 016.78026/6. Index available. **Circ:** 200.
**Desc:** A listing of classical and broadway musical CD's releases commercially in the US with indexes by composor, performer, and musical geure.

CN/0710-5398
**ANNUAIRE (CANADIAN UNIVERSITY MUSIC SOCIETY).** (ANNUAIRE / SOCIETE DE MUSIQUE DES UNIVERSITES CANADIENNES.). [Annu. - Soc. music. univ. can.]. **Added/Corp** Canadian University Music Society. **VFOAT** Directory. (1980/1981)-. English (French). be (1 issue every 2 years). 35.00Can$. Canadian University Music Society, c/o School of Music, University of Windsor, Windsor Ontario N9B 3P4 Canada. **Tel** (519)253-4232 Ext. 2784. **DD** 780/.7/2971. Each issue contains an index to its own contents (no volume index)--loose.

SZ
**ANNUAIRE SUISSE DU FOLK : MUSICIENS. SCHWEIZER FOLK-KALENDAR : MUSIKER.**
**Added/Corp** Vereinigung Schweizer Folk-Clubs. **VFOAT** Schweizer Folk-Kalendar Musiker. (1978)-. English (French and German). an. Association Suisse des Folk-Clubs, Freigutstr 22, 8002 Zurich Switzerland. **LC** ML3720; .A56. **DD** 781.7/092/2.

SZ
**ANNUAIRE SUISSE DU FOLK: ORGANISATEURS. SCHWEIZER FOLK-KALENDER: VERANSTALTER.**
**Added/Corp** Vereinigung Schweizer Folk-Clubs. **VFOAT** Schweizer Folk-Kalender : Veranstalter. (1978)-. English (French and German). an. Akaderuische Buckhandlung, Falken Platz 14, 30001 Bern Switzerland. **LC** ML21.S9; A5. **DD** 781.7/025/494.

SZ
**ANNUAIRE SUISSE FOLK & CHANSON. MUSICIENS, ORGANISATEURS.** **VFOAT** Folk et Chanson; Annuaire Suisse Folk et Chanson. Musiciens, Organisateurs; Schweizer Folk und Chanson Handbuch. Musiker, Veranstalter; Musiciens, Organisateurs; Schweizer Folk & Chanson Handbuch. Musiker, Veranstalter; Annuaire Suisse du Folk et de la Chanson; Folk & Chanson. (19??)-. English (French and German). an. Edition CM, Riedhofstrasse 106, 8408 Winterthur Switzerland. **LC** ML21.S9; .A53. **DD** 781.7/025/494.

UK
**ANNUAL REPORT AND ACCOUNTS FOR ... / ROYAL MUSICAL ASSOCIATION.** **Main/Corp** Royal Musical Association. (19??)-. English. an. British Library, Great Russell Street, London WC1B 3DG England. **LC** ML27.G7; R75. **DD** 780/.6/041.

US/0731-0641
**ANNUAL REVIEW OF JAZZ STUDIES.** [Annu. rev. jazz stud.]. **Added/Corp** Rutgers University. Institute of Jazz Studies. Vol. 1 (1982)-. Periodical. English. ir. 39.50 latest issue. Scarecrow Press Inc., 52 Liberty Street, PO Box 4167, Metuchen NJ 08840. **Tel** (908)548-8600, (800)537-7107. **ED** Dan Morgenstern, Charles Nanry, and David Cayer. **LC** ML3505.8; .A56. **DD** 785.42/05. **[CCC].** available on microfilm and microfiche from University Microfilms International (UMI). ***Continues*** *Journal of Jazz Studies, 0093-3686.*
**Desc:** Publishes research on jazz and related musical forms. Embraces musicology, musical analysis, discography, social history, oral history, and archival practice.
**Ind/Abst** Am. Hist. Life (1982-); Music Index.

UK
**ANNUAL SURVEY OF MUSIC LIBRARIES.** **See** Library and Information Sciences.

GW
**ANSCHLAGE.** **Added/Corp** Archiv fuer Populare Musik. (1978)-. Periodical. German. qt. DM72.00. Archiv fuer Populare Musik, Ostertorsteinweg 3, 2800 Bremen 1 Germany. **LC** ML3469; .A57. **DD** 780/.42/05.

IS
**ANTHROPOLOGY OF YIDDISH FOLKSONGS.** Yiddish (English). Magnes Press, Hebrew University of Jerusalem, PO Box 7695, Jerusalem 91076 Israel. **Tel** 011 972 2 660341, 011 972 2 635291, FAX 011 972 2 633370, telex 25391.
**Desc:** Comprehensive collection of 350 songs.

US/0361-2147
**ANTIQUE PHONOGRAPH MONTHLY, THE.** **See** Antiques.

AU
**ANTON BRUCKNER GESAMTAUSGABE.** (19??)-. German. ir. **(Subscription address:** Broude Brothers Limited, 141 White Oaks Road, Williamstown MA 01267.**)**

SP/0211-3538
**ANUARIO MUSICAL.** (ANUARIO MUSICAL / CONSEJO SUPERIOR DE INVESTIGACIONES CIENTIFICAS, INSTITUTO ESPANOL DE MUSICOLOGIA.). [Anu. music.]. **Main/Corp** Instituto Espanol de Musicologia. **Added/Corp** Instituto Espanol de Musicologia. Vol. 1, (1946)-. Periodical. Spanish. an. Consejo Superior Investigacion Cientificas (CSIC), Vitruvio 8, 28006 Madrid Spain. **Tel** 011 34 1 5612833, FAX 011 34 1 4113077, telex 42182. **LC** ML32.S7; S7.
**Desc:** Articles from Spain and other countries on musicological research of interest to musicologists and ethnomusicologists, this journal provides a point of contract for cultural institutions of the world.
**Ind/Abst** Music Index; RILM Abstr.

UK
**APC NEWSLETTER : JOURNAL OF THE ASSOCIATION OF PROFESSIONAL COMPOSERS.** **Added/Corp** Association of Professional Composers. **VFOAT** A.P.C. Newsletter. (19??)-. Newsletter. English. APC Administration, 81A Priory Road, London NW6 3NL England. **LC** ML27.G7; A9. **DD** 780/.942/0904.

AT
**APRA (AUSTRALASIAN PERFORMING RIGHT ASSOCIATION).** (APRA : MAGAZINE OF THE AUSTRALASIAN PERFORMING RIGHT ASSOCIATION LTD.). **Added/Corp** Australasian Performing Right Association. **VFOAT** A.P.R.A. (19??)-. Periodical. English. Australasian Performing Right Association, 25 27 Albany Street, Crow Nest NSW 2065 Australia. **LC** ML5; .A696. **DD** 780/.994. ***Continues*** *APRA Journal.*
**Ind/Abst** Music Index.

US/0148-5865
**ARABESQUE (NEW YORK, N.Y.).** (ARABESQUE.). [Arabesque]. Vol. 1 (May/June 1975)-. Periodical. English. Six times a year (Jan., Mar., May, July, Sept., Nov.). $25.00 (individuals); $37.00 (institutions). Arabesque, 1 Sherman Square, Suite 22F, New York NY 10023. **Tel** (212)595-1677, FAX (212)595-1677. **ED** Nina Costanza. **LC** GV1703.N36; A7. **DD** 792. **Bk Rev. Ad Acc. Circ:** 6,000 (ctrl).
**Desc:** Focus on ethnic music and dance, primarily from the Middle and Near East but many articles on Spanish, Indian, and other ethnic forms.

GW/0003-9292
**ARCHIV FUER MUSIKWISSENSCHAFT.** [Arch. Musikwiss.]. **Added/Corp** Furstliches Institut fuer Usikwissenschaftliche Forschung (Buckeburg, Germany). Vol. 1 (Oct. 1918)-. Periodical. German (English). qt. DM140.00. Franz Steiner Verlag GmbH, Postfach 101061, D 70009 Stuttgart Germany. **Tel** 011 49 0711 2582372, FAX 011 49 0711 2582290, telex 723636 daz d. **ED** Hans Heinrich Eggebrecht. **LC** ML5; .A63. **DD** 780/.5. **[CCC]. Ad Acc. Circ:** 600. Documents available from The Genuine Article. ***Continues*** *Sammelbande der Internationalen Musikgesellschaft.*
**Desc:** Articles dedicated to the history of music and to problems of musicology.
**Ind/Abst** Arts Humanit. Citation Index [Full Cov.]; Curr. Contents Arts Humanit.; Music Index; Res. Alert [Full Cov.]; RILM Abstr.; Romant. Move.

GW
**ARCHIV FUER MUSIKWISSENSCHAFT. BEIHEFTE.** (1966)-. Monographic series. German. ir. Price varies per volume. Franz Steiner Verlag GmbH, Postfach 101061, D 70009 Stuttgart Germany. **Tel** 011 49

0711 2582372, FAX 011 49 0711 2582290, telex 723636 daz d. **ED** H.H. Eggebrecht. **Ad Acc. Circ:** 700.
**Desc:** Covers musicology.

UK
**ARENA.** English. bm. £18.00 (one year), £34.00 (two year). Alan Wells International, Memberline House, Farndon Road, Market Harbor LE16 9NR England. **Tel** 011 44 858 410510. **(Subscription address:** Alan Wells International, PO box 500, Subscriptions Department, Leicester LE99 0AA England**)**

US/0518-6129
**ARIZONA MUSIC NEWS. Added/Corp** Arizona Music Educators Association. **VFOAT** AMN. (1957)-. Periodical. English. Three times a year (Mar., Oct., Dec.). $15.00. Arizona Music News, 1137 North 7th Avenue, Box 36883, Suite 395, Tucson AZ 85704. **Tel** (602)622-5655. **ED** David Ashcraft. **Bk Rev. Ad Acc. Circ:** 1,000 (ctrl). available on diskette.
**Desc:** Ideas for innovative school and college music programs; "Think Pieces" on arts, education.

IT
**ARMONIA DI VOCI. VFOAT** Armonia de Voci Corali. (19??)-. Periodical. Italian. bm. L21000 Italy; L28000 US. Editrice Elle di Ci, Corso Francia 214, 10090 Rivoli Turin Italy. **Tel** 39 11 9591091, FAX (011)9574048. **LC** M1; .A73. **DD** 783/.026/05. **Circ:** 1,500.
**Desc:** Musical proposals for Christian communities. Each issue is monographical, presenting several items for the choir and the congregation mostly with organ accompaniments.

US/1043-3848
**ARS LYRICA. See** Literature-Poetry.

US/1058-7500
**ARS MUSICA DENVER.** [Ars musica Denver]. **Added/Corp** Lamont School of Music. Vol. 1, No. 1 (Fall 1988)-. Periodical. English. sa (June, Dec.). $10.00. Lamont School of Music, 7111 Montview Boulevard, University of Denver, denver CO 80220. **Tel** (303)871-6920, FAX (303)871-6411, telex 9109310586. **ED** Paul Laird. **LC** IN PROCESS. **DD** 780. **Bk Rev**, (Qty: 2). **Circ:** 75.
**Desc:** The purpose of this publication is to establish a dialogue between the faculty and students of Lamont School of Music and their colleagues in Colorado and across the country concerning all forms of music.

SA
**ARS NOVA. Added/Corp** University of South Africa. Dept. of Musicology. (1969)-. Periodical. Afrikaans (English). an. $6.00. University of South Africa, PO Box 392, Pretoria 0001 South Africa. **Tel** 011 27 12 4298468, FAX 011 (27)12 429 3321, telex (59)350068+. **ED** B. Van der Linde. **LC** ML5; .A652. **DD** 780/.5. **Bk Rev. Ad Acc. Circ:** 500 (ctrl).
**Desc:** Articles on composers and compositions - bibliographical data, contributions from students and musicologists on music.

GW/0004-2919
**ARS ORGANI.** [Ars organi]. **Added/Corp** Gesellschaft der Orgelfreunde. Issue 1 (1953)-. Periodical. German. Four times a year. Verlag Merseburger Berlin GmbH, POB 103880, D 34038 Kassel Germany. **Tel** 011 49 561 772002.
**Ind/Abst** Music Index; RILM Abstr.

CI/0587-5455
**ARTI MUSICES. Added/Corp** Muzicka Akademija u Zagrebu. Muzikoloski Zavod. (1969)-. Serbo-Croatian (Roman) (summaries and/or abstracts in English and German). sa. $24.00. Croatian Musicological Society, Opaticka 18, 41000 Zagreb Croatia. **Tel** 011 38 41 420277. **(Subscription address:** Muzicka Akademija, Muzikoloski Zavod, 41000 Zagreb Berislaviceva 16 Yugoslavia**) ED** Koradjka Kos, Eva Sedak and Lovro Zupanovic. **LC** ML5; .A667. Index available. cum. index. **Bk Rev. Ad Acc. Circ:** 600.
**Desc:** Includes articles on the history of music in Croatia, articles and on musicological research in Yugoslavia; includes articles on the history of music.
**Ind/Abst** Music Index; RILM Abstr.

GW
**ARTIST, DER.** (1883)-. Periodical. German. Twelve times a year. Zeitschriftenverlag RBDV, Postfach 14 02 20, 80452 Muenchen Germany. **Tel** 011 49 211 5050. **LC** ML5; .A673.

US/0197-7849
**ASCAP IN ACTION.** [ASCAP action]. **Main/Corp** American Society of Composers, Authors and Publishers. **Added/Corp** American Society of Composers, Authors and Publishers. **VAT** American Society of Composers, Authors and Publishers in Action. (Fall 1979)-. Periodical. English. Three times a year. American Society of Composers, Authors and Publishers, PO Box 296, Old Chelsea Station, New York NY 10011. **Tel** (718)899-2605. **LC** ML27.U5; A83445. **DD** 338.4/778/0973. available on microfilm and microfiche from University Microfilms International (UMI). ***Continues*** *ASCAP Today, 0001-2424.*
**Ind/Abst** Music Artic. Guide; Music Index.

US/0044-9202
**ASIAN MUSIC.** [Asian music]. **Added/Corp** Society for Asian Music. (Winter 1968/69)-. Academic Scholarly Publication. English (German and French). sa. $35.00 institutions; $100.00 patron. Society for Asian Music, Cornell University, Department of Asian Studies, Ithaca NY 14853. **Tel** (607)255-5049, FAX (607)255-1454. **ED** Martin Hatch. **LC** ML1; .A834. **DD** 780/.95. **[CCC].** Index available. cum. index. **Bk Rev**, (Qty: 10-20). **Pr Rev. Circ:** 600. Documents available from The Genuine Article.
**Desc:** Scholarly articles on all aspects of the performing arts of Asian origins.
**Ind/Abst** Arts Humanit. Citation Index [Full Cov.]; Curr. Contents Arts Humanit.; MLA Int. Bibl. Books Artic. Mod. Lang. Lit.; Music Artic. Guide (?-199?); Music Index; Res. Alert [Full Cov.]; RILM Abstr.

US/0097-8116
**ASTERISK.** (ASTERISK : A JOURNAL OF NEW MUSIC.). (Dec. 1974)-. Periodical. English. sa. $6.00. Asterisk, 1215 Kuchnle Avenue, Ann Arbor MI 48103. **LC** ML1; .A845. **DD** 780/.5.
**Ind/Abst** Comput. Rev.

NE
**AUCTION CATALOGUES OF MUSIC.** (1973)-. Monographic series. English (German, French and Dutch). ir. Price varies per volume. Uitgeverij Frits Knuf B V, PO Box 720, 4116 ZJ Buuren Netherlands. **Tel** 011 31 03449-1255, FAX 011 31 03449-2617. **Circ:** 700.
**Desc:** Facsimile reprints with introductions.

GW
**AUFSATZE UND JAHRESBERICHT - KARL-MARX-UNIVERSITAT MUSIKINSTRUMENTEN-MUSEUM. Main/Corp** Leipzig. Universitat. Musikinstrumenten-Museum. (19??)-. German. Musikinstrumenten-Museum der Karl-Marx-Universitat, 701 Leipzig Taubchenweg 2 C, Leipzig Germany. **LC** ML5; .L38. **DD** 780/.5.

US/1074-0740
**AUSTIN CHRONICLE, THE. See** General Interest-General Interest-North America.

AT
**AUSTRALIAN DIGITAL MUSIC.** (19??)-. Periodical. English. Four times a year. 17.00Aus$ Australia; 29.00Aus$ New Zealand & Papua New Guinea; 31.00Aus$ Singapore, Malaysia, Indonesia; 34.00Aus$ Hong Kong, China, India, Japan; 37.00Aus$ US & Canada; 39.00Aus$ other. Federal Publishing Co Pty Ltd, PO Box 199, 180 Bourke Road, Alexandria New South Wales, 2015 Australia. **Tel** 011 61 2 693 6666, FAX 011 61 2 693 9935. **(Subscription address:** Federal Publishing Co. Pty Ltd., PO Box 199, Alexandria NSW 2015 Australia.**)**

AT/0004-9484
**AUSTRALIAN JOURNAL OF MUSIC EDUCATION.** [Aust. j. music educ.]. **Added/Corp** Australian Society for Music Education. (1967)-. English. sa. 60.00Aus$ (comes with Australian Society of Music Education membership and Monograph Series). Australian Society of Music Education, PO Box 179, Coburg Victoria 3058 Australia. **Tel** 011 61 3 3539244. **LC** ML5; .A698. **DD** 780/.7. available on microfilm and microfiche from University Microfilms International (UMI).
**Ind/Abst** Aust. Educ. Index (1977-1982); Music Index.

AT/1036-9457
**AUSTRALIAN JOURNAL OF MUSIC THERAPY, THE. See** Medical Science and Technology.

AT/0727-4025
**AUSTRALIAN MUSIC STUDIES. Added/Corp** Australian Music Studies Project. (1982)-. Monographic series. English. ir. Price varies per volume.

AT/1033-1352
**AUSTRALIAN RECORD AND MUSIC REVIEW.** [Aust. rec. music rev.]. (1989)-. Periodical. English. Four times a year (Jan., Apr., July, Oct.). 20.00Aus$ Australia; 21.00Aus$ other. Australian Record and Music Review, 15 Lowanna Avenue, Baulkham Hills, New South Wales 2153 Australia. **Tel** 011 61 639 7902. **ED** Mike Sutcliffe. **DD** 780.2660994. **Bk Rev. Circ:** 120 (ctrl).
**Desc:** Discographical magazine for record and music collectors.

AT/0312-9950
**AUSTRALIAN STRING TEACHER.** [Aust. string teach,]. (1976)-. Periodical. English. an (June or July). 40.00Aus$ (individuals); 60.00Aus$ (institutions) Comes with Australian String Teachers Association membership. Australian String Teachers Association, 5 Oakridge Road, Aberfoyle Park, South Australian, 5159 Australia. **Tel** 011 61 8 2701917. **ED** Catherine Milligan, (editor's address: 17 Russell Avenue, Adamstown Heights, New South Wales, 2289 Australia). **DD** 787.007. **Bk Rev. Ad Acc. Pr Rev. Circ:** 1,200 (ctrl).

US/0091-8687
**AUTOHARP. Added/Corp** University of Illinois (Urbana-Champaign campus). Campus Folksong Club. (Apr. 7, 1961)-. Periodical. English. University of Illinois School of Music, 1114 West Nevada, Urbana IL 61801. **Tel** (217)333-1027. **LC** ML1; .A95. **DD** 784.4/005.
**Ind/Abst** Music Index.

US/1071-1619
**AUTOHARP QUARTERLY.** (19??)-. Periodical. English. Four times a year (Jan., Apr., July, Oct.). $18.00 US; $20.00 Canada; $22.00 Europe; $24.00 Asia. Autoharp Quarterly, PO Box A, Newport PA 17074. **Tel** (717)567-9469. **ED** Mary Lou Orthey and Ivan Stiles, (editor's address: Route 1 Box 34F, Newport, PA 17074). **DD** 787. **Ad Acc, Adv Mgr:** Ivan Stiles, **Tel** (215)935-9062.
**Desc:** This magazine is dedicated to the autoharp enthusiast.

US/0736-3796
**AUTOHARPOHOLIC, THE. *Ceased.*** (Spring 1980)-Vol. 14, No. 1, (Jan. 1993). Periodical. English. qt. I.A.D. Publications, PO Box 504, Brisbane CA 94005. **Tel** (415)467-1700. **ED** Becky Blackley. **LC** ML1015.A9; A9. **DD** 787/.8. **Bk Rev. Ad Acc. Circ:** 1,000.
**Desc:** Music and articles pertaining to the autoharp.

US/0148-818X
**AUTOMATIC MUSICAL INSTRUMENTS PRICING GUIDE.** (19??)-. English. WH Edgerton, Box 88, Darien CT 06820. **LC** ML155; .A9. **DD** 789.7/075.

FR
**AVANT SCENE OPERA (PARIS, FRANCE : 1986).** (L'AVANT SCENE OPERA.). **VFOAT** Avant-Scene Opera. No. 90/91 (Sept./Oct. 1986)-. Periodical. French. Six times a year. 550.00F France; 710.00F other. Premieres Loges, 15 rue Tiquetonne, F-75002 Paris France. **Tel** 011 33 1 42335151, FAX 011 33 1 42338091. **ED** Michel Pazdro. **Circ:** 5,000. Documents available from The Genuine Article. ***Continues*** *Avant Scene Opera, Operette.*
**Desc:** Literary comments on the opera.
**Ind/Abst** Arts Humanit. Citation Index [Full Cov.]; Curr. Contents Arts Humanit.; Res. Alert [Full Cov.].

GW
**AWA KONTAKTE. Added/Corp** Anstalt zur Wahrung der Auffuhrungsrechte auf dem Gebiete der Musik. **VFOAT** Kontakte. No. 1 (1985)-. Periodical. German. sa.

US/0193-0850
**AWC NEWS/FORUM. See** Music-Abstracting, Bibliographies and Statistics.

CN/0828-7465
**AXES (RIMOUSKI).** (AXES : BULLETIN D'INFORMATION DU CENTRE DE RECHERCHE G.I.M. INC.). [Axes]. **Added/Corp** Centre de Recherche G.I.M. Inc. Vol. 1, No. 1 (1984)-. Bulletin. French. bm. Centre De Recherche GIM Inc., 167 St-Louis, Local 451, Rimouski Quebec G5L 5R2. **DD** 784.5/005.

CN/0705-9019
**B.C. MUSIC EDUCATOR.** (THE B. C. MUSIC EDUCATOR.). [B.C. music educ.]. Vol. 20, No. 2 (Oct. 1977)-. Periodical. English. ir. British Columbia Music Educators' Association, 22259 48th Avenue, Langley British Columbia V3A 3A7 Canada. **DD** 780/.7. ***Formed by the union of*** *British Columbia Music Educators' Association. Newsletter, 0382-8182* ***and*** *British Columbia Music Educator, 0007-0564.* ***Continued in part by*** *Newsletter (British Columbia Music Educators Association), 0714-7384.*

US/0005-3600
**BACH.** [Bach]. **Added/Corp** Riemenschneider Bach Institute. Vol. 1 (Winter 1970)-. Periodical. English. sa (2 issues). $26.00 institution; $20.00 individual. Riemenschneider Bach Institute, Baldwin Wallace College, 275 Eastland Road, Berea OH 44017. **Tel** (216)826-2207. **ED** Dr. Elinore Barber. **LC** M410.B1; B15. **DD** 780/.92/4. cum. index. **Circ:** 800. Documents available from The Genuine Article.
**Ind/Abst** Arts Humanit. Citation Index [Full Cov.]; Curr. Contents Arts Humanit.; Music Artic. Guide; Music Index; Res. Alert [Full Cov.]; RILM Abstr.

GW/0084-7682
**BACH-JAHRBUCH.** (BACH-JAHRBUCH / IM AUFTRAGW DER NEUEN BACHGESELLSCHAFT.). [Bach-Jahrb.]. **Added/Corp** Neue Bachgesellschaft. **VAT** Bach Jahrbuch. Vol. 1, (1904)-. German (summaries and/or abstracts in English, French, Czech and Russian). an. Evangel Verlagsanstalt Gmbh, Postfach 1467, D 04025 Leipzig Germany. **Tel** 011 49 341 7114122, FAX 49 341 295383. **(Subscription address:** LKG Leipzigler Komm & Grossbuch, Postfach 520, D 04005 Leipzig Germany, phone: 011 49 341 71370**) ED** Hans-Joachim Schulze and Christoph Wolff. **LC** ML410.B1; A6. Index available. cum. index. **Bk Rev. Circ:** 5,000.
**Desc:** Sources and documents enlarging the knowledge of Bach, instructions for acute treatises and issues, expositions promoting the discussion on all subjects of international Bach research.
**Ind/Abst** RILM Abstr.

●US/1072-1924
**BACH PERSPECTIVES.** **Added/Corp** American Bach Society. (1995)-. English. Twice a year (Spring/Summer & Fall/Winter). $20.00 (individuals); $26.00 (institutions). Riemenschneider Bach Institute, Baldwin Wallace College, 275 Eastland Road, Berea OH 44017. **Tel** (216)826-2207.

II
**BAGINA.** (1973/74)-. Periodical. Nepali (Nepali). qt. Narayan Gopal, Narsingh Kyap, Thamel, Narenda Thapa, Kathmandu Nepal. **LC** ML5; .B323.

NO/0332-5148
**BALLADE : TIDSSKRIFT FOR NY MUSIKK.** No. 1 (1977)-. Periodical. Norwegian. qt. Kr335.00 Scandinavia; KR380.00 other. Scandinavian University Press, PO Box 2959 Toeyen, N 0608 Oslo 6 Norway. **Tel** 011 47 2 2575400, FAX 011 47 2 2575353, telex 71896 UROR N. **(Subscription address:** Scandinavian University Press, 200 Meacham Ave., Elmont NY 11003.**)**
**Ind/Abst** Music Index; RILM Abstr.

US/0885-7113
**BALUNGAN.** (BALUNGAN : A PUBLICATION OF THE AMERICAN GAMELAN INSTITUTE.). [Balungan]. **Added/Corp** American Gamelan Institute. Vol. 1, No. 1 (June 1984)-. Periodical. English (Indonesian). Twice a year (Jan., Sept.). $30.00 (institutions), $15.00 (individuals) US; $20.00 (individuals) other. American Gamelan Institute of Music & Education, Box A36, Hanover NH 03755. **Tel** (603)448-8837. **DD** 785.
**Ind/Abst** Music Index (Vol. 5, No. 1, 1991-).

US/0194-5793
**BAM.** (197?)-. Periodical. English. Twenty-five times a year. $25.00 US; $55.00 Canada and Mexico; $60.00 other. Bam Publications, 3470 Buskirk Avenue, Pleasant Hill CA 94523. **Tel** (510)934-3700, FAX (510)934-3958. **ED** Steve Stolder and Bill Holdship. **Ad Acc**, **Adv Mgr:** Marianne Stone. **Circ:** 130,000 (ctrl).
**Desc:** Presents interviews with famous rock stars, record reviews, musical instrument reports, product reviews, and coming events and happenings in California.

US/0735-4711
**BAND & FESTIVAL GUIDE.** (BAND & FESTIVAL GUIDE / TRI-STATE BLUEGRASS ASSOCIATION.). **Added/Corp** Tri-State Bluegrass Association. **VFOAT** Band and Festival Guide. (19??)-. English. an. Tri-State Bluegrass Association, Rural Route 1, Kohoka MO 63445. **Tel** (314)853-4344. **ED** Erma Spray. **LC** ML19; .B36. **DD** 784.5/2/002573. **Ad Acc. Circ:** 5,000 (ctrl).
**Desc:** Bluegrass band pictures and information. Bluegrass festival listings and information music related businesses and agencies.

UK
**BAND INTERNATIONAL : THE JOURNAL OF THE INTERNATIONAL MILITARY MUSIC SOCIETY.** **Added/Corp** International Military Music Society. (Dec. 1978)-. Periodical. English. Three times a year. $11.50. International Military Music Society, 1 Larkspur Court Toftwood, DEREHAM Norfolk NR19 1LB England. **(Subscription address:** International Military Music Society, 5418 Waycross Drive, Alexandria, VA 22310 USA**) ED** Major G. Turner (editor's address: R.M.S.M., Kniller Hall, Twickenham, Middlesex TW2 7DV England). **LC** ML1300; .B27. **DD** 785/.06/7105. **Bk Rev. Ad Acc. Circ:** 1,100 (ctrl).

US
**BAND MUSIC GUIDE.** (1956)-. English. ir. Instrumentalist Company, 200 Northfield Road, Northfield IL 60093. **Tel** (708)446-5000, FAX (708)446-6263.

AT
**BAND NEWS.** (19??)-. English. Twelve times a year. 12.00Aus$ Australia; 24.00Aus$ New Zealand & South Pacific; 42.00Aus$ other. Band News, PO Box 18, Cambridge Park NSW 2750 Australia. **Tel** 011 61 2 47 316235. **Bk Rev. Ad Acc. Circ:** 500 (ctrl).

US/0092-0819
**BANDMASTERS REPORT.** (THE BANDMASTERS REPORT.). (June 1973)-. Periodical. English. qt. $5.00. Bandmasters Report, Box 33, Folcraft PA 19032. **LC** ML1; .B42. **DD** 785.1/2/05.

US/0887-9036
**BANDWORLD.** [Bandworld]. **VFOAT** Band World. (1985)-. Periodical. English. Five times a year (Jan., Mar., May, Aug., Oct.). $18.00 US; $26.00 Canada; $33.00 other. Western International Band Clinic, 407 Terrace Street, Ashland OR 97520. **Tel** (503)482-5030. **(Subscription telephone:** (503)482-1418**) ED** M. Max McKee. **DD** 785.
**Desc:** Practical tools for band directors including tips and complete music arrangements with parts for all instruments.

US/0190-1559
**BANJO NEWSLETTER.** **VFOAT** BNL Master Index. Vol. 1 (Nov. 1973)-. Periodical. English. Twelve times a year. $22.00. Banjo Newsletter, PO Box 3418, Annapolis MD 21403. **Tel** (800)759-7425. **ED** Donald Nitchie (phone: (508)645-3648). **LC** ML1; .B43. **DD** 787/.7/05. Index available. cum. index. **Bk Rev**, (Qty: 5-8). **Ad Acc. Circ:** 5,700. available on microfiche.
**Desc:** A magazine devoted to the 5-string banjo in all its musical styles, articles, reviews, history, collecting and repairing.
**Ind/Abst** Music Index.

US/0748-2728
**BANJO SOUNDSHEET.** (198?)-. Periodical. English. bm. Sacks Robert, 2001 21st Avenue South, Apartment B6, Nashville TN 37212. **LC** ML1015.B3; B36. **DD** 787/.7/05.

SZ
**BASLER JAHRBUCH FUER HISTORISCHE MUSIKPRAXIS : EINE VEROFFENTLICHUNG DER SCHOLA CANTORUM BASILIENSIS AN DER MUSIK-AKADEMIE DER STADT BASEL.** **Added/Corp** Schola Cantorum Basiliensis. (1977)-. German. ir. Amadeus Verlag, AM Iberghang 16, CH 8405 Winterthur Switzerland. **Tel** 011 41 52 282038. **(Subscription address:** Broekmans & Van Popple BV, Van Baerlestraat 92 94, 1071 BB Amsterdam, Netherlands (phone: 011 31 20 6628084)**) LC** ML5; .B34. **DD** 781.6/3/09.
**Ind/Abst** Music Index.

US/1050-785X
**BASS PLAYER.** [Bass play.]. Vol. 1, No. 1 (Spring 1990)-. Periodical. English. Eight times a year. $29.95. Miller Freeman Inc., 600 Harrison Street, San Francisco CA 94107. **Tel** (415)905-2337, FAX (415)905-2240, telex 278273. **(Subscription address:** Neodata / Colorado, PO Box 2606, Boulder Boulder CO 80322.**) DD** 787. **[CCC].** available on microfilm and microfiche from University Microfilms International (UMI). ***Continues in part*** *GPI Collectors' Edition, 1044-6656.*

US/0734-0206
**BASS PLAYER QUARTERLY.** (Feb. 1980)-. Periodical. English. qt. Bass Player Quarterly, 333 Gross Street, Pittsburgh PA 15224. **LC** ML920; .B37. available in microform.

FR/0981-8936
**BATTEUR MAGAZINE.** [Batteur mag.]. (198?)-. Periodical. French. Eleven times a year. 220.00F France; 300.00F other. Carredas, 132 rue du Faubourg St. Denis, 75010 Paris France. **Tel** 011 33 1 40357373. **UDC** 789.

UK
**BBC MUSIC.** English. mo. $36.00. BBC Music Magazine, PO Box 90, Wetherby W YK LS23 7JB England. **Tel** 011 44 937 541574. **(Subscription address:** BBC Classical Music Service, PO Box 60043, Tampa FL 33661.**)**
**Desc:** Features numerous photographs of musicians and reviews of current classical and semipopular CDs. Directed towards beginning CD collectors.

US/0084-8018
**BBC MUSIC GUIDES.** **Added/Corp** British Broadcasting Corporation. (1969)-. Monographic series. English. ir. Price varies per volume. University of Washington Press, Box C-50096, Seattle WA 98145-0096. **Tel** (206)543-8870. **ED** Gerald Abraham.

UK
**BBC SYMPHONY ORCHESTRA. [PROGRAMME].** **Main/Corp** BBC Symphony Orchestra. **VAT** British Broadcasting Corporation Symphony Orchestra. (19??)-. Multiple languages (English, French, German and Latin). wk. British Broadcasting Corporation, Caversham Park, Reading RG4 8TZ England. **Tel** 011 44 734 472742, FAX 011 44 734 463823, telex 848318. **LC** MT125; .B12. **DD** 785/.015.

US
**BDGUIDE.** **VFOAT** BD Guide. (1986)-. English. Five times a year (Jan., Mar., May, Sept., Nov.). $15.00 US; $18.00 others. Village Press, 2779 Aero Park Drive, Traverse City MI 49684. **Tel** (800)447-7367, (616)946-3712.
**Ind/Abst** Music Artic. Guide.

US/1063-5319
**BEAT (LOS ANGELES, CALIF. 1989).** (THE BEAT.). [Beat]. **VFOAT** Reggae & African Beat. Vol. 7, No. 5 (1988)-. Periodical. English. Six times a year (Feb., Apr., June, Aug., Oct., Dec.). $12.00 US; $15.00 Canada & Mexico; $30.00 others. Bongo Productions, PO Box 65856, Los Angeles CA 90065. **Tel** (213)257-2328, FAX (213)257-2461. **LC** ML3469; .B42. **DD** 781.64/09. Index available (back issues, price varies). ***Continues*** *Reggae & African Beat.*
**Desc:** Devoted to reggae, african, and caribbean music. Each issue is a valuable treasure trove of news, interviews, discographies, commentary and original graphics and photos. Coverage of the artist, the music business, concerts, events, recordings, videos and the faith and culture of Tastafari.

GW/0522-5949
**BEETHOVEN-JAHRBUCH.** [Beethoven-Jahrb.]. **Added/Corp** Beethoven-Haus (Bonn, Germany). (1954)-. Monographic series. German. ir. Price varies per volume. Beethoven Archiv, Bonnagasse 24 26, W 5300 Bonn 1 Germany. **Tel** 011 49 228 658245. **ED** P. Mies and J. Schmidt-Gorg. ***Supersedes*** *Neues Beethoven-Jahrbuch.*
**Ind/Abst** RILM Abstr.

GW
**BEETHOVEN / KONVERSATIONSHEFTE.** (19??)-. German. ir. Price varies per volume. Deutscher Verlag fuer Musik Leipzig GmbH, Karlstrasse 10, O 7010 Leipzig Fed Rep Germany. **Tel** 011 49 341 7351. **(Subscription address:** Breitkopf & Haertel Wiesbaden, Postfach 1707, Walkmuehlstrasse 52, W 6200 Wiesbaden FR Germany; telephone: 011 49 611 450080**)**

US/0898-6185
**BEETHOVEN NEWSLETTER, THE.** (THE BEETHOVEN NEWSLETTER / SAN JOSE STATE UNIVERSITY.). [Beethoven newsl.]. **Added/Corp** Ira F. Brilliant Center for Beethoven Studies. American Beethoven Society. **VFOAT** Beethoven. Vol. 1, No. 1 (Spring 1986)-. Periodical. English. Three times a year. $20.00. San Jose State University Foundation, IF Brillant Center of Beethoven Studies, 1 Washington Square, San Jose CA 95192. **Tel** (408)924-4590, FAX (408)924-4365. **ED** William Meredith. **DD** 780. **Bk Rev. Pr Rev. Circ:** 1,000 (ctrl).
**Desc:** Features articles, book and record reviews, auction reports, bibliographies and more about Beethoven.
**Ind/Abst** Music Artic. Guide; Music Index.

SI/0129-0169
**BEFORE I GET OLD.** (BIGO.). [Before I get old]. (1985)-. Periodical. English. Twelve times a year. $60.00 Asia; $65.00 others. Options Publications, PO Box 0663 Robinson Road, Singapore 9013 Singapore. **Tel** (201)694-2327. **ED** Phillop Cheah and Stephen Tan. **DD** 780.5.
**Desc:** Articles, news, and information on music artists and their music.

GW
**BEITRAEGE ZUR GREGORIANIK.** (1985)-. Periodical. German. Twice a year. Con Brio Verlagsgesellschaft, Postfach 100245, D 93002 Regensburg Germany. **LC** ML169.8; .B43. **DD** 783.5/09.

GW/0005-8106
**BEITRAEGE ZUR MUSIKWISSENSCHAFT.** ***Ceased.*** [Beitr. Musikwiss.]. Vol. 1 (1959)-Vol. 34, No. 2. Periodical. German. qt. Deutscher Judo Verband, Redaktion Ippon Segewaldweg 40, D 12557 Berlin Germany. **Tel** 011 49 711 210770, telex 051 678. **LC** ML5; .B352. cum. index. Documents available from The Genuine Article.
**Ind/Abst** Arts Humanit. Citation Index [Full Cov.]; Curr. Contents Arts Humanit.; Music Index; Res. Alert [Full Cov.]; RILM Abstr.

GW
**BEITRAGE ZUR JAZZFORSCHUNG. STUDIES IN JAZZ RESEARCH.** **VFOAT** Studies in Jazz Research. (1969)-. Monographic series. German (English). ir. Price varies per volume. International Society for Jazz Research, Schoenaugasse 6 POB 598, A-8010 Graz Austria. **Tel** 011 43 316 813460. **LC** ML55; .B34. **DD** 785.4,2,08.

GW
**BEITRAGE ZUR MITTELRHEINISCHEN MUSIKGESCHICHTE.** (1962)-. Periodical. German. ir. B. Schotts Soehne Musikverlag, Carl Zeiss Str 1, Postfach 3640, D 55026 Mainz Germany. **Tel** 011 49 6131 505129, 011 49 6131 505122, FAX 011 49 6131 505115, telex 04187821. **(Subscription address:** European / American Music Distribution Corporation, PO Box 850, Valley Forge, PA 19482; telephone: (215)648-0506**) ED** B. Schotts Soehne.

US/0092-8666
**BELL TOWER, THE.** [Bell tower]. **Added/Corp** American Bell Association. (19??)-. Periodical. English. Eight times a year. $22.00. American Bell Association, 7210 Bellbrook Drive, San Antonio TX 78227. **Tel** (210)674-1814. **ED** Eleanor Evans, (editor's address: 12250 Birdhaven Lane, St. Louis, MO 63128). **LC** ML1; .B4925. **DD** 789. **Ad Acc**, **Adv Mgr:** Bill Martin, **Tel** (810)349-4494. **Circ:** 2,000 (ctrl).
**Desc:** About 250-300 pages a year on all categories of collectible bells: figurals, enameled bells, tap bells, sleigh bells, glass and china bells.

IT
**BEQUADRO.** Italian. qt. L20000.00. Centro Ricerca Sperimentazione Didattica Musicale, Via Fontanelle 24, 50016 S Domenico Fiesole Italy. **Tel** 011 39 55 599545. **Bk Rev. Ad Acc.**
**Desc:** Studies on the application of new techniques applied to every branch of music education.

# Music

BE
**BERICHTEN OVER DE BUITENLANDSE HANDEL.** sm. 6000.00F. Ofc Belge du Commerce Exterior, Blvd Emile Jacqmain 162, 1210 Brussels Belgium. **Tel** 11 32 2 2093511.

FR
**BEST.** French. mo. 228.00F France; 350.00F other. Best / France, 23 Rue d'Antin, 75002 Paris France. **Tel** 011 33 1 47423356.

US/1062-6913
**BEST OF METAL, THE.** [Best met.]. (1991)-. Periodical. English. bm. $3.95 (single issue). Ashley Communications, Inc., 19431 Business Center Drive, Northridge CA 91374. **DD** 781. **Continues** Blast! Metal, 1052-0910.

RU
**BIBLIOGRAFICHESKAIA INFORMATSIIA. MUZYKA / MINISTERSTVO KULTURY SSSR, GOSUDARSTVENNAIA ORDENA LENINA BIBLIOTEKA SSSR IMENI V.I. LENINA. Added/Corp** Soviet Union. Ministerstvo Kultury. Gosudarstvennaia Biblioteka SSSR Imeni V.I. Lenina. Informtsentr po Problemam Kultury i Iskusstva (Soviet Union). **VFOAT** Muzyka. (1979)-. Periodical. Russian. mo. Gosudarstvennaia Biblioteka, Informatsionnyi Tsentr, Imeni V. I. Lenina, Prospekt Kalinina 3, 121019 Moscow Russia. **LC** ML5; .N83. **Continues** Novosti Nauchnoi Literatury: Muzyka.

YU/0523-2201
**BIBLIOGRAFIJA JUGOSLAVIJE. KNJIGE, BROSURE I MUZIKALIJE. Added/Corp** Bibliografski Institut FNRJ. Jugoslovenski Bibliografski Institut. **VFOAT** Bibliography of Yugoslavia. Vol. 1, (1950)-. Periodical. Serbo-Croatian (Roman). Twenty-four times a year. 230.00 Din. Jugoslovenski Bibliografski, Tera 2 IJE 26, Belgrade Yugoslavia. **Tel** 011 38 11 687836. **LC** Z2951; .B37. **NLM** Z 2933 B5816. **Continues** Yugoslovenska Bibliografija.

GW
**BIBLIOGRAPHIE DES MUSIKSCHRIFTTUMS. See** Music-Abstracting, Bibliographies and Statistics.

●FR
**BIBLIOGRAPHIE NATIONALE FRANCAISE. MUSIQUE : BIBLIOGRAPHIE ETABLIE PAR LA BIBLIOTHEQUE NATIONALE. Added/Corp** Bibliotheque Nationale (France). **VFOAT** Musique. (1992)-. French. tq. **LC** Z2165; .B5725. **Continues** Bibliographie Nationale Francaise. Supplement III. Musique, 1142-3285.

US
**BIBLIOGRAPHIES IN AMERICAN MUSIC. See** Music-Abstracting, Bibliographies and Statistics.

NE
**BIBLIOTECA CLASSICA. VFOAT** Biblioteca Classica d'Edizioni Originali; Biblioteca Classica E G A. (1984)-. Monographic series. English. ir. Price varies per volume. Biblioteca Classica, Musica Antica, G. Accardi, Rotterdam, Netherlands.

XR/0862-9021
**BIBLIOTHECA MUSICA - NARODNI KNIHOVNA CR.** (1990)-. Czech. ir. Statni Knihovna CSR, Liliova 5, Prague Czech Republic. **UDC** 78.

GW
**BIBLIOTHECA MUSICA THERAPEUTICA.** (19??)-. Monographic series. German. ir. Price varies per volume. Zentralantiquariat der DDR, Talstrasse 29, D 04103 Leipzig Germany. **Tel** 011 49 341 293641.

IT
**BIBLIOTHECA MUSICAE, COLLANA DI CATALOGHI E BIBLIOGRAFIE. Added/Corp** Instituto Editoriale Italiano. (1962)-. Italian. Instituto Editoriale Italiano, Milan Italy. Each issue contains an index to its own contents (no volume index)--loose.

NE
**BIBLIOTHECA ORGANOLOGICA.** English (German, French and Dutch). ir. Uitgeverij Frits Knuf B V, PO Box 720, 4116 ZJ Buuren Netherlands. **Tel** 011 31 03449-1255, FAX 011 31 03449-2617. **ED** Dr Peter Williams. **Circ:** 700.
**Desc:** All about organs.

US/0147-6645
**BIG APPLE JAZZ.** (Winter 1977)-. Periodical. English. F.F.O. Graphics, 888 7th Avenue, New York NY 10019. **LC** ML1; .B509. **DD** 785.4/2/097471.

US/0738-7067
**BIG BANDS, THE.** [Big bands]. (Nov. 1977)-. Periodical. English. mo. $15.00 US; $20.00 other. Studio City Advertising & Publishing, 4914 Lankershim Boulevard/Suite 1, North Hollywood CA 91601.

●US/1042-9263
**BIG CITY MUSIC.** (1991)-. Periodical. English. mo. $18.00. Charles Garcia, 18758-6 Bryant Street, Northridge CA 91324.

US/0006-2510
**BILLBOARD (CINCINNATI, OHIO. 1963).** (BILLBOARD.). [Billboard]. Vol. 75, No. 1 (Jan. 5, 1963)-. Periodical. English. wk (51 issues). $225.00 US, Puerto Rico and Canada; $230.00 other (surface mail). Billboard Publications Inc., 1515 Broadway Billboard, New York NY 10036. **Tel** (212)764-7300, FAX (305)755-7048, telex WU TWX 710-581-6279. **(Subscription address:** Fulfillment Corporation of America, 205 West Center Street, Marion, OH 43302) **ED** Ken Schlager. **LC** PN2000; .B5. **DD** 338. **[CCC]. Ad Acc. Circ:** 48,000. available on microfilm from Xerox; and KTO Microform; available on microfilm and microfiche from University Microfilms International (UMI). Documents available from UMI Article Clearinghouse.
**Continues** Billboard Music Week.
**Desc:** Covers the music and home entertainment industries. Weekly features include the famous Billboard charts. Helps keep music and video retailers, radio programmers and music fans up to date on what the public is buying and listening to in every category.
**Ind/Abst** Acad. Search (July 1993-); Bus. ASAP (1990-) [Full Txt.]; Bus. Index (1985-); Expand. Acad. Index (1992-); Gen. BusinessFile (1985-); Gen. Period. Index (1985-); Index Period. Artic. Relat. Law; INFO-SOUTH Abstr.; Infobank (Jan. 1979-); Infomat Int. Bus.; Mag. Search; Mark. Advert. Ref. Serv.; Music Index; Newsp. Period. Abstr. (1988-); TOM Gen. Index (1993-) [Full Txt.]; Trade Ind. ASAP [Full Txt.]; Trade Ind. Index (1981-) [Full Txt.].

US/0731-9460
**BILLBOARD EN ESPANOL.** [Billboard esp.]. (July 1980)-. Periodical. Spanish. mo. $65.00. Billboard Publications Inc., 1515 Broadway Billboard, New York NY 10036. **Tel** (212)764-7300, FAX (305)755-7048, telex WU TWX 710-581-6279. **LC** ML3486.5; .B54. **DD** 789.9/1245/098.

US
**BILLBOARD. INTERNATIONAL BUYER'S GUIDE OF THE MUSIC-RECORD INDUSTRY.** English. an. $83.00. Billboard Publications Inc., 1515 Broadway Billboard, New York NY 10036. **Tel** (212)764-7300, FAX (305)755-7048, telex WU TWX 710-581-6279.
**Desc:** Lists worldwide contacts in every phase of the music and video industry.
**Ind/Abst** Music Index (-19??).

●US
**BILLBOARD INTERNATIONAL LATIN MUSIC BUYER'S GUIDE. VFOAT** International Latin Music Buyer's Guide. (1992)-. Periodical. English. an (Published in Aug.). $59.00. Billboard Publications Inc., 1515 Broadway Billboard, New York NY 10036. **Tel** (212)764-7300, FAX (305)755-7048, telex WU TWX 710-581-6279. **LC** IN PROCESS.
**Desc:** Essential tool for finding business contacts in the Latin music marketplace. Covers popular music, folk music, sound recordings, and music trade.

US/0732-0124
**BILLBOARD INTERNATIONAL TALENT & TOURING DIRECTORY.** (BILLBOARD'S ... INTERNATIONAL TALENT & TOURING DIRECTORY.). [Billboard's int. talent tour. dir.]. **VFOAT** Billboard's ... International Talent and Touring Directory. (1986/87)-. Directory. English. an. $73.00. Billboard Publications Inc., 1515 Broadway Billboard, New York NY 10036. **Tel** (212)764-7300, FAX (305)755-7048, telex WU TWX 710-581-6279. **(Subscription address:** Billboard Publications, 1695 Oak Street, Lakewood, NJ 08701) **ED** Leslie Shaver. **DD** 780. **Ad Acc. Circ:** 15,000.
**Continues** Billboard International Talent & Touring Directory, 0732-0124.
**Desc:** The music industry's world wide reference source to talent, talent management, booking agencies, promoters, venue facilities, venue services and products.

US
**BILLBOARD ... RECORD RETAILING DIRECTORY. Added/Corp** Billboard Communications, Inc. **VFOAT** Record Retailing Directory; Billboard's Record Retailing Directory. (1991)-. Directory. English. an. $102.00. Billboard Publications Inc., 1515 Broadway Billboard, New York NY 10036. **Tel** (212)764-7300, FAX (305)755-7048, telex WU TWX 710-581-6279. **(Subscription address:** Billboard Publications, 1695 Oak Street, Lakewood, NJ 08701) **LC** IN PROCESS.
**Desc:** Comprehensive directory of independent music stores and chain operations across the US.

US/1042-2544
**BILLBOARD'S COUNTRY MUSIC SOURCEBOOK AND DIRECTORY. Title Change.** [Billboard's ctry. music sourceb. dir.]. **VFOAT** Billboard's Country Music Source Book and Directory; Country Music Source Book and Directory; Country Music Source Book & Directory; Country Music Source Book; Country Music Sourcebook and Directory; Country Music Sourcebook & Directory; Country Music Sourcebook. (198?)-(1992). Directory. English. an. Billboard Publications Inc., 1515 Broadway Billboard, New York NY 10036. **Tel** (212)764-7300, FAX (305)755-7048, telex WU TWX 710-581-6279. **LC** ML18; .B54 PARR Ref. **DD** 781.642/025. **Continues** Country Music Sourcebook, 0889-4949. **Continued by** Billboard's Nashville 615/Country Music Sourcebook.
**Desc:** Personal managers, booking agents, performing artists, radio stations, venues everyone involved in country music.

US/1042-2544
**BILLBOARD'S NASHVILLE 615 / COUNTRY MUSIC SOURCEBOOK.** [Billboard's ctry. music sourceb. dir.]. Directory. English. an. Billboard Publications Inc., 1515 Broadway Billboard, New York NY 10036. **Tel** (212)764-7300, FAX (305)755-7048, telex WU TWX 710-581-6279. **LC** ML18; .B54 PARR Ref. **DD** 781.642/025. **Continues** Billboard's Country Musics Sourcebook and Directory.
**Desc:** Personal managers, booking agents, performing artists, radio stations, venues everyone involved in country music.

YU/0352-7115
**BILTEN SOKOJ.** [Bilt. SOKOJ]. **VFOAT** Bilten Saveza Kompozitora Jugoslavije. (1973)-. Periodical. Serbo-Croatian (Roman). bm. **UDC** 78.
**Ind/Abst** Music Index.

UK
**BING. Added/Corp** International Crosby Circle. (19??)-. Periodical. English. qt. $3.00. Bing, 7 Greenmeadow Close, Monmouthshire NP4 3NR England. **LC** ML420.C93; B5. **DD** 784/.092/4.

US/0742-6968
**BIO-BIBLIOGRAPHIES IN MUSIC.** [Bio-bibliogr. music]. **VFOAT** Biobibliographies in Music. No. 1, (1984)-. Monographic series. English. ir. Price varies per volume. Greenwood Press Inc., PO Box 5007, Westport CT 06881-5007. **Tel** (203)226-3571, FAX (203)222-1502. **LC** UNC. **DD** 016.

●US/1069-5230
**BIO-CRITICAL SOURCE BOOKS ON MUSICAL PERFORMANCE. VFOAT** Bio Critical Source Books on Musical Performance. (1994)-. Periodical. English. Greenwood Press Inc., PO Box 5007, Westport CT 06881-5007. **Tel** (203)226-3571, FAX (203)222-1502.

US/0745-8649
**BLACK BEAT.** Vol. 14, No. 4 (Apr. 1983)-. Periodical. English. mo (12 issues). $20.00 (one year), $38.00 (two year). Sterling Macfadden, 233 Park Avenue South, New York NY 10003. **Tel** (212)979-4800. **LC** ML3478; .B42. **DD** 784.5/008996073. **Continues** Soul Teen, 0277-8114.

US/0276-3605
**BLACK MUSIC RESEARCH JOURNAL.** [Black music res. j.]. **Added/Corp** Fisk University. Institute for Research in Black American Music. **VFOAT** B.M.R. Journal; BMR Journal. (1980)-. Periodical. English. ir (Spring and Fall). $15.00 US; $20.00 other. Center for Black Music Research, Columbia College, 600 South Michigan Avenue, Chicago IL 60605-1996. **Tel** (312)663-1600 Ext. 559. **ED** Samuel A. Floyd Jr., (editor's address: 623 S Wabash, Chicago, IL 60605). **LC** ML3556; .B58. **DD** 781.7/296073/05. **Ad Acc. Circ:** 150. Documents available from The Genuine Article.
**Desc:** Focuses on matters of philosophy, aesthetics, and criticism in researching black music from the 17th century to the present.
**Ind/Abst** Arts Humanit. Citation Index [Full Cov.]; Curr. Contents Arts Humanit.; Music Artic. Guide; Music Index; Res. Alert [Full Cov.].

US/1043-9455
**BLACK SACRED MUSIC.** (BLACK SACRED MUSIC: A JOURNAL OF THEOMUSICOLOGY.). [Black sacred music]. Vol. 3, No. 2 (Fall 1989)-. Periodical. English. sa (2 issues - published in April & October). $20.00 (individuals), $40.00 (institutions) US; add $6.00 for postage other. Duke University Press, PO Box 90660, Durham NC 27708-0660. **Tel** (919)687-3600, (919)688-5134 (orders), FAX (919)688-4574, telex 802829. **ED** Jon Michael Spencer. **LC** ML2999; .J68. **DD** 781.71/0089/96073. available on microfilm and microfiche from University Microfilms International (UMI). **Continues** Journal of Black Sacred Music, 0891-9321.
**Desc:** A journal of theomusicology.
**Ind/Abst** Index Book Rev. Relig.; Music Artic. Guide; Music Index; Relig. Index One Period.

UK
**BLACK WAX MAGAZINE.** (19??)-. Periodical. English. mo. Black Wax Magazine, Flat 3 108 Greyhound Lane, London England. **LC** ML5; .B55. **DD** 784.

GW/0344-8231
**BLASMUSIK, DIE.** **Added/Corp** Bund Deutscher Blasmusikverbande. (1950)-. Periodical. German. mo. **LC** ML5; .B653. **DD** 788/.005.

US/0889-5635
**BLITZ (LOS ANGELES, CALIF.).** (BLITZ.). [Blitz]. No. 26 (May 1978)-. Periodical. English. ir. $9.50 US; $10.50 Canada. Blitz, PO Box 48124, Los Angeles CA 90048. **Tel** (818)761-5456. **DD** 784. ***Continues*** *Ballroom Blitz.*

NE/0921-2558
**BLOCK (ALMELO).** (BLOCK.). (March/April 1975)-. Periodical. Dutch. bm. Fl7 50. Persbureau Bossa Nova, Postbus 244, 7600 Ae Almeo Netherlands. **LC** ML5; .B654. **DD** 784.

US/0748-6294
**BLOSSOM MUSIC CENTER.** (BLOSSOM MUSIC CENTER : [FESTIVAL BOOK].). **Main/Corp** Blossom Music Center. (19??)-. English. an. Blossom Music Center, 1145 West Steels Corners Road, Cuyahoga Falls OH 44223. **LC** MT125; .B59. **DD** 780/.7/3977136.

GW/0936-2479
**BLUEGRASS-BUEHNE.** **VFOAT** Bluegrass Buhne. (19??)-. Periodical. German. Six times a year (Feb., Apr., June, Aug., Oct., Dec.). DM30.00. Eberhard Finke, Eberhardstrasse 14-4, 89073 ULM Germany. **Tel** 011 49 731 28642, FAX 011 49 731 21393. **ED** Eberhard Finke. **LC** ML3519; .B56. **DD** 784.52/005. Index available. cum. index. **Bk Rev**, (Qty: 6 per year). **Ad Acc. Circ:** 600.
**Desc:** Bluegrass and old-time music; biographies, concerts, events, record and book reviews, and much more.

US/0148-7396
**BLUEGRASS DIRECTORY, THE.** (July 1977)-. Directory. English. Mike and Arlene Bailey, 4005 Lara Lane, Chattanooga TN 37416. **LC** ML19; .B6. **DD** 780/.42.

US/0006-5129
**BLUEGRASS MUSIC NEWS.** (BLUEGRASS MUSIC NEWS : OFFICIAL PUBLICATION OF THE KENTUCKY MUSIC EDUCATORS ASSOCIATION.). **Added/Corp** Kentucky Music Educators Association. **VFOAT** K.M.E.A. Bluegrass Music News; KMEA Bluegrass Music News. Vol. 4, No. 1 (Oct. 1952)-. Periodical. English. qt. $10.00 (US); $12.00 (Canada); $14.00 (other). Bluegrass Music News, 1007 Granville Lane, Russellville KY 42276. **Tel** (502)726-6427. **ED** Hazel O Carver. **Ad Acc. Circ:** 2,000. ***Continues*** *K.M.E.A. Newsletter;* ***Absorbed*** *Kentucky Music Teacher.*
**Desc:** Official magazine for the Kentucky Music Educators Association. Articles, news items dealing with all areas of school music education state wide. Includes music education trade items.

US/0361-5774
**BLUEGRASS REFLECTIONS.** **Added/Corp** Southwest Bluegrass Club. (19??)-. Periodical. English. mo. $1.00 per issue. Southwest Bluegrass Club, 2704 Haley Avenue, Ft Worth TX 76117. **LC** ML1; .B5165. **DD** 784.

US
**BLUEGRASS STAR, THE.** (19??)-. Periodical. English. mo. $5.00. The Bluegrass Star, 1206 Bell Grimes Lane, Nashville TN 37207. **LC** ML1; .B5 67. **DD** 780/.42.

US/0006-5137
**BLUEGRASS UNLIMITED.** [Bluegrass unltd.]. Vol. 1 (July 1966)-. Periodical. English. Twelve times a year. $41.00 (one year), $81.00 (two years), $118.00 (three years), first class US & Canada; $21.00 (one year), $40.00 (two years), $58.00 (three years), regular delivery. Bluegrass Unlimited, Box 111, Broad Run VA 22014-0111. **Tel** (703)349-8181, FAX (703)341-0011. **ED** Peter V. Kuykenda II. **LC** ML1; .B517. **DD** 784. **Bk Rev**, (Qty: 30). **Ad Acc, Adv Mgr:** Pat Jeffries **Tel** (703)349-8181. **Circ:** 23,500 (ctrl).
**Desc:** This serves the interests of Bluegrass old-time and traditional country music. Record reviews, book reviews, listing of events including complete festival schedule for each year, regular appearances of Bluegrass, old-time artists, songbook, instruction, help on playing traditional country music instruments, artist profiles, rare photographs, interviews, and instrument repair.
**Ind/Abst** MLA Int. Bibl. Books Artic. Mod. Lang. Lit.; Music Index.

FR
**BLUES.** (Feb. 1970)-. Periodical. French (French). Blues, 39 rue Chambery, 1040 Brussels Belgium. **LC** ML5; .B655. **DD** 784.

US/1066-4068
**BLUES ACCESS.** [Blues access]. (1991)-. Periodical. English. Four times a year (Feb., June, Aug., Nov.). $12.00 US; $14.00 Canada & Mexico; $ 18.00 Asia & Australia; $16.00 other. Blues Access, 1455 Chestnut Drive, Boulder CO 80304. **Tel** (303)443-7245, FAX (303)393-9729. **ED** Cary Wolfson. **DD** _a781. **Bk Rev**, (Qty: 10). **Ad Acc. Circ:** 12,000.
**Desc:** Designed to serve as a resource guide to blues music. The contents includes comprehensive listings of new releases and festivals. Contains articles, interviews, and music reviews. Material is dedicated primarily to blues music fans and industry professions.

UK
**BLUES & SOUL.** **VFOAT** Blues and Soul. No. 412 (July 31-Aug. 13 1984)-. Periodical. English. Twenty-six times a year. £41.60 UK; £60.20 others. Blues & Soul Limited, 153 Praed Street, London W2 1RL England. **Tel** 011 44 71 4026897, FAX 011 44 71 2248227, telex 8951182 GECOMS G. **ED** Bob Killbourn. **LC** ML3469; .B583. **DD** 784.5/005. **Bk Rev. Ad Acc. Circ:** 42,000. ***Absorbed*** *Black Music & Jazz Review (London, England).*
**Desc:** Covers news, reviews, and charts of the soul music scene.

FR
**BLUES AND SWING MAGAZINE.** (1971)-. Periodical. French (French). $5.00. Parc Ste Anne 10 42 Bd de la Fabrique, 13009 Marseille France. **LC** ML5; .B657. **DD** 784.

AU/0250-4421
**BLUES LIFE.** ***Title Change.*** [Blues life]. (1978)-(19??). Periodical. German. qt. Blues Life, F & F Svacina Kegelgasse 40, A 1030 Vienna Austria. **Tel** 11 43 222 723765. **ED** Fritz Svacina. **LC** ML3521; .B63. **DD** 784.5/3/005. **Bk Rev. Ad Acc. Circ:** 2,000. ***Continued by*** *Blues Life Journal.*
**Desc:** Covers articles, reviews, discographies, photos, instruments, and videos on blues and related music.

AU/0250-4421
**BLUES LIFE JOURNAL.** **VFOAT** Blues Life. (19??)-. German (English). Four times a year (Jan., Mar., June, Sept.,). $32.00. Blues Life, F & F Svacina Kegelgasse 40, A 1030 Vienna Austria. **Tel** 11 43 222 723765. **ED** Franziska Svacina. **LC** ML3521; .B63. **DD** 784.5/3/005. **Bk Rev. Ad Acc, Adv Mgr:** Fran. **Circ:** 8,000. ***Continues*** *Blues Life, 0250-4421.*
**Desc:** Todays blues & blues musicians in a very wide sense.

UK/0307-7241
**BLUES-LINK.** (BLUES LINK.). (Aug./Sept. 1973)-. Periodical. English. bm. Blues Link, 94 Puller Road, Herts EN5 4HD England. **LC** ML5; .B6577. **DD** 784. ***Absorbed*** *Blues World.*

AU
**BLUES NOTES.** (Sept. 1969)-. Periodical. German (German). bm. S50.00. Blues Notes, Bischofstrasse 9, A-4020 Linz Austria. **LC** ML5; .B658. **DD** 784.

UK/0006-5153
**BLUES UNLIMITED.** [Blues unltd.]. No. 1 (1963)-. Periodical. English. Four times a year. Blues Unlimited, 1170 Towering B, Greenstreet, St. Louis MO 63163. **ED** B. W. Turner and M. J. Rowe. **LC** ML5; .B659. **Bk Rev. Ad Acc. Circ:** 4,500. available on microfilm and microfiche from University Microfilms International (UMI).
**Desc:** Articles, reviews, and photographs on all areas of black American blues.
**Ind/Abst** MLA Int. Bibl. Books Artic. Mod. Lang. Lit.

UK/0005-321X
**BMG; BANJO, MANDOLIN, GUITAR.** **VFOAT** Banjo, Mandolin, Guitar. (Nov. 1973)-. Periodical. English. mo. $7.50. D K Keogh, 20 Earlham Street, London WC2H 9LR England. **LC** ML5; .B25. **DD** 787/.61/05. ***Continues*** *Guitarist.*

US/0521-9604
**BMI ORCHESTRAL PROGRAM SURVEY.** **Main/Corp** Broadcast Music, Inc. **Added/Corp** American Symphony Orchestra League. **VFOAT** Orchestral Program Survey. **VAT** Broadcast Music Incorporated Orchestral Program Survey. (19??)-. English. ir. Broadcast Music Inc., 320 West 57th Street, New York NY 10019. **LC** ML1; .B74. **DD** 785/.06/610973.

FI
**BN.** **Added/Corp** Finnish Blues Society. Suomen Afroamerikkalaisen Musiikin Yhdistys. **VFOAT** Blues News. (19??)-. Periodical. Finnish. Six times a year (Mar., May, June, Aug., Oct., Dec.). Fmk42.00. Finnish Blues Society, PL257SF-00531, Helsinski 53 Finland. **Tel** 011 358 0 7591160. **ED** Aimo Ollikainen. **LC** ML3556; .B67. **DD** 781.7/296073. Index available. **Ad Acc. Circ:** 1,500. ***Continues*** *Blues News (Helsinki, Finland).*
**Desc:** Covers the rhythm and blues, soul, rock and roll (old), funk, gospel, doo wop, and reggae and other music.

PO
**BOLETIM INFORMATIVO.** **Main/Corp** Liga dos Amigos do Canto Gregoriano. (19??)-. Bulletin. Portuguese. Campo dos Martires DA, Datria 96, 2 Lisbon Portugal. **LC** ML28.L63; L5. **DD** 783.5/05.

PE
**BOLETIN DE MUSICA Y DANZA.** **Added/Corp** Instituto Nacional de Cultura (Peru). Oficina de Musica y Danza. (April 1978)-. Periodical. Spanish. Jr Ancash 390, Lima 1 Peru.

IT/0411-5384
**BOLLETINO DEL CENTRO ROSSINIANO DI STUDI.** **Main/Corp** Centro Rossiniano di Studi, Pesaro. **Added/Corp** Fondazione Rossini di Pesaro. (1955)-. Periodical. Italian. an (Oct.). Fondazione G. Rossini, Piazza Oliviere 5, 61100 Pesaro Italy. **Tel** 011 39 721 30053. **LC** ML5; .C275.
**Ind/Abst** RILM Abstr.

SP/0214-297X
**BOOGIE MADRID.** [BoogieMadr.]. (1988)-. Periodical. Spanish. mo. 3500ptas Spain. Musical Urbana Sa, Embajadores 81, Esc 2 2A, 28012 Madrid Spain. **Tel** 011 34 1 2308702. **UDC** 78.

US/8755-5832
**BOOMBAH HERALD.** Vol. 1, No. 1 (Dec. 1973)-. Periodical. English. sa. $10.00. Loren D. Geiger, 15 Park Boulevard, Lancaster NY 14086. **ED** Loren D. Geiger. **DD** 785. Index available. cum. index. **Bk Rev**, (Qty: 1). **Ad Acc. Circ:** 100.
**Desc:** Devoted to biographies of band composers, new CDs, cassettes, records, and the histories of bands.

CN/0712-645X
**BORGO.** (LE BORGO.). [Borgo]. **Added/Corp** Alliance Chorale Nouveau-Brunswick. No. 1 (June 1979)-. Periodical. French. Aliance Chorale Nouveau-Brunswick, 236, Rue St. Georges, Moncton NV E1C 1W1. **DD** 784.1/006/0715.

US/0524-1170
**BOSTON ORGAN CLUB NEWSLETTER, THE.** **Added/Corp** Organ Historical Society. Boston Organ Club Chapter. (19??)-. Newsletter. English. ir. Boston Organ Club, PO Box 104, Harrisville NH 03450-0104. **Tel** (603)827-3055. **ED** E. A. Boadway. **Bk Rev. Circ:** 200.
**Desc:** Musical and historical study of pipe organ building, especially in New England.

US/0889-230X
**BOSTON ROCK.** (198?)-. Periodical. English. Ten times a year (July/Aug. & Dec./Jan. issues combined). $15.00. Boston Rock, PO Box 371, New Town Branch, Boston MA 02258. **Tel** (617)244-6803. **ED** Tristram Lozam and Lisa M. Moore. **Bk Rev. Ad Acc. Circ:** 30,000.
**Desc:** Internationally recognized resource for modern popular music and allied arts, films, illustration, books and video.

US/0006-8020
**BOSTON SYMPHONY ORCHESTRA.** (BOSTON SYMPHONY ORCHESTRA; PROGRAM.). **Main/Corp** Boston Symphony Orchestra. (19??)-. English. Twenty-four times a year. $120.00 US; $125.00 other. Boston Symphony Orchestra, Symphony Hall, Boston MA 02115. **Tel** (617)638-9332, FAX (617)638-9288. **ED** Marc Mandell. Index available in last issue of volume--attached. **Ad Acc, Adv Mgr:** Steve Ganak, **Tel** (617)542-6913. available on microfilm from University Microfilms International (UMI). ***Continues*** *Boston Symphony Orchestra. Concert Bulletin, 0734-2497.*

●CN/1187-9580
**BOTTIN DE L'INDUSTRIE DE LA MUSIQUE AU QUEBEC.** (LE BOTTIN DE L'INDUSTRIE DE LA MUSIQUE AU QUEBEC / RADIO ACTIVITE.). [Bottin ind. musique Que.]. **Added/Corp** Radio Activite (Firme). (1992/1993)-. French. an. 25.00Can$ Canada; 35.00Can$ others. Radio Activite Inc., 3981 Boulevard St-Laurent, Suite 715, Montreal Quebec H2W 1Y5 Canada. **Tel** (514)849-1236, FAX (514)486-5805. **DD** 338.4/778164/025714. ***Continues*** *Les Pages Jaunes de l'Industrie., 0839-0959.*

US/0145-3165
**BRAILLE SCORES CATALOG. INSTRUMENTAL.** (BRAILLE SCORES CATALOG. INSTRUMENTAL / NATIONAL LIBRARY SERVICE FOR THE BLIND AND PHYSICALLY HANDICAPPED.). **Main/Corp** Library of Congress. National Library Service for the Blind and Physically Handicapped. **VFOAT** Braille Scores Catalog--Instrumental. (19??)-. Catalog. English. National Library Service for the Blind and Physically Handicapped, Library of Congress, 1291 Taylor Street Northwest, Washington DC 20542. **Tel** (800)424-8567, (202)707-5100, (800)424-9100. **LC** ML136.U52; B7. **DD** 016.7808. available in braille.

US/0145-3149
**BRAILLE SCORES CATALOG. ORGAN.** [Braille scores cat., Organ]. **Main/Corp** Library of Congress. National Library Service for the Blind and Physically Handicapped. **VFOAT** Braille Scores Catalog, Organ. **VAT** Music and Musicians. Braille Scores Catalog. Organ. (1978)-. Catalog. English. National Library Service for the Blind and Physically Handicapped, Library of

Congress, 1291 Taylor Street Northwest, Washington DC 20542. **Tel** (800)424-8567, (202)707-5100, (800)424-9100. **LC** ML136.U52; M86. **DD** 016.7868.

US/1051-1016
**BRAILLE SCORES CATALOG. VOCAL.** [Braille scores cat., Vocal]. **Main/Corp** Library of Congress. National Library Service for the Blind and Physically Handicapped. (1983)-. Catalog. English. National Library Service for the Blind and Physically Handicapped, Library of Congress, 1291 Taylor Street Northwest, Washington DC 20542. **Tel** (800)424-8567, (202)707-5100, (800)424-9100. **LC** IN PROCESS. **DD** 780. ***Continues*** *Library of Congress. National Library Service for the Blind and Physically Handicapped. Braille Scores Catalog. Voice, 0145-3157.*

US/1066-4033
**BRANSON'S COUNTRY REVIEW.** [Branson's ctry. rev.]. **VFOAT** Country Review. (19??)-. Periodical. English. Six times a year (Jan., Mar., May, July, Sept., Nov.). $12.97 (one year); $22.97 (two years). Anderson Publishing Incorporated / Branson, PO Box 357, Branson MO 65616. **Tel** (417)334-6627. **ED** Sandy Poneleit. **DD** 781. Index Bound in First Issue ($2.00). **Ad Acc. Circ:** 27,000 (ctrl). ***Continues*** *Ozark Mountain Country Review.*

SZ/0303-3848
**BRASS BULLETIN.** [Brass bull.]. No 1 (Oct. 1971)-. Bulletin. Multiple languages (English, French and German). qt. $70.00. Brass Bulletin, PO Box 576, CH-1630 Bulle Switzerland. **Tel** 011 41 29 24422. **ED** Jean-Pierre Mathez. **LC** ML5; .B6864. **DD** 788/.01/04. Index available. cum. index. **Bk Rev. Ad Acc. Circ:** 7,000 (ctrl). ***Absorbed*** *Brass International, 0952-794X.*
**Desc:** International magazine for brass players with articles (history, inquiries, techniques, biographies), illustrations, correspondence, new publications with reviews (scores, records, books, instruments etc.) Promotes international contacts in 92 countries.
**Ind/Abst** Music Index.

US/0363-454X
**BRASS RESEARCH SERIES.** (19??)-. Monographic series. English. ir. Price varies per volume. 148 Eighth Avenue North, Nashville TN 37203-3798. **Tel** (615)254-8969. **ED** Stephen L. Glover. **LC** unc. **Bk Rev. Ad Acc. Circ:** 700 (ctrl).
**Desc:** Historical and bibliographical texts about the trumpet, horn, trombone, and tuba.

GW/0406-9595
**BRAVO MUNCHEN. See** Motion Picture.

CN/0824-6653
**BREAK-THROUGH (HARTNEY).** (BREAK-THROUGH.). [Break-through]. Issue 1 (Oct./Nov. 1983)-. Periodical. English. bm. Break-Through, PO Box 160, Hartney Manitoba R0M 0X0 Canada. **DD** 784/.092/4.

UK/0007-0173
**BRIO (UNITED KINGDOM BRANCH, INTERNATIONAL ASSOCIATION OF MUSIC LIBRARIES).** (BRIO.). [Brio]. **Added/Corp** International Association of Music Libraries. United Kingdom Branch. Vol. 1, (Spring 1964)-. Periodical. English. Twice a year (May, Nov.). International Association Music Library Woodhouse, 47 Berriedale, Hove E Sussex BN3 4JG England. **Tel** 011 44 273 779129. **ED** John Wagstaff. **Bk Rev. Ad Acc. Circ:** 400 (ctrl). available on microfilm and microfiche from University Microfilms International (UMI).
**Desc:** Journal of the United Kingdom branch of the International Association of Music libraries, archives and documentation centres.
**Ind/Abst** Libr. Inf. Sci. Abstr.; Music Index; RILM Abstr.

UK
**BRISTOL FOLK NEWS. Added/Corp** English Folk Dance and Song Society. **VFOAT** Folk News. (19??)-. Periodical. English. John Maher, Shambee Claremont Avenue, Bishopston 7, Bristol England. **LC** ML5; .B6897. **DD** 781.7/0942.

UK
**BRITISH BANDSMAN.** (1899)-. Periodical. English. wk. $46.00. British Bandsman Ltd, 64 London End, Beaconsfield Bucks HP9 2JD England. **Tel** (049 46) 4411. **ED** Peter Wilson. **Bk Rev. Ad Acc. *Continues*** *British Musician.*
**Desc:** News and views of the world of bands.

UK/0068-1407
**BRITISH CATALOGUE OF MUSIC, THE. Added/Corp** British Library. Bibliographic Services Division. Council of the British National Bibliography. (Jan./March 1957)-. English. Three times a year (May, Aug., Dec.). £69.00 UK & EEC Countries; £75.00 others; $140.00 North America. Bowker Saur Ltd., A Reed Reference Publishing Company, Part of Reed International PLC, 59-60 Grosvenor Street, London WIX 9DA England. **Tel** 011 44 71 4935841, FAX 011 44 71 4991590. **LC** ML120.G7; B7. **DD** 781.971. Index available. cum. index. **Circ:** 600.
**Desc:** Comprehensive listing of printed music available in the UK, covering a wide range of currently available material from western classical to pop and educational music.

UK/0308-4698
**BRITISH COUNTRY MUSIC ASSOCIATION YEARBOOK.** (YEARBOOK - BRITISH COUNTRY MUSIC ASSOCIATION.). **Main/Corp** British Country Music Association. (19??)-. English. an. British Country Music Association, PO Box 2, New Abbot TQ12 4HT England. **LC** ML21; .B73. **DD** 784.

UK
**BRITISH HERITAGE SERIES.** No. 1 (198?)-. Monographic series. English. ir. Price varies per volume. G Schirmer Inc, 24 East 22nd Street, New York NY 10010.

UK/0265-0517
**BRITISH JOURNAL OF MUSIC EDUCATION : BJME. VFOAT** BJME. Vol. 1, No. 1 (March 1984)-. Academic Scholarly Publication. English. Three times a year (March, July and November). $69.00 US, Canada & Mexico; £44.00 other. Cambridge University Press, The Edinburgh Building, Shaftesbury Road, Cambridge CB2 2RU United Kingdom. **Tel** 011 44 223 312393, FAX 011 44 223 325959. **(Subscription address:** Cambridge University Press / North America, 110 Midland Avenue, Port Chester NY 10573.**) ED** John Paynter, Keith Swanwick. **LC** ML5; .B6898. **DD** 780/.7. **[CCC].** available on microfilm from University Microfilms International (UMI).
**Desc:** Aims to provide clear, stimulating and readable accounts of current issues in music education worldwide. The journal strives to strengthen professional development and improve practice within the field of music education. The range of subjects covered is wide: classroom music teaching; individual instrumental teaching and group teaching; music in higher education; international comparative music education and the development of literature in this field. Audio examples included with published articles are supplied on cassette tape Contributors are encouraged to submit recorded material to accompany articles.
**Ind/Abst** Br. Educ. Index; Music Index.

UK
**BRITISH LIBRARY MUSIC FACSIMILES. Added/Corp** British Library. (1980)-. Monographic series. English. ir. Price varies per volume. British Library / Bibliographic Service, Boston Spa, Wetherby West Yorkshire LS23 7BQ England. **Tel** 011 44 937 546160, FAX 011 44 937 546586, telex 557381.

UK/0958-5664
**BRITISH MUSIC. Added/Corp** British Music Society. **VFOAT** Journal of the British Music Society. Vol. 12 (1990)-. English. an (Oct.). £5.00. British Music Society, 7 Tudor Gardens, Upminst Essex, RM14 3DE England. **Tel** 11 44 708 224795. **ED** Robert A. Barnett. **LC** ML5; .B694. **DD** 781.741/05. Index available (every 10 years). cum. index. **Ad Acc. Circ:** 600. ***Continues*** *British Music Society Journal.*

UK/0266-2329
**BRITISH MUSIC EDUCATION YEARBOOK.** (1984)-. English. an. £11.50 UK; £15.00 other. Rhinegold Publishing Ltd, 239-241 Shaftesbury Avenue, London WC2H 8EH England. **Tel** 011 44 71 2405749, FAX 240 0897, telex 264675 GILDED.

UK/0306-5928
**BRITISH MUSIC YEARBOOK.** [Br. music yearb.]. (1975)-. English. an (Nov.). £14.95 UK; £18.45 other. Rhinegold Publishing Ltd, 239-241 Shaftesbury Avenue, London WC2H 8EH England. **Tel** 011 44 71 2405749, FAX 240 0897, telex 264675 GILDED. **LC** ML21; .M89483. **DD** 780/.942. ***Continues*** *Music Yearbook.*

US/0740-7955
**BROADSIDE (NEW YORK, N.Y. 1962).** ***Ceased.*** (BROADSIDE.). [Broadside]. No. 1-1962-Ceased (Winter 1989). Periodical. English. bm. Broadside Magazine, PO Box 20558, New York NY 10011. **Tel** (212)873-2100. **ED** Judith Cohen. **DD** 784. **Bk Rev. Ad Acc. Circ:** 1,000.
**Desc:** Current topical songs with words and music by performers such as Pete Seeger, Arlo Guthrie, Tom Paxton and Holly Near. Topics include the Mideast, Central America and nuclear energy.

US/1075-0371
**BROWBEAT.** English. sa (Nov. & May). $6.00 US; $8.00 Canada & Mexico. Browbeat, PO Box 11124, Oakland CA 94611-1124. **Tel** (510)562-2441. **ED** Mike Burma. **Bk Rev**, (Qty: 5-10). **Ad Acc, Adv Mgr:** Mike Rizzi. **Circ:** 1,000.
**Desc:** Music magazine dedicated to dissonance and noise in its variety of forms - jazz, punk, industrial and experimental. Also contains articles on movies, books, and sexually disenfranchised.

BE
**BRUSSELS MUSEUM OF MUSICAL INSTRUMENTS BULLETIN, THE.** ***Suspended.*** **Main/Corp** Conservatoire Royal de Musique de Bruxelles. Musee Instrumental. Vol. 1 (1971)-Suspended. Bulletin. Multiple languages (Dutch, English, French, German, Russian and Spanish). sa. Fl140.00. Vereniging Voor Nederlandse Muziekgeschiedenis, PO Box 1514, 3500 BM Utrecht Netherlands. **Tel** 011 31 30 23327787, FAX (0)3449-2617. **LC** ML459; .M87. **DD** 781.91/05.
**Desc:** Describes different instruments written by different authors.
**Ind/Abst** Music Index (-19??); RILM Abstr.

GW
**BUCERUS MARTIN OPERA OMNIA.** (19??)-. Monographic series. German. ir. Price varies per volume. VVA Bertelsmann Dist GmbH, Postfach 7600, D 33310 Gutersloh Germany. **Tel** 011 49 5241 803294.

US/0192-9097
**BUDDY (DALLAS, TEX.).** (BUDDY.). (197?)-. Periodical. English. Twelve times a year. $12.00. Buddy Inc., 11218 Goodnight Lane, Suite 102, Dallas TX 75229. **Tel** (214)484-9010. **ED** Stoney Burns. **Bk Rev. Ad Acc. Circ:** 100 (ctrl).
**Desc:** Covers all types of music with emphasis on Texas artists. Extensive calendar section.

AU/0007-3075
**BUEHNE.** No. 1 (Oct. 1958)-. Periodical. German. Eleven times a year. S620.00 Austria; S745.45 other. Orac Verlag, Schoenbrunner Str 58-61, 1050 Vienna Austria.
**Ind/Abst** Music Index.

BU/0204-823X
**BULGARSKO MUZIKOZNANIE (SOFIA, BULGARIA : 1979).** (BULGARSKO MUZIKOZNANIE / [BULGARSKA AKADEMIIA NA NAUKITE, INSTITUT ZA MUZIKOZNANIE].). **Added/Corp** Institut Za Muzikoznanie (Bulgarska Akademiia Na Naukite). (1979)-. Periodical. Bulgarian. qt. Izdatelstvo na Bulgarskata, Akademiia na Naukite, Institut za Muzikoznanie, Ul Dimitur Poliznov 21, 1504 Sofia Bulgaria. **ED** Venelin Krastev. **LC** ML5; .M99155. **Bk Rev. Ad Acc.** ctrl circ. ***Continues*** *Muzikoznanie.*

BU
**BULGARSKOTO MUZIKALNO IZPULNITELSTVO PO SVETA. Added/Corp** Suiuz Na Muzikalnite Deitsi V Bulgariia. (1976)-. Bulgarian. Suiuz na Muzikalnite Deitsi v Bulgaria, Sofia Bulgaria. **LC** ML5; .B85.

AT/0156-5184
**BULLETIN / AUSTRALIAN MUSIC THERAPY ASSOCIATION. VFOAT** Australian Music Therapy Association Bulletin; AMTA Bulletin; A.M.T.A. Bulletin. Vol. 1, No. 1 (Nov. 1977)-. Bulletin. English. Four times a year (Mar., June, Sept., Dec.). 40.00Aus$ Comes with Australian Music Therapy Association Membership. Australian Music Therapy Association, 18 Collins Street, Box Hill, Victoria 3128 Australia. **Tel** 011 61 3 8173129. **NLM** W1; BU478HCAR. ***Continues*** *Australian Music Therapy Association Bulletin.*
**Ind/Abst** Aust. Educ. Index.

UK/0953-7511
**BULLETIN / BRITISH SOCIETY FOR MUSIC THERAPY. Added/Corp** British Society for Music Therapy. No. 1 (Autumn 1987)-. Bulletin. English. Three times a year (Jan., May, Sept.,). £50.00. British Society for Music Therapy, 69 Avondale Avenue, East Barnet Herts EN4 8NB England. **Tel** 011 44 81 368 8879. **LC** ML3919; .B84. **DD** 615.8/5154/05. **Ad Acc. Circ:** 400 (ctrl). ***Continues*** *British Journal of Music Therapy, 0308-244X.*
**Desc:** News, reports of meetings and details of courses for society members.

FR
**BULLETIN - CENTRE D'ETUDES DE MUSIQUE ORIENTALE. Main/Corp** Centre d'Etudes de Musique Orientale. (Dec. 1967)-. Bulletin. French. an. Centre d'Etudes de Musique Orientale, c/o CNRS Ecase 298, 22 rue d'Athenes, 75009 Paris France. **LC** ML5 b .C273. **Circ:** 700.

US/0010-9894
**BULLETIN - COUNCIL FOR RESEARCH IN MUSIC EDUCATION.** [Bull. Counc. Res. Music Educ.]. **Main/Corp** Council for Research in Music Education. **Added/Corp** University of Illinois at Urbana-Champaign. School of Music. **VFOAT** Bulletin of the Council for Research in Music Education. (1963)-. Bulletin. English. qt. $15.00 individual; $22.50 institutions. University of Illinois School of Music, 1114 West Nevada, Urbana IL 61801. **Tel** (217)333-1027. **ED** Marilyn P Zimmerman. **LC** ML1; .C916. **DD** 780. **Bk Rev. Pr Rev.** available on microfilm and microfiche from University Microfilms International (UMI). Documents available from The Genuine Article.
**Desc:** Publishes research-related articles of interest to music educators and critiques of research studies in the field of music education.
**Ind/Abst** Arts Humanit. Citation Index [Full Cov.]; Contents Pages Educ.; Curr. Contents Arts Humanit.; Educ. Index; Middle East Abstr. Index; Music Artic. Guide;

Music Index; Psychol. Abstr. (1974-); Res. Alert [Full Cov.]; Res. High. Educ. Abstr.; RILM Abstr.; Soc. Sci. Cit. Index [Select. Cov.].

CN/1181-9189
**BULLETIN DE LAUDEM.** (BULLETIN DE LAUDEM / L'ASSOCIATION DES ORGANISTES DU DIOCESE DE MONTREAL.). [Bull. LAUDEM]. **Added/Corp** Association des Organistes du Diocese de Montreal. **VFOAT** LAUDEM. Vol. 1, No 1 (1990)-. Bulletin. French. Twice a year (June, Dec.). 10.00Can$ US & Canada; 16.00Can$ others. Association des Organistes Liturgiques, 1085 rue de la Cathedrale, Montreal, Quebec H3B 2V3 Canada. **Tel** (514)767-4074. **DD** 786.5/06/071428.

UK/0419-618X
**BULLETIN - DOLMETSCH FOUNDATION.** (BULLETIN - DOLMETSCH FOUNDATION, HASLEMERE, ENGLAND.). [Bull. - Dolmetsch Found.]. **Main/Corp** Dolmetsch Foundation, Haslemere, England. **Added/Corp** Dolmetsch Foundation. No. 1 (April 1962)-. Bulletin. English. Three times a year. £10.60 Comes with Consort. Dolmetsch Foundation, Lavant Park Farm, West Lavant, Chichester SX PO18 9AH England. **Tel** 011 44 243 528612. **ED** G. Beechy. **LC** ML26; .D64. **DD** 780. Index available. **Ad Acc. Circ:** 750 (ctrl).
**Desc:** Development of early instruments, music and dance, methods of playing, musicology and manuscripts.
**Ind/Abst** Music Index (-19??).

FR/0755-7272
**BULLETIN DU HOT-CLUB DE FRANCE.** (BULLETIN DU HCF.). [Bull. hot-club Fr.]. **Main/Corp** Hot Club de France. **Added/Corp** Hot Club de France. (19??)-. Bulletin. French. **LC** ML5; .H66. **DD** 781.65/0944/05. ***Continues*** *Hot Club de France. Bulletin, 0755-7272.*

FR/0755-7272
**BULLETIN - HOT CLUB DE FRANCE.** ***Title Change.*** [Bull. hot-club Fr.]. **Main/Corp** Hot Club de France. (1950)-?. Bulletin. French. ir. **LC** ML5; .H66. **DD** 789.9/136/54205. ***Continued by*** *Bulletin du HCF, 0755-7272.*

UK/0018-828X
**BULLETIN - HYMN SOCIETY OF GREAT BRITAIN AND IRELAND.** (THE HYMN SOCIETY OF GREAT BRITAIN AND IRELAND BULLETIN.). [Bull. - Hymn Soc. G. B. Irel.]. **Main/Corp** Hymn Society of Great Britain and Ireland. **Added/Corp** Hymn Society of Great Britain and Ireland. (1937)-. Periodical. English. qt (Jan., Apr., July, and Oct.). $18.00 US and Canada; £9.00 other. Hymn Society of Great Britain and Ireland, J. Akroyd, 15 Park Hall Close, W. Midlands WS5 3HQ England. **ED** B. S. Massey. **LC** ML5; .H95. **DD** 783.905. Index available. cum. index. **Bk Rev. Circ:** 500 (ctrl).
**Desc:** Articles, book and record reviews concerning words and music of hymns and related items such as their origins, selection and use, their authors and composers.
**Ind/Abst** Music Index.

US/0094-3258
**BULLETIN - KODALY MUSICAL TRAINING INSTITUTE INC.** (BULLETIN.). **Main/Corp** Kodaly Musical Training Institute. (19??)-. Bulletin. English. Kodaly Musical Training Institute Inc., 525 Worcester Street, Wellesley MS 02181. **LC** MT4.W365; K6. **DD** 780/.729744/7.

US
**BULLETIN / MIDWEST KODALY MUSIC EDUCATORS OF AMERICA.** **VFOAT** M.K.M.E.A. Bulletin; MKMEA Bulletin; Midwest Kodaly Music Educators of America Bulletin. Vol. 10, No. 1 (Sept. 1981)-. Bulletin. English. qt. Lynee Ransom, MKMEA Editor, Department of Music, Iowa State University, Ames IA 50011. **LC** MT1; .O36. **DD** 780/.7/2977. ***Continues*** *Official Magazine (Midwest Kodaly Music Educators of America).*

GW/0433-678X
**BULLETIN / MUSIKRAT DER DEUTSCHEN DEMOKRATISCHEN REPUBLIK, SEKTION DDR DES INTERNATIONALEN MUSIKRATES.** **Main/Corp** Germany (East). Musikrat. **Added/Corp** Germany (East). Kommision fuer Unesco-Arbeit. (1964)-. Bulletin. German (English and French). sa. Musikrat der Deutschen Republik, Sektion DDR des Internationalen Musikrates, Leipziger Strabe 26, Berlin 1086 Germany. **Tel** 2292772.

CN/0703-9999
**BULLETIN - NATIONAL SHEVCHENKO MUSICAL ENSEMBLE GUILD OF CANADA.** **Main/Corp** National Shevchenko Musical Ensemble Guild of Canada. No. 2 (Nov. 1972)-. Bulletin. English (Ukrainian). an. Free. National Shevchenko Musical Ensemble Guild of Canada, 626 Bathurst Street, Toronto Ontario M5S 2R1 Canada. **Tel** (416)533-2725. **ED** Ginger Kautto. **DD** 785.06/2/71. **Circ:** 4,000 (ctrl). ***Continues*** *Shevchenko Ensemble Bulletin, 0703-9980.*

US/0739-5639
**BULLETIN OF HISTORICAL RESEARCH IN MUSIC EDUCATION, THE.** [Bull. hist. res. music educ.]. **Added/Corp** University of Kansas. Dept. of Art and Music Education and Music Therapy. Vol. 1, No. 1 (July 1980)-. Bulletin. English. Three times a year. $20.00. University of Kansas Department of Art and Music Education, 311 Bailey Hall, Lawrence KS 66045. **Tel** (913)864-4784. **ED** George N Heller. **LC** ML1; .B786. **DD** 780/.7/29. **Bk Rev**, (Qty: 5-6). **Pr Rev. Circ:** 200.
**Desc:** Publishes research on a historical nature pertinent in any way to music education. Emphasis is on music education in the United States.
**Ind/Abst** Music Artic. Guide; Music Index.

US/0827-5955
**BULLETIN OF THE GUILD OF CARILLONNEURS IN NORTH AMERICA.** [Bull. Guild Carillonneurs North Am.]. **Main/Corp** Guild of Carillonneurs in North America. No. 1 (Oct. 1940)-. English. an. $4.00. Guild of Carillonneurs, c/o William DeTurk, BOK Tower Gardens, 1151 Tower Boulevard, Lake Wales FL 33853-3412. **Tel** (813)676-1154. **LC** ML1; .G95. **Ad Acc.**

US/0739-1390
**BULLETIN OF THE INTERNATIONAL COUNCIL FOR TRADITIONAL MUSIC.** (BULLETIN OF THE INTERNATIONAL COUNCIL FOR TRADITIONAL MUSIC.). [Bull. Int. Counc. Tradit. Music]. **Main/Corp** International Council for Traditional Music. No. 59 (Oct. 1981)-. Bulletin. English (French and Spanish). Twice a year. The International Council for Traditional Music, Columbia University, 417 Dodge Department of Music, New York NY 10027. **Tel** (212)678-0332. **ED** Dieter Christensen. **LC** ML26; .I546. **DD** 781.7/06/01. **Circ:** 1,200. ***Continues*** *Bulletin of the International Folk Music Council, 0020-6768.*
**Desc:** Reports from national committees and the liaison office of ICTM about events related to music and dance in their respective countries.

US/0736-9549
**BULLETIN OF THE REED ORGAN SOCIETY, INC.** **Added/Corp** Reed Organ Society (U.S.). (198?)-. Bulletin. English. Four times a year. Reed Organ Society, 6 Carswell Circle, Wichita Falls TX 76306. **Tel** (817)855-2414. ***Continues*** *Reed Organ Society Newsletter.*

CN/0838-6730
**BULLETIN / SASKATCHEWAN CHORAL FEDERATION.** [Bull. - Sask. Choral Fed.]. **Added/Corp** Saskatchewan Choral Federation. (1985)-. Bulletin. English. ir. 10.00Can$ (associate members & students); 15.00Can$ (individuals); 30.00Can$ (groups);. Saskatchewan Choral Federation, 1871 Lorne Street, Regina Saskatchewan S4P 2L7 Canada. **Tel** (306)359-9730. **ED** Gwin Edey. **DD** 784.1/006/07124. **Bk Rev. Circ:** 1,000 (ctrl). ***Continues*** *Saskatchewan Choral Federation Bulletin, 0838-6722.*
**Desc:** A non-profit organization for singers and directors of choral music in Saskatchewan.

SW/0586-0709
**BULLETIN - SVENSKT MUSIKHISTORISKT ARKIV.** [Bull. - Sven. musikhist. ark.]. **Main/Corp** Svenskt Musikhistoriskt Arkiv. No. 1 (1966)-. Bulletin. Swedish. Svenskt Musikhistoriskt Arkiv, Box 16326, Stockholm S 10326 Sweden.
**Ind/Abst** RILM Abstr.

GW
**BUXTEHUDE DIETRICH COLLECTED WORKS SERIES : WERKE GESAMTAUSGABE.** (19??)-. English. ir. Price varies per volume. Deutscher Verlag fuer Musik Leipzig GmbH, Karlstrasse 10, O 7010 Leipzig Fed Rep Germany. **Tel** 011 49 341 7351. **(Subscription address:** Broude Brothers Ltd., 141 White Oaks Road, Williamstown, MA 01267; telephone: (413)458-8132)

US/0092-5063
**C.B.M.S. NEWSLETTER.** (CBMS NEWSLETTER.). [C.B.M.S. newsl.]. **Main/Corp** Colorado Bluegrass Music Society. **VAT** Colorado Bluegrass Music Society Newsletter. (Sept. 1972)-. Newsletter. English. mo. $5.00. Colorado Bluegrass Music Society, 2307 Spruce Street, Boulder CO 80302. **LC** M127.U5; C68. **DD** 780/.42.

US/0162-6973
**CADENCE.** [Cadence]. **VFOAT** Cadence Magazine. (Jan. 1976)-. Periodical. English. Twelve times a year. $30.00. Cadence Jazz & Blues Review, Cadence Building, Rt. 1 Box 345, Redwood NY 13679. **Tel** (315)287-2852. **LC** ML3505.8; .C3. **DD** 781/.57/05. Index available (Bound in Jan. iss., at $4.00). cum. index. **Bk Rev. Ad Acc, Adv Mgr:** Susan. ctrl circ.
**Desc:** Jazz and blues journal, its features includes interviews, oral histories, news and complete coverage of the entire record scene worldwide.
**Ind/Abst** Music Artic. Guide (?-?); Music Index.

US/0007-9405
**CADENZA (LOLO, MONT.).** (CADENZA / MONTANA MUSIC EDUCATORS ASSOCIATION.). [Cadenza]. **Added/Corp** Montana Music Educators Association. **VFOAT** MMEA Cadenza. (1942)-. Periodical. English. Three times a year (Jan., Apr., Oct.). $8.00. MMEA Cadenza, 3833 Audubon Way, Billings MT 59102. **Tel** (406)652-1419. **ED** Ed Harris. **DD** 780. **Ad Acc. Circ:** 1,100 (ctrl).
**Desc:** Montana Music Educators Association newsletter.

CN/0703-8380
**CADENZA (SASKATOON).** (CADENZA.). [Cadenza]. **Added/Corp** Saskatchewan Music Educators Association. Opus 12, No. 2 (Jan. 1977)-. Periodical. English. Three times a year. 30.00Can$. Saskatchewan Teachers Federation, PO Box 1108, Saskatoon Saskatchewan, S7K 3N3 Canada. **Tel** (306)373-1660. **DD** 780.7/05. ***Formed by the union of*** *Saskatchewan Music Educators Association. Journal, 0317-5073* ***and*** *Saskatchewan Music Educators Association. Newsletter, 0381-9051.*

BL
**CADERNO DE MUSICA.** **Added/Corp** Federacao Paulista de Conjuntos Corais. Universidade de Sao Paulo. Escola de Comunicacoes e Artes. Sociedade Brasileira de Musica Contemporanea. Universidade de Sao Paulo. Escola de Comunicacoes e Artes. Servico de Biblioteca e Documentacao. No. 1 (Sept. 1980)-. Periodical. Portuguese. Federacao Paulista de Conjuntos Corais, rua Domingos de Morias 2452, 04036 Sao Paulo SP Brazil. **LC** ML1499; .C3. **DD** 784.1/00981.

FR/0294-6939
**CAHIERS DE LA GUITARE, LES.** No. 1 (1982)-. Periodical. French. Four times a year (Jan., Apr., July, Oct.). 170.00F (France); 180.00F (other). Les Cahiers de la Guitare, BP 83, 94472 Boissy St Leger France. **Tel** 33 1 45981291, FAX 011 33 1 45991649.
**Ind/Abst** Music Index.

CN/0821-1817
**CAHIERS DE L'ARMUQ, LES.** [Cah. ARMuQ]. **Added/Corp** Association pour L'Avancement de la Recherche en Musique du Quebec. **VFOAT** Cahier. **VAT** Cahiers de l'Association pour l'Avancement de la Recherche en Musique du Quebec; Cahier - Association pour l'Avancement de la Recherche en Musique du Quebec. No. 1, (April 1983)-. Periodical. French. ir. $60.00 (corporation memberships), $30.00 (individual memberships). ARMUQ, C P 695 Tour de la Bourse, Montreal Quebec H4Z 1J9 Canada. **DD** 781.7714/07/2. cum. index. ctrl circ.

SZ
**CAHIERS DE MUSIQUES TRADITIONNELLES.** **Added/Corp** Ateliers d'Ethnomusicologie (Geneva, Switzerland). (1988)-. French. an. **LC** ML3797.6; .C33. **DD** 780/.89.

FR/0395-1200
**CAHIERS DEBUSSY.** [Cah. Debussy]. **Added/Corp** Centre de Documentation Claude Debussy. No. 1-3, (1974-76)-; New Series No. 1 (1977)-. Academic Scholarly Publication. French (English). an. 120.00F. Centre de Documentation, Claude Debussy, IRCAM, 31 rue Saint-Merri, 75004 Paris France. **Tel** 011 33 1 42770639. **LC** ML410.D28; C18. **DD** 780/.92/4; B. Index available. cum. index. **Ad Acc.**
**Desc:** Scholarly journal about Debussy, his life, works, relationships with his contemporaries and aesthetic analysis.
**Ind/Abst** RILM Abstr.

FR
**CAHIERS DU JAZZ.** (19??)-. Periodical. French. Three times a year. 280.00F France; 330.00F other. Presses Universitaires de France, Department des Revues, 14 Avenue du Bois de l'Epine, BP 90, 91003 Evry Cedex France. **Tel** (1)60 77 82 05, FAX (1) 60 79 20 45, telex PUF 600 474 F.

US/0886-4594
**CALENDAR FOR NEW MUSIC, THE.** (1981)-. Periodical. English. Eight times a year. Sound Art Foundation, 31 Linden Street, Brooklyn NY 11221-3712. **Tel** (718)443-2611. **ED** William Hellermann. **Ad Acc. Circ:** 6,500. ***Continues*** *New Music Calendar.*
**Desc:** Contains advertising on music.

CN/0821-2791
**CALGARY FOLK CLUB.** (CALGARY FOLK CLUB : BROCHURE.). [Calg. Folk Club]. **Added/Corp** Alberta. Alberta Culture. Calgary Folk Club. (1978)-. English. an. **DD** 781.7/06/071233.

US/1067-5213
**CALIFORNIA JAZZ NOW.** [Calif. jazz now]. **VFOAT** Jazz Now. Vol. 1, No. 1 (May. 1991)-. Periodical. English. Eleven times a year (Except January). $15.00 US; $30.24 others. California Jazz Now, PO Box 31742, Oakland CA 94604. **Tel** (510)531-2389, FAX (510)531-8875. **ED** Haybert King Houston and Stella Cheung Brandt. **DD** 781. Index available (publish separately). cum. index. **Bk Rev**, (Qty: 12). **Ad Acc. Circ:** 4,000 (ctrl).
**Desc:** We provide our readers with information on who's who in the West Coast Jazz world, covering the hottest up and coming stars on the West Coast. Giving the latest

updates on today's legendary greats and those other than musicians who have promoted and contributed to the Jazz blues and Latin Jazz Communities.

US
**... CALIFORNIA MUSIC DIRECTORY, THE.** ***Suspended.*** (1985)-Suspended with (1987). Directory. English. an. $34.50. Music Industry Resources, PO Box 190, San Anselmo CA 94960. **Tel** (415)457-0215. **LC** ML14.C26; C3. **DD** 338.4/778/025747. available on CD-ROM.

TR
**CALYPSO.** (19??)-. Periodical. English. $2.75. Unique Services, 17 Cassia Avenue, Pleasantville Trinidad. **LC** ML5; .C146. **DD** 784.7/6/96072983.

UK/0954-5867
**CAMBRIDGE OPERA JOURNAL.** Vol. 1, No. 1 (March 1989)-. Academic Scholarly Publication. English. Three times a year (March, July and November). $75.00 US, Canada & Mexico; £47.00 other. Cambridge University Press, The Edinburgh Building, Shaftesbury Road, Cambridge CB2 2RU United Kingdom. **Tel** 011 44 223 312393, FAX 011 44 223 325959. **(Subscription address:** Cambridge University Press / North America, 110 Midland Avenue, Port Chester NY 10573.**) ED** Roger Parker and Arthur Groos. **LC** ML1699; .C35. available on microfilm from University Microfilms International (UMI).
**Desc:** Interdisciplinary journal devoted to opera. It addresses audiences from a wide variety of disciplines ranging from musicology to literature, theatre and history. Strives to avoid narrowly musicological or philological modes of enquiry. Issues contain four to six articles and occasional commentaries and review articles.
**Ind/Abst** Music Index.

US
**CAMBRIDGE READINGS IN THE LITERATURE OF MUSIC.** Monographic series. English. ir. Price varies per volume. Cambridge University Press / New York, 40 West 20th Street, New York NY 10011-4211. **Tel** (212)924-3900, (800)221-4512. **(Subscription address:** Cambridge University Press / Outside of North America, Journal Fulfillment Department, The Edinburgh Building, Cambridge CB2 2RU United Kingdom.**)**
**Desc:** Series covering various writings on music. Editions have covered subjects such as music analysis.

CN/0711-6659
**CANADIAN ACOUSTICS.** (ACOUSTIQUE CANADIENNE.). [Can. acoust.]. **Added/Corp** Association Canadienne de l'Acoustique. **VFOAT** Acoustique Canadienne. Vol. 10, No. 1 (Jan. 1982)-. Periodical. French (English). Four times a year (Jan., Apr., July, Oct.). 35.00Can$. Canadian Acoustical Association, 2410 Old Pheasant Road, Mississauga, Ontario L5A 2S1, Canada. **Tel** (905)949-2164. **DD** 363.7/4/05. ***Continues*** *Acoustics and Noise Control in Canada., 0229-2238.*
**Ind/Abst** Ind. Hyg. Dig. (19??-).

CN/0831-0203
**CANADIAN BAND JOURNAL.** [Can. band j.]. (1984)-. Periodical. English. Four times a year. 18.00Can$ Comes with Canadian Band Directors Association membership. CBDA Journal, PO Box 5005, Red Deer Alta T4N 5H5 Canada. **Tel** (403)342-3216, FAX (403)341-5474. **ED** Keith Mann. **DD** 785.06710971. **Circ:** 3,500. ***Continues*** *CBDA Journal, 0703-9077.*
**Desc:** A national organization dedicated to the promotion and development of the musical and educational values of the band.

CN/1180-3762
**CANADIAN COMPOSER.** ***Title Change.*** [Can. compos.]. **Added/Corp** Society of Composers, Authors and Music Publishers of Canada. Vol. 1, No. 1 (Spring 1990)-(Dec. 1993). Periodical. English. qt. Performing Rights Organization of Canada, 41 Valleybrook Drive, Don Mills Ontario M3B 2S6 Canada. **DD** 780/.971/05. Documents available from Magazine Collection. ***Separated from*** *Compositeur Canadien, 0008-3259.* ***Merged into*** *Probe.*
**Ind/Abst** Acad. Search (Jan. 1992-Sept. 1993); Gen. Period. Index (1985-); Humanit. Source (Jan. 1992-); INFO-SOUTH Abstr.; Mag. Index Plus (1989-); Mag. Search; TOM Gen. Index (1989-) [Full Txt.].

CN/0008-3259
**CANADIAN COMPOSER, THE.** ***Ceased.*** [Can. compos.]. **Added/Corp** Composers, Authors and Publishers Association of Canada. **VFOAT** Canadian Composer. No. 1 (May 1965)-(19??). Periodical. English (French). mo. Creative Arts Co, 1240 Bay Street/Suite 303, Toronto Ontario M5R 2A7 Canada. **Tel** (416)925-5138. **LC** ML27.C3; C6. **DD** 780/.971. available on microfilm and microfiche from University Microfilms International (UMI); and Micromedia Limited. Documents available from UMI Article Clearinghouse. ***Continued in part by*** *Canadian Composer (Society of Composers, Authors and Music Publishers of Canada), 1180-3762.*
**Ind/Abst** Acad. Abstr. Full Text Elite (Jan. 1992-); Acad. Abstr. (Jan. 1992-); Can. Index; Can. Period. Index; Music Index; Newsp. Period. Abstr. (1991-); Point Repere (1990-); RILM Abstr.; Mag. Index (1983-).

CN/0008-3259
**CANADIAN COMPOSER.** (LE COMPOSITEUR CANADIEN [MICROFORM].). [Can. compos.]. **Added/Corp** Composers, Authors and Publishers Association of Canada. **VFOAT** Canadian Composer. No. 1 (May 1965)-. English (French). an. 20.00 (microfiche). Micromedia Limited, 20 Victoria Street, Toronto Ontario M5C 2N8 Canada. **Tel** (416)362-5211, (800)387-2689, FAX (416)362-6161, telex 06524668. **DD** 780/.971/05.

CN/0829-5344
**CANADIAN FOLK MUSIC BULLETIN.** [Can. folk music bull.]. **Added/Corp** Canadian Folk Music Society. Canadian Society for Musical Traditions. **VFOAT** Bulletin de Musique Folklorique Canadienne. Vol. 16, No. 2 (April 1982)-. Bulletin. English (French). Four times a year. Canadian Folk Music Society, Box 4232 Station C, Calgary Alberta T2T 5N1 Canada. **Tel** (403)230-0340. **ED** John Leeder. **LC** ML3563; .C37. **DD** 781.771/05. cum. index. **Bk Rev. Ad Acc. Circ:** 1,000 (ctrl). ***Continues*** *Canadian Folk Music Society. Bulletin, 0820-0742;* ***Absorbed*** *Canadian Folk Festival Directory, 0827-2492.*
**Desc:** Articles, features, songs, news, and reviews on the subject of Canadian folk music.
**Ind/Abst** MLA Int. Bibl. Books Artic. Mod. Lang. Lit.; Music Index.

CN/0318-2568
**CANADIAN FOLK MUSIC JOURNAL.** **Added/Corp** Canadian Folk Music Society. Vol. 1, (1973)-. Academic Scholarly Publication. English (French). an. $15.67 (individuals), $19.58 (institutions) Comes with Canadian Society for Musical Traditions Membership. Canadian Society for Music Traditions, Box 4232, Station C, Calgary ALTA T2T 5N1 Canada. **Tel** (403)230-0340. **ED** Edith Fowke. **DD** 781.7/71. **Bk Rev. Circ:** 800.
**Desc:** Contains scholarly articles devoted to various aspects of traditional folk music in Canada.
**Ind/Abst** MLA Int. Bibl. Books Artic. Mod. Lang. Lit.; Music Index.

CN/0008-4549
**CANADIAN MUSIC EDUCATOR, THE.** [Can. music educ.]. **Added/Corp** Canadian Music Educators' Association. **VFOAT** Canadian Journal of Research in Music Education; Musicien Educateur au Canada. Vol. 1 (June 1959)-. Periodical. English (French). Three times a year. 35.00Can$ Canada; 47.00Can$ US; 52.00Can$ others Comes with Canadian Music Educators Association membership. Canadian Music Educators Association, 16 Royaleigh Avenue, Etobicoke Ontario M9P 2J5 Canada. **Tel** (416)244-3745, FAX (416)235-1833. **ED** Brian Roberts (editor's address: Faculty of Education, Memorial University of Newfoundland, St. John's Newfoundland, Canada, A1B 3X8 Canada). **LC** ML5; .C25. **Bk Rev. Ad Acc. Circ:** 2,600 (ctrl). ***Absorbed*** *Newsletter. Canadian Music Educators' Association, 0045-5172.*
**Ind/Abst** Can. Educ. Index; Music Index.

CN/0319-6283
**CANADIAN MUSIC THERAPY JOURNAL.** **Added/Corp** Canadian Music Therapy Association. Vol. 1, No. 3 (Dec. 1973)-. Periodical. English. sa. Oxford Mental Health Centre, PO Box 310, Woodstock Ontario N4S 7X9 Canada. **DD** 615/.837/05. ***Continues*** *Canadian Music Therapy Bulletin, 0319-6275.*

CN/0225-9435
**CANADIAN MUSIC TRADE.** [Can. music trade]. (Aug. 1979)-. Periodical. English. Six times a year. 10.00Can$ Canada; 16.00Can$ other. Norris-Whitney Communications Inc., 23 Hannover Drive Unit 7, St. Catharine Ontario L2W 1A3 Canada. **Tel** (905)641-3471, FAX (905)641-1648. **DD** 338.4/778/0971. available on microfiche (from Micromedia : Toronto, Ont.).

CN
**CANADIAN MUSICAL HERITAGE, THE.** **Added/Corp** Canadian Musical Heritage Society. **VFOAT** Patrimoine Musical Canadien. Vol. 1 (1983)-. Monographic series. English (French). ir. Price varies per volume. Canadian Musical Heritage Society, PO Box 262, Station A, Toronto, Ontario K1N 8V2 Canada. **Tel** (613)232-3406.

CN/0708-9635
**CANADIAN MUSICIAN.** [Can. music.]. Vol. 1, No. 1 (March/April 1979)-. Periodical. English. Six times a year (Jan., Mar., May, July, Sept., Nov.). 16.00Can$ Canada; 21.00Can$ other. Norris-Whitney Communications Inc., 23 Hannover Drive Unit 7, St. Catharine Ontario L2W 1A3 Canada. **Tel** (905)641-3471, FAX (905)641-1648. **ED** Shauna Kennedy (phone: (416)533-8303). **LC** ML3848; .C36. **DD** 780/.5. **Bk Rev. Ad Acc, Adv Mgr:** Jan Smith, **Tel** (905)641-1512. **Circ:** 30,000. available on microfiche.
**Desc:** Exposure of Canadian music, to aid in the development of Canadian music and Canadian music trade.
**Ind/Abst** Can. Index; Can. Period. Index (19??-); Music Index.

CN/0710-2666
**CANADIAN OPERA COMPANY.** (CANADIAN OPERA COMPANY : [YEARBOOK].). [Can. Opera Co.]. **Added/Corp** Canadian Opera Company. (1980)-. English. an. Controlled Media Communications, 160 Bedford Road, Toronto Ontario M5R 2K9. **DD** 782.1/05.

CN/0820-4896
**CANADIAN OPERA COMPANY NEWS (1986).** (CANADIAN OPERA COMPANY NEWS.). [Can. Opera Co. news]. **Added/Corp** Canadian Opera Company. Vol. 4, No. 4 (Dec. 1986)-. Periodical. English. qt. Canadian Opera Guild, 227 Front Street East, Toronto Ontario M5A 1E8, Canada. **DD** 782.1/06/071. ***Continues*** *COC News, 0822-8922.*

CN/1189-9956
**CANADIAN ORCHESTRAS AND YOUTH ORCHESTRAS DIRECTORY.** (CANADIAN ORCHESTRAS AND YOUTH ORCHESTRAS DIRECTORY / ANNUAIRE DES ORCHESTRES CANADIENS ET DES ORCHESTRES DE JEUNES.). [Can. orch. youth orch. dir.]. **Added/Corp** Association of Canadian Orchestras. Ontario Federation of Symphony Orchestras. **VFOAT** Annuaire des Orchestres et des Orchestres de Jeunes. (199?)-. Directory. English (French). Association of Canadian Orchestras / OFSO Secretariat, 56 The Esplanade / Suite 311, Toronto Ontario M5E 1A7 Canada. **Tel** (416)366-8834, FAX (416)366-1780. **ED** M. Fiala. **DD** 784.2/025/71. **Bk Rev. Ad Acc. Circ:** 750. ***Continues*** *Directory of Canadian Orchestras and Youth Orchestras., 0705-6249.*
**Desc:** Listings and contacts of key personnel in Canadian orchestras and youth orchestras.

CN/0714-8070
**CANADIAN RECORD CATALOGUE.** ***Ceased.*** [Can. rec. cat.]. **Added/Corp** Canadian Independent Record Production Association. Association du Disque et de L'Industrie du Spectacle Quebecoise. CIRPA/ADISQ Foundation. **VFOAT** Catalogue de Disques Canadiens. (1982)-(198?). English (French). ir. CIRPA ADISQ Foundation, Front Street West, Suite 330 144, Toronto Ontario M5J 2L7 Canada. **Tel** (416)593-4545. **DD** 016.7899/12/0971. available in microform.

CN/0710-0353
**CANADIAN UNIVERSITY MUSIC REVIEW.** [Can. univ. music rev.]. **Added/Corp** Canadian University Music Society. **VFOAT** Revue de Musique des Universites Canadiennes. (1980)-. English (French). an. $35.00. University of Toronto Press, 5201 Dufferin Street, Downsview Ontario M3H 5T8 Canada. **Tel** (416)667-7781, (416)667-7782, FAX (416)667-7803. **ED** M. Cyr and M. A. Roberge. **LC** ML5; .C1557. **DD** 780/.5. **Bk Rev. Circ:** 450. available on microfilm and microfiche from University Microfilms International (UMI). ***Continues*** *Journal (Canadian Association of University Schools of Music), 0315-3541.*
**Desc:** Publishes research by Canadian scholars in music, both French and English, who represent the fields of musicology, ethnomusicology, theory, aesthetics, criticism and music education. Emphasis is given to scholarship relating to Canadian music and music in Canada, but writing on subjects of a more general nature is also welcomed.
**Ind/Abst** Music Index; RILM Abstr.

GW
**CANTANTIBUS ORGANIS; SAMMLUNG VON ORGELSTUCKEN ALTER MEISTER.** (1958)-. Monographic series. German. ir. Price varies per volume. Heinrichshofen Verlag, Liebigstrasse 16, D 26389 Wilhelmshaven Germany. **Tel** 011 49 04421 202004, FAX 011 49 04421 202007. **(Subscription address:** C.F. Peters Corporation, 373 Park Avenue South, New York, NY 10016 USA; telephone: (212)686-4147**) ED** Eberhard Kraus. **LC** M7; .C23.

US/0898-8463
**CANTIGUEIROS (LEXINGTON, KY.).** **See** Literature.

GW
**CANTIO SACRA.** (1955)-. Monographic series. German. ir. Price varies per volume.

AT/0812-1494
**CAPITAL NEWS.** (197?)-. Periodical. English. Twelve times a year. 30.00Aus$ Australia; 60.00Aus$ New Zealand; 100.00Aus$ other. Capital News, PO Box 497, Tamworth NSW 2340 Australia. **Tel** 011 61 67 650300, FAX 011 61 67 650345, telex 163166. **ED** Jim Hynes. **Ad Acc, Adv Mgr:** Terry Hill, **Tel** 067-650300. **Circ:** 6,000.
**Desc:** News of country music around Australia and the world.

US/0730-5001
**CARILLON NEWS.** (CARILLON NEWS : NEWSLETTER OF THE GUILD OF CARILLONNEURS IN NORTH AMERICA.). **Added/Corp** Guild of Carillonneurs in North America. No. 21 (Oct. 1979)-. Newsletter. English. sa. The Guild of Carillonneurs in North America, 900 Burtm Tower, Ann Arbor MI 48109. **Tel** (313)764-2539. **ED** Margo Halsted. **LC** ML1039; .C37. **DD** 789/.5/05. **Bk Rev. Circ:** 500 (ctrl). ***Continues***

*Randschriften, 0092-4105.*
**Desc:** Newsletter of the Guild of Carillonneurs in North America.

CN/0315-3916
**CARNET MUSICAL.** [Carnet music.]. **Added/Corp** Ensemble Claude Gervaise. (June 1971)-. Periodical. French. qt. Ensemble Glaude Gervaise, CP 91, Chambly Quebec Canada. **LC** ML5; .C19. **DD** 780/.5. cum. index.
**Ind/Abst** Music Index (-19??).

IT/1120-4621
**CARTELLINA, LA. Added/Corp** Edizioni Suvini Zerboni. Notiziario. No. 1 (1974)-. Italian. bm (6 issues). L50000 Italy; L60000 others. Edizioni Suvini Zerboni, Via MF Quintiliano 40, 20138 Milan Italy. **Tel** 011 39 2 5084365, FAX 011 39 2 5084261, telex 321063. **ED** Suvini Zerboni. **LC** ML5; .C193. Index available (published separately). **Bk Rev**, (Qty: 15-20). **Ad Acc**, **Adv Mgr:** Paola Mazzini, **Tel** same as publisher. **Circ:** 3,000 (ctrl).
**Desc:** Covers music, teaching and directing of choirs.

US/1053-7694
**CAS JOURNAL.** [CAS j.]. **Added/Corp** Catgut Acoustical Society. **VFOAT** CASJ. **VAT** Catgut Acoustical Society Journal. Ser. 2, Vol. 1, No. 5 (May 1990)-. Periodical. English. Twice a year. $50.00 (libraries), $45.00 (individuals) US; add $5.00 postage other. Catgut Acoustical Society, 112 Essex Avenue, Montclair NJ 07042. **Tel** (201)744-4029. **ED** Daniel W. Haines, 142 Greenridge Avenue, White Plains, NY 10605. **LC** ML1; .C329. **DD** 787/.1923/05. Index available (published separately). cum. index. **Bk Rev**, (Qty: 2-4). **Ad Acc**. **Pr Rev. Circ:** 800 (ctrl). ***Continues*** *Journal of the Catgut Acoustical Society.*

US/0008-7289
**CASH BOX, THE. See** Sound Recordings and Systems.

JA
**CATALOG OF PUBLICATIONS - THE JAPAN FEDERATION OF COMPOSERS.** **Main/Corp** Nihon Sakkyokuka Kyogikai. (1970/71)-. Catalog. English (Japanese). Japan Federation of Composers, 602 Shinano-machi Building, 33 Shinanao-machi, Shinjuku-Ku Tokyo 160 Japan. **Tel** 011 81 03 3359 3916, FAX 011 81 03 3359 2927. **LC** ML120.J3; N54.

FR
**CATALOGUE DISQUES. Main/Corp** Centre Regional de Documentation Pedagogique de Besancon. (19??)-. French. CRDP, 20 rue Daniel Casanova, 94170 Le Perr S Marne France. **Tel** 011 31 1 48727070. **LC** ML156.2; .C457. **DD** 016.7899/12.

UK
**CATALOGUE : FOR THE INDEPENDENT MUSIC TRADE.** English. mo (11 issues). $62.50 US and Canada. Catalogue, 61 Collier Street, London N1 9BE England. **Tel** 011 44 71 833 2843.

UK
**CATALOGUE OF PRINTED MUSIC IN THE BRITISH LIBRARY : ACCESSIONS.** **Main/Corp** British Library. (19??)-. English. **ED** Laureen Baillie. **LC** ML136.L8; B73. **DD** 016.78.

GW/0069-116X
**CATALOGUS MUSICUS. Added/Corp** International Association of Music Libraries. International Musicological Society. Vol. 1, (1963)-. Monographic series. German. ir. Price varies per volume. Baerenreiter-Verlag, KGA Verlagssvc PF 100329, D 34003 Kassel Germany. **Tel** 011 49 561 31050, telex 99504. **(Subscription address:** Kasseler Grossauslieferung, KGA Verlagssvc GmbH PF 102180, W 3500 Kassel F R Germany, phone: 011 49 561 8070346) **LC** ML113; .C35.
**Desc:** A series of important music bibliographies. Catalogues and inventories of the sixteenth century.

●US/1059-9088
**CATHOLIC MUSIC EDUCATOR.** (CATHOLIC MUSIC EDUCATOR: A PUBLICATION OF THE NATIONAL ASSOCIATION OF PASTORAL MUSICIANS.). [Cathol. music educ.]. **Added/Corp** National Association of Pastoral Musicians (U.S.). Vol. 1, No. 1 (May 1992)-. Periodical. English. qt. $22.00. National Association of Pastoral Musicians, 225 Sheridan Street Northwest, Washington DC 20011. **Tel** (202)723-5800, FAX (202)723-2262. **DD** 782.

CN/0712-3272
**CAYO PUBLICATION.** [CAYO publ.]. **Main/Corp** Canadian Association of Youth Orchestras. **VFOAT** Publication AOJC. **VAT** Canadian Association of Youth Orchestras Publication; Publication Association des Orchestres de Jeunes du Canada. (1980)-. Periodical. English (French; summaries and/or abstracts in French). Three times a year. Canadian Association of Youth Orchestras, Box 1020, Banff Alberta T0L 0C0 Canada. **Tel** (403)762-6278, telex ARTSBANFF 03-826657. **DD** 785/06/271. ***Continues*** *Canadian Association of Youth Orchestras. C A Y O News and Views., 0709-6739.*

CN/0713-1283
**CBC CLASSICAL CATALOGUE.** (CBC CLASSICAL RECORD CATALOGUE.). [CBC classical rec. cat.]. **Main/Corp** Canadian Broadcasting Corporation. Merchandising. **Added/Corp** Canadian Broadcasting Corporation. **VAT** Canadian Broadcasting Corporation Classical Record Catalogue. (197?)-. English (French; summaries and/or abstracts in French). an. Free. Canadian Broadcasting Corporation, CP 6000, Montreal Quebec H3C 3A8 Canada. **Tel** (514)597-7666. **DD** 016.7899/12. ctrl circ.

CN/0713-1291
**CBC JAZZ AND POPULAR RECORD CATALOGUE.** [CBC jazz pop. rec. cat.]. **Main/Corp** Canadian Broadcasting Corporation. Merchandising. **Added/Corp** Canadian Broadcasting Corporation. **VAT** Canadian Broadcasting Corporation Jazz and Popular Record Catalogue. (197?)-. English (French; summaries and/or abstracts in French). an. Free. Canadian Broadcasting Corporation, CP 6000, Montreal Quebec H3C 3A8 Canada. **Tel** (514)597-7666. **DD** 016.7899/12. ctrl circ.

US/1043-1241
**CBMR DIGEST.** [CBMR dig.]. **Added/Corp** Columbia College (Chicago, Ill.). Center for Black Music Research. **VFOAT** Center for Black Music Research Digest. **VAT** Center for Black Music Research Digest. Vol. 1, No. 1 (Summer 1988)-. Periodical. English. sa (Spring & Fall). Free. Center for Black Music Research, Columbia College, 600 South Michigan Avenue, Chicago IL 60605-1996. **Tel** (312)663-1600 Ext. 559. **ED** Suzanne Flandreau. **Bk Rev.** ***Continues*** *Inside CBMR.*
**Desc:** Broad range of research in Black music.

US/1042-8836
**CBMR MONOGRAPHS.** [CBMR monogr.]. **Added/Corp** Columbia College (Chicago, Ill.) Center for Black Music Research. **VAT** Center for Black Music Research Monographs. No. 1 (1989)-. Monographic series. English. ir. Price varies per volume. Center for Black Music Research, Columbia College, 600 South Michigan Avenue, Chicago IL 60605-1996. **Tel** (312)663-1600 Ext. 559. **ED** Samuel A. Floyd Jr. **DD** 781. Index available. **Circ:** 450 (ctrl).
**Desc:** Covers the broad range of research in black music.

UK
**CBS MAIN ALPHABETICAL & NUMERICAL CATALOGUE. Main/Corp** Columbia Broadcasting System, Inc. CBS Records Division. **Added/Corp** Columbia Broadcasting System, Inc. CBS Records Division. CBS Catalogue. **VFOAT** CBS Catalogue. **VAT** Columbia Broadcasting System Main Alphabetical & Numerical Catalogue. (19??)-. English. CBS Records, 28 Theobalds Road, London WCLX 8PB England. **LC** ML156; .C56. **DD** 016.7899/12.

US
**CD INTERNATIONAL. AMERICAN CD REFERENCE GUIDE. VFOAT** American CD Reference Guide. Fall (1991)-. English. CDI Publishing Corporation, PO Box 22014, Milwaukie OR 97222. **LC** ML156.4.P6; C28. **DD** 016.78164/0266.

CN/0843-9532
**CD PLUS COMPACT DISC CATALOGUE.** [CD plus compact disc cat.]. **Main/Corp** CD Plus (Firm). **VFOAT** Compact Disc Catalogue. **VAT** Compact Disc Plus Compact Disc Catalogue. (Winter 1989)-. Periodical. English. Twice a year (Feb., Oct.). 10.00Can$. CD Plus, 766 Gordon Baker Road, Willowdale Ontario M2H 3B4 Canada. **Tel** (416)490-8850, FAX (416)490-9662. **(Subscription address:** CD Plus, 1825 Dundas Street Unit B, Mississauga Ontario L4X 2X1 Canada.) **ED** John Ellis Thomson (telephone: (416)629-9255 or (800)263-4020). **DD** 016.78026/6. **Ad Acc, Adv Mgr:** Mary Thomson with Sheperd Media, **Tel** (416)485-2098. **Circ:** 35,000.
**Desc:** Contains over 30,000 titles to choose from, including over 2,000 laser discs. Also contains interviews, reviews and feature articles on popular artists and the latest information on Consumer Electronics advances.

US
**CD REVIEW DIGEST ANNUAL. CLASSICAL. VFOAT** Classical; Compact Disc Review Digest Annual. Classical. Vol. 2 (1988)-. English. an. $59.00 US; $69.00 other. Peri Press, PO Box 348, Voorheesville NY 12186. **Tel** (518)765-3163, FAX (518)765-3158. ***Continues*** *CD Review Digest Annual, 0893-5173.*

US/1045-0114
**CD REVIEW DIGEST. CLASSICAL.** [CD rev. dig. Class.]. **VFOAT** Classical. **VAT** Compact Disc Review Digest. Classical. (1989)-. Periodical. English. qt. $79.00 US; $92.00 other. Peri Press, PO Box 348, Voorheesville NY 12186. **Tel** (518)765-3163, FAX (518)765-3158. **ED** Janet Grimes. **LC** ML156.9; .C363. **DD** 781.6/80266/05. **Ad Acc.** ***Continues in part*** *CD Review Digest, 0890-0213.*
**Desc:** Detailed information on each release, citations with excerpts to reviews of classical recordings including video on compact disc from over 35 magazines, multiple indexes to record label numbers, reviewers, performers and awards. Highlighted notice of special recognition.

US/1045-0122
**CD REVIEW DIGEST. JAZZ, POPULAR, ETC.** [CD rev. dig. Jazz, pop., etc.]. **VFOAT** Jazz, Popular, etc. **VAT** Compact Disc Review Digest. Jazz, Popular, Et Cetera. (1989)-. English. qt. $79.00 US; $92.00 other. Peri Press, PO Box 348, Voorheesville NY 12186. **Tel** (518)765-3163, FAX (518)765-3158. **ED** Janet Grimes. **LC** ML156.4.J3; C45. **DD** 781.64/0266/05. **Ad Acc.** ***Continues in part*** *CD Review Digest, 0890-0213.*
**Desc:** Coverage of reviews of all music except classical from 30 magazines. Includes additional index to titles.

US/1044-1700
**CD REVIEW (HANCOCK, N.H.).** (CD REVIEW.). **VAT** Compact Disc Review. Vol. 5, No. 8 (April 1989)-. Periodical. English. Twelve times a year. $19.97 (one year), $34.95 (two year), $49.95 (three year). Music Publishing Inc., 86 Elm Street, Forest Road, Petersborough NH 03458. **Tel** (603)924-7271. **(Subscription address:** Kable Publishers Aide, 308 East Hitt Street, Subscription Department, Mt. Morris IL 61054-1473.) **LC** ML156.9; .D525. **DD** 780.26/6/05. available on microfilm from University Microfilms International (UMI). ***Continues*** *Digital Audio's CD Review, 1041-8342.*
**Desc:** Classical, jazz, pop, country, rock'n'roll, and folk. For millions of CD buying costumers who are looking to grow their CD collections.

US
**CENTRAL TEXAS BLUEGRASS BULLETIN. Added/Corp** Central Texas Bluegrass Association. (Aug/Sept 1987)-. Bulletin. English. bm. $10.00 (US); $15.00 (other). Central Texas Bluegrass Association, PO Box 1303, Austin TX 78767. **Tel** (512)346-0746, (512)454-6424, FAX (512)467-0027.

CN/0227-3233
**CENTREGRAMME.** (CENTREGRAMME : THE NEWSLETTER OF THE B.C. REGIONAL BRANCH OF THE CANADIAN MUSIC CENTRE.). [Centregramme]. **Added/Corp** Canadian Music Centre. B.C. Regional Branch. (Feb. 1981)-. Newsletter. English. Four times a year. Free on request. Canadian Music Centre BC, 2021 West 4th Avenue Suite 200, Vancouver British Columbia V6J 1N3 Canada. **Tel** (604)734-4622. **ED** Colin Miles. **DD** 780/.971. **Circ:** 1,300. ***Continues*** *Canadian Music Centre. Vancouver Region. Newsletter, 0225-7688.*
**Desc:** News about Canadian composers and their music, new library acquisitions, performers and broadcasts of Canadian music, and information about competitions for composers and performers.

XR/0323-1569
**CESKE HUDEBNINY A GRAMOFONOVE DESKY. Added/Corp** Prague. Narodni Knihovna. Prague. Statni Knihovna CSSR. Statni Knihovna CSR. (1955)-. Periodical. Czech. qt. **(Subscription address:** Artia Pegas Press Ltd., Palac Metro Narodni Trida 25, 11210 Prague 1 Czech Republic.) ***Supersedes in part*** *Ceske a Slovenske Hudebniny.*

US/1071-1791
**CHAMBER MUSIC (NEW YORK, N.Y.).** (CHAMBER MUSIC.). [Chamb. music]. **Added/Corp** Chamber Music America. Vol. 3, No. 3 Fall (1986)-. Periodical. English. ir. $60.00 Comes with Chamber Music Magazine & Membership Directory & CMA Matters. Chamber Music America, 545 8th Avenue, New York NY 10018. **Tel** (212)244-2772, FAX (212)244-2776. **ED** Philip Kennicott. **LC** ML1; .C353. **DD** 785/.005. **Ad Acc.** ***Continues*** *Chamber Music Magazine, 8755-0725.*
**Desc:** Aimed at professional musicians, interested amateur players, concert management, concert goers, and music educators. Serves as a 'trade journal' by including articles of practical information for chamber musicians and concert managers.
**Ind/Abst** Music Index.

US
**CHAMPLAIN VALLEY FIDDLERS CLUB, INC. [NEWS LETTER], THE. Main/Corp** Champlain Valley Fiddlers Club. **Added/Corp** Champlain Valley Fiddlers Club. News Letter. (April 1972)-. Periodical. English. mo. Champlain Valley Fiddlers Club Inc, Box 501, Middlebury VT 05753. **LC** ML1; .C355. **DD** 781.7/73.

CN/0227-5023
**CHANSONS D'AUJOURD'HUI.** ***Title Change.*** (CHANSONS D'AUJOURD'HUI / REUNIES PAR GUY TREPANIER.). [Chansons aujourd'hui]. Vol. 1, No. 1, Record 1 (Nov. 1977)-(1992). Periodical. French. bm. Office Des Communications Sociales, 1340 Boulevard St. Joseph EST, Montreal QUE H2J 1M3 Canada. **Tel** (514)524-8223, FAX (514)524-8522. **DD** 784.5/009714. **Ad Acc.** ***Continued by*** *Chansons (Montreal, Quebec : 1992).*
**Desc:** Evaluation of songs written in French.

CN/1193-9249
**CHANSONS (MONTREAL. 1992).** (CHANSONS.). [Chansons]. (1992)-. Periodical. French.

Six times a year. 18.00Can$ (institutions), 15.00Can$ (individuals) Canada; 24.00Can$ other. Office Des Communications Sociales, 1340 Boulevard St. Joseph EST, Montreal QUE H2J 1M3 Canada. **Tel** (514)524-8223, FAX (514)524-8522. **DD** 782.42164/09714/05. ***Continues** Chansons d'Aujourd'Hui., 0227-5023.*

●CN/1192-1900
**CHANTER (MONTREAL).** (CHANTER.). [Chanter]. **Added/Corp** Alliance des Chorales du Quebec. Vol. 19, No 1 (Sept. 1992)-. Periodical. French. qt. Free. Alliance des Chorales du Quebec, 4545 Pierre-de-Coubertin, PO Box 1000 Postal Station M, Montreal Quebec H1V 3R2 Canada. **Tel** (514)252-3020, FAX (514)251-8038. **DD** 782.5/06/0714. ***Continues** A l'Ecoute., 0700-3900.*

US/0731-4051
**CHAPTER NEWSLETTER - BIG BAND SOCIETY. ED WALKER CHAPTER.** (CHAPTER NEWSLETTER / BIG BAND SOCIETY, WASHINGTON D.C. METRO AREA, ED WALKER CHAPTER, INC.). **Added/Corp** Big Band Society. Ed Walker Chapter. **VFOAT** Newsletter, Big Band Society, Washington D.C. Metro Area, Ed Walker Chapter, Inc. (198?)-. Newsletter. English. mo. The Big Band Society, Ed Walker Chapter, PO Box 6103, Silver Spring MD 20906. **Tel** (202)244-2263. **ED** Carol and Tom Lukas. **LC** Discard. **Ad Acc. Circ:** 750 (ctrl).

CN
**CHART MAGAZINE.** (19??)-. English. Twelve times a year. 35.00Can$ Canada; 40.00Can$ US; 60.00Can$ others. National Chart Publishing, PO Box 332, Willowdale Station A, North York Ontario M2N 5S9 Canada. **Tel** (416)363-3101, FAX (905)928-1357. **ED** Edward Skira. Index available. cum. index. **Bk Rev**, (Qty: 12). **Ad Acc. Circ:** 2,000. ***Continues** National Chart Magazine, 1193-4069.*
**Desc:** Focusing on alternative and campus music in Canada and other related lifestyles.

CN/0229-1509
**CHEER.** [Cheer]. (June 1979)-. Periodical. English. Cheer Productions, 24 Ryerson Avenue, Toronto Ontario M5T 2P3, Canada. **DD** 780/.42/05.
**Desc:** Rock music publication.

UK/0952-8407
**CHELYS (VIOLA DA GAMBA SOCIETY).** (CHELYS : THE JOURNAL OF THE VIOLA DA GAMBA SOCIETY.). [Chelys]. **Added/Corp** Viola da Gamba Society (Great Britain). Vol. 1 (1969)-. English. an. Free to members, £14.00 nonmembers. Viola da Gamba Society, 6 Bramshill Gardens, London NW5 1JH England. **Tel** 071 263 0613, 0904 706 959. **(Subscription address:** 56 Hunters Way, Dringhouses, York Y02 2JJ England**) ED** Lynn Hulse. **LC** ML749.5; .C5. **DD** 787/.42/05. **Bk Rev. Ad Acc. Circ:** 600 (ctrl). ***Continues** Viola da Gamba Society Bulletin (Great Britain).*
**Ind/Abst** Br. Humanit. Index; RILM Abstr.

IT
**CHI E - DOV' E; ANNUARIO DELL'INDUSTRIA FONOGRAFICA E DELL'EDITORIA MUSICALE IN ITALIA.** **See** Sound Recordings and Systems.

IT/0069-3391
**CHIGIANA.** [Chigiana]. **Added/Corp** Accademia Musicale Chigiana. Vol. 1 (1939)-; New Ser. Vol. 1 (1964)-. Italian (French, German and English). an. Casa Editrice Leo S. Olschki, Viuzzo del Pozzetto, Casella Postale 66, 50126 Florence Italy. **Tel** 011 39 55 6530684, FAX 011 39 55 6530214. **DD** 780.
**Ind/Abst** Music Index; RILM Abstr.

US/0192-3749
**CHINESE MUSIC.** [Chin. music]. **Added/Corp** Chinese Music Society of North America. Vol. 2, No. 2 (June 1979)-. Periodical. English. Four times a year (Mar., June, Sept., Dec.). $41.00 (institution), $25.00 (individual), surface mail; $37.00 (individuals), $53.00 (institutions) airmail. Chinese Music Society of North America, PO Box 5275, One Heritage Plaza, Woodbridge IL 60517. **Tel** (708)910-1551, FAX (708)910-1561. **ED** Sin-yan Shen. **LC** ML336; .C498. **DD** 781.751. Index available. cum. index. **Bk Rev. Ad Acc. Pr Rev. Circ:** 1,200. available on microfilm and microfiche from University Microfilms International (UMI). ***Supersedes** Chinese Music General Newsletter, 0190-4086.*
**Desc:** Covers all phases of research and performance activities in Chinese music. It also contains news items and book and record reviews. The first and only journal published in the United States devoted wholly to Chinese music.
**Ind/Abst** Music Artic. Guide (?-?); Music Index; RILM Abstr.

IT
**CHITARRE.** (19??)-. Italian. mo. L800000 Italy; L12000000 Europe. Lakota SRL, via P Mascagni 3/5, 00199 Rome Italy. **Tel** 011 39 6 8608913, FAX 011 39 6 8608930. **ED** Andrea Carpi. **Bk Rev. Ad Acc. Circ:** 20,000 (ctrl).
**Desc:** Articles and interviews on guitar and bass players, information about instruments, musical exercises and transcriptions.

●UK/0968-7262
**CHOIR & ORGAN.** **VFOAT** Choir and Organ. Vol. 1, No. 1 (Feb. 1993)-. Periodical. English. qt (Feb., May, Aug., Nov.). $27.00 (one year), $32.40 (two year) US and Canada; £13.50 (one year), $23.40 (two year) UK & Ireland; £18.00 (one year), £32.40 (two year), Europe; £21.00 (one year), £37.00 (two year) other. Orpheus Publications, 7 St. Johns Road, Harrow Middlesex HA1 2EE England. **Tel** 011 44 81 863-4040, FAX 011 44 81 424-9945. **(Subscription address:** Orpheus Subscriptions Departmenmt, PO Box 648, Harrow, Middlesex, HA1 2NW; England.**) LC** ML5; .C46. ***Separated from** Musical Times (London, England : 1957), 0027-4666.*

CN/0822-4749
**CHOIRS ONTARIO.** (CHOIRS ONTARIO : THE NEWSLETTER OF THE ONTARIO CHORAL FEDERATION.). [Choirs Ont.]. **Added/Corp** Ontario Choral Federation. V. 12, No. 2 (Dec. 1982/Jan. 1983)-. Periodical. English. Four times a year (Sept./Oct., Oct./Nov., Dec./Jan., Jan., Feb.). 20.00Can$ (institutions). Ontario Choral Federation, 100 Richmond Street East, Suite 200, Toronto Ontario M5C 2P9 Canada. **Tel** (416)363-7488. **ED** Bev Jahnke. **DD** 784.1/006/0713. **Ad Acc, Adv Mgr:** Bev Jahnke. **Circ:** 1,500 (ctrl). ***Continues** Ontario Choral Federation. Newsletter., 0317-0497.*

US/0009-5028
**CHORAL JOURNAL, THE.** [Choral j.]. **Added/Corp** American Choral Directors Association. Vol. 1 (May 1959)-. Periodical. English. Ten times a year (Except June and July). $25.00 (individuals) schools & libraries, $75.00 (institutions) others, (surface mail); $75.00 (individuals) schools & libraries, $112.00 (institutions) others (airmail). American Choral Directors Association, PO Box 6310, Lawton OK 73506-0310. **Tel** (405)355-8161, FAX (405)248-1465. **ED** Wesley Coffman. **LC** ML1; .C656. **DD** 784.1/005. Index available. **Bk Rev. Ad Acc. Circ:** 16,000 (ctrl). available on microfilm and microfiche from University Microfilms International (UMI). ***Absorbed** Texas Choirmaster.*
**Desc:** Manuscripts related to the historical, the practical, or the informative aspects of choral music. Reviews of choral music and books, and general information about the American Choral Directors Association.
**Ind/Abst** Music Artic. Guide; Music Index; RILM Abstr.

US
**CHORAL MUSIC IN PRINT.** (1974)-. English. Choral Music in Print, 18 West Chelten Avenue, Philadelphia PA 19144. **ED** T.R. Nardone, J.H. Nye and M. Resnick.
**Desc:** Includes secular and sacred choral music.

US/0360-2443
**CHORAL OVERTONES.** **Added/Corp** Southern Baptist Convention. Sunday School Board. Vol. 1 (Oct./Dec. 1970)-. Periodical. English. qt. $2.25. Southern Baptist Convention, 901 Commerce, Suite 750, Nashville TN 37203. **Tel** (615)244-2355, FAX (615)742-8919. **(Subscription address:** Sunday School Board - Customer Service, 127 Ninth Avenue North, Nashville, TN 37234 USA; telephone: (800)458-2772**) LC** ML1; .C658. **DD** 783.

US/0360-2524
**CHORAL TONES.** **Added/Corp** Southern Baptist Convention. Sunday School Board. (Oct./Dec. 1970)-. Periodical. English. qt. Southern Baptist Convention, 901 Commerce, Suite 750, Nashville TN 37203. **Tel** (615)244-2355, FAX (615)742-8919. **(Subscription address:** Sunday School Board - Customer Service, 127 Ninth Avenue North, Nashville, TN 37234 USA; telephone: (800)458-2772**) LC** ML1; .C665. **DD** 783.

UK
**CHORALE.** Vol. 1. No. 1 (July/Aug. 1980)-. Periodical. English. bm. **LC** ML1499; .C5. **DD** 784.1/005.

US/0069-3758
**CHORD AND DISCORD.** **Added/Corp** Bruckner Society of America. Chord and Dischord. Vol. 1, (Feb. 1932)-. Periodical. English. ir (every 3 to 4 years). Free. Bruckner Society of America, 2150 Dubuque Road, Iowa City IA 52240-9632. **Tel** (319)351-5758. **LC** ML1; .C675. **DD** 780.5. Index available. cum. index. **Circ:** 750.
**Desc:** Articles dealing with the composers Mahler and Bruckner and their works.

US/0412-2801
**CHORISTERS GUILD LETTERS.** **Main/Corp** Choristers' Guild. **VFOAT** Letters. Vol. 1 (1949)-. Periodical. English. Ten times a year (Except June and July). $40.00 Comes with Choristers Guild Membership. Choristers Guild, 2834 West Kingsley Road, Garland TX 75041. **Tel** (214)271-1521. **ED** Donald Jensen. **LC** ML1; .C692. Index available. cum. index. **Bk Rev. Ad Acc. Circ:** 9,000 (ctrl). available on audiocassette.
**Desc:** A journal for directors of childrens and youth choirs with supplements of music and materials.
**Ind/Abst** Music Artic. Guide (?-?).

GW
**CHORSANGER, DER.** **Added/Corp** Mitteldeutscher Sangerbund. (19??)-. Periodical. German. qt. Mitteldeutscher Sangerband, Ulmestrasse 16, 35 Kassel Germany. **LC** ML27.G3; M6.

US/1044-7857
**CHORUS! (DULUTH, GA.).** (CHORUS!). Vol. 1, No. 1 (June 1989)-. Periodical. English. Twelve times a year. $19.95 (one year); $38.95 (two years). DSC Publishing, 2131 Pleasant Hill Road, Suite 151 121, Duluth GA 30136. **Tel** (404)497-1902. **ED** Mark Gresham. **DD** 784. Index available. cum. index. **Bk Rev. Ad Acc. Circ:** 5000.
**Ind/Abst** Music Artic. Guide.

CN/0821-1108
**CHORUS (HALIFAX).** (CHORUS : NOVA SCOTIA CHORAL FEDERATION NEWSLETTER.). [Chorus]. **Added/Corp** Nova Scotia Choral Federation. Vol. 6, No. 1 (1981)-. Newsletter. English. Four times a year. 20.00Can$. Nova Scotia Choral Federation, 1809 Barrington Street / Suite 901, Halifax Nova Scotia B3J 3K8 Canada. **Tel** (902)423-4688. **ED** D. Simon. **DD** 784.9/6/060716. **Bk Rev. Ad Acc. Circ:** 350 (ctrl). ***Continues** NSCF News., 0712-6352.*
**Desc:** Aimed towards members with news of Nova Scotia Choral Federation programs, member news and articles of interest.

NE/0009-5176
**CHRISTELIJKE MUZIEKBODE, DE.** **Added/Corp** Nederlandse Federatie van Christelijke Muziekbonden. (1932)-. Periodical. Dutch. mo. W J Timmer, PO Box 204, Winterswijk Netherlands.

US/0883-4210
**CHRISTIAN ACTIVITIES CALENDAR (MIDDLE ATLANTIC ED.).** **See** Religion and Theology.

UK
**CHRISTIAN MUSIC.** ***Title Change.*** (1???)-(1993)-. English. qt. Herald House Publishing, 96 Dominion Road, Worthing West Sussex, BN14 8JP England. **Tel** 011 44 903 821082, FAX 011 44 903 821081. **ED** Jane Hicks. **Bk Rev. Ad Acc. Circ:** 4,000. ***Continued by** DEO.*
**Desc:** Information and encouragement for those involved across a wide spectrum of Christian music.

US
**CHRISTIAN MUSIC DIRECTORIES. PRINTED MUSIC, THE.** **VFOAT** Printed Music. (1990)-. English. Four times a year (Directory published in June). $160.00 Includes basic volume with 3 supplements (supplements not available separately). Resource Publications, 160 East Virginia Street, Suite 290, San Jose CA 95112. **Tel** (408)286-8505. **Ad Acc. Circ:** 1,000. ***Continues** Music Locator, 0899-0115.*
**Desc:** Lists songs, composers and cross indexes songs with song books.

CC
**CHUNG-KUO YIN YUEH NIEN CHIEN / CHUNG-KUO I SHU YEN CHIU YUAN YIN YUEH YEN CHIU SO PIEN.** **Added/Corp** Chung-kuo i Shu Yen Chiu Yuan. Yin Yueh Yen Chiu So. (1987)-. Chinese. an. $10.00 (latest edition). China National Publishing Import & Export Corporation, 16 Gongti E Rd., Chaoyang Dist., Beijing 100704, People's Republic of China. **Tel** 011 8601 50630169, 5066688, FAX 011 8601 5063101, 5063010, telex 22313. **LC** ML5; .C565. **DD** 780/.951.

UK/0307-6334
**CHURCH MUSIC QUARTERLY.** [Church music q.]. **Added/Corp** Royal School of Church Music (London, England). (19??)-. Periodical. English. Four times a year (Jan., Apr., July, Oct.). £8.00 UK; £13.00 other. Royal School of Church Music, Addington Palace, Croydon CR9 5AD England. **Tel** 011 44 81 6547676. **ED** Richard Morrison. **LC** ML5; .C573. **DD** 783/.026/305. **Bk Rev. Ad Acc. Circ:** 16,500 (ctrl).
**Desc:** Articles and new information concerning all aspects of church music.

US/1071-9903
**CHURCH MUSIC REPORT : TCMR, THE.** [Church music rep.]. **VFOAT** TCMR; T.C.M.R. (198?)-. Periodical. English. mo. $39.95 (1 year), $59.95 (2 year), $79.95 (3 year) US; $44.95 (1 year), $69.95 (2 year), $94.95 (3 year) Canada; $49.95 (1 year), $79.95 (2 year), $109.95 (3 year) other. TCMR Communications, PO Box 1179, Grapevine TX 76051. **Tel** (817)488-0141, FAX (817)481-4191. **ED** William H. Rayborn. **DD** 246. **Bk Rev**, (Qty: 12). **Ad Acc, Adv Mgr:** D. Yarlott, **Tel** (800)969-2670. ctrl circ.

US/0009-6466
**CHURCH MUSICIAN, THE.** **Added/Corp** Southern Baptist Convention. Sunday School Board. Vol. 1 (Oct. 1950)-. Periodical. English. Four times a year. $23.90. Southern Baptist Convention, 901 Commerce, Suite 750, Nashville TN 37203. **Tel** (615)244-2355, FAX (615)742-8919. **(Subscription address:** Sunday School Board - Customer Service, 127 Ninth Avenue North, Nashville, TN 37234 USA; telephone: (800)458-2772**) ED**

William M. Anderson. **LC** ML1; .C74. **DD** 783.8. **Bk Rev. Ad Acc. Circ:** 19,000. available on microfilm and microfiche from University Microfilms International (UMI). ***Superseded in part by*** *Choral Tones, 0360-2524* ***and*** *Choral Overtones, 0360-2443.*
**Desc:** Magazine for church music leaders in the local Baptist church. Includes human interest and success stories on ministering through music.
**Ind/Abst** Christ. Period. Index (-19??); South. Baptist Period. Index.

US/0890-9032
**CHURCH PIANIST, THE. VFOAT** CP. (1984)-. Periodical. English. Six times a year (Jan., Mar., May, July, Sept., Nov.). $16.95 one year; $30.95 two year; $44.95 three year. Lorenz Publishing Company, PO Box 802, Dayton OH 45401. **Tel** (513)228-6118. **LC** M21; .C523.
**Desc:** It the newest addition to Lorenz line of useful practical church music periodicals. Idea for church use or home enjoyment, each 32-page issue is filled with attractive, melodious preludes, ollerlories, and postiudes.

UK
**CINEMA ORGAN. Added/Corp** Cinema Organ Society. (19??)-. Periodical. English. qt. Cinema Organ Society, 3 Dorthy Farm Road, Raleigh Essex SS6 8RE England. **LC** ML5; .C576. **DD** 786.6/05.

●CN/1183-1693
**CIRCUIT (MONTREAL. 1991).** (CIRCUIT.). [Circuit]. Vol. 1, No 1 (1991)-. Periodical. French. Twice a year (Apr., Nov.). 50.00Can$. Periodica Inc, PO Box 444, Outremont Quebec H2V 4R6 Canada. **Tel** (514)274-5468, FAX (514)274-0201. **DD** 780./9/0405.

US/0009-7365
**CIRCUS (NEW YORK, N.Y. 1979).** (CIRCUS.). [Circus]. (Oct. 1979)-. Periodical. English. Twelve times a year. $22.00 US; $28.00 other. Circus Enterprise Corp., 805 Third Avenue 28th Floor, New York NY 10020. **Tel** (212)633-9042. **(Subscription address:** Kable Publishers Aide, 308 East Hitt Street, Subscription Department, Mt. Morris IL 61054-1473.**) ED** Gerald Rothberg and Ben Liemer. **LC** ML3533.8; .C58. **DD** 784.5/4/005. **Ad Acc. Circ:** 270,000. available on microfilm and microfiche from University Microfilms International (UMI). ***Supersedes*** *Circus Weekly, 0164-9248.*
**Desc:** Popular music magazine covering music news and rock & roll personalities.

US/0740-7858
**CIRCUS ROCK IMMORTALS.** No. 1 (1980)-. Periodical. English. Circus Enterprise Corp., 805 Third Avenue 28th Floor, New York NY 10020. **Tel** (212)633-9042. **LC** ML3533.8; .C6. **DD** 784.5/4/00922.

US/0737-8009
**CITY OPERA SPOTLIGHT.** (CITY OPERA SPOTLIGHT : THE MAGAZINE OF THE NEW YORK CITY OPERA GUILD.). **Added/Corp** New York City Opera. Guild. **VFOAT** Spotlight. (19??)-. Periodical. English. qt. New York City Opera Guild, New York State Theater, Lincoln Center, New York NY 10023. **Tel** (212)870-5640. **ED** June Wolfberg. **LC** ML1699; .C57. **DD** 782.1/09747/1. **Circ:** 5,000 (ctrl).
**Desc:** Opera topics related to performances of New York City Opera.

UK
**CLARINET AND SAXOPHONE. Added/Corp** Clarinet & Saxophone Society (Great Britain) Clarinet and Saxophone Society of Great Britain. **VFOAT** Clarinet & Saxophone. Vol. 5, No. 3 (July 1980)-. Periodical. English. Four times a year. £20.00 UK; £23.00 Europe; £25.00 other. Clarinet & Saxophone Society, 167 Ellerton Road, Tolworth Surrey KT6 7UB England. **Tel** 011 44 325 469 438. **LC** ML929; .C6. **DD** 788/.6/05. ***Continues*** *CASS News.*

US/0361-5553
**CLARINET (POCATELLO, IDAHO), THE.** (THE CLARINET.). [Clarinet]. **Added/Corp** International Clarinet Society. Idaho State University. Dept. of Music. (Oct. 1973)-. Periodical. English. Four times a year (Feb., May, July, Nov.). $30.00 US & Canada & Mexico, $40.00 other. International Clarinet Association, PO Box 7683, Shawnee Mission KS 66207. **Tel** (913)268-3064, FAX (913)268-3064. **ED** James Gillespie (editor's address: 405 Santiago PL., Denton, TX 76205). **LC** ML1; .C787. **DD** 788/.62/05. Index available. **Bk Rev. Ad Acc. Pr Rev. Circ:** 3,000.
**Desc:** Articles about the clarinet, music, book, concert reviews.
**Ind/Abst** Music Artic. Guide; Music Index.

FR/0761-9553
**CLARINETTE MAGAZINE.** No. 1 (1984)-. Periodical. French. qt. 100.00F. Clarinette Magazine, c/o Jean-Marie Paul, 47 rue de l'Yser, 67000 Strasbourg France. **LC** ML929; .C62. **DD** 788/.62/05.

US/0733-3544
**CLARINETWORK. *Ceased.*** Vol. 1, No. 1 (1982)-Vol. 7 ?. English. Clarinetwork International Inc., 550 Phair Road NE/Suite 614, Atlanta GA 30305. **LC** ML929; .C63. **DD** 788/.62/05.

●US/1070-4574
**CLASSIC CD (U.S. ED.).** (CLASSIC CD.). [Class. CD]. **VFOAT** Classic Compact Disc. Issue 11 (Mar. 1991)-. Periodical. English. Twelve times a year. $59.95 US, $85.07 Canada (American issues); £42.00 UK, £80.00 others (English issues). Musical Heritage Society, 1710 Highway 35, Ocean NJ 07712. **Tel** (908)531-7003, (908)531-4990. **LC** IN PROCESS; ML1; .C52. **DD** 780. Documents available from UMI Article Clearinghouse. ***Continues*** *Classical (Rahway, N.J.), 1048-4507.*
**Ind/Abst** Newsp. Period. Abstr. (1990-).

AT
**CLASSICAL. *Suspended.*** (19??)-Suspended (19??). English. bm. 30.00Aus$ Australia; 45.00Aus$ other. Downies Pty Ltd., 308, Kew Victoria 3101 Australia. **Tel** 011 63 03 853 0500, FAX 011 63 03 853 0050.
**Ind/Abst** Music Index.

US
**CLASSICAL ACCORDIONIST.** English. 202 East Cypress Avenue, Monrovia CA 91016.
**Ind/Abst** Music Artic. Guide (19??-19??).

UK/0961-5237
**CLASSICAL CATALOGUE. *Title Change.* See** Sound Recordings and Systems.

UK/0950-429X
**CLASSICAL GUITAR. See** Classical Studies.

UK
**CLASSICAL MUSIC.** (June 16, 1979)-. Periodical. English. bw. £36.00 UK; £42.00 other. Rhinegold Publishing Ltd, 239-241 Shaftesbury Avenue, London WC2H 8EH England. **Tel** 011 44 71 2405749, FAX 240 0897, telex 264675 GILDED. **ED** Graeme Kay. **LC** ML5; .C583. **DD** 780/.5. **Bk Rev. Ad Acc. Circ:** 20,000. ***Continues*** *Classical Music & Album Reviews.*
**Desc:** The newsmagazine for music, opera and dance, serving Britain and the world.

CN/1185-9717
**CLASSICAL MUSIC MAGAZINE (MISSISSAUGA).** (CLASSICAL MUSIC MAGAZINE.). [Class. music mag.]. **VFOAT** Music Magazine. Vol. 14, No. 3 (July 1991)-. Periodical. English. Five times a year (Feb., Apr., June, Sept., Nov.). $25.00 US; $42.00 others; 18.69Can$ Canada; 33.64Can$ others. Music Magazine, 121 Lakeshore Road East, Suite 207, Mississauga Ontario L5G 1E5 Canada. **Tel** (905)271-0339. **LC** ML5; .M6513. **DD** 780. ***Continues*** *Music Magazine, 0705-4009.*
**Ind/Abst** Music Index.

CU
**CLAVE (HAVANA, CUBA).** (CLAVE / ORGANO DE LA DIRECCION DE MUSICA, MINISTERIO DE CULTURA.). **Added/Corp** Cuba. Direccion de Musica. Vol. 1 (1986)-. Periodical. Spanish. Calve, Unidad Presupuestada de Musica, Amistad No. 416, Entre Neptuno Y San Miguel, Habana 2.

US/0009-854X
**CLAVIER.** [Clavier]. Vol. 1 (March/April 1962)-. Periodical. English. mo (except June and Aug.). $18.00 (one year), $30.00 (two year), $41.00 (three year) US;. Instrumentalist Company, 200 Northfield Road, Northfield IL 60093. **Tel** (708)446-5000, FAX (708)446-6263. **ED** Kingsley Day. **LC** ML1; .C79. **DD** 786/.05. **Bk Rev. Ad Acc. Circ:** 21,000 (ctrl). available on microfilm from University Microfilms International (UMI). Documents available from The Genuine Article. ***Absorbed*** *Piano Teacher.*
**Desc:** International magazine for pianists and organists; noted for interviews with famous performers, master classes and practical teaching articles.
**Ind/Abst** Acad. Search (July 1993-); Am. Bibliogr. Slavic East Europ. Stud.; Arts Humanit. Citation Index [Full Cov.]; Curr. Contents Arts Humanit.; Educ. Index; INFO-SOUTH Abstr.; Mag. Search; Music Artic. Guide; Music Index; Ref. Sources; Res. Alert [Full Cov.]; RILM Abstr.; Soc. Sci. Cit. Index [Select. Cov.].

US/0279-0858
**CLAVIER'S PIANO EXPLORER. VFOAT** Piano Explorer. (198?)-. Periodical. English. mo (except June and Aug.). $6.00 US; $8.00 other. Instrumentalist Company, 200 Northfield Road, Northfield IL 60093. **Tel** (708)446-5000, FAX (708)446-6263. **ED** Ann Rohner and Bill Rohner. **LC** ML3930.A2; C49. **DD** 786.1/05. **Ad Acc. Circ:** 85,000 (ctrl).
**Desc:** Each issue contains a cover story, a featured composer and instrument, compositions, and music games and puzzles.

US
**CLEVELAND ORCHESTRA AT SEVERANCE HALL, THE. Main/Corp** Cleveland Orchestra. 1st Program (1982/83 Season)-. English. ir. Musical Arts Association, 11001 Euclid Avenue, Cleveland OH 44106. **Tel** (216)231-7300. ***Continues*** *Cleveland Orchestra. Program.*

US/1050-9887
**CMA MATTERS.** (CMA MATTERS : THE TECHNICAL BULLETIN OF CHAMBER MUSIC AMERICA.). [CMA matters]. **Added/Corp** Chamber Music America. **VAT** Chamber Music America Matters. (19??)-. Bulletin. English. Four times a year. $60.00 (includes membership for business/institution). Chamber Music America, 545 8th Avenue, New York NY 10018. **Tel** (212)244-2772, FAX (212)244-2776. **LC** ML1100; .C6. **DD** 785/.005.

US/0007-8638
**CMEA NEWS. Main/Corp** California Music Educators Association. **VAT** California Music Educators Association News. Vol. 1, (Feb. 1948)-. Periodical. English. Four times a year (Feb., May, Sept., Nov.). $10.00. California Music Educators, 3924 Cottonwood Drive, Concord CA 94519. **Tel** (415)685-3237. **ED** Jerri Burke. **Bk Rev. Ad Acc. Circ:** 2,700 (ctrl).
**Desc:** Information applicable to public schools and college music teachers.
**Ind/Abst** Music Artic. Guide (?-?).

CN/1188-1518
**CMJ CANADA.** [CMJ Can.]. Issue 1 (Nov. 1, 1991)-. Periodical. English. wk. $95.00 per year. CMJ Canada, 61 Jefferson Avenue, Toronto Ontario M6K 1Y3 Canada. **DD** 782.42164/0971/05.

US
**CMJ NEW MUSIC MONTHLY.** English. mo. $29.95 US; $39.95 Canada; $49.95 other. CMJ New Music Report, 245 Great Neck Road, 3rd Floor, Great Neck NJ 11021. **Tel** (516)466-6000, FAX (516)466-7159. **(Subscription address:** Subscription Office, PO Box 11806, Birmingham, AL 35202-1806; telephone: (800)633-4931 or (205)995-1567; FAX: (205)466-7159**)**
**Desc:** Comprehensive consumer guide to the latest alternative music. Subscription includes 12 free full-length compilation CD's. Each monthly CD serves as a companion to the information in each issue and features the latest releases from both new and established alternative music artists.

US/0890-0795
**CMJ NEW MUSIC REPORT.** [CMJ new music rep.]. **VFOAT** New Music Report. **VAT** College Media Journal New Music Report. (19??)-. Periodical. English. Forty-eight times a year. $295.00 US; $395.00 Canada; $550.00 other (includes Progressive Media). CMJ New Music Report, 245 Great Neck Road, 3rd Floor, Great Neck NJ 11021. **Tel** (516)466-6000, FAX (516)466-7159. **(Subscription address:** Subscription Office, PO Box 11806, Birmingham, AL 35202-1806; telephone: (800)633-4931 or (205)995-1567; FAX: (205)466-7159**) ED** Robert K. Haber and Scott L. Byron. **DD** 784. **Ad Acc. Circ:** 3,000. ***Continues*** *CMJ, Progressive Media, 0731-5708.*

US/1053-9794
**CMS PROCEEDINGS.** (CMS PROCEEDINGS : THE NATIONAL AND REGIONAL MEETINGS.). [CMS proc.]. **Main/Corp** College Music Society. **VAT** College Music Society Proceedings. (1983/84)-. Proceedings. English. an. College Music Society / CMS Publications, 202 West Spruce Street, Missoula MT 59802. **Tel** (406)728-2002, (800)729-0235. **DD** 780.

CN/0826-3140
**COAST TO COAST COUNTRY.** [Coast coast ctry.]. Vol. 2, Issue 1 (Feb. 1984)-. Periodical. English. bm. Coast to Coast Country, Suite 300/11821-1123 Street, Edmonton Alberta T5L 0G7 Canada. **DD** 784.5/2/00971. ***Continues*** *Alberta Country, 0826-3132.*

CN/0820-926X
**CODA MAGAZINE.** [Coda mag.]. **VFOAT** Coda. **VAT** Coda (1981). Issue No. 177 (1981)-. Periodical. English. Six times a year. $24.00. Coda Publications / Canada, PO 1002 Station O, Toronto Ontario M4A 2N4 Canada. **Tel** (416)593-7230. **ED** William E. Smith. **LC** ML5; .C595. **DD** 785.42/05. **Bk Rev. Ad Acc. Circ:** 4,000. available on microfilm and microfiche from Micromedia Limited. ***Continues*** *Coda, 0010-017X.*
**Desc:** A leading voice of jazz and improvised music. Contents consist of oral interviews, articles, essays, record and book reviews, and news columns from around the world. The goal is to approach jazz with a seriousness and dedication comparable to that of the musicians who create it.
**Ind/Abst** Can. Period. Index; Music Index.

IT/0069-5211
**COLLANA DI STUDI PALESTRINIANI.** (1960)-. Periodical. Italian. Via Giovanni Pascoli 55, 20133 Milan Italy. **DD** 780.

US/0742-8480
**COLLEGE BAND DIRECTORS NATIONAL ASSOCIATION JOURNAL. Added/Corp** College Band Directors National Association. **VFOAT** CBDNA Journal. Vol. 1, No. 1 (Spring 1984)-. Periodical. English. ir. $7.50 (per issue). Yale University / 3A Yale Station, Thomas Duffey, New Haven CT 06520. **Tel** (203)432-4111. **ED** Thomas Duffy. **LC** ML1299; .C64. **DD** 785/.06/705. **Bk Rev. Pr Rev. Circ:** 1000.
**Desc:** Articles covering the latest in research into wind music.
**Ind/Abst** Music Artic. Guide (?-?).

US/0069-5696
**COLLEGE MUSIC SYMPOSIUM.** [Coll. music symp.]. **Added/Corp** College Music Society. Vol. 1, (1961)-. Periodical. English. Twice a year. $25.00 Comes with College Music Symposium Membership. College Music Society Inc., 202 West Spruce Street, Missoula MT 59802. **Tel** (406)721-9616. **ED** H. Lee Riggins. **LC** ML1; .C825. **DD** 780/.5. **Bk Rev**, (Qty: 6 per year). **Ad Acc. Circ:** 4,500. available on microfilm and microfiche from University Microfilms International (UMI). Documents available from The Genuine Article.
**Ind/Abst** Arts Humanit. Citation Index (19??-19??) [Full Cov.]; Curr. Contents Arts Humanit.; Music Artic. Guide; Music Index; Res. Alert [Full Cov.]; RILM Abstr.

US/0010-1672
**COLORADO MUSIC EDUCATOR.** **Added/Corp** Colorado Music Educators Association. (19??)-. Periodical. English. qt. Colorado Music Educator, 1309 Rollingwood Lane, Fort Collins CO 80525.
**Ind/Abst** Music Artic. Guide.

US/0270-4609
**COME FOR TO SING.** [Come sing]. **Added/Corp** Old Town School of Folk Music. (Jan. 1975)-. Periodical. English. qt. Come for to Sing, 917 West Wolfram, Chicago IL 60657. **LC** ML3551; .C59. **DD** 784.4/977311/05.
**Desc:** Folk music journal.

FR
**COMPACT: LA REVUE DU DISQUE LASER.** Medialink Compact, 60 rue Etienne Dolet, 92240 Malakoff France.

US/0894-5950
**COMPOSER NEWS.** (COMPOSER NEWS / TEXAS COMPOSERS FORUM.). [Compos. news]. **Added/Corp** Texas Composers Forum. (1986)-. Periodical. English. Three times a year (Jan., June, Sept.). $30.00. Texas Composers Forum, PO Box 744022, Dallas TX 75374. **Tel** (214)231-1666. **ED** Mary Durin (phone: (214)731-1666). **DD** 781. **Ad Acc. Circ:** 2,500 (ctrl).

US
**COMPOSER/USA.** **Added/Corp** National Association of Composers, U.S.A. (Oct. 1975)-. Periodical. English. Three times a year (Jan., Apr., Oct.). $15.00. National Association of Composers USA, PO Box 49652, Barrington Station, Los Angeles CA 90049. **Tel** (310)541-8213. **ED** Charles Dvorak, (phone: (310)454-8091). **Bk Rev. Ad Acc. Circ:** 600-700. ***Supersedes** Composer and Conductor, 0573-1968.*
**Desc:** This composer's newsletter is filled with notices of performances of the members's music as well as feature articles about subjects of interest of classical composers.
**Ind/Abst** Music Artic. Guide.

CN/0709-8219
**COMPOSERS WEST.** **Added/Corp** Alberta Composers' Association. Vol. 2, No. 3 (Sept. 1979)-. Periodical. English. qt. Alberta Composers' Association University of Calgary, Suite 2920 / 24 Avenue NW, Calgary Alberta T2N 1N4 Canada. **Tel** (403)220-7350. **DD** 780/.97123. ***Continues** A C A Newsletter, 0705-1557.*

NE
**COMPOSERS' WORKLISTS.** English (German, French and Dutch). ir. Uitgeverij Frits Knuf B V, PO Box 720, 4116 ZJ Buuren Netherlands. **Tel** 011 31 03449-1255, FAX 011 31 03449-2617. **Circ:** 700.

CN/0008-3259
**COMPOSITEUR CANADIEN.** (LE COMPOSITEUR CANADIEN.). [Compos. can.]. **Added/Corp** Association des Compositeurs, Auteurs et Editeurs du Canada. Societe Canadienne des Auteurs, Compositeurs et Editeurs de Musique. **VFOAT** Canadian Composer. No. 1 (May 1965)-. Periodical. French (English). mo. Compositeur Canadien, Bureau 501, 1407 Rue Yonge, Toronto, Ontario M4T 1Y7 Canada. **DD** 780/.971. ***Absorbed** Scene Musicale, 0380-514X. **Continued in part by** Canadian Composer (Societe Canadienne des Auteurs, Compositeurs et Editeurs de Musique).*
**Ind/Abst** Can. Period. Index (19??-); Music Index (?-19??); Point Repere (1981-1989); RILM Abstr.; Mag. Index (1977-?).

US/0093-0253
**COMPUTATIONAL MUSICOLOGY NEWSLETTER.** (Oct. 1973)-. Newsletter. English. J. Wenker, 11 Carlton Club Drive, Piscataway NJ 08854. **LC** ML1; .O856. **DD** 780/.01/02854.

US/1046-1744
**COMPUTERS IN MUSIC RESEARCH.** [Comput. music res.]. **Added/Corp** Wisconsin Center for Music Technology. **VFOAT** CMR. Vol. 1 (Fall 1989)-. English. an (May or June of the following year). $16.00 (institutions); $12.00 (individuals). Computers in Music Research, School of Music, 455 North Park Street, University of Wisconsin, Madison WI 53706. **Tel** (608)263-1898. **LC** ML73; .C64. **DD** 780/.285.
**Ind/Abst** Music Artic. Guide; Music Index.

US/0277-9560
**CONCERT MAGAZINE (WALPOLE, MASS.).** (CONCERT MAGAZINE.). **Added/Corp** New Sound Concerts (Firm). Vol. 1, No. 1 (March/April '81)-. Periodical. English. bm. Free. New Sound Concerts, 545 High Street, Walpole MA 02081. **LC** ML3533.8; .C65. **DD** 784.5/4/005.
**Desc:** Rock music magazine.

US
**CONCERT NOTES; CARL FISCHER NEWSLETTER.** **Added/Corp** Carl Fischer Inc. (Winter 1972)-. Newsletter. English. Carl Fischer, 62 Cooper Square, New York NY 10003. **LC** ML1; .C876. **DD** 780/.65.

US
**CONCERTINA & SQUEEZEBOX.** **VFOAT** Concertina and Squeezebox. (1983)-. English. Three times a year (May, Sept., Dec.). $20.00 North America; $25.00 Europe; $35.00 others. Concertina and Squeezebox, PO Box 6706, Ithaca NY 14851. **ED** Joel M. Cowan. **LC** ML1083; .C66. **DD** 786.9/7. Index available. **Bk Rev. Ad Acc. Circ:** 750 (ctrl). ***Continues** Concertina, 0740-0993.*
**Desc:** An international journal for musicians interested in free reed instruments of all varieties.

GW
**CONCERTO : DAS MAGAZIN FUER ALTE MUSIK.** **VFOAT** Magazin fuer Alte Musik. Vol. 1, No. 1 (Nov. 1983)-. Periodical. German. Ten times a year. DM65.37 Germany; DM81.50 other. Concerto Verlag, PO Box 420157, W-5000 Cologne 41 Germany. **Tel** 011 49 221 515110. **LC** ML169.8; .C66. **DD** 780/.9. Index available (bound in issue).
**Ind/Abst** Music Index.

GW
**CONCERTO VOCALE.** (19??)-. German. ir. Price varies per volume. Baerenreiter-Verlag, KGA Verlagssvc PF 100329, D 34003 Kassel Germany. **Tel** 011 49 561 31050, telex 99504.

UK
**CONFERENCE PROCEEDINGS - INTERNATIONAL SOCIETY FOR MUSIC EDUCATION.** (19??)-. Proceedings. English. sa. International Society for Music Education, Music Education Centre, University of Reading, Bulmershe Court, Reading RG6 1H4 England. **Tel** 011 44 734 318846, FAX 011 44 834 352080, 011 44 734 318846. Index available. cum. index. **Circ:** 2,000 (ctrl). ***Continues** ISME Yearbook, 0172-0597.*
**Desc:** Selected papers from conferences of the International Society for Music Education.

US/0010-6038
**CONNCHORD.** **Main/Corp** Conn Corporation. **VFOAT** Conn Chord. (1958)-. Periodical. English. Three times a year. **DD** 788.

US
**CONNECTICUT ASSESSMENT OF EDUCATIONAL PROGRESS. ART AND MUSIC. / PREPARED FOR CONNECTICUT STATE DEPARTMENT OF EDUCATION, BUREAU OF RESEARCH, PLANNING, AND EVALUATION; PREPARED BY NATIONAL EVALUATION SYSTEMS, INC.** **See** The Arts-Art.

UK/0268-9111
**CONSORT (DOLMETSCH FOUNDATION), THE.** (THE CONSORT.). [Consort]. **Added/Corp** Dolmetsch Foundation. No. 1 (Oct. 1929)-. Periodical. English. Twice a year (march, Sept.). £17.50 UK; £22.00 (surface mail), £24.50 (air mail) other. Dolmetsch Foundation, Lavant Park Farm, West Lavant, Chichester SX PO18 9AH England. **Tel** 011 44 243 528612. **(Subscription address:** PO Box 106, Haslemere Surrey England**) ED** Dr. Julie Ann Sadie. cum. index. **Bk Rev**, (Qty: 15). **Ad Acc, Adv Mgr:** Jeremy Stewart. **Circ:** 600 (ctrl).
**Ind/Abst** Br. Humanit. Index; Music Index; RILM Abstr.

CN/0823-8278
**CONSORT (HALIFAX).** (CONSORT / EARLY MUSIC SOCIETY OF NOVA SCOTIA.). [Consort]. **Added/Corp** Early Music Society of Nova Scotia. Vol. 4, No. 1 (Sept. 1983)-. Academic Scholarly Publication. English. ir. 10.00Can$. Early Music Society of Nova Scotia, c/o Department of Music, Dalhousie University, Halifax Nova Scotia B3H 3J5 Canada. **Tel** (902)424-2418. **ED** David F. Wilson. **DD** 780/.902. **Bk Rev. Ad Acc. Circ:** 150 (ctrl). ***Continues** Early Music Society of Nova Scotia Newsletter.*
**Desc:** Semi-scholarly and popular articles on early music.

US/1049-3379
**CONTEMPORARY CHRISTIAN MUSIC (1986).** (CONTEMPORARY CHRISTIAN MUSIC : CCM.). [Contemp. Christ. music]. **VFOAT** CCM; C.C.M. (1986)-. Periodical. English. Twelve times a year. $19.95 US; $27.00 Canada; $33.00 other. CCM Communications, 107 Kenner Avenue, Nashville TN 37205. **Tel** (615)386-3011. **(Subscription address:** Contemporary Christian Music, PO Box 55995, Boulder CO 80322.**) DD** 783. **Bk Rev. Ad Acc. Circ:** 32,000. ***Continues** Contemporary Christian Magazine, 0746-0066.*
**Desc:** Designed to provide both the consumers and producers of contemporary Christian music with profiles of artists, album reviews, charts, industry news and concert listings.
**Ind/Abst** Christ. Period. Index (19??-).

US
**CONTEMPORARY COMPOSERS.** (1992)-. English. $125.00. St. James Press, PO Box 33477, Detroit MI 48232-5477. **Tel** (800)345-0392.
**Desc:** Presents biographical and analytical information on nearly 500 of the greatest contemporary composers from around the world.

US/0196-6200
**CONTEMPORARY MUSIC ALMANAC.** [Contemp. music alm.]. **VFOAT** Music Almanac. (19??)-. Periodical. English. ir. Macmillan Publishing Company, 100 Front Street, Box 500, Riverside NJ 08075-7500. **Tel** (800)257-5755, (609)461-6500, FAX (609)461-7070. **LC** ML3533.8; .C66. **DD** 784.5/4/00973.

US/1065-4712
**CONTEMPORARY MUSIC FORUM.** (CONTEMPORARY MUSIC FORUM : PROCEEDINGS OF THE BOWLING GREEN STATE UNIVERSITY NEW MUSIC & ART FESTIVAL PAPER SESSIONS.). [Contemp. music forum]. **Added/Corp** MidAmerican Center for Contemporary Music. **VFOAT** Proceedings of the Bowling Green State University New Music & Art Festival 10 Paper Sessions. Vol. 1 (1989)-. Proceedings. English. Free. MidAmerican Center for Contemporary Music, College of Musical Arts, Bowling Green State University, Bowling Green OH 43403-0290. **DD** 781.

UK/0749-4467
**CONTEMPORARY MUSIC REVIEW.** [Contemp. music rev.]. Vol. 1, Pt. 1 (Oct. 1984)-. Periodical. English. £58.00. Harwood Academic Publishers, PO Box 90, Reading RG1 8JL England. **Tel** 011 44 734 560080. **(Subscription address:** International Publishers Distributor at one of the following addresses: 820 Town Center Drive, Langhorne, PA 19047; or PO Box 90, Reading Berkshire RG1 8JL UK; or Kent Ridge PO Box 1180, Singapore 9111, Republic of Singapore**) ED** Nigel Osborne. **LC** ML197; .C7514. **DD** 780/.904. **[CCC].** Index available. **Bk Rev. Ad Acc.**
**Desc:** A contemporary musician's journal; provides a forum where new tendencies in composition can be discussed in both breadth and depth.

SZ/0891-5415
**CONTEMPORARY MUSIC STUDIES.** [Contemp. music stud.]. Vol. 1 (1989)-. Monographic series. English. Price varies per volume. Harwood Academic Publishers / New York, PO Box 786, Cooper Station, New York NY 10276. **Tel** (212)206-8900, (201)643-7500. **(Subscription address:** International Publishers Distributor at one of the following addresses: 820 Town Center Drive, Langhorne, PA 19047; or PO Box 90, Reading Berkshire RG1 8JL UK; or Kent Ridge PO Box 1180, Singapore 9111, Republic of Singapore**) DD** 780.
**Desc:** Explores the rapid expansion and diversification of contemporary music. Leading experts and practitioners present composition today in all its aspects and use the series to communicate actual musical materials.

US/1044-2197
**CONTEMPORARY MUSICIANS.** [Contemp. music.]. **Added/Corp** Gale Research Inc. Vol. 1 (1989)-. English. sa. $59.00. Gale Research Inc., 835 Penobscot Building, Detroit MI 48226. **Tel** (800)877-GALE, (313)961-2242, FAX (313)961-6083, telex TWX 810-221-7086. **ED** Julia M. Rubiner. **LC** ML385; .C615. **DD** 780/.92/2. available on magnetic tape; available on diskette; available on an online database (File GALBIO in the PEOPLE, ENTERTAINMENT and SPORTS Libraries) from NEXIS.
**Desc:** A biographical and critical guide to performers and writers from a diverse range of musical genres who are active and influential in music today.

CN/0316-893X
**CONTEMPORARY SHOWCASE. SYLLABUS.** (SYLLABUS - CONTEMPORARY SHOWCASE.). **Main/Corp** Contemporary Showcase (Festival). **Added/Corp** Contemporary Music Showcase Association. Canadian Music Centre. (1970)-. Periodical. English. be. Free. Contemporary Music Showcase Association, 3296 Cindy Crescent, Mississauga Ontario L4Y 3J6 Canada. **DD** 780.7/9/713541.
**Desc:** Scholarship adjudication-workshop-concert on contemporary music for teaching and performance in conjunction with the Canadian Music Centre.

CN/0705-6656
**CONTINUO.** Vol. 1, No. 7 (April 1978)-. Periodical. English. bm. $30.00 (US), $35.00 (Canada); $36.00 (other); $35.00 (US), $39.00 (other) library. Continuo, PO Box 327, Hammondsport NY 14840. **Tel** (607)569-2489,

(800) 231-2489. **(Subscription address:** PO Box 10, Bath, NY 14810**) ED** Matthew J Redsell. **DD** 780/.5. Index available. cum. index. **Bk Rev**, (Qty: 60 /yr). **Ad Acc. Circ:** 1,000. ***Continues*** *Early Music Directory, 0705-6648.*
**Desc:** Informative magazine about the performers, builders and teachers of music before 1850, as it is currently practised in North America.

AT/0310-6802
**CONTINUO (BRISBANE, QLD.).**
(CONTINUO : NEWSLETTER OF THE INTERNATIONAL ASSOCIATION OF MUSIC LIBRARIES ARCHIVES AND DOCUMENTATION CENTRES (AUSTRALIA AND NEW ZEALAND BRANCH) .). **Added/Corp** International Association of Music Libraries, Archives, and Documentation Centres (Australia and New Zealand Branch) International Association of Music Libraries, Archives, and Documentation Centres (Australian Branch). (19??)-. Newsletter. English. Twice a year (May, Nov.). 8.50Aus$ (individuals), 14.50Aus$ (institutions) Comes with International Association of Music Libraries Membership. Treasurer IAML Australia, Wigmore Music Libraries, University of WA, Nedlands WA 6009 Australia. **ED** Mary O'Mara and Gordon Abbott. **LC** PAR. **Bk Rev. Ad Acc. Circ:** 80 (ctrl).
**Desc:** A journal of all aspects of music librarianship.
**Ind/Abst** Music Artic. Guide.

FR
**CONTRECHAMPS.** ***Ceased.*** No. 1 (Sept. 1983)-(19??). Periodical. French. sa. Editions l'Age d'Homme / France, 5 rue Ferou, 75006 Paris France. **Tel** 011 33 1 46341851, FAX 011 33 1 40517102. **LC** ML197; .C755. **DD** 780/.904.

US/0190-4922
**CONTRIBUTIONS TO MUSIC EDUCATION.** [Contrib. music educ.]. No. 1 (1972)-. English. an (Oct.). $5.00 (individuals), $7.50 (institutions) US; $7.50 (individuals), $10.00 (institutions) other. Case Western Reserve University / Music, Department of Music, Cleveland OH 44106. **Tel** (216)368-2431. **ED** John Kratus. **LC** ML1; .C9154. **DD** 780/.72. **Pr Rev. Circ:** 500.
**Desc:** Contributions to music education. Publishes research reports pertinent to instruction in music.
**Ind/Abst** Music Artic. Guide; Music Index.

US/0193-9041
**CONTRIBUTIONS TO THE STUDY OF MUSIC AND DANCE.** [Contrib. study music dance]. No. 1, (1981)-. Monographic series. English. ir. Price varies per volume. Greenwood Press Inc., PO Box 5007, Westport CT 06881-5007. **Tel** (203)226-3571, FAX (203)222-1502. **LC** UNC.
**Desc:** This series is devoted to an examination of music and dance throughout the world. Historical as well as contemporary concerns are treated.

IT/0070-0363
**CORPUS MENSURABILIS MUSICAE.**
**Added/Corp** American Institute of Musicology in Rome. Vol. 1, (1947)-. Monographic series. Latin. ir. Price varies per volume. Haenssler Verlag, Postfach 1220, D-73762 Neuhausen Germany. **Tel** 011 49 07158 1770, telex 715816 HAENSR.

GW/0070-0371
**CORPUS OF EARLY KEYBOARD MUSIC.** **Added/Corp** American Institute of Musicology. (1963)-. English. ir (Published 1 - 3 books per year). Haenssler Verlag, Postfach 1220, D-73762 Neuhausen Germany. **Tel** 011 49 07158 1770, telex 715816 HAENSR. **ED** John Caldwell. **Bk Rev. Ad Acc.**
**Desc:** Early music for keyboards.

GW/0070-0460
**CORPUS SCRIPTORUM DE MUSICA.**
[Corpus scr. musica]. **Added/Corp** American Institute of Musicology. (1950)-. Monographic series. German. ir. Price varies per volume. Haenssler Verlag, Postfach 1220, D-73762 Neuhausen Germany. **Tel** 011 49 07158 1770, telex 715816 HAENSR. **LC** ML170; .C6.

CN/0709-7166
**COUNTERPOINT CLASSICAL RECORD REVIEW.** [Counterpoint classical rec. rev.]. (June 1979)-. Periodical. English. ir. Counterpoint Publishing Company, Postal Station Z, Box 186, Toronto Ontario M4N 2Z4 Canada. **Tel** (416)486-8134. **DD** 789.9/131/05.

CN/0709-7158
**COUNTERPOINT'S BASIC CLASSICAL RECORD LIBRARY GUIDE.** (1978)-. English. be. Counterpoint Publishing Company, Postal Station Z, Box 186, Toronto Ontario M4N 2Z4 Canada. **Tel** (416)486-8134. **DD** 789.9/131/05.

US/1043-4488
**COUNTRY AMERICA.** [Ctry. Am.]. (1989)-. Periodical. English. Ten times a year. $19.00. Meredith Corporation, Locust at 17th, Des Moines IA 50309. **Tel** (515)284-3000. **(Subscription address:** Neodata / Colorado, PO Box 2606, Boulder Boulder CO 80322.**) ED** Danita Allen. **DD** 051. **Circ:** 400,000 (ctrl).
**Desc:** A lifestyle magazine for country music fans and those who enjoy the country way of life. Regular features include visits off-stage and at home with top country music personalities. A TNN (The Nashville Network) guide is included.

●US/1066-0453
**COUNTRY FEVER.** [Ctry. fever]. Vol. 1 No. 1 (Aug 1992)-. Periodical. English. bm (6 issues). $9.95. LFP Inc., 9171 Wilshire Boulevard/Suite 300, Beverly Hills CA 90210. **Tel** (310)858-7100, FAX (310)274-7985. **(Subscription address:** Kable Publishers Aide, 308 East Hitt Street, Subscription Department, Mt. Morris IL 61054-1473.**) LC** ML3523; .C68. **DD** 781.642/05.
**Desc:** Covers country music.

US/0733-8759
**COUNTRY HERITAGE.** [Ctry. herit.]. Vol. 8, No. 10 (May 1982)-. Periodical. English. bm. $9.25 US; $10.75 other. Country Heritage, Rural Route 1 Box 320, Madill OK 73446. **Tel** (405)795-2117. **ED** Matt Nozzolio. **LC** ML459 .D6. **DD** 784.5/2/005. Index available (bound in July/Aug. issue). cum. index (annually in July/Aug. issue). **Ad Acc, Adv Mgr:** Beverly King. **Circ:** 300 (ctrl). ***Continues*** *Resophonic Echoes, 0273-3242; The Dobro Nut.*
**Desc:** Centers around Resophonic (Dobro) guitar and traditional country music in general. Interviews with Dobroists, tablatures, ads, historical (on Dobro), instrument technical information.

US/0090-4007
**COUNTRY MUSIC.** [Ctry. music]. Vol. 1, No. 1 (Sept. 1972)-. Periodical. English. Six times a year (Jan., Mar., May, July, Sept., Nov.). $15.98. Country Music, 329 Riverside Avenue, Building C, Westport CT 06880. **Tel** (203)222-6662. **(Subscription address:** Fulfillment Corp of America, 205 West Center Street, Marion, OH 43302**) ED** Russell Barnard. **LC** ML1; .C9177. **DD** 784. **Bk Rev. Ad Acc. Circ:** 350,000. available on microfilm and microfiche from University Microfilms International (UMI). Documents available from UMI Article Clearinghouse, Magazine Collection.
**Desc:** Covers the country music scene.
**Ind/Abst** Access (1984-); Gen. Period. Index (1985-); Mag. Index Plus (1989-); Newsp. Period. Abstr. (1988-); Mag. Index (1977-1982, Jan. 1985-).

US/0360-8131
**COUNTRY MUSIC BOOKING GUIDE.**
(19??)-. English. Country Music Booking Guide, 1717 West End Avenue, Nashville TN 37203. **LC** ML19; .C67. **DD** 338.4/7/784.

US/1066-3312
**COUNTRY MUSIC CITY NEWS.** ***Title Change.*** [Ctry. music city news]. **VFOAT** Music City News. (19??)-(1994). Periodical. English. mo. Music City News Inc, PO Box 22975, Nashville TN 37202. **Tel** (615)329-2200, FAX (615)327-2726. **LC** ML3523; .C663. **DD** 781.642/05. ***Continues*** *Music City News, 0027-4291.* ***Continued by*** *Music City News (Nashville, Tenn. : 1994), 1078-5558.*

US/0360-8697
**COUNTRY MUSIC EXPLORER.** [Ctry. music explor.]. **Added/Corp** International Association of Country Music. (19??)-. Periodical. English. mo. $5.00. International Association of Country Music, PO Box 147, Hamilton OH 45012. **LC** ML1; .C91773. **DD** 784.

CN/0714-8356
**COUNTRY MUSIC NEWS (OTTAWA).**
(COUNTRY MUSIC NEWS.). [Ctry. music news]. Vol. 2, No. 10 (Jan. 1982)-. Periodical. English. mo. 26.75Can$ Canada; 40.00Can$ US; 42.00Can$ other. Country Music News, Box 7323 Vanier Terminal, Ottawa Ontario K1L 8E4 Canada. **Tel** (613)745-6006, FAX (613)745-0576. **ED** Larry DeLaney. **DD** 784.5/2/00971. **Bk Rev. Ad Acc. Pr Rev. Circ:** 9,500. ***Continues*** *Capital Country News, 0228-0191.*
**Desc:** Coverage of Canada's country music industry and artists. Includes interviews, reviews, photos, and columns on Nashville stars.

US/0098-9037
**COUNTRY MUSIC NEWS (TURBOTVILLE, PA.).** (COUNTRY MUSIC NEWS.). [Ctry. music news]. (19??)-. Periodical. English. mo. $5.00. Country Music Society of America, PO Box 2000, Marion OH 43305. **Tel** (800)743-4429. **LC** ML1; .C917814. **DD** 784/.0973.

AT
**COUNTRY MUSIC NEWSLETTER, THE.**
**Added/Corp** Earl Heywood Fan Club. (Jan. 1970)-. Newsletter. English. qt. Earl Heywood Fan Club, PO Box 186, Murwillimbah 2484 New South Wales Australia. **LC** ML5.G725; C7. **DD** 784.

UK/0591-2237
**COUNTRY MUSIC PEOPLE.** (1970)-. Periodical. English. Twelve times a year. £24.00 UK, £30.00 others (surface mail); £42.00 (airmail). Music Farm Ltd., 225A Lewisham Way, London SE4 1UY England. **Tel** 011 44 81 6921106. **ED** Bob Powel. **LC** ML5; .C7055. **DD** 784. **Bk Rev. Ad Acc. Circ:** 13,000.
**Desc:** Covers all areas of country music from country rock to country gospel.

UK
**COUNTRY MUSIC REVIEW.** **VFOAT** CMR. (19??)-. Periodical. English. Twelve times a year. Country Music Review, 10 North Tenter Street, London E1 8DL England. **LC** ML5; .C7056. **DD** 784.

UK/0140-5721
**COUNTRY MUSIC ROUND UP.** (1976)-. Newspaper. English. mo. £13.20 UK; £21.50 Europe; £28.00 other. CMRU Publishing Company, PO Box 111 Waltham, Grimsby DN37 0YN England. **Tel** 011 44 522 750150, 011 44 472 821707, FAX 011 44 472 821808. **ED** John Emptage. **Bk Rev. Ad Acc, Adv Mgr:** Doreen Holder. Documents available from BLDSC.
**Desc:** Contains news, reviews, and comments on both international UK country music.

AT
**COUNTRY MUSIC TIMES.** **Added/Corp** Modern Country Music Association. (19??)-. Periodical. English. bm. PO Box 35, North Quay, Queensland Australia 4000. **LC** ML5; .C7057. **DD** 784.

US/0094-1344
**COUNTRY MUSIC WORLD.** (July/Aug. 1972)-. Periodical. English. Dobson Publishing Company, Box 3693, Arlington VA 22203. **LC** ML1; .C91827. **DD** 784.

US
**COUNTRY MUSICAL TRAILS LESS TRAVELED.** (19??)-. English. bm (6 issues). $12.00. Taylor Publishing / North Carolina, PO Box 143, Marshville NC 28103. **Tel** (704)233-4502. **ED** P. Jay Taylor. cum. index. **Circ:** 300.
**Desc:** Featuring artists and information pertinent to those interested in traditional country music.

US/0092-4059
**COUNTRY RECORDING VOICE.** (19??)-. Periodical. English. mo. Country Recording Voice, PO Box 1393, Nashville TN 37202. **LC** ML1; .C9187. **DD** 784.

US/0732-5614
**COUNTRY RHYTHMS.** ***Ceased.*** (1981)-(August 1985). Periodical. English. mo. Starlog Press Inc., 475 Park Avenue South, New York NY 10016. **Tel** (212)689-2830, FAX (212)889-7933. **ED** Dan Fields. **DD** 780. **Ad Acc. Circ:** 250,000.
**Desc:** Country lifestyle and music including interviews with country music stars.

US/0011-0248
**COUNTRY SONG ROUNDUP.** [Ctry. song roundup]. (1950)-. Periodical. English. Twelve times a year. $25.00 one year; $40.00 two years. Country Song Roundup Inc., 63 Grand Avenue, River Edge NJ 07661. **Tel** (201)487-6124. **ED** William T. Anderson. **DD** 781. **Ad Acc. Circ:** 102,464.

US/0277-3554
**COUNTRY SONG ROUNDUP. SPECIAL.**
(19??)-. English. an. Charlton Publications Inc., PO Box 158, 60 Division Street, Derby CT 06418. **Tel** (203)732-4797. **LC** M1630.18; .C6759.
**Desc:** A country music journal.

US/0147-5738
**COUNTRY SOUNDS OF THE SOUTHWEST.** (Mar. 1973)-. Periodical. English. mo. Country Sounds of the Southwest / Circulation Department, 5326 West Bellfort / Suite 215, Houston TX 77035. **LC** ML1; .C91915. **DD** 784.

US/0092-0991
**COUNTRY SQUIRE.** (19??)-. Periodical. English. Country Squire, PO Box 4551, Rochester NY 14513. **LC** ML1; .C9192. **DD** 784.

US/0364-0078
**COUNTRY STYLE MONTHLY.** (COUNTRY STYLE.). (19??)-. Periodical. English. mo. Country Style Publications Company, 11058 West Addison Street, Franklin Park IL 60131. **LC** ML1; .C9193. **DD** 780/.42.

CN/0821-7971
**COUNTRY TIMES (THORNHILL).**
(COUNTRY TIMES / ACADEMY OF COUNTRY MUSIC ENTERTAINMENT.). [Ctry. times]. **Added/Corp** Academy of Country Music Entertainment. Issue 1983 # 1 (Dec. 1982)-. Periodical. English. Academy of Country Music Entertainment, PO Box 574, Thornhill Ontario L3T 4A2 Canada. **ED** Mary Quartarone. **DD** 780/.42/06. **Bk Rev. Circ:** 1,000 (ctrl). ***Continues*** *Country Music News (Thornhill, Ont.), 0225-5863.*
**Desc:** News on the activities of academy members -- artists, record company and broadcasting personnel. Updates on the business of the academy.

CN/1180-8047
**COUNTRY (TORONTO).** (COUNTRY.). [Country]. Vol. 1, No. 1 (Nov./Dec. 1989)-. Periodical. English. Six times a year. 14.00Can$. Canadian Country Music Authority, RR #1, Holstein Ontario N0G 2A0 Canada. **Tel** (519)334-3246, FAX (519)334-3366. **ED** Jim Baine. **DD** 781.642/05. **Bk Rev**, (Qty: 12/year). **Ad Acc. Circ:** 12,000.

US/0093-4566
**COUNTRYSIDE (BLAINE).** (COUNTRYSIDE.). (19??)-. Periodical. English. mo. $5.50. Countryside, Box 677, Minneapolis MN 55440. **LC** ML1; .C9196. **DD** 784. ***Continues*** *Country & Western News Scene.*
**Ind/Abst** Index Inf.

US/0092-5454
**COUNTRYWIDE ANNUAL YEARBOOK.** (COUNTRYWIDE ANNUAL YEAR BOOK.). (1973/74)-. English. ir. $2.00. The Country Publishers Inc., PO Box 778, Berryville VA 22611. **Tel** (703)955-1298. **LC** ML1; .C9197. **DD** 784.

US
**COURANT (ANN ARBOR, MICH.).** (THE COURANT.). **Added/Corp** Academy for the Study and Performance of Early Music. Vol. 1, No. 1 (Jan. 1983)-. Periodical. English. qt. $15.00. Academy of Early Music, School of Music, 2221 Moore Building, University of Michigan, Ann Arbor MI 48109. **LC** ML457; .C78. **DD** 780/.902.

●US/1076-9102
**CRANK (PHILADELPHIA, PA.).** (CRANK.). [Crank]. (1994)-. Periodical. English. qt. $2.00 (single issue). Crank, POB 1646, Philadelphia PA 19105-1646. **Tel** (215)476-4647. **ED** Jeff Koyen. **DD** 051. **Ad Acc, Adv Mgr:** Jeff Koyen. Full Page (B&W) $80.00. Half Page (B&W) $45.00. **Circ:** 1,000 (ctrl). available via Internet from the publisher.
**Desc:** Reviews and commentary pertaining to underground pop culture, music, art and literature.

US/0092-8887
**CREATIVE GUITAR INTERNATIONAL.** [Creat. guitar int.]. (Fall 1973)-. Periodical. English. Three times a year. $5.00. Mockingbird Press, 1407 North 9th, Alpine TX 79830. **LC** ML1; .C927. **DD** 787/.61/05.
**Ind/Abst** Music Index (19??-19??).

US/0360-7135
**CREATIVE WORLD.** (19??)-. English. Stan Kenton's Creative World, 1012 S Robertson Boulevard, Box 35216, Los Angeles CA 90035. **LC** ML1; .C928. **DD** 785/.06/72.

US/1045-0815
**CREATOR (WICHITA, KAN.).** (CREATOR.). **Added/Corp** Creative Church Music Society. Church Music Associates. **VFOAT** Creator Magazine. (1978)-. Periodical. English. Six times a year (Jan., Mar., May, July, Sept., Nov.). $32.95 one year; $55.95 two year; $73.95 three year. Church Music Associates, PO Box 100, Dublin OH 43017. **Tel** (614)777-7774, FAX (614)792-3585. **ED** Marshall Sanders. **LC** ML2999; .C74. **DD** 781.71/005. cum. index. **Bk Rev**, (Qty: 25). **Ad Acc, Adv Mgr:** M. Sanders. **Circ:** 6,500 (ctrl).
**Desc:** For church musicians, directors and staff. Contains educational articles, interviews, two pages of music "clip art," entertaining cartoons, appropriate advertising, music reviews; all designed to inspire creative thinking for every aspect of church music programs.

US/0737-1918
**CREEM CLOSEUP.** (19??)-. Periodical. English. Twelve times a year. $27.00. Creem Magazine Inc, 8150 Beverly Boulevard, Suite 200, Los Angeles CA 90048. **Tel** (213)653-8687. **LC** ML3533.8; .C73. **DD** 784.5/4/005.

●US/0011-1147
**CREEM (NEW YORK, N.Y.).** ***Suspended.*** (CREEM: AMERICA'S ONLY ROCK & ROLL MAGAZINE.). [Creem]. **VFOAT** Creem Magazine. Vol. 1, No. 3 (March 1992)-(March 1994). Periodical. English. Ten times a year. $17.50. Raven Press / Wisconsin, West 227 North 6355 Sussex Road, Sussex WI 53089. **Tel** (414)246-7082. **DD** 784. ***Continues*** *Creem, 0011-1147.*
**Ind/Abst** Med. Rev. Dig.; Music Index (19??-19??).

●UK/0962-7472
**CRESCENDO & JAZZ MUSIC.** **VFOAT** Crescendo and Jazz Music. Vol. 28, Issue 1 (May 1991)-. Periodical. English. bm (Feb., Apr., June, Aug., Oct., Dec.). £15.00 Great Britain; £35.00 others. Crescendo & Jazz Music, 28 Lambs Conduit Street, London WC1N 3LE England. **Tel** 011 44 71 405 6556, FAX 011 44 71 405 6505. **ED** Dennis H. Matthews. **LC** ML3505.8; .C73. **DD** 781.65/05. **Bk Rev**, (Qty: varies). **Ad Acc, Adv Mgr:** 1071 405 8911. **Circ:** 5,000. ***Continues*** *Crescendo International, 0011-118X.*
**Ind/Abst** Music Index.

CN/0225-9370
**CRESCENDO (CHARLOTTETOWN).** (CRESCENDO : JOURNAL OF THE PRINCE EDWARD ISLAND MUSIC EDUCATORS' ASSOCIATION.). [Crescendo]. **Added/Corp** Prince Edward Island Music Educators' Association. **VFOAT** Newsletter. (1974)-. Periodical. English. ir. Free to members. Prince Edward Island Music Educators' Association, c/o P. Campbell, APT.2, 44 Mount Edward Road, Parkdale, P.E.I. C1A 5S3. **DD** 780/.7.

IT
**CRESCERE CON LA MUSICA.** (19??)-. Italian. Four times a year. L18000. Ctro Educazione Musicale Base, Viale Brianza 14, 20127 Milan Italy. **Tel** 011 39 2 26111938.

AT
**CROSBY VOICE : NEWSLETTER OF THE VICTORIAN BING CROSBY SOCIETY, THE.** **Added/Corp** Victorian Bing Crosby Society. (19??)-. Newsletter. English. Victorian Bing Crosby Society, PO Box 422, South Melbourne Victoria 3205 Australia. **LC** ML420.C93; C8. **DD** 784.5/0092/4.

UK
**CROSS RHYTHMS.** English. bm. £14.50. Cross Rhythms, Cornerstone House, 28 Old Park Road, Peverell Plymouth, Devon PL3 4PY England. **Circ:** 4,000.
**Desc:** Covers the spectrum of contemporary Christian music from praise and worship through to rap and heavy metal. Articles on Christian musicians and bands, music reviews, Christian music festivals and concerts.

SP/0213-0815
**CUADERNOS DE SECCION. MUSICA / EUSKO-IKASKUNTZA, SOCIEDAD DE ESTUDIOS VASCOS.** **Added/Corp** Sociedad de Estudios Vascos (San Sebastian, Spain). **VFOAT** Musica. Vol. 1 (198?)-. Periodical. Spanish (Basa; summaries and/or abstracts in English). ir. Eusko-Ikaskuntza, Legazpi 10-1o, 20004 San Sebastian Spain. **Tel** 425111, FAX 422250. **LC** ML315.7.B37; C8. **DD** 780/.946/6.

US/0888-9015
**CUE SHEET, THE.** (THE CUE SHEET : THE NEWSLETTER OF THE SOCIETY FOR THE PRESERVATION OF FILM MUSIC.). [Cue sheet]. **Added/Corp** Society for the Preservation of Film Music (Los Angeles, Calif.). **VFOAT** Newsletter of the Society for the Preservation of Film Music. (198?)-. Newsletter. English. Four times a year (Jan., Apr., July, Sept.,). $35.00 (members) Comes with Society Preservation of Film Music Membership. Society for the Preservation of Film Music, PO Box 93536, Hollywood CA 93536. **Tel** (818)248-5775. **ED** Leslie T. Zador, William Rosar, Clifford McCarty, Fred Steiner and Tony Thomas. **LC** ML2074; .C83. **DD** 780. **Bk Rev**. ctrl circ.
**Desc:** Covers current affairs in film music scoring, recording, and publications. Publishes discographies and obituaries as well as articles about and interviews with film composers and others in the field.
**Ind/Abst** Film Lit. Index (19??-); Music Index.

CN/0229-1533
**CUE TRACK.** (CUE TRACK : THE CANADIAN RECORD & TAPE GUIDE.). (1980)-. Periodical. English (French). qt. Cue Track, PO Box 2309, Winnipeg Manitoba R3C 4A6 Canada. **LC** ML156.2; .C84. **DD** 016.7899/12.

IT
**CULTURE MUSICALI : SEMESTRALE DELLA SOCIETA ITALIANA DI ETNOMUSICOLOGIA.** **Added/Corp** Societa Italiana di Etnomusicologia. Vol. 1, No. 1 (Jan./June 1982)-. Periodical. Italian (summaries and/or abstracts in English). ir. Edizioni Unicopli SPA, Via Soperga 13, 20127 Milan Italy. **Tel** 011 39 2 66984682. **LC** ML3797.8; .C84.

US
**CURRENT ISSUES IN MUSIC EDUCATION.** **Added/Corp** Ohio State University. Vol. 1, (1963)-. Monographic series. English. ir. Price varies per volume. Ohio State University / School of Music, 105B Hughes Hall/1899 College, Columbus OH 43210. **Tel** (614)422-7940. **ED** James Major. **Circ:** 300 (ctrl).
**Desc:** A summary of the Current Issues Symposia held annually on announced topic. The series began in the late 1960's and continues today.

US/0011-3735
**CURRENT MUSICOLOGY.** [Curr. musicol.]. **Added/Corp** Columbia University. Dept. of Music. No. 1, (1965)-. Periodical. English. Twice a year. $16.00 (individual), $24.00 (institution), $13.00 (student). Current Musicology, Columbia University, Department of Music, New York NY 10027. **Tel** (212)854-1632. **ED** Anthony Barone and A. Clarkson (1965). **LC** ML1; .C98. **DD** 780/.01/05. Index available. cum. index. **Bk Rev. Ad Acc. Circ:** 1,000 (ctrl). available on microfilm and microfiche from University Microfilms International (UMI). Documents available from The Genuine Article, UMI Article Clearinghouse.
**Desc:** Musicology and musical research; reviews of recent literature, reports from major musicological institutions.
**Ind/Abst** Acad. Search (Jan. 1993-); Arts Humanit. Citation Index (19??-19??) [Full Cov.]; Curr. Contents Arts Humanit.; Expand. Acad. Index (1989-); Humanit. Index; Humanit. Source (Jul. 1993-); INFO-SOUTH Abstr.; Mag. Search; Middle East Abstr. Index; Music Artic. Guide; Music Index; Newsp. Period. Abstr. (1991-); Res. Alert [Full Cov.]; RILM Abstr.

US/0731-8529
**DALLAS OPERA MAGAZINE, THE.** **Added/Corp** Dallas Civic Opera Company. Vol. 4, No. 1 (1981)-. Periodical. English. qt. Dallas Opera Office, 3000 Turtle Creek Plaza, Dallas TX 75219. **LC** ML1699; .D34. **DD** 782.1/09764/2812. ***Continues*** *Dallas Civic Opera Magazine, 0277-0113.*

US/0883-1122
**DANCE MUSIC REPORT.** ***Ceased.*** [Dance music rep.]. **VFOAT** DMR. (19??)-(Nov. 1992). Periodical. English. Twelve times a year. Disco Music Report, 636 Broadway, Suite 804, New York NY 10012. **Tel** (212)677-6770. **ED** Andy Man and Darren Ressler. **DD** 784. **Ad Acc, Adv Mgr Tel** (212)677-6770.
**Desc:** A dance/disco music publication covering the latest in club music, hip-hop, and alternative music.

●CN/1183-4048
**DANCEHALL (TORONTO).** (DANCEHALL.). [DanceHall]. **VFOAT** Dance Hall. Vol. 1, No. 1 (Mar. 14/27, 1991)-. Periodical. English. bw. Dancehall, 2573 Eglinton Avenue West, Toronto Ontario M6M 1T3 Canada. **DD** 780.

US/0418-3290
**DANIEL BLUM'S OPERA WORLD.** **VFOAT** Opera World. (1954)-. English. be. G P Putnam's Sons, 200 Madison Avenue, New York NY 10016. **LC** ML1705; .D3. **DD** 782.058.

DK/0416-6884
**DANSK AARBOG FOR MUSIKFORSKNING.** [Dan. arb. musikforsk.]. **Added/Corp** Dansk Selskab for Musikforskning. (19??)-. English (Danish, English, French and German). ir. kr18.75. Dan Fog Musikforlag, 7 Graabrodretorv DK 1154, Copenhagen K Denmark. **LC** ML5; .D109.
**Ind/Abst** BHA : Biblio. Hist. Art.

DK
**DANSK AMATRMUSIK.** **Added/Corp** Dansk Amatr-Orkester Union. (19??)-. Periodical. Danish. Holbaekvej 34, 4571 Gravienge Denmark. **LC** ML5; .D12.

DK
**DANSK MUSIKFORTEGNELSE.** **Added/Corp** Dansk Musikhandlerforening. Kongelige Bibliotek (Denmark). Musikafdelingen. **VFOAT** Danish National Bibliography, Music. (1931)-. Danish (English). an. Dansk BiblioteksCenter AS, Tempovej 7-11, DK-2750 Ballerup, Denmark. **Tel** 011 45 42974000. **LC** ML120.D3; D3. **DD** 016.7817489.
**Ind/Abst** Music Index.

DK/0107-4857
**DANSK ORGELAARBOG.** **Added/Corp** Danske Orgelselskab. **VFOAT** Danish Organ Yearbook; Danisches Orgeljahrbuch. Vol. 1, (1982)-. Danish (summaries and/or abstracts in English and German). be. Kr127.00 (two year). Dansk Orgelaarbog, Det Danske Orgelselskab, c/o Forlaget Syrinx, Norrevoldgade 54 4th, DK-1350 Copenhagen Denmark. **Tel** 01 32 06 36. **ED** Det Danske Orgelselskab. **LC** ML549.8; .D36. **DD** 786.6/2489/05.
**Desc:** History of Danish and European organ building.

US/0898-1558
**DARIUS MILHAUD SOCIETY NEWSLETTER, THE.** [Darius Milhaud Soc. newsl.]. **Added/Corp** Darius Milhaud Society. (1985)-. Newsletter. English. ir (2 or 3 per year). $18.00 US; $19.00 Canada and Mexico; $25.00 other. Darius Milhaud Society, 15715 Chadbourne Road, Cleveland OH 44120. **LC** ML410.M674; D3. **DD** 780. **Circ:** 2,000.

GW/0418-3878
**DARMSTADTER BEITRAEGE ZUR NEUEN MUSIK.** [Darmst. Beitr. neuen Musik]. **Added/Corp** Internationale Ferienkurse feur Neue Musik. Vol. 1, (1958)-. German. ir. DM30.00 (latest volume). B. Schotts Soehne Musikverlag, Carl Zeiss Str 1, Postfach 3640, D 55026 Mainz Germany. **Tel** 011 49 6131 505129, 011 49 6131 505122, FAX 011 49 6131 505115, telex 04187821. **ED** Ernst Thomas. **LC** ML5; .D24. **DD** 780.
**Desc:** Principally texts of seminars held at the Internationale Ferienkurse feur Neue Musik.
**Ind/Abst** RILM Abstr.

US
**DCMEA NEWSLETTER.** Newsletter. English. Substance, 8500 New Hampshire Avenue #129.
**Ind/Abst** Music Artic. Guide (?-?).

UK
**DEE JAY AND RADIO MONTHLY.** **See** Communication-Broadcasting.

US
**DELANEY'S SONG BOOK.** No. 1 (189?)-. Periodical. English. Three times a year. Delaney's Song Book, WM. W. Delaney, New York NY.

UK/0306-0373
**DELIUS SOCIETY JOURNAL, THE.** [Delius Soc. j.]. **Main/Corp** Delius Society. **Added/Corp** Delius Society. Journal. No. 43 (April 1974)-. English. Four times a year (Jan., Apr., July, Oct.). £31.00. Delius Society, 85A

Farley Hill, Luton Lubief Bedfordsh England. **Tel** 0582-20075. **ED** S. Lloyd. **LC** ML410.D35; D47. **DD** 780/.92/4. **Ad Acc. Circ:** 450 (ctrl).
**Desc:** Life and works of Frederick Delius.
**Ind/Abst** Music Index.

GW
**DENKMAELER DER TONKUNST IN BAYERN. NEUE FOLGE.** (19??)-. Monographic series. German. ir. Price varies per volume. Breitkopf and Haertel, Obere Waldstr 30, D 65232 Taunusstein Germany. **Tel** 11 49 611 49030.
**Desc:** Historic music editions related to Bolvaria.

GW
**DENKMALER DER MUSIK IN SALZBURG / HERAUSGEGEBEN VOM INSTITUT FUER MUSIKWISSENSCHAFT AN DER+ UNIVERSITAT SALZBURG. Added/Corp** Universitat Salzburg. Institut fuer Musikwissenschaft. Vol. 1 (1977)-. Monographic series. German. ir. Price varies per volume. Musikverlag Katzbichler, Munich Germany. **LC** UNC. ***Continues*** *Publicationen / Universitat Salzburg. Instituut fur Musikwissenschaft.*

AU
**DENKMALER DER TONKUNST IN OSTERREICH. Added/Corp** Gesellschaft zur Herausgabe der Denkmaler der Tonkunst in Osterreich. Austria. Ministerium feur Cultus und Unterricht. Austria. Bundesministerium feur Inneres und Unterricht. **VFOAT** Publikationen der Gesellschaft zur Herausgabe der Denkmaler der Tonkunst in Osterreich. (1894)-. Monographic series. German. ir. Price varies per volume. Akademische Druck & Verlagsanstalt, Schoenaugasse 6, Postfach 598, A 8010 Graz Austria. **Tel** 011 43 316 813460. **ED** Guido Adler and Eric Schenck. **LC** M2; .D36.

GW/0416-9816
**DENKMALER RHEINISCHER MUSIK.** (1951)-. Monographic series. German. ir. Price varies per volume. CF Peters Corporation, 373 Park Avenue South, New York NY 10016. **Tel** (212)686-4147, FAX (212)689-9412. **ED** Waldstein, Neefe, Miles and De Castro. **DD** 780. **Circ:** 10.
**Desc:** A series of critical editions dealing with early music from the Rhineland.

UK
**DEO.** (1993)-. Consumer Publication. English. qt. £9.50 UK; £12.00 (surface mail), £17.00 (air mail). Herald House Publishing, 96 Dominion Road, Worthing West Sussex, BN14 8JP England. **Tel** 011 44 903 821082, FAX 011 44 903 821081. **ED** Jane Hicks. **Bk Rev. Ad Acc, Adv Mgr:** Sue Mills. **Circ:** 4,000. ***Continues*** *Christian Music.*
**Desc:** Serves interests in music in worship.

US
**DETROIT MONOGRAPHS IN MUSICOLOGY.** No. 1 (1971)-. Monographic series. English. ir. Price varies per volume. Harmonie Park Press, 23630 Pinewood, Warren MI 48091. **Tel** (313)755-3080, (800)886-3080, FAX (313)755-4213. **Circ:** 175.

US/0070-3885
**DETROIT STUDIES IN MUSIC BIBLIOGRAPHY. See** Music-Abstracting, Bibliographies and Statistics.

GE/0012-0502
**DEUTSCHE MUSIKBIBLIOGRAPHIE.** ***Ceased.*** **Added/Corp** Leipzig. Deutsche Bucherei. (1829)-Vol. 162 (Dec. 1990). Periodical. German. mo. Deutscher Judo Verband, Redaktion Ippon Segewaldweg 40, D 12557 Berlin Germany. **Tel** 011 49 711 210770, telex 051 678. **LC** ML113; .H72. ***Supersedes*** *Handbuch der Musikalischen Literatur.*

●GW/0939-0642
**DEUTSCHE NATIONALBIBLIOGRAPHIE UND BIBLIOGRAPHIE DER IM AUSLAND ERSCHIENEN DEUTSCHSPRACHIGEN VEROFFENTLICHUNGEN. REIHE T, MUSIKTONTRAGER MONATLICHES VERZEICHNIS. Added/Corp** Deutsche Bibliothek (Frankfurt am Main, Germany). **VFOAT** Musiktontrager Monatliches Verzeichnis. (Jan. 1991)-. German (Multiple languages). Twelve times a year. Buchhandler Vereinigung GmbH, Grosser Hirschgraben 17-21, D 60311 Frankfurt 1 Germany. **Tel** 011 49 69 1306243, telex 413573 BUCH VOL. ***Continues*** *Deutsche Bibliothek. Musiktontrager-Verzeichnis.*

GW/0418-8896
**DEUTSCHES MOZARTFEST DER DEUTSCHEN MOZART-GESELLSCHAFT.** (DEUTSCHES MOZARTFEST DER DEUTSCHEN MOZART-GESELLSCHAFT.). [Dtsch. Mozartfest Dtsch. Mozart-Ges.]. **Main/Conf** Deutsches Mozartfest der Deutschen Mozart-Gesellschaft. **Added/Corp** Deutsche Mozart-Gesellschaft. (19??)-. German. an. Deutsche Mozart Gesellschaft, Karlstrasse 6, D 86150 Augsburg Germany. **Tel** 011 49 821 518588. **LC** ML410.M9; D5. **DD** 780/.92/4; B.
**Ind/Abst** Music Index.

US/0092-0789
**DEVIL'S BOX.** (THE DEVIL'S BOX.). [Devil's box]. **Added/Corp** Tennessee Valley Old Time Fiddlers' Association. No. 8 (March 1969)-. Periodical. English. qt. $2.00. Tennessee Valley Old Time Fiddlers' Association, Route 11 / 16 Bond Street, Clarksville TN 37040. **LC** ML1; .D325. **DD** 787/.1/05. ***Continues*** *Tennessee Valley Old Time Fiddlers' Association. Newsletter.*
**Ind/Abst** MLA Int. Bibl. Books Artic. Mod. Lang. Lit.

US/0197-7784
**DEVOTEE.** [Devotee]. (Spring 1979)-. Periodical. English (English). qt. $9.00 US; $12.00 other. Devotee, 28-24th Street, New York NY 12180. **LC** ML1100; .D48. **DD** 785.7/005.
**Ind/Abst** Music Artic. Guide (?-?); Music Index (?-19??).

US/0147-7544
**DIALOGUE IN INSTRUMENTAL MUSIC EDUCATION.** [Dialogue instrum. music educ.]. Vol. 1, (Winter 1977)-. Periodical. English. Twice a year (May, Oct.). $8.00. Dialogue in Instrumental Music, Humanities Building, University of Wisconsin, Madison WI 53706. **Tel** (608)263-3220. **ED** David Nelson. **LC** ML1; .D39. **DD** 780/.7. Index available. cum. index. **Bk Rev. Ad Acc. Circ:** 400 (ctrl).
**Desc:** The purpose of DIME is to provide a medium that will aid in improving instruction and the preparation of music teachers.
**Ind/Abst** Music Artic. Guide; Music Index.

FR
**DIAPASON.** (199?)-. Periodical. French. mo. Editions Mondiales, 9 11 13 Rue du Col Pierre Avia, 75754 Paris Cedex 15 France. **Tel** 011 33 1 46622162. **(Subscription address:** Diapason, Service Abonnements, BP 53, F-77932 Perthes Cedex France.**) LC** ML5; .D5. **DD** 780/.5. ***Continues*** *Diapason Harmonie, 0765-5983.*
**Ind/Abst** Music Index.

US/0012-2378
**DIAPASON (CHICAGO), THE.** (THE DIAPASON.). [Diapason]. **Added/Corp** American Guild of Organists. Hymn Society of America. Organ Builders' Association of America. National Association of Organists. Canadian College of Organists. No. 10 (Dec. 1909)-. Periodical. English. mo. $18.00 (one year) $27.00 (two year), $36.00 (three year) US and possessions; $28.00 (one year), $43.00 (two year), $60.00 (three year) other. Scranton Gillette Communications Inc., 380 East Northwest Highway, Des Plaines IL 60016-2282. **Tel** (708)298-6622, FAX (708)390-0408. **ED** Jerome Butera and Wesley Vos. **LC** ML1; .D41. **DD** 786.5/05. **[CCC].** Index available. **Bk Rev. Ad Acc. Circ:** 6,000 (ctrl). available on microfilm and microfiche from University Microfilms International (UMI).
**Desc:** Devoted to the organ, harpsichord and church music. Each issue includes feature articles, news, new organs, reviews of new music, recordings and books, carillon news, an international calendar and extensive classified advertising.
**Ind/Abst** Music Artic. Guide; Music Index; RILM Abstr.

FR/0765-5983
**DIAPASON HARMONIE.** ***Title Change.*** Issue 1 (Mar. 1985)-(199?). Periodical. French. Eleven times a year. Editions Mondiales, 9 11 13 Rue du Col Pierre Avia, 75754 Paris Cedex 15 France. **Tel** 011 33 1 46622162. **(Subscription address:** Diapason, Service Abonnements, BP 53, F-77932 Perthes Cedex France.**) LC** ML5; .D5. **DD** 780/.5. ***Formed by the union of*** *Diapason (Boulogne, France), 0419-0912* ***and*** *Harmonie, Panorama, Musique, 0756-0189.* ***Continued by*** *Diapason (Paris, France : 1994).*
**Ind/Abst** Music Index.

NE/0419-1129
**DICTIONARIUM MUSICUM.** (1965)-. Monographic series. English. ir. Price varies per volume. Vereniging Voor Nederlandse Muziekgeschiedenis, PO Box 1514, 3500 BM Utrecht Netherlands. **Tel** 011 31 30 23327787, FAX (0)3449-2617. **DD** 780.
**Desc:** A series of early music dictionaries.

VE
**DIRECTORIO MUSICAL VENEZOLANO / DIVISION DE MUSICA Y FONOTECA. Added/Corp** Instituto Autonomo Biblioteca Nacional y de Servicios de Bibliotecas (Venezuela). Division de Musica y Fonoteca. (19??)-. Spanish. an. Instituto Autonomo Biblioteca Nacional y de Services de Bibliotecas, Oficina de Informacion Calle Paris con Caroni, Edif. Macanao, 4O Piso Las Mercedes, Caracas Venezuela.

US
**DIRECTORY / AMERICAN MUSICOLOGICAL SOCIETY. Main/Corp** American Musicological Society. (1987)-. Directory. English. ir. $40.00 Comes with AMS Newsletter & AMS Directory Doctoral Dissertations in Musicology. American Musicological Society, 201 South 34th Street, Philadelphia PA 19104. **Tel** (215)898-8698. **LC** IN PROCESS. **Circ:** 4,500 (ctrl). ***Continues*** *American Musicological Society. Directory of Members and Subscribers - American Musicological Society, 0192-8368.*
**Desc:** Listing of members and subscribers. Also contains by-laws, organization, and guidelines for competitions and prizes.

US
**DIRECTORY / COMPOSERS' FORUM, INC, THE. Main/Corp** Composers' Forum (U.S.). (1982)-. Directory. English. an. $20.00. Composers' Forum Inc., 596 Broadway / Suite 602A, New York NY 10012. **Tel** (212)334-0216. **ED** Bernadette Speach. **LC** ML13; .C64a. **Ad Acc. Circ:** 2,000 (ctrl).

US/0547-4175
**DIRECTORY - NATIONAL ASSOCIATION OF SCHOOLS OF MUSIC.** (DIRECTORY.). **Main/Corp** National Association of Schools of Music. **VFOAT** NASM Directory. (1967)-. Directory. English. an (Mar.). $15.00 Comes with National Association of Schools of Music Library. National Association of Schools of Music, 11250 Roger Bacon Drive, Suite 21, Reston VA 22090. **Tel** (703)437-0700. **ED** David Bading. **LC** ML27.U5; N2633. **DD** 780/.72973. **Circ:** 1,500. ***Continues*** *National Association of Schools of Music. List of Members.*
**Desc:** List accredited institutions and approved major degree programs. Includes address, telephone numbers and music executives for each member institution.

US/0196-9757
**DIRECTORY - NATIONAL BAND ASSOCIATION.** [Dir. - Natl. Band Assoc.]. **Main/Corp** National Band Association (U.S.). (19??)-. Directory. English. PO Box 6, Ada OH 45810. **LC** ML17; .N34. **DD** 785.1/2/06073.

AT/0815-5232
**DIRECTORY OF AUSTRALIAN COMPOSERS.** [Dir. Aust. compos.]. **Added/Corp** Australia Music Centre. (1985)-. English. ir. Sounds Australian, PO Box N690, Grosvenor Place, Sydney NSW 2000 Australia. **Tel** 011 61 2 2474677, FAX 011 61 2 241-2873. **DD** 780.9202594. **Circ:** 1,000.
**Desc:** Names and essential data about selected Australian composers.

UK
**DIRECTORY OF BRITISH BRASS BANDS. Added/Corp** British Federation of Brass Bands. (19??)-. Directory. English. British Federation of Brass Bands, 28 Marigold Street, Rochdale Lancs England. **LC** ML27.G7; B73 1978. **DD** 785/.06/71.

CN/0705-6249
**DIRECTORY OF CANADIAN ORCHESTRAS AND YOUTH ORCHESTRAS / ANNUAIRE CANADIEN DES ORCHESTRES ET ORCHESTRES DES JEUNES.** ***Title Change.*** [Dir. Can. orch. youth orch.]. **Added/Corp** Association of Canadian Orchestras. Ontario Federation of Symphony Orchestras. **VFOAT** Annuaire des Orchestres et Orchestres des Jeunes Canadiens; Annuaire Canadien des Orchestres et Orchestres des Jeunes. (1975/1976)-(199?). Directory. English (French). an. Association of Canadian Orchestras / OFSO Secretariat, 56 The Esplanade / Suite 311, Toronto Ontario M5E 1A7 Canada. **Tel** (416)366-8834, FAX (416)366-1780. **ED** M. Fiala. **DD** 785/.06/6102571. **Bk Rev. Ad Acc. Circ:** 750. ***Continued by*** *Canadian Orchestras and Youth Orchestras Directory, 1189-9956.*
**Desc:** Listings and contacts of key personnel in Canadian orchestras and youth orchestras - boards and committees and government granting bodies.

US
**DIRECTORY OF MEMBERS AND FRIENDS / RSCM. Main/Corp** Royal School of Church Music (Warren, Conn.). **VFOAT** R.S.C.M. Directory of Affiliated Choirs and Friends in the U.S.A.; RSCM Directory of Affiliated Choirs and Friends in the U.S.A. (1983)-. Directory. English. **LC** MT4.W28; R697. **DD** 783.8/025/73.

US/0197-9949
**DIRECTORY OF MEMBERS & MUSEUMS. Main/Corp** Musical Box Society International, Morgantown, Ind. **VAT** Directory of Members and Museums. (19??)-. Directory. English. $20.00 (membership). Musical Box Society, Hughes M. Ryder, 495 Springfield Avenue, Summit NJ 07901. **(Subscription address:** Musical Box Society, Box 202 Rt. #3, Morgantown, IN 46160 USA**) LC** ML26; .M873. **DD** 789/.8/025.

US/0098-664X
**DIRECTORY OF MUSIC FACULTIES IN COLLEGES AND UNIVERSITIES, U.S. AND CANADA. Added/Corp** College Music Society. **VAT** Directory of Music Faculties in Colleges and Universities, United States and Canada. Vol. 1 (1972)-. Directory. English. an. $55.00 (two years). College Music Society, PO Box 8208, Missoula MT 59807. **Tel**

(406)728-2002, (800)729-0235, FAX (406)721-9419. **ED** Robby D. Gunstream. **LC** ML13; .D57. **DD** 780/.92/2. **Circ:** 3,500. ***Continues*** *Directory of Music Faculties in American Colleges and Universities.*
**Desc:** Contains 26,666 music faculty members in 1,545 institutions. Indexed by area of teaching interest.

US
**DIRECTORY OF SPOKEN-VOICE AUDIO-CASSETTES.** (1972)-. Directory. English. an. Price varies per volume. **LC** ML157.32; .D6. **DD** 011.

US
**DIRECTORY OF SUMMER CHAMBER MUSIC WORKSHOPS, SCHOOLS & FESTIVALS, A.** **Added/Corp** Chamber Music America. (19??)-. Directory. English. be (every 2 years in March). $12.00. Chamber Music America, 545 8th Avenue, New York NY 10018. **Tel** (212)244-2772, FAX (212)244-2776. **ED** Dorothy Sasser.

CN/0317-2155
**DIRECTORY OF THE CANADIAN ASSOCIATION OF UNIVERSITY SCHOOLS OF MUSIC.** (DIRECTORY OF THE CANADIAN ASSOCIATION OF UNIVERSITY SCHOOLS OF MUSIC. ANNUAIRE DE L'ASSOCIATION CANADIENNE DES ECOLES UNIVERSITAIRES DE MUSIQUE.). **Main/Corp** Canadian Association of University Schools of Music. **VFOAT** Annuaire de l'Asscciation Canadienne des Ecoles Universitaires de Musicue. (1974/75)-. Directory. Multiple languages (English and French). Free. Department of Music, c/o B Ellard, Ottawa Ontario K1S 5B6 Canada. **DD** 780.7/2971.

US/0893-3065
**DIRECTORY OF TRADITIONAL MUSIC.** [Dir. tradit. music]. **Added/Corp** International Council for Traditional Music. Columbia University. Dept. of Music. (1987)-. Directory. English. an. $10.00 (subscribers); $20.00 (non-subscribers). International Council for Traditional Music, Department of Music, Columbia University, 417 Dodge, New York NY 10027. **Tel** (212)678-0332. **ED** Nerthus and Dieter Christensen. **LC** ML26; .I528. **DD** 781.7/025. **Circ:** 1,200. ***Continues*** *International Council for Traditional Music. ICTM Directory of Interests & Projects.*
**Desc:** Contains an address listing of International Council for Traditional Music members and institution subscribers. Also lists ICTM members' interests and projects.

US/1047-4315
**DIRTY LINEN.** (DIRTY LINEN : THE JOURNAL OF FOLK, FOLK-ROCK, AND TRADITIONAL MUSIC.). [Dirty linen]. No. 23 (Summer 1988)-. Periodical. English. Six times a year. $20.00 (one year), $38.00 (two years). Dirty Linen, PO Box 66600, Baltimore MD 21239-6600. **Tel** (410)583-7973, FAX (410)337-6735. **ED** Paul Hartman. **LC** ML3551; .D57. **DD** 781.62/00973/05. Index available. cum. index. **Bk Rev**, (Qty: 12-20). **Ad Acc, Adv Mgr:** Linda Cohn, **Tel** (410)768-9261. **Circ:** 10,000. available on an online database (from Newgrass City BBS (reviews only)). ***Continues*** *Fairport Fanatics.*
**Desc:** Contains interviews, record reviews, personality sketches, and news of concerts on "folk, folk-rock, and traditional music." Coverage is international, although most interest is in American rockers.

US/0731-843X
**DIS COLLECTOR (CHESWOLD, DEL. : 1981).** (DISC COLLECTOR.). No. 100 (Jan. 1981)-. Periodical. English. mo. Disc Collector Publishing, POB 315, Cheswold DE 19936. **Tel** (302)674-3149. **ED** Lou Deneumoustier. **LC** ML1; .D483. **DD** 016.7899/12. **Bk Rev. Ad Acc. Circ:** 950 (ctrl). ***Continues*** *Disc Collector Newsletter, 0360-8700.*
**Desc:** Reviews and sales of old time country, bluegrass, cowboy and Western music records, tapes, and books.

US/0092-0436
**DISC AND THAT.** (July/Aug. 1973)-. Periodical. English. mo. Pruitt/Scott Publications, PO Box 228 Kingsbridge Station, New York NY 10463. **LC** ML1; .D47. **DD** 338.4/7/7899105.

UK
**DISCO 45.** (19??)-. Periodical. English. **LC** ML1.; D487. **DD** 789.9/12.

CN/0706-7763
**DISCO FEVER.** (1978)-. English (French). an. Canadian Association of Professional D.J.'s, Suite 1, 7148 St. Laurent Blvd., Montreal Quebec H2S 3E2 Canada. **DD** 780/.42/05. ***Continues*** *Disco, 0703-7740.*

●GW
**DISCO-MAGAZIN.** **VFOAT** Disco Magazin. (1992)-. Periodical. German. mo. **LC** ML5; .M9475. **DD** 781.64/0943/05. ***Continues*** *Sigert's Fachmagazin fur die Unterhaltungs-Gastronomie.*

US/0192-334X
**DISCOGRAPHIES (WESTPORT).** (DISCOGRAPHIES.). (1979)-. Monographic series. English. ir. Price varies per volume. Greenwood Press Inc., PO Box 5007, Westport CT 06881-5007. **Tel** (203)226-3571, FAX (203)222-1502. **ED** Michael Gray. **LC** UNC.

IT
**DISCOTECA HI-FI.** ***Suspended.*** **See** Sound Recordings and Systems.

US/0896-8322
**DISCOVERIES (PORT TOWNSEND, WASH.).** **See** Hobbies.

SW
**DISSONANZ.** **Added/Corp** Schweizerischer Tonkunstlerverein. **VFOAT** Dissonance; Neue Schweizerische Musikzeitschrift; Nouvelle Revue Musicale Suisse. No. 1 (Aug. 1984)-. Periodical. German (French). qt. 35.00F. Dissonanz, Postfach 160, 3000 Bern Switzerland.
**Ind/Abst** Music Index.

US/0192-6128
**DIVISIONS.** ***Ceased.*** (19??)-(19??). Periodical. English. qt. Divisions, PO Box 18647, Cleveland Heights OH 44118. **LC** ML1; .D53. **DD** 780/.5.
**Ind/Abst** Music Artic. Guide (?-?).

NE
**DIVITIAE MUSICAE ARTIS.** English (German, French and Dutch). ir. Uitgeverij Frits Knuf B V, PO Box 720, 4116 ZJ Buuren Netherlands. **Tel** 011 31 03449-1255, FAX 011 31 03449-2617. **Circ:** 700.

US
**DMA DANCE MUSIC AUTHORITY.** (19??)-. English. mo. $30.00 US; $36.00 Canada; $60.00 other. Dance Music Authority, 7943 Paxton Avenue, Tunley Park IL 60477. **Tel** (708)614-8417, FAX (708)429-7830. **ED** Gary Hayslett. **Ad Acc. Circ:** 6,000.
**Desc:** Source for dance music industry news, music reviews, and information. Of interest to the industry and consumers.

DK/0106-5629
**DMT. DANSK MUSIK TIDSSKRIFT.** (DMT. DANSK MUSIKTIDSSKRIFT.). [Dmt, Dan. musik tidsskr.]. **Added/Corp** Unge Tonekunstnerselskab. Dansk Komponistforening. Dansk Tonekunstnerforening. Dansk Musikpdagogisk Forening. **VFOAT** Dansk Musiktidsskrift. Vol. 41 (1966)-. Periodical. Danish. Eight times a year. kr225.00 Scandinavia; kr291.00 Europe; kr357.00 other. Musikvidenskabeligt Institut, Klerkegabe 2, DK-1308 Copenhagen Denmark. **Tel** 011 45 33 150726. **ED** Anders Beyer. Index available. **Bk Rev**, (Qty: 6). **Ad Acc, Adv Mgr:** Anders Beyer. **Circ:** 1,200 (ctrl). ***Continues*** *Dansk Musiktidsskrift.*
**Desc:** Includes interviews, profiles, analyses, reviews, etc.
**Ind/Abst** Music Index; RILM Abstr.

US
**DOCTORAL DISSERTATIONS IN MUSICOLOGY (PHILADELPHIA, PA. : 1984).** (DOCTORAL DISSERTATIONS IN MUSICOLOGY.). **Added/Corp** American Musicological Society. International Musicological Society. (April 1984)-. English. an (Feb., (every 5 years)). $15.00 (members); $20.00 (non-members) Comes with Journal of the American Musicological Society. American Musicological Society, 201 South 34th Street, Philadelphia PA 19104. **Tel** (215)898-8698. **ED** Cecil Adkins. **LC** ML128.M8; D62. **DD** 016.78. **Circ:** 1,000.

GW/0419-5205
**DOCUMENTA MUSICOLOGICA. 1. REIHE. DRUCKSCHRIFTEN-FAKSIMILES.** (19??)-. Periodical. German. ir. Baerenreiter-Verlag, KGA Verlagssvc PF 100329, D 34003 Kassel Germany. **Tel** 011 49 561 31050, telex 99504. **DD** 780. ***Continues*** *Documenta Musicologica.*
**Desc:** Facsimile editions of important sources in musicology, music theory and performance practice from the Renaissance to the 18th Century.

GW/0417-805X
**DOCUMENTA MUSICOLOGICA. 2. REIHE: HANDSCHRIFTEN-FAKSIMILES.** **Added/Corp** International Association of Music Libraries. (1955)-. German. Kasseler Grossauslieferung KGA Verlagssvc GmbH, Postfach 102180, 3500 Kassel Germany. **Tel** 011 49 561 8070346. **DD** 780.

UK/0307-1448
**DONIZETTI SOCIETY JOURNAL.** **Added/Corp** Donizetti Society. **VFOAT** Journal; Journal of the Donizetti Society. (1974)-. Periodical. English. an. $6.00. Donizetti Society, 56 Harbut Road, London SW11 2RB England. **LC** ML410.D7; A4. **DD** 782.1/092/4.

US/0198-8654
**DOUBLE PLATINUM CIRCUS.** (19??)-. Periodical. English. Circus Enterprises, 805 Third Avenue / 28th Floor, New York NY 10020. **Tel** (212)633-9042. **LC** ML3533.8; .D68. **DD** 784.5/4/005.

US/0741-7659
**DOUBLE REED, THE.** [Double reed]. **Added/Corp** International Double Reed Society. Vol. 1, No. 1 (Mar. 1978)-. Periodical. English (French and Spanish). Four times a year (includes annual journal). $30.00. International Double Reed Society, 626 Lakeshore Drive, c/o Dr L Riggins, Monroe LA 71203-4032. **Tel** (318)343-5715. **ED** Ronald Klimko and Daniel Stolper. **LC** ML929; .D69. **DD** 788/.056. Index available. cum. index. **Bk Rev. Ad Acc. Circ:** 2,900 (ctrl). ***Formed by the union of*** *To the World's Oboists, 0091-9683* ***and*** *To the World's Bassoonists, 0828-1475.*
**Desc:** Specializes in Double Reeds: oboe, English horn, Bassoon, and Contra-bassoon.
**Ind/Abst** Music Artic. Guide; Music Index (Vol. 14, No. 2, 1991-).

US/0012-5768
**DOWN BEAT.** [Down beat]. **VAT** Downbeat. Vol. 1, (July 1934)-. Periodical. English. Twelve times a year. $29.00. Maher Publications Inc, 180 West Park Avenue, Elmhurst IL 60126. **Tel** (312)941-2030, (800)515-7496. **(Subscription address:** Down Beat, PO Box 906, Elmhurst IL 60126.) **ED** Art Lange. **LC** ML1; .D72. **DD** 780/.5. **Bk Rev. Ad Acc. Circ:** 91,000 (ctrl). available on microfilm from University Microfilms International (UMI). Documents available from The Genuine Article, UMI Article Clearinghouse.
**Desc:** Published for contemporary musicians.
**Ind/Abst** Acad. Abstr. Full Text Elite (Jan. 1984-); Acad. Abstr. (Jan. 1984-); Acad. Ind. [Computer File] (1984-); Acad. Search (Jan. 1984-); Arts Humanit. Citation Index [Full Cov.]; Book Rev. Index; Curr. Contents Arts Humanit.; Expand. Acad. Index (1984-); Gen. Period. Index (1985-); Mag. Artic. Summar. Elite (Jan. 1984-); Mag. Artic. Summar. Select (Jan. 1984-); Mag. Artic. Summar. CD-ROM (Jan. 1984-); Mag. Express (1988-) [Full Txt.]; Mag. Index Plus (1989-); Mag. Index. Sel. (1986-); Mag. Search; Music Artic. Guide; Music Index; Newsp. Period. Abstr. (1988-); Read. Guide Abstr. Select Ed.; Read. Guide Period. Lit.; Res. Alert [Full Cov.]; Resource/One Ondisc; RILM Abstr.; Mag. Index (1977-); Vocat. Search (Jan. 1984-).

CN/0703-458X
**DOWN HOME.** **VFOAT** Downhome. (Sept. 1976)-. Periodical. English. bm. Down Home / Orangeville, 66 Carlton Drive, Orangeville, Ontario L9W 2X9 Canada. **DD** 780/.42/05.

US/0095-3717
**DRIVING WHEEL.** Vol. 1 (Dec. 1973)-. English. Driving Wheel, 82 Clematis Avenue, Waltham MA 02154. **LC** ML1; .D744. **DD** 780/.5.

US/0012-6748
**DRUM CORPS NEWS.** ***Ceased.*** Periodical. English. ir. Tri Star Enterprises Inc, Box 108, Boston MA 02199. **Tel** (617)289-8571.
**Ind/Abst** Music Artic. Guide (?-?).

US/0094-3649
**DRUM CORPS REVIEW.** (19??)-. English. Government Printing Office / Brooklyn, PO Box 495, Brooklyn NY 11201. **LC** ML1; .D748. **DD** 785/.06/71. ***Continues*** *Eastern Review.*

US/0164-3223
**DRUM CORPS WORLD (MADISON).** (DRUM CORPS WORLD.). **Added/Corp** Drum Corps Sights and Sounds. (19??)-. Periodical. English. Twenty times a year (monthly Sept.-May; 3 issues June; 4 issues July and Aug.). $63.00 US & Canada, $83.00 (airmail) Europe, $121.00 (airmail); other $43.00 US, $53.00 Canada (second class mail). Drum Corps World, PO Box 8052, Madison WI 53708-8052. **Tel** (608)241-2292, FAX (608)241-4974. **ED** Steve Vickers. **LC** ML1306; .D78. **DD** 785/.06/7105. **Ad Acc, Adv Mgr:** Jeff Collins, **Tel** (916)392-6994. **Circ:** 5,000.
**Desc:** The most complete coverage of drum and bugle corps and color guard activities available today.

US
**DRUM MAJOR.** (Aug. 1, 1971)-. Periodical. English. Eleven times a year. $12.00. Drum Major Publishing, P.O.Box 266, Janesville WI 53547. **Tel** (608)754-2238. **ED** Don Sartell. **DD** 301.45.

US/1052-3324
**DRUMS & DRUMMING.** ***Title Change.*** [Drums drum.]. **VFOAT** Drums and Drumming; D & D. Vol. 1, No. 6 (Oct./Nov. 1989)-(1992). Periodical. English. bm. Modern Drummer Publications, 870 Pompton Avenue, Cedar Grove NJ 07009. **Tel** (201)239-4140, (800)221-1988, FAX (201)239-7139. **LC** ML1030; .D78. **DD** 786.9/05. ***Continues in part*** *GPI Collector's Edition, 1044-6656.* ***Merged into*** *Modern Drummer, 0194-4533.*

US/0098-3527
**DULCIMER PLAYER NEWS, THE.** Vol. 1 (Jan. 1975)-. Periodical. English. qt. $15.00 (1 year), $27.00 (2 year) US; $17.00 other. Dulcimer Player News, PO Box 2164, Winchester VA 22604. **Tel** (703)678-1305. **ED** Madeline MacNeil. **LC** ML1; .D78. **DD** 787/.9. **Bk Rev**, (Qty: 6 /year). **Ad Acc. Circ:** 2,200 (ctrl).
**Desc:** Contains information on hammer and fretted dulcimers for builders and players. Includes an events calendar, reviews, interviews and musical arrangements.
**Ind/Abst** Music Index.

US/0893-9500
**EAR (NEW YORK, N.Y.).** ***Ceased.*** (EAR.). [Ear]. Vol. 9, No. 1 (May/June 1984)-(1992). Periodical. English. mo. $20.00 (individuals), $40.00 (institutions) US; $40.00 (individuals), $40.00 (institutions) other. Ear Magazine, 131 Varrick Street/Room 905, New York NY 10013-0323. **Tel** (212)807-7944. **ED** Carol E Tuynman, Iris Brooks, and David L L Laskin. **LC** ML197; .E2. **DD** 780/.904. Index available. cum. index. **Bk Rev. Ad Acc. Circ:** 20,000. ***Continues*** *Ear Magazine (New York, N.Y. : 1983), 0748-4291.*
**Desc:** Covers experimental, avant-garde, and world music from a multi-media perspective, EAR strives to foster appreciation and understanding of new music and sound art worldwide.
**Ind/Abst** Music Index.

UK/0424-0359
**EARLY ENGLISH CHURCH MUSIC.** **Added/Corp** British Academy. (1963)-. Monographic series. English. ir. Price varies per volume. Stainer & Bell, 23 Gruneisen Road, Victoria House, London N3 1DZ England. **Tel** 011 44 81 343 3303. **(Subscription address:** Stainer & Bell Ltd., PO Box 110, London N3 1DZ England.**) ED** Frank L. Harrison. ctrl circ.
**Desc:** Contains music with introduction and textual commentary.

US/0899-8132
**EARLY KEYBOARD JOURNAL.** (EARLY KEYBOARD JOURNAL / SOUTHEASTERN HISTORICAL KEYBOARD SOCIETY.). [Early keyboard j.]. **Added/Corp** Southeastern Historical Keyboard Society (U.S.) University of Georgia. School of Music. Vol. 1 (1983)-. English. an (Summer and Fall). $30.00 (institutions); $25.00 (individuals). Southeastern Historical Keyboard Society, PO Box 32022, Charolette NC 28232. **Tel** (704)334-3468. **ED** Lilian Pruett and Tom MacCracken (phone: (202)547-7402). **LC** ML549.8; .E2. **DD** 786/.05. Index available. cum. index. **Bk Rev**, (Qty: 5-10). **Ad Acc, Adv Mgr:** K. Jacob, **Tel** (704)334-3468. **Pr Rev. Circ:** 500-600.
**Desc:** This journal is about the early keyboard music and instruments prior to 1860.
**Ind/Abst** Music Index.

US/0882-0201
**EARLY KEYBOARD STUDIES NEWSLETTER.** (EARLY KEYBOARD STUDIES NEWSLETTER : A PUBLICATION OF THE WESTFIELD CENTER FOR EARLY KEYBOARD STUDIES, INC.). [Early keyboard stud. newsl.]. **Added/Corp** Westfield Center for Early Keyboard Studies (Easthampton, Mass.). Vol. 1, No. 1 (Dec. 1984)-. Newsletter. English. qt (Jan., Apr., July, Oct.). Free to members; $40.00 (nonmembers) US; $45.00 (nonmembers) Canada; $48.00 (nonmembers) other. Westfield Center for Early Keyboard Studies Inc, 1 Cottage Street, Easthampton MA 01027. **Tel** (413)527-7664. **ED** Gregory Hayes. **DD** 786. **Bk Rev. Ad Acc. Circ:** 550.
**Desc:** Includes articles of interest to performers and scholars of early keyboard music, including 19th-century piano. Emphasis is on organology and performance practice, but bibliographical studies and reviews of books and editions are included.

UK/0306-1078
**EARLY MUSIC.** [Early music]. Vol. 1 (Jan. 1973)-. Periodical. English. qt. £49.00 UK and Europe; $85.00 other. Oxford University Press, Walton Street, Oxford OX2 6DP England. **Tel** 011 44 865 56767, FAX 011 44 865 267773, telex 837330 OXPRES G. **(Subscription address:** Oxford University Press / USA, Journals Marketing Department, Oxford University Press, 2001 Evans Road, Cary NC 27513.**) ED** Nicholas Kenyon. **LC** ML5; .E18. **DD** 780/.5. **[CCC]**. Index available. **Bk Rev. Ad Acc**. available on microfilm and microfiche from University Microfilms International (UMI). Documents available from The Genuine Article, UMI Article Clearinghouse.
**Desc:** Offers a comprehensive fully illustrated guide to every aspect of medieval, renaissance, baroque, and classical music. Covers reviews of books, music and recordings, correspondence and saleroom reports.
**Ind/Abst** Acad. Search (July 1993-); Am. Hist. Life (1986-); Art Archaeol. Tech. Abstr.; Arts Humanit. Citation Index [Full Cov.]; BHA : Biblio. Hist. Art; Br. Humanit. Index; Curr. Contents Arts Humanit.; Expand. Acad. Index (1989-); Humanit. Index; Humanit. Source (Jul. 1993-); INFO-SOUTH Abstr.; Mag. Search; Music Index; Newsp. Period. Abstr. (1991-); Res. Alert [Full Cov.]; RILM Abstr.

UK/0261-1279
**EARLY MUSIC HISTORY.** (1981)-. Academic Scholarly Publication. English. an (January). $92.00 US, Canada & Mexico; £50.00 other. Cambridge University Press, The Edinburgh Building, Shaftesbury Road, Cambridge CB2 2RU United Kingdom. **Tel** 011 44 223 312393, FAX 011 44 223 325959. **(Subscription address:** Cambridge University Press / North America, 110 Midland Avenue, Port Chester NY 10573.**) ED** Iain Fenlon. **LC** ML169.8; .E15. **DD** 780/.902/05. **[CCC]. Bk Rev**. available on microfilm and microfiche from University Microfilms International (UMI). Documents available from The Genuine Article.
**Desc:** Devoted to the study of music from the early Middle Ages to the seventeenth century. Gives preference to studies pursuing interdisciplinary approaches and those developing new methodological ideas. The scope is broad and includes manuscript studies, textual criticism, iconography, studies of the relationship between words and music, and the relationship between music and society. The aim is to bring together British, European and North American scholarship.
**Ind/Abst** Am. Hist. Life (1985-); Arts Humanit. Citation Index (19??-19??) [Full Cov.]; Curr. Contents Arts Humanit.; Res. Alert [Full Cov.].

UK
**EARLY MUSIC NEWS.** No. 1, (Aug. 1977)-. Periodical. English. Eleven times a year (July/Aug. issue combined). £21.50 EEC countries; £19.50 UK; £28.00 US; £34.00 Australia and Japan. Early Music News, Sutton House 2-4 Homerton High, London E9 6JQ England. **Tel** 011 44 71 727 6339. **LC** ML5; .E19. **DD** 780/.5. **Ad Acc. Circ:** 1,000 (ctrl). available on an online database, CD-ROM, magnetic tape, and microfilm; available on CD-ROM and an online database.

NE
**EARLY MUSIC THEORY IN THE LOW COUNTRIES.** English (German, French and Dutch). ir. Uitgeverij Frits Knuf B V, PO Box 720, 4116 ZJ Buuren Netherlands. **Tel** 011 31 03449-1255, FAX 011 31 03449-2617. **Circ:** 700.

US
**EAST COAST ROCKER.** (19??)-. English. wk (Wed.). $100.00 (one year); $175.00 (two years). Arts Weekly, PO Box 137, Montclair NJ 07042. **Tel** (201)783-4346, FAX (201)783-5057. **ED** Robert Makin. **Ad Acc, Adv Mgr:** D. Hein. **Circ:** 40,000.

US/0147-345X
**EASTMAN NOTES.** **Main/Corp** Eastman School of Music. (19??)-. English. Four times a year. Free. University Rochester, Eastman School of Music, 26 Gibbs Street, Rochester NY 14604. **Tel** (716)274-1550. **ED** Albert Rodenald. **LC** MT4.R6; E263. **DD** 780/.729747/89. **Bk Rev. Circ:** 8,000 (ctrl).
**Desc:** Information and articles of interest to Eastman School alumni and friends.
**Ind/Abst** Music Artic. Guide.

UK
**EASY LISTENING.** No. 1 (Jan. 1973)-. Periodical. English. mo. Cardfont Publishers, 7 Carnaby Street, London W1V 1PG London England. **LC** ML5; .E2. **DD** 780/.42/05.

FR/0013-1415
**EDUCATION MUSICALE, L'.** [Educ. music.]. (1945)-. Periodical. French. mo. 350.00F (France); 425.00F (other). L'Education Musicale, 23 rue Benard, 75014 Paris France. **Tel** 11 33 1 45423407. **ED** Charles Negiar. Index available. **Ad Acc. Circ:** 7,000 (ctrl).
**Desc:** Review centers on musical subjects: history, musicology, psychology, pedagogy, techniques and instruments.
**Ind/Abst** RILM Abstr.

FR/0013-2357
**EGLISE QUI CHANTE.** ***Ceased.*** No. 1 (1957)-(19??). Periodical. French. Six times a year (Jan., Mar., May, July, Sept., Nov.). Editions du CERF, BP 65, 77932 Perthes Cedex France. **Tel** 011 33 1 44181212. **DD** 783.
**Desc:** Chants for Liturgical Assemblies.

IE/0332-298X
**EIGSE CHEOL TIRE.** **See** Music-Abstracting, Bibliographies and Statistics.

US
**ELDERSONG.** English. bm (Jan., Mar., May, July, Sept., Nov.). $15.00 (one year), $26.00 (two year). Eldersong Publications, PO Box 74, Mt. Airy MD 21771. **Tel** (301)829-0533, FAX (301)829-5249. **ED** Beckie Karras. **Bk Rev. Circ:** 400.
**Desc:** Publishes information and ideas for music therapists working with the elderly.

UK
**ELECTROACOUSTIC MUSIC.** **Added/Corp** Electro-Acoustic Music Association of Great Britain. **VFOAT** Electro-Acoustic-Music. Vol. 1, No. 1 (Sept. 1984)-. Periodical. English. qt. Electro Acoustic Music Assn, 10 Stratford Place, London W1N 9AE England. **Tel** 011 44 71 499 2576. **LC** ML73; .E38. **DD** 786.7/05. ***Continues*** *Electro-Acoustic Music Association of Great Britain. EMAS Newsletter.*

US/1044-3150
**ELECTRONIC MUSIC EDUCATOR.** **See** Computers-Computer Music.

US/0884-4720
**ELECTRONIC MUSICIAN.** [Electron. music.]. Vol. 1, No. 1 (June 1985)-. Periodical. English. Twelve times a year. $25.98 New York; $24.00 other US; $39.00 Canada; $54.00 other. Cardinal Business Media, Inc., 6400 Hollis Street, Suite 12, Emeryville CA 94608. **Tel** (510)653-3307, FAX (510)653-5142. **ED** Michael Molenda. **LC** ML1380; .E4. **DD** 789.9/9/05. **Ad Acc, Adv Mgr:** Robin Boyce. **Circ:** 60,381. ***Continues*** *Polyphony, 0163-4534.*
**Desc:** This professional's magazine on using technology to make and record music. These articles help readers choose and use the instruments, software and recording equipment for today's technically advanced industry.
**Ind/Abst** ACM Guide Comput. Lit.; Comput. Rev.; Music Index (-19??).

US/0160-1148
**ELECTRONOTES.** [Electronotes]. **Added/Corp** Musical Engineering Group. Vol. 5, No. 33 (Jan. 1974)-. Periodical. English. ir. Electronotes, 203 Snyder Hill Road, Ithaca NY 14850. **Tel** (607)273-8030. ***Continues*** *Electronotes Newsletter.*
**Ind/Abst** RILM Abstr.

NE
**ELVIS COSTELLO INFORMATION SERVICE.** (19??)-. English (Dutch). Six times a year. $21.78. Elvis Costello Information Service, Primulastaat 46, 1441 HC Purmerend Netherlands. **Tel** 011 31 29 9024256. **ED** Richard Groothuizen. Index available. cum. index. **Bk Rev. Ad Acc. Pr Rev. Circ:** 700 (ctrl).
**Desc:** A magazine dedicated to to the music of Elvis Costello. Information on releases worldwide, concerts, radio, TV, videos, research and more.

UK/0013-6484
**ELVIS MONTHLY.** [Elvis mthly.]. (1958)-. Periodical. English. Twelve times a year. £19.20. Heanor Record Centre Ltd., 6 Empire Road, Leicester England. **Bk Rev. Ad Acc. Circ:** 20,000.
**Desc:** Written by its readership. Illustrated in colour and black and white.

CN/0712-631X
**ENCORE (EDMONTON).** (ENCORE.). [Encore]. **Added/Corp** Edmonton Symphony Society. Alberta Ballet Company. Vol. 1, No. 1 (Sept. 14, 1979)-. Periodical. English. bm. Free. Association ICC Practitioners, 1112 ICC Building, Washington DC 20423. **DD** 785/.06/271233. ***Continues*** *Arts Edmonton, 0712-6301.*

FR
**ENSEIGNEMENT MUSICAL.** (19??)-. Periodical. French. mo. EGP, 9 rue Coetlogon, 75006 Paris France. **LC** ML5; .E6. **DD** 780/.5.

IT
**ENTE RASSEGNE MUSICALI N.S. DI LORETO.** (1981)-. Monographic series. Italian. ir. Price varies per volume.

CN
**ENTRE NOUS (MONTREAL, QUEBEC : 1981).** (ENTRE NOUS : C.I.O.F.F. BULLETIN.). **Added/Corp** C.I.O.F.F. Canadian Folk Arts Council. **VFOAT** Entre Nous. (19??)-. Bulletin. English (French). an. Canadian Folk Arts Council / Montreal, 1499 de Bleury, Suite 200, Montreal, Quebec H3A 2H5 Canada. **DD** 791/.6.

US/1050-7868
**EQ (CUPERTINO, CALIF.).** (EQ.). [EQ]. (Mar./Apr. 1990)-. Periodical. English. Six times a year (Feb., Apr., June, Aug., Oct., Dec.). $27.97 (one year); $55.94 (two years); $83.91 (three years). PSN Publications, 2 Park Avenue, Suite 1820, New York NY 10016. **Tel** (212)213-3444, FAX (212)213-3484. **(Subscription address:** EQ, PO Box 0532, Baldwin NY 11510.**) LC** WMLC 93/1279. **DD** 789.

GW/0425-1695
**ERBE DEUTSCHER MUSIK. SONDERREIHE / HERAUSGEGEBEN IM AUFTRAGE DES STAATLICHEN INSTITUTS FUER MUSIKFORSCHUNG, DAS.** **Added/Corp** Staatliche Institut fur Musikforschung. **VFOAT** Sonderreihe. Vol. 1 (1954)-. Monographic series. German. ir. Price varies per volume. Breitkopf and Haertel, Obere Waldstr 30, D 65232 Taunusstein Germany. **Tel** 11 49 611 49030. **(Subscription address:** Foreign Music Distributors, 13 Elkay Drive, Chester, New York 10918, (phone: (914)469-5790)**) DD** 780.
**Desc:** A series of music monuments divided among several publishers. Baereneiter's divisions: chamber music, middle ages, oratorio and cantata.

FR
**ESCARGOT, L'.** **Added/Corp** Folk Song International. (19??)-. Periodical. French. mo. Folk Song International, 43 rue Leon Frot, Paris 75011 France. **LC** ML5; .E777. **DD** 784.4/005.

FR
**ESCARGOT FOLK?, L'.** **Added/Corp** Folk Song International. No. 43 (May 1977)-. Periodical. French. mo. Folk Song International, 43 rue Leon Frot, Paris 75011 France. **LC** ML5; .E777. **DD** 784.4/005. ***Continues*** *L'Escargot.*

GW
**ESSAYS ON MUSIC IN AFRICA.** **Added/Corp** IWALEWA-Haus. Vol. 1, (1988)-. English. Essays on Music in Africa, IEALEWA-Haus, Universitat of Bayreuth, Bayreuth W Germany. **LC** ML5; .E79. **DD** 780/.96/05.

US
**ETC / EXECUTIVE TRAVEL COLLECTION.** (19??)-. English. an. $39.00. Network Magazine Group, 120 North Victory Boulevard, Burbank CA 91502. **Tel** (818)955-4000, (800)222-4382, FAX (818)955-8048.

US/0014-1836
**ETHNOMUSICOLOGY.** [Ethnomusicology]. **Added/Corp** Society for Ethnomusicology. Vol. 1, No. 9 (Jan. 1957)-. Periodical. English. Three times a year. $50.00. Society for Ethnomusicology, Morrison Hall 005, Indiana University, Bloomington IN 47405. **Tel** (812)855-6672, FAX (812)855-6673. **ED** Jeff Liton. **LC** ML1; .E77. **[CCC].** Index available in last issue of volume--attached. cum. index. **Bk Rev. Ad Acc. Circ:** 2,000 (ctrl). available on microfilm and microfiche from University Microfilms International (UMI). Documents available from The Genuine Article, UMI Article Clearinghouse. ***Continues** Ethno-Musicology, 0014-1836.*
**Desc:** Advancement of research and study in all cultural contexts.
**Ind/Abst** Abstr. Anthropol.; Acad. Search (July 1993-); Am. Bibliogr. Slavic East Europ. Stud.; Anthropol. Lit.; Arts Humanit. Citation Index [Full Cov.]; Curr. Contents, Agric. Biol. Environ. Sci.; Curr. Contents Life Sci.; Ethnoarts Index; Expand. Acad. Index (1989-); Humanit. Index; Humanit. Source (Jul. 1993-); INFO-SOUTH Abstr.; Mag. Search; Middle East Abstr. Index; MLA Int. Bibl. Books Artic. Mod. Lang. Lit.; Music Artic. Guide; Music Index; Newsp. Period. Abstr. (1991-); Res. Alert [Full Cov.]; RILM Abstr.; Soc. Sci. Cit. Index [Select. Cov.].

●US
**ETHNOMUSICOLOGY AND SYSTEMATIC MUSICOLOGY AT UCLA.** **Added/Corp** University of California, Los Angeles. Dept. of Ethnomusicology and Systematic Musicology. Vol. 7, No. 1 (Spring/Summer 1991)-. Periodical. English. sa. UCLA / Department of Ethnomusicology, Los Angeles CA 90024. **Tel** (310)825-5947. ***Continues** Ethnomusicology at UCLA.*

US/0749-4033
**ETHNOMUSICOLOGY AT UCLA.** ***Title Change.*** (ETHNOMUSICOLOGY AT UCLA : NEWSLETTER OF THE PROGRAM IN ETHNOMUSICOLOGY, UCLA DEPARTMENT OF MUSIC.). [Ethnomusicol. UCLA]. **Added/Corp** University of California, Los Angeles. Program in Ethnomusicology. University of California, Los Angeles. Dept. of Ethnomusicology and Systematic Musicology. **VFOAT** Ethnomusicology at U.C.L.A. **VAT** Ethnomusicology at University of California, Los Angeles. Vol. 1, No. 1 (1983)-(199?). Newsletter. English. sa. UCLA / Department of Ethnomusicology, Los Angeles CA 90024. **Tel** (310)825-5947. **ED** Eran Fraenkel. **DD** 781. **Circ:** 2,000. ***Continued by** Ethnomusicology and Systematic Musicology at UCLA.*
**Desc:** Reports on the activities and research conducted by the program in ethnomusicology at UCLA.

US/1054-1624
**ETHNOMUSICOLOGY RESEARCH DIGEST.** (ETHNOMUSICOLOGY RESEARCH DIGEST : [COMPUTER FILE].). [Ethnomusicol. res. dig.]. Vol 1, No 1 (Dec. 20, 1989)-. Periodical. English. Free. Karl Signell, 7208 Wells Parkway West, Hyattsville MD 20782-1038. **LC** ML3797.6; .E84. **DD** 780.
**Desc:** Available through BITNET and other networks.

NE
**EURO FILE MUSIC INDUSTRY DIRECTORY.** Directory. English. an. Fl135.00 Benelux; DM120.00 Germany, Switzerland, and Austria; £40.00 UK; 420.00F France; $90.00 other. Music & Media, PO Box 9027, 1006 AA Amsterdam Netherlands. **Tel** 31 20 669 1961, FAX 31 20 669 1941. **ED** Cesco Van Gool. **Ad Acc, Adv Mgr:** Ron Betist.
**Desc:** Provides information on 11,000 companies in the European music industry. Includes names and positions of thousands of top executives, a cross-index by company name and country-by-country factfiles.

CN/0276-6795
**EX TEMPORE.** (EX TEMPORE : ANALYTICAL AND THEORETICAL PAPERS FROM THE DEPARTMENT OF MUSIC, THE UNIVERSITY OF CALIFORNIA AT SAN DIEGO.). **Added/Corp** University of California, San Diego. Dept. of Music. University of Alberta. Dept. of Music. Vol. 1 (Jan. 1981)-. Periodical. English. ir. $15.00. University of Colorado at Denver, Department of Music, PO Box 173364, Campus Box 162, Denver CO 80217-3364. **Tel** (303)556-2727, FAX (303)556-2335. **ED** John W. MacKay. **LC** ML1; .E9. **DD** 780/.5. **Bk Rev. Ad Acc. Circ:** 50.
**Desc:** Theoretical and analytical research in contemporary music and contemporary music theory.
**Ind/Abst** Music Index (-19??).

NE
**EXEMPLA MUSICA NEERLANDICA.** Vol. 1 (1964)-. Monographic series. Dutch. ir. Price varies per volume. Vereniging voor Nederlandse Muziekgeschiedenis, PO Box 1514, 3500 BM Utrecht Netherlands. **Tel** 011 31 30 23327787.

US/0883-0754
**EXPERIMENTAL MUSICAL INSTRUMENTS.** Vol. 1, No. 1 (June 1985)-. Periodical. English. Four times a year (Mar., June, Sept., Dec.). $24.00 US; $27.00 Canada and Mexico; $34.00 other. Experimental Musical Instruments, PO Box 784, Nicasio CA 94946. **Tel** (415)662-2182.
**Ind/Abst** Music Artic. Guide.

US
**EXPLORATIONS IN MUSIC LIBRARIANSHIP.** ***Ceased.* See** Library and Information Sciences.

RU
**EZHEGODNIK PAMIATNYKH MUZYKALNYKH DAT I SOBYTII.** (19??)-. Russian. an. **LC** ML5; .E99.

UK/0263-1210
**FACE (LONDON, ENGLAND).** (THE FACE.). No. 1 (1980)-. Periodical. English. Twelve times a year. £22.00 UK, £36.00 Europe, £28.00 others (surface mail); £60.00 (airmail). MRM Promotional Services Ltd., Premier House, Farndon Road, Market Hrbr. LEI LE16 9NR England. **Tel** 011 44 858 410510. **(Subscription address:** MRM Promotional Services Ltd., PO Box 500, Subscriptions Department, Leicester LE99 0AA England.**)** **LC** WMLC 93/1292.

US/0882-2921
**FACES ROCKS.** ***Suspended.*** [Faces rocks]. **VFOAT** Faces. Vol. 1, No. 2 (Dec. 1983)-Suspended (1993). Periodical. English. Four times a year. Faces Magazine, 63 Grand Avenue / Suite 230, River Edge NJ 07661. **Tel** (201)487-6124, FAX (201)487-9360. **ED** Lorena Alexander and Greg Fasolino. **LC** ML3533.8; .F3. **DD** 784.5/4/005. **Bk Rev. Ad Acc.** ***Continues** Faces (New York, N.Y.), 0883-8658.*

NE
**FACSIMILE OF DUTCH SONGBOOKS.** (19??)-. Monographic series. Dutch. ir. Price varies per volume. Uitgeverij Frits Knuf B V, PO Box 720, 4116 ZJ Buuren Netherlands. **Tel** 011 31 03449-1255, FAX 011 31 03449-2617. **Circ:** 700.

NE
**FACSIMILIA MUSICA NEERLANDICA.** **Added/Corp** Vereniging voor Nederlandse Muziekgeschiedenis. (1979)-. Monographic series. English (Latin). ir. Price varies per volume. Uitgeverij Frits Knuf B V, PO Box 720, 4116 ZJ Buuren Netherlands. **Tel** 011 31 03449-1255, FAX 011 31 03449-2617. **LC** M2; .F17.

GW/0430-0246
**FAKSIMILE-REIHE BACHSCHER WERKE UND SCHRIFTSTUCKE.** **Added/Corp** Bach-Archiv, Leipzig. (1955)-. Monographic series. German. ir. Price varies per volume. Baerenreiter-Verlag, KGA Verlagssvc PF 100329, D 34003 Kassel Germany. **Tel** 011 49 561 31050, telex 99504. **(Subscription address:** KGA Kasseler Grossauslieferung, Postfach 102180, D 34021 Kassel Germany.**)** **ED** W. Neumann.

US/8755-268X
**FALLEN LEAF MUSIC REFERENCE BOOKS.** ***Title Change.*** (FALLEN LEAF REFERENCE BOOKS IN MUSIC.). [Fallen Leaf music ref. books]. **Added/Corp** Fallen Leaf Press. (1984)-?. Monographic series. English. ir. Fallen Leaf Press, PO Box 10034, Berkeley CA 94709. **Tel** (510)848-7805. **ED** Ann Basart. **DD** 780. ***Continued by** Fallen Leaf Reference Books in Music.*
**Desc:** Reference books in music.

US/8755-2698
**FALLEN LEAF PUBLICATIONS IN CONTEMPORARY MUSIC.** (1985)-. Monographic series. English. ir. Price varies per volume. Fallen Leaf Press, PO Box 10034, Berkeley CA 94709. **Tel** (510)848-7805. **ED** Ann Basart. **LC** UNC. **DD** 780. **Circ:** 60.
**Desc:** Series of musical scores by contemporary American composers.

US/0148-9364
**FANFARE (TENAFLY, N.J.).** (FANFARE.). [Fanfare]. Vol. 1, (Sept. 1977)-. Periodical. English. Six times a year (Jan., Mar., May, July, Sept., Nov.). $34.00 (one year); $67.00 (two years); $99.00 (three years). Fanfare, PO Box 720, Tenafly NJ 07670. **Tel** (201)567-3908. **ED** Joel Flegler. **LC** ML156.9; .F36. Index available. **Bk Rev. Ad Acc. Circ:** 20,000 (ctrl).
**Desc:** Largest record review magazine in the world concentrating mostly on classical reviews. Equipment and book reviews also.
**Ind/Abst** Music Artic. Guide (?-?); Music Index.

IT
**FARE MUSICA.** (19??)-. Italian. mo. 7000000L. Ediscreen, Via G Calderini 68, 00196 Rome Italy. **Tel** 011 39 6 3233212.

US/8755-9137
**FAST FOLK MUSICAL MAGAZINE.** [Fast folk music. mag.]. Vol. 1, No. 1 (Jan. 1984)-. Periodical. English. Ten times a year (includes 10 magazines and 10 records per year). $65.00. Fast Folk Musical Magazine, PO Box 938 Village Station, New York NY 10014. **Tel** (718)935-0389. **ED** Richard Meyer. **LC** ML3551; .F26. **DD** 781.773/05. Index available ($1.00). cum. index. **Bk Rev. Ad Acc. Circ:** 1,500 (ctrl).
**Desc:** A unique full-length album/magazine. Each issue contains 12 recorded songs with accompanying magazine listing lyrics and related written articles.

GW
**FASZINATION MUSIK / ZDF.** **Added/Corp** Zweites Deutsches Fernsehen. (1986)-. German. Faszination Musik/ZDF, Zweites Deutsches Fernsehen, Information und Presse, Offentlichkeitsarbeit, Mainz Germany. **LC** PN1992.8.M87; F37. **DD** 791.45/657.

SZ
**FEDERATION MONDIALE DES CONCOURS INTERNATIONAUX DE MUSIQUE : BROCHURE.** **Added/Corp** World Federation of International Music Competitions. (198?)-. French. an. Federation Mondiale des Concours Internationaux de Musique, 104 rue de Carouge, CH-1205 Geneve Switzerland. **Tel** (4122)213620, FAX (4122)7811418. **LC** ML75.5; .F43. **DD** 780/.79.

CN/0822-4978
**FESTIVAL OF FRIENDS.** (FESTIVAL OF FRIENDS : [PROGRAM].). [Festiv. Friends]. **Main/Conf** Festival of Friends (Hamilton, Ont.). **Added/Corp** Hamilton-Wentworth Creative Arts. (1976)-. Periodical. English. ir. Hamilton-Wentworth Creative Arts, 21 Augusta Street, Hamilton Ontario L8N 1P6 Canada. **DD** 780/.7/971352.

AG
**FICTA.** Vol. 1, Nov./Dec. (1976)-. Periodical. Spanish. ir. Mexico 1208, Buenos Aires 1097 Argentina. **LC** ML5; .F52. **DD** 780/.5.

US/0160-0850
**FIDDLE & A BOW.** ***Suspended.*** **VAT** Fiddle and a Bow. (19??)-Suspended. Periodical. English. mo. Fiddle & a Bow, 1008 North Monterey Street, Alhambra CA 91801. **LC** ML1; .F24. **DD** 780/.42.
**Desc:** Bluegrass music.

US/0196-187X
**FIGA.** **Main/Corp** Fretted Instrument Guild of America. **VAT** Fretted Instrument Guild of America. (May/June 1978)-. Periodical. English. Six times a year. $18.00 (membership). Fretted Instrument Guild of America, 2344 South Oakley Avenue, Chicago IL 60608. **Tel** (312)376-1143. **ED** Glen Lemmer. **LC** ML1; .F679. **DD** 787/.005. **Ad Acc. Circ:** 2,000 (ctrl). ***Continues** FIGA Review, 0196-1861.*
**Desc:** Music news on banjo, mandolin, guitar and kindred instruments. International information and music for these instruments and their artists.

US/1055-081X
**FILM COMPOSERS GUIDE. See** Motion Picture.

US/0091-7591
**FIND CATALOG.** (Oct. 1971)-. Catalog. English. $14.00. Find Service International, PO Box 775, Terre Haute IN 47808. **LC** ML156.2; .F54. **DD** 381/.45/789912.

FI/0782-1069
**FINNISH MUSIC QUARTERLY.** **Added/Corp** Performing Music Promotion Centre (Finland) Luovan Saveltaiteen Edistamissaatio (Finland) Sibelius-Akatemia (Helsinki, Finland). **VFOAT** FMQ. (1985)-. Periodical. English (French). Four times a year (Feb., May, Sept., Dec.). Fmk120.00 Finland and Scandinavia; Fmk150.00 other. Finnish Music Quarterly, Hietaniemenkatu 2, 00100 Helsinki Finland. **Tel** 011/358/0/490525, FAX 011/358/0/441224. **ED** Ainomaija Pennanen and Antero Kartiunen. **LC** ML3619; .F55. **DD** 781.74897/05. Index available. cum. index. **Ad Acc. Circ:** 3,000 (ctrl).
**Ind/Abst** Music Index.

NE
**FIRE-BALL MAIL.** (19??)-. English. bm (6 issues). $20.00. Fire-Ball Mail, Jan Hendrikxstraat 22, 5684 XJ Best Netherlands. **ED** Wim de Boer.
**Desc:** Publication of the Jerry Lee Lewis International Fan Club.

US/0090-7308
**FLAG.** (FLAG; THE MUSIC SCENE.). Vol. 2, No. 8/9 (Nov./Dec. 1972)-. Periodical. English. mo. $6.00. F.P.B. Enterprises, 310 Evesham Road, Glendora NJ 08029. **LC** ML1; .F327. **DD** 784. ***Continues** Freedoms Country Flag.*

US/0046-4155
**FLORIDA MUSIC DIRECTOR.** **Added/Corp** Florida Music Educators Association. Florida State Music Teachers Association. Vol. 23, (Aug. 1969)-. English. Ten times a year. $12.00. Florida Music Educators Association, Florida Music Director, 207 Office Plaza Drive, Tallahassee FL 32301. **Tel** (904)878-6844. **ED** Reid Poole. **LC** ML1; .M2325. **DD** 780/.729759. **Bk Rev. Ad Acc. Circ:** 4,200 (ctrl). ***Continues** Music Director.*

**Desc:** Carries articles and news of interest to music educators, music teachers and music students in Florida. Includes reviews of band, orchestra, piano and choral music.
**Ind/Abst** Music Artic. Guide.

NE
**FLUTE LIBRARY, THE.** (1973)-. German (English, French and Dutch). ir. Uitgeverij Frits Knuf B V, PO Box 720, 4116 ZJ Buuren Netherlands. **Tel** 011 31 03449-1255, FAX 011 31 03449-2617. **ED** Rien de Reede. **Circ:** 700.
**Desc:** Books about the flute.

US/0744-6918
**FLUTE TALK.** [Flute talk]. **Added/Corp** Instrumentalist Publishing Company. Instrumentalist Co. Vol. 1, No. 1 (Sept. 1981)-. Periodical. English. mo (except June and Aug.). $15.00 (one year), $26.00 (two year), US; $20.00 (one year), $36.00 (two year) other. Instrumentalist Company, 200 Northfield Road, Northfield IL 60093. **Tel** (708)446-5000, FAX (708)446-6263. **ED** Kathleen Goll-Wilson. **LC** ML929; .F6. **DD** 788/.51/05. **Ad Acc. Circ:** 13,000.
**Desc:** The art of flute playing including interviews with classical and jazz flutists, performance guides on standard pieces in flute repertoire, and other flute related topics.
**Ind/Abst** Music Artic. Guide; Music Index.

US/0737-8459
**FLUTE WORKER, THE.** [Flute worker]. **Added/Corp** Flute Works, Etc. (Firm). (19??)-. Periodical. English. sa. The Flute Works, 1146 Biltmore Drive Northeast, Atlanta GA 30329. **LC** ML929; .F65. **DD** 788/.51/05.

US/8756-8667
**FLUTIST QUARTERLY, THE.** (THE FLUTIST QUARTERLY : THE OFFICIAL MAGAZINE OF THE NATIONAL FLUTE ASSOCIATION.). **Added/Corp** National Flute Association. Vol. 9, No. 3 (Spring 1984)-. Periodical. English. Four times a year. $12.50 students, $20.00 NFA membership. National Flute Association Inc., 805 Laguna Drive, Denton TX 76201. **Tel** (817)387-9472. **ED** Glennis M. Stout. **LC** ML27.U5; N3676. **DD** 788/.5/05. cum. index. **Ad Acc. Circ:** 4,600 (ctrl). ***Continues*** *Newsletter (National Flute Association).*
**Desc:** Articles and information on flutes and flutists: history, teaching, performing, music, flute clubs, competitions, classes, conventions, flute making and design; includes biographies and interviews.
**Ind/Abst** Music Artic. Guide (?-?); Music Index.

●US/1065-4631
**FLY! (BALDWIN, N.Y.).** (FLY!.). [Fly!]. **VFOAT** Fly Magazine. No. 1 (1992)-. Periodical. English. bm. $14.00. Jack/Howard Publishing Co., 807 Vivian Court, Baldwin NY 11510. **DD** 781.

US
**FOLIO-DEX VOCAL, PIANO AND ORGAN FINDING LIST.** (1963)-. English. bm. $225.00. **ED** Darlene Poole. **Circ:** 1,100.
**Desc:** Music reference book, including song titles, composers, copyright owners and publishers; covers all types of music.

UK/0430-876X
**FOLK DIRECTORY, THE.** **See** Societies and Clubs.

US/0094-8934
**FOLK HARP JOURNAL.** [Folk harp j.]. Vol. 1 (June 1973)-. Periodical. English. Four times a year (Mar., June, Sept., Dec.). $16.00 U.S.; $22.00 other. International Society Folk Harpers Crafts, 4718 Maychelle Drive, Anaheim CA 92807. **Tel** (714)998-5717. **(Subscription address:** ISFHC, 4718 Maychelle Drive, Anaheim, CA 92807**)** **ED** Nadine Bunn (editor's address: 1034 Santa Barbara St. Santa Barbara, CA 93101; phone: (805)962-0930). **LC** ML1; .F4138. **DD** 787/.5/05. Index available. cum. index. **Bk Rev**, (Qty: 5). **Ad Acc. Pr Rev. Circ:** 1,400.
**Desc:** Concerns all aspects of the harp. Folk harp history, current events, music, plans for building, book and record reviews, and technical aspects to the harpists and harp makers.
**Ind/Abst** Music Index.

US/0145-3734
**FOLK LETTER, THE.** [Folk lett.]. **Added/Corp** Folk Song Society of Greater Boston. (Mar. 1971)-. English. mo. Folk Song Society of Greater Boston, 11 Sunset Road, Newton MA 02158. **LC** ML1; .F4143. **DD** 781.7/05.

GW/0934-6449
**FOLK MICHEL.** Vol. 1, (1988)-. Periodical. German. bm. **LC** ML3544; .M5. **DD** 781.62/005. ***Continues*** *Michel (Bonn, Germany), 0176-0378.*

●CN/1186-7523
**FOLK MUSIC CATALOGUE.** (FOLK MUSIC CATALOGUE : LP'S, CASSETTES AND BOOKS / THE CANADIAN SOCIETY FOR MUSICAL TRADITIONS.). [Folk music cat.]. **Main/Corp** Canadian Society for Musical Traditions. (1991)-. English. CMST Mail Order Service, #510, 1701 Centre Street NW, Calgary Alberta T2E 8A4 Canada. **DD** 016.78162/00971. ***Continues*** *Canadian Society for Musical Traditions. Catalogue of LP's, Cassettes, and Books., 1186-7515.*

UK/0531-9684
**FOLK MUSIC JOURNAL.** [Folk music j.]. **Added/Corp** English Folk Dance and Song Society. Vol. 1 (1965)-. Periodical. English. an. £30.00 UK; £35.00 others Available in combination of English Folk Dance & Song Society only. English Folk Dance and Song Society, Cecil Sharp House, 2 Regents Park Road, London NW1 7AY England. **Tel** 011 44 71 485 2206. **ED** Ian Russell. Index available. cum. index. **Bk Rev. Ad Acc. Circ:** 8,000 (ctrl). available on microfilm and microfiche from University Microfilms International (UMI). Documents available from The Genuine Article. ***Supersedes*** *Journal of the English Folk Dance & Song Society.*
**Desc:** Covers all aspects of English folk music heritage.
**Ind/Abst** Annu. Bibliogr. Engl. Lang. Lit.; Arts Humanit. Citation Index (19??-19??) [Full Cov.]; Br. Humanit. Index; Curr. Contents Arts Humanit.; MLA Int. Bibl. Books Artic. Mod. Lang. Lit.; Music Index; Res. Alert [Full Cov.]; Soc. Sci. Cit. Index [Select. Cov.].

US/0190-6577
**FOLK MUSIC MAGAZINE.** Vol. 1 (Sept. 1978)-. Periodical. English. bm. $10.00. Folk Music Magazine Inc, 6730 East McDowell #117, Scottsdale AZ 85257. **LC** ML1; .F4147. **DD** 781.7/05.

US/0276-6655
**FOLK MUSIC MINISTRY.** [Folk music minist.]. Vol. 1, No. 1 (July 1981)-. Periodical. English. Six times a year. $24.00. Folk Music Ministry, PO Box 3443, Annapolis MD 21403. **Tel** (301)263-4030. **LC** ML2999; .F64. **DD** 783.7.

UK
**FOLK NEWS.** **Added/Corp** British Federation of Folk Clubs. No. 1, (Jan. 1971)-. Periodical. English. bm. British Federation of Folk Clubs, Cecil Sharp House, 2 Regents Park Road, London NW1 7AY England. **LC** ML5; .F6515. **DD** 781.7/42.

US
**FOLK NEWS (WASHINGTON, D.C.).** (FOLK NEWS / WORLD FOLK MUSIC ASSOCIATION.). **Added/Corp** World Folk Music Association. (1985)-. Periodical. English. Four times a year. $25.00. World Folk Music Association, PO Box 40553, Washington DC 20016. **Tel** (202)302-2225, FAX (202)244-1543. **LC** ML1; .N768. **DD** 781.7/05. **Bk Rev. Circ:** 5,000 (ctrl). available on audiocassette. ***Continues*** *Newsletter (World Folk Music Association).*
**Desc:** Features popular folk music, interviews and new LP, tape and CD releases.

UK
**FOLK REVIEW.** (Mar. 1972)-. Periodical. English. Twelve times a year. Folk Review, Austin House, Hospital Street, Nantwich/Cheshire England. ***Continues*** *Folk & Country.*

UK/0951-1326
**FOLK ROOTS.** (1985)-. Periodical. English. Twelve times a year. £25.50 UK; £31.00 other. Southern Rag Ltd., PO Box 337, London N4 1TW England. **Tel** 11 44 340 9651, FAX 11 44 348 5626. **ED** Ian Anderson. **LC** ML3544; .F64. **DD** 781.7/05. **Bk Rev**, (Qty: 6). **Ad Acc, Adv Mgr:** Gina Jennings. **Circ:** 13,000. ***Continues*** *Southern Rag.*
**Desc:** Features British, American and European folk music along with roots-based popular music from other parts of the world.
**Ind/Abst** Music Index.

US/0146-9169
**FOLKNIK, THE.** **Added/Corp** San Francisco Folk Music Club. College of Marin. Folk Music Club. Vol. 1 (Oct. 1964)-. Periodical. English. bm. $5.00. San Francisco Folk Music Club, 885 Clayton Street, San Francisco CA 94117. **Tel** (415)661-2217. **ED** Nick Holbrook. **LC** ML1; .F416. **DD** 781.7/05. **Bk Rev. Circ:** 1,200 (ctrl).
**Desc:** Information on local, state and national events of interest to folk musicians and afficionados, songs, articles, record and book reviews, detailed schedule of local music and dance.

UK
**FOMRHI QUARTERLY.** **Added/Corp** Fellowship of Makers and Restorers of Historical Instruments (Great Britain). **VFOAT** FOMRHIQ. **VAT** Fellowship of Makers and Restorers of Historical Instruments Quarterly. Vol. 1 (July 1978)-. Periodical. English. qt. £5.00 (membership). Fellowship of Makers and Restorers of Historical Instruments, St. Aldates Faculty of Music, Jeremy Montagu, Oxford OX1 1DB England. **LC** ML26; .F4863. **DD** 781.91/05. ***Continues*** *Bulletin and Communications.*

GW/0015-6140
**FONO FORUM.** (1956)-. Periodical. German. Twelve times a year. DM120.00. PC Moderner Verlags GmbH, Schellingstr 39 43, D 80799 Munich Germany. **Tel** 011 49 89 23726. **(Subscription address:** Waso VVH GmbH & Co KG, Postfach 290180, D 47261, Duisburg Germany; telephone: 011 49 203 769080**)** **LC** ML5; .F657.
**Ind/Abst** RILM Abstr.

SZ/0015-6191
**FONTES ARTIS MUSICAE.** [Fontes artis music.]. **Added/Corp** International Association of Music Libraries. Vol. 1, (1954)-. Periodical. English (French and German). Four times a year (Jan., Apr., July, Oct.). $48.00 (institutions); $33.00 (individual) Comes with International Association of Music Libraries & Canadian Association of Music Libraries Memberships. Association International Bibliothe Musicales, Heinrich Schuetz Allee 29, D 34131 Kassel Germany. **ED** Brian Redferu. **LC** ML5; .F66. Index available. **Bk Rev. Ad Acc. Circ:** 2,000 (ctrl). Documents available from The Genuine Article.
**Ind/Abst** Arts Humanit. Citation Index [Full Cov.]; Curr. Contents Arts Humanit.; Libr. Inf. Sci. Abstr.; Libr. Lit.; Music Index; Res. Alert [Full Cov.]; RILM Abstr.; Romant. Move.; Soc. Sci. Cit. Index [Select. Cov.].

IT/1120-8260
**FONTI MUSICALI IN ITALIA, LE.** [Fonti mus. ital.]. (1987)-. Italian. an. Price varies per volume. Cidim, Via Vittoria Colonna 18 Santoro, 00193 Rome Italy. **Tel** 011 39 6 68802900. **UDC** 78.

GW
**FORCES FOLK.** (19??)-. Periodical. English. mo. Christine Lewis-Jones, c/o PS2 Sub-Sect Sy Wing, Int & Sy Gp Germany Bfpo 33, Hannover Germany. **LC** ML5; .F675. **DD** 784.4/005.

GW/0532-226X
**FORSCHUNGSBEITRAGE ZUR MUSIKWISSENSCHAFT.** Vol. 1 (1954)-. Monographic series. German. ir. Price varies per volume. Gustav Bosse Verlag GmbH & Company KG, Postfach 417, W-8400 Regensburg 1 Germany. **Tel** 011 49 941 794091.

US/0893-2220
**FORTE (MILWAUKEE, WIS.).** (FORTE). [Forte]. **Added/Corp** Midwest Music, Inc. Vol. 1, No. 1 (Sept. 1984)-. Periodical. English. Four times a year. $6.00. Midwest Music Inc., 207 East Buffalo Street, Suite 545, Milwaukee WI 53212. **Tel** (414)278-0066. **DD** 780. ***Continues*** *Women's Music News.*

FR/0760-7245
**FORUM DES AUDIOPHILES PARIS.** [Forum audiophiles Paris]. (1983)-. Periodical. French. bm. 270.00F France; 315.00F other. Editions Frequences, 1 Boulevard Ney, 75018 Paris France. **Tel** 011 33 1 40360197, FAX 011 33 1 40361196. **ED** Jean Hiraga & Gerard Chretien. **UDC** 681.84. **Ad Acc.**

GW/0173-5187
**FORUM MUSIKBIBLIOTHEK.** **See** Library and Information Sciences.

US/0883-0223
**FRANKIE CROCKER'S MUSIC TRACK.** [Frankie Crocker's Music track]. **VFOAT** Music Track. (198?)-. Periodical. English. ir. Big Apple Music, PO Box 6570, New York NY 10150. **DD** 784.

CN/0826-5984
**FREE MUSIC MAGAZINE.** [Free music mag.]. **VFOAT** Free Music. Vol. 1, No. 1 (Nov. 1983)-. Periodical. English. ir. Free. Free Music Magazine, 4 Walmsley Boulevard, Toronto Ontario M4V 1X5 Canada. **DD** 784.5/4/00971.

US/0886-9596
**FRESH!.** [Fresh]. (198?)-. Periodical. English. Twelve times a year. $20.00. Ashley Communications, PO Box 91878, Los Angeles CA 90006. **Tel** (818)885-6800. **DD** 789. ***Continues*** *Record Review, 0198-8573.*

US/0892-2500
**FRIENDS OF FLORIDA FOLK.** **See** Folklore.

US
**FROM THE PAGES OF EXPERIMENTAL MUSICAL INSTRUMENTS.** English. Four times a year. $8.00 (subscribers to Experimental Musical Instruments), $11.00 (nonsubscribers). Experimental Musical Instruments, PO Box 784, Nicasio CA 94946. **Tel** (415)662-2182.
**Desc:** Features instruments which have appeared in Experimental Musical Instruments.

IT
**FRONIMO; RIVISTA TRIMESTRALE DI CHITARRA E LIUTO, IL.** Vol. 1, (Oct. 1972)-. Periodical. Italian (Italian). Four times a year (Jan., Apr., July, Oct.). L30000.00 Italy; L40000.00 others. Edizioni Suvini Zerboni, Via MF Quintiliano 40, 20138 Milan Italy. **Tel** 011 39 2 5084365, FAX 011 39 2 5084261, telex 321063. **ED** Ruggero Chiesa. **LC** ML5; .F76. **DD** 787/.61/05. Index available. cum. index. **Bk Rev. Ad Acc. Circ:** 3,000.
**Desc:** Devoted to the guitar and the lute and to their literature. It handles problems of these instruments. It contains book and scores reviews.
**Ind/Abst** Art Archaeol. Tech. Abstr.; RILM Abstr.

CN/0702-8393
**FUGUE.** [Fugue]. (Sept. 1976)-. Periodical. English. Twelve times a year. Watts & Johnson Publications, York

# Music

Square 49 Avenue Road, Toronto Ontario M5R 2G3 Canada. **Tel** (416)960-5889. **DD** 780/.5. **Ind/Abst** Music Index (-19??).

US/0191-1953
**FULL BLAST.** (Winter 1979)-. English. Full Blast Enterprises, 1800 Austin, Oklahoma City OK 73127. **LC** ML1; .F84. **DD** 784.

CN/0821-509X
**GA PLAINSONG NOTES.** (GA PLAINSONG NOTES : NEWSLETTER OF THE GREGORIAN ASSOCIATION OF CANADA.). **Added/Corp** Gregorian Association of Canada. **VFOAT** G.A. Newsletter. **VAT** Gregorian Association of Canada Plainsong Notes; Gregorian Association of Canada Newsletter; Plainsong Notes. (Aug. 1982)-. Newsletter. English. ir. Free. Gregorian Association of Canada, Suite 506, 2221 Yonge Street, Toronto Ontario M4S 2B4. **DD** 783.5/06/071.

GW
**GABRIELI.** (19??)-. Monographic series. English. ir. Price varies per volume. Haenssler Verlag, Postfach 1220 D-73762 Neuhausen Germany. **Tel** 011 49 07158 1770, telex 715816 HAENSR.

US
**GAMUT (GEORGIA ASSOCIATION OF MUSIC THEORISTS).** (GAMUT : JOURNAL OF THE GEORGIA ASSOCIATION OF MUSIC THEORISTS.). **Added/Corp** Georgia Association of Music Theorists. (19??)-. Periodical. English. an. Georgia State University School of Music, University Plaza, Atlanta GA 30303. **Tel** (404)651-2000, (404)651-3676.

US
**GAVIN REPORT.** (19??)-. English. wk (50 issues). $295.00. Gavin Report, 140 2nd Street, San Francisco CA 94105. **Tel** (415)495-1990.

GW
**GEMEINSCHAFTSKATALOG.** (1972/73)-. German. Josef Keller GmbH & Co. Verlags KG, Postfach 1455, D 82317 Starnberg Germany. **Tel** 011 49 (08151)771-0, FAX 011 49 (08151)771-152, telex 566438. **LC** ML156.2; .G37. **DD** 016.7899/12.

US/0270-7101
**GEMSHORN.** [Gemshorn]. **Added/Corp** Church Music Institute. Office of Divine Worship. (19??)-. Periodical. English. qt. $6.00. Church Music Institute, Office of Divine Worship, PO Box 2018, Milwaukee WI 53201.
**Ind/Abst** Music Artic. Guide (?-?).

US/8755-5905
**GENERAL MUSIC JOURNAL.** Ceased. [Gen. music j.]. Ceased (1989). Academic Scholarly Publication. English. Three times a year. Martha J Waters, PO Box 181, Oxford OH 45056. **Tel** (513)523-6508. **ED** Martha J Waters. **DD** 372. **Bk Rev**. **Circ**: 650.
**Desc**: Mix of scholarly pieces and how-to articles for teachers of classroom music. Forum for instructional problems, research findings.

US/1048-3713
**GENERAL MUSIC TODAY.** (GENERAL MUSIC TODAY : THE JOURNAL OF THE SOCIETY FOR GENERAL MUSIC, MUSIC EDUCATORS NATIONAL CONFERENCE.). [Gen. music today]. **Added/Corp** Society for General Music. **VFOAT** General Music. Vol. 1, No. 1 (Fall 1987)-. Periodical. English. Three times a year. $12.00 US; $14.00 Canada & Mexico; $16.00 other. Music Educators National Conference, 1806 Robert Fulton Drive, Reston VA 22091. **Tel** (703)860-4000, (800)336-3768. **LC** MT1; .G375. **DD** 780/.7/073.
Continues Soundings, 1048-3705.

GW
**GEORGE PHILIPP TELEMANN MUSIKALISCHE WERKE.** (19??)-. German. ir. Price varies per volume. Baerenreiter-Verlag, KGA Verlagssvc PF 100329, D 34003 Kassel Germany. **Tel** 011 49 561 31050, telex 99504.

US/0046-5798
**GEORGIA MUSIC NEWS.** **Added/Corp** Georgia Music Educators Association. (19??)-. Periodical. English. Four times a year (Mar., May, Sept., Nov.). $16.00. Georgia Music News, PO Box 422, Marietta GA 30061. **Tel** (404)427-2466. **ED** Mary Leglar. **LC** ML1; .G27. **Bk Rev**. **Ad Acc**. **Circ**: 2,400 (ctrl).
**Desc**: Primary readership is teachers of music in Georgia. Editorial focus on instructional articles.
**Ind/Abst** Music Artic. Guide.

GW
**GERMAN BLUES GUIDE.** **Added/Corp** German Blues Circle. (19??)-. English (German). German Blues Circle, Postfach 180212, W-6000 Frankfurt 18 Germany. **LC** ML12; .G47. **DD** 784.5/3/0025.
**Desc**: A blues music publication.

US/1070-7794
**GIA QUARTERLY.** (GIA QUARTERLY / GREGORIAN INSTITUTE OF AMERICA.). [GIA q.]. **Added/Corp** Gregorian Institute of America. **VFOAT** Gregorian Institute of America Quarterly; GIAQ. Vol. 1 (Spring 1990)-. Periodical. English. Four times a year (Mar., June, Sept., Dec.). $14.00. GIA Publications Inc., 7404 South Mason Avenue, Chicago IL 60638. **Tel** (708)496-3800. **ED** Fred Moleck, (editor's address: P. O. Box 490, Loughlintown, PA 15655, telephone; (412)834-2200). **DD** 782. **Bk Rev**, (Qty: 4). **Ad Acc**, **Adv Mgr**: Alec Harris, **Tel** (708)496-3800. **Circ**: 23,000.
**Desc**: News and information for the Roman Catholic Church musicians.

IT/1120-6195
**GIORNALE DELLA MUSICA, IL.** (1985)-. Periodical. Italian. Eleven times a year. L60.000 Italy; L95.000 other. EDT SRL, Via Alfieri 19, 10121 Turin Italy. **Tel** 011 39 11 5621496. **ED** Enzo Peruccio. **LC** IN PROCESS. Index available. cum. index. **Circ**: 20,000 (ctrl).
**Desc**: Music news, billboard of music performances throughout Europe.

US
**GIRL GROUPS GAZETTE, THE.** English. Four times a year. $20.00. Fan Club Publishing, PO Box 69A04, West Hollywood CA 90069. **Tel** (213)650-5112. **ED** Louis Wendruck. **Bk Rev**. **Ad Acc**. **Circ**: 1,000.
**Desc**: Publications of the Girls Groups Fan Club. Newsletter for fans of the 1960s female singers and female singing groups such as The Supremes, Martha & The Vandellas, The Ronettes, The Marvelettes, etc. Offers photos, post cards, t-shirts, videos, records, and articles about girl groups & singers.

GW/0172-9683
**GITARRE + LAUTE.** **VAT** Gitarre und Laute. (1979)-. Periodical. German. bm. DM39.00. Gitarre & Laute Verlagsgesselschaft MBH, Postfach 410408, 5000 Koln 41 Germany. **Tel** 011 49 0221 49377. **ED** Peter Paffgen.
**Ind/Abst** Music Index.

US/0731-0781
**GLORY SONGS.** **Added/Corp** Southern Baptist Convention. Sunday School Board. **VFOAT** Easy Choir Music. (198?)-. Periodical. English. Four times a year. $9.20. Southern Baptist Convention, 901 Commerce, Suite 750, Nashville TN 37203. **Tel** (615)244-2355, FAX (615)742-8919. (**Subscription address**: Sunday School Board, Customer Service, 127 9th Avenue North, Nashville TN 37234.)

US/1055-2685
**GOLDMINE (1985).** **See** Hobbies.

US/0017-2235
**GOPHER MUSIC NOTES.** **Added/Corp** Minnesota Music Educators Association. Minnesota Public School Music League. (19??)-. Periodical. English. Four times a year (Feb., Apr., Oct., Dec.). $10.00. Gopher Music Notes, 1104 Pine View Road, Alexandria MN 56308. **Tel** (612)763-6135.
**Ind/Abst** Music Artic. Guide.

US/0362-7330
**GOSPEL MUSIC ASSOCIATION ANNUAL DIRECTORY & YEARBOOK.** **Main/Corp** Gospel Music Association. **Added/Corp** Gospel Music Association. Annual Directory & Yearbook. **VAT** Gospel Music Association Annual Directory and Yearbook. (19??)-. Directory. English. an. Gospel Music Association, PO Box 23201, Nashville TN 37202. **Tel** (615)242-0303. **LC** ML19; .G68. **DD** 783.7. Continues Gospel Music Directory & Yearbook.

US/0739-604X
**GOSPEL MUSIC OFFICIAL DIRECTORY.** Ceased. **Added/Corp** Gospel Music Association. (1983)-(198?). Directory. English. Gospel Music Association, PO Box 23201, Nashville TN 37202. **Tel** (615)242-0303. **LC** ML3186.8; .G64. **DD** 783.7/025/73.

US
**GOSPEL VOICE.** English. mo. $18.00 (US); $28.00 (Canada); $30.00 (other). Music City News Inc, PO Box 22975, Nashville TN 37202. **Tel** (615)329-2200, FAX (615)327-2726. **ED** Lydia Harden. **Ad Acc, Adv Mgr**: Rick Francis. **Circ**: 10,000 (ctrl).
**Desc**: News, charts, reviews, artist concert itineraryes, and interviews on southern gospel music.

US/0278-3436
**GOSPEL WORLD.** [Gospel world]. Vol. 1, No. 1 (April 1980)-. Periodical. English. mo. $12.00 US; $14.00 other. C. Dick, PO Box T, Cambria Heights NY 11411. **LC** ML3186.8; .G67. **DD** 783.7.
**Desc**: Gospel music publication.

GW/0017-2499
**GOTTESDIENST UND KIRCHENMUSIK.** (GOTTESDIENST UND KIRCHENMUSIK : G + K.). [Gottesd. Kirchenmusik]. **Added/Corp** Lutherische Liturgische Konferenz in Bayern. **VFOAT** G + K; G und K. (Jan. 1950)-. Periodical. German. Six times a year. DM18.00. Friedemann Haessler, Martin Luther Str 2, D 97616 Bad Neustadt Germany. **Tel** 011 49 9771 5812. **LC** ML5; .G56. **DD** 783/.02/605.
**Ind/Abst** Music Index; RILM Abstr.

UK/0141-5085
**GRAINGER SOCIETY JOURNAL, THE.** (19??)-. Periodical. English. sa. £8.00 UK; $20.00 US. Barry Peter Ould, 6 Fairfax Crescent, Aylesbury Buckinghamshire HP20 2ES United Kingdom. **Tel** (0296)28609. **ED** Barry Peter Ould. **LC** ML410.G75; G7. **DD** 786.2/092. Index available. **Bk Rev**. **Ad Acc**. **Circ**: 500. Continues Grainger Journal, 0141-5085.
**Desc**: Contains articles on and about the life and music of Percy Aldridge Grainger. Also includes work by Grainger himself through the medium of his many writings.
**Ind/Abst** Music Index.

UK/0017-310X
**GRAMOPHONE.** (19??)-. Periodical. English. Twelve times a year. £30.80, $75.00. General Gramophone Publishers Ltd., 177-179 Kenton Road, Harrow Middlesex HA3 0HA England. **Tel** 011 44 81 907 4476, FAX 011 44 81 907 0073, telex 265871 MONREF G MUS027. **LC** ML5; .G65. **DD** 780.26/6/05. Index available (£7.50, $12.90). available on microfilm and microfiche from University Microfilms International (UMI). Continues Gramophone Including Compact Disc News and Reviews, 0017-310X.
**Ind/Abst** Music Index.

US/0147-8494
**GRAMOPHONE NEWS, THE.** **See** Sound Recordings and Systems.

UK
**GRAMOPHONE, WIRELESS & TALKING MACHINE NEWS.** **See** Sound Recordings and Systems.

US/0434-3336
**GRAND BATON, LE.** **Added/Corp** Sir Thomas Beecham Society. (1964)-. Periodical. English. ir. $10.00 (includes Sir Thomas Beecham Society Membership). Sir Thomas Beecham Society, PO Box 340, Camden NC 27921. **Tel** (919)335-1025. **DD** 780.
**Ind/Abst** Music Artic. Guide (?-?).

US/0092-0592
**GRAPEVINE (SARATOGA).** (THE GRAPEVINE.). (Nov. 1972)-. Periodical. English. $3.20 / 5 issues. L. Ransil, 19801 Braemar Drive, Saratoga CA 95070. **LC** ML1; .G926. **DD** 784.

AU
**GRAZER MUSIKWISSENSCHAFTLICHE ARBEITEN.** **Added/Corp** Universitaet Graz. Institut fuer Musikwissenschaft. Vol. 1 (1975)-. Monographic series. German. ir. Price varies per volume. Akademische Druck & Verlagsanstalt, Schoenaugasse 6, Postfach 598, A 8010 Graz Austria. **Tel** 011 43 316 813460.

US/0272-0264
**GREENWOOD ENCYCLOPEDIA OF BLACK MUSIC, THE.** (1981)-. Monographic series. English. ir. Price varies per volume. Greenwood Press Inc., PO Box 5007, Westport CT 06881-5007. **Tel** (203)226-3571, FAX (203)222-1502. **Bk Rev**. **Ad Acc**.

NE
**GREGORIUS NYSSENUS OPERA.** (19??)-. English. ir. Price varies per volume. E. J. Brill, Postbus 9000, 2300 PA Leiden Netherlands. **Tel** 011 31 71 312624, FAX 011 31 71 317532, telex 39296 BRILL NL.

NE
**GREGORIUSBLAD.** Ceased. **Added/Corp** Nederlandse Sint-Gregoriusvereniging. Vol. 1 (Jan. 1876)-(19??). Periodical. Dutch. qt. Nederlandse Sint-Gregoriusver, Oudwijk 21, 3581 TG Utrecht Netherlands. **Tel** (030)5137 39. **LC** ML5; .S574. Index available. cum. index. **Bk Rev**. **Ad Acc**.
**Desc**: Covers liturgy and liturgical music.
**Ind/Abst** Music Index.

AU/0533-3067
**GROSSEN DARSTELLUNGEN DER MUSIKGESCHICHTE IN BAROCK UND AUFKLARUNG, DIE.** (1964)-. German. Akademische Druck & Verlagsanstalt, Schoenaugasse 6, Postfach 598, A 8010 Graz Austria. **Tel** 011 43 316 813460. **ED** Von Othmar Wessely. **DD** 780.

BE
**GUIDE DE LA MUSIQUE, LE.** French. 750F Belgium & Luxembourg; 220F France; 1450F other. Edimedia ASBL, rue de la Constitution 22, 1030 Brussels Belgium. **Tel** 011 32 2 2180031. **Bk Rev**. **Ad Acc**.

BE
**GUIDE DU PRODUCTEUR DE DISQUES, LE.** **See** Sound Recordings and Systems.

CN/0823-7875
**GUILD GAZETTE.** (THE GUILD GAZETTE : A MEMBERSHIP NEWSLETTER OF REGINA GUILD OF FOLK ARTS.). [Guild gaz.]. **Added/Corp** Regina Guild of Folk Arts. (1982)-. Newsletter. English. bm. 10.00Can$. Regina Guild of Folk Arts, PO Box 1203, Regina Saskatchewan S4P 3B4 Canada. **Tel** (306)757-7684. **ED**

Paul Wilson. **DD** 781.7/06/071244.
**Desc:** A publication of record reviews, up-coming events and music-related articles.

CN/0834-1656
**GUILD NEWS (TORONTO. 1979).** (GUILD NEWS.). [Guild news]. **Added/Corp** Canadian Opera Guild. (Fall 1979)-. Periodical. English. qt. Canadian Opera Guild, 227 Front Street East, Toronto Ontario M5A 1E8, Canada. **DD** 782.1/06/071. ***Supersedes** Overtures (Toronto, Ont.)., 0382-778X.*

US/0199-9117
**GUITAR & LUTE.** [Guitar lute]. **VFOAT** Guitar & Lute Magazine. **VAT** Guitar and Lute. No. 1 (April/June 1974)-. Periodical. English. Four times a year. $15.00. Gailliard Press, 8939 Keith, Los Angeles CA 90069.
**Ind/Abst** Music Artic. Guide; Music Index (-19??).

US/0270-9325
**GUITAR & MANDOLIN.** ***Suspended.*** [Guitar mandol.]. **VAT** Guitar and Mandolin. Vol. 2, No. 2 (March 1980)-Suspended. Periodical. English. Five times a year. $12.00. Mugwumps C O MIH Publ. Inc., 15 Arnold Place, New Bedford MA 02740. **LC** ML1; .M122. **DD** 787.6/1/05. ***Continues** Mandolin Notebook, 0148-5482.*

CN/0830-8721
**GUITAR CANADA.** ***Ceased.*** [Guitar Can.]. Vol. 1, No. 1 (Spring 1986)-(1990). Periodical. English. qt. Guitar Canada, 525 Balliol Street/Unit 6, Toronto Ontario M4S 1E1 Canada. **DD** 787.6/1/0971.
**Desc:** Canada's national publication concerned with the world of classical guitar. Interviews, features, book and record reviews, cover performers, composers, guitar makers and events on a national and international scale are featured. Articles also cross into jazz, flamenco and other guitar styles. Informative columns keep readers up-to-date on classical guitar news.

●US/1061-4400
**GUITAR CLASSICS, THE.** (1992)-. Periodical. English. bm. Cherry Lane Music Company Inc., PO Box 430, Port Chester NY 10573. **Tel** (914)935-5200, FAX (914)937-0614.

US
**GUITAR FOR THE PRACTICING MUSICIAN.** **Added/Corp** Cherry Lane Music Company. **VFOAT** Guitar. (198?)-. Periodical. English. mo. $27.95 (one year), $45.95 (two year) US; $42.95 (one year), $75.95 (two year) Canada; $52.95 (one year), $95.95 (two year) other. Cherry Lane Music Company Inc., PO Box 430, Port Chester NY 10573. **Tel** (914)935-5200, FAX (914)937-0614. **ED** John Stix, 10 Midland Ave, Port Chester, NY 10573. **Ad Acc, Adv Mgr:** Barbara Seerman, **Tel** (914)935-5243. **Circ:** 180,000. ***Continues** Guitar (Port Chester, N.Y.), 0738-937X.*
**Desc:** Features note-for-note guitar and bass transcriptions to classic rock and metal songs and profiles, interviews, instructional columns and advice from top guitarists.

UK
**GUITAR INTERNATIONAL.** **Added/Corp** Musical New Services. Vol. 13, No. 1 (Aug. 1984)-. Periodical. English. Twelve times a year. Purestop Ltd., Manor Road Mere, Wiltshire BA12 6HZ England. **Tel** 011 44 747 861033. **LC** ML5; .G828. **DD** 787.6/1/05. **Bk Rev. Ad Acc.** ***Continues** Guitar.*
**Desc:** With its international readership and contributors, it is the most highly respected and influential magazine for classical guitarists.

UK/0962-2640
**GUITAR MAGAZINE.** [Guitar mag.]. (1990)-. Periodical. English. Thirteen times a year (Published monthly with 1 special issue). £19.50 UK; £38.00 Europe; £55.00 others. United Leisure Magazines Ltd., 4 Seosdon Way City Harbor, E Surr London E14 9ZR England. **(Subscription address:** Stonehart Subscriptions Services, Hainault Road Little Heath, Bromford, RM6 5NP England**)** **DD** 787.87.

US/0017-5463
**GUITAR PLAYER.** [Guitar play.]. **VFOAT** Guitar Player Magazine. Vol. 1 (1967)-. Periodical. English. mo. $29.95 US; $44.95 Canada; $44.95 (surface mail), $69.95 (airmail) other. Miller Freeman Inc., 600 Harrison Street, San Francisco CA 94107. **Tel** (415)905-2337, FAX (415)905-2240, telex 278273. **(Subscription address:** Neodata / Colorado, PO Box 2606, Boulder Boulder CO 80322.**)** **ED** Tom Wheeler, Tom Mulhern, Jas Obrecht, Jim Ferguson, Jon Sievert, and Joe Gore. **LC** ML1; .G965. **DD** 787. **[CCC].** Index available. cum. index. **Ad Acc. Circ:** 135,000. available on microfilm and microfiche from University Microfilms International (UMI). Documents available from UMI Article Clearinghouse.
**Desc:** Edited for acoustic, electric and synth guitar players of all styles. Covers performers, techniques, equipment, electronics and repair, with how-to articles. Each issue includes a flexible record.
**Ind/Abst** Gen. Period. Index (1985-); Mag. Index Plus (1989-); Music Artic. Guide (19??-); Music Index (19??-); Newsp. Period. Abstr. (1988-); Mag. Index (1977-).

US/0884-7517
**GUITAR PLAYER LEGENDS OF GUITAR.** [Guitar play. legends guitar]. **VFOAT** Legends of Guitar; Guitar Player Collector's Edition; Guitar Players Magazine's Legends of Guitar; Guitar Player Magazine Collector's Edition. Vol. 1, No. 1 (1984)-. Periodical. English. GPI Publications, 20085 Stevens Creek Boulevard, Cupertino CA 95014. **Tel** (408)446-1105, FAX (408)446-1088, telex 4994425. **LC** ML1; .G967. **DD** 787.6/1/0922.

US/0017-5471
**GUITAR REVIEW, THE.** [Guitar rev.]. **Added/Corp** Society of the Classic Guitar (U.S.). **VFOAT** GR. No. 1 (Oct./Nov. 1946)-. Periodical. English. Four times a year (Jan., Apr., July, Oct.). $24.00 US; $28.00 others. Albert Augustine Ltd, 40 West 25th Street, 12th Floor, New York NY 10010. **Tel** (212)924-4651, FAX (212)242-2220, (212)924-9388. **ED** Rose Augustine. **LC** ML1; .G97. **DD** 787.6/1/05. **Bk Rev. Ad Acc. Circ:** 4,000 (ctrl).
**Desc:** International magazine devoted to the classic guitar. Contains in-depth articles, interviews with prominent artists, book, music and concert reviews, and rare music supplements.
**Ind/Abst** Music Artic. Guide; Music Index; RILM Abstr.

US/1058-0220
**GUITAR SCHOOL.** [Guitar sch.]. (1989)-. Periodical. English. bm. $11.94. Harris Publications, 1115 Broadway/8th Floor, New York NY 10010. **Tel** (212)807-7100. **DD** 787.

US/1045-6295
**GUITAR WORLD.** [Guitar world]. (1980)-. Periodical. English. mo. $19.94. Harris Publications, 1115 Broadway/8th Floor, New York NY 10010. **Tel** (212)807-7100. **LC** ML1015.G9; .G854. **DD** 787.87/166/05.

FR
**GUITARE ET CLAVIERS.** French. Eleven times a year. 238.00F France; 335.00F other. Carredas, 132 rue du Faubourg St. Denis, 75010 Paris France. **Tel** 011 33 1 40357373. **(Subscription address:** Guitare & Claviers, BP 701, Service Abonnements, 60732 Ste Genevieve Cedex France**)**

US/0434-9350
**GUITARRA MAGAZINE.** ***Ceased.*** [Guitar. mag.]. **VFOAT** Guitarra. (Mar./Apr. 1963)-(19??). Periodical. English. bm. Flamencos International Association, 3145 West 63rd Street, Chicago IL 60629.
**Desc:** Interviews with performing guitarists, publication (music) reviews, record reviews, calendar of events, where and when artists are performing, technique and history.
**Ind/Abst** Music Artic. Guide; Music Index (-19??).

US/1046-3879
**GUITARS & MUSICAL INSTRUMENTS.** [Guitars music. instrum.]. **Added/Corp** Orion Research Corporation. **VFOAT** Orion Blue Book Guitars & Musical Instruments; Guitars and Musical Instruments. (1989)-. Periodical. English. an. $149.00. Orion Research Corporation, 14555 North Scottsdale Road, Suite 330, Scottsdale AZ 85260. **Tel** (800)844-0759, (602)951-1114, FAX (602)951-1117. **LC** ML155; .P76. **DD** 784.19/029/473. ***Continues in part** Professional Sound & Musical Instruments.*

UK
**HALLE YEARBOOK.** **Main/Corp** Halle Concerts Society. **VFOAT** Halle Year Book. (1982)-. English. an. Halle Concerts Society, 30 Cross Street, Manchester M2 7BA England. **Tel** 061-834-8363, FAX 061-832-1669, telex 666140. **ED** C. F. Smart. **LC** ML28.M19; H33. **DD** 785/.06/242733. **Bk Rev. Ad Acc. Circ:** 7,000 (ctrl).
**Desc:** Contains details of all Manchester concerts, related articles, plus diary of Orchestra's complete concert schedule for season, photographs and repertoire.

GW
**HALLISCHE HANDEL AUSGABE.** (19??)-. German. ir. Baerenreiter-Verlag, KGA Verlagssvc PF 100329, D 34003 Kassel Germany. **Tel** 011 49 561 31050, telex 99504. **(Subscription address:** North America/ Foreign Music Distributors, 13 Elkay Drive, Chester, NY 10918; telephone: (914)469-5790**)**

GW
**HAMBURGER JAHRBUCH FUER MUSIKWISSENSCHAFT.** (1974)-. German. an. Laaber Verlag, Regensburger Strasse 19, W 93164 Laaber Germany. **Tel** 011-49-9498-2307. **ED** Peter Petersen. **LC** ML5; .H16. **DD** 780/.5.
**Desc:** Research in music history.
**Ind/Abst** RILM Abstr.

GW
**HAMBURGER JAHRBUCH FUER THEATER UND MUSIK.** **See** Theater.

US/8756-7407
**HANDBELLS FOR DIRECTORS AND RINGERS.** **Added/Corp** Southern Baptist Convention. Sunday School Board. **VFOAT** Handbells. Vol. 1, No. 1 (Oct./Nov./Dec. 1985)-. Periodical. English. qt. $19.30 (one year), $38.00 (two year). Baptist Sunday School Board, 127 9th Avenue North, Nashville TN 37324. **Tel** (615)251-2289. **LC** M147; .H.

US/0164-2847
**HANDBOOK - NATIONAL ASSOCIATION OF SCHOOLS OF MUSIC.** **Main/Corp** National Association of Schools of Music. **Added/Corp** National Association of Schools of Music. NASM Handbook. **VFOAT** NASM Handbook. (1974)-. English. an. $14.00 Comes with National Association of Schools of Music Library Subscription. National Association of Schools of Music, 11250 Roger Bacon Drive, Suite 21, Reston VA 22090. **Tel** (703)437-0700. **ED** David Bading. **LC** ML27.U5; N26334. **DD** 780/.7/2973. **Circ:** 1,500.
**Desc:** List standards for music curricular at nondegree granting junior college and baccalaureate level as well as the associations constitution, by laws, rules of practice and procedure and code of ethics.

US/0732-2321
**HANDBOOK TO THE SEASON / CINCINNATI SYMPHONY ORCHESTRA.** **Main/Corp** Cincinnati Symphony Orchestra. (1982)-. English. an. Cincinnati Symphony Orchestra, 1241 Elm Street, Cincinnati OH 45210. **Tel** (513)621-1919. **ED** Denis Wagner. **LC** MT125; .C58. **DD** 785/.07/3977178. Index available. **Ad Acc. Circ:** 7,000 (ctrl).
**Desc:** Complete program notes for the Cincinnati Symphony Orchestra.

GW
**HANDEL JAHRBUCH.** (19??)-. German. ir. Buchexport, Postfach 160, DDR-7010 Leipzig Germany. **Tel** 011 37 41 71370.

US/0270-0832
**HARMONICA HAPPENINGS.** [Harmonica happen.]. **Added/Corp** Society for the Preservation and Advancement of the Harmonica. Vol. 1 (Sept. 1967)-. Periodical. English. qt. $10.00. Harmonica Happenings, Box 865, Troy MI 48084. **LC** ML990.M7; H33. **DD** 788/.9.

US
**HARMONICA HORIZONS.** (19??)-. Periodical. English. qt. J. McKenzie, PO Box 1952, Orange CA 92668. **LC** IN PROCESS. ***Continues** Harmonica Hospital Newsletter.*

US
**HARMONICA HOSPITAL NEWSLETTER.** ***Title Change.*** Newsletter. English. qt. **LC** ML1088; .H37. **DD** 788.8/21928/05. ***Continued by** Harmonica Horizons.*

CN/0713-8059
**HARMONIE-QUEBEC : BULLETIN OFFICIEL, FEDERATION DES HARMONIES DU QUEBEC.** [Harmonie-Que.]. **Added/Corp** Federation des Harmonies du Quebec. (1978)-. Bulletin. French. Three times a year. $8.00. Federation des Harmonies du Quebec, CP 1000 Succursale M, Montreal QUE H1V 3R2 Canada. **Tel** (514)252-3026, FAX (514)251-8038. **DD** 785/.06/7. **Ad Acc. Circ:** 1,000.

GW
**HARMONIKA INTERNATIONAL.** **Added/Corp** Deutscher Harmonika-Verband. Vol. 2, (1989)-. Periodical. German. qt. Harmonika-International, Postfach 1150, 7218 Trossingen Germany. **LC** PAR. ***Continues** Harmonika-Revue.*

US/0017-7849
**HARMONIZER (KENOSHA, WIS.), THE.** (THE HARMONIZER.). [Harmonizer]. **Added/Corp** Society for the Preservation and Encouragement of Barber Shop Quartet Singing in America. (194?)-. Periodical. English. Six times a year. $18.00 US; $27.00 other. Society for the Preservation and Encouragement of Barber Shop Quartet Singing in America, 6315 3rd Avenue, Box 575, Kenosha WI 53143. **Tel** (414)653-8440, FAX (414)654-4048. **ED** Dan Daily. **DD** 784.06273. Index available. **Ad Acc. Circ:** 37,000 (ctrl). ***Continues** Barber Shop Re-Chordings.*
**Desc:** News and information about the barbershop quartet singing.

SZ/1017-1142
**HARPA.** **Added/Corp** International Harp Center. Historical Harp Society. Swiss Society for Harp Music. (1991)-. Periodical. English (French and German). qt. **LC** IN PROCESS.

UK
**HARPSICHORD AND FORTEPIANO MAGAZINE, THE.** Vol. 4, No. 3 (April 1987)-. Periodical. English. Twice a year (Apr., Oct.). Harpsichord & Fortepiano Mag, PO Box 129, Cheltenham GL52 3BZ England. ***Continues** English Harpsichord Magazine.*

US/0073-0629
**HARVARD PUBLICATIONS IN MUSIC.** Vol. 1, (1967)-. Monographic series. English. ir. Price varies per volume. Harvard University Press, 79 Garden Street, Cambridge MA 02138. **Tel** (617)496-1344, (800)448-2242.

GW/0440-5323
**HAYDN-STUDIEN.** [Haydn-Stud.]. **Added/Corp** Joseph Haydn-Institut. Vol. 1, (June 1965)-. Periodical. German. ir. G Henle USA Inc., POB 1753, 2446 Centerline Industrial Drive, St Louis MO 63043. **Tel** (314)991-0487.
**Ind/Abst** Arts Humanit. Citation Index (19??-19??) [Full Cov.]; RILM Abstr.

UK/0073-1390
**HAYDN YEARBOOK, THE.** ***Ceased.*** [Haydn yearb.]. **VFOAT** Haydn Jahrbuch. Vol. 1 (1962)-Ceased ?. English (German). an. Cardiff Press University College, PO Box 78, Cathys Park, Cardiff CF1 1XL Wales. **Tel** 011 44 222 2874833. **LC** ML410.H4; H45.
**Ind/Abst** Music Index; RILM Abstr.

US/0892-6913
**HAZARD'S PAVILION.** **Added/Corp** Society for the Preservation of Southern California Musical Heritage (Lomita, Calif.). Vol. 1, No. 1 (Summer 1986)-. Periodical. English. Four times a year. $20.00 Comes with Society Preservation of Southern California Musical Heritage Membership. Society for the Preservation at Southern California Musical Heritage, PO Box 374, Lomita CA 90717. **Tel** (310)631-1322. **DD** 780. **Bk Rev**. **Circ:** 275.
**Desc:** Publishes articles on Southern California musical heritage.

US/0739-4306
**HEAVY METAL TIMES.** (19??)-. Periodical. English. qt. $8.50 US; $12.50 other. Heavy Metal Times, 216 Vernon Castle, Benbrook TX 76126. **LC** ML3533.8; .H4. **DD** 784.5/4/005.

MX/0018-1137
**HETEROFONIA.** [Heterofonia]. Vol. 1, No. 1 (July 1968)-. Periodical. Spanish. Twice a year. $35.00. Cenidim Inba, Liverpool 16 Col Juarez, 06600 Mexico DF Mexico. **Tel** 011 52 5 5925953. **ED** Esperanza Pulido and Juan Jose Escorza. **LC** ML5; .H49. **DD** 780/.5. **Bk Rev**. **Ad Acc**. **Circ:** 1,000 (ctrl).
**Desc:** Fights for real musical understanding between all the countries of America. Encourages research into the little-known colonial music of Mexico.
**Ind/Abst** Arts Humanit. Citation Index (19??-19??) [Full Cov.]; Music Index (-19??); RILM Abstr.

FR/0337-1891
**HIFI STEREO, VIDEO.** **Added/Corp** Societe des Publications Radio-Electriques et Scientifiques (Paris, France). **VFOAT** HiFi Stereo; HiFi Video. No. 131 (Nov. 1986)-. Periodical. French. mo. 262.00F. Societe des Publications Radio-Electriques et Scientifiques, 2A 12 rue de Bellevue, 75940 Paris Cedex 19 France. **LC** ML5; .H5. **DD** 789.9/1/05. ***Continues*** *HiFi Stereo, Video, Loisirs, 0337-1891.*

UK/0018-1846
**HILLANDALE NEWS, THE.** [Hillandale news]. **Main/Corp** City of London Phonograph and Gramophone Society. **VFOAT** Hillandale. (1960)-. Periodical. English. Six times a year. £12.00 Europe; £13.00 ($25.00) US. City of London Phonograph & Gramophone Society : CLPGS, "Ardlarich" 2, Kirklands Park, Cuper FIFE KY15 4EP Scotland. **Tel** 11 44 334 54390. **ED** Chris Hamilton. **DD** 780. Index available (published separately).

CN
**HISTOIRE DU ROCK.** (1973)-. Periodical. French. wk. Messageries Dynamiques Inc, 775 Boulevard Lebeau, Saint-Laurent Quebec H4N 1S5 Canada. **Tel** (800)463-4645, (514)332-0680. **DD** 780/.42/09.

US/1045-4616
**HISTORIC BRASS SOCIETY JOURNAL.** [Hist. Brass Soc. j.]. **Added/Corp** Historic Brass Society. Vol. 1 (1989)-. English. an. $15.00 (individual); $25.00 (institution), membership. Historic Brass Society, 148 West 23rd Street #2A, New York NY 10011. **Tel** (212)627-3820, FAX (212)627-3820. **ED** Jeff Nussbaum. **LC** ML933; .H57. **DD** 788.9/19/05. cum. index. **Bk Rev**, (Qty: 10-20). **Ad Acc**, **Adv Mgr:** Jeff Nussbaum, **Tel** (212)627-3820. **Pr Rev. Circ:** 800.
**Desc:** Presents scholarly research articles on all aspects of early brass music from the period of antiquity through the 19th century.
**Ind/Abst** Music Artic. Guide; Music Index.

US/1045-4594
**HISTORIC BRASS SOCIETY NEWSLETTER.** [Hist. Brass Soc. newsl.]. **Added/Corp** Historic Brass Society. **VFOAT** HBS Newsletter. Issue No. 1 (Summer 1989)-. Newsletter. English. an. $15.00 (individual); $25.00 (institution), membership. Historic Brass Society, 148 West 23rd Street #2A, New York NY 10011. **Tel** (212)627-3820, FAX (212)627-3820. **ED** Jeff Nussbaum. **LC** ML929.5; .H58. **DD** 788.9/05. cum. index. **Bk Rev**, (Qty: 10-20). **Ad Acc**, **Adv Mgr:** Jeff Nussbaun. **Pr Rev. Circ:** 800.
**Desc:** Presents articles dealing with all aspects of early brass music. Interviews with leading musicians in the field, articles on early brass instrument makers, reviews of books, music, recordings and a news in the field section.

UK
**HISTORICAL ORGAN BROADSHEETS.** (188?)-. English. $12.00 Includes Historical Organs Information Newsletter & Historical Organ Broadsheets. Martin Renshaw, North Lyminge Folkestone, Kent CT18 8EE England. **ED** M. Renshaw. **LC** ML549.8; .H57. **DD** 786.5/1923/05.

UK
**HISTORICAL ORGAN NOTES.** No. 1 (Feb. 1987)-. Periodical. English. $12.00 Includes Historical Organs Information Newsletter & Historical Organ Broadsheets. Martin Renshaw, North Lyminge Folkestone, Kent CT18 8EE England. **ED** M. Renshaw. **LC** ML549.8; .H574. **DD** 786.5/1923.

US/0898-8587
**HISTORICAL PERFORMANCE.** (HISTORICAL PERFORMANCE : THE JOURNAL OF EARLY MUSIC AMERICA.). [Hist. perform.]. **Added/Corp** Early Music America (Organization). Vol. 1, No. 1 (Spring 1988)-. Periodical. English. Twice a year. $30.00. Early Music America, 11421 1 2 Bellflower Road, Cleveland OH 44106. **Tel** (216)229-1685. **LC** ML1; .H46. **DD** 780/.973. **Bk Rev**. **Ad Acc**. **Circ:** 3,000 (ctrl).
**Desc:** Offers articles on the cutting edge of performance practice issues, interviews with early-music notables, editorials on topical concerns of the field, reviews of books, records, and musical editions, chronicles of events, and regular features about education, marketing, and Early Music America, the national service organization.
**Ind/Abst** Music Artic. Guide; Music Index.

NE
**HITKRANT.** (19??)-. Dutch. wk (published on Wed.). Fl118.50. BV Uitgeversmaatschappij Bonaventura, PO Box 2158, 1000 CD Amsterdam Netherlands. **Tel** 011 31 20 6914111, 011 31 20 5674911.

US/0737-7959
**HITMEN.** (HITMEN / BY SAM BRADLEY.). [Hitmen]. Vol. 1, No. 1 (1982)-. Periodical. English. S Y Bradley, 5909 Wilkinson Avenue, North Hollywood CA 91607. **LC** MT662; .H6. **DD** 789/.1.

US
**HITS.** **VFOAT** Hits Magazine. Vol. 1, No. 1 (August 4, 1986)-. Periodical. English. wk (50 issues - published on Thursdays). $300.00. Hits Magazine, 14958 Ventura Boulevard, Sherman Oaks CA 91403. **Tel** (818)501-7900. **LC** ML3533.8; .H57. **DD** 784.5/005.

XR/0323-1283
**HMM.** **VFOAT** Hudebni Nastroje; Musical Instruments; Musikinstrumente. (1991)-. Periodical. Czech (English and German). qt. kcs12.00 (single issue). Charles University / Univerzita Karlova, Ovocnytrh 5, 116 36 Prague 1 Czech Republic. **Tel** 228441. **(Subscription address:** Artia Pegas Press Ltd., Palac Metro Narodni Trida 25, 11210 Prague 1 Czech Republic.**)** ***Continues*** *Hudebni Nastroje.*

US/0886-1862
**HOGAKU.** ***Ceased.*** [Hogaku]. Vol. 1, No. 1 (Spring 1983)-Ceased Vol. 3, No. 2 (Winter 1989). Academic Scholarly Publication. English. sa. Traditional Japanese Music Society, Aaron Copland School of Music, Queens College, Flushing NY 11367. **Tel** (718)520-7340. **ED** H Burnett. **LC** ML340; .H63. **DD** 781.752/05. cum. index. **Bk Rev**. **Ad Acc**. **Circ:** 300.
**Desc:** Scholarly journal devoted to all aspects of traditional Japanese music. Important articles by recognized Japanese musicologists (in English translation) and American scholars.
**Ind/Abst** Music Index (?-?); RILM Abstr. (?-?).

US/0046-7928
**HORN CALL, THE.** **Added/Corp** International Horn Society. (Feb. 1971)-. Periodical. English (German and Spanish). Four times a year. $30.00. International Horn Society, 2220 North 1400 East, Provo UT 84604. **Tel** (801)377-3026. **ED** Paul Mansur. **LC** ML1; .H617. Index available in last issue of volume--attached. cum. index. **Bk Rev**. **Ad Acc**. **Pr Rev. Circ:** 3,000 (ctrl).
**Desc:** Historical and technical research reports, music and record reviews, reprints, horn pedagogy, biographical sketches of noted hornists, humor, etc., in regard to the horn.
**Ind/Abst** Music Artic. Guide.

GW
**HORTUS MUSICUS.** (1950)-. Monographic series. Undetermined. ir. Price varies per volume. Baerenreiter-Verlag, KGA Verlagssvc PF 100329, D 34003 Kassel Germany. **Tel** 011 49 561 31050, telex 99504. **(Subscription address:** Foreign Music Distributors, 13 Elkay Drive, Chester, NY 10918, phone: (914)469-5790**)**
**Desc:** A series of interesting and important works for string and wind instruments with various instrumentation - solo instruments, chamber music, orchestral works, of the Renaissance to the Early Classical period.

UK/0302-0762
**HOT BUTTERED SOUL.** [Hot buttered soul]. (19??)-. Periodical. English. mo. C. Savory, 36 Scrapsgate Road, Minster Sheppey England. **LC** ML5; .H65. **DD** 784.

US
**HOT HOUSE.** English. mo. $13.00. Hot House, 18 Whippoorwill Lane, Rockaway Township NJ 07866. **Tel** (201)627-5349. **ED** Gene Kalbacher. **Ad Acc**. **Circ:** 40,000.
**Desc:** Jazz nightlife guide for the New York-New Jersey metropolitan area. Includes concert schedules, CD reviews and artist profiles.

CN/0714-864X
**HOT WACKS.** [Hot wacks]. **VFOAT** Hot Wax. (1975)-. Periodical. English. sa. Hot Wacks, Blue Flake Productions, Box 2666 Station B, Kitchener Ontario N2H 6N2 Canada. **LC** ML156.2; .H68. **DD** 016.78242166/0266.

XR/0018-6996
**HUDEBNI ROZHLEDY.** (HUDEBNI ROZHLEDY : MESICNIK PRO HUDEBNI KRITIKU VYDAVA SVAZ CESKYCH SKLADATELU A KONCERTNICH UMELCU.). [Hudeb. rozhl.]. **Added/Corp** SCSKU. Vol. 1, No. 1 (1948)-. Periodical. Czech. Twelve times a year. $82.50. **(Subscription address:** Artia Pegas Press Ltd., Palac Metro Narodni Trida 25, 11210 Prague 1 Czech Republic.**)**
**Ind/Abst** Music Index; RILM Abstr.

XR/0018-7003
**HUDEBNI VEDA.** [Hudeb. veda]. **Added/Corp** Ustav Hudebni Vedy (Ceskoslovenska Akademie Ved) Ustav Teorie a Dejin Umeni CSAV v Praze. Sekce Hudebni Vedy. Vol. 1, No. 1 (1964)-. Periodical. Czech (summaries and/or abstracts in Russian and German). Four times a year. DM141.00. Academia, Publishing House of the Czechoslovak Academy of Sciences, Czech AC SCI, Vodickova 40, PO Box 896, 112 29 Prague 1, Czech Republic. **Tel** 011 42 2 245117. **(Subscription address:** Kubon & Sagner, ABT Zeitschriftenimport, D 80328 Munich Germany.**)** Index available. **Bk Rev**. Documents available from The Genuine Article. ***Continues*** *Hudebni Veda (Prague, Czechoslovakia : 1961), 0018-7003.*
**Desc:** A journal of scientific studies of music. Deals with a great variety of branches of musicology, such as the history of music, aesthetics and theory of musical art, theory of musical composition and structure, the sociology of music and popular music.
**Ind/Abst** Arts Humanit. Citation Index [Full Cov.]; Curr. Contents Arts Humanit.; Music Index; Res. Alert [Full Cov.]; RILM Abstr.

XO
**HUDOBNY ARCHIV.** **Added/Corp** Matica Slovenska. (1974)-. Slovak (summaries and/or abstracts in German and Russian). Matica Slovenska, Slovenska Narodna Kniznica Bibliograficke Oddelenie, Novomeskeho 32, 036 52 Martin Slovakia. **Tel** (842)313-71, FAX (842)331-88, telex 75331. **LC** ML247.1; .H82.

CN/0229-6659
**HUGH LE CAINE PROJECT NEWSLETTER, THE.** [Hugh Le Caine Proj. newsl.]. **Added/Corp** Hugh Le Caine Project. Issue No. 1 (June 1979)-. Newsletter. English. qt. Free. Hugh Le Caine Project, 27 Davies Avenue, Toronto Ontario M4M 2A9. **DD** 789.9/9/0924.

HU/0238-9401
**HUNGARIAN MUSIC QUARTERLY.** ***Ceased.*** Vol. 1, No. 1 (1989)-(1991). Periodical. English. qt. **(Subscription address:** Kultura, PO Box 149, H 1389 Budapest 62 Hungary Telephone:011 36 1 359370**)** **LC** ML248; .H86. **DD** 780/.9439/05. ***Absorbed*** *Hungarian Music News (Budapest, Hungary : 1984).*

US/0191-6785
**HURDY GURDY.** [Hurdy gurdy]. **Added/Corp** Amateur Organists Association International. (19??)-. Periodical. English. Six times a year (Jan., Mar., May, July, Sept., Nov.). $16.50. Amateur Organist Association International, 5101 Parkdale Drive, Minneapolis MN 55416. **Tel** (612)593-0692. **DD** 786.

US/0018-8271
**HYMN, THE.** [Hymn]. **Added/Corp** Hymn Society of America. Vol. 1 (Oct. 1949)-. Academic Scholarly Publication. English. qt (Jan., Apr., July, Oct.). $22.00 student, $40.00 other. The Hymn Society of America and Canada, National Headquarters, Texas Christian University, PO Box 30854, Fort Worth TX 76129. **Tel** (817)921-7608, 1-800-843-4966, FAX (817)921-7333. **ED** David Music. **LC** ML1; .H92. **DD** 783.9/05. Index available. cum. index. **Bk Rev**. **Ad Acc**. **Circ:** 3,500 (ctrl). available on microfilm and microfiche from University Microfilms International (UMI).
**Desc:** Journal of congregational songs for church musicians, clergy and institutional libraries; contains practical and scholarly articles reflecting diverse cultural and theological identities and provides hymn texts and tunes in various styles.
**Ind/Abst** Christ. Period. Index (19??-); Index Book Rev. Relig.; Music Artic. Guide; Music Index; Relig. Index One Period. (1979-); Relig. Theol. Abstr.

DK/0106-4940
**HYMNOLOGISKE MEDDELELSER.** [Hymnol. medd.]. **Added/Corp** Salmehistorisk Selskab (Kbenhavns Universitet). (1971)-. Periodical. Danish (Norwegian and Swedish). qt. Salmehistorisk Selskab, Kobenhavns Universitet, Institut for Kirkehistorie Koebmagergade 44-46, DK-1150 Kobenhavn K, Denmark. **Tel** 45-35-32-36-23. **ED** Peter Balslev-Clausen,

Vagner Lund and Henrik Fibiger Norfeld. **LC** ML3142; .H9. **Bk Rev**. **Circ:** 500.
**Desc:** Articles on hymnology in its historical, literary, theological and sociological settings; emphasis on Scandinavian hymnology.
**Ind/Abst** MLA Int. Bibl. Books Artic. Mod. Lang. Lit.

US/1054-7495
**HYMNOLOGY ANNUAL, THE.** [Hymnol. annu.]. **Added/Corp** Hymn Society in the United States and Canada. Hymn Society of Great Britain and Ireland. International Fellowship for Research in Hymnology. Vol. 1 (1991)-. English. an (April). $48.50 US; $51.50 other. Vande Vere Publishing, Ltd., PO Box 226, 8744 College Avenue, Berrien Springs MI 49103. **Tel** (616)695-3442, FAX (616)695-6515. **LC** IN PROCESS; ML3270; .H956. **DD** 782.

US/0097-6539
**HYPE.** (19??)-. English. Hype, PO Box 14001, Washington DC 20044. **LC** ML1; .H95. **DD** 784.

●US/1064-9859
**I/E (CHANDLER, ARIZ.).** (I/E : THE MAGAZINE OF PROGRESSIVE AND ELECTRONIC MUSIC.). [i/e]. **VFOAT** I E; I.E.; IE. Vol. 1, No. 1 (Fall 1992)-. Periodical. English. qt. $10.00. Think Tank Tomes, 2300 North Yucca, Chandler AZ 85224. **DD** 786.

US
**I.S.A.M. MONOGRAPHS.** **Main/Corp** Brooklyn College. Institute for Studies in American Music. **Added/Corp** Brooklyn College. Institute for Studies in American Music. **VFOAT** Institute for Studies in American Music Monographs; ISAM Monographs. (1973)-. Monographic series. English. ir. Price varies per volume. Institute for Studies in American Music, Brooklyn College, Conservatory of Music, Brooklyn NY 11210. **Tel** (718)780-5655, FAX (718)951-6140. **ED** H. Wiley Hitchcock.
**Desc:** A series of bibliographies, discographies, extended essays, and reference works covering all aspects of American music.
**Ind/Abst** RILM Abstr.

US/0098-9487
**IAJRC JOURNAL.** [IAJRC j.]. **Main/Corp** International Association of Jazz Record Collectors. **Added/Corp** International Association of Jazz Record Collectors. Journal. **VAT** International Association of Jazz Record Collectors Journal. (19??)-. Periodical. English. qt. $40.00. International Association of Jazz Record Collectors, 127 Briarcliff LA, Bell Air MD 21014. **Tel** (410)838-7542, FAX (410)638-0497. **ED** Phil Oldham. **LC** ML156.9; .I6. **DD** 785/.06/7205. **Bk Rev**. **Ad Acc**. **Circ:** 1,300.
**Desc:** Information of importance to jazz record collectors including results of research concerning recordings, labels and musicians; also record and book reviews, and new products of interest to jazz collectors.
**Ind/Abst** Jazz Index; Music Index.

KO
**IHWA UMAK.** **Added/Corp** Ihwa Yoja Taehakkyo. Umak Taehak. Haksaenghoe. **VFOAT** Journal of Music, Ewha Women's University. (1972)-. Periodical. Korean. an. EWHA Women's University / Music, Department of Music, Seoul 120 South Korea. **LC** ML5; .I3.

US/0889-8723
**IJS JAZZ REGISTER.** [IJJ jazz reg.]. **Main/Corp** Rutgers University. Institute of Jazz Studies. **VFOAT** Jazz Register. **VAT** Institute of Jazz Studies Jazz Register. (June 1979)-. English. qt. $35.00. Institute of Jazz Studies, Bradley Hall Room 135 Rutgers, Newark NJ 07102. **Tel** (201)648-5595. **DD** 785. Each issue contains an index to its own contents (no volume index)--loose. cum. index.

US/0098-3535
**ILLINOIS MUSIC COUNTRY MAGAZINE.** (19??)-. Periodical. English. qt. $4.50. New Salem Country Opry, Rural Route 1 Box 246B, Petersburg IL 62675. **LC** ML1; .I48. **DD** 784.

US/0019-2147
**ILLINOIS MUSIC EDUCATOR, THE.** **Added/Corp** Illinois Music Educators Association. (19??)-. Periodical. English. Three times a year (May, Oct., Dec.). $10.00. Illinois Music Educators Association, 807 LaSalle Street/Suite 105, Ottawa IL 61350. **Tel** (815)434-3774. **ED** Don Davis. **Ad Acc**. **Circ:** 6,000 (ctrl).
**Desc:** Information and articles directly related to Music Education in Illinois and information on activities sponsored by the Illinois Music Educators Association.
**Ind/Abst** Music Artic. Guide.

US
**IMA BULLETIN : THE NEWSLETTER OF THE INTERNATIONAL MIDI ASSOCIATION, THE.** **See** Computers-Computer Systems.

US/0162-6450
**IMAGINE (WATERBURY, CONN.).** (IMAGINE.). [Imagine]. (1978)-. Periodical. English. bm. Gorman Bechard, Box 2715, Waterbury CT 06720. **LC** ML3476.8; .I4. **DD** 780/.42/05.
**Ind/Abst** Chicano Index.

US/0892-1911
**IMPROVISOR.** [Improvisor]. (198?-. Periodical. English. ir (Fall). $10.00. The Improvisor, 1705 12th Street South, Birmingham AL 35205. **Tel** (205)-930-0914. **ED** LaDonna Smith and Daney Williams. **DD** 700. **Bk Rev**, (Qty: 2). **Ad Acc**, **Adv Mgr:** LaDonna Smith, **Tel** (205)930-0914. **Circ:** 1,000.
**Desc:** This well read journal celebrating and promoting the art of free improvisation. Articles, reviews, interviews, essays and philisophical comentaries.

US/0360-4365
**IN THEORY ONLY.** ***Suspended.*** [In theory only]. **Added/Corp** Michigan Music Theory Society. (19??)-(1992). Periodical. English. ir. In Theory Only, 700 Burton Memorial Tower, University of Michigan, School of Music, Ann Arbor MI 48109-1270. **Tel** (313)764-0583, 764-1817. **ED** Eric McKee. **LC** ML1; .I59. **DD** 781/.05. Index available. **Bk Rev**. **Ad Acc**. **Circ:** 500 (ctrl). available on microfilm and microfiche from University Microfilms International (UMI). Documents available from The Genuine Article.
**Desc:** Publishes papers, articles, comments on any music theory related topic.
**Ind/Abst** Arts Humanit. Citation Index (19??-19??) [Full Cov.]; Curr. Contents Arts Humanit.; Music Artic. Guide; Music Index; Res. Alert [Full Cov.]; RILM Abstr.

CN/1186-6055
**IN TUNE (EDMONTON).** ([IN TUNE : WORDS ON MUSIC].). [In tune]. **Added/Corp** University of Alberta. Dept. of Music. **VFOAT** In Tune, Words on Music. Vol. 1, No. 1 (Sept./Oct. 1990)-. Periodical. English. bm. University of Alberta Department of Music, 3-82 Fine Arts Building, Edmonton, Alberta T6G 2C9 Canada. **DD** 780/.71/1712334.

II/0019-5995
**INDIAN MUSIC JOURNAL.** [Indian music j.]. **Added/Corp** Delhi Sangita Samaj. Tyaga Bharati (Association). **VFOAT** Indian Music Journal of the Delhi Sangita Samaj; IMJ. No. 1 (1964)-. Periodical. English. an. $12.50. Delhi Sangita Samaj, New Delhi, India. **(Subscription address:** Prints India, 11 Darya Ganj, New Delhi 110002 India.) **LC** ML5; .I413.

US/0273-9933
**INDIANA MUSICATOR.** (INDIANA MUSICATOR : OFFICIAL PUBLICATION OF THE INDIANA MUSIC EDUCATORS ASSOCIATION.). **Added/Corp** Indiana Music Educators Association. Vol. 1 (Mar. 1946)-. Periodical. English. qt (Mar., May, Sept., Nov.). $15.00. Indiana Music Educator Association, School of Music, Ball State University, Muncie IN 47306. **Tel** (317)285-1137, FAX (317) 285-1139. **ED** JoDee Marshall. **LC** ML1; .I623. **Bk Rev**. **Ad Acc**. **Pr Rev**. **Circ:** 2,000 (ctrl).
**Desc:** Presents timely articles dealing with music education. Also presents information dealing with the work of the Music Educators National Conference and the Indiana Musicator.
**Ind/Abst** Music Artic. Guide.

US/0271-8022
**INDIANA THEORY REVIEW.** [Indiana theory rev.]. **Added/Corp** Indiana University, Bloomington. School of Music. Graduate Theory Association. Vol. 1 (Sept. 1977)-. Periodical. English. sa. $15.00 (one year), $26.00 (two year) US; $18.00 (one year), $32.00 (two year) other. Indiana University Foundation, School of Music, Indiana University, Bloomington IN 47405. **Tel** (812)885-0168. **ED** Eric Lai, Clair Sellars. **LC** MT6; .I52. **DD** 781/.05. **Bk Rev**, (Qty: 3-4). **Ad Acc**. **Circ:** 200.
**Desc:** Operated by the Graduate Theory Association of Indiana University, this biannual journal features articles by prominent theorists in North America, and by graduate students in the US and Canada.
**Ind/Abst** Music Artic. Guide; Music Index; RILM Abstr.

US
**INDIANAPOLIS SYMPHONY ORCHESTRA : [PROGRAMS].** **Main/Corp** Indianapolis Symphony Orchestra. (1930)-. English. an. Indianapolis Symphony, 45 Monument Circle, Indianapolis IN 46204-2901. **Tel** (317)924-6321.

CN/0822-8167
**INFO-COMPTOIR MUSICAL.** (INFO-COMPTOIR MUSICAL / ALLIANCE CHORALE ALBERTA.). **Main/Corp** Alliance Chorale Alberta. Vol. 1, No. 1 (Nov. 1981)-. Periodical. French. ir. Free. Alliance Chorale Alberta, 102, 9942-82 Avenue, Edmonton Alberta T6E 1Y9 Canada. **DD** 016.7841/06. ctrl circ.

GW
**INFO / GERMAN BLUES CIRCLE.** **Main/Corp** German Blues Circle. No. 1 (Aug. 1976)-. Periodical. German (English). mo. German Blues Circle, Postfach 180212, W-6000 Frankfurt 18 Germany. **LC** ML3520.8; G47. **DD** 781.643/05.
**Desc:** A blues music journal.

IT/0393-2915
**INFORMAZIONI E STUDI VIVALDIANI.** (INFORMAZIONI E STUDI VIVALDIANI : BOLLETTINO DELL'ISTITUTO ITALIANO ANTONIO VIVALDI, VENEZIA, FONDAZIONE GIORGIO CINI.). [Inf. studi vivaldiani]. **Added/Corp** Istituto Italiano Antonio Vivaldi. Fondazione "Giorgio Cini". (1980)-. Periodical. English (French and Italian). an. $15.00. G. Ricordi & Co. S.p.A., Via Berchet 2, 20121 Milan Italy. **Tel** 011 39 2 8881204, FAX 011 39 2 8881212. **LC** ML410.V82; I56. **DD** 780/.92/4.
**Ind/Abst** Music Index; RILM Abstr.

FR/0987-6960
**INHARMONIQUES.** **Added/Corp** IRCAM (Research institute : France). **VFOAT** In Harmoniques. No. 1 (Dec. 1986)-. Periodical. French. sa. Editions du Centre Pompidou, Service Commerical, 75191 Paris Cedex 04 France. **Tel** 011 33 1 44784288, 011 33 1 44781233, FAX 011 33 1 42725650, telex CNAC GP 212 726. **LC** ML5; .I. **DD** 780.5.

US/0891-0537
**INSIDE BLUEGRASS.** [Inside bluegrass]. **Added/Corp** Minnesota Bluegrass and Old-Time Music Association. Vol. 12, No. 6 (June 1986)-. Periodical. English. Twelve times a year. $15.00. MN Bluegrass & Old Time Music, PO Box 11419, St. Paul MN 55111. **Tel** (612)721-8026. **ED** Douglas Lohman. **LC** ML3519; .I57. **DD** 784.4/3/009. **Bk Rev**. **Ad Acc**. **Circ:** 1,000 (ctrl). ***Continues*** *Minnesota Bluegrass & Old-Time Music Ass'n, 0737-0857.*
**Desc:** Music magazine, specifically Bluegrass and associated styles of american music.

IT/0073-8611
**INSTITUTA ET MONUMENTA. SERIE 2: INSTITUTA.** (1967)-. Monographic series. Italian. ir. Price varies per volume. Fondazione Claudio Monteverdi, Via Ugolani Dati 4, 26100 Cremona Italy. **Tel** 011 39 372 26580.

US/0145-2525
**INSTRUCTIONAL CASSETTE RECORDINGS CATALOG.** [Instr. cassette rec. cat.]. **Main/Corp** Library of Congress. National Library Service for the Blind and Physically Handicapped. **VFOAT** Instructional Cassette Recordings Catalog. **VAT** Music and Musicians. Instructional Cassette Recording Catalog. (19??)-. Catalog. English. ir. Free. National Library Service for the Blind and Physically Handicapped, Library of Congress, 1291 Taylor Street Northwest, Washington DC 20542. **Tel** (800)424-8567, (202)707-5100, (800)424-9100. **LC** ML156.2; .N39. **DD** 016.7899/12. ***Continues*** *Library of Congress. Division for the Blind and Physically Handicapped. Instructional Cassette Recordings Catalog.*
**Desc:** List of instructional music recordings available on loan to eligible individuals.

US/0145-2517
**INSTRUCTIONAL DISC RECORDINGS CATALOG.** [Instr. disc rec. cat.]. **Main/Corp** Library of Congress. National Library Service for the Blind and Physically Handicapped. **VFOAT** Instructional Disc Recordings Catalog. **VAT** Music and Musicians. Instructional Disc Recordings Catalog. (19??)-. Catalog. English. an. National Library Service for the Blind and Physically Handicapped, Library of Congress, 1291 Taylor Street Northwest, Washington DC 20542. **Tel** (800)424-8567, (202)707-5100, (800)424-9100. **LC** ML156.2; .U6. **DD** 016.7899/12/07. ***Continues*** *Music & Musicians. Instructional Disc Recordings Catalog, 0145-2517.*

US/0020-4331
**INSTRUMENTALIST, THE.** [Instrumentalist]. Vol. 1, No. 1 (Sept./Oct. 1946)-. Periodical. English. mo. $22.00 (one year), $37.00 (two year) US; $31.00 (one year), $55.00 (two year) other. Instrumentalist Company, 200 Northfield Road, Northfield IL 60093. **Tel** (708)446-5000, FAX (708)446-6263. **ED** Judy Nelson. **DD** 780. Index available. **Bk Rev**. **Ad Acc**. **Circ:** 21,000. Documents available from UMI Article Clearinghouse.
**Desc:** Contains practical professional information for school band and orchestra directors and professional performers.
**Ind/Abst** Acad. Abstr. Full Text Elite (July 1989-); Acad. Abstr. (July 1989-); Acad. Search (July 1989-); Educ. Index; Humanit. Source (Jul. 1989-); INFO-SOUTH Abstr.; Mag. Artic. Summar. Elite (July 1989-); Mag. Artic. Summar. Select (July 1989-); Mag. Artic. Summar. CD-ROM (July 1989-); Mag. Search; Mid. Search (Jul. 1989-); Music Artic. Guide; Music Index; Newsp. Period. Abstr. (1989-); Prim. Search (Jul. 1989-); Vocat. Search (July 1989-).

GW/0934-3962
**INSTRUMENTENBAU ZEITSCHRIFT, MUSIK INTERNATIONAL : IZ.** **VFOAT** Instrumentenbau Zeitschrift; Musik International; A.IZ; A.Instrumentenbau-Zeitschrift, Musik international. (1990)-. Periodical. German (summaries and/or abstracts in English). Ten times a year. DM88.20. Verlag Franz Schmitt, Kaiserstrasse 99-101, D 53721 Siegburg Germany. **Tel** 011 49 2241 64039, FAX 011 49 2241 53891. **ED** Carsten Durer. **LC** ML5; .I57. **DD** 781.91/05. Index available (bound in issue). **Bk Rev**. **Ad Acc**, **Adv Mgr:** T Leugendorf, **Tel** 224 64039. **Circ:** 4300.

***Continues** Musik International, 0720-0439.*
**Desc:** Information on new products, marketing, monthly focal points; plus reviews on books, records and CD's.

GW/0936-014X
**INSTRUMENTENBAUREPORT.**
[Instrumentenbaureport]. **VFOAT** Instrumentenbau-Report. (1984)-. Periodical. German. sa. DM12.00. Instrumentenbau Report, Wilhelm Erlewein, Laerchenstr 23, W-8077 Zorneding Germany. **Tel** 08106 22476. **UDC** 78. **Bk Rev.** ctrl circ.
**Desc:** Reconstruction of historical musical instruments.

US
**INTEGRAL.** English. an. $16.00 (institutions); $12.00 (individuals). University Rochester, Eastman School of Music, 26 Gibbs Street, Rochester NY 14604. **Tel** (716)274-1550.
**Ind/Abst** Music Artic. Guide; Music Index.

US/0195-6655
**INTER-AMERICAN MUSIC REVIEW.**
[Inter-Am. music rev.]. (Fall 1978)-. Academic Scholarly Publication. English (Portuguese and Spanish). Twice a year. $18.00. Theodore Front Musical Literature, 16122 Cohasset Street, Van Nuys CA 91406. **Tel** (818)994-1902, FAX (818)994-0419. **ED** Robert Stevenson. **LC** ML1; .I7173. **DD** 780/.5. **Bk Rev.**
**Desc:** Articles on aspects of music in the Americas. Emphasis on the scholarly subject.
**Ind/Abst** HAPI Hisp. Am. Period. Index; Music Index; RILM Abstr.

US
**INTER NOS. Added/Corp** South Dakota. University. Dept. of Classics. (19??)-. Periodical. English. NATS / National Association of Teachers of Singing Inc., 2800 University Blvd., North JU Station, Jacksonville FL 32211. **Tel** (904)744-9022.
**Ind/Abst** Music Artic. Guide (?-?).

US
**INTERCOMPANY ANNOUNCEMENTS / OPERA AMERICA.** ***Title Change.*** **Added/Corp** OPERA America. **VFOAT** OPERA America Intercompany Announcements; OPERA America. (1972)-(19??). Periodical. English. Information Service OPERA America, 777 14th Street Northwest, Suite 520, Washington DC 20005. **Tel** (202)347-2800, FAX (202)393-0735.
***Continued by** OPERA America Newsline, 1062-7243.*

NE/0303-3902
**INTERFACE (AMSTERDAM).** ***Title Change.*** (INTERFACE.). [Interface]. Vol. 1 (April 1972)-(199?). Periodical. English. qt. Swets & Zeitlinger BV, Heereweg 347B PO Box 825, 2160 SZ Lisse Holland. **Tel** 011 31 2521 35111, FAX 02521-15888, telex 41325. **ED** Marc Leman, Herman Sabbe, Frits C Weiland, Paul Berg. **LC** ML5; .I578. **DD** 780/.5. **CODEN** IFCEBC. **[CCC]. Bk Rev. Ad Acc. Circ:** 600. Documents available from The Genuine Article, Ask*IEEE. ***Formed by the union of*** *Electronic Music Reports* ***and*** *Seminarie voor Musicologie. Jaarboek.* ***Continued by*** *Journal of New Music Research.*
**Desc:** A journal devoted to discussions of all questions that fall into the borderline area between music and the physical and human sciences. New fields of research, as well as new methods of investigation in known fields, receive special emphasis. In addition, communications on the description of new apparatus, compositional devices, interviews, are eligible for publication.
**Ind/Abst** Arts Humanit. Citation Index [Full Cov.]; INSPEC (April 1972-); Music Index; Res. Alert [Full Cov.]; RILM Abstr.; Soc. Sci. Cit. Index [Select. Cov.].

US
**INTERNATIONAL BUYER'S GUIDE.**
**VFOAT** Billboard International Buyer's Guide. (198?)-. English. an. $83.00. Billboard Publications Inc., 1515 Broadway Billboard, New York NY 10036. **Tel** (212)764-7300, FAX (305)755-7048, telex WU TWX 710-581-6279. **LC** ML18; .B5. **DD** 338.4/778/025.
***Continues** Billboard International Buyer's Guide.*

US/0896-0968
**INTERNATIONAL CHORAL BULLETIN.**
[Int. choral bull.]. **Added/Corp** International Federation for Choral Music. (19??)-. Periodical. English (French, German and Spanish). Four times a year. $15.00. International Federation for Choral Music, University of Illinois At Chicago, Dept. of Performing Arts, 1040 West Harrison Street, Chicago IL 60607-7130. **Tel** (312)996-8744, FAX (312)996-0954. **ED** Michael Anderson. **DD** 784. Index available. cum. index. **Bk Rev.** (Qty: 4-6). **Ad Acc. Pr Rev. Circ:** 2,500.
**Ind/Abst** Music Artic. Guide.

UK
**INTERNATIONAL COUNTRY MUSIC NEWS.** English. mo. £12.75 UK; £16.00 Europe; £18.00 US and Canada. Business Unit, Leicester House, 67 Derby Road, Kegworth Derby DE7 2EN England. **Tel** 0509 673724.

US
**INTERNATIONAL DIRECTORY OF APPROVED MUSIC EDUCATION DOCTORAL DISSERTATIONS IN PROGRESS. Added/Corp** Council for Research in Music Education. University of Illinois at Urbana-Champaign. Graduate Program in Music Education. **VFOAT** Doctoral Dissertations in Progress; Directory of International Music Education Dissertations in Progress. (1989)-. Directory. English. be. $10.00. University of Illinois School of Music, 1114 West Nevada, Urbana IL 61801. **Tel** (217)333-1027. **LC** ML128.I64; I6.
***Continues** International Institutional Directory of Approved Music Education Doctoral Dissertations in Progress.*

●US/1054-6669
**INTERNATIONAL DIRECTORY OF CONTEMPORARY MUSIC. COMPOSERS.** [Int. dir. contemp. music, Compos.]. **Added/Corp** Contemporary Music International Information Service. **VFOAT** Composers. (1991)-. Directory. English. an. $395.00 (two years) Comes also in combination with International Directory of Comtemporary Music Instrumentation. CMIIS, 215 East 12th Street, New York NY 10003. **LC** ML118; .I452. **DD** 780.

●US/1054-6677
**INTERNATIONAL DIRECTORY OF CONTEMPORARY MUSIC. INSTRUMENTATION.** [Int. dir. contemp. music, Instrum.]. **Added/Corp** Contemporary Music International Information Service. **VFOAT** Instrumentation. (1991)-. Directory. English. an. $395.00 (two years) Comes also in combination with International Directory of Comtemporary Music Composers. CMIIS, 215 East 12th Street, New York NY 10003. **LC** ML118; .I45. **DD** 780. ***Continues*** *International Directory of Contemporary Music to ..., 1047-7454.*

●US
**INTERNATIONAL DIRECTORY OF OPERA.** (1992)-. Directory. English. $250.00. St. James Press, PO Box 33477, Detroit MI 48232-5477. **Tel** (800)345-0392.
**Desc:** Evaluates the most important operas and biographies of composers, librettists, producers, designers, performers, and conductors who made them great.

GW/0538-8007
**INTERNATIONAL INVENTORY OF MUSICAL SOURCES.** No. 1, (1960)-. Multiple languages (English, French and German). ir. Baerenreiter-Verlag, KGA Verlagssvc PF 100329, D 34003 Kassel Germany. **Tel** 011 49 561 31050, telex 99504. **(Subscription address:** Foreign Music Distributors, 13 Elkay Drive, Chester, NY 10918 phone: (914)469-5790**) LC** ML113; .I6.

UK
**INTERNATIONAL JOURNAL OF MUSIC EDUCATION / INTERNATIONAL SOCIETY FOR MUSIC EDUCATION.**
**VFOAT** Music Education; IJLME. No. 1 (May 1983)-. Periodical. English. be. $18.00. International Society for Music Education, Music Education Centre, University of Reading, Bulmershe Court, Reading RG6 1H4 England. **Tel** 011 44 734 318846, FAX 011 44 834 352080, 011 44 734 318846. **ED** Jack P B Dobbs and Anthony Kemp. **LC** ML5; .I5785. **DD** 780/.7. Index available (every 6 issues). **Bk Rev. Ad Acc, Adv Mgr:** Elizabeth Smith. **Pr Rev. Circ:** 1,800. available on microfilm from University Microfilms International (UMI).
**Desc:** Publishes articles of interest to music educators around the would, also reviews books, sheet music and teacher aids in the comprehensive review section of the journal.
**Ind/Abst** Aust. Educ. Index (1984-); Music Index.

US/0020-8051
**INTERNATIONAL MUSICIAN.**
(INTERNATIONAL MUSICIAN : OFFICIAL JOURNAL OF THE AMERICAN FEDERATION OF MUSICIANS OF THE UNITED STATES AND CANADA.). [Int. music.]. **Added/Corp** American Federation of Musicians of the United States and Canada. American Federation of Musicians. Vol. 1, (1901)-. Periodical. English. Twelve times a year. $20.00 US; $25.00 Canada; $30.00 (surface mail) other. American Federation of Musicians / New York, 1500 Broadway, Suite 600 Paramount Building, New York NY 10036. **Tel** (212)869-1330. **LC** ML1; .I8. available on microfilm and microfiche from University Microfilms International (UMI).
**Ind/Abst** Music Artic. Guide (1984-); Music Index (1984-).

UK
**INTERNATIONAL MUSICIAN AND RECORDING WORLD.** (19??)-. English. Independent Magazine Ltd, Bridge House, 181 Queen Victoria Street, London EC4V 400 England. **LC** ML5; .I6834. **DD** 780/.42/05.

UK
**INTERNATIONAL PIPER, THE.** (May 1978)-. Periodical. English. mo. International Piper Ltd., Seaton Works, Edinburgh Road, Cockenzie, East Lothian EH32 CHQ Scotland. **LC** ML980; .I6. **DD** 788/.92/05.
**Desc:** Bagpipe music.

CI/0351-5796
**INTERNATIONAL REVIEW OF THE AESTHETICS AND SOCIOLOGY OF MUSIC.** [Int. rev. aesth. sociol. music]. **Main/Corp** International Committee for Aesthetic Studies. **Added/Corp** Muzicka Akademija u Zagrebu. Muzikoloski Zavod. International Committee for Aesthetic Studies. **VFOAT** International Review of the Esthetics and Sociology of Music. Vol. 2, (1971)-. Periodical. English (French, German and Italian; summaries and/or abstracts in French, German, Italian and Serbo-Croatian (Roman)). Twice a year (June, Dec.). $40.00. Muzicka Akademija u Zagrebu, Muzikoloski Zavod, Berlislaviceva 16, 41001 Zagreb Croatia. **(Subscription address:** Mladost Export Import, PO Box 1028, Ilica 30, 41000 Zagreb Croatia.**)** Documents available from The Genuine Article.
***Continues** International Review of Music Aesthetics and Sociology.*
**Ind/Abst** Art Archaeol. Tech. Abstr.; Arts Humanit. Citation Index (19??-19??) [Full Cov.]; Curr. Contents Arts Humanit.; Music Index; Res. Alert [Full Cov.]; RILM Abstr.; Soc. Plann. Policy Dev. Abstr.

UK/0172-0597
**INTERNATIONAL SOCIETY FOR MUSIC EDUCATION YEARBOOK.** ***Title Change.*** (ISME YEARBOOK.). [Int. music educ.]. **Main/Corp** International Society for Music Education. **VFOAT** I.S.M.E. Yearbook; International Music Education. Vol. 1 (1973)-?. English. an. International Society for Music Education, Music Education Centre, University of Reading, Bulmershe Court, Reading RG6 1H4 England. **Tel** 011 44 734 318846, FAX 011 44 834 352080, 011 44 734 318846. **ED** Jack Dobbs. **LC** ML5; .I745. **DD** 780/.7. Index available. cum. index. **Circ:** 2,000 (ctrl). ***Continues*** *International Music Educator.* ***Continued by*** *Conference Proceedings - International Society for Music Education.*
**Desc:** Selected papers from conferences and seminars of the International Society for Music Education.
**Ind/Abst** Music Index; RILM Abstr.

US/0892-0532
**INTERNATIONAL SOCIETY OF BASSISTS.** (INTERNATIONAL SOCIETY OF BASSISTS : MAGAZINE.). [Int. Soc. Bass.]. **Added/Corp** International Society of Bassists. **VFOAT** International Society of Bassists Magazine. (1982)-. Periodical. English. Three times a year. $30.00 (1 year), $55.00 (2 year), $80.00 (3 year) North America; $35.00 (1 year), $65.00 (2 year), $95.00 (3 year) other. International Society of Bassists, 4020 McEwen Suite, Dallas TX 75244. **Tel** (214)233-9107, FAX (214)490-4219. **ED** Don Bowyer. **LC** ML920; .I58. **DD** 787/.41/05. Index available. cum. index. **Bk Rev. Ad Acc. Circ:** 1,600 (ctrl).
***Continues** Newsletter (International Society of Bassists : 1977), 0197-7946.*
**Desc:** For bass performers, teachers, students, and enthusiasts.
**Ind/Abst** Music Artic. Guide; Music Index.

US/0363-5708
**INTERNATIONAL TROMBONE ASSOCIATION SERIES. Main/Corp** International Trombone Association. (1974)-. Monographic series. English. ir. Price varies per volume. 148 Eighth Avenue North, Nashville TN 37203-3798. **Tel** (615)254-8969. **ED** Stephen L Glover. **Bk Rev. Ad Acc. Circ:** 600 (ctrl).
**Desc:** Trombone music series.

UK/0307-2894
**INTERNATIONAL WHO'S WHO IN MUSIC AND MUSICIANS' DIRECTORY.**
**See** Biographies.

SZ
**INTERPRETATION DE LA MUSIQUE FRANCAISE.** French. ir. 100.00F. Slatkine Editions, PO Box 765, 1211 Geneva 3 Switzerland. **Tel** 011 41 22 762551.

US/0276-3052
**INTERVAL (SAN DIEGO, CALIF.).**
***Suspended.*** (INTERVAL.). [Interval]. Vol. 1, May 1978-Suspended with Vol. 5, No. 4. Periodical. English. qt. $18.00. Interval, PO Box 8027, San Diego CA 92102. **Tel** (619)295-9023. **ED** Jonathan Glasier. **Bk Rev. Ad Acc. Circ:** 350.
**Desc:** New music research in new instruments, scales, computers. Works by Dartch, Harrison, Darreg Ben Johnston and microtonal composers and theorists from US and abroad.
**Ind/Abst** Music Index.

GW
**INTERVALLE. Added/Corp** Arbeitskreis fuer Musik in der Jugend (Wolfenbuttel, Germany). (Feb./March 1969)-. Periodical. German. qt. DM10.00 Germany; $6.00 US. Arbeitskreis fuer Musik in der Jugend, Deutsche Federation Junger Chore und Instrumentalgruppen,

Adersheimer Strabe 60, Postfach 16 61, W-3340 Wolfenbuettel Germany. **Tel** 011 49 05331 46016. **ED** Elke Jacobs. **LC** ML5; .I76. **DD** 780/.5. **Bk Rev**. **Ad Acc**. **Circ:** 2,500 (ctrl).
**Desc:** Magazine for members of AMJ and interested nonmembers. Contains notices, festival documentation, articles on music and music education.

CN/1181-7739
**INTERVENTIONS SONORES.** [Interv. son.]. Vol. 1, No. 1 (Winter 1991)-. Periodical. French. Three times a year. 17.00Can$ (institutions), 14.00Can$ (individuals) Canada; 21.00Can$ (institutions), 20.00Can$ (individuals) other. Interventions Sonores, 2080 rue Becancour BP 2, Lyster, Quebec G0S 1V0 Canada. **Tel** (819)389-5774, FAX (819)389-5969. **ED** Sylvie Ouellet. **DD** 615.8/5154/05. **Bk Rev**, (Qty: 12). **Ad Acc**. **Circ:** 800 (ctrl).
**Desc:** A publication on and about music therapy.

US/0889-6607
**INVENTORY OF MUSIC ICONOGRAPHY.** (INVENTORY OF MUSIC ICONOGRAPHY / INTERNATIONAL REPERTORY OF MUSICAL ICONOGRAPHY.). [Inventory music iconogr.]. **Added/Corp** International Repertory of Musical Iconography (Organization) Research Center for Musical Iconography (U.S.). No. 1 (1986)-. Periodical. English. ir. Research Center for Music Iconography, 33 West 42nd Street, Room 1009, New York NY 10036. **Tel** (212)642-2709. **ED** Terence Ford. **LC** ML85; .I6. **DD** 704.9/4978/05. Index available. **Circ:** 400 (ctrl).
**Desc:** Each issue is devoted to an individual museum or collection, and consists of a list of all that collection's artworks that show a musical scene, including instruments, singing, and dancing. Each work is described and detailed indexes to performer, instrument, artist, and subject matter are provided.

CN/1188-0759
**INVITATION A L'OPERA.** **See** The Arts-Performing Arts.

CN/1188-0759
**INVITATION A L'OPERA.** **See** The Arts-Performing Arts.

US/0270-7098
**IOWA JOURNAL OF RESEARCH IN MUSIC EDUCATION.** ***Ceased.*** [Iowa j. res. music educ.]. **Added/Corp** Iowa Music Educators Association. **VFOAT** Journal of Research in Music Education. No. 1 (1976)-(19??). Periodical. English. an. University of Iowa School of Music, Iowa City IA 52242. **Tel** (319)353-3715.

IE
**IRISH MUSICAL STUDIES.** (1990)-. Monographic series. English. ir. Price varies per volume. Irish Academic Press, Kill Lane, Blackrock County Dublin Ireland. **LC** ML287.9; .I74.

GW/0579-5613
**ISO INFORMATION.** [ISO inf.]. **Main/Corp** International Society of Organbuilders. No. 1 (Feb. 1969)-. Periodical. English (German). Three times a year. International Society of OrganBuilders, Martelarenplein 6, B 3000 Leuven Belgium. **Tel** 011 32 6 221252. **LC** ML5; .I686. **DD** 786.6/3.
**Ind/Abst** Music Index.

●BE/1017-7515
**ISO NEWS : THE QUARTERLY MAGAZINE OF THE INTERNATIONAL SOCIETY OF ORGANBUILDERS.** **Added/Corp** International Society of Organbuilders. No. 1 (1991)-. English (French and German). Four times a year. International Society of Organbuilders, Martelarenplein 6 Leuven, B-3000 Leuven Belgium. **Tel** 011 32 6 221252. **LC** IN PROCESS.

IS
**ISRAEL STUDIES IN MUSICOLOGY.** **Added/Corp** Igud ha-Yisreeli le-Musikologyah. Universitah ha-Ivrit bi-Yerushalayim. Merkaz le-Heker ha-Musikah ha-Yehudit. **VFOAT** Mehkarim Be-Musikologyah. (1978)-. Monographic series. English. ir. Price varies per volume. Israel Music Publications, PO Box 7681, Jerusalem Israel. **Tel** 02 241377 8. **LC** ML5; .I833. **DD** 780/.5.

US/0145-3513
**ITA JOURNAL.** **Added/Corp** International Trombone Association. **VFOAT** International Trombone Association Journal. Vol. 11, No. 1 (Jan. 1983)-. Periodical. English. Four times a year (Jan., Apr., July, Oct.,). $30.00 (one year), $50.00 (two years), $70.00 (three years). North Texas State University / Music, School of Music, Denton TX 76203. **Tel** (817)267-3731. **LC** ML1; .I86. **DD** 788/.2/05. ***Continues*** *International Trombone Association. Journal - International Trombone Association, 0145-3513.*
**Ind/Abst** Music Index.

US/0363-2849
**ITG JOURNAL.** [ITG j.]. **Main/Corp** International Trumpet Guild. **Added/Corp** International Trumpet Guild. Journal. **VFOAT** Journal of the International Trumpet Guild. **VAT** International Trumpet Guild Journal. Vol. 1 (Oct. 1976)-. English. qt (4 issues). $26.00. International Trumpet Guild, School of Music, Florida State University, Tallahassee FL 32306. **Tel** (904)644-3424, FAX (904)386-8613. **ED** Anne F. Hardin. **LC** ML1; .I87. **DD** 788/.1/05. Index available. **Bk Rev**. **Ad Acc**. **Circ:** 3,500 (ctrl). ***Absorbed*** *International Trumpet Guild. ITG Newsletter, 0363-2857.* ***Continued in part by*** *Trumpet and Brass Programs, 1061-8856.*
**Desc:** Covers trumpet performance and teaching.
**Ind/Abst** Music Artic. Guide; Music Index (-19??).

IS
**IYUNIM BE-MUSIKAH.** **Added/Corp** League of Composers in Israel. **VFOAT** Musical Prose. (19??)-. Periodical. Hebrew. Israel Composers' League, Nordau Boulevard 73, PO Box 11180, Tel-Aviv Israel. **LC** ML5; .I98. **DD** 780/.95694.

RU/0021-3454
**IZVESTIJA VYSSIH UCEBNYH ZAVEDENIJ. PRIBOROSTROENIE.** (IZVESTIIA VYSSHIKH UCHEBNYKH ZAVEDENII. PRIBOROSTROENIE / MINISTERSTVO VYSSHEGO OBRAZOVANIIA SSSR.). [Izv. vyss. ucebn. zaved., Priborostro.]. **Added/Corp** Soviet Union. Ministerstvo Vysshego Obrazovaniia. Soviet Union. Ministerstvo Vysshego i Srednego Spetsialnogo Obrazovaniia. Soviet Union. Gosudarstvennyi Komitet po Narodnomu Obrazovaniiu. **VFOAT** Priborostroenie; Izvestiia Vysshikh Uchebnykh Zavedenii MV i SSO SSSR. Priborostroenie. (1958)-. Periodical. Russian (table of contents in English). mo. $159.95. **(Subscription address:** East View Publications Inc., 3020 Harbor Lane North, Suite 110, Minneapolis MN 55447.**) CODEN** IVUBAY. Documents available from Article Express International, Ask*IEEE, CASDDS. ***Absorbed in part*** *Nauchnye Doklady Vysshei Shkoly. Mashinostroenie i Priborostroenie.*
**Desc:** Information on instrument making.
**Ind/Abst** Bioeng. Abstr.; Ceram. Abstr. (19??-); Chem. Abstr.; Ei Page One; Eng. Index Annu.; INSPEC (1973-1989); Int. Aerosp. Abstr.

US/0363-8367
**J & F RECORD SPECIAL.** **Added/Corp** J & F Southern Record Sales (Firm). **VAT** J and F Record Special. (Apr./May 1976)-. Periodical. English. bm. J & F Southern Record Sales, 44 North Lake, Pasadena CA 91101. **LC** ML156.9; .J2. **DD** 789.9/131/05.

SZ
**JAHRBUCH.** **Main/Corp** Opernhaus Zurich. (19??)-. German. Jahrbuch, Opernhaus, Zurich Switzerland. **LC** ML1749.8.Z8; O6.

GW
**JAHRBUCH DER BAYERISCHEN STAATSOPER / ANLASSLICH DER MUNCHNER OPERNFESTSPIELE ... HERAUSGEGEBEN VON DER GESELLSCHAFT ZUR FORDERUNG DER MUNCHNER OPERNFESTSPIELE ZUSAMMEN MIT DER INTENDANZ DER BAYERISCHEN STAATSOPER.** **Added/Corp** Bayerische Staatsoper Munchen. Gesellschaft zur Forderung der Munchner Opernfestspiele. (19??)-. German. an. **LC** ML5; .J128. **DD** 782/.0943/36.

GW
**JAHRBUCH DER DEUTSCHEN MUSIKORGANISATION.** **Added/Corp** Germany. Reichsministerium des Innern. Prussia (Germany). Ministerium feur Wissenschaft, Kunst und Volksbildung. (1931)-. German. **LC** ML21; .J2.

GW
**JAHRBUCH DER MUSIKBIBLIOTHEK PETERS.** **Added/Corp** Leipzig. Musikbibliothek Peters. (1894)-. Periodical. German. **LC** ML5; .J15.

GW/0572-6239
**JAHRBUCH DES STAATLICHEN INSTITUTS FUER MUSIKFORSCHUNG PREUSSISCHER KULTURBESITZ.** [Jahrb. Staatl. Inst. Musikforsch. Preuss. Kulturbes.]. **Main/Corp** Staatliches Institut feur Musikforschung. **Added/Corp** Staatliches Institut feur Musikforschung Preussischer Kulturbesitz. (1968)-. Periodical. German. ir. Verlag Merseburger Berlin GmbH, POB 103880, D 34038 Kassel Germany. **Tel** 011 49 561 772002. **LC** ML5; .S74.
**Ind/Abst** RILM Abstr.

GW/0075-2681
**JAHRBUCH FUER LITURGIK UND HYMNOLOGIE.** [Jahrb. Liturg. Hymnol.]. (1955)-. German. an. Price varies. Baerenreiter-Verlag, KGA Verlagssvc PF 100329, D 34003 Kassel Germany. **Tel** 011 49 561 31050, telex 99504. **ED** Konrad Ameln and Alexander Volker. **LC** ML3168; .J3. **Bk Rev**.
**Desc:** Essays and miscellany on liturgy and hymn by international and ecumenical authors. Comprehensive reports on international literature.
**Ind/Abst** RILM Abstr.

GW/0075-2703
**JAHRBUCH FUER MUSIKALISCHE VOLKS- UND VOLKERKUNDE.** [Jahrb. musik. Volks- Volkerkd.e]. **Added/Corp** Gesellschaft feur Musikforschung (Founded 1946). Kommission feur Musikalische Volks- und Volkerkunde. Vol. 1 (1963)-. Multiple languages (German, French and English). an. Breitkopf and Haertel, Obere Waldstr 30, D 65232 Taunusstein Germany. **Tel** 11 49 611 49030. **(Subscription address:** Kasseler Grossauslieferung, KGA Verlagssvc GmbH, PF 102180, W 3500 Kassel F R Germany, phone: 011 49 561 8070346**) ED** F. Bose. **LC** ML5; .J24.
**Ind/Abst** Anthropol. Index; Anthropol. Lit.; RILM Abstr.

GW/0724-8156
**JAHRBUCH FUER OPERNFORSCHUNG.** (1985)-. Monographic series. English (French and German). ir. Price varies per volume. Verlag Peter Lang GmbH, Eschborner Landstrasse 42-50, D 60489 Frankfurt Germany. **Tel** 011 49 69 7807050. **(Subscription address:** Verlag Peter Lang AG, Jupiterstrasse 15, CH-3000 Bern 15 Switzerland.**) LC** ML1699; .J33. **DD** 782.1/05.
**Ind/Abst** Music Index.

GW/0075-2789
**JAHRBUCH FUER VOLKSLIEDFORSCHUNG.** [Jahrb. Volksliedforsch.]. Vol. 1 (1928)-. German. an. Price varies per volume. Erich Schmidt Verlag GmbH, Postfach 304240, D 10724 Berlin Germany. **Tel** 011 49 30 25008525. **ED** John Meier. **LC** ML3630; .J2. **Bk Rev**. **Ad Acc**. Documents available from The Genuine Article.
**Desc:** Concerned with folk song research.
**Ind/Abst** Arts Humanit. Citation Index [Full Cov.]; Curr. Contents Arts Humanit.; MLA Int. Bibl. Books Artic. Mod. Lang. Lit.; Res. Alert [Full Cov.]; RILM Abstr.; Romant. Move.; Soc. Sci. Cit. Index [Select. Cov.].

GW/0323-3693
**JAHRESVERZEICHNIS DER MUSIKALIEN UND MUSIKSCHRIFTEN.** **Added/Corp** Deutsche Bucherei (Germany). Vol. 118, (1969)-. Monographic series. German. ir. Price varies per volume. Broude Brothers Limited, 141 White Oaks Road, Williamstown MA 01267. **Tel** (413)458-8132, (800)525-8559. ***Continues*** *Jahresverzeichnis der Deutschen Musikalien und Musikschriften, 0075-2959.*

US/0890-8672
**JALEO.** [Jaleo]. **Added/Corp** Flamenco Association of San Diego. (19??)-. Periodical. English. ir. $20.00. Jaleo, Box 4706, San Diego CA 92104. **Tel** (619)444-3050. **LC** ML3712; .J28. **DD** 785.4/1/0946. Index available (free).

CN/0229-2203
**JAMBOREE COUNTRY MUSIC MAGAZINE.** [Jamboree ctry. music mag.]. **VFOAT** Jamboree. Vol. 1, No. 7 (Oct. 1980)-. Periodical. English. mo. Jamboree Country Music Magazine, PO Box 452, St Catharines Ontario L2R 6V9 Canada. **DD** 784.5/2/005. ***Continues*** *Fan Fair Country Music Magazine, 0229-219X.*

US/0092-0525
**JAZZ DIGEST.** (19??)-. Periodical. English. mo. $5.00. Jazz Digest, 79 Lincoln Avenue, Bergenfield NJ 07621. **LC** ML1; .J236. **DD** 789.9/136/54205. ***Supersedes*** *Hip; The Jazz Record Digest.*

US/0730-9791
**JAZZ EDUCATORS JOURNAL.** (JAZZ EDUCATORS JOURNAL : OFFICIAL MAGAZINE OF THE NATIONAL ASSOCIATION OF JAZZ EDUCATORS.). [Jazz educ. j.]. **Added/Corp** National Association of Jazz Educators. Vol. 13, No. 2 (Dec. 1980/Jan. 1981)-. Periodical. English. Five times a year. $25.00 US; $35.00 other. International Association of Jazz Educators, Box 724, Manhattan KS 66502. **Tel** (913)776-8744. **ED** John Kuzmich Jr. **LC** ML1; .N12. **DD** 785.42/05. Index available ($15.00). cum. index. **Bk Rev**. **Ad Acc**, **Adv Mgr Tel** (913)776-8744. **Circ:** 7,000 (ctrl). available on microfilm. ***Continues*** *NAJE Educator.*
**Desc:** Educational and historical articles, sources for up-to-date teaching and performing material, graded music lists, and other necessary aids for jazz education.
**Ind/Abst** Music Artic. Guide; Music Index.

US/0882-0368
**JAZZ FESTIVALS INTERNATIONAL DIRECTORY.** (JAZZ FESTIVALS INTERNATIONAL DIRECTORY / COMPILED BY JAN A. BYRCZEK.). [Jazz festiv. int. dir.]. **Added/Corp** Jazz World Society. **VFOAT** Festivals International Directory. (198?)-. Directory. English. an. Jazz World Society, 1697 Broadway Suite 1203, New York NY 10019. **Tel** (201)939-0836. **LC** ML3505.8; .J376. **DD** 785.42/07/9. ***Continues*** *World Jazz Calendar of Festivals & Events, 0275-973X.*

US/0021-5635
**JAZZ FORUM.** ***Ceased.*** [Jazz forum]. Vol. for (1967)-(1992). Periodical. English. bm. Jazz World Society, 1697 Broadway Suite 1203, New York NY 10019. **Tel** (201)939-0836. **ED** Jan A Byrczek. **LC** ML3505.8; .J38. **DD** 785.42/05. **Bk Rev**. **Ad Acc**. **Circ:**

6,000. available on microfilm and microfiche from University Microfilms International (UMI).
**Desc:** Market place for jazz industry offering opportunities for communication and cooperation worldwide.
**Ind/Abst** Music Index.

UK/0140-2285
**JAZZ JOURNAL INTERNATIONAL.** [Jazz j. int.]. Vol. 30, No. 5 (May 1977)-. Periodical. English. mo. £28.00 UK; £36.00 other Europe (surface sea-mail), $84.00 (airmail) US. Jazz Journal Ltd., 1/5 Clerkenwell Road, London EC1M 5PA England. **Tel** 011 44 71 608 1348, 011 44 71 608 1362, FAX 011 44 71 608 1292. **ED** Eddie Cook. **LC** ML5; .J316. Index available. **Bk Rev. Ad Acc. Circ:** 12,000. available on microfilm and microfiche from University Microfilms International (UMI). ***Continues** Jazz Journal.*
**Desc:** Jazz music: records, musicians, books, films, profiles, interviews, previews, and reviews.
**Ind/Abst** Music Index.

FR/0021-566X
**JAZZ MAGAZINE (PARIS).** (JAZZ MAGAZINE.). [Jazz mag.]. No. 1 (Dec. 1954)-. Periodical. French. Eleven times a year. 259.55F France; 327.00 others. Publications Filipacchi, 63-65 Champs Elysees, 75008 Paris France. **Tel** 011 33 1 40747000, telex 651-294. **LC** ML5; .J318. available on microfilm and microfiche from University Microfilms International (UMI).
**Ind/Abst** Music Index.

CN/0383-9206
**JAZZ OTTAWA. VFOAT** Jazz Messenger; Jazz Notes. Vol. 1, (Mar. 1975)-. Periodical. English. Six times a year (Feb., Apr., June, Aug., Oct., Dec.). 6.00Can$. Jazz Ottawa, 1702-500 Laurier Avenue West, Ottawa Ontario K1R 5E1 Canada. **Tel** (613)232-9387. **ED** Janet Matthews. **DD** 785.4/2/0971384. Index available. **Bk Rev. Ad Acc. Circ:** 250 (ctrl).
**Desc:** Local live jazz listings. Profiles on local musicians. Information and news releases of the International Jazz World and club news and activities.

GW/0021-5686
**JAZZ-PODIUM.** (JAZZ PODIUM.). [Jazz-Podium]. Vol. 1 (1952)-. Periodical. German. Twelve times a year. Jazz Podium, Vogelsangstrasse 32, W 7000 Stuttgart 1 Germany. **Tel** 011 49 0711 631530. **ED** Dieter Zimmerle. **LC** ML5; .J337. **Bk Rev. Ad Acc. Circ:** 10,500.
**Desc:** All about jazz music: radio and club programs, concerts, news, portraits, reports, interviews, etc.
**Ind/Abst** Music Index; RILM Abstr.

US/0270-4048
**JAZZ RAG.** [Jazz rag]. (19??)-. Periodical. English. mo. Jazz Rag, PO Box 1124, Berkeley CA 94701. **LC** ML156.9; .J4. **DD** 016.78899/12542.

CN/0843-3151
**JAZZ REPORT (TORONTO).** (THE JAZZ REPORT.). [Jazz rep]. Vol. 1, No. 1 (Aug./Sept. 1987)-. Periodical. English. qt. 15.00Can$ Canada; 18.00Can$ other. Jazz Report, 22 Helena Avenue, Toronto ONT M6G 2H2 Canada. **Tel** (416)656-7366, FAX (416)656-7366. **ED** Greg Sutherland. **DD** 785.42/05. Index available. cum. index. **Bk Rev**, (Qty: 8). **Ad Acc, Adv Mgr:** Bill King, **Tel** (416)656-7366. **Pr Rev.**
**Desc:** Guide to improvised music featuring interviews, profiles, columns, pictorials, record reviews, new releases, compositions, and radio and club listings.

US
**JAZZ RESEARCH PAPERS. Added/Corp** National Association of Jazz Educators. (1984)-. English. IAJE Publications, PO Box 724, Manhattan KS 66502. **LC** ML3505.8; .P76. **DD** 785.42/05. ***Continues** Proceedings of NAJE Research.*
**Ind/Abst** Music Index.

US/1060-670X
**JAZZ REVIEW AND COLLECTOR'S DISCOGRAPHY, THE.** [Jazz rev. collect. discog.]. **VFOAT** Jazz Review. (1991)-. Periodical. English. mo. $19.80 US; $29.80 others. Jazz Review, 2005 Palo Verde Avenue, Suite 158, Long Beach CA 90815. **Tel** (213)493-6136. **DD** 781.

US
**JAZZ SCENE, LA.** (19??)-. English. Twelve times a year. $20.00. La Jazz Scene, 12439 Magnolia Boulevard, Suite 254, North Hollywood CA 91607. **Tel** (818)504-2115. **ED** Myrna Daniels. **Bk Rev**, (Qty: 15). **Ad Acc. Circ:** 38,000 (ctrl).
**Desc:** A guide to jazz activities in the Los Angeles area; contains reviews, profiles, interviews, and calendar.

US
**JAZZ SPOTLITE NEWS.** (1979)-. Periodical. English. Four times a year. $15.00. Jazz Spotlite Productions, 701 7th Avenue/Suite 9W, New York NY 10036.

US/0272-572X
**JAZZ TIMES (WASHINGTON).** (JAZZ TIMES.). [Jazz times]. **VFOAT** Jazztimes. (June 1980)-. Periodical. English. Ten times a year (Except Jan. and Aug.). $21.95 US; $31.95 Canada; $59.95 other. Jazz Times, 7961 Eastern Avenue, Suite 303, Silver Spring MD 20910. **Tel** (301)588-4114, FAX (301)588-5531. **ED** Mike Joyce. **LC** ML1; .R232. **DD** 785.42/05. cum. index. **Bk Rev. Ad Acc, Adv Mgr:** Lee Mergner. **Circ:** 73,000 (ctrl). available on microfiche from University Microfilms International (UMI). ***Continues** Radio Free Jazz, 0145-5125.*
**Desc:** Reviews and promotes jazz in all its varieties; also concerts, books, recordings, and musicians.
**Ind/Abst** Music Artic. Guide; Music Index.

US/0749-4564
**JAZZ WORLD (NEW YORK, N.Y. 1984).** (JAZZ WORLD.). [Jazz world]. **Added/Corp** Jazz World Society. Vol. 14, No. 59 (1984)-. Periodical. English. ir. $25.00 individual members. Jazz World Society, 1697 Broadway Suite 1203, New York NY 10019. **Tel** (201)939-0836. **ED** Jan A. Byrczek. **LC** ML3505.8; .J37. **DD** 785.42/05. **Bk Rev. Circ:** 6,000. ***Continues** Jazz World Index, 0886-1927.*
**Desc:** As an organ of the Jazz World Society, it serves as a market place for the whole jazz industry, offering worldwide opportunities for communication and cooperation.

AG
**JAZZBAND.** (March/April 1972)-. Periodical. Spanish. bm. $2.00 single issue. Yerbal No 2291, Dpto 62, Buenos Aires Argentina. **LC** ML5; .J345. **DD** 785.4/2/05.

AU/0075-3572
**JAZZFORSCHUNG (GRAZ).** (JAZZFORSCHUNG.). [Jazzforschung]. **Added/Corp** Hochschule feur Musik und Darstellende Kunst in Graz. Institut feur Jazzforschung. International Society for Jazz Research. **VFOAT** Jazz Research. Vol. 1, (1969)-. German (English; summaries and/or abstracts in English). an. Akademische Druck & Verlagsanstalt, Schoenaugasse 6, Postfach 598, A 8010 Graz Austria. **Tel** 011 43 316 813460. **LC** ML5; .J35. **DD** 785.42/05.
**Ind/Abst** Music Index; RILM Abstr.

GW/0021-5724
**JAZZFREUND (MENDEN), DER.** (DER JAZZFREUND.). [Jazzfreund]. (1959)-. Periodical. German. qt. Gerhard Conrad, Von-Stauffenburg Str 24, W-5750 Menden Germany. **Tel** 02373-63776. **ED** Gerhard Conrad. **LC** ML5; .J355. **Bk Rev. Ad Acc. Circ:** 500.

US/0741-5885
**JAZZIZ (GAINESVILLE, FLA.).** (JAZZIZ.). [Jazziz]. Vol. 1, No. 1 (Jan./Feb. 1984)-. Periodical. English. bm. $12.95 (one year), $25.00 (two years), $37.00 (three years) US; $18.00 (Canada & Mexico); $30.00 (other) airmail. Meg Inc., 3620 NW 43rd Street, Suite D, Gainesville FL 32606. **Tel** (904)375-3705, FAX (904)375-7268. **ED** Mike Fagien, Will Kinnally, Tom Gillen. **DD** 785. **Bk Rev. Ad Acc. Circ:** 60,000 (ctrl). available on microfilm and microfiche from University Microfilms International (UMI).
**Desc:** Contains articles for new and old music enthusiasts, practicing musicians and professionals in the music industry. Primary awareness is on artist profiles, new releases, labels, new age and Brazilian music, new products (audio, video, instruments, accessories). Reviews: books, records, CDs, videos.
**Ind/Abst** Music Artic. Guide (?-?).

US/0890-6440
**JAZZLETTER.** (GENE LEES JAZZLETTER.). [Jazzletter]. **VFOAT** Gene Lees Jazz Letter; Jazz Letter. Vol. 1, No. 1 (Aug. 15, 1981)-. Periodical. English. mo. $75.00. Gene Lee's Jazzletter, PO Box 240, Ojai CA 93024. **LC** ML3505.8; .G45. **DD** 785.42/05.

SW/0332-7248
**JAZZNYTT.** (JAZZ-NYTT.). [Jazznytt]. **Added/Corp** Svenska Jazzriksforbundet. (1960)-. Periodical. Swedish. ir. Svenska JazzriksForbundet, Box 570, 107271 Stockholm Sweden. **LC** ML5; .J335.

US/0198-6805
**JAZZOLOGIST, THE.** [Jazzologist]. **Added/Corp** New Orleans Jazz Club of Calif. (19??)-. English. ir. New Orleans Jazz Club of California, PO Box 1225, Kerrville TX 78028. available on microfilm.

SW/0345-5653
**JEFFERSON.** [Jefferson]. **Added/Corp** Scandinavian Blues Association. (1969)-. Periodical. Swedish (English). qt. Kr130.00 (surface mail), Kr180.00 (airmail). Scandinavian Blues Association, c/o I. Westergren, Skaeftingebacken 21, S-16364 Spanga Sweden. **Tel** 011 46 8 7612687, FAX 011 46 8 7022118. **ED** Tommy Lofgren. **LC** ML5; .J36. **DD** 784. **Bk Rev. Ad Acc. Circ:** 2000 (ctrl).
**Desc:** Covers blues and folk music.
**Ind/Abst** Jazz Index.

FR/0021-6208
**JEUNESSE ET ORGUE. *Ceased.*** [Jeun. orgue]. No. 1, April/May 1970-Ceased with No. 70. Periodical. French. qt. Rev Jeunesse Orgue, La Canterane, B17 rue J Verne, 33270 Floirac France. **Tel** 011 33 56 863738. **LC** ML5; .J39. **DD** 786.5/05.
**Ind/Abst** Music Index (-19??).

CN/0317-0489
**JMC BULLETIN. Main/Corp** Jeunesses Musicales of Canada. (Jan. 1974)-. Bulletin. English. ir. Jeunesses Musicales of Canada, 462 Cote Ste-Catherine Road, Montreal Quebec H2V 2B4 Canada. **DD** 785.06/2/71.

US/0195-4040
**JOEL WHITBURN'S TOP POP SINGLES.** **See** Music-Abstracting, Bibliographies and Statistics.

US/1061-5032
**JOR QUARTERLY.** [JOR q.]. **Added/Corp** Universal World Communications. **VFOAT** Journal of Rap Expression and Hip Hop Culture. Vol. 1, No. 1 (Fall 1991)-. Periodical. English. qt. JOR Quarterly, 2214 North 18th Street, Philadelphia PA 19132. **LC** ML3531; .J68. **DD** 782.42164.

US/0735-1585
**JOSLIN'S JAZZ JOURNAL.** [Joslin's jazz j.]. Vol. 1, No. 1 (Feb. 1982)-. Periodical. English. Four times a year. $18.00. Joslin's Jazz Journal, Box 213, Parsons KS 67357. **Tel** (316)421-4114. **ED** Gene Voslin. **LC** ML156.4.J3; J7. **DD** 789.9/12542/05. **Bk Rev. Ad Acc. Circ:** 1,300 (ctrl).
**Desc:** Contains information pertaining to jazz record history and research, popular and country recordings of the twenties, thirties and nineties.

US
**JOTS AND TITLES. Added/Corp** University of Colorado, Boulder. Music Library. **VFOAT** Jots & Titles. Vol. 2, No. 3 (Nov. 1977)-. Periodical. English. ir. Free on request. University of Colorado Library, Music Library, Boulder CO 80918. **Tel** (303)492-8093. ***Continues** Music Library Newsletter.*

CN/0838-9349
**JOURNAL DE MUSIQUE ANCIENNE.** [J. musique anc.]. **Added/Corp** Studio de Musique Ancienne de Montreal. Vol. 9, No. 1 (Oct. 1987)-. Periodical. French (English). Four times a year. 15.00Can$ US & Canada; 20.00Can$ other. Journal Musique Ancienne Montreal, 3575 Boul St. Laurent Bureau 422, Montreal Quebec H2X 2T7 Canada. **Tel** (514)845-2707. **ED** Francois Filiatrault. **DD** 780/.5. Index available. **Bk Rev. Ad Acc. Circ:** 1,000. ***Continues** Tic-Toc-Choc, 0227-4299.*
**Desc:** Familiarizes music lovers with music before 1800's. Articles on books, records reviews, historical and practical aspects of early music.

UK/0072-0127
**JOURNAL - GALPIN SOCIETY.** (THE GALPIN SOCIETY JOURNAL.). [J. - Galpin Soc.]. **Main/Corp** Galpin Society. No. 1 (March 1948)-. English. an. £15.00 (individual) UK; £20.00 (individuals), £25.00 (institutions) other Comes with Galpin Society membership. The Galpin Society, 7 Perceval Avenue, London NW3 4PY England. **Tel** 011 44 71 4350370. **ED** Dr. David Rycroft. **LC** ML5; .G26. **DD** 781.91/05. cum. index. **Bk Rev**, (Qty: varies). **Ad Acc. Circ:** 1,500 (ctrl). available on microfilm and microfiche from University Microfilms International (UMI).
**Desc:** Musical instrument research.
**Ind/Abst** BHA : Biblio. Hist. Art; Br. Humanit. Index; Music Index; RILM Abstr.

US/1048-2482
**JOURNAL OF AMERICAN ORGANBUILDING.** [J. Am. Organbuild.]. **Added/Corp** American Institute of Organbuilders. **VFOAT** Journal of American Organ Building. (1986)-. Periodical. English. Four times a year (Mar., June, Sept., Dec.). $12.00. American Institute of Organbuilders, PO Box 130982, Houston TX 77219. **Tel** (713)529-2212. **ED** Howard Maple. **LC** ML549.8; .J69. **DD** 786.5/1923/097305. **Bk Rev**, (Qty: 2). **Ad Acc, Adv Mgr:** Howard Maple, **Tel** (713)529-2212. ctrl circ. ***Continues** AIO Newsletter.*
**Desc:** Technical articles and product reviews for builders and maintaining of pipe organs.

US/0021-9207
**JOURNAL OF BAND RESEARCH.** [J. band res.]. **Added/Corp** American Bandmasters Association. **VFOAT** ABA Journal of Band Research. Vol. 1 (Autumn 1964)-. Academic Scholarly Publication. English. sa. $7.00 (one year), $13.50 (two year), $20.00 (three year) US; $10.00 (one year), $19.50 (two year), $29.00 (three year) other. Journal of Band Research, Troy State University Press, Troy AL 36082. **Tel** (205)670-3258. **ED** Frances Conner. **LC** UNC. **DD** 785. **Circ:** 1,200. available on microfilm and microfiche from University Microfilms International (UMI). Documents available from The Genuine Article.
**Desc:** A scholarly journal encompassing the whole spectrum of band/wind ensemble research, serves as a stimulus and outlet for valid scholarly research.
**Ind/Abst** Arts Humanit. Citation Index (19??-19??) [Full Cov.]; Curr. Contents Arts Humanit.; Music Artic. Guide; Music Index; Res. Alert [Full Cov.]; RILM Abstr.

UK/0951-5038
**JOURNAL OF BRITISH MUSIC THERAPY. Added/Corp** British Society for Music Therapy. Association of Professional Music Therapists (Great Britain). **VFOAT** JBMT. Vol. 1, No. 1 (1987)-. Periodical. English. Twice a year (Apr., Oct.). £50.00. British Society for Music Therapy, 69 Avondale Avenue,

East Barnet Herts EN4 8NB England. **Tel** 011 44 81 368 8879. **ED** J. Robarts. **LC** ML3919; .J68. **DD** 615.8/5154/05. **NLM** W1; JO57JK. Index available. cum. index. **Bk Rev**. **Ad Acc**. **Circ:** 800 (ctrl).

US/0092-0517
**JOURNAL OF COUNTRY MUSIC, THE.** [J. ctry. music]. **Added/Corp** Country Music Foundation. Vol. 2, No. 4 (Winter 1971)-. Periodical. English. Three times a year (Apr., Aug., Dec.). $18.00 (individuals); $28.00 (institutions). Country Music Foundation, 4 Music Square East, Nashville TN 37203. **Tel** (615)256-1639, (800)255-2357. **ED** Paul Kingsbury. **LC** ML1; .C91774. **DD** 784. Index available. **Bk Rev**. **Circ:** 1,000. Documents available from The Genuine Article. ***Continues*** *Country Music Foundation. News Letter.*
**Desc:** Articles and reviews by leading scholars and pertaining to country music.
**Ind/Abst** Arts Humanit. Citation Index [Full Cov.]; Curr. Contents Arts Humanit.; MLA Int. Bibl. Books Artic. Mod. Lang. Lit.; Music Index (Vol. 14, No. 1, 1991-); Res. Alert [Full Cov.]; RILM Abstr.

US/0735-4371
**JOURNAL OF GUITAR ACOUSTICS.** (Dec. 1980)-. Periodical. English. qt. $38.00. Journal of Guitar Acoustics, 146 Lull Road, New Boston NH 03070. **Tel** (313)665-7808. **LC** ML1015.G9; J68. **DD** 787.6/12/01534. Index available in last issue of volume--attached.

UK
**JOURNAL OF JAZZ DISCOGRAPHY.** (Nov. 1976)-. Periodical. English. C. Evans, 83 Church Road Newport Ghent, South Wales NPT 7EH England. **LC** ML156.9; .J6. **DD** 016.7899/12.

US/0197-0100
**JOURNAL OF JEWISH MUSIC AND LITURGY.** [J. Jew. music liturg.]. **Added/Corp** Cantorial Council of America. Vol. 1, No. 1 (June 1976)-. Periodical. English (Hebrew). an. $8.00 US; $9.00 Canada; $11.00 other. Yeshiva University, Cantorial Council of America, 500 West 185th Street, New York NY 10033. **Tel** (212)960-5359, (212)960-5353. **ED** Macy Nulman, 7460 Andorra Place, Boca Raton, FL 33433; (407)362-0385. **LC** ML3195; .J69. **DD** 783/.02/9605. **Bk Rev**. **Circ:** 1,000.
**Desc:** An analytical study of Jewish music and the liturgy of the synagogue services. Related articles concerning the cantorial profession.

US/1057-0837
**JOURNAL OF MUSIC TEACHER EDUCATION.** (JOURNAL OF MUSIC TEACHER EDUCATION : JMTE.). [J. music teach. educ.]. **Added/Corp** Society for Music Teacher Education (Music Educators National Conference (U.S.)). **VFOAT** JMTE. Vol. 1, No. 1 (Fall 1991)-. Periodical. English. sa. $12.00 US; $14.00 Canada & Mexico; $16.00 other. Music Educators National Conference, 1806 Robert Fulton Drive, Reston VA 22091. **Tel** (703)860-4000, (800)336-3768. **LC** IN PROCESS. **DD** 370.

US/0022-2909
**JOURNAL OF MUSIC THEORY.** [J. music theory]. V. 1- March 1957-. Periodical. English. sa (2 issues). $21.00 (individuals), $27.00 (institutions) one year, $54.00 (individuals), $70.00 (institutions) two year. The Journal of Music Theory, Yale School of Music, New Haven CT 06520. **Tel** (203)787-8372. **LC** ML1; .J68. **DD** 781. available on microfilm and microfiche from University Microfilms International (UMI). Documents available from The Genuine Article.
**Ind/Abst** Acad. Search (Jan. 1993-); Arts Humanit. Citation Index (19??-19??) [Full Cov.]; Curr. Contents Arts Humanit.; Humanit. Source (Jul. 1993-); INFO-SOUTH Abstr.; Mag. Search; Music Artic. Guide; Music Index; Res. Alert [Full Cov.]; RILM Abstr.; Soc. Sci. Cit. Index [Select. Cov.].

US/0891-7639
**JOURNAL OF MUSIC THEORY PEDAGOGY, THE.** **Added/Corp** University of Oklahoma. School of Music. Gail Boyd de Stwolinski Center for Music Theory Pedagogy. Vol. 1, No. 1 (Spring 1987)-. Periodical. English. an (Oct.). $15.00 Student & retired faculty; $20.00 (individual); $30.00 (institutions). Journal of Music Theory Pedagogy, School of Music, University of Oklahoma, Norman OK 73019. **Tel** (405)325-2081, (405)325-5001. **ED** Mary Wennerstrom. **LC** MT10; .J85. **DD** 781/.07. **Bk Rev**, (Qty: 2-4). **Ad Acc**, **Adv Mgr:** A. Lanning, **Tel** (405)364-7328. **Pr Rev. Circ:** 800.
**Desc:** A journal devoted exclusively to the problems of teaching and learning music theory.
**Ind/Abst** Music Artic. Guide; Music Index.

US/0022-2917
**JOURNAL OF MUSIC THERAPY.** [J. music ther.]. **Added/Corp** National Association for Music Therapy. Vol. 1 (March 1964)-. Periodical. English. qt. $95.00 US; $100.00 other. National Association for Music Therapy Inc., 8455 Colesville Road, Suite 930, Silver Spring MD 20910. **Tel** (301)589-3300, FAX (301)589-5175. **ED** Jayne Standley. **LC** ML1; .J685. **DD** 615/.837/05. **NLM** W1 JO776. **CODEN** JMUTA2. Index available in last issue of volume--attached. **Bk Rev**. **Pr Rev**. **Acid Free**. **Circ:** 4,500 (ctrl). available on microfilm and microfiche from University Microfilms International (UMI). Documents available from The Genuine Article. ***Supersedes*** *Bulletin of NAMT.*
**Desc:** Forum for authoritative articles of current music therapy research and theory. Articles explore the use of music in the behavioral sciences and include book reviews and guest editorials.
**Ind/Abst** Arts Humanit. Citation Index [Full Cov.]; Curr. Contents Arts Humanit.; Curr. Contents Soc. Behav. Sci.; Educ. Index; Except. Child Educ. Resour.; Health Plan. Adminis.; Hospit. Health Admin. Index; Music Artic. Guide; Music Index; Psychol. Abstr. (1964-); PsycINFO; PsycLit; Res. Alert [Full Cov.]; RILM Abstr.; Soc. Sci. Cit. Index [Full Cov.].

US/0141-1896
**JOURNAL OF MUSICOLOGICAL RESEARCH, THE.** [J. musicol. res.]. Vol. 3 (Oct. 1979)-. Periodical. English. Four times a year. £76.00. Gordon & Breach Science Publishers, PO Box 90, Reading RG1 8JL England. **Tel** 011 44 734 560080, FAX 011 44 734 568211. **(Subscription address:** International Publishers Distributor at one of the following addresses: 820 Town Center Drive, Langhorne, PA 19047; or PO Box 90, Reading Berkshire RG1 8JL UK; or Kent Ridge PO Box 1180, Singapore 9111, Republic of Singapore) **ED** Ralph P. Locke. **LC** ML5; .M6415. **DD** 780/.5. **[CCC]**. **Bk Rev**. **Ad Acc**. Documents available from The Genuine Article. ***Continues*** *Music & Man, 0306-2082.*
**Desc:** Publishes original articles representing a wide range of approaches to the study of music, including historical and archival studies, theory and analysis, ethnomusicology, interdisciplinary explorations, critical and interpretive essays, and reports and reflections on the current state of musical scholarship.
**Ind/Abst** Arts Humanit. Citation Index [Full Cov.]; Br. Humanit. Index; Curr. Contents Arts Humanit.; Music Artic. Guide; Music Index; Res. Alert [Full Cov.].

US/0277-9269
**JOURNAL OF MUSICOLOGY (ST. JOSEPH, MICH.), THE.** (THE JOURNAL OF MUSICOLOGY : JM.). [J. musicol.]. **VFOAT** JM; J.M. Vol. 1, No. 1 (Jan. 1982)-. Periodical. English. qt (Jan., Apr., July, Oct.). $32.00 (individuals), $65.00 (institutions), $23.00 (students). University of California Press, 2120 Berkeley Way, Berkeley CA 94720. **Tel** (510)642-4191, (510)642-3907, FAX (510)642-9917. **ED** Marian Green. **LC** ML1; .J693. **DD** 780/.5. **[CCC]**. **Bk Rev**. **Ad Acc**. **Circ:** 1,500 (ctrl). available on microfilm and microfiche from University Microfilms International (UMI). Documents available from The Genuine Article, UMI Article Clearinghouse.
**Desc:** Music history, criticism, analysis, performance practice.
**Ind/Abst** Acad. Search (July 1993-); Am. Hist. Life (1989-); Am. Bibliogr. Slavic East Europ. Stud.; Arts Humanit. Citation Index [Full Cov.]; Curr. Contents Arts Humanit.; Expand. Acad. Index (1989-); Humanit. Index; Humanit. Source (Jul. 1993-); INFO-SOUTH Abstr.; Mag. Search; Music Artic. Guide; Music Index; Newsp. Period. Abstr. (1991-); Res. Alert [Full Cov.]; Romant. Move.; Soc. Sci. Cit. Index [Select. Cov.].

NE/0929-8215
**JOURNAL OF NEW MUSIC RESEARCH.** English. Four times a year. Fl445.00 (institutions). Swets & Zeitlinger BV, Heereweg 347B PO Box 825, 2160 SZ Lisse Holland. **Tel** 011 31 2521 35111, FAX 02521-15888, telex 41325. **(Subscription address:** Swets Publishing Service, PO Box 825, 2160 SZ Lisse The Netherlands) ***Continues*** *Interface: Journal of New Music Research.*

US/0022-4294
**JOURNAL OF RESEARCH IN MUSIC EDUCATION.** [J. res. music educ.]. **Added/Corp** Music Educators National Conference (U.S.). Vol. 1 (Spring 1953)-. Periodical. English. qt. $24.00 US; $26.00 Canada and Mexico; $28.00 other. Music Educators National Conference, 1806 Robert Fulton Drive, Reston VA 22091. **Tel** (703)860-4000, (800)336-3768. **ED** Jack Taylor. **LC** ML1; .J63. **DD** 780.7. **CODEN** JRMEAX. Index available. **Circ:** 3,800 (ctrl). available on microfilm and microfiche from University Microfilms International (UMI). Documents available from The Genuine Article, Ask*IEEE.
**Desc:** Publishes reports of research studies in the field of music and music education.
**Ind/Abst** Arts Humanit. Citation Index [Full Cov.]; Contents Pages Educ.; Curr. Contents Arts Humanit.; Curr. Index J. Educ.; Educ. Index; INSPEC (Spring 1972-Spring 1982); Music Artic. Guide; Music Index; Psychol. Abstr. (1957-); Res. Alert [Full Cov.]; RILM Abstr.; Soc. Sci. Cit. Index [Select. Cov.].

US
**JOURNAL OF RESEARCH IN SINGING AND APPLIED VOCAL PEDAGOGY.** **Added/Corp** International Association for Research in Singing. **VFOAT** JRS. Vol. 10, No. 1 (Dec. 1986)-. Periodical. English. sa (June & Dec.). $25.00 US; $30.00 other. International Association Research in Singing, Box 32887, Department of Music, Fort Worth TX 76129. **Tel** (817)921-7602, FAX (817)921-7333. **ED** Dr. Vincent Russo. ***Continues*** *Journal of Research in Singing.*
**Desc:** For the increase and diffusion of knowledge of the singing voice and the practical application of that knowledge.
**Ind/Abst** Music Artic. Guide; Music Index; RILM Abstr.

US/0449-5128
**JOURNAL OF SYNAGOGUE MUSIC.** **Added/Corp** Cantors Assembly of America. Vol. 1, (Feb. 1967)-. Periodical. English (German, Hebrew and Spanish). Twice a year (Jan., July). $15.00. Jewish Theological Summary America, Cantor Assembly, 3080 Broadway, New York NY 10027. **Tel** (212)678-8834. **ED** Jack Chomsky. **LC** ML1; .J73. **DD** 783/.029/605. **Bk Rev**. **Circ:** 650.
**Desc:** Devoted exclusively to Jewish liturgical music.
**Ind/Abst** Music Artic. Guide.

US/1054-3872
**JOURNAL OF THE AMERICAN ACADEMY FOR THE PRESERVATION OF OLD-TIME COUNTRY MUSIC, THE.** (THE JOURNAL / AMERICAN ACADEMY FOR THE PRESERVATION OF OLD TIME COUNTRY MUSIC.). [J. Am. Acad. Preserv. Old-Time Ctry. Music]. **Added/Corp** American Academy for the Preservation of Old-Time Country Music. Country Music Society of America. **VFOAT** Journal of the American Academy for the Preservation of Old Time Country Music. Vol. 1, No. 1 (1991)-. Periodical. English. Six times a year. $7.99. Country Music Social of America, PO Box 2000, Marion OH 43305. **Tel** (800)669-1002. **LC** ML3523; .J69. **DD** 781.642/0973/05.

US/0147-4413
**JOURNAL OF THE AMERICAN LISZT SOCIETY.** [J. Am. Liszt Soc.]. **Main/Corp** American Liszt Society. Vol. 1, (June 1977)-. Periodical. English. Twice a year (July & Dec.). $36.33 (one year) Comes with American Liszt Society Membership. American Liszt Society, 9212 Villia Drive, Bethesda MD 20817. **Tel** (301)530-7348. **ED** Michael Saffle. **LC** ML410.L7; A68. **DD** 780/.92/4. **Bk Rev**. **Ad Acc**. **Circ:** 500. available on microfilm and microfiche from University Microfilms International (UMI).
**Desc:** Covers the life, music and contributions of Franz Liszt. Includes areas such as piano, composition, conducting, criticism, teaching and literary writing.
**Ind/Abst** Music Artic. Guide; Music Index; RILM Abstr.

US/0362-3300
**JOURNAL OF THE AMERICAN MUSICAL INSTRUMENT SOCIETY.** [J. Am. Mus. Instrum. Soc.]. **Main/Corp** American Musical Instrument Society. Vol. 1 (1975)-. Academic Scholarly Publication. English. Four times a year. $35.00. American Musical Instrument Society, R. D. #3, Box 205-B, Franklin PA 16323. **Tel** (814)374-4119, FAX (814)374-4563. **ED** Martha Novak Clinkscale. **LC** ML1; .A527. **DD** 780/.5. **Bk Rev**. **Ad Acc**. **Pr Rev. Circ:** 800. Documents available from The Genuine Article.
**Desc:** Scholarly articles concerning musical instruments in all cultures and from all periods, their design, use, and history.
**Ind/Abst** Arts Humanit. Citation Index [Full Cov.]; BHA : Biblio. Hist. Art; Curr. Contents Arts Humanit.; Music Artic. Guide; Music Index; Res. Alert [Full Cov.]; RILM Abstr.

US/0003-0139
**JOURNAL OF THE AMERICAN MUSICOLOGICAL SOCIETY.** [J. Am. Musicol. Soc.]. **Main/Corp** American Musicological Society. Vol. 1, (Spring 1948)-. Periodical. English. Three times a year. $40.00. American Musicological Society, 201 South 34th Street, Philadelphia PA 19104. **Tel** (215)898-8698. **ED** William F. Prizer and Jan W. Herlinger. **LC** ML27.U5; A83363. **DD** 780.5. Index available. cum. index. **Bk Rev**. **Ad Acc**. **Circ:** 4,500 (ctrl). Documents available from The Genuine Article, UMI Article Clearinghouse.
**Desc:** Articles concerning research in all branches of music.
**Ind/Abst** Acad. Search (July 1993-); Arts Humanit. Citation Index [Full Cov.]; BHA : Biblio. Hist. Art; Curr. Contents Arts Humanit.; Expand. Acad. Index (1989-); Humanit. Index; Humanit. Source (Jul. 1993-); INFO-SOUTH Abstr.; Mag. Search; Music Artic. Guide; Music Index; Newsp. Period. Abstr. (1991-); Res. Alert [Full Cov.]; RILM Abstr.

US/0898-5987
**JOURNAL OF THE AMERICAN VIOLA SOCIETY.** [J. Am. Viola Soc.]. **VFOAT** AVS Journal. Vol. 1, No. 1 (Aug. 1985)-. Periodical. English. tq. $30.00 (US); $35.00 (others). American Viola Society, 11640 Amanda Drive, Studio city CA 91604. **Tel** (801) 378-4953. **DD** 787. ***Continues*** *Newsletter / American Violoa Society.*
**Ind/Abst** Music Artic. Guide; Music Index.

US/0146-5856
**JOURNAL OF THE ARNOLD SCHOENBERG INSTITUTE.** [J. Arnold Schoenberg Inst.]. **Main/Corp** Arnold Schoenberg Institute. Vol. 1 (Oct. 1976)-. English. Twice a year (June and November). $20.00 (individual); $32.00 (institution). Arnold Schoenberg Institute, University of Southern California, University Park MC 1101, Los Angeles CA 90089-1101. **Tel** (213)740-4096, FAX (213)746-4507. **ED**

Paul Zukofsky. **LC** ML410.S283; A77. **DD** 780/.92/4; B. Index Bound in First Issue (1st issue in June, 1990.). cum. index. **Ad Acc. Circ:** 1,000. Documents available from The Genuine Article. ***Continues*** *Bulletin - Arnold Schoenberg Institute.*
**Desc:** The journal brings to light the multi-faceted genius of Arnold Schoenberg through the publication of newly discovered and translated materials from his archives.
**Ind/Abst** Arts Humanit. Citation Index (19??-19??) [Full Cov.]; Curr. Contents Arts Humanit.; Music Artic. Guide; Music Index; Res. Alert [Full Cov.]; RILM Abstr.

US/0734-1032
**JOURNAL OF THE CONDUCTORS' GUILD.** [J. Conduct. Guild]. **Added/Corp** American Symphony Orchestra League. Conductors' Guild (American Symphony Orchestra League). Vol. 1, No. 1 (Winter 1980)-. Academic Scholarly Publication. English. sa. $30.00 US; $35.00 Canada; $40.00 other. Conductors Guild Inc, PO Box 3361, West Chester PA 19381. **Tel** (610)430-6010, FAX (610)430-6010. **ED** Jacques Voois. **LC** ML457; .J7. **DD** 781.6/35/05. Index available. **Bk Rev**, (Qty: 10-12). **Ad Acc, Adv Mgr:** Judy Voois. **Circ:** 1,500 (ctrl).
**Desc:** Scholarly articles of interest to conductors and musicologists, reviews and definitive articles on errata in the scores and parts of standard orchestral masterworks.
**Ind/Abst** Music Artic. Guide.

II/0251-012X
**JOURNAL OF THE INDIAN MUSICOLOGICAL SOCIETY.** [J. Indian Musicol. Soc.]. **Main/Corp** Indian Musicological Society. Vol. 2 (Jan./Mar. 1971)-. Periodical. English. sa. $15.00. Indian Musicological Society, Jambu Bet-Dandia Bazar, Baroda 390001 India. **Tel** 55 53 88. **(Subscription address:** Prints India, 11 Darya Ganj, New Delhi 110002 India.) **ED** R C Mehta. **LC** ML5; .I415. **DD** 781.754/05. cum. index. **Bk Rev. Ad Acc. Circ:** 700. available on microfilm and microfiche from University Microfilms International (UMI). Documents available from The Genuine Article. ***Continues*** *Sangeet Kala Vihar. English Supplement.*
**Desc:** Devoted to several areas of musicology: aesthetics of music, psychology of music, music in education, psychomusicology, music analysis, discussions on forms and styles, historical musicology concerning Indian music in main, etc.
**Ind/Abst** Abstr. Anthropol.; Arts Humanit. Citation Index [Full Cov.]; Curr. Contents Arts Humanit.; Music Index; Res. Alert [Full Cov.]; RILM Abstr.

US/0076-1524
**JOURNAL OF THE LUTE SOCIETY OF AMERICA, INC.** (JOURNAL OF THE LUTE SOCIETY OF AMERICA.). [J. Lute Soc. Am. Inc.]. **Main/Corp** Lute Society of America. No. 1 (1968)-. English. an. $33.00 (one year) Comes with Lute Society of America Membership. Lute Society of America, PO Box 1328, Lexington VA 24450. **Tel** (703)463-5812. **LC** ML1; .L75. **DD** 789/.67/05.
**Ind/Abst** Music Index (-19??); RILM Abstr.

II
**JOURNAL OF THE MUSIC ACADEMY, MADRAS, THE.** **Main/Corp** Music Academy (Madras, India). Vol. 1 (Jan. 1930)-. English. an. $10.00. Journal of the Music Academy, 306 T T K Road, Madras 14 India. **(Subscription address:** Prints India, 11 Darya Ganj, New Delhi 110002 India.) **ED** T S Parthasarathy. **LC** ML5; .M124. **Bk Rev. Circ:** 400.
**Desc:** Concerns music and dance.

UK/0269-0403
**JOURNAL OF THE ROYAL MUSICAL ASSOCIATION.** **Added/Corp** Royal Musical Association. Vol. 112 (1987)-. Periodical. English. sa. £45.00 UK and Europe; $82.00 other. Oxford University Press, Walton Street, Oxford OX2 6DP England. **Tel** 011 44 865 56767, FAX 011 44 865 267773, telex 837330 OXPRES G. **(Subscription address:** Oxford University Press / USA, Journals Marketing Department, Oxford University Press, 2001 Evans Road, Cary NC 27513.) **ED** David Greer. **LC** ML28.L8; M8. **DD** 780/.9. **[CCC].** cum. index. **Bk Rev. Ad Acc.** available on microfilm and microfiche from University Microfilms International (UMI). Documents available from The Genuine Article. ***Continues*** *Royal Musical Association. Proceedings of the Royal Musical Association, 0080-4452.*
**Desc:** New research into all branches of musical scholarship - historical musicology and ethnomusicology, theory and analysis, textual criticism, archival research, organology and performing practice.
**Ind/Abst** Br. Humanit. Index; Curr. Contents Arts Humanit.; Music Index; Res. Alert [Full Cov.].

US/0507-0252
**JOURNAL OF THE VIOLA DA GAMBA SOCIETY OF AMERICA.** [J. Viola Gamba Soc. Am.]. **Main/Corp** Viola da Gamba Society of America. Vol. 1, (1964)-. English. an (Dec.). $20.00 Comes with VDASGA News & Membership. Viola da Gamba Society of America, 1308 Jackson Avenue, Charleston IL 61920. **Tel** (217)348-8260. **LC** ML1; .V295.
**Ind/Abst** Music Index; RILM Abstr.

US/0148-6845
**JOURNAL OF THE VIOLIN SOCIETY OF AMERICA.** [J. Violin Soc. Am.]. **Main/Corp** Violin Society of America. Vol. 2, No. 2 (Spring 1976)-. Periodical. English. ir (Approx. 3 issues per volume). $45.00 Comes with Violin Society of America Membership. Violin Society of America, 614 Lerew Road, Boiling Springs PA 17007. **Tel** (717)258-3203, FAX (717)258-3201. **ED** Albert Mehl (editor's address: 157-18 Oak Avenue, Flushing, NY 11355, phone: (718)353-9039). **LC** ML1; .V298. **DD** 787/.1/05. Index available (bound in issue, ($20.00)). cum. index. **Bk Rev**, (Qty: varies). **Ad Acc, Adv Mgr:** Rachel Goodkind. **Pr Rev. Circ:** 1,400. ***Continues*** *News Bulletin - The Violin Society of America, 0193-6352.*
**Desc:** A broad range of interests and concerns that include the making and restoring of instruments and bows, the history of instruments and performers, technique performance practice, repertory and the acoustics of bowed stringed instruments. The society hopes to bring together people from various fields to exchange ideas and skills.
**Ind/Abst** Music Artic. Guide; Music Index; RILM Abstr.

II
**JOURNAL (SANGEET RESEARCH ACADEMY (CALCUTTA, INDIA)).** (JOURNAL / SANGEET RESEARCH ACADEMY.). **Added/Corp** Sangeet Research Academy (Calcutta, India). **VFOAT** Sangeet Research Academy Journal. Vol. 1, No. 1 (July 1980)-. Periodical. English (Bengali and Hindi). an. Free. Sangeet Research Academy, 1 Netaji Subhas Chandra Bose Road, Calcutta 700040 India. **Tel** 46-3395/7642. **LC** MT3.I48; J7. **DD** 781.754/05. **Bk Rev. Circ:** 300 (ctrl).

US/0897-6473
**JOURNAL SEAMUS : THE JOURNAL OF THE SOCIETY FOR ELECTRO-ACOUSTIC MUSIC IN THE UNITED STATES.** [J. SEAMUS]. **Added/Corp** Society for Electro-Acoustic Music in the United States. **VAT** Journal Society for Electro-Acoustic Music in the United States. Vol. 1, No. 1 (Apr. 1986)-. Periodical. English. Three times a year. $25.00 (individuals and libraries), $15.00 (student), $50.00 (institutions) US; $30.00 other. Society for Electro - Acoustic Music in the United States, 2550 Beverly Boulevard, Los Angeles CA 90057. **Tel** (213)388-0476. **ED** Rodney Oakes. **DD** 780.

IT/0022-5711
**JUCUNDA LAUDATIO; RASSEGNA DI MUSICA ANTICA.** **Added/Corp** Fondazione "Giorgio Cini". (1963)-. Italian.

UK
**JUKE BLUES.** (19??)-. Periodical. English. Four times a year (Spring, Summer, Fall & Winter). £13.50 England; $25.00 other. Juke Blues, PO Box 148, London W9 1DY England. **Tel** 011 44 71 2862993, FAX 011 44 71 2862993. **(Subscription address:** Juke Blues, 3S 321 Winfield Road, Warrenville IL 60555.) **ED** Cilla Huggins. **LC** ML3520.8; .J84. **DD** 781.643/09. **Bk Rev**, (Qty: 17). **Ad Acc. Circ:** 4,000.
**Desc:** Covers popular and academic. Coverage of Black American blues music, including rhythm and blues and deep-soul.

US/1053-6884
**JUKEBOX COLLECTOR.** [Jukebox collect.]. **VFOAT** Jukebox Collector Newsletter. (19??)-. Trade Publication. English. mo. $30.00. Jukebox Collector, Attn: Rick Botts, 2545 SE 60th Court, Des Moines IA 50317-5099. **ED** Rick Botts. **DD** 621. **Ad Acc, Adv Mgr:** Rick Botts. **Circ:** 3200. ***Continues*** *Jukebox Collector Newsletter, 0882-4908.*
**Desc:** Collectors of jukeboxes from the '30s, '40s, and '50s use this magazine to buy, sell and trade their jukeboxes, parts, records and service manuals.

CN
**JUST ABOUT MUSIC.** **VFOAT** JAM; J A M. English. mo. Bargain Hunters Press, 593 Yonge Street, Toronto Ontario M4Y 1Z4 Canada. **Tel** (416)964-8700, FAX (416)964-8403.

US/0022-8702
**KANSAS MUSIC REVIEW.** **Added/Corp** Kansas Music Educators Association. Kansas Music Teachers' Association. (19??)-. Periodical. English. Five times a year (Feb., Mar., Sept., Oct., Dec.). Kansas Music Education Association, School of Music, 3904 West Murdock / Hollowell, Wichita KS 67203. **Tel** (316)943-8143. **ED** J. Hardy. **LC** ML1; .M22. **DD** 780.72781. **Bk Rev. Ad Acc.** ctrl circ.
**Ind/Abst** Music Artic. Guide.

GW
**KATALOG DER FILMSAMMLUNG.** **Main/Corp** Kassel. Deutsches Musikgeschichtliches Archiv. Vol. 1, No. 1 (Spring 1955)-. Monographic series. German. ir. Price varies per volume. Baerenreiter-Verlag, KGA Verlagssvc PF 100329, D 34003 Kassel Germany. **Tel** 011 49 561 31050, telex 99504. **(Subscription address:** Foreign Music Distributors, 13 Elkay Drive, Chester, NY 10918 phone: (914)469-5790) **ED** Harald Heckmann and Guergen Kindermann. **LC** ML120.G3; K3. **DD** 781.97.
**Desc:** A general catalogue on the known sources of German music history. Prints and manuscripts for Musica Practica and Musica Theoretica.

US/0098-0668
**KEEPING UP WITH KODALY CONCEPTS IN MUSIC EDUCATION.** **Added/Corp** Keeping Up With Music Education (Firm). (Sept./Oct. 1974)-. Periodical. English. bm (during the school year). $10.00. Keeping Up With Music Education, 1220 Ridge Road, Muncie IN 47304. **LC** ML1; .K228. **DD** 780/.7.

UK
**KEMPS INTERNATIONAL MUSIC BOOK.** **VFOAT** International Music Book; Kemps International Music and Recording Industry Year Book; Kemps International Music & Recording Industry Year Book. 21st Ed. (1989)-. English. an. £30.00. Showcase Publications Ltd., 12 Felix Avenue, London N8 9TL United Kingdom. **Tel** 01 348 2332. **LC** ML12; .K45. **DD** 338.4/778/025. ***Continues*** *Kemps International Music & Recording Industry Year Book.*

JA
**KENKYU KIYO - KUNITACHI ONGAKU DAIGAKU.** **Main/Corp** Kunitachi Ongaku Daigaku. **Added/Corp** Kunitachi Ongaku Daigaku. Memoirs of Kunitachi Music College. **VFOAT** Memoirs of Kunitachi Music College. (1966)-. Japanese (Japanese). Kunitachi Ongaku Daigaku, 12-19 Nishi 2-chome, Kunitachi 186 Japan. **LC** ML5; .K94.

US/0735-8660
**KERAULOPHON, THE.** (THE KERAULOPHON / GREATER NEW YORK CITY CHAPTER, O H S.). **Added/Corp** Organ Historical Society. Greater New York City Chapter. (19??)-. Periodical. English. Four times a year (Jan., Apr., July, Oct.). $5.00. Greater New York City Chapter of OHS Inc, PO Box 104, Harrisville NH 03450-0104. **Tel** (603)827-3055, FAX (603)827-3750. **ED** John K. Ogasapian. **LC** ML552; .K4. **DD** 786.6/2/05. **Bk Rev. Circ:** 60 (ctrl).
**Desc:** Musical and historical study of pipe organ building, especially in New York City and environs.

NE
**KEY NOTES MUSICAL LIFE IN THE NETHERLANDS.** English. Four times a year (Jan., Apr., July, Oct.). F42.50 (individuals); F52.50 (institutions). Donemus Amsterdam, Paulus Potterstraat 16, 1017 CZ Amsterdam The Netherlands. **Tel** 011 31 20 676 4436, FAX 011 31 20 673 3588. **ED** S. Smith and F. V. Rossum. **Bk Rev. Ad Acc. Circ:** 4,000.
**Desc:** Information and news about serious music in the Netherlands.

AT/0310-8260
**KEY VIVE.** (19??)-. Periodical. English. Three times a year (Jan., May, Sept.). 8.00Aus$. Australian Society for Keyboard Music, 6A/8-12 Sutherland Road, Chatswood NSW 2067 Australia. **Tel** 02/417-5131. Index available. **Bk Rev. Ad Acc.** ctrl circ.
**Desc:** Keyboard music journal.

UK
**KEYBOARD.** (19??)-. Periodical. English. bm. $5.00. Music Industry Publications, 10 A High Street, Tunbridge Wells Kent England. **LC** ML5; .K39. **DD** 786/.05.

US/0090-3361
**KEYBOARD ARTS.** ***Ceased.*** [Keyboard arts]. Vol. 1 (1972)-Vol. 17 ( ). Periodical. English. Three times a year. Keyboard Arts Magazine, Box 24 C 54, Los Angeles CA 90024. **Tel** (310)474-8966, (800)824-5087. **ED** Thomas McBeth. **LC** ML1; .K253. **DD** 780/.5. **Ad Acc. Circ:** 1,000 (ctrl).
**Desc:** Relates to research and practical, down to earth help for progressive piano teaching methods and materials.
**Ind/Abst** Music Artic. Guide (?-?).

US/1044-3266
**KEYBOARD CLASSICS.** ***Title Change.*** [Keyboard class.]. Vol. 3, No. 2 (Mar./Apr. 1983)-Vol. 13, No. 1 (Jan./Feb. 1993). Periodical. English. bm. Keyboard Classics, Subscription Department, 351 Evelyn Street, Paramus NJ 07652. **LC** ML649.8; .K5. **DD** 786.2/05. ***Continues*** *Keyboard Classics & Virtuoso, 0744-3218.* ***Merged with*** *Piano Stylist & Jazz Workshop, 1041-2492* ***to form*** *Keyboard Classics & Piano Stylist, 1069-4285.*
**Ind/Abst** Music Artic. Guide; Music Index.

●US/1069-4285
**KEYBOARD CLASSICS & PIANO STYLIST.** [Keyboard class. piano stylist]. **VFOAT** Keyboard Classics; Keyboard Classics and Piano Stylist; Piano Stylist. Vol. 13, No. 2 (Mar./Apr. 1993)-. Periodical. English. bm. $16.97. **LC** IN PROCESS; ML649.8; .K55. **DD** 786. ***Separated from*** *Keyboard Classics, 1044-3266* ***and*** *Piano Stylist & Jazz Workshop, 1041-2492.*

US
**KEYBOARD COMPANION.** (19??)-. English. Four times a year. $15.95. Keyboard Companion Inc., Box 24-C-54, Los Angeles CA 90025. **Tel** (213)474-8966, (800)824-5087, FAX (213)475-0092. **ED** Richard

# Music

Chronister. **Ad Acc, Adv Mgr:** Elizabeth Van Ness. **Circ:** 15,000 (ctrl).
**Desc:** Practical magazine on early-level piano study.

US/0730-0158
**KEYBOARD (CUPERTINO, CALIF.).** (KEYBOARD.). [Keyboard]. Vol. 7, No. 7 (July 1981)-. Periodical. English. mo. $29.95 US; $44.95 Canada & Mexico; $44.95 (surface mail), $69.95 (airmail) other. Miller Freeman Inc., 600 Harrison Street, San Francisco CA 94107. **Tel** (415)905-2337, FAX (415)905-2240, telex 278273. **(Subscription address:** Neodata / Colorado, PO Box 2606, Boulder Boulder CO 80322.) **ED** Dominic Milano, Jim Aiken, Bob Doerschuk, David Leytze and Mark Vail. **LC** ML1; .C9153. **DD** 786.1/05. **[CCC].** Index available. cum. index. **Bk Rev. Ad Acc. Circ:** 92,431. available on microfilm and microfiche from University Microfilms International (UMI). **Continues** Contemporary Keyboard, 0361-5820.
**Desc:** Edited for keyboard musicians interested in piano, electric piano, electronic keyboards, synthesizers, samplers and computers. Covers performers, techniques, electronics, MIDI, equipment, computers and music software.
**Ind/Abst** Music Artic. Guide (19??-); Music Index (19??-).

SP
**KEYBOARD MUSICA Y TECNOLOGIA.** Spanish. mo. 3850.00ptas Spain. Musica y Tecnologia, C Bobilla 53 Bajos, 08915 Hosp de Llobregat Spain. **Tel** 011 34 93 3338429. **UDC** 78.

NE
**KEYBOARD STUDIES.** English (German, French and Dutch). ir. Uitgeverij Frits Knuf B V, PO Box 720, 4116 ZJ Buuren Netherlands. **Tel** 011 31 03449-1255, FAX 011 31 03449-2617. **Circ:** 700.
**Desc:** Reprints and first editions for the widening circle of discerning pianists and harpsichordists.

US/0199-3313
**KEYBOARD WORLD. Suspended. Added/Corp** Young Organists' Association International International Association of Organ Teachers. Young Organists' Association. National Association of Organ Teachers. (Jan. 1972)-Suspended. Periodical. mo. $8.00. Keyboard World, PO Box 4399, Downey CA 90241. **Tel** (213)949-5600. **LC** ML549; .K5. **DD** 786./05. **Continues** Organist Magazine.
**Ind/Abst** Music Artic. Guide (?-?).

GW/0178-4641
**KEYBOARDS.** (KEYBOARDS : HOMERECORDING AND COMPUTER.). (19??)-. Periodical. German. mo. DM71.00 Germany; DM85.00 other Europe; DM142.10 other. MM Musik Media Verlag GmbH, Aindlinger Strasse 17 19, D 86167 Augsburg Germany. **Tel** 011 821 79040. **UDC** 789.9.

CN/0317-5855
**KEYNOTE (VANCOUVER).** (KEYNOTE.). **Added/Corp** Junior Symphony Society of Vancouver - Community Music School of Greater Vancouver. (1966)-. English. ir. Free. Junior Symphony Society of Vancouver, 557 West 12th Avenue, Vancouver BC V5Z 3X7 Canada. **DD** 780/.9711/33.

US/0895-948X
**KEYS (NORTHFIELD, ILL.).** (KEYS.). **VFOAT** Keys Piano Music Magazine. (1986)-. Periodical. English. bm. $15.00 US; $18.00 other. Instrumentalist Company, 200 Northfield Road, Northfield IL 60093. **Tel** (708)446-5000, FAX (708)446-6263. **DD** 786.

US/0882-6811
**KILT AND HARP, THE.** (THE KILT AND HARP: JOURNAL OF THE SCOTTISH HARP SOCIETY OF AMERICA). [Kilt harp]. **Added/Corp** Scottish Harp Society of America. (19??)-. Periodical. English. ir. $15.00 membership. Tourin Musica, PO Box 48, Jericho Center VT 05465-0048. **DD** 782.

US/0147-1384
**KING'S LETTER, THE.** (19??)-. English. The King's Letter, PO Box 42, Zavalla TX 75980. **LC** ML1; .K47. **DD** 786.6/05.

GW/0023-1800
**KIRCHENCHOR, DER.** (DER KIRCHENCHOR / IM AUFTRAGE DES VERBANDES EVANGELISCHER KIRCHENCHORE DEUTSCHLANDS HERAUSGEGEBEN.). [Kirchenchor]. **Added/Corp** Verband Evangelischer Kirchenchore Deutschlands. Vol. 9, No. 1 (Jan./Feb. 1949)-. Periodical. German. Six times a year. $12.00. Baerenreiter-Verlag, KGA Verlagssvc PF 100329, D 34003 Kassel Germany. **Tel** 011 49 561 31050, telex 99504. (Foreign Music Distributors, 13 Elkay Drive, Chester NY 10918.) **LC** ML5; .K583; ML5; .M9043. **DD** 783.8/0943. **[CCC].** Index available (bound in issue). **Formed by the union of** Kirchenchordienst **and** Nun Freut Euch, Lieben Christen Gmein.
**Desc:** Magazine for the Association of Church Choirs in Germany.
**Ind/Abst** Music Index.

GW/0075-6199
**KIRCHENMUSIKALISCHES JAHRBUCH.** [Kirchenmusik. Jahrb.]. **Added/Corp** Allgemeiner Cacilien-Verband feur die Lander der Deutschen Sprache. Gorres-Gesellschaft. Allgemeiner Cacilien-Verein feur Deutschland, Osterreich und die Schweiz. Musikwissenschaftliche Kommission. Allgemeiner Caecilien-Verband feur Deutschland, Osterreich und die Schweiz. (1886)-. German. an. DM50.00 Germany; DM57.00 others. Allgemeiner Caecilien Verband, Andreasstrasse 9, D 93059 Tegensburg Germany. **Tel** 011 49 941 84339. **Circ:** 400. **Continues** Caecilienkalendar.
**Ind/Abst** Music Index; RILM Abstr.

GW/0023-1819
**KIRCHENMUSIKER, DER.** (DER KIRCHENMUSIKER : MITTEILUNGEN DER ZENTRALSTELLE FUER EVANGELISCHE KIRCHENMUSIK.). [Kirchenmusiker]. **Added/Corp** Verband Evangelischer Kirchenmusiker Deutschlands. **VFOAT** Kirchen Musiker. Issue No. 1 (Mar./Apr. 1950)-. Periodical. German. Six times a year (Feb., Apr., June, Aug., Oct., Dec.). DM30.00. Verlag Merseburger Berlin GmbH, POB 103880, D 34038 Kassel Germany. **Tel** 011 49 561 772002. **ED** Christiane Bernsdorff Engelbrecht, Horst Christoph Diehl and Hermann Rau. **[CCC].** Index available. cum. index. **Bk Rev. Ad Acc. Circ:** 4,800 (ctrl).
**Desc:** Periodical of the society evangelical sacred music of Germany.
**Ind/Abst** Music Index; RILM Abstr.

US
**KLACTO JAZZ MAGAZINE.** (June/July 1981)-. Periodical. English. sa. Mike Bloom, 916 McCully Street, Honolulu HI 96826. **Continues** Klacto (Honolulu, Hawaii).

US
**KODALY ENVOY. Added/Corp** Organization of American Kodaly Educators. (19??)-. English. Four times a year. $25.00. Organization of American Kodaly Educators, 823 Old Westtown Road, West Chester PA 19382. **ED** Alan Strong. **LC** ML1; .K64. **DD** 780/.7. Index available. cum. index. **Bk Rev.** (Qty: 4/yr). **Ad Acc, Adv Mgr:** Jim Lovell. **Circ:** 1,600 (ctrl).
**Desc:** Information regarding the Kodaly concept in music education.
**Ind/Abst** Music Index.

II
**KOLAHAL.** Vol. 1, No. 1 (July 1984)-. Periodical. English (English). qt. **LC** ML5; .K645. **DD** 781.754/09.

GW
**KOLNER BEITRAGE ZUR MUSIKFORSCHUNG.** Vol. 1 (1938)-. Periodical. German. ir. Gustav Bosse Verlag GmbH & Company KG, Postfach 417, W-8400 Regensburg 1 Germany. **Tel** 011 49 941 794091.

GW
**KONZERTE / PHILHARMONISCHES ORCHESTER DER STADT DORTMUND. Main/Corp** Philharmonisches Orchester der Stadt Dortmund. (19??)-. German. an. **LC** ML42.D7; P55. **DD** 784.2/078/435633.

SW
**KOUNTRY KORRAL MAGAZINE.** (19??)-. Periodical. Swedish (Swedish). Kr50.00. Kountry Korral Magazine, Box 8014, 720 08 Vasteras 8 Sweden. **ED** Lillies Ohlsson. **LC** ML5; .K73. **DD** 784. **Bk Rev. Ad Acc. Circ:** 2,500.
**Desc:** Country and Rockabilly music.

RU
**KRITIKA I MUZYKOZNANIE.** (1975)-. Periodical. Russian. Izdatelstvo Muzyka Leningradskoe Otdelenie, izhenernaia Ulitsa 9, 191011 St. Petersburg Russia. **LC** ML3880; .K74.
**Desc:** A publication of musical criticism.

US/0899-6407
**KURT WEILL NEWSLETTER.** [Kurt Weill newsl.]. **Added/Corp** Kurt Weill Foundation for Music. (Fall 1983)-. Newsletter. English. Twice a year. Free on request. The Kurt Weill Foundation for Music, 7 East 20th Street, New York NY 10003-1106. **Tel** (212)505-5240. **ED** David Farneth. **DD** 780. **Bk Rev. Circ:** 5,000.
**Desc:** Specializes in Kurt Weill's life and works. Includes feature articles; book, recording, and performance reviews; news, and bibliographies.
**Ind/Abst** Music Artic. Guide; Music Index.

SW/0281-286X
**KYRKOMUSIKERNAS TIDNING. Added/Corp** Kyrkomusikernas Riksforbund. (19??)-. Periodical. Swedish. Seventeen times a year. kr225.00 (Sweden); Kr325.00 (other). Jerker Sjoqvist Krykomusikerna, Riksfoerbund Box 2100, S 44202 Ytterby, Sweden. **Tel** 11 46 303 92172. **LC** ML5; .K987. **DD** 783.02/609485. **Formed by the union of** Svensk Kyrkomusik uppl. A/B **and** Svensk Kyrkomusik uppl. B.

IT
**LABORATORIO MUSICA. Ceased.** (19??)-(19??). Italian. Four times a year. Laboratorio Musica, Via Berchet 2, 20121 Milan Italy.

US/0363-8472
**LARGE-PRINT SCORES AND BOOKS CATALOG.** [Large-print scores books cat.]. **Main/Corp** Library of Congress. National Library Service for the Blind and Physically Handicapped. **VFOAT** Large Print Scores and Books Catalog. (1978)-. Catalog. English. National Library Service for the Blind and Physically Handicapped, Library of Congress, 1291 Taylor Street Northwest, Washington DC 20542. **Tel** (800)424-8567, (202)707-5100, (800)424-9100. **LC** ML136.U52; M9. **DD** 016.7808. **Continues** Library of Congress. Division for the Blind and Physically Handicapped. Large-Print Scores and Books Catalog, 0363-8472.

US/0278-7989
**LATIN MUSIC YEARBOOK, THE.** (1981)-. English. Applause Publications, 2234 South Shady Hills Drive, Diamond Bar CA 91765. **LC** ML3486.5; L37. **DD** 789.9/13617268/05.

US/1056-5329
**LEAD BELLY LETTER.** [Lead Belly lett.]. **Added/Corp** Lead Belly Society. **VFOAT** Leadbelly Letter. Vol. 1, No. 1 (Autumn 1990)-. Periodical. English. Four times a year (Jan., Apr., July, Oct.). $15.00. Lead Belly Society, PO Box 6679, Ithaca NY 14851. **Tel** (607)273-6615, FAX (607)844-4810. **ED** Sean Killeen. **LC** ML420.L277; L4. **DD** 787.87/092. Index available. **Bk Rev,** (Qty: 4-5). **Pr Rev. Circ:** 2,000 (ctrl).
**Desc:** Provides news and information on Lead Belly music.

US
**LEBLANC BELL.** English. G Leblanc Corporation, 7019 30th Avenue, Kenosha WI 53141.
**Ind/Abst** Music Artic. Guide.

CN/0700-3900
**L'ECOUTE, A.** *Title Change.* [A ecoute]. **Added/Corp** Alliance des Chorales du Quebec. Vol. 1 (Sept. 1976)-(1992). Periodical. French. bm. Alliance des Chorales du Quebec, 4545 Pierre-de-Coubertin, PO Box 1000 Postal Station M, Montreal Quebec H1V 3R2 Canada. **Tel** (514)252-3020, FAX (514)251-8038. **DD** 784/.96. **Bk Rev. Ad Acc. Circ:** 6,500 (ctrl) **Continued by** Chanter (MontReal, Quebec), 1192-1900.

US/0892-1830
**LEFSETZ LETTER, THE.** [Lefsetz lett.]. (Oct. 1986)-. Periodical. English. Twenty-four times a year. $110.00. The Lefsetz Letter, 2128 Oak Street, Suite B, Santa Monica CA 90405. **Tel** (310)450-3798, FAX (310)450-8332. **DD** 780.

UK/0961-1215
**LEONARDO MUSIC JOURNAL : LMJ : JOURNAL OF THE INTERNATIONAL SOCIETY FOR THE ARTS, SCIENCES AND TECHNOLOGY.** *Title Change.* **Added/Corp** International Society for the Arts, Sciences, and Technology. **VFOAT** LMJ. Vol. 1, No. 1 (1991)-. Periodical. English. Massachusetts Institute of Technology (MIT) Press, 55 Hayward Street, Cambridge MA 02142-1399. **Tel** (617)253-2889, (617)625-8481, FAX (617)258-6779. **LC** ML3807; .L52. **Merged into** Leonardo, 0024-094X.
**Ind/Abst** Music Artic. Guide.

AT
**LIBRARY BULLETIN. See** Library and Information Sciences.

●US/1070-6690
**LIGHTHOUSE (UNIVERSITY PARK, PA.), THE.** (THE LIGHTHOUSE.). [Lighthouse]. (1992)-. Periodical. English. mo. $10.00 US; $29.00 other. The Lighthouse, 256 East College Avenue, Suite 302, State College PA 16801. **Tel** (814)238-6730, FAX (814)238-6730. **ED** Beth Blinn, J. Warner Soditus. **DD** 781. **Bk Rev. Ad Acc. Circ:** 1,000.
**Desc:** Provides artist interviews, album reviews, and more focusing on contemporary Christian music.

CG
**LIKEMBE; REVUE ZAIROISE DE MUSIQUE.** (19??)-. Periodical. French. Likembe, 46 rue de Lubaki, Kin-Bumbu BP 9624, Kinshasa 1 Zaire. **LC** ML5; .L47. **DD** 781.7/675/1.

UK
**LINFOLKB2S : MAGAZINE FOR THE LINCOLNSHIRE AND SOUTH HUMBERSIDE DISTRICT OF THE E.F.D.S.S. Added/Corp** English Folk Dance and Song Society. Lincolnshire and South Humberside District. No. 1 (Feb./March 1983)-. Periodical. English. qt. £1.48 (non-members). Lincolnshire and South Humberside District, District Secretary, 49 Broadway, Lincoln LN2 1SG England. **LC** ML3544; .L56. **DD** 781.7425/3/05. **Continues** Linfolk.

CC
**LING NAN YIN YUEH.** **VFOAT** Lingnanyinyue; Lingnan Music. (19??)-. Periodical. Chinese. mo. Ling Nan Yin Yueh, Post Office, Canton, People's Republic of China. **LC** ML5; .L4736. **DD** 780/.951/27.

US/0893-620X
**LIP SERVICE.** [Lip serv.]. **VFOAT** Lip Service Magazine. Vol. 1, No. 1 (Spring/Fall 1987)-. Periodical. English. mo. $15.00 one year, $27.00 two year, $40.00 three year. Macey Lipman Marketing, 8739 Sunset Boulevard, Los Angeles CA 90069. **Tel** (213)652-0818, 800-333-4487, FAX (213)652-0907. **ED** Don Coleman. **DD** 811. **Bk Rev. Ad Acc. Circ:** 5,500 (ctrl).
**Desc:** A newsletter of potentially worthless gossip and news about music and musicians.

IT
**LIRICA NEL MONDO.** Vol. 1, (Dec. 1971)-. Periodical. Italian. mo. Lirica Nel Mondo, CP 7246, Rome Italy. **LC** ML5; .L485. **DD** 782.1/05.

AU
**LIST OF MEMBERS - INTERNATIONAL SOCIETY FOR JAZZ RESEARCH. MITGLIEDERLISTE - INTERNATIONALE GESELLSCHAFT FUER JAZZFORSHCUNG. LISTE OF MEMBRES - SOCIETE INTERNATIONALE DE RECHERCHES SCIENTIFIQUE POUR LE JAZZ.** **Main/Corp** International Society for Jazz Research. **Added/Corp** International Society for Jazz Research. Mitgliederliste - Internationale Gesellschaft fuer Jazzforschung. International Society for Jazz Research. Liste of Membres - Societe Internationale de Recherches Scientifique pour le Jazz. **VFOAT** Mitgliederliste - Internationale Gesellschaft fuer Jazzforschung; Liste of Membres - Societe Internationale de Recherches Scientifique pour le Jazz. (1977)-. Periodical. English. ir. S420.00 (membership). International Society for Jazz Research, Schoenaugasse 6 POB 598, A-8010 Graz Austria. **Tel** 011 43 316 813460.

●US/1054-3104
**LISTEN (NEW YORK, N.Y. 1991).** (LISTEN : THE WORLDWIDE MUSIC TIPSHEET.). [Listen]. Vol. 1, Issue 1 (Jan. 11, 1991)-. Periodical. English. Twelve times a year. $50.00. Listen, 143 Avenue B, Number 5A, New York NY 10009. **Tel** (212)529-5881. **DD** 781.

US/0147-0388
**LISTENERS' GUIDE - WGMS.** (LISTENERS' GUIDE.). **Added/Corp** Washington, D.C. Radio Station WGMS. Vol. 1, (March 1977)-. Periodical. English. Four times a year. $15.00. WSSU, Sangamon State University, Springfield IL 62794. **Tel** (317)786-6600. **LC** ML1; .L55. **DD** 780/.5.

US/0148-3544
**LISTENING POST (CITY OF INDUSTRY).** (LISTENING POST.). (1970)-. Periodical. English. mo. $12.50. Bro-Dart, 1236 South Hatcher Street, City of Industry CA 91749. **LC** ML156.9; L57. **DD** 789.9/131.

SW
**LISZT SAECULUM.** **Added/Corp** International Liszt Centre for 19th Century Music. No. 23 (1978)-. Periodical. Undetermined. Twice a year. Kr250.00 Comes with International Liszt Centre Membership. International Liszt Centre, Toredalsvagen 2 M Kagebeck, S 144 63 Ronnlnge Sweden. **Tel** 011 46 8 532 52960. **ED** L. Rabes. **LC** ML410.L7; I6. **DD** 780/.92/4. ***Continues*** *I.L.C. Quarterly.*

UK
**LISZT SOCIETY JOURNAL, THE.** **Main/Corp** Liszt Society (London, England). **Added/Corp** Liszt Society (London, England) Journal. (197?)-. Periodical. English (French and German). an. £15.00 UK; £18.00 other. The Liszt Society, 135 Stevenage Road, Fulham London SW6 6PB England. **ED** Dudley Newton. **LC** M1410.L7; L6. **DD** 780/.92/4. Index available. cum. index. **Bk Rev. Ad Acc. Circ:** 350 (ctrl). ***Continues in part*** *Newsletter (Liszt Society, London, England : 1971).*

IT
**LIUTERIA MUSICA E CULTURA.** ***Ceased.*** (19??)-(Dec. 1992). Italian. Three times a year. Editrice Turris, Corso Garibaldi 215, 26100 Cremona Italy. **Tel** 011 39 372 413084.

CN/0713-4991
**LIVE (LAVAL).** (LIVE JOURNAL ROCK.). [Live]. Vol. 1, No. 1 (May 1980)-. Periodical. French. ir (Every three weeks). Live Canada, CP 281, Laval-des-Rapides, Laval Quebec H7N 4Z9 Canada. **Tel** (514)687-1428. **ED** Marie-France Remillard. **DD** 784.5/4/005. **Ad Acc.** ctrl circ.
**Desc:** Covers news, interviews, albums and concert reviews.

●US/1059-4809
**LIVE WIRE (NEW YORK, N.Y. 1991).** (LIVE WIRE.). [Live wire]. **VFOAT** Livewire; Livewire Magazine. Vol. 1, No. 9 (Sept. 1991)-. Periodical. English. bm. $2.95 single issue US; $3.50 single issue Canada. J. Q. Adams Production, 519 8th Avenue, New York NY 10018. **DD** 781.

US/0024-5232
**LIVING BLUES.** [Living blues]. **Added/Corp** University of Mississippi. Center for the Study of Southern Culture. **VFOAT** Living Blues Magazine; LB. No. 1 (Spring 1970)-. Periodical. English. Six times a year. $18.00 (one year), $35.00 (two year), $50.00 (three year) US; $22.00 (one year), $43.00 (two year), $62.00 (three year) Canada; $28.00 (one year), $55.00 (two year), $80.00 (three year) other. University of Mississippi, Sam Hall Room 206, University MS 38677. **Tel** (601)232-5742, FAX (601)232-7842. **ED** David Nelson. **LC** ML1; .L57. **DD** 784. **Bk Rev. Ad Acc, Adv Mgr:** Brett Bonner. **Circ:** 11,000. available on microfilm and microfiche from University Microfilms International (UMI). ***Absorbed*** *Living Bluesetter.*
**Desc:** Journal of Black American Blues tradition - includes interviews, feature articles, record and book reviews, obituaries, photographs, festival dates and club dates.
**Ind/Abst** MLA Int. Bibl. Books Artic. Mod. Lang. Lit.; Music Index; RILM Abstr.

US/1044-1026
**LIVING BLUES BLUES DIRECTORY.** [Living blues blues dir.]. **Added/Corp** University of Mississippi. Center for the Study of Southern Culture. Blues Foundation. **VFOAT** Blues Directory. (1989)-. Directory. English. an. $7.00. Living Blues Magazine, Sam Hall Room 206, University of Mississippi, University MS 38677. **LC** ML12; .L58. **DD** 781.643/025/73.

US/8755-092X
**LIVING MUSIC.** [Living music]. Vol. 1, No. 1 (Fall 1983)-. Periodical. English (Spanish and French). qt. $10.00 US; $11.25 Canada and Pan America; $14.40 other. Minuscule University Press, 66358 Buena Vista Avenue, Desert Hot Springs CA 92240-3914. **Tel** (619)329-8463. **ED** Charles Mason (editor's address: 900 Arkadelphia Road, Birmingham AL 35254; editor's phone: (205)226-4952). **DD** 780. Index available. cum. index. **Bk Rev**, (Qty: 1). **Ad Acc, Adv Mgr:** same as editor. **Pr Rev. Circ:** 600 (ctrl). Documents available.
**Desc:** Original articles and news of interest to composers and performers of 'New Music', biographical information and publicity.
**Ind/Abst** Music Artic. Guide; RILM Abstr.

CN/0381-5730
**LLOYD'S CANADIAN MUSIC DIRECTORY.** 40th Ed. (1964)-. Directory. English. an (Dec.). 30.00Can$ Canada; 50.00Can$ US; 60.00Can$ others. Sentinel Business Publications, 7575 Trans Canada Highway, Suite 500, St. Laurent Quebec H4T 1V6 Canada. **Tel** (514)333-1116, FAX (514)631-8858. **ED** Carol Clifford. **DD** 338.4/7/681802571. **Ad Acc. Circ:** 3,800 (ctrl). ***Continues*** *Willson's Canadian Music Directory.*
**Desc:** A directory of product listings and suppliers to the retail and wholesale music trade in Canada.

US/1049-4340
**LOOK BACK AT BOB DYLAN.** [Look back Bob Dylan]. **VFOAT** Look Back. (19??)-. Periodical. English. qt. $20.00 North America; $30.00 other. Look Back, PO Box 857, Chardon OH 44024. **DD** 780. **Bk Rev. Ad Acc. Circ:** 800 (ctrl).
**Desc:** All matters concerning Bob Dylan.

CN/1189-3540
**LOOKING AHEAD (VANCOUVER).** (LOOKING AHEAD.). [Look. ahead]. **Added/Corp** Coastal Jazz & Blues Society. (Feb./Mar. 1991)-. Periodical. English. bm. Coastal Jazz & Blues Society, 435 West Hastings Street, Vancouver BC V6B 1L4 Canada. **DD** 781.65/09711/33.

US
**LOS ANGELES FLUTE NEWS NETWORK.** **VFOAT** Flute News Network. (198?)-. Periodical. English. mo. Los Angeles Flute News Network, 4100 Warner Boulevard L, Burbank CA 91505.

RM
**LUCRARI DE MUZICOLOGIE.** **Added/Corp** Conservatorul de Muzica G. Dima. (1965)-. Romanian (summaries and/or abstracts in French, Russian and German). an. Gheorge Dima Academy of Music, Str IC Bratianu 25, 3400 Cluj-Napoca Romania. **ED** Dan Voiculescu. **LC** ML5; .L83. **Circ:** 300.
**Ind/Abst** RILM Abstr.

NE/0024-7286
**LUISTER.** [Luister]. (1952)-. Periodical. Dutch. mo. Wegener Tijl Tijdschriften Group, Postbus 9943, 1006 AP Amsterdam Netherlands. **Tel** 011 31 20 5182828. **(Subscription address:** Wegener NV, Vandenbusschestraat 14 Abonnement, 1030 Brussels Belgium.) **UDC** 78.

UK
**LUTE NEWS : THE LUTE SOCIETY NEWSLETTER.** **Added/Corp** Lute Society (Great Britain). (19??)-. Newsletter. English. qt.

US
**LUTE SOCIETY OF AMERICA QUARTERLY.** **Added/Corp** Lute Society of America. **VFOAT** Quarterly (Lute Society of America); LSA Quarterly; Lute Society of America, Inc. Quaraterly; LSA Newsletter. Vol. 25 (Feb. 1989)-. Periodical. English. Four times a year (Feb., May, Aug., Nov.). $33.00 (one year); $63.00 (two years); $93.00 (three years) Comes with Lute Society of America Membership. Lute Society of America, PO Box 1328, Lexington VA 24450. **Tel** (703)463-5812. **LC** ML1; .L87. ***Continues*** *Newsletter (Lute Society of America), 0882-0155.*
**Ind/Abst** Music Artic. Guide.

CN/0226-868X
**LUTRIN.** (LE LUTRIN.). [Lutrin]. **Added/Corp** Orchestre Symphonique de Quebec. (Sept. 1979)-. Periodical. French. qt. Free. Orchestre Symphonique Quebec, 350 S Boulevard St, Cyrille OFC 201, Quebec City Quebec G1R 2B4 Canada. **Tel** (418)643-5598. **DD** 785/.06/2714471.

NO
**LYD & [I.E. OG] BILDE.** (1978)-. Norwegian. Forlaget Pem-Inform, Postboks 3073, Elisenberg 2, Oslo 2 Norway. **LC** ML5; .L98.

US/0093-0164
**LYONS TEACHER-NEWS.** **Added/Corp** Lyons Band Instrument Company, Chicago. (19??)-. Periodical. English. Three times a year. Lyons Teacher-News, 530 Riverview Avenue, Elkhart IN 46514. **LC** ML1; .L79. **DD** 780/.7.

US
**LYRIC OPERA OF CHICAGO ANNUAL REPORT, THE.** **Main/Corp** Lyric Opera of Chicago. (19??)-. English. an. Lyric Opera of Chicago, 20 North Wacker Drive, Chicago IL 60606. **Tel** (312)332-2244, telex 190252.
**Desc:** An attractive brochure of the company's productions, finances, and activities, with valuable illustrations.

US/0740-5812
**MADAMINA.** [MadAminA]. **Added/Corp** Music Associates of America. (Fall 1980)-. Periodical. English. sa. Baerenreiter-Verlag, KGA Verlagssvc PF 100329, D 34003 Kassel Germany. **Tel** 011 49 561 31050, telex 99504. **ED** George Sturm. **Ad Acc. Circ:** 5,000 (ctrl).
**Desc:** Includes news, interviews with personalities in the arts, and articles of general interest on music-related themes.
**Ind/Abst** Music Artic. Guide.

IT
**MADRIGALISTI DELL'ITALIA SETTENTRIONALE / UNIVERSITA DI BOLOGNA, INSTITUTO DI DISCIPLINE DELLA MUSICA.** **Added/Corp** Universita di Bologna. Istituto di Discipline Della Musica. Universita di Bologna. Dipartimento di Musica e Spettacolo. (1980)-. Monographic series. Italian. ir. Price varies per volume. **LC** UNC.

US/0541-8771
**MAESTRO, THE.** **Added/Corp** Arturo Toscanini Society. (Jan./July 1969)-. Periodical. English. ir. Arturo Toscanini Society, 812 Dumas Avenue, Dumas TX 79029. **LC** ML422.T67; M18. **DD** 785/.092/4; B.

PL/0021-5600
**MAGAZYN MUZYCZNY : MM.** **VFOAT** MM; M.M. (19??)-. Periodical. Polish. mo. Price on Request. **(Subscription address:** ARS Polona, PO Box 1001, 00068 Warsaw Poland.) **LC** ML5; .J277. **DD** 780/.42/05. ***Continues*** *Jazz.*

HU/0025-0384
**MAGYAR ZENE.** [M. zene]. (1960)-. Periodical. English. qt (4 issues). $18.00. **(Subscription address:** Kultura, PO Box 149, H 1389 Budapest 62 Hungary.) **LC** ML5; .M14.
**Ind/Abst** Music Index; RILM Abstr.

US/0360-1935
**MAIN TITLE.** **Added/Corp** Entr'acte Recording Society. (19??)-. Periodical. English. qt. Entr'acte Recording Society, PO Box 2319, Chicago IL 60690. **LC** ML1; .M118. **DD** 782.8/5.

UK
**MANCHESTER FOLK DIRECTORY.** (19??)-. Directory. English. an. T & C Hicks, 12 Winster Avenue, Stretford M32 95E England. **LC** ML21; .M2. **DD** 781.7/42.

US/0199-6533
**MANDOLIN WORLD NEWS.** (19??)-. Periodical. English. qt. $10.00 US; $12.00 other. Mandolin World, 107 Watson Street, Ripon WI 54971.

CN/0824-7358
**MANITOBA COMPOSERS' ASSOCIATION.** (MANITOBA COMPOSERS' ASSOCIATION : NEWSLETTER.). **Added/Corp** Manitoba Composers' Association. Vol. 1, No. 1 (Summer

1984)-. Newsletter. English. qt. Free. Manitoba Composers' Association, 3rd Floor, 374 Donald Street, Winnipeg Manitoba R3B 2J2. **DD** 780/.92/2.

CN/0315-9116
**MANITOBA MUSIC EDUCATOR.** [Manit. music educ.]. **Added/Corp** Manitoba Music Educators' Association. (1961)-. Periodical. English. Four times a year. 15.00Can$. Manitoba Music Educators Association, 191 Harcourt Street, Winnipeg Manitoba R3J 3H2 Canada. **Tel** (204)888-7961, FAX (204)831-0877. **DD** 780.7297127005.

US/0363-6585
**MANUSCRIPTS FOR TUBA SERIES.** (197?)-. Monographic series. English. ir. Price varies per volume. 148 Eighth Avenue North, Nashville TN 37203-3798. **Tel** (615)254-8969. **ED** Stephen L. Glover. **Bk Rev**. **Ad Acc**. **Circ:** 400 (ctrl).
**Desc:** Tuba music series.

UK
**MAPA MUNDI; RENAISSANCE PERFORMING SCORES. SERIES A: SPANISH CHURCH MUSIC.** **VFOAT** Spanish Church Music. (1978)-. English (Latin). Bruno Turner, 72 Brewery Road, King's Cross, London N79NE England.

GW/0542-6502
**MARBURGER BEITRAGE ZUR MUSIKFORSCHUNG.** (1967)-. Monographic series. German. ir. Price varies per volume. Baerenreiter-Verlag, KGA Verlagssvc PF 100329, D 34003 Kassel Germany. **Tel** 011 49 561 31050, telex 99504. **ED** Heinrich Hueschen.
**Desc:** An irregularly appearing series of dissertations of the Musicological Institute of the University of Marburg.

CN/0712-6263
**MARIPOSA FOLK FESTIVAL.** (MARIPOSA FOLK FESTIVAL : [PROGRAMME].). [Mariposa Folk Fest]. **VFOAT** Mariposa. (19??)-. English. an. Mariposa Folk Foundation, 95 Lavinia Avenue/Suite 10, Toronto Ontario M6S 2H9 Canada. **Tel** (416)363-4009. **DD** 780/.7/9713541. **Bk Rev**. **Ad Acc**. **Circ:** 25,000 (ctrl).
**Desc:** Newsletter providing information regarding the folk arts, including articles on dance, singing-songwriting, crafts, instrument making, etc. Also interviews with artists, folk calendar and reviews.

US/0364-815X
**MARQUEE (NORWALK), THE.** (THE MARQUEE.). (19??)-. Periodical. English. mo. National Singles Register, PO Box 509, Norwalk CA 90650. **Tel** (310)864-2741. **LC** ML1; .M124. **DD** 780/.42/05.

US
**MARYLAND MUSIC EDUCATOR.** **Added/Corp** Maryland Music Educators Association. (195?)-. Periodical. English. qt (Jan., May, Sept., Nov.). $8.00 US; $13.00 Canada; $18.00 other. Maryland Music Educators, Thomas W. Fugate, 27 Meadow Lane, Thurmont MD 21788-1737. **Tel** (301)271-7269, FAX (301)271-7032. **ED** Thomas W. Fugate. **LC** UNC. **Ad Acc**. **Circ:** 1,400 (ctrl).

US/0147-2550
**MASSACHUSETTS MUSIC NEWS.** **Added/Corp** Massachusetts Music Educators Association. Vol. 22, (Fall 1973)-. Periodical. English. Four times a year (Mar., Jun., Sep., Dec.). $8.00 one year; $12.00 two years; $16.00 three years. Mass Music Educators Association, C/O J. A. Digiore, PO Box 532, West Springfield MA 01090-0532. **Tel** (413)739-9065, FAX (413)788-9251. **ED** J. Anthony DiGiore. **Bk Rev**, (Qty: 6800). **Ad Acc**. **Circ:** 1,600 (ctrl). ***Continues*** *MMEA Music News.*
**Desc:** A documentation of the progress of music education in the state of Massachusetts.
**Ind/Abst** Music Artic. Guide.

US/8756-0828
**MASTERS AND MONUMENTS OF THE RENAISSANCE.** [Masters monum. Renaiss.]. (1980)-. Monographic series. English. ir. Price varies per volume. Broude Brothers Limited, 141 White Oaks Road, Williamstown MA 01267. **Tel** (413)458-8132, (800)525-8559. **LC** M2; .M276. **DD** 780.

SW
**MATRIKEL.** **Main/Corp** Kungl. Musikaliska Akademien (Sweden). (19??)-. Swedish. an. Valhallavagen 103-109, 115 31 Stockholm Sweden. **LC** MT5.S88; M8425.

US/0360-8484
**MATTHAY NEWS, THE.** **Added/Corp** American Matthay Association. (19??)-. Periodical. English. Three times a year. $5.00. American Matthay Association, 63 West Water Street, Gettysburg PA 17325. **LC** ML423.M42; M4. **DD** 786.2/1/06273.

US/0743-3530
**MAXIMUM ROCKNROLL.** **VFOAT** Maximum Rock and Roll; M.R.R.; MRR; Maximum Rock 'N' Roll. (1982)-. Periodical. English. mo. $18.00. Maximum Rock 'N' Roll, PO Box 288, Berkeley CA 94701. **Tel** (415)658-5756. **Ad Acc**. **Circ:** 16,000.
**Desc:** A semi-coherent look at the international punk scene, analyzing and criticizing itself and the environment which spawned it.

UK/0768-8172
**MBI MUSIC BUSINESS INFORMATIONS.** **VFOAT** Music Business Informations. (1987)-. Periodical. French. Six times a year. £75.00. Spotlight Publications, 245 Blackfriars Road, 8th Floor, London SE1 9UR England. **Tel** 011 44 71 6203636, FAX 011 44 71 4018036. **UDC** 534.32. **Ad Acc**. **Circ:** 10,000 (ctrl).
**Desc:** In depth news, feature coverage and analysis of the global music industry.
**Ind/Abst** Infomat Int. Bus.

CN/0848-9645
**ME. MUSIC EXPRESS MAGAZINE.** ***Ceased.*** (MUSIC EXPRESS MAGAZINE : ME.). [ME, Music express mag.]. **VFOAT** Music Express; ME. Vol. 14, No. 143 (Jan. 1990)-(Jan. 1993). Periodical. English. Twelve times a year. K Sharp Music Enterprises Inc., 219 Dufferin Street / Suite 100, Toronto Ontario M6K 3J1 Canada. **DD** 781.66/05. ***Continues*** *Music Express (Toronto, Ont.)., 0848-9637.*

US/0195-6191
**MEAN MOUNTAIN MUSIC.** **Added/Corp** Mean Mountain Music (Firm). (19??)-. Periodical. English. bm. $12.00. Mean Mountain Music, 926 West Oklahoma Avenue, Milwaukee WI 53215. **LC** ML156; .M4. **DD** 016.7899/12454.

US/0094-0321
**MECCA (NEW ORLEANS).** (MECCA.). (Jan. 1974)-. Periodical. English. mo. $12.00. Mecca, 611 Gravier Street/Room 913, New Orleans LA 70130. **LC** ML1; .M137. **DD** 785.4/2/05.

US/1045-795X
**MECHANICAL MUSIC.** [Mech. music]. **Added/Corp** Musical Box Society International. **VFOAT** Journal of Mechanical Music. Vol. 34, No. 3 (Winter 1988)-. Periodical. English. ir. $42.00 (latest edition). Christies Catalogue, 21 24 44th Avenue, Long Island City NY 11101. **Tel** (718)784-1480. **ED** Angelo Rulli. **LC** ML1; .M395. **DD** 786.6/19/05. Index available. cum. index. **Bk Rev**. **Ad Acc**. ctrl circ. ***Continues*** *Journal of Mechanical Music.*
**Ind/Abst** Music Index.

GW
**MEISTERWERKE DER MUSIK.** (1965)-. Monographic series. German. ir. Price varies per volume. Wilhelm Fink Verlag, Ohmstrasse 5, D 80802 Munich Germany. **Tel** 011 49 89 348017, 348018. **ED** Stephan Kunze.
**Desc:** Monographic series on the history of music; examines different compositions and their composers.

GW
**MELODIE.** **Added/Corp** Bertelsmann Schallplattenring. (19??)-. Periodical. German. mo. Panorama / Czech Republic, 1 Halkova, 12072 Prague 2 Czech Republic. **Tel** (2)2361391. **(Subscription address:** Artia Pegas Press Ltd., Palac Metro Narodni Trida 25, 11210 Prague 1 Czech Republic.**)** **LC** ML156.9; .M45. ***Continues*** *Schallplattenring Illustrierte.*

GW/0025-9004
**MELODIE UND RHYTHMUS.** [Melodie Rhythm.]. (1957)-. Periodical. German. mo. Deutscher Judo Verband, Redaktion Ippon Segewaldweg 40, D 12557 Berlin Germany. **Tel** 011 49 711 210770, telex 051 678.
**Ind/Abst** RILM Abstr.

UK/0025-9012
**MELODY MAKER (LONDON).** (MELODY MAKER.). [Melody mak.]. (1926)-. English. Fifty-one times per year. £33.00 UK; £63.00 others; $150.00 US & Canada (airmail). IPC Magazines Ltd., Perrymount Road, Haywards Heath, West Sussex RH16 3DH England. **Tel** 011 44 444 440421. **LC** ML5; .M17. **DD** 780/.5. **[CCC]**. available on microfilm from University Microfilms International (UMI). Documents available from UMI Article Clearinghouse. ***Absorbed*** *Rhythm.*
**Ind/Abst** Mag. Search; Music Index; Newsp. Period. Abstr. (1988-).

CN/0250-765X
**MEMBERS - INTERNATIONAL FOLK MUSIC COUNCIL.** [Memb. - Int. Folk Music Counc.]. **Main/Corp** International Folk Music Council. (1970)-. English. International Folk Music Council, Department of Music, Queen's University, Kingston Ontario K7L 3N6 Canada. **Tel** (613)545-2553. **DD** 784.4/06/01.

US/1055-3010
**MEMBERSHIP DIRECTORY.** (MEMBERSHIP DIRECTORY / AMERICAN MUSICAL INSTRUMENT SOCIETY.). [Membshp. dir. - Am. Music. Instrum. Soc.]. **Main/Corp** American Musical Instrument Society. (1988)-. Directory. English. an. $35.00 Includes American Musical Instrument Society Newsletter. American Musical Instrument Society, R. D. #3, Box 205-B, Franklin PA 16323. **Tel** (814)374-4119, FAX (814)374-4563. **LC** ML27.U5; A8333953. **DD** 784.19/025/73. ***Continues*** *American Musical Instrument Society. Membership Roster, Geographic Index, Interest Index.*

US/0277-4054
**MEMBERSHIP DIRECTORY / CHAMBER MUSIC AMERICA.** [Membsh. dir. - Chamb. Music Am.]. **Main/Corp** Chamber Music America. (1978)-. Directory. English. an. $25.00 US; $50.00 other. Chamber Music America, 545 8th Avenue, New York NY 10018. **Tel** (212)244-2772, FAX (212)244-2776. **ED** Daniel J. Myers. **LC** ML19; .C5. **DD** 785.7/0025/73. Index available. **Circ:** 10,000 (ctrl).
**Desc:** Lists members of Chamber Music America. Voting members are listed geographically by state and include description of activities. Associate organizations are listed by discipline. Associate individuals are listed alphabetically. Indices pertain to voting members.

US/8755-5964
**MEMBERSHIP DIRECTORY / INTERNATIONAL TRUMPET GUILD.** [Membsh. dir. - Int. Trumpet Guild]. **Main/Corp** International Trumpet Guild. **VFOAT** Directory of the International Trumpet Guild; ITB Membership Directory. (19??)-. Directory. English. an (Dec.). Membership: $26.00 US; $41.00 Europe; $46.00 other (airmail). International Trumpet Guild, School of Music, Florida State University, Tallahassee FL 32306. **Tel** (904)644-3424, FAX (904)386-8613. **LC** ML17; .I57. **DD** 788/.1/025. **Circ:** 3,500. ***Continues*** *ITG Journal, 0363-2845.*

US/8755-2892
**MEMBERSHIP DIRECTORY / NATIONAL ASSOCIATION FOR MUSIC THERAPY.** [Membsh. dir. - Natl. Assoc. Music Ther.]. **Main/Corp** National Association for Music Therapy. (19??)-. Directory. English. an. $25.00. National Association for Music Therapy Inc., 8455 Colesville Road, Suite 930, Silver Spring MD 20910. **Tel** (301)589-3300, FAX (301)589-5175. **LC** ML3919; .N37. **DD** 615.8/5154/06073. **Ad Acc**. **Circ:** 4,000.

US
**MEMBERSHIP DIRECTORY / THE AMERICAN BELL ASSOCIATION.** **Main/Corp** American Bell Association. (19??)-. Directory. English. an. $1.50. American Bell Association, 7210 Bellbrook Drive, San Antonio TX 78227. **Tel** (210)674-1814. **LC** ML27.U5; A593. **DD** 789/.5/06073. ***Continues*** *American Bell Association. Directory.*

US
**MEMBERSHIP HANDBOOK.** **Main/Corp** Music Library Association. (1993)-. Periodical. English. an. $10.00 (nonmembers), $5.00 (members). Music Library Association, PO Box 487, Canton MA 02021. **Tel** (617)828-8450, FAX (617)828-8915. ***Continues*** *Music Library Association. Membership Directory, 0884-982X.*

CN/0828-7007
**MEMBERSHIP LIST - CANADIAN ASSOCIATION OF MUSIC LIBRARIES (1984).** **See** Library and Information Sciences.

CN/0823-955X
**MEMBERSHIP LIST / CAPAC.** [Membsh. list - CAPAC]. **Main/Corp** Composers, Authors and Publishers Association of Canada. **VFOAT** Liste des Membres. **VAT** Membership List - Composers, Authors and Publishers Association of Canada; Liste des Membres - Composers, Authors and Publishers Association. (1983)-. English (French). an. Composers Authors and Publishers Association of Canada, 1240 Bay Street, Toronto Ontario M5R 2C2 Canada. **DD** 780/.6/071. ***Continues*** *Composers, Authors and Publishers Association of Canada. Membres de la C A P A C, 0319-4035.*

UK
**MEMBERSHIP LIST - THE GALPIN SOCIETY.** **Main/Corp** Galpin Society. (1948)-. Academic Scholarly Publication. English. an. The Galpin Society, 7 Perceval Avenue, London NW3 4PY England. **Tel** 011 44 71 4350370. **(Subscription address:** Membership Secretary's address: c/o P. Holden, 2, Quinton Rise, Oadby, Leicester LE2 5PN, England, telephone: 0533 711808**)** **ED** Dr. David Rycroft. **LC** ML27.E8; G333. **DD** 781.9/1/0621. Index available. **Bk Rev**, (Qty: varies). **Ad Acc**, **Adv Mgr:** T.K. Diblet, **Tel** 0304 374772. **Acid Free**. **Circ:** 1,100 (ctrl). available on diskette.
**Desc:** News and information of the members and about the society.

UK/0266-8033
**MEMORY LANE (LEIGH-ON-SEA, ESSEX).** (MEMORY LANE.). [Mem. lane]. (19??)-. Periodical. English. qt (Feb., May, Aug., Nov.). $35.00. Memory Lane / England, 226 Station Road, Leigh-On-Sea Essex, 559 4HJ England. **ED** Ray Pallett. Index available (ú4.00). **Bk Rev**. **Ad Acc**. **Circ:** 2,000.
**Desc:** Popular music, dance bands, big bands, vocalists, jazz, etc.

# Music

US/0272-8214
**MEMPHIS MUSIC DIRECTORY, THE.**
**Added/Corp** National Academy of Recording Arts and Sciences (U.S.). Memphis Chapter. (1980)-. Directory. English. an. Ward Archer Jr., Memphis Music Directory, PO Box 41072, Memphis TN 38104. **LC** ML19; .M45. **DD** 780/.25/76819.
**Desc:** Country music directory.

GW
**MENDELSSOHN STUDIEN. Added/Corp** Mendelssohn-Gesellschaft. Vol. 1 (1972)-. Multiple languages (English and German). Duncker und Humblot Verlag, Postfach 410329, D-12113 Berlin Germany. **Tel** 011 49 30 79000612, 011 49 30 79000613. **LC** ML410.M5; M6. **DD** 780/.92/4; [B].
**Ind/Abst** RILM Abstr.

NE/0025-9462
**MENS & MELODIE.** (MENS EN MELODIE.). [Mens melod.]. **VFOAT** Mens & Melodie. Vol. 3, No. 1 (Jan. 1948)-. Periodical. Dutch. Ten times a year. Fl62.00 Netherlands; Fl119.00 other. Uitgeverij Scala, Postbus 28009, 3828 Hoogland Netherlands. **Tel** 011 31 33 806896. **ED** John Kasander. Index available (free). **Bk Rev. Ad Acc. Circ:** 4,000 (ctrl). **Continues** Mensch en Melodie.
**Desc:** Articles about classical music: performances, composers, and analyses.
**Ind/Abst** Music Index; RILM Abstr.

●US/1056-554X
**MESSAGE IN THE MUSIC.** [Message music]. **VFOAT** M.I.T.M. Magazine; M.I.T.M. (1991)-. Periodical. English. qt. $7.00. Dove Photography, 2497 Glenrock Drive, Atlanta GA 30032. **DD** 782.

●UK/0967-442X
**METAL CD.** (1992)-. English. mo. £70.00 for six issues. Northern & Shell Publications, PO Box 381, Mill Harbour, London E14 9TW England. **Tel** 011 44 71 987 5090, FAX 011 44 71 987 2160. **ED** Kirk Blows. **Ad Acc, Adv Mgr:** Elspeth Thomson. **Circ:** 100,000.

US/1068-2872
**METAL EDGE.** [Met. edge]. **VFOAT** TV Picture Life Metal Edge; TV Picture Life. (199?)-. Periodical. English. mo. $22.95 (one year), $38.95 (two year). Sterling Macfadden, 233 Park Avenue South, New York NY 10003. **Tel** (212)979-4800. **DD** 782. **Continues** TV Picture Life, Metal Edge, 1059-8006.

CN/0824-7056
**METAL K.O.** [Met. K.O.]. Vol. 1, No. 1 (Jan. 1984)-. Periodical. French. mo. Metal K.O., CP 237, Succursale Delorimer, Montreal Quebec, H2H 2N6. **DD** 784.5/4.

US
**METAL MANIACS.** English. bm. $15.00 (one year), $28.00 (two year). Sterling Macfadden, 233 Park Avenue South, New York NY 10003. **Tel** (212)979-4800.

US/1045-6392
**METAL MUSCLE.** (METAL MUSCLE : MM.). [Met. muscle]. **VFOAT** MM. (1989)-. Periodical. English. bm. Faces Magazine Inc., 63 Grand Avenue, Suite 230, River Edge NJ 07661-1912. **Tel** (201)487-6124. **DD** 780.

US/0736-4229
**METROPOLITAN OPERA BOX.** [Metrop. Opera box]. **Added/Corp** Metropolitan Opera Guild. (1981)-. Monographic series. English. ir. Price varies per volume. Education at the Met, 70 Lincoln Center, New York NY 10023-6593. **Tel** (212)769-7000. **LC** UNC.

US
**METROPOLITAN OPERA SEASON ANNUAL SOUVENIR BOOK.** Periodical. English. an. $13.50 US; $17.00 Canada; $20.50 other. Metropolitan Opera Guild Inc., 70 Lincoln Center Plaza, New York NY 10023. **Tel** (212)769-7080.

US/0160-9483
**MICHIGAN MUSIC.** Vol. 2, No. 3 (Dec. 1977)-. Periodical. English. mo. Michigan Music, Box 724, Detroit MI 48232. **LC** ML1; .M171. **DD** 780/.9774. **Continues** Michigan Musician.

BE/0771-0461
**MINUTES / OCIC. See** Motion Picture.

UK
**MIRO : MUSIC INDUSTRY RESEARCH ORGANISATION. VFOAT** Music Industry Research Organisation. English. mo. Music Industry Research Organisation, Studio 5, RVPB Trinity Road, London SW18 3SX England.

AT/0076-9355
**MISCELLANEA MUSICOLOGICA (ADELAIDE).** (MISCELLANEA MUSICOLOGICA; ADELAIDE STUDIES IN MUSICOLOGY.). [Misc. music.]. **Added/Corp** Libraries Board of South Australia. University of Adelaide. Dept. of Music. **VFOAT** Adelaide Studies in Musicology. Vol. 1 (March 1966)-. English. an. University of Adelaide, Associate Editor, Misc Musicological, Adelaide 5005 South Australia. **Tel** 228-5333, telex 89141 UNIVAD AA. **(Subscription address:** Music Department, University of Adelaide, GPO Box 498, Adelaide 5001 South Australia) **ED** Andrew D. McCredie. **LC** ML5; .M34. **Bk Rev. Ad Acc. Circ:** 200 (ctrl).
**Desc:** A periodic publication of musicological essays covering a variety of topics with most volume centered around a defined theme.
**Ind/Abst** APAIS, Aust. Public Aff. Inf. Ser. (1986-); Music Index; RILM Abstr.

US/0742-4612
**MISSISSIPPI RAG, THE.** [Miss. rag]. No. 1 (Nov. 1973)-. Periodical. English. mo. $18.00 (one year), $34.00 (two years) US; $20.00 (one year), $38.00 (two years) other. Mississippi Rag, Firstar Bank Building, 6500 Nicollet Avenue South, Minneapolis MN 55423. **Tel** (612)920-0312, FAX 9612)861-4621. **ED** Leslie Johnson (editor's phone: (612)861-2446). Index available. cum. index. **Bk Rev**, (Qty: Varies). **Ad Acc, Adv Mgr:** same as editor. **Circ:** 4000.
**Desc:** Articles on traditional jazz, ragtime topics and performers, historical features, festival coverage, book and record reviews, photo features, current jazz and ragtime news.
**Ind/Abst** Jazz Index; Music Index.

US/1061-7019
**MISSISSIPPI SAXOPHONE.** [Miss. saxophone]. Vol. 1, Issue 1 (Sept. 1991)-. Periodical. English. bm. $12.00. Potential Publications, 23 School Street, Brunswick ME 04011. **DD** 788.

US/0085-350X
**MISSOURI JOURNAL OF RESEARCH IN MUSIC EDUCATION. Added/Corp** Missouri. Dept. of Education. Missouri Music Educators Association. Vol. 1, No. 1 (Autumn 1962)-. English. an (Summer). $2.00. Missouri Journal of Research in Music and Education, Dr. Randall Pembrook, 4949 Cherry, Conservatory of Music, University of Missouri Kansas City, Kansas City MO 64110. **Tel** (816)235-2945. **ED** Dr. Randall Pembrook. **LC** ML1; .M176. **DD** 780/.7/073. Index available. **Circ:** 250-300.
**Ind/Abst** Music Artic. Guide; Music Index.

US
**MISSOURI SCHOOL MUSIC MAGAZINE. Added/Corp** Missouri Music Educators Association. **VFOAT** Missouri School Music. (1946)-. Periodical. English. Four times a year. $8.00. Missouri Music Educators Association, PO Box 690, Marshfield MO 65706. **Tel** (417)468-2555.
**Ind/Abst** Music Artic. Guide.

GW
**MITTEILUNGEN DER ARBEITSGEMEINSCHAFT FUER MITTELRHEINISCHE MUSIKGESCHICHTE. Main/Corp** Arbeitsgemeinschaft fuer Mittelrheinische Musikgeschichte. (Aug. 1961)-. Periodical. German. ir. Arbeitsgemeinschaft fur Mittelrheinische Musikgeschichte, Postfach 3980, 65 Mainz Germany. **LC** ML275.7.R5; A7. **DD** 780/.943/4.

GW/0417-2051
**MITTEILUNGEN DER DEUTSCHEN GESELLSCHAFT FUER MUSIK DES ORIENTS.** (MITTEILUNGEN.). [Mitt. Dtsch. Ges. Musik Orients]. **Main/Corp** Deutsche Gesellschaft fuer Musik des Orients. (1962)-. Multiple languages (English and German). Four times a year. DM160.00. Duncker und Humblot Verlag, Postfach 410329, D-12113 Berlin Germany. **Tel** 011 49 30 79000612, 011 49 30 79000613. **LC** ML5; .D36. **DD** 780/.95.
**Ind/Abst** Anthropol. Index; RILM Abstr.

GW/0440-2863
**MITTEILUNGEN DER HANS PFITZNER-GESELLSCHAFT.** [Mitt. Hans-Pfitzner-Ges.]. **Main/Corp** Hans Pfitzner-Gesellschaft. (1954)-. Periodical. German. ir. Hans Pfitzner Gesellschaft, Mozartstrasse 8, W 8132 Tutzing Fed Rep Germany. **Tel** 011 49 8158 3050. **LC** ML410.P32; H295.
**Ind/Abst** Music Index; RILM Abstr.

AU/0541-2331
**MITTEILUNGEN DER INTERNATIONALEN STIFTUNG MOZARTEUM.** [Mitt. Int. Stift. Mozart.]. **Main/Corp** Internationale Stiftung Mozarteum Salzburg. (1953)-. Periodical. German. qt. Internationale Stiftung Mozarteum, 26 Schwarzstr., A 5020 Salzburg Austria. **LC** ML26; .M656. **DD** 780/.92/4.
**Ind/Abst** Music Index; RILM Abstr.

AU
**MITTEILUNGEN DER OSTERREICHISCHEN GESELLSCHAFT FUER MUSIKWISSENSCHAFT. Main/Corp** Osterreichische Gesellschaft fur Musikwissenschaft. (Nov. 1973)-. German. Postfach 1461, A-1011 Vienna Austria. **LC** ML27.A9; O39.
**Ind/Abst** RILM Abstr.

NE
**MIXTUUR, DE.** No. 1 (Nov. 1970)-. Periodical. Dutch. ir. De Mixtuur, Vincent Van Goghlaan 29, Schagen Netherlands. **LC** ML549.8; .M59.

US/0094-6478
**MLA INDEX AND BIBLIOGRAPHY SERIES.** [MLA index bibliogr. ser.]. **Main/Corp** Music Library Association. **VFOAT** Index and Bibliography Series. **VAT** Music Library Association Index and Bibliography Series. No. 12 (1975)-. Bibliography. English. ir. Price varies per volume. Music Library Association, PO Box 487, Canton MA 02021. **Tel** (617)828-8450, FAX (617)828-8915. **DD** 780. **Continues** Music Library Association. MLA Index Series, 0077-2445.

US
**MLA TECHNICAL REPORTS. Added/Corp** Music Library Association. **VFOAT** Music Library Association Technical Reports; MLA Technical Report; Technical Reports. No. 4 (1977)-. Monographic series. English. ir. Price varies per volume. Music Library Association, PO Box 487, Canton MA 02021. **Tel** (617)828-8450, FAX (617)828-8915. **LC** ML27.U5; M861. **Continues** Music Library Association Technical Reports, 0094-5099.

DK/0105-6972
**MM.** [MM]. (19??)-. Periodical. Danish. mo. Kr216.00 Denmark; Kr300.00 other. Gothersgade 21 1 TV, DK-1123 Copenhagen K Denmark. **Tel** 01 323331, 21316 DANSIN, FAX 01324057. **ED** Svend Rasmussen and Soren Friis. **LC** ML5; .M06. Index available. **Bk Rev. Ad Acc. Circ:** 15,000.
**Desc:** Trend-setting magazine on rock and jazz in Denmark; attempts to combine the qualities of Musician, Down Beat and Rolling Stone.

●US/1058-0212
**MOBILE BEAT INTERNATIONAL.** (MOBILE BEAT INTERNATIONAL : THE OFFICIAL TRADE NEWSMAGAZINE FOR PROFESSIONAL MOBILE DISC JOCKEYS.). [Mob. beat int.]. **VFOAT** Mobile Beat. (1991)-. Periodical. English. bm. $12.95 (institution), $19.95 (individual) US; $19.95 (institution), $24.95 (individual) Canada and Mexico. Mobile Beat, PO Box 309, 533 West Commercial Street, East Rochester NY 14445. **Tel** (716)385-9920, FAX (716)385-3637. **ED** Michael Buonaccorso. **LC** WMLC 91/1476. **DD** 780. **Ad Acc, Adv Mgr:** Bob Lindquist. **Circ:** 10,000. **Continues** Mobile Beat Entertainment.
**Desc:** Music news, equipment reviews, trade news, marketing and managing information for the mobile entertainer, including disc jockeys and karioke mc's.

US/0194-4533
**MODERN DRUMMER.** (MODERN DRUMMER : MD.). [Mod. drum.]. **VFOAT** MD; M.D. (Jan. 1977)-. Periodical. English. mo. $29.95 (one year), $51.95 (two years) US and Canada; $36.95 (one year), $58.95 (two years) other. Modern Drummer Publications, 870 Pompton Avenue, Cedar Grove NJ 07009. **Tel** (201)239-4140, (800)221-1988, FAX (201)239-7139. **(Subscription address:** PO Box 480, Mt Morris, IL 61054) **ED** Ronald Spagnardi. **LC** ML1035; .M6. **DD** 789/.1/05. **Bk Rev. Ad Acc, Adv Mgr:** Robert Berenson. **Circ:** 102,000. available on microfilm and microfiche from University Microfilms International (UMI). **Absorbed** Modern Percussionist, 8750-7838.
**Desc:** A publication for drummers and percussionists.
**Ind/Abst** Jazz Index; Music Index.

US/0097-2533
**MODERN HI-FI AND MUSIC. See** Sound Recordings and Systems.

US/0273-8511
**MODERN RECORDING & MUSIC.**
**Suspended. See** Sound Recordings and Systems.

US/0276-9239
**MODERN RECORDING & MUSIC'S BUYER'S GUIDE. See** Sound Recordings and Systems.

●US/1070-5104
**MODERN SCREEN'S COUNTRY MUSIC.** [Mod. screen's ctry. music]. **VFOAT** Country Music. Vol. 87, No. 6 (May 1993)-. Periodical. English. mo. $19.95 (one year), $36.95 (two year). Sterling Macfadden, 233 Park Avenue South, New York NY 10003. **Tel** (212)979-4800. **DD** 781. **Continues** Modern Screen's Country Music Special, 1068-0373.

DK/0105-9238
**MODSPIL.** No. 1 (1978)-. Periodical. Danish. Four times a year. kr128.00. Rhodos, 36 Strandgade, 1401 Copenhagen K Denmark. **Tel** 011 45 31543020, FAX 011 45 954742, telex 31 502. **LC** ML5; .M45. **Bk Rev. Circ:** 1,500.
**Desc:** Non-conventional music review. Each number has a special theme, such as 'Music and Magic', 'Latin', and 'The Experience of Music'.

CN/0827-2387
**MOLE.** (THE MOLE.). [Mole]. (March 1984)-. Periodical. English. ir. B. Mowat, 169 Locke Street South, Hamilton Ontario L8P 4B2 Canada. **ED** B. F. Mowat. **DD** 784.5/4/005. **Bk Rev**. **Ad Acc**. **Circ:** 1,000 (ctrl).

FR/0181-7949
**MONDE DE LA MUSIQUE, LE.** No. 1, (June 1978)-. Periodical. French. Eleven times a year. 282.08F France; 375.00F others. Loft International, 1 Rue Lord Byron, 75008 Paris France. **Tel** 011 33 1 42256520. **(Subscription address:** Service Abonnements B700, 60732 Ste Genevieve Cedex France, Telephone: 011 33 44 034414**)**
**Ind/Abst** Point Repere (1992-).

CN/0823-0498
**MONDE DU ROCK.** (LE MONDE DU ROCK.). [Monde rock]. (1980)-. Periodical. French. mo. Monde du Rock, 558 6E rue, Quebec Quebec G1J 2S4 Canada. **Tel** (418)524-2731. **ED** Michel Jacques. **DD** 784.5/4/005. **Bk Rev**. **Ad Acc**. **Circ:** 20,000 (ctrl).
**Desc:** Covers the rock music scene of Eastern Canada, especially in the Quebec Province. We work in French and try to promote local talents.

US
**MONOGRAPH SERIES IN ETHNOMUSICOLOGY.** **Added/Corp** University of California, Los Angeles. Program in Ethnomusicology. **VFOAT** UCLA Monograph Series in Ethnomusicology; U.C.L.A. Monograph Series in Ethnomusicology. (1980)-. Monographic series. English. ir. Price varies per volume. UCLA / Department of Ethnomusicology, Los Angeles CA 90024. **Tel** (310)825-5947. **ED** Eran Fraenkel. **LC** UNC. **Circ:** 600 (ctrl).
**Desc:** In-depth scholarly studies in the field of ethnomusicology.

US/0093-6642
**MONOGRAPHS ON MUSIC IN HIGHER EDUCATION.** **Added/Corp** National Association of Schools of Music. No. 1 (1973)-. English. National Association of Schools of Music, 11250 Roger Bacon Drive, Suite 21, Reston VA 22090. **Tel** (703)437-0700. **ED** David Bading. **LC** MT1; .M8. **DD** 780/.72.

US/0147-6653
**MONOLITH.** (Nov. 1976/Feb. 1977)-. Periodical. English. bm. Monolith Publications Inc, 1411 Bellevue Avenue, Seattle WA 98122. **LC** ML1; .M182. **DD** 780/.42/09795.

SP/0210-4083
**MONSALVAT.** ***Ceased.*** [Monsalvat]. No. 1, (Dec. 1973)-(Jan. 1994). Spanish. Eleven times a year (July/Aug., issues combined). Editorial Labor, Aragon 390 6 Planta, 08013 Barcelona Spain. **Tel** 011 34 3 2322211. **LC** ML5; .M537.
**Ind/Abst** Music Index; RILM Abstr.

UK
**MONTHLY GUIDE TO RECORDED MUSIC, THE.** (19??)-. Periodical. English. Twelve times a year. £12.00 Europe; £20.00 US & Canada; £18.50 Pan America; £22.00 others. Monthly Guide to Recorded Music, 26 Arundel Drive, Bedford MK41 8JF England. **LC** ML156.2; .M64. **DD** 016.7899/13.

US/1056-2877
**MONTHLY MUSIC REPORT.** (MONTHLY MUSIC REPORT : M.M.R. / ALL GENRE.). [Mon. music rep.]. **Added/Corp** All Genre (Firm). **VFOAT** M.M.R. Vol. 1, Rep. 1 (Feb. 1991)-. Periodical. English. mo. $50.00. All Genre, 738 Main Street, Suite 387, Waltham MA 02254-9038. **DD** 782.

GW/0544-9987
**MONUMENTA MONODICA MEDII AEVI. HRSG. IM AUFTRAG DES INSTITUTS FUER MUSIKFORSCHUNG REGENSBURG MIT UNTERSTUTZUNG DER MUSIKGESCHICHTLICHEN KOMMISSION VON BRUNO STABLEIN.** (1956)-. Monographic series. Latin. ir. Price varies per volume. Baerenreiter-Verlag, KGA Verlagssvc PF 100329, D 34003 Kassel Germany. **Tel** 011 49 561 31050, telex 99504. **(Subscription address:** Foregin Music Distributors, 13 Elkay Drive, Chester NY 10918.**)** **LC** M2; .M48193.
**Desc:** Presents the repertoire of monodic music from antiquity to the end of the middle ages.

FR/0545-0004
**MONUMENTA MUSICAE SACRAE.** Vol. 1, (1952)-. Monographic series. Latin. ir. Price varies per volume. Protat Freres Imprimerie, 1 rue de la Barre, F-71000 Macon France. **ED** Publiee Sous la Direction de Dom Hesbert. **LC** M2; .M483.

SW/0077-1473
**MONUMENTA MUSICAE SVECICAE / SVENSKA SAMFUNDET FOR MUSIKFORSKNING.** **Added/Corp** Svenska Samfundet for Musikforskning. Kungl. Musikaliska Akademien (Stockholm,Sweden). (1958)-. Monographic series. English (German and Swedish). ir. Price varies per volume. Edition Reimers AB, Fack 30, S-16 115 Broma-Stockholm Sweden. **LC** M2; .M4833. **Bk Rev**. **Circ:** 1,000.
**Desc:** A philological and practical documentation of old Swedish music.

SP
**MONUMENTOS DE LA MUSICA ESPANOLA.** **Added/Corp** Instituto Espanol de Musicologia. (1941)-. Monographic series. Spanish. ir. Price varies per volume. Consejo Superior Investigacion Cientificas (CSIC), Vitruvio 8, 28006 Madrid Spain. **Tel** 011 34 1 5612833, FAX 011 34 1 4113077, telex 42182.

US/0077-1503
**MONUMENTS OF RENAISSANCE MUSIC.** (1964)-. Monographic series. English. ir. Price varies per volume. University of Chicago Press / Book Department, 11030 South Langley Avenue, Chicago IL 60628. **Tel** (800)621-2736, (312)568-1550, FAX (312)753-0811, telex 23933.

US/0278-0763
**MORAVIAN MUSIC JOURNAL.** [Morav. music j.]. **Added/Corp** Moravian Music Foundation. Vol. 26, No. 1 (Spring 1981)-. Periodical. English. sa. $10.00. Moravian Music Foundation, 20 Cascade Avenue, Winston Salem NC 27127. **Tel** (910)725-0651, FAX (910)725-4514. **ED** Nola Reed Knouse. **LC** ML1; .M192. **DD** 780/.5. **Circ:** 1,200. ***Continues*** *Bulletin (Moravian Music Foundation), 0027-1020.*
**Desc:** Articles and information on research and composers of Moravian music and early American music.
**Ind/Abst** Music Artic. Guide; Music Index.

US/0273-2114
**MOTIF (SPRINGFIELD).** (MOTIF.). **Added/Corp** Assemblies of God. Music Dept. Vol. 1 (Aug. 1979)-. Periodical. English. qt. $13.50. Motif, 1445 Boonville, Springfield MO 65802. **Tel** (417)862-2781. **ED** Carmen Wassam. **LC** ML3000; .M68. **DD** 783/.02/605. Index available. cum. index. **Circ:** 400 (ctrl).
**Desc:** Primarily an inspirational and informational publication to the ministers of music in the General Council of the Assemblies of God denomination.

●GW
**MOTIV.** (Jan. 1991)-. Periodical. German. Twelve times a year (Some issues are double). DM93.60. Verlag Constructiv Berlin, Hermann Matern STR 58 60, 0 1040 Berlin Fed Rep Germany. **Tel** 011 37 30 2878324. **LC** ML5; .M9033. ***Continues*** *Musik und Gesellschaft, 0027-4755.*

US/0149-8096
**MOUNTAIN MUSIC AND WHERE TO FIND IT.** **Added/Corp** Cut Cane Asssociates. (1971)-. Periodical. English. Cut Cane Associates, PO Box 98, Mineral Bluff GA 30559. **LC** ML1; .M1933. **DD** 784.

CN/0380-0601
**MOUTHPIECE (TORONTO).** (THE MOUTHPIECE.). **Added/Corp** Canadian National Institute for the Blind. Music Dept. (Feb. 1970)-. Periodical. English. qt. Free. Canadian National Institute for the Blind, 1929 Bayview Avenue, Toronto Ontario M4G 3E8 Canada. **Tel** (416)480-7584. **Circ:** 250 (ctrl). available on magnetic tape.
**Desc:** A series of articles relating to the Canadian music scene.

GW/0077-1805
**MOZART-JAHRBUCH.** **Added/Corp** Mozarteum, Salzburg. (19??)-. German. ir. Baerenreiter-Verlag, KGA Verlagssvc PF 100329, D 34003 Kassel Germany. **Tel** 011 49 561 31050, telex 99504. Index Available Published separately--free--upon request.
**Desc:** Essays on the music, life, environment, and performance practice of Mozart's works and bibliographies on the writings.

IT
**MUCCHIO SELVAGGIO, IL.** (Oct. 1977)-. Periodical. Italian. Eleven times a year. L70000 Italy; L100000 elsewhere Europe. Lakota SRL, Via Pietro Mascagni 3 5, 00199 Rome Italy. **Tel** 011 39 06 8608913. **LC** ML3533.8; .M8. **Bk Rev**. **Ad Acc**. **Circ:** 40,000 (ctrl).

US/0149-8517
**MUGWUMPS.** ***Suspended.*** [Mugwumps]. Vol. 1, Jan. 1972-?. Periodical. English. bm. $12.00. MIH Publications, 15 Arnold Place, New Bedford MA 02740. **Tel** (617)993-0156. **LC** ML1; .M1947. **DD** 781.9/1.
**Ind/Abst** Music Index (-19??).

GW
**MUNCHNER EDITIONEN ZUR MUSIKGESCHICHTE.** (1979)-. Monographic series. German. ir. Price varies per volume. Broude Brothers Limited, 141 White Oaks Road, Williamstown MA 01267. **Tel** (413)458-8132, (800)525-8559.

GW
**MUNCHNER VEROFFENTLICHUNGEN ZUR MUSIKGESCHICHTE.** (1959)-. Monographic series. German. ir. Price varies per volume. Dr. Hans Schneider Verlag GmbH, Mozartstrasse 6, W 82327 Tutzing Germany. **Tel** 011 49 8158 3050.

US/1054-2639
**MUSE, MUSIC SEARCH.** (MUSE, MUSIC SEARCH [COMPUTER FILE].). [MUSE MUsic SEarch]. **Added/Corp** National Information Services Corporation. International Repertory of Music Literature (Organization). **VFOAT** Music Search; MUSE. NISC MSL 199103-01 (1970-1984)-. English. an. $1,211.00 US; $1,225.00 other. National Information Services Corp, 3100 St Paul Street, Wyman Towers, Suite 6, Baltimore MD 21218. **Tel** (410)243-0797, FAX (410)243-0982. **LC** ML113; .M87. **DD** 780.

US/0736-6949
**MUSELETTER (WASHINGTON, D.C.).** (MUSELETTER.). **Added/Corp** Washington Performing Arts Society. (19??)-. Periodical. English. W A P S, 425 13th Street NW/Suite 712, Washington DC 20004. **LC** ML28.W2; .W227. **DD** 790.2/09753. ***Continues*** *WPAS Museletter, 0092-4113.*

**MUSI-STAFF.** (19??)-. Periodical. English. mo. **LC** ML5; .M9843. **DD** 780/.5.

UK/0960-6033
**MUSIC.** English. mo. £23.40 UK; £37.00 Europe; £46.00 other. Orpheus Publications, 7 St. Johns Road, Harrow Middlesex HA1 2EE England. **Tel** 011 44 81 863-4040, FAX 011 44 81 424-9945.

CN/1186-2378
**MUSIC '91 (VANCOUVER).** (MUSIC '91 : BRITISH COLUMBIA'S YEAR OF MUSIC 1991 NEWSLETTER.). [Music '91]. **Added/Corp** British Columbia's Year of Music Society. **VFOAT** Music '91 Newsletter. (Jan. 1990)-. Newsletter. English. qt. Limited free distribution. British Columbia's Year of Music Society, Suite 201-1110 Hamilton Street, Vancouver, British Columbia V6B 2B2 Canada. **DD** 380.1/4591711/005.

US/1051-8975
**MUSIC ALIVE.** [Music alive]. (19??)-. Periodical. English. Eight times a year. $175.00 US; $225.00 other. Cherry Lane Music Company Inc., PO Box 430, Port Chester NY 10573. **Tel** (914)935-5200, FAX (914)937-0614. **ED** Cathy Carr, 10 Midland Ave, Port Chester, NY 10573. **LC** MT3.U5; M73. **DD** 780/.71/2. **Circ:** 70,000.
**Desc:** Intended for use with general grades 5-12.

UK
**MUSIC ANALYSIS.** Vol. 1, No. 1 (March 1982)-. Academic Scholarly Publication. English. Three times a year. £98.00 UK & Europe; $191.00 North America; £123.00 other. Basil Blackwell Publishers Ltd, 108 Cowley Road, Oxford 0X4 1JF England. **Tel** 011 44 865 791100, FAX 011 44 865 791347, telex 837022 OXBOOK G. **(Subscription address:** Blackwell Publishers / UK, Marston Book Services, PO Box 87, Oxford OX2 0DT England.**)** **ED** Derrick Puffett. **LC** ML1; .M2125. **DD** 781/.05. **Bk Rev**. **Ad Acc**. available on microfilm and microfiche from University Microfilms International (UMI). Documents available from The Genuine Article.
**Ind/Abst** Arts Humanit. Citation Index [Full Cov.]; Curr. Contents Arts Humanit.; Music Index; Res. Alert [Full Cov.]; Soc. Sci. Cit. Index [Select. Cov.].

UK/0262-8260
**MUSIC & AUTOMATA.** **VFOAT** Music and Automata. Vol. 1, No. 1 (Mar. 1983)-. Periodical. English. sa. £15.00 UK; $25.00 US. Arthur W J G Ord-Hume, 24 Shepherds Lane, Guildford Surrey GU2 6SL England. **Tel** 0483 574460, FAX 0730 895298. **ED** Arthur W. J. G. Ord-Hume. **LC** ML1049.8; .M9. **DD** 786.6/05. Index available. **Bk Rev**. **Ad Acc**. **Circ:** 2,500.
**Desc:** Concerned with mechanical musical instruments and the music they play.

IT
**MUSIC AND COMMUNICATION.** (1970)-. Monographic series. English. ir. Price varies per volume. Casa Editrice Leo S. Olschki, Viuzzo del Pozzetto, Casella Postale 66, 50126 Florence Italy. **Tel** 011 39 55 6530684, FAX 011 39 55 6530214.

UK/0027-4224
**MUSIC & LETTERS.** [Music lett.]. **VFOAT** Music and Letters. **VAT** Music and Letters. Vol. 1 (Jan. 1920)-. Periodical. English. qt. £48.00 UK and Europe; $90.00 other. Oxford University Press, Walton Street, Oxford OX2 6DP England. **Tel** 011 44 865 56767, FAX 011 44 865 267773, telex 837330 OXPRES G. **(Subscription address:** Oxford University Press / USA, Journals Marketing Department, Oxford University Press, 2001 Evans Road, Cary NC 27513.**)** **ED** Nigel Fortune and John Whenham. **LC** ML5; .M64. **[CCC]**. Index available. cum. index. **Bk Rev**. **Ad Acc**. available on microfilm and microfiche from University Microfilms International (UMI). Documents available from The Genuine Article, UMI Article Clearinghouse.
**Desc:** Journal for musicologists, educators, students, and all classical music lovers. Each issue contains comprehensive, diverse, and interpretative articles with book reviews, biographies and complete indexes.
**Ind/Abst** Abstr. Engl. Stud.; Acad. Search (July 1993-); Am. Hist. Life (1991-); Annu. Bibliogr. Engl. Lang. Lit.; Arts Humanit. Citation Index [Full Cov.]; Br. Humanit. Index; Curr. Contents Arts Humanit.; Expand. Acad. Index (1989-); Humanit. Index; Humanit. Source (Jul. 1993-);

INFO-SOUTH Abstr.; Mag. Search; MLA Int. Bibl. Books Artic. Mod. Lang. Lit.; Music Index; Newsp. Period. Abstr. (1991-); Res. Alert [Full Cov.]; RILM Abstr.; Soc. Sci. Cit. Index [Select. Cov.].

UK/0305-4438
**MUSIC AND LITURGY.** [Music and liturgy]. **Added/Corp** Society of St. Gregory. Church Music Association. Vol.1 (Autumn 1974)-. Periodical. English. Six times a year. £18.00 UK; £19.00 Europe; £21.00 other. Society of Saint Gregory, 33 Brockenhurst Road, P. Moynihan, Croydon Surrey CR0 7DR England. **Tel** 081-654 3379. **ED** Stephen Dean. **LC** ML5; .M6413. **DD** 783/.026/205. **Bk Rev**, (Qty: 15/yr). **Ad Acc. Circ:** 750. available on microfilm and microfiche from University Microfilms International (UMI). ***Formed by the union of*** *Life and Worship, 0024-5119* ***and*** *Church Music.*
**Desc:** A magazine of information and practical assistance to Roman Catholic musicians, principally in the British Isles.
**Ind/Abst** Abr. Cathol. Period. Lit. Index; Cathol. Period. Lit. Index.

NE
**MUSIC & MEDIA.** ir (50 issues per year). $270.00. Billboard Publications Inc., 1515 Broadway Billboard, New York NY 10036. **Tel** (212)764-7300, FAX (305)755-7048, telex WU TWX 710-581-6279. **(Subscription address:** Music & Media, PO Box 9027, 1006 AA Amsterdam, The Netherlands**)** available on an online database (file 16/Full-Text) from DIALOG.
**Desc:** Covers the broadcasting and home entertainment industries. Provides the most complete coverage of the 18 most important European markets.
**Ind/Abst** Infomat Int. Bus.

US
**MUSIC AND RECORDINGS.** (1955)-. English. an. Oxford University Press, Walton Street, Oxford OX2 6DP England. **Tel** 011 44 865 56767, FAX 011 44 865 267773, telex 837330 OXPRES G. **LC** ML1; .M22743. **DD** 780.973.

US
**MUSIC & SOUND BUYER'S GUIDE.** **VFOAT** Music and Sound Buyer's Guide. (1982)-. English. an. $4.95. Testa Communications, 25 Willowdale Avenue, Port Washington NY 11050. **Tel** (516)767-2500, FAX (516)767-9335. **LC** ML459; .M9. **DD** 789/.0029/4. Index available (bound in issue).

US/0894-1238
**MUSIC & SOUND RETAILER, THE.** [Music sound retail.]. **VFOAT** Music and Sound Retailer. Vol. 3, No. 7 (Oct. 1, 1986)-. Periodical. English. Twelve times a year (Except Feb., July). $18.00 (one year); $26.00 (two years). Professional Recording Sound Publ. Inc., 25 Willowdale Avenue, Port Washington NY 11050. **Tel** (516)767-2500, FAX (516)767-9335. **ED** Jon Maye (phone: (516)767-2500). **LC** ML1092; .M85. **DD** 789.9/9/05. **Ad Acc.** ctrl circ. ***Continues*** *Music & Sound Electronics Retailer, 0746-8067.*
**Desc:** The news magazine for musical instrument and sound products merchandisers produced with the philosophy of the right people.

AT/0047-8431
**MUSIC AND THE TEACHER.** (19??)-. English. Four times a year (Mar., June, Sept., Dec.). 20.00Aus$. Victorian Music Teachers Association, 49 Earl Street, East Kew VIC 3101 Australia. **Tel** 011 61 03 853 7861. **ED** Vera Jeppesen. Index Available, published separately, free-automatically sent ($5.00). cum. index. **Bk Rev**, (Qty: 12). **Ad Acc, Adv Mgr:** J. Thomas, **Tel** 03 853-7861. **Circ:** 1,250 (ctrl).
**Desc:** Contains articles and news about music and music teachers.
**Ind/Abst** Aust. Educ. Index (?-?).

US/0027-4240
**MUSIC ARTICLE GUIDE.** **See** Music-Abstracting, Bibliographies and Statistics.

US/0146-096X
**MUSIC AT YALE.** **Main/Corp** Yale University. Music Executive Committee. (Fall/Winter 1971/72)-. Periodical. English. qt. $5.00. Yale University Music Executive Committee, School of Music, 96 Wall Street, New Haven CT 06520. **Tel** (203)787-8372. **LC** ML1; .Y3. **DD** 780/.9746/8.

US/0360-1943
**MUSIC BOOK GUIDE.** (19??)-. English. an. GK Hall & Co, 100 Front Street, Riverside NJ 08075. **Tel** (800)257-5755 ext. 2223. **LC** ML113; .M88. **DD** 016.78.

UK
**MUSIC BOX, THE.** **Added/Corp** Musical Box Society of Great Britain. (Winter 1962)-. Periodical. English. qt. Musical Box Society of Great Britain, Landbeach Cambridge CB4 4DT England. **Tel** 01-462-1181. **ED** G. Whitehead. **LC** ML5; .M643. **DD** 789.7/05. Index available. cum. index. **Bk Rev. Ad Acc. Circ:** 1,500 (ctrl).
**Desc:** The society's objective is the restoration and preservation of all forms of mechanical musical instruments.

US/0747-6655
**MUSIC BUSINESS DIRECTORY.** [Music bus. dir.]. **Added/Corp** Music Business Directory (Firm). 1st Ed. (1984)-. Directory. English. sa. Music Business Directory, 1100 16th Avenue South, Nashville TN 37212. **LC** ML15.N2; M9. **DD** 338.4/778/02576855. available on CD-ROM.

FR
**MUSIC BUSINESS INTERNATIONAL.** (MBI : MUSIC BUSINESS INTERNATIONAL.). (1991)-. Trade Publication. English. Six times a year. £75.00. Spotlight Publications, 245 Blackfriars Road, 8th Floor, London SE1 9UR England. **Tel** 011 44 71 6203636, FAX 011 44 71 4018036. **ED** Ajax Scott. **Ad Acc, Adv Mgr:** Rudi Blackett, **Tel** 011 44 71 921 5981. **Circ:** 9,000 (ctrl).
**Desc:** In depth news, feature coverage and analysis of the global music industry.
**Ind/Abst** Infomat Int. Bus.

US/0092-1041
**MUSIC CAPITOL NEWS. COUNTRYWIDE.** **VFOAT** Countrywide. Vol. 1 (Summer 1971)-. Periodical. English. Music Capitol News, PO Box 186, Fairfax VA 22030. **LC** ML1; .M2298. **DD** 784.

US/1055-5536
**MUSIC CATALOG (WASHINGTON, D.C.), THE.** (THE MUSIC CATALOG [MICROFORM].). [Music cat.]. **Added/Corp** Library of Congress. Cataloging Distribution Service. (1990)-. Catalog. English. Four times a year. $110.00 North America; $125.00 others. Advanced Library Systems, PO Box 246, Andover MA 01810. **Tel** (508)470-0610, FAX (508)475-1072. **LC** ML136.U5; N9. **DD** 016. available on microfiche. ***Formed by the union of*** *Music, Books on Music, and Sound Recordings, 0092-2838* ***and*** *Music, Books on Music, and Sound Recordings, 0092-2838.*

US
**MUSIC CATALOG. [COMPUTER FILE].** **See** Bibliographies.

US/0027-4283
**MUSIC CATALOGING BULLETIN.** **Added/Corp** Music Library Association. (1970)-. Periodical. English. mo. $25.00. Music Library Association, PO Box 487, Canton MA 02021. **Tel** (617)828-8450, FAX (617)828-8915. **LC** ML111; .M75. **DD** 025.3/48.

US/0278-9051
**MUSIC CIRCULAR.** (CIRCULAR / NATIONAL LIBRARY SERVICE FOR THE BLIND AND PHYSICALLY HANDICAPPED, THE LIBRARY OF CONGRESS.). **Added/Corp** Library of Congress. National Library Service for the Blind and Physically Handicapped. No. 1 (Dec. 1980)-. English. National Library Service for the Blind and Physically Handicapped, Library of Congress, 1291 Taylor Street Northwest, Washington DC 20542. **Tel** (800)424-8567, (202)707-5100, (800)424-9100. **LC** ML63; .M88. **DD** 780.

US/0027-4291
**MUSIC CITY NEWS.** ***Title Change.*** [Music city news]. (1963)-(19??). Periodical. English. mo. Music City News Inc, PO Box 22975, Nashville TN 37202. **Tel** (615)329-2200, FAX (615)327-2726. **ED** John Sturdivant and Lydia Dixon-Harden. **LC** UNC. **DD** 781. **Ad Acc. Circ:** 120,000 (ctrl). ***Continued by*** *Country Music City News, 1066-3312.*
**Desc:** Feature articles deal with country music personalities and various aspects of the industry record charts and reviews.

●US/1078-5558
**MUSIC CITY NEWS (1994).** (MUSIC CITY NEWS.). [Music city news]. (1994)-. Periodical. English. mo. Music City News Inc, PO Box 22975, Nashville TN 37202. **Tel** (615)329-2200, FAX (615)327-2726. **DD** 781. ***Continues*** *Country Music City News, 1066-3312.*

US/0161-2654
**MUSIC CLUBS MAGAZINE (1963).** (MUSIC CLUBS MAGAZINE.). [Music clubs mag.]. **Added/Corp** National Federation of Music Clubs. Vol. 43, No. 2 (Dec. 1963)-. Periodical. English. Four times a year (Feb., May, Oct., Dec.). $6.00. National Federation of Music Clubs, 1336 North Delaware Street, Indianapolis IN 46202. **Tel** (317)638-4003. **ED** Mrs. Bryan L. Blackwell (editor's address: PO Box 418, Hartsville, SC 29550, phone: (803)332-8573). **LC** ML1; .M2299. **DD** 780/.973. **Bk Rev. Ad Acc.** available on microfilm and microfiche from University Microfilms International (UMI). ***Continues*** *Showcase (Mount Morris, Ill.).*
**Ind/Abst** Music Artic. Guide; Music Index.

US/0896-4750
**MUSIC, COMPUTERS & SOFTWARE.** **See** Computers-Computer Music.

US
**MUSIC CONNECTION.** (19??)-. English. bw. $40.00. Music Connection, 6640 Sunset Boulevard, 1st Floor, Hollywood CA 90028. **Tel** (213)462-5772, FAX (213)462-3123.
**Desc:** Music industry trade publication. Contains news items, interviews and articles that relate to and affect the music industry, including columns and guides specifically for musicians and songwriters.

CN/0820-0416
**MUSIC DIRECTORY CANADA.** [Music dir. Can.]. (1983)-. Directory. English. be (every 2 years). 29.95Can$. Norris-Whitney Communications Inc., 23 Hannover Drive Unit 7, St. Catharine Ontario L2W 1A3 Canada. **Tel** (905)641-3471, FAX (905)641-1648. **ED** David Henman. **LC** ML21.C3; M9. **DD** 780/.25/71. **Ad Acc.**
**Desc:** The directory of the Canadian music industry - a comprehensive guide book containing information for anyone involved in music in Canada.

UK
**MUSIC EDUCATION REVIEW.** (1977)-. English. an. Chappell, 50 New Bond Street, London W1 England. **LC** ML5; .M644234. **DD** 780/.72.

US/0027-4321
**MUSIC EDUCATORS JOURNAL.** [Music educ. j.]. **Added/Corp** Music Educators National Conference (U.S.). Vol. 21 (1934)-. Periodical. English. mo. $60.00 US (includes Teaching Music). Music Educators National Conference, 1806 Robert Fulton Drive, Reston VA 22091. **Tel** (703)860-4000, (800)336-3768. **ED** Maribeth Rose. **LC** ML1; .M234. **DD** 780. Index available. cum. index. **Bk Rev. Ad Acc. Circ:** 56,600 (ctrl). available on microfilm and microfiche from University Microfilms International (UMI). ***Continues*** *Music Supervisors' Journal.*
**Desc:** Offers timely articles on teaching approaches and philosophy, current trends and issues in music education, classroom techniques and the latest in products and services available to music educators.
**Ind/Abst** Acad. Search (July 1993-); Book Rev. Index; Contents Pages Educ.; Curr. Index J. Educ.; Educ. Index; Except. Child Educ. Resour.; Humanit. Source (Jul. 1993-); INFO-SOUTH Abstr.; Mag. Search; Music Artic. Guide; Music Index; RILM Abstr.; Spec. Educ. Needs Abstr.

US/0898-8757
**MUSIC FOR THE LOVE OF IT.** [Music love it]. Vol. 1, No. 1 (March 1988)-. Periodical. English. Six times a year (Feb., Apr., June, Aug., Oct., Dec.). $20.00 (individuals), $30.00 (institutions). Music for the Love of It, 67 Parkside Drive, Berkeley CA 94705. **Tel** (510)654-9134. **ED** Ted Rust. **DD** 780. **Bk Rev**, (Qty: 5). **Ad Acc. Circ:** 500.
**Desc:** About making your own music.
**Ind/Abst** Music Artic. Guide.

US/0885-503X
**MUSIC FORUM, THE.** [Music forum]. (1967)-. English. Four times a year. Joint Council of NSW Music Organ, Box N42, Grosvenor STR PO, Sydney 2000 Australia. **Tel** 90 1638.
**Ind/Abst** Music Index; RILM Abstr.

US/1071-2801
**MUSIC FROM CHINA NEWSLETTER.** (MUSIC FROM CHINA NEWSLETTER = CHANG FENG YUEH HSUN.). [Music China newsl.]. **Added/Corp** Music from China (Organization). **VFOAT** Chang Feng Yueh Hsun. (1991)-. Newsletter. English (Chinese). qt. $10.00 US; $14.00 other. Music from China, 170 Park Row, Suite 12-D, New York NY 10038. **Tel** (212)962-5698. **ED** Chen Yi, Paul Shackman. **DD** 780. **Bk Rev**, (Qty: 2). **Circ:** 2,500 (ctrl).
**Desc:** Designed to encourage interest in Chinese music, traditional and modern, through the dissemination of information and the exchange of ideas.

UK
**MUSIC HALL.** No. 9 (Oct. 1979)-. Periodical. English. bm. Music Hall Records, 50 Reporton Road, London SW6 England. **ED** Tony Barker. **LC** PN1968.G7; M87. **DD** 792.7/0941. **Bk Rev.** ***Continues*** *Music Hall Records.*
**Desc:** Presents detailed biographies of music hall artists, with lists of their song recordings and etc.

NZ/0113-7441
**MUSIC IN NEW ZEALAND.** (1988)-. Periodical. English. Four times a year (Seasonally). 28.00NZ$ New Zealand; 43.00NZ$ other. Music in New Zealand, 29 Prospect Terrace, Mt Eden Auckland 3 New Zealand. **LC** ML5.; M64454. **DD** 780/.993/05.
**Ind/Abst** Music Index.

US/0146-7883
**MUSIC-IN-PRINT SERIES.** **VFOAT** Music in Print Series. Vol. 1, (1974)-. Monographic series. English. ir. Price varies per volume. Musicdata Inc, PO Box 48010, Philadelphia PA 19144-8010. **Tel** (215)842-0555. **LC** UNC. Index available. **Bk Rev. Ad Acc.**
**Desc:** Reference catalog listing various categories of printed music published worldwide.

AU
**MUSIC IN THE MEDIA : IMZ BULLETIN.** **Added/Corp** International Music Centre. (19??)-. Bulletin. English. **LC** ML68; .M85. **DD** 780. ***Continues*** *International Music Centre. IMZ Bulletin Information.*

IS
**MUSIC IN TIME.** **Added/Corp** Akademyah Le-Musikah U-Mahol Bi-Yerushalayim a. sh. Rubin. **VFOAT** Etim Le-Musikah. (19??)-. English. an (Nov.). Free. Jerusalem Rubin Academy of Music & Dance, Givat Ram Campus, Jerusalem 91904 Israel. **Tel** 011 972 2 636232, FAX 011 972 2 527713. **ED** Tzui Avui. **LC** ML5; .M6447. **DD** 780/.5. **Circ:** 1,000.

UK
**MUSIC IN WORSHIP.** No. 1 (Sept. 1977)-. Periodical. English. Music in Worship, 78 Trevellance Way, Garston Hertfordshire WD2 6LZ England. **LC** ML3001; .M85. **DD** 783/.02/605.

US/1050-1681
**MUSIC INC.** [Music inc.]. Vol. 1, No. 1 (March 1990)-. Periodical. English. Ten times a year. $15.00 U.S.; $24.00 others. Maher Publications Inc, 180 West Park Avenue, Elmhurst IL 60126. **Tel** (312)941-2030, (800)515-7496. **DD** 381. ***Continues*** *Up Beat Monthly, 0892-113X.*

US/0027-4348
**MUSIC INDEX, THE.** **See** Music-Abstracting, Bibliographies and Statistics.

US/1066-1514
**MUSIC INDEX ON CD-ROM, THE.** (THE MUSIC INDEX ON CD-ROM [COMPUTER FILE].). [Music index CD-ROM]. (19??)-. English. an. $1,305.00. Chadwyck-Healey Limited, The Quorum Barnwell Road, Cambridge CB5 8SW England. **Tel** 011 44 223 215512, telex 9312102281 CH G. **(Subscription address:** Chadwyck Healey Inc. / US Subscriptions, 1101 King Street, Suite 380, Alexandria VA 22314.**)** **LC** ML118; ML118; .M845. **DD** 780.

US/0270-3203
**MUSIC INDUSTRY BULLETIN.** [Music ind. bull.]. **Added/Corp** National Association of Pastoral Musicians (U.S.). (June 1980)-. Bulletin. English. qt. National Association of Pastoral Musicians, 225 Sheridan Street Northwest, Washington DC 20011. **Tel** (202)723-5800, FAX (202)723-2262.

US/0740-3755
**MUSIC INDUSTRY PRODUCTS.** [Music ind. prod.]. Vol. 1, No. 1 (Oct./Nov./Dec. 1983)-. Periodical. English. qt. $24.00 US; $34.00 Canada. Music Industry Products, PO Box 24169, Los Angeles CA 90024.

US/1048-1494
**MUSIC INTERNATIONAL (RUSSIAN ED.).** (MUSIC INTERNATIONAL.). (1991)-. Periodical. Russian. Four times a year. $20.00. Kompass Publishing Inc., 418 Commonwealth Avenue, Boston MA 02215. **Tel** (617)266-1214.

US
**MUSIC K 8.** English. ir (5 issues per year). $39.95. Plank Road Publishing, PO Box 26627, Wauwatosa WI 53226. **Tel** (414)771-0771, FAX (414)771-1384. cum. index. available on audiocassette.

US/0027-4372
**MUSIC LEADER, THE.** **Added/Corp** Southern Baptist Convention. Sunday School Board. (Oct./Dec. 1970)-. Periodical. English. Four times a year (Jan., Apr., July, Oct.). $11.40. Southern Baptist Convention, 901 Commerce, Suite 750, Nashville TN 37203. **Tel** (615)244-2355, FAX (615)742-8919. **(Subscription address:** Sunday School Board - Customer Service, 127 Ninth Avenue North, Nashville, TN 37234 USA; telephone: (800)458-2772**)** **ED** Derrell Billingsley. **LC** ML1; .M249. **DD** 783. **Bk Rev. Ad Acc. Circ:** 50,000 (ctrl).
**Desc:** For church music leaders of boys and girls ages four through eleven. Contents include guidance materials, training aids, and enrichment for leaders of preschoolers and other children.
**Ind/Abst** Music Artic. Guide (?-?); South. Baptist Period. Index (1991-).

US/1065-1179
**MUSIC LIBRARIAN.** [Music libr.]. **Added/Corp** CD One Stop (Firm). **VFOAT** Music Librarian Monthly Buying Guide; CD One Stop ... Music Librarian. (19??)-. Periodical. English. Twelve times a year. $50.00. CD One Stop, 13 Francis J. Clarke Circle, Bethel CT 06801. **Tel** (203)798-6590. **ED** Darryl Ohrt. **DD** 025. **Ad Acc. Pr Rev. Circ:** 4,000 (ctrl).
**Desc:** An updated to yearly catalogs for all new music releases.

US
**MUSIC LIBRARY ASSOCIATION JOB LIST.** (19??)-. Periodical. English. mo. Music Library Association, PO Box 487, Canton MA 02021. **Tel** (617)828-8450, FAX (617)828-8915.

●US/1061-8376
**MUSIC MADNESS MAGAZINE.** (1992)-. Periodical. English. bm. $19.95. Nice/Love Entertainment Publishing, PO Box 849, New York NY 10268-0849.

US/0162-4377
**MUSIC MAKERS (NASHVILLE).** (MUSIC MAKERS.). **Added/Corp** Southern Baptist Convention. Sunday School Board. Vol. 1, (Oct./Dec. 1970)-. Periodical. English. Four times a year (Jan., Apr., July, Oct.). $5.60 (one year); $10.90 (two years). Southern Baptist Convention, 901 Commerce, Suite 750, Nashville TN 37203. **Tel** (615)244-2355, FAX (615)742-8919. **LC** ML1; .M2657.

UK
**MUSIC MASTER.** **See** Sound Recordings and Systems.

CN/0702-9012
**MUSIC MCGILL.** **Added/Corp** McGill University. Faculty of Music. (Summer 1976)-. Periodical. English. sa. McGill University / Faculty of Music, 853 Sherbrooke Street West, Montreal Quebec H3A 2T6 Canada. **Tel** (514)398-4850. **DD** 780.7/29714/281.

US
**MUSIC. MUSIC PROFESSIONAL TRAINING, CAREER DEVELOPMENT ORGANIZATIONS, MUSIC RECORDING, SERVICES TO COMPOSERS, CENTERS FOR NEW MUSIC RESOURCES, SPECIAL PROJECTS.** **VFOAT** Music Professional Training, Career Development Organizations, Music Recording, Services to Composers, Centers for New Music Resources, Special Projects. (1985)-. English. an. Free. National Endowment for the Arts, 1100 Pennsylvania Avenue Northwest, Washington DC 20506. **Tel** (202)682-5400, (202)682-5435. **Circ:** 1,000. ***Formed by the union of*** *Music Professional Training* ***and*** *Music Recording.*
**Desc:** Funding guidelines for the organization.

XR/0027-4410
**MUSIC NEWS FROM PRAGUE.** [Music news Prague]. **Added/Corp** Cesky Hudebni Fond Praha. Hudebni Informacni Stredisko. Guild of Czechoslovak Composers. (19??)-. Periodical. English (German, French, Spanish and Russian). Six times a year (Jan., Mar., May, July, Sept., Nov.). $20.00 Europe; $25.00 other. Music Information Center, Czech Music Fund, Besedni 3, 11800 Prague 1 Czech Republic. **Tel** 011 42 2 539720 or 530546. **ED** Nina Vseteckova. **LC** ML5; M6527. **DD** 780/.9437/12. **Bk Rev. Circ:** 15,000 (ctrl).
**Desc:** Contemporary Czech music culture.
**Ind/Abst** Music Index.

US/0027-4437
**MUSIC NOW.** **Added/Corp** Southeastern Composer's League. (19??)-. Periodical. English. Four times a year (Jan., May, Sept., Nov.). $20.00. Southeastern Composer's League, Mississippi University for Women, Box W-70, Columbus MS 39701. **Tel** (601)329-7203. **ED** Richard Montalto (phone: (601)329-3606). **LC** UNC. **Circ:** 85.
**Desc:** News and information on Southeastern Composer's League.
**Ind/Abst** Music Artic. Guide (?-?).

●US/1057-0934
**MUSIC OF THE BABA ALLAUDDIN GHARANA AS TAUGHT BY ALI AKBAR KHAN AT THE ALI AKBAR COLLEGE OF MUSIC, THE.** [Music Baba Allauddin Gharana taught Ali Akbar Khan Ali Akbar Coll. Music]. **VFOAT** Music of the Baba Allauddin Gharana as Taught by Ali Akbar Khan. (1991)-. Monographic series. English. ir. Price varies per volume. East Bay Books, PO Box 1165, Staunton VA 24401. **DD** 780.

US/0892-2721
**MUSIC OF THE SPHERES.** **See** New Age Publications.

US
**MUSIC PAPER, THE.** **VFOAT** Music Paper of New York. Vol. 14, No. 12 (June 1986)-. Periodical. English. Twelve times a year. $12.00. Sound Resources Ltd, PO Box 304, Manhasset NY 11030. **Tel** (516)883-8898. ***Continues*** *Music Paper of New York.*

US/0730-7829
**MUSIC PERCEPTION.** [Music percept.]. Vol. 1, No. 1 (Fall 1983)-. Periodical. English. qt (Mar., June, Sept., Dec.). $46.00 (individuals), $98.00 (institutions). University of California Press, 2120 Berkeley Way, Berkeley CA 94720. **Tel** (510)642-4191, (510)642-3907, FAX (510)642-9917. **ED** Diana Deutsch. **LC** ML1; .M2735. **DD** 780/.5. **[CCC]. Bk Rev. Ad Acc. Pr Rev. Circ:** 900 (ctrl). available on microfilm from University Microfilms International (UMI). Documents available from The Genuine Article.
**Desc:** Approaches by scientists and musicians to the study of musical phenomena.
**Ind/Abst** Arts Humanit. Citation Index [Full Cov.]; Curr. Contents Arts Humanit.; Curr. Contents Soc. Behav. Sci.; Music Index; Psychol. Abstr. (1983-); PsycINFO; PsycLit; Res. Alert [Full Cov.]; Soc. Plann. Policy Dev. Abstr.; Soc. Sci. Cit. Index [Full Cov.].

US/0896-1352
**MUSIC PERFORMANCE RESOURCES.** ***Ceased.*** [Music perform. resour.]. (Fall/Winter 1987)-(19??). Periodical. English. sa. SMS Publications, 1418 Lake Street, Evanston IL 60201. **Tel** (312)328-3386. **ED** Steven Plattner and Tom Gillette. **LC** ML1; .M2737. **DD** 780/.7/2. **Ad Acc. Circ:** 50,000 (ctrl).
**Desc:** Provides a balanced editorial view of new products and current educational trends in the band, orchestra, and choral areas through feature articles with recognized leaders in these respective fields, as well as many other topics of practical interest to the music educator. Music festivals, study and performance opportunities are a regular feature as well as the latest in instruments, uniforms, etc.

US
**... MUSIC RADIO DIRECTORY, THE.** ***Suspended.*** **Added/Corp** Music Industry Resources. (1988)-(1990). Directory. English. ir. Music Industry Resources, PO Box 190, San Anselmo CA 94960. **Tel** (415)457-0215. **LC** PN1991.67.M86; M87. **DD** 384.54/025/73. available on CD-ROM.

US/0736-7740
**MUSIC REFERENCE COLLECTION, THE.** [Music ref. collect.]. No. 1, (1983)-. Monographic series. English. ir. Price varies per volume. Greenwood Press Inc., PO Box 5007, Westport CT 06881-5007. **Tel** (203)226-3571, FAX (203)222-1502. **LC** UNC.

●US/1058-8167
**MUSIC REFERENCE SERVICES QUARTERLY.** [Music ref. serv. q.]. Vol. 1, No. 1 (1992)-. Periodical. English. qt. $45.00 US; $63.00 other. The Haworth Press Inc, 10 Alice Street, Binghamton NY 13904-1580. **Tel** (607)722-5857, (800)3-HAWORTH, FAX (607)722-1424. **ED** William Studwell. **LC** IN PROCESS. **DD** 780. **Bk Rev. Ad Acc. Pr Rev. Acid Free.** available on microfiche. Documents available from Haworth Document Delivery Service.
**Desc:** Includes the entire range of interests of music librarians. Coverage includes administration, collection development, cataloging, online services, and bibliographies.
**Ind/Abst** Inf. Sci. Abstr.; Music Artic. Guide.

US/1042-1262
**MUSIC RESEARCH FORUM.** [Music res. forum]. **Added/Corp** University of Cincinnati. College-Conservatory of Music. Vol. 1, (Winter 1986)-. Periodical. English. an (Winter). $6.00 (individuals); $8.00 (institutions). College Conservatory of Music, Box 49, University of Cincinnati, Cincinnati OH 45221. **Tel** (513)556-1970. **LC** ML1; .M279. **DD** 780/.5.
**Ind/Abst** Music Index.

CN/0700-3838
**MUSIC RESEARCH NEWS.** **Added/Corp** Canadian Music Research Council. Bulletin 1 (Spring 1976)-. Periodical. English. sa. Canadian Music Research Council, Faculty of Education, Simon Fraser University, Burnaby British Columbia Canada. **DD** 780/.01.

US/0271-5163
**MUSIC RESEARCHER'S EXCHANGE, THE.** [Music res. exch.]. **Added/Corp** Indiana University. School of Music. Vol. 1, (May 1974)-. Periodical. English. Five times a year (Jan., Mar., May, Sept., Nov.). $5.00 (individuals), $6.00 (institutions) surface mail; $12.00 airmail. Columbia University Teachers College, Box 139, Music & Arts Education, New York NY 10027. **Tel** (212)678-3283. **ED** Harold F. Abeles. **Bk Rev. Circ:** 724.
**Desc:** A newsletter for active researches in music education, psychology of music and acoustics.

US/1051-1822
**MUSIC RETAILING.** [Music retail.]. No. 1 (Sept. 1990)-. Periodical. English. Twenty-four times a year. $95.00. Wayne Green Enterprises, 70 Route 202 North, Peterborough NH 03458. **Tel** (603)924-0058. **ED** Mark Lo. **LC** ML3790; .M75. **DD** 381/.4780266/097305. ctrl circ.
**Desc:** Targets record retailers and covers on how to manage a business.

US/0882-8229
**MUSIC REVELATION.** (19??)-. Periodical. English. mo (10 issues -not published in June or Aug.). $32.00 US; $37.00 Canada. Music Revelation, 7 Elmwood Court, Rockville MD 20850. **Tel** (301)424-2956. **ED** C. Harry Causey. **DD** 783. Index available. cum. index. **Bk Rev**, (Qty: varies). **Circ:** 1,500 (ctrl).
**Desc:** Variety of articles by an variety of writers on worship and the music ministry of the local church. Designed to equip, inform, motivate, and inspire.

UK/0027-4445
**MUSIC REVIEW, THE.** [Music rev.]. Vol. 1, (Feb. 1940)-. Periodical. English. Four times a year (Feb., May, Aug., Nov.). $110.00 US & Canada (surface mail). Black Bear Press Ltd, King's Hedges Road, Cambridge CB4 2PQ England. **Tel** 011 44 223 424571. **ED** A. E. Leighton-Thomas. **LC** ML5; .M657. **DD** 780/.5. Index available. **Bk Rev. Ad Acc. Circ:** 1,500 (ctrl). available on microfilm and microfiche from University Microfilms International (UMI). Documents available from The Genuine Article, UMI Article Clearinghouse.
**Ind/Abst** Acad. Search (July 1991-); Arts Humanit. Citation Index (19??-19??) [Full Cov.]; Br. Humanit. Index; Curr. Contents Arts Humanit.; Expand. Acad. Index

(1989-); Humanit. Index; Humanit. Source (Jul. 1993-); INFO-SOUTH Abstr.; Mag. Search; Music Index; Newsp. Period. Abstr. (1991-); Res. Alert [Full Cov.]; RILM Abstr.

US/0745-5054
**MUSIC ROW.** **VFOAT** Music Row Directory. (19??)-. Periodical. English. Twenty-three times a year. Music Row, PO Box 158542, Nashville TN 37215. **Tel** (615)321-3617. **ED** David M. Ross (editor's address: 1804 Grand Avenue, Nashville, TN 37212). **Bk Rev**. **Ad Acc**. **Circ:** 14,000.
**Desc:** Nashville music industry publication.

SZ
**MUSIC SCENE (DIETIKON, SWITZERLAND).** (MUSIC SCENE.). No. 1 (1982)-. Periodical. French (German). mo. MSM Music Sales & Management AG, Gjuchtstrasse 15, 8953 Dietikon Switzerland. **Tel** 01-740 00 00, FAX 01-740 05 58, telex 828365 MSM CH. **ED** Paul Casutt. **LC** ML3469; .M87. **DD** 784.5/005. **Bk Rev**. **Ad Acc**. **Circ:** 14,000 (ctrl).
**Desc:** This magazine lists the information source for musicians as well as the business.

UK/0027-4461
**MUSIC TEACHER.** [Music teach.]. Vol. 47, No. 1 (Jan. 1968)-. English. mo. $28.85. Rhinegold Publishing Ltd, 239-241 Shaftesbury Avenue, London WC2H 8EH England. **Tel** 011 44 71 2405749, FAX 240 0897, telex 264675 GILDED. **ED** Karin Brookes. **LC** ML5; .M67. **DD** 780/.5. **Bk Rev**. **Ad Acc**. **Circ:** 6,000. available on microfilm and microfiche from University Microfilms International (UMI). ***Continues*** *Music Teacher and Piano Student.*
**Desc:** Magazine for primary and secondary school music teachers. New music, examination set works, teaching notes, and book reviews.
**Ind/Abst** Br. Educ. Index; Music Index.

UK/0957-6606
**MUSIC TECHNOLOGY (ELY).** (MUSIC TECHNOLOGY.). [Music technol.]. (Nov. 1986)-. Periodical. English. Twelve times a year. £22.00 UK; £27.00 others. Music Maker Publications, Alexander House, Forehill, Ely Cambridgeshire CB7 4AF England. **Tel** 011 44 353 665577, FAX 011 44 353 662489. Index available. **Bk Rev**. **Ad Acc**. ***Continues*** *E & MM.*
**Desc:** Reviews of current musical equipment for musicians, interviews with professional musicians with reference to the ways in which they use their equipment, and technical features for the hi-tech musician.

US/0027-447X
**MUSIC TEMPO.** (19??)-. Periodical. English. Four times a year. Kings Enterprise, c/o Walter Kosakowski, 4136 Peak Street, Toledo OH 43612. **LC** ML1; .M3265.

US/0195-6167
**MUSIC THEORY SPECTRUM.** [Music theory spectr.]. **Added/Corp** Society for Music Theory. **VFOAT** Spectrum. Vol. 1, (1979)-. Periodical. English. Twice a year (Apr., Oct.). $40.00 North America; $50.00 other Comes with Society for Music Theory Membership. Society Music Theory, Florida State University, School of Music, c/o J. Clendinning, Tallahassee FL 32306. **Tel** (904)644-5786, FAX (904)644-6100. **ED** James Baker. **LC** MT6; .M9622. **DD** 781/.05. Index available. cum. index. **Bk Rev**. **Ad Acc**, **Adv Mgr:** James Baker, **Tel** (401)863-3234. **Pr Rev**. **Circ:** 1,200 (ctrl). Documents available from The Genuine Article.
**Desc:** Articles and book reviews on all aspects of music theory (analytical, historical, pedagogical).
**Ind/Abst** Arts Humanit. Citation Index [Full Cov.]; Curr. Contents Arts Humanit.; Music Artic. Guide; Music Index; Res. Alert [Full Cov.]; RILM Abstr.

US/0541-4024
**MUSIC THEORY TRANSLATION SERIES.** Vol. 1, (1963)-. Monographic series. English. ir. Price varies per volume. Yale University Press, PO Box 209040, New Haven CT 06520. **Tel** (203)432-0940, (800)987-7323, FAX (203)432-0948.

US/0734-7367
**MUSIC THERAPY (NEW YORK, N.Y.).** (MUSIC THERAPY : THE JOURNAL OF THE AMERICAN ASSOCIATION FOR MUSIC THERAPY.). [Music ther.]. **Added/Corp** American Association for Music Therapy. Vol. 1, No. 1 (Summer 1981)-. Periodical. English. an (November). $32.50 (institutions), $22.50 (individuals) US and Canada; $34.33 (institutions), $24.33 (individuals) Europe; $35.58 (institutions), $25.58 (individuals) Asia; $35.69 (institutions), $25.69 (individuals) other. American Association of Music Therapy, PO Box 80012, Valley Forge PA 19484. **Tel** (215)265-4006. **LC** ML3920; .M8975. **DD** 615.8/5154/05. **NLM** W1; MU972F. Index available. cum. index. **Pr Rev**. **Circ:** 1,000 (ctrl).
**Desc:** A publication which examines the therapeutic use of music in a variety of educational and clinical settings; written for students and professionals in the field.
**Ind/Abst** Music Index; Psychol. Abstr.; PsycINFO; PsycLit.

US/0734-6875
**MUSIC THERAPY PERSPECTIVES.** [Music ther. perspect.]. **Added/Corp** National Association for Music Therapy. Vol. 1, No. 1 (Spring/Summer 1982)-. English. sa. $85.00 US; $90.00 other. National Association for Music Therapy Inc., 8455 Colesville Road, Suite 930, Silver Spring MD 20910. **Tel** (301)589-3300, FAX (301)589-5175. **ED** Mary Scovel and Brian Wilson. **LC** ML3920; .M8995. **DD** 615.8/5154/05. **NLM** W1; MU972FK. Index available. **Ad Acc**. **Circ:** 4,000 (ctrl).
**Desc:** Designed to appeal to a wide readership, both inside and outside the profession of music therapy. Articles focus on music therapy practice, as well as academic and administration.
**Ind/Abst** Music Index; Psychol. Abstr. (1987-); PsycINFO (1990-); PsycLit.

US/0027-4488
**MUSIC TRADES.** [Music trades]. Vol. 1 (1890)-. Periodical. English. mo. $14.00. Music Trades Corporation, PO Box 432, 80 West Street, Englewood NJ 07631. **Tel** (201)871-1965. **LC** ML1; .M35. available on microfilm and microfiche from University Microfilms International (UMI); available on an online database (file 648/Full-Text) from DIALOG.
**Ind/Abst** F&S Index Plus Text, Int. [Full Txt.] [Select. Cov.]; Music Index; Trade Ind. ASAP [Full Txt.]; Trade Ind. Index [Full Txt.].

UK
**MUSIC TRADES INTERNATIONAL.** Vol. 60, No. 708 (Aug. 1972)-. Periodical. English. mo. Trade Papers, 157 Hagden Lane, Watford Herts WD1 8LW England. **LC** ML5; .P45. **DD** 380.1/45/78191. ***Continues*** *Piano World and Music Trades Review.*

UK/0307-8523
**MUSIC TRADES INTERNATIONAL DIRECTORY.** (MTI, MUSIC TRADES INTERNATIONAL DIRECTORY.). **VFOAT** Music Trades International Directory. (19??)-. Directory. English. an. Trade Papers London Ltd., 902 High Road, London N12 95B England. **LC** ML12; .M2. **DD** 338.4/7/78025.

UK
**MUSIC TRADES INTERNATIONAL YEARBOOK.** 3rd Ed. (1973)-. English. Trade Papers London Ltd., 902 High Road, London N12 95B England. **LC** ML21; .M894815. **DD** 380.1/45/7802542. ***Continues*** *Piano World and Music Trades Review Yearbook.*

US/0197-4173
**MUSIC USA.** (MUSIC USA; REVIEW OF THE MUSIC INDUSTRY AND AMATEUR MUSIC PARTICIPATION.). [Music USA]. **Added/Corp** American Music Conference (U.S.). **VAT** Music United States of America. (19??)-. English. an. $10.00 (non-member), $5.00 (member). American Music Conference, 303 E Wacker Drive/Suite 1214, Chicago IL 60601. **Tel** (312)856-8820. **ED** Jerry Derloshen. **LC** ML3795; .M8903. **DD** 338.4/778/0973. ctrl circ.
**Desc:** Provides an annual statistical review of the U.S. music products industry tracking manufacturer shipments (units) to retailers by dollar volume.
**Ind/Abst** Predicasts Forecasts.

●US/1065-0229
**MUSIC VIDEO MAGAZINE.** (1994)-. Periodical. English. qt. $9.95. David Bernstein, PO Box 17705, Irvine CA 92713.

US/8750-569X
**MUSIC VIDEO RETAILER.** (MUSIC / VIDEO RETAILER.). [Music video retail.]. **VFOAT** Music Video Retailer. Vol. 10, No. 2 (Aug. 1981)-. Periodical. English. mo. Music Video Retailer, 210 Boyleston Street, Chestnut Hill MA 02167. **DD** 621. ***Continues*** *Music Retailer, 0192-818X.*

UK/0265-1548
**MUSIC WEEK (1983).** (MUSIC WEEK.). [Music week]. (Sept. 3, 1983)-. Periodical. English. wk (52 issues). $349.00 (airmail). Link House Magazines Ltd., Link House, Dingwall Avenue, Croydon Surrey CR9 2TA England. **Tel** 011 44 81 686 2599, FAX 011 44 81 760 5154, telex 947709. **(Subscription address:** Spotlight Publishing, 120 126 Lavender Avenue, Mitcham Surrey CR4 3HP England; telephone: 011 44 81 646 1031**)** **LC** IN PROCESS. available on an online database (file 16/Full-Text) from DIALOG. ***Continues in part*** *Music & Video Week, 0261-0817;* ***Absorbed*** *Record Mirror (London, England : 1990).*

UK/0267-3290
**MUSIC WEEK DIRECTORY.** **VFOAT** Music Week Directory. No. 15 (1984)-. English. an (Jan.). £36.00 UK; £41.00 others. Spotlight Publications, 245 Blackfriars Road, 8th Floor, London SE1 9UR England. **Tel** 011 44 71 6203636, FAX 011 44 71 4018036. **ED** Steve Redmond. **Ad Acc**. ctrl circ. ***Continues*** *Music & Video Week Directory.*

UK
**MUSIC WEEK INDUSTRY YEAR BOOK.** (19??)-. English. an. Music Week Industry Year Book, 7 Carnaby Street, London W1V 1PG England. **LC** ML21; .M89482. **DD** 338.4/7/780942.

US/0193-5127
**MUSIC WORKS (SAN FRANCISCO, CALIF.).** (MUSIC WORKS.). [Music works]. (Apr. 1976)-. Periodical. English. sa. $5.00. D.S. Rapaport and D.T. Wills, 83 McAllister Street, Room 403, San Francisco CA 94102. **ED** E. Sergeant and D.T. Wills. **LC** ML1; .M3538. **DD** 338.4/7/780973.

US/0090-3663
**MUSIC WORLD MAGAZINE (LOS ANGELES).** (MUSIC WORLD MAGAZINE.). [Music world mag.]. (Nov. 1972)-. Periodical. English. mo. $5.00. Music World Magazine, 6472 Santa Monica Boulevard, Hollywood CA 90038. **LC** ML1; .M356. **DD** 780/.5.

UK
**MUSIC WORLD YEAR BOOK.** **VFOAT** Music World Yearbook; Music World Directory and Yearbook; Music World Directory & Yearbook; Music World. (1985)-. English. an. Turret Wheatland Ltd, PO Box 64, Rickmansworth Herts WD3 1SN England. **Tel** 011/44/923/777000, FAX 011/44/923/771297, telex 888095. **LC** ML21.G7; M87. **DD** 338.4/778/0942. ***Continues*** *Music World Directory.*

GW/0027-4518
**MUSICA.** [Musica]. Vol. 1, (Jan./Feb. 1947)-. Periodical. German. Six times a year (Jan., Mar., May, July, Sept., Nov.). $56.00. Baerenreiter-Verlag, KGA Verlagssvc PF 100329, D 34003 Kassel Germany. **Tel** 011 49 561 31050, telex 99504. **(Subscription address:** Foregin Music Distributors, 13 Elkay Drive, Chester NY 10918.**)** **ED** Clemens Kuhn. **LC** ML5; .M71357. **DD** 780.5. **[CCC]**. **Ad Acc**. **Circ:** 6,500 (ctrl). available on microfilm and microfiche from University Microfilms International (UMI). Documents available from The Genuine Article.
**Desc:** Magazine for all areas of classical music.
**Ind/Abst** Arts Humanit. Citation Index [Full Cov.]; Music Index; Res. Alert [Full Cov.]; RILM Abstr.

IT
**MUSICA.** (May/June 1977)-. Periodical. Italian. Six times a year. L49000 Italy; L112000 other. Edizioni Diapason, Via Ampere 60, 20131 Milan Italy. **Tel** 011 39 02 2367615. **ED** Umberto Masini. **LC** ML5; .M713595. **DD** 780/.5. Index available (free). cum. index. **Bk Rev**. **Ad Acc**. **Circ:** 35,000 (ctrl).
**Desc:** Devoted entirely to classical music. Includes record and book reviews, with various articles about musicians and performers.

BE/0771-7016
**MUSICA ANTIQUA : ACTUELE INFORMATIE OVER OUDE MUZIEK.** **Added/Corp** Vlaams Centrum voor Oude Muziek. (198?)-. Periodical. Dutch. qt. Vlaams Centrum voor Vlksntwikk, Visverkopersstraat 13 Bus 2, B-1000 Brussels Belgium.
**Ind/Abst** Music Index.

UK/0140-6078
**MUSICA ASIATICA.** [Music. Asiat.]. (1977)-. Academic Scholarly Publication. English (Japanese). ir. Cambridge University Press, The Edinburgh Building, Shaftesbury Road, Cambridge CB2 2RU United Kingdom. **Tel** 011 44 223 312393, FAX 011 44 223 325959. **(Subscription address:** US / 110 Midland Avenue, Port Chester, NY 10573; telephone: (800)431-1580; (914)937-9600**)** **LC** ML330; .M83. **DD** 780/.95.
**Ind/Abst** RILM Abstr.

UK/0580-2954
**MUSICA BRITANNICA.** **Added/Corp** Royal Musical Association. Vol. 1 (1951)-. Monographic series. English. ir. Price varies per volume. Stainer & Bell, 23 Gruneisen Road, Victoria House, London N3 1DZ England. **Tel** 011 44 81 343 3303. **(Subscription address:** Stainer & Bell, PO Box 110, London N3 1DZ England, phone: 011 44 81 343 3303**)** **ED** Paul Doe.

CU
**MUSICA (CASA DE LAS AMERICAS: 1980).** (MUSICA / CASA DE LAS AMERICAS.). **Added/Corp** Casa de las Americas. **VFOAT** Boletin de Musica. (19??)-. Periodical. Spanish. Casa de las Americas, 3RA Y G Vedado, La Habana Cuba. **LC** ML5; .M7139. **DD** 780/.5. ***Continues*** *Boletin de Musica.*

IT/0077-2461
**MUSICA DISCIPLINA.** [Musica discip.]. **Added/Corp** American Institute of Musicology. Vol. 2 (1948)-. English. ir. $45.00. Haenssler Verlag, Postfach 1220, D-73762 Neuhausen Germany. **Tel** 011 49 07158 1770, telex 715816 HAENSR. **ED** A. Carapetyan. cum. index. **Bk Rev**. **Ad Acc**. Documents available from The Genuine Article. ***Continues*** *Journal of Renaissance and Baroque Music.*
**Ind/Abst** Arts Humanit. Citation Index [Full Cov.]; Curr. Contents Arts Humanit.; Music Index; Res. Alert [Full Cov.]; RILM Abstr.

IT/0391-4380
**MUSICA DOMANI : ORGANO DELLA SOCIETA ITALIANA PER L'EDUCAZIONE MUSICALE.** **Added/Corp** Societa Italiana per l'Educazione Musicale. (19??)-. Periodical. Italian. qt. L30000.00 Italy; L35000.00 other. G. Ricordi & Co. S.p.A., Via Berchet 2, 20121 Milan Italy. **Tel** 011 39 2 8881204, FAX 011 39 2 8881212. **LC** MT3.I8; M7. **DD** 780/.7/245. **Bk Rev**, (Qty: 10). **Ad Acc**. **Circ:** 4,000.
**Desc:** About culture and educational music, official organ

of SIEM, (International Society for the Music Education). Faces institutional problems of the music instruction and formation of all grades.

IT
**MUSICA E DOSSIER.** ***Ceased.*** **VFOAT** Musica Dossier. Vol. 1, No. 1 (Nov. 1986)-(Dec. 1993). Periodical. Italian. mo. Giunti Editore, Via Bolognese 165, 50139 Florence Italy. **Tel** 011 39 55 6679267, FAX 011 39 55 268312, telex 571438. **LC** ML5; .M7255. **DD** 780/.9.

NE
**MUSICA (HILVERSUM, NETHERLANDS).** ***Ceased.*** (MUSICA.). **Added/Corp** Algemene Nedelandse Unie van Muziekverenigingen. ( )-Ceased (1987). Periodical. Dutch. mo. Tijdschriftenfonds JJ Lispet, Postbus 338, Bussum Netherlands.

SP
**MUSICA HISPANA. SER. A: CANCION POPULAR.** **Added/Corp** Spain. Consejo Superior de Investigaciones Cientificas. Instituto Espanol de Musicologia. **VFOAT** Cancion Popular. (1952)-. Periodical. Spanish. Instituto Espanol de Musicologia, Consejo Superior de Investigaciones Cientificas, Barcelona Spain.

SP
**MUSICA HISPANA. SER. B: POLIFONIA.** **Added/Corp** Spain. Consejo Superior de Investigaciones Cientificas. Instituto Espanol de Musicologia. **VFOAT** Polifonia. (1953)-. Periodical. Spanish. Instituto Espanol de Musicologia, Consejo Superior de Investigaciones Cientificas, Barcelona Spain.

SP
**MUSICA HISPANA. SER. C: MUSICA DE CAMARA.** **Added/Corp** Spain. Consejo Superior de Investigaciones Cientificas. Instituto Espanol de Musicologia. **VFOAT** Musica de Camara. (1952)-. Periodical. Spanish. Instituto Espanol de Musicologia, Consejo Superior de Investigaciones Cientificas, Barcelona Spain.

IT
**MUSICA IN URSS. (ITALIAN EDITION).** Italconcert, C So Buenos Aires 19/7 SC B, 16129 Genoa Italy.

IT/0027-4542
**MUSICA JAZZ.** [Musica jazz]. **VFOAT** Jazz. (1945)-. Periodical. Italian. mo. L230000 (Italy); L144000 (other). Rusconi Editore Spa, Servicio Abbonements, V Le Sarca 235, 20126 Milan Italy. **Tel** 011 39 2 66192634. **LC** ML5; .M732. **DD** 785.42/05. ***Continues*** *Musica e Jazz.*

US/0147-7536
**MUSICA JUDAICA.** [Music. jud.]. (1976)-. Academic Scholarly Publication. English (French, German and Hebrew). an. $15.00. American Society for Jewish Music, 129 West 67th Street, New York NY 10023. **Tel** (212)362-8060 ext. 307. **ED** Neil W Levin (editor's address: 170 West 74th Street New York NY 10023; editor's phone: (212)874-4456). **LC** ML1; .M3565. **DD** 781.7/2/92405. **Bk Rev. Circ:** 500.
**Desc:** Publishes scholarly articles pertaining to all facets of Jewish secular and liturgical music.
**Ind/Abst** Music Index; RILM Abstr.

PL/0077-247X
**MUSICA MEDII AEVI.** (MUSICA MEDII AEVI / INSTYTUT SZTUKI POLSKIEJ AKADEMII NAUK.). [Musica medii aevi]. **Added/Corp** Pracownia Historii Muzyki (Polska Akademia Nauk) Zakad Historii i Teorii Muzyki (Polska Akademia Nauk). No. 1, (1965)-. Monographic series. Polish (English). ir. Price varies per volume. **(Subscription address:** ARS Polona, PO Box 1001, 00068 Warsaw Poland.**)** **ED** J. Morawski. **LC** ML170; .M88. **DD** 780/.9/02/2 19.
**Ind/Abst** RILM Abstr.

IT
**MUSICA POPOLARE, LA.** **Added/Corp** Amicizia Musicale Italiana. (Summer 1975)-. Periodical. Italian. qt. Amicizia Musicale Italiana, Conto Corrente Postale 3/20838 Popolare, Via Giulini 5, Milan 20123 Italy. **LC** ML5; .M737.

IT
**MUSICA/REALTA.** **Added/Corp** Istituto Musicale "A. Peri.". Vol. 1, No. 1 (April 1980)-. Periodical. Italian. Three times a year (Apr., Aug., Dec.). L70000 Italy; L90000 other. Enrico Mucchi Editore SRL, Via Emilia Est 1527, 41100 Modena Italy. **Tel** 011 39 59 374094, FAX 059/374096. **LC** ML5; .M739. **DD** 780/.5. Index available. **Bk Rev. Ad Acc. Circ:** 1,500.
**Desc:** Studies and essays on music in general classic, rock and modern music.
**Ind/Abst** Music Index.

IT
**MUSICA (ROME, ITALY : 1985).** ***Suspended.*** (LA MUSICA.). Vol. 1, No. 1, Jan. 1985-Suspended with No. 19, 1988. Periodical. Italian (English and French). qt. L50000 Italy; L100000 other. La Musica, Viale Mazzini 6, 00195 Rome Italy. **Tel** 06/360.59.52. **LC** ML5; .M7395. **DD** 780/.904. **Bk Rev.**

IT
**MUSICAE SACRAE MINISTERIUM (ROME).** (MUSICAE SACRAE MINISTERIUM.). (1964)-. Periodical. German (English and French). an. $25.00. Consociatio Internationalis, Via di Torre Rossa 21, 00165 Rome Italy. **Tel** 011 39 6 66000173. **Bk Rev. Circ:** 600.
**Desc:** Church music and liturgy, bulletin of information for members of Consociatio Internationalis Musicae Sacrae.
**Ind/Abst** RILM Abstr.

US/1042-3443
**MUSICAL AMERICA (1987).** ***Title Change.*** (MUSICAL AMERICA.). [Music. Am.]. Vol. 107, No. 1 (March 1987)-Vol. 112, No. 1 (Jan./Feb. 1992). Periodical. English. bm. Musical America Publications, 21625 Prairie Street, Chatsworth CA 91311. **Tel** (818)998-8830, FAX (818)718-8482. **(Subscription address:** PO Box 10759, Des Moines, IA 50340**)** **ED** Shirley Fleming. **LC** ML1; .M385. **DD** 780/.43/0973. **Bk Rev. Ad Acc.** available on microfilm. Documents available from UMI Article Clearinghouse. ***Continues*** *High Fidelity (Musical America Ed. : 1980), 0735-777X;* ***Absorbed*** *Opus (Harrisburg, PA.), 8750-488X.* ***Absorbed by*** *American Record Guide, 0003-0716.*
**Desc:** Classical music magazine with a dual focus, including reviews of live performances as well as reviews of recordings and books.
**Ind/Abst** Acad. Abstr. Full Text Elite (June 1987-Dec. 1991); Acad. Abstr. (June 1987-Dec. 1991); Acad. Search (June 1987-Dec. 1991); Gen. Period. Index (1986-); Humanit. Source (Jan. 1988-Feb. 1992); INFO-SOUTH Abstr.; Mag. Artic. Summar. Elite (June 1987-Dec. 1991); Mag. Artic. Summar. Select (Jan. 1988-Feb. 1992); Mag. Artic. Summar. CD-ROM (June 1987-Dec. 1991); Mag. Index Plus (1989-); Mag. Index. Sel. (1986-); Mag. Search; Music Artic. Guide (1991-?); Music Index; Newsp. Period. Abstr. (1988-1992); Read. Guide Abstr. Select Ed.; Mag. Index (1987-); TOM Gen. Index (1987-).

US/0735-7788
**MUSICAL AMERICA. INTERNATIONAL DIRECTORY OF THE PERFORMING ARTS.** **See** The Arts-Performing Arts.

US
**MUSICAL AMERICA'S FESTIVALS.** ***Ceased.*** **VFOAT** Festivals. (1991)-(1991 ed.). Periodical. English. ABC Consumer Magazine, 825 7th Avenue, New York NY 10019. **Tel** (212)887-8469. **LC** ML35; .M9. ***Continues*** *Festivals (New York, N.Y.).*

US/0192-8627
**MUSICAL HERITAGE REVIEW.** **Added/Corp** Musical Heritage Society. Vol. 1, No. 13 (Oct. 17, 1977)-. Periodical. English. Eighteen times a year. Musical Heritage Society, 1710 Highway 35, Ocean NJ 07712. **Tel** (908)531-7003, (908)531-4990. ***Continues*** *Musical Heritage Review Magazine, 0160-3876.*

NE
**MUSICAL INSTRUMENT COLLECTIONS OF THE WORLD.** English (German, French and Dutch). ir. Uitgeverij Frits Knuf B V, PO Box 720, 4116 ZJ Buuren Netherlands. **Tel** 011 31 03449-1255, FAX 011 31 03449-2617. **Circ:** 700.
**Desc:** Catalogues, guides and other descriptive matter collected from the museums of the world and issued as a series.

US/0364-7501
**MUSICAL MAINSTREAM, THE.** (THE MUSICAL MAINSTREAM / NATIONAL LIBRARY SERVICE FOR THE BLIND AND PHYSICALLY HANDICAPPED, LIBRARY OF CONGRESS.). [Music. mainstream]. **Added/Corp** Library of Congress. National Library Service for the Blind and Physically Handicapped. Library of Congress. Division for the Blind and Physically Handicapped. Vol. 1, (Jan./Feb. 1977)-. Periodical. English. ir. Division for the Blind and Physically Handicapped, Library of Congress, Washington DC 20001. **LC** ML1; .M632. **DD** 780/.5. available in braille. ***Continues*** *New Braille Musician, 0093-2817.*

US/0027-4615
**MUSICAL MERCHANDISE REVIEW.** [Music. merch. rev.]. **VFOAT** MMR. Vol. 117 (Jan. 1958)-. Periodical. English. mo. $24.00 (one year), $30.00 (two years) US; $48.00 (one year), $72.00 (two years) other. Larkin Group, 100 Wells Avenue, Newton MA 02159. **Tel** (617)964-5100, 800-869-7469, FAX (617)964-2752. **ED** Don Johnson. **LC** ML1; .M6373. **Ad Acc. Circ:** 13,500 (ctrl). ***Formed by the union of*** *Musical Merchandise Magazine* ***and*** *Piano & Organ Review.*

US/0748-9293
**MUSICAL NEWS (SAN FRANCISCO, CALIF.).** (THE MUSICAL NEWS.). **Added/Corp** American Federation of Musicians. Local 6 (San Francisco, Calif.). **VFOAT** MN. (19??)-. Periodical. English. Twelve times a year. $15.00. Musicians Union Local Six of the American Federation of Musicians, 230 Jones Street, San Francisco CA 94102. **Tel** (415)775-8118. **ED** Don Menary. **LC** ML1; .M69. **DD** 331.881178. **Ad Acc. Circ:** 4,500 (ctrl).

CN/0709-7174
**MUSICAL NEWS (TORONTO).** (MUSICAL NEWS.). (Apr. 1979)-. Periodical. English. ir. Counterpoint Publishing Company, Postal Station Z, Box 186, Toronto Ontario M4N 2Z4 Canada. **Tel** (416)486-8134. **DD** 780/.5.

UK/0027-4623
**MUSICAL OPINION.** [Music. opin.]. **VFOAT** Musical Opinion and Music Trade Review. Vol.51, No. 601 (Oct. 1927)-. Periodical. English. mo. £23.00 UK; £35.00 other. Musical Opinion Ltd, 2 Princes Road, St Leonards-on-Sea, East Sussex TN37 6EL England. **Tel** 44 424 715167, FAX 44 424 712214. **ED** Denby Richards. **LC** ML5; .M78. **DD** 780/.9. **Bk Rev**, (Qty: 25-30). **Ad Acc, Adv Mgr:** Liz Biddle, **Tel** 44 81 6690011. **Circ:** 5,500. available on microfilm and microfiche from University Microfilms International (UMI). ***Continues*** *Musical Opinion and Music Trade Review.*
**Desc:** MUSICAL OPINION is one of the oldest existing classical music magazines in the world. It covers articles on current musical events and musicians, reviews concerts, opera and dance internationally and also CDs, music and books published in the UK. There is a special section devoted to Organ.
**Ind/Abst** Br. Humanit. Index; Music Index; RILM Abstr.

●SZ/1049-8869
**MUSICAL PERFORMANCE.** (1993)-. Periodical. English. ir. $42.00 (individuals), $138.00 (corporate). Harwood Academic Publishers, PO Box 90, Reading RG1 8JL England. **Tel** 011 44 734 560080. **(Subscription address:** International Publishers Distributor at one of the following addresses: 820 Town Center Drive, Langhorne, PA 19047; or PO Box 90, Reading Berkshire RG1 8JL UK; or Kent Ridge PO Box 1180, Singapore 9111, Republic of Singapore**)**

US/0027-4631
**MUSICAL QUARTERLY, THE.** [Music. q.]. Vol. 1 (Jan. 1915)-. Periodical. English. qt (4 issues). $53.00 institutions, $35.00 individuals US; $68.00 institutions, $50.00 individuals other. Oxford University Press / New York, 200 Madison Avenue, New York NY 10016. **Tel** (212)679-7300, (919)677-0977, (800)451-7556, (800)445-9714, FAX (919)677-1303. **(Subscription address:** Oxford University Press / USA, Journals Marketing Department, Oxford University Press, 2001 Evans Road, Cary NC 27513.**)** **ED** Eric Salzman. **LC** ML1; .M725. **DD** 780. **[CCC].** cum. index. **Bk Rev. Ad Acc. Circ:** 4,000 (ctrl). available on microfilm and microfiche from University Microfilms International (UMI). Documents available from The Genuine Article, UMI Article Clearinghouse, Magazine Collection.
**Desc:** Musicological and general essays on all subjects pertaining to music. Book reviews usually in essay format.
**Ind/Abst** Acad. Abstr. Full Text Elite (July 1990-); Acad. Abstr. (July 1990-); Acad. Ind. [Computer File] (1984-); Acad. Search (July 1990-); Annu. Bibliogr. Engl. Lang. Lit.; Arts Humanit. Citation Index [Full Cov.]; Book Rev. Index; Curr. Contents Arts Humanit.; Expand. Acad. Index (1984-); Gen. Period. Index (1985-); Humanit. Index; Humanit. Source (Jul. 1990-); INFO-SOUTH Abstr.; Mag. Index Plus (1989-); Mag. Search; Music Artic. Guide; Music Index; Newsp. Period. Abstr. (1991-); Read. Guide Period. Lit.; Res. Alert [Full Cov.]; RILM Abstr.; Romant. Move.; Mag. Index (1977-).

UK
**MUSICAL SALVATIONIST, THE.** (19??)-. Periodical. English. qt. Salvationist Publishing and Supplies, 117-121 Judd St Kings Cross, London WC1H 9NN England. **Tel** 11 44 71 3871656, FAX 11 44 71 3873768. **LC** M2198; .M977. **Circ:** 20,000.

IE
**MUSICAL SOURCES.** Vol. 10 (1978)-. Monographic series. English. ir. Price varies per volume. Severinus Press, 24 Trefaenor Comins Coch, Dyfed SY23 3UB Wales. **LC** UNC. ***Formed by the union of*** *Early Music in Facsimile; Reproductions of Early Music* ***and*** *Early Music Reprinted.*

UK/0027-4666
**MUSICAL TIMES (LONDON, ENGLAND : 1957).** (MUSICAL TIMES.). [Music. times]. Vol. 98, No. 1367 (Jan. 1957)-. Periodical. English. Twelve times a year. £22.20 UK; £39.00 Europe; £60.00 (one year), £108.00 (two years) US & Canada; £45.00 other. Orpheus Publications, 7 St. Johns Road, Harrow Middlesex HA1 2EE England. **Tel** 011 44 81 863-4040, FAX 011 44 81 424-9945. **(Subscription address:** Orpheus Subscriptions Departmenmt, PO Box 648, Harrow, Middlesex, HA1 2NW; England.**)** **ED** Andrew Clements. **LC** ML5; .M85. Index available. **Bk Rev. Ad Acc. Circ:** 6,600. available on microfilm from University Microfilms International (UMI). Documents available from

The Genuine Article. ***Continues*** *Musical Times & Singing Class Circular (London, England : 1810).* ***Continued in part by*** *Choir & Organ, 0968-7262.*
**Desc:** For the serious musician, covering all aspects of music in UK and abroad.
**Ind/Abst** Arts Humanit. Citation Index [Full Cov.]; Br. Humanit. Index; Curr. Contents Arts Humanit.; Music Index; Res. Alert [Full Cov.]; RILM Abstr.; Soc. Sci. Cit. Index [Select. Cov.].

UK/0265-5063
**MUSICAL TRADITIONS.** No. 1 (Mid 1983)-. English. ir. Musical Traditions, 98 Ashingdon Road, Rochford Essex SS4 1RE England. **Tel** 011 44 702 548876. **ED** Keith Summers. **LC** ML3544; .M87.

US/0737-0032
**MUSICAL WOMAN, THE.** [Mus. woman]. (1983)-. English. ir. Greenwood Press Inc., PO Box 5007, Westport CT 06881-5007. **Tel** (203)226-3571, FAX (203)222-1502. **LC** ML82; .M8. **DD** 780/.88042.

IT/1121-0494
**MUSICALIA LUCCA.** (MUSICALIA). [MusicaliaLucca]. (1991)-. Monographic series. Italian. bm. Price varies per volume. Musicalia, Via Alatri 30, 00171 Rome Italy. **Tel** 06-215-51-22, FAX 06-215-51-22. **ED** Enrico Castiglione. **UDC** 78.072.2.

US/0733-5253
**MUSICIAN (GLOUCESTER, MASS.).** (MUSICIAN.). [Musician]. No. 42 (Apr. 1982)-. Periodical. English. mo (12 issues). $19.97 (one year), $34.97 (two years). Billboard Publications Inc., 1515 Broadway Billboard, New York NY 10036. **Tel** (212)764-7300, FAX (305)755-7048, telex WU TWX 710-581-6279. **(Subscription address:** Musician, PO Box 1923, Marion, OH 43305**)** **ED** Jock Baird. **LC** ML1; .M212. **DD** 780/.42/05. **[CCC]**. cum. index. **Bk Rev.** available on microfilm and microfiche from University Microfilms International (UMI). ***Continues*** *Musician, Player, and Listener, 0161-9543.*
**Desc:** Written for the rock and jazz musician, from amateur to semi-pro to professional, and serious music fans. Interview with today's leading musicians. Articles on instruments, equipment, recording techniques, the business of music, record reviews, buys, industry news, etc.
**Ind/Abst** Acad. Search (May 1987-June 1989); Humanit. Source (Jan. 1988-Jun. 1989); INFO-SOUTH Abstr.; Mag. Artic. Summar. Elite (May 1987-June 1989); Mag. Artic. Summar. Select; Mag. Artic. Summar. CD-ROM (May 1987-June 1989); Mag. Search; Music Index.

●US/1064-5411
**MUSICIAN MAGAZINE SPECIAL EDITION SERIES.** **VFOAT** Musician Magazine Special Edition; Musician Special Edition. (1992)-. English. qt. $3.95 (single issue). Musician Magazine, 33 Commercial Street, Gloucester MA 01930.

AT
**MUSICIAN OF THE SALVATION ARMY IN AUSTRALIA.** Periodical. English. sm. Salvation Army Auxiliary Company Australia, 69 Bourke Street, Melbourne Victoria Australia.

US/0362-2959
**MUSICIAN'S GUIDE (BOSTON).** (MUSICIAN'S GUIDE.). **Added/Corp** New England Musician's Guild. Vol. 2, No. 8 (Aug. 1975)-. Periodical. English. mo. $5.00. New England Musician's Guild, 739 Boylston Street, Boston MA 02116. **LC** ML1; .N337. **DD** 780/.5. ***Continues*** *New England Musician's Guide.*

●US/1062-4759
**MUSICIANS GUIDE TO TOURING & PROMOTION, THE.** (1993)-. Periodical. English. $5.95. BPI Inc., 33 Commercial Street, Gloucester MA 01930.

CN/0226-8620
**MUSICK.** [Musick]. **Added/Corp** Vancouver Society for Early Music. (Summer 1979)-. Periodical. English. qt (Jan., Mar., July, Oct.). 10.00Can$ (one year), 17.00Can$ Canada; 12.00Can$ (one year), 20.00Can$ (two year) other. Early Music Vancouver, 1254 West 7th Avenue, Vancouver British Columbia V6H 1B6 Canada. **ED** John R. Burgess, Peter Slemon, J. Evan Kreider, and John E. Sawyer. **DD** 780/.9711/33. Index available. cum. index. **Bk Rev.** **Ad Acc.** **Circ:** 4,500 (ctrl).
**Desc:** Journal with articles on all aspects of early music, instruments and performance practice, book and record reviews; Vancouver Society for Early Music Newsletter outlining society activities, concerts, etc.

AU
**MUSICOLOGICA AUSTRIACA.** **Added/Corp** Osterreichische Gesellschaft fuer Musikwissenschaft. (1977)-. Monographic series. German (English and French). an. Price varies per volume. Verlag E Stiglmayr, Wienerstrasse 141, A 2822 Foehrenau Austria. **Tel** 011 43 2627 6236. **LC** ML5; .M8963. **DD** 750/.5.
**Ind/Abst** Music Index (-19??).

GW/0077-2496
**MUSICOLOGICAL STUDIES & DOCUMENTS.** (MUSICOLOGICAL STUDIES AND DOCUMENTS.). [Musicol. stud. & doc.]. **Added/Corp** American Institute of Musicology. **VFOAT** Musicological Studies & Documents. No. 2 (1957)-. Monographic series. English. ir. Price varies per volume. Haenssler Verlag, Postfach 1220, D-73762 Neuhausen Germany. **Tel** 011 49 07158 1770, telex 715816 HAENSR. **ED** Armen Carapetyan. **LC** UNC. **Bk Rev.** **Ad Acc.** ***Continues*** *Studies and Documents (American Institute of Musicology).*
**Desc:** Translations, reproductions, facsimile and critical editions of musicological documents of 13th century.

US/0275-5866
**MUSICOLOGY.** **VFOAT** Musicology Book Series. Vol. 5 (1988)-. Monographic series. English. Price varies per volume. Harwood Academic Publishers / New York, PO Box 786, Cooper Station, New York NY 10276. **Tel** (212)206-8900, (201)643-7500. **(Subscription address:** International Publishers Distributor at one of the following addresses: 820 Town Center Drive, Langhorne, PA 19047; or PO Box 90, Reading Berkshire RG1 8JL UK; or Kent Ridge PO Box 1180, Singapore 9111, Republic of Singapore**)** **ED** F. Joseph Smith, Ralph P. Locke. ***Continues*** *Musicology Series.*
**Desc:** Features a wide range of approaches, from the traditional life-and-works monograph to essays on music's place in intellectual history.

CN/0846-426X
**MUSICOLOGY AND ETHNOMUSICOLOGY AT YORK.** [Musicol. ethnomusicol. York]. **Added/Corp** York University (Toronto, Ont.). Graduate Programme in Music. No. 1 (Spring 1985)-. Periodical. English. an. Graduate Programme in Music, York University, 4700 Keele Street, Downsview Ontario M3J 1P3 Canada. **LC** ML5; .M89713. **DD** 780/.01.

AT/0814-5857
**MUSICOLOGY AUSTRALIA.** **Added/Corp** Musicological Society of Australia. (1985)-. English. an. 35.00Aus$. Musicological Society of Australia, GPO Box 2404, Canberra ACT 2601 Australia. **Tel** 011 61 7 3444611, FAX 011 61 3 3445346. **ED** Stephen A. Wild. **LC** ML5; .M897. **DD** 780/.5. **[CCC]**. cum. index. **Bk Rev.** **Ad Acc.** **Pr Rev.** **Circ:** 500. ***Continues*** *Musicology, 0077-250X.*
**Desc:** Contains musicological articles, book reviews, a register of members' publications, and a register of Australian undergraduate theses in music.
**Ind/Abst** APAIS, Aust. Public Aff. Inf. Ser.; Music Index.

SA
**MUSICUS.** **Added/Corp** University of South Africa. Dept. of Music Examinations. (19??)-. Periodical. Afrikaans (English). Twice a year. R20.00. University of South Africa, Department of Semitics, PO Box 392, Pretoria 0001 South Africa. **Tel** 011 27 12 4298468. **ED** John Roos. **LC** ML5; .M898. **DD** 780/.5. **Ad Acc.** **Circ:** 1,500 (ctrl).
**Desc:** Aspects of music teaching and performance, South African musicians and composers, church music, articles for examination candidates and analyses of prescribed work.

CN/0225-686X
**MUSICWORKS.** (MUSICWORKS.). **VFOAT** Music Works. (Mar. 1978)-. Periodical. English. Three times a year. 30.00Can$. MusicWorks, 179 Richmond Street West, Toronto Ontario M5V 1V3 Canada. **Tel** (416)977-3546. **ED** Gayle Young. **LC** ML5; .M8984. **DD** 780/.971. Index available (bound in issue). cum. index. **Bk Rev.** **Ad Acc.** **Circ:** 1,200. available on microfilm; available on audiocassette.
**Desc:** Presents a sounding of the world from a Canadian perspective. Its format, combining journal with cassette, offers lively, multi-faceted explorations of innovative and traditional music as it is practiced in Canada and the world today.
**Ind/Abst** Can. Index.

US/1042-6736
**MUSICWORLD (NEW YORK, N.Y.).** (MUSICWORLD.). [MusicWorld]. **Added/Corp** Broadcast Music, Inc. **VFOAT** Music World; BMI Music World; BMI MusicWorld. (Winter 1988)-. Periodical. English (French and Spanish). Four times a year. Broadcast Music Inc., 320 West 57th Street, New York NY 10019. **LC** ML3469; .M9. **DD** 781.64/05. available on microfilm from Xerox. ***Continues*** *Many Worlds of Music, 0045-317X.*
**Ind/Abst** Music Index.

US
**MUSIGRAM / NATIONAL SHEET MUSIC SOCIETY.** (1963)-. Periodical. English. mo. National Sheet Music Society, Covina CA. **LC** ML27.U5; N37.

FI
**MUSIIKKI.** **Added/Corp** Suomen Musiikkitieteellinen Seura. Helsingin Yliopisto. Musiikkitieteen Laitos. (1971)-. Periodical. Finnish (summaries and/or abstracts in English). ir. Musiikki, Vironkatu 1 C 17, 00170 Helsinki 17 Finland. **LC** ML5; .M8994. **DD** 780/.5.

GW/0930-8954
**MUSIK-ALMANACH (KASSEL, GERMANY).** (MUSIK-ALMANACH / DEUTSCHER MUSIKRAT.). **Added/Corp** Deutscher Musikrat. **VFOAT** Musik Almanach. (1986/87)-. German. be. Gustav Bosse Verlag GmbH & Company KG, Postfach 417, W-8400 Regensburg 1 Germany. **Tel** 011 49 941 794091. **LC** ML21.G3; M9. **DD** 780/.25/43. **Ad Acc.**

DK/0903-188X
**MUSIK & FORSKNING.** (MUSIK & [I.E. OG] FORSKNING.). [Musik & forsk.]. **Main/Corp** Kobenhavns Universitet. Musikvidenskabeligt Institut. (1975)-. Multiple languages (Danish and English). Akademisk Forlag, Finsensvej 82, DK 2000 Frederiksberg Denmark. **Tel** 011 45 38 334212. **LC** ML5; .C678. **DD** 780/.5.
**Ind/Abst** RILM Abstr.

SZ
**MUSIK & THEATER (SAINT GALL, SWITZERLAND).** (MUSIK & THEATER.). **VFOAT** Musik und Theater. (19??)-. Periodical. German. mo. Verlag Musik & Theater, Postfach 926, 9001 St Gallen Switzerland. **LC** ML5; .M9016. **DD** 782/.05.

GW/0580-3225
**MUSIK DES OSTENS.** [Musik Ostens]. **Added/Corp** Johann-Gottfried-Herder-Forschungsstelle fuer Musikgeschichte. (1962)-. Monographic series. German. ir. Price varies per volume. Baerenreiter-Verlag, KGA Verlagssvc PF 100329, D 34003 Kassel Germany. **Tel** 011 49 561 31050, telex 99504. **(Subscription address:** Foreign Music Distributors, 13 Elkay Drive, Chester, NY 10918, (phone: (914)469-5790)**)** **ED** Fritz Feldmann and Hubert Unverricht. **LC** ML240; .M88.
**Desc:** Collected essays on music in Eastern Europe and Byzantium.
**Ind/Abst** RILM Abstr.

SZ
**MUSIK EXPRESS/SOUNDS.** **VFOAT** Musik Express Sounds. No. 325 (Feb. 1983)-. Periodical. German. mo. Christian Krummer Verlag GmbH, Winterhuder Weg 29, 2 Hamburg 76 Germany. **LC** ML5; .M9017. **DD** 781/42166/09. ***Continues*** *Musik Express.*

GW
**MUSIK IN BAYERN : HALBJAHRESSCHRIFT DER GESELLSCHAFT FUER BAYERISCHE MUSIKGESCHICHTE E.V.** **Added/Corp** Gesellschaft fuer Bayerische Musikgeschichte. (1975)-. Monographic series. German. ir (approx. 2 issues per year). Price varies per volume. Dr. Hans Schneider Verlag GmbH, Mozartstrasse 6, W 82327 Tutzing Germany. **Tel** 011 49 8158 3050. **LC** ML275.7.B4; M9. **DD** 780/.943/305. **Bk Rev.** **Ad Acc.** Documents available from The Genuine Article. ***Continues*** *Mitteilungsblatt der Gesellschaft fuer Bayerische Musikgeschichte.*
**Ind/Abst** Arts Humanit. Citation Index [Full Cov.]; Curr. Contents Arts Humanit.; Res. Alert [Full Cov.]; RILM Abstr.

GW/0027-4704
**MUSIK IN DER SCHULE.** [Musik Sch.]. **Added/Corp** Germany (East). Ministerium fur Volksbildung. (Nov. 1949)-. Periodical. German. Six times a year. DM57.00. Paedagogischer Zeitschriftenverlag GmbH, Postfach 269, D 10107 Berlin, Germany. **Tel** 011 49 30 20343431. **LC** ML5; .M901.
**Ind/Abst** Music Index; RILM Abstr.

GW/0931-3311
**MUSIK-KONZEPTE.** [Musik-Konzepte]. **VFOAT** Reihe Musik-Konzepte. (1977)-. Monographic series. German. Four times a year. DM74.00 Germany; DM83.60 other. Edition Text & Kritik GmbH, Levelingstrasse 6A, Postfach 800529, D 81605 Munich Germany. **Tel** 011 49 89 432929, FAX 011 49 89 433997. **UDC** 78.

GW/0930-7591
**MUSIK MAGAZIN.** Vol. 1 No. 1 (Feb. 1987)-. Periodical. German. sa. B. Schotts Soehne Musikverlag, Carl Zeiss Str 1, Postfach 3640, D 55026 Mainz Germany. **Tel** 011 49 6131 505129, 011 49 6131 505122, FAX 011 49 6131 505115, telex 04187821. **LC** ML1; .M9938. **DD** 780/.5.

GW/0177-350X
**MUSIK PSYCHOLOGIE : JAHRBUCH DER DEUTSCHEN GESELLSCHAFT FUER MUSIKPSYCHOLOGIE.** **Added/Corp** Deutsche Gesellschaft feur Musikpsychologie. **VFOAT** Musikpsychologie; Jahrbuch Musikpsychologie. Vol. 1 (1984)-. German (summaries and/or abstracts in English). an. Florian Noetzel Verlag, Heinrichshofen BKS, PO Box 580, D-26353 Wilhelmshaven Germany. **Tel** 011 49 4421 43003, FAX 011 49 4421 42985. **(Subscription address:** VVA Bertelsmann Distributors GmbH, Postfach 7777, D-33310 Guetersloh Germany.**)** **LC** ML3830; .M987. **DD** 781/.15/05.
**Ind/Abst** Music Index.

GW
**MUSIK REPORT; DAS KRITISCHE HANDBUCH DER KLASSISCHEN MUSIKSCHALLPLATTE.** (1971)-. German. **ED** I. Harden. **LC** ML5; .M9029. **DD** 789.9/136.

GW/0933-6885
**MUSIK-, TANZ- UND KUNSTTHERAPIE.** **VFOAT** Zeitschrift fuer Musik-, Tanz- und Kunsttherapie. (1988)-. Periodical. Multiple languages. qt (4 issues). DM92.00. Verlag fur Angewandte Psychologie, Rohnsweg 25, Postfache 3751, D 27085 Gottingen Germany. **Tel** 011 49 551 496090, FAX 011 49 551 4960988. **ED** Karl Hormann. **UDC** 793.3 :616-085. **Circ:** 1,600.

GW/0027-4747
**MUSIK UND BILDUNG.** [Musik Bild.]. Vol. 1, (1969)-. Periodical. German. Six times a year (Jan., Mar., May, July, Sept., Nov.). DM59.90 Germany, DM74.73 other (surface mail); DM101.90 (airmail). B. Schotts Soehne Musikverlag, Carl Zeiss Str 1, Postfach 3640, D 55026 Mainz Germany. **Tel** 011 49 6131 505129, 011 49 6131 505122, FAX 011 49 6131 505115, telex 04187821. **ED** Richard Jacoby, Christoph Richter, Haus Bapler and Karl Heinz Elsenfort. **LC** ML5; .M90323. **DD** 780/.72. **Bk Rev. Ad Acc. Circ:** 8,200. ***Supersedes*** *Musik im Unterricht.*
**Desc:** Recent didactic attempts in music teaching, specialized technical developments, practical examples for the preparation of teachers, information on practical new book, music, record and CD releases. Reports on the didactic of the rock and pop music as well as developments in the field of new music technologies.
**Ind/Abst** Music Index; RILM Abstr.

SZ/0027-4755
**MUSIK UND GESELLSCHAFT (BERLIN, DDR).** ***Title Change.*** (MUSIK UND GESELLSCHAFT.). [Musik Ges.]. **Added/Corp** Verband Deutscher Komponisten und Musikwissenschaftler. Verband der Komponisten und Musikwissenschaftler der DDR. (March 1951)-(19??). Periodical. German. mo. Deutscher Judo Verband, Redaktion Ippon Segewaldweg 40, D 12557 Berlin Germany. **Tel** 011 49 711 210770, telex 051 678. **LC** ML5; .M9033. ***Continued by*** *Motiv.*
**Ind/Abst** Music Index (-19??); RILM Abstr.

SZ/1015-6798
**MUSIK UND GOTTESDIENST.** [Musik Gottesd.]. (Jan. 1947)-. Periodical. German. Six times a year. 70.00F. Gotthelf Verlag, Badenstrasse 69, CH-8026 Zurich Switzerland. **Tel** 011 41 01 2428155. **LC** ML5; .M9042. **DD** 783.05. **Bk Rev. Ad Acc. Circ:** 3,700. ***Continues*** *Evangelische Kirchenchor.*
**Desc:** Organ of the organist and church choir of Switzerland.
**Ind/Abst** Music Index; RILM Abstr.

GW/0027-4771
**MUSIK UND KIRCHE.** [Musik Kirche]. **Added/Corp** Neue Schutz-Gesellschaft. Vol. 1 (Jan./Feb.1929)-. Periodical. German. Six times a year (Jan., Mar., May, July, Sept., Nov.). $56.00. Baerenreiter-Verlag, KGA Verlagssvc PF 100329, D 34003 Kassel Germany. **Tel** 011 49 561 31050, telex 99504. **(Subscription address:** Foregin Music Distributors, 13 Elkay Drive, Chester NY 10918.**) ED** Walker Blankenburg, Renate Glinger and Gerhard Schuhmucher. **LC** ML5; .M9043. **DD** 783.05. **[CCC].** Index available. **Bk Rev. Ad Acc. Circ:** 2,200 (ctrl). Documents available from The Genuine Article. ***Absorbed*** *Zeitschrift fur Evangelische Kirchenmusik.*
**Desc:** Discusses church music within the framework of ecumenical questions-including liturgy and organ playing.
**Ind/Abst** Arts Humanit. Citation Index [Full Cov.]; Curr. Contents Arts Humanit.; Music Index; Res. Alert [Full Cov.]; RILM Abstr.

GW
**MUSIK UND UNTERRICHT : ZEITSCHRIFT FUER MUSIKPADAGOGIK.** **VFOAT** Zeitschrift fuer Musikpadagogik. (Jan. 1990)-. Periodical. German. Six times a year. Erhard Friedrich Verlag, Postfach 100150, D 30917 Seelze Germany. **Tel** 011 49 511 4000452. **LC** ML5; .Z44. **DD** 780/.72943. ***Continues*** *ZfMP, Zeitschrift fuer Musikpadagogik.*

DK
**MUSIKALIER I DANSKE BIBLIOTEKER.** **Added/Corp** Denmark. Rigsbibliotekarembedet. Bibliotekscentralen (Denmark). **VFOAT** Music in Danish Libraries. (1970)-. Periodical. Danish. an. Dansk Bibliotekscenter AS, Tempovej 7 11, DK-2750 Ballerup Denmark. **Tel** 011 45 42 974000.
**Desc:** This catalogue lists Danish and foreign printed music acquired by Danish public libraries and Danish research libraries during a year's period.

GW/0077-2526
**MUSIKALISCHE DENKMALER.** **Added/Corp** Akademie der Wissenschaften und der Literatur (Germany). Kommission feur Musikwissenschaft. Vol. 1, (1955)-. Monographic series. German. ir. Price varies per volume. B. Schotts Soehne Musikverlag, Carl Zeiss Str 1, Postfach 3640, D 55026 Mainz Germany. **Tel** 011 49 6131 505129, 011 49 6131 505122, FAX 011 49 6131 505115, telex 04187821.

●RU
**MUSIKALNAIA AKADEMIIA.** (1992)-. Russian. Four times a year. $89.95. Sovetskii Kompozitor, 14-12, Sadovaya-Triumfalnaya St., 103006 Moscow Russia. **(Subscription address:** East View Publications Inc., 3020 Harbor Lane North, Suite 110, Minneapolis MN 55447.**)** ***Continues*** *Sovetskaia Muzyka, 0038-5085.*

DK
**MUSIKBRANCHENS ARBOG.** Issue 1 (1982)-. Danish. an. Musikbranchens Arbog, Kroghsgade 1 2100 Denmark. **Tel** 0451268040. **ED** Uffe Egekvist and Regnar Egekvist. **LC** ML21.D29; M9. Index available. **Ad Acc. Circ:** 7,500.
**Desc:** Contains practical and laws information about the branch of music. A complete index of the total branch is added to this publication.

SW/0027-478X
**MUSIKERN.** [Musikern]. **Added/Corp** Svenska Musikerforbundet. (1908)-. Periodical. Swedish. Ten times a year. Kr150.00. Svenska Musikerfoerbundet, Box 43, S-10120 Stockholm Sweden. **Tel** 011 46 8 247860. **LC** ML5; .M9426.
**Ind/Abst** Music Index.

AU/0027-4798
**MUSIKERZIEHUNG.** Vol. 1, (Dec. 1947)-. Periodical. German. Five times a year (Feb., Apr., June, Oct., Dec.). S410.00. Oesterreichischer Bundesverlag, Schwarzenbergstr 5, Postfach 79, A-1015 Vienna Austria. **Tel** 011 43 1 51405. **LC** ML5; .M9435. **DD** 780/.7/29436.
**Ind/Abst** Art Archaeol. Tech. Abstr.; Music Index; RILM Abstr.

GW
**MUSIKETHNOLOGISCHE SAMMELBANDE.** **Added/Corp** Hochschule fuer Musik und Darstellende Kunst in Graz. Institut fuer Musikethnologie. (1977)-. Monographic series. German (English). ir. Price varies per volume. Akademische Druck & Verlagsanstalt, Schoenaugasse 6, Postfach 598, A 8010 Graz Austria. **Tel** 011 43 316 813460. **ED** Wolfgang Suppan.
**Desc:** A monographic series on European folk music, historical research, rhythm and metrics in the European folk songs and folk dances.

US/0895-1543
**MUSI*KEY.** (MUSI KEY.). [Musi*key]. **VFOAT** Musi Key. (198?)-. English. Six times a year (Feb., Apr., June, Aug., Oct., Dec.). $300.00. Musi-Key, 10260 North Alder Springs Drive, Tucson AZ 85737. **Tel** (602)742-0880, FAX (602)742-1881. **ED** Randy and Linda Rucker. **LC** ML128.P63; M87. **DD** 784.5/0016. **Circ:** 1,000 (ctrl).
**Desc:** Publishes music currently in print, sheet music and folio collections. Includes pop, rock, broadway, jazz, country, folk, blues, gospel, ethnic, standards, novelty, nostalgic, and Christmas music.

GW/0027-4801
**MUSIKFORSCHUNG.** [Musikforschung]. **Added/Corp** Gesellschaft fuer Musikforschung (1946)- Landesinstitut fuer Musikforschung in Kiel. Institut fuer Musikforschung Berlin. Vol. 1, (1948)-. Periodical. German. Four times a year (Jan., Apr., July, Oct.). $110.00. Baerenreiter-Verlag, KGA Verlagssvc PF 100329, D 34003 Kassel Germany. **Tel** 011 49 561 31050, telex 99504. **(Subscription address:** Foregin Music Distributors, 13 Elkay Drive, Chester NY 10918.**) LC** ML5; .M9437. **DD** 780/.5. **[CCC]. Bk Rev. Ad Acc. Circ:** 2,500 (ctrl). Documents available from The Genuine Article. ***Supersedes*** *Gesellschaft fuer Musikforschung (Founded 1946) Mitteilung.*
**Desc:** Articles on musicological themes and reviews of musicological books and music.
**Ind/Abst** Arts Humanit. Citation Index [Full Cov.]; Curr. Contents Arts Humanit.; Music Index; Res. Alert [Full Cov.]; RILM Abstr.; Soc. Sci. Cit. Index [Select. Cov.].

GW/0323-5106
**MUSIKFORUM.** [Musikforum]. **Added/Corp** Zentralhaus fuer Kulturarbeit der DDR. (Jan. 1971)-. Periodical. German. bm. Deutscher Judo Verband, Redaktion Ippon Segewaldweg 40, D 12557 Berlin Germany. **Tel** 011 49 711 210770, telex 051 678. **LC** ML5; .M94375. **DD** 780/.5. ***Continues*** *Volksmusik, 0042-8558.*
**Ind/Abst** Music Index (-19??); RILM Abstr.

GW/0935-2562
**MUSIKFORUM : REFERATE UND INFORMATIONEN DES DEUTSCHEN MUSIKRATES.** **Main/Corp** Deutscher Musikrat. (June 1988)-. Periodical. German. ir. B. Schotts Soehne Musikverlag, Carl Zeiss Str 1, Postfach 3640, D 55026 Mainz Germany. **Tel** 011 49 6131 505129, 011 49 6131 505122, FAX 011 49 6131 505115, telex 04187821. **LC** ML5.I579; R4. **DD** 780/.6/043. ***Continues*** *Deutscher Musikrat. Referate und Informationen, 0538-8791.*

GW
**MUSIKHANDEL.** **Added/Corp** Deutscher Musikverleger-Verband. (Sept. 1949)-. Periodical. German. Eight times a year. DM35.00 Germany; DM40.00 other. Musikhandel Verlagsges MBH, Friedrich Wilhelm Strasse 31, 5300 Bonn Germany. **Tel** (0228)238565, FAX 235916. **LC** ML5; .M9438. Index available. **Ad Acc. Circ:** 2,400.
**Desc:** The official journal for the German music publishers and the German music dealers.
**Ind/Abst** Music Index; RILM Abstr.

GW/0027-4828
**MUSIKINSTRUMENT, DAS.** [Musikinstrument]. (1952)-. Periodical. German (English, French and Italian). Twelve times a year. DM112.00. Verlag E Bochinsky GMBH & CO KG, Muenchener Strasse 45, W-6000 Frankfurt Germany. **Tel** 11 49 69 239521, FAX 11 49 69 233301. **ED** Rita Otgel. **LC** ML5; .M90225. **[CCC].** Index available. cum. index. **Bk Rev. Ad Acc. Circ:** 6,000 (ctrl).
**Desc:** International magazine specializing in manufacturing, trade, handicraft and research in musical instruments and musical electronics.
**Ind/Abst** Art Archaeol. Tech. Abstr.; RILM Abstr.

GW/0047-8474
**MUSIKMARKT, DER.** (19??)-. Periodical. German. Twenty-six times a year. DM236.40 Germany; DM288.00 other. Josef Keller GmbH & Co. Verlags KG, Postfach 1455, D 82317 Starnberg Germany. **Tel** 011 49 (08151)771-0, FAX 011 49 (08151)771-152, telex 566438. **LC** ML5; .M954. **DD** 780/.5. **[CCC].**

SW/0027-4844
**MUSIKREVY.** [Musikrevy]. Vol. 1, (Oct./Nov. 1946)-. Periodical. Swedish. Six times a year. Kr350.00 Nordic Countries; Kr370.00 Europe; Kr460.00 others. Musikrevy Tidskriftsaktiebolag, Box 144, S-233 23 Stockholm Sweden. **Tel** 011 46 40 405665. **ED** Bengt Pleijel. **LC** ML5; .M9635. Index available. cum. index. **Bk Rev. Ad Acc. Circ:** 5,000.
**Desc:** Article subjects include composers, performing artists, instruments, sections for review, music books, sheet music and records.
**Ind/Abst** Music Index.

GW
**MUSIKTEXTE.** **VFOAT** Musik Texte. No. 1 (Oct. 1983)-. Periodical. German. Five times a year. DM68.00. Verlag Musiktexte GBR, Postfach 101348, W-5000 Cologne 1 Germany. **Tel** 011 49 221 525934. **LC** ML197; .M83. **DD** 780/.9/04.

GW
**MUSIKTHEATER.** **Added/Corp** Universitat Bayreuth. Forschungsinstitut fuer Musiktheater. (19??)-. Periodical. German. Forschungsinstitut fuer Musiktheater, Universitat Bayreuth, Bayreuth Germany. **LC** ML128.O4; M9. **DD** 016.7821.

GW/0177-4182
**MUSIKTHEORIE.** Vol. 1, No. 1 (Jan. 1986)-. Periodical. German (English, Italian and French). Three times a year (Jan., May and Sept.). DM98.90. Laaber Verlag, Regensburger Strasse 19, W 93164 Laaber Germany. **Tel** 011-49-9498-2307. **LC** ML5; .M96358. **DD** 781/.05. Index available. cum. index. **Bk Rev. Ad Acc. Circ:** 1,400. Documents available from The Genuine Article. ***Continues*** *Zeitschrift Fuer Musiktheorie.*
**Desc:** Three to five essays per issue on musical theory; texts from the history of music reproduced and discussed. Includes yearly bibliography and a list of events.
**Ind/Abst** Arts Humanit. Citation Index [Full Cov.]; Curr. Contents Arts Humanit.; Music Index; Res. Alert [Full Cov.].

GW/0172-5505
**MUSIKTHERAPEUTISCHE UMSCHAU.** [Musikther. Umsch.]. **Added/Corp** Deutsche Gesellschaft fuer Musiktherapie. (19??)-. Academic Scholarly Publication. German (summaries and/or abstracts in English). qt. $66.00. Gustav Fischer Verlag Stuttgart, Postfach 720143, Wollgrasweg 49, D 70577 Stuttgart Germany. **Tel** 011 49 711 458030, FAX 0711-4580334, telex 2627-7111488. **LC** ML3920; .M96. **DD** 615.8/5154/05. **NLM** W1; MU972JF. **[CCC]. Bk Rev. Circ:** 1,500 (ctrl).
**Desc:** Leading German journal in the growing field of music therapy and official journal of the German Society of the Music Therapy.
**Ind/Abst** EMBASE; Music Index (Vol. 12, No. 1, 1991-); PsycINFO.

SW
**MUSIKTIDNINGEN.** (19??)-. Periodical. Swedish. bm. Forlags AB Musiktidningen, Radarvagen 7 183 61, Taby Sweden. **LC** ML5; .M9636.

GW
**MUSIKWISSENSCHAFTLICHE STUDIENBIBLIOTHEK.** (1???)-. Periodical. German. ir. Haenssler Verlag, Postfach 1220, D-73762 Neuhausen Germany. **Tel** 011 49 07158 1770, telex 715816 HAENSR. **Bk Rev. Ad Acc.**

FR/0750-2079
**MUSIQUE ET CULTURE STRASBOURG.** [Musique cult. Strasbourg]. **VFOAT** Musique & Culture Mensuel (Strasbourg); Musique & Culture (Strasbourg). (1955)-. Periodical.

French. ir (9 issues). 347.87F France; 422.00F other. Musique et Culture, 15 Rue Hechner, 67000 Strasbourg France. **Tel** 011 33 88 310322. **UDC** 78.

FR
**MUSIQUE ET INSTRUMENTS.** **Added/Corp** Federation Nationale des Industries et Commerces de la Musique (France). (Sept./Oct. 1964)-. Periodical. French. Six times a year. $15.96. EGP, 9 rue Coetlogon, 75006 Paris France. **LC** ML5; .M9815. ***Supersedes** Musique et Radio.*

CN/0702-9160
**MUSIQUE PERIODIQUE.** (LA MUSIQUE PERIODIQUE.). (Nov. 1976)-. Periodical. French. mo. Editions Rogemo, CP 307 Succursale Beaconsfield, Quebec H9W 5T7 Canada. **DD** 780/.9714.

FR/1141-5177
**MUSIQUE SACREE 1947, LA.** [Musique sacree 1947]. **VFOAT** Musique Sacree, L'Organiste. (1947)-. Periodical. French. qt. 190.00F France; 240.00F US and Canada; 225.00F other. Association Jeanne d'Arc Longchamp, F-88000 Longchamp France. **Tel** 011 33 29346005, FAX 33 29 34 73 25. **UDC** 783. ***Continues** Les Cahiers de la Musique Sacree (Paris), 1153-558X.*

CN/1188-1496
**MUSIQUE VIVANTE.** [Musique vivante]. Vol. 1, No 1 (Oct./Nov./Dec. 1991)-. Periodical. French. qt. 2.50Can$. F Guerette, 1433 Rue de Callieres, Quebec Quebec G1S 2C2 Canada. **DD** 780/.9714/47.

FI
**MUUSIKKO.** **Added/Corp** Suomen Muusikkojen Liitto. (19??)-. Periodical. Finnish. mo. Muusikko, Uudenmaankatu 36, D 21, Helsinki 00120 Finland. **Tel** 011 358 90640362. **LC** ML5; .M985.

●US
**MUZE / EBSCO CD-ROM.** (1993)-. English. an. $299.00 (annual), $499.00 (quarterly). EBSCO Publishing / Boston, 83 Pine Street, Peabody MA 01960. **Tel** (800)653-2726 North America, (508)535-8500, FAX (508)535-8545.
**Desc:** Combines Muze, Inc.'s comprehensive electronic music catalog with the user-friendly and efficient EBSCO-CD Search Software. Muze includes all categories of music, from rock to classical and allows users to identify recordings by performer, song titles, album titles or specialized category. Songs can be searched in three ways: by title, by keyword in a title, or by an alphabetical list of one performer's recordings. One can search Muze through specialized categories including musical genres, formats, and record companies - 28 categories in all. Classical information can be accessed by any combination of composer, conductor, ensemble, genre, soloist, label and catalog number, instrument, or a word in the title of the work.

RM/0580-3713
**MUZICA.** (MUZICA : REVISTA UNIUNII COMPOZITORILOR DIN R.P.R. SI A COMITETULUI DE STAT PENTRU CULTURA SI ARTA.). [Muzica]. **Added/Corp** Uniunea Compozitorilor din R.P.R. Romania. Comitetul de Stat Pentru Cultura si Arta. Uniunea Compozitorilor din Republica Socialista Romania. Consiliul Culturii si Educatiei Socialiste. Uniunea Compozitorilor si Muzicologilor din Romania. (1951)-. Periodical. Romanian (summaries and/or abstracts in Russian, English, French and German). qt. DM169.00. **(Subscription address:** Kubon & Sagner, ABT Zeitschriftenimport, D 80328 Munich Germany.**)** **LC** ML5; .M988. cum. index.
**Ind/Abst** RILM Abstr.

NE/0166-0535
**MUZIEK & DANS.** (MUZIEK & [I.E. EN] DANS.). [Muziek dans]. **Added/Corp** Stichting Kunstpublikaties. **VFOAT** Muziek en Dans. (197?)-. Academic Scholarly Publication. Dutch. mo. Fl70.00 Netherlands; Fl90.00 other. Openbaar Kunstbezit, Vondelstraat 120, Postbus 5555, 1007 AN Amsterdam the Netherlands. **Tel** 020-854511. **ED** Sytze Smit. **LC** ML5; .M98917. **DD** 780/.5. **Bk Rev. Ad Acc. Circ:** 5,000. ***Continues** MD.*
**Desc:** Dutch magazine with articles on music and dance.
**Ind/Abst** EMBASE.

YU/0580-373X
**MUZIKOLOSKI ZBORNIK.** (MUZIKOLOSKI ZBORNIK. MUSICOLOGICAL ANNUAL.). [Muzik. zb.]. **Added/Corp** Univerza v Ljubljani. Oddelek za Muzikologijo. **VFOAT** Musicological Annual. (1965)-. Slovenian (summaries and/or abstracts in English). an. **(Subscription address:** Jugoslovenska Knjiga, PO Box 36, YU 11001 Belgrade Yugoslovia.**)**
**Ind/Abst** Music Index; RILM Abstr.

HU/0027-5336
**MUZSIKA.** [Muzsika]. (1958)-. Periodical. Hungarian. Twelve times a year. $30.00. Pallas Lap es Konyvkiado Vallalat, Lenin korut 9-11, H-1906 Budapest, Hungary. **Tel** 36 1 2210285. **(Subscription address:** Kultura, PO Box 149, H-1389 Budapest 62 Hungary**)** **ED** Maria Feuer, Kristof Csengery, Andras Szekely and Andrea Felvegi. Index available. cum. index (yearly). **Bk Rev. Ad Acc. Circ:** 4,500-6,000 (ctrl).
**Ind/Abst** Music Index; RILM Abstr.

PL/0027-5344
**MUZYKA (1956).** (MUZYKA.). [Muzyka]. **Added/Corp** Panstwowy Instytut Sztuki (Poland) Instytut Sztuki (Polska Akademia Nauk). Vol. 1, No. 1 (1956)-. Periodical. Polish. qt. Price on Request. **(Subscription address:** ARS Polona, PO Box 1001, 00068 Warsaw Poland.**)** **LC** ML5; .M9918. **DD** 780/.9438. ***Continues** Muzyka (Warsaw, Poland : 1950), 0541-4830.*
**Ind/Abst** Music Index.

RU/0303-5689
**MUZYKA I ZIZN.** (MUZYKA I ZHIZN.). (19??)-. Russian. Izdatelstvo Sovetskii Kompozitor / St Petersburg, D-65 Nevskii Prospekt 11, St. Petersburg Russia. **LC** ML300.5; .M765.

UN/0131-2367
**MUZYKA (KIEV, UKRAINE).** (MUZYKA.). **Added/Corp** Ukraine. Ministerstvo Kultury. Spilka Kompozytoriv Ukrainy. Muzychne Tovarystvo URSR. (1923)-. Periodical. Ukrainian. bm. **LC** ML5; .M9923.

PL
**MUZYKA RELIGIJNA W POLSCE : MATERIAY I STUDIA.** **Added/Corp** Akademia Teologii Katolickiej (Warsaw, Poland). Vol. 1 (1975)-. Polish (summaries and/or abstracts in French). Akademia Teologii Katolickiej, Ul Dewajtis 3, 01-653 Warsawa Poland. **LC** ML3051.P64; M9.

RU
**MUZYKALNAIA FOLKLORISTIKA.** **Added/Corp** Soiuz Kompozitorov RSFSR. Folklornaia Komissiia. Vol. 1 (1973)-. Russian (English; summaries and/or abstracts in English and German). ir (every five years). 1.90rub single issue. Sovetskii Kompozitor, 14-12, Sadovaya-Triumfalnaya St., 103006 Moscow Russia. **LC** ML3547.1; .M89.
**Desc:** Information on ethnomusicology and Russian folk music.
**Ind/Abst** MLA Int. Bibl. Books Artic. Mod. Lang. Lit.

RU/0131-2383
**MUZYKALNAIA ZHIZN.** **Added/Corp** Soviet Union. Ministerstvo Kultury. Soiuz Kompozitorov SSSR. Vol. 1, (1958)-. Periodical. Russian. mo. $89.95. **(Subscription address:** East View Publications Inc., 3020 Harbor Lane North, Suite 110, Minneapolis MN 55447.**)**

RU
**MUZYKALNOE VOSPITANIE Y SHKOLE.** (19??)-. Russian. 0.57rub each issue. Izdatelstvo Muzyku, Neglinnaia Ul., 14, K-45, Moscow Russia. **LC** MT3.R8; M94.

RU
**MUZYKALNYI SOVREMENNIK.** **Added/Corp** Soiuz Kompozitorov SSSR. (1973)-. Periodical. Russian. Sovetskii Kompozitor, 14-12, Sadovaya-Triumfalnaya St., 103006 Moscow Russia. **LC** ML300.5; .M88.

US/0027-576X
**N.A.C.W.P.I JOURNAL.** (NACWPI JOURNAL.). [N.A.C.W.P.I j.]. **Main/Corp** National Association of College Wind and Percussion. Instructors. Vol. 19 (Fall 1970)-. Periodical. English. Four times a year (Feb., Aug., Oct. and Nov.). $25.00. Northeast Missouri State University, Division of Fine Arts, Kirksville MO 63501. **Tel** (816)785-4442. **ED** Richard Weerts. **LC** ML27.U5; N17. **DD** 788/.006/273. Index available ($25.00). cum. index. **Bk Rev**, (Qty: 4). **Ad Acc. Pr Rev. Circ:** 6,000 (ctrl). available on microfilm and microfiche from University Microfilms International (UMI). ***Continues** NACWPI Bulletin.*
**Desc:** A forum for communication within the profession of woodwind, brass and percussion music on the college and university campus.
**Ind/Abst** Music Artic. Guide; Music Index; RILM Abstr.

US/0027-5913
**N.A.M.M. MUSIC RETAILER NEWS.** (NAMM MUSIC RETAILER NEWS.). [N.A.M.M. music retail. news]. **Main/Corp** National Association of Music Merchants (U.S.). **Added/Corp** National Association of Music Merchants (U.S.). **VFOAT** Music Retailer News; National Association of Music Merchants Music Retailer News; MR News. (Jan. 1971)-. Periodical. English. Four times a year. National Association of Music Merchants, 5140 Avenida Encinas, Carlsbad CA 92008. **Tel** (619)438-8001, FAX (619)438-7327. **LC** ML3790; .N39. **DD** 338.4/778/0973. ***Continues** Members' Monthly Bulletin (National Association of Music Merchants (U.S.)), 1068-6630.*

US/0147-4618
**NAAM.** **Main/Corp** National Association of Awareness in Music. **VAT** National Association of Awareness in Music. (Jan. 1977)-. Periodical. English. mo. National Association of Awareness in Music, 11441 California Avenue, Lynwood CA 90262. **LC** ML1; .N118. **DD** 786.6/05.

GW
**NAGELS MUSIK-ARCHIV.** (1927)-. Monographic series. German. ir. Price varies per volume. Baerenreiter-Verlag, KGA Verlagssvc PF 100329, D 34003 Kassel Germany. **Tel** 011 49 561 31050, telex 99504. **(Subscription address:** Foregin Music Distributors, 13 Elkay Drive, Chester NY 10918.**)** **LC** M2; .N25.
**Desc:** A series of instrumental music for solo instruments, chamber music and orchestral works from the Renaissance to the 18th Century.

US/0163-612X
**NAMIT JOURNAL.** **Main/Corp** National Association of Musical Instrument Technicians. **Added/Corp** National Association of Musical Instrument Technicians. Journal. **VAT** National Association of Musical Instrument Technicians Journal. (Jan. 1977)-. English. mo. NAMIT Publications Inc., PO Box 1824, South Bend IN 46634. **LC** ML1; .N126. **DD** 781.9/1/028.

US
**NASHVILLE WEST.** (Sept. 1975)-. Periodical. English. mo. Nashville West Enterprises, PO Box 14722, Austin TX 78761. **LC** ML1; .N114. **DD** 784.

US/0147-9938
**NATIONAL BLUEGRASS MUSIC NEWS, THE.** **Added/Corp** Bluegrass Music Association. Society for the Preservation of Bluegrass Music of America. (April 1977)-. Periodical. English. mo. Bluegrass Music Association, Route 3, Box 364, Claremore OK 74017. **LC** ML1; .N128. **DD** 784. ***Supersedes** National Bluegrass News, 0099-0035.*

CN/1193-4069
**NATIONAL CHART.** ***Title Change.*** [Natl. chart]. (1990)-(19??). Periodical. English. Twelve times a year. National Chart Publishing, PO Box 332, Willowdale Station A, North York Ontario M2N 5S9 Canada. **Tel** (416)363-3101, FAX (905)928-1357. **DD** 781.660971. ***Continued by** Chart Magazine, 1198-7235.*

US
**NATIONAL SACRED HARP NEWSLETTER.** ***Ceased.*** (1985)-(Oct. 1993). Newsletter. English. Hugh McGraw, PO Box 185, Bremen GA 30110. **Tel** (404)832-1195. **ED** Hugh W McGraw, Richard L DeLong, W H Denney Jr. **LC** PAR. Index available. **Ad Acc. Circ:** 600 (ctrl).
**Desc:** Pretains to folk religious music known as "Sacred Harp" or "Fa-Sol-La" singing.

US/0884-8106
**NATS JOURNAL / NATIONAL ASSOCIATION OF TEACHERS OF SINGING JOURNAL, THE.** [NATS j.]. **VAT** National Association of Teachers of Singing Journal. Vol. 42, No. 1 (Sept./Oct. 1985)-. Periodical. English. Five times a year (Jan, Mar, May, Sep, Nov). $23.00 US; $25.00 Canada and Mexico; $27.00 other. NATS / National Association of Teachers of Singing Inc., 2800 University Blvd., North JU Station, Jacksonville FL 32211. **Tel** (904)744-9022. **ED** James McKinney. **LC** ML27.U5; N2652. **DD** 784/.05. **Ad Acc. Circ:** 5,700. available on microfilm and microfiche from University Microfilms International (UMI). ***Continues** NATS Bulletin, 0027-6073.*
**Desc:** Official publication of the National Association of Teachers of Singing. Only nationally distributed magazine devoted exclusively to the art of singing, the teaching of singing, care of the professional voice, vocal literature, vocal function, and voice science.
**Ind/Abst** Music Artic. Guide; Music Index; RILM Abstr.

US/0732-1503
**NEBRASKA MUSIC EDUCATOR, THE.** **Added/Corp** Nebraska Music Education Association. Nebraska Music Educators' Association. (19??)-. Periodical. English. qt (Feb., Apr., Aug., Oct.). $10.00. Nebraska Music Educator, PO Box 83046, Lincoln NE 68501-3046. **Tel** (402)435-6913, FAX (402)474-3250. **ED** Michael H. Veak. **LC** UNC. **Ad Acc. Circ:** 1,500.
**Desc:** News of the association, officer columns, convention news, major news happenings in state, music reviews, college calendars and advertising. Also articles on music.
**Ind/Abst** Music Artic. Guide.

US
**NETWORK FORTY.** (19??)-. English. Fifty times a year. $300.00. Network Magazine Group, 120 North Victory Boulevard, Burbank CA 91502. **Tel** (818)955-4000, (800)222-4382, FAX (818)955-8048.
**Desc:** Covers current top 40 music.

GW
**NEUE AUSGABE SAEMTLICHER WERKE. FRANZ LISZT.** (19??)-. Monographic series. German. ir. Price varies per volume. Baerenreiter-Verlag, KGA Verlagssvc PF 100329, D 34003 Kassel Germany. **Tel** 011 49 561 31050, telex 99504. **(Subscription address:** Foreign Music Distributors, 13 Elkay Drive, Chester, NY 10918**)**
**Desc:** A new critical edition of the musical works of Franz Liszt.

GW
**NEUE AUSGABE SAEMTLICHER WERKE. HEINRICH SCHUTZ.** Monographic series. German. ir. Price varies per volume. Baerenreiter-Verlag, KGA Verlagssvc PF 100329, D 34003 Kassel Germany. **Tel** 011 49 561 31050, telex 99504. **(Subscription address:** Foreign Music

# Music

**GW**
### NEUE AUSGABE SAEMTLICHER WERKE. WOLFGANG AMADEUS MOZART. (19??)-. Monographic series. German. ir. Price varies per volume. Baerenreiter-Verlag, KGA Verlagssvc PF 100329, D 34003 Kassel Germany. **Tel** 011 49 561 31050, telex 99504. **(Subscription address:** Foreign Music Distributors, 13 Elkay Drive, Chester, NY 10918**)**
  **Desc:** A new critical edition of the musical works of Mozart. All music volumes have been published, but some have gone out of print and are being reissued.

**GW**
### NEUE AUSGABE SAMTLICHER WERKE JOHANN SEBASTIAN BACH. (19??)-.
Monographic series. German. ir. Price varies per volume. Baerenreiter-Verlag, KGA Verlagssvc PF 100329, D 34003 Kassel Germany. **Tel** 011 49 561 31050, telex 99504. **(Subscription address:** Foreign Music Distributors, 13 Elkay Drive, Chester, NY 10918**)**

**GW**
### NEUE AUSGABE SAMTLICHER WERKE SCHUBERT. Monographic series. German. ir. Price varies per volume. Baerenreiter-Verlag, KGA Verlagssvc PF 100329, D 34003 Kassel Germany. **Tel** 011 49 561 31050, telex 99504. **(Subscription address:** Foreign Music Distributors, 13 Elkay Drive, Chester, NY 10918; Phone: (914)469-5790**)**

**GW/0548-2879**
### NEUE MUSIK IN DER BUNDESREPUBLIK DEUTSCHLAND.
(NEUE MUSIK IN DER BUNDESREPUBLIK DEUTSCHLAND. DOKUMENTATION.). **Added/Corp** International Society for Contemporary Music. German Section. (1957/58)-. German. be. **LC** ML275.5; .N5.

**GW**
### NEUE MUSIKZEITUNG. Added/Corp
Musikalische Jugend Osterreichs. (19??)-. Periodical. German. Six times a year. Con Brio Verlagsgesellschaft, Postfach 100245, D 93002 Regensburg Germany. **LC** ML5; .N367. Index available (free).
  **Ind/Abst** Music Index.

**GW**
### NEUE ZEITSCHRIFT FUER MUSIK.
**Added/Corp** Robert-Schumann-Gesellschaft (Frankfurt am Main, Germany). **VFOAT** NZ. (Jan. 1991)-. Periodical. English. bm. DM101.90 (airmail); DM70.40 (Germany), DM75.80 (other) surface mail. B. Schotts Soehne Musikverlag, Carl Zeiss Str 1, Postfach 3640, D 55026 Mainz Germany. **Tel** 011 49 6131 505129, 011 49 6131 505122, FAX 011 49 6131 505115, telex 04187821. Documents available from The Genuine Article. **Continues** NZ : Neue Zeitschrift fur Musik.
  **Ind/Abst** Arts Humanit. Citation Index (19??-19??) [Full Cov.]; Music Index; Res. Alert [Full Cov.].

**UK**
### NEW CONSENSUS AND REVIEW OF THE LATEST ISSUES OF RECORDED CLASSICAL MUSIC, THE. (19??)-. Periodical. English. mo. Henry Stave & Company, Record Specialties, 9 Dean Street, London W1 England. **LC** ML156.9; .N5. **DD** 789.9/131. **Continues** Consensus and Review of the Latest Issues of Recorded Classical Music.

**GW**
### NEW EDITION OF THE COMPLETE WORKS OF HECTOR BERLIOZ.
Monographic series. German. Price varies per volume. **(Subscription address:** Broude Brothers Limited, 141 White Oaks Road, Williamstown, MA 01267; Phone: (413)458-8132, (800)525-8559**)**
  **Desc:** A critical edition of the musical works of Hector Berlioz.

**US/0732-4820**
### NEW ENGLAND FOLK DIRECTORY, THE. (THE NEW ENGLAND FOLK DIRECTORY / COMPILED AND EDITED BY WAYNE LICWON.). (19??)-. Directory. English. an. New England Folk Directory, c/o Alcazar Inc, PO Box 429, Waterbury VT 05676. **LC** ML14.N33; N5. **DD** 781.7/025/74.

**US/0098-3381**
### NEW ENGLAND MUSICIAN'S GUIDE, THE. Added/Corp New England Musician's Guild. (19??)-. Periodical. English. mo. New England Musician's Guild, 739 Boylston Street, Boston MA 02116. **LC** ML1; .N337. **DD** 780/.5.

**US/0362-7357**
### NEW GOSPEL TREASURE SELECT-A-SONG. (1976)-. English. an. New Gospel Treasure Select-a-Song, 201 Grizzard R-12, Nashville TN 37207. **LC** ML128.V7; N46. **DD** 016.7836/75.

**US/0028-5315**
### NEW HAMPSHIRE QUARTER NOTES.
**Added/Corp** New Hampshire Music Educators' Association. (19??)-. English. Five times a year (Jan., Mar., May, Sept., Nov.) $10.00. New Hampshire Music Education Association, Elaine Hashem, Rt 5 Box 240, Penacook NH 03303. **LC** ML1; .N34. **DD** 780/.729742.
  **Ind/Abst** Music Artic. Guide.

**US/0742-8278**
### NEW MEXICO MUSICIAN, THE. Added/Corp
New Mexico Music Educators Association. Music Educators National Conference (U.S.). Vol. 1, No. 1 (Oct. 1953)-. Periodical. English. tq (Apr., Sept., Nov.) $7.00. The New Mexico Musician, 93 Mimbres Drive, c/o Don Gerheart, Los Alamos NM 87544. **Tel** (505)672-9840. **ED** Don Gerheart. **Ad Acc. Circ:** 1,600 (ctrl).
  **Desc:** Official publication of the New Mexico Music Education Association.

**CN/0706-7984**
### NEW MUSIC. (THE NEW MUSIC.). (Aug. 1978)-. Periodical. English. mo. Free. New Music Publishing Company, Box 430, Station A, Toronto Ontario M5W 1C2. **DD** 780/.42/05.

**US/0197-5994**
### NEW MUSIC NEWS. [New music news].
**Added/Corp** Composers' Forum (U.S.). (Nov. 1979)-. Periodical. English. mo. Composers' Forum Inc., 596 Broadway / Suite 602A, New York NY 10012. **Tel** (212)334-0216. **LC** ML197; .N39. **DD** 780/.904.

**US**
### NEW MUSIC PERFORMANCE AND CHAMBER MUSIC / NATIONAL ENDOWMENT FOR THE ARTS. Main/Corp
National Endowment for the Arts. **VFOAT** New Music Performance and Chamber Music Application Guidelines. (1979/80/81)-. English. be. National Endowment for the Arts, 1100 Pennsylvania Avenue Northwest, Washington DC 20506. **Tel** (202)682-5400, (202)682-5435.

**US/0276-7031**
### NEW ON THE CHARTS. [New charts]. Vol. 1, No. 1 (Jan. 1976)-. English. Twelve times a year. $185.00. Music Business Reference Inc, 70 Laurel Place, New Rochelle NY 10801. **Tel** (914)632-3349, FAX (914)633-7690. **ED** Leonard Kalikow. **LC** ML18; .N48. **DD** 338.4/778/02573. Index available. cum. index. **Ad Acc. Circ:** 6,000 (ctrl).
  **Desc:** Addresses and phone numbers for companies involved with current hit pop, country, and rhythm and blues, records and music videos. Includes a cumulative index of every hit single and album.

**UK/0308-1990**
### NEW ORLEANS MUSIC. Vol. 1, No. 1 (Oct./Nov. 1989)-. Periodical. English. bm. £6.00 UK; $15.00 US. New Orleans Music, Bayou Press, 117 High Street, Wheatley, Oxford OX9 1VE United Kingdom. **Tel** (0763)60823. **ED** Mike Hazeldine. **LC** IN PROCESS. Index available. cum. index. **Bk Rev. Ad Acc. Circ:** 1,500 (ctrl). **Continues** Footnote.
  **Desc:** Covers the field of New Orleans and traditional jazz including ragtime. We run articles on past and present musicians.
  **Ind/Abst** Music Index.

**UK**
### NEW RECORD MIRROR. Title Change.
(19??)-(19??). English. Punch Subscriptions, Unit 8, Grove Ash, Bletchley, Milton Keyes MK1 1BV England. **Absorbed by** Music Week.

**US/0887-7335**
### NEW YORK REGGAE TIMES. VFOAT
Reggae Times. (1985)-. Periodical. English. bm. $6.50. Reggae Times, 577 Albany Avenue, Brooklyn NY 11203. **DD** 784.

**US**
### NEW YORK ROCKER. (1977)-. Periodical. English. bm. **ED** A. Betrock.

● **US/1071-0191**
### NEWS BULLETIN / THE MUSICAL BOX SOCIETY INTERNATIONAL. [News bull. - Music. Box Soc. Int.]. **Added/Corp** Musical Box Society International. (199?)-. Bulletin. English. Six times a year. Musical Box Society International, 887 Orange Avenue East, St Paul MN 55106. **Tel** (612)774-2590. **LC** ML26; .M879. **DD** 786.6/5. **Continues** MBSI News Bulletin, 1058-7241.

**CN/1181-6023**
### NEWS FROM THE CANADIAN MUSICAL HERITAGE SOCIETY. [News Can. Music. Herit. Soc.]. **Added/Corp** Canadian Musical Heritage Society. **VFOAT** News; Nouvelles; Nouvelles de la Societe pour le Patrimoine Musical Canadien. Vol. 1, No. 1 (Summer 1990)-. Periodical. English (French). sa. Free to members. Canadian Musical Heritage Society, PO Box 262, Station A, Toronto, Ontario K1N 8V2 Canada. **Tel** (613)232-3406. **DD** 780/.6/071.

**US/0735-7079**
### NEWSBRIEF / AMERICAN CONSERVATORY OF MUSIC. [Newsbr. - Am. Consev. Music]. **Main/Corp** American Conservatory of Music. (Oct. 1981)-. Periodical. English. ir. American Conservatory of Music, Chicago IL 60602-3315. **Tel** (312)263-4161.

**US/0015-5950**
### NEWSLETTER. Main/Corp Folklore Society of Greater Washington. (Oct. 23, 1964)-. Newsletter. English. Twelve times a year. $16.00. Folklore Society of Greater Washington, 307 Broadleaf Drive, Vienna VA 22180. **Tel** (703)281-2228. **LC** ML1; .F4155. **DD** 784.4/006/2754.

**US**
### NEWSLETTER. Main/Corp Boston Area Friends of Bluegrass & Old-Time Country Music. (19??)-. Newsletter. English. mo. Boston Area Friends of Bluegrass & Old-Time Country Music, 238 Putnam Avenue, Cambridge MA 02139. **LC** ML28.C18; B7. **DD** 784/.06/274461.

**US**
### NEWSLETTER. Main/Corp Texas Bluegrass Association. (19??)-. Newsletter. English. mo. Texas Bluegrass Association, 6544 Balcer Boulevard, Fort Worth TX 76118. **LC** ML27.U5; T5. **DD** 780/.42.

**US/0160-2365**
### NEWSLETTER - AMERICAN MUSICAL INSTRUMENT SOCIETY. [Newsl. Am. Music. Instrum. Soc.]. **Main/Corp** American Musical Instrument Society. Vol. 1, (Nov. 1971)-. Newsletter. English. Three times a year (Feb., June, Oct.). $35.00 Includes American Musical Instrument Society Membership & Newsletter. American Musical Instrument Society, R. D. #3, Box 205-B, Franklin PA 16323. **Tel** (814)374-4119, FAX (814)374-4553. **ED** Andre P. Larson. **LC** ML1; .A53. **DD** 781.9/1/06273. **Bk Rev. Ad Acc. Circ:** 800.
  **Desc:** A vehicle for communication between all AMIS members, with or without scholarly pretensions.
  **Ind/Abst** Music Index.

**US**
### NEWSLETTER. AMERICAN RECORDER SOCIETY. Main/Corp American Recorder Society. No. 1 (Jan. 20, 1950)-. Newsletter. English. ir. $30.00 US & Canada; $35.00 others Comes with American Recorder Society Membership & Newsletter. American Recorder Society, PO Box 1067, Jackson NJ 08527. **Tel** (908)363-5656. **ED** Martha Bixler and Valerie Horst. **LC** ML27.U5; A8343. **DD** 788.5306273. **Circ:** 4,000 (ctrl).
  **Desc:** Calendar of events for recorder and early music world-wide and news of society activities.

**US/1071-0639**
### NEWSLETTER - ASSOCIATION FOR CHINESE MUSIC RESEARCH.
(NEWSLETTER.). [Newsl. - Assoc. Chin. Music Res.]. **Added/Corp** Association for Chinese Music Research. **VFOAT** ACMR Newsletter. (19??)-. Newsletter. English (Chinese). Twice a year (Jan., & June). $10.00. University of Pittsburgh - Music Department, Pittsburgh PA 15260. **Tel** (412)624-4126. **ED** Bell Yung (phone: (412)624-4061). **DD** 780. **Bk Rev. Circ:** 150 (ctrl).
  **Desc:** News on chinese music, periodical, and ethnomusicology.

**US/0098-3632**
### NEWSLETTER - BLUEGRASS CLUB OF NEW YORK. Main/Corp Bluegrass Club of New York. (19??)-. Newsletter. English. Bluegrass Club of New York, PO Box 1B, 417 East 89 Street, New York NY 10028. **LC** ML28; .N5B5. **DD** 780/.42.

**US/0006-7598**
### NEWSLETTER - BOOSEY AND HAWKES INC. Main/Corp Boosey and Hawkes, Inc., New York. Vol. 1, (Fall 1965)-. Newsletter. English. ir. Free. Boosey and Hawkes, 295 Regent Street, London W1A 1BR England. **Tel** 011 44 71 5802060, FAX 011 44 71 4365675.

**CN/0822-8175**
### NEWSLETTER / BRITISH COLUMBIA CHORAL FEDERATION. [Newsletter - B.C. Choral Fed.]. **Added/Corp** British Columbia Choral Federation. **VAT** B.C.C.F. Newsletter; BCCF Newsletter; British Columbia Choral Federation Newsletter. (19??)-. Periodical. English. ir (3 or 4 issues per year). 20.00Can$ (individuals), 30.00Can$ (institutions) US & Canada; 35.00Can$ (individuals), 45.00Can$ (institutions) others. British Columbia Choral Federation, PO Box 4397, Vancouver British Columbia V6B 3Z8 Canada. **Tel** (604)733-9687, FAX (604)733-4026. **DD** 784.1/006/0711.

**CN/0714-7384**
### NEWSLETTER (BRITISH COLUMBIA MUSIC EDUCATORS ASSOCIATION).
(NEWSLETTER / BRITISH COLUMBIA MUSIC EDUCATORS ASSOCIATION OF THE BRITISH COLUMBIA TEACHERS' FEDERATION.). [Newsl. - B.C. Music Educ. Assoc. B.C. Teach. Fed.]. **Added/Corp** British Columbia Music Educators' Association. (Summer 1981)-. Newsletter. English. qt. Free to Members.

# Music

BCMEA Newsletter, c/o British Columbia Teachers Federation, 2235 Burrard Street, Vancouver British Columbia V6J 3H9 Canada. **DD** 780/.7. **Separated from** B.C. Music Educator, 0705-9019.

CN/0383-1299
**NEWSLETTER / CANADIAN ASSOCIATION OF MUSIC LIBRARIES.**
See Library and Information Sciences.

CN/0833-9503
**NEWSLETTER (CANADIAN BAND ASSOCIATION. ONTARIO CHAPTER).** (NEWSLETTER / CANADIAN BAND ASSOCIATION (ONTARIO) INC.). [Newsl. - Can. Band Assoc. Ont. Chapter]. **Added/Corp** Canadian Band Association. Ontario Chapter. (July/Aug. 1985)-. Newsletter. English. bm. Canadian Band Association (Ontario) Inc, 21 Tecumshe Street, Brantford Ontario N3S 2B3 Canada. **Tel** (519)753-1858. **ED** Frank McKinnon. **DD** 785/.06/7109713. **Circ:** 110. **Continues** Canadian Band Directors' Association. Ontario Chapter. Newsletter - Canadian Band Directors' Association., 0381-9159.

US
**NEWSLETTER - COLLEGE MUSIC SOCIETY. Main/Corp** College Music Society. (19??)-. Newsletter. English. ir. $37.00 Comes with College Music Society Membership & College Music Symposium. College Music Society Inc., 202 West Spruce Street, Missoula MT 59802. **Tel** (406)721-9616.

US
**NEWSLETTER : CONCERT RECORDINGS. Main/Corp** Symposium at Guerneville. **Added/Corp** Symposium at Guerneville. Concert Recordings. **VFOAT** Concert Recordings. (Sept. 1973)-. Newsletter. English. mo. $7.50. Newsletter : Concert Recordings, Box 465, Guerneville CA 95446. **LC** ML156 9; .S9. **DD** 789.9/131.

US/0160-5119
**NEWSLETTER - FLORIDA FRIENDS OF BLUEGRASS SOCIETY.** (NEWSLETTER - THE FLORIDA FRIENDS OF BLUEGRASS SOCIETY.). **Main/Corp** Florida Friends of Bluegrass Society. (19??)-. Newsletter. English. bm. The Florida Friends of Bluegrass Society, 7318 Sequaia Drive, Tampa FL 33617. **LC** ML1; .F329. **DD** 784.

US/0091-9764
**NEWSLETTER - HUNTSVILLE ASSOCIATION OF FOLK MUSICIANS.** (NEWSLETTER.). **Main/Corp** Huntsville Association of Folk Musicians. No. 1 (July 1968)-. Newsletter. English. Huntsville Association of Folk Musicians, PO Box 1444, Huntsville AL 35807. **LC** ML28.H9; H85. **DD** 781.7/06/276197.

US/0145-8396
**NEWSLETTER - INSTITUTE FOR STUDIES IN AMERICAN MUSIC. Main/Corp** Brooklyn College. Institute for Studies in American Music. **Added/Corp** Brooklyn College. Institute for Studies in American Music. I.S.A.M. Newsletter. **VFOAT** I.S.A.M. Newsletter. **VAT** Institute for Studies in American Music Newsletter. Vol. 1, (Nov. 1971)-. Newsletter. English. Twice a year (May, Nov.). Free. Institute Studies in American Music, Brooklyn College, Conservatory of Music, Brooklyn NY 11210. **Tel** (718)780-5655, FAX (718)951-6140. **ED** H. Wiley Hitchcock. **LC** ML28.B81; B75. **DD** 781.7/73. **Bk Rev. Ad Acc. Circ:** 3,700.
**Desc:** Includes essays, book and record reviews, research reports, and information on all aspects of American music.
**Ind/Abst** Music Artic. Guide; Music Index; RILM Abstr.

US/0161-1704
**NEWSLETTER - MUSIC OCLC USERS GROUP. Main/Corp** Music OCLC Users Group. **VFOAT** MOUG Newsletter; Music OCLC Users Group Newsletter. No. 1 (1977)-. Newsletter. English. Three times a year (usually May, Aug., Nov.). $10.00 (individual), $15.00 (institution), North America; $25.00 (individual & institution) other. Music OCLC Users Group, 1299 University or Knight Library, C/O C. Grandy, Eugene OR 97403-1299. **Tel** (503)346-1850. **ED** Judy Weidow (phone: (512)495-4191). **Circ:** 560.
**Desc:** Covers issues in music cataloging and bibliographic control.

AT/0155-0543
**NEWSLETTER / MUSICOLOGICAL SOCIETY OF AUSTRALIA. Main/Corp** Musicological Society of Australia. Vol. 1, No. 1 (Dec. 1977)-. Newsletter. English. Three times a year. 40.00Aus$ Australia; 50.00Aus$ other. Musicological Society of Australia, GPO Box 2404, Canberra ACT 2601 Australia. **Tel** 011 61 7 3444611, FAX 011 61 3 3445346. **ED** Georgina Binns. **Ad Acc. Circ:** 300 (ctrl).
**Desc:** Contains information about musicological events w thin Australia and overseas to its members and subscribers.

US/0888-8701
**NEWSLETTER OF THE AMERICAN HANDEL SOCIETY.** [Newsl. Am. Handel Soc.]. **Added/Corp** American Handel Society. Vol. 1, No. 1 (Apr. 1986)-. Periodical. English. Three times a year (Apr., Aug., Dec.). $30.00 Comes with American Handel Society membership. American Haendel Society / Department of Music, University of Maryland, College Park MD 20742. **Tel** (301)405-5523. **DD** 780. **Bk Rev. Ad Acc.**
**Desc:** Articles, events, calendar, and reviews of sound recordings, life and works of George Fridenc Handel.

US/1053-9948
**NEWSLETTER OF THE ERNST KRENEK ARCHIVE.** [Newsl. Ernst Krenek Arch.]. **Added/Corp** Ernst Krenek Archive. **VFOAT** Ernst Krenek Newsletter. Vol. 1, No. 1 (spring 1990)-. Periodical. English. tq. $10.00. Ernst Krenek Archive, 0175Q, University of California San Diego, La Jolla CA 92093. **Tel** (619)534-2759. **LC** ML410.K7365; N5. **DD** 780/.92.
**Desc:** Discusses the performances and compositions of Ernst Krenek.

US/0198-8921
**NEWSLETTER OF THE MUSIC CRITICS ASSOCIATION, INC. Main/Corp** Music Critics Association (U.S.). **VAT** Newsletter of the Music Critics Association, Incorporated. (19??)-. Newsletter. English. Music Critics Association Inc., 6201 Tuckerman Lane, Rockville MD 20852. **LC** ML3880; .M87. **DD** 780/.9.

CN/1187-0362
**NEWSLETTER - OPERA LYRA OTTAWA.** See The Arts-Performing Arts.

US/0736-6876
**NEWSLETTER / OPERA ORCHESTRA OF NEW YORK. Added/Corp** Opera Orchestra of New York. **VFOAT** Opera Orchestra Newsletter. Vol. 1, No. 1 (Spring 1982)-. Newsletter. English. qt. OONY, 211 West 56th Street, New York NY 10019. **LC** ML1699; .N48. **DD** 782.1/09747/1.

CN/0829-4291
**NEWSLETTER (ROYAL CANADIAN COLLEGE OF ORGANISTS).** (NEWSLETTER / THE ROYAL CANADIAN COLLEGE OF ORGANISTS.). [Newsl. - R. Can. Coll. Organists]. **Added/Corp** Royal Canadian College of Organists. (March 1985)-. Newsletter. English. Three times a year. Royal Canadian College of Organists, Suite 300A / 212 King Street West, Toronto Ontario M5H 1K5 Canada. **DD** 786.5/06/071. **Continues** College Newsletter (Royal Canadian College of Organists), 0826-2950.

US/0748-0148
**NEWSLETTER (ROYAL SCHOOL OF CHURCH MUSIC (WARREN, CONN.).** (NEWSLETTER / ROYAL SCHOOL OF CHURCH MUSIC.). **Added/Corp** Royal School of Church Music (Warren, Conn.). (19??)-. Newsletter. English. Royal School of Church Music In America, PO Box 176, Warren CT 06754. **LC** ML1; .N767. **DD** 783/.02/605.

US/0191-1791
**NEWSLETTER - SALT CITY SONG MINERS TRADITIONAL FOLK MUSIC CLUB OF CENTRAL NEW YORK.** (NEWSLETTER - THE SALT CITY SONG MINERS TRADITIONAL FOLK MUSIC CLUB OF CENTRAL NEW YORK.). **Main/Corp** Salt City Song Miners Traditional Folk Music Club of Central New York. (19??)-. Newsletter. English. mo. The Salt City Song Miners Traditional Folk Music Club of Central New York, 723 Broad Street, Syracuse NY 13210. **LC** ML1; .S214. **DD** 781.7/73.

AT/0726-2183
**NEWSLETTER - SUZUKI TALENT EDUCATION ASSOCIATION OF AUSTRALIA (VICTORIA).** [Newsl. - Suzuki Talent Education Assoc. Aust. (Vic.)]. (1981)-. Newsletter. English. Four times a year. 40.00Aus$. Suzuki Talent Education Association, 2 Denham Street, Hawthorn VIC 3122 Australia. **Tel** 011 61 3 8197330, FAX 011 61 3 8169441. **DD** 786.21070945.

US/8756-8357
**NEWSLETTER / THE AMERICAN BRAHMS SOCIETY.** [Newsl. - Am. Brahms Soc.]. **Added/Corp** American Brahms Society. **VFOAT** American Brahms Society Newsletter. Vol. 1, No. 1 (Spring 1983)-. Periodical. English. Twice a year (Spring & Fall). $25.00. The American Brahms Society, School of Music / DN 10, University of Washington, Seattle WA 98195. **Tel** (206)543-1200. **ED** Virginia Hancock (editor's address: Reed College, Department of Music, Portland, OR 97202, phone: (503)771-1112). **LC** ML410.B81; N38. **DD** 780/.92/4. **Bk Rev. Circ:** 1,500.
**Desc:** A newsletter with feature articles and reviews, as well as announcements of current research on Brahms.
**Ind/Abst** Music Artic. Guide.

US/0732-8966
**NEWSLETTER - UNIVERSITY OF SOUTHERN CALIFORNIA. ARMENIAN MUSICAL STUDIES.** (NEWSLETTER / UNIVERSITY OF SOUTHERN CALIFORNIA, ARMENIAN MUSICAL STUDIES, SCHOOL OF PERFORMING ARTS.). [Newsl. - Univ. South. Calif., Armen. Music. Stud.]. **Main/Corp** University of Southern California. Aemenian Musical Studies. Vol. 1, No. 1 (Summer 1980)-. Newsletter. English. sa. Elise Tashjian, 610 Prospect Boulevard, Pasadena CA 91103. **LC** MT4; .L7572. **DD** 781.7/2922/06079494.

US
**NEWSLETTER - WESTERN PENNSYLVANIA BLUEGRASS COMMITTEE. Main/Corp** Western Pennsylvania Bluegrass Committee. (19??)-. Newsletter. English. mo. $5.00. Western Pennsylvania Bluegrass Committee, PO Box 5295, Pittsburgh PA 15206-5295. **LC** ML1; .W29. **DD** 784.

US/1051-0788
**NEWSLETTER - WILLEM MENGELBERG SOCIETY.** (NEWSLETTER / THE WILLEM MENGELBERG SOCIETY.). [Newsl. - Willem Mengelberg Soc.]. **Added/Corp** Willem Mengelberg Society. No. 1 (1970)-. Newsletter. English. qt. $6.50 (institutions), $6.00 (individuals) one year; $13.00 (institutions), $12.00 (individuals) two year (US); $7.00 (insitutions), $6.50 (individuals) one year; $14.00 (institutions), $13.00 (individuals) two year (Canada & Mexico); $7.50 (institutions), $7.00 (individuals) surface mail; $9.00 (institutions), $8.50 (individuals) airmail (Europe & Orient). Willem Mengelberg Society, 1408-A Marshall Street, Manitowoc WS 54220. **ED** Ronald Klett. **DD** 786. **Bk Rev.**
**Desc:** Covers all aspects of the life, recordings, and concerts of the orchestral and choral conductor.

US/1063-1909
**NHAC VIET.** [Nhac viet]. **Added/Corp** Association for Research in Vietnamese Music. **VFOAT** Nhac Viet Newsletter. Vol. 1, No. 1 (Spring 1990)-. Periodical. English. Twice a year (Spring and Fall). $10.00 (individual); $20.00 (institutions). Association for Research in Vietnamese Music, Box 16, Kent OH 44240. **ED** Tuyen Tonnu, (phone: (216)677-9703). **LC** ML345.V5; N52. **DD** 780/.9597/05. **Bk Rev**, (Qty: 10). **Ad Acc, Adv Mgr:** Tonnu, **Tel** (216)677-9703. **Circ:** 500 (ctrl).

NR
**NIGERIAN MUSIC AWARDS ANNUAL, THE. Main/Corp** Nigerian Music Awards. (1990)-. English. **LC** ML5; .N68.

CN/0824-6718
**NIGHTMOVES.** [Nightmoves]. Issue 1, (1983)-. Periodical. English. Nightmoves, 66 Ashburn Drive, Nepean Ontario K2E 6N3 Canada. **DD** 784.5/4/00971384.

CN/0384-5842
**NIGHTOUT.** (Jan. 26/Feb. 15, 1976)-. Periodical. English. bm. Nightout, 75 Sherbourne Street, Toronto Ontario M5A 2P9 Canada. **DD** 780/.9713/541.
**Desc:** Metro Toronto's complete club listing.

JA
**NIHON ONGAKU BUNKEN YOSHI MOKUROKU. Added/Corp** International Repertory of Music Literature (Organization). Kokunai linkai. (1973)-. Multiple languages (Japanese, English, French and German). Rilon Kokunai linkai, c/o Nanki Ongaku Bunko, Nihon Kindai Bungakukan, 4-3-55 Komabu Meguro-ku, Tokyo 153 Japan. **LC** ML113; .N59.

JA
**NIHON SHIYO KYOKUSHU / NIHON SHIJIN RENMEI HEN. Added/Corp** Nihon Shijin Renmei. (19??)-. Japanese. an. Tokyo Gakufu Shuppansha, 5-22 Obinta 1, Bunkyo-ku, Tokyo-TU 112 Japan. **LC** M1812; .N5474.

US/0749-9345
**NOA NEWSLETTER.** (NOA NEWSLETTER : OFFICIAL ORGAN, NATIONAL OPERA ASSOCIATION.). [NOA newsl.]. **Added/Corp** National Opera Association. **VFOAT** N.O.A. Newsletter. **VAT** National Opera Association Newsletter. (19??)-. Newsletter. English. Four times a year. National Opera Association Inc., Northwestern University, School of Music, 711 Elgin Road, Evanston IL 60208-1200. **Tel** (708)467-2422, FAX (708)491-5260. **DD** 782.

DK
**NORDIC SOUNDS / NORDIC COUNCIL OF MINISTERS/NOMUS, THE SECRETARIAT FOR NORDIC CULTURAL COOPERATION. Added/Corp** NOMUS (Organization) Nordic Council of Ministers. Secretariat for Nordic Cultural Co-operation. (1982)-. Periodical. English. qt. MIC Dansk Musik Information Center, Vimmelskaftet 48 DK 1161, Copenhagen K

Denmark. **Tel** 01 11 47 11. **LC** ML5; .N689. **DD** 780/.948/05. ***Continues*** *Nomus Nytt.*
**Ind/Abst** Music Index.

NO/0800-9805
**NORSK BOKFORTEGNELSE. MUSIKKTRYKK. THE NORWEGIAN NATIONAL BIBLIOGRAPHY / UTARBEIDET VED NORSK MUSIKKSAMLING, UNIVERSITETSBIBLIOTEKET I OSLO.**
**Added/Corp** Norsk Musikksamling (Universitetsbiblioteket i Oslo). **VFOAT** Musikktrykk; The Norwegian National Bibliography. (1983)-. Bibliography. Norwegian. an. Norwegian Booksellers Association, Ovre Vollgate 15, 0158 Oslo 1 Norway. **Tel** 011 47 2 410 760. **LC** ML120.N6; N67. **DD** 016.7817481. available in microform (under title: Norske Musikktrykk). ***Continues in part*** *Norsk Bokfortegnelse.*

NO/0029-2044
**NORSK MUSIKERBLAD.** [Nor. musikerbl.]. **Added/Corp** Norsk Musikerforbund. (1914)-. Periodical. English (Norwegian). Eleven times a year. Kr160.00 Scandinavia; Kr280.00 other. Norsk Musikerforbund, Youngsgt 11, 0181 Oslo 1 Norway. **Tel** 011 47 2 401492. **Ad Acc. Circ:** 2,600 (ctrl).
**Desc:** A trade union for musicians; Nebotiatsins results and bits and pieces from culture life in Norway.
**Ind/Abst** Music Index.

NO
**NORSK MUSIKKGRANSKNING; MEDDELELSER FRA NORSK SAMFUND FOR MUSIKKGRANSKNING, NORSK MUSIKKSAMLINGS VENNER. ARBOK.**
**Added/Corp** Norsk Samfund for Musikkgranskning--Norsk Musikksamlings Venner. (1937)-. Norwegian. **LC** ML312; .N86.

NO/0332-5482
**NORSK MUSIKKTIDSSKRIFT.** [Nor. musikktidsskr.]. **Added/Corp** Norsk Musikklreres Landsforbund. **VFOAT** Norsk Musikk Tidsskrift. (1964)-. Periodical. Norwegian. qt. Nicolai Dirdal, Schonings Gt 42, Oslo 3 Norway. **Tel** 42-25989. **ED** Jorg Johnsen. **Bk Rev. Ad Acc. Circ:** 1,600.
**Desc:** Information and news for music teachers, composers, musicians, and libraries.
**Ind/Abst** RILM Abstr.

US/0734-1741
**NORTH & CENTRAL AMERICAN DIRECTORY.** (NORTH & CENTRAL AMERICAN DIRECTORY / AMATEUR CHAMBER MUSIC PLAYERS, INC.). **Main/Corp** Amateur Chamber Music Players. **VFOAT** North and Central American Directory. 27th (1982)-. Directory. English. Amateur Chamber Music Players, 545 Eighth Avenue, New York NY 10018. **Tel** (212)244-2778. **LC** ML26; .A4535. **DD** 785.7/0025/7. ***Continues*** *Amateur Chamber Music Players. North American Directory, 0364-5975.*

US/0029-2753
**NORTH DAKOTA MUSIC EDUCATOR.**
**Added/Corp** North Dakota Music Educators Association. Vol. 1, (Oct. 1960)-. Periodical. English. Four times a year (Mar., May Sept., Dec.). $10.00. Caroyln Italiano, 4450 San Juan Drive, Fargo ND 58103-1092. **Tel** (701)258-0360. **ED** Mark A. Dimond. Index available. **Bk Rev. Ad Acc. Circ:** 800. ***Continues*** *N D M E A Newsletter.*
**Desc:** Official state music magazine of MENC in North Dakota.

US/0092-2021
**NORTH STAR.** (19??)-. Periodical. English. North Star, 270 Fort Wash. Avenue, New York NY 10032. **LC** ML1; .N78. **DD** 784.

CN/0830-8411
**NOTES - CANADIAN ASSOCIATION OF YOUTH ORCHESTRAS.** (NOTES.). [Notes - Can. Assoc. Youth Orch.]. **Added/Corp** Canadian Association of Youth Orchestras. (Jan. 1985)-. Periodical. English (French). ir. Free. Canadian Association of Youth Orchestras, Box 1020, Banff Alberta T0L 0C0 Canada. **Tel** (403)762-6278, telex ARTSBANFF 03-826657. **ED** Dolya Konoval. **DD** 785/.06/271. **Circ:** 3,500.
**Desc:** Designed as a forum for the exchange of information about youth orchestra development in Canada.

US
**NOTES FROM EASTMAN.** **Added/Corp** Eastman School of Music. (197?)-. Periodical. English. Four times a year. Free on request. Notes from Eastman, 12 de Paul, East Rochester NY 14445. **Tel** (716)275-3160. **LC** UNC. ***Continues*** *Eastman Notes, 0147-345X.*

US/0027-4380
**NOTES (PHILADELPHIA, PA.).** (NOTES.). [Notes]. **Main/Corp** Music Library Association. No. 1-15, (July 1934-Dec. 1942) Series 2 Vol. 1 (Dec. 1943)-. Periodical. English. qt. $65.00 (institutions), $60.00 (individuals). Music Library Association, PO Box 487, Canton MA 02021. **Tel** (617)828-8450, FAX (617)828-8915. **LC** ML27.U5; M695. **DD** 026.78. cum. index. available on microfilm and microfiche from University Microfilms International (UMI). Documents available from The Genuine Article, UMI Article Clearinghouse.
**Ind/Abst** Acad. Search (Jan. 1994-); Am. Bibliogr. Slavic East Europ. Stud.; Arts Humanit. Citation Index [Full Cov.]; Book Rev. Digest; Book Rev. Index; Humanit. Index; Humanit. Source (Jul. 1993-); INFO-SOUTH Abstr.; Libr. Inf. Sci. Abstr.; Libr. Lit.; Mag. Search; Music Artic. Guide; Music Index; Newsp. Period. Abstr. (1991-); Res. Alert [Full Cov.]; RILM Abstr.; Soc. Sci. Cit. Index [Select. Cov.].

US
**NOTES. SUPPLEMENT FOR MEMBERS.**
**Main/Corp** Music Library Association. (Sept. 1947)-. Periodical. English. Music Library Association, PO Box 487, Canton MA 02021. **Tel** (617)828-8450, FAX (617)828-8915. **LC** ML27.U5; M6952.

RU
**NOTNAIA LETOPIS.** **Added/Corp** Vsesoiuznaia Knizhnaia Palata. Soviet Union. Komitet po Pechati. Gosudarstvennyi Komitet Soveta Ministrov SSSR po Delam Izdatelstv, Poligrafii i Knizhnoi Torgovli. Gosudarstvennyi Komitet SSSR po Delam Izdatelstv, Poligrafii i Knizhnoi Torgovli. (1967)-. Periodical. Russian. mo. $129.95. Izdatelstvo Kniga, 50 Gorky Ulitsa, 125047 Moscow Russia. **(Subscription address:** East View Publications Inc., 3020 Harbor Lane North, Suite 110, Minneapolis MN 55447.**)** ***Continues*** *Letopis Muzykalnoi Literatury.*

CN/0828-6035
**NOUVELLES DE CAMMAC MONTREAL.** (NOUVELLES DE CAMMAC MONTREAL / MUSICIENS AMATEURS DU CANADA.). [Nouv. CAMMAC Montr.]. **Main/Corp** CAMMAC Montreal. **VFOAT** CAMMAC Montreal News. Vol. 15, No. 4, (April 1984)-. Periodical. English (French). CAMMAC Montreal, Apt 214/300 rue St-Georges, St-Lambert Quebec J4P 3P9 Canada. **DD** 780/.6/0714281. ***Continues*** *Cammac Montreal. CAMMAC Montreal Bulletin., 0708-7853.*

BU
**NOVA BULGARSKA MUZIKA / SUIUZ NA BULGARSKITE KOMPOZITORI.**
**Added/Corp** Suiuz na Bulgarskite Kompozitori. (19??)-. Bulgarian. Tsentur za Propaganda i Informatsiia pri Durzhavno Obedinenie Teatur i Muzika, Sofia Bulgaria. **LC** ML390; .N84.

RU
**NOVAIA SOVETSKAIA I INOSTRANNAIA LITERATURA PO KULTURA I ISKUSSTVU: MUZYKA.** **Added/Corp** Informtsentr po Problemam Kultury i Iskusstva (Soviet Union) Nauchnaia Muzykalnaia Biblioteka Im. S.I. Taneeva. Vsesoiuznaia Gosudarstvennaia Bilioteka Inostrannoi Literatury (Soviet Union). (19??)-. Periodical. Multiple languages (Russian and Multiple languages). mo. Gosudarstvennaia Biblioteka, Informatsionnyi Tsentr, Imeni V. I. Lenina, Prospekt Kalinina 3, 121019 Moscow Russia. **LC** ML5; .N83.

XR
**NOVINKY HUDEBNI LITERATURY.**
**Added/Corp** Prague. Mestska Knihovna. Hudebni Oddeleni. (19??)-. Multiple languages (Czech and Multiple languages). Mestska Knihovna, Nam Dr V Vack C 1, V Praze Czechoslovakia. **LC** ML113; .N73. **DD** 016.78.

UK
**NOW DIG THIS.** English. mo. £36.00 UK; £39.00 other. Now Dig This, 2 Ferndale Avenue, WALLSEND, Tyne and Wear, NE28 7NA England. **Tel** 011 44 91 2624006, FAX 011 44 91 2342496. **ED** Trevor Cajiao. **Bk Rev**, (Qty: 12). **Ad Acc, Adv Mgr Tel** (091) 2624006. **Pr Rev. Circ:** 2,500 (ctrl).
**Desc:** A publication concerned with the coverage of the rock and roll music of the 1950's.

CN/0821-3283
**NSMEA NOTES.** (NSMEA NOTES / NOVA SCOTIA MUSIC EDUCATORS' ASSOCIATION.). [NSMEA notes]. **Added/Corp** Nova Scotia Music Educators' Association. Nova Scotia Teachers Union. **VFOAT** N.S.M.E.A. Newsletter. **VAT** Nova Scotia Music Educators' Association Notes; Nova Scotia Music Educators' Association Newsletter. (1981)-. Periodical. English. ir. NSMEA Notes, c/o Terrance E Hill, Head of Department of Music, Breton Education, New Waterford Nova Scotia B1H 3T4 Canada. **DD** 780/.7/29716. ***Continues*** *Nova Scotia Music Educators' Association. Newsletter, 0382-0785.*

US/0146-9975
**NSOA BULLETIN.** [NSOA bull.]. **Main/Corp** National School Orchestra Association. **Added/Corp** National School Orchestra Association. Bulletin. **VAT** National School Orchestra Association Bulletin. (1960)-. Bulletin. English. qt. $12.00 (one year). National School Orchestra Assn, c/o Norman Mellion, 801 Louisville Ward, Starkville MS 39759. **Tel** (601)324-7569. **ED** Glenn Cooper. **LC** ML1; .N175. **DD** 785/.06/6. **Bk Rev. Circ:** 1,850 (ctrl).
**Desc:** Information of public school orchestra field including articles on pedagogy, music reviews, and professional information on orchestra events.
**Ind/Abst** Music Artic. Guide (?-?); Music Index (-19??).

US
**NUMERICAL LISTING OF SUPRAPHON LP RECORDS / SUPRAPHON.** **Main/Corp** Supraphon. (19??)-. English. Qualiton Imports Ltd, 39-28 Crescent Street, Long Island City NY 11101. **LC** ML156.S9; .N8. **DD** 016.7899/12.

IT/0029-6228
**NUOVA RIVISTA MUSICALE ITALIANA.**
[Nuova riv. music. ital.]. (19??)-. Periodical. Italian. Four times a year (Mar., June, Sept., Dec.). L60000 Italy; L85000 other. Nuova Eri Edizioni RAI, Via Arsenale 41, 10121 Turin Italy. **Tel** 011 39 11 8102238. **LC** ML5; .R8. **DD** 780/.94. Index available. cum. index. **Bk Rev. Ad Acc. Circ:** 4,000 (ctrl). Documents available from The Genuine Article. ***Continues*** *Rivista Musicale Italiana.*
**Desc:** Historical and musicological studies on music history, criticism, actuality, book music, record reviews, musical events, calendar and obituary.
**Ind/Abst** Arts Humanit. Citation Index [Full Cov.]; Curr. Contents Arts Humanit.; Music Index; Res. Alert [Full Cov.]; RILM Abstr.

SW/0029-6597
**NUTIDA MUSIK.** [Nutida musik]. **Added/Corp** Sveriges Radio Aktiebolag. Vol. 1, (1958)-. Periodical. Swedish. Four times a year (Mar., May, Sept., Nov.). Kr200.00. Nutida Musik, C/O S. Rikskonserter, PO Box 1225, S 111 82 Stockholm Sweden. **Tel** 011 46 8 7914600, FAX 011 46 8 213468. **ED** Bo Rydberg. **LC** ML5; .N96. **DD** 780/.904. Index available. **Bk Rev. Circ:** 2,000 (ctrl).
**Desc:** A new Swedish and international contemporary music is presented in all its different forms of expression. It contains portraits and interviews with composers and musicians, novelties and debates.
**Ind/Abst** Music Index; RILM Abstr.

GW/0170-8791
**NZ. NEUE ZEITSCHRIFT FUER MUSIK (1979).** (NEUE ZEITSCHRIFT FUER MUSIK : NZ.). [NZ, Neue Z. Musik]. **Added/Corp** Robert-Schumann-Gesellschaft (Frankfurt am Main, Germany). **VFOAT** NZ. Vol. 140 (Jan./Feb. 1979)-. Periodical. German. Six times a year (Jan., Mar., May, July, Sept., Nov.). DM59.90 Germany, DM74.73 other (surface mail); DM101.90 (airmail). B. Schotts Soehne Musikverlag, Carl Zeiss Str 1, Postfach 3640, D 55026 Mainz Germany. **Tel** 011 49 6131 505129, 011 49 6131 505122, FAX 011 49 6131 505115, telex 04187821. ***Continues*** *Melos/NZ, 0343-0138.*
**Ind/Abst** Curr. Contents Arts Humanit.; Music Index (-19??); RILM Abstr.

MX
**OAXACA CULTURAL: SU MUSICA.** (Jan. 1978)-. Spanish. mo. $20.00 each issue. Ediciones Culturales, Oaxaca Mexico. **LC** M1682; .O2. **DD** 780/.972/7.

GW/0933-4556
**OBOE, FAGOTT.** [Oboe Fagott]. (198?)-. Periodical. German. qt. DM30.00 Germany; DM45.00 other. Winfried Baumbach, Hildastrasse 5, W-6200 Wiesbaden F R Germany. **Tel** 011 49 611 308096. **UDC** 788.

GW
**OBOE, KLARINETTE, FAGOTT.** ***Title Change.*** (Nov. 1988)-(1992). Periodical. German (table of contents in English and French). qt. Verlag Karl Hofmann, Postfach 1360, D-73603 Schorndorf Germany. **Tel** 011 49 7181 4020. **LC** ML929; .K6. **DD** 788/.05. ***Continues*** *Klarinette.* ***Continued by*** *Rohrblatt, 0944-0291.*

CN/0823-8162
**OCSM NEWSLETTER.** [OCSM newsl.]. **Added/Corp** Organization of Canadian Symphony Musicians. **VAT** Organization of Canadian Symphony Musicians Newsletter (1980); O.C.S.M. Newsletter (1980). (1980)-. Newsletter. English (French; summaries and/or abstracts in French). ir. Free. OCSM Newsletter, c/o Murray Ginsberg, Apt 216/4000 Yonge Street, Toronto Ontario M4N 2N9 Canada. **DD** 785/.06/071. ctrl circ. ***Continues*** *Newsletter (Organization of Canadian Symphony Musicians), 0229-2211.*

AU
**OESTERRIECHISCHE BIBLIOGRAPHIE. SONDERHEFT - PRAKTISCHE MUSIK (AUSWAHL).** **Added/Corp** Hauptverband des Osterreichischen Buchhandels. Osterreichische Nationalbibliothek. **VFOAT** Sonderheft--Praktische Musik (Auswahl); Praktische Musik. (19??)-. German. an. Morawa & Company, Wollzeile 11, Postfach 159, 1011 Vienna Austria. **Tel** 011 43 1 51562404. **LC** ML120.A9; O5. **DD** 016.78/09436.

GW
**OFFENE TOR, DAS.** **VFOAT** Open Gate. Vol. 1 (1950/51)-. German. mo. DM20.00 Germany; DM30.00

other. Stadt Offenburg, Postfach 2450 Germany. **Tel** 07801/82271, FAX 07807/82582. Index available. **Circ:** 10,000.

US/0162-3540
**OFFICIAL MUSIC & RECORD DIRECTORY.** **VAT** Official Music and Record Directory. (19??)-. Directory. English. Kay-May Enterprises, 45 Oakland Street, Irvington NJ 07111. **LC** ML18; .O28. **DD** 338.4/7/780973.
**Desc:** Music trade.

US/8756-4955
**OFFICIAL PRICE GUIDE TO COLLECTIBLE RECORDS, THE.** [Off. price guide collect. rec.]. **Added/Corp** House of Collectibles. **VFOAT** Collectible Records; Records. 1st Ed. (1983)-. English. Random House Inc., 400 Hahn Road, Westminster MD 21157. **Tel** (800)726-0600, (800)733-3000, FAX (800)659-2436. **ED** T. E. Hudgeons. **LC** ML156.4; .P6O34. **DD** 789.9/1245/0750973.

US/0748-111X
**OFFICIAL PRICE GUIDE TO MUSIC COLLECTIBLES (ORLANDO, FLA. : 1984), THE.** (THE OFFICIAL PRICE GUIDE TO MUSIC COLLECTIBLES.). **Added/Corp** House of Collectibles. **VFOAT** Music Collectibles; Music. 3rd Ed. (1984)-. English. ir. Random House Inc., 400 Hahn Road, Westminster MD 21157. **Tel** (800)726-0600, (800)733-3000, FAX (800)659-2436. **LC** ML152; .O35. **DD** 780/.75/0973. ***Continues** Official Price Guide to Music Machines & Instruments.*

US/0747-7392
**OFFICIAL PRICE GUIDE TO RECORDS, THE.** [Off. price guide rec.]. **Added/Corp** House of Collectibles. **VFOAT** Records. 4th Ed. (1983)-. English. an. $20.00. Random House Inc., 400 Hahn Road, Westminster MD 21157. **Tel** (800)726-0600, (800)733-3000, FAX (800)659-2436. **LC** ML156.4.P6; O35. **DD** 789.9/1245/0750973. ***Continues** Official Price Guide to Collectible Rock Records.*

US/1044-3649
**OKLAHOMA BLUEGRASS GAZETTE.** (OKLAHOMA BLUEGRASS GAZETTE : OFFICIAL NEWSPAPER OF THE OKLAHOMA BLUEGRASS CLUB.). [Okla. bluegrass gaz.]. **Added/Corp** Oklahoma Bluegrass Club. (Sept. 1975)-. Periodical. English. mo. $8.00. Oklahoma Bluegrass Club, 8700 Hillview, Midwest City OK 73150. **DD** 781.

US/1044-1042
**OLD TIME COUNTRY.** ***Ceased.*** [Old time ctry.]. **Added/Corp** University of Mississippi. Center for the Study of Southern Culture. Jimmie Rodgers Memorial Association. Vol. 5, No. 1 (Spring 1988)-(Oct. 1994). Periodical. English. Four times a year. University of Mississippi, Sam Hall Room 206, University MS 38677. **Tel** (601)232-5742, FAX (601)232-7842. **ED** David Nelson. **DD** 781. **Bk Rev. Ad Acc. Circ:** 1,000. available on microfilm. ***Absorbed** Jimmie Rodgers Memorial Association Newsletter.*
**Desc:** Deals with traditional acoustic country music. Each issue includes artist profiles, song histories, feature articles, etc.

US/1040-3582
**OLD-TIME HERALD.** [Old-time her.]. **VFOAT** Old Time Herald. (1987)-. Periodical. English. Four times a year (Feb., May, Aug., Nov., (each volume consists of 8 issues covering 2 years)). $18.00 (individuals); $21.00 (institutions). Old Time Music Group Inc, 1812 House Avenue, Durham NC 27717. **Tel** (919)490-6578, FAX (919)490-6578. **(Subscription address:** Old Time Music Group Inc., PO Box 51812, Durham NC 27705.**)** **ED** Alice Gerrard. **DD** 780. Index available. cum. index. **Bk Rev. Ad Acc, Adv Mgr:** L. Copulsky.
**Desc:** Dedicated to the support and promotion of old-time music.
**Ind/Abst** Music Index.

●US/1061-9763
**OLDTIMERS (AUGUSTA, GA.).** (OLDTIMERS: HARRISBURG'S OLDTIME MUSIC EPISODICAL.). [Oldtimers]. Vol. 1, No. 1 (Feb. 1992)-. Periodical. English. qt. $10.00. Richard A. Hathaway, 1840 Ellis Street, Augusta GA 30904. **DD** 781.

US/0734-0281
**ON KEY.** No. 1 (Sept. 1982)-. Periodical. English. mo. $15.00. JDL Publications, PO Box 1213, Montclair NJ 07042. **Tel** (201)746-8967. **LC** MT745; .O5. **DD** 372.87.
**Ind/Abst** Music Artic. Guide (?-?).

US/0889-0536
**ONE, TWO, THREE, FOUR.** ***Suspended.*** [One two three four]. **VFOAT** 1234. No. 1 (Summer 1984)-?. Periodical. English. ir. $24.00 (individuals), $35.00 (institutions). Strong Sounding Thought Press Inc, 1854 West 84th Place, Los Angeles CA 90047-3001. **Tel** (310)750-5399. **ED** Brenda Johnson-Grau. **DD** 784. **Bk Rev. Pr Rev. Circ:** 300.

JA/0030-2600
**ONGAKU GEIJUTSU.** (1???)-. Periodical. English. Twelve times a year. $148.00. **(Subscription address:** Kyowa Book Company Inc., 1 38 Kanda Jinbocho Chiyoda-ku, Tokyo 101 Japan.**)**

JA
**ONGAKUGAKU. JOURNAL OF THE JAPANESE MUSICOLOGICAL SOCIETY.** **Main/Corp** Ongaku Gakkai. **Added/Corp** Ongaku Gakkai. Journal. **VFOAT** Journal of Japanese Musicological Society; Journal of Musicology. (1954)-. Periodical. Japanese (summaries and/or abstracts in English, French and German). Three times a year. **(Subscription address:** Maruzen Company Ltd., PO Box 5050, Import & Export Department, Tokyo 100 31 Japan.**)** **LC** ML5; .O5.
**Desc:** Organ paper of Tokyo Artistic University.
**Ind/Abst** RILM Abstr.

NE
**OOR.** Vol. 14, No. 6 (24 March 1984)-. Periodical. Dutch. Twenty-six times a year. Fl125.00. BV Uitgeversmaatschappij Bonaventura, PO Box 2158, 1000 CD Amsterdam Netherlands. **Tel** 011 31 20 6914111, 011 31 20 5674911. **LC** ML5; .M9894. **DD** 784.5/009492. ***Continues** Muziekkrant Oor.*

MX
**OP. CIT. (MEXICO CITY, MEXICO).** (OP. CIT.). **VAT** Opere Citato. Vol. 1, No. 1, (Jan. 6-19, 1981)-. Periodical. Spanish. bw. Yucalpeten No 2 Manzana 166, Col Padierna Tlalpan, Mexico 20 DF Mexico. **ED** Jamie A. Mendoza.

GW
**OPER.** (1966)-. German. Friedrich Verlag, Velber Bei, Hannover Germany. **LC** ML5; .O65. **DD** 782.105.

GW
**OPER HEUTE.** (1978)-. German. an. Henschelverlag Kunst & GES, Oranienburger Str. 67 68, D 10117 Berlin Germany. **LC** ML1699; .O63. **DD** 782.1/09/04. ***Continues** Musikbuhne.*

AU
**OPER UND BALLETT IM FILM.** **Added/Corp** Gesellschaft fuer Musiktheater. **VFOAT** Opera and Ballet on Film. (19??)-. Multiple languages (English, French and German). Gesellschaft fuer Musiktheater, Briete Gasse 12, A 1070 Vienna Austria. **LC** ML2075; .O6. **DD** 016.7821/073.

GW/0030-3518
**OPER UND KONZERT (MUNCHEN).** (OPER UND KONZERT.). [Oper Konzert]. (1963)-. Periodical. German. Four times a year. DM83.00. Industrie und Handelswerbung, Ungerer Str 19, App 601, W-80802 Munich Germany. **Tel** 011 49 89 391442. **ED** A. Hanuschik. **LC** ML5; .O652. **Bk Rev. Ad Acc. Circ:** 4,150.
**Desc:** Opera reviews of Germany and abroad, book and disk reviews, information of the opera-scene, interviews, etc.
**Ind/Abst** Music Index.

US/1062-7243
**OPERA AMERICA NEWSLINE.** **See** The Arts-Performing Arts.

US/0899-3645
**OPERA ANNUAL U.S.** [Opera annu. U. S.]. **VFOAT** Opera Annual US; Opera Annual. (1985)-. English. an (Apr.). $48.00. Jerome S. Ozer Publishing, 340 Tenafly Road, Englewood NJ 07631. **Tel** (201)567-7040, FAX (201)641-8062. **ED** Jerome S. Ozer. **LC** ML1699; .O6. **DD** 792.5/45/0973. Index available. **Pr Rev. Circ:** 800.
**Desc:** A review of opera performances in the US with programs and illustrations.

AT
**OPERA AUSTRALIA.** (19??)-. Periodical. English. mo. 38.00Aus$ Australia; 57.00Aus$ New Zealand, Papua New Guinea; 60.00Aus$ Fiji, Indonesia, Malaysia, Singapore; 64.00Aus$ China, Hong Kong, India, Japan; 69.00Aus$ US, Canada, Mexico; 75.00Aus$ Europe, Africa, South America. Pellinor Pty Ltd, PO Box R-361, Royal Exchange, New South Wales 2000 Australia. **Tel** 011 61 2 2472264, FAX 011 61 2 2472269. **ED** David E. Gyger. Index available. cum. index. **Bk Rev. Ad Acc. Circ:** 2,247.
**Desc:** Tabloid newspaper covering opera and music theatre in Australasia with some reference to international scene.

CN/0030-3577
**OPERA CANADA.** [Opera Can.]. **Added/Corp** Canadian Opera Association. Canadian Opera Guild. Vol. 4, No. 3 (1963)-. Periodical. English. qt (Published March, June, Sept., and Dec.). 20.00Can$ (individuals), 30.00Can$ (institutions) Canada; 28.00Can$ (individuals), 35.00Can$ (institutions) other. Opera Canada, 366 Adelaide Street East, Suite 433 Toronto, Ontario M5A 3X9 Canada. **Tel** (416)363-0395, FAX (416)363-0396. **ED** Jocelyn Laurence (Editor's phone: (416)538-0047). Index available. cum. index. **Bk Rev**, (Qty: varies). **Ad Acc, Adv Mgr:** Robert de Vrij, **Tel** 538-0395. **Circ:** 5,800. available on microfiche from University Microfilms International (UMI); available on microfilm; available on an online database from Canadian Business and Public Affairs Database. ***Continues** Opera in Canada, 0030-3577.*
**Desc:** National magazine devoted to opera and opera lovers. Has followed the development and growth of Canadian opera companies and professionals. Each issue brings interesting articles, special features, an international calendar of opera performances, reviews of books, records and compact discs, and on-the-spot reports of opera in Canada and around the world.
**Ind/Abst** Can. Index (?-?); Can. Period. Index; Music Index; RILM Abstr.

US/0889-9398
**OPERA COMPANION, THE.** ***Ceased.*** [Opera companion]. ( )-(Dec. 1990). Periodical. English. mo. The Opera Companion, 40 Museum Way, San Francisco CA 94114. **DD** 782.
**Ind/Abst** Music Artic. Guide (?-?).

US/0891-3757
**OPERA FANATIC.** (Spring 1986)-. Periodical. English. an. $20.00. Bel Canto Society Inc, 11 Riverside Drive, New York NY 10023. **Tel** (212)877-1595. **ED** Stefan Zucker. **DD** 782. **Bk Rev. Ad Acc. Circ:** 9,850.

FR
**OPERA INTERNATIONAL.** No. 1 (Oct. 1977)-. Periodical. French. Eleven times a year (monthly except August). 372.18F France; 450.00F other. Opera International, 122 Avenue des Champs Elysees, 75008 Paris France. **Tel** 011 33 1 42253162, telex 649609F. **LC** ML1699; .O633. **DD** 782.1/05. ***Continues** Opera.*

US/0030-3585
**OPERA JOURNAL, THE.** [Opera j.]. **Added/Corp** National Opera Association. Vol. 1 (Winter 1968)-. Academic Scholarly Publication. English. Four times a year (Mar., June, Sept., Dec.). $30.00 Comes with National Opera Association Membership, $45.00 individual, $60.00 institutions. National Opera Association Inc., Northwestern University, School of Music, 711 Elgin Road, Evanston IL 60208-1200. **Tel** (708)467-2422, FAX (708)491-5260. **ED** Carol Kimball (phone: (702)895-3735) (address: University of Nevada Las Vegas, Department of Music, 4505 Maryland Parkway, Las Vegas, NV 89154-5025). **LC** ML1; .O46. Index available. **Bk Rev. Ad Acc. Pr Rev. Circ:** 1,000 (ctrl). available on microfilm and microfiche from University Microfilms International (UMI).
**Desc:** A scholarly journal with about three articles in each issue. Some issues contain reviews of performances and books.
**Ind/Abst** Am. Bibliogr. Slavic East Europ. Stud.; Music Index.

UK/0030-3526
**OPERA (LONDON).** (OPERA.). [Opera]. Vol. 1 (Feb. 1950)-. Periodical. English. Thirteen times a year. £37.00 UK, £43.50 other (surface & airmail). Data Services Bureau, 2A Sopwith Cres Hurricane Way, Wickford Essex SS118YU England. **Tel** 011 44 268 766330, FAX 011 44 268 766229. **ED** Rodney Milnes. **LC** ML5; .O66. **DD** 782.1/05. Index available. **Bk Rev. Ad Acc. Circ:** 14,000. available on microfilm and microfiche from University Microfilms International (UMI). Documents available from The Genuine Article.
**Desc:** Reviews of books, magazines and opera performances worldwide; articles on opera and opera people; details of coming events.
**Ind/Abst** Arts Humanit. Citation Index [Full Cov.]; Br. Humanit. Index; Humanit. Index; Music Index; Res. Alert [Full Cov.]; RILM Abstr.

IT/1121-4112
**OPERA MILANO. 1987, L'.** (L'OPERA.). [Opera Milano, 1987]. (1987)-. Periodical. Multiple languages. mo. L90000.00 Italy; L110000.00 other. Opera SL Edizioni, Via Carlo Botta 4, 20135 Milan Italy. **Tel** 011 39 2 5460154, FAX 011 39 2 5460154. **UDC** 782. Index available. **Ad Acc, Adv Mgr:** Sabino Lenoci. ctrl circ.

US/0897-6554
**OPERA MONTHLY.** [Opera mon.]. Issue 1 (May 1988)-. Periodical. English. Six times a year. $12.00. That New Magazine Inc., 28 West 25th Street, 4th Floor, New York NY 10159. **Tel** (212)627-2120, FAX (212)727-9321. **(Subscription address:** PO Box 816, Madison Square Station, New York, NY 10159**)** **ED** Thomas Steele. **LC** ML1699; .O636. **DD** 782.1/05. **Bk Rev. Ad Acc. Circ:** 8,000 (ctrl).
**Desc:** Interviews and features on singers, directors, composers, and conductors of opera around the world. Also reviews of important operatic videos, books and compact discs.

US/8756-856X
**OPERA-MUSICAL THEATER.** (OPERA-MUSICAL THEATER / NATIONAL ENDOWMENT FOR THE ARTS.). [Opera-music. theater]. **Added/Corp** National Endowment for the Arts. **VFOAT** Opera, Musical Theater. (1980)-. English. an (May). Free. National Endowment for the Arts, 1100 Pennsylvania Avenue Northwest, Washington DC 20506. **Tel** (202)682-5400, (202)682-5435. **LC** ML1699; .O64. **DD** 782/.079. ***Continues** Opera Orchestra.*

US/0030-3607
**OPERA NEWS.** [Opera news]. **Added/Corp** Metropolitan Opera Guild. (Dec. 1936)-. Periodical. English. Seventeen times a year (Monthly May-November; biweekly Dec.-April). $30.00. Metropolitan Opera Guild Inc., 70 Lincoln Center Plaza, New York NY 10023. **Tel** (212)769-7080. **ED** Patrick O'Connor. **LC** ML1; .O482. **DD** 782. Index available. **Bk Rev. Ad Acc. Circ:** 120,000. available on microfilm and microfiche from University Microfilms International (UMI); available on an online database (file 647/Full-Text) from DIALOG. Documents available from The Genuine Article, UMI Article Clearinghouse, Magazine Collection.
**Desc:** Features singers and related aspects of the field; reviews from around the world and TV and radio operatic coverage.
**Ind/Abst** Acad. Abstr. Full Text Elite (Oct. 1984-); Acad. Abstr. (Oct. 1984-); Acad. Search (Oct. 1984-); Annu. Bibliogr. Engl. Lang. Lit.; Arts Humanit. Citation Index [Full Cov.]; Book Rev. Index; Curr. Contents Arts Humanit.; Expand. Acad. Index (1984-); Gen. Period. Index (1985-); Humanit. Index; Humanit. Source (Jan. 1988-); INFO-SOUTH Abstr.; Mag. Artic. Summar. Elite (Oct. 1984-); Mag. Artic. Summar. Select (Oct. 1984-); Mag. Artic. Summar. CD-ROM (Oct. 1984-); Mag. Index Plus (1989-); Mag. Index. Sel. (1986-); Mag. Search; Music Artic. Guide; Music Index; Newsp. Period. Abstr. (1988-); Read. Guide Abstr. Select Ed.; Read. Guide Period. Lit.; Res. Alert [Full Cov.]; RILM Abstr.; Romant. Move.; Mag. Index (1977-).

UK/0958-501X
**OPERA NOW.** English. Twelve times a year. Rhinegold Publishing Ltd, 239-241 Shaftesbury Avenue, London WC2H 8EH England. **Tel** 011 44 71 2405749, FAX 240 0897, telex 264675 GILDED.

US/0736-0053
**OPERA QUARTERLY, THE.** [Opera q.]. Vol. 1, No. 1 (Spring 1983)-. Periodical. English. qt. $72.00 (institutions), $36.00 (individuals) US; $84.00 (institutions), $48.00 (individuals) other. Duke University Press, PO Box 90660, Durham NC 27708-0660. **Tel** (919)687-3600, (919)688-5134 (orders), FAX (919)688-4574, telex 802829. **ED** William Ashbrook. **LC** ML1699; .O65. **DD** 782.1/05. **Bk Rev. Ad Acc. Circ:** 5,300 (ctrl). available on microfilm and microfiche from University Microfilms International (UMI). Documents available from The Genuine Article, UMI Article Clearinghouse.
**Desc:** Each issue contains five to eight original articles, written by noted authorities in both the performing and academic and worlds; in-depth reviews of 35-50 books, recordings and videotapes, featuring one comprehensive book review and one important recording (reviewed).
**Ind/Abst** Acad. Search (July 1993-); Am. Hist. Life (1989-); Arts Humanit. Citation Index [Full Cov.]; Curr. Contents Arts Humanit.; Expand. Acad. Index (1989-); Humanit. Index; Humanit. Source (Jul. 1993-); INFO-SOUTH Abstr.; Mag. Search; Music Artic. Guide; Music Index; Newsp. Period. Abstr. (1991-); Res. Alert [Full Cov.]; Romant. Move.

US/0146-6062
**OPERA REVIEW.** (June/July 1977)-. Periodical. English. bm. Washington Opera Inc., c/o Craver, Mathews, Smith and Company, 1501 Wilson Boulevard / Suite 1004, Arlington VA 22209. **LC** ML1; .O483. **DD** 782.1/05.

US
**OPERA SCENE.** (1990)-. Periodical. English. Six times a year. $12.00. Opera Scene, PO Box 492 Gracie Station, New York NY 10028. **Tel** (212)685-8118.

US/1056-6791
**OPERA SCENE (DURHAM, N.C.).** **See** The Arts-Performing Arts.

GW/0030-3690
**OPERNWELT.** [Opernwelt]. Vol. 1, (Oct. 1960)-. Periodical. German. Twelve times a year. DM203.40. Erhard Friedrich Verlag, Postfach 100150, D 30917 Seelze Germany. **Tel** 011 49 511 4000452. **(Subscription address:** Erhard Friedrich Verlag, Postfach 100150, W 3016 Seelze Germany, phone: 011 49 511 400040**)** **LC** ML5; .O672. **[CCC].**
**Ind/Abst** Music Index; RILM Abstr.

US/0882-178X
**OPTION (LOS ANGELES, CALIF.).** (OPTION.). [Option]. **Added/Corp** Sonic Options Network. **VFOAT** Option Magazine. (Mar./Apr. 1985)-. Periodical. English. Six times a year. $15.95 US; $21.00 Canada & Mexico; $36.00 Europe & South America; $42.00 Asia & Australia. Sonic Options Network, 1522 B Cloverfield Boulevard, Santa Monica CA 90404. **Tel** (310)449-0120, FAX (310)449-1153. **ED** Scott Becker and Richie Unterberger. **LC** ML1; .O488. **DD** 780/.5. **Bk Rev. Ad Acc, Adv Mgr:** Scott Becker. **Circ:** 15,000. ***Continues*** *Op (Olympia, Wash.), 0276-8747.*
**Desc:** Covers the broadest possible spectrum of 'alternative' music, including jazz, folk, experimental, blues, reggae, underground rock and more.

DK/0107-2919
**OPUS (COPENHAGEN, DENMARK).** (OPUS.). **Added/Corp** Dansk Musikpdagogisk Forening. Vol. 1, No. 1, (March 1981)-. Periodical. Danish. bm. kr110.00. Opus DMPF, St Kongensgade 65 B, 1264 Kbenhavn K Denmark. **LC** MT3.D4; .O7.

CN/0700-5318
**OPUS (LONDON, ONT.).** (OPUS.). **Added/Corp** University of Western Ontario. Faculty of Music. (1???)-. Periodical. English. Opus, c/o Faculty of Music, University of Western Ontario, London Ontario N6A 3K7 Canada. **DD** 780.7/29713/26.

XR/0231-7362
**OPUS MUSICUM.** [Opus music.]. **Added/Corp** Moravska Galerie v Brne. Svaz Ceskoslovenskych Skladatelu. Statni Filharmonie Brno. (1969)-. Periodical. Czech (Czech). mo. Statni Filharmonie Brno, 10 Radnicka, 60200 Brno Czech Republic. **(Subscription address:** Artia Pegas Press Ltd., Palac Metro Narodni Trida 25, 11210 Prague 1 Czech Republic.**)** **LC** ML5; .O674.
**Ind/Abst** Music Index; RILM Abstr.

CN/0225-6355
**OPUS (ST. JOHN'S).** (OPUS.). [Opus]. **Added/Corp** Newfoundland Teachers' Association. Music Council. Newfoundland Teachers' Association. Music Special Interest Council. (197?)-. Periodical. English. ir. Free to members. Music Council, Newfoundland Teachers Association, 3 Kenmount Road, St John's Newfoundland A1B 1W1 Canada. **DD** 780/.7. ***Continues*** *Newsletter (Newfoundland Teachers' Association. Music Council), 1196-1597.*

IT
**ORATORII, GLI.** (19??)-. Italian. ir. $125.00. **(Subscription address:** Broude Brothers Ltd., 141 White Oak Road, Williamstown, MA 01267**)**
**Desc:** First modern edition of the oratorios of Alessandro Stradella.

IS/0303-3937
**ORBIS MUSICAE.** (ORBIS MUSICAE; STUDIES IN MUSICOLOGY.). [Orbis music.]. **Added/Corp** Universitat Tel-Aviv. Hug le-Musikologyah. Universitat Tel-Aviv. Faculty of Visual and Performing Arts. **VFOAT** Assaph: Studies in Arts. Vol. 1 (Aug. 1971)-. Academic Scholarly Publication. English (French and German). ir. Tel Aviv University / Musicology, Department of Musicology, Ramat Aviv Israel. **Tel** 011 972 3 420332. **(Subscription address:** Theodore Front, Musical Literature Inc., 16122 Cohasset St, Van Nuys, CA 91406**)** **ED** Shai Burstyn. **Bk Rev. Circ:** 600 (ctrl).
**Desc:** Scholarly essays in the history and theory of music, ethnomusicology and musicology in the Middle East.
**Ind/Abst** Music Index.

GW/0030-4468
**ORCHESTER, DAS.** [Orchester]. **Added/Corp** Deutsche Orchestervereinigung. Vol. 1 (1953)-. Periodical. German. Eleven times a year (July/Aug. issues combined). DM102.00 Germany, DM117.90 other (surface mail); DM176.00 (airmail). B. Schotts Soehne Musikverlag, Carl Zeiss Str 1, Postfach 3640, D 55026 Mainz Germany. **Tel** 011 49 6131 505129, 011 49 6131 505122, FAX 011 49 6131 505115, telex 04187821. **ED** Rolf Dmennsold and Guenther Engelmann. **LC** ML5; .O68. **DD** 785/.05; 785. Index Available in last issue of each volume--loose separately paged. **Bk Rev. Ad Acc. Circ:** 14,500.
**Desc:** Includes articles on music history, record reviews, current musical events in theater, concerts and broadcast media, instrument building and the new generation of orchestras.
**Ind/Abst** Music Index.

CN/0380-1799
**ORCHESTRA CANADA.** **Added/Corp** Ontario Federation of Symphony Orchestras. Association of Canadian Orchestras. **VFOAT** Orchestres Canada. Vol. 1, (Oct. 1973)-. Periodical. English (French). Eight times a year (Apr./May & Sept./Oct. issues combines). 22.00Can$ North America; 32.00Can$ others. Association of Canadian Orchestras, 56 Esplanade, Suite 311, Toronto Ontario M5E 1A7 Canada. **Tel** (416)366-8834, FAX (416)366-1780. **ED** Jack Edds. **Ad Acc. Circ:** 3,000. ***Supersedes*** *Orchestra Letter, 0380-1780.*
**Desc:** Topics include government communications, fund raising ideas, workshops, conferences, summer programs and orchestra news.

CN/0824-3654
**ORCHESTRA RESOURCE GUIDE.** [Orch. resour. guide]. **Added/Corp** Ontario Federation of Symphony Orchestras. Ontario Arts Council. (19??)-. English. an. Ontario Federation of Symphony Orchestras, The Esplanade, Suite 311 56, Toronto Ontario M5E 1A7 Canada. **Tel** (416)366-8834. **DD** 785/.06/61.
**Desc:** A reference manual of orchestra management.

US
**OREGON MUSIC EDUCATOR.** **Added/Corp** Oregon Music Educators' Association. (Jan./Feb. 1954)-. Periodical. English. Three times a year. $5.00. Oregon Music Educator, 995 Morningside SE, Salem OR 97302. **LC** ML27.U5; O8. **DD** 780.7. ***Continues*** *Oregon Music Educators News.*
**Ind/Abst** Music Artic. Guide.

US/0095-2613
**ORFF ECHO, THE.** [Orff echo]. **Added/Corp** American Orff Schulwerk Association. (19??)-. English. qt (Jan., Mar., June, Sept.). $40.00. American Orff Schulwerk Association, PO Box 391089, Cleveland OH 44139. **Tel** (216)543-5366, FAX (216)543-4057. **ED** Tossi Aaron. **LC** ML1; .O57. **DD** 780/.7. Index available. **Bk Rev. Ad Acc. Circ:** 4,500 (ctrl).
**Desc:** Orff-Schulwerk, its use in music education, music therapy, church music and practical applications.
**Ind/Abst** Music Artic. Guide.

UK/0030-4883
**ORGAN (BOURNEMOUTH).** (THE ORGAN.). [Organ]. Vol. 1, (1921)-. Periodical. English. Four times a year (Jan., Apr., July, Oct.). £15.00 UK; £20.00 others. Musical Opinion Ltd, 2 Princes Road, St Leonards-on-Sea, East Sussex TN37 6EL England. **Tel** 44 424 715167, FAX 44 424 712214. **ED** Douglas Carrington. **Bk Rev. Ad Acc. Circ:** 700.
**Desc:** Classical music and pipe organ journal.
**Ind/Abst** Music Index; RILM Abstr.

US/0882-2085
**ORGAN HANDBOOK.** [Organ handb.]. **Main/Corp** Organ Historical Society. National Convention. **Added/Corp** American Guild of Organists. Regional Convention. 28th (1983)-. English. an. $25.00 North America; $30.00 other. Organ Historical Society Inc, PO Box 26811, Richmond VA 23261. **Tel** (804)353-9226. **ED** Alan M. Laufman. **LC** ML549.8; .O67. **DD** 786.6/05. **Circ:** 3,000. ***Continues*** *Organ Historical Society. Annual National Convention of the Organ Historical Society, 0148-3099.*
**Desc:** Annual convention program with historical sketches of organs, biographies of builders, and recital programs and other information.

NE/0920-3192
**ORGAN YEARBOOK, THE.** [Organ yearb.]. Vol. 1, (1970)-. English (French and German). an (Dec. of the following year). Uitgeverij Frits Knuf B V, PO Box 720, 4116 ZJ Buuren Netherlands. **Tel** 011 31 03449-1255, FAX 011 31 03449-2617. **ED** Peter Williams. **LC** ML5; .O875. **DD** 786.5/05. Index available. **Bk Rev. Ad Acc. Circ:** 1,000 (ctrl).
**Desc:** A journal for the players and historians of keyboard instruments.
**Ind/Abst** Music Index; RILM Abstr.

AU
**ORGANA AUSTRIACA.** (1976)-. German. ir. W. Braumuller Universitat Verlagsbuchhandlung, A-1092 Vienna Austria. **Tel** 011 43 0222 34 81 24. **ED** Rudolf Scholz. **LC** ML5; .O877.
**Desc:** Publication of the Institute for Organological Research and Documentation at the Academy of Music and Theater in Vienna.

US/0749-3533
**ORGANIST'S COMPANION, THE.** [Organist's companion]. (Dec. 1978)-. Periodical. English. bm. $21.95 (1 year), $40.95 (2 year) US; $24.95 (1 year), $44.95 (2 year) other. McAfee Music Corp., 501 East Third Street, PO Box 802, Dayton OH 45401. **Tel** (516)293-3400. **(Subscription address:** CPP/Belwin Inc., 15800 Northwest 48th Avenue, Miami FL 33014.**)** **ED** Wayne Leupold. **LC** M7; .O679. **DD** 786. **Ad Acc, Adv Mgr:** J. Atwood. **Circ:** 2,800.
**Desc:** Collection of organ music by the masters and contemporary composers, containing service music; edited for specific church seasons.

UK/0048-2161
**ORGANISTS' REVIEW.** [Organists' rev.]. **Added/Corp** Incorporated Association of Organists. (1913)-. Periodical. English. qt (Feb., May, Aug., Nov.). £14.00 UK, Isle of Man, Channel Islands; £16.50 other. Incorporated Association of Organists, 18 Duffins Close, Rochdale, Lancs 0L12 6XA United Kingdom. **Tel** 011 44 706 43575. **ED** Paul Hale (editor's address: 4 Vicar's Court, Southwell, Notts NG25 OHP). **Bk Rev. Ad Acc, Adv Mgr:** Marcus Knight. **Circ:** 5,500. available on microfilm from University Microfilms International (UMI).
**Desc:** Dedicated to organ and choir music, and related matters.
**Ind/Abst** Music Index; Philip. Sci. Technol. Abstr.

IT
**ORGANO, L'.** **Added/Corp** Gruppo Musicale "Girolamo Frescobaldi". (1960)-. Periodical. Italian. an. L75000 Italy; L85000 other. Patron Editore SRL, Via Badini 12, 40050 Quarto Inf. Bologna Italy. **Tel** 011 39 51 767003. **LC** ML5; .O8813. **Bk Rev. Ad Acc. Circ:** 1,000.
**Desc:** The review subject is about the technology and the history of the European organ tradition. Each volume has three sections: papers, notations, and discussions.

NE
**ORGEL (AMERSFOORT, NETHERLANDS).** (HET ORGEL.). **Added/Corp** Nederlandse Organistenvereniging. (19??)-. Periodical. Dutch. mo. Nederlandse Organistenvereniging, Juliettestraat 41, 3816 RB Amersfoort Netherlands. **Tel** 033-723814. **ED** Paul Peeters (editor's address: Bouriciusstraat 1, 6814 CS Arnhem Netherlands). **LC** ML549.8; .O7. **DD** 786.5/05. **Bk Rev. Ad Acc. Circ:** 2,100 (ctrl).
**Desc:** Information on organ building and restoration;

articles on organ-playing, repertoire and church music; musicological articles, reviews of music and books; news of new gramophone recordings.

FR/0985-3642
**ORGUE FRANCOPHONE : BULLETIN DE LIAISON DE LA FEDERATION FRANCOPHONE DES AMIS DE L'ORGUE, L'.** **Added/Corp** Federation Francophone des Amis de L'Orgue. No. 1 (Dec. 1986)-. Bulletin. French. sa. 200.00F France; $35.00 other. L'Orgue Francophone, Sarupt/St.-Leonard, F 88230 Fraize France. **Tel** 29.50.04.84. **LC** PAR. **Bk Rev**. **Ad Acc. Circ:** 1,000.

FR/0030-5170
**ORGUE (PARIS), L'.** (L'ORGUE.). [Orgue]. **Added/Corp** Association des Amis de l'Orgue. (1928)-. Periodical. French. Four times a year. 342.80F, 391.77F (combined with Cahiers et Memoires) France; 380.00F, 430.00F (combined with Cahiers et Memoires) Europe; 420.00F, 470.00F (combined with Cahiers et Memoires) other. Les Amis de l'Orgue, 3 Square Latour Maubourg, 75007 Paris France. **Tel** 011 33 1 47053930. **LC** ML5; .O883. cum. index. **Bk Rev**. **Ad Acc**. **Pr Rev**. ctrl circ.
**Ind/Abst** RILM Abstr.

SW/0030-5642
**ORKESTER JOURNALEN.**
[Orkesterjournalen]. **VFOAT** OJ. (1933)-. Periodical. Swedish. Eleven times a year (July/Aug. issues combined). Kr160.00 Sweden; Kr290.00 Scandinavia; Kr320.00 others. Orkester Journalen AB, Box 4204, 102 63 Stockholm Sweden. **Tel** 011 46 8 426464. **ED** Lars Westin and Bo Scherman. **LC** ML5; .O895. Index available. **Bk Rev**. **Ad Acc. Circ:** 3,000 (ctrl).
**Desc:** Live and recorded jazz articles, reviews, interviews and pictures. Covers both the Swedish and the international scenes.
**Ind/Abst** Music Index.

GW/0932-6111
**ORPHEUS BERLIN.** [Orpheus Berl.]. (1973)-. Periodical. German. Thirteen times a year. DM137.00 Germany; DM152.00 other. Neue Ges F Musikinfo GmbH, Livlaendische Str 27, D 10715 Berlin Germany. **Tel** 011 49 30 8533287. **UDC** 78/792. Index available.

AU/0029-9316
**OSTERREICHISCHE MUSIKZEITSCHRIFT.** [Oesterr. Musikz.]. Vol. 1, (Jan. 1946)-. Periodical. German. mo. S450.00 Austria; S570.00 other. Oesterreichische Musikzeitsch, Hegelgasse 13, A1010 Vienna Austria. **Tel** 011 43 15126869. **ED** Marion Diederichs Lafite and Elisabeth Lafite. **LC** ML5; .O1983. **DD** 780/.9436. Index available. **Ad Acc. Circ:** 3,000. Documents available from The Genuine Article.
**Ind/Abst** Arts Humanit. Citation Index [Full Cov.]; Music Index; Res. Alert [Full Cov.]; RILM Abstr.

US
**OVERTONES.** **Added/Corp** American Guild of English Handbell Ringers. (1955)-. Periodical. English. Six times a year. $45.00. AGEHR / American Guild of English Handbell Ringers, 1055 East Centerville Station, Dayton OH 45459. **Tel** (513)438-0085. **ED** Helen K. Flanagan. **LC** ML1; .O979.
**Desc:** Handbell ringing.

US/0030-7556
**OVERTURE (LOS ANGELES).**
(OVERTURE.). **Added/Corp** American Federation of Musicians. Musicians' Union, Local 47 (Los Angeles, Calif.) Musicians Mutual Protective Association (Los Angeles, Calif.). (1924)-. Periodical. English (Spanish). Twelve times a year. Free on request. Musicians Union, Local 47 AF Of M / 817 Vine St., Los Angeles CA 90038. **Tel** (213)462-2161 ext. 260. **ED** Serena Kay Williams. **LC** ML1; .O985. **DD** 331.881178. **Ad Acc. Circ:** 12,000 (ctrl).
**Desc:** News for members of Musicians' Union Local 47 of Los Angeles.

CN/0846-3530
**PACIFIC MUSIC.** ***Title Change.*** [Pac. music]. **Added/Corp** PMIA. (June 1991)-(Spring 1992). Periodical. English. sa. Pacific Music Industry Association, 504-402 West Pender Street, Vancouver British Columbia V6B 1T6 Canada. **DD** 782.42164/09711. ***Continued by** Pacific Music Newsletter, 1193-6681.*

US/0097-8035
**PAID MY DUES.** (1974)-. Periodical. English. qt. Calliope Publishing Inc, PO Box 6517, Chicago IL 60680. **Tel** (312)929-5592. **LC** ML1; .P1052. **DD** 780/.5.

CN/0319-8421
**PALMARES LA QUEBECOISE.** **Added/Corp** Association Quebecoise des Producteurs de Disques. (June 23, 1975)-. Periodical. French. bw. Association Quebecoise des Producteurs des Disques Inc, 7033 Route Trans-Canadienne, Ville St-Laurent Quebec H4T 1S2 Canada. **DD** 016.7899/12.

US/0889-7581
**PAN PIPES.** [Pan pipes]. **Added/Corp** Sigma Alpha Iota. **VFOAT** Sigma Alpha Iota Quarterly. Vol. 73, No. 1 (Fall 1980)-. Periodical. English. Four times a year (Jan., Mar., May, Nov.). $15.00. Sigma Alpha Iota / National Executive Office, 34 Wall Street, Suite 515, Asheville NC 28801. **Tel** (704)251-0606, FAX (704)251-0606. **ED** Margaret Maxwell (editor's address: 8466 North Lockwood Ridge Road, Suite 312, Sarasota, FL 34243). **LC** ML1; .P1055. **DD** 780/.5. **Bk Rev**, (Qty: varies). **Ad Acc, Adv Mgr:** M. Maxwell. **Circ:** 20,000 (ctrl). ***Continues** Pan Pipes of Sigma Alpha Iota, 0031-0611.*
**Ind/Abst** Music Artic. Guide (?-?); Music Index (?-19??).

FR
**PANORAMA MUSIQUES.** (19??)-. Periodical. French. bm. $12.64. Panorama Musiques, 20 Avenue Kleber, 75116 Paris France. **LC** ML5; .P119. **DD** 780/.5.

CN/0712-290X
**PAR SI PAR LA.** **Added/Corp** Alliance Chorale Alberta. Vol. 1, No. 1, (Spring 1980)-. Periodical. French. Three times a year. Free. Alliance Chorale Alberta, 102, 9942-82 Avenue, Edmonton Alberta T6E 1Y9 Canada. **DD** 784.9/6/0607123.

CN
**PARADES AND PAGEANTRY.** (19??)-. Newsletter. English. Twelve times a year. 25.00Can$. Ontario Drum Corps Associations, 122 King Street South, Suite 201, Waterloo Ontario N2J 1PS Canada. **Tel** (519)746-0042, FAX (519)746-4936. **ED** Betty Schmidt. **Ad Acc. Circ:** 200.
**Desc:** Newsletter containing information about drum corps.

HU/0133-2767
**PARLANDO.** [Parlando]. **Added/Corp** Muveszeti Szakszervezetek Szovetsege (Hungary). (19??)-. Periodical. Hungarian. mo. VI Gorkij Fasor 38, Budapest Hungary. **LC** ML5; .P15.
**Ind/Abst** RILM Abstr.

FR/0247-0357
**PAROLES ET MUSIQUE MENSUEL.**
***Suspended.*** [Paroles musique Mensuel]. **VFOAT** Paroles Musique (Mensuel); Paroles & Musique (Mensuel). (1980)-(1991). Periodical. French. mo (11 issues). Paroles & Musique, Herville 28270, Brezolles France. **Tel** 011 33 16 44033250. **UDC** 784.4.

CN/0712-5062
**PASSING TONES.** [Passing tones]. **Added/Corp** Winnipeg Jazz Society. (1973)-. Periodical. English. mo. Free. Passing Tones, c/o Winnipeg Jazz Society, 911 Valour Road, Winnipeg Manitoba R3G 3B6 Canada. **DD** 785.4/2/0971274.

RU
**PASSKAZY O'MUZYKE.** **Added/Corp** Pionerskii Muzykalnyi Klub. Vol. 1 (1968)-. Russian. Muzkya, Neglinnaia 14, Moscow Russia. **LC** ML63; .R28.

US/0363-6569
**PASTORAL MUSIC.** [Pastor. music]. **Added/Corp** National Association of Pastoral Musicians (U.S.). Vol. 1 (Oct./Nov. 1976)-. Periodical. English. bm. $27.00 (institutions), $24.00 (individuals). National Association of Pastoral Musicians, 225 Sheridan Street Northwest, Washington DC 20011. **Tel** (202)723-5800, FAX (202)723-2262. **ED** Dr. Gordon E. Truitt. **LC** ML1; .P1057. **DD** 783/.026/205. **Bk Rev**. **Ad Acc. Circ:** 7,200 (ctrl). available on microfilm and microfiche from University Microfilms International (UMI). ***Continues** Musart, 0027-3724.*
**Desc:** The journal of the National Association of Pastoral Musicians, an organization dedicated to fostering the art of musical liturgy.
**Ind/Abst** Index Book Rev. Relig.; Music Artic. Guide; Music Index; Abr. Cathol. Period. Lit. Index; Cathol. Period. Lit. Index.

US/0145-6636
**PASTORAL MUSIC NOTEBOOK.**
(PASTORAL MUSIC NOTEBOOK : A PUBLICATION OF THE NATIONAL ASSOCIATION OF PASTORAL MUSICIANS.). **Added/Corp** National Association of Pastoral Musicians (U.S.). **VFOAT** Pastoral Musicians Notebook. Vol. 1, No. 1 (May 1977)-. Newsletter. English. bm. $38.00 (membership) includes the journal Pastoral Music. National Association of Pastoral Musicians, 225 Sheridan Street Northwest, Washington DC 20011. **Tel** (202)723-5800, FAX (202)723-2262. **ED** Gordon E. Truitt. **LC** ML2999; .P37. **DD** 783/.02/605. **Bk Rev**, (Qty: 10). **Circ:** 8,500 (ctrl).
**Desc:** One central theme per issue dealing with music, the arts, and worship. Includes music and book reviews, calendar of events and job referrals.
**Ind/Abst** Music Artic. Guide (?-?).

●US/1057-039X
**PAUL MCCARTNEY MAGAZINE.** (1991)-. Periodical. English. mo. $32.70. V3 Publications, 53 Nahant Avenue, Winthrop MA 02152.

US/0360-2109
**PAUL'S RECORD MAGAZINE.** (19??)-. Periodical. English. mo. $5.00. P.E. Bezanker, 105 Preston Street, Hartford CT 06114. **LC** ML156.9; .P38. **DD** 789.9/12.

MX
**PAUTA.** **Added/Corp** Universidad Autonoma Metropolitana. Unidad Iztapalapa. Instituto Nacional de Bellas Artes (Mexico). Vol. 1, No. 1 (Jan./March 1982)-. Periodical. Spanish. Four times a year (Jan., Apr., July, Oct.). $35.00. Cenidim Inba, Liverpool 16 Col Juarez, 06600 Mexico DF Mexico. **Tel** 011 52 5 5925953. **LC** ML5; .P2. **DD** 780/.5. **Bk Rev**. **Circ:** 4,000.
**Desc:** Presents musical articles, critiques of musical events, classic and contemporary, as well as literary news.
**Ind/Abst** Music Index (?-19??).

US/1042-4350
**PEABODY ESSAYS IN MUSIC HISTORY.**
[Peabody essays music hist.]. **Added/Corp** Johns Hopkins University. Peabody Institute. Vol. 1 (Apr. 1986)-. English. ir. Johns Hopkins University Press, 2715 North Charles Street, Baltimore MD 21218-4319. **Tel** (410)516-6987, FAX (410)516-6968. **LC** ML160; .P3. **DD** 780/.9.

US/0272-9199
**PEDALPOINT.** [Pedalpoint]. **Added/Corp** Southern Baptist Convention. Sunday School Board. Vol. 1, No. 1 (Oct./Nov./Dec. 1981)-. Periodical. English. Four times a year. $29.20. Southern Baptist Convention, 901 Commerce, Suite 750, Nashville TN 37203. **Tel** (615)244-2355, FAX (615)742-8919. **(Subscription address:** Sunday School Board - Customer Service, 127 9th Avenue North, Nashville, TN 37234 USA; telephone: (800)458-2772) **LC** ML2999; .P42. **DD** 783.1.

US/1046-0292
**PENN SOUNDS.** (PENN SOUNDS : SERVING PENNSYLVANIA COMPOSERS.). [Penn sounds]. **Added/Corp** Delaware Valley Composers. Vol. 1, No. 1 (Fall 1989)-. Periodical. English. tq (Sept., Jan., May,). $10.00. Penn Sounds, 345 South 19th Street, Suite 3A, Philadelphia PA 19103. **Tel** (215)985-0963. **ED** Harry and Betty Hewitt. **LC** IN PROCESS. **DD** 780. Index available. cum. index. **Bk Rev**, (Qty: 3-4). **Ad Acc. Circ:** 200.
**Ind/Abst** Music Artic. Guide.

US
**PERCUSSION NEWS / P.A.S., PERCUSSIVE ARTS SOCIETY,.**
**Added/Corp** Percussive Arts Society. (19??)-. Periodical. English. bm. Percussion Arts Society, PO Box 25, Lawton OK 73502. **LC** ML1; .P4.

US/0553-6502
**PERCUSSIVE NOTES.** [Percuss. notes]. **Added/Corp** Percussive Arts Society. **VFOAT** Percussive Notes. Research Edition; Magazine: Percussive Notes. (1962)-. Periodical. English. Six times a year (Feb., Apr., June, Aug., Oct., Dec.). $40.00 Comes with a Percussive Arts Society Membership. Percussive Arts Society, PO Box 25, Lawton OK 73502. **Tel** (405)353-1455, FAX (405)353-1456. **ED** James Lambert. **LC** ML1; .P1087. **DD** 789/.01/05. **Bk Rev**. **Ad Acc. Circ:** 6,000 (ctrl). available on microfilm and microfiche from University Microfilms International (UMI). ***Continues** Percussive Notes. Research Edition.*
**Desc:** Includes information on symphonic jazz, drum set, corps, timpani, mallet-key board, publications, new products, recordings, personalities and research in the percussion field.
**Ind/Abst** Music Artic. Guide; Music Index.

UK
**PERFORM.** **Added/Corp** PERFORM (Organization). (19??)-. Periodical. English. ir. Free to Members. Perform, 10 Chapelfield Place Thorpe Hesley Rotherham, S Yorkshire S61 2TN United Kingdom. **LC** ML3650; .P47. **DD** 781.742/05.

US/0882-9314
**PERFORMANCE (FORT WORTH, TEX.).**
**See** The Arts-Performing Arts.

US/1044-1638
**PERFORMANCE PRACTICE REVIEW.**
[Perform. pract. rev.]. **Added/Corp** Claremont Graduate School. **VFOAT** PPR. Vol. 1, No. 1&2 (Spring-Fall 1988)-. Periodical. English. sa. $36.00 US; $39.00 other. Performance Practice Review, Claremont Graduate School, Music Department, Claremont CA 91711. **Tel** (909)621-8081. **ED** Roland Jackson. **LC** ML1; .P10876. **DD** 781.4/3/05. **Bk Rev**. **Ad Acc. Circ:** 500 (ctrl).
**Ind/Abst** Music Artic. Guide; Music Index.

US/0191-1554
**PERFORMING WOMAN, THE.** (June 1978)-. English. sa. $5.00. The Performing Woman, Subscription Department, Grand View Avenue, Hayward CA 94542. **LC** ML1; .P1088. **DD** 780/.25/73.

CN/0822-7594
**PERIODICA MUSICA.** ***Ceased.*** (PERIODICA MUSICA : NEWSLETTER OF THE REPERTOIRE INTERNATIONAL DE LA PRESSE MUSICALE DU XIXE SIECLE, CENTRES INTERNATIONAUX DE RECHERCHE SUR LA PRESSE MUSICALE.). [Period. musica]. **Added/Corp** University of British Columbia. Centre for Studies in Nineteenth-Century Music. **VAT** RIPMXIX Newsletter; Repertoire International de la Presse Musicale du XIXe Siecle Newsletter. Vol. 1, No. 1 (Spring 1983)-(1993). Newsletter. English (Italian). an.

Center for Studies in Nineteenth Century Music, University of Maryland, College of Arts and Humanities, 2101 Skinner Boulevard, College Park MD 20742. **Tel** (301)405-7780. **ED** H. Robert Cohen, Peter Loeffler and Zolton Roman. **DD** 780/.5. **Bk Rev. Circ:** 250.
**Desc:** Periodical dealing with research into the musical press of the nineteenth century.

US/0031-6016
**PERSPECTIVES OF NEW MUSIC. See** Computers-Computer Music.

BL
**PESQUISA BRASILEIRA DO DISCO. See** Sound Recordings and Systems.

BL
**PESQUISA NACIONAL DO SUCESSO.** (19??)-. Periodical. Portuguese. mo. Pesquisa Nacional do Sucesso, Sociedade Civil Ltda, rua Timbiras No 502 30 Andar c/307-310, Sao Paulo Brazil. **LC** ML5; .P26. **DD** 780/.42/05.

US/0364-5487
**PETERS NOTES. Added/Corp** C.F. Peters Corporation. (Fall/Winter 1976/77)-. Periodical. English. sa. CF Peters Corporation, 373 Park Avenue South, New York NY 10016. **Tel** (212)686-4147, FAX (212)689-9412. **LC** ML1; .P12. **DD** 780/.5. ***Supersedes** Peters Notes, 0364-5487.*

US
**PHILADELPHIA FOLKSONG SOCIETY NEWSLETTER.** (1994)-. Newsletter. English. Nine times a year (Oct.-June). Comes free with membership: $20.00 regular; $30.00 family; $15.00 student and senior citizen. Philadelphia Folksong Society, 7113 Emlen Street, Philadelphia PA 19119. **Tel** (215)247-1300, FAX (215)247-0293. **ED** Ed Halpern and Rosemarie Urbano. **Ad Acc.**
**Desc:** Covers local events and interests in the folk music scene of the Philadelphia area.

●US/1063-5734
**PHILOSOPHY OF MUSIC EDUCATION REVIEW.** [Philos. music educ. rev.]. **Added/Corp** Indiana University. School of Music. Vol. 1, No. 1 (Spring 1993)-. Periodical. English. sa. $18.00. Indiana University School of Music Education Department, Bloomington IN 47405. **Tel** (812)855-2051, FAX (812)855-4936. **ED** Estelle R. Jorgenson. **DD** 378. Index available. **Bk Rev**, (Qty: 2). **Pr Rev. Circ:** 100. ***Continues** Philosophy of Music Education Newsletter.*
**Desc:** Scholarly articles which reflect on the theoretical and practical issues of the teaching and learning of music in all its settings.

AU
**PHONO. See** Sound Recordings and Systems.

GW
**PHONO PRESS. See** Sound Recordings and Systems.

US
**PHONOLOG LIST-O-TAPES. VFOAT** List-O-Tapes. **VAT** Phonolog List of Tapes. Vol. 1 (June 1964)-. Periodical. English. qt. Trade Service Publications, Phonolog Publishing Division, 2720 Beverly Boulevard, Los Angeles CA 90057. **(Subscription address:** PO Box 3308, Terminal Annex, Los Angeles, CA 90051**) LC** ML157.32; .P5.
**Desc:** Audiotape listings.

US
**PHONOLOG REPORTER.** (1948)-. Periodical. English. wk. $402.00. Trade Service Corporation, PO Box 85007, San Diego CA 92138. **Tel** (619)457-5920, (800)854-1527, FAX (619)457-1320. **ED** Ronnie Duddley.
**Desc:** This 6,000 page loose-leaf publication contains over 1,000,000 current listings of pop titles, pop artists, pop albums, classical titles, classical artists and composers.

US/0279-6562
**PHONOLOG REPORTS.** (19??)-. English. wk. $592.00. Trade Service Corporation, PO Box 85007, San Diego CA 92138. **Tel** (619)457-5920, (800)854-1527, FAX (619)457-1320.

●US/1067-3881
**PIANO & KEYBOARD.** (PIANO & KEYBOARD : THE BIMONTHLY PIANO QUARTERLY.). [Piano keyboard]. **VFOAT** Piano and Keyboard. No. 160 (Jan./Feb. 1993)-. Periodical. English. Six times a year (Jan., Mar., May, July, Sept., Nov.). $36.00. String Letter Press Publishers, 412 Red Hill Avenue 15, San Anselmo CA 94960. **Tel** (415)485-6946, (800)827-6837. **(Subscription address:** String Letter Press Publishers Subscriber Services Desk, PO Box 767, San Anselmo, CA 94979**) LC** ML1; .P66. **DD** 786. ***Continues** Piano Quarterly, 0031-9554.*
**Ind/Abst** Arts Humanit. Citation Index [Full Cov.]; Music Artic. Guide.

US
**PIANO & ORGAN.** English. an. $79.00. Orion Research Corporation, 14555 North Scottsdale Road, Suite 330, Scottsdale AZ 85260. **Tel** (800)844-0759, (602)951-1114, FAX (602)951-1117.
**Desc:** Gives used pricing information on 6,056 products.

US/0031-9546
**PIANO GUILD NOTES. Added/Corp** National Guild of Piano Teachers. (1945)-. Periodical. English. Six times a year (Jan., Mar., May, July, Sept., Nov.). $15.00. National Guild of Piano Teachers, PO Box 1807, Austin TX 78767. **Tel** (512)478-5775. **ED** Barbara Stooksberry. **LC** UNC. **Bk Rev. Ad Acc. Circ:** 14,000 (ctrl). available on microfilm and microfiche from University Microfilms International (UMI).
**Desc:** Publishes works of piano teachers and their students. A common bond between organization teachers and their students.

GW/0173-8607
**PIANO-JAHRBUCH. VFOAT** Piano Jahrbuch. (1980)-. Periodical. German. an. Piano-Verlag, Kornerplatz 8, W-4350 Recklinghausen Germany. **ED** Rainer M. Klaas. **LC** ML650; .P5. **DD** 786.1/05.

UK/0267-7253
**PIANO JOURNAL / EUROPEAN PIANO TEACHERS ASSOCIATION. Added/Corp** European Piano Teachers Association. (19??)-. Periodical. English. tq (Feb., June, Oct.). £6.00. European Piano Teachers Association, 28 Emperor's Gate, London SW7 4HS England. **Tel** 011 44 071 373 7307. **(Subscription address:** EPTA UK Ltd., 7 Blenheim Close, London SW20 9BC England.**) ED** Carola Grindea and Malcolm Troup. **LC** ML5; .P385. **DD** 786.4/041/05. **Bk Rev. Ad Acc. Circ:** 3,250 (ctrl).
**Desc:** Topics relating to piano teaching and interpretation.

●US/1066-1530
**PIANO (PORT TOWNSEND, WASH.).** (PIANO.). [Piano]. Issue #1 (Jan. 1993)-. Periodical. English. mo. $10.00. First Person Publishing, 871 H Street, Port Townsend WA 98368. **DD** 784.

US/0031-9554
**PIANO QUARTERLY, THE.** ***Title Change.*** [Piano q.]. **VFOAT** Essential Piano Quarterly. No. 25 (Fall 1958)-(1992). Periodical. English. qt. String Letter Press Publishers, 412 Red Hill Avenue 15, San Anselmo CA 94960. **Tel** (415)485-6946, (800)827-6837. **ED** Robert Joseph Silverman. **LC** ML1; .P66. **DD** 786.1/05. Index available. **Bk Rev. Ad Acc. Circ:** 13,000 (ctrl). available on microfilm and microfiche from University Microfilms International (UMI). Documents available from The Genuine Article. ***Continues** Piano Quarterly Newsletter, 0735-7125.* ***Continued by** Piano & Keyboard, 1067-3881.*
**Desc:** Interviews with great pianists and composers. First publication of diaries of pianists of the past. Articles, reviews of new music, books, records and much more.
**Ind/Abst** Arts Humanit. Citation Index (19??-19??) [Full Cov.]; Music Artic. Guide (?-?); Music Index; Res. Alert [Full Cov.]; RILM Abstr.

US/1041-2492
**PIANO STYLIST & JAZZ WORKSHOP, THE.** ***Title Change.*** [Piano stylist jazz workshop]. **VFOAT** Piano Stylist and Jazz Workshop; Piano Stylist. (Oct./Nov. 1988)-(19??). English. bm. Shacor Inc, 352 Evelyn Street, Paramus NJ 07652. **LC** M20; .P375. **DD** 786. ***Continues** Jazz & Keyboard Workshop, 0893-4797.* ***Merged with** Keyboard Classics, 1044-3266 **to form** Keyboard Classics & Piano Stylist, 1069-4285.*

US/0031-9562
**PIANO TECHNICIAN'S JOURNAL.** [Piano tech. j.]. **Added/Corp** Piano Technicians' Guild. **VFOAT** Piano Technicians Journal. Vol. 1, (Jan. 1958)-. Periodical. English. Twelve times a year. $85.00 (one year); $155.00 (two years). The Piano Technicians Guild, 4510 Belleview, Suite 100, Kansas City MO 64111. **Tel** (816)753-7747. **ED** Larry Goldsmith. **LC** ML1; .P68. **DD** 786. **Bk Rev. Ad Acc. Circ:** 4,000. ***Formed by the union of** Tuner's Journal **and** Piano Technician.*
**Desc:** A technical journal for those interested in the tuning, maintenance and repairs or rebuilding of fine pianos.
**Ind/Abst** Music Index.

US/0733-429X
**PIERCE PIANO ATLAS.** [Pierce piano atlas]. **VFOAT** Piano Atlas. (196?)-. English. ir. Pierce Piano Atlas, 1880 Termino, Long Beach CA 90815. **Tel** (213)597-8245. **ED** Bob Pierce. cum. index. **Ad Acc.** ***Continues** Michel's Piano Atlas.*
**Desc:** Piano business worldwide - used by dealers, toners, manufacturers and libraries.

US/0710-3034
**PIG PAPER, THE.** [Pig. pap.]. **VFOAT** Schweine Zeitung; Cochonnerie. (1975)-. Periodical. English. ir. Pig Productions, PO Box 2700, Huntington Beach CA 92647. **DD** 780/.42/05.

RU
**PIONERSKII MUZYKALNYI KLUB.** Vol. 1 (1959)-. Periodical. Russian. Muzykalnoe Izdatelstvo, Moscow Russia. **LC** ML5; .P56.

UK
**PIPE BAND.** Periodical. English. bm. £4.50 UK; $20.00 (airmail) US; $25.00 (airmail) Canada. Royal Scottish Pipe Band Association, 45 Washington Street, Glasgow G3 9AZ Scotland. **Tel** 041-221-5414. **Ad Acc.** ctrl circ.

US/0882-214X
**PITCH PIPE, THE.** [Pitch pipe]. **Added/Corp** Sweet Adelines, Inc. (19??)-. Periodical. English. qt. $4.00. Sweet Adelines Inc., PO Box 470168, Tulsa OK 74147. **Tel** (918)622-1444, FAX (918)665-0894. **ED** Janet Weberling. **LC** ML1; .P69207. **DD** 781. **Ad Acc. Pr Rev. Circ:** 30,000.
**Desc:** Educational articles relating to the art form of four-part harmony, barbershop style; administrative activities at various levels of the organization; plus coverage of organizational events and activities; member-related news.

US
**PITTSBURGH MUSICIAN. Added/Corp** American Federation of Musicians. Local No. 60, Pittsburgh. (May 1949)-. Periodical. English. ir. Pittsburgh Musician Society, Local No 60 471, 709 Forbes Avenue, Pittsburgh PA 15219. **LC** ML1; .P6922.

●UK/0961-1371
**PLAINSONG AND MEDIEVAL MUSIC. Added/Corp** Plainsong and Mediaeval Music Society (Great Britain). **VFOAT** Plainsong and Medieval Music. **VAT** Plainsong and Medieval Music. Vol. 1, Pt. 1 (Apr. 1992)-. Academic Scholarly Publication. English. sa. $62.00 US, Canada and Mexico; £38.00 other. Cambridge University Press, The Edinburgh Building, Shaftesbury Road, Cambridge CB2 2RU United Kingdom. **Tel** 011 44 223 312393, FAX 011 44 223 325959. **(Subscription address:** Cambridge University Press / North America, 110 Midland Avenue, Port Chester NY 10573.**) ED** John Caldwell and Christopher Page. **LC** ML169.8; .P54. **DD** 780/.9/0205. ***Continues** Plainsong and Mediaeval Music Society (Great Britain). **and** Journal of the Plainsong & Mediaeval Music Society.*
**Desc:** Covers the whole field of plainchant and medieval music, monophonic and polyphonic, in both East and West, and will embrace the liturgical chant of any period.

US/1048-8243
**PLAY METER MAGAZINE. See** Recreation, Leisure-Games and Amusements.

CN/0048-4415
**PLAYBOARD. See** The Arts-Performing Arts.

US/0030-8102
**PMEA NEWS. Main/Corp** Pennsylvania Music Educators Association. **Added/Corp** Pennsylvania Music Educators Association. News. **VAT** Pennsylvania Music Educators Association News. (19??)-. Periodical. English. Four times a year (Jan. Mar., May, Nov.). $8.00. Pennsylvania Music Educators Association, 823 Old Westtown Road, West Chester PA 19382. **Tel** (610)436-9281, FAX (610)430-2169. **ED** Richard C. Merrell. **LC** UNC. **Bk Rev. Ad Acc.** Full Page (B&W) $275.00. Half Page (B&W) $200.00 (island); $175.00 (horizontal). **Circ:** 5,000 (ctrl). ***Continues** Bulletin of Research in Music Education.*
**Desc:** Music education in the schools of Pennsylvania.
**Ind/Abst** Music Artic. Guide.

US/0886-1897
**PODIUM (CHICAGO, ILL.), THE.** ***Ceased.*** (THE PODIUM : MAGAZINE OF THE FRITZ REINER SOCIETY.). [Podium]. Vol. 1, No. 1 (1976)-Ceased Vol. 1 (1989). Periodical. English. sa. 1525 Lunt Avenue, Chicago IL 60626. **LC** ML422.R38; P6. **DD** 785/.092/4.
**Ind/Abst** Music Index (-19??).

RU
**POEM I TANTSUEM.** (19??)-. Periodical. Russian. **LC** M1757.18; .P636.

SP
**POLIFONIA ARAGONESA. Added/Corp** Institucion "Fernando el Catolico." Seccion de Musica Antigua. (1984)-. Monographic series. Spanish. ir. Price varies per volume. Inst Fernando El Catolico, Plaza de Espana 2, Zaragoza 50004 Spain. **Tel** 011 34 76 229652, FAX 22.18.42.

PL/0032-2946
**POLISH MUSIC.** ***Suspended.*** (POLISH MUSIC. POLNISCHE MUSIK.). [Pol. music]. **VFOAT** Polnische Musik. (1966)- Suspended Vol. 27, No. 4 (1992). Periodical. English. qt. Price on Request. **(Subscription address:** ARS Polona, PO Box 1001, 00068 Warsaw Poland.**) LC** ML5; .P64. **DD** 780/.9438.
**Ind/Abst** Music Index; RILM Abstr.

US/0273-6454
**POLKA NEWS, THE. See** Dance.

US/1067-6945
**POLLSTAR (FRESNO, CALIF.).** (POLLSTAR.). [Pollstar]. (19??)-. Periodical. English. wk. $295.00 (one year), $495.00 (two year). Promoters On-Line Listings Inc., 4333 North West Avenue, Fresno

CA 93705. **Tel** (209)224-2631, (800)344-7383, FAX (209)224-2674. **LC** ML13; .P64. **DD** 338.4/778164/097305.

US/0556-5189
**POP DIRECTORY.** (Summer 1970)-. Directory. English. Daisy Publishing Inc., 3824 Smith Avenue, Everett WA 98201-4548. **LC** ML17; .P66. **DD** 780/.42/02573.

US
**POP MUSIC SURVEY.** English. wk (50 issues). $195.00. Pop Music Survey, 4818 Chevy Chase Drive, Chevy Chase MD 20815. **Tel** (301)951-1215.

CN/0713-8121
**POP ROCK.** [Pop rock]. (1971)-. Periodical. French. ir. Editions De L'Ultra Monde, 408 St. Gabriel, Montreal Quebec H2Y 2Z9. **DD** 784.5/4/005.

US/0886-442X
**POPULAR MUSIC : AN ANNOTATED INDEX OF AMERICAN POPULAR SONGS.** Vol. 7 (1970/1974)-. English. ir. $63.00. Gale Research Inc., 835 Penobscot Building, Detroit MI 48226. **Tel** (800)877-GALE, (313)961-2242, FAX (313)961-6083, telex TWX 810-221-7086. **ED** Bruce Pollock. **LC** ML120.U5; S5 Suppl. **DD** 784.5/00973. ***Continues*** *Popular Music.*
**Desc:** Each volume in the series contains indexes of lyricists and composers, important performances, and awards.

US/0300-7766
**POPULAR MUSIC AND SOCIETY.** [Pop. music soc.]. **Added/Corp** Bowling Green State University. Dept. of Sociology. Vol. 1 (Fall 1971)-. Periodical. English. qt. $30.00 (4 issues). Popular Press Journals Area, Bowling Green State University, Bowling Green OH 43403. **Tel** (419)372-7866, (419)372-7865. **ED** R. Serge Denisoff. **LC** ML1; .P69457. **DD** 780/.42. **Bk Rev. Ad Acc.** available on microfilm and microfiche from University Microfilms International (UMI). Documents available from The Genuine Article, UMI Article Clearinghouse.
**Ind/Abst** Am. Hist. Life (1989-); Arts Humanit. Citation Index [Full Cov.]; Book Rev. Index; Commun. Abstr.; Curr. Contents Arts Humanit.; Expand. Acad. Index (1992-); Music Index; Newsp. Period. Abstr. (1989-); Res. Alert [Full Cov.]; RILM Abstr.; Soc. Sci. Cit. Index [Select. Cov.].

UK/0261-1430
**POPULAR MUSIC (CAMBRIDGE UNIVERSITY PRESS).** (POPULAR MUSIC.). [Pop. music]. (1981)-. Academic Scholarly Publication. English. Three times a year. $99.00 US, Canada and Mexico; £56.00 other. Cambridge University Press, The Edinburgh Building, Shaftesbury Road, Cambridge CB2 2RU United Kingdom. **Tel** 011 44 223 312393, FAX 011 44 223 325959. **(Subscription address:** Cambridge University Press / North America, 110 Midland Avenue, Port Chester NY 10573.**) ED** Richard Middleton and David Horn. **LC** ML3469; .P66. **DD** 780/.42/05. **[CCC]. Bk Rev.** available on microfilm from University Microfilms International (UMI). Documents available from UMI Article Clearinghouse.
**Desc:** A multi-disciplinary journal which covers all aspects of popular music, broadly defined from Abba to zydeco, from broadside ballads to hip-hop. It presents the results of scholarly work in an accessible form, while at the same time responding to current events. Each issue contains substantial articles, shorter topical pieces, news, correspondence and review. Annotated bibliographies of recent publications in the field and discographies are published.
**Ind/Abst** Music Index; Newsp. Period. Abstr. (1992-).

US/0198-8158
**POPULAR MUSIC MAGAZINE.** [Pop. music mag.]. Vol. 7 (Dec./Jan. 1979)-. Periodical. English. bm. The Heritage Music Press, 501 East Third Street, PO Box 802, Dayton OH 45401. **LC** M1630.18; .P647. ***Formed by the union of*** *Best of Popular Music Magazine: Piano, Vocal, Guitar, 0198-814X* ***and*** *Best of Popular Music Magazine: Organ, Vocal, 0198-8131.*

US/0092-4741
**POPULAR MUSIC NEWS.** (19??)-. Periodical. English. Eastend Music & Art Workshop, 1842 West Avenue, Miami Beach FL 33139. **LC** ML1; .P69463. **DD** 780/.5.

UK
**POPULAR MUSIC PERIODICALS INDEX (LONDON, ENGLAND).** (POPULAR MUSIC PERIODICALS INDEX : POMPI.). **Added/Corp** British Library. National Sound Archive. **VFOAT** POMPI. No. 1-2 (Sept. 1986)-. English. an. British Library National Sound Archive, 29 Exhibition Road, London SW7 2A5 England. **Tel** 0937 546060, FAX 0937 546333, telex 557381. **(Subscription address:** British Library Publications Sales Unit, Boston Spa, Wetherby West Yorkshire LS23 7BQ England**) ED** Chris Clark and Andy Linehan. **LC** ML3470; .P683. **DD** 016.78164/05. Index available. **Ad Acc. Circ:** 500.
**Desc:** Devoted exclusively to the indexing of articles relevant to research into pop and jazz, from performers, fashion and popular culture to technological developments, films and the media.

CN/0705-8780
**POURQUOI CHANTER?. Added/Corp** Association Action-Chanson du Quebec. Vol. 1 (Mar 1977)-. Periodical. French. ir. Association Action-Chanson du Quebec, C P 205 Succursale G, Montreal Quebec H2W 2M9 Canada. **DD** 780/.5.

CN/0822-7500
**PRAIRIE SOUNDS.** (PRAIRIE SOUNDS : NEWSLETTER OF THE CANADIAN MUSIC CENTRE, PRAIRIE REGION.). [Prairie sounds]. **Added/Corp** Canadian Music Centre. Prairie Region. Vol. 1, No. 2 (Oct. 1980)-. Newsletter. English. Three times a year. Free on request. Canadian Music Centre, Prairie Region, 911 Library Tower, 2500 University Drive Northwest, Calgary Alberta T2N 1N4 Canada. **Tel** (403)220-7403, FAX (403)282-6837. **DD** 780/.9712. ***Continues*** *Canadian Music Centre (Newsletter), 0822-7497.*

CN/0381-890X
**PRELUDE (CALGARY).** (PRELUDE.). **Added/Corp** Calgary Philharmonic Society. (Fall 1975)-. Periodical. English. Three times a year. Philharmonic Society, 210, 320-9th Avenue SW, Calgary Alta T2P 1K6 Canada. **DD** 785.06/2/71233. ***Supersedes*** *Bravura, 0381-8918.*

NE
**PRELUDIUM. Added/Corp** Nederlandse Vereniging "Concertgebouw-Vrienden.". **VFOAT** Concertgebouw-Nieuws. (19??)-. Periodical. Dutch. ir. WYT Uitgeefgrouep, Postbus 6438, 3000 AG Rotterdam Netherlands. **Tel** 011 31 10 4762566, 4255944. **LC** ML5; .P706.

SZ
**PREMIERS PRIX ... DES CONCOURS MEMBRES DE LA FEDERATION, LES. Main/Corp** World Federation of International Music Competitions. **VFOAT** Premiers Prix; First Prize-Winners; First Prize Winners ... of the Competitions Members of the Federation; First Prize-Winners ... of the Competitions Members of the Federation. (198?)-. English (French). Federation Mondiale des Concours Internationaux de Musique, 104 rue de Carouge, CH-1205 Geneve Switzerland. **Tel** (4122)213620, FAX (4122)7811418. **LC** ML385; .F33. **DD** 780/.92/2; B. ***Continues*** *Federation of International Music Competitions.; First Prizes.*

CN/0228-0868
**PRENONS NOTRE MUSIQUE EN MAIN!. Added/Corp** Syndicat de la Musique du Quebec. (Feb. 1979)-. Periodical. French. mo. Free to members. Syndicat de la Musique du Quebec, 938 Est, Rachel Montreal Quebec H2J 2J1, Canada. **DD** 780/.6/0714.

US/0079-5259
**PRINCETON STUDIES IN MUSIC.** No. 1, (1964)-. Monographic series. English. ir. Price varies per volume. Princeton University Press, 41 William Street, Princeton NJ 08540. **Tel** (609)258-4900.

US/0363-5244
**PRO MUSICA MAGAZINE.** (Jan./Feb. 1976)-. Periodical. English. bm. Pro Musica Magazine, 861 Arlington Boulevard, El Cerrito CA 94530. **LC** ML1; .P747. **DD** 780/.902. ***Supersedes*** *Westcoast Early Music Magazine.*

US/0361-9559
**PRO MUSICA SANA. Added/Corp** Miklos Rozsa Society. (Spring 1972)-. Periodical. English (English). qt. Miklos Rozsa Society, 303 East 8th Street, Apartment 12, Bloomington IN 47401. **LC** ML1; .P754. **DD** 782.8/5/05.

RU
**PROBLEMY MUZYKALNOI NAUKI.** Vol. 1 (1972)-. Russian. 1.97rub. **LC** MT6; .P935.

US/0066-0701
**PROCEEDINGS OF THE ANNUAL CONFERENCE - AMERICAN SOCIETY OF UNIVERSITY COMPOSERS.** (PROCEEDINGS OF THE ANNUAL CONFERENCE.). **Main/Corp** American Society of University Composers. **Added/Corp** Summer Institute in Compositional Studies. (19??)-. Proceedings. English. an. American Society of University Composers, PO Box 296, Old Chelsea Station, New York NY 10011-9998. **Tel** (718)899-2605. **LC** ML1; .A7256. **DD** 780. available on microfilm and microfiche from University Microfilms International (UMI).
**Ind/Abst** Music Artic. Guide.

US/0190-6615
**PROCEEDINGS OF THE ANNUAL MEETING - NATIONAL ASSOCIATION OF SCHOOLS OF MUSIC.** (PROCEEDINGS OF THE ... ANNUAL MEETING.). [Proc. annu. meet. - Natl. Assoc. Sch. Music]. **Main/Corp** National Association of Schools of Music. Meeting. (1960)-. Proceedings. English. an. $20.00. National Association of Schools of Music, 11250 Roger Bacon Drive, Suite 21, Reston VA 22090. **Tel** (703)437-0700. **ED** David Bading. **LC** ML27.U5; N25 subser. **DD** 780. **Circ:** 1,500. ***Continues*** *National Association of Schools of Music. Meeting. Annual Meeting.*
**Desc:** Proceedings includes papers, addresses and committee reports presented at annual meetings.
**Ind/Abst** Music Index.

AT/0314-528X
**PROCEEDINGS OF THE ... NATIONAL CONFERENCE OF THE AUSTRALIAN MUSIC THERAPY ASSOCIATION HELD IN ..., THE.** ***Title Change.*** **Main/Corp** Australian Music Therapy Association. National Conference. (1975)-(19??). Proceedings. English. an. Australian Music Therapy Association, 18 Collins Street, Box Hill, Victoria 3128 Australia. **Tel** 011 61 3 8173129. **NLM** W1; AU642. ***Continued by*** *Australian Journal of Music Therapy.*

●US/1068-5391
**PRODUCER REPORT.** [Prod. rep.]. (23 Feb. 1993)-. Periodical. English. bw. $50.00. Mojave Music Inc, 115 South Topanga Canyon, Suite 114, Topanga CA 90290. **Tel** (310)455-0888, FAX (310)455-0894. **ED** Pat Neslon. **DD** 780.

CN/0829-8998
**PROFESSIONAL MUSICIAN (DOWNSVIEW).** (PROFESSIONAL MUSICIAN.). [Prof. music.]. (May 1985)-. Periodical. English. ir. KRM Communications Inc., 2817 Keele Street, Toronto ONT M3M 2G6 Canada. **Tel** (416)635-5530. **DD** 780/.42/0971.

US
**PROGRAM / CHICAGO SYMPHONY ORCHESTRA. Main/Corp** Chicago Symphony Orchestra. 58th Season, 1st Program (Oct. 7 & 8, 1948)-. English. an. $85.00. Chicago Symphony Orchestra, 220 South Michigan Avenue, Chicago IL 60604. **Tel** (312)435-8122, telex 25 3866. Index available. cum. index. **Circ:** 30 (ctrl). ***Continues*** *Chicago Symphony Orchestra. Program Notes, 0740-6290.*

US
**PROGRESS REPORTS IN ETHNOMUSICOLOGY. Added/Corp** University of Maryland, Baltimore County. SEMPOD Laboratory. Vol. 1, No. 1 (1984)-. Periodical. English. Progress Reports, Department of Music, University of Maryland, 5401 Wilkins Avenue, Baltimore County, Baltimore MD 21228. **LC** ML3797.6; .P76. **DD** 780/.89.

US/0738-8861
**PROGRESSIVE PLATTER.** (197?)-. Periodical. English. Ten times a year. $15.00. Progressive Platter, PO Box 638, Boston MA 02215. **Tel** (617)247-1144. Index available ($1.00).

US/0737-0776
**PROPAGANDA (NEW HYDE PARK, N.Y.).** (PROPAGANDA.). Issue 1 (Winter 1982)-. Periodical. English. $20.00. Propaganda, PO Box 296, New Hyde Park NY 11040. **Tel** (516)248-1795. **ED** Fred Berger. **LC** ML3533.8; .P76. **DD** 784.5/4. **Ad Acc. Circ:** 4,500.
**Desc:** Punk avant-garde underground music, fashion, personalities, clubs, movies. Lots of top quality unusual photos, and fast lively text. Large format glossy paper, and slick layout.

UK/0309-0884
**PRS YEARBOOK. Added/Corp** Performing Right Society. **VAT** Performing Right Society Yearbook. (1988/89)-. English. an. Performing Right Society, 29/33 Berners Street, London W1P 4AA England. **Tel** 01 580 5544, FAX 01 631 4138, telex 892678. **LC** ML27.G7; P45. **DD** 380.1/4578/060421. ***Continues*** *Performing Right Yearbook.*

AG/0033-2542
**PSALLITE.** [Psallite]. (19??)-. Periodical. Spanish. qt. $2.00. Parroquia San Roque, Calle 40 N 577, La Plata Argentina. **LC** ML5; .P8. **DD** 783/.05.
**Ind/Abst** RILM Abstr.

US/0031-9627
**PSG NEWSLETTER.** (PSG NEWSLETTER / PICK'N & SING'N' GATHER'N.). **Added/Corp** Pick'n & Sing'n' Gather'n, Inc. **VFOAT** P.S.G. Newsletter. (1967)-. Newsletter. English. ir. $8.00. Carol Moseley, 24 Brookline Avenue, Albany NY 12203.

UK/0305-7356
**PSYCHOLOGY OF MUSIC.** [Psychol. music]. **Added/Corp** Society for Research in Psychology of Music and Music Education. Vol. 1 (Jan. 1973)-. Periodical. English. sa. £25.00. SRPMME - Society for Research in Psychology and Music Education, 38 Westfield Road Horbury, West Yorkshire WF4 6EA England. **LC** ML5; .P82. **DD** 781/.15.
**Ind/Abst** Br. Educ. Index; Commun. Abstr. (?-?); Music Index; Psychol. Abstr. (1976-); PsycINFO; PsycLit; RILM Abstr.

US/0275-3987
**PSYCHOMUSICOLOGY.** [Psychomusicology]. Vol. 1, No. 1 (Spring 1981)-. Periodical. English. Twice a year. $21.00. Illinois State University / Music, Department of Music, Normal IL 61761. **Tel** (309)438-5447. **ED** Dr.

David B. Williams. **LC** ML3830; .P93. **DD** 781/.11/05. **Bk Rev. Circ:** 400 (ctrl).
**Ind/Abst** Music Index; Psychol. Abstr. (1981-); PsycINFO (1990-); PsycLit.

SP
**PUBLICACIONES. Main/Corp** Barcelona. Biblioteca Central. Seccion de Musica. (1920)-. Periodical. Spanish. ir. Free. Biblioteca Cataluna, Department of Music, Carrer del Carme 47, 08001 Barcelona Spain. **Tel** 011 34 3 3170778.

US
**PUBLICATIONS. Main/Corp** North Carolina. University. Library. Hanes Foundation for the Study of the Origin and Development of the Book. English. ir. $28.00 US; $32.00 other. University of North Carolina Press, 116 South Boundary Street, PO Box 2288, Chapel Hill NC 27515-2288. **Tel** (919)966-3561, FAX (919)966-3829. **ED** Irene and Sherwin Sloan. **Bk Rev. Ad Acc. Circ:** 4,500.
**Desc:** Presents 6-10 original articles in each issue on all aspects of opera. Reviews books, recordings and videotapes. Back issues are available.

FR
**PUBLICATIONS DU CENTRE D'ETUDES DE LA MUSIQUE FRANCAISE AUX XVIIIE & XIXE SIECLES. Added/Corp** Centre D'Etudes de la Musique Francaise aux XVIIIe & XIXe Siecles. Vol. 1, (1981)-. Monographic series. French. ir. Price varies per volume. **LC** UNC.

US/1047-4528
**PUNCTURE (SAN FRANCISCO, CALIF.).** (PUNCTURE : A MAGAZINE OF MUSIC AND THE ARTS.). [Puncture]. (1982)-. Periodical. English. qt. $10.00 US; $20.00 other. Puncture Publications, 4020 SE Grant Street, Portland OR 97214. **Tel** (503)236-8270. **DD** 705.

US
**PURCHASER'S GUIDE TO THE MUSIC INDUSTRIES, THE.** (1???)-. English. an. Music Trades Corporation, PO Box 432, 80 West Street, Englewood NJ 07631. **Tel** (201)871-1965. ***Continues*** *Piano and Organ Purchaser's Guide.*

UK/0955-4955
**Q (LONDON).** (Q : THE MODERN GUIDE TO MUSIC AND MORE.). [Q]. **VFOAT** Modern Guide to Music and More. (1986)-. Periodical. English. Twelve times a year. £24.00 UK, £44.50 others (surface mail); £47.50 Europe, £84.00 Southeast Asia & Mexico & Oceania, £76.50 others (airmail). EMAP Metro, 20 Orange Street, London WC2H 7ED England. **Tel** 011 44 71 4361515. **(Subscription address:** Tower Publishing, Tower House, Sovereign Park Market Harborough, Leicester LE16 9EF England.**) LC** ML3533.8; .Q2. **DD** 781.66/05.

●US/1060-8931
**QRM (WASHINGTON, D.C.).** (QRM: THE SOUTHEAST'S ALTERNATIVE MUSIC REVIEW.). [QRM]. Vol. 1, No. 1 (Jan./Feb. 1992)-. Periodical. English. bm. $10.00. Wickham & Associates, 1700 K Street NW, Suite 1202, Washington DC 20006. **DD** 781. ***Continues*** *In Your Ear.*

IT/0394-4395
**QUADERNI DELLA RIVISTA ITALIANA DI MUSICOLOGIA / A CURA DELLA SOCIETA ITALIANA DI MUSICOLOGIA. Added/Corp** Societa Italiana di Musicologia. **VFOAT** Rivista Italiana di Musicologia. Quaderni; RIDM. Qd. (1966)-. Monographic series. Italian. ir. Price varies per volume. Casa Editrice Leo S. Olschki, Viuzzo del Pozzetto, Casella Postale 66, 50126 Florence Italy. **Tel** 011 39 55 6530684, FAX 011 39 55 6530214.

IT/0065-0714
**QUADERNI DELL'ACCADEMIA CHIGIANA. Main/Corp** Siena. Accademia Musicale Chigiana. **Added/Corp** Accademia Musicale Chigiana. (1942)-. Monographic series. Italian. ir. Price varies per volume. Accademia Musicale Chigiana - Siena, Via di Citta 89, 53100 Siena Italy. **Tel** 011 39 55 635068. **LC** ML5; .S5.

IT
**QUADERNI VIVALDIANI. Added/Corp** Istituto Italiano Antonio Vivaldi. (1980)-. Monographic series. Italian. ir. Price varies per volume. Casa Editrice Leo S. Olschki, Viuzzo del Pozzetto, Casella Postale 66, 50126 Florence Italy. **Tel** 011 39 55 6530684, FAX 011 39 55 6530214. **LC** ML410.V82; Q3. **DD** 780/.92/4.

US/0360-4071
**QUALITY ROCK READER.** (Sept. 1975)-. Periodical. English. qt. $5.00. K. Seebacher, Government Printing Office / Box 1201, New York NY 10001. **LC** ML1; .Q34. **DD** 784.

CN/0711-0170
**QUARTER NOTES (TORONTO).** (QUARTER NOTES / Y.M.C.). [Quart. notes]. **Added/Corp** Youth and Music Canada. **VFOAT** Youth and Music. Vol. 1, No. 1 (Summer 1981)-. Periodical. English. ir. Free. Youth and Music Canada, 57 Adelaide Street East, Toronto Ontario M5C 1K6. **DD** 780/.6/071.

US/1066-0437
**QUARTERLY JOURNAL OF MUSIC TEACHING AND LEARNING, THE.** [Q. j. music teach. learn.]. **Added/Corp** University of Northern Colorado. School of Music. **VFOAT** Journal of Music Teaching and Learning; Quarterly. Vol. 2, No. 3 (Fall 1991)-. Periodical. English. Four times a year (Mar., June, Sept., Dec.). $45.00 institutions; $26.00 individuals. University of Northern Colorado School of Music, School of Music, Greeley CO 80639. **Tel** (303)351-2254, FAX (303)351-1923. **ED** Manny Brad and Porce Pitkin. **LC** ML1; .Q37. **DD** 780. **Bk Rev**, (Qty: 2-3). **Circ:** 400. ***Continues*** *Quarterly (University of Northern Colorado. School of Music), 1066-0429.*
**Ind/Abst** Music Artic. Guide.

AT/0155-5367
**QUARTERLY MAGAZINE / MUSIC TEACHERS' ASSOCIATION OF NEW SOUTH WALES. Added/Corp** Music Teachers' Association of New South Wales. (Feb. 1983)-. Periodical. English. qt.

AT/0810-7211
**QUARTERLY MAGAZINE - MUSIC TEACHERS' ASSOCIATION OF NEW SOUTH WALES.** [Q. mag. - Music Teach. Assoc. N.S.W.]. (1983)-. Periodical. English. qt. **DD** 780.5. ***Continues*** *Quarterly Magazine - Federation of Australian Music Teachers Associations, 0155-5367.*
**Ind/Abst** Aust. Educ. Index.

CN/0226-7187
**QUEBEC ROCK.** [Que. rock]. (April 1977)-. Periodical. French. Twelve times a year. $21.67. Quebec Rock, 3510 St. Laurent/Suite 404, Montreal Quebec H2X 2V2 Canada. **Tel** (514)845-3707. **DD** 780/.42/05.
**Ind/Abst** Point Repere (1985-1986).

GW/0079-905X
**QUELLENKATALOGE ZUR MUSIKGESCHICHTE.** (1966)-. Monographic series. German. ir. Price varies per volume. CF Peters Corporation, 373 Park Avenue South, New York NY 10016. **Tel** (212)686-4147, FAX (212)689-9412. **ED** Richard Schaal. **Circ:** 10.
**Desc:** A series of source catalogues for music history, cloth-bound.

CN/0826-4996
**QUIRES.** (QUIRES / ALBERTA CHORAL FEDERATION.). [Quires]. **Added/Corp** Alberta Choral Federation. Vol. 11, No. 1 (March 1, 1983)-. Periodical. English. ir. Alberta Choral Federation, 609 McLeod Building 10136 100th Street, Edmonton Alta T5J 0P1 Canada. **Tel** (403)428-1096. **DD** 784.9/6. ***Continues*** *Newsletter (Alberta Choral Federation), 0821-7076.*

US
**R AND B MAGAZINE.** Vol. 1, No. 4 & 5 (July/Oct. 1970)-. Periodical. English. bm. $3.00. Hauptverband der Osterreichischen Sozialversicherungstrager, Kundmanngasse 21, 1030 Vienna Austria. **LC** ML1; .R15. **DD** 784/.05. ***Formed by the union of*** *R and B Collector* ***and*** *Quartette.*

UK/0033-684X
**R.C.M. MAGAZINE.** (THE R.C.M. MAGAZINE.). [R.C.M. mag.]. **Added/Corp** Royal College of Music (Great Britain). Union. **VFOAT** RCM Magazine; Royal College of Music Magazine. (1904)-. Periodical. English. Three times a year. £10.00. Royal College of Music Society, Prince Consort Road, London 2BS SW7 England. **Tel** 11 44 71 5893643 Ext. 13. **ED** Angela Escott; Telephone: 11 44 71 5893643 Ext. 4328. **LC** ML5; .R13. **Bk Rev. Ad Acc. Circ:** 7,500.
**Ind/Abst** Music Index (-19??).

CN/0033-7064
**R P M WEEKLY.** Vol. 9, (Mar. 2, 1968)-. Periodical. English. Fifty times a year. 195.33Can$ (one year), 350.47Can$ (two years) 1st class mail Canada; 149.53Can$ (one year) 2nd class mail US & Canada; 209.00Can$ US, 300.00Can$ other (1st class mail) others. R P M Music Weekly, 6 Brentcliff Road, Toronto Ontario M4G 3Y2 Canada. **Tel** (416)425-0257. **ED** Walter Girealis. **Bk Rev. Ad Acc.** ***Continues*** *R P M Music Weekly, 0315-6001.*
**Desc:** Music industry news, singles, LP charts and classified ads section.

CN/0229-9844
**RACKETT.** (THE RACKETT : A JOURNAL OF EARLY MUSIC NEWS AND INFORMATION.). [Rackett]. **Added/Corp** Towne Waytes Society. Vol. 1, No. 1 (Summer 1978)-. Periodical. English. qt. Rackett, c/o Towne Waytes Society, 1921 West 4th Avenue, Vancouver British Columbia V6J 1M7 Canada. **DD** 780/.903/1.

US
**RAD! : REVIEW AND DISCUSSION OF ROCK & ROLL CULTURE.** English. Twelve times a year. $25.00 (institutions), $18.00 (individuals). Conspiracy M.E.D.I.A., 826 Old Charlotte Pike East, Franklin TN 37064. **Tel** (615)791-1624. **ED** Keith A. Gordon. **Bk Rev**, (Qty: 12). **Ad Acc. Circ:** 3,000. available on an online database from Internet.
**Desc:** Review and discussion of rock and roll music and related culture.

UK
**RADIO & MUSIC.** English. EMAP Readerlink, Audit House, 260 Field End Road, Ruislip Middlesex HA4 9LT England. **Tel** 011 44 081 868 4499, FAX 011 44 081 429 3117.

CN/0822-7926
**RADIO ATIVITE INC.** [Radio act. inc.]. (1982)-. Periodical. French (English). Forty-eight times a year (published weekly except 2 weeks in July and 2 weeks in Dec.). 350.00Can$ Canada and US; 500.00Can$ other. Radio Activite Inc., 3981 Boulevard St-Laurent, Suite 715, Montreal Quebec H2W 1Y5 Canada. **Tel** (514)849-1236, FAX (514)486-5805. **ED** Luc Martel. **DD** 016.7899/1245. **Ad Acc. Circ:** 400 (ctrl).
**Desc:** Music industrial tip sheet. Includes music reviews and charts.

US
**RAG: THE ALL MUSIC MAGAZINE.** (1977)-. English. mo. $15.00 one year, $25.00 two year. RAG, PO Box 24308, Ft. Ldle FL 33307. **Tel** (305)463-5799. **ED** Dino Fedele.

US/0090-4570
**RAG TIMES.** [Rag times]. **Added/Corp** Maple Leaf Club. (1967)-. Periodical. English. Six times a year. $17.00 US; $20.00 other. Maple Leaf Club, 15522 Ricky Court, Grass Valley CA 95949. **ED** Richard Zimmerman. **LC** ML1; .R233. **DD** 785.4/2. **Bk Rev. Ad Acc. Circ:** 550 (ctrl).
**Desc:** The latest news about ragtime - past and present.

CN/0033-8672
**RAGTIMER, THE.** [Ragtimer]. **Added/Corp** Ragtime Society. (Apr. 1967)-. Periodical. English. Six times a year. The Ragtime Society, PO Box 520, Station A, Weston Ontario M9N 3N3 Canada. **LC** ML5; .R144. **DD** 786.2/1. **Circ:** 450 (ctrl). ***Continues*** *Ragtime Society Dedicated to the Preservation of Classic Ragtime.*
**Desc:** Dedicated to the preservation of classical ragtime.
**Ind/Abst** Music Index (-19??).

US/1056-4705
**RAP MASTERS.** [Rap masters]. **VFOAT** Word Up! Presents Rap Masters. (1988)-. Periodical. English. Twelve times a year. $29.00. Word Up! Publications, 63 Grand Avenue, Suite 230, River Edge NJ 07661. **Tel** (201)487-6124. **DD** 781.

●US/1063-1283
**RAPPAGES (BEVERLY HILLS, CALIF.).** (RAPPAGES.). [Rappages]. **VFOAT** Rap Pages. Vol. 1, No. 1 (Oct. 1991)-. Periodical. English. Nine times a year. $19.95. LFP Inc., 9171 Wilshire Boulevard/Suite 300, Beverly Hills CA 90210. **Tel** (310)858-7100, FAX (310)274-7985. **(Subscription address:** Kable Publishers Aide, 308 East Hitt Street, Subscription Department, Mt. Morris IL 61054-1473.**) LC** ML3531; .R36. **DD** 782.42164.
**Desc:** Cover rap music and rap musicians.

IT/0033-9806
**RASSEGNA MUSICALE CURCI.** [Rass. music. Curci]. (1956)-. Periodical. Italian. Three times a year (Jan., May, Sept.). Free. Edizioni Curci Srl, Galleria del Corso 4, 20122 Milan Italy. **Tel** 011 39 2 794746, FAX 011 39 2 7601 4504, telex 332.638. **ED** Giuseppe Gramitto Ricci. Index available. **Bk Rev. Circ:** 21,000 (ctrl). ***Continues*** *Rassegna Musicale Delle Edizioni Curci.*
**Desc:** Information and culture of classical music.
**Ind/Abst** Music Index; RILM Abstr.

●UK/0965-190X
**RCD. ROCK COMPACT DISC MAGAZINE.** [RCD, Rock compact disc mag.]. **VFOAT** Rock Compact Disc Magazine. (1992)-. Periodical. English. mo. £70.00 for six issues. Northern & Shell Publications, PO Box 381, Mill Harbour, London E14 9TW England. **Tel** 011 44 71 987 5090, FAX 011 44 71 987 2160. **ED** Paul Trynka. **DD** 781.6605. **Ad Acc, Adv Mgr:** Elspeth Thomson. **Circ:** 60,000.

US/0147-0078
**RECENT RESEARCHES IN AMERICAN MUSIC.** Vol. 1, (1977)-. Monographic series. English. ir. Price varies per volume. A-R Editions Inc., 801 Deming Way, Madison WI 53717. **Tel** (800)736-0700, (608)836-9000. **LC** UNC.

US/0484-0828
**RECENT RESEARCHES IN THE MUSIC OF THE BAROQUE ERA.** Vol. 1, (1964)-. Monographic series. English. ir. Price varies per volume. A-R Editions Inc., 801 Deming Way, Madison WI 53717. **Tel** (800)736-0700, (608)836-9000. **LC** M2; .R238.

US/0147-0086
**RECENT RESEARCHES IN THE MUSIC OF THE CLASSICAL ERA.** **VFOAT** Recent Researches in the Music of the Pre-Classical, Classical, and Early Romantic Eras. (1975)-. Monographic series. English. ir. Price varies per volume. A-R Editions Inc., 801 Deming Way, Madison WI 53717. **Tel** (800)736-0700, (608)836-9000. **LC** M2; .R2381.

US/0362-3572
**RECENT RESEARCHES IN THE MUSIC OF THE MIDDLE AGES AND EARLY RENAISSANCE.** Vol. 1, (1975)-. English. ir. A-R Editions Inc., 801 Deming Way, Madison WI 53717. **Tel** (800)736-0700, (608)836-9000. **LC** M2; .R2383. **DD** 780.9.

US/0193-5364
**RECENT RESEARCHES IN THE MUSIC OF THE NINETEENTH AND EARLY TWENTIETH CENTURIES.** (1979)-. Monographic series. English. qt. Price varies per volume. A-R Editions Inc., 801 Deming Way, Madison WI 53717. **Tel** (800)736-0700, (608)836-9000. **LC** M2; .R23834. **DD** 780/.904.

US/0486-123X
**RECENT RESEARCHES IN THE MUSIC OF THE RENAISSANCE.** Vol. 1, (1964)-. Monographic series. English. ir. Price varies per volume. A-R Editions Inc., 801 Deming Way, Madison WI 53717. **Tel** (800)736-0700, (608)836-9000. **LC** M2; .R2384.

CN/0844-5923
**RECHERCHE EN EDUCATION MUSICALE AU QUEBEC.** **See** Education.

UK
**RECORD COLLECTOR.** English. mo. $110.00. Parker Publishing, 43 45 St. Mary's Road, London W5 5RQ England. **Tel** 011 44 81 5791082.

UK/0034-155X
**RECORD COLLECTOR, THE.** (19??)-. Periodical. English. Four times a year (Mar., June, Sep., Dec.). £20.00 UK; £27.00 other. Record Collector, 111 Longshots Close Broomfield, Cheslmsford ESX CM1 5DU England. **Tel** 44 245 441661. **LC** ML156.9; .R35. Index available (bound in Dec. issue). **Bk Rev. Ad Acc.**
**Desc:** Each issue contains at least 10 articles on collectable popular artists complete with discographies and current values, plus thousands of records for sale. Extensive reviews cover latest CD's and Re - issues, videos, book reviews and fanzines.

US/8755-6154
**RECORD COLLECTOR'S MONTHLY.** **See** Hobbies.

US/0034-1592
**RECORD RESEARCH.** [Rec. res.]. Vol. 1, (Feb. 1955)-. Periodical. English. ir. Len Kunstadt Record Research, 65 Grand Avenue, Brooklyn NY 11205. **Tel** (718)857-7003. **LC** ML1; .R293. **DD** 789.9/12/05.
**Ind/Abst** Music Index.

US/1071-4170
**RECORD ROUNDUP (NORTH CAMBRIDGE, MASS.).** (RECORD ROUNDUP.). [Rec. roundup]. (19??)-. Periodical. English. bm. Free upon request. Round Up Records, PO BOX 154, North Cambridge MA 02140. **Tel** (617)661-6308. **ED** Mark Cardigan. **DD** 780. **Bk Rev**, (Qty: 5-20). **Ad Acc, Adv Mgr:** Leland Stern. **Circ:** 40,000.

CN/0712-8290
**RECORD (TORONTO).** (THE RECORD.). [Record]. (1981)-. Periodical. English. Forty-eight times a year. 225.00Can$ Canada; $325.00 other. David Farnell and Associates, PO Box 201 Station M, Toronto Ontario M6S 4T3 Canada. **Tel** (416)533-9417, FAX (416)533-0367. **ED** Lee Silversidos. **DD** 380.1/45789912. **Ad Acc. Circ:** 1,600 (ctrl). available on an online database.
**Desc:** Used for recording industry. Contains charts, statistics, business news, recording releases and reviews.

US/0034-1622
**RECORD WORLD.** **See** Sound Recordings and Systems.

UK
**RECORDER, THE.** **VFOAT** RMM. Vol. 8, No. 1 (Mar. 1984)-. Periodical. English. Four times a year. £10.00. Peacock Press, Scout Bottom Farm, Mytholmroyed Hebden Bridge, West Yorkshire HX7 5JS England. **Tel** 44 422 882751, FAX 44 422 886157. **ED** Andrew Mayes (editor's address: 52 Woking Road, Cheadle Hulme, Cheadle, Cheshire SK8 6NU England; editor's phone: 44 61 485 6477). **Bk Rev. Ad Acc, Adv Mgr:** J. Burbidge. ***Continues** Recorder & Music Magazine.*

UK/0306-4409
**RECORDER MAGAZINE, THE.** ***Ceased.*** Vol. 10, No. 1 (Mar. 1990)-(1993). Periodical. English. qt. Magnamusic Distributors Inc, Sharon CT 06069. **Tel** (203)364-5431. **LC** ML5; .R189. **DD** 788.3/6/05. **Bk Rev. Ad Acc. Circ:** 150 (ctrl). ***Continues** Recorder & Music, 0306-4409.*
**Desc:** Articles concerning musical performances and courses offered in England, interviews with well-known performers and composers.
**Ind/Abst** Music Index.

CN/0704-7231
**RECORDER (TORONTO).** ***Ceased.*** (THE RECORDER.). [Recorder]. **Added/Corp** Ontario Music Educators' Association. (Sept. 1958)-Ceased (1990). Periodical. English. qt. Ontario Music Educators Association, 7 Riviera Drive, Scarborough Ontario M1N 1J9 Canada. **Tel** (416)681-2436. **ED** Kenneth Peglar. **DD** 780.7. **Bk Rev. Ad Acc. Circ:** 900 (ctrl).
**Desc:** Journal of the Ontario music educators association. Theory, practice, and commentary on music in Ontario schools.

US/0362-0476
**REFORMED LITURGY AND MUSIC.** **See** Religion and Theology.

US/1065-3023
**REGGAE REPORT.** [Reggae rep.]. (198?)-. Periodical. English. mo. $23.43 Florida residents (includes sales tax); $22.00 US; $38.00 Canada; $42.00 other. Reggae Report, PO Box 2722, Hallandale FL 33008. **Tel** (305)933-1178, FAX (305)933-1077. **ED** M. Peggy Quattro. **LC** IN PROCESS. **DD** 782. **Bk Rev**, (Qty: 2). **Ad Acc. Circ:** 15,000.
**Desc:** Covers reggae music and musicians.
**Ind/Abst** Music Index.

US
**REGGAE YEARBOOK.** English. an. $4.00. Reggae Report, PO Box 2722, Hallandale FL 33008. **Tel** (305)933-1178, FAX (305)933-1077.

US/1044-1034
**REJOICE! (UNIVERSITY, MISS.).** ***Ceased.*** (REJOICE!). [Rejoice!]. **Added/Corp** University of Mississippi. Center for the Study of Southern Culture. (Winter 1987)-(19??). Periodical. English. Four times a year. University of Mississippi, Sam Hall Room 206, University MS 38677. **Tel** (601)232-5742, FAX (601)232-7842. **ED** W. K. McNeil. **LC** ML3186.8; .R44. **DD** 782.25/05. **Ad Acc, Adv Mgr:** Brett Bonner. **Circ:** 1,000. available on microfilm.
**Desc:** Features articles and columns on all types of gospel music from contemporary to traditional - focuses on the gospel sounds of today as well as the rich heritage of gospel's past.

CN/1182-3976
**RELEASE (VANCOUVER).** (RELEASE.). [Release]. **VFOAT** Release Magazine. (July/Aug./Sept. 1990)-. Periodical. English. Six times a year (Jan., Mar., May, July, Sept., Nov.). 10.00Can$ (one year); 18.00Can$ (two years). Royal Magazine Group, 404 BNA Drive, Building 200, Suite 600, Nashville TN 37217. **Tel** (615)872-8080, FAX (615)889-0437. **ED** Roberta Croteau. **DD** 781.71. **Ad Acc, Adv Mgr:** Frank Chimento, **Tel** (615)872-8080 ext. 2159. **Circ:** 170,000. ***Continues** Gospel Music Today Magazine., 0836-4540.*

US/0146-3489
**RELIX.** (1974)-. Periodical. English. Six times a year (Feb., Apr., June, Aug., Oct., Dec.). $27.00. Relix Magazine, PO Box 94, Brooklyn NY 11229. **Tel** (718)258-0009, FAX (718)692-4345. **ED** Toni A. Brown and William Ruhlmann. **Bk Rev. Ad Acc. Circ:** 60,000. ***Continues** Dead Relix.*
**Desc:** Psychedelic/classic rock music magazine specializing in Bay area rock. Grateful Dead are frequently the main focus, with additional focus on new bands, reggae, rock and blues.

US/0889-8790
**REMEMBER THAT SONG.** [Rememb. song]. (1981)-. Periodical. English. Twelve times a year. Remember That Song, 5821 North 67th Avenue, Suite 103 306, Glendale AZ 85301. **Tel** (602)435-2136. **ED** Lois Cordrey. **LC** ML3469; .R45. **DD** 781.64/075. **Bk Rev. Ad Acc. Circ:** 300.
**Desc:** An illustrated newsletter for sheet music collectors.

GW/0196-7037
**RENAISSANCE MANUSCRIPT STUDIES.** [Renaiss. manuscr. stud.]. **Added/Corp** American Institute of Musicology. (1979)-. Monographic series. English. ir. Price varies per volume. Haenssler Verlag, Postfach 1220, D-73762 Neuhausen Germany. **Tel** 011 49 07158 1770, telex 715816 HAENSR. **LC** ML169.8; .R46. **DD** 780/.903/1. **Bk Rev. Ad Acc.**

US
**RENASCENCE.** **See** Literature.

CN/1184-6097
**RENDEZ-VOUS (QUEBEC).** (RENDEZ-VOUS ..). [Rendez-vous]. **Added/Corp** Publications Ye Ye. Publications SARMA. **VFOAT** Rendez Vous. (1991)-. Periodical. French. Les Publications Ye Ye/Sarma, CP 1051, Succursale Haute-Ville, Quebec G1R 4V2 Canada. **DD** 781.63/09714/05.

GW
**REPERTOIRE INTERNATIONAL DES SOURCES MUSICALES. INTERNATIONALES QUELLENLEXICON DER MUSIK. SER. B: SERIE METHODIQUE.** **Added/Corp** International Musicological Society. International Association of Music Libraries. **VFOAT** International Inventory of Musical Scores; Internationales Quellenlexicon der Musik. Vol. 1 (1960)-. Monographic series. French (German and English). ir. Price varies per volume. Baerenreiter-Verlag, KGA Verlagssvc PF 100329, D 34003 Kassel Germany. **Tel** 011 49 561 31050, telex 99504. **(Subscription address:** Broude Brothers Ltd., 141 White Oaks Road, Williamstown, MA 01267 USA; telephone: (413)458-8132) Index available. cum. index. **Circ:** 1,000.
**Desc:** International inventory of musical sources up to 1800.

GW
**REPERTOIRE INTERNATIONAL DES SOURCES MUSICALES. SERIES A. EINZELDRUCKE VOR 1800.** **Added/Corp** International Musicological Society. International Association of Music Libraries. **VFOAT** RISM; International Inventory of Musical Sources; Internationales Quellenlexikon der Musik; Einzeldrucke vor 1800. Vol. 1 (1971)-. Monographic series. English (French and German). ir. Price varies per volume. Baerenreiter-Verlag, KGA Verlagssvc PF 100329, D 34003 Kassel Germany. **Tel** 011 49 561 31050, telex 99504. **(Subscription address:** Foreign Music Distributors, 13 Elkay Drive, Chester, NY 10918, (phone: (914)469-5790))

US
**REPLAY.** **VFOAT** RePlay Magazine. (19??)-. Periodical. English. mo. $60.00. Replay Publishing Inc., PO Box 2550, Woodland Hills CA 91365. **Tel** (818)347-3820. **LC** TJ1557; R47. ***Continues** Replay Magazine, 0360-7348.*

US/1045-0084
**REQUEST (MINNEAPOLIS, MINN.).** (REQUEST.). [Request]. (July 1989)-. Periodical. English. Twelve times a year. $12.95. Request, 7630 Excelsior Boulevard, Minneapolis MN 55426. **Tel** (612) 932-7740, FAX (612) 932-7797. **LC** ML476.8; .R45. **DD** 781.64/0973/05.
**Desc:** Provides fresh, exciting, up-to-the-minute coverage of today's new music, from rap and metal to blues and pop. Reviews a wide range of new albums every month. Also features interviews with both established and emerging artists, as well as the latest music news.

US/0883-9700
**RESEARCH AND APPLICATIONS IN MUSIC EDUCATION.** ***Ceased.*** [Res. appl. music educ.]. **VFOAT** RAME. Vol. 1 (1985)-?. English. an. 108 Brandywine Avenue, Dr Campbell, Schenectady NY 12307. **LC** ML1; .R535. **DD** 780/.7.

UK
**RESEARCH CHRONICLE.** **Added/Corp** Royal Musical Association. (1978)-. English. ir. £16.00. Royal Musical Association, Brian Jordan, 10 Green Street, Cambridge CB2 3JU England. **Tel** 011 44 0223-322368. **ED** J. Milsom. **LC** ML5; .R14. **DD** 780/.5. Index available. cum. index. ***Continues** R.M.A. Research Chronicle, 0080-4460.*
**Desc:** Unique among English-language journals by its emphasis on the raw materials of musicology - lists, indexes, catalogues, inventories, etc.
**Ind/Abst** Music Index (-19??).

US/0749-2472
**RESOUND.** (RESOUND : A QUARTERLY OF THE ARCHIVES OF TRADITIONAL MUSIC.). [Resound]. **Added/Corp** Indiana University, Bloomington. Archives of Traditional Music. Vol. 1, No. 1 (Jan. 1982)-. Periodical. English. Four times a year (Jan., Apr., July, Oct.). $20.00. Archives of Traditional Music, Morrison Hall/Room 117, Indiana University, Bloomington IN 47405. **Tel** (812)855-4679, FAX (812)855-6673. **ED** Ruth Stone. **LC** IN PROCESS. **DD** 781. Index available. cum. index. **Circ:** 500.
**Desc:** Includes articles about collections of sound recording recently added to the archives (written by the collectors), and articles about some of the more interesting older collections. The publication primarily is of interest to sound archivists, ethnomusicologists, and anthropologists.

BL/0486-6398
**REVISTA BRASILEIRA DE MUSICA.** **Added/Corp** Universidade do Rio de Janeiro. Instituto Nacional de Musica. Escola Nacional de Musica (Brazil). (March 1934)-. Periodical. Portuguese. qt. Universidade do Brasil, Avenida Vancelan Braz 95, Rio de Janeiro Brazil. **LC** ML5; .R198. **DD** 780/.5. ***Supersedes** Associacao Brasileira de Musica. Revista.*
**Ind/Abst** Music Index.

US/0163-0350
**REVISTA DE MUSICA LATINOAMERICANA.** (REVISTA DE MUSICA LATINOAMERICANA. LATIN AMERICAN MUSIC REVIEW.). [Rev. musica latinoam.]. **VFOAT** Latin American Music Review. Vol. 1 (Spring/Summer 1980)-. Periodical. English (Portuguese and Spanish). sa. $35.00 (institutions), $20.00 (individuals) US; add $4.00 postage other. University of Texas Press, PO Box 7819, Austin TX 78713. **Tel** (512)471-4531, FAX (512)320-0668, telex 776453 UTEXPRES AUS. **ED** Gerard Behague. **LC** ML199; .R48. **DD** 781.781/05. **[CCC].** Index available. **Bk Rev. Ad Acc. Circ:** 450 (ctrl). available on microfilm and microfiche from University Microfilms International (UMI). Documents available from The Genuine Article. ***Continues*** *Anuario Interamericano de Investigacion Musical, 0886-2192.*
**Desc:** A unique periodical that examines all aspects of the diverse written and oral musical traditions of Latin America, including the music of such cultural groups as Mexican Americans, Puerto Ricans, Cubans, and Portuguese in the United States.
**Ind/Abst** Arts Humanit. Citation Index (19??-19??) [Full Cov.]; Curr. Contents Arts Humanit.; HAPI Hisp. Am. Period. Index; MLA Int. Bibl. Books Artic. Mod. Lang. Lit.; Music Index; Res. Alert [Full Cov.]; RILM Abstr.; Soc. Sci. Cit. Index [Select. Cov.].

SP
**REVISTA DE MUSICOLOGIA / SOCIEDAD ESPANOLA DE MUSICOLOGIA.** **Added/Corp** Sociedad Espanola de Musicologia. (1978)-. Periodical. Spanish. Twice a year. Sociedad Espanola Musicologia, JA Medizabal 65 Dup 3, 28008 Madrid Spain. **Tel** 011 34 1 2470190. **(Subscription address:** Editorial Alpuerto SA, Canos del Peral 7 1, 28013 Madrid Spain; telephone: 011 34 91 2470190) **LC** ML5; .R212. **DD** 780/.5.
**Ind/Abst** RILM Abstr.

BL
**REVISTA DO MUSICO.** (Sept. 1974)-. Periodical. Portuguese. mo. Irmanaultson Realizacoes, Av 13 de Maio 47/S 1713, Rio de Janeiro Brazil. **LC** ML5; .R215.

VE
**REVISTA INIDEF.** **Main/Corp** Instituto Interamericano de Etnomusicologia y Folklore. **VAT** Revista Instituto Interamericano de Etnomusicologia y Folklore. No. 1 (April 1975)-. Periodical. Spanish. Instituto Nacional de Cultura y Bellas Artes, Apartado 6238, Caracus Venezuela. **LC** ML5; .I47. **DD** 781.7/05.
**Desc:** Concentrates on ethnomusicology and folklore.

CL/0716-2790
**REVISTA MUSICAL CHILENA.** [Rev. music. chil.]. **Added/Corp** Chile. Universidad, Santiago. Instituto de Extension Musical. Universidad de Chile. Facultad de Artes. Universidad de Chile. Facultad de Ciencias y Artes Musicales. Universidad de Chile. Facultad de Ciencias y Artes Musicales y de la Representacion. Vol.1, No.1 (May 1945)-. Periodical. Spanish (English). sa (Jan. and July). $45.00. Facultad de Artes / Universidad de Chile, Casilla 2100, Compania 1264 Santiago Chile. **Tel** 011 56 2 6965767, FAX 11 561 6711435. **ED** Luis Merino Montero. **LC** ML5; .R283. Each issue contains an index to its own contents (no volume index)--loose. **Bk Rev. Ad Acc, Adv Mgr Tel** 11 56 2 6713326. **Pr Rev. Circ:** 500 (ctrl). available on microfiche.
**Desc:** Dedicated to the study of Chilean and Latin American music from colonial epoch to 20th century music.
**Ind/Abst** HAPI Hisp. Am. Period. Index; Music Index; RILM Abstr.

VE
**REVISTA MUSICAL DE VENEZUELA / INSTITUTO LATINOAMERICANO DE INVESTIGACIONES Y ESTUDIOS MUSICALES VICENTE EMILIO SOJO.** **Added/Corp** Instituto Latinoamericano de Investigaciones y Estudios Musicales Vicente Emilio Sojo. Consejo Nacional de la Cultura. Vol. 1, No. 1 (May/Aug. 1980)-. Periodical. Spanish. ir. Fundacion Vicente Emilio Sojo, Apartado 70537, Caracas 1071 Venezuela. **LC** ML238; .R49. **DD** 780/.987/05.
**Ind/Abst** HAPI Hisp. Am. Period. Index.

SP
**REVOLUCIONES POR MINUTO : RPM.** Spanish. mo. 1500.00ptas Spain; 2650.00ptas Europe; 3800.00ptas other. Editorial Zona Diez Sa, Bruc 65 3A-2A, 08009 Barcelona Spain. **Tel** 34-3-3016659, 34-3-302 4294. **Bk Rev. Ad Acc.**
**Desc:** Music reviews, critics, articles and interviews.

BE/0771-6788
**REVUE BELGE DE MUSICOLOGIE.** **VFOAT** Belgisch Tijdschrift voor Muziekwetenschap. Vol. 1, (1947)-. Multiple languages (French, Dutch, English, German and Italian). an. 1270F Belgium; 1550F other. Societe Belge de Musicologie, 30 rue de la Regence, Brussels Belgium. **ED** Robert Wangermee and Henri Vanhulst. **Bk Rev. Circ:** 500.
**Ind/Abst** Arts Humanit. Citation Index (19??-19??) [Full Cov.]; Music Index; RILM Abstr.; Romant. Move.

FR/0035-1601
**REVUE DE MUSICOLOGIE.** (REVUE DE MUSICOLOGIE / PUBLIEE PAR LA SOCIETE FRANCAISE DE MUSICOLOGIE.). [Rev. musicol.]. **Added/Corp** Societe Francaise de Musicologie. (March 1922)-. Periodical. French. Twice a year. 230.00F. Societe Francaise Musicologie, 2 rue Louvois, F 75002 Paris France. **Tel** 011 33 1 47038126. available on microfilm and microfiche from University Microfilms International (UMI). ***Continues*** *Bulletin de la Societe Francaise de Musicologie.*
**Ind/Abst** Arts Humanit. Citation Index [Full Cov.]; Music Index; RILM Abstr.

SZ
**REVUE MUSICALE DE SUISSE ROMANDE.** Vol. 16 (Mar. 1963)-. Periodical. French. qt (4 issues). 36.00F Switzerland; 50.00F Europe; 60.00F other. Revue Musicale de Suisse, Case Postale 3074, 1401 Yverdon-les-Bains Switzerland. **Tel** 011 41 24 212606, FAX 011 41 24 217310. Index available. **Bk Rev. Ad Acc. Circ:** 6,500. ***Continues*** *Feuilles Musicales.*
**Desc:** Includes articles on music and certain musicians and information concerning recordings and musical manifestations.
**Ind/Abst** Music Index; RILM Abstr.

CN/0820-9626
**RHYTHM (SASKATOON).** (RHYTHM.). [Rhythm]. (Jan./Feb. 1982)-. Periodical. English. bm. Rhythm Publishing and Productions, PO Box 7950, Saskatoon Sask. S7K 6C7. **DD** 784.5/005.

AU
**RICHARD STRAUSS-BLATTER.** **Added/Corp** Internationale Richard Strauss-Gesellschaft. No. 1 (June 1971)-. Periodical. German (English). International Richard Strauss Society, Staatsoper, A-1010 Vienna Austria. **DD** 780/.924. ***Supersedes*** *Internationale Richard Strauss-Gesellschaft. Mitteilungen.*

US/0360-8727
**RIDIM/RCMI NEWSLETTER.** **See** The Arts-Art.

US/0747-5977
**RIGHT ON POSTER BOOK.** (RIGHT ON! POSTER BOOK.). **VFOAT** Right on Annual Poster Book. (198?)-. Periodical. English. an. D S Magazines Inc., 1086 Teaneck Road, Teaneck NJ 07666. **Tel** (201)833-1800. **ED** Cynthia Horner. **Bk Rev. Ad Acc.**
**Desc:** Huge 16x22 inch posters with information of favorite TV and music stars. A must for every teenage dreamer's bedroom walls.

US/0033-6955
**RILM ABSTRACTS.** **See** Music-Abstracting, Bibliographies and Statistics.

US/0098-1788
**RING (WASHINGTON), THE.** (THE RING.). **Added/Corp** Opera Society of Washington. (19??)-. English. The Ring, Suite 5089, 1629 K Street NW, Washington DC 20006. **LC** ML1; .R565. **DD** 782.1/05.

UK
**RINGING WORLD, THE.** (1911)-. English. Fifty-two times a year. £45.50. Ringing World Ltd., Penmark House, Woodbridge Meadows, Guildford GU1 1BL England. **Tel** 69535.

US/0889-5791
**RIP (LOS ANGELES, CALIF.).** (RIP.). [Rip]. (Dec. 1986)-. Periodical. English. mo. $24.95 (one year), $44.95 (two year). LFP Inc., 9171 Wilshire Boulevard/Suite 300, Beverly Hills CA 90210. **Tel** (310)858-7100, FAX (310)274-7985. **(Subscription address:** Kable Publishers Aide, 308 East Hitt Street, Subscription Department, Mt. Morris IL 61054-1473.) **LC** ML3533.8; .R47. **DD** 784.5/4/005.
**Desc:** Covers rock music.

IT
**RISVEGLIO MUSICALE : RM.** **Added/Corp** Anbima (Association). **VFOAT** RM; R.M. Vol. 1, (Feb. 1, 1982)-. Periodical. Italian. Via Marianna Dionigi, 43-00193 Rome Italy. **LC** ML5; .R748. **DD** 780/.5. ***Continues*** *Risveglio Bandistico.*

SP
**RITMO.** **VFOAT** Revista Musical Ilustrada. Vol. 1, No. 1 (1929)-. Periodical. Spanish. Eleven times a year. $95.00. Lira Editorial SA, Virgen de Aranzazu 21, 28034 Madrid Spain. **Tel** 011 34 1 3580267, 3580363.

MX
**RITMO (MEXICO CITY, MEXICO).** ***Ceased.*** (RITMO.). Yearly V. 1, No. 1, (April 21, 1982)-Ceased (Dec. 1991). Periodical. Spanish. sm. Editorial America SA / Iowa, PO Box 10950, Des Moines IA 50340-0950. **Tel** (800)288-6677. **ED** Benjamin Bustamante. **LC** ML3485; .R57. **DD** 784.5/00972. Index available. **Ad Acc. Circ:** 7,147.
**Desc:** Latest on stars and personalities of the Latin music and rock and roll.

US/0360-4381
**RIVER CITY (WICHITA, KAN.).** (RIVER CITY.). [River city]. (19??)-. Periodical. English. qt. River City, Old Flatiron Building, 2148 North Broadway, Wichita KS 67214. **LC** ML1; .R57; M1630.18; ML54.6. **DD** 784.
**Ind/Abst** Am. Humanit. Index (199?-).

IT/0394-6282
**RIVISTA INTERNAZIONALE DI MUSICA SACRA.** [Riv. int. musica sacra]. **VFOAT** International Church Music Review. Vol. 1, No. 1 (Jan./March 1980)-. Periodical. English (French and Italian). Four times a year. L60000 Italy; L75000 other. EIMA, Viale Gorizia 5, 20144 Milan Italy. **Tel** 011 39 2 837 3064. **LC** ML2999; .R59. **DD** 783/.02/605.
**Ind/Abst** Music Index; RILM Abstr.

IT/0035-6867
**RIVISTA ITALIANA DI MUSICOLOGIA.** [Riv. ital. musicol.]. **Added/Corp** Societa Italiana di Musicologia. Vol. 1 (1966)-. Periodical. Italian. Twice a year. L7000.00 Italy; L9000.00 others. Casa Editrice Leo S. Olschki, Viuzzo del Pozzetto, Casella Postale 66, 50126 Florence Italy. **Tel** 011 39 55 6530684, FAX 011 39 55 6530214. **LC** ML5; .R79. Documents available from The Genuine Article.
**Ind/Abst** Arts Humanit. Citation Index (19??-19??) [Full Cov.]; Curr. Contents Arts Humanit.; Music Index; Res. Alert [Full Cov.]; RILM Abstr.

FR/0048-8445
**ROCK & FOLK PARIS. 1966.** (ROCK & FOLK.). [Rock folk Paris, 1966]. **VFOAT** Rock and Folk (Paris. 1966). (1966)-. Periodical. French. mo. 235.00F (one year), 440.00F (two years) France; 275.00F (one year), 500.00F (two years) other. Editions Lariviere Naryse Menn, 15 17 Quai de l Oise Sec. Abonn., 75166 Paris Cedex 19 France. **Tel** 011 33 1 40342207, FAX 33 1 40358441, telex 211678. **UDC** 78.
**Ind/Abst** Point Repere (1991-).

●US/1068-7653
**ROCK & RAP CONFIDENTIAL.** [Rock rap confid.]. **VFOAT** Rock and Rap Confidential; RRC. No. 101 (Oct. 1992)-. Periodical. English. mo. $36.00 (1 year), $60.00 (2 year), $80.00 (3 year) US; $38.00 (1 year), $64.00 (2 year), $86.00 (3 year) Canada; $48.00 (1 year), $80.00 (2 year), $110.00 (3 year) other. Rock and Rap Confidential, Box 341305, Los Angeles CA 90034. **Tel** (213)204-0827. **LC** ML3533.8; .R52. **DD** 784.5/4/005. ***Continues*** *Rock & Roll Confidential, 0891-9372.*

US/0891-9372
**ROCK & ROLL CONFIDENTIAL.** ***Title Change.*** [Rock roll confid.]. **VFOAT** Rock and Roll Confidential. (1983)-(1992). Periodical. English. mo. Rock and Rap Confidential, Box 341305, Los Angeles CA 90034. **Tel** (213)204-0827. **ED** Dave Marsh. **LC** ML3533.8; .R52. **DD** 784.5/4/005. **Bk Rev,** (Qty: 12). ***Continues*** *Dave Marsh's Rock & Roll Confidential, 0740-2058.* ***Continued by*** *Rock & Rap Confidential, 1068-7653.*
**Ind/Abst** Altern. Press Index (199?-); Music Index.

NE
**ROCK & ROLL INTERNATIONAL MAGAZINE.** (Sept. 1975)-. Periodical. Multiple languages (Dutch and English). mo. Fl35.00. Rock & Roll International Magazine, PO Box 712, Hengelo 7700 The Netherlands. **LC** ML5; .R847. **DD** 784.

US/8756-3487
**ROCK & SOUL.** ***Ceased.*** [Rock soul]. **VFOAT** Rock and Soul. Ceased Vol. 31 (Oct. 1987). Periodical. English. bm. Dilo Inc, 1037 Rosedale Road, Woodmere NY 11581-2704. **LC** ML3533.8; .R55. **DD** 784.5/4/00973. ***Continues*** *Rock & Soul Songs, 0035-743X.*

SP
**ROCK DE LUX.** (19??)-. Spanish. Twelve times a year. 5600ptas Spain; 7200ptas other. Ediciones Rock de Lux SA, C Deu I Mata 152, Entr 4A, 08029 Barcelona Spain. **Tel** 011 34 93 3210144.

●US/1059-5279
**ROCK HEROES PRESENTS ... .** [Rock heroes presents]. **VFOAT** Rock Heroes Magazine. Vol. 1, No. 11 (Nov. 1991)-. Periodical. English. bm. $3.50 (single issue). J. Q. Adams Productions, 519 8th Avenue, New York NY 10018. **DD** 782.

US/0739-408X
**ROCK MAGAZINE (BEVERLY HILLS, CALIF.).** (ROCK MAGAZINE.). [Rock mag.]. (19??)-. Periodical. English. bm. $9.00 US; $12.00 Canada. Jolson Publications, 1112 La Cienega Blvd., Los Angeles CA 90069. **LC** ML3533.8; .R6. **DD** 784.5/4/00973.

US/0092-0401
**ROCK (NEW YORK).** (ROCK.). (19??)-. Periodical. English. Four times a year. Rev. Peter P. S. Ching, 144-25 Roosevelt Avenue, Flushing NY 11354. **LC** ML1; .R58. **DD** 784.

# Music

US/1045-6376
**ROCK-OUT! (RIVER EDGE, N.J.).** (ROCK-OUT!). [Rock-out!]. **VFOAT** Rock Out!. (198?)-. Periodical. English. qt. Rock-Out Magazine Inc., 63 Grand Avenue, Suite 230, River Edge NJ 07661. **DD** 780.

US/8755-8661
**ROCK POSTER MAGAZINE.** [Rock poster mag.]. (1983)-. Periodical. English. qt. Rock Poster Magazine, 475 Park Avenue South, New York NY 10016. **DD** 784.

US/0090-3353
**ROCK SCENE. Suspended.** (Mar. 1973)-(Suspended 1981). Periodical. English. Six times a year. $4.00. Four Seasons Publications, 358 Fairwood Road, Bethany CT 06525. **Tel** (203)393-3082. **LC** ML1; .R63. **DD** 784.

US/0735-8326
**ROCK STAR BAZAAR.** (19??)-. English. Rock Star Bazaar, 114 West Bayaud, Denver CO 80223. **LC** ML3533.8; .R62. **DD** 784.5/4/005.

US/0883-6469
**ROCKAMERICA GUIDE TO VIDEO/MUSIC, THE.** [Rockamerica guide video/music]. **VFOAT** Rock America Guide to Video/Music; Guide. (1985)-. English. Rockamerica Inc, 27 East 21st Street, New York NY 10010. **LC** PN1992.8.M87; R63. **DD** 789.9/12454.

US/0890-460X
**ROCKBILL. Ceased.** [RockBill]. **VFOAT** Rock Bill; Rockbill Magazine. Periodical. English. mo. Rave Publ Inc, 40 Prince Street, New York NY 10012. **LC** ML3533.8; .R64. **DD** 784.5/4/00973.

IT
**ROCKERILLA.** (19??)-. Italian. mo (11 issues). L55000 Italy; L68000 other. Edizioni Rockerilla Snc, Via Pighini 24, 17014 Cairomontenotte Italy. **Tel** 011 39 19 520514.

JM
**ROCKERS (KINGSTON, JAMAICA).** (ROCKERS.). (19??)-. Periodical. English. bm. Rockers Productions, PO Box 46 Hagley Park PO, Kingston 11 Jamaica West Indies. **LC** ML3533.8; .R65. **DD** 784.5/4/0097292.

US
**ROCKET (SEATTLE, WA).** (19??)-. English. Twelve times a year. $15.00. Rocket Magazine, 2028 5th Ave., Seattle WA 98121. **Tel** (206)728-7625, FAX (206)728-8827. **ED** Grant Alden. **Bk Rev**, **(Qty**: 24). **Ad Acc**, **Adv Mgr**: Courtney Miller, **Tel** (206)728-7625. **Circ**: 76,000.
**Desc**: Music and contemporary culture of the Pacific Northwest United States. Primarily alternative and college music.

US/0738-7717
**ROCKIN' 50'S. VFOAT** Rockin' Fifties. (1986)-. Periodical. English. Six times a year (Feb., Apr., June, Aug., Oct., Dec.). $25.00 US & Canada; $35.00 Europe & South America; $38.00 others. William F. Griggs, 3806 55th Street, Lubbock TX 79413. **Tel** (806)799-4299. **LC** ML3533.8; .R66. **DD** 784.5/4/009045. **Bk Rev**. **Ad Acc**. **Circ**: 5,400.
**Desc**: Devoted to the music and events of the rock 'n roll era of the 1950's.

US/0146-1885
**ROCKINGCHAIR.** (Apr. 1977)-. Periodical. English. mo. Cupola Productions, PO Box 27, Philadelphia PA 19105.

IT
**ROCKSTAR.** (19??)-. Italian. mo. L60000 Italy; L80000 Europe; L140000 other. Actual Media Srl, L Go Antonelli 27, 00145 Rome Italy. **Tel** 011 39 6 5417100.

NE
**ROCKVILLE INTERNATIONAL.** (19??)-. Periodical. Multiple languages (Dutch and English). mo. $9.00. Middelburg, Postbus 3, The Netherlands. **LC** ML5; .R85. **DD** 784.

US/0148-7493
**ROCKY MOUNTAIN MUSICAL EXPRESS.** (19??)-. Periodical. English. mo. Rocky Mountain Musical Express, Box B, Boulder CO 80306. **LC** ML1; .R64. **DD** 780/.42/0978.

GW/0944-0291
**ROHRBLATT : MAGAZIN FUER OBOE, KLARINETTE, FAGOTT UND SAXOPHON. Added/Corp** International Double Reed Society. Deutschland. (1993)-. Periodical. German. qt. Verlag Karl Hofmann, Postfach 1360, D-73603 Schorndorf Germany. **Tel** 011 49 7181 4020. **LC** ML929; .K6. **DD** 788/.05. **Continues** Oboe, Klarinette, Fagott.

US/0035-791X
**ROLLING STONE.** [Roll. stone]. No. 1 (Nov. 9, 1967)-. Periodical. English. Twenty-six times a year (Published every other Thurs.). $25.95. Wenner Media Inc., 1290 Avenue of the Americas, 2nd Floor, New York NY 10104. **Tel** (212)484-1616, FAX (212)759-2966. **(Subscription address:** Neodata / Colorado, PO Box 2606, Boulder Boulder CO 80322.) **ED** Robert B. Wallace and James Henke. **LC** AP2; .R73. **DD** 784. **Bk Rev**. **Ad Acc**. available in braille; available on microfilm and microfiche from University Microfilms International (UMI); available on an online database (file 647/Full-Text) from DIALOG. Documents available from UMI Article Clearinghouse.
**Desc**: Information on rock music and popular culture.
**Ind/Abst** Abr. Read. Guide Period. Lit.; Acad. Abstr. Full Text Elite (Jan. 1984-) [Full Txt.]; Acad. Abstr. (Jan. 1984-); Acad. Ind. [Computer File] (1984-); Acad. Search (Jan. 1984-); Expand. Acad. Index (1984-); Film Lit. Index; Gen. Period. Index (1985-); Index Period. Artic. Relat. Law; INFO-SOUTH Abstr.; Mag. Artic. Summar. Elite (Jan. 1984-) [Full Txt.]; Mag. Artic. Summar. Select (Jan. 1984-) [Full Txt.]; Mag. Artic. Summar. CD-ROM (Jan. 1984-); Mag. Express (1986-) [Full Txt.]; Mag. Index Plus (1989-); Mag. Index. Sel. (1986-); Mag. Search; Med. Rev. Dig.; Mid. Search (Jan. 1984-) [Full Txt.]; Music Index; Newsp. Period. Abstr. (1986-); Point Repere; Pop. Period. Index; Read. Guide Abstr. Select Ed.; Read. Guide Period. Lit.; Resource/One Ondisc; Mag. Index (1977-); TOM Gen. Index (1985-); Vocat. Search (Jan. 1984-) [Full Txt.].

US/8755-6324
**ROLLING STONE REVIEW, THE.** [Roll. Stone rev.]. **VFOAT** Rollingstone Review. (1985)-. English. ir. $22.50 hardbound. Charles Scribner's Sons, 115-5th Avenue, New York NY 10003. **LC** ML3533.8; .R67. **DD** 784.5/4/005.
**Desc**: Information on rock music and popular culture.

UK
**ROYAL COLLEGE OF MUSIC MAGAZINE. Main/Corp** Royal College of Music (Great Britain). **VFOAT** RCM Magazine. (1904)-. Periodical. English. Three times a year. £10.00. Royal College of Music Society, Prince Consort Road, London 2BS SW7 England. **Tel** 11 44 71 5893643 Ext. 13. **ED** Angela Escott. Index available. **Bk Rev**. **Ad Acc**. **Circ**: 2,500. (ctrl)
**Desc**: For students, past students and staff of the Royal College of Music, and others who wish to subscribe.
**Ind/Abst** Music Index.

UK
**ROYAL OPERA HOUSE PRESENTS, THE. Main/Corp** Royal Opera House (London, England). (Oct. 13, 1982)-. English. ir. Friends of Covent Garden Limited, Royal Opera House, Covent Garden, London WC2E 9DD England. **Tel** 011 71 2401200 Ext. 268. **Continues** Royal Opera House (London, England). Royal Opera House Covent Garden Limited Presents ... .

PL/0035-9610
**RUCH MUZYCZNY (WARSAW, POLAND).** (RUCH MUZYCZNY.). [Ruch muzycz.]. (May 1957)-. Periodical. Polish. sm. $52.00. **(Subscription address:** ARS Polona, PO Box 1001, 00068 Warsaw Poland.) **LC** ML5; .R855. **DD** 780/.5.
**Ind/Abst** Music Index; RILM Abstr.

PL
**RYTMY.** (19??)-. Periodical. Polish. Z10.00 single issue. Polksie Wydawn Muzyczne, Senatorska 13/15, Warszana Poland. **LC** ML5; .R983.

US/0739-9103
**S.E.M. NEWSLETTER (1981).** (S.E.M. NEWSLETTER.). [S.E.M. newsl.]. **Added/Corp** Society for Ethnomusicology. **VFOAT** SEM Newsletter. **VAT** Society for Ethnomusicology Newsletter. Vol. 15, No. 2 (May 1981)-. Newsletter. English. Four times a year. Society for Ethnomusicology, Morrison Hall 005, Indiana University, Bloomington IN 47405. **Tel** (812)855-6672, FAX (812)855-6673. **DD** 781. **Continues** on microfilm and microfiche from University Microfilms International (UMI). **Continues** Society for Ethnomusicology Newsletter (1981).

●CN/1191-2642
**SABIAN NEWS BEAT CATALOG.** [Sabian news beat cat.]. **Added/Corp** Sabian Ltd. **VFOAT** Sabian Newsbeat Catalog; News Beat Catalog. No. 1 (1992)-. Catalog. English. Free. Sabian Ltd., Meductic N B E0H 1LO Canada. **DD** 786.8. **Continues** News Beat (Meductic, N.B.), 0847-7795.

US/0036-2255
**SACRED MUSIC.** See Religion and Theology-Catholicism.

US/0036-2263
**SACRED ORGAN JOURNAL, THE.** (19??)-. Periodical. English. Six times a year (Jan., Mar., May, July, Sept., Nov.). $16.95 one year; $30.95 two year; $44.95 three year. Lorenz Publishing Company, PO Box 802, Dayton OH 45401. **Tel** (513)228-6118.

**Desc**: The primary purpose for this journal is to supplement the well-trained church organist's repertoire of practical and worthwhile service music.

GW
**SAEMTLICHE WERKE. ANTON BRUCKNER.** (19??)-. Monographic series. German. ir. Price varies per volume. **(Subscription address:** Broude Brothers Limited, 141 White Oaks Road, Williamstown, MA 01267)
**Desc**: The first critical edition of the musical works of Anton Bruckner.

GW
**SAEMTLICHE WERKE. ARNOLD SCHOENBERG.** (19??)-. Monographic series. German. ir. Price varies per volume. **(Subscription address:** Broude Brothers Limited, 141 White Oaks Road, Williamstown, MA 01267)
**Desc**: A critical edition of the musical works of Arnold Schoenberg.

GW
**SAEMTLICHE WERKE. GUSTAV MAHLER.** (19??)-. Monographic series. German. ir. Price varies per volume. **(Subscription address:** Broude Brothers Limited, 141 White Oaks Road, Williamstown, MA 01267)
**Desc**: A critical edition of the musical works of Gustav Mahler.

GW
**SAEMTLICHE WERKE. ORLANDO DE LASSUS.** (19??)-. Monographic series. German. ir. Price varies per volume. **(Subscription address:** Broude Brothers Limited, 141 White Oaks Road, Williamstown, MA 01267)
**Desc**: A critical edition of the works of Orlando di Lassus, completing the project left unfinished with the termination of the Saemtliche Werke, Alte Reihe.

GW
**SAEMTLICHE WERKE. RICHARD WAGNER.** German. $500.00. Broude Brothers Limited, 141 White Oaks Road, Williamstown MA 01267. **Tel** (413)458-8132, (800)525-8559.
**Desc**: A critical edition of the musical works of Richard Wagner.

CN/0715-4976
**SAINT JOHN FOLK CLUB RAG, THE.** [St. John Folk Club rag]. **Added/Corp** Saint John Folk Club. (1977)-. Periodical. English. bm. Free. Saint John Folk Club, 176 Germain Street, Saint John New Brunswick E2L 2G3 Canada. **DD** 781.7715/32.

GW
**SAITENSPIEL. Added/Corp** Deutscher Zithermusik-Bund. (19??)-. German. ir. Resonanz, Fach-Mitteilungsblatt, des Zither-u Volksmusik Landesverbandes Bayern, Germany. **LC** ML5; .S15. **DD** 787/.8/05.

GE/0557-1634
**SAMMELBANDE DER ROBERT-SCHUMANN-GESELLSCHAFT. Main/Corp** Robert-Schumann-Gesellschaft. No. 1, (1961)-. German. ir. LKG Leipziger Kommissions & Grossbuchhandel, Leinenstrasse 16, Postfach 520, D 04005 Leipzig, Germany. **Tel** 011 49 341 71370. **LC** ML410.S4; R55. **Circ**: 500.
**Desc**: A scientific congress for the life and work of Robert Schumann.

GE
**SAMMELBANDE ZUR MUSIKGESCHICHTE DER DEUTSCHEN DEMOKRATISCHEN REPUBLIK.** Vol. 1, (1969)-. German. ir. Broude Brothers Ltd, 141 White Oaks Road, Williamstown MA 01267. **Tel** (413)458-8132, (800)525-8559. **LC** ML275.5; S3. **DD** 780/.943/1.

GW
**SAMUEL SCHEIDT WERKE.** (19??)-. German. ir. $54.00 Volume 16. **(Subscription address:** Broude Brothers Ltd., 141 White Oaks Road, Williamstown, MA 01267)
**Desc**: A critical edition of the musical works of Samuel Scheidt.

US/0036-407X
**SAN DIEGO SOUND POST, THE. Added/Corp** Musician's Association of San Diego County. (19??)-. Periodical. English. mo. $5.00 (non-members). American Federation of Musicians / San Diego, 1717 Morena Boulevard, San Diego CA 92110.

US/0892-7189
**SAN FRANCISCO OPERA.** [San Franc. opera]. **VFOAT** San Francisco Opera Magazine. (198?)-. Periodical. English. ir. San Francisco Opera Magazine, War Memorial Opera House, San Francisco CA 94102. **Tel** (415)861-4008. **DD** 782. **Continues** San Francisco Opera Magazine.
**Ind/Abst** Music Index.

US
**SAN FRANCISCO SYMPHONY MAGAZINE.** (19??)-. Periodical. English. Six times a year. $25.00. San Francisco Symphony Orchestra Association, Davies Symphony Hall, San Francisco CA 94102. **Tel** (415)552-8000.

II/0036-4339
**SANGEET NATAK.** **See** The Arts-Performing Arts.

GW/0036-2328
**SANGER UND MUSIKANTENZEITUNG.** [Sanger - Musikantenztg.]. (1958)-. Periodical. German. bm. BLV Verlagsgesellschaft MBH, Lothstrasse 29, D80797 Munich Germany. **Tel** 011 49 89 12705214. **LC** ML5; .S135.
**Ind/Abst** RILM Abstr.

CY
**SAWT AL-FANNANIN.** **VFOAT** Sot Elfananin. (1990)-. Periodical. Arabic. mo. Niqosiya, Qubrus, Dar Sawt al-Fannanin, Lil-Tabaah Wa-al-Nashr, Wa-al-Ilan. ***Continues*** *Musiqa al-Arabiyah.*

US/0276-4768
**SAXOPHONE JOURNAL.** No. 24 (Winter 1980)-. Periodical. English. Six times a year. $27.00 US; $34.00 other. Saxophone Journal, PO Box 206, Medfield MA 02052. **Tel** (508)359-4417. **LC** IN PROCESS. **Bk Rev**. **Ad Acc**. ***Continues*** *Saxophone Sheet.*
**Desc:** Presents technical information and news for saxophonists to improve playing skills, with regular columns on jazz improvisation, playing techniques, tips on doubling, career management, news publications, writing for saxophones, teaching techniques, saxophone repair, vintage saxophones revisited, the saxophone mouthpiece, reviews of new recordings, coming artist performances, and new product announcements. Also added is the feature front cover interviews with leading jazz, pop, and classical artists, transcribed jazz solos, and sheet music.
**Ind/Abst** Music Artic. Guide; Music Index.

US/0271-3705
**SAXOPHONE SYMPOSIUM, THE.** [Saxophone symp.]. **Added/Corp** World Saxophone Congress. North American Saxophone Alliance. Vol. 1, (Winter 1976)-. Periodical. English. Four times a year (Jan., Apr., July, Oct.). $25.00 Comes with North American Saxophone Alliance Membership. North American Saxophone Alliance, Indiana State University, Department of Music, Terra Haute IN 47809. **Tel** (812)237-2730. **DD** 788. ***Supersedes*** *World Saxophone Congress Newsletter.*

XR
**SBORNIK. UMENI.** **Main/Corp** Pedagogicka Fakulta V Plzni. **Added/Corp** Pedagogicky Institut v Plzni. Sbornik. Umeni. (1960)-. Czech (summaries and/or abstracts in German and Russian). Statni Pedagogicke Nakladatelstvi, Ostrovni 30, 113 01 Prague 1 Czech Republic. **Tel** (2)203787, FAX (2)293883. **LC** ML247; .P63. ***Continues in part*** *Sbornik. Umeni.*

US/1064-6116
**SCENE ENTERTAINMENT WEEKLY.** **See** The Arts.

GW
**SCHALLPLATTEN ABC. SINGLE SCHALLPLATTEN, GESAMTVERZEICHNIS, DAS.** **VFOAT** Schallplatten A.B.C. Single Schallplatten, Gesamtverzeichnis; Single Schallplatten, Gesamtverzeichnis. (19??)-. German. Three times a year. Helmut Sander Verlag, Hohenfriedbergweg 1, W-4950 Minden Germany. **LC** ML156.4.P6; S3. **DD** 016.7899/1245/00943.

US/1048-2180
**SCHERZO.** (SCHERZO : A MAGAZINE FOR MUSIC STUDENTS.). [Scherzo]. Vol. 1, No. 1 (May 1989)-. English. qt. $10.00 US; (add $2.50 for postage) other. Jimm Omodt Music Studio, 3016 Northeast 19th Street, Portland OR 97212. **Tel** (503)287-7009. **ED** Jimm A. Omodt and Mary B. Omodt. **DD** 780. Index available. cum. index. **Circ:** 500 (ctrl).
**Desc:** Music magazine for beginning to intermediate music students with puzzles, music math activities, articles, music history and music cartoons to aid in learning about music.

US/0036-6668
**SCHOOL MUSIC NEWS, THE.** [Sch. music news]. **Added/Corp** New York State School Music Association. **VFOAT** New York State School Music News. (19??)-. Periodical. English. Eight times a year. $16.00. School Music News, 167 Middleville Road, Northport NY 11768. **Tel** (516)261-1534, FAX (516)261-1537. **ED** Thomas Gellert. **LC** ML1; .S4. **DD** 780.7205. **Bk Rev**. **Ad Acc**. **Circ:** 50,000 (ctrl). available on microfilm and microfiche from University Microfilms International (UMI).
**Desc:** Articles, reviews of music, education oriented materials, listing of NYSSMA sponsored activities.
**Ind/Abst** Music Artic. Guide.

AU
**SCHRIFTEN ZUR VOLKSMUSIK.** Periodical. German. ir. Verlag Dr. A. Schendl Mbh Co KG, Postfach 29, Karlsgasse 15, A 1041 Vienna Austria. **Tel** 011 49 222 655593, 655596.

GW
**SCHUTZ-JAHRBUCH.** [Schutz-Jahrb.]. **Added/Corp** Internationale Heinrich Schutz-Gesellschaft. (1979)-. Monographic series. German (summaries and/or abstracts in English, French and Swedish). ir. Price varies per volume. Baerenreiter-Verlag, KGA Verlagssvc PF 100329, D 34003 Kassel Germany. **Tel** 011 49 561 31050, telex 99504. **(Subscription address:** Foreign Music Distributors, 13 Elkay Drive, Chester, NY 10918 USA) **LC** ML410.S35; .S39. **DD** 780/.92/4; B.
**Desc:** Essays on the music, life, environment, and performance practice of Schuet's works with bibliographies on the writings.
**Ind/Abst** Music Index.

US
**SCHUTZ SOCIETY REPORTS : NEWSLETTER OF THE AMERICAN HEINRICH SCHUTZ SOCIETY.** ***Title Change.*** **Added/Corp** American Heinrich Schutz Society. Vol. 6, Issue 1 (Fall 1989)-(199?). Newsletter. English. sa. International Heinrich Schutz Society, American Section, c/o Paul Walker, Chelsea Drive, Charlottesville VA 22903. **Tel** (804)293-5339. **LC** ML410.S35; A72. **Bk Rev**. **Circ:** 120 (ctrl). ***Continues*** *Archer (Princeton, N.J.).* ***Continued by*** *17th Century Music, 1054-6022.*
**Desc:** Brief articles, reviews and general information on the music of Heinrich Schutz and other music of the 17th-century German and Italy.

SZ
**SCHWEIZER JAHRBUCH FEUR MUSIKWISSENSCHAFT.** **Added/Corp** Schweizerische Musikforschende Gesellschaft. **VFOAT** Annales Suisses de Musicologie. Vol. 1 (1981)-. Monographic series. French (German). ir. Price varies per volume. Verlag Paul Haupt, Falkenplatz 11, CH-3001 Bern Switzerland. **Tel** 011 41 31 3012435, FAX 011 41 30 243023, telex 912 906 HAUP CH. **LC** ML5; .S325. **DD** 780/.5. ***Continues*** *Schweizer Beitrage zur Musikwissenschaft.*

SZ
**SCHWEIZER MUSIK AUF SCHALLPLATTEN. MUSIQUE SUISSE SUR DISQUES. SWISS MUSIC ON RECORDS.** **Added/Corp** Schweizerisches Musik-Archiv. **VFOAT** Musique Suisse sur Disques; Swiss Music on Records. (1975/76)-. Periodical. French (German). be. Free. Schweizerisches Musik-Archiv, Bellariastrasse 82, CH-8038 Zurich Switzerland. **Tel** 01 482 66 66, FAX 01 482 4333, telex 59 876 CAEZ. **ED** Hans Steinbeck. **LC** ML156.2; .S4. **DD** 016.7899/12. **Circ:** 2,500 (ctrl).
**Desc:** Lists all commercial records known in US of serious Swiss music.

SZ
**SCHWEIZERISCHE BLASMUSIKZEITUNG.** **VFOAT** Revue des Musiques Suisses; Rivista Bandistica Svizzera. (1???)-. Periodical. Multiple languages (German, French and Italian). Eleven times a year. 23.00F (members) Brassband Clubs in Switzerland; 28.00F (non-members) Switzerland; 33.00F others. Zollikofer AG, Fuerstenlandstr 122, CH-9001 St. Gallen Switzerland. **Tel** 011 41 71 297777, FAX 011 41 71 257487, telex 77537. **Ad Acc**. **Circ:** 24,000.

US
**SCIMITAR AND SONG ANTHOLOGY.** (1976)-. English. an. Scimitar and Song, PO Box 151, Edgewater MD 21037. Each issue contains an index to its own contents (no volume index)--loose.

US/1074-5769
**SCORE (NASHVILLE, TENN.).** (SCORE.). [Score]. **VFOAT** Score Magazine. (1989)-. Periodical. English. bm (6 issues). $20.00. Score, 2201 Murfreesboro Road, Suite C206, Nashville TN 37217. **Tel** (615)360-9444, FAX (615)361-1274. **DD** 781. **Bk Rev**, (Qty: 36). **Ad Acc**, **Adv Mgr:** Mr. Nowlin, **Tel** same as publisher. **Circ:** 30,000.
**Desc:** Covers gospel music.

UK
**SCOTTISH FOLK DIRECTORY.** (1973)-. Directory. English. S. Douglas, 12 Mansfield Road, Perth Scotland. **LC** ML21; .S28. **DD** 781.7/411/025411.

US
**SEATTLE OPERA MAGAZINE.** **Added/Corp** Seattle Opera Association. (19??)-. Periodical. English. bm. Seattle Opera Association, PO Box 9248, Seattle WA 98109. **LC** ML1699; .S4. **DD** 782.1.09797/77.

US/0037-0576
**SECOND LINE, THE.** [Second line]. **Added/Corp** New Orleans Jazz Club. Vol. 1, (1950)-. Periodical. English. Four times a year (Jan., Apr., July, Oct.). $25.00 Comes with New Orleans Jazz Club Membership. New Orleans Jazz Club, 828 Royal Street, Suite 265, New Orleans LA 70116. **Tel** (504)455-6847. **LC** ML1; .S495. **DD** 780.973; 785.42*.
**Ind/Abst** Music Index.

US/1052-5025
**SECONDS (NEW YORK, N.Y.).** (SECONDS.). [Seconds]. (Feb. 1987)-. Periodical. English. Six times a year. $20.00. Seconds Magazine, 24 5th Avenue, Suite 405, New York NY 10011. **Tel** (212)260-0481. **ED** George Petros (phone: (212)260-0440). **LC** ML3533.8; .S43. **DD** 781.66. **Bk Rev**. **Ad Acc**, **Adv Mgr:** Ken Senudato. **Circ:** 75,000.
**Desc:** State of the art mag devoted to pop culture icons.

●US/1065-2981
**SECRET GUIDE TO MUSIC AND OTHER GREAT STUFF YOU'RE UNLIKELY TO FIND ANYWHERE ELSE, THE.** **VFOAT** Secret Guide to Music; Secret Guide. (July 1992)-. Periodical. English. Twelve times a year. $12.97. Wayne Green Enterprises, 70 Route 202 North, Peterborough NH 03458. **Tel** (603)924-0058. **DD** 780.

CN/0826-5216
**SEE THE MUSIC.** [See music]. **Added/Corp** Toronto Musicians' Association. **VFOAT** Live Music Talent Directory. No. 1, (1981)-. Periodical. English. be. Free. Toronto Musicians Association, 101 Thorncliffe Park Drive, Toronto Ontario M4H 1M2 Canada. **Tel** (416)421-1020. **ED** Hazel Walker. **DD** 780/.25/713541. **Bk Rev**. **Ad Acc**. **Circ:** 15,000 (ctrl).
**Desc:** A catalogue of musical services available for large or small parties and other events. Music listings for every occasion plus suggestions to prompt your imagination.

US/0361-6622
**SELECTED REPORTS IN ETHNOMUSICOLOGY.** [Sel. rep. ethnomusicol.]. **Added/Corp** University of California, Los Angeles. Dept. of Ethnomusicology. University of California, Los Angeles. Institute of Ethnomusicology. University of California, Los Angeles. Dept. of Music. Vol. 2, No. 1 (1974)-. Monographic series. English. ir. Price varies per volume. UCLA / Department of Ethnomusicology, Los Angeles CA 90024. **Tel** (310)825-5947. **ED** Eran Fraenkel. **LC** ML3799; .C34. **DD** 781.7/05. **Pr Rev**. **Circ:** 400-500 (ctrl). ***Continues*** *University of California, Los Angeles. Institute of Ethnomusicology. Selected Reports, 0575-4712.*
**Desc:** Articles of depth and breadth on ethnomusicological theory, methods, world areas and comparative analyses.
**Ind/Abst** Anthropol. Index; MLA Int. Bibl. Books Artic. Mod. Lang. Lit.; Music Index; RILM Abstr.

US
**SENIOR MUSICIAN.** English. Southern Baptist Convention, 901 Commerce, Suite 750, Nashville TN 37203. **Tel** (615)244-2355, FAX (615)742-8919. **(Subscription address:** Sunday School Board - Customer Service, 127 Ninth Avenue North, Nashville, TN 37234 USA; telephone: (800)458-2772)
**Ind/Abst** South. Baptist Period. Index (1990-).

US
**SENZA SORDINO.** **Added/Corp** International Conference of Symphony & Opera Musicians. Vol. 1, (1963)-. Periodical. English. Six times a year (Feb., Apr., June, Aug., Oct., Dec.). $10.00. Senza Sordino, c/o Robert Levine, 7680 North Longview Drive, Glendale WI 53209. **ED** Deborah L.Torch. **Bk Rev**. **Circ:** 6,000 (ctrl).
**Desc:** Official publication of the International Conference of Symphony and Opera Musicians.

US/0588-490X
**SERIES A. MASTERWORKS OF YESTERDAY.** **Main/Corp** Colorado College Music Press. (1955)-. Periodical. English. Colorado College Music Department, Box 10, Colorado Springs CO 80903. **DD** 784.

CN/1181-8522
**SFP (MONTREAL).** (SFP : SFORZANDO, BULLETIN DE LA FACULTE DE MUSIQUE.). [SFP]. **Main/Corp** Universite de Montreal. Faculte de Musique. **VFOAT** Sforzando. Vol. 1, No 1 (Oct. 1990)-. Bulletin. French. sa. Free. EBSI Universite de Montreal, CP 6128 Succursale A, Montreal Quebec H3C 3J7 Canada. **Tel** (514)343-7422, (514)343-6444, FAX (514)343-2283, telex 05267389. **DD** 780.

CN/0228-3115
**SHADES.** [Shades]. (Feb. 1978)-. Periodical. English. mo. $11.14. Shady Publications, Box 310 Station B, Toronto Ontario M5T 2W2 Canada. **Tel** (416)929-9493. **ED** Sheila Wawanash. **DD** 784.5/4/009713541. **Bk Rev**. **Ad Acc**. **Circ:** 7,000.
**Desc:** An attempt to analyze and articulate, by demonstration, the leading tips of culture and thought.

US/0741-7780
**SHEET MUSIC EXCHANGE, THE.** **VFOAT** SMX. (1982)-. Periodical. English. Six times a year (Feb., Apr., June, Aug., Oct., Dec.). $20.00. Sheet Music Exchange, 1202 12th Street, Key West FL 33040-4031.

Tel (703)740-3080. **(Subscription address:** SMX, PO Box 2114, Key West, FL 33045) **ED** Pat Cleveland. Index available. **Bk Rev. Ad Acc.**

US/1045-3911
**SHEET MUSIC MAGAZINE. EASY PLAY.** [Sheet music mag. Easy play]. **VFOAT** Easy Play. (198?)-. Periodical. English. Six times a year. $16.97 (one year), $29.97 (two year), $43.00 (three year) US, Canada and Mexico. Sheet Music Magazine Inc., 223 Katonah Avenue, Katonah NY 10536. **Tel** (800)759-3036. **(Subscription address:** Neodata / Colorado, PO Box 2606, Boulder Boulder CO 80322.) **LC** M1630.18; .S5184. **DD** 784. ***Formed by the union of*** *Sheet Music Magazine. Easy Organ, 0197-3487* ***and*** *Sheet Music Magazine. Easy Piano/Guitar, 0273-6470.*

US/0273-6462
**SHEET MUSIC MAGAZINE. STANDARD PIANO/GUITAR.** [Sheet music mag., Stand. piano/guitar]. **VFOAT** Standard Piano Guitar; Sheet Music Magazine. Standard Piano Edtion. **VAT** Sheet Music Magazine. Standard Piano Guitar. (19??)-. Periodical. English. Six times a year. $16.97 (one year), $29.97 (two year), $43.00 (three year) US, Canada and Mexico. Sheet Music Magazine Inc., 223 Katonah Avenue, Katonah NY 10536. **Tel** (800)759-3036. **(Subscription address:** Neodata / Colorado, PO Box 2606, Boulder Boulder CO 80322.) **ED** Edward Shanaphy, Josephine Sblendorio. **LC** ML1; .S555. **DD** 784.5/06/05. **Ad Acc, Adv Mgr:** Josephine Sblendorio, **Tel** (914)232-8108. **Circ:** 200,000 (ctrl). ***Continues*** *Sheet Music Magazine. Standard Piano, 0197-3525.*

US/0093-1950
**SHINDIG IN THE BARN.** (THE SHINDIG IN THE BARN.). (19??)-. English. The Shindig in the Barn, 434 Strasburge Pike, Lancaster PA 17602. **LC** ML1; .S5617. **DD** 784.

●US/1059-4817
**SHOUT! (NEW YORK, N.Y.).** (SHOUT!.). [Shout!]. **VFOAT** Shout! Magazine. Vol. 1, No. 10 (Oct. 1991)-. Periodical. English. bm. $2.95 (U.S., single issue), $3.50 (Canada, single issue). J. Q. Adams Productions, 519 8th Avenue, New York NY 10018. **DD** 781.

US/8755-9560
**SHOW MUSIC.** [Show music]. **Added/Corp** Goodspeed Opera House Foundation. **VFOAT** Showmusic. (19??)-. Periodical. English. Four times a year (Mar., June, Sept., Dec.). $17.00. Show Music, PO Box 466, East Haddam CT 06423. **Tel** (203)873-8664 Ext. 303. **ED** Max O. Preeo. **LC** ML1699; .S56. **DD** 782.81/05. **Bk Rev. Ad Acc. Circ:** 4,000 (ctrl).
**Desc:** Reviews new original cast albums and related interest records and books from USA and around the world.

SP
**SHOW PRESS.** Trade Publication. Spanish. mo. $80.00 North America; $60.00 Europe (except Spain); $85.00 other. Show Press Sa, Cerdena 229 6-3A, 08013 Barcelona Spain. **Tel** 347 5036, FAX 456 1729. **ED** Jordi Rueda. **Circ:** 12,000.
**Desc:** Trade magazine for the music industry and show business.

US/0196-1586
**SHOWCASE (MINNEAPOLIS).** (SHOWCASE : MAGAZINE OF THE MINNESOTA ORCHESTRA.). **Added/Corp** Minnesota Orchestral Association. Minnesota Orchestra. **VFOAT** Show Case. (19??)-. Periodical. English. ir. Minnesota Orchestra Hall, 1111 Nicollet Mall, Minneapolis MN 55403. **Tel** (612)371-5639. **ED** Mary Ann Feldman and Jack El-Hai. **LC** MT125.M5; S95. **DD** 785/.06/776579. **Bk Rev. Ad Acc. Circ:** 55,000 (ctrl). ***Continues*** *Symphony.*
**Desc:** Contains music features, news items, as well as program listings and full program notes.

GW
**SIGERT'S FACHMAGAZIN FUER DIE UNTERHALTUNGS-GASTRONOMIE.** ***Title Change.*** **VFOAT** Sigert's. (May 1986)-(1992). Periodical. German. mo. Sigert-Verlag GmbH, Ekbertstrasse 14, W-3300 Braunschweig Germany. **LC** ML5; .M9475. **DD** 781.64/0943/05. ***Continues*** *Musik Info.* ***Continued by*** *Disco-Magazin.*

●US/1070-2199
**SIN INTERNATIONAL.** [Sin int.]. **VFOAT** Sin; Sin Magazine. (1992)-. Periodical. English. mo. $32.00. Sin, 4640 Cass Street, Suite 9428, San Diego CA 92109. **Tel** (619)239-9746. **ED** Rex Edlund. **DD** 051.

US/8750-5347
**SINFONIAN (1980), THE.** (THE SINFONIAN.). [Sinfonian]. **Added/Corp** Phi Mu Alpha Sinfonia Fraternity. **VFOAT** Sinfonian Magazine. Vol. 30, No. 1 (Sept. 1980)-. Periodical. English. Twice a year. $25.00. Phi Mu Alpha Sinfonia Fraternity, 10600 Old State Road, Evansville IN 47711. **Tel** (812)867-2433, FAX (812)867-2433. **ED** Scott Sanders. **LC** ML27.U5; S414. **DD** 780/.973. **Ad Acc. Pr Rev. Circ:** 25,000 (ctrl). ***Continues*** *Sinfonian Newsletter, 0037-5594.*
**Desc:** Contains musical and fraternal articles, and news of the national, chapter, and alumni activities of the nation's largest music fraternity.

US/0037-5624
**SING OUT.** [Sing out]. Vol. 1 (May 1950)-. Periodical. English. Four times a year (Feb., May, Aug., Nov.). $18.00 (individuals); $25.00 (institutions). The Sing Out Corporation, PO Box 5253, 125 East Third Street, Bethlehem PA 18015. **Tel** (215)865-5366, FAX (215)865-5129. **ED** Mark D. Moss (editor's address: 360 16th Avenue, Bethlehem, PA 18018, phone: (610)691-1744). **LC** ML1; .S588. **DD** 784/.05. **Bk Rev**, (Qty: varies). **Ad Acc. Circ:** 10,000 (ctrl). available on microfilm and microfiche from University Microfilms International (UMI).
**Desc:** Dedicated to preserving the diversity and heritage of all traditional folk music. Supports all creators of new folk music from all countries and cultures.
**Ind/Abst** Access (1976-1987); Altern. Press Index (-199?); MLA Int. Bibl. Books Artic. Mod. Lang. Lit.; Music Artic. Guide (1959-?); Music Index; Mag. Index (1977-Dec. 1984).

US/0737-1705
**SING OUT BULLETIN, THE.** (Aug. 1982)-. Bulletin. English. mo. Sing Out Bulletin, Box 1480, New York NY 10023. **LC** ML1; .S589. **DD** 780/.973.

AT/0818-0555
**SING OUT EAST DONCASTER.** [Sing out East Doncaster]. **Added/Corp** Australian Choral Association. (1984)-. Periodical. English. Four times a year (Mar., June, Sept., Dec.). 20.00Aus$ (consessional), 50.00Aus$ (institution), 35.00Aus$ (individual) Comes with Australian National Choral Association Membership. Australian National Choral Association, PO Box 384, Ashgrove Queensland, 4060 Australia. **Tel** 11 44 07 3692778, FAX 11 44 07 3717451. **ED** Blanka West and Katie Purvis. **DD** 784.0994. **Bk Rev. Ad Acc, Adv Mgr Tel** 03 568-7374. **Pr Rev. Circ:** 800 (ctrl).
**Desc:** Promotes choral music in Australia, encourages the development of choral conductors, singers and composers and represents musicians at all levels of choral music.

AU/0037-5721
**SINGENDE KIRCHE.** [Sing. Kirche]. **Added/Corp** Arbeitsgemeinschaft der Kirchenmusik-Kommissionen und - Referenten der Osterreichischen Bistumer. (Sept. 1953)-. Periodical. German. Four times a year. S150.00. Zeitschrift Diozesancomm-Kirch, Stock IM Eisen Platz 3, A 1010 Vienna Austria. **LC** ML5; .S5728. **Bk Rev. Ad Acc. Circ:** 4,000 (ctrl).
**Desc:** Spiritual leading articles, interesting facts on the history of church music, worth-knowing-about organ builders and organs, new built organs and restoration and review of performances.
**Ind/Abst** Music Index; RILM Abstr.

US/1060-3956
**SINGING NEWS MAGAZINE, THE.** [Sing. news mag.]. (1983)-. Periodical. English. mo. $19.00 US; $30.00 Canada; $38.00 other. Singing News Inc., PO Box 2810, Boone NC 28607. **Tel** (800)255-2810. **ED** Jerry Kirksey and Deana Surles. **DD** 782. **Ad Acc, Adv Mgr:** Rick Templeton, **Tel** same as publisher. **Circ:** 150,000 (ctrl). ***Continues*** *Singing News.*
**Desc:** Covers southern gospel music.

●US/1055-0135
**SLIDE GUITARIST.** [Slide guitar.]. Vol. 1 No. 1 (Jan. 1991)-. Periodical. English. mo. $29.00. Educational Services, 230 12th Street, Suite 110, Miami Beach FL 33139. **DD** 787.

XO/0862-0407
**SLOVAK MUSIC.** [Slovak music]. **Added/Corp** Slovensky Hudobny Fond. Music Information Centre. (1969)-. Periodical. English (German, French and Russian). Slovak Music Fund, Music Information Centre, Fucikova 29, CS-811 02 Bratislava Slovakia. **Tel** 333 569. **ED** Viera Polakovicova. **LC** ML5; .S57665. **DD** 781.7/437/305. **Bk Rev. Ad Acc.**
**Desc:** Promotional bulletin for the Slovak music culture with the stress on the Slovak music creation. Includes reviews, articles about the main musical events, about first performances, records, analysis of music creation.
**Ind/Abst** Music Index.

US/8756-8861
**SOCIETY NEWS (BROOMALL, PA.).** (SOCIETY NEWS.). [Soc. news]. **Added/Corp** CRS (Organization). **VFOAT** Society News Magazine; Society. (198?)-. Periodical. English. Twice a year. $20.00 US; $40.00 other. Contemporary Record Society, 724 Winchester Road, Broomall PA 19008. **Tel** (215)544-5920. **ED** Caroline Hunt. **LC** ML28.B815; C767. **DD** 780/.5. **Bk Rev. Ad Acc. Circ:** 100,000 (ctrl). ***Continues*** *Society Newsletter, 0748-5867.*
**Desc:** Assists in developing various funding for the support of performances, phonograph recordings, lectures and composer commissions for recordings. Generating public interest and international appreciation of the performers and composers.

PE
**SOL MAYOR : REVISTA DE MUSICA.** **Added/Corp** Taller Harawi. No. 1 (July 1981)-. Periodical. Spanish. Sol Mayor, Huascar 1908, Jesus Maria, Lima Peru.

CN/0821-4743
**SOLSTICE NEWS.** **Added/Corp** Summer Solstice Festival. Issue 38 (Aug. 1982)-. Periodical. English. mo. Summer Solstice Festival, 14-210 South Algoma Street, Thunder Bay Ontario P7A 5A1 Camada. **DD** 780/.7/971312. ***Continues*** *Solstice News & Program, 0821-4743.*

CN/0712-2438
**SONANCES.** ***Ceased.*** [Sonances]. Vol. 1, No. 1 (Oct. 1981)-(199?). Periodical. French. qt. Sonances, 857 Avenue du Chanoine Martin, Sainte Foy Quebec G1V 3P6 Canada. **Tel** (418)651-1967. **ED** Jean Michel Boulay. **DD** 780/.5. **Bk Rev. Ad Acc. Circ:** 900.
**Desc:** An information quarterly for musicians and music lovers alike which contains leading articles and commentaries on musical events and reviews.
**Ind/Abst** Music Index (-19??); Point Repere.

●US/1053-7791
**SONG HITS' HEARTBREAKERS.** [Song hits' heartbreak.]. **VFOAT** Heartbreakers. Vol. 55, No. 278 (Feb. 1991)-. Periodical. English. bm. $25.00. Charlton Publications Inc., PO Box 158, 60 Division Street, Derby CT 06418. **Tel** (203)732-4797. **DD** 782. ***Continues*** *Song Hits, 0038-1365.*

US/0274-5917
**SONGWRITER (HOLLYWOOD).** (SONGWRITER.). (197?)-Suspended. Periodical. English. mo. Songwriter Magazine, PO Box 3510, Hollywood CA 90028. **Tel** (213)464-7664. **ED** Rick Wiseman. ***Continues*** *Songwriter Magazine, 0362-7373.*

US/0161-5971
**SONGWRITER'S MARKET.** **VFOAT** Song Writer's Market. (1979)-. English. an (published in Sept. of the prior year). $24.99. Writer's Digest Books, 1507 Dana Avenue, Cincinnati OH 45207. **Tel** (513)531-2222, (800)289-0963, FAX (513)531-4744. **ED** Brian Rushing. **LC** MT67; .S657. **DD** 338.4/7/784. Index available (free).
**Desc:** Contains listings of 2,000 song buyers. Includes contact names, address, pay rates, submission requirements, types of songs wanted, and business tips. Contains articles and interviews on current trends. Also includes annual reports on the music industry, articles on how to market songs and listings of contests, competition and workshops.

US/0038-1373
**SONGWRITER'S REVIEW.** ***Suspended.*** (SONGWRITER'S REVIEW : THE GUIDING LIGHT TO TIN PAN ALLEY.). **VFOAT** Song Writer's Review. (Jan. 1946)-(19??). Periodical. English. SN, 1697 Broadway, New York NY 10019. **DD** 784.
**Ind/Abst** Music Artic. Guide (19??-19??); Music Index (-19??).

US/0734-2896
**SONIDO (NEW YORK, N.Y.).** (SONIDO.). [Sonido]. **Added/Corp** Harbor Performing Arts Center (New York, N.Y.). Vol. 1, No. 1 (May 1981)-. Periodical. English (English). qt. Boys Harbor Inc, 1 East 104th Street, New York NY 10029. **LC** ML3475; .S64. **DD** 780/.42/098.

US
**SONNECK SOCIETY BULLETIN, THE.** **Added/Corp** Sonneck Society. Vol. 13, No. 1 (Spring 1987)-. Bulletin. English. Three times a year (Feb., July, Sept.). $75.00 Comes with Sonneck Society for American Music Membership. Sonneck Society, PO Box 476, Canton MA 02021. **Tel** (617)828-8450. **ED** Susan L. Porter. **LC** ML27.U5; S76. **DD** 780/.5. Index available. cum. index. **Bk Rev. Ad Acc. Circ:** 1,500 (ctrl). available on microfilm from University Microfilms International (UMI). ***Continues*** *Sonneck Society Newsletter, 0196-7967.*
**Desc:** Timely information, articles, reviews and news about all aspects of American music.
**Ind/Abst** Music Artic. Guide; Music Index.

US/0739-229X
**SONUS.** [Sonus]. Vol. 1, No. 1 (Fall 1980)-. Periodical. English. sa (Jun., Dec.). $25.00 institutions; $20.00 individuals. Sonus, 24 Avon Hill, Cambridge MA 02140. **Tel** (617)868-0215, (617)492-5493. **ED** Pozzi Escot. **LC** ML1; .S815. **DD** 780/.5. Index available (bound in Dec. issue). cum. index. **Bk Rev**, (Qty: 500). **Circ:** 300. available on microfiche.
**Desc:** A journal of investigations into global and interdisciplinary musical possibilities.
**Ind/Abst** Music Artic. Guide; Music Index; RILM Abstr.

CN/0229-6640
**SORT IT OUT.** (1980)-. Periodical. English. Three times a year. Sort It Out, c/o D. Meyer, 11 Virgil Road, Ottawa Ontario K2H 6B2 Canada. **DD** 784.5/4/005.
**Desc:** Punk rock music.

US/0361-2619
**SOUL & JAZZ RECORD, THE.** (THE SOUL AND JAZZ RECORD.). (19??)-. Periodical. English. mo. The Soul and Jazz Record, 1680 Vine Street, Suite 1017, Hollywood CA 90028. **LC** ML1; .S816. **DD** 784.

US/0098-0730
**SOUL IN REVIEW.** (Feb. 1975)-. English. Soul In Review Publication, 572 West 125 Street, New York NY 10027. **LC** ML1; .S818. **DD** 784.

US/1050-2777
**SOUND & IMAGE.** [Sound image]. **VFOAT** Sound and Image. Vol. 1, No. 1 (Summer 1990)-. English. Four times a year. $14.97. Hachette Magazines Inc., 1633 Broadway, New York NY 10019. **Tel** (212)767-6000. **ED** Michael Riggs. **LC** TK7881.7; .S673. **DD** 621.388. **Ad Acc.**
**Desc:** Covers a wide variety of videos and recordings, includes the performer profiles and articles on custom installations.

NE
**SOUND CHECK.** ***Ceased.*** (19??)-Vol. 11 (1993). ir (8 issues). AV Press BV, Postbus 155, 6500 AD Nijmegen Netherlands. **Tel** 011 31 80 787444.

US/0749-0755
**SOUND POST (GRANITE FALLS, MINN.).** (SOUND POST.). **Added/Corp** Hardanger Fiddle Association of America. Vol. 1, No. 1 (Jan. 1984)-. Periodical. English. qt. $10.00. Hardanger Fiddle Association of America, Granite Falls MN 56241. **Tel** (612)564-3408. **ED** Carl and Amy Narvestad. **LC** ML1; .S8195. **DD** 787/.4. cum. index. **Bk Rev. Ad Acc. Circ:** 250 (ctrl).
**Desc:** Music and sagas of Norwegian 8-stringed hardanger fiddle, other Scandinavian folk instruments and old dances. News of current performers, work shops, reviews and learning aids.

US/0163-4607
**SOUND TRAX.** Vol. 1, No. 2 (Dec. 1978)-. Periodical. English. bm. $7.50. Sound Trax, 630 Third Avenue, New York NY 10017. ***Continues*** *Modern Hi-Fi & Music's Sound Trax.*

US/0145-6237
**SOUNDBOARD.** [Soundboard]. **Added/Corp** Guitar Foundation of America. **VFOAT** Guitar Foundation of America Soundboard; GFA Soundboard. Vol. 1, (Feb. 1974)-. Periodical. English. qt (Feb., May, Aug., Nov.). $30.00 (one year); $55.00 (two years); $80.00 (three years) includes Directory of Guitar Foundation of America Membership. Guitar Foundation of America, PO Box 1240, Claremont CA 91711. **Tel** (818)914-8585. **ED** Peter Danner. Index available. cum. index. **Bk Rev. Ad Acc, Adv Mgr:** Gunnar Eisel. **Circ:** 3,000 (ctrl).
**Desc:** Classical guitar information, including techniques, performances, pedogogy, music, records, events, calendar, construction and reviews.
**Ind/Abst** Music Artic. Guide; Music Index.

●CN/1183-7659
**SOUNDNOTES (TORONTO).** (SOUNDNOTES.). [SoundNotes]. **VFOAT** Sound Notes. (Fall/Winter 1991)-. Periodical. English. Twice a year (Mar., Oct.). Free Universities & Libraries, 10.00Can$ (individuals), 15.00Can$ (institutions) Canada. Soundnotes, Box 793, Station P, Toronto Ontario M5S 2Z1 Canada. **Tel** (416)975-5185. **DD** 780/.971.

UK/0144-5774
**SOUNDS.** ***Ceased.*** [Sounds]. (1970)-(1992). Periodical. English. wk. United Magazine Subscriptions, 1st Floor Stephenson House, Brunel C, Milton Keynes MK2 2EW England. **Tel** 011 44 908 747008. **DD** _a780.

AT/0811-3149
**SOUNDS AUSTRALIAN : AUSTRALIAN MUSIC CENTRE JOURNAL. Added/Corp** Australian Music Centre. No. 15 (Oct. 1987)-. Periodical. English. Four times a year. 55.00Aus$ (institutions), 40.00Aus$ (individuals) Australia; 70.0Aus$ (institutions), 55.00Aus$ (individuals) New Zealand; 85.00Aus$ (institutions), 70.00Aus$ (individuals) other. The Australia Music Centre, PO Box N690, Grosvenor Place, Sydney New South Wales 2000 Australia. **Tel** 011 61 2 2474677, FAX 011 61 2 2412873. **ED** Catherine Brown-Watt. **LC** IN PROCESS. **Bk Rev**, (Qty: 6). **Ad Acc, Adv Mgr:** F. Harvey. **Circ:** 1,100 (ctrl). ***Continues*** *AMC News.*
**Desc:** National music quarterly that covers issues of Australian composition, music education, and musical life. Recordings, books, and publications are frequently reviewed.

US/1042-0649
**SOUNDTRACK (RINGWOOD, N.J.). See** Sound Recordings and Systems.

NE
**SOURCE MATERIALS AND STUDIES IN ETHNOMUSICOLOGY.** English (German, French and Dutch). ir. Uitgeverij Frits Knuf B V, PO Box 720, 4116 ZJ Buuren Netherlands. **Tel** 011 31 03449-1255, FAX 011 31 03449-2617. **Circ:** 700.

SA/0258-509X
**SOUTH AFRICAN JOURNAL OF MUSICOLOGY. Added/Corp** Musicological Society of South Africa. Southern African Music Rights Organisation. **VFOAT** Suid-Afrikaanse Tydskrif Vir Musiekwetenskap; SAMUS. Vol. 1 (1981)-. Afrikaans (English). an. R30.00. Musicological Society of South Africa, Box 29958, Sunnyside 0132 Pretoria South Africa. **Tel** 011 27 12 4296686, 11 7163834. **ED** R. Walton. **LC** ML5; .S667. **DD** 780/.9. cum. index. **Bk Rev. Circ:** 200 (ctrl).
**Desc:** Any articles on musicology and ethnomusicology with preference to those on subjects relevant to southern Africa.
**Ind/Abst** Music Index (Vol. 11, 1991-); RILM Abstr.

SA/0038-2493
**SOUTH AFRICAN MUSIC TEACHER.** (THE SOUTH AFRICAN MUSIC TEACHER. DIE SUID-AFRIKAANSE MUSIEKONDERWYSER.). [S. Afr. music teach.]. **Added/Corp** South African Society of Music Teachers. **VFOAT** Suid-Afrikaanse Musiekonderwyser. (1931)-. Periodical. English. Twice a year. $9.00. South African Society of Music Teachers, 3 Bantry Steps Bantry Way, Capetown 8001 South Africa. **ED** M. Whiteman. **LC** ML5; .S669. **Bk Rev. Ad Acc. Circ:** 1,800 (ctrl).
**Desc:** Informative articles on music teaching in general and activities of the South African Society of Music Teachers; also list of members.
**Ind/Abst** Music Index.

US/0038-3341
**SOUTH DAKOTA MUSICIAN. Added/Corp** South Dakota Music Educators. South Dakota Bandmasters Association. South Dakota Music Teachers National Association. Vol.1 (Oct. 1966)-. Periodical. English. Three times a year. $4.00. Northern State College, Aberdeen SD 57401. **Tel** (605)622-2497. ***Supersedes*** *South Dakota Music Educator;* ***Continues*** *South Dakota Bandmasters Journal.*

US/1047-9635
**SOUTHEASTERN JOURNAL OF MUSIC EDUCATION.** [Southeast. j. music educ.]. **Added/Corp** Georgia Center for Continuing Education. **VFOAT** SJME. Vol. 1 (1989)-. English. an. $15.00 (institutions), $10.00 (individuals). University of Georgia Georgia Center for Continuing Education, Suite 295, Athens GA 30602. **Tel** (706)542-1226. **LC** ML1; .S826. **DD** 780/.7/073.

US/0749-4106
**SOUTHERN CALIFORNIA EARLY MUSIC SOCIETY NEWSLETTER.** [South. Calif. Early Music Soc. newsl.]. **Added/Corp** Southern California Early Music Society. (198?)-. Newsletter. English. mo. Southern California Early Music Society, 6000 Sunset Boulevard, Suite 209, Los Angeles CA 90028. **DD** 780. ***Continues*** *Southern California Early Music Society.*

US
**SOUTHWESTERN MUSICIAN COMBINED WITH THE TEXAS MUSIC EDUCATOR, THE. Added/Corp** Texas Music Educators Association. Texas Music Teachers Association. (Dec. 1934)-. Periodical. English. Ten times a year (August through May). $15.00. Texas Music Educators Association, PO Box 49469, Austin TX 78765. **Tel** (512)452-0710. **ED** Bill Cormack. **LC** ML1; .S85. **Ad Acc. Circ:** 7,005 (ctrl). available on microfilm. ***Absorbed*** *Texas Music Educator;* ***Supersedes*** *Southwestern Musicale.*
**Desc:** Means of communication between members, promoting the field of music education throughout the state.

GW
**SOZIALISTISCHES MUSIKSCHAFFEN DER DEUTSCHEN DEMOKRATISCHEN REPUBLIK. Added/Corp** Sachsische Landesbibliothek (Dresden, Germany). (19??)-. German. an. Sachsisches Landesbibliothek, Marienallee 12, Dresden 806 Germany. **Tel** 5 26 77. **ED** Ludwig Muller. **LC** ML120.G3; S68. **DD** 016.78/09431. **Circ:** 750 (ctrl).
**Desc:** Index of first performances.

US/0270-1766
**SPECIAL SERIES / SOCIETY FOR ETHNOMUSICOLOGY.** [Spec. ser. - Soc. Ethnomusicol.]. **Main/Corp** Society for Ethnomusicology. **Added/Corp** Society for Ethnomusicology. (19??)-. Monographic series. English. ir. Price varies per volume. Society for Ethnomusicology, Morrison Hall 005, Indiana University, Bloomington IN 47405. **Tel** (812)855-6672, FAX (812)855-6673. **LC** UNC.

US/1047-2371
**SPECTRUM (CHATSWORTH, CALIF.).** ***Title Change.*** (SPECTRUM.). [Spectrum]. **VFOAT** Schwann Spectrum. Vol. 1 No. 1 (Spring 1990)-Vol. 3 No. 4 (Fall 1992). Periodical. English. qt. Schwann Publications, PO Box 5529, Santa Fe NM 87502. **Tel** (800)446-3563, (505)982-2366, FAX (818)718-8482. **(Subscription address:** Schwann, PO Box 55442, Boulder CO, 80322**) ED** Jane Hart. **LC** ML156.2; .S69. **DD** 016.78026/605. **Ad Acc. Circ:** 52,000 per year. ***Continues in part*** *Schwann, 0893-0449; Schwann CD, 1042-5047.* ***Continued by*** *Schwann Spectrum, 1065-9161.*
**Desc:** List over 50,000 non-classical recordings currently available on CD, LP, cassette tape and CD-Video.

NO/0333-0370
**SPELEMANNSBLADET. Added/Corp** Landslaget for Spelemenn. (19??)-. Periodical. Norwegian. bm. Landslaget for Spellmenn, Stavangergt, 25 OSLO 4. **LC** ML3704; .S63. **DD** 781.7481/05.

US/0886-3032
**SPIN (NEW YORK, N.Y.).** (SPIN.). [Spin]. Vol. 1, No. 1 (May 1985)-. Periodical. English. mo. $11.95 (one year), $19.95 (two year) US; $30.00 Canada; $50.00 other. Camouflage Publishing Inc, 6 West 18th Street, New York NY 10011. **Tel** (212)633-8200. **(Subscription address:** Palm Coast Data, PO Box 420235, Agency Department, Palm Coast FL 32142.**) LC** ML3533.8; .S64. **DD** 784.5/4/005. available on microfilm and microfiche from University Microfilms International (UMI).
**Ind/Abst** Access (1986-); Music Index.

CN/0229-7930
**SPIRIT CANADA.** [Spirit Can.]. (May 1979)-. Periodical. English. mo. $3.00 for 10 issues. Spirit Canada, PO Box 6812 Station A, Toronto Ontario M5W 1X6 Canada. **DD** 784.5/4/00971.

US/0889-3276
**STACCATO (TERRE HAUTE, IND.).** (STACCATO.). [Staccato]. **Added/Corp** WE Educational Music Publications (Terre Haute, Ind.). **VFOAT** New Staccoto. (19??)-. Periodical. English. an. WE Educational Music Publishers Inc., 1313 Wabash Avenue, Terre Haute IN 47807. **Tel** (812)466-1950. **DD** 780.

US/0146-5791
**STAFF NOTES. Added/Corp** University Society, New York. (197?)-. Periodical. English. University Society, 25 Cottage Street, Milland Park NJ 07432. ***Continues*** *International Library of Music Staff Notes.*

US/0092-0398
**STANYAN NEWS.** (19??)-. Periodical. English. Cheval/Stanyan Company, PO Box 2783, Hollywood CA 90028. **LC** ML1; .S873. **DD** 784/.05.

UK
**STAR FILE ANNUAL.** (19??)-. English. an. The Hamlyn Publishing Group, Astronaut House, Feltham, Middlesex England. **LC** ML156.4.R6; S7. **DD** 016.7899/12454/00941.

US
**STEEL GUITAR INTERNATIONAL NEWSLETTER.** Newsletter. English. Four times a year (published Jan., Apr., July, Oct.). $20.00 US; $25.00 other. Steel Guitar International, PO Box 2413, St. Louis MO 63114. **Tel** (314)427-7794, FAX (314)427-0516. **ED** Dewitt A. Scott Sr. **Ad Acc. Circ:** 2,200.
**Desc:** Steel guitar information and instruction.

US
**STEINWAY NEWS. Added/Corp** Steinway & Sons. (19??)-. Periodical. English. ir. Steinway & Sons, Steinway Place, Long Island City NY 11105. **Tel** (718)721-2600. **ED** Leo Spellman. **LC** ML1; .S883. **DD** 786.205. **Circ:** 50,000.

CN/1181-6805
**STEPPIN' OUT (SUDBURY).** (STEPPIN OUT.). [Steppin' out]. **Added/Corp** Northern Lights Festival (Sudbury, Ont.). **VFOAT** Stepping Out. (1990)-. Periodical. English (summaries and/or abstracts in French). mo. $28.00 per year. Northern Lights Festival, 3rd Floor/136 Larch Street, Sudbury Ontario P3E 1C2 Canada. **DD** 784.4/007/9713133. ***Continues*** *Northern Lights Festival (Sudbury, Ont.) Northern Lights Festival., 0827-3995.*

GW/0340-0778
**STEREO. See** Sound Recordings and Systems.

US/1048-7468
**STEVENSON CLASSICAL COMPACT DISC GUIDE.** [Stevenson class. compact disc guide]. **VFOAT** Classical Compact Disc Guide; Classical, Stevenson Compact Disc Review Guide; Stevenson Classical Disc Guide; Stevenson Classical Guide; Classical Disc Guide; Stevenson; Stevenson Compact Disc Review Guide. Vol. 5, No. 3 (Sept. 1989)-. Periodical. English. Four times a year. $26.00. Stevenson Classical CD Guide, PO Box 53286, Indianapolis IN 46253. **Tel** (317)293-7778. **LC** ML156.9; .S82. **DD** 780. ***Continues*** *Stevenson Compact Disc Review Guide, 0890-8907.*

UK/0039-2030
**STORYVILLE (CHIGWELL).** (STORYVILLE.). [Storyville]. (Oct. 1965)-. Periodical. English. Four times a year (Mar., June, Sept., Dec.). £8.40 UK; £10.00 others. Storyville Publication Company Essex IG7 6HS England, 66 Fairview Drive, Chigwell Essex IG7 6HS England. **Tel** 011/44/1/500/6098. **ED** Laurie Wright. **LC** ML5; .S87. **DD** 785.4/2/05. **Bk Rev. Ad Acc. Circ:** 2,500.
**Desc:** Covers the earlier forms of jazz and blues with interviews, articles, record and book reviews and discographical research featured. Always includes rare photographs from its period.

UK/0039-2049
**STRAD, THE.** [Strad]. Vol. 1, No. 1 (May 1890)-. Periodical. English. Twelve times a year. $75.00 (one year), $135.00 (two year), US, and Canada; £35.00 (one year), £63.00 (two year) UK; £55.00 (one year), £99.00 (two year) other. Orpheus Publications, 7 St. Johns Road, Harrow Middlesex HA1 2EE England. **Tel** 011 44 81 863-4040, FAX 011 44 81 424-9945. **(Subscription address:** Orpheus Subscriptions Departmenmt, PO Box 648, Harrow, Middlesex, HA1 2NW; England.) **ED** Eric Wen. **LC** ML5; .S89. **DD** 787/.01/05. **Bk Rev. Ad Acc. Circ:** 10,000 (ctrl). Documents available from The Genuine Article.
**Desc:** For those interested in the stringed instruments player, manufacturer, collector, student, and teacher.
**Ind/Abst** Arts Humanit. Citation Index [Full Cov.]; Br. Humanit. Index; Curr. Contents Arts Humanit.; Music Index; Res. Alert [Full Cov.].

CN/0841-2650
**STREETSOUND (TORONTO).** (STREETSOUND.). [Streetsound]. (Nov. 1986)-. Periodical. English. Twelve times a year. $29.00. Street Media Ventures Inc., 333 West 52nd Street, Suite 1003, New York NY 10019. **Tel** (212)397-6203. **DD** 780/.42/05.

US/0888-3106
**STRINGS (SAN ANSELMO, CALIF.).** (STRINGS.). Vol. 1, No. 1 (1986)-. Periodical. English. Six times a year (Jan., Mar., May, July, Sept., Nov.). $36.00. String Letter Press Publishers, 412 Red Hill Avenue 15, San Anselmo CA 94960. **Tel** (415)485-6946, (800)827-6837. **(Subscription address:** PO Box 767, San Anselmo, CA 94960) **ED** David A. Lusterman. **LC** ML749.5; .S87. **DD** 787/.05. **Bk Rev. Ad Acc. Circ:** 8,000.
**Desc:** For players and makers of bowed stringed instruments with practical articles on techniques of performance plus how to care for and evaluate instruments and bows.
**Ind/Abst** Music Artic. Guide; Music Index.

AT/0157-7832
**STRINGYBARK & GREENHIDE. VFOAT** Stringybark and Greenhide. Vol. 1, No. 1 (1979)-. Periodical. English. qt. S & G, PO Box 424, Newcastle NSW 2300 Australia. **LC** ML3544; .S77. **DD** 781.794/05.

IT/0392-890X
**STRUMENTI MUSICALI.** [Strum. music.]. (1979)-. Periodical. Italian. Eleven times a year. L46200.00 Italy; L92400.00 other. Gruppo Editoriale Jackson Spa, Via Gorki 69, 20092 Cinisello Balsamo Italy. **Tel** 011 39 2 66034401. **ED** Paolo Reine. **UDC** 681.8. **Bk Rev. Ad Acc. Circ:** 22,000 (ctrl).

IT
**STUDI DONIZETTIANI. Added/Corp** Centro di Studi Donizettiani. (1962)-. Italian (English). Centro di Studi Donizettiani, 24100 Bergamo Italy.

IT/0391-7789
**STUDI MUSICALI.** (STUDI MUSICALI / ACCADEMIA NAZIONALE DI SANTA CECILIA, ROMA.). [Studi music.]. **Added/Corp** Accademia di Santa Cecilia. Vol. 1, (1972)-. Periodical. Multiple languages (English, French, German and Italian). Twice a year. L7000.00 Italy; L9000.00 others. Casa Editrice Leo S. Olschki, Viuzzo del Pozzetto, Casella Postale 66, 50126 Florence Italy. **Tel** 011 39 55 6530684, FAX 011 39 55 6530214. **LC** IN PROCESS. Documents available from The Genuine Article. ***Continues** Santa Cecilia.*
**Ind/Abst** Arts Humanit. Citation Index (19??-19??) [Full Cov.]; Curr. Contents Arts Humanit.; Music Index; Res. Alert [Full Cov.]; RILM Abstr.

IT
**STUDI VERDIANI. Added/Corp** Istituto di Studi Verdiani. (1982)-. Periodical. English (French, German, Italian and Spanish). ir. L30000. 1st Nazion Studi Verdiani, Strada Della Repubblica 56, 43100 Parma Italy. **Tel** 011 39 521 286044. **(Subscription address:** EDT SRL; Via Alfieri 19, 10121 Turin Italy; telephone: 011 39 11 5621496) **LC** ML410.V4; S85. **DD** 782.1/092/4.
**Ind/Abst** Music Index.

HU/0039-3266
**STUDIA MUSICOLOGICA. ACADEMIAE SCIENTIARUM HUNGARICA.** (STUDIA MUSICOLOGICA.). [Stud. musicol. Acad. Sci. Hung.]. **Added/Corp** Magyar Tudomanyos Akademia. Vol. 1 (1961)-. Academic Scholarly Publication. English (French, Italian and Russian). qt. $96.00. Akademiai Kiado, Publishing House of the Hungarian Academy of Sciences, Prielle Kornelia u. 19-35, H-1117 Budapest Hungary. **Tel** 011 36 1 1811991, FAX 011 36 1 1811991, telex 22-6228 AKNYO H. **ED** Jozsef Ujfalussy (editor's address: Studia Musicologica, H-1014 Budapest, Tancsics U 7 Hungary). **[CCC].** cum. index.
**Desc:** Publishes papers in the field of Hungarian musicology, including questions of the history of Hungarian music and of universal music history from a Hungarian angle.
**Ind/Abst** MLA Int. Bibl. Books Artic. Mod. Lang. Lit.; Music Index; RILM Abstr.

NO/0332-5024
**STUDIA MUSICOLOGICA NORVEGICA.** [Stud. musicol. Norv.]. Vol. 1 (1968)-. Norwegian (English). an. Kr235.00, $41.00. Scandinavian University Press, PO Box 2959 Toeyen, N 0608 Oslo 6 Norway. **Tel** 011 47 2 2575400, FAX 011 47 2 2575353, telex 71896 UROR N. **(Subscription address:** Scandinavian University Press, 200 Meacham Ave., Elmont NY 11003.) **ED** O K Sundberg Oversand and Arvid O Vollsness. **LC** ML3797.1; S87. **[CCC]. Bk Rev. Ad Acc. Circ:** 150 (ctrl).
**Desc:** Contains articles on music studies, both general and Norwegian.
**Ind/Abst** Music Index; RILM Abstr.

GW/0081-7341
**STUDIEN ZUR MUSIKGESCHICHTE DES 19. JAHRHUNDERTS.** Vol. 1 (1965)-. Monographic series. German. ir. Price varies per volume. Gustav Bosse Verlag GmbH & Company KG, Postfach 417, W-8400 Regensburg 1 Germany. **Tel** 011 49 941 794091.

GW/0081-3222
**STUDIEN ZUR MUSIKWISSENSCHAFT.** (1913)-. German. ir. B. Schotts Soehne Musikverlag, Carl Zeiss Str 1, Postfach 3640, D 55026 Mainz Germany. **Tel** 011 49 6131 505129, 011 49 6131 505122, FAX 011 49 6131 505115, telex 04187821. **(Subscription address:** European American Music District Corporation, PO Box 850, Valley Forge, PA 19482; telephone: (215)648-0506) **ED** B. Schotts Soehne. **LC** ML55; .S9.

GW
**STUDIEN ZUR TRADITIONELLEN MUSIK JAPANS.** (1977)-. Monographic series. German. ir. Price varies per volume. Baerenreiter-Verlag, KGA Verlagssvc PF 100329, D 34003 Kassel Germany. **Tel** 011 49 561 31050, telex 99504. **ED** Robert Guenter.
**Desc:** Publications are issued irregularly and examine special themes of Japanese music traditions which have rapidly fallen into oblivion.

GW
**STUDIEN ZUR WERTUNGSFORSCHUNG. Added/Corp** Akademie fuer Musik und Darstellende Kunst in Graz. Institut fuer Wertungsforschung. Hochschule fuer Musik und Darstellende Kunst in Graz. Institut fuer Wertungsforschung. Vol. 2, No. 1 (1969)-. Monographic series. German (English). ir. Price varies per volume. Institut fur Wertungsforschung Darstellende Kunst, Graz Austria. **Tel** 43 316 32053 525. **ED** Otto Kolleritsch. **LC** ML55; .S92. **DD** 780. **Circ:** 700.
**Desc:** Presents written versions of papers given at yearly symposia during "Styrian Autumn." The general subject, on musical criticism and aesthetic research, changes from year to year.

US
**STUDIES AND DOCUMENTS. Main/Corp** American Musicological Society. No. 1, (1947)-. Monographic series. English. ir. Price varies per volume. Galaxy Music Corporation, 138 Ipswich Street, Boston MA 02215. **Tel** (617)236-1935, (800)777-1919.
**Desc:** Monographs and historical editions.

HU
**STUDIES IN CENTRAL AND EASTERN EUROPEAN MUSIC.** Vol. 1, (1986)-. Academic Scholarly Publication. English. ir. Price varies per volume. Akademiai Kiado, Publishing House of the Hungarian Academy of Sciences, Prielle Kornelia u. 19-35, H-1117 Budapest Hungary. **Tel** 011 36 1 1811991, FAX 011 36 1 1811991, telex 22-6228 AKNYO H.

AT/0081-8267
**STUDIES IN MUSIC. *Ceased.*** [Stud. music]. No. 1, (1967)-Vol. 26 (1992). English. ir. University of Western Australia / University Bookshop, PO Box 656, Nedlands WA 6009 Australia. **Tel** 011 61 9 3802069. **ED** Frank Callaway, D. Tunley and D. Symons. **LC** ML5; .S9255. **DD** 780/.5. **Bk Rev. Ad Acc.**
**Desc:** Report of the results of musicological studies in Australia and New Zealand, with contributions from scholars in other countries, for all facts of musical thought.
**Ind/Abst** APAIS, Aust. Public Aff. Inf. Ser. (1968-); Music Index; RILM Abstr.

CN/0703-3052
**STUDIES IN MUSIC FROM THE UNIVERSITY OF WESTERN ONTARIO.** [Stud. music Univ. West. Ont.]. **Main/Corp** University of Western Ontario. Dept. of Music History. (1976)-. English. Department of Music History / Talbot College, Faculty of Music, London Ontario N6A 3K7 Canada. **LC** ML5; .U597. **DD** 780/.5. ctrl circ.
**Ind/Abst** Music Index; RILM Abstr.

US/0743-9822
**STUDIES IN THE HISTORY OF MUSIC.** [Stud. hist. music]. **VFOAT** S.H.M.; SHM. (1983)-. Monographic series. English. ir. Price varies per volume. Broude Brothers Limited, 141 White Oaks Road, Williamstown MA 01267. **Tel** (413)458-8132, (800)525-8559. **LC** ML1; .S899. **DD** 780/.9.

SW/0346-8119
**SUMLEN.** [Sumlen]. **Added/Corp** Samfundet for Vvisforskning. Svenskt Visarkiv. (1976)-. German (Swedish; summaries and/or abstracts in English). an. Kr100.00 Sweden; Kr150.00 other. Svenskt Visarkiv, Hagagatan 23 A, S-113 47 Stockholm Sweden. **Tel** 340935. **ED** Bengt R. Jonsson. **LC** ML3545; .S85. **DD** 781.7/05. **Bk Rev. Circ:** 1,000 (ctrl).
**Desc:** Vocal and instrumental folk music; folk and medieval poetry in Scandinavia.
**Ind/Abst** MLA Int. Bibl. Books Artic. Mod. Lang. Lit.; RILM Abstr.

GW/0585-9158
**SUMMA MUSICAE MEDII AEVI.** (1957)-. Monographic series. German. ir. Price varies per volume. Haenssler Verlag, Postfach 1220, D-73762 Neuhausen Germany. **Tel** 011 49 07158 1770, telex 715816 HAENSR. **DD** 780. **Bk Rev. Ad Acc.** ctrl circ.

CN/1182-6630
**SUMMERFOLK MUSIC & CRAFTS FESTIVAL.** [Summerfolk music crafts festiv.]. **Added/Corp** Georgian Bay Folk Society. **VFOAT** Summerfolk Music and Crafts Festival. 15th (Aug. 17/18/19, 1990)-. English. Limited free distribution. Georgian Bay Folk Society, PO Box 521, Owen Sound Ontario N4K 5R1 Canada. **Tel** 371-2995. **DD** 780/.7/971318. ***Continues** Annual Summerfolk Music & Crafts Festival., 0845-8057.*

FI/0782-1875
**SUOMALAISTEN ANITTEIDEN LUETTELO. CATALOGUE OF FINNISH RECORDINGS. Added/Corp** Jyvaskylan Yliopisto. Kirjasto. **VFOAT** Catalogue of Finnish Recordings. (1983)-. Finnish. **LC** ML156.4.N3; F57. **DD** 016/78/094897. ***Continues** Suomalaisten Aanilevyjen Luettelo.*

US
**SUPPLEMENT TO THE INDEX OF FLUTE MUSIC. VFOAT** Supplement to Index of Flute Music. (1974)-. English. ir. Music Register, 105 South Battery, Little Rock AR 72205.

US
**SURVEY OF OPERATING PERFORMANCE FOR MUSIC DEALERS. Added/Corp** National Association of Music Merchants (U.S.) Industry Insights, Inc. **VFOAT** NAMM's Cost of Doing Business Survey; Cost of Doing Business Survey. (1988)-. Periodical. English. National Association of Music Merchants, 5140 Avenida Encinas, Carlsbad CA 92008. **Tel** (619)438-8001, FAX (619)438-7327. ***Continues** Retail Music Products Industry Report.*

UK
**SUSSEX FOLK DIARY.** No. 20 (Mar./Apr. 1973)-. Periodical. English. bm. Vic Smith, 7 Stanmer Villas, BN7 7HQ Sussex England. **LC** ML5; .B6892. **DD** 781.7/025/4225. ***Continues** Brighton Folk Diary.*

SW/0081-9816
**SVENSK TIDSKRIFT FOR MUSIKFORSKNING.** (SVENSK TIDSKRIFT FOR MUSIKFORSKNING. SWEDISH JOURNAL OF MUSICOLOGY.). [Sven. tidskr. musikforsk.]. **Added/Corp** Svenska samfundet for Musikforskning. **VFOAT** Swedish Journal of Musicology. Vol. 1, (1919)-. Periodical. Swedish (English and German). Twice a year. Kr325.00 Europe; Kr345.00 others. Swedish Society for Musicology, Box 5439, S 402 29 Goteborg Sweden. **Tel** 011 31 7734086, 7734087. **ED** Hans Bernskiold and Ola Stockfelt. **LC** ML5; .S968. Index available. cum. index. **Bk Rev. Circ:** 500. Documents available from The Genuine Article.
**Desc:** Presents articles covering various fields of musicology, with reports of unpublished theses, research projects, congresses, etc. Includes a review section, listings of Swedish music literature.
**Ind/Abst** Arts Humanit. Citation Index (19??-19??) [Full Cov.]; Curr. Contents Arts Humanit.; Music Index; Res. Alert [Full Cov.]; Soc. Sci. Cit. Index [Select. Cov.].

US/0147-5282
**SWEET POTATO.** (19??)-. Periodical. English. Twenty-six times a year. $9.00. Sweet Potato Inc, Box 385, Portland ME 04112. **Tel** (207)775-5991. **ED** Bennie Green and Richard Cromonic. **LC** ML1; .S923. **DD** 784. **Bk Rev. Ad Acc. Circ:** 45,000.
**Desc:** A music and entertainment magazine for Southern Maine. Includes club listings, calendar of events, and local coverage of events.

US/1052-7648
**SYMPHONIUM (PITTSBURGH, PA.).** (SYMPHONIUM : A NEWSLETTER FOR AND ABOUT THE BLACK SYMPHONY MUSICIAN.). [Symphonium]. **Added/Corp** Black Symphony Musician (Group). Vol. 1, No. 1 (Fall/Winter 1988)-. Newsletter. English. Symphonium, c/o Patricia P Jennings, 1349 North Sheridan Avenue, Pittsburgh PA 15206. **LC** ML394; .S97. **DD** 785.
**Ind/Abst** Music Artic. Guide.

US/1046-3232
**SYMPHONY (WASHINGTON, D.C.).** (SYMPHONY.). [Symphony]. **Added/Corp** American Symphony Orchestra League. **VFOAT** Symphony Magazine. Vol. 40, No. 4 (July/Aug. 1989)-. Periodical. English. Six times a year (Feb., Apr., June, Aug., Oct.,

Dec.). $50.00 Includes the American Symphony Orchestra League Membership. American Symphony Orchestra League, 777 14th Street Northwest, Suite 500, Washington DC 20005. **Tel** (202)628-0099. **DD** 785. available on microfilm and microfiche from University Microfilms International (UMI). ***Continues** Symphony Magazine, 0271-2687.*
**Ind/Abst** Music Index.

US/0145-5435
**SYNAPSE (SAN FERNANDO).** (SYNAPSE.). (19??)-. Periodical. English. bm. Schill and Schill Pub, PO Box 359, North Hollywood CA 91603. **LC** ML1; .S995. **DD** 789.9.

US/0890-9687
**SYNTHESIS (MINNEAPOLIS, MINN.).** (SYNTHESIS.). [Synthesis]. Vol. 1, Issue 1 (1970)-. Periodical. English. qt. Scully-Cutter Publishing, 1315 4th Street SE, Minneapolis MN 55414. **DD** 789.
**Ind/Abst** Music Artic. Guide (?-?); Music Index (-19??).

US/0363-4787
**T.U.B.A. JOURNAL. Main/Corp** Tubists Universal Brotherhood Association. **Added/Corp** Tubists Universal Brotherhood Association. Journal. **VAT** Tubists Universal Brotherhood Association Journal. Vol. 4 (Fall 1976)-. Periodical. English. qt. $35.00 US; $45.00 other. University Texas Austin, Department of Music, Austin TX 78712. **Tel** (512)471-0504. **ED** Karen Cotton (editor's address: 133 Stagecrest Drive, Raleigh NC 27603; editor's phone: (919)779-5178). **LC** ML1; .T82. **DD** 788/.48/05. Index available. cum. index. **Bk Rev**, (Qty: 4). **Ad Acc**, **Adv Mgr:** Jim Shearer, **Tel** (505)646-2601. **Circ:** 2,500. ***Continues** T.U.B.A. Newsletter, 0363-4779.*
**Desc:** A quarterly journal of interest to tuba and euphonium players and teachers.

US/0163-5360
**T.U.B.A. MEMBERSHIP ROSTER.**
**Main/Corp** Tubists Universal Brotherhood Association. **Added/Corp** Tubists Universal Brotherhood Association. Membership Roster. **VFOAT** TUBA ... Membership Roster. **VAT** Tubists Universal Brotherhood Association Membership Roster. (19??)-. English. an. $25.00 US; $35.00 other. School of Music, University of North Carolina at Greensboro, c/o David G. Lewis, Greensboro NC 27403. **ED** Jerry Young. **LC** ML26; .T83 1977. **DD** 788/.48. **Ad Acc. Circ:** 2,300 (ctrl).

MY
**TA MA KO YU CHIH SHENG. VFOAT** Sound of Malaysian's Musician. (1971)-. Periodical. Chinese (Chinese). sa. $0.30 each issue. Ta Ma Ko Yu Pan She, 18 Dato Koyah Road, Penang Malaysia. **LC** ML5; .T1.

US/0194-1771
**TALENT & BOOKING'S DISCO.** (TALENT & BOOKING'S DISCO, THE BOOK.). **VFOAT** Disco, the Book. **VAT** Talent and Booking's Disco. (19??)-. English. an. $20.00. Talent & Booking Publishing Company, PO Box 2772, Palm Springs CA 92263. **LC** ML3526; .T34. **DD** 785.4/1.

US/0889-4175
**TALENT EDUCATION JOURNAL. *Ceased.*** [Talent educ. j.]. -Ceased Jan. 1990. Periodical. English (Japanese). qt. Talent Education of St Louis, 236 Spring Avenue, St Louis MO 63119. **LC** ML1; .T18. **DD** 372.
**Ind/Abst** Music Artic. Guide (?-?).

US/0738-7911
**TALKIN' UNION (TAKOMA PARK MD.).**
***Ceased.* See** Economics-Labor.

US/0272-9520
**TARAKAN MUSIC LETTER, THE.** (19??)-. Periodical. English. qt. $22.50. Sound Advice Enterprises, 40 Holly Lane, East Hills NY 11577. **Tel** (516)621-2445.

●US/1069-7446
**TEACHING MUSIC.** [Teach. music]. **Added/Corp** Music Educators National Conference (U.S.). Vol. 1 No. 1 (Aug. 1993)-. Periodical. English. bm. $60.00 US (includes Music Educators Journal). Music Educators National Conference, 1806 Robert Fulton Drive, Reston VA 22091. **Tel** (703)860-4000, (800)336-3768. **LC** IN PROCESS; ML1; .T38. **DD** 780.
**Desc:** Emphasis is on news and brief practical features.

●US
**TECHNOLOGY DIRECTORY / ASSOCIATION FOR TECHNOLOGY IN MUSIC INSTRUCTION. Added/Corp** Association for Technology in Music Instruction. **VFOAT** ATMI Technology Directory. **VAT** Association for Technology in Music Instruction Technology Directory. (1991)-. Directory. English. ir. $30.00 Comes with Courseway Directory. Association Technology Music Instruction, 1866 College Road, Ohio State University, San Francisco CA 94114. **Tel** (614)292-2138. **LC** ML74.35; .T4. **DD** 016.78/078. ***Continues** Courseware Directory.*

US/1056-0505
**TEEN BEAT ALL STARS. See** Children and Youth Interests.

GW
**TEILTON : SCHRIFTENREIHE DER HEINRICH-STROBEL-STIFTUNG.**
**Added/Corp** Suedwestfunk (Baden-Baden, Germany). Heinrich-Strobel-Stiftung. **VFOAT** Schriftenreihe der Heinrich-Strobel-Stiftung. (1978)-. Monographic series. German. ir. Price varies per volume. Baerenreiter-Verlag, KGA Verlagssvc PF 100329, D 34003 Kassel Germany. **Tel** 011 49 561 31050, telex 99504. **ED** Heinrich Strobel-Stiftung Baden. **LC** ML1379; .T44. **DD** 789.9/9/0943.
**Desc:** Studies questions about music and frequency technique, and electric/electronic music experiments in the dimension of music and radio.

UK/0040-2982
**TEMPO (LONDON).** (TEMPO.). [Tempo]. No. 1-15 (Jan. 1939-June 1946); New Ser. No. 1 (Sept. 1946)-. Periodical. English. qt. 20.00Can$ Canada; £13.00 UK; £14.50 other. Boosey and Hawkes, 295 Regent Street, London W1A 1BR England. **Tel** 011 44 71 5802060, FAX 011 44 71 4365675. **ED** Calum MacDonald. **LC** ML5; .T317. **DD** 780.5. cum. index. **Bk Rev**. Documents available from The Genuine Article.
**Desc:** A review of modern music.
**Ind/Abst** Arts Humanit. Citation Index [Full Cov.]; Br. Humanit. Index; Curr. Contents Arts Humanit.; Music Index; Res. Alert [Full Cov.]; RILM Abstr.

US/0040-3016
**TEMPO (ROCKAWAY, N.J.).** (TEMPO.). **Added/Corp** New Jersey Music Educators Association. (1960)-. Periodical. English. qt. $8.00. New Jersey Music Educators Association, 14 Lum Avenue, c/o Chic Hansen, Chatham NJ 07928. **Tel** (201)635-2122, (201)635-0091, FAX (201)635-4523. **ED** Chic Hansen. **DD** 780. ***Continues** Bulletin (New Jersey Music Educators Association).*
**Ind/Abst** Music Artic. Guide.

US/0040-3334
**TENNESSEE MUSICIAN.** [Tenn. music.]. **Added/Corp** Tennessee Music Educators Association. Vol. 1 (1948)-. Periodical. English. qt. $6.00. The Tennessee Musician, 500 Holly Hill Court, Nashville TN 37221. **DD** 780.

US
**TEXAS COUNTRY WESTERN MAGAZINE.** (19??)-. Periodical. English. mo. Ransehc Publishing, PO Box 966, Alief TX 77411. **LC** ML1; .T333. **DD** 784.

US/0148-270X
**TEXAS FIDDLER, THE. Main/Corp** Texas Old Time Fiddlers Association. Vol. 1, No. 2 (May 1973)-. Periodical. English. mo. Texas Old Time Fiddlers Association, Route 2, Box 726, Burleson TX 76028. **LC** ML27.U5; T536. **DD** 787/.1/062764. ***Continues** Texas Fiddler, 0148-270X.*

●US/1062-6646
**TEXAS MUSIC INDUSTRY DIRECTORY, THE.** (THE TEXAS MUSIC INDUSTRY DIRECTORY : A REFERENCE BOOK FOR THE TEXAS MUSIC INDUSTRY.). [Tex. music ind. dir.]. **Added/Corp** Texas Music Office. 1st Ed. (Mar. 1991)-. Directory. English. an. Texas Music Office, Texas Department of Commerce, PO Box 12728, Austin TX 78711. **Tel** (512)472-5059. **LC** ML14.T3; T55. **DD** 338.4/778/025764.

US/0892-0796
**THEATRE JOBLIST. See** The Arts-Performing Arts.

US/0040-5531
**THEATRE ORGAN (1970).** (THEATRE ORGAN.). [Theatre organ]. **Added/Corp** American Theatre Organ Society. Vol. 12 (Feb. 1970)-. Periodical. English. bm (6 issues). $25.00 US; $30.00 other. American Theatre Organ Society, PO Box 417490, Sacramento CA 95841. **Tel** (916)962-1019, FAX (916)966-3172. **ED** Grace McGinnis, 4833 SE Brookside Drive #58, Milwawkie, OR, 97222, (503)654-5823. **DD** 786. cum. index. **Bk Rev**, (Qty: 3). **Ad Acc**, **Adv Mgr Tel** (503)233-7276. **Circ:** 6,000. ***Continues** Theatre Organ/Bombarde.*
**Desc:** Describes theatre organs with emphasis on restoration, preservation, recordings available and artists now being featured.

US
**THEORIA (DENTON, TEX.).** (THEORIA / COMPILED AND EDITED ANNUALLY BY GRADUATE STUDENTS AT THE SCHOOL OF MUSIC, NORTH TEXAS STATE UNIVERSITY.). **Added/Corp** North Texas State University. School of Music. Vol. 1 (1985)-. English. an. $7.00 individuals, $10.00 institutions. Theoria, School of Music, North Texas State University, PO Box 13887, Denton TX 76203. **Tel** (817)565-2791. **ED** John Covach & Robin Miller. **LC** ML1; .T3344. **DD** 781/.05. Index available. **Ad Acc**. ctrl circ.

US/0741-6156
**THEORY AND PRACTICE : JOURNAL OF THE MUSIC THEORY SOCIETY OF NEW YORK STATE.** [Theory pract.]. **Added/Corp** Music Theory Society of New York State. Vol. 1, No. 1 (June 1975)-. Periodical. English. an. $30.00 US; $35.00 other. Music Theory Society of New York State, Howard Cinnamon, Treasurer, Department of Music, Emily Lowe Hall 101B, 112 Hofstra University, Hempstead NY 11550-1090. **Tel** (516)463-5298. **ED** Severing Neff. **Bk Rev**, (Qty: 4). **Pr Rev. Circ:** 300.
**Desc:** Reviews, analyses, bibliographies, pedagogical information, articles.
**Ind/Abst** INFO-SOUTH Abstr.; Music Artic. Guide; Music Index; RILM Abstr.

GW
**TIBIA.** (1976)-. Periodical. German. qt. DM38.30 Europe; DM47.80 other. Moeck Verlag, Postfach 143, W 3100 Celle F R Germany. **Tel** 011 49 5141 885333, FAX 011 49 5141 885342. **ED** Nikolaus Delius, Gerhard Baun, Hermann Moeck, Christian Schneider. **LC** ML929; .T5. **DD** 788/.005. Index available. **Bk Rev. Ad Acc. Circ:** 4,000 (ctrl).
**Ind/Abst** Music Index; RILM Abstr.

US/0040-7380
**TIGER BEAT. See** Children and Youth Interests.

NE/0042-3874
**TIJDSCHRIFT VAN DE VERENIGING VOOR NEDERLANDSE MUZIEKGESCHIEDENIS.** [Tijdschr. Ver. Ned. Muziekgesch.]. **Added/Corp** Vereniging voor Nederlandse Muziekgeschiedenis. Vol. 19, Nos. 1, 2 (1960/61)-. Dutch (German, English and French). Twice a year. Fl88.00. Vereniging Voor Nederlandse Muziekgeschiedenis, PO Box 1514, 3500 BM Utrecht Netherlands. **Tel** 011 31 30 23327787, FAX (0)3449-2617. **(Subscription address:** Swets Publishing Service, PO Box 825, 2160 SZ Lisse, the Netherlands.**) ED** Arend Jan Gierveld. cum. index. **Bk Rev. Ad Acc**. Documents available from The Genuine Article. ***Continues** Tijdschrift voor Muziekwetenschap.*
**Desc:** Publishes research on the life and work of major and minor composers, particularly those who have some significance in the history of music in the Netherlands.
**Ind/Abst** Arts Humanit. Citation Index [Full Cov.]; Curr. Contents Arts Humanit.; Music Index; Res. Alert [Full Cov.]; RILM Abstr.

NE/0920-0649
**TIJDSCHRIFT VOOR OUDE MUZIEK.** [Tijdschr. oude muziek]. (1986)-. Periodical. Dutch. Four times a year. Fl40.00. Organisatie Oude Muziek, PO Box 734, NL 3500 Utrecht Netherlands. **Tel** 011 31 30 362236. **UDC** 783.3 (492). ***Formed by the union of** Cornemuse, 0920-3494 **and** Stimulus (Utrecht), 0166-7386.*

US/8750-782X
**TIMBRE (WOODINVILLE, WASH.).** (TIMBRE : EVERGREEN DISTRICT BULLETIN OF THE SOCIETY FOR THE PRESERVATION AND ENCOURAGEMENT OF BARBER SHOP QUARTET SINGING IN AMERICA, INC.). **Added/Corp** Society for the Preservation and Encouragement of Barber Shop Quartet Singing in America. Evergreen District. (19??)-. Bulletin. English. bm. S P E B S Q S A Inc, 6315 3rd Avenue, Kenosha WI 53140-5199.

US/0099-0396
**TIME BARRIER EXPRESS.** (197?)-. Periodical. English. bm. $9.00. Time Barrier Express, PO Box 206, Yonkers NY 10710. **LC** ML1; .T34. **DD** 784.

UK/0049-397X
**TOCHER; TALES, SONGS, TRADITION.** **Added/Corp** University of Edinburgh. School of Scottish Studies. No. 1 (Spring 1971)-. Periodical. English (Gaelic (Scots)). Twice a year (Apr., Oct.). £6.00. School of Scottish Studies, 27 George Square, Edinburgh EH8 9LD Scotland. **Tel** 011 44 31 6503060. **ED** A. Bruford. **LC** ML5; .T59. **DD** 784.4/941. Index available. **Bk Rev. Ad Acc. Circ:** 1,500.
**Desc:** Tales, legends and personal memories of ordinary and extraordinary Scots, recalling customs and superstitions, clan feuds, and Gaelic folksongs and ballads.
**Ind/Abst** Annu. Bibliogr. Engl. Lang. Lit.; Museum Abstr.

UK/0260-7425
**TONIC (ROBERT SIMPSON SOCIETY).** (TONIC : THE JOURNAL OF THE ROBERT SIMPSON SOCIETY.). **Added/Corp** Robert Simpson Society. (19??)-. Periodical. English. Twice a year. Robert Simpson Society, 3 Engel Park, London NW7 2HE England. **Tel** 011 441 346 3073. **ED** Martin Anderson, Christine Skinner and Graham Melville Mason. **LC** ML410.S587; T6. **DD** 780/.92/4. **Ad Acc. Circ:** 160 (ctrl).
**Desc:** To members of the Robert Simpson Society.

US
**TOP 10'S AND TRIVIA OF ROCK & ROLL AND RHYTHM & BLUES. *Ceased.***
**VFOAT** Top 10's & Trivia of Rock & Roll and Rhythm & Blues. **VAT** Top Tens and Trivia of Rock & Roll and Rhythm & Blues. (19??)-(1991). English. an. Blueberry Hill Publishing Company, 6504 Delmar, St Louis MO 63130. **Tel** (314)727-0880. **ED** Joe Edwards. **Bk Rev. Ad Acc.**
**Desc:** Complete monthly and yearly charts plus indexes

of every record and artist that made Billboard's weekly top 10 singles and top five albums charts. Artist, record, title, label, and serial number of each top ten record.

FR
**TOP MUSIQUE.** (19??)-. Periodical. French. sm. Top Musique, 45 rue Richer, 75009 Paris France. **LC** ML5; .T78.

CN/0844-5818
**TORONTO CHILDREN'S CHORUS.** (TORONTO CHILDREN'S CHORUS : NEWSLETTER.). [Tor. Child. Chorus]. **Main/Corp** Toronto Children's Chorus. (198?)-. Newsletter. English. ir. Free to members. Toronto Childrens Chorus, 60 St. Clair Avenue West, Suite 5A, Toronto Ontario M4V 1M7 Canada. **ED** Nancy MacArthur. **DD** 784.1/006/0713541. **Circ:** 1,000 (ctrl). available on diskette. ***Continues*** *Toronto Children's Chorus. Newsletter, 0844-5826.*

CN/0049-4208
**TORONTO MUSIC GUIDE.** (June 1971)-. Periodical. English. mo. Toronto Music Guide Magazine Subscription Department, 130 Glenforest Road, Toronto Ontario M4N 1Z9 Canada. **DD** 780/.9713/541.

JA/0039-3851
**TOYO ONGAKU KENKYU. Added/Corp** Toyo Ongaku Gakkai. **VFOAT** Journal of the Society for the Research of Asiatic Music. (Nov. 1937)-. Japanese (English). ir. **(Subscription address:** Japan Publications Trading Company, Ltd., PO Box 5030, Tokyo International, Tokyo 100-31 Japan.**) LC** IN PROCESS.
**Ind/Abst** RILM Abstr.

US/0041-0330
**TRACKER, THE.** [Tracker]. **Added/Corp** Organ Historical Society. (1956)-. Periodical. English. Four times a year (Feb., May, Aug., Nov.). $27.00 US; $35.00 other. Organ Historical Society Inc, PO Box 26811, Richmond VA 23261. **Tel** (804)353-9226. **ED** John Ogasapian. **LC** ML1; .T49. Index Available in first issue of next volume--attached. cum. index. **Bk Rev**, (Qty: 4-5). **Ad Acc. Circ:** 3,600. available on microfilm from University Microfilms International (UMI).
**Desc:** Musical and historical study of pipe organ building in North America.
**Ind/Abst** Music Artic. Guide; Music Index.

FR/0980-8493
**TRADITION MAGAZINE.** (1987)-. Periodical. French. Twelve times a year. 320.00F France; 390.00F other. Histoire et Collections, 19 Avenue de la Republique, F-75011 Paris France. **Tel** 33 1 43578383. **ED** Tesu Louis Vias (editor's phone: 33 1 40211820). **UDC** 379.824 : 623.444. Index available. **Bk Rev**, (Qty: 1). **Ad Acc, Adv Mgr:** Sbraire, **Tel** 33 1 40211829. **Circ:** 26,000 (ctrl).

US/1071-1864
**TRADITION (WALNUT, IOWA).** (TRADITION.). [Tradition]. **Added/Corp** National Traditional Country Music Association. (1976)-. Periodical. English. Six times a year. $15.00. Tradition, PO Box 438, Walnut IA 51577. **Tel** (712)784-3001, FAX (712)784-2010. **ED** Robert Everhart. **DD** 781. **Bk Rev**, (Qty: 8-10). **Ad Acc. Circ:** 2,500 (ctrl).

UK/0306-7440
**TRADITIONAL MUSIC.** [Tradit. music]. No. 1 (1975)-. Periodical. English. Three times a year. **LC** ML5; .T786. **DD** 781.741/05.
**Ind/Abst** MLA Int. Bibl. Books Artic. Mod. Lang. Lit.; Music Index (-19??).

US/1059-5953
**TRADITIONAL MUSICLINE, THE.** (THE TRADITIONAL MUSICLINE : THE MONTHLY MUSIC CALENDAR FOR NY/NJ/CT/PA/RI/DE.). [Tradit. musicline]. **VFOAT** Traditional Music Line. (19??)-. English. mo. $17.50 (one year); $32.00 (two year). Traditional Musicline, PO Box 10598, New Brunswick NJ 08906. **Tel** (908) 699-0665. **ED** Stephanie P Legin. **LC** IN PROCESS. **DD** 780. **Ad Acc. Circ:** 1500.
**Desc:** Comprehensive concert, festival, & dance listings for traditional acoustic music events in the Northeast.

US/1041-7494
**TRAVERSO (CLAVERACK, N.Y.).** (TRAVERSO.). [Traverso]. (1989)-. Periodical. English. qt. $12.00. Traverso, HCR Box 83, Claverack NY 12513. **Tel** (518)851-3680, telex (23) 650 3624777 MCIUW. **ED** Ardal Powell. **LC** ML935; .T7. **DD** 788.3/2/0903305. **Bk Rev.**
**Desc:** A newsletter of information and ideas for all interested in the baroque flute and its music.
**Ind/Abst** Music Artic. Guide.

IE/0790-004X
**TREOIR.** [Treoir]. **Added/Corp** Comhaltas Ceoltoiri Eireann. (19??)-. Periodical. English (Irish). Four times a year (Mar., June, Sept., Dec.). $20.00. Comhaltas Director General, Belgrave Square, Dublin Ireland. **Tel** 011 353 1 2800295. **(Subscription address:** Treoir, 244 Wardwell Road, Mineola, NY 11501, phone: (516)248-7809**) LC** ML5; .T79. **DD** 781.7/415.

US/0041-2511
**TRIAD (OHIO MUSIC EDUCATION ASSOCIATION).** (TRIAD : OFFICIAL PUBLICATION OF THE OHIO MUSIC EDUCATION ASSOCIATION.). **Added/Corp** Ohio Music Education Association. (1933)-. Periodical. English. Six times a year. $15.00. Scheide Music Center, University of Beall, Avenue College Wooster, Wooster OH 44691. **Tel** (216)263-2052. **ED** Joan K. Lehr. **LC** ML1; .T51. **DD** 780/.7/29771. **Ad Acc. Circ:** 4,500 (ctrl).
**Desc:** This publication addresses the issues concerning music education.

US/0041-2600
**TRIANGLE OF MU PHI EPSILON, THE.** [Triangle Mu Phi Epsil.]. **Main/Corp** Mu Phi Epsilon. (1905)-. Periodical. English. qt. $10.00. Mu Phi Epsilon National Executive Office, 730 Waukegan Road, Deerfield IL 60015. **Tel** (708)940-1222. **ED** Gerri Flynn. **LC** ML1; .T52. **DD** 780.6273. **Bk Rev. Circ:** 10,000 (ctrl).
**Desc:** International professional music fraternity magazine.
**Ind/Abst** Music Index.

SZ/1013-6835
**TRIBUNE DE L'ORGUE, LA.** [Trib. orgue]. (1948)-. Periodical. French. Four times a year (Mar., June, Sep., Dec.). 37.80F (libraries), 42.00F (others). Morisod Dominique, CH Des Dailles 40 B, CH 1870 Monthey Switzerland. **Tel** 41 25 717856. **ED** Morisod Dominique. **LC** ML5; .T799. **DD** 786.6/05. Index available. cum. index. **Bk Rev. Ad Acc. Circ:** 2,000 (ctrl).
**Ind/Abst** Music Index.

CN/0713-8113
**TROUBADOUR (FREDERICTON).** (THE TROUBADOUR.). [Troubadour]. **Added/Corp** New Brunswick Choral Federation. (1979)-. Periodical. English. qt. Free with NBCF membership. Troubadour, New Brunswick Choral Federation, Department of Education, PO Box 6000, Kings Place, Fredericton New Brunswick E3B 5H1 Canada. **Tel** (506)453-3731. **DD** 784.9/060715. **Bk Rev. Ad Acc. Circ:** 300 (ctrl).
**Desc:** Contains news of member choirs, music reviews, articles relating to choral music. Information on other national and international events, and on the NBCF events and projects.

US/0161-3081
**TUNE UP. Added/Corp** Philadelphia Folksong Society. (19??)-(19??). Periodical. English. ir. Philadelphia Folksong Society, 7113 Emlen Street, Philadelphia PA 19119. **Tel** (215)247-1300, FAX (215)247-0293. **LC** ML1; .T85. **DD** 781.7/05.

US/0362-6091
**TUNING BOARD, THE.** (Sept. 1974)-. Periodical. English. mo. Baker Enterprises, 2300 Fairview Road, Costa Mesa CA 92626. **LC** ML1; .T915. **DD** 781.7/73.

US/1052-3170
**TUROK'S CHOICE.** [Turok's choice]. No. 1 (May 1990)-. Periodical. English. mo (except Aug.). $13.95 US; $20.00 (air mail) other. Turok's Choice, PO Box 202, Old Chelsea Station, New York NY 10113-0202. **Tel** (212)691-9229. **ED** Paul Turok. **LC** ML156.9; .T87. **DD** 781/.6/80266/05. Index available. **Circ:** 1000.
**Desc:** This publication provides reviews of classical music and performing artists and groups.

US/0731-4469
**TWIN FIDDLE TREASURY, THE.** [Twin fiddle treas.]. (Jan. 1978)-. Periodical. English. mo. Twin Fiddle Treasury, PO Box 3776, Santa Rosa CA 95402. **ED** Tim Rued. **LC** ML3544; .T95. **DD** 787.1/52/05.

GW
**UBEN & MUSIZIEREN. VFOAT** Uben und Musizieren. (198?)-. German. Six times a year (Jan., Mar., May, July, Sept., Nov.). DM45.00 Germany, DM54.30 other (surface mail); DM84.00 (airmail). B. Schotts Soehne Musikverlag, Carl Zeiss Str 1, Postfach 3640, D 55026 Mainz Germany. **Tel** 011 49 6131 505129, 011 49 6131 505122, FAX 011 49 6131 505115, telex 04187821. **LC** MT3.G3; U2. **DD** 780/.71/043.

●US/1059-7182
**UCGM (NORTH CHARLESTON, S.C.).** (UCGM : URBAN CONTEMPORARY GOSPEL MAGAZINE.). [UCGM]. **VFOAT** Urban Contemporary Gospel Magazine; UCG Magazine. (June/July 1991)-. Periodical. English. bm. $12.00. UCG Magazine, PO Box 72186, North Charleston SC 29415-2186. **LC** ML3186.8; .U25. **DD** 782.25.

DK
**UDVALGSLISTE OVER ORKESTERMATERIALE. Main/Corp** Copenhagen. Kongelige Bibliotek. (19??)-. Danish. **LC** ML136.C78; K65.

UN/0566-6155
**UKRAINSKE MUZYKOZNAVSTVO. Added/Corp** Akademiia Nauk Ukrainskoi RSR. Ukraine. Ministerstvo Kultury. **VFOAT** Ukrainskoe Muzykovedenie. Vol. 1, (1964)-. Ukrainian (Russian). **LC** ML308.U4; U4.

KO
**UMAK NONDAN. JOURNAL OF THE SCIENCE AND PRACTICE OF MUSIC. Added/Corp** Hanyang Taehakkyo. Umak Yonguso. **VFOAT** Journal of the Science and Practice of Music. Vol. 1, (1984)-. Periodical. Korean (English). Hanyang Taehakkyo Chulpanwon, 17 Hyangdang-Dong, Songdong-ku, Seoul Korea. **LC** ML5; .U562.

KO
**UMAK SEGYE. Added/Corp** Chungang Ilbosa. **VFOAT** Music World. (19??)-. Periodical. Korean. mo. **LC** ML3469; .U42.

KO
**UMAK TONGA. Added/Corp** Tong Ilbosa. **VFOAT** Eumak Dong-A. Vol. 1, (1984)-. Periodical. Korean (Korean). mo. Tonga Ilbosa, PO Box 400, Kwanghwamun Ucheguk, Seoul 110 Korea. **LC** ML5; .U563.

KO
**UMAK YONGU. Added/Corp** Hanguk Umak Hakhoe. **VFOAT** Hanguk Umak Hakhoe Nonmunjip; Music Research. Vol. 1, Series (Feb. 1982)-. Periodical. Korean (summaries and/or abstracts in English). Hanguk Umak Hakhoe, 232-32 Sogye-dong, Yongsan-ku, Seoul South Korea. **LC** ML5; .U567.

UK
**UNIVERSITY FOLK.** ***Title Change.*** Periodical. English. University Union, Oxford Road, M13 9PP Manchester England. **LC** ML28.M19; U5. **DD** 784.4/006/24272. ***Continued by*** *Mancunion : The Official Newspaper of Manchester University Students Union.*

UK
**UNKNOWN PUBLIC.** English. qt. £50.00 (compact disc), £40.00 (cassette) Europe; $80.00 (compact disc), $65.00 (cassette) US. Gordon & Breach Science Publishers, PO Box 90, Reading RG1 8JL England. **Tel** 011 44 734 560080, FAX 011 44 734 568211. **(Subscription address:** International Publishers Distributor at one of the following addresses: 820 Town Center Drive, Langhorne, PA 19047; or PO Box 90, Reading Berkshire RG1 8JL UK; or Kent Ridge PO Box 1180, Singapore 9111, Republic of Singapore**) ED** John L. Walters, Laurence Aston.
**Desc:** Audio journal named after its subscribers- the unknown international audience that would like to engage with all kinds of creative music by listening to it on CD or tape.

US/8755-1233
**UPDATE - UNIVERSITY OF SOUTH CAROLINA. DEPT. OF MUSIC.** (UPDATE.). [Update - Univ. S.C., Dep. Music]. **Added/Corp** University of South Carolina. Dept. of Music. **VFOAT** Applications of Research in Music Education. Vol. 1, No. 1 (May 1982)-. Periodical. English. Twice a year. $12.00 US; $14.00 Canada and Mexico; $16.00 other. Music Educators National Conference, 1806 Robert Fulton Drive, Reston VA 22091. **Tel** (703)860-4000, (800)336-3768. **ED** Charles A. Elliott. **LC** ML1; .U56. **DD** 780/.7. **Bk Rev. Ad Acc. Circ:** 500.
**Desc:** The applications of research in public school music instruction. Research findings presented in a jargon-free manner.
**Ind/Abst** Music Artic. Guide.

US
**URBAN NETWORK.** (19??)-. English. Fifty times a year. $280.00. Network Magazine Group, 120 North Victory Boulevard, Burbank CA 91502. **Tel** (818)955-4000, (800)222-4382, FAX (818)955-8048.
**Desc:** Covers urban contemporary music.

US/0502-871X
**UTAH MUSIC EDUCATOR. Added/Corp** Utah Music Educators Association. (195?)-. Periodical. English. Three times a year. $6.00. Utah Music Educator Association, Robert Coleman / 5084 S. 150 E., Ogden UT 84405. **Bk Rev. Ad Acc. Circ:** 450 (ctrl).

US/0191-1635
**UTAH SYMPHONY.** (UTAH SYMPHONY. [PROGRAM].). **Main/Corp** Utah Symphony Orchestra. (19??)-. Periodical. English. Utah Symphony Orchestra, 55 West 1 Street South, Salt Lake City UT 84101. **ED** Gilbert W. Scharffs. **LC** MT125; .U8. **DD** 785/.015. **Ad Acc. Circ:** 4,500 (ctrl). ***Continues*** *Utah Symphony Orchestra. Utah Symphony Orchestra (1968).*
**Desc:** Notes on programs, intermission notes, player profiles.

NE/0566-4632
**UTRECHTSE BIJDRAGEN TOT DE MUZIEKWETENSCHAP. Main/Corp** Utrecht. Rijksuniversiteit. Instituut voor Miziekwetenschap. Vol. 1 (1958)-. Dutch. ir. **DD** 780.

●FI
**UUSI KANSANMUSIIKKI. Added/Corp** Kansanmusiikki-Instituutti (Kaustinen, Finland). (1991)-. Periodical. Finnish. bm. Kansanmusiikkii Instituutti, Kaustinen Finland. **LC** ML3619; .K35. ***Continues*** *Kansanmusiikki, 0355-9335.*

# Music

US/0733-8562
**V.M.E.A. NOTES.** [VMEA notes]. **Main/Corp** Virginia Music Educators Association. **Added/Corp** Virginia Music Educators Association. Notes. **VFOAT** VMEA Notes. **VAT** Virginia Music Educators Association Notes. (Jan./Feb. 1949)-. Periodical. English. ir. Virginia Music Education Education, 14 Martell Road, Newark DE 19713. **LC** ML27.U5; V45. **DD** 780/.7/29755.

US/0506-306X
**VDGSA NEWS.** [VdGSA news]. **Main/Corp** Viola da Gamba Society of America. **Added/Corp** Viola da Gamba Society of America. News. **VAT** Viola da Gamba Society of America News. (19??)-. Periodical. English. Four times a year (Mar., June, Sept., Dec.). $20.00 Includes Journal of Viola da Gamba Society of America & VDSGA News. Viola da Gamba Society of America, 1308 Jackson Avenue, Charleston IL 61920. **Tel** (217)348-8260.

US/0160-2667
**VERDI NEWSLETTER.** [Verdi newsl.]. **Added/Corp** American Institute for Verdi Studies. No. 3, (June 1977)-. Newsletter. English (Italian and French). an. $15.00. American Institute for Verdi Studies, New York University, Department of Music, 24 Waverly Place/Room 268, New York NY 10003. **Tel** (212)998-8300. **ED** Martin Chusid. **LC** ML410.V4; A64. **DD** 782.1/092/4; B. **Bk Rev**, (Qty: 1-2). **Ad Acc**. **Circ:** 500. **Continues** American Institute for Verdi Studies. AIVSnewsletter, 0148-0383.
**Desc:** Articles, reviews, and other information relating to the music and life of Giuseppe Verdi, composer of operas.
**Ind/Abst** RILM Abstr.

US/0042-4188
**VERMONT MUSIC NEWS.** Vol. 1, (1959)-. Periodical. English. qt. Vermont Music News, Harwood Union High School, Moutown VT 05401.

GW/0435-8112
**VEROFFENTLICHUNG - GESELLSCHAFT DER ORGELFREUNDE.** **Main/Corp** Gesellschaft der Orgelfreunde. (1952)-. English. Verlag Merseburger Berlin GmbH, POB 103880, D 34038 Kassel Germany. **Tel** 011 49 561 772002. **DD** 786.

GW/0418-3827
**VEROFFENTLICHUNGEN DES INSTITUTS FUER NEUE MUSIK UND MUSIKERZIEHUNG DARMSTADT.**
**Added/Corp** Institut fuer Neue Musik und Musikerziehung Darmstadt. (1961)-. Monographic series. German. ir. Price varies per volume. B. Schotts Soehne Musikverlag, Carl Zeiss Str 1, Postfach 3640, D 55026 Mainz Germany. **Tel** 011 49 6131 505129, 011 49 6131 505122, FAX 011 49 6131 505115, telex 04187821. **DD** 780.

GW
**VEROFFENTLICHUNGEN. NEUE FOLGE, REIHE 4. SCHRIFTEN ZUR BEETHOVENFORSCHUNG.** **Main/Corp** Bonn. Beethovenhaus. (1957)-. Periodical. German. **(Subscription address:** G. Henle USA Inc., PO Box 1753, 2446 Centerline Industrial Drive, St. Louis, MO 63043 USA; telephone: (314)991-0487) **Continues** Bonn. Beethovenhaus. Veroffentlichungen.

US/0270-6350
**VIBES (NEW YORK).** (VIBES.). (Mar. 1978)-. Periodical. English. bm. Ideal Publishing Corporation, 2 Park Avenue, New York NY 10016. **LC** ML3469; .V5. **DD** 784.5/005.
**Desc:** Popular music journal.

CN/0703-9883
**VIBRATIONS (MONTREAL).** (VIBRATIONS.). Vol. 1 (June 1977)-. Periodical. English (French). mo. Starfish Publishing, Suite 108, 5871 Victoria Avenue, Montreal Quebec A3W 2R7 Canada. **DD** 780/.42/05.

AT/0310-4834
**VICTORIAN ORGAN JOURNAL.** [Vic. organ j.]. (1972)-. Periodical. English. Six times a year. 22.00Aus$. Society of Organists Victoria Inc., PO Box 952 G, Melbourne Victoria 3001 Australia. **Tel** 011 61 3 8732583. **ED** Bill Smith (editor's address: 17 Creswick Street, Glen Iris Victoria 3146 Australia). **DD** _a786.605.
**Bk Rev**, (Qty: varies). **Ad Acc**.

US
**VICTORY MUSIC REVIEW.** English. mo. $20.00 US; $28.00 Canada; $36.00 other. Victory Music, PO Box 7515, Bonney Lake WA 98390. **Tel** (206)863-6617.
**Desc:** Publishes 100 CD, video, cassette, book and magazine reviews per month. Also includes classifieds, music ads and columns on folk music, songwriting, jazz, blues, traditional jazz, Irish and kids' music, etc.

FR/0080-0139
**VIE MUSICALE EN FRANCE SOUS LES ROIS BOURBONS. 2EME SERIE. RECHERCHES SUR LA MUSIQUE FRANCAISE CLASSIQUE, LA.**
(RECHERCHES SUR LA MUSIQUE FRANCAISE CLASSIQUE.). [Vie music. Fr. rois Bourbons, 2eme ser. Rech. musique fr. class.]. (1960)-. French (English). an. Editions A et J Picard, 82 rue Bonaparte, 75006 Paris France. **Tel** 011 33 1 43269778. **LC** ML270; .R43.
**Ind/Abst** RILM Abstr.

FR/0083-6109
**VIE MUSICALE EN FRANCE SOUS LES ROIS BOURBONS. ETUDES.** Vol. 1, (1954)-. Monographic series. French (English). ir. Price varies per volume. Editions A et J Picard, 82 rue Bonaparte, 75006 Paris France. **Tel** 011 33 1 43269778. **ED** A. J. Picard.

●US/1056-8581
**VINTAGE GUITAR.** [Vintage guitar]. **Added/Corp** Orion Research Corporation. **VFOAT** Vintage Guitar Blue Book; Orion Vintage Guitar Blue Book. (1991)-. English. Four times a year. $184.80. Orion Research Corporation, 14555 North Scottsdale Road, Suite 330, Scottsdale AZ 85260. **Tel** (800)844-0759, (602)951-1114, FAX (602)951-1117. **LC** IN PROCESS. **DD** 784.

UK/0042-6369
**VINTAGE JAZZ MART.** (Jan. 1963)-. Periodical. English. Four times a year (Jan., Apr., May, Dec.). $22.00 North and South America and Asia; £12.00 other. Vintage Jazz Mart, PO Box R 184, Radnor PA 19087. **Tel** (215)688-4842. **(Subscription address:** Vintage Jazz Mart, 1 Station Cottage Moore Road, Nottingham NG6 8S England.) **ED** Russell Shor. **Bk Rev**. **Ad Acc**. **Circ:** 2,000. **Continues** Palaver.
**Desc:** The primary medium for record collectors to sell and exchange worldwide. All advents and articles pertain to jazz, modern and traditional, blues and dance bands.

US/0278-5455
**VINYL EDITION, THE.** Vol. 1, No. 1 (Mar. 1978)-. English. mo. H.B. Plunkett Inc., Buffalo NY. **LC** ML3476.8; .V56. **DD** 784.5/4/005.

GW/0172-9098
**VIOLA : JAHRBUCH DER INTERNATIONALEN VIOLA-FORSCHUNGSGESELLSCHAFT, DIE.** **Added/Corp** International Viola Research Society. **VFOAT** Viola. (1979)-. German (English). Baerenreiter-Verlag, KGA Verlagssvc PF 100329, D 34003 Kassel Germany. **Tel** 011 49 561 31050, telex 99504. **LC** ML900; .V55. **DD** 787/.2/05.
**Desc:** Viola journal from Kassel, Germany.
**Ind/Abst** Music Index.

US/0892-5437
**VIOLEXCHANGE, THE.** [Violexchange]. **Added/Corp** L.S.F. Publications, Inc. **VFOAT** Viol Exchange. Vol. 1, No. 1 (Jan. 1986)-. Periodical. English. Four times a year (Feb., June, and double issues in Oct.). $25.00. The Violexchange, Carnegie Mellon University, Department of Music, 5000 Forbes Avenue, Pittsburgh PA 15213. **Tel** (412)268-2383. **LC** ML749.5; .V55. **DD** 787/.005. Index available. cum. index. **Bk Rev**. **Ad Acc**. **Circ:** 5,000. available on microfilm.
**Desc:** News and interviews on music inserts (rare material), musicological discussions and discographies.
**Ind/Abst** Music Artic. Guide.

DK
**VIVALDI INFORMATIONS.** **Added/Corp** International Antonio Vivaldi Society. Vol. 2 (1973)-. French (German and English). ir. Societe Intl Antonio Vivaldi, c/o Institute Ital Cultura, Gjoerlingsvejii Hellerup Denmark. **Continues** International Antonio Vivaldi Society. Informations.

US/1074-0805
**VOICE OF CHORUS AMERICA, THE.** [Voice Chorus Am.]. **Added/Corp** Chorus America. **VFOAT** Voice. Vol. 14, No. 1 (Fall 1990)-. Periodical. English. Four times a year (Mar., June, Sept., Dec.). $25.00 (members) Professional Vocal Ensembles & American Choral Directors Association; $30.00 US: $32.50 Canada; $35.00 others. American Choral Foundation, 2111 Sansom Street, Philadelphia PA 19103. **Tel** (215)563-2430, FAX (215)563-2431. **ED** Alfred Mann. **LC** ML1499; .V65. **DD** 782. **Circ:** 1,000. **Continues** Voice (Philadelphia, Pa.) **and** American Choral Review and Research Memorandum Series; **Absorbed** Research Memorandum Series.
**Ind/Abst** Music Artic. Guide; Music Index.

US/0147-4367
**VOICE OF WASHINGTON MUSIC EDUCATORS.** **Added/Corp** Washington Music Educators' Association. Vol.17 (Sept. 1971)-. Trade Publication. English. qt. Washington Music Educator Association, 817 East 3rd Avenue, Ellensburg WA 98926. **Tel** (509)925-3210, FAX (509)925-7150. **ED** Tom Bourne. **LC** ML1; W172. **DD** 780/.729797. **Ad Acc**. **Circ:** 1,700 (ctrl). **Continues** Washington Music Educator.
**Desc:** A journal for music educators, with emphasis upon trends in methodology, governmental relations and trade news.
**Ind/Abst** Music Artic. Guide.

UK
**VOICES OF THE PAST.** (1956)-. Periodical. English. Oakwood Press. **LC** ML156.4 .V7; V6. **DD** 789.913.

AU
**VOLKSMUSIK, DIE.** **Added/Corp** Verband der Arbeiter-Musikvereine Osterreichs. (August 1946)-. Periodical. German. mo. **LC** ML5; .V787.
**Desc:** Folk music journal from Vienna, Austria.

RU/0507-3723
**VOPROSY MUZYKALNOI FORMY.** Vol 1 (1966)-. Russian. **LC** ML448; .V56.

UK
**VOX.** English. mo. $100.00 US and Canada. IPC Magazines Ltd., Perrymount Road, Haywards Heath, West Sussex RH16 3DH England. **Tel** 011 44 444 440421. **Circ:** 106,000.

AU
**VOX (VIENNA, AUSTRIA).** (VOX.). (Sept. 1979)-. Periodical. German. mo. Technischer Verlag ERB, Eichenstrasse 38, A-1120 Vienna Austria. **Tel** 011 43 1 81120. **LC** ML5; .V95. **DD** 780/.9.

UK
**WAGNER.** **Added/Corp** Wagner Society (London, England). Vol. 1, No 1 (Nov. 1980)-. Periodical. English. Four times a year. (Membership) £12.00 UK; £16.00 Europe; £17.00 other. Wagner Society, 4 Lucastes Road Haywards Heath, West Sussex RH16 1JL England. **Tel** 011 44 444 450829. **ED** Stewart Spencer. **LC** ML410.W1; A585. **DD** 782.1/092/4. **Bk Rev**. **Ad Acc**. **Circ:** 1,200 (ctrl).
**Desc:** Articles on the music, life, thought, and reception of Richard Wagner.

PL
**WARSAW AUTUMN.** **Main/Conf** International Festival of Contemporary Music. (19??)-. English. an. **LC** ML36; .I59578. **DD** 780/.79/438.

US/0196-3236
**WASHINGTON OPERA MAGAZINE, THE.** **Added/Corp** Washington Opera Guild. (19??)-. Periodical. English. Five times a year. Free on request. Washington Opera Guild, Kennedy Center, Washington DC 20566. **Tel** (202)416-8700. **LC** ML1699; .W37. **DD** 782.1/09753.

US/0741-2460
**WAVELENGTH (NEW ORLEANS, LA.).** (WAVELENGTH.). **VFOAT** Wave Length. Vol. 1, No. 1 (Nov. 1980)-. Periodical. English. Twelve times a year. $40.00. Wavelength, One Center Street, New York NY 10007. **Tel** (212)669-7800. **ED** Connie Atkinson. **Bk Rev**. **Ad Acc**. **Circ:** 30,000.
**Desc:** New Orleans music magazine, devoted to all types of music from rock to early rhythm and blues. Reviews, articles, calendar, etc.

US/0093-6170
**WEB (WALTHAM).** (THE WEB.). **Added/Corp** Musicians' Workshop. Musicians' Workshop. Workshop Exchange Bulletin. **VFOAT** Workshop Exchange Bulletin. (19??)-. Periodical. English. mo. Musicians' Workshop, 82 Clematis Avenue, Waltham MA 02154. **LC** ML28.W185; M9. **DD** 338.4/7/780974461.

US/0083-7881
**WELLESLEY EDITION, THE.** (1950)-. English. ir. Yesterday Service Inc., 1972 Massachusetts Avenue/4th Floor, Cambridge MA 02140. **ED** Jan La Rue. **LC** M2; .W4.

GW
**WER SPIELTE WAS?.** See Theater.

US
**WERKE JOSEPH HAYDN.** **VFOAT** Joseph Haydn Works. Monographic series. English. ir. Price varies per volume. Broude Brothers Limited, 141 White Oaks Road, Williamstown MA 01267. **Tel** (413)458-8132, (800)525-8559.

CN/0228-8168
**WESTCOAST MUSIC.** Vol. 4, No. 1 (Sept. 1980)-. Periodical. English. mo. Westcoast Music Magazine, 1870 West First Avenue, Vancouver British Columbia V6J 1G5 Canada. **DD** 780/.42/09711.
**Continues** Open Door West Coast Music, 0228-8176.

DK
**WESTERN BULLETIN.** (19??)-. Bulletin. Multiple languages (Danish and English). Western Bulletin, Box 1218, 2300 Copenhagen S. Denmark. **LC** ML5; .W48. **DD** 784.

US/0273-1991
**WESTERN ROUNDUP COUNTRY MUSIC TRADE DIRECTORY & NEWS REPORT.**
**Added/Corp** Western Roundup (Buffalo). **VAT** Western Roundup Country Music Trade Directory and News

Report. (Summer 1974)-. Directory. English. **LC** ML19; .C69. **DD** 784.5/2/002573. ***Continues*** *Western Roundup Country Music Trade Directory, 0273-2009.*
**Desc:** News on country music; published out of Buffalo, NY.

US
**WESTERN ROUNDUP : WESTERN NEW YORK'S COUNTRY MUSIC GUIDE.** **VFOAT** Western New York's Country Music Guide; Western Roundup Country Music Guide. (19??)-. Periodical. English. qt. Western Roundup Country Music Guide, 7168 Rapids Road, Lockport NY 14094. **LC** ML1; .W33. **DD** 784.

UK/0266-030X
**WHAT KEYBOARD?.** [What keyboard?]. (1983)-. Periodical. English. mo. Cover Publications Ltd., 39 41 North Road, London N7 9DP England. **Tel** 011 44 71 6098661. ***Continues*** *Home Organist & Keyboard Update.*

US/0043-4752
**WHEEL OF DELTA OMICRON, THE.** **Main/Corp** Delta Omicron International Music Fraternity. (19??)-. Periodical. English. qt (4 times a year). Free to members; $5.00 other. Delta Omicron, 1352 Redwood Court, Columbus OH 43229. **Tel** (614)888-2640. **ED** Patricia Almon. **LC** ML27.U5; .D4. **Circ:** 5,500 (ctrl).
**Desc:** Organization news.

US/0091-7664
**WHISKEY, WOMEN, AND ... .** ***Ceased.*** [Whiskey women ...]. No. 1 (1971)-(1989). Periodical. English. an. Whiskey, Women & ..., PO Box 1245, Haverhill MA 01831-1645. **Tel** (617)372-0101. **ED** Daniel P Kochakian. **LC** ML1; .W37. **DD** 784. **Bk Rev**. **Ad Acc**. **Circ:** 1,000 (ctrl).
**Desc:** Explores the recordings and artists of black American blues, jazz, gospel and vocal group history. Geared to the collector; vintage label and artist photos abound.

US/0039-7873
**WHO PUT THE BOMP!.** [Who put bomp]. (19??)-. Periodical. English. qt. $8.00. G Shaw, PO Box 7112, Burbank CA 91510. **LC** ML1; .W415. **DD** 784.

AU/0511-9294
**WIENER MUSIKWISSENSCHAFTLICHE BEITRAGE.** **Added/Corp** Gesellschaft zur Herausgabe von Denkmalern der Tonkunst in Osterreich. (1955)-. Monographic series. German. ir. Price varies per volume. Boehlau Verlag GmbH & Co KG, Sachsenplatz 4 6 PF 87, A 1201 Vienna Austria. **Tel** 011 43 222 3302427.

UK/0269-2015
**WINDS : THE JOURNAL OF THE BRITISH ASSOCIATION OF SYMPHONIC BANDS AND WIND ENSEMBLES.** **VFOAT** Journal of the British Association of Symphonic Bands and Wind Ensembles; Winds. Vol. 1, No. 1 (Autumn 1985)-. English. Four times a year (Feb., May, Aug., Nov.). £9.50 Europe; £10.50 others; $17.30 (one year) US & Canada. Egon Publishers Ltd, Royston Road, Baldock Herts, Oxfordshire SG7 6NW England. **Tel** 011 44 462 894498.

US/0737-7789
**WINDSTORM.** **VFOAT** Wind Storm. (June 1983)-. Periodical. English. mo. Windstorm, Inc., 15160 West 8 Mile Road, Suite 309, Oak Park MI 48237. **LC** ML3186.8; .W56. **DD** 783.7/05.

NE
**WINEK INFO.** **Main/Corp** Werkgroep Integratie Nederlandstalige Kerkmuziek. **VAT** Werkgroep Integratie Nederlandstalige Kerkmuziek-Info. (Jan. 1977)-. Periodical. Dutch. bm. Werkgroep Integratie Nederlandstalige Kerkmuziek, Biltstraat 51 Bis, Utrecht Netherlands. **LC** ML5; .W47.

CN/0700-3129
**WINNIPEG FOLK FESTIVAL NEWSLETTER.** (THE WINNIPEG FOLK FESTIVAL NEWSLETTER.). **Main/Corp** Winnipeg Folk Festival. Vol. 1 (April/May 1976)-. Newsletter. English. Winnipeg Folk Festival, 253 Hugo Street North, Winnipeg Manitoba R3M 2N2 Canada. **DD** 781.7/05.

UK/0952-0686
**WIRE (LONDON, ENGLAND).** (THE WIRE.). [Wire]. Issue 1 (Summer 1982)-. Periodical. English. Twelve times a year. $50.00 US; £25.00 UK; £30.00 others. Namara Group, Namara House, 45 46 Poland Street, London W1V 3DF England. **Tel** 011 44 71 439 6422. **ED** Richard Cook. **LC** ML5; .W62. **DD** 785.42/05. **Bk Rev**. **Ad Acc**. **Circ:** 20,000.
**Desc:** Covers reviews and analysis of jazz and new music.

US/0043-6658
**WISCONSIN SCHOOL MUSICIAN, THE.** **Added/Corp** Wisconsin School Music Association. Wisconsin Music Educators' Conference. **VFOAT** Wisconsin School Music Association Handbook. Vol. 1 (Feb. 1930)-. Periodical. English. qt (Feb., Apr., Sep., Nov.). $12.00. The Wisconsin School Musician Association, 4797 Hayes Road/Suite 3, Madison WI 53704. **Tel** (608)249-4566, FAX (608)249-4973. **ED** Michael G. George and Robin Pharo. **LC** ML1; .W48. **DD** 780.72. **Bk Rev**. **Ad Acc**, **Adv Mgr:** Ms. Pharo. **Circ:** 5,000.
**Desc:** Publishes submissions from state music educators, current news in music education and features articles about music education.
**Ind/Abst** Music Artic. Guide.

KO
**WOLGAN UMAK.** **VFOAT** Weolgan Eumag. (19??)-. Periodical. Korean. Wolgan Umak Sa, 60-1 4-Ka Chungmu-Ro, Chung-Ku, Seoul South Korea. **LC** ML5; .W65.

US/0891-9585
**WOODSTOCK SERIES, THE.** [Woodstock ser.]. Vol. 1 (1976)-. Monographic series. English. ir. Price varies per volume. Borgo Press, PO Box 2845, San Bernardino CA 92406. **Tel** (714)884-5813, (714)885-1161. **LC** UNC. **DD** 784.
**Desc:** Monographs on popular musicians and music groups of the twentieth century, with discographies and bibliographies.

US
**WORLD HARP CONGRESS REVIEW : OFFICIAL PUBLICATION OF THE WORLD HARP CONGRESS, INC.** **Added/Corp** World Harp Congress. **VFOAT** Revue du Congres Mondial de la Harpe; WHC Review. Vol. 2, No. 2 (May 1986)-. Periodical. English. sa. Catherine Gotthoffer, 13243-A Fiji Way, Marina-del-Rey CA 90292. **LC** ML1005; .W67. ***Continues*** *World Harp Congress Newsletter.*
**Ind/Abst** Music Artic. Guide.

US/1049-0140
**WORLD MUSIC CONNECTIONS.** [World music connect.]. Vol. 1, No. 1 (Summer/Fall 1988)-. Periodical. English. qt. Free. White Cliffs Media Company, Box 561, Crown Point IN 46307. **Tel** (219)322-5537. **ED** Larry W. Smith. **DD** 781. **Bk Rev**. **Ad Acc**. **Circ:** 5,000.

SZ/0043-8774
**WORLD OF MUSIC (WILHELMSHAVEN).** (THE WORLD OF MUSIC.). [World music]. **Added/Corp** International Institute for Comparative Music Studies and Documentation. International Music Council. International Institute for Traditional Music. Vol. 1, No. 1 (May 1959)-. Periodical. English (German and French). tq. $44.00 (institutions), $38.00 (individuals) Europe; $45.00, $54.00 (air mail), (institutions), $39.00, $48.00 (air mail), (individuals) other. Florian Noetzel Verlag, Heinrichshofen BKS, PO Box 580, D-26353 Wilhelmshaven Germany. **Tel** 011 49 4421 43003, FAX 011 49 4421 42985. **ED** Ivan Vandor. **LC** ML5; .W67. Index available (bound in issue). cum. index. **Bk Rev**. **Ad Acc**. **Circ:** 2,000 (ctrl). Documents available from The Genuine Article.
**Ind/Abst** Arts Humanit. Citation Index [Full Cov.]; BHA : Biblio. Hist. Art; Curr. Contents Arts Humanit.; Music Index; Res. Alert [Full Cov.]; RILM Abstr.; Romant. Move.; Soc. Sci. Cit. Index [Select. Cov.].

US/1042-931X
**WORLD OPERA SCHEDULE.** [World opera sched.]. **VFOAT** World Opera Schedules. (19??)-. English. Four times a year. $75.00 US; $95.00 other. World Opera Schedule, PO Box 298, Elk Grove Village IL 60009. **Tel** (708)259-6878, FAX (708)259-6878. **ED** Barbara Rozanski. **LC** ML1699; .O67. **DD** 782.1. Each issue contains an index to its own contents (no volume index)--loose. **Ad Acc**, **Adv Mgr:** L. Morton, **Tel** (505)983-8786. ***Continues*** *Opera Schedules, 0892-161X.*
**Desc:** Lists opera performance schedules worldwide, including casts, dates, addresses, phone/fax numbers of opera houses and hotel recommendations.

US/0277-4135
**WORLD-WIDE OFFICIAL ORGAN BLUE BOOK.** [World-wide off. organ blue book]. **Added/Corp** Sight & Sound International. **VFOAT** Official Organ Blue Book. **VAT** World Wide Official Organ Blue Book. (19??)-. English (Dutch and German). Hobby Publications Inc., 225 Gordons Corner Road, Box 420, Manalapan NJ 07726. **Tel** (908)446-4900. **LC** ML597; .W67. **DD** 786.9/2/075.
**Desc:** Electronic organ publication.

US/0146-1966
**WWIM. WHO'S WHERE IN MUSIC.** (WHO'S WHERE IN MUSIC: WWIM.). **VFOAT** WWIM. (Dec. 1976/Feb. 1977)-. Periodical. English. qt. Who's Where in Music Corporation, 5410 Wilshire Boulevard/Suite 905, Los Angeles CA 90036. **LC** ML1; .W422. **DD** 784. ***Supersedes*** *Who's Where in Music, 0360-4411.*

US/0098-3330
**XENHARMONIKON.** (Spring 1974)-. English. sa. Xenharmonikon, 10819 Shannon Hills Drive, Houston TX 77099. **LC** ML1; .X4. **DD** 780/.904. available on microfilm from University Microfilms International (UMI).

UK/0260-1702
**YEAR BOOK & REGISTER OF MEMBERS / CLARINET AND SAXOPHONE SOCIETY.** **Main/Corp** Clarinet & Saxophone Society (Great Britain). **VFOAT** Year Book and Register of Members; Yearbook and Register of Members. (19??)-. English. an. Clarinet & Saxophone Society, 167 Ellerton Road, Tolworth Surrey KT6 7UB England. **Tel** 011 44 325 469 438. **LC** ML27.G7; C63. **DD** 788/.6/02541.

US/0190-8685
**YEAR BOOK - CINCINNATI SYMPHONY ORCHESTRA.** **Main/Corp** Cincinnati Symphony Orchestra. **Added/Corp** Cincinnati Symphony Orchestra Association Company. (1895)-. English. an (May). $40.00. Cincinnati Symphony Orchestra, 1241 Elm Street, Cincinnati OH 45210. **Tel** (513)621-1919. **LC** MT125; .C6. **DD** 785/.0739/77178.

UK
**YEARBOOK & REGISTER OF MEMBERS / INCORPORATED SOCIETY OF MUSICIANS.** **Main/Corp** Incorporated Society of Musicians (Great Britain). **VFOAT** Yearbook and Register of Members; Yearbook. (198?)-. English. an. Incorporated Society of Musicians, 10 Stratford Place, London W1N 9AE England. **Tel** (01)629-4302. **ED** David E. Padgett-Chandler. **LC** ML27.G7; I5. **DD** 780/.6/041. **Ad Acc**. **Circ:** 7,000 (ctrl). ***Continues*** *Incorporated Society of Musicians (Great Britain). Handbook and Register of Members.*

US/0740-1558
**YEARBOOK FOR TRADITIONAL MUSIC.** [Yearb. tradit. music]. **Added/Corp** International Council for Traditional Music. Vol. 13 (1981)-. Academic Scholarly Publication. English (German and French). an. $35.00. International Council of Traditional Music, Columbia University, 417 Dodge, Department of Music, New York NY 10027. **Tel** (212)678-0332, FAX (212)749-0397, telex 220094. **ED** Dieter Christensen. **LC** ML1; .I719. **DD** 781.7/05. **Bk Rev**. **Pr Rev**. **Circ:** 1,200. Documents available from The Genuine Article. ***Continues*** *Yearbook of the International Folk Music Council, 0316-6082.*
**Desc:** Scholarly journal for ethnomusicologists.
**Ind/Abst** Am. Bibliogr. Slavic East Europ. Stud.; Anthropol. Index; Arts Humanit. Citation Index (19??-19??) [Full Cov.]; Curr. Contents Arts Humanit.; MLA Int. Bibl. Books Artic. Mod. Lang. Lit.; Music Index; Res. Alert [Full Cov.]; Soc. Sci. Cit. Index [Select. Cov.].

CN/0228-9539
**YEARBOOK - ROYAL CANADIAN COLLEGE OF ORGANISTS (1978).** (YEARBOOK / ROYAL CANADIAN COLLEGE OF ORGANISTS.). [Yearb. - R. Can. Coll. Organists &b 1978]. **Main/Corp** Royal Canadian College of Organists. No. 21 (Oct. 1978)-. English. an. Royal Canadian College of Organists, Suite 300A / 212 King Street West, Toronto Ontario M5H 1K5 Canada. **DD** 786.5/06/071. ***Continues in part*** *Royal Canadian College of Organists Quarterly, 0380-8424.*

UK
**YEAR'S WORK IN MUSIC, THE.** **Added/Corp** British Council. (1947/48)-. English. an. Longman Group Ltd., Fourth Avenue, Longman House, Harlow Essex CM19 5SR England. **Tel** 011 44 279 429655, FAX 011 44 279 431059, telex 81259. **(Subscription address:** Fourth Avenue, Harlow Essex CM19 5AA England**)** **LC** ML5; .Y4. **DD** 780.58.

US
**YELLOW PAGES OF ROCK / THE ALBUM NETWORK.** **Added/Corp** Album Network, Inc. **VFOAT** Album Network Yellow Pages of Rock; Album Network's Yellow Pages of Rock. (198?)-. English. an (includes monthly updates). $90.00. Network Magazine Group, 120 North Victory Boulevard, Burbank CA 91502. **Tel** (818)955-4000, (800)222-4382, FAX (818)955-8048.

US/0098-1796
**YESTERDAY'S MEMORIES.** (1975)-. English. Freebizak Inc, PO Box 1825, FDR Station, New York NY 10022. **LC** ML1; .Y4. **DD** 784.

CH
**YIN YEAH SHENG HUO TSA CHIH.** **VFOAT** Music Life. Chinese. mo. Music Life, Sec 1 Gin-Shan South Rd, Taipei Taiwan. **Tel** 011 886 2 3952598.

HK
**YIN YUEH SHENG HUO.** **VFOAT** Hifi Musical Life. (July 1962)-. Periodical. Chinese (Chinese). mo. $18.00. Chung Kuang Yu Hsien Kung SSU, 907 Takshing House Des Voeux Road, Hong Kong Hong Kong. **LC** ML5; .Y547.

US/0044-0841
**YOUNG MUSICIANS.** **Added/Corp** Southern Baptist Convention. Sunday School Board. (1970)-. Periodical. English. Four times a year. $8.80. Southern Baptist Convention, 901 Commerce, Suite 750, Nashville TN 37203. **Tel** (615)244-2355, FAX (615)742-8919.

**(Subscription address:** Sunday School Board, Customer Service, 127 9th Avenue North, Nashville TN 37234.) **LC** ML1; .Y65. **DD** 783/.026/05.

US/1042-0843
**YOUR FAVORITE COUNTRY STARS.** (1989)-. Periodical. English. sa. $4.95 (single issue) US; $5.95 (single issue) Canada and England; $10.00 (single issue) other. Southeast Magazines Inc, PO Box 24649, 545 Mainstream Road, Suite 101, Nashville TN 37228. **Tel** (615)242-6992, FAX (615)242-2248. **ED** Walt Henney. **Circ:** 20,000.
**Desc:** Photographs and descriptions of the most current country music star performers.

IS/0084-439X
**YUBAL GOBES MEHQARIM SEL HA-MERKAZ LE-HEQER HA-MUSIQAH HA-YHUDIT.** (YUVAL.). [Yubal gobes mehqarim sel ha-merkaz le-heqer ha-musiqah ha-yhudit]. **Added/Corp** Universitah Ha-Ivrit Bi-Yerushalayim. Merkaz Le-Heker Ha-Musikah Ha-Yehudit. (1968)-. Monographic series. English (French and Hebrew; summaries and/or abstracts in Hebrew). ir. Price varies per volume. Magnes Press, Hebrew University of Jerusalem, PO Box 7695, Jerusalem 91076 Israel. **Tel** 011 972 2 660341, 011 972 2 635291, FAX 011 972 2 633370, telex 25391. **LC** ML3776; .Y89.
**Ind/Abst** RILM Abstr.

CC
**YUEH CHI. YUEQI. Added/Corp** Chuan kuo Yueh Chi Kung Yeh Ko Chi Ching Pao Chan (China). **VFOAT** Yueqi; Musical Instruments. (19??)-. Periodical. Chinese. bm. Chung-Kuo Kuo Chi Tu Shu Mao I Tsung Kung SSU, PO Box 2820, Beijing, People's Republic of China. **Tel** 23724. **LC** ML459; .Y84. **DD** 781.91/05.

CC
**YUEH TAN. YUETAN. VFOAT** Yuetan. (19??)-. Periodical. Chinese. mo. Post Office / China, People's Republic of China. **LC** ML5; .Y815. **DD** 780/.5.

PL
**Z DZIEJOW MUZYKI POLSKIEJ. Added/Corp** Bydgoskie Towarzystwo Naukowe. Filharmonia Pomorska im. I. Paderewskiego w Bydgoszczy. (1960)-. Periodical. Polish. Bydgoskie Towarzystwo Naukowe, 4 Jezuicka, Bydgoszcz Poland. **LC** ML5; .Z15.

GW/0232-9387
**ZEITGENOSSISCHES MUSIKSCHAFFEN IN DER DEUTSCHEN DEMOKRATISCHEN REPUBLIK. Added/Corp** Sachsische Landesbibliothek (Dresden, Germany). (1982)-. German. an. Sachsische Landesbibliothek, Marienallee 12, Dresden 806 Germany. **Tel** 52677, telex 2-368. **ED** Ludwig Muller. **LC** ML120.G3; Z35. **DD** 016.78/09431. **Circ:** 650 (ctrl). ***Continues*** *Sozialistisches Musikschaffen der Deutschen Demokratischen Republik.*

GW
**ZEITSCHRIFT FUER SPIELMUSIK.** (19??)-. Periodical. German. mo. $34.00. Magnamusic Distributors Inc, Sharon CT 06069. **Tel** (203)364-5431. **ED** Moeck Verlag. cum. index. **Bk Rev. Circ:** 100 (ctrl). ***Continues*** *Zeitschrift fuer Spielmusik Auf Allerlei Instrumenten.*
**Desc:** Recorder music some with percussion or continuo.

GW/0044-3824
**ZEITSCHRIFTENDIENST MUSIK. Added/Corp** Deutscher Bibliotheksverband. **VFOAT** ZD Musik. (19??)-. German. bm. DM85.00. Deutsches Bibliotheksinstitut, Bundesallee 184 185, D 10717 Berlin Germany. **Tel** 011 49 30 8505186, 011 49 30 8505187, FAX 011 49 30 8505100. **LC** ML118; .Z43. **DD** 780/.5. cum. index. **Circ:** 200.
**Desc:** Index of articles in over 50 German and foreign music periodicals.

CN/0703-4709
**ZOUNDS.** (Mar. 1975)-. Periodical. English. mo. Free. Fancon Productions, Box 214, Station A, Mississauga Ontario L5A 2Z7 Canada. **DD** 780/.42/05.

GW/0176-0971
**ZUPFMUSIK MAGAZIN. Added/Corp** Bund Deutscher Zupfmusiker (Germany). **VFOAT** Zupfmusik. (1984)-. Periodical. German. qt. **LC** ML5; .M159. **DD** 787.6/1/05. ***Continues*** *Zupfmusik, Guitarre, 0722-0545.*

YU/0044-555X
**ZVUK (BEOGRAD).** (ZVUK; JUGOSLOVENSKA MUSICKA REVIJA.). [Zvuk]. **Added/Corp** Savez Kompozitora Jugoslavije. Savez Organizacija Kompozitora Jugoslavije. (1955)-. Periodical. Serbo-Croatian (Roman) (summaries and/or abstracts in English). Four times a year. $55.00. **(Subscription address:** Jugoslovenska Knjiga, PO Box 36, YU 11001 Belgrade Yugoslovia.) **LC** ML5; .Z9.
**Ind/Abst** Music Index; RILM Abstr.

## ABSTRACTING, BIBLIOGRAPHIES AND STATISTICS

US/0193-0850
**AWC NEWS/FORUM. Added/Corp** American Women Composers. **VFOAT** A.W.C. News Forum. Vol. 4, No. 1 & 2 (Feb./May 1983)-. Periodical. English. an (Mar.). $15.00 US; $21.00 Canada & Pan American & Europe; $27.00 others. American Women Composers Inc., 1690 36th Street Northwest, Suite 409, Washington DC 20007. **Tel** (202)342-8179. **ED** Tina Davidson. **Bk Rev. Ad Acc. Circ:** 500. ***Continues*** *AWC News, 0193-0850.*
**Desc:** Covers composers, with biographies and bibliography/discography. Includes reviews of record books, listing of new music in the AWC Music Library, news on competitions, news on AWC chapter programs and activities.
**Ind/Abst** Music Artic. Guide (?-?).

US/0360-2753
**BIBLIOGRAPHIC GUIDE TO MUSIC. Main/Corp** New York Public Library. Music Division. 1975-. English. an. $150.00. GK Hall & Co, 100 Front Street, Riverside NJ 08075. **Tel** (800)257-5755 ext. 2223. **LC** ML136.N5; N5732. **DD** 016.78.

GW
**BIBLIOGRAPHIE DES MUSIKSCHRIFTTUMS. Added/Corp** Staatliches Institut fuer Musikforschung. Staatliches Institut fuer Deutsche Musikforschung (Germany). Institut fuer Musikforschung (Germany). (1936)-. Monographic series. German. ir. Price varies per volume. B. Schotts Soehne Musikverlag, Carl Zeiss Str 1, Postfach 3640, D 55026 Mainz Germany. **Tel** 011 49 6131 505129, 011 49 6131 505122, FAX 011 49 6131 505115, telex 04187821. **ED** B. Schotts Soehne. **LC** ML113; .B54.

GW
**BIBLIOGRAPHIE MUSIK.** 1975-. German. an. Sachsische Landesbibliothek, Marienallee 12, Dresden 806 Germany. **Tel** 52677, telex 2-368. **LC** ML120; .G3B54. **DD** 016.78. ***Continues*** *Neuerwerbungen (Sachsische Landesbibliothek (Dresden, Germany). Musikabteilung).*

US
**BIBLIOGRAPHIES IN AMERICAN MUSIC. Added/Corp** College Music Society. (1974)-. Monographic series. English. ir. Price varies per volume. Harmonie Park Press, 23630 Pinewood, Warren MI 48091. **Tel** (313)755-3080, (800)886-3080, FAX (313)755-4213. **ED** J. Bunker Clark. **Circ:** 300.
**Desc:** Series is published in conjunction with the College Music Society and covers bibliographies of American composers.

US
**BILLBOARD'S MUSIC & VIDEO YEARBOOK. VFOAT** Billboard's Music and Video Yearbook; Music and Video Yearbook; Billboard ... Music and Video Yearbook; Music & Video Yearbook. (1987)-. English. an. $40.00 US; $41.00 other. Record Research Incorporated, PO Box 200, Menomonee Falls WI 53051. **Tel** (414)251-5408, FAX (414)251-9452. **LC** ML156.4.P6; J64. **DD** 016.78164/0973. ***Continues*** *Billboard's Music Yearbook.*

●GW
**CDS ZUM AUSLEIHEN.** (1992)-. Catalog. German. Berliner Stadtbibliothek Phonothek, Breite Str. 32-34, 10178 Berlin Germany. **Tel** 24 42 366 / 369. ***Continues*** *Schallplatten zum Ausleihen.*
**Desc:** A catalog of phonograph records.

US/0070-3885
**DETROIT STUDIES IN MUSIC BIBLIOGRAPHY.** [Detroit stud. music bibliogr.]. (1961)-. Bibliography. English. ir. Price varies per volume. Harmonie Park Press, 23630 Pinewood, Warren MI 48091. **Tel** (313)755-3080, (800)886-3080, FAX (313)755-4213. **DD** 780.

GW
**DEUTSCHE BIBLIOGRAPHIE : MUSIKALIEN-VERZEICHNIS.** German. mo. DM245.00. Buchhandler Vereinigung GmbH, Grosser Hirschgraben 17-21, D 60311 Frankfurt 1 Germany. **Tel** 011 49 69 1306243, telex 413573 BUCH VOL.
**Desc:** Includes scores from West Germany and other German-speaking countries as they are deposited with the Deutsche Musikarchiv.

IE/0332-298X
**EIGSE CHEOL TIRE.** (IRISH FOLK MUSIC STUDIES.). [Eigse cheol tire]. **Added/Corp** Folk Music Society of Ireland. **VFOAT** Irish Folk Music Studies. Vol. 1, (1973)-. Periodical. Multiple languages (English and Irish). ir. 3.00p. Folk Music Society of Ireland, 15 Henrietta Street, Dublin 1 Ireland. **Tel** (01)730093. **ED** Hugh Shields. **LC** ML3654; .I7. **DD** 781.7/415. **Bk Rev. Ad Acc. Circ:** 1,000.
**Desc:** Studies, reviews, current bibliography and discography of Irish folk music.
**Ind/Abst** Annu. Bibliogr. Engl. Lang. Lit.; Music Index (-19??); RILM Abstr.

US/0195-4040
**JOEL WHITBURN'S TOP POP SINGLES. Added/Corp** Record Research, Inc. **VFOAT** Top Pop Singles. (1978)-. English. Record Research Incorporated, PO Box 200, Menomonee Falls WI 53051. **Tel** (414)251-5408, FAX (414)251-9452. **LC** ML156.4.P6; J66. **DD** 016.78164/0973.

GW/0077-1805
**MOZART-JAHRBUCH. See** Music.

US/0027-4240
**MUSIC ARTICLE GUIDE.** Vol. 1 (Winter 1966)-. Abstracting/Indexing Service. English. Four times a year (Mar., June, Sept., Dec.). $52.00. Music Article Guide, PO Box 27066, Philadelphia PA 19118. **Tel** (215)848-3540. **ED** Morris Henken. **LC** ML1; .M22795. available on microfilm and microfiche from University Microfilms International (UMI).
**Desc:** The nation's only annotated guide to signed feature articles in American music magazines geared to the needs of school and college music educators.

US/0027-4348
**MUSIC INDEX, THE.** (MUSIC INDEX.). [Music index]. Vol. 1 (1949)-. Abstracting/Indexing Service. English. mo (with annual cumulation and annual subject heading list). $1295.00 US; $1428.45 (includes GST) Canada; $1335.00 other. Harmonie Park Press, 23630 Pinewood, Warren MI 48091. **Tel** (313)755-3080, (800)886-3080, FAX (313)755-4213. **LC** ML118; .M84. **DD** 016.78. cum. index. **Circ:** 800.
**Desc:** Detailed entries include extensive collation enabling the reader to determine if illustration, biographies, portraits, or specifications are included in the citation. Covers over 350 titles, both popular and academic materials.

CN/0823-1338
**MUSIC SCORE CATALOGUE - CARLETON UNIVERSITY.** (MUSIC SCORE CLASSED CATALOGUE MICROFORM / CARLETON UNIVERSITY.). [Music score cl. cat. - Carleton Univ.]. **Main/Corp** Carleton University. Library. Periodical. English. 3.00Can$. Carleton University Library, Ottawa Ontario K1S 5B6 Canada. **Tel** (613)564-6647. **DD** 016.7808.
**Desc:** Catalogue of all music scores in Carleton University Library's collection, organized by subject headings.

US/0027-4585
**MUSICAL DENMARK.** [Music. Den.]. **Added/Corp** Danske Selskab (Copenhagen, Denmark) Dansk Musik Informations Center (Copenhagen, Denmark). No. 1 (Mar. 1952)-. Periodical. English. an. $4.50. Nordic Books, PO Box 1941, Philadelphia PA 19105. **Tel** (215)464-4186. **ED** Knud Ketting. **LC** UNC; ML27.D4; D36. **Ad Acc. Circ:** 3,000 (ctrl).
**Desc:** Articles about Danish music and musicians. Bibliographies listing first performances, Danish music on disc/tape, published music, books/periodicals.
**Ind/Abst** Music Index.

GW
**MUSIK-INFORMATION; BIBLIOGRAPHISCHE TITELUBERSICHT. Added/Corp** Leitstelle fur Information und Dokumentation "Musik". Vol. 1 (1971)-. Multiple languages (German and Multiple languages). mo. Deutscher Judo Verband, Redaktion Ippon Segewaldweg 40, D 12557 Berlin Germany. **Tel** 011 49 711 210770, telex 051 678. **LC** ML113; .M888. **DD** 016.78.

US/0033-6955
**RILM ABSTRACTS.** [RILM abstr.]. **Main/Corp** International Repertory of Music Literature (Organization). **Added/Corp** International Musicological Society. International Association of Music Libraries. American Council of Learned Societies. **VFOAT** RILM Abstracts of Music Literature. **VAT** Repertoire International de Litterature Musicale Abstracts. Vol. 1, (Jan./April 1967)-. Abstracting/Indexing Service. English. qt. RILM Abstracts, City University of New York, 33 West 42nd Street, New York NY 10036. **Tel** (212)642-2709, FAX (212)642-1900. **ED** Terence Ford. **LC** ML1; .I83. **DD** 780/.5. Index available. cum. index. **Bk Rev. Circ:** 2,000. available on an online database from DIALOG.
**Desc:** Abstracts of music literature published three times per year in addition to a fourth issue containing an index for the year.

GW
**SCHALLPLATTEN ZUM AUSLEIHEN, NEUERWERBUNGEN / PHONOTHEK, BERLINER STADTBIBLIOTHEK.** ***Title Change.*** **Added/Corp** Berliner Stadtbibliothek. Phonothek. (19??)-(1991). Catalog. German. an. Berliner Stadtbibliothek Phonothek, Breite Str. 32-34, 10178 Berlin Germany. **Tel** 24 42 366 / 369. **LC** PAR. ***Continued by*** *CDs zum Ausleihen.*
**Desc:** A catalog of phonograph records.

CN/0822-9783
**TAPES BY MAIL CATALOGUE.** [Tapes mail cat.]. **Main/Corp** Northwestern Regional Library System (Ont.). Periodical. English. Northwestern Regional Library System, 910 Victoria Avenue, Thunder Bay Ontario P7C 1B4 Canada. **DD** 016.78.

## NATURAL HISTORY

GW
**ABHANDLUNGEN AUS DEM LANDESMUSEUM FUER NATURKUNDE ZU MUNSTER IN WESTFALEN.** **See** Museums and Galleries.

GW/0365-7000
**ABHANDLUNGEN DER SENCKENBERGISCHEN NATURFORSCHENDEN GESELLSCHAFT.** ***Title Change.*** [Abh. Senckenb. Naturforsch. Ges.]. Essay 428; 1934-. Monographic series. German (English). ir. Senckenberg Naturforschende, Gesellschaft, Senckenberganlage 25, W-6000 Frankfurt Germany. **Tel** 011 49 069 75421, FAX 069-746238. **LC** QH5; .S38. **CODEN** ASNGA7. Index available. **Pr Rev.** ctrl circ. available on an online database from STN International; CISTI; ORBIT; (file 51) OCLC EPIC; and (GEOREF file 89) DIALOG. Documents available from BIOSIS Document Express. ***Continued by*** *Senckenbergische Naturforschende Gesellschaft. Abhandlungen.*
**Desc:** Strictly scientific treatises (biology, geology).
**Ind/Abst** Biol. Abstr.; Fish Rev.; GeoRef; Wildl. Rev.

GW/0373-7586
**ABHANDLUNGEN UND BERICHTE DES NATURKUNDEMUSEUMS GORLITZ.** [Abh. Ber. Nat.kd.mus. Gorlitz]. **Main/Corp** Gorlitz. Naturkundemuseum. Vol. 1- 1827-. Periodical. German. ir. **LC** QH5; .G65. **CODEN** ABNGAO. Documents available from BIOSIS Document Express.
**Ind/Abst** Biocont. News Inf. (1991-); Biol. Abstr.; GeoRef; Nematol. Abstr.; Rev. Agric. Entomol.; Rev. Med. Vet. Entomol.; Rev. Plant Pathol.; Soils Fert.

GW/0177-9214
**ACTA BIOLOGICA BENRODIS.** [Acta biol. Benrodis]. **Added/Corp** Naturkundliches Heimatmuseum Benrath. **VFOAT** Acta Biologica Benrodis + Mitteilungen aus dem Naturkundlichen Heimatmuseum Benrath; Acta Biologica Benrodis plus Mitteilungen aus dem Naturkundlichen Heimatmuseum Benrath. Vol. 1, No. 1 (1988)-. Periodical. German (English). sa. Naturkundliches Heimatmuseum Benrath, Benrather Schlossallee 102, Schloss Benrath, D-4000 Dusseldorf Germany.
**Ind/Abst** Ecol. Abstr.

IC/0365-4850
**ACTA NATURALIA ISLANDICA.** (ACTA NATURALIA ISLANDICA / MUSEUM RERUM NATURALIUM REYKJAVIKENSIS, NATTURUGRIPASAFNI I REYKJAVIK.). [Acta nat. Isl.]. **Added/Corp** Natturugripasafni i Reykjavik. Nattuurugripasafn Islands. Natturufristofnun Islands. Vol. 1, No. 1 (1946)-. Monographic series. English (French and German). **LC** QH166; .A75. **CODEN** ANIRAE. Documents available from BIOSIS Document Express, CASDDS.
**Ind/Abst** Biol. Abstr.; Chem. Abstr.; Fish Rev. (Jan. 1989-July 1992); GeoRef; Wildl. Rev. (Jan. 1989-July 1992).

CN/0318-5540
**ALBERTA NATURALIST.** **Added/Corp** Federation of Alberta Naturalists. **VFOAT** Newsletter; Federation of Alberta Naturalists Newsletter. (1971)-. Periodical. English. qt. 15.00Can$ (subscribing member); $25.00 (supporting member). Federation Alberta Naturalists, Box 1472, Edmonton Alta T5J 2N5 Canada. **Tel** (403)453-8629, FAX (403)453-8553. **ED** Edrea Daniel. **DD** 500.9/7123. **CODEN** ALNAEC. **[CCC].** Index available. cum. index. **Bk Rev**, (Qty: 4). **Ad Acc. Circ:** 500 (ctrl).
**Desc:** Articles concerning the natural history in Alberta. Coverage and announcements of meetings, field trips and events of interest to Alberta naturalists and conservationists.
**Ind/Abst** Fish Rev.; Key Word Index Wildl. Res.; Wildl. Rev.

GE/0065-6631
**ALTENBURGER NATURWISSENSCHAFTLICHE FORSCHUNGEN.** (1981)-. Periodical. German.
**Ind/Abst** Geogr. Abstr. Phys. Geogr.; GeoRef.

US/0003-0031
**AMERICAN MIDLAND NATURALIST, THE.** [Am. midl. nat.]. **Added/Corp** University of Notre Dame. Vol. 1, No. 5 (Dec. 1909)-. Academic Scholarly Publication. English. qt (4 issues). $75.00 North and South America and the Caribbean; $80.00 other. American Midland Naturalist, University of Notre Dame, Room 285 GLSC, Notre Dame IN 46556. **Tel** (219)631-7481. **ED** R. P. McIntosh. **LC** QH1; .A35. **CODEN** AMNAAF. Index available (free, April). cum. index. **Pr Rev. Acid Free. Circ:** 1,500 (ctrl). available on microfilm and microfiche from University Microfilms International (UMI). Documents available from The Genuine Article, BIOSIS Document Express, UMI Article Clearinghouse, CASDDS. ***Continues*** *Midland Naturalist, 0271-6844.*
**Desc:** A primary journal publishing basic research in biology including animal and plant ecology, systematics and physiology, entomology, mammalogy, ichthyology, parasitology, invertebrate zoology and limnology.
**Ind/Abst** AGRICOLA [Select. Cov.]; Anim. Behav. Abstr.; AQUAREF; Biocont. News Inf.; Biodeter. Abstr.; Biol. Agric. Index; Biol. Abstr.; Chem. Abstr.; Cot. Trop. Fibr. Abstr. Bibliogr.; Curr. Aware. Biol. Sci., CABS; Curr. Contents, Agric. Biol. Environ. Sci.; Curr. Ref. Fish Res.; Ecol. Abstr.; Ecology Abstr.; Energy Res. Abstr.; Entomol. Abstr.; Environ. Period. Bibliogr.; Expand. Acad. Index (1989-); Field Crop Abstr.; Fish Rev.; For. Prod. Abstr.; For. Abstr.; Gen. Sci. Index; Gen. Sci. Source (Jul. 1993-); Geogr. Abstr. Phys. Geogr. (?-?); GeoRef; Grasslands For. Abstr.; Helminthol. Abstr. (1991-); Hortic. Abstr.; INIS Atomindex [Micro.]; Key Word Index Wildl. Res.; Mag. Search; Newsp. Period. Abstr. (1991-); Ornamental Hort. (19??-19??); Life Sci. Collect.; Plant Breed. Abstr.; Plant Genet. Resour. Abstr.; Res. Alert [Full Cov.]; Rev. Agric. Entomol.; Rev. Med. Vet. Entomol.; Rev. Plant Pathol.; Sci. Cit. Index; SCISEARCH; Seed Abstr.; Soc. Sci. Cit. Index [Select. Cov.]; Soils Fert.; Weed Abstr.; Wildl. Rev.

US/0003-0147
**AMERICAN NATURALIST, THE.** [Am. nat.]. **Added/Corp** Essex Institute. American Society of Naturalists. Vol. 1 (March 1867)-. Periodical. English. mo. $63.00 (individuals), $198.00 (institutions), $44.00 (students). University of Chicago Press / Journals Division, PO Box 37005, 5720 South Woodlawn, Chicago IL 60637. **Tel** (312)753-3347, FAX (312)753-0811. **LC** QH1; .A5. **DD** 574/.05. **NLM** W1 AM66. **CODEN** AMNTA4. **[CCC]. Pr Rev.** available on microfilm and microfiche from University Microfilms International (UMI). Documents available from The Genuine Article, BIOSIS Document Express, UMI Article Clearinghouse, CASDDS.
**Desc:** Research in ecology, evolution, and population biology. Drawing upon examinations of all members of the animal kingdom as well as studies of plant life, the naturalist emphasizes sophisticated methodologies and innovative theoretical syntheses - all in the effort to advance the knowledge of organic evolution and other broad biological principals.
**Ind/Abst** Acad. Ind. [Computer File] (1992-); Acad. Search (Jan. 1993-); AGRICOLA [Select. Cov.]; Anim. Behav. Abstr.; Anim. Breed. Abstr.; AQUAREF; Biocont. News Inf.; Biol. Agric. Index; Biol. Abstr.; Chem. Abstr.; Curr. Aware. Biol. Sci., CABS; Curr. Contents, Agric. Biol. Environ. Sci.; Curr. Ref. Fish Res.; Dairy Sci. Abstr.; Ecol. Abstr.; Ecology Abstr.; Energy Res. Abstr.; Entomol. Abstr.; Environ. Period. Bibliogr.; Expand. Acad. Index (1989-); Field Crop Abstr.; Fish Rev. (Jan. 1989-July 1992); For. Prod. Abstr.; For. Abstr.; Gen. Sci. Index; Gen. Sci. Source (Jan. 1993-); Genet. Abstr.; Geol. Abstr.; GeoRef; Grasslands For. Abstr.; INFO-SOUTH Abstr.; INIS Atomindex [Micro.]; Key Word Index Wildl. Res.; Mag. Search; Math. Rev.; Newsp. Period. Abstr. (1989-); Nutr. Abstr. Rev., Ser. B, Live Feeds and Feed.; Nutr. Abstr. Rev., Ser. A, Hum. Exp.; Life Sci. Collect.; Plant Breed. Abstr.; Plant Genet. Resour. Abstr.; Postharvest News Inf.; Potato Abstr.; Poult. Abstr.; Protozoolog. Abstr.; Res. Alert [Full Cov.]; Rev. Agric. Entomol.; Rev. Med. Vet. Entomol.; Rev. Med. Vet. Mycology; Rev. Plant Pathol.; Sci. Cit. Index; SCISEARCH; Seed Abstr.; Soc. Sci. Cit. Index [Select. Cov.]; Stat. Theory Method Abstr. (1959-1963, 1973); Vocat. Search (Jan. 1993-); Weed Abstr.; Wildl. Rev. (Jan. 1989-July 1992).

NE/0926-3543
**AMOEBA AMSTERDAM. 1976.** (AMOEBA.). [Amoeba Amst., 1976]. **VFOAT** Amoebe (Deventer). (1976)-. Periodical. Dutch. Eight times a year. Netherlands Youth Organization for Natural Studies, Schaep en Burgh, Noordereinde 60, 1243 JJs Graveland Netherlands. **UDC** 502.2. Index available. cum. index. **Bk Rev. Circ:** 1,500 (ctrl). ***Continues*** *Trias (Zeist), 0166-8358.*

BL/0071-1276
**ANAIS DA ESCOLA SUPERIOR DE AGRICULTURA LUIZ DE QUEIROZ.** ***Title Change.*** **Main/Corp** Escola Superior de Agricultura "Luiz de Queiroz.". Vol. 1 (1944)-(19??). Portuguese (summaries and/or abstracts in English). an. Universidade de Sao Paulo / Piracicaba, Caixa Postal 9, CEP 13400, Piracicaba SP Brazil. **Tel** 011 55 11 194 330011. **CODEN** AESQAW. Documents available from CASDDS. ***Continued by*** *Scientia Agricola.*
**Ind/Abst** Agrindex; Agrofor. Abstr.; Anim. Breed. Abstr.; Biocont. News Inf.; Chem. Abstr.; Crop Physiol. Abstr.; Field Crop Abstr.; For. Abstr.; Grasslands For. Abstr.; Hortic. Abstr.; Irr. Drain. Abstr.; Maize Abstr.; Nutr. Abstr. Rev., Ser. B, Live Feeds and Feed.; Ornamental Hort.; Plant Breed. Abstr.; Plant Grow. Reg. Abstr.; Postharvest News Inf.; Rev. Agric. Entomol.; Rev. Plant Pathol.; Rice Abstr.; Seed Abstr.; Soils Fert.; Sorghum Mill. Abstr.; Soyabean Abstr.; Sug. Indus. Abstr.

CL/0716-6486
**ANALES DEL INSTITUTO DE LA PATAGONIA. SERIE CIENCIAS NATURALES.** [An. Inst. Patagon., Ser. Cienc. nat.]. **VFOAT** Serie Ciencias Naturales; Anales del Instituto de la Patagonia, Universidad de Magallanes; Anales del Instituto de la Patagonia. Vol. 15 (1984)-. Spanish. an. 2.500Chil$; $10.00 other. Universidad de Magallanes, Punta Arenas, Ave Presidente Bulnes Km 4, Casilla Correo 113-D, Punta Arenas Chile. **Tel** FAX (061)223039, telex 380004 UMAE - CK. **ED** Sr B Mateo Martinic. **LC** QH119; .A53. **DD** 508.83. **CODEN** AIPNE6. Index available. cum. index. **Bk Rev. Circ:** 1,000 (ctrl). Documents available from BIOSIS Document Express. ***Continues in part*** *Anales del Instituto de la Patagonia, 0085-1922.*
**Desc:** Original research articles on social and natural sciences referring to Patagonia, Tierra del Fuego, Antarctica, adjacent islands and the Pacific Ocean.
**Ind/Abst** Biol. Abstr. (1984-).

CL
**ANALES DEL MUSEO DE HISTORIA NATURAL DE VALPARAISO.** **Main/Corp** Museo de Historia Natural de Valparaiso. No. 1 (1968)-. Academic Scholarly Publication. Spanish (Spanish; summaries and/or abstracts in English). an. $15.00. Museo de Historia Natural de Valparaiso, Cassilla 3208 Correo 3, Valparaiso Chile. **Tel** 257441. **ED** Serigo Zunino. **LC** QH119; . V34a. **DD** 574.983/05. Index available. **Circ:** 350 (ctrl).
**Desc:** Covers botany, ecology, zoology (invertebrate and vertebrate), and archaeology.

UY
**ANALES - MUSEO NACIONAL DE HISTORIA NATURAL (URUGUAY).** **Main/Corp** Museo Nacional de Historia Natural (Uruguay). Spanish. Museo Nacional de Historia Natural, Casilla de Correo 399, Montevideo Uruguay. **LC** QH7; .M85A. ***Continues*** *Anales del Museo de Historia Natural de Montevideo.*

●AT
**ANH / THE AUSTRALIAN MUSEUM TRUST.** **See** Museums and Galleries.

FR/0373-7039
**ANNALES DE LA SOCIETE DES SCIENCES NATURELLES ET D'ARCHEOLOGIE DE TOULON ET DU VAR.** **See** Archaeology.

FR/0995-9181
**ANNALES DE LA SOCIETE SCIENTIFIQUE ET LITTERAIRE DE CANNES ET DE L'ARRONDISSEMENT DE GRASSE.** (1929)-. Periodical. French. an. **UDC** 061.22 (449.4). ***Continues*** *Memoires de la Societe des Sciences Naturelles, des Lettres et des Beaux-Arts de Cannes et de l'Arrondissement de Grasse, 0995-9173.*
**Ind/Abst** Numis. Lit.

HU
**ANNALES HISTORICO-NATURALES MUSEI NATIONALIS HUNGARICI (BUDAPEST, HUNGARY : 1965).** (ANNALES HISTORICO-NATURALES MUSEI NATIONALIS HUNGARICI.). [Ann. hist.-nat. Mus. Nat. Hung.]. **Added/Corp** Termeszettudomanyi Muzeum (Hungary). **VFOAT** Termeszettudomanyi Muzeum Enkonyve. Vol. 57 (1965)-. English (German, Italian and French). an. $15.00. Hungarian Natural History Museum, Baross U 13, H-1088 Budapest Hungary. **ED** Dr Z Korsos. **LC** PAR. **CODEN** AHMHAU. **Circ:** 700 (ctrl). Documents available from BIOSIS Document Express. ***Continues*** *Magyar Nemzeti Muzeum Termeszettudomanyi Muzeum Evokonyve.*
**Desc:** Papers on the material of special collections of the Hungarian Natural History Museum.
**Ind/Abst** Biocont. News Inf.; Biol. Abstr.; Field Crop Abstr.; GeoRef; Grasslands For. Abstr.

GR/0302-1033
**ANNALES MUSEI GOULANDRIS.** (EPETERIS MOUSEIOU GOULANDRE. ANNALES MUSEI GOULANDRIS.). [Epet. mous. goulandre]. **Main/Corp** Mouseion Goulandre Physikes Historias. **Added/Corp** Mouseion Goulandre PhysikÂes Historias. Annales Musei Goulandris. **VFOAT** Annales Musei Goulandris. (1973)-. Periodical. English (French, German and Latin; summaries and/or abstracts in Greek, Modern). an. Dr5000.00 Greece; $25.00 US. Goulandris Natural History Museum, Levidou 13, 145 62 Kifissia Greece. **Tel** 8015-870, 01 8086405, FAX 01 8080 674. **ED** William T. Stearn. **LC** QH151; .M68a. **DD** 500.9/495. **CODEN** AMUGAY. **Circ:** 800 (ctrl). Documents available from BIOSIS Document Express.
**Desc:** An international scientific journal primarily devoted

to the natural history of Greece and the Eastern Mediterranean.
**Ind/Abst** AGRICOLA; Biol. Abstr.; GeoRef.

GW/0080-5165
**ANNALES UNIVERSITATIS SARAVIENSIS. REIHE : MATHEMATISCH-NATURWISSENSCHAFTLICHE FAKULTAT.** [Ann. Univ. Sarav., Math.- Naturwiss. Fak.]. **Main/Corp** Universitat des Saarlandes. **Added/Corp** Universitat des Saarlandes. **VFOAT** Reihe Mathematisch-Naturwissenschaftliche Fakultat. No. 1 (1963)-. Academic Scholarly Publication. German (French). ir. Price varies per volume. Gebruder Borntraeger Verlagsbuchhandlung, Johannesstrasse 3-A, D-70176 Stuttgart Germany. **Tel** 0711/62 50 01, FAX (0711)625005, telex 723363 SCHB D. **ED** Fridolin Firtion. **LC** Q49; .S25A25. **CODEN** AUSVAN. **Bk Rev. Ad Acc.** Documents available from CASDDS. ***Continues*** *Universitat des Saarlandes. Annales Universitatis Saraviensis. Scientia.*
**Ind/Abst** Chem. Abstr. (1963-1981); Energy Res. Abstr. (May 1972-); GeoRef; Math. Rev.

IT/0365-4389
**ANNALI DEL MUSEO CIVICO DI STORIA NATURALE GIACOMO DORIA.** [Ann. Mus. civ. stor. nat. Giacomo Doria]. **Added/Corp** Museo Civico di Storia Naturale Giacomo Doria (Genoa, Italy). (1916)-. Periodical. Italian (English; summaries and/or abstracts in French). **CODEN** AMGDAN. cum. index. ***Continues*** *Annali del Museo Civico di Storia Naturale di Genova.*
**Ind/Abst** Biocont. News Inf.

SA/0570-1880
**ANNALS OF THE CAPE PROVINCIAL MUSEUMS. NATURAL HISTORY.** [Ann. Cape prov. mus. nat. hist.]. **VFOAT** Natural History. Began in 1966. English. Albany Museum, Somerset Street, Grahamstown 6140 South Africa. **LC** QH194; .A55. **DD** 508.6. **CODEN** ACPVAI. Documents available from BIOSIS Document Express. ***Continues in part*** *Annals of the Cape Provincial Museums.*
**Ind/Abst** Biol. Abstr.; Fish Rev.; GeoRef; Life Sci. Collect.; Wildl. Rev.

US/0097-4463
**ANNALS OF THE CARNEGIE MUSEUM.** [Ann. Carnegie Mus.]. **Added/Corp** Carnegie Museum. Carnegie Museum of Natural History. **VFOAT** Annals of Carnegie Museum. Vol. 1, No. 1 (1901)-. Monographic series. English. Four times a year (Feb., May, Aug., Nov.). $65.00 (institutions), $25.00 (individuals). Carnegie Museum of Natural History, 4400 Forbes Avenue, Pittsburgh PA 15213. **Tel** (412)622-3315, FAX (412)622-8837. **ED** Mary Ann Schmidt (phone: (412)622-3287). **LC** AS36; .P7. **DD** 500.9/08. **CODEN** CIMUAU. Index available (Bound in 4th issue, publish in November). **Bk Rev**, (Qty: varies). **Pr Rev. Circ:** 590. Documents available from BIOSIS Document Express.
**Desc:** International journal that publishes short and medium-length contributions in organismal biology, earth sciences and anthropology. Specific studies treat fossil and living plants and animals, especially vascular floras, arthropods, molluscs, echinoderms, brachiopods, amphibians, reptiles, birds and mammals. Subjects of major focus include systematics, evolutionary relationships, biogeography, ecology, faunal and floral composition, comparative morphology and karyology, paleontology, paleoecology, palynology, historical geology, biostratigraphy, ethnology and archaeology.
**Ind/Abst** Biol. Abstr.; Ecol. Abstr.; Geogr. Abstr. Human Geogr.; GeoRef; Zool. Rec.; Wildl. Rev.

SA/0304-0798
**ANNALS OF THE NATAL MUSEUM, PIETERMARITZBURG.** (ANNALS OF THE NATAL MUSEUM.). [Ann. Natal Mus., Pietermaritzbg.]. **Main/Corp** Natal Museum, Pietermaritzburg. **VFOAT** Annale van die Natalse Museum. Vol. 1 (June 1906)-. English (German and French). ir (2 or 3 per year). R42.00 South Africa; R43.00 other. Natal Museum, 237 Loop Street, Pietermaritzburg, 3201 South Africa. **Tel** 0331-51404. **(Subscription address:** Library, Private Bag 9070, Pietermaritzburg 3200 South Africa**) ED** Jason Londt. **LC** Q85; .N3. **DD** 574.96/05. **CODEN** ANMUA9. Index available. cum. index. **Pr Rev. Circ:** 350 (ctrl). Documents available from BIOSIS Document Express.
**Desc:** Scientific journal reporting research in systematic zoology, especially arachnology, entomology, and malacology.
**Ind/Abst** Anthropol. Lit.; Biol. Abstr.; Ethnoarts Index; GeoRef; Life Sci. Collect.; Zool. Rec.

SA/0041-1752
**ANNALS OF THE TRANSVAAL MUSEUM.** [Ann. Transvaal Mus.]. **Added/Corp** Transvaal Museum. **VFOAT** Annale van die Transvaal Museum; Annale van die Transvaal-Museum; Mededelingen van het Transvaal Museum. Vol. 1, No. 1 (April 1908)-. Monographic series. English (Afrikaans). ir. Price varies per volume. Transvaal Museum, PO Box 413, Pretoria South Africa 0001. **Tel** (012)322-7632, FAX (012)322-7939. **ED** N. J. Dippenaar. **LC** QH1; .T7. **DD** 574. **CODEN** ATVMA4. Index available. cum. index. **Pr Rev. Circ:** 400 (ctrl). Documents available from BIOSIS Document Express.
**Desc:** Taxonomy, biology, ecology, paleontology of Southern African fauna.
**Ind/Abst** Biol. Abstr.; Fish Rev.; GeoRef; Helminthol. Abstr. (1991-); Wildl. Rev.

FR
**ANNUAIRE DU MUSEUM NATIONAL D'HISTOIRE NATURELLE POUR L'ANNEE.** **Main/Corp** Museum National d'Histoire Naturelle (France). Began with 1939 vol. French. Editions du Museum, 57 rue Cuvier, 75005 Paris Cedex 05 France. **Tel** 011 33 1 40793700. **LC** QH70.F82; P375. **DD** 508/.074/44.

UK/0268-9936
**ANNUAL BIBLIOGRAPHY OF THE HISTORY OF NATURAL HISTORY.** ***Ceased.*** **See** Natural History-Abstracting, Bibliographies and Statistics.

NP
**ANNUAL - NEPAL NATURE CONSERVATION SOCIETY.** **Main/Corp** Nepal Nature Conservation Society. (1977)-. English. an. **LC** QH193.N4; N46a. **DD** 333.9/5/095496.

US/0742-5066
**ANNUAL REPORT - CHESAPEAKE BAY FOUNDATION.** (ANNUAL REPORT.). [Annu. rep. - Chesap. Bay Found.]. **Main/Corp** Chesapeake Bay Foundation. English. an. Chesapeake Bay Foundation, 162 Prince George Street, Annapolis MD 21401. **LC** QH104.5.C45; C44A. **DD** 333.91/816/06075518.

US/0065-9452
**ANTHROPOLOGICAL PAPERS OF THE AMERICAN MUSEUM OF NATURAL HISTORY.** [Anthropol. pap. Am. Mus. Nat. Hist.]. **VFOAT** Anthropological Papers, American Museum of Natural History. Vol. 1, Pt. 1 (Jan. 1907)-. Monographic series. English. ir. Price varies per volume. American Museum of Natural History, Central Park West at 79th Street, New York NY 10024. **Tel** (212)769-5500, (800)234-5252, telex 910 240 8933 MICRO PRESS VQ. **ED** Brenda Jones. **LC** GN2; .A27. **CODEN** APNHAN. **Circ:** 1,500 (ctrl). available on microfilm from University Microfilms International (UMI). Documents available from BIOSIS Document Express.
**Desc:** Each issue devoted exclusively to one report in the field of anthropology or archaeology.
**Ind/Abst** Am. Hist. Life (1963-1970); Art Archaeol. Tech. Abstr.; Biol. Abstr.

SZ/0252-9289
**ARCHIVES DES SCIENCES ET COMPTE RENDU DES SEANCES DE LA SOCIETE.** **Added/Corp** Societe de Physique et d'Histoire Naturelle de Geneve. **VFOAT** Compte Rendu des Seances de la Societe; Archives des Sciences. Vol. 34, (Jan./April 1981)-. Periodical. French (English). Three times a year. F135.00. Soc Physique Historie Naturell, CH-1290 Sauverny, Switzerland. **Tel** 011 41 22 552611. **LC** Q67; .A73. ***Formed by the union of*** *Archives des Sciences, 0003-9705* ***and*** *Compte Rendu des Seances de la Societe de Physique et d'Histoire Naturelle de Geneve (1966).*
**Ind/Abst** Ei Page One.

UK/0260-9541
**ARCHIVES OF NATURAL HISTORY.** [Arch. nat. hist.]. **Added/Corp** Society for the Bibliography of Natural History. Vol. 10, Pt. 1 (Apr. 1981)-. Periodical. English (French and German). Three times a year (3 issues per volume). £95.00 UK, $140.00 other. Society for the History of Natural History, British Museum - Natural History, London SW7 5BD England. **Tel** 011/44/71/5896323 ext.662. **ED** A.C. Wheeler. **LC** Z7403; .S68. **NLM** ZQ 1 S678J. **Bk Rev. Pr Rev. Circ:** 800. ***Continues*** *Journal of the Society for the Bibliography of Natural History, 0037-9778.*
**Desc:** An international journal with original refereed papers on the history and bibliography of natural history, zoology, geology and botany together with book reviews.
**Ind/Abst** Am. Hist. Life (1981-); Fish Rev. (Jan. 1989-July 1992); Wildl. Rev. (Jan. 1989-July 1992).

PO/0870-6581
**ARQUIPELAGO. CIENCIAS DA NATUREZA.** **Added/Corp** Universidade dos Acores. **VFOAT** Ciencias da Natureza; Life and Earth Sciences; Arquipelago. Life and Earth Sciences. No. 8 (1990)-. Periodical. English (French and Portuguese). Universidade Dos Acores, P-9500 Ponta Delgada, Acores, Portugal. ***Continues*** *Arquipelago.*

PO/0871-4843
**ARQUIVOS DO MUSEU BOCAGE. NOVA SERIE.** [Arq. Mus. Bocage (1987)]. Vol. 1, No. 1 (19 Oct. 1987)-. Monographic series. English (Portuguese, Spanish and French). ir. Price varies per volume. Museu Bocage, R Escola Politechnica 58, P-1200 Lisbon Portugal. **LC** PAR. ***Formed by the union of*** *Arquivos do Museu Bocage. Serie A, 0254-0444; Arquivos do Museu Bocage. Serie B, Notas, 0254-0452; Arquivos do Museu Bocage. Serie C, Suplementos, 0254-0460* ***and*** *Arquivos do Museu Bocage. Serie D, Extensao Cultural e Ensino, 0870-0540.*
**Ind/Abst** Fish Rev.; Wildl. Rev.

BL/0102-4272
**ARQUIVOS DO MUSEU DE HISTORIA NATURAL.** [Arq. Mus. Hist. Nat.]. **Main/Corp** Universidade Federal de Minas Gerais. Museu de Historia Natural. Vol. 1 (1971)-. Portuguese (summaries and/or abstracts in English). Universidade Federal de Minas Gerais / Museu de Historia Natural, Museu de Historia Natural, Belo Horizonte Brazil. **LC** QH7; .M89A.
**Ind/Abst** Anthropol. Lit.; GeoRef.

NO
**ARSBERETNING / UNIVERSITETET I TRONDHEIM, VITENSKAPSMUSEET.** **Main/Corp** Universitetet i Trondheim. Vitenskapsmuseet. (1985)-. Norwegian. an. **LC** WMLC L 83/5214.

IT/0037-8844
**ATTI DELLA SOCIETA ITALIANA DI SCIENZE NATURALI E DEL MUSEO CIVICO DI STORIA NATURALE DI MILANO.** [Atti Soc. ital. sci. nat., Mus. civ. stor. nat. Milano]. **Added/Corp** Societa Italiana di Scienze Naturali. Museo Civico di Storia Naturale di Milano. Vol. 36 (Jan. 1896)-. Academic Scholarly Publication. Italian (English). ir. L45000 Italy; L50000 other. Societa Italiana di Scienze Naturali, Corso Venezia 55, 20121 Milan Italy. **Tel** 011 39 2 62025405. **ED** Giovanni Pinna. **LC** Q54; .M6. **DD** 508. **NLM** W1 AT782Q. **CODEN** ASIMAY. Index available. **Circ:** 1,500. Documents available from BIOSIS Document Express, CASDDS. ***Continues*** *Atti della Societa Italiana di Scienze Naturali.*
**Ind/Abst** Biol. Abstr.; Chem. Abstr. (1955-1982); Fish Rev.; GeoRef; Key Word Index Wildl. Res.; Life Sci. Collect.; Zool. Rec.; Wildl. Rev.

US/0888-6555
**AUDUBON NATURALIST NEWS : A PUBLICATION OF THE AUDUBON NATURALIST SOCIETY OF THE CENTRAL ATLANTIC STATES.** [Audubon nat. news]. **Added/Corp** Audubon Naturalist Society of the Central Atlantic States. (197?)-. Periodical. English. Ten times a year. $10.00. Audubon Naturalist Society of the Central Atlantic States, 8940 Jones Mill Road, Chevy Chase MD 20815. **Tel** (301)652-9188, FAX (301)951-7179. **ED** Judith Nierman. **DD** 500. **Bk Rev. Ad Acc. Circ:** 7,400 (ctrl). ***Continues*** *Naturalist Review : A Publication of the Audubon Naturalist Society of the Central Atlantic States.*
**Desc:** Natural history and conservation news and feature articles. The focus is on the Mid-Atlantic States.

AT/0004-9840
**AUSTRALIAN NATURAL HISTORY.** ***Title Change.*** [Aust. nat. hist.]. **Added/Corp** Australian Museum. Vol. 14 (Mar. 1962)-(1992). Periodical. English. qt. Australian Museum, 6 College Street, P.O. Box A285, Sydney South 2000 Australia. **Tel** 011 61 2 3398200, FAX 61-2-3398313. **ED** Fiona Doig, Jenny Sanders and Georgina Hickey. **LC** QH1; .A986. **CODEN** AUNHAO. Index Available, published separately, free-automatically sent. **Bk Rev. Ad Acc, Adv Mgr:** Mike Field, **Tel** 339-8331. **Circ:** 20,000. Documents available from BIOSIS Document Express. ***Continues*** *Australian Museum. Australian Museum Magazine.* ***Continued by*** *ANH.*
**Desc:** Covers all aspects of Australian natural history: plants, animals, anthropology and geology; accredited scientifically.
**Ind/Abst** AESIS Q.; Art Archaeol. Tech. Abstr.; Biol. Abstr.; Environ. Period. Bibliogr.; GeoRef.

GW/0340-4277
**BEITRAEGE ZUR NATURKUNDE NIEDERSACHSENS.** [Beitr. Naturkd. Niedersachs.]. Vol. 1 (1948)-. Periodical. German. Four times a year. DM28.00. Beitrage Naturkunde Niedersach Stettiner, STR 3, D 31241 Ilsede 1 Germany. **Tel** 011 49 5172 4530. **ED** H. Oellee. **LC** QH5; .B38. Index available. **Bk Rev. Ad Acc.** ctrl circ.
**Ind/Abst** Key Word Index Wildl. Res.

US/1063-9241
**BEND OF THE RIVER.** (BEND OF THE RIVER : THE MAGAZINE OF THE HISTORIC MAUMEE VALLEY.). [Bend river]. **VFOAT** Bend of the River Magazine. Vol. 1, No. 1 (Dec. 1972)-. Periodical. English. Twelve times a year. $9.00. Raizk, PO Box 39, 143 West Third Street, Perrysburg OH 43552. **Tel** (419)874-7534, FAX (419)874-1466. **ED** Lee Raizk. **DD** 973. **Bk Rev**, (Qty: 12). **Ad Acc, Adv Mgr:** Sue Hunter, **Tel** (419)874-7534. **Circ:** 3,600 (ctrl).

AU/0302-9654
**BERICHT AUS DEM HAUS DER NATUR IN SALZBURG.** [Ber. Haus Nat. Salzbg.]. **Main/Corp** Salzburg. Haus der Natur. (19??)-. German.

ir. Haus der Natur, Museumsplatz 5, A-5020 Salzburg Austria. **LC** QH5; .S24a.
**Ind/Abst** GeoRef.

GW/0343-7655
**BERICHT DER NATURFORSCHENDEN GESELLSCHAFT AUGSBURG.** [Ber. Naturforsch. Ges. Augsbg.]. **Main/Corp** Naturforschende Gesellschaft, Augsburg. No. 1 (1948)-. German. an. **LC** QH5; .N416. **CODEN** BNGAAW.
**Ind/Abst** GeoRef.

GW/0365-9844
**BERICHT DER NATURHISTORISCHEN GESELLSCHAFT HANNOVER.** [Ber. Naturhist. Ges. Hannover]. **Main/Corp** Naturhistorische Gesellschaft Zu Hannover. **Added/Corp** Naturhistorische Gesellschaft zu Hannover. Festschrift. (1954)-. Academic Scholarly Publication. German. an. DM30.00. Naturhistorische Ges Hannover, Postfach 510153, D 30631 Hannover Germany. **Tel** 0511 643 2456, FAX 0511 643 2304. **LC** QH5; .N44. **CODEN** BENHAP. **Circ:** 900. Documents available from BIOSIS Document Express, CASDDS. ***Continues*** *Naturhistorische Gesellschaft zu Hannover. Jahresbericht der Naturhistorischen Gesellschaft zu Hannover.*
**Desc:** Covers archaeology, botany, earth science, geology, paleontology, geography, science, and zoology.
**Ind/Abst** Biol. Abstr.; Chem. Abstr.; GeoRef.

GW/0505-2793
**BERICHTE DES VEREINS NATUR UND HEIMAT UND DES NATURHISTORISCHEN MUSEUMS ZU LUBECK.** **Main/Corp** Verein Natur und Heimat, Lubeck. Began with No. 1 (1959)-. Periodical. German. te. $10.15. Naturhistorisches Museum, Luebeck/Muhlendamm 1-3, W-2400 Luebeck 1 Germany. **Tel** 0451/1224120. **ED** M Diehl, G V Studnitz. **LC** WMLC L 83/2690. cum. index. **Circ:** 500 (ctrl). ***Continues in part*** *Mitteilungen der Geographischen Gesellschaft Und des Naturhistorischen Museums in Lubeck.*
**Desc:** Biology and ecology of native biotopes.

IT
**BIBLIOTECA DELLA RIVISTA DI STORIA DELLE SCIENZE MEDICHE E NATURALI.** ***Title Change.*** (1947)-(19??). Periodical. Italian. ir. Casa Editrice Leo S. Olschki, Viuzzo del Pozzetto, Casella Postale 66, 50126 Florence Italy. **Tel** 011 39 55 6530684, FAX 011 39 55 6530214. ***Continued by*** *Biblioteca della Storia della Scienza.*

IT/0394-5065
**BIBLIOTECA DI STORIA DELLA SCIENZA.** [Bibl. stor. sci.]. (1986)-. Monographic series. Multiple languages. ir. Price varies per volume. Casa Editrice Leo S. Olschki, Viuzzo del Pozzetto, Casella Postale 66, 50126 Florence Italy. **Tel** 011 39 55 6530684, FAX 011 39 55 6530214. **UDC** 009. ***Continues*** *Biblioteca della Rivista di Storia delle Scienze Mediche e Naturali, 0080-326X.*

US
**BIENNIAL REPORT / IOWA PRESERVES BOARD.** **Main/Corp** Iowa Preserves Board. Began with Vol. for 1975/76. English. be. Iowa Preserves Board, Des Moines IA 50319. **LC** QH105.I8; I59A. **DD** 353.97770082/32.

US
**BIENNIAL REPORT - THE ACCOKEEK FOUNDATION.** **Main/Corp** Accokeek Foundation. 1st (1958/1959)-. English. be. **DD** 333.7.

KZ/0303-4119
**BIOLOGICESKIE NAUKI.** (BIOLOGICHESKIE NAUKI.). [Biol. nauki]. **Added/Corp** Qazaqtyng S.M. Kirov Atyndaghy Memlekettik Universiteti. (1971)-. Academic Scholarly Publication. Russian. ir. $179.95. **(Subscription address:** East View Publications Inc., 3020 Harbor Lane North, Suite 110, Minneapolis MN 55447.**)** **LC** QH191; .B57. **CODEN** BLNKAF. Documents available from BIOSIS Document Express, CASDDS.
**Ind/Abst** Aquat. Sci. Fish. Abstr. (Computer File); Biol. Abstr.; Chem. Abstr. (-1988); Energy Res. Abstr.; Fish Rev. (Jan. 1989-July 1992); Potato Abstr.; Wildl. Rev. (Jan. 1989-July 1992).

RU
**BIOLOGICHESKIE RESURSY I PRIRODNYE USLOVIIA MONGOLSKOI NARODNOI RESPUBLIKI.** **See** Biology.

IC
**BLIKI : TIMARIT UN FUGLA.** **Added/Corp** Natturufristofnun Islands. Fuglaverndarfelag Islands. No. 1 (May 1983)-. Academic Scholarly Publication. Icelandic (summaries and/or abstracts in English). an. $15.00 (each issue). Icelandic Museum of Natural History, PO Box 5320, 125 Reykjavik Iceland. **Tel** 354 1 629822, FAX 354 1 620815. **ED** Aevar Petersen. **Bk Rev**, (Qty: 1-3). **Pr Rev. Circ:** 600.
**Desc:** The primary aim is to act as forum for previously unpublished material and Icelandic birds, in the form of longer or shorter papers and reports.

CN/0006-5099
**BLUE JAY.** [Blue jay]. **Added/Corp** Saskatchewan Natural History Society. (1942/43)-. Periodical. English. Four times a year. $20.00 family membership; $15.00 individual. Saskatchewan Natural History Society, Box 4348, Regina Saskatchewan S4P 3W6 Canada. **Tel** (306)780-9273. **CODEN** BLJYA3. **Bk Rev.** **Ad Acc. Circ:** 2,000 (ctrl).
**Desc:** Articles pertaining to the flora and fauna of the prairie provinces of Canada.
**Ind/Abst** AQUAREF; Key Word Index Wildl. Res.; Wildl. Rev.

CN/0822-9988
**BLUE JAY NEWS.** [Blue jay news]. **Added/Corp** Saskatchewan Natural History Society. Issue No. 63 (May 1983)-. Periodical. English. Four times a year. 15.00Can$ (regular) Canada; 18.00Can$ (regular) others; 30.00Can$ (sustaining); 60.00Can$ (patron) Comes with Saskatchewan Natural History Society membership. Saskatchewan Natural History Society, Box 4348, Regina Saskatchewan S4P 3W6 Canada. **Tel** (306)780-9273. **ED** Lance Irvine and Sheila Lamont. **DD** 508.7124/05. Index available. **Bk Rev.** **Ad Acc. Circ:** 2,000 (ctrl). ***Continues*** *Saskatchewan Natural History Society. Newsletter, 0581-8443.*
**Desc:** News of activities of the Saskatchewan Natural History Society and information on environmental and conservation issues in Saskatchewan.

MX/0417-9455
**BOLETIN DE DIVULGACIONES.** **Main/Corp** Dominican Republic. Direccion General de Estadistica. No. 1- ; Dec., 1958-. Periodical. Spanish. Publ Sociedad Mexicana Hist Nat, Av Dr Vertiz No 724, Mexico 12 DF Mexico.

PE/0378-7699
**BOLETIN / INSTITUTO DEL MAR DEL PERU.** **Added/Corp** Instituto del Mar del Peru. Vol. 1 (1964)-. Monographic series. Spanish (summaries and/or abstracts in English). ir (four or five issues per year). Price varies per volume. Instituto del Mar del Peru, Lima Peru. **Tel** 297630. **LC** QH95.52; .L3. **DD** 574.92/05.

IT/0505-205X
**BOLLETTINO DEL MUSEO CIVICO DI STORIA NATURALE DI VENEZIA.** [Boll. Mus. civ. stor. nat. Ven.]. **Main/Corp** Museo Civico di Storia Naturale di Venezia. Vol. 7 (1954)-. Periodical. Italian (English, French, German and Spanish). an. Museo Civico di Storia Naturale, Lungadige Porta Vittoria 9, 37129 Verona Italy. **LC** QH7; .V4. **DD** 574. **Circ:** 1,000. ***Continues*** *Societa Veneziana di Storia Naturale. Bollettino del Societa Veneziana di Storia Naturale e Museo Civico di Storia Naturale di Venezia,.*
**Ind/Abst** Biocont. News Inf.; Life Sci. Collect.; Rev. Med. Vet. Entomol.

IT/0392-0062
**BOLLETTINO DEL MUSEO CIVICO DI STORIA NATURALE DI VERONA.** **See** Museums and Galleries.

GW/0174-3384
**BRAUNSCHWEIGER NATURKUNDLICHE SCHRIFTEN.** Vol. 1, No. 1 (Nov. 1980)-. Periodical. German (summaries and/or abstracts in English). an. DM20.00. Staatliches Museum Naturkunde, Rosenstein 1, D 70191 Stuttgart Germany. **Tel** (011)49 7 1189360. **LC** QH5; .B73. Index available. **Circ:** 800.
**Ind/Abst** CSA Neuro. Abstr. (?-?); Ecol. Abstr.; Ecology Abstr.; Geogr. Abstr. Phys. Geogr. (?-?).

CR/0304-3711
**BRENESIA.** [Brenesia]. **Added/Corp** San Jose, Costa Rica. Museo Nacional de Costa Rica. Division de Historia Natural. Museo Nacional de Costa Rica. Departamento de Historia Natural. No. 1 (Nov. 1972)-. Monographic series. Spanish (English). ir. Price varies per volume. Museo Nacional de Costa Rica, Biblioteca Apartado 749, San Jose 1000 Costa Rica. **Tel** 011 506 571433. **LC** QH7; .B76. **CODEN** BRNSBE. **Circ:** 1,000. available with illustrations. Documents available from BIOSIS Document Express. ***Supersedes*** *Boletin del Museo Nacional (San Jose, Costa Rica).*
**Ind/Abst** Biocont. News Inf.; Biol. Abstr.; Fish Rev. (Jan. 1989-July 1992); For. Abstr.; Helminthol. Abstr.; Nematol. Abstr.; Life Sci. Collect.; Rev. Agric. Entomol.; Rev. Med. Vet. Entomol.; Wildl. Rev. (Jan. 1989-July 1992).

UK/0952-7583
**BRITISH JOURNAL OF ENTOMOLOGY AND NATURAL HISTORY.** [Br. j. entomol. nat. hist.]. **Added/Corp** British Entomological and Natural History Society. Vol. 1, Pt. 1, (April 1988)-. Periodical. English. qt. £18.00. British Entomological and Natural History Society, 30 Meadowcroft Close Hawkins, Horley Surrey RH6 9EL England. ***Continues*** *Proceedings and Transactions of the British Entomological and Natural History Society, 0525-5252.*
**Ind/Abst** AGRICOLA [Select. Cov.]; Biocont. News Inf. (19??-19??); Curr. Aware. Biol. Sci., CABS; For. Abstr.; Rev. Agric. Entomol.; Rev. Med. Vet. Entomol.; Weed Abstr.

US/0196-1039
**BULLETIN (ALABAMA MUSEUM OF NATURAL HISTORY).** (BULLETIN - ALABAMA MUSEUM OF NATURAL HISTORY.). No. 1-. Bulletin. English. ir. Price varies per volume. University of Alabama Museum of Natural History, Box 870340, Tuscaloosa AL 35487. **Tel** (205)348-7550. **DD** 508. Index available. cum. index. **Bk Rev.** **Ad Acc.** ctrl circ.
**Desc:** Miscellaneous natural history topics.

FR/0164-3940
**BULLETIN DE LA SOCIETE DES SCIENCES HISTORIQUES ET NATURELLES DE L'YONNE.** **See** History(General)-History of Europe.

AE/0374-0994
**BULLETIN DE LA SOCIETE D'HISTOIRE NATURELLE DE L'AFRIQUE DU NORD.** [Bull. soc. hist. nat. Afr. Nord]. **Main/Corp** Societe d'Histoire Naturelle de l'Afrique du Nord, Algiers. Vol. 1 (Nov. 1909)-. Bulletin. English (French and Arabic). qt. Universite d'Algiers, Societe d'Histoire Naturelle de l'Afrique du Nord, 2 rue Didouche Mourad, Algiers Algeria. **LC** QH3; .S49. **CODEN** BHNAAP. cum. index. Documents available from BIOSIS Document Express.
**Ind/Abst** Biol. Abstr.; Field Crop Abstr.; GeoRef; Grasslands For. Abstr.; Soils Fert.

FR/0366-3477
**BULLETIN DE LA SOCIETE D'HISTOIRE NATURELLE DE TOULOUSE.** [Bull. Soc. hist. nat. Toulouse]. **Main/Corp** Societe d'Histoire Naturelle de Toulouse. Vol. 48 (1920)-. Academic Scholarly Publication. French. qt. Universite Paul Sabatier LSI, Lab LSI, 118 Route de Narbonne, 31062 Toulouse Cedex France. **CODEN** BSNTAN. cum. index. Documents available from BIOSIS Document Express, CASDDS. ***Continues*** *Bulletin Trimestriel / Societe d'Histoire Naturelle et des Sciences Biologiques et Energetiques.*
**Ind/Abst** Biol. Abstr.; Chem. Abstr. (1866-1981); GeoRef; Life Sci. Collect.

SZ/0037-9603
**BULLETIN DE LA SOCIETE VAUDOISE DES SCIENCES NATURELLES.** [Bull. Soc. vaudoise sci. nat.]. **Main/Corp** Societe Vaudoise des Sciences Naturelles, Lausanne. Vol. 1 No. 1 (1842/1845)-. Periodical. French. ir. SUSN, Palais de Rumine, 1005 Lausanne Switzerland. **LC** Q67; .L3. **DD** 574.062494. cum. index.
**Ind/Abst** Ecol. Abstr.

ML
**BULLETIN DE L'ASSOCIATION DES NATURALISTES DU MALI.** **Main/Corp** Association des Naturlistes du Mali. Bulletin. French. Association des Naturalistes du Mali, B P 1746, Bamako Mali. **LC** QH195.M475; A85A. **DD** 500.9/66/23.

●FR/1167-9786
**BULLETIN DES NATURALISTES DES YVELINES / PUBLICATION DE L'ASSOCIATION DES NATURALISTES DES YVELINES.** **Added/Corp** Association des Naturalistes des Yvelines. Series 5, Pt. 19, No. 1 (Mar. 1992)-. Periodical. French. Four times a year. 200.00F. Association Naturalists Yveslines, 4 rue Hardy RP 914, 78009 Versailles Cedex France. **(Subscription address:** Association Naturalist Yveslines, 34 Route de Versailles, 78150 Rocquencourt France.**)** ***Continues*** *Bulletin de la Societe Versaillaise de Sciences Naturelles.*

FR/0181-0642
**BULLETIN DU MUSEUM NATIONAL D'HISTOIRE NATURELLE. SECTION C : SCIENCES DE LA TERRE : PALEONTOLOGIE, GEOLOGIE, MINERALOGIE.** [Bull. Mus. natl. hist. nat., Sect. C, Sci. terre paleontol. geol. miner.]. **VFOAT** Sciences de la Terre: Paleontologie, Geologie, Mineralogie. 4. Ser. Vol. 1- March 1979-. Academic Scholarly Publication. French (English). qt. $33.26. Cryptogamie, 12 rue de Buffon, 75005 Paris France. **Tel** 33 1 40793184. **LC** QE1; .B83. **CODEN** BMNMDV. Index Available, published separately, free-automatically sent. Documents available from BIOSIS Document Express, CASDDS. ***Continues*** *Bulletin du Museum National d'Histoire Naturelle. Sciences de la Terre;* ***Absorbed in part*** *Bulletin du Museum National d'Histoire Naturelle. Sciences Physico-Chimiques.*
**Ind/Abst** Biol. Abstr.; Chem. Abstr.; Geogr. Abstr. Phys. Geogr.; GeoRef; Life Sci. Collect.

US/0073-4918
**BULLETIN (ILLINOIS. NATURAL HISTORY SURVEY DIVISION).** (BULLETIN - ILLINOIS NATURAL HISTORY SURVEY.). [Bull. Ill. Nat. Hist. Surv.]. **Added/Corp** Illinois. Natural History Survey Division. Vol. 13 (Sept. 1918)-. Monographic series. English. ir. Price varies per volume. Illinois Natural History Survey Division, Department of Registration and Education, 196 Natural Resources Building, Urbana IL 61801. **LC** QH1; .I25. **CODEN** INHBAF. Documents

available from BIOSIS Document Express, CASDDS. ***Continues*** *Bulletin of the Illinois State Laboratory of Natural History.*
**Ind/Abst** Biol. Abstr.; Chem. Abstr.; Life Sci. Collect.

CN/0823-2911
**BULLETIN / MANITOBA NATURALISTS SOCIETY.** **Added/Corp** Manitoba Naturalists Society. Vol. 1, No. 1 (Sept. 1977)-. Bulletin. English. Eleven times a year. 30.00Can$. Manitoba Naturalists Society, 302-128 James Avenue, Winnipeg Manitoba R3B 0N8 Canada. **Tel** (204)943-9029. **ED** Marty Helgerson and Pat Nichols. **DD** 574.9/06/07127. **Bk Rev. Ad Acc. Circ:** 2.
**Desc:** For members, items of Canada's and Manitoba's environmental concerns, natural history and book reviews, listings of society activities including trips, workshops, and meetings.

FR/0366-1326
**BULLETIN MENSUEL DE LA SOCIETE LINNEENNE DE LYON.** [Bull. mens. Soc. Linn. Lyon]. **Main/Corp** Societe Linneenne de Lyon. Vol. 1 (Jan. 1932)-. Bulletin. French. Ten times a year (monthly except July & Aug.). 150.00F France; 200.00F other. Societe Linneenne de Lyon, 33 rue Bossuet, 69006 Lyon France. **ED** Rolland Allemand. **CODEN** BMSLAG. **Bk Rev. Circ:** 1,500. Documents available from BIOSIS Document Express. ***Supersedes*** *Bulletin Bi-Mensuel de la Societe Linneenne de Lyon et des Societes Botanique de Lyon, d'Anthropologie et de Biologie de Lyon, Reunies.*
**Desc:** Contains articles on natural science, entomology, botany, and biology.
**Ind/Abst** Anthropol. Index; Biol. Abstr.; Life Sci. Collect.; Rev. Med. Vet. Mycology; Rev. Plant Pathol.

US/0145-9058
**BULLETIN OF CARNEGIE MUSEUM OF NATURAL HISTORY.** [Bull. Carnegie Mus. Nat. Hist.]. **Main/Corp** Carnegie Museum of Natural History. No. 1 (1976)-. Monographic series. English. ir. Price varies per volume. Carnegie Museum of Natural History, 4400 Forbes Avenue, Pittsburgh PA 15213. **Tel** (412)622-3315, FAX (412)622-8837. **ED** L. Conard Krishtalka, C. J. McCoy and M. A. Schmidt. **LC** UNC. **CODEN** BCMHD9. **Pr Rev. Circ:** 500 (ctrl). Documents available from BIOSIS Document Express.
**Desc:** Original scientific monographs in zoology, anthropology, botany, ecology, systematics, mineralogy, invertebrate and vertebrate paleontology and archaeology.
**Ind/Abst** Biol. Abstr.; Fish Rev.; GeoRef; Wildl. Rev.

US/0003-0090
**BULLETIN OF THE AMERICAN MUSEUM OF NATURAL HISTORY.** [Bull. Am. Mus. Nat. Hist.]. **Added/Corp** American Museum of Natural History. **VFOAT** Bulletin. Vol. 1 (1881)-. Monographic series. English. ir. Price varies per volume. American Museum of Natural History, Central Park West at 79th Street, New York NY 10024. **Tel** (212)769-5500, (800)234-5252, telex 910 240 8933 MICRO PRESS VQ. **ED** Brenda Jones. **LC** QH1; .A4. **DD** 500.9/05. **CODEN** BUMNAE. **Pr Rev. Circ:** 1,500. available on microfilm and microfiche from University Microfilms International (UMI). Documents available from The Genuine Article, BIOSIS Document Express.
**Desc:** Contains articles in the field of natural sciences relating to zoology, paleontology, geology and mineralogy.
**Ind/Abst** Biol. Abstr.; Curr. Aware. Biol. Sci., CABS; Curr. Contents, Agric. Biol. Environ. Sci.; Curr. Ref. Fish Res.; Fish Rev.; GeoRef; Life Sci. Collect.; Res. Alert [Full Cov.]; Rev. Agric. Entomol.; Rev. Med. Vet. Entomol.; Sci. Cit. Index; SCISEARCH; Zool. Rec.; Wildl. Rev.

US/0097-0298
**BULLETIN OF THE BIOLOGICAL SOCIETY OF WASHINGTON.** [Bull. Biol. Soc. Wash.]. **Added/Corp** Biological Society of Washington. No. 1 (1918)-. Monographic series. English. qt. Price varies per volume. Biological Society of Washington, Room E503B, Smithsonian Natural History, Washington DC 20560. **Tel** (202)357-4990. **ED** Brian Robbins. **LC** QH105.D6; M3. **DD** 574/.05. **CODEN** BBSWA6. **Circ:** 1,000 (ctrl).
**Desc:** Proceedings of the Biological Society of Washington.
**Ind/Abst** GeoRef.

UK
**BULLETIN OF THE BRITISH MUSEUM (NATURAL HISTORY). GEOLOGY SERIES.** ***Title Change.*** **Added/Corp** British Museum (Natural History). **VFOAT** Geology Series. Vol. 29, No. 1 (Nov. 1977)-(1992). Bulletin. English. ir. Intercept Ltd., PO Box 716, Andover Hampshire SP10 1YG England. **Tel** 011 44 264 334748, FAX 011 44 264 334058, telex 41103 PEPSOS G. **LC** QE1; .B65. **CODEN** BUBMAO. Documents available from Petroleum Abstracts Document Delivery Service. ***Continues*** *Bulletin of the British Museum (Natural History). Geology), 0007-1471.* ***Continued by*** *Bulletin of the Natural History Museum. Geology Series, 0968-0462.*
**Ind/Abst** GeoRef; Pet. Abstr.

UK/0068-2306
**BULLETIN OF THE BRITISH MUSEUM (NATURAL HISTORY). HISTORICAL SERIES.** ***Ceased.*** [Bull. Br. Mus., Nat. Hist., Hist. ser.]. Vol. 1, No. 1 (1953)-Ceased ?. Bulletin. English. ir. British Museum of Natural History, Cromwell Road, London SW7 5BD England. **Tel** 011 44 71 9389123. **DD** 574. **CODEN** BBMHAX. cum. index. Documents available from BIOSIS Document Express.
**Desc:** History of natural history.
**Ind/Abst** Biol. Abstr.; GeoRef.

US/0096-4131
**BULLETIN OF THE BUFFALO SOCIETY OF NATURAL SCIENCES.** [Bull. Buffalo Soc. Nat. Sci.]. **Main/Corp** Buffalo Society of Natural Sciences. Vol. 1; April 1873-. Bulletin. English. ir. Price varies per volume. Buffalo Society of Natural Sciences, Humboldt Parkway, Buffalo NY 14211-1293. **Tel** (716)896-5200. **LC** QH1; .B94. **CODEN** BBNSA3. Documents available from BIOSIS Document Express.
**Desc:** Treats anthropology, botany, geology/paleontology, vertebrate and invertebrate zoology.
**Ind/Abst** Biol. Abstr.; GeoRef; Vet. Bull.

US/1052-3669
**BULLETIN OF THE FLORIDA MUSEUM OF NATURAL HISTORY. BIOLOGICAL SCIENCES.** [Bull. Fla. Mus. Nat. Hist., Biol sci.]. **Added/Corp** Florida Museum of Natural History. **VFOAT** Biological Sciences; Bulletin. Biological Sciences. Vol. 35 No. 1 (1990)-. Monographic series. English (Spanish; summaries and/or abstracts in Spanish). ir. Price varies per volume. Florida Museum of Natural History, University of Gainesville, Gainesville FL 32611. **Tel** (904)392-1565. **LC** QH1; .F6. **DD** 574. **CODEN** BFMSEU. Documents available from BIOSIS Document Express. ***Continues*** *Bulletin of the Florida State Museum. Biological Sciences, 0071-6154.*
**Ind/Abst** Biol. Abstr. (1991-).

US/0093-6812
**BULLETIN OF THE UNIVERSITY OF NEBRASKA STATE MUSEUM.** [Bull. Univ. Nebr. State Mus.]. **Added/Corp** University of Nebraska State Museum. Vol. 2, No. 2 (Sept. 1939)-. Monographic series. English. ir. Price varies per volume. University of Nebraska / State Museum, W436 Nebraska Hall, Lincoln NE 68588. **Tel** (402)472-2642. **LC** Q11; .N35. **DD** 505. available on microfilm from University Microfilms International (UMI). ***Continues*** *Bulletin (Nebraska State Museum).*

US/0079-032X
**BULLETIN - PEABODY MUSEUM OF NATURAL HISTORY.** ***Suspended.*** [Bull. - Peabody Mus. Nat. Hist.]. **Main/Corp** Yale University. Peabody Museum of Natural History. **Added/Corp** Peabody Museum of Natural History. No. 1 (1926)-(19??). Monographic series. English (summaries and/or abstracts in German, Russian and Spanish). ir. Price varies per volume. Yale University / Peabody Museum, Peabody Museum of Natural History, PO Box 6666, New Haven CT 06511-8161. **Tel** (203)423-3786. **ED** John H Ostrom. **LC** QH1; .Y3. **DD** 500.9/05. **CODEN** YUPBA8. **Circ:** 500. Documents available from BIOSIS Document Express. ***Absorbed*** *Bulletin of the Bingham Oceanographic Collection, 0097-1375.*
**Desc:** Scientific monographs of research in biology, geology, paleontology, ornithology and anthropology.
**Ind/Abst** Biol. Abstr.; GeoRef; Life Sci. Collect.

US/0095-8638
**BULLETIN - STATE GEOLOGICAL AND NATURAL HISTORY SURVEY OF CONNECTICUT.** **Main/Corp** State Geological and Natural History Survey of Connecticut. **Added/Corp** State Geological and Natural History Survey of Connecticut. **VFOAT** Biennial Report of the Commissioners of the State Geological and Natural History Survey of Connecticut. No. 1 (1904)-. Bulletin. English. ir. Price varies per volume. Natural Resource Center, Publications and Sales, 165 Capitol Avenue, Room 555, Hartford CT 06106. **Tel** (203)566-7719. **LC** QH105.C8; A2. **DD** 508.746. **CODEN** CNGBAC.
**Desc:** The series includes a biennial report of the commissioners of the State Geologicals and History Survey of Connecticut.
**Ind/Abst** GeoRef.

UK/0265-6833
**BULLETIN / YORKSHIRE NATURALISTS' UNION.** **Added/Corp** Yorkshire Naturalists' Union. (198?)-. Bulletin. English. sa. Yorkshire Naturalists Union, D. Bramley, c/o Doncaster Museum, Doncaster DN1 2AE United Kingdom. **Tel** 011 44 302 535246. **ED** A Norris, A Henderson and D T Richardson. **Bk Rev. Ad Acc. Circ:** 500 (ctrl).
**Desc:** The natural history and naturalists (historical and modern) of the county of Yorkshire.
**Ind/Abst** Biodeter. Abstr. (1991-).

CK/0366-5232
**CALDASIA.** [Caldasia]. **Added/Corp** Universidad Nacional de Colombia. Instituto de Ciencias Naturales. Vol. 1 No. 1 (1940)-. Periodical. Spanish (French and Portuguese). Twice a year. $8.00 Colombia; $14.00 others. Inst de Ciencias Naturales, Apartado 7495, Museo Historia, Bogota Colombia. **Tel** 011 57 1 2684336. **LC** QH7; .C25. **CODEN** CALDAK. Documents available from BIOSIS Document Express, CASDDS.
**Ind/Abst** Biol. Abstr.; Chem. Abstr.; Ecol. Abstr.; GeoRef; Grasslands For. Abstr.; Hortic. Abstr.; Rev. Med. Vet. Entomol.; Rev. Plant Pathol.

CN/0008-3550
**CANADIAN FIELD-NATURALIST, THE.** **Added/Corp** Ottawa Field-Naturalists' Club. (1887)-. Periodical. English. Four times a year. 38.00Can$ (institutions), 23.00Can$ (individuals) Canada; 42.00Can$ (institutions), 27.00Can$ (individuals) other. Ottawa Field Naturalist Club Westgate, PO Box 35069, Ottawa Ontario K1Z 1A2 Canada. **Tel** (613)996-1665. **ED** F. R. Cook. **[CCC].** Index available. **Bk Rev. Pr Rev. Circ:** 2,200 (ctrl). Documents available from The Genuine Article, Documents on Demand. ***Continues*** *Ottawa Field-Naturalists' Club. Transactions.*
**Desc:** Natural history-scientific.
**Ind/Abst** AGRICOLA [Select. Cov.]; Anim. Behav. Abstr.; Aquat. Sci. Fish. Abstr. (Computer File); Biocont. News Inf. (1991-); Curr. Aware. Biol. Sci., CABS; Curr. Contents, Agric. Biol. Environ. Sci.; Curr. Ref. Fish Res.; Ecol. Abstr.; Ecology Abstr.; Entomol. Abstr.; Environ. Abstr.; Environ. Period. Bibliogr.; Fish Rev.; Geogr. Abstr. Phys. Geogr. (?-?); GeoRef; Helminthol. Abstr. (1991-); Res. Alert [Select. Cov.]; Rev. Med. Vet. Entomol.; SCISEARCH; Wildl. Rev.

US/0897-3423
**CANYON LEGACY.** **See** History(General).

US
**CAPE NATURALIST, THE.** **Added/Corp** Cape Cod Museum of Natural History. Vol. 1, No. 1 (June 1972)-. English. Four times a year. $4.00 Comes with Cape Cod Museum of Natural History membership. Cape Cod Museum of Natural History, Drawer R, Brewster MA 02631. **Tel** (508)896-3867.

GW/0176-3997
**CAROLINEA.** [Carolinea]. **Added/Corp** Landessammlungen fuer Naturkunde Karlsruhe. Vol. 40 (Oct. 19, 1982)-. German. an. Staatliches Museum Naturkunde, Erbprinzenstrasse 13, D 76133 Karlsruhe Germany. **Tel** 011 49 0721 175152. **CODEN** CAROEJ. ***Continues*** *Beitrage zur Naturkundlichen Forschung in Sudwestdeutschland, 0005-8122.*
**Ind/Abst** GeoRef; Nematol. Abstr.; Life Sci. Collect.

SZ
**CAT NEWS.** **See** Environmental Issues-Conservation and Natural Resources.

US/0885-7083
**CATALOGUE OF FORAMINIFERA. SUPPL.** (CATALOGUE OF FORAMINIFERA. SUPPLEMENT.). [Cat. foraminifer., Suppl.]. **Added/Corp** American Museum of Natural History. (1943)-. Periodical. English. an. $11005.00 corporate membership, $6805.00 associate membership, $4255.00 continuing membership. Micropaleontology Press, American Museum of Natural History, Central Park West at 79th Street, New York NY 10024. **Tel** (212)769-5658, FAX (212)769-5233. **ED** J. A. Van Couvering. **DD** 560. Index available. cum. index. **Circ:** 300 (ctrl).
**Desc:** Extracts and verifies type descriptions of all new species and genus names, mainly for use in oil exploration. In operation since 1800; includes 35,000 names increasing 700 per year in the foraminifera.

SP
**CAZA FOTOGRAFICA.** No. 1- Oct. 1973-. Periodical. Spanish (summaries and/or abstracts in English). bm. 1,500. Caza Fotografica, Incafo Castello 59, Madrid 1 Spain. **LC** QH7; .C36. **DD** 910/.5.

JA/0915-9452
**CHIBA KENRITSU CHUO HAKUBUTSUKAN SHIZENSHI KENKYU HOKOKU.** **Added/Corp** Chiba Kenritsu Chuo Hakubutsukan. **VFOAT** Shizenshi Kenkyu Hokoku; Journal of the Natural History Museum and Institute, Chiba. (1990)-. Japanese (English). **LC** QH7; .C5.
**Ind/Abst** Ecol. Abstr.

US/0073-4926
**CIRCULAR - ILLINOIS NATURAL HISTORY SURVEY.** [Circ. - Ill. Nat. Hist. Surv.]. **Main/Corp** Illinois. Natural History Survey Division. No. 46 (April 1961)-. Monographic series. English. ir. Price varies per volume. Illinois Natural History, Survey Division, 196 Natural Resources Building, Urbana IL 61801. **ED** Audrey Hodgins, Shirley McClellan and Eva Steger. **DD** 574. **CODEN** INHCAI. **Circ:** 2,000. Documents available from BIOSIS Document Express, CASDDS. ***Continues*** *Circular - Natural History Survey Division.*
**Desc:** Covers natural resources subjects: aquatic biology, botany and plant pathology, economic entomology, faunistics and insect identification, wildlife research.

**Ind/Abst** Biol. Abstr. (-1981); Chem. Abstr.; For. Abstr.; Rev. Med. Vet. Mycology; Rev. Plant Pathol.; Soyabean Abstr.

CN/0831-4985
**COLLECTION FORUM (OTTAWA).** (COLLECTION FORUMS.). [Collect. forum]. **Added/Corp** Society for Scientific Collections. Society for the Preservation of Natural History Collections. **VFOAT** Bulletin for the Society for Scientific Collections. Vol. 1, No. 1 (Oct. 1985)-. Periodical. English. sa. Free to members of the Society for the Preservation of Natural History Collections. Society for the Preservation of Natural History Collections, 121 Trowbridge Hall, University of Iowa, Iowa City IA 52242. **Tel** (319)335-1822. **ED** Daniel J. Faber. **DD** 508/.074/011. **Bk Rev. Ad Acc. Circ:** 300 (ctrl).
**Ind/Abst** Museum Abstr.

US/0160-0664
**COLLECTIONS (BUFFALO).** (COLLECTIONS.). [Collect.]. **Added/Corp** Buffalo Society of Natural Sciences. Vol. 56, No. 1/2 (Oct. 1976)-. Periodical. English. Six times a year. Buffalo Society of Natural Science, Humboldt Park, Buffalo NY 14211. **ED** Barbara Park Leggett. **LC** QH1; .C64. **DD** 500.9/05. **Circ:** 7,000. ***Continues*** *Science on the March, 0036-8474.*
**Desc:** Newsletter of the Buffalo Society of Natural Sciences, administrator of the Buffalo Museum of Science and Tifft Farm Nature Preserve.
**Ind/Abst** GeoRef.

SW/0284-8422
**COMPOSITAE NEWSLETTER.** No. 1 (1975)-. Newsletter. English. sa. Free. Compositae Newsletter, Swedish Museum of Natural History, Department of Phanerogamic Botany, PO Box Box 5007, S-104 05 Stockholm Sweden.

UY/0077-1244
**COMUNICACIONES ANTROPOLOGICAS DEL MUSEO DE HISTORIA NATURAL DE MONTEVIDEO.** **See** Museums and Galleries.

SP/0210-3338
**COMUNICACIONES I.N.I.A. SERIE RECURSOS NATURALES.** **See** Agriculture.

US
**CONNECTICUT WARBLER, THE.**
**Added/Corp** Connecticut Audubon Society. Connecticut Ornithological Association. (1981)-. Periodical. English. qt. comes with Connecticut Warbler Orinthological Society Membership. Connecticut Warbler Ornthological Society, 314 Unquowa Road, Fairfield CT 06430. **Tel** (203)838-1649.

US/0459-8113
**CONTRIBUTIONS IN SCIENCE (LOS ANGELES, CALIF.).** (CONTRIBUTIONS IN SCIENCE / LOS ANGELES COUNTY MUSEUM.). [Contrib. sci.]. **Added/Corp** Los Angeles County Museum. Los Angeles County Museum of Natural History. Natural History Museum of Los Angeles County. No. 1 (Jan. 23, 1957)-. Monographic series. English (Spanish). ir. Price varies per volume. Natural History Museum / California, 900 Exposition Boulevard, Publishing Office, Los Angeles CA 90007. **Tel** (214)744-3330. **ED** John M Harris. **LC** Q11; .L52. **DD** 508. **CODEN** LAMSAX. **Circ:** 1,000 (ctrl). available on microfiche. Documents available from BIOSIS Document Express. ***Absorbed*** *Science Bulletin, 0076-0935.*
**Desc:** Original research in taxonomy and systematics.
**Ind/Abst** Biol. Abstr.; Fish Rev.; GeoRef; Wildl. Rev.

UK/0011-023X
**COUNTRY-SIDE.** **See** Environmental Issues-Ecology.

US/0011-3069
**CURATOR (NEW YORK, N.Y.).** **See** Museums and Galleries.

CN/0011-3093
**CURLEW, THE.** ***Ceased.*** **Added/Corp** Willow Beach Field Naturalists. (1???)-?. Periodical. English. mo. Willow Field Naturalist Club, 578 Lakeshore Road, Cobourg Ontario Canada.

GW/0366-872X
**DECHENIANA.** [Decheniana]. Academic Scholarly Publication. German. an. **CODEN** DCNNAH. Documents available from BIOSIS Document Express, CASDDS. ***Continues*** *Verhandlungen des Naturhistorischen Vereins der Preussischen Rheinlande und Westfalens.*
**Ind/Abst** AGRICOLA; Biocont. News Inf.; Biol. Abstr.; Chem. Abstr.; GeoRef; Life Sci. Collect.; Vitis Vitic. Enol. Abstr.

US/0012-3625
**DISCOVERY (NEW HAVEN, CONN.).** **See** Museums and Galleries.

SA/0012-723X
**DURBAN MUSEUM NOVITATES.** [Durban Mus. novit.]. **Main/Corp** Durban Museum. Vol. 1 (June 1914)-. English. ir. Durban Natural Science Museum, PO Box 4085, Durban 4000 South Africa. **Tel** 031 3006211. **LC** QH1. Index available. **Circ:** 400 (ctrl).
**Desc:** Contains scientific information.

KE/0374-7387
**EANHS BULLETIN.** [Bull. - EANHS]. **Main/Corp** East Africa Natural History Society. **Added/Corp** East Africa Natural History Society. **VFOAT** E.A.N.H.S. Bulletin. **VAT** East Africa Natural History Society Bulletin. (Jan. 1971)-. Periodical. English. qt (4 issues). Comes with East Africa Natural History Society membership. East Africa Natural History Society, PO Box 44486, Nairobi Kenya. **Tel** 011 254 2 742161 ext. 278. **ED** D. E. G. Backhurst. **LC** QH195.A23; E37a. **DD** 574.967/05. Index available. **Bk Rev. Pr Rev. Circ:** 1,000 (ctrl). ***Continues*** *East Africa Natural History Society. EANHS Newsletter.*
**Desc:** Exists for rapid publication of short notes, articles, letters and reviews on all natural history subjects.
**Ind/Abst** AGRICOLA.

CN/1184-1877
**ECOZOO.** **See** Zoology.

AU/0013-2373
**EGRETTA : VOGELKUNDLICHE NACHRICHTEN AUS OSTERREICH.**
**Added/Corp** Osterreichische Gesellschaft fur Vogelkunde. Osterreichische Vogelwarte, Verband fur Vogelkunde und Vogelschutz. Vol. 1 (1958)-. Academic Scholarly Publication. German. sa. S300.00. Birdlife Osterreich--Gesellschaft fuer Vogelkunde, c/o Naturhistorisches Museum, Burgring 7, Postfach 417, A-1014 Vienna Austria. **Tel** 011 43 1 93 46 51, FAX 011 43 1 93 52 54. **ED** Gerhard Loupal. Index available. **Bk Rev**, (Qty: 8-10). **Acid Free. Circ:** 1,700. ***Continues*** *Vogelkundliche Nachrichten aus Osterreich, 0504-5827.*
**Desc:** Information on birds and ornithology, mainly in Austria.

JA
**EHIME KENRITSU HAKUBUTSUKAN KENKYU HOKOKU.** **Main/Corp** Ehime Kenritsu Hakubutsukan. **VFOAT** Bulletin of the Ehime Pref. Museum. No. 9 (1978)-. Japanese. Ehime Kenritsu Hakubitsukan, Horinouchi, Matsuyama 790 Japan. **LC** QH188; .E38A.

RU/0367-0597
**EKOLOGIJA.** **See** Environmental Issues-Ecology.

US/0737-108X
**ELEPHANT (DETROIT, MICH.).** **See** Zoology.

US/1046-8641
**ENVIRONMENT WEST.** ***Ceased.*** [Environ. West]. **Added/Corp** San Diego Society of Natural History. San Diego Natural History Museum. (Fall 1989)-Ceased July (1991). Periodical. English. qt. San Diego Natural History Museum, PO Box 1390, San Diego CA 92112. **Tel** (619)232-3821. **DD** 500. ***Continues*** *Environment Southwest, 0090-5097.*
**Ind/Abst** AGRICOLA; Ecol. Abstr.; GeoRef.

CN/1195-5015
**EUSKARIEN (QUEBEC).** **See** Environmental Issues-Conservation and Natural Resources.

US/0014-5009
**EXPLORER, THE.** [Explorer]. **Added/Corp** Cleveland Museum of Natural History. Natural Science Museum (Cleveland Museum of Natural History). No. 55 (Nov./Dec. 1938)-No. 100 (Summer 1949); Vol. 2, No. 1-. Periodical. English. qt. Free to members of museum, $7.50 nonmembers. Cleveland Museum of Natural History, Wade Oval University Circle, Cleveland OH 44106. **Tel** (216)231-4600, FAX (216)231-5919. **ED** Cindy Grahl. **LC** QH1; .E95. **CODEN** EXPOAI. Index available. **Bk Rev. Circ:** 11,000. available on audiocassette. Documents available from BIOSIS Document Express. ***Continues*** *Bulletin of the Cleveland Museum of Natural History.*
**Desc:** Natural history articles written in basic English. Black and white and color photographs are also included. Children's section, museum news and astronomy.
**Ind/Abst** Biol. Abstr.; Biol. Dig.; GeoRef.

US
**FIELD MUSEUM OF NATURAL HISTORY ... BIENNIAL REPORT.** **Main/Corp** Field Museum of Natural History. **VFOAT** Biennial Report. (1989/1990)-. English. be. Field Museum of Natural History, Roosevelt Road at Lake Shore Drive, Chicago IL 60605-2496. **Tel** (312)922-9410 ext. 402, FAX (312)922-0671. **LC** QH70.U52; C4. ***Continues in part*** *Field Museum of Natural History Bulletin.* ***Continued in part by*** *In the Field (Chicago, Ill.).*

UK/0428-304X
**FIELD STUDIES.** [Field stud.]. **Added/Corp** Field Studies Council (Great Britain). (1959)-. English. an. £15.00. The Richmond Publishing Company Ltd, PO Box 963, Slough SL2 3RS England. **Tel** 011 44 281 43104. **ED** Jenifer M. Baker, R. H. L. Disney, P. A. Moxey, R. J. Berry, F. S. Dobson, K. M. Clayton, A. D. Thomas, R. A. D. Cameron, D. A. Job, P. J. Wanstall, J. H. Crothers and S. M. Tilling. **LC** QH137; .F5. **CODEN** FSTUBX. Index available. **Bk Rev. Circ:** 4,000. Documents available from BIOSIS Document Express.
**Ind/Abst** Biol. Abstr.; Br. Archaeol. Bibliogr.; Ecol. Abstr.; Geogr. Abstr. Phys. Geogr. (?-?); Geol. Abstr.; GeoRef; Irr. Drain. Abstr.; Life Sci. Collect.; Rev. Med. Vet. Entomol.; Soils Fert.

HU/0231-035X
**FOLIA MUSEI HISTORICO-NATURALIS BAKONYIENSIS.** (A BAKONYI TERMESZETTUDOMANYI MUZEUM KOZLEMENYEI.). [Folia Mus. Hist.-Nat. Bakony.]. **Added/Corp** Bakonyi Termeszettudomanyi Muzeum. **VFOAT** Folia Musei Historico-Naturalis Bakonyiensis. (1982)-. Periodical. German (Hungarian; summaries and/or abstracts in English). an. **LC** QH178.H8; B34. **DD** 508.439. ***Continues*** *Veszprem Megyei Muzeumok Kozlemenyei, 0230-7235.*
**Ind/Abst** BHA : Biblio. Hist. Art.

NZ
**FOREST AND BIRD.** [For. bird]. **Added/Corp** Royal Forest and Bird Protection Society of New Zealand. Forest and Bird Protection Society of New Zealand. No. 31 (1933)-. Periodical. English. qt. Comes with Royal Forest and Bird Society membership. Royal Forest & Bird Protection Society, PO Box 631, Wellington New Zealand. **Tel** 64 4 857374. **ED** Ian Close. Index available. **Bk Rev. Ad Acc. Circ:** 27,000 (ctrl). ***Continues*** *Birds.*
**Desc:** An independently published magazine combining colour illustrated articles on natural history and the politics of conservation.
**Ind/Abst** Fish Rev.; Wildl. Rev.

AU
**FORSCHUNGSBERICHT / ARBEITSGEMEINSCHAFT GESAMTKONZEPT NEUSIEDLER SEE.**
**Added/Corp** Arbeitsgemeinschaft Gesamtkonzept Neusiedler See. (19??)-. German.

US/0016-2159
**FRONTIERS (PHILADELPHIA).** (FRONTIERS.). [Front.]. V. 1- 1979-. Periodical. English. an. The Academy of Natural Sciences, Nineteenth and the Parkway, Philadelphia PA 19103. **LC** QH1; .F758. **DD** 574/.05. **CODEN** FRNTAQ. ***Supersedes*** *Frontiers, 0016-2159.*
**Ind/Abst** GeoRef.

SP/0212-923X
**GARCILLA.** (LA GARCILLA : BOLETIN-CIRCULAR DE LA SOCIEDAD ESPANOLA DE ORNITOLOGIA.). [Garcilla]. (1984)-. Spanish. an. Boletin-Circular de la SEO, Facultad de Biologia, Tercer Pabellon, Planta IX, Cuidad Universitaria, 28040 Madrid Spain. ***Continues*** *Boletin-Circular, 0210-2617.*

GW/0342-8311
**GEO.** [Geo]. **VFOAT** Geo Magazin; Geo-Magazin. (1978)-. Periodical. German. mo. DM156.00. Gruner und Jahr Ag & Co, Abonnenten Service, D 20080 Hamburg Germany. **Tel** 011 49 40 37030. **(Subscription address:** Deutscher Pressevertrieb Buch, POB 101602 Hansa GMBH, D 20010 Hamburg Germany.**) ED** Gruner Hamburg and Jahr Hamburg. **Ad Acc.**
**Ind/Abst** GeoRef.

UK/0373-241X
**GLASGOW NATURALIST.** (THE GLASGOW NATURALIST.). [Glasg. nat.]. **Added/Corp** Andersonian Naturalists of Glasgow. Natural History Society of Glasgow. Glasgow and Andersonian Natural History and Microscopial Society. Vol. 1 (Nov. 1908/Feb. 1909)-. English. an (5 parts per volume). £7.00. Glasgow Natural History Society, 7 Netherburn Avenue, Glasgow G44 3UF, Scotland. **Tel** 11 44 41 6373476. **ED** Dr. Ronald M. Dobson (editor's address: Glasgow University Glasgow G12 8QQ Scotland; telephone: 11 44 41 3398855 ext. 4432). **CODEN** GGNTAS. Index available (Included in last part of volume). **Bk Rev. Ad Acc. Circ:** 300 (ctrl). Documents available from BIOSIS Document Express. ***Supersedes*** *Transactions of the Natural History Society of Glasgow.*
**Desc:** Covers all aspects of natural history in Scotland.
**Ind/Abst** AGRICOLA; Biol. Abstr.; GeoRef.

IT/0391-5859
**GORTANIA.** [Gortania]. **VFOAT** Atti del Museo Friulano di Storia Naturale. (1979)-. Periodical. Italian. an. **UDC** 93/99.
**Ind/Abst** Geogr. Abstr. Phys. Geogr.

US/0017-3614
**GREAT BASIN NATURALIST, THE.** [Great Basin nat.]. **Added/Corp** Brigham Young University. Dept. of Zoology and Entomology. Vol. 1 (July 25, 1939)-. Academic Scholarly Publication. English. qt. $50.00 (institutions), $25.00 (individual). Great Basin Naturalist, 290 MLBM, Brigham Young University, Provo UT 84602. **Tel** (801)378-5053. **ED** Richard R. Bauman. **LC** QH1; .G7. **DD** 574.978. **CODEN** GRBNAR. Index available. cum. index. **Bk Rev. Pr Rev. Circ:** 500 (ctrl). Documents available from CASDDS.
**Desc:** Biological natural history of Western North America.
**Ind/Abst** AGRICOLA [Select. Cov.]; Biocont. News Inf.; Biol. Abstr.; Chem. Abstr. (1939-1986); Coal Abstr.; Curr. Aware. Biol. Sci., CABS; Curr. Contents, Agric. Biol. Environ. Sci.; Curr. Ref. Fish Res.; Ecol. Abstr.; EMBASE; Energy Res. Abstr.; Entomol. Abstr.; Field Crop Abstr.; Fish Rev.; For. Prod. Abstr. (1991-); For. Abstr.; Geogr.

Abstr. Phys. Geogr. (?-?); Geol. Abstr.; GeoRef; Grasslands For. Abstr.; Irr. Drain. Abstr.; Key Word Index Wildl. Res.; Nematol. Abstr.; Life Sci. Collect.; Protozoolog. Abstr.; Res. Alert [Select. Cov.]; Rev. Agric. Entomol.; SCISEARCH; Soils Fert.; Weed Abstr.; Wildl. Rev.

US/0160-239X
**GREAT BASIN NATURALIST MEMOIRS.** [Gt. Basin nat. mem.]. **Added/Corp** Brigham Young University. No. 1 (1976)-. Academic Scholarly Publication. English. ir. Price varies per volume. Great Basin Naturalist, 290 MLBM, Brigham Young University, Provo UT 84602. **Tel** (801)378-5053. **ED** James R. Barnes. **LC** UNC. **CODEN** GBNMD9. **Circ:** 500 (ctrl). Documents available from BIOSIS Document Express, CASDDS.
**Desc:** Biological natural history of Western North America.
**Ind/Abst** Biol. Abstr.; Chem. Abstr. (1976-1986); Rev. Med. Vet. Entomol.

US/1052-5165
**GREAT PLAINS RESEARCH.** [Gt. Plains res.]. **Added/Corp** University of Nebraska--Lincoln. Center for Great Plains Studies. Vol. 1, No. 1 (Feb. 1991)-. Periodical. English. Twice a year (Feb., Aug.). $50.00 (institutions), $25.00 (individuals). Center for Great Plains Studies, 1215 Oldfather Hall, University of Nebraska, Lincoln NE 68588-0317. **Tel** (402)742-3082, FAX (402)472-1123. **ED** Clare V. McKanna Jr. **LC** QH104.5.G73; G755. **DD** 508.78/05. **CODEN** GPLREB. **Bk Rev**, (Qty: 20-25). **Ad Acc.**
**Ind/Abst** Am. Hist. Life (1991); Meteorol. Geoastrophys. Abstr.

GW/0072-7741
**GROSSE NATURFORSCHER.** Vol. 1 (1947)-. Monographic series. German. ir. Price varies per volume. Wissenschaftliche Verlagsgesellschaft mbH, Postfach 101061, D 70009 Stuttgart Germany. **Tel** 011 49 711 258200, FAX 011 49 711 2582290, telex 723636 DAZ D.

US/0739-2052
**HABITAT (FALMOUTH, ME.).** **See** Environmental Issues-Conservation and Natural Resources.

CN/0715-3627
**HALIFAX FIELD NATURALISTS NEWSLETTER.** [Halifax Field Nat. newsl.]. No. 1 (Nov. 1975)-. Newsletter. English. bm. Free to members. Nova Scotia Museum, 1747 Summer Street, Halifax Nova Scotia B3H 3A6 Canada. **Tel** (902)429-4610, FAX (902)424-0560. **ED** D Butters. **DD** 574.9/06/071622. **Circ:** 300.

US/0737-5867
**HIGH TIDINGS.** **See** Museums and Galleries.

CN/0703-7481
**HINTERLAND WHO'S WHO.** **Added/Corp** Canadian Wildlife Service. (1965)-. English (French). ir. 25.00Can$ Canada; 30.00Can$ other. Canadian Wildlife Service Publications, Environment Canada, Ottawa Ontario K1A 0E7 Canada. **Tel** (819)997-1095, FAX (819)997-0547.
**Desc:** Describes the life histories of birds and mammals and are directed to students and adults with an interest in wildlife.

FR/0396-9681
**HISTOIRE ET NATURE.** [Hist. nat.]. **Added/Corp** Association pour l'Histoire des Sciences de la Nature. Laboratoire d'Ethnobotanique (Museum National d'Histoire Naturelle). **VFOAT** Cahiers de l'Association pour l'Historie des Sciences de la Nature. No. 3 (Sept. 1973)-. Periodical. French (summaries and/or abstracts in English). ir. 300.00F France; 350.00F others. Museum National d'Histoire Naturelle, 57 rue Cuvier, 75005 Paris France. **Tel** 011 33 1 40793700. **(Subscription address:** Bibliotheque du Museum, 38 rue Geoffroy St. Hilaire, 75005 Paris France.**)** **NLM** W1 HI76N. ***Continues*** *Histoire et Biologie, 0441-6732.*
**Ind/Abst** GeoRef.

GT/0018-2346
**HISTORIA NATURAL Y PRO NATURA.** Began in Sept. 1964. Spanish. qt. Historia Natural y Pro Natura, Apartado Postal 987, Guatemala Guatemala.

US/1061-9801
**ILLINOIS AUDUBON.** [Ill. Audubon]. **Added/Corp** Illinois Audubon Society. No. 211, (Winter 1985)-. Periodical. English. qt. $20.00. Illinois Audubon Society, PO Box 608, Wayne IL 60184. **Tel** (312)584-6290. **DD** 598. **Bk Rev. Ad Acc.** ctrl circ. ***Continues in part*** *Illinois Audubon Bulletin.*
**Ind/Abst** Fish Rev. (Jan. 1989-July 1992); Wildl. Rev. (Jan. 1989-July 1992).

US/0536-4132
**ILLINOIS NATURAL HISTORY SURVEY REPORTS, THE.** Periodical. English. mo. Illinois Natural History Survey Division, Department of Registration and Education, 196 Natural Resources Building, Urbana IL 61801.

US/0888-9546
**ILLINOIS NATURAL HISTORY SURVEY SPECIAL PUBLICATION.** [Ill. Nat. Hist. Surv. spec. publ.]. **VFOAT** Special Publication. (1976)-. Monographic series. English. ir. Price varies per volume. Illinois Natural History Survey Division, Department of Registration and Education, 196 Natural Resources Building, Urbana IL 61801. **LC** QH105.I3; I36. **DD** 508.773.

US/1051-4546
**IN THE FIELD (CHICAGO, ILL.).** **See** Museums and Galleries.

RE
**INFO-NATURE : ILE DE LA REUNION.** No. 1/4-12. French. 14.00F. Museum d'Histoire Naturelle, B P 1012, Saint-Denis Reunion. **LC** QH196.R4; I54. **DD** 333.9/5/096981.

UK/0535-0859
**INTERNATIONAL INSTITUTE FOR CONSERVATION OF HISTORIC AND ARTISTIC WORKS.** **Main/Corp** International Institute for Conservation of Historic and Artistic Works. (1954). English. an. $80.00 supporting institutions membership; $60.00 fellow memberships; $40.00 associates-all other individuals. International Institution Conservation, History Art Work, 6 Buckingham Street, London WC2N 6BA England. **Tel** (011)44 71 8395975.

SA/0528-0397
**INVESTIGATIONAL REPORT - DEPARTMENT OF NATURE CONSERVATION.** ***Title Change.*** [Invest. rep., Dep. Nat. Conserv.]. **Main/Corp** Cape of Good Hope (South Africa). Dept. of Nature Conservation. No. 1 (1962)-(19??). English. **LC** QH77.S62; C36a. **DD** 333.7/2/09687. **CODEN** CGIRAL. Documents available from BIOSIS Document Express. ***Continued by*** *Bontebok.*
**Ind/Abst** Aquat. Sci. Fish. Abstr. (Computer File); Biol. Abstr.

UK/0021-1311
**IRISH NATURALISTS' JOURNAL, THE.** [Ir. nat. j.]. **Added/Corp** Armagh Field Naturalists' Club. Belfast Naturalists' Field Club. Vol. 1 (Sept. 1925)-. Academic Scholarly Publication. English. qt. $25.00. Irish Naturalists Journal Ltd., Ulster Museum Botanical Gardens, Belfast BT9 5AB Northern Ireland. **Tel** 011 44 232 381251 ext. 258, FAX 011 44 232 665510. **ED** R.N. Govier. **CODEN** INAJA4. Index available. **Bk Rev. Ad Acc, Adv Mgr:** Catherine Tyrie. **Pr Rev. Circ:** 500. Documents available from BIOSIS Document Express, CASDDS.
**Desc:** Articles on all aspects of Irish natural history.
**Ind/Abst** Biocont. News Inf.; Biol. Abstr.; Chem. Abstr.; Ecol. Abstr.; Ecology Abstr.; Field Crop Abstr.; For. Abstr.; Geogr. Abstr. Phys. Geogr.; Geol. Abstr.; GeoRef; Grasslands For. Abstr.; Helminthol. Abstr. (1991-); Hortic. Abstr.; Index Vet.; Ornamental Hort. (1991-); Life Sci. Collect.; Postharvest News Inf.; Poult. Abstr.; Ref. Sources; Rev. Agric. Entomol.; Rev. Med. Vet. Entomol.; Vet. Bull.; Weed Abstr.

NE/0302-5276
**JAARVERSLAG / RIJKSINSTITUUT VOOR NATUURBEHEER.** [Jaarversl. - Rijksinst. Natuurbeheer]. **Main/Corp** Rijksinstituut voor Natuurbeheer. **VFOAT** Annual Report. (1970/71)-. Dutch (summaries and/or abstracts in English). an. Rijksinstituut voor Natuurbeheer, Postbus 9201, 6800 HB Arnhem Netherlands. **LC** QH77.N4; R54a. ***Separated from*** *Rijksinstituut voor Veldbiologisch Onderzoek. Jaarverslag; Instituut voor Toegepast Biologisch Onderzoek in de Natuur. Jaarverslag.*

●US/1061-1878
**JEFFERSONIANA (MARTINSVILLE, VA.).** (JEFFERSONIANA: CONTRIBUTIONS FROM THE VIRGINIA MUSEUM OF NATURAL HISTORY.). [Jeffersoniana]. **Added/Corp** Virginia Museum of Natural History. No. 1 (Mar. 6, 1992)-. Monographic series. English. Price varies per volume. Virginia Museum of Natural History, 1001 Douglas Avenue, Martinsvulle VA 24112. **DD** 508.

UK/0022-2933
**JOURNAL OF NATURAL HISTORY.** [J. nat. hist.]. Vol. 1 (Jan./March 1967)-. Periodical. English (French and German). bm. £482.00 UK; $795.00 other. Taylor & Francis Ltd., Rankine Road, Basingstoke Hampshire, RG24 8PR United Kingdom. **Tel** 011 44 256 840366, FAX 011 44 256 479438, telex 858540. **(Subscription address:** Taylor & Francis Inc., 1900 Frost Road, Suite 101, Bristol PA 19007-1598.**)** **ED** T. Huddleston (editor's address: The Natural History Museum, Cromwell Road, London SW7 5BD United Kingdom); P. G. Moore (editor's address: University of Marine Biological Station, Millport, Isle of Cumbrae, KA28 0EG United Kingdom). **LC** QH1; .A614. **DD** 574/.05. **CODEN** JNAHA9. **[CCC]**. Index available. **Pr Rev. Circ** 600. available on microfilm and microfiche from University Microfilms International (UMI). Documents available from The Genuine Article, BIOSIS Document Express, Documents on Demand. ***Supersedes*** *Annals and Magazine of Natural History.*
**Desc:** An international journal publishing original research and reviews in systematics and evolutionary and interactive biology. The traditional features of the journal, taxonomic works in entomology and zoology, have been maintained, providing a scientific basis for the application of systematics in biological control, agriculture, aquaculture, and medical and veterinary zoology. Publishes papers on cladistics, experimental taxonomy, parasitology, ecology, behavior and the interaction of organisms with their environment.
**Ind/Abst** AGRICOLA; Anim. Behav. Abstr.; Biocont. News Inf.; Biol. Abstr.; Curr. Aware. Biol. Sci., CABS; Curr. Ref. Fish Res.; Ecol. Abstr.; Ecology Abstr.; Energy Inf. Abstr.; Energy Res. Abstr.; Entomol. Abstr.; Environ. Abstr.; Environ. Period. Bibliogr.; Field Crop Abstr.; Fish Rev.; Geogr. Abstr. Phys. Geogr.; Geol. Abstr.; GeoRef; Grasslands For. Abstr.; Helminthol. Abstr. (19??-19??); Nematol. Abstr.; Life Sci. Collect.; Protozoolog. Abstr.; Ref. Sources; Res. Alert [Full Cov.]; Rev. Agric. Entomol.; Rev. Med. Vet. Entomol.; Sci. Cit. Index; SCISEARCH; Sel. Water Resour. Abstr.; Soils Fert.

JA
**JOURNAL OF RAKUNO GAKUEN UNIVERSITY. NATURAL SCIENCE.** **Added/Corp** Rakuno Gakuen Daigaku. **VFOAT** Natural Science; Shizen Kagaku-Hen; hizen Kagaku Hen; Rakuno Gakuen Daigaku Kiyo. Shizen Kagaku-Hen. Vol. 13, No. 1 (Oct. 1988)-. Periodical. English (Japanese). **CODEN** JRGSE2. Documents available from CASDDS. ***Continues*** *Journal of the College of Dairying. Natural Science, 0388-001X.*
**Ind/Abst** Chem. Abstr.; Index Vet.; Maize Abstr.; Soils Fert.

CH/0256-257X
**JOURNAL OF TAIWAN MUSEUM.** **Added/Corp** Tai-Wan Sheng li Po Wu Kuan. **VFOAT** Tai-Wan Sheng Li Po Wu Kuan Pan Nien Kan. Vol. 36, No. 1 (June 1983)-. Periodical. English (summaries and/or abstracts in Chinese). qt. Free on request. Taiwan Museum, 2 Siangyang Road, Taipei 10014 Taiwan. **LC** QH1; .T15. **DD** 574.951/249. ***Continues*** *Quarterly Journal of the Taiwan Museum, 0254-6914.*
**Ind/Abst** Life Sci. Collect.; Rev. Med. Vet. Entomol.

II/0006-6982
**JOURNAL OF THE BOMBAY NATURAL HISTORY SOCIETY.** [J. Bombay Nat. Hist. Soc.]. **Main/Corp** Bombay Natural History Society. **Added/Corp** Bombay Natural History Society. Vol. 1 (Jan. 1886)-. Periodical. English. Three times a year. $50.00. Bombay Natural History Society India, Hornbill House Shahid Bhagat, 400 023 Bombay India. **Tel** 244085/243869. **(Subscription address:** Prints India, 11 Darya Ganj, New Delhi 110002 India.**)** **LC** QH1; .B61. **DD** 574/.06254. **CODEN** JBOMAA. Index available. cum. index. **Bk Rev. Circ:** 3,000 (ctrl). Documents available from BIOSIS Document Express.
**Ind/Abst** AGRICOLA; Anim. Behav. Abstr.; Biocont. News Inf.; Biol. Abstr.; Ecology Abstr.; EMBASE; Energy Res. Abstr. (Dec. 1981-); Field Crop Abstr.; Fish Rev.; For. Prod. Abstr.; For. Abstr.; GeoRef; Grasslands For. Abstr.; Helminthol. Abstr. (1991-); Hortic. Abstr.; Key Word Index Wildl. Res.; Ornamental Hort.; Life Sci. Collect.; Protozoolog. Abstr.; Rev. Agric. Entomol.; Rev. Med. Vet. Entomol.; Wildl. Rev.

KE/0012-8317
**JOURNAL OF THE EAST AFRICA NATURAL HISTORY SOCIETY AND NATIONAL MUSEUM.** [J. East Afr. Nat. Hist. Soc. Natl. Mus.]. **Added/Corp** East Africa Natural History Society. National Museum (Kenya). Vol. 25, No. 1 (Jan. 1965)-. Periodical. English. ir. East African Natural History Society, PO Box 44486, Nairobi Kenya. **Tel** 011 254 2 742161 Ext. 278. **LC** QH1; .E11. **DD** 574.9676. ***Continues*** *Journal of the East Africa Natural History Society and Coryndon Museum.*
**Ind/Abst** Fish Rev. (Jan. 1989-July 1992); Life Sci. Collect.; Wildl. Rev. (Jan. 1989-July 1992).

AT/0035-922X
**JOURNAL OF THE ROYAL SOCIETY OF WESTERN AUSTRALIA.** [J. R. Soc. West. Aust.]. **Added/Corp** Royal Society of Western Australia. Vol. 11 (1924/1925)-. Academic Scholarly Publication. English. Four times a year. 60.00Aus$. Royal Society of Western Australia, Western Australian Museum, Francis Street, Perth West Australia 6000 Australia. **Tel** 11 61 9 3284411. **ED** Philip Withers. **LC** Q93; .W5. **CODEN** JRSUAU. **Pr Rev. Circ:** 660 (ctrl). Documents available from BIOSIS Document Express, CASDDS. ***Continues*** *Journal and Proceedings of the Royal Society of Western Australia.*
**Desc:** Papers on West Australian natural history or other sciences, including agriculture and forestry.
**Ind/Abst** AESIS Q.; AGRICOLA [Select. Cov.]; Biol. Abstr.; Chem. Abstr. (1925-1983); Ecol. Abstr.; Fish Rev.; Geogr. Abstr. Phys. Geogr. (?-?); Geol. Abstr.; GeoRef; Life Sci. Collect.; Wildl. Rev.

JA/0453-1906
**KANAGAWA KENRITSU HAKUBUTSUKAN KENKYU HOKOKU. SHIZEN KAGAKU.** **Added/Corp** Kanagawa Kenritsu Hakubutsukan. **VFOAT** Shizen Kagaku; Natural Science; Bulletin of the Kanagawa Prefectural Museum.

Natural Science for 1968-1972; Bulletin of the Kanagawa Pref. Museum. Natural Science. (1968)-. Japanese (English). Kanagawa Kenritsu Hakubutsukan, (Kanagawa Prefectural Museum), 5-60, Minami Nakadoori, Nakaku, Yokohamashi, Kanagawaken 231, Japan. **LC** QH188; .K3137. Documents available from BIOSIS Document Express.
**Ind/Abst** Biol. Abstr. (1991-); Ecol. Abstr.; Geogr. Abstr. Phys. Geogr.; GeoRef.

CC
**KAO CHA YU YEN CHIU / SHANG-HAI TZU JAN PO WU KUAN. Added/Corp** Shang-Hai Tzu Jan Po Wu Kuan. **VFOAT** Investigatio et Studium Naturae. Vol. 1 (1983)-. Periodical. Chinese (summaries and/or abstracts in English). ir. RMBY0.35. Shang-Hai Tzu Jan Po Wu Kuan, Shanghai, People's Republic of China. **Tel** 213548, telex 5722. **ED** C C Tan. **LC** QH7; .K29. **DD** 508.51. **CODEN** KYYAEU. **Circ:** 2,500 (ctrl).
**Desc:** Topics include: Botany, Zoology, Anthropology, Astronomy, and Geography.

JA
**KIKAN ANIMA. VFOAT** Anima Quarterly. Summer (1975)-. Periodical. Japanese. mo. ¥14500. Heibonsha Limited Publishers, 5 Sanbancho, Chiyoda-ku Tokyo 102 Japan. **Tel** (03)265-0451, FAX (03)265-0477. **ED** Tokuichi Sawachika. **LC** QL1; .K53. **Bk Rev. Ad Acc. Circ:** 80,000.

US/0075-6245
**KIRTLANDIA.** [Kirtlandia]. **Added/Corp** Cleveland Museum of Natural History. No. 1 (1967)-. Monographic series. English. ir. Price varies per volume. Cleveland Museum of Natural History, Wade Oval University Circle, Cleveland OH 44106. **Tel** (216)231-4600, FAX (216)231-5919. **ED** David S. Brose and Joseph Hannibal. **LC** QH1; .K47. **DD** 508. **CODEN** KIRTA4. Index available. **Pr Rev. Circ:** 500 (ctrl). available on microfilm. Documents available from BIOSIS Document Express.
**Desc:** Contains natural history and sciences.
**Ind/Abst** Biol. Abstr.; GeoRef; Life Sci. Collect.; Zool. Rec.

SA/0075-7780
**LAMMERGEYER, THE.** [Lammergeyer]. **Added/Corp** Natal Parks, Game, and Fish Preservation Board. Vol. 1-3, No. 6 (1960-1966)-. Periodical. English. ir. R15.00. Natal Parks Board, PO Box 662, Pitermaritzburg 3200 Natal South Africa. **Tel** 011 27 (0331)471961, FAX 011 27 (0331)471037. **ED** D. N. Johnson. **LC** QH195.N3; L3. **DD** 500.9. **CODEN** LMGYA3. **Circ:** 400 (ctrl). Documents available from CASDDS.
**Desc:** Nature conservation research in Natal.
**Ind/Abst** Chem. Abstr.; Fish Rev.; Index Vet.; Key Word Index Wildl. Res.

IO
**LAPORAN TAHUNAN DIREKTORAT PERLINDUNGAN DAN PENGAWETAN ALAM. Main/Corp** Indonesia. Direktorat Perlindungan dan Pedgawetan Alam. Indonesian. Direktorat Perlingungan dan Pengawetan Alam, Jalan Ir H Juanda No 9, Bogor Indonesia. **LC** QH186; .I52A.

CN/0227-2377
**LINNEEN, LE.** [Linneen]. Published since Fall 1976?. Periodical. French. qt. Free to members, $1.00 per no. Societe Linneenne du Quebec Aquarium du Quebec, 1675 Av du Parc, Sainte-Foy Quebec G1W 4S3 Canada. **Tel** (418)653-8186. **DD** 509.714. **Circ:** 1,000.
**Desc:** Brief description by the president of the upcoming activities of the society. Progress report concerning the major issues.

US/0024-5283
**LIVING MUSEUM, THE. See** Museums and Galleries.

UK/0076-0579
**LONDON NATURALIST.** (THE LONDON NATURALIST : THE JOURNAL OF THE LONDON NATURAL HISTORY SOCIETY.). [Lond. nat.]. **Added/Corp** London Natural History Society. (1921)-. English. an. £5.00. London Natural History Society, 3 Chatsworth Edwards, West Harrow, Middlesex HA2 0RS England. **Tel** 011 44 0273 654714. **CODEN** LONAAE. ***Continues*** *Transactions / London Natural History Society.*
**Ind/Abst** GeoRef.

FI/0024-7383
**LUONNON TUTKIJA.** [Luonnon tutk.]. **Added/Corp** Suomalainen Elain-ja Kasvitieteellinen Seura Vanamo. (1897)-. Finnish. Five times a year. Fmk70.00. Academic Bookstore Akateeminen, Postilokero 23, FIN-00371 Helsinki Finland. **Tel** 011 358 0 12141. **LC** QH7; .L8. **CODEN** LUTUAA. Documents available from BIOSIS Document Express.
**Ind/Abst** AGRICOLA; Biol. Abstr.; GeoRef; Life Sci. Collect.

SX/1011-5498
**MADOQUA (WINDHOEK. 1975).** (MADOQUA.). [Madoqua]. **Added/Corp** Namibia. Division of Nature Conservation and Tourism. Namibia. Dept. of Agriculture and Nature Conservation. (1975)-. Periodical. English (German). Twice a year (March and Sept.). R25.00. Ministry of Wildlife Cons & Tourisn, Bag 13306, Windhoek 9000 Namibia. **Tel** 011 264 61 63131, FAX 011 264 61 63195. **ED** Dr. C. J. Brown. **CODEN** MADOAL. cum. index. **Bk Rev. Pr Rev. Circ:** 700. Documents available from BIOSIS Document Express. ***Formed by the union of*** *Madoqua. Ser. I, 1010-2299; Madoqua Series II, 1010-2302.*
**Desc:** These are original research findings and reviews which provides new ideas on environmental, wildlife, and biology subjects.
**Ind/Abst** Biol. Abstr.; Life Sci. Collect.

IQ/1017-8678
**MAGALLAT MATHAF AL-TARIH AL-TABII (BAGDAD).** (BULLETIN OF THE IRAQ NATURAL HISTORY MUSEUM.). **Added/Corp** Mathaf Al-Tarikh Al-Tabii Al-Iraqi. **VFOAT** Majallaf Mathaf Al-Tarikh Al-Tabii Al-Iraqi. Vol. 8, No. 1, May (1988)-. Bulletin. English. ir. **CODEN** BINME4. Documents available from BIOSIS Document Express. ***Continues*** *Bulletin of the Natural History Research Centre.*
**Ind/Abst** Biodeter. Abstr.; Biol. Abstr.

US/8756-9620
**MAINE BIRDLIFE.** [Maine birdlife]. **VFOAT** Birdlife. Periodical. English. qt. $10.00 US; $12.50 other. Maine Birdlife, PO Box 18, Winthrop ME 04364. **DD** 508.
**Desc:** Articles and columns on the natural history of the Northeast for professionals and serious amateurs. Also ornithological field notes.

●US/1063-3626
**MAINE NATURALIST (STEUBEN, ME.).** (MAINE NATURALIST.). [Maine nat.]. **Added/Corp** Eagle Hill Wildlife Research Station (Steuben, Me.). Vol. 1, No. 1 (1993)-. Periodical. English. qt (Mar., June, Sept., Dec.). $30.00. Eagle Hill Wildlife Restoration Station, PO Box 99, Steuben ME 04680. **Tel** (207)546-2821, FAX (207)546-2821. **ED** Joerg-Henner Lotze. **DD** 508. **Bk Rev**, (Qty: 60). **Ad Acc. Pr Rev.** ***Continues*** *Maine Field Naturalist.*

MY/0127-0206
**MALAYAN NATURALIST.** [Malay. nat.]. **Added/Corp** Malayan Nature Society. (19??)-. Periodical. English. qt (Feb., May, Aug., Nov.). 110.00Mal$. Malayan Nature Society, PO Box 10750, 50724 Kuala Lumpur Malaysia. **Tel** 011 60 3 753330. **LC** QH185; .M34. **DD** 333.95/16/09595.
**Ind/Abst** Fish Rev.; Wildl. Rev.

MY/0025-1291
**MALAYAN NATURE JOURNAL, THE.** [Malay. nat. j.]. **Added/Corp** Malayan Nature Society. Vol. 1 (Aug. 1940)-. Periodical. English. qt. 60.00Mal$ (ordinary & schools); 110.00Mal$ (corporations). Malayan Nature Society, PO Box 10750, 50724 Kuala Lumpur Malaysia. **Tel** 011 60 3 753330. **ED** Ruth Kiew. **LC** QH1; .M265. **DD** 574.9595. **CODEN** MANJAM. **Bk Rev. Ad Acc. Circ:** 1,500 (ctrl). Documents available from BIOSIS Document Express.
**Desc:** Original articles on natural history, biology and conservation of Malaysia and the surrounding region.
**Ind/Abst** AGRICOLA; Biol. Abstr.; Ecol. Abstr. (?-?); Fish Rev.; For. Abstr.; Helminthol. Abstr.; Index Vet.; Key Word Index Wildl. Res.; Life Sci. Collect.; Rev. Agric. Entomol.; SEA Abstr.; Seed Abstr.; Wildl. Rev.

US/0096-4158
**MARYLAND NATURALIST, THE.** (MARYLAND NATURALIST.). [Md. nat.]. **Added/Corp** Natural History Society of Maryland. Vol. 30 (1948)-. Periodical. English. qt (Mar., June, Sept., Dec.). $20.00 US; $30.00 other. Natural Historical Society of Maryland, 2643 North Charles Street, Baltimore MD 21218. **Tel** (410)235-6116. **ED** Arnold Norden. **LC** QH1; .N314. **DD** 574.062752. Index available. **Bk Rev**, (Qty: 1-6). **Circ:** 500. ***Continues*** *Maryland (Baltimore, Md.), 0896-5587.*
**Ind/Abst** Fish Rev. (Jan. 1989-July 1992); Wildl. Rev. (Jan. 1989-July 1992).

BE
**MEMOIRES. DEUXIEME SERIE (BRUXELLES).** (MEMOIRES. DEUXIEME SERIE.). **Main/Corp** Brussels. Institut Royal des Sciences Naturelles de Belgique. **VFOAT** Verhandelingen. Tweede Reeks. Issue 2, (1949)-. Monographic series. Multiple languages (French). Price varies per volume. Institut Royal des Sciences Naturelles de Belgique, rue Vautier 29, 1040 Brussels Belgium. **Tel** 011 32 2 6482123, FAX 011 32 2 6464433. **LC** QH3; .B852. **DD** 574.062493. ***Continues*** *Musee Royal d'Histoire Naturelle de Belgique. Memoires. Deuxieme Serie.*

●FR/1243-4442
**MEMOIRES DU MUSEUM NATIONAL D'HISTOIRE NATURELLE. Added/Corp** Museum National d'Histoire Naturelle (France). (1993)-. Monographic series. French. ir. Price varies per volume. Museum National d'Histoire Naturelle, 57 rue Cuvier, 75005 Paris France. **Tel** 011 33 1 40793700. **(Subscription address:** Universal Book Services, Warmonderweg 80, 2341 KZ Oegstgeest Netherlands.) ***Formed by the union of*** *Memoires du Museum National d'Histoire Naturelle, 0078-9747; Memoires du Museum National d'Histoire Naturelle, 0078-9755* ***and*** *Memoires du Museum National d'Histoire Naturelle, 0078-9763.*

FR
**MEMOIRES DU MUSEUM NATIONAL D'HISTOIRE NATURELLE. SERIE D, SCIENCES PHYSICO-CHIMIQUES. VFOAT** Sciences Physico-Chimiques. (1960)-. Periodical. French. ir. Museum Natl d Hist Naturelle, 38 rue Geoffroy Saint Hilaire, 75005 Paris France. ***Continues in part*** *Memoires de Museum National d'Histoire Naturelle.*

US/0749-1743
**MEMOIRS OF THE NATURAL HISTORY FOUNDATION OF ORANGE COUNTY.** [Mem. Nat. Hist. Found. Orange County]. Vol. 1-. Academic Scholarly Publication. English. ir. Price varies per volume. Natural History Foundation of Orange County, PO Box 7038, Newport Beach CA 92660. **Tel** (714)640-7120. **ED** Henry Keorper. **Circ:** 2,000. Documents available from CASDDS.
**Ind/Abst** Chem. Abstr.

AT/0079-8835
**MEMOIRS OF THE QUEENSLAND MUSEUM.** [Mem. Queensl. Mus.]. **Main/Corp** Queensland Museum, Brisbane. Vol. 1 (1912)-. English. an. price varies per volume. Royal Society of Queensland, PO Box 21, St Lucia Queensland 4067 Australia. **Tel** 011 44 07 840 7684. **ED** P. A. Jell. **LC** QH1; .Q35. **CODEN** MQUMA8. Index available. **Pr Rev. Circ:** 800. Documents available from BIOSIS Document Express. ***Supersedes*** *Annals of the Queensland Museum.*
**Desc:** Journal is refereed by two independent assessors for each paper. International refereeing is preferred.
**Ind/Abst** Anthropol. Lit.; Biocont. News Inf. (1991-); Biol. Abstr.; Ecol. Abstr.; Geogr. Abstr. Human Geogr.; GeoRef; Life Sci. Collect.; Rev. Med. Vet. Entomol.

PE/0457-9151
**MEMORIAS DEL MUSEO DE HISTORIA NATURAL JAVIER PRADO. Main/Corp** Museo de Historia Natural "Javier Prado.". No. 1 (1951)-. Monographic series. Spanish (summaries and/or abstracts in English). ir. Price varies per volume. Universidad Nacional Mayor de San Marcos, Casilla 454, Lima 1 Peru. **Tel** 71-0117. **ED** Cesar Acleto. **DD** 574. **Pr Rev. Circ:** 1,000.

PE
**MEMORIAS DEL MUSEO DE HISTORIA NATURAL. UNIVERSIDAD NACIONAL MAYOR DE SAN MARCOS.** Spanish (English, French and German). ir. Museo de Historia Natural, Universidad Nacional Mayor de San Marcos, Apartado 14-0434, Lima-14 Peru. **Tel** (5114)71-0117. **ED** Victor Pacheco. cum. index. **Circ:** 1,000.

GU/0026-279X
**MICRONESICA.** [Micronesica]. **Added/Corp** University of Guam. Territorial College of Guam. Vol. 1 (June 1964)-. Periodical. English. Twice a year. $15.00 (individuals); $25.00 (institutions & libraries). University of Guam Press / Office of Graduate School and Research, UOG Station, Mangilao 96923 Guam. **Tel** (671)734-9430, FAX (671)734-3676, telex 7216275. **ED** Robert Richmond. **LC** QH198.M48; M52. **DD** 574.996/5. **CODEN** MCNSBU. **Bk Rev. Circ:** 600. Documents available from BIOSIS Document Express.
**Desc:** Journal of the University of Guam devoted to the natural sciences of Guam, micronesia, and related areas.
**Ind/Abst** AGRICOLA [Select. Cov.]; Anthropol. Index; Biol. Abstr.; Fish Rev.; GeoRef; Life Sci. Collect.; Wildl. Rev.

AG/0074-025X
**MISCELANEA - FUNDACION MIGUEL LILLO.** (MISCELANEA.). [Misc. - Fund. Miguel Lillo]. **Main/Corp** Fundacion Miguel Lillo. **Added/Corp** Fundacion Miguel Lillo. No. 25 (1968)-. Monographic series. Spanish (summaries and/or abstracts in English, French and German). ir. Price varies per volume. Fundacion Miguel Lillo, Miguel Lillo 251, 4000 Tucuman Argentina. **LC** UNC. ***Continues*** *Miscelanea (Instituto Miguel Lillo).*
**Ind/Abst** AGRICOLA.

US/0075-5028
**MISCELLANEOUS PUBLICATION - UNIVERSITY OF KANSAS, MUSEUM OF NATURAL HISTORY.** [Misc. publ. Univ. Kans. Mus. Nat. Hist.]. (1946)-. Monographic series. English. Price varies per volume. University of Kansas Museum of Natural History, Publications Department, Lawrence KS 66045. **Tel** (913)864-4540. **CODEN** UKMPAN. Documents available from BIOSIS Document Express. ***Supersedes in part*** *University of Kansas Publications. Museum of Natural History, 0075-5036.*
**Ind/Abst** Biol. Abstr.; GeoRef.

US/0076-8405
**MISCELLANEOUS PUBLICATIONS - MUSEUM OF ZOOLOGY, UNIVERSITY OF MICHIGAN.** See Zoology.

SX
**MITTEILUNGEN / NAMIBIA WISSENSCHAFTLICHE GESELLSCHAFT.** **Added/Corp** Namibia Scientific Society. **VFOAT** Newsletter. (1990)-. Periodical. English (German). bm. Namibia Scientific Society, Secretariat, PO Box 67, Windhoek, Namibia. **LC** IN PROCESS. **CODEN** MNWGEH. ***Continues*** *Mitteilungen (South West Africa Scientific Society).*

IT
**MONDO VITA.** ***Ceased.*** (19??)-(19??). Italian. bm. Editrice APS, Via Marcona 93, 20129 Milan Italy. **Tel** 2/7383328, FAX 2/7496086.

US/0084-9650
**MONOGRAPH SERIES - DELAWARE MUSEUM OF NATURAL HISTORY.** (MONOGRAPH SERIES.). No. 1-. Monographic series. English. ir. Price varies per volume. Delaware Museum of Natural History, PO Box 3937, Greenville DE 19807. **Tel** (302)658-9111. **CODEN** MDMHDZ.

US/0096-7750
**MONOGRAPHS - ACADEMY OF NATURAL SCIENCES OF PHILADELPHIA.** [Monogr. Acad. Nat. Sci. Philadelphia]. **Main/Corp** Academy of Natural Sciences of Philadelphia. **Added/Corp** Academy of Natural Sciences of Philadelphia. No. 1 (1935)-. Monographic series. English. ir. Price varies per volume. Academy of Natural Sciences, 1900 Benjamin Franklin Parkway, Philadelphia PA 19103. **Tel** (215)299-1130, FAX (215)299-1028. **ED** William F. Smith-Vaniz. **Pr Rev. Circ:** 1,000 (ctrl).
**Desc:** Comparatively long works (often taxonomic treatises) re: natural sciences, biogeography, systematics, evolution and ecology.

NE/0301-6463
**MUSEOLOGIA (AMSTERDAM).** (MUSEOLOGIA.). [Museologia]. Oct. 1973-. Dutch (English; summaries and/or abstracts in Dutch and English). sa. 24.59. Quadriga-Drukwerken, Amstel 21,, Amsterdam. **LC** QH7; .M87. **DD** 500.9/05. **CODEN** MSLGCT.
**Ind/Abst** GeoRef.

CN/0047-9551
**N. B. NATURALIST.** **Added/Corp** New Brunswick Federation of Naturalists. New Brunswick Museum. Natural Science Dept. Vol. 1, (Jan. 1970)-. Periodical. English (French). Four times a year (Mar., June, Sept., Dec.). 10.00Can$. New Brunswick Federation of Naturalists, 277 Douglas Avenue, Saint John New Brunswick E2K 1E5 Canada. **Tel** (506)693-1196. **ED** Mary Majka and David Christie. Index available. **Bk Rev. Ad Acc. Circ:** 500 (ctrl).
**Desc:** Natural history of New Brunswick.

PH/0117-0686
**NATIONAL MUSEUM PAPERS.** **Added/Corp** National Museum (Philippines) Concerned Citizens for the National Museum (Manila, Philippines). Vol. 1, No. 1 (1990)-. Periodical. English. sa. **LC** IN PROCESS.
**Ind/Abst** Int. Bibliogr. Sociol.

IC/0369-5921
**NATTURUFRINGURINN.** [Natturufringurinn]. 1.-Vol.; 1931-. Periodical. Icelandic. qt. Free to members. H Islenska Natturufrifelag, Stefan Stefansson, Storholti 12 Postholf 836, Reykjavik Iceland. **LC** QH166; .N38. **CODEN** NTFDA6. cum. index.
**Ind/Abst** AGRICOLA; GeoRef.

GW/0028-0593
**NATUR UND HEIMAT.** [Natur Heimat]. **Added/Corp** Westfalisches Landesmuseum fuer Naturkunde. Vol. 1 (1934)-. Periodical. German. qt. $26.00. Natur und Heimat, Sentruper Strasse 285, D-48161 Munster West Germany. **LC** QH5; .N22. **CODEN** NTRHAA. Documents available from BIOSIS Document Express.
**Ind/Abst** Biol. Abstr.

GW/0028-0615
**NATUR UND LANDSCHAFT (STUTTGART).** (NATUR UND LANDSCHAFT.). [Nat. Landsch.]. **Added/Corp** Germany (Federal Republic). Bundesanstalt fur Vegetationskunde, Naturschutz und Landschaftspflege. Germany (Federal Republic). Bundesanstalt fur Naturschutz und Landschaftspflege. (19??)-. Periodical. German. mo. DM105.00. W Kohlhammer Verlag GmbH, Postfach 800430, D 70549 Stuttgart Germany. **Tel** 011 49 711 78631, FAX 011 49 711 7863263, telex 7-255820. **LC** QH77.G3; N27. **[CCC].**
**Desc:** Journal for conservation of natural resources, natural preservation and environmental protection.
**Ind/Abst** Agrofor. Abstr.; Coal Abstr.; GeoRef; Key Word Index Wildl. Res.

GW/0028-1301
**NATUR UND MUSEUM (FRANKFURT AM MAIN : 1962).** (NATUR UND MUSEUM.). [Nat. Mus.]. **Added/Corp** Senckenbergische Naturforschende Gesellschaft. Vol. 92, No. 1 (Jan. 1962)-. Periodical. German (English). Twelve times a year. DM60.00. Senckenberg Naturforschende Gesellschaft, Senckenberganlage 25, D 60325 Frankfurt Germany. **Tel** 011 49 611 75421, telex 413129. **ED** Willi Ziegler. **LC** QH5; .S4. **DD** 508/.05. **CODEN** NAMUAR. Index available. **Bk Rev. Ad Acc. Circ:** 7,000 (ctrl). ***Continues*** *Natur und Volk.*
**Desc:** Contains popular articles of natural history.
**Ind/Abst** GeoRef; Life Sci. Collect.; Wildl. Rev. (19??-).

SZ
**NATUR- UND NATIONALPARKE.** **VFOAT** Nature and National Parks. (March 1963)-. Periodical. German. qt. Fed Natur & Nationalparke Eur, Bathausgasse 1, W-8352 Grafenau FR Germany. **Tel** 011 49 8552 2839.

NE/0028-0631
**NATURA.** 1st.- Year; 1906-. Periodical. Dutch. mo. Fl47.50 Netherlands; $27.50 US. K N N V Bureau, Audegracht 237, 3511NK Utrecht Netherlands. **Tel** 030-314797. **ED** A Vaessen. **Bk Rev. Ad Acc.** ctrl circ.

IT/0391-156X
**NATURA BRESCIANA.** [Nat. brescia.]. **Added/Corp** Museo Civico di Storia Naturale, Brescia. Museo Civico di Scienze Naturali di Brescia (Italy). (1965)-. Italian. Museo Civico di Storia Naturale, Lungadige Porta Vittoria 9, 37129 Verona Italy. **LC** QH152; .N34. **DD** 500.9/0945/26.

IT/0369-6243
**NATURA (MILANO).** (NATURA.). [Natura]. **Added/Corp** Societa Italiana di Scienze Naturali. Vol. 1 (Nov. 1909)-. Periodical. Italian. qt. L35000 (membership only). Societa Italiana di Scienze Naturali, Corso Venezia 55, 20121 Milan Italy. **Tel** 011 39 2 62025405. **ED** Giovanni Pinna. **LC** QH7; .S6647. **DD** 574.05. **CODEN** NTRMAP. Index Available, published separately, free-automatically sent. **Circ:** 1,500.
**Ind/Abst** Fish Rev. (Jan. 1989-July 1992); GeoRef; Life Sci. Collect.; Wildl. Rev. (Jan. 1989-July 1992).

US/0028-0712
**NATURAL HISTORY.** [Nat. hist.]. **Added/Corp** American Museum of Natural History. Vol. 19, (Jan. 1919)-. Periodical. English. mo. $28.00 (one year), $38.00 (two year), $48.00 (three year). American Museum of Natural History, Central Park West at 79th Street, New York NY 10024. **Tel** (212)769-5500, (800)234-5252, telex 910 240 8933 MICRO PRESS VQ. **(Subscription address:** CDS Agency Hard Copy, PO Box 4966, Des Moines IA 50340.**) ED** Alan Ternes. **LC** QH1; .N13. **NLM** W1 NA804N. **CODEN** NAHIAX. Index available. **Bk Rev. Ad Acc. Pr Rev. Circ:** 500,000. available on microfilm and microfiche from University Microfilms International (UMI). Documents available from The Genuine Article, BIOSIS Document Express, UMI Article Clearinghouse, Documents on Demand, Magazine Collection. ***Continues*** *American Museum Journal (New York, N.Y.), 1049-1112;* ***Absorbed*** *Nature Magazine.*
**Desc:** Translates the natural sciences into easy reading and color photography. Covers from archaeology to zoology, from inner man to outer space. Strives to explore, explain, define and depict.
**Ind/Abst** ASTIS Curr. Aware. Bull. (1978-); Abr. Read. Guide Period. Lit.; Abstr. Anthropol.; Acad. Abstr. Full Text Elite (Jan. 1984-) [Full Txt.]; Acad. Abstr. (Jan. 1984-); Acad. Ind. [Computer File] (1984-); Acad. Search (Jan. 1984-); AGRICOLA [Select. Cov.]; Anthropol. Index; Anthropol. Lit. (-Vol. Vol. 11, 1989); ASTIS Bibliogr. (1978-); Biogr. Index; Biol. Abstr.; Biol. Dig.; Book Rev. Digest; Book Rev. Index; Curr. Ref. Fish Res.; Environ. Abstr.; Environ. Period. Bibliogr. (?-?); Expand. Acad. Index (1984-); Fish Rev. (Jan. 1989-July 1992); Garden Lit. (1992-); Gen. Period. Index (1985-); Gen. Sci. Index; Gen. Sci. Source (Jan. 1988-) [Full Txt.]; INFO-SOUTH Abstr.; Int. Aerosp. Abstr.; Key Word Index Wildl. Res.; Mag. Artic. Summar. Elite (Jan. 1984-) [Full Txt.]; Mag. Artic. Summar. Select (Jan. 1984-) [Full Txt.]; Mag. Artic. Summar. CD-ROM (Jan. 1984-); Mag. Express (1986-) [Full Txt.]; Mag. Index Plus (1989-); Mag. Index Sel. Microfiche (1986-) [Full Txt.]; Mag. Index. Sel. (1986-); Mag. Search; Middle East Abstr. Index; Mid. Search (Jan. 1984-) [Full Txt.]; Newsp. Period. Abstr. (1986-); Peace Res. Abstr. J. (1969-); Life Sci. Collect.; Protozoolog. Abstr.; Read. Guide Abstr. Select Ed.; Read. Guide Period. Lit.; Res. Alert [Full Cov.]; Resource/One Ondisc; Rev. Med. Vet. Entomol.; Sci. Cit. Index; SCISEARCH; Soc. Sci. Cit. Index [Select. Cov.]; Mag. Index (1977-); TOM Gen. Index (1985-) [Full Txt.]; Vocat. Search (Jan. 1984-) [Full Txt.]; West. Hist. Q.; Wildl. Rev. (Jan. 1989-July 1992).

TH/0080-9462
**NATURAL HISTORY BULLETIN (BANGKOK).** (NATURAL HISTORY BULLETIN.). **Main/Corp** Siam Society. **Added/Corp** Siam Society. Journal. Natural History Supplement. Natural History Society of Siam. Journal. Thailand Research Society. Journal. Natural History Supplement. Thailand Research Society. Journal. Natural History Bulletin. (Feb. 1914)-. Periodical. English. Twice a year. $15.00. Siam Society, PO Box 65, Bangkok Thailand. **Tel** 011 66 2 2583494, 2583491. **ED** Warren Y. Brockelman. **Circ:** 1,500 (ctrl).
**Desc:** The study of the natural history in Thailand and neighbouring countries.
**Ind/Abst** Am. Hist. Life; Fish Rev.; Wildl. Rev.

TH/0080-9462
**NATURAL HISTORY BULLETIN OF THE SIAM SOCIETY.** (THE NATURAL HISTORY BULLETIN OF THE SIAM SOCIETY.). [Nat. hist. bull. Siam Soc.]. **Added/Corp** Siam Society. Vol. 14, No. 2 (May 1947)-. Bulletin. English. sa. Free (to Siam Society Members), $15.00 (U.S., postage included). Siam Society, PO Box 65, Bangkok Thailand. **Tel** 011 66 2 2583494, 2583491. **LC** QH1; .T5. **DD** 508.593. **CODEN** NHSAAC. Documents available from BIOSIS Document Express. ***Continues*** *Natural History Bulletin of the Thailand Research Society.*
**Ind/Abst** Am. Hist. Life (1961-1968); Anim. Breed. Abstr.; Biol. Abstr.; For. Abstr.; Rev. Agric. Entomol.; Rev. Med. Vet. Entomol.

UK
**NATURAL HISTORY OF EGYPT, THE.** Vol. 1 (1986)-. Monographic series. English. ir. Price varies per volume. Aris & Phillips Ltd, Teddington House, Church Street, Wiltshire BA1 28PQ England. **Tel** 011 44 985 213409, FAX 011 44 985 212910.

BL/0101-1944
**NATURALIA (SAO JOSE DO RIO PRETO).** (NATURALIA.). [Naturalia]. Vol. 1 (1975)-. Academic Scholarly Publication. Portuguese (English). an. $30.00. Fundacao Desenvolvimento Unesp, Av Rio Branco 1210, 01206 Sao Paulo SP Brazil. **Tel** 011 55 11 2237088. **LC** QH7. **DD** 505. **CODEN** NTRLDP. **Circ:** 600 (ctrl). Documents available from BIOSIS Document Express, CASDDS.
**Desc:** Publishes original papers and revisions of subjects on the field of biological sciences.
**Ind/Abst** AGRICOLA [Select. Cov.]; Biol. Abstr.; Chem. Abstr. (1975-1982); CSA Neuro. Abstr. (?-?); Curr. Aware. Biol. Sci., CABS; Entomol. Abstr.; GeoRef; Math. Rev.; Life Sci. Collect.

UK/0028-0771
**NATURALIST (LEEDS).** (THE NATURALIST.). [Naturalist]. **Added/Corp** West-Riding Consolidated Naturalists' Society. Yorkshire Naturalists' Union. **VFOAT** Naturalist, and Field Club Journal. No. 1 (May 1, 1864)-. Periodical. English. qt. £15.00 Europe; £18.00 other. Naturalist, D Bramley Doncaster Museum, Chequer Road, Doncaster DN1 2AE England. **Tel** 011 44 302 535246. **ED** M R D Seaword, The University Bradford. **LC** QH1; .N416. **CODEN** NTRLAM. **[CCC].** Index available. **Bk Rev. Ad Acc. Circ:** 800. available on microfilm and microfiche from University Microfilms International (UMI). Documents available from BIOSIS Document Express. ***Continues*** *Naturalist (London, England : 1851).*
**Ind/Abst** Biol. Abstr.; GeoRef.

SA/1013-6444
**NATURALIST PORT ELIZABETH, THE.** (1981)-. Multiple languages. Wildlife Society Southern Africa, P.O.Box 44189 Linden 2104, South Africa. **Tel** 011 27 41 29606. ***Continues*** *Eastern Cape Naturalist, 0012-8724.*
**Ind/Abst** Environ. Period. Bibliogr.

TR
**NATURALIST (TRINIDAD AND TOBAGO).** (THE NATURALIST.). **VFOAT** Naturalist Magazine. English. bm. $30.00, $40.00 (airmail) US. 20 Collens Road, Maraval, Republic of Trinidad and Tobago. **Tel** 1-809-622-6625, telex TRINATMAG. **ED** Stephen Mohammed and Kitty Hannays. **LC** QH77.T75; T74. **DD** 508.7298/3. Index available. **Bk Rev. Ad Acc. Circ:** 12,000 (ctrl). ***Continues*** *Trinidad Naturalist Magazine.*
**Desc:** Promotes and educates people on the natural beauty of Trinidad, Tobago and the Caribbean.
**Ind/Abst** Fish Rev.; Wildl. Rev.

BE/0028-0801
**NATURALISTES BELGES.** (LES NATURALISTES BELGES / BULLETIN DE LA FEDERATION DES SOCIETES BELGES DES SCIENCES DE LA NATURE.). [Nat. belges]. **Added/Corp** Federation des Societes Belges des Sciences de la Nature. Naturalistes Belges. (Jan. 1930)-. Bulletin. French. Twice a year. $20.99 Belgium; $27.00 other. Institut Royal de Sciences Naturelles de Belgique, 29 rue Vautier, 1040 Brussels Belguim. **Tel** 011 32 2 6482123. **LC** QH3; .N26. **CODEN** NTUBA7. Documents available from BIOSIS Document Express. ***Continues*** *Naturalistes Belges. Bulletin Mensuel.*
**Ind/Abst** AGRICOLA; Biol. Abstr.

US
**NATURALISTS' DIRECTORY AND ALMANAC INTERNATIONAL. SUPPLEMENT, THE.** 1980-1981-. Directory. English. Sandhill Crane Press Inc., PO Box 147050, Gainesville FL 32614. **Tel** (904)371-9858, FAX (904)371-9969.

US/0191-2941
**NATURE AND SYSTEM.** ***Ceased.*** [Nat. syst.]. Vol. 1 (March 1979)-Vol. 6 (March 1985). Periodical. English. qt. Nature and System Inc, PO Box 3368,

Tucson AZ 85722. **Tel** (602)624-7849. **LC** QH1; .N487. **DD** 500.9/01.
**Ind/Abst** Philos. Index.

MY/0126-5318
**NATURE MALAYSIANA.** [Nat. Malays.]. Vol. 1 (1976)-. Periodical. English. Four times a year. $12.00 Malaysia; $21.00 other. Tropical Press SDN BHD, 56-2 Jalan Maarof, Bangsar Baru, 59100 Kuala Lumpur, Malaysia. **Tel** 011 60 3 2823233, FAX 011 60 3 2827230. **ED** Prof. Yong Hoi-Sen. **LC** QH185; .N37. **DD** 500.9/595/105. **CODEN** NAMAE5. **Circ:** 2,000 (ctrl).
**Desc:** Concerning the rich and diverse natural heritage of Malaysia in particular and of other parts of the world in general.
**Ind/Abst** AGRICOLA.

CN/0836-4702
**NATURE NORTHWEST.** (NATURE NORTHWEST : THE NEWSLETTER OF THE THUNDER BAY FIELD NATURALISTS.). [Nat. northw.]. Vol. 41, No. 1 (Feb. 1987)-. Newsletter. English. qt. 13.00Can$ $15.00 single. Thunder Bay Field Naturalists, Box 1073, Thunder Bay Ontario P7C 4X8 Canada. **Tel** (807)577-3297. **ED** Bill Addison and Mike Bryan. **DD** 574.9713/11. **Bk Rev. Ad Acc. Circ:** 300 (ctrl). ***Continues*** *Thunder Bay Field Naturalists' Newsletter, 0836-4710.*
**Desc:** Newsletter focuses on the natural history of Northwestern Ontario and the protection of the local environment.

US/1054-9641
**NATURE SOUTH.** (NATURE SOUTH : THE MAGAZINE OF THE ALABAMA NATURAL HISTORY SOCIETY.). [Nat. South]. **Added/Corp** Alabama Natural History Society. Alabama State Museum of Natural History. **VFOAT** Nature/South. Vol. 1, No. 1 (Fall 1990)-. Periodical. English. qt. comes with membership. Alabama Natural History Society, PO Box 870340, Tuscaloosa AL 35487. **Tel** (205)348-2040. **(Subscription address:** Capstone Foundation, PO Box 870340, Tuscaloosa AL 35487.**) DD** 508. **Pr Rev. Circ:** 1,000 (ctrl).

AT
**NATURE WALKABOUT.** ***Ceased.*** Periodical. English. sa. Education Supplies Branch, Department of Education, 23 Miles Road, Kewdale West Australia 6105 Australia. **Tel** (09)353 2033. **LC** QH197; .N4.

NE
**NATUURHISTORISCH MAANBLAD : ORGAAN VAN HET NATUURHISTORISCH GENOOTSCHAP IN LIMBURG. Added/Corp** Natuurhistorisch Genootschap in Limburg. (1924)-. Periodical. Dutch (English; summaries and/or abstracts in English). mo. Fl112.50 Netherlands; $80.00 other. Natuurhistorisch Genootschap Limburg, Bosquetplein 7, G211 KJ Maastricht Netherlands. **Tel** (0)43-213671. **ED** Douwe de Graaf. Index available. cum. index. **Bk Rev. Ad Acc. Circ:** 1,200 (ctrl). ***Continues*** *Natuurhistorisch Genootschap in Limburg. Maandblad.*
**Desc:** Studies on biology, geology and paleontology in the province of Limburg (Netherlands).

BE/0770-1748
**NATUURWETENSCHAPPELIJK TIJDSCHRIFT.** [Natuurwet. tijdschr.]. **Added/Corp** Natuur en Geneeskundige Vennootschap (Belgium). **VFOAT** A.NWT. (1915)-. Periodical. Dutch (English). Four times a year (Jan., Apr., July, Oct.). $40.00. Natuur-en Geneesk Vennootschap, Krijgslaan 281, B-9000 Gent Belgium. **Tel** 011 32 91 644669, FAX 011 32 91 644997. **ED** L. Walschot. **CODEN** NATGAK. Index available. **Bk Rev. Circ:** 300. Documents available from BIOSIS Document Express. ***Continues*** *Tijdschrift van den Wetenschappelijken Kring van Antwerpen.*
**Ind/Abst** Biol. Abstr.; GeoRef; Life Sci. Collect.

US/0085-3887
**NEMOURIA.** (NEMOURIA : OCCASIONAL PAPERS OF THE DELAWARE MUSEUM OF NATURAL HISTORY.). **VFOAT** Occasional Papers of the Delaware Museum of Natural History. Began in 1970. Monographic series. English. ir. Price varies per volume. Delaware Museum of Natural History, PO Box 3937, Greenville DE 19807. **Tel** (302)658-9111. **ED** Rudiger Bieler. **LC** QL1; .N33. **DD** 590/.5. **CODEN** NOPHD2. Index available. cum. index. **Pr Rev.** Documents available from BIOSIS Document Express.
**Ind/Abst** Biol. Abstr.

UK/0951-5305
**NERC NEWS / NATURAL ENVIRONMENT RESEARCH COUNCIL.** **See** Environmental Issues-Ecology.

US/0749-1158
**NEW YORK STATE MUSEUM MEMOIR.** [N.Y. State Mus. memoir]. (1983)-. Academic Scholarly Publication. English. ir. Price varies per volume. New York State Museum, 3140 Cultural Education Center, Albany NY 12230. **Tel** (518)474-3505. **DD** 508. **CODEN** NYSMEZ. **Circ:** 1,000. Documents available from CASDDS. ***Continues*** *Memoir (New York State Museum : 1976), 0898-8846.*
**Desc:** Comprehensive works on topics in New York's natural history and prehistory.
**Ind/Abst** Chem. Abstr. (1983-); GeoRef.

US
**NEWS & INFO / FRIENDS FOR LONG ISLAND'S HERITAGE. Added/Corp** Friends for Long Island's Heritage. Vol. 1, No. 1 (Fall 1991)-. Periodical. English. qt. ***Continues*** *Newsletter (Friends for Long Island's Heritage).*

UK/0029-0076
**NIGERIAN FIELD.** (THE NIGERIAN FIELD.). [Niger. field]. **Added/Corp** Nigerian Field Society. Vol. 1 (July 1931)-. Periodical. English. qt (4 issues). Comes with Nigerian Field Society membership. Nigerian Field Society, 1 Fishers Heron, East Mills, Fordingbridge SP6 2JR England. **ED** Joyce Lowe. **LC** QH195.N5; A15. **DD** 574.966. **CODEN** NIFIAC. Index available. **Bk Rev. Ad Acc. Circ:** 1,000 (ctrl).
**Desc:** Learned articles and book reviews of general interest to members and other readers on the flora, fauna, and culture of Nigeria.
**Ind/Abst** Fish Rev.; GeoRef; Int. Bibliogr. Sociol.; MLA Int. Bibl. Books Artic. Mod. Lang. Lit.; Wildl. Rev.

JA
**NIHON BENTOSU KENKYUKAI SHI. Main/Corp** Nihon Bentosu Kenkyukai. **VFOAT** Benthos Research : Bulletin of Japanese Association o Benthology; Bulletin of Japanese Association of Benthology; Benthos Research. No. 21/22- (Aug. 1981)-. Japanese (summaries and/or abstracts in English). sa. $15.00 US membership. Nihon Bentosu Kenkyukai, c/o Kyudai Rinkai Jikkenjo Tomioka Reihoku-machi Amakusa-gun, Kumanoto-ken 863-25 Japan. **LC** QH90.8.B46; B46A. ***Continues*** *Bentosu Kenkyukai Renrakushi.*

KO
**NONMUNJIP. CHAYON KWAHAKPYON. Added/Corp** Cheju Taehakkyo. **VFOAT** Chayon Kwahakpyon; Cheju University Journal. Natural Sciences. (19??)-. Academic Scholarly Publication. Korean (English). **LC** QH7; .N62. **CODEN** CUJSDS. Documents available from CASDDS. ***Continues in part*** *Nonmunjip (Cheju Taehak).*
**Ind/Abst** Chem. Abstr.

●US/1070-468X
**NORTH CAROLINA NATURALIST. Added/Corp** Friends of the North Carolina State Museum of Natural Sciences. **VFOAT** N.C. Naturalist; Naturalist. (1993)-. Periodical. English. qt. Free. Friends of the North Carolina State Museum of Natural Sciences, Box 27647, Raleigh NC 27611. **Tel** (919)733-7450, FAX (919)733-1573. **Bk Rev. Circ:** 2,000.
**Desc:** Articles deal with the natural history of North Carolina.

AT/0078-1630
**NORTH QUEENSLAND NATURALIST.** (THE NORTH QUEENSLAND NATURALIST.). [North Qld. nat.]. **Added/Corp** North Queensland Naturalists' Club. (1932)-. English. sa. $10.00Aus$. North Queensland Naturalist, Box 991, PO Cairns, 4870 Queenslands Australia. **ED** Les Francis. **CODEN** NQNAAG. **Bk Rev. Circ:** 200 (ctrl). Documents available from BIOSIS Document Express.
**Desc:** Natural history and conservation.
**Ind/Abst** AGRICOLA; Biol. Abstr. (-1987).

US/0277-0997
**NORTHERN RAVEN, THE.** (THE NORTHERN RAVEN : THE QUARTERLY NEWSLETTER OF THE CENTER FOR NORTHERN STUDIES.). [North. raven]. **Added/Corp** Center for Northern Studies. Vol. 3, No. 3 & 4 (Fall & Winter 1974-75)-. Periodical. English. qt. $15.00. Center for Northern Studies, Wolcott VT 05680. **Tel** (802)888-4331. **ED** Debra Mason. **LC** QH84.1; .N67. **DD** 508.11. **Bk Rev. Circ:** 3,200. ***Continues*** *Raven.*
**Desc:** Articles relevant to both physical and social systems of the Arctic and Subarctic; 2-3 substantial reviews of recent northern literature with list of books received.

US/0272-1570
**NORTHWEST DISCOVERY.** [Northwest discov.]. Vol. 1 (June 1980)-. Academic Scholarly Publication. English. mo. $15.00. Northwest Press, 1439 East Prospect Street, Seattle WA 98112. **LC** F851; .N64. **DD** 979.5/005.
**Desc:** Covers the history and natural history of Northwest America; includes prime source materials and bibliographic reference citations.
**Ind/Abst** Am. Hist. Life (1987-1988); GeoRef.

US/1060-4812
**NORTHWEST PARKS & WILDLIFE.** [Northwest parks wildl.]. **VFOAT** Northwest Parks and Wildlife. (1991)-. Periodical. English. Six times a year (Feb., April, June, Aug., Oct., Dec.). $14.95 one year; $26.95 two years. Oregon Coast Magazine, PO Box 18000, Florence OR 97439. **Tel** (503)997-8401, FAX (503)997-1124. **ED** Dave Peden and Judy Fleagle. **LC** WMLC 93/912; QH104.5.N6; N67. **DD** 917. **Bk Rev**, (Qty: 2 per year). **Circ:** 13,000 (ctrl). ***Continues*** *Oregon Coast Getaway Guide, 1053-7538.*
**Desc:** Extensive information on parks, plants, and wildlife in the Pacific Northwest. Lots of full-color, full-page photographs of plants, wildlife and scenery.

US/1051-1733
**NORTHWESTERN NATURALIST : A JOURNAL OF VERTEBRATE BIOLOGY.** [Northwest. nat.]. Vol. 70, No. 1 (Spring 1989)-. Periodical. English. Three times a year. $25.00 (institutions), $15.00 (regular), $8.00 (student), $250.00 (life, individual). Society for Northwestern Vertebrate Biology, Department of Wildlife, 600 Capitol Way North, Olympia WA 98501-1091. **Tel** (206)753-2868. **ED** Frederick F. Gilbert. **CODEN** NNATEP. Index available. cum. index. **Bk Rev. Ad Acc. Pr Rev. Acid Free. Circ:** 600 (ctrl). ***Continues*** *Murrelet.*
**Desc:** Publishes original contributions dealing with the biology of the terrestrial vertebrates of its geographic region. Feature articles and general notes are sent out for manuscript review and accepted on the basis of scientific merit. Book reviews of regional interest are also included.

SZ/0029-3725
**NOS OISEAUX.** [Nos oiseaux]. **Added/Corp** Societe Romande pour l'Etude et la Protection des Oiseaux. Vol. 1 No. 1 (July 1913)-. Periodical. French. Four times a year. 40.00F. Societe Romande pour l'Etude et la Protection des Oiseaux, Musee Historie Naturel, 2300 Chaux D Fonds Switzerland. **Tel** 011 41 39 233976. **CODEN** NOOIAV. Documents available from BIOSIS Document Express.
**Ind/Abst** Biol. Abstr.; Fish Rev. (Jan. 1989-July 1992); Wildl. Rev. (Jan. 1989-July 1992).

RM/0253-4649
**NYMPHAEA. See** Earth Sciences.

IT
**OASIS : BIMESTRALE DI NATURA ECOLOGIA FOTOGRAFIA.** Vol. 1, No. 1 (Jan./Feb. 1985)-. Periodical. Italian. Ten times a year. L59000 Italy; L100000 other. Oasis, Loc America 99, 11020 Quart/AO Italy. **Tel** 011 39 165 765801, FAX 011 39 165 765106.

FR/0029-7615
**OBJETS ET MONDES.** ***Suspended.*** (OBJETS ET MONDES : LA REVUE DU MUSEE DE L'HOMME, MUSEUM NATIONAL D'HISTOIRE NATURELLE.). [Objets mondes]. **Added/Corp** Musee de l'Homme (Museum National d'Histoire Naturelle). (Spring 1961)-Suspended with Vol. 26, Nos. 1/2. Periodical. French. qt (4 issues). Musee de l'Homme, Pal Chaillot Place Trocadero, 75116 Paris France. **Tel** 011 33 1 44057336. **LC** GN1; .O2. **DD** 306/.05.
**Ind/Abst** Abstr. Anthropol.; Am. Hist. Life (1972-1975); Ethnoarts Index; MLA Int. Bibl. Books Artic. Mod. Lang. Lit.

AT/0814-1819
**OCCASIONAL PAPERS FROM THE MUSEUM OF VICTORIA.** [Occas. pap. Mus. Vic.]. **Added/Corp** Museum of Victoria. Vol. 1 Nos. 1 & 2 (1984)-. Periodical. English. ir. 15.00Aus$. National Museum of Victoria, 285 Russell Street, Melbourne Victoria 3000 Australia. **ED** Dr. Gary Poore. **LC** QH197; .R46. **DD** 574.9945/05. **CODEN** OPMVEE. **Circ:** 540 (ctrl). Documents available from BIOSIS Document Express. ***Continues*** *Reports of the National Museum of Victoria.*
**Ind/Abst** Biol. Abstr. (1984-); Fish Rev. (Jan. 1989-July 1992); Wildl. Rev. (Jan. 1989-July 1992).

CN/0068-1636
**OCCASIONAL PAPERS OF THE BRITISH COLUMBIA PROVINCIAL MUSEUM. Main/Corp** British Columbia Provincial Museum. Began publication 1939?. Monographic series. English. ir. Price varies per volume. British Columbia Provincial Museum, 601 Belleville Street, Victoria British Columbia V8W 1A1 Canada. **Tel** (604)384-4425, FAX (604)356-8197. **(Subscription address:** Royal Museum Shop, 675 Belleville Street, Victoria British Columbia V8W 1A1 Canada**)**

US/0196-7703
**OCCASIONAL PAPERS OF THE IDAHO MUSEUM OF NATURAL HISTORY. See** Museums and Galleries.

US/0091-7958
**OCCASIONAL PAPERS OF THE MUSEUM OF NATURAL HISTORY (LAWRENCE).** (OCCASIONAL PAPERS OF THE MUSEUM OF NATURAL HISTORY, THE UNIVERSITY OF KANSAS.). [Occas. pap. Mus. Nat. Hist.]. **Added/Corp** University of Kansas. Museum of Natural History. **VFOAT** Occasional Papers of the Museum of Natural History, University of Kansas. No. 1 (Apr. 29, 1971)-. Monographic series. English. ir. Price varies per volume. Museum of Natural History, University of Kansas, 602 Dyche Hall, Lawrence KS 66045-2454. **Tel** (913)864-4540. **ED** Joseph T. Collins. **LC** QH1; .O28. **DD** 574/.05. **CODEN** OPMNAK. **Circ:** 1,500. Documents available from BIOSIS Document Express. ***Continues***

*University of Kansas. Museum of Natural History. University of Kansas Publications, Museum of Natural History, 0075-5036.*
**Desc:** Scientific information from research.
**Ind/Abst** AGRICOLA [Select. Cov.]; Biol. Abstr.; Fish Rev. (Jan. 1989-July 1992); GeoRef; Wildl. Rev. (Jan. 1989-July 1992).

US/0076-8413
**OCCASIONAL PAPERS OF THE MUSEUM OF ZOOLOGY, UNIVERSITY OF MICHIGAN.** See Zoology.

PL/0078-3250
**OCHRONA PRZYRODY.** [ochr. przyr.]. No. 1 (1920)-. Monographic series. Polish. Price varies per volume. **LC** QH75; .P6. **CODEN** OCPZAE. Documents available from BIOSIS Document Express.
**Ind/Abst** Biol. Abstr.; Wildl. Rev.

RM/0253-1879
**OCROTIREA NATURII SI A MEDIULUI INCONJURATOR.** [Ocrotirea nat. mediu. inconj.]. **VFOAT** Ocrotirea Mediului Inconjurator, Natura, Terra. Vol. 19 (1975)-. Periodical. Romanian (English, French and German; summaries and/or abstracts in English, French and German). sa. DM162.00. **(Subscription address:** Kubon & Sagner, ABT Zeitschriftenimport, D 80328 Munich Germany.**)** **LC** QH7; .O33. ***Continues*** *Ocrotirea Naturii, 0029-8263.*
**Desc:** Studies on natural history and natural monuments.
**Ind/Abst** Ecol. Abstr. (?-?); Fish Rev. (Jan. 1989-July 1992); Geogr. Abstr. Phys. Geogr. (?-?); Geogr. Abstr. Human Geogr. (?-?); GeoRef; Wildl. Rev. (Jan. 1989-July 1992).

XR/0474-2559
**OPERA CORCONTICA.** **VFOAT** Krkonosske Prace. Vol. 1 (1964)-. Multiple languages (Czech). an. **(Subscription address:** Artia Pegas Press Ltd., Palac Metro Narodni Trida 25, 11210 Prague 1 Czech Republic.**)** **LC** QH178.C8.

US/1058-3130
**ORION (NEW YORK, N.Y.).** (ORION.). [Orion]. **Added/Corp** Myrin Institute. Conservation International. **VFOAT** People and Nature; Orion Nature Quarterly. Vol. 10, No. 1 (Winter 1991)-. Periodical. English. qt. $20.00 (one year), $36.00 (two year), $50.00 (three year). Myrin Institute, 136 East 64th Street, New York NY 10021. **Tel** (212)758-6475, FAX (212)758-6784. **ED** R. Emerson Blake. **LC** QH1; .O714. **DD** 574/.05. **Bk Rev. Circ:** 11,000 (ctrl). ***Continues*** *Orion Nature Quarterly, 0732-0876.*
**Desc:** Focuses on the relationship between nature and human culture. Its focus is global and includes nature essays, conservation reporting, interviews, fiction.
**Ind/Abst** Biol. Dig.; Environ. Period. Bibliogr.; Garden Lit. (1992-).

CN/0710-4847
**OSPREY.** (THE OSPREY.). [Osprey]. **Added/Corp** Newfoundland Natural History Society. (1970)-. Periodical. English. Four times a year. 15.00Can$. Natural History Society of Newfoundland & Labrador, PO Box 1013, St John's Newfoundland A1C 5M3 Canada. **DD** 574/.09718.
**Ind/Abst** Fish Rev.; Key Word Index Wildl. Res.; Wildl. Rev.

NO/0030-6703
**OTTAR.** [Ottar]. **Added/Corp** Troms Museum. No. 1 (June 1954)-. Monographic series. Norwegian (Lapp). ir. Price varies per volume. Progek Prospar, Box 31003, S 400-32 Goteborg Sweden. **Tel** 011 46 31 243425. **ED** Helge A. Wold and Arne C. Milssen. **LC** DL401; .O75. **CODEN** OTTADD. Index available. **Bk Rev. Ad Acc.** ctrl circ.
**Desc:** Popular science on cultural and natural history of Northern Norway.
**Ind/Abst** Art Archaeol. Tech. Abstr.; GeoRef.

US/0021-3314
**OUTDOOR AMERICA (1971).** (OUTDOOR AMERICA.). [Outdoor Am.]. **Added/Corp** Izaak Walton League of America. Vol. 36, No. 7 (July 1971)-. Periodical. English. Four times a year (Jan., Mar., July, Oct.). $20.00. Izaak Walton League of America, 1401 Wilson Boulevard, Level B, Arlington VA 22209. **Tel** (703)528-1818, FAX (703)528-1836. **ED** Michael E. Diegel (phone: (703)528-1818). **LC** SK1; .O653. **DD** 799/.0973. **Ad Acc. Circ:** 55,000. Documents available from Documents on Demand. ***Continues*** *Izaak Walton Magazine.*
**Desc:** This magazine is seeking queries and ideas that could be used. Focusing on some aspect of hunting, fishing, camping and similar pursuits that appeals to our readers.
**Ind/Abst** Environ. Abstr.; SportSearch.

US/0030-8641
**PACIFIC DISCOVERY.** See Science and Technology.

CC
**PEI-CHING TZU JAN PO WU KUAN YEN CHIU PAO KAO.** **VFOAT** Memoirs of Beijing Natural History Museum; Memoirs of Peking Natural History Museum. Began in 1979. Monographic series. Chinese (summaries and/or abstracts in English). ir. Price varies per volume. Peking Natural History Museum, 126 Tien Chiao Street, Beijing, People's Republic of China. **LC** QA7; .P24. **DD** 508/.05.

US/0164-7822
**PENNSYLVANIA NATURALIST, THE.** V. 1- Oct./Nov. 1978-. Periodical. English. bm. $6.50. Shafer Publishing Company, Box 47, Huntingdon PA 16652.

MY
**PERHILITAN.** See Zoology.

SP
**PERIPLO.** **Added/Corp** INCAFO. (19??)-. Periodical. Spanish (summaries and/or abstracts in English). bm. 2750ptas. Instituto de la Caza Fotografica y Ciencias de la Naturaleza / INCAFO, Castello 59, 28001 Madrid, Spain. **Tel** (91)431 34 60. **ED** Luis Blas Aritio. **LC** QH7; .P32.
**Desc:** Information on natural history and natural photography.

US
**PETROGLYPH.** **Added/Corp** Utah State University. English Dept. (198?)-. Periodical. English. sa. $8.00. Utah State University / English Department, Logan UT 84322-3200. **Tel** (801)797-1603, FAX (801)797-4099.
**Ind/Abst** Am. Humanit. Index (199?-).

CN/0225-7114
**PICA.** [Pica]. **Added/Corp** Calgary Field Naturalists' Society. Vol. 1 (Fall 1979)-. Periodical. English. qt (4 issues). Comes with Calgary Field Naturalists Society membership. Calgary Field Naturalists' Society, PO Box 981, Calgary Alberta T2P 2K4 Canada. **Tel** (403)246-2028. **ED** Luke Dewit. **DD** 509.7123. **Bk Rev. Circ:** 300 (ctrl). ***Supersedes Calgary Field Naturalist, 0318-8434.***

●US/1065-285X
**PONY EXPRESS (GAINESVILLE, FLA.).** (PONY EXPRESS : FLORIDA FOSSIL HORSE NEWSLETTER.). [Pony express]. **Added/Corp** Florida Museum of Natural History. Vol. 1, No. 2 (2nd Quarter, June 1992)-. Newsletter. English. qt. $20.00 (institutions). Pony Express, Florida Museum of Natural History, University of Florida, Gainesville FL 32611. **DD** 569. ***Continues*** *Florida Fossil Horse Newsletter.*

US/0079-4295
**POSTILLA.** (POSTILLA / YALE PEABODY MUSEUM OF NATURAL HISTORY.). [Postilla]. **Added/Corp** Peabody Museum of Natural History. No. 1 (March 10, 1950)-. Monographic series. English. ir. Price varies per volume. Peabody Museum of Natural History, Yale University, 170 Whitney Avenue, PO Box 666, New Haven CT 06511-8161. **Tel** (203)432-3786, FAX (203)432-9816. **ED** John H. Ostrom. **LC** QH1; .P934. **DD** 574/.05. **CODEN** PSTLAD. cum. index. **Circ:** 450. Documents available from BIOSIS Document Express.
**Desc:** Publishes scientific papers of research in the fields of study encompassed by the Yale Peabody Museum of Natural History: paleontology, evolutionary biology and other aspects of biology, geology and archaeology.
**Ind/Abst** Biol. Abstr.; GeoRef; Life Sci. Collect.

US/0091-0376
**PRAIRIE NATURALIST, THE.** [Prairie nat.]. **Added/Corp** North Dakota Natural Science Society. Vol. 1, (March 1968)-. Periodical. English. Four times a year (Mar., June, Sept., Dec.). $20.00. North Dakota Natural Science Society, PO Box 9019, University Station, Grand Forks ND 58202. **Tel** (701)777-2199, FAX (701)777-2623. **ED** Paul B. Kannowski. **LC** QH540; .P7. **DD** 574.9/784. **CODEN** PRNTBZ. Index Available published separately, bound from publisher, free-automatically sent (4th iss.). cum. index. **Bk Rev**, (Qty: 6-10). **Pr Rev. Circ:** 460 (ctrl). Documents available from BIOSIS Document Express.
**Desc:** Journal for the communication of research on the North American grasslands and their biota.
**Ind/Abst** Agrofor. Abstr. (1991-); Biol. Abstr.; Fish Rev.; For. Abstr.; Grasslands For. Abstr.; Key Word Index Wildl. Res.; Rev. Agric. Entomol.; Weed Abstr.; Wildl. Rev.

GW/0032-6542
**PRAPARATOR.** See Museums and Galleries.

XR
**PRIRODOVEDNE PRACE USTAVU AKADEMIE VED CESKE REPUBLIKY V BRNE.** (19??)-. Czech (English and German; summaries and/or abstracts in Russian and English). ir. Academia, Publishing House of the Czechoslovak Academy of Sciences, Czech AC SCI, Vodickova 40, PO Box 896, 112 29 Prague 1, Czech Republic. **Tel** 011 42 2 245117. **(Subscription address:** Artia Pegas Press Ltd., Palac Metro Narodni Trida 25, 11210 Prague 1 Czech Republic.**)** ***Continues*** *Prirodovedne Prace Ustavu Ceskoslovenske Akademie Ved V Brne, 0032-8758.*

RU/0555-2648
**PROBLEMY ARKTIKI I ANTARKTIKI.** [Prob. Arktiki i Antarktiki]. **Added/Corp** Arkticheskii i Antarkticheskii Nauchno-Issledovatelskii Institut (Leningrad, R.S.F.S.R.). (1959)-. Russian. **LC** G575; .L422. **DD** 998/.005. **CODEN** PBAAA4. Documents available from CASDDS.
**Ind/Abst** Chem. Abstr. (1959-1981); GeoRef; Int. Aerosp. Abstr.

UK/0070-7112
**PROCEEDINGS - DORSET NATURAL HISTORY AND ARCHAEOLOGICAL SOCIETY.** **Main/Corp** Dorset Natural History and Archaeological Society. **Added/Corp** Dorset Natural History and Antiquarian Field Club. Proceedings - Dorset Natural History and Antiquarian Field Club. Vol. 1, (1877)-. English. an. £15.00. Dorset Natural History and Archaeological Society, Dorset County Museum, High W. Street, Dorchester DT1 1XA England. **Tel** 011 44 71 305 262735. **LC** DA670.D69; D6. cum. index.
**Desc:** List of members in each volume.
**Ind/Abst** BHA : Biblio. Hist. Art; Br. Archaeol. Bibliogr.; Br. Humanit. Index; Numis. Lit.

UK
**PROCEEDINGS - ISLE OF MAN NATURAL HISTORY AND ANTIQUARIAN SOCIETY.** **Main/Corp** Isle of Man Natural History and Antiquarian Society. V. 1- Aug. 23, 1906-. Proceedings. English. be. ***Continues*** *Isle of Man Natural History and Antiquarian Society. Journal.*

US/0097-3157
**PROCEEDINGS OF THE ACADEMY OF NATURAL SCIENCES OF PHILADELPHIA.** [Proc. Acad. Nat. Sci. Philadelphia]. **Main/Corp** Academy of Natural Sciences of Philadelphia. Vol. 1 (1841)-. English. an (Nov.). $30.00. Academy of Natural Sciences, 1900 Benjamin Franklin Parkway, Philadelphia PA 19103. **Tel** (215)299-1130, FAX (215)299-1028. **ED** William F. Smith-Vaniz. **LC** QH1; .A2. **CODEN** PANPA5. **Bk Rev. Pr Rev. Circ:** 1,200 (ctrl). Documents available from The Genuine Article, BIOSIS Document Express, CASDDS.
**Desc:** Original research articles on evolution, systematics, ecology, biogeography, and natural history.
**Ind/Abst** AGRICOLA [Select. Cov.]; Anim. Breed. Abstr.; Biol. Abstr.; Chem. Abstr.; Curr. Aware. Biol. Sci., CABS; Curr. Contents, Agric. Biol. Environ. Sci.; Fish Rev. (Jan. 1989-July 1992); GeoRef; Helminthol. Abstr. (1991-); Life Sci. Collect.; Res. Alert [Full Cov.]; Sci. Cit. Index; SCISEARCH; Wildl. Rev. (Jan. 1989-July 1992).

AT/0370-047X
**PROCEEDINGS OF THE LINNEAN SOCIETY OF NEW SOUTH WALES.** [Proc. Linn. Soc. N.S.W.]. **Main/Corp** Linnean Society of New South Wales. Vol. 1 (1875)-. English. ir. 65.00Aus$. Linnean Society of New South Wales, 6/24 Cliff Street, PO Box 457, Milsons Point New South Wales 2061 Australia. **Tel** 011 61 929-0253. **ED** J. R. Merrick. **CODEN** PLSWAQ. Index available. cum. index. **Pr Rev. Circ:** 800. Documents available from BIOSIS Document Express, CASDDS.
**Desc:** Original research in natural history.
**Ind/Abst** AGRICOLA [Select. Cov.]; Biol. Abstr.; Chem. Abstr.; Coal Abstr.; For. Abstr.; Life Sci. Collect.; Rev. Med. Vet. Entomol.; Soils Fert.

US/0079-0745
**PROCEEDINGS OF THE PEORIA ACADEMY OF SCIENCE.** [Proc., Peoria Acad. Sci.]. Began in 1968. Proceedings. English. an. Lakeview Museum of Arts and Sciences, 1125 West Lake Avenue, Peoria IL 61614. **LC** QH105.I3; P76. **DD** 508. **CODEN** PPASDN.

UK/0269-7270
**PROCEEDINGS OF THE ROYAL SOCIETY OF EDINBURGH. SECTION B, BIOLOGICAL SCIENCES.** ***Ceased.*** See Biology.

US/1059-8707
**PROCEEDINGS OF THE SAN DIEGO SOCIETY OF NATURAL HISTORY.** [Proc. S. Diego Soc. Nat. Hist.]. **Added/Corp** San Diego Society of Natural History. No. 1, July 1 (1990)-. Proceedings. English (summaries and/or abstracts in Spanish). ir. Price varies per volume. San Diego Society of Natural History, San Diego Natural History Museum Library, PO Box 1390, San Diego CA 92112. **Tel** (619)232-3821, FAX (619)232-0248. **ED** Philip Unitt. **DD** 508. **CODEN** PSDHER. **Pr Rev. Circ:** 400. ***Formed by the union of*** *Transactions of the San Diego Society of Natural History, 0080-5947* ***and*** *Memoirs of the San Diego Society of*

*Natural History, 0080-5920.*
**Desc:** Original research in botany, paleontology, mammalogy, ornithology, herpetology, marine invertebrates and entomology.
**Ind/Abst** Ecol. Abstr.

US/0511-9456
**PROCEEDINGS - WILDERNESS CONFERENCE.** **Main/Conf** Wilderness Conference. **Added/Corp** Sierra Club. Proceedings. English. be. Price varies per volume. Sierra Club / San Francisco, 730 Polk Street, San Francisco CA 94109. **Tel** (415)776-2211. **LC** QH75; .W5. **DD** 333.7; 574.9.

US
**PROGRESS REPORT - ARKANSAS NATURAL HERITAGE COMMISSION.**
**Main/Corp** Arkansas Natural Heritage Commission. English. Arkansas Natural Heritage Commission, Continental Building/Suite 500, Main and Markham, Little Rock AR 72201. **LC** QH76.5.A6; A74B. **DD** 333.78/2/09767.

PL/0552-430X
**PRZYRODA POLSKA.** [Przyr. pol.]. **Added/Corp** Liga Ochrony Przyrody. (1957)-. Periodical. Polish (summaries and/or abstracts in English and French). mo. $33.00. **(Subscription address:** ARS Polona, PO Box 1001, 00068 Warsaw Poland.**)** **LC** QH7; .P8.
**Ind/Abst** Energy Res. Abstr. (Oct. 1982-).

IT/0428-2396
**PUBBLICAZIONI - FERRARA. CIVICO MUSEO DE STORIA NATURALE.**
**Main/Corp** Ferrara. Civico Museo de Storia Naturale. 1-1952-). Periodical. Italian. Civico Museo de Storia Naturale, Ferrara 50122 Italy.

IT
**QUADERNI DEL MUSEO DI STORIA NATURALE DI LIVORNO (1982).**
(QUADERNI DEL MUSEO DI STORIA NATURALE DI LIVORNO.). **Added/Corp** Museo di Storia Naturale di Livorno. Vol. 3 (1982)-. Italian (summaries and/or abstracts in English). an. Museo Prov. Storia Naturale, Via Roma 234, 50127 Livorno Italy. **Tel** 011 39 586 802294. ***Continues*** *Quaderni di Storia Naturale.*

AT/0079-8843
**QUEENSLAND NATURALIST.** [Queensl. nat.]. **Added/Corp** Queensland Naturalists' Club. Vol. 1 (March 31, 1908)-. Periodical. English. ir (2 to 3 per year). Queensland Naturalists Club, GPO Box 5663, West End Queensland 4101 Australia. **Tel** 011 61 7 3434361. **ED** J. Cribb. **CODEN** QLNAAE. Index available. **Circ:** 450 (ctrl). Documents available from BIOSIS Document Express.
**Desc:** Reports on the activities of the Queensland Naturalists Club and the scientific findings of these natural history activities.
**Ind/Abst** AGRICOLA; Biol. Abstr.; Fish Rev.; GeoRef; Rev. Med. Vet. Entomol.; Wildl. Rev.

US/1059-4566
**QUEST (WASHINGTON, D.C. 1991).**
(QUEST.). [Quest]. **Added/Corp** National Museum of Natural History (U.S.). **VFOAT** Natural History Quest. Vol. 1, No. 1 (Nov. 1991)-. Periodical. English. bm. $20.00. National Museum of Natural History, Smithsonian Institution, Washington DC 20560. **DD** 508.
**Ind/Abst** Annu. Bibliogr. Engl. Lang. Lit.

SW
**RADSRAPPORT.** **Main/Corp** Naturvetenskapliga Forskningsradet (Sweden). (19??)-. Swedish. ir. Naturvetenskapliga Forskningsradet, Swedish Natural Science Research Council, Wenner Gren Center, Box 6711, S-113 85 Stockholm Sweden. **Tel** (0)18 365566. **LC** QH51; .N295.

US/0738-6656
**RANGER RICK.** **See** Children and Youth Interests.

CN/0828-8739
**RANGER RICK (OTTAWA).** (RANGER RICK / CANADIAN WILDLIFE FEDERATION.). [Ranger Rick]. **Added/Corp** Canadian Wildlife Federation. Vol. 18 No. 3 (March 1984)-. Periodical. English. mo. 25.00Can$. Canadian Wildlife Federation, 2740 Queensview Drive, Ottawa Ontario K2B 1A2 Canada. **Tel** (800)563-9453, (613)721-2286. **DD** J591/.05. ***Separated from*** *Ranger Rick, 0738-6656.*
**Ind/Abst** Can. Period. Index.

US
**RANGER RICK'S NATURESCOPE.**
**Added/Corp** National Wildlife Federation. **VFOAT** Ranger Rick's Nature Scope; Nature Scope. Vol. 1, No. 1 (1986)-. English. ir. Price varies per volume. National Wildlife Federation / Virginia, 8925 Leesburg Pike, Vienna VA 22184. **Tel** (703)790-4000, (800)822-9919, FAX (703)442-7332. **LC** WMLC L 83/4136.

AT/0312-3162
**RECORDS OF THE WESTERN AUSTRALIAN MUSEUM.** [Rec. West. Aust. Mus.]. **Main/Corp** Western Australian Museum. V. 3-1974-. English. ir. 5.00Aus$. Western Australian Museum, Francis Street, Perth Western Australia 6000 Australia. **Tel** (09)328 4411, FAX (09)328 8686. **LC** QH1; .W7848A. **DD** 500.9/941. **CODEN** REMUDY. **Circ:** 400 (ctrl). available on diskette. Documents available from BIOSIS Document Express.
**Desc:** Reviews, observations and results of research into all branches of natural science and human studies. Short communications accommodate observations, results and new records of significance.
**Ind/Abst** Biol. Abstr.; Ethnoarts Index.

BL
**RELATORIO - FUNDACAO ZOOBOTANICA DO RIO GRANDE DO SUL.** **Main/Corp** Fundacao Zoobotanica do Rio Grande do Sul. Portuguese. Fundacao Zoobotanica Do Rio Grande Do Sul, Rua Salvador Franca, 1427 Y Botanico, 90610 Porto Alegre RS Brazil. **LC** QH117; .F8A.

UK/0524-6474
**REPORT ON THE BRITISH MUSEUM (NATURAL HISTORY).** [Rep. Br. Mus. Nat. Hist.]. **Main/Corp** British Museum (Natural History). (1965)-. English. ir (Published every 3 year). British Museum of Natural History, Cromwell Road, London SW7 5BD England. **Tel** 011 44 71 9389123. **LC** QH70.G72; L6533a. **DD** 508/.074/421. **NLM** W1 BR716. ***Continues*** *Report - British Museum and British Museum (Natural History).*
**Ind/Abst** GeoRef.

FI/0453-7831
**REPORTS FROM THE KEVO SUBARCTIC RESEARCH STATION.** [Rep. Kevo Sbarct. Res. Stat.]. **Main/Corp** Lapin Tutkimusasema Kevo. (1964)-. Monographic series. English. ir. Price varies per volume. University of Turku, Kevo Subarctic Research Institute, SF 20500 Turku Finland. **Tel** 011 358 21 6335913. **LC** AS262.T84; A28 subser. Documents available from The Genuine Article.
**Ind/Abst** Curr. Contents, Agric. Biol. Environ. Sci.; Ecol. Abstr.; For. Abstr.; Geogr. Abstr. Phys. Geogr.; Life Sci. Collect.; Res. Alert [Select. Cov.]; Rev. Agric. Entomol.; Rev. Plant Pathol.

US/1056-800X
**RESEARCH & EXPLORATION.** (RESEARCH & EXPLORATION : A SCHOLARLY PUBLICATION OF THE NATIONAL GEOGRAPHIC SOCIETY.). [Res. explor.]. **Added/Corp** National Geographic Society (U.S.). **VFOAT** Research and Exploration; National Geographic Research and Exploration; National Geographic Research & Exploration. Vol. 7, No. 1 (Winter 1991)-. Periodical. English. qt. $50.00 (institutions), $40.00 (individuals) US; $56.00 (institutions), $46.00 (individuals) other. National Geographic Society, 11555 Darnestown, Gaithersburg MD 20878. **Tel** (202)857-7000, (800)638-4077, FAX (202)429-5727, telex 64194 NATGEO. **ED** Dr. Anthony de Souza. **LC** QH1; .N113. **DD** 508/.05. **CODEN** REXPE7. available on microfilm and microfiche from University Microfilms International (UMI). Documents available from The Genuine Article. ***Continues*** *National Geographic Research, 8755-724X.*
**Desc:** Interdisciplinary scholarly journal, ranging from anthropology and archaeology to ecology and zoology. Scientists, students, scholars, and well-informed laypeople are the audience. Color graphics support scientific text.
**Ind/Abst** Abstr. Anthropol.; Anim. Behav. Abstr.; Curr. Aware. Biol. Sci., CABS; Curr. Contents, Agric. Biol. Environ. Sci.; Curr. Primate Ref.; Ecol. Abstr.; Ecology Abstr.; Entomol. Abstr.; Fish Rev. (Jan. 1989-July 1992); Gen. Sci. Index; Genet. Abstr.; Geogr. Abstr. Human Geogr.; GeoRef; Ocean. Abstr.; Res. Alert [Full Cov.]; Sci. Cit. Index; SCISEARCH; Soc. Sci. Cit. Index [Select. Cov.]; Wildl. Rev. (Jan. 1989-July 1992).

ZA
**RESEARCH NOTES (LIVINGSTONE MUSEUM).** **See** Museums and Galleries.

CL/0716-078X
**REVISTA CHILENA DE HISTORIA NATURAL (VALPARAISO, CHILE : 1983).** (REVISTA CHILENA DE HISTORIA NATURAL.). [Rev. chil. hist. nat.]. Periodical. Spanish (English). sa. Sociedad de Biologia de Chile, Casilla 16164, Santiago 9 Chile. **Tel** 2713891, FAX (562)496729. Documents available from The Genuine Article. ***Continues*** *Revista Chilena de Historia Natural Pura y Aplicada.*
**Ind/Abst** Curr. Contents, Agric. Biol. Environ. Sci.; Res. Alert [Select. Cov.].

AG/0076-6380
**REVISTA DE LA JUNTA DE ESTUDIOS HISTORICOS DE MENDOZA.** (REVISTA.). [Rev. Junta estud. hist. Mendoza]. **Main/Corp** Junta de Estudios Historicos de Mendoza. (1934)-. Spanish. **LC** F2911; .J85.
**Ind/Abst** Am. Hist. Life (1972).

BO
**REVISTA DE LA SOCIEDAD BOLIVIANA DE HISTORIA NATURAL.** **Main/Corp** Sociedad Boliviana de Historia Natural. Yearly V. 1- Feb. 1974-. Spanish (summaries and/or abstracts in English). Sociedad Boliviana de Historia Natural, Casilla de Correo 538, Cochabamba Bolivia. **LC** QH115; .S6A.

BE/0375-1465
**REVUE VERVIETOISE D'HISTOIRE NATURELLE.** [Rev. vervietoise hist. nat.]. (1949)-. Periodical. French. Four times a year. 300.00F Belgium; 400.00F others. M L Philippe, Rue de Jehanster 89 B, 4800 Verviers Belgium. **Ad Acc.** **Circ:** 300.
**Ind/Abst** GeoRef.

MY
**SABAH MUSEUM AND ARCHIVES JOURNAL.** **Added/Corp** Sabah. Sabah Museum and State Archives Dept. **VFOAT** Sabah Museum and State Archives Journal. Vol. 1, No. 1 (Dec. 1986)-. Periodical. English. an. Sabah Museum and State Archives Department, Jalan Muzium, 88000 Kota Kinabalu Sabah Malaysia. **LC** DS597.33; .S34. **DD** 959.5/3/005. **Circ:** 1,000.

US/0272-8966
**SANCTUARY (LINCOLN, MASS.).**
(SANCTUARY.). [Sanctuary]. **Added/Corp** Massachusetts Audubon Society. Vol. 20 (Aug./Sept. 1980)-. Periodical. English. Six times a year. $50.00. Massachusetts Audubon Society, South Great Road, Lincoln MA 01773. **Tel** (617)259-9500, FAX (617)259-8899. **LC** QH76.5.N45; S25. **DD** 333.73/005. ***Continues*** *Massachusetts Audubon (Lincoln, Mass : 1974), 0887-0225.*
**Ind/Abst** Fish Rev.; Wildl. Rev.

FI
**SAVON LUONTO.** Periodical. Finnish. ir. 15. Kupion Luonnon Ystavain Yhdistys, Kupion Museo Luonnontieteen Osato, Kauppak 23, 70100 Kuopio 10 Finland. **LC** QH178.F5; S28.

XR
**SBORNIK NARODNIHO MUZEA V PRAZE. RADA B, PRIRODNI VEDY.**
**Added/Corp** Narodni Muzeum v Praze. **VFOAT** Prirodni Vedy; Acta Musei Nationalis Pragae. (1977)-. Periodical. Czech (English, German, Latin and Russian; summaries and/or abstracts in English). qt. $42.20. **(Subscription address:** Artia Pegas Press Ltd., Palac Metro Narodni Trida 25, 11210 Prague 1 Czech Republic.**)** **LC** QH7; .P65. **DD** 508/.05. ***Continues*** *Sbornik Narodniho Musea v Praze. Rada B, Prirodni Vedy.*
**Ind/Abst** Rev. Med. Vet. Entomol.

US/0076-0943
**SCIENCE SERIES (LOS ANGELES).**
(SCIENCE SERIES.). [Sci. ser.]. **Added/Corp** Natural History Museum of Los Angeles County. (Apr. 1930)-. Monographic series. English. ir. Price varies per volume. Natural History Museum / California, 900 Exposition Boulevard, Publishing Office, Los Angeles CA 90007. **Tel** (214)744-3330. **ED** Robin A. Simpson. **DD** 505. Index available. **Pr Rev.** **Circ:** 10,000.
**Desc:** Monographs and collections of papers on systematics.
**Ind/Abst** GeoRef.

●BL/0103-9016
**SCIENTIA AGRICOLA.** (1992)-. Periodical. Portuguese (summaries and/or abstracts in English). Twice a year. $45.00. Universidade de Sao Paulo / Piracicaba, Caixa Postal 9, CEP 13400, Piracicaba SP Brazil. **Tel** 011 55 11 194 330011. ***Continues*** *Anais da Escola Superior de Agricultura "Luiz de Queiroz".*

IT/0393-7917
**SCIENZA & VITA NUOVA.** (1979)-. Periodical. Italian. mo. L48000 Italy; L70000 other. Rusconi Editore Spa, Servicio Abbonements, V Le Sarca 235, 20126 Milan Italy. **Tel** 011 39 2 66192634. **UDC** 5.

CN/0227-793X
**SEASONS.** [Seasons]. **Added/Corp** Federation of Ontario Naturalists. Vol. 20, No. 1 (Spring 1980)-. Periodical. English. qt. 25.00Ca$ (libraries), 31.00Can$ (individual and government membership) Canada; 30.00Can$ (libraries), 36.00Can$ (individual and government membership) other. Federation of Ontario Naturalists, 355 Lesmill Road, Don Mills Ontario, M3B 2W8 Canada. **Tel** (416)444-8419, FAX (416)444-9866. **ED** Gail Muir (editor's phone: (416)652-6556). **DD** 574.9713. Index available. **Bk Rev.** **Ad Acc**, **Adv Mgr:** C Davidson, **Tel** (416)477-4297. **Circ:** 16,750. available on microfilm and microfiche from University Microfilms International (UMI). ***Continues*** *Ontario Naturalist, 0030-3046.*
**Desc:** Colorful, readable, insightful outdoors magazine designed to enhance your feeling and knowledge about

the natural world. Educational and filled with the latest facts and information about what's going on in the world from a conservationist's viewpoint, it balances incisive reporting and analysis with well-written articles on all aspects of nature and ecology.
**Ind/Abst** AQUAREF; Can. Environ.; Can. Index; Can. Period. Index.

GW/0037-2102
**SENCKENBERGIANA BIOLOGICA.** [Senckenberg. biol.]. **Added/Corp** Senckenbergische Naturforschende Gesellschaft. Vol. 35 (1954)-. Periodical. German (summaries and/or abstracts in English). ir (2 per year). DM98.00. Verlag Dr. Waldemar Kramer, Postfach 600445, D-60334 Frankfurt Germany. **Tel** 011 49 69 449045. **ED** Willi Ziegler. **LC** QH5; .S33. **DD** 574/.05. **CODEN** SBBOAG. Index available. cum. index. **Circ:** 750 (ctrl). Documents available from BIOSIS Document Express. ***Continues in part*** *Senckenbergiana.*
**Desc:** Papers on zoology and botany (morphology and taxonomy) with references to ecology and phylogeny.
**Ind/Abst** AGRICOLA; Aquat. Sci. Fish. Abstr. (Computer File); Biol. Abstr.; Ecol. Abstr.; Entomol. Abstr.; Fish Rev.; GeoRef; Ocean. Abstr.; Life Sci. Collect.; Rev. Agric. Entomol.; Rev. Med. Vet. Entomol.; Wildl. Rev.

UK/0267-3347
**SERIAL PUBLICATIONS IN THE BRITISH MUSEUM, NATURAL HISTORY LIBRARY ON MICROFICHE.** (SERIAL PUBLICATIONS IN THE BRITISH MUSEUM (NATURAL HISTORY) LIBRARY, ON MICROFICHE. MICROFORM.). [Ser. publ. Br. Mus. Nat. Hist. Libr. microfiche]. **Main/Corp** British Museum (Natural History). Dept. of Library Services. **VFOAT** List of Serial Publications in the British Museum (Natural History) Library; BMNH Serials. (Jan. 1985)-. Periodical. English. Twice a year. £25.00. British Museum of Natural History, Cromwell Road, London SW7 5BD England. **Tel** 011 44 71 9389123.

JA
**SHIZENSHI KENKYU. / OCCASIONAL PAPERS FROM THE OSAKA MUSEUM OF NATURAL HISTORY.** **Main/Corp** Osaka Shiritsu Shizen Kagaku Hakubutsukan. **Added/Corp** Osaka Shiritsu Shizen Kagaku Hakubutsukan. Occasional Papers. **VFOAT** Occasional Papers from the Osaka Museum of Natural History. Vol. 1 (1968)-. Periodical. Japanese. an. Osaka Museum of Natural History, 1-23 Nagai Koen, Higashisumiyoshiku, Osakashi, Osakafu 546 Japan.

GW/0433-8731
**SITZUNGS-BERICHTE DER GESELLSCHAFT NATURFORSCHENDER FREUNDE ZU BERLIN.** **Main/Corp** Gesellschaft Naturforschender Freunde (Berlin, Germany). (1839)-. Periodical. German (summaries and/or abstracts in English). Twice a year. DM80.00. Duncker und Humblot Verlag, Postfach 410329, D-12113 Berlin Germany. **Tel** 011 49 30 79000612, 011 49 30 79000613. **LC** QH5; .G4.

US/0270-2614
**SKENECTADA.** **Added/Corp** Pine Bush Historic Preservation Project. (1979)-. Periodical. English. an. Skenectada, PO Box 22820, 1400 Washington A, Albany NY 12222. **Tel** (518)482-9255. **LC** QH105.N7; S57. **DD** 508.747/42. **CODEN** SKNCD4. Documents available from BIOSIS Document Express.
**Ind/Abst** Biol. Abstr.

US/0037-7333
**SMITHSONIAN.** [Smithsonian]. **Added/Corp** Smithsonian Associates. Vol. 1 (April 1970)-. Periodical. English. mo. $22.00. Smithsonian Institution / Washington DC, 420 Lexington Avenue, Suite 1945, New York NY 10170. **Tel** (212)490-1840, (800)533-7901. **(Subscription address:** Neodata / Colorado, PO Box 2606, Boulder Boulder CO 80322.) **ED** Don Moser. **LC** AS30; .S6. **DD** 505. **CODEN** SMSNA5. **Bk Rev. Ad Acc. Circ:** 2,000,000. available on microfilm from Xerox; available on microfilm and microfiche from University Microfilms International (UMI); available on an online database (file 647/Full-Text) from DIALOG. Documents available from The Genuine Article, UMI Article Clearinghouse, Documents on Demand.
**Desc:** Illustrated, colorful magazine exploring the world of man and nature - past, present, and future.
**Ind/Abst** Abr. Read. Guide Period. Lit.; Abstr. Anthropol.; Acad. Abstr. Full Text Elite (Jan. 1984-) [Full Txt.]; Acad. Abstr. (Jan. 1984-); Acad. Ind. [Computer File] (1984-); Acad. Search (Jan. 1984-); AGRICOLA; Am. Hist. Life (1970-); Am. Bibliogr. Slavic East Europ. Stud.; Annu. Bibliogr. Engl. Lang. Lit.; Art Archaeol. Tech. Abstr.; ARTbibliogr. Mod.; Arts Humanit. Citation Index [Full Cov.]; Biol. Dig.; Book Rev. Digest; Book Rev. Index (1988-); Can. Index (?-?); Child. Lit. Abstr. (19??-); Curr. Contents Arts Humanit.; Environ. Abstr.; Expand. Acad. Index (1984-); Garden Lit. (1992-); Gen. Period. Index (1985-); GeoRef; Guide Soc. Sci. Relig.; Hist. Source (Jan. 1984-) [Full Txt.]; INFO-SOUTH Abstr.; Int. Aerosp. Abstr.; Mag. Artic. Summar. Elite (Jan. 1984-) [Full Txt.]; Mag. Artic. Summar. Select (Jan. 1984-) [Full Txt.]; Mag. Artic. Summar. CD-ROM (Jan. 1984-); Mag. Index Plus (1989-); Mag. Index Sel. Microfiche (1986-) [Full Txt.]; Mag. Index. Sel. (1986-); Mag. Search; Middle East Abstr. Index; Mid. Search (Jan. 1984-) [Full Txt.]; Newsp. Period. Abstr. (1986-); Ocean. Abstr.; Read. Guide Abstr. Select Ed.; Read. Guide Period. Lit.; Res. Alert [Full Cov.]; Resource/One Ondisc (1986-); Soc. Sci. Cit. Index [Select. Cov.]; Mag. Index (1977-); TOM Gen. Index (1985-) [Full Txt.]; Vocat. Search (Jan. 1984-) [Full Txt.]; West. Hist. Q.

US/0037-7473
**SNOWY EGRET.** Vol. 15 (Spring 1941)-. Periodical. English. Twice a year. $24.00. Snowy Egret, PO Box 9, Bowling Green IN 47833. **Tel** (812)819-1910. **ED** Karl Barnebey. cum. index. **Bk Rev. Circ:** 400. ***Continues*** *Animal World.*
**Desc:** Explores literary, artistic, and philosophic aspects of natural history. Fresh nature essays, poetry, fiction and reviews.

AT/0038-2965
**SOUTH AUSTRALIAN NATURALIST; THE JOURNAL OF THE FIELD NATURALISTS' SECTION OF THE ROYAL SOCIETY OF SOUTH AUSTRALIA.** [S. Aust. nat.]. **Added/Corp** Royal Society of South Australia. Field Naturalists' Section. (1919)-. Periodical. English. qt. 20.00Aus$ Australia; 30.00Aus$ other. Field Naturalist Society of South Australia Inc, GPO Box 1594M, Adelaide 5001 South Australia. **Tel** (08)339-4809. **ED** Russell Cook. **LC** QH1; .S675. **CODEN** SANAAR. **Bk Rev**, (Qty: 2-3). **Circ:** 350. Documents available from BIOSIS Document Express.
**Desc:** Natural history.
**Ind/Abst** AESIS Q.; AGRICOLA; Biol. Abstr.

FJ/1013-9877
**SOUTH PACIFIC JOURNAL OF NATURAL SCIENCE, THE.** [S. Pac. j. nat. sci.]. **Added/Corp** University of the South Pacific. School of Natural Resources. Vol. 1 (1980)-. Academic Scholarly Publication. English. sa. 5.00Fij$ institution. South Pacific Journal of Natural Science, University of South Pacific, School of Pure & Applied Sciences, PO Box 1168, Suva, Fiji Islands. **Tel** FAX 679-302-548, telex FJ2276. **CODEN** SPJSEY. Index available. cum. index. **Pr Rev. Circ:** 150 (ctrl). available on diskette. Documents available from BIOSIS Document Express.
**Desc:** Papers pertaining to the natural sciences in the South Pacific Island region.
**Ind/Abst** Biol. Abstr. (-1987); Trop. Dis. Bull.

US/0038-4909
**SOUTHWESTERN NATURALIST, THE.** (THE SOUTHWESTERN NATURALIST.). [Southwest. nat.]. **Added/Corp** Southwestern Association of Naturalists. Vol. 1 (Jan. 1956). Periodical. English (Spanish). qt. $35.00 (institutions), $25.00 (individuals) US; $40.00 (institutions), $30.00 (individuals) other. Southwest Texas State University / Biology Department, San Marcos TX 78666. **Tel** (512)245-7181, FAX (512)245-8095. **ED** Anthony Echelle. **LC** QH1; .S745. **CODEN** SWNAAB. Index available. cum. index. **Pr Rev. Circ:** 1,100. available on microfilm and microfiche from University Microfilms International (UMI). Documents available from The Genuine Article, BIOSIS Document Express.
**Desc:** Field studies of plants and animals, living and fossil, in the Southwestern United States, Mexico and Central America.
**Ind/Abst** AGRICOLA [Select. Cov.]; Agrofor. Abstr. (1991-); Biocont. News Inf. (19??-19??); Biol. Abstr.; Curr. Aware. Biol. Sci., CABS; Curr. Contents, Agric. Biol. Environ. Sci.; Curr. Ref. Fish Res.; Ecol. Abstr. (?-?); Fish Rev.; For. Abstr.; GeoRef; Grasslands For. Abstr.; Helminthol. Abstr. (19??-19??); Index Vet.; Key Word Index Wildl. Res.; Nucl. Sci. Abstr.; Nutr. Abstr. Rev., Ser. B, Live Feeds and Feed.; Life Sci. Collect.; Plant Genet. Resour. Abstr.; Protozoolog. Abstr.; Ref. Sources; Res. Alert [Select. Cov.]; Rev. Agric. Entomol.; Rev. Med. Vet. Entomol.; Seed Abstr.; Sel. Water Resour. Abstr.; Weed Abstr.; Wildl. Rev.

US/0145-9031
**SPECIAL PUBLICATION - CARNEGIE MUSEUM OF NATURAL HISTORY.** [Spec. publ. - Carnegie Mus. Nat. Hist.]. **Added/Corp** Carnegie Museum of Natural History. **VFOAT** Special Publication of Carnegie Museum of Natural History. No. 1 (1975)-. Monographic series. English. ir. Price varies per volume. Carnegie Museum of Natural History, 4400 Forbes Avenue, Pittsburgh PA 15213. **Tel** (412)622-3315, FAX (412)622-8837. **ED** Leonard Krishtalka, C. J. McCoy, M. A. Schmidt. **LC** UNC. **CODEN** SPCHDX. **Pr Rev.** ctrl circ. Documents available from BIOSIS Document Express.
**Desc:** Original scientific publications in zoology, anthropology, botany, ecology, systematics, mineralogy, invertebrate and vertebrate paleontology, archaeology.
**Ind/Abst** Biol. Abstr.; GeoRef.

CN/0080-6552
**SPECIAL PUBLICATION - SASKATCHEWAN NATURAL HISTORY SOCIETY.** **Main/Corp** Saskatchewan Natural History Society. Vol. 1 (1958)-. Monographic series. English. ir (usually one every two years). Price varie per volume. Saskatchewan Natural History Society, Box 4348, Regina Saskatchewan S4P 3W6 Canada. **Tel** (306)780-9273. **ED** Mary Gilliland. **DD** 574; 574.9. **Circ:** 2,000 (ctrl).
**Desc:** Publications on the natural history of the prairie provinces of Canada.

CC/0490-6756
**SSU-CHUAN TA HSUEH HSUEH PAO. TZU JAN KO HSUEH PAN.** [Ssu-chuan ta hsueh hsueh pao. Tzu jan ko hsueh]. **Added/Corp** Ssu-Chuan Ta Hsueh. **VFOAT** Sichuan Daxue Xuebao; Journal of Sichuan University. Natural Science Edition. (1955)-. Periodical. Chinese (summaries and/or abstracts in English). qt. $4.00. Sichuan Daxue, Xuebao Bianjibu, Jiuyanqiao, Chengdu, Sichuan 610064, People's Republic of China. **Tel** 583875. **ED** L. Yingming. **LC** QH7; .S8876. **DD** 508/.05. **CODEN** SCTHAO. **Circ:** 2,100. Documents available from BIOSIS Document Express, CASDDS, BLDSC.
**Ind/Abst** Biol. Abstr. (1988-); Math. Rev.

US/0097-4412
**STUDIES IN NATURAL SCIENCES.** [Stud. nat. sci.]. Monographic series. English. ir. Price varies per volume. Eastern New Mexico University / Museum of Natural Science, Portales NM 88130. **LC** QH1; .S86. **DD** 500.9/05. **CODEN** SNTSBX. Documents available from BIOSIS Document Express.
**Ind/Abst** Biol. Abstr.

GW/0341-0161
**STUTTGARTER BEITRAEGE ZUR NATURKUNDE. SERIES C. ALLGEMEINVERSTAENDLICHE AUFSAETZE.** [Stuttg. Beitr. Naturkd., C]. No. 1 (1974)-. Monographic series. German. ir. Price varies per volume. Staaliches Museum Naturkunde, Rosenstein 1, D 70191 Stuttgart 1 Germany. **Tel** 011 49 7 1189360. **ED** Horst Janus (Editor's address: Hauptkonservator A. D., Rosenstein 1, 7000 Stuttgart 1 Germany). **CODEN** SBNAD3. **Ad Acc.** ctrl circ. Documents available from BIOSIS Document Express.
**Desc:** Special contributions in Natural History on a common base.
**Ind/Abst** Biol. Abstr.; GeoRef.

JA/0913-6800
**SUGADAIRA KOGEN JIKKEN SENTA KENKYU HOKOKU.** **VFOAT** Tsukuba Daigaku Sugadaira Kogen Jikken Senta Kenkyu Hokoku; Bulletin of the Sugadaira Montane Research Center, University Tsukuba. No. 8 (1987)-. Periodical. Japanese (English). Tsukuba Daigaku Sugadaira Kogen Jikken Senta, Showa 62, University of Tsukuba, Tokyo Japan. **LC** QH188. **CODEN** TSJHEX. ***Continues*** *Sugadaira Kogen Seibutsu Jikkenjo Kenkyu Hokoku.*
**Ind/Abst** CSA Neuro. Abstr. (?-?).

CC/0255-7800
**TA TZU JAN.** **Added/Corp** Chung-kuo Tzu Jan ko Hsueh po wu Kuan Hsieh Hui. Chung-kuo Huan Ching ko Hsueh Hsueh Hui. Pei-ching Tzu Jan po wu Kuan. **VFOAT** Nature. (19??)-. Periodical. Chinese. qt. $1.00 (per issue). Beijing Ziran Bowuguan / Beijing Natural History Museum, Daziran Zazhishe, 126 Tianqiao Nandajie, Beijing 100050 People's Republic of China. **Tel** 754431. **ED** J. Jianming. **LC** QH7; .T18. **DD** 508.

US/0892-6476
**TALON (AURORA, COLO.).** **See** Zoology.

NZ/0496-8026
**TANE.** [Tane]. **Added/Corp** Auckland University Field Club. (1950)-. English. an. 16.00NZ$. Auckland University Field Club, c/o Botany Department, University of Auckland, Private Bag, Auckland New Zealand. **Tel** 544-136. **ED** Anthony E Wright. **LC** QH197.5; .T3. **DD** 500.9/931. **Circ:** 500. Documents available from BIOSIS Document Express.
**Desc:** Natural history of Northern New Zealand especially offshore islands.
**Ind/Abst** Biol. Abstr.; Fish Rev. (Jan. 1989-July 1992); GeoRef; Life Sci. Collect. (-1984); Wildl. Rev. (Jan. 1989-July 1992).

AT
**TASMANIAN NATURALISTS, THE JOURNAL OF THE TASMANIAN FIELD NATURALISTS' CLUB, THE.** Vol. 1 (1907)-. English. an. 18.00Aus$ Australia; 20.00Aus$ other. Tasmanian Field Naturalists' Club, GPO Box 68A, Hobart Tasmania 7001 Australia. **Tel** 011 61 2 344293. **ED** Rob Taylor. Index available. cum. index. **Bk Rev**, (Qty: 2-8). **Circ:** 130.
**Desc:** Articles on Tasmanian natural history and articles relating to the conservation of Tasmania's natural history are published.
**Ind/Abst** Life Sci. Collect.

US/0040-0823
**TEBIWA.** [Tebiwa]. **Added/Corp** Idaho Museum of Natural History. No. 1 (Dec. 1, 1976)-. Academic Scholarly Publication. English. ir. Price varies per volume. Idaho Museum of Natural History, Campus Box 8096, Idaho State University, Pocatello ID 83209. **Tel** (208)236-3410, FAX (208)236-4000. **ED** Barry L. Keller

(editor's phone: (208)236-3168). **CODEN** TEBIDX. Index available. cum. index (Index by year only). **Circ:** 250. available on an online database, CD-ROM, magnetic tape, and microfilm from University Microfilms International (UMI). Documents available from CASDDS. ***Supersedes*** *Tebiwa, 0040-0823.*
**Desc:** Contains original papers in anthropology, archaeology, botany, geology, paleontology, zoology and museum methods, usually pertaining to subjects on the Intermountain West.
**Ind/Abst** Anthropol. Index; Chem. Abstr.; Ecol. Abstr. (?-?); Fish Rev. (Jan. 1989-July 1992); GeoRef; Wildl. Rev. (Jan. 1989-July 1992).

US
**TECHNICAL REPORT - STANFORD UNIVERSITY, NATURAL HISTORY MUSEUM.** **Main/Corp** Stanford University. Natural History Museum. **Added/Corp** United States. Office of Naval Research. Arctic Institute of North America. Monographic series. English. Price varies per volume.

US/0040-3733
**TERRA (LOS ANGELES, CALIF.).** ***Ceased.*** (TERRA.). [Terra]. Vol. 9, No. 2 (Fall 1970)-Vol.31, No. 4. Periodical. English. qt. Natural History Museum / California, 900 Exposition Boulevard, Publishing Office, Los Angeles CA 90007. **Tel** (214)744-3330. **ED** Kathy Talley-Jones. **LC** AM101; .L72222. **DD** 069. **CODEN** TRRAB8. Index available. cum. index. **Bk Rev. Ad Acc. Circ:** 22,000 (ctrl). ***Continues*** *Los Angeles County Museum of Natural History. Quarterly.*
**Desc:** Articles on natural history, anthropology and history for a general audience. Sent as a benefit of membership with the Natural History Museum of Los Angeles County.
**Ind/Abst** GeoRef.

FR
**TERRE SAUVAGE.** French. mo. 247.50F (libraries), 275.00 (individuals) France; $329.40 (libraries), $366.00 (individuals) other. Editions Nuit et Jour, 9 rue Christiani, 75018 Paris, France. **Tel** 011 31 1 49251818.

US/0882-5335
**TEXAS NATURAL HISTORY.** [Tex. nat. hist.]. Vol. 1, No. 1 (Spring 1985)-. Periodical. English. qt. $12.74 US; $16.98 other. Texas Natural History Magazine Inc., PO Box 226585, Dallas TX 75222-6585. **DD** 508.

CN/0041-0748
**TRAIL & LANDSCAPE.** **Added/Corp** Ottawa Field-Naturalists' Club. (March/April 1967)-. Periodical. English. Four times a year. 23.00Can$. Ottawa Field Naturalist Club Westgate, PO Box 35069, Ottawa Ontario K1Z 1A2 Canada. **Tel** (613)996-1665. **ED** E. Morton. Index available in last issue of volume--attached. cum. index. **Circ:** 950 (ctrl).
**Desc:** Natural history and conservation of the Ottawa region.
**Ind/Abst** Fish Rev.; Wildl. Rev.

UK/0144-221X
**TRANSACTIONS OF THE NATURAL HISTORY SOCIETY OF NORTHUMBRIA.** [Trans. Nat. Hist. Soc. Northumbria]. **Added/Corp** Natural History Society of Northumbria. (1974)-. Academic Scholarly Publication. English. an. price varies per volume. The Natural History Society of Northumbria, The Hancock Museum, Newcastle upon Tyne NE2 4PT England. **Tel** 011 44 91 2326386, telex TYNESIDE. **ED** R. B. Clark. **LC** QH1; .N34. **DD** 508.428/8. **CODEN** TNHND5. **Circ:** 700 (ctrl). Documents available from BIOSIS Document Express, CASDDS. ***Continues*** *Natural History Society of Northumberland, Durham, and Newcastle-Up on-Tyne. Transactions.*
**Desc:** Covers scientific papers related to the Northeast of England. Subject area covered include, geology, ornithology, botany, mammalogy, entomology and the history of natural history.
**Ind/Abst** Biol. Abstr.; Chem. Abstr.; Ecol. Abstr.; Geol. Abstr.; GeoRef; Life Sci. Collect.

SA/0035-919X
**TRANSACTIONS OF THE ROYAL SOCIETY OF SOUTH AFRICA.** **See** Science and Technology.

UK/0143-5175
**TRANSACTIONS OF THE SHROPSHIRE ARCHAEOLOGICAL AND HISTORICAL SOCIETY.** **See** Archaeology.

FR/0180-961X
**TRAUVUX SCIENTIFIQUES DU PARC NATIONAL DE LA VANOISE.** [Trav. sci. Parc natl. Vanoise]. **Main/Corp** France. Director Generale de la Protection de la Nature. Vol. 1- 1970-. French (summaries and/or abstracts in English, German and Italian). Director Generale de la Protection de la Nature, 15 rue du Docteur-Juliand, Chambery 73000 France. **LC** QH147; .F72A. **DD** 500.9/44/48.
**Ind/Abst** Life Sci. Collect.

RM/0301-9187
**TRAVAUX DE L'INSTITUT DE SPEOLOGIE EMILE RACOVITZA.** (TRAVAUX.). [Trav. Inst. speol. Emile Racovitza]. **Main/Corp** Institutul de Speologie "Emil Racovita.". (1970)-. French. an. DM137.00. **(Subscription address:** Kubon & Sagner, ABT Zeitschriftenimport, D 80328 Munich Germany.) **LC** QH89; .I57a. **DD** 591.9/09/44. **CODEN** TISPBT. Documents available from BIOSIS Document Express. ***Continues*** *Institutul de Speologie "Emil Racovita." Lucrarile Institutului de Speologie "Emil Racovita", 0567-6363.*
**Ind/Abst** Biol. Abstr. (1971-1989, 1991-).

CN/0704-1993
**TRAVAUX DES CAMPEUSES D'ETE AU CAMP ROLLAND-GERMAIN (1976).** ***Title Change.*** (TRAVAUX DES CAMPEUSES DE L'ETE AU CAMP ROLLAND-GERMAIN.). **Main/Corp** Camp Rolland-Germain. 1976-. French. an. Camp Rolland-Germain, Frelighsburg Quebec J0J 1C0 Canada. **DD** 500.9'714'62. ***Continues*** *Rapports des Campeuses, 0704-1977.* ***Continued by*** *Travaux des Stagiaires, Filles, 0709-8499.*

FR
**TRAVAUX ET ACQUISITIONS DU MUSEUM NATIONAL D'HISTOIRE NATURELLE.** **Main/Corp** Museum National d'Histoire Naturelle (France). (1977)-. Periodical. French. Museum Natl d Hist Naturelle, 38 rue Geoffroy Saint Hilaire, 75005 Paris France.

NE
**UITGAVEN VAN DE NATUURWETENSCHAPPELIJKE STUDIEKRING VOOR SURINAME EN DE NEDERLANDSE ANTILLEN. NATUURHISTORISCHE REEKS.** **VFOAT** Natural History Series. No. 1-. Monographic series. Dutch (English). Price varies per volume. Secretariat of the Foundation for Scientific Research in Surinam and the Netherlands Antilles, c/o Zoological Laboratory, Plompetorengracht 9, Utrehct Netherlands. **Tel** (0)30-392478. **ED** P Wagenaar Hummelinck and L J v d Steen. **LC** QH7; .N2842 subser. **Circ:** 1,000 (ctrl).
**Desc:** Publications on natural sciences (in widest sense) of Caribbean region, especially Netherlands Antilles and Surinam.

NE/0470-3995
**UITGAVEN VAN DE NATUURWETENSCHAPPELIJKE WERKGROEP NEDERLANDSE ANTILLEN.** **Main/Corp** Natuurwetenschappelijke Werkgroep Nederlandse Antillen. No. 1 (April 1951)-. Monographic series. Dutch (summaries and/or abstracts in English; table of contents in English). Price varies per volume. **CODEN** UNWNAK. Documents available from BIOSIS Document Express.
**Ind/Abst** Biol. Abstr. (-1976).

UK/0049-5891
**VASCULUM, THE.** Vol. 1 (June 1915)-. Periodical. English. qt. £6.00 UK; £6.20 Europe; £6.36 other. Northern Naturalists Union, c/o Sunderland Museum, Borough Road Sunderland, Tyne & Wear, Sri Ipp England. **Tel** 091 5141235. **ED** A. Coles and L. Jessop. **Bk Rev**, (Qty: 1-2). **Pr Rev. Circ:** 250.
**Desc:** Notes and records of local flora and fauna (natural history) of North-East England.

GW/0173-749X
**VERHANDLUNGEN DES NATURWISSENSCHAFTLICHEN VEREINS IN HAMBURG (1979).** (VERHANDLUNGEN DES NATURWISSENSCHAFTLICHEN VEREINS IN HAMBURG.). [Verh. naturwiss. Ver. Hamburg]. **Added/Corp** Naturwissenschaftlicher Verein in Hamburg. No. 23 (1979)-. German (summaries and/or abstracts in English). an. Naturwissenschaftlicher Verein in Hamburg Zoologischen Institut, Martin-Luther-King Platz 3, D 20146 Hamburg Germany. **LC** Q49; .H44. **DD** 508. Documents available from BIOSIS Document Express. ***Continues in part*** *Abhandlungen und Verhandlungen des Naturwissenschaftlichen Vereins in Hamburg, 0301-2697.*
**Ind/Abst** Biol. Abstr.; GeoRef.

US/0270-5982
**VERMONT NATURAL HISTORY.** [Vt. nat. hist.]. June 1973-. English. an. $15.00 US (membership includes quarterly newsletter and program calendar). Vermont Institute of Natural Sciences, Church Hill Road, Woodstock VT 05091. **Tel** (802)457-2779. **ED** Sarah B Laughlin. **Ad Acc. Circ:** 3,500 (ctrl).
**Desc:** Magazine devoted to the natural history of Vermont.

AU/0378-8202
**VEROFFENTLICHUNGEN AUS DEM NATURHISTORISCHEN MUSEUM WIEN.** [Veroff. Nat.hist. Mus.]. Monographic series. German. ir. Price varies per volume. Naturhistorisches Museum in Wien, Burgring 7, Vienna 1 Austria. **Tel** (043)0222934541254. **Circ:** 5,000 (ctrl).
**Desc:** Covers earth sciences, mineralogy, paleontology, geology, zoology, invertebrate and vertebrate. Anthropology, speleology, history of the natural history museum in Vienna, and Polar exploring expeditions.
**Ind/Abst** GeoRef.

GW/0342-684X
**VEROFFENTLICHUNGEN FUER NATURSCHUTZ UND LANDSCHAFTSPFLEGE IN BADEN-WURTTEMBERG.** [Veroff. naturschutz landschaftspflege Baden-Wurt.]. (1976)-. Periodical. German. ir. Landesanstalt fur Umweltschutz Baden Wurttemberg, Institut fur Okologie und Naturschutz, Postfach 210752, Bannwaldallee 32, 7500 Karlsruhe 21 Germany. **LC** QH77.G3; B35. **DD** 333.7/2/09434605. ***Continues*** *Veroffentlichungen der Landesstelle fur Naturschutz und Landschaftspflege Baden Wurttemberg.*
**Ind/Abst** AGRICOLA.

CN/0049-612X
**VICTORIA NATURALIST, THE.** **Added/Corp** Victoria Natural History Society (B.C.). Vol. 1, (1944)-. Periodical. English. Six times a year (Jan., Mar., May, July, Sept., Nov.). 15.00Can$ Canada; 17.00Can$ other. Victoria Natural History Society, PO Box 5220 Station B, Victoria BC V8R 6N4 Canada. **Tel** (604)361-1694. **ED** Warren Drinnan, (phone: (604)361-3543). Index available (Ten year indexes are available. $3.00 per copies). cum. index. **Bk Rev**, (Qty: 2). **Ad Acc. Pr Rev. Circ:** 800.
**Desc:** Newsletter for members. Articles on local plants, birds and field trips. Lists of first sightings of birds for seasons in the area. Also lists of field trips in the area. Includes reports and special articles.

AT/0042-5184
**VICTORIAN NATURALIST.** (THE VICTORIAN NATURALIST.). [Victorian nat.]. **Added/Corp** Field Naturalists Club of Victoria. Vol. 1 (Jan. 1884)-. Periodical. English. bm (6 issues). 50.00Aus$ Australia; $60.00 other. Field Naturalist Club of Victoria, National Herbarium, Birdwood Avenue, S Yarra Victoria, 3141 Australia. **Tel** 011 61 3 6508661. **ED** Robyn Watson, Ed Grey, & Pat Grey. **LC** QH1; .V55. **DD** 508.94. **CODEN** VICNAW. Index available. cum. index. **Bk Rev. Ad Acc. Pr Rev. Circ:** 800 (ctrl).
**Desc:** Club news and scientific articles on natural history.
**Ind/Abst** AGRICOLA; GeoRef; MLA Int. Bibl. Books Artic. Mod. Lang. Lit.; Wildl. Rev.

FR
**VIE DES BETES, LA.** (19??)-. Periodical. French. mo. 240.00F. Dawson France SA, BP 40, 91121 Palaiseau Cedex France. **Tel** 011 33 1 69104700, telex 220064F. **LC** QL1; 43. **DD** 591/.05. ***Continues*** *Betes et Nature.*
**Ind/Abst** Point Repere.

SP/0210-945X
**VIERAEA.** **Added/Corp** Universidad de La Laguna. Departamento de Botanica. **VFOAT** Folia Scientiarum Biologicarum Canariensium. (1970)-. Periodical. Spanish (English, French, German, Italian and Portuguese; summaries and/or abstracts in Spanish and English). an. 2500ptas Spain; $25.20 other. Museo Ciendas, APDO Corr 853, 38080 Sta Cruz Tenerife, Islas Canarias Spain. **Tel** 34 22 213633, FAX 22 212909. **LC** QH132.C3; V55. **DD** 508.64/9. ctrl circ.
**Desc:** Publishes original contributiuons in the fields of Botany, Zoology, and Ecology in the Macronesian Archipelagos.

US
**VIRGINIA MUSEUM OF NATURAL HISTORY MEMOIR.** **Added/Corp** Virginia Museum of Natural History. **VFOAT** Memoir. No. 1 (1990)-. Monographic series. English. Price varies per volume. **CODEN** VMNMEE.

JA
**VIVA ORIGINO.** **Added/Corp** Seimei no Kigen Oyobi Shinka Gakkai (Japan). (19??)-. Academic Scholarly Publication. Japanese (summaries and/or abstracts in English). Seimei No Kigen Oyobi Shinka Gakkai, c/o Kyoto Daigaku Genshiro Jikkenjo Noda, Kumatori-cho Sennan-gun, Osaka-fu 590-04 Japan. **LC** QH325; .V58. **DD** 577/.05. **CODEN** VIORE6. Documents available from CASDDS.
**Ind/Abst** Chem. Abstr.

TK
**VOPROSY GEOGRAFII TURKMENISTANA.** **Added/Corp** Turkmenskoe Geograficheskoe Obshchestvo. **VFOAT** Turkmenistanyng Geografiiasyng Meseleleri. (19??)-. Periodical. Russian. 1.15rub single issue. Izdatelstvo Ylym, Ulitsa Engelsa 6, 744000 Ashkhabad Turkmenistan. **Tel** 3632 9 04 84. **LC** QH191; .V663.

FR
**WAPITI.** French. mo. 293.83F France; 365.00F Europe; 435.00F other. Milan Presse/Serv Abonnement, 300 Rue Leon Joulin, 31101 Toulouse Cedex France. **Tel** 011 33 1 61766464, FAX 011 33 1 61766400.

AT/0508-4865
**WESTERN AUSTRALIAN NATURALIST, THE.** [West. Aust. nat.]. Vol. 1, (1947)-. Periodical. English. Four times a year. 40.00Aus$. Western Australian Naturalist Club, PO Box 156, Nedlands Western Australia 6009 Australia. **ED** John Dell. **CODEN** WAUNA9. Bound Index published separately, free upon request (free). **Circ:** 500. Documents available from BIOSIS Document Express.
**Desc:** Deals with all matters of natural history science in Western Australia; includes a section on field notes. Only such publication in Western Australia.
**Ind/Abst** Biol. Abstr.; Fish Rev.; Wildl. Rev.

NE
**WETENSCHAPPELIJKE MEDEDELINGEN KNNV.** [Wet. Meded. K.N.N.V. (K. Ned. Natuurhist. Ver.)]. **Main/Corp** Nederlandse Natuurhistorische Vereniging. **VFOAT** Wetenschappelijke Mededelingen van de Koninklijke Nederlandse Natuurhistorische Vereniging. No. 1 (1951)-. Dutch (summaries and/or abstracts in English).

CN/0830-8284
**WILDERNESS ALBERTA.** ***Title Change.*** **See** Environmental Issues-Conservation and Natural Resources.

UK/0262-6608
**WILTSHIRE ARCHAEOLOGICAL AND NATURAL HISTORY MAGAZINE (1982).** **See** Archaeology.

CC/1001-4276
**WUYI KEXUE.** (WU-I KO HSUEH.). [Wuyi kexue]. **VFOAT** Wuyi Science Journal. (1981)-. Periodical. Chinese (Latin; summaries and/or abstracts in English). **LC** QH7; .W9. **DD** 508. **CODEN** WUKEE8. Documents available from BIOSIS Document Express.
**Ind/Abst** Biol. Abstr. (1981-1986); For. Abstr.; Helminthol. Abstr. (1991-); Poult. Abstr.; Protozoolog. Abstr.; Rev. Agric. Entomol.

JA/0385-8766
**YAMANASHI DAIGAKU KYOIKU GAKUBU KENKYU HOKOKU. DAI 2 BUNSATSU, SHIZEN KAGAKU KEI.** **See** Science and Technology.

BW/0136-7595
**ZAPOVEDNIKI BELORUSSII / GOSUDARSTVENNOE ZAPOVEDNO-OKHOTNICHE KHOZIAISTVO BELOVEZHSKAIA PUSHCHA.** Began in 1977. Periodical. Russian. 0.80rub. Uradzhai / Harvest Publishing House, Masherova 11, 220600 Minsk Byelarus. **Tel** 0172 23-64-94. **LC** QH77.S626; Z35. **DD** 914.7/65.

XO
**ZBORNIK VYCHODOSLOVENSKEHO MUZEA V KOSICIACH. PIRIODNE VEDY.** **VFOAT** Prirodne Vedy; Acta Musei Slovaciae Regionis Orientalis Kosice. 20 (1979)-. Periodical. Slovak (summaries and/or abstracts in German and Russian). an. kcs15.00. **LC** QH178.C8; V9A. **DD** 508.437/3/05. ***Continues*** *Zbornik Vychodoslovenskeho Muzea V Kosiciach. Seria AB, Prirodne Vedy.*
**Ind/Abst** Ecol. Abstr.

XR/0044-4812
**ZIVA.** [Ziva]. V. 1 (1953)-. Periodical. Czech. bm. DM65.00. **(Subscription address:** Artia Pegas Press Ltd., Palac Metro Narodni Trida 25, 11210 Prague 1 Czech Republic.) Index Available, published separately, free-automatically sent.
**Ind/Abst** AGRICOLA.

## ABSTRACTING, BIBLIOGRAPHIES AND STATISTICS

UK/0268-9936
**ANNUAL BIBLIOGRAPHY OF THE HISTORY OF NATURAL HISTORY.** ***Ceased.*** (ANNUAL BIBLIOGRAPHY OF THE HISTORY OF NATURAL HISTORY / BRITISH NATURAL HISTORY MUSEUM.). [Annu. bibliogr. hist. nat. hist.]. **Added/Corp** British Museum (Natural History). Dept. of Library Services. Vol. 1 (1982)-(19??). Bibliography. English. ir. British Museum of Natural History, Cromwell Road, London SW7 5BD England. **Tel** 011 44 71 9389123.

UK
**NATURAL HISTORY BOOK REVIEWS.** ***Ceased.*** Vol. 1 (Jan. 1976)-(19??). English. ir. AB Academic Publishers, PO Box 42 Bicester, OXON OX6 7NW England. **Tel** 011 44 869 320949. **ED** Frank Brightman. **LC** QH1; .N137. **DD** 016.5009. Index available. **Bk Rev. Ad Acc.**
**Desc:** A critical international bibliographic review journal invaluable to all those involved in buying books in all fields of natural history.

US/0738-0925
**RECENT PUBLICATIONS IN NATURAL HISTORY.** [Recent publ. nat. hist.]. **VFOAT** R.P.I.N.H.; RPINH. Vol. 1, No. 1 (March 1983)-. Periodical. English. qt. $17.00 US and Canada; $20.00 other. American Museum of Natural History, Central Park West at 79th Street, New York NY 10024. **Tel** (212)769-5500, (800)234-5252, telex 910 240 8933 MICRO PRESS VQ. **ED** Priscilla Watson. **NLM** Z 7401; R295. **Bk Rev. Circ:** 300. ***Continues in part*** *Curator, 0011-3069.*
**Desc:** Bibliographies and reviews of recent books in the natural sciences (including astronomy and anthropology), classified into 25 subject headings with cross-references.

## NAVAL SCIENCE, NAVIGATION

FR/0531-0067
**ACTES - COLLOQUE INTERNATIONAL D'HISTOIRE MARITIME.** **Main/Conf** Colloque International d'Histoire Maritime. **VFOAT** Navire et l'Economie Maritime; Sources de l'Histoire Maritime en Europe, du Moyen Age au Xviiie Siecle; Aspects Internationaux de la Decouverte Oceanique Aux Xve et Xvie Siecles; Oceans Indien et Mediterranee. 1st- 1956-. Periodical. French. 1 rue des Fosses St Jacques, 75005 Paris France.

UK
**ADMIRALTY LIST OF RADIO SIGNALS DIAGRAMS RELATING TO RADIOBEACONS.** **Added/Corp** Great Britain. Hydrographic Dept. English. an. **LC** VK397; .A35. **DD** 623.89/32.

UK
**ADMIRALTY TIDE TABLES.** **VFOAT** European Waters. (1933)-. English. an. £16.00 (comes in combination with Altantic & Indian & Pacific Oceans, not membership title). Royal Navy, Hydrographic Department, Somerst England. **Tel** 011 44 823 337900. **(Subscription address:** Brown & Perrin, 36/44 Tabernacle St Redway Hse, London EC2A 4DT England**)**

US
**AIDS TO NAVIGATION BULLETIN / DEPARTMENT OF TRANSPORTATION, COAST GUARD.** **Added/Corp** United States. Coast Guard. National Aids to Navigation School (U.S.). (19??)-. Periodical. English. bm. Free. National Aids to Navigation Schools, United States Coast Guard RTC, Yorktown VA 23690. **Tel** (804)898-2135.

US/0002-5577
**ALL HANDS (ALEXANDRIA, VA.).** (ALL HANDS.). [All hands]. **Added/Corp** United States. Navy Dept. Office of the Chief of Information. United States. Bureau of Naval Personnel. United States. Navy Internal Relations Activity. No. 339 (June 1945)-. Government Publication. English. mo. $20.00 US; $25.00 other. Superintendent of Documents, US Government Printing Office, Washington DC 20402. **Tel** (202)275-3328, FAX (202)786-2377. **ED** Robin Barnette and Bob Rucker. **DD** 359. Index available. **Circ:** 87,000. available on microfilm and microfiche from University Microfilms International (UMI). ***Continues*** *Information Bulletin (United States. Bureau of Naval Personnel).*
**Desc:** Includes articles of general public interest about the United States Navy and its operations.
**Ind/Abst** Index U.S. Gov. Period.

NE/0002-5674
**ALLE HENS.** [Alle hens]. **Added/Corp** Netherlands (Kingdom, 1815- ). Departement van Marine. Netherlands. Ministerie van Defensie. (19??)-. Dutch. mo. Fl29.50 Netherlands; Fl39.50 other. VWU BV Abonnementenadm, Postbus 30225, 6803 AR Arnhem Netherlands. **Tel** 011 31 85 231123. **ED** J. L. van Zwet. **LC** VA530; .A44. **Bk Rev. Ad Acc. Circ:** 28,000.
**Desc:** Material and personnel matters in relation with the Royal Netherlands Navy and naval allies and developments in the widest sense in this field.

US/0736-3559
**ALMANAC OF SEAPOWER, THE.** [Alm. seap.]. **Added/Corp** Navy League of the United States. **VFOAT** Almanac of Sea Power. (1983)-. English. an (Jan.). $14.95 (softback), $24.95 (hardback). Navy League of the United States, 2300 Wilson Boulevard, Arlington VA 22201. **Tel** (703)528-1775. **ED** Vincent C. Thomas Jr. **LC** V1; .A38. **DD** 359/.005. **[CCC]. Ad Acc.** available on microfilm from University Microfilms International (UMI).

US/0002-9866
**AMERICAN MARINE ENGINEER, THE.** Vol. 1 (Jan. 1906)-. Periodical. English. mo. AFL CIO, 17 Battery Place/Room 1930, New York NY 10004. **LC** VM1; .A45. **DD** 387.5.
**Ind/Abst** Work Relat. Abstr.

US/0065-9207
**AMERICAN MARITIME LIBRARY, THE.** V. 1- 1970-. Monographic series. English. ir. Price varies per volume. Mystic Seaport Museum, 50 Greenmanville Avenue, Mystic CT 06355. **Tel** (203)572-0711.

US/0003-0155
**AMERICAN NEPTUNE, THE.** [Am. neptune]. **Added/Corp** Peabody Museum of Salem. Vol. 1 (Jan. 1941)-. Periodical. English. qt (Jan., Apr., July, Oct.). $32.00 (one year), $52.00 (two year), $72.00 (three year) US; $35.00 (one year), $58.00 (two year), $81.00 (three year) other. Peabody Museum of Salem, East India Square W, Salem MA 01970. **Tel** (508)745-1876. **ED** Timothy J. Runyan. **LC** V1; .A4. **DD** 387.05. cum. index. **Bk Rev. Ad Acc. Circ:** 900. available on microfilm and microfiche from University Microfilms International (UMI). Documents available from The Genuine Article.
**Desc:** Maritime history and marine art.
**Ind/Abst** Am. Hist. Life (1954-); Arts Humanit. Citation Index [Full Cov.]; Curr. Contents Arts Humanit.; Res. Alert [Full Cov.].

AT/1035-6878
**ANNUAL AUSTRALIAN NOTICES TO MARINERS IN FORCE ON 1ST JANUARY.** [Annu. Aust. not. mar. force 1st January]. **Added/Corp** Australia. Royal Australian Navy. Hydrographic Service. (1989)-. English. an. Department of Defense / Hydrographic Service, Royal Australian Navy, Sydney Australia. **Tel** FAX 011 61 2 925 4225. **ED** Mark Bolger. **DD** 623.892. Index available. ***Continues*** *Annual Summary of Australian Notices to Mariners, 0312-6056.*

CN
**ANNUAL EDITION: NOTICES TO MARINERS.** **Main/Corp** Canada. Coast Guard. Aids and Waterways Branch. **Added/Corp** Canada. Guard. Aids and Waterways Branch. Notices to Mariners: Annual Edition. **VFOAT** Notices to Mariners: Annual Edition. (1977)-. English. an. Free. Minister of Supply & Services Canada, 88 Metcalfe Street/5th Floor, Ottawa Ontario K1A 0S9 Canada. **Tel** 990-3021. **LC** VK798; .C3a. **DD** 387.1. **Bk Rev. Ad Acc. Circ:** 15,000 (ctrl). ***Continues*** *Canada. Marine Transportation Administration. Annual Edition: Notices to Mariners.*
**Desc:** Contains information and notices to help mariners navigate safely in Canadian waters.

CN/0704-8343
**ANNUAL REPORT - GEORGETOWN SHIPYARD INC.** (ANNUAL REPORT / GEORGETOWN SHIPYARD INC.). **Main/Corp** Georgetown Shipyard Inc. (P.E.I.). (1976)-. English. an. P E I Georgetown Shipyard Inc, Post Office Box 220, Georgetown Prince Edward Island Canada. **LC** VM301.G44; G45a. **DD** 338.7/62/383097177.

US/0884-9951
**ANNUAL REPORT / U.S. NAVY'S MILITARY SEALIFT COMMAND.** **Main/Corp** United States. Navy. Military Sealift Command. English. an. Military Sealift Command Atlantic, Bayonne NJ 07002. **LC** VA79; .U54A. **DD** 359.9/82/0973.

AT/0312-6056
**ANNUAL SUMMARY OF AUSTRALIAN NOTICES TO MARINERS.** ***Title Change.*** [Ann. summ. of Aust. not. to mar.]. **Main/Corp** Australia. Dept. of the Navy. **Added/Corp** Australia. Dept. of the Navy. Notices to Mariners. (1967)-(19??). English. Department of Defense / Hydrographic Service, Royal Australian Navy, Sydney Australia. **Tel** FAX 011 61 2 925 4225. **LC** VK927; .A86a. **DD** 623.89/05. ***Continued by*** *Annual Australian Notices to Mariners.*

SP
**ANO DE LA NAUTICA, EL.** No. 1- 1976/77-. Spanish. 1.500. Edisport S L, Isaac Peral 12, Madrid 15 Spain. **LC** VK4; .A55.

US/0570-4979
**APPROACH (NORFOLK).** (APPROACH.). [Approach]. **Added/Corp** Naval Safety Center. Naval Aviation Safety Center (U.S.). Vol. 1, No. 1 (July 1955)-. Government Publication. English. mo. $22.00 domestic; $27.50 other. Superintendent of Documents, US Government Printing Office, Washington DC 20402. **Tel** (202)275-3328, FAX (202)786-2377. **LC** VG93; .A9. **DD** 629.13255; 629.126. available on microfilm and microfiche from University Microfilms International (UMI). ***Continues*** *United States Naval Aviation Safety Bulletin.*
**Desc:** Contains stories, editorials, and accurate information currently available on the subject of aviation accident prevention.
**Ind/Abst** Int. Aerosp. Abstr.

UK
**ARCTIC PILOT.** **Main/Corp** Great Britain. Hydrographic Dept. Monographic series. English. Price varies per volume. **LC** VK807. **DD** 656; 623.892.

CN/0842-0866
**ARGONAUTA (POINTE-CLAIRE. 1986).** (ARGONAUTA : THE NEWSLETTER OF THE CANADIAN NAUTICAL RESEARCH SOCIETY.). [Argonauta]. **Added/Corp** Canadian Nautical Research

## Naval Science, Navigation

Society. Memorial University of Newfoundland. Division of University Relations. Memorial University of Newfoundland. Maritime Studies Research Unit. Vol. 3, No. 3 (30 Sept. 1986)-. Newsletter. English. qt. 25.00Can$ individuals, 50.00Can$ institutions (includes membership Canadian Nautical Research Society). Canadian Nautical Research Society, University of Newfoundland, St. Johns NFLD A1C 5S7 Canada. **Tel** (709)737-8424, FAX (709)737-4569. **LC** V1; .A74. **DD** 629.04/5/06071. **Continues** Newsletter of the Canadian Nautical Research Society, 0842-0858.

SI
**ASIAN MISSION.** English. Twice a year (Feb., Sept.). 16.00Sing$. ACTI, 161 Jalan Loyang Besar, Singapore 1750 Singapore. **Tel** 011 65 7536124.

●US/1064-0142
**ATLANTIC TIDE & CURRENT ALMANAC (NORTHEAST ED.).** (ATLANTIC TIDE & CURRENT ALMANAC.). **Added/Corp** Better Boating Association. (1993)-. English. $14.95. Better Boating Association, Box 407, Needham MA 02192.

IT
**ATTI DELL'ISTITUTO ITALIANO DI NAVIGAZIONE.** **Main/Corp** Istituto Italiano di Navigazione. (19??)-. Periodical. Italian. qt. Istituto Italiano di Navigazione, Via Prisciano 42, Rome 00136 Italy. **Tel** 011 39 6 3452841. **LC** VK4; .I85b.
**Ind/Abst** Int. Aerosp. Abstr.

US
**AUDIT REPORT. FLEET ADMIRAL CHESTER W. NIMITZ MEMORIAL NAVAL MUSEUM COMMISSION.** VFOAT Fleet Admiral Chester W. Nimitz Memorial Naval Museum Commission. English. State Auditor, John H Reagan, State Office Building, PO Box 12067, Austin TX 78711. **LC** V13.U6; F733. **DD** 359/.0074/016465.

FR/0180-9938
**AVIS AUX NAVIGATEURS.** **Added/Corp** France. Service Hydrographique. France. French. wk. 13 rue de l'Universite, 7E Arr Paris France. **LC** VK798; .F83a. **DD** 623.89/29.

CN
**AVIS AUX NAVIGATEURS (ED. HEBDOMADAIRE).** (AVIS AUX NAVIGATEURS.). [Avis navig.]. **Main/Corp** Canada. Garde Cotiere. Direction des Aides et des Voies Navigables. **Added/Corp** Canadian Coast Guard. (1983)-. Periodical. French. wk. Canada Communication Group Publishers, Order Processing, Ottawa Ontario K1A 0S9 Canada. **Tel** (819)956-4800, (819)956-4802. **Continues** Avis aux Navigateurs, 0700-1827.

UY
**AVISOS A LOS NAVEGANTES.** **Main/Corp** Uruguay. Servicio de Oceanografia, Hidrografia y Meteorologia. Periodical. Spanish. Capurro 980, Montevideo Uruguay. **LC** VK798; .U73A. **Continues** Avisos a los Navegantes.

●US
**BIBLIOGRAPHY FOR ADVANCEMENT EXAMINATION STUDY.** **Added/Corp** United States. Naval Education and Training Command. (1994)-. Bibliography. English. Naval Education and Training Command, US Government Printing Office, Washington DC 20402. **Continues** Bibliography for Advancement Study.

GW
**BLAUE JUNGS.** German. mo. DM48.00 Germany; DM56.00 other. Bundesministerium der Verteidigung, 1 Postfach 1388, W-53 Bonn 1 Germany. **Tel** 0228/124782, FAX 0228/126759. **Bk Rev. Ad Acc. Circ:** 25,000 (ctrl).

US
**BLUEJACKETS' MANUAL, THE.** **Added/Corp** United States Naval Institute. United States. Navy. (1902)-. English. ir. price varies per volume. U. S. Naval Institute, 2062 Generals Highway, Annapolis MD 21402. **Tel** (301)268-6110, (800)233-8764. **LC** V113; .B552. **DD** 359.
**Desc:** Contains a compendium of information of interest to career Navy men and women. Bibliography offers the reader additional references, both official and unofficial, on hundreds of subjects.

UK/0268-9650
**BMT ABSTRACTS : BRITISH MARITIME TECHNOLOGY ABSTRACTS. See** Naval Science, Navigation-Abstracting, Bibliographies and Statistics.

AG
**BOLETIN DEL CENTRO NAVAL.** **Main/Corp** Argentine Republic. Ministerio de Marina. 1- 1882-. Periodical. Spanish. qt. Centro Naval Florida, 801 Av Cordoba 354, 1054 Buenos Aires Argentina.

UK/0068-290X
**BROWN'S NAUTICAL ALMANAC.** [Brown naut. alm.]. (1878)-. Periodical. English. an (September).

£34.50. Brown Son & Ferguson Ltd, 4/10 Darnley Street, Glasgow G41 2SD Scotland. **Tel** 011 44 41 4291234, FAX 011 44 41 4201694. **ED** T. N. Brown. Index available. cum. index. **Bk Rev. Ad Acc, Adv Mgr:** D. Provan. **Circ:** 12,000 (ctrl).

UK/0068-290X
**BROWN'S NAUTICAL ALMANAC; DAILY TIDE TABLES.** (1858)-. English. an. £33.00 UK and Eire; £37.05 other. Brown Son & Ferguson Ltd, 4/10 Darnley Street, Glasgow G41 2SD Scotland. **Tel** 011 44 41 4291234, FAX 011 44 41 4201694. **ED** T. Nigel Brown. **Ad Acc, Adv Mgr:** D. Provan. **Pr Rev. Acid Free. Circ:** 12,000+.

FR/0066-9814
**BULLETIN DE L'ASSOCIATION TECHNIQUE MARITIME ET AERONAUTIQUE.** [Bull. Assoc. tech. marit. aeronaut.]. **Added/Corp** Association Technique Maritime et Aeronautique. Vol. 25 (1914)-. Bulletin. French. an. 480.00F. Association Technique Maritime Aeronautique, 47 rue du Monceau, 75008 Paris France. **Tel** 011 33 1 45619911, telex 280756. **CODEN** BATMA8. **Circ:** 1,000. Documents available from Article Express International. **Continues** Association Technique Maritime. Bulletin.
**Desc:** Publishes technical papers and corresponding discussions of the members' annual meetings.
**Ind/Abst** Bioeng. Abstr.; Ei Page One; Eng. Index Annu.; Int. Aerosp. Abstr.

FR/0379-2811
**BULLETIN (INTERNATIONAL ASSOCIATION OF LIGHTHOUSE AUTHORITIES).** (BULLETIN / AISM, ASSOCIATION INTERNATIONALE DE SIGNALISATION MARITIME.). VFOAT Bulletin de l'AISM; IALA Bulletin. (1958)-. Bulletin. English (French). qt. 100.00F Switzerland. Association Internationale Signalisation Maritime, 13 rue di Villarceau, 75116 Paris France. **Tel** 33(1)4500 38 60, FAX (1)33(1)45002902, telex 610480 IALAISM F. **ED** Paul Ridgway. **LC** VK1000; .B84. **DD** 387.1/55. Index available. cum. index. **Bk Rev. Ad Acc. Circ:** 600. **Continues** AISM-IALA.
**Desc:** Various techniques related to aids to marine navigation (visual, audible, radio), their powering and maintenance.

BE/0374-1001
**BULLETIN OF THE PERMANENT INTERNATIONAL ASSOCIATION OF NAVIGATION CONGRESSES. See** Engineering-Hydraulic Engineering.

FR/0007-5752
**BULLETIN TECHNIQUE DU BUREAU VERITAS.** [Bull. tech. Bur. Veritas]. **Main/Corp** Bureau Veritas. **Added/Corp** Bureau Veritas. Vol. 45, No. 1 (Jan. 1963)-. Academic Scholarly Publication. French (English). Four times a year. 245.04F France; 290.00F other. Bulletin Tech Bureau Veritas, Cedex 44, 92077 Paris La Defense France. **Tel** 33 1 42915291, FAX 33 1 42915294, telex 615370. **ED** Philippe Boisson (editor's address: 17 bis Place des Reflets, 92400 Conrbevoie France; editor's phone: 33 1 4291587). **LC** TJ2; .B85. **DD** 623.8/1/05. **Circ:** 2,000. **Continues** Bulletin Technique du "Veritas".
**Ind/Abst** BMT Abstr.; EMBASE; Energy Res. Abstr. (April 1982-);; Ship Abstr.

US/0191-9814
**BULLETIN - U.S. COAST GUARD ACADEMY ALUMNI ASSOCIATION. See** College and School Publications-Alumni.

GW
**BUNDESMARINE.** Periodical. German. mo. DM24.00. Bundesministerium der Verteidigung, 1 Postfach 1388, W-53 Bonn 1 Germany. **Tel** 0228/124782, FAX 0228/126759. **LC** V3; .B86.

CN/0822-9481
**CAPT. LILLIE'S BRITISH COLUMBIA COAST GUIDE AND RADIOTELEPHONE DIRECTORY.** [Capt. Lillie's B.C. coast guide radiotelep. dir.]. VFOAT Capt. Lillie's British Columbia, Puget Sound & S.E. Alaska Coast Guide and Radiotelephone Directory. **VAT** Capt. Lillie's British Columbia, Puget Sound & S.E. Alaska Coast Guide and Radiotelephone Directory (1984). 24th (1983/84 Ed.)-. Directory. English. be. $14.00 per volume. Captain Lillie's British Columbia Coast Guide and Radiotelephone Directory, C-310 Marine Building, 355 Burrard Street, Vancouver British Columbia V6C 2G6 Canada. **LC** WMLC L 83/272. **DD** 623.89/229711. **Continues** Capt. Lillie's Coast Guide and Radiotelephone Directory, 0318-3742.

●US/1045-4543
**CAPTN. JACK'S TIDE AND ... CURRENT ALMANAC.** [Capt. Jack's tide current alm.]. VFOAT Almanac; Captn Jack's Almanac. (1991)-. English. $4.95. Marine Trade Publications, PO Box 65119, Port Ludlow WA 98365. **DD** 551.

US
**CENTER FOR NAVAL ANALYSES PUBLICATIONS CLEARED FOR PUBLIC RELEASE.** **Main/Corp** Center for Naval Analyses. English. **Continues** Index of Selected Publications.

JA
**CHOSA KENKYU JIHO - KOKAI KUNRENJO.** **Main/Corp** Kokai Kunrenjo. VFOAT Journal of the Institute for Sea Training. Periodical. Japanese (summaries and/or abstracts in English). Kokai Kunrenjo, 1-3 Kasumigaseki 2-chome Chiyoda-ku, Tokyo 100 Japan. **LC** VK4; .K65A.

KO
**CHOSON KONGOP HYOPHOE PO.** VFOAT Shipbuilding News Service. Periodical. Korean (Korean). mo. **LC** VM298.5; .C52.

CH
**CHUAN PO KUNG CHENG.** VFOAT Chuanbo Gongcheng; Ship Engineering. Periodical. Chinese. bm. Science Press, 16 Donghuangchenggen North Street, Beijing 100707, People's Republic of China. **Tel** 011 86 1 4019821, 011 86 1 4010642, FAX 011 86 1 4012180, 011 86 1 4019810, telex 210147. **ED** Zhu Song. **LC** VM4; .C45. **DD** 623.8/05. **Ad Acc. Circ:** 11,000.
**Desc:** The official journal of the Chinese Society of Naval Architecture and Marine Engineering.
**Ind/Abst** BMT Abstr.

CH
**CHUNG CHUAN CHI KAN.** Chinese. qt. Chung Chuan Chi Kan She, 20 Pa Te Road 3 Section, Taipei Taiwan. **LC** VM4; .T33. **Continues** Tai Chuan Chi Kan.

US/1055-8373
**COAST GUARD LETTER.** (1991)-. Periodical. English. $32.00. Maritime Week, 4665 34th Street South, Suite 2, Arlington VA 22206-1701.

UK
**COASTGUARD.** (1???)-. Periodical. English. qt. Free. Department of Transport / England, 2 Marsham Street, London SW1P 3EB England. **Tel** 011 44 71 2765082. **ED** Ian Fraser. **Bk Rev. Ad Acc. Circ:** 17,000 (ctrl).
**Desc:** Search and rescue at sea, on shore, on cliffs; safety education.

BE
**COLLECTANEA MARITIMA. See** Earth Sciences-Oceanography.

FR
**COLS BLEUS.** (19??)-. French. ir. 377.00F France; $510.00F other. Addim, 6 rue Saint Charles, 75015 Paris France. **Tel** 011 33 1 45770376. **LC** VA500; .C64. **DD** 359/.00944.

US/0740-6029
**COMMAND HISTORY - UNITED STATES. NAVAL FACILITIES ENGINEERING COMMAND.** (COMMAND HISTORY / NAVAL FACILITIES ENGINEERING COMMAND.). **Main/Corp** United States. Naval Facilities Engineering Command. VFOAT Naval Facilities Engineering Command History. (19??)-. English. an. Naval Facilities Engineering Command, 200 Stovall Street, Alexandria VA 22332. **LC** VG593; .U55a. **DD** 359.4/17/0973.

US/0097-9910
**COMMISSARYMAN 1 & C.** [Commis.man 1 C]. **Main/Corp** United States. Naval Training Publications Detachment. **VAT** Commissary Man First Class and Chief Commissary Man. English. Naval Training Command, Betty Sponaugle Code Elex 08TA, Washington DC 20363. **LC** VC353; .A2. **DD** 359.3/41. **Continues** Commisaryman 1 & C, 0097-9910.

US/1062-6506
**CONGRESSIONAL INFORMATION BUREAU.** (C.I.B. DAILY MARITIME NEWSLETTER.). [Congr. Inf. Bur.]. **Added/Corp** Congressional Information Bureau, Inc. VFOAT CIB Daily Maritime Newsletter. (1???)-. Periodical. English. da. $1260.00 US,Canada, and Mexico; $1440.00 other. Congressional Information Bureau, 3030 Clarendon Boulevard, Suite 202, Arlington VA 22201. **Tel** (703)516-4801. **DD** 387. Index available. cum. index. **Circ:** 1,000 (ctrl).
**Desc:** Newsletter covering the industry and government.

FR/0181-3048
**CONNAISSANCE DES TEMPS.** (CONNAISSANCE DES TEMPS / BUREAU DES LONGITUDES.). [Connais. temp.]. **Added/Corp** France. Bureau des Longitudes. France. Service Hydrographique et Oceanographique de la Marine. (19??)-. French (English). an. 140.00F France; 170.00F other. Service Hydrographique et Oceanographique de la Marine / Brest France, BP 426, 29275 Brest Cedex France. **Tel** 011 33 1 98030917. **LC** QB8; .F9. **DD** 528/.01. **Ad Acc. Circ:** 400. **Continues** France. Bureau des Longitudes. Connaissance des Temps ou des Mouvements Celestes a l'Usage des Astronomes et des Navigateurs.

**Desc:** A high precision epheureris for professional and amateur astronomers which gives the coordinates of sun, moon, planets and galileu, satellites of Jupiter.

FR
**CONSTRUCTION NAVALE, LA. Main/Corp** Chambre Syndicale des Constructeurs de Navires et de Machines Marine. (19??)-. French. 47 rue de Monceau, Paris 75008 France. **LC** VM298.5; .C48a. **DD** 354/.44/008775.

US/0740-7602
**CRYPTOLOG.** (CRYPTOLOG / NAVAL CRYPTOLOGIC VETERANS ASSOCIATION.). Periodical. English. qt. Association National Office, 3065 Olive Street, Denver CO 80207. **LC** VB255. **DD** 359.3/432. ***Continues*** *Naval Cryptologic Veterans Association Newsletter.*

US
**DEPARTMENT OF THE NAVY SUPPLEMENT / DISKETTE.** English. Four times a year (Jan., Apr., July, Oct.). $99.00. EZ - Far Systems, 360 Wire Road, York PA 17402. **Tel** 1-800-388-1415, FAX (717)975-2813. **ED** TSA Inc. 2 Market Plaza Way Mechanicsburg, PA 17055 (717)691-5691. **Ad Acc.** ctrl circ. available on CD-ROM.

AG
**DERROTERO ARGENTINO. Main/Corp** Argentine Republic. Direccion General de Navegacion, Hidrografia, Faros y Balizas. (19??)-. Spanish. Opeuser S.A., Buenos Aires Argentina.

GR
**DIARKES KODIX NAUTERGATIKES & NAUTILIAKES NOMOTHESIAS / EKDIDETAI KAI DIEUTHYNETAI HYPO TOU INSTITOUTOU ERGATIKON MELETON, SYNTASSETAI HYOP EPITROPES EIDIKON. See** Law-Maritime Law.

US
**DIRECTORY - U. S. COAST GUARD ACADEMY ALUMNI ASSOCIATION. See** College and School Publications-Alumni.

BE/0538-8643
**DOCUMENTATION - INTERNATIONAL MARITIME COMMITTEE. Main/Corp** International Maritime Committee. (1969)-. English (French). qt. International Maritime Committee, c/o Messrs Henry Voet-Genicto, 17 Borzestraat, B2000 Antwerp Belgium. **Tel** (32)3-232-24-71, telex 31-653 VOET B. ***Supersedes*** *International Maritime Committee. Conference; Constitution, Members, Maritime Conventions, Ratifications and Accessions, Attendance, Minutes, Resolutions.*

AT
**DOG WATCH, THE. Added/Corp** Shiplovers' Society of Victoria. No. 28 (1971)-. English. an. 11.00Aus$. Shiplovers' Society of Victoria, GPO Box 1169K, Melbourne Victoria 3001 Australia. **Tel** 011 61 3 8906070. **LC** V1; .S453. **DD** 623.8/05. Index available. cum. index. **Bk Rev. Ad Acc. Pr Rev. Circ:** 1,500 (ctrl). ***Continues*** *Annual Dog Watch.*
**Desc:** Maritime history generally related to shipping in Australian waters.

UK
**EANS REPORT (EMPIRE AIR NAVIGATION SCHOOL (GREAT BRITAIN)).** (EANS REPORT / EMPIRE AIR NAVIGATION SCHOOL, ROYAL AIR FORCE.). **Added/Corp** Empire Air Navigation School (Great Britain). (19??)-. Monographic series. English. Price varies per volume. Royal Air Force College, Cranwell Sleaford, Lincolnshire NC34 8HB England. **Tel** 011 44 0400 61201 ext 6250. **LC** WMLC L 83/4326.

CN
**EDITION ANNUELLE : AVIS AUX NAVIGATEURS. Main/Corp** Canada. Coast Guard. Aids and Waterways Branch. **VFOAT** Avis aux Navigateurs: Edition Annuelle. French. an. Free. Canada Communication Group Publishers, Order Processing, Ottawa Ontario K1A 0S9 Canada. **Tel** (819)956-4800, (819)956-4802. **LC** VK798; .C33A. **DD** 623.89/2. **Ad Acc. Circ:** 18,000.
**Desc:** Issued to mariners. Contains information, notices to help mariners navigate safely in our waters.

SP
**EFEMERIDES ASTRONOMICAS. Added/Corp** Instituto y Observatorio de Marina (Spain). Vol. 170 (1961)-. Spanish. 200ptas. Instituto y Observatorio de Marina, San Fernando Cadiz, San Fernando Spain. **Tel** 883548. **LC** QB8; .S7. **DD** 528/.05. ***Continues*** *Almanaque Nautico.*

DK
**EFTERRETNINGER FOR SOFARENDE. Main/Corp** Denmark. Frakvandsdirektoratet. (Jan. 1978)-. Government Publication. Danish. wk. kr480.00. Farvandsvaesenet, Farvandsinspektoratet, Overgaden o. Vandet 62B, PO Box 1919, 1023 Koebennhavn K Denmark. **Tel** 31 57 40 50, FAX 31 57 43 41, telex 22204 FRVSKA DK. **ED** Flemming S. Damo. **LC** VK802; .D4. Index available. cum. index. **Acid Free. Circ:** 1,300 (ctrl). ***Continues*** *Denmark. Skortarkivet. Efterretninger for Sofarende.*
**Desc:** Notices to mariners, navigational warning, corrections to Danish charts and nautical publications.

US/1058-3556
**EGREGIOUS STEAMBOAT JOURNAL, THE.** [Egreg. steamb. j.]. **Added/Corp** Steamboat Masters & Associates. **VFOAT** Steamboat Journal; EJS. Premier Issue (May/June 1991)-. Periodical. English. Six times a year. $20.00 US; $24.00 Canada & Mexico; $40.00 others. Steamboat Masters & Associates, PO Box 3046, Louisville KY 40201-3046. **Tel** (502)778-6784. **ED** Jack E. Custer. **LC** VM461; .E35. **DD** 623.8/2436/0973. **Bk Rev**, (Qty: 15-25). **Ad Acc, Adv Mgr:** Sandra Custer. **Circ:** 1,000.
**Desc:** Devoted to the history of steamboats, inland rivers and river people. indispensable for historians and genealogists. Photo essays highlight design and architecture. Emphasis on untold histories.

CN/0822-4056
**ESCALE (QUEBEC).** (L'ESCALE.). [Escale]. Published since spring 1983. Periodical. French. Six times a year. 16.00Can$ Canada; 22.00Can$ US; 25.00Can$ other. La Revue Maritime L'Escale, 20 des Navigateurs, Quebec Quebec G1K 8E4 Canada. **Tel** (418)692-3779. **DD** 623.88/09714. **Bk Rev. Ad Acc.**

US/0149-239X
**EXPERIMENTAL YACHT SOCIETY JOURNAL. Main/Corp** Experimental Yacht Society. Sept. 1977-. Periodical. English. qt. 591 Island Avenue, Tarpon Springs FL 33589. **LC** VM320; .E93A. **DD** 623.82/2/05.

US/1040-807X
**FACEPLATE.** Vol. 1, Issue 1 (July/Aug. 1988)-. Periodical. English. bm. $18.00 US; $30.00 other. Faceplate Publishing Inc, 512 Lehigh Street, Blackwood NJ 08012. **Tel** (202)655-4000, FAX (609)962-9084. **ED** Harry T Dare. **LC** VM975; .F26. **DD** 627/.72/05. **Ad Acc. Circ:** 3,000 (ctrl).
**Desc:** Covers diving research and safety.

US/0739-3229
**FACT BOOK - NAVAL RESEARCH LABORATORY (U.S.).** (FACT BOOK / NAVAL RESEARCH LABORATORY.). [Fact book - Nav. Res. Lab. (U.S.)]. **Main/Corp** Naval Research Laboratory (U.S.). **VFOAT** N.R.L. Fact Book; NRL Fact Book. English. an. Naval Research Lab, Disbursing Officer, SVIC/Code 5804, Washington DC 20375. **Tel** (202)767-3306. **LC** U394.W3; N38A. **DD** 359/.07/073.

UK
**FAIRPLAY MARINE COMPUTING GUIDE.** (1985)-. English. ir. £45.00 UK; £89.00 others. Fairplay International Publications Ltd, PO Box 96, Coulsdon Surrey CRE 2TE England. **Tel** 011 44 81 6602811, FAX 011 44 81 6602824, telex 884595. **LC** VK1; .F35. **DD** 623.89/028/5.
**Desc:** An comprehensive international directory of computing software, systems and services for the marine industry.

US/0014-8822
**FATHOM (NORFOLK).** (FATHOM.). [Fathom]. **Added/Corp** Naval Safety Center. (1969)-. Government Publication. English. bm. $11.00 domestic; $13.75 other. Superintendent of Documents, US Government Printing Office, Washington DC 20402. **Tel** (202)275-3328, FAX (202)786-2377. **LC** V383; .F37. available on microfilm and microfiche from University Microfilms International (UMI).
**Desc:** Published by the Naval Safety Center, this publication presents the most accurate information currently available on the subject of nautical accident prevention.

FR
**FEUX ET SIGNAUX DE BRUME. *Title Change.* Main/Corp** France. Service Hydrographique. (1???)-?. French. Etablissement Principal du Service Hydrographique et Oceanographique de la Marine, 29283 Brest, Paris France. ***Continues*** *Phares et Signaux de Brume.* ***Continued by*** *Feux et Signaux de Brume.*

US
**FOCUS ON FOUR. Main/Corp** United States. Naval Mobile Construction Battalion Four. **VFOAT** Deployment. English. US Department of The Navy Naval Mobile Construction, Battalion Four FPO, San Francisco CA 96601. available on microfiche (Vols. for 1980/81- distributed to depository libraries).

FR
**FORCES SOUS-MARINES. VFOAT** Forces Sous Marines. No. 1 (Dec. 1977)-. Periodical. English (French). qt. 295.00. BP 80 08, 75362 Paris Cedex 08 France. **LC** V859.F7; F67. **DD** 623.8/205.

US/0362-9910
**FORTITUDINE.** (FORTITUDINE : NEWSLETTER OF THE MARINE CORPS HISTORICAL PROGRAM.). **Added/Corp** United States. Marine Corps. History and Museums Division. **VFOAT** Historical Bulletin. (19??)-. Government Publication. English. qt. $5.00 domestic; $6.25 other. Superintendent of Documents, US Government Printing Office, Washington DC 20402. **Tel** (202)275-3328, FAX (202)786-2377. **LC** VE23.A1; F58. **DD** 359.9/6/0973.
**Desc:** Intended to educate and train Marines on active duty in the uses of military and Marine Corps history.

CN/0834-4302
**FRESHWATER.** (FRESH WATER.). [Freshwater]. **Added/Corp** Marine Museum of the Great Lakes at Kingston. Vol. 1 No. 1 (Spring 1986)-. Periodical. English. Twice a year (Mar., Nov.). 20.00Can$ US; 28.04Can$ (corporations), 70.09 (individuals) others, Comes with Jib Gems & Marine Museum Great Lakes membership. Marine Museum of the Great Lakes at Kingston, 55 Ontario Street, Kingston Ontario K7L 2Y2 Canada. **Tel** (613)542-2261. **ED** Maurice D. Smith. **DD** 386.5/09713. **Bk Rev. Circ:** 500 (ctrl).
**Desc:** A journal of Great Lakes marine history, featuring archaeological, economic, social, technological and political articles which help preserve and interpret Great Lakes marine heritage.
**Ind/Abst** Am. Hist. Life (1986-); Can. Period. Index.

UK/0308-6437
**GEARTEST.** [Geartest]. Periodical. English. £8.00. Kenneth Mason Publications Ltd, 12A North Street Emsworth, Hampshire P010 7DD England. **Tel** 011 44 243 377977. **LC** VM320; .G4. **DD** 623.86/05.

NE
**GEGEVENS BETREFFENDE HET NAUTISCH ONDERWIJS. Main/Corp** Netherlands. Ministerie van Onderwijs en Wetenschappen. (19??)-. Dutch. an. Ministerie Van Onderwijs en Wetenschappen, Staatsuitgeverij, 'S-Gravenhage Netherlands. **LC** VK477; .N48a.

GW/0174-4933
**GKSS JAHRESBERICHT. VFOAT** G.K.S.S. Jahresbericht. German. an. GKSS-Forschungszentrum Geesthacht GmbH, Max-Planck-Strasse, Postfach 1160, W-2054 Geesthacht Germany. **LC** VM317; .G53.

US/1072-3080
**GLOBAL POSITIONING & NAVIGATION NEWS.** [Glob. position. navig. news]. **VFOAT** Global Positioning and Navigation News. (1993)-. Periodical. English. bw (25 issues). $497.00 US; $530.00 other. Phillips Business Information, Inc., 1201 Seven Locks Road, Potomac MD 20854. **Tel** (301)424-3338, (800)777-5006, FAX (301)309-3847. **DD** 526. ***Continues*** *GPS Report, 1056-7127;* ***Absorbed*** *Marine Technology News.*

US/1048-5104
**GPS WORLD. See** Geography.

AT/0156-8698
**GREAT CIRCLE.** (THE GREAT CIRCLE : JOURNAL OF THE AUSTRALIAN ASSOCIATION FOR MARITIME HISTORY.). [Great circle]. **Added/Corp** Australian Association for Maritime History. Vol. 1, No. 1 (Apr. 1979)-. Periodical. English. Twice a year (Apr. & Oct.). 30.00Aus$ (individuals), 40.00Aus$ (institutions) Comes with Australian Association for Maritime History membership. Australian Association for Maritime History, c/o Ms. S. May, Department of Maritime History, W.A. Maritime Museum, Cliff Street Fremantle WA 6160 Australia. **Tel** 03 822 5671. **ED** Graydon Henning. **LC** VK15; .G67. **DD** 623.89/05. Index available. cum. index. **Bk Rev**, (Qty: 24). **Pr Rev. Circ:** 420 (ctrl).
**Desc:** History of seafaring, shipping, navies, ports, fishing, whaling and overseas trade. Covers the entire world, with special emphasis on Australia and the Indian and Pacific Oceans.
**Ind/Abst** Am. Hist. Life (1979-); APAIS, Aust. Public Aff. Inf. Ser. (1980-).

FR
**GUIDE DU NAVIGATEUR. Main/Corp** France. Service Hydrographique et Oceanographique de la Marine. No. 1-. French. Service Hydrographique et Oceanographique de la Marine / Brest France, BP 426, 29275 Brest Cedex France. **Tel** 011 33 1 98030917. **LC** VK2; .F73A. **DD** 623.89. ***Supersedes*** *Renseignements Relatifs aux Documets Nautiques et a la Navigation.*

US/0882-2913
**GUIDE FOR THE SELECTION OF TANKERS.** [Guide sel. tankers]. **Added/Corp** Tanker Advisory Center. (1983)-. English. an. $620.00 U.S. and Canada; $680.00 other. Tanker Advisory Center Inc., 217 East 85th Street, Suite 259, New York NY 10028. **Tel** (212)628-7686. **LC** VM455; .G84. **DD** 623.8/245. **Circ:** 250.
**Desc:** Ranks oil tankers on scale of one to five basis age, casualty experience and ownership.

US/1063-1364
**GUIDE TO MARINES IN REUNION.** [Guide mar. reun.]. **Added/Corp** Once a Marine, Always a Marine Society. (1991)-. English. $10.00. Once a Marine Always a Marine Society, PO box 488, College Park MD 27040. **DD** 355.

KO
**HAEGI.** **VFOAT** Monthly Hae Gi; Wolgan Haegi. Periodical. Korean (English). mo. W88000 South Korea; W12000 other. Hanguk Haegisa Hyophoe, 1212-7 Choryang-dong Tong-ku, Pusan Korea. **Tel** (051)463-5030-3, telex K 52327. **ED** Jo Su Eun. **LC** VM595; .H34. Index available. cum. index. **Bk Rev. Ad Acc. Circ:** 10,000 (ctrl).
**Desc:** Provides maritime technique, current news, marine safety, and other information to all members and maritime organization.

US
**HANDBOOK OF THE HOSPITAL CORPS, UNITED STATES NAVY.** **Main/Corp** United States. Bureau of Medicine and Surgery. **Added/Corp** United States Bureau of Naval Personnel. United States Bureau of Navigation. No. 1 (1914)-. Government Publication. English. mo. Superintendent of Documents, US Government Printing Office, Washington DC 20402. **Tel** (202)275-3328, FAX (202)786-2377. **LC** VG463; .A15. **DD** 359.34; 610.2.

UK
**HANDBOOK OF TIDE TABLES, PARTICULARS OF DOCKS, &C.** **Main/Corp** Port of London Authority. 1951-. English. an. **LC** VK638.5; .P67. **DD** 525.6942.

CC
**HANG HAI.** **Added/Corp** Shang-hai Shih Hang Hai Hsueh Hui. **VFOAT** Hanghai. (19??)-. Periodical. Chinese. bm. $8.00. **(Subscription address:** China International Book Trading Corporation, PO Box 399, Library Service Department, Beijing 100044 People's Republic of China.**)** **LC** VK4; .H36. **DD** 623.89/05.

GW/0017-7504
**HANSA.** (HANSA : WOCHENTLICH ERSCHEINENDES ZENTRALORGAN FUER SCHIFFAHRT, SCHIFFBAU, HAFEN.). [Hansa]. (1863)-. Academic Scholarly Publication. German (English). sm. DM278.32 Germany; DM302.30 other. Schiffahrts Verlag Hansa, Schroedter & Co., Postfach 520365, D 22605 Hamburg Germany. **Tel** 011 49 40 8228070. **(Subscription address:** Maximilian Verlagsgruppe, Postfatch 2352, D 32045 Herford Germany.**)** **ED** Claus Wilde. **LC** VK3; .H3. Index available. **Bk Rev. Ad Acc. Circ:** 6,500 (ctrl).
**Desc:** Serves German and international maritime quarters with latest information, topical news, detailed articles on shipping, shipbuilding, marine engineering, port matters and cargo handling.
**Ind/Abst** Alum. Ind. Abstr.; Aquat. Sci. Fish. Abstr. (Computer File); Bibliogr. Mission.; BMT Abstr.; EMBASE; Eng. Mater. Abstr.; Fluid Abstr., Civil Eng.; Fluid Abstr. Proc. Eng.; FLUIDEX (19??-); Met. Abstr.; Saf. Health Work.

JA
**HIROSHIMA SHOSEN KOTO SEMMON GAKKO KIYO.** **Main/Corp** Hiroshima Shosen Koto Semmon Gakko. **VFOAT** The Bulletin of Hiroshima Mercantile Marine College. No. 1 (1979)-. Japanese. Hiroshima Shosen Koto, Semmon Gakko 4272-1 Higashinocho Toyota-gun, Hiroshima-ken Japan. **LC** V5; .H57A.

JA
**HOKKYOKUSEI HOIKAKU HYO.** **VFOAT** Polaris Almanac for Azimuth Determination. Japanese (Japanese). 400. EDI Executive, 1225 Johnson Ferry Road/Suite 230, Marietta GA 30067. **Tel** (404)973-4683, (205)991-6920, FAX (205)991-1479, telex 78-2661. **LC** VK563; .H64.

US/0736-9220
**HOOK (BONITA, CALIF.), THE.** (THE HOOK.). [Hook]. **Added/Corp** Tailhook Association. (19??)-. Periodical. English. Four times a year. $30.00. Tailhook Association, PO Box 40, Bonita CA 92002-0040. **Tel** (619)566-6019, FAX (619)578-8839. **ED** Steve Millikin, PO Box 45308, NAS, Miramar, San Diego, CA 92145; Telephone: (619)689-9227. **Bk Rev. Ad Acc. Circ:** 14,300.
**Desc:** Tells the story of US Navy carrier aviation, past and present. Issues contain carrier and squadron histories along with news from current naval operations.

SP/0020-1073
**INGENIERIA NAVAL (MADRID).** (INGENIERIA NAVAL.). [Ing. nav.]. **Added/Corp** Asociacion de Ingenieros Navales (Spain). (1929)-. Periodical. Spanish. mo (11 issues). 6500ptas, Spain & Portugal; 9500ptas Latin America; 8790ptas other Europe; 12500ptas other. Escuela Tec Sup de Ingenieria Naval, Castello 66, 28001 Madrid Spain. **Tel** 011 34 1 5751024, 011 34 1 5771678. cum. index.
**Ind/Abst** Biodeter. Abstr. (1991-); BMT Abstr. (-199?); Fluid Abstr., Civil Eng.; Fluid Abstr. Proc. Eng.; FLUIDEX (19??-).

US/0737-8181
**INTERNATIONAL DREDGING REVIEW.** **See** Engineering.

CN/0843-8714
**INTERNATIONAL JOURNAL OF MARITIME HISTORY.** [Int. j. marit. hist.]. **Added/Corp** Maritime Economic History Group. Vol. 1, No. 1 (June 1989)-. Periodical. English. Twice a year (June & Dec.). $35.00. International Journal of Maritime Histroy, Memorial University of Newfoundland, Department of History, St Johns Newfoundland A1C 5S7 Canada. **Tel** (709)737-8424, (709)737-2602, FAX (709)737-4569. **ED** Lewis Fischer, Helge W. Nordvik and Margaret Gulliver. **DD** 623.89/09. Index available. cum. index. **Bk Rev. Ad Acc. Pr Rev. Circ:** 500 (ctrl).
**Desc:** A journal for researchers concerned with the economic and social history of the merchant marines, shipbuilding, fishing, ports, trade and maritime societies.
**Ind/Abst** Am. Hist. Life (1989-).

UK/1057-2414
**INTERNATIONAL JOURNAL OF NAUTICAL ARCHAEOLOGY, THE.** **See** Archaeology.

UK/0263-7618
**INTERNATIONAL MARINE SAFETY DIRECTORY.** Directory. English. an. Industrial & Marine Publishing Ltd, Queensway House, 2 Queensway, Redhill Surrey RH1 1QS England. **Tel** 0737 68611. **LC** VK200; .I64. **DD** 623.89/3/029.

US/0363-261X
**INTERNATIONAL NAUTICAL INDEX.** V. 1- Apr. 1976-. English. qt. $10.00. Wilcox Publishing Company, PO box 4227, 2632 North Forgeus Avenue, Tucson AZ 85717. **LC** Z6839.Y2; I58; VM331. **DD** 016.62382/02.

NE/0020-868X
**INTERNATIONAL SHIPBUILDING PROGRESS.** [Int. shipbuild. prog.]. Vol. 1, (1954)-. Academic Scholarly Publication. English. Four times a year (Apr., July, Oct., Dec.). F285.00. Delft University Press, Stevinweg 1, 2628 CN Delft The Netherlands. **Tel** 011 31 15 783254. **CODEN** ISBPAS. Documents available from Article Express International.
**Desc:** News, research and results on the marine oriented studies.
**Ind/Abst** Aquat. Sci. Fish. Abstr. (Computer File); Bioeng. Abstr.; BMT Abstr.; Ei Page One; EMBASE; Eng. Index Annu.; Fluid Abstr., Civil Eng.; Fluid Abstr. Proc. Eng.; FLUIDEX (1973-); Life Sci. Collect.; Pollut. Abstr. Indexes.

US
**INTERNATIONAL YEARBOOK.** **Main/Corp** Naval Stores Review. English. an. $50.00. Kriedt Enterprises LTD, 129 South Cortez Street, New Orleans LA 70119. **Tel** (504)482-3914, FAX (504)482-4205.

US/1061-8244
**ION NEWSLETTER / THE INSTITUTE OF NAVIGATION, THE.** [ION newsl.]. **Added/Corp** Institute of Navigation. **VAT** Institute of Navigation Newsletter. Vol. 1, No. 1 (Spring 1991)-. Newsletter. English. qt. Institute of Navigation, 1800 Diagonal Road, Suite 480, Alexandria VA 22314. **Tel** (703)683-7101, FAX (703)683-7105. **DD** 629.

IE/0791-2137
**IRISH SKIPPER, THE.** [Ir. skipp.]. (1964)-. Periodical. English. mo. 11.04p Ireland; 11.76p UK; 13.80p other. Mac Publishing Ltd., 44 Leinster Road, Rathmines, Dublin 6 Ireland. **Tel** 011 353 1 966000. **DD** 623.82 639.2.

DK
**J. L. NEWS.** **VAT** J. Lauritzen News. (1???)-. Periodical. English. J. Lauritzen Lines, Copenhagen, Denmark. **ED** P.G. Petersen.
**Ind/Abst** BMT Abstr.

GW
**JACHTFUNKDIENST MITTELMEER FUER NICHTAUSRUSTUNGSPFLICHTIGE SCHIFFE.** **Main/Corp** Deutsches Hudrographisches Institut. 1st Ed.; 1977-. German. an. Deutsches Hydrographisches Institut, Bernhard-Nocht-Strasse 78, 2000 Hamburg 4 Germany. **LC** VK397; .G234A.

GW
**JACHTFUNKDIENST NORD- UND OSTSEE FUR NICHTAUSRUSTUNGSPFLICHTIGE SCHIFFE.** **Main/Corp** Deutsches Hydrographisches Institut. German. Deutsches Hydrographisches Institut, Bernhard-Nocht-Strasse 78, 2000 Hamburg 4 Germany. **LC** VK1151; .G47A. **DD** 623.89/32/094.

US/0374-1222
**JAHRBUCH DER SCHIFFBAUTECHNISCHEN GESELLSCHAFT.** **Main/Corp** Schiffbautechnische Gesellschaft. (1900)-. Monographic series. German. ir. price varies per volume. Springer-Verlag New York Inc., 175 5th Avenue, New York NY 10010. **Tel** (212)460-1500, telex 232 235 SPB UR. **(Subscription address:** Springer Verlag New York Inc. / for North America, 44 Hartz Way, Secaucus NJ 07096.**)** **LC** VM3; .S3. **DD** 623.8/1/05.
**Desc:** Numbered series.

UK/0075-3025
**JANE'S FIGHTING SHIPS.** [Jane's fight. ships]. (1916)-. English. an. $245.00 US & Mexico; $300.13 Central & South America. Jane's Information Group, Sentinel House, 163 Brighton Road, Coulsdon Surrey CR3 2NX England. **Tel** 011 44 81 763 1030, FAX 011 44 81 763 1006. **(Subscription address:** Jane's Information Group / US Subscriptions, 1340 Braddock Place, Suite 300, Alexandria VA 22314.**)** **ED** John Moore. **LC** VA40; .J34. **[CCC].** Index available. **Ad Acc. Circ:** 10,000 (ctrl). available on microfiche; available on CD-ROM. ***Continues*** *All the World's Fighting Ships.*
**Desc:** Current information on the world's naval fleets, alphabetically by country, including history, specifications, armament and crew of individual ships, with illustrations.

UK
**JANE'S MERCHANT SHIPS.** ***Ceased.*** **VFOAT** Merchant Ships. 1982-Ceased 1988. English. an. Jane's Information Group, Sentinel House, 163 Brighton Road, Coulsdon Surrey CR3 2NX England. **Tel** 011 44 81 763 1030, FAX 011 44 81 763 1006. **ED** David Greenman. **LC** VM391; .J36. **DD** 623.8/24/05. **Ad Acc.**
**Desc:** Guide to merchant ship identification with 10,000 common scale line drawings. Vessels are classified by Talbot-Booth recognition system. Covers 1,400 ships; updated information.

JA/0021-4647
**JAPAN SHIPBUILDING & MARINE ENGINEERING.** **Added/Corp** Japan Association for Technical Information. **VAT** Japan Shipbuilding and Marine Engineering. V. 1- (1966)-. Periodical. English. qt. $34.00. **(Subscription address:** Japan Publications Trading Company, Ltd., PO Box 5030, Tokyo International, Tokyo 100-31 Japan.**)** **LC** VM105; .J33. **CODEN** JSMEBS. Documents available from Ask*IEEE.
**Ind/Abst** Ei Page One; INSPEC (1972-1979); Life Sci. Collect.

US
**JOURNAL DE LA NAVIGATION FLUVIALE & I.E. ET MARITIME (MICROFICHE).** (JOURNAL DE LA NAVIGATION FLUVIALE & [I.E. ET] MARITIME.). (1903)-. French. ir. **LC** Microfilm 01355HE; HE668.
**Ind/Abst** BMT Abstr. (-199?).

UK/0373-4633
**JOURNAL OF NAVIGATION, THE.** [J. navig.]. **Added/Corp** Royal Institute of Navigation (Great Britain). Vol. 25 (Jan. 1972)-. Academic Scholarly Publication. English. Three times a year. $178.00 US, Canada and Mexico; £96.00 other. Cambridge University Press, The Edinburgh Building, Shaftesbury Road, Cambridge CB2 2RU United Kingdom. **Tel** 011 44 223 312393, FAX 011 44 223 325959. **(Subscription address:** Cambridge University Press / North America, 110 Midland Avenue, Port Chester NY 10573.**)** **ED** John F. Kemp. **LC** VK1; .I5545. **DD** 629.04/5/05. **CODEN** JONVAL. **Bk Rev. Ad Acc.** available on microfilm and microfiche from University Microfilms International (UMI). Documents available from The Genuine Article, Ask*IEEE. ***Continues*** *Journal of the Institute of Navigation, 0020-3009.*
**Desc:** Contains original papers on the science of navigation over land and sea and through air and space, including those papers presented at the meetings of the Institute. Covers every aspect of the subject from the highly technical to the descriptive and historical. Subjects include: electronics, astronomy, mathematics, cartography, command and control, psychology and zoology, operational research, risk analysis, theoretical physics, operation in hostile environments, instrumentation, ergonomics, and financial planning and law.
**Ind/Abst** Aquat. Sci. Fish. Abstr. (Computer File); BMT Abstr. (Sept. 1977-); Curr. Contents Eng. Tech. Appl. Sci.; Curr. Mil. Pol. Lit.; Curr. Technol. Index (1973-); EMBASE; Ergon. Abstr. (Sept. 1977-); Fluid Abstr., Civil Eng.; Fluid Abstr. Proc. Eng. (Sept. 1977-); FLUIDEX (1973-); Geogr. Abstr. Phys. Geogr.; Geol. Abstr.; INSPEC (Sept. 1977-); Int. Aerosp. Abstr.; Life Sci. Collect.; Res. Alert [Select. Cov.]; SCISEARCH.

US/8756-1417
**JOURNAL OF SHIP PRODUCTION, THE.** [J. ship prod.]. **Added/Corp** Society of Naval Architects and Marine Engineers (U.S.). Vol. 1, No. 1 (Feb. 1985)-. Periodical. English. Four times a year (Feb., May, Aug., Nov.). $65.00 US; $75.00 other. Society of Naval Architecture and Marine Engineering, 601 Pavonia Avenue, Suite 400, Jersey City NJ 07306. **Tel** (201)798-4800 Ext.3025. **DD** 623. Documents available from Article Express International.
**Ind/Abst** BMT Abstr.; Ei Page One; Eng. Index Annu.; Shock Vibr. Dig.

US/0022-4502
**JOURNAL OF SHIP RESEARCH.** [J. ship res.]. **Added/Corp** Society of Naval Architects and Marine Engineers (U.S.). Vol. 1, No. 1 (April 1957)-. Periodical. English. qt (Mar., June, Sept., Dec.). $80.00 US; $90.00 other. Society of Naval Architects and Marine Engineers, 601

Pavonia Avenue, Suite 400, Jersey City NJ 07306-2907. **Tel** (201)798-4800 ext. 3025, FAX (201)798-4975. **LC** VM1; .S628. **CODEN** JSRHAR. **[CCC]. Pr Rev. Circ:** 1,700. Documents available from Article Express International, The Genuine Article.
**Desc:** Publication for technical papers on applied research in hydrodynamics, propulsion, ship motions, structures and vibrations.
**Ind/Abst** Acoust. Abstr.; Bioeng. Abstr.; BMT Abstr.; Curr. Contents Eng. Tech. Appl. Sci.; Ei Page One; Eng. Index Annu.; Fluid Abstr., Civil Eng.; Fluid Abstr. Proc. Eng.; FLUIDEX (1973-); Ocean. Abstr.; Pollut. Abstr. Indexes; Res. Alert [Select. Cov.]; SCISEARCH; Shock Vibr. Dig.

AT/0312-5807
**JOURNAL OF THE AUSTRALIAN NAVAL INSTITUTE.** [J. Aust. Nav. Inst.]. (1975)-. Periodical. English. qt. 30.00Aus$ (one year), 55.00Aus$ (two year), 75.00Aus$ (three year). Australian Naval Institute, PO Box 80, Campbell ACT 2600 Australia. **Tel** 011 61 62 801214. **ED** R. Sherwood. **DD** _a359.40094. **Bk Rev. Ad Acc. Pr Rev. Circ:** 1,000 (ctrl).

JA
**KAINAN TOKEI NENPO. Main/Corp** Japan. Unyusho. Daijin Kambo. Joho Kanribu. (19??)-. Japanese. Saiban No Dokuritsu O Mamoru Kai, c/o Seni Boeki Kaikan, 16-9 Uchi Kanda 2-chome, Chiyoda-ku Tokyo Japan. **LC** VK1288.J3; J38a. ***Continues*** *Japan. Unyusho. Daijin Kanbo. Tokei Chosabu. Kainan Tokei Nempo.*

JA
**KIYO - YUGE SHOSEN KOTO SEMMON GAKKO. Main/Corp** Yuge Shosen Koto Semmon Gakko. 1979 Edition -. Multiple languages (English and Japanese). Yuge Shosen Koto Semmon Gakko, Himoyuge Yugemachi, Ochi-gun 794-25, Ehime-ken Japan. **LC** VK4; .Y83A.

GW
**KLASINGS BOOTSMARKT INTERNATIONAL.** Began in 1968. German (German). Delius Klasing & Co GmbH, Siekerwall 21, D 33602 Bielefeld Germany. **Tel** 011 49 521 559291, telex 9 32 934 DEKLA. **LC** VM361; .K58. **DD** 623.8/223/0294.

JA/0450-609X
**KOBE SHOSEN DAIGAKU KIYO. DAI 2-RUI, SHOSEN, RIKOGAKU HEN. VFOAT** Review of Kobe University of Mercantile Marine. Part II, Maritime Studies, and Science and Engineering. Academic Scholarly Publication. English (Japanese). Kobe Shosen Daigaku, 1-1 Fukae Minami-Machi 5-chome Higashinada-ku, Kobe-shi Japan. **LC** VK4; .K63A. **CODEN** KDKRDX. Documents available from CASDDS. ***Continues*** *Kobe Shosen Kaigaku Kiyo. Dai 2-rue, Kokai-Kikan-Genshi Koryoku-Rigaku Hen.*
**Ind/Abst** Chem. Abstr. (1983-); Life Sci. Collect.

US/0565-1557
**LIGHT LIST.** English. an. $175.00. US Department of Transportation / Coast Guard, 2100 Second Street Southwest, Washington DC 20953-0001. **Tel** (202)267-2229. **ED** Frank Parker. **Circ:** 70,000. available on microfiche (Vols. for (1983) distributed to depository libraries); available on an online database.
**Desc:** A listing of federal and privately maintained aids to navigation that are found on the waters of the U.S. and its territories.

US/0096-1280
**LIST OF LIGHTS AND FOG SIGNALS.** [List lights fog signals]. **Main/Corp** United States. Defense Mapping Agency Hydrographic/Topographic Center. English. US Department of Defense Defense Mapping Agency, 8613 Lee Highway, Fairfax VA 22031. **Tel** (703)285-9290, FAX (703)285-9374. **LC** VK1150; .U6. **DD** 623.89/4. ***Continues*** *List of Lights and Fog Signals, 0096-1280.*

US
**LIST OF LIGHTS AND FOG SIGNALS. BALTIC SEA WITH KATTEGAT, BELTS AND SOUND, AND GULF OF BOTHNIA. VFOAT** Baltic Sea with Kattegar Belts and Sound, and Gulf of Bothnia; Lights, Baltic Sea. English. US Department of Defense Defense Mapping Agency, 8613 Lee Highway, Fairfax VA 22031. **Tel** (703)285-9290, FAX (703)285-9374. **LC** VK1185.B34; L58. **DD** 623.89/3/0916334.

US
**LIST OF LIGHTS AND FOG SIGNALS. BRITISH ISLES, ENGLISH CHANNEL, AND NORTH SEA. VFOAT** British Isles, English Channel, and North Sea. English. an. US Department of Defense Defense Mapping Agency, 8613 Lee Highway, Fairfax VA 22031. **Tel** (703)285-9290, FAX (703)285-9374.

CN/0590-9384
**LIST OF LIGHTS, BUOYS AND FOG SIGNALS. ATLANTIC COAST.** (LIST OF LIGHTS, BUOYS AND FOG SIGNALS. ATLANTIC COAST INCLUDING THE GULF AND RIVER ST. LAWRENCE TO MONTREAL.). **Main/Corp** Canada. Coast Guard. **Added/Corp** Canada. Dept. of Transport. Canada. Ministry of Transport. Canada. Transport Canada. Canadian Coast Guard. Aids and Waterways Directorate. **VFOAT** List of Lights, Buoys and Fog Signals, Atlantic Coast; Atlantic Coast, List of Lights, Buoys and Fog Signals. **VAT** Atlantic Coast. List of lights, Buoys and Fog Signals. (19??)-. English. an. Canada Communication Group Publishers, Order Processing, Ottawa Ontario K1A 0S9 Canada. **Tel** (819)956-4800, (819)956-4802. **LC** VK1026; .C33a. ***Continues*** *List of Lights, Buoys and Fog Signals.*

CN/0382-1080
**LIST OF LIGHTS, BUOYS AND FOG SIGNALS. PACIFIC COAST.** (LIST OF LIGHTS, BUOYS AND FOG SIGNALS, PACIFIC COAST, AND THE RIVERS AND LAKES OF BRITISH COLUMBIA.). **Main/Corp** Canada. Coast Guard. **Added/Corp** Canadian Coast Guard. Aids and Waterways Directorate. **VFOAT** Pacific Coast; List of Lights, Buoys and Fog Signals. **VAT** Pacific Coast. List of Lights, Buoys and Fog Signals. (1976)-. English. an. Canada Communication Group Publishers, Order Processing, Ottawa Ontario K1A 0S9 Canada. **Tel** (819)956-4800, (819)956-4802. **LC** VK1027.P3; C36a. **DD** 623.89/4/09711. ***Continues*** *Canada. Ministry of Transport. List of Lights, Buoys and Fog Signals; Pacific Coast and the Rivers and Lakes of British Columbia., 0382-1080.*

CN/0381-3401
**LIST OF LIGHTS, BUOYS AND FOG SIGNALS. INLAND WATERS.** (LIST OF LIGHTS, BUOYS AND FOG SIGNALS; INLAND WATERS, WEST OF MONTREAL AND EAST OF BRITISH COLUMBIA.). **Main/Corp** Canada. Coast Guard. **Added/Corp** Canadian Coast Guard. Aids and Waterways Directorate. **VFOAT** Inland Waters; List of Lights, Buoys and Fog Signals. **VAT** Inland Waters. Lists of Lights, Buoys, Fog Signals. (1976)-. English. an. Canada Communication Group Publishers, Order Processing, Ottawa Ontario K1A 0S9 Canada. **Tel** (819)956-4800, (819)956-4802. **LC** VK1245; .A3. **DD** 623.89/29/71. ***Continues*** *Canada. Ministry of Transport. List of Lights, Buoys and Fog Signals; Inland Waters, West of Montreal and East of British Columbia., 0381-3401.*

FR
**LISTE DES MEMBRES / ASSOCIATION INTERNATIONALE DE SIGNALISATION MARITIME. Main/Corp** International Association of Lighthouse Authorities. **VFOAT** List of Members. English (French). Association Internationale de Signalisation Maritime, 13 rue Yvon Villarceau, 75116 Paris France. **LC** VK1000; .I46A. **DD** 387.1/55/025.

CN/0381-3398
**LIVRE DES FEUX, DES BOUEES ET DES SIGNAUX DE BRUME. EAUX INTERIEURES.** (LIVRE DES FEUX, DES BOUEES ET DES SIGNAUX DE BRUME.). **Main/Corp** Canada. Garde Cotiere. **VFOAT** Eaux Interieures: Livre des Feux, des Bouees et des Signaux de Brume. 1976-. French (French). an. Transport Canada / Canadian Coast Guard, Ottawa Ontario K1A 0S9 Canada. **Tel** 990-3021. **Ad Acc.**
**Desc:** Contains list of all fixed lighted aids in Canada and contiguous waters.

CN
**LIVRE DES FEUX, DES BOUEES ET DES SIGNAUX DE BRUME: EAUX INTERIEURES (A L'OUEST DE MONTREAL ET A L'EST DE LA COLOMBIE-BRITANNIQUE). Main/Corp** Canadian Coast Guard. (19??)-. French. an. Canada Communication Group Publishers, Order Processing, Ottawa Ontario K1A 0S9 Canada. **Tel** (819)956-4800, (819)956-4802. **LC** VK1245; .C34a. **DD** 016.62389/29/71.

CN
**LIVRE DES FEUX, DES BOUEES ET DES SIGNAUX DE BRUME, TERRE-NEUVE, Y COMPRIS LES EAUX COTIERES DU LABRADOR. Main/Corp** Canada. Coast Guard. Aids and Waterways Branch. **Added/Corp** Canada. Coast Guard. Aids and Waterways Branch. Terre-Neuve : Livres des Feux, des Bouees et des Signaux de Brume. **VFOAT** Terre-Neuve : Livre des Feux, des Bouees et des Signaux de Brume. (19??)-. French (English). Canada Communication Group Publishers, Order Processing, Ottawa Ontario K1A 0S9 Canada. **Tel** (819)956-4800, (819)956-4802. **LC** VK1027.N4; C28a. **DD** 623.89/44/09718.

CN/0704-5417
**LIVRE DES FEUX, DES BOUEES ET DES SIGNAUX DU BRUME. COTE DU PACIFIQUE.** (LIVRE DES FEUX, DES BOUEES ET DES SIGNAUX DE BRUME: COTE DU PACIFIQUE ET LES RIVIERES ET LACS DE LA COLOMBIE-BRITANNIQUE.). **Main/Corp** Canada. Coast Guard. Aids and Waterways Branch. **Added/Corp** Canada. Coast Guard. Aids and Waterways Branch. Cote du Pacifique: Lire des Feux, des Bouees et des Signaux de Brume. **VFOAT** Cote du Pacifique : Livre des Feux, des Bouees et des Signaux de Brume. **VAT** Cote du Pacifique. Livres des Feux, des Bouees et des Signaux de Brume. (1977)-. French. an. Canada Communication Group Publishers, Order Processing, Ottawa Ontario K1A 0S9 Canada. **Tel** (819)956-4800, (819)956-4802. **LC** VK1027.P3; C36b. **DD** 623.89/4/09711.

UK
**LLOYD'S INTERNATIONAL MARINE EQUIPMENT GUIDE. VFOAT** International Marine Equipment Guide. (1989)-. English. an (May). $160.00 North America; £70.00 UK; £70.00 others. Lloyd's of London Press Ltd, Sheepen Place, Colchester, Essex, CO3 3LP England. **Tel** 011 44 206 772113, US: (212)529-9500, US: (800)955-6937, FAX 011 44 206 772880, US: (212)529-9826, telex 987321 LLOYDS G. **(Subscription address:** North America/ Lloyds of London Press, Inc., 611 Broadway, Suite 308, New York, NY 10012; telephone: (212)529-9500) **Ad Acc. Circ:** 1500. ***Continues*** *Lloyd's Ship Manager International Marine Equipment Guide.*
**Desc:** Provides the most comprehensive, worldwide list of marine equipment manufacturers available. An invaluable aid for international buyers and sellers of marine and offshore equipment and services. Approximately 380 pages, it contains over 40,000 product entries, 6,300 company listings and other special features.

UK
**LLOYD'S NAUTICAL YEAR BOOK. Added/Corp** Lloyd's of London Press. (1979)-. English. an (October). $85.00. Lloyd's of London Press Ltd, Sheepen Place, Colchester, Essex, CO3 3LP England. **Tel** 011 44 206 772113, US: (212)529-9500, US: (800)955-6937, FAX 011 44 206 772880, US: (212)529-9826, telex 987321 LLOYDS G. **(Subscription address:** Lloyd's of London Press Inc. / North America, 611 Broadway, Suite 308, New York NY 10012.) **ED** P. Cuny. **LC** VK8; .L6. **DD** 623.89/05. Index available. **Ad Acc. Circ:** 3,650. ***Continues*** *Lloyd's Calendar.*
**Desc:** Maritime reference book for companies and individuals involved with shipping ashore or afloat. Annual reviews include: the Shipping Industry Year; Port Developments; Cargo Handling and other matters. Also describes Lloyd's and the Lloyd's Agency system and provides worldwide listings of Agents and Brokers; major maritime cases and legislation; IMO Conventions and other Rules and Regulations; details of holidays; currencies; shipping and insurance terms; conversion and distance tables.

UK/0047-4908
**LLOYD'S WEEKLY CASUALTY REPORTS.** [Lloyd's wkly. casualty rep.]. (1920)-. English. wk. £735.00. Lloyd's of London Press Inc., 611 Broadway/Suite 308, New York NY 10012. **Tel** (212)529-9500, FAX (212)529-9826, telex 7105812659. **ED** Peter Stokes. **DD** 368.2.
**Desc:** Compilation of all marine, non-marine and aviation casualty reports received by Lloyd's Information, together with a "Casualty Briefing" supplement, which contains a weekly summary of major cases and an analysis of casualty trends. A quarterly index assists reference and identification.

UA/0304-2855
**MAGALLA AL-AKADIMIYYA AL-ARABIYYA LI-N-NAQL AL-BAHRI.** (JOURNAL OF ARAB MARITIME TRANSPORT ACADEMY.). [Magalla al-Akadimiyya al-arabiyya li-n-naql al-bahri]. **Added/Corp** Akadimiyah al-Arabiyah lil-Naql al-Bahri (Egypt). Vol. 1, No. 1 (July 1975)-. Periodical. English (Arabic). Twice a year (Jan. & July). $40.00. Arab Maritime Transport Academy, PO Box 1029, Alexandria Egypt. **Tel** 011 20 3 203 5862325, FAX 011 20 3 203 560 2144, telex 54160 ACAD UN. **Circ:** 3,000 (ctrl).

UA
**MAJALLAT AL-AKADEMIYAH AL-ARABIYAH LIL-NAQL AL-BAHARI. Main/Corp** Al-Akadimiyah Al-Arabiyah Lil-Naql Al-Bahari (Egypt). **VFOAT** Journal of Arab Maritime Transport Academy. Periodical. Arabic (English). $12.00. PO Box 1029, Al-Iskandariyah Uruguay. **LC** VK4; .A39A.

US
**MALACCA AND SINGAPORE STRAITS TIDE TABLES. VFOAT** Tide Tables, Malacca and Singapore Straits. English. **LC** VK710; .M34. **DD** 623.89/49/0916565.

US
**MANAGEMENT DATA LIST (ML) BASIC NAVY MICROFORM. VFOAT** Navy Management Data List; ML-N. English. mo. Defense Logistics Agency / Battle Creek, Defense Logistics Services Center, Federal Center, 74 North Washington, Battle Creek MI 49017-3084.

GW
**MARINE.** Periodical. German. DM24.00. Verlag Redaktion Bundesmarine, Postfach 161, 53 Bonn 1 Germany. **LC** VA510; .M36.

US
**MARINE ACCIDENT REPORTS. SUMMARY FORMAT / NATIONAL TRANSPORTATION SAFETY BOARD.** Issue No. 1 (Jan. through June 1978)-. English. $65.00. National Technical Information Service - NTIS, Room 2027S, 5285 Port Royal Road, Springfield VA 22161. **Tel** (703)487-4630, (703)487-4660, (703)487-4650, FAX (703)321-8547, telex 89-9405. available on microfiche (Vols. for (1983-) distributed to depository libraries).

US/0882-1984
**MARINE EQUIPMENT CATALOG.** [Mar. equip. cat.]. 1984-. Catalog. English. an. $65.00. Maritime Activity Reports, Inc., 107 East 31st Street, New York NY 10016. **DD** 623.

CN/0824-8729
**MARINE EQUIPMENT DIRECTORY.** [Mar. equip. dir.]. (Nov./Dec. 1972)-. English. an. 40.00Can$. Shipping Register Publications / Canada, 1056 Chemin de Golf Nuns ISLD, Verdun Quebec H3E 1H4 Canada. **ED** Olaf J. Silva. **LC** VM470; .M35. **DD** 338.4/762386025. **Ad Acc. Circ:** 3,000.
**Desc:** Directory of marine products and services offered.

US
**MARINE SAFETY MANUAL. Main/Corp** United States. Coast Guard. (1977)-. Government Publication. English. ir. $76.00 US; $95.00 other. Superintendent of Documents, US Government Printing Office, Washington DC 20402. **Tel** (202)275-3328, FAX (202)786-2377.

UK
**MARINE STORES INTERNATIONAL. See** Economics-Industry and Production.

UK/0951-8339
**MARINE STRUCTURES.** [Mar. struct.]. Vol. 1, No. 1 (1988)-. Academic Scholarly Publication. English. Six times a year. $455.00 The Americas; £305.00 other. Elsevier Applied Science, An Imprint of Elsevier Science Ltd., The Boulevard, Langford Lane, Kidlington, Oxford OX5 1GB United Kingdom. **Tel** 011 44 865 843000, 011 44 865 843699, FAX 011 44 865 843010. **(Subscription address:** Elsevier Science Ltd. Oxford Fulfillment Centre, PO Box 800, Kidlington, Oxford OX5 1DX United Kingdom.) **[CCC].** Index available. cum. index. **Bk Rev. Ad Acc. Circ:** 400 (ctrl). available on microfilm and microfiche from University Microfilms International (UMI). Documents available from Article Express International.
**Desc:** Presents and discusses the latest developments in research, design, fabrication and inservice experience relating to marine structures.
**Ind/Abst** BMT Abstr.; Corros. Abstr.; Ei Page One; Eng. Index Annu.; Fluid Abstr., Civil Eng.; Fluid Abstr. Proc. Eng.; FLUIDEX (19??-); Health Saf. Sci. Abstr.; Int. Civil Eng. Abstr.; Soft. Abstr. Eng.

US/1071-1333
**MARINE TECHNOLOGY NEWS.** ***Title Change.*** **Added/Corp** Phillips Business Information, Inc. (1993)-(July 1994). Periodical. English. bw (25 issues). Phillips Business Information, Inc., 1201 Seven Locks Road, Potomac MD 20854. **Tel** (301)424-3338, (800)777-5006, FAX (301)309-3847. **[CCC].** ***Merged into*** *Global Positioning & Navigation News.*

UK
**MARINE WEEK MARINE DESIGN INTERNATIONAL. VFOAT** Marine Design International. (1974)-. English. an. Reed Business Publishing / West Sussex, England, Perrymount Road, Haywards Heath, West Sussex RH16 3DH England. **Tel** 011 44 81 6523500. **LC** VM1; .S17. **DD** 623.8/05. ***Continues*** *S & SR Marine Design International.*

NE/0025-3340
**MARINEBLAD.** [Marineblad]. Vol. (1987)-. Academic Scholarly Publication. Dutch (English). Eleven times a year. F81.50. De Boer Mailingservice, Postbus 507, 1200 AM Hiversum Netherlands. **Tel** 011 31 30 258611. **LC** V5; .M3. Index available. **Ad Acc. Circ:** 5,500 (ctrl).
**Ind/Abst** EMBASE.

US/0198-9618
**MARINER'S CATALOG, THE.** [Mar. cat.]. V. 1-1973-. Catalog. English. an. $7.95. International Marine Publishing Company, PO Box 220, Camden ME 04843. **Tel** (207)236-4342. **LC** VM320; .M37. **DD** 623.8/2023/029473. Each issue contains an index to its own contents (no volume index)--loose.

UK/0025-3359
**MARINER'S MIRROR.** (THE MARINER'S MIRROR.). [Mar. mirror]. **Added/Corp** Society for Nautical Research (London, England). **VFOAT** Mariner's Mirror, Wherein May Be Discovered His Art, Craft & Mystery After the Manner of Their Use in all Ages and Among all Nations ... . Vol. 1 (Jan. 1911)-. Periodical. English. qt (Jan., Apr., July, Oct.). $50.00 (individuals); $65.00 (institutions). Society for Nautical Research, c/o Ms. Gould, 5 Goodwood Close, West Sussex GU29 9JG England. **ED** B. H. Dolley. **LC** VK1; .M4. **DD** 623.8/05. cum. index. **Bk Rev. Ad Acc. Circ:** 2,500 (ctrl). Documents available from The Genuine Article.
**Desc:** Nautical history, archaeology and all aspects of maritime activity through the centuries.
**Ind/Abst** Am. Hist. Life (1955-); Arts Humanit. Citation Index [Full Cov.]; BHA : Biblio. Hist. Art; Br. Archaeol. Bibliogr.; Br. Humanit. Index; Numis. Lit.; Res. Alert [Full Cov.]; Soc. Sci. Cit. Index [Select. Cov.].

SI/0303-4445
**MARINERS' (SINGAPORE).** (MARINERS'.). [Mariners']. **Added/Corp** Singapore Polytechnic Marine Engineering Society. Vol. 1 (1973)-. English. Singapore Polytechnic Marine Engineering Society, 9 Prince Edward Road, Singapore Singapore. **LC** VM595; .M37. **DD** 623.8/05.

US/0025-3367
**MARINERS WEATHER LOG. See** Earth Sciences-Meteorology.

SW/0025-3375
**MARINNYTT.** No. 1 (1953)-. Periodical. Swedish. qt. Kr6.00. Marinstaben, Marinnytt, Fack, 104 50 Stockholn Sweden. **LC** V5; .M27. **DD** 359.

DK/0106-7818
**MARITIM KONTAKT.** 1-. Periodical. Danish. Kontaktudvalget for Dansk Maritim Historie, OG Samfundsforskning, Hellerupvej 51 E, 2900 Hellerup Denmark. **LC** VK69; .M3. **DD** 387.5/0948.

UK/0950-558X
**MARITIME DEFENCE.** [Marit. def.]. Vol. 4, No. 10 (Oct. 1979)-. Periodical. English. Ten times a year (monthly with Jan./Feb. and July/Aug. issues combined). $70.00 US & Canada; £43.00 other. Eldon Publications Limited, 292-294 Walton Road, East Molesey Surrey, KT8 0HY England. **Tel** 011 44 81 9417510, FAX 011 44 81 9417449, telex 8814338. **LC** V1; .M34. **DD** 359/.005. **Bk Rev**, (Qty: 2). **Ad Acc. Circ:** 4,000. available on microfilm and microfiche from University Microfilms International (UMI). ***Continues*** *Maritime Defence International.*
**Desc:** Journal of international naval technology embracing all naval hulls, weapons, electronics, aircraft (fixed and rotary wing).
**Ind/Abst** Life Sci. Collect.

UK
**MARITIME STUDIES CURRENT AWARENESS BULLETIN.** Bulletin. English. ir. £20.00 UK; £36.00 other. Learning Resources Centre, Plymouth Polytechnic, Drake Circle, Plymouth PL4 8AA England.

UK
**MARITIME SURVEY.** Began with Vol. for 1973. English. an. £0.60 UK; £2.00 other. **LC** VK8; .M37. **DD** 387/.0941. ***Continues*** *Navy Year Book and Diary.*

AT
**MARITIME WORKER. See** Economics-Labor.

US/0025-6471
**MECH.** [Mech]. **Added/Corp** Naval Safety Center. Naval Aviation Safety Center (U.S.). **VFOAT** Naval Aviation Maintenance Safety Review. (1968)-. Government Publication. English. bm. $11.00 domestic; $13.75 other. Superintendent of Documents, US Government Printing Office, Washington DC 20402. **Tel** (202)275-3328, FAX (202)786-2377. **LC** VG93; .A394. ***Continues*** *Aircraft Mishaps Involving Maintenance and Servicing.*
**Desc:** Presents the most accurate information available on the prevention of maintenance-caused mishaps as well as general aviation ground safety.

UK/0047-5955
**MER. MARINE ENGINEERS REVIEW. See** Engineering.

US/0199-7068
**MODEL SHIP BUILDER.** [Model ship build.]. Sept./Oct. (1979)-. Periodical. English. bm (Jan., Mar., May, July, Sept., Nov.). $24.90 (one year), $46.45 (two year). Phoenix Publications Inc. / Wisconsin, PO Box 128, Cedarsburg WI 53012. **Tel** (414)377-7888. **ED** Jeffrey A. Phillips. **LC** VM298; .M57. **DD** 623.8/201/05. Index available. cum. index. **Bk Rev**, (Qty: 20). **Ad Acc. Circ:** 10,000.
**Desc:** Construction and history of model ships, also location and availability of model ship and nautical books.

RU/0134-9236
**MORSKOI SBORNIK.** [Mor. sb.]. (1848)-. Periodical. Russian. mo. $119.95. **(Subscription address:** East View Publications Inc., 3020 Harbor Lane North, Suite 110, Minneapolis MN 55447.) **CODEN** MORSAV.
**Ind/Abst** Am. Hist. Life (1972-).

US/0147-572X
**MRIS ABSTRACTS. Main/Corp** Maritime Research Information Service. **Added/Corp** National Research Council (U.S.). Transportation Research Board. **VAT** Maritime Research Information Service Abstracts. (June 1973)-. Periodical. English. sa. $50.00. National Research Council, 2101 Constitution Avenue, Washington DC 20418. **LC** Z6837; .M2; VK145. **DD** 016.6238. ***Continues*** *M.R.I.S. Bulletin, 0090-9785.*

NE
**NAAMBOEK VAN OFFICIEREN DER KONINKLIJKE MARINE. Main/Corp** Netherlands. Ministerie van Defensie. Dutch. Ministerie van Defensie, PO Box 20701, 2500 ES Dan, Haag Netherlands. **LC** VB315.N4; N47A.

IT/0392-369X
**NAUTICA.** [Nautica]. (1962)-. Periodical. Italian. mo. L300000.00 America, Asia & Africa; L80000.00 Italy; L160000.00 Europe; L400000.00 other. Nautica, Via Tevere 44, 00198 Rome Italy. **Tel** 011 39 6 8413060. **UDC** 797.2. Index available. cum. index. **Bk Rev. Ad Acc. Circ:** 60,000 (ctrl).
**Desc:** Covers naval science and navigation.

US
**NAUTICAL BRASS, ETC. VFOAT** Nautical Brass, et Cetera. Vol. 2, No. 4 (July/August 1982)-. Periodical. English. bm. $30.00 US; $36.00 other. Nautical Brass, PO Box 3966, North Fort Myers FL 33918. **Tel** (813)997-1458, FAX (813)997-0725. **ED** Bill Momsen, 1003 April Lane, North Ft. Myers, FL 33918. **LC** V745; .N38. **DD** 623.8/6/05. **Bk Rev**, (Qty: 12). **Ad Acc. Circ:** 1,500. ***Continues*** *Nautical Brass, 0882-4401.*
**Desc:** Nautical collectibles, marine brass, steam whistles, flare guns, instruments, scrimshaw, ordnance, marine art, ship models, antique diving helmets and equipment, plus stories of the sea, pirates, treasure salvage, and maritime history.

UK/0028-1336
**NAUTICAL MAGAZINE.** (THE NAUTICAL MAGAZINE: A JOURNAL OF PAPERS ON SUBJECTS CONNECTED WITH MARITIME AFFAIRS.). [Naut. mag.]. Vol. 1, No. 1 (Mar. 1832)-. Periodical. English. Twelve times a year. £30.60. Brown Son & Ferguson Ltd, 4/10 Darnley Street, Glasgow G41 2SD Scotland. **Tel** 011 44 41 4291234, FAX 011 44 41 4201694. **ED** L. Ingram-Brown. Index available. cum. index. **Bk Rev. Ad Acc, Adv Mgr:** D. Provan. **Circ:** 1,100 (ctrl).
**Desc:** Merchant navy and those interested in the sea.

US/0738-7245
**NAUTICAL RESEARCH JOURNAL.** [Naut. res. j.]. **Added/Corp** Nautical Research Guild. (Jan. 1949)-. Periodical. English. qt. $25.00. Nautical Research Guild, 19 Pleasant Street, Everett MA 02149. **Tel** (617)389-2505. **ED** Erik A.B. Ronnberg Jr. **LC** V1; .N27. cum. index. **Bk Rev. Ad Acc. Circ:** 1,600 (ctrl). available on microfilm and microfiche from University Microfilms International (UMI).
**Desc:** Historical data on maritime materials useful for modelers, historians and collectors.
**Ind/Abst** Am. Hist. Life (1965-).

PL/0548-0523
**NAUTOLOGIA. Added/Corp** Polskie Towarzystwo Nautologiczne. Vol. 1 (1966)-. Periodical. Polish. qt. Price on Request. **(Subscription address:** ARS Polona, PO Box 1001, 00068 Warsaw Poland.) **LC** VK4; .N32.

US/0028-1409
**NAVAL AFFAIRS.** [Nav. aff.]. **Added/Corp** Fleet Reserve Association. (1921)-. Periodical. English. mo. $7.00. Fleet Reserve Association, 125 North West Street, Alexandria VA 22314. **Tel** (703)683-1400, FAX (703)549-6610. **ED** James T. McClung. **LC** VA49; .N22. **DD** 359. **Bk Rev. Ad Acc.** ctrl circ.
**Desc:** Primarily concerned with legislation and personnel issues of enlisted active duty, retired, reserve of the US Navy, Marine Corps, and Coast Guard.

JA/0387-5504
**NAVAL ARCHITECTURE AND OCEAN ENGINEERING.** [Nav. archit. ocean eng.]. **Added/Corp** Nihon Zosen Gakkai. Vol. 15 (1977)-. Periodical. English. an. $74.00. Society of Naval Architects of Japan, 15-16 Toranomon 1 chome, Minato-ku Tokyo Japan. **(Subscription address:** Kyowa Book Company Inc., 1-38 Kanda Jinbo-Cho, Chiyoda-Ku, Tokyo 101, Japan) **LC** VM4; .N57. **DD** 623.8/1/08. **[CCC].** Documents available from Article Express International. ***Continues*** *Nihon Zosen Gakkai. Selected Papers from the Society of Naval Architects of Japan.*
**Ind/Abst** Bioeng. Abstr.; Ei Page One; Eng. Index Annu.

US/0028-1425
**NAVAL ENGINEERS JOURNAL.** [Nav. eng. j.]. **Added/Corp** American Society of Naval Engineers. Vol. 74, No. 2, (May 1962)-. Periodical. English. Six times a year (Jan., Mar., May, July, Sept., Nov.). $80.00 US & Canada; $95.00 others. American Society of Naval Engineers, Inc., 1452 Duke Street, Alexandria VA 22314-3458. **Tel** (703)836-6727, FAX (703)836-7491. **LC** VM1; .A5. **DD** 623.8/05. **CODEN** NVEJAX. cum. index. Documents available from Article Express International, The Genuine Article, CASDDS. ***Continues*** *Journal of the American Society of Naval Engineers, Inc., 0099-7056.*
**Desc:** Original technical papers and informative engineering articles by authorities in the design, construction, operation and support of naval ships and maritime auxiliaries.
**Ind/Abst** Acoust. Abstr.; Alum. Ind. Abstr.; Bioeng. Abstr.; BMT Abstr.; Chem. Abstr.; Curr. Contents Eng. Tech. Appl. Sci.; Ei Page One; EMBASE; Energy Res. Abstr.; Eng. Mater. Abstr.; Eng. Index Annu.; Met. Abstr.;

Ocean. Abstr.; Life Sci. Collect.; Pollut. Abstr. Indexes; Res. Alert [Select. Cov.]; SCISEARCH; Shock Vibr. Dig.; Soc. Sci. Cit. Index [Select. Cov.].

UK/0722-8880
**NAVAL FORCES.** [Nav. forces]. Vol. 1, No. 1 (1980)-. Periodical. English. Six times a year. $40.84. Special Publication Service, Karl Mand Str 2, D 56070 Koblenz Germany. **Tel** 011 49 261 807060. **(Subscription address:** US/Can Nautical and Aviation Publishing Company, 101 West Read Street, Room 314, Baltimore MD 21201) **LC** V1; .N35. **DD** 359/.005. **Ad Acc. Circ:** 18,450 (ctrl).
**Desc:** A forum for discussion and focuses attention on the importance of naval forces worldwide. Provides information on hardware, weapons systems, strategy, and modern technology in world's navies.
**Ind/Abst** Air Univ. Libr. Index Mil. Period.; BMT Abstr.; Curr. Mil. Pol. Lit.

US/1042-1920
**NAVAL HISTORY.** [Naval hist.]. **Added/Corp** United States Naval Institute. Vol. 1/1/1 (Apr. 1987)-. Periodical. English. bm. $18.00 (one year), $44.00 (two year), (member); $20.00 (one year), $50.00 (two year), (non-member and non-subscriber to Proceedings of the USNI) surface mail. U. S. Naval Institute, 2062 Generals Highway, Annapolis MD 21402. **Tel** (301)268-6110, (800)233-8764. **ED** Paul Stillwell and Fred H. Rainbow. **LC** V27; .N35. **DD** 359/.00973. Index available. **Bk Rev. Ad Acc. Circ:** 27,187.
**Desc:** Covers a wide range of naval history, including various eras, subjects and countries, as well as services-U.S. Coast Guard, Marine Corps, Merchant Marine and Navy.
**Ind/Abst** Am. Hist. Life (1989-).

US
**NAVAL INSTITUTE GUIDE TO COMBAT FLEETS OF THE WORLD. Added/Corp** United States Naval Institute. **VFOAT** Combat Fleets of the World. (1990/91)-. Periodical. English. be. price varies per volume. U. S. Naval Institute, 2062 Generals Highway, Annapolis MD 21402. **Tel** (301)268-6110, (800)233-8764. ***Continues*** *Combat Fleets of the World, 0364-3263.*

US/0894-069X
**NAVAL RESEARCH LOGISTICS.** [Nav. res. logist.]. **Added/Corp** United States. Office of Naval Research. Vol. 34, No. 1 (Feb. 1987)-. Periodical. English. Eight times a year. $488.00 US; $568.00 Canada and Mexico; $598.00 other. John Wiley & Sons, Inc., 605 Third Avenue, New York NY 10158-0012. **Tel** (212)850-6000, (212)850-6645, FAX (212)850-6088, telex 12-7063. **(Subscription address:** John Wiley & Sons / England, Baffins Lane, Chichester, West Sussex PO19 1UD England.) **ED** Richard E. Rosenthal. **LC** V179; .N3. **CODEN** NRLOEP. **[CCC]. Pr Rev.** available on microfilm and microfiche from University Microfilms International (UMI). Documents available from Article Express International, The Genuine Article, Ask*IEEE. ***Continues*** *Naval Research Logistics Quarterly, 0028-1441.*
**Desc:** Offers research papers that cover operations research topics relevant to theoretical logistics. Articles are published on both theory and applications in key areas including mathematical statistics, economics, tactics and surgery.
**Ind/Abst** Appl. Mech. Rev.; Bioeng. Abstr. (1987-); Compumath Citation Index [Full Cov.]; Curr. Contents Eng. Tech. Appl. Sci.; Curr. Index Stat.; Ei Page One (1987-); Eng. Index Annu. [Select. Cov.]; INSPEC (1987-); Int. Abstr. Oper. Res. [Full Cov.]; Int. Aerosp. Abstr. (1987-); Math. Rev. (1987-); Oper. Res./Manag. Sci.; Qual. Control Appl. Stat.; Res. Alert [Full Cov.]; Sci. Cit. Index; SCISEARCH; Soc. Sci. Cit. Index [Select. Cov.]; Stat. Theory Method Abstr.

US/0028-145X
**NAVAL RESEARCH REVIEWS.** [Nav. res. rev.]. **Added/Corp** United States. Office of Naval Research. **VFOAT** Naval Research. (May 1959)-. Government Publication. English. qt. $9.50 domestic; $11.90 other. Superintendent of Documents, US Government Printing Office, Washington DC 20402. **Tel** (202)275-3328, FAX (202)786-2377. **LC** V393; .R43. **DD** 359/.07/0973. **NLM** W1 UN6983. **CODEN** NARRA9. available on microfilm and microfiche from University Microfilms International (UMI). Documents available from BIOSIS Document Express, Ask*IEEE, CASDDS. ***Continues*** *Research Reviews / United States Division of Naval Research, 0193-1334.*
**Desc:** Publishes articles about research conducted by the laboratories and contractors of the Office of Naval Research and describes important naval experimental activities.
**Ind/Abst** Acoust. Abstr.; Biol. Abstr.; Chem. Abstr.; INSPEC (Jan. 1969-); Int. Aerosp. Abstr.; Life Sci. Collect.; Soc. Plann. Policy Dev. Abstr.

UK
**NAVAL REVIEW.** English. qt. £15.00. Naval Review, Secretary of the Treasury, 32 West Street, Chichester West Sussex PO19 1QS England. **Tel** 011 44 0243 784482. **ED** J.R. Hill. Index available. cum. index. **Bk Rev**, (Qty: 50). **Ad Acc, Adv Mgr:** A. Gorst-Williams, **Tel** 089283-2232. **Circ:** 3,000 (ctrl).
**Desc:** Covers the royal navy present, future, and past.
**Ind/Abst** Am. Hist. Life (1962-1969).

US/0077-6238
**NAVAL REVIEW (ANNAPOLIS).** (NAVAL REVIEW.). [Nav. rev.]. **Added/Corp** United States Naval Institute. (1963)-. English. an (May). $8.00 (member), $10.00 (non-member); Naval Review is the May issue of Proceedings of the US Naval Institute. U. S. Naval Institute, 2062 Generals Highway, Annapolis MD 21402. **Tel** (301)268-6110, (800)233-8764. **LC** V10; .N615. **DD** 359.058.

US/0028-1484
**NAVAL WAR COLLEGE REVIEW.** [Naval War Coll. rev.]. **Added/Corp** Naval War College (U.S.). (1948)-. Periodical. English. ir. Naval War College, Department of the Navy, Newport RI 02841. **Tel** (401)841-4552. **ED** Frank Whlig. **LC** V1; .U48. **DD** 359/.005. Index available. cum. index. **Bk Rev. Circ:** 15,000 (ctrl). available on microfilm and microfiche from University Microfilms International (UMI).
**Desc:** A journal of strategic, naval and political-military thought.
**Ind/Abst** Air Univ. Libr. Index Mil. Period.; Am. Hist. Life (1969-); Am. Bibliogr. Slavic East Europ. Stud.; Curr. Mil. Pol. Lit.; Int. Polit. Sci. Abstr.; Middle East Abstr. Index; Peace Res. Abstr. J. (1979-1985).

JA/0289-6079
**NAVI.** [NAVI]. **VFOAT** Gekkan Nabi; Navigator (Tokyo. 1984). (1984)-. Periodical. Japanese. Twelve times a year. ¥15900.00. Nippon IPS Co. Ltd., 11 6 3 Chome Iidabashi, Chiyodaku Tokyo 102 Japan. **Tel** 011 81 3 3238 0700. **ED** Nigensha (phone: (03)3263-6051). **DD** 388.3.

AT/0077-6262
**NAVIGATION.** [Navigation]. **Added/Corp** Australian Institute of Navigation. (1959)-. English. Four times a year (Mar., June, Sept., Dec.). 20.00Aus$. Australian Institute of Navigation, GPO Box 2250, Sydney New South Wales 2001 Australia. **Tel** 011 61 2 2566354. **ED** Captain K. C. Crompton, (phone: 011 61 2 264 6413). **LC** V1; .N73. **DD** 623.89/05. **Ad Acc. Circ:** 700 (ctrl).
**Desc:** News, information and articles related to navigation and position findings on sea, land and air.
**Ind/Abst** Aquat. Sci. Fish. Abstr. (Computer File); BMT Abstr.; Comput. Inf. Syst. Abstr. J. [Full Cov.]; Int. Aerosp. Abstr.; Mech. Eng. Abstr.; Solid State Supercond. Abstr.

US
**NAVIGATION AND VESSEL INSPECTION CIRCULAR / DEPARTMENT OF TRANSPORTATION, UNITED STATES COAST GUARD.**
**Added/Corp** United States. Coast Guard. (19??)-. Government Publication. English. ir. $23.00 US; $28.75 other. Superintendent of Documents, US Government Printing Office, Washington DC 20402. **Tel** (202)275-3328, FAX (202)786-2377.
**Desc:** Provides information relating to navigation, regulation of ships by the United States and vessel operation.

FR/0028-1530
**NAVIGATION (PARIS).** (NAVIGATION.). [Navigation]. **Added/Corp** Institut Francais de Navigation. Vol. 1, No. (Jan. 1953)-. Periodical. French (English). qt. 298.83F France; 360.00F other. Institut Francais de Navigation, 3 Avenue Octave, Greard 75007 Paris France. **Tel** 011 33 1 42603330 Ext. 27343. **LC** VK2; .N3. **CODEN** NVGNAL. **Bk Rev. Ad Acc. Circ:** 1,500 (ctrl). Documents available from Ask*IEEE.
**Desc:** Technical review of maritime air and space navigation.
**Ind/Abst** Bibliogr. Carto.; INSPEC (Oct. 1971-); Int. Aerosp. Abstr.

US
**NAVIGATION SEASON EXTENSION DEMONSTRATION PROGRAM. DRAFT ENVIRONMENTAL STATEMENT.**
**Main/Corp** United States. Army. Corps of Engineers. Detroit District. Periodical. English. PO Box 1027, Detroit MI 48231.

US/0028-1522
**NAVIGATION (WASHINGTON).** (NAVIGATION.). [Navigation]. **Added/Corp** Institute of Navigation. Vol. 1, (Mar. 1946)-. Periodical. English. Four times a year (Mar., June, Sept., Dec.). $45.00. Institute of Navigation, 1800 Diagonal Road, Suite 480, Alexandria VA 22314. **Tel** (703)683-7101, FAX (703)683-7105. **ED** Ronald Braff. **LC** VK1; .N33. **DD** 527.05. **CODEN** NAVIB3. **[CCC].** Index available. **Bk Rev. Ad Acc. Circ:** 3,000 (ctrl). Documents available from Article Express International, Ask*IEEE.
**Desc:** Covers development and application of navigation systems for aerospace, nautical and land use.
**Ind/Abst** Aquat. Sci. Fish. Abstr. (Computer File); Bibliogr. Carto.; Bioeng. Abstr.; Ei Page One; Elect. Comm. Abstr.; Eng. Index Annu.; INSPEC (Fall 1973-); Int. Aerosp. Abstr.; Ocean. Abstr.; Life Sci. Collect.

FI
**NAVIGATOR (ENGLISH EDITION).** (NAVIGATOR.). English. an. Satamakatu 4, PO Box 161, SF-00161 Helsinki 16 Finland. **LC** VK96.F5; N38. **DD** 387.5/094897.
**Ind/Abst** BMT Abstr.

FR/0028-159X
**NAVIRES, PORTS & CHANTIERS.** ***Title Change.*** [Navires ports chantiers]. **VAT** Navires, Ports et Chantiers. Yearly Volume No. 1 (June 1950)-(1993). Periodical. French (English). mo. Navires Ports and Chantiers, 190 Boulevard Hussmann, Paris 75008 France. **Tel** 1 45 63 11 55, telex NAVIMAR 290131 F. **ED** Didier Dorse, Maine De Leyritz. **LC** VM2; .N35. Index available. cum. index. **Bk Rev. Ad Acc. Circ:** 12,000. ***Merged into*** *Journal de la Marine Marchande et du Transport Multimodal.*
**Ind/Abst** BMT Abstr.; Energy Res. Abstr. (April 1982-); Saf. Health Work.

FR
**NAVIS; ANNUAIRE DE LA MARINE MARCHANDE, DE LA CONSTRUCTION NAVALE ET DES PORTS MARITIMES.**
French. an. 450.00F. NAVIS, 190 Boulevard Haussmann, 75008 Paris France. **Tel** 45-63-11-55, telex NAVIMAR 290 131 F.

US
**NAVORD OD. Main/Corp** United States. Naval Ordnance Systems Command. Periodical. English. US Department of Defense Department of the Navy, Pentagon, Room 4E686, Washington DC 20350. **Tel** (703)695-0911. ***Continues*** *NAVORD Report.*

US/0161-9411
**NAVSEA JOURNAL. Main/Corp** United States. Naval Sea Systems Command. **VAT** Naval Sea Systems Command Journal. Periodical. English. mo. Naval Sea Systems Command, Sea OOD2 Department of the Navy, Washington DC 20362. **LC** V1; .U46A. **DD** 623.8/05.

US
**NAVY CHAPLAIN, THE. Added/Corp** United States. Office of the Navy Chief of Chaplains. United States. Office of the Chief of Naval Operations. Vol. 1, No. 1 (Fall 1986)-. Periodical. English. Four times a year. Free. Chaplins Resource Board, 9591 Maryland Avenue, Norfolk VA 23511. **Tel** (804)444-7665. ***Formed by the union of*** *Porthole* ***and*** *Navy Chaplains Bulletin, 0028-1654.*

US
**NAVY CONTRACTING DIRECTIVES.**
**Main/Corp** United States. Navy Dept. (1979)-. English. mo. US Department of Defense Department of the Navy, Pentagon, Room 4E686, Washington DC 20350. **Tel** (703)695-0911. **(Subscription address:** Superintendent of Documents, US Government Printing Office, Washington DC 20402.) ***Continues*** *Navy Procurement Directives, 0147-7102.*

UK/0144-3194
**NAVY INTERNATIONAL.** [Navy int.]. Vol. 77, (Jan. 1972)-. Periodical. English. Six times a year. £31.50 UK; £45.00 other. Maritime World Ltd, 114 South Street, Dorking Surrey RH4 2EZ England. **Tel** 011 44 306 631442, FAX 011 44 306 631226, telex 859424 INTLX G. **ED** Anthony J. Watts. **LC** V1; .N77. **DD** 359/.005. **Bk Rev. Ad Acc. Circ:** 2,500 (ctrl). available on an online database. ***Absorbed*** *Combat Craft, 0264-4649.*
**Desc:** International coverage in detail, studying all aspects of maritime defense and its importance for maintaining the freedom of the seas.
**Ind/Abst** BMT Abstr.

UK
**NAVY LIST, THE. Main/Corp** Great Britain. Ministry of Defence. English. £8.00. Ministry of Defence, Old Admiral Building, Spring Gardens, London SW1 A 2BE England. **LC** V11.G7; A2. **DD** 359.3/0941. ***Continues*** *Navy List.*

US/0028-1662
**NAVY NEWS.** (19??)-. Periodical. English. mo. Scope Interprises Inc, 3121 Evening Way, La Jolla CA 92037-1614.
**Ind/Abst** BMT Abstr. (-199?).

US/8756-1700
**NAVY NEWS & UNDERSEA TECHNOLOGY.** [Navy news undersea technol.]. **VFOAT** Navy News and Undersea Technology. (1984)-. English. Fifty times a year. $545.00 US; $575.00 other. Pasha Publications Inc., 1616 North Fort Myer Drive, Suite 1000, Arlington VA 22209. **Tel** (800)424-2908, (703)528-1244, FAX (703)528-3742, (703)528-1253. **DD** 359. **[CCC].** available on an online database (files 16,80,636,648/Full-Text) from DIALOG.
**Ind/Abst** PROMT [Full Txt.]; PTS Newsl. Database [Full Txt.].

US/0364-3646
**NAVY TECHNICAL DISCLOSURE BULLETIN / OFFICE OF NAVAL RESEARCH, DEPARTMENT OF THE NAVY.** Bulletin. English. mo. Office of Naval Research, Department of the Navy, Arlington VA 22217. **LC** V1; .U58A. **DD** 623.8/05.

US/0028-1697
**NAVY TIMES.** Vol. 1, No. 1 (Oct. 20, 1951)-. Periodical. English. wk. $48.00 (one year), $88.00 (two year), $132.00 (three year). Army Times Publishing

Company, 6883 Commercial Drive, Springfield VA 22159. **Tel** (800)368-5718, (703)750-8099. **ED** Tom Philpott. **LC** V1; .N88. **[CCC]. Bk Rev. Ad Acc. Pr Rev. Circ:** 88,000. available on microfilm and microfiche from University Microfilms International (UMI). ***Absorbed*** *Armed Force.*
**Desc:** Contains current government information for Navy personnel; also an independent forum for analysis of military policy.

FR
**NEPTUNIA. Added/Corp** Amis de Musees de la Marine. Association des Amis du Musees de la Marine, Paris. No. 1 (1946)-. Periodical. French. Four times a year (Mar., June, Sept., Dec.). 190.00F France; 210.00F other. Amis du Musees de la Marine, Palais Chaillot, 75016 Paris France. **Tel** 011 33 1 47 046763. **ED** Cristina Baron. **LC** V2; .N4. cum. index. **Bk Rev. Circ:** 2,000. ***Supersedes*** *Association des Amis des Musees de la Marine. Bulletin Trimestriel;* ***Absorbed*** *Triton.*
**Desc:** The three main subjects are maritime history, modelism specialized in models 17th and 18th century and underwater archaeology and museums.
**Ind/Abst** Br. Archaeol. Bibliogr. -?.

BE
**NEPTUNUS.** (March 1966)-. Periodical. Dutch (French). bm. $7.30 Belgium; $9.55 other. Neptunus, Postbus 17, B-8400 Oostende Belgium. **Tel** 59-803999. **LC** VA480; .N46. **DD** 359/.009493. **Bk Rev. Ad Acc. Circ:** 3,500 (ctrl).
**Desc:** Covers naval history, ship building, ports, military navy book reviews, bibliographies, fishery, naval vocabulary, and sailing.

US/1056-7348
**NEWS FROM THE OCEANOGRAPHER OF THE NAVY.** (NEWS FROM THE OCEANOGRAPHER OF THE NAVY / DEPARTMENT OF THE NAVY, OFFICE OF THE CHIEF OF NAVAL OPERATIONS.). [News Oceanogr. Navy]. **Added/Corp** United States. Office of the Chief of Naval Operations. (1990)-. Periodical. English. News from the Oceanographer of the Navy, 34th Street and Massachusetts Avenue NW, Washington DC 20392. **DD** 551. ***Continues in part*** *News from the Naval Observatory (1984), 1056-7291.*

US/1065-2329
**NEWSLETTER / NORTH AMERICAN SOCIETY OF OCEANIC HISTORY.** [Newsl. - N. Am. Soc. Ocean. Hist.]. **Main/Corp** North American Society of Oceanic History. **VFOAT** North American Society for Oceanic History Newsletter; NASOH Newsletter. (19??)-. Periodical. English. Three times a year. Comes with North American Society for Oceanic History membership. North American Society for Oceanic History, US Naval Academy, History Department, Annapolis MD 21402. **Tel** (301)267-3101. **ED** William R. Roberts. **DD** 910. **Bk Rev. Circ:** 250 (ctrl).
**Desc:** Publishes information for individuals, both professionals and lay persons, who are interested in maritime history, especially that of North America. The aim is to promote the dissemination of information among individuals interested in the sea and inland waterways and to foster a general awareness of maritime historical matters.

AT/0158-5312
**NEWSLETTER OF THE AUSTRALIAN ASSOCIATION FOR MARITIME HISTORY. Added/Corp** Australian Association for Maritime History. (19??)-. English. Four times a year (Feb., Apr., July, Oct.). 30.00Aus$ (individuals), 40.00Aus$ (institutions) Comes with Australian Association for Maritime History membership. Australian Association for Maritime History, c/o Ms. S. May, Department of Maritime History, W.A. Maritime Museum, Cliff Street Fremantle WA 6160 Australia. **Tel** 03 822 5671. **LC** VK121; .N48. **DD** 387.5/0994.

US/0360-716X
**NEWSLETTER - UNITED STATES. NAVY. SUPPLY CORPS.** (NEWSLETTER / NAVY SUPPLY CORPS.). [Newsl. - U.S., Navy, Supply Corps]. Newsletter. English. bm. Navy Supply Corps Newsletter, Supply Systems Command 091, Navy Department, Washington DC 20376. **LC** VC35; .A44. **DD** 355.6/21. available on microfiche (Vols. for (1986-) distributed to depository libraries). ***Continues*** *Monthly Newsletter (United States. Navy Dept. Bureau of Supplies and Accounts).*

JA
**NIHON HAKUYO KIKAN GAKKAI SHI. JOURNAL OF THE MARINE ENGINEERING SOCIETY IN JAPAN. See** Engineering.

JA/0388-7405
**NIHON KOKAI GAKKAI RONBUNSHU. VFOAT** Journal of Japan Institute of Navigation. (1949)-. Periodical. Japanese. Japan Institute of Navigation, Tokyo Japan. Documents available from Ask*IEEE.
**Ind/Abst** BMT Abstr.; INSPEC (Sept. 1983-).

JA
**NIHON SHOSEN SEMPUKU TOKEI. Added/Corp** Nihon Senshu Kyokai. (1972)-. Japanese. an. Free. Japanese Shipowners' Association, Nihon Senshu Kyokai, Kaiun Building, 6-4 Hirakawa-cho 2-chme Chiyoda-ku, Tokyo 102 Japan. **Tel** 03 262 4760, telex J2322148. **LC** VK105; .N54. **Circ:** 2,800.

JA/0514-8499
**NIHON ZOSEN GAKKAI RONBUNSHU.** [Nihon Zosen Gakkai ronbunshu]. **Added/Corp** Nihon Zosen Gakkai. **VFOAT** Journal of the Society of Naval Architects of Japan. (1???)-. Academic Scholarly Publication. Japanese (summaries and/or abstracts in English; table of contents in English). sa. $256.00. Nihon Zosen Gakkai, (Soc. of Naval Architects of Japan), 15-16, Toranomon 1 Chome, Minatoku, Tokyoto 105, Japan. **(Subscription address:** Kyowa Book Company Inc., 1-38 Kanda Jinbo-Cho Chiyoda-Ku Tokyo 101, Japan**) CODEN** NZGRDU. Documents available from CASDDS.
**Ind/Abst** Alum. Ind. Abstr.; BMT Abstr.; Chem. Abstr. (1968-1983); Coal Abstr.; Met. Abstr.; Life Sci. Collect.

NO/0029-2222
**NORSK TIDSSKRIFT FOR SJOVESEN.** [Nor. tidsskr. sjoves.]. (1882)-. Periodical. Norwegian. bm (6 issues). Kr130.00 Norway; Kr250.00 other. Norsk Tidskift for Sjovesen, PO Box 105, N-5078 Haakonsvern Norway. **Tel** 011 47 51 867000. **LC** V5; .N67.

●CN/1183-112X
**NORTHERN MARINER : JOURNAL OF THE CANADIAN NAUTICAL RESEARCH SOCIETY / LE MARIN DU NORD : REVUE DE SOCIETE CANADIENNE POUR LA RECHERCHE NAUTIQUE, THE. Added/Corp** Canadian Nautical Research Society. Memorial University of Newfoundland. Maritime Studies Research Unit. **VFOAT** Marin du Nord. Vol. 1, No. 1 (Jan. 1991)-. Periodical. English. qt. 25.00Can$ individuals, 50.00Can$ institutions (includes membership Canadian Nautical Research Society). Canadian Nautical Research Society, University of Newfoundland, St. Johns NFLD A1C 5S7 Canada. **Tel** (709)737-8424, FAX (709)737-4569. **LC** VK26; .N67. **DD** 623.89/0971.

US/0092-1262
**NOTICE TO MARINERS.** (NOTICE TO MARINERS / PREPARED JOINTLY WITH THE NATIONAL OCEAN SURVEY AND U.S. COAST GUARD.). **Added/Corp** National Ocean Survey. United States. Coast Guard. United States. Defense Mapping Agency. Hydrographic/Topographic Center. United States. Hydrographic Office. United States. Naval Oceanographic Office. United States. National Ocean Service. (Sept. 23, 1978)-. Periodical. English. Fifty-two times a year. Free on request. National Ocean Service, NOAA Distribution Branch NCG33, Riverdale MD 20737. **Tel** (301)436-6993. **LC** VK798; .U45. **DD** 623.89/2/05.

●US/0700-1789
**NOTICE TO MARINERS (ANNUAL EDITION 1976).** (NOTICES TO MARINERS.). (1992)-. English. an. Canada Communication Group Publishers, Order Processing, Ottawa Ontario K1A 0S9 Canada. **Tel** (819)956-4800, (819)956-4802. ***Continues*** *Canadian Coast Guard Aids and Waterways Directorate Notice to Mariners.*

FR
**NOUVEAUTES TECHNIQUES MARITIMES.** Periodical. French. ir. Nouveautes Techniques, 190 Bd Haussmann, Paris 75008 France. **Tel** 563-1155. **LC** VM2; .J6.

US/0162-2129
**NRA. NAVAL RESERVE ASSOCIATION NEWS. Main/Corp** Naval Reserve Association. **VFOAT** Naval Reserve Association News. (19??)-. Periodical. English. mo. $5.00. Naval Reserve Association, 1619 King Street, Alexandria VA 22314. **Tel** (703)548-5800.

US/0502-3378
**NRL MEMORANDUM REPORT.** [NRL memo. rep.]. **Added/Corp** Naval Research Laboratory (U.S.). **VFOAT** N.R.L. Memorandum Report. **VAT** Naval Research Laboratory Memorandum Report. (19??)-. Monographic series. English. **LC** QC621; .U55a. **DD** 500. **CODEN** XNLMAT. Documents available from CASDDS.
**Ind/Abst** Bioeng. Abstr.; Chem. Abstr.; Ocean. Abstr.

US
**NRL REPORT. Added/Corp** Naval Research Laboratory (U.S.) Naval Postgraduate School (U.S.). **VAT** Naval Research Laboratory Report. (19??)-. Monographic series. English. ir. Superintendent of Documents, US Government Printing Office, Washington DC 20402. **Tel** (202)275-3328, FAX (202)786-2377. **LC** QC453; .U54.
**Ind/Abst** Aquat. Sci. Fish. Abstr. (Computer File); Ocean. Abstr.

US
**NTIS ALERT. NAVIGATION, GUIDANCE & CONTROL. Added/Corp** United States. National Technical Information Service. (19??)-. Periodical. English. Twenty-four times a year. $140.00 US; $195.00 other. National Technical Information Service - NTIS, Room 2027S, 5285 Port Royal Road, Springfield VA 22161. **Tel** (703)487-4630, (703)487-4660, (703)487-4650, FAX (703)321-8547, telex 89-9405.

US/0886-0149
**OCEAN NAVIGATOR. See** Earth Sciences-Oceanography.

UK/0261-6777
**OCEAN VOICE.** [Ocean voice]. **Added/Corp** International Maritime Satellite Organization. Vol. 1, No. 1 (Oct. 1981)-. Periodical. English (summaries and/or abstracts in French and Spanish). Four times a year. International Maritime Satellite Organization, 44 Melton Street, London NW1 2EQ England. **Tel** 011 44 71 3879089, FAX 011 44 71 7281044, telex 297201 INMSAT G. **ED** T. M. Wilding-White, L. Adamson and H. Pytkiewicz. **LC** VK562; .O32. **DD** 621.38/0422. Index available. **Bk Rev. Ad Acc. Circ:** 17,606 (ctrl).
**Ind/Abst** Aquat. Sci. Fish. Abstr. (Computer File); BMT Abstr.

US/0093-2124
**ON SCENE. Added/Corp** United States. Coast Guard. United States. Coast Guard. Office of Navigation Safety and Waterway Services. (1972)-. Periodical. English. qt. US Coast Guard, Office of Navigation Safety and Waterway Services, 2100 Second Street Southwest, Washington DC 20593. **Tel** (202)267-1943. **LC** VK1323; .N35. **DD** 363.3/4. ***Continues*** *National Maritime S.A.R. Review, 0047-8946.*

GW/0474-7550
**ORTUNG UND NAVIGATION.** (196?)-. Periodical. German. Three times a year. DM147.00 Germany; DM169.00 other. Deutsche Gesellschaft fur Ortung und Navigation e.V., PO Box 2622, W 4000 Duesseldorf 1, Germany. **UDC** 621.396:527.
**Ind/Abst** Int. Aerosp. Abstr.

JA/0563-7546
**PAPERS OF SHIP RESEARCH INSTITUTE. Added/Corp** Sempaku Gijutsu Kenkyujo (Tokyo, Japan). **VFOAT** Sempaku Gijutsu Kenkyujo Obun Hokoku. No. 1 (Mar. 1964)-. Monographic series. English. Ship Research Institute, 38-1, 6-Chome, Shinkawa, Mitaka, Tokyo 181 Japan. **LC** VM7; .S45. **DD** 623.8/1/05. **CODEN** PSRIAS. Documents available from Article Express International.
**Ind/Abst** Bioeng. Abstr.; Ei Page One; Eng. Index Annu.

IO
**PERSPEKTIVA ANGKATAN LAUT.** Periodical. Indonesian. Dinas Penerangan Tni-Al, Jln Gunungsahari No 66, Jakarta Indonesia. **LC** V5; .P47.

US
**PILOTING, SEAMANSHIP, AND SMALL BOAT HANDLING / CHARLES F. CHAPMAN ; WITH REVISIONS BY ELBERT S. MALONEY ... [ET AL.]. VFOAT** Piloting, Seamanship & Small Boat Handling; Chapman Piloting, Seamanship, and Small Boat Handling. (1922)-. English. $11.95. Motor Boating & Sailing, 224 West 57th Street, New York NY 10019. **LC** VM341; .C63; VM341; .M9. **DD** 623.88/2.3105. ***Separated from*** *Motor Boating.*

US/0032-4868
**PORT OF TOLEDO NEWS.** (PORT OF TOLEDO NEWS / TOLEDO-LUCAS COUNTY PORT AUTHORITY.). Began with: Jan./Feb. 1967. Periodical. English. qt. Free. Toledo-Lucas County Port Authority, One Maritime Plaza/7th Floor, Toledo OH 43604-1866. **Tel** (419)243-8251, FAX (419)243-1835. **ED** Paula C Wittich. **Circ:** 6,000 (ctrl). ***Continues*** *Port of Toledo Newsletter.*
**Desc:** Details activities of Toledo-Lucas County Port Authority's three main divisions: seaport, aviation and economic development. Editorial copy and layout is for general audience (no technical copy).

BL/0101-5664
**PORTOS E NAVIOS.** [Portos nav.]. Periodical. Portuguese. mo. Rue Leandro Martins, 1 901 02 OX Postal 2791, Rio de Janeiro Brazil. **LC** VM41; .P6.

US/0278-9396
**PROCEEDINGS OF THE ... ANNUAL MEETING / INTERNATIONAL OMEGA ASSOCIATION. Main/Corp** International Omega Association. Meeting. **VFOAT** Annual Meeting, International Omega Association, Inc. Proceedings. English. an. $50.00, $70.00 (photocopies after printing is exhausted). International Omega Association Inc, PO Box 2324, Arlington VA 22202-0324. **LC** VK560; .I59A. **DD** 623.89/32/05. cum. index.
**Desc:** Compilation of technical papers presented at the annual meeting of the International Omega Association.

US
**PROCEEDINGS OF THE INSTITUTE OF NAVIGATION ANNUAL MEETING.** (19??)-. Proceedings. English. an. $70.00 (members), $80.00 (nonmembers). Institute of Navigation, 1800 Diagonal Road, Suite 480, Alexandria VA 22314. **Tel**

(703)683-7101, FAX (703)683-7105. Documents available from Article Express International.
**Ind/Abst** Eng. Index Annu.

US/0364-0981
**PROCEEDINGS OF THE MARINE SAFETY COUNCIL.** [Proc. Mar. Saf. Counc.]. Began with V. 28, No. 5, May 1971. Proceedings. English. bm. Free. Proceedings Magazine, US Coast Guard (G-MP-2), Washington DC 20593-0001. **Tel** (202)267-1483. **ED** Sharon L Chapman. **LC** VK23; .A26. **DD** 614.8/64/05. **Circ:** 6,000 (ctrl). ***Continues*** *Proceedings (United States. Merchant Marine Council).*
**Desc:** Articles relate to all aspects of maritime safety.
**Ind/Abst** BMT Abstr.

US/0276-4849
**PROCEEDINGS OF THE NATIONAL OCEAN SURVEY HYDROGRAPHIC SURVEY CONFERENCE, ... ANNUAL MEETING.** [Proc. Natl. Ocean Surv. Hydrogr. Surv. Conf., annu. meet.]. **Main/Conf** National Ocean Survey Hydrographic Survey Conference. Proceedings. English. an. US Department of Commerce / National Oceanic & Atmospheric Administration NOAA, 6010 Executive Boulevard, Washington Science Center, Building 5, Rockville MD 20852. **Tel** (202)482-6090, FAX (202)482-3154. **LC** VK589; .N38A. **DD** 526.9/9.

US
**PROCEEDINGS OF THE NATIONAL TECHNICAL MEETING / INSTITUTE OF NAVIGATION.** Proceedings. English. $65.00 US and Canada; $70.00 other. Institute of Navigation, 1800 Diagonal Road, Suite 480, Alexandria VA 22314. **Tel** (703)683-7101, FAX (703)683-7105.

US
**PROCEEDINGS OF THE NATIONAL TECHNICAL MEETING / THE INSTITUTE OF NAVIGATION.** **Main/Corp** Institute of Navigation. National Technical Meeting. (198?)-. Proceedings. English. $80.00 (members), $90.00 (nonmembers). Institute of Navigation, 1800 Diagonal Road, Suite 480, Alexandria VA 22314. **Tel** (703)683-7101, FAX (703)683-7105. ***Continues*** *ION National Marine Navigation Meeting. Proceedings.*

US/0198-7194
**PROCEEDINGS OF THE NORTH AMERICAN SOCIETY FOR OCEANIC HISTORY.** [Proc. North Am. Soc. Ocean. Hist.]. **Main/Corp** North American Society of Oceanic History. **VFOAT** Proceedings for the North American Society of Oceanic History. 1977-. Proceedings. English. an. North American Society for Oceanic History, US Naval Academy, History Department, Annapolis MD 21402. **Tel** (301)267-3101. **LC** VK15; .N67A. **DD** 387.5/09.

US
**PROCEEDINGS / SHIP TECHNOLOGY AND RESEARCH (STAR) SYMPOSIUM.** ***Suspended.*** **Main/Conf** Ship Technology and Research (STAR) Symposium. **VFOAT** STAR Proceedings. 1st (1975)-Suspended. Proceedings. English. an. $73.00. Society of Naval Architecture and Marine Engineering, 601 Pavonia Avenue, Suite 400, Jersey City NJ 07306. **Tel** (201)798-4800 Ext.3025. **LC** VM1; .S394A. **DD** 623.8/05. **CODEN** PTRSDY. Documents available from Article Express International.
**Ind/Abst** Bioeng. Abstr.; Ei Page One; Eng. Index Annu.

US/0041-798X
**PROCEEDINGS - UNITED STATES NAVAL INSTITUTE.** (PROCEEDINGS OF THE UNITED STATES NAVAL INSTITUTE.). [Proc. - U.S. Nav. Inst.]. **Added/Corp** United States Naval Institute. **VFOAT** Proceedings; United States Naval Institute Proceedings; Naval Institute Proceedings; Record of the United States Naval Institute. Vol. 5, No. 3 (1879)-. English. mo. $33.00 US (includes APO & FPO); $45.00 other (surface mail); May issue of Proccedings is The Naval Review softbound edition. U. S. Naval Institute, 2062 Generals Highway, Annapolis MD 21402. **Tel** (301)268-6110, (800)233-8764. **ED** Fred H. Rainbow. **LC** V1; .U8. Index available (bound in May issue). cum. index. **Bk Rev. Ad Acc. Circ:** 122,000 (ctrl). available on microfilm and microfiche from University Microfilms International (UMI). ***Continues*** *Record of the United States Naval Institute;* ***Absorbed*** *Naval Review (Annapolis, Md.), 0077-6238.*
**Desc:** Features timely and thought-provoking articles on the naval world of yesterday, today, and tomorrow. Its up-to-date information makes it an invaluable asset for sea service professional and others interested in naval and maritime affairs.
**Ind/Abst** Air Univ. Libr. Index Mil. Period.; Am. Hist. Life (1954-); Am. Bibliogr. Slavic East Europ. Stud.; Int. Aerosp. Abstr. (1954-); Peace Res. Abstr. J. (1969-1972).

●US/1066-2774
**PROFESSIONAL MARINER.** (PROFESSIONAL MARINER : THE JOURNAL OF PROFESSIONAL SEAMANSHIP.). (1993)-. Periodical. English. bm. $21.00. Navigator Publishing Corp, PO Box 569, Portland ME 04112. **Tel** (207)772-2466.

PL
**PRZEGLAD MORSKI.** **Added/Corp** Poland. Marynarka Wojenna. Torun, Poland. Szkoa Podchorazych Marynarki Wojennej. (1928)-. Periodical. Polish. mo. $27.00. **(Subscription address:** ARS Polona, PO Box 1001, 00068 Warsaw Poland.**)** **LC** V5; .P7.

SW
**PUBLIC RESEARCH REPORT.** **See** Architecture.

UK
**PUBLICATIONS OF THE INTERNATIONAL MARITIME ORGANIZATION.** **Main/Corp** International Maritime Organization. (1988)-. Catalog. English. an. Free. Secretariat of the International Maritime Organization, Publications Section, 4 Albert Embankment, London SE1 7SR England. **Tel** 44 71 7357611, FAX 44 71 5873210, telex 23588. **LC** Z6839.S2; I57b; VK200. **DD** 016.62389/028/9. Index available. cum. index. **Bk Rev**, (Qty: 25). **Pr Rev. Acid Free. Circ:** 20,000. ***Continues*** *Publications Catalogue / International Maritime Organization.*

US/0363-5597
**RADIO NAVIGATIONAL AIDS : ATLANTIC AND MEDITERRANEAN AREA.** **Main/Corp** United States. Defense Mapping Agency. Hydrographic Center. **VFOAT** Radio Aids: Atlantic. English. $4.00. US Department of Defense Defense Mapping Agency, 8613 Lee Highway, Fairfax VA 22031. **Tel** (703)285-9290, FAX (703)285-9374. **LC** VK397; .D38A. **DD** 623.89/32/0251821.

US/0161-3715
**RADIONAVIGATION JOURNAL.** **Main/Corp** Wild Goose Association. English. an. Wild Goose Association, PO Box 556, Bedford MA 01730. **LC** VK560; .W48A. **DD** 623.89/32.
**Ind/Abst** Ei Page One.

US
**REGISTER OF COMMISSIONED AND WARRANT OFFICERS OF THE UNITED STATES NAVY AND MARINE CORPS.** **Main/Corp** United States. Bureau of Naval Personnel. **Added/Corp** Navy Department. Bureau of Navigation. (1814)-. Government Publication. English. ir. Superintendent of Documents, US Government Printing Office, Washington DC 20402. **Tel** (202)275-3328, FAX (202)786-2377. **LC** V11; .U4.

US/0364-8753
**REGISTER OF OFFICERS - COAST GUARD.** (REGISTER OF OFFICERS / DEPARTMENT OF TRANSPORTATION, COAST GUARD.). **Main/Corp** United States. Coast Guard. Began with 1 July 1976. English. an. US Department of Transportation / US Coast Guard, 2100 Second Street Southwest, Washington DC 20953-0001. **Tel** (202)267-2229. **LC** VG53; .U53C. **DD** 359.9/7. available on microfiche (Vols. for (1985-) distributed to depository libraries). ***Continues*** *United States. Coast Guard. Register of Officers and Cadets, 0095-2818.*

US/0147-8982
**REGISTER OF RESERVE OFFICERS.** (REGISTER OF RESERVE OFFICERS / COAST GUARD.). **Main/Corp** United States. Coast Guard. **VFOAT** USCG Reserve Register; U.S.C.G. Reserve Register; Coast Guard Register of Reserve Officers. English. an. US Coast Guard, 2100 2nd Street Southwest, Washington DC 20590. **Tel** (202)267-1408. **LC** VG53; .U53D. **DD** 359.9/7/0973. available on microfiche (Vols. for (1981-) distributed to depository libraries). ***Continues*** *Register of Commissioned and Warranted Officers of the Coast Guard Reserve.*

US/0193-3337
**REPORT ON SURVEY OF U.S. SHIPBUILDING AND REPAIR FACILITIES.** **VAT** Report on Survey of United States Shipbuilding and Repair Facilities. English. an. US Department of Transportation / Maritime Administration, 400 7th Street SW, Room 7206, Washington DC 20590. **Tel** (202)366-5812, FAX (202)366-3890. **LC** VM299.6; .U56A. **DD** 338.4/7/623830973. available on microfiche (Vols. for 1981- distributed to depository libraries). ***Continues*** *Report on Survey of Shipbuilding and Repair Industry.*

ML
**REPORT ON THE WORK OF THE BUREAU SINCE THE PREVIOUS CONFERENCE.** **Main/Corp** International Hydrographic Bureau. English. International Hydrographic Bureau, BP 445, 7 Avenue President J. F. Kennedy, MC 98011 Cedex Monaco. **Tel** 011 33 93506587, FAX 011 33 93 25 2003, telex 479164 MC. **LC** VK596; .I56B. **DD** 341.44.

US/0736-4849
**REVIEW - NAVAL RESEARCH LABORATORY (U.S.).** (REVIEW / NAVAL RESEARCH LABORATORY.). **VFOAT** NRL. 1981-. English. an. National Technical Information Service - NTIS, Room 2027S, 5285 Port Royal Road, Springfield VA 22161. **Tel** (703)487-4630, (703)487-4660, (703)487-4650, FAX (703)321-8547, telex 89-9405. **LC** V394.W2. **DD** 623.8/0724. available on microfiche (Vols. for (1981-) distributed to depository libraries). ***Continues*** *NRL Review, 0732-7609.*

BL
**REVISTA DA ADISMAR.** ***Ceased.*** **Main/Corp** Fundacao Estudos do Mar. Associacao dos Diplomados. (19??)-(1992). Portuguese. Associacao dos Diplomados da Fundaco Estudos do Mar, rua Marques de Olinda 18 ZC-02, Rio de Janeiro Brazil. **LC** VK4; .F85A.

SP
**REVISTA DE HISTORIA NAVAL.** Yearly V. 1, No. 1-. Periodical. Spanish. Three times a year. $2.00 single issue. Museo Naval, Montalban, 2 Madrid-14 Espana Spain. **LC** D215; .R48.
**Ind/Abst** Am. Hist. Life (1983-).

PO
**REVISTA DE MARINHA.** (19??)-. Periodical. Portuguese. Twelve times a year. Revista de Marinha, Luis de Almeida e Albuguerque 5, Lisbon 2 Portugal. **LC** V5; .R37. **DD** 359.05.

MX/0188-1477
**REVISTA GENERAL DE MARINA.** [Rev. gen. mar.]. Vol. 1 (Sept. 1940)-. Periodical. Spanish. Banco de Santander, C Alcala 37, Madrid 28014 Spain.
**Ind/Abst** Am. Hist. Life (1958-1986-).

BL/0034-9860
**REVISTA MARITIMA BRASILEIRA.** **Added/Corp** Brazil. Ministerio da Marinha. Bibliotheca. Brazil. Ministerio da Marinha. (1881)-. Periodical. Portuguese. qt. $12.00. Servico de Documentacao Geral da Marinha, rua d Manuel 15 Centro, 20010 Rio de Janeiro RJ Brasil. **Tel** 221-6696. **LC** V5; .R5. **Bk Rev. Ad Acc. Circ:** 3,200 (ctrl).
**Desc:** Subjects connected to naval power and Brazilian Navy. Focuses on aspects of science and technology, history, navigation, strategy and maritime news, etc.

FR/1146-2132
**REVUE MARITIME 1990, LA.** (LA REVUE MARITIME.). (1990)-. Periodical. French. Four times a year. 176.30F France; 244.85F other. Institut Francais de la Mer, 9 Ave du Docteur Gley, 75020 Paris France. **Tel** 011 33 1 40310400, FAX 011 33 1 43643404. **UDC** 656.6. **Bk Rev. Ad Acc. Pr Rev.** ***Continues*** *La Nouvelle Revue Maritime, 0242-780X.*
**Ind/Abst** Am. Hist. Life (1963-1971); PAIS Int. Print.

US/0145-0689
**RIVER CURRENTS (ST. LOUIS, MO. : 1981).** (RIVER CURRENTS.). Vol. 1, No. 1 (Apr./May 1981)-. Periodical. English. bm. Second Coast Guard District, 1430 Olive Street, St Louis MO 63103. **LC** VG53; .R59. **DD** 359.9/7/0973. available on microfilm and microfiche from University Microfilms International (UMI). ***Continues*** *River Currents, 0145-0689.*

IT/0035-6964
**RIVISTA MARITTIMA.** (RIVISTA MARITIIMA.). [Riv. maritt.]. (1868)-. Italian. Eleven times a year. L28000 Italy; L58000 other. Direzione di Commissariato MM, Via Domenico Alberto Azuni 2, 00196 Rome Italy. **Tel** 11 39 6 36805967. **ED** Vincenzo Pellegrino. **LC** V4; .R6. Index available (published separately). cum. index. **Bk Rev. Circ:** 67,000 (ctrl).
**Desc:** Deals with a great variety of subjects connected with the sea.
**Ind/Abst** Am. Hist. Life (1970-1987)(1970-); Int. Aerosp. Abstr.; Recent. Publ. Artic.

PL/0079-2667
**ROCZNIK STATYSTYCZNY GOSPODARKI MORSKIEJ.** **Main/Corp** Poland. Gowny Urzad Statystyczny. 1945/68-. Polish. ir (every five years). Z13.00 Poland; Z16.00 North America; Z15.00 other. Zaklad Wydawnictw Statystycznych, Al Niepodleglosci 208, 00-925 Warszawa Poland. **Tel** 253241, telex 814581A GUS. **LC** HE848.7. **Circ:** 800 (ctrl).
**Desc:** Yearbook of the polish sea economy.

US/1073-9335
**SAFETYLINE / NAVAL SAFETY CENTER.** **Added/Corp** Naval Safety Center. (19??)-. Government Publication. English. bm. $11.00 US; $13.75 other. Superintendent of Documents, US Government Printing Office, Washington DC 20402. **Tel** (202)275-3328, FAX (202)786-2377.
**Desc:** Articles designed to keep people within the Department of the Navy knowledgeable about current safety concerns and emerging development.

●CN
**SAILING DIRECTIONS. GULF OF ST. LAWRENCE.** **Added/Corp** Canada. Dept. of Fisheries and Oceans. **VFOAT** Gulf of St. Lawrence; Gulf of Saint Lawrence. (1992)-. English. Canada Communications Group - Publishing, Ottawa, Ontario K1A 0S9 Canada. **LC** VK988; .S342. ***Continues*** *Sailing Directions. Gulf and River of St. Lawrence.*

●CN
**SAILING DIRECTIONS. ST. LAWRENCE RIVER. CAP-ROUGE TO MONTREAL.** **Added/Corp** Canada. Dept. of Fisheries and Oceans. Canadian Hydrographic Service. **VFOAT** St. Lawrence River. Cap-Rouge to Montreal; Saint Lawrence River. Cap-Rouge to Montreal. 1st ed. (1992)-. Periodical. English. Fisheries & Oceans Canada, Scientific Information & Publications Branch, 200 Kent Street/12th Floor, Ottawa Ontario K1A 0E6 Canada. **Tel** (613)993-0600, (800)267-6677, telex 053-3585. **LC** VK988; .S252.

●CN
**SAILING DIRECTIONS. ST. LAWRENCE RIVER. ILE VERTE TO QUEBEC.** **Added/Corp** Canada. Dept. of Fisheries and Oceans. Canadian Hydrographic Service. **VFOAT** St. Lawrence River. Ile Verte to Quebec; Saint Lawrence River. Ile Verte to Quebec. 1st ed. (1992)-. Periodical. English. Fisheries & Oceans Canada, Scientific Information & Publications Branch, 200 Kent Street/12th Floor, Ottawa Ontario K1A 0E6 Canada. **Tel** (613)993-0600, (800)267-6677, telex 053-3585. **LC** VK988; .S25.

FR
**SAUVETAGE : REVUE DE LA SOCIETE NATIONALE DE SAUVETAGE EN MER.** **See** Public Health and Safety.

US/0194-780X
**SCALE SHIP MODELER.** ***Title Change.*** [Scale ship model.]. (19??)-(19??). Periodical. English. Nine times a year. Challenge Publications Inc., 7950 Deering Avenue, Canoga Park CA 91304. **Tel** (818)887-0550. **LC** VM298; .S32. **DD** 623.8/201/05. ***Merged with*** *R/C Race Boats, 1057-0322* ***to form*** *R/C Model Boats & Racing, 1062-757X.*

GW/0036-6056
**SCHIFFBAUFORSCHUNG.** (SCHIFFBAUFORSCHUNG : WISSENSCHAFTLICH-TECHNISCHE MITTEILUNGEN.). [Schiffbauforschung]. **Added/Corp** Kombinat Schiffbau, VEB. Institut fuer Schiffbau Rostock. Wilhelm-Pieck-Universitat Rostock. Sektion Schiffstechnik. (1962)-. Periodical. German (English and Russian). ir. price varies per volume. Verein Ferderer University Rostock, FB Maschinenbau Schiffstechnik, D-18051 Rostock, Germany. **Tel** 011 49 381 4405254. **LC** VM156; .S355. **Bk Rev. Circ:** 500.
**Desc:** Research and development in shipbuilding, hydrodynamics model testing, vibrational behaviour and strength of ship structures, marine propulsion plants, behaviour of materials, corrosion.
**Ind/Abst** BMT Abstr.

NE/0926-4213
**SCHIP EN WERF DE ZEE.** **VFOAT** SWZ. (Jan. 1991)-. Periodical. Dutch. Twenty-six times a year. Fl142.50. WYT Uitgeefgroeup, Postbus 6438, 3000 AG Rotterdam Netherlands. **Tel** 011 31 10 4762566, 4255944. **LC** VM4; .S36. ***Formed by the union of*** *Schip en Werf* ***and*** *Nautisch Technisch Tijdschrift de Zee.*
**Ind/Abst** Fluid Abstr., Civil Eng.; Fluid Abstr. Proc. Eng.; FLUIDEX (19??-).

US/0048-9867
**SEA CLASSICS.** [Sea class.]. (19??)-. Periodical. English. mo. $35.50. Challenge Publications Inc., 7950 Deering Avenue, Canoga Park CA 91304. **Tel** (818)887-0550. **LC** VM1; .S3. **DD** 387.2/05. ***Absorbed*** *Sea Combat, 0199-087X.*
**Ind/Abst** Am. Hist. Life.

US/0146-9312
**SEA HISTORY.** [Sea hist.]. **Added/Corp** National Maritime Historical Society (U.S.). No. 1 (April 1972)-. Periodical. English. qt. $30.00 (1 year), $51.00 (2 year), $72.00 (3 year) (National Maritime Historical Society membership). National Maritime Historical Society, Charles Point Marina, PO Box 68, Peekskill NY 10566. **Tel** (914)737-7878, FAX (914)737-7816. **LC** VK23; .S42. **DD** 387/.00973.
**Ind/Abst** Am. Hist. Life (1978-); ARTbibliogr. Mod.; Book Rev. Index.

US/0199-1337
**SEA POWER (1971).** (SEA POWER.). [Sea power]. **Added/Corp** Navy League of the United States. Vol. 14, No. 8 (Sept. 1971)-. Periodical. English. Twelve times a year. $25.00 US; $75.00 other. Navy League of the United States, 2300 Wilson Boulevard, Arlington VA 22201. **Tel** (703)528-1775. **ED** James Hessman. **LC** VA49; .N28. **DD** 359. **[CCC].** Index available. cum. index. **Bk Rev. Ad Acc. Circ:** 70,000 (ctrl). available on microfilm and microfiche from University Microfilms International (UMI). ***Continues*** *Navy.*
**Ind/Abst** Air Univ. Libr. Index Mil. Period.; Am. Hist. Life (1972); Am. Bibliogr. Slavic East Europ. Stud.

UK/0037-007X
**SEAFARER (LONDON).** (THE SEAFARER.). [Seafarer]. **Added/Corp** Seafarers' Education Service. No. 1 (Jan. 1934)-. English. Four times a year (Jan., Apr., July, Oct.). £25.00 (individual); £28.00 (institution). Marine Society, 202 Lambeth Road, London SE1 7JW England. **Tel** 01 261 9535, FAX 01 401 2537, telex 934089 MARSOC G. **ED** Michael Moore. **LC** VK1; .S39. **DD** 656. **Bk Rev**, (Qty: 200). **Ad Acc. Circ:** 3,500.
**Desc:** Publishes seafarer works and the work of the marine society.
**Ind/Abst** Ocean. Abstr.

UK/0144-1019
**SEAWAYS (1980).** (SEAWAYS.). [Seaways]. **Added/Corp** Nautical Institute (Great Britain). (March 1980)-. Periodical. English. Twelve times a year. £50.00. Nautical Institute, 202 Lambeth Road, London SE1 7LQ England. **Tel** (071)928-1351. **ED** David J. Sanders. Index available. **Bk Rev. Ad Acc, Adv Mgr:** Tina Scott. **Circ:** 6,000.
**Desc:** Serves the professional interest of qualified mariners.
**Ind/Abst** Am. Hist. Life (1991-); BMT Abstr.; Ocean. Abstr.

●US/1065-8904
**SEAWAYS' SHIPS IN SCALE.** [Seaways' ships scale]. **VFOAT** Ships in Scale. (1992)-. Periodical. English. Six times a year. $24.95. Seaways Publishing Inc., 2271 Constitution Drive, San Jose CA 95124. **Tel** (408)978-5657. **LC** VM298; .S37. **DD** 623.8/201. ***Continues*** *Seaways (Salt Lake City, Utah), 1052-4975.*

JA
**SENIN ROPPO.** **Main/Corp** Japan. **Added/Corp** Kaiji Horei Kenkyukai. Japan. Unyusho. Seninkyoku. (19??)-. Periodical. Japanese. ¥6500. Seizando Shoten, 4-51 Minami-Motocho, Shinjuku-ku 160 Tokyo Japan. **LC** LAW.

JA/0495-775X
**SENPAKU GIJUTSU KENKYUJO HOKOKU.** [Sempaku Gijutsu Kenkyujo Hokoku]. **Main/Corp** Sempaku Gijutsu Kenkyujo (Japan). **VFOAT** Report of Ship Research Institute. Vol. 1, No. 1 (1964)-. Periodical. Japanese. bm. Ship Research Institute, 38-1, 6-Chome, Shinkawa, Mitaka, Tokyo 181 Japan. **CODEN** SPGKAP. Documents available from Article Express International.
**Ind/Abst** Ei Page One; Eng. Index Annu. [Select. Cov.].

UK
**SHIP & BOAT INTERNATIONAL. ANNUAL GUIDE.** ***Title Change.*** **VFOAT** Ship and Boat International. Annual Guide. (1983)-?. English. an. Metal Bulletin PLC, PO Box 28E, Worcester Park, Surrey KT4 7HX England. **Tel** 011 44 71 827 9977, FAX 011 44 81 337 8943. **ED** Richard White. **LC** VM320; .S46. **DD** 623.8/2/005. **Ad Acc.** ***Continued by*** *Ship & Boat. Annual Guide to the International Small Ship and Workboat Industry, 0266-3929.*
**Desc:** Directories of ship builders, diesel engines, ships on order.

US/0488-6720
**SHIPMATE (ANNAPOLIS, MD.).** (SHIPMATE.). [Shipmate]. **Added/Corp** U.S. Naval Academy Alumni Association. (1938)-. Periodical. English. Ten times a year (July/August and January/February issues are combined). $30.00. US Naval Academy Alumni Association, 247 King George Street, Annapolis MD 21402. **Tel** (410)263-4448. **ED** James W. Hammond Jr. **LC** VA49; .S53. **DD** 359.05. **Bk Rev. Ad Acc. Circ:** 30,000.
**Desc:** Alumni magazine of the United States Naval Academy, with alumni news, obituaries, chapters and general articles, historical and current, concerning the United States Navy and the Naval Academy.

US/0080-9292
**SHIPS AND AIRCRAFT OF THE UNITED STATES FLEET, THE.** **See** Military and Defense.

CN/1183-5400
**SHIP'S LOG (AMHERSTBURG).** (THE SHIP'S LOG.). [Ship's log]. **Added/Corp** Project H.M.S. Detroit. (Jan. 1991)-. Periodical. English. qt. Free to members. Project H.M.S. Detroit, PO Box 1812, Amherstberg Ontario N9V 2Z2 Canada. **DD** 623.8/225.

UK/0037-394X
**SHIPS MONTHLY.** [Ships mon.]. (Jan. 1966)-. Periodical. English. Twelve times a year. £21.60 UK; £29.50 other. Waterway Prod Ltd., Kottingham House, Dale Street, Burton-on-Trent Staffs DE14 3TD England. **Tel** 011 44 283 64290, telex 0283 35427. **ED** Robert Shopland. **LC** VM1; .S495. **DD** 623.82/005. **Bk Rev. Ad Acc. Circ:** 21,692 (ctrl).
**Desc:** Photographs and illustrated articles on all kinds of ships: mercantile and naval, sail and steam, past and present.
**Ind/Abst** Ship Abstr.

●US/1061-9224
**SHIPYARD CHRONICLE.** (SHIPYARD CHRONICLE / SHIPBUILDERS COUNCIL OF AMERICA.). [Shipyard chron.]. **Added/Corp** Shipbuilders Council of America. Vol. 1, No. 1 (Jan. 16, 1992)-. Periodical. English. sw. $175.00 US; $250.00 other. Shipbuilders Council of America, 4301 North Fairfax Drive, Suite 330, Arlington VA 22203. **Tel** (703)276-1700, FAX (703)276-1707. **DD** 623. ***Continues*** *Shipyard Weekly, 0737-7428.*

NO
**SJFARTSHISTORISK ARBOK.** **Added/Corp** Bergens Sjfartsmuseum. Foreningen. **VFOAT** Norwegian Yearbook of Maritime History. (19??)-. Multiple languages (English and Norwegian). 10. **LC** V5; .S48.

DK
**SKIBSTILSYNETS MEDDELELSER / STATENS SKIBSTILSYN.** **Main/Corp** Denmark. Direktoratet for Statens Skibstilsyn. Danish. kr40.00. Direktoratet for Statens, Skibstilsyn Snorresgade 19, 2300 Kbenhavn S Denmark. **LC** HE589.D4; A3. ***Continues*** *Denmark. Direktoratet for Statens Skibstilsyn. Meddelelser.*

US/1050-5199
**SKIPPER'S ALMANAC (SOUTHERN U.S. ED.).** (SKIPPER'S ALMANAC.). [Skipp. alm.]. (1990)-. English. $23.95. Marine Market Publishing Co., 1460 Brickell Avenue, No. 312, Miami FL 33131. **LC** WMLC L 83/9154. **DD** 623.

KO
**SOBO.** **Main/Corp** Hanguk Sonbak Yonguso. **Added/Corp** Han'guk Sonbak Yon'guso. Bulletin of KRIS. **VFOAT** Bulletin of Kris. Vol. 1 (1978)-. Periodical. English (Korean). sa. Not for sale. Hanguk Sonbak Yonguso, PO Box 315, Taejon Korea. **LC** VM4; .H36a. **DD** 623.82/005.

SA
**SOUTH AFRICAN TIDE TABLES.** **VFOAT** Suid--Afrikaanse Getytafels. English (Afrikaans). an. Maritime Headquarters, Hydrographic Office, Private Bag X1, Tokal 7966 South Africa. **Tel** 87 2911. **ED** S A Navy. **LC** VK687.1; .S68. **Circ:** 1,000.

US/0094-9892
**SOVIET SHIPBUILDING.** English. Naval Intelligence Support Center, Translation Division, 4301 Suitland Road, Suitland MD 20746. **LC** VM4; .S66. **DD** 623.82/005.

IT
**STATISTICHE DELLA NAVIGAZIONE MARITTIMA.** Vol. 39 (Ed. 1988)-. Italian. an. Istituto Nazionale Statistica, GBP SEZ4 Via Cesare Balbo 16, 00184 Rome Italy. **Tel** 011 39 6 46735118. **LC** HE839; .A15. ***Continues*** *Annuario Statistico della Navigazione Marittima, 0075-1898.*

US/1065-349X
**STEM TO STERN (CLAYTON, CALIF.).** ***Ceased.*** (STEM TO STERN.). **Added/Corp** American Marine Small Craft Association. (1993)-(199?)_. Periodical. English. mo. American Marine Small Craft Association, PO Box 432, Clayton CA 94521-0432.

JA
**SUIKO.** Periodical. Japanese. mo. Suikokai, 5-3 Jingumae 1, Shibuya-ku 150, Tokyo-to Japan. **LC** V69.J3; S93.

JA
**SUIROBU GIHO.** **VFOAT** Technical Bulletin of Hydrography. Vol. 1- (March 1983)-. Periodical. Japanese (Japanese). Kaijo Hoancho Suirobu, (Hydrographic Dept., Maritime Safety Agency), 3-1, Tsukiji 5 Chome, Chuoku, Tokyoto 104 Japan. **LC** VK588; .S93.

FI
**SUOMEN RANNIKON LOISTOT.** **Main/Corp** Finland. Merenkulkuhallitus. **VFOAT** Fyrar vid Finlands Kuster; List of Lights of Finland. 1978-. Finnish (Swedish; summaries and/or abstracts in Swedish and English). Valtion Painatuskeskus, PO Box 516, SF 00101 Helsinki Finland. **Tel** 011 358 0 5660266. **LC** VK1185.F5; F56B. ***Continues*** *Suomen Rannikon Loistot.*

US/0270-8876
**SUPPLEMENTAL TIDAL PREDICTIONS, ANCHORAGE, NIKISHKA, SELDOVIA, AND VALDEZ, ALASKA.** (SUPPLEMENTAL TIDAL PREDICTIONS, ANCHORAGE, NIKISHKA, SELDOVIA, AND VALDEZ, ALASKA / OFFICE OF OCEANOGRAPHY AND MARINE ENVIRONMENTAL SERVICES DIVISION, MARINE PREDICTIONS BRANCH.). [Suppl. tidal predict., Anchorage, Nikishka, Seldovia, Valdez, Alsk.]. English. an. National Ocean Service, NOAA Distribution Branch NCG33, Riverdale MD 20737. **Tel** (301)436-6993. **LC** VK743; .S95. **DD** 623.89/49/09798.

UK/0373-529X
**SUPPLEMENTARY PAPERS - ROYAL INSTITUTION OF NAVAL ARCHITECTS.** [Suppl. pap. - R. Inst. Nav. Archit.]. **Main/Corp** Royal Institution of Naval Architects. English. Royal Institution of Naval Architects, 10 Upper Belgrave Street, London SW1X 8BQ England. **Tel** 011 44 71 2354622, FAX 011 44 71 245 6959, telex 265844 SINAI G. **LC** VM1; .R5817. **DD** 623.8/1/08.
**Ind/Abst** Ei Page One; Life Sci. Collect.

US/0145-1073
**SURFACE WARFARE.** [Surf. warf.]. **Added/Corp** United States. Office of the Chief of Naval Operations. **VFOAT** Surface Warfare Magazine. (Sept. 1975)-. Periodical. English. bm. $9.50; US; $11.90 other.

Chief of Naval Operations, The Pentagon, Washington DC 20350. **Tel** (202)545-6700. **(Subscription address:** Superintendent of Documents, US Government Printing Office, Washington DC 20402.**)** **LC** V1; .S87. **DD** 359/.005. available on microfiche (Vols. for (1986-) distributed to depository libraries).
**Desc:** Provides timely information of interest to the Surface Warfare Community.

SW/0039-6702
**SVENSK SJOFARTSTIDNING.** (SVENSK SJOFARTSTIDNING SWEDISH SHIPPING GAZETTE. UPPL A.). [Sven. sjofartstidn.]. **Added/Corp** Sveriges Redareforening. **VFOAT** Swedish Shipping Gazette. (July 7, 1905)-. Periodical. Swedish. wk. **LC** VK4; .S852.
**Ind/Abst** Selec. Coop. Index Manage. Period.

MX
**TABLAS DE PREDICCION DE MAREAS : PUERTOS DEL OCEANO PACIFICO.** **Main/Corp** Servicio Mareografico Nacional (Mexico). Spanish. an. $20.00. UNAM - Universidad Nacional Autonoma de Mexico / Geofisica, Instituto de Geofisica, Postal 22, 118 Seccion ED, 14000 Mexico DF Mexico. **Tel** 011 52 5 5505215 Ext 4363. **ED** Ismael Herrera-Revilla. **LC** VK749; .M4. **DD** 623.89/49/0972. **Circ:** 1,500. ***Continues*** *Tablas de Prediccion de Mareas: Puertos del Oceano Pacifico.*
**Desc:** Tide tables for different ports on the Pacific Ocean Coast for service of ships, fishing, tourism and harbor constructions.

US
**TECHNICAL DIGEST / NAVAL SURFACE WARFARE CENTER.** **Main/Corp** Naval Surface Warfare Center (U.S.). **VFOAT** Naval Surface Warfare Center Technical Digest. (Sept. 1991)-. Periodical. English. Naval Surface Warfare Center, New Hampshire Avenue, Silver Springs MD 20903. **LC** IN PROCESS.

US/0502-3262
**TECHNICAL REPORT - CIVIL ENGINEERING LABORATORY, NAVAL CONSTRUCTION BATTALION CENTER, PORT HUENEME, CALIFORNIA.** **See** Engineering-Civil Engineering.

US/0040-2702
**TELESCOPE (DETROIT).** (TELESCOPE.). [Telescope]. **Added/Corp** Great Lakes Model Shipbuilders' Guild. Great Lakes Maritime Institute. (June 1952)-. Periodical. English. bm. comes with membership. Great Lakes Maritime Institute, 100 Strand Drive Belle Isle, Detroit MI 48207. **Tel** (313)267-6440. **ED** Kathy McGraw. **LC** VK23.7; .T44. **DD** 386/.5/0977. Index available. **Bk Rev. Circ:** 1,700.

US/0197-4114
**TEXAS CRUISING GUIDE.** [Tex. cruis. guide]. 1980-. English. an. Texas Cruising Guide, 2708 Sackett, Houston TX 77098. **LC** VK975; .S48. **DD** 623.89/29764.

US/0501-8234
**TIDAL CURRENT TABLES. ATLANTIC COAST OF NORTH AMERICA.** [Tidal curr. tables, Atl. coast North Am.]. **Added/Corp** U.S. Coast and Geodetic Survey. National Ocean Survey. United States. National Ocean Service. **VFOAT** Atlantic Coast of North America. (1958)-. English. an. National Ocean Service, NOAA Distribution Branch NCG33, Riverdale MD 20737. **Tel** (301)436-6993. **LC** VK781; .C87. **DD** 623.89/49/091634. ***Continues*** *Current Tables. Atlantic Coast, North America for the Year ..., 0743-7064.*

US
**TIDAL CURRENT TABLES. PACIFIC COAST OF NORTH AMERICA AND ASIA FOR THE YEAR ... .** **VFOAT** Pacific Coast of North America and Asia. (1958)-. English. an. National Ocean Service, NOAA Distribution Branch NCG33, Riverdale MD 20737. **Tel** (301)436-6993. **LC** VK747; .A16. **DD** 623.89/49/09164. available on microfiche (Vols. for (1984) distributed to depository libraries). ***Continues*** *Current Tables. Pacific Coast, North America and Asia for the Year ... .*

UK
**TIDE, DISTANCE AND SPEED TABLES.** **Added/Corp** Brown, Son & Ferguson, Ltd. (1951)-. English. an. £5.30 UK; £22.90 other. Brown Son & Ferguson Ltd, 4/10 Darnley Street, Glasgow G41 2SD Scotland. **Tel** 011 44 41 4291234, FAX 011 44 41 4201694. **ED** T. Nigel Brown. **LC** VK627; .T53. **DD** 525.69. **Ad Acc, Adv Mgr:** D. Provan. **Pr Rev. Acid Free. Circ:** 1,800.

US
**TIDE TABLES ... HIGH AND LOW WATER PREDICTIONS, WEST COAST OF NORTH AND SOUTH AMERICA, INCLUDING THE HAWAIIAN ISLANDS.** **VFOAT** West Coast of North and South America, including the Hawaiian Islands; Tide Tables ... West Coast of North and South America, including the Hawaiian Islands. Began with 1958. English. an. National Ocean Service, NOAA Distribution Branch NCG33, Riverdale MD 20737. **Tel** (301)436-6993. **LC** VK741; .U6. **DD** 623.89/49/091642. ***Continues*** *Tide Tables, West Coast, North and South America, (including the Hawaiian Islands).*

DK
**TIDEVANDSTABELLER. DANMARK.** **Added/Corp** Denmark. Farvandsdirektoratet. Denmark. Farvandsvsenet. (1985)-. Danish (English). Farvandsdirektoratet Nautisk Afdeling, Esplanaden 19, 1263 Copenhagen K Denmark. **LC** VK623; D46a. ***Continues*** *Tidevandstabeller for Danmark, 0106-8334.*

DK/0040-7186
**TIDSSKRIFT FOR SVSEN.** [Tidsskr. svs.]. **Added/Corp** Se-Lieutenant-Selskabet. (1856)-. Periodical. Danish. Ten times a year. $8.45. Tidskriftor Sqvesen, Overgaden OV 62B, 1415 Copenhagen Denmark. **Tel** 01 540552. **LC** V5; .T485.
**Ind/Abst** Ship Abstr.

US/1068-896X
**TILLER (ALEXANDRIA, VA.), THE.** (THE TILLER / VIRGINIA CANALS & NAVIGATIONS SOCIETY, INC.). [Tiller]. **Added/Corp** Virginia Canals and Navigations Society. Vol. 1, No. 1 (Spring 1980)-. Periodical. English. qt. Free to members of the Virginia Canals & Navigation Society. Virginia Canals & Navigation Society, 6826 Rosemont Drive, Mclean VA 22101. **Tel** (703)356-4027. **ED** Richard L. Guild. **DD** 627. Index available. cum. index. **Bk Rev. Circ:** 400.

JA
**TOYAMA SHOSEN KOTO SEMMON GAKKO KENKYU SHUROKU.** **Main/Corp** Toyama Shosen Koto Semmon Gakko. No. 1- 1968-. Multiple languages (English). 1-2 Ebie Neriai Shimminato, Toyama Japan. **LC** VK4; .T67A.

US/0081-1661
**TRANSACTIONS - THE SOCIETY OF NAVAL ARCHITECTS AND MARINE ENGINEERS.** [Trans. - Soc. Nav. Archit. Mar. Eng.]. **Main/Corp** Society of Naval Architects and Marine Engineers (U.S.). **VFOAT** Transactions of the Society of Naval Architects and Marine Engineers. Vol. 1 (1893)-. English. an. $45.00 US; $57.50 other. Society of Naval Architects and Marine Engineers, 601 Pavonia Avenue, Suite 400, Jersey City NJ 07306-2907. **Tel** (201)798-4800 ext. 3025, FAX (201)798-4975. **LC** VM1; .S6. **DD** 623.8/1/05. **CODEN** SNAMAL. Index available. cum. index. **Bk Rev. Ad Acc. Circ:** 4,000 (ctrl). Documents available from Article Express International.
**Desc:** A record of the Society's annual meeting papers for that year.
**Ind/Abst** Bioeng. Abstr.; Civ. Struct. Eng. Abstr.; Comput. Inf. Syst. Abstr. J. [Full Cov.]; Ei Page One; Eng. Index Annu.; Environ. Eng. Abstr.; Mech. Eng. Abstr.

US/0744-8651
**U.S. MARITIME MONTHLY.** (U.S. MARITIME MONTHLY : NATIONAL NEWSPAPER OF THE U.S. MARITIME INDUSTRIES.). **VFOAT** US Maritime Monthly. **VAT** United States Maritime Monthly. Periodical. English. mo. $3.00. Banner News Service, PO Box 9887, Seattle WA 98109-0368. **Tel** (206)284-6176.

US/0363-3209
**UNITED STATES COAST PILOT. 1, ATLANTIC COAST. EASTPORT TO CAPE COD.** (UNITED STATES COAST PILOT. 1, ATLANTIC COAST. EASTPORT TO CAPE COD / U.S. DEPARTMENT OF COMMERCE, COAST AND GEODETIC SURVEY.). [U.S. coast pilot, 1, Atl. Coast, Eastport Cape Cod]. **VFOAT** Atlantic Coast. **VAT** United States Coast Pilot. One, Atlantic Coast. Eastport to Cape Cod. 6th Ed. (1960)-. English. an. National Ocean Service, NOAA Distribution Branch NCG33, Riverdale MD 20737. **Tel** (301)436-6993. **LC** VK982.N43; .U54. **DD** 623.89/2974. available on microfiche (Vols. for (18th ED., Jan. 1982 - 19th Ed. Jan. 1983) distributed to depository libraries). ***Continues*** *United States Coast Pilot. Atlantic Coast. Section A, St. Croix River to Cape Cod.*

US/0363-695X
**UNITED STATES COAST PILOT. 2, ATLANTIC COAST. CAPE COD TO SANDY HOOK.** [U.S. coast pilot, 2, Atl. Coast, Cape Cod Sandy Hook]. **Added/Corp** U.S. Coast and Geodetic Survey. National Ocean Survey. United States. National Ocean Service. **VFOAT** Atlantic Coast. Cape Cod to Sandy Hook; U.S.C.P. 2, Atlantic Coast. Cape Cod to Sandy Hook; USCP. 2, Atlantic Coast. Cape Cod to Sandy Hook. **VAT** United States Coast Pilot. Two, Atlantic Coast. Cape Cod to Sandy Hook. 6th Ed. (1960)-. English. an. National Ocean Service, NOAA Distribution Branch NCG33, Riverdale MD 20737. **Tel** (301)436-6993. **LC** VK981; .U54. **DD** 623.89/2974. available on microfiche. ***Continues*** *United States Coast Pilot. Atlantic Coast. Section B, Cape Cod to Sandy Hook, 8755-2345.*

US/0363-3217
**UNITED STATES COAST PILOT. 3, ATLANTIC COAST. SANDY HOOK TO CAPE HENRY.** [U.S. coast pilot, 3, Atl. Coast, Sandy Hook Cape Henry]. **VFOAT** Atlantic Coast. Sandy Hook to Cape Henry. **VAT** United States Coast Pilot. Three, Atlantic Coast. Sandy Hook to Cape Henry. 6th Ed. (1953)-. English. an. National Ocean Service, NOAA Distribution Branch NCG33, Riverdale MD 20737. **Tel** (301)436-6993. **LC** VK982.M53; U54. **DD** 623.89/2974. available on microfiche (Vols. for (19th Ed., July 1981 - 20th Ed., July 1982) distributed to depository libraries). ***Continues*** *United States Coast Pilot. Atlantic Coast. Section C, Sandy Hook to Cape Henry, 8756-1581.*

US/0362-7713
**UNITED STATES COAST PILOT. 4, ATLANTIC COAST. CAPE HENRY TO KEY WEST.** [U.S. coast pilot, 4, Atl. Coast, Cape Henry Key West]. **Added/Corp** National Ocean Survey. U.S. Coast and Geodetic Survey. United States. National Ocean Service. **VFOAT** Atlantic Coast. Cape Henry to Key West. **VAT** United States Coast Pilot. Four, Atlantic Coast. Cape Henry to Key West. 6th Ed. (1955)-. English. an. National Ocean Service, NOAA Distribution Branch NCG33, Riverdale MD 20737. **Tel** (301)436-6993. **LC** VK982.S68; U54. **DD** 623.89/2976. available on microfiche (Vol. for (19th Ed., July 1981)-20th Ed., July (1982) distributed to depository libraries). ***Continues*** *United States Coast Pilot. Atlantic Coast. Section D, Cape Henry to Key West, 8755-142X.*

US/0360-0149
**UNITED STATES COAST PILOT. 5, ATLANTIC COAST. GULF OF MEXICO, PUERTO RICO, AND VIRGIN ISLANDS.** [U.S. coast pilot, 5, Atl. Coast, Gulf Mex. P.R. Virg. Isl.]. **VFOAT** Atlantic Coast. Gulf of Mexico, Puerto Rico, and Virgin Islands. **VAT** United States Coast Pilot. Five, Atlantic Coast. Gulf of Mexico, Puerto Rico, and Virgin Islands. 6th Ed. (1967)-. English. an. US Department of Commerce / National Oceanic & Atmospheric Administration NOAA, 6010 Executive Boulevard, Washington Science Center, Building 5, Rockville MD 20852. **Tel** (202)482-6090, FAX (202)482-3154. **LC** VK975; .U65. **DD** 623.89/2976. ***Continues*** *United States Coast Pilot. 5, Gulf Coast, Puerto Rico, and Virgin Islands, 8755-1446.*

US/0161-4444
**UNITED STATES COAST PILOT. 6, GREAT LAKES, LAKES ONTARIO, ERIE, HURON, MICHIGAN, AND SUPERIOR AND ST. LAWRENCE RIVER.** [U.S. coast pilot, 6, Great Lakes Lakes Ont. Erie Huron Mich. Super. St. Lawrence River]. **Added/Corp** National Ocean Survey. United States. National Ocean Service. **VFOAT** Great Lakes, Lakes Ontario, Erie, Huron, Michigan, and Superior and St. Lawrence River; Lakes Ontario, Erie, Huron, Michigan, and Superior and St. Lawrence River; USCP. 6, Lakes Ontario, Erie, Huron, Michigan, and Superior and St. Lawrence River. **VAT** United States Coast Pilot. Six, Great Lakes, Lakes Ontario, Erie, Huron, Michigan, and Superior and Saint Lawrence River. (1978)-. English. an. $14.50. National Ocean Service, NOAA Distribution Branch NCG33, Riverdale MD 20737. **Tel** (301)436-6993. **LC** VK597; .U65. **DD** 628.89/29/77. ***Continues*** *United States Great Lakes Pilot. Lakes Ontario, Erie, Huron, Michigan, and Superior, and St. Lawrence River, 0362-8329.*
**Desc:** Covers a wide variety of information important to navigators of coastal and intracoastal waters and the Great Lakes.

US/0163-9471
**UNITED STATES COAST PILOT. 8, PACIFIC COAST. ALASKA, DIXON ENTRANCE TO CAPE SPENCER.** [U.S. coast pilot, 8, Pac. Coast, Alsk. Dixon Entr. Cape Spencer]. **VFOAT** Pacific Coast. Alaska, Dixon Entrance to Cape Spencer. **VAT** United States Coast Pilot. Eight, Pacific Coast. Alaska: Dixon Entrance to Cape Spencer. 11th Ed. (Jan. 6, 1962)-. English. be. National Ocean Service, NOAA Distribution Branch NCG33, Riverdale MD 20737. **Tel** (301)436-6993. **LC** VK943.U7; D5. **DD** 623.89/29/798. available on microfiche (Vols. for 1982 was distributed to depository libraries). ***Continues*** *United States Coast Pilot. Southeast Alaska, Dixon Entrance to Yakutat Bay.*

US/0278-0089
**UNITED STATES COAST PILOT. 9, PACIFIC AND ARCTIC COASTS. ALASKA, CAPE SPENCER TO BEAUFORT SEA.** [U.S. coast pilot, 9, Pac. Arct. coasts, Alsk., Cape Spencer Beaufort Sea]. **VFOAT** Pacific and Arctic Coasts. Alaska, Cape Spencer to Beaufort Sea; USCP. 9, Pacific and Arctic Coasts. Alaska, Cape Spencer to Beaufort Sea. **VAT** United States Coast Pilot. Nine, Pacific and Arctic Coasts. Alaska: Cape Spencer to Beaufort Sea. Began with 7th Ed. in 1964. English. be. US Department of Commerce / National Oceanic & Atmospheric Administration NOAA, 6010 Executive Boulevard, Washington Science Center, Building 5, Rockville MD 20852. **Tel** (202)482-6090, FAX

(202)482-3154. **LC** VK943.U7; Y3. **DD** 623.89/29798. available on microfiche (Vol. for (11th Ed., Jan. 1983) distributed to depository libraries). *Continues* United States Coast Pilot. 9, Alaska. Cape Spencer to Arctic Ocean.

US
**UTILIZATION OF SHIPBUILDING AND REPAIR FACILITIES SERIES. Added/Corp** United Nations. Industrial Development Organization. No. 1 (1972)-. Monographic series. English. United Nations Industrial Development Organization, PO Box 300, A 1400 Vienna Austria. **Tel** 011 43 222 211310. **LC** JX1977; .A2 subser. **DD** 623.82/008 S.

NE
**VERKEERSGEGEVENS. Added/Corp** Netherlands. Rijkswaterstaat. Onderafdeling Permanente Inwinning en Uitvoer. (19??)-. Dutch. an. Rijkswaterstaat Onderafdeling Permanente, Inwinning en Uitvoer, Postbus 20906, 2500 Ex's-Gravenhage Netherlands. **LC** HE674; .A39.

US/0043-0374
**WARSHIP INTERNATIONAL.** [Warsh. int.]. **Added/Corp** Naval Records Club (U.S.) International Naval Research Organization. Vol. 1, (1964)-. Periodical. English. Four times a year (Mar., June, Sept., Dec.). $20.00 US; $22.00 Canada; $25.00 other. International Naval Research Organization, 5905 Reinwood Drive, Toledo OH 43613. **Tel** (419)472-1331. **ED** Christopher C. Wright. **LC** V750; .W37. **DD** 359.8/3; 359. Index available. **Bk Rev. Circ:** 4,500 (ctrl). available on microfilm and microfiche from University Microfilms International (UMI).
**Desc:** Naval history of ships all over the world.
**Ind/Abst** Am. Hist. Life (1966-).

US/0090-712X
**WATERWAY GUIDE. NORTHERN EDITION. See** Boats and Boating.

US/0741-000X
**WEYER'S FLOTTENASCHENBUCH (NORTH AMERICAN ED.).** (WEYER'S WARSHIPS OF THE WORLD.). [Weyer's Flottentaschenbuch]. **Added/Corp** United States Naval Institute. (1968)-. English. be. $104.95. Nautical & Aviation Publishing Company of America, 8 Randall Street, Baltimore MD 21401. **Tel** (410)659-0220. **ED** A. Bredt. **LC** V10; .W47. **DD** 623.82/5/05.

GW
**WEYERS FLOTTENTASCHENBUCH.** Began publication with 1900 issue. German (English). Bernard and Graefe Verlag GmbH 2060, W-5400 Koblenz 1 Germany. **Tel** 011 49 261 803071. **ED** B Weyer and A Bredt. **LC** V10.

US/0882-5610
**WORLD WARSHIPS FORECAST.** [World warsh. forecast]. **Added/Corp** Defense Marketing Services, Inc. (1984)-. English. an. Defense Marketing Services, 1340 Braddock Pl, Alexandria VA 22314-1651. **Tel** (703)683-3700, FAX (703)836-0029, telex 6819193. **LC** V750; .W67. **DD** 623.8/25/025.

BE
**YEARBOOK - INTERNATIONAL MARITIME COMMITTEE. Main/Corp** International Maritime Committee. **VFOAT** Annuaire - Comite Maritime International. (1978)-. Periodical. English (French). an. $85.00. Scandinavian University Press, PO Box 2959 Toeyen, N 0608 Oslo 6 Norway. **Tel** 011 47 2 2575400, FAX 011 47 2 2575353, telex 71896 UROR N. **(Subscription address:** Scandinavian University Press, 200 Meacham Ave., Elmont NY 11003.)

NO
**YEARBOOK, SHIPYARDS, BOATBUILDERS, AND MARINE ENGINEERS. VFOAT** Shipyards, Boatbuilders, and Marine Engineers. English. an. K/S Selvig Publishing A S, PO Box 9070 Vaterland Chr Krohgsgt 16A, Oslo Norway. **LC** VM86.5; .Y4. **DD** 623.8/3/02548.

JA
**YOKYUJO KAINAN TOKEI. Added/Corp** Japan. Kaijo Hoancho. Keibi Kyunanbu. Koko Anzenka. Kaijo Kotsu Kikakushitsu. Japan. Kaijo Hoancho. Keibi Kyunanbu. Koko Anzen Kikakuka. Japan. Kaijo Hoancho. (1970)-. Periodical. Japanese. Japan. Kaijo Hoancho, (Maritime Safety Agency), 5-3-1 Tsukiji, Chuoku Tokyo 104 Japan. **LC** VK1288.J3; Y6.

JA/0387-2203
**ZOSEN GIJUTSU.** [Zosen gijutsu]. **VFOAT** Shipbuilding & Engineering; Shipbuilding and Engineering. Periodical. Japanese (Japanese). mo. ¥15000. Japan Indastoriaru Paburisshingu, c/o Suzuki Building 10-1, Azabu Juaban 3, Minato-ku 106, Tokyo-to Japan. **LC** VM4; .Z59.
**Ind/Abst** Coal Abstr.

---

## ABSTRACTING, BIBLIOGRAPHIES AND STATISTICS

UK/0268-9650
**BMT ABSTRACTS : BRITISH MARITIME TECHNOLOGY ABSTRACTS. Added/Corp** British Maritime Technology Ltd. **VFOAT** British Maritime Technology Abstracts. Vol. 41, No. 1 (Jan. 1986)-. Abstracting/Indexing Service. English. Twelve times a year. £220.00 UK; £238.00 others. BMT Northumbria House Davy Bank, Wallsend, Wallsend Tyne and Wear NE28 6UY England. **Tel** 011 44 91 262 5242, FAX 011 44 91 263 8754, telex 53476. **ED** G. Smith. **LC** VM1; .B7. **DD** 623.8/1. **CODEN** BMABE2. Index available. **Bk Rev. Circ:** 400. available on an online database. *Continues* Journal of Abstracts of the British Ship Research Association, 0141-903X.
**Desc:** Abstracts approximately 3,000 articles from periodicals and conference proceedings that cover all aspects of ship and offshore technology and operation.
**Ind/Abst** World Surf. Coat. Abstr.

NO
**KATALOG OVER NORSKE SJKART OG NAUTISKE PUBLIKASJONER. Main/Corp** Norges Sjkartverk. **VFOAT** Catalogue of Norwegian Charts and Nautical Publications. Multiple languages (English and Norwegian). Kr2.00. Sjkartverket, Box 60, Stavanger Norway. **LC** Z6028; .N76A.

BL
**LIST OF NAUTICAL CHARTS AND ITS CORRECTIONS BY NOTICES TO MARINERS: PERMANENT, PRELIMINARY AND TEMPORARY. Main/Corp** Brazil. Diretoria de Hidrografia e Navegacao. (197?)-. English. Diretoria de Hidrografia E Navegacao, Ministerio da Marinha, ILHA Fiscal, Rio de Janeiro Brazil. **LC** Z6026.H9; B72b; GA359. **DD** 016.62389/2/0222. *Continues* Brazil. Diretoria de Hidrografia e Navegacao. List of Permanent, Preliminary and Temporary Notices to Mariners Affecting Nautical Charts.

JA/0385-1176
**SENPAKU KAIYO KOGAKU GIJUTSU BUNKEN SOKUHO. Added/Corp** Nihon Zosen Shinko Zaidan. Zosen Shiryo Senta. **VFOAT** Marine Technology Research Abstracts & Index (Matrax); Marine Technology Research Abstracts and Index (Matrax); Matrax. (19??)-. English (Japanese). ir. ¥42360.00 Japan; $360.00 US. Japan Foundation for Shipbuilding Advancement, c/o Senpaku Shinko Building, 15-16 Toranomon 1 Minato-ku, Tokyo 105 Japan. **Tel** 03-502-2371, FAX 03-502-2033. **(Subscription address:** Maruzen Company Ltd., PO Box 5050, Import & Export Department, Tokyo 100 31 Japan.) **LC** VM4; .S46. Index available. cum. index. **Circ:** 300 (ctrl) *Continues* Zosen Kankei Gijutsu Shiryo Sokuho.

---

# NEW AGE PUBLICATIONS

US/0002-662X
**ALTERNATIVE PRESS INDEX. See** New Age Publications-Abstracting, Bibliographies and Statistics.

US/0097-1146
**ANIMA (CHAMBERSBURG).** (ANIMA.). [Anima]. Vol. 1 (Fall 1974)-. Periodical. English. sa. $9.95 (US); $11.95 (other). Anima Publications, 1053 Wilson Avenue, Chambersburg PA 17201. **Tel** (717)267-0087, FAX (717)267-0087. **ED** Harry M Buck. **LC** AP2; .A553. **DD** 051. Index available. cum. index. **Bk Rev. Ad Acc. Circ:** 2,000. available in microform.
**Desc:** An experimental journal that concentrates on the quest for wholeness through values traditionally labelled feminine.
**Ind/Abst** Am. Humanit. Index; Except. Hum. Exp.; Index Book Rev. Relig.; Relig. Index One Period. (1974-); Relig. Theol. Abstr.

US
**AT THE CROSSROADS : FEMINISM, SPIRITUALITY AND NEW PARADIGM SCIENCE EXPLORING EARTHLY AND UNEARTHLY REALITY. See** Women's Interests.

US/0895-7657
**BODY, MIND, SPIRIT.** [Body mind spirit]. **VFOAT** Body Mind & Spirit; Body Mind Spirit Magazine; Body Mind and Spirit. Vol. 6, No. 4 (Sept./Oct. 1987)-. Periodical. English. Six times a year (Jan., Mar., May, July, Sept., Nov.). $20.00 (one year); $32.00 (two years); $44.00 (three years). Island Publishing Company Inc, PO Box 701, Providence RI 02901. **Tel** (401)351-4320, FAX (401)272-5767. **ED** Carol Kramer. **DD** 133. **Bk Rev. Ad Acc. Adv Mgr:** Clarke Williams.
**Circ:** 150,000. *Continues* Psychic Guide, 0745-8746.
**Desc:** Leading new age, wholistic, metaphysical, natural living, self-help magazine. We provide practical information for creating a richer, more fulfilling life.

CN/0826-967X
**BORDER/LINES.** [Border/lines]. **VFOAT** Border Lines. No. 1 (Fall 1984)-. Academic Scholarly Publication. English. qt. 20.00Can$ (individuals) 35.00Can$ (institutions). Border/Lines Magazine Society Inc, Bethune College/York University, 4700 Keele Street, North York Ontario M3J 1P3 Canada. **Tel** (416)736-5164, (416)360-5249. **ED** Julie Jenkinson. **DD** 700/.971. **Bk Rev. Ad Acc.** ctrl circ. available in microform from Micromedia Limited.
**Desc:** Magazine which defies classification; concerned with the arts as an aspect of a self-generating culture. Has opinions that are scholarly without being pedantic. About people and places, but is not sycophantic about either. Its style is literary and it is certainly concerned with sports, the outdoors and children, but in a manner that is ecologically aware and politically and sexually curious.
**Ind/Abst** Altern. Press Index; Am. Hist. Life (1984); Can. Index.

US/0164-8594
**CAMEL'S CALF, THE. Added/Corp** Ancient Arabic Order of the Nobles of the Mystic Shrine for North America. (19??)-. Periodical. English. mo. $0.50. Camel's Calf, PO Box 959, Dallas TX 75221.

US/0899-7292
**CHRISTIAN NEW AGE QUARTERLY. See** Religion and Theology.

US/0277-4461
**DAWN (HONESDALE, PA.). Ceased.** (DAWN.). [Dawn]. **Added/Corp** Himalayan International Institute of Yoga Science & Philosophy. **VFOAT** Dawn magazine. Vol. 1, No. 1 (Summer 1981)-?. Periodical. English. qt. Himalayan International Institute, Rural Route 1 Box 400, Honesdale PA 18431. **Tel** (717)253-4929. **ED** Kay Gendron. **LC** B132.Y6; D316. **DD** 158/.1. **Circ:** 10,000. *Continues* Research Bulletin of the Himalayan International Institute/Eleanor N. Dana Laboratory, 0276-4148.
**Desc:** A magazine devoted to yoga, meditation, philosophy, psychology and holistic living.

II
**DIVINE LIFE, THE. Added/Corp** Divine Life Society. (1991)-. Periodical. English. mo. $4.50. Divine Life Society Press, Sivananda Nagar, Tehri-Garhwal 249192, Uttar Pradesh India. **LC** B132.Y6; W56. Index available. **Bk Rev.** available with illustrations. *Continues* Wisdom Light.

US/1058-8981
**EARTH CHANGES REPORT, THE.** (THE EARTH CHANGES REPORT : THE SURVIVAL GUIDE FOR THE NINETIES). [Earth chang. rep.]. **Added/Corp** Matrix Institute (Westmoreland, N.H.). Vol. 1, No. 1 (Oct. 1991)-. Periodical. English. mo. $50.00 US; $60.00 other. Matrix Institute, PO Box 87, Westmoreland NH 03467. **Tel** (603)399-4916, (800)623-7493. **ED** Gordon-Michael Scallion & Cynthia Keyes. **DD** 551. **Acid Free.**
**Desc:** The purpose of this publication is to forecast future trends, using intuitive methodologies, as they relate to Earth changes, Earth consciousness, personal and environmental health and healing, phenomena, and the origin of Mankind.

NE
**ERANOS. VFOAT** Eranos Yearbook Eranos Jahrbuch Eranos Annales. Vol. 39 (1970)-. Monographic series. English (French and German; summaries and/or abstracts in English and French). an. Price varies per volume. Eranos Stiftung, vai Moscia 127, Ch 6612 Ascona Switzerland. **(Subscription address:** International Book Import Services Inc., 2995 Wall Triana Highway, Suite B4, Huntsville AL 35824.) **ED** Adolf Portmann and Rudolf Ritsema. *Continues* Eranos-Jahrbuch, 0071-1055.

US/1046-6029
**FIREHEART (MAYNARD, MASS.).** (FIREHEART : A JOURNAL OF MAGICK AND SPIRITUAL TRANSFORMATION.). [FireHeart]. **Added/Corp** EarthSpirit Community. **VFOAT** Fire Heart. (1988)-. Periodical. English. sa. $8.50. Earth Spirit Community, Box 462, Maynard MA 01754. **Tel** (617)395-1023. **ED** Myrriah Lavin. **DD** 291. **Bk Rev. Ad Acc. Circ:** 3,500.
**Desc:** Devoted to magic and nature spirituality and to exploring various traditions such as Wicca, Paganism, Shamanism and New Age spirituality.

US/1069-3211
**GREEN MAN, THE. See** Parapsychology and Occultism.

US/0896-0801
**HINDUISM TODAY. See** Religion and Theology-Hinduism.

II/0254-3478
**JOURNAL OF RESEARCH IN AYURVEDA & SIDDHA.** [J. res. Ayurveda Siddha]. **Added/Corp** Central Council for Research in

Ayurveda and Siddha (India). **VFOAT** Journal of Research in Ayurveda and Siddha. Vol. 1, No. 1 (March 1980)-. Periodical. English. qt. $30.00. Central Council for Research in Ayurveda and Siddha, S-10 Dharma Bhawan Green Park Extension Market, New Delhi-110016 India. **(Subscription address:** Prints India, 11 Darya Ganj, New Delhi 110002 India.) **LC** R605; .J68. **DD** 615.8/9. **NLM** W1 JO868V. ***Continues*** *Journal of Research in Indian Medicine, Yoga and Homeopathy, 0250-4790.*

AT
**LIFESTYLES SEASON.** English. Queensland Awareness Centre Pty Ltd, POB 356, South Brisbane Queensland 4101 Australia.

US/0147-1201
**MAIN.** **VAT** Mark-Age Inform-Nations. (19??)-. Periodical. English. bm (6 issues). $15.00. Mark Age, PO Box 290368, Ft Lauderdale FL 33329. **Tel** (305)587-5555. **ED** Pauline Sharpe. **Bk Rev**. **Circ:** 1,000 (ctrl).
**Desc:** Publishes news, information, education and guidelines for linking of light workers and groups as a preparation for Second Coming and New Age of Aquarius.

US/0891-5989
**MODERN SCIENCE AND VEDIC SCIENCE.** [Mod. sci. Vedic sci.]. **Added/Corp** Maharishi International University. Vol. 1, No. 1 (Jan. 1987)-. Periodical. English. ir (2 issues per volume). $18.00. MIU Press, 1000 North 4th Street, Department Box 1115, Fairfield IA 52557. **Tel** (515)472-1101, FAX (515)472-1137, telex 286515. **DD** 158. **Bk Rev**. **Circ:** 500.
**Desc:** Reviews some of the most significant and exciting developments in human knowledge today. Each article takes you to the forefront of research- exploration of the unified field of natural law through the sciences, humanities, and arts, in light of Maharishi's Vedic Science.
**Ind/Abst** Math. Rev. (1987-).

US/0892-2721
**MUSIC OF THE SPHERES.** (1990)-. Periodical. English. qt. $15.00. John Patrick Lamkin, PO Box 1751, Taos NM 87571. **ED** John Patrick Lamkin. Index available. cum. index. **Bk Rev**. **Ad Acc**. **Circ:** 10,000 (ctrl).
**Desc:** Contains information on the art and music of the New Age.

●US/1070-762X
**NETWORKER (ASHEVILLE, N.C.), THE.** (THE NETWORKER.). [Networker]. (1992)-. Periodical. English. mo. $16.00 US; $28.00 Canada & Mexico; $40.00 Europe; $52.00 other. Delphi Communications, 20 Battery Park Avenue, Suite 612, Asheville NC 28801. **Tel** (704)254-6852, FAX (704)258-8332. **ED** Robin & Belinda Dunn. **DD** 158. **Bk Rev**, (Qty: 12). **Ad Acc**, **Adv Mgr:** Ken Burke. **Circ:** 5,000 (ctrl).
**Desc:** Includes articles on planetary awakening, holistic healing practices, spirituality, and sustainable technologies.

US/1047-2746
**NEW AGE ENCYCLOPEDIA.** [New age encycl.]. **Added/Corp** Gale Research Inc. (1990)-. Periodical. English. ir. $59.50. Gale Research Inc., 835 Penobscot Building, Detroit MI 48226. **Tel** (800)877-GALE, (313)961-2242, FAX (313)961-6083, telex TWX 810-221-7086. **ED** J. Gordon Melton, Aidan A. Kelly and Jerome Clark. **LC** BP605.N48; N447. **DD** 299/.93.
**Desc:** Chronicles the New Age Movement, bringing its elements together. Introductory overview is followed by entries and discussions of a range of topics, definitions, names, organizations, and sources for further reference.

US/0746-3618
**NEW AGE JOURNAL (1983).** (NEW AGE JOURNAL.). [New age j.]. **VFOAT** New Age. (Oct. 1983)-. Periodical. English. Six times a year (Jan., Mar., May, July, Sept., Nov.). $24.00 (one year), $39.00 (two year), $49.00 (three year). New Age Journal, 42 Pleasant Street, Watertown MA 02172. **Tel** (617)926-0200, (800)234-4556. **(Subscription address:** Neodata / Colorado, PO Box 2606, Boulder Boulder CO 80322.) **ED** Florence Graves. **LC** BP605.N48; N46. **DD** 051. **Bk Rev**. **Ad Acc**. **Circ:** 165,000. available on microfiche from University Microfilms International (UMI). ***Continues*** *New Age (Brookline Village, Brookline, Mass.), 0164-3967.*
**Desc:** A lifestyle magazine exploring health, spiritual growth, personal development, and relationships. Written for people with 'new age' attitudes and a concern for self, others, and our environs.
**Ind/Abst** Altern. Press Index (-199?); Book Rev. Index (Oct. 1983-).

US/1052-8032
**NEW AGE LINK'S LETTER LINK : THE SPIRITUAL AWARENESS NETWORK.** [New Age Link's lett. link]. **Added/Corp** New Age Link Network. **VFOAT** Letter Link. Vol. 2, No. 3 (Winter 1991)-. Periodical. English. Three times a year. $39.00 (includes membership ). New Age Link Network, PO Box 25097, Fort Wayne IN 46925-0097. **DD** 133. ***Continues*** *New Age Link, 1042-7112.*

US/1042-6566
**NEW AGE RETAILER.** [New age retail.]. Vol. 3, No. 1 (Jan.-Feb. 1989)-. Periodical. English. Seven times a year. $15.00. Continuity Publishing Inc, Box 224, Greenback WA 98253. **Tel** (206)678-7772. **ED** Duane Sweney. **DD** 658. **Bk Rev**. **Ad Acc**. **Circ:** 5,000 (ctrl). ***Continues*** *Monthly Report to Booksellers.*
**Desc:** Material of use or interest to retailers of new age and self help information and products. Includes business articles, reviews, etc.

US/1040-2047
**NEW DAY HERALD, THE.** (NEW DAY HERALD.). [New day her.]. Vol. 1, Issue 1 (July 1988)-. Periodical. English. bm. $15.00. Movement, Mandeville Press, 3500 West Adams, Los Angeles CA 90018. **Tel** (310)737-1134. **DD** 291. ***Continues*** *Movement (Los Angeles, Calif.), 0889-776X.*

US/1044-2782
**NEW TIMES (SEATTLE, WASH.).** (THE NEW TIMES.). [New times]. (1985)-. Periodical. English. mo. $9.50. Silver Owl Publications Inc, Box 51186, Seattle WA 98115-1186. **Tel** (206)524-9071. **ED** Krysta Gibson. **DD** 158. **Bk Rev**. **Ad Acc**. **Circ:** 17,000 (ctrl).
**Desc:** Provides information on human potential, peace, spirituality, personal growth.

US/0892-5984
**OF A LIKE MIND.** [Of like mind]. (198?)-. Periodical. English. qt (4 issues). $21.00. Of a Like Mind, PO Box 6021, Madison WI 53716. **Tel** (608)838-8629. **ED** Lynnre Levy. **DD** 299. **Bk Rev**. **Ad Acc**. **Circ:** 12,000.
**Desc:** A women's spiritual newspaper and network dedicated to bring together women following a positive path to spiritual growth. It focuses on women's spirituality, Goddess religions, paganism and our earth connections from a feminist perspective.

●US/1068-2473
**PAGAN MUSE & WORLD REPORT.** (PAGAN MUSE & WORLD REPORT / BAY AREA PAGAN ASSEMBLIES.). [Pagan muse world rep.]. **Added/Corp** Bay Area Pagan Assemblies. **VFOAT** Pagan Muse and World Report; Muse; Pagan Muse. Vol. 2, Issue 4 (1992)-. Periodical. English. bm. $3.95 per issues. BAPA / Bay Area Pagan Assemblies, PO Box 850, Fremont CA 94537-0850. **Tel** (510)656-4242. **ED** Janet Christian. **DD** 292. **Ad Acc**. ***Continues*** *Bay Area Pagan Assemblies Newsletter.*
**Desc:** Serves as a way of distributing information to the Pagan community and as an outlet for the creativity of members of the Bay Area Pagan Assemblies.

●US/1065-3031
**PARAPSYCHOLOGY, NEW AGE, AND THE OCCULT.** See Parapsychology and Occultism.

FR
**REVUE FRANCAISE DE YOGA.** French. sa. 250.00F France; 300.00F other. Fed Francaise et Union Europeenne Yoga, 3 rue Aubriot, 75004 Paris France. **Tel** 011 33 1 42780305.

NE/0169-1341
**SHARE INTERNATIONAL.** [Share int.]. **Added/Corp** Share International Foundation. Vol. 1 (1982)-. Periodical. English (Dutch, French, German, Japanese and Spanish). mo (Jan/Feb & July/Aug are combined issues). $30.00 Australia & New Zealand; $27.50 other; $20.00 libraries. Share International, PO Box 971, c/o Lynne Girdlestone, North Hollywood CA 91603. **Tel** (818)785-6300, FAX (818)994-0383. **ED** Peter Liefhebber & Benjamin Creme. Index available. **Bk Rev**. **Circ:** 5,000. available on an online database (Selected articles available on Compuserve & PeaceNet).
**Desc:** This publication seeks to bring together the political and spiritual aspects of New Age thinking. It shows the synthesis underlying the political, social, economic, and spiritual changes now occurring on a global scale.

PL/0867-2490
**UFO BIAYSTOK.** (UFO.). [UFO Biayst.]. **VFOAT** Unidentified Flying Objects. (1990)-. Periodical. Polish. qt. $17.00. **(Subscription address:** ARS Polona, PO Box 1001, 00068 Warsaw Poland.) **UDC** 001.94. ***Continues*** *NOL (Biaystok), 0866-9309.*

US/1055-7911
**YOGA INTERNATIONAL.** [Yoga int.]. **Added/Corp** Himalayan International Institute of Yoga Science & Philosophy. **VFOAT** Yoga. Vol. 1, No. 1 (July/Aug. 1991)-. Periodical. English. bm. $15.00 (one year), $24.00 (two year) U.S.; $20.00 (one year), $34.00 (two year), Canada; $25.00 (one year), $44.00 (two year) other. Himalayan International, Rural Route 1, Box 400, Honesdale PA 18431. **Tel** (717)253-4929, FAX (717)253-6360, telex 5106001805. **ED** Deborah Willoughby. **LC** B132.Y6; Y574. **DD** 181/.45/05. **Bk Rev**. **Ad Acc**. **Circ:** 20,000.
**Desc:** Dedicated to bringing authentic information on the practice of yoga in our contemporary world. Articles on meditation, personal growth, and holistic health for cultivating a balanced lifestyle that acknowledges our need to integrate body, mind, and spirit.

II/0044-0507
**YOGA-MIMAMSA.** **Added/Corp** Kaivalyadhama. (1958)-. Periodical. Multiple languages (English and Sanskrit). qt. $35.00. Kaivalyadhama, Lonavala, India. **(Subscription address:** Prints India, 11 Darya Ganj, New Delhi 110002 India.) **LC** B132.Y6; Y614. **DD** 181/.45/05.

US/0191-3298
**YOGA RESEARCH.** V. 1- 1978-. English. an. Free to members Yoga Research Society, $5.00 members of Swami Kuvalayananda Yoga Foundation, $7.00 others. 251 South 12th Street, Philadelphia PA 19107. **LC** B132.Y6; Y615. **DD** 158.

## ABSTRACTING, BIBLIOGRAPHIES AND STATISTICS

US/0002-662X
**ALTERNATIVE PRESS INDEX.** [Altern. press index]. **Added/Corp** Alternative Press Centre. Radical Research Center. Vol. 1 (July/Dec. 1969)-. Abstracting/Indexing Service. English. Four times a year (Mar., June, Sept., Dec.). $175.00. Alternative Press Centre, PO Box 33109, Baltimore MD 21218. **Tel** (410)243-2471, FAX (410)235-5325. **ED** Bill Wilson and Les Wade. **LC** AI3; .A27. **DD** 051.016. **NLM** Z 7161.S66 A466. Index available. cum. index. **Circ:** 1,000 (ctrl).
**Desc:** Subject index to alternative, progressive and radical publications, similar in form to the Readers' Guide to Periodical Literature.

# Nutrition and Dietetics

US/0732-9954
**ADA REPORT FOR EDUCATORS.** (ADA REPORT FOR EDUCATORS / THE AMERICAN DIETETIC ASSOCIATION.). [ADA rep. educ.]. **VFOAT** A.D.A. Report for Educators; Report for Educators. Periodical. English. Three times a year. $15.00. The American Dietetic Association, 430 North Michigan Avenue, Chicago IL 60611. **LC** RM218; .A36. **DD** 613.2/071/173.

US/1043-4526
**ADVANCES IN FOOD AND NUTRITION RESEARCH.** [Adv. food nutr. res.]. (1989)-. Academic Scholarly Publication. English. an. $80.00 (Vol. 36). Academic Press, Inc., 6277 Sea Harbor Drive, Orlando FL 32887. **Tel** (800)543-9534, (407)345-4100, FAX (407)363-9661. **LC** TX537; .A25. **DD** 664/.005. **NLM** W1; AD601R. **CODEN** AFNREL. **[CCC].** Documents available from BIOSIS Document Express, CASDDS. ***Continues*** *Advances in Food Research, 0065-2628.*
**Ind/Abst** AGRICOLA [Full Cov.]; Biol. Agric. Index; Biol. Abstr.; Chem. Abstr.; Food Sci. Technol. Abstr.; Foods Adlibra; Index Med.; INIS Atomindex [Micro.]; Physic. Medline Plus; Trop. Dis. Bull.

US/0891-7396
**ADVANCES IN HUMAN NUTRITION.** [Adv. hum. nutr.]. Vol. 2 (1985)-. Monographic series. English. ir. Price varies per volume. Chem Orbital, PO Box 134, Park Forest IL 60466. **Tel** (708)748-0440. **LC** QP141.A1; A29. **DD** 613.2/05. **NLM** W1; AD64N. ***Continues*** *Advances in Modern Human Nutrition, 0270-8957.*
**Ind/Abst** AGRICOLA [Full Cov.].

US/0149-9483
**ADVANCES IN NUTRITIONAL RESEARCH.** [Adv. nutr. res.]. Vol. 1 (1977)-. Monographic series. English. ir. Price varies per volume. Plenum Press, 233 Spring Street, New York NY 10013-1578. **Tel** (212)620-8000, (800)221-9369, FAX (212)463-0742, (212)807-1047, telex 23/421139. **ED** Harold H. Draper. **LC** QP141.A1; A3. **DD** 613.2/05. **NLM** W1 AD685N. **CODEN** ANURD9. Documents available from The Genuine Article, BIOSIS Document Express, CASDDS.
**Ind/Abst** AGRICOLA; Bibliogr. Agric.; Biol. Abstr. (1985-); Chem. Abstr. (1984-); Foods Adlibra; Health Plan. Adminis.; Index Med. (1981-); Res. Alert [Full Cov.]; SCISEARCH.

FR
**AGE & NUTRITION.** **VFOAT** Age et Nutrition. (1990)-. Periodical. French (English; summaries and/or abstracts in English; table of contents in English). Three times a year. 379.15F France; 400.00F all except EEC; 500.00F other. Editions Hervas, 123 Avenue Philippe Auguste, F 75011 Paris France. **Tel** 011 33 1 43791095. **NLM** W1; AG343HH. Index available. **Bk Rev**. ctrl circ.
**Desc:** Information on aging, nutrition and dietetics.
**Ind/Abst** Abstr. Soc. Gerontol.; Dairy Sci. Abstr.; Nutr. Abstr. Rev., Ser. A, Hum. Exp.

GW/0341-0501
**AKTUELLE ERNAHRUNGSMEDIZIN.** [Aktuel. Ernahrungsmed.]. **Added/Corp**

Arbeitsgemeinschaft fuer Klinische Diatetik (Germany). **VFOAT** Aktuelle Ernahrungsmedizin in Klinik und Praxis. Vol. 1 (Sept./Oct. 1976)-. Academic Scholarly Publication. German (summaries and/or abstracts in English). bm (6 issues). $130.00. Georg Thieme Verlag Stuttgart, Postfach 301120, D 70451 Stuttgart Germany. **Tel** 011 49 711 89310, FAX 011 49 711 8931298, telex 7 252 275 GTVD. **(Subscription address:** Thieme Medical Publishers Inc., 381 Park Avenue South, New York NY 10016.**)** **NLM** W1 AK992B. **CODEN** AEKPDQ. **[CCC].** Documents available from CASDDS.
**Ind/Abst** Chem. Abstr.; EMBASE; Hortic. Abstr.; Nutr. Abstr. Rev., Ser. A, Hum. Exp.; Life Sci. Collect.; Potato Abstr.; Wheat Barley Trit. Abstr.

SP/0212-1689
**ALIMENTACION, EQUIPOS Y TECNOLOGIA.** [Aliment. equipos tecnol.]. (1982)-. Academic Scholarly Publication. Spanish. Ten times a year. $113.00 Europe; $220.00 others. Editorial Alcionsa, Triana 53, 28016 Madrid Spain. **Tel** 011 34 1 3456400. **CODEN** AEQTDY. **[CCC].** Documents available from CASDDS.
**Ind/Abst** BioBusiness (1988-); Chem. Abstr.; Food Sci. Technol. Abstr.

IT/0392-7512
**ALIMENTAZIONE, NUTRIZIONE, METABOLISMO (1979).** (ALIMENTAZIONE, NUTRIZIONE, METABOLISMO.). [Alim., nutr., metab.]. Vol. 1 (Oct./Dec. 1979)-. Academic Scholarly Publication. Italian (French and English; summaries and/or abstracts in English). Three times a year (Jan., May, Sept.). L47000 Italy; L94000 others Comes with Clinica Dietologica. Societa Editrice Universo, Via GB Morgagni 1, 00161 Rome Italy. **Tel** 011 39 6 44231171. **ED** Michelangelo Cairella. **NLM** W1 AL378NB. **CODEN** ANMTD9. **Bk Rev. Ad Acc. Circ:** 3,000. Documents available from BIOSIS Document Express, CASDDS. ***Supersedes*** *Alimentazione, Nutrizione, Metabolismo, 0392-8071.*
**Desc:** Clinical dietetics in disorders of metabolism.
**Ind/Abst** Biol. Abstr.; Chem. Abstr.

BL/0103-4235
**ALIMENTOS E NUTRICAO / UNIVERSIDADE ESTADUAL PAULISTA.** **Added/Corp** Universidade Estadual Paulista. Vol. 1 (1989)-. Periodical. Portuguese (summaries and/or abstracts in English; table of contents in English). **NLM** W1; AL38. **CODEN** ALNUE4.
**Ind/Abst** Food Sci. Technol. Abstr.; Foods Adlibra.

FR
**ALISCOPE.** ***Ceased.*** **See** Animal Welfare.

CN/0228-586X
**ALIVE (VANCOUVER).** (ALIVE.). [Alive]. No. 1 (1975)-. Periodical. English (French). Eleven times a year. $26.50 (1 year) US; 21.03Can$ (1 year), 39.25Can$ (2 year), 57.01Can$ (3 year) Canada; 40.00Can$ (1 year) other. Canadian Health Reform Production Ltd, 4728 Byrne Road, Burnaby British Columbia V5J 3H7 Canada. **Tel** (604)435-1919, FAX (604)435-4888. **(Subscription address:** Box 80055, Burnaby British Columbia V5H 4K2 Canada**)** **ED** Hilda Ward. **DD** 641.1. Index available. cum. index. **Bk Rev. Ad Acc. Circ:** 20,000 (ctrl).
**Desc:** Health related topics, information and product knowledge.

US/0002-9165
**AMERICAN JOURNAL OF CLINICAL NUTRITION, THE.** [Am. j. clin. nutr.]. **Added/Corp** American Society for Clinical Nutrition. Vol. 2, No. 4 (July/Aug. 1954)-. Academic Scholarly Publication. English. mo. $135.00 (institution), $90.00 (individual) US; $160.00 (institution), $115.00 (individual) other. American Institute of Nutrition, 9650 Rockville Pike, Room L 2310, Bethesda MD 20814-3998. **Tel** (301)530-7026, FAX (301)530-7001. **LC** RC584; .A5. **NLM** W1 AM45J. **CODEN** AJCNAC. **[CCC].** Index available. **Bk Rev. Ad Acc. Pr Rev. Circ:** 7,000. available on microfilm and microfiche from University Microfilms International (UMI). Documents available from The Genuine Article, BIOSIS Document Express, CASDDS. ***Continues*** *Journal of Clinical Nutrition, 0095-9871.*
**Desc:** Original research articles in clinical nutrition for the research scientist, physician, dietitian and nurse.
**Ind/Abst** Abr. Index Med.; AGRICOLA [Full Cov.]; Agrofor. Abstr. (1991-); Annals Behav. Med.; Biol. Agric. Index; Biol. Abstr.; Calcium Calcif. Tissue Abstr.; Chem. Abstr.; Chicano Index; Curr. Aware. Biol. Sci., CABS; Curr. Contents Life Sci.; Dairy Sci. Abstr.; Dev. Med. Child Neurol. (-1990); EMBASE; Energy Res. Abstr.; Environ. Period. Bibliogr. (?-?); Food Sci. Technol. Abstr.; Foods Adlibra; Health Index (1989-); Health Period. Database; Health Ref. Cent. (Jan. 1989-) [Full Cov.]; Helminthol. Abstr. (1991-); Hospit. Health Admin. Index; Index Med.; Index Vet.; INIS Atomindex [Micro.]; Int. Aerosp. Abstr.; Iowa Drug Inf. Serv.; Leis. Recreat. Tour. Abstr.; Maize Abstr.; Med. Abstr. Newsl.; NAPRALERT; Nutr. Abstr. Rev., Ser. B, Live Feeds and Feed.; Nutr. Abstr. Rev., Ser. A, Hum. Exp.; Nutr. Res. Newsl.; PESTDOC; Physic. Medline Plus; Pig News Inf.; Potato Abstr.; Poult. Abstr.; Protozoolog. Abstr.; Ref. Upd. Basic Ed.; Ref. Upd. Clinical Ed.; Ref. Upd. Deluxe Ed.; Res. Alert [Full Cov.]; Rev. Med. Vet. Mycology; Rev. Plant Pathol.; Rice Abstr.; Risk Abstr. (19??-19??); Rural Dev. Abstr.; Sci. Cit. Index; SCISEARCH; Soc. Sci. Cit. Index [Select. Cov.]; Soyabean Abstr.; SPORT Discus; SportSearch; Stat. Theory Method Abstr.; Sug. Indus. Abstr.; Vet. Bull.; Trop. Dis. Bull.; Wheat Barley Trit. Abstr.; Women Stud. Abstr.; World Agric. Econ.

SP/0003-2492
**ANALES DE BROMATOLOGIA.** [An. bromatol.]. **Added/Corp** Sociedad Espanola de Bromatologia. Consejo Superior de Investigaciones Cientificas. Deparamento de Investigaciones Bromatologicas. Consejo Superior de Investigaciones Cientificas (Spain). (1949)-. Academic Scholarly Publication. Spanish (summaries and/or abstracts in English). qt. 7400ptas. Sociedad Espanola de Bromatologia, Edif Fac de Farmacia Ciudad U, 28040 Madrid Spain. **Tel** 011 34 1 3941801, 011 34 1 3941799. **LC** TX341; .A65. **NLM** W1 AN135. **CODEN** ANBRAD. **[CCC].** cum. index. Documents available from CASDDS.
**Ind/Abst** Anal. Abstr.; Biodeter. Abstr. (1991-); Chem. Abstr.; Dairy Sci. Abstr.; Food Sci. Technol. Abstr.; Hortic. Abstr.; Mass Spect. Bull.; Nutr. Abstr. Rev., Ser. B, Live Feeds and Feed.; Nutr. Abstr. Rev., Ser. A, Hum. Exp.; Potato Abstr.; Vitis Vitic. Enol. Abstr.

SZ/0517-8606
**ANNALES NESTLE.** **Added/Corp** Nestle Nutrition S.A. (195?)-. Periodical. English. tq. NESTEC Ltd., Avenue Nestle 55, CH-1800, Vevey, Switzerland.
**Ind/Abst** EMBASE.

SZ/0250-6807
**ANNALS OF NUTRITION & METABOLISM.** [Ann. nutr. metab.]. **VFOAT** Annals of Nutrition and Metabolism. Vol. 25, No. 1 (Jan./Feb. 1981)-. Academic Scholarly Publication. English (French and German). bm (6 issues). $276.00. S. Karger AG, Allschwilerstrasse 10, PO Box - Postfach - Case Postale, CH-4009 Basel Switzerland. **Tel** 011 41 61 306-1111, FAX 011 41 61 306-1234, telex CH 962 652. **ED** G. Wolfram, G. Debry. **NLM** W1 AN616M. **CODEN** ANUMDS. **[CCC]. Ad Acc. Pr Rev.** available on microfilm and microfiche. Documents available from The Genuine Article, BIOSIS Document Express, CASDDS. ***Formed by the union of*** *Nutrition and Metabolism, 0029-6678* ***and*** *Annales de la Nutrition et de l'Alimentation, 0003-4037.*
**Desc:** The editors of this journal show their dedication to the search for reliable dietary guidelines by carefully selecting basic and clinical reports offering new information relating to human nutrition and metabolic diseases including their molecular genetics. Papers present original findings dealing with problems such as the consequences of specific diets and dietary supplements, nutritional factors in the etiology of metabolic and gastrointestinal disorders, and the epidemiological association between dietary habits and disease incidence.
**Ind/Abst** AGRICOLA [Full Cov.]; Anim. Breed. Abstr.; Biol. Abstr.; Chem. Abstr.; Chem. Titles; Curr. Aware. Biol. Sci., CABS; Curr. Contents, Agric. Biol. Environ. Sci.; Curr. Contents Life Sci.; Dairy Sci. Abstr.; EMBASE; Health Plan. Adminis.; Index Med.; Index Vet.; Leadscan; Maize Abstr.; Nutr. Abstr. Rev., Ser. B, Live Feeds and Feed.; Nutr. Abstr. Rev., Ser. A, Hum. Exp.; Nutr. Res. Newsl.; Life Sci. Collect.; PESTDOC; Pig News Inf.; Poult. Abstr.; Ref. Upd. Deluxe Ed.; Res. Alert [Full Cov.]; Sci. Cit. Index; SCISEARCH; Soyabean Abstr.; SportSearch; Vet. Bull.; Trop. Dis. Bull.; Wheat Barley Trit. Abstr.

US/0732-7013
**ANNUAL REPORT OF THE NATIONAL INSTITUTES OF HEALTH. PROGRAM BEHAVIORAL NUTRITION RESEARCH AND TRAINING.** [Annu. rep. Natl. Inst. Health, Program biomed. behav. nutr. res. train.]. **Main/Corp** National Institutes of Health (U.S.). Nutrition Coordinating Committee. Began with: 1977. English. an. N I H Nutrition Coordinating Committee, Building 31/Room 4B59, National Institutes of Health, Bethesda MD 20814. **LC** QP141.A1; N28A. **DD** 613.2/072073. **NLM** W2 A N203A. available on microfiche (Vols. for (1985-) distributed to depository libraries).

US/0199-9885
**ANNUAL REVIEW OF NUTRITION.** [Annu. rev. nutr.]. Vol. 1 (1981)-. Academic Scholarly Publication. English. an (July). $48.00 US; $53.00 other. Annual Reviews Inc., 4139 El Camino Way, PO Box 10139, Palo Alto CA 94303-0139. **Tel** (415)493-4400, (800)523-8635, FAX (415)855-9815. **ED** Robert E. Olson. **LC** QP141.A1; A64. **DD** 613.2/05. **NLM** W1 AN778D. **CODEN** ARNTD8. **[CCC].** Index available. cum. index. **Pr Rev.** ctrl circ. available on microfilm and microfiche from University Microfilms International (UMI). Documents available from The Genuine Article, BIOSIS Document Express, CASDDS.
**Desc:** Comprehensive, thorough coverage of latest advances in nutrition, written by acknowledged experts in the field. Extensive literature citations included.
**Ind/Abst** AGRICOLA [Full Cov.]; Biol. Agric. Index; Biol. Abstr.; Chem. Abstr.; Curr. Aware. Biol. Sci., CABS; Curr. Contents, Agric. Biol. Environ. Sci.; Curr. Contents Life Sci.; Dairy Sci. Abstr.; EMBASE; Food Sci. Technol. Abstr.; Foods Adlibra; Health Plan. Adminis.; Index Med. (1981-); Index Sci. Rev. [Full Cov.]; Life Sci. Collect.; Potato Abstr.; Ref. Upd. Basic Ed.; Ref. Upd. Clinical Ed.; Ref. Upd. Deluxe Ed.; Res. Alert [Full Cov.]; Sci. Cit. Index; SCISEARCH; SportSearch; Trop. Dis. Bull.

UK/0195-6663
**APPETITE.** [Appetite]. Vol. 1, No. 1 (Mar. 1980)-. Academic Scholarly Publication. English. bm (6 issues). $325.00. Academic Press Ltd., A Division of Harcourt Brace & Company Ltd., 24-28 Oval Road, London NW1 7DX England. **Tel** 071 267 4466, FAX 071 482 2293, 071 485 4752, telex 25775 ACPRES G. **(Subscription address:** Harcourt Brace & Company, Ltd., Foots Cray, High Street, Sidcup Kent DA14 5HP England.**)** **ED** D. A. Booth, S. Nicolaidis, J. Rodin, P. Rozin, J. S. Stern and A. Stunkard. **LC** QP136. **DD** 599/.013. **NLM** W1 AP49H. **CODEN** APPTD4. **[CCC]. Bk Rev. Pr Rev.** Documents available from The Genuine Article, BIOSIS Document Express, CASDDS.
**Desc:** An international research journal covering the determinants and consequences of eating, drinking, and their disorders, with dietary intake, attitudes, and practices in their widest aspects.
**Ind/Abst** AGRICOLA [Full Cov.]; Anim. Behav. Abstr.; Biol. Abstr. (1984-); Chem. Abstr.; Chemorecept. Abstr.; Curr. Contents Life Sci.; Dairy Sci. Abstr.; EMBASE [Select. Cov.]; Food Sci. Technol. Abstr.; Foods Adlibra; Health Plan. Adminis.; Index Med.; Nutr. Abstr. Rev., Ser. B, Live Feeds and Feed.; Nutr. Abstr. Rev., Ser. A, Hum. Exp.; Nutr. Res. Newsl.; Life Sci. Collect.; Potato Abstr.; Psychol. Abstr. (1980-); PsycINFO; PsycLit; Ref. Upd. Deluxe Ed.; Res. Alert [Full Cov.]; Sci. Cit. Index; SCISEARCH; Soc. Sci. Cit. Index [Select. Cov.].

VE/0004-0622
**ARCHIVOS LATINOAMERICANOS DE NUTRICION.** (ARCHIVOS LATINOAMERICANOS DE NUTRICION / ORGANO OFICIAL DE LA SOCIEDAD LATINOAMERICANA DE NUTRICION.). [Arch. latinoam. nutr.]. **Added/Corp** Sociedad Latinoamericana de Nutricion. Vol. 16, No. 1 (Sept. 1966)-. Periodical. Spanish (English, French and Portuguese). Four times a year (Mar., June, Sept., Dec.). $125.00 Americas; $150.00 others. Funcacion Cavendes Edificio, Apartado 62 778 Chacao, Caracas 1060 Venezuela S A. **Tel** FAX 011 58 2 2848543. **ED** Virgilio Bosch. **LC** TX341; .A674. **NLM** W1 AR725V. **CODEN** ALANBH. **[CCC].** Index available. cum. index. **Bk Rev**, (Qty: 6/yr). **Ad Acc. Circ:** 500 (ctrl). Documents available from The Genuine Article, CASDDS. ***Continues*** *Archivos Venezolanos de Nutricion.*
**Desc:** Dissemination of knowledge in food nutrition and allied fields through general articles. Original research papers and reviews, announcements of new books, upcoming conferences and other events.
**Ind/Abst** Agrofor. Abstr. (1991-); Biodeter. Abstr. (1991-); Chem. Abstr.; Curr. Contents, Agric. Biol. Environ. Sci.; Dairy Sci. Abstr.; EMBASE; Field Crop Abstr.; Food Sci. Technol. Abstr.; Health Plan. Adminis.; Index Med.; Maize Abstr.; Nutr. Abstr. Rev., Ser. B, Live Feeds and Feed.; Nutr. Abstr. Rev., Ser. A, Hum. Exp.; Nutr. Res. Newsl.; Life Sci. Collect.; Plant Breed. Abstr.; Potato Abstr.; Poult. Abstr.; Protozoolog. Abstr.; Res. Alert [Select. Cov.]; Rice Abstr.; SCISEARCH; Seed Abstr.; Soc. Sci. Cit. Index [Select. Cov.]; Soyabean Abstr.; Wheat Barley Trit. Abstr.

UK/0964-7058
**ASIA PACIFIC JOURNAL OF CLINICAL NUTRITION.** English. Four times a year. £55.00. Smith Gordon and Company Ltd, 16 Gunter Grove, No. 1, London SE1 0UJ England. **Tel** 011 44 71 3517042, FAX 011 44 71 3511250.

AT/1032-1322
**AUSTRALIAN JOURNAL OF NUTRITION AND DIETETICS.** [Aust. J. nutr. diet.]. **Added/Corp** Dietitians Association of Australia. Vol. 46 No. 1 (March 1989)-. Periodical. English. Four times a year (Mar., June, Sept., Dec.). 45.00Aus$ Australia; 60.00Aus$ other. Dietitians Association of Australia, PO Box 11, Oconnor Act, 2601 Australia. **Tel** 11 61 6 2472555, FAX 011 61 6 2572184. **NLM** W1; AU624E. Index available (Bound 4th issue in December). cum. index. **Bk Rev**, (Qty: varies). **Ad Acc. Circ:** 1,650. ***Continues*** *Journal of Food & Nutrition.*
**Ind/Abst** AGRICOLA [Select. Cov.]; Dairy Sci. Abstr.; Food Sci. Technol. Abstr.; Nutr. Abstr. Rev., Ser. A, Hum. Exp.

US/0270-4978
**BASIC AND CLINICAL NUTRITION.** [Basic clin. nutr.]. Vol. 1 (1980)-. Academic Scholarly Publication. English. Price varies per volume. Marcel Dekker Inc., 270 Madison Avenue, New York NY 10016. **Tel** (212)696-9000, (800)228-1160, FAX (212)685-4540, telex 421419. **(Subscription address:** Marcel Dekker Inc, PO Box 5017, Monticello NY 12701.**)** **LC** UNC. **DD** 599/.013/05. **NLM** W1 BA813U. **CODEN** BCNUDJ. Documents available from BIOSIS Document Express, CASDDS.
**Desc:** Series covering topics in nutrition such as vitamins and dietary fiber.
**Ind/Abst** Biol. Abstr. (?-1981); Chem. Abstr. (1980-1981).

US/0405-668X
**BETTER NUTRITION.** ***Title Change.*** (19??)-. Periodical. English. mo. Argus Business, 6151 Powers Ferry Road, Atlanta GA 30339. **Tel** (404)995-2500, (800)233-3359. **LC** TX341; .B46. **DD** 641.1/05. **[CCC].** available on microfilm from University Microfilms

# Nutrition and Dietetics

International (UMI). *Continued by* Better Nutrition for Today's Living.
**Ind/Abst** Acad. Abstr. Full Text Elite (Jan. 1992-); Health Index (1989-1990); Health Ref. Cent. (Jan. 1989-?) [Full Txt.] [Full Cov.]; Mag. Search.

US
## BETTER NUTRITION FOR TODAY'S LIVING.
(1992)-. English. mo. $24.00 (1 year), $36.00 (2 year). Argus Business, 6151 Powers Ferry Road, Atlanta GA 30339. **Tel** (404)995-2500, (800)233-3359. available on an online database (file 149/Full-Text) from DIALOG.
**Ind/Abst** Acad. Abstr. (Jan. 1992-); Acad. Search (Jan. 1992-); Health Index (1990-); Health Period. Database [Full Txt.]; Health Ref. Cent. (Jan. 1989-) [Full Txt.] [Full Cov.]; Health Source (Jan. 1992-).

SZ/0067-8198
## BIBLIOTHECA NUTRITIO ET DIETA.
[Bibl. nutr. dieta]. **VFOAT** Nutritio et Dieta. Supplement. Vol. 1 (1960)-. Monographic series. English (German). an. 150.00F (approx. per volume). S. Karger AG, Allschwilerstrasse 10, PO Box - Postfach - Case Postale, CH-4009 Basel Switzerland. **Tel** 011 41 61 306-1111, FAX 011 41 61 306-1234, telex CH 962 652. **ED** J. C. Somogyi. **LC** TX341; .B5. **NLM** W1 BI422. **CODEN** BNDSA3. **[CCC].** Documents available from BIOSIS Document Express, CASDDS.
**Desc:** Individual volumes, largely based on symposia, provide a balanced assessment of the latest views on various matters of current interest. Workers in all areas of nutrition and dietetics will consult this series for reference not only to health aspects of alimentation, but also to related social, psychological and economic considerations.
**Ind/Abst** Biol. Abstr.; Chem. Abstr.; Dairy Sci. Abstr.; Food Sci. Technol. Abstr.; Health Plan. Adminis.; Index Med.; Nutr. Abstr. Rev., Ser. B, Live Feeds and Feed.; Nutr. Abstr. Rev., Ser. A, Hum. Exp.; Life Sci. Collect.; Ref. Upd. Deluxe Ed.

US/0884-6081
## BIENNIAL REPORT ON THE SPECIAL SUPPLEMENTAL FOOD PROGRAM FOR WOMEN, INFANTS, AND CHILDREN, AND ON THE COMMODITY SUPPLEMENTAL FOOD PROGRAM.
See Food and Food Industry.

US/0730-7918
## BIOLOGY OF CARBOHYDRATES.
[Biol. carbohydr.]. Vol. 1 (1981)-. Academic Scholarly Publication. English. ir. Price varies. John Wiley & Sons, Inc., 605 Third Avenue, New York NY 10158-0012. **Tel** (212)850-6000, (212)850-6645, FAX (212)850-6088, telex 12-7063. **(Subscription address:** John Wiley & Sons / England, Baffins Lane, Chichester, West Sussex PO19 1UD England.) **ED** Victor Ginsburg and Phillips Robbins. **NLM** W1 BI852M. **CODEN** BICADE. Documents available from BIOSIS Document Express, CASDDS.
**Ind/Abst** Biol. Abstr.; Chem. Abstr.

UK/0141-9684
## BNF NUTRITION BULLETIN.
(NUTRITION BULLETIN.). [BNF nutr. bull.]. **Main/Corp** British Nutrition Foundation. **VAT** British Nutrition Foundation Bulletin. Vol. 4 No. 19 (Jan. 1977)-. Academic Scholarly Publication. English. Three times a year. £24.00 UK; £32.00 other. British Nutrition Foundation, 15 Belgrave Square, London SW1X 8PS England. **Tel** 011/44/71/2354904, FAX 011/44/71/2359336. **ED** Janice Ryley. **CODEN** BNUBD6. **Bk Rev. Circ:** 1,500 (ctrl). Documents available from CASDDS. *Continues BNF Bulletin, 0307-3548.*
**Desc:** News and easy ways to keep up with the developments in nutrition.
**Ind/Abst** AGRICOLA [Select. Cov.]; Chem. Abstr.; EMBASE (?-1986); Food Sci. Technol. Abstr.; Nutr. Abstr. Rev., Ser. A, Hum. Exp.; Trop. Dis. Bull.

BL
## BOLETIM DA SOCIEDADE BRASILEIRA DE CIENCIA E TECNOLOGIA DE ALIMENTOS / SOCIEDADE BRASILEIRA DE CIENCIA E TECNOLOGIA DE ALIMENTOS, SBCTA.
See Food and Food Industry.

SP/0211-1128
## BOLETIN DEL CENTRO NACIONAL DE ALIMENTACION Y NUTRICION.
(BOLETIN DEL CENTRO NACIONAL DE ALIMENTACION Y NUTRICION (C.E.N.A.N.).). [Bol. Cent. Nac. Aliment. Nutr.]. Academic Scholarly Publication. Spanish (Spanish). qt. Servicio de Publicaciones de Publicaciones del Ministerio de Sanidad y Seguridad Social, 14 Spain. **NLM** W1; BO28XB. **CODEN** BCNSDD. Documents available from CASDDS.
**Ind/Abst** Chem. Abstr.

UK/0007-1145
## BRITISH JOURNAL OF NUTRITION, THE.
[Br. j. nutr.]. **Added/Corp** Nutrition Society (Great Britain). Vol. 1, No. 1 (Sept. 1947)-. Academic Scholarly Publication. English. mo. $528.00 US, Canada & Mexico; £282.00 other. Cambridge University Press, the Edinburgh Building, Shaftesbury Road, Cambridge CB2 2RU United Kingdom. **Tel** 011 44 223 312393, FAX 011 44 223 325959. **(Subscription address:** Cambridge University Press / North America, 110 Midland Avenue, Port Chester NY 10573.) **ED** D. A. T. Southgate. **LC** TX501; .B75. **DD** 641.06242. **NLM** W1 BR584. **CODEN** BJNUAV. **[CCC].** **Pr Rev.** available on microfilm and microfiche from University Microfilms International (UMI). Documents available from The Genuine Article, BIOSIS Document Express, CASDDS.
**Desc:** International in scope. Publishes reports of original research aimed to advance nutritional concepts and to provide the kind of information needed to make rational decisions on practical nutritional questions. Includes papers on clinical and physiological human nutrition, the nutrition of farm animals and other animal species, and studies of nutritional metabolism. Topics are discussed critically in a "Letters to the Editor" section. An editorial column highlights publications of exceptional scientific interest and comments on current developments in nutrition.
**Ind/Abst** AGRICOLA [Full Cov.]; Anim. Breed. Abstr.; Annals Behav. Med.; Biol. Agric. Index; Biol. Abstr.; Chem. Abstr.; Chem. Titles; Curr. Aware. Biol. Sci., CABS; Curr. Contents, Agric. Biol. Environ. Sci.; Curr. Contents Life Sci.; Curr. Ref. Fish Res.; Dairy Sci. Abstr.; Dev. Med. Child Neurol. (-1990); EMBASE; Environ. Period. Bibliogr.; Food Sci. Technol. Abstr.; Foods Adlibra; Health Plan. Adminis.; Index Med.; Index Vet.; Maize Abstr.; Nutr. Abstr. Rev., Ser. B, Live Feeds and Feed.; Nutr. Abstr. Rev., Ser. A, Hum. Exp.; Nutr. Res. Newsl.; Life Sci. Collect.; PESTDOC; Pig News Inf.; Potato Abstr.; Poult. Abstr.; Ref. Upd. Deluxe Ed.; Res. Alert [Full Cov.]; Rev. Med. Vet. Mycology; Rice Abstr.; Sci. Cit. Index; SCISEARCH; Soyabean Abstr.; SportSearch; Stat. Theory Method Abstr. (1959-1963); Sug. Indus. Abstr.; Vet. Bull.; Trop. Dis. Bull.; Wheat Barley Trit. Abstr.

CN/0319-7808
## BULLETIN - CORPORATION PROFESSIONNELLE DES DIETETISTES DU QUEBEC.
**Main/Corp** Corporation Professionnelle des Dietetistes du Quebec. First issued in 1973. Bulletin. French (English). Free to members. Corporation Professionnelle Des Dietetistes Du Quebec, bureau 130, 934 Est, Rue Ste-Catherine, Montreal Quebec H2L 2E9. *Continues Corporation des Dietetistes du Quebec. Bulletin, 0319-7794.*

PH
## BULLETIN OF THE NUTRITION FOUNDATION OF THE PHILIPPINES.
Bulletin. English. bm.
**Ind/Abst** Philip. Sci. Technol. Abstr.

UA/0366-1393
## BULLETIN OF THE NUTRITION INSTITUTE OF THE UNITED ARAB REPUBLIC.
[Bull. Nutr. Inst. U. A. R.]. (1965)-. Multiple languages. ir. **CODEN** BNARAJ.
**Ind/Abst** Wheat Barley Trit. Abstr.

CN/0836-6845
## BULLETIN / THE NATIONAL EATING DISORDER INFORMATION CENTRE.
See Medical Science and Technology-Neurology.

FR/0007-9960
## CAHIERS DE NUTRITION ET DE DIETETIQUE.
[Cah. nutr. diet.]. (Jan./March 1966)-. Academic Scholarly Publication. Multiple languages (English and French). bm. $80.00. SPPIF, BP 22, 41350 Vineuil France. **Tel** 011 33 54 439440. **NLM** W1 CA139D. **CODEN** CNDQA8. **[CCC].** Index available. **Bk Rev. Ad Acc.** ctrl circ. Documents available from BIOSIS Document Express, CASDDS.
**Ind/Abst** Biol. Abstr.; Chem. Abstr.; Dairy Sci. Abstr.; EMBASE; Food Sci. Technol. Abstr. Leis. Recreat. Tour. Abstr.; Nutr. Abstr. Rev., Ser. A, Hum. Exp.; Life Sci. Collect.; Point Repere (1979-1980); Postharvest News Inf.; Potato Abstr.; Rice Abstr.; Rural Dev. Abstr.; Soyabean Abstr.; Sug. Indus. Abstr.; Wheat Barley Trit. Abstr.; World Agric. Econ.

JM/0376-7655
## CAJANUS.
[Cajanus]. **Added/Corp** Caribbean Food and Nutrition Institute. No. 1 (Feb. 1968)-. Periodical. English. Four times a year. Free on request in the Caribbean; $12.00 North America, Oceania, USSR, and Europe; $6.00 other. Caribbean Food & Nutrition Institute, Box 140, Mona Kingston 7 Jamaica. **Tel** (809)927-1540-1, (809)927-1927, telex 3705. **ED** C. Forrester. **NLM** W1 CA162M. Index available. cum. index. **Bk Rev. Circ:** 2,500 (ctrl).
**Desc:** Highlights food and nutrition concerns in the English speaking Caribbean. Includes reports, research, articles, topics, and comments.
**Ind/Abst** Dairy Sci. Abstr.; Int. Labour Doc.; Nutr. Abstr. Rev., Ser. B, Live Feeds and Feed.; Nutr. Abstr. Rev., Ser. A, Hum. Exp.

US/1049-1791
## CALORIE CONTROL COMMENTARY.
(CALORIE CONTROL COMMENTARY / CALORIE CONTROL COUNCIL.). [Calor. control comment.]. **Added/Corp** Calorie Control Council (U.S.). **VFOAT** Commentary. (1979)-. Periodical. English. ir. Free. Calorie Control Council, 5775 Peachtree-Dunwoody Road, Suite 5, Atlanta GA 30342. **Tel** (404)252-3663. **DD** 613.

US/1049-4901
## CARNATION NUTRITION EDUCATION SERIES.
(CARNATION NUTRITION EDUCATION SERIES / CARNATION EDUCATION.). [Carnat. nutr. educ. ser.]. **Added/Corp** Carnation Company. Vol. 1 (1989)-. Monographic series. English. The Carnation Company, 5045 Wilshire Boulevard, Los Angeles CA 90036. **DD** 613. **NLM** W1; CA835L. **CODEN** CNSEEH. Documents available from BIOSIS Document Express.
**Ind/Abst** Biol. Abstr. (1990-); Nutr. Abstr. Rev., Ser. A, Hum. Exp.

US/0030-2201
## CHRONICLE (OMAHA, NEB.), THE.
(THE CHRONICLE.). [Chron.]. Periodical. English. mo (except July and August). $10.00. Chronicle / Omaha, 119 North 51st Street, Omaha NE 68132. **Tel** (402)554-1333. **ED** D O de Shazer. **NLM** W1 CH962K. **Bk Rev. Ad Acc. Pr Rev. Circ:** 2,000. *Continues Chronicle of the Omaha District Dental Society.*
**Desc:** Dental and good health nutrition interest, cooking, recipes, and book reviews.
**Ind/Abst** Health Plan. Adminis.; Index Dent. Lit.

BL/0101-2061
## CIENCIA E TECNOLOGIA DE ALIMENTOS.
[Cienc. tecnol. aliment.]. **Added/Corp** Sociedad Brasileira de Ciencia e Tecnologia Alimentos. Vol. 1, No. 1 (Jan./June 1981)-. Academic Scholarly Publication. Portuguese. sa. $40.00. Sociedade Brasileira de Ciencia e Tecnologia de Alimentos, Caixa Postal 271, 13001 Campinas SP Brazil. **Tel** 0192 41 0527. **CODEN** CTALDN. Documents available from BIOSIS Document Express, CASDDS.
**Ind/Abst** Biol. Abstr.; Chem. Abstr.; Food Sci. Technol. Abstr.

IT/0392-7318
## CLINICA DIETOLOGICA, LA.
[Clin. dietol.]. (1970)-. Periodical. Italian (English and French; summaries and/or abstracts in English). bm. L60000 Italy; L120000 other. Societa Editrice Universo, Via GB Morgagni 1, 00161 Rome Italy. **Tel** 011 39 6 44231171. **ED** Michelangelo Cairella. **NLM** W1 CL366K. **CODEN** CLDID7. **Bk Rev. Ad Acc. Circ:** 3,000. Documents available from BIOSIS Document Express.
**Desc:** Covers nutrition dietetics, metabolic diseases, obesity, diabetes, hellitus, and preventive medicine.
**Ind/Abst** Biol. Abstr.; Dairy Sci. Abstr.; Nutr. Abstr. Rev., Ser. A, Hum. Exp.

US/0888-7748
## CLINICAL AND EXPERIMENTAL NUTRITION.
[Clin. exp. nutr.]. Vol. 1 (1984)-. Monographic series. English. ir. Price varies per volume. Marcel Dekker Inc., 270 Madison Avenue, New York NY 10016. **Tel** (212)696-9000, (800)228-1160, FAX (212)685-4540, telex 421419. **(Subscription address:** Marcel Dekker Inc, PO Box 5017, Monticello NY 12701.) **DD** 613. **NLM** W1; CL664BQ. **CODEN** CENUE3.

US/0733-933X
## CLINICAL DISORDERS ON PEDIATRIC NUTRITION.
[Clin. disord. pediotr. nutr.]. (1982)-. Academic Scholarly Publication. English. ir. Price varies per volume. Marcel Dekker Inc., 270 Madison Avenue, New York NY 10016. **Tel** (212)696-9000, (800)228-1160, FAX (212)685-4540, telex 421419. **(Subscription address:** Marcel Dekker Inc, PO Box 5017, Monticello NY 12701.) **ED** Fima Lifshitz. **LC** UNC. **DD** 618.92/39. **NLM** W1 CL694I. **CODEN** CDPNDQ. Documents available from CASDDS.
**Desc:** Covers aspects nutrition and nutrition disorders in children. Topics include nutrition for special needs in infancy and carbohydrate intolerance in infants.
**Ind/Abst** Chem. Abstr.

UK/0261-5614
## CLINICAL NUTRITION.
(CLINICAL NUTRITION : OFFICIAL JOURNAL OF THE EUROPEAN SOCIETY OF PARENTERAL AND ENTERAL NUTRITION.). [Clin. nutr.]. **Added/Corp** European Society of Parenteral and Enteral Nutrition. Vol. 1, No. 1 (March 1982)-. Academic Scholarly Publication. English. Six times a year. £236.00 Europe; £240.00 Other (Institutions). Churchill Livingstone, 1-3 Baxter's Place, Leith Walk, Edinburgh EH1 3AF Scotland. **Tel** 011 44 31 556 2424, FAX 011 44 31 558 1278, telex 727511. **(Subscription address:** Maruzen Company Ltd., PO Box 5050, Import & Export Department, Tokyo 100 31 Japan.) **ED** S P Allison. **NLM** W1 CL739F. **CODEN** CLNUDP. **[CCC].** **Bk Rev. Ad Acc. Pr Rev.** available on microfilm and microfiche from University Microfilms International (UMI). Documents available from The Genuine Article, BIOSIS Document Express, CASDDS.
**Desc:** Original articles and review papers on all the factors in disease which have metabolic and nutritional significance.

**Ind/Abst** Biol. Abstr. (1986-); Chem. Abstr.; Curr. Aware. Biol. Sci., CABS; Curr. Contents Clin. Med.; Curr. Contents Life Sci.; EMBASE; Res. Alert [Select. Cov.]; Soc. Sci. Cit. Index [Select. Cov.].

US
**CLINICAL NUTRITION IN HEALTH AND DISEASE.** Monographic series. English. ir. Price varies per volume. Marcel Dekker Inc., 270 Madison Avenue, New York NY 10016. **Tel** (212)696-9000, (800)228-1160, FAX (212)685-4540, telex 421419. **(Subscription address:** Marcel Dekker Inc, PO Box 5017, Monticello NY 12701.**)**

US/1050-5008
**CLINICAL NUTRITION (PHILADELPHIA, PA.).** (CLINICAL NUTRITION.). [Clin. nutr.]. Vol. 1 (1984)-. Monographic series. English. ir. Price varies per volume. Holt Rinehart and Winston, 6277 Sea Harbor Drive, Orlando FL 32887. **Tel** (407)345-2500, 800 545-2522. **DD** 615. **CODEN** CLNUEQ. Documents available from BIOSIS Document Express.
**Ind/Abst** Biol. Abstr. (1986-); Ref. Upd. Deluxe Ed.

US/1053-0452
**CLINICS IN APPLIED NUTRITION.** ***Ceased.*** [Clin. appl. nutr.]. Vol. 1, No. 1 (Jan. 1991)-(199?). Periodical. English. qt. Andover Medical Publishers Inc., A Subsidiary of Butterworth-Heinemann, 80 Montvale Avenue, Stoneham MA 02180. **Tel** (800)366-2665, (617)438-8464, FAX (617)279-4851. **LC** RM214; .C55. **DD** 616.3/9/005. **NLM** W1; CL831ACK. **[CCC].**
**Desc:** Each issue presents a comprehensive review of a major topic in nutrition, with expert dieticians, physicians, and nutritionists exploring all aspects of that topic and bringing together articles of recent science and clinical advances.

CN/0711-8112
**COMMUNIQUE - CDA.** (COMMUNIQUE / CDA/ACD.). [Commun. - CDA]. **VAT** Communique - ACD; Communique - Canadian Dietetic Association; Communique - Association Canadienne des Dietetistes. Periodical. English. ir. Free. Canadian Dietetic Association, 7 Pleasant Boulevard, Toronto Ontario M4T Canada. **Tel** (416)596-0857. **DD** 641/.023/71. ctrl circ.

US/0883-1963
**CONSUMER HEALTH & NUTRITION INDEX.** **See** Nutrition and Dietetics-Abstracting, Bibliographies and Statistics.

US/1044-6516
**CONSUMER MAGAZINES DIGEST : NUTRITION AND FOOD-RELATED HEALTH TOPICS.** [Consum. mag. dig.]. **VFOAT** Digest. Vol. 1, No. 1 (June 1989)-. Periodical. English. mo. $67.00 US; $72.00 Canada; $97.00 other. Consumer Choices Inc., 2272 Woodview Road #401, Ypsilanti MI 48198-6818. **Tel** (313)485-2442, FAX (313)485-7268. **ED** Kristen McNutt. **DD** 613. **Circ:** 1,200.
**Desc:** Summary of nutrition and food related health articles in more than 45 consumer magazines.

US/0741-7748
**CONSUMING PASSIONS.** (198?)-. Newsletter. English. bm (6 issues). $18.00. Consuming Passions Newsletter, PO Box 77, Norwood NJ 07648. **Tel** (201)768-0201. **ED** Barbara May. **DD** 616. **Bk Rev. Circ:** 5,000 (ctrl).
**Desc:** A newsletter devoted to the conflicting relationship between people and food.

US/0736-4369
**CONTEMPORARY ISSUES IN CLINICAL NUTRITION.** [Contemp. issues clin. nutr.]. Vol. 1 (1981)-. Academic Scholarly Publication. English. ir. Price varies per volume. Wiley Liss, 605 3rd Avenue, New York NY 10158. **Tel** (212)850-8800, (212)850-6645. **(Subscription address:** John Wiley / Philadelphia, PO Box 7247, Philadelphia PA 19170.**) ED** Richard S. Rivlin. **LC** UNC. **NLM** W1 CO769MQH. **Bk Rev. Ad Acc.** Documents available from CASDDS.
**Desc:** Nutrition-clinical book series.
**Ind/Abst** Chem. Abstr.; Nutr. Abstr. Rev., Ser. A, Hum. Exp.

US/0198-0009
**CONTEMPORARY NUTRITION.** [Contemp. nutr.]. **Added/Corp** General Mills, Inc. Nutrition Dept. (19??)-. Monographic series. English. mo. Price varies per volume. General Mills Inc, JFB Technical Center Library, 9000 Plymouth Avenue North, Minneapolis MN 55427. **CODEN** CONUDC. Documents available from CASDDS.
**Ind/Abst** AGRICOLA [Full Cov.]; Chem. Abstr.; Foods Adlibra; SPORT Discus.

US/0886-4446
**COOKING LIGHT (SOUTHERN LIVING, INC.).** (COOKING LIGHT.). [Cook. light]. (Spring 1986)-. Periodical. English. Eight times a year. $15.00. Southern Progress Corporation, PO Box 1748, Birmingham AL 35201. **Tel** (205)877-6000. **(Subscription address:** Cooking Light, PO Box C 549, Birmingham AL 35283.**) ED** Jeffrey C Ward. **DD** 641. Index available. **Bk Rev. Ad Acc. Circ:** 525,000. available on microfilm and microfiche from University Microfilms International (UMI).
**Desc:** Covering food and practical fitness, edited for an audience that is active and dedicated to good nutrition. Presents medical information that promotes a healthy lifestyle.

US/0198-9510
**CORNELL INTERNATIONAL NUTRITION MONOGRAPH SERIES.** [Cornell int. nutr. monogr. ser.]. **Added/Corp** Cornell University. Program on International Nutrition and Development Policy. Cornell University. Program in International Nutrition. No. 1 (1974)-. Monographic series. English. ir. Price varies per volume. Cornell University / Division of Nutritional Science, Ithaca NY 14853. **ED** Michael C. Latham. **LC** UNC. **NLM** W1 CO8596M.
**Ind/Abst** Nutr. Abstr. Rev., Ser. A, Hum. Exp.; Wheat Barley Trit. Abstr.

US/0191-1368
**CRC HANDBOOK SERIES IN NUTRITION AND FOOD. SECTION G : DIETS, CULTURE MEDIA, FOOD SUPPLEMENTS.** ***Ceased.*** **VFOAT** Diets, Culture Media, Food Supplements; Handbook Series in Nutrition and Food. Section G: Diets, Culture Media, Food Supplements. Vol. 1 (1977)-(19??). Periodical. English. CRC Press Inc., 2000 Corporate Boulevard Northwest, Boca Raton FL 33431. **Tel** (407)994-0555, (800)272-7737, FAX (407)998-9784, telex 568689. **ED** M Rechcigl Jr. **NLM** W1 C58D.

US/1040-8398
**CRITICAL REVIEWS IN FOOD SCIENCE AND NUTRITION.** **See** Food and Food Industry.

US/0090-0443
**CURRENT CONCEPTS IN NUTRITION.** [Curr. concepts nutr.]. Vol. 1 (1972)-. Monographic series. English. ir. Price varies per volume. John Wiley & Sons, Inc., 605 Third Avenue, New York NY 10158-0012. **Tel** (212)850-6000, (212)850-6645, FAX (212)850-6088, telex 12-7063. **(Subscription address:** John Wiley & Sons / England, Baffins Lane, Chichester, West Sussex PO19 1UD England.**) NLM** W1 CU788AS. **CODEN** CCNTBP. Documents available from BIOSIS Document Express, CASDDS.
**Ind/Abst** AGRICOLA [Select. Cov.]; Biol. Abstr.; Chem. Abstr.; Energy Res. Abstr. (Aug. 1982-); Health Plan. Adminis.; Index Med.

US/0191-2453
**CURRENT TOPICS IN NUTRITION AND DISEASE.** Vol. 1 (1977)-. Academic Scholarly Publication. English. ir. Price varies per volume. Wiley Liss, 605 3rd Avenue, New York NY 10158. **Tel** (212)850-8800, (212)850-6645. **LC** UNC. **NLM** W1 CU82R. **CODEN** CTNDDU. **[CCC].** Documents available from BIOSIS Document Express, CASDDS.
**Desc:** A scholarly book series concerning all aspects of nutrition and nutritional diseases.
**Ind/Abst** AGRICOLA [Select. Cov.]; Biol. Abstr.; Chem. Abstr.

GW/0340-1960
**CURRENT TOPICS IN NUTRITIONAL SCIENCES.** **VFOAT** Beitraege zur Ernahrungswissenschaft. Vol. 1 (1974)-. Monographic series. Multiple languages (English and German). ir. Price varies per volume. Dr Dietrich Steinkopff Verlag, PO Box 111442, D 64229 Darmstadt Germany. **Tel** 011 49 6151 17450. **ED** K. Lang. **NLM** W1 CU82T. ***Supersedes*** *Beitraege zur Ernahrungswissenschaft, 0067-4982.*
**Desc:** A book serial about current topics in nutritional sciences.

US/0882-7915
**CURRENTS (CHAPEL HILL, N.C.).** (CURRENTS : THE JOURNAL OF FOOD, NUTRITION & HEALTH.). [Currents]. Vol. 1, No. 1 (Winter Quarter, 1985)-. Periodical. English. qt. $20.00. Currents, Institute of Nutrition, University of North Carolina, 311 Pittsboro Street/CB #7410, Chapel Hill NC 27599-7410. **Tel** (919)966-1094. **ED** John Timothy Hesla and Marjorie Ward. **DD** 613. cum. index. **Ad Acc. Circ:** 2,500 (ctrl).
**Desc:** This publication provides a forum for a variety of observations on the many and ever-changing issues which affect food, nutrition and health in contemporary society.
**Ind/Abst** AGRICOLA [Select. Cov.].

US/0011-5568
**DAIRY COUNCIL DIGEST.** **See** Agriculture-Dairy Industry.

JA
**DAIZU TANPAKUSHITSU EIYO KENKYUKAI KAISHI.** [Daizu Tanpakushitsu EiyÂo KenkyÂukai kaishi]. **Added/Corp** Daizu Tanpakushitsu Eiyo Kenkyukai. **VFOAT** Nutritional Science of Soy Protein, Japan. (1980)-. Periodical. Japanese (summaries and/or abstracts in English). an. Daizu Tanpakushitsu Eiyo Kenkyukai, Hachiman-cho 6-1, Fuji Seiyo K K -Nai, Higashi-ku, Osaka-shi 542 Japan. **CODEN** DTEKDH. Documents available from CASDDS.
**Ind/Abst** Chem. Abstr.; Nutr. Abstr. Rev., Ser. A, Hum. Exp.

CN/0848-9068
**DEFI-SANTE.** **See** Health and Personal Fitness.

US
**DELICIOUS!.** Vol. 1 No. 1 (Feb. 1985)-. Periodical. English. mo. $20.00. New Hope Communications, PO Box 600, Boulder CO 80306. **Tel** (303)939-8440, FAX (303)939-9559.

NE/0167-6504
**DEVELOPMENTS IN NUTRITION AND METABOLISM.** [Dev. nutr. metab.]. V. 1-. Academic Scholarly Publication. English. Price varies per volume. Elsevier Science Publishers Ltd, Crown House, Linton Road, Barking Essex IG11 8JU England. **Tel** 011 44 81 5947272, FAX 081-594-5942, telex 896950. **NLM** W1 DE998L. **CODEN** DNMEDV. Documents available from CASDDS.
**Ind/Abst** AGRICOLA; Chem. Abstr.

NE
**DIABC.** **See** Medical Science and Technology.

IT/0394-3402
**DIABETES, NUTRITION & METABOLISM.** **VFOAT** Diabetes, Nutrition and Metabolism. (1988)-. Periodical. English. bm. L100000 (Italy); $80.00 (other). Editrice Kurtis Srl, Via Luigi Zoja 30, 20153 Milan Italy. **Tel** 011 39 2 48202740, FAX 011 39 2 48201219. **UDC** 616.379. **CODEN** _b616-008.
**Ind/Abst** Sci. Cit. Index.

●US/1065-7746
**DIAGNOSTIC NUTRITION NETWORK.** (DIAGNOSTIC NUTRITION NETWORK : DNN.). [Diagn. nutr. netw.]. **VFOAT** DNN. Vol. 1, No. 1 (Apr. 1992)-. Periodical. English. Twice a year (Apr. & Oct.). $10.00. Nutritional Care Enterprises, 1360 Maywood Avenue, Upland CA 91786. **Tel** (909)985-1775. **DD** 613.

US/1048-8391
**DIET AND HEALTH MAGAZINE.** [Diet health mag.]. **VFOAT** Diet and Health Magazine. No. 5 (July 1989)-. Periodical. English. bm. $2.95 (per issue) US; $3.75 (per issue) Canada. Frederick Fell Publishers Inc, 2131 Hollywood Boulevard, Suite 204, Hollywood FL 33020. **Tel** (305)925-5242, FAX (302)925-5244. **ED** Allan Taber. **DD** 613. Index available. **Ad Acc. Pr Rev. Circ:** 45,000. ***Continues*** *Diet & Health Series.*
**Desc:** Contains menu plans, low cholesterol, low sodium, low calorie meals.

●US/1062-9289
**DIET BUSINE$$ BULLETIN, THE.** [Diet busine$$ bulletin]. **VFOAT** Diet Business Bulletin. (1992)-. Periodical. English. qt (4 issues). $99.00 (libraries), $119.00 (institutions) US; $145.00 other. Marketdata Enterprises Inc, 181 South Franklin Avenue, Suite 608, Valley Stream NY 11580. **Tel** (516)791-6579, FAX (516)791-7759. **ED** John S. LaRosa. **DD** 338. Index available. cum. index.
**Desc:** Covers developments and original market research related to US weight loss and diet programs, products, and services.

●US/1062-1121
**DIETARY MANAGER.** [Diet. manag.]. **Added/Corp** Dietary Managers Association (US). (1992)-. Periodical. English. bm. Dietary Managers Association, 400 East, 22nd Street, Lombard IL 60148-6122. **DD** 613.

US/0890-7803
**DIETETIC CURRENTS.** [Diet. curr.]. **Added/Corp** Ross Laboratories. Vol. 1 (Jan./Feb. 1974)-. Periodical. English. bm. Free (to health care professionals). Ross Laboratories, 625 Cleveland Avenue, Columbus OH 43216. **Tel** (614)227-3333. **DD** 613.
**Ind/Abst** AGRICOLA [Full Cov.].

CN/0834-3160
**DIETETIQUE EN ACTION.** (DIETETIQUE EN ACTION : REVUE DE LA CORPORATION PROFESSIONNELLE DES DIETETISTES DU QUEBEC.). [Diet. action]. **Added/Corp** Corporation Professionnelle des Dietetistes du Quebec. Vol. 1, No 1 (Sept. 1986)-. Periodical. French (summaries and/or abstracts in English). qt. 65.43Can$ (institution); 46.73Can$ (individual). Corporation des Dietetistes du Quebec, 1425 rue Rene-Leveque Ouest, bureau 402, Montreal Quebec, H3G 1T7 Canada. **Tel** (514)393-3733, FAX (514)393-3582. **DD** 613.2/05. ***Continues*** *Corporation Professionnelle des Dietetistes du Quebec. La Lettre - Corporation Professionnelle des Dietetistes du Quebec., 0701-1660.*
**Ind/Abst** Point Repere (1989-).

FR/0769-1793
**DIETETIQUE ET MEDICINE.** (1965)-. Periodical. French. Four times a year (Mar., June, Sept., Dec.). 150.00F France; 200.00F other. Societe d'Etudes Therapeutiques et Dietetiques, 32 Boulevard Antoine

Gautier, 33000 Bordeaux France. **Tel** 011 33 56795814. **ED** Docteu Baccalin (phone: 56795815). **UDC** 61 : 641.563. Index available (Dec. iss.).

CN/0701-1350
**DIETETIQUE (MONTREAL).** (DIETETIQUE.). [Dietetique]. V. 1- June 1976-. Periodical. French. 40.00Can$. Corporation Professionnelle des Dietetistes du Quebec, 934 Est rue Ste-Catherine/Bureau 130, Montreal Quebec H2L 2E9 Canada. **Tel** (514)842-7923. **ED** Gisele Fournier. **DD** 613.2/06/2714. **Bk Rev. Ad Acc. Circ:** 1,700.
**Desc:** Professional information - news of the health and food industries - information on the corporation's activities - and so on.

US/0888-286X
**DIRECTIONS IN APPLIED NUTRITION.** ***Ceased.*** [Dir. appl. nutr.]. Vol. 1, No. 1 (Nov. 1986)-Ceased (1988). Periodical. English. mo. Aspen Publishers Inc., 7201 McKinney Circle, Frederick MD 21701. **Tel** (800)234-1660, (301)698-7100, FAX (301)251-5784, telex 5106014543. **DD** 641. **NLM** W1; DI659AB.
**Ind/Abst** AGRICOLA.

US/0898-4905
**DIRECTORY - NATIONAL RESEARCH COUNCIL (U.S.). FOOD AND NUTRITION BOARD (1982).** (DIRECTORY / FOOD AND NUTRITION BOARD.). [Dir. - Natl. Res. Counc. (U.S.), Food Nutr. Board (1982)]. **Main/Corp** National Research Council (U.S.). Food and Nutrition Board. (Jan. 1982)-. Directory. English. Food and Nutrition Board, National Research Council, Washington DC. **DD** 613. **NLM** QU 22; AA1 N2d. ***Continues*** *National Research Council (U.S.). Food and Nutrition Board. Food and Nutrition Board, 0197-0925.*

US
**DIRECTORY OF DIETETIC PROGRAMS : ACCREDITED AND APPROVED.**
**Added/Corp** American Dietetic Association. **VFOAT** Directory of Accredited and Approved Dietetic Programs. (19??)-. English. an. $12.00 (per copy). American Dietetic Association, 216 West Jackson Boulevard, Suite 800, Chicago IL 60606. **Tel** (312)899-0040, (800)877-1600. **(Subscription address:** American Dietetic Association, PO Box 97215, Chicago IL 60678.**) LC** RM218; .D57. **DD** 362.1/76/071173. **Circ:** 5,000.
**Desc:** A complete up-to-date listing of ADA-accredited coordinated and internship programs, and ADA-approved dietetic technician, plan IV/V, and preprofessional practice programs. Advanced degree programs are also listed.

US/1065-4666
**DISCUSSIONS IN DIETETICS.** ***Ceased.*** (DISCUSSIONS IN DIETETICS [SOUND RECORDING].). [Discuss. diet.]. **Added/Corp** Educational Reviews, Inc. Vol. 1, No. 1 (1992)-(1994). Periodical. English. mo. Educational Reviews Inc., 6801 Cahaba Valley Road, Birmingham AL 35242. **Tel** (205)991-5188, (800)633-4743, FAX (205)995-1926. **DD** 613.

SZ
**DOCUMENTS SCIENTIFIQUES. VFOAT** Scientific Review; Documents Scientifiques Guigoz. (1963)-. Periodical. French (English; summaries and/or abstracts in Dutch, German, Italian and Spanish). sa. **NLM** W1; GU789. ***Absorbed in part*** *Scientific Review; Documentation Scientifique Guigoz.*

●US/1073-8169
**DR. ATKINS' HEALTH REVELATIONS.**
**See** Medical Science and Technology.

●SZ
**DYNAMIC NUTRITION RESEARCH.** Vol. 1, (1992)-. Monographic series. English. an. 180.00F (approx. per volume). S. Karger AG, Allschwilerstrasse 10, PO Box - Postfach - Case Postale, CH-4009 Basel Switzerland. **Tel** 011 41 61 306-1111, FAX 011 41 61 306-1234, telex CH 962 652. **ED** M. Paubert-Braquet. **NLM** W1; DY988BE. **CODEN** DNREEN. **Pr Rev.** Documents available from BIOSIS Document Express.
**Desc:** Reflects the increasingly close relationship that is developing between the agro-food sector and health care industries, placing particular emphasis on the influences of foodstuffs on human biology and pathophysiology. Articles are contributed by leading national authorities and comprise both concise general reviews and detailed reports of experimental data.
**Ind/Abst** Biol. Abstr.; Index Med.; Ref. Upd. Deluxe Ed.

US/0891-6977
**EATING DISORDERS DIGEST. See** Public Health and Safety.

US/1048-6984
**EATING DISORDERS REVIEW (VAN NUYS, CALIF.).** (EATING DISORDERS REVIEW.). [Eat. disord. rev.]. Vol. 1, No. 1 (July/Aug. 1990)-. Periodical. English. bm. $79.00. Raven Press, 1185 Avenue of the Americas, 37th Floor, New York NY 10036. **Tel** (212)930-9500, (212)930-9604, FAX (212)869-3495, (212)302-8507, telex 640073. **DD** 613. **NLM** W1; EA872.

US/1046-1639
**EATING WELL.** [Eat. well]. Vol. 1, No. 1 (Sept./Oct. 1990)-. Periodical. English. bm. $18.00. Camden House Publishing Inc, Ferry Road, Charlotte VT 05445. **Tel** (802)425-3961, FAX (802)425-3307. **(Subscription address:** Neodata, PO Box 2606, Boulder, CO 80322**) DD** 641. **CODEN** EAWEE2.
**Ind/Abst** Access (1991-); Foods Adlibra.

US/0367-0244
**ECOLOGY OF FOOD AND NUTRITION.** [Ecol. food nutr.]. Vol. 1 (1971)-. Periodical. English. qt. $678.00 (academic institutions), $1057.00 (corporate institutions). Gordon & Breach Science Publishers, Inc., PO Box 786, Cooper Station, New York NY 10276. **Tel** (212)206-8900, FAX (212)645-2459. **(Subscription address:** Gordon & Breach Science Publishers / England, PO Box 90, Reading RG1 8JL England.**) ED** J. R. K. Robson. **LC** TX341; .E26. **DD** 641.1/05. **NLM** W1 EC917. **CODEN** ECFNBN. **[CCC]. Bk Rev. Ad Acc. Pr Rev.** Documents available from The Genuine Article, BIOSIS Document Express, CASDDS.
**Ind/Abst** Abstr. Anthropol.; AGRICOLA [Select. Cov.]; Anthropol. Index; Biodeter. Abstr. (1991-); Biol. Abstr. (?-1985); Chem. Abstr. (1971-1987); Curr. Aware. Biol. Sci., CABS; Curr. Contents, Agric. Biol. Environ. Sci.; Dairy Sci. Abstr.; Environ. Period. Bibliogr.; Field Crop Abstr.; Food Sci. Technol. Abstr.; Grasslands For. Abstr.; Leadscan; Maize Abstr.; Nutr. Abstr. Rev., Ser. B, Live Feeds and Feed.; Nutr. Abstr. Rev., Ser. A, Hum. Exp.; Life Sci. Collect.; Postharvest News Inf.; Potato Abstr.; Res. Alert [Full Cov.]; Rice Abstr.; Rural Dev. Abstr.; Sci. Cit. Index; SCISEARCH; Soc. Sci. Cit. Index [Select. Cov.]; Soils Fert.; Trop. Dis. Bull.; World Agric. Econ.

JA/0021-5147
**EIYO-GAKU ZASSHI.** (EIYO-GAKU ZASSHI. JAPANESE JOURNAL OF NUTRITION.). [Eiyo-gaku zasshi]. **Added/Corp** Kokumin Eiyo Shinkokai. Kokuritsu Eiyo Kenkyujo (Japan). **VFOAT** Japanese Journal of Nutrition. (Oct. 1941)-. Academic Scholarly Publication. Japanese (English). bm. $62.00. **(Subscription address:** Kyowa Book Company, Inc., 1-38 Kanda Jinbo-Cho, Chiyoda-Ku Tokyo 101, Japan**) NLM** W1; EI698. **CODEN** EYGZAD. Documents available from BIOSIS Document Express, CASDDS.
**Ind/Abst** AGRICOLA; Biol. Abstr.; Chem. Abstr.; Food Sci. Technol. Abstr.; Nutr. Abstr. Rev., Ser. A, Hum. Exp.; Potato Abstr.; Soyabean Abstr.

CN/0707-2406
**EN-TROPHY INSTITUTE REVIEW.** [En-Trophy Inst. rev.]. **Main/Corp** En-Trophy Institute. **VAT** En-Trophy Review. Periodical. English. bm. $19.50. En-Trophy Institute, 20 Hilton Street, Hamilton Ontario L8P 3K2 Canada. **DD** 641.1'05. ***Continues*** *En-Trophy Institute for Advanced Study, 0707-2716.*

US/0893-4452
**ENVIRONMENTAL NUTRITION.** [Environ. nutr.]. Vol. 9 No. 7 (July 1986)-. Periodical. English. Twelve times a year. $24.00. R.L. Polk, 521 Fifth Avenue, 11th Floor, New York NY 10175. **Tel** (212)986-0555. **(Subscription address:** Palm Coast Data, PO Box 420235, Agency Department, Palm Coast FL 32142.**) ED** Densie Webb. **DD** 613. Index available. **Bk Rev. Circ:** 10,000. available on an online database (file 149/Full-Text) from DIALOG. ***Continues*** *Environmental Nutrition Newsletter, 0195-4024.*
**Desc:** Newsletter of diet nutrition and health in easy to read format for consumers and health professionals.
**Ind/Abst** Acad. Abstr. Full Text Elite (Jan. 1992-); Acad. Abstr. (Jan. 1992-); Acad. Search (Jan. 1992-); AGRICOLA [Select. Cov.]; Gen. Sci. Source (Jan. 1992-); Health Index (1989-); Health Period. Database [Full Txt.]; Health Ref. Cent. (Jan. 1989-) [Full Txt.] [Full Cov.]; Health Source (Jan. 1992-); INFO-SOUTH Abstr.; Mag. Search.

AU/0250-1554
**ERNAHRUNG (VIENNA, AUSTRIA).** (ERNAHRUNG.). [Ernahrung]. **Added/Corp** Osterreichische Gesellschaft fur Ernahrungsforschung. **VFOAT** Osterreichische Spirituosen Zeitung; Nutrition. (1977)-. Academic Scholarly Publication. German (summaries and/or abstracts in English). Eleven times a year. S1200.00. Fachzeitschriftenverlag AG, Schwarzenbergplatz 6, A 1030 Vienna Austria. **Tel** 11 43 222 7153193, FAX 011 43 222 7154819. **LC** TX341; .E72. **CODEN** ERNRDC. Index available (Bound in 1st iss.). **Bk Rev**, (Qty: 40-70). **Ad Acc, Adv Mgr:** Ms. Allacher. **Circ:** 2,000. Documents available from CASDDS.
**Desc:** The magazine about science, economy, techniques and law in connection with nutrition.
**Ind/Abst** Chem. Abstr.; Curr. Biotechnol.; Dairy Sci. Abstr.; Field Crop Abstr.; Food Sci. Technol. Abstr.; Nutr. Abstr. Rev., Ser. A, Hum. Exp.; Soyabean Abstr.; Wheat Barley Trit. Abstr.

GW/0014-021X
**ERNAHRUNGS- UMSCHAU.** [Ernahr.-umsch.]. Vol. 1 (1954)-. Academic Scholarly Publication. summaries and/or abstracts in English. mo. DM117.60 Germany; DM125.80 other. Umschau Verlag, Postfach 110262, D-60037 Frankfurt Germany. **Tel** 011 49 69 2600692, FAX 011 49 69 2600223, telex 411964. **NLM** W1 ER6924. **CODEN** ERUMAT. **[CCC].** Documents available from The Genuine Article, CASDDS.
**Ind/Abst** AGRICOLA; Chem. Abstr.; Curr. Contents, Agric. Biol. Environ. Sci.; Dairy Sci. Abstr.; EMBASE; Energy Res. Abstr. (Oct. 1972-); Food Sci. Technol. Abstr.; Nutr. Abstr. Rev., Ser. A, Hum. Exp.; Life Sci. Collect.; Res. Alert [Select. Cov.]; SCISEARCH; Soc. Sci. Cit. Index [Select. Cov.].

GW
**ERNAHRUNGSBERICHT. Main/Corp** Deutsche Gesellschaft fur Ernahrung. German (English). ir (every 4 years). DM24.60 Germany; $35.00 US. Deutsche Gesellschaft fur Ernahrung, Feldbergstrasse 28, 6000 Frankfurt A M Germany. **Tel** 069-72 01 46, FAX 741 0383. **LC** TX341; .D46A. **DD** 613.2/05. **Circ:** 9,000.
**Desc:** Describes the nutritional situation, the psychological evaluation of nutrition, a critical evaluation of diets, toxicological and microbiological aspects of nutrition.

GW/0071-1179
**ERNAHRUNGSFORSCHUNG.** [Ernahrungsforschung]. **Added/Corp** Akademie der Wissenschaft der DDR. Zentralinstitut fuer Ernahrung. Vol. 19 (1974)-. Periodical. German. Four times a year (1 volume). $113.00 (academic institutions), $177.00 (corporate institutions). Harwood Academic Publishers, PO Box 90, Reading RG1 8JL England. **Tel** 011 44 734 560080. **(Subscription address:** International Publishers Distributor at one of the following addresses: 820 Town Center Drive, Langhorne, PA 19047; or PO Box 90, Reading Berkshire RG1 8JL UK; or Kent Ridge PO Box 1180, Singapore 9111, Republic of Singapore**) NLM** W1 ER6922. **CODEN** ERNFA7. **[CCC].** Documents available from CASDDS. ***Continues*** *Ernahrungsforschung. Berichte und Mitteilungen.*
**Ind/Abst** AGRICOLA; Chem. Abstr.; Dairy Sci. Abstr.; EMBASE; Food Sci. Technol. Abstr.; Nutr. Abstr. Rev., Ser. B, Live Feeds and Feed.; Nutr. Abstr. Rev., Ser. A, Hum. Exp.; Life Sci. Collect.; Pig News Inf.; Potato Abstr.

IT
**ETUDE FAO : ALIMENTATION ET NUTRITION / ORGANISATION DES NATIONS UNIES POUR L'ALIMENTATION ET L'AGRICULTURE.**
***Suspended.*** Suspended 1988. Monographic series. French. Price varies per volume. Food and Agriculture Organization (FAO) / Italy, GIPC166 via Terme di Caracalla, 00100 Rome Italy. **Tel** 011 39 6 522 52925, FAX 011 39 6 522 55784.

UK/0954-3007
**EUROPEAN JOURNAL OF CLINICAL NUTRITION.** [Eur. j. clin. nutr.]. Vol. 42, No. 1 (Jan. 1988)-. Academic Scholarly Publication. English. mo. £195.00 UK and EEC; £205.00 (surface mail), £246.00 (airmail) other. Macmillan Magazines Ltd., Houndmills, Basingstoke, Hampshire RG21 2XS England. **Tel** 011 44 256 29242, FAX 011 44 256 812358, telex 858493. **ED** J. S. Garrow and J. G. Hautvast. **NLM** W1; EU72CK. **CODEN** EJCNEQ. **[CCC]. Bk Rev. Ad Acc. Pr Rev. Circ:** 850. available on microfilm and microfiche from University Microfilms International (UMI). Documents available from The Genuine Article, BIOSIS Document Express, UMI Article Clearinghouse, CASDDS. ***Formed by the union of*** *Human Nutrition. Clinical Nutrition, 0263-8290* ***and*** *Human Nutrition. Applied Nutrition, 0263-8495.*
**Desc:** Publishes papers on basic and theoretical aspects of nutrition, relations of function to nutritional status, nutritional causes and effects of disease, community nutrition and education, and determinants of eating behavior for clinical and research workers in nutrition and related fields.
**Ind/Abst** AGRICOLA [Full Cov.]; Biol. Abstr. (1985-); Chem. Abstr.; Curr. Aware. Biol. Sci., CABS; Curr. Contents Clin. Med.; Dairy Sci. Abstr.; EMBASE; Expand. Acad. Index (1992-); Foods Adlibra; Gen. Sci. Index; Health Plan. Adminis.; Index Med. (Jan. 1988-); Maize Abstr.; Newsp. Period. Abstr. (1992-); Nutr. Abstr. Rev., Ser. B, Live Feeds and Feed.; Nutr. Abstr. Rev., Ser. A, Hum. Exp.; Nutr. Res. Newsl.; Pig News Inf.; Potato Abstr.; Res. Alert [Full Cov.]; Rice Abstr.; Sci. Cit. Index; SCISEARCH; Soc. Sci. Cit. Index [Select. Cov.]; Soyabean Abstr.; Trop. Dis. Bull.; Wheat Barley Trit. Abstr.

US/0161-5580
**FALK SYMPOSIUM. See** Medical Science and Technology.

IT/0254-4725
**FAO FOOD AND NUTRITION PAPER.** [FAO food nutr. pap.]. **VFOAT** F.A.O. Food and Nutrition Paper. **VAT** Food and Agriculture Organization of the United Nations Food Nutrition Paper. (197?)-. Monographic series. English. ir. Price varies per volume. Food and Agriculture Organization (FAO) / Italy, GIPC166 via Terme di Caracalla, 00100 Rome Italy. **Tel** 011 39 6 522 52925, FAX 011 39 6 522 55784. **NLM** W1 FA456. ***Continues in part*** *FAO Nutrition Meetings Report Series; FAO Food and Nutrition Series.*
**Ind/Abst** AGRICOLA [Select. Cov.]; Agrofor. Abstr. (1991-); Field Crop Abstr.; Health Plan. Adminis.; Index Med.; Nutr. Abstr. Rev., Ser. B, Live Feeds and Feed.; Nutr. Abstr. Rev., Ser. A, Hum. Exp.; Postharvest News Inf.; Potato Abstr.; Rice Abstr.; World Agric. Econ.

Nutrition and Dietetics

IT
**FAO FOOD AND NUTRITION SERIES.**
**VFOAT** Food and Nutrition Series. No. 1; 1976-. Monographic series. English. Price varies per volume. UNIPUB, 4611-F Assembly Drive, Lanham MD 20706-4391. **Tel** (800)274-4888, FAX (301)459-0056, telex 28787 GATT CH. **NLM** W1 F192C. ***Continues in part*** *FAO Nutritional Studies; FAO Nutrition Meetings Report Series.*

IT/0071-707X
**FAO NUTRITION MEETINGS REPORT SERIES.** [FAO nutr. meet. rep. ser.]. **Main/Corp** Food and Agriculture Organization of the United Nations. **VAT** Food and Agriculture Organization Nutrition Meetings Report Series. No. 1 (1948)-?. Monographic series. Multiple languages (French). ir. Price varies per volume. Food and Agriculture Organization (FAO) / Italy, GIPC166 via Terme di Caracalla, 00100 Rome Italy. **Tel** 011 39 6 522 52925, FAX 011 39 6 522 55784. **LC** S401. **DD** 612; 613. **NLM** W1 F197. **CODEN** FAONAU. Documents available from CASDDS. ***Continued in part by*** *FAO Food and Nutrition Series.*
**Ind/Abst** Chem. Abstr.; Health Plan. Adminis.

CN/0826-2594
**FEELING FINE.** (FEELING FINE : A DIGEST OF INFORMATION AND IDEAS FROM THE FITNESS AND NUTRITION CLUB.). Vol. 2, No. 1 (Mar. 1984)-. Periodical. English. ir. Free to members. F A N Club, 2 203 Beverley Street, Toronto Ontario M5T 1Y5 Canada. **DD** 641.1/05. ***Continues*** *F.A.N. Club Digest, 0827-3170.*

GW/0720-8731
**FETT IN DER PARENTERALEN ERNAHRUNG.** (FETT IN DER PARENTERALEN ERNAHRUNG / SYMPOSIUM IN ROTTACH-EGERN.). [Fett parenter. Ernahr.]. **Main/Conf** Symposium in Rottach-Egern. (Mar 10 1981)-. Academic Scholarly Publication. German. **ED** J Eckart and G Wolfram. **NLM** W3 SY34F. **CODEN** FPEREX. Documents available from CASDDS.
**Ind/Abst** Chem. Abstr. (?-1984).

US/0160-8053
**FNP NEWSLETTER : FOOD, NUTRITION AND HEALTH.** [FNP newsl., Food nutr. health]. **VFOAT** Food, Nutrition and Health. **VAT** Food and Nutrition Press Newsletter. Food, Nutrition and Health. Vol. 1 (Apr. 1977)-. Newsletter. English. mo (12 issues per volume). $76.00 US, Canada & Mexico; $96.00 other. Food & Nutrition Press Inc, 2 Corporate Drive, PO Box 374, Trumbull CT 06611. **Tel** (203)261-8587, FAX (203)261-9724. **ED** Paul A. Lachance and Michele C. Fisher. **NLM** W1 F384. **Bk Rev.**
**Desc:** Doctors Lachance and Fisher draw on their unique backgrounds in nutrition-food science to make clear distinctions between food, nutrition and health research, education and policy issues.
**Ind/Abst** AGRICOLA.

US
**FOOD ANALYST. CD-ROM.** (19??)-. English. ir. $39.95 US and Canada; $42.35 other. Hopkins Technology, 421 Hazel Lane, Suite 120, Hopkins MN 55343. **Tel** (612)931-9376, FAX (612)931-9377.
**Desc:** Complete nutritional analysis software program that breaks down what you eat into specific nutrients such as calories, fat, sugar, protein, cholesterol, vitamins and much more. Direct access to over 80 nutrients and approximately 5,000 foods is provided.

US
**FOOD ANALYST PLUS. CD-ROM.** English. $210.94 Minnesota residents; $199.00 US and Canada; $284.00 Africa, Russia and Eastern Europe; $264.00 India; $249.00 other. Hopkins Technology, 421 Hazel Lane, Suite 120, Hopkins MN 55343. **Tel** (612)931-9376, FAX (612)931-9377.
**Desc:** The most complete nutritional analysis software program which includes the world's largest microcomputer food database.

JA/0379-5721
**FOOD AND NUTRITION BULLETIN.** [Food nutr. bull.]. **Added/Corp** United Nations. Administrative Committee on Co-ordination. Sub-committee on Nutrition. United Nations University. World Hunger Programme. United Nations University. Vol. 1, No. 1 (Oct. 1978)-. Academic Scholarly Publication. English. Four times a year (March, June, Sep., Dec.). $25.00 developing countries; $40.00 other. United Nations University Press, 53-70, Jingumae 5 Chome, Shibuya-ku Tokyo 150, Japan. **Tel** 81 3 34992811, FAX 81 3 34992828, telex J25442. **ED** Nevin S. Scrimshaw. **LC** TX341; .F8134. **DD** 641.3/05. **NLM** W1 FO428M. **CODEN** FNBPDV. Index available. cum. index. **Bk Rev. Pr Rev. Circ:** 2,000. available on microfiche. Documents available from BIOSIS Document Express, CASDDS. ***Continues*** *PAG Bulletin, 0377-760X.*
**Desc:** A forum for scientists and scholars that reports on all aspects of global food and nutrition problems, including world hunger, and the broad programmes and new activities to deal with them.
**Ind/Abst** AGRICOLA [Select. Cov.]; Agrofor. Abstr.; Biol. Abstr.; Chem. Abstr.; Dairy Sci. Abstr.; Food Sci. Technol. Abstr.; Int. Dev. Abstr.; Leis. Recreat. Tour. Abstr.; Maize Abstr.; Nutr. Abstr. Rev., Ser. B, Live Feeds and Feed.; Nutr. Abstr. Rev., Ser. A, Hum. Exp.; Rural Dev. Abstr.; Soyabean Abstr.; Trop. Dis. Bull.; World Agric. Econ.

GH
**FOOD AND NUTRITION IN AFRICA. See** Food and Food Industry.

US/0015-6310
**FOOD & NUTRITION NEWS.** [Food nutr. news]. **VFOAT** Food and Nutrition News. Vol. 45, No. 1 (Oct./Nov. 1973)-. Periodical. English. qt. Free. American Meat Science Association, 444 North Michigan Avenue, Chicago IL 60611. **Tel** (312)467-5520. **ED** Eleanor M Urenos. **Circ:** 57,000. ***Continues*** *Food & Nutrition News, 0015-6310.*
**Desc:** Timely nutrition topics and related topics of current interest are presented in lead and inside articles. Also includes computer nutrition software and short items about nutrition, food and health.
**Ind/Abst** Acad. Abstr. Full Text Elite (Jan. 1992-) [Full Txt.]; Acad. Abstr. (Jan. 1992-); Acad. Search (Jan. 1992-); AGRICOLA [Full Cov.]; Consum. Health Nutr. Index (Jan. 1990); Gen. Sci. Source (Jan. 1992-); Health Index (1989-); Health Period. Database [Full Txt.]; Health Ref. Cent. (Jan. 1989-) [Full Cov.]; Health Source (Jan. 1992-) [Full Txt.]; Index Free Period.; INFO-SOUTH Abstr.; Mag. Artic. Summar. Elite (Jan. 1992-); Mag. Artic. Summar. Select (Jan. 1992-); Mag. Artic. Summar. CD-ROM (Jan. 1992-); Mag. Search; Vocat. Search (Jan. 1992-) [Full Txt.].

US/0887-0535
**FOOD AND NUTRITION QUARTERLY INDEX.** ***Ceased.*** [Food nutr. q. index]. Vol. 1, No. 1-Ceased (Dec. 1987). English. qt. Oryx Press, 4041 North Central Avenue, #700, Phoenix AZ 85012-3397. **Tel** (800)279-ORYX, (602)265-2651, FAX (602)265-6250, (800)279-4663, (800)279-6799. **LC** QP141.A1; F65. **DD** 613.2/05. **NLM** ZQU 145; N271ca. ***Continues*** *Food and Nutrition Bibliography, 0278-2499.*
**Desc:** The most complete and up-to-date source of nutritional information available.

US/0046-4384
**FOOD AND NUTRITION (WASHINGTON. 1971).** (FOOD AND NUTRITION.). [Food nutr.]. **Added/Corp** United States. Food and Nutrition Service. **VFOAT** Food & Nutrition. **VAT** Food and Nutrition. Vol. 1, No. 1 (June 1971)-. Government Publication. English. qt. $5.00; $1.25 (single issues) US; $6.25; $1.56 (single issues) other. Superintendent of Documents, US Government Printing Office, Washington DC 20402. **Tel** (202)275-3328, FAX (202)786-2377. **LC** TX341; .F812. **DD** 362.5. **NLM** W1 FO428. available on microfilm and microfiche from University Microfilms International (UMI). Documents available from UMI Article Clearinghouse, Magazine Collection. ***Continues*** *Food and Nutrition Newsletter.*
**Desc:** Reports on the federal food assistance programs administered by the Food and Nutrition Service. It shows their impact on people, the activities of public and private agencies in helping those in need of food assistance, and outstanding work of individuals or groups of volunteers in furthering the drive to eliminate malnutrition in the United States.
**Ind/Abst** Acad. Search (Jan. 1992-); AGRICOLA; Biol. Agric. Index (1992-); Gen. Sci. Index; Gen. Sci. Source (Jan. 1992-); Health Index (1989-); Health Period. Database [Full Txt.]; Health Ref. Cent. (Jan. 1989-) [Full Txt.] [Full Cov.]; Health Source (Jan. 1992-); INFO-SOUTH Abstr.; Mag. Artic. Summar. Elite (Jan. 1992-) [Full Txt.]; Mag. ASAP Plus [Full Txt.]; Mag. ASAP Sel. [Full Txt.]; Mag. Index Plus (1989-); Mag. Index. Sel. (1986-); Mag. Search; Newsp. Period. Abstr. (1988-).

UK/0308-8146
**FOOD CHEMISTRY. See** Chemistry-Chemical Technology.

GW/0721-6912
**FOOD COMPOSITION AND NUTRITION TABLES / DIE ZUSAMMENSETZUNG DER LEBENSMITTEL, NAEHRWERT-TABELLEN. Added/Corp** Germany (West). Bundesministerium fuer Ernaehrung, Landwirtschaft und Forsten. Deutsche Forschungsanstalt fËur Lebensmittelchemie. **VFOAT** Zusammensetzung der Lebensmittel, Naehrwert-Tabellen; Nutrition Tables. (1982)-. Trade Publication. English (summaries and/or abstracts in French and German). ir. Wissenschaftliche Verlagsgesellschaft mbH, Postfach 101061, D 70009 Stuttgart Germany. **Tel** 011 49 711 258200, FAX 011 49 711 2582290, telex 723636 DAZ D.

IT
**FOOD, NUTRITION AND AGRICULTURE. See** Agriculture.

●US/1063-4169
**FOODS INTELLIGENCE ON COMPACT DISC. See** Food and Food Industry-Abstracting, Bibliographies and Statistics.

US/1065-0067
**FOODTALK (SAN FRANCISCO, CALIF.).** (FOODTALK.). [Foodtalk]. Vol. 1, No. 1, (1978)-. Periodical. English. qt (Mar., June, Sept., Dec.). $18.00 one year; $35.00 two years. Foodtalk, PO Box 6543, San Francisco CA 94101. **Tel** (415)386-3067. **ED** Elaine Douglas-Cahn. **DD** 641. Index available. cum. index. **Bk Rev**, (Qty: 10-12). **Circ:** 10,000.
**Desc:** The art and science of good eating.

JA/0389-5564
**GEKA TO TAISHA, EIYO. See** Medical Science and Technology-Surgery.

CN/0229-5903
**GOOD HEALTH (DON MILLS). See** Consumer Interests.

KO/0253-3154
**HANGUG NYENNYAN SIGRYAN HAGHOI JI.** (HANGUK YONGYANG SINGNYANG HAKHOE CHI.). [Hangug nyennyan sigryan haghoi ji]. **Added/Corp** Hanguk Yongyang Singnyang Hakhoe. **VFOAT** Journal of the Korean Society of Food and Nutrition. (19??)-. Korean (summaries and/or abstracts in English). **LC** TX341; .H36. **CODEN** HYSHDL. Documents available from CASDDS.
**Ind/Abst** Chem. Abstr.; Crop Physiol. Abstr.; Hortic. Abstr.; Plant Grow. Reg. Abstr.; Potato Abstr.; Soyabean Abstr.

CN/0831-8530
**HEALTH & NUTRITION UPDATE. *Title Change.*** [Health nutr. update]. **Added/Corp** Canadian Schizophrenia Foundation. **VAT** Health and Nutrition Update. Vol. 1, Issue 1 (Jan. 1986)-(1993). Periodical. English. qt. Canadian Schizophrenia Foundation / Ontario, 16 Florence Avenue, Toronto Ontario M2N 1E9 Canada. **Tel** (416)733-2117. **DD** 613.2/05. **Bk Rev. Ad Acc. Circ:** 1,000. ***Continues*** *Huxley Institute-CSF Newsletter, 0318-8272.* ***Continued by*** *Nutrition & Mental Health (North York, Ont.), 1199-7699.*

●US/1055-8241
**HEALTH DIET & NUTRITION. VFOAT** Health Diet and Nutrition. (1993)-. Periodical. English. qt. $29.99. Publishing & Business Consultants, PO Box 75392, Los Angeles CA 90075. **Tel** (213)732-3477, FAX (213)732-9123. **ED** Andeson Napoleon Atia. **Ad Acc.** Full Page (B&W) $5750.00. Half Page (B&W) $3575.00. Full Page (Color) $8750.00 (2 color). Half Page (Color) $5500.00 (2 color). **Circ:** 172,000 total.
**Desc:** Of interest to health conscious individuals who actively maintain a productive lifestyle at work and at home. Features articles on nutrition, diet and weight loss, and more.

US/1056-1900
**HEALTH NEWS & REVIEW.** [Health news rev.]. **VFOAT** Health News and Review. Vol. 1, No. 1 (April 1991)-. Periodical. English. Four times a year (Jan., Apr., July, Oct.). $9.95 (one year), $15.95 (two year). Keats Publishing, PO Box 876, New Canaan CT 06840. **Tel** (203)966-8721, FAX (203)972-3991. **ED** Mary Ellen Hehinger. **DD** 362. **Bk Rev. Ad Acc. Circ:** 100,000 (ctrl). available on an online database (file 149/Full-Text) from DIALOG. ***Continues*** *Your Good Health Review & Digest, 0745-7278.*
**Ind/Abst** Acad. Abstr. Full Text Elite (Jan. 1992-); Acad. Abstr. (Jan. 1992-); Acad. Search (Jan. 1992-); Health Index (1989-); Health Period. Database [Full Txt.]; Health Ref. Cent. (Jan. 1989-) [Full Txt.] [Full Cov.]; Health Source (Jan. 1992-); Mag. Search.

US/0883-8216
**HEALTH SCIENCE (1985). See** Public Health and Safety.

US/0737-7568
**HEALTH SPECTRUM. See** Public Health and Safety.

US/0897-9251
**HEALTHWAYS.** (1987)-. Periodical. English (French). Three times a year. $25.00 US; $30.00 other. International Macrobiotic Shiatsu Society, 1122 M Street, Eureka CA 95501-2442. **ED** Patrick McCarty. **DD** 613. **Circ:** 200 (ctrl).

CN/0846-0663
**HEALTHY EATING.** [Healthy eat.]. (July/Aug. 1990)-. Periodical. English. bm. Limited free distribution. Odyssey Publishing, 2135 West 45th Avenue, Vancouver, British Columbia V6M 2J2 Canada. **DD** 613.2.

CN/0823-7352
**HEALTHY HORIZONS. See** Food and Food Industry.

●US/1075-0169
**HEALTHY WEIGHT JOURNAL.** [Healthy weight j.]. **Added/Corp** Healthy Living Institute. Vol. 8, No. 3 (May/June 1994)-. Periodical. English. bm. $59.00. Healthy Weight Journal, 402 South 14th Street, Hettinger ND 58639. **Tel** (800)663-0023, (701)567-2845. **DD** 613. **NLM** W1; HE629. Index available (bound in Jan. issue). ***Continues*** *Obesity & Health, 1044-1522.*
**Desc:** Keeps health professionals up to date on a wide range of issues. Current scientific research and new paradigms in treatment and prevention.
**Ind/Abst** Acad. Search (May 1994-); Bibliogr. Agric.; Mag. Artic. Summar. Elite (May 1994-).

JA/0387-4141
**HISSU AMINOSAN KENKYU.** [Hissu aminosan kenkyu]. **VFOAT** Reports of the Research Committee of Essential Amino Acids (Japan). (1958)-. Periodical. Japanese. qt. Hissu Aminosan Kenku Iinkai, (Research Committee of Essential Amino Acids), Kokuritsu Koshu Eiseiin Eiyo, Seikagakubu, 6-1, Shirokanedai, 4 Chome, Minatoku, Tokyoto 108 Japan. **DD** 547.75. Documents available from CASDDS.
**Ind/Abst** Chem. Abstr.

US/0747-7376
**HOSPITAL FOOD & NUTRITION FOCUS.** [Hosp. food nutr. focus]. **Added/Corp** Aspen Systems Corporation. **VFOAT** Hospital Food and Nutrition Focus. Vol. 1, No. 1 (Sept. 1984)-. Periodical. English. mo. $143.00 US. Aspen Publishers Inc., 7201 McKinney Circle, Frederick MD 21701. **Tel** (800)234-1660, (301)698-7100, FAX (301)251-5784, telex 5106014543. **(Subscription address:** Aspen Publishers Inc., PO Box 990, Frederick MD 21701.**) ED** Darlene Dougherty, MS, RD. **DD** 641. **NLM** W1; HO776H.
**Desc:** Each issue covers proven problem solving techniques and practical methods to gain greater operational efficiency, improved management skills, and greater job satisfaction.
**Ind/Abst** AGRICOLA; Health Plan. Adminis.; Hospit. Health Admin. Index (1986-).

●US/1062-7723
**HOW ON EARTH!.** [How earth!]. **Added/Corp** Vegetarian Education Network. **VFOAT** HOE!. Issue No. 1 (Spring 1992)-. Periodical. English. qt. $12.00. Vegetarian Education Network, PO Box 3347, West Chester PA 19381. **DD** 613.

YU/0018-6872
**HRANA I ISHRANA.** **See** Food and Food Industry.

US/0886-6848
**HUMAN NUTRITION.** [Hum. nutr.]. (1979)-. Monographic series. English. ir. $565.00. Plenum Press, 233 Spring Street, New York NY 10013-1578. **Tel** (212)620-8000, (800)221-9369, FAX (212)463-0742, (212)807-1047, telex 23/421139. **ED** David M. Klurfeld. **LC** QP141.A1; H84. **DD** 613.2. **NLM** QU 145 H9183. **CODEN** HNUTEP. Documents available from BIOSIS Document Express.
**Ind/Abst** AGRICOLA [Full Cov.]; Biol. Abstr.

US/0730-9198
**IFT BASIC SYMPOSIUM SERIES.** [IFT basic symp. ser.]. **VFOAT** I.F.T. Basic Symposium Series. (19??)-. Monographic series. English. ir. Price varies per volume. Marcel Dekker Inc., 270 Madison Avenue, New York NY 10016. **Tel** (212)696-9000, (800)228-1160, FAX (212)685-4540, telex 421419. **(Subscription address:** Marcel Dekker Inc, PO Box 5017, Monticello NY 12701.**)** **CODEN** IBASEJ.

US
**ILSI NEWSLETTER.** (19??)-. Newsletter. English. bm. Free on request. ILSI / International Life Science Institute, 1126 16th Street Northwest, Suite 300, Washington DC 20036. **Tel** (202)659-0074.

II/0022-3174
**INDIAN JOURNAL OF NUTRITION AND DIETETICS, THE.** [Indian j. nutr. diet.]. **Added/Corp** Sri Avinashilingam Home Science College, Coimbatore, India. Sri Avinashilingam Home Science College. Vol. 7 (Jan. 1970)-. Periodical. English. mo. $40.00. SRI Avinashilingam Home Science, College for Women, Coimbatore 641 043 India. **Tel** 40241. **(Subscription address:** Prints India, 11 Darya Ganj, New Delhi 110002 India.**) ED** Rajammal P. Devadas, M. Swaminathan and Usha Chandrasekhar. **LC** TX341; .J594. **DD** 641.1/05. **NLM** W1 IN221K. **CODEN** IJNDAN. cum. index. **Bk Rev**. **Ad Acc**. **Circ:** 700. Documents available from BIOSIS Document Express, CASDDS. ***Continues*** *Journal of Nutrition and Dietetics.*
**Desc:** Original and review papers, book reviews, news, views, announcements, and current literature supplement.
**Ind/Abst** AGRICOLA; Biol. Abstr.; Chem. Abstr.; Crop Physiol. Abstr.; Dairy Sci. Abstr.; Field Crop Abstr.; Food Sci. Technol. Abstr.; Hortic. Abstr.; Int. Aerosp. Abstr.; Maize Abstr.; Nutr. Abstr. Rev., Ser. B, Live Feeds and Feed.; Nutr. Abstr. Rev., Ser. A, Hum. Exp.; Life Sci. Collect.; Plant Breed. Abstr.; Postharvest News Inf.; Poult. Abstr.; Protozoolog. Abstr.; Rice Abstr.; Seed Abstr.; Soyabean Abstr.; Trop. Dis. Bull.

AG/0368-0088
**INFORMACION SOBRE GRASAS Y ACEITES.** [Inf. grasas aceites]. Academic Scholarly Publication. Spanish. bm. Publicacion Tecnio-Econ Iaga, Department Estad and Information, Chile 1192 Buenos Aires 1098 Argentina. **CODEN** ISGAA8. Documents available from CASDDS. ***Continues*** *Informaciones Argentinas Sobre Grasas y Aceites, 0446-1568.*
**Ind/Abst** AGRICOLA; Chem. Abstr.

AT
**INFORMATION BULLETIN / BRI.** **Added/Corp** Bread Research Institute of Australia. Baking Division. No. 434A (Feb. 1991)-. Bulletin. English. ***Continues*** *Industry Bulletin (North Ryde, N.S.W.), 0819-2022.*

FR/0020-0034
**INFORMATION DIETETIQUE COLOMBES, L'.** (INFORMATION DIETETIQUE.). [Inf. diet. Colombes]. **VFOAT** ID. Information Dietetique. (1967)-. Periodical. French. qt. 186.10F France; 290.00F other. Assn Dieteticiens Langue Franc, 35 Allee Vivaldi, 75012 Paris France. **Tel** 011 33 1 40020302. **UDC** 641.563.

US/0742-3799
**INSIDE NUTRITION.** [Inside nutr.]. Issue 1 (Jan. 9, 1984)-. Periodical. English. bw. Clayman Enterprises, 5560 Woodbridge Drive, Columbus OH 43213. **LC** TX341. **DD** 613.2/05.

AT/0813-9008
**INTERNATIONAL CLINICAL NUTRITION REVIEW.** [Int. clin. nutr. rev.]. Vol. 3, No. 1 (Jan. 1983)-. Academic Scholarly Publication. English. qt. $63.00. Integrated Therapies Pty Ltd, PO Box 370, Manly 2095 Australia. **Tel** 011-61-2-977-0771, FAX 011-61-2-977-0267. **ED** Dr. Robert Buist Ph.D. **NLM** W1; IN733LH. **CODEN** ICNRDJ. **[CCC]. Bk Rev**, (Qty: 4-5/yr). **Circ:** 1500. Documents available from CASDDS. ***Continues*** *Orthomolecular Review, 0725-7090.*
**Ind/Abst** Chem. Abstr. (1983-); Hortic. Abstr.; Nutr. Abstr. Rev., Ser. A, Hum. Exp.; Rev. Med. Vet. Mycology.

SZ/0300-9831
**INTERNATIONAL JOURNAL FOR VITAMIN AND NUTRITION RESEARCH.** [Int. j. vitam. nutr. res.]. **VFOAT** Internationale Zeitschrift fur Vitamin- und Ernahrungsforschung; Journal International de Vitaminologie et de Nutrition. (1971)-. Periodical. Multiple languages (English, French and German). Four times a year. 197.00F. Verlag Hans Huber Ag Bern, Laenggass Strasse 76, CH 3000 Bern 9 Switzerland. **Tel** 011 41 31 3004500. **(Subscription address:** Hogrefe & Huber Publishers, Seattle Office, Box 2487, Kirkland WA 98083.**) LC** QP771; .I57. **DD** 612/.399/05. **NLM** W1 IN7652Q. **CODEN** IJVNAP. **[CCC]. Pr Rev.** Documents available from The Genuine Article, BIOSIS Document Express, CASDDS. ***Continues*** *Internationale Zeitschrift fuer Vitaminforschung, 0020-9506.*
**Desc:** Provides an important international forum for scientific advances in the study of nutrition and vitamins. Presents work dealing with basic as well as applied topics.
**Ind/Abst** AGRICOLA [Full Cov.]; Biol. Abstr.; Chem. Abstr.; CSA Neuro. Abstr. (?-?); Curr. Contents, Agric. Biol. Environ. Sci.; Curr. Contents Life Sci.; Dairy Sci. Abstr.; EMBASE; Field Crop Abstr.; Fish Rev. (Jan. 1989-July 1992); Helminthol. Abstr.; Index Med.; Nutr. Res. Newsl.; Life Sci. Collect.; PESTDOC; Protozoolog. Abstr.; Res. Alert [Full Cov.]; Rev. Med. Vet. Entomol.; Rice Abstr.; Sci. Cit. Index; SCISEARCH; Seed Abstr.; Soyabean Abstr.; Trop. Dis. Bull.; Wildl. Rev. (Jan. 1989-July 1992).

SZ/0300-9831
**INTERNATIONAL JOURNAL FOR VITAMIN AND NUTRITION RESEARCH (SUPPLEMENT).** ***Ceased.*** (BEIHEFT ZUR INTERNATIONALE ZEITSCHRIFT FUER VITAMIN- UND ERNAHRUNGSFORSCHUNG.). [Int. j. vitam. nutr. res.]. **VFOAT** International Journal for Vitamin and Nutrition Research. Supplement; Supplement to the International Journal for Vitamin and Nutrition Research. (1972)-(19??). Academic Scholarly Publication. English (German and French). qt. **(Subscription address:** Jugoslovenska Knjiga, PO Box 36, YU 11001 Belgrade Yugoslovia.**) ED** G Ritzer. **LC** QP771. **NLM** W1 IN7652R. **CODEN** IVEBBN. **[CCC]. Bk Rev. Ad Acc. Pr Rev. Circ:** 1,000. Documents available from BIOSIS Document Express, CASDDS. ***Continues*** *Internationale Zeitschrift fur Vitaminforschung. Beiheft.*
**Desc:** Scholarly articles on experimental and applied research in vitaminology and nutrition in humans and animals.
**Ind/Abst** AGRICOLA (?-?) [Full Cov.]; Biol. Abstr. (1986-); Chem. Abstr. (?-?); Dairy Sci. Abstr. (?-?); EMBASE (?-?); Index Med. (?-?); Index Vet. (?-?); Nutr. Abstr. Rev., Ser. B, Live Feeds and Feed. (?-?); Nutr. Abstr. Rev., Ser. A, Hum. Exp. (?-?); Life Sci. Collect. (?-?); PESTDOC (?-?); SportSearch (?-?); Vet. Bull. (?-?).

SZ/0373-0883
**INTERNATIONAL JOURNAL FOR VITAMIN AND NUTRITION RESEARCH. SUPPLEMENT.** [Int. j. vitam. nutr. res., Suppl.]. **VFOAT** Internationale Zeitschrift fuer Vitamin- und Ernahrungschung; Journal International de Vitaminologie et de Nutrition. Supplement. No. 17 (1979)-. Academic Scholarly Publication. English (German). ir. Price varies per volume. Verlag Hans Huber Ag Bern, Laenggass Strasse 76, CH 3000 Bern 9 Switzerland. **Tel** 011 41 31 3004500. **NLM** W1 IN7652R. **CODEN** IVEBBN. Documents available from CASDDS. ***Continues*** *Internationale Zeitschrift fuer Vitamin- und Ernahrungsforschung. Beiheft, 0375-9075.*
**Ind/Abst** Chem. Abstr.; Index Med.

●UK/0963-7486
**INTERNATIONAL JOURNAL OF FOOD SCIENCES AND NUTRITION.** **VFOAT** Food Sciences and Nutrition. Vol. 43, No. 1 (June 1992)-. Periodical. English. Four times a year. Carfax Publishing Company, PO Box 25 Abingdon, Oxfordshire OX14 3UE England. **Tel** 011 44 235 555335, FAX (0279)31067, telex 817484. **CODEN** IJFNEH. ***Continues*** *Food Sciences and Nutrition, 0954-3465.*
**Ind/Abst** Curr. Aware. Biol. Sci., CABS; Gen. Sci. Index.

US/1050-1606
**INTERNATIONAL JOURNAL OF SPORT NUTRITION.** [Int. j. sport nutr.]. **VFOAT** IJSN. (1991)-. Periodical. English. qt (Mar., June, Sept., Dec.). $40.00 (individual), $90.00 (institution) US; $44.00 (individual), $94.00 (institution) other. Human Kinetics Publishers Inc, 1607 North Market Street, PO Box 5076, Champaign IL 61825-5076. **Tel** (217)351-5076, FAX (217)351-2674. **ED** Pricilla M. Clarkson. **LC** RC1235; .I515. **DD** 612.3/08/8796. **[CCC].** Index available (Included in Dec. issue). **Bk Rev**. Documents available from The Genuine Article.
**Desc:** Seeks to advance the understanding of the nutritional aspects of human physical and athletic performance.
**Ind/Abst** Curr. Contents Clin. Med.; Phys. Educ. Index (1991-); Res. Alert [Select. Cov.]; SPORT Discus.

UK/0958-9414
**INTERNATIONAL MONOGRAPHS IN NUTRITION, METABOLISM, AND OBESITY.** **VFOAT** International Monographs in Nutrition, Metabolism, & Obesity. (1990)-. Monographic series. English. Price varies per volume. **NLM** W1; IN8251.

US/0190-8480
**INTERNATIONAL NUTRITION POLICY SERIES.** ***Ceased.*** (1978)-(19??). Monographic series. English. Massachusetts Institute of Technology (MIT) Press, 55 Hayward Street, Cambridge MA 02142-1399. **Tel** (617)253-2889, (617)625-8481, FAX (617)258-6779. **NLM** W1 IN827B. **CODEN** INPSD7. Documents available from BIOSIS Document Express. ***Continues*** *Cornell/MIT International Nutrition Policy Series.*
**Ind/Abst** Biol. Abstr.

US/0883-1904
**JEWISH VEGETARIANS OF NORTH AMERICA : NEWSLETTER.** [Jew. Veg. North Am.]. **Added/Corp** Jewish Vegetarians (Organization). **VFOAT** Jewish Vegetarians. Vol. 1, No. 2 (Fall 1984)-. Newsletter. English. Four times a year (Mar., June, Aug., Dec.). $12.00. Jewish Vegetarians North America, 6938 Relliance Road, Federalsburg MD 21632. **Tel** (410)754-5550. **ED** Shelli Yesenko. **LC** TX392; .A16. **DD** 641.5/676/05. **Bk Rev**, (Qty: 4). **Circ:** 2,000 (ctrl). ***Continues*** *Jewish Vegetarians.*
**Desc:** Relationship between Judaism and vegetarianism including kindness to animals, world hunger, ecology, ethics, recipes, health, issues, animal rights, restaurants, and local Jewish vegetarian contacts.

JA/0286-0511
**JOSHI EIYO DAIGAKU KIYO.** [Joshi Eiyo Daigaku kiyo]. **Added/Corp** Joshi Eiyo Daigaku. **VFOAT** Journal of Kagawa Nutrition College. (1970)-. Periodical. Japanese (summaries and/or abstracts in English). an. Joshi Eiyo Daigaku, (Kagawa Nutrition College), 24-3, Komagome 3 Chome, Toshimaku, Tokyoto 170 Japan. **CODEN** JEDKD7. Documents available from CASDDS.
**Ind/Abst** Chem. Abstr.

NZ/0110-635X
**JOURNAL - NEW ZEALAND DIETETIC ASSOCIATION.** [J. N.Z. Diet. Assoc.]. **Main/Corp** New Zealand Dietetic Association. **Added/Corp** New Zealand Dietetic Association. **VFOAT** Journal. (1947)-. Periodical. English. Twice a year. 41.00NZ$ New Zealand; 48.00NZ$ Australia & the Pacific; 56.00NZ$ other. Journal - New Zealand Dietetic Association, 88 Remuera Road, Auckland 5 New Zealand. **Tel** 011 64 9 5205194, FAX 011 64 9 5205194. **ED** P. Duncan. **NLM** W1; JO941Z. **Bk Rev**, (Qty: 4). **Ad Acc.** ctrl circ.
**Ind/Abst** AGRICOLA; Nutr. Abstr. Rev., Ser. B, Live Feeds and Feed.; Nutr. Abstr. Rev., Ser. A, Hum. Exp.; Potato Abstr.

US/0894-5888
**JOURNAL OF ADVANCEMENT IN MEDICINE.** **See** Medical Science and Technology.

US/0021-8960
**JOURNAL OF APPLIED NUTRITION, THE.** [J. appl. nutr.]. Vol. 6 (1953)-. Academic Scholarly Publication. English. qt. $75.00 US; $100.00 other. International Academy of Nutrition and Preventive Medicine, PO Box 18433, Asheville NC 28814. **Tel** (704)258-3243. **ED** Jim Heffley. **NLM** W1 JO541R. **CODEN** JNAPAX. **[CCC].** Index available. cum. index. **Bk Rev. Ad Acc. Pr Rev. Circ:** 1,100 (ctrl). available on microfilm and microfiche from University Microfilms International (UMI). Documents available from BIOSIS Document Express, CASDDS. ***Continues*** *Journal of the American Academy of Applied Nutrition, 0095-9839.*
**Desc:** The new focus of the Journal of Applied Nutrition is on supplementary macro- and micro-nutrients in the prevention and treatment of disease as well as in the maintenance of optimal health. An enormous, and ever-increasing, volume of data supports the concept that

# Nutrition and Dietetics

increased dietary intakes of nutritional factors are efficacious against numerous human diseases. This is the future of nutrition, and the Journal of Applied Nutrition is the first journal specifically dedicated to this principle.
**Ind/Abst** AGRICOLA; Biol. Agric. Index; Biol. Abstr.; Chem. Abstr.; Dairy Sci. Abstr.; EMBASE; Environ. Period. Bibliogr.; Nutr. Abstr. Rev., Ser. B, Live Feeds and Feed.; Nutr. Abstr. Rev., Ser. A, Hum. Exp.

JA/0912-0009
## JOURNAL OF CLINICAL BIOCHEMISTRY AND NUTRITION. See Biology-Biochemistry.

SP/0214-2880
## JOURNAL OF CLINICAL NUTRITION & GASTROENTEROLOGY, THE. Ceased. See Medical Science and Technology-Gastroenterology.

US/0742-826X
## JOURNAL OF DIETETIC SOFTWARE.
**Suspended.** [J. diet. softw.]. Vol. 1, No. 1 (Winter 1984)-?. Periodical. English. an. $39.00 US; $49.00 other. Journal of Dietetic Software, PO Box 1057, Cordova TN 38018. **Tel** (901)377-9175. **ED** Sara Gill Estabrook. Index available. **Ad Acc. Circ:** 1,000.
**Ind/Abst** AGRICOLA.

II/0022-1155
## JOURNAL OF FOOD SCIENCE AND TECHNOLOGY. [J. food sci. technol.]. Added/Corp Association of Food Technologists. Vol. 1 (Apr. 1964)-. Periodical. English. bm. $125.00. Association of Food Technologists, CFTRI Campus, Mysore 13 India. **Tel** 21747, telex 0846-241. **(Subscription address:** Prints India, 11 Darya Ganj, New Delhi, 110002 India, (Phone: 011 91 11 3268645)) **ED** J R Rangaswamy. **LC** TX341; .J58. **NLM** W1 JO651S. **CODEN** JFSTAB. Index available. **Bk Rev. Pr Rev. Circ:** 2,000 (ctrl). Documents available from The Genuine Article, BIOSIS Document Express, CASDDS.
**Desc:** Food science and technology.
**Ind/Abst** AGRICOLA; Anal. Abstr.; Biodeter. Abstr. (19??-19??); Biol. Abstr. (1990-); Chem. Abstr.; Crop Physiol. Abstr.; Curr. Contents, Agric. Biol. Environ. Sci.; Dairy Sci. Abstr.; EMBASE; Field Crop Abstr.; Fish Rev. (Jan. 1989-July 1992); Food Sci. Technol. Abstr.; Foods Adlibra; Hortic. Abstr.; Int. Packag. Abstr.; Nutr. Abstr. Rev., Ser. A, Hum. Exp.; Life Sci. Collect.; Plant Breed. Abstr.; Plant Grow. Reg. Abstr.; Postharvest News Inf.; Potato Abstr.; Res. Alert [Select. Cov.]; Rev. Med. Vet. Mycology; Rev. Plant Pathol.; Rice Abstr.; SCISEARCH; Soyabean Abstr.; Wildl. Rev. (Jan. 1989-July 1992).

UK/0952-3871
## JOURNAL OF HUMAN NUTRITION AND DIETETICS. [J. hum. nutr. diet.]. Added/Corp British Dietetic Association. **VFOAT** Human Nutrition and Dietetics. Vol. 1, No. 1 (Feb. 1988)-. Academic Scholarly Publication. English. bm (6 issues). $217.00 US & Canada; £127.00 Europe; £140.00 other. Blackwell Scientific Publications Ltd, Marston Book Services, PO Box 87, Oxford OX2 ODT UK. **Tel** 011 44 865 791155, FAX 011 44 865 791927, telex 837 515 MARDIS G. **ED** P. A. Judd. **NLM** W1; JO673VU. **CODEN** JHNDEO. **[CCC].**
**Bk Rev. Ad Acc. Pr Rev. Circ:** 3,200. available on microfilm and microfiche from University Microfilms International (UMI). Documents available from The Genuine Article, BIOSIS Document Express. **Continues in part** Human Nutrition. Applied Nutrition, 0263-8495.
**Desc:** Publishes research and review papers on the science of nutrition in man in health and disease.
**Ind/Abst** AGRICOLA [Full Cov.]; Biol. Abstr. (1988-); Curr. Contents Clin. Med.; Dairy Sci. Abstr.; EMBASE; Food Sci. Technol. Abstr.; Nutr. Abstr. Rev., Ser. A, Hum. Exp.; Potato Abstr.; Res. Alert [Select. Cov.]; SCISEARCH; Soc. Sci. Cit. Index [Select. Cov.]; Sug. Indus. Abstr.; Trop. Dis. Bull.; Wheat Barley Trit. Abstr.

US/0022-3166
## JOURNAL OF NUTRITION, THE. [J. nutr.]. Added/Corp Wistar Institute of Anatomy and Biology American Institute of Nutrition. Vol. 1 (Sept. 1928)-. Academic Scholarly Publication. English. mo. $200.00 (institutions), $90.00 (individuals) US; $215.00 (institutions), $105.00 (individuals) other. Federation of American Societies for Experimental Biology, Room L-2310, 9650 Rockville Pike, Bethesda MD 20814-3998. **Tel** (301)530-7027. **ED** Dr. Willard Visek. **LC** RM214; .J6. **NLM** W1 JO798. **CODEN** JONUAI. **[CCC]. Ad Acc, Adv Mgr Tel** (301)530-7103. **Pr Rev.** available on microfilm and microfiche from University Microfilms International (UMI). Documents available from The Genuine Article, BIOSIS Document Express, UMI Article Clearinghouse, CASDDS, Documents on Demand.
**Desc:** Contains reports of research bearing on the nature of nutrients and their function in a variety of organisms, articles which report the development of new nutritional concepts and interrelationships of importance in human and animal nutrition, and critical reviews, symposia, and essays on issues in nutrition.
**Ind/Abst** Abstr. Anthropol.; Acad. Search (July 1993-); AgBiotech News Inf.; AGRICOLA [Full Cov.]; Anim. Breed. Abstr.; Annals Behav. Med.; Arts Humanit. Citation Index [Select. Cov.]; Biol. Agric. Index; Biol. Abstr.; Biol. Dig.; Calcium Calcif. Tissue Abstr.; Chem. Abstr.; Chem. Titles; CSA Neuro. Abstr. (?-?); Curr. Aware. Biol. Sci.; CABS; Curr. Ref. Fish Res.; Dairy Sci. Abstr.; EMBASE;

Energy Inf. Abstr.; Energy Res. Abstr.; Environ. Abstr.; Expand. Acad. Index (1992-); Fish Rev. (Jan. 1989-July 1992); Food Sci. Technol. Abstr.; Foods Adlibra; Gen. Sci. Index; Gen. Sci. Source (Jul. 1993-); Index Med.; INFO-SOUTH Abstr.; Int. Aerosp. Abstr.; Mag. Search; Maize Abstr.; Med. Abstr. Newsl.; Newsp. Period. Abstr. (1992-); Nutr. Abstr. Rev., Ser. B, Live Feeds and Feed.; Nutr. Abstr. Rev., Ser. A, Hum. Exp.; Nutr. Res. Newsl.; Life Sci. Collect.; PESTDOC; Pig News Inf.; Plant Breed. Abstr.; Potato Abstr.; Poult. Abstr.; Protozoolog. Abstr.; Ref. Upd. Basic Ed.; Ref. Upd. Deluxe Ed.; Res. Alert [Full Cov.]; Rice Abstr.; Small Anim. Abstr. Bibliogr.; Soc. Sci. Cit. Index [Select. Cov.]; Soyabean Abstr.; SportSearch; Stat. Theory Method Abstr. (1959-1963); Trop. Dis. Bull.; Wildl. Rev. (Jan. 1989-July 1992).

US/0022-3182
## JOURNAL OF NUTRITION EDUCATION.
[J. nutr. educ.]. **Added/Corp** Society for Nutrition Education. Vol. 1 (Summer 1969)-. Periodical. English (summaries and/or abstracts in Spanish and French). bm. $126.00 (institutions), $84.00 (individuals) US & Canada; $147.00 (institutions), $115.00 (individuals) other. Decker Periodicals Publishing Inc, PO Box 620, Station A, Hamilton Ontario L8N 3K7 Canada. **Tel** (416)522-7017, (800) 568-7281, FAX (416)522-7839. **LC** QP141.A1; J66. **DD** 613.2/05. **NLM** W1 JO798G. **[CCC].** cum. index. **Bk Rev. Ad Acc. Pr Rev. Circ:** 8,000. available on microfilm and microfiche from University Microfilms International (UMI). Documents available from The Genuine Article, UMI Article Clearinghouse.
**Desc:** Focuses on applied nutritional sciences and positive nutritional practices and policies using reports literature reviews, research articles, special reports, and extensive professional and popular book reviews.
**Ind/Abst** Acad. Ind. [Computer File] (1992-); Acad. Search (July 1993-); AGRICOLA [Full Cov.]; Annals Behav. Med.; Commun. Abstr.; Contents Pages Educ.; Cumul. Index Nurs. Allied Health Lit.; Curr. Contents, Agric. Biol. Environ. Sci.; Curr. Index J. Educ.; Educ. Index; Expand. Acad. Index (1989-); Food Sci. Technol. Abstr.; Foods Adlibra; Gen. Sci. Index; Gen. Sci. Source (Jul. 1993-); INFO-SOUTH Abstr.; Mag. Search; Newsp. Period. Abstr. (1991-); Nutr. Abstr. Rev., Ser. B, Live Feeds and Feed.; Nutr. Abstr. Rev., Ser. A, Hum. Exp.; Nutr. Res. Newsl.; Life Sci. Collect.; Res. Alert [Select. Cov.]; Risk Abstr.; SCISEARCH; Soc. Sci. Cit. Index [Select. Cov.]; Spec. Educ. Needs Abstr.; SportSearch; Stud. Women Abstr.

US/0163-9366
## JOURNAL OF NUTRITION FOR THE ELDERLY. [J. nutr. elder.]. Vol. 1 (Spring 1980)-. Academic Scholarly Publication. English. qt. $225.00 US; $315.00 other. The Haworth Press Inc, 10 Alice Street, Binghamton NY 13904-1580. **Tel** (607)722-5857, (800)3-HAWORTH, FAX (607)722-1424. **ED** Annette B. Natow (editor's address: Box 169, Little Neck, NY 11363). **LC** TX361.A3. **DD** 613.2. **NLM** W1 JO798H. **CODEN** JNELDA. **Bk Rev. Ad Acc. Pr Rev. Acid Free. Circ:** 455. available on microfilm and microfiche from University Microfilms International (UMI). Documents available from Haworth Document Delivery Service.
**Desc:** Covers all the essential aspects of nutrition and publishes research papers from a variety of fields in the biological and social sciences. Also presents critical reviews, new concepts, theories and their application in community and clinical settings.
**Ind/Abst** Abstr. Soc. Gerontol.; AGRICOLA [Full Cov.]; Cumul. Index Nurs. Allied Health Lit.; EMBASE; Food Sci. Technol. Abstr.; Index Med. (Vol. 6, No. 4, 1987-); Int. Nurs. Index; Nutr. Abstr. Rev., Ser. B, Live Feeds and Feed.; Nutr. Abstr. Rev., Ser. A, Hum. Exp.; Nutr. Res. Newsl.; Potato Abstr.; Psychol. Abstr. (1985-); PsycINFO; PsycLit; Soc. Work Abstr. [Select. Cov.].

●US/1055-1379
## JOURNAL OF NUTRITION IN RECIPE & MENU DEVELOPMENT. VFOAT Journal of Nutrition in Recipe and Menu Development. (1992)-. Periodical. English. qt. $60.00 US; $84.00 other. The Haworth Press Inc, 10 Alice Street, Binghamton NY 13904-1580. **Tel** (607)722-5857, (800)3-HAWORTH, FAX (607)722-1424. **ED** Mahmood A. Khan (editor's address: Virginia Polytechnic Institute and State University, Department of Hotel, Restaurant and Inst. Mgt., Blacksburg, VA 24061). **Bk Rev. Ad Acc. Pr Rev. Acid Free.** available on microfiche. Documents available from Haworth Document Delivery Service.
**Desc:** Strives to be at the cutting edge of health and medical issues related to the restaurant and food service field. Does not intend to endorse any medical benefits of specific food products but will provide as one feature an on-going literature review of the medical and nutritional science literature to assist business and industry to keep up with the anticipated expanding "Green Market" for health-focused food product lines.
**Ind/Abst** Food Sci. Technol. Abstr.

US/0955-2863
## JOURNAL OF NUTRITIONAL BIOCHEMISTRY, THE. [J. nutr. biochem.]. VFOAT Nutritional Biochemistry. Vol. 1, No. 1 (Jan. 1990)-. Academic Scholarly Publication. English. mo. $390.00 US; $445.00 other. Butterworth Heinemann / Woburn, MA, 225 Wildwood Avenue, Unit B, Woburn MA 01801. **Tel** (800)366-2665, FAX (617)928-2620, telex 880052. **(Subscription address:** Elsevier Science Inc. / New York Books, 655 Avenue of the Americas, New York NY 10010.**) NLM** W1; JO798HR. **CODEN** JNBIEL. **[CCC].** available on microfilm and microfiche from University Microfilms International (UMI). Documents available from The Genuine Article, BIOSIS Document Express, CASDDS. **Continues** Nutrition Reports International, 0029-6635.
**Ind/Abst** AGRICOLA [Full Cov.]; Biol. Abstr.; Chem. Abstr. (1990-); Curr. Aware. Biol. Sci.; CABS; Curr. Contents, Agric. Biol. Environ. Sci.; Curr. Contents Life Sci.; Dairy Sci. Abstr.; EMBASE [Select. Cov.]; Food Sci. Technol. Abstr.; Foods Adlibra (1990-); Nutr. Abstr. Rev., Ser. B, Live Feeds and Feed.; Nutr. Abstr. Rev., Ser. A, Hum. Exp.; Life Sci. Collect.; Poult. Abstr.; Ref. Upd. Deluxe Ed.; Res. Alert [Full Cov.]; Sci. Cit. Index; SCISEARCH; Wheat Barley Trit. Abstr.

●US/1049-5150
## JOURNAL OF NUTRITIONAL IMMUNOLOGY. [J. nutr. immunol.]. Vol. 1, No. 1 (1992)-. Periodical. English. qt. $90.00 US; $126.00 other. The Haworth Press Inc, 10 Alice Street, Binghamton NY 13904-1580. **Tel** (607)722-5857, (800)3-HAWORTH, FAX (607)722-1424. **ED** Jullian E. Spallholz (Editor's Address: 507 Food Science Building, PO Box 4170, Texas Tech University, Lubbock, TX 79409). **LC** QP141.A1; J685. **DD** 616.97. **NLM** W1; JO798HS. **CODEN** JNUIEE. **Bk Rev. Ad Acc. Pr Rev. Acid Free.** available on microfilm and microfiche from University Microfilms International (UMI). Documents available from Haworth Document Delivery Service.
**Desc:** Has been established to provide a publishing and informational forum for research scientists that bridges the classical disciplines of nutrition and immunology. This journal features original research, brief communications and reviews on all aspects of the effects of nutrients and diets on all basic and clinical aspects of both animal and human immunology.
**Ind/Abst** AGRICOLA; Biostatistica; Curr. Aware. Biol. Sci., CABS; Food Sci. Technol. Abstr.; Foods Adlibra (1992-).

UK/0955-6664
## JOURNAL OF NUTRITIONAL MEDICINE. [J. nutr. med.]. Added/Corp British Society for Nutritional Medicine. Vol. 1, No. 1 (1990)-. Academic Scholarly Publication. English. qt. £174.00. Carfax Publishing Company, PO Box 25 Abingdon, Oxfordshire OX14 3UE England. **Tel** 011 44 235 555335, FAX (0279)31067, telex 817484. **(Subscription address:** US and Canada/ PO Box 2025, Dunnellon, FL 34430-2025; telephone:(904)489-6996) **LC** RM214; .J69. **NLM** W1; JO798HU. **CODEN** JNMEEU. **[CCC].** available on microfiche. Documents available from BIOSIS Document Express.
**Ind/Abst** AGRICOLA; Biol. Abstr.; Dairy Sci. Abstr.; EMBASE; Nutr. Abstr. Rev., Ser. A, Hum. Exp.; Ref. Z.

JA/0301-4800
## JOURNAL OF NUTRITIONAL SCIENCE AND VITAMINOLOGY. [J. nutr. sci. vitaminol.]. Added/Corp Nihon Eiyo Shokuryo Gakkai. Nihon Bitamin Gakkai. Vol. 19 (1973)-. Periodical. English. bm (6 issues). $145.00. Nippon Eiyo Shokuryo Gakkai, (Japanese Soc. of Nutrition & Food Science), 4-16, Yayoi 2 Chome, Bunkyoku, Tokyoto 113 Japan. **(Subscription address:** Maruzen Company Ltd., PO Box 5050, Import & Export Department, Tokyo 100 31 Japan.) **NLM** W1 JO798I. **CODEN** JNSVA5. **Pr Rev.** Documents available from The Genuine Article, BIOSIS Document Express, CASDDS. **Continues** Journal of Vitaminology, 0022-5398.
**Ind/Abst** Biol. Abstr.; Chem. Abstr.; Chem. Titles; Curr. Contents, Agric. Biol. Environ. Sci.; Curr. Contents Life Sci.; Dairy Sci. Abstr.; EMBASE; Food Sci. Technol. Abstr.; Index Med.; NAPRALERT; Nutr. Abstr. Rev., Ser. A, Hum. Exp.; Nutr. Res. Newsl.; Life Sci. Collect.; PESTDOC; Res. Alert [Full Cov.]; Rice Abstr.; Sci. Cit. Index; SCISEARCH; Soyabean Abstr.; Wheat Barley Trit. Abstr.

●US/1061-2130
## JOURNAL OF OPTIMAL NUTRITION, THE. (THE JOURNAL OF OPTIMAL NUTRITION : AN OFFICIAL PUBLICATION OF THE INSTITUTE FOR THE STUDY OF OPTIMAL NUTRITION.). [J. optim. nutr.]. Added/Corp Institute for the Study of Optimal Nutrition. **VFOAT** JON. Vol. 1, No. 1 (1992)-. Periodical. English. Four times a year. $75.00 US; $90.00 other. Journal of Optimal Nutrition, 2552 Regis Drive, Davis CA 95616. **Tel** (916)756-3311, FAX (916)758-7444. **ED** Brian Leibovitz. **LC** QP141.A1; J688. **DD** 612.3/9/05. **NLM** W1; JO803RF. **CODEN** JOTNEV. **Bk Rev. Pr Rev. Acid Free. Circ:** 350.
**Desc:** The primary goal is to shape the future of nutritional science and medicine. The focus is on elucidating the optimal levels of macronutrients and micronutrients for the prevention and treatment of disease as well as for the maintenance of optimal health.

US/8756-6206
## JOURNAL OF PEDIATRIC & PERINATAL NUTRITION. Ceased. See Medical Science and Technology-Pediatrics.

US/0277-2116
**JOURNAL OF PEDIATRIC GASTROENTEROLOGY AND NUTRITION.** See Medical Science and Technology-Pediatrics.

●US/1060-3999
**JOURNAL OF RAPID METHODS AND AUTOMATION IN MICROBIOLOGY.** See Food and Food Industry.

US/0731-5724
**JOURNAL OF THE AMERICAN COLLEGE OF NUTRITION.** [J. Am. Coll. Nutr.]. **Added/Corp** American College of Nutrition (U.S.). Vol. 1, No. 1 (1982)-. Academic Scholarly Publication. English. bm. $150.00 (institutions), $75.00 (individuals) US; $190.00 (institutions), $115.00 (individuals) other. American College of Nutrition, 4802 10th Avenue, Maimonde Dep Ped, Brooklyn NY 11219. **Tel** (718)283-5226. **(Subscription address:** Fulco, 30 Broad Street, Denville NJ 07834.**) ED** Mildred S. Seelig. **LC** RC620.A1; J68. **DD** 613.2/05. **NLM** W1 JO908TR. **CODEN** JONUDL. **[CCC]. Pr Rev.** available on microfilm and microfiche. Documents available from The Genuine Article, CASDDS.
**Desc:** Provides coverage of nutrition research applicable to patient care. Critical reviews in each issue summarize new developments and present proven concepts that affect utilization and the requirements of nutrients. Topics covered include the use of calcium in hypertension, dietary management of diabetes mellitus and the relation of nutrition to cancer metabolism.
**Ind/Abst** AGRICOLA [Full Cov.]; Chem. Abstr.; Curr. Aware. Biol. Sci., CABS; Curr. Contents Life Sci.; Dairy Sci. Abstr.; EMBASE; Index Med.; Index Vet.; Nutr. Abstr. Rev., Ser. A, Hum. Exp.; Nutr. Res. Newsl.; Life Sci. Collect.; Pig News Inf.; Ref. Upd. Deluxe Ed.; Res. Alert [Full Cov.]; Risk Abstr.; Sci. Cit. Index; SCISEARCH; Soc. Sci. Cit. Index [Select. Cov.]; Vet. Bull.

US/0002-8223
**JOURNAL OF THE AMERICAN DIETETIC ASSOCIATION.** [J. Am. Diet. Assoc.]. **Main/Corp** American Dietetic Association. **Added/Corp** American Dietetic Association. American Dietetic Association Reports. Vol. 1 (June 1925)-. Academic Scholarly Publication. English. mo. $100.00 US & possessions; $123.00 Canada; $170.00 other. American Dietetic Association, 216 West Jackson Boulevard, Suite 800, Chicago IL 60606. **Tel** (312)899-0040, (800)877-1600. **(Subscription address:** American Dietetic Association, PO Box 97215, Chicago IL 60678.**) ED** Elaine R. Monsen. **LC** RM214; .A6. **NLM** W1 JO909C. **CODEN** JADAAE. Index available (bound in Dec. issue). cum. index. **Bk Rev. Ad Acc. Pr Rev. Circ:** 61,000. available on microfilm and microfiche from University Microfilms International (UMI). Documents available from The Genuine Article, BIOSIS Document Express, UMI Article Clearinghouse, CASDDS. ***Supersedes*** *Bulletin of the American Dietetic Association.*
**Desc:** The journal publishes reports of original research and other papers covering all aspects of dietetics including nutrition and diet therapy, community nutrition, education and administration.
**Ind/Abst** Abr. Index Med.; Acad. Abstr. Full Text Elite (July 1990-); Acad. Abstr. (July 1990-); Acad. Ind. [Computer File] (1987-); Acad. Search (Jan. 1990-); AGRICOLA [Full Cov.]; Annals Behav. Med.; Biol. Agric. Index; Biol. Abstr.; Chem. Abstr.; Chicano Index; Curr. Contents, Agric. Biol. Environ. Sci.; Curr. Contents Clin. Med.; Dairy Sci. Abstr.; EMBASE; Environ. Period. Bibliogr. (?-?); Expand. Acad. Index (1988-); Foods Adlibra; Gen. Sci. Index; Gen. Sci. Source (Jul. 1990-); Health Index (1989-); Health Period. Database [Full Txt.]; Health Ref. Cent. (Jan. 1989-) [Full Cov.]; Health Source (Jul. 1990-); Index Med.; INFO-SOUTH Abstr.; Mag. Search; Maize Abstr.; Med. Abstr. Newsl.; Newsp. Period. Abstr. (1988-); Nutr. Abstr. Rev., Ser. B, Live Feeds and Feed.; Nutr. Abstr. Rev., Ser. A, Hum. Exp.; Nutr. Res. Newsl.; Physic. Medline Plus; Pig News Inf.; Potato Abstr.; Protozoolog. Abstr.; Res. Alert [Full Cov.]; Rice Abstr.; Sci. Cit. Index; SCISEARCH; Soc. Sci. Cit. Index [Select. Cov.]; Soc. Work Abstr. [Select. Cov.]; SPORT Discus; SportSearch; Sug. Indus. Abstr.; Trop. Dis. Bull.; Wheat Barley Trit. Abstr.

KO
**JOURNAL OF THE KOREAN SOCIETY OF FOOD AND NUTRITION.** English. Korean Society of Food and Nutrition, 599-1 Daeyeon-dong, Nam-gu Puson 608, Korea.
**Ind/Abst** Field Crop Abstr.; Postharvest News Inf.

US/0197-0666
**JOURNAL OF THE NUTRITIONAL ACADEMY.** [J. Nutr. Acad.]. **VFOAT** International Journal of the Nutritional Academy. V. 1- March 1978-. Periodical. English. International Nutritional Academy, 1238 Hayes Street, Eugene OR 97402. **NLM** W1 JO943W.

US/0148-6071
**JPEN, JOURNAL OF PARENTERAL AND ENTERAL NUTRITION.** [JPEN. J. parenter. enteral nutr.]. **Added/Corp** American Society of Parenteral and Enteral Nutrition. **VFOAT** Journal of Parenteral and Enteral Nutrition. Vol. 1 (1977)-. Academic Scholarly Publication. English. bm (6 issues). $115.00 US; $130.00 Canada and Mexico; $145.00 other (institution). American Society of Parenteral and Enteral Nutrition / ASPEN, 8630 Fenton Street, Suite 412, Silver Spring MD 20910-3805. **Tel** (301)587-6315, FAX (301)587-2365. **ED** Harry M. Shizgal. **LC** RM224; .J2. **DD** 615.8. **NLM** W1 J514C. **CODEN** JPENDU. **[CCC]. Ad Acc. Pr Rev. Circ:** 7,900. available in microform. Documents available from The Genuine Article, BIOSIS Document Express, CASDDS.
**Desc:** Clinically oriented research on nutritional deficiency and its treatment, including administration, risks, and complications.
**Ind/Abst** AGRICOLA; Biol. Abstr. (1986-); Chem. Abstr.; Cumul. Index Nurs. Allied Health Lit.; Curr. Contents Clin. Med.; Dairy Sci. Abstr.; EMBASE; Energy Res. Abstr. (March 1982-); Health Devices Alerts (19??-1984); Index Med.; Int. Nurs. Index; Int. Pharm. Abstr.; Iowa Drug Inf. Serv. (1985-); Nutr. Abstr. Rev., Ser. A, Hum. Exp.; Nutr. Res. Newsl. (19??-1988); Life Sci. Collect.; Physic. Medline Plus; Pig News Inf.; Res. Alert [Full Cov.]; Sci. Cit. Index; SCISEARCH; Soc. Sci. Cit. Index [Select. Cov.]; Soyabean Abstr.

US/0024-1288
**LET'S LIVE.** (1959)-. Periodical. English. mo. $19.95 US; $29.95 other. Let's Live, 320 North Larchmont Boulevard, 3rd Floor, Los Angeles CA 90004. **Tel** (213)469-3901, (800)676-4333. **ED** Keith Stepro. **Bk Rev. Ad Acc. Circ:** 125,000. available on microfilm and microfiche from University Microfilms International (UMI).
**Desc:** Information on natural living, preventive medicine, nutrition, diet, longevity, health foods, physical fitness, environmental protection, vitamins, minerals, protein and related food supplements, recipes, exercise, etc.
**Ind/Abst** Health Index (1989-); Health Period. Database; Health Ref. Cent. (Jan. 1989-) [Full Cov.].

US/1051-9467
**LIFELINE (TORRANCE, CALIF.).** (LIFELINE.). **Added/Corp** Overeaters Anonymous, Inc. (U.S.). **VFOAT** Life Line. (198?)-. Periodical. English. mo. $10.00. Overeaters Anonymous, 6075 Zenith Court, Rio Rancho NM 92870. **Tel** (505)891-2664. **(Subscription address:** Lifeline, PO Box 92870, Los Angeles CA 90009.**) DD** 362. ***Continues*** *Box 6190, 0273-5741.*

US/0892-7294
**LOSE WEIGHT NATURALLY NEWSLETTER.** ***Title Change.*** [Lose weight nat. newsl.]. **VFOAT** Lose Weight Naturally. (1987)-?. Newsletter. English. mo. Rodale Press Inc., 400 South 10th Street, Emmaus PA 18098. **Tel** (215)967-5171, (800)666-2503. **DD** 613. ***Continued by*** *Rodale's Food and Nutrition Letter, 1051-6646.*

US/1048-8383
**MAGAZINE OF AMERICA'S BEST RECIPES, THE.** [Mag. Am. best recipes]. **VFOAT** America's Best Recipes. (July 1989)-. Periodical. English. bm. $2.95 (per issue) US; $3.75 (per issue) Canada. Frederick Fell Publishers Inc, 2131 Hollywood Boulevard, Suite 204, Hollywood FL 33020. **Tel** (305)925-5242, FAX (302)925-5244. **ED** Allan Taber. **DD** 641. **Ad Acc. Circ:** 50,000.
**Desc:** Contains recipes.

UK/0953-1424
**MAGNESIUM RESEARCH : OFFICIAL ORGAN OF THE INTERNATIONAL SOCIETY FOR THE DEVELOPMENT OF RESEARCH ON MAGNESIUM.** See Medical Science and Technology.

CN/0714-3761
**MAIGRIR MEDECINE BEAUTE.** [Maigrir med. beaute]. **VFOAT** Maigrir. **VAT** Maigrir (1982). No. 37-. French. mo. $1.95 per no. Maigrir, 3280 Boulevard Ste-Rose, Laval Quebec H7P 5B9 Canada. **DD** 613.2/5/05. ***Continues*** *Maigrir et Rester Belle (Laval, Quebec : 1980), 0710-4472.*

FR/0398-7604
**MEDECINE ET NUTRITON.** See Medical Science and Technology.

●US/1057-9354
**MEDICINE, EXERCISE, NUTRITION, AND HEALTH.** See Medical Science and Technology.

CN/1184-8928
**MEMBERSHIP ROSTER / ALBERTA REGISTERED DIETITIANS ASSOCIATION.** [Membsh. roster - Alta. Regist. Diet. Assoc.]. **Main/Corp** Alberta Registered Dietitians Association. (1990/1991)-. English. Alberta Registered Dietitians Association, Registrar, Wanda Daniels, #370, 4445 Calgary Trail South, Edmonton Alberta T6H 5R7 Canada. **DD** 613.2. ***Continues*** *Current Register for ...., 1184-8936.*

VE
**MEMORIA Y CUENTA.** **Main/Corp** Instituto Nacional de Nutricion (Venezuela). Spanish. Ministerio de Sanidad y Asistencia Social, Direccion General/G-820, Caracas Venezuela.

UK/0957-4360
**MICRONUTRIENT NEWS AND INFORMATION.** [Micronutr. news inf.]. (1990)-. Periodical. English. Four times a year (Jan., Apr., July, Oct.). $213.00 (surface), $225.00 (air) US and Canada; £113.00 UK; £115.00 (surface mail), £117.00 (airmail) Europe; £115.00 (surface), £122.00 (air) other. Micronutrient Bureau, M B House Wigginton Tring, Hertfordshire HP23 6ED England. **Tel** 011 44 282 2720, FAX 011 44 0442 822720. **DD** 631.5. ***Continues*** *Iron in Agriculture, 0264-5998; Zinc in Agriculture, 0261-5452; Boron in Agriculture, 0261-5444; Copper in Agriculture, 0261-5436; Molybdenum in Agriculture, 0261-5045; Manganese in Agriculture, 0261-5010* ***and*** *Micronutrient News, 0261-5002.*

GW/0026-3788
**MILCHWISSENSCHAFT.** See Agriculture-Dairy Industry.

CN/0226-7535
**MINCE ET SVELTE.** [Mince svelte]. No. 1- Sept. 1979-. Periodical. French. mo. $1.50 each number. Quebescope, Distributions Eclair, 8320 Place de la Lorraine, Anjou Quebec H1J 1E6 Canada. **DD** 613.2/5/05.

IT
**MINERVA GASTROENTEROLOGICA E DIETOLOGICA.** See Medical Science and Technology-Gastroenterology.

US
**MISSOURI NUTRITION EDUCATION & TRAINING PROGRAM.** **VFOAT** Missouri Nutrition Education and Training Program. Fiscal Year 1981-. English. an. Free. Missouri Department of Health, Financial Services, PO Box 570, Jefferson City MO 65102. **Tel** (314)751-6279, (314)751-6400. **ED** Julia Noland Chryst. **LC** TX364; .M57. **DD** 641.1/07/10778. ctrl circ.
**Desc:** State plan for nutrition education and training educators, school food service personnel, and children.

US/0164-0585
**MONOGRAPHS OF THE AMERICAN COLLEGE OF NUTRITION.** [Monogr. Am. Coll. Nutr.]. V. 1-. Academic Scholarly Publication. English. an. Price varies per volume. Spectrum Publications Inc, 175-20 Wexford Terrace, Jamaica NY 11432. **Tel** (718)658-0888. **NLM** W1 MO569QP. **CODEN** MACNDG. Documents available from CASDDS.
**Desc:** Consists of the proceedings of the 16th annual meeting of the American College of Nutrition, 1975.
**Ind/Abst** Chem. Abstr.

GW/0027-769X
**NAHRUNG, DIE.** [Nahrung]. **Added/Corp** Akademie der Wissenschaften der DDR. Zentralinstitut fur Ernahrung. **VFOAT** Food. Vol. 1 (1957)-. Academic Scholarly Publication. German (English and German; summaries and/or abstracts in Russian). bm. $325.00. VCH Gesellschaft GmbH, Postfach 101161, D 69451 Weinheim Germany. **Tel** 011 49 6201 606459, FAX 011 49 6201 606184. **(Subscription address:** VCH Publishers Inc., 303 Northwest 12th Avenue, Journals Department, Deerfield FL 33442.**) ED** J. Voigt. **LC** TX341; .N27. **NLM** W1; NA116. **CODEN** NAHRAR. **[CCC].** Index Available, published separately, free-automatically sent. **Pr Rev.** Documents available from The Genuine Article, BIOSIS Document Express, CASDDS.
**Ind/Abst** AGRICOLA; Anal. Abstr.; Anim. Breed. Abstr.; Biodeter. Abstr.; Biol. Abstr.; Chem. Abstr.; Curr. Biotechnol.; Dairy Sci. Abstr.; EMBASE; Field Crop Abstr.; Food Sci. Technol. Abstr.; Helminthol. Abstr. (1991-); Hortic. Abstr.; Index Med.; Leadscan; Maize Abstr.; Nutr. Abstr. Rev., Ser. B, Live Feeds and Feed.; Nutr. Abstr. Rev., Ser. A, Hum. Exp.; Life Sci. Collect.; Pig News Inf.; Postharvest News Inf.; Potato Abstr.; Poult. Abstr.; Res. Alert [Full Cov.]; Rev. Agric. Entomol.; Rev. Med. Vet. Mycology; Rev. Plant Pathol.; Rice Abstr.; Sci. Cit. Index; SCISEARCH; Seed Abstr.; Soc. Sci. Cit. Index [Select. Cov.]; Soyabean Abstr.; Sug. Indus. Abstr.; Vitis Vitic. Enol. Abstr.; Weed Abstr.

SW/0346-7104
**NARINGSFORSKNING. SUPPLEMENT.** (1969)-. Academic Scholarly Publication. Multiple languages (English and Swedish). **NLM** W1 NA106A. **CODEN** NRFSA3. Documents available from CASDDS.
**Ind/Abst** Chem. Abstr.

CN/0830-0887
**NATURAL LIFE MAGAZINE.** [Nat. life mag.]. **VFOAT** Natural Foods Bulletin. (March/April 1984)-. Periodical. English. bm. 18.00Can$ Canada; $23.00 other. Canadian Health Reform Production Ltd, 4728 Byrne Road, Burnaby British Columbia V5J 3H7 Canada. **Tel** (604)435-1919, FAX (604)435-4888. **(Subscription address:** Box 8055, Burnaby British Columbia V5H 4K2 Canada**) ED** Nancy Weatherley. **DD** 641.1/05. Index

available. cum. index. **Bk Rev.** **Ad Acc.** **Circ:** 50,000. ***Continues*** *Natural Foods Bulletin (Burnaby, B.C.), 0830-0879.*

RU
**NAUCHNAIA SESSIIA - GOSUDARSTVENNYI NAUCHNO-ISSLEDOVATELSKII INSTITUT VITAMINOLOGII.** **Added/Corp** Gosudarstvennyi Nauchno-Issledovatelskii Institut Vitaminologii, Moscow. (1960)-. Russian. **NLM** W1 NA941.

NE
**NEDERLANDS TIJDSCHRIFT VOOR DIETISTEN.** **See** Medical Science and Technology.

SZ/0253-0457
**NESTLE FOUNDATION PUBLICATION SERIES.** [Nestle Found. publ. ser.]. **Added/Corp** Nestle Foundation. No. 1 (1980)-. Academic Scholarly Publication. English. **LC** UNC. **NLM** W1 NE227. **CODEN** NFPSD6. Documents available from CASDDS.
**Ind/Abst** AGRICOLA [Select. Cov.]; Chem. Abstr.

US/0742-2806
**NESTLE NUTRITION WORKSHOP SERIES.** [Nestle Nutr. workshop ser.]. **Added/Corp** Nestle Nutrition S.A. Vol. 2 (1983)-. Academic Scholarly Publication. English. ir. Price varies per volume. Raven Press, 1185 Avenue of the Americas, 37th Floor, New York NY 10036. **Tel** (212)930-9500, (212)930-9604, FAX (212)869-3495, (212)302-8507, telex 640073. **ED** Paul R. Swyer and Bernard L. Salle. **NLM** W1; NE228. **CODEN** NNWSDT. Documents available from CASDDS.
**Ind/Abst** AGRICOLA [Full Cov.]; Chem. Abstr. (1983-); Dairy Sci. Abstr.; Nutr. Abstr. Rev., Ser. A, Hum. Exp.; Protozoolog. Abstr.

SZ/1010-0970
**NESTLE RESEARCH NEWS.** ***Ceased.*** [Nestle res. news]. **Added/Corp** Nestle Products Technical Assistance Co. Technical Documentation Centre. (19??)-(19??). English. be.
**Ind/Abst** AGRICOLA [Select. Cov.].

NR/0189-0913
**NIGERIAN JOURNAL OF NUTRITIONAL SCIENCES.** [Niger. j. nutr. sci.]. Vol. 1, No. 1 (Jan./June 1980)-. Academic Scholarly Publication. English. sa. N50.00. University of Ibadan Department of Human Nutrition, Nigerian Journal of Nutritional Sciences, Ibadan Nigeria. **Tel** 022 400 550. **ED** Tola Atinmo. **NLM** W1; NI392F. **CODEN** NJNSEP. **Bk Rev.** **Ad Acc.** **Circ:** 5,000. Documents available from CASDDS.
**Ind/Abst** Chem. Abstr. (1980-1981).

JA/0287-3516
**NIHON EIYO SHOKURYO GAKKAI SHI.** **Added/Corp** Nihon Eiyo Shokuryo Gakkai. **VFOAT** Journal of Japanese Society of Nutrition and Food Science; Nippon Eiyo Shokuryo Gakkaishi. Vol. 36, No. 1 (1983)-. Academic Scholarly Publication. Japanese (summaries and/or abstracts in English; table of contents in English). bm (6 issues). $214.00. Do Gakkai, Keto Tsushin 19-ban 30-go Mita, 2-chome Minato-ku, Tokyo 108 Japan. **(Subscription address:** Kyowa Book Company Inc., 1-38 Kanda Jinbocho Chiyoda-Ku. Tokyo 101 Japan; Telephone: 011 81 3 3293 0727**)** **NLM** W1; NI146GM. **CODEN** NESGDC. Documents available from CASDDS. ***Continues*** *Eiyo to Shokuryo, 0021-5376.*
**Ind/Abst** Chem. Abstr.; Food Sci. Technol. Abstr.; Maize Abstr.; Nutr. Abstr. Rev., Ser. A, Hum. Exp.; Soc. Sci. Cit. Index [Select. Cov.]; Soyabean Abstr.; Sug. Indus. Abstr.

AT
**NUTIRDATE.** **See** Health and Personal Fitness.

US/1053-8887
**NUTRI-TOPICS (CONSUMER).** (NUTRI-TOPICS / FOOD AND NUTRITION INFORMATION CENTER, NATIONAL AGRICULTURAL LIBRARY.). [Nutri-topics]. **Added/Corp** Food and Nutrition Information Center (U.S.). (1991)-. English. Free. National Agricultural Library, 10301 Baltimore Boulevard, Beltsville MD 20705. **DD** 613.

US/1053-8895
**NUTRI-TOPICS / FOOD AND NUTRITION INFORMATION CENTER, NATIONAL AGRICULTURAL LIBRARY.** [Nutri-topics]. **Added/Corp** Food and Nutrition Information Center (U.S.). (1991)-. English. Free. Food and Nutrition Information Center, National Agricultural Library, 10301 Baltimore Boulevard, Beltsville MD 20705. **DD** 613.

US/1053-8879
**NUTRI-TOPICS (HEALTH PROFESSIONAL/RESEARCHER).** (NUTRI-TOPICS / FOOD AND NUTRITION INFORMATION CENTER, NATIONAL AGRICULTURAL LIBRARY.). [Nutri-topics]. **Added/Corp** Food and Nutrition Information Center (U.S.). 91-H1 (1991)-. English. Free. Food and Nutrition Information Center, National Agricultural Library, 10301 Baltimore Boulevard, Beltsville MD 20705. **DD** 613.

SP/0211-6057
**NUTRICION CLINICA DIETETICA HOSPITALARIA.** [Nutr. clin., Diet hosp.]. **VFOAT** Dietetica Hospitalaria. (1981)-. Academic Scholarly Publication. Spanish. Five times a year. 5000ptas Spain; $55.00 Europe; $100.00 others. Alpe Editores SA, C Pedro Rico 27, Oficinas 11 & 12, 28029 Madrid Spain. **Tel** 011 34 1 7338811, FAX 011 34 1 3159652. **NLM** W1; NU839. **CODEN** NUTCDF. **[CCC].** Documents available from CASDDS.
**Ind/Abst** Chem. Abstr. (-1981); EMBASE; Indice Med. Esp.

SP/0212-1611
**NUTRICION HOSPITALARIA.** Periodical. Spanish (summaries and/or abstracts in Spanish and English; table of contents in English and Spanish). Seven times a year. 3.300ptas Spain; 5.000ptas other. Jarpyo Editores SA, Antonio Lopez Aguados 4, 28029 Madrid, Spain. **Tel** 011 34 1 3144338, 011 34 1 3144458. **(Subscription address:** Antonio Lopez Aguado 1-4, 28029 Madrid Spain**)** **ED** J M Culebras Fernandez. **NLM** W1; NU839E. **Ad Acc.** **Circ:** 2,000.
**Ind/Abst** Indice Med. Esp.

CN/0701-1997
**NUTRIGUIDE.** V. 1- Winter 1976/77-. Periodical. French. ir. $1.50 per number. Copunat Inc, Bureau 119/305 East Boulevard Saint-Joseph, Montreal Quebec H2T 1J3 Canada. **DD** 641.1/05.

PH/0115-4516
**NUTRISYON.** (NUTRISYON : A PUBLICATION OF THE PHILIPPINE SOCIETY OF DIETITIANS AND NUTRITIONISTS, INC. (PSDN).). [Nutrisyon]. Periodical. English. Three times a year. P50.00. University of Philippines College of Home Economics, Diliman Quezon City Philippines. **Tel** 816-41-97. **ED** Rachel A Arboleda. **NLM** W1 NU855. **Circ:** 1,000 (ctrl). ***Continues*** *Nutrilite.*
**Desc:** New trends in nutrition, and results of research studies.
**Ind/Abst** Philip. Sci. Technol. Abstr.

UK/0309-1295
**NUTRITION ABSTRACTS AND REVIEWS. SERIES A: HUMAN & EXPERIMENTAL.** **See** Nutrition and Dietetics-Abstracting, Bibliographies and Statistics.

US/0885-7792
**NUTRITION ACTION HEALTH LETTER.** [Nutr. action health lett.]. **Added/Corp** Center for Science in the Public Interest. **VFOAT** Nutrition Action; Nutrition Action Healthletter. Vol. 12, No. 2 (Mar. 1985)-. Periodical. English. Ten times a year. $24.00 US & Possessions; $32.00 other. Center for Science in the Public Interest, 1875 Conn Avenue NW, Suite 300, Washington DC 20009. **Tel** (202)332-9110. **ED** Stephen B Schmidt and Michael Jacobson. **DD** 641. **NLM** W1; NU862G. **CODEN** NAHLED. Index available. cum. index. **Bk Rev.** **Circ:** 210,000. available on an online database (file 149/Full-Text) from DIALOG. Documents available from UMI Article Clearinghouse. ***Continues*** *Nutrition Action, 0199-5510.*
**Desc:** Offers 16 pages of objective data on nutrition and health issues. Carefully illustrated and there are scores of easy to understand items. In one number there is a 200-word note on "fake fat news," a longer article covering food and pesticides, a consumer report on "picking a pasta sauce," and questions and answers about common eating problems. An accurate report for all libraries.
**Ind/Abst** Acad. Abstr. Full Text Elite (Jan. 1992-); Acad. Abstr. (Jan. 1992-); Acad. Search (Jan. 1992-); AGRICOLA [Select. Cov.]; Consum. Health Nutr. Index (?-?); Foods Adlibra; Gen. Period. Index (1992-); Health Index; Health Period. Database [Full Txt.]; Health Ref. Cent. (Jan. 1989-) [Full Txt.] [Full Cov.]; Health Source (Jan. 1992-); INFO-SOUTH Abstr.; Mag. ASAP Plus; Mag. Index Plus (1992-); Mag. Search; Newsp. Period. Abstr. (1992-).

US/0163-5581
**NUTRITION AND CANCER.** [Nutr. cancer]. Vol. 1 (Fall 1978)-. Academic Scholarly Publication. English. Six times a year. $385.00 US & Canada; $425.00 other. Lawrence Erlbaum Associates, 365 Broadway, Suite 102, Hillsdale NJ 07642. **Tel** (201)666-4110, (800)926-6579, FAX (201)666-2394. **ED** Gio B Gori. **DD** 616. **NLM** W1 NU879. **CODEN** NUCADQ. **Bk Rev.** **Ad Acc.** **Pr Rev.** **Circ:** 500. available on microfilm and microfiche from University Microfilms International (UMI). Documents available from The Genuine Article, BIOSIS Document Express, CASDDS.
**Desc:** Reports and reviews current findings on the effects of nutrition on the etiology, therapy, and prevention of cancer.
**Ind/Abst** AGRICOLA [Full Cov.]; Biol. Abstr.; Chem. Abstr.; Curr. Aware. Biol. Sci., CABS; Curr. Contents Life Sci.; Dairy Sci. Abstr.; EMBASE; Foods Adlibra; Index Med.; Index Vet.; Maize Abstr.; NAPRALERT; Nutr. Abstr. Rev., Ser. A, Hum. Exp.; Nutr. Res. Newsl.; Poult. Abstr.; Ref. Upd. Deluxe Ed.; Res. Alert [Select. Cov.]; Rev. Med. Vet. Mycology; Rice Abstr.; Sci. Cit. Index; SCISEARCH; Vet. Bull.; Wheat Barley Trit. Abstr.

US/0360-7259
**NUTRITION AND CLINICAL NUTRITION.** Vol. 1 (1975)-. Monographic series. English. ir. Price varies per volume. Marcel Dekker Inc., 270 Madison Avenue, New York NY 10016. **Tel** (212)696-9000, (800)228-1160, FAX (212)685-4540, telex 421419. **(Subscription address:** Marcel Dekker Inc, PO Box 5017, Monticello NY 12701.**)** **ED** R. Olson. **LC** UNC. **NLM** W1 NU863D. **CODEN** NCNUDF. Documents available from BIOSIS Document Express.
**Desc:** This is an ongoing series. Each title has a different subject.
**Ind/Abst** Biol. Abstr. (?-1976).

US/8750-8370
**NUTRITION & DIETARY CONSULTANT, THE.** [Nutr. dietary consult.]. **VFOAT** Nutrition and Dietary Consulant. (198?)-. Periodical. English. Twelve times a year. $15.96 (one year); $31.20 (two years); $46.80 (three years). American Association of Nutritional Consultants, 1641 East Sunset Road, Suite B 117, Las Vegas NV 89119. **Tel** (702)361-1132, FAX (702)361-1086. **ED** Myra E. Zelikovics. **DD** 613. **Ad Acc.** **Circ:** 15,000. ***Continues*** *Your Nutritional Consultant, 8750-3395.*
**Desc:** A professional journal dedicated to the practice of nutritional consulting with emphasis on private practice and articles written for the professional.

SZ
**NUTRITION AND FOOD SAFETY.** (19??)-. English. $220.00. World Health Organization, Distribution and Sales, 20 Avenue Appia, CH-1211 Geneva 27 Switzerland. **Tel** 011 41 22 7912111, FAX 011 41 22 7880401.
**Desc:** Covers the International Digest of Health Legislation plus all books published by WHO on nutrition, food safety, and food quality control.

UK/0034-6659
**NUTRITION & FOOD SCIENCE.** **VFOAT** Nutrition and Food Science. (199?)-. Periodical. English. bm (Jan., Mar., May, July, Sep., Nov.). $329.00. MCB University Press, 60 62 Toller Lane, Bradford West Yorkshire BD8 9BX England. **Tel** 011 44 274 499821, FAX 011 44 274 547143, telex 51317 MCBUNI G. **(Subscription address:** MCB University Press / US and Canada Subscriptions, PO Box 10812, Birmingham AL 35201-0812.**)** **LC** IN PROCESS. ***Continues*** *Nutrition and Food Science, 0034-6659.*

UK/0034-6659
**NUTRITION & FOOD SCIENCE.** ***Title Change.*** (NUTRITION AND FOOD SCIENCE.). [Nutr. food sci.]. **Added/Corp** British Nutrition Foundation. No. 22 (Jan. 1971)-(19??). Periodical. English. an (Vol. 23 with 6 issues). MCB University Press, 60 62 Toller Lane, Bradford West Yorkshire BD8 9BX England. **Tel** 011 44 274 499821, FAX 011 44 274 547143, telex 51317 MCBUNI G. **ED** Dilys Wells. **CODEN** NFSCD7. Index available. **Bk Rev.** **Circ:** 3,500. Documents available from CASDDS. ***Continues*** *Review of Nutrition and Food Science.* ***Continued by*** *Nutrition & Food Science (Bradford, West Yorkshire, England), 0034-6659.*
**Desc:** Developments in the subject areas are presented in a concisely readable form to provide a link between education and the food science world.
**Ind/Abst** AGRICOLA; BioBusiness (1989-); Biodeter. Abstr. (1991-); Chem. Abstr.; Curr. Technol. Index; Dairy Sci. Abstr.; Food Sci. Technol. Abstr.; Nutr. Abstr. Rev., Ser. A, Hum. Exp.; Nutr. Res. Newsl.; Postharvest News Inf.; Sug. Indus. Abstr.; World Agric. Econ.

UK/0260-1060
**NUTRITION AND HEALTH (BERKHAMSTED).** (NUTRITION AND HEALTH.). [Nutr. health]. (1982)-. Academic Scholarly Publication. English. ir. price varies per volume. AB Academic Publishers, PO Box 42 Bicester, OXON OX6 7NW England. **Tel** 011 44 869 320949. **ED** Kenneth Barlow. **CODEN** NUHEDT. **[CCC].** **Bk Rev.** **Ad Acc.** **Pr Rev.** Documents available from BIOSIS Document Express, CASDDS.
**Desc:** Research and reviews of recent advances on aspects of nutrition with special relevance to health and prevention of disease. Includes book reviews.
**Ind/Abst** AGRICOLA [Select. Cov.]; Appl. Soc. Sci. Index Abstr.; Biol. Abstr.; Chem. Abstr.; EMBASE; Environ. Period. Bibliogr.; Food Sci. Technol. Abstr.; Index Med. Vol. 3, No. 1, 1984-; Physic. Medline Plus; Soc. Plann. Policy Dev. Abstr.; Sociol. Abstr.

US/0270-658X
**NUTRITION AND HEALTH (NEW YORK).** ***Ceased.*** (NUTRITION AND HEALTH.). [Nutr. health]. Vol. 1 (1979)-Vol. 10 (1988). Periodical. English. bm. Nutrition and Health, Institute of Human Nutrition, Columbia University, College of Physicians and Surgeons, 701 West 168th Street, Ms S Silver, Subscription Director, New York NY 10032. **Tel** (212)305-6991. **ED** Myron Winick and Brian Morgan. **NLM** W1 NU863J. **Circ:** 5,000 (ctrl).
**Desc:** Current and informative information on health topics such as heart disease, obesity diabetes, cancer, high blood pressure, stress, vitamins, food intake, nutrition and exercise, etc.
**Ind/Abst** AGRICOLA [Select. Cov.]; Nutr. Abstr. Rev., Ser. A, Hum. Exp.; Nutr. Res. Newsl.; Physic. Medline Plus; Rev. Med. Vet. Mycology.

●CN/1199-7699
**NUTRITION & MENTAL HEALTH.** (NUTRITION & MENTAL HEALTH : THE QUARTERLY NEWSLETTER OF THE CANADIAN SCHIZOPHRENIA FOUNDATION.). [Nutr. ment. health]. **Added/Corp** Canadian Schizophrenia Foundation. **VFOAT** Nutrition and Mental Health. (Autumn 1993)-. Newsletter. English. qt. Free (members). Canadian Schizophrenia Foundation / Ontario, 16 Florence Avenue, Toronto Ontario M2N 1E9 Canada. **Tel** (416)733-2117. **DD** 616.89. ***Continues*** *Health & Nutrition Update., 0831-8530.*

US/0149-2667
**NUTRITION AND THE BRAIN.** [Nutr. brain]. Vol. 1 (1977)-. Academic Scholarly Publication. English. ir. Price varies per volume. Raven Press, 1185 Avenue of the Americas, 37th Floor, New York NY 10036. **Tel** (212)930-9500, (212)930-9604, FAX (212)869-3495, (212)302-8507, telex 640073. **ED** Richard J. Wurtman and Judith J. Wurtman. **LC** QP376; .N86. **NLM** W1 NU8632. **CODEN** NUBRD4. Documents available from CASDDS.
**Ind/Abst** AGRICOLA [Select. Cov.]; Chem. Abstr. (1977-1983).

US/0732-0167
**NUTRITION & THE M.D.** [Nutr. M.D.]. **VFOAT** Nutrition and the M.D.; Nutrition & the MD; Nutrition and the MD. (Nov. 1974)-. Periodical. English. mo. $48.00 US, Canada & Mexico; $73.00 other. Raven Press, 1185 Avenue of the Americas, 37th Floor, New York NY 10036. **Tel** (212)930-9500, (212)930-9604, FAX (212)869-3495, (212)302-8507, telex 640073. **ED** Gerald McKee. Index available. **Bk Rev. Circ:** 10,000.
**Desc:** Clinical nutrition information for those involved in professional health care: registered dietitians, physicians, food service managers, hospitals and federal, state and municipal agencies.
**Ind/Abst** AGRICOLA [Select. Cov.].

US/0899-9007
**NUTRITION (BURBANK, LOS ANGELES COUNTY, CALIF.).** (NUTRITION.). **Added/Corp** Australian Society of Parenteral and Enteral Nutrition. Brazilian Society of Parenteral and Enteral Nutrition. Western Nutrition Education and Cancer Research Foundation. Vol. 3, No. 3 (May/June 1987)-. Periodical. English. Six times a year. $79.00 US; $120.00 other. Nutrition, PO Box 920, Syracuse NY 13210-0920. **Tel** (315)464-6280, FAX (315)464-6238. **LC** QP141.A1; N866. **DD** 612/.3/05. **NLM** W1; NU861. **CODEN** NUTRER. Index available. **Bk Rev. Ad Acc. Pr Rev.** Documents available from The Genuine Article. ***Continues Nutrition International, 0888-1294.***
**Ind/Abst** Curr. Aware. Biol. Sci., CABS; Index Med. (Jan./Feb. 1989-); Index Vet.; Nutr. Abstr. Rev., Ser. A, Hum. Exp.; Res. Alert [Full Cov.]; Rev. Med. Vet. Mycology; Sci. Cit. Index; SCISEARCH; Small Anim. Abstr. Bibliogr.; Soc. Sci. Cit. Index [Select. Cov.].

US/0888-3483
**NUTRITION CLINICS.** ***Title Change.*** [Nutr. clin.]. Vol. 1, No. 1 (June 1986)-(1992). Periodical. English. bm. J.B. Lippincott Company, 227 East Washington Square, Philadelphia PA 19106-3780. **Tel** (215)238-4200 or 4454, FAX (215)238-4227. **ED** Eleanor N. Whitney. **LC** QP141.A1; N864. **DD** 613.2. **NLM** W1; NU8734. **Circ:** 1,100. available on microfilm and microfiche from University Microfilms International (UMI). ***Merged into*** *Topics in Clinical Nutrition.*
**Desc:** Devoted to a single topic in health and nutrition including populations involved, developments in literature, case studies and suggestions for diet-related corrective measures.
**Ind/Abst** AGRICOLA [Full Cov.]; Int. Pharm. Abstr.

FR/0985-0562
**NUTRITION CLINIQUE ET METABOLISME.** (1987)-. Periodical. French (summaries and/or abstracts in English and French; table of contents in English and French). qt. 695.00F (institutions), 550.00F (individuals) France; 750.00F other. Blackwell Scientific Publishers / Arnette, 2 rue Casimir-Delavigne, 75006 Paris France. **Tel** 011 33 1 44860770, FAX 011 33 1 46336797. **NLM** W1; NU8737. **CODEN** NCMEEV. available on microfilm and microfiche from University Microfilms International (UMI).
**Ind/Abst** EMBASE [Select. Cov.]; Food Sci. Technol. Abstr.

US/0748-8165
**NUTRITION FORUM (PHILADELPHIA, PA.).** (NUTRITION FORUM.). [Nutr. forum]. Vol. 1, No. 1 (Oct. 1984)-. Periodical. English. bm. $35.00 (individuals US); $50.00 (institutions US). Nutrition Forum, c/o D. Xu & J. Raso, PO Box 747924, Rego Park NY 11374. **Tel** (718)275-0414, FAX (718)997-8227. **ED** David Xu & Jack Raso. **DD** 613. **NLM** W1; NU8856. Index available. cum. index. **Bk Rev**, (Qty: 6-10). **Circ:** 2,000. available on microfilm and microfiche from University Microfilms International (UMI); available on an online database (file 149/Full-Text) from DIALOG.
**Desc:** Reliable, current information on the latest trends in popular nutritional practices combining information from nutrition, medicine, dentistry, pharmacology, biochemistry and the law.
**Ind/Abst** Acad. Abstr. Full Text Elite (Jan. 1992-); Acad. Abstr. (Jan. 1992-); Acad. Search (Jan. 1992-); AGRICOLA [Select. Cov.]; Consum. Health Nutr. Index; Gen. Sci. Source (Jan. 1992-); Health Index (1989-); Health Period. Database [Full Txt.]; Health Ref. Cent. (Jan. 1989-) [Full Txt.] [Full Cov.]; Health Source (Jan. 1992-); INFO-SOUTH Abstr.; Mag. Search.

US/0892-1474
**NUTRITION FUNDING REPORT, THE.** **Added/Corp** Nutrition Legislation Services (Washington, D.C.). (1986)-. Periodical. English. mo. $45.00 (one year), $80.00 (two year). Nutrition Legislation Service, PO Box 75035, Washington DC 20013. **Tel** (202)488-8879, FAX (202)554-3116. **ED** Lenora Moragne. **DD** 613. **NLM** QU 22; AA1 N9. **Bk Rev.**
**Desc:** Eight-page publication outlining available grants, contracts, scholarships, fellowships, publications, and other information from foundations, corporations, charities and government. Written with nutrition and health professionals in mind.

US/0164-7202
**NUTRITION HEALTH REVIEW.** (1976)-. Periodical. English. Four times a year. $18.00 (two years). Vegetus Publications, 171 Madison Avenue, New York NY 10016. **Tel** (212)679-3590, FAX (212)679-3597. **ED** Frank Ray Rifkin (editor's phone: (215)896-1853). Index available. **Bk Rev. Circ:** 300,000. available on an online database (file 149/Full-Text) from DIALOG; available on microfiche.
**Desc:** Nutrition and health information gleaned from medical and psychiatric publications plus original manuscripts.
**Ind/Abst** Acad. Abstr. Full Text Elite (Jan. 1992-); Acad. Abstr. (Jan. 1992-); Acad. Search (Jan. 1992-); Consum. Health Nutr. Index (?-?); Gen. Sci. Source (Jan. 1992-); Health Index (1989-); Health Period. Database [Full Txt.]; Health Ref. Cent. (Jan. 1989-) [Full Txt.] [Full Cov.]; Health Source (Jan. 1992-); INFO-SOUTH Abstr.; Mag. Search.

US/0884-5336
**NUTRITION IN CLINICAL PRACTICE.** (NUTRITION IN CLINICAL PRACTICE : OFFICIAL PUBLICATION OF THE AMERICAN SOCIETY FOR PARENTERAL AND ENTERAL NUTRITION.). [Nutr. clin. prac.]. **Added/Corp** American Society of Parenteral and Enteral Nutrition. **VFOAT** NCP. Vol. 1, No. 1 (Feb. 1986)-. Periodical. English. bm (6 issues). $70.00 US; $85.00 Canada and Mexico; $90.00 other (institution). American Society of Parenteral and Enteral Nutrition / ASPEN, 8630 Fenton Street, Suite 412, Silver Spring MD 20910-3805. **Tel** (301)587-6315, FAX (301)587-2365. **DD** 613. **NLM** W1; NU887T. **CODEN** NCPREH. **[CCC].** available on microfilm and microfiche from University Microfilms International (UMI). Documents available from BIOSIS Document Express.
**Ind/Abst** Biol. Abstr. (1987-); Cumul. Index Nurs. Allied Health Lit.; Int. Nurs. Index (Vol. 3, No. 1, 1988-); Int. Pharm. Abstr.

US
**NUTRITION LEGISLATION AND REGULATORY NEWS.** Eighteen times a year. $150.00 US, Canada and Mexico; $175.00 other (international air) one year; $250.00 US, Canada and Mexico; $300.00 other (international air) two year. Nutrition Legislation Service, PO Box 75035, Washington DC 20013. **Tel** (202)488-8879, FAX (202)554-3116. **ED** Lenora Moragne.
**Desc:** A report on food, nutrition, and health related initiatives from the US Congress and Federal regulatory agencies. Includes new bills, resolutions, hearings, regulatory actions, committee studies and reports.

US/8756-6060
**NUTRITION LEGISLATION NEWS.** **See** Law.

US/8756-5919
**NUTRITION NEWS (RIVERSIDE, CALIF.).** (NUTRITION NEWS.). [Nutr. news]. Periodical. English. mo. $18.00 US; $28.80 other. Nutrition News, 4108 Watkins Drive, Riverside CA 92507-4752. **Tel** (909)784-7500. **ED** Siri Khalsa. **DD** 613. Index available. cum. index. **Circ:** 80,000.
**Desc:** We publish a four-page newsletter on a particular health topic or on a vitamin or mineral supplement.

US/0369-6464
**NUTRITION NEWS (ROSEMONT).** (NUTRITION NEWS.). [Nutr. news]. **Added/Corp** National Dairy Council. Vol. 1, (Oct. 1937)-. Periodical. English. Three times a year. $6.00 (one year), $11.00 (two year), $16.00 (three year) US; $9.00 other; $15.00 combined subscription with Dairy Council Digest. National Dairy Council, 10255 West Higgins Road, Suite 900, Rosemont IL 60018. **Tel** (708)803-2000, FAX (708)803-2077. **ED** Rebecca Mackler. **LC** TX501; .N85. **DD** 641.105. **NLM** W1 NU908. **Bk Rev. Circ:** 68,000 (ctrl). available on microfilm and microfiche from University Microfilms International (UMI).
**Desc:** Purpose is to integrate nutrition education research, practice, and/or nutrition research.
**Ind/Abst** Acad. Abstr. Full Text Elite (Jan. 1992-); Acad. Abstr. (Jan. 1992-); Acad. Search (Jan. 1992-); AGRICOLA [Select. Cov.]; Consum. Health Nutr. Index (?-?); Gen. Sci. Source (Jan. 1992-); Health Index (1989-); Health Period. Database; Health Ref. Cent. (Jan. 1989-) [Full Cov.]; Health Source (Jan. 1992-); INFO-SOUTH Abstr.; Mag. Search.

US
**NUTRITION NEWSLETTER.** **Added/Corp** Cornell University. Division of Nutritional Sciences. Vol. 10 (Fall 1974)-. Newsletter. English. sa. Free. Cornell University Division of Nutritional Sciences, Ithaca NY 14853. ***Continues*** *Cornell University. Graduate School of Nutrition. Graduate School of Nutrition News.*

US/0898-1604
**NUTRITION NEWSLINE.** ***Ceased.*** [Nutr. newsline]. **VFOAT** Nutrition News Line. Vol. 1, No. 1 (May 1988)-(May 1989). Periodical. English. bm. Nutrition Newsline, PO Box 439, South Elgin IL 60177. **DD** 641.

US
**NUTRITION NOTES.** **Added/Corp** American Institute of Nutrition. (19??)-. Periodical. English. qt (4 issues). $34.00; Also comes with American Institute of Nutrition membership. American Institute of Nutrition, 9650 Rockville Pike, Room L 2310, Bethesda MD 20814-3998. **Tel** (301)530-7026, FAX (301)530-7001. **ED** Phylis Moser-Veillon. **LC** TX341; .N83. **DD** 641.1. **Bk Rev. Circ:** 3,000.
**Desc:** The newsletter of the American Institute of Nutrition. It covers the announcement of nutrition meetings, national and international, new publications in nutritional science, public affairs and items of interest to its members.

US/0892-6042
**NUTRITION NOW.** [Nutr. now]. **Added/Corp** Professional Nutrition Services (Boulder, Colo.). (198?)-. Periodical. English. bm (6 issues). $18.00 (institutions), $12.00 (individuals). Professional Nutrition Services, PO Box 744, Boulder CO 80306. **Tel** (303)440-4246. **DD** 616.

AT/0813-4499
**NUTRITION POLICY STATEMENTS.** (NUTRITION POLICY STATEMENTS / COMMONWEALTH DEPARTMENT OF HEALTH AND NATIONAL HEALTH AND MEDICAL RESEARCH COUNCIL.). [Nutr. policy statements]. **Main/Corp** Australia. Dept. of Health. **Added/Corp** National Health and Medical Research Council (Australia). (19??)-. English. an.

CN
**NUTRITION POST.** (19??)-. English. Four times a year. 35.00Can$ Canada; 48.00Can$ other. MacLean Hunter Ltd. Business Publishers / Canada, Box 9100, Station A, Toronto ONT M5W 1A5 Canada. **Tel** (416)946-8420, (800)567-0444. **(Subscription address:** Indas, 35 Riviera Drive, Building 17, Markham Ontario L3R 8N4 Canada.**)**

CN/0710-166X
**NUTRITION QUARTERLY.** (NUTRITION QUARTERLY / COMPILED BY NUTRITION DIVISION, DAIRY BUREAU OF CANADA.). [Nutr. q.]. **Added/Corp** Dairy Bureau of Canada. Service de la Nutrition. (1977)-. Periodical. English. qt. Free on request. Dairy Nutrition Info Centre, 1981 McGill College Avenue, Room 1320, Montreal Quebec H3A 2X9 Canada. **Tel** (514)284-3214, (800)361-4632. **DD** 641.1/05. ctrl circ.

US/0740-8684
**NUTRITION REPORT, THE.** [Nutr. rep.]. **Added/Corp** Health Media of America (Firm). Vol. 1, No. 1 (Oct. 1983)-. Periodical. English. mo. $48.00. Health Media of America, 11300 Sorrento Valley Road #250, San Diego CA 92121. **Tel** (619)453-3887, (800)331-7807. **ED** Lisa M Moye. Index available. cum. index.
**Desc:** Summaries of research selected from over 6,000 scientific journals. Easy to read, complete, yet concise, latest findings in nutritional pharmacology.
**Ind/Abst** Foods Adlibra.

US/0097-0166
**NUTRITION RESEARCH.** **Added/Corp** Sunkist Growers. (1940)-. Periodical. English. Sunkist Growers Inc, 14130 Riverside Drive, Sherman Oak CA 91423. **NLM** W1 NU942. Documents available from The Genuine Article.
**Ind/Abst** Calcium Calcif. Tissue Abstr.; Curr. Contents Life Sci.; Nutr. Abstr. Rev., Ser. A, Hum. Exp.; Pig News Inf.; Potato Abstr.; Res. Alert [Full Cov.].

US/0271-5317
**NUTRITION RESEARCH (NEW YORK, N.Y.).** (NUTRITION RESEARCH.). [Nutr. res.]. Vol. 1, No. 1 (1981)-. Academic Scholarly Publication. English. mo. $626.00 The Americas; £420.00 other. Pergamon Press, An Imprint of Elsevier Science Ltd., The Boulevard, Langford Lane, Kidlington, Oxford OX5 1GB United Kingdom. **Tel** 011 44 865 843000, 011 44 865 843699, FAX 011 44 865 843010. **(Subscription address:** Elsevier Science Ltd. Oxford Fulfillment Centre, PO Box 800, Kidlington, Oxford OX5 1DX United Kingdom.**) ED** Ranjit Chandra. **LC** QP141.A1; N88. **DD** 616.3/9. **CODEN** NTRSDC. **[CCC]. Bk Rev. Ad Acc. Pr Rev.** available on microfilm and microfiche from University Microfilms International (UMI). Documents available from The Genuine Article, BIOSIS Document Express, CASDDS.

**Ind/Abst** AGRICOLA [Full Cov.]; Biol. Agric. Index; Biol. Abstr. (1986-); Chem. Abstr.; CSA Neuro. Abstr. (?-?); Curr. Aware. Biol. Sci., CABS; Curr. Contents Life Sci.; Dairy Sci. Abstr.; EMBASE; Food Sci. Technol. Abstr.; Foods Adlibra; Index Med.; Index Sci. Rev.; Index Vet.; Maize Abstr.; Nutr. Abstr. Rev., Ser. B, Live Feeds and Feed.; Nutr. Res. Newsl.; Life Sci. Collect.; Poult. Abstr.; Ref. Upd. Deluxe Ed.; Res. Alert [Full Cov.]; Rice Abstr.; Sci. Cit. Index; SCISEARCH; Soc. Sci. Cit. Index [Select. Cov.]; Soyabean Abstr.; Vet. Bull.; Trop. Dis. Bull.

US/0736-0037
**NUTRITION RESEARCH NEWSLETTER.** **See** Nutrition and Dietetics-Abstracting, Bibliographies and Statistics.

UK/0954-4224
**NUTRITION RESEARCH REVIEWS.** [Nutr. res. rev.]. **Added/Corp** Nutrition Society (Great Britain). Vol. 1 (1988)-. Academic Scholarly Publication. English. an. $89.00 US, Canada and Mexico; £49.00 other. Cambridge University Press, The Edinburgh Building, Shaftesbury Road, Cambridge CB2 2RU United Kingdom. **Tel** 011 44 223 312393, FAX 011 44 223 325959. **(Subscription address:** Cambridge University Press / North America, 110 Midland Avenue, Port Chester NY 10573.**) ED** M. I. Gurr. **LC** QP141.A1; N883. **DD** 613.2. **NLM** W1; NU943K. **CODEN** NREREX. available on microfilm from University Microfilms International (UMI). Documents available from BIOSIS Document Express, CASDDS.
**Desc:** Contains reviews of research on a variety of nutritional problems. Contributions are invited from internationally recognized experts and innovators, and provide global reviews of recent research developments in specified areas. Individual topics range widely from those which deal with problems of human nutrition to those which are concerned mainly with the nutrition of domestic and farm animals. The main objective is to encourage the exchange of such fundamental ideas between workers whose principal interests and practical concerns may lie in very different nutritional fields.
**Ind/Abst** AGRICOLA [Full Cov.]; Anim. Breed. Abstr.; Biol. Abstr. (1990-); Chem. Abstr. (1988-); Dairy Sci. Abstr.; Environ. Period. Bibliogr.; Index Vet.; Nutr. Abstr. Rev., Ser. B, Live Feeds and Feed.; Nutr. Abstr. Rev., Ser. A, Hum. Exp.; Poult. Abstr.; Trop. Dis. Bull.

US/0029-6643
**NUTRITION REVIEWS.** [Nutr. rev.]. **Added/Corp** Nutrition Foundation. Vol. 1 (Nov. 1942)-. Academic Scholarly Publication. English. mo. $90.00 (institutions), $55.00 (individuals) North America; $95.00 (institutions), $60.00 (individuals) other. ILSI / International Life Science Institute, 1126 16th Street Northwest, Suite 300, Washington DC 20036. **Tel** (202)659-0074. **(Subscription address:** Nutrition Reviews, PO Box 1897, Lawrence KS 66044-8897.**) ED** Irwin H. Rosenberg. **LC** TX341; .N85. **DD** 641.105. **NLM** W1 NU945. **CODEN** NUREA8. **[CCC].** cum. index. **Pr Rev.** available on microfilm and microfiche from University Microfilms International (UMI). Documents available from The Genuine Article, UMI Article Clearinghouse, CASDDS, Documents on Demand.
**Desc:** Provides critical reviews of discoveries in nutrition science.
**Ind/Abst** Acad. Ind. [Computer File] (1987-); Acad. Search (July 1993-); AgBiotech News Inf.; AGRICOLA [Full Cov.]; Biol. Agric. Index; Chem. Abstr.; Chicano Index; CSA Neuro. Abstr. (?-?); Cumul. Index Nurs. Allied Health Lit.; Curr. Aware. Biol. Sci., CABS; Curr. Contents, Agric. Biol. Environ. Sci.; Curr. Contents Life Sci.; Curr. Ref. Fish Res.; Dairy Sci. Abstr.; EMBASE; Energy Inf. Abstr.; Energy Res. Abstr.; Environ. Abstr.; Expand. Acad. Index (1987-); Food Sci. Technol. Abstr.; Foods Adlibra; Gen. Sci. Index; Gen. Sci. Source (Jul. 1993-); Health Ref. Cent. (1987-) [Select. Cov.]; Health Source (Jul. 1993-); Index Med.; Index Sci. Rev. [Full Cov.]; INFO-SOUTH Abstr.; Leadscan; Mag. Search; Newsp. Period. Abstr. (1989-); Nucl. Sci. Abstr.; Nutr. Abstr. Rev., Ser. A, Hum. Exp.; Nutr. Res. Newsl.; Life Sci. Collect.; Ref. Upd. Basic Ed.; Ref. Upd. Clinical Ed.; Ref. Upd. Deluxe Ed.; Res. Alert [Full Cov.]; Sci. Cit. Index; SCISEARCH; Soc. Sci. Cit. Index [Select. Cov.]; SportSearch; Trop. Dis. Bull.

US/0889-7034
**NUTRITION SAVVY.** [Nutr. savvy]. Vol. 1, No. 1 (Winter 1987)-. Periodical. English. qt. $15.00. Donna Bell and Associates, 3071 Forest Hill Boulevard/Suite 307, West Palm Beach FL 33406. **DD** 613.

US
**NUTRITION (SPRINGFIELD, IL).** (NUTRITION.). Jan. 1980-. Periodical. English. $10.95. Dushkin Publishing Group Inc., Sluice Dock, Guilford CT 06437. **Tel** (203)453-4351, (800)243-6532, FAX (203)453-6000. **ED** Charlotte Cook-Fuller.
**Desc:** Carefully selected articles reflecting timely topics of interest and concern in the area of nutrition. Provides broad coverage in a careful, discriminating fashion.
**Ind/Abst** Nutr. Res. Newsl.

US/0029-666X
**NUTRITION TODAY (ANNAPOLIS).** (NUTRITION TODAY.). [Nutr. today]. **Added/Corp** Florida Citrus Commission. Nutrition Today Society. Vol. 1 (March 1966)-. Periodical. English. bm. $40.00 (individual), $77.00 (institution) US; $60.00 (individual), $97.00 (institution) other. Williams & Wilkins Company, 428 East Preston Street, Baltimore MD 21202-3993. **Tel** (410)528-4000, (800)638-6423, FAX (410)528-8596, telex 87669. **(Subscription address:** Williams & Wilkins, PO Box 64380, Baltimore MD 21264.**) ED** Helen Guthrie. **LC** RA784; .N85. **DD** 613.2. **NLM** W1 NU958. **[CCC]. Ad Acc. Circ:** 9,000. available on microfilm; available on an online database (file 149/Full-Text) from DIALOG. Documents available from UMI Article Clearinghouse, Quick Copies.
**Desc:** Articles on new developments in nutrition for dietitians, nutritionists, and physicians.
**Ind/Abst** Acad. Abstr. Full Text Elite (Jan. 1992-); Acad. Abstr. (Jan. 1992-); Acad. Ind. [Computer File] (1992-); Acad. Search (Jan. 1992-); AGRICOLA [Select. Cov.]; Appl. Sci. Technol. Index; Consum. Health Nutr. Index; Environ. Period. Bibliogr.; Expand. Acad. Index (1988-); Food Sci. Technol. Abstr.; Foods Adlibra; Gen. Sci. Index; Gen. Sci. Source (Jan. 1992-); Health Index (1989-); Health Period. Database [Full Txt.]; Health Ref. Cent. (Jan. 1989-) [Full Txt.] [Full Cov.]; Health Source (Jan. 1992-); INFO-SOUTH Abstr.; Mag. Search; Newsp. Period. Abstr. (1991-); Nutr. Res. Newsl.

US/0735-4762
**NUTRITION UPDATE (NEW YORK, N.Y.).** (NUTRITION UPDATE.). [Nutr. update]. Vol. 1 (1983)-. Academic Scholarly Publication. English. ir. Price varies per volume. John Wiley & Sons, Inc., 605 Third Avenue, New York NY 10158-0012. **Tel** (212)850-6000, (212)850-6645, FAX (212)850-6088, telex 12-7063. **(Subscription address:** John Wiley & Sons / England, Baffins Lane, Chichester, West Sussex PO19 1UD England.**) ED** Jean Weininger and George M. Briggs. **LC** QP141.A1; N89. **DD** 613.2/05. **NLM** W1; NU959. **CODEN** NUUPEQ. Documents available from CASDDS.
**Ind/Abst** AGRICOLA [Full Cov.]; Chem. Abstr. (1983-).

US/0736-0096
**NUTRITION WEEK.** (NUTRITION WEEK / COMMUNITY NUTRITION INSTITUTE.). [Nutr. week]. **Added/Corp** Community Nutrition Institute (Washington, D.C.). Vol. 13, No. 1 (Jan. 6, 1983)-. Periodical. English. wk. $70.00 US; $90.00 Canada; $120.00 other. Community Nutrition Institute, 2001 S Street Northwest, Suite 530, Washington DC 20009. **Tel** (202)462-4700, FAX (202)462-5241. **ED** Rodney E. Leonard. **NLM** W1; NU959F. **Bk Rev. Circ:** 3,100. ***Continues** CNI Weekly Report, 0191-0833.*
**Ind/Abst** AGRICOLA [Select. Cov.]; Foods Adlibra.

US
**NUTRITIONAL BIOCHEMICALS.** **VFOAT** ICN Nutritional Biochemicals Biochemicals. English. ICN Nutritional Biochemicals, PO Box 28050, Cleveland OH 44128.

US/0160-3922
**NUTRITIONAL PERSPECTIVES.** **Added/Corp** American Chiropractic Association. Council on Nutrition. Vol. 1, No. 1 (Jan. 1978)-. Periodical. English. Four times a year (Jan., Apr., July, Oct.). $20.00. Nutritional Perspectives, 231 Randolph Avenue, Front Royal VA 22630. **Tel** (703)635-8844. **ED** Gordon Lawson. **Bk Rev. Ad Acc.** ctrl circ.
**Desc:** Technical articles on nutrition.

CN/0229-1428
**O.N.E. NEWSLETTER.** [O.N.E. newsl.]. **VAT** Organization for Nutrition Education Newsletter. Vol. 1, No. 1 -. Newsletter. English. qt. 30.00Can$. O N E Newsletter, Organization for Nutrition Education, PO Box 818, Guelph Ontario N1H 6L8 Canada. **Tel** (705)748-6466. **ED** Brenda Moher. **DD** 641.1/05. **Bk Rev. Circ:** 250 (ctrl).
**Desc:** Issues on nutrition and latest tips on nutrition education programs and techniques.

US/1044-1522
**OBESITY & HEALTH.** ***Title Change.*** [Obes. health]. **Added/Corp** Healthy Living Institute. **VFOAT** Obesity and Health. Vol. 3, No. 8 (Aug. 1989)-Vol. 8, No. 2 (Mar./Apr. 1994). Periodical. English. bm. Health Living Institute, Rt 2 Box 905, Hettinger ND 58639. **Tel** (701)567-2845. **DD** 613. **NLM** W1; OB402I. **[CCC].** Index available. **Ad Acc. Circ:** 1,400. ***Continues** International Obesity Newsletter. **Continued by** Healthy Weight Journal, 1075-0169.*
**Desc:** Keeps health professionals up to date on a wide range of issues. Current scientific research and new paradigms in treatment and prevention.
**Ind/Abst** Acad. Abstr. Full Text Elite (Jan. 1992-) [Full Txt.]; Acad. Abstr. (Jan. 1992-); Acad. Search (Jan. 1992-April 1994); AGRICOLA; Curr. Index J. Educ.; Health Source (Jan. 1992-); INFO-SOUTH Abstr.; Mag. Artic. Summar. Elite (Jan. 1992-Apr. 1994) [Full Txt.]; Mag. Artic. Summar. CD-ROM (Jan. 1992-); Mag. Search; Soc. Work Abstr. [Select. Cov.].

US
**ONE PEACEFUL WORLD.** **See** Environmental Issues-Ecology.

US/0748-8394
**OUTPOST EXCHANGE.** **See** Consumer Interests.

US/1063-8822
**PENNINGTON CENTER NUTRITION SERIES.** (PENNINGTON CENTER NUTRITION SERIES / SPONSORED BY THE PENNINGTON BIOMEDICAL RESEARCH CENTER.). [Pennington Cent. nutr. ser.]. **Added/Corp** Pennington Biomedical Research Center. Vol. 1 (1991)-. Academic Scholarly Publication. English. Price varies per volume. Louisiana State University Press, PO Box 25053, Baton Rouge LA 70894. **Tel** (504)388-8271, FAX (504)388-6461. **DD** 612. **NLM** W1; PE289. **CODEN** PCNSEW. Documents available from CASDDS.
**Ind/Abst** AGRICOLA; Chem. Abstr. (1991-).

●US/1070-6224
**PERSPECTIVES IN APPLIED NUTRITION.** (1993)-. Periodical. English. qt. $74.95 (institutions), $49.95 (individuals) US; $78.95 (institutions), $53.95 (individuals) Canada; $88.95 (institutions), $63.95 (individuals) other. Mosby Year Book Inc., 11830 Westline Industrial Drive, St Louis MO 63146. **Tel** (800)325-4177, (314)872-8370, FAX (314)432-1380, telex 44-2402.

UK/0142-4857
**PETITS PROPOS CULINAIRES.** Academic Scholarly Publication. English. Three times a year. £11.00 (one year), £21.50 UK; $23.50 (one year), $45.00 (two year) US. PPC North America, 5311 42nd Street NW, Washington DC 20015. **Tel** (202)362-6986. **ED** Alan E Davidson. **LC** TX341; .P43. **DD** 641/.05. cum. index. **Bk Rev. Circ:** 1,000.
**Desc:** A scholarly journal with no advertising dealing with food and food history.

PH/0031-7640
**PHILIPPINE JOURNAL OF NUTRITION.** [Philipp. j. nutr.]. **Added/Corp** Philippine Association of Nutrition. Vol. 15, No. 3 (July/Sept. 1962)-. Academic Scholarly Publication. English. Four times a year. $12.00. Nutrition Foundation of Philippines, 107 East Rodriguez Sr., Boulevard, Quezon City Philippines. **ED** Velona A. Corpus. **LC** TX501; .N87. **DD** 363.8/05. **NLM** W1 PH569D. **CODEN** PJNUAF. **Bk Rev. Circ:** 1,500. Documents available from BIOSIS Document Express, CASDDS. ***Continues** Nutrition News.*
**Desc:** Researches on foods and nutrition and other commentaries related to the subject.
**Ind/Abst** Biol. Abstr.; Chem. Abstr.; EMBASE; Food Sci. Technol. Abstr.; Philip. Sci. Technol. Abstr.

US/1059-8073
**PILLSBURY FAST AND HEALTHY MAGAZINE.** ***Title Change.*** [Pillsbury fast heal. mag.]. **VFOAT** Fast and Healthy. (May 1992)-(199?). Periodical. English. bm. The Pillsbury Co., 200 S 6th St., Minneapolis MN 55402. **Tel** (612)330-5452. **ED** Diane Anderson. **DD** 641. **Ad Acc. Circ:** 100,000 (ctrl). ***Continued by** Fast and Healthy Magazine, 1078-0203.*
**Desc:** A food and lifestyle magazine focusing on low-fat, quick-to-make recipes and articles on wellbeing. Covers anything from nutrition information to how to entertain. The ratio is 50/50 recipes to editorial.

NE/0921-9668
**PLANT FOODS FOR HUMAN NUTRITION (DORDRECHT).** (PLANT FOODS FOR HUMAN NUTRITION.). [Plant foods hum. nutr.]. Vol. 37, No. 3 (1987)-. Periodical. English. Eight times a year. $800.00. Kluwer Academic Publishers, Postbus 322, 3300 AH Dordrecht, The Netherlands. **Tel** 011 (31) 78 524400, FAX 011 31 78 183273, telex 20083. **ED** Constance V Kies. **LC** TX341; .P58. **DD** 641.3/03/05. **NLM** W1; PL105LV. **CODEN** PFHNE8. **[CCC]. Ad Acc. Pr Rev. Acid Free. Circ:** 210. available on microfilm and microfiche from University Microfilms International (UMI). Documents available from The Genuine Article, BIOSIS Document Express. ***Continues** Qualitas Plantarum - Plant Foods for Human Nutrition, 0377-3205.*
**Ind/Abst** AGRICOLA [Full Cov.]; Biodeter. Abstr. (1991-); Biol. Abstr. (1988-); Crop Physiol. Abstr.; Curr. Aware. Biol. Sci., CABS; Curr. Contents, Agric. Biol. Environ. Sci.; Dairy Sci. Abstr.; Field Crop Abstr.; Food Sci. Technol. Abstr.; Hortic. Abstr.; Index Med. (Vol. 37, No. 3, 1987-); Irr. Drain. Abstr.; Maize Abstr.; Nematol. Abstr.; Nutr. Abstr. Rev., Ser. B, Live Feeds and Feed.; Nutr. Abstr. Rev., Ser. A, Hum. Exp.; Plant Breed. Abstr.; Plant Genet. Resour. Abstr.; Postharvest News Inf.; Potato Abstr.; Res. Alert [Select. Cov.]; Rev. Med. Vet. Mycology; Rice Abstr.; SCISEARCH; Seed Abstr.; Soc. Sci. Cit. Index [Select. Cov.]; Soils Fert.; Sorghum Mill. Abstr.; Soyabean Abstr.; Wheat Barley Trit. Abstr.

BU/0205-003X
**PROBLEMI NA HRANENETO.** (PROBLEMI NA KHRANENETO.). [Probl. hran.]. **Added/Corp** Meditsinska Akademiia (Sofia, Bulgaria). Vol. 1 (1979)-. Academic Scholarly Publication. Bulgarian (summaries and/or abstracts in English and Russian). Izdatelstvo Medicina i Fizkult, PL Slavejkov 11, 1000 Sofia Bulgaria. **NLM** W1 PR572ER. **CODEN** PRKHEL. Documents available from CASDDS.
**Ind/Abst** Chem. Abstr.

UK/0029-6651
**PROCEEDINGS OF THE NUTRITION SOCIETY.** [Proc. Nutr. Soc.]. **Main/Corp** Nutrition Society. **Added/Corp** Nutrition Society (Great Britain). Vol. 1, Nos. 1 and 2 (1944)-. Academic Scholarly Publication. English. Three times a year. $240.00 US, Canada and Mexico; £126.00 other. Cambridge University Press, The Edinburgh Building, Shaftesbury Road, Cambridge CB2 2RU United Kingdom. **Tel** 011 44 223 312393, FAX 011 44 223 325959. **(Subscription address:** Cambridge University Press / North America, 110 Midland Avenue, Port Chester NY 10573.**) ED** D. A. T. Southgate and J. C. Mathers. **LC** TX501; .N9. **DD** 641.06242. **NLM** W1 PR586HN. **CODEN** PNUSA4. **[CCC]. Pr Rev.** available on microfilm and microfiche from University Microfilms International (UMI). Documents available from The Genuine Article, BIOSIS Document Express, CASDDS, Documents on Demand.
**Desc:** Contains full versions of papers read at symposia organized by the Society. Invited speakers are nutritional scientists from all over the world. Topics cover a wide variety of nutritional fields, including all aspects of the effect of nutrients upon the health, metabolism and tissue function of man, laboratory and farm animals. Abstracts of short communications, presented at meetings by members of the Society, are also included and provide a means of keeping in touch with current research developments and views.
**Ind/Abst** AGRICOLA [Full Cov.]; Biodeter. Abstr. (1991-); Biol. Agric. Index; Biol. Abstr.; Chem. Abstr.; Curr. Aware. Biol. Sci., CABS; Curr. Contents, Agric. Biol. Environ. Sci.; Curr. Contents Life Sci.; Dairy Sci. Abstr.; Energy Inf. Abstr.; Environ. Abstr.; Food Sci. Technol. Abstr.; Foods Adlibra; Index Med.; Leadscan; Nutr. Abstr. Rev., Ser. B, Live Feeds and Feed.; Nutr. Abstr. Rev., Ser. A, Hum. Exp.; Nutr. Res. Newsl.; Life Sci. Collect.; PESTDOC; Pig News Inf.; Poult. Abstr.; Res. Alert [Full Cov.]; Sci. Cit. Index; SCISEARCH; Soc. Sci. Cit. Index [Select. Cov.]; Sug. Indus. Abstr.; Trop. Dis. Bull.

AT/0314-1004
**PROCEEDINGS OF THE NUTRITION SOCIETY OF AUSTRALIA.** (PROCEEDINGS OF THE NUTRITION SOCIETY OF AUSTRALIA / ... ANNUAL CONFERENCE.). [Proc. nutr. soc. Aust.]. **Main/Corp** Nutrition Society of Australia. Conference. 1st (Aug. 1976)-. Academic Scholarly Publication. English. an (Nov.). 40.00Aus$ Australia & New Zealand; 45.00Aus$ others. Nutrition Society of Australia, 98 Stanley Street, Nedlands WA 6009 Australia. **Tel** 011 61 9 387 4233, FAX 011 61 9 387 6046, telex 92178. **ED** J. R. Mercer. **NLM** W1; NU947. **CODEN** PNSADB. Index available. **Circ:** 800 (ctrl). Documents available from BIOSIS Document Express, CASDDS.
**Desc:** Proceedings of the Annual Scientific Conference of the Nutrition Society of Australia.
**Ind/Abst** AGRICOLA [Full Cov.]; Anim. Breed. Abstr.; Biol. Abstr.; Chem. Abstr.; Nutr. Abstr. Rev., Ser. B, Live Feeds and Feed.; Nutr. Abstr. Rev., Ser. A, Hum. Exp.; Pig News Inf.; Poult. Abstr.; Soyabean Abstr.

II/0253-7567
**PROCEEDINGS OF THE NUTRITION SOCIETY OF INDIA.** [Proc. Nutr. Soc. India]. **Main/Corp** Nutrition Society of India. No. 1-. Proceedings. English. Price varies per volume. **NLM** W3 PR945SL.
**Ind/Abst** Agrofor. Abstr.; Dairy Sci. Abstr.; Rice Abstr.

NZ/0110-4187
**PROCEEDINGS OF THE NUTRITION SOCIETY OF NEW ZEALAND.** [Proc. Nutr. Soc. N. Z.]. **Main/Corp** Nutrition Society of New Zealand. (1977)-. Proceedings. English. an. 30.00NZ$. Lincoln University / New Zealand, Dr. G. P. Savage, PO Box 84, Cantebury New Zealand. **Tel** 011 64 3 3252811. **NLM** W1 PR586HS. ***Continues*** *Nutrition Society of New Zealand. Proceedings of the Nutrition Society.*
**Ind/Abst** Grasslands For. Abstr.; Nutr. Abstr. Rev., Ser. B, Live Feeds and Feed.; Wheat Barley Trit. Abstr.

US/0163-6847
**PROCEEDINGS - WESTERN HEMISPHERE NUTRITION CONGRESS.** ***Ceased.*** **Main/Conf** Western Hemisphere Nutrition Congress. **Added/Corp** American Institute of Nutrition. Council on Foods and Nutrition (American Medical Association) Nutrition Society of Canada. Sociedad Latinoamericana de Nutricion. 1st (1965)-(19??). Proceedings. English. Publishing Sciences Group Inc, 545 Great Road, Littleton MA 01460. **Tel** (617)486-8971. **LC** TX345; .W4. **DD** 338.1/9/1812. **NLM** W3 WE521.

US
**PRODUCT PROFILES NUTRIENT UPDATE.** (19??)-. English. qt (Jan., April, July, Oct.). $26.25. Product Profiles, 10390 Hinton Mill Rd., Marysville OH 43040. **Tel** (614)666-5491. **ED** Gail Crosser. Index available (October issue - free of charge). **Circ:** 300.
**Desc:** Nutrient composition of 525 new convenience foods and fast foods. Includes carbohydrate, protein, fat, saturated fat, polyunsaturated fat, monounsaturated fat, cholesterol, sodium, potassium, dietary fiber, Vitamin A, Vitamin C, iron and calcium.

US/0735-2395
**PROGRAM PLAN - UNITED STATES. FOOD SAFETY AND INSPECTION SERVICE.** (PROGRAM PLAN / FOOD SAFETY AND INSPECTION SERVICE.). [Program plan - U. S. Food Saf. Insp. Serv.]. **Main/Corp** United States. Food Safety and Inspection Service. **VFOAT** Food Safety and Inspection Service Program Plan. Fiscal Year 1982-. English. an. United States Department of Agriculture / Food Safety and Inspection Service, Washington DC 20250. **LC** TX501; .U56A. **DD** 353.0077/82.

UK/0306-0632
**PROGRESS IN FOOD & NUTRITION SCIENCE.** ***Title Change.*** [Prog. food nutr. sci.]. Vol. 1 (1975)-(19??). Periodical. English. bm. Pergamon Press, An Imprint of Elsevier Science Ltd., The Boulevard, Langford Lane, Kidlington, Oxford OX5 1GB United Kingdom. **Tel** 011 44 865 843000, 011 44 865 843699, FAX 011 44 865 843010. **(Subscription address:** US/ 395 Saw Mill River Road, Elmsford, NY 10523; Can/ 150 Consumers Road/Suite 104, Willowdale Ontario M2J 1P9; Aus-NZ/ POB 544, Potts Point NSW 2011**) ED** Ramkot Chandra. **LC** QP141.A1; P73. **DD** 612/.3. **NLM** W1 PR668V. **CODEN** PFNSDI. **[CCC]. Pr Rev.** available on microfilm and microfiche from University Microfilms International (UMI). Documents available from The Genuine Article, BIOSIS Document Express, CASDDS. ***Merged into*** *Nutrition Research.*
**Ind/Abst** AGRICOLA [Select. Cov.]; Biodeter. Abstr. (1991-); Biol. Abstr.; Chem. Abstr.; CSA Neuro. Abstr. (?-?); Curr. Aware. Biol. Sci., CABS; Curr. Contents, Agric. Biol. Environ. Sci.; Dairy Sci. Abstr.; Food Sci. Technol. Abstr.; Foods Adlibra; Index Med.; Index Sci. Rev. [Full Cov.]; Nutr. Abstr. Rev., Ser. A, Hum. Exp.; Life Sci. Collect.; Res. Alert [Full Cov.]; Sci. Cit. Index; SCISEARCH; SportSearch.

FR
**PUBLICATIONS DE L'UNITE DE BIOCHIMIE DE LA NUTRITION.** French. Ten times a year. 800.00F. Univ Catholique Louvain / IRES, Place Montesquieu 3 Bte 4, B-1348 Louvain Belgium. **Tel** 011 32 10 474152.
**Ind/Abst** Soyabean Abstr.

IT/0033-488X
**QUADERNI DELLA NUTRIZIONE.** Periodical. Italian. qt. Ist Nazion Della Nutriz, Citta Universitaria, Rome Italy.
**Ind/Abst** Index Med.

HT
**RAPPORT DES ACTIVITES DU BUREAU DE NUTRITION.** **Main/Corp** Haiti (Republic). Bureau de Nutrition. French. Departement de la Sante Publique et de la Population, Bureau de Nutrition, Port-Au-Prince Haiti. **LC** TX360.H2; H34A. **DD** 354.72940084/1.

UK/0260-8170
**RECENT ADVANCES IN CLINICAL NUTRITION.** (RECENT ADVANCES IN CLINICAL NUTRITION : PROCEEDINGS OF THE ... INTERNATIONAL SYMPOSIUM ON CLINICAL NUTRITION.). [Recent adv. clin. nutr.]. **Main/Conf** International Symposium on Clinical Nutrition. 1st (9-11 July 1980)-. Academic Scholarly Publication. English. John Libbey & Company Ltd, 13 Smiths Yard, Summerley Street, London SW18 4HR England. **Tel** 01-947 2777, FAX 01-947 2664, telex 94013503 JOHN G. **ED** A N Howard and I M Baird. **NLM** W3 IN916VM. **CODEN** RENUD5. Documents available from CASDDS.
**Ind/Abst** Chem. Abstr.

CN/0226-2649
**REPERTOIRE DES MEMBRES - CORPORATION PROFESSIONNELLE DES DIETETISTES DU QUEBEC.** [Repert. membres - Corp. prof. diet. Que.]. **Main/Corp** Corporation Professionnelle des Dietetistes du Quebec. (1978/1979)-. French. be. Corporation Professionnelle des Dietetistes du Quebec, 934 Est rue Ste-Catherine/Bureau 130, Montreal Quebec H2L 2E9 Canada. **Tel** (514)842-7923. **DD** 613.2/06/0714. ***Continues*** *Corporation Professionnelle de Dietetistes du Quebec. Membres, 0318-8175.*

UK/0301-4924
**REPORT BY THE SUB-COMMITTEE ON NUTRITIONAL SURVEILLANCE (LONDON).** (REPORT BY THE SUB-COMMITTEE ON NUTRITIONAL SURVEILLANCE.). **Main/Corp** Great Britain. Committee on Medical Aspects of Food Policy. Subcommittee on Nutritional Surveillance. **VFOAT** Report; Report by the Subcommittee on Nutritional Surveillance. 1st (1973)-. English. **NLM** W1 RE212VM no. 6 etc.

AT/0155-1507
**REPORT / CSIRO, DIVISION OF HUMAN NUTRITION.** [Rep. - CSIRO Div. Hum. Nutr.]. **Main/Corp** Commonwealth Scientific and Industrial Research Organization (Australia). Division of Human Nutrition. (1975/1976)-. English. be. CSIRO Publications, PO Box 89, 314 Albert Street, East Melborne Victoria 3002 Australia. **Tel** 011 61 3 4187333, 4187217, FAX 011 61 3 4190459, telex AA 30236. **NLM** W2; KA8 C78r. ***Continues*** *Research Report - Division of Nutritional Biochemistry, Commonwealth Scientific and Industrial Research Organization, 0069-7532.*

PH
**REPORT OF THE NUTRITION CENTER OF THE PHILIPPINES.** **Main/Corp** Nutrition Center of the Philippines. 1974/75-. English. Nutrition Center of the Philippines, South Superhighway Rizal, Makati Philippines. **LC** TX367; .N87A. **DD** 363.

US
**REPORT TO THE SENATE ON THE JURISDICTION AND A SUMMARY OF ACTIVITIES OF THE COMMITTEE ON AGRICULTURE, NUTRITION, AND FORESTRY FOR THE ... CONGRESS.** **Main/Corp** United States. Congress. Senate. Committee on Agriculture, Nutrition, and Forestry. English. be.

FR
**REPRODUCTION, NUTRITION, DEVELOPMENT.** **Added/Corp** Institut National de la Recherche Agronomique (France). Vol. 29, No. 1 (1975)-. Academic Scholarly Publication. English (French). bm (6 issues). 1490.00F France; 1820.00F other. Editions Scientifique Elsevier, 141 rue de Javel, 75747 Paris Cedex 15 France. **Tel** 011 33 1 47 07 11 22, FAX 011 33 1 43 36 80 93. **(Subscription address:** Editions Scientifiques Elsevier / for North America, PO Box 7247-7576, Philadelphia PA 19170-7576.**) NLM** W1; RE213KN. **CODEN** RNDEE5. **Pr Rev.** Documents available from The Genuine Article, BIOSIS Document Express, CASDDS. ***Continues*** *Reproduction, Nutrition, Developpement, 0181-1916.*
**Ind/Abst** AgBiotech News Inf.; Biol. Abstr.; Chem. Abstr.; Curr. Aware. Biol. Sci., CABS; Curr. Contents, Agric. Biol. Environ. Sci.; Curr. Contents Life Sci.; EMBASE [Select. Cov.]; Grasslands For. Abstr.; Helminthol. Abstr. (1991-); Index Med. (1989-); Nutr. Abstr. Rev., Ser. A, Hum. Exp.; Postharvest News Inf.; Res. Alert [Full Cov.]; Rev. Med. Vet. Entomol.; Sci. Cit. Index; SCISEARCH; Soyabean Abstr.; Sug. Indus. Abstr.; Wheat Barley Trit. Abstr.

US
**RESEARCH PROGRAMS OF THE NATIONAL INSTITUTE OF CHILD HEALTH AND HUMAN DEVELOPMENT. NUTRITION AND ENDOCRINOLOGY.** **Main/Corp** Center for Research for Mothers and Children (U.S.). Nutrition and Endocrinology Section. **VFOAT** Nutrition and Endocrinology. English. be. National Institute of Child Health and Human Development / Mothers and Children, Center for Research for Mothers and Children, Nutrition and Endocrinology Section, 9000 Rockville Pike, Bethesda MD 20014.

GT/0304-4033
**REVISTA CENTROAMERICANA DE NUTRICION Y CIENCIAS DE ALIMENTOS.** V. 1- Jan./March 1976-. Periodical. Spanish. qt. Instituto de Nutricion de Centro America y Panama, Apartado 1188, Carretera Roosevelt Zona 11, Guatemala Guatemala. **LC** TX367; .R48. **NLM** W1 RE3464.

CL/0716-1549
**REVISTA CHILENA DE NUTRICION : ORGANO OFICIAL DE LA SOCIEDAD CHILENA DE NUTRICION, BROMATOLOGIA Y TOXICOLOGIA.** **Added/Corp** Sociedad Chilena de Nutricion, Bromatologia y Toxicologia. (198?)-. Periodical. Spanish (summaries and/or abstracts in English; table of contents in English and Spanish). Three times a year. $25.00. Sociedad Chilena de Nutricion, Guayaquil 34 Dept 3 C, Santiago Chile. **Tel** 011 56 2 335633. **NLM** W1; RE349F. ***Continues*** *Nutricion, Bromatologia, Toxicologia.*
**Ind/Abst** Nutr. Abstr. Rev., Ser. B, Live Feeds and Feed.; Nutr. Abstr. Rev., Ser. A, Hum. Exp.; Poult. Abstr.

CU/0864-2133
**REVISTA CUBANA ALIMENTACION Y NUTRICION.** (198?)-. Spanish. qt. **NLM** W1; RE359BT.
**Ind/Abst** Nutr. Abstr. Rev., Ser. A, Hum. Exp.; Pig News Inf.

SP
**REVISTA DE LA SOCIEDAD ESPANOLA DE NUTRICION PARENTERAL Y ENTERAL.** Spanish. S.E.N.P.E., Villanueva 11, 28001 Madrid Spain.

FR
**REVUE FRANCAISE DE DIETETIQUE.** French. qt. 160.00F, 50.00F (single issue) France; 240.00F, 60.00F (single issue) other. Syndicat Natl Prof Dieteticien, 95 rue de la Loubiere, 13005 Marseille France. **Tel** 011 33 91 481045.
**Ind/Abst** Food Sci. Technol. Abstr.

JA/0485-1412
**RINSHO EIYO.** [Rinsho eiyo]. **VFOAT** Journal of Clinical Nutrition. (1952)-. Periodical. Japanese. Fourteen times a year. $186.00. **(Subscription address:** Kyowa Book Company Inc., 1-38 Kanda Jinbo-Cho, Chiyoda-Ku Tokyo 101, Japan) **CODEN** RNEYAW.

IT/0391-4887
**RIVISTA DELLA SOCIETA ITALIANA DI SCIENZA DELL'ALIMENTAZIONE, LA.** **See** Food and Food Industry.

IT/0393-5582
**RIVISTA ITALIANA DI NUTRIZIONE PARENTERALE ED ENTERALE : ORGANO UFFICIALE DELLA SOCIETA ITALIANA DI NUTRIZIONE PARENTERALE ED ENTERALE, SINPE - GASAPE.** **Added/Corp** Societa Italiana di Nutrizione Parenterale ed Enterale. (198?)-. Periodical. Italian (English). Three times a year. L90000 (Italy); $90.00 (Europe); $120.00 (other). Wichtig Editore, Via Friuli 72 74, 20135 Milan Italy. **Tel** 011 39 2 55195443. **NLM** W1; RI776N.
**Ind/Abst** EMBASE.

US/1051-6646
**RODALE'S FOOD AND NUTRITION LETTER.** ***Ceased.*** [Rodale's food nutr. lett.]. **VFOAT** Food and Nutrition Letter; Food and Nutrition. Vol. 4, No. 10 (Oct. 1990)-Ceased (Jan. 1992). Periodical. English. mo. Rodale Press Inc., 400 South 10th Street, Emmaus PA 18098. **Tel** (215)967-5171, (800)666-2503. **DD** 613. **CODEN** RFNLEK. ***Continues*** *Lose Weight Naturally Newsletter, 0892-7294.*

SA/1013-3666
**SA JOURNAL OF FOOD SCIENCE AND NUTRITION, THE.** [SA j. food sci. nutr.]. **VFOAT** Tydskrif vir Voedselwetenskap en Voeding. (1989)-. Periodical. English (Afrikaans). qt (4 issues). R50.00. South African Journal of Food Science and Nutrition, PO Box 3230, Northcliff 2115 South Africa. **Tel** 011 27 673 9457, FAX 011 27 673 9457. **ED** Professors HJH de Muelenaerg and Pettifur (editors' telephone: 011 12 841 3224). Index available (bound in Vol. 5, No. 1). cum. index (up to Vol. 4, No. 6). **Bk Rev** (Qty: varies). **Ad Acc, Adv Mgr:** J. Sharland, **Tel** same as publisher. **Pr Rev. Circ:** 2,500 (ctrl). Documents available from CASDDS.
**Desc:** Covers food, dairy science and nutrition.
**Ind/Abst** Chem. Abstr.

●SW/1102-6480
**SCANDINAVIAN JOURNAL OF NUTRITION NARINGSFORSKNING.** [Scand. j. nutr.]. **VFOAT** Naringsforskning. (1992)-. Periodical. Multiple languages. Four times a year (Apr., June, Oct., Dec.). Kr216.00. Naringsforskning, IDEON, S-223070 Lund Sweden. **Tel** 011 46 31 400120. **ED** Bo Hallgren. **UDC** 61. **Bk Rev** (Qty: 1-4). **Pr Rev. Circ:** 2,500. ***Continues*** *Naringsforskning, 0027-7878.*

II
**SCIENTIFIC REPORT / NUTRITION FOUNDATION OF INDIA.** **Added/Corp** Nutrition Foundation of India. (1983)-. Monographic series. English. **NLM** W1; SC864HH.
**Ind/Abst** Nutr. Abstr. Rev., Ser. A, Hum. Exp.

US
**SCN NEWS / UNITED NATIONS, ADMINISTRATIVE COMMITTEE ON COORDINATION, SUBCOMMITTEE ON NUTRITION.** **Added/Corp** United Nations. Administrative Committee on Co-Ordination. Sub-Committee on Nutrition. **VAT** Subcommittee on Nutrition News. No. 1 (Mar. 30, 1988)-. Periodical. English. sa. Free upon request. World Health Organization, Distribution and Sales, 20 Avenue Appia, CH-1211 Geneva 27 Switzerland. **Tel** 011 41 22 7912111, FAX 011 41 22 7880401. **NLM** W1; SC875PF.
**Ind/Abst** Int. Dev. Abstr.; Trop. Dis. Bull.

JA/0286-6366
**SEITOKU EIYO TANKI DAIGAKU KIYO.** [Seitoku Eiyo Tanki Daigaku kiyo]. **Added/Corp** Seitoku Eiyo Tanki Daigaku. **VFOAT** Memoirs of Seitoku Junior College of Nutrition; Kiyo. (1965)-. Periodical. Japanese. an. Seitoku Junior College of Nutrition, Nishishinkoiwa 1-4-6, Katsushika-ku, Tokyo 124 Japan. **CODEN** KSTDD5. Documents available from CASDDS.
**Ind/Abst** Chem. Abstr.

US/0898-5995
**SEMINARS IN NUTRITION.** [Semin. nutr.]. Vol. 3, No. 1 (Aug./Sept. 1983)-. Periodical. English. Six times a year. $60.00. Seminars in Nutrition, PO Box 3525, Littleton CO 80161. **Tel** (303)771-6256. **ED** Thersea Beaudette. **DD** 613. **NLM** W1; SE489DB. **Circ:** 4,500 (ctrl). ***Continues*** *Nutrition in Practice.*
**Ind/Abst** AGRICOLA [Full Cov.].

SP/0212-4637
**SENPE. REVISTA DE LA SOCIEDAD ESPANOLA DE NUTRICION PARENTERAL Y ENTERAL.** **VFOAT** Sociedad Espanola de Nutricion Parenteral y Enteral; Revista de S.E.N.P.E.; Revista de la S.E.N.P.E. (1983)-. Periodical. Spanish. bm. Jarpyo Editores SA, Antonio Lopez Aguados 4, 28029 Madrid, Spain. **Tel** 011 34 1 3144338, 011 34 1 3144458. **UDC** 611.14.

SW/0436-2071
**SIK-RAPPORT.** [SIK-rapp.]. **Main/Corp** SIK-Svenska Livsmedelsinstitutet. Academic Scholarly Publication. Swedish. Price varies per volume. SIK, Box 5401, S-40229 Goteborg Sweden. **Tel** +46 31355600, FAX +46 31833782. **LC** TX341; .G63. **CODEN** SIKRDK. Index available. cum. index. ctrl circ. Documents available from CASDDS. ***Continues*** *SIK-Rapport.*
**Desc:** Research report.
**Ind/Abst** AGRICOLA; Chem. Abstr. (1977); Dairy Sci. Abstr.; Food Sci. Technol. Abstr.

US/0744-2343
**SNE COMMUNICATOR.** ***Ceased.*** (SNE COMMUNICATOR : NEWSLETTER OF THE SOCIETY FOR NUTRITION EDUCATION.). **VFOAT** S.N.E. Communicator. **VAT** Society for Nutrition Education Communicator. ?. Newsletter. English. qt. Society for Nutrition Education, 2140 Shattuck Avenue, Suite 1110, Berkeley CA 94704. **Tel** (510)444-7133.

US
**SOURCEBOOK ON FOOD AND NUTRITION.** ***Ceased.*** 1st- Ed.-Ceased with 3rd Ed.-?. English. ir. Marquis Who's Who, A Reed Reference Publishing Company, Part of Reed International PLC, 121 Chanlon Road, New Providence NJ 07974. **Tel** (908)464-6800, (800)521-8110, FAX (908)665-6688, telex 138 755. **NLM** QU 145.3 S724.
**Desc:** Volume presents 400 selected articles on nutritional subjects.

US/8755-9188
**SOYFOODS.** [Soyfoods]. Vol. 1, No. 3 (Summer 1980)-. Periodical. English. qt. $15.00. Soycrafters Association of North America, Sunrise Farm, Heath Road, Colrain MA 01340. **LC** TX558.S7; S693. **DD** 641.3/5655. ***Continues*** *Soycraft.*

GH/0378-2239
**SPECIAL PAPER - JOINT FAO/WHO/OAU REGIONAL FOOD AND NUTRITION COMMISSION FOR AFRICA.** **See** Food and Food Industry.

US/1048-8413
**SPECIALTY COOKING.** [Spec. cook.]. **VFOAT** Specialty Cooking Cookbook Magazine. No. 9 (July 1989)-. Periodical. English. bm. $15.50. Frederick Fell Publishers Inc, 2131 Hollywood Boulevard, Suite 204, Hollywood FL 33020. **Tel** (305)925-5242, FAX (302)925-5244. **ED** Barbara Newman. **DD** 641. Index available. **Ad Acc. Pr Rev. Circ:** 50,000. ***Continues*** *Fell's Cookbook Series.*
**Desc:** Contains recipes and food ideas.

UK
**SPORTS NUTRITION.** (19??)-. English. bm (6 issues). £7.50. National Sports Medicine Institute, c/o Medical College of St. Bartholomew's Hospital, Charterhouse Square, London EC1M 6BQ United Kingdom. **Tel** 011 44 71 251 0583, FAX 011 44 71 251 0774.

US
**STATE PLAN OF SCHOOL NUTRITION PROGRAMS / BUREAU OF FOOD AND NUTRITION SERVICES.** **See** Education-School Organization and Administration.

US/0039-2308
**STRENGTH AND HEALTH.** ***Ceased.*** **See** Health and Personal Fitness.

●US/1067-3768
**SUPPORT LINE (CHICAGO, ILL.).** (SUPPORT LINE : A NEWSLETTER OF DIETITIANS IN NUTRITION SUPPORT.). [Support line]. **Added/Corp** Dietitians in Nutrition Support. (1992)-. Periodical. English. Six times a year. $20.00. American Dietetic Association, 216 West Jackson Boulevard, Suite 800, Chicago IL 60606. **Tel** (312)899-0040, (800)877-1600. **DD** 613. **NLM** W1; SU694. ***Continues*** *Dietitians in Nutrition Support : [Newsletter], 0892-5879.*

SW/0082-0415
**SYMPOSIA OF THE SWEDISH NUTRITION FOUNDATION.** [Symp. Swed. Nutr. Found.]. **Added/Corp** Stiftelsen Svensk Naringsforskning. (1962)-. Academic Scholarly Publication. English. ir. Price varies per volume. Almqvist & Wiksell International, PO Box 4627, S-11691 Stockholm Sweden. **Tel** 011-46-8-6408800. **NLM** W1 SY432M. **CODEN** SSNFAW. Documents available from BIOSIS Document Express, CASDDS.
**Ind/Abst** Biol. Abstr.; Chem. Abstr. (1963-1978).

CC/0253-6080
**TIAOWEI FUSHIPIN KEJI.** (TIAO WEI FU SHIH PIN KO CHI.). [Tiaowei fushipin keji]. **VFOAT** Tiaoweifushipinkeji. Academic Scholarly Publication. Chinese. mo. RMBY0.30. Tiao Wei Fu Shih Pin Ko Chi Tsa Chih, Tai Hao 14-13, Post Office, Harbin, People's Republic of China. **LC** TX553.A3; T5. **DD** 664/.06/05. **CODEN** TFKED5. Documents available from CASDDS.
**Ind/Abst** Chem. Abstr. (1979-1984).

US/0883-5691
**TOPICS IN CLINICAL NUTRITION.** [Topics clin. nutr.]. **VFOAT** TICN. Vol. 1, No. 1 (Jan. 1985)-. Periodical. English. qt. $69.00 US and Canada. Aspen Publishers Inc., 7201 McKinney Circle, Frederick MD 21701. **Tel** (800)234-1660, (301)698-7100, FAX (301)251-5784, telex 5106014543. **(Subscription address:** Aspen Publishers Inc., PO Box 990, Frederick MD 21701.) **ED** Margaret D. Simko, PhD, RD and Judith A. Gillbride, PhD, RD. **DD** 613. **NLM** W1; TO539LG. **[CCC]. Bk Rev. Ad Acc. Pr Rev. Circ:** 4,000. available on microfilm and microfiche from University Microfilms International (UMI). ***Absorbed*** *Nutrition Clinics.*
**Desc:** Serves as a resource for the continuing education and clinical practice of dietitians and nutritionists. Each issue concentrates on a single area of major concern. Offers the latest results of research, case studies, and practical strategies to use immediately.
**Ind/Abst** AGRICOLA [Select. Cov.].

CN/0843-6584
**TRACE MINERALS, FOOD AND HEALTH.** (TRACE MINERALS, FOOD AND HEALTH NEWSLETTER.). [Trace miner. food health]. **VFOAT** Trace Minerals, Food and Health. Vol. 1, No. 1 (Spring 1989)-. Periodical. English. Three times a year. 25.00Can$ Canada; $30.00 US $35.00 other. Argo Elements, 218 Wineva Avenue, Toronto Ontario M4E 2T4 Canada. **Tel** (416)690-8254. **ED** John Hannigan and Ruth Hannigan. **DD** 612/.3924.
**Desc:** A newsletter of special interest to medical and health science libraries in Canada and the US.

US/0747-4105
**TUFTS UNIVERSITY DIET & NUTRITION LETTER.** [Tufts Univ. diet nutr. lett.]. **Added/Corp** Tufts University. **VFOAT** Tufts University Diet and Nutrition Letter; Diet and Nutrition Letter; Diet & Nutrition Letter. Vol. 1, No. 1 (March 1983)-. Periodical. English. mo. $20.00 (1 year), $36.00 (2 year), $50.00 (3 year). W. H. White Publications, Inc., 53 Park Place, 8th Floor, New York NY 10007. **Tel** (212)608-6515. **(Subscription address:** Neodata / Colorado, PO Box 2606, Boulder Boulder CO 80322.) **DD** 613. **NLM** W1; TU64K. **CODEN** TUDLET. available on an online database (file 149/Full-Text) from DIALOG. Documents available from UMI Article Clearinghouse.
**Ind/Abst** Acad. Abstr. Full Text Elite (Jan. 1992-) [Full Txt.]; Acad. Abstr. (Jan. 1992-); Acad. Ind. [Computer File] (1992-); Acad. Search (Jan. 1992-); AGRICOLA [Select. Cov.]; BioBusiness (1990-); Consum. Health Nutr. Index (Jan. 1990); Cumul. Index Nurs. Allied Health Lit.; Expand. Acad. Index (1992-); Foods Adlibra; Gen. Period. Index (1992-); Health Index (1989-); Health Period. Database [Full Txt.]; Health Ref. Cent. (Jan. 1989-) [Full Txt.] [Full Cov.]; Health Source (Jan. 1992-); INFO-SOUTH Abstr.; Mag. Artic. Summar. Elite (Jan. 1992-) [Full Txt.]; Mag. Artic. Summar. CD-ROM (Jan. 1992-); Mag. ASAP Plus [Full Txt.]; Mag. Index Plus (1989-); Mag. Search; Newsp. Period. Abstr. (1992-).

US/0270-7918
**ULTRANUTRITION DIGEST.** [UltraNutr. dig.]. V. 1- July 1980-. Periodical. English. bm. $15.00. Ultranutrition Institute, 1825 NE 149 Street, Miami FL 33161.

CN/0823-8332
**UP-DATE - B.C. NUTRITION COUNCIL.** (UPDATE : B.C. NUTRITION COUNCIL NEWSLETTER.). [Up-date - B.C. Nutr. Counc.]. **Added/Corp** B. C. Nutrition Council. (1975)-. Periodical. English. Four times a year (Jan., Apr., July, Oct.). 14.00Can$ Canada; 16.00Can$ other. British Columbia Nutrition Council, PO Box 459, 916 West Broadway, Vancouver BC V5Z 1K7 Canada. **ED** Laurie Cheung (editor's address: 6649 Dumfries Street, Vancouver, British Columbia V5P 3B6 Canada (phone: (604)325-8905). **DD** 613.2/05. **Bk Rev. Ad Acc. Circ:** 100.
**Desc:** Presents current information on nutrition-related issues and resources. Provides a great opportunity for information sharing, teamwork and networking.

SW/0042-2657
**VAR FODA.** [Var foda]. **Added/Corp** Statens Institut for Folkhalsan (Sweden) Sweden. Statens Livsmedelsverk. (1949)-. Academic Scholarly Publication. Swedish. Ten times a year (monthly except June and July). Kr210.00 Sweden; Kr290.00 other. Var Foda, Statens Livsmedelsverk, POB 622, 751 26 Uppsala Sweden. **Tel** 46 18 175500, FAX 46 18 105848. **LC** TX341; .V37. **CODEN** VAFOAS. Documents available from CASDDS.
**Desc:** The official publication of the Swedish National Food Administration. Contains research reports, articles, and policy matters that concern all areas of food control.

**Ind/Abst** AGRICOLA; Biodeter. Abstr. (1991-); Chem. Abstr.; Dairy Sci. Abstr.; Index Vet.; Nutr. Abstr. Rev., Ser. A, Hum. Exp.; Pig News Inf.; Rev. Med. Vet. Mycology; World Agric. Econ.

UK/0260-3233
**VEGETARIAN (ALTRINCHAM, CHESHIRE : 1980).** (THE VEGETARIAN : OFFICIAL JOURNAL OF THE VEGETARIAN SOCIETY (UK).). **Added/Corp** Vegetarian Society (U.K.). (19??)-. Periodical. English. Four times a year (Spring, Summer, Fall, Winter). £14.00 UK; £21.00 Europe; £21.00 others (surface mail); £24.00 others (airmail). Vegetarian Society Ltd, Parkdale Dunham Road, Altrincham Cheshire England. **Tel** 061 928 0793, FAX 0619269182. **ED** Carol Timperley. **LC** TX392; .A43. **DD** 613.2/62/05. **Bk Rev**, (Qty: 10). **Ad Acc, Adv Mgr:** Sue Stobart. **Circ:** 13,000 (ctrl). ***Continues*** *Alive (Altrincham, Cheshire).*
**Desc:** This magazine contains news, campaigns updates and hard-hitting features on the issues that most concern vegetarians today.

US/0885-7636 #y 0883-1165
**VEGETARIAN JOURNAL.** (1985)-. Periodical. English. Six times a year (Jan., Mar., May, July, Sept., Nov.). $20.00 (member); $30.00 (contributors); $50.00 (supporters); $100.00 (sustaining members). The Vegetarian Resource Group, PO Box 1463, Baltimore MD 21203-1463. **Tel** (410)366-8343. **ED** Debra Wassesman. **Bk Rev. Pr Rev. Circ:** 26,000 (ctrl). available on microfilm; available on an online database from University Microfilms International (UMI). ***Continues*** *Baltimore Vegetarians, 0883-1165.*
**Desc:** The health professionals evaluate current scientific literature and present it in an easy and practical fashion to our readers so that they can apply the information to their own lives.

US/0164-8497
**VEGETARIAN TIMES.** [Veg. times]. (19??)-. Periodical. English. mo. $23.94. Cowles Magazines, PO Box 8200, Harrisburg PA 17105. **Tel** (717)657-9555, (800)435-9610. **ED** Paul Obis. **LC** TX392; .A46. **DD** 613.2/62/05. **Bk Rev. Ad Acc. Circ:** 160,000. available on microfilm and microfiche from University Microfilms International (UMI); available on an online database (file 149/Full-Text) from DIALOG. Documents available from UMI Article Clearinghouse. ***Absorbed*** *Well-Being, 0146-7824.*
**Desc:** The worlds leading authority on vegetarianism. Each issue contains articles on how a vegetarian lifestyle relates to diet, fitness, cooking, health, consumer choices, natural foods, environmental concerns and animal welfare. Also included are meatless recipes, news, celebrity profiles, humor, product reviews, restaurant guides, book reviews and classifieds. A must for school, public and medical libraries.
**Ind/Abst** Acad. Abstr. Full Text Elite (Jan. 1992-); Acad. Abstr. (Jan. 1992-); Acad. Search (Jan. 1992-); AGRICOLA [Select. Cov.]; Consum. Health Nutr. Index (?-?); Health Index (1989-); Health Period. Database [Full Txt.]; Health Ref. Cent. (Jan. 1989-) [Full Txt.] [Full Cov.]; Health Source (Jan. 1992-); INFO-SOUTH Abstr.; Mag. ASAP Plus [Full Txt.]; Mag. Index Plus (1992-); Mag. Search; Newsp. Period. Abstr. (1992-).

UK/0957-6436
**VITAMIN CONNECTION.** ***Ceased.*** [Vitam. connect.]. (1989)-(1993). Periodical. English. bm. Alphavite Publ Ltd, 20 Potters Lane, Kiln Farm, Milton Keyes MK11 3HF England. **Tel** 011 44 0908 569819, FAX 0908 260229. **Bk Rev. Ad Acc. Circ:** 42,000.
**Desc:** Information on current health issues. Includes information on preventative health practices, nutrition and diet, vitamins and minerals as well as personal healthcare tips, exercise and sports, and current lifestyles and trends.

GW/0721-7110
**VITAMIN D.** (VITAMIN D : PROCEEDINGS OF THE ... WORKSHOP ON VITAMIN D.). [Vitam. D]. (1974)-. Academic Scholarly Publication. English. **NLM** W3 WO512C. **CODEN** PWVDDU. Documents available from CASDDS.
**Ind/Abst** Chem. Abstr.

US/0736-9158
**VITAMIN E ... ABSTRACTS.** [Vitam. E abstr.]. **Added/Corp** Henkel Corporation. Fine Chemicals Division. Vitamin E Research & Information Service. **VFOAT** Vitamin E. (1980)-. English. an. Free to qualified subscribers. Henkel Corporation, 5325 South 9th Avenue, LaGrange IL 60525. **Tel** (800)328-6199. **LC** QP772.T6; V573. **DD** 547.19/26/05. **NLM** ZQU 179; V836. **Circ:** 10,000 (ctrl).
**Desc:** Comprehensive Vitamin E abstracts.

GW/0930-4827
**VITAMINE, MINERALSTOFFE, SPURENELEMENTE IN MEDIZIN, ERNAHRUNG UND UMWELT. VFOAT** VitaMinSpur; Vitamine, Mineralstoffe, Spurenelemente. Vol. 1, No. 1 (Oct. 1986)-. Periodical. German (summaries and/or abstracts in English). qt. $69.00. Hippokrates Verlag, Postfach 102263, W 70018 Stuttgart Germany. **Tel** 011 49 711 89310. **(Subscription address:** Thieme Medical Publishers Inc., 381 Park Avenue South, New York NY 10016.) **NLM** W1; VI977M.

NE/0042-7926
**VOEDING.** [Voeding]. **Added/Corp** Stichting Tot Wetenschappelijke Voorlichting op Voedingsgebied. (April 1939)-. Academic Scholarly Publication. Dutch (English; summaries and/or abstracts in French and English). ir. Fl65.00 Netherlands; Fl75.00 other. Keesing Noordervliet Bv, De Molen 82-86, 3995 Ax Houten Netherlands. **Tel** 011 31 3403 58585, FAX 011 31 3403 58500. **(Subscription address:** Keesing Noordervliet BV, Postbus 1118, 1000 BC Amsterdam Netherlands.) **ED** W. Bosman. **LC** TX341; .V54. **DD** 641/.05. **NLM** W1 VO201. **CODEN** VOEDAK. **Bk Rev. Ad Acc. Circ:** 4,500 (ctrl). Documents available from CASDDS.
**Desc:** Scientific journal on nutrition, food and health.
**Ind/Abst** AGRICOLA (19??-); Chem. Abstr. (19??-); Dairy Sci. Abstr. (19??-); Food Sci. Technol. Abstr. (19??-); Nutr. Abstr. Rev., Ser. A, Hum. Exp. (19??-); Life Sci. Collect. (19??-); Rice Abstr. (19??-); Soyabean Abstr. (19??-).

RU/0042-8833
**VOPROSY PITANIIA.** [Vopr. pitan.]. Vol. 1-32, (1932)-(1973); (1974)-. Academic Scholarly Publication. Russian (summaries and/or abstracts in English). Four times a year. $69.95. Izdatelstvo Meditsina / Russian Academy of Medical Sciences, Ulitsa Solyanka 14, 109801 Moscow Russia. **Tel** 011 95 297-05-04. **(Subscription address:** East View Publications Inc., 3020 Harbor Lane North, Suite 110, Minneapolis MN 55447.) **NLM** W1 VO6414. **CODEN** VPITAR. **[CCC].** Documents available from BIOSIS Document Express, CASDDS.
**Ind/Abst** AGRICOLA; Biol. Abstr.; Chem. Abstr.; Food Sci. Technol. Abstr.; Index Med.; Int. Aerosp. Abstr.; Nutr. Abstr. Rev., Ser. B, Live Feeds and Feed.; Life Sci. Collect.; Potato Abstr.; Rev. Med. Vet. Mycology; Rice Abstr.; Soyabean Abstr.

US/1053-1459
**WEIGHT CONTROL DIGEST (CONSUMER ED.), THE.** ***Title Change.*** (THE WEIGHT CONTROL DIGEST.). [Weight control dig.]. **Added/Corp** LEARN Education Center. Vol. 1, No. 1 (Nov./Dec. 1990)-Vol. 2, No. 2 (Mar./Apr. 1992). Periodical. English. bm. Learn Education Center, 1555 West Mockingbird Lane, Suite 205, Dallas TX 75235. **Tel** (214)637-7700, FAX (214)637-0509. **DD** 613. ***Merged with*** *Weight Control Digest (Professional Ed.), 1053-1882* ***to form*** *Weight Control Digest (Dallas, Tex. : 1992), 1075-2889.*

●US/1075-2889
**WEIGHT CONTROL DIGEST (DALLAS, TEX. 1992), THE.** (THE WEIGHT CONTROL DIGEST.). [Weight control dig.]. **Added/Corp** LEARN Education Center. Vol. 2, No. 3 (May/June 1992)-. Periodical. English. bm (6 issues). $32.65. Learn Education Center, 1555 West Mockingbird Lane, Suite 205, Dallas TX 75235. **Tel** (214)637-7700, FAX (214)637-0509. **ED** Kelly D. Brownell. **DD** 613. Index available (Nov./Dec. issue). ctrl circ. ***Formed by the union of*** *Weight Control Digest (Consumer Ed.), 1053-1459* ***and*** *Weight Control Digest (Professional Ed.), 1053-1882.*

UK
**WEIGHTWATCHERS.** (19??)-. English. Eight times a year. £1.35 per issue. Weight Watchers Ltd., Kidwells Park House, Kidwells Park Drive, Maidenhead Berkshire SL6 8YT England. **Tel** (071)836-2619. **ED** Barbara Thompson. **Ad Acc. Pr Rev. Circ:** 160,000 (ctrl).
**Desc:** Publication encompassing the philosophy of the weight watchers organization. Advice and features on healthy eating and lifestyle topics related to sensible eating and weight loss.

US/0279-5604
**WHOLE LIFE TIMES.** [Whole life times]. (1979)-. Periodical. English. ir. Whole Life Times, 18 Shepard Street, Department S, Brighton MA 02135. **Tel** (617)783-8030. **ED** Shelly Kellman. **Bk Rev. Ad Acc. Circ:** 140,000 (ctrl).
**Desc:** Natural lifestyle magazine with articles on health, diet, exercise, nutrition and the environment.
**Ind/Abst** Health Index (1989-); Health Period. Database; Health Ref. Cent. (Jan. 1989-) [Full Cov.].

US/1053-492X
**WORKSITE WELLNESS WORKS.** [Worksite wellness works]. **Added/Corp** Wellness Councils of America. (1985)-. Periodical. English. qt. $12.00 US; $15.00 Canada and Mexico Councils. Community Health Plaza, Suite 311, 7101 Newport Avenue, Omaha NE 68152-2100. **Tel** (402)572-3590, FAX (402)572-3594. **ED** Sandra Wendel. **DD** 363. **Bk Rev**, (Qty: 4/yr). **Pr Rev. Circ:** 10,000 (ctrl).
**Desc:** Covers the people and events that shape corporate health promotion; exclusive updates on corporate health promotion programs; new products for novice and veteran worksite health coordinators; insider reports on policymakers and a Washington perspective on health promotion.

SZ/0084-2230
**WORLD REVIEW OF NUTRITION AND DIETETICS.** [World rev. nutr. diet.]. Vol. 1 (1959)-. English. Three times a year. 230.00F (approx. per volume). S. Karger AG, Allschwilerstrasse 10, PO Box - Postfach - Case Postale, CH-4009 Basel Switzerland. **Tel** 011 41 61 306-1111, FAX 011 41 61 306-1234, telex CH 962 652. **ED** A. P. Simopoulos. **LC** QP141.A1; W59. **DD** 612.3082. **NLM** W1 W0898. **CODEN** WRNDAT. **[CCC].** Documents available from BIOSIS Document Express, CASDDS.
**Desc:** Volumes in this series consist of thorough reviews on topics selected as either fundamental to improved understanding of human and animal nutrition, useful in resolving present controversies, or relevant to problems of social and preventive medicine that depend for their solution on progress in nutrition.
**Ind/Abst** AGRICOLA [Full Cov.]; Biol. Abstr.; Chem. Abstr.; Dairy Sci. Abstr.; Food Sci. Technol. Abstr.; Foods Adlibra; Index Med.; Nutr. Abstr. Rev., Ser. A, Hum. Exp.; Poult. Abstr.; Ref. Upd. Deluxe Ed.; Trop. Dis. Bull.

JA/0916-1139
**YAKUBUTSU DOTAI. VFOAT** Xenobiotic Metabolism and Disposition. (1968)-. Periodical. Multiple languages. bm. **DD** 615. Documents available from CASDDS.
**Ind/Abst** Chem. Abstr.

GW/0084-5337
**ZEITSCHRIFT FUER ERNAEHRUNGSWISSENSCHAFT. SUPPLEMENTUM. VFOAT** Journal of Nutritional Sciences. Supplementum; Journal des Sciences de la Nutrition Supplementum. Vol. 1 (1961)-. Monographic series. German (English and French). Four times a year. DM260.00 (per volume). Springer-Verlag GmbH & Company KG, Heidelberger Platz 3, D 14197 Berlin Germany. **Tel** 011 49 30 8207223, FAX 011 49 30 8214091, telex 183 319 SPBLN D. **(Subscription address:** Springer Verlag New York Inc. / for North America, 44 Hartz Way, Secaucus NJ 07096.) **ED** K H Bassler and A Fricker.
**Desc:** Features original articles on aspects of nutritional science and related fields.
**Ind/Abst** Curr. Aware. Biol. Sci., CABS; Index Med.

GW/0044-264X
**ZEITSCHRIFT FUER ERNAHRUNGSWISSENSCHAFT.** (ZEITSCHRIFT FUER ERNAHRUNGSWISSENSCHAFT. JOURNAL OF NUTRITIONAL SCIENCES. JOURNAL DES SCIENCES DE LA NUTRITION.). [Z. ernaehrungswiss.]. **VFOAT** Journal of Nutritional Sciences; Journal des Sciences de la Nutrition. Vol. 1 (April 1960)-. Academic Scholarly Publication. German (English, French and German). qt. DM298.00. Dr Dietrich Steinkopff Verlag, PO Box 111442, D 64229 Darmstadt Germany. **Tel** 011 49 6151 17450. **(Subscription address:** Springer Verlag New York Inc. / for North America, 44 Hartz Way, Secaucus NJ 07096.) **LC** QP141.A1; Z4. **NLM** W1 ZE322. **CODEN** ZERNAL. **[CCC]. Pr Rev.** Documents available from The Genuine Article, BIOSIS Document Express, CASDDS.
**Ind/Abst** AGRICOLA; Biodeter. Abstr.; Biol. Abstr.; Chem. Abstr.; Curr. Contents, Agric. Biol. Environ. Sci.; EMBASE [Select. Cov.]; Energy Res. Abstr.; Food Sci. Technol. Abstr.; Index Med.; Nutr. Abstr. Rev., Ser. B, Live Feeds and Feed.; Nutr. Abstr. Rev., Ser. A, Hum. Exp.; Life Sci. Collect.; Poult. Abstr.; Res. Alert [Select. Cov.]; Sug. Indus. Abstr.

PL/0209-164X
**ZYWIENIE CZOWIEKA I METABOLIZM.** (ZYWIENIE CZOWIEKA I METABOLIZM / INSTYTUT ZYWNOSCI I ZYWIENIA.). [Zywienie czowieka metab.]. **Added/Corp** Instytut Zywnosci i Zywienia (Poland). **VFOAT** Polish Journal of Human Nutrition and Metabolism; Human Nutrition and Metabolism. Vol. 10, No. 1 (1983)-. Academic Scholarly Publication. English (English and Russian; summaries and/or abstracts in Polish and Russian). qt. $52.00. Zywienie Czowieka I Metabolizm, Panstwowy Zakad Wydawnictw Lekarskich Ul Duga 38/40, 00-238 Warszawa Poland. **Tel** telex 816854 IZZ PL. **(Subscription address:** ARS Polona, PO Box 1001, 00068 Warsaw Poland.) **CODEN** ZCMEDQ. **Circ:** 1,780. Documents available from CASDDS. ***Continues*** *Zywienie Czowieka, 0303-7851.*
**Ind/Abst** Chem. Abstr. (1983-); Dairy Sci. Abstr.; EMBASE [Select. Cov.]; Food Sci. Technol. Abstr.

---

## ABSTRACTING, BIBLIOGRAPHIES AND STATISTICS

---

US/0883-1963
**CONSUMER HEALTH & NUTRITION INDEX.** [Consum. health nutr. index]. **VFOAT** Consumer Health and Nutrition Index. Vol. 1, No. 1 (July 1985)-. Abstracting/Indexing Service. English. Four times a year. $145.00 North America; $160.00 other. Oryx Press, 4041 North Central Avenue, #700, Phoenix AZ 85012-3397. **Tel** (800)279-ORYX, (602)265-2651, FAX (602)265-6250, (800)279-4663, (800)279-6799.

(Subscription address: Eurospan Ltd., Journals and Serials Division, 3 Henrietta Street, Covent Garden, London WC2E 8LU England.) **ED** Alan M. Rees and Cynthia B. Strong. **DD** 613. **NLM** ZWB 130; C758. Index available. **Bk Rev**. **Ad Acc**. ctrl circ. available on CD-ROM from National Information Service Corporation (NISC).
**Desc:** Provides access to top articles in health and general magazines and newsletters (periodicals) that are written for the layperson. This index is designed to help consumers and librarians locate information on subjects such as nutrition, particular diseases, drugs, exercise, and other areas of concern.

US/1056-1900
**HEALTH NEWS & REVIEW. See** Nutrition and Dietetics.

UK/0309-1295
**NUTRITION ABSTRACTS AND REVIEWS. SERIES A: HUMAN & EXPERIMENTAL.** [Nutr. abstr. rev., Ser. A, Hum. exp.]. **Added/Corp** Commonwealth Bureau of Nutrition. Vol. 47 (Jan. 1977)-. Abstracting/Indexing Service. English. mo. $870.00 US. CAB International Centre, Wallingford, Oxon OX10 8DE United Kingdom. **Tel** 44 491 832111, **FAX** 44 491 833508, telex 847964 (COMAGG G). **ED** R. G. Hankin. **LC** QP141.A1; N86. **DD** 613.2/05. **NLM** ZQU 145 N971. **Ad Acc**. **Circ:** 1,500. available on magnetic tape and CD-ROM; available on an online database from Tsukuba Daigaku; CAN/OLE; STN International; JICST; DATA-STAR; DIMDI; ESA-IRS; BRS; and DIALOG. **Continues in part** Nutrition Abstracts and Reviews, 0029-6619.
**Desc:** Scans journals covering the most significant published papers from all countries in the world in the field of human and environmental nutrition.
**Ind/Abst** Anal. Abstr.; Nutr. Abstr. Rev., Ser. B, Live Feeds and Feed.; Nutr. Abstr. Rev., Ser. A, Hum. Exp.; Soyabean Abstr.; Trop. Dis. Bull.

US/0736-0037
**NUTRITION RESEARCH NEWSLETTER.** [Nutr. res. newsl.]. (1982)-. Abstracting/Indexing Service. English. mo. $96.00 US, Canada & Mexico; $106.00 other. Lyda Associates, Inc., PO Box 700, Palisades NY 10964. **Tel** (914)359-8282, **FAX** (914)359-1229. **ED** Lillian Langseth. **DD** 613. Index available. **Circ:** 75,000. available in microform from DIALOG; available on an online database (file 149/Full-Text) from DIALOG.
**Desc:** A comprehensive review of clinical nutrition research, extracted from articles in over 340 biomedical journals. It is summarized clearly and concisely. Full citations and author's addresses are provided, along with listings of pertinent review articles.
**Ind/Abst** Health Index (1989-); Health Period. Database [Full Txt.]; Health Ref. Cent. (Jan. 1989-) [Full Txt.] [Full Cov.]

US/0892-6204
**NUTRITION UPDATE (SAN CLEMENTE, CALIF.). See** Medical Science and Technology.

# OCCUPATIONS AND CAREERS

NE
**ABU MAGAZINE.** (19??)-. English. Five times a year. Free on request. ABU, Postbus 75451, 1070 AL Amsterdam Netherlands. **Tel** 011 020 573783.

US/1062-0249
**ACADEMIC NURSE, THE.** (THE ACADEMIC NURSE : THE JOURNAL OF THE COLUMBIA UNIVERSITY SCHOOL OF NURSING.). [Acad. nurse]. **Added/Corp** Columbia University. School of Nursing. Vol. 7, No. 1 (Spring 1987)-. Periodical. English. Twice a year (Fall & Spring). Free on request. Columbia University / School of Nursing, 630 West 168th Street, New York NY 10032. **Tel** (212)305-8258, **FAX** (212)305-6937. **ED** Gary Goldenberg, (212)305-3417. **DD** 610. **NLM** W1; AC33NJ. **Circ:** 10,000. **Continues** SNC.
**Desc:** Nursing education and practice and research with relevance to activities at Columbia University School of Nursing.
**Ind/Abst** Int. Nurs. Index (1990-).

US
**ACM NO-NONSENSE GUIDE TO COMPUTING CAREERS.** (19??)-. English. $25.00. ACM Association for Computing Machinery, 1515 Broadway, 17th Floor, New York NY 10036. **Tel** (212)869-7440, **FAX** (212)869-0481.

AT
**ACT TAFE COURSE GUIDE.** English. Twice a year. Free. Act Institute Tafe Careers & Course, PO Box 826, Canberra ACT 2601 Australia. **Tel** 011 61 062 520788.

●US/1072-592X
**ADAMS JOBS ALMANAC, THE.** (1994)-. English. an (1 issue). $15.00. Bob Adams Inc., 260 Center Street, Holbrook MA 02343. **Tel** (617)767-8100, (800)872-5627, **FAX** (617)767-0994.

US
**AMERICAN ALMANAC OF JOBS AND SALARIES, THE.** (1982)-. English. ir. $18.50 (latest edition). Avon Books, PO Box 767, Dresden TN 38225. **Tel** (800)238-0658, (800)762-0779 outside of Tennessee. **ED** John W. Wright. **LC** HD8038.U5; A68. **DD** 331.7/02/0973.

US
**ANNUAL REPORT, OCCUPATIONAL AND PROFESSIONAL LICENSING BOARDS / PREPARED BY THE STATE REORGANIZATION COMMISSION AND THE LEGISLATIVE AUDIT COUNCIL IN COOPERATION WITH THE BUDGET AND CONTROL BOARD. Added/Corp** South Carolina. State Reorganization Commission. South Carolina. General Assembly. Legislative Audit Council. South Carolina. State Budget and Control Board. (June 30, 1980)-. English. State Reorganization Commission, 228 Solomon Blatt Building, 1105 Pendleton Street, Columbia SC 29201. **LC** HD3630.U7; A56. **DD** 353.97570082/4/04606.

US/0730-9023
**ARTSEARCH. See** The Arts-Performing Arts.

●US/1061-9925
**AT WORK (SAN FRANCISCO, CALIF.).** (AT WORK : STORIES OF TOMORROW'S WORKPLACE.). [At work]. Vol. 1, No. 1 (May/June 1992)-. Periodical. English. Six times a year. $75.00. Berrett-Koehler Publishers, 155 Montgomery Street, San Francisco CA 94104-4109. **Tel** (415)288-0260, **FAX** (415)362-2512. **ED** Alis Valen, (editor's address: 6433 Westover Drive, Oakland, CA 94611, phone: (510)530-4000). **LC** HD5650; .A88. **DD** 331. **Bk Rev**, (Qty: 20-30). **Ad Acc**. **Circ:** 1,500 (ctrl).
**Desc:** Source of new ideas, practical guidance, and inspiration for to achieve congruence between values and work, and to create more healthy, ethical, and effective organizations and workplaces.
**Ind/Abst** Foods Adlibra.

US/0888-4870
**ATHLETICS EMPLOYMENT WEEKLY.** [Athl. employ. wkly.]. (198?)-. Periodical. English. Forty-eight issues a year (Oct. thru Aug.). $65.00. Athletics Employment Weekly, Route 2 Box 140, Carthage IL 62321. **Tel** (217)357-3615. **ED** Ruth Fugate. **Circ:** 1,000.
**Desc:** A weekly newsletter listing positions in athletics in 2 & 4 year college all over the United States.

CN/0714-4601
**BETWEEN US. See** Education-Higher Education.

US/0199-8730
**BIZ.** Vol. 1, (Winter 1980)-. Periodical. English. bm. Biz, PO Box 10211, Stamford CT 06904. **Tel** (203)965-8400. **ED** Elise Maclay. **Circ:** 25,000.

US
**BOSTON JOB BANK, THE. VFOAT** Boston Jobbank. 1st Edition (1980)-. English. an (Sept.). $15.95. Bob Adams Inc., 260 Center Street, Holbrook MA 02343. **Tel** (617)767-8100, (800)872-5627, **FAX** (617)767-0994. **LC** HF5382.75.U62; B68.

UK
**BRITISH JOURNAL OF EDUCATION AND WORK. See** Education.

US/0744-1797
**BULLDOG (LOS ANGELES, CALIF.). Title Change.** (BULLDOG.). (1979)-(19??). Newsletter. English. sm (24 issues). Intercom Group, 2115 4th Street, Suite B, Box 2189, Berkeley CA 94710. **Tel** (510)596-9300, (800)327-9893. **ED** Michael Horowitz; telephone: (510)549-4332. Index available (free on request). **Circ:** 880 (ctrl). **Continued by** Bulldog Reporter.
**Desc:** The media placement newsletter for PR professionals.

US/0194-0767
**BULLETIN, NATIONAL EMPLOYMENT LISTING SERVICE FOR THE CRIMINAL JUSTICE SYSTEM. Ceased. Main/Corp** National Employment Listing Service (Huntsville, Tex.). **VFOAT** National Employment Listing Service for the Criminal Justice System; NELS Bulletin. (197?)-(Aug. 1994). Bulletin. English. mo (12 issues). Sam Houston State University Criminal Justice Center, Huntsville TX 77341. **Tel** (409)294-1692. **ED** Laure Pegoda. **Circ:** 2,000 (ctrl).
**Desc:** National job listing service for the criminal justice and social service fields. Listing of employment opportunities in law enforcement, corrections, security, community services and academics.

AT/0158-2631
**BULLETIN - STUDENT COUNSELLING AND RESEARCH UNIT, UNIVERSITY OF NEW SOUTH WALES. Title Change.** (1964)-(1986). English. ir. University of New South Wales, PO Box 1, Kensington New South Wales, 2033 Australia. **Tel** 011 61 2 697-3362, **FAX** 011 61 2 662-6616. **Continued by** Counselling and Careers Bulletin, 1036-0638.
**Ind/Abst** Aust. Educ. Index (?-?).

US/0745-4341
**CAM REPORT.** (197?)-. Periodical. English. bw (except one issue in June, July, and Aug.). $65.00 US; $75.00 other. Priam Publishing Inc., Box 1862, East Lansing MI 48823. **Tel** (517)351-4532. **ED** Camille D McKinley.
**Desc:** Specifically designed for those concerned with sound, imaginative career planning. Present relevant facts and reliable forecasting to this end.

US/0898-6916
**CAPITAL SOURCE, THE. See** Public Administration.

CN/0703-5314
**CAREER CANDIDATES.** (CAREER CANDIDATES - CARLETON UNIVERSITY. SCHOOL OF PUBLIC ADMINISTRATION.). **Main/Corp** Carleton University. School of Public Administration. 1975/1976-. English. an. Carleton University / School of Public Administration, Colonel by Drive, Ottawa Ontario K1S 5B6 Canada. **DD** 350/.0007/1171384.

US
**CAREER CENTER BULLETIN, THE.** Vol. 4, No. 1 (1983)-. Bulletin. English. qt. $29.00. Career Center Bulletin, c/o Julie Alig, 316 Uris, Columbia University, New York NY 10027. **Tel** (212)280-2830, **FAX** (212)316-1473. **ED** Peter Erdmann. **Bk Rev**. **Circ:** 2,000 (ctrl). **Continues** Career Development Bulletin.
**Desc:** Serves as a clearing house for important new information and research in the fields of career development and human resource management.
**Ind/Abst** Work Relat. Abstr.

US/0888-2770
**CAREER CHOICES NEWSLETTER, THE.** [Career choices newsl.]. (1985)-. Newsletter. English. mo (except July-Aug.). $48.00 (one year), $80.00 (two year), $110.00 (three year). Career Choices Newsletter, PO Box 962, Forest Hills NY 11375. **Tel** (718)423-8344. **ED** M. Siegel and J. Siegel. **DD** 331. Index available. cum. index. **Circ:** 1,000 (ctrl).
**Desc:** Written for individuals seeking career goals. Discusses high growth occupations, trends affecting the work place, college and vocational training programs. Reports changes in financial assistance.

US/0889-4019
**CAREER DEVELOPMENT QUARTERLY, THE.** [Career dev. q.]. **Added/Corp** National Career Development Association (U.S.). Vol. 35, No. 1 (Sept. 1986)-. Periodical. English. qt (4 issues). $55.00 (institution), $40.00 (individual) US. American Counseling Association, 5999 Stevenson Avenue, Alexandria VA 22304. **Tel** (703)823-9800, (800)347-6647, **FAX** (703)823-0252. (Subscription address: American Counseling Association, Subscription Office, PO Box 2513, Birmingham AL 35201-2513.) **ED** Mark L. Savickas. **LC** HF5381.A1; V55. **DD** 331.7/02/05. **[CCC]**. Index available (bound in last issue). cum. index. **Ad Acc**. **Circ:** 8,085. available on microfilm and microfiche from University Microfilms International (UMI). Documents available from The Genuine Article, UMI Article Clearinghouse. **Continues** Vocational Guidance Quarterly, 0042-7764.
**Desc:** A professional journal concerned with research, theory, and practice in career development, career guidance, career resources, and career education.
**Ind/Abst** Acad. Search (Jan. 1993-); Contents Pages Educ.; Curr. Contents Soc. Behav. Sci.; Curr. Index J. Educ.; Educ. Index; Educ. Adm. Abstr. (?-?); High. Educ. Abstr. (1986-); Hum. Resour. Abstr. (?-?); INFO-SOUTH Abstr.; Int. Labour Doc.; Mag. Search; Newsp. Period. Abstr. (1990-); Psychol. Abstr. (1954-); PsycINFO; PsycLit; PsycScan: Appl. Psych.; Res. Alert [Full Cov.]; Soc. Sci. Cit. Index [Full Cov.]; Soc. Work Abstr. [Select. Cov.]; Stud. Women Abstr.; Vocat. Search (Jan. 1993-); Work Relat. Abstr.

US
**CAREER DIRECTIONS.** Periodical. English. qt. Alumni Hall, University of Tennessee, Knoxville TN 37916. **Continues** Resources for Student Vocational Pursuits.

●CN/0846-3514
**CAREER DIRECTORY (TORONTO. 1992).** (THE CAREER DIRECTORY.). [Career dir.]. (1992)-. Directory. English. $17.95 per v. Encore Publishing Corporation, 39 Eastmount Avenue, Toronto Ont, M4K 1V2. **DD** 331.12/4/025713541.

US
**CAREER EDUCATION DIGEST.** (1973)-. Periodical. English. mo. Pacific Skipper, PO Box 1698, Newport Beach CA 99623. available on microfilm from University Microfilms International (UMI).

US
**CAREER EDUCATION NEWS : CENTRAL NEWS SERVICE FOR THE WORLDS OF WORK AND LEARNING.** ***Ceased.*** Ceased (Sept. 1991). Periodical. English. Twenty-two times a year. Diversified Learning Inc, 72-300 Vallat Road, Rancho Mirage CA 92270. **Tel** (619)346-3336. **ED** Elizabeth Turner. **Bk Rev. Circ:** 1,000.

US/0270-7705
**CAREER EDUCATION (WASHINGTON).** **See** Education-Vocational Education.

US/1049-9954
**CAREER FOCUS FOR TODAY'S RISING BLACK PROFESSIONAL.** ***Title Change.*** [Career focus today's rising Black prof.]. **VFOAT** Career Focus. (198?)-(19??). Periodical. English. bm. Communications Publishing Group, 250 Mark Twain, TWR 106 West 11th Street, Kansas City MO 64105. **Tel** (816)221-4404. **ED** Molly Christiansen and Toni Myles. **DD** 331. **Bk Rev. Ad Acc. Circ:** 750,000 (ctrl). ***Merged with*** *Career Focus for Today's Rising Hispanic Professional, 1049-9946* ***to form*** *Career Focus for Today's Professional.*

US/1049-9946
**CAREER FOCUS FOR TODAY'S RISING HISPANIC PROFESSIONAL.** ***Title Change.*** [Career focus today's rising Hisp. prof.]. **VFOAT** Career Focus. (198?)-(19??). Periodical. English. bm. Communications Publishing Group, 250 Mark Twain, TWR 106 West 11th Street, Kansas City MO 64105. **Tel** (816)221-4404. **ED** Molly Christiansen and Toni Myles. **DD** 331. **Bk Rev. Ad Acc. Circ:** 750,000 (ctrl). ***Merged with*** *Career Focus for Today's Rising Black Professional, 1049-9954* ***to form*** *Career Focus for Today's Professional.*

US
**CAREER FOCUS FOR TODAY'S RISING PROFESSIONAL.** (19??)-. Periodical. English. Six times a year. $28.95 two years. Communications Publishing Group, 250 Mark Twain, TWR 106 West 11th Street, Kansas City MO 64105. **Tel** (816)221-4404. ***Formed by the union of*** *Career Focus for Today's Rising Hispanic Professional, 1049-9946* ***and*** *Career Focus for Today's Rising Black Professional, 1049-9954.*

US/1045-4314
**CAREER FUTURES.** ***Ceased.*** (CAREER FUTURES : A GUIDE TO THE NEW RULES FOR JOB HUNTING.). [Career futures]. Vol. 1, No. 1 (Spring/Summer 1989)-(19??). Periodical. English. qt. Career Information Services Inc, 21 Charles Street, Westport CT 06880. **Tel** (203)227-1775, FAX (203)226-8988. **ED** James Markland. **DD** 331. **Bk Rev,** (Qty: 4-6 per year). **Ad Acc, Adv Mgr:** Glenn Mairano, **Tel** (203)227-1775. **Circ:** 400,000 (ctrl).
**Desc:** Helpful advice on how to get a job, what tasks and salaries are involved in various industries, job outlooks, and employment news.

US
**CAREER GUIDE TO PROFESSIONAL ASSOCIATIONS.** (19??)-. English. $19.95. Carroll Press, PO Box 8113, Cranston RI 02920. **Tel** (401)942-1587.
**Desc:** Full details on nearly 2500 organizations providing key career information on each.

CN/0709-0366
**CAREER NEWS (WATERLOO).** ***Ceased.*** (CAREER NEWS.). Vol. 1 (Sept. 1978)-(1992). Periodical. English. qt. Career Resource Centre, University of Waterloo, Waterloo Ontario N2L 3G1 Canada. **DD** 331.7/02/0971. ***Supersedes*** *Centrepages, 0702-7230.*
**Desc:** In addition to a topical article on career planning and the job search the publication has short notices on the career activities at the University of Waterloo.

US
**CAREER OPPORTUNITIES. CD-ROM.** English. $74.95. Quanta Press, Inc., 1313 Fifth Street Southeast, Suite 208C, Minneapolis MN 55414. **Tel** (612)379-3956, FAX (612)623-4570.
**Desc:** This disc can help individuals and students make career choices. Included are job titles, job descriptions, education levels, chances for advancement, average salaries and working conditions. Available in DOS and MAC formats.

US/0739-5043
**CAREER OPPORTUNITIES NEWS.** **VFOAT** CNews; C News. Vol. 1, No. 1 (Sept. 1983)-. Periodical. English. bm. $30.00 (1 year), $50.00 (2 year), $65.00 (3 year). Garrett Park Press, PO Box 190 F, Garrett Park MD 20896. **Tel** (301)946-2553. Index available. **Bk Rev.**
**Desc:** Presents latest information on occupational forecasts, fields with jobs, sources of free and inexpensive career materials, and information of special interest to women and minorities.

US
**CAREER OPPORTUNITY BULLETIN.** (19??)-. Bulletin. English. Twenty-six times a year (Thurs.). $30.00. Minnesota Documents, 117 University Avenue, St Paul MN 55155. **Tel** (612)297-3000, (800)657-3757, FAX (612)296-2265.

CN
**CAREER OPTIONS.** ACCIS - The Graduate Workforce Professionals, 1209 King Street West 2nd Floor, Toronto Ontario M6K 1G2 Canada.

CN
**CAREER OUTLOOK, UNIVERSITY AND COMMUNITY COLLEGE : ADMINISTRATION/SOCIAL SCIENCES AND SERVICES.** **VFOAT** Perspectives de Carrieres, Universites et Colleges Administration/Sciences Sociales et Services. Multiple languages (English and French). Manpower and Immigration, 222 NePean Street, Ottawa Ontario K1A 0J5 Canada. **LC** HF5382.5.C2; C28. **DD** 331.7/02/0971.

US/0885-7547
**CAREER PATHFINDER, THE.** Periodical. English. mo (nine issues per year). $39.00. Ask Systems Inc, 55 White Road, Shrewsbury NJ 07702. **Tel** (201)842-7740, (800)524-0188. **ED** Don Kuhlman and Jane Matthews. **DD** 371. Index available. cum. index. **Bk Rev. Circ:** 2,000. available on microfiche; available on microfilm.
**Desc:** Provides information and news of interest to any career guidance counselor on any subject which may affect them including student career and occupation information.

US
**CAREER PLANNING.** Periodical. English. mo. $18.00. Susan Cohn, 245 South Robertson Boulevard, Beverly Hills CA 90211.

US/0736-1920
**CAREER PLANNING AND ADULT DEVELOPMENT JOURNAL.** [Career plann. adult dev. j.]. **Added/Corp** Career Planning and Adult Development Network (U.S.). Vol. 1, No. 1 (Spring 1983)-. Periodical. English. qt. $30.00 US; $50.00 other. Career Planning and Adult Development Network, 4965 Sierra Road, San Jose CA 95132. **Tel** (408)559-4946, FAX (408)559-8211. **LC** HF5381.A1; C283. **DD** 331.7/02/05.
**Desc:** Current information for career counselors who work with adults on workshops, seminars, books, films, tests, issues, new developments and model programs.
**Ind/Abst** Work Relat. Abstr. (-19??).

US/0898-1353
**CAREER PLANNING AND ADULT DEVELOPMENT NETWORK NEWSLETTER.** [Career Plan. Adult Dev. Netw. newsl.]. **Added/Corp** Career Planning and Adult Development Network (U.S.). Vol. 6, No. 1 (Jan. 1984)-. Periodical. English. mo. $50.00 US; $70.00 other. Career Planning and Adult Development Network, 4965 Sierra Road, San Jose CA 95132. **Tel** (408)559-4946, FAX (408)559-8211. **DD** 331. ***Continues*** *Career Planning & Adult Development Newsletter, 0898-1345.*

US/0278-1034
**CAREER SCHOOL DIRECTORY.** Began with 1973 Vol. Directory. English. an. EDFAC Publishing Company, 2211 Broadway, Pekin IN 61554. **LC** HD5715.2; .C36. **DD** 331.25/92/02573.

US/1047-4293
**CAREER WAVES.** [Career waves]. (198?)-. Periodical. English. Four times a year (Within the seasons months). $30.00. Directions Publishing, 21 North Henry Street, Edgerton WI 53534. **Tel** (608)884-3367. **DD** 331.
**Desc:** A new, innovative newsletter, invaluable to professionals who assist others in job hunting. The articles can help library staff be more effective in advising and in ordering useful resources.

US/1051-1075
**CAREER WOMAN.** **See** Women's Interests.

US/0744-1002
**CAREER WORLD (HIGHLAND PARK, ILL. 1981).** (CAREER WORLD / CURRICULUM INNOVATIONS, INC.). [Career world]. (Sept. 1981)-. Periodical. English. Nine times a year. $26.95. Weekly Reader Corporation, 3001 Cindel Drive, Delran NJ 08370. **Tel** (609)786-1000, (800)446-3355, FAX (609)786-3360. **LC** HF5381.A1; C2853. **DD** 331.17/02/05. Index available (bound in May issue). available on microfilm and microfiche from University Microfilms International (UMI). ***Formed by the union of*** *Career World 1, 0198-7615* ***and*** *Career World 2, 0198-7623.*
**Ind/Abst** Abr. Read. Guide Period. Lit.; Child. Mag. Guide (1981-); Mag. Artic. Summar. Elite (July 1989-); Mag. Artic. Summar. Select (July 1989-); Mag. Artic. Summar. CD-ROM (July 1989-); Mag. Search; Mid. Search (Jul. 1989-); Prim. Search (Jul. 1989-); Read. Guide Period. Lit.

US
**CAREERISM NEWSLETTER : ZEROING IN ON CAREER AND JOB OPPORTUNITIES.** **Added/Corp** WWWWW/Information Services. (1976)-. Newsletter. English. Twelve times a year. $75.00 (one year); $135.00 (two years). WWWWW / Information Services Inc, Box 10046, Rochester NY 14610. **Tel** (716)482-2022. **ED** Mark Jones. Index available.
**Desc:** Lists and pinpoints current and future career jobs opportunities.

US/1065-9935
**CAREERS & COLLEGES.** [Career coll.]. **VFOAT** Careers and Colleges. (1981)-. Periodical. English. Four times a year. $15.00. E. M. Guild Inc., 989 Avenue of the Americas / 6th Floor, New York NY 10018. **Tel** (212)563-4688, FAX (212)967-2531. **ED** June Rogoznica. **DD** 378. **Bk Rev,** (Qty: 20). **Ad Acc, Adv Mgr:** Colleen Smith. **Circ:** 500,000 (ctrl).
**Desc:** Targeted to high school students and covers college and career preparation--applying to and financing college, career opportunities and personal development.

US/1056-277X
**CAREERS & THE DISABLED.** [Careers disabl.]. **VFOAT** Careers and the Disabled. Vol. 6, No. 2 (Spring 1991)-. Periodical. English. Three times a year. $12.00 (1 year), $22.00 (2 year), $33.00 (3 year). Equal Opportunity Publications Inc, 150 Motor Parkway Suite 420, Hauppage NY 11788. **Tel** (516)273-0066, FAX (516)273-8936. **ED** James Schneider. **LC** HV3018; .C37. **DD** 331.7/02/087. **Bk Rev. Ad Acc. Circ:** 10,000. ***Continues*** *Careers & The Handicapped, 0891-5202.*
**Desc:** The only career publication for people with disabilities. The advertisers are looking to hire the physically challenged.

ZA
**CAREERS BULLETIN (ZAMBIA).** (CAREERS BULLETIN.). (19??)-. Bulletin. English. Three times a year. Free. Republic of Zambia Ministry of Education, Career Unit, Box RW97, Lusaka Zambia.

CN/0229-379X
**CAREERS (EDMONTON).** (CAREERS.). [Careers]. Vol. 3, Issue 1-. Periodical. English. ir. $17.00. Reed Vocational Resource Library, Suite 800, 4445 Calgary Trail South, Edmonton Alta T6H 5C3 Canada. **DD** 331.7/02. ***Continues*** *Reed Career Magazine, 0706-716X.*

CN/0318-6229
**CAREERS FOR GRADUATES.** **VFOAT** Carrieres pour Diplomes. 1974-. Periodical. Multiple languages (English and French). Free to graduating students. Development Publications, POB 84 Succursale A, Willowdale Ontario M2N 5S7 Canada. **Tel** (416)636-2230. **ED** H Kane. **DD** 331.7/02/02571. **Ad Acc. Circ:** 13,000 (ctrl).
**Desc:** Mailed to placement offices in universities across Canada for free distribution to graduating students.

●UK/0969-6431
**CAREERS GUIDANCE TODAY.** **VFOAT** Careers Guidance To-Day. (1992)-. Trade Publication. English. Four times a year. £10.00. Inst of Careers Guidance, 27A Lower High Street, Stourbridge England. **Tel** 011 44 384 376464, FAX 011 44 384 440830. **ED** Sharon Jandu. **Ad Acc, Adv Mgr:** Annie Van Heerden, **Tel** 0223 276737. **Circ:** 3,300 (ctrl). ***Continues*** *Careers Officer, 0958-7489.*

RH
**CAREERS GUIDE.** English. Careers Publications, PO Box 374, Harare Zimbabwe. **LC** HF5382.5.Z55; C37. **DD** 331.7/02/096891.

US/0576-7334
**CAREERS IN BUSINESS.** 1954-. Periodical. English. an. Careers Inc, 1165 Fifth Avenue.

US/0502-0166
**CAREERS IN THE UNITED STATES DEPARTMENT OF THE INTERIOR.** **Main/Corp** United States. Dept. of the Interior. English. ir. US Department of the Interior / Bureau of Mines, Publications Department, PO Box 18070, Cochrans Mill Road, Pittsburgh PA 15236. **Tel** (412)892-6400. **LC** JK864; .A33. **DD** 353.3.
**Desc:** Describes various occupational opportunities available in the department.

●US/1059-3861
**CAREERS INTERNATIONAL.** [Careers int.]. (1992)-. Periodical. English. mo. $38.00 (professionals), $28.00 (students). Heritage Publishers, Inc., 2700 Woodlands Blvd., Suite 300, Flagstaff AZ 86001. **DD** 331.

UK/0958-7489
**CAREERS OFFICER.** ***Title Change.*** [Careers off.]. (19??)-(1992). Periodical. English. Four times a year. Inst of Careers Guidance, 27A Lower High Street, Stourbridge England. **Tel** 011 44 384 376464, FAX 011

44 384 440830. **DD** 371.425. ***Continues*** *Career's Journal, 0260-5694.* ***Continued by*** *Careers Guidance Today, 0969-6431.*

US/0193-1873
**CAREERS (SARATOGA).** (CAREERS.). 1979-. English. an. $5.00. Vitality Associates, PO Box 154, Saratoga CA 95070. **LC** Z7164.V6; M46; HF5382.5.U5. **DD** 331.7/02.

US/1074-3642
**CARETAKER GAZETTE, THE.** (1983)-. English. bm (6 issues). $24.00 US; $30.00 other. The Caretaker Gazette, HC76 Box 4022, Garden Valley ID 83622. **Tel** (208)462-3993, FAX (208)462-3993. **ED** Thea K. Dunn. Index available in last issue of volume--attached. cum. index. **Bk Rev**, (Qty: 6). **Ad Acc**, **Adv Mgr:** Gary C. Dunn, **Tel** same as publisher. **Circ:** 2,500 (ctrl).
**Desc:** Publication dedicated to finding and listing exclusive caretaker job opportunities in the United States and abroad. Free advertising available to landowners hiring caretakers. Contains job listings, reader correspondence, paid classifieds and caretaker profiles detailing location, duties, compensation and benefits.

●US/1072-575X
**CHICAGO JOB BANK, THE.** **VFOAT** Chicago Job Bank. (1994)-. English. an (Nov.). $15.95. Bob Adams Inc., 260 Center Street, Holbrook MA 02343. **Tel** (617)767-8100, (800)872-5627, FAX (617)767-0994. **ED** Carter Smith. ***Continues*** *Greater Chicago Job Bank, 1070-9142.*

US/0276-0355
**CHRONICLE CAREER INDEX.** [Chron. career index]. (1981)-. Periodical. English. an. $14.25. Chronicle Guidance Publications Inc., PO Box 1190, Moravia NY 13118. **Tel** (315)497-0330. **ED** Paul Downes and Harriet Scarry. **LC** Z7164.V6; C38; HF5381.A1. **DD** 016.3317/02. **Bk Rev**. **Ad Acc. Circ:** 6,350. ***Continues*** *Chronicle Career Index Annual, 0190-4663.*
**Desc:** Bibliography of more than 810 listings of occupational and educational information with these helpful features: identifies free materials, cross-reference of categories, cost and ordering information. Most listings annotated.

US
**CHURCH SECRETARYS COMMUNIQUE.** English. Twelve times a year. $24.00 (one year); $39.00 (two year). Christian Ministry Resources, PO Box 2301, Mathews NC 28106. **Tel** (800)222-1840, FAX (704)841-8039. **ED** James F. Cobble. **Circ:** 14,000.

CN
**CLASSIFICATION CANADIENNE DESCRIPTIVE DES PROFESSIONS.** **Added/Corp** Canada. Employment and Immigration Canada (Dept.). (19??)-. French. an. $5.40. Emploi et Immigration Canada, Approvisionnements et Services Canada, Ottawa Ontario K1A 0S9 Canada. **Tel** (819)994-2973. **LC** HB2619; .C55. **DD** 331.7/00971. **Circ:** 25,000.
**Desc:** Formed from the basis of the CCDO and provides a systematic classification structure in which the working population could be categorized.

US/1076-1799
**COLLEGE PLACEMENT COUNCIL DIRECTORY.** ***Title Change.*** **See** Education-Higher Education.

US
**COLORADO JOB FINDER.** (19??)-. English. $38.00. Colorado Municipal League, 1660 Lincoln, Suite 2100, Denver CO 80264. **Tel** (303)831-6411.
**Desc:** Provides information on administrative, technical and professional job openings in state and local government throughout Colorado.

US
**COMMUNICATIONS AND CLERICAL SKILLS PROGRAM; SCHEDULE OF COURSES.** **See** Education-Vocational Education.

US/0882-200X
**COMPUTER & ELECTRONICS GRADUATE, THE.** ***Ceased.*** [Comput. electron. grad.]. **VFOAT** Computer and Electronics Graduate. Vol. 1, No. 1 (Fall 1983)-Ceased Spring 1988 with Vol. 5, No. 3. Periodical. English. Three times a year. The Computer & Electronics Graduate, 44 Broadway, Greenlawn NY 11740. **ED** James Schneider and Anne Kelly. **DD** 621. **Bk Rev**. **Ad Acc. Circ:** 18,000 (ctrl).
**Desc:** A career/recruitment and information technology magazine for electrical/electronics (EE) engineers, computer science (CS) and systems entry level graduates. Career areas : positions within business, industry, the Armed Forces, and government.

US
**CONNECTICUT STATE PLAN FOR CAREER EDUCATION.** **See** Education-Vocational Education.

US/1063-9268
**CONTRACT EMPLOYMENT WEEKLY.** [Contract employ. wkly.]. **VFOAT** C.E. Weekly. (19??)-. Trade Publication. English. wk (Weds.). $55.00 US; $65.00 Canada and Mexico; $215.00 other. C E Publications Inc, PO Box 97000, Kirkland WA 98083. **Tel** (206)823-2222, FAX (206)821-0942. **ED** Jerry Erikson. **DD** 331. **Ad Acc.** ***Continues*** *Contract Engineer.*
**Desc:** A trade magazine for the contract employment industry. Subscribers are engineering and technical employees who work on contract (temporary) assignments throughout the world.

US/0892-5232
**CORPORATE JOBS OUTLOOK!.** [Corp. jobs outlook!]. (198?)-. Periodical. English. bm. $169.99 US; $194.99 Canada; $219.99 other. Corporate Jobs Outlook, PO Box 100, Boerne TX 78006-0100. **Tel** (210)755-8810, FAX (210)755-2410. **ED** Jack W. Plunkett. **LC** HF5382.5.U5; C66. **DD** 331. Index available. cum. index. available on an online database from HRIN file (ABI); and NEWSNET.
**Desc:** Complete, objective reports on job outlook at major firms; salaries, benefits, financial stability, advancement, and career outlook.

US/0749-7474
**CPC ANNUAL, THE.** ***Title Change.*** [CPC annu.]. **Added/Corp** College Placement Council. **VFOAT** College Placement Annual. (1984)-(1993). English. an. College Placement Council Inc., 62 Highland Avenue, Bethlehem PA 18017. **Tel** (610)868-1421, FAX (610)868-0208. **LC** HF5382.5.U5; C6. **DD** 331.7/02/0973. **Circ:** 1,000,000. ***Continues*** *College Placement Annual, 0069-5734.* ***Split into*** *Job Choices; Planning Job Choices (Two-Year College Edition); Job Choices ... in Business; Job Choices ... Healthcare* ***and*** *Job Choices ... in Science & Engineering.*
**Desc:** Three-volume occupational directory for college graduates. Volume One offers advice on the job search. Other volumes include information on job opportunities.

US/8755-8378
**CPC NATIONAL DIRECTORY.** ***Title Change.*** **See** Education-Higher Education.

US/0196-1004
**CPC SALARY SURVEY.** [CPC salary surv.]. **Main/Corp** College Placement Council. **Added/Corp** College Placement Council. Salary Survey. **VFOAT** C.P.C. Salary Survey. **VAT** College Placement Council Salary Survey. (1973/1974)-. Periodical. English. Four times a year. $220.00 North America; $235.00 other. College Placement Council Inc., 62 Highland Avenue, Bethlehem PA 18017. **Tel** (610)868-1421, FAX (610)868-0208. **ED** Dawn Gulick. **DD** 331. ***Formed by the union of*** *Men's Salary Survey* ***and*** *Women's Salary Survey.*
**Desc:** Reporting service on average beginning salaries offered to graduating college students.
**Ind/Abst** Stat. Ref. Index.

US/0272-2216
**CPC SALARY SURVEY FOR REGION MCPA.** **Main/Corp** College Placement Council. **VFOAT** Salary Survey for Region MCPA; MCPA Regional Report. (19??)-. English. an. College Placement Council Inc., 62 Highland Avenue, Bethlehem PA 18017. **Tel** (610)868-1421, FAX (610)868-0208.

US/0278-5277
**CRIMINAL JUSTICE CAREER DIGEST.** Vol. 1, No. 1 (Oct. 1981)-. Periodical. English. mo. $30.00. Checkpoint Inc, PO Box 565, Phoenix AZ 85001. **LC** Discard.

US/0897-909X
**CRS PUBLICATIONS' CAREER OPPORTUNITY INDEX (EAST-SOUTH-CENTRAL).** (CRS PUBLICATIONS' CAREER OPPORTUNITY INDEX.). [CRS Publ. career oppor. index]. **VFOAT** Career Opportunity Index, East-South-Central. **VAT** Career Research Systems Publications' Career Opportunity Index. Vol. 18, No. 1 (1988)-. Periodical. English. sa. $25.00. Career Research Systems Inc, PO Box 28799, Santa Ana CA 92799-8799. **Tel** (714)556-1200, FAX (714)556-6548. **ED** Timothy M Clancy. **LC** HF5382.5.U5; C335. **DD** 331.7/02/02573. **Bk Rev**. **Ad Acc. Circ:** 35,000 (ctrl). ***Continues*** *Career Research Systems' Career Opportunity Index (East-South-Central).*
**Desc:** Employment information.

US/0898-218X
**CRS PUBLICATIONS' CAREER OPPORTUNITY INDEX (WESTERN).** (CRS PUBLICATIONS' CAREER OPPORTUNITY INDEX.). [CRS Publications' career oppor. index]. **Added/Corp** Career Research Systems, Inc. **VFOAT** Career Opportunity Index; Career Opportunity Index, Western. **VAT** Career Research Systems Publications' Career Opportunity Index. Vol. 18, No. 1 (Spring/Summer 1988)-. Periodical. English. sa. $25.00. Career Research Systems Inc, 3621 S. Harbor, Suite 200, Santa Ana CA 92704. **Tel** (714)556-9360. **ED** John Heberling. **LC** HF5382.5.U5; C77. **DD** 331.7/02/097305. **Bk Rev**. **Ad Acc. Circ:** 50,000 (ctrl). ***Continues*** *Career Research Systems' Career Opportunity Index (Western), 0897-795X.*
**Desc:** Employment information.

US/0161-0562
**CURRENT CAREER AND OCCUPATIONAL LITERATURE.** (1977)-. English. be. Price varies per volume. H W Wilson Company, 950 University Avenue, Bronx NY 10452. **Tel** (800)367-6770, (718)588-8400, FAX (718)590-1617, telex 4990003 HWILSON. **LC** Z7164.V6; G65; HF5381.A1. **DD** 016.3317/02/0973.
**Desc:** With more than 1500 references to career literature listed under 700 job titles, this annotated bibliography of reference books, directories, and pamphlets provides complete publication information, description, and recommended audience level.

●US/1055-8292
**CURRENT EMPLOYMENT.** (1993)-. Periodical. English. qt. $29.99. Publishing & Business Consultants, PO Box 75392, Los Angeles CA 90075. **Tel** (213)732-3477, FAX (213)732-9123. **ED** Andeson Napoleon Atia. **Ad Acc.** Full Page (B&W) $5750.00. Half Page (B&W) $3575.00. Full Page (Color) $8750.00 (2 color). Half Page (Color) $5500.00 (2 color). **Circ:** 165,000 total.
**Desc:** Focused on the active employment seeker. Features articles on resume writing, interview tips, and good work attitudes. Also included are sources of job openings within various industries and government agencies.

US/1054-7762
**CURRENT JOBS FOR GRADUATES.** (CURRENT JOBS FOR GRADUATES : THE NATIONAL EMPLOYMENT BULLETIN FOR THE LIBERAL ARTS PROFESSIONS.). [Curr. jobs grad.]. (Oct. 2, 1990)-. Bulletin. English. sm. $79.00. Plymouth Publishing, Box 40550, 5136 MacArthur Boulevard Northwest, Washington DC 20016. **Tel** (703)506-4400. **DD** 331. ***Continues*** *History Careers Hotline, 0887-2821.*

US
**CURRENT RESEARCH ON OCCUPATIONS AND PROFESSIONS.** [Curr. res. occup. prof.]. Vol. 4 (1987)-. English. ir. $73.25. JAI Press Inc., 55 Old Post Road, Suite 2, PO Box 1678, Greenwich CT 06836-1678. **Tel** (203)661-7602, FAX (203)661-0792. **ED** Helena Znaniecka Lopata. ***Continues*** *Research in the Interweave of Social Roles, 0272-2801.*
**Ind/Abst** Soc. Plann. Policy Dev. Abstr.

US/1042-3672
**CV (NEW YORK, N.Y.).** ***Ceased.*** (CV.). [CV]. **VFOAT** CV Magazine. **VAT** Career Vision. Vol. 1, No. 1 (Feb./March 1989)-(Dec. 1990). Periodical. English. bm. Millicom Media Inc, 411 Lafayette Street/4th Floor, New York NY 10003. **LC** AP2; .C96. **DD** 378.

US
**DICTIONARY OF OCCUPATIONAL TITLES.** **Added/Corp** United States Employment Service. (1939)-. English. ir. $40.00. Claitors Law Books, 3165 South Acadian, Baton Rouge LA 70808. **Tel** (504)344-0476, (800)274-1403. **(Subscription address:** Claitors Law Books, PO Box 3333, Baton Rouge, LA 70821**)**

CN
**DIRECTORY OF AMERICAN EMPLOYMENT AGENCIES.** Directory. English. an. $15.00. Overseas Employment Services, 122 Laird Street, Suite 208, Mount Royal Quebec H3P 2T1 Canada. **Tel** (514)739-1108, FAX (514)739-0795.

UK/0143-3482
**DIRECTORY OF JOBS & CAREERS ABROAD.** [Dir. jobs careers abroad]. **VFOAT** Directory of Jobs and Careers Abroad; Jobs and Careers Abroad (Oxford. 1977). (1977)-. English. be. $16.95. Peterson's Guides, 202 Carnegie Center, Department 2342, Princeton NJ 08543. **Tel** (800)338-3282, FAX (609)452-0966. ***Continues*** *Jobs & Careers Abroad (Oxford. 1971).*
**Desc:** Guide to permanent career opportunities abroad. Lists the top trades and professions, as well as necessary qualifications, in Europe, Australia, and New Zealand.

UK
**DIRECTORY OF OVERSEAS SUMMER JOBS.** **VFOAT** Overseas Summer Jobs. (1985)-. English. an. $14.95. Peterson's Guides, 202 Carnegie Center, Department 2342, Princeton NJ 08543. **Tel** (800)338-3282, FAX (609)452-0966. ***Continues*** *Overseas Summer Jobs.*
**Desc:** Provides information on fifty thousand opportunities in over 40 countries, from archaeological digs in France to working in a Norwegian hotel. Gives important facts about visas, work permits, and health insurance.

●US/1072-4656
**DOWN THE ROAD.** (DOWN THE ROAD : A NEWSLETTER FROM MIKE BYRNES AND ASSOCIATES.). (1993)-. Newsletter. English. qt. $10.00. Mike Byrnes & Associates, 2025 North Third St., Suite

155, Phoenix AZ 85004. **Tel** (602)252-4868, FAX (602)252-8120. **ED** Bern C. Roberts. **Bk Rev. Ad Acc. Circ:** 1,500.

CN/0833-7209
**EMPLOI-AVENIR.** (EMPLOI-AVENIR : PERSPECTIVES PROFESSIONNELLES JUSQU'A.). [Empl.-avenir]. **VFOAT** Systeme de Projections des Professions au Canada (SPPC). 1988/89-. French. an. Employment and Immigration Canada, 3rd Floor/Room 358, 305 Rideau Street, Ottawa Ontario K1A 0J9 Canada. **Tel** (819)994-6509. **DD** 331.7/02/0971.

●US
**EMPLOYMENT AND TRAINING PARTNERSHIP : A PUBLICATION OF THE STATE JOB TRAINING COORDINATING COUNCIL, THE. See** Education-Vocational Education.

US/0146-9673
**EMPLOYMENT AND TRAINING REPORTER. Added/Corp** Manpower Information, inc. (Jan. 5, 1977)-. Periodical. English. wk (50 issues). $684.00 one year; $615.60 other. MII Publications Inc, 1211 Connecticut Avenue Northwest, Suite 402, Washington DC 20036. **Tel** (202)293-1740, FAX (202)293-0377. **(Subscription address:** PO Box 830430, Birmingham, AL 35283-0430; telephone: (800)633-4931, FAX: (205)995-1588**) ED** Anne Mytych and Maray Smith. **LC** HD5724; .M239. **DD** 331.1/1/0973. cum. index. **Bk Rev**, (Qty: 35-50). **Circ:** 5,000. ***Continues*** *Manpower Information Service.*
**Desc:** Newsletter that covers job training, vocational education programs for the poor or disadvantaged, related efforts and issues. Includes in-depth stories, statistics, laws, etc.

US/0194-3642
**EMPLOYMENT BULLETIN (AMERICAN SOCIOLOGICAL ASSOCIATION : 1976).** (EMPLOYMENT BULLETIN.). **Main/Corp** American Sociological Association. **VFOAT** ASA Employment Bulletin. Vol. 1 (Nov. 1976)-. Bulletin. English. Twelve times a year. $25.00 US; $33.00 other. American Sociological Association, 1722 North Street Northwest, Washington DC 20036-2981. **Tel** (202)833-3410, FAX (202)785-0146. **ED** Susan Frensilli. **LC** PAR. **Circ:** 3,000.
**Desc:** Provides a comprehensive listing of job opportunities in the field of sociology. In addition to positions in academic settings, the ASA Employment Bulletin also offers fellowship opportunities and positions in applied settings.

CN
**EMPLOYMENT LEADER.** (19??)-. English. wk. Metroland Printing Publishing & Distributing, 3145 Wolfedale Road, Mississauga, Ontario L5C 3A9 Canada. **Tel** (416)273-5680, FAX (416)273-4991.

US
**EMPLOYMENT MARKETPLACE.** (1982)-. English. qt (4 issues). Employment Marketplace, 12015 Robyn Park Drive, St. Louis MD 63131. **Tel** (314)569-3095, FAX (314)569-3095. **ED** Pat Turner.
**Desc:** Focuses on computers and employment information.

CN/0316-8964
**EMPLOYMENT OPPORTUNITIES HANDBOOK CANADA. WESTERN EDITION.** (EMPLOYMENT OPPORTUNITIES HANDBOOK, CANADA.). 1973/74-. Periodical. English. an. Free. University and College Placement Association, 1209 King Street West 2nd Floor, Toronto Ontario M6K 1G2 Canada. **DD** 331.7/02/02571.

●US/1076-4798
**EMPLOYMENT OPPORTUNITIES, USA.** [Employ. oppor. USA]. (Feb. 1995)-. English. Four times a year. $184.00 US; $187.00 other. Washington Research Associates, PO Box 2003, Littleton CO 80161. **Tel** (303)756-9038, FAX (303)758-9203. **ED** Joseph Ryan (editor's address: Washington Research Associates, 1660 South Albion Street, Suite 309, Denver, CO 80222; phone: (303)756-9038). **DD** 331. Index available (bound in first issue - free). ***Continues*** *U.S. Employment Opportunities, 0890-5959.*

US
**ENCYCLOPEDIA OF CAREERS AND VOCATIONAL GUIDANCE, THE.** (1967)-. Periodical. English. te. $129.95. Garrett Park Press, PO Box 190 F, Garrett Park MD 20896. **Tel** (301)946-2553. **ED** W E Hopke. Index Available Published separately--free--upon request.
**Desc:** Reference on occupations for use in school and college career centers, public libraries, etc. Describes 450 occupations in terms of the nature of the work, entry requirements, necessary training and educational background, working conditions, advancement opportunities, beginning and future earnings, and sources of additional information.

FR/0765-5762
**ENTREPRISES FORMATION. Added/Corp** Association Nationale pour la Formation Professionnelle des Adultes. **VFOAT** EF. (1985)-. Periodical. French. Eight times a year. 430.95F France; 470.00F other. Enterprises Formation, 13 Place du Gal de Gaulle, 93108 Montreuil Cedex France. **Tel** 011 33 1 48705007, 011 33 1 48705010. **LC** LC1060; .E56. **DD** 374/.944/05. ***Continues*** *Objectif Formation.*
**Ind/Abst** LABORDOC.

UK
**EUROPEAN GRADUATE RECRUITMENT NEWS.** (19??)-. English. qt. £45.00 UK; £55.00 other. ATS Quest, Somers House Linkfield Corner, Redhill Surrey RH1 1BB England. **Tel** 011 44 737 770013.

US
**EXECUTIVE, THE.** V. 1- Spring 1973-. Periodical. English. Three times a year. University of Alabama / Box J, Box J, University AL 35486.

UK/0955-6230
**EXECUTIVE SECRETARY BRADFORD.** [Exec. secr. Bradf.]. (1989)-. Periodical. English. Four times a year (Mar., June, Sept., Dec.). £74.95 UK, £84.95 others; £159.95 Australia, New Zealand & South Pacific; $239.95 US & Canada. Salisbury House Publishing Ltd, 13 Castle Street, Marriot Building, Buckingham MK18 1BP England. **Tel** 011 44 280 824444, FAX 011 44 280 824444. **(Subscription address:** Salisbury House Publishing Ltd., 182 Hill Top Road, Thornton Bradford BD13 3QL England.**) ED** Jo Denby. **DD** 651.3741. Index available. cum. index. **Bk Rev**, (Qty: 4). ctrl circ.

US
**EXPERIENCED PROFESSIONAL.** English. bm. $72.00. Career Research Systems Inc / Santa Anna, 3621 South Harbor Boulevard, PO Box 28799, Santa Anna CA 92799. **Tel** (714)556-1200. ***Continues*** *Career Opportunity Update.*

US/0739-1684
**FEDERAL JOBS DIGEST.** [Fed. Jobs Dig.]. **VFOAT** Federal Jobs. (19??)-. Periodical. English. bw (25 issues). $110.00 US; $136.00 Canada; $136.75 Mexico; $155.25 South America and Carribean; $168.75 Europe; $181.25 Asia and Africa; $183.25 other (regular edition) Status Edition is also available. Breakthrough Publishers, 310 North Highland Avenue, Ossining NY 10562. **Tel** (914)762-5111 ext. 1109. **ED** Eero Huovinen. **DD** 331. **Bk Rev. Ad Acc. Circ:** 3,100.
**Desc:** Coverage of current job openings in federal civil service. Included in each issue is how-to advice and a salary chart.

●US/1070-9193
**FINANCE (BOSTON, MASS.). See** Business-Banking and Finance.

US/1050-3757
**FINDING A JOB IN THE NONPROFIT SECTOR.** [Find. job nonprofit sect.]. **Added/Corp** Taft Group (Rockville, Md.). 1st Ed. (1991)-. English. ir. $95.00. Taft Group, 835 Penobscott Building, Customer Service, Detroit MI 48226. **Tel** (800)877-8238, FAX (313)961-6083. **(Subscription address:** Taft Group, PO Box 71701, Chicago IL 60694.**) LC** HD2769.2.U6; F56. **DD** 331.7/02/097305.

US/1069-8981
**FLORIDA JOB BANK, THE.** [Fla. job bank]. **VFOAT** Florida Jobbank. (1987)-. Periodical. English. an (Dec.). $15.95. Bob Adams Inc., 260 Center Street, Holbrook MA 02343. **Tel** (617)767-8100, (800)872-5627, FAX (617)767-0994. **ED** Carter Smith. **LC** HF5382.75.U62; F645. **DD** 331.12/8/0975905.

US
**FLORIDA VIEW. CAREERS.** ***Title Change.*** **Added/Corp** Florida. Bureau of Career Development & Educational Improvement. **VFOAT** Careers. **VAT** Florida Vital Information for Education and Work. Careers. (1994)-(1994). English. Florida Bureau of Career Development, Knott Building, Department of Education, Tallahassee FL 32301. **Tel** (904)488-0400. **LC** HF5382.5.U6; F645. **DD** 331.7/02/0975905. ***Continued by*** *Florida VIEW. Career Profiles.*

US/0888-5656
**FSMB HANDBOOK.** [FSMB handb.]. **Main/Corp** Federation of State Medical Boards of the United States. **VAT** Federation of State Medical Boards Handbook. (1985)-. English. an (July of every year). $15.00. Federation of State Medical Boards of the United States, 6000 West Place, Suite 707, Ft Worth TX 76107. **Tel** (817)735-8445, FAX (817)738-6629. **LC** RA396.A3; F43a. **DD** 353.0084/1046/025. **NLM** W 22; AA1 F2f. **[CCC]. *Continues*** *Federation of State Medical Boards of the United States. Directory, Articles of Incorporation and Bylaws.*

●US/1062-9238
**GETTING THE LOW-DOWN ON EMPLOYERS AND A LEG-UP ON THE JOB MARKET.** (1992)-. Periodical. English. $49.95 (single issue). Washington Researchers, PO Box 19005, 20th Street Station, Washington DC 20036. **Tel** (202)333-3533, (202)333-3499, FAX (202)625-0656.

UK
**GRADUATE OPPORTUNITIES (LONDON, ENGLAND : 1987).** (GRADUATE OPPORTUNITIES : GO.). **VFOAT** GO. (198?)-. English. an. £25.00. Newpoint Publishing Company Ltd., Windsor Court East, Grinstead House, West Sussex RH19 1XA England. **Tel** 011 44 342 318011. ***Formed by the union of*** *GO. Volume 1, Graduate Opportunities* ***and*** *GO. Volume 2, Postgraduate Opportunities.*

AT/0314-0679
**GRADUATE OUTLOOK. See** Education-Higher Education.

US/1070-9142
**GREATER CHICAGO JOB BANK, THE.** ***Title Change.*** [Gt. Chic. job bank]. **VFOAT** Chicago Job Bank. (1982)-(1993). Periodical. English. an. Bob Adams Inc., 260 Center Street, Holbrook MA 02343. **Tel** (617)767-8100, (800)872-5627, FAX (617)767-0994. **ED** Carter Smith. **LC** HF5382.5.U6; I53. **DD** 331.12/8/0977311. ***Continued by*** *Chicago Job Bank, 1072-575X.*

CN/0833-9457
**HEALTH CAREER PATHS. See** Medical Science and Technology-Physicians and Medical Personnel.

CN/0701-1210
**HEALTH CAREERS NEWS.** (Winter 1976)-. Periodical. English. Ontario Hospital Association, 150 Ferrand Drive, Don Mills Ontario M3C 1H6 Canada. **Tel** (905)429-2661 ext. 7736. **DD** 610.69. ***Supersedes*** *Hospital Careers News, 0701-1202.*

US/8756-310X
**HELPING OUT IN THE OUTDOORS. See** Public Administration-Parks and Recreation.

●US/1064-1769
**HIDDEN JOB MARKET.** (THE HIDDEN JOB MARKET : A JOB SEEKER'S GUIDE TO AMERICA'S 2,000 LITTLE-KNOWN, FASTEST GROWING HIGH-TECH COMPANIES / COMPILED BY CORPTECH.). [Hidden job market]. **Added/Corp** Corporate Technology Information Services. Peterson's Guides, Inc. **VFOAT** Discover the Hidden Job Market. (1992)-. English. an. $16.95. Peterson's Guides, 202 Carnegie Center, Department 2342, Princeton NJ 08543. **Tel** (800)338-3282, FAX (609)452-0966. **LC** HF5382.75.U6; H53. **DD** 331.7/4/02573.
**Desc:** Sourcebook of companies that are creating not only new technologies and new products, but new jobs as well. Arranged alphabetically by state, allowing easy access to companies within specific geographic locations.

US/0749-2960
**HIGH TECHNOLOGY CAREERS. VFOAT** Careers. (Apr. 15, 1984)-. Periodical. English. Six times a year (Feb., Apr., June, Aug., Oct., Dec.). $29.00 (one year), $56.00 (two year), $79.00 (three year). Westech Expo Corporation, 4701 Patrick Henry Drive, Building #1901, Santa Clara CA 95054. **Tel** (818)702-0442. **ED** Cathy Mickelson.
**Desc:** Carries the most current technical employment offerings from the nation's top companies. Editorial topics include national employment trends and job search skills.

US/1064-0916
**HISPANIC HOTLINE.** (HISPANIC HOTLINE : THE HISPANIC, DISABLED & WOMEN'S JOB FINDER.). [Hisp. hotline]. (1983)-. Periodical. English. mo. $26.00. Hispanic Hotline, PO Box 163510, Sacramento CA 95816. **Tel** (916)448-7594, FAX (916)989-4742. **DD** 331.

US/0892-1369
**HISPANIC TIMES MAGAZINE.** [Hisp. times mag.]. **VFOAT** Hispanic Times. (19??)-. Periodical. English (Spanish). Five times a year. $30.00. Diversity Enterprises, 1550 Yorkshire Road, Birmingham MI 48009. **Tel** (810)433-1947. **DD** 331. **[CCC]. Bk Rev. Ad Acc, Adv Mgr:** D. Lopez. **Circ:** 35,000 (ctrl). ***Continues*** *Hispanic Times, 0199-770X.*
**Desc:** Edited for Hispanic and American Indian professionals and college students. The majority of editorial content concerns information on careers, business and related activities. Also emphasizes the achievements of Hispanics, American Indians and companies who employ them. Covers events and offers articles on how to improve job opportunities and a resume service.
**Ind/Abst** Acad. Abstr. Full Text Elite (July 1993-) [Full Txt.]; Acad. Abstr. (July 1993-); Acad. Search (July 1993-); Mag. Artic. Summar. Elite (July 1993-) [Full Txt.]; Mag. Artic. Summar. CD-ROM (July 1993-).

●US/1063-1143
**HUNT-SCANLON'S EXECUTIVE RECRUITERS OF NORTH AMERICA.** [Hunt-Scanlon's exec. recruit. N. Am.]. **Added/Corp** Hunt-Scanlon Publishing Company, Inc. **VFOAT** Hunt Scanlon's Executive Recruiters of North America; Executive Recruiters of North America. (1993)-. English. an (Jan.). $79.95. Hunt-Scanlon Publishing Company, Two Pickwick Plaza, Greenwich CT 06830. **Tel** (203)629-3629, FAX (203)629-3701. **ED** Christopher

Hunt and Scott A. Scanlon. **LC** HD38.25.U6; H86. **DD** 338.7/61658407111/0257.
**Desc:** Directory of leading executive recruiters based in the US, Canada and Mexico.

US/0091-648X
**INDEX OF EMPLOYMENT OPPORTUNITIES. PROFESSIONAL CAREERS EDITION.** (INDEX OF EMPLOYMENT OPPORTUNITIES.). [Index employ. oppor., Prof. careers ed.]. English. Resource Publications Inc / Princeton, PO Box 2331, Princeton NJ 08540. **LC** HF5382.5.U5; I55. **DD** 331.7/02/0973.

UY
**INDICE DE PROFESIONALES DEL URUGUAY.** **VFOAT** Indice Professional. 1982-. Spanish. $23.00. Fundacion de Cultura Universitaria, 25 de Mayo, 568 Casilla 1155, 11000 Montevideo Uruguay. **Tel** 011 598 2 961152. **LC** HD8038.U8; I53. **Ad Acc. Circ:** 2,000.
**Desc:** Contains information about all the professions, banks and financial houses of entire Uruguay.

US/1058-0506
**INTERNATIONAL EMPLOYMENT GAZETTE.** [Int. employ. gaz.]. **Added/Corp** International Placement Network. (1990)-. Periodical. English. bw. $95.00 (one year), $55.00 (6 months), $35.00 (3 months). International Employment Gazette, 1525 Wade Hampton Boulevard, Greenville SC 29609. **Tel** (803)235-4444, FAX (803)235-3369. **ED** Robert L. Whitmore. **DD** 333. **Bk Rev**, (Qty: varies). **Ad Acc, Adv Mgr:** Del McCaleb. **Circ:** 20,000.
**Desc:** Publishes more than 400+ overseas job openings every 2 weeks in a tabloid newspaper format. It also contains news and articles of interest to overseas job seekers as well as ads for goods and services needed by Americans working abroad.

US/0748-8890
**INTERNATIONAL EMPLOYMENT HOTLINE.** [Int. employ. outlook]. (1980)-. Periodical. English. Twelve times a year. $39.00 (one year); $69.00 (two years). International Employment Hotline, PO Box 3030, Oakton VA 22124. **Tel** (703)620-1972, FAX (703)620-1973. **ED** Will Cantrell. **DD** 331. **Circ:** 5,000.
**Desc:** Newsletter which monitors international job markets. Features current job openings for a wide variety of occupations throughout the world.

HK/0955-6214
**INTERNATIONAL JOURNAL OF CAREER MANAGEMENT, THE.** Vol. 1, No. 1 (1989)-. Periodical. English. Five times a year. $1129.00. MCB University Press, 60 62 Toller Lane, Bradford West Yorkshire BD8 9BX England. **Tel** 011 44 274 499821, FAX 011 44 274 547143, telex 51317 MCBUNI G. **(Subscription address:** MCB University Press / US and Canada Subscriptions, PO Box 10812, Birmingham AL 35201-0812.**)** **ED** Rod Davies. **LC** HF5549.5.C35; I58. **DD** 650.14/05. Index available. **Bk Rev. Ad Acc. Circ:** 200. Documents available from UMI Article Clearinghouse. ***Absorbed*** *Recruitment Selection and Retention.*
**Desc:** The journal facilitates communication between all those who ask the question: How can we help people to develop their careers and talents within that rapidly changing work environment The journal concerns itself with employees at all levels, across a range of industries and at every stage in their career.
**Ind/Abst** ABI/INFORM Glob. Ed.

US
**INTERNSHIP OPPORTUNITIES AT THE SMITHSONIAN INSTITUTION.** **Added/Corp** Smithsonian Institution. Office of Museum Programs. (1990/1991)-. English. Smithsonian Institution, 1100 Jefferson Drive SW, Washington DC 20560. **Tel** (202)357-2605. **LC** Q11.S8; I57.

US/0272-5460
**INTERNSHIPS.** [Internships]. (1981)-. English. an. $29.95. Peterson's Guides, 202 Carnegie Center, Department 2342, Princeton NJ 08543. **Tel** (800)338-3282, FAX (609)452-0966. **ED** Katherine Jobst. **LC** L901; .I66. **DD** 331.25/922. **Bk Rev. Ad Acc.**
**Desc:** Most comprehensive, current information on training opportunities in fields ranging from business to science to theater.

US/0890-1538
**INTERP CENTRAL CLEARINGHOUSE NEWSLETTER.** ***Ceased.*** [Interp Cent. clgh. newsl.]. **Added/Corp** Interpretation Central. (1978)-(19??). Newsletter. English. bm. Interp Central Inc, PO Box 28, Chelsea MI 48118. **Tel** (313)475-7070. **ED** Gabriel J Cherem. **DD** 050. **Bk Rev. Circ:** 150 (ctrl).
**Desc:** Contains literature updates, news bulletins, want ads, product listings, and training and employment opportunities for public contact personnel and interpretive professionals.

SA
**JAARVERSLAG.** **See** Economics-Labor.

●US/1064-7945
**JIM GILREATH'S EXECUTIVE JOB SEARCH GAZETTE.** **VFOAT** Executive Job Search Gazette. (1992)-. Periodical. English. $39.00. Jim Gilreath, PO Box 1483, Manchester-by-the-Sea MA 01944.

US
**JOB BANK GUIDE TO EMPLOYMENT SERVICES, THE.** **VFOAT** Guide to Employment Services; Employment Services. (1986)-. English. an (Sept.). $150.00. Bob Adams Inc., 260 Center Street, Holbrook MA 02343. **Tel** (617)767-8100, (800)872-5627, FAX (617)767-0994. **LC** HD5873; .J6. **DD** 331.12/8/02573.
**Desc:** Over 6,000 employment agencies, temporary help firms, executive recruiters, and career counseling services.

US/0278-5706
**JOB CATALOG, THE.** 1st Ed. (1979)-. Catalog. English. an. $9.00. Mail Order USA, 1255 Wisconsin Avenue NW/#6, Washington DC 20007. **Tel** (202)686-9521. **ED** Dorothy O'Callaghan. **LC** HF5382.75.U6; O26. **DD** 650.1/4/025753. **Circ:** 6,000.
**Desc:** Where to find creative jobs in Washington DC and Baltimore: book, magazine and newspaper publishers; fast news media, public relations, performing arts, conventions; professional organizations to join.

●US
**JOB CHOICES ... IN BUSINESS.** **Added/Corp** College Placement Council. **VFOAT** Job Choices. 37th Ed. (1994)-. Periodical. English. an (Sept.). $45.90 (complete 4 volume set); Also comes with College Placement Council membership. College Placement Council Inc., 62 Highland Avenue, Bethlehem PA 18017. **Tel** (610)868-1421, FAX (610)868-0208. **LC** HF5382.5.U5; J59. ***Continues in part*** *CPC Annual, 0749-7474.*

●US
**JOB CHOICES ... IN HEALTHCARE.** **Added/Corp** College Placement Council. **VFOAT** Job Choices ... in Health Care; Job Choices. 37th Ed. (1994)-. Periodical. English. an (Sept.). $45.90 (complete 4 volume set); Also comes with College Placement Council membership. College Placement Council Inc., 62 Highland Avenue, Bethlehem PA 18017. **Tel** (610)868-1421, FAX (610)868-0208. **LC** HF5382.5.U5; J593. **DD** 362.1/023/73. ***Continues in part*** *CPC Annual, 0749-7474.*

●US
**JOB CHOICES ... IN SCIENCE & ENGINEERING.** **Added/Corp** College Placement Council. **VFOAT** Job Choices ... in Science and Engineering; Job Choices. 37th Ed. (1994)-. Periodical. English. an (Sept.). $45.90 (complete 4 volume set); Also comes with College Placement Council membership. College Placement Council Inc., 62 Highland Avenue, Bethlehem PA 18017. **Tel** (610)868-1421, FAX (610)868-0208. **LC** HF5382.5.U5; J595. **DD** 502/.3/73. ***Continues in part*** *CPC Annual, 0749-7474.*

●US/1065-4658
**JOB FINDER FOR HIGH TECH SILICON VALLEY.** [Job finder high tech Silicon Val.]. 1st Ed. (1992)-. Periodical. English. $39.90. Simon Guides, 1016 East El Camino Real, #465, Sunnyvale CA 94087. **DD** 331.

CN/0833-7195
**JOB FUTURES.** (JOB FUTURES : AN OCCUPATIONAL OUTLOOK TO.). [Job futur.]. **VFOAT** Canadian Occupational Projection System, COPS. 1988/89-. English. an. Employment and Immigration Canada, 3rd Floor/Room 358, 305 Rideau Street, Ottawa Ontario K1A 0J9 Canada. **Tel** (819)994-6509. **DD** 331.7/02/0971. available on an online database.

US/0889-9908
**JOB HUNTER, THE.** (THE JOB HUNTER / CAREER PLANNING & PLACEMENT CENTER, UNIVERSITY OF MISSOURI - COLUMBIA.). [Job hunt.]. **Added/Corp** University of Missouri - Columbia. Career Planning and Placement Center. Vol. 10, No. 12 (June 7, 1985)-. Periodical. English. Twenty-six times a year. $90.00 institutions, $50.00 individuals. University of Missouri at Columbia, Career Planning Center, 100 Noyes Building, Columbia MO 65211. **Tel** (314)882-2097, (314)882-2351, FAX (314)882-5440. **ED** Thom Ralles. **DD** 371. **Ad Acc, Adv Mgr:** Barb Thornton. **Circ:** 400.
**Desc:** A national publication with job listings from across the country, in categories such as arts, business, communications, health, human services, public affairs, etc.

US/1053-1874
**JOB HUNTER'S SOURCEBOOK.** [Job hunt. sourceb.]. **Added/Corp** Gale Research Inc. Detroit Public Library. Career and Employment Information Center. **VFOAT** Job Hunter's Source Book; JHS. 1st Ed. (1991)-. English. be. $49.95. Gale Research Inc., 835 Penobscot Building, Detroit MI 48226. **Tel** (800)877-GALE, (313)961-2242, FAX (313)961-6083, telex TWX 810-221-7086. **LC** HF5382.75.U6; J63; HF5382.7; .J62. **DD** 331.12/8/097305.

US/8756-1670
**JOB INFORMATION LETTER.** **VFOAT** JIL. Periodical. English. bm. $50.00. National Association of Government Communicators, 80 South Early Street, Alexandria VA 22304. **Tel** (703)823-4821. **ED** Deborah M Trocchi. **DD** 331. **Bk Rev. Ad Acc.** ctrl circ.
**Desc:** A report on communication jobs available in federal, state, local government and private industries.

US/1051-9017
**JOB JARGON.** [Job jarg.]. **VFOAT** Johnson-Rudolph Job Jargon. (1989)-. Periodical. English. mo. $46.45 (one year), 69.95 (two year). Southern School Media, PO Box 70219, Bowling Green KY 42101. **Tel** (502)781-1915, (800)736-0288, FAX (502)782-6925. **DD** 650.

US
**JOB MARKET PREVIEWS.** English. Eleven times a year. $35.00. National Clearinghouse for Legal Services, 205 West Monroe Street 2nd Floor, Chicago IL 60606. **Tel** (312)263-3830.

US/0196-1551
**JOB OPENINGS FOR ECONOMISTS.** **Added/Corp** American Economic Association. **VFOAT** JOE. (1974)-. Periodical. English. Seven times a year. $25.00 (non-members), $15.00 (members). American Economic Association / Tennessee, 2014 Broadway, Suite 305, Nashville TN 37203-2418. **Tel** (615)322-2595.

AT/1031-0894
**JOB PROSPECTS AUSTRALIA.** (1988)-. English. be (Oct.). 26.95Aus$. New Hobsons Press, 553 Elizabeth Street, Surry Hills 2010, Australia. **Tel** 11 61 2 3102257, FAX 11 61 2 3102243. **ED** Melody Lord, Catherine Etteridge. **Bk Rev**, (Qty: 4). **Circ:** 2,000 (ctrl).
**Desc:** Resource for job market information in Australia.

US/0742-9223
**JOB SEARCH. A GUIDE FOR UNIVERSITY OF VERMONT STUDENTS.** **Added/Corp** College Placement Council. (1984)-. English. an. Free on request. College Placement Council Inc., 62 Highland Avenue, Bethlehem PA 18017. **Tel** (610)868-1421, FAX (610)868-0208.

US
**JOB SEEKER.** English. bw. $84.00 institutions; $60.00 individuals. Job Seeker, Rt 2 Box 16, Warrens WI 54666. **Tel** (608)378-4290. **ED** Becky Potter. **Circ:** 2,500.
**Desc:** Nationwide vacancy listings in the environmental and natural resources fields.

●US/1061-3285
**JOB SEEKER'S GUIDE TO PRIVATE AND PUBLIC COMPANIES.** [Job seek. guide priv. public co.]. **Added/Corp** Gale Research Inc. **VFOAT** Job Seeker's Guide; JSG. 1st Ed. (1992)-. English. $365.00. Gale Research Inc., 835 Penobscot Building, Detroit MI 48226. **Tel** (800)877-GALE, (313)961-2242, FAX (313)961-6083, telex TWX 810-221-7086. **ED** Peggy Kneffel Daniels, Susan E. Edgar. **LC** HF5382.75.U6; J634. **DD** 338.7/4/02573.
**Desc:** Answers important questions regarding company benefits and employment opportunities and identifies human resources contacts and other corporate officials.

US/1065-6944
**JOBS AVAILABLE (WESTERN ED.).** (JOBS AVAILABLE : JA.). **VFOAT** JA. (19??)-. Periodical. English. bw. $22.00. Jobs Available, PO Box 1040, Modesto CA 95353. **Tel** (209)571-2120, FAX (209)576-1249. **Ad Acc.** ctrl circ. ***Continues in part*** *Jobs Available, 0738-7601.*
**Desc:** A listing of employment opportunities in the public sector.

CN/1195-5325
**JOBS FOR YOUR FUTURE.** (19??)-. English. ir (Every 4 to 5 years). 4.50Can$ (one copy), 17.50Can$ (seven copies), 33.00Can$ (ten copies). Bridging the Gap, 7777 Keele Street, 2nd Floor, Concord Ontario L4K 1Y7 Canada. **Tel** (905)660-1056, FAX (905)660-7450. ***Continues*** *Jobs Canada.*
**Desc:** The guide that gives people a "tool" to help them explore careers and identify the required training, or learn job-seeking skills to help find a job.

●US/1074-5475
**JOBS IN HIGHER EDUCATION.** [Jobs higher educ.]. Vol. 1, No. 1 (Oct. 1990)-. Periodical. English. mo. $48.00. Jobs in Higher Education, PO Box 10100, Colorado Springs CO 80932. **Tel** (719)475-9797, FAX (719)475-9693. **ED** Charles G. Clute. **DD** 331. **Circ:** 3,000. ***Continues*** *The Minority Review, 1053-4229.*
**Desc:** Contains position announcements/jobs available and positions wanted for people with a college education.

US/1069-0727
**JOURNAL OF CAREER ASSESSMENT.** [J. career assess.]. **Added/Corp** Psychological Assessment Resources. Vol. 1, No. 1 (Winter 1993)-. Periodical. English. qt. $40.00 individuals, $120.00

institutions. Psychological Assessment Resources, PO Box 998, Odessa FL 33556. **Tel** (813)968-3003. **DD** 153. **CODEN** JOAAEX.

US/0894-8453
### JOURNAL OF CAREER DEVELOPMENT.
[J. career dev.]. **Added/Corp** University of Missouri-Columbia. College of Education. **VFOAT** Career Development; JDC. Vol. 11, No. 1 (Sept. 1984)-. Periodical. English. qt. £33.00 (individuals), £130.00 (institutions) UK; $175.00 US; $205.00 other. Human Sciences Press, PO Box 735, 233 Spring Street, New York NY 10013. **Tel** (212)620-8000, FAX (212)807-1047, telex 23421139. **(Subscription address:** Eurospan Ltd., Journals and Serials Division, 3 Henrietta Street, Covent Garden, London WC2E 8LU England.**) ED** Norman Gysbers. **LC** LC1037.5; .J68. **DD** 370. **[CCC].** available on microfilm and microfiche from University Microfilms International (UMI). ***Continues*** *Journal of Career Education, 0164-2502.*
**Desc:** Provides the professional, the public, and policymakers with the latest in career development theory, research and practice, while focusing on the impact that theory and research have on practice. Among the topics covered are career education, adult career development, career development of special needs populations, and career and leisure. The journal will help theorists, researchers and practitioners stay abreast of today's issues in career development, and also become knowledgeable about trends that will have an impact on the future of the field.
**Ind/Abst** AGRICOLA; Contents Pages Educ.; Curr. Index J. Educ. (1984-199?); Educ. Index; Educ. Adm. Abstr. (?-?); Except. Child Educ. Resour. (1984-19??); High. Educ. Abstr. (1984-); Hum. Resour. Abstr. (?-?); Psychol. Abstr. (1984-); PsycINFO (1990-); PsycLit; Soc. Work Abstr. [Select. Cov.]; Tech. Educ. Train. Abstr.; Work Relat. Abstr.

US/0884-5352
### JOURNAL OF CAREER PLANNING & EMPLOYMENT.
[J. career plan. employ.]. **Added/Corp** College Placement Council. **VFOAT** Journal of Career Planning and Employment. Vol. 46, No. 1 (Fall 1985)-. Periodical. English. qt (4 issues). $72.00 North America; $87.00 other. College Placement Council Inc., 62 Highland Avenue, Bethlehem PA 18017. **Tel** (610)868-1421, FAX (610)868-0208. **ED** Patricia A. Sinnott. **LC** LB2343.5; .A15. **DD** 378/.194/202573. Index available. **Bk Rev. Ad Acc. Circ:** 4,000. available on microfilm and microfiche from University Microfilms International (UMI). Documents available from UMI Article Clearinghouse. ***Continues*** *Journal of College Placement, 0021-9770.*
**Desc:** Articles on new ideas, techniques, and current issues, book reviews, how-to and reader's views departments.
**Ind/Abst** Curr. Index J. Educ.; Educ. Index; Expand. Acad. Index (1992-); High. Educ. Abstr. (1985-); Newsp. Period. Abstr. (1989-); Person. Manage. Abstr.; Work Relat. Abstr.

US/0022-0787
### JOURNAL OF EMPLOYMENT COUNSELING.
[J. employ. couns.]. **Added/Corp** National Employment Counselors Association (U.S.). (19??)-. Periodical. English. qt (4 issues). $30.00. American Counseling Association, 5999 Stevenson Avenue, Alexandria VA 22304. **Tel** (703)823-9800, (800)347-6647, FAX (703)823-0252. **(Subscription address:** American Counseling Association, Subscription Office, PO Box 2513, Birmingham AL 35201-2513.**) ED** Robert Drummond. **LC** HF5382.5.U5; J68. **DD** 331.702/0973. **CODEN** JECODE. **[CCC]. Ad Acc. Pr Rev. Circ:** 597 (ctrl). available on microfilm and microfiche from University Microfilms International (UMI). Documents available from The Genuine Article.
**Desc:** Covers theory and practice of interest to state employment counselors, vocational counselors, college placement counselors, counselor educators, and counselors in business, industry, and personnel. Articles focus on developing trends in organizational behavior and state-of-the-art personnel practices.
**Ind/Abst** Appl. Soc. Sci. Index Abstr.; Curr. Contents Soc. Behav. Sci.; Curr. Index J. Educ.; Int. Labour Doc.; LABORDOC; Psychol. Abstr. (1969-); PsycINFO; PsycLit; Res. Alert [Full Cov.]; Soc. Sci. Cit. Index [Full Cov.]; Soc. Work Abstr. [Select. Cov.].

JA
### KAIHATSU TO KENSHU.
Periodical. Japanese. Tokyo-to Sogo Gino, Kaihatsu Kenshujo 1-5, Uchi Kanda 1 Tokyo Japan. **LC** HD5715.5.J3; K34.

US/0891-2572
### KENNEDY'S CAREER STRATEGIST.
[Kennedy's career strateg.]. Vol. 1, No. 1 (Jan. 1986)-. Periodical. English. mo. $59.00 (1 year), $100.00 (2 years) US; $69.00 other. Kennedys Career Strategist, 1150 Wilmette Avenue, Wilmette IL 60091. **Tel** (708)251-1661, FAX (708)251-5191. **DD** 331. cum. index.

BE
### KNACK.
Dutch. wk. 2990.00F Belgium; 8190.00F other. Uitg Roularta, Meiboomlaan 33-35, B-8800 Roeselare Belgium. **Tel** 011 32 51 115863.

FR/0150-6439
### MAISON INDIVIDUELLE, LA.
(1974)-. Periodical. French. Ten times a year. 195.89F France; 290.00F other. Le Groupe Moniteur, 17 Rue d'Uzes, 75002 Paris France. **Tel** 011 33 1 19401330. **UDC** 728.3 + 729.

FR/1157-6049
### MAITRISE PARIS.
(MAITRISE.). (1991)-. Periodical. French. Ten times a year. 880.00F. Edition de Medias d'Entreprise, 17 rue Viete, 75854 Paris Cedex 17 France. **Tel** 011 33 1 47636876. **UDC** 658(44).

US/0741-3092
### MANAGEMENT CONSULTING (BOSTON, MASS.).
(MANAGEMENT CONSULTING.). [Manage. consult.]. **Added/Corp** Harvard Business School Management Consulting Club. (19??)-. English. be. $20.00 US; $21.00 (includes postage) Canada; $23.00 (includes postage) other. Harvard Business School Publishing Division, Operations Department, Boston MA 02163. **Tel** (617)495-6192, (617)495-8948, FAX (617)495-6891, telex 6817229. **LC** HD69.C6; M357. **DD** 658.4/6.
**Desc:** Provides advice about approaching a job search in management consulting. Through personal commentaries, academic perspectives, and company profiles, this guide offers key information on the wide range of careers available to MBA students.

US/0882-3979
### MCGRAW-HILL'S COMPUTER CAREERS.
[McGraw-Hill's comput. careers]. **VFOAT** Computer Careers. Vol. 1, No. 1 (May 1985)-. Periodical. English. qt. $16.00. McGraw Hill's Computer Careers, New York NY 10124. **Tel** (212)512-2000. **DD** 001.

US/1054-7355
### MEMBERSHIP DIRECTORY / ALOA, ASSOCIATED LOCKSMITHS OF AMERICA, INC.
[Membersh. dir. - Assoc. Locksmiths Am.]. **Main/Corp** Associated Locksmiths of America. **VFOAT** Membership Directory of the Associated Locksmiths of America Inc.; ALOA Membership Directory. **VAT** Associated Locksmiths of America Membership Directory. (198?)-. Directory. English. Associated Locksmiths of America, 3003 Live Oak Street, Dallas TX 75204. **LC** TS519; .A8218. **DD** 683/.3/06073. ***Continues*** *Who's Who Among Professional Locksmiths, 8755-2329.*

US
### METROPOLITAN NEW YORK JOB BANK, THE.
**VFOAT** New York Job Bank; Metropolitan New York Jobbank; Metro New York Job Bank; Metro New York Jobbank. 1st Ed. (1981)-. English. an (Nov.). $15.95. Bob Adams Inc., 260 Center Street, Holbrook MA 02343. **Tel** (617)767-8100, (800)872-5627, FAX (617)767-0994. **ED** Carter Smith. **LC** HF5382.75.U62; N615.

US/0093-6421
### MICHIGAN LICENSED OCCUPATIONS.
English. 7310 Woodward Avenue, Detroit MI 48202. **LC** HD3630.U7; M55. **DD** 344/.774/017.

US/0148-1851
### MISSOURI OCCUPATIONAL STAFFING PATTERNS OF SELECTED NON-MANUFACTURING INDUSTRIES SURVEYED.
(MISSOURI OCCUPATIONAL STAFFING PATTERNS OF SELECTED NON-MANUFACTURING INDUSTRIES.). [Mo. occup. staff. patterns sel. non-manuf. ind. surv.]. **Main/Corp** Missouri. Division of Employment Security. **VFOAT** Occupational Employment Statistics: Nonmanufacturing Staffing Patterns. English. te. Division of Employment Security / Missouri, PO Box 59, Jefferson City MO 65104. **Tel** (314)751-3602. **ED** Betty Brown. **LC** HD5725.M8; M58C. **DD** 331.1/1/09778. **Circ:** 325.
**Desc:** Provides staffing patterns for selected nonmanufacturing industries.

US
### MLA JOB INFORMATION LIST. ENGLISH ED.
**Added/Corp** Modern Language Association of America. Association of Departments of English. **VFOAT** Job Information List. **VAT** Modern Language Association of America Job Information List. (19??)-. Periodical. English. $35.00. Association of the Departments of English, A Subsidiary of the Modern Language Association, 10 Astor Place, New York NY 10003. **Tel** (212)614-6321. **ED** Roy Chustek. **Bk Rev. Ad Acc. Circ:** 6,000.
**Desc:** Information on teaching positions in English and foreign languages at the college level.

US
### MLA JOB INFORMATION LIST. FOREIGN LANGUAGE EDITION.
**Added/Corp** Modern Language Association of America. Association of Departments of Foreign Languages (U.S.). **VFOAT** M.L.A. Job Information List; Job Information List. Foreign Language Edition. (19??)-. Periodical. English. qt (Feb., April, Oct., Dec.). $35.00. Association of the Departments of English, A Subsidiary of the Modern Language Association, 10 Astor Place, New York NY 10003. **Tel** (212)614-6321.

US/0744-7140
### NATIONAL AD SEARCH, THE.
Vol. 1 (198?)-. Periodical. English. wk. $235.00 (one year), $435.00 (two year), $625.00 (three year). National Ad Search Inc., PO Box 2083, Milwaukee WI 53201. **Tel** (414)351-1398. ***Continues*** *Ad Search, 0744-043X.*
**Desc:** Over 2,000 career opportunities listed in 55 categorized areas of expertise compiled from 75 major newspaper sources from key markets throughout the U.S.

US/1055-9523
### NATIONAL BUSINESS EMPLOYMENT WEEKLY.
[Natl. bus. employ. wkly.]. **Added/Corp** Dow Jones & Co. (19??)-. Periodical. English. wk. $199.00 US; $205.00 Canada; $210.00 Mexico; $237.00 Western Hemisphere; $281.00 Europe; $320.00 Asia and Africa; $324.00 other. Dow Jones and Company Inc, 200 Burnett Road, Chicopee MA 01021. **Tel** (413)592-7761, (800)568-7625. **DD** 331.
**Desc:** Contains job listings from the nation's top employers, plus multiple articles on the basics of researching the job market, interviewing and networking, plus issues and options to consider in starting a business.

US/1044-9841
### NATIONAL DIRECTORY OF INTERNSHIPS, THE.
[Natl. dir. internsh.]. **Added/Corp** National Society for Internships and Experiential Education (U.S.). (1984)-. Directory. English. an. $26.50 two years. National Society for Internships and Experiential Education, 3509 Haworth Avenue, Suite 207, Raleigh NC 27609-7229. **Tel** (919)787-3263. **DD** 378. ***Formed by the union of*** *Directory of Undergraduate Internships; Directory of Washington Internships; State-Sponsored Internship Programs* ***and*** *Directory of Public Service Internships.*
**Desc:** If you want to explore a future career or are interested in a new one, the Directory can help. You'll find thousands of internships opportunities across the country - in nonprofit organizations, government, and business.

US/0899-0212
### NATIONAL DIRECTORY OF PERSONNEL CONSULTANTS BY SPECIALIZATION.
[Natl. dir. pers. consult. spec.]. **Main/Corp** National Association of Personnel Consultants (U.S.). 1987 Ed.-. Directory. English. $19.95. National Association of Personnel Consultants, 3133 Mt. Vernon Avenue, Alexandria VA 22305. **Tel** (703)684-0180. **LC** HD5873; .N37A. **DD** 331.12/8/02573. ***Continues*** *National Association of Personnel Consultants (U.S.). Access.*

US/0194-0805
### NATIONAL EMPLOYMENT LISTING SERVICE FOR THE CRIMINAL JUSTICE SYSTEM. SPECIAL EDITION: EDUCATIONAL OPPORTUNITIES.
**Main/Corp** Sam Houston State University. National Employment Listing Service for the Criminal Justice System. **VFOAT** Special Edition: Educational Opportunities. (19??)-. English. $5.00. Sam Houston State University Criminal Justice Center, Huntsville TX 77341. **Tel** (409)294-1692. **ED** Stephanie Tinsley. **LC** HV8143; .S24a. **DD** 364/.07/1173. **Circ:** 2,500 (ctrl).
**Desc:** Publication of current educational programs in various criminal justice fields.

US/1051-4872
### NATIONAL JOB BANK, THE.
[Natl. job bank]. 1st Ed. (1983)-. English. an (Oct.). $250.00. Bob Adams Inc., 260 Center Street, Holbrook MA 02343. **Tel** (617)767-8100, (800)872-5627, FAX (617)767-0994. **ED** Carter Smith. **LC** HF5382.5.U5; N34. **DD** 331.12/8/02573.
**Desc:** Over 17,000 employer listings, with profiles from all fifty states, including those not covered by local books.

US
### NATIONAL JOB BULLETIN.
(19??)-. Bulletin. English. $35.00 (NRPA members only). National Recreation and Park Association, 2775 South Quincy Street, Suite 300, Arlington VA 22206. **Tel** (703)820-4940, (703)578-5564, FAX (703)671-6772. ***Continues*** *Park & Recreation Opportunities Job Bulletin.*

US/0747-4296
### NATIONAL JOB MARKET.
***Ceased.*** [Natl. job mark.]. ( )-(April 1988). Periodical. English. bw. National Job Market, 1101 King Street/#410, Alexandria VA 22314. **Tel** (301)946-8910. **ED** Walter McGivney. **DD** 331. **Bk Rev. Ad Acc.**
**Desc:** The most complete and the lowest priced national job newspaper in the US. The only job publication that features private, federal and international jobs.

US/0739-2931
### NATIONAL NEWSLETTER - ASSOCIATION OF PART-TIME PROFESSIONALS (U.S.).
(NATIONAL NEWSLETTER / ASSOCIATION OF PART-TIME PROFESSIONALS.). **VFOAT** APTP National Newsletter A.P.T.P. National Newsletter. Began with issue for Spring

# Occupations and Careers

1981. Newsletter. English. mo. $15.00. Association of Part Time, 7655 Old Springhouse Road, McLean VA 22101. **Tel** (703)734-7975. **ED** Diane Rothberg. **Bk Rev**. **Circ**: 1,500 (ctrl).
**Desc**: Trends in part-time employment, profiles of successful part-time professionals, employer use, family and work issues, and older workers.

US
**NEW ENGLAND MINORITY NEWS.** See Ethnic Interests.

●US/1064-8259
**NEW PROFESSIONAL, THE.** (1992)-. Periodical. English. mo. $79.00. The New Professional, PO Box 2120, Amherst MA 01004-2120.

●US/1064-8267
**NEW PROFESSIONAL SURVEY, THE.** (1992)-. Periodical. English. qt. $29.50. The New Professional, PO Box 2120, Amherst MA 01004-2120.

●US
**NEW YORK STATE PLAN FOR COORDINATION OF TRAINING, EMPLOYMENT AND RELATED PROGRAMS.** See Sociology-Social Services and Welfare.

US
**NEWSLETTER : PROFESSIONAL SECRETARIES INTERNATIONAL.** (19??)-. Newsletter. English. ir. $57.00 professional membership; $115.00 associate membership. Professional Secretaries International, 10502 Northwest Ambassador Drive, Kansas City MO 64195. **Tel** (816)891-6600 ext. 235, .

US/1051-3000
**NORTHWESTERN LINDQUIST-ENDICOTT REPORT.** [Northwest. Lindquist-Endicott rep.]. **Added/Corp** Northwestern University (Evanston, Ill.) Placement Center. **VAT** Northwestern Lindquist, Endicott Report. 42nd Annual Report (1988)-. English. an. $40.00. Placement Center, 601 University Place, Evanston IL 60208. **Tel** (708)491-3707, FAX (708)491-2573. **ED** Victor R. Lindquist. **DD** 331. **Continues** Northwestern Endicott-Lindquist Report, 0892-9998.

US/0192-2394
**NURSING CAREER DIRECTORY.** See Medical Science and Technology-Nursing.

US/1064-7333
**OCCUPATIONAL BRIEFS / CGP.** [Occup. briefs - CGP]. **Added/Corp** Chronicle Guidance Publications, inc. **VFOAT** Chronicle Occupational Briefs. **VAT** Occupational Briefs - Chronicle Guidance Publications. No. 1-19 (19??)-. Periodical. English. Eight times a year. $95.50. Chronicle Guidance Publications Inc., PO Box 1190, Moravia NY 13118. **Tel** (315)497-0330. **ED** Paul Downes. **LC** HF5382.5.U5; O283. **DD** 331.7/02/097305. **Bk Rev**. **Ad Acc**. **Circ**: 12,000.
**Desc**: Information on work performed, working conditions, hours and earnings, education and training, licenses, unions, entry methods, advancement, related occupations, and other sources of information.

US/0271-5589
**OCCUPATIONAL DEVELOPMENTS MAGAZINE.** [Occup. dev. mag.] V. 1- Summer 1979-. Periodical. English. qt. Indiana Office of Occupational Development, 10 North Senate/101, Indianapolis IN 46204. **Supersedes** Manpower Developments, 0271-5570.

●US
**OCCUPATIONAL EMPLOYMENT AND OPENINGS, NEW YORK STATE.** **Added/Corp** New York (State). Dept. of Labor. Division of Research and Statistics. (1991/1992)-. English. New York State Department of Labor / Rochester, Division of Research and Statistics, 155 West Main Street, Rochester NY 14614. **Continues** New York State Occupational Needs.

US
**OCCUPATIONAL OUTLOOK AND DEVELOPMENT.** **Main/Corp** Indiana. Employment Security Division. English. Research and Statistics Section / Indianapolis, Indiana Employment Security Division, 10 North Senate Avenue, Indianapolis IN 46204. **LC** HD5725.I6; I53B SUPPL. **DD** 331.11/09772.

US/0082-9072
**OCCUPATIONAL OUTLOOK HANDBOOK.** (OCCUPATIONAL OUTLOOK HANDBOOK / C.U.S. DEPARTMENT OF LABOR, BUREAU OF LABOR STATISTICS.). [Occup. outlook handb.]. **Added/Corp** United States. Bureau of Labor Statistics. (1949)-. English. be. $23.00 (soft cover), $27.00 (hard cover). Claitors Law Books, 3165 South Acadian, Baton Rouge LA 70808. **Tel** (504)344-0476, (800)274-1403. **DD** 331. **NLM** W1 OC588. Index available.
**Desc**: Reference book describing 300 most common occupations in the USA to include working conditions, training requirements, earnings and employment outlook.

US
**OCCUPATIONAL OUTLOOK ... WESTERN NEW YORK REGION OF NEW YORK STATE : ALLEGANY COUNTY, CATTARAUGUS COUNTY, CHAUTAUQUA COUNTY, ERIE COUNTY, NIAGARA COUNTY.** **Added/Corp** New York (State). Dept. of Labor. Division of Research and Statistics. **VFOAT** Western New York Region of New York State. (1996)-. English. **Continues** Occupational Needs. Western New York Region.
**Desc**: Includes employment forecasting and information on the labor supply.

US
**OCCUPATIONAL PATTERNS OF SELECTED NONMANUFACTURING INDUSTRIES IN UTAH.** **Main/Corp** Utah. Dept. of Employment Security. Research and Analysis Section. English. an. Utah Department of Employment Security, 174 Social Hall Avenue, PO Box 11249, Salt Lake City UT 84147. **Tel** (801)533-2400. **LC** HD5725.U8; U82C. **DD** 331.12/5/09792.

US
**OCCUPATIONAL PREFERENCES OF HIGH SCHOOL SENIORS IN TEN COUNTIES IN IDAHO, THE.** English. be. Idaho Department of Employment, 317 Main Street, Boise ID 83735. **Tel** (208)334-6112, FAX (208)334-6430. **LC** HF5382.5.U6; I26. **DD** 331.7/023.

US/0148-2890
**OCCUPATIONAL PROFILES OF SELECTED NON-MANUFACTURING INDUSTRIES IN OREGON.** **Main/Corp** Oregon. Employment Division. Research and Statistics Section. 1973-. English. Oregon Department of Human Resources Development, 155 Cottage Street NE, Salem OR 97310. **LC** HD5725.O7; O67B. **DD** 331.1/1/09795.

US/0731-8650
**OCCUPATIONAL PROGRAMS IN CALIFORNIA PUBLIC COMMUNITY COLLEGES.** English. ir (issued every two or three years). $25.50. Leo A Meyer Associates Inc, 23850 Clawiter Road, Hayward CA 94545. **Tel** (510)785-1091. **Circ**: 1,600.
**Desc**: Directory of occupational programs in California community colleges. Includes general information for each and indexes programs three ways.

US/0273-382X
**OCCUPATIONAL PROJECTIONS AND TRAINING DATA.** **Ceased.** (OCCUPATIONAL PROJECTIONS AND TRAINING DATA / U.S. DEPARTMENT OF LABOR, BUREAU OF LABOR STATISTICS.). (1971)-?. Government Publication. English. Superintendent of Documents, US Government Printing Office, Washington DC 20402. **Tel** (202)275-3328, FAX (202)786-2377. **LC** HD5723. **DD** 331.12/0973. **NLM** W2; A B880a.

US
**OCCUPATIONAL STARTING WAGES IN THE STATE OF UTAH AND UTAH PLANNING DISTRICTS.** English. Utah Department of Employment Security, 174 Social Hall Avenue, PO Box 11249, Salt Lake City UT 84147. **Tel** (801)533-2400. **LC** HD4976.U8; O27. **DD** 331.2/0792.

US
**OCCUPATIONAL SUPPLY AND DEMAND.** **Added/Corp** Alaska. Dept. of Labor. Research and Analysis Section. (July 1978)-. English. an. Alaska Department of Labor, Administrative Services, Research & Analysis Section, PO Box 25501, Juneau AK 99802-5501. **Tel** (907)465-4500. **LC** HD5725.A4; O25. **DD** 331.12/09798.

US/0739-1404
**OCCUPATIONS OF FEDERAL WHITE-COLLAR AND BLUE-COLLAR WORKERS.** [Occup. fed. white-collar blue-collar work.]. **Added/Corp** United States. Office of Personnel Management. Office of Workforce Information. United States. Office of Personnel Management. Survey and Information Branch. (Oct. 31, 1981)-. English. be. US Office of Personnel Management / Personal Systems and Oversight Group, Office of Workforce Information, 1900 E Street NW/Room 7494, Washington DC 20415. **Tel** (202)632-5417. (**Subscription address**: National Technical Information Service, US Department of Commerce, 5285 Port Royal Road, Springfield, VA 22161) **ED** Christine E Steele. **LC** JK639; .A42 subser; JK671. **DD** 353.001; 331.7/95/0973. available on microfiche (Vols. for (1981-) distributed to depository libraries). **Formed by the union of** Occupations of Federal White-Collar Workers, 0146-4906 **and** Occupations of Federal Blue-Collar Workers, 0146-2490.

**Desc**: Full-time federal civilian employment distributions by occupation series/group, agency, major geographic area, gender, pay, system category, grade, average and median grade, average annual base salary, and supervisory status.

UK
**OFFICE BUYER.** (1990)-. Periodical. English. bm (6 issues). £18.50 UK; £30.00 other. Trade Media Ltd / England, Brookmead House, Two Rivers, Station Lane, Witney Oxon OX8 6BH England. **Tel** 011 44 993 775545, FAX 011 44 993 778884. **Ad Acc**. **Circ**: 10,386.

●UK
**OFFICE DEALER.** (1992)-. Periodical. English. bm (6 issues). £18.50 UK; £30.00 other. Trade Media Ltd / England, Brookmead House, Two Rivers, Station Lane, Witney Oxon OX8 6BH England. **Tel** 011 44 993 775545, FAX 011 44 993 778884. **Ad Acc**. **Circ**: 9,340.

UK/0951-6824
**OFFICE SECRETARY.** [Off. secr.]. (1986)-. Periodical. English. qt. £9.50 UK; £15.00 other. Trade Media Ltd / England, Brookmead House, Two Rivers, Station Lane, Witney Oxon OX8 6BH England. **Tel** 011 44 993 775545, FAX 011 44 993 778884. **DD** 651. **Ad Acc**. **Circ**: 60,000.

US
**OFFICIAL GUIDE TO AIRLINE CAREERS.** **Ceased.** (1978)-(19??). English. ir. International Publishing Company of America, 665 La Villa Drive, Miami Springs FL 33166. **Tel** (305)887-1701, FAX (305)885-1923, telex 6811546.

US/8755-044X
**OFFICIAL GUIDE TO FLIGHT ATTENDANT CAREERS.** [Off. guide flight attend. careers]. **VFOAT** Flight Attendant Careers; Flight Attendant Guide. 15th Ed. (1984)-. English. bm. $8.95. International Publishing Company, 665 La Villa Drive, Miami Springs FL 33166. **Tel** (305)887-1701, FAX (305)885-1923, telex 6811546 INTL PUP. **ED** A C Morton. **DD** 387. **Continues** Official Guide to Stewardess and Steward Careers.

US/8755-0431
**OFFICIAL GUIDE TO FOOD SERVICE AND HOSPITALITY MANAGEMENT CAREERS, THE.** **VFOAT** Food Service; Foodservice Careers. (1982)-. English. ir. $9.95. Foodservice Careers International Publishing Company, 665 Lavilla Drive, Miami Springs FL 33166. **Tel** (305)887-1700, FAX (305)885-1923. **ED** Alexander C. Morton. **DD** 642. Index available.
**Desc**: Tells why to choose a career in the foodservice industry. Also includes job classifications throughout the industry.

US/8755-0458
**OFFICIAL GUIDE TO TRAVEL AGENT & TRAVEL CAREERS, THE.** (THE OFFICIAL ... GUIDE TO TRAVEL AGENT & TRAVEL CAREERS / BY ALEXANDER C. MORTON.). [Off. guide travel agent travel careers]. **VFOAT** Travel Agent and Travel Careers; Guide to Travel Agent & Travel Careers; Travel Agent & Travel Careers. 1st Ed. (1980-1981)-. Monographic series. English. ir. Price varies per volume. International Publishing Company, 665 La Villa Drive, Miami Springs FL 33166. **Tel** (305)887-1701, FAX (305)885-1923, telex 6811546 INTL PUP. **ED** Veronica Dennis. **LC** G154; .O37. **DD** 380.1/4591023. Index available.
**Desc**: A list of traveling agent jobs, training, education and information on how to start your own agency.

CN/1180-9183
**ONESTEP FORWARD.** (ONESTEP FORWARD : THE NEWSLETTER OF THE ONTARIO NETWORK OF EMPLOYMENT AND SKILLS TRAINING PROJECTS.). [ONESTeP forw.]. **Added/Corp** Ontario Network of Employment and Skills Training Projects. **VFOAT** One step forward; ONESTP forward. **VAT** Ontario Network of Employment and Skills Training Projects forward. (1989)-. Periodical. English. bm. 32.10 Can$. ONESTeP, 517 Wellington ST W #210, Toronto ONT M5V 1G1 Canada. **Tel** (416)591-7151, FAX (416)591-9126. **DD** 331.25/92/09713. **Circ**: 250. **Continues** Update (Job Development Association of Ontario)., 0838-8091.
**Desc**: Dedicated to strengthening the community-based training network in Ontario. Provides information on member services and advocacy efforts.

FR
**ONISEP COMMUNIQUE.** (19??)-. French. Twenty times a year. 94.50F France; 118.80F other. ONISEP Diffusion, 46 52 rue Albert, 75635 Paris Cedex 13 France. **Tel** 011 33 1 40776000, FAX 45 86 60 85, telex 202962 F ONISEP N.

US/0029-7968
**OOQ, OCCUPATIONAL OUTLOOK QUARTERLY.** **Added/Corp** United States. Bureau of Labor Statistics. **VFOAT** Occupational Outlook Quarterly. Vol. 1 (Feb. 1957)-. Government Publication. English. ir. $6.50; $2.50 (single issues) US; $8.15; $3.13 (single issues) other. Superintendent of Documents, US Government Printing Office, Washington DC 20402. **Tel** (202)275-3328, FAX (202)786-2377. **LC** HF5382.5.U5;

O3. ***Supersedes*** *Occupational Outlook Review.*
**Desc:** Written in nontechnical language and illustrated in color, contains articles on new occupations, training opportunities, salary trends, career counseling programs, and the results of new studies from the Bureau of Labor Statistics. Designed to help young people, employment planners, and guidance counselors keep abreast of current occupational and employment developments.
**Ind/Abst** Curr. Index J. Educ. (March 1990-199?); Read. Guide Period. Lit.

US
**OPENINGS : JOB OPPORTUNITIES FOR SCHOLARS OF RELIGION. Added/Corp** AAR/SBL Placement Assistance Service. (Sept. 1985)-. Periodical. English. bm. $35.00. Scholars Press / Georgia, PO Box 15399, Atlanta GA 30333-0399. **Tel** (404)636-4757, (404)727-2320, FAX (404)727-2348.

US
**OPPORTUNITIES.** (1972)-. Periodical. English. bm (Jan., Mar., May, July, Sept., Nov.). $20.00. Natural Science Youth Foundation, 130 Azalea Drive, Roswell GA 30075. **Tel** (800)992-6793. **ED** Mildred DeScherer. **Circ:** 300 (ctrl).
**Desc:** Employment opportunities available in natural science field-nature centers, museums, etc.

SA
**OPPORTUNITIES FOR GRADUATES. VFOAT** Opportunities for Graduates in Southern Africa; Opportunities for Graduates in South Africa. English (Afrikaans). Management Development Publishers, PO Box 10061, Johannesburg 2000 South Africa.

SA
**OPPORTUNITIES FOR MATRICULANTS AND SCHOOL LEAVERS. VFOAT** Opportunities for Matriculants and School Leavers in Southern Africa. English (Afrikaans). an. R5.50. Bee Books, PO Box 47433, Parklands 2121 Transvaal South Africa. **Tel** 662-1233/1319, FAX 339-3530. **ED** N G Hulley. Index available. **Ad Acc. Circ:** 35,000.
**Desc:** Aimed to act as a guide to matriculants and schoolleavers to further study their interests and requirements needed for positions that are available to them.

CN/0835-3921
**OPTIONS CARRIERES.** [Options carr.]. **Added/Corp** ACCIS (Organisation). **VFOAT** Annuaire d'Orientation Professionnelle. Vol. 1, No. 1 (1987/88)-. French (English). an. 3.95Can$. University and College Placement Association, 1209 King Street West 2nd Floor, Toronto Ontario M6K 1G2 Canada. **DD** 331.7/02/0971. ***Continues*** *Annuaire d'Orientation Professionnelle, 0229-804X.*

CN/1183-3203
**OVERSEAS EMPLOYMENT NEWSLETTER.** [Overseas employ. newsl.]. **Added/Corp** Overseas Employment Services. (1984)-. Newsletter. English. Twenty-six times a year. $105.00. Overseas Employment Services, 122 Laird Street, Suite 208, Mount Royal Quebec H3P 2T1 Canada. **Tel** (514)739-1108, FAX (514)739-0795. **ED** Leonard Simcoe. **DD** 331.12/4. **Circ:** 3,000 (readership).
**Desc:** Lists and describes in detail several hundred currently available job offers for a broad range of career/skills and positions worldwide.

UK/0966-7660
**OVERSEAS JOBS EXPRESS.** [Overseas jobs express]. (1991)-. Newspaper. English. bw. £49.00 Europe; £59.00 other. Island Publishers, PO Box 22 Brighton, East Sussex EN16 HX United Kingdom. **Tel** 011 44 273 440220, FAX 011 44 273 440229. **Bk Rev. Ad Acc.**
**Desc:** For people interested in living and working overseas. Also for individuals and companies involved in international recruiting.

●US/1059-2040
**PBC EMPLOYMENT BRIEFS. VFOAT** Employment Briefs. **VAT** Publishing and Business Consultants Employment Briefs. (1992)-. Newsletter. English. qt. Publishing & Business Consultants, PO Box 75392, Los Angeles CA 90075. **Tel** (213)732-3477, FAX (213)732-9123.

CN/0705-3126
**PCEC. PRIVATE CAREER EDUCATION COUNCIL.** (P C E C.). **Main/Corp** Private Career Education Council. **VFOAT** Membership Directory of Private Career Schools, Ontario; Private Career Education Council. **VAT** Private Career Education Council. Began publication in 197-. English. an. Free. Private Career Education Council, Suite 205/1530 Albion Road, Rexdale Ontario M9V 1B4 Canada. **DD** 374'.013'025713.
**Desc:** Directory of members.

US/0893-2549
**PERSONAL REPORT FOR THE PROFESSIONAL SECRETARY.** [Pers. rep. prof. secr.]. **Added/Corp** National Institute of Business Management (U.S.). (198?)-. Newsletter. English. mo. $42.00 US; $52.00 Canada. National Institute of Business Management, Inc., 1101 King Street, Alexandria VA 22134. **Tel** (800)543-2051, (703)548-3885, (800)543-2049, FAX (703)549-0182. **(Subscription address:** National Institute of Business Management, PO Box 25337, Alexandria VA 22313.**) ED** Barry Lenson. **DD** 651. ***Continues*** *Research Institute Personal Report for the Professional Secretary, 0276-6035.*

US/1049-636X
**PERSPECTIVES.** (PERSPECTIVES: CONCEPTS FOR A CAREER IN COMMUNICATIONS.). [Perspectives]. (1990)-. Periodical. English. mo. $24.00. Loriann Hoff Oberlin, 241 Coxcomb Hill Road/Suite 26, New Kensington PA 15068. **DD** 001.

US/0897-6023
**PETERSON'S GUIDE TO GRADUATE PROGRAMS IN BUSINESS, EDUCATION, HEALTH, AND LAW.** [Peterson's guide grad. programs bus. educ. health law]. **Added/Corp** Peterson's Guides, Inc. **VFOAT** Graduate Programs in Business, Education, Health, and Law; Peterson's Graduate Programs in Business, Education, Health & Law. 23rd Ed. (1989)-. English. an. $24.95. Peterson's Guides, 202 Carnegie Center, Department 2342, Princeton NJ 08543. **Tel** (800)338-3282, FAX (609)452-0966. **LC** L901; .P459. **DD** 378.1/553025/7. **NLM** L 901; P4855.
**Desc:** Covers over 13,000 graduate programs in business, education, health and law.

US/1048-342X
**PETERSON'S JOB OPPORTUNITIES FOR ENGINEERING, SCIENCE, AND COMPUTER GRADUATES.** ***Title Change.*** [Peterson's job oppor. eng. sci. comput. grad.]. **Added/Corp** Peterson's Guides, inc. **VFOAT** Job Opportunities for Engineering, Science, and Computer Graduates. 12th Ed. (1991)-(199?). English. an. Peterson's Guides, 202 Carnegie Center, Department 2342, Princeton NJ 08543. **Tel** (800)338-3282, FAX (609)452-0966. **LC** TA157; .P48. **DD** 650. ***Continues*** *Peterson's Engineering, Science, and Computer Jobs, 0894-9425.* ***Continued by*** *Peterson's Job Opportunities in Engineering and Technology.*

●US/1070-6615
**PETERSON'S JOB OPPORTUNITIES IN BUSINESS.** [Peterson's job oppor. bus.]. **Added/Corp** Peterson's Guides, Inc. **VFOAT** Job Opps ... Business; Job Opportunities in Business. (1994)-. English. an. $18.95. Peterson's Guides, 202 Carnegie Center, Department 2342, Princeton NJ 08543. **Tel** (800)338-3282, FAX (609)452-0966. **LC** HF5382.5.U5; B88. **DD** 331.12/8/097305. ***Continues*** *Peterson's Job Opportunities for Business and Liberal Arts Graduates, 1048-3411.*
**Desc:** Provides information on the 2,000 largest companies the US hiring employees in a number of fields, including financial services, management consulting, and consumer products.

●US/1071-068X
**PETERSON'S JOB OPPORTUNITIES IN ENGINEERING AND TECHNOLOGY.** [Peterson's job oppor. eng. technol.]. **Added/Corp** Peterson's Guides, Inc. **VFOAT** Job Opps ... Engineering and Technology; Job Opportunities in Engineering and Technology. (1994)-. English. an. $18.95. Peterson's Guides, 202 Carnegie Center, Department 2342, Princeton NJ 08543. **Tel** (800)338-3282, FAX (609)452-0966. **LC** TA157; .P48. **DD** 331. ***Continues*** *Peterson's Job Opportunities for Engineering, Science, and Computer Graduates, 1048-342X.*
**Desc:** Provides information on 1,500 companies hiring engineers and /or developing leading-edge technologies such as biotechnology, telecommunications, software and consumer electronics.

●US/1071-0671
**PETERSON'S JOB OPPORTUNITIES IN HEALTH CARE.** [Peterson's job oppor. health care]. **Added/Corp** Peterson's Guides, Inc. **VFOAT** Job Opps ... Health Care; Job Opportunities in Health Care. (1994)-. English. an. $18.95. Peterson's Guides, 202 Carnegie Center, Department 2342, Princeton NJ 08543. **Tel** (800)338-3282, FAX (609)452-0966. **LC** R690; .P45. **DD** 332.12/913621.
**Desc:** Provides information on 1,500 companies hiring health-care professionals for skilled nursing care facilities, hospitals, medical laboratories, home health care and pharmaceuticals.

●US/1071-183X
**PETERSON'S JOB OPPORTUNITIES IN THE ENVIRONMENT.** [Peterson's job oppor. environ.]. **Added/Corp** Peterson's Guides, Inc. **VFOAT** Job Opps ... The Environment; Job Opportunities in the Environment. (1994)-. English. an. $18.95. Peterson's Guides, 202 Carnegie Center, Department 2342, Princeton NJ 08543. **Tel** (800)338-3282, FAX (609)452-0966. **LC** GE60; .P48. **DD** 331.

US
**PLACEMENT NEWS.** ***Suspended.*** Vol. 1 (Sept. 1980)-?. Periodical. English. ir. $15.00. Boston Theological Institute, 11 Garden Street, Cambridge MA 02138. **Tel** (617)492-5622. ***Continues*** *Doctoral Placement Service.*

●US
**PLANNING JOB CHOICES. Added/Corp** College Placement Council. **VFOAT** Job Choices. 37th Ed. (1994)-. Periodical. English. an (Sept.). $45.90 (complete 4 volume set); Also comes with College Placement Council membership. College Placement Council Inc., 62 Highland Avenue, Bethlehem PA 18017. **Tel** (610)868-1421, FAX (610)868-0208. **LC** HF5382.5.U5; P55. **DD** 650.14/0973/05. ***Continues in part*** *CPC Annual, 0749-7474.*

●US
**PLANNING JOB CHOICES (TWO-YEAR COLLEGE ED.).** (PLANNING JOB CHOICES.). **Added/Corp** College Placement Council. **VFOAT** Job Choices. 37th Ed. (1994)-. Periodical. English. an (Sept.). $45.90 (complete 4 volume set); Also comes with College Placement Council membership. College Placement Council Inc., 62 Highland Avenue, Bethlehem PA 18017. **Tel** (610)868-1421, FAX (610)868-0208. **LC** HF5382.5.U5; P553. **DD** 650.14/0973/05. ***Continues in part*** *CPC Annual, 0749-7474.*

US/1059-633X
**PRENTICE HALL CREATIVE SECRETARY'S LETTER, THE.** [Prentice Hall creat. secr. lett.]. **VFOAT** Creative Secretary's Letter. (1988)-. Periodical. English. sm. $134.28 (US); $162.48 (Canada). Bureau of Business Practice, 24 Rope Ferry Road, Waterford CT 06386. **Tel** (800)243-0876, (203)442-4365, (800)876-9105, FAX (203)443-1123. **DD** 651. **CODEN** CRSLEW.

UK
**PRIVATE COMPANY SECRETARY'S MANUAL.** (1988)-. English. an. £77.00 England; £79.00 Europe except England; £81.00 other. Simon & Schuster International Group, Campus 400, Maylands Avenue, Hemel Hempstead Herts HP2 7EZ England. **Tel** 0442-881900, FAX 0442-252544, telex 82445. **(Subscription address:** International Book Distributors Ltd., Campus 400 Maylands Avenue, Hempstead Hert HP2 7EZ England**) ED** Sidney Bunker. **Pr Rev.**
**Desc:** This manual is written specifically as a much needed aid for small and medium-sized companies who may not employ a fully qualified secretary. Useful checklists are provided at the end of each section as a quick reference tool.

●US/1070-3322
**PROFESSIONAL AND OCCUPATIONAL LICENSING DIRECTORY.** [Prof. occup. licens. dir.]. **Added/Corp** Gale Research Inc. **VFOAT** POLD. 1st Ed. (1993)-. Directory. English. be. $89.50. Gale Research Inc., 835 Penobscot Building, Detroit MI 48226. **Tel** (800)877-GALE, (313)961-2242, FAX (313)961-6083, telex TWX 810-221-7086. **ED** David Bianco. **LC** HD3630.U6; P76. **DD** 351. available on magnetic tape; available on diskette.
**Desc:** Provides complete national and state information on the licenses and licensing procedures required for about 500 occupations.

US/1045-9863
**PROFESSIONAL CAREERS SOURCEBOOK.** (PROFESSIONAL CAREERS SOURCEBOOK : AN INFORMATION GUIDE FOR CAREER PLANNING.). [Prof. careers sourceb.]. **Added/Corp** Gale Research Inc. InfoPLACE (Career Information Center). (1990)-. English. be. $85.00. Gale Research Inc., 835 Penobscot Building, Detroit MI 48226. **Tel** (800)877-GALE, (313)961-2242, FAX (313)961-6083, telex TWX 810-221-7086. **ED** Kathleen M. Savage and Joseph M. Palmisano. **LC** HF5382.5.U5; P76. **DD** 331.7/02/05. available on magnetic tape; available on diskette.
**Desc:** Career planning information for students, professionals, vocational counselors, and others. Provides a listing of state professional and occupational licensing agencies and occupational rankings and statistics. Presents over 115 professional career profiles. Each profile includes information on general career guides, professional associations, standards and certification agencies, directories of educational programs, basic reference guides and handbooks related to the profession, professional and trade periodicals, and more.

US/1043-2051
**PROFESSIONAL LICENSING REPORT.** [Prof. licens. rep.]. Vol. 1, No. 1 (July 1988)-. Periodical. English. mo (12 issues). $168.00 (one year), $310.00 (two year). Paxton Associates, 9904 Foxborough Circle, Rockville MD 20850. **Tel** (301)869-4889, FAX (301)869-8327. **ED** Anne Paxton. **DD** 344. **Circ:** 500 (ctrl).
**Desc:** Newsletter on key legislation, court rulings, and actions by state boards and federal agencies on professional licensing and discipline.

CN/0709-2482
**PROFESSIONAL SCHOOLS FACTSHEETS.** See Education-Higher Education.

## Occupations and Careers

**US**
**PROFESSIONAL SECRETARY'S DEVELOPMENT PROGRAM.** English. Forty-eight times a year. $106.92 (US); $131.52 (Canada) Includes: Creative Secretary's Letter, Secretary's Workshop, & Memory Jogger - Deluxe Edition. Bureau of Business Practice, 24 Rope Ferry Road, Waterford CT 06386. **Tel** (800)243-0876, (203)442-4365, (800)876-9105, FAX (203)443-1123.

US/0742-9770
**PRYOR REPORT, THE.** (THE PRYOR REPORT / FRED PRYOR SEMINARS, INC.). [Pryor rep.]. **Added/Corp** Fred Pryor Seminars, Inc. Vol. 1, No. 1 (Sept. 1984)-. Periodical. English. Twelve times a year. $79.00 US; 109.00Can$ Canada; $109.00 other. The Pryor Report, PO Box 1766, Clemson SC 29633. **Tel** (800)237-7967, FAX (803)654-7275. **ED** Patricia Melshimer (editor's address: P.O. Box 101, Clemson, SC 29633; phone: (803)654-5148). **DD** 658. cum. index. **Circ:** 15,500 (ctrl).

●US/1072-3773
**PUBLIC SECTOR JOB BULLETIN.** (1993)-. Bulletin. English. Twenty-six times a year. $26.00. Public Sector Job Bulletin, PO Box 1222, Newton IA 50208. **Tel** (515)791-9019. **ED** Gerald Pecinovsky. **Ad Acc. Circ:** 3,000. **Continues** Jobs Available - Midwest/Eastern Edition.
 **Desc:** Listing of public sector jobs in cities, counties and states throughout the US.

●US/1068-199X
**RECAREERING NEWSLETTER.** [ReCareer. newsl.]. **VFOAT** ReCareering. (Nov. 1992)-. Periodical. English. Twelve times a year. $59.00. Recareering Newsletter, 801 Skokie Boulevard, Suite 221, Northbrook IL 60062. **Tel** (708)498-1981, FAX (708)498-2024. **ED** Sharon B. Schuster. **DD** 331. **Bk Rev**. **Ad Acc. Circ:** 750.

**US**
**REFINING THE CAREER EDUCATION CONCEPT.** See Education-Vocational Education.

**US**
**REPORT OF SOUTH DAKOTA'S PROFESSIONAL AND OCCUPATIONAL LICENSING BOARDS AND COMMISSIONS.** See Public Administration.

**II**
**REPORT ON SHORTAGE OCCUPATIONS.** **Main/Corp** Himachal Pradesh, India. State Employment Market Information Unit. English. State Employment Market Information Unit, Himachal Pradesh, Simla India. **LC** HD5820.H5; H57A. **DD** 331.1/26.

**FR**
**RESSOURCES INFORMATIQUES.** French. CEP Information Professions, 1 Cite Bergere, 75311 Paris Cedex 09 France. **Tel** 011 33 1 44695550.

**US**
**SALARY INFORMATION FOR WORD PROCESSING PERSONNEL, UNITED STATES, CANADA.** See Computers-Word Processing.

**US**
**SAN FRANCISCO BAY AREA JOB BANK.** **VFOAT** San Francisco Bay Area Jobbank. (1982)-. English. an (Oct.). $17.95. Bob Adams Inc., 260 Center Street, Holbrook MA 02343. **Tel** (617)767-8100, (800)872-5627, FAX (617)767-0994.

**NE**
**SECRETARESSE MAGAZINE.** Samson Bedrijfsinformatie, Postbus 4, 2400 HA Alphen Rij Netherlands. **Tel** 011 31 1 72066633.

US/0037-0622
**SECRETARY, THE.** **Added/Corp** National Secretaries Association (International). (19??)-. Periodical. English. Nine times a year. $19.00 US and Canada; $24.00 other. Professional Secretaries International, 10502 Northwest Ambassador Drive, Kansas City MO 64195. **Tel** (816)891-6600 ext. 235, . **LC** HF5547.A2; S395. **DD** 651.06273.
 **Desc:** Authoritative articles directed to the professional secretary on office technology, management skills, career development and future trends.

**US**
**SECRETARY'S ALUMNAE PROGRAM.** English. Twenty-eight times a year. $68.88 US; $83.40 Canada. Bureau of Business Practice, 24 Rope Ferry Road, Waterford CT 06386. **Tel** (800)243-0876, (203)442-4365, (800)876-9105, FAX (203)443-1123.

US/1040-4708
**SECRETARY'S LETTER (ENGLEWOOD, N.J.).** (SECRETARY'S LETTER.). [Secr. lett.]. Vol. 1, No. 1 (Oct. 1988)-. Periodical. English. mo. $69.00. Economics Press Inc, 12 Daniel Road, Fairfield NJ 07004.

**Tel** (201)227-1224, (800)526-2554, FAX (201)227-9742. **DD** 651.
 **Desc:** Monthly coverage includes specific skills, time-managment techniques, stress busters, phone and faxing tips, confidence boosters, model letters and memos, career-advancement tools and more.

**US**
**SECRETARY'S WORKSHOP.** English. $68.88 US; $83.28 Canada. Bureau of Business Practice, 24 Rope Ferry Road, Waterford CT 06386. **Tel** (800)243-0876, (203)442-4365, (800)876-9105, FAX (203)443-1123.

**NE**
**SECRETARY'S WORLD.** **Ceased.** (19??)-(Jan. 1994). Dutch. bm. Impact Publishers, Postbus 322, 6500 AH Nijmegen Netherlands. **Tel** 011 080-604060.

US/0736-5764
**SERVICE BUSINESS.** **Title Change.** See Business.

US/0739-2222
**SITUATIONS WANTED; JOBS WANTED.** Periodical. English. sa. $1.00. Center for Self Sufficiency / Publishing Division, Publishing Division, PO Box 7234, Houston TX 77248. **Tel** (713)866-4027.
 **Desc:** Tips on growing areas, advertisements for those seeking employment, and career word mapping.

US/1054-3384
**SOCIAL SERVICES EMPLOYMENT BULLETIN.** See Sociology-Social Services and Welfare.

US/0162-1068
**SPOTLIGHT ON CAREER PLANNING, PLACEMENT AND RECRUITMENT.** [Spotlight career plan. place. recruit.]. **Added/Corp** College Placement Council. **VFOAT** Spotlight. Vol. 1 (Sept. 1978)-. Periodical. English. bw (except 1 issue in July, Aug. and Dec.). Comes only in combination with Journal of Career Planning & Employment - $72.00 US. College Placement Council Inc., 62 Highland Avenue, Bethlehem PA 18017. **Tel** (610)868-1421, FAX (610)868-0208. **ED** Patricia A. Sinnott.

UK/0143-3490
**SUMMER JOBS, BRITAIN.** **VFOAT** Directory of Summer Jobs in Britain. 16th Ed. (1985)-. English. an. $15.95. Peterson's Guides, 202 Carnegie Center, Department 2342, Princeton NJ 08543. **Tel** (800)338-3282, FAX (609)452-0966. **LC** HF5382.5.G7; D54. **DD** 331.12/8/094105. **Continues** Directory of Summer Jobs in Britain.
 **Desc:** Covers over 30,000 summer positions in the British Isles. Includes details on wages and hours, work conditions, and requirements.

●US/1064-6701
**SUMMER JOBS (PRINCETON, N.J.).** (SUMMER JOBS.). [Summer jobs]. 42nd Ed. (1993)-. English. an. $16.95. Peterson's Guides, 202 Carnegie Center, Department 2342, Princeton NJ 08543. **Tel** (800)338-3282, FAX (609)452-0966. **LC** HF5382.5.U5; S76. **DD** 331.7/02/097305. **Continues** Summer Employment Directory of the United States, 0081-9352.
 **Desc:** Presents information on 20,000 summer jobs offered by more than 400 organizations in the US. Jobs are conveniently arranged by state and provide detailed employer descriptions.

PL/0137-8171
**SZKOLA ZAWODOWA.** (Szk. Zaw.]. (1945)-. Periodical. Polish. mo (10 issues). $60.00. **(Subscription address:** ARS Polona, PO Box 1001, 00068 Warsaw Poland.) **UDC** 377.

US/1047-8388
**TECHNICAL & SKILLS TRAINING.** [Tech. skills train.]. **Added/Corp** American Society for Training and Development. **VFOAT** Technical and Skills Training. Vol. 1, No. 1 (July 1990)-. Periodical. English. Eight times a year. $59.00 (non-member), $50.00 (member). American Society for Training and Development, 1640 King Street, PO Box 1443, Department 840, Alexandria VA 22313. **Tel** (703)683-8100, (703)683-8129, FAX (703)683-8103. **(Subscription address:** Technical & Skills Training, Box 6871, Syracuse NY 13217.) **LC** WMLC 4.8769. **DD** 658. **[CCC]**.
 **Desc:** Each issue reports on current technical and skills training programs and practices; shares new training theories and their applications; and covers national and international issues, legislation, and news related to technical and skills training.

US/0897-5574
**TEMPDIGEST (HOUSTON, TEX.).** (TEMPDIGEST.). [Tempdigest]. (1984)-. Periodical. English. Four times a year (Jan., Apr., July, Oct.). $65.00 one year; $120.00 two years; $165.00 three years. Tempdigest International Inc., 10500 Forum Place Drive, Suite 420, Houston TX 77036. **Tel** (713)541-2468, FAX (713)541-1542. **ED** Mike Kutka. **DD** 338. **Bk Rev**, (Qty: 3-4). **Ad Acc. Circ:** 2,000.
 **Desc:** Temporary help companies can be found, from the

United States to the United Kingdom, Brazil, Australia, Japan, Sweden, South Africa, New Zealand, Canada and elsewhere.

US/1064-3850
**TEXAS JOB FINDER.** **Ceased.** Issue 92-5 (Mar. 10, 1992)-(19??). Periodical. English. sm. Texas Job Finder, PO Box 227416, Dallas TX 75222-7416.

US/0163-299X
**TODAY'S PROFESSIONALS.** Periodical. English. $12.00 US; $14.00 other. Today's Professionals Inc, 3030 W 6th Street, Los Angeles CA 90020.

**UK**
**TOPICS.** English. qt. £15.00. Employment Relations, 80 Newmarket Road, Resource Center, Cambridge CB5 8DZ England. **Tel** 0223 315944.

**UK**
**TRAINING DIRECTORY, THE.** **Added/Corp** British Association for Commercial and Industrial Education. (1989)-. Directory. English. an (Published in March). £25.00. Kogan Page Ltd., 120 Pentonville Road, London N1 9BR England. **Tel** 011 44 71 2780433, FAX 011 44 71 8376348, telex 263088 KOGAN G. **Ad Acc. Circ:** 3,000. **Continues** Directory of Trainer Support Services.
 **Desc:** Directory of providers of training, equipment and services to the training industry. Information on the latest government initiatives and incentives on training.

FR/0397-0264
**TRAVAIL PROTEGE NIORT.** (1976)-. Periodical. French. Twelve times a year. 220.00F. Societe Dialogue, BP 8378, 95805 Cergy Pontoise France. **Tel** 011 33 1 30303233, FAX 011 33 1 30303230. **UDC** 36.

US/1048-1079
**TRAVEL & HOSPITALITY CAREER DIRECTORY.** [Travel hosp. career dir.]. **Added/Corp** Career Press Inc. **VFOAT** Travel and Hospitality Career Directory. 1st Ed. (1989)-. Directory. English. $29.95 (hardcover), $17.95 (softcover). Gale Research Inc., 835 Penobscot Building, Detroit MI 48226. **Tel** (800)877-GALE, (313)961-2242, FAX (313)961-6083, telex TWX 810-221-7086. **LC** G155.A1; T636. **DD** 338.4/791.
 **Desc:** Discusses breaking into the hotel and motel industry, working for a local travel and tourism board, becoming a travel agent, getting started in car rental, convention and meeting planning, working as a pilot and more.

US/0890-5959
**U.S. EMPLOYMENT OPPORTUNITIES.** **Title Change.** [U.S. employ. oppor.]. **VFOAT** US Employment Opportunities. **VAT** United States Employment Opportunities. (1985)-(1994). English. Four times a year (Feb., May, Aug., Oct.). Washington Research Associates, PO Box 2003, Littleton CO 80161. **Tel** (303)756-9038, FAX (303)758-9203. **ED** Joseph Ryan. **LC** HF5382.5.U5; U2. **DD** 331.7/02/0973. Index available in last issue of volume--attached. **Bk Rev**. **Continues** United States Employment Opportunities. **Continued by** Employment Opportunities, USA, 1076-4798.
 **Desc:** Career news service for professionals and paraprofessionals. Covers fourteen major white collar industries.

US/1044-0151
**VICA JOURNAL.** (VICA JOURNAL : OFFICIAL JOURNAL OF THE VOCATIONAL INDUSTRIAL CLUBS OF AMERICA.). [VICA j.]. **Added/Corp** VICA (Association). **VFOAT** Vocational Industrial Clubs of America Journal. (198?)-. Periodical. English. qt. $8.00. Vocational Industrial Clubs of America, PO Box 3000, Leesbury VA 22075. **Tel** (703)777-8810. **ED** Karen N. Perrino. **LC** LC1045; .V49. **DD** 370.11/3/097305. **Bk Rev**. **Ad Acc. Circ:** 280,000 (ctrl). **Continues** VICA, 0042-1839.
 **Desc:** Articles deal with organization programs and projects, leadership, development how-to's, career interests achievements, and hobbies. Includes club and national news.

**SP**
**VOCACIONES.** mo. $23.00 US; $14.00 other. Vocaciones, Alfonso X1 4 10, Madrid 14 Spain.

●US/1060-5630
**VOCATIONAL CAREERS SOURCEBOOK.** [Vocat. careers sourceb.]. **Added/Corp** Gale Research Inc. InfoPLACE (Career information center). (1992)-. English. an. $75.00. Gale Research Inc., 835 Penobscot Building, Detroit MI 48226. **Tel** (800)877-GALE, (313)961-2242, FAX (313)961-6083, telex TWX 810-221-7086. **LC** Z7164.V6; V62; HF5382.5.U5. **DD** 016.3317/02.

●US/1067-0769
**WASHINGTON JOB SOURCE, THE.** (THE ... WASHINGTON JOB SOURCE : INCLUDES NORTHERN VIRGINIA & SURBURBAN MARYLAND.). [Wash. job source]. (1993)-. English. an. $14.95 US;

## Occupations and Careers

$17.95 Canada and Mexico. MetCom Inc., 1708 Surrey Lane NW, Washington DC 20007. **Tel** (202)337-7800, FAX (202)337-3121. **ED** Ben Psillas. **DD** 331. Index available. **Ad Acc. Pr Rev. Circ:** 10,000 (ctrl).
 **Desc:** Authoritative and comprehensive guide to finding entry-level jobs and internships in Washington DC. Lists over 5,000 personnel contacts including CEOs, presidents, vice-presidents, managing supervisors, personnel directors, human resource managers, and internship coordinators. Also provides some ready-to-use applications including SF-171 (Universal Federal Government Application) and both Senate and House Placement Office applications.

US/8755-4658
### WHAT COLOR IS YOUR PARACHUTE?.
(WHAT COLOR IS YOUR PARACHUTE? / RICHARD NELSON BOLLES.). (1971)-. English. an (Nov.). $23.60 (softbound), $30.60 (hardbound) Korea; $18.45 (softbound), $25.45 (hardbound) others. Ten Speed Press, PO Box 7123, Berkeley CA 94705. **Tel** (510)845-8414. **LC** HF5382.7; .B64. **DD** 650.1/4/05.
 **Desc:** A practical manual for job-hunters and career changers.

US/1056-5558
### WISCONSIN CAREER DIRECTIONS. [Wis. career dir.].
**VFOAT** Career Directions. (1990)-. Periodical. English. qt. Free. Directions Publishing, 21 North Henry Street, Edgerton WI 53534. **Tel** (608)884-3367. **DD** 331.

US/0714-7503
### WORK ABROAD. Ceased. [Work abroad].
Vol. 1, No. 1 (Jan. 1984)-(Nov. 1988). English. mo. MR Information, PO Box 955, Ganges British Columbia V0S 1E0 Canada.

US/0730-8884
### WORK AND OCCUPATIONS. [Work occup.].
Vol. 9, No. 1 (Feb. 1982)-. Periodical. English. qt (Feb., May, Aug., Nov.). $149.00. SAGE Periodical Press, 2455 Teller Road, Thousand Oaks CA 91320. **Tel** (805)499-0721, FAX (805)499-0871, telex 100799. **ED** Andrew Abbott (University of Chicago). **LC** HT675; .S6. **DD** 306/.36/05. **[CCC].** **Pr Rev. Acid Free.** available on microfilm and microfiche from University Microfilms International (UMI). Documents available from The Genuine Article, UMI Article Clearinghouse. **Continues** *Sociology of Work and Occupations, 0093-9285.*
 **Desc:** Provides an international forum for sociological research and theory in the substantive areas of work, occupations, leisure - their structures and interrelationships.
 **Ind/Abst** ABI/INFORM Glob. Ed.; ABI Inform Ondisc (Aug. 1983-); Appl. Soc. Sci. Index Abstr.; Curr. Contents Soc. Behav. Sci.; Curr. Index J. Educ.; Ergon. Abstr.; Expand. Acad. Index (1992-); High. Educ. Abstr. (1987-); Hum. Resour. Abstr.; Index Period. Artic. Relat. Law (19??-19??); Int. Bibliogr. Sociol.; Int. Labour Doc.; LABORDOC; Middle East Abstr. Index; Multicult. Educ. Abstr.; Newsp. Period. Abstr. (1992-); Psychol. Abstr. (1982-); PsycINFO; PsycLit; Res. Alert [Full Cov.]; Sage Fam. Stud. Abstr.; Soc. Plann. Policy Dev. Abstr.; Soc. Sci. Cit. Index [Full Cov.]; Sociol. Abstr. [Full Cov.]; Sociol. Educ. Abstr.; SportSearch; Stud. Women Abstr.; Tech. Educ. Train. Abstr.; UMI ABI/Inform—Bus. Period. Ondisc (May 1988-) [Full Txt.]; Work Relat. Abstr.

US/0736-9166
### WORK TIMES. See Business.

US/0884-4615
### YOUR COMPUTER CAREER. Ceased. [Your comput. career].
Vol. 1, No. 1 (Sept. 1985)-?. Periodical. English. Three times a year (spring, fall, and winter). Data Processing Management Association, 505 Busse Highway, Park Ridge IL 60068-3191. **Tel** (708)825-8124 ext.252, FAX (708)825-1693. **ED** Colette Urban. **DD** 004. **Bk Rev. Ad Acc. Circ:** 3,000 (ctrl).
 **Desc:** Designed specifically for the aspiring information processing professional. Featuring articles on career planning, job opportunities and issues affecting the future of the information processing profession.

## ABSTRACTING, BIBLIOGRAPHIES AND STATISTICS

UK/0141-5972
### BRITISH QUALIFICATIONS. (1966)-.
English. an. $85.00. Kogan Page Ltd., 120 Pentonville Road, London N1 9BR England. **Tel** 011 44 71 2780433, FAX 011 44 71 8376348, telex 263088 KOGAN G.
 **(Subscription address:** In US: Taylor and Francis, 1900 Frost Road, Suite 101, Bristol, PA 19007 USA; telephone: (800)821-8312; (215)785-5800) **LC** L915; .B68. **DD** 378/.01/302541.
 **Desc:** A comprehensive listing of all the academic, educational, technical and professional qualifications available in Britain today. Also includes universities and polytechnics.

## OFFICE EQUIPMENT AND SERVICES

US/1061-3269
### ADVANCE FOR HEALTH INFORMATION PROFESSIONALS. [Adv. health inf. prof.].
Vol. 1, No. 12 (Nov. 18, 1991)-. Periodical. English. Twenty-six times a year. Merion Publications, Inc., 650 Park Avenue West, King of Prussia PA 19406. **Tel** (800)355-1088, (215)265-7812. **DD** 651. **Continues** *Advance for Medical Record Professionals, 1061-3188.*

US/1046-6096
### AMERICAN OFFICE DEALER. [Am. off. deal.].
Periodical. English. mo. Free to qualified office supply retailers and wholesalers, office machine and office furniture industries, $24.00 US; $45.00 Canada. American Office Dealer, 6 Piedmont Center/Suite 300, Atlanta GA 30305. **Tel** (404)841-3333. **DD** 658. **Continues** *American Office Dealer Magazine (Western Ed.), 0891-1045.*

US/0885-9965
### AOR OBSERVER, THE. VFOAT Observer. VAT Automated Office Resources Observer. (19??)-.
Periodical. English. bm (6 issues). $95.00. Observer Word Processing News, PO Box 1119, Aptos CA 95003. **Tel** (408)688-4129. **DD** 651. **Continues** *Word Processing News.*

AT
### AUSTRALIAN SHOPFITTING TRADE JOURNAL.
English. Four times a year. 32.00Au$ Australia; 50.00Au$ other. Furnishing Publications Pty, 5 Faigh Street, Mulgrave Victoria 3170 Australia. **Tel** 011 61 3 5625844, FAX 011 61 3 5625412. **ED** Keith Dunn. **Bk Rev. Ad Acc. Circ:** 2,500.

US/0739-8743
### AUTOMATED OFFICE SYSTEMS.
(AUTOMATED OFFICE SYSTEMS : AOS.). [Autom. off. syst.]. **VFOAT** AOS; A.O.S. Began with V. 1 in Jan. 1981. Periodical. English. mo. $125.00. Office Systems Consulting Group, 10 Milk Street, Cambridge MA 02139. **Tel** (617)492-3300.

●US/1078-5809
### B.P.I.A. BUSINESS PRODUCTS INDUSTRY REPORT. [B.P.I.A. bus. prod. ind. rep.].
**Added/Corp** Business Products Industry Association. **VFOAT** Business Products Industry Association Business Products Industry Report; BPIA Business Products Industry Report; Business Products Industry Report; B.P.I.A. Industry Report. Vol. 1, No. 1 (July 12, 1994)-. Periodical. English. bw. $40.00. Business Products Industry Association, 301 North Fairfax Street, Alexandria VA 22314. **DD** 338. **Continues** *NOPA Industry Report, 0746-5467.*
 **Desc:** Covers pertinent news and information of the office supplies and products industry.

US/0733-5059
### BLACK'S GUIDE. HOUSTON OFFICE SPACE MARKET. Added/Corp Black's Guide, Inc. VFOAT Houston Office Space Market; Black's Guide to the Office Space Market. Issue 82 (Jan. 1982)-.
English. sa. $25.00 (single issue). Blacks Guide Inc, 818 West Diamond Avenue, Suite 300, Gaithersburg MD 20878. **Tel** (301)948-0995.
 **Desc:** A directory of office space available.

US/0738-6095
### BLACK'S GUIDE. ORANGE COUNTY OFFICE SPACE MARKET. Added/Corp Black's Guide, Inc. VFOAT Black's Guide. Orange County; Black's Guide; Black's Guide to the Office Space Market. (1983)-.
English. sa. $37.50. Blacks Guide Inc, 818 West Diamond Avenue, Suite 300, Gaithersburg MD 20878. **Tel** (301)948-0995.
 **Desc:** A directory of office space available.

US/0733-5067
### BLACK'S GUIDE. SUBURBAN MANHATTAN OFFICE SPACE MARKET. Added/Corp Black's Guide, Inc. VFOAT Suburban Manhattan Office Space Market. (197?)-.
English. sa. $25.00. Blacks Guide Inc, 818 West Diamond Avenue, Suite 300, Gaithersburg MD 20878. **Tel** (301)948-0995.
 **Desc:** A directory of office space available.

US/0733-2572
### BLACK'S GUIDE TO THE METRO DENVER OFFICE SPACE MARKET.
**VFOAT** Black's Guide. (Fall 1982)-. English. sa. $25.00 (single issue). Blacks Guide Inc, 818 West Diamond Avenue, Suite 300, Gaithersburg MD 20878. **Tel** (301)948-0995.
 **Desc:** A directory of office space available.

US
### BLACK'S OFFICE LEASING GUIDE. CONNECTICUT/NEW YORK SUBURBS.
**Added/Corp** Black's Guide, Inc. **VFOAT** Connecticut/New York Suburbs; Black's Guide to the Office Space Market; Black's Guide. Connecticut/New York Suburbs. (198?)-. English. an. $49.95. Blacks Guide Inc, 818 West Diamond Avenue, Suite 300, Gaithersburg MD 20878. **Tel** (301)948-0995. **ED** David G Hanson. **LC** HD266.C8; B53. **DD** 333.33/875/097471. **Ad Acc. Circ:** 7,500-10,000 (ctrl).
 **Desc:** Directory of available office space.

US
### BLACK'S OFFICE LEASING GUIDE. HOUSTON OFFICE SPACE MARKET.
**Added/Corp** Black's Guide, Inc. **VFOAT** Houston Office Space Market; Black's Guide. Houston; Black's Guide to the Office Space Market. (198?)-. Periodical. English. sa. $49.95. Blacks Guide Inc, 818 West Diamond Avenue, Suite 300, Gaithersburg MD 20878. **Tel** (301)948-0995. **ED** David G Hanson. **Ad Acc. Circ:** 7,500-10,000 (ctrl).
 **Desc:** A directory of office space available.

US
### BLACK'S OFFICE LEASING GUIDE. PHILADELPHIA & SUBURBS, SOUTHERN NEW JERSEY, DELAWARE.
**Added/Corp** Black's Guide, Inc. **VFOAT** Philadelphia & Suburbs, Southern New Jersey, Delaware; Black's Guide to the Office Space Market; Black's Guide. Philadelphia & Suburbs. (198?)-. English. an. $49.95. Blacks Guide Inc, 818 West Diamond Avenue, Suite 300, Gaithersburg MD 20878. **Tel** (301)948-0995. **ED** David G Hanson. **Ad Acc. Circ:** 7,500-10,000 (ctrl).
 **Desc:** Directory of available office space.

US
### BLACK'S OFFICE LEASING GUIDE. WASHINGTON / BALTIMORE METRO AREA.
**Added/Corp** Black's Guide, Inc. **VFOAT** Washington Baltimore Metro Area; Washington/Baltimore Metro Area; Black's Guide. Annual Directory, Washington/Baltimore. (19??)-. English. an. $69.95; $119.95 (combined Spring and Fall issues). Blacks Guide Inc, 818 West Diamond Avenue, Suite 300, Gaithersburg MD 20878. **Tel** (301)948-0995. **ED** David G Hanson. **LC** HD268.W3; B58. **DD** 333.33/8. **Ad Acc. Circ:** 7,500-10,000 (ctrl). **Continues** *Black's Office Leasing Guide.*
 **Desc:** Directory of available office space.

US/0733-5032
### BLACK'S REVIEW (WASHINGTON ED.).
(BLACK'S REVIEW.). **Added/Corp** Black's Guide, Inc. **VFOAT** Black's Review of the Greater Washington, DC Office Development and Leasing Industry. Vol. 1, No. 1 (Spring 1982)-. English. $25.00 per issue. Blacks Guide Inc, 818 West Diamond Avenue, Suite 300, Gaithersburg MD 20878. **Tel** (301)948-0995. **LC** HD1393.5; .B57. **DD** 333.33/8.
 **Desc:** Directory of available office space.

CN/0380-9463
### BRAND RECOGNITION STUDY : OFFICE EQUIPMENT & METHODS. See Business-Marketing.

GW
### BTL. VFOAT B.T.L. 81/5 (Sept. 1981)-. Periodical. German. bm. D Meininger GmbH, Maximilianstr 11-17, Postfach 310, Neustadt an der Weinstrasse Germany. LC HF5548; .B7955. Continues Burorationalisierung, Transport und Lagertechnik.

GW/0935-0276
### BTS : BUERO, TECHNIK, SYSTEME. Title Change. VFOAT Buero, Technik, System. (19??)-(1992).
Periodical. German. mo. Basten Verlag Buerowirtschaft, Eberstrasse 30, West 5120 Herzogenrath, Germany. **Tel** 011-49-2407-50036, FAX 011-49-2407-4958. **LC** HF5548.2; .B768. **Continues** *BTS Buerotechnische Sammlung, Das Rationelle Buero.* **Merged with** *Buro (Aachen, Germany), 0177-7696* **and** *Computer Magazin* **to form** *Buroszene.*

GW/0341-1370
### BTS BUEROTECHNISCHE SAMMLUNG, DAS RATIONELLE BUERO. Title Change.
**VFOAT** Buerotechnische Sammlung; BTS-Das Rationelle Buero. (1987)-(19??). Periodical. German. mo. Basten Verlag Buerowirtschaft, Eberstrasse 30, West 5120 Herzogenrath, Germany. **Tel** 011-49-2407-50036, FAX 011-49-2407-4958. **LC** HF5548.2; .B768. **Formed by the union of** *BTS-Buerotechnische Sammlung* **and** *Rationelle Buero (1985), 0178-0549.* **Continued by** *BTS, 0935-0276.*

SZ
### BUREAU SUISSE. Title Change. See Business.

SZ/0257-8328
### BUREAUX ET SYSTEMES. Title Change. See Business.

UK/0007-6708
**BUSINESS EQUIPMENT DIGEST.** [Bus. equip. dig.]. **VFOAT** BED. Business Equipment Digest. (1961)-. Periodical. English. mo (11 issues per year). £55.00 UK; £75.00 other Europe; £100.00 other. IML Group, Blair House, 184-186 High Street, Tonbridge Kent, TN9 1BQ England. **Tel** 011 44 732 359990, FAX 011 44 732 770049. Documents available from Ask*IEEE.
**Ind/Abst** HILITES; Infomat Int. Bus.; Inf. Manage. Technol.; INSPEC (April 1983-); World Ceram. Abstr.

US/1044-758X
**BUSINESS FORMS, LABELS & SYSTEMS.** [Bus. forms lab. sys.]. **VFOAT** Business Forms, Labels and Systems. (198?)-. Periodical. English. Twenty-four times a year. $49.00. North American Publishing Company, 401 North Broad Street, Philadelphia PA 19108. **Tel** (215)238-5300, (800)777-8074, FAX (215)238-5283. **LC** HF5371; .B86. **DD** 338.4/765129/097305. **CODEN** BFLSEP. available on microfilm and microfiche from University Microfilms International (UMI). Documents available from Ask*IEEE. ***Continues*** *Business Forms & Systems, 0745-3914.*
**Desc:** Published for distributors, designers, and printers of business forms. Regular issues cover significant trends, product developments, design techniques and information on marketing and manufacturing.
**Ind/Abst** Abstr. Bull. Inst. Pap. Sci. Tech.; Graph. Arts Bull. Inst. Pap. Sci. Technol. (Aug. 1989-); INSPEC (May 1989-)(20 May 1989-); Print. Abstr.

US/1055-7822
**BUSINESS MACHINE DEALER.** ***Title Change.*** [Bus. mach. deal.]. Vol. 5, No. 7 (Nov. 1990)-(199?). Periodical. English. mo. Business Electronics Dealer, 464 Central Avenue, Northfield IL 60093. **Tel** (312)441-9144, FAX (312)441-8740. **DD** 651. ***Continues*** *Business Electronics Dealer, 0893-6013.* ***Continued by*** *Business Systems Dealer, 1066-7997.*

UK/0007-7097
**BUSINESS SYSTEMS AND EQUIPMENT (LONDON, 1972).** ***Ceased.*** (BUSINESS SYSTEMS AND EQUIPMENT.). [Bus. syst. equip.]. Ceased (April 1990). Periodical. English. mo. Maclean Hunter Ltd. / UK, Chalk Lane Cockfosters Road, Barnet Herts EN4 0BU England. **Tel** 011 44 81 2423000, FAX 011 44 81 9759753, telex 299072. **CODEN** BSEQA3. Documents available from UMI Article Clearinghouse, Ask*IEEE. ***Continues*** *Business Systems.*
**Ind/Abst** ABI/INFORM Glob. Ed.; Anbar Account. Finan. Abstr. [Full Txt.]; Anbar Mark. Distr. Abstr. [Full Txt.]; Anbar Top Manage. Abstr. [Full Txt.]; Index Bus. Reports; Infomat Int. Bus.; INSPEC (June 1972-March 1990); Manage. Market. Abstr.; Manage. Bibliogr. Rev.; Oper. Prod. Manage. Abstr. [Full Txt.]; Person. Train. Abstr. [Full Txt.]; Women Manage. Rev. [Full Txt.]; World Ceram. Abstr.

US
**CANNATA REPORT.** English. mo. $215.00 (1 year), $390.00 (2 year) US; $260.00 (1 year), $475.00 (2 year) Canada; $235.00 (1 year), $430.00 (2 year) other. Marketing Research Consultants Inc, PO Box 776, 124 Hebron Avenue, Glastonbury CT 06033. **Tel** (203)633-7988. **ED** Frank G. Cannata. Index available. cum. index. ctrl circ. ***Continues*** *CMN, 0889-5880.*

US/0891-0596
**CAREER GUIDE (PARSIPPANY, N.J.), THE.** (THE CAREER GUIDE : DUN'S EMPLOYMENT OPPORTUNITIES DIRECTORY.). **Added/Corp** Dun's Marketing Services. **VFOAT** Dun's Employment Opportunities Directory; Employment Opportunities Directory. (1985)-. English. an. $495.00. Dun & Bradstreet Information Services, 3 Sylvan Way, Parsippany NJ 07054. **Tel** (201)605-6000, (800)526-0651. **LC** HF5382.5.U5; D86. **DD** 331.12/8. ***Continues*** *Dun's Employment Opportunities Directory, 0740-7289.*

CN/1187-1776
**CATALOGUE DES FOURNITURES ET DU MOBILIER.** [Cat. fournit. mobil.]. **Added/Corp** Quebec (Province). Ministere des Approvisionnements et Services. (1991)-. French. **DD** 651. ***Continues*** *Catalogue des Fournitures de Bureau., 0843-7173.*

US/0889-5880
**CMN OFFICE MACHINE NEWS.** ***Title Change.*** [CMN off. mach. news]. **Added/Corp** Marketing Research Consultants (Glastonbury, Conn.). **VFOAT** Office Machine News. **VAT** Copier Marketing Newsletter Office Machine News. Vol. 5, No. 1 (Jan. 1985)-?. Periodical. English. mo. Marketing Research Consultants Inc, PO Box 776, 124 Hebron Avenue, Glastonbury CT 06033. **Tel** (203)633-7988. **ED** Frank G Cannata. **DD** 658. Index available. **Bk Rev. Circ:** 1,750 (ctrl). ***Continues*** *Copier Marketing Newsletter, 8755-0482.* ***Continued by*** *Cannata Report.*
**Desc:** A management report for the office equipment dealer and manufacturer. Also covers technology, marketing strategies, forecast future trends and reports on industry conventions in US and Europe.

US/1051-0680
**COMPUTER & OFFICE PRODUCT EVALUATIONS.** ***Ceased.*** **See** Computers.

CN/1182-9052
**COMPUTER & TELECOM INDUSTRY UPDATE.** [Comput. telecom ind. update]. **Added/Corp** Stanley L. Jacobs Research Inc. **VFOAT** Computer and Telecom Industry Update. Vol. 30.0815 (Aug. 1990)-. Periodical. English. ir. $495.00 Canada. SLJ Research, 356 Erin Street, Oakville, Ontario L6H 4P9 Canada. **DD** 651.8/05. ***Continues*** *Canadian Office Automation Analyst., 0824-250X.*

US
**COMPUTERS AND BUSINESS EQUIPMENT.** (19??)-. English. mo. $225.00. Predicasts Inc., A Ziff Communications Company, 11001 Cedar Avenue, Cleveland OH 44106. **Tel** (800)321-6388, (216)795-3000, FAX (216)229-9944, telex 985 604. **(Subscription address:** Information Access Company, PO Box 61000, Department 1851, San Francisco, CA 94161; Phone: (800)321-6388**)**

US/0744-0170
**COMPUTERS AND OFFICE AND ACCOUNTING MACHINES.** **See** Economics-Industry and Production.

US/0883-9360
**CONTRACT FURNITURE BUYER'S GUIDE.** ***Title Change.*** [Contract furnit. buy. guide]. **VAT** . Began in 1985-(199?). Periodical. English. an. Zig Zag Corporation, PO Box 638, Highland Park IL 60035. **Tel** (708)831-0300. **ED** Liz Wolf. **LC** HD9803.A1; C66. **DD** 684.1/0029/4. ***Continued by*** *Workstation Report's Buyer' Guide, 1062-7650.*
**Desc:** Edited for purchasers of commercial office furniture.

IT
**COPIA.** (19??)-. Periodical. Italian. Nine times a year. L60000 Italy; L110000 other. Edizioni Directa SRL, Via Paolo Sarpi 62 A, 20154 Milan Italy. **Tel** 011 39 2 331690, FAX 011 39 2 3313692. Index available. cum. index. **Ad Acc. Circ:** 16,000.

US
**COPIER.** English. an. $39.00. Orion Research Corporation, 14555 North Scottsdale Road, Suite 330, Scottsdale AZ 85260. **Tel** (800)844-0759, (602)951-1114, FAX (602)951-1117.
**Desc:** Gives information used pricing information on 1,569 products.

US/0899-6164
**COPIER REVIEW.** (19??)-. Periodical. English. mo. $415.00 US (includes Copier Test Reports). Buyers Laboratory Inc., 20 Railroad Avenue, Hackensack NJ 07601. **Tel** (201)488-0404. **DD** 338.

US/1050-978X
**COPIER SPECIFICATION GUIDE.** (COPIER SPECIFICATION GUIDE / BLI.). [Copier specif. guide]. **Added/Corp** Buyers Laboratory. (19??)-. English. sa. $42.00 (office equipment dealers); $73.90 (other). Buyers Laboratory Inc., 20 Railroad Avenue, Hackensack NJ 07601. **Tel** (201)488-0404. **LC** HD9802.3.A1; C66. **DD** 686.4/4.

GW
**COPIERS OF THE WORLD.** German (English). sa. DM94.48 Germany; $109.00 other. Interdata Verlag GmbH, Lahnstrabe 27, W-5429 Katzenelnbogen Germany. **Tel** 49 6486 8085, FAX 49 6486 8000. **ED** Peter Wurr. Index available. **Ad Acc. Circ:** 4,000.
**Desc:** A standard directory for the complete offerings of the copier world market. It includes directly comparable in-depth information about technical features, manufacturers, vendors and prices.

US/0897-9405
**COPY MAGAZINE.** ***Title Change.*** [Copy mag.]. **VFOAT** Copy. (19??)-(Oct. 1993). Periodical. English. mo. Coast Publishing Inc, 1680 Southwest Bayshore Boulevard, Port St Lucie FL 34984. **Tel** (407)879-6666, FAX (407)879-7388. **DD** 686. ***Merged into*** *Quick Printing.*
**Desc:** A journal about imaging and reproduction for librarians who are responsible for copiers and other document processing, equipment and supplies (desktop publishing, electronic printers, etc.).

UK
**CRONER'S OFFICE COMPANION.** (19??)-. Periodical. English. qt. £131.50. Croner Publ Ltd, Croner House, London Road, Kingston upon Thames, Surrey KT2 6SR England. **Tel** 011 44 81 5473333, FAX 081 547-2637.

US
**CURRENT INDUSTRIAL REPORTS. MA-26B, SELECTED OFFICE SUPPLIES AND ACCESSORIES / U.S. DEPARTMENT OF COMMERCE, BUREAU OF THE CENSUS.** **See** Economics-Industry and Production.

US
**CURRENT INDUSTRIAL REPORTS. MA-27A, BUSINESS FORMS, BINDERS, CARBON PAPER, AND INKED RIBBONS / U.S. DEPARTMENT OF COMMERCE, BUREAU OF THE CENSUS.** **See** Economics-Industry and Production.

US/8750-6416
**DATAPRO MANAGEMENT OF OFFICE AUTOMATION.** ***Ceased.*** [Datapro manage. off. autom.]. **Added/Corp** Datapro Research Corporation. **VFOAT** Management of Office Automation. Vol. 8, No. 1 (Jan. 1985)-(June 1994). Periodical. English. mo. Datapro Information Services Group, 600 Delran Parkway, Delran NJ 08075. **Tel** (609)764-0100, (800)328-2776, FAX (609)764-8953. **DD** 651. **CODEN** DMOAEN. ***Continues*** *Datapro Automated Office Solutions, 0730-8833.*

US/0898-4468
**DATAPRO OFFICE PRODUCTS EVALUATION SERVICE.** ***Ceased.*** [Datapro off. prod. eval. serv.]. **Added/Corp** Datapro Research Corporation. **VFOAT** Office Products Evaluation Service. (198?)-(March 1993). Periodical. English. mo. Datapro Information Services Group, 600 Delran Parkway, Delran NJ 08075. **Tel** (609)764-0100, (800)328-2776, FAX (609)764-8953. **DD** 652. **[CCC].** ***Continues*** *Datapro Reports on Copiers & Duplicators, 0730-8825.*
**Desc:** Consists of: twelve parts and a one-page monthly issue, which describes the twelve parts, and all are kept in two loose-leaf binders.

US/0277-4984
**DATAPRO REPORTS ON OFFICE SYSTEMS.** ***Title Change.*** [Datapro rep. off. syst.]. **Added/Corp** Datapro Research Corp. **VFOAT** Office Systems. (1975)-?. Periodical. English. mo. Datapro Information Services Group, 600 Delran Parkway, Delran NJ 08075. **Tel** (609)764-0100, (800)328-2776, FAX (609)764-8953. **ED** Thomas B Holmes. Each issue contains an index to its own contents (no volume index)--loose. cum. index. ***Continued by*** *Datapro Reports on Office Automation.*
**Desc:** Features continuously updated analysis and product information on office automation equipment.

•US
**DESIGNNETWORK'S WORKSTATION REPORT.** **Added/Corp** DesignNetwork International. **VFOAT** Workstation Report. (July/Aug. 1992)-. Periodical. English. ir (9 issues). $196.00 (includes Workstation Reports Buyer's Guide to Office Furniture). Design Network International Ltd., PO Box 638, Highland Park IL 60035. **Tel** (708)831-0300. **LC** HD9803.A1; W67. **DD** 338.4/7684. ***Continues*** *Workstation Report, 1040-7472.*

FR/1148-5566
**ESPACE BUREAU PARIS.** (ESPACE BUREAU.). (1990)-. Periodical. French. Twelve times a year. 350.00F. Publications du Moniteur, 17 rue d'Uzes, 75108 Paris Cedex 02 France. **Tel** 011 33 1 40133030, FAX 011 33 1 40419495 customer service, 40133037 advertising, telex UPRESSE 680876 F. **UDC** 651. ***Continues*** *Bureaux de France (Paris), 0374-1060.*

GW
**EUROPEAN OFFICE FURNITURE.** English. an. Verlagsanstalt Alexander Koch GmbH, PO Box 100256, W-7022 Leinfelden-Echterdingen 1 Germany. ***Continues*** *Office Furniture Made in Europe.*

US/1052-2336
**EXECUTIVE'S MANUAL OF PERSONAL SECRETARIES, THE.** (1991)-. Periodical. English. be. $25.00. Margy Markwood-Vella Publications, 11083 Glenwood Drive, PO Box 8843, Coral Springs FL 33065-8843.

GW
**FAXES OF THE WORLD.** English (German). sa. DM94.48 Germany; DM109.00 other. Interdata Verlag GmbH, Lahnstrabe 27, W-5429 Katzenelnbogen Germany. **Tel** 49 6486 8085, FAX 49 6486 8000. **ED** Peter Wurr. Index available. **Circ:** 4,000 (ctrl).
**Desc:** A standard directory for the complete offerings of the facsimile world market. It includes directly comparable in-depth information about technical features, manufacturers, vendors, and prices.

US
**FLORIDA ATTORNEYS-SECRETARYS HANDBOOK.** **See** Law.

US/0746-8997
**GEYER'S OFFICE DEALER.** ***Ceased.*** [Geyer's off. deal.]. **VFOAT** Office Dealer. Vol. 149, No. 1 (Jan. 1984)-(1992). Periodical. English. Geyer-McAllister Publications Inc, 51 Madison Avenue, New York NY 10010. **Tel** (212)689-4411. **LC** TS1228; .G4. **DD** 680. available on an online database (file 648/Full-Text) from DIALOG. ***Continues*** *Geyers Dealer Topics, 0016-948X.*

NE
**GROTE SECRETARESSE HANDBOEK.** Dutch. sa. Samson Bedrijfsinformatie, Postbus 4, 2400 HA Alphen Rij Netherlands. **Tel** 011 31 1 72066633.

US/0739-3431
**HANSON'S GUIDELINES. VFOAT** Hanson's Guidelines. (19??)-. Periodical. English. Three times a year. $120.00 (1 year), $200.00 (2 year) US; $145.00 (1 year), $250.00 (2 year) other. Perceptual Evaluations, 28 Jones Street, Setauket KY 11733. **Tel** (516)941-9472, (516)941-9476, FAX (516)941-4444.
**Desc:** Covers copier buys for desktop and console model users.

US/0896-3231
**I/S ANALYZER.** [I/S anal.]. **Added/Corp** United Communications Group. **VFOAT** IS Analyzer. **VAT** Information Systems Analyzer. Vol. 25, No. 9 (Sept. 1987)-. Periodical. English. mo. $199.00 US, Canada and Mexico; $209.00 other. United Communications Group, 11300 Rockville Pike, Suite 1100, Rockville MD 20852. **Tel** (301)816-8950 ext. 223, FAX (301)816-8945. **LC** PAR. **DD** 651. **[CCC]**. Index available (bound in all issues). available on microfilm and microfiche from University Microfilms International (UMI). Documents available from UMI Article Clearinghouse, Ask*IEEE. ***Continues*** *EDP Analyzer, 0012-7523.*
**Desc:** Offers concise advice and analysis on how to manage an information systems organization.
**Ind/Abst** ABI/INFORM Glob. Ed.; ABI Inform Ondisc (Sept. 1987-); Acad. Search (July 1993-); Appl. Sci. Technol. Index (Sept. 1987-); Bus. Index (1988-); Bus. Period. Index (Sept. 1987-); Comput. Lit. Index; Data Process. Dig.; Energy Res. Abstr. (Sept. 1987-); Gen. BusinessFile (1988-); Gen. Period. Index (1988-); INSPEC (Sept. 1987-); SCISEARCH; Trade Ind. Index; World Publ. Monit. (Sept. 1987-).

SZ
**IB SUISSE. See** Business.

●US/1060-894X
**IMAGINGWORLD (CAMDEN, ME.).** (IMAGING WORLD.). [ImagingWorld]. **VFOAT** Imaging World. Vol. 1, Issue 1 (Jan. 1992)-. Periodical. English. Twelve times a year. $23.97 US; $48.00 Canada & Mexico; $96.00 other. IW Publishing, 49 Bayview, Suite 200, Camden ME 04843. **Tel** (207)236-8524, FAX (207)236-8524. **ED** Bruce Taylor. **LC** HF5736; .I453. **DD** 651.5/3. Index Bound in First Issue. **Ad Acc**, **Adv Mgr Tel** (207)236-8524. **Circ:** 60,000 (ctrl).
**Desc:** A trade that features important news and information to the electronic imaging industry. Focus is on trends and analysis, new products, and case studies.

US/0019-0012
**IMC JOURNAL.** (IMC JOURNAL / INTERNATIONAL MICROGRAPHIC CONGRESS.). [IMC j.]. **Added/Corp** International Micrographic Congress. International Information Management Congress. **VFOAT** I.M.C. Journal. **VAT** International Micrographic Congress Journal. (Fall 1967)-. Periodical. English. Six times a year (Jan., Mar., May, July, Sept., Nov.). $20.00 (US); $30.00 (other) airmail. International Information Management Congress, 1650 38th Street, Suite 205W, Boulder CO 80301. **Tel** (303)440-7085, FAX (303)440-7234. **ED** Bill MacArthur. **LC** TR835; .I46a. **DD** 001.55/23/05. **CODEN** IMGCB7. **Ad Acc**, **Adv Mgr:** Chris Lacy. **Circ:** 30,000. available on microfilm and microfiche from University Microfilms International (UMI). Documents available from Ask*IEEE, UMI Article Clearinghouse.
**Desc:** Application and technical articles on document-based information systems.
**Ind/Abst** ABI/INFORM Glob. Ed.; ABI Inform Ondisc (Fall 1976-); ACM Guide Comput. Lit.; Anbar Account. Finan. Abstr. [Full Txt.]; Anbar Mark. Distr. Abstr. [Full Txt.]; Anbar Top Manage. Abstr. [Full Txt.]; Bus. Educ. Index; Comput. Lit. Index; Comput. Rev. (1979-); Data Process. Dig.; Ei Page One; Inf. Instruc. Technol.; INSPEC (1979-); Int. Aerosp. Abstr.; Libr. Inf. Sci. Abstr.; Manage. Bibliogr. Rev.; Oper. Prod. Manage. Abstr. (Fall 1976-) [Full Txt.]; Person. Train. Abstr. (1979-) [Full Txt.]; Women Manage. Rev. (1979-) [Full Txt.].

US/1057-5847
**JOURNAL OF COURT REPORTING.** [J. court report.]. **Added/Corp** National Court Reporters Association. Vol. 52, No. 8 (June 1991)-. Periodical. English. Ten times a year (except Sept., Oct.). $35.00. National Court Reporters Association, 8224 Old Courthouse Road, Vienna VA 22182. **Tel** (703)556-6272, FAX (703)556-6291. **LC** Z54; .N24. **DD** 653. Index available. cum. index (in Aug. issue). **Ad Acc**, **Adv Mgr:** A. Glimka. **Circ:** 35,000. ***Continues*** *National Shorthand Reporter, 0274-5860.*

NE
**KANTOOR EN EFFICIENCY.** mo. Fl90.00. Kluwer BV, Postbus 23, 7400 GA Deventer Netherlands. **Tel** 011 31 5700 33155, 011 31 5700 48999, FAX 011 31 5700 11504, telex 42829. **(Subscription address:** Intermedia, PO Box 4 12400 MA Alphen A/D Rijn Netherlands**)** Index available. **Bk Rev**. **Ad Acc**. **Pr Rev**. **Circ:** 10,000.
**Desc:** Information on office equipment and computers.

NE/0169-7285
**KBM. KANTOORMARKT.** (KBM.). (1984)-. Periodical. Dutch. mo. Fl146.80 Benelux; Fl236.00 other. Wegener Tijl Tijdschriften Group, Postbus 9943, 1006 AP Amsterdam Netherlands. **Tel** 011 31 20 5182828. **UDC** 655.42.

US
**LETTERHEADS.** 1- 1977-. English. an. Letterheads, PO Box 2500, Ashland KY 41101. **LC** HF5733.L4; L47. **DD** 651.7/5.

US
**LIVE WIRE / FAX SERVICE.** English. mo. $120.00. Marketing Research Consultants Inc, PO Box 776, 124 Hebron Avenue, Glastonbury CT 06033. **Tel** (203)633-7988. **ED** Frank G. Cannata.
**Desc:** Office machine dealer / manufacturer information that cannot fit in the "Cannata Report," or is late breaking news.

NE/0005-7622
**MAANDBLAD VOOR BEDRIJFSADMINISTRATIE EN-ORGANISATIE.** Vol. 1 No. 1 (1897)-. Periodical. Dutch. Twelve times a year. F66.00 Netherlands; F97.50 others. Infolio BV, Postbus 16500, 2500 BM Den Haag Netherlands. **Tel** 011 31 70 3819900, FAX 011 31 70 3632338.

●US/1070-4051
**MANAGING OFFICE TECHNOLOGY. See** Business-General Management.

GW/0933-8241
**MENSCH & BUERO. VFOAT** Mensch und Buro. (19??)-. German (English, French and Italian). bm. DM110.00. Mensch und Buero Verlag GmbH, Lange Street 94, Postfach 2247, W-7570 Baden-Baden Germany. **Tel** 07221-22416, FAX 07221-26684. **(Subscription address:** Mensch and Buero Verlags GmbH, Lange StraBe 94, Postfach 2247, W-7570 Baden Germany**)** **ED** Hans Ottoman. **Bk Rev**. **Ad Acc**. **Circ:** 30,000 (ctrl).
**Desc:** Covers office equipment, office environment, office structures, office architecture and accessories from a human standpoint. Contains information, news, and design. All mirror the concerns of the user.

GW/0933-8241
**MENSCH UND BUERO.** German (English, French and Italian). bm. DM110.00. Mensch und Buero Verlag GmbH, Lange Street 94, Postfach 2247, W-7570 Baden-Baden Germany. **Tel** 07221-22416, FAX 07221-26684. **(Subscription address:** Mensch and Buero Verlags GmbH, Lange StraBe 94, Postfach 2247, W-7570 Baden Germany**)** **ED** Hans Ottoman. **Bk Rev**. **Ad Acc**. **Circ:** 30,000 (ctrl).
**Desc:** Covers office equipment, office environment, office structures, office architecture and accessories from a human standpoint. Contains information, news, and design. All mirror the concerns of the user.

US/0883-4377
**MINNELLA'S POCKET-GUIDE TO COPIERS. Added/Corp** Minnella Enterprises. **VFOAT** Minnella's Pocket Guide to Copiers; Pocket Guide to Copiers. (19??)-. English. qt. $68.00 US; $76.00 Alaska, Hawaii, Canada and Puerto Rico; $90.00 other. Minnella Enterprises, PO Box 137, Little Falls NJ 07424. **Tel** (201)785-9029, (201)278-3353, FAX (800)726-0902. **ED** Thomas A. Minnella, 19 E. Main Street, Little Falls, NJ 07424, (201)785-3527. **LC** HF5548; .M49. **DD** 681/.65/0294. **Circ:** 7,000.
**Desc:** Copier reference book, specifications, pricing, productivity test results on all currently marketed copiers in the U.S. marketplace.

IT
**MOBILI PER UFFICIO. VFOAT** Office Furniture Annual. (19??)-. Periodical. Italian (English). an (September). Masson S.P.A, Via Statuto 2/4, 20121 Milan Italy. **Tel** 011 39 2 63671, FAX 011 39 2 6367211.
**Desc:** Presents production, design and ergonomic research on office furnishings and fittings. Deals with: office systems, operative and semi-managerial offices, tables and chairs for conference rooms, and other office accessories.

US/0746-3839
**MODERN OFFICE TECHNOLOGY. *Title Change.*** [Mod. off. technol.]. Vol. 28, No. 10 (Oct. 1983)-Vol. 38, No. 5 (May 1993). Periodical. English. mo. Penton Publishing, 1100 Superior Avenue, Cleveland OH 44114-2543. **Tel** (216)696-7000, FAX (216)696-0836. **ED** J. B. Dykeman, L. K. Romei, P. Fernberg, and S. Brindza. **LC** HF5547.A2; M6. **DD** 651/.05. **CODEN** MDOPAW. **[CCC]**. **Ad Acc**. **Circ:** 160,300 (ctrl). available on microfilm and microfiche from University Microfilms International (UMI); available on an online database (files 15,647,648,675/Full-Text) from DIALOG. Documents available from Ask*IEEE, UMI Article Clearinghouse. ***Continues*** *Modern Office Procedures, 0026-8208.* ***Continued by*** *Managing Office Technology, 1070-4051.*
**Desc:** Covers technology, applications, and issues about office automation and information processing for corporate and middle management involved in evaluating, specifying and buying products and services.
**Ind/Abst** ABI/INFORM Glob. Ed.; ABI Inform Ondisc (Oct. 1983-); Abstr. Bull. Inst. Pap. Sci. Tech.; Bus. ASAP (1990-) [Full Txt.]; Bus. Educ. Index; Bus. Index (1985-); Bus. Period. Index; Bus. Source (Jul. 1993-); Comput. ASAP [Full Txt.]; Comput. Database [Full Txt.]; Comput. Lit. Index; Consum. Index Prod. Eval. Inf. Source (Oct. 1983-); Gen. BusinessFile (1985-); Gen. Period. Index (1985-); INSPEC (Oct. 1983-); Mag. ASAP Plus [Full Txt.]; Mag. Index Plus (1989-); Mag. Search; Newsp. Period. Abstr. (1988-); Mag. Index (1983-); Trade Ind. ASAP [Full Txt.]; Trade Ind. Index (1983-) [Full Txt.]; UMI ABI/Inform--Bus. Period. Ondisc (Dec. 1987-) [Full Txt.]; Wilson Bus. Abstr.; Work Relat. Abstr.; World Publ. Monit.

US/1059-9983
**NCR CONNECTION.** [NCR connect.]. **VAT** National Cash Register Connection. (19??)-. Periodical. English. mo. $92.00. Publications & Communications, 12416 Hymeadow Drive, Austin TX 78750. **Tel** (512)250-9023, (800)678-9724, FAX (512)331-3900. **DD** 004. **Circ:** 10,000. ***Continues*** *NCR Monthly, 0892-3817.*

NE
**NEDLLOYD PARADE.** Koninklijke Nedlloyd Groep NV, Red Nedlloyd Parade, POB 487, 3000 AL Rotterdam Netherlands.

US/0749-8608
**NEWSLETTER - AUTOMATED OFFICE CO.** (NEWSLETTER / THE AUTOMATED OFFICE CO.). **Added/Corp** Automated Office Co. (July 1984)-. Newsletter. English. mo. $12.00. Automated Office Company, 253 Bedford Street, Bridgewater MA 02324. **Tel** (617)697-9438, FAX (617)294-0193. **ED** Brad Vachon.

NE
**NIEUWSBRIEF PZ.** Dutch. ir. Kluwer Law and Taxation Publishers, Staverenstraat 32015, PO Box 23, 7400 GA Deventer Netherlands. **Tel** 011 31 5700 47261.

US/1049-3743
**NOPA DEALER OPERATING RESULTS.** [NOPA deal. oper. results]. **Added/Corp** National Office Products Association. National Office Products Association. Research Dept. NOPA Data Processing Center. **VFOAT** Dealer Operating Results. **VAT** National Office Products Association Dealer Operating Results. (19??)-. English. an (Publishes every two years). $40.00 (members); $100.00 (non-members). National Office Products Association / NOPA, 301 North Fairfax Street, Alexandria VA 22314. **Tel** (703)549-9040, (800)542-6672, FAX (703)683-7552. **LC** HD9800.U5; N66. **DD** 381/.4568.

US/0746-5467
**NOPA INDUSTRY REPORT. *Title Change.*** [NOPA ind. rep.]. **Added/Corp** National Office Products Association (U.S.). **VFOAT** National Office Products Association Industry Report. (19??)-(1994). Periodical. English. Twenty-four times a year. National Office Products Association, 301 North Fairfax Street, Alexandria VA 22314. **Tel** (703)549-9040, (800)542-6672, FAX (703)683-7552. **ED** Sandra Selva. **DD** 338. **Circ:** 10,000. ***Continued by*** *B.P.I.A. Business Products Industry Report, 1078-5809.*
**Desc:** Covers pertinent news and information on the office supplies, furnishings and industry as well as news and events of NOPA.

US/0741-3238
**NOPA MANUFACTURER SELLING COSTS SURVEY. Added/Corp** National Office Products Association. **VFOAT** N.O.P.A. Manufacturer Selling Costs Survey; Manufacturer Selling Costs Survey. **VAT** National Office Products Association Manufacturer Selling Costs Survey. (1975)-. English. sa. $20.00 members, $50.00 non-members. National Office Products Association, 301 North Fairfax Street, Alexandria VA 22314. **Tel** (703)549-9040, (800)542-6672, FAX (703)683-7552. **LC** HF5439.O4; N66. **DD** 338.4/368.
**Desc:** A survey on six classifications of selling costs, subdivided into seven sales volume categories, supplies and furniture product lines.

US/1060-3522
**NOPA OFFICE MARKET UPDATE.** [NOPA off. mark. update]. **Added/Corp** National Office Products Association. **VFOAT** Update. **VAT** National Office Products Association Office Market Update. Vol. 1, No. 1 (Jan./Feb. 1990)-. Periodical. English. bm. $40.00 (non-members), $10.00 (members). National Office Products Association, 301 North Fairfax Street, Alexandria VA 22314. **Tel** (703)549-9040, (800)542-6672, FAX (703)683-7552. **DD** 338. ***Continues*** *Special Report to the Office Products Industry.*

US
**NOPA UPDATE.** English. bm. $40.00. National Office Products Association, 301 North Fairfax Street, Alexandria VA 22314. **Tel** (703)549-9040, (800)542-6672, FAX (703)683-7552.

US/0889-9827
**NORTH AMERICAN ELECTRONIC TYPEWRITER GUIDE.** ***Ceased.*** [North Am. electron. typewrit. guide]. **Added/Corp** Info-Market, Inc. (U.S.). **VFOAT** Electronic Typewriter Guide. (April 1985)-(Jan. 1992). Periodical. English. sa. Info-Market, 13935 Rancheros, Reno NV 89511. **Tel** (702)851-0356. **DD** 652.
**Desc:** Guide to all electronic typewriters on market in North America. Shows performance, pictures, US and Canadian prices. For buyers and sellers of facsimile machines.

JA
**OA JOHO.** **VFOAT** O.A. Joho; Office Automation Info. (19??)-. Periodical. Japanese (Japanese). sa. ¥2000. Dempa Publications Inc., 1 11 15 Higashi Gotanda, Shinagawa Ku Tokyo 141 Japan. **Tel** 011 81 3 34456111. **(Subscription address:** Overseas Courier Srvc America Inc, 5 East 44th Street, New York, NY 10017**) LC** HF5548.125; .O24.

CN/0709-5228
**OE&M. OFFICE EQUIPMENT & METHODS (1979).** (O E & M, OFFICE EQUIPMENT & METHODS.). **VAT** OE&M. Office Equipment and Methods (1979); Office Equipment & Methods (1979). V. 25- Jan./Feb. 1979-. Periodical. English. ir. $30.18. Maclean Hunter Canada / Montreal, 1001 bvd. de Maisonneuve W., Montreal, Quebec H3A 3E1 Canada. **Tel** 514-845-5141, FAX 514-845-4302, telex 055-60604. **DD** 651/.05. **[CCC].** available on microfilm and microfiche from University Microfilms International (UMI). Documents available from Ask*IEEE. ***Continues** Office Equipment & Methods, 0030-0179.*
**Ind/Abst** INSPEC.

JA/0387-5245
**OEP : OFFICE EQUIPMENT & PRODUCTS.** [OEP, Off. equip. prod.]. **VFOAT** Office Equipment & Products; Office Equipment and Products. (19??)-. Periodical. English. mo. $145.00 North & Central America; $130.00 Asia & Oceania; $160.00 Africa and South America. Dempa Publications Inc., 1 11 15 Higashi Gotanda, Shinagawa Ku Tokyo 141 Japan. **Tel** 011 81 3 34456111. **(Subscription address:** Dempa Publications, 275 Madison Avenue, New York, NY 10016**) ED** Tetsuo Hirayama. **DD** 338. **CODEN** OEPRA4. **Ad Acc. Circ:** 82,500. Documents available from UMI Article Clearinghouse, Ask*IEEE.
**Desc:** Reports on new products, market trends and industry issues relating to the office and work place automation.
**Ind/Abst** ABI/INFORM Glob. Ed.; ABI Inform Ondisc (1982-); F&S Index Plus Text, Int. [Select. Cov.]; Infomat Int. Bus.; INSPEC (1981-); PROMT.

US/0472-6049
**OFFICE AUTOMATION.** (1955)-. Periodical. English. Larry Lawier, Administrative Management, 1123 Broadway/Suite 1107, New York NY 10010. **Tel** (212)924-8989. **ED** Don Johnson. **LC** HF5548; .O4. **DD** 651.26. **Bk Rev. Ad Acc. Circ:** 300,000 (ctrl).
**Desc:** The administration, management and automation of offices and businesses.

IT
**OFFICE AUTOMATION.** Soiel International, Via Settala 8, 20124 Milan Italy.

US/0272-4855
**OFFICE AUTOMATION CONFERENCE DIGEST.** ***Ceased.*** **Main/Conf** Office Automation Conference. (1980)-(1986). English. an. AFIPS Press, 1899 Preston White Drive, Reston VA 22091. **Tel** (703)620-8900. **ED** John Goldthwaite. **LC** HF5548.125; .O37A. **DD** 651.8/005.
**Desc:** Some areas covered are office workstations, communications technologies and issues, ergonomics of the workplace, productivity and requirements in evaluation, organizational impacts, and networking applications.

US/0882-0198
**OFFICE AUTOMATION NEWS : THE PUBLICATION OF THE OFFICE AUTOMATION SOCIETY INTERNATIONAL.** [Off. autom. news]. **Added/Corp** Office Automation Society International. (19??)-. Periodical. English. bm. $30.00. Office Automation Society International, PO Box 374, McLean VA 22101. **Tel** (703)821-6650. **DD** 651.

US/0886-6767
**OFFICE AUTOMATION REPORT, THE.** ***Suspended.*** [Off. autom. rep.]. Vol. 28, No. 1 (Jan. 1, 1985)-Suspended May 1988. Periodical. English. mo. $45.00. The Automated Office Ltd, 1123 Broadway, New York NY 10010. **Tel** (212)924-8989. **ED** Don S Johnson and Megan Paznik. **DD** 651. **Circ:** 2,000. available on microfilm from University Microfilms International (UMI). ***Continues** Information & Word Processing Report, 0276-587X.*
**Desc:** Covers the world of office automation systems and equipment. Includes equipment analyses and technical reports.

US/1057-8889
**OFFICE COMPUTING REPORT.** ***Title Change.* See** Computers.

CN/0824-4073
**OFFICE CONNECTIONS.** [Off. connect.]. April/May 1983-. Periodical. English. bm. Paul Talbot Enterprises, PO Box 2275, Vancouver British Columbia V6B 3W5 Canada. **DD** 650.1/3/05. ***Continues** PTA Report, 0822-4234.*

CN/0705-5153
**OFFICE EQUIPMENT AND SUPPLIES MARKET IN CANADA, THE.** **VFOAT** The Office Equipment & Supplies Market in Canada. **VAT** Market and Media Report. The Office and Equipment and Supplies Market in Canada. 1977/78-. English. an. 75.00Can$. Maclean Hunter Canada / Montreal, 1001 bvd. de Maisonneuve W., Montreal, Quebec H3A 3E1 Canada. **Tel** 514-845-5141, FAX 514-845-4302, telex 055-60604. **DD** 381/.45/6512. ***Continues** Office Equipment Market in Canada, 0315-9787.*
**Desc:** Reports Canadian production, imports, exports, apparent domestic consumption of office machinery, furniture and supplies, and office building construction.

UK/0305-635X
**OFFICE EQUIPMENT INDEX.** ***Ceased.*** [Off. equip. index]. (1974)-(1994). Periodical. English. mo. O'Connell Reed Publishing, 6 Welden Place, Bradbourne Vale Road, Sevenoaks Kent TN3 3QQ England. **[CCC].** available on microfilm from University Microfilms International (UMI). ***Continues** Index to Office Equipment and Supplies, 0019-4085.*
**Ind/Abst** Infomat Int. Bus.

UK/0030-0187
**OFFICE EQUIPMENT NEWS.** English. mo. AGB Business Publs Ltd, Audit House, Field End Road, Ruislip Middlesex HA4 9LT England. **Tel** 011 44 81 868 4499. available on microfilm from University Microfilms International (UMI); available on an online database (file 771/Full-Text) from DIALOG. Documents available from Ask*IEEE.
**Ind/Abst** HILITES; INSPEC (Feb. 1984-); World Ceram. Abstr.

IT/1120-2386
**OFFICE FURNITURE.** [Off. furnit.]. (1986)-. Periodical. Multiple languages. an. L6000.00 Italy (surface mail); L150000.00 Europe, L200000.00 Africa & Asia & America, L250000.00 other (airmail). Alberto Greco Editore, Via Del Fusaro 8, 20146 Milan Italy. **Tel** 011 39 2 4819086 or 4691895, FAX 011 39 2 4819091, telex 315367. **UDC** 651.2.

US/0733-1266
**OFFICE GUIDE TO ORLANDO.** [Off. guide Orlando]. Vol. 1, No. 1 (Spring 1982)-. Periodical. English. Four times a year (Jan., Apr., July, Oct.). $30.00 (one year); $50.00 (two years); $60.00 (three years). Zink Media Group Ltd., 701 East Washington Street, Orlando FL 32801. **Tel** (407)628-3880, (407)426-9446. **ED** Carey A. Jasa and Warren Miller. **Ad Acc. Circ:** 12,093 (ctrl).
**Desc:** A complete guide to office space, products and services for the greater Orlando area.

IT
**OFFICE LAYOUT.** Soiel International, Via Settala 8, 20124 Milan Italy.

UK/0269-3046
**OFFICE MAGAZINE WILMINGTON, KENT.** ***Ceased.*** [Off mag. Wilmington, Kent]. (1983)-(1992). Periodical. English. Ten times a year. Wilmington Publishing Ltd., PO Box 200, Field End Road, Ruislip Middx HA4 OSY England. **Tel** 011 44 81 841 3970, FAX 011 44 81 841 9676. ***Continues** Office (Stanford-le-Hope), 0263-8312.*

US/0197-4602
**OFFICE PRODUCTS ANALYST, THE.** (THE OFFICE PRODUCTS ANALYST : OPA.). [Off. prod. anal.]. **Added/Corp** Martin Simpson Research Associates. **VFOAT** OPA; O.P.A. Vol. 1, No. 1. (Feb. 1977)-. English. mo. $195.00 (one year), $325.00 (two years), $450.00 (three years) US; $210.00 (one year), $355.00 (two years), $495.00 (three years) airmail other. Office Products Analyst, 50 Chestnut Plaza, Suite 900, Rochester NY 14604. **Tel** (716)232-5320, FAX (716)454-5760. **ED** Louis E Slawetsky. **LC** HF5548; .O518. **DD** 680. Index available. **Circ:** 1,000 (ctrl).
**Desc:** Unbiased source of analysis for users of office equipment such as copier duplicators, mini-computer office systems, electronic typewriters, PBX, lans, facsimile equipment, and laser printers.
**Ind/Abst** Comput. Bus. (19??-19??).

US/0199-1329
**OFFICE PRODUCTS DEALER (WHEATON).** ***Title Change.*** (OFFICE PRODUCTS DEALER.). **VFOAT** OPD. Vol. 107, No. 10 (Oct. 1979)-Vol. 120, No. 1 (Jan. 1992). Periodical. English. mo. Hitchcock Publishing Company, 191 South Gary Avenue, Carol Stream IL 60188. **Tel** (708)665-1000. **(Subscription address:** PO Box 830409, Birmingham, AL 35283-0409; phone: 800-633-4931**) LC** HF5541.T9; O3. **DD** 684.1/0068/8. **[CCC].** available on microfilm and microfiche from University Microfilms International (UMI). ***Continues** Office Products, 0030-0144.* ***Continued by** OPD.*

CN/1184-0536
**OFFICE PRODUCTS GOLD BOOK.** [Off. prod. gold book]. **VFOAT** Gold Book. Vol. 3, Edition 1 (Feb. 1990)-. English (summaries and/or abstracts in French). ir. Free to subscribers to The Office supplies business magazine. Abaco Communications Ltd., 44 Carlton Road, Unionville, Ontario, L3R 1Z5 Canada. **DD** 381/.456512/002571.

US/0163-9935
**OFFICE PRODUCTS, MASTER CATALOG & BUYING GUIDE.** **VAT** Office Products, Master Catalog and Buying Guide. (1972)-. Catalog. English. mo. $62.55. Hitchcock Publishing Company, 191 South Gary Avenue, Carol Stream IL 60188. **Tel** (708)665-1000. **LC** HF5548; .O52. **DD** 381/.45/6512002573. ***Continues** Office Products Buying Guide.*

AT/1034-6686
**OFFICE PRODUCTS NEWS (DARLINGHURST).** (OFFICE PRODUCTS NEWS.). [Off. prod. news]. (1989)-. Periodical. English. mo. Office Products News, 67-72 Wentworth Avenue, Darlinghurst, Sydney, NSW 2010 Australia. **CODEN** OPNED2. ***Continues** Modern Office, 0810-9451.*

US/0030-0128
**OFFICE (STAMFORD. 1936), THE.** ***Title Change.*** (THE OFFICE.). [Office]. (1936)-(Nov. 1993). Periodical. English. mo. Office Publications, Inc., PO Box 120031, Stamford CT 06912-0031. **Tel** (203)972-4155. **ED** William R. Schulhof. **LC** HF5001; .O2. **DD** 651.205. **CODEN** OFISAD. **[CCC]. Ad Acc. Circ:** 165,000. available on microfilm and microfiche from University Microfilms International (UMI). Documents available from Ask*IEEE, UMI Article Clearinghouse. ***Continues** Office Economics.* ***Absorbed by** Managing Office Technology.*
**Desc:** Magazine for the office, administrative, EDP, MIS, systems, executives. Extensive editorial coverage of office related subjects. Introduces over 1,000 new products annually.
**Ind/Abst** ABI/INFORM Glob. Ed.; ABI Inform Ondisc (Dec. 1971-); Abstr. Bull. Inst. Pap. Sci. Tech.; Acad. Abstr. (July 1993-); Acad. Search (July 1993-); Account. Art.; Bus. Index (1985-); Bus. Period. Index; Bus. Source (Jan. 1993-); Comput. Database; Comput. Lit. Index; Consum. Index Prod. Eval. Inf. Source; Gen. BusinessFile (1985-); Gen. Period. Index (1985-); Health Plan. Adminis.; INFO-SOUTH Abstr.; INSPEC (Sept. 1981-); Mag. Index Plus (1992-); Mag. Search; Manage. Contents; Newsp. Period. Abstr. (1989-); Vocat. Search (July 1993-); Wilson Bus. Abstr.; Work Relat. Abstr.; World Publ. Monit.

CN/1184-0528
**OFFICE SUPPLIES BUSINESS MAGAZINE, THE.** [Off. supplies bus. mag.]. Vol. 1, No. 1 (Apr. 1990)-. Periodical. English. qt. Free. Abaco Communications Ltd., 44 Carlton Road, Unionville, Ontario, L3R 1Z5 Canada. **DD** 381/.456512/0097105.

US/8750-3441
**OFFICE SYSTEMS (GEORGETOWN, CONN.).** (OFFICE SYSTEMS : THE MAGAZINE FOR SMALL AND MEDIUM OFFICES.). [Off. syst.]. Vol. 1, No. 1 (July-Aug. 1984)-. Periodical. English. mo. $0.00 small or medium size offices or office equipment dealers, $36.00 other. Office Systems Magazine Inc., 1111 Bethlehem Pike, Cappucio, Springhouse PA 19477. **Tel** (215)646-8700. **ED** William M Hogan (203)544-9526. **LC** HF5548; .O523. **DD** 651. **CODEN** OFSYEH. **Bk Rev. Ad Acc. Circ:** 100,000 (ctrl). available on microfilm and microfiche from University Microfilms International (UMI).
**Desc:** Represents the fastest growing segment of the office products field: small- to medium-size companies (50-500 employees).
**Ind/Abst** Bus. Educ. Index; F&S Index Plus Text, Int. [Select. Cov.]; Law Office Inf. Serv.; PROMT.

US/0733-5164
**OFFICE TECHNOLOGY MANAGEMENT.** ***Ceased.*** [Off. technol. manage.]. **VFOAT** Office Technology. Vol. 1, No. 1 (June 1982)-(19??). Periodical. English. mo. Office Technology Management, 10076 Boca Entrada Boulevard, Boca Raton FL 33433.

US/0164-5951
**OFFICE WORLD NEWS.** [Off. world news]. **VFOAT** Office World News OWN; OWN. (197?)-. Periodical. English. mo. $24.00 US; $30.00 Canada; $110.00 other. FM Business Publications, 342 Madison Avenue, 22nd Floor, New York NY 10173. **Tel** (212)867-2350. **DD** 651. **CODEN** OWNEEH. **[CCC].** available on microfilm and microfiche from University Microfilms International (UMI). Documents available from Ask*IEEE.
**Ind/Abst** INSPEC (1985-).

US/0733-2564
**OFFICEMATION PRODUCT REPORTS.** [Officemation prod. rep.]. **Added/Corp** Management Information Corporation. (1977)-. Periodical. English. mo. $721.00 US; $821.00 other. Management Information Corporation, 1111 Marlkress Road, Cherry Hill NJ 08003. **Tel** (609)424-1100. **ED** David Axner. **LC** HF5548; .O525. **DD** 651.8/05. Index available. ***Continues*** *Officemation Reports, 0161-8768.*
**Desc:** Objective evaluations of office automation products.

US/1070-938X
**OFFICIAL OFFICE MACHINES & BUSINESS EQUIPMENT USED PRICES GUIDE BLUE BOOK, THE.** [Off. off. mach. bus. equip. used prices guide blue book]. **VFOAT** Official Office Machines and Business Equipment Used Prices Guide Blue Book; Office Machines and Business Equipment Used Prices Guide Blue Book; Blue Book; Office Machines & Business Equipment Used Prices Guide Blue Book; Used Prices Guide Blue Book. (19??)-. English. an. $222.00. Asay Publishing Company, PO Box 670, Joplin MO 64802. **Tel** (417)781-9317, FAX (417)781-0427, (800)825-9633. **ED** Gail Evans (phone: (800)947-0225). **DD** 651.

US
**OPD.** ***Ceased.*** **VFOAT** Office Products Distribution; Office Products Dealer. Vol. 120, No. 2 (Feb. 1992)-Vol. 121, No. 11 (Nov. 1993). Periodical. English. mo. Hitchcock Publishing Company, 191 South Gary Avenue, Carol Stream IL 60188. **Tel** (708)665-1000. **LC** HF5541.T9; O3. **DD** 684.1/0068/8. ***Continues*** *Office Products Dealer, 0199-1329.*

US/1054-7576
**PORTABLE OFFICE. BUYER'S GUIDE ...** . [Portable off., Buyer's guide]. **VFOAT** Buyer's Guide ...; Portable Office Buyer's Guide; Buyer's Guide to ... . (1991)-. English. bm. Portable Office, 80 Elm Street, Peterborough NH 03458. **DD** 004.

UK/0965-4739
**PREMISES & FACILITIES MANAGEMENT.** [Premises facil. manag.]. **VFOAT** Premises and Facilities Management. (1991)-. Periodical. English. mo (10 issues per year). £55.00 UK; £75.00 other Europe; £100.00 other. IML Group, Blair House, 184-186 High Street, Tonbridge Kent, TN9 1BQ England. **Tel** 011 44 732 359990, FAX 011 44 732 770049. **ED** Richard Byatt. **Ad Acc**, **Adv Mgr:** Mark Wiles. ***Continues*** *Premises Management & Facility Planning.*

IT
**PROGETTO UFFICIO.** ***Suspended.*** (19??)-(Dec. 1992). Italian. ir. Rima Srl, via V Da Filicaia 7, 20162 Milan Italy. **Tel** 011 39 2 66013539.

CN/0317-6339
**PURCHASING PREFERENCE SURVEY : OFFICE EQUIPMENT AND SUPPLIES.** **See** Business-Purchasing.

CN/0701-7898
**QUARTERLY SHIPMENTS OF OFFICE FURNITURE PRODUCTS.** (QUARTERLY SHIPMENTS OF OFFICE FURNITURE PRODUCTS / MANUFACTURING AND PRIMARY INDUSTRIES DIVISION.). [Q. shipm. off. furnit. prod.]. **Added/Corp** Statistics Canada. Manufacturing and Primary Industries Division. **VFOAT** Livraisons Trimestrielles des Produits du Meuble de Bureau. Vol. 1, No. 1 (Mar. 1972)-. Periodical. English (French). qt. 32.00Can$ Canada; $39.00 US; $45.00 other. Statistics Canada, Publications Sales & Services, Main Building Room 1710, Ottawa Ontario K1A 0T6 Canada. **Tel** (613)951-5078, (800)267-6677, FAX (613)951-1584, telex 053-3585. **DD** 380.1/456841/00971.
**Desc:** Provides detailed information on office furniture products.

US/8755-4038
**SECRETARIAL SERVICES TODAY.** [Secr. serv. today]. Vol. 1, No. 1 (Dec. 1984)-. Periodical. English. mo. $18.00. Secretarial Services Today, PO Box 29203, Shreveport LA 71149-9203. **DD** 651.

US/0279-0548
**SERVICES (VIENNA, VA.).** (SERVICES : THE MAGAZINE OF THE BUILDING SERVICE CONTRACTORS ASSOCIATION INTERNATIONAL.). [Services]. **Added/Corp** Building Service Contractors Association International. Vol. 1, No. 1 (Jan. 1981)-. Periodical. English. mo. $30.00 US; $54.00 other. Services Magazine, 10201 Lee Highway, Suite 225, Fairfax VA 22030-2202. **Tel** (703)359-7090, (800)368-3414, FAX (703)352-0493. **ED** Robert E. Simanski. **LC** TX955; .S47. **DD** 648/.05. Index available. **Ad Acc. Circ:** 13,000 (ctrl).
**Desc:** Management and technical articles for providers and purchasers of contract cleaning services such as office cleaning, carpet and floor care, window cleaning, and exterior maintenance.

US/0738-6516
**SIZZLE SHEET, THE.** **See** Business-Marketing.

US
**SPECCHECK (SAN JOSE, CALIF.).** ***Ceased.*** (SPECCHECK.). Vol. 1, No. 1 Aug. (1985)-Ceased in (1991). Periodical. English. sa. **LC** HF5548; .S647. **DD** 681/.65.

US/1066-0011
**TONER TECHNOLOGY MONTHLY.** [Toner technol. mon.]. **Added/Corp** Toner Technology, Inc. (1984)-. Periodical. English. mo. $950.00 US & Canada; $1,050.00 other. Toner Research Services, 3495 Mustafa Drive, Sharonville OH 45241. **Tel** (513)733-4407, FAX (513)733-4744. **ED** John F. Cooper. **DD** 680. **Circ:** 80.
**Desc:** Consists of six to eight sections providing current technical information related to copier, printer, toner and developer materials.

US/0897-0939
**UPDATE (HACKENSACK, N.J.).** (UPDATE: THE EXECUTIVE'S PURCHASING ADVISOR.). [Update]. **Added/Corp** Buyers Laboratory. (19??)-. Periodical. English. mo. $115.00. Buyers Laboratory Inc., 20 Railroad Avenue, Hackensack NJ 07601. **Tel** (201)488-0404. **ED** Daria Hoffman. Index available. **Circ:** 3,000.
**Desc:** Provides advice, analysis and information to purchasers of office equipment, including copiers, fax machines, typewriters, printers, furniture, mailing equipment, supplies, and etc.

US/0042-3327
**VENDING TIMES.** [Vend. times]. Vol. 1 (1961)-. Periodical. English. mo. $30.00 (1 year), $40.00 (2 year), $55.00 (3 year) US, Canada and Mexico; $80.00 other. Vending Times Inc, 545 8th Avenue, New York NY 10018. **Tel** (212)714-0101, FAX (212)564-0196. **ED** Arthur E Yohalem. **DD** 658.8. **Bk Rev. Ad Acc. Circ:** 15,000 (ctrl). available on microfilm and microfiche from University Microfilms International (UMI). ***Absorbed*** *Vend; V/T Music & Games.*
**Desc:** Covers vending, coin-operated music and amusement machines, and coffee service fields.
**Ind/Abst** Bus. Index (Jan. 1985-Dec. 1985); F&S Index Plus Text, Int. [Select. Cov.]; Foods Adlibra; Gen. BusinessFile (Jan. 1985-Dec. 1985); Gen. Period. Index (Jan. 1985-Dec. 1985); Mag. Search; PROMT; Stat. Ref. Index; Trade Ind. Index (1981-?); Vocat. Search (July 1993-).

US
**VENDING TIMES, CENSUS OF THE INDUSTRY.** English. an. $25.00. Vending Times Inc, 545 8th Avenue, New York NY 10018. **Tel** (212)714-0101, FAX (212)564-0196.
**Ind/Abst** Predicasts Forecasts.

US
**VENDING TIMES. INTERNATIONAL BUYERS GUIDE ISSUE.** **VFOAT** International Buyers Guide Issue; Vending Times Buyers Guide Issue; V/T Buyers Guide. (1988)-. Consumer Publication. English. an (August). $25.00. Vending Times Inc, 545 8th Avenue, New York NY 10018. **Tel** (212)714-0101, FAX (212)564-0196. ***Continues*** *Vending Times. International Buyers Guide and Directory.*

UK
**WHAT TO BUY.** English. mo. £105.00 UK; £170.00 North America; £130.00 Europe. What to Buy, Quadrant House, The Quadrant, Sutton, Surrey SM2 5AS, England. **Tel** 081-661-8700, FAX 081-770-1284. **(Subscription address:** What to Buy, Computer Action, Central House, 27 Park Street, Croydon CR0 1YD, England**) ED** Sarah Frater. Index available. cum. index. **Circ:** 10,000. ***Continues*** *Copier User.*
**Desc:** Independent business consumer report covering office equipment and services. Articles and charts covering everything from fax to finance, copiers to computers, typewriters to telephone systems and software stationary.

UK/0265-296X
**WHAT TO BUY FOR BUSINESS.** [What buy bus.]. **VFOAT** What to Buy. (1980)-. Periodical. English. mo (12 issues per year). £120.00 UK; £143.00 Europe; £187.00 others. Garrard House, 2 6 Homesdale Road, Bromley Kent, BR2 9WL England. **Tel** 011 44 81 4028493. **DD** 651.200294.

US/0886-6163
**WHAT TO BUY FOR BUSINESS (U.S. ED.).** (WHAT TO BUY FOR BUSINESS.). [What buy bus.]. (1981)-. Periodical. English. Ten times a year (published monthly with Jul./Aug. and Dec./Jan. issues combined). $121.00 US; $212.00 other. What to Buy for Business, 924 Anacapa Street, Suite 4G, Santa Barbara CA 93101. **Tel** (805)963-3539, FAX (805)963-3740. **(Subscription address:** Palm Coast Data, PO Box 420285, Agency Department, Palm Coast, FL 32142; telephone: (904)445-4662 ext 817**) LC** HF5548; .W45. **DD** 381/.45/00029473. Documents available from Ask*IEEE.
**Ind/Abst** HILITES; Inf. Manage. Technol.; INSPEC (June 1983-); Mag. Artic. Summar. Elite (July 1994-); Manage. Market. Abstr.; Print. Abstr.; World Ceram. Abstr.; World Publ. Monit.

US/0164-4742
**WORDS (WILLOW GROVE).** ***Ceased.*** (WORDS.). [Words]. Vol. 1 (Spring 1972)-(June 1988). Periodical. English. bm. Association of Information Systems Professionals, 104 Wilmot Road, Suite 201, Deerfield IL 60015. **Tel** (708)940-8800. **ED** Mark Hertzog. **Bk Rev. Ad Acc. Circ:** 49,000 (ctrl). available on microfilm and microfiche from University Microfilms International (UMI). Documents available from Ask*IEEE, UMI Article Clearinghouse.
**Desc:** The leading publication of AISP with a total readership of 49,000 professionals who design, implement, manage and use office information systems and their related products.
**Ind/Abst** ABI/INFORM Glob. Ed.; ABI Inform Ondisc (Dec. 1982-); Bus. Educ. Index; INSPEC (Dec. 1984/Jan. 1985-May/June 1988); Law Office Inf. Serv.

●US/1068-9699
**WORKGROUP COMPUTING REPORT.** [Workgr. comput. rep.]. **Added/Corp** Patricia Seybold Group. Vol. 16, No. 2 (Feb. 1993)-. Periodical. English. mo. $419.00 US; $431.00 Canada; $443.00 other. Patricia Seybolds Office Computing Group, 148 State Street, Suite 700, Boston MA 02109. **Tel** (617)742-5200, (800)826-2424, FAX (617)742-1028. **DD** 651. **CODEN** WOCREX. Documents available from Ask*IEEE. ***Continues*** *Office Computing Report, 1057-8889.*
**Ind/Abst** INSPEC; Print. Abstr.

US/1040-7472
**WORKSTATION REPORT, THE.** ***Title Change.*** [Workstn. rep.]. **Added/Corp** ZigZag Corporation. DesignNetwork International. (Sept./Oct. 1988)-(1992). Periodical. English. Nine times a year. Design Network International Ltd., PO Box 638, Highland Park IL 60035. **Tel** (708)831-0300. **LC** HD9803.A1; W67. **DD** 338.4/7684. ctrl circ. ***Continued by*** *DesignNetwork's Workstation Report.*
**Desc:** Reviews, news and trends on the contracts and furniture industry.

US/1062-7650
**WORKSTATION REPORT'S ... BUYER' GUIDE TO OFFICE FURNITURE, THE.** [Workstn. rep. buy. guide off. furnit.]. **Added/Corp** ZigZag Corporation. **VFOAT** Buyer' Guide to Office Furniture. (199?)-. Periodical. English. an. $79.00. Design Network International Ltd., PO Box 638, Highland Park IL 60035. **Tel** (708)831-0300. **LC** HD9803.U6; W67. **DD** 684.
**Desc:** Analytical publications in the contract furniture industry. The Workstation Report combines insightful reviews, along with pricing comparisons and current industry news. This dynamic combination allows the reader to make informed decisions when purchasing or specifying office furniture products.

AT
**YOUR COMPLETE OFFICE.** ***Title Change.*** (19??)-(19??). English. bm. Practical Marketing Group, PO Box 105, Willoughby New South Wales, 2068 Australia. **Tel** 011 61 2 9581811. Documents available from Ask*IEEE. ***Continued by*** *Your Complete Office Buyer's Guide.*
**Ind/Abst** INSPEC (Aug. 1991-).

## OPTOMETRY

US/0192-1304
**20/20.** **VFOAT** Twenty/Twenty; 20, 20. (19??)-. Periodical. English. bm. $85.00 US; $170.00 Canada; $215.00 Europe; $265.00 Asia; $180.00 other. Jobson Publishing Corporation, 100 Avenue of the Americas, New York NY 10013. **Tel** (212)274-7084, 274-7000, FAX (212)431-0500. **(Subscription address:** Twenty Twenty Magazine, PO Box 7634, Riverton NJ 08077.**) ED** Jody Stone. **Ad Acc. Circ:** 34,000 (ctrl).
**Desc:** Eyecare products and marketing trends for optical retailers.

US
**20 / 20 EUROPE.** (19??)-. Periodical. English. Nine times a year. $300.00. Jobson Publishing Corporation, 100 Avenue of the Americas, New York NY 10013. **Tel** (212)274-7084, 274-7000, FAX (212)431-0500. **(Subscription address:** Jobsons Publishing / England, Jobsons House, Holbrooke Place, Hillrise, Richmond TW10 6UD England.**)**

US
**20/20'S ... ANNUAL REPORT OF THE OPTICAL INDUSTRY AND DISPENSING PROFESSIONS.** **VFOAT** Twenty/Twenty's ... Annual Report of the Optical Industry and Dispensing Professions; Annual Report of the Optical Industry and Dispensing Professions. (19??)-. English. an. Jobson Publishing Corporation, 100 Avenue of the Americas, New York NY 10013. **Tel** (212)274-7084, 274-7000, FAX (212)431-0500.

●CN
**AMERICAN OPTICIAN.** **Added/Corp** Opticians Association of America. Vol. 1, No. 1 (Feb./Mar. 1992)-. Periodical. English. bm. **NLM** W1; AM6692.

US/0094-9620
**AMERICAN OPTOMETRIC ASSOCIATION NEWS.** **Added/Corp** American Optometric Association. American Optometric Association News. Vol. 11 (Jan. 1972)-. Periodical. English. bm (Published the 1st and 15th each month). $42.00 US, $48.00 Canada, $54.00 other. American Optometric Association, 243 North Lindbergh Boulevard, St Louis MO 63141. **Tel** (314)991-4100, FAX (314)441-4101. **ED** Bob Foster and Bob Pieper. **NLM** W1 AM67H. **Ad Acc, Adv Mgr:** Raeber, **Tel** (314)991-4100. **Circ:** 30,390 (ctrl). ***Continues*** *AOA News, 0095-0440.*
**Desc:** News, information and current events in optometry.

SP
**ANUARIO ESPANOL Y PORTUGUES DE OPTICA Y AUDIOMETRIA.** Spanish (Portuguese). 4.500ptas Spain; 9.00ptas North America; 6.500ptas other. Puntex SA, c/ Mare de Deu del Coll 14, 08023 Barcelona Spain. **Tel** (93)237 71 24, FAX (93)217 55 73, telex 97131 GPMM E. **Bk Rev. Ad Acc. Circ:** 7,000.
**Desc:** Optometry business, distributors, and trademarks. Products listed by specialties. Optical businesses, professionals, and related data.

SZ/0004-7910
**AUGENOPTIK.** [Augenoptik]. Periodical. German. bm. Deutscher Judo Verband, Redaktion Ippon Segewaldweg 40, D 12557 Berlin Germany. **Tel** 011 49 711 210770, telex 051 678. **NLM** W1 AU206P. Documents available from Ask*IEEE.
**Ind/Abst** INSPEC (Aug. 1973-Jan./Feb. 1976).

GW/0004-7929
**AUGENOPTIKER, DER.** **See** Medical Science and Technology-Ophthalmology.

US
**BLUE BOOK OF OPTOMETRISTS, THE.** 1932-. English. be. $65.00. Butterworth Heinemann / Woburn, MA, 225 Wildwood Avenue, Unit B, Woburn MA 01801. **Tel** (800)366-2665, FAX (617)928-2620, telex 880052. **LC** RE940. ***Continues*** *Blue Book of Optometrists and Opticians.*
**Desc:** A complete listing of optometrists in the U.S., Canada, and Puerto Rico (over 30,000 names and addresses).

UK
**BRITISH JOURNAL OF OPTOMETRY AND DISPENSING.** (19??)-. English. Twelve times a year. £74.00 (institutions), £44.00 (individuals) UK; £110.00 (institutions), £80.00 (individuals) other. Mark Allen Publishing Ltd., Croxped Mews, 288 Croxped Road, London SE24 9DA England. **Tel** 011 44 1 671 7521.

US/0273-804X
**CALIFORNIA OPTOMETRY.** **Added/Corp** California Optometric Association. Vol. 6 (1980)-. Periodical. English. Six times a year. $35.00. California Optometric Association, 801 12th Street, Suite 2020, Sacramento CA 95812. **Tel** (916)441-3990. **ED** Margaret Clausen. **NLM** W1 CA403CA. **Ad Acc. Pr Rev. Circ:** 4,000. ***Continues*** *California Optometrist, 0361-7025.*

CN/0045-5075
**CANADIAN JOURNAL OF OPTOMETRY.** **Added/Corp** Canadian Association of Optometrists. Ontario. Board of Examiners in Optometry. **VFOAT** Revue Canadienne d'Optometrie. Vol. 1-48, No. 1 (May 1939)-. Periodical. English. qt. 40.00Can$ Canada; 50.00Can$ other. Canadian Journal of Optometry, 1785 Alta Vista Drive Suite 301, Ottawa Ontario K1G 3Y6 Canada. **Tel** (613)738-4412, FAX (613)738-7161. **ED** G. Maurice Belanger. **NLM** W1 CA598C. **Bk Rev. Ad Acc. Circ:** 3,000 (ctrl). ***Absorbed*** *Canadian Association of Optometrists. Bulletin, 0045-4400.*
**Desc:** Official in-house publication of the Canadian Association of Optometrists: original research, association and professional historical news.

US/0147-7633
**CHILTON'S REVIEW OF OPTOMETRY.** [Chilton's rev. optom.]. **VFOAT** Review of Optometry; OJRO. Vol. 114, No. 5 (May 1977)-. Periodical. English. mo. $50.00. Chilton Company, 201 King of Prussia Road, Radnor PA 19089. **Tel** (610)964-4122, (800)695-1214, FAX (610)964-4978, telex 6851035 CHILTON UW. **ED** Richard L Guerrein. **LC** RE1; .O6. **DD** 617.7/5. **NLM** W1 CH739. **[CCC]. Bk Rev. Ad Acc. Circ:** 26,763. available on microfilm and microfiche from University Microfilms International (UMI). ***Continues*** *Optical Journal and Review of Optometry, 0030-3925.*
**Desc:** Serves the practice and patient care needs of optometrists, vision care professionals who are the major dispensers of ophthalmic materials.

CN/0834-2245
**CJO : CANADIAN JOURNAL OF OPTOMETRY.** [CJO, Can. j. optom.]. **VFOAT** Canadian Journal of Optometry; RCO : Revue Canadienne d'Optometrie; RCO. Vol. 48, No. 3 (Autumn 1986)-. Periodical. English (French). qt. Canadian Association of Optometrists, 1785 Alta Vista Drive/Suite 301, Ottawa Ontario K1G 3Y6 Canada. **Tel** (613)738-4412, FAX (613)738-7161. **DD** 617.7/5/05. **NLM** W1; CA598F. ***Continues*** *Optovision, 0834-2237.*

AT/0816-4622
**CLINICAL AND EXPERIMENTAL OPTOMETRY.** (CLINICAL & EXPERIMENTAL OPTOMETRY : JOURNAL OF THE AUSTRALIAN OPTOMETRICAL ASSOCIATION.). [Clin. exp. optom.]. **Added/Corp** Australian Optometrical Association. **VFOAT** Clinical and Experimental Optometry. Vol. 69, No. 1 (Jan. 1986)-. Periodical. English. bm (6 issues). 82.00Aus$ Australia; 95.00Aus$ (surface mail), 140.00Aus$ (airmail). Australian Optometrical Association, PO Box 185, 204 Drummond Street, Carlton Victoria 3053 Australia. **Tel** 011 61 3 6636833, FAX 011 61 3 6637478. **ED** Professor H. Barry Collin. **NLM** W1; CL664CF. **CODEN** CEOPBB. Index available. **Bk Rev. Ad Acc, Adv Mgr:** Sandra Shaw, **Tel** 03 663 6833. **Pr Rev. Circ:** 2,500 (ctrl). ***Continues*** *Australian Journal of Optometry.*
**Desc:** Contains original scientific papers, case studies, reviews and letters dealing with vision science and optometric clinical patient care.

US/0363-1621
**CONTACT LENS FORUM.** ***Title Change.*** [Contact lens forum]. (May 1976)-(19??). Periodical. English. mo. Viscom Publications Inc., 50 Washington Street, Norwalk CT 06854. **Tel** (203)838-9100, FAX (203)838-2550. **ED** James D. Atwood and Carol A. Schwartz. **LC** RE977.C6; C558. **DD** 617.7/523/05. **NLM** W1 CO768CL. Index available. cum. index. **Ad Acc. Circ:** 20,000 (ctrl). ***Merged into*** *Contact Lens Spectrum, 0885-9175.*
**Desc:** Clinical publication offering researched articles on all aspects of contact lens wear and fitting.

UK/0306-9575
**CONTACT LENS JOURNAL (THORNTON HEATH, SURREY), THE.** (THE CONTACT LENS JOURNAL.). [Contact lens j.]. Vol. 5, No. 1 (Sept. 1974)-. Academic Scholarly Publication. English. Eight times a year. £45.00 Europe, £63.00 others (surface mail); £57.00 Europe, £67.00 others (airmail). S. C. Hardy & Company, 3A Wadhurst Business Park, Faircrouch Lane, Wadhurst E SSX TN5 6PT England. **Tel** 011 44 892 782724. **ED** L. Hines and C. Kerr. **NLM** W1 CO768P. Index available. **Bk Rev. Ad Acc. Pr Rev. Circ:** 2,000. ***Continues*** *Contact Lens.*
**Desc:** Publishes original papers from authors worldwide together with commissioned articles, book reviews and abstracts and general news on contact lens related topics.
**Ind/Abst** EMBASE.

US/0885-9175
**CONTACT LENS SPECTRUM.** [Contact lens spectr.]. Vol. 1, No. 1 (Jan. 1986)-. Periodical. English. mo. $38.00 (1 year), $60.00 (2 year) US; $67.00 (1 year), $98.00 (2 year) Canada; $95.00 (1 year), $145.00 (2 year) other. Viscom Publications Inc., 50 Washington Street, Norwalk CT 06854. **Tel** (203)838-9100, FAX (203)838-2550. **(Subscription address:** Contact Lens Spectrum, PO Box 243, Westport CT 06881.) **ED** Neal Bailey, Joseph Barr and Florence Berghane. **DD** 617. **NLM** W1; CO768R. Index available. cum. index. **Ad Acc. Circ:** 26,227 (ctrl). ***Absorbed*** *Contact Lens Forum, 0363-1621.*
**Desc:** Provides clinical and technical information on lenses and solutions, guidelines for effective patient care and problem-solving, news of industry developments and commentaries.

GW
**CONTACT-LINSE, DIE.** (1967)-. Periodical. German. qt. DM86.40. Verlag Willy Schrickel GmbH, Ernst Mey Strasse 8, Postfach 10 02 52, 7022 Leinfelden Germany. **Tel** 0711/7594-0, telex 7 255 421. **ED** Konrad Kohlhammer. **DD** 617.7. **Bk Rev. Ad Acc. Circ:** 3,200.
**Desc:** Journal for the contact lens specialist.

GW/0724-6226
**CONTACTOLOGIA-BUECHEREI.** [Contactol.-Buech.]. **VFOAT** Contactologia Buecherei. Vol. 1 (1983)-. Monographic series. German. ir. Price varies per volume. Ferdinand Enke Verlag, Ruedigerstrasse 14, D-70469 Stuttgart Germany. **Tel** 011 49 711 8931124, 011 49 711 893123. **ED** Wulf Ehrich and Robert Heitz. **NLM** W1; CO769F.

GW/0171-9599
**CONTACTOLOGIA. DEUTSCHE AUSGABE.** (CONTACTOLOGIA.). [Contactol., Dtsch. Ausg.]. Vol. 1 (Sept. 1979)-. Academic Scholarly Publication. German (summaries and/or abstracts in English; table of contents in English). qt. $97.00. Georg Thieme Verlag Stuttgart, Postfach 301120, D 70451 Stuttgart Germany. **Tel** 011 49 711 89310, FAX 011 49 711 8931298, telex 7 252 275 GTVD. **(Subscription address:** Thieme Medical Publishers Inc., 381 Park Avenue South, New York NY 10016.) **ED** P Cochet, W Ehrich, D Epstein,. **NLM** W1 CO769F. **CODEN** CNTCDF. **[CCC].** Documents available from CASDDS.
**Ind/Abst** Chem. Abstr.; EMBASE; Life Sci. Collect.

UK
**CONTAX.** ***Ceased.*** Ceased (1989). Periodical. English. qt. Reed Business Publishing / West Sussex, England, Perrymount Road, Haywards Heath, West Sussex RH16 3DH England. **Tel** 011 44 81 6523500. **NLM** W1; CO769MC.

GW/0344-7103
**DEUTSCHE OPTIKERZEITUNG.** **See** Medical Science and Technology-Ophthalmology.

US/0091-4258
**DIRECTORY OF THE AMERICAN OPTOMETRIC ASSOCIATION.** **Main/Corp** American Optometric Association. 1st- Ed.; 1972-. Directory. English. American Optometric Association, 243 North Lindbergh Boulevard, St Louis MO 63141. **Tel** (314)991-4100, FAX (314)441-4101. **LC** RE940; .A5. **DD** 617.7/5/06273. **NLM** WW 22 AA1 A7D.

UK/0954-3201
**DISPENSING OPTICS.** (DISPENSING OPTICS : THE PROFESSIONAL JOURNAL OF THE ASSOCIATION OF BRITISH DISPENSING OPTICIANS.). [Dispens. opt.]. **Added/Corp** Association of British Dispensing Opticians. Vol. 1, No. 1 (Jan./Feb. 1986)-. Periodical. English. Nine times a year. £30.00 UK; £35.00 others. Association of British Dispensing Optics, 6 Hurlingham Bus Park, Sullivan Road, London SW6 3DO England. **Tel** 011 44 71 736 0088, FAX 011 44 71 731 5531. **(Subscription address:** 6 Hurlingham Business Park, Sulivan Road, London SW6 3D0 England) **ED** J. W. Roskill. **NLM** W1; DI769. **Bk Rev. Ad Acc, Adv Mgr:** I. McGhie, **Tel** 0303 262272. **Circ:** 5,906. ***Continues*** *Dispensing Optician (London, England), 0012-3773.*
**Desc:** The discussion of eye health care in the optical profession and the retail aspects associated with that care.

GW/0936-1928
**EURO-FOCUS RATINGEN.** [Euro-FocusRating.]. (1989)-. Periodical. German (English, French, Italian and Spanish). qt. DM38.00 Europe; DM76.00 other. Spangemacher Verlags GmbH und Co KG, Lintorfer Str 7-9, W-4030 Ratingen 1 Germany. **ED** Heinz Jurgen Haninger. **UDC** 33 :62. **Ad Acc. Circ:** 25,000.
**Desc:** Articles for consumers and opticians on eyewear fashion.

US/0885-9167
**EYECARE BUSINESS.** **VFOAT** Eye Care Business. (Jan. 1986)-. Periodical. English. mo. $40.00 US; $70.00 Canada; $110.00 other. Viscom Publications Inc., 50 Washington Street, Norwalk CT 06854. **Tel** (203)838-9100, FAX (203)838-2550. **ED** Leo Robert, Karen Mazza and Lynn Faught. **DD** 338. Index available. cum. index. **Ad Acc. Circ:** 35,324 (ctrl).
**Desc:** Provides optometrists and opticians with information on managing and marketing their businesses more effectively. Topics include merchandising, pricing, store design/display, dispensing and advertising.

GW
**FACHVORTRAGE DES WVAO-JAHRESKONGRESSES, DIE.** **Main/Corp** Wissenschaftliche Vereinigung fuer Augenoptik und Optometrie (Ger.). (1977)-. German. an. DM35.00. Wissenschaftliche Vereiningung fur Augenoptik und Optometrie Mainz, Adam-Karrillon-Strasse 32, D 55118 Mainz Germany. **Tel** (06131)613061. **ED** Hartmut Glaser. **LC** RE951; .W57a subser. **Ad Acc. Circ:** 10,000 (ctrl). ***Continues*** *Wissenschaftliche Vereinigung fuer Augeoptik und Optoometrie (Germany). Eroffnungsvortrage des WVAO-Jahreskongresses.*
**Desc:** The essays of the annual congresses.

US/1040-8495
**FOREFRONT (COLUMBUS, OHIO).** (FOREFRONT.). [Forefront]. Vol. 1, No. 1 (Sept./Oct. 1988)-. Periodical. English. bm. $36.00 North America; $46.00 other. Anadem Inc, 3620 North High Street, Columbus OH 43214. **Tel** (614)262-2539, (800)633-0055. **(Subscription address:** PO Box 14385, Columbus, OH 43214) **ED** Faith Reidenbach. **DD** 658. Index available.
**Desc:** Summarizes medical and business publications to train optometric employees in patient relations, business management, etc.

US/0894-5810
**HIGH PERFORMANCE OPTOMETRY.** [High perform. optom.]. Vol. 1, No. 1 (Sept./Oct. 1987)-. Periodical. English. Ten times a year. $79.00 (institutions), $69.00 (individuals), US; $86.00 (institutions) $79.00 (individuals) Canada and Mexico; $94.00 (institutions), $84.00 (individuals) other. Anadem Inc, 3620 North High Street, Columbus OH 43214. **Tel** (614)262-2539, (800)633-0055. **ED** Arol Augsburger. **LC** RE1; .H53. **DD** 617. **NLM** W1; HI22P. Index available.
**Desc:** Digests medical and optometry journal articles about diagnosing and managing ocular disease and vision disorders.

US/0748-9307
**HOLISTIC OPTOMETRIST, THE.** Vol. 1, No. 1 (May/June 1983)-. Periodical. English. bm (6 issues). $49.95. The Holistic Optometrist, PO Box 2172, Farmington Hills MI 48018. **Tel** (313)851-8411. **DD** 617.

US/0892-8967
**INTERNATIONAL CONTACT LENS CLINIC (1987).** (INTERNATIONAL CONTACT LENS CLINIC : ICLC.). [Int. contact lens clin.]. **VFOAT** ICLC. Vol. 14, No. 1 (Jan. 1987)-. Periodical. English. bm. $135.00 US; $165.00 other. Butterworth Heinemann / Woburn, MA, 225 Wildwood Avenue, Unit B, Woburn MA 01801. **Tel** (800)366-2665, FAX (617)928-2620, telex 880052. **(Subscription address:** Elsevier Science Inc. / New York Books, 655 Avenue of the Americas, New York NY 10010.) **LC** RE977.C6; I53. **DD** 617.7/523/05. **NLM** W1; IN736K. **CODEN** ICCLEF. **[CCC].** available on microfilm and microfiche from University Microfilms International (UMI). ***Continues*** *International Eyecare, 0884-4577.*
**Desc:** Provides the contact lens practitioner and researcher with up-to-date clinical and scientific research information relating to the rapidly changing contact lens field. Information is provided in a clear, objective fashion through articles and reviews refereed by clinicians and scientists.

US/1045-8395
**JOURNAL OF BEHAVIORAL OPTOMETRY.** [J. behav. optom.]. **Added/Corp** Optometric Extension Program Foundation. **VFOAT** JBO. Vol. 1, No. 1 (1990)-. Periodical. English. bm (Jan., Mar., May, July, Sept., Nov.). $50.00. Optometric Extension Program, 2912 South Daimler Street, Santa Ana CA 92705. **Tel** (714)250-8070, FAX (714)250-8157. **LC** RE960; .J68. **DD** 617. **NLM** W1; JO557. Index available (bound in Nov. issue). **Ad Acc. Pr Rev. Circ:** 2,500.
**Desc:** A 4-color publication featuring professional news, a calendar of events, editorials and limited advertising.

US/0098-6917
**JOURNAL OF OPTOMETRIC EDUCATION.** ***Title Change.*** [J. optom. educ.]. Vol. 1 (Winter 1975)-. Periodical. English. qt. Association of Schools and Colleges of Optometry, 6110 Executive Blvd, Suite 690, Rockville MD 20852. **Tel** (301)231-5944. **ED** John Potter. **LC** RE956; .J63. **DD** 617.7/5/0711. **NLM** W1 JO803RH. Index available. cum. index. **Bk Rev. Ad Acc. Circ:** 3,000 (ctrl). available on microfilm from University Microfilms International (UMI). ***Continued by*** *Optometric Education.*
**Desc:** Publishes reports, papers and other material relative to optometric education.
**Ind/Abst** Curr. Index J. Educ.

US/0149-886X
**JOURNAL OF OPTOMETRIC VISION DEVELOPMENT (1976).** (JOURNAL OF OPTOMETRIC VISION DEVELOPMENT.). **Added/Corp** College of Optometrists in Vision Development. Vol.7, No. 3 (Sept. 1976)-. Periodical. English. Four times a year (Spring, Summer, Fall and Winter). $45.00 (one year), $75.00 (two year). College Optometrists Vision Development, PO Box 285, Chula Vista CA 92012. **Tel** (619)420-3010. **ED** Sidney Groffman. **NLM** W1 JO803RN. **Bk Rev. Ad Acc. Pr Rev. Circ:** 1,600 (ctrl). ***Continues*** *Journal of Optometric Vision Therapy, 0149-8940.*

US/0003-0244
**JOURNAL OF THE AMERICAN OPTOMETRIC ASSOCIATION.** [J. Am. Optom. Assoc.]. **Main/Corp** American Optometric Association. (1929)-. Periodical. English. Twelve times a year. $50.00 US; $65.00 Canada; $75.00 others. American Optometric Association, 243 North Lindbergh Boulevard, St Louis MO 63141. **Tel** (314)991-4100, FAX (314)441-4101. **ED** John Porter and Mary Horner; (editor's address: c/o Vision America, 42 Music Square West, Suite 106, Nashville, TN 37203, phone: (615)297-3937). **LC** RE1; .A47. **DD** 617.706273. **NLM** W1 JO909Y. **CODEN** JAOPBD. Index available (back issues, $5.00). cum. index. **Bk Rev,** (Qty: 30-40 per year). **Ad Acc, Adv Mgr:** Raeber, **Tel** (314)991-4100. **Pr Rev. Circ:** 29,700 (ctrl). available on microfilm from University Microfilms International (UMI). Documents available from BIOSIS Document Express, CASDDS.
**Desc:** Clinical articles on all aspects of eye care. Educational material on current research in the profession of eye care.
**Ind/Abst** Biol. Abstr.; Chem. Abstr.; Cumul. Index Nurs. Allied Health Lit.; EMBASE; Energy Res. Abstr. (July 1982-); Index Med.; INIS Atomindex [Micro.]; Life Sci. Collect. (1985-); Psychol. Abstr.; PsycINFO; PsycLit; Rev. Med. Vet. Entomol.; SportSearch.

US/0279-6422
**JOURNAL OF THE ILLINOIS OPTOMETRIC ASSOCIATION.** [J. Ill. Optom. Assoc.]. **Added/Corp** Illinois Optometric Association. (19??)-. Periodical. English. bm (6 issues). Free to members; $18.00 other. Illinois Optometric Association, 223 East Monroe, Springfield IL 62701. **Tel** (217)525-8012, FAX (217)525-8018. **ED** George A. Lever. **NLM** W1 JO93E. **Ad Acc.** ctrl circ.

US/1041-0384
**JOURNAL OF VISION REHABILITATION (LINCOLN, NEB.).** **See** Medical Science and Technology-Ophthalmology.

US/1063-1623
**KANSAS OPTOMETRIC JOURNAL.** [Kans. optom. j.]. **Main/Corp** Kansas Optometric Association. Vol. 33, No. 1 (June 1960)-. Periodical. English. qt (Mar., Jun., Sep., Dec.). $15.00. Kansas Optometric Association, 1266 Southwest Topeka Boulevard, Topeka KS 66612. **Tel** (913)232-0225. **DD** 617. ***Continues*** *Kansas Optometrist.*

US/0160-1326
**LAWS RELATING TO THE PRACTICE OF OPTOMETRY, WITH RULES AND REGULATIONS.** **See** Law.

US/1071-1627
**MICHIGAN OPTOMETRIST, THE.** (THE MICHIGAN OPTOMETRIST : THE OFFICIAL PUBLICATION OF THE MICHIGAN OPTOMETRIC ASSOCIATION.). [Mich. optom.]. **Main/Corp** Michigan Optometric Association. (1928)-. Periodical. English. mo. $13.00. Michigan Optometric Association, 530 West Ionia Street, Suite A, Lansing MI 48933. **Tel** (517)482-0616, FAX (517)482-1611. **ED** William D. Dansby. **DD** 617. **Ad Acc, Adv Mgr:** Amy Holmes. **Circ:** 850 (ctrl).
**Desc:** News about the profession of optometry in Michigan.

US/0149-9599
**NEBRASKA HEALTH MANPOWER REPORTS : OPTOMETRISTS.** **Main/Corp** Nebraska. Division of Health Data and Statistical Research. English. 301 Centennial Mall South, PO Box 95007, Lincoln NE 68509. **LC** RE943.N2; N4A. **DD** 331.1/1.

US/0028-4807
**NEW ENGLAND JOURNAL OF OPTOMETRY.** [New Engl. j. optom.]. **Added/Corp** New England Council of Optometrists. (19??)-. Periodical. English. qt (4 issues). $35.00. New England Council of Optometrists, 101 Tremont Street, Suite 401, Boston MA 02108. **Tel** (617)542-1233. **ED** Roger Wilson O.D. **DD** 617. **Bk Rev,** (Qty: varies). **Ad Acc, Adv Mgr:** Jon C. Lundell. **Circ:** 1,900 (ctrl). available on microfilm from University Microfilms International (UMI).

US/0896-050X
**NEW IMAGE, THE.** Vol. 8, No. 3 (Summer 1987)-. Periodical. English. qt. Illinois College of Optometry, 3241 South Michigan Avenue, Chicago IL 60616. ***Continues*** *Image (Chicago, Ill. : 1980), 0886-8387.*

US
**NEWSLETTER - OPTOMETRIC HISTORICAL SOCIETY.** **Main/Corp** Optometric Historical Society. Vol. 1 (Jan. 1970)-. Periodical. English. qt. Comes with Optometric Historical Society membership. Optometric Historical Society, 243 North Lindbergh Boulevard, St Louis MO 63141. **Tel** (314)991-0324. **LC** RE951; .O67a. **DD** 617.7/5/09.

NE
**OCULUS.** Nuvo, Honthorststraat 12, 1071 De Amsterdam Netherlands.

UK/0275-5408
**OPHTHALMIC & PHYSIOLOGICAL OPTICS.** (OPHTHALMIC & PHYSIOLOGICAL OPTICS : THE JOURNAL OF THE BRITISH COLLEGE OF OPHTHALMIC OPTICIANS (OPTOMETRISTS).). [Ophthalmic physiolog. opt.]. **Added/Corp** British College of Ophthalmic Opticians (Optometrists). **VFOAT** Ophthalmic and Physiological Optics. Vol. 1, No. 1 (1981)-. Periodical. English. Six times a year. $440.00 The Americas; £295.00 other. Butterworth Heinemann Publishers, Linacre House, Jordan Hill, Oxford OX2 8DP England. **Tel** 011 44 865 310366. **(Subscription address:** Elsevier Science Ltd. Oxford Fulfillment Centre, PO Box 800, Kidlington, Oxford OX5 1DX United Kingdom.) **ED** B. Gilmartin (editor's address: Department of Vision Sciences Aston University, Birmingham United Kingdom). **LC** RE939.2; .O63. **DD** 617.7/5/05. **NLM** W1 OP216. **CODEN** OPOPD5. **[CCC].** Index available. **Bk Rev. Ad Acc. Pr Rev.** available on microfilm and microfiche from University Microfilms International (UMI). Documents available from The Genuine Article, BIOSIS Document Express, Ask*IEEE. ***Continues*** *British Journal of Physiological Optics, 0007-1218.*
**Desc:** An interdisciplinary journal covering both pure and applied visual sciences, with particular emphasis on topics of importance to optometrists.
**Ind/Abst** Biol. Abstr.; Curr. Contents Clin. Med.; EMBASE; Ergon. Abstr.; Index Med.; Index Vet.; INSPEC (1983-); Life Sci. Collect.; Psychol. Abstr. (1981-); PsycINFO; Res. Alert [Select. Cov.]; SCISEARCH; Vet. Bull.

CN/0824-3441
**OPTICAL PRISM.** [Opt. prism]. No. 1 (Apr. 1983)-. Periodical. English. Eight times a year. Free to Canada; $45.00 others. VezCom Inc., 31 Hastings Drive, Unionville Ontario L3R 4Y5 Canada. **Tel** (416)475-9343, FAX (416)477-2821. **ED** Allan K. Vezina. **DD** 617/.0068. **Bk Rev. Ad Acc. Circ:** 7,000 (ctrl).
**Desc:** Independent optical magazine mailed to all ophthalmologists, optometrists, opticians, suppliers and manufacturers across Canada. Emphasizes product news, new developments, contact lenses, clinical studies, management.

US/0066-7609
**OPTICAL SCIENCES CENTER NEWSLETTER.** [Opt. Sci. Cent. newsl.]. **Main/Corp** Arizona. University. Optical Sciences Center. **Added/Corp** University of Arizona. Optical Sciences Center. Newsletter. (196?)-. Academic Scholarly Publication. English. ir. University of Arizona Optical Sciences Center, Tucson AZ 85721. **Tel** (602)621-2587, FAX (602)623-9034. **ED** Maggie Whitney. **CODEN** OSCADN. **Circ:** 1,200. Documents available from CASDDS.
**Desc:** Pertains to research and social activities at the University of Arizona Optical Sciences Center.
**Ind/Abst** Chem. Abstr.; Int. Aerosp. Abstr.

UK/0030-3968
**OPTICIAN, THE.** Vol. 84, No. 2163 (Sept. 9, 1932)-. Periodical. English. wk (52 issues). $128.00. Reed Business Publishing / West Sussex, England, Perrymount Road, Haywards Heath, West Sussex RH16 3DH England. **Tel** 011 44 81 6523500. **NLM** W1 OP861. ***Continues*** *Optician and Scientific Instrument Maker.*

FR
**OPTIQUE FRANCAISE ET L'OPTICIEN LUNETIER, L'.** **VFOAT** Opticien Lunetier et l'Optique Francaise; Optique Francaise & l'Opticien Lunetier. Periodical. French. mo. Editions de Lancry, 45 rue de Lancry, Paris 75010 France.

CN/0227-0730
**OPTO PRESSE.** [Opto presse]. Vol. 1, No 1 (Sept./Oct. 1976)-. Periodical. French. Free to members. Ordre des Optometristes du Quebec, 1080 Boulevard Rosemont, Montreal Quebec H2S 2A1 Canada. **DD** 617.7/5/060714.

US/1052-7346
**OPTOMETRIC ECONOMICS.** [Optom. econ.]. **Added/Corp** American Optometric Association. Vol. 1, No. 1 (Jan. 1991)-. Periodical. English. Twelve times a year. $30.00 US, $33.00 Canada, $55.00 other. American Optometric Association, 243 North Lindbergh Boulevard, St Louis MO 63141. **Tel** (314)991-4100, FAX (314)441-4101. **ED** Jack Runninger and Gene Mitchell, (editor's address: 1 Pine Valley Road, Rome, GA 30165 phone: (706)235-4039). **LC** RE959.3; .O6. **DD** 617. Index available (Back issues, $5.00). **Ad Acc, Adv Mgr:** Raeber, **Tel** (314)991-4100. **Circ:** 30,000. ***Absorbed*** *Professional Enhancement Strategies.*
**Desc:** News and information on practice management and financial planning.

US/0098-6917
**OPTOMETRIC EDUCATION.** **Added/Corp** Association of Schools and Colleges of Optometry (U.S.). Vol. 17, No. 1 (Fall 1991)-. Periodical. English. qt. Association of Schools and Colleges of Optometry, 6110 Executive Blvd, Suite 690, Rockville MD 20852. **Tel** (301)231-5944. **LC** RE956; .J68. **DD** 617.7/5/0711. available on microfilm from University Microfilms International (UMI). ***Continues*** *Journal of Optometric Education, 0098-6917.*

US/0030-4085
**OPTOMETRIC MANAGEMENT.** [Optom. manag.]. **VFOAT** OM. Vol. 1 (Jan. 1965)-. Periodical. English. mo. $34.00 (1 year), $55.00 (2 year) US; $45.00 Canada. Viscom Publications Inc., 50 Washington Street, Norwalk CT 06854. **Tel** (203)838-9100, FAX (203)838-2550. **ED** D Rosner. **DD** 338. **NLM** W1 OP92. Index available. **Ad Acc. Circ:** 26,000 (ctrl). available on microfilm and microfiche from University Microfilms International (UMI).
**Desc:** The national business and practice management publication for optometrists. Topics include fees, collections, promotion, office design, patient relations, taxes, insurance, and practice enjoyment.

US/0030-4107
**OPTOMETRIC WORLD.** (19??)-. Periodical. English. Twelve times a year. Occidental Publishing Company, 67 692 Ramon Road, Cathedral City CA 92234. **Tel** (310)240-3244. **NLM** W1 OP9253. available on microfilm from University Microfilms International (UMI).

GW/0030-4123
**OPTOMETRIE.** **Added/Corp** Wissenschaftliche Vereinigung fur Augenoptik und Optometrie (Germany). (Oct. 1988)-. Periodical. English (German). qt (Mar., July, Oct., Dec.). DM132.00. Median-Verlag, Postfach 103964 Haupstrasse 64, D 69029 Heidelberg 1 Germany. **Tel** 011 49 6221 25731, FAX 011 49 6221 25030. **Bk Rev. Ad Acc, Adv Mgr:** Ball. **Circ:** 2,800 (ctrl). ***Continues*** *Optometrie (Berlin, Germany), 0030-4123.*

CN/0708-3173
**OPTOMETRISTE.** (L'OPTOMETRISTE.). **Added/Corp** Association Professionnelle des Optometristes du Quebec. Vol. 1 (April 1979)-. Periodical.

French. Six times a year (Jan., Mar., May, July, Sept., Nov.). 48.00Can$ Canada: 60.00Can$ other. Association des Optometristes, 133 rue de la Commune, 4th Floor, Montreal Quebec H2Y 2C7 Canada. **Tel** (514)849-8051, FAX (514)849-7201. **DD** 617.7/5/05. Index available. cum. index. **Bk Rev**, (Qty: 8). **Ad Acc**, **Adv Mgr:** Mrs. Lucie English. **Circ:** 2,400.
**Desc:** News and information of the Quebec Association of Optometrists.

US/1040-5488
**OPTOMETRY AND VISION SCIENCE.**
(OPTOMETRY AND VISION SCIENCE : OFFICIAL PUBLICATION OF THE AMERICAN ACADEMY OF OPTOMETRY.). [Optom. vis. sci.]. **Added/Corp** American Academy of Optometry. **VFOAT** Optometry & Vision Science. Vol. 66, No. 1 (Jan. 1989)-. Periodical. English. mo. $105.00 (individual), $136.00 (institution) US; $140.00 (individual), $171.00 (institution) other. Williams & Wilkins Company, 428 East Preston Street, Baltimore MD 21202-3993. **Tel** (410)528-4000, (800)638-6423, FAX (410)528-8596, telex 87669. **(Subscription address:** Williams & Wilkins, PO Box 64380, Baltimore MD 21264.**)** **DD** 617. **NLM** W1; OP935E. **CODEN** OVSCET. **[CCC]**. **Pr Rev.** Documents available from The Genuine Article, BIOSIS Document Express, Ask*IEEE, Quick Copies. ***Continues*** *American Journal of Optometry and Physiological Optics, 0093-7002.*
**Desc:** Articles document research and clinical findings in optometry, plus present case reports and instrument and technique reviews.
**Ind/Abst** Biol. Abstr.; Curr. Contents Clin. Med.; EMBASE; Index Med. (Jan. 1989-); INSPEC (Jan. 1989-); Protozoolog. Abstr.; Res. Alert [Select. Cov.]; SCISEARCH; Soc. Sci. Cit. Index [Select. Cov.].

US/1050-4451
**OPTOMETRY (CHICAGO, ILL.).**
(OPTOMETRY : CURRENT LITERATURE IN PERSPECTIVE.). [Optometry]. (1991)-. Periodical. English. qt. $89.00 (institutions), $69.00 (individuals) US; $93.00 (institutions), $73.00 (individuals) Canada; $103.00 (institutions), $83.00 (individuals) other. Mosby Year Book Inc., 11830 Westline Industrial Drive, St Louis MO 63146. **Tel** (800)325-4177, (314)872-8370, FAX (314)432-1380, telex 44-2402. **ED** John Amos. **DD** 617. **NLM** ZWW 704; O62.
**Desc:** Designed to help optometrists keep up with current developments affecting their practice and the state of eye care. Each issue contains abstracts of practical articles selected national and international journals.

US/1050-6918
**OPTOMETRY CLINICS : THE OFFICIAL PUBLICATION OF THE PRENTICE SOCIETY.** [Optom. clin.]. **Added/Corp** Prentice Society. Vol. 1, No. 1 (1991)-. Periodical. English. qt. $110.00 institution, $77.00 other. Appleton & Lange, (A Subsidiary of Simon & Schuster), 25 Van Zant Street, East Norwalk CT 06855. **Tel** (203)838-4400, (800)423-1359, FAX (203)854-9486. **(Subscription address:** Optometry Clinics, PO Box 3000, Department OP, Denville NJ 07834.**)** **LC** RE1; .O68. **DD** 617. **NLM** W1; OP935J. **Acid Free.**
**Desc:** Intended to express, for the benefit of the primary care practitioner, the state of the art in the clinical practice of optometry. As the official publication of the Prentice Society, it will address a single topic relevant to optometrists' daily practice and contain reviews as well as standard features.
**Ind/Abst** Index Med. (1991-).

US/0890-7080
**OPTOMETRY TIMES.** [Optom. times]. Vol. 1, No. 1 (Oct. 1983)-. Periodical. English. mo. Murray Communications Inc, 1 East 1st Street, Duluth MN 55802. **DD** 617.

II
**OPTOMETRY TODAY.** (19??)-. Periodical. English. qt (Jan., Apr., July, Oct.). $100.00 (includes air mail postage). Optometry Today, C4F/216 Janakpuri, New Delhi 110058, India. **Tel** 011 91 11 5599839. **(Subscription address:** Prints India, 11 Darya Ganj, New Delhi 110002 India.**)** **ED** Dr. Narendra Kumar. **Bk Rev**, (Qty: 4). **Ad Acc**, **Adv Mgr:** same as editor. **Circ:** 1,200. available on microfilm from University Microfilms International (UMI).
**Desc:** India's premier journal for eye care professionals, trade and industry.

UK/0268-5485
**OPTOMETRY TODAY (LONDON).**
(OPTOMETRY TODAY / ASSOCIATION OF OPTICAL PRACTITIONERS.). [Optom. today]. **Added/Corp** Association of Optical Practitioners (Great Britain). Vol. 25, No. 5 (March 2, 1985)-. Periodical. English. Twenty-two times a year. £65.00 UK; £85.00 other. Optometry Today / Scotland, Unit 4 Station Approach Fleet, Hampshire GU13 8QY Scotland. **Tel** 011 44 252 816266. **ED** Ma Callender. **NLM** W1; OP936Z. **Bk Rev. Ad Acc**, **Adv Mgr:** MA Callender. **Circ:** 12,765 (ctrl). ***Continues*** *Ophthalmic Optician, 0030-3739;* ***Absorbed*** *Scottish Optometrist.*
**Desc:** Features interesting clinical articles and information on what is happening in the optical trade for optometrists and dispensing opticians.

US/0274-6549
**OREGON OPTOMETRY.** **Added/Corp** Oregon Optometric Association. Pacific University Optometric Alumni Association. Vol. 47 (Spring 1980)-. Periodical. English. qt. $9.00. Pacific University College of Optometry, Oregon Optometry Journal, 1503 College Way, Forest Grove OR 97116. **Tel** (503)357-6151. **ED** Wanda Laukkanen. **Bk Rev. Ad Acc. Circ:** 2,500 (ctrl). ***Continues*** *Oregon Optometrist, 0030-476X.*
**Desc:** News of professional associations and articles relating to the art and science of vision care.

US/1055-2359
**PEDIATRIC OPTOMETRY & VISION THERAPY.** ***Ceased.*** [Pediatr. optom. vis. ther.]. **VFOAT** Pediatric Optometry and Vision Therapy. Premiere Issue (Mar./Apr. 1991)-(199?). Periodical. English. bm. Anadem Publishing, 3620 North High Street, PO Box 14385, Columbus OH 43214. **DD** 617.

CN/1181-6058
**PRACTICAL OPTOMETRY.** [Pract. optom.]. Vol. 1, No. 1 (Aug. 1990)-. Periodical. English. Six times a year (Jan., Mar., May, July, Sept., Nov.). $60.00 Canada; $72.00 US; $94.00 other. Medicopea International, 3333 Cote Vertu Boulevard, Suite 300, Montreal QUE H4R 2N1 Canada. **Tel** (514)331-4561, FAX (514)336-1129. **DD** 617.7/5/05. Index available. **Circ:** 2,300.
**Desc:** Each issue covers various topics and includes such regular departments as clinical presentation, clinical consultation, news & notes, and new products.

US/1043-6278
**PROBLEMS IN OPTOMETRY.** ***Ceased.*** [Probl. optom.]. (1989)-(1992). Periodical. English. qt. J.B. Lippincott Company, 227 East Washington Square, Philadelphia PA 19106-3780. **Tel** (215)238-4200 or 4454, FAX (215)238-4227. **(Subscription address:** Journal Fulfillment Department, Lippincott/Harper, Downsville Pike, Route 3, Box 20-B, Hagerstown, MD 21740; telephone: (800)638-3030**)** **ED** Richard London. **LC** RE939.2; .P76. **NLM** W1; PR573MK.
**Desc:** Articles focus on significant problems, complications, unexpected findings, difficult situations, and high-risk challenges in clinical practice optometry. Each issue offers ten to twenty articles grouped around a central theme with an emphasis on 'how to'.

UK/0278-4327
**PROGRESS IN RETINAL RESEARCH.**
***Title Change.*** **See** Biology-Physiology.

US/1055-7407
**PROSPECTUS.** [Prospectus]. **Added/Corp** New York State Optometric Association. Periodical. English. qt. New York State Optometric Association, 90 South Swan Street, Albany NY 12210. **DD** 617. ***Continues*** *New York State Optometry, 0199-5731.*

SZ
**SCHWEIZER OPTIKER. L'OPTICIEN SUISSE. L'OTTICO SVIZZERO, DER.**
**Added/Corp** Schweizerische Optiker-Verband. Berufsverband der Schweizer Augenoptiker mit Hoherer Fachausbildung. **VFOAT** L'Opticien Suisse; L'Ottico Svizzero. (19??)-. Periodical. German (French). ir (twelve times a year). 98.00F Switzerland; $66.00 US. Keller Ltd, Printers & Editors, 6002 Lucerne Switzerland. **Tel** CH 041-28 11 11, telex 72522. **Ad Acc.** ctrl circ.
**Desc:** Official organ of the Swiss Opticians Association and the Swiss Guild of Optics and Optometry.

US/0361-3291
**SILENT PARTNER, THE.** Periodical. English. mo. Optometric Extension Program, 2912 South Daimler Street, Santa Ana CA 92705. **Tel** (714)250-8070, FAX (714)250-8157. **ED** D A Frantz. **NLM** W1 SI459.

SA/0378-9411
**SOUTH AFRICAN OPTOMETRIST, SUID-AFRIKAANSE OOGKUNDIGE, THE.** **Added/Corp** South African Optometric Association. **VFOAT** Suid-Afrikaanse Oogkundige. (1932)-. Periodical. English (Afrikaans). qt (Mar., June, Sept., Dec.). R27.50. South African Optemetric Association, PO Box 3966, Petoria 0001 South Africa. **Tel** 011 27 12 3221310, FAX 011 27 12 3221313. **ED** Prof. W. F. Harris (editor's telephone: 011 27 12 4892423). Index available. **Bk Rev. Ad Acc. Circ:** 1,660 (ctrl).
**Desc:** The journal is the official organ of the South African Optometric Association, and carries articles of interest to optometrists in practice in the Republic.

US
**SOUTHERN JOURNAL OF OPTOMETRY (ATLANTA, GA. : 1983).**
(THE SOUTHERN JOURNAL OF OPTOMETRY : OFFICIAL PUBLICATION OF THE SOUTHERN COUNCIL OF OPTOMETRISTS, INC.). **Added/Corp** Southern Council of Optometrists (U.S.). Vol. 1, No. 1 (Jan. 1983)-. Periodical. English. Four times a year. $12.00 (one year), $30.00 (three years). Southern Council of Optometrists, 4661 North Shallowford Road, Atlanta GA 30338. **Tel** (404)451-8206. ***Continues*** *Southern Journal of Optometry.*

US/0738-7644
**TEXAS OPTOMETRY.** [Tex. optom.]. **Added/Corp** Texas Optometric Association. **VFOAT** Journal of the Texas Optometric Association, Inc. Vol. 30 (Jan. 1974)-. Periodical. English. Three times a year. $12.00. Texas Optometric Association, 1016 La Posada, Suite 174, Austin TX 78752. **Tel** (512)451-8476. **DD** 617. ***Continues*** *Journal of the Texas Optometric Association.*

IT/0392-0453
**VEDERE CONTACT INTERNATIONAL.** [V. contact int.]. (1977)-. Periodical. Italian (English, French and German). Five times a year. L45000 Italy; L50000 other. Edizione Ariminum, Via Negroli 51, 20133 Milan Italy. **Tel** 011 39 2 70102026, FAX 011 39 2 717346. **ED** Claudio Morpurgo. **NLM** W1 VE108. **Bk Rev. Ad Acc. Circ:** 5,500.
**Desc:** International magazine on contactology (optics).

IT/0302-6256
**VEDERE INTERNATIONAL.** (19??)-. Periodical. Italian (English, French and Spanish). bm (with two special issues in January and May). L75000 Italy; L110000 other. Edizione Ariminum, Via Negroli 51, 20133 Milan Italy. **Tel** 011 39 2 70102026, FAX 011 39 2 717346. **ED** Claudio Morpurgo. **Bk Rev. Ad Acc. Circ:** 8,500. ***Continues*** *Vedere.*
**Desc:** International journal on optics, frame industry and optical instruments.

NE
**VERPAKKINGS MANAGEMENT.**
Managenent Media BV, Postbus 1932, 1200 BX Hilversum Netherlands.

US/1054-7665
**VISIONMONDAY (NEW YORK, N.Y.).**
(VISIONMONDAY.). [VisionMonday]. **VFOAT** Vision Monday. (19??)-. Periodical. English. Twenty-six times a year. $49.96 US; $156.00 Canada and Mexico; $180.00 UK; $245.00 Asia. Jobson Publishing Corporation, 100 Avenue of the Americas, New York NY 10013. **Tel** (212)274-7084, 274-7000, FAX (212)431-0500. **(Subscription address:** Vision Monday, PO Box 7635, Riverton NJ 08077.**)** **ED** Marge Axelrad. **DD** 338. **Ad Acc**, **Adv Mgr:** Frank Giammanco, **Tel** (212)24-7070. **Pr Rev.** ctrl circ. ***Continues*** *20/20's VisionMonday, 0891-1770.*
**Desc:** Optical industry news.

## PACKAGING

US/0882-5777
**ADVANCING CONVERTING AND PACKAGING TECHNOLOGIES.** [Adv. convert. packag. technol.]. **Added/Corp** Technical Association of the Pulp and Paper Industry. **VFOAT** Advancing Converting and Packaging Technologies; Converting and Packaging; Converting & Packaging. Vol. 1, No. 1, (Sept. 1985)-. Periodical. English. qt. TAPPI - Technical Association of the Pulp and Paper Industry, Technical Park, PO Box 105113, Atlanta GA 30348. **Tel** (404)446-1400 Ext 203, (800)332-8686. **DD** 688.
**Ind/Abst** Abstr. Bull. Inst. Pap. Sci. Tech.; Int. Packag. Abstr.; Pap. Board Abstr.; Print. Abstr.

US
**AEROSOL RELEASE AND TRANSPORT PROGRAM QUARTERLY PROGRESS REPORT / PREPARED FOR THE U.S. NUCLEAR REGULATORY COMMISSION, OFFICE OF NUCLEAR REGULATORY RESEARCH; PREPARED BY THE OAK RIDGE NATIONAL LABORATORY.** **Added/Corp** U.S. Nuclear Regulatory Commission. Office of Nuclear Regulatory Research. Oak Ridge National Laboratory. Engineering Technology Division. (Oct./Dec. 1981)-. Periodical. English. sa. National Technical Information Service - NTIS, Room 2027S, 5285 Port Royal Road, Springfield VA 22161. **Tel** (703)487-4630, (703)487-4660, (703)487-4650, FAX (703)321-8547, telex 89-9405. available on microfiche. ***Continues*** *LMFRB Aerosol Release and Transport Program Quarterly Progress Report for ... .*

UK/0568-062X
**AEROSOL REVIEW.** [Aerosol rev.]. (1966)-. English. an (Aug.). £25.00. Morgan Grampian, 40 Beresford Street Woolwich, London SE18 6BQ England. **Tel** 011 44 81 855 7777, FAX 011 44 81 855 5548, telex 896238. **(Subscription address:** Benn Business Information Services, Riverbank House Angel Lane, Tonbridge Kent TN9 1SE England.**)** ***Continues in part*** *Manufacturing Chemist and Aerosol News.*

HU/0230-5348
**ANYAGMOZGATASI ES CSOMAGOLASI SZAKIRODALMI TAJEKOZTATO.** [Anyagm. csom. szakirod. taj.]. (1982)-. Periodical. Hungarian. mo. 5.500ft. Orszagos Muszaki Informacios Kozpont es Konyvtar (O.M.I.K.K.),

National Technical Information Centre and Library Museum, u 17, PO Box 12, 1428 Budapest, Hungary. **Tel** (361)118-1994, FAX (36-)138-2414, telex 22-4944 OMIKK H. **(Subscription address:** OMIKK Budapest, POB 12, H-1428 Hungary) **ED** Ferenc Hervai and Bela Kertesz. **UDC** 621.79. **Circ:** 185.
**Desc:** Information on packaging and transportation of goods.

AT
**AUSTRALIAN LITHOGRAPHER, PRINTER AND PACKAGER, THE.**
***Suspended.* See** Printing Industry.

AT/0004-9921
**AUSTRALIAN PACKAGING.** [Aust. packag.]. (199?)-. Periodical. English. mo (except Jan.). 50.00 Aus$ Australia; 100.00Aus$ other. Reed Business Publishing Pty Ltd. / Australia, 1 5 Railway Street, Level 12 North Tower, Chatswood W 2067 NSW Australia. **Tel** 011 61 2 3725222, FAX 011 61 2 4197533. **ED** Norman Macleod. **CODEN** AUPAEH. **Ad Acc. Circ:** 5,096 (ctrl).
**Ind/Abst** Abstr. Bull. Inst. Pap. Sci. Tech.; Art Archaeol. Tech. Abstr.; BioBusiness (1988-); Foods Adlibra; Int. Packag. Abstr.

US/0360-8689
**BEST IN PACKAGING, THE.** (1975)-. English. be. $79.50 (includes entire set of Print casebooks: The Best in Advertising; The Best in Annual Reports; The Best in Covers & Posters; The Best in Environmental Graphics; The Best in Exhibition Design; and The Best in Packaging). RC Publications Inc., 3200 Tower Oaks Boulevard, Rockville MD 20852. **Tel** (800)222-2654, (301)770-2900, FAX (301)984-3203. **LC** TS195.A1; B47. **DD** 688.8/05.

GW
**BEST ON QUALITY : YEARBOOK OF INTERNATIONAL ACADEMY FOR QUALITY, THE. Added/Corp** International Academy for Quality. Vol. 1 (1988)-. English. an. DM81.00. Carl Hanser Verlag, Postfach 860420, D 81631 Munich Germany. **Tel** 011 49 89 998300, FAX 011 49 89 984809. **LC** TS156.A1; B47. **DD** 658.5/62.

GW
**BETRIEBSLEITER, DER.** Periodical. German. 6.00 single issue. Verlag Technik und Wirtschaft, Postfach 4026, D 55030 Mainz Germany. **Tel** 011 49 6131 99203. **LC** TS155.A1; 54. ***Continues*** *Betriebs-Management Service.*

FR/0249-5708
**BIC-CODE.** (CONTAINERS BIC CODE.). [Bic-code]. (1970)-. Periodical. English (French). an (March). 130.00F. Bureau Intl des Containers, 167 Rue de Cowecelles, 75017 Paris France. **Tel** 011 33 1 67660390, FAX 011 33 1 47660891. **UDC** 658.788. ***Continues*** *International Register of Container Owners' Code Marks, 0249-6151.*

FR/0366-2284
**BIOS (PARIS). See** Food and Food Industry-Beverage Industry.

US
**BOARD CONVERTING NEWS.** English. wk. $120.00 US and Canada; $170.00 other. NV Publications, 43 Main Street, Avon-by-the-Sea NJ 07717. **Tel** (800)962-3001, (908)280-1900.
**Desc:** Serving the corrugated, folding carton, rigid box industry.

US
**BOARD CONVERTING NEWS ESPANOL.** (19??)-. English (Spanish). $35.00 Latin America, Spain, and Portugal. N V Business Publishers, 2970 Marion Executive Center, Northbrook IL 60062. **Tel** (708)498-5850. **Circ:** 2,850 (ctrl).
**Desc:** Serves the corrugated box and converting industries.

US/0006-8497
**BOXBOARD CONTAINERS.** [Boxboard contain.]. (19??)-. Periodical. English. mo. $28.00 (one year), $42.00 (two year) US; $37.00 (one year), $52.00 (two year) Canada; $95.00 (one year) other. MacLean Hunter Publishing Corporation, Chicago, IL, 29 North Wacker Drive, Chicago IL 60606-3298. **Tel** (312)726-2802, FAX (312)726-3091. **ED** Greg Kishbaugh. **LC** TS1200.A1; S5. **DD** 338.4/7/67628805. **[CCC].** cum. index. **Circ:** 13,529 (ctrl). available on microfilm and microfiche from University Microfilms International (UMI); available on an online database (file 648/Full-Text) from DIALOG. ***Continues*** *Shears.*
**Desc:** Serves the box and carton manufacturing industry including corrugated, folding carton, setup box, fibre drum and tube plants as well as paperboard coating, laminating and other converting operations Consists of reports and interviews on what companies are doing in the development and utilization of new ideas.
**Ind/Abst** Abstr. Bull. Inst. Pap. Sci. Tech.; Abstr. Graphic Arts Tech. Found. (1984); F&S Index Plus Text, Int. [Select. Cov.]; Int. Packag. Abstr.; Pap. Board Abstr.; Print. Abstr.; PROMT.

UK
**BULK HANDLING.** (1984)-. Periodical. English. bm. £63.00 UK; £74.00 other. Turret Group, 177 Hagden Lane, Watford Herts WD1 8LN United Kingdom. **Tel** 011 44 923 228577, FAX 011 44 923 221346. **LC** TS180.8.B8; B86. **DD** 621.8/6/05. ***Continues*** *Bulk, Solids, Storage, Movement, and Control, 0305-3709.*
**Ind/Abst** Fluid Abstr., Civil Eng.; Fluid Abstr. Proc. Eng.; FLUIDEX; Infomat Int. Bus.; World Surf. Coat. Abstr.

US
**CAN TECHNOLOGY INTERNATIONAL.** English. bm. $70.00. Trend Publishing Inc, 625 North Michigan Avenue, Suite 2500, Chicago IL 60611-3109. **Tel** (312)654-2300, FAX (312)654-2323.

CN/0008-4654
**CANADIAN PACKAGING.** [Can. packag.]. (1948)-. Periodical. English. Eleven times a year. 47.00Can$ Canada; 96.00Can$ other. MacLean Hunter Ltd. Business Publishers / Canada, Box 9100, Station A, Toronto ONT M5W 1A5 Canada. **Tel** (416)946-8420, (800)567-0444. **(Subscription address:** Indas, 35 Riviera Drive, Building 17, Markham Ontario L3R 8N4 Canada.) **CODEN** CPAKAN. available on microfilm and microfiche from University Microfilms International (UMI); available on an online database (indexes and full text) from Mead Data Central; BRS; DATA-STAR; and (file 648/Full-Text) DIALOG.
**Ind/Abst** Abstr. Bull. Inst. Pap. Sci. Tech.; Art Archaeol. Tech. Abstr.; BioBusiness; F&S Index Plus Text, Int. [Select. Cov.]; Food Sci. Technol. Abstr.; Int. Packag. Abstr.; PROMT; Trade Ind. ASAP [Full Txt.]; Trade Ind. Index [Full Txt.].

CN
**CANADIAN PACKAGING. BUYERS GUIDE.** Began with 1963/64 issue. Consumer Publication. English. an. 17.00Can$. Maclean Hunter Canada / Montreal, 1001 bvd. de Maisonneuve W., Montreal, Quebec H3A 3E1 Canada. **Tel** 514-845-5141, FAX 514-845-4302, telex 055-60604. **DD** 338.4/7/62175702571.
**Desc:** Provides an index to materials, machinery, and services available to Canada's packaging industry.

UK/0953-8690
**CANMAKER AND CANNER, THE.** [Canmak. cann.]. **VFOAT** Canmaker & Canner; Canmaker (I Field). (1988)-. Periodical. English. Twelve times a year. $220.00 US & Canada & South America & Far East; $175.26 others. Mayo Sayers Ltd., 31 33 Station Road Horley, Surrey RH6 9HW England. **Tel** 011 44 293 820928. **DD** 688.8.

UK
**CANMAKING & CANNING INTERNATIONAL. VFOAT** Canmaking and Canning International; C&CI; Canmaking International. Vol. 3, No. 2 (April 1988)-. Periodical. English. bm. Metals and Minerals Research Services Ltd, 2-4 Henry Street Bath Avon BA1, United Kingdom. **Tel** (44) 225 481585, FAX (44) 225 481573 071-583 9186. **LC** TS197.5; .C35. **DD** 671.8. ***Formed by the union of*** *Canning & Packing* ***and*** *Tin Printer & Box Maker.*
**Ind/Abst** Infomat Int. Bus.; Int. Packag. Abstr.; Trade Ind. ASAP [Full Txt.]; Trade Ind. Index [Full Txt.].

UK
**CARGOWARE INTERNATIONAL.** Vol. 1, No. 1 (April 1989)-. Periodical. English. mo. International Cargo Holding Coordination Association, 71 Bondway, London SW8 1SH England. **Tel** 011 44 71 7931022, FAX 011 44 71 8201703, telex 261106. **Ad Acc. Circ:** 8,000 (ctrl). available on microfilm and microfiche from University Microfilms International (UMI).
**Ind/Abst** Fluid Abstr., Civil Eng.; Fluid Abstr. Proc. Eng.; FLUIDEX (199?-); Int. Packag. Abstr.

FR
**CARTONNAGES EMBALLAGES MODERNES.** (19??)-. French. Fourteen times a year. 440.74F France, 550.00F others (surface mail); 670.00F others (airmail). Editions Technorama, 31 Place St. Ferdinand, 75017 Paris France. **Tel** 011 33 1 45746743, FAX 011 33 1 45726321. **ED** R. Baschet. Index available. **Bk Rev. Ad Acc. Circ:** 3,200. ***Continues*** *Emballage Moderne, 0013-6565; Cartonnages.*
**Desc:** News and information on paper and paperboard packaging.
**Ind/Abst** Abstr. Bull. Inst. Pap. Sci. Tech.

CN/0576-0186
**CONSUMPTION OF CONTAINERS AND OTHER PACKAGING SUPPLIES BY THE MANUFACTURING INDUSTRIES.** (CONSUMPTION OF CONTAINERS AND OTHER PACKAGING SUPPLIES BY THE MANUFACTURING INDUSTRIES / STATISTICS CANADA, INDUSTRY DIVISION.). [Consum. contain. other packag. supplies manuf. ind.]. **Added/Corp** Canada. Dominion Bureau of Statistics. Manufacturing and Primary Industries Division. Statistics Canada. Manufacturing and Primary Industries Division. Statistics Canada. Machinery, Wood and Metal Products Section. Statistics Canada. Census of Manufactures Section. **VFOAT** Consommation de Contenants et Autres Matieres d'Emballage, par Industrie Manufacturiere. (1962)-. English (French). an. 28.00Can$ Canada; $34.00 US; $40.00 other. Statistics Canada, Publications Sales & Services, Main Building Room 1710, Ottawa Ontario K1A 0T6 Canada. **Tel** (613)951-5078, (800)267-6677, FAX (613)951-1584, telex 053-3585. **ED** Bruno Pepin. **LC** HD9839.P33; C256a. **DD** 381/.456888/0971021. **Circ:** 335.
**Desc:** Contains consumption data of the manufacturing industries on containers by industry, as well as a detailed breakdown of this consumption.

FR
**CONTAINERS.** Dawson France SA, BP 40, 91121 Palaiseau Cedex France. **Tel** 011 33 1 69104700, telex 220064F.

US/0364-1783
**CONVERTED FLEXIBLE PACKAGING PRODUCTS.** (CURRENT INDUSTRIAL REPORTS. MQ-26F, CONVERTED FLEXIBLE PACKAGING PRODUCTS.). [Convert. flex. packag. prod.]. **Added/Corp** United States. Bureau of the Census. **VFOAT** Converted Flexible Packaging Products. (19??)-. Government Publication. English. an. $1.25. US Department of Commerce / Bureau of the Census, Data User Services Division, Customer Services, Washington DC 20233-0800. **Tel** (301)763-4100. **(Subscription address:** Superintendent of Documents, US Government Printing Office, Washington DC 20402.) **LC** HD9999.C743; U6324. **DD** 381/.45/.6888/0973.
**Desc:** Presents timely data on the production, inventories, and orders of approximately 5,000 products, which represents forty percent of all US manufacturing.

CN/0380-7037
**CORRUGATED BOXES AND WRAPPERS.** [Corrugat. boxes wrappers]. **Added/Corp** Statistics Canada. Manufacturing and Primary Industries Division. Statistics Canada. Industry Division. **VFOAT** Boites et Emballages en Carton Ondule; Boites et Emballages en Carton. Vol. 1, No. 1 (Sept. 1975)-. Periodical. English (French). mo. 60.00Can$ Canada; $72.00 US; $84.00 other. Statistics Canada, Publications Sales & Services, Main Building Room 1710, Ottawa Ontario K1A 0T6 Canada. **Tel** (613)951-5078, (800)267-6677, FAX (613)951-1584, telex 053-3585. **DD** 338.4/76763/0971.
**Desc:** Manufacturers' shipments of corrugated boxes and wrappers by regions.

US/0890-4227
**CURRENT PACKAGING ABSTRACTS (PISCATAWAY, N.J.).** ***Suspended.*** (CURRENT PACKAGING ABSTRACTS / IRA S. GOTTSCHO PACKAGING INFORMATION CENTER, RUTGERS--THE STATE UNIVERSITY OF NEW JERSEY.). **Added/Corp** Ira S. Gottscho Packaging Information Center. Rutgers University. (19??)-Suspended (1991). Periodical. English. bw. $120.00. IRA S Gottscho Pachaging Information, PO Box 909, College of Engineering, Piscataway NJ 08854. **Tel** (201)932-3044. **DD** 688.

FR
**DAIRY PACKAGING NEWSLETTER. See** Agriculture-Dairy Industry.

UK/0263-3752
**DEVELOPMENTS IN FOOD PACKAGING.** [Dev. food packag.]. (1980)-. Academic Scholarly Publication. English. ir. $61.25. Elsevier Science Publishers Ltd, Crown House, Linton Road, Barking Essex IG11 8JU England. **Tel** 011 44 81 5947272, FAX 081-594-5942, telex 896950. **CODEN** DFPADC. Documents available from CASDDS.
**Ind/Abst** Chem. Abstr. (1980).

●US/1071-9571
**DIRECTORY OF PACKAGING SOURCES.** (1994)-. Directory. English. $69.00. JPC Directories Inc., PO Box 488, Plainview NY 11803. ***Continues*** *Directory of U.S. Flexographic Packaging Sources, 1060-1473.*

JA/0911-3053
**ELECTRONIC PACKAGING TECHNOLOGY.** [Electron. packag. technol.]. **VFOAT** Erekutoronikusu Jisso Gijutsu. (1985)-. Periodical. Japanese. mo. ¥7416.00. Information Research Center Ltd, 8-1 Kudan Kita 1-chome, Chiyodak U Tokyo 102 Japan. **Tel** 011 81 3 3264 4351. **DD** 621.38.

BL/0013-6530
**EMBALAGEM (RIO DE JANEIRO).** (EMBALAGEM.). Periodical. Portuguese. $6.00. Editora Metodos, Caixa Postal 15085, 20 000 Rio de Janeiro Brazil. **LC** HF5770.A1; E49. **DD** 658.5/64/05.

FR/0013-6557
**EMBALLAGE DIGEST.** (1958)-. Periodical. French. mo. 385.00F France; 400.00F other. Sepe, 142 rue d Aguesseau, 92100 Boulogne France. **Tel** 011 33 1 46031554. **UDC** 621.798.
**Ind/Abst** Abstr. Bull. Inst. Pap. Sci. Tech.

FR/0013-6573
**EMBALLAGES.** [Emballages]. (1932)-. Periodical. French. Ten times a year. 391.77F France; 542.00F

other. CEP Information Professions, 1 Cite Bergere, 75311 Paris Cedex 09 France. **Tel** 011 33 1 44695550. **LC** TS158; .E5. **[CCC].**
**Ind/Abst** Abstr. Bull. Inst. Pap. Sci. Tech.; Alum. Ind. Abstr.; Dairy Sci. Abstr.; F&S Index Plus Text, Int. [Select. Cov.]; Infomat Int. Bus.; Int. Packag. Abstr.; Met. Abstr.; PROMT.

FR/0397-8079
**EMBOUTEILLAGE, CONDITIONNEMENT. VFOAT** Revue Mensuelle de l'Embouteillage et des Industries du Conditionnement. No. 164- Oct. 1976-. Periodical. French. ***Continues*** *Revue de l'Embouteillage et des Industries du Conditionnement: Traitement, Distribution, Transport.*
**Ind/Abst** Dairy Sci. Abstr.

GW/0966-4734
**EUROPEAN PACKAGING.** (19??)-. English. bm. DM33.50 (plus DM15.00 postage). Deutscher Fachverlag GmbH, Verlagsgruppe, D 60264 Frankfurt Germany. **Tel** 011 49 69 75951001, telex 411 862.
**Ind/Abst** Foods Adlibra.

GW
**EUROPEAN PACKAGING MAGAZINE (HEUSENSTAMM, GERMANY).** (EUROPEAN PACKAGING MAGAZINE : EPM.). **VFOAT** EPM. (Oct. 1985)-. Periodical. English (French). Twice a year. International Business Press GmbH, Postfach 100606, W-6000 Frankfurt 1 FR Germany. **Tel** 011 49 69 75951542. **ED** Bernd Wasshonn. Index available. cum. index. **Bk Rev**, (Qty: 4). **Ad Acc**, **Adv Mgr:** G. Bitterlich. **Acid Free. Circ:** 15,000.

FR/1052-2131
**EUROPEAN PACKAGING NEWSLETTER AND WORLD REPORT.** [Eur. packag. newsl. world rep.]. **Added/Corp** International Packaging Club. Vol. 200 (April 1983)-. Newsletter. English. Twelve times a year. $240.00 US & Canada & Mexico; $255.00 others. European Packaging Newsletter, 669 South Washington Street, Alexandria VA 22314. **Tel** (800)626-6578, (703)519-3907, FAX (703)519-7732, telex 648838. **ED** Marilyn Berry, Circulation Manager. **DD** 688. **CODEN** EPANEO. **[CCC].** Index available. ***Continues*** *European Packaging Newsletter.*
**Desc:** Serves the packaging industry as a clearinghouse for the latest information on innovative techniques, new machinery, and processes from Europe and Asia.
**Ind/Abst** BioBusiness; Foods Adlibra (1983-).

US/0196-7215
**FIBRE BOX HANDBOOK.** [Fibre box handb.]. **Main/Corp** Fibre Box Association. English. Fibre Box Association, 10 Gould Center/Suite 412, Rolling Meadows IL 60003. **Tel** (312)693-9600. **ED** Bruce Benson. **LC** HF5770.A1; F5A. **Bk Rev. Ad Acc. Circ:** 67,000 (ctrl).
**Desc:** A compendium of the regulations on the construction of corrugated boxes plus information on their proper usage.

UK
**FILM EXTRUSION MATERIALS AND MARKETS BULLETIN.** English. mo (except Aug. and Dec.). £190.00. Data Transcripts, PO Box 14, Dorking Surrey, RH5 4YN England. **Tel** 011 44 306 884473, FAX 011 44 306 884473.

UK
**FLEXPACK MATERIALS & MARKETS BULLETIN.** Bulletin. English. mo (except Aug. and Dec.). £190.00. Data Transcripts, PO Box 14, Dorking Surrey, RH5 4YN England. **Tel** 011 44 306 884473, FAX 011 44 306 884473. **ED** Lynda Crane. **Bk Rev. Ad Acc. Pr Rev.**
**Desc:** All flexible packaging, paper, film, foil, coatings; for all end uses: foods, pharmaceuticals, cosmetics, etc. Industrial markets data, company and product developments.

US/0194-2980
**FNP NEWSLETTER, FOOD PACKAGING AND LABELING.** [FNP newsl., Food packag. label.]. **VFOAT** Food Packaging and Labeling; Food Packaging and Labeling Newsletter. **VAT** Food and Nutrition Press Newsletter. Food Packaging and Labeling. Vol. 1 No. 1 (Jan. 1977)-. Newsletter. English. mo (12 issues per volume). $76.00 US, Canada & Mexico; $96.00 other. Food & Nutrition Press Inc, 2 Corporate Drive, PO Box 374, Trumbull CT 06611. **Tel** (203)261-8587, FAX (203)261-9724. **ED** Stanley Sacharow. **Bk Rev.**
**Desc:** Stan Sacharow, a recognized expert in food packaging, aids and informs readers on the latest trends, emerging, markets, and legislation in food packaging and labeling.

UK/0306-168X
**FOLDING CARTON INDUSTRY.** [Fold. carton ind.]. (1974)-. English. qt. £25.00 UK, £30.00 others (surface mail); £45.00 (airmail). Binsted Publications, Walton House, 90 London Road, Hook Hampshire RG27 9LF England. **Tel** 011 44 256 764180, FAX 011 44 256 766102, telex 859562. **LC** TS1200.A1; F64. **DD** 676/.32.
**Ind/Abst** Abstr. Bull. Inst. Pap. Sci. Tech.; Int. Packag. Abstr.; Pap. Board Abstr.; Print. Abstr.

US/0015-6272
**FOOD AND DRUG PACKAGING.** ***Title Change.*** [Food drug packag.]. **VFOAT** Food and Drug Packaging. Vol. 1 (Nov. 1959)-(1994). Periodical. English. Twelve times a year. Advanstar Communications Inc., 131 West First Street, Duluth MN 55802. **Tel** (218)723-9477, (800)346-0085. **ED** Sophia Dilberakis. **CODEN** FDPGAZ. **Ad Acc. Circ:** 67,876 (ctrl). available on microfilm and microfiche from University Microfilms International (UMI); available on an online database (file 16/Full-Text) from DIALOG. ***Continued by*** *New Food and Drug Packaging.*
**Desc:** Covers new materials as well as the technical and operating aspects involved in packaging food products and pharmaceuticals.
**Ind/Abst** BioBusiness; F&S Index Plus Text, Int. [Full Txt.] [Select. Cov.]; Foods Adlibra; Infomat Int. Bus.; Int. Aerosp. Abstr.; Int. Packag. Abstr.; PROMT [Full Txt.].

UK/0951-4554
**FOOD, COSMETICS AND DRUG PACKAGING 1986.** [Food cosmet. drug packag.1986]. (1986)-. Periodical. English. mo. $467.00 The Americas; £313.00 other. Elsevier Advanced Technology, An Imprint of Elsevier Science Ltd., The Boulevard, Langford Lane, Kidlington, Oxford OX5 1GB United Kingdom. **Tel** 011 44 865 843000, 011 44 865 843699, FAX 011 44 865 843010. **(Subscription address:** Elsevier Science Ltd. Oxford Fulfillment Centre, PO Box 800, Kidlington, Oxford OX5 1DX United Kingdom.**) DD** 688.805. **[CCC].** Index available. available on an online database from DIALOG. ***Continues*** *FCD Packaging, 0265-3583.*
**Desc:** This newsletter helps management to make well informed decisions on the developments, application, planning and forecasting of the role of FCD packaging within their own organizations.
**Ind/Abst** PTS Newsl. Database [Full Txt.].

UK/0957-5189
**FOOD PACKER INTERNATIONAL.** (1986)-. English. ir (8 issues). £85.00. Binsted Publications, Walton House, 90 London Road, Hook Hampshire RG27 9LF England. **Tel** 011 44 256 764180, FAX 011 44 256 766102, telex 859562.
**Ind/Abst** Foods Adlibra.

US/1049-3158
**GOOD PACKAGING MAGAZINE.** [Good packag. mag.]. **VFOAT** Good Packaging. (Jan. 1985)-. Periodical. English. Twelve times a year. $30.00 US and Canada; $80.00 other. Good Packaging Magazine, 1315 East Julian Street, San Jose CA 95116-1094. **Tel** (408)286-1661, FAX (408)275-8071. **ED** Kent W. Hutchings. **LC** TS2301.C8; G6. **DD** 688.8/05. **CODEN** GPMAEX. **Ad Acc, Adv Mgr:** K. Dean. **Circ:** 9700 (ctrl). ***Continues*** *Good Packaging, 0017-2170.*
**Desc:** Targets the Western packaging industry. It focuses on innovation - new products, new equipment, and new methods in the areas of cosmetics, films, food processing, machinery, material handling, paperboard, pharmaceuticals, and plastics. Each issue also incorporates at least one company profile and news about new packaging facilities and personnel.
**Ind/Abst** BioBusiness (1990-); Int. Packag. Abstr.

GW/0017-2243
**GORDIAN (1948).** **See** Food and Food Industry.

●US/1068-4271
**GREENPACKAGING 2000.** [GreenPackag. 2000]. **VFOAT** Green Packaging 2000; GreenPackaging Two Thousand; Green Packaging Two Thousand. Vol. 3, No. 3 (Mar. 1993)-. Newsletter. English. mo. $327.00 (one year), $637.00 (two year) US, Canada & Mexico; %352.00 (one year), $687.00 (two year) other. Packaging Strategies, 122 South Church Street, West Chester PA 19382. **Tel** (215)436-4220, FAX (215)436-6277, telex 757674. **ED** Ben Miyares. **DD** 363. **Circ:** Not disclosed. ***Continues*** *Green2000, 1053-6418.*
**Desc:** Focuses on news and anlysis of technological, legislative and economic issues related to packaging and the environment.

US
**HANDBOOK, CORRUGATED AND SOLID FIBREBOARD BOXES AND PRODUCTS. Main/Corp** Fibre Box Association. **VFOAT** Corrugated and Solid Fibreboard Boxes and Products. English. ir (every two-four years). Fibre Box Association, 10 Gould Center/Suite 412, Rolling Meadows IL 60003. **Tel** (312)693-9600. **LC** TS1200; .F5. **DD** 676.3. ctrl circ.

US/1068-0802
**HEALTHCARE PACKAGING.** ***Ceased.*** [Healthc. packag.]. Vol. 2, No. 5 (Mar. 1993)-(July 1994). Periodical. English. mo. Packaging Strategies, 122 South Church Street, West Chester PA 19382. **Tel** (215)436-4220, FAX (215)436-6277, telex 757674. **ED** Jim Wagner. **DD** 688. **NLM** W1; HE608SM. **Circ:** Not disclosed. ***Continues*** *Pharmaceutical Packaging.*
**Desc:** Covers packaging issues that impact the health care, pharmaceutical, and diagnostics markets.

US/0148-9208
**INDUSTRY WAGE SURVEY. CORRUGATED AND SOLID FIBER BOXES. See** Economics-Labor.

FR/0988-6249
**INNOVATIVE PACKAGING PARIS.** (INNOVATIVE PACKAGING.). (1987)-. Periodical. French. mo. 1200.00F. International Packaging Club, 42 Avenue de Versailles, 75016 Paris France. **Tel** 011 33 1 42882974, FAX 33 1 45250273. **ED** Pierre Louis. **UDC** 658.8. **Bk Rev. Ad Acc.**

AG/0326-8365
**INSTITUTO ARGENTINO DEL ENVASE.** [Inst. Argent. envase]. (1986)-. Periodical. Spanish. qt. Argentine Packaging Institute, Cnel Ramon L Falcon 2120, 1406 Buenos Aires Argentina. **UDC** 621.798.
**Ind/Abst** Abstr. Bull. Inst. Pap. Sci. Tech.

UK/0020-6199
**INTERNATIONAL BOTTLER AND PACKER, THE.** [Int. bottler packer]. **VFOAT** International Bottler & Packer. (19??)-. Periodical. English. Twelve times a year. £94.00. Binsted Publications, Walton House, 90 London Road, Hook Hampshire RG27 9LF England. **Tel** 011 44 256 764180, FAX 011 44 256 766102, telex 859562. **ED** Edward Binsted. **CODEN** IBOPA8. **Bk Rev. Ad Acc. Circ:** 6,178 (ctrl). ***Continues*** *International Beverage News.*
**Desc:** Reports world-wide bottling and packaging developments. Read by top management, technical and production directors, etc. in brewing soft drinks, cider, milk and bottling industries.
**Ind/Abst** BioBusiness; Food Sci. Technol. Abstr.; Int. Packag. Abstr.

●US/1063-1674
**INTERNATIONAL JOURNAL OF MICROCIRCUITS AND ELECTRONIC PACKAGING, THE.** [Int. j. microcircuits electron. packag.]. **Added/Corp** International Society for Hybrid Microelectronics. International Electronics Packaging Society. **VFOAT** International Journal of Microcircuits & Electronic Packaging. Vol. 15, No. 1 (1st Quarter 1992)-. Periodical. English. qt. $75.00 (nonmembers), $60.00 (members). International Society for Hybrid Microelectronics / Virginia, 1850 Centennial Park Drive, Suite 105, Reston VA 22091. **Tel** (703)758-1060, FAX (703)758-1066. **LC** TK7870.15; .I58. **DD** 621.381/046/05. **CODEN** IMEPE5. Index available. Documents available from Article Express International, Ask*IEEE. ***Formed by the union of*** *International Journal for Hybrid Microelectronics, 0277-8270* ***and*** *IEPS Journal.*
**Ind/Abst** Bioeng. Abstr.; Ei Page One; Eng. Index Annu.; INSPEC; Int. Aerosp. Abstr.

UK/0260-7409
**INTERNATIONAL PACKAGING ABSTRACTS. See** Packaging-Abstracting, Bibliographies and Statistics.

JA
**JAPANESE PACKAGING REPORT.** English. Four times a year. $500.00. Packaging Planning Services, Inc., Toyobo Building 4F 17 9 Koamicho, Tokyo 103 Japan. **Tel** 011 81 3 36604897, FAX 011 81 3 36604871. **ED** Yasuko Tagami. **Circ:** 250.
**Desc:** Descriptions of newly-released packaging material products in Japan.
**Ind/Abst** Foods Adlibra.

US/0892-029X
**JOURNAL OF PACKAGING TECHNOLOGY.** ***Title Change.*** [J. packag. technol.]. **VFOAT** Packaging Technology. Vol. 1, No. 1 (Feb. 1987)-(1992). Periodical. English. bm. North American Publishing Company, 401 North Broad Street, Philadelphia PA 19108. **Tel** (215)238-5300, (800)777-8074, FAX (215)238-5283. **ED** Glenn Milvin , Robert Miller, Christine Wieser. **DD** 688. **CODEN** JPATET. **[CCC]. Ad Acc. Pr Rev. Circ:** 30,000 (ctrl). ***Continued by*** *Packaging Technology & Engineering, 1067-411X.*
**Desc:** Original contributions representing advances in the science, technology, and engineering of the packaging industry. Technical information from basic concepts to specialized techniques, plus coverage of the newest materials, machines and methods available.
**Ind/Abst** Abstr. Bull. Inst. Pap. Sci. Tech.; BioBusiness; Food Sci. Technol. Abstr.; Int. Packag. Abstr.

UK/0143-2192
**LABELS & LABELLING INTERNATIONAL.** [Labels labelling int.]. **VFOAT** Labels and Labelling International; Labels & Labelling. (19??)-. Periodical. English. bm (6 issues). $75.00. Cowise International Publishing Group, White House, 60 High Street, Herts EN6 5AB England. **Tel** 011 44 71 707 56828, FAX 011 44 71 707 45322.

BE
**MANUTENTION-EMBALLAGES. VFOAT** Behandeling-Verpakkingen. Dutch (French). Institut Belge de l Emballage, Editeur-Proprietaire S A, Imprimerie et Publicite du Marais N V, rue de Flandre 169, 1000 Bruxelles Belgium. **LC** TS180; .M284.

US
**MARI BOARD CONVERTING NEWS.**
English. bm. $30.00. N V Business Publishers, 2970 Marion Executive Center, Northbrook IL 60062. **Tel** (708)498-5850.
**Ind/Abst** Abstr. Bull. Inst. Pap. Sci. Tech.

UK
**MHBG, MATERIALS HANDLING BUYER'S GUIDE. VFOAT** Materials Handling Buyers' Guide. (19??)-. Periodical. English. an. £33.00 UK; £35.00 Europe; £39.00 other. Turret Group, 177 Hagden Lane, Watford Herts WD1 8LN United Kingdom. **Tel** 011 44 923 228577, FAX 011 44 923 221346. **LC** TS180; .M18. **DD** 338.4/7/6218602541.

HU/0580-4485
**MINOSEG ES MEGBIZHATOSAG.** (MM. MINOSEG ES MEGBIZHATOSAG.). [Minos. megbiz.]. **Added/Corp** KGM Muszaki Tudomanyos Tajekoztato Intezet. **VFOAT** Minoseg es Megbizhatosag. (1967)-. Periodical. Hungarian (summaries and/or abstracts in English, French, German and Russian). bm. $38.50. Prodinform Muszaki Tanacsodo Vallalat, (Prodinform Technical Consulting Company), Munkacsy Mihaly u. 16, PO Box 453, H-1372 Budapest, Hungary. **Tel** 361-317-569. **(Subscription address:** Kultura, PO Box 149, H 1389 Budapest 62 Hungary.**) ED** G. Gyozo. **LC** TS156.A1; M16. **Bk Rev. Ad Acc. Circ:** 4,000. Documents available from Ask*IEEE.
**Ind/Abst** Energy Res. Abstr. (Oct. 1979-); INSPEC (1971-).

NE
**MISSETS MILIEU NIEUWSBRIEF.** Dutch. sm. Misset Uitgeverij BV, Postbus 9000, 6800 DA Arnhem Netherlands. **Tel** 011 31 85 209911.

NE
**MISSETS PAKBLAD.** Misset Uitgeverij BV, Postbus 9000, 6800 DA Arnhem Netherlands. **Tel** 011 31 85 209911.

US/0026-8038
**MODERN MATERIALS HANDLING. See** Manufacturing.

RU/0130-6898
**NADEZHNOST I KONTROL KACHESTVA.** [Nadezn. kontrol kac.]. **Added/Corp** Soviet Union. Komitet Standartov, Mer i Izmeritelnykh Priborov. (1969)-. Periodical. Russian. mo. $189.95. Izdatelstvo Standartov, D-22 Novoprensenskii Per 3, Moscow Russia. **(Subscription address:** East View Publications Inc., 3020 Harbor Lane North, Suite 110, Minneapolis MN 55447.**) LC** TS173; .N32.
**Ind/Abst** Math. Rev.

US/0743-3956
**NATIONAL MEAT PACKER REFERENCE GUIDE. See** Agriculture-Livestock and Poultry.

●US/1075-3028
**NEW FOOD & DRUG PACKAGING, THE.** [New food drug packag.]. **VFOAT** New Food and Drug Packaging; Food & Drug Packaging; Food and Drug Packaging. Vol. 57, No. 2 (Sept. 1993)-. Periodical. English. Twelve times a year. $53.50. Independent Publishing Company, 210 South 5th Street, Suite 202, St. Charles IL 60174. **Tel** (708)377-0100, FAX (708)377-1678. **ED** Lisa Pierce. **LC** TP368; .F6. **DD** 688. **CODEN** NFDPE6. **Ad Acc, Adv Mgr:** Sharon Needham. **Circ:** 74,000 (ctrl). ***Continues** Food & Drug Packaging, 0015-6272.*

GW/0341-0390
**NV; NEUE VERPACKUNG.** [NV. Neue Verpack.]. **Added/Corp** Fachnormenausschuss Verpackung. **VFOAT** Neue Verpackung. (1952)-. Periodical. German. mo. $199.00. Dr. Alfred Huethig Verlag GmbH, Postfach 102869, D 69018 Heidelberg Germany. **Tel** 011 49 6221 489281. **(Subscription address:** Huethig Publishing Inc., 29 Macintosh Drive, Oxford CT 06478.**) ED** Peter Haberstolz, Collin Weber. **LC** TS195.A1; N18. **Bk Rev. Ad Acc. Circ:** 12,792 (ctrl). available on microfiche.
**Desc:** Internationally distributed journal for packaging technology in the food and non-food sectors.
**Ind/Abst** Abstr. Bull. Inst. Pap. Sci. Tech.; Alum. Ind. Abstr.; Energy Res. Abstr. (May 1973-); Food Sci. Technol. Abstr.; Infomat Int. Bus.; Int. Packag. Abstr.; Met. Abstr.

UK/0957-655X
**OIL PACKER INTERNATIONAL.** [Oil pack. int.]. (1988)-. Periodical. English. Four times a year. £28.00 UK; £35.00 others. Binsted Publications, Walton House, 90 London Road, Hook Hampshire RG27 9LF England. **Tel** 011 44 256 764180, FAX 011 44 256 766102, telex 859562. **DD** 338.4766538. **Ad Acc. Circ:** 8,000 (ctrl).
**Desc:** Information on all aspects of oil packaging industry.

SA
**PACK & PRINT. VFOAT** Pack and Print. Periodical. English. mo. $17.35. Thomson Publications Pty, PO Box 56182, Pinegowrie 2123 South Africa. **Tel** 011 27 11 7892144.
**Ind/Abst** Abstr. Graphic Arts Tech. Found. (1979).

US
**PACK INFO NEWSLETTER.** (19??)-. Newsletter. English. bm (6 issues). $90.00 (membership) comes with Institute of Packaging Professionals membership and Packaging Technology and Engineering. Institute of Packaging Professionals, PO Box 79322, Baltimore MD 21279. **Tel** (703)318-8970.

US/0895-1608
**PACKAGE PRINTING AND CONVERTING.** [Package print. convert.]. Vol. 34, No. 7 (July 1987)-. Periodical. English. Twelve times a year. $49.00. North American Publishing Company, 401 North Broad Street, Philadelphia PA 19108. **Tel** (215)238-5300, (800)777-8074, FAX (215)238-5283. **LC** TS196.7; .P3. **DD** 676/.3/05. available on microfilm from Xerox; available on microfilm and microfiche from University Microfilms International (UMI). ***Continues** Package Printing, 0163-9234.*
**Desc:** Focuses on machinery and methods in the specialized field of printing and converting packages, boxes, cartons, bags and tags and labels.
**Ind/Abst** Abstr. Bull. Inst. Pap. Sci. Tech.; Graph. Arts Bull. Inst. Pap. Sci. Technol. (Jan. 1989, April 1989-May 1989, Nov. 1989); Int. Packag. Abstr. (July 1987-); Print. Abstr. (1987-).

US/1052-682X
**PACKAGE TRAVEL.** (1991)-. Periodical. English. mo. $36.00. The Finney Co., PO Box 5500, Scottsdale AZ 85261-5500.

UK/0030-9060
**PACKAGING.** Vol. 1 (April 1930)-. Periodical. English. bm. £59.00 UK; £65.00 other. Turret Group, 177 Hagden Lane, Watford Herts WD1 8LN United Kingdom. **Tel** 011 44 923 228577, FAX 011 44 923 221346. **LC** TS158; .P32. available on microfilm and microfiche from University Microfilms International (UMI). Documents available from UMI Article Clearinghouse. ***Absorbed** European Packaging; Continental Packaging; PCB. Plastics Packaging Paper Converters Bulletin.*
**Ind/Abst** ABI/INFORM Glob. Ed.; ABI Inform Ondisc (Dec. 1987-); Abstr. Bull. Inst. Pap. Sci. Tech.; Bus. Index (1985-); Curr. Technol. Index; F&S Index Plus Text, Int. [Select. Cov.]; Foods Adlibra; Gen. BusinessFile (1985-); Gen. Period. Index (1985-); Graph. Arts Bull. Inst. Pap. Sci. Technol. (April 1989, Oct. 1989); Infomat Int. Bus.; Int. Packag. Abstr.; Mag. Search; Predicasts F&S Index, U. S. Annu. Ed.; PROMT; Trade Ind. ASAP [Full Txt.]; Trade Ind. Index [Full Txt.].

AT
**PACKAGING.** (1960)-. English. mo ((except Jan.)). 50.00Aus$ Australia; 100.00Aus$ other. Reed Business Publishing Pty Ltd. / Australia, 1 5 Railway Street, Level 12 North Tower, Chatswood W 2067 NSW Australia. **Tel** 011 61 2 3725222, FAX 011 61 2 4197533. **ED** Allison Craven. **Ad Acc, Adv Mgr:** Ms Ros Richards, **Tel** 372-5222. **Circ:** 5,050 (ctrl).
**Desc:** Australia's oldest and most widely recognized packaging technology authority. coverage includes industry news, new pack designs, machinery, new products, the environment and a monthly feature on industry segments.

US
**PACKAGING AND CONVERTING TECHNOLOGY.** Monographic series. English. ir. Price varies per volume. Marcel Dekker Inc., 270 Madison Avenue, New York NY 10016. **Tel** (212)696-9000, (800)228-1160, FAX (212)685-4540, telex 421419. **(Subscription address:** Marcel Dekker Inc, PO Box 5017, Monticello NY 12701.**)**
**Desc:** Topics covered have included medical device packaging and plastics in food packaging.

US/0746-3820
**PACKAGING (BOSTON, MASS.).** (PACKAGING.). [Packaging]. Vol. 28, No. 10 (Sept. 1983)-. Periodical. English. mo (13 issues). $85.00 US; $123.00 Canada; $115.00 Mexico; $150.00 (surface mail) other. Cahners Publishing Company, 249 West 17th Street, New York NY 10011. **Tel** (212)645-0067, FAX (212)242-6987. **(Subscription address:** Cahners Publishing Company / Colorado, Paid Subscription Service Center, PO Box 7610, Highlands Ranch CO 80126-7610.**) ED** R. Bruce Holmgren. **LC** TS195.A1; P26. **DD** 688.8/05. **CODEN** PACKD6. **[CCC].** available on microfilm and microfiche from University Microfilms International (UMI). Documents available from Article Express International. ***Continues** Package Engineering Including Modern Packaging, 0747-9999.*
**Desc:** Is of interest to managers in production and engineering, corporate and general management, marketing, package design, R&D and purchasing. It provides business news and information on technical design, product packaging innovations, consumer protection concerns, and marketing/packaging trends.
**Ind/Abst** Abstr. Bull. Inst. Pap. Sci. Tech.; Appl. Sci. Technol. Index; Eng. Index Annu. [Select. Cov.]; F&S Index Plus Text, Int. [Select. Cov.]; Foods Adlibra; Infomat Int. Bus.; Int. Packag. Abstr.; Life Sci. Collect.; PROMT; Stat. Ref. Index; Topicator; Trade Ind. ASAP [Full Txt.]; Trade Ind. Index [Full Txt.]; Vocat. Search (July 1993-).

US/0030-9109
**PACKAGING DESIGN. *Ceased.*** (1960)-(Fall 1975). Periodical. English. an. Art Direction Book Company, 10 East 39th Street/6th Floor, New York NY 10016. **Tel** (212)889-6500.

JA
**PACKAGING DESIGN IN JAPAN. VFOAT** Nenkan Nihon No Pakkeji Dezain. Vol. 1 (1985)-. Japanese (English). be. Nippo Co Ltd, 3-1-5 Misaki-cho, Chiyoda-ku, Tokyo 101 Japan. **Bk Rev. Circ:** 10,000 (ctrl).

US/0030-9117
**PACKAGING DIGEST (CHICAGO, ILL.).** (PACKAGING DIGEST.). [Packag. dig.]. Vol. 1 (1963)-. Periodical. English. mo (13 issues). $75.00 US; $112.00 Canada; $105.00 Mexico; $135.00 (surface mail) other. Cahners Publishing Company, 249 West 17th Street, New York NY 10011. **Tel** (212)645-0067, FAX (212)242-6987. **(Subscription address:** Cahners Publishing Company / Colorado, Paid Subscription Service Center, PO Box 7610, Highlands Ranch CO 80126-7610.**) [CCC].** available on microfilm and microfiche from University Microfilms International (UMI).
**Desc:** Covers the packaging function within the food, pharmaceutical and all other industries where the application of packaging materials and equipment is of vital importance.
**Ind/Abst** Abstr. Graphic Arts Tech. Found. (1984); Bus. ASAP (1992-) [Full Txt.]; Bus. Index (1985-); Gen. BusinessFile (1985-); Gen. Period. Index (1985-); Int. Packag. Abstr.; Mag. Search; Trade Ind. ASAP [Full Txt.]; Trade Ind. Index (1981-) [Full Txt.]; Vocat. Search (Jan. 1993-).

US
**PACKAGING ENCYCLOPEDIA & TECHNICAL DIRECTORY. VFOAT** Packaging Encyclopedia and Technical Directory; Packaging ... Encyclopedia; Packaging's Encyclopedia. (1989)-. English. an. Cahners Publishing Company, 249 West 17th Street, New York NY 10011. **Tel** (212)645-0067, FAX (212)242-6987. ***Continues** Packaging Encyclopedia (Newton, Mass : 1987).*

II/0030-9125
**PACKAGING INDIA.** [Packag. India]. **Added/Corp** Indian Institute of Packaging. (1968)-. Periodical. English. bm. $75.00. Indian Institute of Packaging, Bombay, India. **(Subscription address:** Prints India, 11 Darya Ganj, New Delhi 110002 India.**) CODEN** PINDDS.

UK/0269-9834
**PACKAGING INDUSTRY DIRECTORY.** [Packag. ind. dir.]. (1987)-. English. an. £72.00. Benn Business Information Service Ltd, Riverbank House, Angel Lane, Tonbridge Kent TN9 1SE England. **Tel** 011 44 732 362666, FAX 011 44 732 770483, telex 95454 BBIS. **ED** Cheryl Whitehead. **DD** 338.4768880941. **Circ:** 1,600. ***Continues** Institute of Packaging Directory and Packaging Review Buyers' Guide, 0265-2773.*
**Desc:** Features five buyers' guides cross-referenced to the master alphabetical listing of over 6,000 companies manufacturing, supplying or distributing materials, products and services to the packaging and related industries.

JA/0288-3864
**PACKAGING JAPAN.** [Packag. Jpn.]. (19??)-. Periodical. English. bm. $172.50. Nippo Co Ltd, 3-1-5 Misaki-cho, Chiyoda-ku, Tokyo 101 Japan. **(Subscription address:** Kyowa Book Company Inc., 1-38 Kanda Jinbo-Cho, Chiyoda-Ku Tokyo 101, Japan**) ED** Katsushi Kawamura. **LC** TS195.A1; P252. **DD** 688.8/0952. **CODEN** PAJAEC. **Ad Acc. Circ:** 15,000 (ctrl).
**Desc:** Covers recent trends, products, news, new technology and events concerning the Japanese packaging industry.
**Ind/Abst** BioBusiness (1990-); Infomat Int. Bus.; Int. Packag. Abstr.

US
**PACKAGING MARKETPLACE. *Suspended.*** 1978-?. English. ir. $120.00. Gale Research Inc., 835 Penobscot Building, Detroit MI 48226. **Tel** (800)877-GALE, (313)961-2242, FAX (313)961-6083, telex TWX 810-221-7086. **ED** J F Hanlon.
**Desc:** A directory of over 4,000 manufacturers, distributors, and wholesalers covering sources of packaging information, services, materials and equipment.

AT
**PACKAGING NEWS.** (19??)-. English. Eleven times a year. 38.00Aus$ Australia; 105.00Aus$ other. Yaffa Publishing Group Pty Ltd., GPO Box 606, Sydney NSW 2001 Australia. **Tel** 011 61 2 2812333, FAX 011 61 2 2812750.

UK/0030-9133
**PACKAGING NEWS (LONDON).** (PACKAGING NEWS.). [Packag. news]. (1954)-. Periodical. English. Twelve times a year. £60.00. Maclean Hunter Ltd. / UK, Chalk Lane Cockfosters Road, Barnet Herts EN4 0BU England. **Tel** 011 44 81 2423000, FAX 011 44 81 9759753, telex 299072. **ED** Rosemary Mason.

CODEN PKGNAY. **Bk Rev.** **Ad Acc. Circ:** 18,634 (ctrl).
**Desc:** The leading packaging publication in Europe. Offers a complete news service for buyers of packaging materials, equipment and services.
**Ind/Abst** Abstr. Bull. Inst. Pap. Sci. Tech.; BioBusiness (1990-); Foods Adlibra; Infomat Int. Bus.; Int. Packag. Abstr.; Pap. Board Abstr.

●US/1061-2300
**PACKAGING PRODUCTIVITY.** (PACKAGING PRODUCTIVITY THE TECHNICAL TRAINING JOURNAL OF THE PACKAGING INDUSTRY.). [Packag. product.]. **Added/Corp** Training Process Development, Inc. **VFOAT** Technical Training Journal of the Packaging Industry. Vol. 1, No. 1 (Mar. 1992)- Vol. 2 (Mar. 1993-94)-. Periodical. English. Six times a year (Jan. Mar., May, July, Sept., Nov.). $199.00 one year; $350.00 two year. Trianing Process Development, PO Box 115, Manchester VT 05254. **Tel** (802)362-0062. **ED** Kevin B. Carey. **LC** TS195.A1; P253. **DD** 688.8/05.

US/8755-6189
**PACKAGING STRATEGIES.** [Packag. strategies]. (1983)-. Periodical. English. Twenty-three times a year. $377.00 North America; $419.00 other. Packaging Strategies, 122 South Church Street, West Chester PA 19382. **Tel** (215)436-4220, FAX (215)436-6277, telex 757674. **ED** Ben Miyares. **DD** 658. **CODEN** PASTEC. **Bk Rev. Circ:** Not disclosed.
**Desc:** Newsletter oriented to the packaging industry with a focus on emerging trends and issues. It examines materials, containers, equipment developments and new technology. The newsletter also covers business issues related to the packaging industry.
**Ind/Abst** BioBusiness; Foods Adlibra.

●US/1067-411X
**PACKAGING TECHNOLOGY & ENGINEERING.** [Packag. technol. eng.]. **VFOAT** Packaging Technology and Engineering. Vol. 2, No. 1 (Feb. 1993)-. Periodical. English. Five times a year. $69.00. North American Publishing Company, 401 North Broad Street, Philadelphia PA 19108. **Tel** (215)238-5300, (800)777-8074, FAX (215)238-5283. **DD** 688. **CODEN** PTENEN. ***Continues*** *Journal of Packaging Technology, 0892-029X.*
**Desc:** Written expressly for and by packaging professionals who are involved in purchasing equipment, systems, materials, containers and services.
**Ind/Abst** Abstr. Bull. Inst. Pap. Sci. Tech.

UK/0894-3214
**PACKAGING TECHNOLOGY AND SCIENCE.** [Packag. technol. sci.]. **VFOAT** Packaging technology and science. Vol. 1 (1988)-. Periodical. English. bm. $475.00. John Wiley & Sons Ltd., Baffins Lane, Chichester West Sussex PO19 1UD England. **Tel** 0243 779777, FAX 0243 776128 BTG:JWP001, telex 86290 WIBOOKG. **(Subscription address:** John Wiley / Philadelphia, PO Box 7247, Philadelphia PA 19170.**) ED** F. A. Paine. **LC** TS195.A1; P255. **DD** 688.8/05. **CODEN** PTSCEQ. **[CCC].** available on microfilm and microfiche from University Microfilms International (UMI). Documents available from Article Express International.
**Desc:** Provides a forum for the publication of articles about new developments in this field. Among the topics covered are: packaging of foods, medical and pharmaceutical products, electrical goods, machinery and machine tools, agricultural chemicals, fragile and high value goods and hazardous substances.
**Ind/Abst** Abstr. Bull. Inst. Pap. Sci. Tech.; Ceram. Abstr. (19??-); Dairy Sci. Abstr.; Ei Page One; Eng. Index Annu.; Food Sci. Technol. Abstr.; Foods Adlibra; Int. Packag. Abstr.

UK/0268-0920
**PACKAGING TODAY LONDON.** [Packag. today Lond.]. (1979)-. Periodical. English. mo. $174.00. Angel Publishing Ltd., 361 373 City Road, 5th Floor, London EC1V 1LR England. **Tel** 011 44 71 417 7400, FAX 011 44 71 417 7500. **ED** Giles Maddock. **Ad Acc. Circ:** 16,200 (ctrl).
**Desc:** For the packaging industry, designed for packaging people. Gives a balance of news coverage and feature articles.
**Ind/Abst** Food Sci. Technol. Abstr.; Infomat Int. Bus.

JA
**PACKAGING TRENDS : JAPAN.** English. mo. $220.00. Packaging Planning Services, Inc., Toyobo Building 4F 17 9 Koamicho, Tokyo 103 Japan. **Tel** 011 81 3 36604897, FAX 011 81 3 36604871. **ED** Mitsu Yagisawa. **Circ:** 80.
**Desc:** News on Japanese packaging materials, containers, and equipments.

UK/0267-6117
**PACKAGING WEEK.** [Packag. week]. (May 8, 1985)-. Periodical. English. Forty-six times a year. £76.00 UK; £113.00 other. Benn Publications Ltd., Sovereign Way, Tonbridge TNQ 1RW England. **Tel** 011 44 732 364422, FAX 011 44 732 361534, telex 0732 95132 BENTON G. **ED** Mary Murphy. **CODEN** PAWEEL. Index available. ctrl circ. available on microfilm from University Microfilms International (UMI); available on an online database (files 16,648/Full-Text) from DIALOG. ***Absorbed*** *Packaging Review, 0048-2684.*
**Ind/Abst** Abstr. Bull. Inst. Pap. Sci. Tech.; BioBusiness; F&S Index Plus Text, Int. [Select. Cov.]; Infomat Int. Bus.; Int. Packag. Abstr.; PROMT [Full Txt.]; Trade Ind. ASAP [Full Txt.].

GW/0724-8490
**PACKUNG & TRANSPORT. See** Transportation.

US/0145-434X
**PAL, PACKAGING AND LABELING. FEDERAL LEGISLATIVE AND REGULATORY SUPPLEMENT. VFOAT** Packaging and Labeling. Federal Legislative and Regulatory Supplement. **VAT** Packaging and Labeling, Packaging and Labeling. Federal Legislative and Regulatory Supplement. English. Federal State Reports Inc, PO Box 986 Courthouse Station, Arlington VA 22216. **LC** KF1619.A3692; P15. **DD** 343/.73/082.

UK
**PANORAMA.** (19??)-. Newsletter. English. bm. £25.00 UK; £30.00 other. Institute of Packaging, Sysonby Lodge, Nottingham Road, Melton Mowbray, Leicestershire LE30NU England. **Tel** (0664)500055, FAX (0664)64164. **ED** Moira Hart. **Bk Rev**, (Qty: 6). **Ad Acc, Adv Mgr:** M. Hart, **Tel** 0664 500055. **Acid Free. Circ:** 4,000 (ctrl).
**Ind/Abst** Infomat Int. Bus.

UK/0959-9266
**PAPER & PACKAGING ANALYST.** **Added/Corp** Economist Intelligence Unit (Great Britain). **VFOAT** Paper and Packaging Analyst; EIU Paper & Packaging Analyst. No. 1 (May 1990)-. Periodical. English. qt. $792.00 North America; £495.00 other. Pira International, Randalls Road, Leatherhead, Surrey KT22 7RU England. **Tel** 011 44 372 376161, FAX 011 44 372 377526. **LC** HF5770.A1; P362. ***Continues*** *Paper & Packaging Bulletin, 0142-5307.*
**Ind/Abst** Abstr. Bull. Inst. Pap. Sci. Tech. (19??-); F&S Index Plus Text, Int. (19??-) [Select. Cov.]; PROMT (19??-).

US/0031-1138
**PAPER, FILM AND FOIL CONVERTER. See** Paper and Pulp Industry.

US/0031-1227
**PAPERBOARD PACKAGING.** [Paperboard packag.]. Vol. 44, No. 8 (Aug. 1959)-. Periodical. English. mo. $39.00 US and possessions; $59.00 Canada; $85.00 other. Advanstar Communications Inc., 131 West First Street, Duluth MN 55802. **Tel** (218)723-9477, (800)346-0085. **LC** HF5770; .P4. **[CCC]. Circ:** 13,141. available on microfilm and microfiche from University Microfilms International (UMI); available on an online database (file 16/Full-Text) from DIALOG. ***Continues*** *Fibre Containers and Paperboard Mills, 0097-2770.*
**Ind/Abst** Abstr. Bull. Inst. Pap. Sci. Tech.; Bus. Index (1985-); F&S Index Plus Text, Int. [Full Txt.] [Select. Cov.]; Gen. BusinessFile (1985-); Gen. Period. Index (1985-); Graph. Arts Bull. Inst. Pap. Sci. Technol. (Jan. 1989-May 1989, July 1989, Sept. 1989-Oct. 1989-); Int. Packag. Abstr.; Mag. Search; Pap. Board Abstr.; PROMT [Full Txt.]; Stat. Ref. Index; Trade Ind. Index; Vocat. Search (July 1993-).

US/0741-4129
**PAPERBOARD PACKAGING'S INTERNATIONAL CONTAINER DIRECTORY. VFOAT** International Container Directory. (19??)-. Directory. English. an. $100.00 US; $110.00 others. Advanstar Communications Inc., 131 West First Street, Duluth MN 55802. **Tel** (218)723-9477, (800)346-0085. **(Subscription address:** Advanstar Marketing Service / Ohio, 7500 Old Oak Boulevard, Cleveland OH 44130.**) LC** HD9999.C74; P36. **DD** 688.8/029/4. ***Continues*** *International Container Directory.*

US/0198-8867
**PAPERBOARD PACKAGING'S OFFICIAL CONTAINER DIRECTORY.** [Paperboard packag. off. contain. dir.]. **VFOAT** Official Container Directory. (19??)-. Directory. English. sa. $100.00 US; $110.00 other. Advanstar Communications Inc., 131 West First Street, Duluth MN 55802. **Tel** (218)723-9477, (800)346-0085. **ED** Mark Arzoumanian. **LC** HD9820.1; .P33. **DD** 380.1/456763/02947. **Ad Acc. Circ:** 4,000 (ctrl).
**Desc:** Information about almost all converters of corrugated and solid fibre containers, folding cartons, rigid boxes, fibre drums, fibre cans and tubes, plus packaging machinery.

US
**PERFORMANCE.** Periodical. English. bm. $12.00. Charger Productions, PO Box HH, Capistrano Beach CA 92624. **LC** TS168; .P47. **DD** 658.5/6.

UK
**PIRA PACKAGING ABSTRACTS.** **Main/Corp** Pira (Association). **Added/Corp** Pira (Association) Packaging Abstracts. (19??)-. Periodical. English. mo. $42.00. Pira International, Randalls Road, Leatherhead, Surrey KT22 7RU England. **Tel** 011 44 372 376161, FAX 011 44 372 377526. **ED** Sarah-Jane Sutton. **LC** Z7164.C8; P14; TS195. **DD** 016.6217/57. ***Continues*** *Packaging Abstracts.*
**Ind/Abst** Abstr. Bull. Inst. Pap. Sci. Tech.

US/1046-3046
**PLASTIC WASTE STRATEGIES.** ***Title Change.*** [Plast. waste strateg.]. (1989)-(19??). Periodical. English. mo. Washington Business Information Inc., 1117 North 19th Street, Suite 200, Arlington VA 22209. **Tel** (703)247-3433, (800)426-0416, FAX (703)247-3421. **ED** Jeffrey Yohn and John Sisson. **DD** 363. ***Merged into*** *Plasic Business News.*
**Desc:** Focuses on recycling, degradability, incineration and alternative methods of handling solid waste.

US/8750-6653
**POWDER/BULK SOLIDS.** [Powder/bulk solids]. **VFOAT** Powder Bulk Solids. (19??)-. Periodical. English. mo (13 issues). $35.00 US, Canada & Mexico; $48.00 (surface mail), $96.00 (airmail) other. Cahners Publishing Company, 249 West 17th Street, New York NY 10011. **Tel** (212)645-0067, FAX (212)242-6987. **(Subscription address:** Gordon Publications, Inc., Paid Circulation Department, 301 Gibraltar Drive, Box 650, Morris Plains NJ 07950-0650.**) DD** 338. **[CCC]. Ad Acc. Circ:** 29,000 (ctrl).
**Desc:** Serves industries that process, handle and package dry 'particulate' matter, including chemicals, food, primary metals, mining, electronics, rubber and plastics.

US/0149-144X
**PROCEEDINGS : ANNUAL RELIABILITY AND MAINTAINABILITY SYMPOSIUM.** [Proc., Annu. Reliab. Maintainab. Symp.]. **Main/Conf** Reliability and Maintainability Symposium. **VFOAT** Annals of Assurance Sciences. 1972-. Proceedings. English. an. $56.00. IEEE, Institution of Electrical and Electronics Engineers, Inc., 345 East 47th Street, New York NY 10017-2394. **Tel** (908)981-1393, FAX (908)981-9667. **(Subscription address:** IEEE Service Center, 445 Hoes Lane, Piscataway NJ 08854; telephone: (201)981-1393**) LC** TS173; .R43. **DD** 003. **CODEN** PRMSCS. **[CCC].** Documents available from Article Express International, The Genuine Article, Ask*IEEE. ***Continues*** *Symposium on Reliability. Proceedings.*
**Ind/Abst** Civ. Struct. Eng. Abstr.; Coal Abstr.; Comput. Inf. Syst. Abstr. J. [Full Cov.]; Curr. Contents Eng. Tech. Appl. Sci.; Elect. Comm. Abstr.; Energy Res. Abstr. (Feb. 1979-); Eng. Index Annu.; Environ. Eng. Abstr.; Index IEEE Publ.; INSPEC; Manuf. Process Eng. Abstr.; Mater. Sci. Eng. Abstr.; Mech. Eng. Abstr.; Res. Alert [Select. Cov.]; SCISEARCH; Solid State Supercond. Abstr.

UK
**PROCEEDINGS / INTERNEPCON ELECTRONIC PACKAGING CONFERENCE. Main/Conf** INTERNEPCON Electronic Packaging Conference. **VFOAT** Conference Proceedings. 1987-. Proceedings. English. an. Cahners Exhibitions Ltd, Chatsworth House, 59 London Road, Twickenham Middlesex TW1 3SZ England. ***Continues*** *Conference Proceedings / INTERNEPCON Production Show & Conference.*

US/0162-2919
**PROCEEDINGS PLP. PRODUCT LIABILITY PREVENTION CONVENTION.** (PROCEEDINGS PLP.). [Proc. PLP. Prod. Liabil. Prev. Conf.]. **Main/Conf** Product Liability Prevention Conference. **Added/Corp** New Jersey Institute of Technology. American Society for Quality Control. North Jersey Section. **VAT** Proceedings, Product Liability Prevention. Product Liability Prevention Conference. 1st (1970)-. Proceedings. English. an. $15.00. New Jersey Institute of Technology, Center for Technology Studies, Newark NJ 07102. **Tel** (201)596-3270. **LC** TS175; .P76a. **DD** 658.5/6.

US/0162-279X
**PROCEEDINGS PLP. PRODUCT LIABILITY PREVENTION SEMINAR.** (PROCEEDINGS PLP.). **Main/Conf** Product Liability Prevention Seminar. **VAT** Proceedings Product Liability Prevention. Product Liability Prevention Seminar. 1st-1977-. Proceedings. English. $10.00. New Jersey Institute of Technology, Center for Technology Studies, Newark NJ 07102. **Tel** (201)596-3270. **LC** TS175; .P77A. **DD** 658.5/6.

KO
**PUMJIL KWALLI HAKHOE CHI. VFOAT** Journal of the Korean Society for Quality Control. Periodical. Korean (summaries and/or abstracts in English). Hanguk Pumjil Kwalli Hakhoe, 105-153 Kongdok-dong, Mapo-ku 121, Seoul South Korea. **LC** TS155.A1; P85.

IT
**RASSEGNA DELL IMBALLAGGIO E CONFEZIONAMENTO.** Italian. Twenty times a year. L200.000. Arti Poligrafiche Europee SAS, Via Casella 16, 20156 Milan Italy. **Tel** 011 39 02 330221, FAX 011 39 02 394341, telex 326544 ANTO I. **ED** Giorgio Bianchini. **Ad Acc. Circ:** 12,000 (ctrl).
**Desc:** Packing and packaging in every solution for every purpose.
**Ind/Abst** Food Sci. Technol. Abstr.

US/0740-7297
**RULES FOR CERTIFICATION OF CARGO CONTAINERS.** [Rules certif. cargo contain.]. **Main/Corp** American Bureau of Shipping. **VFOAT** Certification of Cargo Containers. (19??)-. English. an. $75.00. American Bureau of Shipping, 2 World Trade Center, 106th Floor, New York NY 10048. **Tel** (212)839-5000, FAX (201)368-0255, telex RCA 232099. **ED** Donald L. Monroe. **LC** TS195.6; .A45a. **DD** 688.8. **Circ:** 200.
**Desc:** Design and strength requirements for the cargo containers. Also, requirements for the certification of container corner castings, marine container chassis, and tank containers for the carriage of dangerous goods.

SZ
**SCHWEIZER VERPACKUNGSKATALOG. VFOAT** Catalogue Suisse de l'Emballage. German (French). an. 25.00F Switzerland; $20.00 US. Verlag Binkert AG, Baslerstrasse 15, CH-4335 Laufenburg Switzerland. **Tel** 011 41 64 697272, FAX 011 41 64 697333. **ED** M Binkert, W Meier and O Oetterli. **LC** TS158; .S34. **DD** 688.8/05. **Ad Acc. Circ:** 4,100. ***Continues** Schweizer Verpackungs- und Transportkatalog.*
**Desc:** Reference book for the packaging industry of Switzerland.

UK
**SELF ADHESIVE MATERIALS & MARKETS BULLETIN.** Bulletin. English. mo (published monthly except Aug. and Dec.). $190.00. Data Transcripts, PO Box 14, Dorking Surrey, RH5 4YN England. **Tel** 011 44 306 884473, FAX 011 44 306 884473. **ED** L. Crane. **Bk Rev. Ad Acc.** ctrl circ.

US/0889-9193
**SEMICONDUCTOR PACKAGING UPDATE.** [Semicond. packag. update]. Vol. 1, No. 1 (1986)-. Periodical. English. Ten times a year. $425.00. Semiconductor Packaging Update, PO Box 218, Neffs PA 18065. **Tel** (215)799-0919, FAX (215)799-2677. **ED** Subash Khadpe. **DD** 338. ctrl circ.

UK
**SPECIALITY PAPER & BOARD MATERIALS & MARKETS BULLETIN.** Bulletin. English. mo (except Aug. and Dec.). £180.00. Data Transcripts, PO Box 14, Dorking Surrey, RH5 4YN England. **Tel** 011 44 306 884473, FAX 011 44 306 884473. **ED** Lynda Crane. **Bk Rev. Ad Acc. Pr Rev.** ctrl circ.
**Desc:** Focuses on special paper and board materials for all uses, markets, companies, tecanology, and new products developments, raw materials, facestock, etc.

US/1055-2340
**SPRAY TECHNOLOGY & MARKETING.** [Spray technol. mark.]. **VFOAT** Spray Technology and Marketing. Vol. 1, No. 1 April (1991)-. Periodical. English. mo. $20.00. Industry Publications Inc / New Jersey, 389 Passaic Avenue, Fairfield NJ 07004. **Tel** (201)227-5151, FAX (201)227-9219. **LC** TS198.P7; S67. **DD** 660/.294515. **CODEN** STEMEJ. available in microform from ABC Database; available on microfilm and microfiche from University Microfilms International (UMI). ***Continues** Aerosol Age, 0001-9291.*
**Ind/Abst** BioBusiness (1991-); F&S Index Plus Text, Int. [Select. Cov.]; PESTDOC; PROMT.

SZ
**SWISS PACKAGING CATALOGUE.** English. an. 26.00F. Verlag Binkert AG, Baslerstrasse 15, CH-4335 Laufenburg Switzerland. **Tel** 011 41 64 697272, FAX 011 41 64 697333. **Ad Acc.** ctrl circ.
**Desc:** Reference book for packaging and the packaging industry in Switzerland.

●CH
**TAI-WAN PAO CHUANG CHI HSIEH PIEN LAN. VFOAT** Taiwan Packaging Machinery Guide. (1992/1993)-. Chinese (English). Tai-Wan Pao Chuang Kung Yeh Tsa Chih She, 5F-1 Number 95 Fu-Kuo Road, Shih-Lin, Taipei Taiwan.

SZ
**TARA.** (1949)-. mo. $137.00 Switzerland; $175.00 other. Tara Verlag AG, Webergasse 28, PO Box 1012, CH-8640 Rapperswil Switzerland. **Tel** 011 41 055 272874, FAX 011 41 055 274524. **ED** P. Senecky. **Ad Acc, Adv Mgr:** R. Schmuki. **Circ:** 6,000.
**Ind/Abst** Abstr. Bull. Inst. Pap. Sci. Tech.; Food Sci. Technol. Abstr.

US/1051-1636
**TARGET (WHEELING, ILL.).** (TARGET.). [Target]. **Added/Corp** Association for Manufacturing Excellence (U.S.). (198?)-. Periodical. English. bm. $125.00. Association for Manufacturing Excellence, 380 Palatine Road, Wheeling IL 60090. **Tel** (708)520-3282. **LC** TS155.A1; T37. **DD** 658.5/005.

US/0892-7146
**TECHPAK.** [TechPak]. **VFOAT** Tech Pak; McGraw-Hill's Techpak. Vol. 1 (March 1987)-. Periodical. English. bw (25 issues). $460.00. Market Research Inc., 2727 Holland Sylvania Road, Suite A, Toledo OH 43615. **Tel** (419)535-7899. **DD** 338. ***Continues** Packaging Letter, 0277-9722.*

IT
**TECNICHE DELL IMBALLAGGIO.** (19??)-. Italian. mo. L96000 Italy; L140000 other. Franco Angeli Riviste SRL, Viale Monza 106, 20127 Milan Italy. **Tel** 011 39 2 2827651, 011 39 2 289562.

●US/1070-9894
**TRANSACTIONS ON COMPONENTS, PACKAGING & MANUFACTURING TECHNOLOGY PART B : TRANSACTIONS ON COMPONENTS, PACKAGING & ADVANCED PACKAGING.** [IEEE trans. compon. packag. manuf. technol. Part B, Adv. packag.]. **Added/Corp** Institute of Electrical and Electronics Engineers. Lasers and Electro-Optics Society (Institute of Electrical and Electronics Engineers) Components, Packaging & Manufacturing Technology Society. **VFOAT** Transactions on Components, Packaging, and Manufacturing Technology. Part B, Advanced Packaging; Advanced Packaging. (1994)-. Periodical. English. Four times a year. $250.00. IEEE, Institution of Electrical and Electronics Engineers, Inc., 345 East 47th Street, New York NY 10017-2394. **Tel** (908)981-1393, FAX (908)981-9667. **(Subscription address:** IEEE / Institute of Electrical and Electronics Engineers, 445 Hoes Lane, PO Box 1331, Piscataway NJ 08855-1331.**) LC** IN PROCESS; TK7869; .I183. **DD** 621. ***Continues** IEEE Transactions on Components, Hybrids, and Manufacturing Technology, 0148-6411.*

GW/0042-4269
**VERPACKUNG.** (DIE VERPACKUNG.). [Verpackung]. (1960)-. Periodical. German (summaries and/or abstracts in English and Russian). mo. 65.00F. Deutscher Judo Verband, Redaktion Ippon Segewaldweg 40, D 12557 Berlin Germany. **Tel** 011 49 711 210770, telex 051 678. **ED** Ralph Walser. **LC** TS158; .V4. **DD** 658.5/64/05. cum. index. **Ad Acc. Circ:** 4,650.
**Desc:** Package design and marketing, packaging and canning, packaging materials and machinery, product information, and industry information.
**Ind/Abst** Food Sci. Technol. Abstr.; Int. Packag. Abstr.

NE
**VERPAKKEN.** Wegener Tijl Tijdschriften Group, Postbus 9943, 1006 AP Amsterdam Netherlands. **Tel** 011 31 20 5182828.

NE
**VERPAKKING.** 1.- Yearly volume; Sept. 1948-. Periodical. Dutch. mo. Tile and Decorative Surfaces, 20335 Ventura Boulevard/Suite 400, Woodland Hills CA 91364. **Tel** (818)704-5555. **LC** HF5770.A1; V4.

GW/0341-7131
**VR. VERPACKUNGS-RUNDSCHAU.** [VR, Verpack.-Rundsch.]. **Added/Corp** Fachnormenausschuss Verpackung im Deutschen Normenausschuss. **VFOAT** Verpackungs-Rundschau. (1974)-. Academic Scholarly Publication. German. mo. DM428.06 Germany; DM536.49 other. P Keppler KG, Industriestrasse 2, D 63150 Heusenstamm Germany. **Tel** 011 49 6104 6060, telex 410 131. **(Subscription address:** Verlagshaus Heusenstamm, Postfach 1353, D 63131 Heusenstamm Germany.**) CODEN** VPKRAV. Documents available from Article Express International, CASDDS. ***Continues** Verpackungs-Rundschau, 0042-4307.*
**Ind/Abst** BioBusiness (1990-); Chem. Abstr. (19??-); Ei Page One (19??-); Eng. Index Annu. (19??-).

KO
**WOLGAN POJANG SANOP. VFOAT** Monthly Packaging Industry; Packaging Industry; Pojang Sanop. Periodical. Korean (Korean). mo. W20,000. Pojang Sanop, 297-4 Toksan-dong Kuro-ku, Seoul Korea. **LC** TS195.A1; W64.

## ABSTRACTING, BIBLIOGRAPHIES AND STATISTICS

UK/0260-7409
**INTERNATIONAL PACKAGING ABSTRACTS.** [Int. packag. abstr.]. **Added/Corp** International Packaging Information Service. Pira (Association). IPA Vol. 1, No. 1 (Jan. 1981)-. Abstracting/Indexing Service. English. mo. £703.00, $1,150.20. Pira International, Randalls Road, Leatherhead, Surrey KT22 7RU England. **Tel** 011 44 372 376161, FAX 011 44 372 377526. **ED** K Brown (editor's address: PIRA, The Research Association for the Paper and Board, Printing and Packaging Industries, Randalls Road, Leatherhead Surrey KT22 7RU UK). **[CCC]. Bk Rev. Pr Rev. Circ:** 1,000. available on CD-ROM; available on an online database; available on microfilm and microfiche from University Microfilms International (UMI). Documents available. ***Continues** PIRA Packaging Abstract.*
**Desc:** Contains information about the packaging industry, company and market information, plastics, packages, containers, food packaging, bulk packaging and regulations.
**Ind/Abst** Abstr. Bull. Inst. Pap. Sci. Tech. (19??-); World Surf. Coat. Abstr. (19??-); World Text. Abstr. (19??-).

US/0162-8097
**STATISTICAL REVIEW (NEW YORK).** (STATISTICAL REVIEW, GROCERS BAGS, GROCERS SACKS AND MERCHANDISE BAGS.). **Main/Corp** Paper Bag Institute, New York. 1974-. Statistical Publication. English. an. Paper Bag Institute, 41 East 42nd Street, New York NY 10017. **LC** HD9839.P28; P32C. **DD** 338.4/7/676330212. ***Formed by the union of** Grocers Bags and Grocers Sacks, 0091-617X **and** Paper Bag Institute, New York. Merchandise Bags.*

# PAINTS AND PAINTING

IT/0394-8501
**ACHADEMIA LEONARDI VINCI. Added/Corp** Armand Hammer Center for Leonardo Studies at UCLA. **VFOAT** ALV Journal. Vol. 1 (1988)-. Periodical. English (French, German and Italian). an. L20000 (1993). Giunti Editore, Via Bolognese 165, 50139 Florence Italy. **Tel** 011 39 55 6679267, FAX 011 39 55 268312, telex 571438. **LC** N6923.L33; A82.
**Ind/Abst** Avery Index Archit. Period. Suppl. Colum. Univ. (1990-); BHA : Biblio. Hist. Art.

US/0098-5430
**AMERICAN PAINT & COATINGS JOURNAL.** [Am. paint coat. j.]. **VFOAT** American Paint and Coatings Journal. **VAT** American Paint and Coatings Journal. Vol. 58, No. 46 (Apr. 29, 1974)-. Periodical. English. wk (52 issues plus 5 convention issues). $25.00 US, American Samoa, Guam & Virgin Islands; $47.00 Canada & Mexico; $52.00 others. American Paint Journal Company, 2911 Washington Avenue, St. Louis MO 63102. **Tel** (314)534-0301. **ED** Chuck Reitter. **LC** TP934; .A53. **DD** 338.4/7/66790973. **CODEN** APCJDB. **[CCC].** Index available. **Bk Rev. Ad Acc. Circ:** 7,000 (ctrl). available on microfilm from University Microfilms International (UMI). Documents available from CASDDS. ***Continues** American Paint Journal, 0003-0317.*
**Desc:** News, technical, business, marketing, regulatory, production statistics, company features of interest at the paint manufacturing industry.
**Ind/Abst** Art Archaeol. Tech. Abstr.; Bus. ASAP (1992-) [Full Txt.]; Bus. Index (1985-); Chem. Abstr.; Chem. Bus. Bull.; Chem. Bus. NewsBase (1985-); Chem. Bus. Update; Chem. Ind. Notes; F&S Index Plus Text, Int. [Select. Cov.]; For. Prod. Abstr.; Gen. BusinessFile (1985-); Gen. Period. Index (1985-); Infomat Int. Bus.; Mag. Search; PROMT; Trade Ind. ASAP [Full Txt.]; Trade Ind. Index (1981-) [Full Txt.]; World Surf. Coat. Abstr.

US/0097-4749
**AMERICAN PAINT & COATINGS JOURNAL. CONVENTION DAILY.** V. 59-1974-. English. da. $25.00. American Paint Journal Company, 2911 Washington Avenue, St. Louis MO 63102. **Tel** (314)534-0301. **ED** Chuck Reitter. **LC** TP934; .A532. **DD** 667/.9/06273. **Bk Rev. Ad Acc. Circ:** 40,000 (ctrl). ***Continues** American Paint Journal. Convention Daily.*
**Desc:** News technical marketing raw material prices and trades of interest to the paint and resin manufacturing industry.
**Ind/Abst** World Surf. Coat. Abstr.

US/0003-0325
**AMERICAN PAINTING CONTRACTOR.** [Am. paint. contract.]. Vol. 40, No. 6 (June 1963)-. Periodical. English. Twelve times a year. $24.00 US, American Samoa, Guam, Puerto Rico & Virgin Islands; $31.00 others. American Paint Journal Company, 2911 Washington Avenue, St. Louis MO 63102. **Tel** (314)534-0301. **ED** Paul Stoecklein. **[CCC]. Bk Rev. Ad Acc. Circ:** 25,000 (ctrl). ***Continues** American Painter and Decorator, 0096-0918.*
**Desc:** How to, general management, health and safety, industrial maintenance, educational and construction subjects pertinent to the paint contracting and paint maintenance markets.
**Ind/Abst** Art Archaeol. Tech. Abstr.; Constr. Index; Corros. Abstr. (-199?); Mag. Search.

BL
**ANUARIO BRASILEIRO DE TINTAS & I.E. E VERNIZES.** Portuguese. Rua Jaceguai 438-2 Andar Cj 5, 01315 Sao Paulo Brazil. **LC** TP934.5; .A55.

NE
**ATELIER. Main/Corp** Amsterdam. Stedelijk Museum. (1965)-. Periodical. Dutch. Uitgeverij de Doelenpers, Ramen 36, 1811 LC Alkmaar Netherlands. **Tel** 011 31 072 152222.

AT/0816-3596
**AUSTRALASIAN PAINT AND PANEL.** [Australas. paint panel]. (1984)-. Periodical. English. Six times a year. 27.00Aus$ Australia; 77.00Aus$ other. Yaffa Publishing Group Pty Ltd., GPO Box 606, Sydney NSW 2001 Australia. **Tel** 011 61 2 2812333, FAX 011 61 2 2812750. **DD** 629.28705.

IT
**CATALOGO DIPINTI DELL 800 : SEMENZATO.** Italian. ir. L120000. Franco Semenzato Spa, Cannaregio 2292, 30121 Venice Italy. **Tel** 011 39 41 721811.

IT
**CATALOGO DIPINTI MODERNI E ARTE CONTEMPORANIA : SEMENZATO.** (19??)-. Italian. ir. Free on request. Franco Semenzato Spa, Cannaregio 2292, 30121 Venice Italy. **Tel** 011 39 41 721811.

CN/0225-6363
**COATINGS.** [Coatings]. Vol. 1 (Sept. 1979)-. Periodical. English. Six times a year (Jan., Mar., May, July, Sept., Nov.). 22.00Can$ Canada; 35.00Can$ US; 50.00Can$ other. Coatings Magazine, 86 Wilson Street, Oakville Ontario L6K 365 Canada. **Tel** (416)844-9773, FAX (416)844-5672. **ED** G. Barry Kay. **DD** 667/.9/05. **[CCC]. Bk Rev. Ad Acc, Adv Mgr:** L. Bonilowsky, **Tel** (416)844-9773. **Circ:** 7,300 (ctrl).
**Desc:** Edited for management in paint, coatings manufacturing, and industrial finishing.
**Ind/Abst** Alum. Ind. Abstr.; Eng. Mater. Abstr.; F&S Index Plus Text, Int. [Select. Cov.]; Met. Abstr.; PROMT; Trade Ind. ASAP [Full Txt.]; Trade Ind. Index [Full Txt.].

US/1041-9144
**COATINGS, DYES & PIGMENTS.** [Coat. dyes pigments]. **Added/Corp** Predicasts, Inc. **VFOAT** Coatings, Dyes and Pigments. (19??)-. Periodical. English. mo. $240.75 (includes 7% tax) Ohio; $225.00 other. Predicasts Inc., A Ziff Communications Company, 11001 Cedar Avenue, Cleveland OH 44106. **Tel** (800)321-6388, (216)795-3000, FAX (216)229-9944, telex 985 604. **(Subscription address:** Information Access Company, PO Box 61000, Department 1851, San Francisco, CA 94161; Phone: (800)321-6388**) DD** 338.

US
**CURRENT INDUSTRIAL REPORTS. MA28F, PAINT AND ALLIED PRODUCTS.** **VFOAT** Paint and Allied Products. 1981-. Government Publication. English. an. $16.00. US Department of Commerce, 14th Street & Constitution Avenue NW, Washington DC 20230. **Tel** (202)482-2000, FAX (202)482-3772. **LC** HD9660.P253; U624. **DD** 381/.456676/0981.
**Desc:** Presents timely data on the production, inventories, and orders of approximately 5,000 products, which represents 40 percent of all US manufacturing.

US
**CURRENT INDUSTRIAL REPORTS. MQ28F, PAINT, VARNISH, AND LACQUER.** ***Title Change.*** **Added/Corp** United States. Bureau of the Census. **VFOAT** Paint, Varnish, and Lacquer. 1st Quarter (1991)-4th Quarter (1992). Government Publication. English. qt. US Department of Commerce, 14th Street & Constitution Avenue NW, Washington DC 20230. **Tel** (202)482-2000, FAX (202)482-3772. Documents available from Documents on Demand. ***Continues*** *Current Industrial Reports. M28F, Paint, Varnish and Lacquer, 0145-5230.* ***Continued by*** *Current Industrial Reports. MQ28F, Paint, Varnish and Lacquer (Computer file).*
**Ind/Abst** Am. Stat. Index.

US
**CURRENT INDUSTRIAL REPORTS. MQ28F PAINT, VARNISH, LACQUER (COMPUTER FILE).** (1992)-. Government Publication. English. qt. US Department of Commerce, 14th Street & Constitution Avenue NW, Washington DC 20230. **Tel** (202)482-2000, FAX (202)482-3772. ***Continues*** *Currrent Industrial Reports. MQ28F Paint, Varnish, Lacquer.*

DK/0905-6440
**DANSKE MALERMESTRE.** **Added/Corp** Danske Malermestre (Society). (1990)-. Trade Publication. Danish. mo (January). kr285.00. Danske Malermestre, Snaregade 12, DK-1205 Copenhagen K, Denmark. **Tel** 45-33-93-36-00, FAX 45-33-93-42-10. **ED** Adam Pade. **Bk Rev. Circ:** 3,000 (ctrl). ***Continues*** *Malermesteren, 0025-1364.*

GW/0012-009X
**DEFAZET. DEUTSCHE FARBEN-ZEITSCHRIFT.** (DEFAZET.). [DEFAZET. Dtsch. Farben-Z.]. **VFOAT** Deutsche Farben-Zeitschrift. Vol. 27, No. 4 (April 1973)-. Academic Scholarly Publication. German. Twelve times a year. Edition Lack und Chemie Elvira Moeller GmbH, Postfach 1168, W 7024 Filderstadt 1 Germany. **Tel** 011 49 711 704800. **LC** TP934; .D4. **CODEN** DFZTBF. Documents available from CASDDS. ***Continues*** *Defazet-Aktuell, 0366-8975.*
**Ind/Abst** Chem. Abstr.; EMBASE; Energy Res. Abstr. (April 1973-); Saf. Health Work.

GW/0012-0448
**DEUTSCHE MALERBLATT, DAS.** **Added/Corp** Hauptverband des Deutschen Maler- und Lackiererhandwerks. (19??)-. Periodical. German. mo. DM129.60 Germany; DM135.60 other. DVA Deutsche Verlagsanstalt, Neckarstrasse 121, D-70190 Stuttgart Germany. **Tel** 011 49 711 26310. **(Subscription address:** Zenit Pressvertrieb GmbH, Postfach 810640, D 70523 Stuttgart Germany.**) ED** Karl Apel. **LC** TT300; .D4. **DD** 667/.9. **[CCC]. Circ:** 18,700.
**Ind/Abst** Biodeter. Abstr.; World Surf. Coat. Abstr.

FR/0012-5709
**DOUBLE LIAISON.** [Double liaison]. (1954)-. Academic Scholarly Publication. French. mo. 430.00F (French Edition), 520.00F (Bilingual Edition). EREC, 68 rue Jean-Jaures, F-92800 Puteaux France. **Tel** (33 1)47 73 01 23, FAX (33 1) 49 00 05 91. **ED** Annik Chauvel. **CODEN** DOLIA8. Index available. **Bk Rev. Ad Acc.** Documents available from CASDDS. ***Absorbed*** *Chemie des Peintures, 0009-434X.*
**Desc:** Covers paintings, varnish, ink printing, fine paints, glues and adhesives, raw materials and fabricated materials and their applications in artwork.
**Ind/Abst** Alum. Ind. Abstr.; Art Archaeol. Tech. Abstr.; Chem. Abstr.; Met. Abstr.; Print. Abstr.; World Surf. Coat. Abstr.

FR/0012-5709
**DOUBLE LIAISON-CHIMIE DES PEINTURES.** (1954)-. Academic Scholarly Publication. French (English). mo. 416.00F. Double Liaison-Chimie des Peintures, 68 rue Jean Jaures, 92800 Puteaux France. **Tel** (1)47730123, telex (1) 49 00 05 91. **ED** Annik Chauvel. Index available. **Bk Rev. Ad Acc. Circ:** 4,700. Documents available from CASDDS.
**Desc:** The sole French review about paints, inks, and adhesives.
**Ind/Abst** Chem. Abstr.; F&S Index Plus Text, Int. [Select. Cov.]; Predicasts F&S Index, U. S. Annu. Ed.

UK/0143-7208
**DYES AND PIGMENTS.** (DYES AND PIGMENTS : AN INTERNATIONAL JOURNAL.). [Dyes pigm.]. Vol. 1, No. 1 (July/Sept 1980)-. Academic Scholarly Publication. English. Twelve times a year. $701.00 The Americas; £470.00 other. Elsevier Applied Science, An Imprint of Elsevier Science Ltd., The Boulevard, Langford Lane, Kidlington, Oxford OX5 1GB United Kingdom. **Tel** 011 44 865 843000, 011 44 865 843699, FAX 011 44 865 843010. **(Subscription address:** Elsevier Science Ltd. Oxford Fulfillment Centre, PO Box 800, Kidlington, Oxford OX5 1DX United Kingdom.**) ED** A. T. Peters. **LC** TP890; .D964. **DD** 667/.2/05. **CODEN** DYPIDX. **[CCC]. Bk Rev. Ad Acc. Pr Rev. Circ:** 200. available on microfilm and microfiche from University Microfilms International (UMI). Documents available from Article Express International, The Genuine Article, CASDDS.
**Desc:** Covers the scientific and technical aspects of the chemistry and physics of dyes, pigments and their intermediates.
**Ind/Abst** Art Archaeol. Tech. Abstr.; Bioeng. Abstr.; Chem Inform; Chem. Abstr.; Chem. Titles; Curr. Contents Eng. Tech. Appl. Sci.; Ei Page One; Eng. Mater. Abstr.; Eng. Index Annu.; Leadscan; Met. Abstr.; Life Sci. Collect.; Polymer Contents; Res. Alert [Full Cov.]; Sci. Cit. Index; SCISEARCH; Text. Technol. Dig.; World Surf. Coat. Abstr.

NE/0920-2099
**EISMA 'S VAKPERS.** [Eisma 's vakpers]. (1986)-. Trade Publication. Dutch. sm (24 issues per year). Fl149.00 Netherlands; Fl210.00 other. De Uitgevery Eisma BV, Postbus 340, 8901 BC Leewarden Netherlands. **Tel** 058-152545, FAX 058-154000. **ED** F Klaas, C Dijkstra, F P de Vilder and C Winterink. **UDC** 691 75-023. cum. index. **Bk Rev. Ad Acc. Pr Rev. Circ:** 6,765. ***Continues*** *Eisma's Schildersblad, 0013-287X.*
**Desc:** A general professional trade journal for painters and finishing companies. Information about painting, coating, wallcoating and insulation.

UK/0955-2804
**EMULSION POLYMERISATION AND POLYMER EMULSIONS.** (19??)-. English. Twelve times a year. £240.00 (members); £280.00 others. The Paint Research Association, 8 Waldegrave Road, Teddington, Middlesex TW11 8LD England. **Tel** 11 44 81 977 4427, FAX 11 44 81 943 4705, telex 928720. **Circ:** 65 (ctrl). ***Absorbed*** *Application of Polymer Emulsions, 0143-716X.*
**Desc:** Collects together detailed summaries with illustrative formulations and examples of patents, journal articles, conference papers, etc., about polymer emulsions; non-coating uses of polymer emulsions included.
**Ind/Abst** Chem. Abstr.

UK/0264-9047
**EUROPEAN ADHESIVES AND SEALANTS.** [Eur. adhes. sealants]. **VFOAT** European Adhesives and Sealants. (1983)-. Periodical. English. qt. £78.25 UK; £91.35, $141.60 other. Argus Press Group, Queensway House, 2 Queensway Redhill, Surrey RH1 1QS England. **Tel** 011 44 737 768611, 011 44 737 761685, FAX 011 44 737 760510, telex 948669 TOPJNL G. **ED** John Ward. **DD** 668.305. Index available. **Ad Acc. Circ:** 3,200. available on an online database (file 16/Full-Text) from DIALOG.
**Desc:** Technical articles on adhesives and sealant application, latest developments in raw materials, reviews on process applications equipment, general industry news and new product information.
**Ind/Abst** Chem. Bus. Bull.; Chem. Bus. NewsBase; Chem. Bus. Update; F&S Index Plus Text, Int.; Infomat Int. Bus.; PROMT.

GW/0930-3847
**EUROPEAN COATINGS JOURNAL.** [Eur. coat. j.]. (1986)-. Periodical. Multiple languages. Ten times a year. DM219.00. Curt R. Vincentz Verlag, Postfach 6247, D 30062 Hannover Germany. **Tel** 011 49 511 990980, FAX 011 49 511 9909899, telex 923846. **UDC** 678.026.3. **[CCC].**

UK/0266-7800
**EUROPEAN PAINT AND RESIN NEWS.** [Eur. paint resin news]. (1984)-. Periodical. English. mo. £160.00 UK; £205.00 Europe; $413.00 other. Information Research Ltd, 262 Regent Street, London W1R 5DA England. **Tel** 44 71 4344536, FAX 44 71 2879322. **ED** Mrs. Cvetka Fuller. Index available. **Circ:** 200. ***Continues*** *Continental Paint and Resin News, 0010-7735.*
**Desc:** Provides a regular update of significant news items in the coatings industry and includes acquisitions and industry changes; new plants and plant expansions; marketing news and statistics; financial results and comparisons; recent technology developments; forthcoming symposia and exhibitions; European patents review.
**Ind/Abst** Chem. Bus. Bull.; Chem. Bus. NewsBase (1985-); Chem. Bus. Update.

UK/0963-8474
**EUROPEAN POLYMERS PAINT COLOUR JOURNAL.** [Euro. polym. paint. colour. j.]. **Added/Corp** Paintmakers Association of Great Britain. **VFOAT** Polymers Paint Colour Journal. Vol. 180, No. 4260 (May 9, 1990)-. Academic Scholarly Publication. English. bw. £110.80 UK; £138.00, $215.30 other. Argus Press Group, Queensway House, 2 Queensway Redhill, Surrey RH1 1QS England. **Tel** 011 44 737 768611, 011 44 737 761685, FAX 011 44 737 760510, telex 948669 TOPJNL G. **LC** TP934; .P333. **DD** 667/.6/05. **CODEN** EPPJEJ. available on an online database (file 16,648/Full-Text) from DIALOG. Documents available from CASDDS. ***Continues*** *Polymers Paint Colour Journal, 0370-1158.*
**Desc:** Covers paint manufacture and raw materials and additives for plastics, printing inks, adhesives and allied industries.
**Ind/Abst** Chem. Abstr. (1991-); Chem. Ind. Notes; Coal Abstr.; EMBASE; F&S Index Plus Text, Int. [Full Txt.] [Select. Cov.]; Infomat Int. Bus.; Print. Abstr.; PROMT [Full Txt.]; Trade Ind. ASAP [Full Txt.]; Trade Ind. Index [Full Txt.]; World Surf. Coat. Abstr.

GW
**FARBE + I.E. UND LACK ADRESSBUCH MIT BEZUGSQUELLENNACHWEIS.** German. be. Curt R. Vincentz Verlag, Postfach 6247, D 30062 Hannover Germany. **Tel** 011 49 511 990980, FAX 011 49 511 9909899, telex 923846. **ED** Barbara Harms and Renate Weber. **LC** TP934.5; .F37. Index available. **Bk Rev. Ad Acc. Circ:** 1,500 (ctrl).
**Desc:** Gives detailed information on the paints, varnishes, synthetic materials, wallpapers, sealants and adhesives industries on the wholesale and retail trades on the raw materials suppliers and importers as well as on the commercial agents dealing in these fields.

GW/0014-7699
**FARBE + LACK.** [Farbe Lack]. **VFOAT** Farbe und Lack. Vol. 70, No. 1 (Jan. 1964)-. Academic Scholarly Publication. German (summaries and/or abstracts in English and French). mo. DM140.00 Germany; DM174.00 other. Curt R. Vincentz Verlag, Postfach 6247, D 30062 Hannover Germany. **Tel** 011 49 511 990980, FAX 011 49 511 9909899, telex 923846. **ED** Lothar Vincentz and Erlwine Dewald. **[CCC].** Index available. **Bk Rev. Ad Acc. Circ:** 5,268 (ctrl). available on microfilm and microfiche from University Microfilms International (UMI). Documents available from CASDDS. ***Continues*** *Farbe und Lack.*
**Desc:** Provides coverage of the paints and pigments industry. Contains original papers on research, applications and developments in materials and equipment.
**Ind/Abst** Anal. Abstr.; Art Archaeol. Tech. Abstr.; Chem. Abstr.; Chem. Bus. Bull.; Chem. Bus. NewsBase (1985-); Chem. Bus. Update; Chem. Ind. Notes; Coal Abstr.; Ei Page One; EMBASE; Energy Res. Abstr. (Jan. 1971-); F&S Index Plus Text, Int. [Select. Cov.]; For. Prod. Abstr. (19??-19??); Infomat Int. Bus.; Int. Packag. Abstr.; Leadscan; PROMT; Surf. Treat. Technol. Abstr.; World Surf. Coat. Abstr.

DK/0106-7559
**FARG OCH LACK SCANDINAVIA.** [Farg lack Scand.]. (Jan. 1980)-. Periodical. Danish (summaries and/or abstracts in English). mo. kr710.00. Farg Och Lack Scandinavia, Herlev Hovegade 201 B, DK 2730 Herlev Denmark. **Tel** 011 45 42 843398. **CODEN** FLSCDT.

Documents available from CASDDS. ***Continues*** *Skandinavisk Tidskrift for Farg Och Lack.*
**Ind/Abst** Chem. Abstr.

GE/0430-2222
**FATIPEC CONGRESS / ORGANISE PAR L'ASSOCIATION FRANCAISE DES TECHNICIENS DES PEINTURES ET VERNIS (A.F.T.P.V.).** **Added/Corp** L'Association Francaise des Techniciens des Peintures et Vernis (A.F.T.P.V.) Federation d'Associations de Techniciens des Industries des Peintures, Vernis, Emaux et Encres d'Imprimerie de l'Europe Continentale. **VFOAT** Congres FATIPEC; FATIPEC Kongress. (19??)-. French (German and English). **CODEN** FAPVAP. Documents available from CASDDS.
**Ind/Abst** Chem. Abstr.

UK/0264-2506
**FINISHING.** [Finishing]. Vol. 6, No. 6 (June 1982)-. Academic Scholarly Publication. English. mo. £65.00 UK; £81.00 other. Turret Group, 177 Hagden Lane, Watford Herts WD1 8LN United Kingdom. **Tel** 011 44 923 228577, FAX 011 44 923 221346. **ED** Peter De Lacey. **LC** TS670.A1; F56. **DD** 671.7/05. **CODEN** FINIE2. **Bk Rev. Ad Acc. Circ:** 4,200 (ctrl). available on microfilm from University Microfilms International (UMI). Documents available from Article Express International, Ask*IEEE, CASDDS. ***Continues*** *Finishing Industries, 0309-3018.*
**Desc:** All aspects of surface finishing, including electroplating, powder coating and paint finishes, plus associated pretreatments and application equipment.
**Ind/Abst** Alum. Ind. Abstr.; Chem. Abstr. (1982-1985); Curr. Technol. Index; Ei Page One; Eng. Mater. Abstr.; Eng. Index Annu.; INSPEC (June 1982-); Int. Packag. Abstr.; Leadscan; Met. Abstr.; Surf. Treat. Technol. Abstr.; World Surf. Coat. Abstr.

US
**FORMULARY OF PAINTS AND OTHER COATINGS.** Periodical. English. Chemical Publishing Company / New York, 80 Eighth Avenue, Room 1101, New York NY 10011. **Tel** (212)555-1950.

US
**INDUSTRIAL FINISHING. BUYERS' GUIDE.** **VFOAT** Buyers' Guide; Industrial Finishing Buyers Guide. '84-'85-. Consumer Publication. English. an. $30.00 US; $40.00 Canada and Mexico. Hitchcock Publishing Company, 191 South Gary Avenue, Carol Stream IL 60188. **Tel** (708)665-1000. **(Subscription address:** Fulfillment Office, PO Box C-409, Birmingham, AL 35283-0409**) ED** Greg Beels and Joe Schrantz. **LC** TT303; .I53. **DD** 667/.9/02573. **Ad Acc. Circ:** 36,000 (ctrl).
**Desc:** Written for those involved in the manufacture and application of industrial coatings as a source book of suppliers.

US/0019-8323
**INDUSTRIAL FINISHING (WHEATON).** ***Title Change.*** (INDUSTRIAL FINISHING.). [Ind. finish.]. **VFOAT** Finishing, Industrial. Vol. 1 (Nov. 1924)-(1993). Academic Scholarly Publication. English. mo. Chilton Company, 201 King of Prussia Road, Radnor PA 19089. **Tel** (610)964-4122, (800)695-1214, FAX (610)964-4978, telex 6851035 CHILTON UW. **ED** Greg Beels, Joe Schrantz. **LC** TT325.A1; I6. **DD** 667/.9/05. **CODEN** IFIIAJ. **[CCC]. Bk Rev. Ad Acc. Circ:** 36,000 (ctrl). available on microfilm from University Microfilms International (UMI); available on an online database (file 648/Full-Text) from DIALOG. Documents available from Article Express International, CASDDS, Documents on Demand. ***Continued by*** *Industrial Paint & Powder, 1073-4651.*
**Desc:** Reports on advances in manufacturing and application techniques for paint manufacturers, finishers and their suppliers.
**Ind/Abst** Alum. Ind. Abstr.; Appl. Sci. Technol. Index (-1990); Biodeter. Abstr. (1991-); Bioeng. Abstr.; Bus. ASAP (1990-) [Full Txt.]; Bus. Index (1985-); Bus. Source (Jan. 1993-); Ceram. Abstr.; Chem. Abstr. (1924-1984); Ei Page One; EMBASE; Energy Inf. Abstr.; Eng. Mater. Abstr.; Eng. Index Annu. [Select. Cov.]; Environ. Abstr.; Gen. BusinessFile (1985-); Gen. Period. Index (1985-); Mag. Search; Met. Abstr.; Surf. Treat. Technol. Abstr.; Trade Ind. ASAP [Full Txt.]; Trade Ind. Index (1981-) [Full Txt.]; Vocat. Search (July 1993-).

●US/1073-4651
**INDUSTRIAL PAINT & POWDER.** [Ind. paint powder]. **VFOAT** Industrial Paint and Powder; Paint & Powder; Paint and Powder. Vol. 69, No. 10 (Oct. 1993)-. Academic Scholarly Publication. English. mo. $60.00 US. Chilton Company, 201 King of Prussia Road, Radnor PA 19089. **Tel** (610)964-4122, (800)695-1214, FAX (610)964-4978, telex 6851035 CHILTON UW. **LC** TT325.A1; I6. **DD** 667/.9/05. Documents available from Documents on Demand. ***Continues*** *Industrial Finishing, 0019-8323.*
**Ind/Abst** EMBASE; Energy Inf. Abstr.; Environ. Abstr.; Met. Abstr.; Sel. Water Resour. Abstr.; Trade Ind. Index; World Alum. Abstr.

GW/0019-9109
**INDUSTRIE LACKIER BETRIEB.** [Ind.-Lackier-Betrieb]. (1944)-. Academic Scholarly Publication. English. Twelve times a year. DM138.00 Germany; DM162.00 other. Curt R. Vincentz Verlag, Postfach 6247, D 30062 Hannover Germany. **Tel** 011 49 511 990980, FAX 011 49 511 9909899, telex 923846. **ED** Olaf Luckert. **CODEN** ILBEAE. **[CCC].** Index available. cum. index. **Bk Rev. Ad Acc. Pr Rev. Circ:** 2,923 (ctrl). Documents available from CASDDS.
**Desc:** For the organic surface treatment industries. Articles by experts, interviews and reports on all aspects of modern industrial coatings applications.
**Ind/Abst** Art Archaeol. Tech. Abstr.; Chem. Abstr.; CIS Abstr.; EMBASE; Energy Res. Abstr. (April 1978-);; Saf. Health Work; World Surf. Coat. Abstr.

US/0361-8773
**JCT, JOURNAL OF COATINGS TECHNOLOGY.** [JCT, J. coat. technol.]. **Added/Corp** Federation of Societies for Coatings Technology. **VFOAT** Journal of Coatings Technology. Vol. 48 No. 612 (Jan. 1976)-. Periodical. English. Twelve times a year. $30.00 (US & Canada); $60.00 (Europe); $45.00 (other). Federation of Society Coatings Technology, 492 Norristown Road, Blue Bell PA 19422. **Tel** (215)940-0777. **LC** TP934; .F44. **DD** 667/.9/05. **CODEN** JCTEDL. **[CCC].** Index available in last issue of volume--attached. cum. index. **Bk Rev. Ad Acc. Pr Rev.** available on microfilm and microfiche from University Microfilms International (UMI); available on an online database (file 648/Full-Text) from DIALOG. Documents available from Article Express International, The Genuine Article, CASDDS. ***Continues*** *Journal of Paint Technology, 0022-3352.*
**Ind/Abst** Abstr. Graphic Arts Tech. Found. (1984-); Alum. Ind. Abstr.; Appl. Sci. Technol. Index; Art Archaeol. Tech. Abstr.; Biodeter. Abstr. (1991-); Bioeng. Abstr.; Chem. Abstr.; Corros. Abstr. (199?-); Curr. Contents Eng. Tech. Appl. Sci.; Curr. Titles Electrochem.; Ei Page One; EMBASE; Eng. Index Annu.; F&S Index Plus Text, Int. [Select. Cov.]; Graph. Arts Bull. Inst. Pap. Sci. Technol. (Jan. 1989, Nov. 1989); Int. Aerosp. Abstr.; Int. Packag. Abstr.; Mater. Sci. Eng. Abstr.; Met. Abstr.; Pollut. Abstr. Indexes; Print. Abstr.; PROMT; Res. Alert [Full Cov.]; Sci. Cit. Index; SCISEARCH; Trade Ind. ASAP [Full Txt.]; Trade Ind. Index [Full Txt.]; World Surf. Coat. Abstr.

US/0163-4526
**JOURNAL OF WATER BORNE COATINGS.** [J. water borne coat.]. V. 1- Feb. 1978-. Academic Scholarly Publication. English. qt. $78.00 US; $89.00 other. Technology Marketing Corporation, One Technology Plaza, Norwalk CT 06854. **Tel** (203)852-6800, FAX (203)853-2845. **ED** Carolyn Kovachik. **UDC** 667.637.233. **CODEN** JWBCDV. Index available. cum. index. **Bk Rev. Ad Acc. Circ:** 1,500. Documents available from Article Express International, CASDDS.
**Desc:** Features the latest developments and applications of water borne coatings.
**Ind/Abst** Bioeng. Abstr.; Chem. Abstr.; Ei Page One; Eng. Index Annu.

RU/0023-737X
**LAKOKRASOCHNYE MATERIALY I IKH PRIMENENIE.** Vol. 1 (1960)-. Academic Scholarly Publication. Russian. bm. $89.95. Gosudarstvennyi Komitet Soveta Ministrov SSSR, PO Pechati, Moscow Russia. **(Subscription address:** East View Publications Inc., 3020 Harbor Lane North, Suite 110, Minneapolis MN 55447.**) CODEN** LAMAAD. Index available. Documents available from CASDDS.
**Ind/Abst** Anal. Abstr.; Biodeter. Abstr. (1991-); Chem. Abstr.; World Surf. Coat. Abstr.

UK
**LEISURE PAINTER AND CRAFTSMAN.** English. mo. £21.50 UK; $49.00 US; 59.00Can$ Canada; 34.00p Southern Ireland; £25.00 other. Artist Publishing Company Ltd, Caxton House, 63-65 High Street, Tenterden Kent TN30 6BD England. **Tel** 011 44 5806-3315, FAX 011 44 5806-5411. **ED** Irene Briers. Index available. **Bk Rev. Ad Acc, Adv Mgr:** P. Hunter. **Circ:** 23,000.

GW/0938-9865
**MITTEILUNGEN DES VEREINS DEUTSCHER EMAILFACHLEUTE E.V. (1990).** (MITTEILUNGEN DES VEREINS DEUTSCHER EMAILFACHLEUTE E.V.). (1990)-. Academic Scholarly Publication. German. mo. Documents available from CASDDS. ***Continues*** *Mitteilungen des Vereins Deutscher Emailfachleute E.V. und des Deutschen Email-Zentrums E.V., 0723-886X.*
**Ind/Abst** Ceram. Abstr. (199?-); Chem. Abstr.

US/0098-7786
**MODERN PAINT AND COATINGS.** [Mod. paint coat.]. Vol. 65 (Jan. 1975)-. Periodical. English. Twelve times a year. $48.00 (surface mail), $108.00 (airmail) one year. Argus Business, 6151 Powers Ferry Road, Atlanta GA 30339. **Tel** (404)995-2500, (800)233-3359. **LC** TP934; .P25. **DD** 667/.9/05. **CODEN** MPCODM. **[CCC].** available on microfilm and microfiche from University Microfilms International (UMI); available on an online database (files 15,648/Full-Text) from DIALOG. Documents available from CASDDS. ***Continues*** *PVP. Paint and Varnish Production, 0190-9533.*
**Ind/Abst** Anal. Abstr.; Appl. Sci. Technol. Index; Art Archaeol. Tech. Abstr.; Chem. Abstr.; Chem. Ind. Notes; EMBASE; F&S Index Plus Text, Int. [Select. Cov.]; Infomat Int. Bus.; Leadscan; PROMT; Trade Ind. ASAP [Full Txt.]; Trade Ind. Index [Full Txt.]; World Surf. Coat. Abstr.

SZ/0048-1270
**OBERFLACHE - SURFACE.** ***Title Change.*** **See** Metals and Metallurgy.

US/0884-3848
**PAINT & COATINGS INDUSTRY.** [Paint coat. ind.]. **VFOAT** Paint and Coatings Industry; PCI. Vol. 1, No. 1 (Jan./Feb. 1985)-. Trade Publication. English. Nine times a year. $49.00 US; $61.00 Canada; $85.00 other. Business News Publishing Company, 755 West Big Beaver Road, Suite 1000, Troy MI 48084. **Tel** (810)362-3700, FAX (810)362-0317, telex 230295. **DD** 667. **Bk Rev. Ad Acc. Circ:** 12,000 (ctrl). ***Continues in part*** *Western Paint & Decorating, 0274-8703.*
**Desc:** Edited for administrative, production, research and development, engineering, purchasing and marketing personnel in the manufacturing of paints, coatings, adhesives, sealants and printing inks.
**Ind/Abst** Biodeter. Abstr. (1991-); F&S Index Plus Text, Int. [Select. Cov.]; PROMT; Vocat. Search (July 1993-); World Surf. Coat. Abstr.

UK/0953-9891
**PAINT & INK INTERNATIONAL.** **VFOAT** Paint and Ink International. (198?)-. Periodical. English. qt. £78.40 UK; £99.80, $154.75 other. Argus Press Group, Queensway House, 2 Queensway Redhill, Surrey RH1 1QS England. **Tel** 011 44 737 768611, 011 44 737 761685, FAX 011 44 737 760510, telex 948669 TOPJNL G. **ED** Tom Mulligan. Index available. **Bk Rev. Ad Acc. Circ:** 5,504. available on an online database (file 16/Full-Text) from DIALOG.
**Desc:** Development in the coatings industry. Technical articles for the paint and printing ink industry worldwide.
**Ind/Abst** F&S Index Plus Text, Int. [Full Txt.] [Select. Cov.]; PROMT [Full Txt.].

UK/0261-5746
**PAINT & RESIN.** [Paint resin]. **VFOAT** Paint and Resin. Vol. 51, No. 2 (March/April 1981)-. Academic Scholarly Publication. English. bm. £59.00 UK; £82.00 other. Turret Group, 177 Hagden Lane, Watford Herts WD1 8LN United Kingdom. **Tel** 011 44 923 228577, FAX 011 44 923 221346. **ED** Nick Dellow. **LC** TP934; .P33. **DD** 667/.6/05. **CODEN** PTRNDJ. **Bk Rev. Ad Acc. Circ:** 2,000. Documents available from CASDDS. ***Continues*** *Paint Manufacture Incorporating Resin News, 0030-9508.*
**Desc:** Details of developments in raw materials and equipment for the paint, ink and varnish industries, marketing developments, company news, etc.
**Ind/Abst** Biodeter. Abstr.; Chem. Abstr.; Curr. Technol. Index; EMBASE; F&S Index Plus Text, Int. [Select. Cov.]; Infomat Int. Bus.; Leadscan; PROMT; World Surf. Coat. Abstr.

US/0090-5402
**PAINT RED BOOK.** (1968)-. English. an. $54.95. Argus Business, 6151 Powers Ferry Road, Atlanta GA 30339. **Tel** (404)995-2500, (800)233-3359. **LC** TP934.5; .P34. **DD** 338.4/7/66760257. **[CCC].**

II/0556-4409
**PAINTINDIA.** (1951)-. Academic Scholarly Publication. English. Twelve times a year. $50.00. Colour Publications Private, 126A Dhuruwadi Off, c/o Dr. Nariman, Bombay 400025 India. **Tel** 011 91 22 4309318 6319, telex 71242 CEPE. Documents available from CASDDS. ***Superseded in part by*** *Paintindia. Annual, 0030-9540.*
**Desc:** Technical articles, special columns and news reports pertaining to the paint and printing ink manufacturing industries.
**Ind/Abst** Art Archaeol. Tech. Abstr.; Biodeter. Abstr. (19??-19??); Chem. Abstr.; World Surf. Coat. Abstr.

II/0030-9540
**PAINTINDIA. ANNUAL.** (PAINTINDIA.). [Paintindia, Annu.]. **VAT** Paint India. Annual. (1968)-. Academic Scholarly Publication. English. an. Colour Publications Private, 126A Dhuruwadi Off, c/o Dr. Nariman, Bombay 400025 India. **Tel** 011 91 22 4309318 6319, telex 71242 CEPE. **ED** R.V. Raghavan. **LC** TP934; .P37. **DD** 338.4/7/66760954. **CODEN** PIDABZ. **Bk Rev. Ad Acc. Circ:** 4,889. available on microfilm from University Microfilms International (UMI). Documents available from CASDDS. ***Supersedes in part*** *Paintindia.*
**Desc:** Technical articles, special columns and news reports pertaining to the paint and printing ink manufacturing industries.
**Ind/Abst** Art Archaeol. Tech. Abstr.; Biodeter. Abstr. (19??-19??); Chem. Abstr.; World Surf. Coat. Abstr.

UK/0956-9227
**PAINTING & DECORATING (LONDON, ENGLAND).** (PAINTING & DECORATING : JOURNAL OF NATIONAL FEDERATION OF PAINTING AND DECORATING CONTRACTORS.). **VFOAT** Painting and Decorating. Periodical. English. bm. £15.00 (surface mail), £25.50 (airmail) other countries. National Federation of Painting and Decorating Contractors, 82 Cavendish Street, London W1M 8AD England. **LC** NK1160; .J683. ***Continues*** *Painting & Decorating Journal.*
**Ind/Abst** World Surf. Coat. Abstr.

US/0735-9713
**PAINTING & WALLCOVERING CONTRACTOR.** (PAINTING & WALLCOVERING CONTRACTOR : MAGAZINE OF THE PAINTING & DECORATING CONTRACTORS OF AMERICA.). **Added/Corp** Painting & Decorating Contractors of America. **VFOAT** Painting and Wallcovering Contractor; PWC. Vol. 45, No. 2 (Feb. 1983)-. Periodical. English. bm. $15.00 (US); $47.00 (other). Painting and Decorating Contractor of America, 3913 Old Lee Highway, Suite 33B, Fairfax VA 22030. **LC** TT300; .P235. **DD** 698/.1/05. **Bk Rev. Ad Acc. Circ:** 25,000 (ctrl). ***Continues*** *Professional Decorating & Coating Action, 0099-0310.*

UK/0369-9420
**PIGMENT & RESIN TECHNOLOGY.** [Pigm. resin technol.]. **VFOAT** Pigment and Resin Technology. Vol. 1 (Jan. 1972)-. Academic Scholarly Publication. English. bm (6 issues). $154.00. MCB University Press, 60 62 Toller Lane, Bradford West Yorkshire BD8 9BX England. **Tel** 011 44 274 499821, FAX 011 44 274 547143, telex 51317 MCBUNI G. **(Subscription address:** MCB University Press / US and Canada Subscriptions, PO Box 10812, Birmingham AL 35201-0812.**) ED** J E Bean. **LC** TP934; .P342. **DD** 667/.623/05. **CODEN** PGRTBC. **Bk Rev. Ad Acc. Circ:** 1,550. Documents available from CASDDS. ***Supersedes*** *Paint Technology.*
**Desc:** A publication dealing with the formulation and manufacture of paints, printing, inks, and adhesives.
**Ind/Abst** Anal. Abstr.; Art Archaeol. Tech. Abstr.; Biodeter. Abstr. (19??-19??); Chem. Abstr.; Chem. Bus. Bull.; Chem. Bus. NewsBase (1985-); Chem. Bus. Update; Curr. Technol. Index; EMBASE; F&S Index Plus Text, Int. [Select. Cov.]; Graph. Arts Bull. Inst. Pap. Sci. Technol. (March 1989-); Leadscan; Print. Abstr.; PROMT; World Surf. Coat. Abstr.

SP/0031-9953
**PINTURAS Y ACABADOS INDUSTRIALES.** [Pint. acab. ind.]. (1959)-. Academic Scholarly Publication. Spanish. Eight times a year. $120.00. Cedel, PO Box 5326, Barcelona Spain. **Tel** 011 34 3 215 6039. **ED** Jose O. Avila. **LC** TT300; .P55. **CODEN** PACIDY. **Bk Rev. Ad Acc. Circ:** 8,000. Documents available from CASDDS.
**Desc:** News and information on metals, industrial finishing, painting and electroplating.
**Ind/Abst** Art Archaeol. Tech. Abstr.; Chem. Abstr.; Sug. Indus. Abstr.; Surf. Treat. Technol. Abstr.; World Surf. Coat. Abstr.

US/0360-3164
**PLATING AND SURFACE FINISHING.** [Plating surf. finish.]. **Added/Corp** American Electroplaters' Society. American Electroplaters and Surface Finishers Society. Vol. 62, No. 4 (April 1975)-. Academic Scholarly Publication. English. Twelve times a year. $45.00 North America, $65.00 other (surface mail); $180.00 (airmail). American Electroplaters Society, 12644 Research Parkway, Orlando FL 32826-3225. **Tel** (407)281-6441, (800)334-2052, FAX (407)281-6446, telex 510 601 6246. **LC** TS670; .A3. **DD** 671.7/3/05. **CODEN** PSFMDH. **Bk Rev. Ad Acc. Pr Rev. Circ:** 10,000 (ctrl). available on microfilm and microfiche from University Microfilms International (UMI). Documents available from Article Express International, The Genuine Article, Ask*IEEE, CASDDS. ***Continues*** *Plating, 0032-1397;* ***Absorbed*** *AES Research Report, 0361-0411.*
**Desc:** For professionals in the surface finishing industry. Includes articles and technical papers on electronics, pollution control, electroplating, painting and other finishing operations.
**Ind/Abst** Alum. Ind. Abstr.; Appl. Sci. Technol. Index; Bioeng. Abstr.; Chem. Abstr.; Curr. Contents Eng. Tech. Appl. Sci.; Curr. Titles Electrochem.; Ei Page One; EMBASE; Eng. Mater. Abstr.; Eng. Index Annu.; INSPEC (May 1975-); Leadscan; Met. Abstr.; Res. Alert [Full Cov.]; Sci. Cit. Index; SCISEARCH; Soc. Sci. Cit. Index [Select. Cov.]; Surf. Treat. Technol. Abstr.

FR
**POLYMERES PEINTURES BOIS, F24.** French. 1403.88F France; 1460.00F other. Institut de l'Information Scientique et Technique (INIST), 2 Allee du Parc de Brabois, 54514 Vandoeuvre Nancy Cedex France. **Tel** 011 33 83 504600, FAX 011 33 83 504650. ***Continues*** *Pascal Folio, F24. Polymers Peintures Bois.*

UK/0078-7817
**POLYMERS PAINT COLOUR YEAR BOOK.** **VFOAT** Polymers Paint & Colour Year Book. (19??)-. English. an. £96.60 UK; $161.33 other. Argus Press Group, Queensway House, 2 Queensway Redhill, Surrey RH1 1QS England. **Tel** 011 44 737 768611, 011 44 737 761685, FAX 011 44 737 760510, telex 948669 TOPJNL G. **ED** R Robin. **LC** TP934.5; .P64. **DD** 338.4/7/6676025. **Ad Acc. Circ:** 1,126.
**Desc:** Journal for the surface coatings industry keeping readers abreast of technical and commercial developments.

US/0163-4542
**POWDER COATINGS.** ***Ceased.*** [Powder coat.]. Vol. 1 (Mar. 1978)-Ceased Vol. 8, No. 2 (1985). Academic Scholarly Publication. English. qt. Technology Marketing Corporation, One Technology Plaza, Norwalk CT 06854. **Tel** (203)852-6800, FAX (203)853-2845. **UDC** 621.793.8. **CODEN** PCOADG. **Bk Rev. Ad Acc. Circ:** 1,000. Documents available from Article Express International, CASDDS.
**Desc:** Concentrates on practical applications, markets, and research and development news as reported by the International Powder Coatings Community.
**Ind/Abst** Bioeng. Abstr.; Chem. Abstr.; Ei Page One; Eng. Index Annu.

UK/0140-8445
**POWDER COATINGS BULLETIN.** **VFOAT** Powder Coatings. (1978)-. Newsletter. English. mo. $300.00 US; £150.00 EC and other. Royal Society of Chemistry, Thomas Graham House, Science Park, Cambridge CB4 4WF England. **Tel** 011 44 223 420066, FAX 011 44 223 423429, telex 818293 ROYAL. **(Subscription address:** Turpin Distribution Services Limited, Blackhorse Road, Letchworth, Hertfordshire SG6 1HN, United Kingdom.**) ED** S. T. Harris. **Bk Rev. Circ:** 300 (ctrl).
**Desc:** Up-to-date technical and market developments in powder coatings technology.

UK
**PROFESSIONAL PAINTER & DECORATOR.** (19??)-. Periodical. English. Eight times a year. £15.00 UK; £25.00 other. David Pescod Associates, Old Chapel, 69 Primrose Hill, K. Langley Herts WD48HX England. **Tel** 0442 832715, FAX 0923 260085. ***Continues*** *Painting & Decorating Journal.*

SZ/0300-9440
**PROGRESS IN ORGANIC COATINGS.** [Prog. org. coat.]. Vol. 1 (March 1972)-. Periodical. English. Eight times a year (2 vols.). 910.00F. Elsevier Sequoia SA, PO Box 564, CH-1001 Lausanne 1 Switzerland. **Tel** 011 41 21 3207381. **ED** W. Funke, G.P. Bierwagen, A.L.L. Palluei. **CODEN** POGCAT. **Ad Acc, Adv Mgr:** Ms. W van Cattenburch (Amsterdam). **Pr Rev.** available on microfilm from University Microfilms International (UMI). Documents available from Article Express International, The Genuine Article, CASDDS.
**Desc:** Aim is to summarize and analyze the progress and current state of knowledge in the field of organic coatings and related subjects; chemical, physical and technological properties of organic coatings and related material, problems and methods of preparation, manufacture and application of these materials, performance testing and analysis are covered.
**Ind/Abst** Abstr. Graphic Arts Tech. Found. (1979, 1984); Alum. Ind. Abstr.; Art Archaeol. Tech. Abstr.; Biodeter. Abstr.; Bioeng. Abstr.; Chem. Abstr.; Corros. Abstr.; Curr. Contents Eng. Tech. Appl. Sci.; Curr. Titles Electrochem.; Ei Page One; Energy Res. Abstr. (March 1982-); Eng. Mater. Abstr.; Eng. Index Annu.; Index Sci. Rev. [Full Cov.]; Met. Abstr.; Phys. Briefs; Polymer Contents; Res. Alert [Full Cov.]; Sci. Cit. Index; SCISEARCH; World Surf. Coat. Abstr.

UK/0966-9698
**RADNEWS TEDDINGTON.** [RadnewsTeddingt.]. (1992)-. Periodical. English. Four times a year. £75.00. The Paint Research Association, 8 Waldegrave Road, Teddington, Middlesex TW11 8LD England. **Tel** 11 44 81 977 4427, FAX 11 44 81 943 4705, telex 928720. **DD** 338.476602982.
**Desc:** A technical bulletin dedicated to the radiation curing industry. Focuses on research and development through production and to the end users. Features include technical innovations, new products, new legislation and health information.

US/8755-0261
**RAUCH GUIDE TO THE U.S. PAINT INDUSTRY, THE.** [Rauch guide U.S. paint ind.]. **Added/Corp** Rauch Associates. **VFOAT** Rauch Guide to the US Paint Industry; US Paint Industry; U.S. Paint Industry. **VAT** Rauch Guide to the United States Paint Industry. (1984)-. English. ir. $170.00. Rauch Associates, PO Box 6802, Bridgewater NJ 08807. **Tel** (908)231-9548. **ED** James A. Rauch. **LC** HD9660.P253; U665. **DD** 338.4/76676/0973.
**Desc:** Contains industry data on production, uses and suppliers.

UK/0144-6266
**RECENT ADVANCES IN CROSSLINKING & CURING.** [Recent adv. crosslink. curing]. **VFOAT** Recent Advances in Crosslinking and Curing. (1980)-. Periodical. English. Six times a year. £190.00. The Paint Research Association, 8 Waldegrave Road, Teddington, Middlesex TW11 8LD England. **Tel** 11 44 81 977 4427, FAX 11 44 81 943 4705, telex 928720.
**Desc:** Covers polymers with reactive groups, self-crosslinking, radiation cure, autoxidative drying, and siloxanes. Also cure studies, resin types, curing catalysts, curable coatings, etc.

IT/0048-8348
**RIVISTA DEL COLORE, VERNICIATURA INDUSTRIALE, LA.** [Riv. colore vernic. ind.]. **VFOAT** Verniciatura Industriale. (19??)-. Academic Scholarly Publication. Italian. mo. 100000L Italy, 200000L other. La Rivista Del Colore SRL, Via Imbriani #10, 20121 Milan Italy. **Tel** 011 39 2 3761227. **CODEN** RCLRA3. Documents available from CASDDS.
**Ind/Abst** Art Archaeol. Tech. Abstr.; Chem. Abstr.; World Surf. Coat. Abstr.

IT
**SMALTO.** **Added/Corp** Centro Italiano Smalti Porcellanati. Vol. 30, No. 1 (1988)-. Academic Scholarly Publication. Italian. Three times a year. CISP Milan, Via Olona 41, 20016 Pero Mi Italy. **Tel** 011 39 2 38103333. **LC** TS700; .C37. **DD** 666/.2/05. Documents available from CASDDS. ***Continues*** *Notiziario del Centro Italiano Smalti Porcellanati.*
**Ind/Abst** Ceram. Abstr. (19??-); Chem. Abstr.

UK/0268-9766
**SURFACE COATING & RAW MATERIAL DIRECTORY.** [Surf. coat raw mater. div.]. **VFOAT** Surface Coating and Raw Material Directory. (1986)-. Academic Scholarly Publication. English. an (June). £55.00 UK; £61.00 others. Industrial Trade Journals Ltd, Stakes House, Quebec Square, Westerham Kent TN161TD England. **Tel** 011 44 0959 564212, FAX 011 44 0959 562325. **ED** Cathy Neale. **DD** 338.47669094. **Ad Acc, Adv Mgr:** John Lane, **Tel** 011 44 061 442 5828. **Acid Free. Circ:** 3,000. available in print.
**Desc:** A comprehensive publication serving the paint, colour, printing, ink and allied industries throughout Europe and available for worldwide distribution.

UK/0964-928X
**SURFACE COATINGS INTERNATIONAL : JOCCA, JOURNAL OF THE OIL AND COLOUR CHEMISTS' ASSOCIATION.** **Added/Corp** Oil and Colour Chemists' Association (Great Britain) Society of British Printing Ink Manufacturers. Paintmakers Association of Great Britain. **VFOAT** Journal of the Oil and Colour Chemists' Association; JOCCA. Vol. 74, No. 2 (Feb. 1991)-. Academic Scholarly Publication. English. mo. $210.00 North America; £135.00 UK and Europe; £120.00 other. Oil Colour Chemists Association, 967 Harrow Road, Priory House, Wembley Middlesex HA0 2SF England. **Tel** (081)908-1086, FAX (081)908-1219, telex 922670. **ED** Lindsay Gale. **LC** TP934; .O5. **DD** 667/.6/0941. **CODEN** SCOIE6. Index available. Documents available from The Genuine Article, CASDDS. ***Continues*** *Oil and Colour Chemists' Association (Great Britain). Journal of the Oil & Colour Chemists' Association.*
**Desc:** Contains news of the UK surface coating industries and details of technical meetings organized by the Oil & colour Chemists' Association.
**Ind/Abst** Chem. Abstr.; Curr. Contents Eng. Tech. Appl. Sci.; Res. Alert [Full Cov.]; Sci. Cit. Index; SCISEARCH.

FR/0585-9840
**SURFACES.** **See** Metals and Metallurgy.

KO
**TORYO WA TOJANG.** **VFOAT** The Paint & Finish; Paint and Finish; Paint & Finish. Periodical. Korean (Korean). bm. 20,000. Hanguk Toryo Tojang Yonguso, PO Box 7152, Chungang Ucheguk. **LC** TP934; .T67. **UDC** 667.6.

CH/0253-4312
**TULIAO GONGYE.** (TU LIAO KUNG YEH.). [Tuliao gongye]. **VFOAT** Paint & Coatings Industry; P.C.I.; Paint and Coatings Industry; PCI. Academic Scholarly Publication. Chinese (table of contents in English). bm. NT$6.00. Science Press, 16 Donghuangchenggen North Street, Beijing 100707, People's Republic of China. **Tel** 011 86 1 4019821, 011 86 1 4010642, FAX 011 86 1 4012180, 011 86 1 4019810, telex 210147. **UDC** 667.6. **CODEN** TLKYD5. **Ad Acc. Circ:** 13,000. Documents available from CASDDS.
**Desc:** Deals with the research, technology and advance of coatings, pigments and additives in China and outside. Application of coatings also is introduced.
**Ind/Abst** Chem. Abstr.

NE/0042-3904
**VERFKRONIEK.** **See** Printing Industry.

UK/0140-8798
**WATERBORNE & HIGH SOLIDS COATINGS BULLETIN.** [Waterborne high solids coat. bull.]. **VFOAT** Waterborne and High Solids Coatings Bulletin. (1978)-. English. Twelve times a year. £150.00. The Paint Research Association, 8 Waldegrave Road, Teddington, Middlesex TW11 8LD England. **Tel** 11 44 81 977 4427, FAX 11 44 81 943 4705, telex 928720.
**Desc:** A critical survey of recent publications and patents; includes news items.

UK/0043-9088
**WORLD SURFACE COATINGS ABSTRACTS.** **See** Paints and Painting-Abstracting, Bibliographies and Statistics.

## ABSTRACTING, BIBLIOGRAPHIES AND STATISTICS

UK/0967-2508
**CORE. COATINGS, REGULATIONS AND THE ENVIRONMENT.** [CORE. Coat. regul. environ.]. **VFOAT** Coatings, Regulations and the Environment. (1992)-. English. Twelve times a year. £160.00. The Paint Research Association, 8 Waldegrave Road, Teddington, Middlesex TW11 8LD England. **Tel** 11 44 81 977 4427, FAX 11 44 81 943 4705, telex 928720. **DD** 344.10446. ***Supersedes*** *Hazards, Pollution and Legislation in the Coatings Field.*
**Desc:** Legislation from around the world along with literature on toxic materials, atmospheric pollution, waste disposal, transport, paint application, etc., presented in abstract form.

UK/0144-4425
**PAINT TITLES.** [Paint titles]. (1971)-. English. Fifty-two times a year. £440.00. The Paint Research Association, 8 Waldegrave Road, Teddington, Middlesex TW11 8LD England. **Tel** 11 44 81 977 4427, FAX 11 44 81 943 4705, telex 928720. **(Subscription address:** US/ 395 Saw Mill River Road, Elmsford, NY 10523; Can/ 150 Consumers Road/Suite 104, Willowdale Ontario M2J 1P9; Aus-NZ/ POB 544, Potts Point NSW 2011**)** **ED** S C Haworth. **[CCC]. Bk Rev. Circ:** 400. available on microfilm and microfiche from University Microfilms International (UMI).
**Desc:** A bibliographic listing of approximately 230 items each week. Short summaries are provided of European and British patents and titles are extended where necessary.

UK/0043-9088
**WORLD SURFACE COATINGS ABSTRACTS.** [World surf. coat. abstr.]. **Added/Corp** Research Association of British Paint, Colour and Varnish Manufacturers. Vol. 42, No. 319 (Jan. 1969)-. Abstracting/Indexing Service. English. Thirteen times a year. £940.00. The Paint Research Association, 8 Waldegrave Road, Teddington, Middlesex TW11 8LD England. **Tel** 11 44 81 977 4427, FAX 11 44 81 943 4705, telex 928720. **ED** Norman R. Morgan. **LC** Z7914.P15; R48; TP935. **DD** 016.667/9. **[CCC].** Index available. available in microform from ORBIT; available on magnetic tape from ORBIT; available on an online database from ORBIT; available on microfilm and microfiche from University Microfilms International (UMI). ***Continues*** *Review of Current Literature Relating to the Paint, Colour, Varnish and Allied Industries.*
**Desc:** An abstracts journal containing 10,000 abstracts a year on all aspects of paints, from raw materials to formulations, and their uses. Also covers properties, hazards, pollution, legislation, statistics, company activities, standards, etc.
**Ind/Abst** Abstr. Bull. Inst. Pap. Sci. Tech.; Anal. Abstr.; BMT Abstr.; Int. Packag. Abstr.; Pap. Board Abstr.; Print. Abstr.; Surf. Treat. Technol. Abstr.

# PALEONTOLOGY

PL/0567-7920
**ACTA PALAEONTOLOGICA POLONICA.** [Acta Palaeontol. Pol.]. **Added/Corp** Polska Akademia Nauk. Komitet Geologiczny. Zakad Paleobiologii (Polska Akademia Nauk) Zakad Paleozoologii (Polska Akademia Nauk). Vol. 1, No. 1 (1956)-. Periodical. Polish (English; summaries and/or abstracts in French and Russian; table of contents in French and Russian). qt. Price on Request. **(Subscription address:** ARS Polona, PO Box 1001, 00068 Warsaw Poland.**)** **LC** QE755.P7; A6. **CODEN** APGPAC. Documents available from BIOSIS Document Express.
**Ind/Abst** Biol. Abstr.; Life Sci. Collect.

US/0276-444X
**ADDRESS DIRECTORY / SOCIETY OF VERTEBRATE PALEONTOLOGY.** [Address dir. - Soc. Vertebr. Paleontol.]. **Main/Corp** Society of Vertebrate Paleontology. (19??)-. Directory. English. be. $12.50 (two year). Florida Paleontological Society, Florida State Museum, University of Florida, Gainesville FL 32611. **Tel** (904)392-1721. **LC** QE841; .S65a. **DD** 566/.06/01.

AT/0311-5518
**ALCHERINGA (SYDNEY).** (ALCHERINGA.). [Alcheringa]. Vol. 1 (1975)-. Periodical. English. Twice a year (Apr., & Sept.). 65.00Aus$ (individuals); 95.00Aus$ (institutions). Geological Society of Australia, 504 Wynyard House, 301 George Street, Sydney New South Wales 2000 Australia. **Tel** 011 61 2 2902194, FAX 011 61 02 290-2198. **ED** J. Pickett. **LC** QE758.A1; A4. **DD** 560/.99. **UDC** 56(93). **CODEN** ALCHDB. **[CCC].** Index available. cum. index. **Pr Rev. Circ:** 700. Documents available from The Genuine Article, Petroleum Abstracts Document Delivery Service.
**Desc:** Journal of Australasian paleontology.
**Ind/Abst** AESIS Q.; Curr. Contents Phys. Chem. Earth Sci.; Geol. Abstr.; GeoRef; Pet. Abstr.; Res. Alert [Full Cov.]; Sci. Cit. Index; SCISEARCH.

AG/0002-7014
**AMEGHINIANA.** [Ameghiniana]. **Added/Corp** Asociacion Paleontologica Argentina. Vol. 1 (Jan. 1957)-. Spanish (English, French and Portuguese; summaries and/or abstracts in English). Four times a year. Asociacion Paleontologica Argentina, Maipu 645 Piso 1 5047, 1006 Buenos Aires Argentina. **Tel** 011 54 1 3222820. **ED** Gustavo Scillato-Yane. **LC** QE752.A7; A38. **CODEN** AMGHB2. **[CCC].** Index available (volume 1-20). **Bk Rev. Ad Acc. Pr Rev. Circ:** 800 (ctrl). Documents available from BIOSIS Document Express.
**Desc:** Writings on all aspects of palaeontology and related areas such as biostratigraphy palaeobiology.
**Ind/Abst** Biol. Abstr.; GeoRef.

US/0003-0082
**AMERICAN MUSEUM NOVITATES.** **See** Zoology.

FR/0980-157X
**ANNALES DE LA FOUNDATION FYSSEN.** **See** Anthropology.

FR/0767-7367
**ANNALES DE LA SOCIETE GEOLOGIQUE DU NORD.** **See** Earth Sciences-Geology.

FR/0753-3969
**ANNALES DE PALEONTOLOGIE (1982).** (ANNALES DE PALEONTOLOGIE.). [Ann. paleontol.]. Vol. 68, No. 1 (1982)-. French. qt. $340.00. Masson Editeur, Box Postale 22, 41353 Vineuil 16 France. **Tel** 011 33 54 438994. **(Subscription address:** 7A Boulevard de Perolles, CH-1701 Fribourg Switzerland**)** **[CCC].** available on microfilm and microfiche from University Microfilms International (UMI). Documents available from BIOSIS Document Express. ***Formed by the union of*** *Annales de Paleontologie. Invertebres, 0570-1619* ***and*** *Annales de Paleontologie. Vertebres, 0570-1627.*
**Ind/Abst** Biol. Abstr.; Geol. Abstr.; GeoRef; Life Sci. Collect.

GW/0587-5404
**ARGUMENTA PALAEOBOTANICA.** [Argum. palaeobot.]. (1966)-. Monographic series. English (German). ir. Price varies per volume. R A Remy Verlag, Postiege 20, D 48161 Meunster Germany. **Tel** 011 49 251 861623. **LC** QE901; .A75. **CODEN** ARPBCV.
**Ind/Abst** GeoRef.

AU/1017-5563
**BEITRAGE ZUR PALAONTOLOGIE VON OSTERREICH.** (BEITRAEGE ZUR PALAONTOLOGIE VON OSTERREICH / HERAUSGEGEBEN VOM PALAONTOLOGISCHEN INSTITUT DER UNIVERSITAT WIEN.). [Beitr. Palaontol. Osterr.]. **Added/Corp** Universitat Wien. Palaontologisches und Palaobiologisches Institut. Universitat Wien. Institut fuer Palaontologie. No. 1 (1976)-. Monographic series. German. ir. Price varies per volume. Koeltz Scientific Books, PO Box 1360, D 61453 Koenigstein Germany. **Tel** 011 49 6174 4492, 3189, FAX 011 49 6174 1634. **LC** QE755.A8; B44. **CODEN** BPOEDX. ctrl circ. Documents available from BIOSIS Document Express.
**Ind/Abst** Biol. Abstr.; GeoRef.

GW/0172-8784
**BERLINER GEOWISSENSCHAFTLICHE ABHANDLUNGEN. REIHE A. GEOLOGIE UND PALAONTOLOGIE.** **See** Earth Sciences-Geology.

US/0300-7227
**BIBLIOGRAPHY AND INDEX OF MICROPALEONTOLOGY.** **See** Paleontology-Abstracting, Bibliographies and Statistics.

IT/0375-7633
**BOLLETTINO DELLA SOCIETA PALEONTOLOGICA ITALIANA.** [Boll. soc. paleontol. ital.]. **Main/Corp** Societa Paleontologica Italiana. Vol. 1 (1960)-. Bulletin. Italian (English, French, German and Spanish; summaries and/or abstracts in English). Three times a year. L100000 institutions; 60000 (individuals) Italy and EEC; 80000 (individuals) other. Societa Paleontologica Italiana, Via Universita 4, 4100 Modena Italy. **Tel** 011 39 59 217084. **ED** E. Serpagli (editor's address: Istituto di Paleontologia, Via Universita 4, Modena Italy). **LC** QE755.I8; .S6a. **CODEN** BSPIAY. Index available in last issue of volume--attached. cum. index. **Circ:** 800. Documents available from BIOSIS Document Express.
**Ind/Abst** Biol. Abstr.; GeoRef.

US/0897-2451
**BULLETIN OF PALEOMALACOLOGY.** ***Ceased.*** Vol. 1 (1988)-Ceased Vol.2 (1989). Bulletin. English. qt. Coastal Education Research Foundation Inc, PO Box 8068, Charlottesville VA 22906. **DD** 564.

US/0160-4937
**BULLETIN OF THE SOUTHERN CALIFORNIA PALEONTOLOGICAL SOCIETY.** [Bull. South. Calif. Paleontol. Soc.]. **Main/Corp** Southern California Paleontological Society. (1960)-. Bulletin. English. bm. $17.00. Southern California Paleontological Society, Emma King, 1826 9th Street, Manhattan Beach CA 90266-6204. **Tel** (213)379-0496. **ED** Floyd A. Jenkins (editor's address: PO Box 45041, Los Angeles CA 90045; editor's telephone: (213)338-7482). Index available. cum. index (Vol. 19, No. five and six). **Bk Rev. Circ:** 120 (ctrl).
**Desc:** Original articles and reports of society activities and also occasional reprints of articles from other professional and amateur publications.
**Ind/Abst** GeoRef.

US/0007-5779
**BULLETINS OF AMERICAN PALEONTOLOGY.** [Bull. Am. paleontol.]. **Added/Corp** Paleontological Research Institution (Ithaca, N.Y.) Columbia University. Vol. 1, No. 1 (May 1895)-. Monographic series. English. Twice a year. Price varies per volume. Paleontological Research Institution, 1259 Trumansburg Road, Ithaca NY 14850. **Tel** (607)273-6623, FAX (607)273-6620. **LC** UNC. **CODEN** BAPLAJ. Index available. **Circ:** 500 (ctrl). Documents available from Petroleum Abstracts Document Delivery Service.
**Desc:** A publication outlet for longer manuscripts that use fossils as the data base or that provide neontological information for application in paleontological studies.
**Ind/Abst** GeoRef; Int. Aerosp. Abstr.; Pet. Abstr.

FR/0068-5054
**CAHIERS DE MICROPALEONTOLOGIE.** [Cah. micropaleontol.]. 1965-. Monographic series. French (summaries and/or abstracts in English). qt. Price varies per volume. Editions du CNRS, 22 rue Saint Armand, F 75015 Paris France. **Tel** 011 33 1 45075050. **LC** QE719; .C338. **UDC** 56:576.8. **[CCC]. Circ:** 1,500.
**Desc:** Original articles covering the entire field of micropaleontology.
**Ind/Abst** GeoRef.

GW
**CATALOGUE OF CONODONTS.** (1973)-. Monographic series. English. ir. Price varies per volume. E. Schweizerbartsche Verlagsbuchhandlung, Johannesstrasse 3A, D-70176 Stuttgart Germany. **Tel** 011 49 711 625001, FAX 011 49 711 625005, telex 723363 SCHB D. **ED** Willi Ziegler. **Bk Rev. Ad Acc.**

US/0097-3556
**CONTRIBUTIONS FROM THE MUSEUM OF PALEONTOLOGY.** (CONTRIBUTIONS FROM THE MUSEUM OF PALEONTOLOGY / UNIVERSITY OF MICHIGAN.). [Contrib. Mus. Paleontol.]. **Added/Corp** University of Michigan. Museum of Paleontology. Vol. 3, No. 1 (1928)-. Monographic series. English. ir. Price varies per volume. Contributions from the Museum of Paleontology, University of Michigan, Ann Arbor MI 48104. **LC** QE701; .M5. **DD** 560/.5. **CODEN** UMMPA3. Documents available from BIOSIS Document Express. ***Continues*** *Contributions from the Museum of Geology, 0883-8879.*
**Ind/Abst** Biol. Abstr.; GeoRef.

US/0160-8843
**CONTRIBUTIONS SERIES - AMERICAN ASSOCIATION OF STRATIGRAPHIC PALYNOLOGISTS.** **See** Earth Sciences-Geology.

UK/0195-6671
**CRETACEOUS RESEARCH.** [Cretac. res.]. Vol. 1, No. 1 (March 1980)-. Academic Scholarly Publication. English (summaries and/or abstracts in French). Six times a year. $465.00. Academic Press Ltd., A Division of Harcourt Brace & Company Ltd., 24-28 Oval Road, London NW1 7DX England. **Tel** 071 267 4466, FAX 071 482 2293, 071 485 4752, telex 25775 ACPRES G. **(Subscription address:** Harcourt Brace & Company, Ltd., Foots Cray, High Street, Sidcup Kent DA14 5HP England.**)** **ED** D. Batten and N. Mateer. **LC** QE685; .C875. **DD** 551.7/7/05. **UDC** 551.763: 56(116.3). **CODEN** CRRSDD. **[CCC].** Documents available from The Genuine Article, Petroleum Abstracts Document Delivery Service, CASDDS.
**Desc:** Publishes research on all aspects of the Cretaceous period, including its boundaries with the Jurassic and Tertiary. Papers reporting detailed investigations of Cretaceous stratigraphy and palaeontology and studies of regional geological features are complemented by short communications of significant new findings.
**Ind/Abst** AESIS Q.; Chem. Abstr.; Curr. Contents Phys. Chem. Earth Sci.; Geogr. Abstr. Phys. Geogr.; Geol. Abstr.; GeoRef; Pet. Abstr.; Res. Alert [Full Cov.]; Sci. Cit. Index.

US/8755-898X
**CURRENT RESEARCH IN THE PLEISTOCENE.** **See** Anthropology.

US/0886-3806
**CYPRIS.** [Cypris]. (19??)-. Periodical. English. an. Free. North East Louisiana Univ, Dept of Geosciences, Monroe LA 71209. **Tel** (318)342-1000, 342-1878. **DD** 565. ***Continues*** *Ostracodologist, 0085-4573.*

NE/0920-5446
**DEVELOPMENTS IN PALEONTOLOGY AND STRATIGRAPHY.** [Dev. palaeontol. stratigr.]. 1975-. Academic Scholarly Publication. English. Price varies per volume. Elsevier Science Publishers BV, PO Box 211, 1000 AE Amsterdam Netherlands. **Tel** 011 31 20 5803642, FAX 011 31 20 5862696, telex 15682. **UDC** 551.7: 56. **CODEN** DPSTEJ. Documents available from CASDDS.
**Ind/Abst** Chem. Abstr. (1984-); GeoRef.

●US/1060-4006
**DINOSAUR REVIEW (BOULDER, COLO.), THE.** (THE DINOSAUR REVIEW.). (1992)-. Periodical. English. qt. $18.00. Dinosaur Publications, PO Box 2307, Boulder CO 80306.

GW/0174-4224
**EARLY MAN NEWS. Added/Corp** International Union for Quaternary Research. Commission for the Paleology of Early Man. Vol. 1 (1976)-. English. an. Institute fuer Ur und Frueh, Abteilung Aeltere Gesc Schloss, D-72070 Tuebingen Germany. **Tel** 011 49 7071 292416. **LC** GN700; .E17. **DD** 930.1/05.
**Ind/Abst** Anthropol. Lit.

FR
**ETUDES QUATERNAIRES LANGUEDOCIENNES.** Issue No. 1 (1st Semester 1981)-. Periodical. French (English and Spanish). sa. 100.00F France; $15.00 other. Etudes Quaternaires Languedociennes Laboratoire de Prehistoire de Vauvert, 4 Avenue Robert Gourdon, F-30600 Vauvert France. **Tel** 66.88.46.80. **ED** F Bazile. **DD** 560/.1/78. **UDC** 551.79(448.1/.7); 551.583.79(448.1/.7). Index available. cum. index. **Bk Rev. Circ:** 300 (ctrl).
**Desc:** Covering geology, palaeoclimatology, and prehistoric life studies.

FR/0768-3650
**ETUDES QUATERNAIRES. MEMOIRE.**
**See** Earth Sciences-Geology.

RU/0201-9280
**EZHEGODNIK. Main/Corp** Vsesoiuznoe Paleontologicheskoe Obshchestvo. V. 1- ; 1916- . Russian (French). **LC** QE701. **UDC** 56. **CODEN** EVPOA4.
**Ind/Abst** GeoRef.

RU
**EZHEGODNIK VSESOIUZNOGO PALEONTOLOGICHESKOGO OBSHCHESTVA. Added/Corp** Vsesoiuznoe Paleontologicheskoe Obshchestvo. Vol. 16, (1956)-. Russian. ir. **LC** QE701; .V8. **DD** 560/.5. ***Continues*** *Ezhegodnik Vserossiskogo Paleontologicheskogo Obshchestva.*

GW/0172-9179
**FACIES.** [Facies]. **Added/Corp** Friedrich-Alexander-Universitat Erlangen-Nurnberg. Institut fuer Palaontologie. (1979)-. Periodical. German (English; summaries and/or abstracts in English). sa. DM120.00. Institut fur Palaontologie, Loewenichstrasse 28, D91054 Erlangen Germany. **Tel** 011 49 9131 852622. **ED** Erik Flugel and Erentraud Flugel. **LC** QE640; .F33. **DD** 551.7. **Circ:** 300. Documents available from Petroleum Abstracts Document Delivery Service.
**Desc:** Papers on facies analysis, paleoecology, sedimentology and basin analysis.
**Ind/Abst** Ecol. Abstr.; Geogr. Abstr. Phys. Geogr.; Geol. Abstr.; GeoRef; Pet. Abstr.

CN/1183-0298
**FIELD GUIDE TO THE PALEONTOLOGY OF ... / CANADIAN PALEONTOLOGY CONFERENCE, A.** [Field guide paleontol.]. **Added/Corp** Geological Association of Canada. Paleontology Division. Pander Society. 1st (Aug. 1991)-. English. Limited free distribution. Canadian Paleontology Conference, c/o Paleontology Division, Geological Association of Canada, Department of Earth Sciences, Memorial University of Newfoundland, St John's, Newfoundland A1B 3X5 Canada. **DD** 560.

NE
**FORRILIUM CATALOGUS. I: ANIMALIA.** (1913)-. Latin. Kugler Publications BV / Amsterdam, PO Box 11188, 1001 GD Amsterdam Netherlands. **Tel** 011 31 20 6278070. **ED** F Frech and F Westphal. **CODEN** FCANDB.
**Ind/Abst** GeoRef.

NE
**FOSSILIUM CATALOGUS. II: PLANTAE.** (1913)-. Monographic series. English. ir. Price varies per volume. Kugler Publications BV / Amsterdam, PO Box 11188, 1001 GD Amsterdam Netherlands. **Tel** 011 31 20 6278070. **CODEN** FOSCBE.
**Ind/Abst** GeoRef.

FR/0293-843X
**GEOBIOS (LYON, FRANCE).** (GEOBIOS MEMOIRE SPECIAL.). [Geobios, Mem. Spec.]. **VFOAT** Memoire Special. (1977)-. Monographic series. French (English). an. Price varies per volume. Geobios Service Promotion, 43 Boulevard du 11 Novembre, 69622 Villeurbanne France. **Tel** 011 33 72 668000 ext.3881.
**Ind/Abst** GeoRef.

FR/0016-6995
**GEOBIOS (LYON, FRANCE).** (GEOBIOS.). [Geobios]. **Added/Corp** Universite Claude Bernard. Departement de Geologie. Universite de Lyon. Departement des Sciences de la Terre. No. 1, (1968)-. Periodical. French (English). bm. $150.00 EEC countries; $170.00 other. Geobios Service Promotion, 43 Boulevard du 11 Novembre, 69622 Villeurbanne France. **Tel** 011 33 72 668000 ext.3881. **ED** P Racheboeuf (editor's phone: 33 72 668616). **CODEN** GEBSAJ. **Bk Rev**, (Qty: 6). **Pr Rev. Circ:** 500. Documents available from BIOSIS Document Express, Petroleum Abstracts Document Delivery Service.
**Desc:** An important journal of paleontology in all its aspects; paleoecology, biostratigraphy and biogeography.
**Ind/Abst** Biol. Abstr.; Curr. Contents Phys. Chem. Earth Sci.; Ecol. Abstr. (?-?); GeoRef; Pet. Abstr.; Protozoolog. Abstr.; Rev. Med. Vet. Mycology; Rev. Plant Pathol.

GW/0072-1018
**GEOLOGICA ET PALAEONTOLOGICA.**
**See** Earth Sciences-Geology.

HU/0374-1893
**GEOLOGICA HUNGARICA. SERIES PALAEONTOLOGICA.** [Geol. Hung., Ser. palaeontol.]. **Added/Corp** Magyar Tudomanyos Akademia. Magyar Allami Foeldtani Intezet. **VFOAT** Series Palaeontologica. Issue 1 (1929)-. English (French, German, Hungarian and Russian). ir. £45.00. Collets Holdings Ltd, Denington Road, Wellingborough Northamptonshire NN8 2QT, England. **Tel** 011 44 933 224351, FAX 011 44 933 76402, telex 317320 COLLET G. **LC** QE755.H9; G4. **CODEN** GHPADH. Documents available from BIOSIS Document Express. ***Continues in part*** *Palaeontologia Hungarica.*
**Ind/Abst** Biol. Abstr.; GeoRef.

GW/0534-0403
**GOTTINGER ARBEITEN ZUR GEOLOGIE UND PALAONTOLOGIE. See** Earth Sciences-Geology.

CC/1000-3118
**GUJIZHUI DONGWU XUEBAO.** (KU CHI CHUI TUNG WU HSUEH PAO.). [Gujizhui dongwu xuebao]. **Added/Corp** Chung-Kuo Ko Hsueh Yuan. Ku Chi Chui Tung Wu Yu Ku Jen Lei Yen Chiu So. **VFOAT** Vertebrata Palasiatica. (1984)-. Academic Scholarly Publication. Chinese (summaries and/or abstracts in English). qt. $98.00. Science Press, 16 Donghuangchenggen North Street, Beijing 100707, People's Republic of China. **Tel** 011 86 1 4019821, 011 86 1 4010642, FAX 011 86 1 4012180, 011 86 1 4019810, telex 210147. ***Continues*** *Ku Chi Chui Tung Wu Yu Ku Jen Lei.*

CC/0001-6616
**GUSHENG WUXUE BAO.** (KU SHENG WU HSUEH PAO.). [Gusheng wuxue bao]. **VFOAT** Acta Palaeontologica Sinica. (1953)-. Academic Scholarly Publication. Chinese (summaries and/or abstracts in English). bm. $87.60. Science Press, 16 Donghuangchenggen North Street, Beijing 100707, People's Republic of China. **Tel** 011 86 1 4019821, 011 86 1 4010642, FAX 011 86 1 4012180, 011 86 1 4019810, telex 210147. **(Subscription address:** China International Book Trading Corporation, PO Box 399, Library Service Department, Beijing 100044 People's Republic of China.**) LC** QE701. **DD** 560. **UDC** 56(51). **CODEN** KSWHAT.
**Desc:** Contains information on paleontology.
**Ind/Abst** GeoRef.

UK/0255-013X
**INA NEWSLETTER.** [INA newsl.]. **VFOAT** International Nannoplankton Association newsletter. (1979)-. Periodical. English. sa. £15.00. Nicky Hine, Sheffield University, Industrial Palynology Unit, Mappin Street, Sheffield S1 3JD England. **Tel** 011 44 602 363410, FAX 011 44 602 363200, telex 727343. **ED** Dr. J.R. Young. **UDC** 55. **Bk Rev. Ad Acc. Pr Rev. Circ:** 300.
**Desc:** For calcareous nannoplankton.

TU/0256-6672
**INTERNATIONAL QUARTERLY OF ENTOMOLOGY. See** Zoology-Entomology.

SZ/0252-1881
**JAHRBUCH DER SCHWEIZERISCHEN GESELLSCHAFT FUER UR- UND FRUHGESCHICHTE. See** Archaeology.

GW/0078-2947
**JAHRESBERICHTE UND MITTEILUNGEN DES OBERRHEINISCHEN GEOLOGISCHEN VEREINES. See** Earth Sciences-Geology.

UK/0262-821X
**JOURNAL OF MICROPALEONTOLOGY.** (JOURNAL OF MICROPALAEONTOLOGY : THE JOURNAL OF THE BRITISH MICROPALAEONTOLOGICAL SOCIETY.). [J. micropaleontol.]. **Added/Corp** British Micropalaeontological Society. Vol. 1 (1982)-. Periodical. English. sa. £60.00 UK; $100.00 other. Geological Society Publishing House, Unit 7 Brassmill Enterprise Centre, Brassmill Lane, Bath BA1 3JN England. **Tel** 011 44 225 445046, FAX 011 44 225 442836. **ED** Dr M.C. Keen. Index available. **Ad Acc. Pr Rev. Circ:** 1000.
**Desc:** To publish original papers and review articles on all aspects of micropalaeontology.
**Ind/Abst** AESIS Q.; Curr. Aware. Biol. Sci., CABS; Geol. Abstr.; GeoRef; Mar. Sci. Contents Tables.

US/0022-3360
**JOURNAL OF PALEONTOLOGY.** [J. paleontol.]. **Added/Corp** Society of Economic Paleontologists and Mineralogists. Paleontological Society. American Association of Petroleum Geologists. Geological Society of America. Vol. 1 (July 1927)-. Periodical. English. bm. $99.00. Paleontological Society. **(Subscription address:** Journal of Paleontology, PO Box 1897, Lawrence KS 66044-8897.**) ED** Don C. Steinker. **LC** QE701; .J6. **DD** 560. **CODEN** JPALAZ. **[CCC].** Index available. cum. index. **Bk Rev. Pr Rev. Acid Free. Circ:** 2,500 (ctrl). available on microfilm and microfiche from University Microfilms International (UMI). Documents available from The Genuine Article, BIOSIS Document Express, UMI Article Clearinghouse, Petroleum Abstracts Document Delivery Service, CASDDS.
**Desc:** Contributions in any field of paleontology including invertebrates, vertebrates, micropaleontology, and paleobotany. Contributions may emphasize taxonomic, biostratigraphic, paleoecological, paleoclimatological, or paleobiogeographic aspects.
**Ind/Abst** AESIS Q.; Biol. Abstr.; Chem. Abstr.; Coal Abstr.; Curr. Aware. Biol. Sci., CABS; Curr. Contents Phys. Chem. Earth Sci.; Ecol. Abstr. (?-?); Ecology Abstr.; Expand. Acad. Index (1992-); Fish Rev.; Geogr. Abstr. Phys. Geogr. (?-?); Geol. Abstr.; Indian Geosci. Abstr.; Int. Aerosp. Abstr.; Newsp. Period. Abstr. (1992-); Ocean. Abstr.; Life Sci. Collect.; Pet. Abstr.; Res. Alert [Full Cov.]; Sci. Cit. Index; SCISEARCH; Soc. Sci. Cit. Index [Select. Cov.].

II/0552-9360
**JOURNAL OF THE PALAEONTOLOGICAL SOCIETY OF INDIA. Main/Corp** Palaeontological Society of India. Vol. 1 (1956)-. Periodical. English. an. $80.00. Paleontological Society of India, Lucknow, India. **(Subscription address:** Prints India, 11 Darya Ganj, New Delhi 110002 India.**) LC** QE756.I4; P34a. **CODEN** PLSIBJ. **Bk Rev. Circ:** 1,000.
**Ind/Abst** GeoRef.

US/0272-4634
**JOURNAL OF VERTEBRATE PALEONTOLOGY.** [J. vertebr. paleontol.]. Vol. 1, No. 1 (June 1981)-. Periodical. English. qt. $85.00. Society of Vertebrate Paleontology, University of Nebraska, W436 Nebraska Hall, Lincoln NE 68588-0542. **Tel** (402)472-4604, FAX (402)472-8949. **ED** Hans-Dieter Sues and Richard L. Cifelli. **LC** QE841; .J67. **UDC** 566. **CODEN** JVPADK. Index available. **Bk Rev. Circ:** 1,200 (ctrl). Documents available from BIOSIS Document Express.
**Desc:** The journal covers all theoretical and applied aspects of paleontology of the chordates including their origins, evolution, anatomy, taxonomy, biostratigraphy, paleoecology, paleogeography, and paleoanthropology.
**Ind/Abst** Biol. Abstr.; Fish Rev. (Jan. 1989-July 1992); GeoRef; Wildl. Rev. (Jan. 1989-July 1992).

JA/0022-9202
**KASEKI. VFOAT** Fossils. Began publication in 1960. Periodical. Japanese (summaries and/or abstracts in English). Nihon Koseibutsu Gakkai, (Palaeontological Soc. of Japan), Nihon Gakkai Jimu Senta, 4-16, Yayoi 2 Chome, Bunkyoku, Tokyoto 113, Japan. **LC** QE701; .K35. **CODEN** KASKAS. Documents available from BIOSIS Document Express.
**Ind/Abst** Biol. Abstr. (1986-); GeoRef.

NO/0024-1164
**LETHAIA.** (LETHAIA : AN INTERNATIONAL JOURNAL OF PALAEONTOLOGY AND STRATIGRAPHY.). [Lethaia]. **Added/Corp** Universitetsforlaget. International Palaeontological Association. Vol. 1 (Jan. 1968)-. Periodical. English (French and German). qt. Kr860.00, $150.00. Scandinavian University Press, PO Box 2959 Toeyen, N 0608 Oslo 6 Norway. **Tel** 011 47 2 2575400, FAX 011 47 2 2575353, telex 71896 UROR N. **(Subscription address:** Scandinavian University Press, 200 Meacham Ave., Elmont NY 11003.**) ED** Lars Ramskoeld. **LC** QE701; .L5. **CODEN** LETHAT. **[CCC].** cum. index. **Bk Rev. Pr Rev. Circ:** 1,400 (ctrl). available on microfilm

and microfiche from University Microfilms International (UMI). Documents available from The Genuine Article, BIOSIS Document Express, Petroleum Abstracts Document Delivery Service.
**Desc:** A geological journal that specializes in the field of palaeontology, stratography and fossils.
**Ind/Abst** Abstr. Anthropol.; Biol. Abstr.; Coal Abstr.; Curr. Contents Phys. Chem. Earth Sci.; Ecol. Abstr. (?-?); Geogr. Abstr. Phys. Geogr. (?-?); Geol. Abstr.; GeoRef; Life Sci. Collect.; Pet. Abstr.; Res. Alert [Full Cov.]; Sci. Cit. Index; SCISEARCH.

SP/0212-078X
**MAINAKE.** See Archaeology.

NE/0377-8398
**MARINE MICROPALEONTOLOGY.** [Mar. micropaleontol.]. Vol. 1 (July 1976)-. Academic Scholarly Publication. English. Eight times a year (2 volumes). FI908.00. Elsevier Science Publishers BV, PO Box 211, 1000 AE Amsterdam Netherlands. **Tel** 011 31 20 5803642, FAX 011 31 20 5862696, telex 15682. **ED** B U Haq. **LC** QE719; .M27. **DD** 560. **CODEN** MAMIDH. **[CCC]. Pr Rev.** available on microfilm and microfiche from University Microfilms International (UMI). Documents available from The Genuine Article, BIOSIS Document Express, Petroleum Abstracts Document Delivery Service.
**Desc:** Devoted to the publication of results of research in the fields of marine micropaleontology and paleoecology, and for marine microbiological studies with a bearing on these fields.
**Ind/Abst** AESIS Q.; AQUAREF; Aquat. Sci. Fish. Abstr. (Computer File); Biol. Abstr.; Curr. Aware. Biol. Sci., CABS; Curr. Contents Phys. Chem. Earth Sci.; Ecol. Abstr.; Energy Res. Abstr. (Jan. 1980-); Geogr. Abstr. Phys. Geogr.; Geol. Abstr.; GeoRef; Indian Geosci. Abstr.; Mar. Sci. Contents Tables; Ocean. Abstr.; Life Sci. Collect.; Pet. Abstr.; Res. Alert [Full Cov.]; Sci. Cit. Index; SCISEARCH.

NE/0165-280X
**MEDEDELINGEN VAN DE WERKGROEP VOOR TERTIAIRE EN KWARTAIRE GEOLOGIE.** See Earth Sciences-Geology.

AT/0810-8889
**MEMOIR ... OF THE ASSOCIATION OF AUSTRALASIAN PALAEONTOLOGISTS.** [Mem. Assoc. Australas. Palaeontol.]. **Added/Corp** Association of Australasian Palaeontologists. (1983)-. Monographic series. English. ir. Price varies per volume. Geological Society of Australia, 504 Wynyard House, 301 George Street, Sydney New South Wales 2000 Australia. **Tel** 011 61 2 2902194, FAX 011 61 02 290-2198. **[CCC].**

US/0078-8597
**MEMOIR / THE PALEONTOLOGICAL SOCIETY.** [Mem. - Paleontol. Soc.]. 1-. Monographic series. English. Price varies per volume. **UDC** 56. **CODEN** PSMECR. Documents available from BIOSIS Document Express.
**Ind/Abst** Biol. Abstr.; GeoRef.

AT/0077-8699
**MEMOIRS OF THE GEOLOGICAL SURVEY OF NEW SOUTH WALES. PALAEONTOLOGY.** [Mem. Geol. Surv. N.S.W., Palaeontol.]. **VFOAT** Palaeontology. Began with: No. 1, published in 1888. Monographic series. English. ir. Price varies per volume. Geological Survey of New South Wales, Department of Mineral Resources, 8-18 Bent Street, Sydney New South Wales 2000 Australia. **LC** QE758; .A3. **DD** 560/.9944. **UDC** 56:576.8. **CODEN** MGSWAQ.
**Ind/Abst** GeoRef.

GW/0076-7689
**MEYNIANA.** See Earth Sciences-Geology.

US/0026-2803
**MICROPALEONTOLOGY.** [Micropaleontology]. **Added/Corp** American Museum of Natural History. Dept. of Micropaleontology. Vol. 1 (Jan. 1955)-. Periodical. English. qt (plus one supplement). $175.00 library; $90.00 individual. Sheridan Press, PO Box 465, Hanover PA 17331. **Tel** (800)352-2210, (717)632-3535, FAX (717)633-8900. **ED** John Van Couvering. **LC** QE701; .M527. **DD** 560. **CODEN** MCPLAI. **[CCC]. Bk Rev. Pr Rev. Circ:** 1,400 (ctrl). Documents available from The Genuine Article, BIOSIS Document Express, Petroleum Abstracts Document Delivery Service, CASDDS. ***Continues** Micropaleontologist, 1050-0960.*
**Desc:** The leading journal in its field, containing international research on stratigraphy, systematics, morphology, paleobiology, and paleoecology of all microorganisms with fossilized hard parts.
**Ind/Abst** Biol. Abstr.; Chem. Abstr.; Coal Abstr.; Curr. Aware. Biol. Sci., CABS; Curr. Contents Phys. Chem. Earth Sci.; Geol. Abstr.; GeoRef; Int. Aerosp. Abstr.; Life Sci. Collect.; Pet. Abstr.; Res. Alert [Full Cov.]; Sci. Cit. Index; SCISEARCH.

US/0160-2071
**MICROPALEONTOLOGY SPECIAL PUBLICATION.** [Micropaleontol. spec. publ.]. **Added/Corp** American Musuem of Natural History. No. 1 (1975)-. Monographic series. English. ir. Price varies per volume. Micropaleontology Press, American Museum of Natural History, Central Park West at 79th Street, New York NY 10024. **Tel** (212)769-5658, FAX (212)769-5233. **LC** UNC. **CODEN** MSPUDO. **[CCC]. Circ:** 750.
**Desc:** Research monographs and symposia on micropaleontology.
**Ind/Abst** GeoRef.

US/0275-8555
**MISSISSIPPI GEOLOGY.** See Earth Sciences-Geology.

AU/0379-1432
**MITTEILUNGEN DER ABTEILUNG FUER GEOLOGIE, PALAONTOLOGIE UND BERGBAU AM LANDESMUSEUM JOANNEUM. SH.** See Earth Sciences-Geology.

GW/0077-2070
**MITTEILUNGEN DER BAYERISCHE.** (MITTEILUNGEN - BAYERISCHE STAATSSAMMLUNG FUER PALAONTOLOGIE UND HISTORISCHE GEOLOGIE.). [Mitt. Bayer. Staatssamml. Palaontol. Hist. Geol.]. **Main/Corp** Bayerische Staatssammlung fur Palaontologie und Historische Geologie. No. 1- 1961-. German (English and French). an. DM80.00 Germany; $45.00 US. Wissenschaftliche Literatur, Gerhard Trenkle, Jorg Tomlinger Strabe 2, 8033 Planegg Germany. **Tel** 089/52 03 361, FAX 089/5203 286. **ED** Dietrich Herm. **LC** QE701; .B38A. **UDC** 56. **CODEN** BSPGBT. Index available. **Circ:** 500 (ctrl). Documents available from BIOSIS Document Express.
**Ind/Abst** Biol. Abstr.; GeoRef.

JA/0385-0900
**MIZUNAMI-SHI KASEKI HAKUBUTSUKAN KENKYU HOKOKU.** [Mizunami-shi Kaseki Hakubutsukan kenkyu hokoku]. **Main/Corp** Muzunami-Shi Kaseki Hakubutsukan. **VFOAT** Bulletin of the Mizunami Fossil Museum. No. 1- 1974-. English (Japanese). an. Mizunami Fossil Museum, Akeyo-cho Mizunami City, Gifu 509-61 Japan. **Tel** 0572-68-7710. **ED** Junji Itoigawa. **LC** QE756.J29. **UDC** 56. **CODEN** MKHKEZ. Index available. cum. index. **Bk Rev. Circ:** 600 (ctrl).
**Ind/Abst** GeoRef.

NE/0168-6151
**MODERN QUATERNARY RESEARCH IN SOUTHEAST ASIA.** [Mod. quat. res. Southeast Asia]. Periodical. English. an. FI75.00 Netherlands; $40.00 other. AA Balkema, Box 1675, 3000 BR Rotterdam Netherlands. **Tel** 011 31 10 4145822, FAX 011 31 10 4135947, telex 41605. **ED** G Bartstra and W A Casparie. **LC** QE696; .S94A. **DD** 551.7/9/05. **UDC** 551.79(59). **[CCC]. Circ:** 500. ***Continues** Modern Quaternary Research in Southeast Asia.*
**Desc:** Information on research projects and results.
**Ind/Abst** Anthropol. Lit.; GeoRef.

US/0736-3907
**MOSASAUR, THE.** (THE MOSASAUR : THE JOURNAL OF THE DELAWARE VALLEY PALEONTOLOGICAL SOCIETY.). [Mosasaur]. **Added/Corp** Delaware Valley Paleontological Society. Vol. 1 (Jan. 1983)-. English. ir. $18.00. The Mosasaur, PO Box 42078, Philadelphia PA 19101-2078. **ED** William B. Gallagher. **LC** QE701.M68. **DD** 560/.5. **[CCC].** cum. index. **Circ:** 800.
**Desc:** Designed to bridge the gap between the amateur and professional paleontological communities, publishing articles of interest to all.
**Ind/Abst** GeoRef.

AU
**NEUE DENKSCHRIFTEN DES NATURHISTORISCHEN MUSEUMS IN WIEN.** **Main/Corp** Naturhistorisches Museums (Austria). Vol. 1 (1977)-. Monographic series. German (English and German). ir. Price varies per volume. Verlag Ferdinand Berger & Soehne, Wienerstrasse 21-23, A-3580 Horn Austria. **Tel** 011/43/2982/23170, 41610. **Bk Rev.** ***Supersedes** Naturhistorisches Museum (Austria). Denkschriften des Naturhistorischen Museums in Wien.*
**Ind/Abst** GeoRef.

GW/0077-7749
**NEUES JAHRBUCH FUER GEOLOGIE UND PALAONTOLOGIE. ABHANDLUNGEN.** See Earth Sciences-Geology.

GW/0028-3630
**NEUES JAHRBUCH FUER GEOLOGIE UND PALAONTOLOGIE. MONATSHEFTE.** See Earth Sciences-Geology.

US/0749-1158
**NEW YORK STATE MUSEUM MEMOIR.** See Natural History.

NZ
**NEW ZEALAND GEOLOGICAL SURVEY PALEONTOLOGICAL BULLETIN.** See Earth Sciences-Geology.

US/0096-9117
**NEWS BULLETIN (AUSTIN, TEX.).** (NEWS BULLETIN - SOCIETY OF VERTEBRATE PALEONTOLOGY.). [News bull., Soc. Vertebr. Paleontol.]. **Added/Corp** Society of Vertebrate Paleontology. No. 1 (Mar. 20, 1941)-. Bulletin. English. Three times a year (Feb., Jun., Sep.). $25.00 US; $37.00 (airmail) other. Society of Vertebrate Paleontology, University of Nebraska, W436 Nebraska Hall, Lincoln NE 68588-0542. **Tel** (402)472-4604, FAX (402)472-8949. **ED** Mary Ann Schmidt, ESL and David S. Berman. **LC** QE701; .S725. **DD** 566/.05. **CODEN** SVPNAJ. **Circ:** 1,500 (ctrl). available on diskette.
**Desc:** Contains activity reports from vertebrate paleontologists in museums, colleges and universities, announcements of special meetings, publications, job opportunities, and new fossil preparation techniques.
**Ind/Abst** GeoRef.

NE/0078-0421
**NEWSLETTERS ON STRATIGRAPHY.** See Earth Sciences-Geology.

AT/0159-818X
**NOMEN NUDUM.** See Earth Sciences-Geology.

SZ/0253-3251
**NOTES DU LABORATOIRE DE PALEONTOLOGIE DE L'UNIVERSITE DE GENEVA.** (NOTES DU LABORATOIRE DE PALEONTOLOGIE.). [Notes Lab. paleontol. Univ. Geneve]. **Main/Corp** Geneva. Universite. Laboratoire de Paleontologie. No. 1- 1977-. Periodical. French. Universite de Geneva, 13 rue des Manaichers, 1211 Geneva 4 Switzerland. **UDC** 56.
**Ind/Abst** GeoRef.

US
**NOTES - NEW YORK PALEONTOLOGICAL SOCIETY.** **Main/Corp** New York Paleontological Society. English. $0.25 per copy. New York Paleontological Society, PO Box 287 Planetarium Station, 127 West 83rd Street, New York NY 10024. **LC** QE701; .N47A. **DD** 560/.5. **UDC** 56.

HU
**OSLENYTANI VITAK.** **VFOAT** Discussiones Palaeontologicae. Hungarian. **LC** QE701; .O84. **UDC** 56.
**Ind/Abst** GeoRef.

GW/0724-6331
**PALAEO ICHTHYOLOGICA.** **VFOAT** Palaeoichthyologica. 1 (1983)-. Monographic series. German. Price varies per volume. Verlag Dr Friedrich Pfeil, PO Box 65 00 86, W-8000 Munich 65 Germany. **Tel** (0043)89-8888196, FAX (0043)89-8341873.

●US/1063-7176
**PALAEOCLIMATES.** (PALAEOCLIMATES : DATA AND MODELLING.). (1992)-. Periodical. English. Four times a year. $180.00 (academic institutions), $280.00 (corporate institutions). Harwood Academic Publishers / New York, PO Box 786, Cooper Station, New York NY 10276. **Tel** (212)206-8900, (201)643-7500. **(Subscription address:** International Publishers Distributor at one of the following addresses: 820 Town Center Drive, Langhorne, PA 19047; or PO Box 90, Reading Berkshire RG1 8JL UK; or Kent Ridge PO Box 1180, Singapore 9111, Republic of Singapore**)**
**Desc:** Brings together paleoclimate modelling and data studies in one publication. Publishes on both the geological and climatological aspects of paleoclimate research.

NE/0168-6208
**PALAEOECOLOGY OF AFRICA AND THE SURROUNDING ISLANDS.** [Palaeoecol. Afr. surround. isl.]. **VFOAT** Palaeoecology of Africa. Vol. 10 (1978)-. Monographic series. English (French and German). ir. Price varies per volume. AA Balkema, Box 1675, 3000 BR Rotterdam Netherlands. **Tel** 011 31 10 4145822, FAX 011 31 10 4135947, telex 41605. **(Subscription address:** Ashgate Publishing Company, Old Post Road, Brookfield VT 05036.**) LC** QE993; .P28. **DD** 560/.96. **CODEN** PLEABR. **[CCC].** Documents available from BIOSIS Document Express. ***Continues** Palaeoecology of Africa & of the Surrounding Islands & Antarctica, 0078-8538.*
**Ind/Abst** AGRICOLA; Anthropol. Lit.; Biol. Abstr.; GeoRef; Soils Fert.

NE/0031-0182
**PALAEOGEOGRAPHY, PALAEOCLIMATOLOGY, PALAEOECOLOGY.** [Palaeogeogr. palaeoclimatol. palaeoecol.]. **VFOAT** Palaeo. Vol. 1, No. 1 (Mar. 1965)-. Academic Scholarly Publication. English (French and German). Twenty-eight times a year (7 volumes). FI2828.00; FI3438.00 combined subscription with Global and Planetary Change. Elsevier Science Publishers BV, PO Box 211, 1000 AE Amsterdam Netherlands. **Tel** 011 31 20 5803642, FAX 011 31 20 5862696, telex 15682. **LC** QE500; .P25. **DD** 560/.45. **CODEN** PPPYAB. **[CCC].** cum. index. **Pr Rev.** available on microfilm and microfiche from University Microfilms International (UMI). Documents available from The Genuine Article, BIOSIS Document Express, CASDDS.

*Continued in part by* Global and Planetary Change, 0921-8181.
**Ind/Abst** ASTIS Curr. Aware. Bull. (1978-); AESIS Q.; Aquat. Sci. Fish. Abstr. (Computer File); ASTIS Bibliogr. (1978-); Biol. Abstr.; Chem. Abstr.; Coal Abstr.; Curr. Aware. Biol. Sci., CABS; Curr. Contents Phys. Chem. Earth Sci.; Ecol. Abstr.; Ecology Abstr.; Geogr. Abstr. Phys. Geogr.; GeoRef; Indian Geosci. Abstr.; Meteorol. Geoastrophys. Abstr. (199?-); Ocean. Abstr.; Life Sci. Collect.; Res. Alert [Full Cov.]; Sci. Cit. Index; SCISEARCH; Soc. Sci. Cit. Index [Select. Cov.]; Soils Fert.

GW/0375-0442
**PALAEONTOGRAPHICA. ABTEILUNG A : PALAOZOOLOGIE, STRATIGRAPHIE.** [Palaeontogr., Abt. A]. **VFOAT** Palaozoologie, Stratigraphie. Vol. 78 (1933)-. German. Eight times a year. $274.00. E. Schweizerbartsche Verlagsbuchhandlung, Johannesstrasse 3A, D-70176 Stuttgart Germany. **Tel** 011 49 711 625001, FAX 011 49 711 625005, telex 723363 SCHB D. **CODEN** PGABA8. **[CCC].** Documents available from BIOSIS Document Express. ***Continues in part*** *Palaeontographica.*
**Ind/Abst** Biol. Abstr.; GeoRef.

GW/0375-0299
**PALAEONTOGRAPHICA. ABTEILUNG B : PALAOPHYTOLOGIE.** [Palaeontogr., Abt. B]. Vol. 78 (1933)-. English (German). Ten times a year. $274.00. E. Schweizerbartsche Verlagsbuchhandlung, Johannesstrasse 3A, D-70176 Stuttgart Germany. **Tel** 011 49 711 625001, FAX 011 49 711 625005, telex 723363 SCHB D. **ED** H J Schweitzer. **CODEN** PABPAD. **[CCC]. Bk Rev. Ad Acc.** Documents available from BIOSIS Document Express. ***Continues in part*** *Palaeontographica.*
**Desc:** Contains information on paleophytology.
**Ind/Abst** AESIS Q.; Biol. Abstr.; Coal Abstr.; Geol. Abstr.; GeoRef; Indian Geosci. Abstr.

US/0078-8546
**PALAEONTOGRAPHICA AMERICANA.** [Palaeontogr. Am.]. **Added/Corp** Paleontological Research Institution (Ithaca, N.Y.). Vol. 1 (1916)-. Monographic series. English. ir. Price varies per volume. Paleontological Research Institution, 1259 Trumansburg Road, Ithaca NY 14850. **Tel** (607)273-6623, FAX (607)273-6620. **ED** Peter R. Hoover. **LC** QE701; .I82. **CODEN** PALAAI. Index available. **Circ:** 400 (ctrl). Documents available from BIOSIS Document Express.
**Desc:** A publication outlet for longer manuscripts that use fossils as the data base, or that provide neontological information for application in paleontological studies.
**Ind/Abst** Biol. Abstr.; Geol. Abstr.; GeoRef.

CN/0821-7556
**PALAEONTOGRAPHICA CANADIANA.** [Palaeontogr. Can.]. **Added/Corp** Canadian Society of Petroleum Geologists. Geological Association of Canada. (1983)-. Monographic series. English (French). ir. price varies per volume. Memorial University of Newfoundland / Department of Earth Sciences, Geological Association of Canada, St. Johns Newfoundland A1B 3X5 Canada. **Tel** (709)737-7660. **LC** UNC; QE748.A1; P35. **CODEN** PALCES. Documents available from BIOSIS Document Express.
**Ind/Abst** Biol. Abstr. (1985-); Geol. Abstr.; GeoRef.

UK/0376-2734
**PALAEONTOGRAPHICAL SOCIETY MONOGRAPHS.** (MONOGRAPH OF THE PALAEONTOGRAPHICAL SOCIETY.). [Palaeontogr. Soc. Monogr.]. **Main/Corp** Palaeontographical Society (Great Britain). **Added/Corp** Palaeontographical Society (Great Britain). Vol. 1 (1847)-. Monographic series. English. Price varies per volume. Palaeontographical Society, British Geological Survey, Keyworth, Nottingham NG12 599 England. **LC** UNC. **CODEN** PLTSAJ. Documents available from BIOSIS Document Express.
**Ind/Abst** Biol. Abstr.; GeoRef.

SA/0078-8554
**PALAEONTOLOGIA AFRICANA.** [Palaeontol. Afr.]. **Added/Corp** Bernard Price Institute for Palaeontological Research. Vol. 1 (1953)-. Monographic series. English (French). ir. Price varies per volume. Witwatersrand University Press, PO Wits, Education Department, Johannesburg 2050 South Africa. **Tel** 011 27 11 7165088, FAX 011 27 11 4031926 3394386, telex 4-27125 SA. **ED** B. S. Rubidge, C. E. Gow and R. J. Rayner. **LC** QE757.A1; P34. **DD** 560.96. **CODEN** PBPRAS. cum. index. **Circ:** 600 (ctrl). Documents available from BIOSIS Document Express.
**Desc:** All aspects of paleontology: vertebrate, invertebrate, plant, taphonomy, biostratigraphy, phylogeny and systematics.
**Ind/Abst** Art Archaeol. Tech. Abstr.; Biol. Abstr.; GeoRef.

CC
**PALAEONTOLOGIA CATHAYANA.** **Added/Corp** Chung-kuo Ko Hsueh Yuan. Nan-ching Ti Chih Ku Sheng Wu Yen Chiu So. No. 1 (1983)-. Periodical. English. an. $88.00. Science Press, 16 Donghuangchenggen North Street, Beijing 100707, People's Republic of China. **Tel** 011 86 1 4019821, 011 86 1 4010642, FAX 011 86 1 4012180, 011 86 1 4019810, telex 210147. **LC** QE756.C6; P3. **DD** 560.951.

II/0379-5225
**PALAEONTOLOGIA INDICA.** (MEMOIRS OF THE GEOLOGICAL SURVEY OF INDIA. PALAEONTOLOGICA INDICA.). [Palaeontol. Indica]. **Added/Corp** Geological Survey of India. **VFOAT** Palaeontologia Indica. (1899)-. Monographic series. English. ir. Price varies per volume. Geological Survey of India, 29 Jawaharlal Nehru Road, Calcutta 700016 India. **(Subscription address:** Prints India, 11 Darya Ganj, New Delhi 110002 India.**) LC** QE756.I4; A4. **DD** 560/.954.
**Ind/Abst** Indian Geosci. Abstr.

CI/0552-9352
**PALAEONTOLOGIA JUGOSLAVICA.** [Palaeontol. Jugosl.]. **Added/Corp** Jugoslavenska Akademija Znanosti i Umjetnosti. Vol. 1 (1958)-. Periodical. Serbo-Croatian (Cyrillic). ir. Hrvatska Akademija Znanosti i Umjetnosti / Croatian Academy of Sciences & Arts, Zrinski TRG 11, 41000 Zagreb Croatia. **Tel** 011 38 41 433 661, FAX 011 38 41 433 383. **(Subscription address:** Mladost Export Import, PO Box 1028 Ilica 30, 41000 Zagreb Croatia; Phone: 011 385 41 422425**) ED** Mirko Malez. **CODEN** PLJUA9. ctrl circ. Documents available from BIOSIS Document Express.
**Desc:** Covers micropaleontology, nannofossils, biostratigraphy, and vertebrate paleontology.
**Ind/Abst** Biol. Abstr.; Geol. Abstr.; GeoRef.

PL/0078-8562
**PALAEONTOLOGIA POLONICA.** [Palaeontol. pol.]. No. 1 (1929)-. Monographic series. English. ir (1-2 issues per year). Price varies per volume. **(Subscription address:** ARS Polona, PO Box 1001, 00068 Warsaw Poland.**) CODEN** PLPOAL. Documents available from BIOSIS Document Express.
**Ind/Abst** Biol. Abstr.; GeoRef.

UK
**PALAEONTOLOGICAL ASSOCIATION FIELD GUIDES TO FOSSILS.** **Added/Corp** Palaeontological Association. **VFOAT** Field Guides to Fossils. No. 1 (1983)-. Monographic series. English. ir. Price varies per volume. Palaeontological Association, Dep. Geologyqueens Road, Bristol BS8 1RJ England. **Tel** 011 44 272 303778. **CODEN** PAFFE7.

UK/0031-0239
**PALAEONTOLOGY.** [Palaeontology]. Vol. 1 (Nov. 1957)-. Academic Scholarly Publication. English. Four times a year. £180.00 UK and Europe; $344.00 North America; £222.00 other. Basil Blackwell Publishers Ltd, 108 Cowley Road, Oxford 0X4 1JF England. **Tel** 011 44 865 791100, FAX 011 44 865 791347, telex 837022 OXBOOK G. **(Subscription address:** Blackwell Publishers / UK, Marston Book Services, PO Box 87, Oxford OX2 0DT England.**) ED** D E G Briggs, P R Crowther, D Edwards, L B Halstead, R Harland and T J Palmer. **UDC** 56. **CODEN** PONTAD. cum. index. **Bk Rev. Ad Acc. Pr Rev. Circ:** 500 (ctrl). Documents available from The Genuine Article, BIOSIS Document Express, Petroleum Abstracts Document Delivery Service.
**Desc:** Publishes papers on all aspects of paleontology and stratigraphic paleontology. Review articles and short papers are also included and each issue is illustrated.
**Ind/Abst** AESIS Q.; Biol. Abstr.; Coal Abstr.; Curr. Contents Phys. Chem. Earth Sci.; Ecol. Abstr.; Geol. Abstr.; Ocean. Abstr.; Life Sci. Collect.; Pet. Abstr.; Res. Alert [Full Cov.]; Sci. Cit. Index; SCISEARCH.

UK/0954-9900
**PALAEONTOLOGY NEWSLETTER.** **Added/Corp** Palaeontological Association. No. 1 (Autumn 1988)-. Newsletter. English. qt. Free (with membership to the Association). Paleontological Association, The Croft Barn, Church Street, East Hendred Oxon OX12 8LA England. **Tel** 0223 333437, FAX 0223 333450. **(Subscription address:** J A Crame, BAS/NERC, High Cross, Madengley Road, Cambridge CB3 0ET UK**) LC** QE701; .P3422. Index available. **Ad Acc. Pr Rev.** ctrl circ. ***Continues*** *Palaeontological Association. Palaeontological Association Circular.*
**Desc:** It covers everything of interest to paleontologists including global information, advance notices of conferences and reports on meetings.

FR/0031-0247
**PALAEOVERTEBRATA.** [Palaeovertebrata]. **Added/Corp** Universite des Sciences et Techniques du Languedoc. Laboratoire de Paleontologie. Ecole Pratique des Hautes Etudes (France). Laboratoire de Paleontologie des Vertebres. Laboratoire de Paleontologie (Montpellier, France). Vol. 1, No. 1 (June 1967)-. Monographic series. English (French and German). qt. 450.00F France; 500.00F other. Universite Montpellier, Place Eugene Bataillon, 34095 Montpellier Cedex France. **Tel** 011 33 67143890. **ED** Serge Legendre. **LC** QE841; .P3. **DD** 566/.05. **NLM** W1 PA361U. **CODEN** PLVTAW.
**Ind/Abst** GeoRef.

US/0883-1351
**PALAIOS.** [Palaios]. **Added/Corp** Society of Economic Paleontologists and Mineralogists. SEPM (Society for Sedimentary Geology). Vol. 1, No. 1 (Feb. 1986)-. Academic Scholarly Publication. English. bm. $128.00 (non-members), $64.00 (members). Society of Economic Paleontologists and Mineralogists, PO Box 4756, Tulsa OK 74159-0756. **Tel** (918)743-9765, 800 865-9765, FAX (918)743-2498. **ED** David J. Bottjer. **DD** 553. **CODEN** PALAEM. **[CCC]. Bk Rev. Pr Rev. Acid Free. Circ:** 1,800 (ctrl). available on microfilm from University Microfilms International (UMI). Documents available from BIOSIS Document Express, Petroleum Abstracts Document Delivery Service, CASDDS.
**Desc:** Devoted to the applications of paleontology in solving geologic problems and should be of interest to a broad spectrum of international geologists interested in stratigraphy, sedimentology, paleontologic, paleoecology, and paleobiology, as well as to paleontologic specialists. Provides authors and readers with timely publication of significant research that stimulates new developments in applied paleontologic research.
**Ind/Abst** AESIS Q.; Biol. Abstr. (1986-); Chem. Abstr. (1986-); Ecol. Abstr. (?-?); Geogr. Abstr. Phys. Geogr.; Geol. Abstr.; GeoRef; Pet. Abstr.; Sci. Cit. Index.

GW/0031-0220
**PALAONTOLOGISCHE ZEITSCHRIFT.** [Palaontol. Z.]. **Added/Corp** Palaontologische Gesellschaft. Deutsche Palaontologische Gesellschaft. No. 1 (1913)-. Periodical. German. Four times a year. $90.00. E. Schweizerbartsche Verlagsbuchhandlung, Johannesstrasse 3A, D-70176 Stuttgart Germany. **Tel** 011 49 711 625001, FAX 011 49 711 625005, telex 723363 SCHB D. **CODEN** PAZEAW. **[CCC].** cum. index. Documents available from BIOSIS Document Express.
**Ind/Abst** Biol. Abstr.; Coal Abstr.; GeoRef.

US/0094-8373
**PALEOBIOLOGY.** [Paleobiology]. **Added/Corp** Paleontological Society. Vol. 1 (Winter 1975)-. Periodical. English. qt. $65.00. Paleobiology Society. **(Subscription address:** Paleobiology, PO Box 1897, Lawrence KS 66044-8897.**) ED** R. Cowen and P. W. Signor. **LC** QE701; .P17. **DD** 560/.5. **CODEN** PALBBM. **[CCC].** Index available. **Bk Rev. Ad Acc. Pr Rev. Acid Free. Circ:** 2,250 (ctrl). available on microfilm and microfiche from University Microfilms International (UMI). Documents available from The Genuine Article, BIOSIS Document Express, Petroleum Abstracts Document Delivery Service.
**Desc:** Publishes original contributions dealing with any aspect of biological paleontology. Emphasis is placed upon biological or paleobiological processes and patterns.
**Ind/Abst** Abstr. Anthropol.; Biol. Abstr.; Br. Archaeol. Bibliogr.; Curr. Aware. Biol. Sci., CABS; Curr. Contents, Agric. Biol. Environ. Sci.; Ecol. Abstr.; Ecology Abstr.; Fish Rev.; Geogr. Abstr. Phys. Geogr.; Geol. Abstr.; GeoRef; Life Sci. Collect.; Pet. Abstr.; Res. Alert [Full Cov.]; Sci. Cit. Index; SCISEARCH; Wildl. Rev.

US/0031-0298
**PALEOBIOS.** [Paleobios]. **Added/Corp** University of California, Berkeley. Museum of Paleontology. **VFOAT** Paleo Bios. (1967)-. Monographic series. English. ir. $8.00. Museum of Paleontology / California, 3 Earth Sciences Building, University of California, Berkeley CA 97420. **Tel** (510)642-1821, (510)642-3926, FAX (510)642-1822. **ED** Jessica Theodor. **LC** QE701; .P46. **DD** 560/.5. **CODEN** PLBIA. **Pr Rev. Circ:** 300.
**Desc:** Paleontological publication of the University of California Museum of Paleontology. Publishes original papers in paleontology and related fields, especially topics of local or regional interest.
**Ind/Abst** Br. Archaeol. Bibliogr. (?-?); GeoRef.

BL/0100-5472
**PALEOCLIMAS.** [Paleoclimas]. No. 1 (1971)-. Periodical. Portuguese (summaries and/or abstracts in English). Instituto de Geografia, USP Cidade Universitaria, Edificio de Geografia e Historia, Caixa Postal 20.715, Sao Paulo SP 05508 Brazil. **UDC** 551.583.7. **CODEN** PLCLDI.
**Ind/Abst** GeoRef.

MX/0543-7652
**PALEONTOLOGIA MEXICANA.** [Paleontol. mex.]. **Main/Corp** Universidad Nacional Autonoma de Mexico. Instituto de Geologia. No. 1 (1954)-. Monographic series. Spanish (English). ir. Price varies per volume. UNAM - Universidad Nacional Autonoma de Mexico / Geologia, Ciudad Universitaria, PO 70 296, 04510 Mexico DF Mexico. **Tel** 011 52 5 6224033. **ED** Arturo Gomez Caballero. **LC** QE749; .M45. **CODEN** MUGPA9. **Circ:** 1,200 (ctrl). Documents available from BIOSIS Document Express.
**Desc:** Contains the results of research realized by the staff of the Department of Paleontology of the Institute of Geology.
**Ind/Abst** Biol. Abstr. (-1975); GeoRef.

US/0031-0301
**PALEONTOLOGICAL JOURNAL.** [Paleontol. j.]. **Added/Corp** American Geological Institute. Vol. 1 (1967)-. Periodical. English (Russian). Five times a year. $894.00 US; $954.00 Canada and Mexico; $976.75 other. Scripta Technica, A Subsidiary of John Wiley & Sons, Inc., 7961 Eastern Avenue, Silver Spring MD 20910. **Tel** (301)588-0484, FAX (301)588-5278. **(Subscription address:** John Wiley / Philadelphia, PO Box 7247, Philadelphia PA 19170.**) ED** Matthew Nitecki, Field Museum, Chicago, IL. **LC** QE701; .P5443. **DD** 560/.5. **CODEN** PJOUA. **[CCC]. Ad Acc.** available on microfilm and microfiche from University Microfilms International (UMI).

**Desc:** Provides information on the paleontology of Eurasia. Communicates advances in the anatomy, morphology and taxonomy of extinct animals and plants, their relationships, distributions, ecology, origin and evolution as well as the biostratigraphy of Eastern Europe and Asia.
**Ind/Abst** GeoRef.

RU/0031-031X
**PALEONTOLOGICESKIJ ZURNAL.** (PALEONTOLOGICHESKII ZHURNAL.). [Paleontol. z.]. **Added/Corp** Akademiia Nauk SSSR. **VFOAT** Palaeontological Journal. (1959)-. Academic Scholarly Publication. Russian (table of contents in English). Four times a year. $115.95. Izdatelstvo Nauka / Akademiia Nauk, Publishing House of the Russian Academy of Sciences, Leninskii Porspekt 14, 117901 Moscow Russia. **Tel** 011 95 954-21-53, FAX 011 95 938-21-44, telex 411964. **(Subscription address:** East View Publications Inc., 3020 Harbor Lane North, Suite 110, Minneapolis MN 55447.**)** **LC** QE701; .P544. **DD** 560/.5. **CODEN** PAZHA7. **[CCC].** Documents available from The Genuine Article, BIOSIS Document Express.
**Ind/Abst** Biol. Abstr.; GeoRef; Res. Alert [Select. Cov.]; SCISEARCH; Soc. Sci. Cit. Index [Select. Cov.].

US
**PALEONTOLOGY AND GEOLOGY OF THE BADWATER CREEK AREA, CENTRAL WYOMING.** English. Carnegie Museum of Natural History, 4400 Forbes Avenue, Pittsburgh PA 15213. **Tel** (412)622-3315, FAX (412)622-8837. **LC** AS36; .P7 subser. **DD** 500.9/08 S. **UDC** 56(787); 55(787).

US/0256-1670
**PALYNOS.** **See** Biology-Botany.

US/0148-3838
**PAPERS ON PALEONTOLOGY.** [Papers paleontol.]. **Added/Corp** University of Michigan. Museum of Paleontology. (1972)-. Monographic series. English. ir. Price varies per volume. Museum of Paleontology / Michigan, University of Michigan, Ann Arbor MI 48109. **Tel** (313)747-2101. **LC** QE701; .P585. **DD** 560/.5. **CODEN** PPUMD3.
**Ind/Abst** GeoRef.

FR/1146-5247
**PASCAL. F 47, PALEONTOLOGIE.** **VFOAT** PASCAL. F 47, Paleontology; PASCAL. F Quarante-Sept, Paleontologie. (1990)-. Periodical. Multiple languages. mo. 865.00F France; 915.00F other. CNRS / Institut d'Information Scientifique et Technique, (Centre National de la Recherche Scientifique), 15 Quai Anatole France, Paris 75700 France. **Tel** 011 33 1 47531515, telex 299 356 F. **(Subscription address:** 2 Allee du Parc de Brabois, 54514 Vandoeuvre Nancy France, Telephone: 011 33 83 504664**)** **UDC** 011. ***Continues*** *PASCAL Folio F47 Paleontologie., 0761-1889.*

US/0554-288X
**PLASTER JACKET, THE.** ***Ceased.*** [Plaster jacket]. No. 1 (Sept. 1966)-?. English. ir. Florida State Museum, University of Florida, Museum Drive, Gainesville FL 32611. **Tel** (904)392-1721. **LC** QE841; .P68. **DD** 566/.09759. **UDC** 566(759). **CODEN** PLJABI.
**Ind/Abst** GeoRef.

PL/0556-0691
**POMORANIA ANTIQUA.** **Added/Corp** Muzeum Archeologiczne (Gdansk, Poland). (196?)-. Polish (summaries and/or abstracts in English). **LC** GN814.P6; P62. ***Continues*** *Pomerania Antiqua.*
**Ind/Abst** BHA : Biblio. Hist. Art.

CN/1183-028X
**PROGRAM AND ABSTRACTS OF THE CANADIAN PALEONTOLOGY CONFERENCE ... AND PANDER SOCIETY MEETING.** [Program abstr. Can. Paleontol. Conf. Pander Soc. meet.]. **Added/Corp** Geological Association of Canada. Paleontology Division. Pander Society. **VFOAT** Program and Abstracts. **VAT** Program and Abstracts - Canadian Paleontology Conference. 1st (Aug. 1991)-. English. Limited free distribution. Canadian Paleontology Conference, c/o Paleontology Division, Geological Association of Canada, Department of Earth Sciences, Memorial University of Newfoundland, St John's, Newfoundland A1B 3X5 Canada. **DD** 557.1.

FR/1142-2904
**QUATERNAIRE : BULLETIN DE L'ASSOCIATION FRANCAISE POUR L'ETUDE DU QUATERNAIRE : INTERNATIONAL JOURNAL OF THE FRENCH QUATERNARY ASSOCIATION.** **See** Earth Sciences-Geology.

NE/0034-6667
**REVIEW OF PALAEOBOTANY AND PALYNOLOGY.** [Rev. palaeobot. palynol.]. Vol. 1 (March 1967)-. Academic Scholarly Publication. English (French and German). Sixteen times a year (4 volumes). Fl1848.00. Elsevier Science Publishers BV, PO Box 211, 1000 AE Amsterdam Netherlands. **Tel** 011 31 20 5803642, FAX 011 31 20 5862696, telex 15682. **ED** W Punt. **LC** QE993; .R4. **DD** 561/.05. **CODEN** RPPYAX. **[CCC].** cum. index. **Pr Rev.** available on microfilm and microfiche from University Microfilms International (UMI). Documents available from The Genuine Article, BIOSIS Document Express, Petroleum Abstracts Document Delivery Service.
**Desc:** Strives to stimulate wide interdisciplinary cooperation and understanding among workers in the fields of paleobotany and palynology.
**Ind/Abst** ASTIS Curr. Aware. Bull. (1978-); AESIS Q.; AGRICOLA [Full Cov.]; ASTIS Bibliogr. (1978-); Biol. Abstr.; Coal Abstr. (1978-); Curr. Aware. Biol. Sci., CABS; Curr. Contents, Agric. Biol. Environ. Sci.; Ecol. Abstr.; For. Abstr.; Geogr. Abstr. Phys. Geogr.; Geogr. Abstr. Human Geogr.; Geol. Abstr.; GeoRef; Indian Geosci. Abstr.; Life Sci. Collect.; Pet. Abstr.; Res. Alert [Full Cov.]; Rev. Plant Pathol.; Sci. Cit. Index; SCISEARCH; Soils Fert.

SP/0556-655X
**REVISTA ESPANOLA DE MICROPALEONTOLOGIA.** [Rev. esp. micropaleontol.]. **Added/Corp** Empresa Nacional Adaro de Investigaciones Mineras. Centro de Investigacion Juan Gavala. (1969)-. Periodical. Spanish (English, French and Italian). Three times a year (Jan., May, Sept.). 9800ptas Spain; 12100ptas other. Instituto Tecnologico Geominero De Espana, Rios Rosas 23, 28003 Madrid Spain. **Tel** 11 34 1 4416500, FAX 11 34 1 4426216, telex 480541. **LC** QE719; .R445. **CODEN** RTEMB5. **[CCC].** Index available. **Bk Rev.** **Ad Acc.** Documents available from BIOSIS Document Express.
**Ind/Abst** Biol. Abstr.; GeoRef.

SP
**REVISTA ESPANOLA DE PALEONTOLOGIA.** **Added/Corp** Sociedad Espanonola de Paleontologia. Vol. 1 (Nov. 1986)-. Spanish. Twice a year (Jan. & July). 8000ptas. Society Espanola Paleontologia, Departmento Geologia, Faculted de Biologia, c/o Dr. Moliner 50, 46100 Burjasot Spain. **Tel** FAX 011 34 4 4648500. **ED** Marcos Lamolda. **Circ:** 7,600.

FR/0035-1598
**REVUE DE MICROPALEONTOLOGIE.** [Rev. micropaleontol.]. **Added/Corp** Paris. Universite. Laboratoire de Micropaleontologie. Vol. 1 (Jan./Mar. 1958)-. Periodical. French (English). qt. 410.00F France; 470.00F other. Reuve de Micropaleontologie, Maison D Geologie BP 11-705, 75224 Paris Cedex 05 France. **ED** M M Neumann. **CODEN** RMCPAM. cum. index. **Bk Rev.** **Circ:** 650 (ctrl). Documents available from Petroleum Abstracts Document Delivery Service.
**Desc:** Contains information about micropaleontology, microfossils, stratigraphy, ecology, oceanography, palaeoecology, biogeography, systematic geology, petrography and sedimentary evolution.
**Ind/Abst** Geol. Abstr.; GeoRef; Pet. Abstr.

SZ
**REVUE DE PALEOBIOLOGIE.** **Added/Corp** Museum d'Histoire Naturelle de Geneve. Vol. 1, No. 1 (June 1982)-. Periodical. French (English). sa (2 issues). Museum d'Histoire Naturelle de Geneve, CP 434, CH 1211 Geneva 6 Switzerland. **Tel** FAX 011 41 22 7353445. **LC** QE701; .R44. **DD** 560/.5. Index available. **Ad Acc.** ctrl circ.

IT/0035-6883
**RIVISTA ITALIANA DI PALEONTOLOGIA E STRATIGRAFIA.** [Riv. ital. paleontol. stratigr.]. **VFOAT** Rivista Italiana di Paleontologia. (1947)-. Periodical. English (Italian and French). Four times a year (Mar., June, Sept., Dec.). L130000 Italy; L148000 others. Rivista Italiana di Paleontologia Stratigrafia, Dip SC Terra V Mangiagalli 34, 20133 Milan Italy. **Tel** 011 39 2 23698232, FAX 011 39 2 70638261. **LC** QE701; .R6. **DD** 560/.5. **CODEN** RPLSAT. Index available (Bound in 4th issue). cum. index. **Bk Rev**, (Qty: varies). **Pr Rev.** **Circ:** 350. Documents available from BIOSIS Document Express, Petroleum Abstracts Document Delivery Service. ***Continues*** *Rivista Italiana di Paleontologia.*
**Desc:** Covers macropaleontology, micropaleontology, stratigraphy, paleogeography, geology, paleoecology, taxonomy, morphology, and sedimentology.
**Ind/Abst** Biol. Abstr.; Geogr. Abstr. Phys. Geogr.; Geol. Abstr.; GeoRef; Pet. Abstr.

IT/0375-9784
**RIVISTA ITALIANA DI PALEONTOLOGIA E STRATIGRAFIA. MEMORIA.** [Riv. ital. paleontol. stratigr., Mem.]. (1947)-. Monographic series. Italian (summaries and/or abstracts in English). ir. Price varies per volume. Rivista Italiana di Paleontologia Stratigrafia, Dip SC Terra V Mangiagalli 34, 20133 Milan Italy. **Tel** 011 39 2 23698232, FAX 011 39 2 70638261. **CODEN** RVPMA5.
**Ind/Abst** GeoRef.

●RM/1220-5656
**ROMANIAN JOURNAL OF PALEONTOLOGY.** **Added/Corp** Institutul de Geologie si Geofizica. **VFOAT** Paleontology. Vol. 75 (1992)-. Periodical. English (French and Romanian). Institute of Geology and Geophysics, Str. Caransebes 1, 78344 Bucharest 32 Romania. **LC** QE755.R6; I57a. **DD** 560/.5. ***Continues*** *Dari de Seama ale Sedintelor. 3, Paleontologie, 0254-7295.*
**Ind/Abst** GeoRef.

XR/0036-5297
**SBORNIK GEOLOGICKYCH VED. PALEONTOLOGIE.** [Sb. geol. ved, Paleontol.]. **Added/Corp** Ustredni Ustav Geologicky (Czechoslovakia). **VFOAT** Paleontologie; Paleontology; Journal of Geological Sciences. Paleontology; Sbornik Geologickych Ved. Rada P, Paleontologie. (1963)-. Czech (English and German; summaries and/or abstracts in Russian). ir. $7.75. **(Subscription address:** Artia Pegas Press Ltd., Palac Metro Narodni Trida 25, 11210 Prague 1 Czech Republic.**)** **LC** QE755.C95; S25. **CODEN** SGPABC. ***Continues*** *Ustredni Ustav Geologicky (Czechoslovakia). Sbornik Ustredniho Ustavu Geologickeho.*
**Ind/Abst** GeoRef.

SZ/0080-7389
**SCHWEIZERISCHE PALAEONTOLOGISCHE ABHANDLUNGEN.** [Schweiz. palaeontol. Abh.]. **Added/Corp** Schweizerische Naturforschende Gesellschaft. Schweizerischen Palaontologische Gesellschaft. Abhandlungen. **VFOAT** Memoires Suisses de Paleontologie. Vol. 1 (1874)-. Monographic series. German (French). ir. Price varies per volume. Birkhaeuser Verlag Ag, Klosterberg 23, PO Box 133, CH-4010 Basel Switzerland. **Tel** 011 41 61 2717400, FAX 011 41 0 61 2717666, telex 963475 birk ch. **ED** Burkart Engesser. **CODEN** SPAAAX. **[CCC].** available on microfilm and microfiche from University Microfilms International (UMI).
**Desc:** Offers a publication medium for papers in the field of paleontology which require extensive illustrations.

GW/0037-2110
**SENCKENBERGIANA LETHAEA.** [Senckenbergiana lethaea]. **Added/Corp** Senckenbergische Naturforschende Gesellschaft. Vol. 35 (1954)-. Periodical. German (English, French and German). ir (2 per year). DM98.00. Verlag Dr. Waldemar Kramer, Postfach 600445, D-60334 Frankfurt Germany. **Tel** 011 49 69 449045. **ED** Wolfgang Struve. **LC** QE701; .S4. **DD** 560/.5. **CODEN** SLETAE. Index available in last issue of volume--attached. cum. index. **Circ:** 700 (ctrl). Documents available from BIOSIS Document Express, CASDDS. ***Continues in part*** *Senckenbergiana.*
**Desc:** Papers on paleontology (paleozoology and paleobotany) with reference to actuogeology and biochronology are published.
**Ind/Abst** Biol. Abstr.; Chem. Abstr.; GeoRef; Life Sci. Collect.

US
**SEPM JOURNAL.** Monographic series. English. bm (Jan., Mar., May, July, Sept., Nov.). $152.00. Society of Economic Paleontologists and Mineralogists, PO Box 4756, Tulsa OK 74159-0756. **Tel** (918)743-9765, 800 865-9765, FAX (918)743-2498.

US/0731-759X
**SEPM REPRINT SERIES.** [SEPM repr. ser.]. **VFOAT** Reprint Series. **VAT** Society of Economic Paleontologists and Mineralogists Reprint Series. No. 1 (1976)-. Monographic series. English. ir. Price varies per volume. Society of Economic Paleontologists and Mineralogists, PO Box 4756, Tulsa OK 74159-0756. **Tel** (918)743-9765, 800 865-9765, FAX (918)743-2498. **LC** UNC. **CODEN** SERSDU. **Circ:** 2,000. ***Continues*** *Society of Economic Paleontologists and Mineralogists. Reprint Series.*
**Ind/Abst** GeoRef; Life Sci. Collect.

US/1050-9763
**SEPM SHORT COURSE NOTES.** [SEPM short course notes]. **Added/Corp** Society of Economic Paleontologists and Mineralogists. **VAT** Society of Economic Paleontologists and Mineralogists Short Course Notes. (19??)-. Academic Scholarly Publication. English. ir. Price varies per volume. Society of Economic Paleontologists and Mineralogists, PO Box 4756, Tulsa OK 74159-0756. **Tel** (918)743-9765, 800 865-9765, FAX (918)743-2498. **DD** 560. Documents available from BIOSIS Document Express, CASDDS. ***Continues*** *Society of Economic Paleontologists and Mineralogists. SEPM Short Course, 0160-0966.*
**Ind/Abst** Biol. Abstr.; Chem. Abstr.; GeoRef.

US/0081-0266
**SMITHSONIAN CONTRIBUTIONS TO PALEOBIOLOGY.** [Smithson. contrib. paleobiol.]. **Added/Corp** Smithsonian Institution. No. 1 (1969)-. Monographic series. English. ir. Price varies per volume. Smithsonian Institution Press, 470 L'Enfant Plaza, Suite 7100, Washington DC 20560. **Tel** (202)287-3738, (800)782-4612, FAX (202)287-3184. **ED** Barbara Spann. **LC** QE701; .S56. **DD** 560/.8 S. **CODEN** SPBYA8. **Circ:** 2,300 (ctrl). Documents available from BIOSIS Document Express.
**Desc:** Monographs that report the research of

# Paleontology —Abstracting, Bibliographies and Statistics

Smithsonian staff in paleobiology (zoology and botany).
**Ind/Abst** AESIS Q.; Biol. Abstr.; Curr. Aware. Biol. Sci.; CABS; Geol. Abstr.; GeoRef; Life Sci. Collect.

US/1062-161X
**SOCIETY OF VERTEBRATE PALEONTOLOGY MEMOIR.** [Soc. Vertebr. Paleontol. mem.]. **Added/Corp** Society of Vertebrate Paleontology. **VFOAT** Memoir. (1991)-. Periodical. English. Society of Vertebrate Paleontology, University of Nebraska, W436 Nebraska Hall, Lincoln NE 68588-0542. **Tel** (402)472-4604, FAX (402)472-8949. **DD** 566.

UK/0038-6804
**SPECIAL PAPERS IN PALEONTOLOGY.** [Spec. pap. palaeontol.]. No. 1 (1967)-. Monographic series. English. qt. Price varies per volume. Marston Book Services Ltd, PO Box 87, Osney Mead, Oxford OX2 ODT England. **Tel** 011 44 865 791179. **ED** D E G Briggs. **UDC** 56. **CODEN** SPPAB7. **Circ:** 500. Documents available from BIOSIS Document Express.
**Desc:** Publishes papers on all aspects of paleontology. Reviews and short papers are included as well as high quality photographs.
**Ind/Abst** Biol. Abstr.; GeoRef.

II
**SPECIAL PUBLICATION OF THE PALAEONTOLOGICAL SOCIETY OF INDIA.** **Added/Corp** Palaeontological Society of India. **VFOAT** Palaeontological Society of India Special Publication. No. 1 (1982)-. Monographic series. English. Price varies per volume.
**Ind/Abst** Indian Geosci. Abstr.

US
**SPECIAL PUBLICATION. PALEONTOLOGICAL SOCIETY.** **Added/Corp** Paleontological Society. No. 1 (1984)-. Monographic series. English. ir. Price varies per volume. Paleontological Society, University of Tennessee, Department of Geological Science, Knoxville TN 37996. **Tel** (615)974-2366.

US/1060-071X
**SPECIAL PUBLICATION / SOCIETY FOR SEDIMENTARY GEOLOGY.** [Spec. publ. - Soc. Sediment. Geol.]. **Added/Corp** Society for Sedimentary Geology. No. 45 (1991)-. Monographic series. English. **DD** 553. **Continues** Special Publication (Society of Economic Paleontologists and Mineralogists), 0097-3270.

PL
**SWIATOWIT.** See Archaeology.

JA/0082-4658
**TOHOKU DAIGAKU RIGAKUBU CHISHITSUGAKU KOSEIBUTSUGAKU KYOSHITSU KENKYU HOBUN HOKOKU.** See Earth Sciences-Geology.

JA/0031-0204
**TRANSACTIONS AND PROCEEDINGS OF THE PALAEONTOLOGICAL SOCIETY OF JAPAN.** **Main/Corp** Nihon Koseibutsu Gakkai. **Added/Corp** Nihon Koseibutsu Gakkai. Nihon Koseibutsu Gakkai Kiji. **VFOAT** Nihon Koseibutsu Gakkai Hokoku Kiji. No. 1-32, (1935-50); New Series No. 1 (1951)-. Proceedings. English (summaries and/or abstracts in Japanese). Four times a year (Apr., June, Sept., Dec.). $75.00. Nihon Koseibutsu Gakkai, (Palaeontological Soc. of Japan), Nihon Gakkai Jimu Senta, 4-16, Yayoi 2 Chome, Bunkyoku, Tokyoto 113, Japan. **(Subscription address:** Japan Publications Trading Company, Ltd., PO Box 5030, Tokyo International, Tokyo 100-31 Japan.**) LC** QE756.J29; N53. **DD** 560/.952. **CODEN** TPPJAA. Documents available from BIOSIS Document Express.
**Ind/Abst** Biol. Abstr.; GeoRef.

RU/0376-1444
**TRUDY PALEONTOLOGICHESKOGO INSTITUTA.** [Tr. Paleontol. inst.]. **Added/Corp** Paleontologicheskii Institut (Akademiia Nauk SSSR). **VFOAT** Transactions of the Paleontological Institute. Vol. 7, No. 1 (1937)-. Monographic series. Russian (English, French, German and Russian). Price varies per volume. **(Subscription address:** Victor Kamkin, 4956 Boiling Brook Parkway, Rockville, MD 20852**) LC** QE701; .A453. **CODEN** TPIAAG. Documents available from BIOSIS Document Express. **Continues** Trudy Paleozoologicheskogo Instituta.
**Ind/Abst** Biol. Abstr.; GeoRef.

RU/0506-2160
**TRUDY ... SESSII VSESOIUZNOGO PALEONTOLOGICHESKOGO OBSHCHESTVA.** **Main/Corp** Vsesoiuznoe Paleontologicheskoe Obshchestvo. Sessiia. **VFOAT** Tezisy Dokladov ... Sessii Vsesoiuznogo Paleontologicheskogo Obshchestva. (1955)-. Russian. an. **LC** QE701; .V82.
**Ind/Abst** GeoRef.

US/0041-4018
**TULANE STUDIES IN GEOLOGY AND PALEONTOLOGY.** See Earth Sciences-Geology.

●US/1046-8390
**UNIVERSITY OF KANSAS PALEONTOLOGICAL CONTRIBUTIONS (1992), THE.** (THE UNIVERSITY OF KANSAS PALEONTOLOGICAL CONTRIBUTIONS.). [Univ. Kans. paleontol. contrib.]. **Added/Corp** University of Kansas. Paleontological Institute. **VFOAT** Paleontological Contributions. No. 1&2 (Aug. 1992)-. Monographic series. English. University of Kansas / Lars Leon, Exchange Gift Unit, Acquisition Department, Lawrence KS 66045. **Tel** (913)864-4334. **DD** 560. Documents available from BIOSIS Document Express. **Formed by the union of** University of Kansas Paleontological Contributions. Papers, 0075-5044; University of Kansas Paleontological Contributions. Article, 0075-5052 and University of Kansas Paleontological Contributions. Monographs, 0278-9744.
**Ind/Abst** AESIS Q.; Biol. Abstr.; GeoRef.

US/0075-5044
**UNIVERSITY OF KANSAS PALEONTOLOGICAL CONTRIBUTIONS. ARTICLE.** *Title Change.* [Univ. Kans. paleontol. contrib., Artic.]. **Main/Corp** Kansas. University. **Added/Corp** University of Kansas. Paleontological Institute. **VFOAT** Paleontological Contributions. Article. (1969)-(19??). Monographic series. English. ir. Exchange and Gifts Department, University of Kansas Libraries, Lawrence KS 66045. **Tel** (913)864-3338. **ED** Roger L Kaesler. **LC** QE701; .K3. **DD** 560.82. **CODEN** KUPABMUKPAB5. **Circ:** 700 (ctrl). Documents available from BIOSIS Document Express. **Continues** University of Kansas Paleontological Contributions, 0889-0420. **Merged with** University of Kansas Paleontological Contributions. Article, 0075-5044; University of Kansas Paleontological Contributions. Monographs, 0278-9744 and University of Kansas Paleontological Contributions. Papers, 0075-5052 **to form** University of Kansas Paleontological Contributions (Lawrence, Kan. : 1992), 1046-8390.
**Desc:** Principally systematic invertebrate paleontology.
**Ind/Abst** Biol. Abstr.; GeoRef.

US/0278-9744
**UNIVERSITY OF KANSAS PALEONTOLOGICAL CONTRIBUTIONS. MONOGRAPHS.** *Title Change.* [Univ. Kans. paleontol. contrib., Monogr.]. **Added/Corp** University of Kansas. Paleontological Institute. **VFOAT** Monographs. (1975)-(19??). Monographic series. English. ir. Library Sales Office, Exchange & Gifts Department, University of Kansas Libraries, Lawrence KS 66044. **Tel** (913)864-3338. **ED** Roger L Kaesler. **DD** 560. **Circ:** 700. **Merged with** University of Kansas Paleontological Contributions. Article, 0075-5044 and University of Kansas Paleontological Contributions. Papers, 0075-5052 **to form** University of Kansas Paleontological Contributions (Lawrence, Kan. : 1992), 1046-8390.
**Desc:** Systematic paleontology, usually dealing with invertebrates, often with geological implications.
**Ind/Abst** GeoRef.

US/0075-5052
**UNIVERSITY OF KANSAS PALEONTOLOGICAL CONTRIBUTIONS. PAPERS.** *Title Change.* [Univ. Kans. paleontol. contrib. Pap.]. **Added/Corp** University of Kansas. Paleontological Institute. **VFOAT** Paleontological Contributions. Papers; University of Kansas Paleontological Contributions. Paper; Papers; Paper. (1965)-(19??). Monographic series. English. ir. University of Kansas Libraries Department, Library Sales Office, Lawrence KS 66045. **Tel** (913)864-3338. **ED** Roger L Kaesler. **LC** QE701; .K33. **DD** 560/.5. **CODEN** KCPCA3. **Circ:** 750 (ctrl). Documents available from BIOSIS Document Express. **Merged with** University of Kansas Paleontological Contributions. Monographs, 0278-9744 and University of Kansas Paleontological Contributions. Article, 0075-5044 **to form** University of Kansas Paleontological Contributions (Lawrence, Kan. : 1992), 1046-8390.
**Desc:** Principally systematic invertebrate paleontology.
**Ind/Abst** Biol. Abstr.; GeoRef.

US/0275-5513
**UNIVERSITY OF LOUISVILLE STUDIES IN PALEONTOLOGY AND STRATIGRAPHY.** [Univ. Louisville stud. paleontol. stratigr.]. **Main/Corp** Louisville. University. No. 1 (1973)-. Monographic series. English. ir. Price varies per volume. University of Louisville National Science Building, Room 132, Louisville KY 40292. **Tel** (502)588-6821. **UDC** 551.7.
**Ind/Abst** GeoRef.

NE/0083-4963
**UTRECHT MICROPALEONTOLOGICAL BULLETINS.** [Utr. micropaleontol. bull.]. (1969)-. Monographic series. English. ir. Price varies per volume. Faculteit Aardwetenschappen, PO Box 80021, Budapestlaan 4, 3584 CD Utrecht Netherlands. **Tel** 011 31 034 0567558. **(Subscription address:** Utrecht Micropaleontological B, 4 Budapestlaan, 3584 CD Utrecht Netherlands**) ED** T. Van Schaik. **LC** QE719; .U8. **DD** 560/.5. **CODEN** UTMBAA. cum. index. **Pr Rev. Circ:** 500 (ctrl).
**Ind/Abst** GeoRef.

NE/0165-2753
**UTRECHT MICROPALEONTOLOGICAL BULLETINS. SPECIAL PUBLICATION.** [Utrecht micropaleontol. bull., Spec. publ.]. No. 1-. Monographic series. English. ir. Price varies per volume. UMB Special Publications, UMB Singel 105, Odijk The Netherlands. **UDC** 56:576.8. **CODEN** UMBPDJ.
**Ind/Abst** GeoRef.

US
**VIRGINIA MUSEUM OF NATURAL HISTORY MEMOIR.** See Natural History.

GW/0340-5109
**ZENTRALBLATT FUER GEOLOGIE UND PALAEONTOLOGIE. TEIL 1: ALLGEMEINE, ANGEWANDTE, REGIONALE UND HISTORISCHE GEOLOGIE.** See Earth Sciences-Geology.

GW/0044-4189
**ZENTRALBLATT FUER GEOLOGIE UND PALAEONTOLOGIE. TEIL II: PALAONTOLOGIE.** [Zentralbl. Geol. Palaontol., Teil 2]. (1965)-. Periodical. German. Seven times a year. $52.00. E. Schweizerbartsche Verlagsbuchhandlung, Johannesstrasse 3A, D-70176 Stuttgart Germany. **Tel** 011 49 711 625001, FAX 011 49 711 625005, telex 723363 SCHB D. **CODEN** ZGPGA4. Index available in last issue of volume--attached. **Continues** Zentralblatt fuer Geologie und Palaontologie. Teil II: Historische Geologie und Palaontologie.
**Ind/Abst** GeoRef.

## ABSTRACTING, BIBLIOGRAPHIES AND STATISTICS

US/0300-7227
**BIBLIOGRAPHY AND INDEX OF MICROPALEONTOLOGY.** **Added/Corp** American Museum of Natural History. American Geological Institute. Vol. 1 (Jan. 1972)-. Abstracting/Indexing Service. Multiple languages (English and Multiple languages). mo. $75.00, $600.00 (corporate). Micropaleontology Press, American Museum of Natural History, Central Park West at 79th Street, New York NY 10024. **Tel** (212)769-5658, FAX (212)769-5233. **ED** Susan Carrol and Sharon Tahirkheli. **[CCC].** cum. index. **Circ:** 300 (ctrl).
**Desc:** Information service extracted from GEOREF database covering current literature in all fields of micropaleontology; highly relevant to petroleum exploration.

US/0272-8869
**BIBLIOGRAPHY OF FOSSIL VERTEBRATES.** (BIBLIOGRAPHY OF FOSSIL VERTEBRATES / THE AMERICAN GEOLOGICAL INSTITUTE, THE SOCIETY OF VERTEBRATE PALEONTOLOGY.). [Bibliogr. foss. vertebr.]. **Added/Corp** American Geological Institute. Society of Vertebrate Paleontology. University of California, Berkeley. Museum of Paleontology. (1978)-. Bibliography. English. an (September). $135.00. Society of Vertebrate Paleontology, University of Nebraska, W436 Nebraska Hall, Lincoln NE 68588-0542. **Tel** (402)472-4604, FAX (402)472-8949. **ED** Judith A. Backsai. **LC** Z6230.V45; B53; QE841. **DD** 016.566. Index available. ctrl circ.
**Desc:** Designed to provide ready reference to publications on vertebrate paleontology and related disciplines from all countries and in all languages.
**Ind/Abst** GeoRef.

NE
**INA NEWSLETTER / INTERNATIONAL NANNOPLANKTON ASSOCIATION.** **Main/Corp** International Nannoplankton Association. **VFOAT** Newsletter. **VAT** International Nannoplankton Association Newsletter. Vol. 1 (1979)-. Newsletter. English. sa. $25.00. International Nannoplankton Association, Shell Mex House Strand, London WC2R 0DX England. **Tel** 11 44 30 535180. **(Subscription address:** International Nannoplankton Association, Robertson Research Llandudno, Gwynedd LL30 ISA N Wales UK.**) ED** J. Young. **Bk Rev. Ad Acc. Circ:** 300 (ctrl).
**Desc:** Covers nannoplankton, nannofossils and silicoplagellates; includes bibliography, taxonomy, reviews and announcements.
**Ind/Abst** Br. Archaeol. Bibliogr. (?-?); GeoRef.

# PAPER AND PULP INDUSTRY

US
**ABSTRACT BULLETIN OF THE INSTITUTE OF PAPER CHEMISTRY.** ***Title Change.*** **See** Paper and Pulp Industry-Abstracting, Bibliographies and Statistics.

US
**ABSTRACT BULLETIN OF THE INSTITUTE OF PAPER CHEMISTRY. KEYWORD INDEX.** ***Ceased.*** **Main/Corp** Institute of Paper Chemistry (Appleton, Wis.). ( )-(1989). Bulletin. English. mo. Institute of Paper Chemistry, 575 Fourteenth Street NW, Atlanta GA 30318-5403. **Tel** (404)853-9500, FAX (404)853-9510. **UDC** 676(048.3). ***Continues*** *Abstract Bulletin of the Institute of Paper Chemistry. Keyword Supplement.*

US/1047-2088
**ABSTRACT BULLETIN OF THE INSTITUTE OF PAPER SCIENCE AND TECHNOLOGY.** **See** Paper and Pulp Industry-Abstracting, Bibliographies and Statistics.

US/0897-2524
**ALKALINE PAPER ADVOCATE.** **VFOAT** Alk. Pap. Advocate. Vol. 1, No. 1 (Jan. 1988)-. Periodical. English. bm. $35.00 (individuals), $45.00 (institutions) surface mail. Abbey Publications, 7105 Geneva Drive, Austin TX 78723. **Tel** (512)929-3992, FAX (515)929-3995. **ED** Ellen McCrady. **DD** 676. Index available. **Bk Rev**. **Ad Acc**. **Circ:** 500.
**Desc:** Newsletter for the advancement of the production and use of alkaline paper.
**Ind/Abst** Abstr. Bull. Inst. Pap. Sci. Tech.

US/0364-2763
**ALKALINE PULPING CONFERENCE.** [Alkaline Pulping Conf.]. **Main/Corp** Technical Association of the Pulp and Paper Industry. **VFOAT** TAPPI Alkaline Pulping Conference Preprint. Academic Scholarly Publication. English. an. TAPPI - Technical Association of the Pulp and Paper Industry, Technical Park, PO Box 105113, Atlanta GA 30348. **Tel** (404)446-1400 Ext 203, (800)332-8686. **UDC** 676. **CODEN** TAPCDN. Documents available from CASDDS.
**Ind/Abst** Chem. Abstr.

MX/0187-6112
**'AMATL.** **See** College and School Publications.

US/1056-4772
**AMERICAN PAPERMAKER (1991).** (AMERICAN PAPERMAKER.). [Am. papermak.]. **VFOAT** Papermaker. Vol. 54, No. 3 (Mar. 1991)-. Trade Publication. English. Twelve times a year. $45.00 (one year); $67.00 (two years). American Papermaker, 57 Executive Park South, Suite 310, Atlanta GA 30329. **Tel** (404)325-9153, FAX (404)325-9581. **ED** Jerome Koncel; (editor's address: 3419A North Kennicott Avenue, Ablington Heights, IL 60004, phone: (708)307-3716). **LC** TS1080; .A55. **DD** 676. Index available (published separately). cum. index. **Ad Acc**, **Adv Mgr:** Carolyn Benedict, **Tel** (404)325-9153. **Circ:** 32,000 (ctrl). available on microfilm and microfiche from University Microfilms International (UMI). ***Formed by the union of*** *American Papermaker (Great Lakes Ed.), 1046-7122; American Papermaker (Eastern Ed.), 1046-7114; American Papermaker (Pacific Ed.), 1046-7130* ***and*** *American Papermaker (Southern Ed.), 0893-3545.*
**Desc:** Trade magazine for the pulp and paper industry.
**Ind/Abst** Abstr. Bull. Inst. Pap. Sci. Tech.; Pap. Board Abstr.; Trade Ind. ASAP [Full Txt.]; Trade Ind. Index [Full Txt.].

FR/0337-4971
**ANNUAIRE DU PAPIER, L'.** (19??)-. French. an. 225.00F. PACACEL, 18 rue Saint Fiacre, 75002 Paris France. **Tel** 011 33 1 42369559. **ED** Charley Sifaoui. **Bk Rev**. **Ad Acc**. **Circ:** 2,500 (ctrl).

CN/0316-4241
**ANNUAL NEWSPRINT SUPPLEMENT - CANADIAN PULP AND PAPER ASSOCIATION.** [Annu. newspr. suppl.]. **Main/Corp** Canadian Pulp and Paper Association. **VFOAT** Supplement Annuel sur le Papier Journal - Association Canadienne des Producteurs de Pates et Papiers. 1971-. English (French). an. Free. Sun Life Building/19th Floor, Montreal Quebec H3B 4T7 Canada. **LC** HD9839.N4; C3A. **DD** 338.4/7/6762860971. **Circ:** 2,000. ***Continues*** *Annual Newsprint Supplement, 0468-1444.*
**Desc:** Vols. for 1973 include comparative data for previous years.

US/1053-2781
**ANNUAL REPORT - PULP AND PAPER FOUNDATION (1988).** (ANNUAL REPORT / PULP AND PAPER FOUNDATION.). [Annu.l rep. - Pulp Paper Found. (1988)]. **Main/Corp** Pulp and Paper Foundation. English. North Carolina State University / Pulp and Paper, Pulp and Paper Foundation Inc, Robertson Wing/Biltmore Hall, PO Box 5288, Raleigh NC 27650. **LC** TS1111; .P85a. **DD** 676/.06073. ***Continues*** *Report (Pulp and Paper Foundation), 0882-8954.*

CN/0079-7960
**ANNUAL REPORT - PULP AND PAPER RESEARCH INSTITUTE OF CANADA.** ***Ceased.*** [Annu. rep. - Pulp Paper Res. Inst. Can.]. **Main/Corp** Pulp and Paper Research Institute of Canada. **Added/Corp** Pulp and Paper Research Institute of Canada. Paprican. (19??)-(19??). Periodical. English. an. Pulp and Paper Research Institute of Canada, 570 St John's Boulevard, Pointe-Claire Quebec H9R 3J9 Canada. **Tel** (514)630-4100, telex 05-821541. **LC** TS1080; .P8616. **DD** 676/.072071. ***Continues*** *Pulp and Paper Research Institute of Canada. Report.*

US
**ANNUAL STATISTICAL SUMMARY.** **See** Paper and Pulp Industry-Abstracting, Bibliographies and Statistics.

AT
**APPITA JOURNAL : JOURNAL OF THE TECHNICAL ASSOCIATION OF THE AUSTRALIAN AND NEW ZEALAND PULP AND PAPER INDUSTRY.** **Added/Corp** Technical Association of the Australian and New Zealand Pulp and Paper Industry. Vol. 40, No. 1 (Jan. 1987)-. Periodical. English. bm (Jan., Mar., May, July, Sept., Nov.). 60.00Aus$ (plus postage). Australian Pulp and Paper Industry Tech, 191 Royal Parade, Parkville Victoria 3052 Australia. **Tel** 011 61 3 3472377, FAX 011 61 3 3481206, telex 30625. **CODEN** APJOES. Documents available from The Genuine Article, CASDDS. ***Continues*** *Appita, 0003-6757.*
**Ind/Abst** Abstr. Bull. Inst. Pap. Sci. Tech.; AGRICOLA [Select. Cov.]; BioBusiness; Chem. Abstr.; Curr. Contents Eng. Tech. Appl. Sci.; For. Prod. Abstr. (1991-); Res. Alert [Select. Cov.]; SCISEARCH; Sug. Indus. Abstr.

GW/0002-5917
**APR. ALLGEMEINE PAPIER-RUNDSCHAU (1966).** (ALLGEMEINE PAPIER-RUNDSCHAU : APR.). [APR, Allg. Pap.-Rundsch.]. **VFOAT** APR. (1966)-. Periodical. German (English and French). Forty-eight times a year. DM425.91 Germany; DM522.00 other. P Keppler KG, Industriestrasse 2, D 63150 Heusenstamm Germany. **Tel** 011 49 6104 6060, telex 410 131. **(Subscription address:** Verlagshaus Heusenstamm, Postfach 1353, D 63131 Heusenstamm Germany.**)** **[CCC].** ***Formed by the union of*** *Allgemeine Papier-Rundschau (Technische Ausgabe), 0343-5415* ***and*** *Allgemeine Papier-Rundschau M, Marketing Papier, Papierwaren, 0171-1369.*
**Ind/Abst** Abstr. Bull. Inst. Pap. Sci. Tech.; F&S Index Plus Text, Int. [Select. Cov.]; Infomat Int. Bus.; Pap. Board Abstr.; PROMT.

GW/0939-141X
**APR EUROPE.** [Apr Eur.]. **VFOAT** Allgemeine Papier-Rundschau Europe; Paper Magazine for the European Market. (1990)-. Periodical. Multiple languages. P Keppler KG, Industriestrasse 2, D 63150 Heusenstamm Germany. **Tel** 011 49 6104 6060, telex 410 131. **UDC** 66/68 :33.
**Ind/Abst** Abstr. Bull. Inst. Pap. Sci. Tech.

AT/1320-9787
**ASIA PACIFIC PAPERMAKER.** (19??)-. Trade Publication. English. Eight times a year. $130.00 Australia, Asia & the Pacific; $154.00 other. Martin Bayliss Marketing Ltd, PO Box 943, Bondi Junction, Sydney 2022 Australia. **Tel** 011 61 2 6998395, FAX 011 61 2 389 8480. **ED** Martin Bayliss (editor's phone: 011 61 2 3896055). **Ad Acc**, **Adv Mgr:** Jan Henderson. Full Page (Color) $2,950.00. Half Page (Color) $2,240.00. **Pr Rev. Circ:** 6,000 (ctrl). ***Continues*** *Asia Pacific Pulp & Paper.*
**Ind/Abst** Abstr. Bull. Inst. Pap. Sci. Tech.

AT
**ASIA PACIFIC PULP & PAPER.** ***Title Change.*** (????)-(19??). English. qt. Martin Bayliss Marketing Ltd, PO Box 943, Bondi Junction, Sydney 2022 Australia. **Tel** 011 61 2 6998395, FAX 011 61 2 389 8480. ***Continued by*** *Asia Pacific Papermaker.*
**Ind/Abst** Abstr. Bull. Inst. Pap. Sci. Tech. (?-?).

●JA
**ASIA PULP & PAPER, TECHNOLOGY MARKETS.** **VFOAT** Asia Pulp & Paper; Asia Pulp and Paper, Technology Markets; Asia Pulp and Paper. Vol. 30, No. 2 (Sept. 1993)-. Periodical. English. Four times a year (Mar., June,. Sept., Dec.). ¥10300.00 Japan, ¥10400.00 others (surface mail);. Tec Times Company Ltd., Bunsei Building, 9-4 Ginza 3-Chome, Chuo-ku Tokyo 104 Japan. **Tel** 011 81 3 35415350, FAX 011 81 3 35419419. **ED** Show Goto. **Ad Acc**, **Adv Mgr:** Kei Yuhara. **Circ:** 7,500 (ctrl). ***Continues*** *Japan Pulp and Paper, 0285-726X.*

MX
**ATCP.** **Main/Corp** Asociacion Mexicana de Tecnicos de las Industrias de la Celulosa y del Papel. (May 1961)-. Periodical. Spanish (English). Six times a year (Jan., Mar., May, July, Sept., Nov.). $105.00 US & Canada; $135.00 Latin America; $180.00 others. Octavio Tirado - ATCP, Av Insurgentes Sur 3493, Poseidon 504, 14020 Mexico DF Mexico. **Tel** 011 52 5 6650368, 011 52 5 6061622, telex 1773608 CNCPME. **LC** TS1080; .A78. Index available (free). **Bk Rev**. **Ad Acc**. Full Page (B&W) $1,040.00. Half Page (B&W) $940.00. **Pub. Size:** Standard. **Pr Rev. Circ:** 2,250 (ctrl).
**Desc:** Publishes articles on the technology of cellulose and paper.
**Ind/Abst** Abstr. Bull. Inst. Pap. Sci. Tech.

FR/0997-7554
**ATIP. ASSOCIATION TECHNIQUE DE L'INDUSTRIE PAPETIERE 1989.** (ATIP.). **VFOAT** Revue - ATIP (1989); Revue de l'Association Technique de l'Industrie Papetiere. (1989)-. Periodical. Multiple languages. ir. Association Technique de l'Industrie Papetiere, 154 Boulevard Haussmann, 75008 Paris France. **Tel** 33 1 45628707, telex 290563 F ATIP. **UDC** 676. Documents available from CASDDS. ***Continues*** *Revue - A.T.I.P., 0750-7666.*
**Ind/Abst** Abstr. Bull. Inst. Pap. Sci. Tech.; Chem. Abstr.

AG/0325-6901
**ATIPCA. ASOCIACION DE TECNICOS DE LA INDUSTRIA PAPELERA Y CELULOSICA ARGENTINA.** [ATIPCA, Asoc. tec. ind. papel. celul. argent.]. **VFOAT** Asociacion de Tecnicos de la Industria Papelera y Celulosicaargentina. (1962)-. Periodical. Spanish. bm. Asociacion de Tecnicos de la Industria Papelera y Celulosica Argentina, Avda. Belgrano 2850, 1209 Capital Federal, Buenos Aires Argentina. **UDC** 676.
**Ind/Abst** Abstr. Bull. Inst. Pap. Sci. Tech.

GW/0170-4060
**AVR. ALLGEMEINER VLIESSTOFF-REPORT.** [AVR, Allg. Vliesst.-Rep.]. **VFOAT** Allgemeiner Vliesstoff-Report. (1972)-. Periodical. German. Twelve times a year. DM183.86 Germany; DM241.71 others. DPW-Verlagsgesellschaft GmbH, Borsigstr 1 3, D-63150 Heusenstamm Germany. **Tel** 011 49 6104 6060. **(Subscription address:** Verlagshaus Heusenstamm, Postfach 1353, D 63131 Heusenstamm Germany.**)** **UDC** 677-486.6.
**Ind/Abst** Abstr. Bull. Inst. Pap. Sci. Tech.

MY/0005-9145
**BERITA SELULOSA.** [Ber. selul.]. **Added/Corp** Bandung, Indonesia. Laboratorium Projek Balai Rayon dan Selulosa. Lembaga Penelitian Selulosa. (1965)-. Academic Scholarly Publication. Malay (English; summaries and/or abstracts in Malay and English). Four times a year. Free on request. Balai Besar Selulosa, Jl Raya Dayeuhkolot 132, Kotak Pos 1005, Bandung Indonesia. **Tel** 011 61 22 502980. **ED** Ir. Hendayani T. Adisesha, MS. **CODEN** BSELBN. Documents available from CASDDS.
**Desc:** Cellulose industry journal.
**Ind/Abst** Abstr. Bull. Inst. Pap. Sci. Tech.; Chem. Abstr.

GW
**BIRKNER.** (19??)-. English (French, German, Italian, Spanish and Portuguese). an. DM180.00. Birkner & Co. Verlag, Postfach 540750, D 22507 Hamburg Germany. **Tel** 011 49 40 85308 401, FAX 011 49 40 85308 381. **Bk Rev**. **Ad Acc**. available on CD-ROM. ***Continues*** *Europa Birkner.*

US
**BULL AND BRANCH : NEWSLETTER OF THE FRIENDS OF THE DARD HUNTER PAPER MUSEUM.** **Added/Corp** Dard Hunter Paper Museum. Vol. 10, No. 1 (Mar. 1991)-. Newsletter. English. Three times a year. $60.00 (institutions), $25.00 (individuals) US; $76.00 (institutions), $33.00 (individuals) other. Friends of the Dard Hunter Paper Museum, 4517 Pennsylvania Avenue North, Minneapolis MN 55412. **Tel** (612)588-7900. **ED** Doug Stone, 2920 South Wentworth Avenue, Milwaukee, WI 53207 USA; Telephone: (414)744-633. **Bk Rev**, (Qty: 2/year). **Circ:** 400. ***Continues*** *Dard Hunter Paper Museum Newsletter, 0737-4534.*
**Desc:** Hand papermaking news and special articles on paper, paper art, and papermaking techniques.

US/1040-7200
**CA SELECTS: PAPER CHEMISTRY.** **See** Chemistry-Abstracting, Bibliographies and Statistics.

●CN/1193-2988
**CANADIAN MARKET PULP.** [Can. mark. pulp]. **Added/Corp** Canadian Pulp and Paper Association. Woodpulp Section. (Jan. 1992)-. Periodical. English. qt. Limited free distribution. Canadian Market Pulp, The Editor, Suite 3, 2857 Sherwood Hieghts Drive, Oakville Ontario L6J 7J9 Canada. **DD** 338.4.

CN/0836-6756
**CANADIAN MARKET PULP STATISTICS.** [Can. mark. pulp stat.]. **Added/Corp** Canadian Pulp and Paper Association. **VFOAT** Statistiques Canadiennes, Pate Commerciale. (Dec. 1986)-. Periodical. English (French). mo. Free. Canadian Pulp & Paper Association, 1155 Metcalfe Street, 19th

Floor, Montreal Quebec H3B 4T6 Canada. **Tel** (514)866-6621, FAX (514)866-3035, telex 055-60690. **DD** 382/.4567612/0971021.

CN/1186-2033
**CANADIAN MILL PRODUCT NEWS.** [Can. mill prod. news]. Vol. 1, No. 1 (Sept. 1990)-. Periodical. English. bm. $2.00 per issue; $25.00 Canada; $35.00 other. Baum International Media, 831 Helmecken Street, Vancouver, British Columbia V6Z 1B1 Canada. **DD** 676/.05.
**Ind/Abst** Abstr. Bull. Inst. Pap. Sci. Tech.

CN/0705-6710
**CANADIAN PAPER ANALYST.** Vol. 1, (Feb. 1978)-. Periodical. English. Nine times a year. 215.00Can$ Canada; $205.00 other. JDR Publications, PO Box 300 Victoria Station, Westmount Quebec H3Z 2V5 Canada. **Tel** (514)933-8749, FAX (514)849-8367. **ED** Jim Rowland. **DD** 338.4/7/6760971.
**Desc:** Analysis in marketing, prices and costs on Canadian pulp, paper and paperboard industry.

●CN/1191-887X
**CANADIAN PAPERMAKER.** [Can. papermak.]. **VFOAT** Papermaker. Vol. 45, No. 7 (Sept./Oct. 1992)-. Periodical. English. Twelve times a year. 48.00Can$. MacLean Hunter Ltd. Business Publishers / Canada, Box 9100, Station A, Toronto ONT M5W 1A5 Canada. **Tel** (416)946-8420, (800)567-0444. **(Subscription address:** Indas, 35 Riviera Drive, Building 17, Markham Ontario L3R 8N4 Canada.**)** **LC** TS1080; .C35. **DD** 676./05. **CODEN** CPAPE8. available on an online database (file 16/Full-Text) from DIALOG. ***Continues** Pulp & Paper Journal, 0713-5807.*
**Ind/Abst** Abstr. Bull. Inst. Pap. Sci. Tech.

CN/0068-9491
**CANADIAN PULP AND PAPER ASSOCIATION. NEWSPRINT DATA.** (NEWSPRINT DATA.). [Can. Pulp Pap. Assoc., Newspr. data]. **Main/Corp** Canadian Pulp and Paper Association. (1970)-. English. an. Canadian Pulp & Paper Association, 1155 Metcalfe Street, 19th Floor, Montreal Quebec H3B 4T6 Canada. **Tel** (514)866-6621, FAX (514)866-3035, telex 055-60690. **LC** HD9769.W53; C55. **DD** 338.4/7/6762860971. ***Continues** Newsprint Association of Canada. Newsprint Data., 0317-4506.*
**Ind/Abst** Abstr. Bull. Inst. Pap. Sci. Tech.; Pap. Board Abstr.

CN/0823-2873
**CANADIAN PULP AND PAPER CAPACITY.** **Added/Corp** Canadian Pulp and Paper Association. Canadian Pulp and Paper Association. Economic and Statistical Services. **VFOAT** Capacite Canadienne de Production de Pates et Papiers. (197?)-. English (French). an. Free. Canadian Pulp & Paper Association, 1155 Metcalfe Street, 19th Floor, Montreal Quebec H3B 4T6 Canada. **Tel** (514)866-6621, FAX (514)866-3035, telex 055-60690. **DD** 338.4/7676/0971. ***Continues** Canadian Pulp and Paper Industry, 0823-2865.*

IT/0008-8765
**CELLULOSA E CARTA.** (CELLULOSA E CARTA. BOLLETTINO DELL'ENTE NAZIONALE PER LA CELLULOSA E PER LA CARTA.). [Cell. carta]. **Added/Corp** Ente Nazionale per la Cellulosa e per la Carta. **VFOAT** Bollettino dell'Ente Nazionale per la Cellulosa e per la Carta. Vol. 1 (1950)-. Periodical. Italian. Six times a year. L35000 Italy; L50000 others. Ress, Via Assisi 163, 00181 Rome Italy. **Tel** 011 39 6 78051205. **DD** 676. **CODEN** CLCAA9. Documents available from BIOSIS Document Express, CASDDS. ***Supersedes** Cellulosa.*
**Ind/Abst** Abstr. Bull. Inst. Pap. Sci. Tech.; Agrofor. Abstr. (1991-); Biol. Abstr.; Chem. Abstr.; For. Prod. Abstr. (1991-); For. Abstr.; Pap. Board Abstr.

CL/0716-2308
**CELULOSA Y PAPEL.** [Celul. pap.]. (1985)-. Periodical. Spanish. qt. Asociacion Tecnica de la Celulosa y el Papel, Lincoyan 199, 2 piso, Casilla 74-C, Concepcion Chile. **Tel** 56 41 237 679. **UDC** 676.
**Ind/Abst** Abstr. Bull. Inst. Pap. Sci. Tech.

BL
**CELULOSE & PAPEL.** **VFOAT** Celulose e Papel. Vol. 1, No. 1 (April/May 1985)-. Periodical. Portuguese.
**Ind/Abst** Pap. Board Abstr.

BU/0204-6377
**CELULOZA I KHARTIYA.** (TSELULOZA I KHARTIIA.). [Celul. khartiya]. **Added/Corp** Bulgaria. Ministerstvo na Gorite i Gorskata Promishlennost. Nauchno-Tekhnicheski Suiuz po Khimicheska Promishlenost. **VFOAT** Pulp and Paper; Zellstoff und Papier. (19??)-. Academic Scholarly Publication. Bulgarian (table of contents in English, German and Russian). bm (6 issues). $10.00. **(Subscription address:** Hemus Foreign Trade Organization, 6 Tzar Osvoboditel Boulevard, 1000 Sofia Bulgaria.**)** **ED** I. Genev. **CODEN** TKHADD. Documents available from CASDDS.
**Ind/Abst** Abstr. Bull. Inst. Pap. Sci. Tech.; Chem. Abstr. (1970-1984).

RM
**CELULOZA SI HIRTIE (BUCHAREST, ROMANIA : 1986).** (CELULOZA SI HIRTIE : CH.). **Added/Corp** Institutul Central de Chimie (Romania). **VFOAT** Revista Celuloza Si Hirtie. Vol. 35 (1986)-. Academic Scholarly Publication. Romanian. qt. $100.00. Technical Association for Romanian Pulp and Paper Industry, Calea Grivitei 21 Sector 1, Bucharest Romania. **Tel** 50 64 30, FAX 50 60 45. **LC** TS1080; .C43. **CODEN** CEHIED. **Bk Rev. Ad Acc.** Documents available from CASDDS. ***Continues** Revista Padurilor-Industria Lemnului, Celuloza Si Hirtie. Celuloza Si Hirtie, 0258-2287.*
**Ind/Abst** Abstr. Bull. Inst. Pap. Sci. Tech.; Chem. Abstr.; For. Prod. Abstr. (1991-).

US
**COMPETITIVE GRADE FINDER FOR THE PAPER AND GRAPHIC ARTS INDUSTRIES, THE.** **Added/Corp** Grade Finders Inc. **VFOAT** Paper Buyers Guide; Competitive Grade Finder for the Paper Industry; Competitive Grade Finder. (19??)-. English. an. $37.10 Pennsylvania; $35.00 other US; $40.00 Canada. Grade Finders Inc, PO Box 944, 662 Exton Commons, Exton PA 19341. **Tel** (215)524-7070, 800 633-6088, FAX (215)524-8912. **ED** William A. Subers. **LC** TS1088; .C57. **DD** 676/.28/029473. **Ad Acc, Adv Mgr:** Mark Subers. **Circ:** 3,500.

US
**COMPETITIVE GRADE FINDER FOR THE PAPER INDUSTRY, THE.** ***Title Change.*** (19??)-?. English. an. Grade Finders Inc, PO Box 944, 662 Exton Commons, Exton PA 19341. **Tel** (215)524-7070, 800 633-6088, FAX (215)524-8912. **LC** TS1088; .C58. **DD** 338.4/7/676202573. ***Continued by** Competitive Grade Finder for the Paper and Graphic Arts Industry.*

US/1041-7249
**CONFERENCE RECORD OF ... ANNUAL PULP AND PAPER INDUSTRY TECHNICAL CONFERENCE.** [Conf. rec. Annu. Pulp Pap. Ind. Tech. Conf.]. **Added/Corp** Institute of Electrical and Electronics Engineers. IEEE Industry Applications Society. Pulp and Paper Industry Committee. (1985)-. English. ir. IEEE, Institution of Electrical and Electronics Engineers, Inc., 345 East 47th Street, New York NY 10017-2394. **Tel** (908)981-1393, FAX (908)981-9667. **LC** TS1109; .P84. **DD** 676/.05. Documents available from Article Express International. ***Continues** Pulp and Paper Industry Technical Conference. IEEE Conference Record of Annual Pulp and Paper Industry Technical Conference, 0190-2172.*
**Ind/Abst** AGRICOLA [Select. Cov.]; Bioeng. Abstr.; Ei Page One; Eng. Index Annu.; Index IEEE Publ.

UK/0010-8189
**CONVERTER.** (THE CONVERTER.). [Converter]. Jan. 1964-. Periodical. English. mo. £43.00 UK; £50.00 other. Faversham House Group Ltd, Faversham House, 111 Saint James Road, Croydon Surrey CR9 2TH England. **Tel** 011 44 81 684 4082. available on microfilm from University Microfilms International (UMI).
**Ind/Abst** Abstr. Bull. Inst. Pap. Sci. Tech.; Abstr. Graphic Arts Tech. Found. (1979, 1984); Int. Packag. Abstr.; Pap. Board Abstr.; Print. Abstr.

US
**CURRENT INDUSTRIAL REPORTS. MA26A, PULP, PAPER, AND BOARD.** **VFOAT** Pulp, Paper, and Board. 1980-. Government Publication. English. an. US Department of Commerce / Bureau of the Census, Data User Services Division, Customer Services, Washington DC 20233-0800. **Tel** (301)763-4100. **(Subscription address:** Superintendent of Documents, US Government Printing Office, Washington DC 20402.**)** ***Continues** Current Industrial Reports. M26A, Pulp, Paper, and Board, 0146-3527.*

GW/0012-1096
**DEUTSCHER DRUCKER STUTTGART.** [Dtsch Druck.Stuttg.]. (1965)-. Periodical. German. Forty-two times a year. DM241.80 Germany; DM354.60 other. Deutscher Drucker Verlag International, Postfach 4124/Senefelderstr 12, D 73744 Ostfildern 1 Germany. **Tel** 011 49 711 448170, FAX 011 49 711 415299, telex 841 177111490.
**Ind/Abst** Abstr. Bull. Inst. Pap. Sci. Tech.

GW/0070-4296
**DPW. DEUTSCHE PAPIERWIRTSCHAFT.** (DEUTSCHE PAPIERWIRTSCHAFT.). [DPW, Dtsch. Papierwirtsch.]. **VFOAT** DPW; D.P.W. (1961)-. Academic Scholarly Publication. German. Four times a year. DM198.29 Germany; DM282.86 other. DPW-Verlagsgesellschaft GmbH, Borsigstr 1 3, D-63150 Heusenstamm Germany. **Tel** 011 49 6104 6060. **CODEN** DPAWA2. **[CCC].** Documents available from CASDDS.
**Ind/Abst** Abstr. Bull. Inst. Pap. Sci. Tech.; Chem. Abstr.; Pap. Board Abstr.

NE/0924-9303
**ECMA FOLDING CARTON BULLETIN ENGLISH ED.** (ECMA FOLDING CARTON BULLETIN.). [ECMA fold. carton bull. Engl. ed.]. **VFOAT** European Carton Makers Folding Carton Bulletin (English Ed.). (1990)-. Bulletin. English. qt. European Carton Maker's Association, Laan Copes van Cattenburch 79, 2585-EW, The Hague Netherlands. **UDC** 621.798.14 + 676.27.
**Ind/Abst** Abstr. Bull. Inst. Pap. Sci. Tech.

FR/0754-0590
**EMBALLAGES MAGAZINE.** [Emball. mag.]. (983)-. Periodical. French. mo. Emballages Magazine, 1 Cite Bergere, 75009 Paris France. **UDC** 621.798. ***Continues** Emballages (Paris), 0013-6573.*
**Ind/Abst** Abstr. Bull. Inst. Pap. Sci. Tech.

US/0271-9959
**ENGINEERING CONFERENCE.** [Eng. conf.]. **Added/Corp** Technical Association of the Pulp and Paper Industry. (19??)-. Academic Scholarly Publication. English. an. price varies per volume. Technical Association of the Pulp and Paper Industry, PO Box 100113, Atlanta GA 30348. **Tel** 800 332-8686 or, (404)446-1400 ext. 203. **LC** TS1080; .E5. **DD** 676/.2. **CODEN** ECOPD8. **[CCC].** Documents available from Article Express International, CASDDS.
**Ind/Abst** Bioeng. Abstr.; Chem. Abstr.; Ei Page One; Eng. Index Annu.

GW
**EUROPA BIRKNER.** ***Title Change.*** **VFOAT** Papier, Papiererzeugnisse, Zellstoff. (19??)-(19??). English (French, German, Italian, Portuguese and Spanish). an. Birkner & Co. Verlag, Postfach 540750, D 22507 Hamburg Germany. **Tel** 011 49 40 85308 401, FAX 011 49 40 85308 381. **LC** HD9835.A1; E95. **DD** 338.7/6762/0254. ***Continued by** Birkner.*

SW
**EUROPEAN PAPERMAKER.** (19??)-. English. Six times a year. $48.00 (one year); $72.00 (two years). Swedish Pulp and Paper Association, PO Box 5518, S 11485 Stockholm Sweden. **Tel** 011 46 8 7892800, . **(Subscription address:** Arbor Publishing AB, Midskogsgrand 5, S 11543 Stockholm Sweden.**)** ***Continues** Pulp and Paper Magazine.*
**Ind/Abst** Abstr. Bull. Inst. Pap. Sci. Tech.

US/0748-3236
**FADUM REPORT, THE.** [Fadum rep.]. (19??)-. Periodical. English. mo. $320.00 US; $350.00 other. Fadum Enterprises Inc, PO Box 3436, Boulder CO 80307. **Tel** (303)447-1711. **ED** Ole Kristian Fadum. **DD** 676.
**Desc:** Comments on information systems and process control management of the pulp and paper industry.

FI/0781-7789
**FINNPAP WORLD.** [Finnpap world]. (1984)-. Trade Publication. English. Four times a year. Finnpap, PO Box 380, SF-00101 Helsinki Finland. **Tel** 358 0 1324438, FAX 358 0 1324433. **ED** Monica Karske. **UDC** 676. **Circ:** 13,000.
**Ind/Abst** Abstr. Bull. Inst. Pap. Sci. Tech.

CN/0319-762X
**FORET ET PAPIER.** No. 1- Jan. 1975-. French. bm. $33.27. Maclean Hunter Canada / Montreal, 1001 bvd. de Maisonneuve W., Montreal, Quebec H3A 3E1 Canada. **Tel** 514-845-5141, FAX 514-845-4302, telex 055-60604. **DD** 338.4/7/6760971. available on microfilm from University Microfilms International (UMI).

US/0730-8124
**GIDROLIZNAIA I LESOKHIMISCHESKAIA PROMYSHLENNOST.** ***Title Change.*** (HYDROLYSIS AND WOOD CHEMISTRY USSR.). [Hydrolys. wood chem. USSR]. **VFOAT** Hydrolysis and Wood Chemistry U.S.S.R. (1977)-(1992). Academic Scholarly Publication. English (Russian; translations available in Russian). Eight times a year. Allerton Press, Inc., 150 Fifth Avenue, New York NY 10011. **Tel** (212)924-3950, FAX (212)463-9684, telex 427441 ALPRES. **LC** TS1171; .G53. **DD** 676/.12. ***Continued by** Gidroliznaia i Lesokhimicheskaia Promyshlennost. English. Hydrolysis and Wood Chemistry, 1068-3658.*
**Ind/Abst** AGRICOLA (?-?) [Select. Cov.]; EMBASE (?-?); For. Prod. Abstr. (?-?); For. Abstr. (?-?).

NE
**GOLFKARTON- EN KARTONNAGE-INDUSTRIE PRODUKTIESTATISTIEKEN.** **Main/Corp** Netherlands. Centraal Bureau Bureau voor de Statistiek. Hoofdafdeling Statistieken van Industrie en Bouwnijverheid. **VFOAT** Corrugated Board and Folding Carton Converting Production Statistics. Dutch (summaries and/or abstracts in English). Fl8.75. Centraal Bureau voor de Statistiek, AFD ALG Zaken, Postbus 959, 2270 AZ Voorburg Netherlands. **Tel** 011 31 70 3373800, FAX 011 31 038 7429, telex 32692 CBS NL. **LC** HD9839.P33; N446A.

CN/0317-1078
**GREAT LAKER, THE.** No. 1- Sept. 1959-. English. mo. Free to employees, retirees, and individual

requests. Canadian Pacific Forest Products Limited, Great Lakes Region, 2001 Neebing Avenue, Thunder Bay Ontario P7C 4W3 Canada. **Tel** (807)475-2641, telex 073-4576. **ED** Larry Squire. **DD** 071/.13/12. **Circ:** 6,000 (ctrl).
**Desc:** Employee newsletter.

CC/1001-3911
**GUOWAI ZAOZHI.** **VFOAT** World Pulp and Paper. (1982)-. Periodical. Chinese. bm. $24.00. World Pulp and Paper, 12 Guaghua Road, Beijing, China. **Tel** 011 86 5022561 ext. 3106. **DD** 676. Index available (bound in 6th issue).
**Desc:** Covers the paper and pulp industry.
**Ind/Abst** Abstr. Bull. Inst. Pap. Sci. Tech.

US/0887-1418
**HAND PAPERMAKING.** [Hand papermak.]. **VFOAT** Hand Paper Making. Vol. 1, No. 1 (Spring 1986)-. Periodical. English. Six times a year. $25.00 US; $28.00 Canada and Mexico; $30.00 other. Hand Papermaking, PO Box 77027, Washington DC 20013-7027. **Tel** (301)587-3635. **ED** Michael Durgin. **DD** 676. Index available (published separately). cum. index. **Bk Rev**, (Qty: 4-6). **Ad Acc. Circ:** 1,500.
**Desc:** Information on the art and craft of Western and Eastern hand papermaking with a distinctive handmade paper sample in each issue; also an accompanying quarterly newsletter.
**Ind/Abst** Abstr. Bull. Inst. Pap. Sci. Tech.; Index Inf.

RU/0132-7046
**HIMIJA I TEHNOLOGIJA CELLJULOZY.** **See** Chemistry-Chemical Technology.

AU/0018-3849
**HOLZFORSCHUNG UND HOLZVERWERTUNG.** **See** Forestry-Lumber and Wood.

US/1068-3658
**HYDROLYSIS AND WOOD CHEMISTRY.** [Hydrolys. wood chem.]. (1992)-. Periodical. English (translations available in Russian). bm. $825.00. Allerton Press, Inc., 150 Fifth Avenue, New York NY 10011. **Tel** (212)924-3950, FAX (212)463-9684, telex 427441 ALPRES. **LC** TS1171; .G53. **DD** 676/.12. **[CCC].** ***Continues*** *Gidroliznaia I Lesokhimicheskaia Promyshlennost. English. Hydrolysis and Wood Chemistry USSR, 0730-8124.*
**Ind/Abst** EMBASE.

GW/0250-8338
**I P H INFORMATION.** [IPH inf.]. Nos. 1-6, N.F. V. 1 (June 1962-Sept. 1966, Jan. 1967)-. Periodical. German (English and French). qt. International Association of Paper Historians, Wehrdaerstrasse 135, D 35041 Marburg Germany.
**Ind/Abst** Abstr. Bull. Inst. Pap. Sci. Tech.

II
**INDIAN PRINT AND PAPER.** **VFOAT** Indian Print & Paper. Periodical. English. ir. Indian Print and Paper, Chartered Bank Building, Calcutta India.

IT/0392-9108
**INDICATORE CARTARIO : RASSEGNA BIBLIOGRAFICA MENSILE.** [Indic. cart.]. Began in 1980. Periodical. Italian. mo.
**Ind/Abst** Abstr. Bull. Inst. Pap. Sci. Tech.

SP/0376-9933
**INDICE DE TECNICOS PAPELEROS ESPANOLES.** **Added/Corp** Asociacion de Investigacion Tecnica de la Industria Papelera Espanola. (1973)-. Spanish. ir. 500ptas. Asociacion de Investigacion Tecnica de la Industria Papelera Espanola, Plaza de Salamanca 9 6, Madrid Spain. **LC** TS1088; .I53.

IT/0019-7548
**INDUSTRIA DELLA CARTA.** [Ind. carta]. **Added/Corp** Milan. Stazione Sperimentale per la Cellulosa, Carta e Fibre Tessili Vegetali ed Artificiali. (1963)-. Academic Scholarly Publication. Italian. mo. L100000 Italy; 130000 Europe; 240000 other. Arti Poligrafiche Europee SAS, Via Casella 16, 20156 Milan Italy. **Tel** 011 39 02 330221, FAX 011 39 02 394341, telex 326544 ANTO I. **ED** Osvaldo Gigliotti. **CODEN** ICAMA4. Index available. **Bk Rev. Ad Acc. Circ:** 2,900. Documents available from CASDDS.
**Ind/Abst** Abstr. Bull. Inst. Pap. Sci. Tech.; Chem. Abstr.; Pap. Board Abstr.

FR
**INDUSTRIE DES PATES ET PAPIERS.** (L'INDUSTRIE DES PATES ET PAPIERS DANS LES PAYS MEMBRES DE L'OCDE.). **Added/Corp** Organisation for Economic Co-Operation and Development. **VFOAT** Pulp and Paper Industry in the OECD Member Countries. (1968/69)-. English (French). an. $32.00. OECD Publications and Information Center, 2 rue Andre-Pascal, 75775 Paris Cedex 16 France. **Tel** 011 33 1 45248167, US:(202)785-6323, FAX 011 33 1 45248500 OR 45248176, telex 620 160 OCDE. **(Subscription address:** OECD Publications Center, 2001 L Street, Suite 700, Washington DC 20036.**) LC** HD9769.W5; O7. ***Continues*** *Industrie des Pates et Papiers dans les Pays Membres de l'OECD la Finlande, 0474-5485.*

**Desc:** Provides annual quantity data on production and consumption of pulp and paper products, on production capacity and utilization and on foreign trade for thirty-three pulp and paper products or group of products by partner country.

US/0884-8238
**INDUSTRY FACT SHEET.** [Ind. fact sheet]. **Added/Corp** American Paper Institute. (19??)-. Periodical. English. mo. American Forest & Paper Association, 1111 19th Street Northwest, Suite 800, Washington DC 20036. **Tel** (202)463-2721, FAX (202)463-2787, telex 140950 AF+PA DC. **DD** 676.

US/0361-4719
**INSTRUMENTATION IN THE PULP AND PAPER INDUSTRY.** [Instrum. pulp pap. ind.]. **Added/Corp** Instrument Society of America. Pulp & Paper Industry Division. Vol. 9 (1968)-. Monographic series. English. bm. Instrument Society of America, 67 Alexander Drive, Research Triangle NC 27709. **Tel** (919)549-8411, FAX (919)549-8288, telex 802 540. **DD** 676. **CODEN** IPPICOIPPPBA. **[CCC].** Documents available from Article Express International, Ask*IEEE.
**Ind/Abst** Ei Page One; Eng. Index Annu.; INSPEC (1984-).

UK/0020-8191
**INTERNATIONAL PAPER BOARD INDUSTRY.** [Int. pap. board ind.]. (1958)-. Periodical. English. Twelve times a year. £26.00 UK, £32.00 other (surface mail); £60.00 (airmail). Brunton Business Publ Ltd., Thruston Down House, Thruston Down, Hampshire SP11 8PR England. **Tel** 011 44 264 889533, FAX 011 44 264 889622, telex 859562. **LC** TS1135; .I5.
**Ind/Abst** Abstr. Bull. Inst. Pap. Sci. Tech.; F&S Index Plus Text, Int. [Select. Cov.]; Int. Packag. Abstr.; Pap. Board Abstr.; PROMT.

CN
**INTERNATIONAL PAPERMAKER.** English. qt. (Comes with Canadian Papermaker). MacLean Hunter Publ. Limited / Toronto, 777 Bay Street, 8th Floor Agency Control, Toronto Ontario M5W 1A7 Canada. **Tel** (416)596-5000, (800)268-6811, FAX (416)596-5526.
**Ind/Abst** Abstr. Bull. Inst. Pap. Sci. Tech.

US/0097-2509
**INTERNATIONAL PULP & PAPER DIRECTORY.** (1975/1976)-. Directory. English. an. $263.00. Miller Freeman Inc., 600 Harrison Street, San Francisco CA 94107. **Tel** (415)905-2337, FAX (415)905-2240, telex 278273. **ED** Margaret Fennessey. **LC** HD9820.3; .I57. **DD** 338.4/7/676025. **[CCC].** Index available. cum. index. **Ad Acc. Pr Rev. Circ:** 2,800. available on diskette.
**Desc:** Information on the international pulp and paper industry. Containing detailed listings for over 6,000 pulp and paper mills and executive offices. Includes charts, North American paper importers/exporters. A buyers' guide listing over 2,000 industry suppliers.

FI/0784-7289
**INTERNATIONAL PULP & PAPER MARKETS.** **VFOAT** International Pulp and Paper Markets. (1988)-. English. qt (4 issues). $1100.00. Jaakko Poyry Oy, Martinkatu 3, PO Box 4, SF-01621 Vantaa Finland. **Tel** 011 358 0 89471, FAX 358 0 562 6957, telex 121069 JPCON SF. **UDC** 339.5 - 339.7.
**Desc:** A reliable source of information highlights the short-term trends in pulp and paper markets for: market pulp producers, paper and board producers, banks, agents, sales offices, associations, and industries related with pulp and paper making.

AU/0020-9422
**INTERNATIONALER HOLZMARKT.** **See** Forestry-Lumber and Wood.

SP/0368-0789
**INVESTIGACION Y TECNICA DEL PAPEL.** [Invest. tec. pap.]. **Added/Corp** Asociacion de Investigacion Tecnica de la Industria Papelera Espanola. (1964)-. Periodical. Spanish (summaries and/or abstracts in English, French and German). qt. $90.00 South America; $80.00 Spain; $100.00 other. Instituto Papelero Espanol, Avda Padre Huidobro SN, 27949 Madrid Spain. **Tel** 34 1 307 0977, FAX 34 1 357 2828. Index available. **Bk Rev. Ad Acc. Circ:** 1,000. Documents available from CASDDS.
**Ind/Abst** Abstr. Bull. Inst. Pap. Sci. Tech.; Chem. Abstr.

GW/1010-4054
**IPH YEARBOOK.** [IPH yearb.]. **Added/Corp** International Association of Paper Historians. **VFOAT** I.P.H. Yearbook; I.P.H. Jahrbuch; Annuaire IPH. Vol. 1 (1980)-. Periodical. English (French and German). an. 50.00F. International Association of Paper Historians, Wehrdaerstrasse 135, D 35041 Marburg Germany. **LC** TS1090; .I63. **DD** 676/.2/09.
**Ind/Abst** Abstr. Bull. Inst. Pap. Sci. Tech.; Art Archaeol. Tech. Abstr.

II/0379-5462
**IPPTA.** (IPPTA : QUARTERLY JOURNAL OF INDIAN PULP & PAPER TECHNICAL ASSOCIATION.). [IPPTA]. **Added/Corp** Indian Pulp & Paper Technical Association. (19??)-. Periodical. English. qt. **CODEN** IPPTDO.
Documents available from CASDDS.
**Ind/Abst** Abstr. Bull. Inst. Pap. Sci. Tech.; Chem. Abstr.; Cot. Trop. Fibr. Abstr. Bibliogr.

JA/0285-726X
**JAPAN PULP AND PAPER.** ***Title Change.*** [Jpn. pulp pap.]. **VFOAT** Japan Pulp & Paper. (1963)-(19??). Academic Scholarly Publication. English. qt. Tekku Taimusu, (Tech. Times Corp., Ltd.), 9-4, Ginza 3 Chome, Chuoku, Tokyoto 104 Japan. **(Subscription address:** Japan Publications Trading Company, Ltd., PO Box 5030, Tokyo International, Tokyo 100-31 Japan.**) CODEN** JPUPAB. Documents available from CASDDS. ***Continued by*** *Asia Pulp and Paper Technology Markets.*
**Ind/Abst** Abstr. Bull. Inst. Pap. Sci. Tech.; AGRICOLA; Chem. Abstr.; Nonwovens Abstr.; Pap. Board Abstr.

CN/0830-887X
**JOURNAL DES PATES ET PAPIERS.** ***Ceased.*** [J. pates pap.]. (May/June 1985)-Vol. 10 No. 2 (19??). Periodical. French. Four times a year. MacLean Hunter Ltd. Business Publishers / Canada, Box 9100, Station A, Toronto ONT M5W 1A5 Canada. **Tel** (416)946-8420, (800)567-0444. **(Subscription address:** Indas, 35 Riviera Drive, Building 17, Markham Ontario L3R 8N4 Canada.**) DD** 338.4/7676/0971. available on microfilm and microfiche from University Microfilms International (UMI). ***Continues*** *Foret et Papier., 0319-762X.*

CN/0826-6220
**JOURNAL OF PULP AND PAPER SCIENCE.** (JOURNAL OF PULP AND PAPER SCIENCE : TRANSACTIONS OF THE TECHNICAL SECTION.). [J. pulp pap sci.]. **Added/Corp** Canadian Pulp and Paper Association. Technical Section. **VFOAT** JPPS; Transactions of the Technical System; J.P.P.S. Vol. 9, No. 1 (March 1983)-. Academic Scholarly Publication. English (French; summaries and/or abstracts in French). mo. 210.00Can$ US; 175.00Can$ Canada; 235.00Can$ other. Canadian Pulp & Paper Association, 1155 Metcalfe Street, 19th Floor, Montreal Quebec H3B 4T6 Canada. **Tel** (514)866-6621, FAX (514)866-3035, telex 055-60690. **ED** D.H. Paterson. **LC** TS1080; .J677. **DD** 676/.05. **CODEN** JPUSDN. **Pr Rev. Acid Free. Circ:** 6,000. Documents available from Article Express International, The Genuine Article, Ask*IEEE, CASDDS. ***Continues*** *Canadian Pulp and Paper Association. Technical Section. Transactions of the Technical Section, 0317-882X.*
**Desc:** Devoted to the science of pulp and paper. Aim is to publish articles that illuminate the underlying principles of the technology of pulp and paper.
**Ind/Abst** Abstr. Bull. Inst. Pap. Sci. Tech.; Biodeter. Abstr.; Bioeng. Abstr.; Chem. Abstr. (1983-); Curr. Biotechnol.; Curr. Contents Eng. Tech. Appl. Sci.; Ei Page One; Eng. Index Annu.; For. Prod. Abstr. (1983-19??); Graph. Arts Bull. Inst. Pap. Sci. Technol. (Feb. 1989, April 1989, Aug. 1989); INSPEC (March 1983-); Pap. Board Abstr.; Res. Alert [Full Cov.]; Sci. Cit. Index; SCISEARCH.

US/0277-3813
**JOURNAL OF WOOD CHEMISTRY AND TECHNOLOGY.** **See** Chemistry-Physical and Theoretical Chemistry.

JA/0022-815X
**KAMI PA GIKYOSHI.** [Kami pa gikyoshi]. **Added/Corp** Kami Parupu Gijutsu Kyokai. **VFOAT** Journal of the Japanese Technical Association of the Pulp and Paper Industry; Japan TAPPI. Vol. 9 (1955)-. Academic Scholarly Publication. Japanese (English). mo. ¥18000. Japan Tappi, Kami Pulp Kaikan Bldg, 9-11 Ginza 3-Chome, Chuo ku Tokyo 104 Japan. **Tel** 011 81 3 32484841, FAX 011 81 3 32484843. **(Subscription address:** Kyowa Book Company Inc., 1 38 Kanda Jinbocho Chiyoda ku, Tokyo 101 Japan; Phone: 011 81 3 3293 0727**) ED** A. Fuse. **CODEN** KAGIAU. **Ad Acc. Circ:** 4,500 (ctrl). Documents available from CASDDS. ***Continues*** *Parupu Kami Kogyo Zasshi.*
**Ind/Abst** Abstr. Bull. Inst. Pap. Sci. Tech.; Chem. Abstr.; Coal Abstr.; Curr. Biotechnol.

JA/0453-1507
**KAMI, PARUPU GIJUTSU TAIMUSU.** [Kami, parupu gijutsu taimusu]. **VFOAT** Pulping, Papermaking & Converting; Pulping, Papermaking and Converting. (1958)-. Periodical. Japanese. mo. Tekku Taimusu, (Tech. Times Corp., Ltd.), 9-4, Ginza 3 Chome, Chuoku, Tokyoto 104 Japan. **CODEN** KPGTAW. Documents available from CASDDS.
**Ind/Abst** Abstr. Bull. Inst. Pap. Sci. Tech.; Chem. Abstr.

JA
**KAMI PARUPU KOGYO SETSUBI CHOSA HOKOKUSHO.** **Main/Corp** Japan. Tsusho Sangyosho Daijin Kambo. Chosa Tokeibu. (19??)-. Periodical. Japanese. Nihon Seishi Rengokai, (Japan Paper Association), 9-11, Ginza 3 Chome, Chuoku, Tokyoto 104, Japan. **LC** TS1117; .J36a.

JA
**KAMI PARUPU SEIZO SETSUBI CHOSA HOKOKUSHO / TSUSHO SANGYO DAIJIN KAMBO CHOSA TOKEIBU HEN.** Japanese. Nihon Seishi Rengokai, (Japan Paper

Association), 9-11, Ginza 3 Chome, Chuoku, Tokyoto 104, Japan. **LC** TS1117; .J36A. ***Continues*** *Kami Parupu Kogyo Setsubi Shosa Hokokusho.*

JA/0288-5867
**KINOSHI KENKYUKAI SHI / ANNALS OF THE HIGH PERFORMANCE PAPER SOCIETY, JAPAN.** **Added/Corp** Kasenshi Kenkyukai (Japan). **VFOAT** Kinoshi Kenkyu Kaishi; Annals of the High Performance Paper Society, Japan; Kinoshi Kenkyukaishi. No. 21 (Oct. 1982)-. Academic Scholarly Publication. Japanese (English). an. $30.00. Sanshu Paper Company Ltd, 12 1 chome Matsufuku-cho, Takamatsu 760 Japan. **Tel** 81 0878-67-3511. **CODEN** KIKKDD. Documents available from CASDDS. ***Continues*** *Kasenshi Kenkyu Kaishi.*
**Ind/Abst** Abstr. Bull. Inst. Pap. Sci. Tech.; Chem. Abstr.

JA/0911-2316
**KONBATEKKU.** [Konbatekku]. **Added/Corp** Kako Gijutsu Kenkyukai (Tokyo, Japan). **VFOAT** Paper, Film and Foil, Converting Technology; Converting Technology; Paper, Film & Foil, Converting Technology. (1985)-. Periodical. Japanese. mo. Kako Gijutsu Kenkyukai, Tokyo Japan. **CODEN** KONBEA. Documents available from CASDDS. ***Continues*** *Kami to Purasuchikku, 0389-7613.*
**Ind/Abst** Chem. Abstr.

CN/0822-4811
**LISTES - ASSOCIATION CANADIENNE DES PRODUCTEURS DE PATES ET PAPIERS, SECTION TECHNIQUE.** (LISTES : LISTES DE PAPIERS TECHNIQUES DE LA SECTION TECHNIQUE DE L'ACCP PUBLIES AU COURS DE ...). [Listes - Assoc. can. prod. pates pap., Sect. tech.]. **VFOAT** Indices : Indices to Technical Papers of the Technical Section, CPPA, Published During ...; Listes de Papiers Techniques de la Section Technique de l'AACP Publies au Cours de ...; Indices to Technical Papers of the Technical Section, CPPA, Published During ... . **VAT** Indices - Canadian Pulp and Paper Association, Technical Section (English and French Ed.). 1981-. English. an. Free. Canadian Pulp & Paper Association, 1155 Metcalfe Street, 19th Floor, Montreal Quebec H3B 4T6 Canada. **Tel** (514)866-6621, FAX (514)866-3035, telex 055-60690. **DD** 676/.05. ***Continues*** *Indices (Canadian Pulp and Paper Association. Technical Section), 0227-616X.*

US/1046-5359
**LOCKWOOD-POST'S DIRECTORY OF THE PULP, PAPER AND ALLIED TRADES.** [Lockwood-Post's dir. pulp paper allied trades]. **Added/Corp** Miller Freeman Publications, Inc. **VFOAT** Lockwood Post's Directory of the Pulp, Paper and Allied Trades; Lockwood-Post's Directory. **VAT** Lockwood Post's Directory of the Pulp, Paper, and Allied Trades. (1988)-. Directory. English. an. $223.00. Miller Freeman Inc., 600 Harrison Street, San Francisco CA 94107. **Tel** (415)905-2337, FAX (415)905-2240, telex 278273. **(Subscription address:** Miller Freeman / Gilroy, CA, 6600 Silacci Way, Gilroy CA 95020.**)** **LC** TS1088; .L79. **DD** 676/.025/7. **[CCC].** Each issue contains an index to its own contents (no volume index)--loose. ***Formed by the union of*** *Lockwood's Directory of the Paper and Allied Trades, 0076-0277* ***and*** *Post's Pulp and Paper Directory.*

UK
**MEMBERSHIP DIRECTORY - INSTITUTE OF PAPER CONSERVATION.** **Main/Corp** Institute of Paper Conservation. 1977/78-. Directory. English. £56.00 institutions England; £76.00 institutions other; £28.00 individuals England; £38.00 individuals other.

CN/0709-602X
**MONTHLY NEWSPRINT STATISTICS / CANADIAN PULP AND PAPER ASSOCIATION.** **See** Paper and Pulp Industry-Abstracting, Bibliographies and Statistics.

US
**NCASI SPECIAL REPORT.** **Added/Corp** National Council of the Paper Industry for Air and Stream Improvement. (19??)-. Periodical. English. ir. National Council of the Paper Industry for Air and Stream Improvement, 260 Madison Avenue, New York NY 10016. **Tel** (212)532-9000.
**Ind/Abst** Abstr. Bull. Inst. Pap. Sci. Tech.

US
**NCASI TECHNICAL REVIEW : BULLETIN.** **Main/Corp** National Council of the Paper Industry for Air and Stream Improvement. No. 3 (19??)-. Bulletin. English. ir. $1,200. National Council of the Paper Industry for Air and Stream Improvement, 260 Madison Avenue, New York NY 10016. **Tel** (212)532-9000. ***Continues*** *National Council of the Paper Industry for Air and Stream Improvement. National Council Technical Review : Bulletin.*
**Ind/Abst** Abstr. Bull. Inst. Pap. Sci. Tech.

BE
**NEW MAP OF THE EUROPEAN PULP & PAPER INDUSTRY.** (19??)-. Periodical. English. te. 2000F. Miller Freeman Publications / Belgium, 123A Chaussee Charleroi Box 5, B-1060 Brussels Belgium. **Tel** 011/32/2/5386040. **ED** B. Wilkinson. Index available. **Ad Acc. Circ:** 2,000.
**Desc:** Locates every pulp, paper and paperboard mill in Europe with annual capacity of over 10,000 metric tons, about 1,000 mills in 24 countries. Incorporates changes in mill ownership, mill closures, new mills, and mills under construction.

FI/0784-5073
**NORDIC PULP & PAPER.** [Nord. pulp paper]. **VFOAT** Nordic Pulp and Paper. (1987)-. Periodical. English. bm. Ekono Oy, PO Box 27, R Ristolainen, SF-00131 Helsinki Finland. **Tel** 011 358 0 46911. **UDC** 677.
**Ind/Abst** Pap. Board Abstr.

SW/0283-2631
**NORDIC PULP & PAPER RESEARCH JOURNAL.** [Nord. pulp pap. res. j.]. **VFOAT** Nordic Pulp and Paper Research Journal. Vol. 1, No. 1 (April 1986)-. Academic Scholarly Publication. English. Four times a year. Kr2450.00. Swedish Pulp and Paper Association, PO Box 5518, S 11485 Stockholm Sweden. **Tel** 011 46 8 7892800, . **(Subscription address:** Arbor Publishing AB, Midskogsgrand 5, S 11543 Stockholm Sweden.**)** **LC** TS1080; .N57. **DD** 676/.05. **CODEN** NPPJEG. Documents available from CASDDS. ***Continues in part*** *Svensk Papperstidning, 0039-6680.*
**Ind/Abst** Abstr. Bull. Inst. Pap. Sci. Tech.; Chem. Abstr.; Pap. Board Abstr.; Print. Abstr.

SW/0281-6733
**NORDISK CELLULOSA.** (1984)-. Swedish. mo. Svensk Travarutidning AB, Midskogsgrand 5, S-115 43 Stockholm Sweden. **Tel** 011 46 8 664 3400, FAX 011 46 8 664 2124.

BU/0204-9562
**NOVOSTI V TSELULOZNO-KHARTIENATA PROMISHLENOST / MINISTERSTVO NA GORITE I GORSKATA PROMISHLENOST, DSO, "TSELULOZA I KHARTIIA"-NIITSKH.** [Nov. celul.-hartienata prom-st.]. **Added/Corp** Nauchnoizsledovatelski Institut po Tseluloza i Khartiia (Bulgaria). (1971)-. Academic Scholarly Publication. Bulgarian. Nauchnoizsledovatelski Institut po Tseluloza i Khartiia, Sofiia Bulgaria. **CODEN** NTKPD2. Documents available from CASDDS.
**Ind/Abst** Abstr. Bull. Inst. Pap. Sci. Tech.; Chem. Abstr. (1971-1981).

US/0739-2214
**NPTA MANAGEMENT NEWS.** [NPTA manage. news]. **Added/Corp** National Paper Trade Association (U.S.). **VFOAT** Management News. **VAT** National Paper Trade Association Management News. (1983)-. Periodical. English. mo. $20.00 (1 year), $35.00 (2 year). National Paper Trade Association Inc, 111 Great Neck Road, Great Neck NY 11021. **Tel** (516)829-3070, FAX (516)829-3074. **ED** Edward Pasternack. cum. index. **Bk Rev**, (Qty: 4). **Ad Acc**, **Adv Mgr:** Carl Dunby, **Tel** (516)829-3070 ext. 19. **Circ:** 20,000 (ctrl). ***Continues*** *Current (Great Neck, N.Y.), 0737-0067.*
**Ind/Abst** Abstr. Bull. Inst. Pap. Sci. Tech.; Graph. Arts Bull. Inst. Pap. Sci. Technol. (Apr. 1989, Aug. 1989); Stat. Ref. Index.

US/0030-0284
**OFFICIAL BOARD MARKETS.** [Off. board mark.]. **VFOAT** Yellow Sheet. (1925)-. Periodical. English. wk. $130.00 US and possessions, Canada and Mexico; $180.00 other. Advanstar Communications Inc., 131 West First Street, Duluth MN 55802. **Tel** (218)723-9477, (800)346-0085. **ED** Fred Sharring. **DD** 338. **[CCC]. Bk Rev. Ad Acc.**
**Desc:** Newsletter for executives in the paperboard industry.
**Ind/Abst** Abstr. Bull. Inst. Pap. Sci. Tech.

FR/0396-0064
**P.C.C.** [P.C.C.]. **VFOAT** Papiers, Cartons, Films Complexes. (1973)-. Periodical. French. mo. **UDC** 676. ***Continues*** *Papiers, Cartons Complexes, 0035-2802.*
**Ind/Abst** Abstr. Bull. Inst. Pap. Sci. Tech.

BL/0031-1057
**PAPEL, O.** [Papel]. (1939)-. Academic Scholarly Publication. Portuguese. mo. $250.00. Editora Orientador Ltd, Caixa Postal 1430, Sao Paulo Brazil. **Tel** 220-4610. **ED** Paulo Engelberg. **LC** TS1080; .P106. **CODEN** PAPLA3. Index available. **Ad Acc. Circ:** 3,000. Documents available from CASDDS.
**Desc:** Everything concerning the pulp and paper industry and forestry.
**Ind/Abst** Abstr. Bull. Inst. Pap. Sci. Tech.; Art Archaeol. Tech. Abstr.; Chem. Abstr.; Corros. Abstr. (199?-); Pap. Board Abstr.

US/0031-1081
**PAPER AGE.** [Pap. age]. Periodical. English. mo. $65.00 US; $75.00 Canada; $95.00 other. Business Press Inc, 400 Old Hook Road/Suite G-5, Westwood NJ 07675. **Tel** (201)767-6800. **ED** Kenneth A Johnson. **DD** 338. **Bk Rev. Ad Acc. Circ:** 28,000 (ctrl).
**Desc:** Paper Age contains information on paper and pulp industry.
**Ind/Abst** Abstr. Bull. Inst. Pap. Sci. Tech.; F&S Index Plus Text, Int. [Select. Cov.]; Int. Packag. Abstr.; Pap. Board Abstr.; PROMT.

CN/0835-0094
**PAPER AND ALLIED PRODUCTS (OTTAWA).** (PAPER AND ALLIED PRODUCTS INDUSTRIES / STATISTICS CANADA, INDUSTRY DIVISION, CENSUS OF MANUFACTURES SECTION.). [Pap. allied prod.]. **Added/Corp** Statistics Canada. Census of Manufactures Section. Statistics Canada. Industry Division. **VFOAT** Paper and Allied Products; Industries du Papier et Produits Connexes. (1985)-. English (French). an. 38.00Can$ Canada; $46.00 US; $54.00 other. Statistics Canada, Publications Sales & Services, Main Building Room 1710, Ottawa Ontario K1A 0T6 Canada. **Tel** (613)951-5078, (800)267-6677, FAX (613)951-1584, telex 053-3585. **LC** HD9834.C2; P36. **DD** 338.4/76762/0971/021. ***Formed by the union of*** *Pulp and Paper Industries, 0828-9751; Other Converted Paper Products Industries, Including Asphalt Roofing Industry, 0828-976X* ***and*** *Paper Box and Bag Industries, 0828-9778;* ***Continues*** *Pulp and Paper Mills, 0384-4625.*
**Desc:** Annual census of manufacturers.

UK/0307-0778
**PAPER & BOARD ABSTRACTS.** **See** Paper and Pulp Industry-Abstracting, Bibliographies and Statistics.

UK/0959-9266
**PAPER & PACKAGING ANALYST.** **See** Packaging.

US/0031-1103
**PAPER & TWINE JOURNAL.** [Pap. twine j.]. **VFOAT** Paper and Twine Journal. (19??)-. Periodical. English. Ten times a year. Paper and Twine Journal, 1860 Broadway, New York NY 10025. **LC** TS1080; .P117. **DD** 676.
**Ind/Abst** Abstr. Bull. Inst. Pap. Sci. Tech.

SI
**PAPER ASIA.** (1985)-. Periodical. English. Nine times a year. $140.00 (12 issues) surface mail; $170.00 (12 issues) airmail. Toucan Publications PTE Ltd, 322-C King George's Avenue, Singapore 0820. **Tel** 011 65 2997121, FAX 011 65 2997545.
**Ind/Abst** Pap. Board Abstr.

SI/0958-0824
**PAPER ASIA NEWS : THE ASIAN PULP & PAPER NEWSLETTER.** (1994)-. Newsletter. English. mo. $275.00. Toucan Publications PTE Ltd, 322-C King George's Avenue, Singapore 0820. **Tel** 011 65 2997121, FAX 011 65 2997545. **[CCC]. Circ:** 200.
**Desc:** Digest of news, events, developments, personalities and corporations in pulp and paper industry as they relate to Asia.

US
**PAPER BUYERS' ENCYCLOPEDIA : FINE PAPER DIRECTORY AND SAMPLE BOOK, THE.** **Added/Corp** Grade Finders Incorporated. **VFOAT** Fine Paper Directory and Sample Book. 14th ed. (1990/1991)-. English. an. $95.40 Pennsylvania; $90.00 US; $105.00 other. Grade Finders Inc, PO Box 944, 662 Exton Commons, Exton PA 19341. **Tel** (215)524-7070, 800 633-6088, FAX (215)524-8912. **ED** Willam A. Subers. **Ad Acc**, **Adv Mgr:** Mark Subers. **Circ:** 3,000. ***Continues*** *Fine Paper Directory-Sample Book.*

US/0886-8212
**PAPER CLIPP.** (PAPER CLIPP / INSTITUTE OF PAPER CHEMISTRY.). [Pap. CLIPP]. **Added/Corp** Institute of Paper Chemistry (Appleton, Wis.). **VAT** Paper Current Literature in Pulp and Paper. (1986)-. Periodical. English. bw. $200.00 North America; $300.00 other. Institute of Paper Science and Technology, 500 10th Street Northwest, Atlanta GA 30318. **Tel** (404)853-9500, FAX (404)853-9510. **ED** N. Skifstad. **DD** 676. **Circ:** 75 (ctrl).
**Desc:** Contains the table of contents for over 250 pulp, paper, and forestry journals received by the IPC library.

UK/0140-1033
**PAPER CONSERVATION NEWS (LONDON).** (PAPER CONSERVATION NEWS - UNITED KINGDOM CONSERVATORS PAPER GROUP.). [Paper conserv. news]. **Added/Corp** United Kingdom Conservators Paper Group. Institute of Paper Conservation (Great Britain). No. 1 (June 1976)-. Periodical. English. Four times a year. Free to members of the Institute of Paper Conservation; $152.00 (institutions), $76.00 (individuals) membership. Institute of Paper Conservation, Leigh Lodge Leigh, Worcester WR6 5LB England. **Tel** 011 44 886 832323, FAX 011 44 886 833688. **ED** Edward Simpson. **Bk Rev. Ad Acc. Circ:** 1,500 (ctrl).
**Ind/Abst** Art Archaeol. Tech. Abstr.

UK/0309-4227
**PAPER CONSERVATOR.** (THE PAPER CONSERVATOR : JOURNAL OF THE INSTITUTE OF PAPER CONSERVATION.). [Pap. conserv.]. **Added/Corp** Institute of Paper Conservation. (1976)-. Periodical. English. an. Free to members of the Institute of

Paper Conservation; $152.00 (institutions), $76.00 (individuals) membership. The Institute of Paper Conservation, Leigh Lodge, Leigh Worcestershire WR6 5LB England. **Tel** 011 44 886 832323. **LC** TS1109; .P174. **DD** 676/.282/0288. Index available. cum. index. **Bk Rev. Ad Acc. Circ:** 1,500 (ctrl).
**Desc:** The Institute exists to disseminate information on conservation of art on paper, archives and books. Members are all those interested in the subject.
**Ind/Abst** Abstr. Bull. Inst. Pap. Sci. Tech.; Art Archaeol. Tech. Abstr.

UK/0955-7806
**PAPER EUROPE.** [Pap. Eur.]. (1989)-. Trade Publication. English. Twelve times a year. Whitmar Publications, 402 Vale Road, Tonbridge Kent TN9 1SW England. **Tel** 011 44 732 365629, FAX 011 44 732 359160. **ED** Martin White. **DD** 338.476762. **Ad Acc, Adv Mgr:** Jaret Smith. **Circ:** 14,350 (ctrl).
**Ind/Abst** Abstr. Bull. Inst. Pap. Sci. Tech.; Infomat Int. Bus.

UK/0950-4478
**PAPER EUROPEAN DATA BOOK.** [Pap. Eur. data book]. (1986)-. English. an. £190.00. Benn Business Information Service Ltd, Riverbank House, Angel Lane, Tonbridge Kent TN9 1SE England. **Tel** 011 44 732 362666, FAX 011 44 732 770483, telex 95454 BBIS. **ED** Dr. John Vincent. **DD** 338.47676094021. **Circ:** 600.
**Desc:** For all top decision makers involved with the European paper industry. Vital statistical analysis of the economies, raw material resources, and pulp and paper industries of Western Europe in one source.

UK
**PAPER FACTS & FIGURES. VFOAT** Paper Facts and Figures. (1961)-. English. qt. £68.00 UK; £84.00 other. Benn Publications Ltd., Sovereign Way, Tonbridge TNQ 1RW England. **Tel** 011 44 732 364422, FAX 011 44 732 361534, telex 0732 95132 BENTON G. **ED** Janet Seal. **Circ:** 3,500. ***Continues** PaperNews.*
**Desc:** Provides factual information on all aspects of paper and board. Over 1,600 papers and boards are listed carrying details on color range, surface character, recommended print processes, size, grammage and price.
**Ind/Abst** Pap. Board Abstr.

US/0031-1138
**PAPER, FILM AND FOIL CONVERTER.** [Pap. film foil convert.]. Vol. 27, No. 9 (Sept. 1953)-. Periodical. English. mo. $62.50 (one year), $112.50 (two year), $150.00 (three year) US & Canada; $87.50 (one year), $157.50 (two year), $210.00 (three year) other. MacLean Hunter Publishing Corporation / Chicago, IL, 29 North Wacker Drive, Chicago IL 60606-3298. **Tel** (312)726-2802, FAX (312)726-3091. **ED** James R. Martin. **CODEN** PFFCAT. **[CCC]. Ad Acc. Circ:** 32,000 (ctrl). available on microfilm and microfiche from University Microfilms International (UMI). ***Continues** American Paper Converter, 0096-090X.*
**Desc:** Serves the field which fabricates paper, paperboard, plastic films and resins, and foil materials into packaging products.
**Ind/Abst** Abstr. Bull. Inst. Pap. Sci. Tech.; Abstr. Graphic Arts Tech. Found. (1984); BioBusiness (1990-); F&S Index Plus Text, Int. [Select. Cov.]; Graph. Arts Bull. Inst. Pap. Sci. Technol. (Jan. 1989-March 1989, June 1989-July 1989, Oct. 1989, Dec. 1989); Infomat Int. Bus.; Int. Packag. Abstr.; Nonwovens Abstr.; Pap. Board Abstr.; Print. Abstr.; PROMT; Trade Ind. ASAP [Full Txt.]; Trade Ind. Index [Full Txt.].

UK/0950-3420
**PAPER FOCUS.** [Paper focus]. (1986)-. Periodical. English. mo. £72.00 UK; £115.00 other. Paper Publications Ltd., 14 High Street, Kings Langley, Herts WD4 8BH England. **Tel** 0892 45318, FAX 0892 31597. **DD** 338.4767620941.
**Ind/Abst** Abstr. Bull. Inst. Pap. Sci. Tech.; Infomat Int. Bus.

US/1048-8251
**PAPER INDUSTRY (MONTGOMERY, ALA.).** (PAPER INDUSTRY: THE PRODUCT NEWS DIGEST SERVING THE NORTH AMERICAN PULP AND PAPER INDUSTRY.). [Pap. ind.]. **VFOAT** Paper Industry Equipment. (1989)-. Periodical. English. bm. Paper Industry Equipment, PO Box 2268, 610 South McDonough Street, Montgomery AL 36197. **Tel** (205)834-1170, FAX (205)834-4525, telex 782350. **DD** 338. ***Continues** Paper Industry Equipment, 0889-731X.*
**Ind/Abst** Abstr. Bull. Inst. Pap. Sci. Tech.

UK/0306-8234
**PAPER (LONDON).** ***Title Change.*** (PAPER.). [Paper (London)]. (June 1972)- Vol. 217 [i.e. 218], No. 10 (Oct. 1993). Academic Scholarly Publication. English. Twelve times a year. Benn Publications Ltd., Sovereign Way, Tonbridge TNQ 1RW England. **Tel** 011 44 732 364422, FAX 011 44 732 361534, telex 0732 95132 BENTON G. **ED** Martin Bayliss. **LC** TS1080; .P3. **DD** 676/.2/05. **CODEN** PAPRCN. **[CCC]. Bk Rev. Ad Acc. Circ:** 8,600. available on microfilm and microfiche from University Microfilms International (UMI). ***Formed by the union of** Paper Maker; World's Paper Trade Review **and** Disposables International. **Continued by** World Paper (Tonbridge, England), 1353-2677.*

**Desc:** Provides international coverage of commercial and technical developments in pulp and paper. Includes an annual statistical review.
**Ind/Abst** Abstr. Bull. Inst. Pap. Sci. Tech.; Chem. Bus. Bull.; Chem. Bus. NewsBase (1985-); Chem. Bus. Update; Chem. Ind. Notes; Curr. Technol. Index; EMBASE; F&S Index Plus Text, Int. [Select. Cov.]; Graph. Arts Bull. Inst. Pap. Sci. Technol. (Jan. 1989-Feb. 1989, April 1989, June 1989-July 1989, Oct. 1989); Infomat Int. Bus.; Nonwovens Abstr.; Pap. Board Abstr.; PROMT; Trade Ind. ASAP [Full Txt.].

UK
**PAPER MARKET DIGEST.** English. £145.00 UK; £165.00 other. Paper Market Digest Ltd, 14 High Street, Kings Langley, Hertfordshire WD4 8BH England. **Tel** 09232, 61555, FAX 61118. **Pr Rev. Circ:** 500 (ctrl).
**Desc:** Statistical and marketing information specific to the UK market. Includes major news on European and world items relating to paper and pulp.
**Ind/Abst** Abstr. Bull. Inst. Pap. Sci. Tech.

US/0884-6545
**PAPER, PAPERBOARD & WOOD PULP.** **See** Paper and Pulp Industry-Abstracting, Bibliographies and Statistics.

US/1049-6572
**PAPER PILE QUARTERLY.** [Pap. pile q.]. (Apr. 1980)-. Periodical. English. Four times a year (Jan., Apr., July, Oct.). $12.50 one year; $22.50 two year; $30.00 three year. Paper Pile, PO Box 337, San Anselmo CA 94960. **Tel** (415)454-5552. **ED** L. Fitzsimmons, (619)322-3525. **DD** 790. **Ad Acc.**

SA/0254-3494
**PAPER. SOUTHERN AFRICA.** [Pap., South. Afr.]. (1???)-. Periodical. English. Six times a year. R68.40 South Africa; R80.00 APU countries; R96.00 other. George Warman Publications Pty, PO Box 704, Cape Town 8000 South Africa. **Tel** 011 27 21 245320, FAX 011 27 21 261332, telex 5-21849. **UDC** 676. **Bk Rev. Ad Acc. Circ:** 1,400 (ctrl).
**Ind/Abst** Abstr. Bull. Inst. Pap. Sci. Tech.

UK/0958-6024
**PAPER TECHNOLOGY (1989).** (PAPER TECHNOLOGY.). [Pap. technol.]. **Added/Corp** Paper Industry Technical Association. Pira (Association). Vol. 30, No. 2 (Feb. 1989)-. Periodical. English. mo. £80.00 UK; $137.75 US. Pira International, Randalls Road, Leatherhead, Surrey KT22 7RU England. **Tel** 011 44 372 376161, FAX 011 44 372 377526. **LC** TS1080.B73; A26. **DD** 656/.05. Documents available from Article Express International. ***Continues** Paper Technology and Industry, 0306-252X.*
**Ind/Abst** Abstr. Bull. Inst. Pap. Sci. Tech. (19??-); BioBusiness (19??-); Eng. Index Annu. (19??-); Graph. Arts Bull. Inst. Pap. Sci. Technol. (Aug. 1989, Dec. 1989); Pap. Board Abstr. (19??-).

FR/0299-9781
**PAPERCAST.** [Papercast]. (1986)-. Periodical. French. mo (11 issues). 3700.00F. Communication Conseil International, 5 rue des Gravilliers, F 75003 Paris France. **Tel** 011 33 1 42728066. **UDC** 676.
**Ind/Abst** Abstr. Bull. Inst. Pap. Sci. Tech.

FI/0031-1243
**PAPERI JA PUU.** (PAPERI JA PUU. PAPPER OCH TRA. PAPER AND TIMBER.). [Pap. puu]. **Added/Corp** Suomen Paperi Insinoorien Yhdistys. Suomen Puunjalostusteollisuuden Keskusliitto. **VFOAT** Papper Och Tra; Paper and Timber. Vol.32 (1950)-. Periodical. Finnish (English and Swedish). mo (10 issues per year - not published in January & July). Fmk430.00 Findland; Fmk620.00 other (surface mail); Fmk790.00 (airmail). Finnish Paper and Timber Journal Company, PO Box 154, SF-00131 Helsinki 13 Finland. **Tel** 011 358 0 132 6688, FAX 011 358 0 630 365. **ED** Marja Korpivaara. **LC** HD9765.F4; P3. **DD** 338.4/7674/0094897. **CODEN** PAPUAU. Index available (Published separately in December). **Bk Rev. Ad Acc. Pr Rev. Circ:** 4,100 (ctrl). Documents available from The Genuine Article, CASDDS. ***Supersedes in part** Suomen Paperi- Ja Puutavaralehti.*
**Desc:** A scientific-technical journal of the Finnish chemical and mechanical forest industries appearing ten times a year. It publishes scientific-technical articles, results of studies, news and reports relating to the pulp, paper, paperboard, sawn goods, plywood and panel products branches.
**Ind/Abst** Abstr. Bull. Inst. Pap. Sci. Tech.; Abstr. Graphic Arts Tech. Found. (1979, 1984); AGRICOLA; Chem. Abstr.; Energy Res. Abstr.; Graph. Arts Bull. Inst. Pap. Sci. Technol. (Oct. 1989); Pap. Board Abstr.; Res. Alert [Full Cov.]; Saf. Health Work; Sci. Cit. Index; Selec. Coop. Index Manage. Period; SCISEARCH; Soc. Sci. Cit. Index [Select. Cov.].

II/0048-2862
**PAPERPRINTPACK INDIA.** [Paperprintpack India]. **VFOAT** PPP India; Paper Print Pack India. (1963)-. Periodical. English. mo. $15.00. **(Subscription address:** Prints India, 11 Darya Ganj, New Delhi 110002 India.) **UDC** 676.

US/1180-9175
**PAPERTREE LETTER.** [PaperTree lett.]. **VFOAT** Paper Tree Letter. (June 1, 1989)-. Newsletter. English. Twelve times a year. $339.00 North America; $359.00 other. Miller Freeman Inc., 600 Harrison Street, San Francisco CA 94107. **Tel** (415)905-2337, FAX (415)905-2240, telex 278273. **DD** 338.1/749/05. ***Continues** Hay-Roe's Papertree Letter, 0822-8094.*
**Desc:** Market analysis of the worldwide paper and forest products industry.
**Ind/Abst** Abstr. Bull. Inst. Pap. Sci. Tech. (19??-).

FR/0031-1308
**PAPETERIE, LA.** [Papeterie]. Vol. 1, (1878)-. Periodical. French. Ten times a year. 744.37F France; 910.00F other. Grap Groupement Activites Presse, 21 rue d'Hauteville, 75010 Paris France. **Tel** 011 33 1 42463232.
**Ind/Abst** Abstr. Bull. Inst. Pap. Sci. Tech.; F&S Index Plus Text, Int. [Select. Cov.]; Pap. Board Abstr.; PROMT.

FR
**PAPETIER DE FRANCE, LE.** (1946)-. Periodical. French. Eleven times a year (Published tenth of each month). 220.37F France; 440.00F other. Editions Fructidor, 14 Boulevard Montmartre, F 75009 Paris France. **Tel** 011 33 1 42469294, FAX 011 33 1 90882849, telex 432845. **ED** Andre Durrieu. **LC** HD9833.1; .P3. **Bk Rev. Ad Acc. Circ:** 10,333 (ctrl).
**Desc:** Professional review concerning stationery items for retailers, wholesalers and dealers.

CN/0048-2889
**PAPETIER (QUEBEC).** (LE PAPETIER.). [Papetier]. **Added/Corp** Conseil des Producteurs de Pates et Papiers du Quebec. Association des Industries Forestieres du Quebec. Vol. 1 (Jan. 1964)-. Periodical. French. qt. Free. Association des Industries Forestieres du Quebec, 1200 Germain des Pres #102, Ste-Foy Quebec G1V 3M7 Canada. **Tel** (418)651-9352. **Circ:** 25,000.
**Ind/Abst** Point Repere.

CN/0847-2645
**PAPETIERES DU QUEBEC, LES.** [Papet. Que.]. Vol. 1, No 1 (Feb. 1990)-. Periodical. French. bm. 22.00Can$ (one year), 35.00Can$ (two year), 43.00Can$ (three year) Canada; 35.00Can$ (one year), 45.00Can$ (two year) US; 55.00Can$ other. Southam Information and Technology Group Inc., 1450 Don Mills Road, Don Mills Ontario M3B 2X7 Canada. **Tel** (416)445-6641, (800)668-2374, FAX (416)442-2261. **DD** 338.4/7676/0971405.

GW/0031-1340
**PAPIER, DAS.** [Papier]. **Added/Corp** Papiermacherberufsgenossenschaft. Vol. 1, No. 1/2 (July 1947)-. Academic Scholarly Publication. German (summaries and/or abstracts in English). Thirteen times a year. DM302.00. Eduard Roether Verlag KG, PO Box 101205, D 64212 Darmstadt Germany. **Tel** 011 49 6151 300116. **ED** Edward Roether. **LC** TS1080; .P286. **DD** 676. **CODEN** PAERAY. Index available. **Bk Rev. Ad Acc. Pr Rev. Circ:** 4,000 (ctrl). available on microfilm from University Microfilms International (UMI). Documents available from The Genuine Article, CASDDS.
**Desc:** Periodical for the production of wood pulp, cellulose, paper and board; chemical technology of cellulose; joint organ of the German Pulp and Paper Trade Associations.
**Ind/Abst** Abstr. Bull. Inst. Pap. Sci. Tech.; AGRICOLA; Chem. Abstr.; Curr. Contents Eng. Tech. Appl. Sci.; EMBASE; F&S Index Plus Text, Int. [Select. Cov.]; Pap. Board Abstr.; Res. Alert [Full Cov.]; Sci. Cit. Index; SCISEARCH; World Text. Abstr.

AU
**PAPIER & DRUCK. VFOAT** Papier und Druck. Vol. 92, No. 1 (Jan. 1986)-. Periodical. German. Twenty-four times a year. S710.00 Austria; S780.00 other. Brueder Hollinek & Co., Feldgasse 13, A-1238 Vienna Austria. **Tel** 011 43 1 8893646, 8893647. **ED** Karl Patschlea. **Circ:** 4,300 (ctrl). ***Continues** Papier Druck.*
**Desc:** Independent magazine for the paper and pulp industry, and the printing industry.
**Ind/Abst** Abstr. Bull. Inst. Pap. Sci. Tech.

AU/1011-0186
**PAPIER AUS OSETERREICH.** [Pap. Osterr.]. **Added/Corp** Vereinigung Oseterreichischer Papierindustrieller. Fachverband der Papierindustrie (Austria) Fachverband der Papier und Pappe Verarbeitenden Industrie Oesterreichs. No. 1 (July 1984)-. Periodical. German (summaries and/or abstracts in English). Eleven times a year. S1020.00. Austropapier Zietschriften, Gumpendorfer Strasse 6, A 1061 Vienna 6 Austria. **Tel** 011 43 1 588860, FAX 011 53 1 222 58886 222, telex 32213492. **LC** TS1080; .O37. **DD** 338.4/76762/09436. Index available. cum. index. **Bk Rev. Ad Acc. Circ:** 5,000. ***Continues** Osterreichische Papier.*
**Desc:** Reports of the international paper, pulp, and board industry and the wholesale trade and printing industry. Includes news on economy, engineering, forestry, commercial and jurisprudential articles.
**Ind/Abst** Abstr. Bull. Inst. Pap. Sci. Tech.; Int. Packag. Abstr.; Pap. Board Abstr.

FR/0031-1367
**PAPIER, CARTON ET CELLULOSE.** [Pap. carton cellulose]. (Mar./Apr. 1952)-. Academic Scholarly Publication. French (English; summaries and/or abstracts in English, German and Spanish). Twelve times a year

(Jan./Feb. and July/Aug. issues combined). 570.00F France; 669.00F other. Pacacel, 18 rue Saint Fiacre, 75002 Paris France. **Tel** 011 33 1 42369559, FAX 011 33 1 42338324. **ED** Martine Delefosse. **CODEN** PCCLAK. **[CCC].** Index available (Dec. iss.). **Ad Acc, Adv Mgr:** F. Henin, **Tel** 42 3695 59. **Circ:** 5,000 (ctrl). Documents available from CASDDS.
**Desc:** Covers news, investments and life of companies editorial team and correspondents.
**Ind/Abst** Abstr. Bull. Inst. Paper Chem.; Abstr. Bull. Inst. Pap. Sci. Tech.; Art Archaeol. Tech. Abstr.; Chem. Abstr.; EMBASE; Infomat Int. Bus.; Pap. Board Abstr.

GW/0031-1375
**PAPIER UND DRUCK.** ***Ceased.*** [Pap. Druck]. Vol. 1 (1952)-(19??). Periodical. German. mo. Deutscher Judo Verband, Redaktion Ippon Segewaldweg 40, D 12557 Berlin Germany. **Tel** 011 49 711 210770, telex 051 678. **LC** TS1080; .P289. **DD** 676/.2/05. ***Formed by the union of*** *Buchgewerbe* ***and*** *Polygraphische Industrie.*
**Ind/Abst** Abstr. Bull. Inst. Pap. Sci. Tech.; Bibliogr. Carto.; Print. Abstr.

GW/0048-2897
**PAPIER UND KUNSTSTOFF VERARBEITER.** German. mo. DM142.94 Germany; DM171.80 other. Deutscher Fachverlag GmbH, Verlagsgruppe, D 60264 Frankfurt Germany. **Tel** 011 49 69 75951001, telex 411 862.
**Ind/Abst** Abstr. Bull. Inst. Pap. Sci. Tech.

GW/0171-1458
**PAPIER- UND ZELLSTOFF-DIENST.** [Pap.-Zellst. Dienst]. (19??)-. Periodical. German (English and French). wk. DM710.00. Eueopaeischer Wirtschaftsdienst, Postfach 1332, D 76586 Gernsbach Germany. **Tel** 011 49 7224 939724. **UDC** 676:338. **Bk Rev. Ad Acc.** ctrl circ.

GW
**PAPIERMACHER, DER.** German. ir. (Free upon request). Dr. Curt Haefner Verlag GmbH, Bachstrasse 14, Postfach 106060, D 69050 Heidelberg Germany. **Tel** 011 49 6221 49063.
**Ind/Abst** Abstr. Bull. Inst. Pap. Sci. Tech.

XR
**PAPIR A CELUL'OZA : P + C. VFOAT** P + C. Vol. 21, No. 1 (1966)-. Periodical. Czech (summaries and/or abstracts in English, German and Russian). Twelve times a year. $93.20. **(Subscription address:** Artia Pegas Press Ltd., Palac Metro Narodni Trida 25, 11210 Prague 1 Czech Republic.) ***Continues*** *Papir a Celus'osa.*

HU/0031-1448
**PAPIRIPAR.** [Papiripar]. Vol. 1, No. 1 (1957)-. Academic Scholarly Publication. Hungarian (summaries and/or abstracts in Russian and German; table of contents in Russian and German). Six times a year. $29.00. **(Subscription address:** Kultura, PO Box 149, H 1389 Budapest 62 Hungary) **CODEN** PAPIBT. Documents available from CASDDS.
**Ind/Abst** Abstr. Bull. Inst. Pap. Sci. Tech.; Chem. Abstr.; Pap. Board Abstr.

HU/0231-0740
**PAPRIPARI ES NYOMDAIPARI SZAKIRODALMI TAJEKOZTATO.** (1983)-. Periodical. Hungarian. mo. 5.900ft. Orszagos Muszaki Informacios Kozpont es Konyvtar (O.M.I.K.K.), National Technical Information Centre and Library Museum, u 17, PO Box 12, 1428 Budapest, Hungary. **Tel** (361)118-1994, FAX (361)138-2414, telex 22-4944 OMIKK H. **ED** Peter Kalmar. **UDC** 655. **CODEN** 016. Index available. cum. index. **Bk Rev. Ad Acc. Circ:** 165 (ctrl).
**Desc:** Information on the paper and pulp industry and the printing industry.

KO/0253-3200
**PARPU, JONNI GISUR.** (PALPU, CHONGI KISUL.). [Parpu, jonni gisur]. **VFOAT** Journal of the Technical Association of Pulp and Paper Industry of Korea. Academic Scholarly Publication. English (Korean). **LC** TS1080. **CODEN** PCGIDY. Documents available from CASDDS.
**Ind/Abst** Abstr. Bull. Inst. Pap. Sci. Tech.; Chem. Abstr.; Pap. Board Abstr.

UK/0954-8521
**PHILLIPS INTERNATIONAL PAPER DIRECTORY.** [Phillips int. pap. dir.]. **VFOAT** International Paper Directory. (1989)-. English. an. £110.00. Benn Business Information Service Ltd, Riverbank House, Angel Lane, Tonbridge Kent TN9 1SE England. **Tel** 011 44 732 362666, FAX 011 44 732 770483, telex 95454 BBIS. **ED** George Hutton. **LC** TS1088; .P82. **DD** 338.7/676/025. ***Continues*** *Phillips Paper Trade Directory.*
**Desc:** Over 3,700 pulp, paper and board mills, 1,600 paper, board and paper products merchants, 1,800 pulp and paper agents, 6,150 machinery, equipment and materials manufacturers and/or suppliers in one impeccably cross-referenced book giving the most comprehensive coverage available of the world paper industry.

UK
**PHILLIPS INTERNATIONAL PULP & PAPER DIRECTORY.** Directory. English. an. £90.00 UK; £100.00 other. Benn Business Information Service Ltd, Riverbank House, Angel Lane, Tonbridge Kent TN9 1SE England. **Tel** 011 44 732 362666, FAX 011 44 732 770483, telex 95454 BBIS. ***Continues*** *Phillips Paper Trade Directory.*

US/0739-2133
**PIMA CATALOG.** [PIMA cat.]. **VFOAT** P.I.M.A Catalog; PIMA Pulp and Paper Mill Catalog. Catalog. English. an. $35.00. PIMA, 2400 East Oakton Street, Arlington Heights IL 60005. **Tel** (312)956-0250. **ED** Leslie Ross. **LC** TS1088; .P83. **DD** 338.4/76762/02573. **Ad Acc. Circ:** 5,000 (ctrl). ***Continues*** *Pulp and Paper Mill Catalog and Engineering Handbook.*
**Desc:** Information for equipment, materials and services required by pulp and paper manufacturers. Also engineering data and state-of-the-art reports on papermaking processes and production.

US/1046-4352
**PIMA MAGAZINE.** [PIMA mag.]. **Added/Corp** Paper Industry Management Association. **VFOAT** PIMA. **VAT** Paper Industry Management Association Magazine. (198?)-. Periodical. English. Twelve times a year. $40.00 US & Canada & Mexico (trade); $75.00 US & Canada & Mexico (non-trade); $90.00 other. Paper Industry Management Association, 2400 East Oakton Street, Arlington Heights IL 60005. **Tel** (708)956-0250, FAX (708)956-0520. **ED** Alan Rooks. **LC** TS1080; .P14. **DD** 676/.2. **[CCC].** Index available. **Ad Acc. Circ:** 21,000 (ctrl). available on microfilm and microfiche from University Microfilms International (UMI); available on an online database (file 648/Full-Text) from DIALOG. Documents available from Documents on Demand. ***Continues*** *PIMA, 0161-1364.*
**Ind/Abst** Abstr. Bull. Inst. Paper Chem.; Appl. Sci. Technol. Index; Energy Inf. Abstr.; Environ. Abstr.; Graph. Arts Bull. Inst. Pap. Sci. Technol. (Aug. 1989-); Pap. Board Abstr.; Predicasts.

BE
**PPI THIS WEEK.** (19??)-. Newsletter. English. Forty-eight times a year. 25500F. Miller Freeman Publications / Belgium, 123A Chaussee Charleroi Box 5, B-1060 Brussels Belgium. **Tel** 011/32/2/5386040. **ED** Rita Pappens. available via fax (47500F Europe and North America; 60500F other). ***Continues*** *PPI Newswire Service.*
**Desc:** Weekly newsletter for the paper and pulp industry.
**Ind/Abst** Pap. Board Abstr.

XO/0032-7328
**PREHL'AD LESNICKEJ, DREVARSKEJ, CELULOZOVEJ A PAPIERENSKEJ LITERATURY. VFOAT** Forestry, Wood, Pulp and Paper Technology Abstracts. Periodical. Slovak (German, French and Russian). ir. **LC** SD1; .P77.
**Ind/Abst** Abstr. Bull. Inst. Pap. Sci. Tech.

CN/0822-5206
**PREPRINTS A / TECHNICAL SECTION, CANADIAN PULP AND PAPER ASSOCIATION.** [Prepr. A - Tech. Sect., Can. Pulp Pap. Assoc.]. **Main/Corp** Canadian Pulp and Paper Association. Technical Section. Meeting. **VFOAT** Pretires A. 68th Annual Meeting (Jan. 26/27, 1982)-. English (summaries and/or abstracts in French). an. Canadian Pulp & Paper Association, 1155 Metcalfe Street, 19th Floor, Montreal Quebec H3B 4T6 Canada. **Tel** (514)866-6621, FAX (514)866-3035, telex 055-60690. **DD** 676/.05. Documents available from Article Express International. ***Continues in part*** *Canadian Pulp and Paper Association. Technical Section. Preprints of Papers to be Presented at the Annual Meeting, 0316-6732.*
**Ind/Abst** Bioeng. Abstr.; Ei Page One; Eng. Index Annu.

CN/0822-5214
**PREPRINTS B / TECHNICAL SECTION, CANADIAN PULP AND PAPER ASSOCIATION.** [Prepr. B - Tech. Sect., Can. Pulp Pap. Assoc.]. **Main/Corp** Canadian Pulp and Paper Association. Technical Section. Meeting. **VFOAT** Pretires B. 68th Annual Meeting (Jan. 28/29, 1982)-. English. an. Canadian Pulp & Paper Association, 1155 Metcalfe Street, 19th Floor, Montreal Quebec H3B 4T6 Canada. **Tel** (514)866-6621, FAX (514)866-3035, telex 055-60690. **DD** 676/.05. Documents available from Article Express International. ***Continues in part*** *Canadian Pulp and Paper Association. Technical Section. Preprints of Papers to be Presented at the Annual Meeting, 0316-6732.*
**Ind/Abst** Bioeng. Abstr.; Ei Page One; Eng. Index Annu.

CN/0707-8951
**PRETIRES, CONFERENCE TECHNOLOGIQUE ESTIVALE. Main/Corp** Association Canadienne des Producteurs de Pates et Papiers. Section Technique. 1978-. French. an. $20.00 (members), $25.00 (nonmembers). Association Canadienne des Producteurs de Pates et Pariers Section Technique, 1900 Edifice Sun Life, Montreal Quebec H3B 4T6 Canada. **Tel** (514)866-6621, FAX (514)866-3035, telex 055-60690. **(Subscription address:** 1155 Metcalfe, 19 Etage, Montreal Quebec H3B 4T6 Canada) **DD** 676/.0971. **Circ:** 500.
**Desc:** Compilation of pre-published papers presented at the conference technolgique estivale conference.

US
**PROCEEDINGS / EXECUTIVES' CONFERENCE, INSTITUTE OF PAPER SCIENCE AND TECHNOLOGY. Main/Corp** Institute of Paper Science and Technology. Executives' Conference. 54th (1990)-. Proceedings. English. ***Continues*** *Institute of Paper Chemistry (Appleton, Wis.) Executives' Conference.*

US/1061-1452
**PROGRESS IN PAPER RECYCLING.** (PROGRESS IN PAPER RECYCLING : PPR.). [Prog. pap. recycl.]. **Added/Corp** Doshi & Associates. **VFOAT** PPR. Vol. 1, No. 1 (Nov. 1991)-. Periodical. English. qt. $85.00 (one year), $140.00 (two year), $185.00 (three year) US; $95.00 (one year), $160.00 (two year), $215.00 (three year) other. Progress in Paper Recycling, PO Box 2771, Appleton WI 54913. **Tel** (414)832-9101, FAX (414)832-0870. **ED** Marianne Fiscus (managing editor), Mahendra Dashi (technical editor). **LC** TS1120.5; .P75. **DD** 676/.142/05. **[CCC].** Index available (Included in August issue). **Bk Rev. Ad Acc, Adv Mgr:** J. Schiel. **Pr Rev. Circ:** 660 (ctrl).
**Desc:** Technical journal dedicated to paper recycling.
**Ind/Abst** Abstr. Bull. Inst. Pap. Sci. Tech.

IT
**PROJECTED PULP AND PAPER MILLS IN THE WORLD. Added/Corp** Food and Agriculture Organization of the United Nations. (19??)-. English. an. $15.00 (latest edition). Food and Agriculture Organization (FAO) / Italy, GIPC166 via Terme di Caracalla, 00100 Rome Italy. **Tel** 011 39 6 522 52925, FAX 011 39 6 522 55784. **(Subscription address:** UNIPUB, 4611 F Assembly Drive, Lanham MD 20706.) **LC** HD9820.1; .P76. **DD** 338.4/7676/05.
**Desc:** List of pulp and paper mills planned to be established, expanded or closed down in next ten year period.

PL/0033-2291
**PRZEGLAD PAPIERNICZY.** [Prz. pap.]. **Added/Corp** Stowarzyszenie Inzynierow i Technikow i Przemysu Papierniczego w Polsce. **VFOAT** Polish Papers Review; Obzor Bumazhnogo Dela. (1945)-. Academic Scholarly Publication. Polish (summaries and/or abstracts in English and Russian; table of contents in Russian and English). mo. $117.00. **(Subscription address:** ARS Polona, PO Box 1001, 00068 Warsaw Poland.) **LC** TS1080; .P75. **CODEN** PRZPAE. Documents available from CASDDS.
**Ind/Abst** Abstr. Bull. Inst. Pap. Sci. Tech.; Art Archaeol. Tech. Abstr.; Chem. Abstr.; Pap. Board Abstr.

FR/0335-377X
**PULP AND PAPER. Main/Corp** Organisation for Economic Co-operation and Development. **VFOAT** Pates et Papiers. (1974)-. Periodical. Multiple languages (English and French). qt. OECD Publications and Information Center, 2 rue Andre-Pascal, 75775 Paris Cedex 16 France. **Tel** 011 33 1 45248167, US:(202)785-6323, FAX 011 33 1 45248500 OR 45248176, telex 620 160 OCDE.
**Ind/Abst** Abstr. Bull. Inst. Pap. Sci. Tech.; Bus. Index (1985-); Gen. BusinessFile (1985-); Pap. Board Abstr.; Text. Technol. Dig.

US/0033-4081
**PULP & PAPER.** [Pulp pap.]. **VAT** Pulp and Paper. Vol. 21, No. 10 (Sept. 1947)-. Periodical. English. Thirteen times a year. $105.00 US; $130.00 Canada & Mexico; $155.00 (surface mail), $295.00 (airmail) other. Miller Freeman Inc., 600 Harrison Street, San Francisco CA 94107. **Tel** (415)905-2337, FAX (415)905-2240, telex 278273. **(Subscription address:** Pulp & Paper, PO Box 1065, Skokie IL 60076.) **ED** Ken Patrick. **LC** TS1080; .P82. **DD** 338.47676. **CODEN** PUPAA8PUBAA8. **[CCC]. Circ:** 27,115. available on microfilm and microfiche from University Microfilms International (UMI); available on an online database (files 15,648/Full-Text) from DIALOG. Documents available from Article Express International, UMI Article Clearinghouse. ***Continues*** *Pulp & Paper Industry, 0096-4816;* ***Absorbed*** *Paper Mill News, 0096-1892; Paper Trade Journal.*
**Desc:** Covers the North American pulp and paper industry; read by corporate executives, mill managers, engineers and technical and production personnel. Contains news affecting the industry, interpretations of industry trends and practical information on new methods and equipment in use or in the planning stages.
**Ind/Abst** ABI/INFORM Glob. Ed. (19??-); ABI Inform Ondisc (Sept. 1973-July 1976); Abstr. Bull. Inst. Pap. Sci. Tech. (19??-); Abstr. Graphic Arts Tech. Found. (1984); Acad. Search (July 1993-); AGRICOLA (19??-) [Select. Cov.]; AQUAREF (19??-); BioBusiness (1990-); Bus. ASAP (1990-) [Full Txt.]; Bus. Period. Index (19??-); Chem. Ind. Notes (19??-); EMBASE (19??-); Eng. Index Annu. (19??-); F&S Index Plus Text, Int. (19??-) [Select. Cov.]; Gen. Period. Index (1985-); INFO-SOUTH Abstr. (19??-); Infomat Int. Bus. (19??-); Mag. Search (19??-); Pap. Board Abstr. (19??-); PROMT (19??-); Stat. Ref. Index (19??-); Trade Ind. ASAP (19??-) [Full Txt.]; Trade Ind. Index (19??-) [Full Txt.]; UMI ABI/Inform--Bus. Period. Ondisc (Jan. 1991-) [Full Txt.]; Vocat. Search (July 1993-); Wilson Bus. Abstr. (19??-).

US/0197-1069
**PULP & PAPER BULLETIN.** [Pulp pap. bull.]. **VAT** Pulp and Paper Bulletin. Bulletin. English. DRI McGraw Hill, 24 Hartwell Avenue, Lexington MA 02173. **Tel** (617)863-5100. **LC** HD9820.4; .P84. **DD** 338.4/7676/0973.

US
**PULP & PAPER BUYERS GUIDE.** **VAT** Pulp and Paper. Buyers Guide. (1976)-. Trade Publication. English. an. $55.00. Miller Freeman Inc., 600 Harrison Street, San Francisco CA 94107. **Tel** (415)905-2337, FAX (415)905-2240, telex 278273. available on microfilm.

CN/0316-4004
**PULP & PAPER CANADA.** [Pulp pap. Can.]. **VAT** Pulp and Paper Canada. Vol. 75, No. 9 (Sept. 1974)-. Academic Scholarly Publication. English (French). mo. 55.00can$ (one year), 66.00Can$ (two year), 78.00Can$ (three year) Canada; 62.00Can$ (one year), 91.00Can$ (two year) US; 136.00Can$ other. Southam Information and Technology Group Inc., 1450 Don Mills Road, Don Mills Ontario M3B 2X7 Canada. **Tel** (416)445-6641, (800)668-2374, FAX (416)442-2261. **ED** Peter N Williamson. **LC** TS1080; .P85. **DD** 338.4/7/6760971. **CODEN** PPCAAA. **[CCC]. Ad Acc. Pr Rev. Circ:** 9,000 (ctrl). available on microfilm and microfiche from University Microfilms International (UMI); available on microfilm from Micromedia Limited; available on an online database (file 16/Full-Text) from DIALOG. Documents available from Article Express International, The Genuine Article, Ask*IEEE, CASDDS, Documents on Demand. ***Continues*** *Pulp & Paper Magazine of Canada, 0033-4103.*
**Desc:** Covers new developments and experience in the applied science and technology of pulp and paper making for the Canadian industry.
**Ind/Abst** Abstr. Bull. Inst. Pap. Sci. Tech.; Abstr. Graphic Arts Tech. Found. (1979, 1984); AGRICOLA [Select. Cov.]; AQUAREF; Biodeter. Abstr.; Chem. Abstr.; Chem. Ind. Notes; Curr. Biotechnol.; Curr. Contents Eng. Tech. Appl. Sci.; Energy Inf. Abstr.; Eng. Index Annu. [Select. Cov.]; Environ. Abstr.; For. Prod. Abstr.; Graph. Arts Bull. Inst. Pap. Sci. Technol. (Jan. 1989-Feb. 1989, April 1989-Aug. 1989, Nov. 1989); INSPEC (June 1977-); Pap. Board Abstr.; PROMT [Full Txt.]; Res. Alert [Full Cov.]; SEA Abstr.; Soc. Sci. Cit. Index [Select. Cov.].

CN/0709-2563
**PULP & PAPER CANADA ANNUAL AND DIRECTORY.** [Pulp pap. Can. annu. dir.]. **VFOAT** Pulp and Paper Canada Annual and Directory; Pulp and Paper Canada Annual; Pulp & Paper Canada Annual. (1980)-. Directory. English. an. 85.00Can$ Canada; 110.00Can$ other. Southam Information and Technology Group Inc., 1450 Don Mills Road, Don Mills Ontario M3B 2X7 Canada. **Tel** (416)445-6641, (800)668-2374, FAX (416)442-2261. **ED** Peter Williamson. **LC** TS1088; .P94. **DD** 338.4/7676/02571. **Ad Acc.** ***Formed by the union of*** *Pulp & Paper Canada Directory, 0708-501X* ***and*** *Pulp & Paper Canada Reference Manual & Buyer's Guide, 0316-6716.*
**Ind/Abst** Abstr. Bull. Inst. Pap. Sci. Tech.

CN/1181-6562
**PULP & PAPER CANADA GRADE DIRECTORY.** [Pulp pap. Can. grade dir.]. **VFOAT** Pulp and Paper Canada Grade Directory. (1990)-. Directory. English. $99.95. Southam Information and Technology Group Inc., 1450 Don Mills Road, Don Mills Ontario M3B 2X7 Canada. **Tel** (416)445-6641, (800)668-2374, FAX (416)442-2261. **DD** 338.4/7676/02571.

IT
**PULP AND PAPER CAPACITIES.** **Added/Corp** Food and Agriculture Organization of the United Nations. **VFOAT** Capacites de la Pate et du Papier; Capacidades de Pasta y Papel. (19??)-. English (French and Spanish). Food and Agriculture Organization (FAO) / Italy, GIPC166 via Terme di Caracalla, 00100 Rome Italy. **Tel** 011 39 6 522 52925, FAX 011 39 6 522 55784. **LC** TS1080; .P855. **DD** 338.4/7676/021.
**Ind/Abst** F&S Index Plus Text, Int. [Select. Cov.]; Predicasts Forecasts.

US/0898-6886
**PULP & PAPER FORECASTER.** [Pulp pap. forecast.]. **VFOAT** Pulp and Paper Forecaster; Forecaster. (March/April 1988)-. Periodical. English. bm. $1,115.00. Miller Freeman Inc., 600 Harrison Street, San Francisco CA 94107. **Tel** (415)905-2337, FAX (415)905-2240, telex 278273. **ED** Kenneth E. Lowe. **DD** 338. ctrl circ. ***Continues*** *Paper Industry Forecasts, 0890-5827.*
**Desc:** Information for determining the direction of the North American pulp, paper and paperboard industry.

US/0033-409X
**PULP & PAPER INTERNATIONAL.** (PULP AND PAPER INTERNATIONAL.). [Pulp pap. int.]. (19??)-. Periodical. English (Russian and Chinese). mo. $115.00 North America; $205.00 other. Miller Freeman Inc., 600 Harrison Street, San Francisco CA 94107. **Tel** (415)905-2337, FAX (415)905-2240, telex 278273. **(Subscription address:** Pulp & Paper International, PO Box 1069, Skokie IL 60076.**) ED** John Kalish. **DD** 338. **[CCC]. Ad Acc. Circ:** 8,972 (ctrl). available on microfilm and microfiche from University Microfilms International (UMI); available on an online database (file 648/Full-Text) from DIALOG. Documents available from Article Express International.
**Desc:** Serves the interests of the pulp, paper and paperboard manufacturing industry outside North America. Editorial includes news, interpretation of trends, semitechnical and technical information on the industry for executives, management and technical personnel on an international scale.
**Ind/Abst** Abstr. Bull. Inst. Pap. Sci. Tech. (19??-); Eng. Index Annu. (19??-) [Select. Cov.]; F&S Index Plus Text, Int. (19??-) [Select. Cov.]; For. Prod. Abstr. (1991-); Nonwovens Abstr. (19??-); Pap. Board Abstr. (19??-); PROMT (19??-); Trade Ind. ASAP (19??-) [Full Txt.]; Trade Ind. Index (19??-) [Full Txt.].

BE
**PULP & PAPER INTERNATIONAL THIS WEEK.** English. ir. 23153.75F. Miller Freeman Publications / Belgium, 123A Chaussee Charleroi Box 5, B-1060 Brussels Belgium. **Tel** 011/32/2/5386040.

CN/0713-5807
**PULP & PAPER JOURNAL.** ***Title Change.*** [Pulp & paper j.]. **VAT** Pulp and Paper Journal. Vol. 35, No. 1 (Jan. 1982)-Vol. 45 No. 6 (Aug. 1992). Periodical. English. bm (eight times a year). Maclean Hunter Ltd. / UK, Chalk Lane Cockfosters Road, Barnet Herts EN4 0BU England. **Tel** 011 44 81 2423000, FAX 011 44 81 9759753, telex 299072. **LC** TS1080; .C35. **DD** 676./05. **CODEN** PPAJDU. **[CCC].** available on microfilm and microfiche from University Microfilms International (UMI); available on an online database (file 648/Full-Text) from DIALOG. Documents available from Article Express International. ***Continues*** *Canadian Pulp & Paper Industry, 0008-4867.* ***Continued by*** *Canadian Papermaker, 1191-887X.*
**Desc:** Provides a detailed report on the proposed capital spending plans of Canada's pulp and paper mills.
**Ind/Abst** Abstr. Bull. Inst. Pap. Sci. Tech.; AQUAREF; BioBusiness (1990-); Eng. Index Annu.; F&S Index Plus Text, Int. [Select. Cov.]; Health Saf. Sci. Abstr.; Pap. Board Abstr.; PROMT; Trade Ind. ASAP [Full Txt.]; Trade Ind. Index [Full Txt.].

US/0748-1608
**PULP & PAPER PROJECT REPORT.** [Pulp paper proj. rep.]. **Added/Corp** Miller Freeman Publications, Inc. **VFOAT** Pulp and Paper Project Report; Project Report. (198?)-. Newsletter. English. mo (plus two Mill-by-Mill Listings reports). $379.00 North America; $399.00 other. Miller Freeman Inc., 600 Harrison Street, San Francisco CA 94107. **Tel** (415)905-2337, FAX (415)905-2240, telex 278273. **DD** 676. **[CCC].**
**Desc:** Coverage of expansion and modernization projects in the North American pulp and paper industry.

FI
**PULP & PAPER PROJECT REVIEW MONTHLY.** English. mo. Fmk4200, $1,150. Jaakko Poyry Oy, Martinkatu 3, PO Box 4, SF-01621 Vantaa Finland. **Tel** 011 358 0 89471, FAX 358 0 562 6957, telex 121069 JPCON SF.
**Desc:** Essential sources of information on investment plans in pulp and paper industries worldwide for: pulp and paper producers, equipment and machinery suppliers, chemical suppliers, agents, sales offices, and associations.

US/0161-7079
**PULP & PAPER REVIEW.** **Main/Corp** Data Resources, Inc. **VFOAT** Data Resources Pulp and Paper Review; Pulp and Paper Review. Began with: Vol. 1 (Dec. 1977). English. qt. DRI McGraw Hill, 24 Hartwell Avenue, Lexington MA 02173. **Tel** (617)863-5100. **LC** HD9821; .D37A. **DD** 338.4/7/6760973.

JA
**PULP & PAPER STATISTICS.** **See** Paper and Pulp Industry-Abstracting, Bibliographies and Statistics.

US/0738-0917
**PULP & PAPER WEEK.** [Pulp paper week]. **VFOAT** Pulp and Paper Week. (19??)-. Periodical. English. wk (48 per year). $647.00 North America; $677.00 other. Miller Freeman Inc., 600 Harrison Street, San Francisco CA 94107. **Tel** (415)905-2337, FAX (415)905-2240, telex 278273. available via fax ($997.00 North America; $1577.00 other).
**Ind/Abst** Abstr. Bull. Inst. Pap. Sci. Tech. (19??-); Infomat Int. Bus. (19??-).

CN/0575-9536
**PULPWOOD AND WOOD RESIDUE STATISTICS.** **See** Forestry-Lumber and Wood.

US/0748-142X
**PULPWOOD HIGHLIGHTS.** [Pulpwood highl.]. **Added/Corp** American Pulpwood Association. Vol. 1 (May 1979)-. Periodical. English. Twelve times a year. Comes with American Pulpwood Association memebership. American Pulpwood Association, 1025 Vermont Avenue Northwest, Suite 1020, Washington DC 20005. **Tel** (202)347-2900. **DD** 676. ***Supersedes*** *Pulpwood Highlights, 0748-142X.*
**Ind/Abst** Abstr. Bull. Inst. Pap. Sci. Tech.

US
**PULPWOOD PRODUCTION IN THE LAKE STATES BY COUNTY.** English. North Central Forest Experiment Station, Forest Service, US Department of Agriculture, 1992 Folwell Avenue, St Paul MN 55108. **Tel** (612)642-5233. available on microfiche (Vols. for 1977- distributed to depository libraries).

US
**PULPWOOD PRODUCTION IN THE NORTH CENTRAL REGION BY COUNTY.** Began with 1965. English. an. Free. North Central Forest Experiment Station, Forest Service, US Department of Agriculture, 1992 Folwell Avenue, St Paul MN 55108. **Tel** (612)642-5233. **ED** Robert D Wray. **LC** SD11; .A4553 subser; HD9757.A3 A3. **DD** 333.7/5/0977 S; 338.1/749830977. **Circ:** 2,000 (ctrl). available on microfiche (Vols. for 1979- distributed to depository libraries). Documents available from BIOSIS Document Express.
**Desc:** One of a series (research notes) reporting on periodic surveys of pulpwood production.
**Ind/Abst** AGRICOLA; Biol. Abstr.

●US/1061-3757
**PURCHASING PERFORMANCE BENCHMARKS FOR THE PAPER INDUSTRY.** **Added/Corp** Center for Advanced Purchasing Studies (Tempe, Ariz.). **VFOAT** Purchasing Performance Benchmarks. (1992)-. Periodical. English. Free. Center for Advanced Purchasing Studies, PO Box 22160, Tempe AZ 85285. **Tel** (602)752-2277.

US/0486-1140
**REBEL.** **See** Economics-Labor.

US/1051-9831
**RECYCLED PAPER NEWS.** **See** Environmental Issues-Pollution and Waste Management.

CN/0317-0934
**REFERENCE TABLES - CANADIAN PULP AND PAPER ASSOCIATION.** **Main/Corp** Canadian Pulp and Paper Association. (1948)-. Periodical. English (French). an. free. Canadian Pulp & Paper Association, 1155 Metcalfe Street, 19th Floor, Montreal Quebec H3B 4T6 Canada. **Tel** (514)866-6621, FAX (514)866-3035, telex 055-60690. **DD** 338.4/7/6760971. **Circ:** 5,000.
**Desc:** Statistics on the Canadian pulp and paper industry.

BL
**RELATORIO ESTATISTICO - ASSOCIACAO PAULISTA DOS FABRICANTES DE PAPEL E CELULOSE.** **Main/Corp** Associacao Paulista dos Fabricantes de Papel e Celulose. (19??)-. Portuguese. $25.00. Rua Alfonso de Freitas 499, 04006 Sao Paulo Brazil. **Tel** (011)885-1845, telex (011) 32659. **LC** HD9834.B8; A84A. **Circ:** 1,200.
**Desc:** General data of production, sales and consumption of pulp and paper in Brazil by kind of paper and manufacturers.

US/0736-1238
**REPRODUCTION BULLETIN.** [Reprod. bull.]. **Added/Corp** Andrews Paper & Chemical Co. No. 69 (Apr. 1971)-. Periodical. English. Four times a year. Free on request. Andrews Paper & Chemical Company, 1 Channel Drive, Box 509, Port Washington NY 10050. ***Continues*** *Reproduction Paper News Bulletin.*
**Ind/Abst** Abstr. Bull. Inst. Pap. Sci. Tech.

US
**REVIEW OF THE LITERATURE ON PULP AND PAPER EFFLUENT MANAGEMENT.** English. an. National Council of the Paper Industry for Air and Stream Improvement, 260 Madison Avenue, New York NY 10016. **Tel** (212)532-9000. **LC** TD899.P3; N34 subser. **DD** 676.

IT
**RIUNIONE ANNUALE - ATICELCA.** **Main/Corp** Associazione Tecnica Italiana per la Cellulosa e la Carta. Italian. Aticelca Via Botticelli 19, 20133 Milan Italy. **LC** TS1080; .A793B.

RU/0371-3733
**SBORNIK TRUDOV CENTRALNOGO NAUCNO-ISSLEDOVATELSKOGO INSTITUTA BUMAGI.** (SBORNIK TRUDOV / MINISTERSTVO LESNOI, TSELLIULOZNO-BUMAZHNOI I DEREVOOBRABATYVAIUSHCHEI PROMYSHLENNOSTI SSSR, TSENTRALNYI NAUCHNO-ISSLEDOVATELSKII INSTITUT BUMAGI, TSNIIB.). [Sb. tr. - Cent. naucno-issled. inst. bumagi]. **Added/Corp** TSentralnyi Nauchno-Issledovatelskii Institut Bumagi (Soviet Union). **VFOAT** Sbornik Trudov Tsentralnogo Nauchno-Issledovatelskogo Instituta Bumagi; Sbornik Trudov TSNIIB. Vol. 1 (1966)-. Academic Scholarly Publication. Russian (summaries and/or abstracts in English). **LC** TS1080; .S25. **CODEN**

STNBBS. Documents available from CASDDS.
**Ind/Abst** Abstr. Bull. Inst. Pap. Sci. Tech.; Chem. Abstr. (1966-1982).

SW/0284-6454
**SCANDINAVIAN PULP & PAPER MAGAZINE.** ***Title Change.*** (PULP & PAPER MAGAZINE.). [Scand. pulp pap. mag.]. **VFOAT** Scandinavian Pulp and Paper Magazine; Scandinavian Pulp & Paper Magazine; Pulp and Paper Magazine. No. 1 (1988)-(19??). Periodical. English (summaries and/or abstracts in French and German). Swedish Pulp and Paper Association, PO Box 5518, S 11485 Stockholm Sweden. **Tel** 011 46 8 7892800, . **(Subscription address:** Arbor Publishing AB, Midskogsgrand 5, S 11543 Stockholm Sweden.**) LC** TS1080; .S93. ***Continues*** *Swedish Pulp and Paper Journal.* ***Continued by*** *European Papermaker.*
**Ind/Abst** Abstr. Bull. Inst. Pap. Sci. Tech.

SW/0283-0280
**SCPF INFORMATION.** ***Title Change.*** (SCPF INFORMATION / SWEDISH PULP AND PAPER ASSOCIATION.). [SCPF inf.]. **Added/Corp** Svenska Cellulosa- och Pappersbruksfoereningen. (198?)-(19??). Periodical. English. Swedish Pulp and Paper Association, PO Box 5518, S 11485 Stockholm Sweden. **Tel** 011 46 8 7892800, . ***Continues*** *Information (Svenska Cellulosa- och Pappersbruksfoereningen), 0281-4870.* ***Continued by*** *SCPF Information.*
**Ind/Abst** Pap. Board Abstr. (?-?).

UK/0080-9284
**SHIPPING MARKS ON TIMBER.** **See** Transportation-Ships and Shipping.

NO/0800-8582
**SKOG INDUSTRI.** **VFOAT** Skogindustri. Vol. 39, No. 1 (1985)-. Norwegian. mo. Kr375.00 Norway; Kr435.00 other. Selvig Forlag A. S., PO Box 9070 Vaterland, 0134 Oslo 1 Norway. **Tel** 011 47 22 364440, FAX 011 47 22 170620. **ED** Karl Jorgen Gurandsrud. **[CCC].** Index available. **Bk Rev. Ad Acc. Circ:** 3,000 (ctrl). ***Continues*** *Norsk Skogindustri, 0029-2095.*
**Desc:** A journal for paper, cartons, cellulose, wood pulp, timber, fibre boards and particle boards.
**Ind/Abst** Abstr. Bull. Inst. Pap. Sci. Tech.

SW/1101-3354
**SKOGSINDUSTRIERNA.** (1989)-. Periodical. Swedish. bm. Free on request. Swedish Pulp and Paper Association, PO Box 5518, S 11485 Stockholm Sweden. **Tel** 011 46 8 7892800, . **UDC** 6308. ***Continues in part*** *SCPF Information, 0283-0280.*

US/0190-8200
**SOURCES OF SUPPLY : BUYERS GUIDE.** **VFOAT** SOS Buyers Guide. Vol. 54 (1978)-. Consumer Publication. English. an. $85.00. Advertisers & Publishers Service Inc, PO Box 795, Parkridge IL 60068. **Tel** (312)823-3145. **ED** Louise Cowan. **LC** HD9823; .S6. **DD** 338.4/7/676202573. **Ad Acc.** ***Continues*** *Source of Supply Directory.*

CN
**STANDARD TESTING METHODS.** English. ir. 41.50Can$ (nonmembers), 36.50Can$ (members). Canadian Pulp & Paper Association, 1155 Metcalfe Street, 19th Floor, Montreal Quebec H3B 4T6 Canada. **Tel** (514)866-6621, FAX (514)866-3035, telex 055-60690.
**Desc:** Provides the scientific methods for the evaluation of raw materials, processes, and products.

CN/0709-2253
**STATISTICAL BULLETIN - CANADIAN PULP AND PAPER ASSOCIATION.** **Main/Corp** Canadian Pulp and Paper Association. **VFOAT** Bulletin de Statistiques - Association Canadienne des Producteurs de Pates et Papiers. (May 1966)-. Statistical Publication. English (French). mo. Free. Canadian Pulp & Paper Association, 1155 Metcalfe Street, 19th Floor, Montreal Quebec H3B 4T6 Canada. **Tel** (514)866-6621, FAX (514)866-3035, telex 055-60690. **DD** 338.4/7/67620971.
**Desc:** Statistical summary of monthly data on production, shipments, and inventories of various pulp and paper products.
**Ind/Abst** Mag. Search.

US/0731-8863
**STATISTICS OF PAPER, PAPERBOARD AND WOOD PULP.** **See** Paper and Pulp Industry-Abstracting, Bibliographies and Statistics.

SW/0039-6680
**SVENSK PAPPERSTIDNING.** [Sven. papperstidn.]. **VFOAT** Swedish Paper Journal. Began in 1898. Periodical. Swedish. Eighteen times a year. Kr400.00 Sweden; Kr475.00 other. Svensk Papperstidning, Villagatan 1, 114 32 Stockholm Sweden. **Tel** 46 8 789 28 00, 08-115419, telex 19984. **ED** Anders Forsstrom. **LC** TS1080; .S85. **CODEN** SVPAAE. Index available. **Bk Rev. Ad Acc. Circ:** 8,000 (ctrl). Documents available from The Genuine Article. ***Continued in part by*** *Nordic Pulp and Paper Research Journal, 0283-2631.*
**Desc:** Industrial information about technology and research in Sweden and abroad in the pulp and paper field.
**Ind/Abst** Abstr. Bull. Inst. Pap. Sci. Tech.; AGRICOLA; Curr. Contents Eng. Tech. Appl. Sci.; Energy Res. Abstr. (Aug. 1977-); Infomat Int. Bus.; Pap. Board Abstr.; Print. Abstr.; Res. Alert [Full Cov.]; Sci. Cit. Index; SCISEARCH; Soc. Sci. Cit. Index [Select. Cov.]; World Text. Abstr.

SW/1101-766X
**SVENSK PAPPERSTIDNING. NORDISK CELLULOSA.** **Added/Corp** Svenska Pappers- och Cellulosaingeniorsforeningen. Vol. 94 No. 16 (1990)-. Periodical. Swedish. Arbor Publishing AB, Box 26212, S 100 41 Stockholm Sweden. **Tel** 011 46 8 6799011, FAX 011 46 8 6643005. ***Continues*** *Svensk Papperstidning.*

US/0734-1415
**TAPPI JOURNAL.** [Tappi j.]. **Added/Corp** Technical Association of the Pulp and Paper Industry. **VFOAT** Technical Association of the Pulp and Paper Industry Journal. Vol. 65, No. 9 (Sept. 1982)-. Academic Scholarly Publication. English. Twelve times a year. Price varies, Comes with Technical Association of the Pulp and Paper Industry membership. Technical Association of Pulp and Paper Industry, PO Box 105113, Technical Park, Atlanta GA 30348. **Tel** (404)446-1400 Ext. 203, (800)332-8686, FAX (404)446-6947. **ED** Matthew J. Coleman. **LC** TS1080; .T3. **DD** 676/.05. **CODEN** TAJODT. **[CCC].** Index available. **Ad Acc. Pr Rev. Circ:** 28,145 (ctrl). available in microform (from Princeton Microfilm Corp.). Documents available from Article Express International, The Genuine Article, BIOSIS Document Express, CASDDS, Documents on Demand. ***Continues*** *Tappi, 0039-8241.*
**Desc:** Reports technical and engineering advances in the pulp and paper industry of the United States.
**Ind/Abst** Abstr. Bull. Inst. Pap. Sci. Tech.; Acoust. Abstr.; AGRICOLA [Select. Cov.]; Anal. Abstr.; Appl. Sci. Technol. Index; AQUAREF; Art Archaeol. Tech. Abstr.; BioBusiness; Biol. Abstr.; Chem. Abstr.; Chem. Hazards Ind.; Chem. Ind. Notes; Comput. Abstr.; Curr. Biotechnol.; Curr. Contents Eng. Tech. Appl. Sci.; Ei Page One; EMBASE; Energy Inf. Abstr.; Eng. Index Annu.; Environ. Abstr.; Fluid Abstr., Civil Eng.; Fluid Abstr. Proc. Eng.; FLUIDEX (1982-); For. Prod. Abstr.; Graph. Arts Bull. Inst. Pap. Sci. Technol. (Jan. 1989-March 1989, May 1989); HTFS Dig.; Int. Packag. Abstr.; Lab. Hazards Bull.; Mass Spect. Bull.; Nonwovens Abstr.; Pap. Board Abstr.; Print. Abstr.; Proc. Chem. Eng.; Res. Alert [Full Cov.]; Robotics Abstr.; Sci. Cit. Index; SCISEARCH; Shock Vibr. Dig.; Soc. Sci. Cit. Index [Select. Cov.]; Theoret. Chem. Eng.; World Surf. Coat. Abstr.; World Text. Abstr.

US/0097-2169
**TAPPI MONOGRAPH SERIES.** [TAPPI monogr. ser.]. **Main/Corp** Technical Association of the Pulp and Paper Industry. **VAT** Technical Association of the Pulp and Paper Industry Monograph Series. No. 1-. Monographic series. English. Price varies per volume. **DD** 676/.05. **CODEN** TPMSAM. Documents available from CASDDS.
**Ind/Abst** Chem. Abstr.

US
**TAPPI : [PROCEEDINGS].** **Main/Corp** Technical Association of the Pulp and Paper Industry. Meeting. **VFOAT** TAPPI ... Proceedings. (1990)-. English. Technical Association of Pulp and Paper Industry, PO Box 105113, Technical Park, Atlanta GA 30348. **Tel** (404)446-1400 Ext. 203, (800)332-8686, FAX (404)446-6947. ***Continues*** *Technical Association of the Pulp and Paper Industry. Meeting. Annual Meeting (1980).*

US/0886-0882
**TECHNICAL BULLETIN - NATIONAL COUNCIL OF THE PAPER INDUSTRY FOR AIR AND STREAM IMPROVEMENT (U.S.). (1981).** (TECHNICAL BULLETIN / NATIONAL COUNCIL OF THE PAPER INDUSTRY FOR AIR AND STREAM IMPROVEMENT.). [Tech. bull. - Natl. Counc. Pap. Ind. Air Stream Improv. (U. S.)]. **Added/Corp** National Council of the Paper Industry for Air and Stream Improvement (U.S.). **VFOAT** NCASI technical Bulletin. (1981)-. Bulletin. English. ir (10-20 per year). $1500.00. National Council of the Paper Industry for Air and Stream Improvement, 260 Madison Avenue, New York NY 10016. **Tel** (212)532-9000. **LC** TD899.P3; N34. **DD** 676/.042. ***Continues*** *Stream Improvement Technical Bulletin, 0360-8751.*

CN/0068-9521
**TECHNICAL SECTION PROCEEDINGS (MONTREAL).** (TECHNICAL SECTION PROCEEDINGS - CANADIAN PULP AND PAPER ASSOCIATION.). [Tech. Sect. proc.]. **Main/Corp** Canadian Pulp and Paper Association. Technical Section. Began publication in 1915. Proceedings. English. an. $30.00 members, $40.00 nonmembers. Canadian Pulp & Paper Association, 1155 Metcalfe Street, 19th Floor, Montreal Quebec H3B 4T6 Canada. **Tel** (514)866-6621, FAX (514)866-3035, telex 055-60690. **ED** Catharine Findley. **LC** TS1080; .C322A. **DD** 676/.05. **Circ:** 75.
**Desc:** Branch, committee and section annual reports, award winners, all papers published by the section during the year in Pulp and Paper Canada or Journal of Pulp and Paper Science.
**Ind/Abst** Abstr. Bull. Inst. Pap. Sci. Tech.

US/0160-6433
**TIMBER HARVESTING.** **See** Forestry-Lumber and Wood.

CN/0041-2295
**TREND (POINTE-CLAIRE).** (TREND.). [Trend]. No. 1- Autumn 1963-. Periodical. English. ir. Free. Pulp and Paper Research Institute of Canada, 570 St John's Boulevard, Pointe-Claire Quebec H9R 3J9 Canada. **Tel** (514)630-4100, telex 05-821541. **LC** TS1171; .T73. **CODEN** TRNDAU.
**Ind/Abst** Abstr. Bull. Inst. Pap. Sci. Tech.; AGRICOLA; AQUAREF; Pap. Board Abstr.

●RU
**TSELLIULOZA, BUMAGA, KARTON.** **VFOAT** Pulp, Paper, Board. (1992)-. Periodical. Russian. mo. **(Subscription address:** Victor Kamkin, 4956 Boiling Brook Parkway, Rockville MD 20852.**) LC** TS1080; .T79. ***Continues*** *Bumazhnaia Promyshlennost.*
**Ind/Abst** Abstr. Bull. Inst. Pap. Sci. Tech.

US/0741-823X
**U.S. SECONDARY FIBRE STUDY.** [U.S. second. fibre study]. **VFOAT** US Secondary Fibre Study. **VAT** United States Secondary Fibre Study. English. an. DRI McGraw Hill, 24 Hartwell Avenue, Lexington MA 02173. **Tel** (617)863-5100. **LC** HD9839.W33; U68. **DD** 338.4/7676142/0973.

FI/0784-722X
**VALMET PAPER NEWS.** [Valmet pap. news]. (1985)-. English. ir. Free upon request. Valmet Paperikoneet, PL 587, Mr Juha Kinnunen, 40101 Jyvuskylu Finland. **Tel** 358 41 295515. **UDC** 674.
**Ind/Abst** Abstr. Bull. Inst. Pap. Sci. Tech. (19??-).

XO/0139-5033
**VYSKUMNE PRACE Z ODBORU PAPIERA A CELULOZY.** (VYSKUMNE PRACE Z ODBORU PAPIERA A CELULOZY / VYSKUMNY USTAV PAPIERA A CELULOZY.). [Vysk. pr. odboru pap. celul.]. **Added/Corp** Vyskumny Ustav Papiera a Celulozy (Czechoslovakia). (1972)-. Academic Scholarly Publication. Slovak (Czech; summaries and/or abstracts in English, German and Russian). **LC** TS1105; .V96. **CODEN** VPPCAB. Documents available from CASDDS.
**Ind/Abst** Abstr. Bull. Inst. Pap. Sci. Tech.; Chem. Abstr.

JA
**WAGA KUNI NO KOKOGYO: KAMI PARUPU KOGYO HEN.** **Main/Corp** Japan. Tsusho Sangyosho. Daijin Kambo. Chosa Tokeibu. (19??)-. Periodical. Japanese. Daijin Kanbo, 8-9, Ginza 2-chome, Chuo-ku Tokyo 104 Japan. **LC** HD9836.J3; J33a.

US/0731-2571
**WALDEN'S ABC GUIDE AND PAPER PRODUCTION YEARBOOK.** [Walden's ABC guide paper prod. yearb.]. **VFOAT** ABC Guide and Paper Production Yearbook; Walden's ABC Guide. (1885)-. English. an. $107.50 US; $117.50 other. Walden-Mott Corporation, 225 North Franklin Turnpike, Ramsey NJ 07446. **Tel** (201)818-8630, FAX (201)818-8720. **ED** Theresa Dougherty. **Ad Acc. Circ:** 3,500.
**Desc:** Includes names, addresses, etc., of paper manufacturers, converters, and paper merchants in the US and Canada. Lists products manufactured, plant locations, personnel, and equipment. Also includes a classified section of paper items.

US
**WALDEN'S FIBER AND BOARD REPORT.** (19??)-. English. Twenty-six times a year. $210.00 North America; $235.00 other. Walden-Mott Corporation, 225 North Franklin Turnpike, Ramsey NJ 07446. **Tel** (201)818-8630, FAX (201)818-8720. **ED** Gregg Fales. **Circ:** 600.
**Desc:** Industry information about paperboard, corrugated, waste paper and market wood pulp. News and analyses of expansions, acquisitions, mergers and key players.

US
**WALDEN'S PAPER CATALOG.** **Added/Corp** Walden-Mott Corporation. **VFOAT** Paper Catalog. (19??)-. Catalog. English. sa (spring and fall). $75.00 US; $85.00 other. Walden-Mott Corporation, 225 North Franklin Turnpike, Ramsey NJ 07446. **Tel** (201)818-8630, FAX (201)818-8720. **ED** Linda Cohen. **Ad Acc. Circ:** 5,550.
**Desc:** Reference source on printing papers. Includes six different sections to provide paper buyers or specifiers with product information.

US
**WALDEN'S PAPER REPORT.** (19??)-. English. Twenty-six times a year. $185.00 North America; $215.00 other. Walden-Mott Corporation, 225 North Franklin Turnpike, Ramsey NJ 07446. **Tel** (201)818-8630, FAX (201)818-8720. **ED** Sylvia Peremes.
**Desc:** A concise review of news on the North American paper industry. Covers marketing trends with charts and commentary. Also reviews price movements, inventory adjustments, sales and the introduction of major lines by manufacturers.

UK/0956-4683
**WASTE PAPER NEWS.** [Waste pap. news]. **VFOAT** Waste Paper News International. (1989)-. English. Twelve times a year. £35.00 UK; £45.00 others. Brunton Business Publ Ltd., Thruston Down House, Thruston Down, Hampshire SP11 8PR England. **Tel** 011 44 264 889533, FAX 011 44 264 889622, telex 859562. **DD** 676.142.

GW/0043-7131
**WOCHENBLATT FUER PAPIERFABRIKATION.** [Wochenbl. Papierfabr.]. **Added/Corp** Papiermacherberufsgenossenschaft. (1870)-. Academic Scholarly Publication. German. sm. DM148.00. Guentter Staib Verlag, PO Box 14 52, W-7950 Biberach 1 Germany. **Tel** 07351/6969, FAX 07351/72038, telex 719620. **ED** Ulrich Kirchner. **LC** TS1080; .W6. **CODEN** WBPFAZ. Index available. cum. index. **Bk Rev. Ad Acc. Circ:** 3,400. Documents available from CASDDS.
**Desc:** Pulp and paper production from wood to finishing.
**Ind/Abst** Abstr. Bull. Inst. Pap. Sci. Tech.; Chem. Abstr.; Coal Abstr.; EMBASE; F&S Index Plus Text, Int. [Select. Cov.]; Infomat Int. Bus.; Pap. Board Abstr.; PROMT.

US
**WOOD PULP AND FIBER STATISTICS.** ***Ceased.*** **See** Paper and Pulp Industry-Abstracting, Bibliographies and Statistics.

CN
**WOODLANDS SECTION NEWS BULLETIN.** **Main/Corp** Canadian Pulp and Paper Association. Woodlands Section. (19??)-. Bulletin. English.
**Ind/Abst** For. Prod. Abstr. (1991-).

●UK/1353-2677
**WORLD PAPER (TONBRIDGE).** (WORLD PAPER.). [World paper]. Vol. 218, No. 11 (Nov. 1993)-. Academic Scholarly Publication. English. mo. Free to qualified subscribers; £82.00 (non-qualified) UK; £105.00 (non-qualified) other. Benn Publications Ltd., Sovereign Way, Tonbridge TNQ 1RW England. **Tel** 011 44 732 364422, FAX 011 44 732 361534, telex 0732 95132 BENTON G. ***Continues** Paper, 0306-8234.*
**Ind/Abst** Abstr. Bull. Inst. Paper Chem.; Chem. Ind. Notes; EMBASE; Pap. Board Abstr.; Predicasts.

GW/0044-3867
**ZELLSTOFF UND PAPIER.** [Zellst. pap.]. Academic Scholarly Publication. German. mo. $16.13. Deutscher Judo Verband, Redaktion Ippon Segewaldweg 40, D 12557 Berlin Germany. **Tel** 011 49 711 210770, telex 051 678. **LC** TS1080; .Z42. **CODEN** ZLPAAL. Documents available from CASDDS. ***Continues in part** Papier und Druck.*
**Ind/Abst** Abstr. Bull. Inst. Pap. Sci. Tech.; Chem. Abstr.; EMBASE; Pap. Board Abstr.

CC/0254-508X
**ZHONGGUO ZAOZHI.** (CHUNG-KUO TSAO CHIH.). [Zhongguo zaozhi]. **Added/Corp** Chung-kuo Tsao Chih Hsueh Hui. Ching Kung Yeh Pu Tsao Chih Kung Yeh Ko Hsueh Yen Chiu So (China). **VFOAT** China Pulp and Paper. Vol. 1 (1982)-. Academic Scholarly Publication. Chinese (summaries and/or abstracts in English). bm. $30.00. China Pulp and Paper, 12 Guang Hua Road, Beijing, People's Republic of China. **Tel** 011 86 5060022-3105. **ED** Zhu Yin-Ce. **LC** TS1080; .C48. **DD** 676/.0951. **CODEN** ZHZADC. Index available. **Ad Acc. Circ:** 10,000. Documents available from CASDDS.
**Desc:** Contains information on pulp and paper, how it is made, and technology (including process, machinery and fundamental theory, etc.).
**Ind/Abst** Abstr. Bull. Inst. Pap. Sci. Tech.; Chem. Abstr.; Pap. Board Abstr.

---

## ABSTRACTING, BIBLIOGRAPHIES AND STATISTICS

---

US
**ABSTRACT BULLETIN OF THE INSTITUTE OF PAPER CHEMISTRY.** ***Title Change.*** **Main/Corp** Institute of Paper Chemistry (Appleton, Wis.). **Added/Corp** Institute of Paper Chemistry (Appleton, Wis.) Bulletin of the Institute of Paper Chemistry. Vol. 1 (Sept. 1930)-(19??). Abstracting/Indexing Service. English. mo. Institute of Paper Chemistry, 575 Fourteenth Street NW, Atlanta GA 30318-5403. **Tel** (404)853-9500, FAX (404)853-9510. **ED** Francis J Lynch. **CODEN** ABPCAM. **Bk Rev.** available on an online database from Paperchem. ***Continued by** Abstract Bulletin of the Institute of Paper Science and Technology, 1047-2088.*
**Desc:** Pulp and paper science and technology. All aspects of forest products production, from tree to pollution control. Converting industry, packaging and printing.
**Ind/Abst** Anal. Abstr.; For. Prod. Abstr.; For. Abstr.; Int. Packag. Abstr.; Pap. Board Abstr.; Print. Abstr.; World Surf. Coat. Abstr.

US/1047-2088
**ABSTRACT BULLETIN OF THE INSTITUTE OF PAPER SCIENCE AND TECHNOLOGY.** [Abstr. bull. Inst. Pap. Sci. Technol.]. **Added/Corp** Institute of Paper Science and Technology. **VFOAT** Abstract Bulletin; ABIPST. Vol. 60, No. 1 (July 1989)-. Abstracting/Indexing Service. English. mo. $1230.00 North America; $1440.00 other. Institute of Paper Science and Technology, 500 10th Street Northwest, Atlanta GA 30318. **Tel** (404)853-9500, FAX (404)853-9510. **ED** Wayne Witt. **LC** Z7914.P2; A6; TS1105. **DD** 676. **[CCC].** Index available (in 12th Iss., pubd July). available on microfiche; available on an online database from DIALOG. Documents available from CASDDS. ***Continues** Institute of Paper Chemistry (Appleton, Wis.) Abstract Bulletin of the Institute of Paper Chemistry, 0020-3033.*
**Ind/Abst** Chem. Abstr.; Int. Packag. Abstr.; Print. Abstr.; World Surf. Coat. Abstr.; World Text. Abstr.

US
**ANNUAL STATISTICAL SUMMARY.** **Main/Corp** American Paper Institute. Printing-Writing Paper Division. (19??)-. Statistical Publication. English. an. American Forest & Paper Association, 1111 19th Street Northwest, Suite 800, Washington DC 20036. **Tel** (202)463-2721, FAX (202)463-2787, telex 140950 AF+PA DC. **ED** Benjamin Slatin. **LC** HD9822; .A65. **DD** 338.4/7/67620973. **Circ:** 1,200.
**Desc:** Paper industry statistics- long term.

CN/0709-602X
**MONTHLY NEWSPRINT STATISTICS / CANADIAN PULP AND PAPER ASSOCIATION.** [Mon. newspr. stat., Can. Pulp Pap. Assoc.]. **Added/Corp** Canadian Pulp and Paper Association. **VFOAT** Statistiques Mensuelles de Papier Journal. (Jan. 1977)-. Periodical. English (French). Twelve times a year. Free. Canadian Pulp & Paper Association, 1155 Metcalfe Street, 19th Floor, Montreal Quebec H3B 4T6 Canada. **Tel** (514)866-6621, FAX (514)866-3035, telex 055-60690. **LC** HD9839.N43; C364. **DD** 338.4/7676286. ***Continues** Canadian Pulp and Paper Association. Monthly Newsprint Report, 0316-4268.*
**Ind/Abst** Abstr. Bull. Inst. Pap. Sci. Tech.

UK/0307-0778
**PAPER & BOARD ABSTRACTS.** [Pap. board abstr.]. **Added/Corp** Pira (Association). **VFOAT** PIRA Paper & Board Abstracts; Paper and Board Abstracts. (Jan. 1968)-. Abstracting/Indexing Service. English. mo. £550.00, $907.20. Pira International, Randalls Road, Leatherhead, Surrey KT22 7RU England. **Tel** 011 44 372 376161, FAX 011 44 372 377526. **ED** Diana Deavin (editor's Printing and Packaging Industries, Randalls Road, Leatherhead Surrey KT22 7RU UK). **Bk Rev. Pr Rev.** available on microfilm and microfiche from University Microfilms International (UMI); available on an online database. Documents available. ***Continues in part** Kenley Abstracts.*
**Desc:** Contains abstracts of publications and documents issued throughout the world relating to all aspects of paper and board manufacturing including company and market information, processes, technical papers, conference papers, environmental issues and products.
**Ind/Abst** Abstr. Bull. Inst. Pap. Sci. Tech. (19??-); World Text. Abstr. (19??-).

US/0884-6545
**PAPER, PAPERBOARD & WOOD PULP.** **Added/Corp** American Paper Institute. **VFOAT** Paper, Paperboard and Wood Pulp. Vol. 59, No. 9 (Sept. 1981)-. English. Twelve times a year. $470.89 New York residents (including sales tax); $435.00 US and Canada; $465.00 other, includes Fact Sheet. American Forest & Paper Association, 1111 19th Street Northwest, Suite 800, Washington DC 20036. **Tel** (202)463-2721, FAX (202)463-2787, telex 140950 AF+PA DC. **LC** HD9824; .A76a. **DD** 338.4/76762/0973. ***Continues** American Paper Institute. Monthly Statistical Summary, 0003-0341.*
**Desc:** A summary of total paper and paperboard production and how it contributed to that growth.

US/1049-6572
**PAPER PILE QUARTERLY.** **See** Paper and Pulp Industry.

JA
**PULP & PAPER STATISTICS.** **Main/Corp** Nihon Seishi Rengokai. English. an. ¥1600 Japan; $17.00 US. Nihon Seishi Rengokai, (Japan Paper Association), 9-11, Ginza 3 Chome, Chuoku, Tokyoto 104, Japan. **(Subscription address:** Japan Publications Trading Company, Ltd., PO Box 5030, Tokyo International, Tokyo 100-31 Japan.) **LC** HD9836.J3; K3. **DD** 338.4/7/6760952. ***Continues** Pulp & Paper Statistics.*
**Desc:** Comprehensive statistical material about Japanese Pulp and Paper Industry.

US/0731-8863
**STATISTICS OF PAPER, PAPERBOARD AND WOOD PULP.** **Added/Corp** American Paper Institute. 19th Ed. (1981)-. English. an. $365.00 US; $380.00 other. American Forest & Paper Association, 1111 19th Street Northwest, Suite 800, Washington DC 20036. **Tel** (202)463-2721, FAX (202)463-2787, telex 140950 AF+PA DC. **ED** Benjamin Slatin. **LC** HD9839.P33; U55. **DD** 338.4/76762/0973021. **Bk Rev. Ad Acc. Circ:** 1,000. ***Continues** Statistics of Paper and Paperboard, 0097-4730.*
**Desc:** Long term annual statistical data on paper and paperboard industry.
**Ind/Abst** Predicasts Forecasts; Stat. Ref. Index.

US
**WOOD PULP AND FIBER STATISTICS.** ***Ceased.*** **Main/Corp** American Paper Institute. Pulp, Fiber and Raw Materials Group. Vol. 38 (1974)-49th Edition (1984/85). Periodical. English. an. American Forest & Paper Association, 1111 19th Street Northwest, Suite 800, Washington DC 20036. **Tel** (202)463-2721, FAX (202)463-2787, telex 140950 AF+PA DC. ***Continues** American Paper Institute. Pulp and Raw Materials Group. Wood Pulp Statistics.*

---

# PARAPSYCHOLOGY AND OCCULTISM

---

US/1066-5455
**ABRASAX (CORPUS CHRISTI, TEX.).** (ABRASAX.). [Abrasax]. (19??)-. Periodical. English. Four times a year (at Equinoxes and Solstices). $10.00 North America; (add $3.00 airmail postage) other. Ordo Templi Baphe-Metis, Box 1219, Corpus Christi TX 78403-1219. **ED** James M. Martin. **DD** 133. **Circ:** 300.
**Desc:** An occult magazine devoted to mysticism, mythology, divination, Magick, and the so-called "black arts" and so forth. A non-judgmental vis-a-vis on Satanism and Black Magic.

CN/0700-5067
**ACTION (WINDSOR).** (ACTION.). **Added/Corp** Church of Scientology. Mission of Windsor. Vol. 1 (1975)-. Periodical. English. Church of Scientology, Mission of Windsor, 437 Ouelette Avenue, Windsor Ontario N9A 4J2 Canada. **DD** 131/.35/05.

US/0093-089X
**AMERICAN DOWSER.** (THE AMERICAN DOWSER.). **Added/Corp** American Society of Dowsers. Vol. 9, No. 3 (Aug. 1969)-. Periodical. English. Four times a year. $25.00. American Society of Dowsers Inc., PO Box 24, Danville VT 05828. **Tel** (802)684-3417. **LC** BF1628; .A59a. **DD** 133.3/23/05. **Circ:** 3,500. ***Continues** Quarterly Digest - American Society of Dowsers, 0569-8154.*

UK/0308-5406
**ANCIENT MYSTERIES.** Periodical. English. Institute of Geomantic Research, 142 Pheasant Rise, Bar Hill Cambridge CB3 8SD England. ***Continues** Journal of Geomancy.*

BL
**ANUARIO ALLAN KARDEC.** 1975-. Portuguese. an. Librarian Allan Kardec Editora, Cx Postal 15 190, Sao Paulo Brazil. **LC** BF1005; .A56.

FR/0752-2452
**ARIES / ASSOCIATION POUR LA RECHERCHE ET L'INFORMATION SUR L'ESOTERISME.** **Added/Corp** Association pour la Recherche et l'Information sur l'Esoterisme. No 1 (1982)-. Periodical. English (French and German). Twice a year. $30.00. Joscelyn Godwin Music Department, Colgate University, Hamilton NY 12246. **Tel** 315-824-1000. **ED** A Faivre, R Edhigoffer, P Deghaye. **LC** BL624; .A73. **Bk Rev. Circ:** 400.
**Ind/Abst** Index Book Rev. Relig.; Relig. Index One Period.

US
**ASPR NEWSLETTER.** **Added/Corp** American Society for Psychical Research (1906- ). Vol. 1, No. 1 (Nov. 1968)-. Periodical. English. qt. $50.00. American Society for Psychical Research, 5 West 73rd Street, New York NY 10023. **Tel** (212)799-5050. **ED** Patrice Keane. **NLM** W1 A154K. cum. index. **Bk Rev. Circ:** 2,000.
**Desc:** Aimed at laypersons interested in scientific parapsychology. Contains in-depth articles and information about current organizations, publications, educational opportunities and lectures. Available with a cumulative table of contents.
**Ind/Abst** Except. Hum. Exp.

CN/1185-197X
**ASTRO (MONTREAL).** (ASTRO.). [Astro]. Vol. 1, No 1 (1990)-. Periodical. French. qt. 2.50Can$ per issue. Astro, Bureau 2, 1880 Est Rue Ste-Catherine, Montreal, Quebec H2K 2H5 Canada. **DD** 133.5.

US/0885-7148
**ASTROLOGY & PARAPSYCHOLOGY TODAY.** **See** Astrology.

AT/1035-9621
**AUSTRALIAN PARAPSYCHOLOGICAL REVIEW.** (1989)-. Newsletter. English. Three times a year. 15.00Aust$ Australia; $20.00 (surface mail), $26.00

(airmail) other. Australian Institute of Parapsychological Research, Inc, PO Box 176, Annandale New South Wales 2038 Australia. **Tel** 02-6607232. **ED** Harvey Irwin. **Bk Rev**, (Qty: 20). **Circ:** 350. ***Continues*** *A.I.P.R. Bulletin, 0813-2194.*
**Desc:** Scientific study of parapsychological phenomena with focus on Australia and nearby countries.
**Ind/Abst** Except. Hum. Exp.

FR/0984-4759
**AUTRE MONDE (PARIS. 1987), L'.** (L'AUTRE MONDE.). (1987)-. Periodical. French. qt (4 issues). $20.00 France; $30.00 other. Editions Francois de Villac, 10 rue de Crussol, 75011 Paris France. **Tel** 33 1 48 05 41 10. **UDC** 364(1-772).

GW/0939-0154
**BIBLIOGRAPHIE ZUR SYMBOLIK, IKONOGRAPHIE UND MYTHOLOGIE. ERGANZUNGSBAND.** **See** Religion and Theology.

CN/0706-120X
**BULLETIN PSILOG, LE.** [Bull. psilog]. Vol. 1, No. 1 1981-. Bulletin. French. ir. $11.00. Le Bulletin Psilog, St-Francois-du-Lac Quebec J0G 1M0 Canada. **DD** 133/.05.
**Ind/Abst** Except. Hum. Exp. (?-?).

CN/0318-7349
**CAHIERS DE COURS DE L'HOLANTHROPE, LES.** V. 1- Oct. 1975-. Periodical. French. qt. $2.00 per no. Cosmos-Express, CP 3, Jonquiere Quebec G7X 7V8 Canada. **ED** C G Sarrazin. **DD** 133.05.

US/0747-9840
**CHAMP CHANNELS.** **See** Zoology.

UK/0308-6194
**CHRISTIAN PARAPSYCHOLOGIST, THE.** **Added/Corp** Churches' Fellowship for Psychical and Spiritual Studies. (197?)-. Periodical. English. qt. £6.00 UK; $16.00 US; £8.00 other. Churches' Fellowship for Psychical and Spiritual Studies, Rural Workshop, South Road, North Somercotes, New Romney Louth, Lincolnshire LN11 7PT England. **Tel** 011 44 507 358845. **ED** M C Perry (editor's address 7, The College, Durham, DHI 3EQ). Index available. cum. index. **Bk Rev. Circ:** 1,400 (ctrl).
**Ind/Abst** Except. Hum. Exp.

AT
**CONSCIOUSNESS.** (19??)-. Newsletter. English. Six times a year. Australian Transpersonal Association, PO Box 11, Phillip Mall, West Pymble 2073 Australia. **Bk Rev. Circ:** 350 (ctrl). ***Continues*** *A I P R News.*
**Desc:** Current awareness newsletter about parapsychology and transpersonal psychology in Australia.

US/0736-7023
**CRYPTOZOOLOGY.** **See** Zoology.

US
**DARKNERVE.** English. qt. $10.00 North America; $12.00 other. Darknerve, 276 28th Street, San Francisco CA 94131. **Tel** (415)824-2093. **ED** James E Lough. **Bk Rev. Ad Acc. Circ:** 750.
**Desc:** Focuses on the "dark" side. Contains satire, experimentation, and topics of an uncomfortable nature.

CN/0836-5059
**DIMENSIONS.** [Dimensions]. No. 40 (June 1987)-. Periodical. English. mo. $28.00. Toronto Dimensions, 214 Glengarry Avenue, Toronto Ontario M5M 1E4 Canada. **Tel** (416)926-1483. **DD** 133/.09713/541. ***Continues*** *Toronto Dimensions, 0822-8000.*

●US/1065-8181
**DRAGONS' QUEST, THE.** [Dragons' quest]. (Summer 1992)-. Periodical. English. qt. $25.00. Dragon Moon Centre, PO Box 1595, Capitola CA 95010. **DD** 130.

US/0731-7840
**ENCYCLOPEDIA OF OCCULTISM & PARAPSYCHOLOGY.** [Encycl. occult. parapsychol.]. **VFOAT** Encyclopedia of Occultism and Parapsychology. 1st Edition (1978)-. English. ir. Price varies. Gale Research Inc., 835 Penobscot Building, Detroit MI 48226. **Tel** (800)877-GALE, (313)961-2242, FAX (313)961-6083, telex TWX 810-221-7086. **ED** Leslie A. Shepard. **LC** BF1407; .E54. **DD** 133.
**Desc:** A convenient reference guide for research and study of all aspects on the paranormal and the occult. Includes the occult, magic, miracles, and witchcraft, as well as numerous paranormal events previously regarded as supernatural. Prominent individuals and personalities in the field are covered, and entries on particular countries trace the development of occultism and parapsychology in each. New entries cover recent phenomena, concepts, cults, personalities, organizations, and publications. In certain controversial areas, the case both for and against has been indicated, with sources noted for further study.

NE
**ERANOS.** **See** New Age Publications.

CN/0225-543X
**ERE ATLANTEENNE.** (L'ERE ATLANTEENNE.). Vol. 1, No. 1, (Dec. 1979)-. Periodical. French. wk. $18.00. L'Ere Atlanteenne, CP 1223, Belleville Ontario K8N 5E9 Canada. **DD** 133/.05.

NE
**EUROPEAN JOURNAL OF PARAPSYCHOLOGY.** **Added/Corp** Rijksuniversiteit te Utrecht. Parapsychology Laboratory. (19??)-. Periodical. English. an. £12.00. Koestler Chair Parapsychology, Department of Psychology, 7 George Square, Edinburgh EH 8 9JZ Scotland. **Tel** 011 44 31 6503348 6501000.
**Ind/Abst** Except. Hum. Exp. (?-?); Psychol. Abstr. (1983-); PsycINFO (1990-).

US/1053-4768
**EXCEPTIONAL HUMAN EXPERIENCE.** **See** Parapsychology and Occultism-Abstracting, Bibliographies and Statistics.

US/0014-8776
**FATE (MARION).** (FATE.). (1948)-. Periodical. English. mo. $18.00 (one year), $30.00 (two year). Llewellyn Worldwide, 213 East 4th Street, PO Box 64383, St Paul MN 55164. **Tel** (800)843-6666, (612)291-1970, FAX (612)291-1908. **(Subscription address:** Fulfillment Corporation of America, PO Box 1962, Marion OH 43305.**) ED** Phyllis Galde. **LC** BF1995; .F2. **DD** 133.05. **Bk Rev. Ad Acc. Circ:** 120,000. available on microfilm and microfiche from University Microfilms International (UMI).
**Desc:** Reports of unexplainable phenomena.
**Ind/Abst** Access (1975-); Except. Hum. Exp.; Mag. Index (1977-May 1984).

US/1046-6029
**FIREHEART (MAYNARD, MASS.).** **See** New Age Publications.

US/1054-4208
**FOCUS (BURBANK, CALIF.).** (FOCUS : THE QUARTERLY NEWSLETTER OF THE FAIR WITNESS PROJECT INCORPORATED.). Newsletter. English. qt. $25.00 North America; $30.00 other. Fair Witness Project Incorporated, 4219 West Olive Avenue, Suite 247, Burbank CA 91505. **Tel** (818)980-8758. **ED** W L Moore and Jimmy Ward. **DD** 001. Index available. **Bk Rev. Ad Acc. Circ:** 800 (ctrl).
**Desc:** Contains well-researched articles about unexplained phenomena with emphasis on UFOs. Also book reviews, letters, ect.

US
**GEORGIAN ANNUAL.** English. an. $35.00 North America; $50.00 other. Georgian Church, PO Box 41718, Bakersfield CA 93384. **Tel** (805)323-3309. **ED** Fauna and Dean. Index available. **Bk Rev. Pr Rev.** ctrl circ.
**Desc:** Witchcraft and related subjects.

US/0145-885X
**GNOSTICA.** No. 22 (May 1974)-. Periodical. English. bm. $10.00. Llewellyn Worldwide, 213 East 4th Street, PO Box 64383, St Paul MN 55164. **Tel** (800)843-6666, (612)291-1970, FAX (612)291-1908. **ED** Carl. L. Weschcke. **LC** BF1001; .G66. **DD** 133/.05. **Bk Rev. Ad Acc. Circ:** 10,000. available on microfilm and microfiche from University Microfilms International (UMI). ***Continues*** *Gnostica News, 0362-8922.*

US
**GNOSTICA NEWS AND VIEWS.** **Added/Corp** Llewellyn Publications. (1980)-. Periodical. English. ***Continues*** *Gnostica.*

US/1066-7385
**GREEN EGG.** [Green egg]. **Added/Corp** Council of Earth Religions. Church of All Worlds. (1968)-. Periodical. English. Four times a year (Mar., June, Sept., Dec.). $16.00 US; $23.00 Canada & Mexico; $28.00 Europe; $31.00 other. Green Egg, PO Box 1542, Ukiah CA 95482. **Tel** (707)485-7787. **ED** Diane Darling. **DD** 291. **Bk Rev**, (Qty: 30-40). **Ad Acc, Adv Mgr:** Ron Johnson.

US/1069-3211
**GREEN MAN, THE.** (THE GREEN MAN : A MAGAZINE FOR PAGAN MEN.). [Green man]. Issue No. 1 (Spring 1993)-. Periodical. English. qt. $15.00. Green Man, Box 641HC, Point Arena CA 95468. **DD** 299.

BL
**HOMEM, MITO & I.E. E MAGIA.** Vol. 1 (1973)-. Periodical. Portuguese. wk. $180.00. Editoria Tres, Avenue Paulista 2 006, 15 E 16 Andares Caixa Postal 1481, Sao Paulo Brazil. **LC** BF1005; .H65.

CN/1182-6304
**HOROSCOPE (ANDRE MAURICE).** (HOROSCOPE.). [Horoscope]. (1991)-. French. 12.95Can$ per volume. Edimag, Bureau 2, 1880 Est Rue Ste-Catherine, Montreal Quebec H2K 2H5 Canada. **DD** 133.5/4/05.

US/0019-0144
**INFO JOURNAL / INTERNATIONAL FORTEAN ORGANIZATION.** (19??)-. Periodical. English. qt. $12.00 US, APO, and Hawaii; $16.00 other. International Fortean Organization, PO Box 367, Arlington VA 22210-0367. **Tel** (703)522-9232. **ED** Raymond D Manners. Index available. cum. index. **Bk Rev**, (Qty: 20). **Pr Rev. Circ:** 800. available on microfilm from University Microfilms International (UMI).
**Desc:** Often skeptical, usually humorous, always intelligent review of strange phenomena, events, and places that are unexplainable or ignored by conventional science.

US/1068-5340
**INPSIDER (ATLANTA, GA.), THE.** ***Ceased.*** (THE INPSIDER : UNLOCKING THE HUMAN PSYCHE.). [Inpsider]. **Added/Corp** Parapsychological Services Institute. Vol. 1, No. 1 (July 1992)-(199?). Periodical. English. Twelve times a year. Parapsychological Services Institute, 5575 B Chamblee Dunwoody Boulevard, Atlanta GA 30338. **Tel** (404)391-0991. **ED** Judith Winters and W.M. Roll. **DD** 133. **Bk Rev**, (Qty: 80). **Circ:** 150.
**Desc:** This newsletter contains of current experiences from around the world. It tells of unusual experiences they have had. Includes an article from one of our professional guides giving us some perspective on what we are seeing along the way.

US/0273-3749
**INTERNATIONAL DIRECTORY OF ASTROLOGERS & PSYCHICS, THE.** **See** Astrology.

CN/1182-8757
**ISSUES (PENTICTON).** (ISSUES.). [Issues]. Vol. 1, No. 1 (Feb./Mar. 1990)-. Periodical. English. bm. $15.00 per year. Angele Rowe, 2645 McKenzie Street, Penticton, British Columbia V2A 6J1 Canada. **DD** 613.

SZ
**JAHRBUCH DER ESOTERIK.** (1989)-. German. an. Fischer Druck AG, Satz Druck und Verlag, CH 3110 Muensingen Switzerland. **Tel** 011 41 31 7212211, FAX 011 41 31 7214617, telex 845/911600.

CN/0315-5412
**JOURNAL OF AUTOMATIC WRITING, THE.** ***Title Change.*** V. 1- June 1974-. Periodical. English. mo. The Spiritual Press, PO Box 464, Don Mills Ontario M3C 2T3 Canada. ***Continued by*** *Spiritual Press, 0381-6621.*

US/0897-0394
**JOURNAL OF BORDERLAND RESEARCH, THE.** [J. borderl. res.]. **Added/Corp** Borderland Sciences Research Foundation. (19??)-. Periodical. English. bm. $20.00 (membership), $25.00 (supporting membership). Borderland Sciences Research Foundation, PO Box 429, Garberville CA 95440-0429. **DD** 001.
**Ind/Abst** Except. Hum. Exp.

US/0891-4494
**JOURNAL OF NEAR-DEATH STUDIES.** [J. near-death stud.]. **Added/Corp** International Association for Near-Death Studies. **VFOAT** Journal of Near Death Studies. Vol. 6, No. 1 (Fall 1987)-. Periodical. English. qt. £35.00 (individuals), £130.00 (institutions) UK; $175.00 US; $205.00 other. Human Sciences Press, PO Box 735, 233 Spring Street, New York NY 10013. **Tel** (212)620-8000, FAX (212)807-1047, telex 23421139. **(Subscription address:** Eurospan Ltd., Journals and Serials Division, 3 Henrietta Street, Covent Garden, London WC2E 8LU England.**) ED** Bruce Greyson. **LC** BF789.D4; A53. **DD** 155.9/37. **NLM** W1; JO777TF. **CODEN** JNDAE7. **[CCC].** available on microfilm from University Microfilms International (UMI). ***Continues*** *Anabiosis, 0743-6238.*
**Desc:** Internationally acclaimed for its pioneering explorations on the nature and scope of human consciousness as it is affected by the prospect or occurrence of clinical death. The journal publishes articles on near-death experiences, and the empirical effects and theoretical implications of such events.
**Ind/Abst** Abstr. Anthropol.; Abstr. Res. Pastor. Care Couns. (19??-); Except. Hum. Exp.; Psychol. Abstr. (1981-); PsycINFO (1990-); PsycLit; Soc. Work Abstr. [Select. Cov.].

US/0022-3387
**JOURNAL OF PARAPSYCHOLOGY, THE.** [J. parapsychol.]. **Added/Corp** Duke University. Parapsychology Laboratory. Vol. 1 (March 1937)-. Periodical. English. qt (Mar., Jun., Sep., Dec.). $30.00 (individuals), $45.00 (institutions). Foundation for Research on the Nature of Man, 402 North Buchanan Blvd., Durham NC 27701-1728. **Tel** (919)688-8241, FAX (919)683-4338. **ED** K. R. Rao. **LC** BF1001; .J66. **DD** 133.072; 159.961. **NLM** W1 JO827D. **CODEN** JPRPAU. **[CCC].** Index available in last issue of volume--attached. cum. index. **Bk Rev. Ad Acc. Pr Rev. Circ:** 1,000 (ctrl). available on microfilm and microfiche from University Microfilms International (UMI). Documents available from The Genuine Article, BIOSIS Document Express, UMI Article Clearinghouse.
**Desc:** The journal publishes articles on parapsychology, surveys of literature, book reviews, correspondence, and abstracts of reports from unpublished material and other journals.
**Ind/Abst** Acad. Search (July 1993-); Appl. Soc. Sci. Index Abstr.; Biol. Abstr.; Curr. Contents Soc. Behav. Sci.; Except. Hum. Exp.; Expand. Acad. Index (1989-);

INFO-SOUTH Abstr.; Mag. Search; Middle East Abstr. Index; Newsp. Period. Abstr. (1991-); Psychol. Abstr. (1937-); PsycINFO; PsycLit; Res. Alert [Full Cov.]; Soc. Sci. Source (Jul. 1993-); Soc. Sci. Cit. Index [Full Cov.]; Soc. Sci. Index; Soc. Sci. Index Fulltext (March 1988-) [Full Txt.].

US/0731-2148
**JOURNAL OF RELIGION AND PSYCHICAL RESEARCH, THE.** See Religion and Theology.

US/0003-1070
**JOURNAL OF THE AMERICAN SOCIETY FOR PSYCHICAL RESEARCH (1932).** (THE JOURNAL OF THE AMERICAN SOCIETY FOR PSYCHICAL RESEARCH.). [J. Am. Soc. Psych. Res.]. **Added/Corp** American Society for Psychical Research. Vol. 26 (1932)-. Periodical. English. Four times a year. $65.00 (libraries and institutions) US; $75.00 other. American Society for Psychical Research, Inc., 5 West 73rd Street, New York NY 10023. **Tel** (212)799-5050, FAX (212)496-2497. **ED** Rhea White. **NLM** W1 JO911A. Index available in last issue of volume--attached. cum. index. **Bk Rev. Pr Rev. Circ:** 1,500 (ctrl). available on microfilm and microfiche from University Microfilms International (UMI). Documents available from The Genuine Article. ***Continues*** *Psychic Research, 0092-8259.*
**Ind/Abst** Curr. Contents Soc. Behav. Sci.; Except. Hum. Exp.; Middle East Abstr. Index; Psychol. Abstr. (1933-); PsycINFO (1990-); PsycLit; Res. Alert [Full Cov.]; Soc. Sci. Cit. Index [Full Cov.].

UK/0037-9751
**JOURNAL OF THE SOCIETY FOR PSYCHICAL RESEARCH.** [J. Soc. Psych. Res.]. **Main/Corp** Society for Psychical Research (London, England). Vol. 1, No. 1 (Feb. 1884)-. Periodical. English. qt. $27.00 Parapsychological Association members, $36.00 non-members US; £15.00 Parapsychological Association members, £20.00 non-members other. Society for Psychical Research, 49 Marloes Road, Kensington W8 6LA England. **Tel** 011 44 71 937 8984. **ED** John Beloff. **LC** BF1011; .I3. **DD** 133.8/05. **NLM** W1 JO954P. **[CCC]. Bk Rev**, (Qty: 10-12). **Circ:** 1,000 (ctrl).
**Desc:** To examine without prejudice or prepossession, and in a scientific spirit those faculties of man, real or supposed, which appear to be inexplicable in terms of any generally recognized hypotheses.
**Ind/Abst** Br. Humanit. Index; Except. Hum. Exp.; Psychol. Abstr. (1954-); PsycINFO; PsycLit.

IS/0334-6994
**KABBALAH.** [Kabbalah]. Vol. 1, No. 1 (Aug. 1985)-. Periodical. English. Three times a year. $32.00. Kabbalah, 41 Palyam Street, Jerusalem 97 890 Israel. **Tel** 02 817876.

US/1045-103X
**KOOKS MAGAZINE.** English. Twice a year. $17.00 US; $18.00 Canada; $23.00 other. Out-of-Kontrol Data Institute, Box 953, Allston MA 02134. **Tel** (617)782-5602. **ED** Donna Kossy. **Bk Rev. Ad Acc. Circ:** 750.
**Desc:** Extremism in all its splendor, including cults, religious fanatics, lone nuts, UFO's, weird science, channeling, street philosophers and those who have one solution to all the world's problems.

US
**LLEWELLYN'S NEW WORLDS OF MIND AND SPIRIT.** (1993)-. Periodical. English. Six times a year. $10.00 US and Canada; $20.00 other. Llewellyn Worldwide, 213 East 4th Street, PO Box 64383, St Paul MN 55164. **Tel** (800)843-6666, (612)291-1970, FAX (612)291-1908. **ED** Jana Branch. **Bk Rev**, (Qty: 50). **Ad Acc, Adv Mgr:** Nancy Trudelle. **Circ:** 65,000.

IT
**LUCE E OMBRA; RIVISTA DI STUDI METAPSICHICI E DI PROBLEMI DELL'ANIMA E DEL PENSIERO.** (Jan. 1901)-. Italian. **LC** BF1004; .L77.
**Ind/Abst** Except. Hum. Exp.

CH
**LUNG TSAI TIEN.** Began with June 1980 issue. Periodical. Chinese. bm. $20.00 US. Lung Tsai Tien Tsa Chih She, 34 Lane 66 Tung Ming Chieh, Chung-Li Shih Taiwan. **LC** BF1773.2.C5; L86. **DD** 133.3/05.

US/1073-5879
**MAGICAL BLEND (1989).** (MAGICAL BLEND.). Issue 21 (Jan. 1989)-. Periodical. English. qt. $13.00. Magical Blend, PO Box 600, Chico CA 95927. **Tel** (415)673-1001, (916)893-9037. **ED** Michael Peter Langevin. **LC** WMLC 93/3881. **DD** 133. **Bk Rev. Ad Acc. Circ:** 60,000. available on an online database. ***Continues*** *Magical Blend Magazine, 1040-4287.*

US/1040-4287
**MAGICAL BLEND MAGAZINE.** ***Title Change.*** [Magical blend mag.]. (198?)-(199?). Periodical. English. Four times a year (Jan., Apr., July, Oct.). Magical Blend, PO Box 600, Chico CA 95927. **Tel** (415)673-1001, (916)893-9037. **ED** Michael Peter Langevin. **DD** 133. **Bk Rev**, (Qty: 100). **Ad Acc, Adv Mgr:** Neal Powers, **Tel** (916)893-9037. **Circ:** 60,000. available on an online database from Compuserve. ***Continues*** *Magical Blend.* ***Continued by*** *Magical Blend (San Francisco, Calif. : 1989), 1073-5879.*

US/0742-8898
**MAGICK CIRCLE DIRECTORY OF OCCULT GOODS AND SERVICES, THE.** 1984/85 Ed.-. Directory. English. sa. $6.00. Technology Group, PO Box 93124, Pasadena CA 91109. **Tel** (818)794-6013. **ED** Rev White. **LC** BF1409; .M34. **DD** 133/.025/73. **Ad Acc. Circ:** 1,000.
**Desc:** Directory of occult shops, suppliers, and practitioners.

●US/1056-7917
**MEDIEVAL AND EARLY MODERN MYSTICISM.** (1992)-. Monographic series. English. Price varies per volume. Peter Lang Publishing, 62 West 45th Street, 4th Floor, New York NY 10036. **Tel** (212)764-1471, (800)770-5264, telex 6973364 PLNY.

US/0892-5429
**MUTABLE DILEMMA, THE. Added/Corp** Los Angeles Community Church of Religious Science (Calif.). (19??)-. Periodical. English. qt. $16.00 US; $20.00 other. L.A. Community Church Religious Science, 838 5th Avenue, Los Angeles CA 90005. **Tel** (213)487-1000, FAX (213)487-7853. **ED** Mark Pottenger. **DD** 133. **Bk Rev. Circ:** 200.

US
**NEW CONSCIOUSNESS SOURCEBOOK.** 1982-. English. ir. $8.95 (add $2.50 postage). Arcline Publications, 1800 South Robertson Boulevard, Suite 182, Los Angeles CA 90035. **Tel** (213)551-0484, FAX (213)553-3953. **ED** D K Khalsa and P S Khalsa. **LC** WMLC L 83/262. **Circ:** 10,000. ***Continues*** *Spiritual Community Guide, 0160-0354.*
**Desc:** Directory of New Age, holistic health, metaphysical and spiritual groups and individuals. Also contains articles and graphics.

US/0147-3395
**NEW ENGLAND JOURNAL OF PARAPSYCHOLOGY.** V. 1-. Periodical. English. ir. Franklin Pierce College, PO Box 825, Rindge NH 03461. **Tel** (603)899-5111. **LC** BF1001; .N35. **DD** 133.8/05.

CN/0225-8536
**NEW HORIZONS (TORONTO. 1972).** (NEW HORIZONS.). [New horiz.]. V. 1- Summer 1972-. English. an. New Horizons Research Foundation, PO Box 427 Station F, Toronto Ontario M4Y 2L8 Canada. **DD** 133/.05.

PL/0867-3152
**NIE Z TEJ ZIEMI.** (1990)-. Periodical. Polish. mo. $48.00. **(Subscription address:** ARS Polona, PO Box 1001, 00068 Warsaw Poland.**) UDC** 615.89. **CODEN** 159.96.

CN/0380-4127
**NOSTRADAMUS. EDITION QUEBECOISE.** (NOSTRADAMUS.). Yearly V. 2, No. 58- 13/20 Aug. 1973-. Periodical. French. wk. 35.00Can$ per no. Distributions Eclair, 8320 Place de Lorraine, Anjou Quebec H1J 1E6 Canada. **DD** 001.9/4/05.

UK/0969-1375
**OCCULT OBSERVER, THE.** [Occult obs.]. (1991)-. Periodical. English. qt. £11.80. Atlantis Bookshop, 2 Tavistock Chambers, Bloomsbury Way, London WC1A 2SE England. **DD** 133.05.

CN/0838-1550
**PAGANS FOR PEACE.** (PAGANS FOR PEACE : NEWSLETTER.). [Pagans Peace]. **Added/Corp** Pagans for Peace. (Oct. 1983)-. Newsletter. English. ir. $15.00. PO Box 6531, Station A, Toronto Ontario M5W 1X4 Canada. **DD** 299/.05.

SA
**PARAPSYCHOLOGICAL JOURNAL OF SOUTH AFRICA.** English. Twice a year. South African Society for Psychical Research, PO Box 23154, Joubert Park 2044 South Africa.
**Ind/Abst** Psychol. Abstr. (1980-); PsycLit.

US/0078-9437
**PARAPSYCHOLOGICAL MONOGRAPHS.** No. 1-. Monographic series. English (summaries and/or abstracts in French, German, Italian and Spanish). Price varies per volume. Parapsychology Foundation Inc, 228 East 71st Street, New York NY 10021. **Tel** (212)628-1550. **NLM** W1 PA633M.
**Ind/Abst** Except. Hum. Exp. (?-?).

US/0748-0156
**PARAPSYCHOLOGY IN THE USSR.** [Parapsychol. USSR]. **VFOAT** Parapsychology in the U.S.S.R. Pt. 1-. Periodical. English. Washington Research Center, 3101 Washington Street, San Francisco CA 95115. **LC** BF1001; .V54. **DD** 133.8/0947.

●US/1065-3031
**PARAPSYCHOLOGY, NEW AGE, AND THE OCCULT.** (PARAPSYCHOLOGY, NEW AGE, AND THE OCCULT : A SOURCE ENCYCLOPEDIA.). (1992)-. English. $29.50. Reference Press International, PO Box 4126, Greenwich CT 06830.

CN/0227-6119
**PARAPSYCHOLOGY (OTTAWA).** (PARAPSYCHOLOGY.). [Parapsychol.]. Autumn 1978-. Periodical. English. qt. $3.00. Canadian Institute of Parapsychology, PO Box 6147 Station J, Ottawa Ontario K2A 1T2 Canada. **DD** 133/.07/2.

US/0031-1804
**PARAPSYCHOLOGY REVIEW.** ***Ceased.*** [Parapsychol. rev.]. Vol. 1 (Mar./Apr. 1970)-(March 1990). Periodical. English. bm. Parapsychology Foundation Inc, 228 East 71st Street, New York NY 10021. **Tel** (212)628-1550. **ED** Betty Shapin. **LC** BF1001; .P29. **DD** 133/.05. **NLM** W1 PA635S. **CODEN** PAREDT. **Bk Rev. Circ:** 1,500. ***Continues*** *Newsletter of the Parapsychology Foundation, Inc.*
**Desc:** Contains articles covering a wide range of studies by leading authorities from all the sciences, book reviews, reports on conferences, educational notes, and others.
**Ind/Abst** Except. Hum. Exp. (?-?); Psychol. Abstr. (1970-); PsycINFO (?-?); PsycLit (?-?).

NE
**PARAVISIE.** Paravisie BV, Oude Enchweg 24, 1217 JD Hilversum Netherlands.

CN/0701-4945
**PHENOMENA (TORONTO).** (PHENOMENA.). V. 1- Jan. 1977-. Periodical. English. mo. $10.00, $7.50 for groups of 10 or more. Phenomena Publications, Box 6228, Toronto A. Ontartio. **DD** 133.5/05.

US
**PROCEEDINGS OF THE ACADEMY OF RELIGION AND PSYCHICAL RESEARCH ... ANNUAL ACADEMIC CONFERENCE. Main/Corp** Academy of Religion and Psychical Research. Academic Conference. **VFOAT** Annual Conference Proceedings. 10th (1985)-. Proceedings. English. an. Academy of Religion and Psychical Research, PO Box 614, Bloomfield CT 06002. **Tel** (203)242-4593. **LC** BF1021; .A27A. **DD** 133. ***Continues*** *Proceedings of the ... Annual Academic Conference of the Academy of Religion and Psychical Research.*
**Ind/Abst** Except. Hum. Exp.

US/0197-2138
**PSI-M.** [PSI-M]. Periodical. English. mo. $7.00 members of American MENSA, $9.00 associate members. PSI-M, The Psychic Science International Special Interest Group Inc, 7514 Belleplaine Drive, Dayton OH 45424. **Tel** (513)236-0361. **ED** Richard Allen Strong. **Circ:** 250.
**Desc:** A nonprofit scientific research and educational organization for promoting awareness and competency in psychical sciences and arts for benefit of individual and society.

US/0749-2898
**PSI RESEARCH.** [Psi res.]. Vol. 1, No. 1 (Mar. 1982)-. Periodical. English. qt. $28.00. PSI Research, 3101 Washington Street, San Francisco CA 94115. **Tel** (415)563-7780. **ED** Larissa Vilenskaya. **LC** BF1001; .P57. **DD** 133.8. **Bk Rev. Ad Acc. Circ:** 300 (ctrl).
**Desc:** International quarterly on parapsychology and related studies, with emphasis on research in the USSR, Eastern Europe and China.
**Ind/Abst** Except. Hum. Exp.; LABORDOC; Psychol. Abstr. (1982-).

US/1051-6581
**PSYCHIC ALMANAC, THE.** (THE PSYCHIC ALMANAC / BY GARY AND LAUREN LANGFORD.). [Psych. alm.]. 1st World Ed. (1991)-. English. $6.95 (single issue). Forest Light Press, 1089 Tunitas Creek Road, Woodside CA 94062. **DD** 001.

US/0048-573X
**PSYCHIC OBSERVER.** ***Suspended.*** Suspended (July 1981). Periodical. English. ir. ESP Press Inc, PO Box 55482, Washington DC 20011. **Tel** (202)723-4578. **ED** Henry J Nagorka. **Bk Rev. Ad Acc.**
**Desc:** A broadly eclectic journal of spiritual science well respected since 1938, specializing in metaphysics, inner development, psychic phenomena, new age concepts and psychotronics.

US/0033-2798
**PSYCHIC (SAN FRANCISCO).** ***Title Change.*** (PSYCHIC.). [Psychic]. (June/July 1969)-(19??). Periodical. English. bm. Psychic, PO Box 26289, San Francisco CA 94126. **LC** BF1001; .P58. **DD** 133/.05. **NLM** W1 PS359. **CODEN** PSCCB. ***Superseded by*** *New Realities, 0147-7625.*
**Ind/Abst** Mag. Index (?-?).

AU/0379-7449
**PSYCHOTRONIK. Added/Corp** International Association for Psychotronic Research. Vol. 1, (1977)-. Periodical. German. qt. **NLM** W1 PS89.

HK
**PU SHIH HSING HSIANG.** Vol. 1 (1975)-. Periodical. Chinese. mo. $24.00. Wai Chi Lee, 294 King's Road 6th Floor, Hsiang-Kang Hong Kong. **ED** Chien-Li. **LC** BF1868.C5; P79.
 **Desc:** Information on fortune-telling.

US/0033-4685
**PURSUIT (COLUMBIA). *Suspended.*** (PURSUIT.). [Pursuit]. **Added/Corp** Society for the Investigation of the Unexplained. (19??)-Suspended with Vol. 21, No. 1 (19??). Periodical. English. qt. Society for the Investigation of the Unexplained, Box 265, Little Silver NJ 07739. **Tel** (908)842-5229. available on microfilm and microfiche from University Microfilms International (UMI).
 **Ind/Abst** GeoRef.

CN/0843-865X
**QUEBEC SCEPTIQUE.** (LE QUEBEC SCEPTIQUE : BULLETIN D'INFORMATION DES SCEPTIQUES DU QUEBEC.). [Que. scept.]. **Added/Corp** Sceptiques du Quebec. No 9 (Jan. 1989)-. Bulletin. French. Four times a year (Feb., May, Sept., Dec.). 25.00Can$. Les Sceptiques du Quebec, PO Box 202, Succ. Beaubien, Montreal Quebec H2G 3C9 Canada. **Tel** (514)278-7692. **ED** Claude Lafleur. **DD** 133/.05. Index available (Each iss.). cum. index. **Bk Rev**, (Qty: 10). **Circ:** 600. *Continues* Bulletin d'Information (Sceptiques du Quebec)., 0843-266X.
 **Desc:** Devoted to scientific and skeptical views of pseudoscientific and paranormal claims, namely astrology, UFOs, parapsychology, New Age and health pseudo-treatments.

FR
**QUESTION DE SPIRITUALITE, TRADITION, LITTERATURES. Added/Corp** Centre d'Etudes Litteraires et Traditionelles. **VFOAT** Question de. No. 1 (1973)-. Periodical. French. bm. 330.00F (6 issues). Editions Albin Michel, 22 rue Huyghens, 75014 Paris, France. **Tel** 011 33 1 42791000, **FAX** 011 33 1 43272158, telex 203379. **ED** Jean Mouttapa & Marc de Smedt. **Bk Rev**. ctrl circ.

US/0744-432X
**RAYS FROM THE ROSE CROSS. Added/Corp** Rosicrucian Fellowship, Oceanside, Calif. **VFOAT** Rosicrucian Fellowship Magazine. Vol. 66, No. 12 (Dec. 1974)-. Periodical. English. Twelve times a year. $15.00. Rosicrucian Fellowship, PO Box 713, Oceanside CA 92054. **Tel** (619)757-6600. *Continues* Rosicrucian Fellowship, Oceanside, Calif. Rosicrucian Fellowship Magazine.

CN/0384-6016
**REALITE (QUEBEC).** (REALITE.). [Realite]. **Added/Corp** Eglise de Scientologie de Quebec. Vol 1 (April 1975)-. Periodical. French. mo. Eglise de Scientologie de Quebec, 781 Est Boulevard Charest, Quebec Quebec G1K 3J6 Canada. **DD** 131/.35/05. *Supersedes* Connection Francaise.

US/0093-4798
**RESEARCH IN PARAPSYCHOLOGY. Main/Corp** Parapsychological Association. (1972)-. Monographic series. English. an. $25.00 (latest issue). Scarecrow Press Inc., 52 Liberty Street, PO Box 4167, Metuchen NJ 08840. **Tel** (908)548-8600, (800)537-7107. **LC** BF1021; .P28. **DD** 133. **NLM** W1 RE227JK. *Continues* Proceedings of the Parapsychological Association, 0090-5399.
 **Desc:** Volumes for 1972 are the abstracts and papers of the association's 15th-annual conventions.

US/0275-6935
**REVISION (CAMBRIDGE, MASS.). See** Literature.

US/0035-8339
**ROSICRUCIAN DIGEST.** [Rosicrucian dig.]. 1932-. Periodical. English (Spanish, Portuguese, French, Japanese, German and Dutch). bm. $9.00. Rosicrucian Park, San Jose CA 95191. **Tel** (408)287-9171. **ED** Robin Thompson. **LC** BF1623.R7; A28. **DD** 135. **Circ:** 80,000 (ctrl). *Continues* Mystic Triangle.
 **Desc:** Features articles with an up-beat philosophical approach on the subjects of philosophy, psychology, metaphysics, sciences, parapsychology and the arts.

●US/1063-9330
**SKEPTIC (ALTADENA, CALIF.). See** Science and Technology.

US/0194-6730
**SKEPTICAL INQUIRER, THE.** [Skept. inq.]. **Added/Corp** Committee for the Scientific Investigation of Claims of the Paranormal. Vol. 2, No. 2 (Spring/Summer 1978)-. Periodical. English. qt. $25.00 (1 year), $43.00 (2 year), $59.00 (3 year). Skeptical Inquirer, Post Office Box 703, Buffalo NY 14226-0703. **Tel** (716)636-1425, **FAX** (716)636-1733. **ED** Kendrick Frazier. **LC** BF1001; .S47. **DD** 001.9. **NLM** W1 SK583. Index available. cum. index. **Bk Rev**. **Circ:** 35,000. available on microfilm and microfiche from University Microfilms International (UMI). Documents available from UMI Article Clearinghouse. *Continues* Zetetic, 0148-1096.
 **Desc:** Acts as a consumer information organization, serving the public and news media, providing access to facts regarding the scientific investigation of claims of the paranormal from a skeptical point-of-view, enabling readers to separate fact from myth in the flood of occultism and pseudoscientific theories presented in today's culture.
 **Ind/Abst** Except. Hum. Exp.; Expand. Acad. Index (1992-); GeoRef; Newsp. Period. Abstr. (1991-); Pop. Period. Index (1991-); Read. Guide Abstr. Select Ed.; Read. Guide Period. Lit. (1991-); Soc. Plann. Policy Dev. Abstr.; Sociol. Abstr.

GW/0936-9244
**SKEPTIKER.** (1987)-. Periodical. German. Four times a year (Feb., May, Aug., Nov.). DM30.00. GES Wissenschaftl Untersuchung, PF 1222 Von Parawissenschaften, D 64374 Rossdorf Germany. **Tel** 011 49 6154 695021, **FAX** 49 6154 695022. **ED** Prof. Irmgard Oepen (eidtor's address: Inst. Rechtsmedizin, Bahnhoftr. 7, D-35037 Marburg Germany; editor's phone: 49 6421 284048). **UDC** 1. **Bk Rev**, (Qty: 10-20). **Ad Acc**. **Pr Rev. Circ:** 2,000 (ctrl).
 **Desc:** Critically examines paranormal and other extraordinary claims using the scientific method. Critical and rational thinking is encouraged.

US/0275-6501
**SOUL SEARCHER.** [Soul search.]. V. 1-Spring/Summer 1977-. Periodical. English. qt. Free to members, $6.00 nonmembers. Foundation for Christian Psychic Research Inc, 351 Main Street, Ridgefield CT 06877.

CN/0381-6621
**SPIRITUAL PRESS.** (THE SPIRITUAL PRESS.). Vol. 1, No. 14 (Nov. 1975)-. Periodical. English. ir. Spiritual Press, PO Box 464, Don Mills Ontario M3C 2T3 Canada. **DD** 133.9/3.

US/0743-1384
**TALK OF THE MONTH. See** Literature.

US/0894-2528
**THEORETICAL PARAPSYCHOLOGY. *Ceased.*** [Theor. parapsychol.]. Vol. 6, No. 1 (Nov. 1988)-Volume 6 Issue 1. Periodical. English. bm. Gordon & Breach Science Publishers, Inc., PO Box 786, Cooper Station, New York NY 10276. **Tel** (212)206-8900, **FAX** (212)645-2459. **(Subscription address:** International Publishers Distributor at one of the following addresses: 820 Town Center Drive, Langhorne, PA 19047; or PO Box 90, Reading Berkshire RG1 8JL UK; or Kent Ridge PO Box 1180, Singapore 9111, Republic of Singapore) **LC** BF1001; .P85. **DD** 133/.05. **NLM** W1; TH12TB. **CODEN** THPAEX. **[CCC]**. *Continues* Psychoenergetics, 0278-6060.
 **Ind/Abst** Except. Hum. Exp. (?-?).

●US/1062-4643
**THESE CELESTIAL TIMES.** [These celest. times]. Vol. 1, No. 1-(1992)-. Periodical. English. qt. $22.00. These Celestial Times Inc., PO Box 8094, Gaithersburg MD 20898-8094. **DD** 133.

US/0040-6066
**THETA (DURHAM). *Ceased.*** (THETA.). **Added/Corp** Psychical Research Foundation. No. 1 (Apr. 1963)-(199?). Periodical. English. Three times a year. Theta, Psychology Department West Georgia College, Carrollton GA 30118-0001. **Tel** (919)968-4956. **ED** Grace a McGee. **LC** BF1001; .T48. **DD** 133.9/013/05. **Bk Rev. Circ:** 1,000.
 **Desc:** Focuses on the question of whether personality and consciousness extend beyond bodily existence.
 **Ind/Abst** Except. Hum. Exp. (?-?).

NE
**TIJDSCHRIFT VOOR PARAPSYCHOLOGIE. Added/Corp** Studievereniging voor Psychical Research. (19??)-. Periodical. Dutch. qt. Fl40.00. Studievereniging voor Pyschical Research, Postbus 786, NL-35 AT Utrecht Netherlands. **Tel** 030 314282. **ED** D.J. Bierman, J.L.F. Gerding and M.V. Dongen. **LC** BF1008.D8; T5. **NLM** W1 TI715. **Bk Rev. Ad Acc**.
 **Desc:** Philosophical, anthropological and psychological articles on parapsychology including experiments cases and book reviews.
 **Ind/Abst** Except. Hum. Exp. (?-?).

●US/1061-6683
**TRANSCENDING LIMITS.** Vol. 1, No.1 (1992)-. Periodical. English. bm. $17.50. AS Productions,Inc., 15476 NW, 77th Court #350, Miami Lakes FL 33016. **DD** 133.

US
**UNITARIAN UNIVERSALIST PSI SYMPOSIUM : NEWSLETTER. Added/Corp** Unitarian Universalist Psi Symposium. **VFOAT** Newsletter; U.U. Psi Symposium. Vol. 1 Newsletter No. 4 (Jan./Feb. 1970)-. Newsletter. English. qt. $7.00 (membership). Unitarian Universalist Psi Symposium, Unitarian Church of Lancaster, 538 West Chestnut Street, Lancaster PA 17603. *Continues* UU's Interested in ESP.
 **Ind/Abst** Except. Hum. Exp.

US/0748-3406
**VENTURE INWARD / THE MAGAZINE OF THE ASSOCIATION FOR RESEARCH AND ENLIGHTENMENT. See** Religion and Theology.

US/0742-8820
**WHITE LIGHT, THE.** Periodical. English. qt. $5.00 US; $8.00 other. Temple of Truth, PO Box 93124, Pasadena CA 91104-3124. **Tel** (818)794-6013. **ED** Nelson H White. **DD** 133.4/3/05. Index available. cum. index. **Bk Rev. Ad Acc. Circ:** 200.
 **Desc:** Ceremonial magic and related areas: Qaballah, occultism, etc.

GW/0028-3479
**ZEITSCHRIFT FUER PARAPSYCHOLOGIE UND GRENZGEBIETE DER PSYCHOLOGIE.** [Z. Parapsychol. Grenzgeb. Psychol.]. Vol. 1-. Periodical. German (summaries and/or abstracts in English). qt. DM80.00. WGFP-Geschaftsstelle, Hildastabe 64, W-7800 Freiburg 1 Br Germany. **Tel** (0761)77202. **LC** BF1003; .Z45. **DD** 133/.05. **NLM** W1 ZE531T. Index available. cum. index. **Bk Rev. Ad Acc. Pr Rev. Circ:** 1,000 (ctrl).
 **Desc:** Parapsychology
 **Ind/Abst** EMBASE; Except. Hum. Exp.; PsycINFO (?-?); PsycLit.

US/0741-6229
**ZETETIC SCHOLAR.** [Zetet. sch.]. Vol. 1, No. 1-. Periodical. English. ir. $18.00 North America; $20.00 other. Eastern Michigan University / Sociology Dept., Department of Sociology, 1 Wojeik-Andrews, Ypsilanti MI 48197. **Tel** (313)487-0150. **ED** Marcello Truzzi. **LC** BF1001; .Z47. **DD** 133/.05. **Bk Rev. Circ:** 600 (ctrl).
 **Desc:** Scientific exchanges on anomalies and the paranormal between critics and proponents plus reviews and bibliographies.
 **Ind/Abst** Except. Hum. Exp. (?-?); Soc. Plann. Policy Dev. Abstr.; Sociol. Abstr.

## ABSTRACTING, BIBLIOGRAPHIES AND STATISTICS

US/1053-4768
**EXCEPTIONAL HUMAN EXPERIENCE.** [Except. hum. exp.]. **Added/Corp** Parapsychology Sources of Information Center. **VFOAT** EHE. Vol. 8, No. 1/2 (Dec. 1990)-. Abstracting/Indexing Service. English. Twice a year (June and December). $50.00 (institutions), $35.00 (individuals). Parapsychology Sources of Information Center, 2 Plain Tree Lane, Dix Hills NY 11746. **Tel** (516)271-1243, **FAX** (516)271-1243. **ED** Rhea White. **LC** BF1001; .P275. **DD** 016.1338; 133. Index available (Every issue, every 5 years.). **Bk Rev**, (Qty: 120). **Circ:** 350. *Continues* Parapsychology Abstracts International, 0740-7629.
 **Desc:** Information resource for literature recording parapsychology and other unusual phenomena.

US/0277-9870
**INTERNATIONAL GUIDE TO PSI PERIODICALS AND ORGANIZATIONS.** [Int. guide psi period. organ.]. English. an. $4.00. Inner Space Interpreters Services, Po Box 1133, Burbank CA 91507. **LC** Z6878.P8; I57; BF1001. **DD** 016.133/05. *Continues* Guide to PSI Periodicals.

## PEST CONTROL

●PL
**ACTA PARASITOLOGICA / WITOLD STEFANSKI INSTITUTE OF PARASITOLOGY. Added/Corp** Polska Akademia Nauk. Instytut Parazytologii im. Witolda Stefanskiego. Vol. 37, No. 1 (1992)-. Academic Scholarly Publication. English. qt. $90.00. **NLM** W1; AC906J. **CODEN** ACTPEO. Documents available from CASDDS. *Continues* Acta Parasitologica Polonica, 0065-1478.
 **Desc:** Looks at parasites and parasitology.
 **Ind/Abst** Chem. Abstr.

TH
**AGRO-CHEMICALS NEWS IN BRIEF. See** Agriculture.

US/0099-1929
**ANALYSIS OF OFFICIAL PESTICIDE SAMPLES.** (ANALYSIS OF OFFICIAL PESTICIDE SAMPLES; ANNUAL REPORT.). **Main/Corp** Louisiana Dept. of Agriculture. (19??)-. English. an. Louisiana Department of Agriculture & Forestry Department, PO Box 631, Baton Rouge LA 70821. **Tel** (504)922-1234,

FAX (504)922-1289. **LC** SB951; .L65. **DD** 668/.65. ***Continues*** *Louisiana. Dept. of Agriculture and Immigration. Analysis of Pesticides.*

NE
**ANALYTICAL METHODS FOR RESIDUES OF PESTICIDES IN FOODSTUFFS.** (19??)-. English. an. SDU Uitgeverij, Postbus 20014, Christoffel Plan, 2500 EA Den Haag Netherlands. **Tel** 011 31 70 3789911.

US/0098-0196
**ANNUAL CONFERENCE REPORT ON COTTON INSECT RESEARCH AND CONTROL.** [Annu. conf. rep. cotton insect res. control]. **Added/Corp** United States. Agricultural Research Service. Southern Region. United States. Agricultural Research Service. United States. Science and Education Administration. Agricultural Research. Southern Region. (19??)-. English. an. National Technical Information Service - NTIS, Room 2027S, 5285 Port Royal Road, Springfield VA 22161. **Tel** (703)487-4630, (703)487-4660, (703)487-4650, FAX (703)321-8547, telex 89-9405. **LC** SB608.C8; U58. **DD** 633.5/197/0973. available on microfiche (Vols. for (1982-) distributed to depository libraries). ***Continues*** *Conference Report on Cotton Insect Research and Control.*

UK
**ANNUAL REPORT / ADVISORY COMMITTEE ON PESTICIDES.** **Main/Corp** Great Britain. Advisory Committee on Pesticides. (19??)-. English. an. Her Majesty's Stationery Office, 51 Nine Elms Lane, London SW8 5DR England. **Tel** 011 44 71 873 8459, 011 44 71 873 8499, FAX 011 44 71 873 8499, 011 44 71 873 8456, telex 297138. **(Subscription address:** Her Majesty's Stationery Office, PO Box 276, Publications Centre, London SW8 5DT England.**)** **LC** SB950.3.G7; G7a. **DD** 363.7/384.

GW/0340-7330
**ANZEIGER FUER SCHADLINGSKUNDE, PFLANZENSCHUTZ, UMWELTSCHUTZ.** [Anz. Schadlingsk., Pflanzen., Umweltschutz]. Vol. 48 (Jan. 1975)-. Academic Scholarly Publication. German (summaries and/or abstracts in English; table of contents in English). Eight times a year. DM369.00 Europe; DM366.00 other. Blackwell Wissenschafts-Verlag, Kurfuerstendamm 57, D 10707 Berlin Germany. **Tel** 011 49 30 32790623, 011 49 30 32790624, FAX 011 49 30 327 90610. **ED** W. Schwenke. **LC** SB599; .A69. **NLM** W1 AN961. **CODEN** ASUMDTASPUCR. **[CCC].** Index available. cum. index. **Bk Rev. Ad Acc. Circ:** 2,500. Documents available from The Genuine Article, BIOSIS Document Express, CASDDS. ***Continues*** *Anzeiger fuer Schadlingskunde, Pflanzen- und Unweltschutz, 0340-7322.*
**Desc:** Reports on pest control, plant and environmental protection.
**Ind/Abst** Agrofor. Abstr. (1991-); Biocont. News Inf. (19??-19??); Biodeter. Abstr.; Biol. Abstr.; Chem. Abstr.; Chemorecept. Abstr.; Curr. Contents, Agric. Biol. Environ. Sci.; EMBASE; Energy Res. Abstr. (Aug. 1976-); Field Crop Abstr.; For. Prod. Abstr. (19??-19??); For. Abstr.; Grasslands For. Abstr.; Hortic. Abstr.; Maize Abstr.; Nematol. Abstr.; Life Sci. Collect. (1975-); PESTDOC; Postharvest News Inf.; Protozoolog. Abstr.; Res. Alert [Select. Cov.]; Rev. Agric. Entomol.; Rev. Med. Vet. Entomol.; Rev. Plant Pathol.; SCISEARCH; Seed Abstr.; Soils Fert.

●US
**ARTHROPOD MANAGEMENT TESTS.** **VFOAT** AMT. (Effective May 1995)-. English. an (May). $45.00 US; $50.00 other. Entomological Society of America, 9301 Annapolis Road, Suite 300, Lanham MD 20706. **Tel** (301)731-4535, FAX (301)731-4538. **(Subscription address:** ESA, PO Box 177, Hyattsville, MD 20781-0177**)** **ED** Arthur K. Burditt, Jr. Index available. ***Continues*** *Insecticide & Acaracide Test, 0276-3656.*
**Desc:** Presents the results of field and laboratory screenings performed with agricultural chemicals on a variety of crops.

US/1049-9644
**BIOLOGICAL CONTROL.** (BIOLOGICAL CONTROL : THEORY AND APPLICATIONS IN PEST MANAGEMENT.). [Biol. control]. Vol. 1, No. 1 (June 1991)-. Academic Scholarly Publication. English. qt (4 issues). $199.00 US and Canada; $228.00 other. Academic Press, Inc., 6277 Sea Harbor Drive, Orlando FL 32887. **Tel** (800)543-9534, (407)345-4100, FAX (407)363-9661. **ED** Raghavan Charudattan, Harry K. Kaya, W. Joe Lewis and Charlie E. Rogers. **LC** SB925; .B5. **DD** 628. **CODEN** BCIOEB. **[CCC].**
**Desc:** An environmentally sound and effective means of reducing or mitigating pests and pest effects through the use of natural enemies. The aim of the journal is to promote the science and technology of biological control through publication of original research articles and reviews of research and theory. The journal devotes a section to reporting on biotechnologies dealing with the elucidation and use of genes or gene products for the enhancement of biological control agents. Encompasses biological control of viral, microbial, nematode, insect, mite, weed, and vertebrate pests in agriculture, aquatic, forest, natural resource, stored product, and urban environments. Biological control of arthropod pests of human and domestic animals is also included.
**Ind/Abst** Sci. Cit. Index.

US/0149-0907
**BIORESEARCH TODAY. PESTICIDES.** ***Ceased.*** **VFOAT** Pesticides. **VAT** BioResearch Today. Pesticides. Ceased (Dec. 1991). English. mo. BioSciences Information Service, Biological Abstracts / BIOSIS, 2100 Arch Street, Philadelphia PA 19103-1399. **Tel** (800)523-4806 US, (215)587-4800 Pennsylvania and worldwide, FAX (215)587-2016, telex 831739.
**Desc:** Current awareness journal including abstracts and content summaries of studies involving pesticides.

AG
**BOLETIN DE PLAGUICIDAS / CENTRO DE INVESTIGACION Y ASISTENCIA TOXICOLOGICA.** **Added/Corp** Centro de Investigacion y Asistencia Toxicologica. (Argentina). (19??)-. Spanish.

SP/0213-6910
**BOLETIN DE SANIDAD VEGETAL. PLAGAS.** [Bol. sanid. veg., Plagas]. **VFOAT** Plagas; Boletin Plagas; Sanidad Vegetal Plagas. Vol. 12, No. 1; 1986-. Periodical. Spanish. sa. Instituto Nacional de Investigaciones Agrarias, C. Jose Abascal 56, 28003 Madrid Spain. **Tel** 011 34 1 3473906, FAX (91)4423587, telex 48989 INIA E. ***Continues*** *Boletin / Spain. Servicio de Defensa Contra Plagas e Inspeccion Fitopatologica, 0210-8038.*
**Ind/Abst** Biocont. News Inf. (1991-); For. Abstr.; Hortic. Abstr.; Maize Abstr.; Nematol. Abstr.; PESTDOC; Plant Breed. Abstr.; Rev. Agric. Entomol.; Rice Abstr.; Wheat Barley Trit. Abstr.

US/0031-448X
**BULLETIN - PENNSYLVANIA FLOWER GROWERS.** **See** Gardening and Horticulture-Florist Trade.

US/0278-1824
**CHEMICAL SCREENING, INITIAL EVALUATIONS OF SUBSTANTIAL RISK NOTICES, SECTION 8(E).** (CHEMICAL SCREENING, INITIAL EVALUATIONS OF SUBSTANTIAL RISK NOTICES, SECTION 8(E) / OFFICE OF TESTING AND EVALUATION, OFFICE OF PESTICIDES AND TOXIC SUBSTANCES.). **VFOAT** Initial Evaluations, TSCA Section 8(E). Vol. 1 (Jan. 1, 1977-June 30, 1979)-. English. ir. EPA Office of Testing & Evaluations, Office of Pesticides and Toxic Substances, Washington DC 20460. **NLM** W1 CH265.

US
**COMMERCIAL VEGETABLE PRODUCTION RECOMMENDATIONS.** Periodical. English. an. ***Continues in part*** *Cook College. Cooperative Extension Service. Extension Bulletin.*

US/8756-7881
**COMMON SENSE PEST CONTROL QUARTERLY.** [Common sense pest control q.]. **Added/Corp** Bio Integral Resource Center (Berkeley, Calif.). Vol. 1, No. 1 (Fall 1984)-. Periodical. English. Four times a year (Mar., June, Sept., Dec.). $30.00 (individuals), $50.00 (institutions) associate member, $45.00 (individuals), $75.00 (institutions) dual member, Comes with Bio Integral Resource Center membership. Bio Integral Resource Center, PO Box 7414, Berkeley CA 94707. **Tel** (510)524-2567. **ED** William Olkowski, Helga Olkowski and Sheila Daar. **LC** WMLC L 83/8920. **DD** 648. Index available. **Bk Rev. Ad Acc. Circ:** 1,000 (ctrl).
**Desc:** Describes least-toxic methods for managing insect, weed, disease and rodent pests; written for non-technical readers.
**Ind/Abst** AGRICOLA [Select. Cov.]; Garden Lit. (1992-).

UK/0261-2194
**CROP PROTECTION (GUILDFORD, SURREY).** **See** Agriculture-Crop Production and Soil.

US/0733-2068
**CROP PROTECTION RESEARCH.** [Crop prot. res.]. **VFOAT** Crop Protection Research Annual Report. 1980-. Government Publication. English. an. US Department of Agriculture / Science & Education, Administration Building, Room 217-W, Washington DC 20250. **Tel** (202)720-5923, FAX (202)755-7842. **LC** SB950.A1; C76. **DD** 632/.9. ***Continues*** *Crop Protection (United States. Science and Education Administration. National Program Staff).*

LV/0367-0724
**EKSPERIMENTALNAIA VODNAIA TOKSIKOLOGIIA / AKADEMIIA NAUK LATVIISKOI SSR, INSTITUT BIOLOGII.** **Added/Corp** Biologijas Instituts (Latvijas PSR Zinatnu Akademija). **VFOAT** Experimental Water Toxicology. (1970)-. Monographic series. Russian (summaries and/or abstracts in English). Zinatne / Science Publishing House, Turgeneva Iela 19, Riga Latvia 1530. **Tel** 3712 212 797. **LC** SB951; .E475. **CODEN** EKVTA6. Documents available from CASDDS.
**Ind/Abst** Chem. Abstr.

AT
**ENTOMOLOGY BRANCH INSECT PEST BULLETIN.** **Main/Corp** New South Wales. Dept. of Agriculture. Entomology Branch. No. 149 (1974)-. Monographic series. English. Price varies per volume. New South Wales Department of Agriculture / Entomology Branch, Sydney NSW Australia. ***Continues*** *New South Wales. Dept. of Agriculture. Entomology Branch. Insect Pest Bulletin.*

FR/0013-8959
**ENTOMOPHAGA.** [Entomophaga]. **Added/Corp** International Organization for Biological Control. Vol. 1 (July 1956)-. Periodical. Multiple languages (English, French, German, Italian and Spanish; summaries and/or abstracts in French, German, Italian and Spanish). qt. $142.00. Lavoisier Abonnements, 14 rue de Provigny, F 94236 Cachan Cedex France. **Tel** 011 33 1 47406700. **(Subscription address:** VCH Publishers Inc., 303 Northwest 12th Avenue, Journals Department, Deerfield FL 33442.**)** **ED** J.M. Rabasse. **LC** SB599; .E42. **NLM** W1 EN939. **CODEN** ETPGAY. **[CCC].** Index available. cum. index. **Circ:** 1,250 (ctrl). Documents available from The Genuine Article, BIOSIS Document Express, CASDDS. ***Continued in part by*** *Liste d'Identification des Entomophages.*
**Desc:** Official periodical of the International Organization for Biological Control of Noxious Animals and Plants. Includes original research papers on the biological control of crops, forests, and stored products.
**Ind/Abst** AGRICOLA; Agrindex; BioBusiness; Biocont. News Inf. (19??-19??); Biol. Abstr.; Chem. Abstr.; Cot. Trop. Fibr. Abstr. Bibliogr.; Curr. Aware. Biol. Sci., CABS; Curr. Contents, Agric. Biol. Environ. Sci.; Ecol. Abstr.; Ecology Abstr.; Entomol. Abstr.; For. Prod. Abstr.; For. Abstr.; Helminthol. Abstr.; Hortic. Abstr.; Int. Dev. Abstr.; Maize Abstr.; Microbiol. Abstr. Sect. A; Nematol. Abstr.; Life Sci. Collect.; PESTDOC; Potato Abstr.; Poult. Abstr.; Protozoolog. Abstr.; Res. Alert [Full Cov.]; Rev. Agric. Entomol.; Rev. Med. Vet. Entomol.; Rev. Med. Vet. Mycology; Rev. Plant Pathol.; Rice Abstr.; Sci. Cit. Index; SCISEARCH; Seed Abstr.; Soils Fert.; Sorghum Mill. Abstr.; Soyabean Abstr.; Weed Abstr.; Wheat Barley Trit. Abstr.

US/1040-1512
**EPA COMPENDIUM OF REGISTERED PESTICIDES. VOLUME 1. HERBICIDES AND PLANT REGULATORS.** [EPA compend. regist. pestic., 1 Herbic. plant regul.]. **Main/Corp** United States. Environmental Protection Agency. **VFOAT** Herbicides and Plant Regulators. 1973-. Periodical. English. US Environmental Protection Agency / Office of Pesticide Programs, Technical Services Division, 401 Main Street Southwest, Washington DC 20402. **Tel** 800 424-9065. **DD** 632.

US/1040-1520
**EPA COMPENDIUM OF REGISTERED PESTICIDES. VOLUME 2. FUNGICIDES AND NEMATICIDES.** [EPA compend. regist. pestic., 2 Fungic. nematic.]. **Main/Corp** United States. Environmental Protection Agency. **Added/Corp** United States. Environmental Protection Agency. Office of Pesticide Programs. Technical Services Division. **VFOAT** Fungicides and Nematicides. **VAT** Environmental Protection Agency compendium of registered pesticides. Volume 2. Fungicides and nematicides. (1973)-. English. ir. US Environmental Protection Agency / Office of Pesticide Programs, Technical Services Division, 401 Main Street Southwest, Washington DC 20402. **Tel** 800 424-9065. **DD** 632.

US
**EPA COMPENDIUM OF REGISTERED PESTICIDES. VOLUME 3. INSECTICIDES, ACARICIDES, MOLLUSCICIDES AND ANTIFOULING COMPOUNDS.** **Main/Corp** United States. Environmental Protection Agency. **VFOAT** Insecticides, Acaricides, Molluscicides and Antifouling Compounds. 1972-. Periodical. English. US Environmental Protection Agency / Office of Pesticide Programs, Technical Services Division, 401 Main Street Southwest, Washington DC 20402. **Tel** 800 424-9065.

US
**EPA COMPENDIUM OF REGISTERED PESTICIDES. VOLUME 4. RODENTICIDES AND MAMMAL, BIRD AND FISH TOXICANTS.** **Main/Corp** United States. Environmental Protection Agency. **VFOAT** Rodenticides and Mammal, Bird and Fish Toxicants. 1972-. Periodical. English. US Environmental Protection Agency / Office of Pesticide Programs, Technical Services Division, 401 Main Street Southwest, Washington DC 20402. **Tel** 800 424-9065.

US
**EPA COMPENDIUM OF REGISTERED PESTICIDES. VOLUME 5. DISINFECTANTS.** **Main/Corp** United States. Environmental Protection Agency. **Added/Corp** United States. Environmental Protection Agency. Office of Pesticide Programs. Technical Services Division. **VFOAT**

Disinfectants. (1973)-. Periodical. English. US Environmental Protection Agency / Office of Pesticide Programs, Technical Services Division, 401 Main Street Southwest, Washington DC 20402. **Tel** 800 424-9065.

UK
**EUROPEAN DIRECTORY OF AGROCHEMICAL PRODUCTS.**
**Added/Corp** Royal Society of Chemistry (Great Britain). (1984)-. English. Royal Society of Chemistry, Thomas Graham House, Science Park, Cambridge CB4 4WF England. **Tel** 011 44 223 420066, FAX 011 44 223 423429, telex 818293 ROYAL. **(Subscription address:** Royal Society of Chemistry, Distribution Center, Blackhorse Road, Letchworth, SG6 1HN England.**) LC** SB950.3.E85; E93. **DD** 668/.65/0284. available on an online database from DIALOG.
**Desc:** Gives access to over 25,000 agrochemical products registered for use in European countries. Data provided includes product name, country of registration, marketing company, active ingredients plus active ingredient proportions and uses.
**Ind/Abst** Nematol. Abstr.; Rev. Med. Vet. Entomol.

US
**GEORGIA LICENSED NURSERIES. See** Gardening and Horticulture.

US
**HOME, YARD, AND GARDEN PEST NEWSLETTER. Added/Corp** Illinois. University at Urbana-Champaign. Cooperative Extension Service in Agriculture and Home Economics. Illinois. University at Urbana-Champaign. College of Agriculture. Illinois. Natural History Survey Division. (1978)-. English. Twenty times a year. $20.00. Agricultural Newsletter Service, University of Illinois, 116 Mumford Hall, Urbana IL 61801. **Tel** (217)333-2666.

US/0145-6288
**INFOLETTER - INTERNATIONAL PLANT PROTECTION CENTER. See** Agriculture-Crop Production and Soil.

CN/0713-1313
**INSECT AND DISEASE CONTROL IN THE HOME GARDEN.** [Insect des. control home gard.]. 1977/1978-. English. be. $0.50. Ontario Ministry of Agriculture and Food, 801 Bay Street, Toronto Ontario M7A 1B3 Canada. **Tel** (416)965-1064, (416)326-3400. **DD** 635/.049/09713. ***Continues** Insect, Disease and Weed Control in the Home Garden, 0713-1305.*

US
**INSECT CONTROL GUIDE.** (1991)-. Periodical. English. an. $40.50 US; $42.75 Canada; $48.00 other. Meister Publishing Company, 37733 Euclid Avenue, Willoughby OH 44094-5992. **Tel** (216)942-2000, (800)572-7740, FAX (216)942-0662. **LC** SB951.5; .I6. **DD** 632/.951. ***Continues** Insecticide Product Guide, 0891-1878.*
**Desc:** Contains insecticide descriptions, use recommendations, and environmental data.

AT
**INSECT PEST SURVEY / TASMANIAN DEPARTMENT OF AGRICULTURE.**
**Added/Corp** Tasmania. Dept. of Agriculture. (1969)-. Monographic series. English. an. Price varies per volume. Tasmania Department of Agriculture, Hobart Tasmania Australia.
**Ind/Abst** Rev. Med. Vet. Entomol.

US/0276-3656
**INSECTICIDE & ACARICIDE TESTS. *Title Change.*** [Insectic. acaric. tests]. **Added/Corp** Entomological Society of America. **VFOAT** Insecticide & Acaricide Tests. Vol. 6 (1976)-(Effective May 1995)-. English. an. Entomological Society of America, 9301 Annapolis Road, Suite 300, Lanham MD 20706. **Tel** (301)731-4535, FAX (301)731-4538. **ED** Alan C. York. **LC** SB951.5; .I55. **DD** 632/.951/0287. **CODEN** IATEEV. **Circ:** 1,200 (ctrl). Documents available from BIOSIS Document Express. ***Continues** Insecticide and Acaricide Tests, 0276-3656.* ***Continued by** Arthropod Management Test (AMT).*
**Desc:** Gives reports of studies performed in the previous year on efficacy of pesticides on crops.
**Ind/Abst** AGRICOLA; Biol. Abstr. (1985-); PESTDOC; Postharvest News Inf.; Rev. Med. Vet. Entomol.

US
**INSECTICIDE, HERBICIDE, FUNGICIDE QUICK GUIDE, THE. VFOAT** Insecticides, Herbicides, Fungicides Quick Guide. (1971)-. English. an. $17.50. Thomson Publications / California, PO Box 9335, Fresno CA 93791. **Tel** (209)435-2163, FAX (209)435-8319. ***Continues** Insecticide, Herbicide, Fungicide Quick Guide and Date Book.*

●UK/1353-5226
**INTEGRATED PEST MANAGEMENT REVIEWS.** (1995)-. Periodical. English. Four times a year. $240.00 US and Canada; £140.00 Europe; £155.00 Other. Chapman & Hall, 2-6 Boundary Row, London SE1 8HN England. **Tel** 011 44 71 865 0066, FAX 011 44 71 522 9623, telex 290164 Chapmag. **(Subscription address:** Chapman & Hall, Cheriton House, North Way, Andover, Hampshire, SP10 5BE England.**)**

NR
**INTERAFRICAIN PHYTOSANITARY BULLETIN. See** Gardening and Horticulture.

UK/0020-8256
**INTERNATIONAL PEST CONTROL.** [Int. pest control]. Vol. 5 (1962)-. Academic Scholarly Publication. English. Six times a year (Feb., Apr., June, Aug., Oct., Dec.). £50.00 (surface mail); £100.00 (airmail). McDonald Publications of London Ltd, 238A High Street, Uxbridge Middex UB8 1UA England. **Tel** 011 44 81 4268012, FAX 011 44 81 4268012, telex 8954029. **ED** David McDonald. **LC** SB950; .I5. **NLM** W1; IN827L. **CODEN** IPCLBZ. Index available. **Bk Rev. Ad Acc. Pr Rev. Circ:** 2,500. Documents available from BIOSIS Document Express, CASDDS. ***Continues** Pest Technology.*
**Desc:** News and information on pest control in agriculture and public health.
**Ind/Abst** AGRICOLA; Agric. Eng. Abstr.; BioBusiness; Biol. Agric. Index; Biol. Abstr.; Chem. Abstr.; Chem. Bus. Bull.; Chem. Bus. NewsBase (1985-); Chem. Bus. Update; Curr. Aware. Biol. Sci., CABS; EMBASE; Environ. Period. Bibliogr.; F&S Index Plus Text, Int. [Select. Cov.]; Field Crop Abstr.; For. Prod. Abstr.; For. Abstr.; Grasslands For. Abstr.; Hortic. Abstr.; Index Vet.; Nematol. Abstr.; PESTDOC; Pig News Inf.; Predicasts; PROMT; Ref. Sources; Rev. Med. Vet. Entomol.; Rev. Med. Vet. Mycology; Rev. Plant Pathol.; Soils Fert.; Vet. Bull.; Trop. Dis. Bull.; Weed Abstr.; Wildl. Rev.

US/0738-968X
**IPM PRACTITIONER, THE.** (THE IPM PRACTITIONER : THE NEWSLETTER OF INTEGRATED PEST MANAGEMENT.). [IPM pract.]. **Added/Corp** Bio-Integral Resource Center (Winters, Calif.). **VFOAT** I.P.M. Practitioner. **VAT** Integrated Pest Management Practitioner. (1979)-. Periodical. English. Ten times a year. $45.00 (individuals), $75.00 (institutions) Comes with Bio Integral Resource Center membership (dual). Bio Integral Resource Center, PO Box 7414, Berkeley CA 94707. **Tel** (510)524-2567. **ED** William Olkowski, Helga Olkowski, and Sheila Daar. Index available. **Bk Rev. Ad Acc. Circ:** 5,000.
**Desc:** Monitors the field of integrated pest management applied to agricultural, urban, range and forest settings.
**Ind/Abst** AGRICOLA [Select. Cov.]; Art Archaeol. Tech. Abstr.; Biocont. News Inf. (1991-); For. Prod. Abstr.; Garden Lit. (1992-); Helminthol. Abstr.; Hortic. Abstr.; Maize Abstr.; Nematol. Abstr.; Ornamental Hort. (1991-); Rev. Agric. Entomol.; Rev. Med. Vet. Entomol.

RU/0134-7780
**ITOGI NAUKI I TEKHNIKI. SERIIA ZASHCHITA RASTENII / VSESOIUZNYI INSTITUT NAUCHNOI I TEKHNICHESKOI INFORMATSII.** [Itogi nauki teh., Ser. Zasc. rast.]. **Added/Corp** Vsesoiuznyi Institut Nauchnoi i Tekhnicheskoi Informatsii (Soviet Union). **VFOAT** Zashchita Rastenii; Seriia Zashchita Rastenii; Itogi Nauki i Tekhniki. Zashchita Rastenii. (1980)-. Monographic series. Russian. Price varies per volume. VINITI - Vsesoyuznyi Institut Nauchno-Tekhnicheskoi Informatsii, All-Union Scientific and Technical Information Institute, Baltiiskaia Ulitsa 14, 125219 Moscow Russia. **Tel** 238-46-00, FAX 9430060, telex 411160. **LC** SB599; .I88. **CODEN** ITSRDR. Documents available from CASDDS. ***Continues** Itogi Nauki: Zashchita Rastenii.*
**Ind/Abst** Chem. Abstr.

NE/0074-0446
**JAARSVERSLAG - INSTITUUT VOOR PLANTENZEIKTENKUNDIG ONDERZOEK. See** Gardening and Horticulture.

JA/0368-265X
**JAPAN PESTICIDE INFORMATION. *Title Change.*** [Jpn. pestic. inf.]. **Added/Corp** Nihon Shokubutsu Boeki Kyokai. No. 1 (Oct. 1969)-(1994). Periodical. English. sa. Sun Publications Service Ltd, Ishii Building, 3 37 Sakumacho Kanda, Chiyoda-ku Tokyo 101 Japan. **Tel** 011 81 3 3866 9897, FAX 011 81 3 3861 7715. **ED** Kazuo Fukunaga. **LC** SB950.3.J3; J3. **DD** 632/.95/0952. **CODEN** JPIFAN. **Circ:** 6,000. Documents available from BIOSIS Document Express, CASDDS. ***Continued by** Agrochemicals Japan.*
**Ind/Abst** AGRICOLA; Biol. Abstr.; Chem. Abstr.; Chem. Bus. Bull.; Chem. Bus. NewsBase (1989-); Chem. Bus. Update; Crop Physiol. Abstr.; Hortic. Abstr.; Maize Abstr.; Nematol. Abstr.; PESTDOC; Plant Grow. Reg. Abstr.; Potato Abstr.; Protozoolog. Abstr.; Rev. Agric. Entomol.; Rev. Med. Vet. Mycology; Rev. Plant Pathol.; Rice Abstr.; SEA Abstr.; Soils Fert.; Weed Abstr.

II/0970-3810
**JOURNAL OF APHIDOLOGY. See** Zoology-Entomology.

US/0022-0493
**JOURNAL OF ECONOMIC ENTOMOLOGY. See** Zoology-Entomology.

US/0360-1234
**JOURNAL OF ENVIRONMENTAL SCIENCE AND HEALTH. PART B, PESTICIDES, FOOD CONTAMINANTS, AND AGRICULTURAL WASTES. See** Environmental Issues.

US/0893-357X
**JOURNAL OF PESTICIDE REFORM.** (JOURNAL OF PESTICIDE REFORM : A PUBLICATION OF THE NORTHWEST COALITION FOR ALTERNATIVES TO PESTICIDES.). [J. pestic. reform]. **Added/Corp** Northwest Coalition for Alternatives to Pesticides. (1985)-. Periodical. English. Four times a year (Mar., June, Sept., Dec.). $25.00. Northwest Coalition for Alternatives to Pesticides, PO Box 1393, Eugene OR 97440. **Tel** (503)344-5044. **ED** Caroline Cox. **DD** 632. **Bk Rev,** (Qty: 8). **Circ:** 1,700. ***Continues** Northwest Coalition for Alternatives to Pesticides. N.C.A.P. News, 0194-5939.*
**Ind/Abst** AGRICOLA [Full Cov.]; Dairy Sci. Abstr.; Environ. Period. Bibliogr.; Nutr. Abstr. Rev., Ser. A, Hum. Exp.; Rev. Agric. Entomol.; Rev. Med. Vet. Entomol.; Weed Abstr.

JA/0385-1559
**JOURNAL OF PESTICIDE SCIENCE (TOKYO, 1975).** (NIHON NOYAKU GAKKAI SHI.). [J. pestic. sci.]. **Added/Corp** Nihon Noyaku Gakkai. **VFOAT** Journal of Pesticide Science. Vol. 1 (1976)-. Academic Scholarly Publication. Japanese (English; summaries and/or abstracts in English). qt. $182.00. Nihon Noyaku Gakkai, (Pesticide Science Soc. of Japan), Nihon Shokubutsu Boeki Kyokai, 43-11, Komagome 1 Chome, Toshimaku, Tokyoto 170, Japan. **(Subscription address:** Kyowa Book Company Inc., 1 38 Kanda Jinbocho Chiyoda-ku, Tokyo 101 Japan.**) NLM** W1; NI426W. **CODEN** NNGADV. **[CCC]. Pr Rev.** Documents available from BIOSIS Document Express, CASDDS. ***Continues** Noyaku Kagaku.*
**Ind/Abst** AGRICOLA; BioBusiness; Biocont. News Inf.; Biol. Abstr.; Chem. Abstr.; Curr. Ref. Fish Res.; Life Sci. Collect.; PESTDOC; Postharvest News Inf.; Rev. Agric. Entomol.; Rev. Med. Vet. Entomol.

US/8756-971X
**JOURNAL OF THE AMERICAN MOSQUITO CONTROL ASSOCIATION.** [J. Am. Mosq. Control Assoc.]. **Added/Corp** American Mosquito Control Association. **VFOAT** Mosquito News. Vol. 1, No. 1 (March 1985)-. Academic Scholarly Publication. English. Four times a year (Mar., June, Sept., Dec.). $50.00 (individuals), $85.00 (institutions) surface mail; $65.00 (individuals), $100.00 (institutions) Canada, Mexico & APO & AFO Addresses, $70.00 (individuals), $105.00 (institutions) South & Central America & Europe, $80.00 (individuals), $115.00 (institutions) others airmail, Comes with American Mosquito Control Association membership. American Mosquito Control Association, PO Box 5416, Lake Charles LA 70606-5416. **Tel** (318)474-2723, FAX (318)439-8615, (318)478-9434. **ED** Ronald A. Ward. **LC** RA640; .J68. **DD** 614.4/323. **NLM** W1; JO909T. **CODEN** JAMAET. **[CCC].** Index Available in first issue of next volume--attached. **Bk Rev. Ad Acc. Pr Rev. Circ:** 2,000. Documents available from The Genuine Article, BIOSIS Document Express, CASDDS. ***Continues** Mosquito News, 0027-142X.*
**Ind/Abst** AGRICOLA [Full Cov.]; Agric. Eng. Abstr. (1991-); Aquat. Sci. Fish. Abstr. (Computer File); Biocont. News Inf. (19??-19??); Biol. Abstr. (1985-); Chem. Abstr. (1985-); Curr. Contents, Agric. Biol. Environ. Sci.; Dairy Sci. Abstr.; Ecology Abstr.; Entomol. Abstr.; Fish Rev.; For. Abstr.; Helminthol. Abstr. (1991-); Index Med. (Vol.1, No. 1, 1985-);; Index Vet.; Irr. Drain. Abstr.; Microbiol. Abstr. Sect. A; Microbiol. Abstr. Sect. C; Nematol. Abstr.; Protozoolog. Abstr.; Res. Alert [Full Cov.]; Rev. Agric. Entomol.; Rev. Med. Vet. Entomol.; Rice Abstr.; Sci. Cit. Index; SCISEARCH; Trop. Dis. Bull.; Virol. AIDS Abstr.; Weed Abstr.; Wildl. Rev.

US/1055-355X
**JOURNAL OF THE FLORIDA MOSQUITO CONTROL ASSOCIATION. See** Public Health and Safety.

JA
**KAJU BYOGAICHU BOJO HANDOBUKKU. See** Gardening and Horticulture.

JA/0916-9962
**NIPPON NOYAKU GAKKAISHI INTERNATIONAL ED. VFOAT** Journal of Pesticide Science (International Ed.); Nihon Noyaku Gakkaishi (International Ed.). (1992)-. Academic Scholarly Publication. English. qt (1 volume). Fl391.00. Elsevier Science Publishers BV, PO Box 211, 1000 AE Amsterdam Netherlands. **Tel** 011 31 20 5803642, FAX 011 31 20 5862696, telex 15682. Documents available from The Genuine Article. ***Continues** Nippon Noyaku Gakkaishi, 0385-1559.*
**Ind/Abst** Agric. Eng. Abstr. (1991-); Cot. Trop. Fibr. Abstr. Bibliogr.; Crop Physiol. Abstr.; Curr. Aware. Biol. Sci., CABS; Field Crop Abstr.; Food Sci. Technol. Abstr.; Hortic. Abstr.; Maize Abstr.; Potato Abstr.; Res. Alert [Full Cov.]; Rev. Med. Vet. Entomol.; Rev. Plant Pathol.; Rice Abstr.; Sci. Cit. Index; SCISEARCH; Soils Fert.; Soyabean Abstr.; Weed Abstr.; Wheat Barley Trit. Abstr.

CN/0849-2212
**NOTE TO CAPCO.** [Note CAPCO]. **Added/Corp** Canada. Pesticides Directorate. Canadian Association of Pest Control Officials. **VFOAT** Note a l'ACRCP. **VAT** Note to Canadian Association of Pest Control Officials. (1990)-. Periodical. English (French). **DD** 632/.95042/097105. ***Absorbed*** *Note a l'ACRCP., 0849-2220;* ***Continues in part*** *CAPCO Note., 0838-8938.*

US
**NPIRS NEWS / NATIONAL PESTICIDE INFORMATION RETRIEVAL SYSTEM.**
**Main/Corp** National Pesticide Information Retrieval System. Vol. 1, No. 1 (Nov. 1982)-. Periodical. English. qt. Purdue University, Lafayette IN 47907. Documents available from Documents on Demand.
**Ind/Abst** Environ. Abstr.

US
**OFFICIAL PUBLICATION - ASSOCIATION OF AMERICAN PESTICIDE CONTROL OFFICIALS, INC.**
**Main/Corp** Association of American Pesticide Control Officials, Inc. (1964/1965)-. English. an (Mar.). $15.00 Comes with Association of American Pesticide Control Officials membership. Association of American Pesticide Control Officials, Minnesota Department of Agriculture, 90 West Plato Boulevard, St Paul MN 55107. **Tel** (612)296-8547. **Circ:** 250. ***Continues*** *Association of American Pesticide Control Officials, Inc. Proceedings of the Annual Convention - Association of American Pesticide Control Officials, Inc.*
**Desc:** A listing of state pesticide regulatory officials, official minutes of meetings and model pesticide regulations.

US
**PACIFIC NORTHWEST INSECT CONTROL HANDBOOK.** ***Suspended.***
**Added/Corp** University of Idaho. Cooperative Extension Service. Oregon State University. Extension Service. Washington State University. Cooperative Extension. **VFOAT** Insect Control Handbook. (1978)-Suspended. Periodical. English. an. Agricultural Communications, Publications Orders, Oregon State University, Administrative Services/Room 422, Corvallis OR 97331-2119. **Tel** (503)737-2513, FAX (503)737-2400. **ED** Glenn Fisher. **Bk Rev. Ad Acc. Circ:** 1,500 (ctrl). ***Supersedes*** *Oregon Insect Control Handbook.*
**Desc:** Guide to the control of insect pests for Oregon, Washington, and Idaho.

NL/1017-6276
**PEST ADVISORY LEAFLET.** [Pest advis. leafl.]. (1989)-. Periodical. English. South Pacific Commission, PO Box D5, Noumea Cedex New Caledonia. **Tel** (687)26 20 00, FAX (687)26 38 18. **UDC** 631.54.
**Ind/Abst** Nematol. Abstr.

US
**PEST-BANK [COMPUTER FILE].** (19??)-. Periodical. English. qt. $2280.00. Silverplatter Information Inc., 100 River Ridge Drive, Norwood MA 02062. **Tel** (800)343-0064, (617)769-2599, FAX (617)235-1715.
**Desc:** Contains two databanks covering all of the approximately 27,500 currently registered U.S. pesticides used in agriculture, industry, and general commerce and details on about 40,000 cancelled products. Includes pesticide product names and synonyms, registration dates and registering companies, active ingredients, composition and formulation, sites and pests for which the pesticide is registered, permissible residue levels, records for cancelled products.

US/0031-6121
**PEST CONTROL.** [Pest contr.]. (1949)-. Academic Scholarly Publication. English. mo. $32.00 US and possessions; $55.00 Canada; $85.00 other. Advanstar Communications Inc., 131 West First Street, Duluth MN 55802. **Tel** (218)723-9477, (800)346-0085. **ED** Jerry Mix. **LC** TX325. **DD** 648/.7/05. **NLM** W1 PE925. **CODEN** PCONAI. **[CCC]. Circ:** 15,000. available on microfilm and microfiche from University Microfilms International (UMI). Documents available from BIOSIS Document Express, CASDDS. ***Continues*** *Pests and Their Control, 0096-2147.*
**Desc:** Serves professionals involved in industrial and residential pest control.
**Ind/Abst** AGRICOLA; Art Archaeol. Tech. Abstr.; BioBusiness; Biodeter. Abstr.; Biol. Abstr.; Chem. Abstr.; EMBASE; Fish Rev.; For. Prod. Abstr. (1991-); PESTDOC; Rev. Med. Vet. Entomol.; Wildl. Rev.

CN/0833-9090
**PEST CONTROL CANADA.** [Pest contr. Can.]. **Added/Corp** PACS. (1986)-. English. an (Feb.). 59.95Can$. North American Compendiums Ltd., Rural Route 2 Box 39, Hensall Ontario N0M 1X0 Canada. **Tel** (519)263-3000, FAX (519)263-2936. **ED** Ed Clutton (editor's address: PO Box 85506, Burlington Ontario L7R 4K6 Canada, phone: (416)632-7232). **DD** 632/.9/02571. **Circ:** 300. ***Continues*** *Pest Control Chemicals.*

US
**PEST CONTROL LETTER.** (1975)-. Periodical. English. Twelve times a year. Research Endeavors Company, PO Box 26, San Carlos CA 94070. **Tel** (415)593-9311. **ED** Billy B. Gillespie. ctrl circ.
**Desc:** Authoritative publication on technical and regulatory developments affecting the pest control business person.

US/0730-7608
**PEST CONTROL TECHNOLOGY.** (19??)-. Periodical. English. mo. $30.00 (one year), $45.00 (two year) US; $42.00 Canada; $82.00 other. GIE Publishing Company, 4012 Bridge Avenue, Cleveland OH 44113. **Tel** (216)961-4130, (800)456-0707, FAX (216)961-0364. **ED** Dan Moreland. **LC** SB950.A1; P22. **DD** 632/.9/05. **Ad Acc, Adv Mgr:** D Foster. **Circ:** 16,300. ***Continues*** *PCT, Pest Control Technology, 0091-6692.*
**Ind/Abst** Biocont. News Inf. (1991-); Rev. Agric. Entomol.; Rev. Med. Vet. Entomol.

CN/0715-0830
**PEST LEAFLET (VICTORIA).** (PEST LEAFLET.). [Pest leafl.]. **Added/Corp** Pacific Forest Research Centre. No. 64 (1981)-. English. Pacific Forest Research Centre, 506 West Burnside Road, Victoria British Columbia V8Z 1M5 Canada. ***Continues*** *Forest Insect and Disease Survey Pest Leaflet.*
**Ind/Abst** Rev. Plant Pathol.

US/0744-6357
**PEST MANAGEMENT.** (PEST MANAGEMENT / NATIONAL PEST CONTROL ASSOCIATION.). [Pest manage.]. **Added/Corp** National Pest Control Association. Vol. 1, No. 1 (Nov. 1981)-. Trade Publication. English. mo (except Nov./Dec.). $35.00 (nonmembers), $17.00 (members) US; $48.00 (nonmembers), $30.00 (members) includes postage other. National Pest Control Association, 8100 Oak Street, PO Box 377, Dunn Loring VA 22027. **Tel** (703)573-8330, FAX (703)573-4116. **ED** Kathleen H Bova. **LC** HD9718.5.P473; U66. **DD** 338.4/762896/0973. **Ad Acc. Circ:** 6,000 (ctrl).
**Desc:** Trade journal geared to the pest control operator and technician. Contains technical and management articles, association news and information on ways to treat a pest problem.

CN/0710-7935
**PEST MANAGEMENT REPORT ... .** [Pest manage. rep.]. No. 1-. Periodical. English. Ministry of Forests, 1450 Government Street Information Center, Victoria British Columbia V8W 3E7 Canada. **DD** 634.9/676.

US
**PEST RESISTANCE MANAGEMENT.**
English. sa. Michigan State University / 60 Pesticide Research Center, WRCC, East Lansing MI 48824-1311. **Tel** (517)353-0671, FAX (517)353-5598. **ED** Mark E Whalon and Robert Hollingworth. Index available. **Bk Rev. Circ:** 1,800.

AT
**PESTALK.** (19??)-. English. Ten times a year. 75.00Aus$. Australian Environmental Pest Managers, PO Box 349, Turramurra NSW Australia 2074. **Tel** 011 61 2 449 8929, FAX 011 61 2 488 9717. **ED** Ross Blackmore. **Ad Acc.** ctrl circ.

UK
**PESTDOC.** **See** Pest Control-Abstracting, Bibliographies and Statistics.

US
**PESTICIDE ANALYTICAL MANUAL.**
**Main/Corp** United States. Food and Drug Administration. English. ir. Volume 1: $72.95 US, Canada & Mexico; $149.00 other; Volume 2: $205.00 US, Canada & Mexico; $405.00 other. US Food and Drug Administration / FDA, 5600 Fishers Lane, Room 14-71, Rockville MD 20857. **Tel** (301)443-2410, FAX (301)443-0755. **(Subscription address:** National Technical Information Service, 5285 Port Royal Road, Springfield, VA 22161**)**

US/0146-0501
**PESTICIDE & TOXIC CHEMICAL NEWS.**
**VAT** Pesticide and Toxic Chemical News. Vol. 5 (Dec. 1, 1976)-. Periodical. English. wk. $840.00. Food Chemical News Inc, 1101 Pennsylvania Avenue Southeast, Washington DC 20003. **Tel** (202)544-1980, FAX (202)546-3890. **ED** Cathy Cooper. **[CCC].** Index available. available on an online database (files 16,636/Full-Text) from DIALOG. ***Continues*** *Pesticide Chemical News.*
**Desc:** Covers EPA policies and regulations for pesticides, toxic substances, hazardous wastes, toxicological testing, OSHA standards, risk/benefit analysis, congressional and court activities in the areas of environment and wastes.
**Ind/Abst** PROMT [Full Txt.]; PTS Newsl. Database [Full Txt.].

US/0048-3575
**PESTICIDE BIOCHEMISTRY AND PHYSIOLOGY.** [Pestic. biochem. physiol.]. Vol. 1 (Mar. 1971)-. Academic Scholarly Publication. English. Nine times a year. $486.00 US and Canada; $591.00 other. Academic Press, Inc., 6277 Sea Harbor Drive, Orlando FL 32887. **Tel** (800)543-9534, (407)345-4100, FAX (407)363-9661. **ED** Fumio Matsumura. **LC** SB951; .P39. **DD** 632/.95/05. **NLM** W1 PE931. **CODEN** PCBPBS. **[CCC]. Pr Rev.** Documents available from The Genuine Article, BIOSIS Document Express, CASDDS.
**Desc:** Publishes original scientific articles pertaining to the mode of action of plant protection agents such as insecticides, fungicides, herbicides, and similar compounds including nonlethal pest control agents, biosynthesis of pheromones, hormones, and plant-resistant agents.
**Ind/Abst** AgBiotech News Inf.; AGRICOLA [Full Cov.]; AQUAREF; Biocont. News Inf. (19??-19??); Biodeter. Abstr. (1991-); Biol. Agric. Index; Biol. Abstr.; Chem. Abstr.; Chem. Titles; Crop Physiol. Abstr.; CSA Neuro. Abstr.; Curr. Aware. Biol. Sci., CABS; Curr. Contents, Agric. Biol. Environ. Sci.; Curr. Contents Life Sci.; Curr. Ref. Fish Res.; Ecol. Abstr. (?-?); EMBASE; Entomol. Abstr.; Field Crop Abstr.; Fish Rev.; Grasslands For. Abstr.; Hortic. Abstr.; Maize Abstr.; Microbiol. Abstr. Sect. A; Microbiol. Abstr. Sect. C; Nematol. Abstr.; Life Sci. Collect.; PESTDOC; Plant Breed. Abstr.; Plant Grow. Reg. Abstr.; Pollut. Abstr. Indexes; Postharvest News Inf.; Potato Abstr.; Poult. Abstr.; Res. Alert [Full Cov.]; Rev. Agric. Entomol.; Rev. Med. Vet. Entomol.; Rev. Med. Vet. Mycology; Rev. Plant Pathol.; Rice Abstr.; Sci. Cit. Index; SCISEARCH; Seed Abstr.; Soils Fert.; Sorghum Mill. Abstr.; Soyabean Abstr.; Toxicol. Abstr.; Trop. Dis. Bull.; Weed Abstr.; Wildl. Rev.

US
**PESTICIDE CHEMICAL NEWS GUIDE.**
English. mo (12 issues). $687.00. Food Chemical News Inc, 1101 Pennsylvania Avenue Southeast, Washington DC 20003. **Tel** (202)544-1980, FAX (202)546-3890.

UK
**PESTICIDE MANUAL.** (19??)-. English. ir (every 3 to 4 years). £85.00 UK; £95.00 other. BCPC Publications Sales, Bear Farm, Binfield Bracknell, Berks RG12 5QE England. **Tel** 011 44 734 341998. **ED** Charles Worthing, Raymond Hanes. Index available. cum. index. **Bk Rev**, (Qty: 5). **Pr Rev. Acid Free.**
**Desc:** Reference manual for all those working in crop protection concerned with the science, technology and toxicology of pesticides and their effects on target species, on wildlife and the environment.

UK
**PESTICIDE MANUAL, THE.** **See** Agriculture.

UK/0956-1250
**PESTICIDE OUTLOOK.** [Pestc. outlook]. **Added/Corp** Royal Society of Chemistry (Great Britain). Information Services. Vol. 1, No. 1 (1989)-. Academic Scholarly Publication. English. Six times a year. £138.00 EC; $245.50 US; £145.00 other. Royal Society of Chemistry, Thomas Graham House, Science Park, Cambridge CB4 4WF England. **Tel** 011 44 223 420066, FAX 011 44 223 423429, telex 818293 ROYAL. **(Subscription address:** Turpin Distribution Services Limited, Blackhorse Road, Letchworth, Hertfordshire SG6 1HN, United Kingdom.**) CODEN** PEOUEN. **[CCC].** Documents available from CASDDS.
**Desc:** Offers news, reviews, letters, forthcoming events and detailed features. Contains a wide range of informative and well written articles by acknowledged experts. Essential reading for those wishing to keep up-to-date with developments on all aspects of the pesticides business.
**Ind/Abst** Chem. Abstr.; Chem. Bus. Bull.; Chem. Bus. NewsBase (1989-); Chem. Bus. Update; Foods Adlibra; Hortic. Abstr.; Index Vet.; Irr. Drain. Abstr.; Rev. Agric. Entomol.; Rev. Plant Pathol.; Rice Abstr.; Seed Abstr.; Soyabean Abstr.; Weed Abstr.

US/0361-4522
**PESTICIDE-PCB IN FOODS PROGRAM.** (PESTICIDE/PCB IN FOODS PROGRAM: EVALUATION REPORT.). **Main/Corp** United States. Food and Drug Administration. Bureau of Foods. Office of Compliance. **VAT** Pesticide-Polychlorinated Biphemyl in Foods Program; Pesticide/Polychlorinated Biphemyl in Foods Program Evaluation Report. (19??)-. English. an. US Food and Drug Administration / FDA, 5600 Fishers Lane, Room 14-71, Rockville MD 20857. **Tel** (301)443-2410, FAX (301)443-0755. **LC** TX571.P4; U53a. **DD** 664/.07.

UK/0031-613X
**PESTICIDE SCIENCE.** [Pestic. sci.]. **Added/Corp** Society of Chemical Industry (Great Britain). Vol. 1 (1970)-. Academic Scholarly Publication. English. mo. $675.00. John Wiley & Sons Ltd., Baffins Lane, Chichester West Sussex PO19 1UD England. **Tel** 0243 779777, FAX 0243 776128 BTG:JWP001, telex 86290 WIBOOKG. **(Subscription address:** John Wiley / Philadelphia, PO Box 7247, Philadelphia PA 19170.**) ED** C. G. L. Furmidge. **NLM** W1 PE923N. **CODEN** PSSCBG. **[CCC]. Pr Rev.** available on microfilm from University Microfilms International (UMI). Documents available from The Genuine Article, BIOSIS Document Express, CASDDS, Documents on Demand, ADONIS.
**Desc:** A journal of international research and technology on crop protection and pest control.
**Ind/Abst** ADONIS; AgBiotech News Inf.; AGRICOLA [Full Cov.]; Anal. Abstr.; BioBusiness; Biocont. News Inf. (19??-19??); Biodeter. Abstr. (19??-19??); Biol. Agric. Index; Biol. Abstr.; Chem. Abstr.; Chem. Titles; Cot. Trop. Fibr. Abstr. Bibliogr.; Crop Physiol. Abstr.; CSA Neuro. Abstr. (?-?); Curr. Aware. Biol. Sci., CABS; Curr. Biotechnol.; Curr. Contents, Agric. Biol. Environ. Sci.; Curr. Ref. Fish Res.; Dairy Sci. Abstr.; Ecol. Abstr.; EMBASE; Environ. Abstr.; Environ. Period. Bibliogr.; Field Crop Abstr.; Fish Rev.; Food Sci. Technol. Abstr.; For.

Abstr.; Geogr. Abstr. Phys. Geogr.; Hortic. Abstr.; Maize Abstr.; Nematol. Abstr.; Nutr. Res. Newsl.; Life Sci. Collect.; PESTDOC; Plant Breed. Abstr.; Plant Grow. Reg. Abstr.; Pollut. Abstr. Indexes; Postharvest News Inf.; Potato Abstr.; Poult. Abstr.; Protozoolog. Abstr.; Res. Alert [Full Cov.]; Rev. Agric. Entomol.; Rev. Med. Vet. Entomol.; Rev. Med. Vet. Mycology; Rev. Plant Pathol.; Rice Abstr.; Sci. Cit. Index; SCISEARCH; Seed Abstr.; Soils Fert.; Soyabean Abstr.; Vitis Vitic. Enol. Abstr.; Weed Abstr.; Wildl. Rev.

UK
**PESTICIDE USAGE SURVEY REPORT.** **Added/Corp** Great Britain. Ministry of Agriculture, Fisheries and Food. No. 1 (Feb. 1972)-. Periodical. English.
**Ind/Abst** Nematol. Abstr.

US/0896-7253
**PESTICIDES AND YOU.** (PESTICIDES AND YOU / NATIONAL COALITION AGAINST THE MISUSE OF PESTICIDES.). [Pestic. you]. **Added/Corp** National Coalition Against the Misuse of Pesticides (U.S.). **VFOAT** PAY. (19??)-. Periodical. English. qt. $25.00 (individuals), $100.00 (corporations), $50.00 (government). NCAMP, 701 East Street SE, Suite 200, Washington DC 20003. **Tel** (202)543-5450. **DD** 363. Documents available from Documents on Demand.
**Ind/Abst** Environ. Abstr.

II
**PESTICIDES ANNUAL.** English. an. Rs60.00. P V Raghavan, Colour Publications Private Ltd, 126A Dhuruwadi Off Dr Nariman Road 25, Bombay India. **LC** SB951; .P443. **DD** 632/.95/05. ***Supersedes in part*** *Pesticides.*

UK/0258-7602
**PESTICIDES-CIPAC METHODS AND PROCEEDINGS SERIES : COLLABORATIVE INTERNATIONAL PESTICIDES ANALYTICAL COUNCIL PUBLICATIONS.** [Pestic.-CIPAC methods proc. ser.]. **VFOAT** Pesticides, CIPAC Methods and Proceedings Series; Pesticides CIPAC Methods and Proceedings Series. **VAT** Pesticides, Collaborative International Pesticides Analytical Council Methods and Proceedings Series. (1981)-. Academic Scholarly Publication. English. Price varies per volume. CIPAC, St Andrews Lodge, Southdown Road Harpenden, Hertfordshire England. **CODEN** PMPSEA. Documents available from CASDDS. ***Continues*** *CIPAC Proceedings Symposium Series.*
**Ind/Abst** Chem. Abstr. (1981).

US
**PESTICIDES IN THE ENVIRONMENT.** Vol. 1 (1971)-. Monographic series. English. ir. Price varies per volume. Marcel Dekker Inc., 270 Madison Avenue, New York NY 10016. **Tel** (212)696-9000, (800)228-1160, FAX (212)685-4540, telex 421419. **(Subscription address:** Marcel Dekker Inc, PO Box 5017, Monticello NY 12701.**)**
**Desc:** This is an ongoing series. Each title has a different subject.

UK
**PESTICIDES : REFERENCE BOOK. 500 PESTICIDES APPROVED UNDER THE CONTROL OF PESTICIDES RLGULATIONS.** (19??)-. English. an. £5.00. Her Majesty's Stationery Office, 51 Nine Elms Lane, London SW8 5DR England. **Tel** 011 44 71 873 8459, 011 44 71 873 8499, FAX 011 44 71 873 8499, 011 44 71 873 8456, telex 297138. **(Subscription address:** Her Majesty's Stationery Office, PO Box 276, Publications Centre, London SW8 5DT England.**)**

UK/0955-7458
**PESTICIDES REGISTER, THE.** [Pestic. regist.]. (1989)-. Periodical. English. mo. £47.00. Her Majesty's Stationery Office, 51 Nine Elms Lane, London SW8 5DR England. **Tel** 011 44 71 873 8459, 011 44 71 873 8499, FAX 011 44 71 873 8499, 011 44 71 873 8456, telex 297138. **(Subscription address:** Her Majestys Stationery Offic, PO Box 276 Public Centre, London SW8 5DT England**)** **DD** 668.65.
**Desc:** Provides details of all new approvals, both full and provisional, making key information widely available. Wood preservatives, public hygiene and household insecticides, surface biocides and anti-fouling paint are also covered.
**Ind/Abst** Biodeter. Abstr.

AT
**PESTICIDES REVIEW.** **Added/Corp** Australia. Environmental Health Branch. National Health and Medical Research Council (Australia). No. 10 (March 1974)-. English. sa. **LC** RA1270.P4; A8. **DD** 632/.95/05. ***Continues*** *Pesticides Review.*

US/0092-6752
**PESTICIDES (SACRAMENTO).** (PESTICIDES / STATE OF CALIFORNIA, DEPARTMENT OF AGRICULTURE, BUREAU OF CHEMISTRY.). [Pesticides (Sacramento)]. 1953-54-. English. an. California Department of Food and Agriculture, 1220 N Street, Sacramento CA 95814. **Tel** (916)654-0433, FAX (916)324-1681. **LC** SB951; .C18. **DD** 363.1/79. ***Continues*** *Economic Poisons.*

UK
**PESTICIDES TRUST AFFILIATION.** English. ir. £150.00 (corporate); £75.00 (non-commercial). Pesticides Trust, Eurolink Centre, 49 Effra Road, London SW2 1BZ England. **Tel** 011 44 71 2748895, FAX 11 44 71 2749084. **ED** David Buffin. cum. index. **Bk Rev**, (Qty: 40 /yr).

DK/0108-2086
**PESTICIDRESTER I DANSKE LEVNEDSMIDLER.** [Pesticidrester dan. levnedsmidler]. **Added/Corp** Statens Levnedsmiddelinstitut. Centrallaboriets Afdeling B: Pesticider og Forurening. **VFOAT** Pesticide Residues in Danish Food; Pesticidrester. (1979)-. Danish (English). an (Every two years). kr20.00. Ministry of Health / National Food Agency of Denmark, Morkhoj Bygade 19, DK 2860 Soborg Denmark. **Tel** 011 45 39 69 66 00, FAX 011 45 39 66 01 00, telex 16 298 Foodin dk. **LC** TX571.P4; R36. **DD** 363.1/92. ***Continues*** *Rapport Over Pesticidrester i Danske Levnedsmidler.*

II/0970-3012
**PESTOLOGY (BOMBAY).** (PESTOLOGY.). [Pestology]. (1977)-. Periodical. English. mo. $50.00. Scientia Publications Pvt. Ltd., 1/286 Station Road, Matunga, Bombay-19 India. **(Subscription address:** Prints India, 11 Darya Ganj, New Delhi, 110002 India, (Phone: 011 91 11 3268645)**)**
**Ind/Abst** PESTDOC.

GW
**PFLANZENSCHUTZMITTEL-VERZEICHNIS. TEIL 1: ACKERBAU, WIESEN UND WEIDEN, HOPFENBAU, SONDERKULTUREN, NICHTKULTURLAND, GEWASSER.** **Main/Corp** Biologische Bundesanstalt fuer Land- und Forstwirtschaft. Abteilung fuer Pflanzenschutzmittel und -Gerate. (197?)-. Periodical. German. ***Supersedes in part*** *Biologische Bundesanstalt fuer Land- und Forstwirtschaft. Abteilung fuer Pflanzenschutzmittel und -Gerate. Pflanzenschutzmittel-Verzeichnis (SB950.A1B5).*
**Ind/Abst** Hortic. Abstr.; Maize Abstr.; Nematol. Abstr.; Wheat Barley Trit. Abstr.

GW
**PFLANZENSCHUTZMITTEL-VERZEICHNIS. TEIL 2: GEMUSEBAU, OBSTBAU, ZIERPFLANZENBAU.** **Main/Corp** Biologische Bundesanstalt fur Land- und Forstwirtschaft. Abteilung fur Pflanzenschutzmittel und -Gerate. (197?)-. Periodical. German. ***Supersedes in part*** *Biologische Bundesanstalt fur Land- und Forstwirtschaft. Abteilung fur Pflanzenschutzmittel und -Gerate. Pflanzenschutzmittel-Verzeichnis (SB950.A1B5).*
**Ind/Abst** Rev. Plant Pathol.

IS/0032-0897
**PLANT PROTECTION ABSTRACTS.** ***Suspended.*** Vol. 1-1965-?. Periodical. English. Three times a year. Makhteshim Chemical Works Ltd, PO Box 60, Beer Sheva 84 100 Israel. **Tel** 57-666611. **ED** J Y Rein. **Circ:** 1,300.
**Desc:** Abstracts on use of pesticides in agriculture and pest control. Includes toxicological aspects and analytical chemistry.

US/0097-8787
**PLANT PROTECTION AND QUARANTINE PROGRAMS.** **See** Gardening and Horticulture.

PL/0554-8004
**PRACE NAUKOWE INSTYTUT OCHRONY ROSLIN.** (PRACE NAUKOWE.). [Pr. nauk. Inst. Ochr. Rosl.]. **Main/Corp** Instytut Ochrony Roslin. (1959)-. Academic Scholarly Publication. Polish (summaries and/or abstracts in English and Russian). sa. **LC** SB599; .I65b. **CODEN** PNORA5. Documents available from CASDDS.
**Ind/Abst** Biocont. News Inf.; Chem. Abstr.; EMBASE; For. Abstr.; Nematol. Abstr.; Life Sci. Collect.; PESTDOC; Postharvest News Inf.; Protozoolog. Abstr.; Rev. Plant Pathol.

RM/0254-2293
**PROBLEME DE PROTECTIA PLANTELOR.** (PROBLEME DE PROTECTIA PLANTELOR / INSTITUTUL DE CERCETARI PENTRU CEREALE SI PLANTE TEHNICE FUNDULEA.). [Probl. prot. plant.]. **Added/Corp** Institutul de Cercetari Pentru Cereale si Plante Tehnice Fundulea. (19??)-. Academic Scholarly Publication. Romanian (English). ir. DM182.00. **(Subscription address:** Kubon & Sagner, ABT Zeitschriftenimport, D 80328 Munich Germany.**)** **CODEN** PPPLD9. Documents available from CASDDS.
**Ind/Abst** Biocont. News Inf.; Biodeter. Abstr.; Chem. Abstr. (1972-1979); Postharvest News Inf.; Potato Abstr.; Rev. Agric. Entomol.; Seed Abstr.; Soyabean Abstr.; Wheat Barley Trit. Abstr.

UK/0955-1514
**PROC. - BRIGHTON CROP PROT. CONF., PESTS DIS.** **See** Agriculture-Crop Production and Soil.

CN/0227-7980
**PROCEEDINGS OF THE ANNUAL MEETING - CANADIAN PEST MANAGEMENT SOCIETY.** [Proc. annu. meet. - Can. Pest Manage. Soc.]. **Main/Corp** Canadian Pest Management Society. Meeting. 23rd (1976)-. Academic Scholarly Publication. English. an. 25.00Can$. Canadian Pest Management Society, Rural Route 3, Box 420, Woodlawn Ontario K0A 3M0 Canada. **Tel** (613)832-3173. **DD** 632/.9/05. **CODEN** PMCSDC. **Circ:** 225. Documents available from CASDDS. ***Continues*** *Agricultural Pesticide Society. Meeting. Proceedings of the Annual Meeting, 0065-4485.*
**Desc:** Technical papers on pest management using biological, chemical or cultural practices as applied in Canada.
**Ind/Abst** Chem. Abstr. (1976-1978).

●NZ
**PROCEEDINGS OF THE NEW ZEALAND PLANT PROTECTION CONFERENCE.** **See** Biology-Botany.

US/0564-7207
**PROCEEDINGS - TALL TIMBERS CONFERENCE ON ECOLOGICAL ANIMAL CONTROL BY HABITAT MANAGEMENT.** [Proc. Tall Timbers Conf. Anim. Habitat Manage.]. **Main/Conf** Tall Timbers Conference on Ecological Animal Control by Habitat Management. **Added/Corp** Tall Timbers Research Station. University of Florida, Gainesville. Dept. of Entomology. No. 1 (1969)-. Proceedings. English. ir. $7.00. Tall Timbers Research Station, Route 1 Box 678, Tallahassee FL 32312. **Tel** (904)893-4153. **LC** SB950.A1; T34. **DD** 574; 632/.9. **CODEN** TTHMA7. ctrl circ. Documents available from BIOSIS Document Express.
**Desc:** Conferences concern ecologically sound environmental management through physical manipulation of the agro- eco- system and native habitat.
**Ind/Abst** Biol. Abstr.

US/0507-6773
**PROCEEDINGS - VERTEBRATE PEST CONFERENCE.** [Proc., Vertebr. Pest Conf.]. **Main/Conf** Vertebrate Pest Conference. 3rd (1967)-. Academic Scholarly Publication. English. be. $25.00 (two years). Vertebrate Pest Conference, Danr North, Davis CA 95616. **Tel** (916)757-8623, FAX (916)757-8817. **ED** Terrell P. Salmon. **DD** 632. **CODEN** PVPCBM. cum. index. **Circ:** 1,000. Documents available from CASDDS. ***Continues*** *Proceedings.*
**Desc:** Articles dealing with research into and application of vertebrate pest management techniques.
**Ind/Abst** AGRICOLA; Chem. Abstr. (1962-1982); Fish Rev. (19??-199?); Key Word Index Wildl. Res.; PESTDOC; Wildl. Rev. (19??-199?).

UK/0887-6142
**PROGRESS IN PESTICIDE BIOCHEMISTRY AND TOXICOLOGY.** [Prog. pestic. biochem. toxicol.]. **VFOAT** Progress in Pesticide Biochemistry. Vol. 3 (1983)-. Academic Scholarly Publication. English. ir. $128.00. John Wiley & Sons Ltd., Baffins Lane, Chichester West Sussex PO19 1UD England. **Tel** 0243 779777, FAX 0243 776128 BTG:JWP001, telex 86290 WIBOOKG. **(Subscription address:** North, South and Central America/ John Wiley & Sons, Inc., Subscription Department, 605 Third Avenue, New York, NY 10158-0012, USA; telephone: (212)850-6645; FAX: (212)850-6021**)** **ED** D. H. Hutson and T. R. Roberts. **LC** QP801.P38; P76. **DD** 632/.95. **NLM** W1; PR677LJ. **CODEN** PPBTDV. Documents available from CASDDS. ***Continues*** *Progress in Pesticide Biochemistry, 0730-1898.*
**Ind/Abst** AGRICOLA [Full Cov.]; Chem. Abstr. (1983-); Fish Rev. (Jan. 1989-July 1992); Plant Grow. Reg. Abstr.; Rev. Agric. Entomol.; Rev. Plant Pathol.; Soils Fert.; Weed Abstr.; Wildl. Rev. (Jan. 1989-July 1992).

US/0565-243X
**PROGRESS REPORT ON PESTICIDES AND RELATED ACTIVITIES.** **Main/Corp** United States. Dept. of Agriculture. **VFOAT** Report on Pesticides and Related Activities. Government Publication. English. US Department of Agriculture, 14th Street and Independence Avenue SW, Washington DC 20250. **Tel** (202)720-5457. **LC** SB951; .U56A. **DD** 632/.95/05. **NLM** W2 A D6P.

UK/0307-9082
**REPORT - CENTRE FOR OVERSEAS PEST RESEARCH.** ***Title Change.*** (REPORT.). [Rep. - Cent. Overs. Pest Res.]. **Main/Corp** Centre for Overseas Pest Research (Great Britain). (1971/72). English. Centre for Overseas Pest Research, Publications Office, College House, Wrights Lane, London W8 5SJ England. **LC** SB950.A1; G73a. **DD** 354/.421/34008233. ***Continues*** *Report of the Anti-Locust Research Centre.* ***Merged with*** *Report of the Tropical Products Institute* ***to***

*form Report of the Tropical Development and Research Institute.*
**Ind/Abst** Life Sci. Collect.

CN/0704-772X
**REPORT - FOREST PEST MANAGEMENT INSTITUTE.** **See** Forestry.

US/0888-2681
**REPORT OF THE INTERAGENCY TOXIC SUBSTANCES DATA COMMITTEE.** **See** Medical Science and Technology-Toxicology.

UK
**REPORT OF THE WORKING PARTY ON PESTICIDE RESIDUES.** **Main/Corp** Great Britain. Working Party of Pesticide Residues. 1977-1981-. English. **LC** TX571.P4; G678A. **DD** 363.1/922.

●CN/1193-0667
**RESUME D'ENQUETE.** [Investig. summ.]. **Added/Corp** Canada. Direction des Pesticides. **VFOAT** Investigation Summary. (Jan. 17, 1992)-. Periodical. French (English). **DD** 363.17.

US/1062-3965
**REVIEWS IN PESTICIDE TOXICOLOGY.** [Rev. pestic. toxicol.]. **Added/Corp** North Carolina State University. **VFOAT** Reviews in Pesticides Toxicology; RPT. (1991)-. Monographic series. English. ir. $55.00. North Carolina State University / Toxicology, Department of Toxicology, Box 7633, Raleigh NC 27695. **Tel** (919)515-2274, FAX (919)515-7169. **DD** 668. **NLM** W1; RE257CGB. **CODEN** RPETEZ.

JA
**SHIROARI.** **Added/Corp** Nihon Shiroari Taisaku Kyokai. **VFOAT** Termite. (1962)-. Periodical. Japanese. qt. comes with membership. Nihon Shiroari Taisaku Kyokai, (Japan Termite Control Association), 2-9 Shinjuku 1 chome, Shinjukuku Tokyoto 160 Japan. **LC** TA423.7; .S55.

UK/0265-7406
**SUGAR CANE (1983).** **See** Agriculture-Crop Production and Soil.

US/0883-8828
**TECHLETTER.** Vol. 1, No. 1 (Dec. 1, 1985)-. Periodical. English. bw. $42.00 US; $46.00 Canada and Mexico; $63.00 (airmail) other. Pinto & Associates Inc, 155 Oak Road, Mechanicsville MD 20659. **Tel** (301)884-3020. **ED** Sandra Kraft. Index available. **Circ:** 1,400.

US
**TECHNICAL RELEASE - NATIONAL PEST CONTROL ASSOCIATION.** **Main/Corp** National Pest Control Association. Periodical. English. ir. $35.00. National Pest Control Association, 8100 Oak Street, PO Box 377, Dunn Loring VA 22027. **Tel** (703)573-8330, FAX (703)573-4116. Index available. cum. index. **Circ:** 6,000 (ctrl).

UK/0951-4309
**TESTS OF AGROCHEMICALS AND CULTIVARS.** [Tests agrochem. cultiv.]. **Added/Corp** Association of Applied Biologists. (March 1980)-. Academic Scholarly Publication. English. an. $43.00. Association of Applied Biologists, Institute of Horticultural Research, Wellesbourne, Warwick CV35 9EF United Kingdom. **Tel** 011 44 789 470382, FAX 011 44 789 470234. **LC** S587; .T47. **DD** 632/.95. **NLM** W1 AN56P v.94 Suppl. etc. **CODEN** TACUDC. **Circ:** 1,500. Documents available from BIOSIS Document Express, CASDDS.
**Ind/Abst** AGRICOLA [Full Cov.]; Biol. Abstr. (1986-); Chem. Abstr.

UK/0143-6147
**TROPICAL PEST MANAGEMENT.** ***Title Change.*** [Trop. pest manage.]. **Added/Corp** Centre for Overseas Pest Research (Great Britain). Vol. 26, No. 1 (Mar. 1980)-Vol. 38, No. 4 (Oct.-Dec. 1992). Academic Scholarly Publication. English (summaries and/or abstracts in French and Spanish). qt. Taylor & Francis Ltd., Rankine Road, Basingstoke Hampshire, RG24 8PR United Kingdom. **Tel** 011 44 256 840366, FAX 011 44 256 479438, telex 858540. **(Subscription address:** Taylor & Francis Inc., 1900 Frost Road, Suite 101, Bristol PA 19007-1598.**)** **ED** P. T. Haskell (editor's address: Cleppa Park Research Station, University College, PO Box 78, Cardiff CF1 1XL Wales). **LC** SB950.A1; P18. **DD** 632/.0913. **NLM** W1 TR884. **CODEN** TPMAD5. **[CCC].** **Pr Rev.** available on microfilm and microfiche from University Microfilms International (UMI). Documents available from The Genuine Article, BIOSIS Document Express, CASDDS. ***Continues** PANS, 0309-7943.* ***Continued by** International Journal of Pest Management, 0967-0874.*
**Desc:** Covers all spheres of pre- and post-harvest pest management, vector-borne diseases and public health, and the relationship of pest management to the wider aspects of farming systems and rural development.
**Ind/Abst** Abstr. Trop. Agric.; AGRICOLA [Full Cov.]; Agric. Eng. Abstr. (1991-?); Agrofor. Abstr. (1991-?); Apic. Abstr.; BioBusiness; Biocont. News Inf. (19??-19??); Biodeter. Abstr. (1991-?); Biol. Abstr.; Chem. Abstr.; Cot. Trop. Fibr. Abstr. Bibliogr.; Curr. Aware. Biol. Sci., CABS; Curr. Contents, Agric. Biol. Environ. Sci.; Ecol. Abstr.; Entomol. Abstr.; Environ. Period. Bibliogr.; Field Crop Abstr.; Food Sci. Technol. Abstr.; For. Abstr.; Geogr. Abstr. Phys. Geogr.; Hortic. Abstr.; Index Vet.; Int. Dev. Abstr.; Maize Abstr.; Microbiol. Abstr. Sect. A; Microbiol. Abstr. Sect. C; Nematol. Abstr.; Ornamental Hort. (1991-?); Life Sci. Collect.; PESTDOC; Plant Breed. Abstr.; Postharvest News Inf.; Potato Abstr.; Res. Alert [Select. Cov.]; Rev. Agric. Entomol.; Rev. Med. Vet. Entomol.; Rev. Plant Pathol.; Rice Abstr.; Rural Dev. Abstr.; Seed Abstr.; Soils Fert.; Sorghum Mill. Abstr.; Soyabean Abstr.; Vet. Bull.; Trop. Dis. Bull.; Virol. AIDS Abstr.; Weed Abstr.; Wheat Barley Trit. Abstr.; World Agric. Econ.

UK/0952-7788
**UK PESTICIDE GUIDE, THE.** **Added/Corp** British Crop Protection Council. C.A.B. International. **VFOAT** U.K. Pesticide Guide; United Kingdom Pesticide Guide. 1st ed. (1988)-. English. an. $25.20. CAB International Centre, Wallingford, Oxon OX10 8DE United Kingdom. **Tel** 44 491 832111, FAX 44 491 833508, telex 847964 (COMAGG G). **ED** G.W. Ivens. **LC** SB950.3.G7; U54. Index available. **Bk Rev.**

SW/0042-2169
**VAXTSKYDDSNOTISER.** [Vaxtskyddsnotiser]. **Added/Corp** Statens Vaxtskyddsanstalt (Sweden). Sveriges Lantbruksuniversitet. (May 1937)-. Periodical. Swedish (Swedish). bm. Sv Lantbruksuniversitet, Konsulentave/Vaxtskydd, Box 7044, 75007 Uppsala Sweden. **LC** SB605.S9; S8. **DD** 632.05. ***Continues in part** Skrifter Bd. 3-4 / Statens Vaxtskyddsanstalt (Sweden).*
**Ind/Abst** AGRICOLA; Hortic. Abstr.; Nematol. Abstr.; Potato Abstr.; Rev. Agric. Entomol.; Soils Fert.

BE
**VIJANDEN VAN GEWASSEN EN HUN BESTRIJDING.** **Added/Corp** Onderzoek- en Voorlichtingscentrum voor Land- en Tuinbouw (West Flanders, Belgium). (19??)-. Dutch.
**Ind/Abst** Rev. Agric. Entomol.; Rev. Plant Pathol.

US/0272-4219
**WHO'S WHO IN PROFESSIONAL PEST CONTROL.** **See** Biographies.

US
**WISCONSIN COOPERATIVE PEST SURVEY BULLETIN.** **See** Agriculture.

RU/0044-1864
**ZASHCHITA RASTENII.** **See** Biology-Botany.

GW/0044-2291
**ZEITSCHRIFT FUER ANGEWANDTE ZOOLOGIE.** **See** Zoology.

## ABSTRACTING, BIBLIOGRAPHIES AND STATISTICS

UK
**PESTDOC.** Abstracting/Indexing Service. wk. £17440.00. Derwent Publications Ltd., Derwent House 14, Great Queen Street, London WC2B 5DF England. **Tel** 011 44 71 3442800. Index available. cum. index. **Circ:** 17,440 (ctrl). available on an online database.
**Desc:** Deals with all aspects of products (other than fertilizers) and measures which have some beneficial action on plants; protect plants against pests, diseases, or the detrimental effects of weeds; protect stored products, timber, textiles, and other material; or protect man and animals against anthropods and other vectors. All articles giving significant information on one or more pesticides are selected whether the subject of the paper is analysis, chemistry, biological properties, pest control, toxicity, etc. Papers concerned with selection and breeding of crop varieties for resistance to pests and diseases, in vitro plant propagation, studies of endogenous plant or insect hormones, the pharmacology and toxicology of DDT and other "old" pesticides are not included. Items of interest only to Ringdoc (human), Vetdoc (veterinary), or biotechnology are not included.

# PETROLEUM AND NATURAL GAS

●US/1075-038X
**21ST CENTURY FUELS.** [21st cent. fuels]. **VFOAT** Twenty-first Century Fuels. Vol. 11, No. 1 (Jan. 1994)-. Periodical. English. mo. $397.00 US; $422.00 other. Hart Publications Inc, 1900 Grant Street, Suite 400, Denver CO 80203. **Tel** (303)837-1917, (800)832-1917, FAX (303)837-8585. **DD** 662. ***Continues** Alcohol Outlook, 1072-8767.*

US/0149-1423
**AAPG BULLETIN.** [AAPG bull.]. **Added/Corp** American Association of Petroleum Geologists. American Association of Petroleum Geologists. Annual Report and Membership Directory. **VFOAT** American Association of Petroleum Geologists Bulletin; A.A.P.G. Bulletin. **VAT** American Association of Petroleum Geologists Bulletin. Vol. 58 (Jan. 1974)-. Academic Scholarly Publication. English. mo. $135.00 (surface mail). American Association of Petroleum Geologists, PO Box 979, Tulsa OK 74101-0979. **Tel** (918)584-2555, FAX (918)584-0469, telex 49-9432. **ED** June Chronos. **LC** TN860; .A3. **DD** 553.2/82/05. **CODEN** AABUD2. **[CCC].** Index available (bound in Dec. issue). cum. index. **Bk Rev. Ad Acc. Pr Rev. Circ:** 37,000 (ctrl). available on microfilm and microfiche from University Microfilms International (UMI). Documents available from Article Express International, The Genuine Article, BIOSIS Document Express, Petroleum Abstracts Document Delivery Service, CASDDS. ***Continues** American Association of Petroleum Geologists Bulletin, 0002-7464.*
**Desc:** Disseminates information on the geology and associated technology of exploration for and production of petroleum, natural gas and other energy mineral resources. Back issues are available and rental use of mailing list.
**Ind/Abst** AESIS Q.; Appl. Sci. Technol. Index; AQUAREF; Bioeng. Abstr.; Biol. Abstr.; Can. Environ.; Ceram. Abstr.; Chem. Abstr.; Coal Abstr.; Ei Page One; Energy Res. Abstr.; Eng. Index Annu.; Geogr. Abstr. Phys. Geogr. (?-?); Geol. Abstr.; GeoRef; INIS Atomindex [Micro.]; Int. Aerosp. Abstr.; Pet. Abstr.; Res. Alert [Full Cov.]; Sci. Cit. Index; SCISEARCH; Soc. Sci. Cit. Index [Select. Cov.]; Soils Fert.

US/0270-8043
**AAPG CONTINUING EDUCATION COURSE NOTE SERIES.** [AAPG contin. educ. course note ser.]. **Main/Corp** American Association of Petroleum Geologists. **VAT** American Association of Petroleum Geologists Continuing Education Course Note Series. (1975)-. Monographic series. English. ir. Price varies per volume. American Association of Petroleum Geologists, PO Box 979, Tulsa OK 74101-0979. **Tel** (918)584-2555, FAX (918)584-0469, telex 49-9432. **[CCC].**
**Ind/Abst** AESIS Q.; GeoRef.

US/0195-2986
**AAPG EXPLORER.** **See** Earth Sciences-Geology.

US/0271-8529
**AAPG MEMOIR.** [AAPG mem.]. **Added/Corp** American Association of Petroleum Geologists. **VFOAT** A.A.P.G. Memoir. **VAT** American Association of Petroleum Geologists Memoir. Vol. 29 (1979)-. Monographic series. English. ir. Price varies per volume. American Association of Petroleum Geologists, PO Box 979, Tulsa OK 74101-0979. **Tel** (918)584-2555, FAX (918)584-0469, telex 49-9432. **LC** UNC. **[CCC].** Documents available from CASDDS. ***Continues** Memoir (American Association of Petroleum Geologists), 0065-731X.*
**Ind/Abst** AESIS Q.; Chem. Abstr.; GeoRef.

US/0272-1511
**AAPG REPRINT SERIES.** **See** Earth Sciences-Geology.

US/0271-8510
**AAPG STUDIES IN GEOLOGY.** [AAPG stud. geol.]. **Added/Corp** American Association of Petroleum Geologists. **VFOAT** A.A.P.G. Studies in Geology; Studies in Geology. **VAT** American Association of Petroleum Geologists Studies in Geology. No. 8 (Aug. 1979)-. Academic Scholarly Publication. English. ir. Price varies per volume. American Association of Petroleum Geologists, PO Box 979, Tulsa OK 74101-0979. **Tel** (918)584-2555, FAX (918)584-0469, telex 49-9432. **LC** UNC. **CODEN** ASTGD6. Documents available from CASDDS. ***Continues** Studies in Geology (Tulsa, Okla.), 0149-1377.*
**Ind/Abst** AESIS Q.; Chem. Abstr.; GeoRef; Life Sci. Collect.

US/1043-6103
**AAPG TREATISE OF PETROLEUM GEOLOGY. ATLAS OF OIL AND GAS FIELDS.** [AAPG treatise pet. geol. Atlas oil gas fields]. **Added/Corp** American Association of Petroleum Geologists. **VFOAT** Atlas of Oil and Gas Fields; Treatise of Petroleum Geology. Atlas of Oil and Gas Fields. **VAT** American Association of Petroleum Geologists Treatise of Petroleum Geology. Atlas of Oil and Gas Fields. (1989)-. Monographic series. English. ir. Price varies per volume. American Association of Petroleum Geologists, PO Box 979, Tulsa OK 74101-0979. **Tel** (918)584-2555, FAX (918)584-0469, telex 49-9432. **DD** 553.
**Ind/Abst** AESIS Q.

CN/0833-4390
**AAROGRAM.** [Aarogram]. Jan. 28, 1985-. Periodical. English. ir. Ontario Retail Gasoline and Automotive Service Association West, Suite 102, 101 Queensway West, Mississauga Ontario L5B 2P7 Canada. **DD** 381/.45629286/09713. ***Continues** Infoletter - Ontario Retail Gasoline and Automotive Service Association, 0228-0477.*

UK/0956-6333
**ABERDEEN PETROLEUM QUARTERLY.** [Aberd. pet. q.]. (1989)-. Periodical. English. qt. £40.00. Aberdeen Petroleum Publishing Ltd, 35-37 Huntly Street, Aberdeen AB1 1TJ Scotland. **Tel** 011 44 224 644725, FAX 44 224 647574. **DD** 338.27282.

UK/0263-5054
**ABERDEEN PETROLEUM REPORT.** [Aberd. pet. rep.]. (1981)-. Periodical. English. wk (50 issues per year). £385.00 UK; £390.00 Europe; £395.00 other. Aberdeen Petroleum Publishing Ltd, 35-37 Huntly Street, Aberdeen AB1 1TJ Scotland. **Tel** 011 44 224 644725, FAX 44 224 647574. **ED** Ted Strachan. **Ad Acc.** ctrl circ.
**Desc:** Newsletter on North Sea market intelligence.

US/0003-0422
**ABSTRACTS OF REFINING LITERATURE. See** Petroleum and Natural Gas-Abstracting, Bibliographies and Statistics.

US/1050-1347
**ADVANCED RECOVERY WEEK.** ***Title Change.*** [Adv. recovery week]. Vol. 1, No. 1 (Feb. 26, 1990)-Vol. 3, No. 6 (Feb. 10, 1992). Periodical. English. wk. Pasha Publications Inc., 1616 North Fort Myer Drive, Suite 1000, Arlington VA 22209. **Tel** (800)424-2908, (703)528-1244, FAX (703)528-3742, (703)528-1253. **DD** 338. **[CCC].** available on an online database (files 636,648/Full-Text) from DIALOG. ***Continues*** *Enhanced Recovery Week, 0277-9137.* ***Continued by*** *Improved Recovery Week, 1061-3692.*
**Ind/Abst** F&S Index Plus Text, Int. [Select. Cov.]; NEXIS.

TS
**AKHBAR AL-BATRUL WA-AL-SINAAH.** Arabic. PO Box 9, Abu Zaby United Arab Emirates. **LC** HD9576.U5; A4.

KU
**AL-HAFT WA-AL-TAAWUN AL-ARABI. VFOAT** Oil and Arab Cooperation. Periodical. Arabic (English). qt. $40.00. Organization of Arab Petroleum Exporting Countries, PO Box 20501, Safat 13066 Kuwait. **Tel** 2420061, telex 22166. **LC** HC498.A1; N33.
**Ind/Abst** GeoRef.

IQ
**AL-NAFT WA-AL-ALAM. VFOAT** Al Naft Wal Aalam; Oil and the World. Periodical. Arabic (English). .5. Wizarat Al-Naft, PO Box 6118, Mansour Iraq. **LC** HD9576.I7; N33.

IQ
**AL-NAFT WA-AL-TANMIYAH. VFOAT** Oil and Development Magazine. Periodical. Arabic. mo. $30.00. Dar Al-Thawrah Lil-Sihafah Wa-Al-Nashr, PO Box 6124, Baghdad Iraq. **LC** HD9560.1; .N24.

LE
**ALAM AL-NAFT.** Periodical. Arabic. 200.00. PO Box 115079, Beirut Lebanon. **LC** HD9560.1; .A37.

US/0889-7352
**ALASKA OIL & INDUSTRY NEWS.** [Alsk. oil ind. news]. **VFOAT** Alaska Oil and Industry News. (1986)-. Periodical. English. mo. available only with Alaska Journal of Commerce. Pacific Rim Publishing Company, PO Box 99007, Anchorage AK 99509. **Tel** (907)272-7500. **DD** 338. ***Continues*** *Alaska Oil and Gas News.*

US/1045-7070
**ALASKA OIL SPILL REPORTER.** [Alsk. oil spill rep.]. Vol. 1, No. 1 (July 15, 1989)-. Periodical. English. bw. $349.00. Waterfront Press Company, 1115 Northwest 46th Street, Seattle WA 98107. **Tel** (206)789-6506, FAX (206)789-9193, telex 272822 SFL UR. **DD** 363.

US/0065-5813
**ALASKA PETROLEUM & INDUSTRIAL DIRECTORY.** ***Ceased.*** **VAT** Alaska Petroleum and Industrial Directory. Vol. 10 (1970/71)-(1984/85). Directory. English. ir. Manufacturers News Inc., 1633 Central Street, Evanston IL 60201-1569. **Tel** (708)864-7000, FAX (708)332-1100. **ED** Lalla Howell. **LC** HC107.A45; A53. **DD** 338/.0025/798. **Bk Rev. Ad Acc. Circ:** 1,800. ***Continues*** *Alaska Petroleum Directory.*
**Desc:** Directory listing of 25,000 Alaska businesses and their branch offices and personnel. Full index for 240 categories, company names and personnel.

CN/0227-3357
**ALBERTA DRILLING PROGRESS AND PIPELINE RECEIPTS WEEKLY REPORT.** [Alta. drill. prog. pipeline receipt wkly. rep.]. (1???)-. Periodical. English. wk. 325.00Can$. Energy Resources Conservation Board, 640 Fifth Avenue Southwest, Calgary Alberta T2P 3G4 Canada. **Tel** (403)297-8311, (403)297-8190, telex 03-821717. **DD** 622/.3382/097123. **[CCC].** ***Continues*** *Alberta. Energy Resources Conservation Board.* ***and*** *Weekly Production and Drilling Statistics, Alberta Oil and Gas Industry, 0032-9827.*
**Desc:** Summary of oil pipeline gathering operations: drilling activities, defined and undefined fields, release of geological markers, drill-stem test results, new licenses and status changes. Issued every Friday for the week ending the previous Monday.

CN/1183-7004
**ALBERTA FIELD/POOL PRODUCTION AND INJECTION MONTHLY SUPPLEMENT.** [Alta. field/pool prod. inject. mon. suppl.]. **Added/Corp** Alberta. Energy Resources Conservation Board. (Jan. 1991)-. Periodical. English. Twelve times a year. 50.00Can$. Energy Resources Conservation Board, 640 Fifth Avenue Southwest, Calgary Alberta T2P 3G4 Canada. **Tel** (403)297-8311, (403)297-8190, telex 03-821717. **DD** 338.2. ***Continues*** *Alberta. Energy Resources Conservation Board. Alberta Pool Production and Injection Monthly Supplement., 0702-3286.*

CN/0840-6146
**ALBERTA OIL & FORESTRY REVIEW QUARTERLY.** ***Title Change.*** [Alta. oil for. rev.]. **VFOAT** Alberta Oil and Forestry Review Quarterly. **VAT** Alberta Oil and Forestry Review. Vol. 1, No. 1 (Fall 1988)-Vol. 4, No. 2 (Fall 1992). Periodical. English. qt. Alberta Publications, 10234 24th Street/Suite 105, Edmonton Alberta T5N 1P9 Canada. **Tel** (403)488-7484, FAX (403)488-7523. **ED** Michael Walker. **DD** 338.1/749. **Circ:** 8,000. ***Continued by*** *Forestry, Oil & Gas Review, 1196-1376.*
**Desc:** Overview of Western Canada Resource Industries.

●CN/1193-3097
**ALBERTA PETROLEUM EQUIPMENT & SERVICES DIRECTORY.** [Alta. pet. equip. serv. dir.]. **Added/Corp** Southam Business Information and Communications Group. Alberta. Alberta Economic Development and Trade. (1992)-. Directory. English. Southam Information and Technology Group Inc., 1450 Don Mills Road, Don Mills Ontario M3B 2X7 Canada. **Tel** (416)445-6641, (800)668-2374, FAX (416)442-2261. **DD** 338.2/728/02571.

CN/0706-1412
**ALBERTA'S ENERGY RESOURCES. See** Energy.

CN/0837-9750
**ALBERTA'S RESERVES OF CRUDE OIL, OIL SANDS, GAS, NATURAL GAS LIQUIDS, AND SULPHUR.** [Alta. reserv. crude oil oil sands gas nat. gas liq. sulphur]. **Added/Corp** Alberta. Energy Resources Conservation Board. **VFOAT** Alberta's Reserves. 23rd Edition (1983)-. English. an. 250.00Can$. Energy Resources Conservation Board, 640 Fifth Avenue Southwest, Calgary Alberta T2P 3G4 Canada. **Tel** (403)297-8311, (403)297-8190, telex 03-821717. **LC** TN873.C22; A442 Subser. **DD** 553.2/8/097123. ***Continues*** *Alberta's Reserves of Crude Oil, Gas, Natural Gas Liquids, and Sulphur at 31 December ..., 0706-3199.*
**Desc:** Data on trends in initial and remaining established reserves of conventional crude oil and marketable gas.

CN/0229-8546
**ALBERTA'S RESERVES OF GAS.** (ALBERTA'S RESERVES OF GAS : COMPLETE LISTING.). [Alta. reserves gas]. **Added/Corp** Alberta. Energy Resources Conservation Board. **VFOAT** Alberta Reserves of Gas. 1st Ed. (1978)-. English. an. 250.00Can$ (microfiche), 1000.00Can$ (print). Energy Resources Conservation Board, 640 Fifth Avenue Southwest, Calgary Alberta T2P 3G4 Canada. **Tel** (403)297-8311, (403)297-8190, telex 03-821717. **LC** TN873.C22; A442 subser. **DD** 553.2/85/097123. available on microfiche from the publisher.
**Desc:** Contains an expansion of the reserves data reported in ERCB St-86-18, with individual estimates and reservoir factors by pools and areas of all non-confidential established gas reserves.

US/1072-8767
**ALCOHOL OUTLOOK.** ***Title Change.*** (19??)-(19??). English. mo. Information Resources Inc, 499 South Capitol Street SW, Suite 406, Washington DC 20003. **Tel** (202)554-0614, (800)872-3835. ***Continued by*** *21st Century Fuels, 1075-038X.*
**Desc:** A data intensive report on alcohol fuels and oxygenates, with an analysis and news summaries.

NO
**ALL ABOUT BLOWOUT.** English. mo. Kr400.00 Norway; Kr45.00 Europe;Kr40.00 UK; Kr90.00 US. Norwegian Oil Review, PO Box 873, Sentrum 0104 Oslo 1 Norway. **Tel** 02-417200, FAX 02-422410. **ED** John Lager and Hans Kristiansen. **Ad Acc. Circ:** 10,000 (ctrl).

US/1043-0652
**AMERICAN GAS.** (AMERICAN GAS : THE MONTHLY MAGAZINE OF THE AMERICAN GAS ASSOCIATION.). [Am. gas]. **Added/Corp** American Gas Association. Vol. 71, No. 1 (Jan. 1989)-. Periodical. English. Eleven times a year. $39.00. American Gas Association / Virginia, 1515 Wilson Boulevard, Arlington VA 22209. **Tel** (703)841-8400, (703)841-8559, FAX (703)841-8697. **LC** TP700; .A28. **DD** 363.6/3/0973. **CODEN** AMGLEH. Documents available from Documents on Demand. ***Continues*** *AGA Monthly, 0885-2413.*
**Ind/Abst** Ei Page One; Energy Inf. Abstr.; Environ. Abstr.; Environ. Period. Bibliogr.; Gas Abstr.; INIS Atomindex [Micro.]; Trade Ind. Index.

US/0145-9198
**AMERICAN OIL & GAS REPORTER, THE.** [Am. oil gas report.]. **Added/Corp** Liaison Committee of Cooperating Oil & Gas Associations (U.S.). **VFOAT** American Oil and Gas Reporter. (19??)-. Periodical. English. Twelve times a year. $28.00 (one year), $73.00 (three year) US; $99.00 (one year) Canada and Mexico; $250.00 other. American Oil and Gas Reporter, PO Box 343, Derby KS 67037-0343. **Tel** (316)788-6271, FAX (316)788-7568. **ED** Bill Campbell. **LC** TN872; .A3155. **DD** 553.2/8/0973. **Ad Acc, Adv Mgr:** Charlie Cookson, **Tel** (316)788-6271. **Circ:** 11,500 (ctrl). Documents available from Petroleum Abstracts Document Delivery Service.
**Desc:** A business publication for US exploration, drilling and production industries. The magazine carries official notices and news pertaining to oil and gas associations.
**Ind/Abst** Pet. Abstr.

US
**ANALYSES OF NATURAL GASES.** Began with 1961. Government Publication. English. an. US Department of the Interior / Bureau of Mines, 810 7th Street NW, Room 604, Washington DC 20241. **Tel** (202)501-9300. available on microfiche (Vols. for (1980-) distributed to depository libraries).

GW/0342-6947
**ANEP. ANNUAIRE EUROPEEN DE PETROLE.** (ANNUAIRE EUROPEEN DU PETROLE.). [ANEP. Annu. eur. pet.]. **VFOAT** ANEP; European Petroleum Yearbook; European Petroleum Year Book; Jahrbuch der Europaischen Erdolindustrie; European Petroleum Year Book : ANEP. (1974)-. English (French and German). an. DM180.00 Germany; DM168.00 other. Urban Verlag Hamburg Wien GmbH, Neumann Reichardt STR 34, D 22041 Hamburg Germany. **Tel** 011 49 40 6567071. **ED** Thomas Vieth. **LC** HD9575.A1; A15. **DD** 338.2/7282/094. **Ad Acc. Circ:** 3,000. ***Continues*** *Annuaire de l'Europe Petroliere, 0066-1716.*
**Ind/Abst** GeoRef.

BE/0020-2185
**ANNALES DE L'INSTITUT BELGE DU PETROLE. Main/Corp** Institut Belge du Petrole. **VFOAT** Belgisch Petroleum Instituut Annalen. (1967)-. Academic Scholarly Publication. Multiple languages (Dutch, English and French). Four times a year. Institut Belge du Petrole, Avenue Paul Terlinden 25, 1330 Rixensart Belgium. **Tel** 02 653 09 47. **CODEN** AIBPD9. Documents available from CASDDS.
**Ind/Abst** Chem. Abstr. (1967-1982).

US/1042-8364
**ANNUAL BENZENE & DERIVATIVES. Added/Corp** DeWitt & Company. **VFOAT** Annual Benzene and Derivatives; Benzene and Derivatives; Benzene & Derivatives. (19??)-. English. wk. $7500.00. Dewitt & Company Inc, 16800 Greenspoint Park, #120 N, Houston TX 77060. **Tel** (713)875-5525, (713)875-0296, FAX (713)875-0175, telex 762-854. **ED** William P Barry and Dr. Hugh Charman (editor's phone: (713)875-0269). **LC** HD9560.4; .B45. **DD** 338.4/7661816. ctrl circ. ***Continues*** *Benzene Annual, 0091-3529.*
**Desc:** International market/pricing review on Benzene, Styrene and other Derivatives of Benzene.

CN/0078-5040
**ANNUAL CONFERENCE / THE ONTARIO PETROLEUM INSTITUTE.** [Annu. conf. - Ont. Pet. Inst.]. **Main/Corp** Ontario Petroleum Institute. Conference. **VFOAT** Ontario Petroleum Institute, ... Annual Conference : [Proceedings]. 1st (1962)-. Periodical. English. an. 40.00Can$. Ontario Petroleum Institute Inc., 555 Southdale Road East, London Ontario N6E 1A2 Canada. **Tel** (519)680-1620. **DD** 333.8/23/0971. **[CCC]. Ad Acc.** ctrl circ.

US/0273-7000
**ANNUAL ENERGY LITIGATION INSTITUTE : EFFECTIVE STRATEGIES & TECHNIQUES. See** Law.

US/0273-5253
**ANNUAL INSTITUTE ON MINERAL LAW. See** Law.

US/0731-9800
**ANNUAL MEETING - INTERNATIONAL OIL SCOUTS ASSOCIATION.** (ANNUAL MEETING.). [Annu. meet. - Int. Oil Scouts Assoc.]. **Main/Corp** International Oil Scouts Association. English. an. $35.00. International Oil Scouts Association, PO Box 272949, Houston TX 77277. **Tel** (713)439-3514. **LC** TN860; .I58A. **DD** 622/.33/8205. **Ad Acc. Circ:** 600.
**Desc:** Board of directors reports, professional seminars recap, industry overview for year, professional speakers report, photographs.
**Ind/Abst** GeoRef.

# Petroleum and Natural Gas

US/0275-6323
**ANNUAL MEETING PAPERS - AMERICAN PETROLEUM INSTITUTE. PRODUCTION DEPT.** Ceased. (ANNUAL MEETING PAPERS - PRODUCTION DEPARTMENT.). **Main/Corp** American Petroleum Institute. Production Department. **VAT** Annual Meeting Papers - American Petroleum Institute. Production Department. (1976)-?. English. an. American Petroleum Institute, 275 Seventh Avenue, New York NY 10001. **Tel** (212)366-4040, FAX (212)366-4298. **(Subscription address:** 1970 Chain Bridge Road, McLean, VA 22109-6000) **CODEN** AMPDD3. **Continues** Annual Meeting Papers - Division of Production, 0196-9978.

FR
**ANNUAL OIL MARKET REPORT.** Ceased. **VAT** Oil Market Report. (19??)-(19??). English. an. OECD Publications and Information Center, 2 rue Andre-Pascal, 75775 Paris Cedex 16 France. **Tel** 011 33 1 45248167, US:(202)785-6323, FAX 011 33 1 45248500 OR 45248176, telex 620 160 OCDE. **(Subscription address:** US/2001 L Street NW, Suite 700, Washington, DC 20036) **LC** HD9560.1; .A54. **DD** 338.2/7282/05.
  **Desc:** Traces changes in spot and contract prices for different categories of crude oil and petroleum products.

US/0747-5594
**ANNUAL PETROLEUM REVIEW.** [Annu. pet. rev.]. English. an. California Energy Commission, 1516 9th Street, Sacramento CA 95814. **Tel** (916)324-3014. **LC** TN872.C2; A627. **DD** 665.5/09794.

US/0098-4043
**ANNUAL PRODUCTION BY ACTIVE FIELDS, OIL AND GAS DIVISION.** **Main/Corp** Texas. Railroad Commission. Oil and Gas Division. **VFOAT** Oil and Gas Annual Production by Active Fields. English. an. Railroad Commission of Texas, PO Drawer 12967, Capitol Station, Austin TX 78711. **Tel** (512)463-7255. **LC** TN872.T4; T34B. **DD** 338.2/7/2809764.

AT/0314-3171
**ANNUAL REPORT AND STATEMENTS OF ACCOUNT. AUSTRALIAN INSTITUTE OF PETROLEUM.** [Annu. rep. statements acc., Aust. Inst. Pet.]. **VFOAT** Annual Report - Australian Institute of Petroleum. (1977)-. Periodical. English. an. Australian Institute of Petroleum Ltd, 257 Collins Street / 11th Floor, Melbourne Victoria 3000 Australia. **Tel** 011 61 3 6541411, FAX 011 61 3 6541950. **DD** _a665.06294.
  **Ind/Abst** AESIS Q.

IS
**ANNUAL REPORT - DELEK, THE ISRAEL FUEL CORPORATION.** **Main/Corp** Delek, Hevrat Ha-Delek Ha-Yisreelit. (19??)-. English. The Israel Fuel Corporation, 6 Ahuzat Bayit Street, Tel-Aviv Israel. **LC** HD9576.I82; D43. **DD** 338.7/62/233282095694.

NO
**ANNUAL REPORT / DET NORSKE VERITAS.** See Transportation-Ships and Shipping.

II
**ANNUAL REPORT / GOVERNMENT OF INDIA, MINISTRY OF PETROLEUM AND CHEMICALS, DEPARTMENT OF CHEMICALS & PETROCHEMICALS.** **Main/Corp** India. Dept. of Chemicals & Petrochemicals. English. **LC** HD9576.I4; I53a. **DD** 354.540082/42. **Continues** Report.

SP
**ANNUAL REPORT / INH.** **Main/Corp** Instituto Nacional de Hidrocarburos (Spain). (19??)-. English. (Spanish). an. Instituto Nacional de Hidrocarburos, Paseo de la Castellana 89, Madrid 16 Spain. **Tel** 456.53.00, telex 48162. **LC** HD9575.S84; I574a. **DD** 354.460082/388/06.
  **Desc:** The holding company which takes part in all phases of gas and oil production, from exploration and production to refining, marketing and distribution.

KU
**ANNUAL REPORT / KUWAIT PETROLEUM CORPORATION.** **Main/Corp** Kuwait Petroleum Corporation. 1st (1980/81)-. English. Kuwait Petroleum Corporation, Manager Public Relations, PO Box 26565, 13126 Safat Kuwait. **LC** HD9576.K84; K85a. **DD** 354.53/670082388/06.

US/0492-8717
**ANNUAL REPORT - LIQUEFIED PETROLEUM GAS DIVISION OF THE RAILROAD COMMISSION OF TEXAS.** **Main/Corp** Texas. Railroad Commission. Liquefied Petroleum Gas Division. **VFOAT** Annual Report - Railroad Commission of Texas, Liquefied Petroleum Gas Division. Periodical. English. Liquefied Petroleum Gas Division of the Railroad Commission of Texas, Austin TX 78711. **DD** 338.2.

US
**ANNUAL REPORT OF THE OIL AND GAS DIVISION (AUSTIN).** (ANNUAL REPORT OF THE OIL AND GAS DIVISION; TO THE GOVERNOR.). **Main/Corp** Texas. Railroad Commission. Oil and Gas Division. **VFOAT** Oil and Gas Annual; Annual Report of the Oil and Gas Division, the Railroad Commission of Texas. Periodical. English. an. $16.00 (latest edition). Railroad Commission of Texas, PO Drawer 12967, Capitol Station, Austin TX 78711. **Tel** (512)463-7255. **LC** HD9567.T3; A3. available in microform. **Continues** Texas. Railroad Commission. Oil and Gas Division. Annual Report of the Railroad Commission of Texas: Oil and Gas Division.
  **Desc:** Reports and news of oil and gas industries.

US/0362-1243
**ANNUAL REPORT OF THE STATE OIL AND GAS SUPERVISOR.** See Petroleum and Natural Gas-Abstracting, Bibliographies and Statistics.

US/8755-2884
**ANNUAL REPORT / OUTER CONTINENTAL SHELF OIL AND GAS LEASING AND PRODUCTION PROGRAM.** [Annu. rep., Outer Cont. Shelf Oil Gas Leas. Prod. Program]. **Main/Corp** Outer Continental Shelf Oil and Gas Leasing and Production Program (U.S.). (1980)-. English. an. Free. Office of Information and Publications, Minerals Management Service, 381 Elden Street, Herndon VA 22070-4817. **Tel** (703)787-1036. **LC** HD242.5; .U56a. **DD** 353.0082/388. **Circ:** 5,000. **Continues** United States. Dept. of the Interior. OCS Oil and Gas Leasing.

AT/0311-7197
**ANNUAL REPORT - PIPELINE AUTHORITY.** [Annu. rep. - Pipeline Auth.]. (1974)-. Periodical. English. an. The Pipeline Authority, 39 London Circuit, Canberra City Australian Capital Territory Australia. **Tel** (062)435222, FAX (062)497043. **DD** 621.867206194.
  **Ind/Abst** AESIS Q.

SP
**ANNUAL REPORT - REPSOL (FIRM).** **Main/Corp** REPSOL (Firm). (1987)-. English. an. REPSOL, Paseo de la Castellana 89, 28046 Madrid Spain. **LC** HD9575.S84; R467A. **DD** 338.7/6223382/0946.

UK
**ANNUAL REPORT, YEAR TO 31ST MARCH ... / BRITISH-BORNEO PETROLEUM SYNDICATE, P.L.C.** **Main/Corp** British-Borneo Petroleum Syndicate. English. an. British-Borneo Petroleum Syndicate P L C, Registered Office/Pembroke House, 40 City Road, London EC1Y 2AD England. **LC** HD9576.B64; B73. **DD** 338.8/87. **Continues** British-Borneo Petroleum Syndicate. Annual Report.

US/0190-3926
**ANNUAL REVIEW FOR THE YEAR RELATING TO OIL AND GAS.** **Main/Corp** Montana. Oil and Gas Conservation Division. **Added/Corp** Montana. Oil and Gas Conservation Commission. Annual Review for the Year. **VFOAT** Annual Review for the Year. Vol. 15 (1971)-. English. an. Free. Board of Oil and Gas Conservation Dnr, 1520 East Sixth Avenue, Helena MT 59620. **Tel** (406)444-6675. **LC** HD9567.M9; M65a. **DD** 338.2/728/09786. **Continues** Annual Review for the Year Relating to Oil and Gas, 0190-3926.

US/0197-5641
**ANNUAL REVIEW OF CALIFORNIA OIL AND GAS PRODUCTION.** [Ann. rev. Calif. oil gas prod.]. **VFOAT** California Oil and Gas Production. 1965-. English. an. $50.00. Conservation Committee of California Oil Producers, 417 South Hill Street/Suite 930, Los Angeles CA 90013. **Tel** (310)625-7731. **ED** Craig Bowman. **Circ:** 800 (ctrl). **Continues** Annual Review of California Crude Oil Production.
  **Desc:** Over 500 pages of annual and cumulative statistical data on California's oil and gas industry includes breakdowns by company and by field and pool.

AU
**ANNUAL STATISTICAL BULLETIN (ORGANIZATION OF PETROLEUM EXPORTING COUNTRIES).** See Petroleum and Natural Gas-Abstracting, Bibliographies and Statistics.

CN
**AOSTRA JOURNAL OF RESEARCH.** [AOSTRA j. res.]. **VAT** Alberta Oil Sands Technology and Research Authority Journal of Research. Vol. 1, No. 1 (Sept. 1984)-. Academic Scholarly Publication. English. Four times a year. 36.00Can$ Canada; 39.00Can$ US; 44.00Can$ other. AOSTRA Provincial Treasurer, 500 Highfield Place, 10010-106 Street, Edmonton Alberta T5J 3L8 Canada. **Tel** (403)427-7623, FAX (403)427-3198, telex 037-3519. **ED** D. S. Montgomery. **Bk Rev. Ad Acc. Circ:** 250. Documents available from CASDDS.
  **Desc:** The journal covers research and technology associated with bitumens, heavy oils, oil source rocks and recovery of conventional petroleums.
  **Ind/Abst** Chem. Abstr. (1984-); GeoRef; Lit. Pat. Abstr., Oilfield Chem. (1992-); Lit. Abstr., Catal. Catal.; Lit. Abstr., Health Environ.; Lit. Abstr., Pet. Refin. Petrochem.; Lit. Abstr., Pet. Substit.; Lit. Abstr., Transp. Storage.

AT/0084-7534
**APEA JOURNAL, THE.** [APEA j.]. **Main/Corp** Australian Petroleum Exploration Association. **Added/Corp** Australian Petroleum Exploration Association. **VAT** The Australian Petroleum Exploration Association Journal. Vol. 1, (1961)-. Academic Scholarly Publication. English. Twice a year (Apr., Aug.). 100.00Aus$ (members), 135.00Aus$ (non-members) Australia; 95.00Aus$ (members), 130.00Aus$ (non-members) New South Wales; 135.00Aus$ (members), 170.00Aus$ (non-members) others. Australian Petroleum Exploration Association, PO Box H172, Australia Square, New South Wales 2000 Australia. **Tel** 011 62 2 221 4899. **LC** TN271.P4; A84a. **DD** 622/.18/28205. **CODEN** APXJAB. **Ad Acc.** Documents available from Article Express International, Petroleum Abstracts Document Delivery Service, CASDDS.
  **Desc:** Contains the technical papers presented at the APEA Conference in Australia as well as other important information on exploration. Very useful to companies and and people involved in the oil exploration and production industry.
  **Ind/Abst** AESIS Q.; Bioeng. Abstr.; Chem. Abstr.; Coal Abstr.; Ei Page One; Energy Res. Abstr. (Oct. 1977-); Eng. Index Annu.; Geogr. Abstr. Phys. Geogr. (?-?); Geogr. Abstr. Human Geogr. (?-?); Geol. Abstr.; GeoRef; Pet. Abstr.

US
**API ABSTRACTS. HEALTH & ENVIRONMENT.** Title Change. See Environmental Issues-Abstracting, Bibliographies and Statistics.

US
**API ABSTRACTS : OILFIELD CHEMICALS.** Title Change. See Petroleum and Natural Gas-Abstracting, Bibliographies and Statistics.

US/0147-9903
**API INDEXES : INDEX TERM USE STATISTICS.** **Main/Corp** American Petroleum Institute. **VAT** American Petroleum Institute Indexes: Index Term Use Statistics. English. API, 36 West 44th, New York NY 10036. **LC** Z695.1.P43; A44B. **DD** 025.3/3553/282.

US
**API REPORTS OF AMERICAN SHIPMENTS OF CASING, TUBING, & DRILL PIPE.** English. an. Free on request. American Petroleum Institute / Dallas, 2535 One Main Place, Dallas TX 75202. **Tel** (214)748-3841.

US
**APIBIZ [ONLINE DATABASE].** See Petroleum and Natural Gas-Abstracting, Bibliographies and Statistics.

US
**APILIT [ONLINE DATABASE].** See Petroleum and Natural Gas-Abstracting, Bibliographies and Statistics.

HK
**APPI-CRUDE OILS.** English. ir. $3500.00. Seapac Services Limited, 1802 Ruttonjee Hse 11 Duddall, Hong Kong Hong Kong. **Tel** 011 852 5 5257102.

FR/0031-6369
**ARAB OIL & GAS.** **Added/Corp** Arab Petroleum Research Center. **VAT** Arab Oil and Gas. (19??)-. Periodical. English (French). bw. $1,340.00. Arab Petroleum Research Center, 7 Avenue Ingres, 75016 Paris France. **Tel** 011 33 1 45243310, FAX 011 33 1 45201685, telex 642963. **ED** N. Sarkis. **Circ:** 1,850.
  **Desc:** Covers news on Arab oil and gas.

FR/0304-8551
**ARAB OIL & GAS DIRECTORY.** **Added/Corp** Arab Petroleum Research Center. **VAT** Arab Oil and Gas Directory. (1974)-. Directory. English. an. $2460.00F France; $420.00 (surface mail), $440.00 (air mail) other. Arab Petroleum Research Center, 7 Avenue Ingres, 75016 Paris France. **Tel** 011 33 1 45243310, FAX 011 33 1 45201685, telex 642963. **ED** N Sarkis. **LC** HD9578.A55; A74. **DD** 338.2/7/2809174927. **Ad Acc. Circ:** 4,560 (ctrl).
  **Desc:** Provides detailed statistics and information on all aspects of oil and gas production, exploration and developments in the 24 Arab countries of the Middle East and North Africa and in Iran.

UK/1013-5464
**ARAB OIL (ARAB OIL PUB. CO. : 1980.).** (ARAB OIL.). [Arab oil]. Academic Scholarly Publication. English. mo. Arab Oil & Economic Review, 3 Dunraven Street, London W1Y 3FG England. **LC** HC498.A1; A75.

**DD** 338.2/7282/09174927. ***Continues*** *Arab Oil and Economic Review.*
**Ind/Abst** EMBASE.

CN/0316-9707
**ARCTIC GAS. BIOLOGICAL REPORT SERIES.** **See** Biology.

CN/0834-2709
**ARCTIC PETROLEUM REVIEW.** ***Ceased.*** [Arct. pet. rev.]. Vol. 9, No. 1 (Summer 1986)-(199?). Periodical. English. sa. Canadian Petroleum Association, 1809 Barrington Street, Halifax Nova Scotia B3J 3K8 Canada. **Tel** (902)421-1159. **DD** 338.2/7282/097299. **CODEN** APRVEL. ***Continues*** *A.P.O.A. Review, 0709-5686.*

●CN/1199-1801
**AREAS SERVED BY NATURAL GAS.** **See** Public Administration-Public Utilities.

UK
**ARGUS EUROPEAN PRODUCTS.** (19??)-. English. ds. £3625.00 (FAX service), £4103.00 (telex service). Petroleum Argus Ltd, 93 Shepperton Road, London N1 3DF England. **Tel** 011 44 71 359 8792.

US/0044-8893
**ARKANSAS LP NEWS.** Periodical. English. bm. Arkansas Propane Gas Association Inc, 103 East 7th Street/Suite 1012, Little Rock AR 72201. **Tel** (501)374-8396. **ED** J Lybrand Jr. **Circ:** 575.

US/0273-4931
**ARMSTRONG OIL DIRECTORIES, LOUISIANA, TEXAS GULF COAST, EAST TEXAS, ARK. AND MISS.** [Armstrong oil dir., La. Tex. Gulf Coast East Tex. Ark. and Miss.]. **Added/Corp** Oil Men's Association of America. **VAT** Armstrong Oil Directories. Louisiana, Texas Gulf Coast, East Texas, Arkansas and Mississippi. (1980)-. English. an (Oct.). $63.50. Armstrong Oil Directories, PO Box 9660, Amarillo TX 79105. **Tel** (806)374-1818, FAX (806)374-1838. **ED** Alan Armstrong. **LC** TN867; .H28. **DD** 338.7/622338/02576. **Ad Acc.** ***Continues*** *Hank Seale Oil Directory: Louisiana, Texas Gulf Coast, East Texas, Ark. and Miss.*

US/0273-5229
**ARMSTRONG OIL DIRECTORIES, ROCKY MOUNTAIN AND CENTRAL UNITED STATES.** **Added/Corp** Oil Men's Association of America. (1980)-. Periodical. English. an (Oct.). $63.50. Armstrong Oil Directories, PO Box 9660, Amarillo TX 79105. **Tel** (806)374-1818, FAX (806)374-1838. **ED** Alan Armstrong. **LC** TN867; .H3. **DD** 338.7/622338/02578. **Ad Acc.** ***Continues*** *Hank Seale Oil Directory; Rocky Mountain and Central United States.*

US/0277-2280
**ARMSTRONG OIL DIRECTORIES, TEXAS AND SOUTHEASTERN NEW MEXICO.** [Armstrong oil dir. Tex. southeast. N. M.]. **Added/Corp** Oil Men's Association of America. (1980)-. English. an (Oct.). $63.50. Armstrong Oil Directories, PO Box 9660, Amarillo TX 79105. **Tel** (806)374-1818, FAX (806)374-1838. **ED** Alan Armstrong. **LC** TN867; .T4. **DD** 338.7/6223382/025764. **Ad Acc.** ***Continues*** *Texas Oil Directory.*

US/0094-6559
**ASIA & AUSTRALASIA. BASIC OIL LAWS AND CONCESSION CONTRACTS, ORIGINAL TEXTS. SUPPLEMENT (PHOTOCOPY).** (ASIA & AUSTRALASIA : BASIC OIL LAWS AND CONCESSION CONTRACTS. (ORIGINAL TEXTS). SUPPLEMENT.). [Asia Australas., Basic oil laws concess. contracts, Orig. texts, Suppl.]. **Main/Corp** Petroleum Legislation (Firm : New York, N.Y.). No. 1 (1960)-. English. qt. $6350.00. Barrows Company Inc., 116 East 66th Street, New York NY 10021. **Tel** (212)772-1199, (800)227-7697, FAX (212)288-7242, telex 4971238 BARROWS. **DD** 346/.5/04682.

US/0748-4089
**ASIA-PACIFIC AFRICA-MIDDLE EAST PETROLEUM DIRECTORY.** [Asia-Pac. Afr.-Middle East pet. dir.]. **VFOAT** Asia, Pacific, Africa, Middle East Petroleum Directory; Asia-Pacific/Africa-Middle East Petroleum Directory. 1st Edition (1985)-. Directory. English. an (Nov.). $141.00 US & Canada; $185.00 other. PennWell Publishing Company, 1421 South Sheridan, PO Box 1260, Tulsa OK 74101. **Tel** (918)835-3161, (800)331-4463, FAX (918)831-9497. **(Subscription address:** PennWell Books, PO Box 21288, Tulsa OK 74121.**)** **ED** Jonelle Moore. **LC** HD9576.A1; A78. **DD** 358.7/622338/02556. **[CCC].** Index available. **Ad Acc. Circ:** 1,000. ***Formed by the union of*** *Africa-Middle East Petroleum Directory, 0197-7830* ***and*** *Asia-Pacific Petroleum Directory, 0270-1235.*
**Desc:** Lists companies involved in all phases of the oil industry in the Asia-Pacific and Africa-Middle East region, with listings organized by country with company index.

HK
**ASIAN OIL & GAS.** English. Ten times a year. $90.00 Asia; $105.00 other (air postage included). Asian Oil & Gas Publ Ltd, 200 Lockhart Road, 14th Floor, Hong Kong Hong Kong. **Tel** 11 852 5111301, FAX 11 852 5074620. ***Continues*** *Resources Asia.*
**Ind/Abst** AESIS Q.

CN/0825-2483
**ATLAS OF ALBERTA'S CRUDE BITUMEN RESERVES.** [Atlas Alta. crude bitumen reserves]. **Added/Corp** Alberta. Energy Resources Conservation Board. (197?)-. English. ir. 50.00Can$ (1990 latest edition). Energy Resources Conservation Board, 640 Fifth Avenue Southwest, Calgary Alberta T2P 3G4 Canada. **Tel** (403)297-8311, (403)297-8190, telex 03-821717. **LC** TN850; .A87. **DD** 553.2/7.
**Desc:** A reserves report concerning maps utilized to determine the in-place volumes of crude bitumen in the Athabasca, Cold Lake, and Peace River oil sands deposits for the 1984 reserves publication.

GW/0072-1670
**AUSSENHANDEL. REIHE 4: GENERALHANDEL. EIN- UND AUSFUHR VON MINERALOEL.** (AUSSENHANDEL. EIN- UND AUSFUHR VON MINERALOEL. REIHE 4: GENERALHANDEL.). **Main/Corp** Germany (West). Statistisches Bundesamt. **VFOAT** Generalhandel. (Jan. 1962)-. German. mo. Metzler Poeschel Verlag Veroeffen, Statist Bundesamt Kernerstr 43, D 70182 Stuttgart Germany. **Tel** 011 49 7071 935350. **(Subscription address:** Metzler Poeschel H Leins GmbH, Postfach 1152, D 72125 Kusterdingen Germany.**)** **LC** HD9573.1; .A3.
**Desc:** Covers the petroleum industry and trade.

GW
**AUSSENHANDEL. REIHE 4.1 : EIN- UND AUSFUHR VON MINERALOL, GENERALHANDEL.** **Main/Corp** Germany (West). Statistisches Bundesamt. **Added/Corp** Germany (West). Statistisches Bundesamt. Ein-und Ausfuhr von Mineralol, Generalhandel. **VFOAT** Fachserie 7. **VAT** Aussenhandel. Reihe Vier. Eins: Ein- und Ausfuhr von Mineralol, Generalhandel. (Jan. 1977)-. Periodical. German. mo. DM141.60 Germany; DM156.90 other. Metzler Poeschel Verlag Veroeffen, Statist Bundesamt Kernerstr 43, D 70182 Stuttgart Germany. **Tel** 011 49 7071 935350. **(Subscription address:** Metzler Poeschel H Leins GmbH, Postfach 1152, D 72125 Kusterdingen Germany.**)** **LC** HD9573.1; .A3. ***Continues*** *Germany (West). Statistisches Bundesamt. Aussenhandel. Reihe 4: Generalhandel. Ein- und Ausfuhr Von Mineralol.*

UK
**AUSTRALASIA OIL SERVICE.** English. mo. £2,250.00. Wood Mackenzie Consultants Ltd., Kintore House, 74 77 Queen Street, Edinburgh EH2 4NS Scotland. **Tel** 011 44 031 225 8525, FAX 011 44 031 243 4435, telex 72555.

AT
**AUSTRALIAN AND NEW ZEALAND GAS INDUSTRY STATISTICS, THE.** **Added/Corp** Australian Gas Association. **VFOAT** Gas Industry Statistics. (19??)-. Periodical. English. an. 25.00Aus$. Australian Gas Association, GPO Box 323, Gas Industry House / 7 Moore Street, Canberra Australian Capital Territory 2601 Australia. **Tel** 011 61 6 2473955, FAX 011 61 6 2497402. **LC** WMLC 91/2226.
**Ind/Abst** AESIS Q.

AT/0727-3525
**AUSTRALIAN GAS INDUSTRY DIRECTORY, THE.** **Added/Corp** Australian Gas Association. (1978/1979)-. Directory. English. an. 35.00Aus$. Australian Gas Association, GPO Box 323, Gas Industry House / 7 Moore Street, Canberra Australian Capital Territory 2601 Australia. **Tel** 011 61 6 2473955, FAX 011 61 6 2497402. **LC** TP738; .A85a. **DD** 665.7/025/44. ctrl circ. ***Continues*** *Directory of the Australian Gas Industry.*
**Desc:** Information on and listings of members of The Australian Gas Association: utilities, manufacturers, associates, and individuals. Also suppliers to the industry, some overseas gas associations, and a buyer's guide.

AT/0004-9166
**AUSTRALIAN GAS JOURNAL, THE.** [Aust. gas j.]. **Added/Corp** Australian Gas Association. Vol. 27, No. 6 (1963)-. Periodical. English. bm (Mar., June, Sept., Dec.). 45.00Aus$ Australia; 54.50Aus$ Asia & Oceania; 57.00Aus$ others. Australian Gas Association, GPO Box 323, Gas Industry House / 7 Moore Street, Canberra Australian Capital Territory 2601 Australia. **Tel** 011 61 6 2473955, FAX 011 61 6 2497402. **ED** Catherine Rayner. **LC** TP700; .A88. **Ad Acc, Adv Mgr:** L. Trimmings, **Tel** (03)544-2233. Full Page (B&W) 590.00Aus$. Half Page (B&W) 340.00Aus$. **Circ:** 3,000. ***Continues*** *Australian Gas Bulletin.*
**Desc:** Information on all aspects of the gas industry and the energy situation in Australia and overseas. Feature and technical articles, reports on conventions, conferences and seminars, information on government activities, energy statistics and new products, notes on personalities.
**Ind/Abst** Coal Abstr.; GeoRef.

AT/0812-857X
**AUSTRALIAN MINING AND PETROLEUM LAW ASSOCIATION YEARBOOK.** **See** Law.

AT/0157-728X
**AUSTRALIAN OIL & GAS DIRECTORY.** [Aust. oil gas dir.]. (1978)-. Directory. English. an (Nov.). 60.00Aus$. Australian Oil & Gas Directory, PO Box 282, Carlton South Victoria 3053 Australia. **Tel** 011 61 3 6509139. **DD** 338.2728029494. **Ad Acc. Circ:** 9,000.
**Desc:** Information regarding companies involved in supplying good services to major oil companies.

AT
**AUSTRALIAN OIL AND GAS EXPLORERS DIRECTORY.** Directory. English. Twice a year (publlished in Mar. and Oct.). 50.00Aus$. Business Intelligence, PO Box 210, Claremont, West Australia, 6010 Australia. **Tel** 011 61 9 341 8803.
**Desc:** Contact details for oil and gas exploration and technical service companies active in the region.

AT
**AUSTRALIAN PETROLEUM ACCUMULATIONS.** Monographic series. English. Price varies per volume. Bureau of Mineral Resources / Canberra, GPO Box 378, Canberra Australian Capital Territory 2601 Australia. **Tel** (062)499111, FAX 488178, telex AA62109.
**Ind/Abst** Geol. Abstr.

AT/0817-9263
**AUSTRALIAN PETROLEUM ACCUMULATIONS REPORT / DEPARTMENT OF RESOURCES AND ENERGY, BUREAU OF MINERAL RESOURCES, GEOLOGY AND GEOPHYSICS.** **Added/Corp** Australia. Bureau of Mineral Resources, Geology and Geophysics. (1986)-. Monographic series. English. ir. Price varies per volume. Australian Geological Survey, PO Box 378, Queen Victoria Terrace, Parkes Australian Capital Territories, 2601 Australia. **Tel** 011 61 6 2499519, 011 61 6 2499642, FAX 011 61 6 2499982.
**Ind/Abst** AESIS Q.

AT/0310-1258
**AUSTRALIAN PIPELINER.** [Aust. pipeliner]. (1972)-. Trade Publication. English. qt. 52.00Aus$ Papua New Guinea, New Zealand & Southeast Asia; 62.00Aus$ US, Canada & Europe. Pipeline News of Australia Pty Ltd., PO Box 1014, Hartwell Victoria 3125, Australia. **Tel** 011 61 3 8894894, FAX 011 61 3 8893600. **ED** J. Barry Wood. **DD** 621.86720994. **Bk Rev. Ad Acc, Adv Mgr:** Claire Bowley. Full Page (B&W) 1200.00Aus$. Half Page (B&W) 780.00Aus$. Full Page (Color) 1650.00Aus$. **Circ:** 2,200.
**Desc:** Publishes news and information about the pipeline industry activities.
**Ind/Abst** AESIS Q.

AT
**AUSTRALIA'S IDENTIFIED PETROLEUM RESOURCES / BUREAU OF MINERAL RESOURCES, GEOLOGY & GEOPHYSICS.** **Added/Corp** Australia. Bureau of Mineral Resources, Geology and Geophysics. (19??)-. Periodical. English. Australian Bureau of Statistics, PO Box 10, Belconnen Australian Capital Territory, 2616 Australia. **Tel** 011 61 6 2527911, FAX 011 61 6 2516009. **LC** HD9578.A8; A88.
**Ind/Abst** AESIS Q.

US
**AUTOMOTIVE AND MARINE SERVICE STATION CODE.** (19??)-. English. ir. $16.00 nonmembers; $14.50 members. National Fire Protection Association, 1 Batterymarch Park, PO Box 9101, Quincy MA 02269-9101. **Tel** (617)770-3000, (800)344-3555.
**Desc:** Provides information on the latest requirements for piping, fuel dispensing systems, service stations inside buildings, and operations.

US/0146-5236
**AUTOMOTIVE FUEL ECONOMY PROGRAM. ANNUAL REPORT TO THE CONGRESS.** (AUTOMOTIVE FUEL ECONOMY PROGRAM / U.S. DEPARTMENT OF TRANSPORTATION, NATIONAL HIGHWAY TRAFFIC SAFETY ADMINISTRATION.). [Automot. fuel econ. program, Annu. rep. Congr.]. **VFOAT** Annual Automotive Fuel Economy Program Report to the Congress. Began with 1st, 1977. English. an. US Department of Transportation / National Highway Traffic Safety Administration, 400 7th Street SW, Washington DC 20590. **LC** HD9561; .U56A. **DD** 353.0082/42. available on microfiche (Vols. for 1982- distributed to depository libraries).

AJ/0005-2531
**AZERBAIDZHANSKII KHIMICHESKII ZHURNAL / AKADEMIIA NAUK AZERBAIDZHANSKOI SSR.** See Chemistry.

UK
**BASE OILS REPORT. FAX SERVICE.** (19??)-. English. wk (Wed.). £650.00. ICIS Lor Group Ltd., 6 Spring Gardens, Citadel Place Tinworth, London SE11 5EH England. **Tel** 011 44 71 8151100.
**Desc:** Covers price, supply and availability of base oils in Scandinavia. The report will also track the movement of base oils and lubes worldwide, provide market intelligence and key feedstock prices.

US/0730-5621
**BASIC PETROLEUM DATA BOOK (WASHINGTON, D.C. : 1981).** (BASIC PETROLEUM DATA BOOK.). [Basic pet. data book]. Vol. 1, No. 1, (1981)-. Periodical. English. Three times a year. $150.00 (non-member); $165.00 Canada; $195.00 other. American Petroleum Institute, 275 Seventh Avenue, New York NY 10001. **Tel** (212)366-4040, FAX (212)366-4298. **(Subscription address:** 1970 Chain Bridge Road, McLean, VA 22109-6000) **LC** HD9564; .B37. **DD** 338.2/728/021. ctrl circ. ***Continues*** *Basic Petroleum Data Book, 0730-5621.*
**Desc:** Continuing source of information, 1947 to current on domestic and world statistical information. Chapters on energy, reserves, exploration and drilling, production, demand, prices, and refining.
**Ind/Abst** Predicasts Forecasts.

IO
**BERITA MIGAS. Main/Corp** Indonesia. Direktorat Jenderal Minyak Dan Gas Bumi. **VAT** Berita Minyak Dan Gas Bumi. V. 6, No. 3- Mar. 1973-. Periodical. Indonesian. Direktorat Jenderal Minyak Dangas Bumi, Merdeka Selatan 18, Jakarta Indonesia. **LC** HD9576.I5; I52A. ***Continues*** *Berita Migas.*

UK/0016-7053
**BIBLIOGRAPHY OF ECONOMIC GEOLOGY.** See Earth Sciences-Abstracting, Bibliographies and Statistics.

FR/0300-4554
**BIP. BULLETIN DE L'INDUSTRIE PETROLIERE.** [BIP, Bull. ind. pet.]. **VFOAT** Bulletin de l'Industrie Petroliere. (1964)-. Bulletin. French. da. 12300.00F France; 12650.00 other. Bureau d'Info Professionnelles, 142 rue Montmartre, 75073 Paris Cedex 02 France. **Tel** 011 33 1 40268321, FAX 011 33 1 40399752, telex 220528 BIP. **ED** Jacques Marie. **[CCC]. Bk Rev. Circ:** 800.
**Desc:** Reference on hydrocarbon activity in France and the world, covers current events in the fields of petroleum and natural gas.
**Ind/Abst** Coal Abstr.; Pet. Energy Bus. News Index (1981).

BL/0006-6117
**BOLETIM TECNICO DA PETROBRAS.** [Bol. tec. Petrobras]. V. 1 (Oct. 1957)-. Academic Scholarly Publication. Portuguese. qt. Free. Centro Pesquisas Desenvolvimen Cidade, Univ-Quadra 7-Pstl 809 Brazil. **Tel** 011 55 21 5986114. **ED** Affonso Celso M de Paula. **CODEN** BTPEAT. **[CCC]. Circ:** 2,000. Documents available from Petroleum Abstracts Document Delivery Service, CASDDS.
**Desc:** Studies and researches of a technical and scientifical approach, from Brazil and other countries, concerning petroleum and derivatives, exploration and the oil industry in general.
**Ind/Abst** Chem. Abstr.; GeoRef; Lit. Pat. Abstr., Oilfield Chem. (1975-); Lit. Abstr., Catal. Catal.; Lit. Abstr., Health Environ.; Lit. Abstr., Pet. Refin. Petrochem.; Lit. Abstr., Pet. Substit.; Lit. Abstr., Transp. Storage; Ocean. Abstr.; Pet. Abstr.

UY/0253-6005
**BOLETIN TECNICO - ARPEL.** (BOLETIN TECNICO.). [Bol. tec. - ARPEL]. **Main/Corp** Asistencia Reciproca Petrolera Estatal Latinoamericana. **VAT** Boletin Tecnico - Asistencia Reciproca Petrolera Estatal Latinoamericana. Vol. 1 No. 1 (May 1972)-. Periodical. Spanish (Portuguese and Spanish). Four times a year (Mar., June, Sept., Dec.). $75.00. ARPEL, Casilla de Correo 1006, Montevideo Uruguay. **Tel** 011 598 2 407454, FAX 011 598 2 237023, telex 22560. **ED** Maria Rosa Chpo. **Ad Acc.** Documents available from Petroleum Abstracts Document Delivery Service.
**Ind/Abst** Lit. Pat. Abstr., Oilfield Chem. (1980-); Lit. Abstr., Catal. Catal.; Lit. Abstr., Health Environ.; Lit. Abstr., Pet. Refin. Petrochem.; Lit. Abstr., Pet. Substit.; Lit. Abstr., Transp. Storage; Pet. Abstr.

IT/1120-544X
**BOLLETTINO UFFICIALE DEGLI IDROCARBURI E DELLA GEOTERMIA / MINISTERO DELL'INDUSTRIA, DEL COMMERCIO E DELL'ARTIGIANATO, DIREZIONE GENERALE DELLE MINIERE, UFFICIO NAZIONALE MINERARIO PER GLI IDROCARBURI E LA GEOTERMIA. Main/Corp** Italy. Ufficio Nazionale Minerario per Gli Idrocarburi e la Geotermia. (19??)-. Italian. mo. L450000 Italy; L627000 other. Istituto Poligrafico Zecca Stato, Piazza Verdi 10, 00198 Rome Italy. **Tel** 011 39 6 85082307, 011 39 6 85082221. **LC** HD9575.I8; A35. ***Continues*** *Italy. Ufficio Nazionale Minerario per Gli Idrocarburi.* ***and*** *Bollettino Ufficiale Degli Idrocarburi, 0406-6669.*
**Desc:** Information on the petroleum industry and trade, geothermal resources, and petroleum law and legislation.

UK
**BP REVIEW OF WORLD GAS. Added/Corp** British Petroleum Company. **VFOAT** Review of World Gas. (19??)-. English. an. Free on request. British Petroleum Company, Britannic House, 1 Finsbury Circus, London EC2M 7B8 England. **Tel** 011 44 071 4964205. **LC** HD9581.A1; B6. **DD** 333.8/233/021.
**Ind/Abst** F&S Index Plus Text, Int. [Select. Cov.]; Predicasts Forecasts.

UK
**BP SHIELD.** English. qt. Free on request. British Petroleum Company, Britannic House, 1 Finsbury Circus, London EC2M 7B8 England. **Tel** 011 44 071 4964205.
**Ind/Abst** Fluid Abstr., Civil Eng.; Fluid Abstr. Proc. Eng.; FLUIDEX (19??-).

GW/0342-6580
**BRENNSTOFFSPIEGEL.** See Economics-Industry and Production.

US/0197-8098
**BROWN'S DIRECTORY OF NORTH AMERICAN AND INTERNATIONAL GAS COMPANIES.** [Brown's dir. North Am. int. gas co.]. (1978)-. Directory. English. an. $270.00 US and possessions; $280.00 other. Advanstar Communications Inc., 131 West First Street, Duluth MN 55802. **Tel** (218)723-9477, (800)346-0085. **ED** Dean Hale. **LC** TP714; .B8. **DD** 338.7/6223385/02573. **[CCC]. Ad Acc. Circ:** 962. ***Continues*** *Brown's Directory of North American Gas Companies, 0068-2888.*

RM/0376-4516
**BULETINUL INSTITUTULUI DE PETROL SI GAZE.** [Bul. inst. pet. gaze]. **Added/Corp** Institutul de Petrol si Gaze. (1974)-. Academic Scholarly Publication. Romanian (English and Romanian; summaries and/or abstracts in French and German). sa. $6.00. Institutului de Petrol si Gaze 22, 2000 Ploiesti Romania. **Tel** 42451. **ED** Oroveanu Tudor. **LC** TN860; .R7. **CODEN** BIPGDT. Index available. **Bk Rev.** ctrl circ. Documents available from CASDDS. ***Continues*** *Buletinul Institutului de Petrol, Gaze Si Geologie.*
**Ind/Abst** Chem. Abstr.; Energy Res. Abstr. (Oct. 1982-); GeoRef.

FR/0007-4101
**BULLETIN ANALYTIQUE PETROLIER.** [Bull. anal. pet.]. (1953)-. Periodical. French. Twenty-two times a year. 843.17F France; 1000.00F other. Comite Professionnel du Petrol CPDP, BP 282, 92505 Rueil Malmaison France. **Tel** 011 33 1 47169460. **UDC** 665.6.

SZ/0366-4848
**BULLETIN DER VEREINIGUNG SCHWEIZ. PETROLEUM-GEOLOGEN UND- INGENIEURE.** (BULLETIN.). [Bull. Ver. Schweiz. Pet.-Geol. Ing.]. **Main/Corp** Vereinigung Schweiz. Petroleum-Geologen und Ingenieure. (19??)-. Bulletin. English (French and German). Twice a year (May & Nov.). 62.00F. Vereinigung Schweizerischer Petroleum Geol & Ing, Bederstr 66, CH-8021 Zurich Switzerland. **LC** TN860; .V4. **CODEN** BUVSA6. cum. index.
**Ind/Abst** GeoRef.

FR/0290-0556
**BULLETIN MENSUEL D'INFORMATION (FRANCE. SERVICE DE CONSERVATION DES GISEMENTS).** (BULLETIN MENSUEL D'INFORMATION / MINISTERE DE LA RECHERCHE ET DE L'INDUSTRIE, DIRECTION DES HYDROCARBURES, SERVICE DE CONSERVATION DES GISEMENTS.). **Added/Corp** France. Service de Conservation des Gisements d'Hydrocarbures. (1968)-. French. mo. 1,800.00F (includes maps and annual report and postage). Service de Conservation des Gisements D'Hydrocarbures, 366 Avenue Napoleon Bonaparte, 92501 Rueil-Malmaison Cedex France. **Tel** (1)47-49-27-75, FAX (1)47.08.33.70. **LC** TN874.F8; .B85. **DD** 338.2/728/0944. **Circ:** 250.
**Desc:** Provides information on oil and gas exploration and production in France.

CN/0007-4802
**BULLETIN OF CANADIAN PETROLEUM GEOLOGY.** [Bull. Can. pet. geol.]. **Added/Corp** Canadian Society of Petroleum Geologists. Alberta Society of Petroleum Geologists. Edmonton Geological Society. Saskatchewan Geological Society. Vol. 11 (March 1963)-. Bulletin. English (French). qt (Mar., Jun., Sep., Dec.). 75.00Can$ (comes with CSPG Reservoir). Canadian Society of Petroleum Geologists, 206 7th Avenue Southwest, Calgary Alberta T2P 0W7 Canada. **Tel** (403)264-5610, FAX (403)264-5898. **ED** Ashton Embry. **CODEN** BCPGAI. **[CCC].** Index available. cum. index. **Bk Rev. Pr Rev. Circ:** 3,500. Documents available from Article Express International, The Genuine Article, BIOSIS Document Express, Petroleum Abstracts Document Delivery Service, CASDDS. ***Continues*** *Alberta Society of Petroleum Geologists. Journal of the Alberta Society of Petroleum Geologists., 0317-4107.*
**Desc:** Covers sedimentary, petroleum geology, stratigraphy, structural geology and related topics.
**Ind/Abst** ASTIS Curr. Aware. Bull. (1978-); AESIS Q.; AQUAREF; ASTIS Bibliogr. (1978-); Bioeng. Abstr.; Biol. Abstr.; Chem. Abstr. (1963-1983); Coal Abstr.; Curr. Contents Eng. Tech. Appl. Sci.; Curr. Contents Phys. Chem. Earth Sci.; Ei Page One; Energy Res. Abstr. (March 1976-); Eng. Index Annu.; Geogr. Abstr. Phys. Geogr.; Geogr. Abstr. Human Geogr.; Geol. Abstr.; GeoRef; Pet. Abstr.; Res. Alert [Select. Cov.]; SCISEARCH.

II/0537-0094
**BULLETIN OF THE OIL AND NATURAL GAS COMMISSION.** (BULLETIN.). [Bull. Oil Nat. Gas Comm.]. **Main/Corp** India (Republic). Oil and Natural Gas Commission. **Added/Corp** India. Oil and Natural Gas Commission. **VFOAT** Bulletin; ONGC Bulletin; Bulletin of Oil & Natural Gas Commission. **VAT** Oil and Natural Gas Commission bulletin; Bulletin of Oil and Natural Gas Commission. Vol. 1 (Dec. 1964)-. Bulletin. English. sa. $50.00. Oil and Natural Gas Commission, Dehra Dun, UP 248195 India. **(Subscription address:** Prints India, 11 Darya Ganj, New Delhi, 110002 India, (Phone: 011 91 11 3268645)) **LC** TN876.I5; A28. **CODEN** BONCDF.
**Ind/Abst** GeoRef.

IO
**BULLETIN PERTAMINA. Main/Corp** Pertamina (Organization). (19??)-. Periodical. Indonesian. wk. Free on request. Indonesian State Owned Oil and Gas, Merdeka Timur No. 1, Jakarta Indonesia. **Tel** 347615. **ED** Yus Soekidjo and A Sidick N. **LC** HD9576.I54; P45a. **Bk Rev. Circ:** 7,500 (ctrl).
**Desc:** Covers the policy on oil and gas business in Indonesia.

US
**BULLETIN - STATE OF ALASKA, ALASKA OIL AND GAS CONSERVATION COMMISSION.** See Environmental Issues-Conservation and Natural Resources.

US/0739-294X
**BUNKERFUELS REPORT.** [Bunkerfuels rep.]. **Added/Corp** Bunkerfuels Corporation. (Apr. 21, 1981)-. Periodical. English. Fifty-two times a year (Tuesdays). $1,675.00 US, Canada, London; $1,750.00 Europe; $2,150.00 Far East, South Africa, South America, Caribbean and Australia; $2,300.00 others. Bunkerfuels Corporation, PO Box 569, Halsey Reed Road, Cranbury NJ 08512. **Tel** (609)395-8500, FAX (609)395-8070.

US/8755-1489
**BURMASS' TEX-OK-KAN OIL DIRECTORY.** [Burmass' Tex-Ok-Kan oil dir.]. **VFOAT** Tex Ok Kan Oil Directory; Burmass' Tex Ok Kan Oil Directory; Tex-Ok-Kan Oil Directory. Directory. English. an. $20.00. Burmass Publishing Company Inc, Box 1768, Midland TX 79702. **Tel** (800)634-5689, (800)682-1782. **LC** HD9567.T3; B87. **DD** 681/.76.

US/0007-7259
**BUTANE-PROPANE NEWS. VAT** Butane Propane News. Vol. 1 (Sept. 1969)-. Periodical. English. Twelve times a year. $20.00 US, $30.00 Canada, $40.00 other, trade; $30.00 US, $40.00 Canada, $50.00 other, non-trade, surface mail; $84.00 trade; $94.00 non-trade, airmail. Butane-Propane News, Box 660698, Arcadia CA 91006-0698. **Tel** (818)357-2168, FAX (818)303-2854. **ED** Steve Prowler. **LC** TP761.B8; B82. **DD** 665/.773. Index available. **Ad Acc. Circ:** 16,800 (ctrl). available on microfiche from University Microfilms International (UMI). ***Supersedes*** *Butane-Propane News, 0007-7259.*
**Desc:** Covering the safety and regular legislative issues. Subjects on carburetion load building, fuel sales, supply, demands and prices.
**Ind/Abst** Gas Abstr.

US
**CALIFORNIA - ALASKA OIL AND GAS REVIEW.** (1969)-. Periodical. English. an. $47.00. Munger Oil Information Service, 9800 South Sepulveda Boulevard, Suite 723, Los Angeles CA 90045. **Tel** (310)776-3990, FAX (312)645-9147. **ED** Averill H. Munger. ***Continues*** *California Oil and Gas Exploration, 0527-2890.*

CN/0824-4766
**CANADA A-Z.** (CANADA A-Z : OIL, GAS, MINING DIRECTORY.). [Can. A-Z]. **VFOAT** Oil, Gas, Mining Directory; Canada Oil, Gas, Mining. 1983/1984-. Directory. English. an. $70.00. Canadian Trade & Industry Publishing Group, PO Box 597 Station M, Calgary Alberta T2P Canada. **DD** 338.2/728/02571.

CN/0822-8698
**CANADA OFFSHORE BUYERS GUIDE.** [Can. offshore buy. guide]. **VFOAT** Offshore Canada. **VAT** Oilweek. Canada Offshore Buyers Guide. 1983/84-. Consumer Publication. English. an. 10.00Can$. Canada

# Petroleum and Natural Gas

Offshore Buyers Guide, Suite 200/1015 Centre Street North, Calgary Alberta T2E 1P8 Canada. **Tel** (403)276-7881. **ED** Vic Humphreys. **DD** 622/.29/02571. **Ad Acc. Circ:** 6,000 (ctrl).
 **Desc:** Listings of suppliers to the offshore oil and gas industry.

CN/0316-3547
**CANADIAN GAS FACTS. See** Public Administration-Public Utilities.

CN
**CANADIAN GAS PRICE REPORTER.** English. mo. 365.00Can$. Canadian Enerdata Limited, Suite 204 7030 Woodbine Avenue, Markham Ontario L3R 1A2 Canada. **Tel** (905)479-9697.

CN/1194-2967
**CANADIAN GAS RATES. See** Public Administration-Public Utilities.

CN/0847-0316
**CANADIAN NATURAL GAS FOCUS.** [Can. nat. gas. focus]. **Added/Corp** Brent Friedenberg Associates. Vol. 1, Issue 1 (July 1987)-. Periodical. English. Twelve times a year. 995.00Can$. Brent Friedenberg Association, 1052 Memorial Drive Northwest, PO Box G684, Station G, Calgary Alberta T2N 3E2 Canada. **Tel** (403)270-0700, **FAX** (403)262-5458. **ED** Brent Friedenberg. **DD** 338.2/7285/0971. **Circ:** 200 (ctrl).

●CN/1196-0906
**CANADIAN NATURAL GAS MARKET REPORT.** [Can. nat. gas mark. rep.]. **Added/Corp** Canadian Enerdata Limited. **VFOAT** Natural Gas Market Report. Vol. 8, No. 21 (Jan. 4, 1993)-. Periodical. English. ir. $315.00. Canadian Enerdata Limited, Suite 204 7030 Woodbine Avenue, Markham Ontario L3R 1A2 Canada. **Tel** (905)479-9697. **DD** 338.8/233/097105. **Continues** Natural Gas Market Report., 0827-6056.

CN/0384-8965
**CANADIAN OIL AND GAS.** (CANADIAN OIL AND GAS / BY DAVID E. LEWIS AND ANDREW R. THOMPSON.). (1955)-. English. ir. 940.00Can$. Butterworth & Co. Ltd. / Kent, England, Borough Green, Sevenoaks Kent TN15 8PH England. **Tel** 011 44 732-884567, **FAX** 011 44 732-885996. **(Subscription address:** Butterworth Heinemann Publishers, 225 Wildwood Avenue, Unit B, Woburn MA 01801.**)**
 **Desc:** Provides in-depth coverage of oil and gas law in Canada.

CN/0710-622X
**CANADIAN OIL & GAS HANDBOOK.** Ceased. **VFOAT** Canadian Oil and Gas Handbook. 1980-1981-Ceased (1990). English. an. Northern Miner Press Ltd, 7 Labatt Avenue, Toronto Ontario M5A 3P2 Canada. **Tel** 368-3481, **FAX** (416)861-9564. **ED** C D Gardiner. **LC** HD9574.C2; C296. **DD** 338.2/728/0971. **Ad Acc. Circ:** 4,500.
 **Desc:** Directory of oil and gas companies in Canada.
 **Ind/Abst** F&S Index Plus Text, Int. [Select. Cov.].

CN/1181-8077
**CANADIAN OIL INDUSTRY MERGER AND ACQUISITION REPORT.** (CANADIAN OIL INDUSTRY MERGER AND ACQUISITION REPORT / SAYER SECURITIES.). [Can. oil ind. merger acquis. rep.]. **Added/Corp** Sayer Securities. (1990)-. Periodical. English. qt. $800.00. Sayer Securities Limited, Suite 500, 665 Eighth Street Southwest, Calgary Alberta T2P 3K7 Canada. **Tel** (403)266-6133. **DD** 338.2/7282/0971.

CN/0068-9394
**CANADIAN OIL REGISTER.** [Can. oil regist.]. **VFOAT** Nickle's Canadian Oil Register. (1962)-. Periodical. English. an (September). 138.00Can$ Alberta (Canada); 140.00Can$ all other Canada; 141.00Can$ US; 160.00Can$ other. Canadian Oil Register, 300 999-8th Street Southwest, Calgary Alberta T2R 1N7 Canada. **Tel** (403)244-6111, **FAX** (403)245-8666. **ED** Barbara Kerry. **LC** TN867; .C3. **DD** Q38.2/7/2802571. **Ad Acc. Circ:** 4,500 (ctrl). **Continues** Canadian Oil and Gas Directory, 0315-4866.
 **Desc:** Directory of comprehensive information on companies in Canada's oil and gas and related industries.

CN/0838-0961
**CANADIAN PETROLEUM TAX JOURNAL.** [Can. pet. tax j.]. **Added/Corp** Canadian Petroleum Tax Society. Vol. 1, No. 1 (Spring 1988)-. Periodical. English. sa. 35.00Can$. Canadian Petroleum Tax Society, PO Box 2562, Station M, Calgary Alberta T2P 3K8 Canada. **Tel** (403)268-3083. **DD** 343.7105/58228/0971.
 **Ind/Abst** Can. Legal Lit.

US
**CASE HISTORIES OF OIL AND GAS FIELDS IN ASIA AND THE FAR EAST.**
**Main/Corp** United Nations. Economic Commission for Asia and the Far East. 1st Ser. (1963)-. English. United Nations Economic Commission for Asia & the Far East, New York NY 10017. **Tel** (212)754-8302. **LC** JX1977; .A2 subser. **DD** 300/.8 S; 622/.33/8095.

UK
**CATALOGUE : BRITISH SUPPLIERS TO THE OIL, GAS, PETROCHEMICAL, AND PROCESS INDUSTRIES / ENERGY INDUSTRIES COUNCIL. Main/Corp** Energy Industries Council (Great Britain). 1982-. English. be. Energy Industries Council, 178-202 Great Portland Street, London W1N 6 England. **LC** HD9571.3; .C12A. **DD** 381/.456817665/029441. **Continues** CBMPE; CBMPE Catalogue.

FR
**CEDIGAZ NEWS REPORT.** English and French. Cedigaz, 1 4 Ave de Bois Preau, 92506 Rueil Malmaison France.

US
**CENTRAL AMERICA AND CARIBBEAN: BASIC OIL LAWS AND CONCESSION CONTRACTS. ORIGINAL TEXTS. SUPPLEMENT. Added/Corp** Petroleum Legislation, New York. No. 1 (1964)-. Periodical. English. $6350.00. Barrows Company Inc., 116 East 66th Street, New York NY 10021. **Tel** (212)772-1199, (800)227-7697, **FAX** (212)288-7242, telex 4971238 BARROWS.

CN
**CGA DOMESTIC DEMAND FORECAST.** See Public Administration-Public Utilities.

US/0009-2355
**CHEMICAL AND PETROLEUM ENGINEERING. See** Engineering-Chemical Engineering.

US/0191-4170
**CHEMICAL REVIEW. See** Chemistry-Chemical Technology.

US/0009-3092
**CHEMISTRY AND TECHNOLOGY OF FUELS AND OILS. See** Chemistry.

US/0577-6406
**CHEMSPHERE. See** Chemistry-Chemical Technology.

US/0748-6367
**CHEVRON FOCUS.** Ceased. [Chevron focus]. **Added/Corp** Chevron Corporation. Vol. 46, No. 5 (Aug. 1984)-(1992). Periodical. English. bm. Chevron Corporation, Publication Office, 225 Bush Street/Room 1100, San Francisco CA 94104-4289. **Tel** (415)894-2574. **LC** TN860; .S67. **DD** 338. **Continues** Standard Oiler, 0738-2847.

US/0148-3102
**CHEVRON WORLD.** Ceased. [Chevron world]. Vol. 54 (Winter 1977)-(1993). Periodical. English. qt. Chevron Corporation, Publication Office, 225 Bush Street/Room 1100, San Francisco CA 94104-4289. **Tel** (415)894-2574. **ED** Rae Leaper. **LC** HD9569.S82; C2. **DD** 338.7/66/5509794. Index available. cum. index. **Bk Rev. Ad Acc. Circ:** 300,000 (ctrl). **Continues** Bulletin (Standard Oil Company of California).
 **Desc:** Covers domestic and world-wide company operations from exploration, refining, research, transportation, and marketing. Basically, a stockholder and employee's publication.
 **Ind/Abst** Coal Abstr.; Energy Res. Abstr. (Oct. 1978-); Fluid Abstr., Civil Eng.; Fluid Abstr. Proc. Eng.; FLUIDEX; Index Free Period.; INIS Atomindex [Micro.].

UK
**CHINA OIL AND GAS REPORT.** (19??)-. Periodical. English. mo. $495.00. IBC Publishing, 57-61 Mortimer St., London W1N 7TD England. **Tel** 011 44 71 637 4383, **FAX** 011 44 71 636 6314.

HK
**CHUNG-KUO SHIH YU. VFOAT** China Oil; Zhongguo Shiyou; Zhong Guo Shi You. (198?)-. Periodical. English (English). qt. Wen Wei Enterprises Ltd, Vicwood Blding, 19th Floor, Glouceste Wanchai Hong Kong. **Tel** 5738391. **LC** TN876.C5; C516. **DD** 622/.3802/0951.

US
**CIRCULAR - WEST VIRGINIA GEOLOGICAL AND ECONOMIC SURVEY. See** Earth Sciences-Geology.

US/1059-2202
**CLEAN FUEL VEHICLE WEEK.** [Clean fuel veh. week]. (July 5 1991)-. Periodical. English. wk. $395.00. Frank Kester Associates, 1709 Avenue Salvador, San Clemente CA 92672. **Tel** (714)492-1340, **FAX** (714)492-6556. **DD** 363.

US/1051-3116
**CLEAN FUELS REPORT, THE.** [Clean fuels rep.]. **Added/Corp** J.E. Sinor Consultants, Inc. (Sept. 1989)-. Periodical. English. qt. $385.00. J. E. Sinor Consultants, PO Box 649, Niwot CO 80544. **Tel** (303)652-2632, **FAX** (303)652-2772. **LC** TP343; .C623. **DD** 333.79/68.

FR
**CNRS PETROLE ET GAZ.** Ceased. (19??)-(Dec. 1992). French. ir. CNRS / Institut d'Information Scientifique et Technique, (Centre National de la Recherche Scientifique), 15 Quai Anatole France, Paris 75700 France. **Tel** 011 33 1 47531515, telex 299 356 F.

FR
**CNRS PETROLE ET GAZ. INDEX CUMULATIF.** French. 250.15F France; 245.00F other. CNRS / Institut d'Information Scientifique et Technique, (Centre National de la Recherche Scientifique), 15 Quai Anatole France, Paris 75700 France. **Tel** 011 33 1 47531515, telex 299 356 F.

US/0045-723X
**COASTAL ZONE MANAGEMENT.** [Coast. zone manage.]. (Nov. 1970)-. Periodical. English. wk. $355.00. Nautilus Press, 1045 National Press Building, Washington DC 20045. **Tel** (202)347-6643. **ED** John R. Botzum. **DD** 333.91/7/0973. **Bk Rev.** Absorbed World Ecology Report and Environmental Monitor.
 **Desc:** Specializes in reporting federal-state relationships in the US exclusive economic zone, and the outer continental shelf, with special emphasis on offshore oil and gas development.

FR/0073-8360
**COLLECTION COLLOQUES ET SEMINAIRES. INSTITUT FRANCAIS DU PETROLE.** (COLLECTION COLLOQUES ET SEMINAIRES.). [Collect. colloq. semin., Inst. fr. pet.]. **Added/Corp** Institut Francais du Petrole. (1964)-. Monographic series. French. ir. Price varies per volume. Societe des Editions Technip, 27 rue Ginoux, 75737 Paris Cedex 15 France. **Tel** 011 33 1 45771108, telex 200 375 F EDITECP. **LC** TN860; .R68. **CODEN** IPTCBP. **[CCC]**.
 Documents available from CASDDS.
 **Ind/Abst** Chem. Abstr.

FR/0530-7678
**COLLECTION DES DICTIONNAIRES TECHNIQUES.** No. 1- 1963-. Periodical. French (English). ir. 704.00F France; $125.00 US. Societe des Editions Technip, 27 rue Ginoux, 75737 Paris Cedex 15 France. **Tel** 011 33 1 45771108, telex 200 375 F EDITECP.
 **Desc:** Includes the sum of vocabularies in geology, geochemistry, geophysics, drilling, production, well-logging, reservoir engineering, enhanced recovery, offshore technology, refining, petrochemistry, etc.

US
**COMMERCIAL GAS MARKET SURVEY.**
**Added/Corp** American Gas Association. (19??)-. English. ir. price varies per volume. American Gas Association / Virginia, 1515 Wilson Boulevard, Arlington VA 22209. **Tel** (703)841-8400, (703)841-8559, **FAX** (703)841-8697. **LC** HD9581.U49; C66. **DD** 381/.42285/0973.

GW/0341-6852
**COMPENDIUM - DEUTSCHE GESELLSCHAFT FUER MINERALOLWISSENSCHAFT UND KOHLECHEMIE E.V.** [Compend. Dtsch. Ges. Mineraloelwiss. Kohlechem.]. **Main/Corp** Deutsche Gesellschaft fur Mineralolwissenschaft und Kohlechemie. (19??)-. Academic Scholarly Publication. German (German). an. Industrieverlag Hernhaussen, Postfach 100252, Ernst Mey Strasse 8, D 70771 Leinfelden Germany. **Tel** 011 49 711 79080. **LC** TN863; .D48a. **CODEN** CDGKD6. Documents available from CASDDS.
 **Ind/Abst** Chem. Abstr. (1974/1975-1981); Coal Abstr.

US/1042-508X
**COMPOUNDINGS.** [Compoundings]. Periodical. English. mo. $45.00 (members); $800.00 (nonmembers). Independent Lubricant Manufacturers Association, 651 South Washington Street, Alexandria VA 22314. **Tel** (203)648-5574, **FAX** (703)836-8503. **ED** Alice E Green. **DD** 338. **Ad Acc. Circ:** 1,350.
 **Desc:** Tabloid carrying news for and about independent lubricant manufacturers, current affairs, company news and government news.

US
**COMPREHENSIVE INDEX OF PUBLICATIONS OF THE AMERICAN ASSOCIATION OF PETROLEUM GEOLOGISTS. Main/Corp** American Association of Petroleum Geologists. **VFOAT** AAPG Comprehensive Index. (1936)-. English. ir. Price varies per volume. American Association of Petroleum Geologists, PO Box 979, Tulsa OK 74101-0979. **Tel** (918)584-2555, **FAX** (918)584-0469, telex 49-9432. **LC** TN860; .A312. **DD** 553.2806273.
 **Desc:** Index of special publications and the AAPG bulletin.

US/0884-7045
**CONOCO.** [Conoco]. **Main/Corp** Continental Oil Company. **VAT** Continental Oil Company. V. 1-. Periodical. English. qt. Conoco, 1007 Market Street,

Wilmington DE 19898. **Tel** (302)594-3409. **LC** HD9569.C65; C66A. **DD** 665.
**Ind/Abst** Index Free Period.

US/8750-5568
**CPC EAST COAST REPORT, THE.** [CPC East Coast rep.]. **VAT** Computer Petroleum East Coast Report. Periodical. English. wk. CPC Publications, 6949 Valley Creek Road, St Paul MN 55125. **Tel** (612)738-1088. **ED** Douglas E Hartman.
**Desc:** Suppliers posted terminal prices at over 250 locations throughout the US customized for an individual company's needs.

US/8750-5584
**CPC PETRONEWS.** [CPC petronews]. **VAT** Computer Petroleum Corporation Petronews. Periodical. English. wk. CPC Publications, 6949 Valley Creek Road, St Paul MN 55125. **Tel** (612)738-1088. **ED** Douglas E Hartman.
**Desc:** Trends, forecasts of petroleum prices along with general information concerning news events in the petroleum industry.

FR
**CPDP BULLETIN MENSUEL. Main/Corp** Comite Professionel du Petrole. **Added/Corp** Comite Professionel du Petrole. Bulletin Mensuel. **VFOAT** Bulletin Mensuel. (19??)-. French. mo. 843.17F France; 1000.00F other. Comite Professionnel du Petrol CPDP, BP 282, 92505 Rueil Malmaison France. **Tel** 011 33 1 47169460. **LC** HD9572.1; .C62c. **DD** 338.2/728/05.
**Desc:** Statistical data on French and foreign petroleum industry.

US
**CRUDE OIL AND GAS NOMINATIONS.** English. mo. $28.00. Railroad Commission of Texas, PO Drawer 12967, Capitol Station, Austin TX 78711. **Tel** (512)463-7255.

US
**CRUDE OIL NOMINATIONS AND PURCHASES BY DISTRICT.** English. mo. $32.00. Railroad Commission of Texas, PO Drawer 12967, Capitol Station, Austin TX 78711. **Tel** (512)463-7255.

CN/0068-7103
**CRUDE PETROLEUM AND NATURAL GAS INDUSTRY.** (THE CRUDE PETROLEUM AND NATURAL GAS INDUSTRY / PREPARED IN THE MINING, METALLURGICAL AND CHEMICAL SECTION, INDUSTRY AND MERCHANDISING DIVISION, DOMINION BUREAU OF STATISTICS.). [Crude pet. nat. gas ind.]. **Added/Corp** Canada. Dominion Bureau of Statistics. Mining, Metallurgical & Chemical Section. Canada. Dominion Bureau of Statistics. Mineral Statistics Section. Canada. Dominion Bureau of Statistics. Industry Division. Canada. Dominion Bureau of Statistics. Energy and Minerals Section. Canada. Dominion Bureau of Statistics. Manufacturing and Primary Industries Division. Statistics Canada. Manufacturing and Primary Industries Division. Statistics Canada. Energy Section. Statistics Canada. Energy and Minerals Section. **VFOAT** Industrie du Petrole Brut et du Gaz Naturel. (1949)-. English (French). an. 28.00Can$ Canada; $34.00 US; $40.00 other. Statistics Canada, Publications Sales & Services, Main Building Room 1710, Ottawa Ontario K1A 0T6 Canada. **Tel** (613)951-5078, (800)267-6677, FAX (613)951-1584, telex 053-3585. **LC** HD9574.C2; A36. **DD** 338.2/728/0971. ***Formed by the union of*** *Crude Petroleum Industry* ***and*** *Natural Gas Industry (Ottawa, Ont.).*

CN/0702-6846
**CRUDE PETROLEUM AND NATURAL GAS PRODUCTION.** (CRUDE PETROLEUM AND NATURAL GAS PRODUCTION / PREPARED IN THE MINERAL STATISTICS SECTION, INDUSTRY AND MERCHANDISING DIVISION.). [Crude pet. nat. gas prod.]. **Added/Corp** Canada. Dominion Bureau of Statistics. Mineral Statistics Section. Canada. Dominion Bureau of Statistics. Industry and Merchandising Division. Canada. Dominion Bureau of Statistics. Industry Division. Canada. Dominion Bureau of Statistics. Manufacturing and Primary Industries Division. Statistics Canada. Manufacturing and Primary Industries Division. Statistics Canada. Industry Division. Statistics Canada. Energy Section. **VFOAT** Production de Petrole Brut et de Gaz Naturel. Vol. 10, No. 1 (Jan. 1958)-. English (French). mo. 110.00Can$ Canada; $132.00 US; $154.00 other. Statistics Canada, Publications Sales & Services, Main Building Room 1710, Ottawa Ontario K1A 0T6 Canada. **Tel** (613)951-5078, (800)267-6677, FAX (613)951-1584, telex 053-3585. **LC** HD9574.C2; A34. **DD** 338.2/728/0971021. ***Continues in part*** *Crude Petroleum, Natural Gas, and Manufactured Gas, 0702-6838.*
**Desc:** Estimates the production and disposition of crude petroleum and natural gas by province.

US
**CURRENT INDUSTRIAL REPORTS. MA-28C, INDUSTRIAL GASES / U.S. DEPARTMENT OF COMMERCE, BUREAU OF THE CENSUS. VFOAT** Industrial Gases. Began with 1978. Government Publication. English. an. $16.00. US Department of Commerce, 14th Street & Constitution Avenue NW, Washington DC 20230. **Tel** (202)482-2000, FAX (202)482-3772. **LC** HD9581.U49; C87. **DD** 338.4/7667/0973.
**Desc:** Presents timely data on the production, inventories, and orders of approximately 5,000 products, which represents 40 percent of all US manufacturing.

IO
**DAFTAR PERBANDINGAN KONTROLE PENGOLAHAN KELAPA SAWIT.**
**Main/Corp** Sumatra Planters Association. Research Institute. (19??)-. Indonesian. **LC** TP684.P3; S85a.

US
**DAILY GAS PRICE INDEX.** (19??)-. Periodical. English. da. $439.00. Intelligence Press, PO Box 70587, Washington DC 20024-0587. **Tel** (703)318-8848, FAX (703)318-0597.
**Desc:** Information and prices on the natural gas industry in the US and Canada.

US/0276-5934
**DAILY MUNGER OILOGRAM. Added/Corp** Munger Oil Information Service. **VFOAT** Munger Oilogram. (19??)-. Periodical. English. da (260 issues). $670.00. Munger Oil Information Service, 9800 South Sepulveda Boulevard, Suite 723, Los Angeles CA 90045. **Tel** (310)776-3990, FAX (312)645-9147.
**Desc:** Carries information on the majority of California wells actively engaged in the search for oil and gas, as well as details of new locations staked. Details of completions/abandonments and also map revisions and contract rig sheet are included.

UK
**DAILY OIL NEWS DIGEST.** English. da. £485.00. McCarthy Information Ltd, Manor House, Ash Walk, Warminst Wilts BA128PY England. **Tel** (44)985 215151, FAX (44)985-217479. **Circ:** 100.
**Desc:** A summary on a daily basis of what the leading UK press has published on energy matters.

US/8756-5439
**DATA BANKS.** (DATA BANKS / MIDDLE EAST ECONOMIC SERVICE.). [Data banks]. **Main/Corp** Wharton Econometric Forecasting Associates. Middle East Economic Service. **VFOAT** Middle East Economic Service Data Banks. English. WEFA / Philadelphia, PO Box 8500, Suite 1995, Philadelphia PA 19178. **Tel** (215)667-6000, telex 710 6700575. **LC** HD9560.1; .W47A. **DD** 338.2/7282/02854.

US
**DENVER OIL & GAS INDUSTRY SURVEY. VFOAT** Denver Oil and Gas Industry Survey. English. Mountain States Employers Council, 1790 Logan Street, PO Box 539, Denver CO 80201. **LC** HD4976.W38; D46. **DD** 331.2/822338/0978883021.

CN/0383-6762
**DETAILLANT, LE.** No. 1- 1976-. Periodical. French. Gulf Oil Canada, 800 Bay Street, Toronto Ontario M5S 1Y8 Canada. **DD** 338.7/66/550971. ***Continues*** *Nouvelles Gulf Canada, 0380-3465.*

UK
**DEVELOPMENT OF THE OIL AND GAS RESOURCES OF THE UNITED KINGDOM. Main/Corp** Great Britain. Dept. of Energy. (1973)-. English. an. £2.75. Department of Trade and Industry, Room 3 3 15 1 Palace Street, London SW1E 5HE England. **Tel** 011 44 71 238 3576, FAX 011 44 71 238 3121, telex 91877 EZEGY G. **(Subscription address:** Department of Energy Publications, PO Box 30, Alton Hunts GU34 4PX United Kingdom.**) LC** HD9571.1; .G74a. **DD** 333.8/2315/0941.

UK/0260-4248
**DEVELOPMENTS IN PETROLEUM GEOLOGY.** [Dev. pet. geol.]. 1 (1977)-. Academic Scholarly Publication. English. ir. $88.25. Elsevier Science Publishers Ltd, Crown House, Linton Road, Barking Essex IG11 8JU England. **Tel** 011 44 81 5947272, FAX 081-594-5942, telex 896950. **(Subscription address:** Elsevier Science Inc. / New York Books, 655 Avenue of the Americas, New York NY 10010.**) CODEN** DPEGDB. **[CCC].** Documents available from CASDDS.
**Ind/Abst** Chem. Abstr.

NE/0376-7361
**DEVELOPMENTS IN PETROLEUM SCIENCE.** [Dev. pet. sci.]. (1975)-. Academic Scholarly Publication. English. ir. Price varies per volume. Elsevier Science Publishers BV, PO Box 211, 1000 AE Amsterdam Netherlands. **Tel** 011 31 20 5803642, FAX 011 31 20 5862696, telex 15682. **(Subscription address:** Elsevier Science Inc. / New York Books, 655 Avenue of the Americas, New York NY 10010.**) CODEN** DPSCDZ. **[CCC]. Pr Rev.** Documents available from Article Express International, CASDDS.
**Ind/Abst** Bioeng. Abstr.; Chem. Abstr.; Ei Page One; Eng. Index Annu.; GeoRef.

UK
**DIRECTORS' REPORT AND ACCOUNTS / BRITISH GAS. Main/Corp** British Gas (Firm). (19??)-. English. **LC** HD9581.C74; B742. **DD** 338.7/66657/094105. ***Continues*** *British Gas (Firm). Annual Report and Accounts.*
**Desc:** Reports on the British gas industry.

CN/0229-1142
**DIRECTORY / CANADIAN GAS ASSOCIATION. See** Public Administration-Public Utilities.

US
**DIRECTORY / COUNCIL OF PETROLEUM ACCOUNTANTS SOCIETIES. See** Business-Accounting.

US
**DIRECTORY, INTERSTATE OIL AND GAS COMPACT COMMISSION AND STATE OIL & GAS AGENCIES. Main/Corp** Interstate Oil and Gas Compact Commission. **VFOAT** Directory. (199?)-. English. an. $5.00. Interstate Oil & Gas Compact Commission, PO Box 53127, Oklahoma City OK 73152-3127. **Tel** (405)525-3556, FAX (405)525-3592. **LC** TN867; .I5. ***Continues*** *Interstate Oil Compact Commission. Directory, 8755-5956.*

US/8755-5956
**DIRECTORY - INTERSTATE OIL COMPACT COMMISSION. *Title Change.*** (DIRECTORY / INTERSTATE OIL COMPACT COMMISSION AND STATE OIL AND GAS AGENCIES.). **Main/Corp** Interstate Oil Compact Commission. (19??)-(199?). English. an. Interstate Oil & Gas Compact Commission, PO Box 53127, Oklahoma City OK 73152-3127. **Tel** (405)525-3556, FAX (405)525-3592. **LC** TN867; .I5. **DD** 338.2/7282/02573. **Circ:** 2,500. ***Continues*** *Interstate Oil Compact Commission. Directory of the Interstate Oil Compact Commission and Oil and Gas Agencies.* ***Continued by*** *Interstate Oil and Gas Compact Commission. Directory, Interstate Oil and Gas Compact Commission and State Oil & Gas Agencies.*

US/0272-1309
**DIRECTORY OF CERTIFIED PETROLEUM GEOLOGISTS. See** Earth Sciences-Geology.

US/0360-9987
**DIRECTORY OF DIESEL FUEL STATIONS COAST TO COAST, A.** 1976-. Directory. English. $5.95. Diesel Fuel Services Inc, 330 East 33rd Street, New York NY 10016. **LC** TL153; .D54. **DD** 381/.45/629286.

US
**DIRECTORY OF LIMITED MEMBERS / COUNCIL OF PETROLEUM ACCOUNTANTS SOCIETIES. See** Business-Accounting.

CN/1193-1345
**DIRECTORY OF NATURAL GAS COMPANY OPERATIONS. *Title Change.* See** Public Administration-Public Utilities.

US/0889-597X
**DIRECTORY OF OIL REFINERIES. *Title Change.*** (DIRECTORY OF OIL REFINERIES : CONSTRUCTION, ENGINEERS, PETROCHEMICAL AND NATURAL GAS PROCESSING PLANTS.). [Dir. oil refin.]. **Added/Corp** Mideast Oil Register (Firm : US). Directory. English. an. Midwest Register Inc., 1345 East 15th Street, Tulsa OK 74120. **Tel** (800)829-2002, (918)582-2000. **LC** TN867; .D48. **DD** 665. ***Continued by*** *Refining, Construction, Petrochemical and Natural Gas Processing Plants, 1054-951X.*

NO/0800-2355
**DNC OIL NOW. VFOAT** Oil Now. Periodical. English. Free to banks, business men, journalists, civil servants and politicians. Den Norske Creditbank, PO Box 1171, Sentrum Oslo 1 Norway. **LC** HD9575.N6; D57. **DD** 338.2/7282/09481.

CN/0827-4290
**DOIG'S DIGEST.** [Doig's dig.]. **Added/Corp** Ian M. Doig & Associates. (June 1983)-. Periodical. English. mo. 360.00Can$. Doig's Digest, 130 Lake Erie Place SE, Calgary Alberta T2J 2L4 Canada. **Tel** (403)225-1105. **DD** 338.2/728/0971.

CN/0228-5630
**DRILLING ACTIVITY REPORT.** [Drill. act. rep.]. Sept. 1978-. Periodical. English. mo. 120.00Can$. Saskatchewan Energy and Mines, 1914 Hamilton, Regina Saskatchewan, S4P 4V4 Canada. **Tel** (306)787-7643, FAX (306)787-2527. **DD** 622/.338. ***Continues*** *Saskatchewan. Geodata Statistics and Research Branch. Weekly Drilling and Land Report, 0487-4013.*
**Desc:** Lists by production, disposition areas and classifications the well licenses issued, wells finished drilling, well completions, well abandonments, wells brought on production, plugback wells, well name changes, well licenses cancelled, well reclassifications and well amendments.

Petroleum and Natural Gas

US/0046-0702
**DRILLING CONTRACTOR.** (THE DRILLING CONTRACTOR.). [Drill. contract.]. **Added/Corp** International Association of Drilling Contractors. American Association of Oilwell Drilling Contractors. (1944)-. Periodical. English. bm. $30.00. International Association of Drilling Contractors, PO Box 4287, Houston TX 77084. **Tel** (713)578-7171. **ED** Alvaro Franco. **LC** TN860; .A273. **DD** 622.33805. **[CCC]. Ad Acc. Circ:** 18,500 (ctrl). Documents available from Petroleum Abstracts Document Delivery Service.
**Desc:** Covers the drilling and production industry.
**Ind/Abst** Pet. Abstr.

UK/0955-7369
**DRILLING NEWS.** English. mo. £170.00 UK; $330.00 US; £180.00 other. STI, 4 Kings Meadow, Ferry Hinksey Road, Oxford OX2 0DU United Kingdom. **Tel** (0865) 798898, FAX (0865) 798788. **(Subscription address:** STI, The Distribution Centre, Blackhorse Road, Letchworth SG6 1HN United Kingdom**) ED** John Howes. **[CCC]. Bk Rev. Circ:** 200.

UK
**DRILLING WEEKLY.** (19??)-. English. wk. £595.00. EIS / Energy Information Services, Seloduct House, 30 Station Road, Redhill Surrey RH1 1PD United Kingdom. **Tel** 737 772599. Index available. ctrl circ.

GW/0724-7605
**DVGW-NACHRICHTEN. VFOAT** Deutscher Verein des Gas- und Wasserfaches-Nachrichten. (1983)-. Periodical. German. ir (3-4 issues). Free on request. Deutscher Verein Gas Wasserfch, Hauptstrasse 71 79, W 6236 Eschborn FR Germany. **Tel** 011 49 6196 70170. **UDC** 662.95 :338.46.

●US/1067-1013
**E&P HEALTH, SAFETY AND ENVIRONMENT.** (E&P HEALTH, SAFETY AND ENVIRONMENT / PETROLEUM ABSTRACTS, THE UNIVERSITY OF TULSA.). [E&P heal. saf. environ.]. **Added/Corp** Petroleum Abstracts (Organization). **VFOAT** E & P Health, Safety and Environment; E and P Health, Safety and Environment; Health, Safety and Environment. Vol. 1, No. 1 (Jan. 1993)-. English. mo. $175.00 (general subscribers), $195.00 (nonsubscribers). Petroleum Abstracts, University of Tulsa, Information Services Division, 600 South College Avenue, Harwell Hall 101, Tulsa OK 74104-3189. **Tel** (800)247-8678, (918)631-2297, FAX (918)599-9361, telex 49 7543. **DD** 363.
**Desc:** Provides in-depth, published coverage of information about the environment, health and safety, including pollution response, control and recovery technology. Coverage includes worldwide literature and patents related to the exploration, production and transportation of petroleum.

CN/0823-1788
**EAST COAST OFFSHORE.** [East coast offshore]. **VFOAT** Offshore. Periodical. English. ir (seven times a year). $2.00 per no. East Coast Offshore, c/o Anchor Films Ltd, PO Box 9433, St John's Newfoundland A1A 2Y3 Canada. **DD** 38.2/7282/09715. ***Continues*** *Newfoundland Offshore, 0822-6121.*

UK
**EAST EUROPEAN INDUSTRIAL MONITORING SERVICE. OIL AND GAS.** English. mo. £500.00; $850.00 US (per monitor). Business International Ltd, 40 Duke Street, Sales Dept, Helena C, London W1A 1DW England. **Tel** 011 44 71 493 6711.
**Desc:** A monthly monitoring service providing detailed information and data on business and trade developments in 19 chemical and industrial sectors in Eastern Europe and Russia. Sectors covered include: agrochemicals; automotives; basic and general chemicals; beverages; chemical fibre; computers; construction; food; general chemical trends; health service and equipment; mining; oil and gas; petrochemicals; pharmaceuticals; plastics and rubber; telecommunications; textiles and clothing; tobacco; and wood, pulp and paper.

UK
**EASTERN BLOC CHEMICALS. *Ceased.* See** Chemistry.

CN/0710-5142
**EASTERN OFFSHORE NEWS.** (EASTERN OFFSHORE NEWS / EPOA, EASTCOAST PETROLEUM OPERATORS' ASSOCIATION.). [East. offshore news]. Vol. 1, No. 1 (Feb. 1979)-. Periodical. English. qt. Free. Canadian Petroleum Association, 1809 Barrington Street, Halifax Nova Scotia B3J 3K8 Canada. **Tel** (902)421-1159. **DD** 338.2/7282/09715.
**Ind/Abst** GeoRef.

US
**ECONOMIC ANALYSIS.** Monographic series. English. ir. Price varies per volume. American Gas Association / Virginia, 1515 Wilson Boulevard, Arlington VA 22209. **Tel** (703)841-8400, (703)841-8559, FAX (703)841-8697. **LC** HD9581.U49; E25. **DD** 338.2/3.

US/0277-7851
**ENERGY FROM BIOMASS AND WASTES.** [Energy biomass wastes]. **Added/Corp** Institute of Gas Technology. **VFOAT** Energy from Biomass & Wastes. 3 (1978)-. Academic Scholarly Publication. English. ir. $100.00. Institute of Gas Technology, 3424 South State Street, Chicago IL 60616. **Tel** (312)949-3970, (312)949-3650, FAX (312)949-3776, telex 25-6189. **ED** D.L. Klass. **LC** TP360; .C56. **DD** 662/.8. **CODEN** EBWADU. Documents available from Article Express International, CASDDS. ***Continues*** *Clean Fuels from Biomass and Wastes, 0743-7374.*
**Desc:** Proceedings of the symposium on energy from biomass and wastes. Concerned with the production of fuel gases from sewage, garbage, and other biological material.
**Ind/Abst** Bioeng. Abstr.; Chem. Abstr.; Ei Page One; Eng. Index Annu.; Gas Abstr. (?-?).

US/0889-5260
**ENERGY STATISTICS SOURCEBOOK. See** Energy-Abstracting, Bibliographies and Statistics.

JA
**ENERUGI TOKEI GEPPO. Main/Corp** Japan. Tsusho Sangyosho. Chosa Tokeibu. **VFOAT** Tsusho Sangyosho Enerugi Tokei Geppo. (19??)-. Japanese. Tsusho Sangyo Chosakai, (Research Institute on International Trade and Industry), Kobikikan Ginza Biru, 8-9 Ginza 2 chome Chuoku, Tokyoto 104 Japan. **LC** HD9502.J3; J35a.

US/0160-337X
**ENHANCED OIL-RECOVERY FIELD REPORTS. *Ceased.*** [Enhanc. oil-recover. field rep.]. Vol. 3, No. 2 (1977)-(19??). Periodical. English. sa. Mennonite Economic Developmebt Association, 280 Smith Street, Suite 302, Winnipeg Manitoba R3C 1K2 Canada. **Tel** (204)944-1995. Documents available from Petroleum Abstracts Document Delivery Service. ***Continues*** *Improved Oil-Recovery Field Reports, 0147-7897.*
**Ind/Abst** Energy Res. Abstr. (July 1978-); Pet. Abstr. (?-?).

IT
**ENI GROUP IN ..., THE. Main/Corp** Ente Nazionale Idrocarburi. English. an. Ente Nazionale Idrocarburi, Piazzale Enrico Mattei 1, 00144 Rome Italy. **LC** PAR. ***Continues*** *Annual Reports and Financial Statements at December 31 ... .*

US/0748-1527
**ENVIRONMENTAL ASSESSMENT OF THE ALASKAN CONTINENTAL SHELF. ANNUAL REPORTS OF PRINCIPAL INVESTIGATORS FOR THE YEAR ENDING ... . See** Environmental Issues.

US
**ENVIRONMENTAL DEVELOPMENT PLAN (EDP). ENHANCED GAS RECOVERY. Main/Corp** United States. Dept. of Energy. Office of Energy Technology. **VFOAT** Enhanced Gas Recovery. 1977-. English. an. US Department of Energy Office of Energy Technology, 1000 Independence Avenue SW, Washington DC 20585.

CN
**ERCB ST. Added/Corp** Alberta. Energy Resources Conservation Board. **VFOAT** E.R.C.B. S.T.; Reserve Report Series E.R.C.B.; Reserve Report Series ERCB. (198?)-. Monographic series. English. ir. Price varies per volume. Energy Resources Conservation Board, 640 Fifth Avenue Southwest, Calgary Alberta T2P 3G4 Canada. **Tel** (403)297-8311, (403)297-8190, telex 03-821717. **LC** TN873.C22; A442. **DD** 553.2/8/097123. ***Continues*** *ERCB (Series), 0701-8711.*

GW/0014-0058
**ERDOL & KOHLE, ERDGAS, PETROCHEMIE.** [Erdol, Kohle, Erdgas, Petrochem.]. **Added/Corp** Deutsche Gesellschaft fuer Mineralolwissenschaft und Kohlechemie. **VFOAT** Erdol und Kohle, Erdgas, Petrochemie. **VAT** Erdol und Kohle, Erdgas, Petrochemie. Vol. 13, Issue 8 (Aug. 1960)-. Academic Scholarly Publication. German (English). mo. $264.00. VCH Gesellschaft GmbH, Postfach 101161, D 69451 Weinheim Germany. **Tel** 011 49 6201 606459, FAX 011 49 6201 606184. **(Subscription address:** VCH Publishers Inc., 303 Northwest 12th Avenue, Journals Department, Deerfield FL 33442.**) CODEN** EKEPAB. **[CCC]. Pr Rev.** available on an online database (file 648/Full-Text) from DIALOG. Documents available from The Genuine Article, Petroleum Abstracts Document Delivery Service, CASDDS. ***Continues*** *Erdol und Kohle, 0367-1305;* ***Absorbed*** *Brennstoff-Chemie.*
**Ind/Abst** Chem Inform; Chem. Abstr.; Chem. Hazards Ind.; Chem. Ind. Notes; Chem. Titles; Coal Abstr.; Curr. Contents Eng. Tech. Appl. Sci.; Ei Page One; EMBASE; Energy Res. Abstr.; Fluid Abstr., Civil Eng.; Fluid Abstr. Proc. Eng.; FLUIDEX (1973-); Gas Abstr.; GeoRef; Infomat Int. Bus.; Lab. Hazards Bull.; Lit. Pat. Abstr., Oilfield Chem. (1954-); Lit. Abstr., Catal. Catal.; Lit. Abstr., Health Environ.; Lit. Abstr., Pet. Refin. Petrochem.; Lit. Abstr., Pet. Substit.; Lit. Abstr., Transp. Storage; Life Sci. Collect.; Pet. Abstr.; Pollut. Abstr. Indexes; Proc. Chem. Eng.; Res. Alert [Full Cov.]; Saf. Health Work; Sci. Cit. Index; SCISEARCH; Soc. Sci. Cit. Index [Select. Cov.]; Theoret. Chem. Eng.

GW/0179-3187
**ERDOL, ERDGAS, KOHLE.** [Erdol Erdgas Kohle]. **Added/Corp** Deutsche Gesellschaft fur Mineralowissenschaft und Kohlechemie. Deutsche Vereinigung der Erdolgeologen und Erdolingenieure. Osterreichische Gesellschaft fuer Erdolwissenschaften. Vol. 102, No. 1 (Jan. 1986)-. Academic Scholarly Publication. German (summaries and/or abstracts in English). mo. DM374.00 Germany; DM342.00 other. Urban Verlag Hamburg Wien GmbH, Neumann Reichardt STR 34, D 22041 Hamburg Germany. **Tel** 011 49 40 6567071. **ED** Thomas Vieth and Hans Jorg Mager. **LC** TN860; .E68. **DD** 665.5. **CODEN** EEKOEY. **[CCC].** Index available. **Bk Rev. Ad Acc. Circ:** 4,000 (ctrl). Documents available from Article Express International, Petroleum Abstracts Document Delivery Service, CASDDS, Documents on Demand. ***Continues*** *Erdoel, Erdgas (Hamburg, Germany : 1983), 0724-8555.*
**Desc:** Leading technical-scientific engineering periodical in the field of oil and gas: exploration, drilling and production engineering onshore and offshore, treatment, manufacturing/processing, storage, transportation, utilization, gas technology; gasification and liquefaction of coal, petrochemicals.
**Ind/Abst** Bioeng. Abstr. (1986-); Chem. Abstr. (1986-); Coal Abstr. (1986-); Ei Page One (1986-); Energy Inf. Abstr. (1986-); Energy Res. Abstr. (1986-); Eng. Index Annu.; Environ. Abstr. (1986-); Environ. Eng. Abstr.; Gas Abstr.; GeoRef (1986-); Lit. Pat. Abstr., Oilfield Chem. (1978-); Lit. Abstr., Catal. Catal.; Lit. Abstr., Health Environ.; Lit. Abstr., Pet. Refin. Petrochem.; Lit. Abstr., Pet. Substit.; Lit. Abstr., Transp. Storage; Mater. Sci. Eng. Abstr.; Mech. Eng. Abstr.; Pet. Abstr.

GW/0343-6705
**ERDOL-INFORMATIONSDIENST. See** Business.

US/1055-5781
**ERNST & YOUNG'S OIL AND GAS FEDERAL INCOME TAXATION.** [Ernst Young's oil gas fed. income tax.]. **Added/Corp** Ernst & Young. Commerce Clearing House. **VFOAT** Oil and Gas Federal Income Taxation; Ernst and Young's Oil and Gas Federal Income Taxation. (1990)-. English. an (March). $75.00. Commerce Clearing House Inc., 4025 West Peterson Avenue, Chicago IL 60646-6085. **Tel** (312)583-8500, FAX (708)940-4600. **LC** KF6482; .O37. **DD** 343.7305/582282/05; 347.303558228205. Index available. available in Loose-leaf. ***Continues*** *Arthur Young's Oil and Gas Federal Income Taxation, 1055-6303.*
**Desc:** Thorough analysis of the latest pertinent laws, rulings, decisions and regulations on oil and gas taxation, including legislative developments.

UK/0014-1011
**ESSO MAGAZINE.** [Esso mag.]. **Added/Corp** Esso Petroleum Company, Ltd. (1971)-. Periodical. English. qt. **LC** TN860; .E87. **CODEN** ESMAAS. Documents available from UMI Article Clearinghouse.
**Ind/Abst** ABI Inform Ondisc (Fall 1977-Summer 1981); Alum. Ind. Abstr.; Coal Abstr.; Curr. Technol. Index; Met. Abstr.; World Surf. Coat. Abstr.; World Text. Abstr.

CN/0823-7751
**ESSO NORTH.** [Esso North]. **Added/Corp** Esso Resources Canada. Vol. 1, No. 1 (Winter 1982)-. Periodical. English. qt. free. Outcrop Northern Publishers, PO Box 1350, Yellowknife Nortwest Territory, X1A 2N9 Canada. **Tel** (403)920-4652 or, 873-6152. **ED** Ted Bower. **DD** 338.2/728/0607193. **Circ:** 3,200.
**Desc:** A company published periodical for employees and annuitants.

US
**ESTIMATED OIL AND GAS RESERVES, SOUTHERN CALIFORNIA OUTER CONTINENTAL SHELF / UNITED STATES DEPARTMENT OF THE INTERIOR, GEOLOGICAL SURVEY.** Began with Jan. 1, 1977. English. an. US Department of the Interior / Geological Survey, Reston, VA, Reston VA 22092.

GW/0720-6240
**ET. ENERGIEWIRTSCHAFTLICHE TAGESFRAGEN. See** Energy.

NO/0802-9474
**EUROIL. VAT** European Oil. Vol. 1, Iss. 1 (Apr. 1990)-. Periodical. English. mo. Kr65.00 Scandinavia; Kr88.00 Europe; $210.00 other. Noroil Publishing House Ltd. A S, 12 50 Kingsgate Road, Suite F-1, Surrey KT2 5AA England. **Tel** 011 44 81 5472411, FAX 011 44 81 5472157. **(Subscription address:** Richard Fry and Associates, Surrey House, 34 Eden Street, Suite 225, Kingston Thames Surrey KT1 1ER England**) LC** HD9560.1; .E9. **DD** 338.2/728/09405. **CODEN** EUJOE5. **[CCC]. Bk Rev. Ad Acc. Circ:** 13,000. ***Formed by the union of*** *Noroil, 0332-544X* ***and*** *Petrole Informations (Paris, France : 1985), 0755-561X.*
**Desc:** Covers exploration, engineering, new technology,

construction, field development, latest news and politics. This is the top selling European offshore oil and gas magazine.
**Ind/Abst** Corros. Abstr. (199?-); Energy Inf. Abstr.; F&S Index Plus Text, Int. [Select. Cov.]; Fluid Abstr., Civil Eng.; Fluid Abstr. Proc. Eng.; FLUIDEX (199?-); Infomat Int. Bus.; PROMT.

US/0093-5018
**EUROPE : BASIC OIL LAWS AND CONCESSION CONTRACTS. ORIGINAL TEXTS. SUPPLELMENT.** **See** Law.

GW/0014-2824
**EUROPE OIL-TELEGRAM.** (1963)-. Periodical. German. sw (104 issues per year). DM1145.00. Oil Telegram GmbH & Co, Carl Petersen Str 70-76, D-20535 Hamburg Germany. **Tel** 011 49 40 251113, 251114. **UDC** 662.753:339.166.

UK
**EUROPEAN CONTINENTAL SHELF GUIDE.** English. be. £125.00. Oilfield Publications Ltd., PO Box 11, Ledbury Hereford HR8 1BN England.

UK
**EUROPEAN OFFSHORE OIL & GAS.** **Added/Corp** Institution of Civil Engineers (Great Britain). **VFOAT** European Offshore Oil and Gas; European Offshore Oil and Gas Yearbook and Directory. (1985)-. English. an. Thomas Telford Ltd, Thomas Telford House, 1 Heron Quay, London E14 9XF England. **Tel** 011 44 71 987 6999, FAX 011 44 71 538 4101, telex 298105. ***Continues** UK Offshore Oil and Gas Directory.*

NO/0332-5210
**EUROPEAN OFFSHORE PETROLEUM NEWSLETTER.** [Eur. offshore pet. newsl.]. (1976)-. Newsletter. English. wk (except Christmas). $895.00. Hart Europe, Ltd., Rosemount House, Rosemount Avenue, W Byfleet Surrey K614 6NP England. **Tel** 011 44 932 344424. **ED** Dan Rigden. **DD** 665.5. **[CCC]. Bk Rev.**
**Desc:** All aspects of petroleum gas exploration and offshore drilling.

US/0275-3871
**EUROPEAN PETROLEUM DIRECTORY.** [Eur. petrol. dir.]. (1980)-. Directory. English. an. $142.50 US and Canada; $189.50 other. PennWell Publishing Company, 1421 South Sheridan, PO Box 1260, Tulsa OK 74101. **Tel** (918)835-3161, (800)331-4463, FAX (918)831-9497. **(Subscription address:** PennWell Books, PO Box 21288, Tulsa OK 74121.**) ED** Jonelle Moore. **LC** HD9575.A12; E88. **DD** 338.2/7282/0254. **[CCC].** Index available. **Ad Acc. Circ:** 2,000. ***Continues in part** Eastern Hemisphere Petroleum Directory, 0070-8224.*
**Desc:** Lists all countries in all phases of oil industry operating in Europe. Listings organized by country with company index.

FR
**EUROPEAN REFINERY REPORT.** English. mo. $2375.00. ICIS Lor Group Ltd., 3730 Kirby Drive, Suite 850, Houston TX 77098. **Tel** (713)527-8653, (800)628-0860.

US
**EXECUTIVE GAS INDUSTRY STATISTICS.** Periodical. English. mo. American Gas Association / Virginia, 1515 Wilson Boulevard, Arlington VA 22209. **Tel** (703)841-8400, (703)841-8559, FAX (703)841-8697.

US/0537-9741
**EXPLORATION AND ECONOMICS OF THE PETROLEUM INDUSTRY.** [Explor. econ. pet. ind.]. **Main/Conf** Institute on Petroleum Exploration and Economics. **Added/Corp** International Oil and Gas Educational Center (Southwestern Legal Foundation). **VFOAT** Exploration & Economics of the Petroleum Industry. Vol. 10 (1972)-. Periodical. English. an. Matthew Bender & Company Inc., 1275 Broadway, Albany NY 12204. **Tel** (800)833-9844, (518)487-3000. **LC** HD9561; .I6. **DD** 338.2/7282/0973. **CODEN** EEPIA3. ***Continues** Exploration and Economics of the Petroleum Industry.*
**Ind/Abst** Coal Abstr.; GeoRef.

CN/0833-0034
**EXPLORATION, DEVELOPMENT AND CAPITAL EXPENDITURES FOR MINING AND PETROLEUM AND NATURAL GAS WELLS, INTENTIONS.** (EXPLORATION, DEVELOPMENT AND CAPITAL EXPENDITURES FOR MINING AND PETROLEUM AND NATURAL GAS WELLS, INTENTIONS / STATISTICS CANADA, SCIENCE, TECHNOLOGY AND CAPITAL STOCK DIVISION.). [Explor. dev. cap. expend. min. pet. nat. gas wells intent.]. **Added/Corp** Statistics Canada. Science, Technology and Capital Stock Division. Statistics Canada. Investment and Capital Stock Division. **VFOAT** Depenses d'Exploration, de Developpement et d'Immobilisations pour les Mines et les Puits de Petrole et de Gaz Naturel, Perspective. (1987)-. English (French). an. 17.00Can$. Statistics Canada, Publications Sales & Services, Main Building Room 1710, Ottawa Ontario K1A 0T6 Canada. **Tel** (613)951-5078, (800)267-6677, FAX (613)951-1584, telex 053-3585. **LC** HD9506.C2; E94. **DD** 338.2/3/0971/021. ***Continues** Investment Statistics, Exploration, Development, Capital and Repair Expenditures by Mining and Exploration Companies.*
**Desc:** This publication presents data on expenditures for exploration and development and capital expenditures for metal and non-metal mines by province and by industry group.

UK/0960-9989
**EXPLORATION INTERNATIONAL NEWS.** [Explor. int. news]. (1990)-. Periodical. English. Twelve times a year. £175.00 UK; £185.00 other Europe; £195.00 other. Robin Thompson Associates, Choice Hill, Lodge over Norton, Oxon OX7 5PR England. **Tel** 011 44 608 642413, FAX 011 44 608 644002. **ED** Robin Thompson. **DD** 338.2728. **Bk Rev. Ad Acc. Circ:** 150 (ctrl).
**Desc:** Newsletter covering oil and gas exploration worldwide.

NO/0800-7683
**FACT SHEET (NORWAY. OLJE OG ENERGIDEPARTEMENTET).** (FACT SHEET.). English. sa. Royal Ministry of Petroleum and Energy, Oslo Norway. **LC** TN874.N8; F83. **DD** 338.2/7282/09481.

AG
**FAROL.** **Added/Corp** Standard Oil Company. (1947)-. Spanish. **LC** AP63; . .F23. ***Continues** Revista Esso.*
**Ind/Abst** Am. Hist. Life (1959-1975).

US
**FEDERAL POWER COMMISSION NEWS RELEASE. MONTHLY FUEL COST AND QUALITY INFORMATION, FPC ISSUES REPORT ON FUEL COST.** **Main/Corp** United States. Federal Power Commission. **VFOAT** Monthly Fuel Cost and Quality Information, FPC Issues Report on Fuel Cost. (1974)-. Periodical. English. mo. Federal Power Commission, Office of Public Information, Washington DC 20426. ***Continues** Staff Report on Monthly Report of Cost and Quality of Fuels for Steam-Electric Plants.*

US
**FEDERAL TAXATION OF OIL AND GAS TRANSACTIONS.** **See** Public Administration-Public Finance and Taxation.

US
**FERC DATA ON CD-ROM.** **See** Energy.

UK/0141-3228
**FINANCIAL TIMES OIL AND GAS INTERNATIONAL YEAR BOOK.** **VFOAT** Oil and Gas. (1983)-. English. an. $238.00. Longman Group Ltd., Fourth Avenue, Longman House, Harlow Essex CM19 5SR England. **Tel** 011 44 279 429655, FAX 011 44 279 431059, telex 81259. **(Subscription address:** US & Canada: Gale Research Inc., 835 Penobscot Building, Detroit, MI 48226**) LC** HG4821; .O4. **DD** 338.7/622338/025. **[CCC]. *Continues** Oil and Gas International Year Book.*
**Desc:** Provides descriptive detail and production and financial information on 793 major oil and gas companies.

UK/0141-3236
**FINANCIAL TIMES WHO'S WHO IN WORLD OIL AND GAS.** **See** Economics-Industry and Production.

CN/0705-1751
**FLAMBEE, LA.** **Added/Corp** Association des Marchands d'Huile a Chauffage du Quebec. Vol. 3, No. 4 (May/June 1965)-. Periodical. French. bm. Free. Association des Marchands d'Huile a Chauffage du Quebec, 294 Boulevard Desmarchais, Montreal Quebec H4H 1S4 Canada. **DD** 338.4/7/665538409714. ctrl circ. ***Continues** Association des Marchands d'Huile a Chauffage du Quebec. Bulletin, 0705-1743.*

UK
**FORECOURT RETAILING.** **VFOAT** Business Review. (1989)-. English. an. Nexus Business Communications, Warwick House, Azalea Drive, c/o Dr. Swanle, Kent BR8 8HY England. **Tel** 011 44 322 660070.

SZ/0253-0279
**FOREIGN SCOUTING SERVICE. LATIN AMERICA.** [Foreign scout. serv., Lat. Am.]. **Added/Corp** Petroconsultants S.A. **VFOAT** Latin America. (19??)-. English. mo. Petroconsultants SA, PO Box 152, 24 Chemin de la Mairie, 1258 Perly-Geneva, Switzerland. **Tel** (41-22)721 1717, FAX (41-22)721 1919, telex 413 541 PETR CH. ctrl circ.
**Desc:** Reports on petroleum activities (upstream sector) for all countries of the world. Reports on law, taxation, and economics of petroleum production.

US/0749-7377
**FOSTER BULLETIN ON DEREGULATED GAS.** ***Ceased.*** (FOSTER BULLETIN ON DEREGULATED GAS / FA.). **Added/Corp** Foster Associates (Washington, D.C.). (19??)-(Oct. 1993). Bulletin. English. bm. Foster Associates Inc., 1015 15th Street Northwest, Suite 1100, Washington DC 20005-2697. **Tel** (202)408-7710, FAX (202)408-7723. **ED** William G Foster. **LC** HD9581.U49; F67. **DD** 338.2/3. **[CCC]. Circ:** 100.
**Desc:** Carries publicly available information on prices for decontrolled natural gas supplies by pipline and producing area.

US/0095-1587
**FOSTER NATURAL GAS REPORT FROM WASHINGTON.** **Main/Corp** Foster Associates (Washington, D.C.). (19??)-. Periodical. English. Fifty-two times a year. $1065.00 US; $1140.00 Europe; $1160.00 Japan. Foster Associates Inc., 1015 15th Street Northwest, Suite 1100, Washington DC 20005-2697. **Tel** (202)408-7710, FAX (202)408-7723. **LC** KF1870.A15; F66. **DD** 338.2/7/28505. **[CCC].** Index available (quarterly cumulative index included with subscription). cum. index. ***Continues** Foster Associates (Washington, D.C.). Report from Washington to Producers of Natural Gas.*
**Ind/Abst** NEXIS (1981-).

UK
**FT GUIDE TO NORTH SEA OPERATORS.** English. ir. £295.00. Financial Times England, 8 16 Great New Street, London EC4A 3BN England. **Tel** 011 44 71 353 0305, 353 1040, FAX 011 44 353 0846.
**Desc:** Report providing details on all North Sea operators, all fields in production, fields under development and under appraisal, sulphur content and production levels, data on platform drilling, subsea systems and pipelines.

US
**FUEL ECONOMY NEWS : THE NEWSLETTER OF THE VOLUNTARY TRUCK AND BUS FUEL ECONOMY PROGRAM.** Newsletter. English. qt. Voluntary Truck and Bus Fuel Economy Program, US Department of Energy, Washington DC 20461.

UK/0016-2361
**FUEL (GUILFORD).** (FUEL.). [Fuel]. (1948)-. Academic Scholarly Publication. English. mo. $1118.00 The Americas; £750.00 other. Butterworth Heinemann Publishers, Linacre House, Jordan Hill, Oxford OX2 8DP England. **Tel** 011 44 865 310366. **(Subscription address:** Elsevier Science Ltd. Oxford Fulfillment Centre, PO Box 800, Kidlington, Oxford OX5 1DX United Kingdom.**) CODEN** FUELAC. **[CCC].** Index available. **Ad Acc. Pr Rev.** available on microfilm and microfiche from University Microfilms International (UMI). Documents available from Article Express International, The Genuine Article, CASDDS, Documents on Demand. ***Continues** Fuel in Science and Practice.*
**Desc:** Concerned with the nature, conservation, preparation, use, interconversion, physical and nuclear properties and chemical reactions including combustion of gaseous, liquid and solid fuels and associated mineral matter, and with geochemistry. Papers on the less usual sources of fuels including wastes and environmental aspects are welcome.
**Ind/Abst** AESIS Q.; Bioeng. Abstr.; Chem. Abstr.; Coal Abstr.; Curr. Technol. Index; Ei Page One; EMBASE; Energy Inf. Abstr.; Energy Res. Abstr.; Eng. Index Annu.; Environ. Abstr.; Gas Abstr.; GeoRef; HTFS Dig.; Int. Aerosp. Abstr.; Leadscan; Lit. Pat. Abstr., Oilfield Chem. (1954-); Lit. Abstr., Catal. Catal.; Lit. Abstr., Health Environ.; Lit. Abstr., Pet. Refin. Petrochem.; Lit. Abstr., Pet. Substit.; Lit. Abstr., Transp. Storage; Mass Spect. Bull.; Res. Alert [Full Cov.]; Sci. Cit. Index; SCISEARCH; World Ceram. Abstr.

US
**FUEL LINE / DEFENSE FUEL SUPPLY CENTER.** **Added/Corp** United States. Defense Fuel Supply Center. (Winter 1985)-. Periodical. English. qt. Defense Fuel Supply Center, DFSC-DB, Cameron Station, Alexandria VA 22304-6160. ***Continues** DFSC Fuel Line.*

US
**FUEL LINE [MICROFORM] / DEFENSE FUEL SUPPLY CENTER.** **Added/Corp** United States. Defense Fuel Supply Center. Began with Winter (1985)-. Periodical. English. qt. Defense Fuel Supply Center, DFSC-DB, Cameron Station, Alexandria VA 22304-6160. ***Continues** DFSC Fuel Line.*

US
**FUEL OIL IN WORLD MARKETS.** English. Twelve times a year. $2200.00 (Standard Edition); $3300.00 (Premium Edition). Poten & Partners Inc., 885 3rd Avenue, New York NY 10022. **Tel** (212)230-2000, FAX (212)355-0295, telex 177118/420811. **ED** Laurence Axelrod (editor's telephone: (212)230-2062).
**Desc:** Reports and analyzes current developments in world fuel oil markets. Provides rolling outlook for fuel oil prices in key world markets - New York Harbor, Rotterdam, Italy, and Singapore.

US/0016-2396
**FUEL OIL NEWS.** [Fuel oil news]. (19??)-. Periodical. English. Twelve times a year. $24.00 US; $33.00 Canada & Mexico; $74.00 other. Pub Data, 5615 West Cermak Road, Chicago IL 60650. **Bk Rev. Ad Acc.**

**Circ:** 17,500 (ctrl).
**Desc:** Directed to the oil heating retailer to provide assistance in business operation. Reports on competitive conditions, products, industry news, management techniques and technical data.
**Ind/Abst** Stat. Ref. Index.

US/1062-3744
**FUEL REFORMULATION.** [Fuel reformul.]. **Added/Corp** Information Resources Inc. Vol. 1, No. 1 (Sept. 1991)-. Periodical. English. bm. $149.00 US. Hart Publications Inc, 1900 Grant Street, Suite 400, Denver CO 80203. **Tel** (303)837-1917, (800)832-1917, FAX (303)837-8585. **LC** TP692.5; .F83. **DD** 665.5/3827.
**Desc:** Provides coverage on new refining and petrochemical process technology, oxygenates, fuel regulations, automotive technology, emissions research, changing market conditions, and new policy direction.

II/0254-3567
**FUEL SCIENCE AND TECHNOLOGY.** [Fuel sci. technol.]. **Added/Corp** Central Fuel Research Institute (India). Vol. 1, No. 1 (July 1982)-. Academic Scholarly Publication. English. qt. $18.00. Central Fuel Research Institute, PO F R I 828108, Dhanbad Bihar India. **Tel** 60141, telex 0629-201. **(Subscription address:** Prints India, 11 Darya Ganj, New Delhi, 110002 India, (Phone: 011 91 11 3268645)) **ED** R Haque Samir Sen and P C Kumar. **LC** TP315; .F834. **DD** 662.6/05. **CODEN** FSTEDL. Index available. cum. index. **Circ:** 300. Documents available from Petroleum Abstracts Document Delivery Service, CASDDS. ***Continues*** *FRI News.*
**Desc:** Includes all major fuels, coal, oil, gas and their derivatives, their natural resources, conservation beneficiation, combustion, gasification, industrial intermediates and fundamental studies, etc.
**Ind/Abst** Chem. Abstr.; Coal Abstr.; GeoRef; Indian Sci. Abstr.; Pet. Abstr.

US/1060-9725
**FUELOIL & OIL HEAT WITH AIR CONDITIONING.** [Fueloil oil heat air cond.]. **VFOAT** Fuel Oil & Oil Heat with Air Conditioning; Fuel Oil and Oil Heat with Air Conditioning; Fueloil and Oil Heat; Fuel Oil & Oil Heat; Fueloil & Oil Heat. Vol. 50, No. 10 (Oct. 1991)-. Periodical. English. mo. $20.00 US; $30.00 Canada and Mexico; $75.00 other. Industry Publications Inc / New Jersey, 389 Passaic Avenue, Fairfield NJ 07004. **Tel** (201)227-5151, FAX (201)227-9219. **DD** 665. ***Continues*** *Fueloil & Oil Heat (Fairfield, Essex County, N.J. : 1990), 1061-141X.*
**Ind/Abst** Bus. Index (1992-); Bus. Period. Index (1985-); Bus. Source (Jan. 1993-); Energy Res. Abstr. (1985-); Gen. BusinessFile (1992-); Gen. Period. Index (1992-); Mag. Search; Trade Ind. Index (1985-); Vocat. Search (Jan. 1993-); Wilson Bus. Abstr.

NE/0016-4828
**GAS.** (HET GAS; TIJDSCHRIFT VOOR DE GASINDUSTRIE.). [Gas]. **Added/Corp** Vereeniging van Gasfabrikanten in Nederland. Vakgroep Gasbedrijven. (1880)-. Periodical. Dutch (summaries and/or abstracts in English). Eleven times a year (July/Aug. issue combined). Fl130.00. Stichting Tijdschrift Openbaregasvoorz, Postbus 220, 7300 AE Apeldoorn Netherlands. **Tel** 011 31 55 494949, FAX 011 31 55 418963, telex 49456. **ED** L.F. Kop. **LC** TP700; .G12. **Ad Acc. Circ:** 2,700.
**Ind/Abst** Coal Abstr.; Energy Res. Abstr. (1976-).

US
**GAS. Added/Corp** Pacific Coast Gas Association. Vol. 1 (May 1925)-. Periodical. English. mo. **LC** TP700; .P3. ***Continues*** *Oil & Gas Equipment Review.*
**Ind/Abst** Surf. Treat. Technol. Abstr.

US/0016-4844
**GAS ABSTRACTS. See** Petroleum and Natural Gas-Abstracting, Bibliographies and Statistics.

GW/0340-6067
**GAS AKTUELL.** [Gas aktuell]. **Added/Corp** Messer Griesheim GmbH. (19??)-. Periodical. German. Messer Griesheim GMBH. **CODEN** GAAKDX. Documents available from CASDDS.
**Ind/Abst** Chem. Abstr.

JA/0913-283X
**GAS & CHEMICAL REPORTER.** [Gas chem. report.]. (1986)-. Periodical. English. mo. ¥70000.00. KK Gas Review, 10 11 1 Chome Nishitani Building, Minamihorie Nishi, Osaka, Japan. **Tel** 06 533-6197, FAX 06 532-1300, telex 64400. **DD** 338.4.
**Ind/Abst** Infomat Int. Bus.

US
**GAS AND OIL EQUIPMENT DIRECTORY. Added/Corp** Underwriters' Laboratories. (197?)-. Directory. English. an (Oct.). $9.50. Underwriters Laboratories Inc., 333 Pfingsten Road, Northbrook IL 60062. **Tel** (708)272-8800 Ext.3542, FAX (708)272-8129, telex 6502543343. ***Continues*** *Gas and Oil Equipment List.*

SP
**GAS (BARCELONA, SPAIN).** (GAS : DOCUMENTACION ANUAL DE SEDIGAS.). Periodical. Spanish. an. 1000ptas. Ediciones Doyma SA, Travesera de Gracia 17 21, 08021 Barcelona Spain. **Tel** 011 34 3 2000711, 011 34 3 4145706, FAX 011 34 3 2091136, telex 51964 INK E. **ED** Ruben Blanco. **LC** HD9581.S7; G37. **DD** 338.2/7285/0946. Index available. cum. index. **Ad Acc. Pr Rev. Circ:** 10,000.
**Desc:** General information about legislative themes and novelties of equipment in the gas sector and about suppliers of all the products for this sector.

US/0897-8778
**GAS BUYERS GUIDE. *Title Change.*** [Gas buy. guide]. **VFOAT** GBG. (1989-1992). Consumer Publication. English. wk. Spencer Publishing Company, PO Box 27717, Houston TX 77227. **Tel** (713)880-0983. **DD** 338. **CODEN** GBGUEX. **[CCC]. *Continues*** *Inside Gas Markets, 8750-1945.* ***Continued by*** *Gas Daily's Gas Markets Week, 1065-867X.*

UK/0433-1931
**GAS COUNCIL RESEARCH COMMUNICATION.** (1952)-. English. ***Continues*** *Communication - Gas Research Board, 0367-5068.*
**Ind/Abst** Ceram. Abstr. (19??-).

US/0885-5935
**GAS DAILY.** [Gas dly.]. (19??)-. Periodical. English. da. $1047.00 US; $1135.00 other. Pasha Publications Inc., 1616 North Fort Myer Drive, Suite 1000, Arlington VA 22209. **Tel** (800)424-2908, (703)528-1244, FAX (703)528-3742, (703)528-1253. **ED** George Spencer. **[CCC]. Circ:** 2,500. available on an online database (file 636/Full-Text) from DIALOG.
**Ind/Abst** PTS Newsl. Database [Full Txt.].

US/1061-5024
**GAS DAILY NATURAL GAS MARKETING. INDUSTRY DIRECTORY.** [Gas dly. nat. gas mark., Ind. dir.]. **Added/Corp** Pasha Publications (Firm). **VFOAT** Natural Gas Marketing. Industry Directory; Industry Directory; Gas Daily Industry Directory. (1991)-. Directory. English. Twelve times a year. $587.00 US; $754.00 other. Pasha Publications Inc., 1616 North Fort Myer Drive, Suite 1000, Arlington VA 22209. **Tel** (800)424-2908, (703)528-1244, FAX (703)528-3742, (703)528-1253. **LC** HD9581.U49; G315. **DD** 381/.42285/02573. ***Continues*** *Natural Gas Marketing. Industry Directory, 0894-900X.*

●US/1065-867X
**GAS DAILY'S GAS MARKETS WEEK.** [Gas dly. gas mark. week]. **Added/Corp** Pasha Publications (Firm). **VFOAT** Gas Markets Week. Vol. 9, No. 32 (Aug. 17, 1992)-. Periodical. English. wk. $477.00 US; $507.00 other. Pasha Publications Inc., 1616 North Fort Myer Drive, Suite 1000, Arlington VA 22209. **Tel** (800)424-2908, (703)528-1244, FAX (703)528-3742, (703)528-1253. **DD** 333. ***Continues*** *Gas Buyers Guide, 0897-8778.*

US/1057-2279
**GAS DAILY'S GAS STORAGE REPORT.** [Gas Dly.'s gas storage rep.]. **VFOAT** Gas Storage Report. (1991)-. Periodical. English. mo. $457.00 US; $472.00 other. Pasha Publications Inc., 1616 North Fort Myer Drive, Suite 1000, Arlington VA 22209. **Tel** (800)424-2908, (703)528-1244, FAX (703)528-3742, (703)528-1253. **DD** 333. **[CCC].**

●US/1068-1299
**GAS DAILY'S NG.** [Gas dly. NG]. **Added/Corp** Pasha Publications (Firm). **VFOAT** NG. **VAT** Gas Daily's Natural Gas. Vol. 1, No. 1 (Spring 1993)-. Periodical. English. Six times a year. $60.00. Pasha Publications Inc., 1616 North Fort Myer Drive, Suite 1000, Arlington VA 22209. **Tel** (800)424-2908, (703)528-1244, FAX (703)528-3742, (703)528-1253.

US/0433-194X
**GAS DATA BOOK; BRIEF EXCERPTS FROM GAS FACTS.** 1st- Ed.; 1955-. Trade Publication. English. an. $2.00. American Gas Association / Virginia, 1515 Wilson Boulevard, Arlington VA 22209. **Tel** (703)841-8400, (703)841-8559, FAX (703)841-8697. **DD** 338.2. **Circ:** 5,000.
**Desc:** Sales revenues, customers and detailed financial statistics regarding the natural gas industry.

US/0161-4851
**GAS DIGEST.** [Gas dig.]. Periodical. English. mo. Gas Digest, PO Box 35819, Houston TX 77235. **Tel** (713)723-7456. **LC** TP700; .G145. **DD** 338.4/7/665705.
**Ind/Abst** Coal Abstr.; Energy Res. Abstr. (April 1977-).

UK/0307-3084
**GAS DIRECTORY AND WHO'S WHO. VFOAT** Gas Directory. (1975)-. Directory. English. an (Feb.). £70.00 UK; £80.00 other. Benn Publications Ltd., Sovereign Way, Tonbridge TNQ 1RW England. **Tel** 011 44 732 364422, FAX 011 44 732 361534, telex 0732 95132 BENTON G. **(Subscription address:** Benn Business Information Services, Riverbank House Angel Lane, Tonbridge Kent TN9 1SE England.) **ED** John Hedges. **LC** TP714; .G28. **DD** 338.4/76657/02541. **[CCC]. Ad Acc. Circ:** 1,500. ***Formed by the union of*** *Gas Directory and Undertakings of the World, 0307-6733* ***and*** *Who's Who in the Gas Industry.*
**Desc:** The standard reference guide to the United Kingdom gas industry-suppliers to the industry, classified buyers guide, British gas statistics, trade name and trade associations.

AT/1039-8112
**GAS DISTRIBUTION INDUSTRY AND PERFORMANCE INDICATORS.** (19??)-. English. an. 25.00Aus$. Australian Gas Association, GPO Box 323, Gas Industry House / 7 Moore Street, Canberra Australian Capital Territory 2601 Australia. **Tel** 011 61 6 2473955, FAX 011 61 6 2497402.

US/8756-5471
**GAS ENERGY REVIEW.** [Gas energy rev.]. Vol. 7, No. 4 (Jan. 1979)-. Periodical. English. mo. $30.00 members, $35.00 nonmembers. American Gas Association / Virginia, 1515 Wilson Boulevard, Arlington VA 22209. **Tel** (703)841-8400, (703)841-8559, FAX (703)841-8697. **LC** TP700; .G148. **DD** 338.4/76657/05. available on an online database (file 15/Full-Text) from DIALOG. Documents available from UMI Article Clearinghouse. ***Continues*** *Gas Supply Review, 0270-6423.*
**Ind/Abst** ABI/INFORM Glob. Ed.; ABI Inform Ondisc (Nov. 1988-).

UK/0306-6444
**GAS ENGINEERING AND MANAGEMENT.** [Gas eng. manage.]. **Added/Corp** Institution of Gas Engineers. Vol. 14, (Jan. 1974)-. Periodical. English. Ten times a year. £53.00 UK; £78.00 other. Institution of Gas Engineers, 17 Grosvenor Crescent, London SW1 7ES England. **Tel** 011 44 71 2459811. **(Subscription address:** TG Scott Subscriber Services, 6 Bourne Enterprise Centre, Kent TN15 8DG United Kingdom.) **LC** TP700; .I612. **DD** 665/.7/05. **CODEN** GEMABL. available on microfilm and microfiche from University Microfilms International (UMI). Documents available from Article Express International. ***Continues*** *Institution of Gas Engineers, London. Journal.*
**Desc:** Provides the latest information on international gas developments and business issues.
**Ind/Abst** Alum. Ind. Abstr.; Bioeng. Abstr.; Coal Abstr.; Curr. Technol. Index; Ei Page One; EMBASE; Energy Res. Abstr. (April 1976-); Eng. Mater. Abstr.; Eng. Index Annu.; Gas Abstr.; Int. Build. Serv. Abstr.; Lit. Pat. Abstr., Oilfield Chem. (1969-1989); Lit. Abstr., Catal. Catal.; Lit. Abstr., Health Environ.; Lit. Abstr., Pet. Refin. Petrochem.; Lit. Abstr., Pet. Substit.; Lit. Abstr., Transp. Storage; Met. Abstr.; Life Sci. Collect.; World Ceram. Abstr.

US/0194-2468
**GAS INDUSTRIES (1978).** (GAS INDUSTRIES.). [Gas ind.]. (1978)-. Periodical. English. mo. $20.00 US & Canada; $90.00 other. Gas Industries, E & A News Inc, PO Box 558, Park Ridge IL 60068. **Tel** (312)693-3682, FAX (312)696-3445. **ED** Ruth W. Stidgen and Vivian Galbarth. **LC** TP350; .G362. **DD** 665.7/05. **Ad Acc, Adv Mgr:** Bill Dannhausen. **Circ:** 10,000 (ctrl). available on microfilm and microfiche from University Microfilms International (UMI). Documents available from Article Express International. ***Formed by the union of*** *Gas Industries* ***and*** *Gas Industries. (Natural Gas Edition).*
**Desc:** Contains natural gas pipelines; transmission and utility, distribution, construction maintenance operations engineering and marketing.
**Ind/Abst** Coal Abstr.; Corros. Abstr.; Ei Page One; Energy Inf. Abstr.; Eng. Index Annu. [Select. Cov.]; Gas Abstr.

UK/0954-853X
**GAS INDUSTRY DIRECTORY.** [Gas ind. dir.]. (198?)-. English. an (published in November). £79.00. Benn Publications Ltd., Sovereign Way, Tonbridge TNQ 1RW England. **Tel** 011 44 732 364422, FAX 011 44 732 361534, telex 0732 95132 BENTON G. **(Subscription address:** Benn Business Information Services, Riverbank House Angel Lane, Tonbridge Kent TN9 1SE England.) **ED** Ann Black. **DD** 338.4766577. **Circ:** 1,500. ***Continues*** *Gas Directory and Who's Who, 0307-3084.*
**Desc:** Standard reference guide to the UK gas industry. Complete guide to reorganised British Gas PLC with references, regional departments, maps and statistics.

UK/0964-8496
**GAS MATTERS.** [Gas matters]. (1988)-. English. Twelve times a year. £765.00 EEC; $1,020.00 other. EconoMatters, 82 Rivington Street, London EC2A 3AY England. **Tel** 11 44 71 613 0087, FAX 11 44 71 613 0094, telex 8954111 REPLAY G. **DD** 338.27285. **Pr Rev.** ctrl circ.
**Desc:** Monthly analysis of important commercial and political issues facing international gas markets.

GW/0343-2092
**GAS (MUNCHEN).** (GAS.). [Gas]. **Added/Corp** Bundesverband der Deutschen Gas- und Wasserwirtschaft. (1978)-. Periodical. German. bm (6 issues). DM124.00. R Oldenbourg Verlag, Postfach 801360, D 81613 Munich Germany. **Tel** 011 49 89 450190, FAX 011 49 89 45019305. **LC** TN880.A1; G27. **[CCC].** Index available. **Bk Rev. Ad Acc. Circ:** 5,500.
**Desc:** Reports on the significance, progress and future relevance of gas as an energy form, considering its use, economic feasibility and practicality. Serves as an organ of communication between manufacturers, construction engineers, installers, vendors and users.
**Ind/Abst** Coal Abstr.

●US/1067-1021
**GAS PROCESSING AND PIPELINING.** (GAS PROCESSING AND PIPELINING / PETROLEUM ABSTRACTS, THE UNIVERSITY OF TULSA.). [Gas process. pipel.]. **Added/Corp** Petroleum Abstracts (Organization). Vol. 1, No. 1 (Jan. 1993)-. Periodical. English. mo. $150.00 (general subscribers), $175.00 (nonsubscribers). Petroleum Abstracts, University of Tulsa, Information Services Division, 600 South College Avenue, Harwell Hall 101, Tulsa OK 74104-3189. **Tel** (800)247-8678, (918)631-2297, FAX (918)599-9361, telex 49 7543. **DD** 665.
**Desc:** Contains bibliographic entries and abstracts of the worldwide literature related to gas processing and pipelining. In addition to engineering and technology, topics include risk analysis, safety management and environmental impact.

US/0740-5278
**GAS PROCESSORS REPORT.** (GAS PROCESSORS REPORT / SPEARS CONSULTING GROUP.). [Gas process. rep.]. **Added/Corp** Spears Consuting Group. (Jan. 1983)-. Periodical. English. bw. $408.00. Gas Processors Report, 800 Wilcrest Drive #125, Houston TX 77042. **ED** Jack Brewster; Telephone: (713)975-7590. **[CCC].**

US
**GAS PRODUCTION LEDGER.** English. mo. $241.00. Railroad Commission of Texas, PO Drawer 12967, Capitol Station, Austin TX 78711. **Tel** (512)463-7255.

JA/0913-2090
**GAS REVIEW NIPPON.** [Gas rev. Nippon]. (1982)-. Periodical. English. sa. ¥15000.00. KK Gas Review, 10 11 1 Chome Nishitani Building, Minamihorie Nishi, Osaka, Japan. **Tel** 06 533-6197, FAX 06 532-1300, telex 64400. **DD** 338.4.

UK/0950-4214
**GAS SEPARATION & PURIFICATION.** [Gas sep. purif.]. **VFOAT** Gas Separation and Purification. Vol. 1, No. 1 (Sept. 1987)-. Periodical. English. qt. $388.00 The Americas; £260.00 other. Butterworth Heinemann Publishers, Linacre House, Jordan Hill, Oxford OX2 8DP England. **Tel** 011 44 865 310366. **(Subscription address:** Elsevier Science Ltd. Oxford Fulfillment Centre, PO Box 800, Kidlington, Oxford OX5 1DX United Kingdom.**) LC** WMLC 93/325. **[CCC].** Index available. **Bk Rev**. **Ad Acc**. available on microfilm and microfiche from University Microfilms International (UMI). Documents available from Article Express International, CASDDS.
**Desc:** Provides comprehensive coverage of all aspects of gas separation and purification, with particular emphasis on the process aspects. It brings together information on large and small-scale processes and separation and purification systems using physical and chemical methods. It also covers research aspects leading to new processes and the provision of basic data needed in process design and evaluation.
**Ind/Abst** Chem. Abstr.; Coal Abstr.; Ei Page One; Energy Inf. Abstr.; Eng. Index Annu.; Fluid Abstr., Civil Eng.; Fluid Abstr. Proc. Eng.; FLUIDEX; HTFS Dig.

●US/1065-786X
**GAS SHALES TECHNOLOGY REVIEW.** (GAS SHALES TECHNOLOGY REVIEW / GAS RESEARCH INSTITUTE.). [Gas shales technol. rev.]. **Added/Corp** Gas Research Institute. **VFOAT** Devonian Gas Shales Technology Review. Vol. 7, No. 3 (Mar. 1992)-. Periodical. English. Gas Research Institute, c/o Charles F Brandenburg, 8600 West Bryn Mawr Avenue, Chicago IL 60631. **Tel** (312)399-8100. **DD** 622. ***Continues*** *Devonian Gas Shales Technology Review, 1063-8091.*

US/1049-4103
**GAS STATS.** (GAS STATS : MONTHLY GAS UTILITY STATISTICAL REPORT / AMERICAN GAS ASSOCIATION, PLANNING AND ANALYSIS.). [Gas stats]. **Added/Corp** American Gas Association. Planning and Analysis Group. American Gas Association. Dept. of Statistics. **VAT** Gas Statistics. (Dec. 1987)-. Statistical Publication. English. Sixteen times a year. $8.00 (members); $16.00 (non-members). American Gas Association / Virginia, 1515 Wilson Boulevard, Arlington VA 22209. **Tel** (703)841-8400, (703)841-8559, FAX (703)841-8697. **DD** 338. ***Formed by the union of*** *Monthly Gas Utility Statistical Report **and** Quarterly Report of Gas Industry Operations, 0197-503X.*

US/0565-0127
**GAS SUPPLIES OF INTERSTATE NATURAL GAS PIPELINE COMPANIES / FEDERAL POWER COMMISSION, BUREAU OF NATURAL GAS, THE.** [Gas supplies interstate nat. gas pipeline co.]. **Added/Corp** United States. Federal Power Commission. Bureau of Natural Gas. United States. Federal Energy Regulatory Commission. United States. Energy Information Administration. Coal and Electric Power Statistics Division. United States. Energy Information Administration. Office of Oil and Gas. United States. Federal Energy Regulatory Commission. Office of Pipeline and Producer Regulation. United States. Energy Information Administration. Office of Energy Data. United States. Energy Information Administration. Office of Energy Data Operations. (19??)-. Government Publication. English. an. $6.00. Superintendent of Documents, US Government Printing Office, Washington DC 20402. **Tel** (202)275-3328, FAX (202)786-2377. **LC** HD9581.U49; G33. **DD** 553.2/85/0973.

US/1072-5113
**GAS TRANSACTIONS REPORT.** (19??)-. English. bw (25 issues). $547.00 US; $582.00 other. Hart Publications Inc, 1900 Grant Street, Suite 400, Denver CO 80203. **Tel** (303)837-1917, (800)832-1917, FAX (303)837-8585.

●US/1065-8661
**GAS TRANSPORTATION REPORT.** [Gas transp. rep.]. **Added/Corp** Pasha Publications (Firm). (1992)-. Periodical. English. Fifty times a year. $377.00 US; $407.00 other. Pasha Publications Inc., 1616 North Fort Myer Drive, Suite 1000, Arlington VA 22209. **Tel** (800)424-2908, (703)528-1244, FAX (703)528-3742, (703)528-1253. **DD** 333.

GW/0016-4909
**GAS- UND WASSERFACH. GAS, ERDGAS : GWF, DAS.** **Added/Corp** Deutscher Verein von Gas- und Wasserfachmannern. Deutscher Verein des Gas- und Wasserfaches. **VFOAT** Gas, Erdgas; GWF; Gas- und Wasserfach. Gas, Erdgas-Wasser, Abwasser; GWF-Gas/Erdgas. Vol. 111 (1970)-. Academic Scholarly Publication. German (table of contents in English and French). mo. DM354.00. R Oldenbourg Verlag, Postfach 801360, D 81613 Munich Germany. **Tel** 011 49 89 450190, FAX 011 49 89 45019305. **CODEN** GWGEAQ. **[CCC].** Documents available from Article Express International, CASDDS. ***Continues in part*** *GWF, das Gas- und Wasserfach.*
**Desc:** Covers all aspects of gas and natural gas production, discovery, distribution and use. Reports on latest technology, measurement, production safety, marketing and construction.
**Ind/Abst** Bioeng. Abstr.; Chem. Abstr.; Coal Abstr.; Ei Page One; EMBASE; Energy Res. Abstr. (Sept. 1974-); Eng. Index Annu.; Fluid Abstr., Civil Eng.; Fluid Abstr. Proc. Eng.; FLUIDEX (199?-); Gas Abstr. (?-?); GeoRef.

CN/0380-2329
**GAS UTILITIES.** (GAS UTILITIES / PREPARED IN THE PUBLIC UTILITIES SECTION, PUBLIC FIANCE AND TRANSPORTATION DIVISION). [Gas util.]. **Main/Corp** Canada. Statistique Canada. Division des Industries Manufacturieres et Primaires. **Added/Corp** Canada. Bureau Federal de la Statistique. Division des Industries Manufacturieres et Primaires. Statistique Canada. Division des Industries Manufacturieres et Primaires. Statistique Canada. Division de l'Industrie. Statistique Canada. Section de l'Energie. Canada. Bureau Federal de la Statistique. Section des Services d'Utilite Publique. Canada. Bureau Federal de la Statistique. Division de l'Industrie. **VFOAT** Services de Gaz. Vol. 4, No. 1 (Jan. 1962)-. Periodical. French (English). mo. 140.00Can$ Canada; $168.00 US; $196.00 other. Statistics Canada, Publications Sales & Services, Main Building Room 1710, Ottawa Ontario K1A 0T6 Canada. **Tel** (613)951-5078, (800)267-6677, FAX (613)951-1584, telex 053-3585. **DD** 338.4/766573/0971. ***Continues*** *Gas Pipe Line Transport (Mensuel), 0702-682X.*
**Desc:** Receipts and disposition of natural gas by province; Covers commodity distance, sales, revenues, customers by rate structure, imports and exports.

CN/0527-5318
**GAS UTILITIES. TRANSPORT AND DISTRIBUTION SYSTEMS.** (GAS UTILITIES.). [Gas util., Transp. distrib. syst.]. **Added/Corp** Canada. Dominion Bureau of Statistics. Public Utilities Section. Canada. Dominion Bureau of Statistics. Energy Statistics Section. Canada. Dominion Bureau of Statistics. Energy and Minerals Section. Statistics Canada. Energy and Minerals Section. Statistics Canada. Census of Manufactures Section. Statistics Canada. Industry Division. **VFOAT** Gas Utilities; Services de Gaz; Services de Gaz, Reseaux de Transport et de Distribution. (1959)-. English (French). an. 27.00Can$ Canada. Statistics Canada, Publications Sales & Services, Main Building Room 1710, Ottawa Ontario K1A 0T6 Canada. **Tel** (613)951-5078, (800)267-6677, FAX (613)951-1584, telex 053-3585. **LC** HD9581.C3; C27a. **DD** 338.2/7285/0971. ***Formed by the union of*** *Canada. Dominion Bureau of Statistics. Public Utilities Section. Gas Utilities., 0826-7596 **and** Gas Pipe Line Transport, 0380-2876.*
**Desc:** Receipts and disposition of natural gas by month and by province, pipeline distance; balance sheet, property account, income account, employees and earnings.

JA
**GAS UTILITY INDUSTRY IN JAPAN.** **Main/Corp** Nihon Gasu Kyokai. (19??)-. Periodical. English. Japan Gas Association, 1-15-12 Toranomon, Minatoku Tokyo 105 Japan. **Tel** 03 5020111, FAX 03 5020013, telex 222-2374 JGA. **LC** TP735.J3; N5. **DD** 338.4/7/66570942. ***Continues*** *Utility Gas Industry in Japan.*

GW/0020-9384
**GAS WARME INTERNATIONAL.** (GAS WARME INTERNATIONAL. GAZ CHALEUR INTERNATIONAL. GAS HEAT INTERNATIONAL.). [Gas Warme int.]. **VFOAT** Gaz Chaleur International; Gas Heat International. Vol. 16, (1967)-. Academic Scholarly Publication. German (summaries and/or abstracts in English and French). Ten times a year. DM335.00 (airmail), DM323.00 (surface mail). Vulkan-Verlag, Dr. W. Classen, Postfach 103962, D 45039 Essen 1 Germany. **Tel** 011 49 201 8200214, telex 8579008. **ED** Beckervordersandfort, Hering, T. Holle, J. Kentmann, H. P. Niepenberg, H. Simon, Skunca and J. Stephanek. **CODEN** GWINAT. **[CCC].** Index available. cum. index. **Bk Rev**. **Ad Acc. Circ:** 3,550. Documents available from Article Express International, CASDDS. ***Continues*** *Internationale Zeitschrift fur Gaswarme.*
**Desc:** Journal of gas utilization and gas furnace engineering.
**Ind/Abst** Bioeng. Abstr.; Chem. Abstr.; Coal Abstr.; Ei Page One; EMBASE; Energy Res. Abstr. (April 1976-); Eng. Index Annu.; Environ. Eng. Abstr.; Gas Abstr.; Int. Aerosp. Abstr.; Manuf. Process Eng. Abstr.; Mater. Sci. Eng. Abstr.; Mech. Eng. Abstr.; Solid State Supercond. Abstr.

AU/0016-5018
**GAS, WASSER, WARME.** [Gas, Wasser, Waerme]. **Added/Corp** Osterreichischer Verein von Gas- und Wasserfachmannern, Vienna. **VFOAT** GWW. Vol. 1 (1947)-. Academic Scholarly Publication. German. mo. S1532.00. Verlag Lorenz, Ebendorferstrasse 10, A-1010 Vienna Austria. **Tel** 011 43 222 426695, FAX 011 43 222 438693. **CODEN** GAWWA6. Documents available from Article Express International, CASDDS. ***Continues*** *Gas und Wasser.*
**Ind/Abst** Bioeng. Abstr.; Chem. Abstr.; Coal Abstr.; Ei Page One; EMBASE; Eng. Index Annu.; Gas Abstr.; GeoRef.

UK/0960-1635
**GAS WORLD INTERNATIONAL.** [Gas world int.]. (1989)-. Periodical. English. mo. £180.00. Petroleum Economist Ltd., Perrymount Road, Haywards Heath, West Sussex RH16 3DH England. **Tel** 011 44 444 440421. ***Continues*** *Gas World (1975), 0308-7654.*
**Ind/Abst** Curr. Technol. Index; PROMT; Trade Ind. ASAP [Full Txt.]; Trade Ind. Index [Full Txt.].

UK/0308-7654
**GAS WORLD (LONDON, ENGLAND : 1974).** ***Title Change.*** (GAS WORLD.). [Gas world]. Vol. 179, No. 4662 (Jan. 1974)-. Periodical. English. mo. Benn Business Information Service Ltd, Riverbank House, Angel Lane, Tonbridge Kent TN9 1SE England. **Tel** 011 44 732 362666, FAX 011 44 732 770483, telex 95454 BBIS. **ED** Victoria Thomas. **LC** TP700; .G2. **CODEN** GAWOAG. **[CCC]. Bk Rev**. **Ad Acc. Circ:** 3,000 (ctrl). available on microfilm and microfiche from University Microfilms International (UMI); available on an online database (file 648/Full-Text) from DIALOG. Documents available from Article Express International, Petroleum Abstracts Document Delivery Service. ***Continues*** *Gas World and Gas Journal, 0367-5505.* ***Continued by*** *Gas World International.*
**Desc:** For engineering management in the transmission distribution and utilization sectors of the gas industry.
**Ind/Abst** Coal Abstr.; Curr. Technol. Index; Ei Page One; Energy Res. Abstr. (Jan. 1978-); Eng. Index Annu. [Select. Cov.]; F&S Index Plus Text, Int. [Select. Cov.]; Gas Abstr.; PAIS Int. Print; Pet. Abstr.

US/0271-082X
**GASAVERS NEWS.** **VAT** Gas Savers News. V. 1-1980-. Periodical. English. mo. $24.00. Fuel Expanders Inc, 173 E Paularino, Costa Mesa CA 92626. **Tel** (714)641-0833.

SW/0039-6834
**GASNYTT.** [Gasnytt]. (1970)-. Periodical. Swedish. Six times a year. Kr490.00. Gasnytt, Box 6405, S 113 82 Stockholm Sweden. **Tel** 011 46 8 340985. **UDC** 66. ***Continues*** *Svenska Gasfoereningens Manadsblad, 0370-9876.*
**Ind/Abst** Gas Abstr.

GW
**GASSTATISTIK FUR DIE BUNDESREPUBLIK DEUTSCHLAND.** **See** Petroleum and Natural Gas-Abstracting, Bibliographies and Statistics.

UK
**GASTECH : PREPRINTS OF CONFERENCE PAPERS / THE ... INTERNATIONAL LNG/LPG CONFERENCE & EXHIBITION ; ORGANISED BY GASTECH LTD.**
**Added/Corp** Gastech Ltd. 13th (1988)-. Proceedings. English. be. Gastech Ltd, 2 Station Road, Rickmansworth Herts WD3 1QP England. **Tel** (0923)776363, FAX (0923)777206, telex 924312. **Ad Acc.** ctrl circ. ***Continues*** *Gastech LNG & LPG Conference. Gastech, 0265-2870.*
**Ind/Abst** Lit. Pat. Abstr., Oilfield Chem.; Lit. Abstr., Catal.

Catal.; Lit. Abstr., Health Environ.; Lit. Abstr., Pet. Refin. Petrochem.; Lit. Abstr., Pet. Substit.; Lit. Abstr., Transp. Storage.

GW/0016-5182
**GASVERWENDUNG.** Academic Scholarly Publication. German. DM42.20. ZFGW-Verlag GmbH, Postfach 901080, W-6000 Frankfurt Germany. **CODEN** GASVDK. Documents available from CASDDS.
**Ind/Abst** Chem. Abstr.

FR
**GAZ ACTUALITES. Added/Corp** Societe pour le Developpement de L'Industrie du Gaz en France. (19??)-. French. Societe pour le Development de l'Industrie du Gaz, 13 Bis Boulevard Berthier, 75823 Paris France. **LC** TP733.F8; G32. **DD** 338.4/7/66570944.

FR/0016-5328
**GAZ D'AUJOURD'HUI.** (GAZ D'AUJOURD'HUI : REVUE MENSUELLE DE LA SOCIETE DU JOURNAL DES USINES A GAZ.). [Gaz aujourd'hui]. **Added/Corp** Societe du Journal des Usines a Gaz. Association Technique de l'Industrie du Gaz en France. (1967)-. Periodical. French (summaries and/or abstracts in English, German and Russian). Ten times a year. 620.00F (includes VAT) France; 700.00F other. Association Technique de l'Industrie du Gaz en France, 62 rue de Courcelles, 75008 Paris France. **Tel** 011 33 1 47543434, FAX 011 33 1 42274943, telex 642621. **ED** Claude Bureau. **LC** TP700; .A853. **DD** 665.7. **[CCC].** Index available. cum. index. **Bk Rev.** (Qty: 3-4). **Ad Acc**. **Circ:** 6,000. *Continues Journal des Industries du Gaz.*
**Ind/Abst** CIS Abstr.; Coal Abstr.; Energy Res. Abstr. (Feb. 1977-); Gas Abstr.; Predicasts; Saf. Health Work.

RU/0016-5581
**GAZOVAIA PROMYSHLENNOST.**
**Added/Corp** Soviet Union. Ministerstvo Neftianoi Promyshlennosti. Russian S.F.S.R. Ministerstvo Kommunalnogo Khoziaistva. Nauchno-Tekhnicheskoe Obshchestvo Energeticheskoi Promyshlennosti (Soviet Union) Nauchno-Tekhnicheskoe Obshchestvo Neftianoi i Gazovoi Promyshlennosti Imeni I.M. Gubkina. Soviet Union. Glavnoe Upravlenie Gazovoi Promyshlennosti. Gosudarstvennyi Proizvodstvennyi Komitet po Gazovoi Promyshlennosti SSSR. Vsesoiuznoe Nauchno-Tekhnicheskoe Obshchestvo Neftianoi i Gazovoi Promyshlennosti Im. Gubkina. Gosudarstvennyi Gazovyi Kontsern "Gazprom" (Soviet Union). (1956)-. Academic Scholarly Publication. Russian. mo. $96.00. Izdatelstvo Nedra, 3 Pl Belorusskogo Vakzala, 125047 Moscow Russia. **Tel** 250-52-55. **(Subscription address:** Victor Kamkin, 4956 Boiling Brook Parkway, Rockville MD 20852.) **CODEN** GZVPAJ. **[CCC].** Documents available from CASDDS.
**Ind/Abst** Appl. Mech. Rev.; Chem. Abstr.; Gas Abstr.; GeoRef.

RU
**GAZOVAIA PROMYSHLENNOST. SERIIA EKONOMIKA, ORGANIZATSIIA I UPRAVLENIE V GAZOVOI PROMYSHLENNOSTI / MINISTERSTVO GAZOVOI PROMYSHLENNOSTI.**
**Added/Corp** Soviet Union. Ministerstvo Gazovoi Promyshlennosti. Vsesoiuznyi Nauchno-Issledovatelskii Institut Ekonomiki, Organizatsii Proizvodstva i Tekhniko-Ekonomicheskoi Informatsii v Gazovoi Promyshlennosti. **VFOAT** Seriia Ekonomika, Organizatsiia I Upravlenie V Gazovoi Promyshlennosti. (1970)-. Periodical. Russian. mo. Izdatelstvo Ekonomika, Berezhkovskaia Nab., 6, 121864 Moscow Russia. **LC** TP733.S57; G39.

US
**GENERAL RULES AND RULES OF PRACTICE.** (19??)-. English. an (with updates usually every 6 months). $220.00. Oil Law Records Corporation, 8 NW 65th, Oklahoma City OK 73116. **Tel** (405)840-1632, FAX (405)840-1085. **ED** Rick Commer. Index available. cum. index. **Pr Rev. Circ:** 1,000 (ctrl).
**Desc:** Oklahoma oil and gas rules and regulations.

RU/0135-1605
**GEOLOGIJA I NEFTEGAZONOSNOST TURKMENISTANA.** (GEOLOGIIA I NEFTEGAZONOSNOST TURKMENISTANA). [Geol. neftegazonosn. Turkm.]. Began in 1976?. Academic Scholarly Publication. Russian. 0.80rub. Izdatelstvo Ylym, Ulitsa Engelsa 6, 744000 Ashkhabad Turkmenistan. **Tel** 3632 9 04 84. **LC** TN875; .G4725. **CODEN** GNTUDB. Documents available from CASDDS.
**Ind/Abst** Chem. Abstr.

US/0275-3960
**GEOLOGY OF PETROLEUM (NEW YORK, N.Y.).** (GEOLOGY OF PETROLEUM.). [Geol. pet.]. (19??)-. Monographic series. English. ir. Price varies per volume. John Wiley & Sons, Inc., 605 Third Avenue, New York NY 10158-0012. **Tel** (212)850-6000, (212)850-6645, FAX (212)850-6088,

telex 12-7063. **(Subscription address:** John Wiley & Sons / England, Baffins Lane, Chichester, West Sussex PO19 1UD England.)

US/0094-6303
**GLOBAL DIRECTORY OF GAS COMPANIES. VFOAT** Gas Global Directory. (1973)-. Directory. English. $90.00. Editorial and Research Staff of Gas Magazine, 4151 Southwest Freeway, Suite 735, Houston TX 77027. **LC** TP714; .G55. **DD** 338.4/7/665702573.

US
**GLOBAL GAS TURBINE NEWS.** English. bm. Free. International Gas Turbine Institute, 6085 Barfield Road, Suite 207, Atlanta GA 30328. **Tel** (404)847-0072.
**Ind/Abst** Energy Inf. Abstr.

UK
**GLOBAL OIL REPORT.** English. bm. £1300.00. Centre for Global Energy Studies, 17 Knightsbridge, London SW1X 7LY England. **Tel** 011 44 71 2354334, FAX 011 44 71 2354338, telex 919089 CGES G. **ED** Leo Drollas.
**Desc:** An overview of recent oil industry events, an oil market report, and 2 papers on subjects of longer term strategic importance to the industry.

US
**GLOBAL OIL STOCKS & BALANCES.** English. Twelve times a year. $745.00 mail; $1390.00 fax; $995.00 subscription including Data Flash; $475.00 on-line. Petroleum Intelligence Weekly, 575 Broadway, 4th Floor, New York NY 10012-3230. **Tel** (212)941-5500, FAX (212)941-5509, telex 62371 PETROIN. available via fax; available on an online database (updated quarterly).

US/1051-6255
**GOLOB'S OIL POLLUTION BULLETIN.**
See Environmental Issues-Pollution and Waste Management.

UK/0964-8755
**GREEN ENERGY MATTERS. Ceased.** [Green energy matters]. (1991)-(Dec. 1993). English. Four times a year (Mar., June, Sept., Dec.). EconoMatters, 82 Rivington Street, London EC2A 3AY England. **Tel** 11 44 71 613 0087, FAX 11 44 71 613 0094, telex 8954111 REPLAY G. **ED** Rachel Ouseley. **DD** 363.73.

US
**GRID. Added/Corp** Gas Research Institute. **VFOAT** Gas Research Institute Digest. (197?)-. Periodical. English. bm. Gas Research Institute, 8600 West Bryn Mawr Avenue, Chicago IL 60631. **Tel** (312)399-8100, FAX (312)399-8170, telex 253812. **ED** Cheryl G. Drugan. Index available. **Circ:** 14,000. (ctrl). Documents available from Documents on Demand. *Continues Gridigest.*
**Desc:** Intended to keep GRI's members, the gas industry, and the interested public informed of the progress and results of gas research and development sponsored by GRI.
**Ind/Abst** Energy Inf. Abstr.; Environ. Abstr.; Gas Abstr. (?-?).

US/0742-8464
**GUIDE TO PETROLEUM STATISTICAL INFORMATION.** See Petroleum and Natural Gas-Abstracting, Bibliographies and Statistics.

US/0533-9855
**GUIDE TO STATIONARY PHASES FOR GAS CHROMATOGRAPHY.** [Guide station. phases gas chromatogr.]. **VFOAT** Analabs Guide to Stationary Phases for Gas Chromatography. English. be. Foxboro Ct/Analabs, 151 Woodward Avenue, South Norwalk CT 06856-4730.

US/1070-4914
**GULF COAST OIL AND GAS WORLD.**
**Title Change.** [Gulf Coast oil gas world]. (19??)-(Feb. 1994). Periodical. English. mo. Hart Publications Inc, 1900 Grant Street, Suite 400, Denver CO 80203. **Tel** (303)837-1917, (800)832-1917, FAX (303)837-8585. **LC** HD9567.A13; G84. **DD** 338.4/7622338/0976. *Continues Gulf Coast Oil World, 0884-7967.* **Merged with** *Midcontinent Oil and Gas World; Pacific Oil and Gas World; Northeast Oil and Gas World; Southwest Oil and Gas World; Western Oil and Gas World* **to form** *Hart's Oil and Gas World, 1075-5365.*

US/0739-3547
**GULF COAST OIL DIRECTORY.** [Gulf Coast oil dir.]. (1982)-. Directory. English. an. $55.00. IEI Publishing Division, 1635 West Alabama, Houston TX 77006. **Tel** (713)529-1616, FAX (713)529-0936. **ED** Susan Anderson. **LC** HD9567.A13; G83. **DD** 622/.338/029476. **Ad Acc. Circ:** 7,000. *Continues Original Gulf Coast Oil Directory.*
**Desc:** Covers the Gulf Coast area from blowout preventers to workover and well servicing.

US/0884-7967
**GULF COAST OIL WORLD. Title Change.**
[Gulf Coast oil world]. (198?)-(19??). Periodical. English. bm. Hart Publications Inc, 1900 Grant Street, Suite 400, Denver CO 80203. **Tel** (303)837-1917, (800)832-1917, FAX (303)837-8585. **LC** HD9567.A13; G84. **DD** 338.4/7622338/0976. **[CCC].** available on microfilm from University Microfilms International (UMI). *Continues Gulf Coast Oil Staff Reporter, 0744-9070. Continued by Gulf Coast Oil and Gas World, 1070-4914.*

CN/0704-5980
**GULF DEALER. VAT** Gulf Canada Dealer News (1976). V. 34- Mar./April 1979-. Periodical. English. mo. Gulf Oil Canada, 800 Bay Street, Toronto Ontario M5S 1Y8 Canada. **DD** 381/.45/665538270971. *Continues Gulf Canada Dealer News, 0380-3457.*

US/0885-355X
**GULF OF MEXICO REPORT. NEWSLETTER EDITION.** (GULF OF MEXICO REPORT. NEWSLETTER EDITION / Pl.]. [Gulf Mex. rep., Newsl. ed.]. **Added/Corp** Petroleum Information Corporation. (19??)-. Newsletter. English. $83.35 (one year), $151.55 (two year) Houston, Texas; $82.58 (one year), $150.15 (two year) Texas; $77.00 (one year), $140.00 (two year) other. Petroleum Information Corporation, 5333 Westheimer, Suite 100, Houston TX 77056. **Tel** (713)840-8282 ext. 38, FAX (713)599-5100. **DD** 553.

US/0191-9849
**GULF STATES OIL AND GAS DIRECTORY.** Directory. English. an. $25.00. Gulf States Oil And Gas Directory Of LA, 3810 Lakeshore Drive, Shreveport LA 71109. **LC** TN867; .G86. **DD** 338.2/7/2802576.

US
**GULF STATES / PERMIAN BASIN PETROLEUM DIRECTORY.** (19??)-. English. an. $89.00, $895.00 on diskette. Hart Publications Inc, 1900 Grant Street, Suite 400, Denver CO 80203. **Tel** (303)837-1917, (800)832-1917, FAX (303)837-8585. available on diskette. *Continues Gulf States Petroleum Directory.*
**Desc:** Covers the states of Texas, Southeast New Mexico, Louisiana, Mississippi, Alabama, Florida, Georgia and South Carolina.

IS
**HADSHOT HA-NEFT VEHA-ENERGYAH.** No. 155/156- December 1974-. Periodical. Hebrew. 26 Ha-Universitah Street, Ramat Aviv Israel. **LC** HD9576.I78; H33. *Continues Hadshot Ha-Neft.*

●US/1075-5365
**HART'S OIL AND GAS WORLD.** [Hart's oil gas world]. **VFOAT** Oil and Gas World. Vol. 86, No. 2 (Feb. 1994)-. Periodical. English. mo. $59.00 (one year), $99.00 (two year). Hart Publications Inc, 1900 Grant Street, Suite 400, Denver CO 80203. **Tel** (303)837-1917, (800)832-1917, FAX (303)837-8585. **ED** Don Lyle. **LC** TN860; .H37. **DD** 338.2/728/0973. *Formed by the union of Gulf Coast Oil and Gas World, 1070-4914; Midcontinent Oil and Gas World, 1071-4790; Northeast Oil and Gas World, 1070-4469; Pacific Oil and Gas World, 1071-9628; Southwest Oil and Gas World, 1071-4804 and Western Oil and Gas World, 1070-6100.*

US/0884-3007
**HART'S PETROLEUM PROFESSIONALS (ROCKY MOUNTAIN ED.). Ceased.** (HART'S PETROLEUM PROFESSIONALS.). [Hart's petrol. prof.]. 1st Ed. (1984)-(19??). English. an. Hart Publications Inc, 1900 Grant Street, Suite 400, Denver CO 80203. **Tel** (303)837-1917, (800)832-1917, FAX (303)837-8585. **LC** TN867; .H33. **DD** 622/.338/02578.

US/1015-0714
**HEAVY OILER. Suspended.** [Heavy oiler]. **Added/Corp** United Nations Institute for Training and Research/United Nations Development Programme Information Centre for Heavy Crude and Tar Sands. (19??)-Suspended. Periodical. English. qt. Free (to members of the Centre), $60.00 (non-members). UNITAR/UNDP, Information Center for Heavy Crude and Tar Sands, 801 United Nations Plaza, 5th Floor, New York NY 10017. **DD** 665.

US/0149-6409
**HENRY L. DOHERTY SERIES.** [Henry L. Doherty ser.]. **Added/Corp** Society of Petroleum Engineers of AIME. (1967)-. Monographic series. English. Price varies per volume. Society of Petroleum Engineers, PO Box 833836, Richardson TX 75083-3836. **Tel** (214)952-9393 or (214)952-9458, FAX (214)952-9435, telex 163245 (SPEUT). **LC** UNC.
**Ind/Abst** GeoRef.

US
**HEROLD'S COMPARATIVE APPRAISAL REPORTS. Added/Corp** John S. Herold, Inc. **VFOAT** Comparative Appraisal Reports. (19??)-. English. mo. $1500.00 (Sectors 1, 2 or 3). John S. Herold, Inc., 5 Edgewood Avenue, Greenwich CT 06830. **Tel** (203)869-2585, FAX (203)869-4729. ***Continues*** *Oil Industry Comparative Appraisals I, 0276-5993; Oil Industry Comparative Appraisals II, 0886-8662* ***and*** *Oil Industry Comparative Appraisals III, 0276-5993.*
**Ind/Abst** Pet. Energy Bus. News Index (1992).

●US/1062-3485
**HEROLD'S OIL HEADLINER.** [Herold's oil headl.]. **Added/Corp** John S. Herold, Inc. **VFOAT** Oil Headliner. Mar. 31, (1992)-. Periodical. English. da (260 issues). $1095.00. John S. Herold, Inc., 5 Edgewood Avenue, Greenwich CT 06830. **Tel** (203)869-2585, FAX (203)869-4729. **DD** 338.

RU/0204-3998
**HIMICESKAJA PROMYSLENNOST. SERIJA, FOSFORNAJA PROMYSLENNOST. See** Chemistry-Chemical Technology.

RU/0023-1169
**HIMIJA I TEHNOLOGIJA TOPLIV I MASEL.** (KHIMIIA I TEKHNOLOGIIA TOPLIV I MASEL.). [Him. tehnol. topl. masel]. **Added/Corp** Soviet Union. Gosudarstvennyi Komitet po Koordinatsii Nauchno-Issledovatelskikh Rabot. Akademiia nauk SSSR. No. 1 (1958)-. Periodical. Russian. mo. $99.95. **(Subscription address:** East View Publications Inc., 3020 Harbor Lane North, Suite 110, Minneapolis MN 55447.**) CODEN** KTPMAG. **[CCC].** Documents available from Article Express International, CASDDS. ***Continues*** *Khimiia i Tekhnologiia Topliva i Masel.*
**Ind/Abst** Chem. Abstr.; Coal Abstr.; Ei Page One; Energy Res. Abstr. (May 1980-); Eng. Index Annu.; GeoRef; Int. Aerosp. Abstr.; Lit. Pat. Abstr., Oilfield Chem. (1990-); Lit. Abstr., Catal. Catal.; Lit. Abstr., Health Environ.; Lit. Abstr., Pet. Refin. Petrochem.; Lit. Abstr., Pet. Substit.; Lit. Abstr., Transp. Storage.

RU/0023-1177
**HIMIJA TVERDOVO TOPLIVA.** (KHIMIIA TVERDOGO TOPLIVA.). [Him. tverd. topl.]. **Added/Corp** Akademiia Nauk SSSR. (1967)-. Academic Scholarly Publication. Russian. bm. $139.95. Izdatelstvo Nauka / Akademiia Nauk, Publishing House of the Russian Academy of Sciences, Leninskii Porspekt 14, 117901 Moscow Russia. **Tel** 011 95 954-21-53, FAX 011 95 938-21-44, telex 411964. **(Subscription address:** East View Publications Inc., 3020 Harbor Lane North, Suite 110, Minneapolis MN 55447.**) LC** TP315; .K46. **CODEN** KTVTBYKTVTAX. Documents available from CASDDS. ***Continues*** *Khimiia Tverdogo Topliva.*
**Ind/Abst** Chem. Abstr.; Coal Abstr.; Energy Res. Abstr. (Feb. 1981-); GeoRef.

US/0191-6653
**HOSE & NOZZLE (SHREVEPORT).** (HOSE & NOZZLE.). **Added/Corp** Louisiana Oil Marketers Association. **VAT** Hose and Nozzle (Shreveport). (19??)-. Trade Publication. English. Four times a year. Free on request. Louisiana Oil Marketers Association, Box One, Shreveport LA 71161. **Tel** (318)221-4113. **ED** Robert K. Butcher. **Ad Acc. Circ:** 800 (ctrl).
**Desc:** Oil marketing trade association journal.

US/0747-1173
**HOTLINE (WILLISTON, N.D.).** ***Suspended.*** (HOTLINE.). (198?)-(Dec. 1986). Periodical. English. bw. $18.00 North Dakota, South Dakota, Montana; $23.50 other US; $27.50 other. Hotline, Box 208, Williston ND 58801. **Tel** (701)774-8757. ***Continues*** *Oil Patch Hotline, 0279-6333.*

US/0739-3555
**HOUSTON OIL DIRECTORY.** [Houston oil dir.]. (197?)-. English. an. $39.00. IEI Publishing Division, 1635 West Alabama, Houston TX 77006. **Tel** (713)529-1616, FAX (713)529-0936. **ED** Susan Anderson. **LC** TN867; .H68. **DD** 338.2/7282/0257641411. Index available. **Ad Acc. Circ:** 4,000.
**Desc:** Covers the Houston, Dallas and Ft. Worth areas from blowout preventers to workover and well servicing.

US
**HPI MARKET DATA. VFOAT** H.P.I. Market Data. **VAT** Hydrocarbon Processing Industry Market Data32. (199?)-. English. an. $10.00. Gulf Publishing Company / Texas, PO Box 2608, Houston TX 77252. **Tel** (800)231-6275, (713)529-4301, FAX (713)520-4433. ***Continues*** *HPI Outlook.*

US
**HPI OUTLOOK, THE.** ***Title Change.*** **VAT** Hydrocarbon Processing Industry Outlook. (1991)-(199?). English. Gulf Publishing Company / Texas, PO Box 2608, Houston TX 77252. **Tel** (800)231-6275, (713)529-4301, FAX (713)520-4433. ***Continues*** *HPI Market Data.* ***Continued by*** *HPI Market Data (Houston, Tex. : 1993).*

US/0018-8190
**HYDROCARBON PROCESSING (INTERNATIONAL ED.).** (HYDROCARBON PROCESSING.). [Hydrocarbon process.]. (19??)-. Academic Scholarly Publication. English. mo. $24.00 US and Canada; $36.00 other. Gulf Publishing Company / Texas, PO Box 2608, Houston TX 77252. **Tel** (800)231-6275, (713)529-4301, FAX (713)520-4433. **LC** TP690.A1; H89. **DD** 665.5/05. **CODEN** IHPRBSHYPRAX. **[CCC].** available on microfilm and microfiche from University Microfilms International (UMI). Documents available from Article Express International.
**Ind/Abst** Appl. Sci. Technol. Index (Jan. 1975-); Bioeng. Abstr.; Chem. Bus. Bull.; Chem. Bus. NewsBase (1985-); Chem. Bus. Update; Chem. Hazards Ind.; Chem. Ind. Notes; Curr. Contents Eng. Tech. Appl. Sci.; Ei Page One (1973-); EMBASE; Energy Inf. Abstr.; Energy Res. Abstr. (Jan. 1975-); Eng. Index Annu.; Fluid Abstr., Civil Eng.; Fluid Abstr. Proc. Eng.; FLUIDEX (1973-); Lab. Hazards Bull.; Lit. Pat. Abstr., Oilfield Chem. (1954-); Lit. Abstr., Catal. Catal.; Lit. Abstr., Health Environ.; Lit. Abstr., Pet. Refin. Petrochem.; Lit. Abstr., Pet. Substit.; Lit. Abstr., Transp. Storage; Sel. Water Resour. Abstr.; Shock Vibr. Dig.; Soc. Sci. Cit. Index [Select. Cov.]; Soils Fert.

US/0887-0284
**HYDROCARBON PROCESSING (U.S. ED.).** (HYDROCARBON PROCESSING.). [Hydrocarbon process.]. Vol. 45, No. 6 (June 1966)-. Academic Scholarly Publication. English. mo. $24.00 North America; $36.00 other. Gulf Publishing Company / Texas, PO Box 2608, Houston TX 77252. **Tel** (800)231-6275, (713)529-4301, FAX (713)520-4433. **ED** R W Scott, J J McKetta Jr, H L Hoffman, L A Kane, C H Vervalin and P S Stantberg. **LC** PAR. **DD** 665. **CODEN** HYPRAX. Index available. **Ad Acc. Circ:** 28,014. available on microfilm from University Microfilms International (UMI). Documents available from Article Express International, The Genuine Article, Petroleum Abstracts Document Delivery Service, CASDDS. ***Continues*** *Hydrocarbon Processing & Petroleum Refiner, 0096-2406.*
**Desc:** Targets petroleum refining, petrochemical/chemical processing, gas processing and synfuels; reaches key buyers in 97 percent of the world's operating plants and all engineer-constructors.
**Ind/Abst** Acoust. Abstr.; Appl. Sci. Technol. Index; Chem Inform; Chem. Abstr.; Chem. Ind. Notes; Coal Abstr.; Ei Page One; EMBASE; Eng. Index Annu.; F&S Index Plus Text, Int. [Select. Cov.]; Fluid Abstr., Civil Eng.; Fluid Abstr. Proc. Eng.; FLUIDEX; Gas Abstr.; Highw. Res. Abstr.; HTFS Dig.; INIS Atomindex [Micro.]; Pet. Abstr.; Proc. Chem. Eng.; PROMT; Res. Alert [Full Cov.]; Sci. Cit. Index; SCISEARCH; Theoret. Chem. Eng.; Trade Ind. ASAP [Full Txt.]; Trade Ind. Index [Full Txt.].

IT/0390-2358
**ICP.** [ICP]. (1973)-. Periodical. Italian. Eleven times a year. L12000.00 Italy; L110000.00 other. Eris Spa, Via E Tellini 14, 20155 Milan Italy. **Tel** 011 39 2 33103305. **UDC** 66.
**Ind/Abst** Curr. Biotechnol.

US/0270-1022
**IGT GASCOPE.** [IGT gaScope]. **Added/Corp** Institute of Gas Technology. **VFOAT** GaScope. **VAT** Institute of Gas Technology Gas Scope. No. 41 (Winter 1977/1978)-. Periodical. English. ir. Free. Institute of Gas Technology, 3424 South State Street, Chicago IL 60616. **Tel** (312)949-3970, (312)949-3650, FAX (312)949-3776, telex 25-6189. **ED** Carl W. Sauer (phone: (312)949-3732 & FAX (312)949-3776). **CODEN** GASCDV. ***Continues*** *Gas Scope.*
**Ind/Abst** Energy Inf. Abstr.

US/0073-5108
**ILLINOIS PETROLEUM.** [Ill. petrol.]. **Added/Corp** Illinois State Geological Survey. Illinois. Dept. of Registration and Education. No. 1 (1926)-. Monographic series. English. ir. Price varies per volume. Illinois Geological Survey, Natural Resources Building, Urbana IL 61801. **LC** TN872.I3; I44. **DD** 553.2/8/09773. **CODEN** ILGPA4. Documents available from CASDDS.
**Ind/Abst** AESIS Q.; Chem. Abstr.; Geol. Abstr.; GeoRef.

CN/0848-8843
**IMPERIAL OIL REVIEW (1989).** (IMPERIAL OIL REVIEW.). [Imp. Oil rev.]. **Added/Corp** Imperial Oil Limited. Vol. 73, No. 394 (Fall 1989)-. Periodical. English. Four times a year (Seasonally). Free. Imperial Oil Ltd, 111 Sainte Clair Avenue West, Toronto Ontario M5W 1K3 Canada. **Tel** (416)968-4917. **ED** Sarah Lawley. **DD** 051. ***Continues*** *Imperial Oil Limited. Review.*
**Ind/Abst** Can. Period. Index.

US/0360-6236
**INACTIVE OIL AND GAS FIELDS.** [Inact. oil gas fields]. **Main/Corp** Texas. Railroad Commission. Oil and Gas Division. English. R R Commission, Oil and Gas Division, Capital Street, PO Drawer 12967, Austin TX 78711. **LC** TN867; .T38A. **DD** 622/.33/809764.

US/0560-6225
**INDEX OF WELLS SHOT FOR VELOCITY.** [Index wells shot veloc.]. **Main/Corp** Society of Exploration Geophysicists. (19??)-. English. an (published in Jan. of prior year). $65.00. Society of Exploration Geophysicists, PO Box 702740, Tulsa OK 74170-2740. **Tel** (918)493-3516, FAX (918)493-2074, telex 796 392 SEG TUL. **LC** TN271.P4; S62.
**Ind/Abst** GeoRef.

II/0971-2542
**INDIAN JOURNAL OF PETROLEUM GEOLOGY.** [Indian J. Pet. Geol.]. (1992)-. Periodical. English. sa. $80.00. Dehadrun Indian Publishing Company. **(Subscription address:** Prints India, 11 Darya Ganj, New Delhi 110002 India.**) UDC** 553.98.

UK
**INDIAN SUB-CONTINENT SERVICE.** English. qt. £2,500.00. Wood Mackenzie Consultants Ltd., Kintore House, 74 77 Queen Street, Edinburgh EH2 4NS Scotland. **Tel** 011 44 031 225 8525, FAX 011 44 031 243 4435, telex 72555.

II/0376-9968
**INDO-BURMA PETROLEUM COMPANY LIMITED ANNUAL REPORT.** (ANNUAL REPORT.). **Main/Corp** Indo-Burma Petroleum Company. English. an. Indo-Burma Petroleum Company, Gillander House, Netaji Subhas Road, Calcutta-1 India. **LC** HD9576.I54; I523. **DD** 338.7/66/50954. ***Continues*** *Report of Directors and Statement of Accounts.*

SI
**INDONESIAN MONTHLY ACTIVITIES REPORT.** English. mo (Plus 2 synopsis issues). $6200.00. IEDS Ltd., Represnetative Office, 10 Anson Road, 17-10 International Plaza, Singapore 0207 Singapore. **Tel** 011 65 2254166, 2253610, FAX 011 65 2259694. **(Subscription address:** IEDS Field Services Ltd., Enterprise House, Avening Road, Gloucestershire GL6 0BS England**) ED** Ian Cross. **Circ:** 50.
**Desc:** Oil and gas exploration activities, new contracts, seismic discoveries, and new exploration programmes.

US/0094-1646
**INDUSTRIAL ENERGY.** V. 3- May/June 1973-. Periodical. English. bm. £10.00. Gas Industries Equipment and Appliance News, 333 North Michigan Avenue, Chicago IL 60601. **LC** TP345.A1; G35. **DD** 665.7/05. ***Continues*** *Gas in Industry.*

UK
**INFORMATION ABOUT THE OIL INDUSTRY, FOR THE OIL INDUSTRY.** ***Ceased.*** Periodical. English. mo. Associated Octel Company Ltd, PO Box 17, Oil States Road, Ellesmere Port South Wirral L65 4HF England. **Tel** 051-355-3611, telex 629384. ctrl circ.

FR
**INFORMATION / GAZ DE FRANCE.** French (French). Gaz de France, 23 rue Philibert-Delorme, 75840 Paris Cedex 17 France. **LC** HD9581.F7; G39. **DD** 338.2/7285/0944. ***Continues*** *Gaz de France. Departement des Relations Publiques. Information.*

US
**INFORMATION SERVICE / AMERICAN GAS ASSOCIATION. Main/Corp** American Gas Association. (19??)-. English. ir. $600.00 (nonmembers), $300.00 (members). American Gas Association / Virginia, 1515 Wilson Boulevard, Arlington VA 22209. **Tel** (703)841-8400, (703)841-8559, FAX (703)841-8697.

MX
**INFORME DE LABORES.** ***Title Change.*** **Main/Corp** Petroleos Mexicanos. **VFOAT** Informe de Labores, Anexo. (1987/1988)-. Spanish. **LC** HD9574.M62; P412. **DD** 338.2/7282/097205. ***Continues*** *Memoria de Labores - Petroleos Mexicanos.* ***Continued by*** *Memoria de Labores.*

BO
**INFORME PETROLERAS. Main/Corp** Bolivia. Direccion General de Hidrocarburos. Vol. 1 (January 1973)-. Periodical. Spanish. mo. Direccion General de Hidrocarburos, Ave Mariscal Santa Cruz No 1322-5, Piso Casilla 4819, La Paz Bolivia. **LC** HD9574.B6; B57a.

US
**INGAA RATE AND POLICY ANALYSIS DEPARTMENTS REPORTS.** (19??)-. English. bw. $50.00 US & Canada; $100.00 other. Interstate Natural Gas Association of America, 555 13th Street Northwest, Suite 300 West, Washington DC 20004. **Tel** (202)626-3200, FAX (202)626-3250. **ED** Cheryl W. Hoffman. **Ad Acc.**

US/0163-948X
**INSIDE F.E.R.C. See** Energy.

US/8756-3711
**INSIDE F.E.R.C.'S GAS MARKET REPORT.** [Inside F.E.R.C.'s gas mark. rep.]. **VFOAT** Inside FERC's Gas Market Report; Gas Market Report. **VAT** Inside Federal Energy Regulatory Commission's Gas Market Report. (Jan. 11, 1985)-. Newsletter. English. bw. $865.00 US and Canada; $890.00 other. McGraw Hill Publishing Company, Inc., 1221 Avenue of the Americas, New York NY 10020. **Tel** (212)512-6410, (800)525-5003, FAX (212)512-6111. **DD** 333. ***Continues in part*** *Inside F.E.R.C., 0163-948X.*

US/0074-0551
**INSTRUMENTATION IN THE CHEMICAL AND PETROLEUM INDUSTRIES.** [Instrum. chem. pet. ind.]. **Added/Corp** Instrument Society of America. Vol. 1 (1964)-. Monographic series. English. an. Price varies per volume. Instrument Society of America, 67 Alexander Drive, Research Triangle NC 27709. **Tel** (919)549-8411, FAX (919)549-8288, telex 802 540. **LC** TP157; .I55. **DD** 660.2/83. **CODEN** INCPAW. **[CCC].** **Circ:** 250. Documents available from Article Express International, Ask*IEEE, CASDDS.
**Desc:** Proceedings of the annual conference.
**Ind/Abst** Chem. Abstr.; Coal Abstr. (Mar. 1979-); Ei Page One; Energy Res. Abstr.; Eng. Index Annu.; INSPEC.

CY/1010-1179
**INTERNATIONAL CRUDE OIL AND PRODUCT PRICES.** [Int. crude oil prod. prices]. (1971)-. Periodical. English. sa. $570.00 (subscribers to Middle East Economic Survey), $600.00 (nonsubscribers). Middle East Petroleum & Economic Publishers, PO Box 4940, Nicosia Cyprus. **Tel** 011 357 2 445431, FAX 011 357 2 474988, telex 2198 MEES CY.

US/1064-9042
**INTERNATIONAL EXPLORATION NEWSLETTER.** [Int. explor. newsl.]. (198?)-. Newsletter. English. bw (26 issues per year). $134.06 Texas; $125.00 US & Canada; $160.00 other. Geo Services International, PO Box 6662, Kingwood TX 77325. **Tel** (713)358-4061, FAX (713)358-4061. **ED** George Tappan. **DD** 338.

UK
**INTERNATIONAL GAS REPORT.** **Added/Corp** Financial Times Business Information Ltd. **VFOAT** IGR; FT International Gas Report. (19??)-. Periodical. English. Twenty-four times a year (Publishes every other Friday). £599.00. Financial Times England, 8 16 Great New Street, London EC4A 3BN England. **Tel** 011 44 71 353 0305, 353 1040, FAX 011 44 353 0846. **LC** HD9581.A1; I784. ***Absorbed*** *World Gas Report.*
**Ind/Abst** PROMT [Full Txt.]; PTS Newsl. Database [Full Txt.].

US/0276-4040
**INTERNATIONAL GAS TECHNOLOGY HIGHLIGHTS.** [Int. gas technol. highlights]. **Added/Corp** Institute of Gas Technology. **VFOAT** IGT Highlights. (Apr. 26, 1971)-. Periodical. English. Twenty-six times a year. Free, IGT members and international associates; $90.00 US; $100 other. Institute of Gas Technology, 3424 South State Street, Chicago IL 60616. **Tel** (312)949-3970, (312)949-3650, FAX (312)949-3776, telex 25-6189. **ED** Colleen T. Sen. **DD** 333. **Circ:** 2,000. available on an online database.
**Desc:** Brief news articles about the natural gas industry producers pipelines, utilities, research and government--aimed primarily at management.
**Ind/Abst** Coal Abstr.

●US/1059-7816
**INTERNATIONAL OFFSHORE OIL COMPANY DIRECTORY.** (1991)-. Directory. English. $150.00. Offshore Data Services Inc., PO Box 19909, Houston TX 77224. **Tel** (713)781-2713, FAX (713)781-9594, telex 166338.

US/1058-6008
**INTERNATIONAL OFFSHORE RIG OWNERS & PERSONNEL DIRECTORY.** [Int. offshore rig owners pers. dir.]. **Added/Corp** Offshore Data Services, Inc. **VFOAT** International Offshore Rig Owners and Personnel Directory; Offshore Rig Owners and Personnel Directory. (1991)-. Directory. English. an (Aug.). $125.00 North America; $135.00 others. Offshore Data Services Inc., PO Box 19909, Houston TX 77224. **Tel** (713)781-2713, FAX (713)781-9594, telex 166338. **LC** HD9563; .I58. **DD** 338.2/7282/025. Index available. ctrl circ.

US/0535-1634
**INTERNATIONAL OIL AND GAS DEVELOPMENT.** **See** Petroleum and Natural Gas-Abstracting, Bibliographies and Statistics.

US/0535-1634
**INTERNATIONAL OIL AND GAS DEVELOPMENT YEARBOOK. PART 1: EXPLORATION.** (19??)-. English. an. $150.00 US; $153.00 other. Mason Research Consultants, PO Box 338, Austin TX 78767. **Tel** (512)472-7173, FAX (512)472-1057. **ED** Margie Wells and Marilyn Lay. **Pr Rev.**
**Desc:** Worldwide oil and gas production statistics by field. Listed by state and country.

US
**INTERNATIONAL OIL AND GAS DEVELOPMENT YEARBOOK. PART 2: PRODUCTION.** (19??)-. English. an (Nov.). $350.00. Mason Research Consultants, PO Box 338, Austin TX 78767. **Tel** (512)472-7173, FAX (512)472-1057. **Circ:** 250. available on diskette from the publisher. Documents available from the publisher.
**Desc:** Information on oil and gas production and exploration data by field or lease.

US/0043-8855
**INTERNATIONAL OIL NEWS.** [Int. oil news]. (19??)-. Periodical. English. wk (52 issues). $455.00 - incorps International Oil News (Management Edition and Suppliers Edition). William F. Bland Company, PO Box 16666, Chapel Hill NC 27516. **Tel** (919)490-0700. **ED** Glenn Sanislo. **[CCC].**

US/0270-1138
**INTERNATIONAL PETROCHEMICAL DEVELOPMENT.** ***Ceased.*** [Int. petrochem. dev.]. (1980)-Ceased (Dec. 1989). Periodical. English. sm. Rickian Inc, 3501 South Ocean Boulevard/Suite 103, Palm Beach FL 33480. **Tel** (407)585-8593. **ED** H L List. Index available. **Circ:** 100 (ctrl).
**Desc:** A review of products and processes in the international petrochemical industry.

US/0733-009X
**INTERNATIONAL PETROCHEMICAL REPORT, THE.** **See** Chemistry.

UK/0309-4944
**INTERNATIONAL PETROLEUM ABSTRACTS.** ***Title Change.*** **See** Petroleum and Natural Gas-Abstracting, Bibliographies and Statistics.

UK/1052-9292
**INTERNATIONAL PETROLEUM ABSTRACTS INCORPORATING OFFSHORE ABSTRACTS.** [Int. pet. abstr. inc. offshore abstr.]. Vol. 19, No. 1 (March 1991)-. Periodical. English. Four times a year. $995.00. John Wiley & Sons Ltd., Baffins Lane, Chichester West Sussex PO19 1UD England. **Tel** 0243 779777, FAX 0243 776128 BTG:JWP001, telex 86290 WIBOOKG. **(Subscription address:** John Wiley / Philadelphia, PO Box 7247, Philadelphia PA 19170.**)** **LC** TN860; .I593. **DD** 553. **CODEN** IPAAET. ***Continues*** *International Petroleum Abstracts, 0309-4944;* ***Absorbed*** *Offshore Abstracts, 0305-0513.*
**Desc:** Covers petroleum and allied literature concerning oil-field exploration and development, petroleum refining and product and economics. Includes scientific and technical topics such as transport and storage, analysis and testing, geology, geophysics, safety, pollution and education.
**Ind/Abst** Fluid Abstr., Civil Eng.; Fluid Abstr. Proc. Eng.; FLUIDEX.

US/0148-0375
**INTERNATIONAL PETROLEUM ENCYCLOPEDIA.** [Int. pet. encycl.]. (1968)-. Trade Publication. English. an. $130.00 US and Canada; $175.00 other. PennWell Publishing Company, 1421 South Sheridan, PO Box 1260, Tulsa OK 74101. **Tel** (918)835-3161, (800)331-4463, FAX (918)831-9497. **(Subscription address:** PennWell Books, PO Box 21288, Tulsa OK 74121.**)** **ED** John C. McCaslin. **LC** HD9560.1; .I565. **DD** 338.2/7/2805. **[CCC].** Index available (free). **Ad Acc.**
**Desc:** Includes atlases and political information along with reports and articles on global hot spots and industry issues.
**Ind/Abst** Stat. Ref. Index.

US/0193-9270
**INTERNATIONAL PETROLEUM FINANCE.** (197?)-. English. Twenty-four times a year. $645.00 mail; $1290.00 fax. Petroleum Intelligence Weekly, 575 Broadway, 4th Floor, New York NY 10012-3230. **Tel** (212)941-5500, FAX (212)941-5509, telex 62371 PETROIN. **ED** Dillard P. Spriggs. **[CCC].** Index available. ctrl circ.
**Desc:** Analysis of management strategies, earnings and finances of oil companies, and key oil industry developments around the world.
**Ind/Abst** Pet. Energy Bus. News Index (1983).

US/1044-1816
**INTERNATIONAL PETROLEUM STATISTICS REPORT.** [Int. pet. stat. rep.]. **Added/Corp** United States. Office of Energy Markets and End Use. (Jan 1989)-. Periodical. English. mo. $43.00 domestic; $53.75 other. National Energy Information Center, Energy Information Administration, Forrestal Building, Room 1F-048, Washington DC 20585. **Tel** (202)586-8800. **LC** HD9560.1; .I566. **DD** 338.2/728/021. Documents available from Documents on Demand.
**Desc:** Presents data on international oil production, consumption, imports, exports, and stocks.
**Ind/Abst** Am. Stat. Index; Energy Inf. Abstr.

US/1046-2333
**INTERSTATE OIL & GAS COMPACT & COMMITTEE BULLETIN, THE.** [Interstate oil gas compact comm. bull.]. **VFOAT** Interstate Oil and Gas Compact and Committee Bulletin. Vol. 1, No. 1 (June 1987)-. Bulletin. English. sa. Free. Interstate Oil & Gas Compact Commission, PO Box 53127, Oklahoma City OK 73152-3127. **Tel** (405)525-3556, FAX (405)525-3592. **LC** TN872; .A3217. **DD** 333.8/23/160973. **Circ:** 2,000. ***Formed by the union of*** *Interstate Oil Compact Commission Committee Bulletin, 0020-9732* ***and*** *Oil and Gas Compact Bulletin, 0196-7177.*
**Ind/Abst** Coal Abstr.; Energy Res. Abstr.; GeoRef; INIS Atomindex [Micro.].

US
**INTERSTATE PIPELINE RATES ON CRUDE PETROLEUM OIL.** English. mo. $165.00 (one year), $180.00 (two year). Fieldston Publications, 1920 North Street Northwest, Suite 210, Washington DC 20036. **Tel** (202)775-0240, FAX (202)872-8045.

US
**INTERSTATE RATES FOR GASOLINE AND PETROLEUM PRODUCTS.** English. mo. $165.00 (one year), $180.00 (two year). Fieldston Publications, 1920 North Street Northwest, Suite 210, Washington DC 20036. **Tel** (202)775-0240, FAX (202)872-8045.

US
**INTRASTATE PIPELINE RATES ON CRUDE PETROLEUM OIL.** English. mo. $165.00 (one year) $180.00 (two year). Fieldston Publications, 1920 North Street Northwest, Suite 210, Washington DC 20036. **Tel** (202)775-0240, FAX (202)872-8045.

US
**INTRASTATE RATES FOR CRUDE PETROLEUM OIL.** English. mo. $165.00 (one year), $180.00 (two year). Fieldston Publications, 1920 North Street Northwest, Suite 210, Washington DC 20036. **Tel** (202)775-0240, FAX (202)872-8045.

US
**INTRASTATE RATES FOR GASOLINE AND PETROLEUM PRODUCTS.** English. mo. $165.00 (one year), $180.00 (two year). Fieldston Publications, 1920 North Street Northwest, Suite 210, Washington DC 20036. **Tel** (202)775-0240, FAX (202)872-8045.

CN/0845-437X
**IPAC QUARTERLY.** [IPAC q.]. **Added/Corp** Independent Petroleum Association of Canada. **VFOAT** Quarterly. **VAT** Independent Petroleum Association of Canada Quarterly. Vol. 1, No. 1 (Aug. 1988)-. Periodical. English. Four times a year. Free on request. IPAC / Independent Petroleum Association of Canada, 700-707 7th Avenue SW, Calgary Alberta T2P 0Z2 Canada. **Tel** (403)290-1530. **ED** Anne Polistac. **DD** 333.8/23/0971. ctrl circ.

US
**IPI DATA SERVICE. EUROPE.** **Added/Corp** International Petroleum Institute. **VFOAT** International Petroleum Industry. Europe Supplement. (197?)-. Periodical. English. mo. $1650.00. Barrows Company Inc., 116 East 66th Street, New York NY 10021. **Tel** (212)772-1199, (800)227-7697, FAX (212)288-7242, telex 4971238 BARROWS.

US/0276-0061
**IPI DATA SERVICE. EXPLORATION, PRODUCTION, TRANSPORTATION, REFINING & MARKETING (NORTH AMERICA).** (IPI DATA SERVICE. EXPLORATION, PRODUCTION, TRANSPORTATION, REFINING & MARKETING.). [IPI data ser., Explor., prod., transp., refin. mark.]. **Added/Corp** International Petroleum Institute. **VFOAT** International Petroleum Industry. IPI Data Service. North America. **VAT** International Petroleum Institute Data Service. Exploration, Production, Transportation, Refining and Marketing (North America). (1973)-. Periodical. English. mo. $1650.00. Barrows Company Inc., 116 East 66th Street, New York NY 10021. **Tel** (212)772-1199, (800)227-7697, FAX (212)288-7242, telex 4971238 BARROWS. ***Formed by the union of*** *International Petroleum Industry. Refining & Marketing. North America, 0276-0088* ***and*** *International Petroleum Industry. Exploration, Production, Transportation. North America, 0276-007X.*

US/0276-0096
**IPI DATA SERVICE. EXPLORATION, PRODUCTION, TRANSPORTATION, REFINING & MARKETING (WORLD).** (IPI DATA SERVICE, EXPLORATION, PRODUCTION, TRANSPORTATION, REFINING & MARKETING. WORLD. SUPPLEMENT.). [IPI data serv., Explor., prod., transp., refin. mark.]. **Added/Corp** International Petroleum Institute. **VFOAT** International Petroleum Industry. IPI Data Service. World. **VAT** International Petroleum Institute Data Service. Exploration, Production, Transportation, Refining and Marketing (World). (1973)-. Periodical. English. mo. $1650.00. Barrows Company Inc., 116 East 66th Street, New York NY 10021. **Tel** (212)772-1199, (800)227-7697, FAX (212)288-7242, telex 4971238 BARROWS. **DD** 338.2/728. ***Formed by the union of*** *International Petroleum Industry Exploration, Production, Transportation. World. Supplement., 0276-0053* ***and*** *International Petroleum Industry Refining & Marketing. World. Supplement., 0276-010X.*

US
**IPI DATA SERVICE. MIDDLE EAST.** **Added/Corp** International Petroleum Institute. **VFOAT** International Petroleum Industry. Middle East Supplement. (197?)-. Periodical. English. mo. $1650.00. Barrows Company Inc., 116 East 66th Street, New York NY 10021. **Tel** (212)772-1199, (800)227-7697, FAX (212)288-7242, telex 4971238 BARROWS. **ED** G H Barrows, M Guerra. Index available. cum. index. **Bk Rev. Circ:** 5,000 (ctrl).
**Desc:** Provides oil and gas economic data by country and area.

US
**IPI DATA SERVICE. NORTH AMERICA. CONSOLIDATED TABLE OF CONTENTS.** (1979)-. Periodical. English. $1650.00. Barrows Company Inc., 116 East 66th Street, New York NY 10021. **Tel** (212)772-1199, (800)227-7697, FAX (212)288-7242, telex 4971238 BARROWS. **DD** 338.2/728/0973.

US
**IPI DATA SERVICE. WORLD. CONSOLIDATED TABLE OF CONTENTS.** (1979)-. Periodical. English. $1650.00. Barrows Company Inc., 116 East 66th Street, New York NY 10021. **Tel** (212)772-1199, (800)227-7697, FAX (212)288-7242, telex 4971238 BARROWS. **DD** 338.2/728/0212.

IQ
**IRAQ OIL NEWS BULLETIN / MINISTRY OF OIL.** Bulletin. English. Ministry of Oil, Information and Public Relations Division, PO Box 6118, Al-Mansoui, Baghdad Iraq. **LC** HD9576.I7; I73. **DD** 338.2/7282/09567. ***Continues** Iraq Oil News.*

US/0360-036X
**ITOGI, SUMMARIES OF SCIENTIFIC PROGRESS : DEVELOPMENT OF OIL AND GAS DEPOSITS.** **VFOAT** Development of Oil and Gas Deposits; Oil and Gas Deposits; Oil & Gas. Monographic series. English (Russian). Price varies per volume. GK Hall & Co, 100 Front Street, Riverside NJ 08075. **Tel** (800)257-5755 ext. 2223. **LC** TN860; .I82. **DD** 622/.33/8.

AJ/0445-0108
**IZVESTIIA VYSSHIKH UCHEBNYKH ZAVEDENII. NEFT I GAZ / MINISTERSTVO VYSSHEGO I SREDNEGO SPETSIALNOGO OBRAZOVANIIA SSSR.** **Added/Corp** Soviet Union. Ministerstvo Vysshego i Srednego Spetsialnogo Obrazovaniia. Azizbaiov Adyna Azarbaijan Neft va Kimia Institutu. Soviet Union. Ministerstvo Vysshego Obrazovaniia. **VFOAT** Neft i Gaz; Izvestiia Vysshikh Uchebnykh Zavedenii. Vol. 1 (1958)-. Academic Scholarly Publication. Russian. mo. $183.00. **(Subscription address:** Victor Kamkin, 4956 Boiling Brook Parkway, Rockville MD 20852.**)** **LC** TN860; .R78. **CODEN** IVUNA2. **[CCC].** Documents available from Article Express International, Petroleum Abstracts Document Delivery Service, CASDDS.
**Ind/Abst** Bioeng. Abstr.; Chem. Abstr.; Coal Abstr.; Ei Page One; Energy Res. Abstr. (Jan. 1972-); Eng. Index Annu.; GeoRef; Pet. Abstr.

JA
**JAPAN PETROLEUM & ENERGY TRENDS.** **Added/Corp** Nihon Sekiyu Konsarutanto. **VFOAT** Japan Petroleum and Energy Trends; JPET. Vol. 23, No. 14 (April 1, 1988)-. Periodical. English. bw. Y180000. Japan Petro Energy Consultants, PO Box 1185, Tokyo Central, Tokyo Japan. **Tel** 011 81 3 3359 8145. **LC** HD9576.J3; J36. **DD** 333.8/232/0952. ***Continues** Japan Petroleum & Energy Weekly, 0386-6165.*

JA
**JAPAN PETROLEUM & ENERGY TRENDS. MONTHLY STATISTICAL SUPPLEMENT.** **Added/Corp** Nihon Sekiyu Konsarutanto. **VFOAT** Japan Petroleum and Energy Trends. Monthly Statistical Supplement; Monthly Statistical Supplement; JPET (Monthly Statistical Supplement). (December 1987)-. Statistical Publication. English. mo. $1,200.00 (includes subscription to: Japan petroleum & energy trends). Japan Petroleum Consultants Ltd, CPO Box 1185, Tokyo 100-91 Japan. **Tel** (03)359-8145, FAX (03)351-9755, telex J25519. **LC** HD9576.J3; J33. **DD** 333.8/232/0952. ***Continues** Japan Petroleum & Energy Weekly. Monthly Statistical Supplement.*

JA
**JAPAN PETROLEUM & ENERGY YEARBOOK.** ***Suspended.*** **Added/Corp** Nihon Sekiyu Konsarutanto. **VFOAT** Japan Petroleum and Energy Yearbook. **VAT** Japan Petroleum and Energy Yearbook. (1975)-. English. an. $195.00. **(Subscription address:** Maruzen Company Ltd., PO Box 5050, Import & Export Department, Tokyo 100 31 Japan.**)** **LC** HD9576.J3; J35. **DD** 338.4/76655/0952.

JA
**JAPAN PETROLEUM INDUSTRY YEARBOOK.** 1st Ed. (1983)-. English. an. Japan Energy Project, 2 5 19 Sekimae Musashinoshi, Tokyo 180 Japan. **LC** HD9576.J3; J354. **DD** 338.2/7282/0952.

JA
**JAPANESE OIL STATISTICS TODAY.** English. $12.00 Japan; $23.00 other. K K Sekiyu Tsushinsha, 16-1 Shinbashi 2-Chome, Minato Ku Tokyo 105 Japan. **Tel** 011 81 3 3591 8351.

US
**JET FUEL INTELLIGENCE.** English. Fifty-one times per year. $1975.00 mail or fax; $200.00 on-line. Petroleum Intelligence Weekly, 575 Broadway, 4th Floor, New York NY 10012-3230. **Tel** (212)941-5500, FAX (212)941-5509, telex 62371 PETROIN. available via fax; available on an online database (updated quarterly).

JA
**JIS HANDOBUKKU : SEKIYU.** **Added/Corp** Nihon Kikaku Kyokai. (1967)-. Periodical. Japanese. ¥2200. Japanese Standards Association, 1-24 Akasaka 4-chome Minato-ku, Tokyo 107 Japan. **LC** TP691; .J17.

AT
**JOBSON'S WHO'S WHO IN AUSTRALIAN MINING & OIL.** ***Title Change.*** **Main/Corp** Jobson's Financial Services Pty. (19??)-(19??). English. an. Jobson's Financial Services, Box 5338, GPO Sydney New South Wales Australia 2000. **LC** HG5899.M5; J6. **DD** 332.6/322. ***Continued by** Jobson's Mining Year Book, 0075-3777.*

CN/0847-9437
**JOURNAL - CANADIAN FUSION FUELS TECHNOLOGY PROJECT.** (JOURNAL.). [Journal - Can. Fusion Fuels Technol. Proj.]. **Added/Corp** Canadian Fusion Fuels Technology Project. **VFOAT** Canadian Fusion Fuels Technology Project Journal; CFFTP Journal. Vol. 6, No. 1 (Feb. 1989)-. Periodical. English. qt. Free. Canadian Fusion Fuels Technology Project, 2700 Lakeshore Road, Mississauga Ontario L5J 1K3 Canada. **Tel** 823-0200, telex 06-982333. **DD** 621.48/335/05. ***Continues** Fusion Fuels Technology., 0824-3921.*

CN/0021-9487
**JOURNAL OF CANADIAN PETROLEUM TECHNOLOGY, THE.** [J. Can. pet. technol.]. **Added/Corp** Canadian Institute of Mining and Metallurgy. Petroleum and Natural Gas Division. Canadian Institute of Mining and Metallurgy. Petroleum Society. Vol. 1 (Spring 1962)-. Periodical. English (summaries and/or abstracts in French). Ten times a year. 135.00Can$ Canada; $150.00 other. Canadian Institute of Mining, Metallurgy and Petroleum, 3400 de Maisonneuve Boulevard West, Xerox Tower, Suite 1210, Montreal, Quebec H3Z 3B8 Canada. **Tel** (514)939-2710, FAX (514)939-2714, telex 055-62344. **ED** P. Michaud. **CODEN** JCPMAM. **Bk Rev. Ad Acc. Pr Rev. Circ:** 6,400 (ctrl). available on microfilm and microfiche from University Microfilms International (UMI). Documents available from Article Express International, The Genuine Article, Petroleum Abstracts Document Delivery Service, CASDDS.
**Desc:** This journal offers concise, scientific, professionally researched technical articles widely regarded as the finest in the industry. The outstanding quality and exclusive articles in the editorial content ensures that each issue is read thoroughly, referred to often, and targeted to the decision-makers.
**Ind/Abst** ASTIS Curr. Aware. Bull. (1978-); AESIS Q.; AQUAREF; ASTIS Bibliogr. (1978-); Bioeng. Abstr.; Chem. Abstr.; Coal Abstr.; Curr. Contents Eng. Tech. Appl. Sci.; Ei Page One; Energy Inf. Abstr.; Energy Res. Abstr. (June 1975-); Eng. Index Annu.; Gas Abstr. (?-?); INIS Atomindex [Micro.]; Lit. Pat. Abstr., Oilfield Chem. (1982-); Lit. Abstr., Catal. Catal.; Lit. Abstr., Health Environ.; Lit. Abstr., Pet. Refin. Petrochem.; Lit. Abstr., Pet. Substit.; Lit. Abstr., Transp. Storage; Mintec, Min. Technol. Abstr.; Life Sci. Collect.; Pet. Abstr.; Res. Alert [Full Cov.]; SCISEARCH; Soc. Sci. Cit. Index [Select. Cov.].

UK/0141-6421
**JOURNAL OF PETROLEUM GEOLOGY.** [J. pet. geol.]. Vol. 1 (July 1978)-. Academic Scholarly Publication. English. qt. £148.00 UK; $294.00 other. Scientific Press Ltd, PO Box 21, Beaconsfield Bucks HP9 1NS England. **Tel** 011 44 494 675139, 011 44 494 672614, FAX 011 44 494 670155. **ED** E.N. Tiratsoo. **LC** TN870.5; .J68. **DD** 553/.28/05. **CODEN** JPEGD9. cum. index. **Bk Rev. Ad Acc. Pr Rev.** ctrl circ. Documents available from Article Express International, The Genuine Article, Petroleum Abstracts Document Delivery Service, CASDDS.
**Ind/Abst** Aquat. Sci. Fish. Abstr. (Computer File); Bioeng. Abstr.; Chem. Abstr.; Coal Abstr.; Curr. Contents Eng. Tech. Appl. Sci.; Curr. Contents Phys. Chem. Earth Sci.; Ei Page One; Energy Res. Abstr. (July 1979-); Eng. Index Annu.; Geogr. Abstr. Phys. Geogr.; Geol. Abstr.; GeoRef; Life Sci. Collect.; Pet. Abstr.; Res. Alert [Full Cov.]; Sci. Cit. Index; SCISEARCH.

US/1055-5056
**JOURNAL OF PETROLEUM MARKETING : JPM / PMAA, THE.** [J. pet. mark.]. **Added/Corp** PMAA (Association). **VFOAT** JPM. Vol. 4, No. 1 (Jan. 1991)-. Periodical. English. mo. BMT Publications Inc, Seven Penn Plaza, New York NY 10001. **Tel** (800)223-9638, (212)594-4120. **LC** HD9561; .J65. **DD** 665.5/38/0688. ***Continues** P, The Journal of Petroleum Marketing, 1050-1754.*

IQ/1012-8603
**JOURNAL OF PETROLEUM RESEARCH.** (JOURNAL OF PETROLEUM RESEARCH / PETROLEUM RESEARCH CENTER, COUNCIL FOR SCIENTIFIC RESEARCH, BAGHDAD.). [J. pet. res.]. **Added/Corp** Markaz Buhuth Al-Naft (Majlis Al-Bahth Al-Ilmi). **VFOAT** Majallat Buhuth Al-Naft; JPR. Vol. 1, No. 1 (1982)-. Periodical. English (Arabic). Twice a year. $50.00 (institutions), $20.00 (individuals). Petroleum Research Center, PO Box 10039, Jadiriyah Baghdad, Iraq. **LC** TN860; .J66. **DD** 665.5/05. **CODEN** JPREEZ. Documents available from Article Express International, CASDDS.
**Ind/Abst** Chem. Abstr.; Ei Page One; Eng. Index Annu. [Select. Cov.].

NE/0920-4105
**JOURNAL OF PETROLEUM SCIENCE & ENGINEERING.** **VFOAT** Journal of Petroleum Science and Engineering. Vol. 1, No. 1 (Aug. 1987)-. Academic Scholarly Publication. English. Eight times a year (2 vols.). Fl840.00. Elsevier Science Publishers BV, PO Box 211, 1000 AE Amsterdam Netherlands. **Tel** 011 31 20 5803642, FAX 011 31 20 5862696, telex 15682. **ED** George V Chilingarian, Erle C Donaldson, K J Weber. **LC** TN860; .J67. **DD** 665.5. **CODEN** JPSEE6. **[CCC]. Bk Rev. Ad Acc. Pr Rev. Circ:** 400. available on microfilm and microfiche from University Microfilms International (UMI). Documents available from Article Express International, Petroleum Abstracts Document Delivery Service.
**Desc:** Bridges the gap between petroleum engineering and petroleum geology; strives to publish explicitly written articles that are intelligible to readers regardless of specialization. Publishes scientific/technical papers, reviews, short communications, case studies/field reports, comments, book reviews and symposia proceedings.
**Ind/Abst** Ei Page One; Eng. Index Annu.; Fluid Abstr., Civil Eng.; Fluid Abstr. Proc. Eng.; FLUIDEX (19??-); Geogr. Abstr. Phys. Geogr.; Geol. Abstr.; GeoRef; Mech. Eng. Abstr.; Pet. Abstr.

US/0149-2136
**JOURNAL OF PETROLEUM TECHNOLOGY.** (JPT : JOURNAL OF PETROLEUM TECHNOLOGY : OFFICIAL PUBLICATION OF THE SOCIETY OF PETROLEUM ENGINEERS OF AIME.). [J. pet. technol.]. **Added/Corp** Society of Petroleum Engineers of AIME. Society of Petroleum Engineers (U.S.). **VFOAT** Journal of Petroleum Technology. Vol. 31, No. 1 (Jan. 1979)-. Periodical. English. mo. $45.00 North America; $105.00 other. Society of Petroleum Engineers, PO Box 833836, Richardson TX 75083-3836. **Tel** (214)952-9393 or (214)952-9458, FAX (214)952-9435, telex 163245 (SPEUT). **LC** TN860; .J68. **DD** 665.5/05. **CODEN** JPTJAM. **[CCC]. Bk Rev. Ad Acc. Pr Rev. Circ:** 57,500. available on microfilm and microfiche from University Microfilms International (UMI). Documents available from Article Express International, The Genuine Article, CASDDS. ***Continues** Journal of Petroleum Technology, 0149-2136.*
**Desc:** Information on how to improve oil and gas exploration, drilling and production performance; reaches influential petroleum managers and engineers that buy tools, equipment and services.
**Ind/Abst** ASTIS Curr. Aware. Bull. (1978-); AESIS Q.; Appl. Sci. Technol. Index; Aquat. Sci. Fish. Abstr. (Computer File); ASTIS Bibliogr. (1978-); Bibliogr. Mission.; Bioeng. Abstr.; Chem. Abstr.; Coal Abstr.; Comput. Abstr.; Comput. Inf. Syst. Abstr. J. [Full Cov.]; Curr. Contents Eng. Tech. Appl. Sci.; Ei Page One; EMBASE; Energy Res. Abstr. (Nov. 1976-); Eng. Index Annu.; Fluid Abstr., Civil Eng.; Fluid Abstr. Proc. Eng.; FLUIDEX (1973-); Gas Abstr.; GeoRef; HTFS Dig.; INIS Atomindex [Micro.]; Int. Aerosp. Abstr.; Leadscan; Lit. Pat. Abstr., Oilfield Chem. (1972-); Lit. Abstr., Catal. Catal.; Lit. Abstr., Health Environ.; Lit. Abstr., Pet. Refin. Petrochem.; Lit. Abstr., Pet. Substit.; Lit. Abstr., Transp. Storage; Ocean. Abstr.; Res. Alert [Full Cov.]; Risk Abstr.; Sci. Cit. Index; SCISEARCH; Soc. Sci. Cit. Index [Select. Cov.].

II
**JOURNAL OF THE OIL TECHNOLOGISTS' ASSOCIATION OF INDIA, THE.** **Main/Corp** Oil Technologists' Association of India. Vol. 1 (1969)-. Periodical. English. sa. Oil Technologists Assn India, Chemical Technologists Department, Matunga Road, Bombay 400019 India. **LC** TN860; .O447a. **DD** 665/.3/0954. Documents available from CASDDS.
**Ind/Abst** Chem. Abstr.; Cot. Trop. Fibr. Abstr. Bibliogr.; Field Crop Abstr.; Food Sci. Technol. Abstr.; For. Abstr.; Hortic. Abstr.; Plant Breed. Abstr.; Rev. Agric. Entomol.; Rice Abstr.; Seed Abstr.; Soyabean Abstr.

# Petroleum and Natural Gas

LU
**KULBRINTER.** *Title Change.* **Main/Corp** Statistical Office of the European Communities. **VFOAT** Kohlenwasserstoffe; Monatsbulletin; Hydrocarbons; Monthly Bulletin. (1977)-?. English (French and German). mo. Office for Official Publications of the European Communities, 2 Rue Mercier, 2985 Luxembourg Luxembourg. **Tel** 011 352 499281, FAX 011 352 488573. **LC** HD9575.E97; S72B. **DD** 338.2/7/28094. *Supersedes in part* Kvartalsbulletin Energistatistik. *Continued by* Kohlenwasserstoffe (Statistical Office of the European Communities).

US/0892-4465
**KWOC LIST OF PETROLEUM ABSTRACTS' EXPLORATION & PRODUCTION THESAURUS, AND NEW E & P TERMS.** [KWOC list Pet. abstr. explor. prod. thesaurus new E P terms]. **Added/Corp** University of Tulsa. Information Services Division. **VAT** Key Word Out of Context List of Petroleum Abstracts' Exploration and Production Thesaurus and New Exploration and Production Terms. (Jan. 1, 1987)-. English. an. $150.00 (general subscribers), $175.00 (non-subscribers). Petroleum Abstracts, University of Tulsa, Information Services Division, 600 South College Avenue, Harwell Hall 101, Tulsa OK 74104-3189. **Tel** (800)247-8678, (918)631-2297, FAX (918)599-9361, telex 49 7543. **LC** Z695.1.P43; K96. *Continues* KWOC List of Petroleum Abstract's Exploration & Production Thesaurus and Addenda Descriptors From the Supplementary Word List, 0191-2747.
**Desc:** A quick reference to descriptors found in the Exploration and Production Thesaurus and supplemental "new terms".

US/0023-7418
**LAMP (NEW YORK), THE.** (THE LAMP.). [Lamp]. **Added/Corp** Standard Oil Company. Exxon Corporation. (19??)-. Periodical. English. qt. Free on request. Exxon Corporation, 225 East John W. Carpenter Freeway, Irving TX 75062. **Tel** (214)444-1000. **LC** HD9560.1; .L3. **DD** 338.2/7/28205.
**Ind/Abst** Energy Inf. Abstr.; F&S Index Plus Text, Int. [Select. Cov.]; Fluid Abstr., Civil Eng.; Fluid Abstr. Proc. Eng.; FLUIDEX (19??)-; GeoRef; Index Free Period.; Meteorol. Geoastrophys. Abstr.; PROMT.

US/1043-7312
**LAND RIG NEWSLETTER, THE.** [Land rig newsl.]. (19??)-. Newsletter. English. Twelve times a year. $250.00 (new subscription) $200.00 (renewal subscription). RJM Communications, PO Box 6645, Lubbock TX 79493. **Tel** (806)741-1531. **ED** Ricmaro J. Mason. **DD** 338.
**Desc:** Provides market intelligence for onshore drillings industry and includes business news on emerging onshore drilling markets, financial reports, rig sales, and company's performance.

US/0457-088X
**LANDMAN (FT. WORTH).** (THE LANDMAN.). [Landman]. **Added/Corp** American Association of Petroleum Landmen. (19??)-. Periodical. English. Six times a year (Jan., Mar., May, July, Sept. Nov.). $100.00. American Association of Petroleum Landmen, 4100 Fossil Creek Boulevard, Fort Worth TX 76137-2723. **Tel** (817)847-7700. **ED** Le'Ann Pembroke Callihan. **LC** HD9561; .L3. **DD** 382. Index available (bound in issue, Dec.). **Ad Acc, Adv Mgr:** L. Wiert, **Tel** (817)847-7700. **Circ:** 8,200 (ctrl).
**Desc:** Provides information about the petroleum/mineral land profession and news of AAPL its members and local association news.
**Ind/Abst** GeoRef.

US/0272-8370
**LANDMEN'S DIRECTORY.** **Main/Corp** American Association of Petroleum Landmen. (1984/85)-. Directory. English. American Association of Petroleum Landmen, 4100 Fossil Creek Boulevard, Fort Worth TX 76137-2723. **Tel** (817)847-7700. *Continues* Membership Directory - American Association of Petroleum Landmen.

US/0193-8738
**LATIN AMERICA PETROLEUM DIRECTORY.** [Lat. Am. pet. dir.]. **VFOAT** Petroleum Directory : Latin America; Latin America Directory. (1971)-. Directory. English. ir. $150.00 US and Canada; $205.00 other. PennWell Publishing Company, 1421 South Sheridan, PO Box 1260, Tulsa OK 74101. **Tel** (918)835-3161, (800)331-4463, FAX (918)831-9497. **LC** HD9574.L28; L33. **DD** 338.2/7/2820258.
**Desc:** Listings include current companies, branch offices and subsidiaries, individuals and titles, addresses, phone, fax and telex numbers, as well as industry surveys on refining, petrochemicals and construction.

US
**LAW OF OIL AND GAS LEASES.** See Law.

US
**LAWFUL RESERVOIR MARKET DEMAND FOR PRORATED GAS FIELDS.** English. mo. $36.00. Railroad Commission of Texas, PO Drawer 12967, Capitol Station, Austin TX 78711. **Tel** (512)463-7255.

IO/0125-9644
**LEMBARAN PUBLIKASI PUSAT PENGEMBANGAN TEKNOLOGI MINYAK DAN GAS BUMI LEMIGAS.** (LEMBARAN PUBLIKASI LEMIGAS.). [Lembaran publ. Pusat Pengembangan Teknol. Minyak Gas Bumi Lemigas]. **Added/Corp** Pusat Pengembangan Teknologi Minyak dan Gas Bumi (Indonesia). **VFOAT** Lembaran Publikasi PPTM; Lembaran Publikasi PPTMGB. (19??)-. Periodical. English (Indonesian). **LC** TN876.I55; L46. **DD** 665.5/09598. **CODEN** LPLEDQ. Documents available from CASDDS.
**Ind/Abst** Chem. Abstr.

AT/0817-6191
**LIPSCOMBE REPORT.** See Energy.

US/8756-7091
**LIQUEFIED GAS DIRECTORY OF AMERICA INC. WESTERN REGION.** [Liq. Gas Dir. Am. Inc., West. reg.]. **VFOAT** Western Region; Liquefied Gas Directory. Western Region. Directory. English. $5.95. Liquefied Gas Directory of America Inc., 1108 East 33rd South, Salt Lake City UT 84106. **LC** HD9579.P43; U58. **DD** 381/.45665773.

US
**LIQUEFIED PETROLEUM GASES HANDBOOK.** (19??)-. English. ir. $64.75 nonmembers; $58.25 members. National Fire Protection Association, 1 Batterymarch Park, PO Box 9101, Quincy MA 02269-9101. **Tel** (617)770-3000, (800)344-3555.

US
**LIQUID FOSSIL FUEL TECHNOLOGY, QUARTERLY TECHNICAL PROGRESS REPORT.** Periodical. English. qt. Bartlesville US Department of Energy, Project Office, PO Box 1398, Bartlesville OK 74003-1398. **Tel** (918)337-4401, FAX (918)337-4418. **ED** Herbert A Tiedemann. **Circ:** 3,000.
**Desc:** Results of enhanced oil recovery research funded by the Department of Energy.

UK/0305-1803
**LIQUID GAS CARRIER REGISTER.** **Added/Corp** H. Clarkson & Company, Ltd., London. (19??)-. English. mo. £95.00 Europe; £102.00 other. Clarkson Research Studies Ltd., 12 Camomile Street, London EC3A 7BP England. **Tel** 011 44 71 2838955. **LC** HE566.T3; L55. **DD** 387.2/45.
**Desc:** Listing of all registered cargo vessels having at least 5 percent of cargo capacity available for carriage of liquid gas. Over 700 vessels listed, with details on type of vessel, capacity, flag, country and year of build.

UK/0268-9219
**LIQUIDS HANDLING.** [Liq. handl.]. (1985)-. Periodical. English. bm. £45.00 UK; £60.00 other. DMG Trinity Limited, Times House, Station Approach, Ruislip HA48NB England. **Tel** 011 44 895 677677.

US/1065-0539
**LITERATURE ABSTRACTS. CATALYSTS & CATALYSIS.** *Title Change.* See Petroleum and Natural Gas-Abstracting, Bibliographies and Statistics.

●US/1074-6870
**LITERATURE ABSTRACTS. CATALYSTS / ZEOLITES.** See Petroleum and Natural Gas-Abstracting, Bibliographies and Statistics.

●US/1065-0512
**LITERATURE ABSTRACTS. PETROLEUM REFINING & PETROCHEMICALS.** See Petroleum and Natural Gas-Abstracting, Bibliographies and Statistics.

●US/1065-0504
**LITERATURE ABSTRACTS. PETROLEUM SUBSTITUTES.** See Petroleum and Natural Gas-Abstracting, Bibliographies and Statistics.

●US/1065-0520
**LITERATURE ABSTRACTS. TRANSPORTATION & STORAGE.** See Petroleum and Natural Gas-Abstracting, Bibliographies and Statistics.

US/1065-0547
**LITERATURE & PATENT ABSTRACTS. OILFIELD CHEMICALS.** *Ceased.* See Petroleum and Natural Gas-Abstracting, Bibliographies and Statistics.

●US/1065-0431
**LITERATURE INDEX.** (LITERATURE INDEX : INCLUDING SUBJECT INDEX, BIBLIOGRAPHIC LIST, AUTHOR INDEX / CENTRAL ABSTRACTING & INFORMATION SERVICES, AMERICAN PETROLEUM INSTITUTE.). [Lit. index]. **Added/Corp** American Petroleum Institute. Central Abstracting and Information Services. (Jan. 1992)-. English. mo. American Petroleum Institute, 275 Seventh Avenue, New York NY 10001. **Tel** (212)366-4040, FAX (212)366-4298. **DD** 665. *Continues* Literature (New York, N.Y.).

US/0276-5918
**LNG DIGEST.** (LNG DIGEST : THE LIQUEFIED NATURAL GAS NEWSLETTER OF ENERGY RESEARCH ASSOCIATES.). [LNG dig.]. **Added/Corp** Energy Research Associates. **VAT** Liquified Natural Gas Digest. (1975)-. Periodical. English. mo. $625.00 US & Canada; $650.00 other. Energy Research Associates, PO Box 1516, Wall Street Station, New York NY 10005. **Tel** (718)338-5384. **ED** J. L. Birnbaum. [CCC].
**Desc:** Analysis of LNG industry.

US/1053-6949
**LNG OBSERVER, THE.** [LNG obs.]. **Added/Corp** Institute of Gas Technology. **VAT** Liquified Natural Gas Observer. Vol. 1, No. 1 (Spring 1990)-. Periodical. English. Four times a year. Free, IGT members and international associates; $100.00 other. Institute of Gas Technology, 3424 South State Street, Chicago IL 60616. **Tel** (312)949-3970, (312)949-3650, FAX (312)949-3776, telex 25-6189. **ED** Colleen Sen. **DD** 338. **Circ:** 2,300. available on an online database.
**Desc:** Updates on issues that are available for future developments and technology on gas and other projects.
**Ind/Abst** Gas Abstr.

US/0024-581X
**LOG ANALYST, THE.** See Energy.

UK/0143-0114
**LONDON OIL REPORTS.** V. 1 (Jan. 15, 1979)-. Periodical. English. ir. price varies per volume. ICIS Inc, 3730 Kirby Drive, Suite 850, Houston TX 77098. **Tel** (713)527-8511.

US/0735-0716
**LOUISIANA ANNUAL OIL AND GAS REPORT.** *Ceased.* [La. annu. oil gas rep.]. (1976)-(Jan. 1994). English. an. Geodata Inc, Box 44262 Capitol Station, Baton Rouge LA 70804. **Tel** (504)344-1679. **LC** TN872.L8; A32. **DD** 338.2/728/09763. ctrl circ. *Continues* Annual Oil and Gas Report, 0459-8393.
**Ind/Abst** GeoRef.

US/0024-7103
**LP-GAS.** Vol. 1 (Feb. 1941)-. Periodical. English. mo. $30.00 US and possessions; $40.00 Canada; $100.00 other. Advanstar Communications Inc., 131 West First Street, Duluth MN 55802. **Tel** (218)723-9477, (800)346-0085. **LC** TP761.P4; L2. [CCC]. available on microfilm from University Microfilms International (UMI).
**Ind/Abst** Gas Abstr.

UK
**LP GAS REVIEW.** Vol. 1 (Jan. 1977)-. Periodical. English. Six times a year. £33.00 UK; £45.00 other. Bouverie Publishing Company Ltd, 141 147 Temple Chambers, London EC4Y ODT England. **Tel** 011 44 825 765075, 011 44 71 5836463. **ED** Peter Hancox. **LC** TP359.L5; L16. **CODEN** LPGRE7. **Bk Rev. Ad Acc. Circ:** 3,730.
**Desc:** Covers every aspect of liquified petroleum gas from bulk, containerization and transport to automotive, industrial and commercial marketing.

UK
**LPG IN WORLD MARKETS.** **VFOAT** L.P.G. in World Markets. (19??)-. English. mo. $5000.00. Poten & Partners UK Ltd, Devonshire House, Mayfair Place, London W1X 5FH England. **Tel** 011 44 71 493-7272, FAX 011 44 71 629-7078, telex 296321. **LC** HD9579.P4; L65. **DD** 338.4/7665773.
**Desc:** Information on the liquefied petroleum gas industry.

US/0195-4563
**LUNDBERG LETTER.** English. sm. $331.00. Tele-Drop Inc, 12041 Strathern Street, PO Box 3996, North Hollywood CA 91609. **Tel** (818)768-5111. Index available. cum. index. ctrl circ.
**Desc:** Covers the US fuels marketing trends, analysis and statistics.
**Ind/Abst** Pet. Energy Bus. News Index (1981).

HU
**MAGYAR OLAJIPARI MUZEUM EVKONYVE, A.** **Main/Corp** Magyar Olajipari Muzeum. Vol. 1 (1969/74)-. Hungarian. ir. Magyar Olajipari Muzeum, Zalaegerszed, Hungary. **LC** TN862; .M33a. **Circ:** 1,000.

NE
**MAJOR CHEMICAL AND PETROCHEMICAL COMPANIES OF EUROPE.** (19??)-. English. an. Kluwer Academic Publishers, Postbus 322, 3300 AH Dordrecht, The Netherlands. **Tel** 011 (31) 78 524400, FAX 011 31 78 183273, telex 20083. **LC** HD9656.A1; M34. **DD** 338.7/66/00254.
**Desc:** Gives details about the finances, personnel, structure, products, and profitability of the 1,000 or more major chemical and petrochemical companies of Europe.

## Petroleum and Natural Gas

UK
**MANUAL OF LEGISLATIVE ACTS RULES AND GUIDANCE NOTES CONCERNING NORTH SEA OFFSHORE DEVELOPMENTS.** (1979)-. English. Four times a year. £455.00 (manual), £220.00 (updates). Weston Law Manual Services, 25 Regal Close, Kings Road, Ealing, London W5 25B Great Britain. **Tel** 810 7257, FAX 998 7553. **ED** Colin Strachan. Index available. cum. index. **Circ:** 1,000 (ctrl).
 **Desc:** Compilation of Acts of Parliament and guidance notes relation to safety in the UK offshore oil and gas industry.

UK/0264-8172
**MARINE AND PETROLEUM GEOLOGY.** See Earth Sciences-Geology.

US/1059-0641
**MARINE RESPONSE BULLETIN : WEST COAST OIL SPILL PREVENTION AND RESPONSE.** [Mar. response bull.]. (Aug. 1991)-. Bulletin. English. wk. $260.00 US; $285.00 Canada. Marine Publishing, PO Box 3905, Seattle WA 98124. **DD** 363.

CY
**MEESFAX.** (1989)-. English. wk. $875.00 US and Canada; $550.00 other. Middle East Petroleum & Economic Publishers, PO Box 4940, Nicosia Cyprus. **Tel** 011 357 2 445431, FAX 011 357 2 474988, telex 2198 MEES CY.
 **Desc:** Compilation of the main stories and highlights of Middle East Economic Survey, with emphasis on the oil section. Amount of material faxed each week varies, but is likely to average six or seven pages.

US/0741-112X
**MEMBERSHIP AND STATISTICAL DIRECTORY - NEW ENGLAND GAS ASSOCIATION.** See Petroleum and Natural Gas-Abstracting, Bibliographies and Statistics.

CN/0703-1130
**MEMOIR (CANADIAN SOCIETY OF PETROLEUM GEOLOGISTS).** See Earth Sciences-Geology.

MX
**MEMORIA DE LABORES / PETROLEOS MEXICANOS. Main/Corp** Petroleos Mexicanos. (1988)-. Spanish. **Continues** Petroleos Mexicanos. Informe de Labores.

MX
**MEMORIA DE LABORES - PETROLEOS MEXICANOS. Title Change. Main/Corp** Petroleos Mexicanos. Spanish. an. **LC** HD9574.M62; P412. **Continued by** Informe de Labores. Petroleos Mexicanos.

SP
**MEMORIA ESTADISTICA [COMPUTER FILE] / MINISTERIO DE ECONOMIA Y HACIENDA, DELEGACION DEL GOBIERNO EN CAMPSA. Added/Corp** Spain. Delegacion del Gobierno en CAMPSA. (19??)-. Statistical Publication. Spanish. **LC** HD9575.
 **Desc:** Available on 5 1/4" diskettes.

US/0743-0531
**METHODS IN EXPLORATION SERIES.** [Methods explor. ser.]. **Added/Corp** American Association of Petroleum Geologists. (1981)-. Monographic series. English. ir. Price varies per volume. American Association of Petroleum Geologists, PO Box 979, Tulsa OK 74101-0979. **Tel** (918)584-2555, FAX (918)584-0469, telex 49-9432.
 **Ind/Abst** AESIS Q.

US/0543-8470
**MICHIGAN'S OIL AND GAS FIELDS.** 1963-. English. an. Department of Natural Resources / Michigan, Box 30028, Lansing MI 48909. **Tel** (517)373-1257. **LC** TN872.M5; A32. **DD** 333.8/23/09774. **Continues** Summary of Operations, Oil and Gas Fields.

US/0746-5769
**MICHIGAN'S OIL & GAS NEWS (1983).** (MICHIGAN'S OIL & GAS NEWS.). [Mich. oil gas news]. **VFOAT** Michigan's Oil and Gas News. Vol. 89, No. 1 (Jan. 7, 1983)-. Periodical. English. wk (except Christmas week and 1st week of new year). $100.00. Michigan's Oil and Gas News Inc, PO Box 10060, Lansing MI 48961. **Tel** (517)487-0480, FAX (517)773-2970. **ED** Jack Westbrook, PO Box 250, Mt Pleasant, MI 48804-0250, (phone# (517)772-5181. **Ad Acc, Adv Mgr:** Emily, **Tel** (517)772-5181. **Circ:** 2,000. **Continues** Oil & Gas News (Mt. Pleasant, Mich.), 0739-2249.
 **Desc:** This weekly publication reports up-to-date on every hole in Michigan from the "drilling permit applied for" to the well completion state, following the drill bit to the bottom of the hole and reporting the result. Additionally, a separate weekly rig locator, drilling activity in brief, and permit list are regular weekly field features. Also, it provides Michigan petroleum exploration, production, transportation and refining "need to know" rather than "nice to know" information regarding the regulatory, legislative, professional organization and even social events directly related to Michigan's petroleum industry, along with summaries of activity to date through the year.

UK
**MID WEEK PETROLEUM ARGUS.** $750.00 North America; £497.00 other. Petroleum Argus Ltd, 93 Shepperton Road, London N1 3DF England. **Tel** 011 44 71 359 8792. **ED** Adnan Binks and Peter Caddy. cum. index. **Bk Rev. Circ:** 1,000 (ctrl).

US/1071-4790
**MIDCONTINENT OIL AND GAS WORLD. Title Change.** [Midcont. oil gas world]. **VFOAT** Oil and Gas World. Vol. 9, No. 4 (July/Aug. 1993)-(19??). Periodical. English. bm. Hart Publications Inc, 1900 Grant Street, Suite 400, Denver CO 80203. **Tel** (303)837-1917, (800)832-1917, FAX (303)837-8585. **DD** 333. **Continues** Midcontinent Oil World, 0883-7325. **Merged into** Gulf Coast Oil and Gas World, 1070-4914; Northeast Oil and Gas World, 1070-4469; Pacific Oil and Gas World, 1071-9628; Southwest Oil and Gas World, 1071-4804; Western Oil and Gas World, 1070-6100 **and** Hart's Oil and Gas World, 1075-5365.

US/0883-7325
**MIDCONTINENT OIL WORLD. Title Change.** [Midcont. oil world]. (1985)-(19??). Periodical. English. mo. Hart Publications Inc, 1900 Grant Street, Suite 400, Denver CO 80203. **Tel** (303)837-1917, (800)832-1917, FAX (303)837-8585. **DD** 665. **[CCC].** available on microfilm from University Microfilms International (UMI). **Continued by** Midcontinent Oil and Gas World, 1071-4790.

US
**MIDCONTINENT PETROLEUM DIRECTORY.** (19??)-. English. an. $77.00, $895.00 on diskette. Hart Publications Inc, 1900 Grant Street, Suite 400, Denver CO 80203. **Tel** (303)837-1917, (800)832-1917, FAX (303)837-8585. available on diskette. **Continues** Midcontinent Oil World Petroleum Directory.
 **Desc:** Lists over 28,000 contacts from more than 11,000 companies in a seven-state region.

CY/0544-0424
**MIDDLE EAST ECONOMIC SURVEY. Added/Corp** Research and Translation Office (Beirut, Lebanon) Middle East Research and Publishing Center (Nicosia, Cyprus) Middle East Petroleum and Economic Publications (Firm). **VFOAT** MEES. Vol. 1 (Nov. 1957)-. Periodical. English. wk. $983.00 (Schools, Universities, Professors, & Students); $1475.00 (other). Middle East Petroleum & Economic Publishers, PO Box 4940, Nicosia Cyprus. **Tel** 011 357 2 445431, FAX 011 357 2 474988, telex 2198 MEES CY. **ED** Ian Seymour. **LC** HD9576.N36; M47. Index available. **Bk Rev**
 **Desc:** Review of petroleum, finance and banking, and political developments in the Middle East and North Africa.
 **Ind/Abst** Pet. Energy Bus. News Index (1975).

US/0897-6694
**MINERAL LAW NEWSLETTER.** See Law.

PE/0379-170X
**MINERIA Y PETROLEO.** See Earth Sciences-Mineralogy.

US
**MINI BRIEFCASE.** English. an. $103.50. Armstrong Oil Directories, PO Box 9660, Amarillo TX 79105. **Tel** (806)374-1818, FAX (806)374-1838. **ED** Alan Armstrong.

CN/0707-3216
**MINUTES OF PROCEEDINGS AND EVIDENCE OF THE SPECIAL COMMITTEE ON A NORTHERN GAS PIPELINE. Main/Corp** Canada. Parliament. House of Commons. Special Committee on a Northern Gas Pipeline. **VFOAT** Proces-Verbaux et Temoignages du Comite Special sur un Pipe-Line pour le Gaz du Nord. **VAT** Pipe-Line pour le Gaz du Nord; Northern Gas Pipeline. Feb. 23, 1978-. Proceedings. English (French). Receiver General for Canada / Ottawa, Canada Comm Group Publishing, Ottawa Ontario K1A 0S9 Canada. **Tel** (819)956-4802, (800)661-2868. **LC** TN880.5; .C324B. **DD** 388.5.

CN/0707-8978
**MINUTES OF PROCEEDINGS AND EVIDENCE OF THE STANDING COMMITTEE ON NORTHERN PIPELINES. Main/Corp** Canada. Parliament. House of Commons. Standing Committee on Northern Pipelines. **VFOAT** Proces-Verbaux et Temoignages du Comite Permanent sur les Pipe-Lines du Nord. **VAT** Northern Pipelines; Pipe-Lines du Nord. Oct. 31, 1978-. Proceedings. English (French). Receiver General for Canada / Ottawa, Canada Comm Group Publishing, Ottawa Ontario K1A 0S9 Canada. **Tel** (819)956-4802, (800)661-2868. **LC** TN880.5; .C324A. **DD** 388.5.

US
**MISCELLANEOUS PUBLICATION.** See Earth Sciences-Geology.

US/0274-6980
**MISSISSIPPI OIL & GAS PRODUCTION REPORT. Added/Corp** Mississippi State Oil & Gas Production Board. **VAT** Mississippi Oil and Gas Production Report. (19??)-. Periodical. English. Fourteen times a year. $100.00 includes 12 monthly reports & 1 annual report & 1 book of maps. Mississippi State Oil and Gas Board, 500 Greymount Avenue, Suite E, Jackson MS 39202. **Tel** (601)354-7142. **Continues** Mississippi State Oil & Gas Board Bulletin.

US/0885-5056
**MOBIL WORLD.** [Mobil world]. **Added/Corp** Mobil Oil Corporation. Vol. 26 (Mar./Apr. 1960)-. Periodical. English. Ten times a year. Mobil Oil Corporation / Technical Publications, Technical Publications, 3225 Gallows Road, Fairfax VA 22037. **DD** 665. **Circ:** 70,000. **Continues** Flying Red Horse.
 **Desc:** Mobil Oil Corporation employee newspaper.
 **Ind/Abst** Coal Abstr.; Energy Res. Abstr. (Nov. 1977-).

UK
**MONITOR. Added/Corp** British Gas Corporation. No. 1 (1985)-. English. **LC** TP350; .M63. **DD** 665.7/072041. **Ind/Abst** Energy Inf. Abstr. (July 27, 1992-).

US
**MONOGRAM, THE.** Periodical. English. ir. American Petroleum Institute, 275 Seventh Avenue, New York NY 10001. **Tel** (212)366-4040, FAX (212)366-4298. **(Subscription address:** 1970 Chain Bridge Road, McLean, VA 22109-6000**)**

US
**MONTANA OIL AND GAS STATISTICAL BULLETIN / BOARD OF OIL AND GAS CONSERVATION. Main/Corp** Montana. Board of Oil and Gas Conservation. (19??)-. Statistical Publication. English. qt. Free. Board of Oil and Gas Conservation Dnr, 1520 East Sixth Avenue, Helena MT 59620. **Tel** (406)444-6675. **Continues** Montana. Oil and Gas Conservation Commission. Montana Oil and Gas Statistical Bulletin.

US/0047-794X
**MONTANA OIL JOURNAL (1953).** (MONTANA OIL JOURNAL : WITH NEWS OF OIL IN THE WILLISTON BASIN, MONTANA, DAKOTAS AND GREATER ROCKIES.). Vol. 33, No. 2 (Mar. 21, 1953)-. Newspaper. English. wk (52 issues). $34.00 US. Montana Oil Journal, 906 South Pearl Street, Denver CO 80209. **Tel** (303)778-8661. **ED** Roy Boles. **Bk Rev. Ad Acc. Circ:** 3,500 (ctrl). **Continues** Montana Oil and Mining Journal.
 **Desc:** Oil and gas activity in Montana, North and South Dakota.

KU
**MONTHLY BULLETIN / OAPEC, ORGANIZATION OF ARAB PETROLEUM EXPORTING COUNTRIES. Suspended.** **VFOAT** Organization of Arab Petroleum Exporting Countries Monthly Bulletin; OAPEC Bulletin; OAPEC Monthly Bulletin. Vol. 12, No. 4 (April 1986)-?. Bulletin. English (Arabic). mo. $48.00. Organization of Arab Petroleum Exporting Countries, PO Box 20501, Safat 13066 Kuwait. **Tel** 2420061, telex 22166. **LC** HD9578.A55; O74B. **DD** 382/.42282/0601. **Continues** OAPEC, Organization of Arab Petroleum Exporting Countries.
 **Ind/Abst** Middle East Abstr. Index.

US
**MONTHLY MOTOR FUEL REPORTED BY STATES. Added/Corp** United States. Federal Highway Administration. (Jan. 1985)-. Periodical. English. mo. Free on request. US Department of Transportation - Federal Highway Administration, 400 Seventh Street Southwest, Washington DC 20590. **Tel** (202)366-0660. Documents available from Documents on Demand. **Absorbed** Monthly Gasoline Reported by States.
 **Ind/Abst** Am. Stat. Index.

CN/0228-5622
**MONTHLY OIL AND GAS PRODUCTION REPORT.** [Mon. oil gas prod. rep.]. **Added/Corp** Saskatchewan. Saskatchewan Mineral Resources. Saskatchewan. Saskatchewan Energy and Mines. (Nov. 1978)-. Periodical. English. mo. 120.00Can$. Saskatchewan Energy and Mines, 1914 Hamilton, Regina Saskatchewan, S4P 4V4 Canada. **Tel** (306)787-7643, FAX (306)787-2527. **DD** 338.2/728/097124. **Continues** Saskatchewan. Geodata Statistics and Research Branch. Monthly Oil and Gas Report, 0702-9926.
 **Desc:** Lists by production and disposition areas the monthly production of oil, gas and water for units and pools. Cumulative production figures for the current year are included.

UK
**MONTHLY OIL REPORT.** English. mo. £250.00. Centre for Global Energy Studies, 17 Knightsbridge,

London SW1X 7LY England. **Tel** 011 44 71 2354334, FAX 011 44 71 2354338, telex 919089 CGES G. **ED** Leo Drollas. **Bk Rev.**

NR/0549-2513
**MONTHLY PETROLEUM INFORMATION.** **Main/Corp** Nigerian National Petroleum Corporation. Economic Research and Intelligence Dept. (19??)-. Periodical. English. mo. Nigerian National Petroleum Corporation, P M B 12701, Lagos Nigeria. **LC** HD9577.N5; A27. **DD** 338.2/7/28209669. ***Continues*** *Nigeria. Dept. of Petroleum Resources. Monthly Petroleum Information, 0549-2513.*

US
**MONTHLY PRODUCTION REPORT.** English. mo. $12.00. North Dakota State Industrial Commission, Oil and Gas Division, 900 East Boulevard, Bismarck ND 58505. **Tel** (701)224-2969.

US
**MONTHLY STATISTICAL REPORT - AMERICAN PETROLEUM INSTITUTE. STATISTICS DEPT.** **See** Petroleum and Natural Gas-Abstracting, Bibliographies and Statistics.

US
**MOTOR FREIGHT CIRCULAR AND ORDERS.** English. wk. $83.00. Railroad Commission of Texas, PO Drawer 12967, Capitol Station, Austin TX 78711. **Tel** (512)463-7255.

UK
**MRS RELAY.** English. Three times a year. Free. British Gas & Research, 31 Homer Road, Solihull Warwickshire England. **Tel** 011 44 509 282000.

TS
**MUJTAMA AL-BATRUL.** **VFOAT** Petroleum Community. Periodical. Arabic (English). mo. Free. ABU Dhabi National Oil Company, Public Relations, PO Box 898, ABU Dhabi United Arab Emirates. **Tel** 366000, FAX (666000) 3389, telex 22215 ADNOC EM. **ED** Bassam Darkazally. **LC** PAR. **Bk Rev. Circ:** 6,000 (ctrl). available on microfilm.
**Desc:** Petroleum related topics; usually progress oriented, scientific and social.

UK
**N W EUROPE PETROLEUM DATABASE.** English. Seventy-two issues per year. $17.50 UK; $17.85 Europe; $1835 other. Arthur Andersen & Company Petroleum Services Group, 1 Surrey Street, London WC2R 2PS England. **Tel** 011 44 71 4383000. **ED** Timothy H. Shingler and Gary Howorth. ctrl circ.

KU
**NAFT AL-ARAB.** Periodical. Arabic. mo. 10.00KD. Maktab Abd Allah Al-Tariqi Lil-Istishaharat Al-Naftiyah, PO Box 22699 Safat-Kuwait, Al-Kuwayt Kuwait. **LC** HD9578.A55; N34.

CI
**NAFTA (ZAGREB, CROATIA).** (NAFTA : MJESECNIK JUGOSLAVENSKOG KOMITETA SVJETSKIH KONGRESA ZA NAFTU.). Began in 1950. Academic Scholarly Publication. Serbo-Croatian (Roman). bm. Documents available from CASDDS.
**Ind/Abst** Chem. Abstr.; Geogr. Abstr. Human Geogr.

●UN
**NAFTOVA I HAZOVA PROMYSLOVIST.** **Added/Corp** Derzhavnyi Komitet Ukrainy po Heolohii i Vykorystanniu Nadr. **VFOAT** Oil & Gas Industry; Oil and Gas Industry. (1992)-. Periodical. Ukrainian (Russian; summaries and/or abstracts in English). Four times a year. $129.95. **(Subscription address:** East View Publications Inc., 3020 Harbor Lane North, Suite 110, Minneapolis MN 55447.**)** **LC** TN860; .N455. ***Continues*** *Neftianaia i Gazovaia Promyshlennost, 0548-1414.*

US
**NATIONAL EMISSIONS DATA SYSTEM (NEDS) FUEL USE REPORT.** **VFOAT** NEDS Fuel Use Report; National Emissions Data System (N.E.D.S.) Fuel Use Report; N.E.D.S. Fuel Use Report. English. an. National Technical Information Service - NTIS, Room 2027S, 5285 Port Royal Road, Springfield VA 22161. **Tel** (703)487-4630, (703)487-4660, (703)487-4650, FAX (703)321-8547, telex 89-9405. available on microfiche (Vols. for 1974-1975 distributed to depository libraries).

US/1071-1260
**NATIONAL OIL & LUBE NEWS, THE.** [Natl. oil lube news]. **VFOAT** National Oil and Lube News; NOLN. (19??)-. Periodical. English. mo. $27.00 US. National Oil & Lube News, 2541 74th Street, Lubbock TX 79423. **Tel** (806)745-7573. **ED** Barbara Tinsley. **DD** 338. **Ad Acc, Adv Mgr:** B. Tinsley. **Circ:** 11,500 US, 100 other (ctrl).

US/0741-1464
**NATIONAL PETROLEUM COUNCIL.** (NATIONAL PETROLEUM COUNCIL NEWS.). **Main/Corp** National Petroleum Council. **VFOAT** News. Periodical. English. ir. National Petroleum Council, 1625 K Street NW/Suite 601, Washington DC 20006.

US/0149-5267
**NATIONAL PETROLEUM NEWS.** [Natl. pet. news]. **VFOAT** NPN. (Oct. 1, 1909)-. Periodical. English. mo (13 issues). $64.00 US; $74.00 Canada; $80.00 other. Hunter Publishing Company Inc., 25 Northwest Point Boulevard, Suite 800, Elk Grove Village IL 60007-1036. **Tel** (708)427-9512, FAX (708)427-2097. **ED** Peggy Smedley. **DD** 338. **[CCC].** Index available. cum. index. **Bk Rev. Ad Acc. Circ:** 18,000. available on microfilm and microfiche from University Microfilms International (UMI); available on an online database (file 648/Full-Text) from DIALOG. Documents available from UMI Article Clearinghouse. ***Continues*** *National Petroleum News.* ***Continued in part by*** *Petroleum Processing, 0096-6525.*
**Desc:** Serves petroleum marketers with news background on the industry, analysis of emerging trends and events of importance.
**Ind/Abst** ABI/INFORM Glob. Ed. (March 1973-Dec. 1978); ABI Inform Ondisc (March 1973-December 1978);; Acad. Search (July 1993-); Bus. ASAP (1990-) [Full Txt.]; Bus. Index (1985-); Bus. Period. Index (1981-); F&S Index Plus Text, Int. [Select. Cov.]; Gen. BusinessFile (1985-); Gen. Period. Index (1985-); INFO-SOUTH Abstr.; Infobank (1979-); Mag. Search; Mark. Advert. Ref. Serv.; Pet. Energy Bus. News Index (1979); Predicasts; PROMT; Stat. Ref. Index; Trade Ind. ASAP [Full Txt.]; Trade Ind. Index (1981-) [Full Txt.]; UMI ABI/Inform--Bus. Period. Ondisc (Jan. 1991-) [Full Txt.]; Wilson Bus. Abstr.

US
**NATIONAL PETROLEUM NEWS. MARKET FACTS.** (1991)-. English. an. $75.00 US; $90.00 Canada; $105.00 other. Hunter Publishing Company Inc., 25 Northwest Point Boulevard, Suite 800, Elk Grove Village IL 60007-1036. **Tel** (708)427-9512, FAX (708)427-2097. ***Continues*** *National Petroleum News Factbook.*
**Desc:** Reference guide to the petroleum and gasoline-based convenience store markets with information on capital spending, domestic and international pricing, marketing management personnel, service stations and C-store statistics, etc.

US/0470-3219
**NATIONAL STRIPPER WELL SURVEY.** **See** Engineering-Mines and Mining Engineering.

US/0736-9808
**NATURAL GAS ANNUAL.** (NATURAL GAS ANNUAL / ENERGY INFORMATION ADMINISTRATION, OFFICE OF OIL AND GAS, U.S. DEPARTMENT OF ENERGY.). [Nat. gas annu.]. (1980)-. English. an. $17.00 (Volume 1), $18.00 (Volume 2). National Energy Information Center, Energy Information Administration, Forrestal Building, Room 1F-048, Washington DC 20585. **Tel** (202)586-8800. **LC** HD9581.U49; N37. **DD** 338.2/7285/0973. available on CD-ROM (As: Natural Gas Annual [Computer File]). ***Continues*** *Natural Gas Production and Consumption, 0732-6629.*
**Desc:** Consists of two volumes. Volume 1 provides information on the supply and disposition of natural gas. Volume 2 presents historical data for the nation from 1930.
**Ind/Abst** Energy Inf. Abstr.; Predicasts Forecasts.

●CN/1195-5287
**NATURAL GAS EXPORTER.** (1993)-. English. Twelve times a year. 445.00Can$. Bulldog Communications, No. 3 830 19th Avenue Southwest, Calgary Alberta, T2T OH5 Canada. **Tel** (403)228-9861, FAX (403)228-9861.

US/1073-6417
**NATURAL GAS FOCUS.** (19??)-. English. bm. $89.00 US; $169.00 other. Hart Publications Inc, 1900 Grant Street, Suite 400, Denver CO 80203. **Tel** (303)837-1917, (800)832-1917, FAX (303)837-8585.
**Desc:** Targets decision-makers involved in the natural gas industry--geologists and producers, gatherers, transporters, refiners and processors, end users, regulators, and suppliers of equipment and services. Focuses on the new money-making opportunities and alliances born out of Order 636 and its ongoing deregulation.

UK/0140-3222
**NATURAL GAS FOR INDUSTRY AND COMMERCE.** ***Ceased.*** [Nat. gas ind. commer.]. (1975)-(19??). Periodical. English. Six times a year (Jan., Mar., May, July, Sept., Nov.). Petroleum Economist Ltd., Perrymount Road, Haywards Heath, West Sussex RH16 3DH England. **Tel** 011 44 444 440421. **LC** TN880.A1; N26. **DD** 665/.7/05. ***Formed by the union of*** *Natural Gas for Industry, 0305-2028* ***and*** *Natural Gas for Commerce.*
**Ind/Abst** World Surf. Coat. Abstr. (?-?).

US/0272-4863
**NATURAL GAS FROM CALIFORNIA FIELDS.** [Nat. gas from Calif. fields]. English. an. Conservation Committee of California Oil Producers, 417 South Hill Street/Suite 930, Los Angeles CA 90013. **Tel** (310)625-7731. **LC** TN881.C2; N37. **DD** 553.2/85/09794.

US/0744-6500
**NATURAL GAS HANDBOOK.** ***Ceased.*** [Nat. gas handb.]. **Added/Corp** Federal Programs Advisory Service. (19??)-(1992). Periodical. English. mo. Federal Programs Advisory Service, 1725 K Street NW/Suite 200, Washington DC 20037. **Tel** (202)872-1766.

US/0739-1811
**NATURAL GAS INTELLIGENCE.** (NATURAL GAS INTELLIGENCE : A WEEKLY NEWSLETTER.). [Nat. gas intell.]. Vol. 1, No. 1 (June 15, 1981)-. Newsletter. English. wk. $790.00 North America; $870.00 other. Intelligence Press, PO Box 70587, Washington DC 20024-0587. **Tel** (703)318-8848, FAX (703)318-0597. **ED** Ellen Beswick. **[CCC].** Index available. cum. index. **Circ:** 1,000.
**Desc:** Information and prices on the natural gas industry in the US and Canada. Carries political and financial reports.

US/1052-3413
**NATURAL GAS LAWYER'S JOURNAL, THE.** **See** Law.

CN/0827-6056
**NATURAL GAS MARKET REPORT.** ***Title Change.*** [Nat. gas mark. rep.]. **Added/Corp** Canadian Enerdata Limited. Vol. 1, No. 1 (Jan. 15, 1985)-(1992). Periodical. English. bw. Canadian Enerdata Limited, Suite 204 7030 Woodbine Avenue, Markham Ontario L3R 1A2 Canada. **Tel** (905)479-9697. **DD** 380.1/42285/0971. ***Continued by*** *Canadian Natural Gas Market Report, 1196-0906.*

CN/1185-5304
**NATURAL GAS MARKET UPDATE.** **See** Business-Commerce.

US/0894-9018
**NATURAL GAS MARKETING. END USER DIRECTORY.** [Nat. gas mark., End user dir.]. **VFOAT** End User Directory. (1987)-. Directory. English. an. Comes with Natural Gas Marketing. Atlantic Information Services Inc., 1050 17th Street Northwest, Suite 480, Washington DC 20036. **Tel** (202)775-9008, (800)521-4323, FAX (202)331-9542. **DD** 338.

US/0894-900X
**NATURAL GAS MARKETING ... INDUSTRY DIRECTORY.** ***Title Change.*** [Nat. gas mark., Ind. dir.]. **Added/Corp** Atlantic Information Services. **VFOAT** Industry Directory. (1987)-(19??). Directory. English. an. Atlantic Information Services Inc., 1050 17th Street Northwest, Suite 480, Washington DC 20036. **Tel** (202)775-9008, (800)521-4323, FAX (202)331-9542. **DD** 338. ***Continued by*** *Gas Daily Natural Gas Marketing. Industry Directory, 1061-5024.*

US/0737-1713
**NATURAL GAS MONTHLY (WASHINGTON, D.C.).** (NATURAL GAS MONTHLY.). [Nat. gas mon.]. **Added/Corp** United States. Energy Information Administration. Office of Oil and Gas. **VFOAT** NGM. (Oct. 1982)-. Academic Scholarly Publication. English. mo. $78.00; US; $97.50 other. National Energy Information Center, Energy Information Administration, Forrestal Building, Room 1F-048, Washington DC 20585. **Tel** (202)586-8800. **LC** TN880.A1; N314. **DD** 338.2/7285/0973021. **CODEN** NGMODK. available on microfiche (Vols. for (1986-) distributed to depository libraries). Documents available from CASDDS, Documents on Demand. ***Formed by the union of*** *Natural Gas Monthly Report, 0731-9479; Underground Natural Gas Storage in the United States, 0275-9535; U.S. Imports and Exports of Natural Gas* ***and*** *Main Line Sales of Natural Gas to Industrial Users.*
**Desc:** Provides information at the state and national levels on the supply and disposition of natural gas, including production, storage, imports, exports, and consumption data. Contains selected data on major interstate pipeline companies and on filings with the Federal Energy Regulatory Commission.
**Ind/Abst** Am. Stat. Index; Chem. Abstr. (1982-1984); Energy Inf. Abstr.

US/0743-5665
**NATURAL GAS (NEW YORK, N.Y.).** (NATURAL GAS.). [Nat. gas]. Vol. 1, No. 1 (Aug. 1984)-. Periodical. English. mo. $295.00 US & Canada; $345.00 other. John Wiley & Sons, Inc., 605 Third Avenue, New York NY 10158-0012. **Tel** (212)850-6000, (212)850-6645, FAX (212)850-6088, telex 12-7063. **(Subscription address:** John Wiley & Sons Inc / New Jersey, PO Box 2575, Secaucus NJ 07096-2575.**)** **ED** Jane G. Bensahel. **DD** 338. **[CCC].** Index available. **Ad Acc.** available on microfilm from University Microfilms International (UMI). ***Continues*** *Oil and Gas Analyst, 0744-5725.*
**Desc:** Covers the financial and regulatory concerns of the national gas industry, leading industry observers of contracts, pricing, purchasing, mergers/acquisitions, financing and financial analysts.
**Ind/Abst** Curr. Technol. Index; Gas Abstr.

US/0891-4230
**NATURAL GAS PRODUCER PRICES.** [Nat. gas prod. prices]. **Added/Corp** Federal Programs Advisory Service. Vol. 2, No. 1 (June 1985)-. Periodical. English. sm. $649.00. Thompson Publishing Group / Washington DC, PO Box 76927, Washington DC 20013. **DD** 338. ***Absorbed*** *Natural Gas Producer Prices (Gulf*

*Coast Edition), 0747-6280; Natural Gas Producer Prices (Western Edition), 0747-6299; Natural Gas Producer Prices (Appalachian Edition), 0747-6272.*

●CN
**NATURAL GAS UTILITY DIRECTORY.**
**See** Public Administration-Public Utilities.

US/8756-3037
**NATURAL GAS WEEK.** [Nat. gas week]. Vol. 1, No. 1 (Jan. 7, 1985)-. Newsletter. English. wk. $847.00. The Oil Daily, 1401 New York Avenue Northwest, Suite 500, Washington DC 20005-2150. **Tel** (800)621-0050, (800)368-5803, (202)662-0700, FAX (202)662-0739, telex 89472. **ED** John H. Jennrich. **DD** 333. **[CCC]. Bk Rev**. available on an online database; available via fax ($1197.00 US; $1347.00 Canada); available via electronic mail ($1297.00).
**Desc:** Current and historical natural gas price information plus news and analysis about developments that affect prices; covers natural gas from exploration to end-use.
**Ind/Abst** GeoRef; Pet. Energy Bus. News Index (1991).

US
**NATURAL GAS WEEK INTERNATIONAL.** English. Twelve times a year. $250.00. The Oil Daily, 1401 New York Avenue Northwest, Suite 500, Washington DC 20005-2150. **Tel** (800)621-0050, (800)368-5803, (202)662-0700, FAX (202)662-0739, telex 89472. available via fax ($300.00); available via electronic mail ($375.00).
**Ind/Abst** Pet. Energy Bus. News Index (1991).

US
**NATURAL GAS WEEK'S BID WEEK REPORT.** (19??)-. English. Twelve times a year. $99.00 (US), $109.00 (Canada) via fax; $99.00 via electronic mail. The Oil Daily, 1401 New York Avenue Northwest, Suite 500, Washington DC 20005-2150. **Tel** (800)621-0050, (800)368-5803, (202)662-0700, FAX (202)662-0739, telex 89472.
**Desc:** A news service providing the average bid-week prices that appear in Natural Gas Week. Also includes news stories covering the natural gas market as well as a wrap-up of the month's gas market activities.

US
**NATURAL GAS WEEK'S DAILY PRICELINE.** (19??)-. English. da. $1297.00 (available via fax or electronic mail only). The Oil Daily, 1401 New York Avenue Northwest, Suite 500, Washington DC 20005-2150. **Tel** (800)621-0050, (800)368-5803, (202)662-0700, FAX (202)662-0739, telex 89472.
**Desc:** A news report of market activities and volume-weighted gas prices for 10 popular price points and regions, including bid-week prices for the current and previous months. Also includes near-month gas future prices and oil prices for reference.

RU
**NEFT I GAZ. Added/Corp** Kazakhskii Politekhnicheskii Institut. (19??)-. Academic Scholarly Publication. Russian. bm. $99.95. **(Subscription address:** East View Publications Inc., 3020 Harbor Lane North, Suite 110, Minneapolis MN 55447.**) LC** TN860; .N44. **CODEN** NEGAD2. Documents available from CASDDS.
**Ind/Abst** Chem. Abstr. (-1974); Gas Abstr.

RU/0028-2421
**NEFTEHIMIJA.** (NEFTEKHIMIIA.). [Neftehim.]. **Added/Corp** Akademiia Nauk SSSR. Otdelenie Khimicheskikh Nauk. (1961)-. Academic Scholarly Publication. Russian (table of contents in English). Six times a year. $144.00. Izdatelstvo Nauka / Akademiia Nauk, Publishing House of the Russian Academy of Sciences, Leninskii Porspekt 14, 117901 Moscow Russia. **Tel** 011 95 954-21-53, FAX 011 95 938-21-44, telex 411964. **(Subscription address:** East View Publications Inc., 3020 Harbor Lane North, Suite 110, Minneapolis MN 55447.**) LC** TP690.A1; A413. **CODEN** NEFTAH. **[CCC].** Documents available from Article Express International, CASDDS.
**Ind/Abst** Chem Inform; Chem. Abstr.; Ei Page One; Energy Res. Abstr.; Eng. Index Annu.; Lit. Pat. Abstr., Oilfield Chem. (1965-); Lit. Abstr., Catal. Catal.; Lit. Abstr., Health Environ.; Lit. Abstr., Pet. Refin. Petrochem.; Lit. Abstr., Pet. Substit.; Lit. Abstr., Transp. Storage.

RU/0131-1670
**NEFTEPERERABOTKA, NEFTEHIMIJA I SLANCEPERERABOTKA.** ***Title Change.*** (NEFTEPERERABOTKA, NEFTEKHIMIIA, SLANTSEPERERABOTKA.). Vol. 1/2; 1976-. Academic Scholarly Publication. Russian. M-35 Ul T Makarovoi, Moscow 12 Russia. **LC** TP690.A1; N43. **CODEN** NNNSAF. Documents available from CASDDS. ***Continues*** *Neftepererabotka i Neftekhimiia (Moscow, R.S.F.S.R. : 1963).* ***Continued by*** *Neftepererabotka i Neftekhimiia (Moscow, R.S.F.S. R. : 1976).*
**Ind/Abst** Chem. Abstr.

RU
**NEFTIANAIA PROMYSHLENNOST. SERIIA NEFTEPROMYSLOVOE STROITELSTVO. Added/Corp** Vsesoyuznyi Nauchno-Issledovatelskii Institut Organizatsii, Uprovleniya i Ekonomiki Neftegazovoi Promyshlennosti. **VFOAT** Seriia Neftepromyslovoe Stroitelstvo. (1980)-. Academic Scholarly Publication. Russian. bw. $21.60. **(Subscription address:** Victor Kamkin, 4956 Boiling Brook Parkway, Rockville MD 20852.**) CODEN** NPNSDW. Documents available from CASDDS. ***Continues*** *Neftepromyslovoe Stroitel'Stvo, 0321-2580.*
**Ind/Abst** Chem. Abstr. (1983-).

RU/0028-243X
**NEFTJANIK.** (NEFTIANIK.). [Neft.]. **Added/Corp** Soviet Union. Ministerstvo Neftianoi Promyshlennosti. Profsoiuz Rabochikh Neftianoi i Gazovoi Promyshlennosti. Tsentralnyi Komitet. (1956)-. Academic Scholarly Publication. Russian. Twelve times a year. $61.00. Izdatelstvo Nedra, 3 Pl Belorusskogo Vakzala, 125047 Moscow Russia. **Tel** 250-52-55. **(Subscription address:** Victor Kamkin, 4956 Boiling Brook Parkway, Rockville MD 20852.**) LC** TN860; .N46. **CODEN** NFTYA7. **[CCC].** Documents available from CASDDS.
**Ind/Abst** Chem. Abstr. (1956-1983); Energy Res. Abstr. (Jan. 1976-); GeoRef.

US
**NEW FUELS REPORT.** (19??)-. English. Fifty-two times a year. $706.20 Washington, DC residents; $660.00 others. Inside Washington Publishers, PO Box 7167, Benjamin Franklin Station, Washington DC 20044. **Tel** (703)416-8500, (800)424-9068. ***Continues*** *Alcohol Week, 0277-4895.*

US
**NEW ORLEANS OIL DIRECTORY.** Directory. English. an (published in Feb.). $40.00. New Orleans Oil Directory, 4450 General de Gaulle, Suite 1207, New Orleans LA 70114. **Tel** (504)392-5323, FAX (504)392-5332. **Ad Acc, Adv Mgr:** Fran Hart.

NE/0169-3956
**NEWSLETTER ON THE OIL EMBARGO AGAINST SOUTH AFRICA.** ***Ceased.*** **Added/Corp** Shipping Research Bureau. Vol. 1, No. 1 (Feb. 1985)-(19??). Newsletter. English. qt (Jan., April, July, Oct.). Shipping Research Bureau, PO Box 11898, 1001 GW Amsterdam Netherlands. **Tel** 011 31 20 6266073, FAX 011 31 20 6220130, telex 10236.
**Ind/Abst** Hum. Rights Intern. Rep.

DK
**NGC NEWS.** ***Ceased.*** (19??)-Vol. 20. qt. Nordic Gas Technology Centre, DR Neergaards VEJ 5A, DK-2970 Horsholm Denmark.

US
**NGI'S GAS PRICE INDEX.** (19??)-. Periodical. English. wk. $490.00 North America; $525.00 other. Intelligence Press, PO Box 70587, Washington DC 20024-0587. **Tel** (703)318-8848, FAX (703)318-0597. **ED** Ellen Beswick. Index available. cum. index. **Circ:** 1,000.
**Desc:** Information and prices on the natural gas industry in the US and Canada.

●US/1065-3422
**NGV NEWS.** [NGV news]. **VAT** Natural Gas Vehicle News. (Sept. 1992)-. Periodical. English. mo. $267.00 US; $282.00 other. Pasha Publications Inc., 1616 North Fort Myer Drive, Suite 1000, Arlington VA 22209. **Tel** (800)424-2908, (703)528-1244, FAX (703)528-3742, (703)528-1253. **DD** 629.

CN/0709-681X
**NICKLE'S DAILY OIL BULLETIN.** [Nickle's dly. oil bull.]. **VFOAT** Daily Oil Bulletin. (1937)-. Bulletin. English. da. 912.00Can$ Canada; 928.00Can$ US. C.O. Nickle Publications, 999 8th Street Southwest, Suite 300, Calgary, Alberta T2R 1N7 Canada. **Tel** (403)244-6111. **DD** 338.272820971.
**Desc:** Delivers the latest oil and gas industry news, land sales and drilling reports to the industry's need to know people. Provides details on oil and gas exploration, drilling, production, transportation and prices.
**Ind/Abst** Pet. Energy Bus. News Index (1982-1983); PROMT [Full Txt.]; PTS Newsl. Database [Full Txt.].

NR/0189-7233
**NIGERIAN PETROLEUM NEWS.** [Niger. pet. news]. **VFOAT** Petronews. (1984)-. Periodical. English. mo. $200.00 US; $250.00 all others except Nigeria. Energy Publication Ltd/Nigeria, PO Box 1790, Lagos, Nigeria. **Tel** 011 234 1 2636999. **ED** Chief M.O. Feyide. **DD** 338.27'282'09'669. **Ad Acc.**

JA/0029-0211
**NIHON GASU KYOKAISHI.** [Nihon Gasu Kyokaishi]. **Added/Corp** Nihon Gasu Kyokai. **VFOAT** Journal of the Japan Gas Association. (1948)-. Academic Scholarly Publication. Japanese. mo. Nihon Gasu Kyokai, (Japan Gas Assoc.), 15-12, Toranomon 1 Chome, Minatoku, Tokyoto 105, Japan. **(Subscription address:** Kyowa Book Company Inc., 1 38 Kanda Jinbocho Chiyoda ku, Tokyo 101 Japan**) CODEN** NIPGAM. Documents available from CASDDS.
**Ind/Abst** Chem. Abstr.; Gas Abstr.

NO/0332-544X
**NOROIL.** ***Title Change.*** [Noroil]. **VFOAT** Norsk Oljetidskrift; Norwegian Journal for Oil and Gas Matters. Vol. 1 (1973)-(19??). Periodical. Norwegian (English). mo. Richard Fry and Associates, Surrey House, 34 Eden Street, Kingston Upon Thames, Surrey KT1 1ER England. **Tel** 081-546-2411, FAX 081-547-2471, telex 027602. **ED** Sveinung Sletten. **[CCC]. Bk Rev. Ad Acc. Circ:** 13,000. Documents available from Petroleum Abstracts Document Delivery Service. ***Merged with*** *Petrole Informations (Paris, France : 1985)* ***to form*** *Euroil.*
**Desc:** Top selling European offshore oil and gas magazine. Covers exploration, engineering, new technology, construction, field development, latest news and politics.
**Ind/Abst** BMT Abstr.; Curr. Technol. Index; Energy Res. Abstr. (Oct. 1975-); Fluid Abstr., Civil Eng.; Fluid Abstr. Proc. Eng.; FLUIDEX; Gas Abstr.; GeoRef; Life Sci. Collect.; Pet. Abstr.; Selec. Coop. Index Manage. Period (19??-199?).

UK/0964-4636
**NOROIL CONTACTS.** (NOROIL CONTACTS OFFSHORE DIRECTORY.). [Noroil contacts]. (1976)-. Periodical. English. tq (April, August and December). £75.00. Noroil Publishing House Ltd. A S, 12 50 Kingsgate Road, Suite F-1, Surrey KT2 5AA England. **Tel** 011 44 81 5472411, FAX 011 44 81 5472157.

NO/0332-5490
**NORSK OLJEREVY.** [Nor. oljerevy]. **VFOAT** Norwegian Oil Review. (1975)-. Periodical. Norwegian (English). mo. $140.00. Norsk Oljerevy A/S, PO Box 93, Slemdal 0321, Oslo 3 Norway. **Tel** 011 47 2 490500, FAX 011 47 2 490710. **ED** Hans Henrikramm. **DD** 665.5. **[CCC]. Ad Acc.** ctrl circ. ***Continues in part*** *Weekly Norwegian Oil Report, 0332-7310.*
**Ind/Abst** Selec. Coop. Index Manage. Period.

US
**NORTH DAKOTA INDUSTRIAL COMMISSION HEARING NOTICES AND ORDERS.** English. ir. $120.00. North Dakota State Industrial Commission, Oil and Gas Division, 900 East Boulevard, Bismarck ND 58505. **Tel** (701)224-2969.

UK
**NORTH SEA OIL & GAS DIRECTORY. VFOAT** North Sea Oil and Gas Directory. (19??)-. Directory. English. an (June). £75.00. Benn Business Information Service Ltd, Riverbank House, Angel Lane, Tonbridge Kent TN9 1SE England. **Tel** 011 44 732 362666, FAX 011 44 732 770483, telex 95454 BBIS. **ED** Judith Patten. **LC** TN874.N78; N673. **DD** 338.2/728/02516336. Index available. **Ad Acc. Circ:** 3,500. available on diskette.
**Desc:** Comprehensive guide to operating companies, official organizations, and manufacturers and suppliers in the oil and gas industries in and around the North Sea.

UK
**NORTH SEA RIG REPORT.** (19??)-. English. mo. £660.00. Petrodata, Dock Gate House, York Place, Waterloo Quay, Aberdeen AB2 1DF Scotland. **Tel** 011 44 224 572247, FAX 011 44 224 580320. **(Subscription address:** Petrodata Limited Accounts Office, Lamdin Road Bury Street, Edmunds IP32 6NU England.**) ED** Iain Mitchell. **Circ:** 45.

UK
**NORTH SEA SERVICE.** English. mo. £3250.00. County Natwest Securities Ltd, Kintore House, 74-77 Queen Street, Edinburgh EH2 4NS Scotland. **Tel** 031 225-8525, FAX 031 243-4435. Documents available. ***Continues*** *North Sea Service Monthly Report.*
**Desc:** Research database of the UK Upstream oil & gas industry.

UK
**NORTH SEA SEVICE.** English. mo. £3,300.00. Wood Mackenzie Consultants Ltd., Kintore House, 74 77 Queen Street, Edinburgh EH2 4NS Scotland. **Tel** 011 44 031 225 8525, FAX 011 44 031 243 4435, telex 72555.

UK
**NORTH SEA VALUATION SERVICE.** English. an. £3,300.00. Wood Mackenzie Consultants Ltd., Kintore House, 74 77 Queen Street, Edinburgh EH2 4NS Scotland. **Tel** 011 44 031 225 8525, FAX 011 44 031 243 4435, telex 72555.

UK
**NORTH WEST EUROPE COMPANY REPORT.** English. sa. £1000.00 (first copy), £500.00 (additional). James Capel and Company, Petroleum Services Department, Wardley House, 7 Devonshire Square, London EC2M 4HN England. **Tel** 011 44 71 626 0866. **ED** Tim Shinger. **Pr Rev.**
**Desc:** Gives summary of exploration and product interests for CGO's most active companies with oil and gas interest in the North Sea and onshore UK. Includes information on : licenses, reserves, production , cash flow table, charts and graphs, and an A3 location map.

UK
**NORTH WEST EUROPE SERVICE.** English. mo. £3,500.00. Wood Mackenzie Consultants Ltd., Kintore House, 74 77 Queen Street, Edinburgh EH2 4NS Scotland. **Tel** 011 44 031 225 8525, FAX 011 44 031 243 4435, telex 72555.

Petroleum and Natural Gas

UK
**NORTH WEST EUROPE SERVICE.** (19??)-. English. mo. £3500.00. Wood Mackenzie Consultants Ltd., Kintore House, 74 77 Queen Street, Edinburgh EH2 4NS Scotland. **Tel** 011 44 031 225 8525, FAX 011 44 031 243 4435, telex 72555. **ED** Douglas Montgomery. **Circ:** 400 (ctrl). Documents available.
**Desc:** Reference work and database covering the upstream oil and gas industry in North West Europe excluding the UK.

US/1070-4469
**NORTHEAST OIL AND GAS WORLD.** ***Title Change.*** [Northeast oil gas world]. **VFOAT** Oil and Gas World. Vol. 13, No. 6 (June 1993)-(Feb. 1994). Periodical. English. mo. Hart Publications Inc, 1900 Grant Street, Suite 400, Denver CO 80203. **Tel** (303)837-1917, (800)832-1917, FAX (303)837-8585. **LC** TN860; .N586. **DD** 553.2/82/0974. ***Continues*** *Northeast Oil World, 0884-4771.* ***Merged with*** *Gulf Coast Oil and Gas World; Southwest Oil and Gas World; Western Oil and Gas World; Midcontinent Oil and Gas World; Pacific Oil and Gas World* ***to form*** *Hart's Oil and Gas World, 1075-5365.*

US/0884-4771
**NORTHEAST OIL WORLD.** ***Title Change.*** [Northeast oil world]. Vol. 5, No. 7 (Aug. 1985)-Vol. 13, No. 5 (May 1993). Periodical. English. mo. Hart Publications Inc, 1900 Grant Street, Suite 400, Denver CO 80203. **Tel** (303)837-1917, (800)832-1917, FAX (303)837-8585. **LC** TN860; .N586. **DD** 553.2/82/0974. **[CCC].** available on microfilm from University Microfilms International (UMI). ***Continues*** *Northeast Oil Reporter, 0279-7798.* ***Continued by*** *Northeast Oil and Gas World, 1070-4469.*

US
**NORTHEAST PETROLEUM DIRECTORY.** (19??)-. English. an. $67.00, $595.00 diskette. Hart Publications Inc, 1900 Grant Street, Suite 400, Denver CO 80203. **Tel** (303)837-1917, (800)832-1917, FAX (303)837-8585.
**Desc:** Over 7,000 company listings that cover a twenty-one state region from Illinois to Maine and Tennessee to Michigan; also includes South Ontario listings.

UK
**NORTHWEST EUROPE UPSTREAM PETROLEUM DATABASE.** English. sa. £1750.00 UK; £1860.00 North America; £1810.00 other. Petroleum Services Dept, Wardley House, 7 Devonshire Square, London 1C2M 4HN England. **ED** Tim Shingler. **Pr Rev.**
**Desc:** Information on licenses, drilling activity, and reserves for offshore Norway, Netherlands, Denmark, Ireland and West Germany. Onshore Denmark and Ireland included. Also includes a total company interests volume and one A3 quadrant map book.

US/0739-0262
**NORTHWEST OIL REPORT.** [Northw. oil rep.]. (19??)-. Periodical. English. sm. $400.00. Northwest Oil Report, 4204 Southwest Condor Avenue, Portland OR 97201. **Tel** (503)224-2156.

NO/0377-1806
**NORWEGIAN OFFSHORE INDEX.** **Added/Corp** Scanpet Scandinavian Petroleum A/S. Norges Industriforbund. Norges Eksportrad. (1974)-. English. Scanpet Scandinavian Petroleum, PO Box 1779, 1 Oslo Norway. **LC** TN867; .N62. **DD** 338.4/7/622338025481.

FR/1156-2560
**NOTE D'INFORMATION ECONOMIQUE - COMITE PROFESSIONNEL DU PETROLE.** (NOTE D'INFORMATION ECONOMIQUE.). **VFOAT** Note d'Information Economique - CPDP. (1990)-. Periodical. French. an. 800.00F. Comite Professionnel du Petrol CPDP, BP 282, 92505 Rueil Malmaison France. **Tel** 011 33 1 47169460. **UDC** 665.6.

US/1040-0354
**NPGA REPORTS.** [NPGA rep.]. **Added/Corp** National Propane Gas Association (U.S.). **VAT** National Propane Gas Association Reports. (198?)-. Periodical. English. wk. $25.00 (members only). National Propane Gas Association, 1600 Eisenhower Lane, Suite 100, Lisle IL 60532. **Tel** (708)515-0600. **ED** James K. Burnham. **DD** 338. ***Continues*** *NPLGA Reports, 0744-4273.*
**Desc:** Information and trends for producers and marketers of liquified petroleum gas.

US
**NPRA FOREIGN TRADE STATISTICS ON SELECTED PETROCHEMICALS.** English. mo. Free. National Petroleum Refiners Association, 1899 L Street NW, Suite 1000 Hamilton, Washington DC 20036. **Tel** (202)457 0480 ext. PUBLS.

CN/0383-9028
**O R G A NEWS.** **Main/Corp** Ontario Retail Gasoline and Automotive Service Association. (Nov. 1985)-. Periodical. English. ir. Free to members. Gasoline and Automotive Service Association, Suite 210, 312 Dolomite Drive, Downsview Ontario M3J 2N2. **DD** 338.4/7/6292860971. ***Supersedes*** *Voice of the Ontario Gasoline Retailer, 0380-7142.*

US/0029-8026
**OCEAN INDUSTRY.** ***Ceased.*** [Ocean ind.]. Vol. 1 (1966)-(Nov. 1992). Academic Scholarly Publication. English (Russian). mo. Ocean Industry, PO Box 2608, Houston TX 77252. **Tel** (713)529-4301, FAX (713)520-4433, telex 287330 GULF UR. **ED** Robert E Snyder. **LC** GC1; .O22. **CODEN** OCIDAF. **[CCC]. Bk Rev. Ad Acc. Circ:** 32,000 (ctrl). available in microform from University Microfilms International (UMI); available on an online database (file 648/Full-Text) from DIALOG. Documents available from Article Express International, UMI Article Clearinghouse, Petroleum Abstracts Document Delivery Service, Documents on Demand.
**Desc:** Targets marine gas and oil operating companies, engineer-constructors and service companies.
**Ind/Abst** ABI/INFORM Glob. Ed.; ABI Inform Ondisc (Feb. 1975-May 1975); AESIS Q.; AQUAREF; Aquat. Sci. Fish. Abstr. (Computer File); Bioeng. Abstr.; Coal Abstr.; Ei Page One; EMBASE; Energy Inf. Abstr.; Energy Res. Abstr. (April 1976-); Eng. Index Annu. [Select. Cov.]; Environ. Abstr.; Fluid Abstr., Civil Eng.; Fluid Abstr. Proc. Eng.; FLUIDEX (1973-); Lit. Pat. Abstr., Oilfield Chem. (1975-1991); Lit. Abstr., Catal. Catal.; Lit. Abstr., Health Environ.; Lit. Abstr., Pet. Refin. Petrochem.; Lit. Abstr., Pet. Substit.; Lit. Abstr., Transp. Storage; Ocean. Abstr.; Life Sci. Collect.; Pet. Abstr.; Pollut. Abstr. Indexes; Risk Abstr.; Trade Ind. ASAP [Full Txt.]; Trade Ind. Index [Full Txt.].

US
**OCEAN OIL WEEKLY REPORT.** (19??)-. Periodical. English. Fifty-two times a year. $395.00 North America; $465.00 other. PennWell Publishing Company, 1421 South Sheridan, PO Box 1260, Tulsa OK 74101. **Tel** (918)835-3161, (800)331-4463, FAX (918)831-9497. **(Subscription address:** Ocean Oil Weekly Report, Publishing Services, PO Box 1260, Tulsa OK 74101.**) ED** Tim Cornitius.
**Desc:** Worldwide activities of the offshore petroleum and supporting marine service industries. Includes oil and gas discoveries and rig construction reports.

CN/0835-1740
**OCTANE.** [Octane]. Vol. 1, No. 1 (Jan. 1987)-. Periodical. English. qt. Free. Energy Equipment News, 200-1015 Centre Street North, Calgary Alberta T2E 2P8 Canada. **Tel** (403)276-7881. **ED** Jim Lyon. **DD** 381/.45553282/0971. **Bk Rev. Ad Acc. Circ:** 5,500 (ctrl).

US/1072-8740
**OCTANE WEEK.** (19??)-. English. wk (50 issues). $1,095.00 US; $1,195.00 other. Hart Publications Inc, 1900 Grant Street, Suite 400, Denver CO 80203. **Tel** (303)837-1917, (800)832-1917, FAX (303)837-8585.

US
**OFFICIAL IPLOCA DIRECTORY.** **Main/Corp** International Pipe Line & Offshore Contractors Association. **VFOAT** International Pipe Line & Offshore Contractors Association ... Directory/Yearbook; International PLOCA Directory/Yearbook; International PLOCA ... Annual Membership Directory. (1991)-. Directory. English. Energy Communications, PO Box 1589, Dallas TX 75221. **LC** TN879.5; .I55a. **DD** 621.8/672/0601. ***Continues*** *Official IPLOCA Directory/Yearbook.*

UK/0952-7125
**OFFSHORE CENTRES REPORT.** [Offshore cent. rep.]. (1989)-. Periodical. English. Ten times a year. £100.00 Uk and Ireland; $175.00 other. World Reports Ltd., 108 Horse Ferry Road, Westminster, London SW1P 2EF United Kingdom. **Tel** 011 44 71 222 3836, FAX 11 44 71 233 0185. **DD** 342.34.

US/0030-0608
**OFFSHORE (CONROE, TEX.).** (OFFSHORE.). [Offshore]. **VFOAT** Off Shore. Vol. 1 (Sept. 1954)-. Periodical. English. Twelve times a year. Offshore Edition: $62.00 US; $82.00 other; Euro/Asia Edition: $62.00 North America; $102.00 Europe and Far East. PennWell Publishing Company, 1421 South Sheridan, PO Box 1260, Tulsa OK 74101. **Tel** (918)835-3161, (800)331-4463, FAX (918)831-9497. **(Subscription address:** Offshore Magazine, PO Box 2895, Tulsa OK 74101.**) ED** Robert G. Burke. **LC** TN871.3; .O3. **DD** 622/.338. **CODEN** OFSHAU. **[CCC]. Bk Rev. Ad Acc.** ctrl circ. available on microfilm and microfiche from University Microfilms International (UMI). Documents available from Petroleum Abstracts Document Delivery Service, Documents on Demand. ***Continues*** *Offshore Operations;* ***Absorbed*** *Oilman, 0264-0759.*
**Ind/Abst** Appl. Sci. Technol. Index; BMT Abstr.; Bus. ASAP (1990-) [Full Txt.]; Bus. Index (1985-); Energy Inf. Abstr.; Energy Res. Abstr. (Feb. 1977-); Environ. Abstr.; Environ. Period. Bibliogr. (?-?); Fluid Abstr., Civil Eng.; Fluid Abstr. Proc. Eng.; FLUIDEX; Gen. BusinessFile (198?-); GeoRef; NEXIS (Jan. 1980-); Ocean. Abstr.; Pet. Abstr.; Trade Ind. ASAP [Full Txt.]; Trade Ind. Index [Full Txt.].

US/0895-3023
**OFFSHORE DRILLING MONTHLY.** ***Title Change.*** (OFFSHORE DRILLING MONTHLY / SALOMON BROTHERS INC.). [Offshore drill. mon.]. **Added/Corp** Salomon Brothers. **VFOAT** Stock Research. Oil Service. (19??)-(19??). Periodical. English. mo. Salomon Brothers Center Finance, 7 World Trade Center, 36th Floor, New York NY 10004. **Tel** (212)747-7000. **DD** 332. ***Merged into*** *Oil Services & Drilling Monthly.*

CN/0712-0745
**OFFSHORE INDUSTRIAL DIRECTORY.** ***Title Change.*** [Offshore ind. dir.]. **Added/Corp** Newfoundland. Dept. of Industrial Development. Newfoundland. Dept. of Development. (1979)-(1992). Directory. English. an. Department of Development / Newfoundland, Confederation Building, St John's Newfoundland A1C 5T7 Canada. **Tel** (709)576-5064, FAX (709)576-5936, telex 016-4949. **ED** Mathew Shinkle. **LC** HD9574.C23; N486. **DD** 381/.458176. Index available. **Circ:** 15,000 (ctrl). ***Continued by*** *Offshore Petroleum Directory, 1196-2747.*

UK
**OFFSHORE INSTALLATIONS : GUIDANCE ON DESIGN, CONSTRUCTION AND CERTIFICATION.** (1986)-. English. ir. £40.00 (consolidated edition). Health & Safety Executive, Room 414 St Hughs House Stanley, Btle Merseyside L20 3QY England. **Tel** 011 44 51 951 4000, FAX 011 44 51 922 5394, telex 628235.

UK
**OFFSHORE INTELEX DRILLING WORLDWIDE.** (19??)-. English. ir (208 issues). £2496.00. Petrodata, Dock Gate House, York Place, Waterloo Quay, Aberdeen AB2 1DF Scotland. **Tel** 011 44 224 572247, FAX 011 44 224 580320.

US/1058-5842
**OFFSHORE INTERNATIONAL NEWSLETTER, THE.** **See** Economics-Industry and Production.

UK
**OFFSHORE LICENCE REPORT.** James Capel and Company, Petroleum Services Department, Wardley House, 7 Devonshire Square, London EC2M 4HN England. **Tel** 011 44 71 626 0866.

UK/0309-4189
**OFFSHORE RESEARCH FOCUS.** [Offshore res. focus]. (1977)-. Periodical. English. Six times a year. Free. Techword Services, 153-155 London Road Hemel, Hempstead Herts HP3 9SQ England. **Tel** 011 44 442 257635, FAX 011 44 442 252519. **ED** M. J. Wright. Index available. cum. index. **Bk Rev**, (Qty: 12). **Circ:** 7,000 (ctrl).
**Desc:** News and information of research programs in the offshore engineering sponsored by the UK Health and Safety Executives.
**Ind/Abst** Fluid Abstr., Civil Eng.; Fluid Abstr. Proc. Eng.; FLUIDEX (19??-); Int. Civil Eng. Abstr.

CN/0820-0858
**OFFSHORE RESOURCES.** ***Ceased.*** [Offshore resour.]. Vol. 1, No. 1 (Spring 1983)-(1986). Periodical. English. qt. Offshore Resources, PO Box 91760, West Vancouver British Columbia V7V 4S1 Canada. **DD** 622/.29/0971.

US/0733-0928
**OFFSHORE RIG LOCATION REPORT, THE.** ***Title Change.*** [Offshore rig locat. rep.]. **Added/Corp** Offshore Rig Data Services. **VFOAT** Offshore Rig Newsletter. (19??)-(19??). Periodical. English. mo. Offshore Rig Data Services Inc, PO Box 19909, Houston TX 77224. **Tel** (713)781-2173. **DD** 622. **Ad Acc.** available on diskette. ***Continued by*** *Offshore Rig Locator.*
**Desc:** Worldwide listing of offshore rigs and their status.

US
**OFFSHORE RIG LOCATOR.** (19??)-. English. Twelve times a year. $485.00 North America; $525.00 others. Offshore Data Services Inc., PO Box 19909, Houston TX 77224. **Tel** (713)781-2713, FAX (713)781-9594, telex 166338. ***Continues*** *Offshore Rig Location Rig Report.*

US/0147-1481
**OFFSHORE RIG NEWSLETTER, THE.** [Offshore rig newsl.]. **Added/Corp** Offshore Rig Data Services. Vol. 1 (Feb. 1974)-. Newsletter. English. mo. $190.00 North America; $205.00 other. Offshore Data Services Inc., PO Box 19909, Houston TX 77224. **Tel** (713)781-2713, FAX (713)781-9594, telex 166338. **ED** Tom Marsh. **Circ:** 1,650.
**Desc:** Reports on the offshore drilling rig market.

US/0734-9386
**OFFSHORE SERVICE VESSELS. A GUIDE TO THE FOREIGN FLEET.** **VFOAT** Guide to the Foreign Fleet. (1987)-. English. an. $150.00 US; $160.00 other. Fleet Data Service, PO Box 2576, Nacogdoches TX 75963-2576.

Petroleum and Natural Gas

●US/1067-103X
**OFFSHORE TECHNOLOGY (TULSA, OKLA.).** (OFFSHORE TECHNOLOGY.). [Offshore technol.]. **Added/Corp** Petroleum Abstracts (Organization). Vol. 1, No. 1 (Jan. 1993)-. Periodical. English. mo. $175.00 (general subscribers), $195.00 (nonsubscribers). Petroleum Abstracts, University of Tulsa, Information Services Division, 600 South College Avenue, Harwell Hall 101, Tulsa OK 74104-3189. **Tel** (800)247-8678, (918)631-2297, FAX (918)599-9361, telex 49 7543. **DD** 665.
**Desc:** Covers the worldwide literature on all aspects of offshore exploration and production, including offshore platforms, offshore storage, deep-water/deep-sea drilling, offshore construction and offshore pipelines.

US/0094-9124
**OFFSHORE TECHNOLOGY YEARBOOK.** [Offshore technol. yearb.]. English. Energy Communications, PO Box 1589, Dallas TX 75221. **LC** TN871.3; .O37. **DD** 622/.33/8.

US/0887-6835
**OFFSHORE TUGS. A GUIDE TO THE AMERICAN FLEET.** [Offshore tugs, guide Am. fleet]. **VFOAT** Offshore Tugs, American; Guide to the American Fleet. (1983)-. English. an. Fleet Data Service, PO Box 2576, Nacogdoches TX 75963-2576. **DD** 387. ***Continues*** *Guide to American Offshore Fleets. Tugs, 0197-1123.*

UK/0950-1045
**OIL & ENERGY TRENDS.** [Oil energy trends]. **Main/Corp** Energy Economics Research Ltd. (197?)-. Academic Scholarly Publication. English. Twelve times a year. £460.00 UK and Europe; $782.00 other. Basil Blackwell Publishers Ltd, 108 Cowley Road, Oxford 0X4 1JF England. **Tel** 011 44 865 791100, FAX 011 44 865 791347, telex 837022 OXBOOK G. **(Subscription address:** Blackwell Publishers / UK, Marston Book Services, PO Box 87, Oxford OX2 0DT England.**) LC** HD9560.4; .E56A. **DD** 338.2/02/12. **[CCC].**
**Ind/Abst** Pet. Energy Bus. News Index (1981-1982).

AT/0727-6842
**OIL & GAS AUSTRALIA.** [Oil gas Aust.]. (1981)-. English. mo (11 issues per year). 60.00Aus$ (one year), 90.00Aus$ (two year), 130.00Aus$ (three year) Australia and New Zealand; $100.00 (one year), $170.00 (two year), $260.00 (three year) other. Energy Publications / Australia, Energy House, 103 Scarborough Road, Mt. Hawthorn WA 6016 Australia. **Tel** 011 61 09 4433400, FAX 011 61 09 2421811, telex 95431.
**Ind/Abst** AESIS Q.

US
**OIL AND GAS DEVELOPMENTS IN PENNSYLVANIA.** **Main/Corp** Pennsylvania. Bureau of Topographic and Geologic Survey. 1950-. English. an. price varies. Bureau of Topographic and Geologic Survey, PO Box 2357, Harrisburg PA 17105. **Tel** (717)787-2169. **ED** John Harper. **LC** QE157; .A293. **DD** 553.28.
**Desc:** Review of oil and gas activity in Pennsylvania.

US
**OIL & GAS DIRECTORY (HOUSTON, TEX. 1970).** (THE OIL & GAS DIRECTORY.). **VFOAT** Oil and Gas Directory. (1970/71)-. English. an. $70.36 Texas; $65.00 other. Oil & Gas Directory, PO Box 130508, Houston TX 77219. **Tel** (713)529-8789, FAX (713)529-3646. **LC** TN867; .O4953. **DD** 338.2/7/28025. **Bk Rev. Ad Acc. Circ:** 5,000.
**Desc:** List of contractors, suppliers and oil and gas companies engaged in petroleum exploration, drilling and producing.

CN/0833-9422
**OIL & GAS EXPLORATION JOURNAL (CALGARY, ALTA.).** (OIL & GAS EXPLORATION JOURNAL.). [Oil gas explor. j.]. **VFOAT** Exploration Journal. **VAT** Oil and Gas Exploration Journal. Vol. 19, Issue 6 (March 6, 1986)-. Periodical. English. bw. 600.00Can$. Oil & Gas Exploration Journal, 3005 505 6th Street Southwest, Calgary Alberta T2P 1X5 Canada. **Tel** (403)237-0318. **DD** 333.8/23. ***Continues*** *Petroleum Land Journal, 0315-8411.*

US/0474-0076
**OIL AND GAS FEDERAL INCOME TAX MANUAL.** **Added/Corp** Arthur Andersen & Co. Periodical. English. Arthur Andersen & Company / Chicago, 33 West Monroe Street, Chicago IL 60603. **Tel** (312)580-0033. **DD** 336.278622338.

US/0738-9809
**OIL AND GAS FIELD CODE MASTER LIST.** (OIL AND GAS FIELD CODE MASTER LIST / ENERGY INFORMATION ADMINISTRATION, OFFICE OF OIL AND GAS.). **Added/Corp** United States. Energy Information Administration. Office of Oil and Gas. (1982)-. English. an (Dec.). $27.00. National Energy Information Center, Energy Information Administration, Forrestal Building, Room 1F-048, Washington DC 20585. **Tel** (202)586-8800. **LC** TN872; .A323. **DD** 553.2/8/0973. available on microfiche (Vols. for (1984-) distributed to depository libraries).
**Desc:** Provides standardized field name spellings and unique six-digit codes for all identified oil and/or gas fields in the United States.

US/0161-0961
**OIL AND GAS FIELD STUDIES.** [Oil gas field stud.]. Began with: No. 1, published in 1972. English. Utah Geological and Mineralogical Survey, University of Utah, 606 Blackhawk Way, Salt Lake City UT 84108. **CODEN** OSUSDV. **Bk Rev. Circ:** 500 (ctrl).
**Desc:** Descriptions of oil and gas fields with history, production, and geologic structure.
**Ind/Abst** GeoRef.

UK/0902-3752
**OIL & GAS FINANCE & ACCOUNTANCY.** **See** Business-Accounting.

UK/0962-3752
**OIL & GAS FINANCE AND ACCOUNTING.** **See** Business-Accounting.

AT/1038-1317
**OIL AND GAS GAZETTE.** (1991)-. Periodical. English. mo. 105.00Aus$ Australia; 145.00Aus$ Papua, New Guinea, New Zealand, Asia; 170.00Aus$ other. Resource Information Unit, 100 Ahy Street Suite 8 10, R Louthean, Subiaco WA 6008 Australia. **Tel** 011 61 9 3823955.
**Ind/Abst** AESIS Q.

FR
**OIL AND GAS INFORMATION.** **Added/Corp** International Energy Agency. **VFOAT** Donnees sur le Petrole et sur le Gaz. (1988)-. English (French). an. $125.00. OECD Publications and Information Center, 2 rue Andre-Pascal, 75775 Paris Cedex 16 France. **Tel** 011 33 1 45248167, US:(202)785-6323, FAX 011 33 1 45248500 OR 45248176, telex 620 160 OCDE. **LC** HD9560.1; .O33. **DD** 333.8/23/05. ***Continues*** *Annual Oil and Gas Statistics and Main Historical Series.*

US/1073-0265
**OIL & GAS INTERESTS NEWSLETTER.** (OIL & GAS INTERESTS NEWSLETTER : BUSINESS NEWS FOR THE OIL & GAS EXECUTIVE.). (1986)-. Newsletter. English. mo (12 issues per year). $427.00. Hart Publications Inc, 1900 Grant Street, Suite 400, Denver CO 80203. **Tel** (303)837-1917, (800)832-1917, FAX (303)837-8585. **ED** Jack Stevenson. Index available (Index - $20.00 extra). **Circ:** 1,250.
**Desc:** Monthly summary of business news of the domestic North American oil and gas industry. Emphasis is on exploration and production companies. Unique newsletter edited by former oil and gas independent operator that includes producing property sales, joint ventures, bankruptcies, financing, mergers, restructuring, etc.

US/0744-5881
**OIL & GAS INVESTOR.** [Oil gas investor]. **VFOAT** Oil and Gas Investor. Vol. 1, No. 1 (Aug. 1981)-. Periodical. English. mo. $195.00 US & Canada; $287.00 other. Hart Publications Inc, 1900 Grant Street, Suite 400, Denver CO 80203. **Tel** (303)837-1917, (800)832-1917, FAX (303)837-8585. **ED** David R. Webster. **LC** HD9561; .O49. **DD** 332.6/722. **[CCC].** Index available. **Ad Acc. Circ:** 10,500. available on microfilm and microfiche from University Microfilms International (UMI); available on an online database (file 15/Full-Text) from DIALOG. Documents available from UMI Article Clearinghouse.
**Desc:** Identifies and interprets trends and opportunities for executives and investors in the oil and gas and financial communities. It links the companies that explore for oil and gas with the capital sources that provide funding for this activity.
**Ind/Abst** ABI/INFORM Glob. Ed.; ABI Inform Ondisc (Aug. 1983-); Bus. Index (1992-); Gen. BusinessFile (1992-); UMI ABI/Inform--Bus. Period. Ondisc (Nov. 1987-) [Full Txt.].

US/0030-1388
**OIL & GAS JOURNAL.** [Oil gas j.]. **VFOAT** Oil and Gas Journal. Vol. 9, No. 1 (June 16, 1910)-. Academic Scholarly Publication. English. wk. $74.00 US; $81.00 Canada and Latin America; $118.00 other. PennWell Publishing Company, 1421 South Sheridan, PO Box 1260, Tulsa OK 74101. **Tel** (918)835-3161, (800)331-4463, FAX (918)831-9497. **(Subscription address:** Oil & Gas Journal, Publishing Services, PO Box 2002, Tulsa OK 74101.**) LC** TN860; .O4. **CODEN** OIGJAV. **[CCC]. Ad Acc. Pr Rev. Circ:** 60,000. available on microfilm and microfiche from University Microfilms International (UMI). Documents available from Article Express International, The Genuine Article, UMI Article Clearinghouse, CASDDS, Petroleum Abstracts Document Delivery Service, Documents on Demand. ***Continues*** *Oil Investors Journal.*
**Desc:** Publishes news of the worldwide petroleum industry and technical operating information about all phases of petroleum operations.
**Ind/Abst** ASTIS Curr. Aware. Bull. (1978-); AESIS Q.; Alum. Ind. Abstr.; Anal. Abstr.; Appl. Sci. Technol. Index; Aquat. Sci. Fish. Abstr. (Computer File); ASTIS Bibliogr. (1978-); Bioeng. Abstr.; Bus. ASAP (1990-) [Full Txt.]; Bus. Index (1985-); Bus. Period. Index; Chem Inform; Chem. Abstr.; Chem. Bus. Bull.; Chem. Bus. NewsBase (1985-); Chem. Bus. Update; Chem. Hazards Ind.; Chem. Ind. Notes; Civ. Struct. Eng. Abstr.; Coal Abstr.; Comput. Inf. Syst. Abstr. J. [Full Cov.]; Corros. Abstr.; Curr. Contents Eng. Tech. Appl. Sci.; Ei Page One; EMBASE; Energy Res. Abstr.; Eng. Mater. Abstr.; Eng. Index Annu.; Environ. Abstr.; Environ. Eng. Abstr.; Expand. Acad. Index (1992-); F&S Index Plus Text, Int. [Select. Cov.]; Fluid Abstr., Civil Eng.; Fluid Abstr. Proc. Eng.; FLUIDEX (1973-); Gas Abstr.; Gen. BusinessFile (1985-); Gen. Period. Index (1985-); GeoRef; Highw. Res. Abstr.; HTFS Dig.; Index Period. Artic. Relat. Law (19??-19??); Infobank (Jan. 1969-); Int. Aerosp. Abstr.; Lab. Hazards Bull.; Lit. Pat. Abstr., Oilfield Chem. (1954-); Lit. Abstr., Catal. Catal.; Lit. Abstr., Health Environ.; Lit. Abstr., Pet. Refin. Petrochem.; Lit. Abstr., Pet. Substit.; Lit. Abstr., Transp. Storage; Mag. Search; Manuf. Process Eng. Abstr.; Mater. Sci. Eng. Abstr.; Mech. Eng. Abstr.; Met. Abstr.; Newsp. Period. Abstr. (1992-); NEXIS (Jan. 2, 1978-); Ocean. Abstr.; Life Sci. Collect.; Pet. Abstr.; Pet. Energy Bus. News Index (1978); Pollut. Abstr. Indexes; Proc. Chem. Eng.; PROMT; Res. Alert [Select. Cov.]; Risk Abstr.; Saf. Health Work; SCISEARCH; Soc. Sci. Cit. Index [Select. Cov.]; Soils Fert.; Stat. Ref. Index; Theoret. Chem. Eng.; Trade Ind. ASAP [Full Txt.]; Trade Ind. Index (1981-) [Full Txt.]; UMI ABI/Inform--Bus. Period. Ondisc (Jan. 1991-) [Full Txt.]; Wilson Bus. Abstr.

US
**OIL AND GAS LAW.** **See** Law.

SI/0217-6602
**OIL & GAS NEWS YEARBOOK.** **VFOAT** Oil and Gas News Yearbook; ; Oil & Gas news year book. (19??)-. English. Fifty times a year. 540.00Sing$. Al Hilal Publishing Fe Pte Ltd., 50 Jalan Sultan, 20-06 JS Centre, Singapore 0719 Singapore. **Tel** 011 65 2939233. **LC** HD9560.1; .O342. **DD** 338.2/728/05.

US
**OIL AND GAS NOTICE AND FORMS.** English. ir. $12.00. Railroad Commission of Texas, PO Drawer 12967, Capitol Station, Austin TX 78711. **Tel** (512)463-7255.

UK/0263-5070
**OIL & GAS (OXFORD, OXFORDSHIRE).** **See** Law.

US
**OIL & GAS PRODUCING INDUSTRY IN YOUR STATE, THE.** **VFOAT** Oil and Gas Producing Industry in Your State. (1984)-. English. an. $35.00. Petroleum Independent Publishers Inc, 1101 16th Street NW, Washington DC 20036. **Tel** (202)857-4775. **ED** Joseph Taylor. **Ad Acc. Circ:** 12,000. ***Continues*** *Oil Producing Industry in Your State, 0191-0396.*
**Desc:** Petro-gas production stats for US petro industry by state and other petro industry data i.e. labor, capital expended, invested.

US/0273-3811
**OIL AND GAS PRODUCTION IN KANSAS.** [Oil gas prod. Kans.]. English. an. Kansas Geological Survey, 1930 Constant Avenue, University of Kansas, Lawrence KS 66046. **Tel** (913)864-3965. **LC** TN872.K2; O38. **DD** 338.2/728/09781.

CN/0702-8202
**OIL AND GAS PRODUCTION REPORT.** **Added/Corp** British Columbia. Dept. of Mines and Petroleum Resources. British Columbia. Ministry of Mines and Petroleum Resources. British Columbia. Ministry of Energy, Mines and Petroleum Resources. (1???)-. Periodical. English. Twelve times a year. 135.00Can$. Crown Publications Inc., 521 Fort Street, Victoria, British Columbia, V8W 1E7 Canada. **Tel** (604)386-4636, FAX (604)386-0221.
**Desc:** Includes a statistical summary of the drilling activity, well count, production, and injection of all fluids on a pool basis, disposition of production, gas plant and refinery operations, and nominations and estimated requirements by the refineries.

US/0270-5400
**OIL AND GAS PRODUCTION REPORT. NORTHERN ROCKIES.** [Oil gas prod. rep., North. Rockies]. English. an. Petroleum Information Corporation, 5333 Westheimer, Suite 100, Houston TX 77056. **Tel** (713)840-8282 ext. 38, FAX (713)599-5100. **LC** HD9567.A17; O38. **DD** 338.2/728/0978.

US/0270-5419
**OIL AND GAS PRODUCTION REPORT. SOUTHERN ROCKIES.** [Oil gas prod. rep., South. Rockies]. English. an. Petroleum Information Corporation, 5333 Westheimer, Suite 100, Houston TX 77056. **Tel** (713)840-8282 ext. 38, FAX (713)599-5100. **LC** HD9567.A165; O38. **DD** 338.2/728/0978.

US
**OIL AND GAS PRODUCTION REPORT [MICROFORM] / NORTH DAKOTA STATE INDUSTRIAL COMMISSION.** **Added/Corp** North Dakota Industrial Commission. Oil and Gas Division. (Jan. 1990)-. Periodical. English. mo. $12.00 US, $24.00 other. North Dakota State Industrial Commission, Oil and Gas Division, 900 East Boulevard, Bismarck ND 58505. **Tel** (701)224-2969. **LC** Microfiche (o) 93/6595. ***Continues*** *Oil Production Report.*

CN/0831-4799
**OIL & GAS REPORT (NORTH VANCOUVER, B.C.).** (OIL & GAS REPORT.). [Oil gas rep.]. **VAT** Oil and Gas Report (North Vancouver). Vol. 2, No. 3 (Summer 1985)-. Periodical. English. bm. 15.00Can$, 4.00Can$ each number. Oil & Gas Report, PO Box 91760 Columbia V7V 4S1 Canada. **DD** 338.2/728/0971. ***Continues*** *Resource Technology Oil & Gas Report, 0824-4952.*

US/0735-7583
**OIL & GAS REPORT (TALLAHASSEE, FLA.).** (OIL & GAS REPORT.). [Oil gas rep.]. **Added/Corp** Florida Petroleum Council. **VFOAT** Florida Petroleum Report. **VAT** Oil and Gas Report (Tallahassee, Fla.). Vol. 3, No. 7 (Aug. 18, 1972)-. Periodical. English. wk. $84.00. Oil & Gas Report, PO Box 10151, Tallahassee FL 32302. **Tel** (904)222-0228. ***Continues*** *Florida Petroleum Council. News.*

US/0364-2984
**OIL AND GAS REPORT (UNIVERSITY OF ALA.).** (OIL AND GAS REPORT.). [Oil gas rep.]. **Added/Corp** Geological Survey of Alabama. Alabama. State Oil and Gas Board. (19??)-. Monographic series. English. ir. Price varies per volume. Geological Survey of Alabama, PO Box O, Tuscaloosa AL 35486. **Tel** (205)349-2852. **LC** UNC. **CODEN** OGRADE.
**Ind/Abst** GeoRef.

US/0472-7630
**OIL AND GAS REPORTER.** [Oil gas report.]. **Added/Corp** Southwestern Legal Foundation. **VFOAT** Oil & Gas Reporter. (1952)-. Periodical. English. mo (4 volumes annually with monthly updates). $127.50. Matthew Bender & Company Inc., 1275 Broadway, Albany NY 12204. **Tel** (800)833-9844, (518)487-3000. **LC** KF1845.A2; O38. **DD** 343.

US/0894-5322
**OIL & GAS RESERVE DISCLOSURES.** (OIL & GAS RESERVE DISCLOSURES / ARTHUR ANDERSEN & CO.). [Oil gas reserve discl.]. **Added/Corp** Arthur Andersen & Co. **VFOAT** Oil and Gas Reserve Disclosures. (19??)-. English. an. Arthur Andersen & Company / Texas, 711 Louisiana Street/Suite 1300, Houston TX 77002. **Tel** (713)237-2469. **DD** 333.

●UK/0967-537X
**OIL & GAS RUSSIA & POST SOVIET REPUBLICS. HYDROCARBONS BRIEF.** [Hydrocarb. brief]. **VFOAT** Oil & Gas Newsletter. Hydrocarbons Brief. (1992)-. English. Four times a year (Jan., Apr., July, Oct.). $180.00. Arguments & Facts International, PO Box 35, Hastings, East Sussex, TN34 2Ux England. **Tel** 011 44 0424 444142, FAX 011 44 0424 717498. **(Subscription address:** Business Center, 12 50 Kingsgate Road, G9 Surrey KT2 5AA England, telephone: 011 41 81 5472411**) ED** Nick Terdrls. **Bk Rev**, (Qty: 16). **Ad Acc**. **Acid Free. Circ:** 5,000 (ctrl).

US/0736-8372
**OIL & GAS STOCKS HANDBOOK / STANDARD & POOR'S CORPORATION.** ***Ceased.*** **See** Business-Investments.

US/0030-1396
**OIL & GAS TAX QUARTERLY.** [Oil gas tax q.]. **VAT** Oil and Gas Tax Quarterly. V. 1- Oct. 1951-. Periodical. English. qt. $125.00. Matthew Bender & Company Inc., 1275 Broadway, Albany NY 12204. **Tel** (800)833-9844, (518)487-3000. **LC** K15; .I55. **DD** 336.2786655. cum. index. available on microfilm and microfiche from University Microfilms International (UMI).
**Ind/Abst** Account. Tax Datab. (1990-); Coal Abstr.; Curr. Law Index (1980-); Energy Res. Abstr. (May 1980-); Fed. Tax Artic.; Index Leg. Period.; Leg. Resour. Index (1980-); LegalTrac (1980-).

US
**OIL & GAS TAXES NATURAL RESOURCES.** **VFOAT** Oil and Gas Taxes-- Natural Resources Report. (19??)-. Periodical. English. mo. Maxwell Macmillan Professional Business Division, 910 Sylvan Avenue, Englewood Cliffs NJ 07632-3310. **Tel** (800)431-9025. ***Continues*** *Oil and Gas Taxes.*

US/8750-4804
**OIL & GAS TECHNOLOGY.** **VFOAT** Oil and Gas Technology. Vol. 7, No. 9 (Oct. 1984)-. Periodical. English. bm. $6.00. Gordon Publications Inc, A Subsidiary of Cahners Publishing Company, 301 Gibraltar Drive, Box 650, Morris Plains NJ 07950. **Tel** (201)292-5100. **DD** 338. ***Continues*** *Petrochemical Equipment News, 0192-8554.*

US/0747-5306
**OIL AND GAS (URBANA, ILL.).** (OIL AND GAS.). [Oil gas]. **Added/Corp** Illinois State Geological Survey. (July 1979)-. English. mo. Illinois Geological Survey, Natural Resources Building, Urbana IL 61801. **LC** TN872.I3; A28. **DD** 338.2/728/09773. ***Continues*** *Illinois State Geological Survey. Oil and Gas Drilling in Illinois, 0193-3531.*

US
**OIL & NATURAL GAS PRODUCING INDUSTRY IN YOUR STATE, THE.** Petroleum Independent Publishers Inc, 1101 16th Street NW, Washington DC 20036. **Tel** (202)857-4775.

UK
**OIL CITY NEWS LETTER.** English. mo. £18.00. Oilnews and Gas International, PO Box 5, Subs Dept, Haddington, East Lothian EH41 3NQ Scotland. **Tel** 011 44 062 0822578.

US/0030-1434
**OIL DAILY, THE.** [Oil daily]. **VFOAT** Oil Daily's Terminals; Terminals. No. 1 (1951)-. Periodical. English. da (Monday-Friday). $947.00. The Oil Daily, 1401 New York Avenue Northwest, Suite 500, Washington DC 20005-2150. **Tel** (800)621-0050, (800)368-5803, (202)662-0700, FAX (202)662-0739, telex 89472. **ED** Marshall Thomas. **LC** HD9561; .O53. **DD** 338.27282. **[CCC]. Ad Acc. Circ:** 5,000. available on microfilm and microfiche from University Microfilms International (UMI); available on an online database (file 648/Full-Text) from DIALOG; available via fax; available via electronic mail.
**Desc:** The newspaper of the petroleum industry. Reports on politics and energy, corporate events, product prices, oil finance and economics, exploration updates, and environmental issues.
**Ind/Abst** Bus. ASAP (1990-) [Full Txt.]; Bus. Index (1985-); Gen. BusinessFile (1985-); Gen. Period. Index (1985-); Infobank (Jan. 1969-); Mag. Search; Pet. Energy Bus. News Index (1975); Trade Ind. ASAP [Full Txt.]; Trade Ind. Index (1981-) [Full Txt.].

US/1066-3002
**OIL DAILY'S LUBRICANTS WORLD, THE.** (OIL DAILY'S LUBRICANTS WORLD.). [Oil daily's lubr. world]. **VFOAT** Lubricants World. (Apr. 29, 1991)-. Periodical. English. Twelve times a year. $65.00 US, Canada and Mexico; $110.00 other. The Oil Daily, 1401 New York Avenue Northwest, Suite 500, Washington DC 20005-2150. **Tel** (800)621-0050, (800)368-5803, (202)662-0700, FAX (202)662-0739, telex 89472. **DD** 338.
**Ind/Abst** Pet. Energy Bus. News Index (1992).

US
**OIL DIRECTORY OF LOUISIANA AND PRODUCTION SURVEY.** **VFOAT** Oil and Gas Directory and Production Survey of Louisiana; Oil & Gas Directory and Production Survey of Louisiana. (19??)-. English. an. $24.00. R. W. Byram & Company, PO Drawer 1867, Austin TX 78767. **Tel** (512)478-2551, (800)252-3201. **LC** HD9567.L8; O37. **DD** 338.2/728/025763.

US/0471-3893
**OIL DIRECTORY OF TEXAS.** **VFOAT** Oil Directory of Texas and Production Survey. (1???)-. English. an (Apr.). $40.00 Texas residents: $38.00 others. R. W. Byram & Company, PO Drawer 1867, Austin TX 78767. **Tel** (512)478-2551, (800)252-3201. **DD** 338.2; 665.
**Desc:** News and information about the oil and gas producers in Texas. Also feature is production fact sheets for one month.

US/0195-0576
**OIL EXPRESS.** [Oil express]. (19??)-. Periodical. English. wk (50 issues). $297.00 (one year), $584.00 (two year). United Communications Group, 11300 Rockville Pike, Suite 1100, Rockville MD 20852. **Tel** (301)816-8950 ext. 223, FAX (301)816-8945. **DD** 338. **[CCC].** ctrl circ. available on an online database (files 16,636/Full-Text) from DIALOG.
**Ind/Abst** PROMT [Full Txt.]; PTS Newsl. Database [Full Txt.].

GW/0342-5622
**OIL GAS.** (OIL GAS : EUROPEAN MAGAZINE.). [Oil, gas]. (1977)-. Periodical. English. qt. DM94.00 Germany; DM104.60 other. Urban Verlag Hamburg Wien GmbH, Neumann Reichardt STR 34, D 22041 Hamburg Germany. **Tel** 011 49 40 6567071. **ED** Thomas Vieth, Hans Jorg Mager. **LC** TN860; O436. **DD** 553/.28/05. **[CCC]. Bk Rev. Ad Acc. Circ:** 5,000. Documents available from Petroleum Abstracts Document Delivery Service, Documents on Demand.
**Desc:** International edition of the scientific/technical monthly ERDOL-ERDGAS-KOHLE, publishing features of international interest.
**Ind/Abst** Coal Abstr.; Ei Page One; Energy Inf. Abstr.; Energy Res. Abstr. (May 1978-); Environ. Abstr.; Fluid Abstr., Civil Eng.; Fluid Abstr. Proc. Eng.; FLUIDEX; Gas Abstr.; GeoRef; Life Sci. Collect.; Pet. Abstr.

US/0030-1353
**OIL, GAS & PETROCHEM EQUIPMENT.** **VAT** Oil, Gas and Petrochem Equipment. Vol. 15, No. 9 (July 1969)-. Trade Publication. English. mo. $32.00 US; $70.00 Canada, Central & South America and Europe; $89.00 Asia, Africa & Middle East. PennWell Publishing Company, 1421 South Sheridan, PO Box 1260, Tulsa OK 74101. **Tel** (918)835-3161, (800)331-4463, FAX (918)831-9497. **(Subscription address:** Oil, Gas & Petrochem Equipment, Publishing Services, PO Box 2367, Tulsa OK 74101.**) ED** J.B. Avants. **LC** TN871.5; .O37. **DD** 622/.33/8028. **[CCC]. Ad Acc.** ctrl circ. available on microfilm from University Microfilms International (UMI). Documents available from Petroleum Abstracts Document Delivery Service.
**Desc:** Target audience includes qualified engineers, operating managers, supervisory and purchasing personnel engaged in design, engineering, construction, operations, and maintenance of oil, gas, and petrochemical operations and facilities.
**Ind/Abst** Pet. Abstr.

US/0162-5675
**OIL, GAS, MARINE DIRECTORY OF THE GULF SOUTH/ATLANTIC COAST.** Directory. English. an. Oil Gas Marine Publ Comp, PO Box 8313, Metarrie LA 70011. **LC** TN867; .O53. **DD** 338.4/7/62233802573.

US/0279-6325
**OIL IN CALIFORNIA.** [Oil Calif.]. **Added/Corp** Petroleum Information Corporation. (19??)-. Periodical. English. mo. $264.00. Petroleum Information Corporation, 5333 Westheimer, Suite 100, Houston TX 77056. **Tel** (713)840-8282 ext. 38, FAX (713)599-5100. **DD** 338.

US/0276-5985
**OIL IN THE ROCKIES.** [Oil Rockies]. **Added/Corp** Petroleum Information Corporation. (19??)-. Periodical. English. mo. $33.50 (monthly rate). Petroleum Information Corporation, 5333 Westheimer, Suite 100, Houston TX 77056. **Tel** (713)840-8282 ext. 38, FAX (713)599-5100.
**Desc:** Regional activity summation comprised of a report section and PI's exclusive Wildcat Activity Map. The report features exploration highlights, land and leasing information, pipeline and refining activity, completion statistics, production data and news, rotary and rig counts and special news stories.

US/0743-6289
**OIL INDUSTRY NEWS.** [Oil ind. news]. **VFOAT** OIN; O.I.N. Periodical. English. mo. $12.00 US; $30.00 other. Oil Industry News, 2328 Quincy, Bakersfield CA 93305-4038.

US/1051-6565
**OIL INDUSTRY OUTLOOK.** [Oil ind. outl.]. **Added/Corp** PennWell Publishing Company. 3rd Ed. (1987-1991)-. Directory. English. an (Dec.). $181.00 US and Canada; $245.75 other. PennWell Publishing Company, 1421 South Sheridan, PO Box 1260, Tulsa OK 74101. **Tel** (918)835-3161, (800)331-4463, FAX (918)831-9497. **(Subscription address:** PennWell Books, PO Box 21288, Tulsa OK 74121.**) LC** HD9561; .O56. **DD** 338.2/7282/097305. ***Continues*** *U.S.A. Oil Industry Outlook, 1051-6557.*
**Desc:** A presentation of the expectations for the worldwide oil and gas industry, prepared by the Oil and Gas Journal's economics editor. Includes recent events that have had an impact on the industry, a discussion of key events that will shape the future of the industry, and the editor's specific forecast of major factors that describe the industry.

US/0030-1310
**OIL, LIFESTREAM OF PROGRESS.** [Oil, lifestream of prog.]. **Added/Corp** California Texas Oil Corporation. Caltex Petroleum Corporation. **VFOAT** Oil Progress. Vol. 1 (July 1951)-. Periodical. English. qt (4 issues). Free on request. Caltex Petroleum Corporation, PO Box 619500, Dallas TX 75261. **Tel** (214)830-1000. **LC** HD9560.1; .O4. **DD** 338.2728.
**Ind/Abst** AESIS Q.; Index Free Period.

FR
**OIL MARKET REPORT.** **Added/Corp** International Energy Agency. **VFOAT** Monthly Oil Market Report. (December 1990)-. English. mo. IEA Oil Market Report, 2nd Floor/Tower House, Southampton Street, London WC2E 7YA England. **LC** HD9560.1; .I38. **DD** 338.2/7282/05. ***Continues*** *IEA Oil Market Report.*

UK
**OIL MARKET TRENDS.** English. mo. £795.00 UK; $1295.00 US. Oil Price Services Ltd, Walton Court, Station Avenue, Walton-on-Thames, Surrey KT12 1SH England. **Tel** 0932-221822, FAX 0932-222895. **ED** R Olle. **Circ:** 100 (ctrl). ***Continues*** *CRU Energy Monitor.*
**Desc:** Tells you what crude and products are worth in main European consuming countries, comparing such values with those based on international spot quotation. Assessments of consumer prices, inland market product values netted back to refineries are complemented by latest demand data and a brief review of market developments.

CN/1184-1664
**OIL MARKET UPDATE.** [Oil mark. update]. **Added/Corp** British Columbia. Ministry of Energy, Mines and Petroleum Resources. No. 1 (Oct. 23, 1990)-. Periodical. English. **DD** 338.2/3282/09711.

UK/0957-655X
**OIL PACKER INTERNATIONAL.** **See** Packaging.

CN/0838-6366
**OIL PATCH MAGAZINE.** [Oil patch mag.]. **VFOAT** Oil Patch. Vol. 10, No. 1 (Sept./Oct. 1987)-. Periodical. English. bm. $18.50. **DD** 338.2/7282/09712. ***Continues** Oil Patch (Edmonton, Alta.)., 0821-5162.*

CN/0410-5591
**OIL PIPE LINE TRANSPORT (ANNUAL ED.).** (OIL PIPE LINE TRANSPORT.). [Oil pipe line transp.]. **Main/Corp** Statistics Canada. Manufacturing and Primary Industries Division. **Added/Corp** Canada. Dominion Bureau of Statistics. Transportation and Public Utilities Section. Canada. Dominion Bureau of Statistics. Public Utilities Section. Canada. Dominion Bureau of Statistics. Energy Statistics Section. Canada. Dominion Bureau of Statistics. Energy and Minerals Section. Statistics Canada. Manufacturing and Primary Industries Division. Statistics Canada. Energy and Minerals Section. Statistics Canada. Energy Section. **VFOAT** Transport du Petrole par Pipe-Lines. (1958)-. English (French). an. 24.00Can$ Canada; $29.00 US; $34.00 other. Statistics Canada, Publications Sales & Services, Main Building Room 1710, Ottawa Ontario K1A 0T6 Canada. **Tel** (613)951-5078, (800)267-6677, FAX (613)951-1584, telex 053-3585. **ED** Gary Smalldridge. **LC** HD9580.C3; A2. **DD** 338.4/7665544/0971. **Circ:** 390. ***Continues** Pipe Lines (Oil) Statistics.*
**Desc:** Cubic meters of oil carried by gathering and trunk lines by province; receipts and deliveries, cubic-meter kilometers, pipe line distance; balance sheet, property account revenues, expenses, income, employees, salaries and wages.

CN/0380-4615
**OIL PIPE LINE TRANSPORT (MONTHLY ED.).** (OIL PIPE LINE TRANSPORT / PREPARED IN THE TRANSPORTATION AND PUBLIC UTILITIES SECTION, PUBLIC FINANCE AND TRANSPORTATION DIVISION.). [Oil pipe line transp.]. **Main/Corp** Canada. Statistique Canada. Division des Industries Manufacturieres et Primaires. **Added/Corp** Canada. Bureau Federal de la Statistique. Section des Transports et des Services d'Utilite Publique. Canada. Bureau Federal de la Statistique. Section des Services d'Utilite Publique. Canada. Bureau Federal de la Statistique. Division de l'Industrie. Canada. Bureau Federal de la Statistique. Division des Industries Manufacturieres et Primaires. Statistique Canada. Division des Industries Manufacturieres et Primaires. Statistique Canada. Section de l'Energie et des Mineraux. Statistique Canada. Section de l'Energie. **VFOAT** Transport du Petrole par Pipe-Lines. Vol. 22, (Jan. 1972)-. French (English). mo. 110.00Can$ Canada; $132.00 US; $154.00 other. Statistics Canada, Publications Sales & Services, Main Building Room 1710, Ottawa Ontario K1A 0T6 Canada. **Tel** (613)951-5078, (800)267-6677, FAX (613)951-1584, telex 053-3585. **DD** 338.4/7665544/0971. ***Continues** Canada. Bureau Federal de la Statistique. Division des Industries Manufacturieres et Primaires. Pipe Lines (Oil) Statistics., 0380-4615.*
**Desc:** Receipts and deliveries by source and by movement of crude oil, and refined petroleum products by gathering and trunk lines, by provinces; barrel-miles, operating revenues.

US/0193-4171
**OIL PRICE DATABOOK.** **VFOAT** Oil Buyers' Guide Oil Price Databook. English. $125.00. PO Box 998, Lakewood NJ 08701. **LC** HD9564; .O54. **DD** 338.4/3665/50973.

US/0279-7801
**OIL PRICE INFORMATION SERVICE.** [Oil price inf. serv.]. Vol. 1, No. 1 (Jan. 12, 1981)-. Periodical. English. wk (52 issues). $1,995.00 complete service; $645.00 single pad. United Communications Group, 11300 Rockville Pike, Suite 1100, Rockville MD 20852. **Tel** (301)816-8950 ext. 223, FAX (301)816-8945. **DD** 338. available on an online database (files 16,636/Full-Text) from DIALOG.
**Desc:** Comprehensive market-by-market petroleum price reporting service that gives over 20,000 actual wholesale and spot gasoline, distillate and propane prices each week for 250 US and Canadian markets. Also identifies important trends and short term supply and price forecasts.
**Ind/Abst** Pet. Energy Bus. News Index (1992); PROMT [Full Txt.]; PTS Newsl. Database [Full Txt.].

US/0191-0396
**OIL PRODUCING INDUSTRY IN YOUR STATE, THE.** ***Title Change.*** **Added/Corp** Independent Petroleum Association of America. English. an. I P A A National Headquarters, 1101 16th Street NW, Washington DC 20036. **Tel** (202)587-4760. **ED** Deborah Rowell. **LC** HD9564; .I55. **DD** 338.2728. **Ad Acc. Circ:** 20,000. ***Continues** Oil Industry in Your State.* ***Continued by** Oil & Gas Producing Industry in Your State.*
**Desc:** Statistical profile of the 33 oil and gas producing states - including maps, tables and graphs covering drilling prices, production, reserves, etc. Also summarizes total US data in tables.

US
**OIL PRODUCTION LEDGER.** English. mo. $225.00. Railroad Commission of Texas, PO Drawer 12967, Capitol Station, Austin TX 78711. **Tel** (512)463-7255.

IE
**OIL REPORT MEDITERRANEAN.** (19??)-. English. mo. Offshore Intelligence Ltd, Marion Hse 3 Lr Fitzwilliam St, Dublin 2 Ireland.

US/0742-7263
**OIL SCOUTS DIRECTORY.** [Oil scouts dir.]. **Main/Corp** International Oil Scouts Association. Directory. English. $35.00. International Oil Scouts Association, PO Box 272949, Houston TX 77277. **Tel** (713)439-3514. **LC** HD9560.3; .I57A. **DD** 622/.1828/02573.

US
**OIL SERVICES & DRILLING MONTHLY.** (19??)-. English. Twelve times a year. $1,800.00. Salomon Brothers Center Finance, 7 World Trade Center, 36th Floor, New York NY 10004. **Tel** (212)747-7000. ***Absorbed** Offshore Drilling Monthly, 0895-3023.*

US/0271-0315
**OIL SHALE SYMPOSIUM PROCEEDINGS.** [Oil Shale Symp. proc.]. **Added/Corp** Colorado School of Mines. Laramie Energy Research Center. Laramie Energy Technology Center. 10th (1977)-. Proceedings. English. **LC** TN858.A1; O37a. **DD** 622/.3382. **CODEN** OSSPDC. Documents available from Article Express International, CASDDS. ***Continues** Oil Shale Symposium. Proceedings of the ... Oil Shale Symposium.*
**Ind/Abst** Bioeng. Abstr.; Chem. Abstr.; Ei Page One; Eng. Index Annu.; GeoRef; Lit. Pat. Abstr., Oilfield Chem.; Lit. Abstr., Catal. Catal.; Lit. Abstr., Health Environ.; Lit. Abstr., Pet. Refin. Petrochem.; Lit. Abstr., Pet. Substit.; Lit. Abstr., Transp. Storage.

US/0195-3524
**OIL SPILL INTELLIGENCE REPORT.** [Oil spill intell. rep.]. **Added/Corp** Center for Short-lived Phenomena (Cambridge, Mass.). Vol. 1, No. 1 (Oct. 6, 1978)-. Periodical. English. wk. $567.00 North America; $667.00 other. Cutter Information Corporation, 37 Broadway, Arlington MA 02174-5539. **Tel** (617)648-8700, (800)964-5118, FAX (617)648-8707, (617)648-1950, telex 650 100 9891. **LC** TD427.P4; O387. **DD** 363.7/382. **[CCC].** Index available. available on an online database (files 16,636/Full-Text) from DIALOG.
**Desc:** Newsletter on oil spills and spill clean-up technology, legislation and regulations. Read by government agencies, oil companies, spill control equipment companies and environmentalists.
**Ind/Abst** PROMT; PTS Newsl. Database [Full Txt.].

UK
**OIL TAXATION ACTS.** (19??)-. English. an (Feb.). £325.00 (volume set). Her Majesty's Stationery Office, 51 Nine Elms Lane, London SW8 5DR England. **Tel** 011 44 71 873 8459, 011 44 71 873 8499, FAX 011 44 71 873 8499, 011 44 71 873 8456, telex 297138. **(Subscription address:** Her Majesty's Stationery Office, PO Box 276, Publications Centre, London SW8 5DT England.**)**

UK/0306-770X
**OIL WORLD STATISTICS.** **See** Petroleum and Natural Gas-Abstracting, Bibliographies and Statistics.

US/0923-1730
**OILFIELD REVIEW / SCHLUMBERGER.** **Added/Corp** Schlumberger Limited. **VFOAT** Oil Field Review. Vol. 1, No. 1 (April 1989)-. Academic Scholarly Publication. English. qt (1 volume). Fl395.00. Elsevier Science Publishers BV, PO Box 211, 1000 AE Amsterdam Netherlands. **Tel** 011 31 20 5803642, FAX 011 31 20 5862696, telex 15682. **LC** TN860; .O55. **CODEN** OIREE7. **[CCC].** available on microfilm and microfiche from University Microfilms International (UMI). ***Formed by the union of** Technical Review (Schlumberger Limited) **and** Drilling and Pumping Journal.*
**Ind/Abst** Ei Page One; Fluid Abstr., Civil Eng.; Fluid Abstr. Proc. Eng.; FLUIDEX (19??-); GeoRef.

SP
**OILGAS.** Spanish. mo. 7.500ptas Spain; $115.00 Europe; $140.00 US. Oilgas, Paseo de la Habana 48, 28036 Madrid Spain. **Tel** 1-5632893, FAX 1-5635234. Index available. **Ad Acc.**
**Desc:** Dealing with oil petrochemicals and gas.
**Ind/Abst** Gas Abstr.

UK/0263-1024
**OILMAN. NEWSLETTER.** (THE OILMAN NEWSLETTER.). [Oilman. Newsl.]. **VFOAT** Oilman. Weekly Newsletter. (1982)-. Newsletter. English. Fifty-two times a year. £395.00 Europe; $465.00 other. PennWell Publishing Company, 1421 South Sheridan, PO Box 1260, Tulsa OK 74101. **Tel** (918)835-3161, (800)331-4463, FAX (918)831-9497. **(Subscription address:** Oilman Weekly Newsletter, PO Box 1260, Tulsa OK 74101.**)** ***Continues** Oilman. News Bulletin, 0143-6708.*
**Desc:** Contains the latest news of developments concerning the North Sea and European oil and gas businesses.

CN/0030-1515
**OILWEEK.** [Oilweek]. **VFOAT** Energy Environment Report. Vol. 8, No. 51 (Feb. 7, 1958)-. Periodical. English. Forty-nine times a year. 99.00Can$ Canada; 155.00Can$ other. MacLean Hunter Ltd. Business Publishers / Canada, Box 9100, Station A, Toronto ONT M5W 1A5 Canada. **Tel** (416)946-8420, (800)567-0444. **(Subscription address:** Indas, 35 Riviera Drive, Building 17, Markham Ontario L3R 8N4 Canada.**)** **ED** Jim Lyon. **CODEN** OLWKAX. **[CCC].** Index available. **Bk Rev. Ad Acc. Circ:** 16,000 (ctrl). available on microfilm and microfiche from University Microfilms International (UMI); available on an online database (file 648/Full-Text) from DIALOG. ***Continues** Myers' Oilweek, 0318-0387;* ***Absorbed** Oil in Canada, 0318-0379.*
**Ind/Abst** ASTIS Curr. Aware. Bull. (1978-); ASTIS Bibliogr. (1978-); Coal Abstr.; F&S Index Plus Text, Int. [Select. Cov.]; GeoRef; Lit. Pat. Abstr., Oilfield Chem. (1975-); Lit. Abstr., Catal. Catal.; Lit. Abstr., Health Environ.; Lit. Abstr., Pet. Refin. Petrochem.; Lit. Abstr., Pet. Substit.; Lit. Abstr., Transp. Storage; MINPROC; Mintec, Min. Technol. Abstr.; Predicasts Forecasts; Trade Ind. ASAP [Full Txt.]; Trade Ind. Index [Full Txt.].

CN/1185-3794
**OILWEEK PULSE.** [Oilweek pulse]. Vol. 42, No. 7 (Apr. 1, 1991)-. Periodical. English. wk. Comes with subscription to Oilweek. MacLean Hunter Ltd. Business Publishers / Canada, Box 9100, Station A, Toronto ONT M5W 1A5 Canada. **Tel** (416)946-8420, (800)567-0444. **(Subscription address:** Indas, 35 Riviera Drive, Building 17, Markham Ontario L3R 8N4 Canada.**)** **DD** 338.2.

US/0745-2268
**OKLAHOMA OIL REPORTER, THE.** (THE OKLAHOMA OIL REPORTER / EDITED BY LEROY A. RITTER.). (193?)-. Periodical. English. wk. $480.00 (weekly edition), $600.00 (daily edition). Oklahoma Business News Company, 605 Northwest 13th Street, Suite C, PO Box 1177, Oklahoma City OK 73101. **Tel** (405)521-1405, FAX (405)521-0457. **ED** Leroy A. Ritter. ctrl circ.
**Desc:** Oil industry, insurance filings, liquor licenses and laws, legislation, energy and environment.

US/0733-0227
**OLIPHANT WASHINGTON SERVICE. DIGEST AND CALENDAR OF ACTIVITIES OF THE...CONGRESS ... SESSION OF POSSIBLE INTEREST.** [Oliphant Washington service. Dig. cal. act. possible interest]. Periodical. English. wk. $250.00. Armenian Canadians, PO Box 1211, Station A, Montreal Quebec H3C 2Z1.

FI
**OLJYPOSTI.** Finnish. qt. Free. Neste Oy, Keilaniemi, 02150 Espoo Finland. **Tel** 358-0-4501, telex 124 641 NESTE SF. **ED** Helena Haapalinna. **LC** TP315; .O33. **Ad Acc. Circ:** 35,000 (ctrl).
**Desc:** Covers oil, refining, plastics, energy, exploration, petroleum, natural gas, shipping, environment, new technology, research.

GW
**OLWELT. OIL WORLD.** **Added/Corp** International Seed Testing Association. **VFOAT** Oil World. (19??)-. Periodical. English. sa. Ista Mielke GmbH, Langenberg 25, 2100 Hamburg 90 Germany. **LC** HD9490.A1; O44. **DD** 338.2/7282/05.
**Ind/Abst** Infomat Int. Bus.

UK
**ON SHORE WEEKLY.** (19??)-. English. wk. EIS / Energy Information Services, Seloduct House, 30 Station Road, Redhill Surrey RH1 1PD United Kingdom. **Tel** 737 772599. Index available. ctrl circ.

II
**ONGC BULLETIN.** **Added/Corp** India. Oil and Natural Gas Commission. **VFOAT** Bulletin of Oil & Natural Gas Commission. Vol. 13, No. 1-2 (June & Dec. 1976)-. Bulletin. English. Twice a year (July, Dec.). $30.00. Keshava Deva Malaviya Institute Oil & Natural Gas, Comm Kaulagarh Road, Dehradun India. **Tel** 011 91 27101. **CODEN** BONCDF. ***Continues** Bulletin of the Oil & Natural Gas Commission, 0537-0094.*
**Ind/Abst** Indian Geosci. Abstr.

UK
**ONSHORE WELL RESULTS SERVICE.** (19??)-. English. wk. Oil Publications Dept, Gilozentrale Gilbert Eliott, Salisbury House, London EC2M 5SB England. ctrl circ.
**Desc:** Hardcopy database system on drilling onshore Europe.

AU/0474-6279
**OPEC BULLETIN.** [OPEC bull.]. **Added/Corp** Organization of Petroleum Exporting Countries. **VAT** Organization of the Petroleum Exporting Countries bulletin. (196?)-. Periodical. English. mo (except Jan.). Free on request. OPEC Fund for International Development, PO Box 995 Parkring 8, 1011 Vienna Austria. **Tel** 011 43 1 515640, FAX 011 43 1 214 98 27. **ED** Keith Jinks. **LC** HD9560.1; .O54. **DD** 341.7/5472282/0601. **Bk Rev**, (Qty: 5). **Ad Acc. Circ:** 8,000 (ctrl).
**Desc:** Articles and updates regarding the petroleum industry.
**Ind/Abst** Coal Abstr.; Energy Inf. Abstr.; GeoRef; PAIS Int. Print (1991-).

Petroleum and Natural Gas

US/0277-0180
**OPEC REVIEW.** [OPEC rev.]. **Added/Corp** Organization of Petroleum Exporting Countries. **VFOAT** O.P.E.C. Review. **VAT** Organization of Petroleum Exporting Countries Review. (Oct. 1976)-. Academic Scholarly Publication. English. qt. $147.00 The Americas; £98.00 other. Pergamon Press, An Imprint of Elsevier Science Ltd., The Boulevard, Langford Lane, Kidlington, Oxford OX5 1GB United Kingdom. **Tel** 011 44 865 843000, 011 44 865 843699, FAX 011 44 865 843010. **(Subscription address:** Elsevier Science Ltd. Oxford Fulfillment Centre, PO Box 800, Kidlington, Oxford OX5 1DX United Kingdom.**)** **ED** Keith Marchant. **LC** HD9560.1; .O55. **DD** 338.2/7282/05. **CODEN** OPECDI. **[CCC]. Bk Rev. Ad Acc.** available on microfilm and microfiche from University Microfilms International (UMI). Documents available from CASDDS, Documents on Demand.
**Ind/Abst** AESIS Q.; Chem. Abstr.; Coal Abstr.; Contents Recent Econ. J.; Energy Inf. Abstr.; Energy Res. Abstr. (Dec. 1982-); Environ. Abstr.; Environ. Period. Bibliogr.; Geogr. Abstr. Human Geogr. (?-?); GeoRef; Int. Dev. Abstr. (?-?); PAIS Int. Print (1991-?).

US/0362-4994
**OPERATING SECTION PROCEEDINGS.** [Oper. Sect. proc.]. **Main/Corp** American Gas Association. Operating Section. **Added/Corp** American Gas Association. Operating Section. Proceedings. **VFOAT** Proceedings; AGA Operating Section Proceedings. (19??)-. Academic Scholarly Publication. English. an. $55.00 (members), $110.00 (nonmembers). American Gas Association / Virginia, 1515 Wilson Boulevard, Arlington VA 22209. **Tel** (703)841-8400, (703)841-8559, FAX (703)841-8697. **LC** TN880.A1; A595a. **DD** 665/.7/05. **CODEN** POAGAB. Documents available from Article Express International, CASDDS.
**Ind/Abst** Chem. Abstr.; Coal Abstr.; Ei Page One; Energy Res. Abstr. (Oct. 1976-); Eng. Index Annu.; Gas Abstr.

CN/0842-2982
**OWNERSHIP STRUCTURE OF PRINCIPAL PETROLEUM COMPANIES IN CANADA.** [Ownersh. struct. princ. pet. co. Can.]. **Added/Corp** Petroleum Monitoring Agency Canada. **VFOAT** Ownership Structures of Principal Petroleum Companies in Canada. (1984)-. Periodical. English. an. 90.00Can$ Canada; 93.00Can$ US; 97.00Can$ other. Canadian Oil Register, 300 999-8th Street Southwest, Calgary Alberta T2R 1N7 Canada. **Tel** (403)244-6111, FAX (403)245-8666. **DD** 338.7/6223382/0971.

US/1072-8759
**OXY-FUEL NEWS.** (19??)-. English. wk (50 issues). $895.00 US; $995.00 other. Hart Publications Inc, 1900 Grant Street, Suite 400, Denver CO 80203. **Tel** (303)837-1917, (800)832-1917, FAX (303)837-8585. available on an online database (file 16/Full-Text) from DIALOG.
**Desc:** Covers news and trends in alcohol fuels and oxygenates, and highlights legislative and regulatory developments.

US
**OXY TODAY.** ***Ceased.*** **Added/Corp** Occidental Petroleum Corporation. Began publication with: No. 1 (Winter 1973)-(19??). English. qt. Occidental Petroleum Corporation, 10889 Wilshire Boulevard, Los Angeles CA 90024.

US
**P/E NEWS INDEX GUIDE AND KEYWORD LIST / AMERICAN PETROLEUM INSTITUTE.** **Added/Corp** American Petroleum Institute. (19??)-. English. an. $40.00. American Petroleum Institute, 275 Seventh Avenue, New York NY 10001. **Tel** (212)366-4040, FAX (212)366-4298. **LC** Z6033.P4; P4; TN870. **DD** 553.2/82/016.

US
**PACE PETROLEUM COKE QUARTERLY.** (1983)-. English. qt (with monthly updates). $7000.00. Pace Company, PO Box 53473, Houston TX 77052. **Tel** (713)669-7828, FAX (713)661-8476, telex 4933676. **Pr Rev.** ctrl circ.
**Desc:** Provides objective analyses for the petroleum coke industry. Used to support marketing, purchasing, and strategic decisions by domestic and international producers, marketers, traders and end users of both green and calcined coke.

US
**PACIFIC COAST OIL DIRECTORY.** ***Title Change.*** **VFOAT** Pacific Oil World. (1984)-(19??). Directory. English. an. Hart Publications Inc, 1900 Grant Street, Suite 400, Denver CO 80203. **Tel** (303)837-1917, (800)832-1917, FAX (303)837-8585. **ED** Jack M. Rider. **Ad Acc.**

US
**PACIFIC COAST PETROLEUM DIRECTORY.** (19??)-. English. an. $67.00, $595.00 on diskette. Hart Publications Inc, 1900 Grant Street, Suite 400, Denver CO 80203. **Tel** (303)837-1917, (800)832-1917, FAX (303)837-8585. available on diskette. ***Continues*** *Pacific Coast Oil Directory.*
**Desc:** Company listings for Alaska, California, Oregon and Washington.

US/1071-9628
**PACIFIC OIL AND GAS WORLD.** ***Title Change.*** [Pac. oil gas world]. (June 1993)-(19??). Periodical. English. mo. Hart Publications Inc, 1900 Grant Street, Suite 400, Denver CO 80203. **Tel** (303)837-1917, (800)832-1917, FAX (303)837-8585. **LC** TN860; .C3. **DD** 553/.282/0979. ***Continues*** *Pacific Oil World, 0008-1329.* ***Merged into*** *Gulf Coast Oil and Gas World, 1070-4914; Midcontinent Oil and Gas World, 1071-4790; Northeast Oil and Gas World, 1070-4469; Southwest Oil and Gas World, 1071-4804; Western Oil and Gas World, 1070-6100* ***and*** *Hart's Oil and Gas World, 1075-5365.*

US/0008-1329
**PACIFIC OIL WORLD.** ***Title Change.*** [Pac. oil world]. Vol. 64 (1971)-(June 1993). Periodical. English. mo. Hart Publications Inc, 1900 Grant Street, Suite 400, Denver CO 80203. **Tel** (303)837-1917, (800)832-1917, FAX (303)837-8585. **ED** Jack Rider. **LC** TN860; .C3. **DD** 553/.282/0979. **[CCC]. Ad Acc. Circ:** 3,000. available on microfilm and microfiche from University Microfilms International (UMI). Documents available from Petroleum Abstracts Document Delivery Service. ***Continues*** *California Oil World, 0161-9950.* ***Continued by*** *Pacific Oil and Gas World, 1071-9628.*
**Ind/Abst** Calif. Period. Index (19??-); Calif. Period. Microfi. (19??-); GeoRef; Pet. Abstr.

TI/0570-5274
**PAPERS AND DISCUSSIONS.** **Main/Conf** Arab Petroleum Congress. **Added/Corp** Arab League League of Arab States. Al-Amanah Al-Ammah. (1959)-. English. **LC** TN863; .A69.

CN/1187-8320
**PARTNERS (CALGARY).** (PARTNERS / PETROLEUM RECOVERY INSTITUTE.). [Partners]. **Added/Corp** Petroleum Recovery Institute. Vol. 1, Issue 1 (Jan. 1991)-. Periodical. English. Free. Petroleum Recovery Institute, 3512-33rd Street NW, Calgary Alberta T2L 2A6 Canada. **DD** 622.

●US/1065-0466
**PATENT ABSTRACTS. PETROLEUM & SPECIALTY PRODUCTS.** **See** Copyright, Intellectual Property.

●US/1065-0458
**PATENT ABSTRACTS. PETROLEUM PROCESSES.** **See** Copyright, Intellectual Property.

●US/1065-044X
**PATENT ABSTRACTS. PETROLEUM SUBSTITUTES.** **See** Copyright, Intellectual Property.

●US/1065-0423
**PATENT INDEX.** (PATENT INDEX : INCLUDING BIBLIOGRAPHIC LIST, PATENT NUMBER LIST, ASSIGNEE INDEX / CENTRAL ABSTRACTING & INFORMATION SERVICES, AMERICAN PETROLEUM INSTITUTE.). [Pat. index]. **Added/Corp** American Petroleum Institute. Central Abstracting and Information Services. **VFOAT** American Petroleum Institute Patent Index. (Jan. 1992)-. English. mo. American Petroleum Institute, 275 Seventh Avenue, New York NY 10001. **Tel** (212)366-4040, FAX (212)366-4298. **DD** 608. ***Continues*** *Patents Alphabetical Subject Index.*

US/0275-6129
**PCH. PETROLEUM CONCESSION HANDBOOK.** [PCH]. **VFOAT** Petroleum Concession Handbook. (19??)-. English. mo. $4400.00. Barrows Company Inc., 116 East 66th Street, New York NY 10021. **Tel** (212)772-1199, (800)227-7697, FAX (212)288-7242, telex 4971238 BARROWS. **LC** HD9560.65; .P37. **DD** 333.33/9.
**Desc:** Worldwide oil and gas contracts summaries, with maps.

FR
**PEGAZ.** French. bm (6 issues). 310.00F (includes VAT) France; 310.00F other. Association Technique de l'Industrie du Gaz en France, 62 rue de Courcelles, 75008 Paris France. **Tel** 011 33 1 47543434, FAX 011 33 1 42274943, telex 642621. **ED** Claude Bureau. **Circ:** 300.

NO
**PERSPEKTIVANALYSEN / OLJEDIREKTORATET.** Norwegian. an. Oljedirektoratet, PO Box 600, 4000 Stavanger Norway. **LC** HD9575.N6; P47.

AT/0729-4069
**PESA JOURNAL.** **Added/Corp** Petroleum Exploration Society of Australia. **VAT** Petroleum Exploration Society of Australia Journal. No. 1 (Aug. 1982)-. Periodical. English. sa. 50.00Aus$. Petroleum Exploration Society of Australia, PO Box 2576, Adelaide SA 5001 Australia. **Tel** 011 61 8 223 4711. **LC** TN878; .A4.
**Ind/Abst** AESIS Q.

JA/0386-2763
**PETOROTEKKU.** [Petorotekku]. **VFOAT** Petrotech. (1978)-. Academic Scholarly Publication. Japanese. mo. $230.00. Noguchi kenkyujo, (Noguchi Inst.), 8-1, Kaga 1 Chome, Itabashiku, Tokyoto 173, Japan. **(Subscription address:** Maruzen Company Ltd., PO Box 5050, Import & Export Department, Tokyo 100 31 Japan.**)** **CODEN** PTRTD3. Documents available from Article Express International, CASDDS. ***Continues in part*** *Sekiyu Gakkai Shi, 0582-4664.*
**Ind/Abst** Bioeng. Abstr.; Chem. Abstr.; Coal Abstr.; Ei Page One; Energy Res. Abstr. (July 1980-); Eng. Index Annu.; Lit. Pat. Abstr., Oilfield Chem. (1991-); Lit. Abstr., Catal. Catal.; Lit. Abstr., Health Environ.; Lit. Abstr., Pet. Refin. Petrochem.; Lit. Abstr., Pet. Substit.; Lit. Abstr., Transp. Storage.

BL/0103-5266
**PETROBRAS NEWS.** (PETROBRAS NEWS / PETROLEO BRASILEIRO, S.A.). [Petrobras news]. **Added/Corp** Petroleo Brasileiro, S.A. Petroleo Brasileiro, S.A. Servico de Relacoes Publicas. **VFOAT** Petrobras. (197?)-. Periodical. English. Twelve times a year. Free. Petroleo Brasileiro SA International, RELTNS Avenue Chile 65, 20035 Rio de Janeiro RJ Brazil. **Tel** 011 55 21 5341299, telex (021)23335. **ED** Angela Lemos. Index available. **Circ:** 6,000 (ctrl).
**Desc:** Newsletter on oil operations in Brazil as well as abroad, exports, petrochemicals, non oil mining, marketing, fertilizers, energy, alternatives.
**Ind/Abst** Energy Inf. Abstr.

US/0031-6342
**PETROCHEMICAL NEWS.** (1963)-. Periodical. English. wk. $597.00. William F. Bland Company, PO Box 16666, Chapel Hill NC 27516. **Tel** (919)490-0700. **ED** Susan Bland Zaro. **[CCC].**
**Desc:** Report of significant current news about the worldwide petrochemical business.

US
**PETROCHEMICAL REPORT.** (19??)-. English. be (Published in March of odd-numbered years). $10.00 each, three for $25.00. Gulf Publishing Company / Texas, PO Box 2608, Houston TX 77252. **Tel** (800)231-6275, (713)529-4301, FAX (713)520-4433.
**Desc:** Contains descriptions and schematics of the most important petrochemical processes.

SI
**PETROCHEMICALS & REFINING.** (Dec. 1990)-. English. mo. $100.00 Asia and Australia; $175.00 Japan. Petrochemicals & Refining, 41 Middle Road #01-00, Singapore 0718 Singapore. **Tel** 3361728, FAX 3367919. **Ad Acc.**
**Desc:** Journal dedicated to the downstream sector of the dynamic and rapidly expanding Pacific Rim market.
**Ind/Abst** Pet. Energy Bus. News Index (1992).

US/0749-2863
**PETROCONSULTANTS INTERNATIONAL OIL LETTER.** [Petroconsultants int. oil lett.]. **VFOAT** International Oil Letter. (1984)-. Periodical. English. wk. $1050.00, $720.00 (multi-copy rate) US and Canada; $1150.00, $820.00 (multi-copy rate) other. Petroconsultants Inc, PO Box 740619, Houston TX 77274. **Tel** (713)995-1764, FAX (713)995-8593, telex 4620521. **ED** Jay Gallagher. **DD** 665.

AT
**PETROFAX.** Newsletter. English. wk. $1380.00Aus$ per year, $415.00Aus$ per quarter. Pex Publications Pty Ltd, PO Box 158, Claremont Western Australia 6010. **Tel** (09)383-3477, FAX (09)385 1485. **ED** Don Lipscombe, 09 383 3477.
**Desc:** Thursday-night faxed exploration scouting service, an easily-scanned but highly informative indicator of upcoming events with a unique graphical status summary of every well in the region.

US/1060-5258
**PETROGRAM (TALLAHASSEE, FLA.).** (PETROGRAM / FLORIDA PETROLEUM MARKETERS ASSOCIATION.). **Added/Corp** Florida Petroleum Marketers Association. (19??)-. Periodical. English. mo (July/Aug issue combined). Free (members) Florida Petroleum Marketers Association; $40.00 (non-members). Florida Petroleum Marketers, 209 Office Plaza, Tallahassee FL 32301. **Tel** (904)877-5178.

FR/0069-6552
**PETROLE. ELEMENTS STATISTIQUES (1968).** (PETROLE.). [Petrole]. (1968)-. French. Comite Professionnel du Petrol CPDP, BP 282, 92505 Rueil Malmaison France. **Tel** 011 33 1 47169460. **LC** HD9572.2; .A22. **DD** 338.2/7/280944. ***Separated from*** *Activite de l'Industrie Petroliere, 0515-3468.*
**Ind/Abst** Energy Res. Abstr. (Feb. 1983-).

FR/0755-7981
**PETROLE ET ENTERPRISE.** (OIL & ENTERPRISE.). [Oil enterpr.]. **VAT** Oil and Enterprise. No. 1 (Aug. 1983)-. Periodical. French. mo. Societe des Editions Technip, 27 rue Ginoux, 75737 Paris Cedex 15 France. **Tel** 011 33 1 45771108, telex 200 375 F EDITECP. **LC** TN860.P364. **DD** 338.2/7282/05.

***Continues in part*** *Industrie du Petrole. Gaz-Chimie.*
**Ind/Abst** Fluid Abstr., Civil Eng.; Fluid Abstr. Proc. Eng.; FLUIDEX (1983-).

FR
**PETROLE ET GAZ EN AFRIQUE.** French. ir. 1190.00F. IC Publications Ediafric, 10 rue Vineuse, 75116 Paris France. **Tel** 011 33 1 44308100.

FR/0150-6463
**PETROLE ET LE GAZ ARABES.** French (English). Twenty-four times a year. $1320.00. Arab Petroleum Research Center, 7 Avenue Ingres, 75016 Paris France. **Tel** 011 33 1 45243310, FAX 011 33 1 45201685, telex 642963. Index available.

FR/0152-5425
**PETROLE ET TECHNIQUES.** [Pet. tech.]. **Added/Corp** Association Francaise des Techniciens du Petrole. No.241 (Feb. 1977)-. Academic Scholarly Publication. French. mo. 585.00F France; 625.00F other. Association Francaise des Techniciens du Petrole, (45 rue Louis Blanc, 92400 Courbevoie), Cedex 72, 92038 Paris la Defense, France. **Tel** 011 47 17 67 32, FAX 011 47 17 67 44. **LC** TN860; .A7. **DD** 665/.5/05. **CODEN** PETEDX. Documents available from Petroleum Abstracts Document Delivery Service, CASDDS. ***Continues*** *Revue de l'Association Francaise des Techniciens du Petrole.*
**Ind/Abst** Chem. Abstr.; Coal Abstr.; Energy Res. Abstr. (March 1979-); GeoRef; Lit. Pat. Abstr., Oilfield Chem. (1954-); Lit. Abstr., Catal. Catal.; Lit. Abstr., Health Environ.; Lit. Abstr., Pet. Refin. Petrochem.; Lit. Abstr., Pet. Substit.; Lit. Abstr., Transp. Storage; Pet. Abstr.

MX
**PETROLEO, EL. Main/Corp** Petroleos Mexicanos. Spanish. Petroleos Mexicanos, Marina Nacional No 329, Edificio 1810-1 Piso, Mexico City Mexico. **LC** TN873.M6; P47A.

US/0093-7851
**PETROLEO INTERNACIONAL.** [Pet. int.]. (19??)-. Academic Scholarly Publication. Spanish. Six times a year. $45.00 US; $120.00 other. Keller Publishing Corporation, 150 Great Neck Road, Great Neck NY 11021. **Tel** (516)829-9210, FAX (516)829-5414, telex 221574 KELLE. **LC** TN860; .P38. **CODEN** PTRIB2. **[CCC].** Documents available from Petroleum Abstracts Document Delivery Service, CASDDS. ***Continues*** *Petroleo y Petroquimica Internacional.*
**Ind/Abst** Chem. Abstr.; GeoRef; Pet. Abstr.

VE/0083-5390
**PETROLEO Y OTROS DATOS ESTADISTICOS.** (PETROLEO Y OTROS DATOS ESTADISTICOS / MINISTERIO DE MINAS E HIDROCARBUROS, DIVISION DE ECONOMIA PETROLERA.). Began with 1958. Spanish. an. Ministerio de Minias, Hidrocarburos, Division de Economia Petrolera, Caracas Venezuela. **LC** HD9574.V4; A32.

VE
**PETROLEUM.** Spanish. mo. $180.00 North America; $140.00 Latin America (except Venezuela); $280.00 other. Petroleum Editores SA, Apartado 379, Maracaibo 4001A Venezuela. **Tel** 011 58 61 529435, FAX 011 58 61 522302, telex 64336. **Bk Rev. Ad Acc, Adv Mgr:** Aristides Villalobos. **Circ:** 5,000 (ctrl).
**Desc:** Specializing in petroleum and gas. Themes include exploration, perforation, exploitation, transport, refining and marketing of hydrocarbons; covers the field of energy in its entirety.

US/0031-6423
**PETROLEUM ABSTRACTS (TULSA, OKLA.). See** Petroleum and Natural Gas-Abstracting, Bibliographies and Statistics.

US
**PETROLEUM ACCOUNTING AND FINANCIAL MANAGEMENT JOURNAL.** **Added/Corp** North Texas State University. Institute of Petroleum Accounting. North Texas State University. College of Business Administration. Professional Development Institute. Vol. 8, No. 1 (Spring 1989)-. Periodical. English. Three times a year. $130.00 US; $160.00 other. Institute of Petroleum Accounting, PO Box 13677, University of North Texas, Denton TX 76203. **Tel** (817)565-3170, FAX (817)565-2599. **ED** Charles Boynton IV. **LC** HF5686.P3; J67. Index available. **Pr Rev.** ***Continues*** *Journal of Petroleum Accounting, 0890-8141.*
**Ind/Abst** Account. Tax Datab. (1982-).

US/0360-974X
**PETROLEUM ACTIVITY REPORT.** **Main/Corp** Louisiana. Office of Conservation. Engineering Division. Periodical. English. mo. Louisiana Office of Conservation, Engineering Division, Baton Rouge LA. **LC** TN872.L8; L68A. **DD** 353.9/763/008232. ***Continues*** *Petroleum Activity Report, 0360-974X.*

IO
**PETROLEUM & NATURAL GAS INDUSTRY OF INDONESIA.** English. Direktorat Jenderal Minyak Dangas Bumi, Merdeka Selatan 18, Jakarta Indonesia. **LC** HD9576.I5; P47. **DD** 338.2/7/2809598.

UK
**PETROLEUM ARGUS FUNDAMENTALS MONTHLY.** (19??)-. English. mo (12 issues). $995.00. Petroleum Argus Ltd, 93 Shepperton Road, London N1 3DF England. **Tel** 011 44 71 359 8792.

II/0970-3098
**PETROLEUM ASIA JOURNAL.** [Pet. Asia j.]. **VFOAT** Petroleum Asia. Vol. 1 (Dec. 1978)-. Periodical. English. Four times a year (Jan., Apr., July, Oct.). $230.00. Academic & Law Serials, F-22 B/3 Laxmi Nagar, Delhi 110092 India. **Tel** 11 91 11 2413394, 011 91 11 2420827, FAX 11 91 11 2223543. **(Subscription address:** Prints India, 11 Darya Ganj, New Delhi 110002 India.**) LC** TP690.2.A78; P47. **DD** 622/.338/095.
**Ind/Abst** Life Sci. Collect.

US/0899-6369
**PETROLEUM/C-STORE PRODUCTS.** ***Title Change.*** [Pet./c-store prod.]. **VFOAT** Petroleum, C-Store Products; Petroleum Equipment. (19??)-(1993). Periodical. English. mo. Hunter Publishing Company Inc., 25 Northwest Point Boulevard, Suite 800, Elk Grove Village IL 60007-1036. **Tel** (708)427-9512, FAX (708)427-2097. **DD** 338. ***Continues*** *Petroleum Equipment, 0195-3125.* ***Continued by*** *Station & Store Products, 1071-8419.*

UK/0965-5441
**PETROLEUM CHEMISTRY. VFOAT** Neftekhimiya. Vol. 31, No. 1 (1991)-. Periodical. English (translations available in Russian). Six times a year. $1483.00 The Americas; £995.00 other. Pergamon Press, An Imprint of Elsevier Science Ltd., The Boulevard, Langford Lane, Kidlington, Oxford OX5 1GB United Kingdom. **Tel** 011 44 865 843000, 011 44 865 843699, FAX 011 44 865 843010. **(Subscription address:** Elsevier Science Ltd. Oxford Fulfillment Centre, PO Box 800, Kidlington, Oxford OX5 1DX United Kingdom.**) ED** Kh.M. Minachev. **LC** TP690.A1; P34. **CODEN** PHEME4. Documents available from Article Express International, The Genuine Article. ***Continues*** *Petroleum Chemistry: U.S.S.R., 0031-6458.*
**Desc:** Cover-to-cover translation of the Russian journal Meftekhimiya, dealing mainly with the chemistry of petroleum and its use as a base for the manufacture of industrial products.
**Ind/Abst** Curr. Contents Eng. Tech. Appl. Sci.; Ei Page One; Eng. Index Annu.; Res. Alert [Full Cov.]; Sci. Cit. Index; SCISEARCH.

UK/0306-395X
**PETROLEUM ECONOMIST (ENGLISH EDITION).** (THE PETROLEUM ECONOMIST.). [Pet. econ.]. Vol. 41, No. 1 (Jan. 1974)-. Periodical. English (Japanese). Twelve times a year. £195.00 UK; $385.00 (surface mail), $425.00 (airmail). Petroleum Economist Ltd., Perrymount Road, Haywards Heath, West Sussex RH16 3DH England. **Tel** 011 44 444 440421. **ED** Bryan Cooper. **LC** HD9560.1; .P63. **DD** 338.2/7/2805. **CODEN** PEECDK. Index available. **Bk Rev. Ad Acc. Circ:** 6,000. available on microfilm and microfiche from University Microfilms International (UMI). Documents available from UMI Article Clearinghouse. ***Continues*** *Petroleum Press Service;* ***Absorbed*** *Petroleum Management.*
**Desc:** Worldwide coverage of the economic and financial implications of energy development, particularly oil, but including coal, gas and nuclear.
**Ind/Abst** ABI/INFORM Glob. Ed.; ABI Inform Ondisc (Feb. 1975-Dec. 1978); Acad. Search (Jan. 1993-); AESIS Q.; Bus. Index (1985-); Bus. Period. Index; Coal Abstr.; F&S Index Plus Text, Int. [Select. Cov.]; Gas Abstr.; Gen. BusinessFile (1985-); Gen. Period. Index (1985-); Index Period. Artic. Relat. Law (1981-); INFO-SOUTH Abstr.; Mag. Search; PAIS Int. Print (1991-); Pet. Energy Bus. News Index (1975); PROMT; Trade Ind. ASAP [Full Txt.]; Trade Ind. Index (1981-) [Full Txt.]; Vocat. Search (Jan. 1993-); Wilson Bus. Abstr.

US/0098-7743
**PETROLEUM/ENERGY BUSINESS NEWS INDEX. See** Petroleum and Natural Gas-Abstracting, Bibliographies and Statistics.

US/0164-8322
**PETROLEUM ENGINEER INTERNATIONAL.** [Pet. eng. int.]. (June 1967)-. Periodical. English. mo (except semimonthly in July). $59.00 US & Canada; $97.00 other. Hart Publications Inc, 1900 Grant Street, Suite 400, Denver CO 80203. **Tel** (303)837-1917, (800)832-1917, FAX (303)837-8585. **ED** Seven D. Moore. **LC** TN860; .P43. **DD** 622/.3382/05. **CODEN** PENGA6. **[CCC].** Index available. **Bk Rev. Ad Acc. Circ:** 37,000 (ctrl). available on microfilm and microfiche from University Microfilms International (UMI). Documents available from Article Express International, UMI Article Clearinghouse, Petroleum Abstracts Document Delivery Service, Documents on Demand. ***Continues*** *Petroleum Engineer.*
**Desc:** Helps petroleum industry engineers and related technical people to build profits in oil and gas drilling and producing on land or offshore worldwide; emphasizes technical, methods, operating and engineering advances.
**Ind/Abst** ABI/INFORM Glob. Ed.; ABI Inform Ondisc (March 1975-Nov. 1976);; Appl. Sci. Technol. Index; Bioeng. Abstr.; Ei Page One; EMBASE; Energy Inf. Abstr.; Energy Res. Abstr. (Dec. 1979-); Eng. Index Annu. [Select. Cov.]; Environ. Abstr.; Gas Abstr.; GeoRef; Health Saf. Sci. Abstr.; Ocean. Abstr.; Life Sci. Collect.; Pet. Abstr.; Ref. Sources; Ship Abstr.; Stat. Ref. Index.

US
**PETROLEUM EXPLORATION, DEVELOPMENT, AND PRODUCTION IN INDIANA DURING ... . Added/Corp** Indiana. Geological Survey. (1989)-. English. Indiana Geological Survey, 611 North Walnut Grove, Bloomington IN 47405. **Tel** (812)885-9350. **LC** TN24; .I39. ***Continues*** *Oil Development and Production in Indiana during ... .*

NZ/0113-0501
**PETROLEUM EXPLORATION IN NEW ZEALAND NEWS.** [Pet. explor. N.Z. news]. **VFOAT** News. (1982)-. Periodical. English. Four times a year. 80.00NZ$ (institutions), 45.00NZ$ (individuals). Crown Minerals Operations Group, Publicity Department, Ministry of Commerce, 33 Bown Street, PO Box 1473, Wellington, New Zealand. **Tel** 011 64 4 4720030, FAX 011 64 4 4990968. **DD** 622.1828099305. **Ad Acc, Adv Mgr:** R. Gregg, **Tel** (04)4720 030. **Circ:** 750 (ctrl).
**Desc:** Publishes information on petroleum exploration, natural gas, and related topics.

US/0277-6650
**PETROLEUM EXPLORATION MAP.** [Pet. explor. map]. **Added/Corp** Indiana. Geological Survey. (19??)-. English. an. $122.00. Indiana Geological Survey, 611 North Walnut Grove, Bloomington IN 47405. **Tel** (812)885-9350.
**Ind/Abst** GeoRef.

US/0743-5274
**PETROLEUM FEEDSTOCKS IN ... . VFOAT** Feedstocks. English. an. Poten & Partners Inc., 885 3rd Avenue, New York NY 10022. **Tel** (212)230-2000, FAX (212)355-0295, telex 177118/420811. **ED** Carol Cole and George Gale. **LC** HD9579.C3; P47. **DD** 338.4/7661804/05. ctrl circ.

US/1077-5285
**PETROLEUM FINANCE WEEK.** (19??)-. English. wk (50 issues). $697.00 US; $797.00 other. Hart Publications Inc, 1900 Grant Street, Suite 400, Denver CO 80203. **Tel** (303)837-1917, (800)832-1917, FAX (303)837-8585. ***Continues*** *PetroMoney.*

US/0740-1817
**PETROLEUM FRONTIERS.** [Petrol. front.]. **Added/Corp** Petroleum Information Corporation. Vol. 1, No. 1 (1983)-. Periodical. English. qt. $200.00, $55.00 (single issues). Petroleum Information Corporation, 5333 Westheimer, Suite 100, Houston TX 77056. **Tel** (713)840-8282 ext. 38, FAX (713)599-5100. **LC** TN872; .A328. **DD** 553.2/8/0973. Documents available from Petroleum Abstracts Document Delivery Service.
**Desc:** Examines selected hydrocarbon provinces or horizons in the initial phases of discovery and development.
**Ind/Abst** Ei Page One; Geol. Abstr.; GeoRef; Pet. Abstr.

AT/0048-3591
**PETROLEUM GAZETTE (MELBOURNE).** (PETROLEUM GAZETTE.). [Pet. gaz.]. **Added/Corp** Australian Institute of Petroleum. Petroleum Information Bureau (Australia). (1952)-. Periodical. English. Four times a year. Free. Australian Institute of Petroleum Ltd, 257 Collins Street / 11th Floor, Melbourne Victoria 3000 Australia. **Tel** 011 61 3 6541411, FAX 011 61 3 6541950. **ED** Rick Wilkinson. **LC** TN860; .P49. **Circ:** 23,000 (ctrl).
**Desc:** Articles on aspects of the upstream and downstream petroleum industry written for schools and general public consumption/readership.
**Ind/Abst** AESIS Q.; Coal Abstr.; GeoRef.

US/0553-8882
**PETROLEUM GEOLOGY. VFOAT** Geologiia Nefti i Gaza. Vol. 2 (1958)-. Periodical. English. bm. $65.00 US; $73.00 other. Petroleum Geology, Box 171, McLean VA 22101. **Tel** (703)648-6503, (703)759-4487, FAX (703)759-3754. **ED** James Clarke. **LC** TN860; .G4135. **DD** 553.280947. Documents available from Petroleum Abstracts Document Delivery Service.
**Desc:** Digest of soviet geological literature on oil and gas.
**Ind/Abst** AESIS Q.; Pet. Abstr.

●UK/1354-0793
**PETROLEUM GEOSCIENCE.** (1995)-. English. Four times a year. £95.00 UK; $171.00 US; £114.00 other. Geological Society Publishing House, Unit 7 Brassmill Enterprise Centre, Brassmill Lane, Bath BA1 3JN England. **Tel** 011 44 225 445046, FAX 011 44 225 442836. Index available.

US/0747-2528
**PETROLEUM INDEPENDENT.** [Pet. indep.]. **Added/Corp** Independent Petroleum Association of America. Vol. 41, No. 11 (Mar./Apr. 1971)-. Periodical. English. bm (6 issues). $100.00. Independent Petroleum Association of America, 1101 16th Street NW, Washington DC 20036. **Tel** (201)857-4775. **ED** Bruce Wells. **LC** HD9561; .P38. **DD** 338.2/7282/0973. **Ad Acc, Adv Mgr:** Rick Carbo, **Tel** (202)857-4775. **Circ:** 8,000. available on an online database (file 648/Full-Text) from

DIALOG. ***Continues*** *Independent Petroleum Monthly.*
**Desc:** Covers the domestic petroleum industry and US independent producers. Emphasis is placed on political developments in taxes and safety, that bear on the industry.
**Ind/Abst** Gas Abstr.; Trade Ind. ASAP [Full Txt.]; Trade Ind. Index [Full Txt.].

US/1064-1807
**PETROLEUM INDUSTRY PROFILES.**
[Pet. ind. profiles]. (1988)-. Periodical. English. an. $795.00. Kirkpatrick Energy Association, Inc, 1725 TWR/ 600 17th Street, Denver CO 80202. **Tel** (303)893-6633, FAX (303)534-5850. **ED** C W MacLeod. **DD** 338.

US/0730-7632
**PETROLEUM INFORMATION INTERNATIONAL.** ***Ceased.*** **VFOAT** PII. Vol. 1, No. 1 (Oct. 5, 1981)-(August 1985). Periodical. English. wk. Petroleum Information Corporation, 5333 Westheimer, Suite 100, Houston TX 77056. **Tel** (713)840-8282 ext. 38, FAX (713)599-5100. **ED** James C Tanner. **Bk Rev.**
**Desc:** Covers daily briefings on world oil and gas exploration.

PP/1021-3600
**PETROLEUM INFORMATION SERVICE.**
**VFOAT** Petroleum Information Report; IMPS Petroleum Information Report. (1988)-. Periodical. English. mo. $750.00. IMPS Research, PO Box 986 Port Moresby, Papua New Guinea. **Tel** 011 675 213283, FAX 011 675 217360. **ED** J. Kassam. **UDC** 553.98. ctrl circ.
**Desc:** Contains factual, public domain information only. Researched by monitoring press and stock exchange releases, and other public sources, but mostly by direct telephone or face-to-face interviews with the key personnel of the relevant organizations.

US/0899-7543
**PETROLEUM INFORMATION'S NATIONAL EXPLORATION DAILY.** [Pet. Inf. natl. explor. dly.]. **Added/Corp** Petroleum Information Corporation. **VFOAT** National Exploration Daily; Exploration Daily. (19??)-. Periodical. English. da. $50.00 (monthly). Petroleum Information Corporation, 5333 Westheimer, Suite 100, Houston TX 77056. **Tel** (713)840-8282 ext. 38, FAX (713)599-5100. **DD** 622.
**Desc:** Reports the most significant exploration stories every business day. News on wildcats, new discoveries, land plays - who is doing what, where, and when.

US/0744-8007
**PETROLEUM INFORMATION'S NATIONAL WILDCAT MONTHLY.**
(NATIONAL WILDCAT MONTHLY : AN ANALYSIS OF NEW FIELD EXPLORATION IN THE U.S.). **Added/Corp** Petroleum Information Corporation. **VFOAT** Petroleum Information's National Wildcat Monthly. (198?)-. Periodical. English. mo. $40.00 (monthly). Petroleum Information Corporation, 5333 Westheimer, Suite 100, Houston TX 77056. **Tel** (713)840-8282 ext. 38, FAX (713)599-5100. **ED** William H. Cobban. **Circ:** 50 (ctrl).
**Desc:** Lists all completed new field discovery wells with the month's most significant discoveries and new locations discussed in detail.

US/0480-2160
**PETROLEUM INTELLIGENCE WEEKLY.**
(1961)-. English. Fifty-one times per year. $1475.00 mail; $2950.00 fax. Petroleum Intelligence Weekly, 575 Broadway, 4th Floor, New York NY 10012-3230. **Tel** (212)941-5500, FAX (212)941-5509, telex 62371 PETROIN. **ED** Sarah Miller. **LC** HD9560.1; .P62. **DD** 338.2/7/28205. **[CCC].** available via fax; available on diskette; available via electronic mail.
**Desc:** Features a weekly analysis of major developments, issues and market news of oil and natural gas.
**Ind/Abst** Pet. Energy Bus. News Index (1975).

US/0884-4550
**PETROLEUM MANAGEMENT (HOUSTON, TEX.).** ***Title Change.*** (PETROLEUM MANAGEMENT.). [Pet. manage.]. **VFOAT** Petroleum Management, International Business Report. Vol. 7, No. 7 (July 1985)-(19??). Periodical. English. Twelve times a year. Management Publishing Services Inc, 7887 San Felipe, Suite 100, Houston TX 77063. **Tel** (713)789-7887, FAX (713)789-0742. **ED** Thelma Marlowe. **LC** HD9560.1; .P636. **DD** 622/.338/068. **[CCC]. Bk Rev. Ad Acc. Circ:** 25,000 (ctrl). Documents available from Ask*IEEE, Petroleum Abstracts Document Delivery Service. ***Continues*** *OGD Publishing Co.'s Oil & Gas Digest, 0744-9399.* ***Merged into*** *Petroleum Economists.*
**Desc:** International oil and gas industry business magazine published specifically for upper management personnel.
**Ind/Abst** GeoRef; INSPEC (Oct. 1989-); Pet. Abstr.; Pet. Energy Bus. News Index (1991).

US
**PETROLEUM MARKET DATA.** **VFOAT** Market Data. (19??)-. Periodical. English. Fifty-two times a year. $192.00. Petroleum Market Data, 962 University Avenue, St Paul MN 55014. **Tel** (612)645-2913.

US/1047-630X
**PETROLEUM MARKET INTELLIGENCE.**
(PETROLEUM MARKET INTELLIGENCE : PIW'S MONTHLY MARKET REPORT.). [Pet. mark. intell.]. Vol. 1, No. 1 (Feb. 1987)-. Periodical. English. mo. $695.00 mail; $1390.00 fax; $475.00 on-line. Petroleum Intelligence Weekly, 575 Broadway, 4th Floor, New York NY 10012-3230. **Tel** (212)941-5500, FAX (212)941-5509, telex 62371 PETROIN. **ED** Sarah Miller. **LC** HD9560.1; .P637. **DD** 338.2/7282/05. available via fax; available on an online database (updated monthly).
**Desc:** Provides analysis of regional pricing and production figures and key statistics on the oil market. Included are overviews of regional markets, crude output, spot prices and netbacks.
**Ind/Abst** Pet. Energy Bus. News Index (1987).

US/0362-7799
**PETROLEUM MARKETER (NEW HAVEN).** (PETROLEUM MARKETER.). 1933. Periodical. English. bm. $18.00 (one year), $30.00 (two year), $40.00 (three year) US; $24.00 (one year), $40.00 (two year), $60.00 (three year) surface mail, $54.00 (one year), $100.00 (two year), $150.00 (three year) airmail other. McKeand Publications Inc, 636 First Avenue, PO Box 507, West Haven CT 06516. **Tel** (203)934-5288, telex 963453. **ED** Keith B Tuerk. **LC** HD9561; .P36. **DD** 338.2/7/2820973. **Ad Acc. Circ:** 14,900 (ctrl). available on microfilm and microfiche from University Microfilms International (UMI). ***Continues*** *Petroleum & TBA Marketer.*

US/0747-5721
**PETROLEUM MARKETERS' HANDBOOK.** ***Title Change.*** (PETROLEUM MARKETERS' HANDBOOK / COMPILED BY THE EDITORS OF OIL BUYERS' GUIDE.). [Petrol. mark. handb.]. (19??)-(19??). Consumer Publication. English. wk (52 issues). Bloomberg Financial Markets, 100 Business Park Drive, Princeton NJ 08542. **Tel** (609)279-4261. **LC** HD9563; .P47. **DD** 338.7/6223382/02573. ***Continued by*** *Bloomberg Energy Handbook.*

US
**PETROLEUM MARKETING ANNUAL / ENERGY INFORMATION ADMINISTRATION, OFFICE OF OIL AND GAS, U.S. DEPARTMENT OF ENERGY.**
**Added/Corp** United States. Energy Information Administration. Office of Oil and Gas. (19??)-. English. an (July). National Energy Information Center, Energy Information Administration, Forrestal Building, Room 1F-048, Washington DC 20585. **Tel** (202)586-8800. **LC** HD9561; .P424. **DD** 338.4/36655/0973021. ***Continued in part by*** *Fuel Oil and Kerosene Sales.*
**Desc:** Petroleum product marketing data is reported by state and Petroleum Administration for Defense (PAD) District. National level statistics on crude oil and petroleum products are also given.
**Ind/Abst** Energy Inf. Abstr.; Predicasts Forecasts.

US/0741-9643
**PETROLEUM MARKETING MONTHLY.**
**See** Business-Marketing.

NO
**PETROLEUM MONITOR FAX SERVICE.**
English. da. Kr9500.00. Hart Europe, Ltd., Rosemount House, Rosemount Avenue, W Byfleet Surrey K614 6NP England. **Tel** 011 44 932 344424.

SI/0253-0775
**PETROLEUM NEWS.** ***Ceased.*** [Pet. news]. (Dec. 1978)-(19??). Periodical. English. Twelve times a year. Petroleum News Publishing Pte Ltd, 43 Middle Road/04 00, 0718 Singapore. **Tel** 011 33 88524. **ED** Matthew Siva. **LC** HD9576.S65; P47. **DD** 338.2/7282/0959. ***Continues*** *Petroleum News, Southeast Asia.*
**Ind/Abst** AESIS Q.; GeoRef.

AT/0312-9837
**PETROLEUM NEWSLETTER, THE.** [Pet. newsl.]. **Added/Corp** Australia. Bureau of Mineral Resources, Geology and Geophysics. (1962)-. Periodical. English. Twice a year (Jan. & July). Free. Australian Geological Survey, PO Box 378, Queen Victoria Terrace, Parkes Australian Capital Territories, 2601 Australia. **Tel** 011 61 6 2499519, 011 61 6 2499642, FAX 011 61 6 2499982. **LC** TN878.A1; P47. **DD** 338.2/7/280994. **CODEN** PNGGD3. **Circ:** 1,000.
**Desc:** Covers petroleum exploration and development in Australia; includes seismic surveys, rigs, well names and status, wells and meters drilled.
**Ind/Abst** AESIS Q.; GeoRef.

US/0031-6490
**PETROLEUM OUTLOOK.** [Pet. outlook]. **Added/Corp** John S. Herold, Inc. Vol. 1 (1948)-. Periodical. English. mo (12 issues). $520.00. John S. Herold, Inc., 5 Edgewood Avenue, Greenwich CT 06830. **Tel** (203)869-2585, FAX (203)869-4729. **LC** HG6047.P47; P48. **DD** 338.7/622338/05. **[CCC].** ***Absorbed*** *Herold's Oil Share Market Performance.*
**Ind/Abst** Energy Res. Abstr. (Dec. 1980-); Pet. Energy Bus. News Index (1983).

US/1050-866X
**PETROLEUM POLITICS.** [Pet. polit.]. Vol. 1, No. 1 (Jan. 1990)-. Periodical. English. qt (Jan., Apr., July, Oct.). $100.00 North America; $125.00 other. Energy Securirty Analysis Inc, 1300 L Street Northwest, Suite 1200, Washington DC 20005. **Tel** (202)682-9101, FAX (202)682-1810. **LC** HD9560.1; .P639. **DD** 338.2/7282/05.

CN/0821-8544
**PETROLEUM PROCESSING IN CANADA.** [Pet process. Can.]. **Added/Corp** Canada. Petroleum Sector. Canada. Energy, Mines and Resources Canada. (Dec. 1981)-. English. an. **LC** TN867; .P39. **DD** 338.4/56655/30971021. ***Continues*** *Petroleum Refineries in Canada, 0079-1296.*

US
**PETROLEUM REFINING AND PETROCHEMICALS.** ***Title Change.*** **Added/Corp** American Petroleum Institute. Central Abstracting and Indexing Service. **VFOAT** Petroleum Refining and Petrochemicals Literature. Vol. 25 (Jan. 9, 1978)-(1992). Abstracting/Indexing Service. English. wk. American Petroleum Institute, 275 Seventh Avenue, New York NY 10001. **Tel** (212)366-4040, FAX (212)366-4298. ***Continues*** *Petroleum Refining and Petrochemicals Literature.* ***Continued by*** *Literature Abstracts. Petroleum Refining & Petrochemicals, 1065-0512.*

UK/0020-3076
**PETROLEUM REVIEW (LONDON. 1978).**
(PETROLEUM REVIEW.). [Pet. rev.]. **Added/Corp** Institute of Petroleum (Great Britain). Vol. 22 No. 253 (Jan 1968)-. Academic Scholarly Publication. English. Twelve times a year. £65.00 UK, £80.00 other (surface mail); £135.00 (airmail). Institute of Petroleum, 61 New Cavendish Street, London W1M 8AR England. **Tel** 011 44 71 636 1004, FAX 011 44 71 255 1472. **ED** Geoffrey Mayhen. **LC** TP690.A1; I553. **DD** 665/.5/05. **CODEN** PETRB2. Index available. **Bk Rev. Ad Acc. Circ:** 9,100. available on microfilm and microfiche from University Microfilms International (UMI). Documents available from Article Express International, Petroleum Abstracts Document Delivery Service, CASDDS. ***Continues*** *Review (Institute of Petroleum (Great Britain)), 0367-9810.*
**Desc:** Magazine of the Institute of Petroleum containing news, features and other technical articles about oil, gas and petrochemicals, internationally.
**Ind/Abst** AESIS Q.; Aquat. Sci. Fish. Abstr. (Computer File); Bioeng. Abstr.; BMT Abstr.; Chem. Abstr.; Coal Abstr.; Curr. Technol. Index; Ecol. Abstr. (?-?); Ei Page One; EMBASE; Energy Res. Abstr. (July 1974-); Eng. Index Annu. [Select. Cov.]; Fluid Abstr., Civil Eng.; Fluid Abstr. Proc. Eng.; FLUIDEX (1973-); GeoRef; Highw. Res. Abstr.; Lit. Pat. Abstr., Oilfield Chem. (1954-); Lit. Abstr., Catal. Catal.; Lit. Abstr., Health Environ.; Lit. Abstr., Pet. Refin. Petrochem.; Lit. Abstr., Pet. Substit.; Lit. Abstr., Transp. Storage; Pet. Abstr.

UK
**PETROLEUM SERVICES ANNUAL PETROLEUM REVIEW.** ***Ceased.*** (1986)-(19??). English. Arthur Andersen & Company Petroleum Services Group, 1 Surrey Street, London WC2R 2PS England. **Tel** 011 44 71 4383000.

UK
**PETROLEUM SERVICES WEEKLY SCOUTING SERVICE - OFF SHORE.**
English. wk. £1530.00 UK; £1570.00 Europe; £1679.00 other. James Capel and Company, Petroleum Services Department, Wardley House, 7 Devonshire Square, London EC2M 4HN England. **Tel** 011 44 71 626 0866. **ED** Simon Roper and Tim Shinaler. **Pr Rev.**
**Desc:** Provides latest information on drilling activity, rig movements and license changes in the offshore regions of the North Sea.

UK
**PETROLEUM SERVICES WEEKLY SERVICE.** English. wk. £1400.00 Europe; £1100.00 Offshore. James Capel and Company, Petroleum Services Department, Wardley House, 7 Devonshire Square, London EC2M 4HN England. **Tel** 011 44 71 626 0866. ctrl circ.
**Desc:** Weekly scouting services for Northwest Europe.

UK
**PETROLEUM SERVICES WEEKLY SERVICE ONSHORE REPORT.** James Capel and Company, Petroleum Services Department, Wardley House, 7 Devonshire Square, London EC2M 4HN England. **Tel** 011 44 71 626 0866.

US
**PETROLEUM SOFTWARE DIRECTORY.**
**VFOAT** Software. 2nd Ed. (1986)-. Directory. English. an. $189.50 US and Canada; $240.00 other. PennWell Publishing Company, 1421 South Sheridan, PO Box 1260, Tulsa OK 74101. **Tel** (918)835-3161, (800)331-4463, FAX (918)831-9497. **(Subscription address:** PennWell Books, PO Box 21288, Tulsa OK 74121.) **ED** Carol Schaefer. **LC** TN860; .P54. **DD** 665.5/028/55369. Each issue contains an index to its own contents (no volume index)--loose. **Ad Acc. Circ:** 1,500. ***Continues*** *Petroleum Software Worldwide Directory,*

0743-6750.
**Desc:** Lists worldwide computer problems related to the petroleum industry under name of owner and/or distributor. Indices provided by company name and program application.

US
**PETROLEUM SOFTWARE SOURCEBOOK FOR PERSONAL COMPUTERS.** 2nd Ed. (1988)-. English. $45.00. Stalsby Wilson Associates, PO Box 19976, Houston TX 77224. **Tel** (713)496-1734, FAX (713)531-7229, telex 401428 SWPRESS. **LC** TN860; .S668. **DD** 665.5/0285/5369. ***Continues*** *Stalsby/Wilson's Petroleum Software Sourcebook for personal computers, 0894-6515.*

US
**PETROLEUM SUBSTITUTES.** ***Title Change.*** **See** Petroleum and Natural Gas-Abstracting, Bibliographies and Statistics.

US
**PETROLEUM SUPPLY ANNUAL / ENERGY INFORMATION ADMINISTRATION, OFFICE OF OIL AND GAS, U.S. DEPARTMENT OF ENERGY.** **Added/Corp** United States. Energy Information Administration. Office of Oil and Gas. (1981)-. English. an. $40.00. National Energy Information Center, Energy Information Administration, Forrestal Building, Room 1F-048, Washington DC 20585. **Tel** (202)586-8800. **LC** HD9561; .P428. **DD** 338.4/76655/0973. ***Formed by the union of*** *Crude Petroleum, Petroleum Products, and Natural Gas Liquids, 0162-623X; Petroleum Refineries in the United States and U.S. Territories, 0197-3711; Sales of Liquefied Petroleum Gases and Ethane in ..., 0162-900X* ***and*** *Deliveries of Fuel Oil and Kerosene in ..., 0744-0510.*
**Desc:** Volume 1 contains annual supply, disposition and stock data beginning in 1973. Volume 2 contains supply and disposition data for each month of the current year.
**Ind/Abst** Energy Inf. Abstr.; Predicasts Forecasts.

US/0733-0553
**PETROLEUM SUPPLY MONTHLY.** (PETROLEUM SUPPLY MONTHLY / ENERGY INFORMATION ADMINISTRATION, OFFICE OF OIL AND GAS, U.S. DEPT. OF ENERGY.). [Pet. supply mon.]. **Added/Corp** United States. Energy Information Administration. Office of Oil and Gas. United States. Energy Information Administration. **VFOAT** PSM; Energy Information Administration/Petroleum Supply Monthly. (March 1982)-. Academic Scholarly Publication. English. mo. $80.00 domestic; $100.00 other. National Energy Information Center, Energy Information Administration, Forrestal Building, Room 1F-048, Washington DC 20585. **Tel** (202)586-8800. **LC** HD9561; .P43. **DD** 338.2/7282/0973. **CODEN** PSMODO. Documents available from CASDDS. ***Formed by the union of*** *Monthly Petroleum Statement, 0731-0188; Availability of Heavy Fuel Oils by Sulfur Level* ***and*** *Monthly Petroleum Statistics Report, 0364-0205.*
**Desc:** Consist chiefly of tables and statistics. Provides articles to help the reader understand and interpret the petroleum statistics.
**Ind/Abst** Chem. Abstr. (1982-1984); Energy Inf. Abstr.

US/0733-6241
**PETROLEUM TAXATION, PETROLEUM LEGISLATION REPORT.** [Pet. tax. pet. legis. rep.]. **VFOAT** World Petroleum Taxation and Legislation Report; World Petroleum Taxation & Legislation Report. No. 1- (1972)-. Periodical. English. bm. $1500.00. Barrows Company Inc., 116 East 66th Street, New York NY 10021. **Tel** (212)772-1199, (800)227-7697, FAX (212)288-7242, telex 4971238 BARROWS. ***Formed by the union of*** *Petroleum Taxation Report* ***and*** *Petroleum Legislation Report.*
**Desc:** Letter on oil and law changes.

US/0897-2001
**PETROLEUM TERMINAL ENCYCLOPEDIA.** [Pet. termin. encycl.]. **VFOAT** Stalsby/Wilson's Petroleum Terminal Encyclopedia. (1988)-. Periodical. English. an. $125.00. Stalsby Wilson Associates, PO Box 19976, Houston TX 77224. **Tel** (713)496-1734, FAX (713)531-7229, telex 401428 SWPRESS. **ED** Kathleen A Sauve, Theresa Williamson and Maria Horn. **LC** HE199.5.P4; S73. **DD** 338.7/665542/025. Index available. cum. index. **Ad Acc. Circ:** 750. ***Continues*** *Stalsby's Petroleum Terminal Encyclopedia, 0882-1747.*
**Desc:** Complete registry of oil company terminals, and independent terminal operators in the United States, Canada and major ports throughout the world.

UK
**PETROLEUM TIMES, A BUSINESS REVIEW.** **VFOAT** Petroleum Times Business Review; Business Review. Vol. 1 (July 1988)-. Periodical. English. bw. £154.00. Nexus Business Communications, Warwick House, Azalea Drive, c/o Dr. Swanle, Kent BR8 8HY England. **Tel** 011 44 322 660070. **LC** TN860; .I62. **DD** 333.8/23/05. ***Continues*** *Petroleum Times (London, England : 1981), 0263-3590.*
**Ind/Abst** Lit. Pat. Abstr., Oilfield Chem. (1988-); Lit. Abstr., Catal. Catal.; Lit. Abstr., Health Environ.; Lit. Abstr., Pet. Refin. Petrochem.; Lit. Abstr., Pet. Substit.; Lit. Abstr., Transp. Storage.

US/0031-6555
**PETROLEUM TODAY.** [Pet. today]. V. 1- Autumn 1959-. Periodical. English. qt. American Petroleum Institute, 275 Seventh Avenue, New York NY 10001. **Tel** (212)366-4040, FAX (212)366-4298. **(Subscription address:** 1970 Chain Bridge Road, McLean, VA 22109-6000) **LC** TN860; .A552. **DD** 338.2/7282/0973. **CODEN** PTTDAU. available on microfilm from University Microfilms International (UMI). ***Continues*** *American Petroleum Institute. Quarterly.*
**Ind/Abst** Coal Abstr.; GeoRef.

IT/0391-9919
**PETROLIERE INTERNATIONAL (MILANO).** (PETROLIERI INTERNATIONAL.). [Pet. int.]. **VFOAT** Petrolieri d'Italia. (19??)-. Academic Scholarly Publication. Multiple languages (English and Italian). Twelve times a year. L60000. Interpetrol, Via Andrea Doria 3, Milan 20124 Italy. **Tel** 011 39 2 6691600. **LC** TN860; .P625. **CODEN** PTITDQ. Documents available from CASDDS.
**Ind/Abst** Chem. Abstr.

SI/0129-1122
**PETROMIN (SINGAPORE).** (PETROMIN.). [Petromin]. (Jan. 1983)-. Periodical. English. mo. 67.00Sing$ Singapore; 98.00Mal$ Malaysia; $63.00 (airmail) Asia/Pacific and Europe; $74.00 other. AP Energy Business Publications PTE LTD, 24 Peck Seah Street 03 00 Nehsons, Singapore 0207 Singapore. **Tel** 011 65 2223422, FAX 011 65 2225587. **LC** HD9576.S652; P47. **DD** 338.2/7282/095. ***Continues*** *Petromin Asia, 0129-5462.*
**Ind/Abst** AESIS Q.; Fluid Abstr., Civil Eng.; Fluid Abstr. Proc. Eng.; FLUIDEX (1983-).

FR/0298-9507
**PETROSTRATEGIES (FRENCH EDITION).** (PETROSTRATEGIES.). French. wk (except Aug.). 1,250.00F other. Petrostrategies, 4 rue Boulitte, 75014 Paris France. **Tel** 011 33 1 40446667, FAX 40446672.
**Desc:** Exclusive information and analysis on world oil and gas.

●US/1073-6425
**PETROSYSTEMS WORLD.** **See** Computers-Hardware.

AT/0310-4184
**PEX.** [Pex]. **VFOAT** Australia's Petroleum Exploration Newsletter. (1972)-. Periodical. English. mo (except Christmas). $200.00 per year. Pex Publications Pty Ltd, PO Box 158, Claremont Western Australia 6010. **Tel** (09)383-3477, FAX (09)385 1485. **ED** Don Lipscombe, 09 383 3477. **DD** 553.280994.
**Desc:** Australia's petroleum exploration newsletter since 1972. News views, comments and analysis.

US/0161-2697
**PHILLIPS SHIELD.** [Phillips shield]. Oct. 1976-. Periodical. English. qt. **LC** HD9569.P53; P48. **DD** 338.7/62/233805.
**Ind/Abst** Coal Abstr.

UK
**PIPELINE.** (19??)-. English. Three times a year (published approx. in Spring, Summer and Winter). Free on request. International Petroleum Exchange London Ltd, 1 St Katharines Way, London E1 9UN England. **Tel** 011 44 71 4810643.

US/0032-0188
**PIPELINE & GAS JOURNAL.** [Pipeline gas j.]. **VFOAT** Pipeline and Gas Journal. **VAT** Pipeline and Gas Journal. Vol. 197, No. 6; (May 1970)-. Periodical. English. mo. $22.00 (1 year), $33.00 (2 year) qualified subscribers (pipeline or gas distribution or transmission companies), $75.00 (non-qualified) US; $37.00 (1 year), $49.00 (2 year) (qualified subscriber) Canada; $60.00 (1 year), $70.00 (2 year) (qualified subscriber), $100.00 (1 year) (non-qualified) other. Pipeline and Gas Journal, PO Box 1589, Dallas TX 75221. **Tel** (214)691-3911, FAX (214)987-3940. **ED** Jim Watts and Ludonna Jackson. **LC** TP757; .P55. **DD** 665/.74/05. **CODEN** PLGJAT. **[CCC].** Index available. cum. index. **Bk Rev. Ad Acc. Circ:** 24,000 (ctrl). available on microfilm and microfiche from University Microfilms International (UMI); available on an online database (file 16/Full-Text) from DIALOG. Documents available from Article Express International, Petroleum Abstracts Document Delivery Service, Documents on Demand. ***Formed by the union of*** *American Gas Journal, 0096-4409* ***and*** *Pipeline Engineer.*
**Desc:** Serves the worldwide energy pipeline and gas distribution business. Feature articles deal with engineering, operating and construction methods relative to cross-country pipelines that transport crude oil products and natural gas, plus facilities that distribute natural gas.
**Ind/Abst** Acad. Search (July 1993-); Alum. Ind. Abstr.; Appl. Sci. Technol. Index; Bioeng. Abstr.; Bus. Index (1985-); Coal Abstr.; Ei Page One; Energy Inf. Abstr.; Energy Res. Abstr. (May 1974-); Eng. Mater. Abstr.; Eng. Index Annu. [Select. Cov.]; Environ. Abstr.; F&S Index Plus Text, Int. [Full Txt.] [Select. Cov.]; Fluid Abstr., Civil Eng.; Fluid Abstr. Proc. Eng.; FLUIDEX (1973-); Gas Abstr.; Gen. BusinessFile (1985-); Gen. Period. Index (1985-); GeoRef; Int. Aerosp. Abstr.; Lit. Pat. Abstr., Oilfield Chem. (1972-); Lit. Abstr., Catal. Catal.; Lit. Abstr., Health Environ.; Lit. Abstr., Pet. Refin. Petrochem.; Lit. Abstr., Pet. Substit.; Lit. Abstr., Transp. Storage; Mag. Search; Met. Abstr.; Life Sci. Collect.; Pet. Abstr.; Predicasts; PROMT [Full Txt.]; Ref. Sources; Stat. Ref. Index; Trade Ind. Index (1981-); World Alum. Abstr.

US/0197-1506
**PIPELINE DIGEST.** [Pipeline dig.]. (1963)-. Trade Publication. English. sm. $57.00 US; $67.00 other. Hart Publications Inc, 1900 Grant Street, Suite 400, Denver CO 80203. **Tel** (303)837-1917, (800)832-1917, FAX (303)837-8585. **ED** Judy R. Clark. **LC** TJ930; .P555. **DD** 621.8/672/05. **[CCC]. Ad Acc. Circ:** 9,000 (ctrl).
**Desc:** Covers design, construction and operation of pipelines and related facilities, worldwide. Includes details of proposed projects, contracts awarded, and industry news.
**Ind/Abst** Corros. Abstr.; Fluid Abstr., Civil Eng.; Fluid Abstr. Proc. Eng.; FLUIDEX (1973-).

US
**PIPELINE ENGINEERING : PRESENTED AT THE ... ANNUAL ENERGY-SOURCES TECHNOLOGY CONFERENCE AND EXHIBITION / SPONSORED BY THE PETROLEUM DIVISION, ASME.** **Added/Corp** American Society of Mechanical Engineers. Petroleum Division. (1991)-. English. The American Society of Mechanical Engineers, United Engineering Center, 345 East 47th Street, New York NY 10017. ***Continues*** *Pipeline Engineering Symposium.*

US
**PIPELINE INTELLIGENCE REPORT.** English. sm. $300.00. Pipeline Intelligence Co., PO Box 1132, Bellaire TX 77402. **Tel** (713)669-9538, FAX (713)666-1381. **ED** Margie Moses. **Ad Acc, Adv Mgr:** Margie Moses. **Circ:** 700.
**Desc:** Tabular listing of upcoming pipeline projects in the continental United States. Pipeline company name, length of project, pipe diameter, location, bid date, awarded contractor.

US
**PIPELINE SAFETY ADVISORY BULLETIN.** **Main/Corp** United States. Materials Transportation Bureau. No. 78, (July 1978)-. Bulletin. English. US Department of Transportation / Research and Special Programs Administration / Materials Transportation Bureau, 400 Seventh Street SW, Washington DC 20590. ***Continues*** *United States. Office of Pipeline Safety Operations. Advisory Bulletin - Office of Pipeline Safety Operations.*

UK/0032-020X
**PIPES & PIPELINES INTERNATIONAL (1965).** (PIPES & PIPELINES INTERNATIONAL.). [Pipes pipelines int.]. **VAT** Pipes and Pipelines International. Vol. 10, No. 12 (Nov. 1965)-. Periodical. English. bm. £75.00 UK; $150.00 other. Scientific Press Ltd, PO Box 21, Beaconsfield Bucks HP9 1NS England. **Tel** 011 44 494 675139, 011 44 494 672614, FAX 011 44 494 670155. **ED** John Tiratsoo. **LC** TS280; .P5. **DD** 621.8/672/05. **CODEN** PPIIAU. Index available. **Bk Rev. Ad Acc.** ctrl circ. ***Continues*** *International Pipes & Pipelines.*
**Ind/Abst** Alum. Ind. Abstr.; Bibliogr. Mission. (1973-); Coal Abstr.; Curr. Technol. Index; Curr. Titles Electrochem.; EMBASE; Fluid Abstr., Civil Eng.; Fluid Abstr. Proc. Eng.; FLUIDEX (1973-); Gas Abstr.; HTFS Dig.; Lit. Pat. Abstr., Oilfield Chem. (1991-); Lit. Abstr., Catal. Catal.; Lit. Abstr., Health Environ.; Lit. Abstr., Pet. Refin. Petrochem.; Lit. Abstr., Pet. Substit.; Lit. Abstr., Transp. Storage; Met. Abstr.; Life Sci. Collect.; World Surf. Coat. Abstr.

US
**PL, PETROLEUM LEGISLATION.** **VFOAT** Petroleum Legislation. (1970)-. Periodical. English. mo. $4,800.00. Barrows Company Inc., 116 East 66th Street, New York NY 10021. **Tel** (212)772-1199, (800)227-7697, FAX (212)288-7242, telex 4971238 BARROWS. **ED** Gordon Barrows and Marta Guerra. cum. index. **Circ:** 2,000.
**Desc:** Worldwide analysis by country.

US/0277-0415
**PLATT'S OIL MARKETING BULLETIN.** **See** Business-Marketing.

US/0160-4457
**PLATT'S OIL PRICE HANDBOOK AND OILMANAC.** **Added/Corp** Platt's Price Service, Inc. McGraw-Hill Publishing Co., Inc. **VFOAT** Oil Price Handbook and Oilmanac. 29th Ed. (1952)-. English. an. $180.00. McGraw Hill Publishing Company, Inc., 1221 Avenue of the Americas, New York NY 10020. **Tel** (212)512-6410, (800)525-5003, FAX (212)512-6111. **LC** HD9564.A1; P5. **DD** 338.2/3; 338.2. ***Continues*** *Platt's Oil Price Handbook.*

US/0163-1284
**PLATT'S OILGRAM NEWS.** [Platt's oilgram news]. **VFOAT** Oilgram News. (19??)-. Periodical. English. da. $1647.00 US, Canada, and Mexico; $1887.00 other. McGraw Hill Publishing Company, Inc., 1221 Avenue of the Americas, New York NY 10020. **Tel** (212)512-6410, (800)525-5003, FAX (212)512-6111. **LC** HD9561; .P53. **DD** 338.2/728/05. available on microfilm and microfiche from University Microfilms International (UMI); available on an online database (file 624/Full-Text) from DIALOG. ***Continues*** *Platt's Oilgram News Service, 0032-1427.*
**Desc:** An international news report serving executives in all branches of the petroleum industry (as well as officers of governmental agencies and financial institutions with interests in oil) throughout the world.
**Ind/Abst** Bus. Index (1985-); Gen. BusinessFile (1985-); Gen. Period. Index (1985-); INFO-SOUTH Abstr.; Infomat Int. Bus.; Mag. Search; NEXIS (Jan. 5, 1981-); Pet. Energy Bus. News Index (1975); Trade Ind. Index.

US/0163-1292
**PLATT'S OILGRAM PRICE REPORT.**
**VFOAT** Oilgram Price Report. (19??)-. Periodical. English. da. $1747.00 US, Canada, and Mexico; $1997.00 other. McGraw Hill Publishing Company, Inc., 1221 Avenue of the Americas, New York NY 10020. **Tel** (212)512-6410, (800)525-5003, FAX (212)512-6111. **LC** HD9561; .P54. **DD** 338.2/3. available on microfilm and microfiche from University Microfilms International (UMI); available on an online database (file 624/Full-Text) from DIALOG. ***Continues*** *Platt's Oilgram Price Service, 0149-581X.*
**Desc:** Report on world oil prices, covering prices of crude oil and products in detail. Crude oil prices are reported in all principal wholesale centers.
**Ind/Abst** NEXIS (1982-).

XR/0032-1761
**PLYN.** [Plyn]. **Added/Corp** Ceske Plynarenske Podniky. (1967)-. Periodical. Czech (summaries and/or abstracts in English, German and Russian). mo. **CODEN** PVZTAK. ***Continues*** *Paliva.*
**Ind/Abst** Gas Abstr.

XR/0139-763X
**PRACE VYZKUMNEHO USTAVU GEOLOGICKEHO INZENYRSTVI.** [Pr. vyzk. ustavu geol. inz]. **Main/Corp** Vyzkumny Ustav Geologickeho Inzenyrstvi. SV. 32-. Academic Scholarly Publication. Czech (summaries and/or abstracts in Russian, English and German). Vyzumny Ustav Geologickeho Inzenyrstvi, Mozartova 1, Brno 601 88 Czech Republic. **LC** TN860; .C47A. **CODEN** PVUIDX. **Ad Acc. Circ:** 500. Documents available from CASDDS. ***Continues*** *Prace Ustavu Geologickeho Inzenyrstvi, 0370-2421.*
**Ind/Abst** Chem. Abstr.; GeoRef.

US/0569-3799
**PREPRINTS - AMERICAN CHEMICAL SOCIETY. DIVISION OF PETROLEUM CHEMISTRY.** **See** Chemistry-Chemical Technology.

US/0569-3772
**PREPRINTS OF PAPERS PRESENTED - AMERICAN CHEMICAL SOCIETY. DIVISION OF FUEL CHEMISTRY.** **See** Chemistry.

US/0096-8870
**PROCEEDINGS, ANNUAL CONVENTION - GAS PROCESSORS ASSOCIATION.** [Proc. Annu. conv. Gas Process. Assoc.]. **Main/Corp** Gas Processors Association. 53rd (1974)-. Academic Scholarly Publication. English. an (June). $25.00. Gas Processors Association, 6526 East 60th Street, Tulsa OK 74145. **Tel** (918)493-3872. **LC** TN880.A1; N33. **DD** 665/.73. **CODEN** PGPAAC. Documents available from Article Express International, CASDDS. ***Continues*** *Proceedings. Annual Convention - Natural Gas Processors Association, 0097-2363.*
**Ind/Abst** Bioeng. Abstr.; Chem. Abstr.; Ei Page One; Energy Res. Abstr. (July 1977-); Eng. Index Annu.; Lit. Pat. Abstr., Oilfield Chem.; Lit. Abstr., Catal. Catal.; Lit. Abstr., Health Environ.; Lit. Abstr., Pet. Refin. Petrochem.; Lit. Abstr., Pet. Substit.; Lit. Abstr., Transp. Storage.

US/0278-3711
**PROCEEDINGS - JOINT SPE/DOE SYMPOSIUM ON ENHANCED OIL RECOVERY.** (PROCEEDINGS / JOINT SPE/DOE SYMPOSIUM ON ENHANCED OIL RECOVERY, TULSA, OKLA., ETC.). [Proc. - Jt. SPE/DOE Symp. Enhanc. Oil Recovery]. **Main/Conf** Joint SPE/DOE Symposium on Enhanced Oil Recovery. **VFOAT** SPE/DOE Symposium on Enhanced Oil Recovery; Symposium on Enhanced Oil Recovery. **VAT** Proceedings - Joint Society of Petroleum Engineers/Department of Energy Symposium on Enhanced Oil Recovery; Proceedings - Joint SPE, DOE Symposium on Enhanced Oil Recovery. 1st-. Proceedings. English. Society of Petroleum Engineers of The American Institute of Mechanical Engineers, 6200 North Central Expressway, Dallas TX 75206.
**Ind/Abst** GeoRef.

US/0146-6267
**PROCEEDINGS OF ... SYNTHETIC PIPELINE GAS SYMPOSIUM.** [Proc. Synth. Pipeline Gas Symp.]. **Main/Conf** Synthetic Pipeline Gas Symposium. **Added/Corp** American Gas Association. United States. Office of Coal Research. International Gas Union. United States. Energy Research and Development Administration. Gas Research Institute. (19??)-. Monographic series. English. ir. Price varies per volume. American Gas Association / Virginia, 1515 Wilson Boulevard, Arlington VA 22209. **Tel** (703)841-8400, (703)841-8559, FAX (703)841-8697. **LC** TP345.A1; S96a. **DD** 665.7/7/05. **CODEN** PSGSD6. Documents available from CASDDS.
**Ind/Abst** Chem. Abstr.

IO/0126-1126
**PROCEEDINGS OF THE ANNUAL CONVENTION - INDONESIAN PETROLEUM ASSOCIATION.** [Proc. Annu. Conv. - Indones. Pet. Assoc.]. **Main/Corp** Indonesian Petroleum Association. Vol. 1 (1972)-. Proceedings. English. ir. $27.00 US. Indonesian Petroleum Association, 3 Jalan Menteng Raya, Jakarta Indonesia. **LC** TN863; .I53A. **DD** 553/.28/09598. **CODEN** PCIADK. Documents available from CASDDS.
**Ind/Abst** Chem. Abstr.; GeoRef.

US/0733-6098
**PROCEEDINGS OF THE ANNUAL INSTITUTE - EASTERN MINERAL LAW FOUNDATION (U.S.). ANNUAL INSTITUTE.** **See** Law.

US/0895-1578
**PROCEEDINGS OF THE ... ANNUAL INSTITUTE OF OIL AND GAS LAW AND TAXATION.** **See** Law.

US/0361-5987
**PROCEEDINGS OF THE ANNUAL SOUTHWESTERN PETROLEUM SHORT COURSE.** [Proc. annu. Southwest. Pet. Short Course]. **Main/Conf** Southwestern Petroleum Short Course. **Added/Corp** Southwestern Petroleum Short Course Association. Texas Technological College. Dept. of Petroleum Engineering. Texas Tech University. Dept. of Petroleum Engineering. (1964)-. Proceedings. English. an (Published in April). $35.00. Southwestern Petroleum Short Course, PO Box 4099, Tech Station, STP 3112, Lubbock TX 79409. **Tel** (806)742-1727. **ED** D A Crawford. **LC** TN863; .S68a. **DD** 665.5. **CODEN** PSPCD3. Index available. cum. index. **Circ:** 500. Documents available from Article Express International, CASDDS. ***Continues*** *West Texas Oil Lifting Short Course. Proceedings.*
**Desc:** State-of-the-art technical papers on petroleum drilling, production reservoir operations and surface facilities with emphasis on artificial lift.
**Ind/Abst** Bioeng. Abstr.; Chem. Abstr.; Ei Page One; Eng. Index Annu.

UK/0950-8708
**PROCEEDINGS OF THE INSTITUTE OF PETROLEUM.** (PROCEEDINGS OF THE INSTITUTE OF PETROLEUM, LONDON.). [Proc. Inst. Pet.]. **Added/Corp** Institute of Petroleum (Great Britain). (1981)-. Academic Scholarly Publication. English. **CODEN** PILODH. Documents available from CASDDS.
**Ind/Abst** Chem. Abstr.

US/0736-5721
**PROCEEDINGS OF THE INTERNATIONAL GAS RESEARCH CONFERENCE.** (PROCEEDINGS OF THE ... INTERNATIONAL GAS RESEARCH CONFERENCE / INTERNATIONAL GAS RESEARCH CONFERENCE ; SPONSORED BY GAS RESEARCH INSTITUTE ... [ET AL.].). [Int. Gas. Res. Conf.]. **Added/Corp** Gas Research Institute. 1st (June 9-12, 1980)-. Academic Scholarly Publication. English. be. $225.00. Governments Institutes Inc., 4 Research Place, Suite 200, Rockville MD 20850. **Tel** (301)921-2300, (301)921-2355. **LC** TP345.A1; I58a. **CODEN** PGRCDV. Documents available from CASDDS.
**Ind/Abst** Chem. Abstr.; Lit. Pat. Abstr., Oilfield Chem.; Lit. Abstr., Catal. Catal.; Lit. Abstr., Health Environ.; Lit. Abstr., Pet. Refin. Petrochem.; Lit. Abstr., Pet. Substit.; Lit. Abstr., Transp. Storage.

US/0887-6746
**PROCEEDINGS OF THE LAURANCE REID GAS CONDITIONING CONFERENCE.** [Proc. Laurance Reid Gas Cond. Conf.]. **Added/Corp** University of Oklahoma. Continuing Engineering Education. (Mar. 4-6, 1985)-. Academic Scholarly Publication. English. an. $50.00. University of Oklahoma / 1700 Asp Avenue, Norman OK 73037. **Tel** (405)325-3136. **LC** TP345.A1; G32a. **DD** 665.7. **CODEN** PLRCEX. Documents available from CASDDS. ***Continues*** *Gas Conditioning Conference. Proceedings of the Gas Conditioning Conference, 0474-067X.*
**Ind/Abst** Bioeng. Abstr. (1985-); Chem. Abstr. (1985-); Coal Abstr. (1985-); Energy Res. Abstr. (1985-).

US/0547-7441
**PROCEEDINGS OF THE NATIONAL INSTITUTE FOR PETROLEUM LANDMEN.** **Main/Corp** National Institute for Petroleum Landmen. **Added/Corp** American Association of Petroleum Landmen. Southwestern Legal Foundation. International Oil and Gas Educational Center. **VFOAT** National Institute for Petroleum Landmen. No.1 (1959)-. Proceedings. English. Matthew Bender & Company Inc., 1275 Broadway, Albany NY 12204. **Tel** (800)833-9844, (518)487-3000. **LC** HD9561; .N35. **DD** 333.8.

SI
**PROCEEDINGS OF THE SOUTHEAST ASIA PETROLEUM EXPLORATION SOCIETY.** **Main/Corp** Southeast Asia Petroleum Exploration Society. **VFOAT** SEAPEX Proceedings. (19??)-. Proceedings. English. ir. 30.00Sing$ members; 35.00Sing$ non-members. Southeast Asia Petro Explr Soc, PO Box 423, Tanglin Post Office, Singapore 9124 Singapore. **LC** TN271.P4; S665a. **DD** 338.2/782/0959. ***Continues*** *Proceedings of the South East Asia Petroleum Exploration Society, 0129-377X.*

CN/0707-8994
**PROCEEDINGS OF THE SPECIAL COMMITTEE OF THE SENATE ON A NORTHERN GAS PIPELINE.** **Main/Corp** Canada. Parliament. Senate. Special Committee on a Northern Gas Pipeline. **VFOAT** Deliberations du Comite Special du Senat sur un Pipe-Line pour la Gaz du Nord. **VAT** Northern Gas Pipeline (Senate of Canada); Pipe-Line pour le Gaz du Nord (Senat du Canada). Mar. 21, 1978-. Proceedings. English (French). Receiver General for Canada / Ottawa, Canada Comm Group Publishing, Ottawa Ontario K1A 0S9 Canada. **Tel** (819)956-4802, (800)661-2868. **LC** TN880.5; .C326A. **DD** 388.5.

CN/0707-9001
**PROCEEDINGS OF THE SPECIAL COMMITTEE OF THE SENATE ON THE NORTHERN PIPELINE.** **Main/Corp** Canada. Parliament. Senate. Special Committee on the Northern Pipeline. **VFOAT** Deliberations du Comite Special du Senat sur le Pipe-Line du Nord. **VAT** Northern Pipeline; Pipe-Line du Nord. Nov. 15, 1978-. Proceedings. English (French). Receiver General for Canada / Ottawa, Canada Comm Group Publishing, Ottawa Ontario K1A 0S9 Canada. **Tel** (819)956-4802, (800)661-2868. **LC** TN880.5; .C326B. **DD** 388.5.

US/0364-4030
**PROCEEDINGS - REFINING DEPARTMENT.** ***Ceased.*** [Proc. - Am. Pet. Inst., Refin. Dep.]. **Main/Corp** American Petroleum Institute. Refining Dept. Vol. 56 (1977)-?. Academic Scholarly Publication. English. an. American Petroleum Institute, 275 Seventh Avenue, New York NY 10001. **Tel** (212)366-4040, FAX (212)366-4298. **(Subscription address:** 1970 Chain Bridge Road, McLean, VA 22109-6000**)** **LC** TP690.A1; A746. **DD** 665/.53. **CODEN** PAPDDG. **[CCC].** Documents available from Article Express International, CASDDS. ***Continues*** *Proceedings - American Petroleum Institute, Refining Department, 0364-4030.*
**Ind/Abst** Bioeng. Abstr. (?-?); Chem. Abstr. (?-?); Coal Abstr. (?-?); Ei Page One (?-?); Energy Res. Abstr. (Aug. 1978-); Eng. Index Annu.; Lit. Pat. Abstr., Oilfield Chem. (1961-); Lit. Abstr., Catal. Catal. (?-?); Lit. Abstr., Health Environ. (?-?); Lit. Abstr., Pet. Refin. Petrochem. (?-?); Lit. Abstr., Pet. Substit. (?-?); Lit. Abstr., Transp. Storage (?-?).

UK/0084-2176
**PROCEEDINGS / WORLD PETROLEUM CONGRESS.** [Proc., World Pet. Congr.]. **VFOAT** Actes et Documents; Proceedings of the ... World Petroleum Congress. (1933)-(1991). Academic Scholarly Publication. English (French, German, Italian, Russian and Spanish). ir. John Wiley & Sons, Inc., 605 Third Avenue, New York NY 10158-0012. **Tel** (212)850-6000, (212)850-6645, FAX (212)850-6088, telex 12-7063. **(Subscription address:** John Wiley & Sons / England, Baffins Lane, Chichester, West Sussex PO19 1UD England.**)** **LC** TN863; .W57. **CODEN** WPCPAU. **[CCC].** Documents available from CASDDS.
**Ind/Abst** Chem. Abstr. (?-?); Life Sci. Collect. (?-?).

US
**PRODUCTION AND ACTIVITY REPORT.** (19??)-. Periodical. English. ir. $200.00 includes weekly activity reports, monthly production reports and notice & results of monthly oil & gas board meetings. State Oil and Gas Board of Alabama, PO Box O, 420 Hackberry Lane, Tuscaloosa AL 35486. **Tel** (205)349-2852. Index available (free on request).

CN/0033-1260
**PROPANE CANADA.** Vol. 61, No. 1 (Summer 1968)-. Periodical. English. bm. 30.00Can$ (one year), 50.00Can$ (two years), 75.00Can$ (three years) Canada; $35.00 (one year), $55.00 (two years) US, $65.00 other. Northern Star Communication, 1609700 4th Avenue SW, Calgary Alberta T2P 3J4 Canada. **Tel** (403)265-4750, FAX (408)263-6886. **ED** Scott Jeffrey. **[CCC].** **Bk Rev.**

# Petroleum and Natural Gas

Ad Acc, Adv Mgr: Jim Graham. Circ: 5,600 (ctrl). Continues in part Canadian Gas Journal, 0366-5925.
Desc: Edited for the Canadian LP Gas industry, devoting its energies to the promotion and well-being of the oil and gas marketplace.
Ind/Abst Gas Abstr.

US
**PROPOSED RULES AND FINAL RULES ADOPTED.** English. ir. $25.00. Railroad Commission of Texas, PO Drawer 12967, Capitol Station, Austin TX 78711. Tel (512)463-7255.

TH/0857-7749
**PTIT FOCUS.** [PTIT Focus]. VFOAT Petroleum Institute of Thailand Focus. (1987)-. Periodical. English. mo (plus 1 annual issue). $260.00. Petroleum Institute Thailand, 18 TH FL PTT Boulevard, 555 Vibhavadi RA Road, Bangkok 10900 Thailand. Tel 011 66 2 5373591, FAX 011 66 2 5373591. ED Konthi Kulachol. DD 665.5.
Bk Rev. Ad Acc.

US/1045-4020
**QUARTERLY COMPLETION REPORT.** [Q. complet. rep.]. Added/Corp American Petroleum Institute. Dept. of Statistics. VFOAT A.P.I. Quarterly Completion Report; API Quarterly Completion Report; American Petroleum Institute Quarterly Completion Report. Vol. 1, No. 1 (1st Quarter 1985)-. Periodical. English. qt. $150.00 (non-member); $165.00 Canada; $195.00 other. American Petroleum Institute, 275 Seventh Avenue, New York NY 10001. Tel (212)366-4040, FAX (212)366-4298. (Subscription address: 1970 Chain Bridge Road, McLean, VA 22109-6000) DD 553. Continues Quarterly Review of Drilling Statistics for the United States, 0033-5789.

UK/0269-1183
**QUARTERLY JOURNAL OF TECHNICAL PAPERS.** Suspended. Added/Corp Institute of Petroleum (Great Britain). VFOAT Technical Papers. (Jan./March 1986)-(1993). Periodical. English. qt. £65.00. Institute of Petroleum, 61 New Cavendish Street, London W1M 8AR England. Tel 011 44 71 636 1004, FAX 011 44 71 255 1472. Documents available from Petroleum Abstracts Document Delivery Service. Continues Institute of Petroleum, 0309-1880.
Ind/Abst Ei Page One; GeoRef; Lit. Pat. Abstr., Oilfield Chem. (1991-); Lit. Abstr., Catal. Catal.; Lit. Abstr., Health Environ.; Lit. Abstr., Pet. Refin. Petrochem.; Lit. Abstr., Pet. Substit.; Lit. Abstr., Transp. Storage; Pet. Abstr.

US/0888-7799
**QUARTERLY OIL COMPANY PERFORMANCE.** Ceased. [Q. oil co. perform.]. Added/Corp Petroleum Analysis Ltd. ( )-Ceased (1991). Periodical. English. qt. Petroleum Analysis Ltd, P.O.Box 130, F.D.R. Station, New York NY 10150. Tel (212)755-7484. DD 338. Continues Quarterly Oil Company Performers and Industry Review.
Desc: Review and analysis of major oil company financial and operating performance in the quarter and year to date.

US
**QUARTERLY REPORT. SUN COMPANY.** (19??)-. English. Four times a year. Free. Sun Company, 1801 Market Street, Philadelphia PA 19103. Tel (215)977-3000. Continues Sun Magazine.

US/0033-5789
**QUARTERLY REVIEW OF DRILLING STATISTICS FOR THE UNITED STATES.** Title Change. See Petroleum and Natural Gas-Abstracting, Bibliographies and Statistics.

AT
**QUENTIN CAMERON'S OIL & GAS BULLETIN.** Bulletin. English. sm. 168.00Aus$ Australia; 180.00Aus$ New Zealand and Papua New Guinea; 190.00Aus$ 190.00 other. Quentin Cameron, PO Box 376, Hamilton CNT, Queensland, 4007 Austarlia. Tel 011 61 7 2681217, FAX 011 61 7 2684742.
Desc: Updates investment opportunities and drilling results in the Australian oil patch.

BE
**RAPPORT ANNUEL - COMITE DE CONCERTATION ET DE CONTROLE DU PETROLE.** Main/Corp Belgium. Comite de Concertation et de Controle du Petrole. English. an. Ministere des Affaires Economiques Comite de Concertation et du Controle du Petrole, Rue de Mot, 1040 Brussels Belgium. LC HD9575.B4; B44A. DD 354.4930082/388/06.

IT
**RASSEGNA DEL BITUME.** (19??)-. Periodical. Italian. ir. Free on request. SITEB, C SO Trieste 38/4, 00198 Rome, Italy. Tel 011 39 6 6631374.

IT/0390-587X
**RASSEGNA PETROLIFERA.** [Rass. pet.]. (1935)-. Periodical. Italian. wk. Rassegna Petrolifera, Lungomare Paolo Toscanelli 166, 00120 Ostia Lido Rome Italy. UDC 665.6.

GW
**RECHT UND STEUERN IM GAS- UND WASSERFACH : R+S / HERAUSGEGEBEN VOM BUNDESVERBAND DER DEUTSCHEN GAS- UND WASSERWIRTSCHAFT E.V.** Added/Corp Bundesverband der Deutschen Gas- und Wasserwirtschaft. VFOAT R+S; R und S. (19??)-. Periodical. German. bm. DM54.00. R Oldenbourg Verlag, Postfach 801360, D 81613 Munich Germany. Tel 011 49 89 450190, FAX 011 49 89 45019305.

CN/0835-0175
**REFINED PETROLEUM AND COAL PRODUCTS INDUSTRIES.** (REFINED PETROLEUM AND COAL PRODUCTS INDUSTRIES / STATISTICS CANADA, INDUSTRY DIVISION, CENSUS OF MANUFACTURES SECTION.). [Refin. pet. coal prod. ind.]. Added/Corp Statistics Canada. Census of Manufactures Section. Statistics Canada. Industry Division. Statistics Canada. Annual Survey of Manufactures Section. VFOAT Industries de Produits Raffines du Petrole et du Charbon. (1985)-. English (French). an. 38.00Can$ Canada; $46.00 US; $54.00 other. Statistics Canada, Publications Sales & Services, Main Building Room 1710, Ottawa Ontario K1A 0T6 Canada. Tel (613)951-5078, (800)267-6677, FAX (613)951-1584, telex 053-3585. LC HD9574.C2; R43. DD 338.4/7665538/0971021. Continues Refined Petroleum and Coal Products, 0319-9045.
Desc: Annual census of manufacturers.

CN/0380-8629
**REFINED PETROLEUM PRODUCTS (MONTHLY ED.).** (REFINED PETROLEUM PRODUCTS / PREPARED IN THE MINING, METALLURGICAL AND CHEMICAL SECTION OF THE INDUSTRY AND MERCHANDISING DIVISION, DOMINION BUREAU OF STATISTICS, ...). [Refin. pet. prod.]. Main/Corp Statistics Canada. Manufacturing and Primary Industries Division. Added/Corp Canada. Dominion Bureau of Statistics. Mining, Metallurgical & Chemical Section. Canada. Dominion Bureau of Statistics. Metal and Chemical Products Section. Canada. Dominion Bureau of Statistics. Industry and Merchandising Division. Canada. Dominion Bureau of Statistics. Industry Division. Canada. Dominion Bureau of Statistics. Manufacturing and Primary Industries Division. Statistics Canada. Manufacturing and Primary Industries Division. Statistics Canada. Energy Section. VFOAT Produits Petroliers Raffines. (Sept. 1949)-. Periodical. English (French). mo. 200.00Can$ Canada; $240.00 US; $280.00 other. Statistics Canada, Publications Sales & Services, Main Building Room 1710, Ottawa Ontario K1A 0T6 Canada. Tel (613)951-5078, (800)267-6677, FAX (613)951-1584, telex 053-3585. DD 338.2/7282/0971. Absorbed Refined Petroleum Products; Continues Refined Petroleum Products in Canada.
Desc: Covers crude oil received by refineries (imports by source of supply), production, inventories and net sales of refined petroleum products by province or region.

CN/0575-9587
**REFINED PETROLEUM PRODUCTS. VOLUME 2. CONSUMPTION OF PETROLEUM PRODUCTS.** (REFINED PETROLEUM PRODUCTS: CONSUMPTION OF PETROLEUM PRODUCTS.). Main/Corp Statistics Canada. Manufacturing and Primary Industries Division. Added/Corp Statistics Canada. Manufacturing and Primary Industries Division. Produits Petroliers Raffines: Consommation des Produits Petroliers. VFOAT Produits Petroliers Raffines: Consommation des Produits Petroliers. (1970)-. English (French). mo. 200.00Can$ Canada; $240.00 US; $280.00 other. Statistics Canada, Publications Sales & Services, Main Building Room 1710, Ottawa Ontario K1A 0T6 Canada. Tel (613)951-5078, (800)267-6677, FAX (613)951-1584, telex 053-3585. LC HD9574.C2; C28a. DD 338.9/7/66550971. Supersedes Canada. Bureau of Statistics. Manufacturing and Primary Industries Division. Refined Petroleum Products; Consumption of Petroleum Products, 0575-9587.

US/1062-5658
**REFINING & GAS PROCESSING INDUSTRY : WORLDWIDE.** [Refin. gas process. ind.]. Added/Corp Midwest Register, Inc. VFOAT Refining and Gas Processing Industry. (1991)-. English. $40.00. Midwest Register Inc., 1345 East 15th Street, Tulsa OK 74120. Tel (800)829-2002, (918)582-2000. DD 338. Continues Refining, Construction, Petrochemical and Natural Gas Processing Plants, 1054-951X.

UK
**REGISTER OF VALVES.** (1988)-. Directory. English. £58.00 UK; £68.00 other. BSI Testing, Maylands Avenue, Hemel Hempstead, Herts HP2 4SQ England. Tel 011 44 442 230442, FAX 011 44 442 231442. ED R. J. Wells.
Desc: A register of kitemark certified valves for all services and fire tested valves for the petroleum, petrochemical and allied industries.

BL
**RELATORIO DAS ATIVIDADES DE ... E PROGRAMACAO PARA ... .** Main/Corp Instituto Brasileiro de Petroleo. VFOAT Relatorio das Atividades de ... . Portuguese. an. Instituto Brasileiro de Petroleo, Av rio Branco 156-10O Andar-Gr 1035, 20043 Rio de Janeiro RJ Brazil. LC HD9574.B8; I57A. Continues Instituto Brasileiro de Petroleo. Relatorio das Atividades em ... .

UK
**REMOTE SENSING: AN OPERATIONAL TECHNOLOGY FOR THE MINING AND PETROLEUM INDUSTRIES.** Institution of Mining and Metallurgy, 44 Portland Place, London W1N 4BR England. Tel 011 44 71 580-3802, FAX 011 44 71 436-5388, telex 261410.

US/0271-6984
**REPORT - CALIFORNIA DIVISION OF OIL & GAS.** (REPORT; TR TECHNICAL REPORT.). [Rep. - Calif. Div. Oil Gas]. Main/Corp California. Division of Oil and Gas. VAT Report - California Division of Oil and Gas. No. 1- . Monographic series. English. Price varies per volume.
Ind/Abst GeoRef.

US/0272-4774
**REPORT ORO.** See Energy.

US/0190-8715
**REPORTS ON RESEARCH ASSISTED BY THE PETROLEUM RESEARCH FUND.** See Chemistry-Chemical Technology.

US/0091-2786
**RESEARCH AND DEVELOPMENT - AMERICAN GAS ASSOCIATION.** (RESEARCH AND DEVELOPMENT.). Main/Corp American Gas Association. (19??)-. English. American Gas Association / Virginia, 1515 Wilson Boulevard, Arlington VA 22209. Tel (703)841-8400, (703)841-8559, FAX (703)841-8697. LC TP723; .A73a. DD 665./7/072073.

US
**RESEARCH AND DEVELOPMENT PROGRAM FOR OUTER CONTINENTAL SHELF OIL AND GAS OPERATIONS, TECHNICAL REPORT.** Main/Corp United States. Geological Survey. English. an. US Department of the Interior / Geological Survey, Reston, VA, Reston VA 22092.

CN/0707-2562
**RESERVOIR ANNUAL (1977).** (RESERVOIR ANNUAL / SASKATCHEWAN ENERGY AND MINES, PETROLEUM AND NATURAL GAS.). [Reserv. annu.]. Added/Corp Saskatchewan. Petroleum and Natural Gas. VFOAT Saskatchewan Reservoir Annual. (1977)-. English. an. 75.00Can$. Saskatchewan Energy and Mines, 1914 Hamilton, Regina Saskatchewan, S4P 4V4 Canada. Tel (306)787-7643, FAX (306)787-2527. LC TN873.C22; S263. DD 553.2/8/097124. Continues Petroleum & Natural Gas Reservoir Annual, 0704-5743.
Desc: Contains oil and gas reserves data, development and production data, information concerning enhanced recovery projects and related reservoir information. Includes pages of tables, graphs, maps and figures.
Ind/Abst GeoRef.

CN
**RESERVOIR ENGINEERING DIGEST. GAS FIELDS.** English. mo. 927.00Can$. Petroleum Digests, 5112 Third Street Southwest, Calgary Alberta T2H 1J6 Canada. Tel (403)255-9400, FAX (403)255-4786.

CN
**RESERVOIR ENGINEERING DIGEST. OIL FIELDS.** English. mo. 884.00Can$. Petroleum Digests, 5112 Third Street Southwest, Calgary Alberta T2H 1J6 Canada. Tel (403)255-9400, FAX (403)255-4786.
Desc: Contains oil and gas well information.

CN
**RESERVOIR PERFORMANCE CHARTS: GAS POOLS.** Main/Corp Alberta. Energy Resources Conservation Board. (1971)-. Periodical. English. an. 75.00Can$. Energy Resources Conservation Board, 640 Fifth Avenue Southwest, Calgary Alberta T2P 3G4 Canada. Tel (403)297-8311, (403)297-8190, telex 03-821717. LC TN873.C22; A442 subser. DD 333.7 S; 338.2/7/285097123. Continues Alberta. Oil and Gas Conservation Board. Reservoir Performance Charts; Gas Pools.
Desc: Index of pools; average gas-oil and water-oil ratios; static bottom hole pressure, number of wells capable of production, daily average oil production, cumulative oil production, daily average water injection and disposal, cumulative water injection and disposal, daily average gas injection, and cumulative gas injection.

CN
**RESERVOIR PERFORMANCE CHARTS: OIL POOLS.** **Main/Corp** Alberta. Energy Resources Conservation Board. (1971)-. Periodical. English. an. 90.00Can$ US and Canada; 97.50Can$ other. Energy Resources Conservation Board, 640 Fifth Avenue Southwest, Calgary Alberta T2P 3G4 Canada. **Tel** (403)297-8311, (403)297-8190, telex 03-821717. **LC** TN873.C22; A442 subser. **DD** 333.7 S; 338.2/7/282097123. ***Continues*** *Alberta. Oil and Gas Conservation Board. Reservoir Performance Charts; Oil Pools.*
**Desc:** Index of pools; number of wells capable of production; cumulative and average daily gas production; static bottom hole pressure; cumulative data for: gas injected, marketable gas for sale or reinjection, water production; graph of total alberta production and disposition.

US
**RESIDENTIAL GAS MARKET SURVEY.** **Added/Corp** American Gas Association. 42nd (1989)-. English. American Gas Association / Virginia, 1515 Wilson Boulevard, Arlington VA 22209. **Tel** (703)841-8400, (703)841-8559, FAX (703)841-8697. **LC** HD9581.U49; G32. ***Continues*** *Gas Househeating Survey, 0749-6907.*

CN/0849-2409
**RESOURCE GUIDE AND DIRECTORY - ALBERTA CHAMBER OF RESOURCES.** (RESOURCE GUIDE AND DIRECTORY.). [Resour. guide dir. - Alta. Chamb. Resour.]. **Added/Corp** Alberta Chamber of Resources. **VFOAT** Alberta Chamber of Resources Directory. Vol. 1, No. 2 (1989)-. Directory. English. **DD** 338.7/622/0257123. ***Continues*** *Alberta Chamber of Resources Directory., 0845-4728.*

US/0276-6043
**RESPONSE (WASHINGTON, D.C.).** (RESPONSE / API.). **Added/Corp** American Petroleum Institute. (19??)-. Periodical. English. wk. Free on request. American Petroleum Institute, 275 Seventh Avenue, New York NY 10001. **Tel** (212)366-4040, FAX (212)366-4298. **(Subscription address:** American Petroleum Institute, 1970 Chain Bridge Road, McLean, VA 22109; Phone: (202)682-8378**)**

US/0270-7527
**RESUME (DENVER).** (RESUME.). [Resume]. **Main/Corp** Petroleum Information Corporation. (1978)-. English. an (Spring of the following year). $99.00. Petroleum Information Corporation, 5333 Westheimer, Suite 100, Houston TX 77056. **Tel** (713)840-8282 ext. 38, FAX (713)599-5100. **ED** Tom Chevey and Dana Cain. **LC** TN860; .P437a. **DD** 622/.338/0973.
**Desc:** Authoritive source book for annual oil & gas statistics.

AU
**REVIEW / QUEENSLAND ENERGY ADVISORY COUNCIL.** **See** Energy.

MX/0538-1428
**REVISTA DEL INSTITUTO MEXICANO DEL PETROLEO.** [Rev. Inst. Mex. Pet.]. **Main/Corp** Instituto Mexicano del Petroleo. **Added/Corp** Instituto Mexicano del Petroleo. Vol. 1, No. 1 (Jan. 1969)-. Periodical. Spanish (summaries and/or abstracts in English). qt (Jan., Apr., July, Oct.). $40.00 US; $50.00 Central & South America; $55.00 Africa & Europe; $60.00 other. Instituto Mexicano del Petroleo, Apartado Postal 14-805, 07730 Mexico DF Mexico. **Tel** 011 52 5 3685911, 011 52 5 3689333. **ED** Armando Comaduran. **LC** TN873.M6; I5. **CODEN** RVMPAX. **Bk Rev. Circ:** 5,500 (ctrl). Documents available from Article Express International, CASDDS.
**Desc:** Petroleum science and technology.
**Ind/Abst** Bioeng. Abstr.; Chem. Abstr.; Ei Page One; Eng. Index Annu.; Gas Abstr.; GeoRef; Lit. Pat. Abstr., Oilfield Chem. (1975-); Lit. Abstr., Catal. Catal.; Lit. Abstr., Health Environ.; Lit. Abstr., Pet. Refin. Petrochem.; Lit. Abstr., Pet. Substit.; Lit. Abstr., Transp. Storage.

BL
**REVISTA DO GAS.** Periodical. Portuguese. Associgas, Av Paulista 1009 - 16, Sao Paulo Brazil. **LC** TP700; .G1025. ***Continues*** *GLP.*

RM
**REVISTA MINELOR.** **See** Engineering-Mines and Mining Engineering.

VE/0251-4478
**REVISTA TECNICA INTEVEP.** ***Title Change.*** [Rev. tec. INTEVEP]. **Added/Corp** INTEVEP, S.A. Centro de Informacion Tecnica. **VFOAT** Revista Tecnica de INTEVEP; Revista Tecnica I.N.T.E.V.E.P. Vol. 1, No. 1 (Jan. 1981)-(199?). Academic Scholarly Publication. Spanish (English; summaries and/or abstracts in English). sa. Revista Tecnica INTEVEP, Centro de Informacion Tecnica, Apartado Postal 76343, Caracas 1070A Venezuela. **Tel** 011 58 2 9086111, telex 28-831 INTVP VC. **ED** Roberto Callarotti. **LC** WMLC 93/4329; TN873.V4; R485. **CODEN** RTEIDT. **Circ:** 5,000 (ctrl). available on microfilm from University Microfilms International (UMI). Documents available from Article Express International, Petroleum Abstracts Document Delivery Service, CASDDS. ***Continued by*** *Vision Tecnologica.*
**Desc:** A multidisciplinary journal that covers original research and development developed within the Venezuelan petroleum industry.
**Ind/Abst** Bioeng. Abstr.; Chem. Abstr.; Coal Abstr.; Ei Page One; Eng. Index Annu.; GeoRef; Lit. Pat. Abstr., Oilfield Chem. (1982-); Lit. Abstr., Catal. Catal.; Lit. Abstr., Health Environ.; Lit. Abstr., Pet. Refin. Petrochem.; Lit. Abstr., Pet. Substit.; Lit. Abstr., Transp. Storage; Pet. Abstr.

CN/0848-8835
**REVUE DE LIMPERIALE.** [Rev. Imp.]. **Added/Corp** Compagnie Petroliere Imperiale. (1989)-. Periodical. French. qt. Compagnie Petroliere Imperiale Ltee, 111 Ouest Avenue, St. Clair, Toronto, Ontario M5W 1K3 Canada. **DD** 051. ***Continues*** *Revue - Compagnie Petroliere Imperiale., 0700-5148.*
**Ind/Abst** Can. Period. Index (19??-).

FR/0020-2274
**REVUE DE L'INSTITUT FRANCAIS DU PETROLE.** [Rev. Inst. fr. pet.]. **Main/Corp** Rueil-Malmaison, France. Institut Francais du Petrole. Vol. 29, No. 1 (Jan/Feb. 1974)-. Periodical. French (English; summaries and/or abstracts in English and Spanish). Six times a year. 1250.00F EEC countries; 1450.00F other. Societe des Editions Tecnip, 27 rue Ginoux, 75737 Paris Cedex 15 France. **Tel** 33 1 45771108, FAX 33 1 45743711, telex 200 375F EDITECP. **ED** P Leprince. **LC** TP690.A1; P322. **DD** 665/.5. **CODEN** RFPTBH. **[CCC].** Index available (last issue). cum. index. **Circ:** 1,700. Documents available from Article Express International, The Genuine Article, Petroleum Abstracts Document Delivery Service, CASDDS. ***Continues*** *Revue de l'Institut Francais du Petrole et Annales des Combustibles Liquides, 0020-2274.*
**Desc:** Includes studies in fields linked to prospection, processing and use of hydrocarbons, oil, natural gas and their derivatives or alternative products.
**Ind/Abst** Aquat. Sci. Fish. Abstr. (Computer File); Bioeng. Abstr.; Chem. Abstr.; Civ. Struct. Eng. Abstr.; Coal Abstr.; Comput. Inf. Syst. Abstr. J. [Full Cov.]; Curr. Contents Eng. Tech. Appl. Sci.; Ei Page One; Elect. Comm. Abstr.; EMBASE; Energy Res. Abstr. (Aug. 1976-); Eng. Index Annu.; Environ. Eng. Abstr.; Geogr. Abstr. Phys. Geogr.; GeoRef; Int. Aerosp. Abstr.; Lit. Pat. Abstr., Oilfield Chem. (1954-); Lit. Abstr., Catal. Catal.; Lit. Abstr., Health Environ.; Lit. Abstr., Pet. Refin. Petrochem.; Lit. Abstr., Pet. Substit.; Lit. Abstr., Transp. Storage; Mater. Sci. Eng. Abstr.; Mech. Eng. Abstr.; Pet. Abstr.; Res. Alert [Full Cov.]; Sci. Cit. Index; SCISEARCH.

BE/0373-5001
**REVUE GENERALE DU GAZ.** ***Ceased.*** [Rev. gen. gaz]. **Added/Corp** Association Royale des Gaziers Belges. (19??)-(Dec. 1992). Periodical. French. mo. Association Royale des Gaziers Belges, Avenue Palmerston 4, B-1040 Brussels Belgium. **LC** TP700; .R46.
**Ind/Abst** Coal Abstr.; Gas Abstr.; Saf. Health Work.

CN/0711-0901
**RIG LOCATOR.** [Rig locat.]. **Added/Corp** C.O. Nickle Publications. Southam Business Publications. Southam Business Information and Communications Group. Southam Information & Technology Group. Canadian Association of Oilwell Drilling Contractors. (1957)-. Periodical. English. wk. 246.00Can$. C.O. Nickle Publications, 999 8th Street Southwest, Suite 300, Calgary, Alberta T2R 1N7 Canada. **Tel** (403)244-6111. **DD** 622.
**Desc:** Lists rigs and rig status.

UK/0960-7315
**RIG MARKET FORECAST.** [Rig mark. forecast]. **VFOAT** NSL Rig Market Forecast; North Sea Letter Rig Market Forecast. (198?)-. Periodical. English. Financial Times Business Information Ltd., Tower House, Southampton Street, London WC2E 7HA England. **Tel** 011 44 71 353 1040. **DD** 339.4862233819.
**Ind/Abst** PROMT [Full Txt.]; PTS Newsl. Database [Full Txt.].

LE
**RISALAT AL-BATRUL AL-ARABI.** **Main/Corp** Muassasat Risalat Al-Batrul Al-Arabi. Periodical. Arabic. Muassasat Risalat Al-Batrul Al-Arabi, PO Box 6732, 3 Bayrut Lebanon. **LC** HD9578.A55; M8A.

IT/0370-5463
**RIVISTA DEI COMBUSTIBILI.** [Riv. combust.]. (1947). Academic Scholarly Publication. Italian (English). Ten times a year. L70000.00. Stazione Sperimentale per I Combustibili, Viale Alcide de Gasperi 3, 20097 San Donato Milan Italy. **Tel** 2 510031, FAX 2 514286, telex 321622 SSC. **CODEN** RICOAP. Index available. cum. index. **Bk Rev. Ad Acc. Circ:** 2,000. Documents available from Article Express International, CASDDS.
**Ind/Abst** Chem. Abstr.; Coal Abstr.; Elect. Comm. Abstr.; Energy Res. Abstr. (Aug. 1976-); Eng. Index Annu.; Environ. Eng. Abstr.; Gas Abstr.; GeoRef; Lit. Pat. Abstr., Oilfield Chem. (1966-); Lit. Abstr., Catal. Catal.; Lit. Abstr., Health Environ.; Lit. Abstr., Pet. Refin. Petrochem.; Lit. Abstr., Pet. Substit.; Lit. Abstr., Transp. Storage; Mech. Eng. Abstr.; Proc. Chem. Eng.; Saf. Health Work; Solid State Supercond. Abstr.; Theoret. Chem. Eng.

US/0278-9299
**ROCKY MOUNTAIN PETROLEUM DIRECTORY.** [Rocky Mt. petrol. dir.]. **VFOAT** Rocky Mountain Petroleum Sales and Service Directory; Rocky Mountain Petroleum Sales & Service Directory. (19??)-. Directory. English. an. $77.00, $895.00 on diskette. Hart Publications Inc, 1900 Grant Street, Suite 400, Denver CO 80203. **Tel** (303)837-1917, (800)832-1917, FAX (303)837-8585. **ED** Dori Harrell. **LC** TN867; .K5. **DD** 338.7/622338/02578. **Ad Acc. Circ:** 12,000 (ctrl). available on labels; available on diskette. ***Continues*** *Kirkland's Rocky Mountain Petroleum Directory.*
**Desc:** Directory of Rockies exploration, production, land companies, pipelines, refiners, gas processors, supply and service companies, locations, field locations, key personnel and business activity description.

XO/0035-8231
**ROPA A UHLIE.** [Ropa uhlie]. Began in 1959-. Academic Scholarly Publication. Slovak (table of contents in English, French, German and Russian). mo. $102.00. **(Subscription address:** Slovart GTG Ltd., Krupinska 4, 852 99 Bratislava Slovakia.**) CODEN** ROUHAY. Documents available from CASDDS.
**Ind/Abst** Alum. Ind. Abstr.; Chem. Abstr.; Coal Abstr.; Curr. Biotechnol.; Eng. Mater. Abstr.; Fluid Abstr., Civil Eng.; Fluid Abstr. Proc. Eng.; FLUIDEX; Gas Abstr.; Met. Abstr.

CN/0048-864X
**ROUGHNECK, THE.** (1???)-. Periodical. English. Twelve times a year. 31.00Can$ North America; 41.00Can$ other. Roughneck Publications Ltd., 1600 700 4th Avenue Southwest, Calgary Alberta T2P 3J4 Canada. **Tel** (403)263-6881, FAX (403)263-6886. **ED** Scott Jefferys. **CODEN** ROUGEZ. **Ad Acc, Adv Mgr:** J. Graham. ctrl circ.

●US/1064-9697
**RUSSIAN OIL & GAS GUIDE.** [Russ. oil gas guide]. **Added/Corp** Atlantis International (Firm). **VFOAT** Russian Oil and Gas Guide. Vol. 1, No. 1 (Oct. 1992)-. English. Four times a year. $800.00. PennWell Publishing Company, 1421 South Sheridan, PO Box 1260, Tulsa OK 74101. **Tel** (918)835-3161, (800)331-4463, FAX (918)831-9497. **(Subscription address:** Russian Oil & Gas Guide, PO Box 2002, Tulsa OK 74101.**) LC** HD9575.R8; R87. **DD** 338.7/622338/02547.
**Desc:** Published for companies participating in or interested in the oil and gas industry joint venture operations in the republics of the former Soviet Union.

US/1072-155X
**RUSSIAN PETROLEUM INVESTOR.** [Russ. pet. invest.]. (199?)-. Periodical. English. mo. $2500.00. Almanac Press Inc., 501 South Fairfax Avenue, Suite 206, Los Angeles CA 90036. **Tel** (818)981-7194. **ED** Patricia Szymczas. **DD** 333. **Ad Acc, Adv Mgr:** Moira Brennan. ***Continues*** *Russian Petroleum Intelligence.*

US
**S P E REPRINT SERIES.** **Main/Corp** Society of Petroleum Engineers of Aime. (1968)-. Monographic series. English. ir. Price varies per volume. Society of Petroleum Engineers, PO Box 833836, Richardson TX 75083-3836. **Tel** (214)952-9393 or (214)952-9458, FAX (214)952-9435, telex 163245 (SPEUT).

XR
**SBORNIK PRACI UVP.** **Added/Corp** Ustav pro Vyzkum a Vyuziti Paliv. (196?)-. Periodical. Czech (summaries and/or abstracts in English, German and Russian). **LC** TP315; .P7. **CODEN** SPUVBR. Documents available from CASDDS. ***Continues*** *Prace Ustavu pro Vyzkum a Vyuziti Paliv.*
**Ind/Abst** Chem. Abstr.

XR/0554-9736
**SBORNIK VYSOKE SKOLY CHEMICKO-TECHNOLOGICKE V PRAZE. D, TECHNOLOGIE PALIV.** [Sb. vys. sk. chem.-technol. Praze, Technol. paliv]. **Added/Corp** Vysoka Skola Chemicko-Technologicka v Praze. **VFOAT** Technologie Paliv; Tekhnologiia Topliv; Technology of Fuel; Sbornik Khimiko-Tekhnologicheskogo Instituta, Praga, D, Tekhnologiia Topliv; Scientific Papers of the Institute of Chemical Technology, Prague. D, Technology of Fuel. (196?)-. Czech (German and Russian; summaries and/or abstracts in English, German and Russian). Statni Pedagogicke Nakladatelstvi, Ostrovni 30, 113 01 Prague 1 Czech Republic. **Tel** (2)203787, FAX (2)293883. **LC** TP315; .S26. **CODEN** SVCTA6. Documents available from CASDDS. ***Continues*** *Sbornik Vysoke Skoly Chemicko-Technologicke v Praze. Technologie Paliv, 0554-9736.*
**Ind/Abst** Chem. Abstr.

NO/0332-5334
**SCANDINAVIAN OIL-GAS MAGAZINE.** [Scand. oil-gas mag.]. (1973)-. Periodical. English. Six times a year. Kr360.00 Scandinavia; Kr500.00 Europe; Kr600.00 other. Scandinavian Oil Gas Publishing, PO Box 6865, Oslo 1 Norway. **Tel** 011 47 2 447270. **DD** 665.5. **[CCC].**
**Ind/Abst** Fluid Abstr., Civil Eng.; Fluid Abstr. Proc. Eng.; FLUIDEX (199?-); Selec. Coop. Index Manage. Period.

Petroleum and Natural Gas

UK
**SCOTTISH PETROLEUM ANNUAL.** (1982)-. English. an. Aberdeen Petroleum Publishing Ltd, 35-37 Huntly Street, Aberdeen AB1 1TJ Scotland. **Tel** 011 44 224 644725, FAX 44 224 647574.

JA/0582-4664
**SEKIYU GAKKAI SHI.** [Sekiyu Gakkai shi]. **Added/Corp** Sekiyu Gakkai (Japan). **VFOAT** Journal of the Japan Petroleum Institute; Sekiyu Gakkaishi. (1958)-. Academic Scholarly Publication. Japanese (English). bm. $195.00. Sakiyu Gakkai, (Japan Petroleum Inst.), Chiyoda Seimei Ikebukuro Biru, 27-12, Nishiikebukuro 3 Chome, Toshimaku, Tokyoto 171, Japan. **(Subscription address:** Maruzen Company Ltd., PO Box 5050, Import & Export Department, Tokyo 100 31 Japan.**) CODEN** SKGSAE. **[CCC].** Documents available from CASDDS. ***Absorbed*** *Bulletin of the Japan Petroleum Institute, 0582-4656.* ***Continued in part by*** *Petorotekku, 0386-2763.*
**Ind/Abst** Chem. Abstr.; Chem. Titles; Coal Abstr.; Curr. Biotechnol.; Energy Res. Abstr. (March 1976-); Lit. Pat. Abstr., Oilfield Chem. (1969-1991); Lit. Abstr., Catal. Catal.; Lit. Abstr., Health Environ.; Lit. Abstr., Pet. Refin. Petrochem.; Lit. Abstr., Pet. Substit.; Lit. Abstr., Transp. Storage.

JA/0370-9868
**SEKIYU GIJUTSU KYOKAISHI.** [Sekiyu Gijutsu Kyokaishi]. **Main/Corp** Sekiyu Gijutsu Kyokai. **Added/Corp** Sekiyu Gijutsu Kyokai. **VFOAT** Journal of the Japanese Association of Petroleum Technologists. (Oct. 1933)-. Academic Scholarly Publication. Japanese (English; summaries and/or abstracts in Japanese and English). Six times a year. $144.00. Sekiyu Gijutsu Kyokai, (Japanese Assoc. for Petroleum Technology), 9-4, Otemachi 1 Chome, Chiyodaku, Tokyoto 100, Japan. **(Subscription address:** Kyowa Book Company Inc., 1 38 Kanda Jinbocho Chiyoda-ku, Tokyo 101 Japan.**) CODEN** SGKYAO. **Circ:** 2,500 (ctrl). Documents available from CASDDS.
**Desc:** Report of research and monographs about petroleum technology.
**Ind/Abst** Chem. Abstr.; Coal Abstr.; GeoRef.

JA
**SEKIYU NENKAN.** 1980-. Japanese. an. ¥9200. Marunouchi Shuppan, Maru Biru 5-kai, Marunouchi 2-4-1 Chiyoda-ku, Tokyo-to 100 Japan.

JA
**SEKIYU SHUNJU.** Periodical. Japanese. mo. ¥12000. Sekiyu Bunkasha, 4-9, Nihonbashi Honcho 1 Chome, Chuoku, Tokyoto 103 Japan. **LC** HD9576.J3; S465.

JA
**SEKIYU TO SHOHI DOTAI TOKEI NENPO, SHO-KO-KOGYO / TSUSHO SANGYO DAIJIN KANBO CHOSA TOKEIBU HEN.** **Added/Corp** Japan. Tsusho Sangyosho. Chosa Tokeibu. **VFOAT** Yearbook of the Current Survey of Oil Consumption in Commerce, Mining and Manufacturing. (1983)-. Japanese. an. Tsusan Tokei Kyokai, (International Trade & Industry Statistics Assoc.), 8-9, Ginza 2 Chome, Chuoku, Tokyoto 104, Japan. **LC** HC462.9; .E473. ***Continues*** *Energi Shohi Dotai Tokei Nenpo. Sho-Ko-Kogyo.*

US/0488-3896
**SERVICE STATION MANAGEMENT.** ***Title Change.*** **See** Transportation-Automobiles.

US/0582-8872
**SEVENTY SIX.** **Added/Corp** Union Oil Company of California. Vol. 1, (1957)-. Periodical. English. bm. Free. Union Oil Company, 1201 West 5th Street, Los Angeles CA 90017. **Tel** (213)486-6823.
**Ind/Abst** Energy Inf. Abstr.

US/0037-3257
**SHALE SHAKER.** **See** Earth Sciences-Geology.

US/0275-3243
**SHELL NEWS.** [Shell news]. **Added/Corp** Shell Oil Company. Shell Oil Company, Inc. (19??)-. Periodical. English. bm. must order direct. Shell Oil Company, 1544 One Shell Plaza, PO Box 2463, Houston TX 77252. **Tel** (713)241-5350. **LC** TP690.A1; S5. **DD** 665.5065.
**Ind/Abst** GeoRef.

US
**SHIELD : THE INTERNATIONAL MAGAZINE OF THE BP GROUP.** ***Ceased.*** **Added/Corp** BP America (Firm). **VFOAT** Shield Magazine. Spring (1991)-(1993). Periodical. English. qt. ***Continues*** *Scene (Cleveland, Ohio), 1051-2683.*
**Ind/Abst** Ecol. Abstr.

CC
**SHIH YU TI CHIU WU LI KAN TAN.** **See** Engineering-Mines and Mining Engineering.

CC/1000-8144
**SHIYOU HUAGONG.** (SHIH YU HUA KUNG.). [Shiyou huagong]. **Added/Corp** Pei-Ching Hua Hsueh Kung Yeh Yen Chiu Yuan. **VFOAT** Petrochemical Technology. (19??)-. Academic Scholarly Publication. Chinese. Twelve times a year. $5.00. The Scientific and Technical Information Research Institute of the Ministry of Chemical Industry, Huaxue Gongye Bu, Beijing Huagong Yanjiuyuan, PO Box 1442, Hepingli, Beijing People's Republic of China. **Tel** 4216131, FAX 4228661. **LC** TP692.3; .S566. **DD** 661/.804/05. **CODEN** SHHUE8. Documents available from CASDDS.
**Ind/Abst** Chem. Abstr. (1985-).

CC/1000-0747
**SHIYOU KANTAN KAIFA.** (SHIH YU KAN TAN YU KAI FA.). [Shiyou kantan kaifa]. **Added/Corp** Shih yu Kan Tan Kai fa Ko Hsueh yen Chiu Yuan (China). **VFOAT** Petroleum Exploration and Development. Began in (1974). Academic Scholarly Publication. Chinese (English; summaries and/or abstracts in English). bm. RMBY15.00. Science Press, 16 Donghuangchenggen North Street, Beijing 100707, People's Republic of China. **Tel** 011 86 1 4019821, 011 86 1 4010642, FAX 011 86 1 4012180, 011 86 1 4019810, telex 210147. **ED** Ain Tong-Loa. **LC** TN870.5; .S473. **DD** 553.2/82/05. **CODEN** SKYKEG. **Ad Acc. Circ:** 25,000. Documents available from CASDDS.
**Desc:** Involved in petroleum geology: oil-gas development, reservoir, engineering, seismic survey and well logging, etc.
**Ind/Abst** Chem. Abstr.; GeoRef.

CH/1001-4101
**SHIYOU LIANZHI.** **VFOAT** Petroleum Processing. (1957)-. Periodical. Chinese. mo. **DD** 665.5.
**Ind/Abst** Lit. Pat. Abstr., Oilfield Chem.; Lit. Abstr., Catal. Catal.; Lit. Abstr., Health Environ.; Lit. Abstr., Pet. Refin. Petrochem.; Lit. Abstr., Pet. Substit.; Lit. Abstr., Transp. Storage.

CC/0253-2697
**SHIYOU XUEBAO.** (SHIH YU HSUEH PAO.). [Shiyou xuebao]. **Added/Corp** Chung-Kuo Shih yu Hsueh Hui (Peking, China). **VFOAT** Acta Petrolei Sinica. Vol. 1, No. 1 (Jan. 1980)-. Academic Scholarly Publication. Chinese (summaries and/or abstracts in English; table of contents in English). qt. $19.60. **(Subscription address:** China International Book Trading Corporation, PO Box 399, Library Service Department, Beijing 100044 People's Republic of China.**) LC** TN860; .S476. **DD** 665/.5/05. **CODEN** SYHPD9. Documents available from Petroleum Abstracts Document Delivery Service, CASDDS.
**Ind/Abst** Chem. Abstr.; Ei Page One; Energy Res. Abstr. (Feb. 1981-); Fluid Abstr., Civil Eng.; Fluid Abstr. Proc. Eng.; FLUIDEX (1980-1989); GeoRef; Lit. Pat. Abstr., Oilfield Chem.; Lit. Abstr., Catal. Catal.; Lit. Abstr., Health Environ.; Lit. Abstr., Pet. Refin. Petrochem.; Lit. Abstr., Pet. Substit.; Lit. Abstr., Transp. Storage; Pet. Abstr.

CC/1001-8719
**SHIYOU XUEBAO. SHIYOU JIAGONG.** (SHIH YU HSUEH PAO. SHIH YU CHIA KUNG.). [Shiyou xuebao, Shiyou jiagong]. **Added/Corp** Chung-kuo Shih yu Hsueh Hui (Peking, China). Shih yu Lien Chih Wei Yuan Hui. **VFOAT** Shih yu Chia Kung; Acta Petrolei Sinica. Petroleum Processing Section. (198?)-. Academic Scholarly Publication. Chinese. qt. **CODEN** SXSHEY. Documents available from CASDDS.
**Ind/Abst** Chem. Abstr. (1985-).

CC/0253-9985
**SHIYOU YU TIANRANQI DIZHI.** (SHIH YU YU TIEN JAN CHI TI CHIH.). [Shiyou yu tianranqi dizhi]. **Added/Corp** China. Shih yu pu Cha Kan tn Chu. Chung Kuo ti Chih Hsueh Hui (Peking, China). Shih yu ti Chih Chuan Yeh Wei Yuan Hui. **VFOAT** Oil and Gas Geology; Oil & Gas Geology. (1980)-. Academic Scholarly Publication. Chinese (summaries and/or abstracts in English). qt. $14.66 (surface mail). **(Subscription address:** China International Book Trading Corporation, PO Box 399, Library Service Department, Beijing 100044 People's Republic of China.**) LC** TN876.C5; S49. **DD** 553.2/8/05. **CODEN** SYYCDL. Documents available from CASDDS.
**Ind/Abst** Chem. Abstr.; GeoRef.

US/1049-488X
**SITUATION AND OUTLOOK REPORT. OIL CROPS.** [Situat. outlook rep., Oil crops]. **VFOAT** Oil Crops; Situation and and Outlook Yearbook. Oil Crops; Oil Crops Situation and Outlook. OCS-11 (July 1986)-. Periodical. English. qt. $19.00. U.S. Department of Agriculture, ERS-NASS, 341 Victory Drive, Herndon VA 22070. **Tel** (800)999-6779. **LC** HD9490.U5; A33. **DD** 338.1/7385/0973021. **CODEN** OCSRE9. ***Continues*** *Outlook and Situation Report. Oil Crops, 0738-4890.*
**Ind/Abst** BioBusiness; F&S Index Plus Text, Int. [Select. Cov.]; Foods Adlibra; Trade Ind. ASAP [Full Txt.]; Trade Ind. Index [Full Txt.]; World Agric. Econ.

UK
**SOFTWARE DIRECTORY FOR THE OFFSHORE INDUSTRY.** **See** Computers-Software.

KO
**SOGYU.** **VFOAT** Petroleum. Periodical. Korean (Korean). qt. Free. Hanguk Sogyu Kaebal Kongsa, 45 Mugyo-dong, Chung-ku, Seoul South Korea. **LC** HD9560.1; .S65.

KO
**SOGYU YONBO.** 1982-. English. Taehan Sogyu Hyophoe, 10 Kwanchol-dong, Chongno-ku, Seoul South Korea. **LC** HD9576.K6; S65.

US/0273-1843
**SOHIO NEWS.** Periodical. English. mo. The Standard Oil Company Ohio, 1762 Guildhall Building, J Eppink, Cleveland OH 44115. **Tel** (216)575-5568.
**Ind/Abst** Predicasts F&S Index, U. S. Annu. Ed.

SI
**SOUTH EAST ASIA ACTIVITY REPORT.** English. mo. $85.00. Lyndon West, IEDS Ltd, Enterprise House, Cirencester Road, Ilsom Tetbury, 9 LOS 9L8 8RX UK. **Tel** 0666-505151, FAX 0666-504704, telex 43605 BRISK G. Index available (bound in each issue). ctrl circ.
**Desc:** A monthly publication illustrated by maps, detailing oil industry exploration activity within 11 countries in South East Asia. Detailed schedules of contracts awarded and wells drilled.

UK
**SOUTH EAST ASIA OIL SERVICE.** English. mo. £4,750.00. Wood Mackenzie Consultants Ltd., Kintore House, 74 77 Queen Street, Edinburgh EH2 4NS Scotland. **Tel** 011 44 031 225 8525, FAX 011 44 031 243 4435, telex 72555.

US/1071-4804
**SOUTHWEST OIL AND GAS WORLD.** ***Title Change.*** [Southwest oil gas world]. **VFOAT** Oil and Gas World. Vol. 42, No. 3 (June/July 1993)-(Feb. 1994). Periodical. English. bm. Hart Publications Inc, 1900 Grant Street, Suite 400, Denver CO 80203. **Tel** (303)837-1917, (800)832-1917, FAX (303)837-8585. **DD** 333. ***Continues*** *Southwest Oil World, 0884-6219.* ***Merged with*** *Gulf Coast Oil and Gas World; Western Oil and Gas World; Northeast Oil and Gas World; Midcontinent Oil and Gas World; Pacific Oil and Gas World* ***to form*** *Hart's Oil and Gas World, 1075-5365.*
**Ind/Abst** GeoRef (19??-19??).

US/0884-6219
**SOUTHWEST OIL WORLD.** ***Title Change.*** [Southwest oil world]. Vol. 34, No. 8 (Aug. 1985)-(1993). Periodical. English. mo. Hart Publications Inc, 1900 Grant Street, Suite 400, Denver CO 80203. **Tel** (303)837-1917, (800)832-1917, FAX (303)837-8585. **ED** Don Lyle. **LC** TN860; .D65. **DD** 338. **[CCC].** Index available. **Ad Acc. Circ:** 4,332. available on microfilm from University Microfilms International (UMI). Documents available from Petroleum Abstracts Document Delivery Service. ***Continues*** *Drill Bit, 0012-6225.* ***Continued by*** *Southwest Oil and Gas World, 1071-4804.*
**Ind/Abst** GeoRef; Pet. Abstr.

US/0584-8016
**SPAN (CHICAGO, ILL.).** **See** Business-Investments.

US/1064-9778
**SPE COMPUTER APPLICATIONS.** [SPE comput. appl.]. **Added/Corp** SPE Microcomputer Users Group. **VFOAT** Computer Applications; Society of Petroleum Engineers Computer Applications. (Mar./Apr. 1989)-. Periodical. English. bm. $45.00 North America, $57.00 other. Society of Petroleum Engineers, PO Box 833836, Richardson TX 75083-3836. **Tel** (214)952-9393 or (214)952-9458, FAX (214)952-9435, telex 163245 (SPEUT). **LC** TN871; .S656. **DD** 665.5/0285. **CODEN** SCAPEP. **[CCC].**
**Desc:** Abstracts of programs, program listings, detailed reports on computer applications in petroleum engineering, hardware and software reviews, details on petroleum-computing activities, programming tips, and general computer application news.

●US/1064-6671
**SPE DRILLING AND COMPLETIONS.** [SPE drill. & complet.]. **Added/Corp** Society of Petroleum Engineers (U.S.). **VFOAT** SPE Drilling and Completion. **VAT** Society of Petroleum Engineers Drilling and Completions. (1993)-. Periodical. English. qt (Mar., June, Sept., Dec.). $60.00 North America, $75.00 other. Society of Petroleum Engineers, PO Box 833836, Richardson TX 75083-3836. **Tel** (214)952-9393 or (214)952-9458, FAX (214)952-9435, telex 163245 (SPEUT). **LC** TN871.2; .S65. **DD** 622/.3381. **CODEN** SDCOE5. **[CCC].** ***Continues*** *PE Drilling Engineering, 0885-9744.*
**Desc:** Technical papers covering bit technology, case histories, casing, cementing, completions, deviation control, directional drilling, drilling fluids, drilling operations, equipment and instrumentation, measurement-while-drilling techniques, offshore drilling, perforation, sand control, simulation of drilling systems, tubulars, and well control.
**Ind/Abst** AESIS Q.; Appl. Sci. Technol. Index.

US/0885-9744
**SPE DRILLING ENGINEERING.** ***Title Change.*** (SPE DRILLING ENGINEERING : AN OFFICIAL PUBLICATION OF THE SOCIETY OF PETROLEUM ENGINEERS.). [SPE drill. eng.]. **Added/Corp** Society of Petroleum Engineers (U.S.). **VFOAT** Drilling Engineering. **VAT** Society of Petroleum Engineers Drilling Engineering. Vol. 1 No. 1 (Feb. 1986)-Vol. 7 No. 4 (Dec. 1992). Periodical. English. qt. Society of Petroleum Engineers, PO Box 833836,

Richardson TX 75083-3836. **Tel** (214)952-9393 or (214)952-9458, FAX (214)952-9435, telex 163245 (SPEUT). **ED** Keith Millheim. **LC** TN871.2; .S65. **DD** 622/.3381. **CODEN** SDENEC. **[CCC].** Index available. cum. index. **Ad Acc. Circ:** 9,000. available on microfilm and microfiche from University Microfilms International (UMI). Documents available from Article Express International, Petroleum Abstracts Document Delivery Service. ***Continues in part*** *Society of Petroleum Engineers Journal, 0197-7520.* ***Continued by*** *SPE Drilling & Completion, 1064-6671.*
**Desc:** Covers oilfield tools, services, materials and equipment that the industry's top oil and gas engineers use every day.
**Ind/Abst** Appl. Sci. Technol. Index; Ei Page One; Eng. Index Annu.; Fluid Abstr., Civil Eng.; Fluid Abstr. Proc. Eng.; FLUIDEX; GeoRef; Pet. Abstr.

US/0885-923X
**SPE FORMATION EVALUATION.** (SPE FORMATION EVALUATION : AN OFFICIAL PUBLICATION OF THE SOCIETY OF PETROLEUM ENGINEERS.). [SPE form. eval.]. **Added/Corp** Society of Petroleum Engineers (U.S.). **VFOAT** Formation Evaluation. **VAT** Society of Petroleum Engineers Formation Evaluation. Vol. 1 No. 1 (Feb. 1986)-. Academic Scholarly Publication. English. qt (Mar., June, Sept., Dec.). $60.00 North America; $75.00 other. Society of Petroleum Engineers, PO Box 833836, Richardson TX 75083-3836. **Tel** (214)952-9393 or (214)952-9458, FAX (214)952-9435, telex 163245 (SPEUT). **ED** Hossein Kazemi. **LC** TN871.35; .S66. **DD** 622/.3382. **CODEN** SFEVEG. **[CCC].** Index available. cum. index. **Ad Acc. Circ:** 8,000. available on microfilm and microfiche from University Microfilms International (UMI). Documents available from Article Express International, Petroleum Abstracts Document Delivery Service, CASDDS. ***Continues in part*** *Society of Petroleum Engineers Journal, 0197-7520.*
**Desc:** Engineering reports on well logging, well testing, geological methods, and other ways to define the nature of oil and gas-bearing formations.
**Ind/Abst** AESIS Q.; Appl. Sci. Technol. Index (-1990); Chem. Abstr. (1986-); Ei Page One; Eng. Index Annu.; Fluid Abstr., Civil Eng.; Fluid Abstr. Proc. Eng.; FLUIDEX; GeoRef; Pet. Abstr.

US/1059-4507
**SPE MEMBERSHIP DIRECTORY.** (SPE ANNUAL MEMBERSHIP DIRECTORY.). **Main/Corp** Society of Petroleum Engineers (U.S.). **Added/Corp** Society of Petroleum Engineers (U.S.). **VFOAT** Membership Directory. **VAT** Society of Petroleum Engineers Annual Membership Directory. (1992)-. English. an (Published in May). $150.00 North America; $155.00 other. Society of Petroleum Engineers, PO Box 833836, Richardson TX 75083-3836. **Tel** (214)952-9393 or (214)952-9458, FAX (214)952-9435, telex 163245 (SPEUT). **LC** TN867; .S64a. **DD** 665.5/025/73. ***Continues*** *JPT. Annual Review and Membership Directory.*
**Desc:** Alphabetical listing of more than 52,000 Society members with addresses, titles, phone or telex numbers, plus company listing of these members sorted by employer and company name.

●US/1064-668X
**SPE PRODUCTION AND FACILITIES.** [SPE prod. facil.]. **Added/Corp** Society of Petroleum Engineers (U.S.). **VFOAT** SPE Production and Facilities. **VAT** Society of Petroleum Engineers Production and Facilities. (1993)-. Academic Scholarly Publication. English. qt (Feb., May, Aug., Nov.). $60.00 North America; $75.00 other. Society of Petroleum Engineers, PO Box 833836, Richardson TX 75083-3836. **Tel** (214)952-9393 or (214)952-9458, FAX (214)952-9435, telex 163245 (SPEUT). **LC** TN870; .S557. **DD** 622/.3382. **CODEN** SPRFEZ. **[CCC].** Documents available from CASDDS. ***Continues*** *SPE Production Engineering, 0885-9221.*
**Desc:** Technical and field reports on acidizing, artificial lift, case histories, design and operation of surface facilities, downhole equipment design and operation, drillstem testing, formation damage control, fracturing, gas production, gas storage, measurement of production streams, multiphase flow in tubulars, offshore operations, pipelines, production logging, production metering and control systems, production optimization systems, sand control, separation and processing, and workovers.
**Ind/Abst** Chem. Abstr. (1993-).

US/0885-9221
**SPE PRODUCTION ENGINEERING.** ***Title Change.*** (SPE PRODUCTION ENGINEERING : AN OFFICIAL PUBLICATION OF THE SOCIETY OF PETROLEUM ENGINEERS.). [SPE prod. eng.]. **Added/Corp** Society of Petroleum Engineers (U.S.). **VFOAT** Production Engineering. **VAT** Society of Petroleum Engineers Production Engineering. Vol. 1 No. 1 (Jan. 1986)-Vol. 7 No. 4 (Nov. 1992). Academic Scholarly Publication. English. qt. Society of Petroleum Engineers, PO Box 833836, Richardson TX 75083-3836. **Tel** (214)952-9393 or (214)952-9458, FAX (214)952-9435, telex 163245 (SPEUT). **ED** Ali Daneshy. **LC** TN870; .S557. **DD** 622/.3382. **CODEN** SPENES. **[CCC].** Index available. cum. index. **Bk Rev. Ad Acc. Circ:** 14,000. available on microfilm and microfiche from University Microfilms International (UMI). Documents available from Article Express International, Petroleum Abstracts Document Delivery Service, CASDDS. ***Continues in part*** *Society of Petroleum Engineers Journal, 0197-7520.* ***Continued by*** *SPE Production & Facilities, 1064-668X.*
**Desc:** Engineering and management reports on oil and gas well completions, producing methods and equipment, cementing, stimulation, casing, logging, and operation.
**Ind/Abst** AESIS Q.; Appl. Sci. Technol. Index; Chem. Abstr. (1986-); Ei Page One; Eng. Index Annu.; Fluid Abstr., Civil Eng.; Fluid Abstr. Proc. Eng.; FLUIDEX; GeoRef; Pet. Abstr.

US/0885-9248
**SPE RESERVOIR ENGINEERING.** [SPE reserv. eng.]. **Added/Corp** Society of Petroleum Engineers (U.S.). **VFOAT** Reservoir Engineering. **VAT** Society of Petroleum Engineers Reservoir Engineering. Vol. 1, No. 1 (Jan. 1986)-. Academic Scholarly Publication. English. qt (Feb., May, Aug., Nov.). $60.00 North America; $75.00 other. Society of Petroleum Engineers, PO Box 833836, Richardson TX 75083-3836. **Tel** (214)952-9393 or (214)952-9458, FAX (214)952-9435, telex 163245 (SPEUT). **ED** Donald W. Peaceman. **LC** TN871; .S66. **DD** 622/.3382. **CODEN** SREEEF. **[CCC].** Index available. **Ad Acc. Circ:** 12,000. available on microfilm and microfiche from University Microfilms International (UMI). Documents available from Article Express International, Petroleum Abstracts Document Delivery Service, CASDDS. ***Continues in part*** *Society of Petroleum Engineers Journal, 0197-7520.*
**Desc:** Engineering reports on oil and gas reservoirs, including computer simulation and measurement and prediction of their producing characteristics and potential.
**Ind/Abst** Appl. Sci. Technol. Index (-1990); Chem. Abstr. (1986-); Ei Page One; Eng. Index Annu.; GeoRef; Lit. Pat. Abstr., Oilfield Chem. (1990-); Lit. Abstr., Catal. Catal.; Lit. Abstr., Health Environ.; Lit. Abstr., Pet. Refin. Petrochem.; Lit. Abstr., Pet. Substit.; Lit. Abstr., Transp. Storage; Pet. Abstr.; Sug. Indus. Abstr.

US/0560-642X
**SPE : SOCIETY OF PETROLEUM ENGINEERS OF AIME.** [SPE - Soc. Pet. Eng. AIME]. **Added/Corp** Society of Petroleum Engineers of AIME. Society of Petroleum Engineers of AIME. Papers. Society of Petroleum Engineers Of AIME Preprints. (19??)-. Monographic series. English. ir. Society of Petroleum Engineers, PO Box 833836, Richardson TX 75083-3836. **Tel** (214)952-9393 or (214)952-9458, FAX (214)952-9435, telex 163245 (SPEUT).
**Ind/Abst** Civ. Struct. Eng. Abstr.; Environ. Eng. Abstr.; GeoRef; Manuf. Process Eng. Abstr.; Mater. Sci. Eng. Abstr.; Mech. Eng. Abstr.

US/0163-1969
**SPEARS REPORT, DRILLING.** **Main/Corp** Spears and Associates. **VFOAT** Drilling. 1978-. English. an. Jamie M Spear, 4608 South Garnett Road/#510, Tulsa OK 74146-5207. **LC** HD9561. **DD** 380.1/45/6817665.

US/0193-2438
**SPEARS REPORT, PRODUCTION.** **Main/Corp** Spears and Associates. **VFOAT** Production. English. Spears and Associates Inc, 5525 East 51st Street, Tulsa OK 74135. **LC** HD9569.S67; S66A. **DD** 338.4/7/68176650973.

IT
**STAFFETTA QUOTIDIANA PETROLIFERA.** Began with 29 Ott. 1980 issue. Periodical. Italian. da. Rivista Italiana del Petrolio, Via Aventina 19, 00153 Rome Italy. **LC** TN860; .R57. ***Continues*** *Staffetta Quotidiana Petrolifera e Delle Altre Fonti di Energia.*

US/1043-0369
**STALSBY/WILSON'S PETROLEUM SUPPLY AMERICAS.** [Stalsby/Wilson's pet. supply Am.]. **Added/Corp** Stalsby/Wilson. **VFOAT** Stalsby Wilson's Petroleum Supply Americas; Petroleum Supply Americas. 22nd Ed. (Apr. 1989)-. English. sa. $125.00 US; $135.00 other. Stalsby Wilson Associates, PO Box 19976, Houston TX 77224. **Tel** (713)496-1734, FAX (713)531-7229, telex 401428 SWPRESS. **LC** HD9563; .S73. **DD** 338.7/6655/02573. ***Continues*** *Stalsby/Wilson's Who's Who in Petroleum Supply, 1043-0148.*

US/1043-0377
**STALSBY/WILSON'S PETROLEUM SUPPLY EUROPE.** [Stalsby/Wilson's pet. supply Eur.]. **VFOAT** Stalsby Wilson's Petroleum Supply Europe; Petroleum Supply Europe. (Mar. 1989)-. English. sa (March and Sept.). $115.00. Stalsby Wilson Associates, PO Box 19976, Houston TX 77224. **Tel** (713)496-1734, FAX (713)531-7229, telex 401428 SWPRESS. **LC** HD9575.A1; S7. **DD** 338.7/6655/0254.

US/0897-2028
**STALSBY/ WILSON'S WHO'S WHO IN NATURAL GAS SUPPLY.** [Who's who nat. gas supply]. **VFOAT** Stalsby Wilson's Who's Who in Natural Gas Supply; Who's Who in Natural Gas Supply. **VAT** Stalsby Wilson's who's who in natural gas supply. (1988)-. English. sa. $125.00 US; $135.00 other. Stalsby Wilson Associates, PO Box 19976, Houston TX 77224. **Tel** (713)496-1734, FAX (713)531-7229, telex 401428 SWPRESS. **ED** Kathleen A Sauve, Theresa Williamson and Lanna Little. **LC** HD9581.U49; W47. **DD** 338.7/6223385/02573. Index available. cum. index. **Ad Acc. Circ:** 500.
**Desc:** Complete registry of gas producers, processors, transporters, marketers and major buyers. Includes titles, names and addresses.

US
**STANDARD FOR THE STORAGE AND HANDLING OF LIQUEFIED PETROLEUM GASES.** (19??)-. English. ir. $25.50 nonmembers; $23.00 members. National Fire Protection Association, 1 Batterymarch Park, PO Box 9101, Quincy MA 02269-9101. **Tel** (617)770-3000, (800)344-3555.

US
**STANDARD GAS CODE AMENDMENTS.** English. $19.50 (nonmembers), $13.00 (members). Southern Building Code Congress International, 900 Montclair Road, Birmingham AL 35213. **Tel** (205)591-1853.

UK
**STANDARD METHODS FOR ANALYSIS AND TESTING OF PETROLEUM AND RELATED PRODUCTS.** **Added/Corp** Institute of Petroleum (Great Britain). **VFOAT** Methods for Analysis and Testing of Petroleum and Related Products. (1987)-. English. an. £195.00. John Wiley & Sons Ltd., Baffins Lane, Chichester West Sussex PO19 1UD England. **Tel** 0243 779777, FAX 0243 776128 BTG:JWP001, telex 86290 WIBOOKG. **ED** John Phipps. **LC** TP691; .I5. **DD** 665.5/028/7. Index available. cum. index. **Ad Acc.** ***Continues*** *IP Standards for Petroleum and its Products.*

US/0739-5205
**STANGER'S DRILLING FUND YEARBOOK.** [Stanger's Drill. fund yearb.]. English. an. Robert A Stanger and Company, PO Box 7490, Shrewsbury NJ 07702. **Tel** (201)389-3600, (800)631-2291, FAX (201)389-1751. **LC** HD9561; .S74. **DD** 338.2/3.

US/0749-8527
**STATE ACTION REPORTER, NATURAL GAS AND ELECTRIC POWER. ABSTRACTS/INDEX.** (STATE ACTION REPORTER ... NATURAL GAS AND ELECTRIC POWER. ABSTRACTS/INDEX / RIS, REGULATORY INFORMATION SERVICE.). [State action rep. nat. gas electr. power, Abstr./index]. **VFOAT** State Action Reporter Abstracts/Index; Natural Gas and Electric Power. Abstracts/Index; State Action Reporter. Vol. 1, No. 1 (July 1984)-. English. mo. RIS, 4520 East-West Highway Suite 800, Bethesda MD 20814. **DD** 016.

US/1071-8419
**STATION & STORE PRODUCTS.** ***Ceased.*** [Station store prod.]. **VFOAT** Station and Store Products. (1993)-(Feb. 1994). Periodical. English. mo (10 issues). Hunter Publishing Company Inc., 25 Northwest Point Boulevard, Suite 800, Elk Grove Village IL 60007-1036. **Tel** (708)427-9512, FAX (708)427-2097. **DD** 338. ***Continues*** *Petroleum/C-Store Products, 0899-6369.*

US
**STATISTICAL BULLETIN.** Statistical Publication. English. mo. Free upon request. Arkansas Oil & Gas Commission, 314 East Oak, El Dorado AR 71730. **Tel** (501)862-4965. **ED** Shirley Knight. **Circ:** 350. ***Continues*** *Arkansas Oil and Gas Statistical Bulletin.*
**Desc:** Monthly crude oil and natural gas production.

US
**STATISTICAL REPORT.** **See** Petroleum and Natural Gas-Abstracting, Bibliographies and Statistics.

FR
**STATISTIQUES DE L'INDUSTRIE GAZIERE EN FRANCE.** **See** Petroleum and Natural Gas-Abstracting, Bibliographies and Statistics.

FR
**STATISTIQUES F. O. A. : DISTRIBUTION DES FUELS-OILS.** **See** Petroleum and Natural Gas-Abstracting, Bibliographies and Statistics.

PH
**STATUS OF THE CONSUMER PRICE EQUALIZATION FUND ... / MINISTRY OF ENERGY.** English. Ministry of Energy, 7901 Makati Avenue, Makati Metro Manila Philippines. **LC** HD9576.P6; S75. **DD** 354.5990072/47.

BE
**STATUTS, LISTE DES MEMBRES - INSTITUT BELGE DU PETROLE.** **Main/Corp** Institut Belge du Petrole. **Added/Corp** Institut Belge du Petrole. Statuten, Ledenlijst - Belgisch Petroleum Instituut. **VFOAT** Statuten, Ledenlijst - Belgisch Petroleum Instituut. (19??)-. Multiple languages (Flemish and French). Institut Belge du Petrole, rue de la Science 4, 1040 Bruxelles Belgium. **LC** HD9575.B42; I57a. **DD** 338.2/7/282062493.

RU/0039-2448
**STROITELSTVO TRUBOPROVODOV.** **Added/Corp** Soviet Union. Ministerstvo Stroitelstva Predpriiatii Neftianoi Promyshlennosti. Soviet Union. Glavnoe Upravlenie Gazovoi Promyshlennosti. Soviet Union. Gosudarstvennyi Proizvodstvennyi Komitet po Gazovoi Promyshlennosti. Soviet Union. Ministerstvo Gazovoi Promyshlennosti. Soviet Union. Ministerstvo Stoitelstvo redpriatii Neftianoi i Gazovoi Promyshlennosti. Vol. 1, (March 1956)-. Academic Scholarly Publication. Russian. mo. $79.95. Izdatelstvo Nedra, 3 Pl Belorusskogo Vakzala, 125047 Moscow Russia. **Tel** 250-52-55. **(Subscription address:** East View Publications Inc., 3020 Harbor Lane North, Suite 110, Minneapolis MN 55447.**)** **LC** TN879.5; .S75. **CODEN** STTRA3. **[CCC].** Documents available from CASDDS. ***Continues*** *Stroitelstvo Predriiatii Neftianoi Promyshlennosti.*
**Ind/Abst** Chem. Abstr. (1958-1983); Gas Abstr.

US
**SUMMARY OF NATURAL GAS STATISTICS / OHIO DEPARTMENT OF ENERGY.** **See** Petroleum and Natural Gas-Abstracting, Bibliographies and Statistics.

US/0276-8453
**SUMMARY OF OIL FIELDS WELL CHANGES.** (SUMMARY OF ... OIL FIELDS WELL CHANGES / CONSERVATION COMMITTEE OF CALIFORNIA OIL PRODUCERS.). English. Conservation Committee of California Oil Producers, 417 South Hill Street/Suite 930, Los Angeles CA 90013. **Tel** (310)625-7731.

US/0889-3497
**SUN MAGAZINE.** ***Title Change.*** [Sun mag.]. **Added/Corp** Sun Company. **VFOAT** Sun. Vol. 43 (Winter 1978)-(19??). Periodical. English. Three times a year. Sun Company, 1801 Market Street, Philadelphia PA 19103. **Tel** (215)977-3000. **ED** Peter E. Brakman. **DD** 665. **Circ:** 80,000 (ctrl). ***Continues*** *Our Sun.* ***Merged with*** *Quarterly Report. Sun Company.*
**Desc:** Reports on Sun's business directions; executive and employee profiles; energy industry trends; social, cultural and educational programs supported by Sun.
**Ind/Abst** Fluid Abstr., Civil Eng.; Fluid Abstr. Proc. Eng.; FLUIDEX (19??-); Index Free Period.

FR/0249-0420
**SUPPLEMENT AU BULLETIN ANALYTIQUE PETROLIER.** ***Title Change.*** [Suppl. Bull. anal. pet.]. (1960)-(1993). Periodical. French. Twenty-three times a year. Comite Professionnel du Petrol CPDP, BP 282, 92505 Rueil Malmaison France. **Tel** 011 33 1 47169460. **UDC** 665.6. **Bk Rev**. **Circ:** 700. ***Split into*** *Notes D Information Economique* ***and*** *Bulletin Analytique Petrolier, 0007-4101.*
**Desc:** Contains abstracts of articles about oil and energy.

US
**SURVEY OF FINANCIAL REPORTING AND ACCOUNTING DEVELOPMENTS IN THE PETROLEUM INDUSTRY, A.** **See** Business-Accounting.

US/0161-5920
**SURVEY OF SECONDARY AND ENHANCED RECOVERY OPERATIONS IN TEXAS, A.** **Main/Corp** Railroad Commission of Texas. Oil and Gas Division. Engineering Research and Inspection. **Added/Corp** Texas Petroleum Research Committee. (1976)-. English. an. $32.00. Railroad Commission of Texas, PO Drawer 12967, Capitol Station, Austin TX 78711. **Tel** (512)463-7255. **LC** TN864; .T42 subser; TN872; .T4. **DD** 665/.5/09764 S; 622/.33/8209764. ***Continues*** *Railroad Commission of Texas. Oil and Gas Division. Engineering Research and Inspection. Survey of Enhanced Recovery Operations in Texas.*

US
**SYMPOSIUM ON PETROLEUM ECONOMICS AND EVALUATION.** **Main/Corp** Symposium on Petroleum Economics and Evaluation. English. ir. Society of Petroleum Engineers, PO Box 833836, Richardson TX 75083-3836. **Tel** (214)952-9393 or (214)952-9458, FAX (214)952-9435, telex 163245 (SPEUT).

US/0732-1120
**SYNFUELS HANDBOOK.** [Synfuels hand.]. **VAT** Synfuels Hand Book. 1980-. English. an. $67.00. Coal Week, McGraw Hill, 1221 Avenue of the Americas, New York NY 10020. **Tel** (212)512-2000, (800)525-5003, FAX (212)512-6111. **LC** TP360; .S9397. **DD** 662/.66/05.

US/0273-2971
**SYNTHETIC FUELS UPDATE.** [Synth. fuels update]. SFU-81/1 (Jan. 1981)-. English. mo. $45.00 US; $90.00 other. National Technical Information Service - NTIS, Room 2027S, 5285 Port Royal Road, Springfield VA 22161. **Tel** (703)487-4630, (703)487-4660, (703)487-4650, FAX (703)321-8547, telex 89-9405. **LC** TP360; .S955. **DD** 662/.66/05.

CN/0704-9811
**TAR PAPER (EDMONTON).** (THE TAR PAPER.). [Tar pap.]. **Added/Corp** Alberta Research Council. Oil Sands Information Centre. Alberta Oil Sands Technology and Research Authority. (May 1978)-. Periodical. English. Four times a year. Free on request. AOSTRA Provincial Treasurer, 500 Highfield Place, 10010-106 Street, Edmonton Alberta T5J 3L8 Canada. **Tel** (403)427-7623, FAX (403)427-3198, telex 037-3519. **ED** J.D. Alton. **Circ:** 3,000 (ctrl).
**Desc:** Information on and about oil sand, heavy oil and enhanced recovery processes. Contains listing of relevant meetings, courses, etc.
**Ind/Abst** MINPROC; Mintec, Min. Technol. Abstr.

GW
**TASCHENBUCH FUER DAS GAS-UND WASSERFACH.** **See** Water Resources.

CN/1182-5847
**TAXES FEDERALES ET PROVINCIALES SUR LES PRODUITS PETROLIERS.** [Taxes fed. prov. prod. pet.]. **Added/Corp** Canada. Division du Marche Canadien du Petrole et de la Planification d'Urgence. (June 1990)-. Periodical. French. sa. **DD** 343.7105/582282/05.

AG
**TECNICO COMERCIAL.** Spanish. Departamento de Difusion y Ceremonial, Esmeralda 255 Piso 8, Buenos Aires Argentina. **LC** TP690.2.A7; T43.

US/0883-7449
**TENTATIVE ... OIL AND GAS UNIT OF PRODUCTION VALUES.** English. an. New York State Board of Equalization and Assessment Agency, Building 4, Governor Nelson A Rockefeller, Empire State Plaza, Albany NY 12223. **LC** HD9560.8.U53; N57. **DD** 336.22/5.

US/1060-5304
**TERM FREQUENCY LIST.** [Term freq. list]. **Added/Corp** Petroleum Abstracts (Organization). **VFOAT** TFL. (Jan. 1965/Dec. 31, 1991)-. English. sa (2 issues). $75.00 general subscribers; $95.00 nonsubscribers. Petroleum Abstracts, University of Tulsa, Information Services Division, 600 South College Avenue, Harwell Hall 101, Tulsa OK 74104-3189. **Tel** (800)247-8678, (918)631-2297, FAX (918)599-9361, telex 49 7543. **LC** Z695.1.P43; P47. **DD** 025.4/95532/82. ***Continues*** *Descriptor Frequency list, 0884-7819.*
**Desc:** Alphabetic list of terms from both thesauri and their supplemental term lists. Enumerates how many times a descriptor has been used to index material for the TULSA database, with a separate count for each use as a weighted term.

US
**TERMINALS MAGAZINE.** (19??)-. English. Six times a year. $30.00. The Oil Daily, 1401 New York Avenue Northwest, Suite 500, Washington DC 20005-2150. **Tel** (800)621-0050, (800)368-5803, (202)662-0700, FAX (202)662-0739, telex 89472.
**Desc:** Covers liquid storage and distribution. Contains news and feature articles about marine and pipeline terminals and tank farms, with emphasis on the services they provide. Also market forecasts, regulatory news, new equipment and services, operations management, engineering and construction, etc.

US/0197-2340
**TEXAS NATURAL RESOURCES REPORTER.** Vol. 1 (Jan. 1977)-. Periodical. English. Twenty-four times a year. $1,228.04 Texas; $1,145.00 others. RPC Publications, 7600 Chevy Chase Drive, Building 2, Austin TX 78752. **Tel** (512)371-8100. **ED** Bonnie Sonnek. Index available. cum. index. **Circ:** 250 (ctrl).
**Desc:** Covers seven state agencies that regulate natural resources and rules for the agencies.

US/0272-8915
**TEXAS OIL REGISTER.** English. qt. $270.00. Howell Publishing, PO Box 1030, Castle Rock CO 80104-1030. **LC** HD9567.T3; T39. **DD** 338.7/622338/025764.

US/0039-8403
**TIPRO REPORTER.** [TIPRO report.]. **Main/Corp** Texas Independent Producers and Royalty Owners Association. **Added/Corp** Texas Independent Procedures and Royalty Owners Association. **VAT** Texas Independent Producers and Royalty Owners Association Reporter. (19??)-. Periodical. English. qt (Jan., May, Aug., Oct.). $25.00. Texas Independent Producers Royalty Owners, 1770 Austin National Bank Tower, Austin TX 78701. **LC** HD9567.T3; T5.
**Ind/Abst** Energy Res. Abstr. (Oct. 1978-).

US/1048-0935
**TODAY'S REFINERY.** [Today's refin.]. (April 1987)-. English. mo. $25.00. Percy Publishing Company Inc, PO Box 287, Chappaqua NY 10514. **Tel** (914)238-0205. **ED** James D. Wall. **DD** 338. **Bk Rev**. **Ad Acc**. **Circ:** 6,300 (ctrl).
**Desc:** Publishes abstracts and reviews of papers and items of interest to petroleum refiners; for petroleum refiners in the US and Canada.

FR
**TOTAL COMPAGNIE FRANCAISE DES PETROLIS IN ... .** **Main/Corp** Total Compagnie Francaise des Petroles. (1985)-. Periodical. English. Compagnie Francaise des Petroles, 5 rue Michel Ange, 75781 Cedex 16 Switzerland. **LC** HD9572.9.C58; C64b. ***Continues*** *Compagnie Francaise des Petroles and the Total Group.*

FR/0152-6189
**TOTAL INFORMATION.** **Added/Corp** Compagnie Francaise des Petroles. (19??)-. Periodical. English. qt. Free. Compagnie Francaise des Petroles, 5 rue Michel Ange, 75781 Cedex 16 Switzerland. **LC** HD9572.9.C58; T67. **DD** 338.2/7282/0944.
**Ind/Abst** AESIS Q.

FR
**TP, TECHNIQUES PETROMONDE.** **VFOAT** Techniques Petromonde. New Series, No. 1- 8 Sept. 1977-. Periodical. French. 350. **LC** TP690.A1; T18. **DD** 338.4/7/665505. ***Formed by the union of*** *Techniques du Petrole* ***and*** *Petromonde.*

US/8756-8152
**TRANSACTIONS OF THE SOCIETY OF PETROLEUM ENGINEERS.** [Trans. Soc. Pet. Eng.]. **Added/Corp** Society of Petroleum Engineers of AIME. **VFOAT** Transactions. Vol. 267 (1979)-. Periodical. English. an. $90.00 North America; $138.00 other. Society of Petroleum Engineers, PO Box 833836, Richardson TX 75083-3836. **Tel** (214)952-9393 or (214)952-9458, FAX (214)952-9435, telex 163245 (SPEUT). **LC** TN1; .A5. **DD** 665.5/05. Index available. cum. index. **Pr Rev. Circ:** 6,000. ***Continues*** *Transactions of the Society of Petroleum Engineers of the American Institute of Mining, Metallurgical, and Petroleum Engineers, Inc., 0081-1696.*
**Desc:** Bound volume of selected papers published during previous year, plus summaries of other papers published that year in the Society's five journals. The binding reflects the year the papers were published; mailing occurs the following year.

US/0081-1718
**TRANSACTIONS OF THE SPWLA ANNUAL LOGGING SYMPOSIUM.** [Trans. SPWLA Annu. Logging Symp.]. **Main/Corp** Society of Professional Well Log Analysts. **Added/Corp** Society of Professional Well Log Analysts. **VFOAT** Annual Logging Symposium Transactions; SPWLA Logging Symposium Transactions. **VAT** Transactions of the Society of Professional Well Log Analysts Annual Logging Symposium. (1960)-. Academic Scholarly Publication. English. an. $75.00. Society of Professional Well Log Analysts, 8866 Gulf Freeway, Suite 320, Houston TX 77023. **Tel** (713)947-8727, FAX (713)928-9061. **LC** TN871.35; .L63a. **CODEN** SPWLA6. Index available. **Circ:** 3,000 (ctrl). Documents available from CASDDS.
**Desc:** Technical articles on formation evaluation.
**Ind/Abst** AESIS Q.; Chem. Abstr. (1960-1983); GeoRef.

US
**TRANSPORTATION AND STORAGE.** ***Title Change.*** **See** Energy-Abstracting, Bibliographies and Statistics.

US
**TRANSPORTATION NOTICE OF HEARING.** English. sm. $31.00. Railroad Commission of Texas, PO Drawer 12967, Capitol Station, Austin TX 78711. **Tel** (512)463-7255.

US/1046-0144
**TREATISE OF PETROLEUM GEOLOGY REPRINT SERIES.** (TREATISE OF PETROLEUM GEOLOGY REPRINT SERIES / AMERICAN ASSOCIATION OF PETROLEUM GEOLOGISTS.). [Treatise pet. geol. repr. ser.]. **Added/Corp** American Association of Petroleum Geologists. No. 1 (1987)-. Monographic series. English. ir. Price varies per volume. American Association of Petroleum Geologists, PO Box 979, Tulsa OK 74101-0979. **Tel** (918)584-2555, FAX (918)584-0469, telex 49-9432. **DD** 553.
**Ind/Abst** AESIS Q.

RU/0131-1689
**TRUDY - GOSUDARSTVENNYJ NAUCNO-ISSLEDOVATELSKIJ I PROEKTNYJ INSTITUT NEFTJANOJ PROMYSLENNOSTI.** (TRUDY - GOSUDARSTVENNYI NAUCHNO-ISSLEDOVATELSKII I PROEKTNYI INSTITUT NEFTIANOI PROMYSHLENNOSTI.). **Main/Corp** Gosudarstvennyi Nauch Noissledovatelskii i Proektnyi Institut Neftianoi Promyshlennosti. (1967)-. Academic Scholarly Publication. Russian. Izdatelstvo Nedra, 3 Pl Belorusskogo Vakzala, 125047 Moscow Russia. **Tel** 250-52-55. **CODEN** TPNPDL. Documents available from CASDDS.
**Ind/Abst** Chem. Abstr. (?-1974).

RU
**TRUDY - VSESOIUZNYI NAUCHNO-ISSLEDOVATELSKII INSTITUT PO PERERABOTKE NEFTI.** **Main/Corp** Vsesoiuznyi Nauchno-Issledovatelskii Institut Po Pererabotke Nefti. (19??)-. Monographic series. Russian. Price varies per volume. **LC** TP690.A1; M66. ***Continues*** *Moscow. Vsesoiuznyi Nauchno-Issledovatelskii Institut po Pererabotke Nefti I Gaza i Polucheniiu Iskusstvennogo Zhidkogo Topliva. Trudy.*

US/0193-9467
**TULSALETTER (1976).** (TULSALETTER.). **Added/Corp** Petroleum Equipment Institute. **VAT** Tulsa Letter. (1976)-. Periodical. English. Thirty-six times a year. $72.00. Petroleum Equipment Institute, PO Box 2380, Tulsa OK 74101. **Tel** (918)494-9696, FAX (918)491-9895. ***Continues*** *PEI Newsletter.*

US/1048-4825
**TWENTIETH CENTURY PETROLEUM STATISTICS.** **See** Petroleum and Natural Gas-Abstracting, Bibliographies and Statistics.

UK/0141-4305
**U.K. PETROLEUM INDUSTRY STATISTICS. CONSUMPTION AND REFINERY PRODUCTION.** **See** Petroleum and Natural Gas-Abstracting, Bibliographies and Statistics.

UK
**U K UPSTREAM PETROLEUM DATABASE.** James Capel and Company, Petroleum Services Department, Wardley House, 7 Devonshire Square, London EC2M 4HN England. **Tel** 011 44 71 626 0866.

•US/1056-795X
**U.S.A. GULF COAST OIL & GAS INDUSTRY DIRECTORY.** [U.S.A. gulf Coast oil gas ind. dir.]. **Added/Corp** PennWell Publishing Company. **VFOAT** U.S.A. Gulf Coast Oil and Gas Industry Directory; USA Gulf Coast Oil and Gas Industry Directory. **VAT** United States of America Gulf Coast Oil & Gas Industry Directory. (1992)-. Directory. English. ir. $95.00 US and Canada; $125.00 other. PennWell Publishing Company, 1421 South Sheridan, PO Box 1260, Tulsa OK 74101. **Tel** (918)835-3161, (800)331-4463, FAX (918)831-9497. **(Subscription address:** PennWell Books, PO Box 21288, Tulsa OK 74121.) **LC** HD9567.A13; U17. **DD** 338.7/622338/029476.
**Desc:** Industry changes specific to the Gulf Coast region, including Texas, Louisiana, Mississippi, Alabama, and Florida. Each listing will feature company name, address, phone, fax, telex, and cable information. Descriptions of each company and a list of executives, subsidiaries, and branch offices are included.

US/0082-8599
**U.S.A. OIL INDUSTRY DIRECTORY.** [U.S.A. oil ind. dir.]. **VAT** United States of America Oil Industry Directory. (1970)-. Directory. English. an. $159.50 US and Canada; $209.50 other. PennWell Publishing Company, 1421 South Sheridan, PO Box 1260, Tulsa OK 74101. **Tel** (918)835-3161, (800)331-4463, FAX (918)831-9497. **(Subscription address:** PennWell Books, PO Box 21288, Tulsa OK 74121.) **ED** Carol Schaefer. **LC** HD9563; .U54. **DD** 338.2/7/2802573. **[CCC]**. Index available. **Bk Rev.** **Ad Acc. Circ:** 6,000 (ctrl). ***Continues*** *Personnel Directory of U.S.A. Oil Industry.*
**Desc:** Includes major integrated oil companies, independent oil producers, fund companies, government agencies, and associations listed geographically. Cross-referenced with subject index and company index.

•US/1062-0605
**U.S.A. OIL INDUSTRY'S ENVIRONMENTAL DIRECTORY.** [U.S.A. oil ind. environ. dir.]. **Added/Corp** PennWell Publishing Company. **VFOAT** USA Oil Industry's Environmental Directory. **VAT** United States of America Oil Industry's Environmental Directory. (1992)-. Directory. English. ir. $175.00. PennWell Publishing Company, 1421 South Sheridan, PO Box 1260, Tulsa OK 74101. **Tel** (918)835-3161, (800)331-4463, FAX (918)831-9497. **(Subscription address:** PennWell Books, PO Box 21288, Tulsa OK 74121.) **LC** HD9718.U6; U17. **DD** 363.73/82/029473.
**Desc:** Designed as a comprehensive resource for use by all levels of petroleum professionals for any environmental need; lists company name, address, phone, fax, a brief company history, services provided, materials handled, and areas served.

US
**U.S.A. OILFIELD SERVICE, SUPPLY, AND MANUFACTURERS DIRECTORY.** **VFOAT** U.S.A. Oilfield Service, Supply & Manufacturers Directory; USA Oilfield Service, Supply, and Manufacturers Directory; USA Oilfield Service, Supply & Manufacturers Directory; Oilfield Service, Supply, and Manufacturers Directory; OSSM. (1985)-. Directory. English. an. $135.00 US and Canada; $185.00 other. PennWell Publishing Company, 1421 South Sheridan, PO Box 1260, Tulsa OK 74101. **Tel** (918)835-3161, (800)331-4463, FAX (918)831-9497. **(Subscription address:** PennWell Books, PO Box 21288, Tulsa OK 74121.) **ED** Carol Schaefer. **LC** HD9560.3; .O37. **DD** 338.7/68176. Index available. **Bk Rev.** **Ad Acc. Circ:** 1,500 (ctrl). ***Continues*** *Oilfield Service, Supply and Manufacturers Worldwide Directory, 0736-038X.*
**Desc:** Complete listing of companies providing oilfield services, wholesale and/or retail sale of oilfield products or engaged in design, manufacture and construction of oilfield facilities.

US/0740-9966
**U.S. CRUDE OIL DISTILLATION REFINING CAPACITY SURVEY FOR ... .** ***Ceased.*** [U.S. crude oil distill. refin. capacity surv.]. **VFOAT** US Crude Oil Distillation Refining Capacity Survey for ... . **VAT** United States Crude Oil Distillation Refining Capacity Survey. (19??)-(1992). English. $10.00 US; $13.00 other. American Petroleum Institute, 275 Seventh Avenue, New York NY 10001. **Tel** (212)366-4040, FAX (212)366-4298. **(Subscription address:** 1970 Chain Bridge Road, McLean, VA 22109-6000) **LC** TP690.3; .U23. **DD** 338.4/766553/0973.

US/0731-924X
**U.S. CRUDE OIL, NATURAL GAS, AND NATURAL GAS LIQUIDS RESERVES, ANNUAL REPORT.** (U.S. CRUDE OIL, NATURAL GAS, AND NATURAL GAS LIQUIDS RESERVES ... ANNUAL REPORT.). [U.S. crude oil nat. gas nat. gas liq. reserves annu. rep.]. **Added/Corp** United States. Office of the Oil and Gas Information System. United States. Energy Information Administration. Office of Oil and Gas. **VFOAT** US Crude Oil, Natural Gas, and Natural Gas Liquids Reserves, Annual Report; United States Crude Oil, Natural Gas, and Natural Gas Liquids Reserves, Annual Report. (1979)-. English. an. $11.00. National Energy Information Center, Energy Information Administration, Forrestal Building, Room 1F-048, Washington DC 20585. **Tel** (202)586-8800. **LC** TN872.A5; U65a. **DD** 553.2/8/0973. available on diskette (As: U.S. Crude Oil, Natural Gas, and Natural Gas Liquids Reserves [Computer File]). ***Continues*** *U.S. Crude Oil and Natural Gas Reserves, 0272-3670.*
**Desc:** Proved reserves of crude oil, natural gas, and natural gas liquids in the United States are reported by state, with US totals. A national summary is given, along with a discussion of areas of notable developments in the industry.
**Ind/Abst** Predicasts Forecasts.

US
**U.S. CRUDE OIL, NATURAL GAS, AND NATURAL GAS LIQUIDS RESERVES [COMPUTER FILE] / U.S. DEPARTMENT OF ENERGY.** **Added/Corp** United States. Dept. of Energy. United States. Energy Information Administration. **VFOAT** U.S. Crude Oil Nat. Gas Liquid. (1989)-. English. an. $19.50. National Energy Information Center, Energy Information Administration, Forrestal Building, Room 1F-048, Washington DC 20585. **Tel** (202)586-8800. available in print (As: U.S. Crude Oil and Natural Gas Reserves ... Annual Report).
**Desc:** Contains data on proved reserves of liquid hydrocarbons in the U.S. Data are state specific and cover ten specific hydrocarbon types. System requirements: IBM PC or compatible. Disk characteristics: double sided, high density, soft sectored.

US/0502-9767
**U.S. OIL WEEK.** [U.S. oil week]. **VFOAT** Oil Week. **VAT** United States Oil Week. (19??)-. Periodical. English. wk (50 times a year). $259.00. Capitol Publications, 1101 King Street, Suite 444, Alexandria VA 22314. **Tel** (703)683-4100, (800)655-5597. **ED** Tom Guay. **DD** 380. **[CCC]**. ctrl circ. available on an online database (files 16,636/Full-Text) from DIALOG. ***Absorbed*** *C-Store Week, 0887-4700.*
**Desc:** Provides information on regulations, litigation, alcohol fuels, storage tanks, major oil companies, fuel oil, refiners' gas and heating oil terminal prices and price changes, and convenience store marketing.
**Ind/Abst** Pet. Energy Bus. News Index (1983); PROMT [Full Txt.]; PTS Newsl. Database [Full Txt.].

UK
**UK OFFSHORE LEGISLATION UPDATES.** English. bm. £225.00. Tolley Publishing Company Ltd, Tolley House, 2 Addiscombe Road, Croydon, Surrey CR9 5AF United Kingdom. **Tel** 011 44 81 6869141, FAX 011 44 81 6863155, 011 44 81 7600588.

UK
**UK OFFSHORE OIL & GAS DIRECTORY.** **VFOAT** U.K. Offshore Oil & Gas Directory; Offshore Oil & Gas Directory; UK Offshore Oil and Gas Directory. (19??)-. Directory. English. an. Thomas Telford Ltd, Thomas Telford House, 1 Heron Quay, London E14 9XF England. **Tel** 011 44 71 987 6999, FAX 011 44 71 538 4101, telex 298105. **LC** TN874.G7; U37. **DD** 622/.338/029441.

UK
**UK OIL & GAS LAW.** **See** Law.

US/0193-5658
**UNDERGROUND STORAGE OF NATURAL GAS BY INTERSTATE PIPELINE COMPANIES.** (UNDERGROUND STORAGE OF NATURAL GAS BY INTERSTATE PIPELINE COMPANIES FOR ...). Government Publication. English. an. US Department of Energy, 1000 Independence Avenue SW, Washington DC 20585. **Tel** (202)586-5000, FAX (202)586-4073. **LC** TP756; .U53. **DD** 665.7/42/0973.

US
**UNIFORM SYSTEM OF ACCOUNTS PRESCRIBED FOR NATURAL GAS COMPANIES.** Jan. 1, 1940-. English. $12.60 US; $15.65 other. Federal Power Commission, Office of Public Information, Washington DC 20426.
**Desc:** Systems of accounts applicable to Class A, B, C, and D, utilities.

UK/0963-8156
**UNITED KINGDOM OIL AND GAS.** [U.K. oil gas]. (1983)-. English. ir (two loose leaf updates). £295.00. Chiltern Publishing, 18 Burgess Wood Road, Beaconsfield Bucks HP9 1EQ England. **Tel** 011 44 494 673062, FAX 011 44 494 678914. **ED** Hazel Powell.
**Desc:** Comprehensive analysis and information on taxation and accounting for UK oil and gas industries.

US/0883-2757
**UNIVERSITY MONOGRAPHS.** [Univ. monogr.]. **Added/Corp** American Gas Association. Policy Evaluation & Analysis Group. Vol. 1, No. 1 (Feb. 1985)-. Periodical. English. ir. American Gas Association / Virginia, 1515 Wilson Boulevard, Arlington VA 22209. **Tel** (703)841-8400, (703)841-8559, FAX (703)841-8697. **LC** TP345.A1; U54. **DD** 665.7/05.

US/0148-2157
**UPPER TEXAS COAST REPORT.** V. 1- July 26, 1977-. Periodical. English. wk. $432.00. Petroleum Information Corporation, 5333 Westheimer, Suite 100, Houston TX 77056. **Tel** (713)840-8282 ext. 38, FAX (713)599-5100.

II/0971-2038
**URJA OIL AND GAS INTERNATIONAL.** [Urja Oil Gas Int.]. (1992)-. Periodical. English. mo. **UDC** 620.9.
**Ind/Abst** Energy Inf. Abstr.

CN/1186-7973
**VANCOUVER ISLAND GAS PIPELINE UPDATE.** [Vanc. Isl. gas pipeline update]. **Added/Corp** British Columbia. Ministry of Energy, Mines and Petroleum Resources. No. 1 (May 1991)-. Periodical. English. British Columbia Ministry of Energy, Mines and Petroleum Resources, Parliament Buildings, Victoria British Columbia V8V 1X4 Canada. **DD** 363.6.

UK
**VIETNAM OIL AND GAS REPORT.** (19??)-. Newsletter. English. mo. $495.00. IBC Publishing, 57-61 Mortimer St., London W1N 7TD England. **Tel** 011 44 71 637 4383, FAX 011 44 71 636 6314.

•VE/1315-0855
**VISION TECNOLOGICA / PUBLICACION DE INTEVEP, S.A.** **Added/Corp** INTEVEP, S.A. Centro de Informacion Tecnica. Vol. 1, No. 1 (1993)-. Periodical. English (Spanish; summaries and/or abstracts in Spanish). Twice a year. Free. Revista Tecnica INTEVEP, Centro de Informacion Tecnica, Apartado Postal 76343, Caracas 1070A Venezuela. **Tel** 011 58 2 9086111, telex 28-831 INTVP VC. **LC** TN873.V4; R4852. ***Continues*** *Revista Tecnica INTEVEP.*

JA
**WAGA KUNI SEKIYU KAIHATSU NO GENJO.** **Main/Corp** Sekiyu Kogyo Remmei. Kikaku Chosabu. **Added/Corp** Sekiyu Kogyo Remmei. (19??)-. Periodical. Japanese. an. ¥2,000. Jekiyu Kogyo Remmei Kikaku Chosabu, c/o Keidanren Kaikan Building, 9-4 Otemachi 1, Chiyoda-ku 100 Tokyo Japan. **Tel** (03)279-5841, FAX (03)279-5844. **ED** Sekiyu Kogyo Renmei. **LC** HD9576.J3; S457a. ctrl circ.

US
**WASHINGTON REPORT INGAA.** ***Ceased.*** (19??)-Number 1628 (Dec. 1993). English. Twice a year (Spring and Fall). Interstate Natural Gas Association of America, 555 13th Street Northwest, Suite 300 West, Washington DC 20004. **Tel** (202)626-3200, FAX (202)626-3250. **Bk Rev**, (Qty: 8).
**Desc:** Covers congressional and regulatory developments of interest to the natural gas pipeline industry. Includes company news.

US/0193-4724
**WEEKLY BPN PROPANE NEWSLETTER.** **VFOAT** Weekly Propane Newsletter; BPN. **VAT** Weekly Butane Propane News Newsletter. (19??)-. English. wk. $175.00. Butane-Propane News, Box 660698, Arcadia CA 91006-0698. **Tel** (818)357-2168, FAX (818)303-2854. **ED** Hal McWilliams. Index available (Free). ctrl circ.

UK
**WEEKLY EUROPEAN LPG REPORT.** (19??)-. English. ICIS Lor Group Ltd., 6 Spring Gardens, Citadel Place Tinworth, London SE11 5EH England. **Tel** 011 44 71 8151100.

UK/0268-7844
**WEEKLY PETROLEUM ARGUS.** [Wkly. pet. argus]. (1985)-. Periodical. English. wk. $1540.00. Petroleum Argus Ltd, 93 Shepperton Road, London N1 3DF England. **Tel** 011 44 71 359 8792. ***Continues** Europ-Oil Prices (London).*

US/1057-5790
**WEEKLY PETROLEUM STATUS REPORT / U.S. DEPARTMENT OF ENERGY, ENERGY INFORMATION ADMINISTRATION.** **See** Petroleum and Natural Gas-Abstracting, Bibliographies and Statistics.

US
**WEEKLY STATISTICAL BULLETIN (AMERICAN PETROLEUM INSTITUTE. STATISTICS DEPT.).** **See** Petroleum and Natural Gas-Abstracting, Bibliographies and Statistics.

US/0043-2393
**WELL SERVICING.** **Added/Corp** Association of Oilwell Servicing Contractors. Vol. 1 (Jan./Feb. 1961)-. Periodical. English. Six times a year (Jan., Mar., May, July, Sept., Nov.). Free. Associated OilWell Servicing Contractors, 6060 North Central Expsy, Suite 428, Dallas TX 75206. **Tel** (214)692-0771. **ED** Polly Fisk. **LC** TN860; .A732. **Ad Acc**, **Adv Mgr:** Katherine Leidy, **Tel** (214)692-0771. **Circ:** 10,000 (ctrl). Documents available from Petroleum Abstracts Document Delivery Service.
**Desc:** Covering the news, trends, technology, legislative issues affecting the oil & gas well servicing industry.
**Ind/Abst** Pet. Abstr.

UK
**WEST AFRICA OIL SERVICE.** English. ir. £3,500.00. Wood Mackenzie Consultants Ltd., Kintore House, 74 77 Queen Street, Edinburgh EH2 4NS Scotland. **Tel** 011 44 031 225 8525, FAX 011 44 031 243 4435, telex 72555.

UK
**WEST AFRICA OIL SERVICE.** English. an. £2750.00. County Natwest Securities Ltd, Kintore House, 74-77 Queen Street, Edinburgh EH2 4NS Scotland. **Tel** 031 225-8525, FAX 031 243-4435. **Circ:** 100 (ctrl).
**Desc:** Economic analysis of all individual oil fields within West Africa. Also commentary on exploration, production, fiscal regimes and licensing.

US/1070-6100
**WESTERN OIL AND GAS WORLD.** ***Title Change.*** [West. oil gas world]. Vol. 50, No. 6 (June 1993)-(Feb. 1994). Periodical. English. mo. Hart Publications Inc, 1900 Grant Street, Suite 400, Denver CO 80203. **Tel** (303)837-1917, (800)832-1917, FAX (303)837-8585. **LC** TN822; .A325. **DD** 338.4/76655/0978. ***Continues** Western Oil World, 0884-7592. **Merged with** Gulf Coast Oil and Gas World; Southwest Oil and Gas World; Northeast Oil and Gas World; Midcontinent Oil and Gas World; Pacific Oil and Gas World **to form** Hart's Oil and Gas World, 1075-5365.*

US/0884-7592
**WESTERN OIL WORLD.** ***Title Change.*** [West. oil world]. Vol. 42, No. 8 (Aug. 1985)-Vol. 50, No. 5 (May 1993). Periodical. English. mo. Western Oil World, PO Box 1917, Denver CO 80201-1917. **Tel** (303)837-1917. **ED** Russ Rountree. **LC** TN872; .A325. **DD** 553.2/8/0978. **[CCC].** Index available. **Ad Acc. Circ:** 6,209. available on microfilm from University Microfilms International (UMI). Documents available from Petroleum Abstracts Document Delivery Service. ***Continues** Western Oil Reporter (Denver, Colo.), 0043-3985. **Continued by** Western Oil and Gas World, 1070-6100.*
**Ind/Abst** GeoRef; Pet. Abstr.

US/0273-1762
**WESTERN PETROLEUM REGISTER.** (1977)-. Directory. English. ir. $40.00. Frank M Chapman Publications Services, PO Box 4185, Glendale CA 91202. **Tel** (213)245-1889. **ED** Frank Chapman. **Ad Acc. Circ:** 1,000 (ctrl). ***Continues** California Petroleum Register, 0198-7526.*
**Desc:** Directory of Western oil, gas and energy industries, including companies, refineries, plants, personnel, associations, governmental agencies, contractors, manufacturers, distributors, services companies plus buyers guide.

US/0148-3609
**WHOLE WORLD OIL DIRECTORY, THE.** ***Ceased.*** [Whole world oil dir.]. (1979)-(Feb. 1993). Directory. English. an. Whole World Publishing Inc, 400 Lake Cook Road/Suite 207, Deerfield IL 60015. **Tel** (312)945-8050. ***Continues** Whole Oil World Oil Directory, 0276-1068.*

AT/0159-1878
**WHO'S DRILLING.** [Who's drilling]. (1980)-. Periodical. English. wk. 700.00Aus$ (Australia); 880.00Aus$ (New Zealand); 915.00Aus$ (Singapore); 960.00Aus$ (Japan); 1005.00Aus$ (US); 1045.00Aus$ (other). Pex Publications Pty Ltd, PO Box 158, Claremont Western Australia 6010. **Tel** (09)383-3477, FAX (09)385 1485. **ED** Don Lipscombe, 09 383 3477. **DD** 622.1828209941. Index available.
**Desc:** National exploration newsletter analysing comprehensively all current and pending wells, rig and boat movements, and seismic surveys.

AT/0817-6353
**WHO'S PEGGING.** Newsletter. English. wk. $460.00 per year, $140.00 per quarter. Pex Publications Pty Ltd, PO Box 158, Claremont Western Australia 6010. **Tel** (09)383-3477, FAX (09)385 1485. **ED** J Lipscombe.
**Desc:** Australia's prospecting newsletter listing all mineral tenements by applicant, location and number.

US
**WHO'S WHO GUIDE OF PETROCHEMICAL & PLASTICS COMPANIES.** **See** Plastics.

US
**WHO'S WHO IN PIPELINING.** (19??)-. English. an. $77.00, $595.00 on diskette. Hart Publications Inc, 1900 Grant Street, Suite 400, Denver CO 80203. **Tel** (303)837-1917, (800)832-1917, FAX (303)837-8585. available on diskette.
**Desc:** Provides worldwide coverage of over 5,550 companies and 15,000 key personnel, including pipeline operators, contractors, subcontractors, and service and supply companies.

CN/1192-2958
**WOODSIDE REPORT, THE.** **See** Energy.

US
**WORLD AUTOMOTIVE ALTERNATIVE ENERGY & FUELS BULLETIN.** **See** Energy.

CN/0843-2295
**WORLD ENERGY NEWS (CALGARY).** (WORLD ENERGY NEWS.). [World energy news]. **Added/Corp** Landman's Petroleum Gazette Ltd. (Aug. 1986)-. Periodical. English. Twenty-four times a year. Landman's Petroleum Gazette Ltd., Box 48/Suite 2S#3, Calgary Alberta T3C 3N9 Canada. **DD** 338.2/7282/097123. ***Continues** L. P. G., 0709-9029.*

US
**WORLD GAS INTELLIGENCE : PIW'S GAS MARKET REPORT.** **Added/Corp** Petroleum Intelligence Group. Vol. 1, No. 1 (Jan. 1990)-. Periodical. English. Twenty-four times a year. $795.00 mail; $1590.00 fax; $400.00 on-line. Petroleum Intelligence Weekly, 575 Broadway, 4th Floor, New York NY 10012-3230. **Tel** (212)941-5500, FAX (212)941-5509, telex 62371 PETROIN. **ED** Pactrick Heren. **LC** IN PROCESS. available via fax; available on an online database (updated quarterly).
**Desc:** Offers news and analysis of gas industry developments worldwide. Explores pipeline gas supply and use, along with current and historical information for eight key markets. Data on competitive pricing provides overviews and options for alternative fuels.

US/1053-9859
**WORLD GEOPHYSICAL NEWS.** [World geophys. news]. **Added/Corp** Petroleum Information Corporation. (19??)-. Periodical. English. Twenty-three times a year (Published 1st & 15th each month with no issue on 1st of January.). $240.00. Petroleum Information Corporation, 5333 Westheimer, Suite 100, Houston TX 77056. **Tel** (713)840-8282 ext. 38, FAX (713)599-5100. **ED** Tom Chevey and Dana Cain, (303)740-7100. **DD** 333.
**Desc:** Geophysical activity reports.

US/0195-6965
**WORLD NATURAL GAS.** Began with 1976. Government Publication. English. an. US Department of Energy, 1000 Independence Avenue SW, Washington DC 20585. **Tel** (202)586-5000, FAX (202)586-4073. **LC** HD9581.A1; U54A. **DD** 333.8/233/05. ***Continues** World Natural Gas, Annual.*

US/0043-8790
**WORLD OIL (HOUSTON, TEX.).** (WORLD OIL.). [World oil]. Vol. 126, No. 6 (July 1947)-. Academic Scholarly Publication. English. mo. $24.00 North and Latin America; $30.00 other. Gulf Publishing Company / Texas, PO Box 2608, Houston TX 77252. **Tel** (800)231-6275, (713)529-4301, FAX (713)520-4433. **ED** Thomas R Wright. **LC** TN860; .O5. **DD** 665.505. **CODEN** WOOIAS. **[CCC].** Index available. **Ad Acc. Pr Rev. Circ:** 37,582 (ctrl). available on microfilm and microfiche from University Microfilms International (UMI). Documents available from Article Express International, The Genuine Article, Petroleum Abstracts Document Delivery Service, CASDDS. ***Continues** Oil Weekly.*
**Desc:** Engineering/operational articles for engineers, supervisors and management.
**Ind/Abst** Acad. Search (July 1993-); AESIS Q.; Appl. Sci. Technol. Index; Aquat. Sci. Fish. Abstr. (Computer File); Bioeng. Abstr.; Bus. ASAP (1990-) [Full Txt.]; Bus. Index (1988-); Bus. Period. Index; Bus. Source (Jan. 1993-); Chem. Abstr.; Chem. Ind. Notes; Ei Page One; EMBASE; Energy Res. Abstr. (April 1974-); Eng. Index Annu. [Select. Cov.]; Environ. Period. Bibliogr. (?-?); F&S Index Plus Text, Int. [Select. Cov.]; Fluid Abstr., Civil Eng.; Fluid Abstr. Proc. Eng.; FLUIDEX; Gas Abstr.; Gen. BusinessFile (1988-); Gen. Period. Index (1988-); GeoRef; INFO-SOUTH Abstr.; Lit. Pat. Abstr., Oilfield Chem. (1981-); Lit. Abstr., Catal. Catal.; Lit. Abstr., Health Environ.; Lit. Abstr., Pet. Refin. Petrochem.; Lit. Abstr., Pet. Substit.; Lit. Abstr., Transp. Storage; Mag. Search; Middle East Abstr. Index; Mintec, Min. Technol. Abstr.; Ocean. Abstr.; Pet. Abstr.; Pet. Energy Bus. News Index (1988); Predicasts Forecasts; Res. Alert [Select. Cov.]; Soc. Sci. Cit. Index [Select. Cov.]; Trade Ind. ASAP [Full Txt.]; Trade Ind. Index [Full Txt.]; Vocat. Search (July 1993-); Wilson Bus. Abstr.

CN/0824-5533
**WORLD OIL MARKET ANALYSIS.** (WORLD OIL MARKET ANALYSIS / CANADIAN ENERGY RESEARCH INSTITUTE.). [World oil mark. anal.]. **Added/Corp** Canadian Energy Research Institute. (June 1983)-. Periodical. English. qt (with 8 monthly updates in between). 435.00Can$. Canadian Energy Research Institute, 3512 33rd Street Northwest #150, Calgary Alberta T2L 2A6 Canada. **Tel** (403)282-1231, FAX (403)284-4181, (403)289-2344. **ED** Tony Reinsch and Jennifer Considine. **DD** 338.2/7282. **Circ:** 400.
**Desc:** Provides informative coverage of economic and political developments in the world oil market.
**Ind/Abst** Energy Res. Abstr.

UK/0950-1029
**WORLD OIL TRADE.** [World oil trade]. (1979)-. Academic Scholarly Publication. English. an. £259.00 UK & Europe; $454.00 other. Basil Blackwell Publishers Ltd, 108 Cowley Road, Oxford 0X4 1JF England. **Tel** 011 44 865 791100, FAX 011 44 865 791347, telex 837022 OXBOOK G. **(Subscription address:** Blackwell Publishers / UK, Marston Book Services, PO Box 87, Oxford OX2 0DT England.) **[CCC].**

UK
**WORLD SOLID FUELS, ELECTRICITY, GAS, IRON AND STEEL AND PETROLEUM STATISTICS.** **See** Energy.

US/0890-2976
**WORLD TRADE IN LIQUIFIED PETROLEUM GASES.** [World trade liq. pet. gases]. **Added/Corp** Poten & Partners. (19??)-. English. Fifteen times a year. $12,000.00. Poten & Partners Inc., 885 3rd Avenue, New York NY 10022. **Tel** (212)230-2000, FAX (212)355-0295, telex 177118/420811. **ED** Gabriel F. Avgerines and Christine J. Gorzanski. **LC** HD9579.P4; W67. **DD** 382/.45665773.
**Desc:** A long-range study concerning the supply and demand of liquified petroleum gases worldwide, price relationships, gas carrier supply and demand outlook and important terminal requirements.

US/1051-3973
**WORLDWIDE NATURAL GAS INDUSTRY DIRECTORY.** [Worldw. nat. gas ind. dir.]. (1991)-. Directory. English. an. $156.00 US and Canada; $205.00 other. PennWell Publishing Company, 1421 South Sheridan, PO Box 1260, Tulsa OK 74101. **Tel** (918)835-3161, (800)331-4463, FAX (918)831-9497. **(Subscription address:** PennWell Books, PO Box 21288, Tulsa OK 74121.) **LC** TP714; .W67. **DD** 338.2/7285/025.

US/1058-9686
**WORLDWIDE OFFSHORE CONTRACTORS & EQUIPMENT DIRECTORY.** **See** Petroleum and Natural Gas-Abstracting, Bibliographies and Statistics.

US/0084-2583
**WORLDWIDE PETROCHEMICAL DIRECTORY.** [Worldw. petrochem. dir.]. **VFOAT** Petrochemical Worldwide Directory; Petrochemical Directory. 11th Ed. (1973)-. English. an. $156.00 US and Canada; $209.50 other. PennWell Publishing Company, 1421 South Sheridan, PO Box 1260, Tulsa OK 74101. **Tel** (918)835-3161, (800)331-4463, FAX (918)831-9497. **(Subscription address:** PennWell Books, PO Box 21288, Tulsa OK 74121.) **ED** Carol Schaefer. **LC** TP692.3; .P47. **DD** 338.4/7661804/025. **[CCC]. Bk Rev. Ad Acc. Circ:** 2,500 (ctrl). ***Continues** Petrochemical Directory, 0090-9904.*
**Desc:** Directory of petrochemical plant operators worldwide. Included is a survey of plant feedstocks and the products produced from these feedstocks.

US/1054-7959
**WORLDWIDE PETROLEUM PHONE/FAX/TELEX DIRECTORY.** [Worldw. pet. phone/fax/telex dir.]. **VFOAT** Worldwide Petroleum Phone Fax Telex Directory; Worldwide Petroleum Phone Fax Telex; Worldwide Petroleum Phone/Fax/Telex. (1991)-. English. be. $105.00. PennWell Publishing Company, 1421 South Sheridan, PO Box 1260, Tulsa OK 74101. **Tel** (918)835-3161, (800)331-4463, FAX (918)831-9497. **(Subscription address:** PennWell Books, PO Box 21288, Tulsa OK 74121.) **LC** HD9560.3; .W63. **DD** 338.7/622338/025.
**Desc:** Lists companies and their subsidiaries in locations from Alaska to Zaire, whether their operations are in exploration, production, refining, transportation,

petrochemicals, etc., offshore or on land. The listings are organized by country, with the companies listed in alphabetical order. Country codes for telephone, fax or telex are provided.

US/0277-0962
**WORLDWIDE REFINING AND GAS PROCESSING DIRECTORY (1978).** (WORLDWIDE REFINING AND GAS PROCESSING DIRECTORY.). [Worldw. refin. gas process. dir.]. **Added/Corp** PennWell Publishing Company. Petroleum Publishing Co. **VFOAT** Refining & Gas Processing Worldwide Directory; Worldwide Directory, Refining and Gas Processing; Refining and Gas Processing, Worldwide Directory; Worldwide Refining & Gas Processing Directory; Refining and Gas Processing. 36th Ed. (1978/79)-. Directory. English. an. $156.00 US and Canada; $205.00 other. PennWell Publishing Company, 1421 South Sheridan, PO Box 1260, Tulsa OK 74101. **Tel** (918)835-3161, (800)331-4463, FAX (918)831-9497. **(Subscription address:** PennWell Books, PO Box 21288, Tulsa OK 74121.**) ED** William R. Leek. **LC** TN867; .O497. **DD** 665. **[CCC]**. Index available. **Ad Acc. Circ:** 2,500. ***Continues*** *Gas Processing, Refining, and Worldwide Directory.*
**Desc:** Directory of refining and gas processing companies worldwide. Includes plant operators, engineering and construction companies, several surveys for refinery, and gas capacities, etc.

UK
**WORLDWIDE SURVEY OF MOTOR GASOLINE QUALITY.** English. an. not available for subsription. Associated Octel Co Ltd, 20 Berkeley Square, London W1 England. ctrl circ.

US/0360-2923
**WYOMING OIL AND GAS STATISTICS.** **See** Petroleum and Natural Gas-Abstracting, Bibliographies and Statistics.

US/0044-0205
**YANKEE OILMAN.** **Added/Corp** New England Fuel Institute. (1955)-. Trade Publication. English. Twelve times a year. $12.00. New England Fuel Institute, PO Box 457, Swampscott MA 01907. **Tel** (617)598-2074. **ED** Lee Yaft. **Bk Rev. Ad Acc. Circ:** 4,500 (ctrl).
**Desc:** Feature copy is primarily devoted to New England and oil heating and the related heating contracting industry.

NO
**YEAR BOOK FOR NORWEGIAN PETROLEUM SOCIETY.** **Main/Corp** Norsk Petroleumsforening. (1979)-. English. Norwegian Petroleum Society, Kronprinsensgt 17, 0251 Oslo 2 Norway. **LC** TN860; .N584.

CC
**YU TIEN KAI FA LUN WEN CHI / CHUNG-KUO SHIH YU HSUEH HUI SHIH YU KUNG CHENG HSUEH HUI PIEN.** **VFOAT** Symposium on Oil Field Development. Vol. 1- (March 1982)-. Periodical. Chinese (summaries and/or abstracts in English). 1.10. Shih Yu Kung Yeh Chu Pan She, Beijing, People's Republic of China. **LC** TN870; .Y8 . **DD** 622/.338.

VE
**ZUMAQUE.** Periodical. Spanish. Sociedad Venezolana de Ingenieros de Petroleo, Los Caobos Apartado 20006, Caracas Venezuela. **LC** TN860; .Z85A. **DD** 338.2/7/280987.

## ABSTRACTING, BIBLIOGRAPHIES AND STATISTICS

US/0003-0422
**ABSTRACTS OF REFINING LITERATURE.** [Abstr. refin. lit.]. **Added/Corp** American Petroleum Institute. **VFOAT** API Abstracts of Refining Literature. Vol. L8 (Jan. 1961)-. Periodical. English. Fifty-two times a year. Price varies. American Petroleum Institute, 275 Seventh Avenue, New York NY 10001. **Tel** (212)366-4040, FAX (212)366-4298. **ED** M. Pronin. **LC** TP690.A1; A82. **DD** 665/.53/08. ***Continues*** *API Technical Abstracts, 0096-5073;* ***Continues in part*** *Petroleum Refining and Petrochemicals Literature Abstracts; Abstracts of Air and Water Conservation Literature; Abstracts of Transportation and Storage Literature;* ***Continues*** *Abstracts of Petroleum Substitutes Literature.*
**Desc:** Articles and documents relating to the petroleum refining and petrochemical business. Technical reports, meetings, papers of research, and trade magazine articles are also included.

US/0066-3824
**ANNUAL BULLETIN OF GAS STATISTICS FOR EUROPE.** (ANNUAL BULLETIN OF GAS STATISTICS FOR EUROPE. BULLETIN ANNUEL DE ATATISTIQUES DU GAZ POUR L'EUROPE. EZHEGODNYÊI BIULLETEN EVROPEISKOI STATISTIKI GAZA.). **Added/Corp** United Nations. Economic Commission for Europe. **VFOAT** Bulletin Annuel de Statistiques du Gaz pour l'Europe; Ezhegodnyi; Biulleten Evropeiskoi Statistiki Gaza. Vol. 1 (1957)-. Government Publication. English (French and Russian). an. $35.00. United Nations Publications, 2 United Nations Plaza, Room DC2 0853, Department 007C, New York NY 10017. **Tel** (212)963-8303, (800)253-9646. **LC** HD9581.E8; U55a. **DD** 338.2/7/285094.
**Desc:** Provides basic data on development and trends, consumption and production of gas in Europe, Canada, and the United States.

US/0362-1243
**ANNUAL REPORT OF THE STATE OIL AND GAS SUPERVISOR.** [Annu. rep. State Oil Gas Superv.]. **Main/Corp** California. Division of Oil and Gas. **VFOAT** Annual Report of the State Oil & Gas Supervisor. (197?)-. Statistical Publication. English. an. Free. Division of Oil & Gas, 801 K Street, 20th Floor MS 20, Sacramento CA 95814. **Tel** (916)445-9686, FAX (916)323-0424. **ED** Susan F. Hodgson. **LC** TN872.C2; C2b. **DD** 354.97940082/388/05. **CODEN** CDOOAL. **Circ:** 2,500. ***Supersedes in part*** *Summary of Operations (California. Division of Oil and Gas), 0888-8248.*
**Desc:** California oil, gas, and geothermal production and injection statistics.

AU
**ANNUAL STATISTICAL BULLETIN (ORGANIZATION OF PETROLEUM EXPORTING COUNTRIES).** (ANNUAL STATISTICAL BULLETIN.). **Added/Corp** Organization of Petroleum Exporting Countries. **VFOAT** OPEC Annual Statistical Bulletin. (1979)-. Statistical Publication. English. an (Nov.). S350.00. Organization of the Petroleum Exporting Countries / OPEC, Obere Donaustrasse 93, A1020 Vienna 2 Austria. **Tel** 011 43 1 211120, FAX 011 43 1 264320, telex 134 474. **LC** HD9560.4; .O735a. **DD** 338.2/7282/021. **Circ:** 1,300. ***Continues*** *Organization of Petroleum Exporting Countries. Statistics Unit. Annual Statistical Report, 0475-0608.*
**Desc:** Statistics on oil and gas exploration, production, refining, consumption, exports, imports, transportation, prices and major oil companies.

US
**API ABSTRACTS : OILFIELD CHEMICALS.** ***Title Change.*** **VFOAT** Oilfield Chemicals. Vol. 28, No. 1 (Jan. 1981)-(19??). Abstracting/Indexing Service. English. mo. American Petroleum Institute, 275 Seventh Avenue, New York NY 10001. **Tel** (212)366-4040, FAX (212)366-4298. ***Continued by*** *Literature & Patent Abstracts. Oilfield Chemicals., 1065-0547.*

US
**APIBIZ [ONLINE DATABASE].** Abstracting/Indexing Service. English. $95.00 (connect time/hour), $0.20 (online types/citation), $0.25 (offline prints/citation), $3.45 (SDI) for supporters via ORBIT; $96.00 (connect time/hour), $0.20 (online types/citation), $0.25 (offline prints/citation), $4.95 (SDI) for supporters via DIALOG; $74.00 (connect time/hour), $0.16 (online types/citation), $0.30 (offline prints/citation) for supporters via DATA-STAR; $97.00 (connect time/hour), $0.30 (online types/citation), $0.35 (offline prints/citation), $4.95 (SDI) for non-supporters via ORBIT; $96.00 (connect time/hour), $0.30 (online types/citation), $0.35 (offline prints/citation), $4.95 (SDI) for non-supporters via DIALOG; $74.00 (connect time/hour), $0.26 (online types/citation), $0.43 (offline prints/citation) for non-supporters via DATA-STAR. American Petroleum Institute, 275 Seventh Avenue, New York NY 10001. **Tel** (212)366-4040, FAX (212)366-4298. available in print.
**Desc:** Online database covering industry news and business information. Twenty-two major newsletters and magazines are indexed cover-to-cover. Available via the online vendors DATA-STAR, DIALOG and ORBIT.

US
**APILIT [ONLINE DATABASE].** Abstracting/Indexing Service. English. mo. $110.00 (connect time/hour), $0.35 (online types/citation), $0.40 (offline prints/citation), $3.45 (SDI) for supporters via ORBIT, STN International, or DIALOG; $200.00 (connect time/hour), $0.60 (online types/citation), $0.65 (offline prints/citation) for non-supporters via ORBIT, STN International, or DIALOG. American Petroleum Institute, 275 Seventh Avenue, New York NY 10001. **Tel** (212)366-4040, FAX (212)366-4298. available in print.
**Desc:** Bibliographic database covering world-wide journal articles, trade magazine articles, meeting papers, dissertations, and technical reports on the technology of petroleum refining, petroleum products, and petrochemicals.

AT/0813-3514
**AUSTRALIAN PETROLEUM SERVICES INDEX.** [Aust. pet. serv. index]. (1982)-. English. an (Published in February). 50.00Aus$. Energy Publications / Australia, Energy House, 103 Scarborough Road, Mt. Hawthorn WA 6016 Australia. **Tel** 011 61 09 4433400, FAX 011 61 09 2421811, telex 95431. **DD** 338.2728029494 338.27280294931 338.27280294953.

AT/1037-9886
**ELECTRICITY AND GAS, AUSTRALIA.** **See** Energy-Abstracting, Bibliographies and Statistics.

US/0016-4844
**GAS ABSTRACTS.** [Gas abstr.]. **Added/Corp** Institute of Gas Technology. Vol. 1 (April 1945)-. Abstracting/Indexing Service. English. mo. $140.00 (surface mail), $170.00 (airmail). Institute of Gas Technology, 3424 South State Street, Chicago IL 60616. **Tel** (312)949-3970, (312)949-3650, FAX (312)949-3776, telex 25-6189. **ED** John Schaeffer. **LC** TP700; .G13. **DD** 665.705. **CODEN** GAABA3. **Bk Rev. Circ:** 800. available on microfilm and microfiche from University Microfilms International (UMI). Documents available from CASDDS.
**Desc:** Gas industry: drilling, gasification, appliances, heating, LNG, purification, process, research and development, energy pipeline, distribution system, regulation, supply, methane, natural gas, geology, and analytical methods.
**Ind/Abst** Chem. Abstr.; Corros. Abstr.

US/0361-4298
**GAS FACTS.** **Main/Corp** American Gas Association. Dept. of Statistics. 1945/1946-. Trade Publication. English. an. $50.00 (nonmembers); $25.00 (members). American Gas Association / Virginia, 1515 Wilson Boulevard, Arlington VA 22209. **Tel** (703)841-8400, (703)841-8559, FAX (703)841-8697. **ED** Patrick J Curley. **LC** TP722; .A59. **DD** 338.4/7/6657097. **Circ:** 3,500. available on microfiche (from Research Publications). ***Formed by the union of*** *Annual Statistics of the Natural Gas Utility Industry* ***and*** *Annual Statistics of the Manufactured Gas Utility Industry.*
**Desc:** A statistical yearbook of the natural gas industry. A must for anyone researching or studying the natural gas industry.
**Ind/Abst** Predicasts Forecasts.

GW
**GASSTATISTIK FUR DIE BUNDESREPUBLIK DEUTSCHLAND.** **VFOAT** Gasstatistik. German. ir. ZFGW-Verlag GmbH, Postfach 901080, W-6000 Frankfurt Germany. ***Continues*** *Zusammenstellung der Statistischen Angaben der Gasversorgungsunternehmen in der Bundesrepublik Deutschland und in West-Berlin.*

US/0742-8464
**GUIDE TO PETROLEUM STATISTICAL INFORMATION.** [Guide pet. stat. inf.]. **Added/Corp** American Petroleum Institute. (1983)-. Statistical Publication. English. an. $55.00. American Petroleum Institute, 275 Seventh Avenue, New York NY 10001. **Tel** (212)366-4040, FAX (212)366-4298. **(Subscription address:** 1970 Chain Bridge Road, McLean, VA 22109-6000**) ED** Kevin Kaczmar. **LC** Z6972; .G88; HD9560.1. **DD** 016.3382/7282. Index available. **Circ:** 250.
**Desc:** Describes all recurring statistical features in 40 petroleum industry periodicals, giving frequency of appearance and sample tables or graphs.

UK
**INSTITUTE OF PETROLEUM. STATISTICS SERVICE.** English. Four times a year. £30.00 UK and Europe; £35.00 other. Institute of Petroleum, 61 New Cavendish Street, London W1M 8AR England. **Tel** 011 44 71 636 1004, FAX 011 44 71 255 1472. **ED** C.M. Cosgrove. **Circ:** 200.
**Desc:** Consumption and production figures for the UK, Scotland and the Netherlands.

US/0535-1634
**INTERNATIONAL OIL AND GAS DEVELOPMENT.** (INTERNATIONAL OIL AND GAS DEVELOPMENT; REVIEW.). [Int. oil gas dev.]. **Added/Corp** International Oil Scouts Association. Society of Petroleum Engineers of AIME. **VFOAT** Yearbook; International Oil and Gas Development Year Book; Review. Vol. 30 (1959)-. English. an. $150.00 (Exploration Edition), $350.00 (Production Edition). Mason Research Consultants, PO Box 338, Austin TX 78767. **Tel** (512)472-7173, FAX (512)472-1057. **ED** Margie Wells. **Circ:** 600 (ctrl). ***Formed by the union of*** *Oil and Gas Field Development in the United States and Canada* ***and*** *Statistics of Oil and Gas Development and Production.*
**Desc:** A yearbook of petroleum statistics, part exploration and part production.
**Ind/Abst** GeoRef.

UK/0309-4944
**INTERNATIONAL PETROLEUM ABSTRACTS.** ***Title Change.*** [Int. pet. abstr.]. **VFOAT** IPA. Vol. 1 (March 1973)-(19??). Abstracting/Indexing Service. English. qt. John Wiley & Sons Ltd., Baffins Lane, Chichester West Sussex PO19 1UD England. **Tel** 0243 779777, FAX 0243 776128 BTG:JWP001, telex 86290 WIBOOKG. **(Subscription address:** North, South and Central America/ John Wiley & Sons, Inc., PO Box 7247-8491, Philadelphia, PA 19170-8491**) ED** Gretchen Taylor, E G Hancock, N J H Small, and G E Taylor. **LC** TN860; .I59. **DD** 665/.5/08. **CODEN** IPMABI. **Circ:** 1,250. available on microfilm and microfiche from University Microfilms International (UMI). ***Supersedes*** *Abstracts (Institute of Petroleum (Great Britain)), 0020-305X.* ***Continued by*** *International*

*Petroleum Abstracts Incorporating Offshore Abstracts, 1052-9292.*
**Ind/Abst** Fluid Abstr., Civil Eng.; Fluid Abstr. Proc. Eng.; FLUIDEX (1973-1990).

US/1065-0539
**LITERATURE ABSTRACTS. CATALYSTS & CATALYSIS.** ***Title Change.*** (LITERATURE ABSTRACTS. CATALYSTS & CATALYSIS / CENTRAL ABSTRACTING & INFORMATION SERVICES, AMERICAN PETROLEUM INSTITUTE.). [Lit. abstr., Catal. catal.]. **Added/Corp** American Petroleum Institute. Central Abstracting & Information Services. **VFOAT** Catalysts & Catalysis; Catalysts and Catalysis. Vol. 39, No. 5 (Feb. 3, 1992)-(1994). Abstracting/Indexing Service. English. wk. American Petroleum Institute, 275 Seventh Avenue, New York NY 10001. **Tel** (212)366-4040, FAX (212)366-4298. **DD** 665. Index available. cum. index. ctrl circ. available on an online database (as APILIT) from DIALOG; (as APILIT) STN International (Math) Database; and (as APILIT) ORBIT. ***Continues*** *Catalysts & Catalysis.* ***Continued by*** *Literature Abstracts. Catalysts/Zeolites, 1074-6870.*
**Desc:** Covers developments in science and technology and general news relating to the uses of catalysts.

●US/1074-6870
**LITERATURE ABSTRACTS. CATALYSTS / ZEOLITES.** **Added/Corp** American Petroleum Institute. Central Abstracting & Information Services. **VFOAT** Catalysts / Zeolites; Catalysts Zeolites. (1994)-. Periodical. English. wk. $80.00 (available to supporters only). American Petroleum Institute, 275 Seventh Avenue, New York NY 10001. **Tel** (212)366-4040, FAX (212)366-4298. **DD** 665. ***Continues*** *Literature Abstracts. Catalysts & Catalysis, 1065-0539.*

●US/1065-0512
**LITERATURE ABSTRACTS. PETROLEUM REFINING & PETROCHEMICALS.** [Lit. abstr., Pet. refin. petrochem.]. **Added/Corp** American Petroleum Institute. Central Abstracting & Information Services. **VFOAT** Petroleum Refining & Petrochemicals; Petroleum Refining and Petrochemicals; Petroleum Refining and Petrochemicals/Literature; American Petroleum Institute Literature Abstracts. Petroleum Refining & Petrochemicals; Petroleum Refining & Petrochemicals/Literature. Vol. 39, No. 5 (Feb. 3, 1992)-. Abstracting/Indexing Service. English. wk. American Petroleum Institute, 275 Seventh Avenue, New York NY 10001. **Tel** (212)366-4040, FAX (212)366-4298. **DD** 665. Index available. cum. index. ctrl circ. available on an online database (as APILIT) from DIALOG; (as APILIT) STN International (Math) Database; and (as APILIT) ORBIT. ***Continues*** *Petroleum Refining and Petrochemicals.*

●US/1065-0504
**LITERATURE ABSTRACTS. PETROLEUM SUBSTITUTES.** [Lit. abstr., Pet. substit.]. **Added/Corp** American Petroleum Institute. Central Abstracting & Information Services. **VFOAT** Petroleum Substitutes; American Petroleum Institute Literature Abstracts. Petroleum Substitutes; Petroleum Substitutes/Literature. Vol. 39, No. 2 (Feb. 1992)-. Abstracting/Indexing Service. English. mo. $35.00 (supporters only). American Petroleum Institute, 275 Seventh Avenue, New York NY 10001. **Tel** (212)366-4040, FAX (212)366-4298. **DD** 665. Index available. cum. index. ctrl circ. available on an online database (as APILIT) from DIALOG; (as APILIT) STN International (Math) Database; and (as APILIT) ORBIT. ***Continues*** *Petroleum Substitutes.*

●US/1065-0520
**LITERATURE ABSTRACTS. TRANSPORTATION & STORAGE.** [Lit. abstr., Transp. storage]. **Added/Corp** American Petroleum Institute. Central Abstracting & Information Services. **VFOAT** Transportation & Storage; Transportation and Storage; Transportation and Storage/Literature; American Petroleum Institute Literature Abstracts. Transportation & Storage; Transportation & Storage/Literature. Vol. 39, No. 2 (Feb. 1992)-. Abstracting/Indexing Service. English. mo. $40.00 (supporters only). American Petroleum Institute, 275 Seventh Avenue, New York NY 10001. **Tel** (212)366-4040, FAX (212)366-4298. **DD** 665. Index available. cum. index. ctrl circ. available on an online database (as APILIT) from DIALOG; (as APILIT) STN International (Math) Database; and (as APILIT) ORBIT. ***Continues*** *Transportation and Storage.*

US/1065-0547
**LITERATURE & PATENT ABSTRACTS. OILFIELD CHEMICALS.** ***Ceased.*** (LITERATURE & PATENT ABSTRACTS. OILFIELD CHEMICALS / CENTRAL ABSTRACTING & INFORMATION SERVICES, AMERICAN PETROLEUM INSTITUTE.). [Lit. pat. abstr., Oilfield chem.]. **Added/Corp** American Petroleum Institute. Central Abstracting & Information Services. **VFOAT** Literature and Patent Abstracts. Oilfield Chemicals; Oilfield Chemicals. (Feb. 1992)-(199?). Abstracting/Indexing Service. English. mo. American Petroleum Institute, 275 Seventh Avenue, New York NY 10001. **Tel** (212)366-4040, FAX (212)366-4298. **DD** 665. available on an online database (as APILIT) from DIALOG; (as APILIT) STN International (Math) Database; and (as APILIT) ORBIT. ***Continues*** *API Abstracts. Oilfield Chemicals.* ***Continued in part by*** *Literature Abstracts. Oilfield Chemicals, 1074-6862* ***and*** *Patent Abstracts. Oilfield Chemicals, 1074-7036.*
**Desc:** Technical literature abstract bulletin of interest to the petroleum refining and petrochemicals industries. Includes literature and patent abstracts.

US/0741-112X
**MEMBERSHIP AND STATISTICAL DIRECTORY - NEW ENGLAND GAS ASSOCIATION.** (MEMBERSHIP AND STATISTICAL DIRECTORY.). [Membsh. stat. dir. - New Engl. Gas Assoc.]. **Main/Corp** New England Gas Association. **VFOAT** New England Gas Association Directory. (19??)-. Statistical Publication. English. be. New England Gas Association, 1427 Statler Office Building, Boston MA 02116. **LC** TP700; .N433. **DD** 363.6/3/02574. ***Continues*** *New England Gas Association. Membership Directory.*

FR
**MONTHLY OIL AND GAS STATISTICS.** **VFOAT** Statistiques Mensuelles du Petrole and du Gaz Naturel. English (French). mo. $2,945.00 (magnetic tape). OECD Publications and Information Center, 2 rue Andre-Pascal, 75775 Paris Cedex 16 France. **Tel** 011 33 1 45248167, US:(202)785-6323, FAX 011 33 1 45248500 OR 45248176, telex 620 160 OCDE. **(Subscription address:** OECD Publications Center, 2001 L Street, Suite 700, Washington DC 20036.**)** available on magnetic tape.

US
**MONTHLY STATISTICAL REPORT - AMERICAN PETROLEUM INSTITUTE. STATISTICS DEPT.** **Main/Corp** American Petroleum Institute. Statistics Dept. Vol. 1, (1977)-. Statistical Publication. English. mo. $60.00 (non-member); $66.00 Canada; $78.00 other. American Petroleum Institute, 275 Seventh Avenue, New York NY 10001. **Tel** (212)366-4040, FAX (212)366-4298. **(Subscription address:** 1970 Chain Bridge Road, McLean, VA 22109-6000**)** **Bk Rev**.
**Desc:** This report will analyze and comment on the significance of trends reflected in the weekly data.

●US/1074-6730
**NATURAL GAS STATISTICS SOURCEBOOK.** [Nat. gas stat. sourceb.]. (Feb. 1994)-. English. an. $185.00. PennWell Publishing Company, 1421 South Sheridan, PO Box 1260, Tulsa OK 74101. **Tel** (918)835-3161, (800)331-4463, FAX (918)831-9497. **(Subscription address:** PennWell Books, PO Box 21288, Tulsa OK 74121.**)** **LC** HD9581.U5; N3458. **DD** 338.4/76657/0973021.

CN/1184-1761
**NICKLE'S OIL AND GAS STATISTICS QUARTERLY.** [Nickle's oil gas stat. q.]. **Added/Corp** Southam Energy Group. **VFOAT** Oil and Gas Statistics Quarterly. (3rd Quarter 1990)-. Periodical. English. qt. 360.00Can$. C.O. Nickle Publications, 999 8th Street Southwest, Suite 300, Calgary, Alberta T2R 1N7 Canada. **Tel** (403)244-6111. **DD** 338.2/728/0971021.
**Desc:** Statistical overview of the quarter most recently completed. Financial results for the top 100 operators in Canada plus cash flow, capital expenditures, net income, and the 50 top spenders.

UK/0953-1033
**OIL & ENERGY TRENDS ANNUAL STATISTICAL REVIEW.** [Oil energy trends annu. stat. rev.]. **VFOAT** Oil and Energy Trends Annual Statistical Review. (1986)-. Academic Scholarly Publication. English. an. £227.00 UK & Europe; $410.00 other. Basil Blackwell Publishers Ltd, 108 Cowley Road, Oxford 0X4 1JF England. **Tel** 011 44 865 791100, FAX 011 44 865 791347, telex 837022 OXBOOK G. **(Subscription address:** Blackwell Publishers / UK, Marston Book Services, PO Box 87, Oxford OX2 0DT England.**)** **DD** 338.4762104205. **[CCC]**. ***Continues*** *Oil & Energy Trends. Statistics Review.*

UK/0306-770X
**OIL WORLD STATISTICS.** [Oil world stat.]. **Added/Corp** Institute of Petroleum, London. Information Services. (1963)-. English. an. Institute of Petroleum, 61 New Cavendish Street, London W1M 8AR England. **Tel** 011 44 71 636 1004, FAX 011 44 71 255 1472. **ED** Lyn Nevin. **LC** HD9560.4; .O34. **DD** 338.2/7/2805.

US/0031-6423
**PETROLEUM ABSTRACTS (TULSA, OKLA.).** (PETROLEUM ABSTRACTS.). [Pet. abstr.]. **Added/Corp** University of Tulsa. Information Services Division. University of Tulsa. Information Services Dept. **VFOAT** PA. (1961)-. Abstracting/Indexing Service. English. ir. $1000.00 companies & consulting firms with assets of less than $250 million; $500.00 universities outside the US & Canada and all government agencies. Petroleum Abstracts, University of Tulsa, Information Services Division, 600 South College Avenue, Harwell Hall 101, Tulsa OK 74104-3189. **Tel** (800)247-8678, (918)631-2297, FAX (918)599-9361, telex 49 7543. **LC** TN860; .P398. **DD** 665. Index available (annual). **Circ:** 2,000 (ctrl). available in microform; available on CD-ROM (as DIALOG OnDisc Petroleum Abstracts) from DIALOG; available on an online database.
**Desc:** Abstracts of articles, monographs, and patents relating to petroleum exploration and production.
**Ind/Abst** Coal Abstr.

US/0098-7743
**PETROLEUM/ENERGY BUSINESS NEWS INDEX.** [Pet./energy bus. news index]. **Added/Corp** American Petroleum Institute. Central Abstracting and Indexing Service. (Jan. 1975)-. Abstracting/Indexing Service. English. Twelve times a year. $825.00. American Petroleum Institute, 275 Seventh Avenue, New York NY 10001. **Tel** (212)366-4040, FAX (212)366-4298. **ED** Monica Pronin (Director). **LC** Z6972; .P39; HD9560.1. **DD** 016.3337. Index available. cum. index. **Circ:** 250 (ctrl). available on an online database (as APIBIZ).
**Desc:** An index to social, political, and economic news having bearing on the petroleum and energy industries, worldwide.

US
**PETROLEUM SUBSTITUTES.** ***Title Change.*** **Added/Corp** American Petroleum Institute. Vol. 25 (Jan. 1978)-(1992). Abstracting/Indexing Service. English. mo. American Petroleum Institute, 275 Seventh Avenue, New York NY 10001. **Tel** (212)366-4040, FAX (212)366-4298. ***Continues*** *Abstracts of Petroleum Substitutes Literature.* ***Continued by*** *Literature Abstracts. Petroleum Substitutes, 1065-0504.*

US/0033-5789
**QUARTERLY REVIEW OF DRILLING STATISTICS FOR THE UNITED STATES.** ***Title Change.*** [Q. rev. drill. stat. U. S.]. Periodical. English. qt. American Petroleum Institute, 275 Seventh Avenue, New York NY 10001. **Tel** (212)366-4040, FAX (212)366-4298. **(Subscription address:** 1970 Chain Bridge Road, McLean, VA 22109-6000**)** **CODEN** QRDSB. ***Continued by*** *Quarterly Completion Report, 1045-4020.*
**Ind/Abst** GeoRef.

US
**STATISTICAL REPORT.** **VFOAT** Oil and Gas Statistical Report. Statistical Publication. English. an. $10.00. West Virginia Department of Energy, Charleston WV 25305. **Tel** (304)348-3741. **LC** HD9567.W4; S7. **DD** 338.7/622338/09753021.

AT/0466-2865
**STATISTICAL YEAR BOOK - THE AUSTRALIAN GAS INDUSTRY.** **Main/Corp** National Gas Association of Australia. **VFOAT** The Australian Gas Industry: Statistical Year Book; NGA: Statistical Year Book; National Gas Association: Year Book; Statistical Year Book - The National Gas Association of Australia. (1958)-. Statistical Publication. English. **LC** TP738; .N3. **DD** 338.476657. ***Continues*** *Statistical Year Book of the Gas Industry in Australia.*

FR
**STATISTIQUES DE L'INDUSTRIE GAZIERE EN FRANCE.** **Main/Corp** France. Direction du Gaz, de l'Electricite et du Charbon. (19??)-. French. Ministere de l'Industrie et de la Recherche, 280, BD Saint-Germain, Paris 75700 France. **LC** TP733.F8; A32. **DD** 338.4/7/66570944. ***Continues*** *France. Direction du Gaz et de L'Electricite. Statistiques Officielles de L'Industrie Gaziere en France.*

FR
**STATISTIQUES F. O. A. : DISTRIBUTION DES FUELS-OILS.** **Main/Corp** Comite Professionnel du Petrole, Paris. **VAT** Statistiques Fuel-Oils A(?): Distribution des Fuel-Oils. Periodical. French. Comite Professionnel du Petrol CPDP, BP 282, 92505 Rueil Malmaison France. **Tel** 011 33 1 47169460. **LC** HD9572.4; .C63. **DD** 381/.42/282. ***Continues*** *Statistique Mensuelles de la Distribution des Fuel-Oils.*

US
**SUMMARY OF NATURAL GAS STATISTICS / OHIO DEPARTMENT OF ENERGY.** English. an. Public Utilities Commission / Ohio, 180 East Broad Street, 11th Floor, Columbus OH 43266. **Tel** (614)466-0327. **LC** HD9581.U52; O37. **DD** 338.2/7285/09771.

US/0190-2997
**SUMMARY OF RATE SCHEDULES OF NATURAL GAS PIPELINE COMPANIES AS FILED WITH THE FEDERAL ENERGY REGULATORY COMMISSION AND THE NATIONAL ENERGY BOARD OF CANADA.** [Summ. rate sched. nat. gas pipeline co. filed Fed. Energy Regul. Comm. Nat. Energy Board Can.]. **Main/Corp** H. Zinder & Associates. (19??)-. English. Four times a year. $395.00. H. Zinder and

Associates Inc., 1828 L Street NW, Washington DC 20036. **Tel** (202)862-3400. **ED** Joseph Blackburn. **LC** HD9581.U53; Z5. **DD** 338.4/3. ***Continues*** *Summary of Rate Schedules of Natural Gas Pipeline Companies as Filed with Federal Power Commission, 0146-1907.*

US/1048-4825
**TWENTIETH CENTURY PETROLEUM STATISTICS.** [Twent. century pet. stat.]. **Added/Corp** DeGolyer and MacNaughton. United States. Office of Naval Petroleum and Oil Shale Reserves. (1945)-. English. an. $35.00. Degolyer & MacNaughton, One Energy Square, Dallas TX 75206. **Tel** (214)368-6391, telex 73-0485. **ED** Norman Bodes. **DD** 338. **Circ:** 1,000 (ctrl). ***Continues*** *Twentieth Century Petroleum Statistics.*
**Desc:** Information regarding world wide oil and gas production.

UK/0141-4305
**U.K. PETROLEUM INDUSTRY STATISTICS. CONSUMPTION AND REFINERY PRODUCTION.** **Added/Corp** Institute of Petroleum (Great Britain). **VFOAT** UK Petroleum Industry Statistics. Consumption and Refinery Production. (1950)-. English. an. Institute of Petroleum, 61 New Cavendish Street, London W1M 8AR England. **Tel** 011 44 71 636 1004, FAX 011 44 71 255 1472. **ED** Lyn Nevin. **LC** HD9571.1; .U16. **DD** 338.4/7665538/0941.

US/1057-5790
**WEEKLY PETROLEUM STATUS REPORT / U.S. DEPARTMENT OF ENERGY, ENERGY INFORMATION ADMINISTRATION.** **Added/Corp** United States. Energy Information Administration. (June 19, 1981)-. Periodical. English. wk. $61.00. National Energy Information Center, Energy Information Administration, Forrestal Building, Room 1F-048, Washington DC 20585. **Tel** (202)586-8800. available on microfiche (Vols. for (1986-) distributed to depository libraries). Documents available from Documents on Demand. ***Continues*** *Energy Information Administration Weekly Petroleum Status Report.*
**Desc:** Provides timely information on the petroleum supply situation in the context of historical information, selected prices, and forecasts.
**Ind/Abst** Am. Stat. Index (19??-); Energy Inf. Abstr. (19??-).

US
**WEEKLY STATISTICAL BULLETIN (AMERICAN PETROLEUM INSTITUTE. STATISTICS DEPT.).** (WEEKLY STATISTICAL BULLETIN / STATISTICS DEPARTMENT, AMERICAN PETROLEUM INSTITUTE.). **Added/Corp** American Petroleum Institute. Dept. of Statistics. (1975)-. Statistical Publication. English. ir. $110.00. American Petroleum Institute / Washington DC, 1220 L Street Northwest, Washington DC 20005. **Tel** (202)682-8378. **(Subscription address:** American Petroleum Institute / Virginia, 1970 Chain Bridge Road, McLean VA 22109.**) LC** HD9561; .W37. ***Continues*** *Weekly Statistical Bulletin - American Petroleum Institute. Division of Statistics and Economics.*

US/1058-9686
**WORLDWIDE OFFSHORE CONTRACTORS & EQUIPMENT DIRECTORY.** [Worldw. offshore contract. equip. dir.]. **VFOAT** Worldwide Offshore Contractors and Equipment Directory. 19th (1987)-. Directory. English. an. $159.50 US and Canada; $209.50 other. PennWell Publishing Company, 1421 South Sheridan, PO Box 1260, Tulsa OK 74101. **Tel** (918)835-3161, (800)331-4463, FAX (918)831-9497. **(Subscription address:** PennWell Books, PO Box 21288, Tulsa OK 74121.**) ED** Carol Schaefer. **LC** TN871.3; .O33. **DD** 622/.3382/025. **Bk Rev**. **Ad Acc. Circ:** 2,500 (ctrl). ***Continues*** *Offshore (Tulsa, Okla. : Annual), 1058-9694.*
**Desc:** Provides a complete listing of all contractors and equipment involved in the offshore petroleum industry. Includes offshore drilling contractors and rig owners; workover and well servicing contractors; construction equipment contractors and diving contractors, etc.

US/0360-2923
**WYOMING OIL AND GAS STATISTICS.** [Wyo. oil gas stat.]. **Main/Corp** Wyoming Oil and Gas Conservation Commission. (19??)-. Statistical Publication. English. an (Aug.). Free on request. Wyoming Oil & Gas Conservation Commission, PO Box 2640, Casper WY 82602. **Tel** (307)234-7147. **LC** TJ163.4.U6; W9a. **DD** 338.2/7/2809787.

## PETS

US/0744-9631
**ACFA BULLETIN.** (ACFA BULLETIN : OFFICIAL PUBLICATION OF THE AMERICAN CAT FANCIERS ASSOCIATION.). **VFOAT** A.C.F.A. Bulletin. **VAT** American Cat Fanciers Association Bulletin. Bulletin. English. mo. American Cat Fanciers Association, PO Box 203, Point Lookout MO 65726.

US/1040-2225
**ADVOCATE (DENVER, COLO.).** (ADVOCATE.). [Advocate]. **Added/Corp** American Humane Association. American Humane Association. Animal Protection Division. Vol. 1 No. 1 (Nov. 1983)-. Periodical. English. qt. $15.00. American Humane Association, 63 Inverness Drive East, Englewood CO 80112. **Tel** (303)792-9900, FAX (303)695-6348. **ED** Susan W Halberstandt. **LC** WMLC 93/214. **DD** 179. **Bk Rev. Circ:** 28,500 (ctrl). ***Continues in part*** *National Animal Protection Newsletter, 0738-582X.*
**Desc:** Reports American Humane Association's animal protection activities and legislative activities from the Washington DC office. Includes reviews concerning the treatment of animals in entertainment as well as pet care and health topics.
**Ind/Abst** AGRICOLA [Select. Cov.].

KO
**AEGYON UI OL.** Periodical. Korean. Taehan Kunyonggyon Hyophoe, 108-1 4-ka Chungmu-ro, Chung-ku Seoul Korea. **LC** SF421; .A33.

US/0199-543X
**AFA WATCHBIRD, THE.** [A.F.A. watchb.]. **Main/Corp** American Federation of Aviculture. **VFOAT** Watchbird. **VAT** American Federation of Aviculture Watchbird. Vol. 1 (1974)-. Periodical. English. Six times a year. $24.00 Comes with American Federation Aviculture membership. American Federation Aviculture, PO Box 56218, Phoenix AZ 85073-6218. **Tel** (602)484-0931. **ED** Jerry Jennings. **LC** WMLC 93/1358. **DD** 636. **CODEN** AFAWE5. Index available. cum. index. **Bk Rev**. **Ad Acc. Circ:** 10,100 (ctrl).

US/8750-9776
**AFGHAN HOUND REVIEW, THE.** [Afghan hound rev.]. (19??)-. Periodical. English. Six times a year (Feb., Apr., June, Aug., Oct., Dec.). $40.00 US; $72.00 other. The Afghan Hound Review, PO Box 30430, Santa Barbara CA 93130. **Tel** (805)966-7270, FAX (805)682-1771. **ED** Bo N. Bengtson. **LC** SF429.A4; A35. **DD** 636.7/53. **Bk Rev**, (Qty: 2-3). **Ad Acc. Circ:** 2,000.
**Desc:** News and information for the hounds such as show racing, obedience, grooming, care and other news.

XR
**AKVARIUM, TERARIUM.** Periodical. Czech. ir. 30.00. PNS-Ustredni Expedice A, Dovoz Tisku Kafkova 19, 160 00 Prague 6 Czech Republic. **LC** SF456; .A37. **DD** 639.3/4/05. ***Continues*** *Akvarium a Terarium.*

US/1059-4477
**AMERICAN AIREDALE, THE.** (THE AMERICAN AIREDALE : OFFICIAL NEWSLETTER OF THE AIREDALE TERRIER CLUB OF AMERICA, INC.). [Amer. Airedale]. **Added/Corp** Airedale Terrier Club of America. No. 5 (Oct.-Nov. 1991)-. Newsletter. English. bm. Airedale Terrier Club of America, Phyllis Madaus, Assistant Secretary, 205 Satsuma Drive, Sanford FL 32771. **LC** WMLC 91/3430. **DD** 636. ***Continues*** *ATCA Newsletter.*

US/0002-774X
**AMERICAN BULLMASTIFF, THE.** Periodical. English. qt. $2.00. The Greeleys, Box 13201, Syracuse NY 13261. **LC** SF429.B86; A44. **DD** 636.7/3.

US/0002-7782
**AMERICAN CAGE-BIRD MAGAZINE.** ***Title Change.*** [Am. cage-bird mag.]. **VFOAT** American Cage Bird Magazine. (1951)-(Feb. 1994). Periodical. English. mo. Audubon Publishing Company, One Glamore Court, Smithtown NY 11787. **Tel** (516)979-7962, FAX (516)979-8681. **ED** Arthur Freud. **LC** SF461.A1; N3. **DD** 636.68605. Index available. **Bk Rev. Ad Acc. Circ:** 50,000. ***Continues*** *American Canary Magazine.* ***Continued by*** *Bird Breeder, 1073-5186.*
**Desc:** Information by internationally known authors on the breeding, feeding, maintenance, taming and health care of parrots, cockatiels, budgies, canaries, finches and other pet birds.
**Ind/Abst** Fish Rev.; Wildl. Rev.

US/0194-5173
**AMERICAN CHOW CHOW INC, THE.** **Main/Corp** The American Chow Chow Inc. (19??)-. Periodical. English. qt. American Chow Chow, 3524 Linda Drive, Dallas TX 75220.

US/0888-627X
**AMERICAN KENNEL CLUB AWARDS.** [Am. Kennel Club awards]. **Added/Corp** American Kennel Club. Vol. 6, No. 7 (July 1986)-. Periodical. English. Twelve times a year. $40.00. American Kennel Club, 5580 Center View Drive, Raleigh NC 27606. **Tel** (919)233-9780. **DD** 636. **Ad Acc. Circ:** 12,800. ***Continues*** *American Kennel Club Show, Obedience and Field Trial Awards, 0272-4383.*

US/0162-2013
**AMERICAN KENNEL CLUB STUD BOOK REGISTER.** **Added/Corp** National American Kennel Club. American Kennel Club. Vol. 1 (1879)-. Periodical. English. Twelve times a year. $75.00. American Kennel Club, 5580 Center View Drive, Raleigh NC 27606. **Tel** (919)233-9780. **LC** SF423; .A5. **Circ:** 500. available on microfilm and microfiche from University Microfilms International (UMI).

CN/0824-8494
**AMI DES BETES, L'.** [Ami betes]. Vol. 1, No. 1 (Jan. 1984)-. Periodical. French. mo. $1.00. **DD** 636/.009714.

CN/0709-4116
**ANIMAG.** V. 1- June 1978-. Periodical. French. Three times a year. 35.00Can$. Animag, CP 2024 Succ, Sherbrooke Quebec J1J 3Y1 Canada. **DD** 636.08/87/05.

US
**ANIMAL FINDERS' GUIDE.** (198?)-. Periodical. English. Eighteen times a year. $25.00. Animal Finders Guide, PO Box 99, Prairie Creek IN 47869. **Tel** (812)898-2701. **ED** Patrick D. Hoctor (phone: (812)898-2678). **Bk Rev**, (Qty: varies). **Ad Acc, Adv Mgr:** Sharon Hoctor, **Tel** (812)898-2678. **Circ:** 5,000.
**Desc:** Articles, classified ads, and display ads pertaining to exotic animals and alternative livestock.

CN/0710-9148
**ANIMAL MAGAZINE, L'.** [Anim. mag.]. Vol. 1, No. 1 (March 1981)-. Periodical. French. bm. $10.00. L'Animal Magazine, CP 388 Succursale A, Longueuil Quebec J4H 3Z2 Canada. **DD** 636.08/87/05.

SP/0214-3151
**ANIMALIA (BARCELONA).** (ANIMALIA.). [Animalia]. (1988)-. Periodical. Spanish. Eleven times a year. $100.00. Elsevier Prensa SA, Avenida Paral Lel 180, 08015 Barcelona Spain. **Tel** 011 34 3 3255350, FAX 011 34 3 4252880. **Ad Acc.** Full Page (B&W) 160000ptas. Half Page (B&W) 10000ptas. Full Page (Color) 20000ptas. Half Page (Color) 130000ptas. **Circ:** 7,000.
**Desc:** Dedicated to pets, including health care, medicine, diet, and show activities.

FR/0151-6981
**AQUARAMA.** **Added/Corp** Association pour la Vulgarisation de l'Aquariophilie et Terrariophilie. (19??)-. Periodical. French. Six times a year. 210.00F France; 246.00F others. Aquarama, 24 rue de Verdun, 67000 Strasbourg France. **Tel** 011 33 88 619608, FAX 011 33 88 411074. **ED** Didie Prevot. **LC** SF456; .A76. **DD** 639/.34/05. Index available. cum. index. **Bk Rev. Ad Acc, Adv Mgr:** A. Saegel. **Pr Rev. Circ:** 10,000 (ctrl).
**Ind/Abst** Aquat. Sci. Fish. Abstr. (Computer File).

US/0899-045X
**AQUARIUM FISH MAGAZINE.** [Aquar. fish mag.]. **VFOAT** Aquarium Fish. (1988)-. Periodical. English. bm. $24.97. Fancy Publications, PO Box 6050, Mission Viejo CA 92690. **Tel** (714)855-8822, (800)426-2516, FAX (714)855-3045. **(Subscription address:** Neodata / Colorado, PO Box 2606, Boulder Boulder CO 80322.**) DD** 639.

CN/0317-5650
**AVICULTURAL JOURNAL, THE.** ***Ceased.*** **See** Zoology-Ornithology.

US/0094-9744
**BASENJI, THE.** [Basenji]. Periodical. English. mo. $18.00. The Basenji, 789 Linton Hill Road, Newtown PA 18940. **Tel** (215)860-8254. **ED** Susan Coe. **LC** SF429.B15; B36. **DD** 636.7/53. **Bk Rev**. **Ad Acc. Circ:** 1,500.
**Desc:** Publication for Basenji (dog) breeders, fanciers and pet owners. Sharing information.

US/0736-9743
**BETTER BEAGLING MAGAZINE.** **VFOAT** Better Beagling. (1982)-. Periodical. English. Twelve times a year. $12.00 (one year), $24.00 (two year). Better Beagling, PO Box 142, Essex VT 05451. ***Continues*** *Large Pack.*

US/0199-8315
**BICHON FRISE REPORTER, THE.** [Bichon frise report.]. Vol. 1 (Oct./Nov. 1979)-. Periodical. English. qt. The Bichon Frise Reporter, PO Box 827, Culver City CA 90232. **DD** 636.

●US/1073-5186
**BIRD BREEDER.** [Bird breed.]. Vol. 66, No. 3/4 (Mar./Apr. 1994)-. Periodical. English. mo. $29.97. Fancy Publications, PO Box 6050, Mission Viejo CA 92690. **Tel** (714)855-8822, (800)426-2516, FAX (714)855-3045. **(Subscription address:** Palm Coast Data, PO Box 420235, Agency Department, Palm Coast FL 32142.**) DD** 636. ***Continues*** *American Cage-Bird Magazine, 0002-7782.*
**Desc:** Authoritative information by internationally known authors on the breeding, feeding, maintenance, taming and health care of parrots, cockatiels, budgies, canaries, finches and other pet birds. A favorite of bird owners since 1928. Each issue is 104 pages with many color and black and white illustrations. Annual annotated index in January issue.

US/0891-771X
**BIRD TALK.** [Bird talk]. (198?)-. Periodical. English. mo. $25.97. Fancy Publications, PO Box 6050, Mission Viejo CA 92690. **Tel** (714)855-8822, (800)426-2516, FAX

(714)855-3045. **(Subscription address:** Neodata / Colorado, PO Box 2606, Boulder Boulder CO 80322.**) ED** Linda Lewis. **LC** WMLC L 83/2744. **DD** 636. **Circ:** 72,000. ***Continues*** *International Bird Talk, 0742-8359.*
**Ind/Abst** Fish Rev.; Wildl. Rev.

US/0199-5979
**BIRD WORLD (NORTH HOLLYWOOD).** **See** Zoology-Ornithology.

US/0890-8923
**BLOODLINES :.** [Bloodlines]. **Added/Corp** United Kennel Club. (1913)-. Periodical. English. Six times a year (Jan., Mar., May, July, Sept., Nov.). $12.00. United Kennel Club Inc, 100 East Kilgore Road, Kalamazoo MI 49001. **Tel** (616)343-9020, FAX (616)343-7037. **ED** Kerry Knudsen, (phone: (616)343-9020 Ext. 107). **DD** 636. Index available (Bound in next issue.). **Bk Rev. Ad Acc, Adv Mgr:** T. Birdsong, **Tel** (616)343-9020. **Circ:** 4,000.
**Desc:** Devoted principally to working and show dogs, obedience training and trials. Includes information on health care, training and events.

US/0190-0226
**BOARDING KENNEL PROPRIETOR.** Periodical. English. mo. $12.50. Boarding Kennel Proprietor, 2785 North Speer Blvd., Denver CO 80211. **LC** SF428; .B6. **DD** 646.7/08.

US/0746-2875
**BORZOI QUARTERLY (WHEAT RIDGE, COLO.), THE.** (THE BORZOI QUARTERLY.). [Borzoi q.]. (19??)-. Periodical. English. bm. $40.00 (one year), $76.00 (two year). Hoflin Publishing Ltd, 4401 Zephyr Street, Wheat Ridge CO 80033-3299. **Tel** (303)934-5656. **ED** Donald R. Hoflin. **DD** 636. **Ad Acc, Adv Mgr:** Cindy Kerstiens. **Circ:** 398.

US/1059-0625
**BREEDER FORUM.** [Breed. forum]. **Added/Corp** Kal Kan Foods. Vol. 1, No. 1 (1991)-. Periodical. English. qt. Free. Kal Kan Foods Inc Professional Services, 3386 East 44th Street, Vernon CA 90058. **DD** 636. ***Formed by the union of*** *Pedigree Forum, 1042-9107* ***and*** *Kal Kan Forum (Vernon, Calif. : 1988), 1043-1772.*

US/0746-1410
**CANINE CHRONICLE.** (19??)-. Periodical. English. mo. $80.00 (one year), $135.00 (two year). Canine Chronicle, 605 2nd Avenue North, Columbus MS 39701. **Tel** (601)327-1124.

US/0069-1003
**CAT FANCIERS' NEWS.** (1984)-. Periodical. English. an. $84.50. Cat Fancier's Association, 1309 Allaire Avenue, Ocean NJ 07712. **Tel** (201)531-2390. **ED** Marna Fogarty. **Ad Acc. Circ:** 2,000.
**Desc:** Articles on cats and cat shows.

US/0892-6514
**CAT FANCY (SAN JUAN CAPISTRANO, CALIF.).** (CAT FANCY.). **VFOAT** Cat Fancy Magazine. Vol. 29, No. 1 (Jan. 1986)-. Periodical. English. mo. $25.97. Fancy Publications, PO Box 6050, Mission Viejo CA 92690. **Tel** (714)855-8822, (800)426-2516, FAX (714)855-3045. **(Subscription address:** Neodata / Colorado, PO Box 2606, Boulder Boulder CO 80322.**) ED** Linda Lewis. **LC** SF441; .I57. **DD** 636.8/005. **Bk Rev. Ad Acc. Circ:** 237,528. ***Continues*** *International Cat Fancy.*

●US/1074-7788
**CAT INDUSTRY NEWSLETTER.** [Cat ind. newsl.]. Vol. 1, No. 1 (July 25, 1992)-. Periodical. English. mo. $206.50. Good Communications, Inc, PO Box 31292, Charleston SC 29417. **Tel** (803)795-9555, FAX (803)795-2930. **ED** Ross Becker. **DD** 636.
**Desc:** Covers new products and marketing and products for cats. Special emphasis is given to cat food and cat litter, both supermarket and specialty brands.

US/1055-8438
**CAT LOVERS : THE OFFICIAL CLA CLUB MAGAZINE.** [Cat lovers]. **Added/Corp** Cat Lovers of America. **VFOAT** Cat Lovers Magazine. Vol. 1, No. 1 (Fall 1991)-. Periodical. English. qt. $29.00 (membership included). Cat Lovers of America, PO Box 5050, El Toro CA 92630. **DD** 636.

US/0163-1926
**CAT WORLD.** Periodical. English. bm. $7.95 US; $8.95 other. Cat World, PO Box 35635, Phoenix AZ 85069.

US/0008-8544
**CATS MAGAZINE.** [Cats mag.]. **VFOAT** Cats. (1945)-. Periodical. English. mo. $21.97. Cats Magazine, PO Box 290037, Port Orange FL 32129. **Tel** (904)788-2770. **ED** Linda J. Walton. **Bk Rev. Ad Acc. Circ:** 189,697. available on microfilm and microfiche from University Microfilms International (UMI). Documents available from UMI Article Clearinghouse.
**Desc:** Articles, care and health information, poems, photos, columns for all cat people.
**Ind/Abst** Newsp. Period. Abstr. (1988-).

AT
**CLUMBER SPANIEL CORRESPONDENCE.** English. mo. 24Aus$ Australia; 36Aus$ other. Erinrac Enterprises, Foott Road, Upper Beaconsfield Victoria 3808 Australia. **Tel** (059)44 3383, FAX (059)44 3384. **ED** Jan Irving. **Bk Rev**, (Qty: 6-12). **Ad Acc. Circ:** 5000.
**Desc:** Breed specialists worldwide.

US/0744-0731
**COLLIE REVIEW.** (19??)-. Periodical. English. mo. $30.00 (one year), $50.00 (two year) US; $45.00 (one year), $60.00 (two year) other. Drucker Publications, 8760 Appian Way, Los Angeles CA 90046. **Tel** (310)553-9277. **ED** M D Drucker. **Bk Rev. Ad Acc. Circ:** 5,000. ***Continues*** *Collie & Shetland Sheepdog Review.*
**Desc:** Appearing monthly in the review are many features such as: Area News, Educational Articles, Show Stoppers, People Are Talking About. Area News are columnists from various parts of the country to see that your news of show wins, new champions, litters, etc. is printed monthly. Educational Articles feature writers appear on a monthly basis with original articles and exclusive to the Review. Show Stoppers are great publicity world-wide at a minimum cost. The Review donates the space. People are Talking About is for clubs that want that great post-show publicity showing the tremendous amount of work they have donw done their recent specialty.

CN/0317-1965
**CYNOMAG.** **Added/Corp** Club Canin de Montreal. Vol. 1, No. 3 (May 1973)-. French. Club Canin de Montreal, 12337 Charles Renard, Riviere des Prairies Quebec Canada. **DD** 636.7/006/2714281. ***Continues*** *Information, 0317-1973.*

US/1045-1757
**DOBERMAN QUARTERLY.** [Doberman q.]. **VFOAT** DQ. Periodical. English. qt. Doberman Quarterly, 739 Edgemar, Pacifica CA 94044. **LC** SF429.D6; D64. **DD** 636.7/3.

US/0892-6522
**DOG FANCY (LOS ANGELES, CALIF.).** (DOG FANCY.). [Dog fancy]. **VFOAT** Dog Fancy Magazine; Dogfancy. Vol. 17, No. 1 (Jan. 1986)-. Periodical. English. mo. $23.97. Fancy Publications, PO Box 6050, Mission Viejo CA 92690. **Tel** (714)855-8822, (800)426-2516, FAX (714)855-3045. **(Subscription address:** Neodata / Colorado, PO Box 2606, Boulder Boulder CO 80322.**) ED** Linda Lewis. **LC** SF421; .D625. **DD** 636. **Bk Rev. Ad Acc. Circ:** 135,320. ***Continues*** *International Dog Fancy.*

US/1074-777X
**DOG INDUSTRY NEWSLETTER.** [Dog ind. newsl.]. (199?)-. Periodical. English. mo. $206.50. Good Communications, Inc, PO Box 31292, Charleston SC 29417. **Tel** (803)795-9555, FAX (803)795-2930. **ED** Ross Becker. **DD** 636.
**Desc:** Covers new products and the business of marketing products for dogs. Special emphasis is given to dog food, both supermarket and specialty brands.

US/0279-4144
**DOG SPORTS.** [Dog sports]. **VFOAT** Dog Sports Magazine. (19??)-. Periodical. English. mo. $44.00 (one year), $80.00 (two year). Dog Sports, 32 Cherokee Trail, Douglas WY 82633. **Tel** (307)358-1000. ***Continues*** *Dog Sports Magazine, 0194-6706.*

US/1062-0699
**DOG WATCH (STUDIO CITY, CALIF.).** (DOG WATCH : A WEEKLY NEWSPAPER FOR THE PUREBRED DOG FANCY.). [Dog watch]. Vol. 1, Issue 1 (Oct. 4, 1991)-. Periodical. English. wk. $120.00. Dog Watch, 11331 Ventura Boulevard, Suite 301, Studio City CA 91604-3155. **LC** WMLC 91/3373. **DD** 636.

US/0012-4893
**DOG WORLD.** (DOG WORLD; THE COMPLETE ALL-BREED MAGAZINE.). [Dog world]. **VFOAT** Dog World Magazine. Vol. 1 (Jan. 1916)-. Periodical. English. mo. $28.00 (one year), $50.00 (two year), $70.00 (three year) US; $38.00 (one year), $70.00 (two year), $100.00 (three year) Canada; $43.00 (one year), $80.00 (two year), $115.00 (three year) other. MacLean Hunter Publishing Corporation / Chicago, IL, 29 North Wacker Drive, Chicago IL 60606-3298. **Tel** (312)726-2802, FAX (312)726-3091. **ED** Enid S. Bergstrom. **DD** 636. **[CCC]. Bk Rev. Ad Acc. Circ:** 63,000. available on microfilm and microfiche from University Microfilms International (UMI). Documents available from UMI Article Clearinghouse.
**Desc:** For breeders, exhibitors, hobbyists and professionals in kennel operations, grooming, veterinarians, animal hospitals/clinics and pet supplies. Includes articles on health care, veterinary medical research, grooming, legislation show awards, training, show schedules, junior showmanship, kennel operations, breed qualities and histories.
**Ind/Abst** Newsp. Period. Abstr. (1988-).

UK
**DOG WORLD.** English. wk. $165.50. Press House, 9 Tufton Street, Ashford Kent TN23 1QN England. **Tel** 0233 621877.
**Desc:** Covers everything about dogs including dog sport news (including showing), training and breed history.

CN/0012-4915
**DOGS IN CANADA.** [Dogs Can.]. V. 28, No. 6-Mar. 1940-. Periodical. English. mo (13 issues per year). 22.00Can$ Canada; 27.00Can$ US; 35.00Can$ other. Dogs in Canada, 43 Railside Road, Don Mills Ontario M3A 3L9 Canada. **Tel** (416)441-3228. **Bk Rev. Ad Acc. Circ:** 21,000. ***Continues*** *Kennel and Bench;* ***Absorbed*** *Dogs Annual, 0317-1485.*
**Desc:** For breeders, exhibitors and people with a serious interest in dogs. "The Annual," released each November, is for every dog lover, particularly those who are planning to get a puppy. Choosing a breed, training, health, grooming and a "Breeders' Directory" are rounded out with beautiful color photos and heartwarming articles about every aspect of the dogs.
**Ind/Abst** Can. Index (?-?).

GW
**DU UND DAS TIER.** **Added/Corp** Deutscher Tierschutzbund. (1971)-. Periodical. German. bm. DM29.50 Germany; DM43.40 other. Verlag M & H Schaper GmbH & Co, Postfach 16 42, D 31046 Alfeld Leine Germany. **Tel** 011 49 5181 80090. ***Supersedes*** *Tier-Illustrierte.*
**Ind/Abst** Index Vet.; Pig News Inf.; Vet. Bull.

CN/0849-3405
**FANCIERS DIGEST, THE.** [Fanciers dig.]. **VFOAT** Fancier's Digest. (Jan. 1990)-. Periodical. English. mo. Limited free distribution. Real Press, 97-53431 Range Road 221, Androssan Alberta T0B 0E0 Canada. **DD** 636/.0097123/05. ***Continues*** *Western Canada Rabbit News., 0844-5419.*

US
**FRONT AND FINISH.** (19??)-. English. mo. $20.00 (one year); $37.00 (two year). Front and Finish, PO Box 333, Galesburg IL 61402. **ED** Robert T. Self.
**Ind/Abst** Mag. Search.

US/0746-5483
**GORDON QUARTERLY, THE.** (THE GORDON QUARTERLY : GQ.). [Gordon q.]. **VFOAT** GQ; G.Q. Vol. 1, No. 1 (Fall 1983)-. Periodical. English. qt. $36.00 US; $40.00 other. The Gordon Quarterly, 4401 Zephyr Street, Wheat Ridge CO 80033-3299. **Tel** (303)420-2222, FAX (303)422-7000. **Circ:** 480.
**Desc:** Publication about Gordon Setters.

US/0191-7633
**GREYHOUND BREEDER'S JOURNAL.** Vol. 1 (1977)-. English. Greyhound Breeder's Journal, 304 Northwest 17th Street, Abilene KS 67410. **LC** SF429.G8; G8.

US/0199-8366
**GROOM & BOARD.** [Groom board]. **VFOAT** Groom and Board. V. 1, No. 1 (Jan./Feb. 1980)-. Periodical. English. Nine times a year. $25.00. H. H. Backer Associates Inc, 20 East Jackson Boulevard, Chicago IL 60604. **Tel** (312)663-4040, FAX (312)663-5676. **ED** Karen Long Machead. **LC** SF427.5; .G76. **DD** 636.7/083/05. **Ad Acc. Circ:** 16,000 (ctrl).
**Desc:** The only national magazine for professional groomers and kennel operators, with news, technical articles and money-making ideas.

US/0018-6384
**HOUNDS AND HUNTING.** (1903)-. Periodical. English. Twelve times a year. $14.00 US; $26.00 other. Hounds and Hunting, Box 372, Bradford PA 16701. **Tel** (814)368-6154, 368-6155, FAX (814)368-3522. **ED** R.F. Slike. **Bk Rev. Ad Acc. Circ:** 12,000 (ctrl).
**Desc:** Devoted to field trial beagling and gun-dog trials and the beagle hound.

US/0899-9570
**I LOVE CATS.** [I love cats]. Vol. 1, Issue 1 (Jan./Feb. 1989)-. Periodical. English. bm. $24.00. Hochman Associates, 950 Third Avenue, 16th Floor, New York NY 10022. **Tel** (212)371-4932. **(Subscription address:** CDS Agency Hard Copy, PO Box 4966, Des Moines IA 50340.**) DD** 636.

●US
**INTERACTIONS / DELTA SOCIETY.** **Added/Corp** Delta Society. (1992)-. Periodical. English. qt. $15.00. Delta Society, 321 Burnett Avenue South, Suite 303, Renton WA 98055-2569. **Tel** (206)226-7357, FAX (206)235-1076. ***Continues*** *People, Animals, Environment, 8755-5875.*

US/0735-8504
**ITALIAN GREYHOUND, THE.** Periodical. English. bm. $20.00 US; $38.00 (air mail) other. The Italian Greyhound, 8414 Kingsgate Road, Potomac MD 20854. **Tel** (301)299-6269. **ED** William Cooper, Joan Cooper and Annette Norton. **LC** SF429.I89; I87. **DD** 636.7/6. Index available. **Bk Rev. Ad Acc. Circ:** 800.

UK/0022-4510
**JOURNAL OF SMALL ANIMAL PRACTICE, THE.** **See** Veterinary Sciences.

UK
**KENNEL GAZETTE, THE.** (19??)-. Periodical. English. mo. £30.00 overseas surface mail; £36.00 (Europe), £50.00 (other) airmail. Kennel Club, 1-5 Charles Strasse/Piccadilly, London W1Y 8AB England. **Tel** 01 493 6651.

US/0164-4289
**KENNEL REVIEW.** [Kennel rev.]. Began with Jan. 1898 issue. Periodical. English. mo. $45.00 (second class), $75.00 (first class) US; $65.00 (second class), $105.00 (first class) Canada and Mexico; $75.00 (second class), $165.00 (first class) other. B & E Publications, 11331 Ventura Boulevard, Studio City CA 91604. **Tel** (818)761-3647. **ED** Richard Beauchamp. **LC** SF425.15; .K46. **DD** 636.7/08/1105. **Bk Rev. Ad Acc. Circ:** 10,000 (ctrl). ***Absorbed*** *Collie; Dogology.*

US/8750-3557
**LABRADOR QUARTERLY : LQ, THE.** [Labrador q.]. **VFOAT** LQ. Vol. 1, No. 1; Summer 1984-. Periodical. English. qt. $40.00 (one year), $76.00 (two year). Hoflin Publishing Ltd, 4401 Zephyr Street, Wheat Ridge CO 80033-3299. **Tel** (303)934-5656. **ED** Donald R. Hoflin. **Ad Acc, Adv Mgr:** Cindy Kerstiens. **Circ:** 2,678.

US/1071-2593
**LIBRARY CAT NEWSLETTER, THE.** [Libr. cat newsl.]. **Added/Corp** Library Cat Society (Sauk Centre, Minn.). Vol. 2, No. 1 (Jan./Feb. 1988)-. Newsletter. English. qt. $5.00. Library Cat Society, PO Box 274, Morhead MN 56560. **Tel** (618)236-7205. **DD** 022. ***Continues*** *Newsletter (Library Cat Club of America).*

US/0746-4002
**MALAMUTE QUARTERLY, THE.** [Malamute q.]. (19??)-. Periodical. English. qt. $40.00 (one year), $76.00 (two year). Hoflin Publishing Ltd, 4401 Zephyr Street, Wheat Ridge CO 80033-3299. **Tel** (303)934-5656. **ED** Donald R. Hoflin. **Ad Acc, Adv Mgr:** Cindy Kerstiens. **Circ:** 916.

CN/0707-4360
**MY PET.** V. 1- Winter 1979-. Periodical. English. qt. 8.49Can$ (for 2 years). My Pet Magazine, 160 Eglinton Avenue East/Suite 302, Toronto Ontario Canada M4P IJ3. **DD** 636.08/87/05.

US/1050-8457
**NATIONAL DOG REVIEW.** [Natl. dog rev.]. Vol. 1, No. 1 (Dec. 1991)-. Periodical. English. mo. $45.00. National Dog Review, PO Box 568, Rochester PA 15074. **DD** 636.

US/0028-0267
**NATIONAL STOCK DOG MAGAZINE.** [Natl. stock dog mag.]. (19??)-. Periodical. English. bm (6 issues). $18.00 (one year), $25.00 (two year), $35.00 (three year). National Stock Dog Registry, PO Box 402, Butler IN 46721-0402. **Tel** (219)868-2670. **ED** J. R. Russell. Index available. cum. index. **Bk Rev. Ad Acc. Circ:** 5,000.
**Desc:** For the preservation and advancement of the livestock working breeds of America and the world.

US/0583-1776
**NEWSLETTER - SIBERIAN HUSKY CLUB OF AMERICA.** (NEWSLETTER.). [Newsl. - Sib. Husky Club Am.]. **Main/Corp** Siberian Husky Club of America. Newsletter. English. bm. Cingel, 118 Young Street, East Hampton Ct 06424-1844. **LC** SF429.S65; S52A. **DD** 636.7/3.

US
**NORTH AMERICAN DIRECTORY OF EXOTIC ANIMAL & BIRD OWNERS.** **VFOAT** North American Directory of Exotic Animal and Bird Owners. (1990)-. Directory. English. $30.00. Pat and Connie Corbett, Department NA, Skaar Route, Box 4028, Sidney MT 59270. ***Continues*** *Directory of North American Exotic Animal and Bird Owners.*

US/0094-0186 #y 0094-0816
**OFF-LEAD.** **VAT** Off Lead. (1971)-. Periodical. English. mo. $20.00 US; $23.50 other. Arner Publications, 100 Bouck Street, Rome NY 13440. **Tel** (315)339-2033. **ED** Lorenz D Arner. **LC** SF431; .O35. **DD** 636.7/08/3. Index available. **Bk Rev. Ad Acc. Circ:** 5,000 (ctrl).
**Desc:** Includes more than 10,000 dog owners actively engaged in dog care and training, including professional trainers, dog training clubs, sportsmen, government agencies, individual competitors, and house pet owners.

UK/0955-9469
**OUR DOGS MANCHESTER.** (1895)-. Newspaper. English. wk. £65.00 UK; £90.00 Europe;. Our Dogs Publishing, 5 Oxford Road Station Approach, Manchester M60 1SX England. **Tel** 011 44 61 23262660, FAX 011 44 61 2365534. **(Subscription telephone:** (061 237 1272) (fax: 061 236 5534))

US/0030-6851
**OUR FOURFOOTED FRIENDS.** **Added/Corp** Animal Rescue League of Boston. (19??)-. Periodical. English. qt (4 issues). $4.00. Animal Rescue League of Boston, PO Box 265, Boston MA 02117. **Tel** (617)426-9170.

US/0098-5406
**PET AGE.** Vol. 1 (July 1971)-. Periodical. English. mo. $25.00. H. H. Backer Associates Inc, 20 East Jackson Boulevard, Chicago IL 60604. **Tel** (312)663-4040, FAX (312)663-5676. **ED** Karen M. Long. **LC** SF414.7; .P45. **DD** 381/.41/6088705. **Ad Acc. Circ:** 17,000 (ctrl).
**Desc:** A magazine for pet shop owners, managers, distributors and manufacturers. Focuses on management and sales techniques, animal care and industry issues through news and features.

US/0731-468X
**PET ANIMAL HEALTH LETTER, THE.** **See** Veterinary Sciences.

US/0191-4766
**PET BUSINESS.** [Pet bus.]. **Added/Corp** Western World Pet Supply Association. **VFOAT** Pet Business Magazine. (March 1978)-. Periodical. English. Twelve times a year. $24.00 (one year); $36.00 (two years); $50.00 (three years). Pet Business Inc, 5400 Northwest 84th Avenue, Miami FL 33166. **Tel** (305)592-9890. **ED** Amy Jordan Smith. **DD** 338. Index available. **Ad Acc. Circ:** 14,500 (ctrl). ***Continues Aquarium Industry.***
**Desc:** News magazine for the pet industry.

US/1047-3815
**PET CARE REPORT.** [Pet care rep.]. (1983)-. Periodical. English. bm. Whittle Communications, 333 Main Avenue, Knoxville TN 37902. **Tel** (615)595-5000, FAX (615)595-5877. **ED** Mardy Fones. **DD** 636.

US/0553-8572
**PET DEALER.** Vol. 1 (Feb. 1927)-. Periodical. English. Twelve times a year. $25.00 US; $29.00 Canada; $50.00 other. PTN Publishing Company, 445 Broad Hollow Road, Melville NY 11747. **Tel** (516)845-2700, FAX (516)845-7109. **LC** SF411; .P3. **DD** 658.896366. **Bk Rev. Ad Acc. Circ:** 15,500 (ctrl). ***Absorbed*** *Pet Shop.*
**Desc:** Geared to the pet shop retailer/buyer of supplies and/or livestock.

US/0553-8572
**PET DEALER ANNUAL GUIDE.** (19??)-. English. an. $38.00. PTN Publishing Company, 445 Broad Hollow Road, Melville NY 11747. **Tel** (516)845-2700, FAX (516)845-7109. **ED** Gina Geslewitz. **Bk Rev**, (Qty: 52/yr). **Ad Acc, Adv Mgr:** Arline Wasserman. **Pr Rev. Circ:** 17,000.

US/1046-2112
**PET FOCUS.** [Pet focus]. Vol. 1, No. 1 (Nov./Dec. 1989)-. Periodical. English. Twelve times a year. $10.50. Focus Publications, 20 Church Street, Montclair NJ 07042. **DD** 636.
**Desc:** Provides up-to-date, reliable and practical information about pet health care. This information is relayed in simple, easy-to-understand and well-illustrated articles. All medical articles are reviewed by board-certified veterinarians. Also includes a column in which veterinary specialists answer readers' questions.
**Ind/Abst** Index Vet.; Nutr. Abstr. Rev., Ser. B, Live Feeds and Feed.; Small Anim. Abstr. Bibliogr.

US/0742-9746
**PET LOVERS' GAZETTE.** **VFOAT** Pet Lovers'. Periodical. English. mo. $10.00. Pet Lovers Gazette, 31 West Main Street, Marlton NJ 08053.

US/0031-6245
**PETFOOD INDUSTRY.** [Petfood ind.]. **VFOAT** Pet Food Industry. Vol. 1 (1959)-. Periodical. English. bm. $36.00. Watt Publishing Company, 122 South Wesley Avenue, Mount Morris IL 61054. **Tel** (815)734-4171, FAX (815)734-7021, telex TWX 910-642-2891. **ED** Marcella Sadler. **DD** 338. **CODEN** PEINE6. **[CCC]. Ad Acc. Circ:** 5,000 (ctrl). available on microfilm from University Microfilms International (UMI).
**Desc:** Serves individuals and firms manufacturing pet foods.
**Ind/Abst** BioBusiness.

CN/0831-2621
**PETS MAGAZINE (1985).** (PETS MAGAZINE.). [Pets mag.]. Vol. 2, No. 6 (May/June 1985)-. Periodical. English. bm. 15.00Can$ Canada; 18.00Can$ US; 20.00Can$ other. Moorshead Publications, 797 Don Mills Road, Tenth Floor, North York, Ontario M3C 3S5 Canada. **Tel** (416)696-5488. **ED** Marie Hubbs. **DD** 636.08/87/05. **Ad Acc. Circ:** 60,000. ***Continues*** *Pets (Toronto, Ont.), 0715-8947.*
**Desc:** Information of healthcare, behavior, nutrition and human/animal bonding for pet owners.

CN/0710-0361
**PLAYBOAR MAGAZINE.** [Playboar mag.]. Periodical. English. qt. $2.50 per. no. Pigskin Productions, PO Box 353, Station A, Kingston Ontario K7M 6R7 Canada. **DD** 636.4/002/07.

US/1058-3637
**POMERANIAN REGISTRY, THE.** (1990)-. Periodical. English. bm. $25.00. The Pomerian Registry, 6902 East 1st Street, Tucson AZ 85710-1221. **DD** 636.

US/0744-8546
**POMERANIAN REVIEW.** (POMERANIAN REVIEW / AMERICAN POMERANIAN CLUB.). **Added/Corp** American Pomeranian Club. **VFOAT** Pomeranian Review of the American Pomeranian Club, Inc. (19??)-. Periodical. English. qt. American Pomeranian Club, PO Box 31927, Tucson AZ 85751.

US/0477-5449
**POODLE REVIEW, THE.** [Poodle rev.]. (19?)-. Periodical. English. bm. $42.00 (one year), $80.00 (two year). Poodle Review, 4401 Zephyr Street, Wheat Ridge CO 80033. **ED** Donald R. Hoflin & Cindy Kerstiens. **LC** SF429.P85; P67. **DD** 636.7/2. **Ad Acc. Circ:** 1,739.

US/0882-2816
**POODLE VARIETY.** (19??)-. Periodical. English. Five times a year. $40.00 US; $48.00 other. Poodle Variety, PO Box 30430, Santa Barbara CA 93130. **Tel** (805)966-7270. **ED** Bo N. Bengtson. **DD** 636. **Bk Rev**, (Qty: 1). **Ad Acc. Circ:** 2,000.
**Desc:** Specialist interest magazine for poodle fanciers interested in breeding, showing, obedience, etc.

UK/0262-5849
**PPM. PET PRODUCT MARKETING.** [PPM. Pet prod. mark.]. **VFOAT** Pet Product Marketing. (1980)-. Periodical. English. mo. EMAP National Publications Ltd, Farndon Road, Market Harborough, Leicestershire, LE16 9NR England. **Tel** 011 44 733 555161. **DD** 636. ***Continues*** *Pet Product Marketing and Garden Supplies, 0031-6202.*
**Ind/Abst** Infomat Int. Bus.

UK
**PRACTICAL FISHKEEPING.** **See** Fish and Fisheries.

US/0033-4561
**PURE-BRED DOGS, AMERICAN KENNEL GAZETTE.** [Pure bred dogs Am. kennel gaz.]. **Added/Corp** American Kennel Club. **VFOAT** Pure-Bred Dogs/American Kennel Gazette. **VAT** Pure Bred Dogs, American Kennel Gazette. (1952)-. Periodical. English. Twelve times a year. $28.00 (one year); $52.00 (two years). American Kennel Club, 5580 Center View Drive, Raleigh NC 27606. **Tel** (919)233-9780. **ED** Diane Vesey, (editor's address: 51 Madison Avenue, New York, NY 10010, phone: (212)696-8291). **LC** SF421; .A52. **DD** 636.7/0973. Index available (Bound in Mar. issue). **Bk Rev**, (Qty: 12). **Ad Acc, Adv Mgr Tel** (212)696-8261. **Circ:** 53,500. available on microfilm and microfiche from University Microfilms International (UMI). ***Continues*** *American Kennel Gazette, Pure-Bred Dogs, 0737-8807.* ***Continued in part by*** *American Kennel Club Show, Obedience and Field Trial Awards, 0272-4383.*
**Desc:** Contains a wide range of articles of interest to the pure-bred dog fancier. Reports vital information in all areas of pure-bred dog breeding and showing.

US/0731-0366
**PURRRRR!.** Vol. 1, No. 1 (Apr. 1982)-. Periodical. English. mo. $18.00. Meow Company, 118 Massachusetts Avenue, Suite 187, Boston MA 02115.

CN/0828-4865
**QUARTERLY - CANADIAN CAT ASSOCIATION.** (THE QUARTERLY / CCA.). [Q. - Can. Cat. Assoc.]. **VAT** CCA Quarterly (1984); Canadian Cat Association Quarterly (1984). Vol. 21, No. 1 (Winter 1984)-. Periodical. English (French). qt. 18.00Can$ Canada; 20.00Can$ other. Canadian Cat Association, 3 Greenside Avenue, London Ontario N6J 2X5 Canada. **Tel** (519)433-2947. **ED** Elaine Gleason. **DD** 636.8/006/071. Index available. cum. index. **Bk Rev. Ad Acc. Circ:** 1,000 (ctrl). ***Continues*** *CCA Quarterly, 0711-074X.*
**Desc:** Contains articles of interest for all cat fanciers; proper care, grooming and health of cats, as well as poetry and stories about cats.

●US/1068-1965
**REPTILES (IRVINE, CALIF.).** (REPTILES : GUIDE TO KEEPING REPTILES AND AMPHIBIANS.). (1993)-. Periodical. English. mo. $27.97. Fancy Publications, PO Box 6050, Mission Viejo CA 92690. **Tel** (714)855-8822, (800)426-2516, FAX (714)855-3045. **(Subscription address:** Neodata / Colorado, PO Box 2606, Boulder Boulder CO 80322.)

FR/0397-6866
**REVUE CHIEN 2000.** [Rev. chien]. **VFOAT** Revue Chien Deux Mille; Revue Chiens 2000. (1976)-. Periodical. French. Eleven times a year. 176.30F France; 251.00F other. Revue Chien 2000, 8 10 rue Pierre Brossolette, 92300 Levallois Perr France. **Tel** 011 33 1 40874015. **UDC** 63. ***Continues*** *Revue du Chien, Chiens 2000, 0397-6874.*

US/8750-3549
**RHODESIAN RIDGEBACK QUARTERLY, THE.** **VFOAT** RRQ. Vol. 1, No. 1 (Fall 1984)-. Periodical. English. qt. Hoflin Publishing Ltd, 4401 Zephyr Street, Wheat Ridge CO 80033-3299. **Tel** (303)934-5656.

US/0161-0651
**SAMOYED QUARTERLY, THE.** (1977)-. Periodical. English. qt. $40.00 (one year), $76.00 (two year). Hoflin Publishing Ltd, 4401 Zephyr Street, Wheat Ridge CO 80033-3299. **Tel** (303)934-5656. **ED** Donald R. Hoflin and Cindy Kerstiens. **LC** SF429.S35; S25. **DD**

**Pets**

636.7/3. **Ad Acc, Adv Mgr:** Cindy Kerstiens. **Circ:** 1,100.
**Desc:** Articles on all areas of interest to the Samoyed Fancier.

US/0276-1521
**SCHNAUZER SHORTS.** (19??)-. Periodical. English. Seven times a year. $24.00. Dan Kiedrowski Company, Drawer A, La Honda CA 94020. **Tel** (415)747-0549. **Ad Acc, Adv Mgr:** Dan Kiedrowski. **Pr Rev. Circ:** 900.
**Desc:** Reports on show results on miniature schnauzers and breeding, litters available, health interests, and profiles of particular dogs.

US/0747-3532
**SCOTTISH TERRIER QUARTERLY, THE.** Vol. 1, No. 1 (Spring 1984)-. Periodical. English. bm. The Scottish Terrier Quarterly, Wheat Ridge CO 80033-3299.

US/0164-372X
**SETTER MAGAZINE, THE.** Periodical. English. bm. $12.50. Gerry Roberts, 2254 Wyandotte Street, Mountain View CA 94043.

US/0734-3078
**SHELTER SENSE.** See Sociology-Social Services and Welfare.

US/0745-2012
**SHELTIE INTERNATIONAL.** [Sheltie int.]. (1982)-. Periodical. English. Six times a year (Feb., Apr., June, Aug., Oct., Dec.). $43.00 Canada & Mexico; $58.00 others. Sheltie International, PO Box 6369, Los Osos CA 93412. **Tel** (805)528-2007. **ED** Jean Fergus (editor's address: 1456 14th Street, Slo, CA 93402). **LC** WMLC L 83/9704. **DD** 636. Index available. cum. index. **Bk Rev**, (Qty: 2). **Ad Acc. Circ:** 1,700.
**Desc:** A magazine about the care training, showing and betterment of the Shetland Sheepdog.

US/0744-6608
**SHELTIE PACESETTER.** (19??)-. Periodical. English. Six times a year. $124.00 (airmail); $44.00 US, $59.00 Canada & Mexico, $64.00 others (surface mail); $63.00 (first class mail) US & Canada & Mexico. Sheltie Pacesetter, PO Box 3310, Palos Verdes CA 90274. **Tel** (213)547-7820. **(Subscription address:** PO Box 3230, Palos Verdes Peninsula, CA 90274) **ED** Nancy Lee Marshall. **LC** WMLC L 83/8847. Index available. cum. index. **Bk Rev. Ad Acc. Circ:** 3,500 (ctrl).
**Desc:** The magazine that color covers. Packed with informative articles. Hundreds of photos.

US/1040-5801
**SHIH TZU REPORTER, THE.** [Shih tzu report.]. (19??)-. Periodical. English. Six times a year (Jan., Mar., May, July, Sept., Nov.). $42.00 US; $52.00 Canada & Mexico; $60.00 others. Reporter Publications, PO Box 6369, Los Osos CA 93412. **ED** Jean Fargus (editor's address: 1456 14th Street, Slo, CA 93402, phone: (805)528-7229). **DD** 636. **Bk Rev. Ad Acc.**

CN/0701-0001
**SHOW RING.** July/Aug. 1976-. Periodical. English. bm. $15.00. Show Ring Publications, PO Box 2077, New Westminster British Columbia V3L 5A3 Canada. **DD** 636.7/08/88.

US/0274-7286
**SIBERIAN QUARTERLY, THE.** [Sib. q.]. (1980)-. Periodical. English. qt. $40.00 US; $44.00 other. Hoflin Publishing Ltd, 4401 Zephyr Street, Wheat Ridge CO 80033-3299. **Tel** (303)934-5656. **ED** Donald R. Hoflin. **Ad Acc, Adv Mgr:** Cindy Kerstiens. **Circ:** 1,350.

US/8750-1953
**SIGHTHOUND REVIEW.** [Sighthound rev.]. Vol. 1, No. 1 (May/June 1984)-. Periodical. English. bm (6 review). $40.00 (one year), $72.00 (two year). The Afghan Hound Review, PO Box 30430, Santa Barbara CA 93130. **Tel** (805)966-7270, FAX (805)682-1771. **ED** Bo N. Bengtson. **DD** 636. **Bk Rev. Ad Acc. Circ:** 2,000.
**Continues** Sighthound, 0744-3323.
**Desc:** For Sighthound/Greyhound type breed fanciers. Covers showing, racing, coursing, obedience, care, training, etc.

US/0561-1245
**SOUTHERN DOG LOVERS DIGEST.** Vol. 1, (Fall 1964)-. Periodical. English. PO Box 9270, Shreveport LA 71139. **LC** SF421; .S48. **DD** 636.7/005.

US/0163-7649
**STABLE & KENNEL NEWS OF THE SOUTH.** See Horses and Horsemanship.

US/1062-6425
**TALKING BETTAS.** (TALKING BETTAS / BETTA BUFFS OF PITTSBURGH.). [Talking bettas]. **Added/Corp** Betta Buffs of Pittsburgh (Organization). (1991)-. Periodical. English. mo. $12.00 (member). Beta Buffs of Pittsburgh, 146 Willow Drive, Freedom PA 15042. **DD** 639.

US/1056-6759
**WACKY WORLD OF PEAFOWL REPORT, THE.** See Zoology-Ornithology.

US/0164-6478
**WHIPPET, THE.** [Whippet]. (1978)-. Periodical. English. bm. $12.00. The Whippet, 3967 Anastasia Street, San Diego CA 92111.

US/0883-7686
**YORKIE TALES.** (19??)-. Periodical. English. Four times a year. $28.00. Yorkie Tales, 731 Paso Robles Street, Unit D, Paso Robles CA 93446. **Tel** (805)239-8406. **DD** 636.

US
**YORKSHIRE TERRIER QUARTERLY, THE.** V. 1- May 1968-. Periodical. English. ir. Yorkshire Terrier Quarterly, Box 256, Times Square Station, New York NY 10036. **LC** SF429.Y6; Y67. **DD** 636.7/55.

US/0278-744X
**YOUR FAMILY PET. Ceased. VFOAT** Family Pet. (19??)-(19??). Periodical. English. an. Meredith Publications / Special Interest Section, 1716 Locust Street, Des Moines IA 50309. **Tel** (515)284-3000. **LC** SF411; .Y68. **DD** 636.08/87/05.

# PHARMACY AND PHARMACOLOGY

US
**483 VALIDATION MONITOR FOR STERILE, NON-STERILE AND MEDICAL DEVICES.** See Medical Science and Technology.

US
**AACP NEWS / AMERICAN ASSOCIATION OF COLLEGES OF PHARMACY. Added/Corp** American Association of Colleges of Pharmacy. **VAT** American Association of Colleges of Pharmacy news. Vol. 1, No. 1 (Dec. 1972)-. Periodical. English. mo. $25.00. American Association of Colleges of Pharmacy, 1426 Prince Street, Alexandria VA 22314-2815. **Tel** (703)739-2330.

US/0197-6176
**ABSTRACTS ON MANAGEMENT & ADMINISTRATION OF PHARMACY.** [Abstr. manage. adm. pharm.]. **Added/Corp** American Society of Hospital Pharmacists. **VFOAT** Management & Administration of Pharmacy. **VAT** Abstracts on Management and Administration of Pharmacy. (1978)-. English. $15.00 single issue. American Society of Hospital Pharmacists, 7272 Wisconsin Avenue, Bethesda MD 20814. **Tel** (301)657-3000, (301)657-4383, FAX (301)652-8278. **NLM** ZQA 737 A164.

US/0098-6437
**ABSTRACTS. SYMPOSIA PAPERS PRESENTED BEFORE THE APHA ACADEMY OF PHARMACEUTICAL SCIENCES AT THE ANNUAL MEETING OF THE AMERICAN PHARMACEUTICAL ASSOCIATION. Added/Corp** Academy of Pharmaceutical Sciences. American Pharmaceutical Association. **VFOAT** Symposia Papers Presented Before the APHA Academy of Pharmaceutical Sciences ... . (1960)-. Monographic series. English. ir (2 issues). Price varies per volume. American Pharmaceutical Association, 2215 Constitution Avenue Northwest, Washington DC 20037-2985. **Tel** (202)628-4410, (800)237-2742, FAX (202)783-2351. **NLM** W1 AB92S.

US/0199-6037
**ACADEMY REPORTER (WASHINGTON).** (ACADEMY REPORTER.). **Added/Corp** Academy of Pharmaceutical Sciences. (19??)-. Periodical. English. bm. $25.00 US; $30.00 Canada and Mexico; $85.00 Europe; $91.00 other. American Pharmaceutical Association, 2215 Constitution Avenue Northwest, Washington DC 20037-2985. **Tel** (202)628-4410, (800)237-2742, FAX (202)783-2351. **[CCC]**.

FR
**ACIP: REVUE DE L'ASSOCIATION DES CADRES DE L'INDUSTRIE PHARMACEUTIQUE.** (19??)-. Periodical. French. Eight times a year. 132.22F (member of ACIP), 186.09F (non-member) France; 135.00F (member of ACIP), 190.00F (non-member) other. Editions de Sante, 5 rue Las Cases, 75007 Paris, France. **Tel** 011 33 1 45519494.

SP
**ACOFAR : REVISTA DEL MUNDO FARMACEUTICO.** (1962)-. Spanish (summaries and/or abstracts in English). 30.00ptas Europe; 35.00ptas other. Editorial Garsi SA, Juan Bravo 46, 28006 Madrid, Spain. **Tel** 011 34 1 4021212, telex 98358 GARSI E.

LH/0001-4958
**ACONCAGUA (VADUZ).** (ACONCAGUA.). [Aconcagua]. **Added/Corp** Centro Europeo de Documentacion e Informacion. Vol. 1 (1965)-. Periodical. German.
**Ind/Abst** Am. Hist. Life (1965-1971); Int. Pharm. Abstr.

XO/0301-2298
**ACTA FACULTATIS PHARMACEUTICAE UNIVERSITATIS COMENIANAE.** [Acta Fac. Pharm. Univ. Comen.]. **Main/Corp** Univerzita Komenskeho v Bratislave. Farmaceuticka Fakulta. (1973)-. Periodical. Slovak (Czech, English, German and Slovak; summaries and/or abstracts in Russian). **CODEN** AFPCAG. Documents available from BIOSIS Document Express, CASDDS. **Continues** Univerzita Komenskeho v Bratislava. Farmaceuticka Fakulta. Acta Fakultatis Pharmaceuticae Bohemoslovenicae.
**Ind/Abst** Biol. Abstr.; Chem. Abstr.

AG/0326-2383
**ACTA FARMACEUTICA BONAERENSE.** (ACTA FARMACEUTICA BONAERENSE : PUBLICACION DEL COLEGIO DE FARMACEUTICOS DE LA PROVINCIA DE BUENOS AIRES (ARGENTINA).). [Acta farm. bonaerense]. **Added/Corp** Colegio de Farmaceuticos de la Provincia de Buenos Aires (Argentina). Vol. 1, No. 1 (1982)-. Academic Scholarly Publication. Spanish (summaries and/or abstracts in English). Three times a year (Apr., Aug., Dec.). $53.50. Acta Farmaceutica Bonaerense, Calle No 5 966, La Plata 1900 Argentina. **Tel** 011 54 21 258603 04 05, FAX 011 54 21 258603. **ED** Nestor Oscar Caffini. **NLM** W1; AC803F. **CODEN** AFBODJ. Index available. cum. index. **Bk Rev. Ad Acc. Pr Rev. Circ:** 1,000 (ctrl). Documents available from BIOSIS Document Express, CASDDS. **Continues** Revista del Colegio de Farmaceutucos de la Provincia de Buenos Aires.
**Desc:** Original articles, reviews and scientific comments. Remarks about pharmaceutical sciences.
**Ind/Abst** Biol. Abstr. (1984-); Chem. Abstr.; EMBASE; Food Sci. Technol. Abstr.; Int. Pharm. Abstr.; Sug. Indus. Abstr.

IO/0125-9407
**ACTA PHARMACEUTICA. Title Change.** [Acta pharm.]. **Added/Corp** Institut Teknologi Bandung. Lembaga Penelitian Farmasi. (1970)-(19??). Periodical. Indonesian. qt. **NLM** W1 AC917. **CODEN** ACPHCC. Documents available from The Genuine Article, CASDDS. **Continued by** Acta Pharmaceutica Indonesia, 0216-616X.
**Ind/Abst** Chem. Abstr.; Int. Pharm. Abstr.; Res. Alert [Full Cov.].

●CI
**ACTA PHARMACEUTICA : A QUARTERLY JOURNAL OF CROATIAN PHARMACEUTICAL SOCIETY AND SLOVENIAN PHARMACEUTICAL SOCIETY, DEALING WITH ALL BRANCHES OF PHARMACY AND ALLIED SCIENCES. Added/Corp** Hrvatsko Farmaceutsko Drustvo Slovenian Pharmaceutical Society. **VFOAT** Acta Pharm. Vol. 42, No. 1 (1992)-. Periodical. English (summaries and/or abstracts in Serbo-Croatian (Roman); table of contents in Serbo-Croatian (Roman)). Four times a year. $40.00. Savez Sarmaceut Skih Prustava, Masatykova Yugoslav Mastatyk 2, 4100 Zagreb Croatia. **LC** RS1; .A28. **NLM** W1; AC917B. **Continues** Acta Pharmaceutica Jugoslavica, 0001-6667.
**Ind/Abst** Sci. Cit. Index.

FI/0356-3456
**ACTA PHARMACEUTICA FENNICA. Title Change.** [Acta pharm. fenn.]. **Added/Corp** Suomen Farmaseuttinen Yhdistys. Vol. 86 (1977)-Vol. 101 (1992). Academic Scholarly Publication. Multiple languages (English and Finnish). qt. Farmasian Laitos, Fabianinkatu 35, SF-00170 Helsinki 17 Finland. **Tel** 90-1912782. **ED** Kirsi-Marja Oksman-Caldentey. **NLM** W1; AC917D. **CODEN** APHFDO. Index available. cum. index. **Bk Rev. Ad Acc. Circ:** 1,000 (ctrl). Documents available from BIOSIS Document Express, CASDDS. **Continues** Farmaseuttinen Aikakauslehti, 0367-259X. **Absorbed by** European Journal of Pharmaceutical Sciences.
**Desc:** Publishes original papers, review articles and short communications in various branches of pharmacy with the understanding that they are subject to editorial revision.
**Ind/Abst** Anal. Abstr.; Biol. Abstr. (1988-); Chem. Abstr.; EMBASE; Int. Pharm. Abstr.; Nat. Prod. Updates; PESTDOC.

HU/0001-6659
**ACTA PHARMACEUTICA HUNGARICA (BUDAPEST. 1953).** (ACTA PHARMACEUTICA HUNGARICA.). [Acta pharm. hung.]. **Added/Corp** Orvos-Egeszsegugyi Szakszervezet. Gyogyszeresz Szakcsoport. Vol. 23 (1953)-. Academic Scholarly Publication. Hungarian (summaries and/or abstracts in Russian and German). Six times a year. $38.00. **(Subscription address:** Kultura, PO Box 149, H 1389 Budapest 62 Hungary; telephone: 011 36 1 359370) **NLM** W1 AC917R. **CODEN** APHGAO. Documents available from BIOSIS Document Express, CASDDS. **Continues**

*Magyar Gyogyszeresztudomanyi Tarsasag. Ertesitoje.*
**Ind/Abst** Anal. Abstr.; Biol. Abstr.; Chem. Abstr.; EMBASE; Index Med.; Int. Pharm. Abstr.; Nat. Prod. Updates; PESTDOC; Sug. Indus. Abstr.

IO/0216-616X
**ACTA PHARMACEUTICA INDONESIA.** (ACTA PHARMACEUTICA INDONESIA / JURUSAN FARMASI MIPA, INSTITUT TEKNOLOGI BANDUNG.). [Acta pharm. Indones.]. **Added/Corp** Institut Teknologi Bandung. Jurusan Farmasi. (1982)-. Periodical. Indonesian. qt. **CODEN** APINEK. Documents available from BIOSIS Document Express, CASDDS. ***Continues*** *Acta Pharmaceutica, 0125-9407.*
**Ind/Abst** Biol. Abstr. (1984-); Chem. Abstr.

DK/0400-4116
**ACTA PHARMACEUTICA INTERNATIONALIA.** [Acta Pharm. Int.]. (1950)-. Periodical. Multiple languages. ir. **DD** _a615. **CODEN** APINAGAPINAG.
**Ind/Abst** Int. Pharm. Abstr.

SW/1100-1801
**ACTA PHARMACEUTICA NORDICA.** ***Title Change.*** [Acta pharm. Nord.]. **Added/Corp** Danmarks Apotekerforening. Norges Apotekerforening. Apotekarsocieteten. Vol. 1, No. 1 (1989)-(Jan. 1993). Periodical. English. qt. Swedish Pharmaceutical Press, PO Box 1136, S 111 81 Stockholm Sweden. **Tel** 011 46 8 345080, FAX 011 46 8 149580. **LC** RS1; .A17724. **NLM** W1; AC9176N. **CODEN** APNOEE. **Pr Rev.** available on microfilm and microfiche from University Microfilms International (UMI). Documents available from The Genuine Article, BIOSIS Document Express, CASDDS. ***Formed by the union of*** *Acta Pharmaceutica Suecica, 0001-6675; Farmaci (Scientific Ed.), 0904-0897* ***and*** *Norvegica Pharmaceutica Acta, 0800-2606.* ***Merged into*** *European Journal of Pharmaceutical Sciences.*
**Ind/Abst** Biol. Abstr.; Chem. Abstr.; CSA Neuro. Abstr. (?-?); Curr. Chem. React.; Curr. Contents Life Sci.; EMBASE; Index Chem.; Index Med.; Index Vet.; Int. Pharm. Abstr.; NAPRALERT; PESTDOC; Res. Alert [Full Cov.]; Rev. Med. Vet. Mycology; Sci. Cit. Index (19??-19??); SCISEARCH; Vet. Bull.

TU/1010-0849
**ACTA PHARMACEUTICA TURCICA.** **Added/Corp** Istanbul Universitesi. Fen Fakultesi. Vol. 26, No. 1 (1984)-. Academic Scholarly Publication. Turkish (English). Three times a year (Apr., Aug. and Dec.). $10.00. Anadol University Faculty of Phar., PharmaTech Prof. Dr. Erden Guler, 26470 Eskisehir Turkey. **Tel** 011 90 222 3350581. **ED** Professor Dr. Erden Guler. **CODEN** APTUES. Index available (Bound last iss.). **Ad Acc.** ctrl circ. Documents available from CASDDS. ***Continues*** *Eczacilik Bulteni.*
**Ind/Abst** Anal. Abstr.; Chem. Abstr. (1984-); EMBASE; Food Sci. Technol. Abstr.; Int. Pharm. Abstr.; Nat. Prod. Updates; Life Sci. Collect. (1984-).

BU/0323-9950
**ACTA PHYSIOLOGICA ET PHARMACOLOGICA BULGARICA.** **See** Biology-Physiology.

AG
**ACTA PHYSIOLOGICA, PHARMACOLOGICA ET THERAPEUTICA LATINOAMERICANA : ORGANO DE LA ASOCIACION LATINOAMERICANA DE CIENCIAS FISIOLOGICAS Y [DE] LA ASOCIACION LATINOAMERICANA DE FARMACOLOGIA.** **See** Biology-Physiology.

PL/0001-6837
**ACTA POLONIAE PHARMACEUTICA.** [Acta Pol. pharm.]. **Added/Corp** Polskie Towarzystwo Farmaceutyczne. (1937)-. Academic Scholarly Publication. Polish. bm. Price on Request. **(Subscription address:** ARS Polona, PO Box 1001, 00068 Warsaw Poland.**)** **NLM** W1 AC927. **CODEN** APPHAX. Documents available from CASDDS.
**Ind/Abst** Anal. Abstr.; Chem. Abstr.; EMBASE; Index Med.; Index Dent. Lit.; Int. Pharm. Abstr.; Methods Organ. Synth.; NAPRALERT; Nat. Prod. Updates; PESTDOC.

BE/0378-0619
**ACTA THERAPEUTICA.** [Acta ther.]. Vol. 1 (1975)-. Academic Scholarly Publication. English (French, Dutch and German). Four times a year (Jan., Apr., July, Oct.). $90.00 (surface mail); $105.00 (airmail) others. Acta Therapeutica, PO Box 215, 1200 Brussels 20 Belgium. **Tel** 11 32 2 7594045, FAX 011 32 2 7599980, telex 25 387 AVVAL B. **ED** L. van Keer, (editor's address: Galgenstraat 43, 3078 Everberg Belgium, phone: 011 32 2 759 9980). **NLM** W1 AC95K. **CODEN** ACTTDZ. Bound Index published separately, free upon request (publish every 3 years). cum. index. **Pr Rev. Circ:** 3,000. Documents available from The Genuine Article, BIOSIS Document Express, CASDDS.
**Desc:** Research papers relating to studies and development of drugs for human use.
**Ind/Abst** Biol. Abstr. (1987-); Chem. Abstr.; Curr. Contents Clin. Med.; EMBASE; PESTDOC; Protozoolog. Abstr.; Res. Alert [Select. Cov.]; SCISEARCH.

CN
**ACTUALITE PHARMACEUTIQUE, L'.** (19??)-. English. mo. 35.00Can$ Canada; 72.00Can$ other. MacLean Hunter Ltd. Business Publishers / Canada, Box 9100, Station A, Toronto ONT M5W 1A5 Canada. **Tel** (416)946-8420, (800)567-0444. **(Subscription address:** Indas, 35 Riviera Drive, Building 17, Markham Ontario L3R 8N4 Canada.**)** ***Continues*** *Le Pharmacien.*

BE/0373-9805
**ACTUALITES DE CHIMIE ANALYTIQUE, ORGANIQUE, PHARMACEUTIQUE ET BROMATOLOGIQUE.** **See** Chemistry.

FR/0338-8999
**ACTUALITES DE CHIMIE THERAPEUTIQUE.** **Added/Corp** Societe de Chimie Therapeutique (France). (1971)-. Periodical. French (English and German). **NLM** W1 AC991HT. **CODEN** ACHTD9. Documents available from CASDDS.
**Ind/Abst** Chem. Abstr.

BE/1370-0464
**ACTUALITES JURIDIQUES PHARMACEUTIQUES.** **VFOAT** Juridisch Farmaceutische Actualiteiten. (19??)-. French (German). Algemene Pharmaceutische Bond - Association Pharmaceutique Belge, Archimedestraat 11 rue Archimede, 1040 Brussels Belgium. **Tel** 011 32 2 2302685.

FR/0515-3700
**ACTUALITES PHARMACEUTIQUES.** [Actual. pharm.]. (1961)-. Periodical. French. mo (except Aug.). 800.00F French overseas depts. and territories; 646.43F France; 880.00F other EEC; 900.00F other. Sutip, 175 rue Faubourg Poissonniere, 75009 Paris France. **Tel** 33 1 42801175, FAX 33 1 42829800. **ED** Danielle Roquier-Charles. **UDC** 61.
**Ind/Abst** Int. Pharm. Abstr.; PESTDOC.

FR/0567-8854
**ACTUALITES PHARMACOLOGIQUES.** [Actual. pharm.]. Vol. 1 (1949)-. Academic Scholarly Publication. French (English). ir. Price varies. Scientific & Medical Publishers of France, 100 East 42nd Street, Suite 1002, New York NY 10017-5613. **Tel** (212)983-6278. **ED** R. Hazard. **NLM** W1 AC997D. **CODEN** ACPMAP. **[CCC]. Circ:** 2,000. Documents available from BIOSIS Document Express, CASDDS. ***Continues*** *Pharmaco, 0395-966X.*
**Desc:** Contains research in all fields of pharmacology.
**Ind/Abst** Biol. Abstr.; Chem. Abstr.; PESTDOC (?-?).

NE/0169-409X
**ADVANCED DRUG DELIVERY REVIEWS.** [Adv. drug deliv. rev.]. Vol. 1, Iss. 1 (May 1987)-. Academic Scholarly Publication. English. Nine times a year (3 volumes). Fl1770.00. Elsevier Science Publishers BV, PO Box 211, 1000 AE Amsterdam Netherlands. **Tel** 011 31 20 5803642, FAX 011 31 20 5862696, telex 15682. **NLM** W1; AD402C. **CODEN** ADDREP. **[CCC].** available on microfilm and microfiche from University Microfilms International (UMI). Documents available from Article Express International, The Genuine Article, BIOSIS Document Express, CASDDS, ADONIS.
**Desc:** Publishes comprehensive yet critical review articles describing current and emerging aspects of research on the design and development of advanced drug delivery systems and their applications in experimental and clinical therapeutics.
**Ind/Abst** ADONIS; Biol. Abstr. (1987-); Chem. Abstr.; Curr. Aware. Biol. Sci., CABS; Curr. Contents Life Sci.; Ei Page One; EMBASE; Eng. Index Annu.; PESTDOC; Ref. Upd. Deluxe Ed.; Res. Alert [Full Cov.]; Sci. Cit. Index; SCISEARCH.

US/0065-2229
**ADVANCES IN BIOCHEMICAL PSYCHOPHARMACOLOGY.** **See** Medical Science and Technology-Neurology.

US
**ADVANCES IN CNS DRUG-RECEPTOR INTERACTIONS.** **VFOAT** Advances in CNS Drug Receptor Interactions; Advances in Central Nervous System Drug-Receptor Interactions. Vol. 1 (1991)-. Academic Scholarly Publication. English. ir. $90.25. JAI Press Inc., 55 Old Post Road, Suite 2, PO Box 1678, Greenwich CT 06836-1678. **Tel** (203)661-7602, FAX (203)661-0792. **LC** RM315; .A414. **DD** 615/.78/05. **NLM** W1; AD5HV. **CODEN** ACDIEP. Documents available from CASDDS.
**Ind/Abst** Chem. Abstr.

UK/0065-2490
**ADVANCES IN DRUG RESEARCH.** [Adv. drug res.]. Vol. 1 (1964)-. Monographic series. English. ir. Price varies per volume. Academic Press Ltd., A Division of Harcourt Brace & Company Ltd., 24-28 Oval Road, London NW1 7DX England. **Tel** 071 267 4466, FAX 071 482 2293, 071 485 4752, telex 25775 ACPRES G. **(Subscription address:** Academic Press Inc., PO Box 620000, Orlando FL 32891-8340.**)** **ED** N. J. Harper and A. B. Simmonds. **LC** RS1; .A287. **DD** 615.1072. **NLM** W1 AD549R. Documents available from CASDDS.
**Ind/Abst** Chem. Abstr.; EMBASE; Health Plan. Adminis.; Index Vet.; Life Sci. Collect.; PESTDOC; Vet. Bull.

US/0272-068X
**ADVANCES IN HUMAN PSYCHOPHARMACOLOGY.** [Adv. human psychopharmacol.]. Vol. 1 (1980)-. Academic Scholarly Publication. English. ir. Price varies per volume. Jessica Kingsley Publishers, 118 Pentonville Road, London N1 9JN England. **Tel** 011 44 71 833 2307, FAX 011 44 71 837 2917. **(Subscription address:** Taylor & Francis Inc., 1900 Frost Road, Suite 101, Bristol PA 19007-1598.**)** **ED** Graham D. Burrows and John S. Werry. **LC** RC483; .A284. **DD** 615/.78. **NLM** W1 AD64P. **CODEN** AHPSDD. Documents available from CASDDS.
**Ind/Abst** Chem. Abstr.; EMBASE; Psychol. Abstr. (1980-); PsycINFO.

US/1041-004X
**ADVANCES IN PARENTERAL SCIENCES.** [Adv. parenter. sci.]. (1985)-. Monographic series. English. Price varies per volume. Marcel Dekker Inc., 270 Madison Avenue, New York NY 10016. **Tel** (212)696-9000, (800)228-1160, FAX (212)685-4540, telex 421419. **(Subscription address:** Marcel Dekker Inc, PO Box 5017, Monticello NY 12701.**)** **DD** 615. **NLM** W1; AD714. **CODEN** AVPSEA. Documents available from CASDDS.
**Ind/Abst** Chem. Abstr.

UK/0065-3136
**ADVANCES IN PHARMACEUTICAL SCIENCES.** [Adv. pharm. sci.]. Vol. 1 (1964)-. Academic Scholarly Publication. English. ir. $78.00 (Vol. 6). Academic Press, Inc., 6277 Sea Harbor Drive, Orlando FL 32887. **Tel** (800)543-9534, (407)345-4100, FAX (407)363-9661. **ED** H. S. Bean, A. H. Beckett and J. E. Carless. **LC** RS1; .A29. **UDC** 615. **NLM** W1 AD774. **CODEN** APHMA8. **[CCC].** Documents available from BIOSIS Document Express.
**Ind/Abst** Biol. Abstr. (-1975); Health Plan. Adminis.; Int. Pharm. Abstr.; PESTDOC.

US/1054-3589
**ADVANCES IN PHARMACOLOGY.** [Adv. pharmacol.]. Vol. 21 (1990)-. Academic Scholarly Publication. English. ir. $74.95 (Vol. 29, Part B). Academic Press, Inc., 6277 Sea Harbor Drive, Orlando FL 32887. **Tel** (800)543-9534, (407)345-4100, FAX (407)363-9661. **LC** RM30; .A4. **DD** 615/.1/05. **NLM** W1; AD78F. **CODEN** ADPHEL. **[CCC].** Documents available from BIOSIS Document Express, CASDDS. ***Continues*** *Advances in Pharmacology and Chemotherapy, 0065-3144.*
**Ind/Abst** Biol. Abstr. (1990-); Chem. Abstr.; EMBASE (1990-); Index Med. (1991-); Life Sci. Collect.; PESTDOC.

SZ/0253-2093
**ADVANCES IN PHARMACOTHERAPY.** [Adv. pharmacother.]. Vol. 1 (1982)-. Academic Scholarly Publication. English. ir. Price varies per volume. S. Karger AG, Allschwilerstrasse 10, PO Box - Postfach - Case Postale, CH-4009 Basel Switzerland. **Tel** 011 41 61 306-1111, FAX 011 41 61 306-1234, telex CH 962 652. **ED** G. Stille, W. Wagner and W. M. Herrmann. **NLM** W1 AD78N. **CODEN** ADPHDK. **[CCC].** Documents available from BIOSIS Document Express, CASDDS.
**Desc:** References to international work in areas of pharmacology selected for their importance to clinical medicine and improved patient care. Key findings from leading research groups are drawn together for critical comparison, allowing balanced appraisal of advances in pharmacotherapy.
**Ind/Abst** Biol. Abstr.; Chem. Abstr.

UK/0964-198X
**ADVERSE DRUG REACTIONS AND TOXICOLOGICAL REVIEWS.** **See** Medical Science and Technology-Toxicology.

●GW
**ADVERSE EFFECTS OF HERBAL DRUGS.** **Added/Corp** World Health Organization. Regional Office for Europe. Pharmaceuticals Programme. (1992)-. Monographic series. English. ir. Price varies per volume. Springer-Verlag GmbH & Company KG, Heidelberger Platz 3, D 14197 Berlin Germany. **Tel** 011 49 30 8207223, FAX 011 49 30 8214091, telex 183 319 SPBLN D. **ED** P.A.G.M Smet. **NLM** QV 766; A2435.
**Desc:** Series published in collaboration with Pharmaceuticals Programme of the World Health Organization Regional Office for Europe.

NR
**AFRICAN JOURNAL OF PHARMACY AND THE PHARMACEUTICAL SCIENCES.** (19??)-. Periodical. English. Four times a year. $100.00 North America, Japan & Europe; $120.00 others. Nigerian Pharmaceutical Medical Company, 21 Wharf Road, PO Box 399, Apapa Lagos Nigeria.
**Ind/Abst** Int. Pharm. Abstr.

SZ/0065-4299
**AGENTS AND ACTIONS.** ***Title Change.*** [Agents actions]. **Added/Corp** European Biological Research Association. European Workshop on

Inflammation. European Histamine Research Society. Vol. 1 (July 1969)-(19??). Academic Scholarly Publication. English. mo. Birkhaeuser Verlag Ag, Klosterberg 23, PO Box 133, CH-4010 Basel Switzerland. **Tel** 011 41 61 2717400, FAX 011 41 0 61 2717666, telex 963475 birk ch. **(Subscription address:** Birkhauser Verlag AG, PO Box 151, CH 4106, Therwil Switzerland**)** **ED** M. J. Parnham. **LC** RM1; .A3. **DD** 615. **NLM** W1 AG33. **CODEN** AGACBH. **[CCC]. Bk Rev. Ad Acc. Pr Rev. Circ:** 900 (ctrl). available on microfilm and microfiche from University Microfilms International (UMI). Documents available from The Genuine Article, BIOSIS Document Express CASDDS, ADONIS. ***Continued by*** *Inflammation Research, 1023-3830.*
**Desc:** Specializes in four areas of pharmacological research: allergy, histamine and kinins; inflammation and imunomodulation; pain and analgesics; platelets and thrombosis. Publishes research reports and survey articles with the action of agents.
**Ind/Abst** ADONIS; Biol. Abstr.; Calcium Calcif. Tissue Abstr.; Chem. Abstr.; Chem. Titles; Curr. Aware. Biol. Sci., CABS; Curr. Contents Life Sci.; Dairy Sci. Abstr.; EMBASE; Health Plan. Adminis.; Helminthol. Abstr. (1991-); Immunol. Abstr.; Index Med.; NAPRALERT; Nutr. Abstr. Rev., Ser. B, Live Feeds and Feed.; Nutr. Abstr. Rev., Ser. A, Hum. Exp.; Life Sci. Collect.; PESTDOC; Protozoolog. Abstr.; Ref. Upd. Basic Ed.; Ref. Upd. Deluxe Ed.; Res. Alert [Full Cov.]; Sci. Cit. Index; SCISEARCH.

US/1063-8792
**AHFS DRUG INFORMATION.** [AHFS drug inf.]. **Added/Corp** American Society of Hospital Pharmacists. **VFOAT** American Hospital Formulary Service. **VAT** American Hospital Formulary Service Drug Information. (1989)-. Academic Scholarly Publication. English. Four times a year. $120.00 US; $140.19 Canada; $190.00 other. American Society of Hospital Pharmacists, 7272 Wisconsin Avenue, Bethesda MD 20814. **Tel** (301)657-3000, (301)657-4383, FAX (301)652-8278. **ED** Gerald K McEvoy. **DD** 615. **NLM** QV 740; AA1 A53a. **CODEN** ADINE4. **Circ:** 45,000. available on CD-ROM; available on an online database (file 229/Full Text) from DIALOG. Documents available from CASDDS. ***Continues*** *American Hospital Formulary Service Drug Information, 8756-6028.*
**Desc:** Drug information monographs.
**Ind/Abst** Chem. Abstr. (1989-).

UA/0013-2438
**AL-NASRA AS-SAYDALIYYA AL-MISRIYYA.** (THE EGYPTIAN PHARMACEUTICAL JOURNAL.). **Added/Corp** Gamiet Al-Savdala Al-Masria. **VFOAT** Journal of Egyptian Pharmacy. Vol. 50 (Jan. 1968)-. Periodical. Multiple languages (Arabic and English). bm. **NLM** W1 EG923. ***Continues in part*** *Egyptian Pharmaceutical Bulletin.*
**Ind/Abst** Int. Pharm. Abstr.

US/0735-519X
**ALASKA PHARMACIST.** [Alsk. pharm.]. **Added/Corp** Alaska Pharmaceutical Association. Alaska Society of Hospital Pharmacists. Vol. 1, No. 1 (Fall 1973)-. Periodical. English. qt.
**Ind/Abst** Int. Pharm. Abstr.

UK/0269-2813
**ALIMENTARY PHARMACOLOGY & THERAPEUTICS.** [Aliment. pharmacol. ther.]. **VFOAT** Alimentary Pharmacology and Therapeutics. Vol. 1, No. 1 (Feb. 1987)-. Academic Scholarly Publication. English. bm (6 issues). $232.00 (institutions), $77.00 (individuals) US & Canada; £150.00 (institutions), £49.50 (individuals) other. Blackwell Scientific Publications Ltd, Marston Book Services, PO Box 87, Oxford OX2 ODT UK. **Tel** 011 44 865 791155, FAX 011 44 865 791927, telex 837 515 MARDIS G. **NLM** W1; AL375. **CODEN** APTHEN. **[CCC]. Pr Rev.** available on microfilm and microfiche from University Microfilms International (UMI). Documents available from The Genuine Article, BIOSIS Document Express, CASDDS, ADONIS.
**Ind/Abst** ADONIS; Biol. Abstr. (1987-); Chem. Abstr. (1987-); Curr. Aware. Biol. Sci., CABS; Curr. Contents Life Sci.; EMBASE; Health Plan. Adminis.; Helminthol. Abstr.; Nutr. Abstr. Rev., Ser. A, Hum. Exp.; PESTDOC; Res. Alert [Select. Cov.]; Sci. Cit. Index; SCISEARCH; Trop. Dis. Bull.

UK/0953-0673
**ALIMENTARY PHARMACOLOGY & THERAPEUTICS SUPPLEMENT.** [Aliment. pharmacol. ther., Suppl.]. **VFOAT** Alimentary Pharmacology and Therapeutics. Supplement. (1987)-. Academic Scholarly Publication. English. Free to subscribers of Alimentary Pharmacology & Therapeutics. Blackwell Scientific Publications Ltd, Marston Book Services, PO Box 87, Oxford OX2 ODT UK. **Tel** 011 44 865 791155, FAX 011 44 865 791927, telex 837 515 MARDIS G.
**Ind/Abst** EMBASE.

US/1053-0649
**ALLIANCE ALERT. MEDICAL/HEALTH. See** Medical Science and Technology-Hospital Administration and Medical Centers.

US
**ALSHP NEWSLETTER.** Newsletter. English. Nine times a year. $50.00 (membership Alabama Society of Hospital Pharmacists). Alabama Society of Hospital Pharmacists, PO Box 20663, Birmingham AL 35216. **Tel** (205)979-6674. **ED** David Collette. **Ad Acc. Circ:** 750 (ctrl).

US/0065-8111
**AMERICAN DRUG INDEX.** [Am. drug index]. (1956)-. English. an. $41.95 (hardbound edition) US; $52.50 other. Facts and Comparisons Inc, 111 West Port Plaza, Suite 400, St Louis MO 63146-3098. **Tel** (314)878-2515, (800)223-0554, FAX (314)878-5563. **ED** C. O. Wilson and T. E. Jones. **LC** RS355; .A48. **DD** 615. **NLM** QV 772 A511. **[CCC].**
**Desc:** Lists drug names in a time-saving dictionary style. Over 20,000 entries with cross-indexing of brands, generics and chemical names.

US/0190-5279
**AMERICAN DRUGGIST (1974).** (AMERICAN DRUGGIST.). [Am. drug.]. (Jan. 1974)-. Academic Scholarly Publication. English. mo (except semimonthly in Oct.). $44.00. Hearst Business Communications, 1790 Broadway, New York NY 10019. **Tel** (212)969-7500, FAX (212)969-7564. **ED** Stanley Siegelman and Kenneth Moss. **LC** RS1; .A4. **DD** 338.4/7615/405. **NLM** W1 AM393. **CODEN** AMDREK. **Ad Acc. Circ:** 92,000 (ctrl). available on microfilm and microfiche from University Microfilms International (UMI). ***Continues*** *American Druggist Merchandising, 0090-6638.*
**Desc:** Articles and departments as well as columns for pharmacy managers. Continuing education section for credit is included.
**Ind/Abst** Acad. Search (July 1993-); BioBusiness (1989-); Bus. Index (1985-); EMBASE; Gen. BusinessFile (1985-); Gen. Period. Index (1985-); INFO-SOUTH Abstr.; Int. Pharm. Abstr.; Mag. Search; Predicasts; Trade Ind. Index (1981-).

US/0002-9289
**AMERICAN JOURNAL OF HOSPITAL PHARMACY.** [Am. j. hosp. pharm.]. **Added/Corp** American Society of Hospital Pharmacists. **VFOAT** AJHP. Vol. 15 (Jan. 1958)-. Academic Scholarly Publication. English. sm (24 issues). $137.00 US; $159.81 Canada; $162.00 other; Also comes with American Society for Hospital Pharmacists membership. American Society of Hospital Pharmacists, 7272 Wisconsin Avenue, Bethesda MD 20814. **Tel** (301)657-3000, (301)657-4383, FAX (301)652-8278. **DD** 615. **NLM** W1 AM456. **CODEN** AJHPA9AJHPA. **[CCC].** Index available. **Bk Rev. Ad Acc. Pr Rev. Circ:** 25,000. available on microfiche; available on microfilm; available on an online database. Documents available from The Genuine Article, CASDDS. ***Continues*** *Bulletin / American Society of Hospital Pharmacists.*
**Desc:** The official publication of the American Society of Hospital Pharmacists, AJHP covers all facets of pharmaceutical care in hospitals and other organized health-care settings. It has received international acclaim as an outstanding journal in pharmacy. ACPE approved continuing education credit is available for selected articles.
**Ind/Abst** Abstr. Clin. Care Guidel.; Chem. Abstr.; Cumul. Index Nurs. Allied Health Lit.; Curr. Contents Life Sci.; Dairy Sci. Abstr.; EMBASE; Health Devices Alerts; Health Plan. Adminis.; Index Med.; Int. Nurs. Index; Int. Pharm. Abstr.; Iowa Drug Inf. Serv. (1966-); Nutr. Abstr. Rev., Ser. B, Live Feeds and Feed.; Nutr. Abstr. Rev., Ser. A, Hum. Exp.; Life Sci. Collect.; PESTDOC; Physic. Medline Plus; Protozoolog. Abstr.; Ref. Upd. Deluxe Ed.; Res. Alert [Full Cov.]; Sci. Cit. Index; SCISEARCH; Soc. Sci. Cit. Index [Select. Cov.].

US/0002-9459
**AMERICAN JOURNAL OF PHARMACEUTICAL EDUCATION.** [Am. j. pharm. educ.]. **Added/Corp** American Association of Colleges of Pharmacy. Vol. 1 (Jan. 1937)-. Periodical. English. qt (4 issues). $100.00 institution, $40.00 individual. American Association of Colleges of Pharmacy, 1426 Prince Street, Alexandria VA 22314-2815. **Tel** (703)739-2330. **ED** George H. Cocolas. **LC** RS110; .A33. **DD** 615.071173. **NLM** W1 AM498C. **CODEN** AJPDAD. Index available. **Bk Rev. Ad Acc. Pr Rev. Circ:** 2,200 (ctrl). available on microfilm and microfiche from University Microfilms International (UMI). Documents available from The Genuine Article, BIOSIS Document Express, CASDDS.
**Desc:** Provides articles on methods, techniques and innovations in pharmaceutical education and informs educators of trends, events and developments in the various areas of specialization in the pharmaceutical sciences.
**Ind/Abst** Biol. Abstr.; Chem. Abstr.; Contents Pages Educ.; Curr. Contents Life Sci.; Curr. Index J. Educ.; EMBASE; Health Plan. Adminis.; Hospit. Health Admin. Index; Int. Pharm. Abstr.; Iowa Drug Inf. Serv. (1976-); NAPRALERT; Life Sci. Collect.; Res. Alert [Full Cov.]; Sci. Cit. Index; SCISEARCH; Soc. Sci. Cit. Index [Select. Cov.].

US/0730-7780
**AMERICAN JOURNAL OF PHARMACY AND THE SCIENCES SUPPORTING PUBLIC HEALTH (1981).** (AMERICAN JOURNAL OF PHARMACY AND THE SCIENCES SUPPORTING PUBLIC HEALTH.). [Am. j. pharm. sci. support. public health]. **Added/Corp** Philadelphia College of Pharmacy and Science. **VFOAT** American Journal of Pharmacy. Vol. 153, No. 1, (Oct./Dec.1981)-. Academic Scholarly Publication. English. an. $12.00 US & Canada; $15.00 others. Philadelphia College of Pharmacy & Science, 600 South 43rd Street, Philadelphia PA 19104. **Tel** (215)596-8800. **NLM** W1 AM498H. **CODEN** APSHDH. available on microfilm and microfiche from University Microfilms International (UMI). Documents available from BIOSIS Document Express, CASDDS. ***Continues*** *PM. Pharmacy Management, 0163-464X.*
**Ind/Abst** Biol. Abstr.; Chem. Abstr. (1981-1982); EMBASE; Int. Pharm. Abstr.

US/0160-3450
**AMERICAN PHARMACY.** [Am. pharm.]. Vol. 18 (Jan. 1978)-. Academic Scholarly Publication. English. mo. $75.00 (institution), $50.00 (individual) US. American Pharmaceutical Association, 2215 Constitution Avenue Northwest, Washington DC 20037-2985. **Tel** (202)628-4410, (800)237-2742, FAX (202)783-2351. **ED** Marlene Z. Bloom. **LC** RS1; .A522. **DD** 362.1. **NLM** W1 AM699K. **CODEN** AMPHDF. **[CCC].** Index available. **Bk Rev. Ad Acc. Pr Rev. Circ:** 49,000. available on microfilm and microfiche from University Microfilms International (UMI). Documents available from BIOSIS Document Express, CASDDS. ***Continues*** *Journal of the American Pharmaceutical Association, 0003-0465.*
**Desc:** Articles on health care, research and practices relating to pharmacy. Also special reports, editorials and news.
**Ind/Abst** Biol. Abstr.; Chem. Abstr.; EMBASE; Energy Res. Abstr. (Aug. 1982-); Index Med.; Int. Pharm. Abstr.; Iowa Drug Inf. Serv. (1966-); NAPRALERT; Life Sci. Collect.; Protozoolog. Abstr.

US/1060-5576
**AMERICAN PHARMACY TECHNICIAN JOURNAL, THE.** ***Ceased.*** (THE AMERICAN PHARMACY TECHNICIAN JOURNAL : OFFICIAL PUBLICATION OF THE AMERICAN ASSOCIATION OF PHARMACY TECHNICIANS.). [Am. pharm. tech. j.]. **Added/Corp** American Association of Pharmacy Technicians. Vol. 1, No. 1 (Sept./Oct.1991)-(1992). Periodical. English. bm. Association of Pharmacy Technicians, PO Box 1109, Madison WI 53701. **Tel** (800)762-8979. **ED** Julie Piotraschle. **DD** 615. Index available. cum. index. **Ad Acc. Circ:** 2500.
**Desc:** Includes scientific and socio-economical issues affecting the practice of pharmacy technology. Subject matter includes, but is not limited to, scientific and managerial aspects of pharmacy practice, pharmaceutical hardware and computer applications, and development of professional skills.
**Ind/Abst** Int. Pharm. Abstr.

●UK
**ANAESTHETIC PHARMACOLOGY REVIEW. See** Medical Science and Technology-Anesthesiology.

PO/0003-2425
**ANAIS AZEVEDOS.** [An. Azevedos]. (1949)-. Portuguese. ir. **CODEN** ANAZAW.
**Ind/Abst** Int. Pharm. Abstr.

BL/0003-2441
**ANAIS DE FARMACIA E QUIMICA DE SAO PAULO. Added/Corp** Sociedade de Farmacia e Quimica de Sao Paulo. Sociedade de Farmacia e Quimica de Sao Paulo. Anais. Vol. 1 (1924)-. Periodical. Multiple languages (Portuguese; summaries and/or abstracts in English). bm. Documents available from CASDDS.
**Ind/Abst** Chem. Abstr.; Int. Pharm. Abstr.

SP/0034-0618
**ANALES. Main/Corp** Academia de Farmacia, Madrid. **Added/Corp** Academia Nacional de Farmacia. Real Academia de Farmacia. (1932)-. Periodical. Spanish (English, French and Portuguese). Six times a year. Real Academia de Farmacia, Calle de Farmacia 11, 28004 Madrid Spain. **Tel** 011 34 915 310307. **ED** Manuel Ortega. **NLM** W1 AC156. **CODEN** ARAFAY. **[CCC].** Index available. **Bk Rev. Pr Rev. Circ:** 800. Documents available from BIOSIS Document Express, CASDDS.
**Desc:** Research works on problems concerning synthesis, analysis and pharmacological effects of drugs; pharmacognosy, pharmaceutical chemistry, clinical biochemistry, microbiology, physiology, nutrition, botany, pharmaceutical history.
**Ind/Abst** Bibliogr. Mission.; Biol. Abstr.; Chem. Abstr.; Curr. Biotechnol.; EMBASE; GeoRef; Int. Pharm. Abstr.; PESTDOC.

US/0099-5428
**ANALYTICAL PROFILES OF DRUG SUBSTANCES.** ***Title Change.*** **See** Chemistry-Physical and Theoretical Chemistry.

●US
**ANALYTICAL PROFILES OF DRUG SUBSTANCES AND EXCIPIENTS.** Vol. 21 (1992)-. Academic Scholarly Publication. English. ir. $95.00 (Vol. 23). Academic Press, Inc., 6277 Sea Harbor Drive, Orlando FL 32887. **Tel** (800)543-9534, (407)345-4100, FAX (407)363-9661. **NLM** QV 740; AA1 A55. **CODEN** APDEE2. ***Continues*** *Analytical Profiles of Drug Substances, 0099-5428.*

TU/1015-3918
**ANKARA UNIVERSITESI ECZACILIK FAKULTESI DERGISI.** [Ankara Univ. Eczacilik Fak. derg.]. **VFOAT** Journal of Faculty of Pharmacy of Ankara University. (1984)-. Periodical. Turkish. Documents available from CASDDS. ***Continues*** *Ankara Universitesi Eczacilik Fakultesi Mecmuasi, 0377-9734.*
**Ind/Abst** Chem. Abstr.

PL/0365-5539
**ANNALES PHARMACEUTICI.** [Ann. Pharm.]. (1965)-. Periodical. Polish. an. Society of Science & Letters Poznan UL SEW, Mielzynskiego 27 29, Poznan Poland. **UDC** 615. ***Continues*** *Prace Komisji Farmaceutycznej, 0370-2251.*
**Ind/Abst** Int. Pharm. Abstr.

BE
**ANNALES PHARMACEUTIQUES BELGES.** (1950)-. French. mo. Association Pharmaceutique Belgium, 11 rue Archimede, B-1040 Brussels Belgium.
**Ind/Abst** Int. Pharm. Abstr.

FR/0003-4509
**ANNALES PHARMACEUTIQUES FRANCAISES.** [Ann. pharm. fr.]. **Added/Corp** Academie de Pharmacie (France) Societe de Pharmacie de Paris. Vol. 1 (Jan. 1943)-. Academic Scholarly Publication. French. bm. $256.00. Masson Editeur, Box Postale 22, 41353 Vineuil 16 France. **Tel** 011 33 54 438994. **(Subscription address:** 7A Boulevard de Perolles, CH-1701 Fribourg Switzerland**) LC** RS1; .A615. **DD** 615.105. **NLM** W1 AN465. **CODEN** APFRAD. **[CCC].** available on microfilm and microfiche from University Microfilms International (UMI). Documents available from BIOSIS Document Express, CASDDS. ***Formed by the union of*** *Journal de Pharmacie et de Chimie* ***and*** *Bulletin des Sciences Pharmacologiques.*
**Ind/Abst** Anal. Abstr.; Biol. Abstr.; Chem. Abstr.; Chem. Titles; Curr. Biotechnol.; Dairy Sci. Abstr.; EMBASE; Energy Res. Abstr.; Health Plan. Adminis.; Index Med.; Int. Pharm. Abstr.; Methods Organ. Synth.; Nat. Prod. Updates; Life Sci. Collect.; PESTDOC; Protozoolog. Abstr.; Saf. Health Work; Vitis Vitic. Enol. Abstr.

FR/0224-5264
**ANNALES SCIENTIFIQUES DE L'UNIVERSITE DE FRANCHE-COMTE-BESANCON. MEDECINE ET PHARMACIE.** Issue No. 1-. Academic Scholarly Publication. French. ir. Price varies per volume. **UDC** 615. **NLM** W1 AN47KL. **CODEN** AUFPDB. Documents available from CASDDS. ***Supersedes*** *Annales Scientifiques de l'Universite de Bescanon. 3E Serie. Medecine.*
**Ind/Abst** Chem. Abstr.

●US/1060-0280
**ANNALS OF PHARMACOTHERAPY, THE.** [Ann. pharmacother.]. Vol. 26, No. 1 (Jan. 1992)-. Academic Scholarly Publication. English. mo. $120.00 (institutions), $177.00 (libraries) US; $135.00 (institutions), $192.00 (libraries) other. Harvey Whitney Books Company, PO Box 42696, Cincinnati OH 45242. **Tel** (513)793-3555, FAX (513)793-3600. **LC** RM300; .D79. **DD** 615.5/8/05. **NLM** W1; AN6170. **CODEN** APHRER. available on microfilm and microfiche from University Microfilms International (UMI). Documents available from BIOSIS Document Express, CASDDS. ***Continues*** *DICP, 1042-9611.*
**Ind/Abst** Biol. Abstr.; Chem. Abstr.; Cumul. Index Nurs. Allied Health Lit.; Curr. Contents Clin. Med.; EMBASE (1992-); Hospit. Health Admin. Index; Index Med. (1992-); Int. Pharm. Abstr.; Life Sci. Collect.; PESTDOC (?-?); Physic. Medline Plus; Sci. Cit. Index.

US/8755-3252
**ANNALS OF THE INSTITUTE FOR ORGONOMIC SCIENCE.** **Added/Corp** Institute for Orgonomic Science (U.S.). Vol. 1, No. 1 (Sept. 1984)-. English. an. $15.00 US; $17.00 other. Institute for Orgonomic Science, PO Box 304, Gwynedd Valley PA 19437. **LC** RZ460; .A56. **DD** 615.

FR/0997-0509
**ANNUAIRE DE L'INDUSTRIE PHARMACEUTIQUE EN FRANCE.** (1985)-. French. an. 360.00F. SEQP / Societe Edn. Quotidien Paris, 140 rue Jules Guesde, 92593 Levallois Perret, France. **Tel** 011 33 1 47307800. **UDC** 615.

II/0376-5563
**ANNUAL ADMINISTRATION REPORT - FOOD AND DRUG ADMINISTRATION, MAHARASHTRA STATE.** **See** Public Administration.

SP/0379-4121
**ANNUAL DRUG DATA REPORT.** (DRUG DATA REPORT.). [Annu. drug data rep.]. Vol. 7, No. 1 (Feb. 1985)-. Periodical. English. mo. $900.00. Prous Science Publishers, Apartado de Correos 540, 08080 Barcelona Spain. **Tel** 011 34 3 4592220, FAX 011 34 3 4581535. **ED** J. R. Prous. **NLM** QV 772; A615. **[CCC].** Index available. cum. index. **Ad Acc. Circ:** 3,000. available in microform. ***Continues*** *Annual Drug Data Report, 0379-4121.*
**Desc:** Drugs presented in condensed monograph form, classified by pharmacological properties, compunds selected mainly from patent literature, also current literature congresses and manufacturers communications.

SP
**ANNUAL DRUG DATA REPORT.** Vol. 1 (1971)-. English. an. $900.00. Prous Science Publishers, Apartado de Correos 540, 08080 Barcelona Spain. **Tel** 011 34 3 4592220, FAX 011 34 3 4581535.

●US/1068-3178
**ANNUAL OF DRUG THERAPY.** (1994)-. English. an. $57.00 (nonsubscriber), $42.00 (subscriber) US; $57.00 (nonsubscriber), $52.00 (subscriber) other. W.B. Saunders Company, A Subsidiary of Harcourt Brace Jovanovich, Inc., The Curtis Center/Suite 300, Independence Square West, Philadelphia PA 19106-3399. **Tel** (215)238-7800 or, 5587, FAX (215)238-7883, telex 173146. **(Subscription address:** W. B. Saunders Company / North America Subscriptions, c/o Periodicals, 6277 Sea Harbour Drive, 4th Floor, Orlando FL 32887.**) NLM** W1; AN755S.

US
**ANNUAL REPORT - NORTH DAKOTA STATE BOARD OF PHARMACY.** **Main/Corp** North Dakota. State Board of Pharmacy. (19??)-. English. an. State Board of Pharmacy, PO Box 1354, Bismarck ND 58501. **LC** RS75; .N67a. **DD** 353.9/784/008243.

US/0899-8612
**ANNUAL REPORT OF THE BOARD OF PHARMACY OF THE STATE OF ARIZONA.** [Annu. rep. Board Pharm. State Ariz.]. **Main/Corp** Board of Pharmacy of the State of Arizona. **VFOAT** Annual Report; Directory of Arizona Professional Pharmacists; Arizona Pharmacist Directory; Pharmacists Directory. English. an. **LC** RS5.A6; A77a. **DD** 615/.1/09791.

US/0098-0099
**ANNUAL REPORT OF THE MARYLAND BOARD OF PHARMACY.** **Main/Corp** Maryland. Board of Pharmacy. (18??)-. English. an. Maryland Board of Pharmacy. **LC** RS67.U7; M35a. **DD** 615/.4/09752.

US
**ANNUAL REPORT / OFFICE OF OKLAHOMA STATE BOARD OF PHARMACY.** **Main/Corp** Office of Oklahoma State Board of Pharmacy. (19??)-. English. an. Joe Schwemin Secretary, Suite 112/North Terrace, Lincoln Plaza Office Center, 4545 Lincoln Boulevard, Oklahoma City OK 73105. **LC** R55; .O5. **DD** 353.7660077/84. ***Continues*** *Oklahoma. Board of Pharmacy. Report.*

US/0065-7743
**ANNUAL REPORTS IN MEDICINAL CHEMISTRY.** (1965)-. Academic Scholarly Publication. English. ir. $70.00 (Vol. 28). Academic Press, Inc., 6277 Sea Harbor Drive, Orlando FL 32887. **Tel** (800)543-9534, (407)345-4100, FAX (407)363-9661. **ED** Cornelius K. Cain. **LC** RS402; .A65. **DD** 615.08. **UDC** 615.31. **NLM** W1 AN769G. **CODEN** ARMCBI. **[CCC]. Pr Rev.** Documents available from The Genuine Article, BIOSIS Document Express, CASDDS.
**Ind/Abst** Biol. Abstr.; Chem. Abstr.; Curr. Biotechnol.; Dairy Sci. Abstr.; Index Sci. Rev. [Full Cov.]; Res. Alert [Full Cov.]; Rev. Med. Vet. Entomol.; Rev. Med. Vet. Mycology; Sci. Cit. Index (19??-19??); SCISEARCH.

UK/0743-9539
**ANNUAL REVIEW OF CHRONOPHARMACOLOGY.** ***Title Change.*** [Annu. rev. chronopharmacol.]. **VFOAT** Chronopharmacology. Vol. 1 (1984)-(1992). Academic Scholarly Publication. English. an. Pergamon Press, An Imprint of Elsevier Science Ltd., The Boulevard, Langford Lane, Kidlington, Oxford OX5 1GB United Kingdom. **Tel** 011 44 865 843000, 011 44 865 843699, FAX 011 44 865 843010. **(Subscription address:** US/ 395 Saw Mill River Road, Elmsford, NY 10523; Can/ 150 Consumers Road/Suite 104, Willowdale Ontario M2J 1P9; Aus-NZ/ POB 544, Potts Point NSW 2011**) ED** A Reinberg, M Smolensky, and G Labrecque. **LC** RS201.C64. **DD** 615/.7. **UDC** 615.22. **NLM** W1; AN77GE. **CODEN** ANRCEI. **[CCC].** available on microfilm and microfiche from University Microfilms International (UMI). Documents available from BIOSIS Document Express, CASDDS. ***Continued by*** *Chronobiology International.*
**Desc:** Focuses on the biological rhythms and medications in human beings and also takes into consideration the many disciplines which contribute to the study of biological rhythms.
**Ind/Abst** Biol. Abstr. (1986-); Chem. Abstr. (1984-).

US/0362-1642
**ANNUAL REVIEW OF PHARMACOLOGY AND TOXICOLOGY.** [Annu. rev. pharmacol. toxicol.]. Vol. 16 (1976)-. English. an (April). $47.00 US; $52.00 other. Annual Reviews Inc., 4139 El Camino Way, PO Box 10139, Palo Alto CA 94303-0139. **Tel** (415)493-4400, (800)523-8635, FAX (415)855-9815. **ED** Authur K. Cho. **LC** RM16; .A63. **DD** 615/.05. **NLM** W1 AN778K. **CODEN** ARPTDI. **[CCC].** Index available. cum. index. **Pr Rev.** ctrl circ. available on microfilm and microfiche from University Microfilms International (UMI). Documents available from The Genuine Article, BIOSIS Document Express, CASDDS. ***Continues*** *Annual Review of Pharmacology, 0066-4251.*
**Desc:** Comprehensive, thorough coverage of latest advances in pharmacology and toxicology, written by acknowledged experts in the field. Extensive literature citations included.
**Ind/Abst** AGRICOLA [Select. Cov.]; BioBusiness (-1990); Biol. Abstr.; Chem. Abstr.; CSA Neuro. Abstr.; Curr. Contents Life Sci.; EMBASE; Energy Res. Abstr. (Jan. 1980-); Health Period. Database; Index Med.; Index Sci. Rev. [Full Cov.]; Index Vet.; Life Sci. Collect.; PESTDOC; Protozoolog. Abstr.; Psychol. Abstr. (1976-); PsycINFO; PsycLit; Ref. Upd. Basic Ed.; Ref. Upd. Clinical Ed.; Ref. Upd. Deluxe Ed.; Res. Alert [Full Cov.]; Rev. Med. Vet. Entomol.; Risk Abstr.; Sci. Cit. Index; SCISEARCH; Soc. Sci. Cit. Index [Select. Cov.]; Vet. Bull.; Toxicol. Abstr.

CN/0829-2078
**ANNUAL SURVEY OF COMMUNITY PHARMACY OPERATIONS.** [Annu. surv. community pharm. oper.]. **Added/Corp** Canadian Pharmaceutical Association. University of Toronto. Faculty of Pharmacy. 4th (1983)-. English. an. 50.00Can$. Canadian Pharmaceutical Association, 1785 Alta Vista Drive, Ottawa Ontario K1G 3Y6 Canada. **Tel** (613)523-7877, FAX (613)523-0445. **ED** H. Segal. **DD** 381/.456154/0971. **Circ:** 1,000 (ctrl). ***Continues*** *Survey of Community Pharmacy Operations, 0834-0390.*
**Desc:** National and provincial financial data on community pharmacy operations. Includes income statements, balance sheets, financial rates and management information.

US
**ANNUAL SURVEY OF FACULTY SALARIES.** (19??)-. English. an. $25.00. American Association of Colleges of Pharmacy, 1426 Prince Street, Alexandria VA 22314-2815. **Tel** (703)739-2330.

●CN/1196-5290
**ANNUAL SURVEY OF PRESCRIPTION AND OVER-THE-COUNTER DRUGS.** [Annu. surv. prescr. over-the-count. drugs]. **Added/Corp** Actmedia Retail Resource Group. InfoMation Resources. **VFOAT** Pharmacist News; Survey of Prescription & Over-the-Counter Drugs. (Aug. 1993)-. Periodical. English. an. Maclean Hunter Canada / Montreal, 1001 bvd. de Maisonneuve W., Montreal, Quebec H3A 3E1 Canada. **Tel** 514-845-5141, FAX 514-845-4302, telex 055-60604. **DD** 381/.456151/0971021. ***Continues*** *Survey of Drug Store Trends, 0832-8692.*

UK/0959-4973
**ANTI-CANCER DRUGS.** **See** Medical Science and Technology-Toxicology.

SZ/0066-4758
**ANTIBIOTICS AND CHEMOTHERAPY.** [Antibiot. chemother.]. Vol. 17 (1971)-. Monographic series. English. an. 220.00F (approx. per volume). S. Karger AG, Allschwilerstrasse 10, PO Box - Postfach - Case Postale, CH-4009 Basel Switzerland. **Tel** 011 41 61 306-1111, FAX 011 41 61 306-1234, telex CH 962 652. **ED** H. Schonfeld. **LC** RM260; .A55. **DD** 615/.58/08S. **NLM** W1 AN855G. **CODEN** ANBCB3. **[CCC].** Documents available from BIOSIS Document Express, CASDDS. ***Continues*** *Antibiotica et Chemotherapia.*
**Desc:** Each volume in this series gives thorough coverage to a specific problem undergoing investigation in the field of antibiotics and chemotherapy. In every case, the studies reported have made great contributions towards finding new and better ways of treating infectious, parasitic, and malignant diseases. Authors focus on different aspects of their particular areas of study in order to make highly specialized information available to clinicians as well as researchers.
**Ind/Abst** Biol. Abstr.; Chem. Abstr.; Health Plan. Adminis.; Index Med.; NAPRALERT; Life Sci. Collect.; Ref. Upd. Deluxe Ed.

US
**ANTIBIOTICS. ANTIBIOTIKI.** **Added/Corp** Consultants Bureau Enterprises. **VFOAT** Antibiotiki. Vol. 4, No. 1, Jan./Feb. (1959)-. Periodical. English (Russian; translations available in Russian). bm. MAIK Nauka / Interperiodica, Ulitsa Profsoyuznaya 90, Moscow 117864 Russia. **LC** RM265; .R523. **DD** 615.329.

US/0097-4668
**ANTIBIOTICS (NEW YORK. 1967).** ***Ceased.*** (ANTIBIOTICS.). No. 1 (1967)-Series complete. Monographic series. English. ir. Springer-Verlag New York Inc., 175 5th Avenue, New York NY 10010. **Tel** (212)460-1500, telex 232 235 SPB UR. **(Subscription address:** Springer Verlag New York Inc. / for North America, 44 Hartz Way, Secaucus NJ 07096.**) NLM** W1 AN854B. **CODEN** ANTBDO. Documents available from BIOSIS Document Express, CASDDS.
**Desc:** Study of antibiotics
**Ind/Abst** Biol. Abstr.; Chem. Abstr.

RU/0235-2990
**ANTIBIOTIKI I HIMIOTERAPIA.** (ANTIBIOTIKI I KH MIOTERAPIIA.). [Antibiot. himioter.]. **Added/Corp** Soviet Union. Ministerstvo Meditsinskoi i Mikrobiologicheskoi Promyshlennosti. **VFOAT** Antibiotics and Chemotherapy. Vol, 33 No. 1 (1988)-. Periodical. Russian (summaries and/or abstracts in English; table of contents in English). mo. $129.95. Izdatelstvo Meditsina / Russian Academy of Medical Sciences, Ulitsa Solyanka 14, 109801 Moscow Russia. **Tel** 011 95 297-05-04. **(Subscription address:** East View Publications Inc., 3020 Harbor Lane North, Suite 110, Minneapolis MN 55447.**) NLM** W1; AN859BS. **CODEN** ANKHEW. **[CCC].** Documents available from The Genuine Article, BIOSIS Document Express, CASDDS. ***Continues** Antibiotiki i Meditsinskaia Biotekhnologiia, 0233-7525.*
**Desc:** Information on antibiotics.
**Ind/Abst** Anal. Abstr.; Biol. Abstr. (1988-); Chem. Abstr. (?-?); Curr. Biotechnol.; Curr. Chem. React.; Curr. Contents Life Sci.; Dairy Sci. Abstr.; EMBASE; Helminthol. Abstr. (1991-); Index Chem.; Index Med. (1988-); PESTDOC; Protozoolog. Abstr.; Res. Alert [Full Cov.]; Sci. Cit. Index (19??-19??); SCISEARCH.

SP
**ANUARIO ESPANOL DE PARA-FARMACIA.** Spanish. an. 4.500ptas Spain; 9.00ptas North America; 6.500ptas other. Puntex SA, c/ Mare de Deu del Coll 14, 08023 Barcelona Spain. **Tel** (93)237 71 24, FAX (93)217 55 73, telex 97131 GPMM E. **Bk Rev. Ad Acc. Circ:** 20,000.
**Desc:** Distributors for foreign businesses. Trademarks, products listed by specialty, wholesalers, pharmacy offices, and useful data.

US/0003-6560
**APOTHECARY (BOSTON), THE.** (THE APOTHECARY.). [Apothecary]. (19??)-. Periodical. English. Twelve times a year. The Health Care Marketing Service, 95 1st Street, Suite 100, Los Altos CA 94022. **Tel** (415)941-3955, FAX (415)941-2303. **ED** Jerold K. Karabensh. **NLM** W1 AP236F. **Circ:** 67,400 (ctrl). available on microfilm and microfiche from University Microfilms International (UMI). ***Continues** Apothecary and New England Druggist.*
**Desc:** Covers business topics of interest to the pharmacist, including management, merchandising, records processing, patient service and interaction, and community involvement in health education.
**Ind/Abst** Int. Pharm. Abstr.

NE/0924-4107
**APOTHEEK IN PRAKTIJK.** ***Ceased.*** [Apoth. prakt.]. (1989)-(1992). Periodical. Dutch. mo. Bohn Stafleu Van Loghum BV, Postbus 246, 3990 GA Houten Netherlands. **Tel** 011 31 3403 95782. **UDC** 615.1.

GW/0177-9591
**APOTHEKE UND KRANKENHAUS : ZEITSCHRIFT DES VERBANDES DER KRANKENHAUSVERSORGENDEN OFFIZIN-APOTHEKER E.V.** **Added/Corp** Verband der Krankenhausversorgenden Offizin-Apotheker (Germany). Vol. 1, No. 1 (1985)-. Periodical. German. qt. DM54.60. Deutscher Apotheker Verlag, Postfach 101061, D 70009 Stuttgart Germany. **Tel** 011 49 711 25820, INLAND:0711/2582, FAX 011 49 711 2582 290, telex 723636 daz d. **ED** Klaus Grimm. **NLM** W1; AP237F.

GW
**APOTHEKENHELFERIN, DIE.** ***Title Change.*** Vol. 1, July (1953)-(19??). Periodical. German. bm. Deutscher Apotheker Verlag, Postfach 101061, D 70009 Stuttgart Germany. **Tel** 011 49 711 25820, INLAND:0711/2582, FAX 011 49 711 2582 290, telex 723636 daz d. **ED** Renate Weber. **Bk Rev. Ad Acc. Circ:** 22,000 (ctrl). ***Continued by** PKA Aktuell.*

GW/0939-3331
**APOTHEKENHELFERIN HEUTE.** ***Title Change.*** (1990)-(1994). German. bm. Deutscher Apotheker Verlag, Postfach 101061, D 70009 Stuttgart Germany. **Tel** 011 49 711 25820, INLAND:0711/2582, FAX 011 49 711 2582 290, telex 723636 daz d. **ED** Michael Schmidt. ***Continued by** PK Aktuell, 0944-7032.*

GW/0066-5347
**APOTHEKER-JAHRBUCH.** (1949)-. German. an. Wissenschaftliche Verlagsgesellschaft mbH, Postfach 101061, D 70009 Stuttgart Germany. **Tel** 011 49 711 258200, FAX 011 49 711 2582290, telex 723636 DAZ D. **Ad Acc. Circ:** 4,000 (ctrl).

GW/0341-0110
**APOTHEKER UND KUNST.** ***Ceased.*** [Apoth. Kunst]. (1955)-(Dec. 1988). Periodical. German. ir. Deutscher Apotheker Verlag, Postfach 101061, D 70009 Stuttgart Germany. **Tel** 011 49 711 25820, INLAND:0711/2582, FAX 011 49 711 2582 290, telex 723636 daz d. **UDC** 615. **NLM** W1 AP261. **Circ:** 24,000.

GW/0178-4862
**APOTHEKER-ZEITUNG STUTTGART.** [Apoth.-Ztg.Stuttg.]. (1985)-. Periodical. German. wk. No separate subscriptions. Deutscher Apotheker Verlag, Postfach 101061, D 70009 Stuttgart Germany. **Tel** 011 49 711 25820, INLAND:0711/2582, FAX 011 49 711 2582 290, telex 723636 daz d. **ED** Peter Ditzel. **UDC** 615.1. Index available. cum. index. **Bk Rev. Ad Acc. Circ:** 30,000 (ctrl).
**Desc:** Covers pharmacy news, health policy and drug information.

BE/0003-6579
**APOTHEKERSBLAD, HET.** [Apothekersblad]. (1942)-. Periodical. French. Ten times a year. 2650.94F. Algemene Pharmaceutische Bond - Association Pharmaceutique Belge, Archimedestraat 11 rue Archimede, 1040 Brussels Belgium. **Tel** 011 32 2 2302685. **UDC** 615.

•US/1064-8542
**APPLIED CLINICAL TRIALS.** (1992)-. English. mo. $59.00 US & Possessions; $79.00 Canada; $117.00 other. Advanstar Communications Inc., 131 West First Street, Duluth MN 55802. **Tel** (218)723-9477, (800)346-0085. **NLM** W1; AP522B. **[CCC].**
**Desc:** Offers practical, hands-on information that helps clinical research scientists develop, execute, and file new drug applications and expedite the drug approval process.

US
**APPM UPDATE.** (19??)-. English. qt. $25.00. American Pharmaceutical Association, 2215 Constitution Avenue Northwest, Washington DC 20037-2985. **Tel** (202)628-4410, (800)237-2742, FAX (202)783-2351. ***Continues** Pharmacy Practice.*

US
**APPROVED BIOEQUIVALENCY CODES.** English. mo. $73.95 US; $92.50 other (loose-leaf edition). Facts and Comparisons Inc, 111 West Port Plaza, Suite 400, St Louis MO 63146-3098. **Tel** (314)878-2515, (800)223-0554, FAX (314)878-5563.
**Desc:** Contains information on the FDA's current data on bioequivalency evaluations.

US/1048-5996
**APPROVED DRUG PRODUCTS WITH THERAPEUTIC EQUIVALENCE EVALUATIONS.** [Approv. drug prod. ther. equiv. eval.]. **Added/Corp** Center for Drugs and Biologics (U.S.) Center for Drug Evaluation and Research (U.S.) Center for Drug Evaluation and Research (U.S.). Office of Management. 6th Ed. (1985)-. Government Publication. English. mo. $55.00 domestic; $68.75 other. Superintendent of Documents, US Government Printing Office, Washington DC 20402. **Tel** (202)275-3328, FAX (202)786-2377. **LC** RM301.45 .A66. **DD** 615/.1. ***Continues** Approved Prescription Drug Products with Therapeutic Equivalence Evaluations, 0733-4036.*
**Desc:** Lists current marketed prescription drug products that have been approved on the basis of their safety and effectiveness by the Food and Drug Administration.

US
**APUA NEWSLETTER / ALLIANCE FOR THE PRUDENT USE OF ANTIBIOTICS.** **Added/Corp** Alliance for the Prudent Use of Antibiotics. Vol. 1, No. 1 (Summer 1983)-. Periodical. English (Spanish). Four times a year. $45.00 (individuals), $80.00 (institutions); $100.00 (institutions & libraries). Alliance For the Prudent Use of Antibiotics, PO Box 1372, Boston MA 02117. **Tel** (617)956-6765, FAX (617)956-0458. **ED** Stuart B. Levy M. D. and Anne Levy. **NLM** W1; AP898. cum. index (members only). **Circ:** 1,000 (ctrl).
**Desc:** Dedicated to promoting the effective use of antibiotics worldwide through education and research.

GW/0365-6233
**ARCHIV DER PHARMAZIE (WEINHEIM).** (ARCHIV DER PHARMAZIE.). [Arch. Pharm.]. **Added/Corp** Arbeitsgemeinschaft der Berufsvertretungen Deutscher Apotheker. Deutsche Pharmazeutische Gesellschaft. Vol. 305 (Jan. 1972)-. Academic Scholarly Publication. German. mo. $498.00. VCH Gesellschaft GmbH, Postfach 101161, D 69451 Weinheim Germany. **Tel** 011 49 6201 606459, FAX 011 49 6201 606184. **(Subscription address:** VCH Publishers Inc., 303 Northwest 12th Avenue, Journals Department, Deerfield FL 33442.**) NLM** W1 AR163C. **CODEN** ARPMAS. **[CCC]. Pr Rev.** Documents available from The Genuine Article, BIOSIS Document Express, CASDDS. ***Continues** Archiv der Pharmazie und Berichte der Deutschen Pharmazeutischen Gesellschaft, 0376-0367.*
**Ind/Abst** Anal. Abstr.; Biol. Abstr.; Chem. Abstr.; Curr. Chem. React.; Curr. Contents Life Sci.; EMBASE; Energy Res. Abstr. (Nov. 1975-); Food Sci. Technol. Abstr.; Helminthol. Abstr.; Hortic. Abstr.; Index Chem.; Index Med.; Int. Pharm. Abstr.; Mass Spect. Bull.; Methods Organ. Synth.; NAPRALERT; Nat. Prod. Updates; Nematol. Abstr.; Life Sci. Collect.; PESTDOC; Protozoolog. Abstr.; Res. Alert [Full Cov.]; Rev. Med. Vet. Mycology; Sci. Cit. Index; SCISEARCH.

BE/0003-9780
**ARCHIVES INTERNATIONALES DE PHARMACODYNAMIE ET DE THERAPIE.** [Arch. int. pharmacodyn. ther.]. **Added/Corp** Heymans Institute of Pharmacology. Vol. 6 (1899)-. Academic Scholarly Publication. English. bm. 8000F. Heymans Institute of Pharmacology, de Pintelaan 185, 9000 Ghent Belgium. **NLM** W1 AR393R. **CODEN** AIPTAK. **[CCC].** cum. index. **Pr Rev.** available on microfilm and microfiche from University Microfilms International (UMI). Documents available from The Genuine Article, BIOSIS Document Express, CASDDS. ***Continues** Archives Internationales de Pharmacodynamie, 0301-4533.*
**Desc:** Original papers in the field of experimental and clinical pharmacology, in particular experimental work on mechanisms of action.
**Ind/Abst** Anim. Breed. Abstr.; Biol. Abstr.; Calcium Calcif. Tissue Abstr.; Chem. Abstr.; CSA Neuro. Abstr. (?-?); Curr. Aware. Biol. Sci., CABS; Curr. Chem. React.; Curr. Contents Life Sci.; Dairy Sci. Abstr.; EMBASE; Health Plan. Adminis.; Index Chem.; Index Med.; Index Vet.; Life Sci. Collect.; PESTDOC; Protozoolog. Abstr.; Res. Alert [Full Cov.]; Sci. Cit. Index; SCISEARCH; Vet. Bull.

KO/0253-6269
**ARCHIVES OF PHARMACAL RESEARCH.** (ARCHIVES OF PHARMACAL RESEARCH : A PUBLICATION OF THE PHARMACEUTICAL SOCIETY OF KOREA.). [Arch. pharm. res.]. **Added/Corp** Taehan Yakhakhoe. Vol. 1, No. 1 (Dec. 1978)-. Periodical. English. sa. W30000.00. Pharmaceutical Society Korea, 1489 3 Seocho 3 Dong Seocho, Seoul 137 073 Korea. **Tel** 011 82 2 5843257. **NLM** W1 AR472. **CODEN** APHRDQ. Documents available from BIOSIS Document Express, CASDDS.
**Ind/Abst** Bibliogr. Mission. (19??-1990); Biol. Abstr.; Chem. Abstr.; EMBASE; Int. Pharm. Abstr.; NAPRALERT; Rev. Med. Vet. Mycology.

SP/0304-8616
**ARCHIVOS DE FARMACOLOGIA Y TOXICOLOGIA.** ***Ceased.*** [Arch. farmacol. toxicol.]. Vol. 1 (March 1975)-(October 1987). Academic Scholarly Publication. Spanish (English). qt. Editorial Garsi SA, Juan Bravo 46, 28006 Madrid, Spain. **Tel** 011 34 1 4021212, telex 98358 GARSI E. **UDC** 615; 615.9. **NLM** W1 AR662M. **CODEN** AFTOD7. cum. index. **Ad Acc. Circ:** 600. Documents available from BIOSIS Document Express, CASDDS. ***Supersedes** Archivos del Instituto de Farmacologia Experimental.*
**Desc:** Medical toxicology, pharmacology and allied sciences.
**Ind/Abst** Biol. Abstr.; Chem. Abstr.; EMBASE; Index Med.; Indice Med. Esp.

YU/0004-1963
**ARHIV ZA FARMACIJU.** **VFOAT** Archives de Pharmacie. (1951)-.
**Ind/Abst** Int. Pharm. Abstr.

US/0004-1602
**ARIZONA PHARMACIST, THE.** [Ariz. pharm.]. **Added/Corp** Arizona Pharmacy Association. Arizona Pharmaceutical Association. (19??)-. Periodical. English. bm. $25.00. Arizona Pharmacist, 2202 North 7th Street, Phoenix AZ 85006. **Tel** (602)258-8121. **ED** Daniel J Boesen and Carrie Hartze. **NLM** W1 AR801. **Bk Rev. Ad Acc. Circ:** 1,400 (ctrl).
**Desc:** Current Arizona news and continuing education.
**Ind/Abst** Int. Pharm. Abstr.

PO/0412-8877
**ARQUIVOS.** **Main/Corp** Coimbra. Universidade. Instituto de Farmacologia e Terapeutica Experimental. (1931)-. Periodical. Portuguese. Arquivos, 5 rua de d'Francasico Manelme, Lisbon 1 Portugal. **DD** 615.

SP/0004-2927
**ARS PHARMACEUTICA.** (ARS PHARMACEUTICA; REVISTA DE LA FACULTAD DE FARMACIA DE LA UNIVERSIDAD DE GRANADA.). [Ars pharm.]. **Added/Corp** Granada. Universidad. Facultad de Farmacia. (1960)-. Academic Scholarly Publication. Spanish (summaries and/or abstracts in English). qt. Universidad de Granada / Facultad de Farmacia, Campus Cartuja, Ser Publicaciones, 18071 Granada Spain. **Tel** 011 34 281356. **NLM** W1 AR941. **CODEN** APHRAN. Documents available from CASDDS.
**Ind/Abst** Biodeter. Abstr.; Chem. Abstr.; EMBASE; Helminthol. Abstr. (1991-); Indice Med. Esp.; Int. Pharm. Abstr.; Maize Abstr.; Nutr. Abstr. Rev., Ser. B, Live Feeds and Feed.; Ornamental Hort.; Life Sci. Collect.

US/0731-3047
**ART OF MEDICATION, THE.** [Art med.]. **Added/Corp** Roche Laboratories. Vol. 1, No. 1 (Sept. 1980)-. English. The Art of Medication, 120 Brighton Road, Clifton NJ 07012. **NLM** W1 AR948G.

GW/0066-8192
**ARZNEI-TELEGRAMM : FAKTEN UND VERGLEICHE FUR DIE RATIONALE THERAPIE.** **Added/Corp** Institut Fur Arzneimittelinformation. **VFOAT** Arznei Telegramm. (197?)-. Periodical. German. Twelve times a year. DM88.00 (individual); DM156.00 (institutions). Arzneimittelinformation Berlin, GMBH Petzower STR 7, West 1000 Berlin 39 F R, Germany. **Tel** 011 49 30 8054044, FAX 011 49 30 8054046. **NLM** W1; AR969KC.

GW/0004-4172
**ARZNEIMITTEL FORSCHUNG.** [Arzneim.-Forsch.]. **VFOAT** Drug Research; Arzneimittel-Forschung. **VAT** Arzneimittel-Forschung.

Vol. 1 (April 1951)-. Academic Scholarly Publication. English (German). mo. DM558.00. Editio Cantor, Postfach 1255, D 88322 Aulendorf Germany. **Tel** 011 49 7525 9400, FAX 011 49 7525 9401. **ED** Hans Georg Classen, Victor Schramm. **LC** RM301.25; .A79. **NLM** W1 AR966. **CODEN** ARZNAD. **[CCC].** Index available. **Bk Rev**. **Ad Acc**. **Pr Rev. Circ:** 5,100 (ctrl). Documents available from The Genuine Article, BIOSIS Document Express, CASDDS, ADONIS. ***Continues*** *Pharmazie.*
**Desc:** Reports on research and test results of drugs which are to be newly developed. In addition, the latest scientific findings on drugs already marketed are also discussed.
**Ind/Abst** ADONIS; AgBiotech News Inf.; Anal. Abstr.; Biol. Abstr.; Chem Inform; Chem. Abstr.; Chem. Titles; CSA Neuro. Abstr. (?-?); Curr. Aware. Biol. Sci., CABS; Curr. Biotechnol.; Curr. Chem. React.; Curr. Contents Life Sci.; Dairy Sci. Abstr.; EMBASE; Health Plan. Adminis.; Helminthol. Abstr. (1991-); Index Chem.; Index Med.; Index Vet.; Int. Pharm. Abstr.; Mass Spect. Bull.; Methods Organ. Synth.; Microbiol. Abstr. Sect. A; Nat. Prod. Updates; Nutr. Abstr. Rev., Ser. B, Live Feeds and Feed.; Nutr. Abstr. Rev., Ser. A, Hum. Exp.; Life Sci. Collect.; PESTDOC; Protozoolog. Abstr.; Ref. Upd. Deluxe Ed.; Res. Alert [Full Cov.]; Rev. Med. Vet. Entomol.; Rev. Med. Vet. Mycology; Rev. Plant Pathol.; Sci. Cit. Index; SCISEARCH; Soc. Sci. Cit. Index [Select. Cov.]; Vet. Bull.

SZ/0250-4669
**ARZNEIMITTEL-KOMPENDIUM DER SCHWEIZ.** **Added/Corp** Schweizerische Gesellschaft fur Chemische Industrie. **VAT** Arzneimittel Kompendium der Schweiz. (1978)-. German (French and German). **(Subscription address:** Jugoslovenska Knjiga, PO Box 36, YU 11001 Belgrade Yugoslovia.**)** **ED** J Neugebauer. **NLM** QV 738 GS9 A7.

GW/0723-6913
**ARZNEIMITTELTHERAPIE.**
[Arzneimitteltherapie]. Year 1, No. 1 (Jan./Feb. 1983)-. Periodical. German. mo. DM44.40. Wissenschaftliche Verlagsgesellschaft mbH, Postfach 101061, D 70009 Stuttgart Germany. **Tel** 011 49 711 258200, FAX 011 49 711 2582290, telex 723636 DAZ D. **ED** S. Heinzl. **NLM** W1 AR969G. **[CCC].**
**Ind/Abst** Int. Pharm. Abstr.

US/0001-2483
**ASHP NEWSLETTER.** [ASHP newsletter]. **Main/Corp** American Society of Hospital Pharmacists. **Added/Corp** American Society of Hospital Pharmacists. ASHP Signal. **VAT** American Society of Hospital Pharmacists Newsletter. Vol. 1 Jan. (1968)-. Newsletter. English. mo. Comes with membership. American Society of Hospital Pharmacists, 7272 Wisconsin Avenue, Bethesda MD 20814. **Tel** (301)657-3000, (301)657-4383, FAX (301)652-8278.

SI/0217-9687
**ASIA PACIFIC JOURNAL OF PHARMACOLOGY.** [Asia Pac. j. pharmacol.]. **VFOAT** Ya Tai Yao li Hsueh Tsa Chih. Vol. 1, No. 1 (July 1986)-. Periodical. English. ir. $250.00. Singapore University Press Pte Ltd, Yusof Ishak House, National University of Singapore, 10 Kent Ridge Crescent, Singapore 0511 Republic of Singapore. **Tel** 011 65 7761148, FAX 011 65 7740652. **NLM** W1; AS139J. **CODEN** APJPEV. Documents available from The Genuine Article, BIOSIS Document Express, CASDDS.
**Ind/Abst** Biol. Abstr. (1986-); Chem. Abstr. (1986-); Curr. Contents Life Sci.; EMBASE; Res. Alert [Select. Cov.]; SCISEARCH; Trop. Dis. Bull.

SI/0129-4172
**ASIAN JOURNAL OF PHARMACEUTICAL SCIENCES.** [Asian j. pharm. sci.]. Vol. 1 (June 1979)-. Academic Scholarly Publication. English. ir. Medical Book Center, Crawford PO Box 666, Singapore 9199 Republic of Singapore. **NLM** W1 AS139V. **CODEN** AJSCDS. Documents available from CASDDS.
**Ind/Abst** Chem. Abstr.

PH/0066-8419
**ASIAN JOURNAL OF PHARMACY.** [Asian j. pharm.]. V. 1- 1967-. Academic Scholarly Publication. English. an. Federation of Asian Pharmaceutical Associations, 29 Queen Boulevard, Quezon City Philippines. **UDC** 615. **NLM** W1 AS1391. **CODEN** ASJPCG. Documents available from CASDDS.
**Ind/Abst** Chem. Abstr. (-1978); Int. Pharm. Abstr.

AT/0310-6810
**AUSTRALIAN JOURNAL OF HOSPITAL PHARMACY.** [Aust. j. hosp. pharm.]. **Added/Corp** Society of Hospital Pharmaceutical Chemists of Australia. Vol. 1 (1971)-. Periodical. English. bm. 85.00Aus$ Australia & New Zealand; 100.00Aus$ other. Society of Hospital Pharmacists of Australia, 31 Coventry Street, Suite 2, South Melbourne Victoria 3205 Australia. **Tel** 61 3 6906733, FAX 61 3 6967634. **ED** Jenni Johnstone. **NLM** W1 AU612. **CODEN** AUHPAI. **[CCC].** Index available (bound in Dec. issue). **Bk Rev**, (Qty: 15). **Ad Acc**, **Adv Mgr:** B Parsons. **Pr Rev. Circ:** 2,100 (ctrl). Documents available from BIOSIS Document Express, CASDDS.
**Desc:** Coverage of contemporary hospital regular practice. Features include clinical case discussion, drug information answers, critically reviewed original research articles, pharmacy practice guidelines and standards, editorials, review articles and conference proceedings.
**Ind/Abst** Biol. Abstr.; Chem. Abstr.; EMBASE; Int. Pharm. Abstr.; Iowa Drug Inf. Serv.; PESTDOC; Pollut. Abstr. Indexes.

AT/0311-8002
**AUSTRALIAN JOURNAL OF PHARMACY.** (AJP. THE AUSTRALIAN JOURNAL OF PHARMACY.). [Aust. j. pharm.]. **VFOAT** AJP. Vol. 58, No. 683 (Jan. 1977)-. Academic Scholarly Publication. English. mo. 69.00Aus$ Australia; 100.00Aus$ other; 25.00Aus$ (students) Australia; 58.00Aus$ New Zealand Soc.; 6.00Aus$ (single issue) Australia; 10.00Aus$ (single issue) other. Australia Pharmaceutical Publishing Company Limited, 40 Burwood Road, PO Box 777, Hawthorn Victoria 3122 Australia. **Tel** 61 3 8109800, FAX 61 3 8191706. **ED** S Dickson. **NLM** W1 A117GN. Index available. cum. index. **Ad Acc. Circ:** 8,500 (ctrl). available on microfilm and microfiche from University Microfilms International (UMI). ***Continues*** *Australian Journal of Pharmacy, 0311-8002.*
**Desc:** Latest drugs on the market, matters of pharmaceutical interest.
**Ind/Abst** EMBASE; Int. Pharm. Abstr.

AT/0728-4632
**AUSTRALIAN PHARMACIST / PHARMACEUTICAL SOCIETY OF AUSTRALIA.** **Added/Corp** Pharmaceutical Society of Australia. (1981)-. Periodical. English. Eleven times a year (Except Jan.). Free (members) of the Pharmaceutical Society in Australia, 60.00Aus$ (non-members); 75.00Aus$ New Zealand; $85.00Aus$ others. Pharmaceutical Society of Australia, PO Box 21, Curtin ACT 2605 Australia. **Tel** 011 61 06 2811366, FAX 011 61 06 2852869. **ED** Bill Kelly. **NLM** W1; AU643L. **Bk Rev**, (Qty: 3-4). **Ad Acc. Circ:** 9,500 (ctrl).
**Desc:** News and information of scientific and biomedical papers, original pharmacy practice research, society policies and guidelines.

SP/0210-3397
**AVANCES EN TERAPEUTICA.** [Av. ter.]. Academic Scholarly Publication. Spanish. an. Salvat Editores SA, Calle Mallorca 45-49, Barcelona 08029 Spain. **Tel** 011 34 3 2010911, FAX 011 34 3 321-0565, telex SAEDI E 53132. **(Subscription address:** Salvat Publicaciones Cientificas SA, Avda Burgos 19 50 D, Madrid 28036 Spain**)** **CODEN** AVTPBI. Documents available from CASDDS.
**Ind/Abst** Chem. Abstr.

BG/0301-4606
**BANGLADESH PHARMACEUTICAL JOURNAL.** [Bangladesh pharm. j.]. **Added/Corp** Bangladesh Pharmaceutical Society. University of Dacca. Dept. of Pharmacy. Vol. 1, No. 1 (Oct. 1972)-. Periodical. English. qt. University of Dacca Department of Pharmacy, Dacca 2 Bangladesh. **NLM** W1 BA644K. **CODEN** BPJLAQ. Documents available from CASDDS.
**Ind/Abst** Bibliogr. Mission.; Chem. Abstr. (1972-1978); Int. Pharm. Abstr.

US/0361-8900
**BASIC DRUG LIST.** **Main/Corp** United Mine Workers of America Health and Retirement Funds. (1975)-. English. $2.50. United Mine Workers of America Health and Retirement Funds, 2021 K Street NW, Washington DC 20006. **LC** RS1; .U53a. **DD** 615/.1/05.

CN/0843-168X
**BC PHARMACIST.** (BC PHARMACIST : THE OFFICIAL JOURNAL OF THE BC PHARMACISTS' SOCIETY.). [BC pharm.]. **Added/Corp** BC Pharmacists' Society. **VAT** British Columbia Pharmacist. Vol. 1, No. 1 (Winter 1988)-. Periodical. English. qt. 16.00Can$. British Columbia Pharmacy Association, 150 3751 Shell Road, Richmond BC V6X 2W2 Canada. **Tel** (604)279-2053. **DD** 615.4/09711.

UK/0955-8810
**BEHAVIOURAL PHARMACOLOGY.**
(1989)-. Periodical. English. Eight times a year. $470.00 US; £275.00 other. Rapid Communications of Oxford Ltd, The Old Malthouse, Paradise Street, Oxford OX1 1LD England. **Tel** 011 44 0865 790447, FAX 011 44 0865 244012, telex 9403712. **ED** Paul Willner. **NLM** W1; BE135G. **CODEN** BPHAEL. **[CCC].** Index available. **Bk Rev**. **Ad Acc**. **Acid Free.** Documents available from The Genuine Article.
**Desc:** Covers areas ranging from ethopharmacology to the pharmacology of schedule controlled operant behavior, provided that their primary focus is behavioral.
**Ind/Abst** Curr. Aware. Biol. Sci., CABS; Curr. Contents Life Sci.; Psychoanal. Abstr.; Psychol. Abstr. (1989-); PsycINFO; PsycScan: Appl. Exp. Eng. Psych.; PsycScan: LD/MR; PsycScan: Neuropsych.; Res. Alert [Full Cov.]; Sci. Cit. Index; SCISEARCH; Soc. Sci. Cit. Index [Select. Cov.].

GW/0341-0099
**BEITRAEGE ZUR GESCHICHTE DER PHARMAZIE.** ***Title Change.*** [Beitr. Gesch. Pharm.]. (1969)-(199?). Periodical. German. qt. Deutscher Apotheker Verlag, Postfach 101061, D 70009 Stuttgart Germany. **Tel** 011 49 711 25820, INLAND:0711/2582, FAX 011 49 711 2582 290, telex 723636 daz d. **ED** Wolf-Dieter Muller-Jahncke. ***Continued by*** *Geschuchte der Pharmazie.*
**Ind/Abst** Am. Hist. Life.

GW/0172-6897
**BERLINER SEMINAR.** (1977)-. Monographic series. German. Price varies per volume. Perimed, Verlag Dr Med D Straube, W-8520 Erlangen Germany. **NLM** W3 BE679S.

UK/0006-2952
**BIOCHEMICAL PHARMACOLOGY.**
[Biochem. pharmacol.]. Vol. 1 (July 1958)-. Academic Scholarly Publication. English. Twenty-four times a year. $2966.00 The Americas; £1990.00 other. Pergamon Press, An Imprint of Elsevier Science Ltd., The Boulevard, Langford Lane, Kidlington, Oxford OX5 1GB United Kingdom. **Tel** 011 44 865 843000, 011 44 865 843699, FAX 011 44 865 843010. **ED** P. Alexander, J. Gielen and A. C. Sartorelli. **LC** QP901; .B5. **DD** 615.7. **NLM** W1 BI622. **CODEN** BCPCA6. **[CCC].** cum. index. **Pr Rev.** available on microfilm and microfiche from University Microfilms International (UMI). Documents available from The Genuine Article, BIOSIS Document Express, CASDDS, ADONIS.
**Desc:** Devoted to research into the development of biologically active substances and their modes of action at the biochemical and subcellular levels.
**Ind/Abst** ADONIS; AgBiotech News Inf.; AGRICOLA; Anim. Breed. Abstr.; Biodeter. Abstr. (1991-); Biol. Abstr.; Calcium Calcif. Tissue Abstr.; Chem. Abstr.; Chem. Titles; CSA Neuro. Abstr.; Curr. Aware. Biol. Sci., CABS; Curr. Biotechnol.; Curr. Contents Life Sci.; Dairy Sci. Abstr.; EMBASE; Genet. Abstr.; Health Plan. Adminis.; Helminthol. Abstr. (19??-19??); Immunol. Abstr.; Index Med.; Index Vet.; INIS Atomindex [Micro.]; Int. Aerosp. Abstr.; Maize Abstr.; Mass Spect. Bull.; Microbiol. Abstr. Sect. B (19??-19??); Microbiol. Abstr. Sect. A; Microbiol. Abstr. Sect. C; NAPRALERT; Nematol. Abstr.; Nucl. Acids Abstr.; Nutr. Abstr. Rev., Ser. B, Live Feeds and Feed.; Nutr. Abstr. Rev., Ser. A, Hum. Exp.; Oncog. Growth Factors Abstr.; Life Sci. Collect.; PESTDOC; Protozoolog. Abstr.; Psychol. Abstr.; Ref. Upd. Basic Ed.; Ref. Upd. Deluxe Ed.; Res. Alert [Full Cov.]; Rev. Agric. Entomol.; Rev. Med. Vet. Entomol.; Rev. Med. Vet. Mycology; Rev. Plant Pathol.; Saf. Health Work; Sci. Cit. Index; SCISEARCH; Soc. Sci. Cit. Index [Select. Cov.]; Vet. Bull.; Toxicol. Abstr. (19??-); Virol. AIDS Abstr.; Weed Abstr.

●JA/0918-6158
**BIOLOGICAL & PHARMACEUTICAL BULLETIN.** **Added/Corp** Nihon Yakugakkai. **VFOAT** Biological and Pharmaceutical Bulletin. Vol. 16, No. 1 (Jan. 1993)-. Bulletin. English. mo. $550.00 combination price with Chemical and Pharmaceutical Bulletin. **(Subscription address:** Kyowa Book Company Inc., 1-38 Kanda Jinbo-Ch0, Chiyoda-Ku Tokyo 101, Japan**)** **NLM** W1; BI738G. **CODEN** BPBLEO. **[CCC].** ***Continues*** *Journal of Pharmacobio-Dynamics, 0386-846X.*
**Ind/Abst** Sci. Cit. Index.

FR/0753-3322
**BIOMEDICINE & PHARMACOTHERAPY.**
**See** Medical Science and Technology.

GW
**BIOMETRIE IN DER CHEMISCH-PHARMAZEUTISCHEN INDUSTRIE.** (1983)-. Monographic series. German. ir. Price varies per volume. Gustav Fischer Verlag Stuttgart, Postfach 720143, Wollgrasweg 49, D 70577 Stuttgart Germany. **Tel** 011 49 711 458030, FAX 0711-4580334, telex 2627-7111488. **NLM** W1 BI859P.
**Desc:** Series providing information on biometry and pharmaceutical chemistry.

US/1040-8304
**BIOPHARM (EUGENE, OR.).** (BIOPHARM.). [Biopharm]. Vol. 1, No. 8 (Sept. 1988)-. Academic Scholarly Publication. English. Nine times a year. $59.00 US and possessions; $79.00 Canada; $117.00 other. Advanstar Communications Inc., 131 West First Street, Duluth MN 55802. **Tel** (218)723-9477, (800)346-0085. **ED** Jane M Ganter. **DD** 615. **NLM** W1; BI876MC. **CODEN** BPRME5. **[CCC].** Index available. cum. index. **Bk Rev**. **Ad Acc**. **Pr Rev. Circ:** 20,000 (ctrl). available on microfilm from University Microfilms International (UMI). Documents available from The Genuine Article, CASDDS. ***Continues*** *Biopharm Manufacturing, 1040-8045.*
**Desc:** Meets the growing need in the biopharmaceutical, diagnostics and intermediates industries for an authoritative source of information regarding scale-up from the research and development stage to full-scale manufacturing. Contains articles and columns from practitioners in the field and at the FDA, new product and literature showcases, a meeting and conference calendar, book reviews, and editorials.
**Ind/Abst** Abstr. BioCommer.; AGRICOLA [Select. Cov.]; BioBusiness; Chem. Abstr.; Res. Alert [Full Cov.]; Soc. Sci. Cit. Index [Select. Cov.]; Trade Ind. Index.

UK/0142-2782
**BIOPHARMACEUTICS & DRUG DISPOSITION.** [Biopharm. drug dispos.]. **VAT** Biopharmaceutics and Drug Disposition. Vol. 1 (July/Sept.

1979)-. Academic Scholarly Publication. English. Nine times a year. $745.00. John Wiley & Sons Ltd., Baffins Lane, Chichester West Sussex PO19 1UD England. **Tel** 0243 779777, FAX 0243 776128 BTG:JWP001, telex 86290 WIBOOKG. **(Subscription address:** John Wiley / Philadelphia, PO Box 7247, Philadelphia PA 19170.**) ED** G. L. Mattok, S. H. Curry, P. Collier, and Y. Sugiyama. **DD** 615. **NLM** W1 BI876MF. **CODEN** BDDID8. **[CCC]. Bk Rev. Ad Acc. Pr Rev. Circ:** 750. available on microfilm and microfiche from University Microfilms International (UMI). Documents available from The Genuine Article, BIOSIS Document Express, CASDDS, ADONIS.
**Desc:** Original reports of studies in biopharmaceutics, drug disposition and pharmacokinetics, especially those which have a direct relation to the therapeutic use of drugs. Research on factors affecting the disposition of clinical response to drugs, and on the design of drug dosage regimens and the treatment of overdose, based on pharmacokinetic principles.
**Ind/Abst** ADONIS; Anal. Abstr.; Biol. Abstr. (1985-); Chem. Abstr.; Chem. Titles; Coal Abstr.; Curr. Aware. Biol. Sci., CABS; Curr. Contents Life Sci.; Dairy Sci. Abstr.; EMBASE; Health Plan. Adminis.; Index Med. (1979-); Index Vet.; Int. Pharm. Abstr.; Iowa Drug Inf. Serv. (1981-); Mass Spect. Bull.; Life Sci. Collect.; PESTDOC; Ref. Upd. Deluxe Ed.; Res. Alert [Full Cov.]; Saf. Health Work; Sci. Cit. Index; SCISEARCH; Vet. Bull.

US
**BLUE BOOK, AMERICAN DRUGGIST.**
**VFOAT** Blue Book; American Druggist Blue Book. (1987-88)-. English. Hearst Business Communications, 1790 Broadway, New York NY 10019. **Tel** (212)969-7500, FAX (212)969-7564. **NLM** QV 772; A512. ***Continues** American Druggist Blue Book, 0364-7471.*

US/0162-3605
**BLUE SHEET, THE.** [Blue sheet]. **VFOAT** Drug Research Reports; DRR; Drug Research Reports. Vol. 19, No. 29/July 21, (1976)-. Government Publication. English. wk. $420.00. FDC Reports Inc., 5550 Friendship Boulevard/Suite 1, Chevy Chase MD 20815. **Tel** (301)657-9830. **ED** Cole Palmer Werble and Brenda Sandburg. **DD** 615. **NLM** W1 BL925. **CODEN** DRRSAL. **[CCC].** Documents available from UMI Article Clearinghouse. ***Continues** Drug Research Reports, 0012-6608.*
**Desc:** Covers health policy and biomedical research, including issues relating to Medicare/Medicaid, public health, health professions education and supply, health planning and federal programs affecting the nation's health care system and industry. Focuses on university and biomedical research by the FDA.
**Ind/Abst** Pharm. News Index (Dec. 1985-).

JA/0385-5201
**BOKIN BOBAI : NIHON BOKIN BOBAI GAKKAI SHI. Added/Corp** Nihon Bokin Bobai Gakkai. **VFOAT** Journal of Antibacterial and Antifungal Agents, Japan. (19??)-. Academic Scholarly Publication. Japanese (summaries and/or abstracts in English). mo. $184.00. Nihon Bokin Bobai Gakkai, c/o Shin-Kosan Building, 13-38 Nishi Hon-machi 1-chome Nishi-ku, Osaka-shi 550 Japan. **Tel** 06-538-2166, FAX 06-538-2169. **(Subscription address:** Kyowa Book Company Inc., 1-38 Kanda Jinbo-Cho, Chiyoda-Ku Tokyo 101, Japan**) ED** K. Arai. **LC** RM409; .B64. **CODEN** BOBODP. **[CCC].** Index available. **Bk Rev. Ad Acc. Circ:** 8,300. Documents available from CASDDS.
**Ind/Abst** Chem. Abstr.; EMBASE [Select. Cov.]; Food Sci. Technol. Abstr.

PO/0378-9608
**BOLETIM DA FACULDADE DE FARMACIA DE COIMBRA.** [Bol. Fac. farm. Coimbra]. **Added/Corp** Universidade de Coimbra. Faculdade de Farmacia. Vol. 1 (Jan./Dec.1976)-. Bulletin. Portuguese (summaries and/or abstracts in English and French). **NLM** W1 BO158L. **CODEN** BFFCDE. Documents available from CASDDS. ***Supersedes** Boletim da Faculdade de Farmacia - Universidade de Coimbra.*
**Ind/Abst** Chem. Abstr.; Int. Pharm. Abstr.

SP/0583-7472
**BOLETIN DE LA SOCIEDAD ESPANOLA DE HISTORIA DE LA FARMACIA.** [Bol. Soc. esp. hist. farm.]. **Main/Corp** Sociedad Espanola de Historia de la Farmacia. Vol. 1, No. 1 (March 1950)-. Bulletin. Spanish. qt. $15.00. Sociedad Espanola Historia Farmacia, Farmacia 11, Madrid 4 Spain. **NLM** W1 BO249.
**Ind/Abst** Am. Hist. Life (1962, 1964-); Int. Pharm. Abstr.

IT/0006-6648
**BOLLETTINO CHIMICO FARMACEUTICA.** [Boll. chim. farm.]. **Added/Corp** Societa Editoriale Farmaceutica. (1892)-. Academic Scholarly Publication. Italian. Twenty-one times a year. $310.00. Societa Editoriale Farmaceutica, Via Ausonio 12, 20132 Milan Italy. **Tel** 011 39 2 89404545. **NLM** W1 BO46. **CODEN** BCFAAI. Documents available from CASDDS. ***Continues** Bolletino Farmaceutica.*
**Ind/Abst** Chem. Abstr.; EMBASE; Health Plan. Adminis.; Index Med.; Int. Pharm. Abstr.; PESTDOC.

IT/0037-8798
**BOLLETTINO DELLA SOCIETA ITALIANA DI FARMACIA OSPEDALIERA.** [Boll. Soc. Ital. Farm. Osp.]. **Added/Corp** Societa Italiana di Farmacia Ospedaliera. **VFOAT** Bollettino SIFO. (1955)-. Periodical. Italian. Six times a year. L110000 (institutions), L75000 (individuals). Il Pensiero Scientifico Editore s.r.l., Via Bradano 3C, 00199 Rome Italy. **Tel** 011 39 6 86207158, 86207159, 86207168, 86207169, FAX 011 39 6 86207160. **ED** N. Martini. **CODEN** BSFOB3. **Ad Acc, Adv Mgr:** Dott Dalla, **Tel** 06-86207165. Full Page (B&W) L1.850.000. **Circ:** 2,100.
**Desc:** Society news and information on the pharmaceutical industry and developments in the field of pharmacy.
**Ind/Abst** Int. Pharm. Abstr.; PESTDOC.

US/0894-4024
**BOSTON BULLETIN ON CHEMICALS AND DISEASE.** [Boston bull. chem. dis.]. **Added/Corp** ChemoPathology ResourCenter. **VFOAT** BBCD. Vol. 1, No. 1 (1985)-. Periodical. English. qt. $50.00. Chemopathology Resource Center, 30 Worthington Street, Boston MA 02120. **Tel** (617)731-0778. **LC** RA1190; .B67. **DD** 615.9/005.

GW/0722-7159
**BRAUNSCHWEIGER VEROEFFENTLICHUNGEN ZUR GESCHICHTE DER PHARMAZIE UND DER NATURWISSENSCHAFTEN.** (198?)-. Monographic series. German. ir. Price varies per volume. Deutscher Apotheker Verlag, Postfach 101061, D 70009 Stuttgart Germany. **Tel** 011 49 711 25820, INLAND:0711/2582, FAX 011 49 711 2582 290, telex 723636 daz d. **ED** Wolfgang Schneider. **LC** UNC. **NLM** W1 BR132. ***Continues** Technische Universitaet Braunschweig. Pharmaziegeschichtliches Seminar. Veroeffentlichungen aus dem Pharmaziegeschichtlichen Seminar der Technischen Universitaet Braunschweig.*

UK
**BRITISH APPROVED NAMES / BRITISH PHARMACOPOEIA COMMISSION.**
**Main/Corp** British Pharmacopoeia Commission. (19??)-. English. Four times a year. £45.00. Her Majesty's Stationery Office, 51 Nine Elms Lane, London SW8 5DR England. **Tel** 011 44 71 873 8459, 011 44 71 873 8499, FAX 011 44 71 873 8499, 011 44 71 873 8456, telex 297138. **(Subscription address:** Her Majesty's Stationery Office, PO Box 276, Publications Centre, London SW8 5DT England.**) LC** Discard.

UK/0264-2689
**BRITISH ASSOCIATION FOR PSYCHOPHARMACOLOGY MONOGRAPH. See** Medical Science and Technology-Psychiatry.

UK/0306-5251
**BRITISH JOURNAL OF CLINICAL PHARMACOLOGY.** [Br. j. clin. pharmacol.]. **Added/Corp** British Pharmacological Society. Vol. 1 (Feb. 1974)-. Academic Scholarly Publication. English. mo. $541.00 US & Canada; £317.00 Europe; £349.00 other. Blackwell Scientific Publications Ltd, Marston Book Services, PO Box 87, Oxford OX2 ODT UK. **Tel** 011 44 865 791155, FAX 011 44 865 791927, telex 837 515 MARDIS G. **ED** C. F. George. **NLM** W1 BR519RI. **CODEN** BCPHBM. **[CCC]. Ad Acc. Pr Rev. Circ:** 2,000 (ctrl). available on microfilm and microfiche from University Microfilms International (UMI). Documents available from The Genuine Article, BIOSIS Document Express, CASDDS, ADONIS.
**Desc:** Contains papers on all aspects of drug action in man.
**Ind/Abst** ADONIS; Biol. Abstr.; Chem. Abstr.; Curr. Aware. Biol. Sci., CABS; Curr. Contents Life Sci.; Dairy Sci. Abstr.; EMBASE; Health Plan. Adminis.; Helminthol. Abstr. (1991-); Index Med.; Int. Pharm. Abstr.; Iowa Drug Inf. Serv. (1976-); Med. Abstr. Newsl.; NAPRALERT; Nutr. Abstr. Rev., Ser. B, Live Feeds and Feed.; Nutr. Abstr. Rev., Ser. A, Hum. Exp.; Life Sci. Collect.; PESTDOC; Protozoolog. Abstr.; Ref. Upd. Basic Ed.; Ref. Upd. Deluxe Ed.; Res. Alert [Full Cov.]; Rev. Med. Vet. Mycology; Sci. Cit. Index; SCISEARCH; Soc. Sci. Cit. Index [Select. Cov.]; Sug. Indus. Abstr.

UK/0007-0947
**BRITISH JOURNAL OF CLINICAL PRACTICE, THE. See** Medical Science and Technology.

UK/0262-8767
**BRITISH JOURNAL OF CLINICAL PRACTICE. SYMPOSIUM SUPPLEMENT. See** Medical Science and Technology.

UK/0007-1188
**BRITISH JOURNAL OF PHARMACOLOGY.** [Br. j. pharmacol.]. **Added/Corp** British Pharmacological Society. Vol. 34 (Sept. 1968)-. Academic Scholarly Publication. English. Twenty-four times a year. £620.00 UK and EEC; £685.00 (surface mail), £822.00 (airmail) other. Macmillan Magazines Ltd., Houndmills, Basingstoke, Hampshire RG21 2XS England. **Tel** 011 44 256 29242, FAX 011 44 256 812358, telex 858493. **ED** Margaret Day and C. V. Wedmore. **NLM** W1 BR601. **CODEN** BJPCBM. **[CCC].** cum. index. **Ad Acc. Pr Rev. Circ:** 3,000. available on microfilm and microfiche from University Microfilms International (UMI). Documents available from The Genuine Article, BIOSIS Document Express, CASDDS, ADONIS. ***Continues** British Journal of Pharmacology and Chemotherapy.*
**Desc:** Publishes up-to-date articles from all parts of the world on all aspects of pharmacology.
**Ind/Abst** ADONIS; Anim. Behav. Abstr.; Biol. Abstr.; Calcium Calcif. Tissue Abstr.; Chem. Abstr.; Chem. Titles; Chemorecept. Abstr.; CSA Neuro. Abstr.; Curr. Aware. Biol. Sci., CABS; Curr. Chem. React.; Curr. Contents Life Sci.; Dairy Sci. Abstr.; EMBASE; Health Plan. Adminis.; Helminthol. Abstr. (19??-19??); Immunol. Abstr.; Index Chem.; Index Med.; Index Vet.; Int. Aerosp. Abstr.; Int. Pharm. Abstr.; Iowa Drug Inf. Serv. (1967-); NAPRALERT; Life Sci. Collect.; PESTDOC; Pig News Inf.; Protozoolog. Abstr.; Ref. Upd. Basic Ed.; Ref. Upd. Deluxe Ed.; Res. Alert [Full Cov.]; Rev. Med. Vet. Entomol.; Rev. Med. Vet. Mycology; Saf. Health Work; Sci. Cit. Index; SCISEARCH; Soc. Sci. Cit. Index [Select. Cov.]; Vet. Bull.

UK
**BRITISH NATIONAL FORMULARY (LONDON, ENGLAND : 1966).** (BRITISH NATIONAL FORMULARY.). (1966)-. English. an (updated twice yearly). £8.95. The Pharmaceutical Press, 1 Lambeth High Street, London High Street, London SE1 7JN. **LC** RS125; .B92. **DD** 615/.1. **UDC** 615.1(410). ***Formed by the union of** British National Formulary (Standard Edition) **and** British National Formulary (Alternative Edition).*
**Desc:** Contains information on all prescribable drugs and medicines available in the UK with notes on prescribing them, indications, cautions, contra-indications, dose, side-effects and relative costs. Each chapter is related to one system of the body or to another main subject, such infections or vaccines.

UK
**BRITISH PHARMACEUTICAL INDUSTRY.** (19??)-. English. an. £195.00. Jordan & Sons Ltd, 21 St Thomas Street, Bristol BS1 6JS England. **Tel** 011 44 272 230600, FAX 0272 230063, telex 499119. **Ad Acc.** available on diskette; available on labels.
**Desc:** Financial and marketing information on the industry and top companies in it.

UK
**BRITISH PHARMACOPIA, THE.**
**Added/Corp** General Medical Council (Great Britain) Great Britain. Medicines Commission. Great Britain. Dept. of Health and Social Security. (19??)-. English. ir. £70.00. Her Majesty's Stationery Office, 51 Nine Elms Lane, London SW8 5DR England. **Tel** 011 44 71 873 8459, 011 44 71 873 8499, FAX 011 44 71 873 8499, 011 44 71 873 8456, telex 297138. **(Subscription address:** Her Majesty's Stationery Office, PO Box 276, Publications Centre, London SW8 5DT England.**) LC** RS141.3; .B75. **DD** 615.11.

US/0898-3070
**BUCKEYE OSTEOPATHIC PHYSICIAN.** [Buckeye osteopath. physician]. **Added/Corp** Ohio Osteopathic Association. (19??)-. Periodical. English. mo. $25.00. Ohio Osteopathic Association, 53 West Third Avenue, Columbus OH 43210. **Tel** (614)299-2107, FAX (614)294-0457. **ED** Kathryn Cheek. **DD** 615. **Ad Acc, Adv Mgr:** same as editor. **Circ:** 2,700 (ctrl). ***Continues** Buckeye Osteopath.*

FR/0037-9093
**BULLETIN DE LA SOCIETE DE PHARMACIE DE BORDEAUX.** [Bull. Soc. pharm. Bordeaux]. **Added/Corp** Societe de Pharmacie de Bordeaux. No. 1 (Jan. 1951)-. Bulletin. French. sa. 150.00F France; 250.00F other. Faculte de Medicine Pharmacie, 91 rue Layteire, 33076 Bordeaux France. **CODEN** BSPBAD. Documents available from CASDDS. ***Continues** Bulletin des Travaux de la Societe de Pharmacie de Bordeaux.*
**Ind/Abst** Bibliogr. Mission.; Chem. Abstr.; GeoRef; Int. Pharm. Abstr.; PESTDOC.

FR/0366-3507
**BULLETIN DE LA SOCIETE DE PHARMACIE DE LILLE.** [Bull. Soc. pharm. Lille]. **Added/Corp** Societe de Pharmacie de Lille. (1945)-. Bulletin. French. qt. Societe Pharmacie de Lille, 3, Rue Professeur, Laguesse France. **CODEN** BSPLA9. Documents available from CASDDS.
**Ind/Abst** Bibliogr. Mission.; Chem. Abstr.; EMBASE; Int. Pharm. Abstr.; PESTDOC.

FR/0291-8374
**BULLETIN DE LA SOCIETE DE PHARMACIE DE L'OUEST.** [Bull. Soc. pharm. ouest]. (1959)-. Bulletin. French. bm. **UDC** 615.
**Ind/Abst** Int. Pharm. Abstr.

# Pharmacy and Pharmacology

FR/0037-9107
**BULLETIN DES TRAVAUX DE LA SOCIETE DE PHARMACIE DE LYON.** Vol. 1 (1957)-. Bulletin. French. mo. Publ Periodiques Specialisees, 11 rue d'Algerie, 69001 Lyon France. **Tel** 28 82 25. **UDC** 615. **NLM** W1 BU621. **CODEN** BTSLAV. Documents available from CASDDS.
**Ind/Abst** Chem. Abstr.; Int. Pharm. Abstr.

SZ
**BULLETIN D'INFORMATION - ASSOCIATION INTERNATIONALE DE STANDARDISATION BIOLOGIQUE. NEWSLETTER - INTERNATIONAL ASSOCIATION OF BIOLOGICAL STANDARDIZATION.** **Main/Corp** International Association of Biological Standardization. **Added/Corp** International Association of Biological Standardization. Newsletter. **VFOAT** Newsletter - International Association of Biological Standardization. No. 15, Jan. (1973)-. Bulletin. English (French). International Association of Biological Standardization, 1211 Geneva 4 Switzerland. **LC** RS189; .I46a. **DD** 610/.28. **CODEN** BAIBDP.

SW/0281-0999
**BULLETIN FROM SADRAC.** [Bull. SADRAC]. **Added/Corp** Swedish Adverse Drug Reactions Advisory Committee. **VFOAT** Bulletin from Swedish Adverse Drug Reactions Advisory Committee. (1982)-. Bulletin. English. ir. Medical Products Agency, PO Box 26, S-751 03 Uppsala Sweden. **Tel** (18)174600. **UDC** 615.
**Ind/Abst** EMBASE.

FR/0153-288X
**BULLETIN INTERNATIONAL D'INFORMATIONS.** **Added/Corp** Droit et Pharmacie (Group). Service International. **VFOAT** Bulletin de Droit et Pharmacie. No 5 (May 1977)-. Bulletin. French. mo. 12000.00F. Droit et Pharmacie, 19 rue Louis le Grand, 75002 Paris France. **Tel** 011 33 1 47428430, FAX 011 33 1 42650966. **NLM** W1; BU664F.
**Desc:** Information bulletin on the pharmaceutical industry. Covers new products, firms, economy and the legal aspects and research.

JA
**BULLETIN OF JAPANESE SOCIETY OF PHYCOLOGY, THE.** **Main/Corp** Japanese Society of Phycology. Vol. 1, No. 1 (Mar. 1953)-. Bulletin. Japanese. qt. Japanese Society of Pharmacology, c/o Faculty of Pharmaceutical, Kyoto University, Kyoto 606 Japan.

UA
**BULLETIN OF PHARMACEUTICAL SCIENCES.** Bulletin. sa. Assiut University Press Ed Secy, Assiut University, Faculty of Pharmacy, Assiut Egypt. Documents available from CASDDS.
**Ind/Abst** Chem. Abstr.

TU/0367-0236
**BULLETIN OF PHARMACY.** **VFOAT** Bulletin of Pharmacy. (1959)-. Bulletin. Turkish. ir. **CODEN** ECBUAN. Documents available from CASDDS.
**Ind/Abst** Chem. Abstr. (1959-1983); Int. Pharm. Abstr. (1959-1993).

UA/0575-1373
**BULLETIN OF THE FACULTY OF PHARMACY.** (BULLETIN OF THE FACULTY OF PHARMACY, CAIRO UNIVERSITY.). **Added/Corp** Jamiat Al-Qahirah. Faculty of Pharmacy. (19??)-. Bulletin. English (summaries and/or abstracts in Arabic). **NLM** W1 BU846T. **CODEN** BFPHA8. Documents available from CASDDS.
**Ind/Abst** Chem. Abstr. (1961/1962-1980); Int. Pharm. Abstr.; NAPRALERT.

UK/0260-0099
**BUTTERWORTHS INTERNATIONAL MEDICAL REVIEWS. CLINICAL PHARMACOLOGY AND THERAPEUTICS.** [Butterworths int. med. rev., Clin. pharmacol. ther.]. **VFOAT** Clinical Pharmacology and Therapeutics. (1982)-. Academic Scholarly Publication. English. ir. Price varies per volume. Butterworth Heinemann / Woburn, MA, 225 Wildwood Avenue, Unit B, Woburn MA 01801. **Tel** (800)366-2665, FAX (617)928-2620, telex 880052. (**Subscription address:** Reed International Book Services, P. O. Box 5 Rushden, Northants, NN10 9YX England, telephone: 011 44 0933 58521) **NLM** W1 BU98N. **CODEN** CPTHDA. Documents available from BIOSIS Document Express, CASDDS.
**Ind/Abst** Biol. Abstr.; Chem. Abstr. (1982).

JA/0389-9098
**BYOIN YAKUGAKU.** (BYOIN YAKUGAKU / JOURNAL OF THE NIPPON HOSPITAL PHARMACISTS ASSOCIATION.). [Byoin yakugaku]. **Added/Corp** Nihon Byoin Yakuzaishikai. **VFOAT** Japanese Journal of Hospital Pharmacy; Journal of the Nippon Hospital Pharmacists Association. (1975)-. Academic Scholarly Publication. Japanese (summaries and/or abstracts in English). Six times a year. $104.00. Yakuji Nipposha, 1-11 Izumi-cho Kanda Chiyoda-ku, Tokyo 101 Japan. **Tel** 011 8 13 862-2141, 011 8 13 58218757, FAX 011 8 13 866-8408. **NLM** W1; BY995S. **CODEN** BYYADW. **Ad Acc. Circ:** 5,000 (ctrl). Documents available from CASDDS, BLDSC, CASDDS.
**Desc:** Japanese journal of hospital pharmacy.
**Ind/Abst** Chem. Abstr.; Curr. Biotechnol.; EMBASE; Int. Pharm. Abstr.

US/0148-2394
**CA SELECTS: ANTI-INFLAMMATORY AGENTS & ARTHRITIS.** See Chemistry-Abstracting, Bibliographies and Statistics.

US/0148-2386
**CA SELECTS: ANTITUMOR AGENTS.** See Chemistry-Abstracting, Bibliographies and Statistics.

US/0148-2378
**CA SELECTS: ATHEROSCLEROSIS & HEART DISEASE.** See Chemistry-Abstracting, Bibliographies and Statistics.

US/0148-2459
**CA SELECTS: B-LACTAM ANTIBIOTICS.** See Chemistry-Abstracting, Bibliographies and Statistics.

US/0162-7775
**CA SELECTS: DRUG & COSMETIC TOXICITY.** See Chemistry-Abstracting, Bibliographies and Statistics.

US/1040-7162
**CA SELECTS: DRUG DELIVERY SYSTEMS & DOSAGE FORMS.** See Chemistry-Abstracting, Bibliographies and Statistics.

US/1051-3914
**CA SELECTS. FOOD, DRUGS, & COSMETICS.** See Chemistry-Abstracting, Bibliographies and Statistics.

US/0162-7813
**CA SELECTS: FOOD TOXICITY.** See Chemistry-Abstracting, Bibliographies and Statistics.

US/0890-1880
**CA SELECTS: FORMULATION CHEMISTRY.** See Chemistry-Abstracting, Bibliographies and Statistics.

US/0895-5875
**CA SELECTS: NEW ANTIBIOTICS.** See Chemistry-Abstracting, Bibliographies and Statistics.

US/0890-1902
**CA SELECTS: PHARMACEUTICAL ANALYSIS.** See Chemistry-Abstracting, Bibliographies and Statistics.

US/0890-1910
**CA SELECTS: PHARMACEUTICAL CHEMISTRY (JOURNALS).** See Chemistry-Abstracting, Bibliographies and Statistics.

US/0890-1929
**CA SELECTS: PHARMACEUTICAL CHEMISTRY (PATENTS).** See Chemistry-Abstracting, Bibliographies and Statistics.

UK
**CALENDAR / ROYAL PHARMACEUTICAL SOCIETY OF GREAT BRITAIN.** **Main/Corp** Royal Pharmaceutical Society of Great Britain. (1988/89)-. English. an. £19.50. Pharmaceutical Press, 1 Lambeth High Street, London SE1 7JN England. **Tel** 011 44 71 735 9141, FAX 011 44 71 735 7629, telex 265871, (MONREF G). **NLM** W1; RO727. *Continues* Calendar of the Pharmaceutical Society of Great Britain.

US/0739-0483
**CALIFORNIA PHARMACIST.** (CALIFORNIA PHARMACIST : OFFICIAL PUBLICATION OF THE CALIFORNIA PHARMACISTS ASSOCIATION.). [Calif. pharm.]. **Added/Corp** California Pharmacists Association. (1952)-. Periodical. English. mo. $30.00. California Pharmacists Association, 1112 I Street/#300, Sacramento CA 95814. **Tel** (916)444-7811. **ED** Michael Ishii (phone: ext.302). **DD** 362. **NLM** W1 CA408C. Index available. **Ad Acc, Adv Mgr:** Lisa Clode, **Tel** (916)444-7811 ext.335. **Circ:** 6,300 (ctrl).
**Desc:** Pharmacy news, new drug information, clinical information and management news for the community; for chain, hospital and long-term care pharmacists in California.
**Ind/Abst** Int. Pharm. Abstr.

US
**CALIFORNIA PHARMACY LAWS, WITH RULES AND REGULATIONS.** See Law.

CN/0824-2666
**CANADIAN DRUG IDENTIFICATION CODE.** (CANADIAN DRUG IDENTIFICATION CODE / STATISTICS AND INFORMATION SCIENCE DIVISION, HEALTH PROTECTION BRANCH, DEPARTMENT OF NATIONAL HEALTH AND WELFARE.). [Can. drug identif. code]. **Added/Corp** Canada. Drug Information Division. Canada. Health and Welfare Canada. Canada. Health Protection Branch. Statistics and Information Science Division. **VFOAT** Code Canadien d'Identification des Drogues. (1972)-. Monographic series. English (French). an. Price varies per volume. Canada Communication Group Publishers, Order Processing, Ottawa Ontario K1A 0S9 Canada. **Tel** (819)956-4800, (819)956-4802. **DD** 615/.1/029471.

CN/0008-4123
**CANADIAN JOURNAL OF HOSPITAL PHARMACY.** (JOURNAL CANADIEN DE LA PHARMACIE HOSPITALIERE.). [Can. j. hosp. pharm.]. **Added/Corp** Canadian Society of Hospital Pharmacists. **VFOAT** Canadian Journal of Hospital Pharmacy. Vol. 37, No. 1 (Spring 1984)-. Periodical. English (summaries and/or abstracts in French). bm. 44.86Can$ Canada; 52.00Can$ US; 54.00Can$ other. Canadian Society of Hospital Pharmacists, 1145 Hunt Club Road, Suite 350, Ottawa Ontario K1V 0Y3 Canada. **Tel** (613)736-9733. **DD** 615/.05. [**CCC**]. *Continues* Canadian Journal of Hospital Pharmacy., 0008-4123.

CN/0008-4212
**CANADIAN JOURNAL OF PHYSIOLOGY AND PHARMACOLOGY.** See Biology-Physiology.

US/0528-1725
**CAROLINA JOURNAL OF PHARMACY, THE.** [Carol. j. pharm.]. **Added/Corp** North Carolina Pharmaceutical Association. North Carolina. Board of Pharmacy. Annual report. North Carolina Pharmaceutical Association. Year book. North Carolina Pharmaceutical Association. Proceedings of the annual meeting. Vol 1 (1915)-. Periodical. English. mo. $25.00 (US); $37.00 (Canada); $41.00 (other). North Carolina Pharmaceutical Association, PO Box 151, Chapel Hill NC 27514. **Tel** (919)967-2237. **ED** Alfred H Mebane III. **DD** 615. **NLM** W1 CA876. cum. index. **Ad Acc. Circ:** 3,000.
**Desc:** Includes the Annual report of the North Carolina Board of Pharmacy, as well as the Year book and Proceedings of the annual meeting of the North Carolina Pharmaceutical Association.
**Ind/Abst** Int. Pharm. Abstr.

US/0884-7487
**CAS BIOTECH UPDATES. PHARMACEUTICAL APPLICATIONS.** [CAS bioTech updates, Pharm. appl.]. **Added/Corp** American Chemical Society. Chemical Abstracts Service. **VFOAT** Pharmaceutical Applications. **VAT** Chemical Abstracts Service Biotech Updates. Pharmaceutical Applications. No. 1 (1987)-. Periodical. English. bw. $215.00. Chemical Abstracts Service, (Subsidiary of The American Chemical Society), 2540 Olentangy River Road, PO Box 3012, Columbus OH 43210-0012. **Tel** (614)447-3731, (800)753-4227, FAX (614)447-3751. (**Subscription address:** Chemical Abstracts Service, Customer Service Department, PO Box 3012, Columbus OH 43210.) **DD** 615. **CODEN** CBUAEX.

US/1051-3957
**CAS BIOTECH UPDATES. SLOW-RELEASE PHARMACEUTICALS.** [Chem. Abstr. Serv. biotech updates, Slow release pharm.]. **Added/Corp** American Chemical Society. Chemical Abstracts Service. **VFOAT** Slow-Release Pharmaceuticals. **VAT** Chemical Abstract Service Biotech Updates. Slow-Release Pharmaceuticals. Issue 21 (Oct. 15, 1990)-. Periodical. English. bw. $215.00. Chemical Abstracts Service, (Subsidiary of The American Chemical Society), 2540 Olentangy River Road, PO Box 3012, Columbus OH 43210-0012. **Tel** (614)447-3731, (800)753-4227, FAX (614)447-3751. (**Subscription address:** Chemical Abstracts Service, Customer Service Department, PO Box 3012, Columbus OH 43210.) **DD** 615. **CODEN** CBUPEA.

SP/0302-4296
**CATALOGO DE ESPECIALIDADES FORMACEUTICOS.** [Cat. espec. farm.]. **Added/Corp** Consejo General de Colegios Officiales de Farmaceuticos (Spain). (197?)-. Catalog. Spanish. an. Consejo General Colegios Ofic Farmaceuticos, Villanueva 11, 28001 Madrid Spain. **Tel** 011 34 1 4312560.

●UK/1351-3214
**CELLULAR PHARMACOLOGY.** Vol. 1, No. 1 (Nov. 1993)-. Periodical. English. bm. £129.00 UK; £140.00 (surface); £168.00 (air mail) other. Macmillan Magazines Ltd., Houndmills, Basingstoke, Hampshire RG21 2XS England. **Tel** 011 44 256 29242, FAX 011 44 256 812358, telex 858493. **NLM** W1; CE1292.

US
**CERVELLO E FARMACI.** See Medical Science and Technology-Psychiatry.

●XR/1210-7816
**CESKA A SLOVENSKA FARMACIE : CASOPIS CESKE FARMACEUTICKE SPOLECNOSTI A SLOVENSKE FARMACEUTICKE SPOLECNOSTI.** **Added/Corp** Ceska Farmaceuticka Spolecnost.

Slovenska Farmaceuticka Spolecnost. **VFOAT** Czech and Slovak Pharmacy. (1994)-. Periodical. Czech (summaries and/or abstracts in English; table of contents in English). Six times a year. $102.70. **(Subscription address:** Artia Pegas Press Ltd., Palac Metro Narodni Trida 25, 11210 Prague 1 Czech Republic.**)** **NLM** W1; CE685. ***Continues*** *Ceskoslovenska Farmacie, 0009-0530.*
**Ind/Abst** Index Med. (1994-).

XR/0009-0530
**CESKOSLOVENSKA FARMACIE.** ***Title Change.*** [Cesk. farm.]. **Added/Corp** Ceskoslovenska Farmaceuticka Spolecnost. **VFOAT** Cesko-Slovenska Farmacie; Czech-Slovak Pharmacy. Vol. 1 (1952)-Vol. 42 (1993). Academic Scholarly Publication. Czech (summaries and/or abstracts in Russian and English). Ten times a year. **(Subscription address:** Artia Pegas Press Ltd., Palac Metro Narodni Trida 25, 11210 Prague 1 Czech Republic.**)** **ED** J. Hubik. **DD** 615. **NLM** W1; CE881. **CODEN** CKFRAY. **[CCC]. Bk Rev. Ad Acc. Circ:** 2,500. Documents available from CASDDS. ***Continued by*** *Ceska a Slovenska Farmacie.*
**Desc:** Covers pharmaceutical substances and preparations; synthesis or isolation analysis; pharmacology; pharmacokinetics; standardization of drugs; pharmacies; the pharmaceutical industry; and new preparations.
**Ind/Abst** Anal. Abstr.; Chem. Abstr.; Chem. Titles; Curr. Biotechnol.; EMBASE; Helminthol. Abstr. (19??-19??); Index Med.; Int. Pharm. Abstr.; PESTDOC; Protozoolog. Abstr.; Saf. Health Work.

JA/0009-2363
**CHEMICAL & PHARMACEUTICAL BULLETIN. Added/Corp** Nihon Yakugakukai. Vol. 1 (Mar. 1958)-. Bulletin. English (French and German). mo. $500.00. Pharmaceutical Society of Japan, Tokyo, Japan. **(Subscription address:** Maruzen Company Ltd., PO Box 5050, Import & Export Department, Tokyo 100 31 Japan.**)** **LC** RS1.N56; A15. **DD** 543; 615. **NLM** W1 CH245N. **CODEN** CPBTAL. **[CCC].** ***Continues*** *Pharmaceutical Bulletin.*
**Ind/Abst** Chem Inform; Rev. Agric. Entomol.; Rev. Med. Vet. Entomol.; Sci. Cit. Index; Seed Abstr.

UK
**CHEMINDEX PLUS.** (19??)-. Trade Publication. English. an. £3,000.00. IMS World Publications Ltd, 7 Harwodd Avenue, london NW1 6JB England. **Tel** 011 44 71 393 5000, FAX 011 44 393 5900.
**Desc:** Links pharmaceutical ingredients with brand names and manufacturers worldwide.

UK/0009-3033
**CHEMIST & DRUGGIST.** (CHEMIST AND DRUGGIST. THE NEWSWEEKLY FOR PHARMACY.). [Chem. drug.]. (1859)-. Periodical. English. wk. £89.00. Benn Business Information Service Ltd, Riverbank House, Angel Lane, Tonbridge Kent TN9 1SE England. **Tel** 011 44 732 362666, FAX 011 44 732 770483, telex 95454 BBIS. **ED** John Skelton. **NLM** W1; CH314R. **CODEN** CHDRAJ. **[CCC]. Bk Rev. Ad Acc.** available on microfilm and microfiche from University Microfilms International (UMI). Documents available from CASDDS.
**Desc:** Aims to improve the profitability of its subscribers by keeping them up-to-date with news and latest developments in the pharmaceutical and allied industries and by providing them with authoritative features which extend their commercial, professional and technical knowledge.
**Ind/Abst** Chem. Abstr.; EMBASE; Infomat Int. Bus.; Int. Pharm. Abstr.; PROMT [Full Txt.].

UK/0262-5881
**CHEMIST & DRUGGIST DIRECTORY.**
**VAT** Chemist and Druggist Directory. (1972)-. Directory. English. an (Nov.). £89.00 UK; £104.00 other. Benn Publications Ltd., Sovereign Way, Tonbridge TNQ 1RW England. **Tel** 011 44 732 364422, FAX 011 44 732 361534, telex 0732 95132 BENTON G. **(Subscription address:** Benn Business Information Services, Riverbank House Angel Lane, Tonbridge Kent TN9 1SE England.**)** **ED** Sarah Walker. **NLM** QV 22 FA1 C5. Index available. **Ad Acc. Circ:** 2,900. ***Absorbed*** *Chemist and Druggist Tablet and Capsule Identification Guide;* ***Continues*** *Chemist and Druggist Year Book.*
**Desc:** Products cross-referenced with an alphabetical listing of their manufacturers, suppliers or agents. Prescription drugs, over-the-counter medicines, herbal remedies, cosmetics, fragrances and toiletries, light electrical, and photography.

UK
**CHEMIST & DRUGGIST DIRECTORY AND TABLET & CAPSULE IDENTIFICATION GUIDE. VFOAT** Chemist and Druggist Directory and Tablet and Capsule Identification Guide; Chemist and Druggist Directory; Chemist & Druggist Directory. (1972)-. Periodical. English. an. $61.30. Benn Business Information Service Ltd, Riverbank House, Angel Lane, Tonbridge Kent TN9 1SE England. **Tel** 011 44 732 362666, FAX 011 44 732 770483, telex 95454 BBIS. **ED** John Hedges. **LC** HD9667.3; .C48. **DD** 615.1/029/441; 615. **Ad Acc. Circ:** 2,600. ***Absorbed*** *Chemist and Druggist Tablet and Capsule Identification Guide;* ***Continues*** *Chemist and Druggist Yearbook.*
**Desc:** The directory of the pharmaceutical, drug, essential oil and cosmetic industries of the United Kingdom including the unique tablet and capsule identification guide.

US/0737-8033
**CHEMISTRY AND PHARMACOLOGY OF DRUGS. See** Chemistry.

KO
**CHEYAK KISUL CHONGBO. Added/Corp** Taehan Yakpum Kongop Hyophoe. **VFOAT** Technical Information for Pharmaceutical Industry. (19??)-. Periodical. Korean (Korean). mo. **LC** RM1; .C46.

US/0899-0042
**CHIRALITY (NEW YORK, N.Y.). See** Chemistry.

KO
**CHONG / ILSONG SINYAK CHUSIK HOESA. Added/Corp** Ilsong Sinyak Chusik Hoesa. (19??)-. Periodical. Korean. mo. Not for sale. Ilsong Sinyak Chusik Hoesa, 44-7 Wonhyo-ro Yongsan-ku, Seoul Korea. **LC** RS1; .C54.

SP/0210-0819
**CIENCIA & INDUSTRIA FARMACEUTICA.** ***Ceased.*** [Cienc. ind. farm.]. **VFOAT** Ciencia y Industria Farmaceutica. Academic Scholarly Publication. Spanish. mo. Ciencia e Industria Farmaceutica, Avda Diagonal 361 3 2, 08037 Barcelona Spain. **NLM** W1; CI218L. **CODEN** CIDFA8. Documents available from CASDDS.
**Ind/Abst** Chem. Abstr. (?-?); EMBASE (?-?); Indice Med. Esp. (?-?); Int. Pharm. Abstr. (?-?); PESTDOC.

SP
**CIENCIA PHARMACEUTICA.** (19??)-. Spanish. bm. 5000.00ptas. Alpe Editores SA, C Pedro Rico 27, Oficinas 11 & 12, 28029 Madrid Spain. **Tel** 011 34 1 7338811, FAX 011 34 1 3159652. **ED** Angel Alvarez. Index available. **Ad Acc. Pr Rev. Circ:** 6000 (ctrl). ***Continues*** *Pharmaklinik.*
**Ind/Abst** EMBASE; Int. Pharm. Abstr.

FR/0294-7390
**CIRCULAIRES DE LA FEDERATION NATIONALE DES PROMOTEURS-CONSTRUCTEURS.** [Circ. Fed. natl. promot.-constr.]. (19??)-. Periodical. French. ir. 10290.00F. Droit et Pharmacie, 19 rue Louis le Grand, 75002 Paris France. **Tel** 011 33 1 47428430, FAX 011 33 1 42650966. **UDC** 71 + 333. Index available.

SP/0366-6425
**CIRCULAR FARMACEUTICA.** [Circ. farm.]. **Added/Corp** Colegio Oficial de Farmaceuticos de la Provincia de Barcelona. (1943)-. Periodical. Spanish (summaries and/or abstracts in English, French, German and Spanish). qt. Colegio Oficial de Farmaceuticos de Barcelona, Pau Claris 92 94, 08010 Barcelona Spain. **NLM** W1 CI701. **CODEN** CIFAA3. Documents available from CASDDS.
**Ind/Abst** Bibliogr. Mission.; Chem. Abstr.; EMBASE; Int. Pharm. Abstr.

US/0069-4770
**CLIN-ALERT. See** Medical Science and Technology.

US/1043-3031
**CLINICAL ABSTRACTS/CURRENT THERAPEUTIC FINDINGS.** (CLINICAL ABSTRACTS/CURRENT THERAPEUTIC FINDINGS : CA / CTF.). [Clin. abstr./curr. ther. find.]. **VFOAT** Clinical Abstracts, Current Therapeutic Findings; CA/CTF; CA / CTF. Vol. 8, No. 1 (Jan. 1989)-. Periodical. English. mo. $56.00 US; $71.00 other. Harvey Whitney Books Company, PO Box 42696, Cincinnati OH 45242. **Tel** (513)793-3555, FAX (513)793-3600. **ED** Harvey A. K. Whitney. **DD** 615. **CODEN** CCTFEG. Index available. cum. index. **Ad Acc. Circ:** 1,000. ***Continues*** *Clinical Abstracts, 0894-7368.*
**Desc:** Contains abstracts on drug therapy from the world's latest medical literature. It is concisely edited with up-to-date information in the areas of previously unreported drug interactions, nondrug factors affecting drug action, adverse reactions, and drug use and comparisons.

AT/0305-1870
**CLINICAL AND EXPERIMENTAL PHARMACOLOGY & PHYSIOLOGY.** [Clin. exp. pharmacol. physiol.]. **Added/Corp** Australian Society for Medical Research. Australasian Society of Clinical and Experimental Pharmacologists. **VAT** Clinical and Experimental Pharmacology and Physiology. Vol. 1 (Jan./Feb. 1974)-. Academic Scholarly Publication. English. Twelve times a year. 570.00Aus$ Australia; 814.00Aus$ other. Blackwell Scientific Publications Australia, 54 University Street, PO Box 378, Carlton Victoria 3053 Australia. **Tel** 011 61 3 3470300, FAX 011 61 3 3475001, telex 10716421. **ED** A.E. Doyle. **NLM** W1 CL664E. **CODEN** CEXPB9. **[CCC]. Ad Acc. Pr Rev. Circ:** 750. available on microfilm and microfiche from University Microfilms International (UMI). Documents available from The Genuine Article, CASDDS, ADONIS. ***Formed by the union of*** *Proceedings of the Australian Society for Medical Research, 0067-2130.*
**Desc:** Publishes research work on the clinical and experimental aspects of pharmacology and physiology.
**Ind/Abst** ADONIS; Calcium Calcif. Tissue Abstr.; Chem. Abstr.; CSA Neuro. Abstr.; Curr. Aware. Biol. Sci., CABS; Curr. Contents Life Sci.; EMBASE; Index Med.; Nutr. Abstr. Rev., Ser. B, Live Feeds and Feed.; Nutr. Abstr. Rev., Ser. A, Hum. Exp.; Life Sci. Collect.; PESTDOC; Ref. Upd. Deluxe Ed.; Res. Alert [Full Cov.]; Rev. Med. Vet. Mycology; Sci. Cit. Index; SCISEARCH.

UK/0143-9294
**CLINICAL AND EXPERIMENTAL PHARMACOLOGY & PHYSIOLOGY. SUPPLEMENT.** [Clin. exp. pharmacol. physiol., Suppl.]. (1974)-. Academic Scholarly Publication. English. Blackwell Scientific Publications Ltd, Marston Book Services, PO Box 87, Oxford OX2 ODT UK. **Tel** 011 44 865 791155, FAX 011 44 865 791927, telex 837 515 MARDIS G. **NLM** W1 CL664EA. **CODEN** CEPSDE. Documents available from CASDDS.
**Ind/Abst** Chem. Abstr.; Index Med.

US/0009-9147
**CLINICAL CHEMISTRY (BALTIMORE, MD.). See** Chemistry.

●NZ/1172-7039
**CLINICAL IMMUNOTHERAPEUTICS.** (1994)-. English. mo (12 issues - 2 volumes per annum). 870.00F Europe; $540.00 other. ADIS International Ltd, 41 Centorian Drive, Private Bag 65901, Mairangi Bay, Auckland 10 New Zealand. **Tel** 011 64 9 4798100, FAX 011 64 9 4791418. **(Subscription address:** Japan Publications Trading Company, Ltd., PO Box 5030, Tokyo International, Tokyo 100-31 Japan.**)**

US/0362-5664
**CLINICAL NEUROPHARMACOLOGY.** [Clin. neuropharmacol.]. Vol. 1 (1976)-. Academic Scholarly Publication. English. bm (6 issues). $135.00 (individuals), $216.00 (institutions) US; $176.00 (individuals), $264.00 (institutions) other. Raven Press, 1185 Avenue of the Americas, 37th Floor, New York NY 10036. **Tel** (212)930-9500, (212)930-9604, FAX (212)869-3495, (212)302-8507, telex 640073. **ED** Harold L. Klawans. **LC** RM315; .C548. **DD** 616.8/04/6105. **NLM** W1; CL731U. **CODEN** CLNEDB. **[CCC]. Pr Rev.** available on microfilm and microfiche from University Microfilms International (UMI). Documents available from The Genuine Article, BIOSIS Document Express, CASDDS.
**Desc:** Devoted to the pharmacology of the nervous system in the broadest sense, with topics ranging from basic mechanisms of action, structure - activity relationships, drug metabolism, and pharmacokinetics, to such practical clinical problems as drug interactions, drug toxicity, and the therapeutics of specific syndromes or symptoms.
**Ind/Abst** Biol. Abstr. (1989-); Chem. Abstr.; Curr. Contents Life Sci.; EMBASE; Index Med. (1980-); Index Sci. Rev. [Full Cov.]; Life Sci. Collect.; PESTDOC; Psychoanal. Abstr.; Psychol. Abstr. (1990-); PsycINFO; PsycLit; PsycScan: Appl. Exp. Eng. Psych.; PsycScan: LD/MR; PsycScan: Neuropsych.; Ref. Upd. Deluxe Ed.; Res. Alert [Full Cov.]; Sci. Cit. Index; SCISEARCH; Soc. Sci. Cit. Index [Select. Cov.].

US/0312-5963
**CLINICAL PHARMACOKINETICS.** [Clin. pharmacokinet.]. Vol. 1 (1976)-. Academic Scholarly Publication. English. mo. 940.00F Europe; $595.00 other. ADIS International Ltd, 41 Centorian Drive, Private Bag 65901, Mairangi Bay, Auckland 10 New Zealand. **Tel** 011 64 9 4798100, FAX 011 64 9 4791418. **(Subscription address:** Japan Publications Trading Company, Ltd., PO Box 5030, Tokyo International, Tokyo 100-31 Japan.**)** **ED** Rennie C. Heel. **DD** 615. **NLM** W1 CL764. **CODEN** CPKNDHCPKND. **[CCC]. Bk Rev. Ad Acc. Pr Rev. Circ:** 1,500 (ctrl). Documents available from The Genuine Article, BIOSIS Document Express, CASDDS.
**Desc:** Aims to assist in the further development of clinical pharmacokinetics, to promote communication and increased awareness within this specialty area and to further postgraduate education in clinical pharmacology and therapeutics. Places particular emphasis on review articles but also welcomes original research articles
**Ind/Abst** Biol. Abstr.; Chem. Abstr.; Curr. Contents Clin. Med.; Curr. Contents Life Sci.; Dairy Sci. Abstr.; EMBASE; Energy Res. Abstr. (Dec. 1981-); Health Plan. Adminis.; Helminthol. Abstr.; Index Med.; Index Sci. Rev. [Full Cov.]; Int. Pharm. Abstr.; Iowa Drug Inf. Serv. (1976-); Nutr. Abstr. Rev., Ser. A, Hum. Exp.; Life Sci. Collect.; PESTDOC; Ref. Upd. Deluxe Ed.; Res. Alert [Full Cov.]; Rev. Med. Vet. Mycology; Sci. Cit. Index; SCISEARCH; Soc. Sci. Cit. Index [Select. Cov.].

NZ/0114-0892
**CLINICAL PHARMACOKINETICS. DRUG DATA HANDBOOK.** ***Ceased.*** **VFOAT** Drug Data Handbook. (1989)-(199?). English. an. ADIS International Ltd, 41 Centorian Drive, Private Bag 65901, Mairangi Bay, Auckland 10 New Zealand. **Tel** 011 64 9 4798100, FAX 011 64 9 4791418.

GW/0937-0978
**CLINICAL PHARMACOLOGY. VFOAT** Klinische Pharmakologie. (1989)-. Monographic series.

English. W Zuckschwerdt Verlag, Kronwinkler Strasse 24, W 8000 Munich 60 F R Germany. **Tel** 49 89 8649490, FAX 011 49 89 86494950. **NLM** W1; CL764M. Documents available from CASDDS.
**Ind/Abst** Chem. Abstr.

US/0009-9236
**CLINICAL PHARMACOLOGY AND THERAPEUTICS.** [Clin. pharmacol. ther.]. **Added/Corp** American Therapeutic Society. American Society for Clinical Pharmacology and Therapeutics. American Society for Pharmacology and Experimental Therapeutics. **VFOAT** Clinical Pharmacology & Therapeutics. Vol. 1 (Jan./Feb. 1960)-. Academic Scholarly Publication. English. mo. $219.00 (institutions), $118.00 (individuals) US; $244.00 (institutions), $143.00 (individuals) other. Mosby Year Book Inc., 11830 Westline Industrial Drive, St Louis MO 63146. **Tel** (800)325-4177, (314)872-8370, FAX (314)432-1380, telex 44-2402. **ED** Marcus M. Reidenberg. **LC** RM1; .C55. **NLM** W1 CL765. **CODEN** CLPTAT. **[CCC]**. Index available. **Ad Acc. Pr Rev. Circ:** 5,570. available on microfilm and microfiche from University Microfilms International (UMI). Documents available from The Genuine Article, BIOSIS Document Express, CASDDS, ADONIS.
**Desc:** Devoted to the clinical study of the nature, action, efficacy and total evaluation of drugs, both new and established, as they are used in man.
**Ind/Abst** Abr. Index Med.; ADONIS; Annals Behav. Med.; Biol. Abstr.; Biostatistica (19??-19??); Chem. Abstr.; Curr. Aware. Biol. Sci., CABS; Curr. Contents Life Sci.; Dairy Sci. Abstr.; EMBASE; Energy Res. Abstr.; Health Plan. Adminis.; Helminthol. Abstr. (1991-); Index Med.; INIS Atomindex [Micro.]; Int. Pharm. Abstr.; Iowa Drug Inf. Serv. (1966-); Mod. Med.; NAPRALERT; Nutr. Abstr. Rev., Ser. A, Hum. Exp.; Life Sci. Collect.; PESTDOC; Physic. Medline Plus; Protozoolog. Abstr.; Ref. Upd. Basic Ed.; Ref. Upd. Deluxe Ed.; Res. Alert [Full Cov.]; Sci. Cit. Index; SCISEARCH.

US/0898-6037
**CLINICAL PHARMACOLOGY AND TOXICOLOGY CONSULTANT.** ***Ceased.*** [Clin. pharmacol. toxicol. consult.]. Vol. 8, No. 1 (1986)-Vol. 8, No. 4 (1986). Academic Scholarly Publication. English. qt. Memphis Pharmacotherapy and Clinical Research Center, 910 Madison Avenue/Suite 906, Memphis TN 38103. **DD** 615. **NLM** W1; CL765JE. Documents available from CASDDS. ***Continues*** *Clinical Toxicology Consultant, 0196-3384.*
**Ind/Abst** Chem. Abstr. (1986-).

US/0892-001X
**CLINICAL PHARMACOLOGY (NEW YORK, N.Y.).** (CLINICAL PHARMACOLOGY.). [Clin. pharmacol.]. Vol. 1 (1983)-. Monographic series. English. Sixteen times a year (2 vols.). Price varies per volume. Marcel Dekker Inc., 270 Madison Avenue, New York NY 10016. **Tel** (212)696-9000, (800)228-1160, FAX (212)685-4540, telex 421419. **(Subscription address:** Marcel Dekker Inc, PO Box 5017, Monticello NY 12701.**) ED** Murray Weiner. **DD** 615. **NLM** W1; CL764H. **CODEN** CLPHEV. available on microfilm from University Microfilms International (UMI). Documents available from BIOSIS Document Express.
**Desc:** Each title covers a different topic in clinical pharmacology. Topics include pharmacology in the elderly and drug stereochemistry.
**Ind/Abst** Biol. Abstr. (1986-); Rev. Med. Vet. Mycology.

US/0278-2677
**CLINICAL PHARMACY.** ***Title Change.*** [Clin. pharm.]. **Added/Corp** American Society of Hospital Pharmacists. Vol. 1, No. 1 Jan./Feb. (1982)-(199?). Academic Scholarly Publication. English. bm. American Society of Hospital Pharmacists, 7272 Wisconsin Avenue, Bethesda MD 20814. **Tel** (301)657-3000, (301)657-4383, FAX (301)652-8278. **NLM** W1 CL764K. **CODEN** CPHADV. **[CCC]**. Index available. **Bk Rev. Ad Acc. Pr Rev. Circ:** 8,000. available on microfilm and microfiche from University Microfilms International (UMI). Documents available from The Genuine Article, BIOSIS Document Express, CASDDS. ***Absorbed by*** *American Journal of Hospital Pharmacy, 0002-9289.*
**Desc:** Publishes the latest information on the clinical use of new drugs, current thinking about drug therapy in selected diseases, clinical trials evaluating drug effects and adverse drug reactions.
**Ind/Abst** Biol. Abstr.; Chem. Abstr.; Curr. Contents Clin. Med.; Dairy Sci. Abstr.; EMBASE; Health Plan. Adminis.; Helminthol. Abstr. (1982-); Index Med. (1982-); Int. Pharm. Abstr.; Iowa Drug Inf. Serv. (1982-); Mod. Med.; Nutr. Abstr. Rev., Ser. A, Hum. Exp.; PESTDOC; Physic. Medline Plus; Protozoolog. Abstr.; Res. Alert [Select. Cov.]; Rev. Med. Vet. Entomol.; Rev. Med. Vet. Mycology; SCISEARCH.

●US/1060-1333
**CLINICAL RESEARCH AND REGULATORY AFFAIRS.** [Clin. res. regul. aff.]. Vol. 9, No. 1 (Mar. 1992)-. Academic Scholarly Publication. English. qt. $435.00 US; $449.00 other. Marcel Dekker Inc., 270 Madison Avenue, New York NY 10016. **Tel** (212)696-9000, (800)228-1160, FAX (212)685-4540, telex 421419. **(Subscription address:** Marcel Dekker Inc, PO Box 5017, Monticello NY 12701.**) LC** RS122; .C57. **DD** 615/.1/072. **NLM** W1; CL778AD. **CODEN** CRRAES. **[CCC]**. ***Continues*** *Clinical Research Practices and Drug Regulatory Affairs, 0735-7915.*
**Ind/Abst** EMBASE; Int. Pharm. Abstr.; Ref. Upd. Deluxe Ed.

US/0149-2918
**CLINICAL THERAPEUTICS.** [Clin. ther.]. Vol. 1 (1977)-. Academic Scholarly Publication. English. Six times a year. $84.00 US; $98.00 other. Excerpta Medica / US, PO Box 3085, Princeton NJ 08543-3085. **Tel** (908)874-8550, FAX (908)874-5611. **(Subscription address:** Clinical Therapeutics, PO Box 3000, Denville NJ 07834.**) ED** George E. Farrar Jr. **LC** RM260; .C56. **DD** 615/.58/05. **NLM** W1 CL796I. **CODEN** CLTHDG. **[CCC]**. Index available. **Pr Rev. Circ:** 2,000 (ctrl). Documents available from The Genuine Article, BIOSIS Document Express, CASDDS, ADONIS.
**Desc:** Publishes original papers on laboratory and clinical investigations, with an emphasis on studies of pharmaceuticals in humans. Distributed to medical schools, teaching hospitals, and individuals worldwide.
**Ind/Abst** ADONIS; Biol. Abstr.; Chem. Abstr.; Curr. Contents Clin. Med.; EMBASE; Health Plan. Adminis.; Index Med. (1980-); Int. Pharm. Abstr.; Mod. Med.; Nutr. Abstr. Rev., Ser. B, Live Feeds and Feed.; Nutr. Abstr. Rev., Ser. A, Hum. Exp.; Life Sci. Collect.; PESTDOC; Protozoolog. Abstr.; Res. Alert [Select. Cov.]; Rev. Med. Vet. Entomol.; Rev. Med. Vet. Mycology; SCISEARCH; Soc. Sci. Cit. Index [Select. Cov.]; SportSearch.

NE/0927-5401
**CLINICAL TRIALS AND META-ANALYSIS.** ***Ceased.*** Vol. 28, No. 1 (June 1992)-Vol. 29. Academic Scholarly Publication. English. Four times a year (one volume). Elsevier Science Publishers BV, PO Box 211, 1000 AE Amsterdam Netherlands. **Tel** 011 31 20 5803642, FAX 011 31 20 5862696, telex 15682. **NLM** W1; CL799M. **[CCC]**. ***Continues*** *Clinical Trials Journal, 0009-9325.*
**Ind/Abst** Curr. Aware. Biol. Sci., CABS.

UK/0264-6404
**CLINICIAN (MACCLESFIELD, ENGLAND).** (CLINICIAN.). (1983)-. Periodical. English. ir. Gardiner Caldwell Communications Ltd., The Old Ribbon Mill, Pitt Street, Macclesfield Cheshire, SK11 7PT England. **Tel** 011 44 625 618507, FAX 011 44 625 610260. **NLM** W1; CL805C.

●NZ/1172-7047
**CNS DRUGS : THE CLINICAL REVIEW OF DRUGS AND THERAPEUICS IN PSYCHIATRY AND NEUROLOGY.** (1994)-. English. mo (12 issues - 2 volumes per annum). 870.00F Europe; $540.00 other. ADIS International Ltd, 41 Centorian Drive, Private Bag 65901, Mairangi Bay, Auckland 10 New Zealand. **Tel** 011 64 9 4798100, FAX 011 64 9 4791418. **(Subscription address:** Japan Publications Trading Company, Ltd., PO Box 5030, Tokyo International, Tokyo 100-31 Japan.**)**

●US/1066-3703
**CODE OF FEDERAL REGULATIONS UPDATE. 21 CFR, DRUGS AND MEDICAL DEVICES. VFOAT** Drugs and Medical Devices. (1993)-. English. qt. $300.00. Deanco Ltd., 189 Happ Road, Northfield IL 60093-3449.

SZ
**COLLEGAMENTO.** Periodical. English.
**Ind/Abst** Int. Pharm. Abstr.

US/0010-163X
**COLORADO JOURNAL OF PHARMACY, THE.** ***Ceased.*** **VFOAT** CJP. Vol. 1 (1958)-?. Periodical. English. qt. University of Colorado School of Pharmacy, Boulder CO 80309. **Tel** (303)492-6278. **ED** James A Ruth. **UDC** 615. **NLM** W1 CO249.
**Desc:** Pharmaceutical sciences.

CN/0707-1035
**COMMON USAGE DRUG SCHEDULE.** (COMMON USAGE DRUG SCHEDULE. LISTE DES PRODUITS DE PRESCRIPTION COURANTE.). **Added/Corp** Nouveau-Brunswick. Ministere de la Sante. Nouveau-Brunswick. Plan de Medicaments sur Ordonnance. Nouveau-Brunswick. Comite de Selection des Produits Medicamenteux. Association des Pharmaciens du Nouveau-Brunswick. **VFOAT** Liste des Produits de Prescription Courante. Vol. 1 Oct./Dec. (1975)-. Periodical. French (English). sa. Ministere de la Sante Plan de Medicaments sur Ordonnance, CP 690, Moncton New Brunswick E1C 8M7 Canada.

US/0746-3979
**COMMUNICATOR OF PHI DELTA CHI FRATERNITY, THE.** **See** Societies and Clubs.

UK/0960-376X
**COMMUNITY PHARMACY LONDON.** (COMMUNITY PHARMACY.). [Community pharm. Lond.]. (1986)-. Periodical. English. mo. £33.00 UK; £40.00 others. Benn Publications Ltd., Sovereign Way, Tonbridge TNQ 1RW England. **Tel** 011 44 732 364422, FAX 011 44 732 361534, telex 0732 95132 BENTON G. available on an online database (file 16/Full-Text) from DIALOG. ***Continues*** *O. T. C. Medication, 0260-518X;* ***Absorbed*** *Chemist and Pharmacy Update, 0956-2729.*
**Ind/Abst** Infomat Int. Bus.; PROMT [Full Txt.].

UK/0742-8413
**COMPARATIVE BIOCHEMISTRY AND PHYSIOLOGY. C, COMPARATIVE PHARMACOLOGY AND TOXICOLOGY.** ***Title Change.*** [Comp. biochem. physiol. C, Comp. pharmacol. toxicol.]. **VFOAT** Comparative Pharmacology and Toxicology. Vol. 74C, No. 1 (1983)-Vol. 106C, No. 3 (Nov. 1993). Academic Scholarly Publication. English. Nine times a year (3 volumes). Pergamon Press, An Imprint of Elsevier Science Ltd., The Boulevard, Langford Lane, Kidlington, Oxford OX5 1GB United Kingdom. **Tel** 011 44 865 843000, 011 44 865 843699, FAX 011 44 865 843010. **ED** G. A. Kerkut. **LC** QP33; .C665. **DD** 591.1/05. **NLM** W1 CO435CD. **CODEN** CBPCEE. available on microfilm and microfiche from University Microfilms International (UMI); available on microfiche from the publisher. Documents available from The Genuine Article, CASDDS, ADONIS. ***Continues*** *Comparative Biochemistry and Physiology. C: Comparative Pharmacology, 0306-4492.* ***Continued by*** *Comparative Biochemistry and Physiology. C, Pharmacology, Toxicology & Endocrinology.*
**Desc:** Publishes papers on action of drugs on animals, tissues and enzymes. Topics include the effects of heavy-metal poisoning, insecticides, pesticides and herbicides, neurotransmitters, anaesthetics and acid rain on invertebrates and vertebrates. This section will interest workers on insecticides, molluscicides, antiprotozoan drugs, and the effects of pollutants.
**Ind/Abst** ADONIS; AGRICOLA [Select. Cov.]; Anim. Breed. Abstr.; AQUAREF; Aquat. Sci. Fish. Abstr. (Computer File); Calcium Calcif. Tissue Abstr.; Chem. Abstr. (1983-); Chem. Titles; CSA Neuro. Abstr.; Curr. Aware. Biol. Sci., CABS; Curr. Contents Life Sci.; Dairy Sci. Abstr.; Ecol. Abstr. (?-?); EMBASE; Entomol. Abstr.; Helminthol. Abstr. (1991-); Index Med.; Index Vet.; Microbiol. Abstr. Sect. C; Nutr. Abstr. Rev., Ser. B, Live Feeds and Feed.; Ocean. Abstr.; Life Sci. Collect.; Pollut. Abstr. Indexes; Postharvest News Inf.; Poult. Abstr.; Protozoolog. Abstr.; Ref. Upd. Basic Ed.; Ref. Upd. Deluxe Ed.; Res. Alert [Full Cov.]; Rev. Agric. Entomol.; Rev. Med. Vet. Entomol.; Rev. Med. Vet. Mycology; Risk Abstr.; Sci. Cit. Index; SCISEARCH; Vet. Bull.; Wildl. Rev.

CN/0715-3066
**COMPENDIUM OF PHARMACEUTICALS AND SPECIALTIES.** [Compend. pharm. spec.]. **Added/Corp** Canadian Pharmaceutical Association. **VFOAT** CPS. **VAT** CPS (1974). 9th Ed. (1974)-. English. an. 71.00Can$ Canada; $66.00 other. Canadian Pharmaceutical Association, 1785 Alta Vista Drive, Ottawa Ontario K1G 3Y6 Canada. **Tel** (613)523-7877, FAX (613)523-0445. **DD** 615/.11/71. **Ad Acc. Circ:** 78,000 (ctrl). ***Continues*** *Compendium of Pharmaceuticals and Specialties (Canada), 0069-7966.*
**Desc:** Monographs on Canadian pharmaceutical products with therapeutic index, index of generic and brand name products, manufacturers index plus reference section.

US/1063-6498
**COMPLETE DRUG REFERENCE, THE.** [Complete drug ref.]. **Added/Corp** Consumer Reports Books. United States Pharmacopeial Convention. (1991)-. English. an. $39.95 US; $44.95 other. Consumer Reports Books, 9180 Le Saint Drive, Fairfield OH 45014. **Tel** (800)272-0722. **LC** RS51; .U65. **DD** 615/.1. ***Continues*** *United States Pharmacopeia Drug Information for the Consumer.*

FR/0293-9908
**COMPTES RENDUS DE THERAPEUTIQUE ET DE PHARMACOLOGIE CLINIQUE.** [Cir. ther. pharmacol. clin.]. V. 1, No. 1 (Sept. 1982)-. Academic Scholarly Publication. French (summaries and/or abstracts in English). Eleven times a year. 200.00F France; 360.00F other. D & D Medical, 6 rue Emile Verhaeren, 92215 Saint Cloud Cedex France. **Tel** 33 1 47712718, FAX 33 1 46027255. **ED** Mr. Serge Dard. **NLM** W1 CO455D. **CODEN** CRTCD9. **[CCC]**. Index available (bound in Feb. issue). cum. index. **Bk Rev**, (Qty: 11). **Ad Acc, Adv Mgr:** Delorme. **Pr Rev. Circ:** 1,500. Documents available from CASDDS.
**Desc:** Publishing of experimental and clinical trials; analysis and synthesis on drugs by a staff of specialists in every area of human medicine. Facilities to realize fast reports and off-prints about pharmaceutical events or congress.
**Ind/Abst** Chem. Abstr.; EMBASE.

US/0736-3893
**COMPUTERTALK FOR THE PHARMACIST.** (COMPUTER TALK FOR THE PHARMACIST.). [Comput. Talk pharm.]. **VFOAT** Computertalk for the Pharmacist. Vol. 1, No. 1 (Jan. 1981)-. Periodical. English. Six times a year. $45.00 (one year), $70.00 (two years). Computertalk Associates, 482 Norristown Road, Suite 112, Blue Bell PA 19422. **Tel** (215)825-7686, FAX (215)825-7641. **ED** Neil R. Bauman. cum. index. **Ad Acc, Adv Mgr:** W.A. Lockwood Jr., **Tel** (215)825-7686. **Circ:** 50,000 (ctrl).

**Desc:** Journal with emphasis on computer applications in pharmacy management.
**Ind/Abst** Int. Pharm. Abstr.

GW/0932-3791
**CONSILIUM CEDIP PRACTICUM.** [Cons. CEDIP pract.]. **Added/Corp** CEDIP Medizinisch-Technische Verlags- und Handelsgesellschaft. **VFOAT** Memento Consilium Cedip Practicum. 13th Edition (84/85)-. German. an. CEDIP, Medizinisch - Technische, Verlags und Handelsgesellschaft. **NLM** WB 39; C755. ***Continues*** *Consilium Cedip, 0343-8376.*

US/0888-5109
**CONSULTANT PHARMACIST, THE.** (THE CONSULTANT PHARMACIST : THE JOURNAL OF THE AMERICAN SOCIETY OF CONSULTANT PHARMACISTS.). [Consult. pharm.]. **Added/Corp** American Society of Consultant Pharmacists. Vol. 1, No. 1 (May/June 1986)-. Periodical. English. mo. $45.00 (individuals), $65.00 (institutions). American Society of Consultant Pharmacists, 1321 Duke Street, Alexandria VA 22314. **Tel** (703)739-1300, FAX (703)739-1321. **ED** L Michael Posey (editor's address: PO Box 6565, Athens GA 30604; editor's phone: (706)613-0100). **DD** 615. **NLM** W1; CO753G. Index available (December). cum. index. **Ad Acc, Adv Mgr:** Mark Piluigi, **Tel** (215)348-4351. **Pr Rev. Circ:** 11,100 (ctrl).
**Desc:** Explores issues, problems and possibilities relevant to consultant pharmacists, including profiles, research and commentary.
**Ind/Abst** Abstr. Soc. Gerontol.; Int. Pharm. Abstr.

US/0738-0615
**CONSUMER PHARMACIST, THE.** [Consum. pharm.]. (1982)-. Periodical. English. Six times a year. $48.00. Elba Medical Foundation, PO Box 1403, 1818 North Turnbull Drive, Metairie LA 70004-1403. **Tel** (504)833-3600. **ED** John F. Dimaggio. **Bk Rev. Ad Acc. Circ:** 6,000 (ctrl).

US/0892-1865
**CONTEMPORARY WRITINGS ON LONG TERM CARE PHARMACY.** (CONTEMPORARY WRITINGS ON LONG TERM CARE PHARMACY / ASCP, AMERICAN SOCIETY OF CONSULTANT PHARMACISTS.). [Contemp. writ. long term care pharm.]. **Added/Corp** American Society of Consultant Pharmacists. Vol. 1, (1978)-. English. ir. American Society of Consultant Pharmacists, 1321 Duke Street, Alexandria VA 22314. **Tel** (703)739-1300, FAX (703)739-1321. **DD** 615. **NLM** W1; CO772.

CN/0318-5141
**CONTINUING EDUCATION (TORONTO).** (CONTINUING EDUCATION - UNIVERSITY OF TORONTO. FACULTY OF PHARMACY.). **Main/Corp** University of Toronto. Faculty of Pharmacy. (1975)-. Monographic series. English. qt. Price varies per volume. Ontario College of Pharmacists, 483 Huron Street, Toronto Ontario M5R 2R4 Canada. **Tel** (416)962-4861, FAX (416)962-1619. **ED** Bernard DesRoches and Lana Parn. **DD** 615/.4/05. **UDC** 615. Index available. cum. index. **Bk Rev. Circ:** 7,200 (ctrl). available on microfilm. ***Supersedes*** *University of Toronto. Faculty of Pharmacy. Continuing Education Programme, 0318-515X.*
**Desc:** New and review articles on drug therapy and social issues affecting pharmacy, book reviews, section on new drugs.
**Ind/Abst** Int. Pharm. Abstr. (19??-19??).

US/0888-773X
**CONTROLLED DRUG BIOAVAILABILITY.** [Control. drug bioavailab.]. Vol. 1-. Academic Scholarly Publication. English. Price varies per volume. John Wiley & Sons, Inc., 605 Third Avenue, New York NY 10158-0012. **Tel** (212)850-6000, (212)850-6645, FAX (212)850-6088, telex 12-7063. **(Subscription address:** John Wiley & Sons / England, Baffins Lane, Chichester, West Sussex PO19 1UD England.**) DD** 615. **UDC** 615.07. **NLM** W1; CO779H. **CODEN** CDBIEA. Documents available from CASDDS.
**Ind/Abst** Chem. Abstr. (1984-).

US
**CONTROLLED SUBSTANCES HANDBOOK.** (1972)-. English. qt. $254.50. Government Information Services / Virginia, 4301 North Fairfax Drive, Suite 875, Arlington VA 22203. **Tel** (703)528-1082, FAX (703)528-6060, telex RCA 263591 GIS UR. **ED** Ken Baumgartner.
**Desc:** Describes in detail Drug Enforcement Administration requirements for manufacturing, storing, securing, shipping and distributing controlled substances.

US/0007-8816
**COPNIP LIST.** Began with 1, Sept. 1953. English. qt. Committee of Pharmaceutical, Nonserial Industrial Publications, 235 Park Avenue South, New York NY 10003. **UDC** 615.

IT
**COSMESI IN FARMACIA.** Italian. Ten times a year. Mediprint Srl, Via Corsica 6/8, 00198 Rome Italy. **Tel** 011 39 6 8845351, FAX 011 39 6 8845354.

CN/0828-6914
**CPJ : CANADIAN PHARMACEUTICAL JOURNAL.** [CPJ, Can. pharm. j.]. **Added/Corp** Canadian Pharmaceutical Association. **VFOAT** RPC; Canadian Pharmaceutical Journal; Revue Pharmaceutique Canadienne. **VAT** Canadian Pharmaceutical Journal (1984); RCP. Revue Pharmaceutique Canadienne; Revue Pharmaceutique Canadienne (1984). Vol. 117, No. 5 (May 1984)-. Periodical. English (French; summaries and/or abstracts in French). Ten times a year (includes index). 60.00Can$. Clifford K. Goodman Inc., 1382 Hurontario Street, Mississauga Ontario L5G 3H4 Canada. **Tel** (705)689-8990. **ED** Jane Dewar. **DD** 615/.05. **[CCC].** Index Available Published separately--free--upon request. **Bk Rev. Ad Acc. Circ:** 12,200 (ctrl). ***Continues*** *Canadian Pharmaceutical Journal, 0317-199X.*
**Ind/Abst** EMBASE; Health Plan. Adminis.; Int. Pharm. Abstr.

US/0577-6392
**CRIB : CHEMOTHERAPY RESEARCH BULLETIN. Added/Corp** Chemotherapy Research Institute. **VFOAT** Chemotherapy Research Bulletin. **VAT** Chemotherapy Research Institute Bulletin. (196?)-. Bulletin. English. mo. Chemotherapy Research Institute, 1315 Walnut Street, Philadelphia PA 19107. **LC** RM260; .C7. ***Continues*** *Chemotherapy Research Bulletin.*

US/1069-4110
**CRITICAL REVIEWS IN PHARMACOLOGY.** ***Ceased.*** (1994)-(1994). Periodical. English. qt. CRC Press Inc., 2000 Corporate Boulevard Northwest, Boca Raton FL 33431. **Tel** (407)994-0555, (800)272-7737, FAX (407)998-9784, telex 568689. **ED** Mannfred A. Hollinger.
**Desc:** A comprehensive publication that will provide reviews of recent developments in major area of pharmacology.

US/0743-4863
**CRITICAL REVIEWS IN THERAPEUTIC DRUG CARRIER SYSTEMS.** [Crit. rev. ther. drug carr. syst.]. **VFOAT** C.R.C. Critical Reviews in Therapeutic Drug Carrier; CRC Critical Reviews in Therapeutic Drug Carrier Systems. **VAT** Chemical Rubber Company Critical Reviews in Therapeutic Drug Carrier Systems. Vol. 1, Issue 1 (1984)-. Academic Scholarly Publication. English. Four times a year. $265.00. Begell House Inc., PO Box 1109, Pearl River NY 10965. **Tel** (212)725-1999. **ED** Stephen D. Bruck. **LC** RS201.V43; C74. **DD** 615. **NLM** W1; CR216ZF. **CODEN** CRTSEO. **[CCC]. Pr Rev.** Documents available from The Genuine Article, BIOSIS Document Express, CASDDS.
**Desc:** Publishes authoritative, objective, and comprehensive multidisciplinary critical review papers which encompass the basic biological, medical, and pharmaceutical sciences.
**Ind/Abst** Biol. Abstr. (1984-); Chem. Abstr. (1984-); Curr. Aware. Biol. Sci., CABS; Curr. Contents Life Sci.; EMBASE; Index Med. (Vol. 1, No. 1, 1984-); Index Sci. Rev. [Full Cov.]; Res. Alert [Full Cov.]; Sci. Cit. Index; SCISEARCH; Soc. Sci. Cit. Index [Select. Cov.].

IT/0011-1783
**CRONACHE FARMACEUTICHE.** (CRONACHE FARMACEUTICHE: PUBBLICAZIONE BIMESTRALE DELLA SOCIETBA ITALIANA DI SCIENZE FARMACEUTICHE].). [Cron. farm.]. **Added/Corp** Societba Italiana di Scienze Farmaceutiche. (1958)-. Academic Scholarly Publication. Italian (English, French and Italian). Six times a year. L60000 Italy; $60.00 other. Societa Italiana di Scienze Farmaceutiche, Via Giorgio Jan 18, 20129 Milan Italy. **Tel** 011 39 2 29513303. **ED** Piero Sensi. **CODEN** CRFMAY. Index available. **Bk Rev. Ad Acc. Circ:** 1,100. Documents available from CASDDS.
**Ind/Abst** Bibliogr. Mission.; Chem. Abstr.; EMBASE; Int. Pharm. Abstr.; PESTDOC.

SP
**CUADERNOS DE FARMACIA.** Spanish. mo. Colegio Oficial de Farmaceuticos, Conde Montornes 7, 46003 Valencia Spain.

US
**CURRENT CONCEPTS IN COMMUNITY PHARMACY.** English. Three times a year. $39.00 US; $45.54 other. Macmillan Professional Journal, 30 Vreeland Road, Florham Park NJ 07932. **Tel** (201)822-1622, FAX (201)822-2498.

●US/1065-7630
**CURRENT DRUG THERAPY.** [Curr. drug ther.]. (1992)-. Periodical. English. mo. $85.00 US, Canada & Mexico; $108.00 other. McLaurine & Co., 515 Marlborough Road, Brooklyn NY 11226. **Tel** (718)693-2087. **DD** 615.

KO
**CURRENT INDEX TO JOURNALS IN SCIENCE & TECHNOLOGY, BIOLOGY, AGRICULTURE, PHARMACY.** **See** Biology.

UK/0958-9384
**CURRENT MEDICAL LITERATURE / HOSPITAL PHARMACY.** [Curr. med. lit., Hosp. pharm.]. (1990)-. English. qt. $40.00. Current Medical Literature Ltd., 40-42 Osnaburgh Street, London NW1 3ND England. **Tel** 011 44 71 4658377, FAX 011 44 71 4658380. **(Subscription address:** Royal Society Medicine Services, 1 Wimpole Street, London W1M 8AE England.**) DD** 016.615105.

UK/0967-8298
**CURRENT OPINION IN INVESTIGATIONAL DRUGS.** ***Title Change.*** (1992)-(19??). English. Twelve times a year. Current Science / England, Middlesex House, 34-42 Cleveland Street, London W1P 5FB England. **Tel** 011 44 71 580 8393, 011 44 71 323 0323, FAX 011 44 81 580 1938. **(Subscription address:** Current Science, 20 North 3rd Street, Philadelphia PA 19106.**) NLM** W1; CU799GEH. ***Continued by*** *Expert Opinion on Investigational Drugs.*

US/0097-8620
**CURRENT PRESCRIBING.** V. 1- Mar. 1975-. Periodical. English. mo. $16.00 US; $20.00 other. Medical Economics Data, Five Paragon Drive, PO Box 27, Montvale NJ 07645. **Tel** (800)442-6657, (201)358-7200. **LC** RM1; .C86. **DD** 615/.58/05. **UDC** 615.15. **NLM** W1 CU8033.

US/0192-7736
**CURRENT STATUS OF MODERN THERAPY.** Vol. 1 (1978)-. Academic Scholarly Publication. English. ir. Price varies per volume. University Park Press, PO Box 4034, New York NY 10163. **NLM** W1 CU81S. **CODEN** CSMTDW. Documents available from CASDDS.
**Ind/Abst** Chem. Abstr.

US/0011-393X
**CURRENT THERAPEUTIC RESEARCH.** [Curr. ther. res.]. Vol.1 (Sept. 1959)-. Academic Scholarly Publication. English. mo. $114.00 US; $129.00 other. Excerpta Medica / US, PO Box 3085, Princeton NJ 08543-3085. **Tel** (908)874-8550, FAX (908)874-5611. **(Subscription address:** Current Therapeutic Research, PO Box 3000, Denville NJ 07834.**) ED** Keyo S. Ross. **DD** 615. **NLM** W1 CU815. **CODEN** CTCEA9. **[CCC].** Index available. **Pr Rev. Circ:** 1,100. Documents available from The Genuine Article, BIOSIS Document Express, CASDDS, ADONIS.
**Desc:** Prompt publication of accepted manuscripts describing results of original research in the broad field of medical therapy.
**Ind/Abst** ADONIS; Biol. Abstr. (1986-); Calcium Calcif. Tissue Abstr.; Chem. Abstr.; CSA Neuro. Abstr. (?-?); Curr. Aware. Biol. Sci., CABS; Curr. Contents Clin. Med.; Curr. Contents Life Sci.; Dairy Sci. Abstr.; EMBASE; Health Plan. Adminis.; Int. Pharm. Abstr.; Iowa Drug Inf. Serv.; Microbiol. Abstr. Sect. B (19??-19??); Microbiol. Abstr. Sect. A; Microbiol. Abstr. Sect. C; Mod. Med.; Nutr. Abstr. Rev., Ser. B, Live Feeds and Feed.; Nutr. Abstr. Rev., Ser. A, Hum. Exp.; Life Sci. Collect.; PESTDOC; Protozoolog. Abstr.; Psychol. Abstr. (1964-); PsycINFO; PsycLit; Res. Alert [Full Cov.]; Rev. Med. Vet. Mycology (1964-); Rev. Plant Pathol.; Sci. Cit. Index; SCISEARCH; Soc. Sci. Cit. Index [Select. Cov.]; SportSearch; Sug. Indus. Abstr.

AT/0311-905X
**CURRENT THERAPEUTICS.** [Curr. ther.]. (1972)-. Periodical. English. mo (12 issues). 110.00Aus$ Australia; 206.00Aus$ US, Israel & Canada; 161.00Aus$ New Zealand, Papua & New Guinea; 175.00Aus$ Fiji, Indonesia & Malaysia; 189.00Aus$ India, Japan, Hong, Kong & Korea; 222.00Aus$ other. ADIS International Ltd, 41 Centorian Drive, Private Bag 65901, Mairangi Bay, Auckland 10 New Zealand. **Tel** 011 64 9 4798100, FAX 011 64 9 4791418. **(Subscription address:** Adis International Pty. Ltd., 9 Rodborough Road, Frenchs Forest, N.S.W. 2086 Australia.**) NLM** W1 CU815T. **[CCC].** Index available. cum. index. **Ad Acc. Circ:** 21,000 (ctrl). ***Continues*** *New Ethicals, 0028-5064.*
**Desc:** A journal of practical drug treatment.
**Ind/Abst** EMBASE; Rev. Med. Vet. Mycology; Rev. Plant Pathol.

US/0196-4143
**D-LIST.** [D-list]. **VFOAT** Facts and Comparisons. **VAT** Discontinued List. 1979-. English. an. $3.95. Facts and Comparisons Inc, 111 West Port Plaza, Suite 400, St Louis MO 63146-3098. **Tel** (314)878-2515, (800)223-0554, FAX (314)878-5563. **DD** 615. **UDC** 615.11. ***Continues*** *Discontinued Drug Products, 0270-0549.*

JA
**DAIICHI YAKKA DAIGAKU KENKYU NENPO. THE ANNUAL REPORT OF THE DAIICHI COLLEGE OF PHARMACEUTICAL SCIENCES.** **Added/Corp** Daiichi Yakka Daigaku. **VFOAT** Annual Report of the Daiichi College of Pharmaceutical Sciences. (1970)-. Periodical. Japanese (summaries and/or abstracts in English). Daiichi Yakka Daigaku, (Daiichi College of Pharmaceutical Sciences), 22-1, Tamagawacho, Minamiku, Fukuokashi, Fukuokaken 815

Japan. **NLM** W1 DA234K. **CODEN** DYDNDM. Documents available from CASDDS.
**Ind/Abst** Chem. Abstr.

US
**DE HAEN NEW PRODUCT SURVEY.** **Main/Corp** Paul de Haen, Inc. **VFOAT** New Product Survey. Monographic series. English. an. Price varies per volume. Paul de Haen International Inc, 2750 South Shoshone Street, Englewood CO 80110. **Tel** (800)438-0296, FAX (303)789-2534. **ED** Janis I Halzel. Index available. **Bk Rev. Circ:** 300 (ctrl).
**Desc:** Listing and brief description of new drugs introduced for marketing.

US
**DE HAEN'S DRUG PRODUCT INDEX. USA.** **Added/Corp** Paul de Haen International. **VFOAT** Drug Product Index. P.U.S.A. Vol. 1 (1987/88)-. English. an. $500.00. Paul de Haen International, 2750 South Shoshone Street, Englewood CO 80110. **Tel** (800)438-0296, FAX (303)789-2534. **NLM** QV 772; D3222. **Circ:** 1,000 (ctrl). ***Continues*** *New Drug Analysis, U.S.A.;* ***Continues in part*** *De Haen Nonproprietary Name Index.*
**Desc:** Includes information on drug trade names, manufacturers and therapeutic class.

US
**DEHAEN'S NEW PRODUCT SURVEY. MONTHLY SUPPLEMENT.** **VFOAT** De Haen's New Product Survey. Began with Jan. 1983. Periodical. English. mo (with annual cumulative edition). $325.00. Paul de Haen International Inc, 2750 South Shoshone Street, Englewood CO 80110. **Tel** (800)438-0296, FAX (303)789-2534. **ED** Janis I Halzel. **UDC** 615.12. **NLM** QV 772; D3223. **Bk Rev. Circ:** 300 (ctrl). ***Continues*** *New Product Survey. Monthly Supplement.*
**Desc:** Listing and brief description of new drugs introduced for marketing.

US/0418-5420
**DELAWARE PHARMACIST.** (1967)-. English. **DD** 615.
**Ind/Abst** Int. Pharm. Abstr.

US/0276-5675
**DES LITIGATION REPORTER.** **See** Law.

GW/0366-8622
**DEUTSCHE APOTHEKER, DER.** [Dtsch. Apoth.]. (19??)-. Periodical. German. mo. DM100.00 Germany; DM120.00 other. Der Deutsche Apotheker, Postfach 1650, 61406 Oberursel, Hans-Thoma-Str. 1, 61440 Oberursel Germany. **Tel** 011 49 6171 55012, FAX 011 49 6171 55142. **ED** Siegfried Beyer-Enke. **NLM** W1 DE592. **CODEN** DAPOAG. Documents available from BIOSIS Document Express, CASDDS.
**Ind/Abst** Biol. Abstr.; Chem. Abstr. (1949-1983); Int. Pharm. Abstr.

GW/0011-9857
**DEUTSCHE APOTHEKER-ZEITUNG.** [Dtsch. Apoth.Ztg.]. **VFOAT** Deutsche Apotheker-Zeitung (Stuttgart). (1950)-. Periodical. German. wk. DM175.20. Deutscher Apotheker Verlag, Postfach 101061, D 70009 Stuttgart Germany. **Tel** 011 49 711 25820, INLAND:0711/2582, FAX 011 49 711 2582 290, telex 723636 daz d. **ED** Klaus G. Brauer, Peter Ditzel. **UDC** 615. **[CCC].** Index available. Documents available from CASDDS. ***Continues*** *Suddeutsche Apotheker-Zeitung, 0370-8527.*
**Ind/Abst** Chem. Abstr.; Int. Pharm. Abstr.; PESTDOC.

GW
**DEUTSCHE APOTHEKER-ZEITUNG, VEREINIGT MIT SUDDEUTSCHE APOTHEKER-ZEITUNG.** Vol. 1 (1861)-. Academic Scholarly Publication. German. wk. DM217.20 (inclusive 7 supplements and weekly delivery of the Apotheker Zeitung); DM138.00 (students). Deutscher Apotheker Verlag, Postfach 101061, D 70009 Stuttgart Germany. **Tel** 011 49 711 25820, INLAND:0711/2582, FAX 011 49 711 2582 290, telex 723636 daz d. **ED** Wolfgang Wessinger, Peter Ditzel and Klaus G Brauer. Documents available from CASDDS. ***Absorbed*** *Deutsche Apotheker-Zeitung.*
**Ind/Abst** Chem. Abstr.; EMBASE; Nat. Prod. Updates.

GW
**DEUTSCHE DROGISTEN ZEITUNG.** Periodical. German. sm. Verlag Luitpold Lang, Theresienhohe 10, 8 Munich 12 Germany. **UDC** 615.19(430.1).

SZ/0379-8305
**DEVELOPMENTAL PHARMACOLOGY AND THERAPEUTICS.** ***Ceased.*** [Dev. pharmacol. ther.]. Vol. 1, No. 1 (1980)-Vol. 21 (1993). Academic Scholarly Publication. English. Six times a year. S. Karger AG, Allschwilerstrasse 10, PO Box - Postfach - Case Postale, CH-4009 Basel Switzerland. **Tel** 011 41 61 306-1111, FAX 011 41 61 306-1234, telex CH 962 652. **ED** J V Aranda and S J Yaffe. **NLM** W1 DE997UNE. **CODEN** DPTHDL. **[CCC]. Ad Acc. Pr Rev.** available on microfilm; available on microfiche. Documents available from The Genuine Article, BIOSIS Document Express, CASDDS. ***Absorbed*** *Pediatric Pharmacology (New York, N.Y.), 0270-322X.*
**Desc:** Publishes papers on the effects of drugs in the perinatal-pediatric population. Included are original papers reporting basic animal studies relevant to general developmental pharmacology; preliminary clinical and laboratory studies characterizing the effects of drugs as related to human developmental events; and clinical trials observing pharmacodynamic, pharmacokinetic and metabolic properties of drugs. Discussions on current controversies have their place in the journal as well as reviews on recent advances in drug therapy.
**Ind/Abst** Biol. Abstr. (1987-); Chem. Abstr.; CSA Neuro. Abstr. (?-?); Curr. Aware. Biol. Sci., CABS; Dairy Sci. Abstr.; Dev. Med. Child Neurol.; EMBASE; Health Plan. Adminis.; Index Med. (1980-); Index Vet.; Life Sci. Collect.; PESTDOC; Ref. Upd. Deluxe Ed.; Res. Alert [Full Cov.]; Sci. Cit. Index; SCISEARCH; Soc. Sci. Cit. Index [Select. Cov.].

US/0885-159X
**DICKINSON'S FDA.** ***Title Change.*** **See** Public Administration.

US/1063-2433
**DICKINSON'S FDA INSPECTION.** ***Title Change.*** **See** Public Administration.

●US/1073-4414
**DICKINSON'S FDA REVIEW.** **See** Public Administration.

US/1063-2441
**DICKINSON'S PHARMACY.** [Dickinson's pharm.]. **Added/Corp** Dickinson, James G. **VFOAT** Pharmacy. (1989)-. Periodical. English. Twelve times a year. $175.00 US & Canada & Mexico; $200.00 other. Ferdic Inc., PO Box 367, Las Cruces NM 88004. **Tel** (505)527-8634, FAX (505)527-8858. **ED** James G. Dickinson. **DD** 658. ***Continues*** *Dickinson's PSAO, 0889-5953.*

US/0889-5953
**DICKINSON'S PSAO.** **See** Business.

FR/0419-1153
**DICTIONNAIRE VIDAL.** (1961)-. French. an. 497.47F France; 700.00F other. Office Vulgarisation Pharmaceutiq, 11 rue Quentin Bauchart, 75384 Paris Cedex 08 France. **Tel** 011 33 1 4723 90 91, FAX 011 33 1 4720 72 89. available on CD-ROM. ***Continues*** *Dictionnaire de Specialites Pharmaceutiques.*

HK
**DIMS. DRUG INDEX FOR MALAYSIA & SINGAPORE.** **VFOAT** Drug Index for Malaysia & Singapore. Vol. 3 (Jan. 1973)-. Periodical. English. Three times a year (Feb., June, Oct.). 110.00Sing$ (airmail), 60.00Sing$ (surface mail). MIMS Asia, 135 Cecil Street, 13-00 LKN Building, Singapore 0106 Singapore. **Tel** 011 65 2233788, FAX 011 65 2214788. **ED** Jenny Oo. Index available. **Ad Acc. Circ:** 7,200 (ctrl). ***Continues*** *Drug Index for Malaysia and Singapore.*
**Desc:** A listing of drugs containing information on contents, dosage, indication, presentation and packing.

US/0191-2550
**DIRECTORY - AMERICAN SOCIETY FOR CLINICAL PHARMACOLOGY AND THERAPEUTICS.** **Main/Corp** American Society for Clinical Pharmacology and Therapeutics. (1970)-. Directory. English. an. $135.00 (members); $75.00 (associate); $50.00 (associate in training) Comes with the Journal of American Society of Clinical Pharmacology & Therapeutics. American Society for Clinical Pharmacology and Therapeutics, 1718 Gallagher Road, Norristown PA 19401. **Tel** (215)825-3838. **NLM** WB 22.1 A512.

●US
**DIRECTORY OF DRUG STORES & HBC CHAINS.** **VFOAT** Drug Stores & HBC Chains; Drug Store and Health Beauty Chains; Drug Stores and Health Beauty Chains; Drug Store and HBC Chains; Directory of Drug Store and HBC Chains. (1992)-. Directory. English. an. $295.00 continental US; $305.00 Alaska, Hawaii, Puerto Rico, and Canada; $320.00 other. Lebhar Friedman Inc., 3922 Coconut Palm Drive, Tampa FL 33619. **Tel** (800)927-9292, (813)664-6707. **LC** HD9666.3; .C5. ***Continues*** *Directory of Drug Store & HBA Chains Includes Drug Wholesalers, 0730-2703.*

US
**DISCOVERIES IN PHARMACOLOGY.** Vol. 1-. Academic Scholarly Publication. English. ir. Price varies per volume. Elsevier Science Publishing Company Inc, Madison Square Station, PO Box 882, New York NY 10159-0882. **Tel** (212)633-3950, FAX (212)633-3990. **UDC** 615. **CODEN** DIPHDK. Documents available from BIOSIS Document Express, CASDDS.
**Ind/Abst** Biol. Abstr. (1986-); Chem. Abstr. (1983-).

TU/1010-7584
**DOGA. TURK TIP VE ECZACILIK DERGISI.** **See** Medical Science and Technology.

FR/0223-5242
**DOSSIER DU CENTRE NATIONAL D'INFORMATION SUR LE MEDICAMENT HOSPITALIER.** [Doss. Cent. natl. inf. medicam. hosp.]. (1979)-. Periodical. French. bm (6 issues). 783.55F (hospitals & individuals), 1469.15F (pharmaceutical laboratories) France; 990.00F (hospitals & individuals), 1690.00F (pharmaceutical laboratories). Centre National d'Information sur Medicament Hospitalier, 7 rue du Fer a Moulin, 75005 Paris France. **Tel** 011 33 1 43364700, FAX 011 33 1 43367649. **UDC** 615.
**Ind/Abst** Int. Pharm. Abstr.

US/0012-5881
**DRAGOCO REPORT (FLAVORS EDITION. ENGLISH).** (DRAGOCO REPORT.). [Dragoco rep.]. Vol. 1 (1954)-. Periodical. English. ir. Free. Dragoco Inc, PO Box 261, Totowa NJ 07511. **DD** 664. **CODEN** DRFSDW. Documents available from CASDDS.
**Ind/Abst** Bibliogr. Mission.; BioBusiness; Chem. Abstr.; Foods Adlibra; Int. Pharm. Abstr.; Life Sci. Collect.

US/0012-6527
**DRUG & COSMETIC INDUSTRY.** [Drug cosmet. ind.]. **VFOAT** D&CI; DCI, Drug & Cosmetic Industry. **VAT** Drug and Cosmetic Industry. Vol. 30, No. 2 (Feb. 1932)-. Periodical. English. mo. $32.00 US and possessions; $57.00 Canada; $90.00 other. Advanstar Communications Inc., 131 West First Street, Duluth MN 55802. **Tel** (218)723-9477, (800)346-0085. **ED** Donald A. Davis. **LC** RS1; .D63. **NLM** W1 DR514. **CODEN** DCINAQ. **[CCC]. Circ:** 11,592. available on microfilm and microfiche from University Microfilms International (UMI); available on an online database (files 16,648/Full-Text) from DIALOG. Documents available from CASDDS. ***Continues*** *Drug Markets;* ***Absorbed*** *Drug & Cosmetic Catalog, 0732-0760.*
**Desc:** Serves manufacturers of cosmetics, pharmaceuticals, proprietary medicines, flavor and allied packaged chemical products.
**Ind/Abst** BioBusiness; Bus. Index (1985-); Bus. Period. Index; Chem. Abstr.; Chem. Bus. Bull.; Chem. Bus. NewsBase (1989-); Chem. Bus. Update; Chem. Ind. Notes; EMBASE; F&S Index Plus Text, Int. [Full Txt.] [Select. Cov.]; Gen. BusinessFile (1985-); Gen. Period. Index (1985-); Int. Packag. Abstr.; Int. Pharm. Abstr.; Leadscan; Mag. Search; NAPRALERT; Life Sci. Collect.; PESTDOC; PROMT [Full Txt.]; Trade Ind. ASAP [Full Txt.]; Trade Ind. Index (1981-) [Full Txt.]; Vocat. Search (July 1993-); Wilson Bus. Abstr.

US/8756-5935
**DRUG AND DEVICE RECALL BULLETIN.** (Jan. 1985)-. Bulletin. English. mo. $40.00. RX Data Pac Service, PO Box 42020, Cincinnati OH 45242. **Tel** (513)489-0943. **ED** I H Goodman. **DD** 363. **Circ:** 5,000 (ctrl).
**Desc:** Complete data about drug and device recalls including generic recalls. Compiled from FDA enforcement reports. Helps satisfy JCAHO recall activity documentation.

US/1053-1564
**DRUG & MARKET DEVELOPMENT.** [Drug mark. dev.]. **VFOAT** Drug and Market Development. (1990)-. Periodical. English. mo (12 issues). $768.00 US; $792.00 other. Drug & Market Development - D&MD, PO Box 187, Lake Forest CA 92630. **Tel** (714)830-4012, FAX (714)830-2153. **DD** 615.
**Desc:** Provides pharmaceutical, biotechnology, and other health care industry professionals with comprehensive analysis of technical, clinical, and market developments in human therapeutics.

UK/0012-6543
**DRUG AND THERAPEUTICS BULLETIN.** [Drug & ther. bull.]. **Added/Corp** Consumers' Association. Vol. 1 (May 3, 1963)-. Academic Scholarly Publication. English. Twenty-six times a year. £42.00 (airmail), £35.00 (surface mail). Consumers Association, Castlemead, Gascoyne Way, Hertford SG14 1LH England. **Tel** 011 44 992 587773. **ED** Andrew Herxheimer. **DD** 615. **NLM** W1 DR518. Index available. cum. index. **Bk Rev. Circ:** 80,000 (ctrl). available on microfilm from University Microfilms International (UMI). ***Supersedes*** *Medical Letter.*
**Desc:** Impartial reviews for the prescribers of drugs and other treatments.
**Ind/Abst** EMBASE; Health Plan. Adminis.; Hospit. Health Admin. Index; Index Med.; Int. Pharm. Abstr.; Iowa Drug Inf. Serv. (1969-).

UK
**DRUG AND THERAPEUTICS BULLETIN. (ITALIAN EDITION).** Bulletin. Italian. Twenty-six times a year. L70000.00. Consumers Association, Castlemead, Gascoyne Way, Hertford SG14 1LH England. **Tel** 011 44 992 587773. **(Subscription address:** Farmacie Comunali Riunite, Via Doberdo 9, 42100 Reggio Emilia Italy**)** Index available. **Ad Acc.**

●US/1071-7544
**DRUG DELIVERY.** (1993)-. Academic Scholarly Publication. English. qt (4 issues). $144.00 US and Canada. Academic Press, Inc., 6277 Sea Harbor Drive,

Orlando FL 32887. **Tel** (800)543-9534, (407)345-4100, FAX (407)363-9661. **NLM** W1; DR519F. **[CCC].** ***Continues*** *Drug Targeting and Delivery.*

JA/0913-5006
**DRUG DELIVERY SYSTEM.** [Drug deliv. syst.]. (1986)-. Periodical. Japanese. sa. Iyaku Janarusha, Medicine & Drug Journal Co., Ltd., 3-28, Hiranocho, Higashiku, Osakashi, Osakafu 541 Japan. **DD** 615. Documents available from CASDDS.
**Ind/Abst** Chem. Abstr.

SZ/1055-9612
**DRUG DESIGN AND DISCOVERY.** [Drug des. discov.]. Vol. 8, No. 1 (Nov. 1991)-. Periodical. English. Four times a year. $508.00 (academic institutions), $792.00 (corporate institutions). Harwood Academic Publishers, PO Box 90, Reading RG1 8JL England. **Tel** 011 44 734 560080. **(Subscription address:** International Publishers Distributor at one of the following addresses: 820 Town Center Drive, Langhorne, PA 19047; or PO Box 90, Reading Berkshire RG1 8JL UK; or Kent Ridge PO Box 1180, Singapore 9111, Republic of Singapore**) LC** RS420; .D78. **DD** 615/.19. **NLM** W1; DR521BB. **CODEN** DDDIEV. **[CCC].** ***Continues*** *Drug Design and Delivery, 0884-2884.*

US/0363-9045
**DRUG DEVELOPMENT AND INDUSTRIAL PHARMACY.** [Drug dev. ind. pharm.]. Vol. 3 (1977)-. Academic Scholarly Publication. English. Twenty times a year. $1,295.00 US; $1,365.00 other. Marcel Dekker Inc., 270 Madison Avenue, New York NY 10016. **Tel** (212)696-9000, (800)228-1160, FAX (212)685-4540, telex 421419. **(Subscription address:** Marcel Dekker Inc, PO Box 5017, Monticello NY 12701.**) ED** Christopher T. Rhodes. **LC** RS402; .D76. **DD** 615/.1/05. **NLM** W1 DR521BL. **CODEN** DDIPD8DDIP8. **[CCC]. Bk Rev. Ad Acc. Pr Rev.** ctrl circ. available on microfiche. Documents available from The Genuine Article, BIOSIS Document Express, CASDDS, ADONIS. ***Continues*** *Drug Development Communications, 0095-5183.*
**Desc:** Covering aspects of the development, production, and evaluation of drugs and pharmaceutical products, this international journal highlights both the technical and regulatory facets of industrial pharmacy. Topics addressed within this continually evolving discipline include computerization of production, quality control, export problems, pharmacokinetics and biopharmaceutics, drug regulatory affairs, and successful manufacturing practices.
**Ind/Abst** ADONIS; BioBusiness; Biol. Abstr.; Chem. Abstr.; Chem. Titles; Curr. Biotechnol.; Curr. Contents Life Sci.; EMBASE; Int. Pharm. Abstr.; NAPRALERT; Life Sci. Collect.; PESTDOC; Protozoolog. Abstr.; Ref. Upd. Deluxe Ed.; Res. Alert [Full Cov.]; Rev. Med. Vet. Mycology; Sci. Cit. Index; SCISEARCH.

US/0272-4391
**DRUG DEVELOPMENT RESEARCH.** [Drug dev. res.]. Vol. 1, No. 1 (1981)-. Academic Scholarly Publication. English. Twelve times a year. $1,644.00 (US); $1,764.00 (Canada and Mexico); $1,809.00 (other). John Wiley & Sons, Inc., 605 Third Avenue, New York NY 10158-0012. **Tel** (212)850-6000, (212)850-6645, FAX (212)850-6088, telex 12-7063. **(Subscription address:** John Wiley & Sons / England, Baffins Lane, Chichester, West Sussex PO19 1UD England.**) ED** Harbans Lal and Stuart Fielding. **DD** 615. **NLM** W1 DR521CM. **CODEN** DDREDK. **[CCC]. Bk Rev. Pr Rev.** Documents available from The Genuine Article, BIOSIS Document Express, CASDDS, ADONIS.
**Desc:** Publishes original research reports and comprehensive reviews on systematic studies in pharmacology and toxicology, as related to the development of safe and efficacious drugs.
**Ind/Abst** ADONIS; Biol. Abstr.; Chem. Abstr.; Chem. Titles; CSA Neuro. Abstr.; Curr. Aware. Biol. Sci., CABS; Curr. Contents Life Sci.; EMBASE; Int. Pharm. Abstr.; NAPRALERT; Life Sci. Collect.; PESTDOC; Ref. Upd. Deluxe Ed.; Res. Alert [Full Cov.]; Sci. Cit. Index; SCISEARCH; Soc. Sci. Cit. Index [Select. Cov.].

US
**DRUG EVALUATIONS ANNUAL : DE / PREPARED BY THE DEPARTMENT OF DRUGS, DIVISION OF DRUGS AND TOXICOLOGY, AMERICAN MEDICAL ASSOCIATION. Added/Corp** American Medical Association. Division of Drugs and Technology. **VFOAT** DE; DE Annual. (1991)-. English. an (Dec.). $98.95 (hardbound). American Medical Association, 515 North State Street, Chicago IL 60610. **Tel** (312)464-5000, (800)262-2350, FAX (312)464-5831. **(Subscription address:** American Medical Association, PO Box 109050, Chicago IL 60610.**) LC** RM300; .D772. **NLM** QV 740; AA1 A17. ***Continues*** *Drug Evaluations, 0898-7467.*

CN/1184-695X
**DRUG FACT SHEET.** [Drug fact sheet]. **Added/Corp** New Brunswick. Prescription Drug Program. No. 1 (Jan. 1991)-. English. **DD** 615.

US/0277-9714
**DRUG FACTS AND COMPARISONS.** [Drug facts comp.]. **VFOAT** Facts and Comparisons. (1982)-. English. an. $99.50 (hardbound) US; $124.50 (hardbound) other. Facts and Comparisons Inc, 111 West Port Plaza, Suite 400, St Louis MO 63146-3098. **Tel** (314)878-2515, (800)223-0554, FAX (314)878-5563. **LC** RM300; .F33. **DD** 615/.1. **NLM** QV 772 D7924. ***Continues*** *Facts and Comparisons (Annual Edition), 0162-1491.*

US/0160-6697
**DRUG FATE AND METABOLISM.** [Drug fate metab.]. **VFOAT** Drug Fate & Metabolism. Vol. 1 (1977)-. Academic Scholarly Publication. English. ir. Price varies per volume. Marcel Dekker Inc., 270 Madison Avenue, New York NY 10016. **Tel** (212)696-9000, (800)228-1160, FAX (212)685-4540, telex 421419. **(Subscription address:** Marcel Dekker Inc, PO Box 5017, Monticello NY 12701.**) ED** Edward R. Garrett and Jean L. Hirtz. **LC** RS189; .D78. **DD** 615/.7/05. **NLM** QV 38 D792. **CODEN** DFMED9. Documents available from CASDDS.
**Ind/Abst** Chem. Abstr.

US/0892-2373
**DRUG FILES, THE.** [Drug files]. **VFOAT** Drug Files. Vol. 1, No. 1 (Feb. 1987)-. Periodical. English. mo. Free to center subscribers, $10.00 other. St Louis Drug Information Center, 4588 Parkview Place, ST Louis MO 63110. **Tel** (314)454-8399. **DD** 615. ***Continues*** *Drug Therapy Report, 0739-5248.*

●US/1061-2335
**DRUG GMP REPORT.** [Drug GMP rep.]. **Added/Corp** Washington Business Information, Inc. (1992)-. English. Twelve times a year. $447.00 North America; $472.00 other. Washington Business Information Inc., 1117 North 19th Street, Suite 200, Arlington VA 22209. **Tel** (703)247-3433, (800)426-0416, FAX (703)247-3421. **ED** Dennis Melamed. **DD** 363. **[CCC].**

CN/0317-2627
**DRUG INDEX (TORONTO).** (DRUG INDEX.). Began with 1948 issue. Periodical. English. an. $7.74. Maclean Hunter Canada / Montreal, 1001 bvd. de Maisonneuve W., Montreal, Quebec H3A 3E1 Canada. **Tel** 514-845-5141, FAX 514-845-4302, telex 055-60604. **DD** 338.4/7/615102571. **UDC** 615.11(71).

NE/0921-2582
**DRUG-INDUCED DISORDERS.** [Drug-induc. disord.]. **VFOAT** Drug Induced Disorders. Vol. 1 (1985)-. Monographic series. English. Elsevier Science Publishers BV, PO Box 211, 1000 AE Amsterdam Netherlands. **Tel** 011 31 20 5803642, FAX 011 31 20 5862696, telex 15682. **LC** UNC. **NLM** W1; DR522H. **CODEN** DRDIER. Documents available from BIOSIS Document Express, CASDDS.
**Ind/Abst** Biol. Abstr.; Chem. Abstr.

US/0092-8615
**DRUG INFORMATION JOURNAL.** [Drug inf. j.]. **Added/Corp** Drug Information Association. Vol. 6 (Jan./June 1972)-. Academic Scholarly Publication. English. Four times a year. $65.00 (academic), $225.00 other. Drug Information Association, PO Box 3113, Maple Glen PA 19002. **Tel** (215)628-2288, FAX (215)641-1229. **ED** Thomas Teal. **LC** RM1; .D78. **DD** 615.1/05. **NLM** W1 DR523P. **CODEN** DGIJB9. **[CCC].** Index available in last issue of volume--attached. **Ad Acc. Circ:** 13,000. available on microfilm and microfiche from University Microfilms International (UMI). Documents available from CASDDS, ADONIS. ***Continues*** *Drug Information Bulletin, 0012-656X.*
**Desc:** The official publication of the Drug Information Association. Includes 30-40 articles in each issue dealing with all aspects of new drug development.
**Ind/Abst** ADONIS; Biol. Abstr.; Chem. Abstr.; Curr. Aware. Biol. Sci., CABS; EMBASE; Health Plan. Adminis.; Hospit. Health Admin. Index; Inf. Sci. Abstr.; Int. Pharm. Abstr.; Life Sci. Collect.; Risk Abstr.; Toxicol. Abstr.

US
**DRUG INTERACTION FACTS / THE MEDIPHOR EDITORIAL GROUP, DIVISION OF CLINICAL PHARMACOLOGY, STANFORD UNIVERSITY SCHOOL OF MEDICINE.** **Added/Corp** Mediphor Editorial Group (Stanford University). (1983)-. Periodical. English. qt. $89.95 (loose-leaf edtition) US; $112.50 (loose-leaf edition) other. Facts and Comparisons Inc, 111 West Port Plaza, Suite 400, St Louis MO 63146-3098. **Tel** (314)878-2515, (800)223-0554, FAX (314)878-5563. **DD** 615/.7045/05.
**Desc:** Comprehensive reference which includes information on drug interactions of clinical significance, as well as interactions which are suspected but unsubstantiated.

US/1041-5041
**DRUG INTERACTION PROGRAM FOR IBM-PC AND COMPATIBLES.** (DRUG INTERACTION PROGRAM FOR IBM-PC AND COMPATIBLES [COMPUTER FILE] / THE MEDICAL LETTER INC.). [Drug interact. program IBM-PC compat.]. **Added/Corp** Medical Letter, Inc. **VFOAT** Medical Letter on Drugs and Therapeutics Drug Interactions Program for the IBM-PC; Medical Letter Inc. Drug Interaction Program for IBM-PC and Compatibles; Drug Interactions Program. (June 1987)-. Periodical. English. an. $60.00. The Medical Letter Inc, 1000 Main Street, New Rochelle NY 10801. **Tel** (914)235-0500. **DD** 615.

US/1044-7083
**DRUG INTERACTIONS AND SIDE EFFECTS INDEX.** ***Title Change.*** [Drug interact. side eff. index]. **Added/Corp** Medical Economics Company. **VFOAT** Physicians' Desk Reference Drug Interactions and Side Effects Index; PDR Drug Interactions and Side Effects Index; PDR's Index of Drug Interactions and Side Effects. (1988)-(1992). English. an. Medical Economics Data, Five Paragon Drive, PO Box 27, Montvale NJ 07645. **Tel** (800)442-6657, (201)358-7200. **(Subscription address:** PO Box 10689, Des Moines, IA 50336**) ED** E Barnhart. **LC** RS75; .D78. **DD** 615/.704. **NLM** QV 772; P5781. available on diskette. ***Merged with*** *Indications Index, 1060-4057* ***to form*** *PDR Guide to Drug Interactions, Side Effects, Indications.*
**Desc:** Offers information to look up potential interactions by generic category and side effects listed by symptom.

US/1055-0186
**DRUG INTERACTIONS AND SIDE EFFECTS SYSTEM.** (DRUG INTERACTIONS AND SIDE EFFECTS SYSTEM [COMPUTER FILE].). [Drug interact. side eff. syst.]. **VFOAT** PDR Drug Interactions and Side Effects System; Drug Interactions and Side Effects Diskettes. (1989)-. English. Three times a year. $219.00, $159.00 (interactions and side effects only). Medical Economic Data, PO Box 824, Mahwah NJ 07430. **DD** 615.

US/0271-8707
**DRUG INTERACTIONS NEWSLETTER.** (DRUG INTERACTIONS NEWSLETTER / PHILIP D. HANSTEN.). [Drug interact. newsl.]. Vol. 1 No. 1 (1980)-. Periodical. English. Four times a year (Jan., apr., July, Oct.). $80.00 US; $90.00 other. Applied Therapeutics Inc., PO Box 5077, Vancouver WA 98668. **Tel** (206)253-7123, FAX (206)253-8475. **ED** Philip D. Hansten and John R. Horn. **NLM** W1 DR525. **CODEN** DINEE2. **Circ:** 10,000 (ctrl). Documents available from BIOSIS Document Express.
**Desc:** Provides current information for those who need to know the clinical implications of drug interactions. Analyzes reported interactions and assesses their significance.
**Ind/Abst** Biol. Abstr. (1984-1988); Int. Pharm. Abstr.

NZ/0114-2402
**DRUG INVESTIGATION.** [Drug investig.]. Vol. 1, No. 1 (Oct. 1989)-. Academic Scholarly Publication. English. mo (12 issues). 220.00F Europe; $150.00 other. ADIS International Ltd, 41 Centorian Drive, Private Bag 65901, Mairangi Bay, Auckland 10 New Zealand. **Tel** 011 64 9 4798100, FAX 011 64 9 4791418. **(Subscription address:** Japan Publications Trading Company, Ltd., PO Box 5030, Tokyo International, Tokyo 100-31 Japan.**) LC** RM301.27; .D78. **DD** 615/.1901/05. **NLM** W1; DR5255. **CODEN** DRUIEA. **Pr Rev.** Documents available from The Genuine Article, BIOSIS Document Express.
**Desc:** Committed to the rapid publication of peer-reviewed original research. Aims to assist in the dissemination of original findings from all aspects of drug research - both animal and human.
**Ind/Abst** Biol. Abstr. (1991-); Curr. Contents Clin. Med.; EMBASE; Int. Pharm. Abstr.; PESTDOC; Res. Alert [Select. Cov.]; SCISEARCH.

UK
**DRUG LAUNCHES.** Trade Publication. English. mo. £2,500.00. IMS World Publications Ltd, 7 Harwodd Avenue, london NW1 6JB England. **Tel** 011 44 71 393 5000, FAX 011 44 393 5900. available on CD-ROM.
**Desc:** Covers information on pharmaceutical introductions in 60 countries from 1982 to the present.

UK
**DRUG LICENSE OPPORTUNITIES.** ***Title Change.*** (19??)-(19??). English. wk. IMSWorld Publications Ltd, 11-13 Melton Street, London NW1 2EH England. **Tel** 01387 9880, FAX 388 0036, telex 295526. ***Continued by*** *R&D Focus.*

CN/0012-6586
**DRUG MERCHANDISING.** ***Title Change.*** [Drug merch.]. Vol. 6 (1925)-(19??). Periodical. English. mo. MacLean Hunter Ltd. Business Publishers / Canada, Box 9100, Station A, Toronto ONT M5W 1A5 Canada. **Tel** (416)946-8420, (800)567-0444. **NLM** W1 DR533. available on microfilm from University Microfilms International (UMI). ***Continues*** *Druggists' Weekly.* ***Continued by*** *Pharmacist News.*
**Ind/Abst** Int. Pharm. Abstr.

US/0090-9556
**DRUG METABOLISM AND DISPOSITION.** (DRUG METABOLISM AND DISPOSITION : THE BIOLOGICAL FATE OF CHEMICALS.). [Drug metab. dispos.]. **Added/Corp** American Society for Pharmacology and Experimental Therapeutics. Vol. 1 (Jan./Feb. 1973)-. Academic Scholarly Publication. English. bm. $140.00 (institution) $85.00 (individual), US; $105.00 (individual), $160.00 (institution) other. Williams & Wilkins Company, 428 East Preston Street, Baltimore MD 21202-3993. **Tel** (410)528-4000, (800)638-6423, FAX (410)528-8596, telex 87669. **(Subscription address:** Williams & Wilkins,

PO Box 64380, Baltimore MD 21264.) **ED** Vincent G. Zannoni. **LC** RM301; .D75. **DD** 615/.7/05. **NLM** W1; DR533M. **CODEN** DMDSAI. **[CCC]**. **Ad Acc. Pr Rev. Circ:** 1,200. available on microfilm. Documents available from The Genuine Article, BIOSIS Document Express, CASDDS, Quick Copies.
**Desc:** The official journal of The American Society for Pharmacology and Experimental Therapeutics, Inc. Covers metabolism of pharmacologist agents or drugs and environmental chemicals, reactants, and preservatives for pharmacologists, toxicologists, and medicinal chemists.
**Ind/Abst** AGRICOLA [Select. Cov.]; Anal. Abstr.; BioBusiness (19??-1990); Biol. Abstr.; Chem. Abstr.; Chem. Titles; CSA Neuro. Abstr. (?-?); Curr. Contents Life Sci.; Dairy Sci. Abstr.; EMBASE; Energy Res. Abstr. (Feb. 1976-); Health Plan. Adminis.; Helminthol. Abstr.; Index Med.; INIS Atomindex [Micro.]; Iowa Drug Inf. Serv.; Nutr. Abstr. Rev., Ser. B, Live Feeds and Feed.; Nutr. Abstr. Rev., Ser. A, Hum. Exp.; Life Sci. Collect.; PESTDOC; Pig News Inf.; Protozoolog. Abstr.; Ref. Upd. Basic Ed.; Ref. Upd. Deluxe Ed.; Res. Alert [Full Cov.]; Rev. Med. Vet. Entomol.; Rev. Med. Vet. Mycology; Sci. Cit. Index; SCISEARCH; SportSearch.

US/0199-7912
**DRUG METABOLISM NEWSLETTER.** [Drug metab. newsl.]. **Added/Corp** American Society for Pharmacology and Experimental Therapeutics. Drug Metabolism Division. (19??)-. Newsletter. English. Four times a year. $5.00 US; $7.00 other. American Society for Pharmaceutical and Experimental Therapeutics, 9650 Rockville Pike, Bethesda MD 20814. **Tel** (301)530-7060. **ED** Mitchell Cayen.

US/0360-2532
**DRUG METABOLISM REVIEWS (SOFTCOVER ED.).** (DRUG METABOLISM REVIEWS.). [Drug metab. rev.]. Vol. 1 (1972)-. Academic Scholarly Publication. English. qt. $885.00 US; $899.00 other. Marcel Dekker Inc., 270 Madison Avenue, New York NY 10016. **Tel** (212)696-9000, (800)228-1160, FAX (212)685-4540, telex 421419. **(Subscription address:** Marcel Dekker Inc, PO Box 5017, Monticello NY 12701.) **ED** Frederick J. Di Carlo. **DD** 615. **CODEN** DMTRAR. **[CCC]. Pr Rev.** available on microfiche. Documents available from The Genuine Article, BIOSIS Document Express, CASDDS, ADONIS.
**Desc:** This in-depth, authoritative journal consistently provides critically needed reviews of an impressive array of drug metabolism research. Topics include: established, new, and potential drugs; environmentally toxic chemicals; absorption; metabolism and excretion; and enzymology of all living species. Moreover, 'Drug Metabolism Reviews' offers new hypotheses vital to medicine and toxicology.
**Ind/Abst** ADONIS; AGRICOLA [Select. Cov.]; Biol. Abstr.; Chem. Abstr.; Curr. Aware. Biol. Sci., CABS; Curr. Contents Life Sci.; Dairy Sci. Abstr.; EMBASE; Energy Res. Abstr. (April 1982-); Index Med.; Index Sci. Rev. [Full Cov.]; Index Vet.; Int. Pharm. Abstr.; Nutr. Abstr. Rev., Ser. A, Hum. Exp.; Life Sci. Collect.; PESTDOC; Protozoolog. Abstr.; Ref. Upd. Deluxe Ed.; Res. Alert [Full Cov.]; Rev. Agric. Entomol.; Sci. Cit. Index; SCISEARCH; Vet. Bull.

SP/0214-0934
**DRUG NEWS & PERSPECTIVES.** [Drug news perspect.]. **VFOAT** Drug News and Perspectives; NB : Drug News & Perspectives. Vol. 1, No. 1 (March 1988)-. Periodical. English. ir. $600.00. Prous Science Publishers, Apartado de Correos 540, 08080 Barcelona Spain. **Tel** 011 34 3 4592220, FAX 011 34 3 4581535. **ED** J. R. Prous. **NLM** W1; DR539. **CODEN** DNPEED. **[CCC]**. Index available. cum. index. **Bk Rev. Ad Acc. Circ:** 15,000. Documents available from BIOSIS Document Express.
**Desc:** International drug news magazine designed for top management and scientific personnel in the pharmaceutical industry, regulatory agencies and academia.
**Ind/Abst** Bibliogr. Mission. (1989-); BioBusiness; Biol. Abstr. (1988-); EMBASE; F&S Index Plus Text, Int. [Select. Cov.]; Int. Pharm. Abstr.; PROMT.

US/0731-5163
**DRUG NEWSLETTER (ST. LOUIS, MO.).** (DRUG NEWSLETTER / FACTS AND COMPARISONS.). [Drug newsl.]. **VFOAT** Facts and Comparisons Drug Newsletter. Vol. 1, No. 1 (April 1982)-. Newsletter. English. mo. $59.50 US; $67.50 other. Facts and Comparisons Inc, 111 West Port Plaza, Suite 400, St Louis MO 63146-3098. **Tel** (314)878-2515, (800)223-0554, FAX (314)878-5563.
**Desc:** Summarizes information on new findings and recent developments in drug therapy, new drugs and drug products, OTC drug products, etc.

US/0272-3530
**DRUG-NUTRIENT INTERACTIONS.** ***Ceased.*** [Drug-nutr. interact.]. Ceased Vol. 5 (1987). Academic Scholarly Publication. English. qt. John Wiley & Sons, Inc., 605 Third Avenue, New York NY 10158-0012. **Tel** (212)850-6000, (212)850-6645, FAX (212)850-6088, telex 12-7063. **(Subscription address:** John Wiley & Sons / England, Baffins Lane, Chichester, West Sussex PO19 1UD England.) **ED** Daphne A Roe. **LC** RM302.4; .D78. **DD** 615/.7045. **CODEN** DNIND4. **[CCC]**. Documents available from BIOSIS Document Express, CASDDS.
**Ind/Abst** Biol. Abstr.; Chem. Abstr.; EMBASE; Health Plan. Adminis.; Index Med. (Vol. 1, No. 1, 1982-Vol. 5, No. 4, 1987); Int. Pharm. Abstr.; Life Sci. Collect.

CN/0836-6314
**DRUG PROTOCOL.** ***Suspended.*** [Drug protoc.]. Vol. 1, No. 1 (Oct. 1986)-Suspended iwth Vol. 4, No. 6 (1990). Periodical. English. mo. Limited free distribution to primary care physicisns, $40.00 others. Trimel Corporation, 5915 Airport Road/Suite 700, Mississauga Ontario L4V 1T1 Canada. **DD** 615.5/8. **NLM** W1; DR514C.
**Ind/Abst** Int. Pharm. Abstr.

●US
**DRUG RESISTANCE WEEKLY.** (1993)-. English. Forty-eight times a year. $995.00 US, Canada and Mexico; $1,195.00 other. CW Henderson, PO Box 5528, Atlanta GA 30307-0528. **Tel** (404)377-8895, FAX (404)378-5411. **(Subscription address:** CW Henderson, Subscription Office, PO Box 830409, Birmingham AL 35283-0409.)
**Desc:** Concentrates on therapeutic drug resistance in disease treatments as well as symptom relief from illness. Topics include the effects of drug resistance in prevention, diagnosis and treatment of the disease, the degree of drug immunity measured in clinical trial results and multiple drug resistance.

NZ/0114-5916
**DRUG SAFETY.** (DRUG SAFETY : AN INTERNATIONAL JOURNAL OF MEDICAL TOXICOLOGY AND DRUG EXPERIENCE.). [Drug safety]. Vol. 5, No. 1 (Jan./Feb. 1990)-. Academic Scholarly Publication. English. mo (12 iaaues). 920.00F Europe; $575.00 other. ADIS International Ltd, 41 Centorian Drive, Private Bag 65901, Mairangi Bay, Auckland 10 New Zealand. **Tel** 011 64 9 4798100, FAX 011 64 9 4791418. **(Subscription address:** Japan Publications Trading Company, Ltd., PO Box 5030, Tokyo International, Tokyo 100-31 Japan.) **ED** Rennie C. Heel, Roderick H. Sayce, Eugene M. Sorkin, and Paul C. Jinks. **NLM** W1; DR607S. **CODEN** DRSAEA. **[CCC]**. Documents available from The Genuine Article, CASDDS. ***Continues*** *Medical Toxicology and Adverse Drug Experience, 0112-5966.*
**Desc:** Reflects the need to extend the existing editorial coverage to include: avoidance of adverse reactions, postmarketing surveillance, and quality of life studies.
**Ind/Abst** Chem. Abstr. (1990-); Curr. Aware. Biol. Sci., CABS; Curr. Contents Clin. Med.; EMBASE; Health Plan. Adminis.; Index Med. (1990-); Int. Pharm. Abstr.; PESTDOC; Res. Alert [Select. Cov.]; Rev. Med. Vet. Mycology; SCISEARCH; Soc. Sci. Cit. Index [Select. Cov.]; Weed Abstr.

US/0277-3716
**DRUG STORE MARKET GUIDE.** [Drug store mark. guide]. **VFOAT** Drugstore Market Guide. (1981)-. Periodical. English. an. $269.00. Drug Store Market Guide, 1739 Horton Avenue, Mohegan Lake NY 10547. **Tel** (914)528-7147, FAX (914)528-1369. **ED** Melanie Buse. **LC** HD9666.3; .D78. **DD** 381/.456151/02573.
**Desc:** A market-by-market analysis of the chain and wholesale drug store industry to help manufacturers and other suppliers sell more to drug stores.

US/0191-7587
**DRUG STORE NEWS.** [Drug store news]. (Jan. 8, 1979)-. Periodical. English. Twenty-three times a year. $45.00 (manufacturers), $95.00 (other) (nontrade) US and Canada; $19.50 (pharmacists in retail & wholesale) (trade) US and Canada; $125.00 other. Lebhar Friedman Inc., 3922 Coconut Palm Drive, Tampa FL 33619. **Tel** (800)927-9292, (813)664-6707. **ED** Bruce Buckly. **LC** HD9666.1; .D74. **DD** 381/.45/61510973. **[CCC]. Ad Acc. Circ:** 41,537. available on microfilm and microfiche from University Microfilms International (UMI); available on an online database (files 16,570,648/Full-Text) from DIALOG. ***Absorbed*** *Chain Store Age.*
**Desc:** Provides reportage on pharmaceutical developments for sighted technology in operational and financial news.
**Ind/Abst** F&S Index Plus Text, Int. [Full Txt.] [Select. Cov.]; Infobank (Jan. 1979-); Mark. Advert. Ref. Serv. [Full Txt.]; PROMT (Jan. 1979-) [Full Txt.]; Stat. Ref. Index; Trade Ind. ASAP [Full Txt.]; Trade Ind. Index [Full Txt.].

US/1055-2952
**DRUG STORE NEWS FOR THE PHARMACIST.** [Drug store news pharm.]. **VFOAT** Journal of Retail Pharmacy. Vol. 1 No. 1 (Jan. 21, 1991)-. Periodical. English. mo. Free on request (trade); $36.00 (nontrade) US; $65.00 (nontrade) Canada; $125.00 (nontrade) other. Lebhar Friedman Inc., 3922 Coconut Palm Drive, Tampa FL 33619. **Tel** (800)927-9292, (813)664-6707. **LC** HD9666.1; .D88. **DD** 615. ***Continues*** *Drug Store News, Inside Pharmacy, 0891-9828.*
**Desc:** Mixes national news with longer news features and columns targeted to pharmacists.

US/0891-9828
**DRUG STORE NEWS, INSIDE PHARMACY.** ***Title Change.*** [Drug store news inside pharm.]. **VFOAT** Inside Pharmacy. (July 1986)-?. Periodical. English. mo. Lebhar Friedman Inc., 3922 Coconut Palm Drive, Tampa FL 33619. **Tel** (800)927-9292, (813)664-6707. **(Subscription address:** 3922 Coconut Palm Drive, Tampa, FL 33619) **ED** Harold Cohen and Diane Sterne. **DD** 615. **Ad Acc. Circ:** 56,537 (ctrl). ***Continued by*** *Drug Store News for the Pharmacist, 1055-2952.*
**Desc:** Edited for chains, volume independents, pharmacies, pharmaceutical buyers and professional directors of drug at supermarket, discount and combo chains with pharmacies. It features an ACPE accredited continuing education program.

US
**DRUG STORE NEWS. REFERENCE FOR PHARMACY PRACTICE.** **VFOAT** Reference for Pharmacy Practice. 1979-. English. bw. $14.00. Lebhar Friedman Inc., 3922 Coconut Palm Drive, Tampa FL 33619. **Tel** (800)927-9292, (813)664-6707. **(Subscription address:** 3922 Coconut Palm Drive, Tampa, FL 33619) ***Continues*** *Chain Store Age.*

UK/0952-0317
**DRUG TARGETING.** [Drug target.]. (1988)-. Periodical. English. bw. £115.00. SUBIS, Mansion House, 19 Kingfield Road, Sheffield S11 9AS England. **Tel** 011 44 114 255 4433, FAX 011 44 114 255 4626. **Bk Rev. Ad Acc.**
**Desc:** Current awareness service for researchers and clinicians.

US/0163-1705
**DRUG THERAPEUTICS.** 1979-. Academic Scholarly Publication. English. an. Elsevier Science Publishing Company Inc, Madison Square Station, PO Box 882, New York NY 10159-0882. **Tel** (212)633-3950, FAX (212)633-3990. **LC** RM260; .D77. **DD** 615/.58/05. **NLM** W1 DR609.
**Ind/Abst** Health Plan. Adminis.; Index Med. (1982-).

US/0882-6684
**DRUG THERAPY TOPICS.** (DRUG THERAPY TOPICS / DEPARTMENT OF PHARMACY SERVICES, UNIVERSITY HOSPITAL/HARBORVIEW MEDICAL CENTER.). [Drug ther. top.]. **Added/Corp** University of Washington. Drug Information Service. University of Washington. Hospital. Dept. of Pharmacy Services. University of Washington/Harborview Medical Center Drug Information Center. (19??)-. Periodical. English. mo. $10.00. Drug Information Center University of Washington, 1959 Northeast Pacific Street RC-32, Seattle WA 98195. **ED** Nelda Murri. **DD** 615. **Bk Rev. Ad Acc. Pr Rev. Circ:** 1,930.
**Desc:** Newsletter containing information on the use of medications and the treatment of disease. Also, contains news items regarding the University of Washington Pharmacy and P & T Committee.

US/1055-2057
**DRUG THERAPY (WALTHAM, MASS.).** (DRUG THERAPY.). [Drug ther.]. Vol. 8 (1991)-. Monographic series. English. ir. $52.95. New England Journal of Medicine, 1440 Main Street, Waltham MA 02154-1649. **Tel** (617)893-3800, (800)843-6356, FAX (617)647-5785, telex 5106015660 NEJM BOS UQ. **DD** 615. ***Continues*** *Articles from the New England Journal of Medicine on Drug Therapy.*

US/0012-6616
**DRUG TOPICS.** [Drug top.]. Vol. 1-56, No. 52, (1883)-(Dec. 23, 1940); Vol. 85 (Jan. 6, 1941)-. Periodical. English. Twenty-three times a year. $58.00 US; $104.00 other. Medical Economics Publishing, Five Paragon Drive, Second Floor, Montvale NJ 07645. **Tel** (800)432-4570, (201)358-2210. **(Subscription address:** Medical Economics Publishing, 120 Cross Street, Winchester MA 01890.) **ED** Val Cardinale. **NLM** W1 DR611. **CODEN** DGTNA7. **[CCC]. Ad Acc. Circ:** 85,000 (ctrl). available on microfilm; available on an online database (files 15,648/Full-Text) from DIALOG. Documents available from UMI Article Clearinghouse. ***Absorbed*** *Druggist Circular.*
**Desc:** Latest ideas, trends and developments affecting the pharmacy field. Includes merchandising, government affairs, management, and clinical news.
**Ind/Abst** ABI/INFORM Glob. Ed.; ABI Inform Ondisc (April 1974-); Acad. Search (July 1993-); BioBusiness; Bus. ASAP (1990-) [Full Txt.]; Bus. Index (1985-); Bus. Period. Index; F&S Index Plus Text, Int. [Select. Cov.]; Gen. BusinessFile (1985-); Gen. Period. Index (1985-); Health Ref. Cent. (1987-) [Full Txt.] [Select. Cov.]; INFO-SOUTH Abstr.; Int. Pharm. Abstr.; Mag. Search; PROMT; Trade Ind. ASAP [Full Txt.]; Trade Ind. Index (1981-) [Full Txt.]; UMI ABI/Inform--Bus. Period. Ondisc [Full Txt.]; Wilson Bus. Abstr.

US
**DRUG TOPICS RED BOOK.** ***Title Change.*** **Added/Corp** Topics Publishing Company. Medical Economics Company. **VFOAT** Drug Topics Redbook; Red Book. (1945)-(1992). English. an. Medical Economics Data, Five Paragon Drive, PO Box 27, Montvale NJ 07645. **Tel** (800)442-6657, (201)358-7200. **NLM** QV 772; D794. ***Continues*** *Drug Topics Price Book.* ***Continued by*** *Red Book (Montvale, N.J.).*

US/0731-8596
**DRUG TOPICS REDBOOK UPDATE.** ***Title Change.*** [Drug top. redbook update]. **Added/Corp** Medical Economics Company. **VFOAT** Redbook Update; Red Book Update; Drug Topics Red Book Update;

Update. Vol. 1, No. 1 (Dec. 1981)-(19??). English. mo. Medical Economics Data, Five Paragon Drive, PO Box 27, Montvale NJ 07645. **Tel** (800)442-6657, (201)358-7200. **LC** Discard. cum. index. **Bk Rev. Ad Acc. Circ:** 8,100 (ctrl). ***Continued by*** *Red Book Update.*

US/0897-1757
**DRUG UTILIZATION IN THE U.S.** [Drug util. U. S.]. **Added/Corp** United States. Food and Drug Administration. Drug Use Analysis Branch. National Center for Drugs and Biologics (U.S.). Drug Use Analysis Branch. **VFOAT** Drug Utilization; Annual Review of Drug Utilization. **VAT** Drug Utilization in the United States. 1st Annual Review (1979)-. English. an. $25.50. US Food and Drug Administration / FDA, 5600 Fishers Lane, Room 14-71, Rockville MD 20857. **Tel** (301)443-2410, FAX (301)443-0755. **(Subscription address:** National Technical Information Service, 5285 Port Royal Road, Springfield, VA 22161**)** **DD** 615.

US/0884-8521
**DRUG UTILIZATION REVIEW. *Ceased.*** [Drug util. rev.]. Vol. 1, No. 1 (Jan. 1985)-(Dec. 1994). Periodical. English. mo. American Health Consultants, 3525 Piedmont Road, Suite 400, Atlanta GA 30305. **Tel** (800)688-2421, (404)262-7436. **DD** 615. **NLM** W1; DR892E.
**Ind/Abst** Cumul. Index Nurs. Allied Health Lit.

NZ/1170-229X
**DRUGS & AGING.** **VFOAT** Drugs and Aging. Vol. 1, No. 1 (Jan. 1991)-. Periodical. English. mo (12 issues). 585.00F (individuals), 940.00F (institutions) Europe; $370.00 (individuals), $595.00 (institutions) other. ADIS International Ltd, 41 Centorian Drive, Private Bag 65901, Mairangi Bay, Auckland 10 New Zealand. **Tel** 011 64 9 4798100, FAX 011 64 9 4791418. **(Subscription address:** Japan Publications Trading Company, Ltd., PO Box 5030, Tokyo International, Tokyo 100-31 Japan.**)** **LC** RC953.7; .D775. **DD** 615.5/8/0846. **NLM** W1; DR458. **CODEN** DRAGE6. **[CCC].** Documents available from The Genuine Article.
**Ind/Abst** Curr. Aware. Biol. Sci., CABS; Curr. Contents Clin. Med.; Curr. Contents Life Sci.; Index Med. (Jan. 1991-); Int. Pharm. Abstr.; Res. Alert [Full Cov.]; Sci. Cit. Index; SCISEARCH; Soc. Sci. Cit. Index [Select. Cov.].

CN/0823-7786
**DRUGS & DEVICES.** (DRUGS & DEVICES / UNIVERSITY OF TORONTO, CONTINUING MEDICAL EDUCATION.). [Drugs devices]. **VFOAT** Drogues & Dispositifs. Vol. 1, No. 1 (May 1983)-. Periodical. English (French). qt. Continuing Medical Education Programme, 70 Bond Street Suite 200, Toronto Ontario M5B 1X3 Canada. **DD** 615/.1/05.

II/0250-6912
**DRUGS AND PHARMACEUTICALS, CURRENT HIGHLIGHTS (R & D).** [Drugs pharm., Curr. highlights]. **Added/Corp** National Information Centre for Drugs and Pharmaceuticals (India). (19??)-. English. mo. **NLM** ZQV 55 D7945.
**Ind/Abst** NAPRALERT.

II/0250-6920
**DRUGS AND PHARMACEUTICALS. INDUSTRY HIGHLIGHTS.** [Drugs pharm., Ind. highlights]. (1978)-. Periodical. English. mo. $60.00. **(Subscription address:** Prints India, 11 Darya Ganj, New Delhi 110002 India.**)** **UDC** 615.

US/0360-2583
**DRUGS AND THE PHARMACEUTICAL SCIENCES.** [Drugs pharm. sci.]. Vol. 1 (1975)-. Monographic series. English. ir. Price varies per volume. Marcel Dekker Inc., 270 Madison Avenue, New York NY 10016. **Tel** (212)696-9000, (800)228-1160, FAX (212)685-4540, telex 421419. **(Subscription address:** Marcel Dekker Inc, PO Box 5017, Monticello NY 12701.**)** **ED** J. Swarbrick. **NLM** W1 DR893B. **CODEN** DPHSDS. Documents available from CASDDS.
**Desc:** Each volume presents a different aspect of drugs and/or the pharmaceutical sciences. Topics covered include drug delivery, pharmacokinetics, and pharmaceutical statistics.
**Ind/Abst** Chem. Abstr.; Curr. Biotechnol.; Microbiol. Abstr. Sect. A.

CN/0705-291X
**DRUGS AND THERAPEUTICS FOR MARITIME PRACTITIONERS.** Vol. 1 (Jan. 1978)-. Periodical. English. bm. 15.00Can$. Dalhousie University / Department of Pharmacology, Halifax Nova Scotia B3H 4H7 Canada. **Tel** (902)494-3435. **ED** J D Gray and C B Tuttle. **DD** 615/.7/05. **Circ:** 5,100 (ctrl).
**Desc:** Reviews of the properties and clinical uses of drugs; their side effects and toxicities, reviews and guidelines for the approach to drug management of various disease states.

●NZ/1172-0360
**DRUGS & THERAPY PERSPECTIVES : FOR RATIONAL DRUG SELECTION AND USE.** **VFOAT** Drugs and Therapy Perspectives; Drugs & Therapy Perspectives for Rational Drug Selection and Use; Drugs and Therapy Perspectives for Rational Drug Selection and Use. (1993)-. English. sm (24 issues). 270.00F (institutions), 135.00F (individuals), 85.00F (students) Europe; $195.00 (institutions), $95.00 (individuals), $60.00 (students/residents) other. ADIS International Ltd, 41 Centorian Drive, Private Bag 65901, Mairangi Bay, Auckland 10 New Zealand. **Tel** 011 64 9 4798100, FAX 011 64 9 4791418. **(Subscription address:** Japan Publications Trading Company, Ltd., PO Box 5030, Tokyo International, Tokyo 100-31 Japan.**)**

●US/1066-7008
**DRUGS IN DEVELOPMENT.** (1993)-. Periodical. English. qt. $195.00 (institutions). Neva Press, PO Box 347, Branford CT 06405. **Tel** (203)272-5338, FAX (203)272-5338.

US/0897-6112
**DRUGS IN PREGNANCY AND LACTATION.** [Drugs pregnancy lact.]. 1st Ed. (1983)-. English. qt. $49.00 (individual), $79.00 (institution) US; $58.00 (individual), $100.00 (institution) other. Williams & Wilkins Company, 428 East Preston Street, Baltimore MD 21202-3993. **Tel** (410)528-4000, (800)638-6423, FAX (410)528-8596, telex 87669. **(Subscription address:** Williams & Wilkins, PO Box 64380, Baltimore MD 21264.**)** **ED** Gerald G. Briggs. **LC** RG627.6.D79; D798. **DD** 618.3/2071. **NLM** WQ 39; B854d. Documents available from Quick Copies.
**Desc:** Contains new information on prescription and OTC drugs in the monograph format of the parent text.

CN/0824-7102
**DRUGS IN PSYCHIATRY (POINTE-CLAIRE).** (DRUGS IN PSYCHIATRY.). Vol. 1, No. 1 (1982)-. Periodical. English. sm. 50.00Can$. STA Communications Inc., 955 St. John Boulevard, Suite 306, Pt Claire, Quebec H9R 5K3 Canada. **Tel** (514)695-7623. **ED** Paul Brand. **DD** 615/.78. Index available. **Ad Acc. Circ:** 2,600 (ctrl). Documents available from CASDDS.
**Desc:** Drug reference manuals.
**Ind/Abst** Chem. Abstr.

US/0739-8824
**DRUGS IN RESEARCH.** (DRUGS IN RESEARCH [MICROFORM] / PAUL DEHAEN INFORMATION SYSTEMS, A DIVISION OF MICROMEDEX, INC.). [Drugs res.]. **Added/Corp** Paul deHaen Information Systems. (197?)-. Periodical. English. bm (6 issues). $795.00. Paul de Haen International, 2750 South Shoshone Street, Englewood CO 80110. **Tel** (800)438-0296, FAX (303)789-2534. **NLM** QV 772 D3215. available on microfiche. ***Continues*** *De Haen Drugs in Research.*

GW/0012-6683
**DRUGS MADE IN GERMANY.** [Drugs made Ger.]. Vol. 1 (1958)-. Academic Scholarly Publication. English. qt. DM45.00. Editio Cantor, Postfach 1255, D 88322 Aulendorf Germany. **Tel** 011 49 7525 9400, FAX 011 49 7525 9401. **ED** Viktor Schramm. **LC** RS1; .D78. **NLM** W1 DR894. **CODEN** DRMGAS. **[CCC]. Bk Rev. Ad Acc. Circ:** 5,500 (ctrl). Documents available from BIOSIS Document Express, CASDDS.
**Desc:** Technical periodical for pharmaceutical production and marketing of special preparations, as well as raw materials, elements, auxiliary materials, chemicals and diagnostic materials.
**Ind/Abst** Bibliogr. Mission.; BioBusiness; Biol. Abstr.; Chem. Abstr.; EMBASE; Int. Pharm. Abstr.; PESTDOC.

US/0012-6667
**DRUGS (NEW YORK, N.Y.).** (DRUGS.). [Drugs]. Vol. 1 (1971)-. Academic Scholarly Publication. English. mo (12 issues). $845.00 North & South America; 1360.00F Europe; $845.00 other. ADIS International Ltd, 41 Centorian Drive, Private Bag 65901, Mairangi Bay, Auckland 10 New Zealand. **Tel** 011 64 9 4798100, FAX 011 64 9 4791418. **(Subscription address:** Japan Publications Trading Company, Ltd., PO Box 5030, Tokyo International, Tokyo 100-31 Japan.**)** **ED** Rennie C. Heel. **LC** RM1; .D8. **DD** 615/.1/05. **NLM** W1 DR892G. **CODEN** DRUGAY. **[CCC].** cum. index. **Pr Rev. Circ:** 3,000. Documents available from The Genuine Article, BIOSIS Document Express, CASDDS.
**Desc:** A key reference journal for libraries with evaluations of new drugs, coverage of practical therapeutics, review articles, selected summaries, guide charts and tables on efficiency, the properties, and hazards of drugs.
**Ind/Abst** Biol. Abstr.; Chem. Abstr.; Curr. Contents Clin. Med.; Curr. Contents Life Sci.; EMBASE; Health Plan. Adminis.; Index Med.; Int. Pharm. Abstr.; Med. Abstr. Newsl.; Life Sci. Collect.; PESTDOC; Ref. Upd. Basic Ed.; Ref. Upd. Deluxe Ed.; Res. Alert [Full Cov.]; Rev. Med. Vet. Mycology; Sci. Cit. Index; SCISEARCH; Soc. Sci. Cit. Index [Select. Cov.].

US/0070-7406
**DRUGS OF CHOICE. *Ceased.*** [Drugs choice]. (1958/59)-Ceased (1984/85). English. be. Mosby Year Book Inc., 11830 Westline Industrial Drive, St Louis MO 63146. **Tel** (800)325-4177, (314)872-8370, FAX (314)432-1380, telex 44-2402. **ED** W Modell. **LC** RM101; .D75. **NLM** W1 DR895. **CODEN** DRCHAF. Documents available from CASDDS.
**Ind/Abst** Chem. Abstr.

US/1065-6596
**DRUGS OF CHOICE FROM THE MEDICAL LETTER.** [Drugs choice Med. Lett.]. **VFOAT** Drugs of Choice; Medical Letter on Drugs and Therapeutics. (1977)-. English. be. $11.50. The Medical Letter Inc, 1000 Main Street, New Rochelle NY 10801. **Tel** (914)235-0500. **DD** 615.

SP/0377-8282
**DRUGS OF THE FUTURE.** [Drugs future]. Vol. 1 (Jan. 1976)-. Periodical. English. mo. $900.00. Prous Science Publishers, Apartado de Correos 540, 08080 Barcelona Spain. **Tel** 011 34 3 4592220, FAX 011 34 3 4581535. **ED** J. R. Prous. **LC** RM1; .D83. **DD** 615/.1/05. **NLM** W1 DR897. **CODEN** DRFUD4. **[CCC].** Index available. cum. index. **Ad Acc. Circ:** 3,000. available on diskette; available on an online database; available in microform. Documents available from BIOSIS Document Express.
**Desc:** Tracing drugs from the first phases of development up to their marketing. Provides essential information in comprehensive monograph form.
**Ind/Abst** BioBusiness; Biol. Abstr.; EMBASE; Int. Pharm. Abstr.; NAPRALERT.

UK/0964-8313
**DRUGS PREVENTION INITIATIVE PROGRESS REPORT / HOME OFFICE ; [PREPARED BY THE HOME OFFICE CENTRAL DRUGS PREVENTION UNIT].** **Added/Corp** Great Britain. Home Office. Central Drugs Prevention Unit. **VFOAT** Progress Report. (1991)-. English. **LC** WMLC 91/4457.

SP/0378-6501
**DRUGS UNDER EXPERIMENTAL AND CLINICAL RESEARCH.** [Drugs exp. clin. res.]. Vol. 1 (April 1977)-. Academic Scholarly Publication. English (French; summaries and/or abstracts in French). bm. 412.00F Europe; 425.00F other. Bioscience Ediprint Inc, rue Alexandre Gavard 16, 1227 Carouge Geneva Switzerland. **Tel** 011 41 22 3003383. **NLM** W1 DR897N. **CODEN** DECRDP. **[CCC]. Pr Rev.** available on microfilm and microfiche from University Microfilms International (UMI). Documents available from The Genuine Article, CASDDS.
**Ind/Abst** Chem. Abstr.; CSA Neuro. Abstr. (?-?); Curr. Aware. Biol. Sci., CABS; Curr. Contents Eng. Tech. Appl. Sci.; EMBASE; Health Plan. Adminis.; Helminthol. Abstr.; Index Med.; Int. Pharm. Abstr.; Microbiol. Abstr. Sect. B; Microbiol. Abstr. Sect. A; NAPRALERT; Life Sci. Collect.; PESTDOC; Protozoolog. Abstr.; Res. Alert [Full Cov.]; Rev. Med. Vet. Mycology; Sci. Cit. Index; SCISEARCH.

VM
**DUC HOC.** **Added/Corp** Vietnam (Democratic Republic). Bo y Te. (19??)-. Periodical. Vietnamese. mo. Bo Y Te, 7 Trinh Hoai Duc, Ha-Noi Vietnam. **LC** RM1; .D9.

II/0012-8872
**EASTERN PHARMACIST.** Periodical. English. mo. $60.00. Eastern Pharmacist, 507 Ashok Bhawan, 93 Nehru Place, New Delhi 110 024 India. **Tel** 6433315. **(Subscription address:** Prints India, 11 Darya Ganj, New Delhi 110002 India.**)** **ED** Mohan C Bazaz. **Bk Rev. Ad Acc. Circ:** 5,000. Documents available from CASDDS.
**Desc:** Pharmaceutical subjects and medical information.
**Ind/Abst** Chem. Abstr.; Int. Pharm. Abstr.

CN/0821-7785
**ECHO (OTTAWA. 1977).** (ECHO / OTTAWA VALLEY REGIONAL DRUG INFORMATION CENTRE.). [Echo]. **VFOAT** Echo. Periodical. English (French). $90.00. Ottawa Valley Regional Drug Information Service, 501 Smyth, Ottawa Ontario K1H 8L6 Canada. **Tel** (613)737-9347, FAX (613)737-8951. **DD** 615.5/8/05.

IT
**EDIMED.** Org Edit Medico Farmaceutica, CP 10434, 20110 Milan Italy. **Tel** 011 39 2 675051.

UA/0301-5068
**EGYPTIAN JOURNAL OF PHARMACEUTICAL SCIENCES.** [Egypt. j. pharm. sci.]. **Added/Corp** Markaz al-Qawmi Lil-Ilam Wa-al-Tawthiq. Jamiyah al-Saydaliyah al-Misriyah. **VFOAT** Majallah Al-Misriyah Lil-Ulum Al-Saydaliyah. Vol. 13 (1972)-. Periodical. English (summaries and/or abstracts in Arabic). ir. $82.00. National Information & Documentation Center, A1-Tahrir St Dokki AGWAF, Cairo Egypt. **Tel** 011 20 2 701696, telex 93069. **LC** [RS1; .J68]. **DD** 615/.1/05. **NLM** W1 EG914J. **CODEN** EJPSBZ. Documents available from CASDDS. ***Continues*** *United Arab Republic Journal of Pharmaceutical Sciences, 0301-5076.*
**Ind/Abst** Chem. Abstr.; Food Sci. Technol. Abstr.; Helminthol. Abstr. (1991-); Hortic. Abstr.; Int. Pharm. Abstr.; Nutr. Abstr. Rev., Ser. B, Live Feeds and Feed.; Nutr. Abstr. Rev., Ser. A, Hum. Exp.; Life Sci. Collect.; Protozoolog. Abstr.; Rev. Agric. Entomol.; Rev. Med. Vet. Mycology; Seed Abstr.; Weed Abstr.

GW/0992-4663
**EJHP, EUROPEAN JOURNAL OF HOSPITAL PHARMACY.** (EUROPEAN JOURNAL OF HOSPITAL PHARMACY : EJHP.). [EJHP. Eur. j. hosp. pharm.]. **Added/Corp** European Association of Hospital Pharmacists. **VFOAT** EJHP; Revista Europea de Farmacia de Hospital; Europaische Zeitschrift der Krankenhauspharmazie; Journal Europeen de la Pharmacie Hospitaliere. No. 1 (March 1984)-. Academic Scholarly Publication. English (French and German). qt. DM48.00. Medpharm Scientific Publishers, Postfach 101061, D 70009 Stuttgart Germany. **Tel** 011 49 711 25820, FAX 0711/2582-290, telex 723636 daz d. **ED** Jochen Kotwas. **CODEN** EJHPEN. **Bk Rev. Ad Acc, Adv Mgr Tel** 0711-2582-245. Documents available from CASDDS.
**Ind/Abst** Chem. Abstr. (1984-); Int. Pharm. Abstr.

●RU/0869-2092
**EKSPERIMENTALNAIA I KLINICHESKAIA FARMAKOLOGIIA.** **Added/Corp** Rossiiskaia Akademiia Meditsinskikh Nauk. Nauchnoe Obshchesvo Farmakologov. **VFOAT** Experimental and Clinical Pharmacology; Eksperimentalnaya i Klinicheskaya Farmakologiya. (Jan./Febr. 1992)-. Academic Scholarly Publication. Russian (summaries and/or abstracts in English; table of contents in English). bm. $112.95. Izdatelstvo Meditsina / Russian Academy of Medical Sciences, Ulitsa Solyanka 14, 109801 Moscow Russia. **Tel** 011 95 297-05-04. **(Subscription address:** East View Publications Inc., 3020 Harbor Lane North, Suite 110, Minneapolis MN 55447.) **ED** D. A. Kharkevich. **LC** RS1; .F25. **NLM** W1; EK2837. **CODEN** EKFAE9. Documents available from CASDDS. ***Continues*** *Farmakologiia i Toksikologiia (Moscow, R.S.F.S.R.), 0014-8318.*
**Ind/Abst** Chem. Abstr.

●US/1061-6098
**EMERGING PHARMACEUTICALS.** [Emerg. pharm.]. Vol. 1, No. 1 (June 1992)-. Periodical. English. mo. $457.00 US & Canada; $477.00 other. CTB International Publishing Inc., PO Box 218, Maplewood NJ 07040. **Tel** (201)379-7749, FAX (201)379-1158. **DD** 615. **NLM** W1; EM664MG.

IT/0392-6699
**EOS (ROMA).** **See** Medical Science and Technology-Allergy and Immunology.

GR
**EPITHEORESE KLINIKES FARMAKOLOGIAS KAI FARMAKOKINETIKES ELLENIKE EKD.** **VFOAT** Review of Clinical Pharmacology and Pharmacokinetics (Ellenike Edition). (1983)-. Greek, Modern. qt. Pharmakon Press, 20 Daskalaki Street, 11526 Athens Greece. Documents available from CASDDS.
**Ind/Abst** Chem. Abstr.; EMBASE.

GR/1011-6583
**EPITHEORESE KLINIKES FARMAKOLOGIAS KAI FARMAKOKINETIKES INTERNATIONAL ED.** [Epitheor. Klin. farmakol. farmakokinet.Int. ed.]. **VFOAT** Review of Clinical Pharmacology and Pharmacokinetics (International Ed.). (1987)-. Periodical. English. qt. Pharmakon Press, 20 Daskalaki Street, 11526 Athens Greece. Documents available from CASDDS.
**Ind/Abst** Chem. Abstr.

GT
**ESCUELA DE FARMACIA. ORGANO DE LA FACULTAD DE C.C.N.N. FARMACIA.** Periodical. Spanish.
**Ind/Abst** Int. Pharm. Abstr.

UK/0147-0205
**ESSAYS IN NEUROCHEMISTRY AND NEUROPHARMACOLOGY.** **See** Medical Science and Technology-Neurology.

US/0894-7058
**ESSENTIAL GUIDE TO PRESCRIPTION DRUGS, THE.** [Essent. guide prescr. drugs]. (1977)-. English. an (Dec.). $16.00 (softcover); $35.00 (hardcover). Harper Collins Publishers, Keystone Industrial Park, Scranton PA 18512. **Tel** (800)242-7737, (800)233-4727, FAX (800)822-4090. **ED** Erica Spaberg (editor's address: 10 East 53rd Street, New York, NY 10024, phone: (212)207-7206). **LC** RS51; .E85. **DD** 615. Index available. **Bk Rev. Ad Acc, Adv Mgr:** Kathy Lynch, **Tel** (212)207-7000.
**Desc:** Everything you need to know about safe drug use. Valuable information on the major prescription drugs in use today.

AT/0157-9509
**ETHICAL TABLET & CAPSULE HANDBOOK.** [Ethical tablet handb.]. **VFOAT** Ethical Tablet and Capsule Handbook; E.T.C.H.; ETCH; Ethical Tablet Capsule Handbook; ETCH Identification Handbook. 1st Ed. (1980)-. English. an. **ED** R A Wailes. **NLM** QV 772 E86.

US/1056-179X
**EUROPE DRUG & DEVICE REPORT.** [Eur. drug device rep.]. **VFOAT** Europe Drug and Device Report. Vol. 1, No. 1 (Apr. 1991)-. Periodical. English. bw. $847.00 North America; $902.00 other. Washington Business Information Inc., 1117 North 19th Street, Suite 200, Arlington VA 22209. **Tel** (703)247-3433, (800)426-0416, FAX (703)247-3421. **ED** Sara Lewis. **DD** 344. **[CCC].**

GW/0031-6970
**EUROPEAN JOURNAL OF CLINICAL PHARMACOLOGY.** [Eur. j. clin. pharmacol.]. Vol. 3 (1970)-. Academic Scholarly Publication. English. Twelve times a year. DM1496.00. Springer-Verlag GmbH & Company KG, Heidelberger Platz 3, D 14197 Berlin Germany. **Tel** 011 49 30 8207223, FAX 011 49 30 8214091, telex 183 319 SPBLN D. **(Subscription address:** Springer Verlag New York Inc. / for North America, 44 Hartz Way, Secaucus NJ 07096.) **ED** J K Aronson, H J Dengler, and L Dettli. **NLM** W1 EU72D. **CODEN** EJCPAS. **[CCC]. Bk Rev. Pr Rev.** available on microfilm and microfiche from University Microfilms International (UMI). Documents available from The Genuine Article, BIOSIS Document Express, CASDDS, ADONIS. ***Continues*** *Pharmacologica Clinica.*
**Desc:** Publishes original papers as well as short communications and letters to the editor on all aspects of clinical pharmacology and drug therapeutics.
**Ind/Abst** ADONIS; Biol. Abstr.; Chem. Abstr.; Curr. Aware. Biol. Sci., CABS; Curr. Contents Life Sci.; Dairy Sci. Abstr.; EMBASE; Energy Res. Abstr. (May 1972-); Health Plan. Adminis.; Helminthol. Abstr. (1991-); Index Med.; Iowa Drug Inf. Serv. (1971-); Med. Abstr. Newsl.; NAPRALERT; Nutr. Abstr. Rev., Ser. A, Hum. Exp.; Life Sci. Collect.; PESTDOC; Protozoolog. Abstr.; Ref. Upd. Basic Ed.; Ref. Upd. Deluxe Ed.; Res. Alert [Full Cov.]; Rev. Med. Vet. Mycology; Saf. Health Work; Sci. Cit. Index; SCISEARCH; Soc. Sci. Cit. Index [Select. Cov.].

FR/0398-7639
**EUROPEAN JOURNAL OF DRUG METABOLISM AND PHARMACOKINETICS.** [Eur. j. drug metab. pharmacokinet.]. Vol. 1 (Jan./Mar. 1976)-. Periodical. English (French and German). qt. $100.00. Medecine et Hygiene, Case Postale 456, CH-1211 Geneve 4 Switzerland. **Tel** 011 41 22 3469355, 011 41 22 3469356. **LC** RM301; .E87. **DD** 615/.7/05. **NLM** W1 EU72DD. **CODEN** EJDPD2. **Pr Rev.** Documents available from The Genuine Article, BIOSIS Document Express, CASDDS.
**Desc:** Information on pharmacokinetics.
**Ind/Abst** Biol. Abstr.; Chem. Abstr.; Curr. Contents Life Sci.; EMBASE; Energy Res. Abstr. (April 1982-); Health Plan. Adminis.; Helminthol. Abstr.; Index Med.; Int. Pharm. Abstr. (19??-19??); NAPRALERT; Life Sci. Collect.; PESTDOC; Ref. Upd. Deluxe Ed.; Res. Alert [Full Cov.]; Sci. Cit. Index; SCISEARCH.

●NE/0928-0987
**EUROPEAN JOURNAL OF PHARMACEUTICAL SCIENCES.** **Added/Corp** European Federation for Pharmaceutical Sciences. Vol. 1/1 (Mar. 1993)-. Academic Scholarly Publication. English. bm (6 issues). Fl515.00. Elsevier Science Publishers BV, PO Box 211, 1000 AE Amsterdam Netherlands. **Tel** 011 31 20 5803642, FAX 011 31 20 5862696, telex 15682. **LC** RM301.25; .E87. **DD** 615/.1/05. **NLM** W1; EU72DPI. **CODEN** EPSCED. **[CCC].** ***Absorbed*** *Acta Pharmaceutica Nordica, 1100-1801* ***and*** *Acta Pharmaceutica Fennica, 0356-3456.*

GW/0939-6411
**EUROPEAN JOURNAL OF PHARMACEUTICS AND BIOPHARMACEUTICS : OFFICIAL JOURNAL OF ARBEITSGEMEINSCHAFT FUER PHARMAZEUTISCHE VERFAHRENSTECHNIK E.V.** **Added/Corp** Arbeitsgemeinschaft fuer Pharmazeutische Verfahrenstechnik. Vol. 37, No. 1 (Mar. 1991)-. Periodical. English (French and German). bm (6 issues). DM297.00. Medpharm Scientific Publishers, Postfach 101061, D 70009 Stuttgart Germany. **Tel** 011 49 711 25820, FAX 0711/2582-290, telex 723636 daz d. **ED** Robert Gurny. **NLM** W1; EU72DPK. **CODEN** EJPBEL. **[CCC].** Documents available from The Genuine Article, CASDDS. ***Continues*** *Acta Pharmaceutica Technologica, 0340-3157.*
**Ind/Abst** Chem. Abstr.; Curr. Contents Eng. Tech. Appl. Sci.; EMBASE; Int. Pharm. Abstr. (19??-19??); PESTDOC; Res. Alert [Select. Cov.]; SCISEARCH.

NE/0014-2999
**EUROPEAN JOURNAL OF PHARMACOLOGY.** [Eur. j. pharmacol.]. Vol. 1 (Jan. 1967)-. Academic Scholarly Publication. English (summaries and/or abstracts in French, German and Spanish). ir (70 times a year, 23 volumes). Fl8694.00. Elsevier Science Publishers BV, PO Box 211, 1000 AE Amsterdam Netherlands. **Tel** 011 31 20 5803642, FAX 011 31 20 5862696, telex 15682. **ED** D de Wied. **NLM** W1 EU72E. **CODEN** EJPHAZ. **[CCC].** cum. index. **Pr Rev.** available on microfilm and microfiche from University Microfilms International (UMI). Documents available from The Genuine Article, BIOSIS Document Express, CASDDS, ADONIS. ***Absorbed*** *Acta Physiologica et Pharmacologica Neerlandica.*
**Desc:** Publishes full length papers, short communications and rapid communications concerning animal and human pharmacology.
**Ind/Abst** ADONIS; AGRICOLA; Biol. Abstr.; Calcium Calcif. Tissue Abstr.; Chem. Abstr. (1989-); Chem. Titles; Chemorecept. Abstr.; CSA Neuro. Abstr.; Curr. Aware. Biol. Sci., CABS; Curr. Contents Life Sci.; Dairy Sci. Abstr.; EMBASE; Health Plan. Adminis.; Helminthol. Abstr.; Index Med.; Index Vet.; NAPRALERT; Oncog. Growth Factors Abstr.; Life Sci. Collect.; PESTDOC; Protozoolog. Abstr.; Psychol. Abstr.; Ref. Upd. Basic Ed.; Ref. Upd. Deluxe Ed.; Res. Alert [Full Cov.]; Rev. Med. Vet. Entomol.; Sci. Cit. Index; SCISEARCH; Soc. Sci. Cit. Index [Select. Cov.]; Vet. Bull.

●NE/0926-6917
**EUROPEAN JOURNAL OF PHARMACOLOGY : ENVIRONMENTAL TOXICOLOGY AND PHARMACOLOGY SECTION.** **VFOAT** Environmental Toxicology and Pharmacology. Vol. 228 (1992)-. Academic Scholarly Publication. English. Eight times a year (2 volumes). Fl920.00; Fl8694.00 combination subscription with Molecular Pharmacology Section. Elsevier Science Publishers BV, PO Box 211, 1000 AE Amsterdam Netherlands. **Tel** 011 31 20 5803642, FAX 011 31 20 5862696, telex 15682. **CODEN** EPEPEG. **[CCC].** Documents available from The Genuine Article, ADONIS.
**Ind/Abst** ADONIS; Curr. Aware. Biol. Sci., CABS; Curr. Contents Life Sci.; Ref. Upd. Basic Ed.; Ref. Upd. Deluxe Ed.; Res. Alert [Full Cov.]; Sci. Cit. Index.

NE/0922-4106
**EUROPEAN JOURNAL OF PHARMACOLOGY. MOLECULAR PHARMACOLOGY SECTION.** [Eur. j. pharmacol., Mol. pharmacol. sect.]. **VFOAT** Molecular Pharmacology Section. Vol. 172 No. 1 (Mar. 1989)-. Academic Scholarly Publication. English. Twelve times a year (4 volumes). Fl1840.00; Fl8694.00 combination subscription with Environmental Toxicology and Pharmacology Section. Elsevier Science Publishers BV, PO Box 211, 1000 AE Amsterdam Netherlands. **Tel** 011 31 20 5803642, FAX 011 31 20 5862696, telex 15682. **CODEN** EJPPET. **[CCC]. Pr Rev.** available on microfilm and microfiche from University Microfilms International (UMI). Documents available from The Genuine Article, BIOSIS Document Express, CASDDS, ADONIS.
**Ind/Abst** ADONIS; Biol. Abstr. (1991-); Chem. Abstr. (1989-); Curr. Aware. Biol. Sci., CABS; Curr. Contents Life Sci.; EMBASE; PESTDOC; Ref. Upd. Basic Ed.; Ref. Upd. Deluxe Ed.; Res. Alert [Full Cov.]; Sci. Cit. Index; SCISEARCH.

NE/0924-977X
**EUROPEAN NEUROPSYCHOPHARMACOLOGY : THE JOURNAL OF THE EUROPEAN COLLEGE OF NEUROPSYCHOPHARMACOLOGY.** **See** Medical Science and Technology-Neurology.

FR
**EUROPEAN PHARMACOPOEIA.** Monographic series. English (English and French). ir. Price varies per volume. **(Subscription address:** Rittenhouse Book Distributors, 511 Feheley Drive, King of Prussia, PA 19406) **ED** James Reynolds. available on CD-ROM; available on diskette.
**Desc:** Provides a concise summary of the properties, actions and uses of drugs and medicines for the practicing pharmacist and medical practitioner.

US/0090-6654
**EVALUATIONS OF DRUG INTERACTIONS.** **Main/Corp** American Pharmaceutical Association. (1973)-. English. bm. $229.00 (textbook with 6 updates). Professional Drug System Inc., 530 Maryville Center Drive, Suite 250, St Louis MO 63141. **Tel** (314)275-8848, FAX (314)275-8819. **ED** Frederic J Zucchero, Mark J Hogan. **LC** RM302; .A44. **DD** 615/.7/04. **NLM** W1 EV13M.
**Desc:** 459 Monographs covering drug interactions, including discussions of their mechanism and recommendations for alternative therapy or management.

US/0094-8640
**EVALUATIONS OF DRUG INTERACTIONS. SUPPLEMENT.** **Main/Corp** American Pharmaceutical Association. English. $2.00. Mosby Year Book Inc., 11830 Westline Industrial Drive, St Louis MO 63146. **Tel** (800)325-4177, (314)872-8370, FAX (314)432-1380, telex 44-2402. **LC** RM302; .A45A. **DD** 615/.7/04.

●NE
**EXCERPTA MEDICA. SECTION 30. CLINICAL AND EXPERIMENTAL PHARMACOLOGY.** **See** Medical Science and Technology-Abstracting, Bibliographies and Statistics.

NE/0167-9171
**EXCERPTA MEDICA. SECTION 37. DRUG LITERATURE INDEX.** ***Ceased.*** **See** Medical Science and Technology-Abstracting, Bibliographies and Statistics.

NE/0167-9090
**EXCERPTA MEDICA. SECTION 38. ADVERSE REACTIONS TITLES.** **See** Medical Science and Technology-Abstracting, Bibliographies and Statistics.

US/0071-3309
**EXECUTIVE DIRECTORY OF THE U.S. PHARMACEUTICAL INDUSTRY.** 1st- Ed.; 1966-. Directory. English. ir. Chemical Economic Services, PO Box 468, Princeton NJ 08540. **Tel** (609)921-8468. **ED** K R Kern. **NLM** QV 22 AA1 E9.

US/1065-7118
**EXECUTIVE PHARMACY REPORT.** [Exec. pharm. rep.]. (19??)-. Periodical. English. mo. $120.00. Executive Pharmacy Report, 78-365 Highway 111, Suite 361, La Quinta CA 92253. **Tel** (619)564-4940, FAX (619)564-4092. **DD** 615.
**Desc:** Guidelines for effective pharmacy management.

●US/1064-1297
**EXPERIMENTAL AND CLINICAL PSYCHOPHARMACOLOGY.** **See** Psychology.

UK
**EXPERT OPINION ON INVESTIGATIONAL DRUGS.** (19??)-. English. Twelve times a year. $2,160.00. Ashley Publications Ltd., Lib 1 Shepherds Hill, 1st Floor, London N6 5QJ England. **Tel** 011 44 81 3475030. ***Continues*** *Current Opinion on Investigational Drugs.*

UK
**EXPERT OPINION ON THERAPEUTIC PATENTS.** **See** Copyright, Intellectual Property.

UK
**EXTRA PHARMACOPOEIA, THE.** (19??)-. Monographic series. English. ir. Pharmaceutical Press, 1 Lambeth High Street, London SE1 7JN England. **Tel** 011 44 71 735 9141, FAX 011 44 71 735 7629, telex 265871, (MONREF G). **(Subscription address:** Rittenhouse Book Distributors, 511 Feheley Drive, King of Prussia PA 19406.**)** available on an online database from DIALOG.

●US/1068-5316
**F-D-C REPORTS. NONPRESCRIPTION PHARMACEUTICALS AND NUTRITIONALS.** [F-D-C rep., Nonprescr. pharm. nutr.]. **Added/Corp** F-D-C Reports, Inc. **VFOAT** Nonprescription Pharmaceuticals and Nutritionals; FDC Reports. Nonprescription Pharmaceuticals and Nutritionals; ATan Sheet. Vol. 1, No. 1 (Mar. 1, 1993)-. Government Publication. English. wk. $670.00. FDC Reports Inc., 5550 Friendship Boulevard/Suite 1, Chevy Chase MD 20815. **Tel** (301)657-9830. **DD** 615. ***Continues*** *FDC Reports. Prescription and OTC Pharmaceuticals, 0734-6514.*
**Desc:** Provides coverage of non-prescription pharmaceuticals and nutritionals. Includes regulatory activities of FDA and FTC, product testing, new product introductions, advertising and executive changes, and financial news such as company stock index, sales and earnings reports and listings of trademarks.

US/0014-6617
**FACTS AND COMPARISONS (MONTHLY ED.).** (FACTS AND COMPARISONS.). [Facts comp.]. **Main/Corp** Facts and Comparisons, Inc., Saint Louis. **VFOAT** Drug Facts and Comparisons. (1953)-. English. mo. $99.50 (hardbound edition), $200.00 (loose-leaf edition with monthly updates) US; $124.50 (hardbound edition), $250.00 (loose-leaf edition with monthly updates) other). Facts and Comparisons Inc, 111 West Port Plaza, Suite 400, St Louis MO 63146-3098. **Tel** (314)878-2515, (800)223-0554, FAX (314)878-5563. **ED** Bennie R. Olin and Erwin K. Kastrup. available on microfiche.
**Desc:** Compendium of drug information. Lists more than 11,000 prescribed and 4,000 over-the-counter products by therapeutic class. Contains monographs, charts and comparisons.

US/0190-5406
**FAMILY PHARMACY NEWSLETTER, THE.** V. 1- Aug. 1977-. Newsletter. English. mo. $6.00. The Family Pharmacy Newsletter, 3311 West 2400 S, Salt Lake City UT 84119. **Tel** (801)972-5184. **NLM** W1 FA4507.

XO/0014-8172
**FARMACEUTICKY OBZOR.** [Farm. obz.]. **Added/Corp** Slovakia. Ministerstvo Zdravotnictva. Institut Pre Dalsie Vzdelavanie Lekarov a Farmaceutov. **VFOAT** Casopis pre Farmaceuticku Vedu a Prax. (1961)-. Periodical. Slovak (summaries and/or abstracts in English, German and Russian). Twelve times a year. **(Subscription address:** Artia Pegas Press Ltd., Palac Metro Narodni Trida 25, 11210 Prague 1 Czech Republic.**) NLM** W1 FA6904. **CODEN** FAOBAS. Documents available from BIOSIS Document Express, CASDDS.
**Ind/Abst** AGRICOLA; Anal. Abstr.; Biol. Abstr.; Chem. Abstr.; EMBASE; Int. Pharm. Abstr.

SP/0214-4697
**FARMACEUTICO HOSPITALES, EL.** (198?)-. Periodical. Spanish (summaries and/or abstracts in English). ir (approximately every two months). Ediciones Mayo SA, Muntaner 374 4TA Planta, 08006 Barcelona Spain. **Tel** 011 34 3 209 0255, FAX 34-3-202 0643. **ED** Jose Mayoral and Josep M Ferrando. **NLM** W1; FA677JD. **Ad Acc. Circ:** 2,000.
**Desc:** Specially designed for the pharmacy service in hospitals.
**Ind/Abst** Int. Pharm. Abstr.

NE
**FARMACEUTISCH NIEUWS.** ***Ceased.*** (19??)-(199?). Dutch. ir. Axioma Communicatie BV, Hettenheuvelweg 37-39, 1101 DM Amsterdam Netherlands. **Tel** 011 31 20 913141.

BE/0369-9714
**FARMACEUTISCH TIJDSCHRIFT VOOR BELGIE.** [Farm. tijdschr. Belg.]. (1971)-. Academic Scholarly Publication. Dutch (summaries and/or abstracts in French, English and German). bm. $119.22 Belgium; $133.96 other. Association Pharmaceutique, Rue Archimede 11, 1040 Brussel Belgium. **Tel** 03/312.10.94. **ED** Paul M M Nys (editor's address: 15 Dorp Street, B-2153 Zoersel Belgium). **NLM** W1 FA679. **CODEN** FMTBB2. Index available. **Bk Rev. Pr Rev. Circ:** 2,850 (ctrl). Documents available from BIOSIS Document Express, CASDDS. ***Continues*** *Pharmaceutisch Tijdschrift voor Belgie, 0369-9714.*
**Ind/Abst** Biol. Abstr. (1987-); Chem. Abstr.; EMBASE; Int. Pharm. Abstr.

BE/0771-2367
**FARMACEUTISCH TIJDSCHRIFT VOOR BELGIE 1971.** [Farm. tijdschr. Belg. 1971]. (1971)-. Periodical. Dutch. Six times a year. 2650.94F. Algemene Pharmaceutische Bond - Association Pharmaceutique Belge, Archimedestraat 11 rue Archimede, 1040 Brussels Belgium. **Tel** 011 32 2 2302685. **UDC** 615. ***Continues*** *Farmaceutisch Tijdschrift voor Belgie, 0369-9714.*

CI/0014-8202
**FARMACEUTSKI GLASNIK.** [Farm. Glas.]. **Added/Corp** Farmaceutsko Drustvo Hrvatske. (1945)-. Periodical. Serbo-Croatian (Roman) (summaries and/or abstracts in English, French and German; table of contents in English, French and German). mo. $100.00. Hrvatsko Farmaceutsko Drustvo, Masarykova 2, 41000 Zagreb Croatia. **Tel** 011 385 41 427944, FAX 011 385 41 431301. **CODEN** FAGLAI. Index available. **Bk Rev. Ad Acc. Circ:** 1,600. available on an online database; available with charts; available with illustrations. Documents available from CASDDS. ***Continues*** *Farmaceutski Vjesnik.*
**Ind/Abst** Bibliogr. Mission.; Chem. Abstr.; EMBASE; Int. Pharm. Abstr.; PESTDOC.

SW/0014-8210
**FARMACEVTISK REVY.** [Farm. revy]. (1902)-. Periodical. Swedish. Eleven times a year. Kr425.00. Sveriges Farmeceutforbund, Box 613, 101 28 Stockholm Sweden. **Tel** 46 8 140840, FAX 46 8 211672. **ED** Lindfors. **NLM** W1 FA683. Index available. **Bk Rev. Ad Acc. Circ:** 6,700 (ctrl).
**Desc:** Pharmacy and union policy in the same field.
**Ind/Abst** AGRICOLA; Int. Pharm. Abstr.

XV/0014-8229
**FARMACEVTSKI VESTNIK (LJUBLJANA).** (FARMACEVTSKI VESTNIK.). [Farm. vestn.]. (1950)-. Periodical. Slovenian (summaries and/or abstracts in English and German; table of contents in English and Slovenian). mo. **(Subscription address:** Mladost Export Import, PO Box 1028, Ilica 30, 41000 Zagreb Croatia.**) NLM** W1 FA6895. Documents available from CASDDS.
**Ind/Abst** Bibliogr. Mission.; Chem. Abstr.; EMBASE; Int. Pharm. Abstr.; PESTDOC.

UN/0367-3057
**FARMACEVTYCNYJ ZURNAL (KIIV. 1928).** (FARMATSEVTYCHNYI ZHURNAL.). [Farm. z.]. **Added/Corp** Ukraine. Ministerstvo Okhorony Zdorovia. (1930)-. Academic Scholarly Publication. Ukrainian (Russian; summaries and/or abstracts in English and Russian). bm. Poligrafkniga, Via Lenin 19, 252030 Kiev 30 Ukraine. **NLM** W1 FA89. **CODEN** FRZKAP. Documents available from BIOSIS Document Express, CASDDS. ***Continues*** *Farmatsevticheskii Zhurnal.*
**Ind/Abst** Anal. Abstr.; Biol. Abstr.; Chem. Abstr.; EMBASE; Index Med.; Int. Pharm. Abstr.; NAPRALERT; PESTDOC.

IT
**FARMACI.** (19??)-. Italian. mo. L220000. Mediprint Srl, Via Corsica 6/8, 00198 Rome Italy. **Tel** 011 39 6 8845351, FAX 011 39 6 8845354. **ED** Pietro Ferrara. **Bk Rev. Ad Acc.** ctrl circ.
**Ind/Abst** Int. Pharm. Abstr.; PESTDOC.

IT/0393-9693
**FARMACI E TERAPIA.** [Farm. terap.]. (1984)-. Periodical. Multiple languages. Four times a year. L60000 Italy; $60.00 other. Scrit Srl, Via Galliano 135, 50144 Florence Italy. **Tel** 011 39 55 331766, FAX 011 39 55 331641. **ED** Mary Forrest. **UDC** 615. **[CCC]. Pr Rev.**

IT
**FARMACIA; BOLLETTINO UFFICIALE DEL SINDACATO NAZIONALE FASCISTA DEI FARMACISTI, LA.** ***Ceased.*** Periodical. Italian.

RM/0014-8237
**FARMACIA (BUCURESTI).** (FARMACIA : REVISTA A SOCIETATII DE FARMACIE / UNIUNEA SOCIETATILOR DE STIINTE MEDICALE DIN REPUBLICA SOCIALISTA ROMANIA.). [Farmacia]. **Added/Corp** Societatii de Farmacie. Uniunea Societatilor de Stiinte Medicale din Republica Socialista Romania. Societatii Stiintelor Medicale din Republica Populara Romina. (1953)-. Periodical. Romanian (summaries and/or abstracts in French and Russian). qt. DM225.00. **(Subscription address:** Kubon & Sagner, ABT Zeitschriftenimport, D 80328 Munich Germany.**) CODEN** FRMBAZ.
**Ind/Abst** Bibliogr. Mission.; Int. Pharm. Abstr.; PESTDOC.

SP/0212-6583
**FARMACIA CLINICA.** [Farm. clin.]. Vol. 1, No. 1 (April/May 1983)-. Periodical. Spanish (summaries and/or abstracts in English). mo (10 issues). $160.00. Rasgo Editorial, Llansa 16, 08015 Barcelona Spain. **Tel** 011 34 3 4238098. **NLM** W1; FA719. **CODEN** FACLE2. **[CCC].** Documents available from BIOSIS Document Express, CASDDS.
**Ind/Abst** Biol. Abstr. (1985-); Chem. Abstr.; EMBASE; Indice Med. Esp.; Int. Pharm. Abstr.

SP/1130-6343
**FARMACIA HOSPITALARIA.** (1990)-. Multiple languages. bm. $120.00 institutions; $100.00 individuals. Sociedad Espanola de Farmacia Hospitalaria, Calle Echegaray 13, 3, 28014 Madrid Spain. **Tel** 011 34 1 4296354. Documents available from CASDDS. ***Continues*** *Revista de la Sociedad Espanola de Farmacia Hospitalaria.*
**Ind/Abst** Chem. Abstr.; EMBASE; Int. Pharm. Abstr.

RU/0430-0947
**FARMACIJA.** (FARMATSIIA.). **Added/Corp** Soviet Union. Ministerstvo Zdravookhraneniia. (1967)-. Periodical. Russian (summaries and/or abstracts in English; table of contents in English). Six times a year. $43.00. **(Subscription address:** Victor Kamkin, 4956 Boiling Brook Parkway, Rockville, MD 20852**) NLM** W1 FA891A. **CODEN** FRMTAL. Documents available from BIOSIS Document Express. ***Continues*** *Aptechnoe Delo.*
**Ind/Abst** Biol. Abstr.; NAPRALERT.

BU/0428-0296
**FARMACIJA.** (FARMATSIIA.). [Farmacija]. **VFOAT** Farmacija. (1951)-. Periodical. Bulgarian (summaries and/or abstracts in English and Russian; table of contents in English and Russian). Six times a year. Izdatelstvo Meditsina i Fizkultura, 11 Pl. Slaveikov, Sofiia Bulgaria. **(Subscription address:** Hemus Foreign Trade Organization, 6 Tzar Osvoboditel Boulevard, 1000 Sofia Bulgaria.**) NLM** W1 FA892. **CODEN** FMTYA2. Documents available from CASDDS.
**Ind/Abst** Bibliogr. Mission.; Chem. Abstr.; EMBASE; Int. Pharm. Abstr.; NAPRALERT.

RU/0367-3014
**FARMACIJA.** (FARMATSIIA.). [Farmacija]. **Added/Corp** Vsesoiuznyi Nauchno-Issledovatelskii Institut Meditsinskoi i Mediko-Tekhnicheskoi Informatsii. (1970)-. Periodical. Russian. bm. $99.95. Izdatelstvo Meditsina / Russian Academy of Medical Sciences, Ulitsa Solyanka 14, 109801 Moscow Russia. **Tel** 011 95 297-05-04. **(Subscription address:** East View Publications Inc., 3020 Harbor Lane North, Suite 110, Minneapolis MN 55447.**) NLM** W1 FA892DE. Documents available from CASDDS.
**Ind/Abst** Chem. Abstr.; Curr. Biotechnol.; EMBASE; Int. Pharm. Abstr.

UN/0301-5394
**FARMACIJA (KIEV).** (FARMATSIIA.). (1973)-. Periodical. Russian. **NLM** W1 FA892D. **CODEN** FMTSBJ. Documents available from CASDDS.
**Ind/Abst** Chem. Abstr. (-1973); PESTDOC.

PL/0014-8261
**FARMACJA POLSKA.** (FARMACJA POLSKA / POLSKIEGO TOWARZYSTWA FARMACETYCZNEGO.). [Farm. Pol.]. **Added/Corp** Polskie Towarzystwo Farmaceutyczne. (Oct. 1945)-. Academic Scholarly Publication. Polish (table of contents in English, French and Russian). Twenty-four times a year. Price on Request. **(Subscription address:** ARS

Polona, PO Box 1001, 00068 Warsaw Poland.) **NLM** W1 FA814. **CODEN** FAPOA4. Documents available from CASDDS.
**Ind/Abst** Chem. Abstr.; EMBASE; Int. Pharm. Abstr.; PESTDOC.

IT
**FARMACO (SOCIETA CHIMICA ITALIANA : 1989).** (IL FARMACO.). **Added/Corp** Societa Chimica Italiana. Vol. 44, No. 1 (Jan. 1989)-. Academic Scholarly Publication. English (French and Italian). mo. L330000 (Italy); L500000 (Mediterranean Countries & Europe); L550000 (other). Societa Chimica Italiana, Viale Liegi 48, 00198 Rome Italy. **Tel** (06)8549691. **NLM** W1; FA826F. **CODEN** FRMCE8. Index available. Documents available from The Genuine Article, CASDDS. ***Formed by the union of** Farmaco (Edizione Practica), 0430-0912 **and** Farmaco (Edizione Scientifica), 0430-0920.*
**Ind/Abst** Anal. Abstr.; BioBusiness; Chem. Abstr.; EMBASE; Index Chem.; Index Med. (1989-); Int. Pharm. Abstr.; PESTDOC; Res. Alert [Full Cov.]; Sci. Cit. Index; SCISEARCH.

SP/0214-8935
**FARMACOTERAPIA MADRID.** [FarmacoterapiaMadr.]. (1984)-. Periodical. Spanish. bm. 8000ptas Europe; 8225ptas other. Editores Medicos SA, Calle Gabriela Mistral 2, 28035 Madrid Spain. **Tel** 011 34 1 3860033, 34 1 3860366, FAX 34 1 3739907. **ED** A. Garcia Garcia. **UDC** 615. **[CCC].** Index available. **Bk Rev. Ad Acc. Pr Rev.** ctrl circ.

RU/0430-0939
**FARMAKOLOGIJA I TOKSIKOLOGIJA (KIEV).** (FARMAKOLOGIIA I TOKSIKOLOGIIA / MINISTERSTVO ZRAVOOKHRANENIIA USSR.). [Farmakol. toksikol.]. **Added/Corp** Ukraine. Ministerstvo Okhorony Zdorovia. (1964)-. Periodical. Russian. **CODEN** FATOBP. Documents available from CASDDS.
**Ind/Abst** Chem. Abstr.

XR/0533-0300
**FARMAKOTERAPEUTICKE ZPRAVY SPOFA. SUPPLEMENTUM.** Academic Scholarly Publication. Czech. Price varies per volume. **NLM** W1 FA877A. **CODEN** FTZSAT. Documents available from CASDDS.
**Ind/Abst** Chem. Abstr. (1963-1978).

NO/0014-8326
**FARMAKOTERAPI.** [Farmakoterapi]. Vol. 1 (1945)-. Periodical. Norwegian (English). qt. Nycomed AS., Nycoveien 1-2, Postboks 4220 Torshov, 0401 Oslo 4 Norway. **NLM** W1 FA879. **CODEN** FMKTAA.
**Ind/Abst** PESTDOC.

SP
**FARMATELEX.** Spanish. Twenty-four times a year. 60,000ptas. Biomedical Systems, c/o Padilla 236, 08013 Barcelona Spain. **Tel** 011 34 3 4333604.

JA/0014-8601
**FARUMASHIA.** [Farumashia]. **Added/Corp** Nihon Yakugakkai. (1965)-. Periodical. Japanese. mo. $308.00. Nihon Yakugakkai, (Pharmaceutical Soc. of Japan), 12-15, Shibuya 2 Chome, Shibuyaku, Tokyoto 150, Japan. **(Subscription address:** Kyowa Book Company, Inc., 1-38 Kanda Jinbo-Cho, Chiyoda-Ku Tokyo 101, Japan) **CODEN** FARUAW. Documents available from CASDDS.
**Ind/Abst** Chem. Abstr.

JA
**FARUMASHIA REBYU.** [Farumashia rebyu]. **Added/Corp** Nihon Yakugakkai. (1978)-. Periodical. Japanese. qt. Nihon Yakugakkai, (Pharmaceutical Soc. of Japan), 12-15, Shibuya 2 Chome, Shibuyaku, Tokyoto 150, Japan. **CODEN** FREBDW. Documents available from CASDDS.
**Ind/Abst** Chem. Abstr.

●US/1064-5055
**FAX-STAT ON DRUGS. Added/Corp** Facts and Comparisons. **VFOAT** Fax Stat on Drugs. (1992)-. Periodical. English. wk. $79.95. Facts and Comparisons Inc, 111 West Port Plaza, Suite 400, St Louis MO 63146-3098. **Tel** (314)878-2515, (800)223-0554, FAX (314)878-5563.

US
**FDA DRUG AND DEVICE PRODUCT APPROVALS / CENTER FOR DRUGS AND BIOLOGICS, CENTER FOR DEVICES AND RADIOLOGICAL HEALTH, CENTER FOR VETERINARY MEDICINE. Added/Corp** Center for Drugs and Biologics (U.S.) Center for Devices and Radiological Health (U.S.) Center for Veterinary Medicine (U.S.) Center for Drug Evaluation and Research (U.S.). Division of Drug Information Resources. **VFOAT** Drug and Device Product Approvals. (197?)-. Periodical. English. mo. $80.00. FOI Services, 12315 Wilkins Avenue, Rockville MD 20852. **Tel** (301)881-0410, FAX (301)881-0415. **ED** John Carey. **NLM** QV 772; F287. **Circ:** 75 (ctrl).

US
**FDA DRUG AND DEVICE PRODUCT APPROVALS LIST / (U.S.) FOOD AND DRUG ADMINISTRATION. Added/Corp** United States. Food and Drug Administration. Bureau of Drugs. Center for Drug Evaluation and Research (U.S.). **VFOAT** F.D.A. Drug and Device Product Approvals List; Drug and Device Product Approvals List. **VAT** Federal Drug Administration Drug and Device Product Approvals List. (197?)-. Periodical. English. mo. $9.00 US; $18.00 other. US Food and Drug Administration / FDA, 5600 Fishers Lane, Room 14-71, Rockville MD 20857. **Tel** (301)443-2410, FAX (301)443-0755. **(Subscription address:** National Technical Information Service, 5285 Port Royal Road, Springfield, VA 22161**)**

US/1063-8067
**FDA MEDICAL BULLETIN.** [FDA med. bull.]. **Added/Corp** United States. Food and Drug Administration. **VAT** Food and Drug Administration Medical Bulletin. Vol. 21, No. 1 (Mar. 1991)-. English. ir. US Food and Drug Administration / FDA, 5600 Fishers Lane, Room 14-71, Rockville MD 20857. **Tel** (301)443-2410, FAX (301)443-0755. **DD** 615. **NLM** W1; FD332. available on an online database (file 636/Full-Text) from DIALOG. ***Continues** FDA Drug Bulletin, 0361-4344.*
**Ind/Abst** PTS Newsl. Database [Full Txt.].

●US/1069-5109
**FDA NEWS. See** Food and Food Industry.

US/0734-6514
**FDC REPORTS. PRESCRIPTION AND OTC PHARMACEUTICALS. *Title Change.*** [FDC rep., Prescr. OTC pharm.]. **Added/Corp** F-D-C Reports, Inc. **VFOAT** Prescription and OTC Pharmaceuticals; F.D.C. Reports. Prescription and O.T.C. Pharmaceuticals; Pink Sheet. **VAT** FDC Reports. Prescription and Over the Counter Pharmaceuticals. Vol. 44, No. 3 (Jan. 18, 1982)-(199?). Government Publication. English. wk. FDC Reports Inc., 5550 Friendship Boulevard/Suite 1, Chevy Chase MD 20815. **Tel** (301)657-9830. **DD** 615. **NLM** W1 FD411. **[CCC].** Documents available from UMI Article Clearinghouse. ***Continues** FDC Reports. Ethical and OTC Pharmaceuticals, 0272-913X. **Split into** F-D-C Reports. Prescription Pharmaceuticals and Biotechnology, 1068-5324 **and** F-D-C Reports. Nonprescription Pharmaceuticals and Nutritionals, 1068-5316.*
**Desc:** Provides in-depth coverage of the pharmaceutical industry, both prescription and over-the-counter drugs. Its spectrum of coverage includes: regulatory activities of FDA, FTC and Congress, as well as other federal and state agencies with jurisdiction in the drug area; developments within industry such as acquisitions and mergers, new product introductions, executive changes, etc.
**Ind/Abst** Pharm. News Index (Jan. 1982-); Trade Ind. Index (?-?).

US/0734-6506
**FDC REPORTS. PRESCRIPTION AND OTC PHARMACEUTICALS. MID-WEEK REPORT. *Ceased.*** [FDC rep., Prescr. OTC pharm., Mid-week rep.]. **Added/Corp** F-D-C Reports, Inc. **VFOAT** Prescription and OTC Pharmaceuticals. Mid-Week Report; F.D.C. Reports. Prescription and O.T.C. Pharmaceuticals. Mid-Week Report; Pink Sheet. Vol. 1, No. 1 (Jan. 13, 1982)-?. Government Publication. English. wk. FDC Reports Inc., 5550 Friendship Boulevard/Suite 1, Chevy Chase MD 20815. **Tel** (301)657-9830. **ED** Cole Palmer. **NLM** W1 FD411C. **[CCC].** Index available. **Bk Rev.** Documents available from UMI Article Clearinghouse.
**Desc:** Update is designed to augment the in-depth, end-of-the-week coverage of "The Pink Sheet".
**Ind/Abst** Pharm. News Index (Dec. 1984-); PROMT.

US/0428-1179
**FEDERAL PHARMACIST.** English. Federal Wholesale Druggists Association, PO Box 238, Alexandria VA 22313. **DD** 615.

US
**FIRST DATA BANK BLUE BOOK.** (199?)-. English. an. $55.00 US; $72.00 other. Hearst Business Communications, 1790 Broadway, New York NY 10019. **Tel** (212)969-7500, FAX (212)969-7564. ***Continues** Blue Book, American Druggist.*

US/0897-4616
**FLORIDA PHARMACY TODAY.** (FLORIDA PHARMACY TODAY: THE JOURNAL OF THE FLORIDA PHARMACY ASSOCIATION.). [Fla. pharm. today]. **Added/Corp** Florida Pharmacy Association. Vol. 52, No. 1 (Jan. 1988)-. Periodical. English. mo. $10.00 members, $20.00 nonmembers. Florida Pharmacy Association, 610 North Adams Street, Tallahassee FL 32301. **DD** 615. **NLM** W1; FL79H. ***Continues** Florida Pharmacy Journal, 0161-746X.*
**Ind/Abst** Int. Pharm. Abstr.

XR/0139-939X
**FOLIA PHARMACEUTICA (PRAHA).** (FOLIA PHARMACEUTICA / UNIVERSITAS CAROLINA PRAGENSIS.). [Folia pharm.]. **Added/Corp** Universita Karlova. (1977)-. Periodical. Czech. **CODEN** FOLPDK. Documents available from CASDDS.
**Ind/Abst** Chem. Abstr.; Int. Pharm. Abstr.; NAPRALERT.

JA/0015-5691
**FOLIA PHARMACOLOGICA JAPONICA.** Vol. 1 (1925)-. Academic Scholarly Publication. Multiple languages (English, German and Japanese). mo. $206.00. Nihon Yakuri Gakkai, (Japanese Pharmacological Society), c/o Kyoto Daigaku Igakubu, Yakurigaku Kyoshitsu, Yoshida Konoecho, Sakyoku,, Kyotoshi, Kyotofu 606 Japan. **(Subscription address:** Kyowa Book Company Inc., 1 38 Kanda Jinbocho Chiyoda-ku, Tokyo 101 Japan.) **CODEN** NYKZAU. **Pr Rev.** Documents available from The Genuine Article, CASDDS.
**Ind/Abst** Chem. Abstr.; CSA Neuro. Abstr. (?-?); Dairy Sci. Abstr.; EMBASE; Index Med.; Maize Abstr.; NAPRALERT; Nutr. Abstr. Rev., Ser. B, Live Feeds and Feed.; Nutr. Abstr. Rev., Ser. A, Hum. Exp.; PESTDOC; Protozoolog. Abstr.; Res. Alert [Full Cov.]; Sci. Cit. Index (19??-19??); SCISEARCH.

US/0362-6466
**FOOD & DRUG LETTER, THE. See** Food and Food Industry.

CN/1188-2344
**FORRUM (MONTREAL).** (FORRUM : BULLETIN DU RESEAU DE REVUE D'UTILISATION DES MEDICAMENTS.). [FoRRUM]. **Added/Corp** Reseau de Revue d'Utilisation des Medicaments. **VAT** FoReseau de Revue d'Utilisation des Medicaments (Montreal). Vol. 1, No 1 (1991)-. Bulletin. French. bm. Free for members. Reseau de Revue d'Utilisation des Medicaments, Bureau 400, 505 Ouest Boulevard de Maisonneuve, Montreal, Quebec H3A 3C2. **DD** 615.

FR/0767-3981
**FUNDAMENTAL & CLINICAL PHARMACOLOGY.** [Fundam. clin. pharmacol.]. **Added/Corp** Association des Pharmacologistes. **VFOAT** Fundamental and Clinical Pharmacology; FCP. Vol. 1, No. 1 (1987)-. Academic Scholarly Publication. English. bm (1 volume). 1830.00F France; 2160.00F other. Editions Scientifique Elsevier, 141 rue de Javel, 75747 Paris Cedex 15 France. **Tel** 011 33 1 47 07 11 22, FAX 011 33 1 43 36 80 93. **(Subscription address:** Editions Scientifiques Elsevier / for North America, PO Box 7247-7576, Philadelphia PA 19170-7576.) **ED** S. Z. Langer, P. Meyer and J. F. Giudicelli. **NLM** W1; FU538TS. **CODEN** FCPHEZ. **[CCC].** Index available. **Bk Rev. Ad Acc. Pr Rev. Circ:** 3,000 (ctrl). available on microfilm and microfiche from University Microfilms International (UMI). Documents available from The Genuine Article, BIOSIS Document Express, ADONIS. ***Continues** Journal de Pharmacologie, 0021-793X.*
**Desc:** Contains full length articles covering the entire field of pharmacology, from molecular studies to clinical investigations. Short communications reporting new results are encouraged. All fields of pharmacology receive the same attention.
**Ind/Abst** ADONIS; Biol. Abstr. (1988-); Curr. Aware. Biol. Sci., CABS; Curr. Contents Life Sci.; EMBASE; Health Plan. Adminis.; Index Med. (1987-); PESTDOC; Ref. Upd. Deluxe Ed.; Res. Alert [Full Cov.]; Sci. Cit. Index; SCISEARCH.

TU/1015-9592
**GAZI UNIVERSITESI, ECZACILIK FAKULTESI DERGISI.** [Gazi univ. Eczacilik fak. derg.]. **VFOAT** Journal of Faculty of Pharmacy of Gazi University; Eczacilik Fakultesi Dergisi, Gazi Universitesi. (1985)-. Periodical. Turkish. sa. Free, Turkey; $50.00 other. Gazi Universitesi Merkez Yayin, Eczacilik Facultesi Dekanligi, 06330 Ankara, Turkey. **Tel** 011 90 312 2126840 ext. 3381. **UDC** 615. Documents available from CASDDS.
**Ind/Abst** Chem. Abstr.; EMBASE; Int. Pharm. Abstr.; Rev. Med. Vet. Mycology.

UK/0962-9335
**GC/MS UPDATE PART B BIOMEDICAL, CLINICAL, DRUGS.** [GC/MS update. Part B, Biomed., clin., drugs]. (1991)-. English. bm (6 issues). £147.00. HD Science LImited, 4A Bessell Lane Stapleford, Nottingham NG9 7BX England. **Tel** 011 44 602 491704, FAX 011 44 602 491703. **DD** 543.0896.

JA
**GEKKAN YAKUJI.** [Gekkan yakuji]. **Added/Corp** Yakuji Kenkyukai (Japan). **VFOAT** Pharmaceuticals Monthly. (1959)-. Academic Scholarly Publication. Japanese. mo. $286.00. Yakuji Kenkyukai (Pharmaceutical Research Association), Yakugyo Jiho Co. Ltd., 2-36 Kanda Jimbo-cho, Chiyoda-ku, Tokyo 101 Japan. **(Subscription address:** Kyowa Book Company, Inc., 1-38 Kanda Jinbo-Cho, Chiyoda-Ku Tokyo 101, Japan) **CODEN** YAKUD5. Documents available from CASDDS.
**Ind/Abst** Chem. Abstr.; Curr. Biotechnol.; Int. Pharm. Abstr.

NE/0304-4629
**GENEESMIDDELENBULLETIN.** [Geneesmiddelenbulletin]. (1967)-. Periodical. Dutch. mo. Fl110.90. Wegener Tijl Tijdschriften Group, Postbus 9943, 1006 AP Amsterdam Netherlands. **Tel** 011 31 20 5182828. **ED** W. Toenderes. **UDC** 615.012. **Pr Rev.**

**Circ:** 48,000.
**Desc:** Information bulletin for medicine prescription.
**Ind/Abst** EMBASE.

UK/0306-3623
**GENERAL PHARMACOLOGY.** [Gen. pharmacol.]. (March 1975)-. Academic Scholarly Publication. English. Eight times a year. $1394.00 The Americas; £935.00 other. Pergamon Press, An Imprint of Elsevier Science Ltd., The Boulevard, Langford Lane, Kidlington, Oxford OX5 1GB United Kingdom. **Tel** 011 44 865 843000, 011 44 865 843699, FAX 011 44 865 843010. **(Subscription address:** Elsevier Science Ltd. Oxford Fulfillment Centre, PO Box 800, Kidlington, Oxford OX5 1DX United Kingdom.**) ED** Gerald A. Kerkut. **LC** RM1; .C63. **DD** 615/.1/05. **NLM** W1 GE255. **CODEN** GEPHDP. **[CCC]. Pr Rev.** available on microfilm and microfiche from University Microfilms International (UMI). Documents available from The Genuine Article, BIOSIS Document Express, CASDDS, ADONIS. ***Continues*** *Comparative and General Pharmacology, 0010-4035.*
**Desc:** Publishes original research papers on all aspects of pharmacology, although special consideration is given to articles dealing with the subject from a comparative point of view.
**Ind/Abst** ADONIS; Biol. Abstr.; Calcium Calcif. Tissue Abstr.; Chem. Abstr.; Chem. Titles; CSA Neuro. Abstr.; Curr. Aware. Biol. Sci., CABS; Curr. Contents Life Sci.; Dairy Sci. Abstr.; EMBASE; Index Med.; Index Vet.; Life Sci. Collect.; PESTDOC; Pig News Inf.; Ref. Upd. Deluxe Ed.; Res. Alert [Full Cov.]; Rev. Med. Vet. Entomol.; Rev. Med. Vet. Mycology; Sci. Cit. Index; SCISEARCH; Sug. Indus. Abstr.; Vet. Bull.

US/0742-308X
**GENERICS MAGAZINE.** ***Ceased.*** **VFOAT** Generics. Vol. 1, Issue 1 (Spring 1984)-?. Periodical. English. qt. Generics Magazine Inc, 200 Madison Avenue, Suite 2404, New York NY 10016. **Tel** (212)683-1881. **DD** 615.

US/1061-2270
**GENESIS REPORT/RX, THE.** (THE GENESIS REPORT / RX : BUSINESS IMPLICATIONS OF TECHNOLOGY INNOVATION IN PHARMACEUTICALS.). [Genes. rep./Rx]. **VFOAT** Genesis Report Rx. Vol. 1, No. 1 (Nov./Dec. 1991)-. Periodical. English. bm. $950.00 US; $995.00 other. Genesis Group, 29 Park Street, Montclair NJ 07042. **Tel** (201)509-7735 or, 509-7740. **DD** 338.

US
**GEORGIA JOURNAL OF HOSPITAL PHARMACY.** **Added/Corp** Georgia Society of Hospital Pharmacists. Vol. 1, No. 1 (Spring 1987)-. Periodical. English. qt. Georgia Pharmaceutical Society, Atlanta GA. ***Continues*** *Newsletter of the Georgia Society of Hospital Pharmacists.*
**Ind/Abst** Int. Pharm. Abstr.

US/0194-4290
**GEORGIA PHARMACEUTICAL JOURNAL.** ***Title Change.*** **Added/Corp** Georgia Pharmaceutical Association. Vol. 1, No. 1 (Nov. 1978)-(198?). Periodical. English. mo. Georgia Pharmaceutical Society, Atlanta GA. **LC** RS1; .G467. ***Continued by*** *Journal (Georgia Pharmaceutical Association).*
**Ind/Abst** Int. Pharm. Abstr.

GW/0939-334X
**GESCHICHTE DER PHARMAZIE.** (19??)-. German. qt. DM12.00. Deutscher Apotheker Verlag, Postfach 101061, D 70009 Stuttgart Germany. **Tel** 011 49 711 25820, INLAND:0711/2582, FAX 011 49 711 2582 290, telex 723636 daz d.

GW/0016-9307
**GESUNDHEITSPOLITISCHE UMSCHAU.** (GESUNDHEITSPOLITISCHE UMSCHAU. GU.). **VFOAT** GU. Vol. 23 (Jan. 1972)-. Periodical. German. mo. DM79.00 Germany; DM89.00 other. Albert Amann Verlag, Richterstrasse 2, D 63916 Amorbach Germany. **Tel** 011 49 9373 3031. **NLM** W1 GE916B. ***Continues*** *Gesundheitspolitische Umschau.*

JA/0434-0094
**GIFU YAKKA DAIGAKU KIYO.** (GIFU YAKKA DAIGAKU KIYO. ANNUAL PROCEEDINGS OF THE GIFU COLLEGE OF PHARMACY.). [Gifu Yakka Daigaku kiyo]. **Main/Corp** Gifu Yakka Daigaku. **VFOAT** Annual Proceedings of the Gifu College of Pharmacy. (1951)-. Proceedings. Japanese (summaries and/or abstracts in English). **NLM** W1 GI131. **CODEN** GYDKA9. Documents available from BIOSIS Document Express, CASDDS.
**Ind/Abst** Bibliogr. Mission.; Biol. Abstr.; Chem. Abstr.; Int. Pharm. Abstr.

IT/0393-8476
**GIORNALE DEL FARMACISTA, IL.** (1986)-. Periodical. Italian. ir (20 issues). L15000 Italy. Masson S.P.A, Via Statuto 2/4, 20121 Milan Italy. **Tel** 011 39 2 63671, FAX 011 39 2 6367211. **UDC** 615.7.

IT/0391-9048
**GIORNALE DI NEUROPSICOFARMACOLOGIN.** [G. neuropsicofarmacol.]. (1979)-. Periodical. Italian. bm. L60000, $42.64. CIC Edizioni Internazionali, Via L Spallanzani 11, 00161 Rome Italy. **Tel** 011 39 6 841-2673, FAX 011 39 6 844-3365, telex 622099 CIC I. **UDC** 616. **[CCC].** Index available (Free).
**Ind/Abst** Psychoanal. Abstr.; PsycINFO (1989-); PsycScan: Appl. Exp. Eng. Psych.; PsycScan: LD/MR; PsycScan: Neuropsych.

IT/1120-3749
**GIORNALE ITALIANO DI FARMACIA CLINICA.** [G. ital. farm. clin.]. **VFOAT** Italian Journal of Clinical Pharmacy. (1987)-. Periodical. Multiple languages. Four times a year. L80000 (individuals), L140000 (institutions). Il Pensiero Scientifico Editore s.r.l., Via Bradano 3C, 00199 Rome Italy. **Tel** 011 39 6 86207158, 86207159, 86207168, 86207169, FAX 011 39 6 86207160. **ED** Nello Martini. **UDC** 615. **Circ:** 2,100.
**Ind/Abst** EMBASE.

US/0734-9505
**GMP AWARENESS REPORT.** **VFOAT** G.M.P. Awareness Report. (1980)-. English. qt. Interpharm Press, Inc., 1358 Busch Parkway, Buffalo Grove IL 60089.

US/1047-6555
**GMP TRENDS.** **See** Manufacturing.

HU/0017-6036
**GYOGYSZERESZET.** (GYOGYSZERESZET / SOCIETAS PHARMACEUTICA HUNGARICA.). [Gyogyszereszet]. **Added/Corp** Orvos-Egeszsegugyi Szakszervezet. Gyogyszeresz Szakcsoport. Magyar Gyogyszereszeti Tarsasag. (1957)-. Periodical. Hungarian. Twelve times a year. $83.00 Austria, Croatia, Czech and Slovak Republics, Romania, Yugoslavia, Slovenia and Ukraine; $92.00 other. **(Subscription address:** Kultura, PO Box 149, H 1389 Budapest 62 Hungary.**) CODEN** GYOGAI. Documents available from CASDDS. ***Continues*** *Gyogyszeresz.*
**Ind/Abst** Bibliogr. Mission.; Chem. Abstr.; EMBASE; Int. Pharm. Abstr.; PESTDOC.

US/0190-3454
**HANDBOOK OF ANTIMICROBIAL THERAPY.** [Handb. antimicrob. ther.]. **VFOAT** Medical Letter Handbook of Antimicrobial Therapy. (1972)-. Periodical. English. be. $11.50 (comes with Drugs of Choice on alternate years - free with new subscription). The Medical Letter Inc, 1000 Main Street, New Rochelle NY 10801. **Tel** (914)235-0500. **LC** RM265; .H36. **DD** 616.9/0461. **NLM** W1 HA51H.

GW/0171-2004
**HANDBOOK OF EXPERIMENTAL PHARMACOLOGY.** [Handb. exp. pharmacol.]. Vol. 50 (1978)-. Academic Scholarly Publication. English. ir. Price varies per volume. Springer-Verlag GmbH & Company KG, Heidelberger Platz 3, D 14197 Berlin Germany. **Tel** 011 49 30 8207223, FAX 011 49 30 8214091, telex 183 319 SPBLN D. **(Subscription address:** Springer Verlag New York Inc. / for North America, 44 Hartz Way, Secaucus NJ 07096.**) ED** G. V. R. Born. **NLM** W1 HA51L. **CODEN** HEPHD2. **[CCC].** Documents available from CASDDS. ***Continues*** *Handbuch der Experimentellen Pharmakologie. New Series, 0073-0033.*
**Ind/Abst** Chem. Abstr.; Index Vet.; Life Sci. Collect.

US/0889-7816
**HANDBOOK OF NON-PRESCRIPTION DRUGS.** [Handb. nonprescr. drugs]. **Added/Corp** American Pharmaceutical Association. **VFOAT** Handbook of Nonprescription Drugs; Hand Book of Nonprescription Drugs; Hand Book of Non-Prescription Drugs. (1967)-. English. ir (every three years). $95.00 (member), $109.00 (nonmember). American Pharmaceutical Association, 2215 Constitution Avenue Northwest, Washington DC 20037-2985. **Tel** (202)628-4410, (800)237-2742, FAX (202)783-2351. **LC** RM671.A1; H34. **DD** 615. **NLM** W1 HA513.

GW/0073-0033
**HANDBUCH DER EXPERIMENTELLEN PHARMAKOLOGIE.** ***Title Change.*** (1920)-(19??). German. ir. Springer-Verlag GmbH & Company KG, Heidelberger Platz 3, D 14197 Berlin Germany. **Tel** 011 49 30 8207223, FAX 011 49 30 8214091, telex 183 319 SPBLN D. **(Subscription address:** Springer Verlag New York Inc. / for North America, 44 Hartz Way, Secaucus NJ 07096.**) ED** G. V. R. Born. **Circ:** 300. Documents available from CASDDS. ***Continued by*** *Handbook of Experimental Pharmacology, 0171-2004.*
**Desc:** Provides critical and comprehensive discussions of the most significant areas of pharmacological research, written by leading international authorities.
**Ind/Abst** Chem. Abstr.

US
**HAYES DRUGGIST DIRECTORY.** Directory. English. an. $350.00. Edward N Hayes, 4229 Birch Street, Newport Beach CA 92660. **Tel** (714)756-9063. **ED** James E Hayes and Jay D Hayes. **Bk Rev. Ad Acc.** ***Continues*** *Hayes' Druggists' Directory.*
**Desc:** Lists all retail drug stores in US with address, financial strength, and credit rating. Separate listings of all larger wholesale druggists. Mailing labels available by individual selection.

RU/0023-1134
**HIMIKO-FARMACEVTICESKIJ ZURNAL.** (KHIMIKO-FARMATSEVTICHESKII ZHURNAL.). [Him.-farm. z.]. **Added/Corp** Soviet Union. Ministerstvo Zdravookhraneniia. Soviet Union. Ministerstvo Meditsinskoi Promyshlennosti. Vol. 1 (Jan. 1967)-. Academic Scholarly Publication. Russian (table of contents in English). mo. $189.95. Izdatelstvo Meditsina / Russian Academy of Medical Sciences, Ulitsa Solyanka 14, 109801 Moscow Russia. **Tel** 011 95 297-05-04. **(Subscription address:** East View Publications Inc., 3020 Harbor Lane North, Suite 110, Minneapolis MN 55447.**) LC** RS402; .K46. **NLM** W1 KH508. **CODEN** KHFZAN. **Pr Rev.** Documents available from The Genuine Article, BIOSIS Document Express, CASDDS.
**Desc:** Information on pharmaceutical chemistry.
**Ind/Abst** AGRICOLA; Anal. Abstr.; Biol. Abstr.; Chem Inform; Chem. Abstr.; Curr. Biotechnol.; Curr. Chem. React.; Curr. Contents Life Sci.; EMBASE; Helminthol. Abstr. (19??-19??); Index Chem.; Index Vet.; Int. Pharm. Abstr.; Life Sci. Collect.; PESTDOC; Plant Breed. Abstr.; Protozoolog. Abstr.; Res. Alert [Full Cov.]; Rev. Med. Vet. Mycology; Rev. Plant Pathol.; Sci. Cit. Index; SCISEARCH.

II/0018-1935
**HINDUSTAN ANTIBIOTICS BULLETIN.** [Hind. antibiot. bull.]. **Main/Corp** Hindustan Antibiotics, Pimpri, India. **Added/Corp** Hindustan Antibiotics, Pimpri, India. Bulletin. (Aug. 1958)-. Academic Scholarly Publication. English. qt. $15.00. Hindustan Antibiotics Ltd, Pimpri Library, Pune 411 018 India. **(Subscription address:** Prints India, 11 Darya Ganj, New Delhi 110002 India.**) ED** P S Borkar. **LC** RM265; .H55. **DD** 615/.329/05. **NLM** W1 HI407. **CODEN** HINAAU. **Bk Rev. Ad Acc. Circ:** 350. Documents available from BIOSIS Document Express, CASDDS.
**Desc:** Biotechnology-fermentation process, pharmacology and clinical trials of new drugs, reviews and bibliography on antibiotics.
**Ind/Abst** AGRICOLA; Biodeter. Abstr. (1991-); Biol. Abstr.; Chem. Abstr.; Curr. Biotechnol.; EMBASE; Health Plan. Adminis.; Index Med.; Life Sci. Collect.; Rev. Med. Vet. Mycology; Rev. Plant Pathol.

US/0098-6909
**HOSPITAL FORMULARY.** [Hosp. formul.]. Vol. 10, No. 6 (June 1975)-. Academic Scholarly Publication. English. mo. $55.00 US and possessions; $80.00 Canada; $110.00 other. Advanstar Communications Inc., 131 West First Street, Duluth MN 55802. **Tel** (218)723-9477, (800)346-0085. **ED** Jane Hovanec-Brown. **NLM** W1 HO779. **CODEN** HOFODY. **[CCC]. Pr Rev. Circ:** 27,000. available on microfilm and microfiche from University Microfilms International (UMI). Documents available from The Genuine Article, BIOSIS Document Express, CASDDS. ***Continues*** *Hospital Formulary Management, 0018-5655.*
**Ind/Abst** Biol. Abstr.; Chem. Abstr.; Cumul. Index Nurs. Allied Health Lit.; Curr. Contents Clin. Med.; EMBASE; Health Plan. Adminis.; Hospit. Health Admin. Index; Int. Pharm. Abstr.; Iowa Drug Inf. Serv. (1969-); PESTDOC; Protozoolog. Abstr.; Res. Alert [Select. Cov.]; Rev. Med. Vet. Mycology; SCISEARCH; Soc. Sci. Cit. Index [Select. Cov.].

●UK/1352-7967
**HOSPITAL PHARMACIST, THE.** (February 1994)-. English. Six times a year. £26.00 UK; £31.00 other. Pharmaceutical Press, 1 Lambeth High Street, London SE1 7JN England. **Tel** 011 44 71 735 9141, FAX 011 44 71 735 7629, telex 265871, (MONREF G).
**Desc:** Aimed solely at pharmacists working in hospitals. Each issue includes a specifically commissioned feature covering an aspect of hospital pharmacy. The features are supplemented by general interest articles, original papers and illustrated reports, including floor plans.

US/1052-3146
**HOSPITAL PHARMACIST REPORT.** [Hosp. pharm. rep.]. (1987)-. Periodical. English. mo. $39.00 US; $55.00 other. Medical Economics Publishing, Five Paragon Drive, Second Floor, Montvale NJ 07645. **Tel** (800)432-4570, (201)358-2210. **(Subscription address:** Medical Economics Publishing, 120 Cross Street, Winchester MA 01890.**) DD** 615. **NLM** W1; HO869AR. **CODEN** HPRPEC.
**Ind/Abst** BioBusiness (1990-).

US/0739-957X
**HOSPITAL PHARMACY DIRECTOR'S MONTHLY MANAGEMENT SERIES.** [Hosp. pharm. dir. mon. manage. ser.]. **VFOAT** Monthly Management Series. (19??)-. Periodical. English. Twelve times a year. $50.00. RX Data Pac Service, PO Box 42020, Cincinnati OH 45242. **Tel** (513)489-0943. **ED** I. H. Goodman. ctrl circ.

US/0018-5787
**HOSPITAL PHARMACY (PHILADELPHIA).** (HOSPITAL PHARMACY.). [Hosp. pharm.]. **VFOAT** Lippincott's Hospital Pharmacy. Vol. 1 (Jan. 1966)-. Academic Scholarly Publication. English. mo. $94.00 (individuals), $119.00 (institutions) US; $129.00 (individuals), $139.00 (institutions) other. J.B. Lippincott Company, 227 East Washington Square, Philadelphia PA 19106-3780. **Tel** (215)238-4200 or 4454, FAX (215)238-4227. **(Subscription address:** J.B.

Lippincott, PO Box 350, Hagerstown MD 21740.) **ED** Neil M. Davis. **DD** 615. **NLM** W1 HO869B. **CODEN** HOPHAZ. **[CCC]. Ad Acc. Circ:** 27,800. available on microfilm and microfiche from University Microfilms International (UMI). Documents available from BIOSIS Document Express.
**Desc:** Deals with areas of interest to pharmacists serving hospital inpatients and outpatients.
**Ind/Abst** Biol. Abstr.; EMBASE; Health Plan. Adminis.; Hospit. Health Admin. Index; Int. Pharm. Abstr.; Iowa Drug Inf. Serv.

US/0739-9561
**HOSPITAL PHARMACY SERVICE "INSTANT UP-DATE".** [Hosp. pharm. serv. "instant up-date"]. **VFOAT** Instant Update. (19??)-. Periodical. English. Twelve times a year. $70.00. RX Data Pac Service, PO Box 42020, Cincinnati OH 45242. **Tel** (513)489-0943. **ED** I. H. Goodman. ctrl circ.
**Desc:** Covers new products, recalls, discontinued products, FDA, Washington up-dates, news briefs and research information.

UK/0885-6222
**HUMAN PSYCHOPHARMACOLOGY.** [Hum. psychopharmacol.]. **VFOAT** Human Psychopharmacology Clinical and Experimental. Vol. 1, No. 1 (Sept. 1986)-. Academic Scholarly Publication. English. Six times a year. $395.00. John Wiley & Sons Ltd., Baffins Lane, Chichester West Sussex PO19 1UD England. **Tel** 0243 779777, FAX 0243 776128 BTG:JWP001, telex 86290 WIBOOKG. **(Subscription address:** John Wiley / Philadelphia, PO Box 7247, Philadelphia PA 19170.) **ED** Guy Edwards. **DD** 615. **NLM** W1; HU46PE. **CODEN** HUPSEC. **[CCC].** available on microfilm and microfiche from University Microfilms International (UMI). Documents available from The Genuine Article, BIOSIS Document Express, CASDDS, ADONIS.
**Desc:** Aims to communicate the results of clinical and experimental studies relevant to the understanding of new and established psychotropic drugs. Covers topics on experimental human psychopharmacology, efficacy studies in humans, especially large scale and placebo-controlled trials, volunteer studies, relevant animal studies, effects of psychotropic drugs on physiological systems, i.e. unwanted effects, plus psychotropic drug use and dependence.
**Ind/Abst** ADONIS; Biol. Abstr. (1989-); Chem. Abstr. (1986-); CSA Neuro. Abstr. (?-?); Curr. Aware. Biol. Sci., CABS; Curr. Contents Life Sci.; EMBASE; PESTDOC; Psychol. Abstr.; PsycINFO; PsycLit; Res. Alert [Full Cov.]; Sci. Cit. Index; SCISEARCH; Soc. Sci. Cit. Index [Select. Cov.].

US/0019-1221
**IDAHO PHARMACIST, THE. Added/Corp** Idaho State Pharmaceutical Association. Vol. 1 (1964)-. Periodical. English. mo. Idaho State Pharmaceutical Association, 21 North Vinson, Boise ID 83704.
**Ind/Abst** Int. Pharm. Abstr.

US/0891-8511
**IDIS.** (IDIS. MICROFORM.). [IDIS]. **Added/Corp** Iowa Drug Information Service. **VFOAT** Drug Literature Microfilm File. **VAT** Iowa Drug Information Service. (1966)-. English. mo. $1700.00 US, Canada, and Mexico; $1870.00 other. Iowa Drug Information Service, The University of Iowa, 100 Oakdale Campus, N330 OH, Iowa City IA 52242-5000. **Tel** (319)335-4800, (800)525-4347, FAX (319)335-4077. **DD** 615. Index available. cum. index. **Bk Rev. Circ:** 1,000 (ctrl). available on CD-ROM; available on an online database.
**Desc:** Offers a bibliographic indexing service to over 260,000 complete journal articles discussing human drug therapy. The articles indexed come from over 160 English language medical journals.

US
**IDIS SYSTEM / CD-ROM. See** Pharmacy and Pharmacology-Abstracting, Bibliographies and Statistics.

SI/0300-4147
**IIMS, INDONESIA INDEX OF MEDICAL SPECIALITIES. VFOAT** Indonesia Index of Medical Specialities. Vol. 1 (Aug. 1972)-. Periodical. English. Three times a year. 110.00Sing$ (airmail), 60.00Sing$ (surface mail). MIMS Asia, 135 Cecil Street, 13-00 LKN Building, Singapore 0106 Singapore. **Tel** 011 65 2233788, FAX 011 65 2214788. **ED** Jenny Oo. **NLM** QV 772 I11. Index available. **Ad Acc. Circ:** 10,500 (ctrl).
**Desc:** A listing of drugs with information on contents, dosage, indication, presentation and packing.

US/0195-2099
**ILLINOIS PHARMACIST (1979).** (ILLINOIS PHARMACIST.). **Added/Corp** Illinois Pharmacists Association. Vol. 41 (Sept. 1979)-. Periodical. English. mo. $36.00. Illinois Pharmacists Association, 223 West Jackson Boulevard #1000, Chicago IL 60606. **Tel** (312)236-1135. **ED** Jim Flanigan. **NLM** W1 IL433B. **Bk Rev. Ad Acc. Circ:** 3,000 (ctrl). available on microfilm. ***Continues*** *Illinois Journal of Pharmacy, 0147-8222.*
**Desc:** News and clinical information of interest to pharmacists.
**Ind/Abst** Int. Pharm. Abstr.

US
**IMMUNOFACTS.** English. sa. $89.95 (loose-leaf edition) US; $112.50 (loose-leaf edition) other. Facts and Comparisons Inc, 111 West Port Plaza, Suite 400, St Louis MO 63146-3098. **Tel** (314)878-2515, (800)223-0554, FAX (314)878-5563.
**Desc:** Comprehensive updatable reference on vaccines and immunologic drugs. Contains both pediatric and adult dosages.

US
**IMMUNOPHARMACOLOGY REVIEWS. See** Medical Science and Technology-Allergy and Immunology.

SZ
**INDEX NOMINUM / ELBORE PAR LE CENTRE SCIENTIFIQUE DE LA SOCIETE SUISSE DE PHARMACIE. Main/Corp** Schweizerischer Apotheker-Verein. Wissenschaftliche Zentralstelle. **Added/Corp** Schweizerischer Apotheker-Verein. Wissenschaftliche Zentralstelle. Vol. 1 (1970/1971)-. French (English, French and German). be. DM398.00. Medpharm Scientific Publishers, Postfach 101061, D 70009 Stuttgart Germany. **Tel** 011 49 711 25820, FAX 0711/2582-290, telex 723636 daz d. **ED** M Mesnil. **LC** RC55; .I47. **DD** 615/.1/014. **NLM** QV 740 GS9 I4. cum. index.
**Desc:** An alphabetical listing of generic and trade names of internationally available drugs.

UK/0019-3925
**INDEX OF NEW PRODUCTS. See** Pharmacy and Pharmacology-Abstracting, Bibliographies and Statistics.

II/0019-462X
**INDIAN DRUGS.** [Indian drugs]. **Added/Corp** Indian Drug Manufacturers' Association. (1963)-. Academic Scholarly Publication. English. mo. $300.00. Indian Drug Maufacturers' Association, Bombay, India. **(Subscription address:** Prints India, 11 Darya Ganj, New Delhi 110002 India.) **LC** HD9672.I5; I47. **DD** 338.4/7/6151900954. **NLM** W1 IN204C. **CODEN** INDRBA. Documents available from BIOSIS Document Express, CASDDS.
**Ind/Abst** AGRICOLA; Anal. Abstr.; Biodeter. Abstr. (1991-); Biol. Abstr. (19??-1987); Chem. Abstr.; Curr. Biotechnol.; EMBASE; Hortic. Abstr.; Int. Pharm. Abstr.; NAPRALERT; Nat. Prod. Updates; Rev. Med. Vet. Mycology.

II/0019-526X
**INDIAN JOURNAL OF HOSPITAL PHARMACY.** (INDIAN JOURNAL OF HOSPITAL PHARMACY : OFFICIAL PUBLICATION OF THE INDIAN HOSPITAL PHARMACISTS' ASSOCIATION.). [Indian j. hosp. pharm.]. **Added/Corp** Indian Hospital Pharmacists' Association. Vol. 1, No. 1 (May 1964)-. Academic Scholarly Publication. English. bm. $20.00. Indian Hospital Pharmacist Association, R-566 New Rajinder, New Delhi 60 India. **Tel** 583371. **(Subscription address:** Prints India, 11 Darya Ganj, New Delhi 110002 India.) **ED** B D Miglani. **LC** RA975.5.P5; I5. **NLM** W1 IN209J. **CODEN** IJHPBU. Index available. **Bk Rev. Ad Acc. Circ:** 3,000. Documents available from BIOSIS Document Express, CASDDS.
**Desc:** Ideas in the areas on pharmaceutical services in hospitals. Continued education, programmed for pharmacists, drug information and pharmaceutical research.
**Ind/Abst** Biol. Abstr.; Chem. Abstr.; EMBASE; Int. Pharm. Abstr.

II/0970-129X
**INDIAN JOURNAL OF NATURAL PRODUCTS.** [Indian j. nat. prod.]. **Added/Corp** Indian Society of Pharmacognosy. (1985)-. Periodical. English. sa. $20.00. Indian Society of Pharmacognosy, Department of Pharmaceutical Sciences, Sagar MP 470003 India. **(Subscription address:** Prints India, 11 Darya Ganj, New Delhi 110002 India.) **NLM** W1; IN219G. **CODEN** IJNPET. Documents available from BIOSIS Document Express, CASDDS.
**Ind/Abst** Anal. Abstr.; Biol. Abstr. (1985-); Chem. Abstr. (1985-); Int. Pharm. Abstr.

II/0019-5464
**INDIAN JOURNAL OF PHARMACEUTICAL EDUCATION.** (INDIAN JOURNAL OF PHARMACEUTICAL EDUCATION : OFFICIAL PUBLICATION OF ASSOCIATION OF PHARMACEUTICAL TEACHERS OF INDIA.). [Indian j. pharm. educ.]. **Added/Corp** Association of Pharmaceutical Teachers of India. Vol. 1, No. 1 (Jan./June 1967)-. Periodical. English. qt. $20.00. Department of Pharmaceutical Sciences, Panjab University, Chandigarh 160 014 India. **Tel** 20061-69. **(Subscription address:** Prints India, 11 Darya Ganj, New Delhi, 110002 India, (Phone: 011 91 11 3268645)) **ED** P Gundu Rao. **LC** RS119.I5; I5. **DD** 615/.071/154. **NLM** W1 IN224P. **CODEN** IJPEB3. **Circ:** 1,000. Documents available from CASDDS.
**Desc:** Covers pharmaceutical education only.
**Ind/Abst** Chem. Abstr.; Int. Pharm. Abstr.

II/0250-474X
**INDIAN JOURNAL OF PHARMACEUTICAL SCIENCES.** [Indian j. pharm. sci.]. **Added/Corp** Indian Pharmaceutical Association. Vol. 40, No. 2 (Mar./Apr. 1978)-. Academic Scholarly Publication. English. bm. $50.00. Indian Pharmaceutical Association, Kalina Santa Cruz East, Bombay 400 098 India. **Tel** 6122401. **(Subscription address:** Prints India, 11 Darya Ganj, New Delhi, 110002 India, (Phone: 011 91 11 3268645)) **ED** R S Baichwal and C L Kaul. **NLM** W1 IN224V. **CODEN** IJSIDW. Index available. cum. index. **Bk Rev. Ad Acc. Circ:** 2,000 (ctrl). available on microfilm from University Microfilms International (UMI). Documents available from BIOSIS Document Express, CASDDS. ***Continues*** *Indian Journal of Pharmacy, 0019-5472.*
**Desc:** Contains scientific and technological reviews and research papers describing results of original research, and reviews of scientific books. Includes abstracts of papers from foreign journals. Subscribers include colleges, universities and others engaged in pharmaceutical education and research.
**Ind/Abst** AGRICOLA; Anal. Abstr.; Biol. Abstr.; Chem. Abstr.; EMBASE; Field Crop Abstr.; For. Prod. Abstr. (1991-); Helminthol. Abstr. (19??-19??); Hortic. Abstr.; Int. Pharm. Abstr.; Mass Spect. Bull.; Nat. Prod. Updates; PESTDOC; Plant Breed. Abstr.; Rev. Med. Vet. Mycology; Rev. Plant Pathol.; Soils Fert.

II/0253-7613
**INDIAN JOURNAL OF PHARMACOLOGY.** [Indian j. pharmacol.]. **Added/Corp** Indian Pharmacological Society. Jawaharlal Institute of Post-Graduate Medical Education & Research. Dept. of Pharmacology. (196?)-. Academic Scholarly Publication. English. qt. $80.00. Department Pharmacology & Therapy, C O Chief Editor Adithan, Pondicherry 605 006 India. **Tel** 11 91 413 36380 ext 419, FAX 11 91 413 38132. **(Subscription address:** Prints India, 11 Darya Ganj, New Delhi, 110002 India, (Phone: 011 91 11 3268645)) **ED** K C Singhal. **NLM** W1 IN2251. **CODEN** INJPD2. Index available. cum. index. **Bk Rev**, (Qty: 6-8). **Ad Acc. Pr Rev. Circ:** 1,400. Documents available from BIOSIS Document Express, CASDDS.
**Desc:** Pharmacology, medicinal chemistry, chemotherapy, clinical toxicology, drugs, drug development, drug kinetics, pharmacodynamics and clinical trials.
**Ind/Abst** Biol. Abstr.; Chem. Abstr.; EMBASE; NAPRALERT.

II/0019-5499
**INDIAN JOURNAL OF PHYSIOLOGY AND PHARMACOLOGY. See** Biology-Physiology.

II/0073-6635
**INDIAN PHARMACEUTICAL GUIDE.** (1963)-. English. an. $80.00. Pamposh Publication, New Delhi, India. **(Subscription address:** Prints India, 11 Darya Ganj, New Delhi 110002 India.) **LC** PS76.I4; I5.

US
**INDIANA PHARMACIST.** (1919)-. Periodical. English. mo (12 issues per year). $15.00 US; $25.00 other. Indiana Pharmaceutical Association, 729 North Pennsylvania, Indianapolis IN 46204. **Tel** (317)634-4968, FAX (317)632-1219. **ED** Lawrence J. Sage. **Ad Acc.** ctrl circ.
**Ind/Abst** Int. Pharm. Abstr.

IT/0446-0243
**INDUSTRIA DEI FARMACI.** [Ind. Farm.]. (1955)-. Periodical. Italian. mo. **CODEN** INFAB3INFAB3.
**Ind/Abst** Int. Pharm. Abstr.

SP/0213-5574
**INDUSTRIA FARMACEUTICA.** [Ind. farm.]. **VFOAT** Industria Farmaceutica, Investigacion y Tecnologia. (1986)-. Periodical. Spanish. bm. $103.00 Europe; $164.00 other. Editorial Alcion SA, Triana 53, 28016 Madrid Spain. **Tel** 011 34 1 345-6400. **UDC** 615.

SP
**INFORMACION TERAPEUTICA DEL SISTEMA NACIONAL DE SALUD. Added/Corp** Instituto Nacional de la Salud (Spain). Vol. 14, No. 6 (1990)-. Periodical. Spanish (summaries and/or abstracts in English). mo. Ministerio de Sanidad y Seguridad Social, Instituto Nacional de la Salud, Madrid Spain. **NLM** W1; IN413N. ***Continues*** *Informacion Terapeutica de la Seguridad Social, 0210-9417.*

IT
**INFORMATICA DEL FARMACO E DEL PARAFARMACO.** Italian. mo. L198000. Org Edit Medico Farmaceutica, CP 10434, 20110 Milan Italy. **Tel** 011 39 2 675051.

AU/0378-2220
**INFORMATION LETTER / UNITED NATIONS, DIVISION OF NARCOTIC DRUGS.** [Inf. let. - U. N., Div. Narc. Drugs]. **Added/Corp** United Nations. Division of Narcotic Drugs. (1971)-. Periodical. English. Six times a year. Free. United Nations Division of Narcotic Drugs, Vienna International Center, PO Box 500, A-1400 Vienna Austria. **Tel** 011 43 222 211310. **NLM** W1; IN4209.

FR
**INFORMATION PHARMACEUTIQUES. Added/Corp** Ordre National des Pharmaciens (France). **VFOAT** Bulletin de L'Ordre National des Pharmaciens.

No. 156 (March 1973)-. Periodical. French. ir (24 issues). 210.00F. Conseil Natl de l Ordre des Pharmaciens, 4 Av Ruysdael, F-75008 Paris France. **Tel** 011 33 1 40537400. **NLM** W1 IN431H. ***Continues*** *Bulletin - Ordre National des Pharmaciens.*
**Ind/Abst** Int. Pharm. Abstr.

IT/0392-3010
**INFORMATORE FARMACEUTICO : ANNUARIO ITALIANO DEI MEDICAMENTI E DEI LABORATORI, L'.** **VFOAT** Italian Directory of Drugs and Manufacturers. (1968)-. Italian (English). an. L385000.00 Italy; L425000.00 Europe; L450000.00 other. Org Edit Medico Farmaceutica, CP 10434, 20110 Milan Italy. **Tel** 011 39 2 675051. **ED** Lucio Marini. **NLM** QV 22 GI8 I4. Index available. **Circ:** 25,000. available on microfiche. ***Continues*** *Informatore Farmaceutico Italiano, 0443-1839.*
**Desc:** Italian list of 25,000 drugs, 6,000 pharmaceutical raw materials and more than 2,000 manufacturer's addresses, updated every two months.

IT/1121-1644
**INFORMAZIONI SUI FARMACI.** [Inf. farm.]. (1977)-. Periodical. Italian. qt. L80000 Italy; L120000 other. Farmacie Comunali Riunite, Via Doberdo 9, 42100 Reggio Emilia Italy. **Tel** 011 39 522 555431, FAX 011 39 522 550146. **UDC** 615. Index available. cum. index. **Circ:** 4,500.
**Desc:** Covers topics in clinical pharmacology for physicians and pharmacists.

US/0730-6628
**INFORMED. BLUE BANNER EDITION.** ***Ceased.*** (INFORMED.). [InforMED. Blue banner ed.]. **VAT** Infor Med. Blue Banner Edition. Periodical. English. wk (except August). MDT Publications, PO Box 581, Sheffield MA 01257. **Tel** (713)668-6700. **ED** M D Tatkon, M Trachtenberg. Index available. **Bk Rev.**

CN/0824-8281
**INHALO-SCOPE.** ***Suspended.*** (L'INHALO-SCOPE : PUBLICATION OFFICIELLE DE LA CORPORATION DES INHALOTHERAPEUTES DU QUEBEC.). [Inhalo-scope]. **Added/Corp** Corporation des Inhalotherapeutes du Quebec. Vol. 1, No. 1 (Oct. 1983)-(19??). Periodical. French (English). Four times a year. 18.00Can$ Canada. Corporation Professionnelle des Inhalotherapeutes du Quebec, 1610 St. Catherine West, Suite 409, Montreal Quebec H3H 2S2 Canada. **Tel** (514)931-2900. **DD** 615.8/36. **Ad Acc. Circ:** 2,000 (ctrl). ***Continues*** *Corporation des Inhalotherapeutes du Quebec. Bulletin, 0712-9610.*

NZ/0156-2703
**INPHARMA WEEKLY.** **VFOAT** ADIS Inpharma Weekly. No. 719 (13 Jan. 1990)-. Periodical. English. wk (50 issues). 2695.00F Europe; $1640.00 other. ADIS International Ltd, 41 Centorian Drive, Private Bag 65901, Mairangi Bay, Auckland 10 New Zealand. **Tel** 011 64 9 4798100, FAX 011 64 9 4791418. **(Subscription address:** Japan Publications Trading Company, Ltd., PO Box 5030, Tokyo International, Tokyo 100-31 Japan.**)** **[CCC].** available on CD-ROM from SilverPlatter (UK); and Micromedia Limited. ***Continues*** *Inpharma, 0156-2703.*
**Desc:** Rapid alerts to news on drugs and drug therapy. Covers drug prescribing trends, new product and development trends, new product therapeutic developments, clinically important adverse reaction reports, health care policy and drug economic issues.

●SZ
**INTERNATIONAL ACADEMY FOR BIOMEDICAL AND DRUG RESEARCH.** **Added/Corp** International Academy for Biomedical and Drug Research. Vol. 1 (1992)-. Monographic series. English. Twice a year. 150.00F (approx. per volume). S. Karger AG, Allschwilerstrasse 10, PO Box - Postfach - Case Postale, CH-4009 Basel Switzerland. **Tel** 011 41 61 306-1111, FAX 011 41 61 306-1234, telex CH 962 652. **ED** S. Z. Langer, J. Mendlewicz, G. Racagni. **NLM** W1; IN701D. Documents available from BIOSIS Document Express.
**Desc:** Addresses new developments and future strategies in drug treatment of human diseases; this series will record the proceedings of international workshops devoted to updating information on several important therapeutic areas each year.
**Ind/Abst** Biol. Abstr.; Ref. Upd. Deluxe Ed.

UK/0268-1315
**INTERNATIONAL CLINICAL PSYCHOPHARMACOLOGY.** Vol. 1, No. 1 (Jan. 1986)-. Periodical. English. qt. $330.00 US; £195.00 other. Rapid Communications of Oxford Ltd, The Old Malthouse, Paradise Street, Oxford OX1 1LD England. **Tel** 011 44 0865 790447, FAX 011 44 0865 244012, telex 9403712. **ED** Dr S A Montgomery and Prof T Silverstone. **NLM** W1; IN733LS. **CODEN** ICLPE4. **[CCC].** Index available. cum. index. **Bk Rev. Ad Acc. Pr Rev. Acid Free.** ctrl circ. Documents available from The Genuine Article.
**Desc:** Largely concerned with psychotropic drugs, covering phase I-IV studies, clinical studies, side effects and epidemiology.
**Ind/Abst** Curr. Aware. Biol. Sci., CABS; Curr. Contents Life Sci.; Helminthol. Abstr.; Index Med. (1986-); PESTDOC; Psychol. Abstr. (1986-); PsycINFO; PsycLit; Res. Alert [Full Cov.]; Rev. Med. Vet. Entomol.; Sci. Cit. Index; SCISEARCH; Soc. Sci. Cit. Index [Select. Cov.].

US/0888-6393
**INTERNATIONAL DRUG & DEVICE REGULATORY MONITOR.** ***Title Change.*** [Int. drug device regul. monit.]. **VFOAT** International Drug and Device Regulatory Monitor; Monitor. No. 111 (Aug. 1982)-(19??). Periodical. English. mo. Monitor Publishers, 1545 New York Avenue NE, Washington DC 20002. **DD** 344. **NLM** W1; IN746D. ***Continues*** *International Drug Regulatory Monitor, 0198-7402.* ***Split into*** *International Pharmaceutical Regulatory Monitor* ***and*** *International Medical Device Monitor.*

US/0734-9084
**INTERNATIONAL DRUG REVIEW.** ***Title Change.*** [Int. drug rev.]. **Added/Corp** Paregian Associates. Vol. 1, No. 1 (Apr. 1982)-(19??). Periodical. English. Nine times a year (nine to ten issues per year). Paregian Associates, 250 Davenport Avenue, New Rochelle NY 10805. **Tel** (914)235-8035. **ED** Philip Paregian. **NLM** QV 772; I61. ***Merged into*** *New Drug Commentary.*
**Desc:** Covers new drugs under development in Europe, Japan, USSR, and India giving stage of progress, description, chemistry, clinical evaluations, markets, patents, licensees, etc.

US/0020-6571
**INTERNATIONAL DRUG THERAPY NEWSLETTER.** (1966)-. Periodical. English. mo (except July and Aug.). $45.00 US; $53.00 Canada and Mexico; $57.00 other. Ayd Medical Communications, 1130 East Cold Spring Lane, Baltimore MD 21239. **Tel** (301)433-9220, FAX (301)532-5419. **ED** Frank J. Ayd Jr. **NLM** W1 IN747. Index available. cum. index. **Bk Rev. Ad Acc. Circ:** 7,000 (ctrl).
**Desc:** Information on psychopharmacotherapy and psychoactive drug therapy and use.
**Ind/Abst** Int. Pharm. Abstr.

UK
**INTERNATIONAL ENCYCLOPEDIA OF PHARMACOLOGY AND THERAPEUTICS.** (19??)-. Monographic series. English. ir. Price varies per volume. Pergamon Press, An Imprint of Elsevier Science Ltd., The Boulevard, Langford Lane, Kidlington, Oxford OX5 1GB United Kingdom. **Tel** 011 44 865 843000, 011 44 865 843699, FAX 011 44 865 843010. **(Subscription address:** US/ 395 Saw Mill River Road, Elmsford, NY 10523; Can/ 150 Consumers Road/Suite 104, Willowdale Ontario M2J 1P9; Aus-NZ/ POB 544, Potts Point NSW 2011**)**

●GW/0946-1965
**INTERNATIONAL JOURNAL OF CLINICAL PHARMACOLOGY AND THERAPEUTICS.** **VFOAT** Clinical Pharmacology and Therapeutics. Vol. 32, No. 1 (Jan. 1994)-. Periodical. English. mo. $165.00 (individuals), $198.00 (institutions). Dustri-Verlag, Dr Karl Feistle, Postfach 49, D 82032 Deisenhofen Germany. **Tel** 011 49 89 6138610, FAX 011 49 89 6135412. **LC** RM1; .I55. **DD** 615/.1/05. **NLM** W1; IN766DJM. **CODEN** ICTHEK. ***Continues*** *International Journal of Clinical Pharmacology, Therapy, and Toxicology (International Symposia on Clinical Pharmacology : 1980), 0174-4879.*
**Ind/Abst** Index Med. (1994-).

SZ/0251-1649
**INTERNATIONAL JOURNAL OF CLINICAL PHARMACOLOGY RESEARCH.** [Int. j. clin. pharmacol. res.]. **Added/Corp** Societa Italiana di Farmacologia Clinica. **VFOAT** Clinical Pharmacology Research. (1981)-. Academic Scholarly Publication. English. bm. 342.00F Europe; 355.00F other. Bioscience Ediprint Inc, rue Alexandre Gavard 16, 1227 Carouge Geneva Switzerland. **Tel** 011 41 22 3003383. **NLM** W1 IN766DKH. **CODEN** CPHRDE. **[CCC]. Pr Rev.** available on microfilm and microfiche from University Microfilms International (UMI). Documents available from The Genuine Article, CASDDS.
**Ind/Abst** Chem. Abstr.; Curr. Contents Life Sci.; EMBASE; Index Med.; Int. Pharm. Abstr.; Life Sci. Collect.; PESTDOC; Res. Alert [Full Cov.]; Sci. Cit. Index; SCISEARCH.

GW/0174-4879
**INTERNATIONAL JOURNAL OF CLINICAL PHARMACOLOGY, THERAPY AND TOXICOLOGY (1980).** ***Title Change.*** (INTERNATIONAL JOURNAL OF CLINICAL PHARMACOLOGY, THERAPY AND TOXICOLOGY.). [Int. j. clin. pharmacol., ther. toxicol.]. **Added/Corp** International Symposia on Clinical Pharmacology. Vol. 18, No. 1 (Jan. 1980)-(19??). Academic Scholarly Publication. English. mo. Dustri-Verlag, Dr Karl Feistle, Postfach 49, D 82032 Deisenhofen Germany. **Tel** 011 49 89 6138610, FAX 011 49 89 6135412. **ED** H.P. Kuemmerle. **LC** RM1; .I55. **DD** 615/.1/05. **NLM** W1 IN766DL. **[CCC].** Index available in last issue of volume--attached. **Bk Rev.** Documents available from The Genuine Article, CASDDS. ***Continues*** *International Journal of Clinical Pharmacology and Biopharmacy, 0340-0026.* ***Continued by*** *International Journal of Clinical Pharmacology and Therapeutics, 0174-4879.*
**Desc:** Information on the latest developments and topics of current interest pertaining to pharmacology and toxicology.
**Ind/Abst** Chem. Abstr.; Curr. Aware. Biol. Sci., CABS; Curr. Contents Life Sci.; Dairy Sci. Abstr.; EMBASE; Hospit. Health Admin. Index; Index Med.; Int. Pharm. Abstr. (19??-19??); NAPRALERT; Life Sci. Collect.; PESTDOC; Protozoolog. Abstr.; Psychol. Abstr. (1980-); PsycINFO; PsycLit; Res. Alert [Full Cov.]; Sci. Cit. Index; Soc. Sci. Cit. Index [Select. Cov.].

UK/0192-0561
**INTERNATIONAL JOURNAL OF IMMUNOPHARMACOLOGY.** [Int. j. immunopharmacol.]. Vol. 1 (1979)-. Academic Scholarly Publication. English. Twelve times a year. $640.00 The Americas; £429.00 other. Pergamon Press, An Imprint of Elsevier Science Ltd., The Boulevard, Langford Lane, Kidlington, Oxford OX5 1GB United Kingdom. **Tel** 011 44 865 843000, 011 44 865 843699, FAX 011 44 865 843010. **(Subscription address:** Elsevier Science Ltd. Oxford Fulfillment Centre, PO Box 800, Kidlington, Oxford OX5 1DX United Kingdom.**)** **ED** P. W. Mullen, J. W. Hadden and F. Spreafico. **NLM** W1 IN768K. **CODEN** IJIMDS. **[CCC]. Pr Rev.** available on microfilm and microfiche from University Microfilms International (UMI). Documents available from The Genuine Article, BIOSIS Document Express, CASDDS, ADONIS.
**Desc:** Publishes original high-quality scientific contributions, particularly those of obvious clinical relevance which interrelate pharmacology and immunology.
**Ind/Abst** ADONIS; Biol. Abstr.; Chem. Abstr.; Chem. Titles; Curr. Aware. Biol. Sci., CABS; Curr. Contents Life Sci.; EMBASE; Helminthol. Abstr.; Immunol. Abstr.; Index Med.; NAPRALERT; Life Sci. Collect.; PESTDOC; Protozoolog. Abstr.; Ref. Upd. Basic Ed.; Ref. Upd. Deluxe Ed.; Res. Alert [Full Cov.]; Rev. Med. Vet. Mycology; Sci. Cit. Index; SCISEARCH.

US/1044-0003
**INTERNATIONAL JOURNAL OF ORIENTAL MEDICINE.** (INTERNATIONAL JOURNAL OF ORIENTAL MEDICINE / KUO CHI HAN FANG I YAO TSA CHIH.). [Int. j. orient. med.]. **Added/Corp** Oriental Healing Arts Institute of U.S.A. **VFOAT** International Journal of Chinese Medicine; Kuo Chi Han Fang i Yao Tsa Chih. Vol. 14, No. 1 (March 1989)-. Periodical. English. Four times a year. $60.00. Oriental Healing Arts Institute, 1945 Palo Verde Avenue, Suite 208, Long Beach CA 90815. **Tel** (213)431-3544, FAX (213)594-6513. **DD** 615. **NLM** W1; IN77W. ***Continues*** *Oriental Healing Arts International Bulletin, 0888-9341.*
**Desc:** Seeks to stimulate an interest in and appreciation of Chinese medicine in an audience which might never be exposed to its principles and practices.

UK/0260-6267
**INTERNATIONAL JOURNAL OF PHARMACEUTICAL TECHNOLOGY & PRODUCT MANUFACTURE.** ***Ceased.*** [Int. j. pharm. technol. prod. manuf.]. **VFOAT** International Journal of Pharmaceutical Technology and Product Manufacture. Vol. 1, No. 1 (Autumn 1979)-(19??). Academic Scholarly Publication. English. ir (4 times a year). Childwall University Press Ltd, PO Box 78, London NW11 0PG England. **Tel** 011 41 81 14551040, telex 8954242 POWDER G. **ED** A S Goldberg. **NLM** W1 IN771S. **CODEN** IPTMDN. **Bk Rev. Ad Acc. Circ:** 1,500 (ctrl). Documents available from BIOSIS Document Express, CASDDS.
**Desc:** Pharmaceutical technology and manufacturing, including analysis, manufacture, process, stability, etc.
**Ind/Abst** BioBusiness; Biol. Abstr.; Chem. Abstr.; EMBASE; Int. Pharm. Abstr.; PESTDOC (?-?).

NE/0378-5173
**INTERNATIONAL JOURNAL OF PHARMACEUTICS.** [Int. j. pharm.]. Vol. 1 (Jan./Feb. 1978)-. Academic Scholarly Publication. English. Twenty-eight times a year (14 vols.). Fl5712.00. Elsevier Science Publishers BV, PO Box 211, 1000 AE Amsterdam Netherlands. **Tel** 011 31 20 5803642, FAX 011 31 20 5862696, telex 15682. **ED** P F D'Arcy, W I Higuchi, and J H Rytting. **NLM** W1 IN771T. **CODEN** IJPHDE. **[CCC]. Pr Rev.** available on microfilm and microfiche from University Microfilms International (UMI). Documents available from The Genuine Article, BIOSIS Document Express, CASDDS, ADONIS.
**Desc:** Provides a medium for the publication of research results dealing with all aspects of pharmaceutics including physical, chemical, analytical, biological and engineering studies related to drug delivery in its broadest sense.
**Ind/Abst** ADONIS; AGRICOLA; BioBusiness (-1990); Biol. Abstr.; Chem. Abstr.; Chem. Titles; Curr. Biotechnol.; Curr. Contents Life Sci.; Dairy Sci. Abstr.; EMBASE; Int. Pharm. Abstr.; NAPRALERT; Nutr. Abstr. Rev., Ser. B, Live Feeds and Feed.; Life Sci. Collect.; PESTDOC; Potato Abstr.; Protozoolog. Abstr.; Ref. Upd. Deluxe Ed.; Res. Alert [Full Cov.]; Rev. Med. Vet. Mycology; Rice Abstr.; Sci. Cit. Index; SCISEARCH; Soyabean Abstr.

NE/0925-1618
**INTERNATIONAL JOURNAL OF PHARMACOGNOSY.** (INTERNATIONAL JOURNAL OF PHARMACOGNOSY : A JOURNAL OF CRUDE DRUG RESEARCH.). [Int. j. pharmacogn.]. Vol. 29 No. 1 (Feb. 1991)-. Academic Scholarly Publication. English (French, German and Spanish). qt. Fl719.00 (Institutions). Swets & Zeitlinger BV, Heereweg 347B PO Box 825, 2160 SZ Lisse Holland. **Tel** 011 31 2521 35111, FAX 02521-15888, telex 41325. **(Subscription address:** Swets Publishing Service, PO Box 825, 2160 SZ Lisse The Netherlands**) ED** John M Pezzuto. **NLM** W1; IN771W. **CODEN** IJPYEW. **[CCC].** Documents available from BIOSIS Document Express, CASDDS. ***Continues*** *International Journal of Crude Drug Research, 0167-7314.*
**Desc:** Publishes original research concerning the validation of folk medicines by scientific means. This includes studies in chemistry, pharmacology, toxicology, and ethnobotany. The journal aims to provide a forum for facilitating collaborations between scientists who may not have access to other disciplines crucial to the exploration of the full potential of plant medicines.
**Ind/Abst** AGRICOLA [Select. Cov.]; Biol. Abstr. (1991-); Chem. Abstr.; EMBASE; Int. Pharm. Abstr.; PESTDOC; Plant Genet. Resour. Abstr.

UK/0961-7671
**INTERNATIONAL JOURNAL OF PHARMACY PRACTICE. Added/Corp** Royal Pharmaceutical Society of Great Britain. Vol. 1, No. 1 (Mar. 1991)-. Periodical. English. qt. £66.00 UK; £74.00 other. Pharmaceutical Press, 1 Lambeth High Street, London SE1 7JN England. **Tel** 011 44 71 735 9141, FAX 011 44 71 735 7629, telex 265871, (MONREF G). **ED** Douglas Simpson. **NLM** W1; IN771WL. **Bk Rev. Ad Acc. Pr Rev.**
**Desc:** Research papers in the field of pharmacy practice; review articles, news and notes.
**Ind/Abst** Int. Pharm. Abstr.

UK/0266-0512
**INTERNATIONAL MONOGRAPHS ON RISK. See** Medical Science and Technology-Toxicology.

SZ
**INTERNATIONAL NONPROPRIETARY NAMES (INN) FOR PHARMACEUTICAL SUBSTANCES / DENOMINATIONS COMMUNES INTERNATIONALES (DCI) POUR LES SUBSTANCES PHARMACEUTIQUES. Main/Corp** World Health Organization. **Added/Corp** World Health Organization. **VFOAT** Denominations Communes Internationales (DCI) pour les Substances Pharmaceutiques. Liste Recapitulative. Cumulative List No. 4 (1976)-. Monographic series. English (French, Latin, Russian and Spanish). ir. Price varies per volume. World Health Organization, Distribution and Sales, 20 Avenue Appia, CH-1211 Geneva 27 Switzerland. **Tel** 011 41 22 7912111, FAX 011 41 22 7880401. **(Subscription address:** World Health Organization, 49 Sheridan Avenue, Albany NY 12210.**) LC** RS55; .W6. **DD** 615/.1/03. Index available. cum. index. ***Continues*** *Cumulative List of Proposed International Non-Proprietary Names for Pharmaceutical Preparations.*
**Desc:** A cumulative list covering all current proposed and recommended international nonproprietary names for pharmaceutical substances. The list in intended as an aid for drug manufacturers, prescribers, and regulartory authorities who must work with generic names and need an authoritative reference that helps them keep track of newly introduced names.

US/0020-8264
**INTERNATIONAL PHARMACEUTICAL ABSTRACTS. See** Pharmacy and Pharmacology-Abstracting, Bibliographies and Statistics.

US
**INTERNATIONAL PHARMACEUTICAL REGULATORY MONITOR.** (19??)-. English. mo. $495.00. Newsletter Services Inc, 9700 Philadelphia Court, Lanham MD 20706. **Tel** (800)345-2611.
***Separated from*** *International Drug & Device Regulatory Monitor.*

UK/0264-2247
**INTERNATIONAL PHARMACEUTICAL TECHNOLOGY & PRODUCT MANUFACTURE ABSTRACTS. *Ceased.*** [Int. pharm. technol. prod. manuf. abstr.]. **VFOAT** International Pharmaceutical Technology and Product Manufacture Abstracts; IPT & PM Abstracts. No. 1 (July 1983)-(19??). Periodical. English. qt. Childwall University Press Ltd, PO Box 78, London NW11 0PG England. **Tel** 011 41 81 14551040, telex 8954242 POWDER G. **NLM** ZQV 778; I61.

NE/1010-0423
**INTERNATIONAL PHARMACY JOURNAL.** (INTERNATIONAL PHARMACY JOURNAL : OFFICIAL JOURNAL OF F.I.P..). [Int. pharm. j.]. **Added/Corp** Federation Internationale Ppharmaceutique. Vol. 1, No. 1 (Jan./Feb. 1987)-. Periodical. English (French; summaries and/or abstracts in German and Spanish). bm (6 issues). DM145.15 Germany; DM145.50 Europe; DM167.46 other. Federation International Pharmaceutique, Andries Bickerweg 5, 2517 JP The Hague Netherlands. **NLM** W1; IN827LN. **CODEN** IPHJEN. ***Continues*** *Pharmacy International.*
**Ind/Abst** EMBASE; Int. Pharm. Abstr.; Iowa Drug Inf. Serv.

SZ/1013-9222
**INTERNATIONAL SYMPOSIUM ON THE PHARMACOLOGY OF THERMOREGULATION. *Ceased.*** (THERMOREGULATION.). [Int. Symp. Pharmacol. Thermoregul.]. (1973)-Volume 8 (1992). Periodical. English. an. S. Karger AG, Allschwilerstrasse 10, PO Box - Postfach - Case Postale, CH-4009 Basel Switzerland. **Tel** 011 41 61 306-1111, FAX 011 41 61 306-1234, telex CH 962 652. Documents available from BIOSIS Document Express.
**Desc:** A forum for the discussion of new knowledge on the management and prevention of thermoregulatory disorders, this series records the proceedings of international symposia on the pharmacology of thermoregulation featuring up-to-date information on research into all aspects of temperature regulation, focusing particularly on the correlation of advances in basic research with their immediate or potential clinical applications. Providing unique access to worldwide investigations, the series serves as an important account of progress being made in both general areas and specific problems, as a guide for further research.
**Ind/Abst** Biol. Abstr.; Ref. Upd. Deluxe Ed.

●US/1065-9412
**INTERPHARMACY FORUM.** [InterPharm. forum]. **Added/Corp** Facts and Comparisons (Firm). **VFOAT** Inter Pharmacy Forum. Vol. 1, Issue 1 (Jan. 1993)-. Periodical. English. mo. $39.95 US; $50.00 other. Facts and Comparisons Inc, 111 West Port Plaza, Suite 400, St Louis MO 63146-3098. **Tel** (314)878-2515, (800)223-0554, FAX (314)878-5563. **DD** 615.

US
**IOWA DRUG INFORMATION SERVICE. See** Pharmacy and Pharmacology-Abstracting, Bibliographies and Statistics.

US/0889-7735
**IOWA PHARMACIST.** [Iowa pharm.]. **Added/Corp** Iowa Pharmacists Association. Iowa Pharmaceutical Association. Vol. 1 (Nov. 1946)-. Periodical. English. mo. $30.00. Iowa Pharmacists Association, 8515 Douglas Street/Suite 16, Des Moines IA 50322. **Tel** (515)270-0713. **DD** 615. **NLM** W1 IO379.
**Ind/Abst** Int. Pharm. Abstr.; Iowa Drug Inf. Serv. (1977-).

IE/0332-2130
**IPU REVIEW.** [IPU rev.]. **Added/Corp** Irish Pharmaceutical Union. **VAT** Irish Pharmaceutical Union Review. (1976)-. Periodical. English. mo. **NLM** W1 I268D.
**Ind/Abst** Int. Pharm. Abstr.

IE/0332-0707
**IRISH PHARMACY JOURNAL. Added/Corp** Pharmaceutical Society of Ireland. Jan. (1972)-. Periodical. English. mo. 18.00p Ireland, 30.00p other. Kenlis Publications Ltd., 37 Northumberland Road, Dublin, 4 Ireland. **Tel** 011 353 1 600551. **LC** RS1; .I75. **DD** 615/.1/05. **NLM** W1 IR458. ***Continues*** *Irish Chemist & Druggist.*
**Ind/Abst** Int. Pharm. Abstr.

IS/0334-2603
**ISRAEL PHARMACEUTICAL JOURNAL.** (JOURNAL DE L'ASSOCIATION PHARMACEUTIQUE D'ISRAEL.). [Isr. pharm. j.]. **Added/Corp** Histadrut Ha-Rokkim Be-Yisrael. **VFOAT** Harokeach Haivri; Journal de l'Association Pharmaceutique D'Israel; Rokeah Ha-Ivri. Vol. 15, No. 1 (Mar. 1972)-. Periodical. English (French and Hebrew). **CODEN** IPHJAJ. Documents available from CASDDS. ***Continues*** *Harokeach Haivri, 0017-7865.*
**Ind/Abst** Bibliogr. Mission.; Chem. Abstr. (19??-1987); Int. Pharm. Abstr.

●US/1061-3439
**ISSX PROCEEDINGS.** [ISSX proc.]. **Main/Corp** International Society for the Study of Xenobiotics. **Added/Corp** International Society for the Study of Xenobiotics. **VFOAT** International Society for the Study of Xenobiotics Proceedings. **VAT** International Society for the Study of Xenobiotics Proceedings. Vol. 1 (1992)-. English. Twice a year. $30.00. International Society for Study Xenobiotics, 9650 Rockville Pike, Bethesda MD 20814-3998. **Tel** (301)983-2434, FAX (301)983-5357. **ED** Nancy Holahan. **LC** QP529; .I58a. **DD** 615.9. **NLM** W1; IS669K. **Ad Acc. Pr Rev. Circ:** 1,800.
**Desc:** Full-page abstracts from all oral and poster presentations at ISSX Scientific meetings, with international representation.

TU/0367-7524
**ISTANBUL UNIVERSITESI ECZACLK FAKULTESI MECMUAS.** (ISTANBUL UNIVERSITESI ECZACLK FAKULTESI MECMUAS / JOURNAL OF FACULTY OF PHARMACY OF ISTANBUL UNIVERSITY.). [Istanbul Univ. Eczaclk Fak. mecm.]. **Added/Corp** Istanbul Universitesi. Eczaclk Fakultesi. **VFOAT** Mecmuas (Istanbul Universitesi. Eczaclk Fakultesi.); Journal of Faculty of Pharmacy of Istanbul University. (1965)-. Periodical. Turkish. **NLM** W1 IS799. **CODEN** IEFMA9. Documents available from BIOSIS Document Express, CASDDS.
**Ind/Abst** Biol. Abstr.; Chem. Abstr.; Int. Pharm. Abstr.

JA/0385-5015
**IYAKUHIN SOGO SAYO KENKYU.** [Iyakuhin sogo sayo kenkyu]. **VFOAT** Research on Drug Interactions. (1976)-. Periodical. Japanese. sa. Iyakuhin Sogo Sayo Kenkyukai, (Research Soc. of Drug Interactions), c/o Tohoku Daigaku Byoin Yakuzaibu, 1-1, Seiryomachi, Sendaishi, Miyagiken 980 Japan. **DD** _a615. Documents available from CASDDS.
**Ind/Abst** Chem. Abstr.

GW/0932-7770
**JAHRBUCH PHARMALABOR.** (1987)-. German. an. VCH Gesellschaft GmbH, Postfach 101161, D 69451 Weinheim Germany. **Tel** 011 49 6201 606459, FAX 011 49 6201 606184. **(Subscription address:** VCH Publishers Inc., 303 Northwest 12th Avenue, Journals Department, Deerfield FL 33442.**) NLM** W1; JA198L.

NE/0165-8352
**JANSSEN RESEARCH FOUNDATION SERIES.** [Janssen Res. Found. ser.]. V. 1-. Academic Scholarly Publication. English. ir. Price varies per volume. Elsevier Science Publishing Company Inc, Madison Square Station, PO Box 882, New York NY 10159-0882. **Tel** (212)633-3950, FAX (212)633-3990. **NLM** W1 JA82. **CODEN** JRFSDU. Documents available from CASDDS.
**Ind/Abst** Chem. Abstr.; Life Sci. Collect.

US
**JANSSEN RESEARCH NEWS. VFOAT** Research News. Periodical. English. bm. Janssen Pharmaceutica, 501 George Street, New Brunswick NJ 08903.
**Ind/Abst** Index Vet.; Vet. Bull.

JA/0368-2781
**JAPANESE JOURNAL OF ANTIBIOTICS, THE.** [Jpn. j. antibiot.]. **Added/Corp** Nihon Koseibusshitsu Gakujutsu Kyogikai. Vol. 21 (Feb. 1968)-. Academic Scholarly Publication. Japanese (summaries and/or abstracts in English). mo. $220.00 Asia; $250.00 Canada & US, West Indies, Oceania, Europe; $270.00 other. Japan Antibiotics Research Association, 2-20-8 Kamiosaki Shinagawa-ku, Tokyo 141 Japan. **Tel** 011 81 3 34910181, FAX 03-491-0179. **ED** K. Maeda, K. Shimizu, T. Ichikawa, and O. Kitamoto. **NLM** W1 JA95N. **CODEN** JJANAX. Index available. **Ad Acc. Circ:** 1,200. available on microfilm from University Microfilms International (UMI). Documents available from CASDDS. ***Continues*** *Journal of Antibiotics. Series B.*
**Desc:** A journal publishing reports on the efficacy and safety of new antibiotics and related chemotherapeutics.
**Ind/Abst** Chem. Abstr.; EMBASE; Index Med.; Life Sci. Collect.; PESTDOC.

JA/0021-5198
**JAPANESE JOURNAL OF PHARMACOLOGY.** (THE JAPANESE JOURNAL OF PHARMACOLOGY : OFFICIAL PUBLICATION OF THE JAPANESE PHARMACOLOGICAL SOCIETY.). [Jpn. j. pharmacol.]. **Added/Corp** Nihon Yakuri Gakkai. Vol. 1 (April 1951)-. Academic Scholarly Publication. English. mo (13 issues). $330.00. Nihon Shoyaku Gakkai, (Japanese Soc. of Pharmacognosy), Nihon Gakkai Jimu Senta, 4-16, Yayoi 2 Chome, Bunkyoku, Tokyoto 113, Japan. **(Subscription address:** Kyowa Book Company Inc., 1 38 Kanda Jinbocho Chiyoda-ku, Tokyo 101 Japan.**) LC** QP901; .J3. **DD** 615/.05. **NLM** W1 JA971. **CODEN** JJPAAZ. **[CCC]. Pr Rev.** available on microfilm and microfiche from University Microfilms International (UMI). Documents available from The Genuine Article, BIOSIS Document Express, CASDDS. ***Continues*** *Japanese Journal of Medical Sciences. Section 4, Pharmacology, 0368-3745.*
**Ind/Abst** Anim. Behav. Abstr.; Biol. Abstr.; Calcium Calcif. Tissue Abstr.; Chem. Abstr.; Chem. Titles; CSA Neuro. Abstr.; Curr. Aware. Biol. Sci., CABS; Curr. Contents Life Sci.; EMBASE; Immunol. Abstr.; Index Med.; NAPRALERT; Nutr. Abstr. Rev., Ser. B, Live Feeds and Feed.; Nutr. Abstr. Rev., Ser. A, Hum. Exp.; Life Sci. Collect.; PESTDOC; Protozoolog. Abstr.; Psychol. Abstr.; Ref. Upd. Deluxe Ed.; Res. Alert [Full Cov.]; Sci. Cit. Index; SCISEARCH.

JA
**JAPANESE PHARMACEUTICAL BUSINESS REPORT: JPB.** English. $120.00. JPB Info, 16-14 Nihonbashi Kodenma Cho, Chuo-ku Tokyo 103 Japan. **Tel** 011 81 3 3661 0881.

JA/0385-8502
**JITCHUKEN ZENRINSHO KENKYUHO.** (JITCHUKEN ZENRINSHO KENKYU HO. CIEA PRECLINICAL REPORTS.). [Jitchuken zenrinsho kenkyuho]. **Added/Corp** Jikken Dobutsu Chuo Kenkyujo (Kawasaki-Shi, Japan) Jikken Dobutsu Chuo Kenkyujo (Kawasaki-Shi, Japan). Jikken Dobutsu Chuo Kenkyujo Nempo. Jikken Dobutsu Chuo Kenkyujo (Kawasaki-Shi,

Japan). CIEA Preclinical Reports. **VFOAT** CIEA Preclinical Reports. Vol. 1 (1975)-. Periodical. English (Japanese). Jikken Dobutsu Chou Kenkyujo, Kawasaki Japan. **NLM** W1 JI67. **CODEN** JZKEDZ. Documents available from BIOSIS Document Express, CASDDS.
**Ind/Abst** Biol. Abstr.; Chem. Abstr.

FR/0291-1981
### JOURNAL DE PHARMACIE CLINIQUE.
[J. pharm. clin.]. **VFOAT** International Journal of Clinical Pharmacy. Vol. 1 (1982)-. Academic Scholarly Publication. French (English; summaries and/or abstracts in English). Four times a year. 783.55F (institutions), 470.13F (individuals) France; 840.00F (institutions), 520.00F (individuals) other EEC; 860.00F (institutions), 565.00F (individuals) other. John Libbey Eurotext Ltd, 6 rue Blanche, Isabelle Trope, 92120 Montrouge France. **Tel** 011 33 1 47358552. **(Subscription address:** ATEI John Libbey Eurotext, 23 25 rue Fernand Combette, 93100 Montreuil France.**)** **NLM** W1; JO327B. **CODEN** JPCLDE. **[CCC].** Index available. cum. index. **Bk Rev. Ad Acc. Circ:** 1,250 (ctrl). Documents available from CASDDS.
**Desc:** Publishes papers on all aspects of pharmaceutical sciences applied to man such as biopharmacy, analytical chemistry, pharmacokinetics, adverse drug reactions and toxicology, therapeutics and clinical pharmacology.
**Ind/Abst** Chem. Abstr.; EMBASE; Int. Pharm. Abstr.; PESTDOC.

BE/0047-2166
### JOURNAL DE PHARMACIE DE BELGIQUE.
[J. pharm. Belg.]. **Added/Corp** Nationale Pharmaceutique, Brussels. Association Pharmaceutique Belge. (1919)-. Academic Scholarly Publication. French. bm. $158.00. Masson Editeur, Box Postale 22, 41353 Vineuil 16 France. **Tel** 011 33 54 438994. **(Subscription address:** 7A Boulevard de Perolles, CH-1701 Fribourg Switzerland**)** **CODEN** JPBEAJ. **[CCC].** Documents available from BIOSIS Document Express, CASDDS. ***Continues** Journal de Pharmacie, 0368-3613.*
**Ind/Abst** AGRICOLA; Biol. Abstr.; Chem. Abstr.; Curr. Biotechnol.; EMBASE; Helminthol. Abstr. (1991-); Hortic. Abstr.; Index Med.; Int. Pharm. Abstr.; Nutr. Abstr. Rev., Ser. A, Hum. Exp.; Life Sci. Collect.; PESTDOC; Protozoolog. Abstr.

FR/0301-4762
### JOURNAL DE PHARMACOLOGIE CLINIQUE.
[J. pharm. clin.]. **VFOAT** Human Pharmacology and Drug Research. V. 1- Jan./Mar. 1973-. Academic Scholarly Publication. English. ir. Edifor, 49 rue Saint-Andre-des-Artes, 75006 Paris France. **NLM** W1 JO328UK. **CODEN** JPCCBJ. Documents available from BIOSIS Document Express, CASDDS.
**Ind/Abst** Biol. Abstr. (-1976); Chem. Abstr.

US/1045-6481
### JOURNAL MICHIGAN PHARMACIST.
[J. Mich. pharm.]. **Added/Corp** Michigan Pharmacists Association. **VFOAT** Michigan Pharmacist. Vol. 27, No. 1 (Jan. 1989)-. Periodical. English. Twelve times a year. $40.00. Michigan Pharmacists Association, 815 North Washington Avenue, Lansing MI 48906. **Tel** (517)484-1466, FAX (517)484-4893. **ED** Debra McGuire. **DD** 615. **NLM** W1; JO52G. Index available in last issue of volume--attached. cum. index. **Ad Acc, Adv Mgr:** Bryan Deutsch. **Pr Rev. Circ:** 3,900. available on microfilm from University Microfilms International (UMI). ***Continues** Michigan Pharmacist, 0026-2404.*
**Desc:** Edited for registered practicing pharmacists and is distributed among Association members and other subscribers.

US/0027-9897
### JOURNAL - NATIONAL PHARMACEUTICAL ASSOCIATION.
[J. - Natl. Pharm. Assoc.]. **Main/Corp** National Pharmaceutical Association. **VFOAT** NPHA Journal. (1954)-. Periodical. English. qt. $35.00 US; $45.00 other (institutions); $20.00 US; $30.00 other (individuals). Altier Maynard Communications, 59 Oakwood Drive, Madison CT 06443. **Tel** (203)421-3494, FAX (203)421-3250. **NLM** W1 JO941P.
**Ind/Abst** Int. Pharm. Abstr.

JA/0021-8820
### JOURNAL OF ANTIBIOTICS (NIHON KOSEIBUSSHITSU GAKUJUTSU KYOGIKAI : 1968).
(JOURNAL OF ANTIBIOTICS.). [J. antibiot.]. **Added/Corp** Nihon Koseibusshitsu Gakujutsu Kyogikai. Vol. 21, (Jan. 1968)-. Academic Scholarly Publication. English. Twelve times a year. $390.00 Asia, $420.00 US & Canada, Europe, West Indies & Oceania; $440.00 others. Japan Antibiotics Research Association, 2-20-8 Kamiosaki Shinagawa-ku, Tokyo 141 Japan. **Tel** 011 81 3 34910181, FAX 03-491-0179. **ED** M. Yagisawa, E. Abraham, V. Prelog, K. E. Rinehart and A. L. Demain. **NLM** W1 JO537. **CODEN** JANTAJ. Index available. **Ad Acc. Pr Rev. Circ:** 2,500. available on microfilm and microfiche from University Microfilms International (UMI). Documents available from The Genuine Article, BIOSIS Document Express, CASDDS. ***Continues** Journal of Antibiotics. Series A.*
**Desc:** An international journal devoted to the research on antibiotics and other types of microbial products.
**Ind/Abst** Anal. Abstr.; BioBusiness; Biocont. News Inf.; Biol. Abstr.; Biotechnol. Res. Abstr.; Chem. Abstr.; Curr. Aware. Biol. Sci., CABS; Curr. Biotechnol.; Curr. Chem. React.; Curr. Contents Life Sci.; EMBASE; Genet. Abstr.; Helminthol. Abstr. (19??-19??); Immunol. Abstr.; Index Chem.; Index Med.; Index Vet.; Iowa Drug Inf. Serv.; Mass Spect. Bull. (?-?); Microbiol. Abstr. Sect. B; Microbiol. Abstr. Sect. A; Microbiol. Abstr. Sect. C; NAPRALERT; Nat. Prod. Updates; Nematol. Abstr.; Oncog. Growth Factors Abstr.; Life Sci. Collect.; PESTDOC; Pig News Inf.; Postharvest News Inf.; Poult. Abstr.; Protozoolog. Abstr.; Res. Alert [Full Cov.]; Rev. Agric. Entomol.; Rev. Med. Vet. Entomol.; Rev. Med. Vet. Mycology; Rev. Plant Pathol.; Sci. Cit. Index; SCISEARCH; SEA Abstr.; Sug. Indus. Abstr.; Vet. Bull.; Virol. AIDS Abstr.; Weed Abstr.

UK/0144-1795
### JOURNAL OF AUTONOMIC PHARMACOLOGY.
[J. auton. pharmacol.]. Vol. 1, No. 1 (Nov. 1980)-. Academic Scholarly Publication. English. bm (6 issues). $473.00 (institutions), $152.00 (individuals) US & Canada; £277.00 (institutions), £89.00 (individuals) Europe; £305.00 (institutions), £98.00 (individuals) other. Blackwell Scientific Publications Ltd, Marston Book Services, PO Box 87, Oxford OX2 ODT UK. **Tel** 011 44 865 791155, FAX 011 44 865 791927, telex 837 515 MARDIS G. **ED** K. J. Broadley. **NLM** W1 JO547P. **CODEN** JAPHDU. **[CCC].** Index available (bound in last issue). **Ad Acc. Pr Rev. Circ:** 650 (ctrl). available on microfilm and microfiche from University Microfilms International (UMI). Documents available from The Genuine Article, BIOSIS Document Express, CASDDS, ADONIS.
**Desc:** Covers the effect of drugs and related substances on the structure and functioning of the mammalian autonomic nervous system, including man's.
**Ind/Abst** ADONIS; Biol. Abstr.; Chem. Abstr.; Chem. Titles; CSA Neuro. Abstr.; Curr. Aware. Biol. Sci., CABS; Curr. Contents Life Sci.; EMBASE; Index Med.; NAPRALERT; Life Sci. Collect.; PESTDOC; Ref. Upd. Deluxe Ed.; Res. Alert [Full Cov.]; Sci. Cit. Index; SCISEARCH.

UK/0334-1534
### JOURNAL OF BASIC AND CLINICAL PHYSIOLOGY AND PHARMACOLOGY.
**See** Biology-Physiology.

US/1054-3406
### JOURNAL OF BIOPHARMACEUTICAL STATISTICS.
[J. biopharm. stat.]. **VFOAT** JBS. Vol. 1, No. 1 (1991)-. Periodical. English. Three times a year. $295.00 US; $305.50 other. Marcel Dekker Inc., 270 Madison Avenue, New York NY 10016. **Tel** (212)696-9000, (800)228-1160, FAX (212)685-4540, telex 421419. **(Subscription address:** Marcel Dekker Inc, PO Box 5017, Monticello NY 12701.**)** **ED** Karl E. Peace. **LC** RS57; .J68. **DD** 615/.1/072. **NLM** W1; JO564VL. **CODEN** JBSTEL. **[CCC].**
**Desc:** Contains high-quality applications of statistics in biopharmaceutical research and development and expositions of statistical methodology with clear and immediate applicability to such work. Publishes full-length and short manuscripts on statistical applications and methods in the biopharmaceutical sciences, significant review articles, selected conference papers, and letters to the editor, making it an ideal forum for statistical applications in pharmaceutical research and development.
**Ind/Abst** Math. Rev.

US/0160-2446
### JOURNAL OF CARDIOVASCULAR PHARMACOLOGY.
[J. cardiovasc. pharmacol.]. Vol. 1, No. 1 (Jan./Feb. 1979)-. Academic Scholarly Publication. English. mo. $310.00 (individuals), $560.00 (institutions) US; $394.00 (individuals), $685.00 (institutions) other. Raven Press, 1185 Avenue of the Americas, 37th Floor, New York NY 10036. **Tel** (212)930-9500, (212)930-9604, FAX (212)869-3495, (212)302-8507, telex 640073. **ED** Paul M. Vanhoutte. **LC** RM345; .J68. **DD** 616.1/061. **NLM** W1 JO576. **CODEN** JCPCDT. **[CCC]. Pr Rev.** available on microfilm and microfiche from University Microfilms International (UMI). Documents available from The Genuine Article, CASDDS.
**Desc:** A journal for clinical as well as non-clinical departments of pharmacology.
**Ind/Abst** Calcium Calcif. Tissue Abstr.; Chem. Abstr.; Chem. Titles; Chicano Index; CSA Neuro. Abstr. (?-?); Curr. Aware. Biol. Sci., CABS; Curr. Contents Clin. Med.; Curr. Contents Life Sci.; EMBASE; Index Med.; INIS Atomindex [Micro.]; Life Sci. Collect.; PESTDOC; Ref. Upd. Basic Ed.; Ref. Upd. Deluxe Ed.; Res. Alert [Full Cov.]; Sci. Cit. Index; SCISEARCH.

US
### JOURNAL OF CELLULAR PHARMACOLOGY.
***Ceased.*** (1992)- ceased publication after Vol. 3, No. 1 (1992). English. bm. Springer-Verlag New York Inc., 175 5th Avenue, New York NY 10010. **Tel** (212)460-1500, telex 232 235 SPB UR. **(Subscription address:** Springer Verlag New York Inc. / for North America, 44 Hartz Way, Secaucus NJ 07096.**)** **NLM** W1; JO579J. available on microfilm and microfiche.
**Desc:** Featuring research on the mechanisms of drug action. Scope encompasses: biochemistry, molecular and cellular pharmacology and biology, toxicology and pharmacology of anticancer agents and chemotherapy, characterization of drug properties, the role of drugs in cell growth inhibition and differentiation.

US/0091-2700
### JOURNAL OF CLINICAL PHARMACOLOGY, THE.
[J. clin. pharmacol.]. **Added/Corp** American College of Clinical Pharmacology. Vol. 13. No. 5/6 (May/June 1973)-. Periodical. English. mo. $195.00 (individuals), $240.00 (institutions) US; $250.00 (individuals), $295.00 (institutions) other. J.B. Lippincott Company, 227 East Washington Square, Philadelphia PA 19106-3780. **Tel** (215)238-4200 or 4454, FAX (215)238-4227. **(Subscription address:** J.B. Lippincott, PO Box 350, Hagerstown MD 21740.**)** **DD** 615. **NLM** W1 JO5899. **CODEN** JCPCBR. **[CCC].** available on microfilm and microfiche from University Microfilms International (UMI). Documents available from The Genuine Article, BIOSIS Document Express, CASDDS. ***Continues** Journal of Clinical Pharmacology and New Drugs, 0021-9754.*
**Ind/Abst** Biol. Abstr.; Chem. Abstr.; CSA Neuro. Abstr. (?-?); Curr. Aware. Biol. Sci., CABS; Curr. Contents Clin. Med.; Curr. Contents Life Sci.; EMBASE; Energy Res. Abstr. (Aug. 1982-); Health Saf. Sci. Abstr.; Index Med.; INIS Atomindex [Micro.]; Int. Pharm. Abstr.; Iowa Drug Inf. Serv. (1969-); Med. Abstr. Newsl.; Mod. Med.; Life Sci. Collect.; PESTDOC; Pollut. Abstr. Indexes; Protozoolog. Abstr.; Psychol. Abstr. (Aug. 1982-); Ref. Upd. Deluxe Ed.; Res. Alert [Full Cov.]; Sci. Cit. Index; SCISEARCH; Soc. Sci. Cit. Index [Select. Cov.]; Sug. Indus. Abstr.

UK/0308-6593
### JOURNAL OF CLINICAL PHARMACY.
***Title Change.*** [J. clin. pharm.]. Vol. 1 (Mar. 1976)-(19??). Academic Scholarly Publication. English. qt. Blackwell Scientific Publications Ltd, Marston Book Services, PO Box 87, Oxford OX2 ODT UK. **Tel** 011 44 865 791155, FAX 011 44 865 791927, telex 837 515 MARDIS G. **NLM** W1 JO5899I. available on microfilm from University Microfilms International (UMI). ***Continued by** Journal of Clinical and Hospital Pharmacy, 0143-3180.*
**Ind/Abst** Bibliogr. Mission.; Int. Pharm. Abstr.

UK/0269-4727
### JOURNAL OF CLINICAL PHARMACY AND THERAPEUTICS.
[J. clin. pharm. ther.]. Vol. 12, No. 1 (Feb. 1987)-. Academic Scholarly Publication. English. bm (6 issues). $353.00 (institutions), $99.50 (individuals) US & Canada; £207.00 (institutions), £58.00 (individuals) Europe; £228.00 (institutions), £64.00 (individuals) other. Blackwell Scientific Publications Ltd, Marston Book Services, PO Box 87, Oxford OX2 ODT UK. **Tel** 011 44 865 791155, FAX 011 44 865 791927, telex 837 515 MARDIS G. **ED** A. Li Wan Po. **NLM** W1; JO5899IE. **CODEN** JCPTED. **[CCC].** Index available. **Bk Rev. Ad Acc. Pr Rev. Circ:** 450. available on microfilm and microfiche from University Microfilms International (UMI). Documents available from The Genuine Article, BIOSIS Document Express, CASDDS, ADONIS. ***Continues** Journal of Clinical and Hospital Pharmacy, 0143-3180.*
**Desc:** Concerns the manufacture quality control and formulation of medicine, drug information services, pharmacokinetics, radiopharmacy and drug distribution systems.
**Ind/Abst** ADONIS; Biol. Abstr. (1987-); Chem. Abstr. (1987-); Cumul. Index Nurs. Allied Health Lit.; Curr. Contents Clin. Med.; EMBASE; Index Med. (Feb. 1987-); Int. Pharm. Abstr.; Iowa Drug Inf. Serv.; PESTDOC; Physic. Medline Plus; Protozoolog. Abstr.; Res. Alert [Full Cov.]; Sci. Cit. Index; SCISEARCH; Soc. Sci. Cit. Index [Select. Cov.].

US/0271-0749
### JOURNAL OF CLINICAL PSYCHOPHARMACOLOGY.
[J. clin. psychopharmacol.]. **VFOAT** Clinical Psychopharmacology. Vol. 1, No. 1 (Jan. 1981)-. Academic Scholarly Publication. English. bm. $98.00 (individual), $145.00 (institution) US; $50.00 (individual), $125.00 (institution). Williams & Wilkins Company, 428 East Preston Street, Baltimore MD 21202-3993. **Tel** (410)528-4000, (800)638-6423, FAX (410)528-8596, telex 87669. **(Subscription address:** Williams & Wilkins, PO Box 64380, Baltimore MD 21264.**)** **ED** Richard I. Shader. **NLM** W1 JO592M. **CODEN** JCPYDR. **[CCC]. Bk Rev. Ad Acc. Pr Rev. Circ:** 4,300. available on microfilm. Documents available from The Genuine Article, BIOSIS Document Express, CASDDS, ADONIS, Quick Copies.
**Desc:** Leading clinical papers in this field, with perspectives for psychiatrists on antipsychotics, antianxiety agents, antidepressants, and stimulants.
**Ind/Abst** ADONIS; Biol. Abstr. (1987-); Chem. Abstr.; Curr. Aware. Biol. Sci., CABS; Curr. Contents Clin. Med.; Curr. Contents Life Sci.; EMBASE; Index Med.; Int. Pharm. Abstr.; Iowa Drug Inf. Serv. (1981-); PESTDOC; Physic. Medline Plus; Psychol. Abstr. (1988-); PsycINFO (1990-); PsycLit; Ref. Upd. Deluxe Ed.; Res. Alert [Full Cov.]; Sci. Cit. Index; SCISEARCH; Soc. Sci. Cit. Index [Select. Cov.].

●US/1066-7865
**JOURNAL OF CLINICAL RESEARCH AND DRUG DEVELOPMENT (1993).** (JOURNAL OF CLINICAL RESEARCH AND DRUG DEVELOPMENT : OFFICIAL PUBLICATION OF THE ASSOCIATES OF CLINICAL PHARMACOLOGY.). [J. clin. res. drug dev.]. **Added/Corp** Associates of Clinical Pharmacology. Vol. 7, No. 1 (Mar. 1993)-. Academic Scholarly Publication. English. qt (1 volume). $185.00 US; $215.00 other. Elsevier Science Publishing Company Inc, Madison Square Station, PO Box 882, New York NY 10159-0882. **Tel** (212)633-3950, FAX (212)633-3990. **DD** 615. **NLM** W1; JO592VK. **CODEN** JCDDE7. Documents available from BIOSIS Document Express, ADONIS. ***Continues*** *Journal of Clinical Research and Pharmacoepidemiology, 1047-0336.*
**Ind/Abst** ADONIS; Biol. Abstr.

US/1047-0336
**JOURNAL OF CLINICAL RESEARCH AND PHARMACOEPIDEMIOLOGY.** ***Title Change.*** [J. clin. res. pharmacoepidemiol.]. **Added/Corp** Associates of Clinical Pharmacology. Vol. 4, No. 1 (March 1990)-(1993). Academic Scholarly Publication. English. qt. Elsevier Science Publishing Company Inc, Madison Square Station, PO Box 882, New York NY 10159-0882. **Tel** (212)633-3950, FAX (212)633-3990. **DD** 615. **NLM** W1; JO592Y. **CODEN** JCRPEB. **[CCC].** available on microfilm and microfiche from University Microfilms International (UMI). Documents available from BIOSIS Document Express. ***Continues*** *Journal of Clinical Research and Drug Development, 0889-5813.* ***Continued by*** *Journal of Clinical Research and Drug Development (New York, N.Y. : 1993), 1066-7865.*
**Ind/Abst** Biol. Abstr. (1990-); EMBASE; Int. Pharm. Abstr.; PESTDOC; Ref. Upd. Deluxe Ed.

US/0163-481X
**JOURNAL OF CONTINUING EDUCATION IN HOSPITAL & CLINICAL PHARMACY, THE.** **VFOAT** J.C.E. Hospital & Clinical Pharmacy. **VAT** Journal of Continuing Education in Hospital and Clinical Pharmacy. V. 1- Jan./Mar. 1979. Periodical. English. qt. $10.00. Medical Digest, 444 Frontage Road, PO Box 8021, Northfield IL 60093.

UK/0952-9500
**JOURNAL OF DRUG DEVELOPMENT.** [J. drug dev.]. Vol. 1, No. 1 (April 1988)-. Periodical. English. Four times a year (Feb., May., Aug., Nov.). £175.00 North America; £105.00 others. Gardiner Caldwell Communications Ltd., The Old Ribbon Mill, Pitt Street, Macclesfield Cheshire, SK11 7PT England. **Tel** 011 44 625 618507, FAX 011 44 625 610260. **ED** David Caldwell. **LC** RM300; .J63. **DD** 615/.1/05. **NLM** W1; JO622T. **CODEN** JDDVEY. cum. index. **Ad Acc, Adv Mgr:** Kathryn Wilkinson, **Tel** 44 625 618507. **Pr Rev. Circ:** 300. Documents available from BIOSIS Document Express, CASDDS.
**Desc:** Offers publication of original research papers and reviews on subjects relevant to pharmaceutical medicine. Areas of particular interest include pharmacology, microbiology, pharmacy, clinical and allied sciences.
**Ind/Abst** Biol. Abstr. (1988-); Chem. Abstr.; EMBASE; PESTDOC.

UA/0368-1866
**JOURNAL OF DRUG RESEARCH.** (JOURNAL OF DRUG RESEARCH / DRUG RESEARCH AND CONTROL CENTRE.). [J. drug res.]. **Added/Corp** Hayah Al-Qawmiyah Lil-Raqabah Wa-Al-Buhuth Al-Dawaiyah (Egypt) Markaz Al-Abhath Waal-Raqabah Al-Dawaiyah (Muassasah Al-Misriyah Al-Ammah lil-Adwiyah). **VFOAT** Journal of Drug Research of Egypt; Majallat Abhath Al-Dawa. (1969)-. Periodical. English (Arabic; summaries and/or abstracts in Arabic). **LC** RS122; .J67. **DD** 615/.1/05. **NLM** W1 JO625. **CODEN** JDGRAX. Documents available from BIOSIS Document Express, CASDDS. ***Continues*** *Drug Research.*
**Ind/Abst** Bibliogr. Mission.; Biol. Abstr. (19??-1989); Chem. Abstr.; Int. Pharm. Abstr.; Mass Spect. Bull.; NAPRALERT; PESTDOC.

●US/1061-186X
**JOURNAL OF DRUG TARGETING.** [J. drug target.]. Vol. 1, No. 1 (Mar. 1993)-. Periodical. English. Four times a year. $364.00 university & hospital libraries, $567.00 other institutions. Harwood Academic Publishers / New York, PO Box 786, Cooper Station, New York NY 10276. **Tel** (212)206-8900, (201)643-7500. **(Subscription address:** International Publishers Distributor at one of the following addresses: 820 Town Center Drive, Langhorne, PA 19047; or PO Box 90, Reading Berkshire RG1 8JL UK; or Kent Ridge PO Box 1180, Singapore 9111, Republic of Singapore**)** **DD** 615. **CODEN** JDTAEH.
**Desc:** Publishes papers and reviews on all aspects of drug delivery and targeting, and the design and characterization of carrier systems, with an emphasis on in vivo evaluation.

●US
**JOURNAL OF DRUG THERPAY IN NEUROLOGICAL DISORDERS.** **See** Medical Science and Technology-Neurology.

SZ/0378-8741
**JOURNAL OF ETHNOPHARMACOLOGY.** [J. ethnopharmacol.]. **VFOAT** Ethnopharmacology. Vol. 1 (Jan. 1979)-. Academic Scholarly Publication. English. Twelve times a year (4 vols.). $813.00. Elsevier Science Ireland Ltd., Bay 15, Shannon Industrial Estate, Co Clare Ireland. **Tel** 011 353 61 471944. **ED** Laurent Rivier, Marvin H. Malone, and T. Plowman. **NLM** W1 JO644CH. **CODEN** JOETD7. **[CCC].** Index available. **Bk Rev. Ad Acc. Pr Rev.** available on microfilm and microfiche from University Microfilms International (UMI). Documents available from The Genuine Article, BIOSIS Document Express, CASDDS.
**Desc:** Publishes original articles concerned with the observation and experimental investigation of the biological activities of plant and animal substances used in the traditional medicine of past and present cultures.
**Ind/Abst** AGRICOLA [Select. Cov.]; Agrofor. Abstr. (1991-); Anthropol. Lit.; Biol. Abstr.; Chem. Abstr.; CSA Neuro. Abstr. (?-?); Curr. Aware. Biol. Sci., CABS; Curr. Contents Life Sci.; Dairy Sci. Abstr.; EMBASE; For. Prod. Abstr. (1991-); For. Abstr.; Helminthol. Abstr. (19??-19??); Hortic. Abstr.; Index Med.; Index Vet.; Int. Pharm. Abstr.; NAPRALERT; Life Sci. Collect.; Plant Genet. Resour. Abstr.; Postharvest News Inf.; Protozoolog. Abstr.; Ref. Upd. Deluxe Ed.; Res. Alert [Full Cov.]; Rev. Med. Vet. Entomol.; Rev. Med. Vet. Mycology; Sci. Cit. Index; SCISEARCH; Seed Abstr.; Soc. Sci. Cit. Index [Select. Cov.]; Vet. Bull.

US/8756-4629
**JOURNAL OF GERIATRIC DRUG THERAPY.** **See** Medical Science and Technology-Geriatrics.

●US/1068-7777
**JOURNAL OF INFECTIOUS DISEASE PHARMACOTHERAPY.** (1995)-. Periodical. English. qt. $75.00 US; $105.00 other. The Haworth Press Inc, 10 Alice Street, Binghamton NY 13904-1580. **Tel** (607)722-5857, (800)3-HAWORTH, FAX (607)722-1424. **ED** Steven L. Barriere. **Pr Rev. Acid Free.** Documents available from Haworth Document Delivery Service.
**Desc:** Integrates principles of pharmaceutical care with the management of infectious diseases. Provides information for pharmacists on the most recent advances in the management of infectious diseases. It is a forum in which practitioners/investigators may relate their experiences and research in the area of infectious disease pharmacotherapy.

US/0194-5106
**JOURNAL OF KANSAS PHARMACY, THE.** **Added/Corp** Kansas Pharmacists Association. Kansas Pharmaceutical Association. **VFOAT** Journal of Kansas Pharmacy Update Newsletter; Update Newsletter; Update; Kansas Pharmacy. Vol.39 (Jan. 1964)-. Periodical. English. qt (with monthly updates). $18.00. Kansas Pharmacists Association, 1308 Southwest 10th Avenue, Topeka KS 66604-1299. **Tel** (913)232-0439. **ED** Jenith Hoover. **Ad Acc. Circ:** 1,200 (ctrl). ***Continues*** *KPA News.*
**Desc:** Contains statewide pharmacy news; association news, reports, and minutes; hospital pharmacy news, original articles, and president's and executive director's editorials.
**Ind/Abst** Int. Pharm. Abstr.

NR/0331-0124
**JOURNAL OF MEDICAL AND PHARMACEUTICAL MARKETING.** ***Suspended.*** [J. med. pharm. mark.]. (1972)-(19??). Periodical. English. bm. Journal of Medical Pharmaceutical Marketing, Plot 25 Kekere Ekum Box 7313, Orile Iganmu Lagos Nigeria.
**Ind/Abst** Int. Pharm. Abstr.

US/0022-2623
**JOURNAL OF MEDICINAL CHEMISTRY.** **See** Biology-Biochemistry.

UK/0265-2048
**JOURNAL OF MICROENCAPSULATION.** [J. microencapsul.]. **VFOAT** J. Microencapsulation. Vol. 1, No. 1 (Jan.-March 1984)-. Academic Scholarly Publication. English. bm (6 issues). £216.00 UK; $357.00 other. Taylor & Francis Ltd., Rankine Road, Basingstoke Hampshire, RG24 8PR United Kingdom. **Tel** 011 44 256 840366, FAX 011 44 256 479438, telex 858540. **(Subscription address:** Taylor & Francis Inc., 1900 Frost Road, Suite 101, Bristol PA 19007-1598.**)** **ED** J. R. Nixon (editor's address: Chelsea Department of Pharmacy, King's College London, Manresa Road, London SW3 6LX). **LC** RS201.C3; J68. **DD** 615/.191. **NLM** W1; JO763D. **CODEN** JOMIEF. **[CCC]. Pr Rev.** available on microfilm from University Microfilms International (UMI). Documents available from The Genuine Article, BIOSIS Document Express, CASDDS.
**Desc:** Scope extends beyond microcapsules to all other small particulate systems which involve preparative manipulation. Covers the chemistry of encapsulating materials; the physics of such matters as release through the capsule walls; the techniques of preparation of the microcapsules; its content and storage; and the many uses to which microcapsules are put.
**Ind/Abst** BioBusiness; Biol. Abstr. (1987-); Chem. Abstr. (1984-); CSA Neuro. Abstr. (?-?); Curr. Contents Eng. Tech. Appl. Sci.; Ei Page One; EMBASE; Food Sci. Technol. Abstr.; Index Med. (1984-); PESTDOC; Res. Alert [Select. Cov.]; SCISEARCH.

●US/1058-8108
**JOURNAL OF NATURAL TOXINS.** [J. nat. toxins]. Vol. 1, No. 1 (Mar. 1992)-. Academic Scholarly Publication. English. sa (March, Sept.). $100.00 (individuals), $200.00 (institutions) US; $115.00 (individuals), $215.00 (institutions) Pan American Nations; $125.00 (individuals), $225.00 (institutions) other. Alaken, Inc., 305 West Magnolia Street, Suite 196, Fort Collins CO 80521. **Tel** FAX (303)491-1591. **ED** Anthony T. Tu & William Gaffield. **DD** 615. **NLM** W1; JO777TB. **CODEN** JNTOER. **Bk Rev. Pr Rev.** Documents available from CASDDS.
**Ind/Abst** Chem. Abstr.

US/8756-3320
**JOURNAL OF OCULAR PHARMACOLOGY.** **See** Medical Science and Technology-Ophthalmology.

US/0279-7976
**JOURNAL OF PARENTERAL SCIENCE AND TECHNOLOGY.** ***Title Change.*** [J. parenter. sci. technol.]. **Added/Corp** Parenteral Drug Association. Vol. 35, No. 1 (Jan./Feb. 1981)-Vol.. 47, No. 6 (Nov./Dec. 1993). Academic Scholarly Publication. English. bm. Parenteral Drug Association, 7500 Old Georgetown Road, Suite 620, Bethesda MD 20814. **Tel** (301)986-0293. **(Subscription address:** Parenteral Drug Association Inc., PO Box 630810, Baltimore MD 20814.**)** **ED** Joseph B. Schwartz. **DD** 615. **NLM** W1 JO827Q. **CODEN** JPATDS. cum. index. **Bk Rev. Ad Acc. Pr Rev. Circ:** 3,000 (ctrl). Documents available from The Genuine Article, BIOSIS Document Express, CASDDS. ***Continues*** *Journal of the Parenteral Drug Association, 0161-1933.* ***Continued by*** *Journal of Pharmaceutical Science and Technology, 1076-397X.*
**Desc:** Vehicle for publication of scientific/technical papers recognized as significant contributions to field of parenteral science and technology.
**Ind/Abst** Biol. Abstr.; Chem. Abstr.; Curr. Contents Eng. Tech. Appl. Sci.; EMBASE; Energy Res. Abstr. (Aug. 1982-); Index Med.; Int. Pharm. Abstr.; Iowa Drug Inf. Serv. (1969-); PESTDOC; Res. Alert [Full Cov.]; SCISEARCH.

UK/0731-7085
**JOURNAL OF PHARMACEUTICAL AND BIOMEDICAL ANALYSIS.** [J. pharm. biomed. anal.]. **VFOAT** Journal of Pharmaceutical & Biomedical Analysis. Vol. 1 No. 1 (1983)-. Academic Scholarly Publication. English. mo. $842.00 The Americas; £565.00 other. Pergamon Press, An Imprint of Elsevier Science Ltd., The Boulevard, Langford Lane, Kidlington, Oxford OX5 1GB United Kingdom. **Tel** 011 44 865 843000, 011 44 865 843699, FAX 011 44 865 843010. **(Subscription address:** Elsevier Science Ltd. Oxford Fulfillment Centre, PO Box 800, Kidlington, Oxford OX5 1DX United Kingdom.**)** **ED** Anthony Fell and Christopher Riley. **NLM** W1; JO828T. **CODEN** JPBADA. **[CCC]. Pr Rev.** available on microfilm and microfiche from University Microfilms International (UMI). Documents available from The Genuine Article, BIOSIS Document Express, CASDDS, ADONIS.
**Desc:** Covers the interdisciplinary aspects of analysis in the pharmaceutical and biomedical sciences, including relevant developments in analytical methodology, instrumentation, computation and interpretation.
**Ind/Abst** ADONIS; Anal. Abstr.; Biol. Abstr. (1985-); Chem. Abstr. (1983-); Chem. Titles; CSA Neuro. Abstr. (?-?); Curr. Aware. Biol. Sci., CABS; Curr. Contents Life Sci.; EMBASE; Health Plan. Adminis.; Helminthol. Abstr. (19??-19??); Index Med. (1989-); Index Vet.; Int. Pharm. Abstr.; Mass Spect. Bull.; Nutr. Abstr. Rev., Ser. A, Hum. Exp.; Life Sci. Collect.; PESTDOC; Pig News Inf.; Poult. Abstr.; Protozoolog. Abstr.; Res. Alert [Full Cov.]; Rev. Med. Vet. Entomol.; Rev. Med. Vet. Mycology; Sci. Cit. Index; SCISEARCH; Vet. Bull.

●US/1056-4950
**JOURNAL OF PHARMACEUTICAL CARE IN PAIN & SYMPTOM CONTROL.** **VFOAT** Journal of Pharmaceutical Care in Pain & Symptom Control. (1993)-. Periodical. English. qt. $60.00 US; $84.00 other. The Haworth Press Inc, 10 Alice Street, Binghamton NY 13904-1580. **Tel** (607)722-5857, (800)3-HAWORTH, FAX (607)722-1424. **ED** Arthur Lipman. **NLM** W1; JO829J. **Bk Rev. Ad Acc. Acid Free.** available on microfiche. Documents available from Haworth Document Delivery Service.
**Desc:** Forum for sharing the most current information on new drug development, evaluation, and use in the management of pain and other symptoms of chronic and acute disease.
**Ind/Abst** Int. Pharm. Abstr. (199?-199?).

US/0883-7597
**JOURNAL OF PHARMACEUTICAL MARKETING & MANAGEMENT.** [J. pharm. mark. manage.]. **VFOAT** Journal of Pharmaceutical Marketing and Management. Vol. 1, No. 1 (Fall 1986)-.

Periodical. English. qt. $135.00 US; $189.00 other. The Haworth Press Inc, 10 Alice Street, Binghamton NY 13904-1580. **Tel** (607)722-5857, (800)3-HAWORTH, FAX (607)722-1424. **ED** Mickey Smith (editor's address: Health Services Research Division, Research Institute of Pharmaceutical Sciences, University of Mississippi School of Pharmacy, University, MS 38677). **DD** 615. **NLM** W1; JO829H. **CODEN** JPMMEY. **Bk Rev. Ad Acc. Pr Rev. Acid Free. Circ:** 230. available on microfilm and microfiche from University Microfilms International (UMI). Documents available from UMI Article Clearinghouse, Haworth Document Delivery Service.
**Desc:** Devoted to solving problems of management and the marketing of pharmaceutical products and services. It is a refereed, multidisciplinary periodical that pursues a vigorous policy of publishing quality research reports of interest to a wide variety of professionals in the industry.
**Ind/Abst** ABI/INFORM Glob. Ed.; Biostatistica (19??-19??); Hospit. Health Admin. Index (1986-); Hospit. Manage. Rev. (19??-19??); Hum. Resour. Abstr. (?-?); Int. Pharm. Abstr.; Manage. Market. Abstr.; PAIS Int. Print (1991-?); Trade Ind. Index.

UK/0958-0581
### JOURNAL OF PHARMACEUTICAL MEDICINE : THE OFFICIAL JOURNAL OF THE SOCIETY OF PHARMACEUTICAL MEDICINE.
**Added/Corp** Society of Pharmaceutical Medicine. Vol. 1, No. 1 (1991)-. Academic Scholarly Publication. English. qt (4 issues). $222.00 US & Canada; £130.00 Europe; £143.00 other. Blackwell Scientific Publications Ltd, Marston Book Services, PO Box 87, Oxford OX2 ODT UK. **Tel** 011 44 865 791155, FAX 011 44 865 791927, telex 837 515 MARDIS G. **ED** Brian Dickson and Michael Young. **NLM** W1; JO829K. **CODEN** JPMDE7. **[CCC].** available on microfilm and microfiche from University Microfilms International (UMI). Documents available from ADONIS.
**Desc:** Provides a unique forum for the exchange of scientific information between professionals in academic, regulatory agencies and industry, whose work is connected with the development and assessment of medicines.
**Ind/Abst** ADONIS; EMBASE.

US/1076-397X
### JOURNAL OF PHARMACEUTICAL SCIENCE AND TECHNOLOGY. *Title Change.*
(JOURNAL OF PHARMACEUTICAL SCIENCE AND TECHNOLOGY : THE OFFICIAL JOURNAL OF PDA.). [J. pharm. sci. technol.]. **Added/Corp** Parenteral Drug Association. **VFOAT** Journal of Pharmaceutical Science & Technology. Vol. 48, No. 1 (Jan./Feb. 1994)-Vol. 48, No. 3 (May/June 1994). Academic Scholarly Publication. English. bm. Parenteral Drug Association, 7500 Old Georgetown Road, Suite 620, Bethesda MD 20814. **Tel** (301)986-0293. **DD** 615. **NLM** W1; JO829L. **CODEN** JPHTEU. ***Continues*** *Journal of Parenteral Science and Technology, 0279-7976.* ***Continued by*** *PDA Journal of Pharmaceutical Science and Technology.*
**Ind/Abst** Biol. Abstr.; Chem. Abstr.; EMBASE; Energy Res. Abstr.; Index Med. (1994-); PESTDOC; RINGDOC; VETDOC.

US
### JOURNAL OF PHARMACEUTICAL SCIENCE AND TECHNOLOGY.
(19??)-. English. bm (6 issues). $70.00 US; $90.00 other. Parenteral Drug Association, 7500 Old Georgetown Road, Suite 620, Bethesda MD 20814. **Tel** (301)986-0293. ***Continues*** *Journal of Parenteral Science and Technology.*

US/0022-3549
### JOURNAL OF PHARMACEUTICAL SCIENCES.
[J. pharm. sci.]. **Added/Corp** American Pharmaceutical Association. Vol. 50 (Jan. 1961)-. Academic Scholarly Publication. English. mo. $310.00 (nonmember/institution), $85.00 (nonmember/individual), $30.00 (member) US. American Pharmaceutical Association, 2215 Constitution Avenue Northwest, Washington DC 20037-2985. **Tel** (202)628-4410, (800)237-2742, FAX (202)783-2351. **(Subscription address:** American Chemical Society / Ohio, Department L 0011, Columbus OH 43268-0011.**) ED** Sharon G. Boots. **LC** RS1; .A52. **NLM** W1 JO829. **CODEN** JPMSAE. **[CCC].** Index available (bound in last issue). **Bk Rev. Ad Acc. Pr Rev. Circ:** 8,601 (ctrl). available on microfilm and microfiche from University Microfilms International (UMI). Documents available from The Genuine Article, BIOSIS Document Express, CASDDS. ***Formed by the union of*** *Journal of the American Pharmaceutical Association. Scientific Edition, 0095-9553* ***and*** *Drug Standards, 0096-0225.*
**Desc:** Devoted to covering the latest developments in pharmaceutical research, including biopharmaceutics, pharmacokinetics, medicinal chemistry, novel analytical methods, etc. Co-published by the American Chemical Society.
**Ind/Abst** AGRICOLA; Anal. Abstr.; Biol. Abstr.; Chem Inform; Chem. Abstr.; Chem. Titles; CSA Neuro. Abstr. (?-?); Curr. Biotechnol.; Curr. Chem. React.; Curr. Contents Life Sci.; Dairy Sci. Abstr.; EMBASE; Energy Res. Abstr.; Helminthol. Abstr. (1991-); Hortic. Abstr.; Index Chem.; Index Med.; INIS Atomindex [Micro.]; Int. Aerosp. Abstr.; Int. Packag. Abstr.; Int. Pharm. Abstr.; Iowa Drug Inf. Serv. (1967-); Nutr. Abstr. Rev., Ser. A, Hum. Exp.; Life Sci. Collect.; PESTDOC; Protozoolog. Abstr.; Psychol. Abstr.; Ref. Upd. Basic Ed.; Ref. Upd. Deluxe Ed.; Res. Alert [Full Cov.]; Rev. Med. Vet. Mycology; Sci. Cit. Index; SCISEARCH.

JA/0386-846X
### JOURNAL OF PHARMACOBIO-DYNAMICS. *Title Change.*
[J. pharmacobio-dyn.]. **Added/Corp** Nihon Yakugakkai. Vol. 1 (March 1978)-(1992). Academic Scholarly Publication. English. mo. **(Subscription address:** Maruzen Company Ltd., PO Box 5050, Import & Export Department, Tokyo 100 31 Japan.**) ED** Yutaka Kasuya. **NLM** W1 JO829N. **CODEN** JOPHDQjpbd. **[CCC]. Pr Rev. Circ:** 2,000 (ctrl). Documents available from The Genuine Article, BIOSIS Document Express, CASDDS. ***Continued by*** *Biological & Pharmaceutical Bulletin, 0918-6158.*
**Desc:** Monographs about dynamic mutual effect of medicine and organism, and the main point of a public performance, concerned with related field of this journal.
**Ind/Abst** Biol. Abstr.; Chem. Abstr.; Chem. Titles; CSA Neuro. Abstr. (?-?); Curr. Biotechnol.; EMBASE; Helminthol. Abstr.; Index Med.; Microbiol. Abstr. Sect. B (19??-19??); NAPRALERT; Nutr. Abstr. Rev., Ser. A, Hum. Exp.; Life Sci. Collect.; PESTDOC; Pollut. Abstr. Indexes; Protozoolog. Abstr.; Res. Alert [Full Cov.]; Rev. Med. Vet. Mycology; Sci. Cit. Index; SCISEARCH.

US/0090-466X
### JOURNAL OF PHARMACOKINETICS AND BIOPHARMACEUTICS.
[J. pharmacokinet. biopharm.]. Vol. 1 (Feb. 1973)-. Periodical. English. Six times a year. $395.00 institutions, $87.00 individuals US; $460.00 institutions, $102.00 individuals other. Plenum Press, 233 Spring Street, New York NY 10013-1578. **Tel** (212)620-8000, (800)221-9369, FAX (212)463-0742, (212)807-1047, telex 23/421139. **ED** Leslie Z. Benet and Malcolm Rowland. **LC** RM1; .J7. **DD** 615/.1/05. **NLM** W1 JO829P. **CODEN** JPBPBJ. **[CCC]. Pr Rev.** available on microfilm and microfiche from University Microfilms International (UMI). Documents available from The Genuine Article, BIOSIS Document Express, CASDDS, ADONIS.
**Desc:** A journal devoted to illustrating the importance of pharmacokinetics and biopharmaceutical applications.
**Ind/Abst** ADONIS; Biol. Abstr.; Chem. Abstr.; Curr. Contents Life Sci.; EMBASE; Energy Res. Abstr. (Aug. 1982-); Index Med.; Int. Pharm. Abstr.; Iowa Drug Inf. Serv. (1974-); Life Sci. Collect.; PESTDOC; Res. Alert [Full Cov.]; Sci. Cit. Index; SCISEARCH; Soc. Sci. Cit. Index [Select. Cov.].

●US/1056-8719
### JOURNAL OF PHARMACOLOGICAL AND TOXICOLOGICAL METHODS.
[J. pharmacol. toxicol. methods]. Vol. 27, No. 1 (Mar. 1992)-. Academic Scholarly Publication. English. Eight times a year (2 volumes). $520.00 US; $565.00 other. Elsevier Science Publishing Company Inc, Madison Square Station, PO Box 882, New York NY 10159-0882. **Tel** (212)633-3950, FAX (212)633-3990. **LC** QP901; .J68. **DD** 615/.1/028. **NLM** W1; JO829PQ. **CODEN** JPTMEZ. **[CCC].** available on microfilm and microfiche from University Microfilms International (UMI). Documents available from The Genuine Article, BIOSIS Document Express, CASDDS, ADONIS. ***Continues*** *Journal of Pharmacological Methods, 0160-5402.*
**Ind/Abst** ADONIS; Biol. Abstr.; Chem. Abstr.; Curr. Aware. Biol. Sci., CABS; Curr. Contents Life Sci.; EMBASE; Index Med. (1992-); INIS Atomindex [Micro.]; Life Sci. Collect.; PESTDOC; Ref. Upd. Deluxe Ed.; Res. Alert [Full Cov.]; Sci. Cit. Index; SCISEARCH.

US/0022-3565
### JOURNAL OF PHARMACOLOGY AND EXPERIMENTAL THERAPEUTICS, THE.
[J. pharmacol. exp. ther.]. **Added/Corp** American Society for Pharmacology and Experimental Therapeutics. Vol. 1 (June 1909)-. Academic Scholarly Publication. English. mo. $190.00 (individual), $340.00 (institution) US; $255.00 (individual), $405.00 (institution) other. Williams & Wilkins Company, 428 East Preston Street, Baltimore MD 21202-3993. **Tel** (410)528-4000, (800)638-6423, FAX (410)528-8596, telex 87669. **(Subscription address:** Williams & Wilkins, PO Box 64380, Baltimore MD 21264.**) ED** Eva K. Killam. **LC** RS1; .J85. **DD** 615/.7/05. **NLM** W1 JO83. **CODEN** JPETAB. **[CCC].** cum. index. **Ad Acc. Circ:** 3,200. available on microfilm. Documents available from The Genuine Article, BIOSIS Document Express, CASDDS, Quick Copies. ***Superseded in part by*** *Pharmacological Reviews, 0031-6997.*
**Desc:** Broad coverage of all aspects of the interactions of chemicals with biological systems for pharmacologists, toxicologists, and biochemists.
**Ind/Abst** AGRICOLA; Biol. Abstr.; Calcium Calcif. Tissue Abstr.; Chem. Abstr.; Chem. Titles; CSA Neuro. Abstr.; Curr. Aware. Biol. Sci., CABS; Curr. Biotechnol.; Curr. Contents Life Sci.; Dairy Sci. Abstr.; EMBASE; Energy Res. Abstr.; Helminthol. Abstr.; Index Med.; Index Vet.; Int. Aerosp. Abstr.; Int. Pharm. Abstr.; Iowa Drug Inf. Serv. (1966-); NAPRALERT; Nucl. Sci. Abstr.; Nutr. Abstr. Rev., Ser. A, Hum. Exp.; Life Sci. Collect.; PESTDOC; Pig News Inf.; Protozoolog. Abstr.; Psychol. Abstr. (1968-); PsycINFO (1990-); PsycLit; Ref. Upd. Basic Ed.; Ref. Upd. Deluxe Ed.; Res. Alert [Full Cov.]; Rev. Med. Vet. Entomol.; Rev. Med. Vet. Mycology; Sci. Cit. Index; SCISEARCH; Soc. Sci. Cit. Index [Select. Cov.]; Stat. Theory Method Abstr. (1959-1963); Vet. Bull.; Toxicol. Abstr. (19??-); Weed Abstr.

PK/0253-8288
### JOURNAL OF PHARMACY.
(JOURNAL OF PHARMACY / FACULTY OF PHARMACY, UNIVERSITY OF THE PUNJAB.). [J. pharm.]. **Added/Corp** University of the Punjab. Faculty of Pharmacy. (1979)-. Periodical. English. sa. **CODEN** JOUPD7. Documents available from BIOSIS Document Express, CASDDS.
**Ind/Abst** Bibliogr. Mission.; Biol. Abstr. (1985-); Chem. Abstr. (1979-1987); Int. Pharm. Abstr.

●US/1062-4546
### JOURNAL OF PHARMACY & LAW, THE.
(THE JOURNAL OF PHARMACY & LAW / OHIO NORTHERN UNIVERSITY, THE PHARMACY-LAW INSTITUTE.). [J. pharm. law]. **Added/Corp** Ohio Northern University. Pharmacy-Law Institute. **VFOAT** Journal of Pharmacy and Law. Vol. 1, No. 1 (1992)-. Periodical. English. Twice a year (June & Dec.). $53.00. Ohio Northern University Law School, PO Box 153, Ada OH 45810. **Tel** (419)772-2248, FAX (419)772-1932. **(Subscription address:** Journal of Pharmacy & Law, Ohio Northern University, Pharmacy & Law Institute, Ada OH 45810.**) DD** 344. **NLM** W1; JO83TG.
**Ind/Abst** Index Leg. Period. (1993-).

UK/0022-3573
### JOURNAL OF PHARMACY AND PHARMACOLOGY.
[J. pharm. pharmacol.]. **Added/Corp** Pharmaceutical Society of Great Britain. British Pharmaceutical Conference. **VFOAT** Journal of Pharmacy & Pharmacology. Vol. 1 (Jan. 1949)-. Academic Scholarly Publication. English. mo. $450.00 US & Japan; £258.00 UK & EC countries; £258.00 other. Pharmaceutical Press, 1 Lambeth High Street, London SE1 7JN England. **Tel** 011 44 71 735 9141, FAX 011 44 71 735 7629, telex 265871, (MONREF G). **ED** John R. Fowler. **NLM** W1 JO831. **CODEN** JPPMAB. **[CCC].** Index available. **Ad Acc. Pr Rev.** Documents available from The Genuine Article, BIOSIS Document Express, CASDDS. ***Supersedes*** *Quarterly Journal of Pharmacy and Pharmacology, 0370-2979.*
**Desc:** Reviews, papers, communications on research in the sciences contributing to the development and evaluation of medicinal substances.
**Ind/Abst** AGRICOLA; Anal. Abstr.; Biol. Abstr.; Chem. Abstr.; Chem. Titles; CSA Neuro. Abstr.; Curr. Aware. Biol. Sci., CABS; Curr. Biotechnol.; Curr. Chem. React.; Dairy Sci. Abstr.; EMBASE; Helminthol. Abstr. (19??-19??); Hortic. Abstr.; Index Chem.; Index Med.; Int. Pharm. Abstr. (19??-19??); Iowa Drug Inf. Serv. (1966-); NAPRALERT; Nat. Prod. Updates; Nutr. Abstr. Rev., Ser. A, Hum. Exp.; Life Sci. Collect.; PESTDOC; Protozoolog. Abstr.; Res. Alert [Full Cov.]; Rev. Med. Vet. Mycology; Sci. Cit. Index; SCISEARCH; Soc. Sci. Cit. Index [Select. Cov.]; Trop. Dis. Bull.

UK/0373-1022
### JOURNAL OF PHARMACY AND PHARMACOLOGY. SUPPLEMENT.
**VFOAT** British Pharmaceutical Conference. (1958)-. English. an. Pharmaceutical Press, 1 Lambeth High Street, London SE1 7JN England. **Tel** 011 44 71 735 9141, FAX 011 44 71 735 7629, telex 265871, (MONREF G). ***Continues*** *Transactions of the British Pharmaceutical Conference.*
**Ind/Abst** EMBASE.

US/0897-1900
### JOURNAL OF PHARMACY PRACTICE.
[J. pharm. pract.]. (1988)-. Periodical. English. bm. $83.00 (individual), $112.00 (institution), $66.00 (student) US; $152.00 (individual), $164.00 (institution) other. W.B. Saunders Company, A Subsidiary of Harcourt Brace Jovanovich, Inc., The Curtis Center/Suite 300, Independence Square West, Philadelphia PA 19106-3399. **Tel** (215)238-7800 or, 5587, FAX (215)238-7883, telex 173146. **(Subscription address:** W. B. Saunders Company / North America Subscriptions, c/o Periodicals, 6277 Sea Harbour Drive, 4th Floor, Orlando FL 32887.**) ED** James T O'Donnell. **LC** RS1; .J886. **DD** 615. **NLM** W1; JO8315. **CODEN** JPPREU. **[CCC].**
**Desc:** Devoted to exploring new practice areas and types of therapies that will enhance the practicing pharmacist's professional skills and help to provide better patient care.
**Ind/Abst** Int. Pharm. Abstr.

US/1044-0054
### JOURNAL OF PHARMACY TEACHING.
[J. pharm. teach.]. Vol. 1, No. 1 (1990)-. Periodical. English. qt. $75.00 US; $105.00 other. The Haworth Press Inc, 10 Alice Street, Binghamton NY 13904-1580. **Tel** (607)722-5857, (800)3-HAWORTH, FAX (607)722-1424. **ED** Mickey Smith (editor's address: Research Professor, School of Pharmacy, University of Mississippi, University, MS 38677). **DD** 615. **NLM** W1; JO831BK. **CODEN** JOPTET. **Bk Rev. Ad Acc. Pr Rev. Acid Free. Circ:** 153. available on microfilm and microfiche from University Microfilms International (UMI). Documents available from Haworth Document Delivery Service.
**Desc:** Devoted to the communication of information with

the goal of improved teaching in pharmacy. Describes successful and/or innovative activities in undergraduate teaching in classroom, laboratory, and clinical settings; graduate education; postgraduate education as continuing education, extension and in-service programs; and education of pharmacy support personnel, other professions, and the general public.
**Ind/Abst** Int. Pharm. Abstr.; Ref. Z.

US/8755-1225
**JOURNAL OF PHARMACY TECHNOLOGY, THE.** (THE JOURNAL OF PHARMACY TECHNOLOGY : JPT.). [J. pharm. technol.]. **Added/Corp** Association of Pharmacy Technicians (U.S.). **VFOAT** JPT. Vol. 1, No. 1 (Jan./Feb. 1985)-. Academic Scholarly Publication. English. bm. $68.00 institution; $99.00 library. Harvey Whitney Books Company, PO Box 42696, Cincinnati OH 45242. **Tel** (513)793-3555, FAX (513)793-3600. **ED** Harvey A. K. Whitney. **DD** 615. **NLM** W1; JO831C. **CODEN** JPTEEB. Index available. **Bk Rev. Ad Acc. Pr Rev. Circ:** 6,000. available on microfilm and microfiche from University Microfilms International (UMI). Documents available from BIOSIS Document Express, CASDDS.
**Desc:** Reviews of drugs and disease states, education and training articles, and topics relevant to practice.
**Ind/Abst** Biol. Abstr. (1985-); Chem. Abstr. (1985-); EMBASE; Health Plan. Adminis.; Int. Pharm. Abstr. (1985-19??); Iowa Drug Inf. Serv. (1985-).

PL
**JOURNAL OF PHYSIOLOGY AND PHARMACOLOGY : AN OFFICIAL JOURNAL OF THE POLISH PHYSIOLOGICAL SOCIETY. See** Biology-Physiology.

US/0163-3759
**JOURNAL OF POSTGRADUATE PHARMACY. COMMUNITY EDITION, THE.** (THE JOURNAL OF POSTGRADUATE PHARMACY.). **Added/Corp** Council of Ohio Colleges of Pharmacy. Vol. 1 (Jan./Feb. 1979)-. Periodical. English. bm. $48.00 (including registration and certification of continuing education credits by the Council of Ohio Colleges of Pharmacy). Journal of Postgraduate of Pharmacy, 110 Hillside Avenue, Springfield NJ 07081. **NLM** W1 JO839.

US/0163-3910
**JOURNAL OF POSTGRADUATE PHARMACY. HOSPITAL EDITION, THE.** (THE JOURNAL OF POSTGRADUATE PHARMACY.). V. 1- Jan./Feb. 1979-. Periodical. English. bm. $48.00 including registration and certification of continuing education credits by the Council of Ohio Colleges of Pharmacy. Journal of Postgraduate of Pharmacy, 110 Hillside Avenue, Springfield NJ 07081. **LC** RS1; .J69. **DD** 615.1/05. **NLM** W1 JO839C.

US/0449-3044
**JOURNAL OF PSYCHOPHARMACOLOGY. *Ceased.*** (1966)-(1992). Periodical. English. qt. **LC** RC483; .J6. **DD** 616.89/18/05. **NLM** W1 JO858J. available in microform from University Microfilms International (UMI). Documents available from The Genuine Article.
**Ind/Abst** Curr. Aware. Biol. Sci., CABS; PsycLit; Ref. Upd. Deluxe Ed.; Res. Alert [Full Cov.]; Soc. Sci. Cit. Index [Select. Cov.].

UK/0269-8811
**JOURNAL OF PSYCHOPHARMACOLOGY (OXFORD, ENGLAND).** (JOURNAL OF PSYCHOPHARMACOLOGY / BRITISH ASSOCIATION FOR PSYCHOPHARMACOLOGY.). [J. psychopharmacol.]. **Added/Corp** British Association for Psychopharmacology. (1987)-. Periodical. English. qt. £105.00 UK and Europe; $185.00 other. Oxford University Press, Walton Street, Oxford OX2 6DP England. **Tel** 011 44 865 56767, FAX 011 44 865 267773, telex 837330 OXPRES G. **(Subscription address:** Oxford University Press / USA, Journals Marketing Department, Oxford University Press, 2001 Evans Road, Cary NC 27513.**) ED** G. J. Everitt (editor's address: Department of Anatomy, University of Cambridge, Downing Street, Cambridge CB2 3DY), R. Maggs, B. Leonard, M. H. Lader, S. A. Checkley, T. J. Crow, A. R. Green, S. D. Iversen, I. L. Martin, S. A. Montgomery and I. P. Stolerman. **NLM** W1; JO858JK. **CODEN** JOPSEQ. **[CCC].** Index available. **Bk Rev. Ad Acc.** available on microfilm and microfiche from University Microfilms International (UMI). Documents available from BIOSIS Document Express, CASDDS.
**Desc:** Seeks to provide a forum in which research and review papers of the highest quality will be published, covering the entire range of psychopharmacology from drug effects on molecular systems to epidemiological studies. Research papers form the bulk of each issue, but critical review papers are welcome. Papers describing clinical trials are accepted on their merits and papers from all over the world are encouraged.
**Ind/Abst** Biol. Abstr.; Chem. Abstr.; EMBASE; PESTDOC; Psychol. Abstr. (1987-); PsycINFO (1990-).

US/0896-6621
**JOURNAL OF RESEARCH IN PHARMACEUTICAL ECONOMICS.** [J. res. pharm. econ.]. **Added/Corp** University of Mississippi. Research Institute of Pharmaceutical Sciences. Health Services Research Division. **VFOAT** Pharmaceutical Economics. Vol. 1, No. 1 (1989)-. Periodical. English. qt. $95.00 US; $133.00 other. The Haworth Press Inc, 10 Alice Street, Binghamton NY 13904-1580. **Tel** (607)722-5857, (800)3-HAWORTH, FAX (607)722-1424. **ED** Mickey C. Smith (editor's address: Health Services Research Division, Research Institute of the Pharmaceutical Sciences, School of Pharmacy, University of Mississippi, University, MS 38677). **LC** HD9666.1; .J68. **DD** 338.4/76151/097305. **NLM** W1; JO869V. **CODEN** JRPEE5. **Bk Rev. Ad Acc. Pr Rev. Acid Free. Circ:** 252. available on microfilm and microfiche from University Microfilms International (UMI). Documents available from Haworth Document Delivery Service.
**Desc:** Under the editorship of an acclaimed researcher/writer, this journal is devoted to the analysis of economic questions and concerns related to the use of pharmaceutical products and services. It is a valuable forum for the pharmaceutical manufacturing industry, academic researchers and theorists, health care financing organizations, insurers, consumer groups and other organizations interested in health benefits, health professional organizations and government policymakers at the international, national and state levels.
**Ind/Abst** BioBusiness; Econ. Lit. Index; Index Period. Artic. Relat. Law; Int. Pharm. Abstr.; Soc. Work Abstr. [Select. Cov.].

SW/0281-0662
**JOURNAL OF SOCIAL AND ADMINISTRATIVE PHARMACY : JSAP.** [J. soc. adm. pharm.]. **VFOAT** JSAP. Vol. 1, No. 1 (1983)-. Periodical. English. Four times a year. Kr350.00 Scandinavia; Kr450.00 other. Swedish Pharmaceutical Press, PO Box 1136, S 111 81 Stockholm Sweden. **Tel** 011 46 8 345080, FAX 011 46 8 149580. **NLM** W1; JO877JH. Index available. **Bk Rev. Circ:** 350.
**Desc:** Covers fundamental aspects of the practice of pharmacy (in pharmacies, industry, universities, administration). Covers all aspects of research in social and administrative pharmacy.
**Ind/Abst** EMBASE; Int. Pharm. Abstr.; Soc. Plann. Policy Dev. Abstr.

US/0022-4901
**JOURNAL OF TEXTURE STUDIES. See** Food and Food Industry.

TU
**JOURNAL OF THE FACULTY OF PHARMACY GAZI UNIVERSITY.** Gazi Universitesi Merkez Yayin, Eczacilik Facultesi Dekanligi, 06330 Ankara, Turkey. **Tel** 011 90 312 2126840 ext. 3381.
**Ind/Abst** PESTDOC.

UK/0140-7783
**JOURNAL OF VETERINARY PHARMACOLOGY AND THERAPEUTICS.** [J. vet. pharmacol. ther.]. **Added/Corp** American College of Veterinary Pharmacology and Therapeutics. Association for Veterinary Clinical Pharmacology and Therapeutics. European Association for Veterinary Pharmacology and Toxicology. American Academy of Veterinary Pharmacology and Therapeutics. Vol. 1 (March 1978)-. Academic Scholarly Publication. English. bm (6 issues). $415.00 US & Canada; £245.00 Europe; £269.50 other. Blackwell Scientific Publications Ltd, Marston Book Services, PO Box 87, Oxford OX2 ODT UK. **Tel** 011 44 865 791155, FAX 011 44 865 791927, telex 837 515 MARDIS G. **ED** Charles Short and Peter Lees. **NLM** W1 JO97Q. **CODEN** JVPTD9. **[CCC].** Index available (bound in last issue). **Bk Rev. Pr Rev. Circ:** 650. available on microfilm and microfiche from University Microfilms International (UMI). Documents available from The Genuine Article, BIOSIS Document Express, CASDDS, ADONIS.
**Desc:** Clinical aspects of veterinary pharmacology and pharmacological topics of veterinary relevance.
**Ind/Abst** ADONIS; AGRICOLA [Full Cov.]; Biol. Abstr.; Chem. Abstr.; Curr. Biotechnol.; Curr. Contents, Agric. Biol. Environ. Sci.; Dairy Sci. Abstr.; EMBASE; Helminthol. Abstr. (19??-19??); Index Med.; Index Vet.; Nutr. Abstr. Rev., Ser. B, Live Feeds and Feed.; PESTDOC; Pig News Inf.; Poult. Abstr.; Protozoolog. Abstr.; Res. Alert [Full Cov.]; Rev. Med. Vet. Entomol.; Sci. Cit. Index; SCISEARCH; Small Anim. Abstr. Bibliogr.; Vet. Bull.

US
**JOURNAL : THE OFFICIAL PUBLICATION OF THE GEORGIA PHARMACEUTICAL ASSOCIATION.** **Added/Corp** Georgia Pharmaceutical Association. **VFOAT** Georgia Pharmaceutical Journal. (1989)-. Periodical. English. mo. **NLM** W1; JO22M. ***Continues*** *Georgia Pharmaceutical Journal, 0194-4290.*

CC/0254-6116
**KANG SHENG SU. *Title Change.*** [Kangshengsu]. **VFOAT** Kangshengsu; Chinese Journal of Antibiotics. (1979)-(19??). Academic Scholarly Publication. Chinese (summaries and/or abstracts in English). bm. Editorial Office C J A, Shan-Ban-Qiao Chengdu, Sichuan, People's Republic of China. **Tel** 4464I. **ED** Chen Xiao-Qing. **LC** RM265; .K36. **DD** 612/.01576/05. **CODEN** KANGDS. Index available. cum. index. **Bk Rev. Ad Acc. Circ:** 6,500. Documents available from BIOSIS Document Express, CASDDS. ***Continues*** *Kang Chun Su.* ***Continued by*** *Zhongguo Kangshengsu Zazhi, 1001-8689.*
**Ind/Abst** Biol. Abstr. (1984-19??); Chem. Abstr. (?-?); Curr. Biotechnol. (?-?); EMBASE (?-?); Microbiol. Abstr. Sect. B (19??-19??); Microbiol. Abstr. Sect. A (?-?); Life Sci. Collect. (?-?).

US/0194-567X
**KENTUCKY PHARMACIST, THE.** **Added/Corp** Kentucky Pharmaceutical Association. (19??)-. Periodical. English. Twelve times a year. $30.00. Kentucky Pharmacists Association, PO Box 715, Frankfort KY 40602. **Tel** (502)227-2303. **ED** Robert L. Barnett Jr. **NLM** W1 KE722. Index available. **Bk Rev. Ad Acc. Circ:** 1,800 (ctrl).
**Desc:** News, educational articles and laws-regulations affecting the practice of pharmacy in Kentucky.
**Ind/Abst** Int. Pharm. Abstr.

UK
**KEYNOTES PRESCRIBED PHARMACEUTICALS.** English. an. £155.00. ICC Business Publications Ltd, Field House, Old Field Road, Hampton Middlesex TW12 2HQ England. **Tel** 011 44 81 783 0755.

GW/0138-5798
**KOMMENTARE ZUM ARZNEIBUCH DER DEUTSCHEN DEMOKRATISCHEN REPUBLIK.** [Komment. Arzneib. Dtsch. Demokr. Repub.]. 1977-. Academic Scholarly Publication. German. ir. Price varies per volume. Akademie-Verlag GmbH, Muehlenstrasse 33 34, D 13162 Berlin Germany. **Tel** 011 49 30 47889300, FAX 011 49 30 47889357. **(Subscription address:** VCH Publishers Inc., 303 Northwest 12th Avenue, Journals Department, Deerfield FL 33442.**) NLM** W1 KO501. **CODEN** KADRDB. Documents available from CASDDS.
**Ind/Abst** Chem. Abstr. (1976-1985).

KO
**KOREAN JOURNAL OF PHARMACOLOGY : OFFICIAL JOURNAL OF THE SOCIETY OF PHARMACOLOGY, REPUBLIC OF KOREA, THE.** **Added/Corp** Taehan Yangni Hakhoe. **VFOAT** Taehan Yangnihak Chapchi. Vol. 21, No. 1 (June 1985)-. Periodical. English (summaries and/or abstracts in Korean). Korean Society of Pharmacology, Seoul National University, 120 752 Seoul Korea. **Tel** 011 82 2 3615214. **LC** RM1; .T25. **DD** 615/.1. **NLM** W1; KO608H. Documents available from CASDDS. ***Continues*** *Taehan Yangnihak Chapchi, 0377-9459.*
**Ind/Abst** Chem. Abstr.; NAPRALERT.

GW/0173-7597
**KRANKENHAUSPHARMAZIE.** (KRANKENHAUSPHARMAZIE / ZEITSCHRIFT DER ARBEITSGEMEINSCHAFT DEUTSCHER KRANKENHAUSAPOTHEKER.). [Krankenhauspharmazie]. **Added/Corp** Arbeitsgemeinschaft Deutscher Krankenhausapotheker. Vol. 1 (July, Aug., Sept. 1980)-. Academic Scholarly Publication. German. mo. DM186.00. Deutscher Apotheker Verlag, Postfach 101061, D 70009 Stuttgart Germany. **Tel** 011 49 711 25820, INLAND:0711/2582, FAX 011 49 711 2582 290, telex 723636 daz d. **ED** Susanne Heinzl. **NLM** W1; KR26T. **CODEN** KRANDZ. **[CCC]. Bk Rev. Ad Acc. Circ:** 2,500 (ctrl). Documents available from CASDDS. ***Continues*** *Krankenhaus-Apotheke.*
**Desc:** Covers the whole field of hospital pharmacy and pharmacotherapy in the clinic.
**Ind/Abst** Chem. Abstr. (1980-1983); EMBASE [Select. Cov.]; Int. Pharm. Abstr.; PESTDOC.

JA/0287-6485
**KUSIRI NO CHISHIKI.** [Kusiri no chishiki]. **Added/Corp** Sumitomo Kagaku Kogyo. Iyaku Jigyobu. **VFOAT** Pharmaceutical Review. (19??)-. Periodical. Japanese. mo. Hoken Dojinsha, (Hoken Dojinsha Inc.), 12-2, Fujimi 2 Chome, Chiyodaku, Tokyoto 102, Japan. **CODEN** KNCHDX. Documents available from CASDDS.
**Ind/Abst** Chem. Abstr.

JA/0452-9731
**KYORITSU YAKKA DAIGAKU KENKYU NENPO.** [Kyoritsu Yakka Daigaku kenkyu nempo]. **Added/Corp** Kyoritsu Yakka Daigaku. **VFOAT** Annual Report of the Kyoritsu College of Pharmacy. (1955)-. Japanese (summaries and/or abstracts in English). Kyoritsu College of Pharmacy, Tokyo Japan. **NLM** W1 KY978. **CODEN** KYDKAJ. Documents available from CASDDS.
**Ind/Abst** Chem. Abstr.

US/0734-4961
**LAWRENCE REVIEW OF NATURAL PRODUCTS, THE.** [Lawrence rev. nat. prod.]. **Added/Corp** Pharmaceutical Information Associates. (19??)-. Monographic series. English. mo. $54.95 US; $69.00 other. Facts and Comparisons Inc, 111 West Port Plaza, Suite 400, St Louis MO 63146-3098. **Tel** (314)878-2515, (800)223-0554, FAX (314)878-5563. **CODEN** LRNSEP. Documents available from BIOSIS Document Express.
**Desc:** Source of current natural product information in monthly monographs.
**Ind/Abst** Biol. Abstr.

LE
**LEBANESE PHARMACEUTICAL JOURNAL. LA REVUE PHARMACEUTIQUE LIBANAISE, THE.** **Added/Corp** Ordre des Pharmaciens du Liban. **VFOAT** Revue Pharmaceutique Libanaise. Vol. 1 (Jan. 1953)-. Periodical. English. qt.
**Ind/Abst** Int. Pharm. Abstr.

US/0191-8516
**LEGAL ASPECTS OF PHARMACY PRACTICE.** **See** Law.

FR
**LETTRE DU PHARMACOLOGUE, LA.** French. ir. 360.00F France; 480.00F other. Edimark, 207 rue Gallieni, 92100 Boulogne France. **Tel** 011 33 1 48251159.

US
**LETTRE MEDICALE SUR LES MEDICAMENTS ET LA THERAPEUTIQUE, LA.** (19??)-. Periodical. French. bw. $37.50 (one year), $61.50 (two year). The Medical Letter Inc, 1000 Main Street, New Rochelle NY 10801. **Tel** (914)235-0500.

FR/1145-4881
**LETTRE MENSUELLE DE FRANCE PHARMACIE LABORATOIRES, LA.** (1989)-. Periodical. French. Eleven times a year (Double issues June/July). 527.50F France; 690.00F other. France Pharmacie, 41 rue Gambetta, 92100 Boulogne France. **Tel** 011 33 46 045246. **ED** M. Roger Baert. **UDC** 615. cum. index. **Bk Rev**. **Ad Acc**. **Circ:** 2,000 (ctrl).

UK/0024-3205
**LIFE SCIENCES (1973).** (LIFE SCIENCES.). [Life sci.]. Vol. 13 (July 1, 1973)-. Academic Scholarly Publication. English. wk. $2325.00 The Americas; £1560.00 other. Pergamon Press, An Imprint of Elsevier Science Ltd., The Boulevard, Langford Lane, Kidlington, Oxford OX5 1GB United Kingdom. **Tel** 011 44 865 843000, 011 44 865 843699, FAX 011 44 865 843010. **(Subscription address:** Elsevier Science Ltd. Oxford Fulfillment Centre, PO Box 800, Kidlington, Oxford OX5 1DX United Kingdom.**)** **ED** Rubin Bressler. **LC** QH301; .L554. **NLM** W1 LI4067. **CODEN** LIFSAK. **[CCC]**. **Pr Rev.** available on microfilm and microfiche from University Microfilms International (UMI); available on microfiche from the publisher. Documents available from The Genuine Article, BIOSIS Document Express, CASDDS, ADONIS. ***Formed by the union of*** *Life Sciences. Part I, Physiology and Pharmacology, 0300-9653* ***and*** *Life Sciences. Part II, Biochemistry, General and Molecular Biology, 0300-9637.*
**Desc:** Publishes papers concerning the pharmacological aspects of biochemistry, chemistry, endocrinology, immunology, medicinal chemistry, microbiology, molecular biology, pathology, physiology and toxicology.
**Ind/Abst** ADONIS; AGRICOLA (Vol. 51, No. 20, 1992.) [Select. Cov.]; Anim. Behav. Abstr.; Anim. Breed. Abstr.; Biol. Agric. Index; Biol. Abstr.; Chem. Abstr.; Chem. Titles; Chemorecept. Abstr.; CSA Neuro. Abstr.; Curr. Aware. Biol. Sci., CABS; Curr. Contents Life Sci.; Curr. Ref. Fish Res.; Dairy Sci. Abstr.; EMBASE; Energy Res. Abstr.; Fish Rev. (Jan. 1989-July 1992); Helminthol. Abstr. (1991-); Immunol. Abstr.; Index Chem.; Index Med.; Int. Aerosp. Abstr.; Nematol. Abstr.; Nutr. Abstr. Rev., Ser. B, Live Feeds and Feed.; Nutr. Res. Newsl.; Oncog. Growth Factors Abstr.; Life Sci. Collect.; PESTDOC; Pig News Inf.; Poult. Abstr.; Protozoolog. Abstr.; Psychol. Abstr.; PsycINFO; PsycLit; Ref. Upd. Basic Ed.; Ref. Upd. Deluxe Ed.; Res. Alert [Full Cov.]; Rev. Med. Vet. Entomol.; Sci. Cit. Index; SCISEARCH; Soc. Sci. Cit. Index [Select. Cov.]; SportSearch; Wildl. Rev. (Jan. 1989-July 1992).

US/0193-5097
**LILLY DIGEST.** **Main/Corp** Lilly (Eli) and Company. Pharmaceutical Division. 1955-. English. an. Eli Lilly & Company, 307 East McCarty Street, Lilly Corporate Center, Indianapolis IN 46285. **Tel** (317)276-2000. ***Continues*** *Lilly Digest of Retail Drug-Store Income and Expense Statements.*

US
**LILLY DIGEST OF THE STATEMENTS OF ... RETAIL DRUG STORES.** **Added/Corp** Eli Lilly and Company. (19??)-. English. an (Oct.). $30.00. Eli Lilly & Company, 307 East McCarty Street, Lilly Corporate Center, Indianapolis IN 46285. **Tel** (317)276-2000. **LC** HD9666.4; .L55. **DD** 615.1065.

UK/0954-1381
**LITHIUM (EDINBURGH).** (LITHIUM.). [Lithium Edinb.]. (1990)-. Periodical. English. qt. £184.00 UK; £185.00 Europe; $405.00 US; £186.00 other (institution). Churchill Livingstone, 1-3 Baxter's Place, Leith Walk, Edinburgh EH1 3AF Scotland. **Tel** 011 44 31 556 2424, FAX 011 44 31 558 1278, telex 727511. **(Subscription address:** Maruzen Company Ltd., PO Box 5050, Import & Export Department, Tokyo 100 31 Japan.**)** **DD** 615.78. **[CCC]**. **Bk Rev**. **Ad Acc**. **Circ:** 250. available on microfilm and microfiche from University Microfilms International (UMI). Documents available from The Genuine Article.
**Ind/Abst** Curr. Aware. Biol. Sci., CABS; EMBASE; Res. Alert [Full Cov.]; Soc. Sci. Cit. Index [Select. Cov.].

CN/0068-8452
**LLOYD'S CANADIAN CHEMICAL, PHARMACEUTICAL, AND PRODUCT DIRECTORY.** ***Ceased.*** **VFOAT** Canadian Chemical, Pharmaceutical, and Product Directory. Ceased (1991). Directory. English. an. Sentinel Business Publications, 7575 Trans Canada Highway, Suite 500, St. Laurent Quebec H4T 1V6 Canada. **Tel** (514)333-1116, FAX (514)631-8858. **ED** Carole Clifford. **LC** HD9655.C2; W5. **DD** 338.4/7/66002571. **Ad Acc**. **Circ:** 5,000 (ctrl). ***Continues*** *Lloyd's Canadian Chemical Directory, 0381-5749.*
**Desc:** A directory of product listings and suppliers to Canada's chemical and pharmaceutical industries.

NZ/1170-814X
**LMS ALERT. NEUROPSYCHOTHERAPEUTICS.** ***Ceased.*** [LMS alert, Neuropsychother.]. **VFOAT** Literature Monitoring and Evaluation Service Alert. Neuropsychotherapeutics. (1991)-(199?). Abstracting/Indexing Service. English. mo. ADIS International Ltd, 41 Centorian Drive, Private Bag 65901, Mairangi Bay, Auckland 10 New Zealand. **Tel** 011 64 9 4798100, FAX 011 64 9 4791418. **(Subscription address:** ADIS International Inc., 940 Town Center Drive, Suite F-10, Langhorne PA 19047.**)** **DD** 016.6157805. ***Continues*** *LMS Neuropsychotherapeutics. Monthly Alert, 0113-5201.*
**Desc:** Designed to meet the pharmaceutical industry's needs for independent, objective drug intelligence. Incorporating in-depth literature review and systematic trend analysis by therapeutic area. Together with clinical trial design, the LMS contains strategic planning leads, rapid identification of licensing, research and promotional opportunities and competitive drug intelligence.

US/0192-3838
**LOUISIANA PHARMACIST, THE.** **Added/Corp** Louisiana Pharmacists Association. Louisiana State Pharmaceutical Association. (19??)-. Periodical. English. mo. $8.00. Louisiana Pharmacists Association, 2337 St Claude Avenue, New Orleans LA 70117. **Tel** (504)949-7545. **ED** Linda M Foreman. **NLM** W1 LO915F. Index available. **Ad Acc**. **Circ:** 2,000 (ctrl).
**Desc:** Contains educational, promotional, and business information to registered pharmacists in the state of Louisiana. Legislative and regulatory information is also included.
**Ind/Abst** Int. Pharm. Abstr.

FR/0024-7804
**LYON PHARMACEUTIQUE.** [Lyon pharm.]. (1923)-. Academic Scholarly Publication. French. Eight times a year. 750.00F France; 840.00F other. Editions Scientifique Elsevier, 141 rue de Javel, 75747 Paris Cedex 15 France. **Tel** 011 33 1 47 07 11 22, FAX 011 33 1 43 36 80 93. **(Subscription address:** Editions Scientifiques Elsevier / for North America, PO Box 7247-7576, Philadelphia PA 19170-7576.**)** **NLM** W1 LY538. **CODEN** LYPHAD. **[CCC]**. Documents available from CASDDS.
**Ind/Abst** Chem. Abstr.; Int. Pharm. Abstr.; NAPRALERT; PESTDOC.

UK/0460-2390
**M & B PHARMACEUTICAL BULLETIN.** [M B pharm. bull.]. **Added/Corp** May & Baker, ltd. **VAT** M and B Pharmaceutical Bulletin. (1952)-. Bulletin. English. qt. **NLM** W1 M109.
**Ind/Abst** AGRICOLA; Int. Pharm. Abstr.

FR/0266-0245
**M & M, D & D.** (MALADIES ET MEDICAMENTS : M&M. DRUGS AND DISEASES : D&D.). [M & M D & D]. **VFOAT** M&M; M et M; D&D; D and D; Drugs and Diseases. Vol. 1, No. 1 (1984)-. Academic Scholarly Publication. French (English). Four times a year. John Libbey Company Ltd, 13 Smith Yard, Summerley Street, London SW18 4HR England. **Tel** 011 44 81 9472777. **NLM** W1; MA498E. **CODEN** MMDDE8. Documents available from CASDDS.
**Ind/Abst** Chem. Abstr. (1984-1989).

IR/0254-4547
**MAJALLAH-I DANISHKADAH-I DARUSAZI.** **VFOAT** Journal of the School of Pharmacy. University of Tehran. (1972)-. Periodical. Arabic. **UDC** 615.1. **CODEN** MDTDDO. Documents available from CASDDS.
**Ind/Abst** Chem. Abstr.

UK/0951-3175
**MARKET LETTER.** [Mark. lett.]. **VFOAT** Marketletter. (1986)-. Periodical. English. wk (50 issues per year). £490.00. Marketletter Publications Ltd, 54-55 Wilton Road, London SW1V 1DE England. **Tel** 011 44 71 8287272, FAX 011 44 71 8280415. **ED** Barbara Obstoj. **Bk Rev**. **Ad Acc**, **Adv Mgr:** Joan Kairis, **Tel** (071)828-7272. available on an online database from Predicasts, Inc.; and DATA-STAR. ***Continues*** *IMS Pharmaceutical Marketletter, 0140-4288.*
**Desc:** Newsletter on world healthcare industry, primarily pharmaceuticals, covering company news, markets, legislation, new products, research and personal appointments. For and about the pharmaceutical and health care industry worldwide, including financial, legislative, products and research aspects.
**Ind/Abst** Abstr. BioCommer.; PROMT [Full Txt.].

TU/1011-3398
**MARMARA UNIVERSITESI ECZACILIK DERGISI.** [Marmara Univ. eczac. derg.]. **VFOAT** Journal of Pharmacy of University of Marmara. (1985)-. Periodical. Turkish. Marmara University, Faculty of Pharmacy, Istanbul Turkey. Documents available from CASDDS.
**Ind/Abst** Chem. Abstr.

US/0025-4347
**MARYLAND PHARMACIST, THE.** **Added/Corp** Maryland Pharmaceutical Association. **VFOAT** MP. The Maryland Pharmacist. (19??)-. Periodical. English. Twelve times a year. $10.00. Maryland Pharmacist, 650 West Lombard Street, Baltimore MD 21201. **Tel** (301)727-0746. **NLM** W1 MA766.
**Ind/Abst** Int. Pharm. Abstr.

US/1052-6986
**MASSACHUSETTS PHARMACY JOURNAL.** [Mass. pharm. j.]. **Added/Corp** Massachusetts State Pharmaceutical Association. **VFOAT** Massachusetts Pharmacy. Vol. 2, No. 3 (May/June 1990)-. Periodical. English. Six times a year. $12.00. Massachusetts State Pharmaceutical Association, 5 Lexington Street, Suite 5, Waltham MA 02154. **Tel** (508)875-1774. **DD** 615. ***Continues*** *Massachusetts Pharmacist, 1050-0081.*
**Ind/Abst** Int. Pharm. Abstr.

PL/0025-5246
**MATERIA MEDICA POLONA (ENGLISH EDITION).** (MATERIA MEDICA POLONA.). [Mater. Med. Pol.]. **VFOAT** The Polish Journal of Medicine and Pharmacy. Vol. 1 (Jan./June 1969)-. Academic Scholarly Publication. English. qt. Price on Request. Foreign Trade Publicity Publ Agpol, POB 726, Marszalkowska 124, 00 950 Warsaw Poland. **Tel** 26 92 21. **ED** Edward Ruzytto. **NLM** W1 MA937N. **CODEN** MMDPA6. Index available. cum. index. **Ad Acc**. **Circ:** 3,000 (ctrl). Documents available from BIOSIS Document Express, CASDDS.
**Desc:** Clinical medicine, pharmacy, physiology, pathology, pharmacology, public health, history of medicine and medical education.
**Ind/Abst** Biol. Abstr.; Chem. Abstr.; EMBASE [Select. Cov.]; Index Med.; Life Sci. Collect.; Trop. Dis. Bull.

US/1067-733X
**MED AD NEWS.** (MED AD NEWS : AN EXECUTIVE BRIEFING ON PHARMACEUTICAL BUSINESS AND MARKETING.). [Med Ad News]. (19??)-. Periodical. English. mo. $85.00 US, Canada, and Mexico; $195.00 other. Engel Communication Inc, 820 Bear Tavern Road, West Trenton NJ 08628. **Tel** (609)530-0044, FAX (609)530-0207. **DD** 610. available on an online database (file 570/Full-Text) from DIALOG. ***Continues*** *Medical Advertising News, 0745-0907.*

CN/0838-2433
**MEDECINES NOUVELLES (QUEBEC).** (LES MEDECINES NOUVELLES.). [Med. nouv.]. Vol. 1, No 1 (Feb. 1988)-. Periodical. French. bm. 19.65Can$ (one year); 34.67Can$ (two year). Ideo-Productions Inc, 2095 Boulevard Charest Ouest #226, Sainte-Foy Quebec, G1N 4L8 Canada. **Tel** (418) 682-3443, FAX (418) 683-3494. **DD** 615.5.

US/0897-5418
**MEDICAL LETTER HANDBOOK OF ADVERSE DRUG INTERACTIONS, THE.** [Med. lett. handb. adverse drug interact.]. **VFOAT** Handbook of Adverse Drug Interactions; Medical Letter on Drug and Therapeutics Handbook of Adverse Drug Interactions. (1985)-. Periodical. English. be. $12.95. The Medical Letter Inc, 1000 Main Street, New Rochelle NY 10801. **Tel** (914)235-0500. **LC** RM302; .M43. **DD** 615/.7045. ***Continues*** *Medical Letter Handbook of Drug Interactions.*

SZ/0253-8512
**MEDICAL LETTER ON DRUGS AND THERAPEUTICS EDITION FRANCAISE, THE.** (MEDICAL LETTER.). [Med. Lett. drugs ther. Ed. fr.]. (1978)-. Periodical. French. bw. 86.00F Switzerland; 90.00F other. Medecine et Hygiene, Case Postale 456, CH-1211 Geneve 4 Switzerland. **Tel** 011 41 22 3469355, 011 41 22 3469356. **UDC** 615.3. Index available. cum.

index. **Pr Rev. Circ:** 4,050.
**Desc:** A French translation of the international review on clinical pharmacology.

US/0025-732X
**MEDICAL LETTER ON DRUGS AND THERAPEUTICS (ENGLISH ED.), THE.** (THE MEDICAL LETTER ON DRUGS AND THERAPEUTICS.). [Med. lett. drugs ther.]. Vol. 1, No. 1 (Jan. 23, 1959)-. Academic Scholarly Publication. English (French, Spanish, Japanese and Italian). bw. $37.50 (one year), $61.00 (two year). The Medical Letter Inc, 1000 Main Street, New Rochelle NY 10801. **Tel** (914)235-0500. **ED** Mark Abramowicz. **DD** 615. **NLM** W1 ME366. Index available. cum. index. **Circ:** 160,000. available on diskette; available on microfilm and microfiche from University Microfilms International (UMI).
**Desc:** Medical letter on drugs and therapeutics.
**Ind/Abst** Abr. Index Med.; Cumul. Index Nurs. Allied Health Lit.; EMBASE; Energy Res. Abstr. (Aug. 1982-); Health Index (1989-); Health Period. Database; Health Ref. Cent. (Jan. 1989-) [Full Cov.]; Index Med.; Int. Pharm. Abstr.; Iowa Drug Inf. Serv. (1966-); Life Sci. Collect.; Physic. Medline Plus; Ref. Upd. Deluxe Ed.

UK/0736-0118
**MEDICAL ONCOLOGY AND TUMOR PHARMACOTHERAPY.** See Medical Science and Technology-Neoplasma, Neoplastic.

HK/0377-9963
**MEDICAL PROGRESS (HONG KONG).** (MEDICAL PROGRESS.). [Med. prog. (Hong Kong)]. (197?)-. Academic Scholarly Publication. English. Twelve times a year. $60.00. MediMedia Pacific Limited, 8 F Pacific Plaza, 410 Dex Voeux Road West, Hong Kong. **Tel** 11 65 5701231, FAX 11 65 5705076, telex 83358 IMSPL HX. **ED** Kristen Fox. **NLM** W1; ME4197H. **CODEN** MEPRDJ. Index available. cum. index. **Bk Rev. Circ:** 23,000. Documents available from CASDDS.
**Desc:** Continuing medical education in drugs and therapeutics.
**Ind/Abst** Chem. Abstr.

US/0199-4905
**MEDICAL SCIENCES BULLETIN.** [Med. sci. bull.]. **Added/Corp** Pharmaceutical Information Associates. (1979)-. Bulletin. English. Twelve times a year. $30.00. Pharmaceutical Information Association Limited, 2761 Trenton Road, Levittown PA 19056. **Tel** (215)949-0490, FAX (215)949-2594. **ED** Robert P. Hand. **DD** 610. **NLM** W1; ME46RF. Index available. **Circ:** 1,800 (ctrl).
**Desc:** Provides accounts of new developments in the fields of pharmacology and therapeutics.
**Ind/Abst** Consum. Health Nutr. Index.

SP/0025-7656
**MEDICAMENTOS DE ACTUALIDAD.** [Med. actual.]. **VFOAT** Drugs of Today. Vol. 8 (Jan. 1965)-. Academic Scholarly Publication. English (Spanish). ir. $425.00. Prous Science Publishers, Apartado de Correos 540, 08080 Barcelona Spain. **Tel** 011 34 3 4592220, FAX 011 34 3 4581535. **ED** J. R. Prous. **NLM** W1 ME55. **CODEN** MDACAP. **[CCC].** Index available. cum. index. **Ad Acc. Circ:** 3,000. Documents available from BIOSIS Document Express, CASDDS.
**Desc:** Describes in monograph form, drugs recently launched on international market. Features review articles on specific drug groups and treatment of particular diseases.
**Ind/Abst** Bibliogr. Mission.; BioBusiness (19??-1990); Biol. Abstr.; Chem. Abstr.; EMBASE; Int. Pharm. Abstr.

CN/0702-8970
**MEDICAMENTS D'AUJOURD'HUI.** V. 1- Sept. 1976-. Periodical. French. mo. $15.00. Monsieur Lucien Fontaine, 5115 rue St Dennis, Montreal Quebec H2J 2M1 Canada. **DD** 615/.1/05.

US/1054-2523
**MEDICINAL CHEMISTRY RESEARCH.** [Med. chem. res.]. Vol. 1, No. 1 (1991)-. Academic Scholarly Publication. English. Nine times a year. 581.90F Switzerland; 592.40F other. Birkhauser Boston, Inc., c/o Springer Publishers New York Inc., Customer Service Department, 333 Meadowlands Parkway, Secaucus NJ 07096-2491. **Tel** (201)348-4033, (800)777-4643. **ED** Richard A. Glennon. **LC** RS400; .M44. **DD** 615/.19/005. **NLM** W1; M64B. **CODEN** MCREEB. **[CCC].** Documents available from The Genuine Article, CASDDS, ADONIS.
**Desc:** Provides prompt disclosure of novel experimental achievements in the many facets of drug design, drug discovery, and the elucidation of mechanisms of action of biologically active compounds.
**Ind/Abst** ADONIS; Chem. Abstr.; Res. Alert.

US/0076-6062
**MEDICINAL RESEARCH.** **VFOAT** Medicinal Research Series. Vol. 1 (1967)-. Monographic series. English. ir. Price varies per volume. Marcel Dekker Inc., 270 Madison Avenue, New York NY 10016. **Tel** (212)696-9000, (800)228-1160, FAX (212)685-4540, telex 421419. **(Subscription address:** Marcel Dekker Inc, PO Box 5017, Monticello NY 12701.**) ED** G. L. Gronewald. **NLM** W1 ME64H. **CODEN** MRSMA.
**Desc:** Series covering topics such as drugs and the nervous system, drug design and drug research.

US/0198-6325
**MEDICINAL RESEARCH REVIEWS.** [Med. res. rev.]. Vol. 1, No. 1 (Spring 1981)-. Academic Scholarly Publication. English. Six times a year. $498.00 (US); $558.00 (Canada and Mexico); $580.50 (other). John Wiley & Sons, Inc., 605 Third Avenue, New York NY 10158-0012. **Tel** (212)850-6000, (212)850-6645, FAX (212)850-6088, telex 12-7063. **(Subscription address:** John Wiley & Sons / England, Baffins Lane, Chichester, West Sussex PO19 1UD England.**) ED** George deStevens. **LC** RM300; .M434. **DD** 615/.1/05. **NLM** W1 ME64J. **CODEN** MRREDD. **[CCC]. Ad Acc. Pr Rev. Circ:** 700. available on microfilm and microfiche from University Microfilms International (UMI). Documents available from The Genuine Article, BIOSIS Document Express, CASDDS, ADONIS.
**Desc:** Covers all aspects of research addressing the study of disease and the consequent development of therapeutic agents. Features developments in specific areas of medicinal research, including a total review of the history leading up to the introduction of a new pharmaceutical.
**Ind/Abst** ADONIS; Biol. Abstr. (1986-); Chem Inform; Chem. Abstr.; Curr. Aware. Biol. Sci., CABS; Curr. Contents Life Sci.; EMBASE; Index Med.; NAPRALERT; PESTDOC; Res. Alert [Full Cov.]; Sci. Cit. Index; SCISEARCH; Soc. Sci. Cit. Index [Select. Cov.].

IO/0126-0901
**MEDIKA.** [Medika]. **Added/Corp** Gabungan Perusahaan Farmasi Indonesia. (1975)-. Periodical. Indonesian. bm. **NLM** W1 ME788H. **CODEN** MEDKD6. Documents available from CASDDS.
**Ind/Abst** Chem. Abstr.

NE/0168-7670
**MEDISCH-FARMACEUTISCHE MEDEDELINGEN.** [Med.-farm. meded.]. (1963)-. Periodical. Dutch. mo. Fl201.10. Wegener Tijl Tijdschriften Group, Postbus 9943, 1006 AP Amsterdam Netherlands. **Tel** 011 31 20 5182828. **ED** A L M Kerremans. **UDC** 615. Index available. cum. index. **Circ:** 2,600.

GW/0939-351X
**MEDIZIN, GESELLSCHAFT, UND GESCHICHTE : JAHRBUCH DES INSTITUTS FUER GESCHICHTE DER MEDIZIN DER ROBERT BOSCH STIFTUNG.** See Medical Science and Technology.

GW/0939-6292
**MEDIZIN OHNE NEBENWIRKUNGEN.** [Med. Nebenwirk.]. **VFOAT** MoN. Medizin ohne Nebenwirkungen. (1991)-. Periodical. German. qt. DM74.00. Vieweg Publishing, PO Box 5829, D 65048 Wiesbaden Germany. **Tel** 011 49 611 160230, FAX 011 49 611 160229. **UDC** 61.

GW/0342-9601
**MEDIZINISCHE MONATSSCHRIFT FUER PHARMAZEUTEN.** [Med. Monatsschr. Pharm.]. Vol. 1 (Jan. 1978)-. Academic Scholarly Publication. German. mo. DM149.40. Deutscher Apotheker Verlag, Postfach 101061, D 70009 Stuttgart Germany. **Tel** 011 49 711 25820, INLAND:0711/2582, FAX 011 49 711 2582 290, telex 723636 daz d. **ED** Susanne Heinzl. **NLM** W1 ME8286. **CODEN** MMPHDB. **[CCC]. Bk Rev. Ad Acc. Circ:** 13,000 (ctrl). Documents available from CASDDS.
**Desc:** Journal for continuing the education of pharmacists, particularly in pharmacology and drug therapy.
**Ind/Abst** Chem. Abstr.; EMBASE [Select. Cov.]; Index Med.; Int. Pharm. Abstr.; Life Sci. Collect.; PESTDOC.

JA/0289-3371
**MEN'EKI YAKURI SHINPOJUMU.** [Men'eki Yakuri Shinpojumu]. **VFOAT** Proceedings of the Symposium on Immunopharmacology; Immunopharmacology, Reviews of Symposium. (1983)-. Periodical. Multiple languages. an. De Emu Be Japan, (D. M. B. Japan), Reburon Biru, 9-12, Roppongi 6 Chome, Minatoku, Tokyoto 106, Japan. **DD** 616.97. Documents available from CASDDS.
**Ind/Abst** Chem. Abstr.

US/0076-6518
**MERCK INDEX; AN ENCYCLOPEDIA OF CHEMICALS AND DRUGS, THE.** 1st Ed. (1889)-. Monographic series. English. ir. Price varies per volume. Merck & Company, PO Box 2000, Rahway NJ 07065. **Tel** (908)594-4600.

●UK/0793-0291
**METAL-BASED DRUGS.** See Chemistry.

SP/0379-0355
**METHODS AND FINDINGS IN EXPERIMENTAL AND CLINICAL PHARMACOLOGY.** [Methods find. exp. clin. pharmacol.]. Vol. 1 (April 1979)-. Academic Scholarly Publication. English. Ten times a year. $425.00. Prous Science Publishers, Apartado de Correos 540, 08080 Barcelona Spain. **Tel** 011 34 3 4592220, FAX 011 34 3 4581535. **ED** J. R. Prous. **NLM** W1 ME9613G. **CODEN** MFEPDX. **[CCC].** Index available. **Bk Rev. Ad Acc. Circ:** 3,000. Documents available from The Genuine Article, BIOSIS Document Express, CASDDS.
**Desc:** A forum for presentation of methodologies used and results obtained in assessment of drugs in animals and man.
**Ind/Abst** Biol. Abstr.; Chem. Abstr.; Curr. Aware. Biol. Sci., CABS; Curr. Contents Life Sci.; EMBASE; Index Med.; Indice Med. Esp.; NAPRALERT; Life Sci. Collect.; PESTDOC; Ref. Upd. Deluxe Ed.; Res. Alert [Full Cov.]; Sci. Cit. Index; SCISEARCH.

US/0091-3030
**METHODS IN PHARMACOLOGY.** [Methods pharmacol.]. Vol. 1 (1971)-. Monographic series. English. ir. Price varies per volume. Plenum Press, 233 Spring Street, New York NY 10013-1578. **Tel** (212)620-8000, (800)221-9369, FAX (212)463-0742, (212)807-1047, telex 23/421139. **LC** QP905; .M45. **DD** 615/.7. **NLM** W1 ME9616N. **CODEN** MTPHBO. Documents available from BIOSIS Document Express, CASDDS.
**Ind/Abst** Biol. Abstr.; Chem. Abstr.

NE/0376-7396
**MEYLER'S SIDE EFFECTS OF DRUGS.** [Meyler's side eff. drugs]. V. 8- 1972/75-. Academic Scholarly Publication. English. 258.75Aus$ Australia. Elsevier Science Publishers BV, PO Box 211, 1000 AE Amsterdam Netherlands. **Tel** 011 31 20 5803642, FAX 011 31 20 5862696, telex 15682. **LC** RM302.5; .S52. **DD** 615/.7042/05. **NLM** W1 ME996S. **CODEN** MSEFDQ. **[CCC].** available on an online database (file 70/Full-Text) from DIALOG. Documents available from BIOSIS Document Express, CASDDS. ***Continues*** *Side Effects of Drugs, 0583-1881.*
**Ind/Abst** Biol. Abstr.; Chem. Abstr. (1972/1975-1980).

US/0163-8084
**MILL'S PHARMACY STATE BOARD REVIEW.** [Mill's pharm. state board rev.]. 29th Ed. (1977)-. English. Medical Exam Publishing Company, 52 Vanderbilt Avenue Elsevier, New York NY 10017-3808. **Tel** (212)463-1052. **ED** J A Romano and M B Wiener. **LC** RS97; .M54. **DD** 615/.1/076. **NLM** QV 18 P538. ***Continues*** *Pharmacy State Board Questions and Answers and Review, 0163-8106.*

UK/0027-0431
**MIMS.** **VFOAT** Monthly Index of Medical Specialties. **VAT** Monthly Index of Medical Specialties. (1959)-. Periodical. English. mo (12 issues). £62.00 UK; £80.00 Eire & Europe; £134.00 America, Middle East, Africa & India; £147.00 Australia, New Zealand & Japan; £91.00 other. Haymarket Publishing Ltd., 12 14 Ansdell Street, London W8 5TR England. **Tel** 011 44 483 733800, FAX 011 44 483 776573. **(Subscription address:** Haymarket Publishing Ltd, PO Box 219, Subscriptions Department, Woking Surrey GU21 1ZW, United Kingdom.**) ED** Pieter Joubert. Index available. **Ad Acc. Circ:** 9,000 (ctrl).
**Desc:** Index of ethical medicines for prescription use by registered medical doctors in South Africa. Medicines placed in pharmacological order.

UK/0140-4415
**MIMS AFRICA.** Vol. 16 (1976)-. Trade Publication. English. bm. £22.00. A E Morgan Publications Ltd, Stanley House, 9 West Street, Epsom Surrey KT18 7RL England. **Tel** 011 44 3727 41411, FAX 0372 744493, telex 291561 VIA SOS G. **ED** Frances Wilson. **NLM** QV 772 M105. **Ad Acc. Circ:** 8,500 (ctrl). ***Continues*** *African MIMS.*
**Desc:** A professionally edited index of ethical preparations circulating to all doctors and hospitals in Central, East, and West Africa.

AT/0725-4709
**MIMS ANNUAL, AUSTRALIAN EDITION.** (THE MIMS ANNUAL.). [MIMS annu., Aust. ed.]. (1977)-. English. an. 82.00Aus$ Australia; 119.05Aus$ New Zealand and Papua, New Guinea; 150.05Aus$ other. Mims Australia, 98 Albany Street, Crows Nest NSW 2065 Australia. **Tel** 011 61 2 9067966, FAX 011 61 2 9063955. **ED** Linda Badewitz-Dodd. **NLM** QV 772 M662. Index available. **Ad Acc. Circ:** 25,000. ***Absorbed*** *Australian Drug Compendium.*
**Desc:** Full disclosure prescribing information of ethical and significant over-the-counter pharmaceuticals. Listed by therapeutic class, combined proprietary, generic, action, and indications index, and other medical information.

UK
**MIMS CARIBBEAN.** (1970)-. Trade Publication. English. bm. £20.90. A E Morgan Publications Ltd, Stanley House, 9 West Street, Epsom Surrey KT18 7RL England. **Tel** 011 44 3727 41411, FAX 0372 744493, telex 291561 VIA SOS G. **ED** Frances Wilson. **Ad Acc. Circ:** 2,600.
**Desc:** Provides a listing of available prescription drugs.

UK
**MIMS COLOUR INDEX.** **VAT** Monthly Index of Medical Specialties Colour Index. (1974)-. English. Haymarket Publishing Ltd., 12 14 Ansdell Street, London W8 5TR England. **Tel** 011 44 483 733800, FAX 011 44 483 776573. **(Subscription address:** Haymarket Publishing Ltd, PO Box 219, Subscriptions Department, Woking Surrey GU21 1ZW, United Kingdom.**) NLM** QV 772; M111AB.

AT/1035-5723
**MIMS CROWS NEST.** [MIMS Crows Nest]. (196?)-. Periodical. English. bm. 66.00Aus$ Australia; 106.70Aus$ New Zealand, Papua, New Guinea, Indonesia, Malaysia; 143.15Aus$ other. Mims Australia, 98 Albany Street, Crows Nest NSW 2065 Australia. **Tel** 011 61 2 9067966, FAX 011 61 2 9063955. **ED** Linda Badewitz-Dodd. **DD** 615.03. Index available. **Ad Acc. Circ:** 25,000 (ctrl).
**Desc:** Abbreviated prescribing information of pharmaceutical products available on the market. Indexes pharmaceutical benefits scheme information and abbreviated warnings, etc.

SA/0076-8847
**MIMS DESK REFERENCE.** **VFOAT** MIMS Lessenaarhandboek; MDR; Medical Information Management System Desk Reference. (19??)-. English. an (Oct.). R320.00 US; R200.00 South Africa; R338.00 others. MIMS Pty Ltd., PO Box 2059, Pretoria 0001 South Africa. **Tel** 011 27 12 348-5010, FAX 011 27 12 477716. **ED** Deo Botha and Pieter Joubert. **Ad Acc. Circ:** 5,266 (ctrl).
**Desc:** Detailed product information on medicines alphabetically in firm order.

II/0970-1036
**MIMS INDIA.** [MIMS India]. **VFOAT** Monthly Index of Medical Specialities India. (1980)-. Periodical. English. Twelve times a year. $70.00. A. E. Morgan Publications India, 90 Nehru Place, New Delhi 110019 India. **Tel** 6433115, FAX 6424016, telex 3170230 MIMS IN. **ED** Dr. C. M. Giulhati. **UDC** 615.1. Index available. cum. index. **Bk Rev. Ad Acc, Adv Mgr:** Pooja Sharma. **Circ:** 280,000.

UK
**MIMS MAGAZINE.** [MIMS mag.]. **VFOAT** Monthly Index of Medical Specialities Magazine. (1974)-. English. wk (52 issues). £81.00 UK; £104.00 Eire & Europe; £174.00 America, Middle East, Africa & India; £190.00 Australia, New Zealand & Japan; £104.00 other. Haymarket Publishing Ltd., 12 14 Ansdell Street, London W8 5TR England. **Tel** 011 44 483 733800, FAX 011 44 483 776573. **(Subscription address:** Haymarket Publishing Ltd, PO Box 219, Subscriptions Department, Woking Surrey GU21 1ZW, United Kingdom.**)**
**Ind/Abst** Int. Pharm. Abstr.

SA/0027-0431
**MIMS MEDICAL SPECIALTIES.** English. mo. R143.30 South Africa; R275.30 North America; R251.30 other. MIMS Pty Ltd., PO Box 2059, Pretoria 0001 South Africa. **Tel** 011 27 12 348-5010, FAX 011 27 12 477716. **(Subscription address:** PO Box 2059, Pretoria 0001 South Africa**) ED** Deo Botha and Pieter Joubert. **NLM** QV 772; M113. **Ad Acc. Circ:** 8,100 (ctrl).
**Desc:** Ethical medicines listed in pharmacological order alphabetically.

UK
**MIMS UK.** English. mo. £66.00. Haymarket Publishing Ltd., 12 14 Ansdell Street, London W8 5TR England. **Tel** 011 44 483 733800, FAX 011 44 483 776573. **(Subscription address:** Tower Subscription, Sovereign Park, Market Harborough, Leics LE16 9EF**) ED** Colin Duncan. Index available. **Ad Acc, Adv Mgr:** Kate Locks. **Circ:** 60 (ctrl).
**Desc:** Lists major prescription medicines according to therapeutic use. It also provides details of manufacturer, ingredients, indications, dosage and side effects.

US/0026-5616
**MINNESOTA PHARMACIST.** [Minn. pharm.]. **Added/Corp** Minnesota Pharmacists Association. Minnesota. State Board of Pharmacy. Twin City Retail Druggists Association. Vol. 1 (Oct. 1946)-. Periodical. English. mo. Minnesota Pharmacists Association, Court International N, Suite 320, 2550 University Avenue W, St. Paul MN 55114. **DD** 615. ***Supersedes*** *Minnesota Pharmacist, 0026-5616.*
**Ind/Abst** Int. Pharm. Abstr.

FR/0294-0671
**MISES AU POINT DE BIOCHIMIE PHARMACOLOGIQUE.** [Mises point biochim. pharmacol.]. **VFOAT** Advances in Biochemical Pharmacology. 1- Series. Academic Scholarly Publication. French (English). Editions Masson, 120 BD Street Germain, 75280 Paris Cedex 06 France. **Tel** (1)46342760, FAX (1)45872999. **ED** G Siest and C Heusghem. **DD** 615. **NLM** W1 MI791QP. **CODEN** MPBPDK. Documents available from CASDDS.
**Ind/Abst** Chem. Abstr.; Life Sci. Collect.

US/0161-3189
**MISSISSIPPI PHARMACIST.** (19??)-. Periodical. English. bm. Mississippi State Pharmaceutical Association, Suite 204, Barnette Bldg., North Congress Street, Jackson MS 39205.
**Ind/Abst** Int. Pharm. Abstr.

US/0026-6663
**MISSOURI PHARMACISTS.** [Mo. pharm.]. **Added/Corp** Missouri. Board of Pharmacy. Missouri Center for Health Statistics. National Center for Health Statistics (U.S.). (1974)-. Periodical. English. mo. **NLM** W2 AM8 C4M.
**Ind/Abst** Int. Pharm. Abstr.

GW/0934-4640
**MITTEILUNGEN - DEUTSCHE GESELLSCHAFT FUR PHARMAKOLOGIE UND TOXIKOLOGIE.** (MITTEILUNGEN.). [Mitt. - Dtsch. Ges. Pharmakol. Toxikol.]. **VFOAT** DGPT-Mitteilungen. (1988)-. Periodical. German. ir. DM24.00. Wissenschaftliche Verlagsgesellschaft mbH, Postfach 101061, D 70009 Stuttgart Germany. **Tel** 011 49 711 258200, FAX 011 49 711 2582290, telex 723636 DAZ D. **ED** W. Braun. **UDC** 615. **Ad Acc. Circ:** 2,500.
**Desc:** Contains information on pharmacology and toxicology.

US/1044-0704
**MODELL'S DRUGS IN CURRENT USE AND NEW DRUGS.** [Modell's drugs curr. use new drugs]. **VFOAT** Drugs in Current Use and New Drugs; Modell's Drugs. 34th Ed. (1988)-. English. an. $18.95. Springer-Verlag New York Inc., 175 5th Avenue, New York NY 10010. **Tel** (212)460-1500, telex 232 235 SPB UR. **(Subscription address:** Springer Verlag New York Inc. / for North America, 44 Hartz Way, Secaucus NJ 07096.**) LC** RS79; .D7. **DD** 615/.1/05. **NLM** QV 740; AA1 D75. ***Continues*** *Drugs in Current Use and New Drugs, 0070-7392.*

US/0732-7218
**MODERN METHODS IN PHARMACOLOGY.** [Mod. methods pharmacol.]. Vol. 1 (1982)-. Academic Scholarly Publication. English. ir. Price varies per volume. John Wiley & Sons, Inc., 605 Third Avenue, New York NY 10158-0012. **Tel** (212)850-6000, (212)850-6645, FAX (212)850-6088, telex 12-7063. **(Subscription address:** John Wiley & Sons / England, Baffins Lane, Chichester, West Sussex PO19 1UD England.**) ED** Sydney Spector and Nathan Back. **LC** RM301; .M63. **DD** 615/.1/072. **NLM** W1 MO166M. **CODEN** MMEPDE. **[CCC].** Documents available from BIOSIS Document Express, CASDDS.
**Desc:** A book series concerning modern methods used in pharmacology.
**Ind/Abst** Biol. Abstr.; Chem. Abstr.; Index Book Rev. Relig.

US/0098-6925
**MODERN PHARMACOLOGY-TOXICOLOGY.** [Mod. pharmacol.-toxicol.]. Vol. 2 (1975)-. Monographic series. English. ir. Price varies per volume. Marcel Dekker Inc., 270 Madison Avenue, New York NY 10016. **Tel** (212)696-9000, (800)228-1160, FAX (212)685-4540, telex 421419. **(Subscription address:** Marcel Dekker Inc, PO Box 5017, Monticello NY 12701.**) ED** Bousquet and Palmer. **LC** UNC. **NLM** W1 MO167T. **CODEN** MPTOD5. Documents available from CASDDS. ***Continues*** *Modern Pharmacology, 0092-0150.*
**Desc:** Each title features a different topic in pharmacology and/or toxicology.
**Ind/Abst** Chem. Abstr.; Life Sci. Collect.

SZ/0077-0094
**MODERN PROBLEMS OF PHARMACOPSYCHIATRY.** **See** Medical Science and Technology-Psychiatry.

UK/0959-5244
**MOLECULAR NEUROPHARMACOLOGY.** ***Ceased.*** **See** Medical Science and Technology-Neurology.

US/0026-895X
**MOLECULAR PHARMACOLOGY.** [Mol. pharmacol.]. **Added/Corp** American Society for Pharmacology and Experimental Therapeutics. Vol. 1 (July 1965)-. Academic Scholarly Publication. English. mo. $105.00 (individual), $230.00 (institution) US; $135.00 (individual), $260.00 (institution) other. Williams & Wilkins Company, 428 East Preston Street, Baltimore MD 21202-3993. **Tel** (410)528-4000, (800)638-6423, FAX (410)528-8596, telex 87669. **(Subscription address:** Williams & Wilkins, PO Box 64380, Baltimore MD 21264.**) ED** William A. Catterall. **LC** QP901; .M65. **DD** 615/.7/05. **NLM** W1 MO197. **CODEN** MOPMA3. **[CCC]. Ad Acc. Pr Rev. Circ:** 1,500. available on microfilm. Documents available from, The Genuine Article, BIOSIS Document Express, CASDDS, Quick Copies.
**Desc:** Covers research on drug action and selective toxicity at the molecular level for pharmacologists and biochemists.
**Ind/Abst** AGRICOLA; Biol. Abstr.; Calcium Calcif. Tissue Abstr.; Chem. Abstr.; Chem. Titles; CSA Neuro. Abstr.; Curr. Aware. Biol. Sci., CABS; Curr. Contents Life Sci.; EMBASE; Energy Res. Abstr.; Index Med.; Microbiol. Abstr. Sect. A; Nucl. Sci. Abstr.; Life Sci. Collect.; PESTDOC; Protozoolog. Abstr.; Ref. Upd. Basic Ed.; Ref. Upd. Deluxe Ed.; Res. Alert [Full Cov.]; Sci. Cit. Index; SCISEARCH; Virol. AIDS Abstr.

FR/0026-9689
**MONITEUR DES PHARMACIES ET DES LABORATOIRES.** [Monit. pharm. lab.]. (1947)-. Periodical. French. Fifty times a year (Includes 4 special issues). 835.00F France; 1,020.00F other. Moniteur Pharmac Laboratoires, 11 17 rue Godefroy Cavaignac, 75541 Paris Cedex 11 France. **Tel** 011 33 1 43790630, FAX 011 33 1 43791775. **UDC** 615.

FR/0994-4478
**MONITEUR INTERNAT PARIS, LE.** ***Ceased.*** (LE MONITEUR INTERNAT.). [Monit. intern. Paris]. (1987)-Series complete with Issue 32 (19??). Periodical. French. bm. Moniteur Pharmac Laboratoires, 11 17 rue Godefroy Cavaignac, 75541 Paris Cedex 11 France. **Tel** 011 33 1 43790630, FAX 011 33 1 43791775. **UDC** 372.861.

SP
**MONITOR DE LA FARMACIA Y DE LA TERAPEUTICA, EL.** **Added/Corp** Asociacion de Centros Farmaceuticos de Espana. Vol. 1 (Oct. 4, 1895)-. Periodical. Spanish. mo. 3000ptas Spain; 6000ptas North America; 5000ptas other. Centro Farmaceutico Nacional SA, Julian Camarillo 37, 28037 Madrid Spain. **Tel** (91)754 43 84, FAX (91)754 56 59. **NLM** W1 MO445. **CODEN** MFTEA4. Index available. **Ad Acc. Circ:** 17,000 (ctrl). Documents available from BIOSIS Document Express.
**Ind/Abst** Biol. Abstr. (19??-1985); Int. Pharm. Abstr.

US/0085-3100
**MONOGRAPHS OF THE MARIO NEGRI INSTITUTE FOR PHARMACOLOGICAL RESEARCH.** [Monogr. Mario Negri Inst. Pharmacol. Res.]. **Main/Corp** Istituto di Richerche Farmacologiche Mario Negri. (19??)-. Monographic series. English. ir. Price varies per volume. Raven Press, 1185 Avenue of the Americas, 37th Floor, New York NY 10036. **Tel** (212)930-9500, (212)930-9604, FAX (212)869-3495, (212)302-8507, telex 640073. **ED** Silvio Garattini.

US/8755-3082
**MOST-PRESCRIBED DRUGS.** (MOST-PRESCRIBED DRUGS : MPD / RONALD J. TALLARIDA.). **VFOAT** MPD; Most Prescribed Drugs. (1985)-. English. an. price varies per volume. W.B. Saunders Company, A Subsidiary of Harcourt Brace Jovanovich, Inc., The Curtis Center/Suite 300, Independence Square West, Philadelphia PA 19106-3399. **Tel** (215)238-7800 or, 5587, FAX (215)238-7883, telex 173146. **(Subscription address:** W. B. Saunders Company / North America Subscriptions, c/o Periodicals, 6277 Sea Harbour Drive, 4th Floor, Orlando FL 32887.**) LC** RM301; .T345. **DD** 615/.1. **NLM** QV 772; T147t. ***Continues*** *Top 200, 0723-872X.*

US/0162-1602
**N.A.R.D. JOURNAL.** [NARD newsl.]. **Main/Corp** National Association of Retail Druggists (U.S.). **Added/Corp** National Association of Retail Druggists (U.S.). Newsletter. **VAT** National Association of. Vol. 100 (Aug. 1977)-. Periodical. English. Twenty-three times a year. $50.00 North America; $70.00 other. National Association of Retail Druggists, 205 Dangerfield Road, Alexandria VA 22314. **Tel** (703)683-8200. **ED** Todd Dankmyer. **LC** HD9666.1; .N2. **DD** 381/.45/61510973. Index available. **Ad Acc. Circ:** 29,238 (ctrl). ***Continues in part*** *NARD Journal, 0027-5972.*
**Desc:** Represents the owners of nearly 30,000 independent retail pharmacies in the US, where 75,000 pharmacists practice their profession.

●US/1064-9786
**N.D.A. (SKOKIE, ILL.), THE.** (THE N.D.A. : NEW DRUGS ANNOTATED.). [N.D.A.]. **VFOAT** NDA; New Drugs Annotated. No. 1 (July 1992)-. Periodical. English. Biomega Corporation, 8707 Skokie Boulevard, Suite 107, Skokie IL 60077. **Tel** (708)982-1400, FAX (708)982-1420. **DD** 615.

US/8756-4483
**NABP NEWSLETTER.** [NABP newsl.]. **Added/Corp** National Association of Boards of Pharmacy. **VAT** Newsletter - National Association of Boards of Pharmacy; National Association of Boards of Pharmacy Newsletter. Vol. 1 (Oct. 1971)-. Newsletter. English. mo (10 issues). $25.00. National Association Boards of Pharmacy, 700 Busse Highway, Park Ridge IL 60068. **Tel** (708)698-6227. **DD** 615. ***Continues*** *NABP Quarterly, 0027-5700.*
**Ind/Abst** Int. Pharm. Abstr.

JA/0369-5611
**NAGOYA SHIRITSU DAIGAKU YAKUGAKUBU KENKYU NENPO.** [Nagoya Shiritsu Daigaku Yakugakubu kenkyu nempo]. **Main/Corp** Nagoya Shiritsu Daigaku. Yakugakubu. **VFOAT** Annual Report of the Faculty of Pharmaceutical Sciences, Nagoya City University. 12 (1964)-. Academic Scholarly Publication. English. Nagoya Shiritsu Daigaku Yakugakubu, (Faculty of Pharmaceutical Sciences, Nagoya City University), 3-1, Tanabe Doori, Mizuhoku, Nagoyashi, Aichiken 467, Japan. **NLM** W1 NA1157. **CODEN** NSDYAI. Documents available from BIOSIS Document Express, CASDDS. ***Continues*** *Nagoya Shiritsu Daigaku. Yakugakubu. Nagoya Shiritsu Daigaku Yakugakubu Kiyo.*
**Ind/Abst** Biol. Abstr.; Chem. Abstr.

US
**NAPRALERT [ONLINE DATABASE].** **See** Pharmacy and Pharmacology-Abstracting, Bibliographies and Statistics.

US/1013-3453
**NARCOTIC DRUGS : ESTIMATED WORLD REQUIREMENTS FOR ..., STATISTICS FOR ... .** **Added/Corp** International Narcotics Control Board. **VFOAT** Stupefiants. (Nov. 1988)-. Government Publication. English (French and Spanish). an. price varies per volume. United Nations Publications, 2 United Nations Plaza, Room DC2 0853, Department 007C, New York NY 10017. **Tel** (212)963-8303, (800)253-9646. **LC** HV5800; .N29. **DD** 338.4/76157822/021. **NLM** W2; MU5 I2n. ***Formed by the union of*** *Estimated World Requirements of Narcotic Drugs in ... (1978); Statistics on Narcotic Drugs for ... Furnished by Governments in Accordance with the International Treaties and Maximum Levels of Opium Stocks **and** Comparative Statement of Estimates and Statistics on Narcotic Drugs for ... Furnished by Governments in Accordance with the International Treaties.*
**Desc:** Provides analysis of recent trends and statistics for estimated requirements and actual movements of narcotic drugs. Data is provided for specific groups of drugs and countries is provided for specific groups of drugs and countries.

US/0027-5972
**NARD JOURNAL.** (N.A.R.D. JOURNAL.). **Added/Corp** National Association of Retail Druggists (U.S.). **VFOAT** NARD Journal. **VAT** National Association of Retail Druggists Journal. Vol. 19, No. 14 (Jan. 7, 1915)-. Periodical. English. mo. National Association of Retail Druggists, 205 Dangerfield Road, Alexandria VA 22314. **Tel** (703)683-8200. **LC** HD9666.1; .N2. **NLM** W1 N119. ***Continues*** *Journal of the National Association of Retail Druggists, 0276-2595.* ***Continued in part by*** *National Association of Retail Druggists (U.S.). NARD Newsletter, 0162-1602.*
**Ind/Abst** Int. Pharm. Abstr.

XO
**NASE LIECIVE RASTLINY.** **VFOAT** Liecive Rastliny. Periodical. Czech. bm. kcs21.00. **(Subscription address:** Slovart GTG Ltd., Krupinska 4, 852 99 Bratislava Slovakia.**)** **LC** RS164; .N34. **NLM** W1 NA181H.
**Ind/Abst** Nutr. Abstr. Rev., Ser. B, Live Feeds and Feed.

US/0027-8890
**NATIONAL CAPITAL PHARMACIST, THE.** **Added/Corp** District of Columbia Pharmaceutical Association. Vol. 1 (Sept. 1939)-. Periodical. English. bm. $20.00. District of Columbia Pharmaceutical Association, 6400 Georgia Avenue NW/Suite 6, Washington DC 20015. **Tel** (202)829-1515. **ED** Cari W Pao. **LC** HD9666.8.W3; D5. **DD** 658.916154. **NLM** W1 NA347. **Ad Acc. Circ:** 300 (ctrl).
**Desc:** Publication for the pharmacists of Washington, DC and the metropolitan area.
**Ind/Abst** Int. Pharm. Abstr.

US
**NATIONAL DRUG CODE DIRECTORY.** ***Ceased.*** **Added/Corp** United States. Food and Drug Administration. Science Information Facility. United States. Food and Drug Administration. Bureau of Drugs. Office of Scientific Coordination. United States. Food and Drug Administration. Drug Listing Branch. **VFOAT** Drug Code Directory. (Oct. 1969)-(1993). Directory. English. ir. Superintendent of Documents, US Government Printing Office, Washington DC 20402. **Tel** (202)275-3328, FAX (202)786-2377. **LC** RS53; .N35. **DD** 615/.1/0285425. **NLM** QV 772 N2763.
**Desc:** Contains an alphabetical index by product trade name, numeric index of products by drug class, and national drug code, and an alphabetical index by short name.

US/0145-5451
**NATIONAL PRESCRIPTION AUDIT: THERAPEUTIC CATEGORY REPORT.** **Main/Corp** IMS America Ltd. (19??)-. English. mo. IMS America Ltd, Butler Pike & Maple Avenue, Ambler PA 19002. **LC** HD9666.1; .I18a. **DD** 381/.45/61510973.

RU
**NAUCHNYE TRUDY / VSESOIUZNYI NAUCHNO-ISSLEDOVATELSKII INSTITUT FARMATSII.** ***Title Change.*** **Added/Corp** Vsesoiuznyi Nauchno-Issledovatelskii Institut Farmatsii (Soviet Union) Soviet Union. Ministerstvo Zdravookhraneniia. (1978)-(19??). Academic Scholarly Publication. Russian. **CODEN** NTVFES. Documents available from CASDDS. ***Continued by*** *Trudy Vsesoiuznogo Nauchno-Issledovatelskogo Instituta Farmatsii.*
**Ind/Abst** Chem. Abstr.

GW/0028-1298
**NAUNYN-SCHMIEDEBERG'S ARCHIVES OF PHARMACOLOGY.** [Naunyn-Schmiedeberg's arch. pharmacol.]. **VFOAT** Archives of Pharmacology. Vol. 272 (1972)-. Academic Scholarly Publication. English. Twelve times a year. DM1798.00. Springer-Verlag GmbH & Company KG, Heidelberger Platz 3, D 14197 Berlin Germany. **Tel** 011 49 30 8207223, FAX 011 49 30 8214091, telex 183 319 SPBLN D. **(Subscription address:** Springer Verlag New York Inc. / for North America, 44 Hartz Way, Secaucus NJ 07096.**)** **ED** K Starke. **NLM** W1 NA987. **CODEN** NSAPCC. **[CCC]. Pr Rev.** available on microfilm and microfiche from University Microfilms International (UMI). Documents available from The Genuine Article, BIOSIS Document Express, CASDDS, ADONIS. ***Continues*** *Naunyn-Schmiedeberg's Archiv fur Pharmakologie, 0340-5249.*
**Desc:** Publishes original papers on the molecular effects of drugs within the cell and observations of the effect of drugs on the whole organism.
**Ind/Abst** ADONIS; AGRICOLA; Anim. Behav. Abstr.; Biol. Abstr.; Chem. Abstr.; Chem. Titles; CSA Neuro. Abstr.; Curr. Aware. Biol. Sci., CABS; Curr. Chem. React.; EMBASE; Index Chem.; Index Med.; NAPRALERT; Life Sci. Collect.; PESTDOC; Ref. Upd. Basic Ed.; Ref. Upd. Deluxe Ed.; Res. Alert [Full Cov.]; Sci. Cit. Index; SCISEARCH.

US
**NCI INVESTIGATIONAL DRUGS. CHEMICAL INFORMATION.** **Added/Corp** National Institutes of Health (U.S.) Developmental Therapeutics Program (U.S.). Pharmaceutical Resources Branch. **VFOAT** Chemical Information. **VAT** National Cancer Institute investigational drugs. Chemical information. (1984)-. Periodical. English. ir. Free on request. National Cancer Institute, NCI Building Room, 10A 18, Bethesda MD 20892. **Tel** (800)422-6237, (301)496-8774. **LC** RS431.A64; N38. **DD** 615/.1901.

US/0890-6610
**NDA PIPELINE, THE.** [NDA pipeline]. **Added/Corp** F-D-C Development Corporation. **VAT** New Drug Application Pipeline. (1982)-. Government Publication. English. an (May). $595.00. FDC Reports Inc., 5550 Friendship Boulevard/Suite 1, Chevy Chase MD 20815. **Tel** (301)657-9830. **LC** RS189; .N36. **DD** 615/.1/0973. **NLM** QV 772; N337.
**Desc:** A reference source of Rx drug development activity in the U.S. Gives information on recently introduced new drugs and products under development.

US/0028-1891
**NEBRASKA MORTAR & PESTLE.** **Added/Corp** Nebraska Pharmaceutical Association. **VAT** Nebraska Mortar and Pestle. (19??)-. Periodical. English. mo.
**Ind/Abst** Int. Pharm. Abstr.

US/1056-8956
**NEONATAL PHARMACOLOGY QUARTERLY.** ***Ceased.*** (1992)-(July 1993). Periodical. English. qt. Neonatal Network, 1304 Southpoint Boulevard, Suite 280, Petaluma CA 94954. **Tel** (707)762-2646. **NLM** W1; NE19WN.
**Ind/Abst** Cumul. Index Nurs. Allied Health Lit.

GW/0724-567X
**NEUE ARZNEIMITTEL.** (NEUE ARZNEIMITTEL : BEILAGE DER DEUTSCHEN APOTHEKER ZEITUNG.). [Neue Arzneim.]. Vol. 27, 1/2 (Jan./Feb. 1982)-. German. mo. DM18.00. Deutscher Apotheker Verlag, Postfach 101061, D 70009 Stuttgart Germany. **Tel** 011 49 711 25820, INLAND:0711/2582, FAX 011 49 711 2582 290, telex 723636 daz d. **ED** Susanne Heinzl. **NLM** W1 NE239G. **Circ:** 24,000.

GW
**NEUES MANUAL FUER DIE PRAKTISCHE PHARMAZIE.** German. Springer-Verlag GmbH & Company KG, Heidelberger Platz 3, D 14197 Berlin Germany. **Tel** 011 49 30 8207223, FAX 011 49 30 8214091, telex 183 319 SPBLN D. **(Subscription address:** Springer Verlag New York Inc. / for North America, 44 Hartz Way, Secaucus NJ 07096.**)**

UK/0028-3908
**NEUROPHARMACOLOGY.** [Neuropharmacology]. Vol. 9 (Jan. 1970)-. Periodical. English. mo. $1282.00 The Americas; £860.00 other. Pergamon Press, An Imprint of Elsevier Science Ltd., The Boulevard, Langford Lane, Kidlington, Oxford OX5 1GB United Kingdom. **Tel** 011 44 865 843000, 011 44 865 843699, FAX 011 44 865 843010. **(Subscription address:** Elsevier Science Ltd. Oxford Fulfillment Centre, PO Box 800, Kidlington, Oxford OX5 1DX United Kingdom.**)** **ED** P. B. Bradley and E. Costa. **LC** RM315; .I55. **DD** 615/.78/05. **NLM** W1 NE337T. **CODEN** NEPHBW. **[CCC]. Pr Rev.** available on microfilm and microfiche from University Microfilms International (UMI). Documents available from The Genuine Article, BIOSIS Document Express, CASDDS, ADONIS. ***Continues*** *International Journal of Neuropharmacology, 0375-9458.*
**Desc:** Publishes original research papers concerned with the actions of drugs and other biologically active substances on the central and peripheral nervous systems in animals and man.
**Ind/Abst** ADONIS; Biol. Abstr.; Calcium Calcif. Tissue Abstr.; Chem. Abstr.; Chem. Titles; CSA Neuro. Abstr.; Curr. Contents Life Sci.; EMBASE; Helminthol. Abstr.; Index Med.; Int. Aerosp. Abstr. (1983-); Nutr. Abstr. Rev., Ser. A, Hum. Exp.; Life Sci. Collect.; PESTDOC; Psychol. Abstr. (1970-); PsycINFO; PsycLit; Ref. Upd. Basic Ed.; Ref. Upd. Deluxe Ed.; Res. Alert [Full Cov.]; Sci. Cit. Index; SCISEARCH; Toxicol. Abstr. (19??-19??).

IT/0394-9540
**NEUROPSICOFARMACOLOGIA DEL COMPORTAMENTO.** [Neuropsicofarmacol. compont.]. **VFOAT** Behavioral Neuro-Psychopharmacology. (1988)-. Periodical. Italian. qt. L40000, $28.43. CIC Edizioni Internazionali, Via L Spallanzani 11, 00161 Rome Italy. **Tel** 011 39 6 841-2673, FAX 011 39 6 844-3365, telex 622099 CIC I. **UDC** 615.21.

●US/1063-360X
**NEW DEVELOPMENTS IN MEDICINE & DRUG THERAPY.** [New dev. med. drug ther.]. **VFOAT** New Developments in Medicine and Drug Therapy. Vol. 1, Iss. 1 (Sept./Oct 1992)-. Periodical. English. bm. $32.00 (one year), $57.00 (two years) US; $45.00 (one year), $70.00 (two years) Canada; $50.00 (one year), $75.00 (two years) other. Physicians & Scientists Publ, PO Box 435, Glenview IL 60025. **Tel** (708)559-0605. **DD** 615. Index Available Published separately--free--upon request (Nov).
**Desc:** Highlights important advances in at least 15 fields of medicine in every issue and includes an in-depth feature article. Each issue contains the New Developments Guide written by physician-scientists on staff at Chicago's most outstanding medical centers as well as other major medical centers in the United States.

US/0734-1989
**NEW DRUG COMMENTARY.** [New drug comment.]. **Added/Corp** Paregian Associates. (1973)-. Periodical. English. Eight times a year (eight or more issues per year). $640.00. Paregian Associates, 250 Davenport Avenue, New Rochelle NY 10805. **Tel** (914)235-8035. **ED** Philip Paregian. Index available. cum. index. ctrl circ.
**Desc:** Covers new drugs under development in the US giving stage of progress, description, chemistry, clinical evaluations, markets, patents, licensees, etc.

UK/0958-9422
**NEW DRUGS AND NOVEL COMPOUNDS IN MEDICINE AND PHARMACOLOGY.** (1990)-. Monographic series. English. Price varies per volume. **NLM** W1; NE374HN.

JA
**NEW DRUGS SURVEY.** ***Suspended.*** (19??)-(19??). an. $105.00. Drug Business Research Co Ltd, 1-25-2 Koishikawa, Bunkyo-ku Tokyo 112 Japan. **Tel** 011 81 3 38130018. **ED** Hiroyuki Kosuge. **Ad Acc, Adv Mgr:** Kiyonori Shiina.

NZ/0111-0020
**NEW ETHICALS (AUCKLAND. 1976).** (NEW ETHICALS.). [New ethicals]. **VFOAT** New Ethicals and Medical Progress. Vol. 13, No. 10 (Oct. 1976)-. Periodical. English. mo (12 issues). 105.00NZ$ New Zealand; 135.00NZ$ Australia and South Pacific; 180.00NZ$ US, Canada and Asia; 193.00NZ$ other. ADIS International Ltd, 41 Centorian Drive, Private Bag 65901, Mairangi Bay, Auckland 10 New Zealand. **Tel** 011 64 9 4798100, FAX 011 64 9 4791418. **NLM** W1 NE395K. **CODEN** NEETEG. ***Continues*** *New Ethicals and Medical Progress.*
**Ind/Abst** Int. Pharm. Abstr.

NZ/0110-9510
**NEW ETHICALS CATALOGUE.** **See** Pharmacy and Pharmacology-Abstracting, Bibliographies and Statistics.

US/0028-5773
**NEW JERSEY JOURNAL OF PHARMACY, THE.** **Added/Corp** New Jersey Pharmaceutical Association. New Jersey Pharmaceutical Association. Proceedings. Vol. 1 (Jan. 1928)-. Periodical. English. mo (11 issues - July/Aug. combined issue). $12.00. N J Pharmaceutical Association, 118 West State Street, Trenton NJ 08608. **Tel** (609)394-5596. **ED** Diana S. Herman. **LC** RS1; .N47. **DD** 615.05. **NLM** W1 NE446L. **Circ:** 4,200. available on microfilm from University Microfilms International (UMI).
**Desc:** Current news articles of interest to pharmacists.
**Ind/Abst** Int. Pharm. Abstr.

US
**NEW MEDICINES IN DEVELOPMENT FOR CHILDREN / PRESENTED BY THE PHARMACEUTICAL MANUFACTURERS ASSOCIATION.** **Added/Corp** Pharmaceutical Manufacturers Association. (Fall 1990)-. Periodical. English. **NLM** W1; NE457J.

SP/0213-411X
**NEW METHODS IN DRUG RESEARCH.** [New methods in drug res.]. (1985)-. Academic Scholarly Publication. English. be (1 issue). Price varies per volume. Prous Science Publishers, Apartado de Correos 540, 08080 Barcelona Spain. **Tel** 011 34 3 4592220, FAX 011 34 3 4581535. **ED** A. Makriyannis. **LC** RS122; .N48. **DD** 615/.1/072. **NLM** W1; NE457K. **CODEN** NMDRER. Documents available from CASDDS.
**Ind/Abst** Chem. Abstr.

# Pharmacy and Pharmacology

IT/0393-5345
**NEW TRENDS IN CLINICAL NEUROPHARMACOLOGY : OFFICIAL JOURNAL OF THE EUROPEAN ASSOCIATION FOR CLINICAL NEUROPHARMACOLOGY. See** Medical Science and Technology-Neurology.

AU/0938-9245
**NEW VISTAS IN DRUG RESEARCH.** Vol. 1 (1990)-. Monographic series. English. Price varies per volume. Springer-Verlag Wien, Sachsenplatz 4 6, PO Box 89, A-1201 Vienna Austria. **Tel** 011 43 1 3302415. **(Subscription address:** Springer Verlag New York Inc. / for North America, 44 Hartz Way, Secaucus NJ 07096.) **NLM** W1; NE513M.

US/0279-8778
**NEW YORK STATE JOURNAL OF PHARMACY, THE.** *Title Change.* (THE NEW YORK STATE JOURNAL OF PHARMACY : OFFICIAL JOURNAL OF THE NEW YORK STATE COUNCIL OF HOSPITAL PHARMACISTS.). [N.Y. State j. pharm.]. **Added/Corp** New York State Council of Hospital Pharmacists. No. 1, No. 1 (Feb. 1981)-(19??). Periodical. English. qt. New York State Council of Hospital Pharmacists, 14 Vanderventer Avenue #145, Port Washington NY 11050. **Tel** (516)944-5250. **ED** Ted S Friedman. **DD** 615. **NLM** W1; NE885P. cum. index. **Ad Acc. Circ:** 2,000 (ctrl). *Continues* Newsletter - New York State Council of Hospital Pharmacists, 0199-6169. *Continued by* News Letter (New York State Council of Hospital Pharmacists), 1066-5617.
**Desc:** Covers institutional practice, laws and regulations, professional standards, research and review articles.
**Ind/Abst** Int. Pharm. Abstr.

US/0739-7062
**NEW YORK STATE PHARMACIST, CENTURY II.** (NEW YORK STATE PHARMACIST, CENTURY II / PHARMACEUTICAL SOCIETY OF THE STATE OF NEW YORK.). **Added/Corp** Pharmaceutical Society of the State of New York. **VFOAT** NY State Pharmacist-Century II; N.Y. State Pharmacist-Century II. Vol. 57, No. 1 (Fall 1982)-. Periodical. English. bm. Pharmaceutical Society of the State of New York, 1975 Linden Boulevard, Elmont NY 11003. **Tel** (516)285-8822. **NLM** W1 NE898F. *Continues* NY State Pharmacist, 0163-1586.
**Ind/Abst** Int. Pharm. Abstr.

NZ/0111-431X
**NEW ZEALAND PHARMACY.** (198?)-. Periodical. English. mo. 70.00NZ$ (surface), 90.00NZ$ (air) Australia; 70.00NZ$ (surface), 140.00NZ$ (air) other. Regatta Group Ltd, PO Box 99141, Auckland New Zealand. **Tel** 011 64 9 5222007, **FAX** 011 64 9 5221991. **ED** Leonie Eriksen. **NLM** W1; NE978L. **[CCC]. Ad Acc. Adv Mgr:** Kerry McKenzie, **Tel** 09 523 1754. **Circ:** 3,026.
**Ind/Abst** Int. Pharm. Abstr.

US/0196-7061
**NEWSLETTER - PHARMACEUTICAL MANUFACTURERS ASSOCIATION.**
**Main/Corp** Pharmaceutical Manufacturers Association. (19??)-. Newsletter. English. wk. **NLM** W1 P651H.
**Ind/Abst** Trade Ind. Index.

NE/0927-0574
**NIEUWE DROGIST.** [Nieuwe drog.]. (1991)-. Periodical. Dutch. bw. Fl71.13. Keesing Noordervliet Bv, De Molen 82-86, 3995 Ax Houten Netherlands. **Tel** 011 31 3403 58585, FAX 011 31 3403 58500. **UDC** 615.1. *Continues* Drogist (Scheveningen), 0012-6330.

NR/0189-322X
**NIGERIAN JOURNAL OF PHARMACEUTICAL SCIENCES.** [Niger. j. pharm. sci.]. **Added/Corp** Ahmadu Bello University. Faculty of Pharmaceutical Sciences. (198?)-. Academic Scholarly Publication. English. qt. Ahmadu Bello University Press Ltd, Ahmed Talis Building, PMB 1094 Zaria Nigeria. **Tel** 011 234 50064. **CODEN** NJPSEZ. Documents available from BIOSIS Document Express, CASDDS.
**Ind/Abst** Biol. Abstr. (-1986); Chem. Abstr. (1986-1988).

NR/0331-670X
**NIGERIAN JOURNAL OF PHARMACY.**
(THE NIGERIAN JOURNAL OF PHARMACY : THE OFFICIAL ORGAN OF THE PHARMACEUTICAL SOCIETY OF NIGERIA.). [Niger. j. pharm.]. **Added/Corp** Pharmaceutical Society of Nigeria. (197?)-. Academic Scholarly Publication. English. bm. $48.00. **NLM** W1; NI394. **CODEN** NJPHDZ. Documents available from CASDDS. *Continues* Journal of Pharmacy (Yaba, Nigeria).
**Ind/Abst** Chem. Abstr.; Int. Pharm. Abstr.; NAPRALERT.

JA/0369-4321
**NIHON DAIGAKU YAKUGAKU KENKYU HOKOKU.** [Nihon Daigaku yakugaku kenkyu hokoku]. **Added/Corp** Nihon Daigaku. Yakugakubu. **VFOAT** Pharmaceutical Bulletin of Nihon University; Yakugaku Kenkyu Hokoku. (1957)-. Academic Scholarly Publication. Japanese (summaries and/or abstracts in English). Nihon Daigaku Rikogakubu Yakugakka, (Dept. of Pharmacy, College of Science & Technology, Nihon University), 1-8, Kanda Surugadai, Chiyodaku, Tokyoku 101, Japan. **CODEN** NIPYA8. Documents available from CASDDS.
**Ind/Abst** Chem. Abstr.

JA/0015-5691
**NIHON YAKURIGAKU ZASSHI.** [Nihon yakurigaku zasshi]. **VFOAT** Folia Pharmacologica Japonica. Vol. 40 (1944)-. Academic Scholarly Publication. Japanese (summaries and/or abstracts in English). mo. $206.00. Nihon Yakuri Gakkai, (Japanese Pharmacological Society), c/o Kyoto Daigaku Igakubu, Yakurigaku Kyoshitsu, Yoshida Konoecho, Sakyoku,, Kyotoshi, Kyotofu 606 Japan. **(Subscription address:** Kyowa Book Company Inc., 1 38 Kanda Jinbocho Chiyoda-ku, Tokyo 101 Japan.) **CODEN** NYKZAU. Documents available from BIOSIS Document Express, CASDDS. *Continues* Nihon Yakubutsugaku Zasshi.
**Ind/Abst** Biol. Abstr.; Chem. Abstr.; Index Med.

JA/0285-3663
**NIIGATA YAKKA DAIGAKU KENKYU HOKOKU.** [Niigata Yakka Daigaku kenkyu hokoku]. **Added/Corp** Niigata Yakka Daigaku. **VFOAT** Bulletin of the Niigata College of Pharmacy. (1981)-. Academic Scholarly Publication. Japanese (English). Niigata Yakka Daigaku, (Niigata College of Pharmacy), 5829, Kamishineicho, Niigatashi, Niigataken 950-21, Japan. **CODEN** NYDHDC. Documents available from CASDDS.
**Ind/Abst** Chem. Abstr.

JA/0369-674X
**NIPPON YAKUZAISHIKAI ZASSHI.** (NIHON YAKUZAISHIKAI ZASSHI.). [Nippon Yakuzaishikai zasshi]. **Added/Corp** Nihon Yakuzaishikai. **VFOAT** Journal of the Japan Pharmaceutical Association. (1962)-. Academic Scholarly Publication. Japanese (summaries and/or abstracts in English). mo. Nihon Yakuzaishikai, Showa 37 01962, Tokyo Japan. **NLM** W1 NI954. **CODEN** NYZZA3. Documents available from CASDDS. *Continues* Nihon Yakuzaishi Kyokai Zasshi.
**Ind/Abst** Chem. Abstr.; Int. Pharm. Abstr.

US
**NODAK PHARMACIST.** (1966)-. Periodical. English.
**Ind/Abst** Int. Pharm. Abstr.

NO/0029-1668
**NORGES APOTEKERFORENINGS TIDSSKRIFT.** (NORGES APOTEKERFORENINGS TIDSSKRIFT / NORGES APOTEKERFORENINGS.). [Nor. apotekerforen. tidsskr.]. **Added/Corp** Norges Apotekerforenings. (19??)-. Periodical. Norwegian (English). Fourteen times a year. Kr450.00 (Norway). Norges Apotekerforenings, PO Box 5070 Majorstva, 0301 Oslo 3 Norway. **Tel** 22 696040, FAX 22 608173. **Circ:** 2000.
**Ind/Abst** Energy Res. Abstr. (May 1980-); Int. Pharm. Abstr.

IT
**NORMATIVA SUL SERVIZIO FARMACEUTICO.** Italian. ir. Org Edit Medico Farmaceutica, CP 10434, 20110 Milan Italy. **Tel** 011 39 2 675051.

DK/0029-1935
**NORSK FARMACEUTISK TIDSSKRIFT.**
[Nor. farm. tidsskr.]. **Added/Corp** Norges Farmaceutiske Forening. (1916)-. Periodical. Danish. Sixteen times a year. Norges Farmaceutiske Forening, Stenersgt. 4,, 0184 Oslo 1 Norway. **Tel** FAX 02 170960. **ED** Kari Bremer. **NLM** W1 NO261. **CODEN** NFTDAC. Index available. **Bk Rev. Ad Acc Acc. Circ:** 2,400. available with charts; available with illustrations. Documents available from CASDDS.
**Ind/Abst** Chem. Abstr.; Int. Pharm. Abstr.

IT
**NUOVA BOLLETTINO DI FARMACOLOGIA CLINICA.** (19??)-. Italian. Usl 37 Nuovo Bollettino di Farmaco Clinica, Via Manzoni 249, 80122 Naples Italy.

US/0273-320X
**NURSING ... DRUG HANDBOOK. See** Medical Science and Technology-Nursing.

CN/0315-1042
**O C P, ON CONTINUING PRACTICE.**
[OCP, On contin. pract.]. **Main/Corp** Ontario College of Pharmacy. **VFOAT** On Continuing Practice. Vol. 1 (Oct. 1973)-. Academic Scholarly Publication. English. Four times a year. Ontario College of Pharmacists, 483 Huron Street, Toronto Ontario M5R 2R4 Canada. **Tel** (416)962-4861, FAX (416)962-1619. **ED** Bernard Desroches and Lana Parn. **NLM** W1 O225. Index available. cum. index. **Bk Rev. Circ:** 7,200 (ctrl). available on microfilm.
**Desc:** New and review articles on drug therapy, social issues affecting pharmacy, book reviews and a section on new drugs.
**Ind/Abst** EMBASE [Select. Cov.]; Int. Pharm. Abstr.; PESTDOC.

AU/0253-5238
**OAZ, OSTERREICHISCHE APOTHEKER-ZEITUNG.** [OAZ, Osterr. Apoth.-Ztg.]. **Added/Corp** Osterreichische Apothekerkammer. **VFOAT** Osterreichische Apotheker-Zeitung. Yearly Volume (Jan. 2, 1971)-. Academic Scholarly Publication. German. wk. S1,103.96. Oesterr Apotheker Verlags GES, Spitalgasse 31, A-1094 Vienna Austria. **Tel** 011 43 1 4023588. **ED** Mag Pharm G Zimmermann. **NLM** W1 O23S. **CODEN** OAZEAL. Index available. cum. index. **Bk Rev. Ad Acc. Circ:** 4,500 (ctrl). Documents available from CASDDS. *Continues* Osterreichische Apotheker Zeitung.
**Desc:** Journal of the Austrian Pharmacists, dealing with pharmaceutical sciences, drug related problems in every aspect, politics of the profession, health authorities, communication platform.
**Ind/Abst** Chem. Abstr.; Int. Pharm. Abstr.; PESTDOC (?-?).

SP/0212-047X
**OFFARM.** [Offarm]. (1982)-. Periodical. Spanish. mo. **UDC** 615.
**Ind/Abst** Int. Pharm. Abstr.

SP
**OFFARM: REVISTA DE LA OFICINA DE FARMACIA.** Spanish. ir. Haymarket SA, Calle Aribau 168 170, 08036 Barcelona Spain. **Tel** 011 34 3 238-1742.

GW/0930-2115
**OFFIZIN : PHARMAZIE IN DER PRAXIS, DIE.** Vol. 1 (1986)-. Academic Scholarly Publication. German. qt. DM80.00. Georg Thieme Verlag Stuttgart, Postfach 301120, D 70451 Stuttgart Germany. **Tel** 011 49 711 89310, FAX 011 49 711 8931298, telex 7 252 275 GTVD. **(Subscription address:** Thieme Medical Publishers Inc., 381 Park Avenue South, New York NY 10016.) **NLM** W1; OF709K. **CODEN** OFFIE6. Documents available from CASDDS. *Continues* Offizinpharmazie, 0171-9971.
**Ind/Abst** Chem. Abstr. (-1986).

CN/0829-741X
**OPERATING RESULTS. RETAIL DRUG STORES. See** Pharmacy and Pharmacology-Abstracting, Bibliographies and Statistics.

NE/0920-2110
**OPTIMA FARMA.** Dutch. mo. Axioma Communicatie BV, Hettenheuvelweg 37-39, 1101 DM Amsterdam Netherlands. **Tel** 011 31 20 913141.

CN/0710-6130
**ORDONNANCE. DOSSIER. Added/Corp** Ordre des Pharmaciens du Quebec. **VFOAT** Dossier. 1 (Sept. 1976)-. Periodical. French. ir. Ordre Dex Pharmaciens Du Quebec, Bureau 160, 1253 Avenue McGill College, Montreal Quebec H3B 2Y5. **DD** 615/.4/09714.

CN/0710-6122
**ORDONNANCE (MONTREAL).**
(ORDONNANCE : BULLETIN DE L'ORDRE DES PHARMACIENS DU QUEBEC.). [Ordonnance]. 1 (Sept. 1976)-. Bulletin. French. ir. Free to members. Ordre Des Pharmaciens Du Quebec, Bureau 160, 1253 AV McGill College, Montreal Quebec H3B 2Y5 Canada. **DD** 615/.4/060714.

US/0473-2456
**OREGON PHARMACIST.** [Or. pharm.]. **Added/Corp** Oregon State Pharmaceutical Association. Oregon State Pharmacists Association. Vol. 1 (1954)-. Periodical. English. mo. Oregon State Pharmaceutical Association, 1460 State Street, Salem OR 97301-4296. **DD** 615. **NLM** W1 OR535A.
**Ind/Abst** Int. Pharm. Abstr.

US/0272-7064
**OSTEOPATHIC PHYSICIAN'S COMPENDIUM OF DRUG THERAPY, THE.** [Osteopath. phys. compend. drug ther.]. **VFOAT** Compendium of Drug Therapy. 1980/81-. English. an. Biomedical Information Corporation, 800 Second Avenue, New York NY 10017. **Tel** (212)262-9662. **LC** RM300; .O85. **DD** 615.1.

UK/0956-2559
**OTC NEWS & MARKET REPORT.** [OTC news mark. rep.]. **VFOAT** Over the Counter News and Market Report. (1988)-. Periodical. English. mo. £695.00 UK; £750.00 other. Nicholas Hall & Company, 35 Alexandra Street, Southend-on-Sea, Essex SS1 1BW England. **Tel** 011 44 702 433422, FAX 011 44 702 430787. **ED** R. Baines and K. Waters. **DD** 338.476151094. Index available. **Ad Acc. Circ:** 4,000. available on an online database from DIALOG; and Predicasts, Inc.
**Desc:** Provides professional information on the European OTC market, giving company profiles, news coverage, and news from industry specialists.
**Ind/Abst** Informat Int. Bus.; Mark. Advert. Ref. Serv. [Full Txt.]; PROMT [Full Txt.]; PTS Newsl. Database [Full Txt.].

US
**OUTCOMES MEASUREMENT AND MANAGEMENT.** See Medical Science and Technology.

JA/0300-8533
**OYO YAKURI.** [Oyo yakuri]. **Added/Corp** Oyo Yakuri Kenyukai. **VFOAT** Pharmacometrics. Vol. 1 (Sept. 1967)-. Academic Scholarly Publication. Japanese (English). mo. $168.00. Oyo Yakuri Kenkyukai, (Japanese Soc. of Pharmacometrics), 6-22, Ichibancho 1 Chome, Sendaishi, Miyagiken 980-91, Japan. **(Subscription address:** Maruzen Company Ltd., PO Box 5050, Import & Export Department, Tokyo 100 31 Japan.**)** **ED** Hikaru Ozawa. **NLM** W1 OY65. **CODEN** OYYAA2. Index available. cum. index. **Bk Rev. Ad Acc. Circ:** 1,200. Documents available from BIOSIS Document Express, CASDDS.
**Desc:** Topics on pharmacology, pharmacodynamics, pharmacokinetics, toxicology, drug screening test.
**Ind/Abst** Biol. Abstr. (1986-); Chem. Abstr.; Chem. Titles; EMBASE; Int. Pharm. Abstr. (19??-19??).

US/0148-5733
**PACIFIC INFORMATION SERVICE ON STREET-DRUGS.** Periodical. English. bm. $3.00. John K Brown, c/o School of Pharmacy, University of the Pacific, Stockton CA 95211. cum. index.

CN/0823-7492
**PAGIDEX.** [Pagidex]. **VFOAT** Pagidex Drugs, Cosmetics. No. 1 (1981)-. English (French). an. $115.00. Infotech, PO Box 7272, Ottawa Ontario K1L 8E3. **ED** G.E. Hendren. **DD** 615/.1/0212. **Circ:** 7,100 (ctrl).
**Desc:** Index of drugs, cosmetics, disinfectants and valuable timesaver for QC/R&D/regulatory affairs.

PK/0030-9680
**PAKISTAN CHEMIST AND DRUGGIST.** Periodical. English.
**Ind/Abst** Int. Pharm. Abstr.

PK/1011-601X
**PAKISTAN JOURNAL OF PHARMACEUTICAL SCIENCES.** [Pak. j. pharm. sci.]. **Added/Corp** University of Karachi. Faculty of Pharmacy. Vol. 1 (Jan. 1988)-. Periodical. English. sa. $25.00. University of Karachi Faculty of Pharmacy, Karachi-32, Pakistan. **CODEN** PJPSEN. Documents available from BIOSIS Document Express. ***Continues*** *Journal of Pharmacy, University of Karachi, 0257-3865.*
**Ind/Abst** Biol. Abstr.

PK/0030-9850
**PAKISTAN JOURNAL OF PHARMACY.** Periodical. English.
**Ind/Abst** Int. Pharm. Abstr.

US/1061-6322
**PARTNERS IN PHARMACEUTICAL CARE.** [Partn. pharm. care]. **Added/Corp** Philadelphia College of Pharmacy and Science. Office of Professional Programs. Vol. 1, No. 1 (Mar. 1991)-. Periodical. English. qt. $40.00. Philadelphia College of Pharmacy and Science, 600 South 43rd Street, Philadelphia PA 19104. **DD** 615.

FR/1146-5301
**PASCAL. F 70, PHARMACOLOGIE, TRAITEMENTS MEDICAMENTEUX.** **VFOAT** PASCAL. F 70, Pharmacology, Drug Treatments; PASCAL. F Soixante-dix, Pharmacologie, Traitements Medicamenteux. (1990)-. Periodical. Multiple languages. Eleven times a year. 1945.00F France; 2055.00F other. CNRS / Institut d'Information Scientifique et Technique, (Centre National de la Recherche Scientifique), 15 Quai Anatole France, Paris 75700 France. **Tel** 011 33 1 47531515, telex 299 356 F. **UDC** 011. ***Continues*** *Pascal Folio. F70, Pharmacologie Traitements Medicamenteux, 0761-1943.*

FR/0761-1943
**PASCAL FOLIO. F70, PHARMACOLOGIE, TRAITEMENTS MEDICAMENTEUX.** ***Title Change.*** [PASCAL folio, F70 Pharmacol. trait. medicam.]. **VFOAT** Pharmacologie, Traitements Medicamenteux; Pharmacology Drug Treatments. No. 1 (1984)-?. Periodical. French (English). mo. Institut de l'Information Scientique et Technique (INIST), 2 Allee du Parc de Brabois, 54514 Vandoeuvre Nancy Cedex France. **Tel** 011 33 83 504600, FAX 011 33 83 504650. **NLM** ZQ 1; P278. ***Continues in part*** *Bulletin Signaletique. 330, Sciences Pharmcoalogiques, Toxicologie.* ***Continued by*** *Pharmacologie Traitements Medicamenteux. F70.*

US
**PDA JOURNAL OF PHARMACEUTICAL SCIENCE AND TECHNOLOGY.** (19??)-. English. ir. Parenteral Drug Association, 7500 Old Georgetown Road, Suite 620, Bethesda MD 20814. **Tel** (301)986-0293. **(Subscription address:** Parenteral Drug Association Inc., PO Box 630810, Baltimore MD 20814.**)** ***Continues*** *Journal of Pharmaceutical Science and Technology : The Official Journal of PDA, 1076-397X.*

US
**PDR FAMILY GUIDE TO PRESCRIPTION DRUGS.** English. an. $24.95. Medical Economics Data, Five Paragon Drive, PO Box 27, Montvale NJ 07645. **Tel** (800)442-6657, (201)358-7200.

●US
**PDR GUIDE TO DRUG INTERACTIONS, SIDE EFFECTS, INDICATIONS.** **VFOAT** Guide to Drug Interactions, Side Effects, Indications; Drug Interactions, Side Effects, Indications; Physicians' Desk Reference Guide to Drug Interactions, Side Effects, Indications. (1993)-. English. an. $46.95. Medical Economics Data, Five Paragon Drive, PO Box 27, Montvale NJ 07645. **Tel** (800)442-6657, (201)358-7200. **LC** RS75; .P37. **NLM** QV 772; P5781. ***Formed by the union of*** *Indications Index, 1060-4057* ***and*** *Drug Interactions and Side Effect Index, 1044-7083.*

●US/1068-6924
**PDR LIBRARY ON CD ROM WITH THE MERCK MANUAL.** **VFOAT** Physicians' Desk Reference Library on CD ROM with the Merck Manual; Physicians' Desk Reference Library with the Merck Manual. (1993)-. English. Three times a year. $895.00. Medical Economics Data, Five Paragon Drive, PO Box 27, Montvale NJ 07645. **Tel** (800)442-6657, (201)358-7200.

US/0892-6980
**PDS UPDATE.** [PDS updat.]. **Added/Corp** Pharmaceutical Data Services (Phoenix, Ariz.). **VAT** Pharmaceutical Data Services Update. (198?)-. Periodical. English. mo. $550.00. Pharmaceutical Data Services, PO Box 52115, Phoenix AZ 85072-2115. **Tel** (602)381-9330. **DD** 615. **NLM** ZQV 771; P348.

UK/0265-9743
**PEM NEWS.** ***Suspended.*** [PEM news]. **VFOAT** Prescription-Event Monitoring News. (1983)- Suspended (19??). Periodical. English. an. Free (general practitioners in England); $8.00 other. Drug Safety Research Unit, Bursledon Hall, Southampton SO3 8BA England. **Tel** 011 44 703 4061223. **DD** 615.7.

US/0031-4633
**PENNSYLVANIA PHARMACIST.** **Added/Corp** Pennsylvania Pharmaceutical Association. (19??)-. Periodical. English. mo. $75.00. Pennsylvania Pharmaceutical Association, 508 North Third Street, Harrisburg PA 17101. **Tel** (717)234-6151. **ED** Carmen A Decello and Ann Fettro. **Ad Acc. Circ:** 2,200 (ctrl).
**Desc:** The official publication of the Pennsylvania Pharmaceutical Association. It contains information interesting to practicing pharmacists and articles of a scientific nature. This publication is provided for members as a benefit of membership.
**Ind/Abst** Int. Pharm. Abstr.

NE
**PERSPECTIVES IN DRUG DISCOVERY & DESIGN.** (19??)-. English. Three times a year. Fl554.38 Netherlands; $291.00 US & Canada; Fl523.00 other. ESCOM Science Publishers B V, PO Box 214, 2300 AE Leiden The Netherlands. **Tel** 011 31 71 127052.
**Desc:** Aimed at drug designers, molecular modelists, medicinal chemists and all biochemists and chemists concerned with the application of computer-based methods in drug discovery and design.

CN/0841-6109
**PERSPECTIVES PHARMACEUTIQUES.** [Perspect. pharm.]. Vol. 1, No. 1 (June 1987)-. Periodical. French. bm. STA Communications Inc., 955 St. John Boulevard, Suite 306, Pt Claire, Quebec H9R 5K3 Canada. **Tel** (514)695-7623. **DD** 615/.05.

US/1043-5905
**PHARM-AID (CHATHAM, N.J.).** (PHARMACEUTICAL ACTIVITIES INDEX-DIRECTORY : PHARM-AID.). **VFOAT** Pharm-AID; Pharmaceutical Activities Index Directory. **VAT** Pharm AID. (1985)-. Directory. English. be. $570.00. Pharmaco Medical Documentation, PO Box 429, Chatham NJ 07928. **Tel** (201)822-9200, FAX (201)765-0722. **LC** RS356; .P53. **DD** 615/.1.
**Desc:** Worldwide drug-reference encyclopedia profiling investigational drugs and pharmaceutical products and their active ingredients, each under up to four categories: pharmacologic activities; specific human clinical or veterinary uses; devices; diagnostics; medicinal plants; (other) natural products; antibiotics and close analogs; prostaglandins and derivatives, etc.

UK
**PHARMA BUSINESS.** (19??)-. Periodical. English. $135.00. Euromoney Publications PLC, Nestor House, Playhouse Yard, London EC4Z 5EX England. **Tel** 011 44 71 779 8888, FAX 011 44 71 779 8617, telex 290700 EUROMON G. **(Subscription address:** Euromoney Publications Plc, Perrymount Road Haywards Heath, West Sussex RH16 3DH England.**)**

GW/0172-0104
**PHARMA DIALOG.** 1-. Monographic series. German. Price varies per volume. Bundesverband der Pharmazeutischen Industrie, Karlstrasse 21, Frankfurt Am Main Germany. **NLM** W1 PH105T.

SZ/0378-7958
**PHARMA-FLASH.** [Pharma-Flash]. (1974)-. Periodical. French. Eight times a year. 42.00F, Switzerland; 73.00F other. Medecine et Hygiene, Case Postale 456, CH-1211 Geneve 4 Switzerland. **Tel** 011 41 22 3469355, 011 41 22 3469356. **[CCC].**

SZ/0301-1348
**PHARMA INTERNATIONAL (TRI-LINGUAL EDITION).** (PHARMA INTERNATIONAL.). [Pharma int.]. (1973)-. Academic Scholarly Publication. English (French and German). Six times a year (Feb., Apr., June, Aug., Oct., Dec.). 178.00F Switzerland; 190.00F others. Verlag Coating Thomas & Company, Bankgasse 8, CH-9001 St. Gallen Switzerland. **Tel** 011 41 71 223239, telex 719220 COAT CH. **ED** Ursula Cantner, E. A. Scheuermann and Friedhelm Heydorn. **CODEN** PHAID5. **Ad Acc. Circ:** 9,000. Documents available from CASDDS. ***Formed by the union of*** *Pharma International (English Ed.), 0301-1356; Pharma International (French Ed.)* ***and*** *Pharma International (German Ed.).*
**Desc:** A broad spectrum information resource with international circulation, as requested by the pharmaceutical industry in trying to keep up with latest standards. Includes columns on industrial news, industrial reports and personalities.
**Ind/Abst** Chem. Abstr.; PESTDOC.

JA/0285-4937
**PHARMA JAPAN.** English. wk (Published on Mondays). $980.00 Europe; $970.00 US & Canada; $960.00 Asia & Oceania; $900.00 others. Yakugyo Jiho Company Ltd, 36 Jinbo Cho 2 Chon Inaoka Bld, Chiyoda Ku Tokyo 101 Japan. **Tel** 011 81 3 3261 8527, FAX 011 81 3 3232 6573. **ED** Ro Midorikawa. Index available. cum. index. **Circ:** 1,000 domestic, 1,000 foreign (ctrl). Documents available from UMI Article Clearinghouse.
**Desc:** Provides the current situation and trends of Japanese pharmaceutical regulartory and Japanese pharmaceutical industry.
**Ind/Abst** Abstr. BioCommer.; Chem. Bus. Bull.; Chem. Bus. NewsBase (1990-); Chem. Bus. Update; Pharm. News Index (Dec. 1982-).

GR
**PHARMA KEFTIKON DELTION.** mo. $50.00 Europe, North America and South Africa; $65.00 Australia, South America and Canada. Leonidas Papathanassopoulos, Album Publs Avagelistrias 10, Kalithea 17671 Athens Greece.

IT
**PHARMA MIX.** Mediamix, Via Abbondio San Giorgio 12, 20145 Milan Italy.

NE/0169-6882
**PHARMA SELECTA.** [Pharma sel.]. (1985)-. Periodical. Dutch. bw. Fl141.51. HR Gerbrands, Postbus 122, 8430 AC Oosterwolde Netherlands. **Tel** 011 31 05115 42623. **UDC** 615.

GW/0931-9700
**PHARMA TECHNOLOGIE JOURNAL.** [Pharma-Technol.-J.]. **VFOAT** Pharma Technologie; Pharmatechnologie Journal. (19??)-. Academic Scholarly Publication. German. ir. DM64.00. Concept Heidelberg, Postfach 101764, W-6900 Heidelberg 1 Germany. **Tel** 011 49 6221 84440. **CODEN** PTJOEH. Documents available from CASDDS. ***Continues*** *Memo Script.*
**Ind/Abst** Chem. Abstr. (1984-).

CI/0031-6857
**PHARMACA.** [Pharmaca]. Academic Scholarly Publication. Serbo-Croatian (Roman) (English). qt. 300.00 Din Yugoslavia; $70.00 US. Zajednica Zdravstvenih Organizacija Sr Hrvatska, P P 913, Zagreb Croatia. **Tel** 041 539-011. **ED** Bozidar Vrhovac. **CODEN** PHAMBF. Index available. **Bk Rev. Circ:** 3,300 (ctrl). Documents available from CASDDS. ***Continues*** *Lijekove.*
**Ind/Abst** Chem. Abstr.; EMBASE.

UK
**PHARMACEASED.** (19??)-. English. £950.00 UK; $1,900.00 US. PJB Publications, 18-20 Hill Rise, Richmond Surrey TW10 6UA England. **Tel** 011 44 81 948 3262.

SZ/0031-6865
**PHARMACEUTICA ACTA HELVETIAE.** [Pharm. acta Helv.]. **Added/Corp** Schweizerische Apotheker-Verein. Vol. 1 (1926)-. Academic Scholarly Publication. German. Four times a year (1 volume). Fl353.00. Elsevier Science Publishers BV, PO Box 211, 1000 AE Amsterdam Netherlands. **Tel** 011 31 20 5803642, FAX 011 31 20 5862696, telex 15682. **NLM** W1 PH127. **CODEN** PAHEAA. **Bk Rev. Ad Acc. Pr Rev. Circ:** 5,000. Documents available from The Genuine Article, CASDDS.
**Desc:** A scientific journal of the Swiss Pharmaceutical Association of interest to industry, universities and hospitals. Covers the total area of pharmacy.
**Ind/Abst** Anal. Abstr.; Chem Inform; Chem. Abstr.;

Chem. Titles; Curr. Chem. React.; EMBASE; Index Chem.; Index Med.; Int. Pharm. Abstr.; Nat. Prod. Updates; Life Sci. Collect.; PESTDOC; Res. Alert [Full Cov.]; Sci. Cit. Index (19??-19??); SCISEARCH.

US
**PHARMACEUTICAL AND BIOTECH DAILY. See** Medical Science and Technology-Biotechnology.

US/1074-8636
**PHARMACEUTICAL & BIOTECH DAILY.** ***Title Change.*** **See** Medical Science and Technology-Biotechnology.

SA/1015-4760
**PHARMACEUTICAL & COSMETIC REVIEW.** [Pharm. cosmet. rev.]. **VFOAT** Pharmaceutical and Cosmetic Review. (19??)-. Periodical. English. Six times a year (Jan., Mar., May, July, Sept., Nov.). R70,00 South Africa & Namibia & Homelands; R130,00 others. National Publishing Pty Ltd, 155 2nd Avenue Kenilworth 7700, PO Box 2271, Clareinch 7740 South Africa. **Tel** (021)61-1140, FAX (021)611389, telex 9555542+. **ED** Gill Loubser. **CODEN** PCRVDQ. **Ad Acc, Adv Mgr:** G Wells. **Circ:** 1500 (ctrl). ***Continues*** *South African Pharmaceutical & Cosmetic Review, 0257-2028.*
**Ind/Abst** BioBusiness (1989-); Int. Pharm. Abstr.

GW/0939-9488
**PHARMACEUTICAL AND PHARMACOLOGICAL LETTERS.** Vol. 1 (1991)-. Periodical. English. Six times a year. DM360.00. Springer-Verlag GmbH & Company KG, Heidelberger Platz 3, D 14197 Berlin Germany. **Tel** 011 49 30 8207223, FAX 011 49 30 8214091, telex 183 319 SPBLN D. **(Subscription address:** Springer Verlag New York Inc. / for North America, 44 Hartz Way, Secaucus NJ 07096.) **ED** G. Franz. **NLM** W1; PH135. **[CCC].** available in microform from University Microfilms International (UMI).
**Desc:** Designed for rapid publication of the latest results in all areas of pharmacy and pharmacology.

UK/0956-0661
**PHARMACEUTICAL BUSINESS NEWS.** [Pharm. bus. news]. (1984)-. Periodical. English. sm (24 issues per year). £385.00 UK; £446.00 other. Financial Times England, 8 16 Great New Street, London EC4A 3BN England. **Tel** 011 44 71 353 0305, 353 1040, FAX 011 44 353 0846. **CODEN** PBNEEH. available on an online database (files 16,636/Full-Text) from DIALOG.
**Ind/Abst** Abstr. BioCommer.; PROMT [Full Txt.]; PTS Newsl. Database [Full Txt.].

US/0091-150X
**PHARMACEUTICAL CHEMISTRY JOURNAL.** [Pharm. chem. j.]. **Added/Corp** Consultants Bureau. No. 1 (Jan. 1967)-. Periodical. English (Russian). mo. $1155.00 US; $1350.00 other. Consultants Bureau, A Division of Plenum Publishing Corporation, 233 Spring Street, New York NY 10013. **Tel** (212)620-8000, (212)620-8466, FAX (212)463-0742, telex 23/421139. **ED** R. G. Glushkov. **LC** RS402; .K4613. **DD** 615/.19/005. **NLM** W1 PH161D. **CODEN** PCJOAU. **[CCC].** Index available. available on microfilm and microfiche from University Microfilms International (UMI). Documents available from BIOSIS Document Express, CASDDS.
**Desc:** Presents latest research concerned in pharmaceutical chemistry by scientists in USSR.
**Ind/Abst** Biol. Abstr. (?-1984); Chem. Abstr.; Chem. Titles; Int. Pharm. Abstr.

UK
**PHARMACEUTICAL CODEX, THE.** 11th-Ed.; 1979-. English. Each issue contains an index to its own contents (no volume index)--loose. ***Continues*** *British Pharmaceutical Codex.*

UK
**PHARMACEUTICAL COMPANY PROFILES.** (19??)-. Trade Publication. English. mo. £2,900.00 - £11,600.00 depending on number of companies purchased. IMS World Publications Ltd, 7 Harwodd Avenue, london NW1 6JB England. **Tel** 011 44 71 393 5000, FAX 011 44 393 5900. available on CD-ROM.
**Desc:** Covers 110 key pharmaceutical companies worldwide. Contains in depth analysis of Corporate Structure, R&D pipeline, product portfolio, sales analysis and reviews financial status and major events.

US/1071-5096
**PHARMACEUTICAL DAILY.** ***Title Change.*** **See** Medical Science and Technology-Biotechnology.

US/0273-8139
**PHARMACEUTICAL ENGINEERING.** [Pharm. eng.]. **Added/Corp** International Society of Pharmaceutical Engineers. Vol. 1, (Jan. 1981)-. Periodical. English. Six times a year (Feb., Apr., June, Aug., Oct., Dec.). Free - US; $48.00 other. International Society Pharmaceutical Engineering, 3816 West Linebaugh Avenue, Suite 412, Tampa FL 33624-4702. **Tel** (813)960-2105, FAX (813)264-2816. **ED** Gloria Esoda. **NLM** W1; PH161DF. Index available (For members only.). **Ad Acc, Adv Mgr:** David Hall. **Pr Rev. Circ:** 14,500 (ctrl).
**Desc:** Application and specification editorials for the construction, supervision and maintenance of process equipment, plant systems, instrumentation and facilities in health care manufacturing.
**Ind/Abst** BioBusiness (1990-); Int. Pharm. Abstr.

US/0279-6570
**PHARMACEUTICAL EXECUTIVE.** [Pharm. exec.]. Vol. 1, No. 1 (Jan. 1981)-. Periodical. English. mo. $59.00 US and possessions; $79.00 Canada; $117.00 other. Advanstar Communications Inc., 131 West First Street, Duluth MN 55802. **Tel** (218)723-9477, (800)346-0085. **ED** Wayne Koberstein. **LC** RS1. **DD** 338.4/76151/0973. **CODEN** PHEXD2. **[CCC].** Index available. cum. index. **Ad Acc. Circ:** 11,000 (ctrl). available on microfilm from University Microfilms International (UMI).
**Desc:** A global business and marketing publication designed to meet the management and marketing needs of professionals in the pharmaceutical industry worldwide. Delivers balanced coverage of the latest marketing techniques, industry trends, sales, promotional strategies, and the legal and regulatory issues influencing product development and management.
**Ind/Abst** AGRICOLA [Select. Cov.]; BioBusiness; Int. Pharm. Abstr.

UK/0079-1393
**PHARMACEUTICAL HISTORIAN.** (PHARMACEUTICAL HISTORIAN : NEWSLETTER OF THE BRITISH SOCIETY FOR THE HISTORY OF PHARMACY.). [Pharm. hist.]. **Added/Corp** British Society for the History of Pharmacy. Vol. 1, No. 1 (Oct. 1967)-. Newsletter. English. qt. £4.60 UK; $£5.00 other. British Society of Historical Pharmacy, 36 York Place, Edinburgh EH1 3HU Scotland. **Tel** 031 556-4386. **LC** RS61; .P485. **NLM** W1 PH161M.
**Ind/Abst** Int. Pharm. Abstr.

US/1078-2885
**PHARMACEUTICAL INDUSTRY WEEKLY.** (19??)-. English. wk (48 issues). $995.00 US, Canada and Mexico; $1195.00 other. CW Henderson, PO Box 5528, Atlanta GA 30307-0528. **Tel** (404)377-8895, FAX (404)378-5411. **(Subscription address:** CW Henderson, Subscription Office, PO Box 830409, Birmingham AL 35283-0409.)
**Desc:** Offers a fresh alternative to industry press releases and press release newswire feeds. Original reporting by staff writers covers the frontiers of drug research.

UK/0031-6873
**PHARMACEUTICAL JOURNAL (1933).** (PHARMACEUTICAL JOURNAL.). [Pharm. j.]. **Added/Corp** Pharmaceutical Society of Great Britain. Vol. 131 (July 1, 1933)-. Academic Scholarly Publication. English. wk. £69.00 UK; $89.00 other. Pharmaceutical Press, 1 Lambeth High Street, London SE1 7JN England. **Tel** 011 44 71 735 9141, FAX 011 44 71 735 7629, telex 265871, (MONREF G). **ED** D Simpson. **NLM** W1 PH162. **CODEN** PHJOAV. Index available. **Bk Rev.** Documents available from BIOSIS Document Express, CASDDS. ***Continues*** *Pharmaceutical Journal and Pharmacist, 0301-5432.*
**Desc:** The official journal of The Pharmaceutical Society of Great Britain. Provides news coverage of all aspects of pharmacy in Great Britain and abroad. Publishes technical articles and reviews on pharmaceutical and similar subjects as well as letters. Classified and display advertisements are included.
**Ind/Abst** Abstr. BioCommer.; AgBiotech News Inf.; BioBusiness; Biodeter. Abstr. (1991-); Biol. Abstr.; Chem. Abstr.; Curr. Biotechnol.; Health Serv. Abstr.; Index Vet.; Int. Pharm. Abstr.; NAPRALERT; Nutr. Abstr. Rev., Ser. A, Hum. Exp.; PESTDOC; Poult. Abstr.; Protozoolog. Abstr.; Sug. Indus. Abstr.

KE/0378-228X
**PHARMACEUTICAL JOURNAL OF KENYA. Added/Corp** Pharmaceutical Society of Kenya. (1970)-. Periodical. English. qt. Free. Pharmaceutical Society of Kenya, PO Box 44290, Nairobi Kenya. **Tel** 726770. **ED** F A Ndemo. **NLM** W1 PH163K. **CODEN** PJKEEO. **Bk Rev. Ad Acc. Circ:** 5,000.
**Desc:** Information pertaining to professors of pharmacy, lecturers of pharmacy, and pharmacist form private sector.
**Ind/Abst** Int. Pharm. Abstr.

US/0887-7815
**PHARMACEUTICAL LITIGATION REPORTER. See** Law.

US/0747-3796
**PHARMACEUTICAL MANUFACTURING.** [Pharm. manuf.]. Vol. 1, No. 1 (March 1984)-. Periodical. English. mo. Free to qualified individuals, $18.00 other. Canon Communications Inc, 3340 Ocean Park Boulevard, Suite 1000, Santa Monica CA 90405. **Tel** (310)392-5509, (312)762-2193, FAX (310)453-2584. **NLM** W1; PH163M. ***Continues*** *Particulate & Microbial Control, 0745-0990.*
**Ind/Abst** Int. Pharm. Abstr.

UK/0955-3894
**PHARMACEUTICAL MANUFACTURING REVIEW. See** Manufacturing.

UK
**PHARMACEUTICAL MARKETING.** English. mo. £48.00 UK; £96.00 other. Ethical Publications Ltd, Vincent House, Vincent Lane, Dorking Surrey RH4 3JD England. **Tel** 011 44 306 740777, FAX 011 44 306 741069. **ED** David Ball. Index available. **Bk Rev**, (Qty: 10 or more). **Ad Acc, Adv Mgr:** Ben Brazelle. **Pr Rev. Circ:** 6,500 (ctrl).
**Desc:** Aimed at pharmaceutical marketing personnel in the pharmaceutical industry.

UK/0265-0673
**PHARMACEUTICAL MEDICINE (BASINGSTOKE).** (PHARMACEUTICAL MEDICINE.). [Pharm. med.]. Vol. 1, No. 1 (Dec. 1984)-. Academic Scholarly Publication. English. qt. $225.00 US and Canada; £130.00 Europe; £145.00 other. Chapman & Hall, 2-6 Boundary Row, London SE1 8HN England. **Tel** 011 44 71 865 0066, FAX 011 44 71 522 9623, telex 290164 Chapmag. **(Subscription address:** Chapman & Hall, Cheriton House, North Way, Andover, Hampshire, SP10 5BE England.) **ED** J. C. Petrie, R. N. Smith, P. L. Keen, A. H. Watt. **NLM** W1; PH164I. **CODEN** PHMDEH. **[CCC]. Bk Rev. Ad Acc. Circ:** 600. available on microfilm from University Microfilms International (UMI). Documents available from BIOSIS Document Express, CASDDS, ADONIS.
**Desc:** An international journal for the clinical assessment of new and tried methods employed to test drugs in humans. Publishes papers on methods used in human pharmacology, clinical trials, adverse reaction monitoring, data management and data analysis. Each issue contains: lively editorials; penetrating commentaries; original articles and thorough coverage of the regulatory scene, etc.
**Ind/Abst** ADONIS; Biol. Abstr. (1984-); Chem. Abstr. (1984-); EMBASE; Index Med. (1984-1988); Int. Pharm. Abstr.; PESTDOC.

US/0891-2793
**PHARMACEUTICAL NEWS CAPSULE, THE.** (PHARMACEUTICAL NEWS CAPSULE.). [Pharm. news capsule]. Vol. 1, No. 1 (Jan. 1984)-. Periodical. English. qt (4 issues). $400.00. Scott-Levin Associates, 60 Blacksmith Road, Newtown PA 18940. **Tel** (215)860-0440, FAX (215)860-5477. **ED** Charles Miller and Tom Marcinko. **DD** 338. ctrl circ.
**Desc:** A unique compiled update on pharmaceutical companies, products and research and development activities. A comprehensive yet concise time saving way to keep current on all facets of the complex, ever-changing pharmaceutical environment.

US/1040-0931
**PHARMACEUTICAL NEWS CAPSULE (SPECIAL ED.).** (PHARMACEUTICAL NEWS CAPSULE.). [Pharm. news capsule (Spec. ed.)]. **VFOAT** Year-End Summary; Year in Review; Pharmaceutical News Capsule. Supplement. (1984)-. English. an (March). $600.00. Scott-Levin Associates, 60 Blacksmith Road, Newtown PA 18940. **Tel** (215)860-0440, FAX (215)860-5477. **DD** 338.
**Desc:** Covers every component of the pharmaceutical industry, from the pipelines of large brandname companies to potential competition from generics companies and emerging biotech firms.

US/0362-4439
**PHARMACEUTICAL NEWS INDEX. See** Pharmacy and Pharmacology-Abstracting, Bibliographies and Statistics.

US
**PHARMACEUTICAL PERSPECTIVES.** English. ir (Includes a minimum of 3 reports per month). $2,150.00. Kidder Peabody & Company, 10 Hanover Square, New York NY 10005. **Tel** (212)747-2802.

UK/0960-6548
**PHARMACEUTICAL PHYSICIAN.** [Pharm. physician]. (1989)-. Periodical. English. bm. £30.00 Europe; £42.00 other. British Association of Pharmaceutical Physicians, 1 Wimpole Street, London W1M 8AE England. **Tel** 011 44 71 491-8610. **DD** 615.58.

UK
**PHARMACEUTICAL POLICY AND PRACTICE.** English. mo. £350.00. Aslan Services Ltd, Parvel House, Guildford Road, Loxwood West Sussex, RH14 0QW England. **Tel** 011 44 403 753152. **(Subscription address:** Dawson UK, Cannon House, Parkfarm Road, Folkstone Kent CT1 5EE United Kingdom.)

US/0732-8419
**PHARMACEUTICAL PREPARATIONS, EXCEPT BIOLOGICALS.** (CURRENT INDUSTRIAL REPORTS. MA-28G, PHARMACEUTICAL PREPARATIONS, EXCEPT BIOLOGICALS / U.S. DEPARTMENT OF COMMERCE, BUREAU OF THE CENSUS.). **Added/Corp** United States. Bureau of the Census. **VFOAT** Pharmaceutical Preparations, Except Biologicals. (19??)-. Government Publication. English.

Five times a year. Superintendent of Documents, US Government Printing Office, Washington DC 20402. **Tel** (202)275-3328, FAX (202)786-2377. **LC** HD9666.1; .C87. **DD** 380.1/456151/0973.
**Desc:** Presents data on the production, inventories, and orders of approximately 5,000 products, which represents 40 percent of all US manufacturing.

US/1049-9156
**PHARMACEUTICAL PROCESSING.** [Pharm. process.]. (19??)-. Periodical. English. mo. $36.00 US, Canada & Mexico; $53.00 (surface mail), $90.00 (airmail) other. Cahners Publishing Company, 249 West 17th Street, New York NY 10011. **Tel** (212)645-0067, FAX (212)242-6987. **(Subscription address:** Gordon Publications, Inc., Paid Circulation Department, 301 Gibralter Drive, Box 650, Morris Plains NJ 07950-0650.) **DD** 615. **CODEN** PLPREY. **[CCC].** ***Continues*** *Pharmaceutical and Cosmetic Equipment, 0895-2795.*
**Desc:** Focus is on the processors and packagers of pharmaceuticals, biologicals, cosmetics and toiletry products.
**Ind/Abst** BioBusiness (1991-).

US/0891-9461
**PHARMACEUTICAL PRODUCTION TECHSOURCE.** [Pharm. prod. techSource]. **VFOAT** Pharmaceutical Production Tech Source. (1986)-. Periodical. English. mo. $195.00 US; $215.00 other. Pharmaceutical Production, PO Box 1145, Ann Arbor MI 48106. **Tel** (313)487-5989. **ED** Leonard Hattosiak. **DD** 338. **Circ:** 500.
**Desc:** Dedicated exclusively to pharmaceutical information. Provides articles related to pharmaceutical R&D, manufacturing and packaging for both solid dosage and liquid pharmaceuticals.

US/0724-8741
**PHARMACEUTICAL RESEARCH.** [Pharm. res.]. **Added/Corp** American Association of Pharmaceutical Scientists. No. 1 (Jan. 1984)-. Academic Scholarly Publication. English. Twelve times a year. $525.00 institutions, $125.00 individuals US; $615.00 institutions, $146.00 individuals other. Plenum Press, 233 Spring Street, New York NY 10013-1578. **Tel** (212)620-8000, (800)221-9369, FAX (212)463-0742, (212)807-1047, telex 23/421139. **ED** Wolfgang Sadee. **DD** 615. **NLM** W1; PH167H. **CODEN** PHREEB. **[CCC]. Pr Rev. Circ:** 2,000. available on microfilm and microfiche from University Microfilms International (UMI). Documents available from The Genuine Article, BIOSIS Document Express, CASDDS, ADONIS.
**Desc:** Original and review articles in pharmacology and medicinal chemistry.
**Ind/Abst** ADONIS; Biol. Abstr. (1986-); Chem. Abstr. (1984-); Curr. Biotechnol.; Curr. Contents Life Sci.; Dairy Sci. Abstr.; EMBASE; Index Med.; Int. Pharm. Abstr.; NAPRALERT; PESTDOC; Protozoolog. Abstr.; Res. Alert [Full Cov.]; Sci. Cit. Index; SCISEARCH; Sug. Indus. Abstr.

UK/1351-6337
**PHARMACEUTICAL SCIENCE COMMUNICATIONS.** (19??)-. English. bm. $295.00 US; £175.00 other. Rapid Communications of Oxford Ltd, The Old Malthouse, Paradise Street, Oxford OX1 1LD England. **Tel** 011 44 0865 790447, FAX 011 44 0865 244012, telex 9403712.

US
**PHARMACEUTICAL STRTEGIC ALLIANCE.** English. an. $1,495. Windhover Information, PO Box 360, South Norwalk CT 06856. **Tel** (203)838-4401.

US/0147-8087
**PHARMACEUTICAL TECHNOLOGY.** [Pharm. technol.]. Vol. 1 (June 1977)-. Academic Scholarly Publication. English. mo. $59.00 US and possessions; $79.00 Canada; $117.00 other. Advanstar Communications Inc., 131 West First Street, Duluth MN 55802. **Tel** (218)723-9477, (800)346-0085. **ED** Stefan Schuber. **LC** RS1. **DD** 615/.19/005. **NLM** W1 PH178J. **CODEN** PTECDN. **[CCC].** Index available. cum. index. **Bk Rev. Ad Acc. Circ:** 30,000 (ctrl). available on microfilm and microfiche from University Microfilms International (UMI). Documents available from CASDDS.
**Desc:** Offers practical hands-on information about the manufacture of pharmaceutical products, focusing on applied technology. Features columns on process control/computer-integrated manufacturing, biotechnology and the pharmaceutical industries, technical management, guest editorials, and a monthly report from Washington. A "What's New" section features products, services and literature, book reviews, summaries of current technical literature, news briefs, a calendar of events, a classified directory, and recruitment advertisements.
**Ind/Abst** AgBiotech News Inf.; AGRICOLA [Select. Cov.]; BioBusiness; Chem. Abstr.; Curr. Biotechnol.; Ei Page One; EMBASE; Int. Pharm. Abstr.; PESTDOC.

US/0164-6826
**PHARMACEUTICAL TECHNOLOGY INTERNATIONAL.** [Pharm. technol. int.]. (1989)-. Periodical. English. mo. £32.00 Europe; £80.00 other. Advanstar Communications Inc., 131 West First Street, Duluth MN 55802. **Tel** (218)723-9477, (800)346-0085. **(Subscription address:** Advanstar Communications / UK Subscriptions, Park West, Sealand Road, Circulation Department, Chester CH1 4RN England.) **ED** Stefan Schuber. **DD** 615. **[CCC].** Index available. cum. index. **Bk Rev. Ad Acc. Circ:** 20,000 (ctrl). available on microfilm from University Microfilms International (UMI). ***Continues*** *Pharmaceutical Technology International, 0164-6826.*
**Desc:** Targeted specifically for the pharmaceutical industry in Western Europe.
**Ind/Abst** Abstr. BioCommer.; Int. Pharm. Abstr.

UK
**PHARMACEUTICAL TIMES.** (1988)-. Trade Publication. English. mo. £56.00 UK; £89.00 other. Europharm Management Education Ltd., 75 Sheen Lane, East Sheen, London SW14 8AD England. **Tel** 011 44 81 878 8566, FAX 011 44 81 876 8834. **ED** Geoff Frew. **Bk Rev.** (Qty: 10-15). **Ad Acc, Adv Mgr:** Angela Fernandez. **Pr Rev. Circ:** 7,400 (ctrl).
**Desc:** Pharmaceutical Industry Management magazine.
**Ind/Abst** Abstr. BioCommer.; Chem. Bus. Bull.; Chem. Bus. NewsBase (1989-); Chem. Bus. Update.

SZ
**PHARMACEUTICALS & BIOLOGICALS.** (19??)-. English (French). ir. $312.00. World Health Organization, Distribution and Sales, 20 Avenue Appia, CH-1211 Geneva 27 Switzerland. **Tel** 011 41 22 7912111, FAX 011 41 22 7880401. Index available.
**Desc:** Includes WHO Drug Information and the International Digest of Health Legislation, plus all books published by WHO concerned with pharmaceutical drugs and biologicals.

FR/1240-0866
**PHARMACEUTIQUES PARIS.** (PHARMACEUTIQUES). (1992)-. Periodical. French. mo. 750.00F. PR Edition, 22 Ave. d' Eylau, 75116 Paris France. **Tel** 011 33 1 47270139, FAX 011 33 1 47277775. **ED** Philippe Cherel. **UDC** 331.885(44). **Bk Rev. Ad Acc. Circ:** 7,000.

NE/0031-6911
**PHARMACEUTISCH WEEKBLAD.** [Pharm. weekbl.]. **Added/Corp** Nederlandsche Maatschappij ter Bevordering der Pharmacie. (1955)-. Periodical. Dutch. wk. Fl185.00. KNMP Koninklijke Ned Maat Phar, PB 30460, 2500GL Gravenhage, Netherlands. **Tel** 011 31 70 3624111. ***Continues*** *Pharmaceutisch Weekblad voor Nederland.*
**Ind/Abst** Anal. Abstr.; Curr. Biotechnol.; EMBASE; Int. Pharm. Abstr.; Iowa Drug Inf. Serv. (1979-); PESTDOC; Saf. Health Work.

NE/0167-6555
**PHARMACEUTISCH WEEKBLAD. SCIENTIFIC EDITION.** ***Title Change.*** [Pharm. weekbl., sci. ed.]. **Added/Corp** Koninklijke Nederlandse Maatschappij ter Bevordering der Pharmacie. European Society of Clinical Pharmacy. Vol. 1-14 (Feb. 23, 1979)-(1992). Academic Scholarly Publication. English. bm. KNMP Koninklijke Ned Maat Phar, PB 30460, 2500GL Gravenhage, Netherlands. **Tel** 011 31 70 3624111. **NLM** W1; PH187H. **CODEN** PWSEDI. **Pr Rev.** Documents available from The Genuine Article, CASDDS. ***Continued by*** *Pharmacy World & Science.*
**Ind/Abst** AGRICOLA; Anal. Abstr.; Chem. Abstr.; Curr. Contents Life Sci.; EMBASE; Index Med.; Int. Pharm. Abstr.; PESTDOC; Res. Alert [Full Cov.]; Rev. Med. Vet. Mycology; Sci. Cit. Index; SCISEARCH.

FR
**PHARMACIE MONDIALE.** No. 87- Oct. 1976-. Periodical. French. mo. $11.97. Production Mondiale, 70 rue de l'Aqueduc, 75010 Paris France. **NLM** W1 PH268EC. ***Formed by the union of*** *Pharmacie Mondiale; Officine Hopital, 0151-8895* ***and*** *Pharmascopie.*
**Ind/Abst** Int. Pharm. Abstr.

FR/0994-4370
**PHARMACIE RURALE PARIS.** (PHARMACIE RURALE.). (1989)-. Periodical. French. qt. Assn de Pharmacie Rurale, 24 rue de Vintimille, 75009 Paris France. **Tel** 011 33 1 48746426. **UDC** 615. ***Continues*** *Pharmacien Rural (Paris), 0031-6954.*

CN/0031-692X
**PHARMACIEN, LE.** ***Title Change.*** **Added/Corp** College des Pharmaciens de la Province de Quebec. Vol. 1, (1930)-(19??). French. Twelve times a year. MacLean Hunter Ltd. Business Publishers / Canada, Box 9100, Station A, Toronto ONT M5W 1A5 Canada. **Tel** (416)946-8420, (800)567-0444. **NLM** W1 PH2683. available on microfilm and microfiche from University Microfilms International (UMI). ***Continued by*** *L'Actualite Pharmaceutique.*

FR/0031-6938
**PHARMACIEN DE FRANCE.** [Pharm. Fr.]. (1936)-. Periodical. French. Twenty times a year. 430.00F France; 735.00F other. Le Pharmacien de France, 13 rue Ballu, 75009 Paris France. **Tel** 011 33 1 44531925, FAX 011 33 1 49950341. **CODEN** PHAFAR. ctrl circ.

FR
**PHARMACIEN HOPITAL, LE.** French. Eleven times a year. 320.00F. Soc Edn Quotidien Paris SEQP, 2 rue Ancelle, 92521 Neuilly Seine Cedex France. **Tel** 011 33 1 47471335.

FR/0768-9179
**PHARMACIEN HOSPITALIER, LE.** (1968)-. Periodical. French. qt. 313.42F France; 372.18F other. Syndicat National des Pharmaciens Gerants d'Etablissements Hospitaliers, 31 rue du Terrage, 75010 Paris France. **Tel** 011 33 1 46072325, FAX 011 33 1 42 09 09 10. **ED** Idea Papeterie Dunkerque. **UDC** 615.1 : 331.88.
**Ind/Abst** Int. Pharm. Abstr.

CN
**PHARMACIST NEWS.** (19??)-. English. mo. 38.00Can$ Canada; 82.00Can$ other. MacLean Hunter Ltd. Business Publishers / Canada, Box 9100, Station A, Toronto ONT M5W 1A5 Canada. **Tel** (416)946-8420, (800)567-0444. **(Subscription address:** Indas, 35 Riviera Drive, Building 17, Markham Ontario L3R 8N4 Canada.) ***Continues*** *Drug Merchandising.*

NE/0165-7208
**PHARMACOCHEMISTRY LIBRARY.** [Pharmacochemistry library]. Vol. 1 (1977)-. Academic Scholarly Publication. English. ir. Price varies per volume. Elsevier Science Publishers BV, PO Box 211, 1000 AE Amsterdam Netherlands. **Tel** 011 31 20 5803642, FAX 011 31 20 5862696, telex 15682. **(Subscription address:** Elsevier Science Inc. / New York Books, 655 Avenue of the Americas, New York NY 10010.) **NLM** W1 PH272L. **CODEN** PHLIDQ. Documents available from BIOSIS Document Express, CASDDS.
**Ind/Abst** Biol. Abstr. (1985-); Chem. Abstr.

●NZ/1170-7690
**PHARMACOECONOMICS.** Vol. 1, No. 1 (Jan. 1992)-. Periodical. English. mo (12 issues). 940.00F Europe; $595.00 other. ADIS International Ltd, 41 Centorian Drive, Private Bag 65901, Mairangi Bay, Auckland 10 New Zealand. **Tel** 011 64 9 4798100, FAX 011 64 9 4791418. **(Subscription address:** Japan Publications Trading Company, Ltd., PO Box 5030, Tokyo International, Tokyo 100-31 Japan.) **NLM** W1; PH272N. **[CCC].**
**Desc:** Features the latest knowledge on economic evaluations of drug therapy. This journal contains pharmacoeconomic evaluations of new drugs and discusses methods of pharmacoeconomic assessment and study.
**Ind/Abst** Int. Pharm. Abstr.; Soc. Sci. Cit. Index [Select. Cov.].

●UK/1053-8569
**PHARMACOEPIDEMIOLOGY AND DRUG SAFETY.** [Pharmacoepidemiol. drug saf.]. Vol. 1 No. 1 (Jan.-Feb. 1992)-. Academic Scholarly Publication. English. bm. $335.00. John Wiley & Sons Ltd., Baffins Lane, Chichester West Sussex PO19 1UD England. **Tel** 0243 779777, FAX 0243 776128 BTG:JWP001, telex 86290 WIBOOKG. **(Subscription address:** John Wiley / Philadelphia, PO Box 7247, Philadelphia PA 19170.) **ED** Dr. Ronald Mann. **DD** 615. **NLM** W1; PH272Q. **CODEN** PDSAEA. available on microfilm and microfiche from University Microfilms International (UMI). Documents available from CASDDS.
**Desc:** Provides an international forum for the communication and evaluation of data, methods and opinions in the emerging discipline of pharmacoepidemiology. Publishes reports of original research, invited reviews and a variety of guest editorials and commentaries embracing scientific, medical, statistical and legal aspects of pharmacoepidemiology and post-marketing surveillance of drug safety.
**Ind/Abst** Chem. Abstr.; Curr. Aware. Biol. Sci., CABS; Int. Pharm. Abstr.

UK/0960-314X
**PHARMACOGENETICS.** Vol. 1, No. 1 (Oct. 1991)-. Periodical. English. bm. $299.00 US and Canada; £175.00 Europe; £190.00 other. Chapman & Hall, 2-6 Boundary Row, London SE1 8HN England. **Tel** 011 44 71 865 0066, FAX 011 44 71 522 9623, telex 290164 Chapmag. **(Subscription address:** Chapman & Hall, Cheriton House, North Way, Andover, Hampshire, SP10 5BE England.) **ED** J. Idle, F. J. Gonzales, A. G. Motulsky. **NLM** W1; PH272QH. **[CCC].** Documents available from ADONIS.
**Desc:** Publishes information on genetic variation in response to drugs and other chemicals in humans and animals. Provides a forum for the sharing of information and participation in debate on all aspects of the genetic variation in response to exogenous chemicals, from the clinical to the gene level.
**Ind/Abst** ADONIS; Curr. Aware. Biol. Sci., CABS; Soc. Sci. Cit. Index [Select. Cov.].

US
**PHARMACOGNOSY TITLES.** ***Ceased.*** (197?)- Ceased (198?). Periodical. English. University of Illinois at Chicago, Program for Collaborative Research in the Pharmaceutical Sciences (M/C 877), College of Pharmacy, Box 6998, Chicago IL 60680. **Tel** (312)996-7253, telex 206243.

GW/0233-237X
**PHARMACOKINETICS.** ***Ceased.***
[Pharmacokinetics]. Vol. 1, No. 1 (Jan. 1986)-Vol. 5, No. 4 (?). Periodical. English. bm. VCH Publishers Inc, 220 East 23rd Street, New York NY 10010. **Tel** (212)683-8333, , FAX (212)481-0897. **(Subscription address:** 303 NW 12th Avenue, Deerfield Beach FL 33442; telephone: (305)428-5566**) NLM** ZQV 38; P535. **CODEN** PHKIEM. available on microfilm.
**Desc:** An abstracts collection covering: drugs and theory, bioavailability, factors influencing pharmacokinetics, pharmacokinetic drug interactions, biotransformation, reviews, and conference proceedings.

FI/0358-4828
**PHARMACOLOGICA ET PHYSIOLOGICA (OULU).**
(PHARMACOLOGICA ET PHYSIOLOGICA.). No. 1-. Monographic series. English (Finnish). ir. Price varies per volume. Professor Leo Hirvonen, University of Oulu, 90100 Oulu 10 Finland. **Tel** 358-81-332133. **ED** Leo Hirvonen. **NLM** W1 AC954NM no.20 etc. cum. index. **Ad Acc. Circ:** 450 (ctrl).
**Desc:** Monographs, reviews, and dissertations in the fields of physiology and pharmacology.

UK/1043-6618
**PHARMACOLOGICAL RESEARCH.**
[Pharmacol. res.]. Vol. 21, No. 1 (Jan./Feb. 1989)-. Academic Scholarly Publication. English. mo. $499.00. Academic Press Ltd., A Division of Harcourt Brace & Company Ltd., 24-28 Oval Road, London NW1 7DX England. **Tel** 071 267 4466, FAX 071 482 2293, 071 485 4752, telex 25775 ACPRES G. **(Subscription address:** Harcourt Brace & Company, Ltd., Foots Cray, High Street, Sidcup Kent DA14 5HP England.**) ED** R. Paoletti, S. Nicosa, R. Kato and J. McGiff. **DD** 615. **NLM** W1; PH275U. **CODEN** PHMREP. **[CCC].** Documents available from The Genuine Article, BIOSIS Document Express, ADONIS. ***Continues*** *Pharmacological Research Communications, 0031-6989.*
**Desc:** Provides a rapid information exchange medium for specialists whose research techniques differ, and whose fields of study vary widely within the discipline of pharmacology. Publishes papers on basic and applied pharmacological research in both animals and man, and aims at rapid publication of all accepted papers. Invited and unsolicited review articles on aspects of pharmacology undergoing rapid change are also featured.
**Ind/Abst** ADONIS; Biol. Abstr. (1989-); Curr. Aware. Biol. Sci., CABS; Curr. Contents Life Sci.; EMBASE; Helminthol. Abstr. (1991-); Index Med.; Index Vet.; Nutr. Abstr. Rev., Ser. A, Hum. Exp.; PESTDOC; Protozoolog. Abstr.; Res. Alert [Full Cov.]; Sci. Cit. Index; SCISEARCH; Vet. Bull.

US/0031-6997
**PHARMACOLOGICAL REVIEWS.**
[Pharmacol. rev.]. **Added/Corp** American Society for Pharmacology and Experimental Therapeutics. Nordisk Selskab foer Farmakologi. British Pharmacological Society. Vol. 1 (April 1949)-. Academic Scholarly Publication. English. qt. $60.00 (individual), $107.00 (institution) US; $75.00 (individual), $122.00 (institution) other. Williams & Wilkins Company, 428 East Preston Street, Baltimore MD 21202-3993. **Tel** (410)528-4000, (800)638-6423, FAX (410)528-8596, telex 87669. **(Subscription address:** Williams & Wilkins, PO Box 64380, Baltimore MD 21264.**) ED** James A. Bain. **LC** RS1; .P655. **DD** 615. **NLM** W1 PH277. **CODEN** PAREAQ. **[CCC]. Ad Acc. Pr Rev. Circ:** 2,800. available on microfilm. Documents available from The Genuine Article, BIOSIS Document Express, CASDDS, Documents on Demand, Quick Copies. ***Separated from*** *Journal of Pharmacology and Experimental Therapeutics, 0022-3565.*
**Desc:** Important review articles on topics of high current interest for pharmacologists, toxicologists, and biochemists.
**Ind/Abst** Biol. Abstr.; Chem. Abstr.; Curr. Aware. Biol. Sci., CABS; Curr. Contents Life Sci.; EMBASE; Energy Inf. Abstr.; Energy Res. Abstr.; Environ. Abstr.; Index Med.; Index Sci. Rev. [Full Cov.]; Int. Aerosp. Abstr.; Iowa Drug Inf. Serv. (1968-); Nucl. Sci. Abstr.; Life Sci. Collect.; PESTDOC; Ref. Upd. Basic Ed.; Ref. Upd. Deluxe Ed.; Res. Alert [Full Cov.]; Sci. Cit. Index; SCISEARCH; Soc. Sci. Cit. Index [Select. Cov.].

IT
**PHARMACOLOGICAL TREATMENT OF THE CLIMACTERIC SYNDROME.** (19??)-. Academic Scholarly Publication. Italian. Four times a year. Free on request. Lakemedelsverket Med Prod Agen, Husargatan 8, S-751 03 Uppsala, Sweden. **Tel** 011 46 18 174600.

CN/0316-7526
**PHARMACOLOGIE PRATIQUE.** V. 1-1969/70-. Periodical. French. Hotel-Dieu, 5 rue Quesnel, Arthabaska Quebec Canada. **DD** 615/.1/05.

US/0031-7004
**PHARMACOLOGIST, THE.** [Pharmacologist]. V. 1- Spring 1959-. Periodical. English. qt. $25.00 US; $30.00 other. American Society for Pharmacology and Experimental Therapeutics, 9650 Rockville Pike, Bethesda MD 20814. **Tel** (703)941-6600. **ED** Kay Croner. **LC** RM1; .P47. **DD** 615/.1/05. **NLM** W1 PH281. **CODEN** PHMCAA. **Circ:** 2,000. available on microfilm and microfiche from University Microfilms International (UMI). Documents available from BIOSIS Document Express, CASDDS.
**Desc:** A complete and timely news service for law enforcement and criminal justice agencies. Provides broad coverage on key court decisions affecting law enforcement, federal and state legislation, and federal government programs.
**Ind/Abst** Biol. Abstr.; Chem. Abstr.; EMBASE; NAPRALERT; PESTDOC.

SZ/0031-7012
**PHARMACOLOGY.** [Pharmacology]. Vol. 1 (1968)-. Academic Scholarly Publication. English. mo. $650.00. S. Karger AG, Allschwilerstrasse 10, PO Box - Postfach - Case Postale, CH-4009 Basel Switzerland. **Tel** 011 41 61 306-1111, FAX 011 41 61 306-1234, telex CH 962 652. **ED** R. Kato, K. F. Sewing and E. S. Vesell. **LC** RM1; .P473. **DD** 615/.1/05. **NLM** W1 PH283. **CODEN** PHMGBN. **[CCC]. Ad Acc. Pr Rev.** available on microfilm from University Microfilms International (UMI). Documents available from The Genuine Article, BIOSIS Document Express, CASDDS. ***Supersedes in part*** *Medicina et Pharmacologia Experimentalis.*
**Desc:** Communicates basic and clinical research in general pharmacology and related fields. It covers biochemical pharmacology, molecular pharmacology, immunopharmacology, drug metabolism, pharmacogenetics, analytical toxicology, neuropsychopharmacology, pharmacokinetics, and clinical pharmacology. In addition to original papers, the journal contains short and rapid communications of investigative findings and pharmacological profiles.
**Ind/Abst** Biol. Abstr.; Chem. Abstr.; Curr. Aware. Biol. Sci., CABS; EMBASE; Index Med.; NAPRALERT; Life Sci. Collect.; PESTDOC; Ref. Upd. Deluxe Ed.; Res. Alert [Full Cov.]; Sci. Cit. Index; SCISEARCH.

SZ/1011-291X
**PHARMACOLOGY AND THE SKIN.** **See** Medical Science and Technology-Dermatology.

UK/0163-7258
**PHARMACOLOGY & THERAPEUTICS (OXFORD).** (PHARMACOLOGY & THERAPEUTICS.). [Pharmacol. ther.]. **Added/Corp** International Union of Pharmacology. **VFOAT** Pharmacology and Therapeutics. Vol. 4 (1979)-. Academic Scholarly Publication. English. mo. $2116.00 The Americas; £1420.00 other. Pergamon Press, An Imprint of Elsevier Science Ltd., The Boulevard, Langford Lane, Kidlington, Oxford OX5 1GB United Kingdom. **Tel** 011 44 865 843000, 011 44 865 843699, FAX 011 44 865 843010. **(Subscription address:** Elsevier Science Ltd. Oxford Fulfillment Centre, PO Box 800, Kidlington, Oxford OX5 1DX United Kingdom.**) ED** A. Sartorelli. **LC** RM1; .P477. **DD** 615/.1/05. **NLM** W1 PH283S. **CODEN** PHTHDT. **[CCC]. Pr Rev.** available on microfilm and microfiche from University Microfilms International (UMI). Documents available from The Genuine Article, BIOSIS Document Express, CASDDS, ADONIS. ***Formed by the union of*** *Pharmacology and Therapeutics. Part A. Chemotherapy, Toxicology and Metabolic Inhibitors, 0362-5478; Pharmacology and Therapeutics. Part B, 0306-039X* ***and*** *Pharmacology and Therapeutics. Part C. Clinical Pharmacology and Therapeutics, 0362-5486.*
**Desc:** Presents lucid, critical and authoritative reviews of currently important topics in pharmacology including chemotherapy, toxicology, metabolic inhibitors, clinical pharmacology and therapeutics and general and systematic pharmacology.
**Ind/Abst** ADONIS; Biol. Abstr.; Chem. Abstr.; CSA Neuro. Abstr. (?-?); Curr. Aware. Biol. Sci., CABS; Curr. Contents Life Sci.; EMBASE; Index Med.; Index Sci. Rev. [Full Cov.]; Int. Pharm. Abstr.; NAPRALERT; Life Sci. Collect.; PESTDOC; Protozoolog. Abstr.; Ref. Upd. Basic Ed.; Ref. Upd. Deluxe Ed.; Res. Alert [Full Cov.]; Rev. Med. Vet. Entomol.; Sci. Cit. Index; SCISEARCH; Soc. Sci. Cit. Index [Select. Cov.].

DK/0901-9928
**PHARMACOLOGY & TOXICOLOGY.**
[Pharm. & toxicol.]. **VFOAT** Pharmacology and Toxicology. Vol. 60, No. 1 (Jan. 1987)-. Academic Scholarly Publication. English. Twelve times a year. kr1885.00 US, Canada and Japan; kr1830.00 other. Munksgaard International Publishers Ltd, PO Box 2148, DK-1016 Copenhagen K Denmark. **Tel** 011 45 33 12 70 30, FAX 011 45 33 12 93 87, telex 19431 MUNKS DK. **ED** Jen S Schou. **LC** QP901. **DD** 615/.1. **NLM** W1; PH2834D. **CODEN** PHTOEH. **[CCC].** Index available. **Ad Acc. Pr Rev. Circ:** 1,000 (ctrl). Documents available from The Genuine Article, BIOSIS Document Express, CASDDS, ADONIS. ***Continues*** *Acta Pharmacologica et Toxicologica, 0001-6683.*
**Desc:** Forensic medicine, pharmacology and toxicology.
**Ind/Abst** ADONIS; Biol. Abstr. (1987-); Chem. Abstr. (1987-); Chem. Titles; Curr. Aware. Biol. Sci., CABS; Curr. Contents Life Sci.; EMBASE; Energy Res. Abstr. (1987-); Health Saf. Sci. Abstr.; Helminthol. Abstr.; Index Med. (1987-); Index Vet.; NAPRALERT; Nutr. Res. Newsl.; Life Sci. Collect. (1987-); PESTDOC (1987-); Pig News Inf.; Poult. Abstr.; Protozoolog. Abstr.; Res. Alert [Full Cov.]; Saf. Health Work (1987-); Sci. Cit. Index; SCISEARCH; Soc. Sci. Cit. Index [Select. Cov.]; Soyabean Abstr.; Vet. Bull.; Weed Abstr.

DK/0901-9936
**PHARMACOLOGY & TOXICOLOGY. SUPPLEMENT.** [Pharm. & toxicol., Suppl.]. **Added/Corp** Nordisk Selskab for Farmakologi. **VFOAT** Pharmacology and Toxicology. Supplement. Vol. 60, Suppl. 1 (1987)-. Academic Scholarly Publication. English. kr1885.00 US and Canada; kr1830.00 other (comes with subscription to Pharmacology & Toxicology). Munksgaard International Publishers Ltd, PO Box 2148, DK-1016 Copenhagen K Denmark. **Tel** 011 45 33 12 70 30, FAX 011 45 33 12 93 87, telex 19431 MUNKS DK. **CODEN** PTSUEC. Documents available from BIOSIS Document Express, CASDDS. ***Continues*** *Acta Pharmacologica et Toxicologica. Supplement, 0065-1508.*
**Ind/Abst** Biol. Abstr. (1987-); Chem. Abstr. (1987-); EMBASE; Energy Res. Abstr. (1987-); Life Sci. Collect. (1987-).

US/0091-3057
**PHARMACOLOGY, BIOCHEMISTRY AND BEHAVIOR.** [Pharmacol. biochem. behav.]. **VFOAT** Pharmacology, Biochemistry & Behavior. Vol. 1 (Jan./Feb. 1973)-. Academic Scholarly Publication. English. mo. $1580.00 The Americas; £1060.00 other. Pergamon Press, An Imprint of Elsevier Science Ltd., The Boulevard, Langford Lane, Kidlington, Oxford OX5 1GB United Kingdom. **Tel** 011 44 865 843000, 011 44 865 843699, FAX 011 44 865 843010. **(Subscription address:** Elsevier Science Ltd. Oxford Fulfillment Centre, PO Box 800, Kidlington, Oxford OX5 1DX United Kingdom.**) ED** Matthew J. Wayner. **LC** QP901; .P53. **DD** 615/.78. **NLM** W1 PH284F. **CODEN** PBBHAU. **[CCC]. Bk Rev. Ad Acc. Pr Rev.** ctrl circ. available on microfilm and microfiche from University Microfilms International (UMI). Documents available from The Genuine Article, BIOSIS Document Express, CASDDS, ADONIS.
**Desc:** Publishes original reports of systematic studies in pharmacology, biochemistry, toxicology and behavior in which the primary emphasis and theoretical context are behavioral.
**Ind/Abst** ADONIS; Biol. Abstr.; Chem. Abstr.; Chem. Titles; Chemorecept. Abstr.; CSA Neuro. Abstr.; Curr. Contents Life Sci.; Dairy Sci. Abstr.; EMBASE; Energy Res. Abstr. (March 1979-); Fish Rev.; Index Med.; NAPRALERT; Nutr. Abstr. Rev., Ser. A, Hum. Exp.; Life Sci. Collect.; PESTDOC; Psychol. Abstr. (1973-); PsycINFO; PsycLit; Ref. Upd. Basic Ed.; Ref. Upd. Deluxe Ed.; Res. Alert [Full Cov.]; Sci. Cit. Index; SCISEARCH; Soc. Sci. Cit. Index [Select. Cov.]; Wildl. Rev.

US
**PHARMACOLOGY BIOCHEMISTRY & BEHAVIOR. SUPPLEMENT.** **VAT** Pharmacology Biochemistry and Behavior. Supplement. Vol. 1 (19??)-. Monographic series. English. ir. Price varies per volume. Pergamon Press, An Imprint of Elsevier Science Ltd., The Boulevard, Langford Lane, Kidlington, Oxford OX5 1GB United Kingdom. **Tel** 011 44 865 843000, 011 44 865 843699, FAX 011 44 865 843010. **ED** Matthew J. Wayner.

●SZ/1060-4456
**PHARMACOLOGY COMMUNICATIONS.**
(PHARMACOLOGY COMMUNICATIONS.). [Pharmacol. commun.]. Vol. 1, No. 1 (Apr. 1992)-. Periodical. English. ir (2 volumes). $484.00 (university and hospital libraries); $756.00 other. Harwood Academic Publishers, PO Box 90, Reading RG1 8JL England. **Tel** 011 44 734 560080. **DD** 615. **NLM** W1; PH284K. **CODEN** PCMME9. **[CCC].**
**Desc:** Provides publications of quality research data for academic and industrial pharmacologists.

US/0737-8882
**PHARMACOLOGY IN NURSING.** **See** Medical Science and Technology-Nursing.

US
**PHARMACOLOGY RESEARCH ASSOCIATE PROGRAM OF THE NATIONAL INSTITUTE OF GENERAL MEDICAL SCIENCES, NATIONAL INSTITUTES OF HEALTH.** English. an. Pharmacology Research Associate Program, National Institute of General Medical Sciences, National Institutes of Health, Westwood Building/Room 919, Bethesda MD 20014.

●US/1063-8946
**PHARMACOLOGY, TOXICOLOGY & THERAPEUTICS.** **VFOAT** Pharmacology, Toxicology and Therapeutics; Pharmacology and Toxicology and Therapeutics. (1992)-. Periodical. English. qt. $60.00. Professional Audience Communications, PO Box 243, Yardley PA 19067. **Tel** (215)493-7400.

US/0363-4655
**PHARMACOPEIAL FORUM.** [Pharmacop. forum]. **Added/Corp** United States Pharmacopeial Convention. Pharmacopeia of the United States of America. National Formulary. **VFOAT** Pharmacopeial Forum, with USP-NF Comment Proof. Vol. 1 (Jan./Feb. 1975)-. Periodical. English. bm. $345.50 (includes sales tax) Maryland residents; $330.00 other. U. S.

Pharmacopeial Convention, 12601 Twinbrook Parkway, Rockville MD 20852. **Tel** (301)881-0666, (800)227-8772, telex 710 8289787. **NLM** QV 738 AA1 P45. **Pr Rev.** Documents available from The Genuine Article. ***Supersedes*** *USP Comment Proof.*
**Desc:** Serves as a forum for the exchange of ideas and information relating to the development of drug standards and analytical methods and to the revision and improvement of existing US Pharmacopeia and NF text.
**Ind/Abst** Anal. Abstr.; Curr. Contents Life Sci.; Index Vet.; Int. Pharm. Abstr.; Life Sci. Collect.; Res. Alert [Full Cov.]; Rev. Med. Vet. Entomol.; Sci. Cit. Index; SCISEARCH.

GW/0176-3679
**PHARMACOPSYCHIATRY.**
[Pharmacopsychiatry]. Vol. 17, No. 1 (Jan. 1984)-. Academic Scholarly Publication. English (German; summaries and/or abstracts in German and English). bm. $208.00. Georg Thieme Verlag Stuttgart, Postfach 301120, D 70451 Stuttgart Germany. **Tel** 011 49 711 89310, FAX 011 49 711 8931298, telex 7 252 275 GTVD. **(Subscription address:** Thieme Medical Publishers Inc., 381 Park Avenue South, New York NY 10016.**)** **ED** B Muller-Oerlinghausen. **LC** RM315; .P48. **DD** 615/.78. **NLM** W1; PH289V. **CODEN** PHRMEZ. **[CCC]. Bk Rev. Ad Acc. Circ:** 1,100. Documents available from The Genuine Article, BIOSIS Document Express, CASDDS, ADONIS. ***Continues*** *Pharmacopsychiatria, 0720-4280.*
**Desc:** Presents latest advances in clinical psychopharmacology. It is of interest for biologically interested psychiatrists and pharmacologists as well as for neurophysiologists.
**Ind/Abst** ADONIS; Biol. Abstr. (1991-); Chem. Abstr. (1984-); Curr. Aware. Biol. Sci., CABS; Curr. Contents Life Sci.; EMBASE; Index Med.; Life Sci. Collect.; PESTDOC; Psychoanal. Abstr.; Psychol. Abstr. (1989-); PsycINFO; PsycLit; PsycScan: Appl. Exp. Eng. Psych.; PsycScan: LD/MR; PsycScan: Neuropsych.; Res. Alert [Full Cov.]; Sci. Cit. Index; Soc. Sci. Cit. Index [Select. Cov.].

GW/0936-9589
**PHARMACOPSYCHIATRY SUPPLEMENT.** [Pharmacopsychiatry, Suppl.]. **VFOAT** Pharmacopsychiatry. Special Issue. Multiple languages. ir. Georg Thieme Verlag Stuttgart, Postfach 301120, D 70451 Stuttgart Germany. **Tel** 011 49 711 89310, FAX 011 49 711 8931298, telex 7 252 275 GTVD. **(Subscription address:** Thieme Medical Publishers Inc., 381 Park Avenue South, New York NY 10016.**)** **UDC** 61. ***Continues*** *Pharmacopsychiatria. Special Issue, 0722-2807.*
**Ind/Abst** EMBASE.

II/0970-3926
**PHARMACOPSYCHOECOLOGIA VARANASI.** **See** Psychology.

●NZ/1172-8299
**PHARMACORESOURCES : WORLD PHARMACOECONOMIC NEWS, VIEWS, AND PRACTICAL APPLICATION.** (1994)-. English. Twenty-four times a year. 725.00F Europe; $495.00 other. ADIS International Ltd, 41 Centorian Drive, Private Bag 65901, Mairangi Bay, Auckland 10 New Zealand. **Tel** 011 64 9 4798100, FAX 011 64 9 4791418. **(Subscription address:** Japan Publications Trading Company, Ltd., PO Box 5030, Tokyo International, Tokyo 100-31 Japan.**)**

II/0369-951X
**PHARMACOS CHANDIGARH.** (THE PHARMACOS.). [PharmacosChandigarh]. **Added/Corp** Punjab University, Pharmaceutical Society. (1956)-. Periodical. English. an.
**Ind/Abst** Int. Pharm. Abstr.

US/0277-0008
**PHARMACOTHERAPY.** [Pharmacotherapy]. **Added/Corp** American College of Clinical Pharmacy. Vol. 1, No. 1 (July/Aug. 1981)-. Academic Scholarly Publication. English. bm. $95.00 (1 year), $175.00 (2 year), $255.00 (3 year) US; $110.00 (1 year), $205.00 (2 year), $300.00 (3 year) other. Pharmacotherapy Publications Inc, New England Medical Center, Box 806, 750 Washington Street, Boston MA 02111. **Tel** (617)956-5390, FAX (617)956-5318. **ED** Richard T. Scheife. **NLM** W1 PH291E. **CODEN** PHPYDQ. **[CCC].** Index available (available in last copy of year). **Bk Rev. Ad Acc. Pr Rev. Acid Free. Circ:** 3,200. available on microfilm from University Microfilms International (UMI). Documents available from The Genuine Article, BIOSIS Document Express, CASDDS.
**Desc:** Devoted to the publication of original research articles and review articles on all aspects of human pharmacology and drug therapy. The journal is known for its "Evaluations of New Drugs" department, where all new drugs introduced in the United States are rigorously reviewed by recognized experts.
**Ind/Abst** Biol. Abstr. (?-1987); Chem. Abstr.; Curr. Aware. Biol. Sci., CABS; Curr. Contents Clin. Med.; EMBASE; Index Med.; Int. Pharm. Abstr.; NAPRALERT; PESTDOC; Protozoolog. Abstr.; Res. Alert [Full Cov.]; Rev. Med. Vet. Mycology; Sci. Cit. Index; SCISEARCH; Soc. Sci. Cit. Index [Select. Cov.].

CN/0834-065X
**PHARMACTUEL.** [Pharmactuel]. **Added/Corp** Association des Pharmaciens des Etablissements de Sante du Quebec. Vol. 19, No. 3 (June 1986)-. Periodical. French. bm. 50.00F. L'A.P.E.S., 50 boul Cremazie Ouest, bureau 505, Montreal Quebec H2P 2T2. **Tel** (514)381-7904, FAX (514)381-2781. **ED** Lucie Robitaille. **DD** 615/.4/09714. **Ad Acc. *Continues*** *Association des Pharmaciens des Etablissements de Sante du Quebec. Bulletin d'Information Officiel de l'Association des Pharmaciens des Etablissements de Sante du Quebec., 0713-5033.*

US/0195-542X
**PHARMACY & THERAPEUTICS FORUM.** (PHARMACY & THERAPEUTICS FORUM : THE BULLETIN OF THE HOSPITAL PHARMACY AND DRUG INFORMATION ANALYSIS SERVICE.). **VFOAT** Pharmacy and Therapeutics Forum. Began with: Vol. 26, No. 7 (Nov./Dec. 1978). Bulletin. English. bm. Free. Drug Information Analysis Service, Box 0622, Division of Clinical Pharmacy, University of California, San Francisco CA 94143-0622. **Tel** (415)476-4240. **ED** Linda L Hart, Kellie D M'Queen, and Susan Heath. **NLM** W1 PH293H. **Circ:** 4,500. ***Continues*** *Bulletin of the Hospital Pharmacy and the Drug Information Analysis Service.*
**Desc:** Recent drug monographs, excerpts from P&T meetings.

US/1060-4537
**PHARMACY BUSINESS.** [Pharm. bus.]. (1990)-. Periodical. English. qt. $19.95. **DD** 615.
**Ind/Abst** Int. Pharm. Abstr.

●US/1064-797X
**PHARMACY CADENCE. Added/Corp** Pharmacy Association Services. (1992)-. English. Pharmacy Association Services, PO Box 6565, Athens GA 30604. **NLM** W1; PH296.

US/0739-9596
**PHARMACY HEALTH-LINE. VAT** Pharmacy Health Line. Vol. 1; 1982-. Periodical. English. mo. $40.00. RX Data Pac Service, PO Box 42020, Cincinnati OH 45242. **Tel** (513)489-0943. **ED** I H Goodman. ctrl circ.

US/0031-7047
**PHARMACY IN HISTORY.** [Pharm. hist.]. **Added/Corp** American Institute of the History of Pharmacy. Vol. 4, No. 1 (1959)-. Academic Scholarly Publication. English. Four times a year (Jan., Apr., July, Oct.). $50.00. American Institute of the History of Pharmacy, 425 North Charter Street, Pharmacy Building, Madison WI 53706. **Tel** (608)262-5378. **ED** Gregory J. Higby. **LC** RS61; .P49. **DD** 615/.05. **NLM** W1 PH298. **CODEN** PHHIB4. Index available. cum. index. **Bk Rev** (Qty: 20). **Circ:** 1,200 (ctrl). available on microfilm and microfiche from University Microfilms International (UMI). Documents available from CASDDS. ***Continues*** *A.I.H.P. Notes (Madison, Wis. : 1955).* ***Continued in part by*** *A.I.H.P. Notes (Madison, Wis. : 1965).*
**Desc:** History of pharmacy, drugs, drug therapy--articles, notes, reviews and departments.
**Ind/Abst** Acad. Search (July 1993-); Am. Hist. Life (1972-); Chem. Abstr. (1972); Hist. Source (July 1993-); INFO-SOUTH Abstr.; Int. Pharm. Abstr.; Mag. Search.

US/0149-1717
**PHARMACY LAW DIGEST.** **See** Law.

US
**PHARMACY LAWS UPDATE SERVICE.** (19??)-. English. $49.00. Michigan Pharmacists Association, 815 North Washington Avenue, Lansing MI 48906. **Tel** (517)484-1466, FAX (517)484-4893. **ED** Debra McGuire.

US/8750-4790
**PHARMACY NEWS AND REVIEW.** (PHARMACY NEWS AND REVIEW : AN OFFICIAL PUBLICATION OF THE PENNSYLVANIA PHARMACEUTICAL ASSOCIATION / PENNSYLVANIA PHARMACEUTICAL ASSOCIATION.). [Pharm. news rev.]. **Added/Corp** Pennsylvania Pharmaceutical Association. **VFOAT** Pharmacy News & Review. (198?)-. Periodical. English. mo. $75.00. Pennsylvania Pharmaceutical Association, 508 North Third Street, Harrisburg PA 17101. **Tel** (717)234-6151. **ED** Carmen A. Dicello and Ann Fettro. **DD** 615. **Circ:** 2,600 (ctrl). ***Continues*** *PPA Newsletter.*

CN/0829-2809
**PHARMACY PRACTICE (MISSISSAUGA).** ***Title Change.*** (PHARMACY PRACTICE.). [Pharm. pract.]. **Added/Corp** Thomson Healthcare Communications. Vol. 1, No. 1 (Feb. 1985)-(19??). Periodical. English. ir. Thomson Healthcare, 1120 Birchmount Road, Suite 200, Scarborough Ontario M1K 5G4 Canada. **Tel** (905)750-8900. **DD** 615/.05. **CODEN** PHRPEA. ***Continued by*** *Hospital Pharmacy Practice.*
**Ind/Abst** Int. Pharm. Abstr. (?-?).

US/0886-988X
**PHARMACY PRACTICE NEWS.** [Pharm. pract. news]. Vol. 12, No. 11 (Nov. 1985)-. Periodical. English. mo. $50.00 US; $74.00 other. McMahon Publishing Company, 148 West 24th Street, 8th Floor, New York NY 10011. **Tel** (212)620-4600, FAX (212)620-5928. **DD** 615. available on microfilm and microfiche from University Microfilms International (UMI). ***Continues*** *Intravenous Therapy News, 8750-3182.*
**Ind/Abst** Health Devices Alerts; Int. Pharm. Abstr.

US/0149-1113
**PHARMACY SCHOOL ADMISSION REQUIREMENTS.** [Pharm. sch. admiss. requir.]. **Main/Corp** American Association of Colleges of Pharmacy. Office Student Affairs. 1st Ed. (1974)-. Monographic series. English. ir. Price varies per volume. American Association of Colleges of Pharmacy, 1426 Prince Street, Alexandria VA 22314-2815. **Tel** (703)739-2330. **ED** Janet R Holsopple. **LC** RS110; .A63a. **DD** 615/.1/071173. **NLM** QV 19; A511p.
**Desc:** Provides general school information and specific admission requirements for the seventy-two colleges of pharmacy in the US and Puerto Rico.

US/0279-5272
**PHARMACY STUDENT, THE.** (THE PHARMACY STUDENT / STUDENT AMERICAN PHARMACEUTICAL ASSOCIATION.). **Added/Corp** Student American Pharmaceutical Association. (19??)-. Periodical. English. qt. $25.00 US; $30.00 Canada and Mexico; $85.00 Europe; $91.00 other. American Pharmaceutical Association, 2215 Constitution Avenue Northwest, Washington DC 20037-2985. **Tel** (202)628-4410, (800)237-2742, FAX (202)783-2351. **ED** Stacey Ferguson. **[CCC]. Circ:** 15,100.
**Ind/Abst** Int. Pharm. Abstr.

US/0003-0627
**PHARMACY TIMES.** [Pharm. times]. Vol. 35, No. 9 (Sept. 1969)-. Periodical. English. Twelve times a year. $30.00 (trade), $18.00 (non-trade) US; $75.00 (trade), $50.00 (non-trade) others. Romaine Pierson Publishing Inc., 80 Shore Road, Port Washington NY 11050. **Tel** (516)883-6350. **ED** Irving Rubin. **LC** RS1; .A596. **DD** 615/.05. **NLM** W1 PH301T. **Ad Acc. Circ:** 93,666 (ctrl). available on microfilm and microfiche from University Microfilms International (UMI). ***Continues*** *American Professional Pharmacist, 0096-0349.*
**Desc:** A mass publication designed to help independent, chain drug, hospital pharmacists, and others interested or involved in pharmacy. Scope is only health-related.
**Ind/Abst** Hospit. Health Admin. Index (1977-1987); Int. Pharm. Abstr.; NAPRALERT.

●US/1077-2839
**PHARMACY TODAY.** Newspaper. English. Twenty-three times a year. $170.00 (individual), $205.00 (institution). Slack Inc., 6900 Grove Road, Thorofare NJ 08086. **Tel** (609)848-1000, (800)257-8290, FAX (609)853-5991, telex 517108 SLACK INC VD.

UK/0968-042X
**PHARMACY TODAY LONDON.** [Pharm. today Lond.]. (1985)-. Periodical. English. Six times a year. £38.00 UK; £53.00 other. Benn Publications Ltd., Sovereign Way, Tonbridge TNQ 1RW England. **Tel** 011 44 732 364422, FAX 011 44 732 361534, telex 0732 95132 BENTON G.

US/1042-0991
**PHARMACY TODAY (WASHINGTON, D.C.).** (PHARMACY TODAY : NEWSLETTER OF THE AMERICAN PHARMACEUTICAL ASSOCIATION.). [Pharm. today]. **Added/Corp** American Pharmaceutical Association. Vol. 1, No. 1 (Jan. 6, 1989)-. Newsletter. English. ir. $75.00 (institution), $50.00 (individual) US. American Pharmaceutical Association, 2215 Constitution Avenue Northwest, Washington DC 20037-2985. **Tel** (202)628-4410, (800)237-2742, FAX (202)783-2351. **DD** 615. ***Continues*** *Pharmacy Weekly, 0883-9387.*
**Ind/Abst** Int. Pharm. Abstr.

AT
**PHARMACY TRADE.** English. mo. 45.00Aus$ Australia; 120.00Aus$ other. Reed Business Publishing Pty Ltd. / Australia, 1 5 Railway Street, Level 12 North Tower, Chatswood W 2067 NSW Australia. **Tel** 011 61 2 3725222, FAX 011 61 2 4197533.

UK/0267-7334
**PHARMACY UPDATE.** ***Title Change.*** Vol. 1, No. 1 (April 1985)-(19??). Periodical. English. ir. Quadrant Subscription Services Ltd, Oakfield House, Perrymount Road, Haywards Heath, West Sussex RH16 3DH England. **Tel** (01)828-5571. **NLM** W1; PH301V. ***Merged into*** *Beauty Counter & Community Pharmacy.*
**Ind/Abst** Int. Pharm. Abstr.

US/0191-6394
**PHARMACY WEST.** [Pharm. west]. Vol. 88 No. 2 (Feb. 1976)-. Periodical. English. Twelve times a year. $18.00 (one year), $27.00 (two years), US; $60.00 other. Western Communications, 333 West Hampden Avenue, Suite 1050, Englewood CO 80110-2340. **Tel** (303)761-8818, FAX (303)761-2440. **ED** Elroy Fitzsenry. **DD** 615. **Ad Acc. Circ:** 16,000 (ctrl). ***Continues*** *West Coast/Rocky Mountain Druggist.*
**Desc:** Covers news and events, particularly C.E. courses, with an events calendar and people items.
**Ind/Abst** Int. Pharm. Abstr.

NR/0189-7705
**PHARMACY WORLD.** [Pharm. world]. (1984)-. Periodical. English. bm. **DD** _a615.1'05.
**Ind/Abst** Int. Pharm. Abstr.

●NE/0928-1231
**PHARMACY WORLD & SCIENCE : PWS.** **Added/Corp** Koninklijke Nederlandse Maatschappij ter Bevordering der Pharmacie. European Society of Clinical Pharmacy. **VFOAT** Pharmacy World and Science; PWS. Vol. 15, No. 1 (19 Feb. 1993)-. Periodical. English. bm. **NLM** W1; PH301VK. **CODEN** PWSCED. ***Continues*** *Pharmaceutisch Weekblad. Scientific Edition, 0167-6555.*
**Desc:** Information on drugs and drug therapy.
**Ind/Abst** Index Med. (1993-); Sci. Cit. Index; Soc. Sci. Cit. Index [Select. Cov.].

SP/1011-4386
**PHARMAKLINIK (MADRID).** ***Title Change.*** (PHARMAKLINIK / ORGANIZACION DE FARMACEUTICOS IBERO-LATINOAMERICANOS (O.F.I.L.).). [Pharmaklinik]. **Added/Corp** Organizacao Farmaceutica Ibero-Latinoamericana. Vol. 1, No. 1 (1987)-(19??). Periodical. Spanish (summaries and/or abstracts in English). bm. Alpe Editores SA, C Pedro Rico 27, Oficinas 11 & 12, 28029 Madrid Spain. **Tel** 011 34 1 7338811, FAX 011 34 1 3159652. **NLM** W1; PH302L. **CODEN** PHKLEV. Documents available from BIOSIS Document Express. ***Continues*** *Boletin de la O.F.I.L.* ***Continued by*** *Ciencia Pharmaceutica.*
**Ind/Abst** Biol. Abstr.; Indice Med. Esp.

GW/0344-7154
**PHARMAKOTHERAPIE.** ***Suspended.*** [Pharmakotherapie]. Vol. 1- 1978-Suspended 1984. Academic Scholarly Publication. German. bm. Price varies per volume. Dustri-Verlag, Dr Karl Feistle, Postfach 49, D 82032 Deisenhofen Germany. **Tel** 011 49 89 6138610, FAX 011 49 89 6135412. **NLM** W1 PH306T. **CODEN** PHKTDK. Documents available from CASDDS.
**Ind/Abst** Chem. Abstr.; EMBASE.

UK/0959-3853
**PHARMAKRITIK INTERNATIONAL.** [PharmaKrit. int.]. (1990)-. Periodical. English. bw. $55.80. Linacre Medical & Business Ser, PO Box 23, Melton Mowbry LE13 0YA England. **Tel** 011 44 664 62528. **DD** 615.1.

US/0278-6850
**PHARMALERT (BALTIMORE, MD.).** (PHARMALERT.). [Pharmalert]. **Added/Corp** University of Maryland at Baltimore. Student Committee on Drug Abuse Education. Vol. 8, No. 1 (Sept. 1976)-. Periodical. English. Four times a year (Jan., Apr., July, Oct.). $8.50. University Maryland School Pharmacy, 20 North Pine Street, C/O T. Tschirgi, Baltimore MD 21201. **Tel** (410)706-7513, FAX (410)706-7184. **ED** Trent Tschirgi. **NLM** W1 PH306W. Index available (Separately). cum. index. **Circ:** 4,500.
**Desc:** This is directed at the educators and health care workers to supplement their knowledge of drug information. Listed are articles on address pharmacological, clinical and social issues on drug use.

UK
**PHARMAPROJECTS.** **VFOAT** Pharma Projects. Vol. 1 (May 1980)-. English. Twelve times a year. £2,750.00 UK; $5,120.00 US. PJB Publications, 18-20 Hill Rise, Richmond Surrey TW10 6UA England. **Tel** 011 44 81 948 3262.

US
**PHARMASCOPE.** (19??)-. Periodical. English. Twelve times a year. $575.00. Transpharma Inc., 13072 Camino del Valle, Poway CA 92064. **Tel** (619)487-3868. **ED** Elvera R. Richardson. Index Available, published separately, free-automatically sent. ctrl circ.

US/0730-1278
**PHARMASOURCES.** [PharmaSources]. 82-. English. an. $85.00. Flexible Software Inc, Box 47, Prairie View IL 60069.

UK
**PHARMASTRUCTURES IN PRINT.** (19??)-. English. PJB Publications, 18-20 Hill Rise, Richmond Surrey TW10 6UA England. **Tel** 011 44 81 948 3262.

UK/0308-051X
**PHARMATHERAPEUTICA.** ***Suspended.*** [Pharmatherapeutica]. Vol. 1 (1976)-Vol. 5 No. 6 (19??)-. Academic Scholarly Publication. English (Multiple languages). ir. $35.00. Clayton-Wray Publishers Ltd., 1A High Street, Alton Hants GU34 1BA England. **Tel** 011 44 420 87293. **NLM** W1 PH307. **CODEN** PHARDW. Documents available from BIOSIS Document Express, CASDDS.
**Ind/Abst** Biol. Abstr.; Chem. Abstr.; EMBASE; Index Med.; Int. Pharm. Abstr.; NAPRALERT; Life Sci. Collect.; PESTDOC; SCISEARCH; SportSearch; Trop. Dis. Bull.

II/0031-6849
**PHARMATIMES BOMBAY.** [Pharmatimes Bombay]. **VFOAT** Pharma Times. (1969)-. Periodical. English. mo. **UDC** 615.
**Ind/Abst** Int. Pharm. Abstr.

GW/0031-711X
**PHARMAZEUTISCHE INDUSTRIE, DIE.** [Pharm. Ind.]. **Added/Corp** Arbeitsgemeinschaft Pharmazeutische Industrie. (1933)-. Academic Scholarly Publication. German (summaries and/or abstracts in English). mo. DM338.00. Editio Cantor, Postfach 1255, D 88322 Aulendorf Germany. **Tel** 011 49 7525 9400, FAX 011 49 7525 9401. **ED** Viktor Schremm. **NLM** W1 PH312. **CODEN** PHINAN. **[CCC].** cum. index. **Bk Rev. Ad Acc. Pr Rev. Circ:** 4,500 (ctrl). Documents available from The Genuine Article, CASDDS.
**Desc:** Publications on all questions concerning the manufacture and distribution of pharmaceutical products.
**Ind/Abst** Chem. Abstr.; Curr. Biotechnol.; Curr. Contents Eng. Tech. Appl. Sci.; EMBASE; Energy Res. Abstr.; F&S Index Plus Text, Int. [Select. Cov.]; Infomat Int. Bus.; Int. Aerosp. Abstr.; Int. Packag. Abstr.; Int. Pharm. Abstr.; PESTDOC; PROMT; Res. Alert [Select. Cov.]; SCISEARCH.

GW/0031-7128
**PHARMAZEUTISCHE RUNDSCHAU.** [Pharm. Rundsch.]. (March 1959)-. Academic Scholarly Publication. German. Twelve times a year. DM230.40 Germany; DM281.91. P Keppler KG, Industriestrasse 2, D 63150 Heusenstamm Germany. **Tel** 011 49 6104 6060, telex 410 131. **(Subscription address:** Verlagshaus Heusenstamm, Postfach 1353, D 63131 Heusenstamm Germany.**)** **LC** RS1; .P667. **NLM** W1 PH315C. **CODEN** PHMRAL. **[CCC].**
**Ind/Abst** EMBASE.

GW/0173-1890
**PHARMAZEUTISCHE VERFAHRENSTECHNIK HEUTE.** ***Ceased.*** [Pharm. Verfahrenstech. Heute]. Vol. 1 (July 1980)-(Dec. 1988). Academic Scholarly Publication. German. qt. Deutscher Apotheker Verlag, Postfach 101061, D 70009 Stuttgart Germany. **Tel** 011 49 711 25820, INLAND:0711/2582, FAX 011 49 711 2582 290, telex 723636 daz d. **NLM** W1; PH321TR. **CODEN** PVHEDO. Documents available from CASDDS.
**Ind/Abst** Chem. Abstr. (1980-1984).

GW/0031-7136
**PHARMAZEUTISCHE ZEITUNG.** [Pharm. Ztg.]. **Added/Corp** Arbeitsgemeinschaft der Berufsvertretungen Deutscher Apotheker. **VFOAT** Apotheker-Zeitung. Vol. 118 (July 5, 1973)-. Periodical. German. wk. DM142.80 Germany; DM176.20 other. Govi Verlag GmbH, Ginnheimer Str 26, D 65760 Eschborn Germany. **Tel** 011 49 6196 928242. **NLM** W1 PH317B. **CODEN** PHZIAP. Index available. cum. index. **Bk Rev. Ad Acc. Circ:** 27,500 (ctrl). Documents available from CASDDS. ***Continues*** *Pharmazeutische Zeitung, Vereinigt Mit Apotheker-Zeitung, 0031-7136.*
**Ind/Abst** Bibliogr. Mission.; Chem Inform; Chem. Abstr.; Curr. Biotechnol.; EMBASE; Energy Res. Abstr. (July 1973-); Int. Pharm. Abstr.; PESTDOC.

GW/0031-7144
**PHARMAZIE, DIE.** [Pharmazie]. **Added/Corp** Pharmazeutische Gesellschaft der DDR. Deutsche Arzneibuch-Kommission. (June 1946)-. Academic Scholarly Publication. German. mo. DM240.00. Govi Verlag GmbH, Ginnheimer Str 26, D 65760 Eschborn Germany. **Tel** 011 49 6196 928242. **LC** RS1; .P673. **NLM** W1 PH3255. **CODEN** PHARAT. **[CCC]. Pr Rev.** Documents available from The Genuine Article, BIOSIS Document Express, CASDDS.
**Ind/Abst** AgBiotech News Inf.; Anal. Abstr.; Bibliogr. Mission.; BioBusiness; Biol. Abstr.; Chem Inform; Chem. Abstr.; Chem. Titles; Curr. Biotechnol.; Curr. Chem. React.; Curr. Contents Life Sci.; EMBASE; Helminthol. Abstr.; Hortic. Abstr.; Index Chem.; Index Med.; Int. Pharm. Abstr.; Methods Organ. Synth.; NAPRALERT; Nat. Prod. Updates; Nutr. Abstr. Rev., Ser. A, Hum. Exp.; Ornamental Hort. (19??-19??); Life Sci. Collect.; PESTDOC; Plant Breed. Abstr.; Plant Grow. Reg. Abstr.; Postharvest News Inf.; Protozoolog. Abstr.; Res. Alert [Full Cov.]; Rev. Agric. Entomol.; Rev. Med. Vet. Mycology; Rev. Plant Pathol.; Sci. Cit. Index; SCISEARCH; Seed Abstr.

GW/0369-979X
**PHARMAZIE HEUTE.** [Pharm. Heute]. Vol. 1 (Oct. 1971)-. Academic Scholarly Publication. German. ir. Deutscher Apotheker Verlag, Postfach 101061, D 70009 Stuttgart Germany. **Tel** 011 49 711 25820, INLAND:0711/2582, FAX 011 49 711 2582 290, telex 723636 daz d. **NLM** W1 PH3256E. **CODEN** PHZHAM. **[CCC]. Circ:** 24,000 (ctrl). Documents available from CASDDS.
**Ind/Abst** Chem. Abstr.

GW/0048-3664
**PHARMAZIE IN UNSERER ZEIT.** [Pharm. unserer Zeit]. **Added/Corp** Deutsche Pharmazeutische Gesellschaft. Vol. 1, No. 1 (Jan. 1972)-. Academic Scholarly Publication. German. bm. $75.00. VCH Gesellschaft GmbH, Postfach 101161, D 69451 Weinheim Germany. **Tel** 011 49 6201 606459, FAX 011 49 6201 606184. **(Subscription address:** VCH Publishers Inc., 303 Northwest 12th Avenue, Journals Department, Deerfield FL 33442.**)** **NLM** W1 PH3256H. **CODEN** PHUZBI. **[CCC].** Index Available, published separately, free-automatically sent. Documents available from CASDDS. ***Continues*** *Deutsche Pharmazeutische Gesellschaft. Mitteilungen.*
**Ind/Abst** Chem. Abstr.; EMBASE; Index Med.; PESTDOC.

US/0146-3128
**PHARMCHEM NEWSLETTER, THE.** [Pharmchem newsl.]. **Added/Corp** PharmChem Laboratories. PharmChem Research Foundation. (Jan. 1972)-. Academic Scholarly Publication. English. Four times a year. PharmChem Laboratories, 3925 Bohannon Drive, Menlo Park CA 94025. **Tel** (415)328-6200. **ED** Elizabeth Roosma. **CODEN** PHNEDO. Documents available from CASDDS.
**Ind/Abst** Chem. Abstr.

INT/1013-5294
**PHARMEUROPA ED. FRANCAISE.** [Pharmeuropa Ed. fr.]. (1988)-. Periodical. French. Four times a year. 900.00F (France); 1000.00F (other). Council of Europe / Group Pact ED, Pharmacopoeia BP 907, 67029 Strasbourg Cedex 01 France. **Tel** 011 33 88 412036, FAX 011 33 88 41277181, telex 880388. Index available. cum. index.

US/0031-7152
**PHARMINDEX.** ***Ceased.*** [Pharmindex]. (Oct. 1958)-Vol. 35 (1993). Academic Scholarly Publication. English. mo. Skyline Publishers Inc, Box 1029, Portland OR 97207. **Tel** (503)235-0071. **ED** Grant Gordash. **NLM** W1 PH3267. **CODEN** PMDXAT. Index available. cum. index. **Ad Acc.** Documents available from CASDDS.
**Desc:** New and changed products package sizes, drug prices, discontinued items and investigational drugs. A continuing education review article, with index.
**Ind/Abst** Chem. Abstr.; EMBASE.

II/0379-556X
**PHARMSTUDENT.** [Pharmstudent]. **Added/Corp** Pharmaceutical Society (Banaras Hindu University). Periodical. English. **CODEN** PMSDBB. Documents available from CASDDS.
**Ind/Abst** Chem. Abstr. (1952-1980); Int. Pharm. Abstr.

US/1056-5671
**PHASE III PROFILES.** (PHASE III PROFILES : A MONTHLY REVIEW OF PHARMACEUTICALS IN CLINICAL TRIALS.). [Phase III profiles]. **Added/Corp** BIOMEGA Corporation. **VFOAT** Phase 3 Profiles; Phase Three Profiles. Vol. 1, No. 1 (Jan. 1991)-. Periodical. English. Ten times a year. $295.00. Biomega Corporation, 8707 Skokie Boulevard, Suite 107, Skokie IL 60077. **Tel** (708)982-1400, FAX (708)982-1420. **DD** 615. **NLM** W1; PH328P. **CODEN** PPOFEL.
**Desc:** Provides comprehensive clinical information on drugs waiting approval by the FDA, and timely follow-up with the FDA's own description of its basis for approval. Reviews the pharmacology, adverse effects, pharmacokinetics, dose and administration, latest clinical data and anticipated costs for each drug.
**Ind/Abst** Int. Pharm. Abstr.

US/0031-7306
**PHILADELPHIA MEDICINE.** **See** Medical Science and Technology.

FR/0369-9560
**PHOTOGRAPHE, LE.** [Photographe]. (1910)-. Periodical. French. mo. 330.00F France; 510.00F other. Photovision, Svc Abonnement, 103 Boulevard Saint Michel, 75005 Paris Cedex 19 France. **ED** Bernard Perrine. **Circ:** 10,000.
**Ind/Abst** Point Repere (1983-).

US/1046-2694
**PHYSICIANS' DESK REFERENCE (COMPACT DISK ED.).** (PHYSICIANS' DESK REFERENCE [COMPUTER FILE] : PDR.). [Physicians' desk ref.]. **VFOAT** PDR. (Jan. 1988)-. English. Three times a year. $595.00. Medical Economics Data, Five Paragon Drive, PO Box 27, Montvale NJ 07645. **Tel** (800)442-6657, (201)358-7200. **DD** 615. available in print (Physicians' Desk Reference); available on diskette (Pocket PDR [Computer File]).
**Desc:** System requirements: IBM PC or compatible with 640K RAM, Microsoft extension 1.01 or higher, MS-DOS 3.1 or higher, CD-ROM drive.

US
**PHYSICIANS' DESK REFERENCE DRUG INTERACTIONS & SIDE EFFECTS INDEX.** (19??)-. English. an. $46.95. Medical Economics Data, Five Paragon Drive, PO Box 27, Montvale NJ 07645. **Tel** (800)442-6657, (201)358-7200. **(Subscription address:** Physicians' Desk Reference, Box 10688, Trade Department KL Grove, Des Moines, IA 50336**)**

US/1044-1395
**PHYSICIANS' DESK REFERENCE FOR NONPRESCRIPTION DRUGS.** [Physicians' desk ref. nonprescr. drugs]. **Added/Corp** Medical Economics Company. **VFOAT** PDR for Nonprescription Drugs. 1st Ed. (1980)-. English. an. $39.95. Medical Economics Data, Five Paragon Drive, PO Box 27, Montvale NJ 07645. **Tel** (800)442-6657, (201)358-7200. **(Subscription address:** Physicians' Desk Reference, 111 10th Street, Des Moines, IA 50309**)** **LC** RM671.A1; P48. **DD** 615/.1/05. **NLM** QV 772 P575.

**Desc:** A most comprehensive, up-to-date volume on over-the-counter drugs. This edition features four complete indices for fast, accurate use...color photographs of most commonly used products for immediate identification...plus a special section on the diagnostics and devices sold for home use.

US/0093-4461
**PHYSICIANS' DESK REFERENCE (PRINT ED.).** (PHYSICIANS' DESK REFERENCE : PDR.). [Physicians' desk ref.]. **VFOAT** PDR. (1974)-. English. an. $56.95 (pre-pub), $59.95 (post-pub). Medical Economics Data, Five Paragon Drive, PO Box 27, Montvale NJ 07645. **Tel** (800)442-6657, (201)358-7200. **(Subscription address:** Physicians' Desk Reference, 111 10th Street, Des Moines, IA 50309**) ED** Edward R Barnhart. **LC** RS75; .P5. **DD** 615/.1. **NLM** QV 772 P578. **[CCC].** Index available. **Ad Acc.** ctrl circ. available on CD-ROM (Physicians' Desk Reference (Compact Disc Ed.)); available on diskette (Pocket PDR [Computer File]). ***Continues*** *Physicians' Desk Reference to Pharmaceutical Specialties and Biologicals, 0093-447X.*
**Desc:** The source for prescription drug information. Contains more drug listings, drug manufacturers and must-know information and product illustration drawings within individual listings whenever possible.

US
**PHYSICIANS DESK REFERENCE : SUPPLEMENT.** English. Twice a year. $18.95. Medical Economics Data, Five Paragon Drive, PO Box 27, Montvale NJ 07645. **Tel** (800)442-6657, (201)358-7200.

●US/1064-7783
**PHYSICIANS' GENRX.** (1993)-. English. an (Jan.). $77.00 North America; $124.00 others. Data Pharmaceutica Inc., 425 Madison Avenue, Suite 605, New York NY 10017. **Tel** (212)888-0967, FAX (212)751-8033. **LC** RS55.2; .P48. **Bk Rev.** available on CD-ROM. ***Continues*** *Physicians' Generix, 1064-7783.*
**Desc:** Covers all prescription drugs, brand names, generic, prices, and therapeutic equivalencies.

US/0736-4326
**PHYSIOLOGIC AND PHARMACOLOGIC BASES OF DRUG THERAPY.** [Physiol. pharmacol. bases drug ther.]. (1980)-. Monographic series. English. ir. Price varies per volume. Academic Press, Inc., 6277 Sea Harbor Drive, Orlando FL 32887. **Tel** (800)543-9534, (407)345-4100, FAX (407)363-9661. **ED** Gesina L. Logenecker. **NLM** W1 PH925N.

US
**PHYSIOLOGICAL PHARMACOLOGY : A COMPREHENSIVE TREATISE.** (1963)-. Monographic series. English. ir. Price varies per volume. Academic Press, Inc., 6277 Sea Harbor Drive, Orlando FL 32887. **Tel** (800)543-9534, (407)345-4100, FAX (407)363-9661. **ED** W. S. Root and F. G. Hofmann.

GW/0944-7032
**PKA AKTUELL.** (19??)-. German. Six times a year. DM9.00. Deutscher Apotheker Verlag, Postfach 101061, D 70009 Stuttgart Germany. **Tel** 011 49 711 25820, INLAND:0711/2582, FAX 011 49 711 2582 290, telex 723636 daz d. **ED** Michael Schmidt. ***Continues*** *Apothekenhelferin Heute.*

GW/0032-0943
**PLANTA MEDICA.** [Planta med.]. **Added/Corp** Gesellschaft fuer Arzneipflanzenforschung (Germany). Deutsche Gesellschaft fuer Arzneipflanzenforschung. (June 1953)-. Academic Scholarly Publication. German (English, French and German). bm. $288.00. Georg Thieme Verlag Stuttgart, Postfach 301120, D 70451 Stuttgart Germany. **Tel** 011 49 711 89310, FAX 011 49 711 8931298, telex 7 252 275 GTVD. **(Subscription address:** Thieme Medical Publishers Inc., 381 Park Avenue South, New York NY 10016.**) ED** E Reinhard. **LC** RS164; .P7. **DD** 615/.32/05. **NLM** W1 PL106. **CODEN** PLMEAA. **[CCC]. Bk Rev. Ad Acc. Pr Rev. Circ:** 800 (ctrl). Documents available from The Genuine Article, BIOSIS Document Express, CASDDS, ADONIS.
**Desc:** Publishes full papers, communications, letters and reviews about pharmacology, phytochemistry, biochemistry, physiology and genetics of medicinal plants.
**Ind/Abst** ADONIS; AgBiotech News Inf.; AGRICOLA [Full Cov.]; BioBusiness; Biol. Abstr.; Chem. Abstr.; Chem. Titles; Chemorecept. Abstr.; Crop Physiol. Abstr.; CSA Neuro. Abstr. (?-?); Curr. Aware. Biol. Sci., CABS; Curr. Biotechnol.; Curr. Contents Life Sci.; EMBASE; Energy Res. Abstr. (June 1972-); Food Sci. Technol. Abstr.; For. Prod. Abstr. (19??-19??); For. Abstr.; Helminthol. Abstr. (19??-19??); Hortic. Abstr.; Index Med.; Int. Pharm. Abstr.; Microbiol. Abstr. Sect. A; Microbiol. Abstr. Sect. C; NAPRALERT; Nat. Prod. Updates; Nematol. Abstr.; Nutr. Abstr. Rev., Ser. B, Live Feeds and Feed.; Ornamental Hort. (19??-19??); Life Sci. Collect.; PESTDOC; Plant Breed. Abstr.; Plant Grow. Reg. Abstr.; Postharvest News Inf.; Protozoolog. Abstr.; Res. Alert [Full Cov.]; Rev. Agric. Entomol.; Rev. Med. Vet. Entomol.; Rev. Med. Vet. Mycology; Sci. Cit. Index; SCISEARCH; Seed Abstr.; Weed Abstr.

GW
**PLANTA MEDICA. SUPPLEMENT.** **Added/Corp** Gesellschaft fuer Arzneipflanzenforschung. (19??)-. Periodical. English (French and German). ir. Comes with Planta Medica. Georg Thieme Verlag Stuttgart, Postfach 301120, D 70451 Stuttgart Germany. **Tel** 011 49 711 89310, FAX 011 49 711 8931298, telex 7 252 275 GTVD. **(Subscription address:** Thieme Medical Publishers Inc., 381 Park Avenue South, New York NY 10016.**)** Documents available from CASDDS.
**Ind/Abst** Chem. Abstr.; Index Med.; NAPRALERT.

FR/0032-0994
**PLANTES MEDICINALES ET PHYTOTHERAPIE.** ***Ceased.*** **See** Biology-Botany.

US/1058-1189
**PLANTS FOR TOXICITY ASSESSMENT.** [Plants toxic. assess.]. **Added/Corp** ASTM Committee E-47 on Biological Effects and Environmental Fate. Subcommittee E47.11 on Plant Toxicity. Vol. 1 (1990)-. English. ASTM - American Society fo Testing and Materials, 1916 Race Street, Philadelphia PA 19103. **Tel** (215)299-5585. **DD** 615. Documents available from BIOSIS Document Express.
**Ind/Abst** Biol. Abstr.

GW
**PM REPORT.** English. Fifteen times a year. E. Habrich Verlag GmbH, Kollwitzstrasse 2, D 10405 Berlin Germany. **Tel** 011 49 30 282656761.

US
**PMA NEWSLETTER.** Newsletter. English. Pharmaceutical Manufacturing Association, 1100 15th Street NW, Washington DC 20005. **Tel** (202)835-3420. Documents available from UMI Article Clearinghouse.
**Ind/Abst** Pharm. News Index (Dec. 1975-Nov. 1977).

US
**PMA STATISTICAL FACTBOOK.** **Added/Corp** Pharmaceutical Manufacturers Association. **VFOAT** Statistical Factbook; PMA Statistical Fact Book; Statistical Fact Book. (Oct. 1984)-. Statistical Publication. English. an. $21.50. Pharmaceutical Manufactur Association, 1100 15th Street Northwest, Washington DC 20005. **Tel** (202)835-3420, FAX (202)835-3429. ***Continues*** *Prescription Drug Industry Fact Book, 0553-9226.*

US/0149-0885
**PMD, PHARMACEUTICAL MARKETERS DIRECTORY.** **VFOAT** Pharmaceutical Marketers Directory. 1977-. Directory. English. an. $109.00. CPS Communications Inc, 7200 West Camino Road, Suite 215, Boca Raton FL 33433. **Tel** (407)368-9301, FAX (407)368-7870. **ED** John C Banghart. **LC** HD9666.3. **DD** 381/.45/615102573. **NLM** QV 22; AA1 P536. **Ad Acc. Circ:** 3,100.
**Desc:** Marketing personnel of pharmaceutical companies, advertising agencies with clients in the medical field, and medical and pharmacy publications. Also includes an alphabetical list of publishers' representatives and a list of industry suppliers.

US/8755-5476
**POCKETBOOK OF PEDIATRIC ANTIMICROBIAL THERAPY.** [Pocketb. pediatr. antimicrob. ther.]. **VFOAT** Pocket Book of Pediatric Antimicrobial Therapy. 1st Ed.-. Periodical. English. be. $3.50. Jodone Publishing Company, 3226 Oliver Street, Dallas TX 75205. **ED** John D Nelson. **DD** 615. **UDC** 616-053.2-085. **NLM** QV 39; N427p.

●PL
**POLISH JOURNAL OF PHARMACOLOGY.** **Added/Corp** Zakad Farmakologii (Polska Akademia Nauk). Vol. 45, No. 1 (Jan./Feb. 1993)-. Periodical. English. **NLM** W1; PO23LS. ***Continues*** *Polish Journal of Pharmacology and Pharmacy, 0301-0244.*

PL/0301-0244
**POLISH JOURNAL OF PHARMACOLOGY AND PHARMACY.** ***Title Change.*** [Pol. j. pharmacol. pharm.]. **Added/Corp** Polska Akademia Nauk. Zakald Farmakologii. Vol. 25 (Jan./Feb. 1973)-Vol. 44, No. 6, (Nov./Dec. 1992). Academic Scholarly Publication. English (summaries and/or abstracts in Polish). bm. Institute of Pharmacology, Polish Academy of Sciences, Smetna 12, 31-343, Cracow, Poland. **(Subscription address:** ARS Polona, PO Box 1001, 00068 Warsaw Poland.**) NLM** W1; PO23M. **CODEN** PJPPAA. **Pr Rev.** Documents available from BIOSIS Document Express, CASDDS. ***Continues*** *Dissertationes Pharmaceuticae et Pharmacologicae, 0012-3870.* ***Continued by*** *Polish Journal of Pharmacology.*
**Desc:** This journal continues to be the comprehensive forum for basic and clinical aspects of developing technologies in computer assisted imaging, including nuclear magnetic resonance, computed tomography, PET scanning, and ultrasound CT.
**Ind/Abst** Anal. Abstr.; Biol. Abstr.; Chem. Abstr.; CSA Neuro. Abstr.; EMBASE; Index Med.; Int. Pharm. Abstr. (199?-); NAPRALERT; Life Sci. Collect.; PESTDOC; Sci. Cit. Index (19??-19??); SCISEARCH.

US/0161-8415
**PR. PHARMACEUTICAL REPRESENTATIVE.** **VFOAT** Pharmaceutical Representative; PR. Vol. 8, No. 7 (July 1978)-. Periodical. English. mo. $24.95. McKnight Medical Communications Inc, 1419 Lake Cook Road, Suite 110, Deerfield IL 60015. **Tel** (708)647-0259, (800)451-7838. **(Subscription address:** Pharmaceutical Representative, PO Box 1165, Skokie IL 60076.**) ED** James Bowe. **[CCC]. Circ:** 17,000. ***Continues*** *Pharmaceutical Salesman.*
**Desc:** For sales representatives of pharmaceutical companies.

NE/0169-1910
**PRAKTIJKMANAGEMENT.** [Praktijkmanagement]. **VFOAT** PM. Praktijkmanagement. (1985)-. Periodical. Dutch. Eight times a year. Fl85.00. Mediselect Management Product, Postbus 28091, 3838 ZH Hoogland Netherlands. **Tel** 011 31 33 808020. **UDC** 614.2.

UK/0032-7611
**PRESCRIBERS' JOURNAL.** [Prescr. j.]. Vol. 1, No. 1 (Mar. 1961)-. Periodical. English. bm (6 issues). £11.60. Her Majesty's Stationery Office, 51 Nine Elms Lane, London SW8 5DR England. **Tel** 011 44 71 873 8459, 011 44 71 873 8499, FAX 011 44 71 873 8499, 011 44 71 873 8456, telex 297138. **(Subscription address:** Her Majestys Stationery Offic, PO Box 276 Public Centre, London SW8 5DT England**) ED** D. Shenton. **NLM** WI; PR434F. **CODEN** PRJOBY. **[CCC].** ***Continues*** *Prescribers' Notes.*
**Desc:** Contains features on the research and development of drugs, progress in the medical treatment of specific illnesses and conditions, and effective prescribing practices.
**Ind/Abst** EMBASE; Int. Pharm. Abstr.; Trop. Dis. Bull.

US/0882-8628
**PRESCRIPTION DRUG NEWS.** [Prescr. drug news]. Began in 1984?. Periodical. English. bm. $26.00. FC&A Publishing, 103 Clover Green, Peachtree City GA 30269. **DD** 615.

US/8756-8950
**PRESCRIPTION DRUGS.** (PRESCRIPTION DRUGS / BY THE EDITORS OF CONSUMER GUIDE.). [Prescr. drugs]. (19??)-. English. an. Prescription Drugs, 3841 West Oakton Street, Skokie IL 60076. **LC** RM301.15; .P73. **DD** 615/.1.

US/1068-5324
**PRESCRIPTION PHARMACEUTICALS AND BIOTECHNOLOGY.** **VFOAT** The Pink Sheet. (19??)-. Government Publication. English. wk. $790.00. FDC Reports Inc., 5550 Friendship Boulevard/Suite 1, Chevy Chase MD 20815. **Tel** (301)657-9830.

AT/0818-4445
**PRESCRIPTION PRODUCTS GUIDE.** **VFOAT** P.P. Guide. 16th Ed. (1987)-. English. an. 99.00Aus$ Australia; 124.00Aus$ (surfacemail) other; 140.00Aus$ (airmail) Asia & Oceania; 165.00Aus$ (airmail) other. Australia Pharmaceutical Publishing Company Limited, 40 Burwood Road, PO Box 777, Hawthorn Victoria 3122 Australia. **Tel** 61 3 8109800, FAX 61 3 8191706. **ED** Stuart Dickson. **NLM** QV 772; P933. **Bk Rev. Ad Acc.** ctrl circ. ***Continues*** *Prescription Proprietaries Guide, 0729-2333.*
**Desc:** Describes the latest drugs on the market, their uses and side effects, in alphabetical order; includes the names of the manufacturers.

●US/1061-0359
**PRIMARY CARE MEDICINE DRUG ALERTS.** [Prim. care med. drug alerts]. Vol. 13, No. 1 (Jan. 1992)-. Periodical. English. Twelve times a year. $59.00 US; $76.00 Canada; $83.00 other. M. J. Powers and Company Publishers, 374 Millburn Avenue, Millburn NJ 07041. **Tel** (201)467-4556. **DD** 616. ***Formed by the union of*** *Drug Alerts for Internal Medicine, 1040-4589* ***and*** *Physicians' Drug Alert, 0277-4194.*

US/0094-9264
**PRINCIPLES AND TECHNIQUES OF HUMAN RESEARCH AND THERAPEUTICS.** Vol. 1 (1974)-. Monographic series. English. ir. $17.00. Futura Publishing Company Inc., 135 Bedford Road, PO Box 418, Armonk NY 10504-0418. **Tel** (914)273-1014, (800)877-8761, FAX (914)273-1015, (914)273-1016. **ED** F. G. McMahon. **NLM** W1 PR524E.

IT
**PRO PHARMACOPOEA.** Istituto Poligrafico Zecca Stato, Piazza Verdi 10, 00198 Rome Italy. **Tel** 011 39 6 85082307, 011 39 6 85082221.

NE/0069-5769
**PROCEEDINGS - INTERNATIONAL CONGRESS OF NEURO-PSYCHOPHARMACOLOGY.** **See** Medical Science and Technology-Neurology.

US
**PROCEEDINGS OF THE ANNUAL MEETING.** **Main/Corp** National Association of Boards of Pharmacy. (19??)-. Proceedings. English. an. $15.00. National Association Boards of Pharmacy, 700 Busse Highway, Park Ridge IL 60068. **Tel** (708)698-6227.
**Ind/Abst** Int. Pharm. Abstr. (199?-).

AT/0067-2084
**PROCEEDINGS OF THE AUSTRALIAN PHYSIOLOGICAL AND PHARMACOLOGICAL SOCIETY.** **See** Biology-Physiology.

US/0083-8969
**PROCEEDINGS OF THE WESTERN PHARMACOLOGY SOCIETY.** [Proc. West. Pharmacol. Soc.]. **Main/Corp** Western Pharmacology Society. Vol. 1 (1958)-. Academic Scholarly Publication. English. an. $25.00. Western Pharmacology Society, Department Pharmacy, School of Medicine, University of Arizona, Tucson AZ 85724. **Tel** (602)626-7843. **ED** Ryan J. Huxtable. **NLM** W1 PR587HN. **CODEN** PWPSA8. **Bk Rev**, (Qty: 4 per year). **Ad Acc, Adv Mgr:** same as Editor. **Circ:** 500. available on microfilm and microfiche from University Microfilms International (UMI). Documents available from BIOSIS Document Express, CASDDS.
**Desc:** Papers presented at the annual meeting of the Society.
**Ind/Abst** Biol. Abstr.; Chem. Abstr.; Cumul. Index Nurs. Allied Health Lit.; EMBASE; Energy Res. Abstr.; Index Med.; Int. Aerosp. Abstr.; NAPRALERT; Life Sci. Collect.; Ref. Upd. Deluxe Ed.

●UK
**PROFESSIONAL NURSE. DRUG UPDATE.** **VFOAT** Drug Update. Ed. 1 (Jan. 1992)-. Periodical. English. sa. Free with subscription of Professional nurse. **NLM** QV 39; P9637.

US
**PROFESSIONAL'S GUIDE TO PATIENT DRUG FACTS.** English. qt. $69.95 (loose-leaf edition) US; $87.50 (loose-leaf edition) other. Facts and Comparisons Inc, 111 West Port Plaza, Suite 400, St Louis MO 63146-3098. **Tel** (314)878-2515, (800)223-0554, FAX (314)878-5563.
**Desc:** An essential reference to aid in patient education, counseling and drug therapy management.

US
**PROFILES IN HOSPITAL PHARMACY.** English. Six times a year. $78.00 US; $91.08 other. Macmillan Professional Journal, 30 Vreeland Road, Florham Park NJ 07932. **Tel** (201)822-1622, FAX (201)822-2498.

SP/0211-8351
**PROGRESOS EN PSICOARMACOLOGIA.** [Prog. psicoform acol.]. Academic Scholarly Publication. Spanish. Price varies per volume. **NLM** W1 PR6648. **CODEN** PRPSDA. Documents available from CASDDS.
**Ind/Abst** Chem. Abstr. (-1980); EMBASE.

SZ/1011-0267
**PROGRESS IN BASIC AND CLINICAL PHARMACOLOGY.** Vol. 1 (1988)-. Monographic series. English. an. 200.00F (approx. per volume). S. Karger AG, Allschwilerstrasse 10, PO Box - Postfach - Case Postale, CH-4009 Basel Switzerland. **Tel** 011 41 61 306-1111, FAX 011 41 61 306-1234, telex CH 962 652. **ED** P. Lomax, E. S. Vesell, C. Scarpignato. **NLM** W1; PR666GK. **[CCC].** Index available. ctrl circ. available in microform. Documents available from BIOSIS Document Express.
**Desc:** Individual volumes in this series review current therapeutic practice world-wide, with a focus on new drugs and new applications of established drugs. Devoted to promoting a rational approach to therapy, each volume discusses clinical applications of drugs in the light of their fundamental mechanisms of action and the pathogenesis of the disorder being treated. The texts also include drug treatment experience with compounds not yet widely available.
**Ind/Abst** Biol. Abstr.; Ref. Upd. Deluxe Ed.

US/0079-6085
**PROGRESS IN BIOCHEMICAL PHARMACOLOGY.** [Prog. biochem. pharmacol.]. Vol. 1 (1965)-. Monographic series. English. an. 170.00F (approx. per volume). S. Karger AG, Allschwilerstrasse 10, PO Box - Postfach - Case Postale, CH-4009 Basel Switzerland. **Tel** 011 41 61 306-1111, FAX 011 41 61 306-1234, telex CH 962 652. **ED** R. Paoletti. **NLM** W1 PR666H. **CODEN** PBPHAW. **[CCC].** Documents available from BIOSIS Document Express, CASDDS.
**Desc:** Volumes in this series consider drugs as therapeutic agents and curative measures for dealing with various conditions of human health. Contributions of high distinction provide general reviews, specific studies based on original work, and discussions of technical data in highly controversial areas.
**Ind/Abst** Biol. Abstr.; Chem. Abstr.; Index Med.; Nutr. Abstr. Rev., Ser. A, Hum. Exp.; PESTDOC; Ref. Upd. Deluxe Ed.

GW/0721-4049
**PROGRESS IN CLINICAL PHARMACOLOGY.** [Prog. clin. parmacol.]. **VFOAT** Fortschritte der Klinischen Pharmakologie. (1980)-. Academic Scholarly Publication. English (German). ir. Price varies per volume. Dustri-Verlag, Dr Karl Feistle, Postfach 49, D 82032 Deisenhofen Germany. **Tel** 011 49 89 6138610, FAX 011 49 89 6135412. **ED** H.P. Kuemmerle. **NLM** W1; PR668GI. **CODEN** PCPHD8. Documents available from CASDDS.
**Ind/Abst** Chem. Abstr.; PESTDOC (?-?).

NE/0167-5028
**PROGRESS IN CLINICAL PHARMACY.** (PROGRESS IN CLINICAL PHARMACY : PROCEEDINGS OF THE ... EUROPEAN SYMPOSIUM ON CLINICAL PHARMACY.). [Prog. clin. pharm.]. **VFOAT** Proceedings of the ... European Symposium on Clinical Pharmacy. (1978)-. Proceedings. English. Elsevier Science Publishers BV, PO Box 211, 1000 AE Amsterdam Netherlands. **Tel** 011 31 20 5803642, FAX 011 31 20 5862696, telex 15682. **NLM** W3 EU938B. **CODEN** PCPYDP.
**Ind/Abst** PESTDOC.

SZ/0071-786X
**PROGRESS IN DRUG RESEARCH.** [Prog. drug res.]. **VFOAT** Fortschritte der Arzneimittelforschung; Progres des Recherches Pharmaceutiques. Vol. 12 (1968)-. Academic Scholarly Publication. English (French and German). an. Price varies per volume. Birkhaeuser Verlag Ag, Klosterberg 23, PO Box 133, CH-4010 Basel Switzerland. **Tel** 011 41 61 2717400, FAX 011 41 0 61 2717666, telex 963475 birk ch. **(Subscription address:** Birkhauser Verlag AG, PO Box 151, CH 4106 Therwil Switzerland; Phone: 011 41 61 7217740**) ED** E. Jucker. **NLM** W1 PR668Q. **CODEN** FAZMAE. **[CCC].** Documents available from BIOSIS Document Express, CASDDS. ***Continues*** *Fortschritte der Arzneimittelforschung.*
**Desc:** Contains review articles on biochemical, biological, immunological, physiological, clinical and medicinal aspects of drug research.
**Ind/Abst** Biol. Abstr.; Chem. Abstr.; EMBASE; Index Med.; Int. Pharm. Abstr.; NAPRALERT; Life Sci. Collect.; PESTDOC; Protozoolog. Abstr.

NE/0079-6468
**PROGRESS IN MEDICINAL CHEMISTRY.** **See** Chemistry.

UK/0278-5846
**PROGRESS IN NEURO-PSYCHOPHARMACOLOGY & BIOLOGICAL PSYCHIATRY.** [Progr. neuro-psychopharmacol. biol. psychiatr.]. **VFOAT** Progress in Neuro-Psychopharmacology and Biological Psychiatry; P.N.P. & BP Journal; PNP and BP Journal; P.N.P. and B.P. Journal; PNP & BP Journal. Vol. 6, No. 1 (1982)-. Academic Scholarly Publication. English. Eight times a year. $805.00 The Americas; £540.00 other. Pergamon Press, An Imprint of Elsevier Science Ltd., The Boulevard, Langford Lane, Kidlington, Oxford OX5 1GB United Kingdom. **Tel** 011 44 865 843000, 011 44 865 843699, FAX 011 44 865 843010. **(Subscription address:** Elsevier Science Ltd. Oxford Fulfillment Centre, PO Box 800, Kidlington, Oxford OX5 1DX United Kingdom.**) ED** C. Radouco-Thomas, P. Bedard and M. Radouco-Thomas. **LC** RM315; .P714. **DD** 615/.78/05. **NLM** W1 PR6745E. **CODEN** PNPPD7. **[CCC]. Pr Rev.** available on microfilm and microfiche from University Microfilms International (UMI). Documents available from The Genuine Article, BIOSIS Document Express, CASDDS, ADONIS. ***Continues*** *Progress in Neuro-Psychopharmacology, 0364-7722.*
**Ind/Abst** ADONIS; Biol. Abstr.; Chem. Abstr.; CSA Neuro. Abstr.; Curr. Aware. Biol. Sci., CABS; Curr. Contents Life Sci.; EMBASE; Energy Res. Abstr. (Aug. 1982-); Index Med.; Index Sci. Rev. [Full Cov.]; Life Sci. Collect.; PESTDOC; Psychol. Abstr. (1982-); PsycINFO; PsycLit; Res. Alert [Full Cov.]; Sci. Cit. Index; SCISEARCH; Soc. Sci. Cit. Index [Select. Cov.].

GW/0934-9545
**PROGRESS IN PHARMACOLOGY AND CLINICAL PHARMACOLOGY.** [Prog. pharmacol. clin. pharmacol.]. Vol. 7 No. 1 (1989)-. Academic Scholarly Publication. English. ir. Price varies per volume. Gustav Fischer Verlag Stuttgart, Postfach 720143, Wollgrasweg 49, D 70577 Stuttgart Germany. **Tel** 011 49 711 458030, FAX 0711-4580334, telex 2627-7111488. **ED** F.M. Eichelbaum, W. Forth, U. Meyer, P.A. van Zwieten. **NLM** W1; PR677N. **CODEN** PPCPEP. **[CCC].** Documents available from BIOSIS Document Express, CASDDS. ***Continues*** *Progress in Pharmacology, 0340-465X.*
**Ind/Abst** Biol. Abstr. (1989-); Chem. Abstr.; EMBASE.

GW/0944-6877
**PSYCHO PHARMAKO THERAPIE.** (1994)-. German. qt. DM36.00. Wissenschaftliche Verlagsgesellschaft mbH, Postfach 101061, D 70009 Stuttgart Germany. **Tel** 011 49 711 258200, FAX 011 49 711 2582290, telex 723636 DAZ D. **ED** Susanne Heinzl.

GW/0033-3158
**PSYCHOPHARMACOLOGIA.** (PSYCHOPHARMACOLOGY.). [Psychopharmacologia]. Vol. 47, No. 1 (1986)-. Academic Scholarly Publication. English (French and German). Twenty-four times a year. DM4200.00. Springer-Verlag GmbH & Company KG, Heidelberger Platz 3, D 14197 Berlin Germany. **Tel** 011 49 30 8207223, FAX 011 49 30 8214091, telex 183 319 SPBLN D. **(Subscription address:** Springer Verlag New York Inc. / for North America, 44 Hartz Way, Secaucus NJ 07096.**) ED** D E Casey and J Gerlach. **LC** RM315; .P747. **DD** 615/.78. **NLM** W1 PS7725. **CODEN** PSCHDL. **[CCC]. Pr Rev.** available on microfilm and microfiche from University Microfilms International (UMI). Documents available from BIOSIS Document Express, CASDDS, ADONIS. ***Continues*** *Psychopharmacologia, 0033-3158.*
**Desc:** Intended to provide a medium for the prompt publication of scientific contributions concerned with the analysis and synthesis of the effects of drugs on behavior, in the broadest sense of the term.
**Ind/Abst** ADONIS; Biol. Abstr.; Chem. Abstr.; EMBASE; Index Med.; NAPRALERT; Life Sci. Collect.; PESTDOC; Psychol. Abstr. (1976-).

NE/0167-9198
**PSYCHOPHARMACOLOGY (AMSTERDAM).** ***Ceased.*** (PSYCHOPHARMACOLOGY : A BIENNIAL CRITICAL SURVEY OF THE INTERNATIONAL LITERATURE.). [Psychopharmacology]. 1, Pt. 1 (1983)-Series complete. Academic Scholarly Publication. English. be. Elsevier Science Publishers BV, PO Box 211, 1000 AE Amsterdam Netherlands. **Tel** 011 31 20 5803642, FAX 011 31 20 5862696, telex 15682. **ED** D. G. Grahame-Smith, H. Hippius, and G. Winokur. **LC** RC483; .P7773. **DD** 615/.78/05. **NLM** W1 PS772. **CODEN** PSYCEF. Documents available from CASDDS.
**Ind/Abst** Chem. Abstr.

US/0048-5764
**PSYCHOPHARMACOLOGY BULLETIN.** **See** Psychology.

US/0161-0139
**PSYCHOPHARMACOLOGY (NEW YORK).** (PSYCHOPHARMACOLOGY.). [Psychopharmacology]. **VFOAT** Psychopharmacology Series. Vol. 1 (1976)-. Academic Scholarly Publication. English. ir. Price varies per volume. Marcel Dekker Inc., 270 Madison Avenue, New York NY 10016. **Tel** (212)696-9000, (800)228-1160, FAX (212)685-4540, telex 421419. **(Subscription address:** Marcel Dekker Inc, PO Box 5017, Monticello NY 12701.**) NLM** W1 PS7727. **CODEN** PSPHDI. Documents available from The Genuine Article, BIOSIS Document Express, CASDDS.
**Ind/Abst** Biol. Abstr. (-1977); Chem. Abstr.; CSA Neuro. Abstr.; Curr. Contents Life Sci.; PsycINFO (1990-); PsycLit; Ref. Upd. Deluxe Ed.; Res. Alert [Full Cov.]; Sci. Cit. Index; SCISEARCH; Soc. Sci. Cit. Index [Select. Cov.].

GW/0931-6795
**PSYCHOPHARMACOLOGY SERIES.** [Psychopharmacol. ser.]. Vol. 3 (1987)-. Academic Scholarly Publication. English. Price varies per volume. Springer-Verlag GmbH & Company KG, Heidelberger Platz 3, D 14197 Berlin Germany. **Tel** 011 49 30 8207223, FAX 011 49 30 8214091, telex 183 319 SPBLN D. **(Subscription address:** Springer Verlag New York Inc. / for North America, 44 Hartz Way, Secaucus NJ 07096.**) NLM** W1; PS773J. **CODEN** PSSEEP. Documents available from BIOSIS Document Express, CASDDS. ***Continues*** *Psychopharmacology (Berlin, Germany). Supplementum, 0179-8456.*
**Ind/Abst** Biol. Abstr. (1986-); Chem. Abstr. (1987-); Index Med. (1987-).

US/1068-5308
**PSYCHOPHARMACOLOGY UPDATE.** (PSYCHOPHARMACOLOGY UPDATE : A MONTHLY ADVISORY FOR MENTAL HEALTH PROFESSIONALS.). [Psychopharmacol. update]. **Added/Corp** Manisses Communications Group. (1990)-. Periodical. English. mo. $99.00 (institutions), $69.00 (individuals). Manisses Communications Group Inc., PO Box 3357, Providence RI 02906-0757. **Tel** (401)831-6020, (800)333-7771, FAX (401)861-6370. **ED** Frank Tornatore. **DD** 615. Index available.

GW/0302-167X
**PTA HEUTE.** [PTA heute]. **VAT** Pharmazeutisch-Techischer Assistent Heute. Vol. 20 (Jan. 1974)-. Periodical. German. mo. DM48.00. Deutscher Apotheker Verlag, Postfach 101061, D 70009 Stuttgart Germany. **Tel** 011 49 711 25820, INLAND:0711/2582, FAX 011 49 711 2582 290, telex 723636 daz d. **ED** Reinhild Berger. **NLM** W1 P978H. **CODEN** PTAHAF. **Circ:** 24,000. Documents available from CASDDS. ***Continues*** *Apothekerpraktikant und Pharmazeutisch-Technischer Assistent, 0303-6219.*
**Ind/Abst** Chem. Abstr.

GW/0722-1029
**PTA IN DER APOTHEKE.** [PTA Apoth.]. **VFOAT** P.T.A. in der Apotheke. **VAT** Pharmazeutisch-Technische Assistenten in der Apotheke. 1981-. Academic Scholarly Publication. German. mo. Umschau Verlag, Postfach 110262,

D-60037 Frankfurt Germany. **Tel** 011 49 69 2600692, FAX 011 49 69 2600223, telex 411964. **CODEN** PTAED9. Documents available from CASDDS.
**Ind/Abst** Chem. Abstr. (1981-1983).

US/0270-0611
**PUBLICATION - AMERICAN INSTITUTE OF THE HISTORY OF PHARMACY.** [Publ. - Am,. Inst. Hist. Pharm.]. No. 1-. Monographic series. English. Price varies per volume. American Institute of the History of Pharmacy, 425 North Charter Street, Pharmacy Building, Madison WI 53706. **Tel** (608)262-5378. **NLM** W1 PU673.

UK/0954-3333
**PULMONARY PHARMACOLOGY SHEFFIELD.** (PULMONARY PHARMACOLOGY.). [Pulm. pharmacol.Sheff.]. (1989)-. English. Twelve times a year. £75.00. SUBIS, Mansion House, 19 Kingfield Road, Sheffield S11 9AS England. **Tel** 011 44 114 255 4433, FAX 011 44 114 255 4626. **[CCC].**

GW/0935-5901
**PZ WISSENSCHAFT : PHARMAZEUTISCHE ZEITUNG, WISSENSCHAFTSAUSGABE.** (1988)-. Academic Scholarly Publication. German (summaries and/or abstracts in English; table of contents in English). bm. Govi-Verlag, PO Box 97 01 08, Beethovenplatz 1-3, W-6000 Frankfurt Germany. **NLM** W1; PZ22. Documents available from CASDDS. ***Continues*** *Pharmazeutische Zeitung (Scientific Ed.), 0724-6315.*
**Ind/Abst** Chem. Abstr.; EMBASE; Int. Pharm. Abstr.

US/0163-2418
**QUALITY CONTROL REPORTS. See** Manufacturing.

GW/0931-8771
**QUANTITATIVE STRUCTURE-ACTIVITY RELATIONSHIPS.** (QUANTITATIVE STRUCTURE-ACTIVITY RELATIONSHIPS INCLUDING MOLECULAR MODELLING AND APPLICATIONS OF COMPUTER GRAPHICS IN PHARMACOLOGY, CHEMISTRY, AND BIOLOGY.). [Quant. struct.-act. relatsh.]. **VFOAT** QSAR; Quantitative Structure-Activity Relationships. Vol. 4, No. 3 (Sept. 1985)-. Academic Scholarly Publication. English. qt. $550.00. VCH Gesellschaft GmbH, Postfach 101161, D 69451 Weinheim Germany. **Tel** 011 49 6201 606459, FAX 011 49 6201 606184. **(Subscription address:** VCH Publishers Inc., 303 Northwest 12th Avenue, Journals Department, Deerfield FL 33442.) **LC** RM301.42; Q35. **DD** 615/.7. **NLM** W1; QU158MGF. **[CCC]. Pr Rev.** Documents available from The Genuine Article, BIOSIS Document Express, CASDDS. ***Continues*** *Quantitative Structure-Activity Relationships in Pharmacology, Chemistry, and Biology, 0722-3676.*
**Ind/Abst** Biol. Abstr. (Sept. 1985-); Chem. Abstr. (Sept. 1985-); Curr. Aware. Biol. Sci., CABS; Curr. Contents Life Sci.; EMBASE; PESTDOC; Res. Alert [Full Cov.]; Rev. Med. Vet. Entomol.; Sci. Cit. Index; SCISEARCH.

CN/0048-6280
**QUEBEC PHARMACIE.** No. 146- Feb. 1967-. Periodical. French. mo. Association Quebec Pharmaciens Prop, 1031 rue St Denis, Montreal Quebec H2X 3P9 Canada. **Tel** (514)842-0515. ***Continues*** *Association des Pharmaciens Detaillants de Montreal et de la Province of Quebec. Bulletin, 0380-7231.*

CN/0826-9874
**QUEBEC PHARMACIE (MONTREAL, 1981).** (QUEBEC PHARMACIE.). [Que. pharm.]. (1981)-. Periodical. French. Ten times a year. 30.00Can$ (1 year), $50.00Can$ (2 year) Canada; 65.00Can$ (1 year) other. Publications Codex, 4378 Pierre de Coubertin, Montreal QUE H1V 1A6 Canada. **Tel** (514)254-0346, FAX (514)254-1288. **ED** Manon Lambert. **DD** 615/.1/09714. **Bk Rev**, (Qty: 5). **Ad Acc, Adv Mgr:** Y. LaCroix, **Tel** (514)626-0024. **Circ:** 6,700 (ctrl). ***Absorbed in part*** *Bulletin d'Information a l'Attention des Pharmaciens des Etablissements de Sante., 0845-3063.*
**Desc:** Main objectives are to gather pharmacists working in different areas,emphasizing the professional content of social events and to provide scientifical information with a definite clinical bias.

FR/0764-5104
**QUOTIDIEN DU PHARMACIEN, LE.** [Quotid. pharm.]. (1985)-. Periodical. French. da. 620.00F France; 1372.00F other. Quotidien du Pharmacien, 140 rue Jules Guesde, 92593 Levallois Cedex France. **Tel** 011 33 1 47307500, FAX 011 33 1 47307575. **ED** Richard Liscia. **UDC** 615. **Ad Acc.** Full Page (Color) 5000.00F. Half Page (Color) 3000.00F. **Circ:** 22,000 (ctrl).
**Desc:** News and information of concern to pharmacists.

US/0748-6111
**RADIOPHARMACY AND RADIOPHARMACOLOGY YEARBOOK. See** Medical Science and Technology-Nuclear Medicine.

UK
**R&D FOCUS.** (19??)-. Trade Publication. English. mo. £3,650. IMS World Publications Ltd, 7 Harwodd Avenue, london NW1 6JB England. **Tel** 011 44 71 393 5000, FAX 011 44 393 5900. available on CD-ROM.
**Desc:** Contains information on therapeutic drugs under development or available for licensing worldwide from 1977 to the present.

NZ/0114-9954
**REACTIONS WEEKLY.** [React. wkly.]. **Added/Corp** IS(Firm). **VFOAT** Reactions. (1990)-. English. wk (50 issues per year). 1070.00F Europe; $675.00 other. ADIS International Ltd, 41 Centorian Drive, Private Bag 65901, Mairangi Bay, Auckland 10 New Zealand. **Tel** 011 64 9 4798100, FAX 011 64 9 4791418. **(Subscription address:** Japan Publications Trading Company, Ltd., PO Box 5030, Tokyo International, Tokyo 100-31 Japan.) available on CD-ROM from Micromedia Limited; and SilverPlatter (UK). ***Continues*** *Reactions (Auckland), 0157-7271.*
**Desc:** Rapid alerts to adverse drug experience. Covers drug interaction reports, tolerability of new drugs, drug abuse and dependence, drug overdose and poisoning, adverse drug reaction reports, risk benefit assessments of new drugs, comparative safety within drug classes and epidemiology.

UK/0957-5545
**RECENT ADVANCES IN CLINICAL PHARMACOLOGY AND TOXICOLOGY.** [Recent adv. clin. pharmacol. toxicol.]. No. 4 (1989)-. English. Longman Group Ltd., Fourth Avenue, Longman House, Harlow Essex CM19 5SR England. **Tel** 011 44 279 429655, FAX 011 44 279 431059, telex 81259. **LC** RM300; .R38. **DD** 615/.7/05. **NLM** W1; RE105TR. ***Continues*** *Recent Advances in Clinical Pharmacology, 0143-8735.*

●US
**RED BOOK. Added/Corp** Medical Economics Data (Firm). **VFOAT** Redbook. (1993)-. English. an. $44.00. Medical Economics Data, Five Paragon Drive, PO Box 27, Montvale NJ 07645. **Tel** (800)442-6657, (201)358-7200. **LC** HD9666.4; .R4. **NLM** QV 772; D794. ***Continues*** *Drug Topics Red Book.*

US
**RED BOOK UPDATE.** English. Twelve times a year. $99.00. Medical Economics Data, Five Paragon Drive, PO Box 27, Montvale NJ 07645. **Tel** (800)442-6657, (201)358-7200. ***Continues*** *Red Book Drug Topics Update.*

RU/0134-580X
**REFERATIVNYI ZHURNAL FARMAKOLOGIYA OBSHCHAYA FARMAKOLOGIYA NERVNOI SISTEMY. See** Biology.

UK/0950-3374
**REGULATORY AFFAIRS BULLETIN.** [Regul. aff. bull.]. (1980)-. Periodical. English. qt. £290.00. Inveresk Research International Limited, Regulatory Affairs Department, Tranent EH33 2NE Scotland. **Tel** 011 44 875 614545, FAX 011 44 875 614555, telex 727228. **DD** 363.1946. cum. index. **Circ:** 300.
**Desc:** Regulatory guidelines and legislation pertaining to the human and veterinary pharmaceutical, agrochemical, and chemical industries worldwide.

UK/0960-7889
**REGULATORY AFFAIRS JOURNAL. See** Medical Science and Technology.

●UK
**REGULATORY AFFAIRS JOURNAL (DEVICES), THE. See** Medical Science and Technology.

US/0273-2300
**REGULATORY TOXICOLOGY AND PHARMACOLOGY.** (REGULATORY TOXICOLOGY AND PHARMACOLOGY : RTP.). [Regul. toxicol. pharmacol.]. **Added/Corp** International Society of Regulatory Toxicology and Pharmacology. **VFOAT** RTP; R.T.P. Vol. 1, No. 1 (June 1981)-. Academic Scholarly Publication. English. bm (6 issues). $263.00 US and Canada; $333.00 other. Academic Press, Inc., 6277 Sea Harbor Drive, Orlando FL 32887. **Tel** (800)543-9534, (407)345-4100, FAX (407)363-9661. **ED** Frederick Coulston, Albert C. Kolbye Jr. and C. Jelleff Carr. **LC** RA1190; .R44. **DD** 363.7/384. **NLM** W1; RE173JM. **CODEN** RTOPDW. **[CCC]. Pr Rev.** Documents available from The Genuine Article, CASDDS.
**Desc:** Reports the concepts and problems involved with the generation, evaluation, and interpretation of experimental and human data in the larger perspective of the societal considerations of protecting human health and the environment.
**Ind/Abst** AGRICOLA [Select. Cov.]; BioBusiness; Biodeter. Abstr.; Chem. Abstr.; Chem. Hazards Ind.; Curr. Biotechnol.; Curr. Contents Life Sci.; EMBASE; Foods Adlibra; Index Med.; Index Vet.; Ind. Hyg. Dig. (19??-); Lab. Hazards Bull.; Nutr. Abstr. Rev., Ser. B, Live Feeds and Feed.; Res. Alert [Full Cov.]; Risk Abstr.; Sci. Cit. Index; SCISEARCH; Toxicol. Abstr. (19??-19??).

US/0065-9983
**REHABILITATION PUBLICATION.** Monographic series. English. Price varies per volume. Rehabilitation Publication, Chicago Avenue at 27th Street, Minneapolis MN 55407. **LC** RM930.A1; A53. **DD** 615/.5/08. ***Continues*** *Rehabilitation Publication, 0065-9983.*

BL
**RELATORIO ANUAL - ASSOCIACAO BRASILEIRA DA INDUSTRIA FARMACEUTICA. Main/Corp** Associacao Brasileira da Industria Farmaceutica. **VFOAT** Industria Farmaceutica Brasileira. 1977/78-. Periodical. Portuguese. Departamento de Comunicacoes, Av Beira Mar 262 70 Andar, 20021 Rio de Janeiro Brazil. ***Continues*** *Relatorio da Presidencia - Associacao Brasileira da Industria Farmaceutica.*

CN/1184-6968
**RENSEIGNEMENTS SUR LES MEDICAMENTS.** [Renseign. medicam.]. **Added/Corp** Nouveau-Brunswick. Plan de Medicaments sur Ordonnance. No 1 (Jan. 1991)-. French. **DD** 615.

IT
**REPERTORIO FARMACEUTICO ITALIANO : REFI. *Ceased.* VFOAT** REFI. (1986)-(1993). Periodical. Italian. an. Org Edit Medico Farmaceutica, CP 10434, 20110 Milan Italy. **Tel** 011 39 2 675051. **NLM** QV 738; GI8 R425.

NE
**REPERTORIUM (UTRECHT, NETHERLANDS).** (REPERTORIUM.). **Added/Corp** Nefarma. College ter Beoordeling van Geneesmiddelen (Netherlands). (1985/1986)-. Dutch. an. Fl84.50. SDU Uitgeverij, Postbus 20014, Christoffel Plan, 2500 EA Den Haag Netherlands. **Tel** 011 31 70 3789911. **NLM** QV 772; R424. ***Continues*** *Repertorium Farmaceutische Specialites, 0165-8301.*

US/0095-3164
**REPORT OF THE SOUTH DAKOTA STATE PHARMACEUTICAL ASSOCIATION AND THE SOUTH DAKOTA BOARD OF PHARMACY. Main/Corp** South Dakota Pharmaceutical Association. English. South Dakota Pharmaceutical Association, PO Box 518, Pierre SD 57501. **LC** RS5; .S88A. **DD** 615/.1/062783.

CN/0315-6311
**REPORT ON THE CANADIAN DRUG STORE MARKET, A. VFOAT** Canadian Drug Store Market. Began with 1963 issue?. Periodical. English. an. 125.00Can$. Maclean Hunter Canada / Montreal, 1001 bvd. de Maisonneuve W., Montreal, Quebec H3A 3E1 Canada. **Tel** 514-845-5141, FAX 514-845-4302, telex 055-60604. **DD** 381/.45/6154.

US/0034-5164
**RESEARCH COMMUNICATIONS IN CHEMICAL PATHOLOGY AND PHARMACOLOGY. *Title Change.*** [Res. commun. chem. pathol. pharmacol.]. **VFOAT** Chemical Pathology and Pharmacology. Vol. 1 (Jan. 1970)-(1994). Academic Scholarly Publication. English. mo. PJD Publications Ltd., PO Box 966, Westbury NY 11590. **Tel** (516)626-0650, FAX (516)626-5546. **LC** RM1; .R4. **DD** 615/.1/05. **NLM** W1 RE216K. **CODEN** RCOCB8. **[CCC]. Pr Rev.** Documents available from The Genuine Article, BIOSIS Document Express, CASDDS. ***Continued by*** *Research Communications in Molecular Pathology & Pharmacology.*
**Ind/Abst** Biol. Abstr.; Chem. Abstr.; Chem. Titles; Chicano Index; CSA Neuro. Abstr.; Curr. Aware. Biol. Sci., CABS; Curr. Contents Life Sci.; Dairy Sci. Abstr.; EMBASE; Energy Res. Abstr. (Feb. 1972-); Index Med.; NAPRALERT; Nutr. Abstr. Rev., Ser. A, Hum. Exp.; Life Sci. Collect.; PESTDOC; Pig News Inf.; Poult. Abstr.; Res. Alert [Full Cov.]; Rev. Med. Vet. Mycology; Sci. Cit. Index; SCISEARCH.

●US
**RESEARCH COMMUNICATIONS IN MOLECULAR PATHOLOGY & PHARMACOLOGY.** (1994)-. Periodical. English. Twelve times a year. $240.00 US; $280.00 other. PJD Publications Ltd., PO Box 966, Westbury NY 11590. **Tel** (516)626-0650, FAX (516)626-5546. ***Continues*** *Research Communcations in Chemical Pathology & Pharmacology, 0034-5164.*

US
**RESIDENCY DIRECTORY.** (1982)-. Directory. English. an. $25.00. American Society of Hospital Pharmacists, 7272 Wisconsin Avenue, Bethesda MD 20814. **Tel** (301)657-3000, (301)657-4383, FAX (301)652-8278. **NLM** QV 20; R433. Index available. **Circ:** 1,000. ***Continues*** *Directory of Pharmacy Residency Programs in Hospitals Accredited by the American Society of Hospital Pharmacists and Directory of Pharmacy Residency Programs Participating in the ASHP Resident Matching Program.*
**Desc:** The directory provides uniform information about each ASHP accredited pharmacy residency and identifies the institutions that are participating the ASHP Resident Matching Program.

GR
**REVIEW OF CLINICAL PHARMACOLOGY AND PHARMACOKINETICS.** English. sa. $40.00. Pharmakon Press, 20 Daskalaki Street, 11526 Athens Greece.
**Ind/Abst** EMBASE.

UK/0954-8602
**REVIEWS IN CONTEMPORARY PHARMACOTHERAPY.** Vol. 1, No. 1 (1990)-. Periodical. English. Four times a year (Mar., June, Sept., Dec.). £130.00 UK; $330.00 US; £180.00 other. Marius Press, Box 15, Carnforth, Lancs LA6 1HW England. **Tel** 011 44 0 524 733027, FAX 011 44 524 736659. **ED** S. Johnson and F. N. Johnson. **NLM** W1; RE252J. **Circ:** 1,000.
**Desc:** Each issue provides an up-to-date and critical survey of the published work in some important aspect of applied pharmacology. The purpose is to examine the current state of knowledge, to indicate where there are deficiencies in that knowledge, and then, whenever possible, to establish guidelines for safe and rational therapy and patient management.

GW/0303-4240
**REVIEWS OF PHYSIOLOGY, BIOCHEMISTRY AND PHARMACOLOGY.** See Biology-Physiology.

BL/0370-372X
**REVISTA BRASILEIRA DE FARMACIA.** [Rev. bras. farm.]. (1940)-. Academic Scholarly Publication. Portuguese (English and French). qt. $50.00. Associacao Brasiliera de Farmacia, Rua Andradas 96 10 Andar, 20051 Rio de Janeiro Brazil. **Tel** (021)263-0791. **ED** Joao Ciribelli Guimaraes. **NLM** W1 RE318. **CODEN** RBFAAH. **Ad Acc. Circ:** 2,000. Documents available from CASDDS. ***Continues*** *Revista da Associacao Brasileira de Farmaceuticos, 0370-3126.*
**Desc:** Scholarly articles for the pharmaceutical professional. Focuses on theory and administration of pharmaceuticals, medical diagnosis, chemistry and morphology of medicines. Each article is summarized and illustrated with photographs and charts, and accompanied with a bibliography.
**Ind/Abst** Chem. Abstr.; EMBASE; Int. Pharm. Abstr.

CK/0034-7418
**REVISTA COLOMBIANA DE CIENCIAS QUIMICO-FARMACEUTICAS.** See Chemistry.

CU/0034-7515
**REVISTA CUBANA DE FARMACIA.** [Rev. cub. farm.]. **Added/Corp** Centro Nacional de Informacion de Ciencias Medicas. Vol. 1 (April 30, 1967)-. Academic Scholarly Publication. Spanish (summaries and/or abstracts in English, French and Russian). ir. $38.30 North America; $35.74 South America; $40.85 other. Ediciones Cubanas, Obispo 527, Altos ESQ Bernaza, CP 10100 Havana Cuba. **Tel** 011 632980, 631942, FAX 011 631011, telex 512337, 6540. **NLM** W1 RE359Q. **CODEN** RCUFAC. **Circ:** 50,000 (ctrl). Documents available from CASDDS.
**Desc:** Contains articles on pharmacology and other related sciences in this field.
**Ind/Abst** Chem. Abstr.; EMBASE; Int. Pharm. Abstr.

BL/0101-3793
**REVISTA DE CIENCIAS FARMACEUTICAS.** [Rev. cienc. farm.]. **Added/Corp** Universidade Estadual Paulista. Faculdade de Ciencias Farmaceuticas. Vol. 2 (1979/80)-. Periodical. Portuguese (summaries and/or abstracts in English). an. $30.00. Fundacao Desenvolvimento Unesp, Av Rio Branco 1210, 01206 Sao Paulo SP Brazil. **Tel** 011 55 11 2237088. **CODEN** RCIFDN. Documents available from BIOSIS Document Express, CASDDS. ***Continues*** *Revista da Faculdade de Ciencias Farmaceuticas, 0101-370X.*
**Ind/Abst** Bibliogr. Mission.; Biol. Abstr.; Chem. Abstr.; EMBASE [Select. Cov.]; Int. Pharm. Abstr.

BL/0301-7052
**REVISTA DE FARMACIA E BIOQUIMICA BELO HORIZONTE.** (REVISTA DE FARMACIA E BIOQUIMICA.). [Rev. farm. bioquim. Belo Horizonte]. **VFOAT** Revista de Farmacia e Bioquimica da UFMG. (1969)-. Periodical. Multiple languages. sa. **UDC** 61. Documents available from CASDDS.
**Ind/Abst** Chem. Abstr.; Int. Pharm. Abstr.; Trop. Dis. Bull.

BL/0370-4726
**REVISTA DE FARMACIA E BIOQUIMICA DA UNIVERSIDADE DE SAO PAULO.** [Rev. farm. bioquim. Univ. Sao Paulo]. **Main/Corp** Universidade de Sao Paulo. Faculdade de Ciencias Farmaceuticas. (19??)-. Academic Scholarly Publication. Portuguese (summaries and/or abstracts in English). sa. Free. Faculdade de Ciencias Farmaceuticas, Caixa Postal 30786, Sao Paula Brazil. **Tel** 210-2122, FAX 8155579. **LC** RS1; .S27. **DD** 615/.1/05. **NLM** W1 RE396F. **CODEN** RFBUBI. **Bk Rev.** ctrl circ. Documents available from BLDSC, UMI Article Clearinghouse, BIOSIS Document Express, CASDDS. ***Continues*** *Sao Paulo, Brazil (City). Universidade. Faculdade de Farmacia e Bioquimica. Revista, (OCoLC)11930372.*
**Desc:** Has an editorial board constituted of teachers of the Faculdade de Ciencias Farmaceuticas and other universities and specialists.
**Ind/Abst** AGRICOLA; Anal. Abstr.; Biol. Abstr.; Chem. Abstr.; EMBASE; Food Sci. Technol. Abstr.; Index Med.; Index Vet.; Int. Pharm. Abstr.; Nutr. Abstr. Rev., Ser. B, Live Feeds and Feed.; Nutr. Abstr. Rev., Ser. A, Hum. Exp.; PESTDOC; Protozoolog. Abstr.; Wheat Barley Trit. Abstr.

SP
**REVISTA DE FARMACOLOGIA CLINICA Y EXPERIMENTAL.** ***Ceased.*** Vol. 1, No. 1 (Oct. 1984)-Ceased (Jan. 1991). Periodical. English (Spanish). qt. Prous Science Publishers, Apartado de Correos 540, 08080 Barcelona Spain. **Tel** 011 34 3 4592220, FAX 011 34 3 4581535. **ED** A Badia, J Gonzalez Macias, and J L Tamargo. **NLM** W1; RE397H. Index available. **Ad Acc. Pr Rev.** Documents available from CASDDS.
**Ind/Abst** Chem. Abstr.; Indice Med. Esp.

SP/0210-6329
**REVISTA DE LA ASOCIACION ESPANOLA DE FARMACEUTICOS DE HOSPITALES.** **VFOAT** Revista AEFH; Revista A.E.F.H. Vol. 1 (1977)-. Periodical. Spanish. qt. Sociedad Espanola de Farmacia Hospitalaria, Calle Echegaray 13, 3, 28014 Madrid Spain. **Tel** 011 34 1 4296354. **NLM** W1; RE406GK. **CODEN** RAEHDT.
**Ind/Abst** Indice Med. Esp.

VE/0041-8307
**REVISTA DE LA FACULTAD DE FARMACIA.** **Main/Corp** Venezuela. Universidad Central, Caracas. Facultad de Farmacia. No. 1 (1959)-. Periodical. Spanish. ir. Revista de la Facultad de Farmacia, Universidad de Los Andes, Merida, Venezuela. **ED** Jose A. Reinosa Fuller, Leo M. Hernandez. **NLM** W1 RE408T. **CODEN** RFFVA6. Documents available from CASDDS.
**Ind/Abst** Chem. Abstr. (1959-1980); Int. Pharm. Abstr.; Protozoolog. Abstr.

SP/0375-9709
**REVISTA DE LA REAL ACADEMIA DE FARMACIA DE BARCELONA.** [Rev. R. Acad. Farm. Barc.]. **Added/Corp** Academia de Farmacia. Barcelona. **VFOAT** aPublicaciones de la Real Academia de Farmacia. Revista de la Real Academia de Farmacia. (1957)-. Periodical. Spanish. sa. **UDC** 615.
**Ind/Abst** Int. Pharm. Abstr.

BL/0370-6907
**REVISTA DE QUIMICA E FARMACIA RIO DE JANEIRO.** [Rev. Quim. Farm.Rio de J.]. (1935)-. Portuguese. mo. **CODEN** RQFAAK.
**Ind/Abst** Int. Pharm. Abstr.

BL
**REVISTA DO INSTITUTO DE ANTIBIOTICOS.** **Main/Corp** Pernambuco, Brazil (State). Universidade Federal. Instituto de Antibioticos. Vol. 6 (Dec. 1966)-. Periodical. Portuguese. sa. Cedade Universetaria Engenho de Meio, Recife Periambuco Brazil. **NLM** W1 RE521D. Documents available from BIOSIS Document Express. ***Continues*** *Recife, Brazil. Universidade. Instituto de Antibioticos. Revista do Instituto de Antibioticos.*
**Ind/Abst** Biol. Abstr. (?-1971).

SP
**REVISTA EL MONITOR DE LA FARMACIA.** Spanish. mo. 1000.00ptas. Asociacion Centros Farmaceutco de Espana, Sa General Oraa 70, Madrid 6 Spain.

PR/1070-5015
**REVISTA FARMACEUTICA (SAN JUAN, P.R.).** (REVISTA FARMACEUTICA : ORGANO OFICIAL DEL COLEGIO DE FARMACEUTICOS DE PUERTO RICO.). [Rev. farm.]. **Added/Corp** Colegio de Farmaceuticos de Puerto Rico. **VFOAT** Revista Farmaceutica de Puerto Rico. (19??)-. Periodical. Spanish. qt. $15.00. Colegio de Farmaceuticos, GPO Box 360206, San Juan PR 00936. **Tel** (809)759-9794, FAX (809)759-9793. **ED** Pedro Vonga. **DD** 615. **Ad Acc, Adv Mgr:** Janet James, **Tel** (809)759-9794. **Circ:** 3,000 (ctrl). ***Continues*** *Revista Farmaceutica de Puerto Rico.*

RM/0034-995X
**REVISTA MEDICALA (TIRGU-MURES).** (REVISTA MEDICALA.). [Rev. med.]. **Added/Corp** Institutul Medico-Farmaceutic. (1955)-. Periodical. Romanian. Twice a year. DM170.00. **(Subscription address:** Kubon & Sagner, ABT Zeitschriftenimport, D 80328 Munich Germany.**)** **NLM** W1 RE65. **CODEN** REMTAS. Documents available from CASDDS.
**Ind/Abst** Chem. Abstr.

PO/0484-811X
**REVISTA PORTUGUESA DE FARMACIA.** [Rev. port. farm.]. (1951)-. Periodical. Multiple languages. qt. Ordem dos Farmaceuticos, Rua da Sociedado Farmaceutica 18, 1199 Lisbon Portugal. **UDC** 615(469). Documents available from CASDDS. ***Continues*** *Jornal dos Farmaceuticos, 0368-2129.*
**Ind/Abst** Chem. Abstr.; EMBASE [Select. Cov.]; Food Sci. Technol. Abstr.; Int. Pharm. Abstr.; Sug. Indus. Abstr.

FR
**REVUE D'HISTOIRE DE LA PHARMACIE.** **Added/Corp** Societe d'Histoire de la Pharmacie. (Feb. 1930)-. Periodical. French. qt. 400.00F. Dawson France SA, BP 40, 91121 Palaiseau Cedex France. **Tel** 011 33 1 69104700, telex 220064F. ***Continues*** *Bulletin de la Societe d'Histoire de la Pharmacie.*
**Ind/Abst** Int. Pharm. Abstr.

CN/0821-5987
**REVUE PHARMACOCINETIQUE.** (REVUE PHARMACOCINETIQUE PHARMACOKINETIC REVIEW / PREPARE PAR SERVICE DE PHARMACOCINETIQUE.). [Rev. pharmacocinet.]. **VFOAT** Pharmacokinetic Review. Periodical. English. ir. Free. Pharmacokinetic Information Centre, Ottawa General Hospital, 501 Smyth Road, Ottawa Ontario K1H 8L6 Canada. **DD** 615/.7/05.

UK
**RINGDOC.** See Pharmacy and Pharmacology-Abstracting, Bibliographies and Statistics.

JA/0388-1601
**RINSHO YAKURI.** [Rinsho yakuri]. **Added/Corp** Nihon Rinsho Yakuri Gakkai. **VFOAT** Japanese Journal of Clinical Pharmacology and Therapeutics. (1970)-. Periodical. Japanese. Four times a year. $72.00. Japanese Society of Clinical Pharmacology, 3-10 Kanda-Surugadai 2-Chome, Chiyoda-ku 101 Tokyo Japan. **(Subscription address:** Kyowa Book Company Inc., 1 38 Kanda Jinbocho Chiyoda-ku, Tokyo 101 Japan.**)** **CODEN** RIYADS. Documents available from CASDDS.
**Ind/Abst** Chem. Abstr.; EMBASE.

IT/0392-291X
**RIVISTA EUROPEA PER LE SCIENZE MEDICHE E FARMACOLOGICHE.** [Riv. eur. sci. med. farmacol.]. **VFOAT** European Review for Medical and Pharmacological Sciences. Vol. 1, No. 1 (Dec. 1979)-. Academic Scholarly Publication. Italian (summaries and/or abstracts in English and French). Six times a year. L60000 Italy; L120000 other. Verduci Editore, Via Gregorio VII 186, 00165 Rome Italy. **Tel** 011 39 6 39375224. **NLM** W1 RI661P. **CODEN** RESFDJ. Documents available from BIOSIS Document Express, CASDDS.
**Ind/Abst** Biol. Abstr.; Chem. Abstr. (-1984); EMBASE; Index Med.

US
**ROCHE HANDBOOK OF DIFFERENTIAL DIAGNOSIS.** **Added/Corp** Hoffmann LaRoche, Inc. (196?)-. English. ir. Free on request. Roche Laboratories, 340 Kingsland Street, Nutley NJ 07110. **Tel** (201)235-2478.

US
**ROSTER OF TEACHING PERSONNEL IN COLLEGES OF PHARMACY.** **Main/Corp** American Association of Colleges of Pharmacy. **VFOAT** Teaching Personnel in Colleges of Pharmacy. (19??)-. English. ir. $100.00. American Association of Colleges of Pharmacy, 1426 Prince Street, Alexandria VA 22314-2815. **Tel** (703)739-2330.

GW
**ROTE LISTE.** (1935)-. German. an. DM102.50. Editio Cantor, Postfach 1255, D 88322 Aulendorf Germany. **Tel** 011 49 7525 9400, FAX 011 49 7525 9401. ***Continues*** *Preisverzeichnis Deutscher Pharmazeutischer Spezial Praeparate.*
**Desc:** List of pharmaceutical products by the members of Bundesverband der Pharmazeutischen Industrie e.v.

UK/0036-0325
**RUSSIAN PHARMACOLOGY AND TOXICOLOGY.** (RUSSIAN PHARMACOLOGY AND TOXICOLOGY INCORPORATING NEW DRUG SCREENING REPORTS.). [Russ. pharmacol. toxicol.]. Vol. 42, No. 1 (1979)-. Academic Scholarly Publication. English. bm. $325.00, (add $25.00 for airmail postage). Euromed Publications, 33 Woodlands Road, Surbiton Surrey KT6 6PR England. **Tel** 011 44 399 3839. **NLM** W1 RU828F. ***Continues*** *Russian Pharmacology and Toxicology Incorporating Chemico--Pharmaceutical Journal and New Drugs in the USSR, 0036-0325.*
**Ind/Abst** EMBASE.

US/0886-9766
**RX BEING WELL.** [Rx being well]. Periodical. English. bm. Biomedical Information Corporation, 800 Second Avenue, New York NY 10017. **Tel** (212)262-9662. **DD** 616. ***Continues*** *Your Doctor's RX Being Well Well, 0746-6005.*

US/1066-7741
**RX CONSULTANT, THE.** [Rx consult.]. (1991)-. Periodical. English. mo (except Aug.). $69.00. Rx Consultant, PO Box 1516, Martinez CA 94553. **Tel** (510)229-3353. **ED** Terry Baker. **DD** 615. Index available (published separately). **Pr Rev.**

US/0744-7736
**RX ET CETERA.** (RX ET CETERA : NEWSLETTER OF THE WASHINGTON STATE PHARMACEUTICAL ASSOCIATION.). Newsletter. English. mo. $150.00 (with membership only). Washington State Pharmacist Association, 1420 Maple Avenue S W/Suite 101, Renton WA 98055. **ED** Sheri Ray and Ray Olson. **Ad Acc.** ctrl circ. available on microfilm and microfiche from University Microfilms International (UMI).

US/1056-4985
**RX REPORT.** [Rx rep.]. Vol. 1.1 (July 1991)-. Periodical. English. mo. $72.00. Rx Report, PO Box 471, Danville PA 17821. **DD** 615. **NLM** W1; RX99DK.

FR/1157-1497
**S.T.P. PHARMA PRATIQUES : TECHNIQUES REGLEMENTATIONS.** **Added/Corp** Societe Francaise des Sciences et Techniques Pharmaceutiques. **VFOAT** STP Pharma Pratiques. Vol. 1, No. 1 (Jan./Feb. 1991)-. Periodical. French (English). Six times a year. 974.53F France; 1020.00F other. Editions de Sante, 5 rue Las Cases, 75007 Paris, France. **Tel** 011 33 1 45519494. **NLM** W1; ST6973. **CODEN** SPPRER. ***Continues in part*** *S.T.P. Pharma, 0758-8703.*
**Ind/Abst** EMBASE; Int. Pharm. Abstr.; PESTDOC.

FR
**S.T.P. PHARMA SCIENCES.** **Added/Corp** Societe Francaise des Sciences et Techniques Pharmaceutiques. Association de Pharmacie Galenique Industrielle. **VFOAT** STP Pharma Sciences. Vol. 1, No. 1 (Jan.-Feb. 1991)-. Academic Scholarly Publication. English (summaries and/or abstracts in French). Six times a year. 979.43F France; 1050.00F other. Editions de Sante, 5 rue Las Cases, 75007 Paris, France. **Tel** 011 33 1 45519494. **NLM** W1; ST698. **CODEN** STSSE5. Documents available from CASDDS. ***Continues in part*** *S.T.P. Pharma, 0758-8703.*
**Ind/Abst** Chem. Abstr.; EMBASE; Int. Pharm. Abstr.; PESTDOC.

US/0273-0820
**SAFE, EFFECTIVE AND THERAPEUTICALLY EQUIVALENT PRESCRIPTION DRUGS.** **Main/Corp** New York (State). Office of Health Systems Management. **VFOAT** Therapeutically Equivalent Prescription Drugs. 1977-. English. an. $3.00. Health Education Service, PO Box 7126, Albany NY 12224. **Tel** (518)439-7286. cum. index. ***Continues*** *Safe, Effective, and Interchangeable Prescription Drugs.*
**Desc:** Publication lists drug products certified or approved by the Commissioner of the FDA. Cross-referenced and indexed listing contains generic and brand drugs, with strengths, dosage forms and approved manufacturers.

AG/0558-1265
**SAFYBI.** [SAFYBI]. (1959)-. Periodical. Spanish. tq. **UDC** 615. **CODEN** SAFYA. Documents available from CASDDS.
**Ind/Abst** Chem. Abstr.; Int. Pharm. Abstr.

KO/0253-3073
**SAINNYAG HAGHOI JI (SENUR).** (SAENGYAK HAKHOE CHI.). [Sainnyag haghoi ji]. **Added/Corp** Hanguk Saengyak Hakhoe. **VFOAT** Korean Journal of Pharmacognosy. (19??)-. Academic Scholarly Publication. Korean (summaries and/or abstracts in English). qt. $30.00 Korea; $40.00 other. Hanguk Saengyak Hakhoe, 28 Yungun-dong Jongro-gu, Natural Products Research Institute, Seoul National University, Seoul 110-460 Korea. **Tel** (02)745-6701, FAX 742-9951. **ED** Kuk Hyun Shin. **LC** RS160; .S23. **DD** 615/.321/09519. **CODEN** SYHJAM. Index available. cum. index. **Ad Acc. Circ:** 600 (ctrl). Documents available from CASDDS.
**Desc:** Original research reports on review on botanical drugs and natural products: chemistry, pharmacology, toxicology, mechanism of action, botany, taxonomy, and Oriental drug preparations.
**Ind/Abst** Chem. Abstr.; EMBASE [Select. Cov.].

US/1060-5703
**SANKOFA JOURNAL : THE AUTHENTIC VOICE OF THE TRADITIONAL HEALERS OF AFRICA.** [Sankofa j.]. **Added/Corp** International Organisation of Traditional & Medical Practitioners & Researchers. Vol. 1, No. 1 (Summer 1991)-. Periodical. English. qt. $20.00 US; $25.00 Canada. Sanfoka Journal (IOTMPR), PO Box 27555, San Francisco CA 94127. **DD** 615.

CN
**SARNIA PHARMACY BULLETIN.** Bulletin. English. 18.00Can$. Sarnia Pharmacy Ltd., 206 Maxwell Street, Sarnia Ontario N7T 5C4 Canada. **Tel** (519)337-3215.

GW/0721-1457
**SCHRIFTENREIHE DER BUNDESAPOTHEKERKAMMER ZUR WISSENSCHAFTLICHEN FORTBILDUNG. GRUNE REIHE.** [Schriftenr. Bundesapothekekerkammer Wiss. Fortbild., Grune Reihe]. V. 1-. Academic Scholarly Publication. German. Price varies per volume. **NLM** W1; SC329AF. **CODEN** SBWGDW. Documents available from CASDDS.
**Ind/Abst** Chem. Abstr.

SZ/0036-7508
**SCHWEIZERISCHE APOTHEKER-ZEITUNG. GIORNALE SVIZZERO DI FARMACIA.** **Added/Corp** Schweizerischer Apotheker-Verein. Verein Schweizerischer Analytischer Chemiker. **VFOAT** Journal Suisse de Pharmacie; Giornale Svizzero di Farmacia. Vol. 1 (1863)-. Academic Scholarly Publication. Multiple languages (German, French and Italian). Twenty-five times a year. 160.00F Switzerland; 175.00F other. Schweizerisch Apothekerverein, Stationsstrasse 12, CH-3097 Bern Liebe Switzerland. **Tel** 011 41 31 9715858. **Bk Rev. Ad Acc. Circ:** 4,800. Documents available from CASDDS. ***Continues*** *Schweizerische Zeitschrift fuer Pharmacie.*
**Ind/Abst** Chem. Abstr.; EMBASE [Select. Cov.]; Int. Pharm. Abstr.; PESTDOC.

AU/0036-8709
**SCIENTIA PHARMACEUTICA.** (SCIENTIA PHARMACEUTICA / OSTERREICHISCHE APOTHEKERSCHAFT.). [Sci. pharm.]. **Added/Corp** Osterreichische Apothekerschaft. (1930)-. Academic Scholarly Publication. German. Four times a year. S359.00. Oesterr Apotheker Verlags GES, Spitalgasse 31, A-1094 Vienna Austria. **Tel** 011 43 1 4023588. **ED** H. Bartsch and J. Jurenitsch. **NLM** W1 SC819. **CODEN** SCPHA4. **Bk Rev. Ad Acc. Circ:** 600 (ctrl). Documents available from CASDDS.
**Desc:** Research in pharmacy, pharmaceutical chemistry, pharmaceutical technology, pharmaceutical biology, pharmaceutical analysis, analytical chemistry and pharmaceutical botany.
**Ind/Abst** AGRICOLA; Anal. Abstr.; Chem. Abstr.; EMBASE; Int. Pharm. Abstr.; Methods Organ. Synth.; Nat. Prod. Updates; PESTDOC.

UK
**SCRIP MAGAZINE.** (19??)-. English. £90.00 UK & Europe; £125.00 N. Africa/Mid East; ¥36,500 Japan; $235.00 US & Canada; £125.00 other. PJB Publications, 18-20 Hill Rise, Richmond Surrey TW10 6UA England. **Tel** 011 44 81 948 3262.

UK/0143-7690
**SCRIP (RICHMOND).** (SCRIP.). [Scrip]. (1972)-. Periodical. English. sw. £440.00 UK; £505.00 Europe; £505.00 N.Africa/Mid East; $980.00 US & Canada; ¥177,000 Japan; £550.00 other. PJB Publications, 18-20 Hill Rise, Richmond Surrey TW10 6UA England. **Tel** 011 44 81 948 3262. **ED** Philip J. Brown. **CODEN** SCRIDK. **[CCC]. Bk Rev. Ad Acc. Circ:** 60,000 (ctrl). Documents available from UMI Article Clearinghouse.
**Desc:** World's leading international news journal on the ethical pharmaceutical market. Products, finance, world markets and people reported by scientific staff to keep decision makers well informed.
**Ind/Abst** AGRICOLA [Select. Cov.]; Chem. Ind. Notes (-1987); Curr. Biotechnol.; Pharm. News Index (Dec. 1979-); Trade Ind. Index; Trop. Dis. Bull.

US/0895-7479
**SECOND MESSENGER AND PHOSPHOPROTEINS.** **See** Biology-Physiology.

FI/0049-0164
**SEMINA.** [Semina]. **VFOAT** Semina. (1917)-. Periodical. Finnish (summaries and/or abstracts in Swedish). sm. Suomen Farmasialiitto, (Finnish Pharmacists' Association), Rautatielaisenkatu 6,, 00520 Helsinki 52, Finland. **Tel** FAX 011 358 0 1496354. **UDC** 615.

KO/0250-3336
**SENUR DAIHAGGYO NYAGHAG KOMMUNJIB.** (SOUL TAEHAKKYO YAKHAK NONMUNJIP.). [Senur Daihaggyo Nyaghag Konmunjib]. **Main/Corp** Soul Taehakkyo. Yakhak Taehak. **VFOAT** Seoul University Journal of Pharmaceutical Sciences; Yakhak Nonmunjip. Vol. 1- No.; 1976-. Academic Scholarly Publication. English (Korean). Seoul National University / South Korea, Sinlim Dong, Kwanack Ku Seoul 151 South Korea. **Tel** 011 82 2 7408358. **LC** RM1; .S66A. **CODEN** STYNDJ. Documents available from BIOSIS Document Express, CASDDS.
**Ind/Abst** Biol. Abstr.; Chem. Abstr.

IT
**SERINFAR : A REGISTRAZIONE E PRODUZIONE SPECIALITA MEDICINALI.** (19??)-. Italian. ir. L1300000. IDMA SRL, Via Gradisca 8, 20151 Milan Italy. **Tel** 39 2 3087137.

IT
**SERINFAR : B, PRESIDI MEDICO CHIRURGICI REGISTRAZIONE PRODUZIONE PUBBLICITA.** IDMA Divisione Serinfar, Via G Frua 11, 20146 Milan Italy.

IT
**SERINFAR DIETETICI : AUTORIZZAZIONE PRODUZIONE PUBBLICITA.** IDMA SRL, Via Gradisca 8, 20151 Milan Italy. **Tel** 39 2 3087137.

SP/0515-1147
**SESION INAUGURAL - REAL ACADEMIA DE FARMACIA DE BARCELONA.** (REAL ACADEMIA DE FARMACIA DE BARCELONA. SESION INAUGURAL DEL CURSO.). [Ses. inaug. - R. Acad. Farm. Barc.]. **VFOAT** Publicaciones de la Real Academia de Farmacia. A: Anuarios, Memorias y Discursos Inaugurales de Curso; Real Academia de Farmacia de Barcelona. A: Sesion Inaugural. 1979-. Periodical. Spanish. an. Anales de la Real Academia, Arrieta 12, 28013 Madrid Spain. **Tel** 011 34 1 2470318. **NLM** W1 RE105FI. ***Continues*** *Real Academia de Farmacia de Barcelona. Sesion Inaugural, 0515-1147.*

CC/1000-1727
**SHENYANG YAOXUEYUAN XUEBAO.** (SHEN-YANG YAO HSUEH YUAN HSUEH PAO.). [Shenyang yaoxueyuan xuebao]. **Added/Corp** Shen-yang yao Hsueh Yuan. **VFOAT** Journal of Shenyang College of Pharmacy. (1984)-. Academic Scholarly Publication. English. qt. **CODEN** SYXUE3. Documents available from CASDDS.
**Ind/Abst** Chem. Abstr.; NAPRALERT; Nutr. Abstr. Rev., Ser. A, Hum. Exp.

JA/0288-1012
**SHIKA YAKUBUTSU RYOHO.** [Shika yakubutsu ryoho]. **VFOAT** Oral Therapeutics and Pharmacology. (1982)-. Academic Scholarly Publication. Multiple languages. Three times a year. $120.50. Japanese Society of Oral Therapeutics and Pharmacology, 4-16 Yayoi 2-chome, Bunkyo-ku 113 Tokyo Japan. **(Subscription address:** Japan Publications Trading Company, Ltd., PO Box 5030, Tokyo International, Tokyo 100-31 Japan.**)** **DD** 617.6. Documents available from CASDDS.
**Ind/Abst** Chem. Abstr.; EMBASE.

JA/0388-7588
**SHINKEI SEISHIN YAKURI.** **See** Medical Science and Technology-Neurology.

JA/0037-4377
**SHOYAKUGAKU ZASSHI.** [Shoyakugaku zasshi]. **Added/Corp** Nihon Shoyaku Gakkai. **VFOAT** Syoyakugaku Zasshi; Japanese Journal of Pharmacognosy. (1947)-. Academic Scholarly Publication. Japanese (summaries and/or abstracts in English). Four times a year. $168.00. Nihon Shoyaku Gakkai, (Japanese Soc. of Pharmacognosy), Nihon Gakkai Jimu Senta, 4-16, Yayoi 2 Chome, Bunkyoku, Tokyoto 113, Japan. **(Subscription address:** Kyowa Book Company Inc., 1-38 Kanda Jinbo-Cho, Chiyoda-Ku, Tokyo 101, Japan**)** **CODEN** SHZAAY. Documents available from CASDDS. ***Continues*** *Yakuyo Shokubutsu to Skoyaku.*
**Ind/Abst** BioBusiness; Chem. Abstr.; EMBASE; Helminthol. Abstr. (1991-); NAPRALERT; Plant Breed. Abstr.

NE/0378-6080
**SIDE EFFECTS OF DRUGS ANNUAL.** [Side eff. drugs annu.]. **Added/Corp** Excerpta Medica Foundation. (1977)-. Academic Scholarly Publication. English. an. $200.00. Elsevier Science Publishers BV, PO Box 211, 1000 AE Amsterdam Netherlands. **Tel** 011 31 20 5803642, FAX 011 31 20 5862696, telex 15682. **(Subscription address:** Elsevier Science Inc. / New York Books, 655 Avenue of the Americas, New York NY 10010.**)** **LC** RM302.5; .S53. **DD** 615/.7/042. **NLM** W1 SI255B. **CODEN** SEDAD8. **[CCC].** available on an online database (file 70/Full-Text) from DIALOG. Documents available from BIOSIS Document Express, CASDDS.
**Ind/Abst** Biol. Abstr.; Chem. Abstr. (1977-1979).

US/0891-5180
**SOCIAL PHARMACOLOGY.** [Soc. pharmacol.]. Vol. 1, No. 1 (1987)-. Periodical. English. qt. $65.00 (indidividuals), $115.00 (institutions) US; $75.00 (individuals), $125.00 (institutions) other. Decisions Issues Alternatives / Atlanta, 864 Somerset Drive Northwest, Atlanta GA 30327. **DD** 615. **NLM** W1; SO121H.

KO
**SOUL YAKSAHOE CHI / JOURNAL OF THE SEOUL PHARMACEUTICAL ASSOCIATION.** **Added/Corp** Soul Tukpyolsi Yaksahoe. **VFOAT** Journal of the Seoul Pharmaceutical Association. (19??)-. Periodical. Korean (Korean). qt. Soul Tukpyolsi Yaksahoe, 549 Pangbae 2-dong Kangnam-ku, Seoul Korea. **LC** RS1; .S768.

US/0192-5792
**SOUTHERN PHARMACY JOURNAL.** Vol. 71, No. 3 (Jan. 1979)-. Periodical. English. Ten times a year. $18.00. Southern Pharmacy, 333 West Hampden Avenue, Suite 1050, Englewood CO 80110. **Tel** (303)761-8818. **ED** Max Ginsberg. **NLM** W1 SO957P. **Circ:** 18,000 (ctrl). ***Continues*** *Southeastern*

*Drug/Southern Pharmaceutical Journal, 0193-9971.*
**Desc:** A business and professional magazine covering news and events of and about pharmacy in the Southeast and Southwest. Publishes ACPE-approved continuing education programs.
**Ind/Abst** Int. Pharm. Abstr. (199?-).

SZ/0896-8306
**SOVIET MEDICAL REVIEWS. SECTION G, NEUROPHARMACOLOGY REVIEWS.** ***Ceased.*** [Sov. med. rev., G Neuropharmacol. rev.]. **Added/Corp** Soviet Medical Reviews (Firm : Chur, Switzerland). **VFOAT** Neuropharmacology Reviews; Neuropharmacology; Soviet Medical Reviews. Neuropharmacology. Vol. 1 (1990)-(1993). English. an. Harwood Academic Publishers, PO Box 90, Reading RG1 8JL England. **Tel** 011 44 734 560080. **(Subscription address:** International Publishers Distributor at one of the following addresses: 820 Town Center Drive, Langhorne, PA 19047; or PO Box 90, Reading Berkshire RG1 8JL UK; or Kent Ridge PO Box 1180, Singapore 9111, Republic of Singapore**)** **LC** RM315; .S637. **DD** 615/.78/05. **NLM** W1; SO996LAH. **CODEN** SMGRET. **[CCC].**

AT/1032-6898
**STANDARD FOR THE UNIFORM SCHEDULING OF DRUGS AND POISONS.** [Stand. unif. sched. drugs poisons]. **Added/Corp** Australia. Dept. of Health. (1986)-. Government Publication. English. Five times a year. 50.00Aus$. Australian Government Publishing Service, GPO Box 84, Canberra ACT 2601 Australia. **Tel** 011 61 6 2954411, FAX 011 61 6 2954455. **DD** 615.105.

CN/1187-3787
**STRAIGHT FACTS ON PHARMACEUTICAL PRICES, MANUFACTURING AND RESEARCH, THE.** [Straight facts pharm. prices manuf. res.]. **Added/Corp** Canadian Drug Manufacturers' Association. **VFOAT** Straight Facts. No. 1 (Apr. 1, 1991)-. Periodical. English. mo. Limited free distribution. Canadian Drug Manufacturers' Association, Suite 604, 1120 Finch Avenue West, Downsview Ontario M3J 3H7 Canada. **DD** 338.4.

US
**STREET PHARMACOLOGIST NEWSLETTER.** Newsletter. English. Up Front Drug Information, 5701 Biscayne Boulevard/Suite 602, Miami FL 33137. **Tel** (305)757-2566.

GW/0721-8672
**STUDENT UND PRAKTIKANT.** [Stud. Prakt.]. (1982)-. Periodical. German. qt. Deutscher Apotheker Verlag, Postfach 101061, D 70009 Stuttgart Germany. **Tel** 011 49 711 25820, INLAND:0711/2582, FAX 011 49 711 2582 290, telex 723636 daz d. **ED** Reinhild Berger. **UDC** 615.15:378.14.

FR/0256-4378
**SUBSTANCES ET SPECIALITES PHARMACEUTIQUES CLASSEES COMME STUPEFIANTS EN VENTE DANS 16 PAYS EUROPEENS. VFOAT** Proprietary and other Pharmaceuticals Classified as Narcotic Substances and on Sale in 16 European Countries. French (English). Pour l'Education en Europe, Conseil de l'Europe, Strasbourg France. **LC** RM328; .S8.

SA/0038-2558
**SUID-AFRIKAANSE TYDSKRIF VIR APTEEKWESE.** (SOUTH AFRICAN PHARMACEUTICAL JOURNAL.). [S. Afr. tydskr. apteekwese]. **Added/Corp** Pharmaceutical Society of South Africa. **VFOAT** S.A. Pharmaceutical Journal; Suid-Afrikaanse Tydskrif vir Apteekwese. Vol. 1 (1934)-. Periodical. English (Afrikaans). mo. R86.00. Pharmaceutical Society of South Africa, PO Box 31360, Braamfontein 2017 South Africa. **Tel** 011 27 11 3391752, FAX 011 27 11 4031309. **ED** Hayley Cameron. **NLM** W1 SO908E. Index available. cum. index. **Bk Rev. Ad Acc, Adv Mgr:** Felicity Wilson. **Circ:** 5,931 (ctrl). ***Absorbed*** *African Chemist and Druggist.*
**Desc:** News and views on all sectors of pharmacy; industrial, retail, hospital and academic including drug and product news and clinical features.
**Ind/Abst** PESTDOC.

FI/0355-533X
**SUOMEN APTEEKKARILEHTI.** [Suom. apteekkaril.]. **VFOAT** Finlands Apotekartidning. (1956)-. Periodical. Multiple languages. sm. **UDC** 615. ***Continues*** *Suomen Apteekkariyhdistyksen Aikakauslehti, 0786-499X.*
**Ind/Abst** Int. Pharm. Abstr.

CN/0832-8692
**SURVEY OF DRUG STORE TRENDS, A.** ***Title Change.*** [Surv. drug store trends]. **Added/Corp** Maclean-Hunter Research Bureau. (1985)-(199?). English. an. Maclean Hunter Canada / Montreal, 1001 bvd. de Maisonneuve W., Montreal, Quebec H3A 3E1 Canada. **Tel** 514-845-5141, FAX 514-845-4302, telex 055-60604. **DD** 381/.456151/0971. ***Continues*** *A Survey on Prescriptions, 0316-9901.* ***Continued by*** *Annual Survey of Prescription and Over-the-Counter Drugs, 1196-5290.*

US/0098-714X
**SURVEY OF PHARMACY LAW. See** Law.

SW/0039-6524
**SVENSK FARMACEUTISK TIDSKRIFT.** [Sven. farm. tidskr.]. **VFOAT** Farmaceutisk Tidskrift. (1897)-. Academic Scholarly Publication. Swedish (Danish and Norwegian). Eleven times a year. Kr320.00 Scandinavia; Kr420.00 other. Swedish Pharmaceutical Press, PO Box 1136, S 111 81 Stockholm Sweden. **Tel** 011 46 8 345080, FAX 011 46 8 149580. **NLM** W1 SV253. **CODEN** SFTIAE. Index available. **Bk Rev. Ad Acc. Circ:** 8,700 (ctrl). Documents available from CASDDS.
**Ind/Abst** Chem. Abstr.; EMBASE; Int. Pharm. Abstr.; PESTDOC.

SZ/0251-1673
**SWISS PHARMA.** [Swiss pharma]. (19??)-. Academic Scholarly Publication. German (English). Ten times a year (Jan/Feb. & July,/Aug. issued combined). 100.00F Switzerland; 120.00F Europe; 160.00F other. Verlag Dr Felix Wuest AG, Seestrasse 5/Postfach, CH-8700 Kuesnacht Switzerland. **Tel** 011 41 1 9110055, FAX (01)9106080, telex 825705. **NLM** W1 SW406P. Index available. ctrl circ.
**Ind/Abst** EMBASE; Int. Pharm. Abstr.

US/0733-9321
**SYMPOSIA ON FRONTIERS OF PHARMACOLOGY.** [Symp. front. pharmacol.]. Vol. 1-. Academic Scholarly Publication. English. Price varies per volume. **DD** 615/.1. **NLM** W3 SY107. **CODEN** SFPHDS. Documents available from CASDDS.
**Ind/Abst** Chem. Abstr.

BE/0770-1772
**TARIF DES SPECIALITES PHARMACEUTIQUES.** [Tarif spec. pharm.]. **VFOAT** Tarief der Pharmaceutische Specialiteiten. Periodical. Multiple languages (Dutch and French). an (with monthly supplements). 6901F Belgium; 7460F other. Algemene Pharmaceutische Bond - Association Pharmaceutique Belge, Archimedestraat 11 rue Archimede, 1040 Brussels Belgium. **Tel** 011 32 2 2302685. **NLM** W1 TA605. **Ad Acc.** available in microform.

US/0736-0681
**TECHNICAL INFORMATION BULLETIN - PARENTERAL DRUG ASSOCIATION.** (TECHNICAL INFORMATION BULLETIN.). [Tech. inf. bull. - Parenter. Drug. Assoc.]. **Added/Corp** Parenteral Drug Association. (19??)-. Bulletin. English. Parenteral Drug Association, 7500 Old Georgetown Road, Suite 620, Bethesda MD 20814. **Tel** (301)986-0293.
**Ind/Abst** Int. Pharm. Abstr.

US/0271-325X
**TECHNICAL METHODS BULLETIN - PARENTERAL DRUG ASSOCIATION.** (TECHNICAL METHODS BULLETIN.). [Tech. methods bull. - Parenter. Drug Assoc.]. **Added/Corp** Parenteral Drug Association. No. 1 (1980)-. Bulletin. English. Parenteral Drug Association, 7500 Old Georgetown Road, Suite 620, Bethesda MD 20814. **Tel** (301)986-0293. **DD** 615.
**Ind/Abst** Int. Pharm. Abstr.

US/0196-3619
**TECHNICAL MONOGRAPH - PARENTERAL DRUG ASSOCIATION, INC.** ***Title Change.*** **Main/Corp** Parenteral Drug Association. No. 1 (1978)-(19??). Monographic series. English. Parenteral Drug Association, 7500 Old Georgetown Road, Suite 620, Bethesda MD 20814. **Tel** (301)986-0293. ***Continued by*** *Technical Report, 0277-3406.*
**Ind/Abst** Int. Pharm. Abstr.

US/0277-3406
**TECHNICAL REPORT - PARENTERAL DRUG ASSOCIATION.** (TECHNICAL REPORT.). [Tech. rep. - Parent. Drug Assoc.]. **Added/Corp** Parenteral Drug Association. No. 3 (1981)-. Monographic series. English. Parenteral Drug Association, 7500 Old Georgetown Road, Suite 620, Bethesda MD 20814. **Tel** (301)986-0293. ***Continues*** *Parenteral Drug Association. Technical Monograph - Parenteral Drug Association, 0196-3619.*
**Ind/Abst** Int. Pharm. Abstr.

US/1047-0166
**TENNESSEE PHARMACIST.** [Tenn. pharm.]. **Added/Corp** Tennessee Pharmaceutical Association. Tennessee Pharmacists Association. Vol. 1 (Feb. 1965)-. Periodical. English. mo. Free to Association members. Tennessee Pharmacists Association, 276 Capitol Blvd., Suite 810, Nashville TN 37219. **DD** 615. **NLM** W1 TE417AT.
**Ind/Abst** Int. Pharm. Abstr.

RU/0040-3660
**TERAPEVTICESKIJ ARHIV. See** Medical Science and Technology.

US/0362-7926
**TEXAS PHARMACY.** [Tex. pharm.]. **Added/Corp** Texas Pharmaceutical Association. Vol. 78 (Jan. 1959)-. Periodical. English. mo. $30.00 US; $60.00 other. Texas Pharmacy, PO Box 14709, Austin TX 78761-4709. **Tel** (512)836-8350, FAX (512)836-0308. **ED** Luther R Parker. **NLM** W1 TE83. **CODEN** TXPDAE. **Bk Rev. Ad Acc. Circ:** 4,500 (ctrl). Documents available from CASDDS. ***Continues*** *Texas Druggist.*
**Desc:** News and articles of interest to community and institutional pharmacists.
**Ind/Abst** Chem. Abstr.; Int. Pharm. Abstr.

NE/0921-562X
**TGO. TIJDSCHRIFT VOOR THERAPIE, GENEESMIDDEL EN ONDERZOEK.** (TIJDSCHRIFT VOOR THERAPIE, GENEESMIDDEL, EN ONDERZOEK.). [TGO. Tijdschr. ther. geneesm. onderz.]. **VFOAT** TGO; JDR; Journal for Drug Therapy and Research; Journal for Drugtherapy and Research. Vol. 9, No. 1 (Jan./Feb. 1984). Academic Scholarly Publication. Dutch (summaries and/or abstracts in English). mo. Reed Healthcare Communications Leiderdorp, Postbus 1126, 1000 BC Amsterdam Netherlands. **Tel** 011 31 20 5153352. **NLM** W1; TI788S. **CODEN** TTTOE9. Documents available from CASDDS. ***Continues*** *Tijdschrift voor Geneesmiddelenonderzoek, 0166-2384.*
**Ind/Abst** Chem. Abstr. (1984-); EMBASE; Helminthol. Abstr.; Protozoolog. Abstr.; Rev. Med. Vet. Entomol.; Rev. Med. Vet. Mycology.

US/0163-4356
**THERAPEUTIC DRUG MONITORING.** [Ther. drug monit.]. Vol. 1, No. 1 (1979)-. Academic Scholarly Publication. English. bm (6 issues). $188.00 (individuals), $318.00 (institutions) US; $232.00 (individuals), $394.00 (institutions) other. Raven Press, 1185 Avenue of the Americas, 37th Floor, New York NY 10036. **Tel** (212)930-9500, (212)930-9604, FAX (212)869-3495, (212)302-8507, telex 640073. **ED** Steven J. Soldin and Folke Sjoqvist. **LC** RM301.5; .T44. **DD** 615/.7. **NLM** W1 TH138. **CODEN** TDMODV. **[CCC]. Bk Rev. Pr Rev.** available on microfilm and microfiche from University Microfilms International (UMI). Documents available from The Genuine Article, BIOSIS Document Express, CASDDS.
**Desc:** Fosters the exchange of knowledge among the various disciplines--clinical pharmacology, pathology, toxicology, analytical chemistry--that share a common interest in therapeutic drug monitoring. Regular features includes review articles on given classes of drugs; original articles and case reports; editorials; technical notes; letters to the editor; continuing education articles; and book reviews.
**Ind/Abst** Anal. Abstr.; Biol. Abstr.; Chem. Abstr.; Curr. Aware. Biol. Sci., CABS; Curr. Contents Clin. Med.; Curr. Contents Life Sci.; EMBASE; Helminthol. Abstr. (1991-); Index Med.; Int. Pharm. Abstr.; Iowa Drug Inf. Serv. (1979-); Med. Abstr. Newsl.; Nutr. Abstr. Rev., Ser. A, Hum. Exp.; Life Sci. Collect.; PESTDOC; Protozoolog. Abstr.; Res. Alert [Full Cov.]; Sci. Cit. Index; SCISEARCH.

FR/0040-5957
**THERAPIE.** (THERAPIE. REVUE DE THERAPEUTIQUE ET DE PHARMACOLOGIE CLINIQUE.). [Therapie]. **Added/Corp** Societe de Therapeutique et de Pharmacodynamie. Vol. 1 (1946)-. Academic Scholarly Publication. French (summaries and/or abstracts in English and French). bm (6 issues). $189.00. Doin Editeurs, 8 Place de l'Odeon, F 75006 Paris France. **Tel** 011 33 1 46332237. **(Subscription address:** Subscription Office, PO Box 830399, Birmingham, AL 35283-0399; telephone: (800)633-4931 or (205)991-6920 (outside US and Canada); FAX: (205)995-1588**)** **ED** A. Pradalier, P. Jaillon, J. C. Evreux, G. Babany, M. O. Richard. **NLM** W1 TH641. **CODEN** THERAP. **[CCC].** Index available. **Bk Rev. Ad Acc. Pr Rev.** available on microfilm from University Microfilms International (UMI). Documents available from The Genuine Article, BIOSIS Document Express, CASDDS.
**Desc:** Publishes original articles, comments and letters to the editor on such subjects as clinical pharmacology, therapeutics and pharmacovigilance. The official organ of the French Society of Therapeutics and Clinical Pharmacology.
**Ind/Abst** Biol. Abstr.; Chem. Abstr.; Curr. Contents Life Sci.; EMBASE; Index Med.; Int. Pharm. Abstr.; Life Sci. Collect.; PESTDOC; Ref. Upd. Deluxe Ed.; Res. Alert [Full Cov.]; Rev. Med. Vet. Mycology; Sci. Cit. Index; SCISEARCH; Soc. Sci. Cit. Index [Select. Cov.].

CC/0253-9896
**TIANJIN YIYAO. See** Medical Science and Technology.

US/8755-1063
**TODO NATURAL DE NUEVA YORK.** [Todo nat. N. Y.]. Vol. 1 No. 1 (Sept. 1984)-. Periodical. Spanish. mo. $12.95. Editorial Mezquita, 20 West 22 Street/Room 1000, New York NY 10010. **DD** 615.

FR
**TONUS PHARMACIE PRATIQUE.** French. bm. 100.00F (one year), 150.00F (two year). Tonus, 29 rue FG Poissonniere, 75009 Paris France. **Tel** 011 33 1 42471317.

UK/0140-0843
**TOPICS IN ANTIBIOTIC CHEMISTRY.** ***Ceased.*** [Topics antibiot. chem.]. Vol. 1-?. Academic Scholarly Publication. English. ir. Halsted Press, 605 Third Avenue, New York NY 10016. **Tel** (718)658-0888. **LC** RS431.A6; T66. **DD** 615/.329. **NLM** W1 TO539C. **CODEN** TACHD7. Documents available from BIOSIS Document Express, CASDDS.
**Ind/Abst** Biol. Abstr. (-1979); Chem. Abstr.

US/0271-1206
**TOPICS IN HOSPITAL PHARMACY MANAGEMENT.** [Topics hosp. pharm. manage.]. **Added/Corp** Aspen Systems Corporation. **VFOAT** THPM; T.H.P.M. Vol. 1, No. 1 (May 1981)-. Periodical. English. qt. $110.00 US and Canada. Aspen Publishers Inc., 7201 McKinney Circle, Frederick MD 21701. **Tel** (800)234-1660, (301)698-7100, FAX (301)251-5784, telex 5106014543. **(Subscription address:** Aspen Publishers Inc., PO Box 990, Frederick MD 21701.**) ED** Andrew Wilson. **NLM** W1 TO539MSF. **[CCC]. Bk Rev. Circ:** 2,266. available on microfilm and microfiche from University Microfilms International (UMI).
**Desc:** Each issue will focus on a specific area of vital concern to hospital pharmacy managers. It is filled with practical information and guidelines and will help you plan for the future more confidently.
**Ind/Abst** Health Plan. Adminis.; Hospit. Health Admin. Index; Int. Pharm. Abstr.

NE/0167-7101
**TOPICS IN MOLECULAR PHARMACOLOGY.** [Top. mol. pharmacol.]. (1981)-. Academic Scholarly Publication. English. ir. $105.25. Elsevier Science Publishing Company Inc, Madison Square Station, PO Box 882, New York NY 10159-0882. **Tel** (212)633-3950, FAX (212)633-3990. **(Subscription address:** Elsevier Science Inc. / New York Books, 655 Avenue of the Americas, New York NY 10010.**) ED** Arnold S. V. Burgen and Gordon C. K. Roberts. **LC** RM1; .T67. **DD** 615/.1/05. **NLM** W1 TO54C. **CODEN** TMPHDK. **[CCC]. Pr Rev.** Documents available from BIOSIS Document Express, CASDDS.
**Ind/Abst** Biol. Abstr. (1986-); Chem. Abstr.

US/0041-008X
**TOXICOLOGY AND APPLIED PHARMACOLOGY.** **See** Medical Science and Technology-Toxicology.

UK/0041-0101
**TOXICON (OXFORD).** (TOXICON.). [Toxicon]. **Added/Corp** International Society on Toxinology. Vol. 1 (Oct. 1962)-. Academic Scholarly Publication. English (French and German; summaries and/or abstracts in French and German). Twelve times a year. $962.00 The Americas; £645.00 other. Pergamon Press, An Imprint of Elsevier Science Ltd., The Boulevard, Langford Lane, Kidlington, Oxford OX5 1GB United Kingdom. **Tel** 011 44 865 843000, 011 44 865 843699, FAX 011 44 865 843010. **(Subscription address:** Elsevier Science Ltd. Oxford Fulfillment Centre, PO Box 800, Kidlington, Oxford OX5 1DX United Kingdom.**) ED** Alan Harvey and Gerhard Habermehl. **LC** QP631; .T6. **DD** 615.37305. **NLM** W1 TO95J. **CODEN** TOXIA6. **[CCC].** cum. index. **Pr Rev.** available on microfilm and microfiche from University Microfilms International (UMI). Documents available from The Genuine Article, BIOSIS Document Express, CASDDS, Documents on Demand, ADONIS.
**Desc:** Covers papers on the chemical, biochemical, pharmacological, zootoxicological and immunological properties of natural poisons, clinical observations on poisoning where a new therapeutic principle or a decidedly superior clinical result has been obtained, material on the use of toxins in studying biological processes, and on subjects related to venom-antivenom problems.
**Ind/Abst** ADONIS; AgBiotech News Inf.; AGRICOLA [Select. Cov.]; Aquat. Sci. Fish. Abstr. (Computer File); Biol. Abstr.; Chem. Abstr.; Chem. Titles; CSA Neuro. Abstr.; Curr. Aware. Biol. Sci., CABS; Curr. Contents Life Sci.; EMBASE; Energy Inf. Abstr.; Environ. Abstr.; Field Crop Abstr.; Fish Rev.; Grasslands For. Abstr.; Index Med.; Maize Abstr.; Microbiol. Abstr. Sect. B; Microbiol. Abstr. Sect. A; Microbiol. Abstr. Sect. C; NAPRALERT; Nutr. Abstr. Rev., Ser. B, Live Feeds and Feed.; Life Sci. Collect.; Pig News Inf.; Pollut. Abstr. Indexes; Ref. Upd. Deluxe Ed.; Res. Alert [Full Cov.]; Rev. Agric. Entomol.; Rev. Med. Vet. Entomol.; Rev. Med. Vet. Mycology; Sci. Cit. Index; SCISEARCH; Seed Abstr.; Toxicol. Abstr.; Trop. Dis. Bull.; Wildl. Rev.

UK/0190-5368
**TOXICON. SUPPLEMENT (OXFORD).** (TOXICON. SUPPLEMENT.). (1978)-. Monographic series. English. **NLM** W1 TO95JA.
**Ind/Abst** NAPRALERT.

UK/0143-4241
**TRANSMITTERS RECEPTORS & SYNAPSES.** [Transmitters recept. synapses]. (1980)-. English. Twenty-four times a year. £130.00. SUBIS, Mansion House, 19 Kingfield Road, Sheffield S11 9AS England. **Tel** 011 44 114 255 4433, FAX 011 44 114 255 4626. **DD** 016.61281. **[CCC].**

UK
**TREATMENT : HANDBOOK OF DRUG THERAPY.** English. £80.00 (new), £48.00 (renewal). Longman Group Ltd., Fourth Avenue, Longman House, Harlow Essex CM19 5SR England. **Tel** 011 44 279 429655, FAX 011 44 279 431059, telex 81259. **(Subscription address:** Fourth Avenue, Harlow Essex CM19 5AA England**)**

US/1061-6314
**TRENDS, BIOTECHNOLOGY : INFORMATION AND ISSUES FOR PHARMACISTS.** [Trends biotech.]. **Added/Corp** Philadelphia College of Pharmacy and Science. Office of Professional Programs. **VFOAT** Biotechnology; Trends in Biotechnology. Vol. 1, No. 1 (May 1991)-. Periodical. English. qt. Philadelphia College of Pharmacy and Science, 600 South 43rd Street, Philadelphia PA 19104. **DD** 615.

UK/0167-7691
**TRENDS IN PHARMACOLOGICAL SCIENCES (REFERENCE ED.).** (TRENDS IN PHARMACOLOGICAL SCIENCES.). [Trends pharmacol. sci.]. **Added/Corp** International Union of Pharmacology. International Union of Toxicology. Vol. 1 (1979/80)-. Periodical. English. mo. $110.00. Elsevier Trends Journals, An Imprint of Elsevier Science Ltd., The Boulevard, Langford Lane, Kidlington, Oxford OX5 1GB United Kingdom. **Tel** 011 44 865 843000, 011 44 865 843699, FAX 011 44 865 843010. Documents available from CASDDS, ADONIS.
**Ind/Abst** ADONIS; Chem. Abstr.; Expand. Acad. Index (1992-); PESTDOC; Ref. Upd. Basic Ed.; Ref. Upd. Deluxe Ed.

UK/0165-6147
**TRENDS IN PHARMACOLOGICAL SCIENCES (REGULAR ED.).** (TRENDS IN PHARMACOLOGICAL SCIENCES.). [Trends pharmacol. sci.]. **Added/Corp** International Union of Pharmacology. International Union of Toxicology. **VFOAT** TIPS. Vol. 1 (April 1979)-. Academic Scholarly Publication. English. mo. $514.00 The Americas; £345.00 other. Elsevier Trends Journals, An Imprint of Elsevier Science Ltd., The Boulevard, Langford Lane, Kidlington, Oxford OX5 1GB United Kingdom. **Tel** 011 44 865 843000, 011 44 865 843699, FAX 011 44 865 843010. **(Subscription address:** Elsevier Science Ltd. Oxford Fulfillment Centre, PO Box 800, Kidlington, Oxford OX5 1DX United Kingdom.**) ED** A. C. Abbott. **NLM** W1 TR341F. **CODEN** TPHSDY. **[CCC].** Index available. **Pr Rev.** available on microfilm and microfiche from University Microfilms International (UMI). Documents available from The Genuine Article, BIOSIS Document Express, UMI Article Clearinghouse, CASDDS, ADONIS.
**Desc:** Aimed to provide up-to-date information for pharmacologists, toxicologists, clinical pharmacologists, medicinal chemists and related scientists.
**Ind/Abst** ADONIS; Biol. Abstr.; Calcium Calcif. Tissue Abstr.; Chem. Abstr.; CSA Neuro. Abstr.; Curr. Aware. Biol. Sci., CABS; Curr. Contents Life Sci.; EMBASE; Index Med.; Int. Pharm. Abstr. (199?-); NAPRALERT; Newsp. Period. Abstr. (1992-); Life Sci. Collect.; Res. Alert [Full Cov.]; Sci. Cit. Index; SCISEARCH.

BL/0371-6619
**TRIBUNA FARMACEUTICA.** [Trib. Farm.]. **Added/Corp** Universidade Federal do Parana. Departamento de Tecnologia Farmaceutica. Vol. 1 (1932)-. Periodical. Portuguese (English; summaries and/or abstracts in English). an. Free. Universidade de Fed'l do Parana, ru Cel Dulcidio 638, C Postal 888, 80000 Curitiba Parana Brazil. **NLM** W1 TR45. **CODEN** TFBRAU. Index available. **Circ:** 500 (ctrl). Documents available from CASDDS.
**Ind/Abst** Bibliogr. Mission.; Chem. Abstr. (1932-1985); Int. Pharm. Abstr. (19??-19??); Life Sci. Collect.

US/0090-6816
**U.S.A.N. AND THE U.S.P. DICTIONARY OF DRUG NAMES.** (USAN AND THE USP DICTIONARY OF DRUG NAMES.). [USAN USP dict. drug names]. **Added/Corp** United States Pharmacopeial Convention. **VFOAT** USP Dictionary of Drug Names. No. 10 (1971)-. English. an. $110.25 (includes sales tax) Maryland Residents; $105.00 other. U. S. Pharmacopeial Convention, 12601 Twinbrook Parkway, Rockville MD 20852. **Tel** (301)881-0666, (800)227-8772, telex 710 8289787. **ED** William M. Heller. **LC** RS55; .U54. **DD** 615/.1/014. **NLM** QV 772 U11. **Bk Rev.** ***Continues*** *United States Adopted Names (USAN).*
**Desc:** The authoritative list of "established" names for drugs in the United States.

US/0275-5181
**U.S. PHARMACEUTICAL MARKET. DRUG STORES.** (U.S. PHARMACEUTICAL MARKET. DRUG STORES / IMS AMERICA.). **VFOAT** U.S. Drug Stores. English. IMS America Ltd, Butler Pike & Maple Avenue, Ambler PA 19002. **LC** HD966.1; .U17. **DD** 381/.456151/0973.

US/0148-4818
**U.S. PHARMACIST.** **VFOAT** US Pharmacist. **VAT** United States Pharmacist. Vol. 1, No. 1 (Oct. 1976)-. Periodical. English. Twelve times a year. $25.00 US; $35.00 Canada; $60.00 Europe; $70.00 other. Jobson Publishing Corporation, 100 Avenue of the Americas, New York NY 10013. **Tel** (212)274-7084, 274-7000, FAX (212)431-0500. **(Subscription address:** US Pharmacist, PO Box 7632, Riverton NJ 08077.**) ED** Allen Schwartz. **LC** RS1; .U2. **DD** 615/.1/05. **NLM** W1 UN724. Index available. **Ad Acc. Circ:** 90,000 (ctrl).
**Desc:** Reviews of drugs and disease for pharmacists.
**Ind/Abst** EMBASE; Int. Pharm. Abstr.; Mod. Med.

US/0749-5005
**U.S. REGULATORY REPORTER.** **See** Sociology-Social Services and Welfare.

KO
**UIYAK CHONGBO.** **VFOAT** Drug Information; Wolgan Uiyak Chongbo. Periodical. Korean (Korean). mo. W30,000. Yagop Sinmunsa, 100-1 2-ka Chongpa-dong Yongsan-ku, Seoul Korea. **LC** RS1; .U45. **NLM** W1; UI33P.

US/0195-7996
**UNITED STATES PHARMACOPEIA, THE.** **Added/Corp** United States Pharmacopeial Convention. Committee of Revision. **VFOAT** US Pharmacopeia; U.S. Pharmacopeia. (20th Revision 1980)- 15th Ed. English. ir (quinquennial). $450.00 other. U. S. Pharmacopeial Convention, 12601 Twinbrook Parkway, Rockville MD 20852. **Tel** (301)881-0666, (800)227-8772, telex 710 8289787. **LC** RS141.2; .P5. **DD** 615/.11/73. **NLM** QV 738 AA1 P5. **CODEN** USPFDX. Index available. cum. index. ***Continues*** *Pharmacopeia of the United States of America.*

US
**UNITED STATES PHARMACOPEIA DRUG INFORMATION FOR THE CONSUMER.** **Added/Corp** United States Pharmacopeial Convention. Consumer Reports Books. Consumers Union of United States. **VFOAT** Drug Information for the Consumer. (1987)-. English. an. $39.95. Consumer Reports Books, 9180 Le Saint Drive, Fairfield OH 45014. **Tel** (800)272-0722. **LC** RS51; .U65. **DD** 615/.1.

US/0190-5384
**UNITED STATES PHARMACOPEIA. NATIONAL FORMULARY. SUPPLEMENT, THE.** (THE UNITED STATES PHARMACOPEIA. SUPPLEMENT. NATIONAL FORMULARY.). **Added/Corp** United States Pharmacopeial Convention. Board of Trustees. United States Pharmacopeial Convention. Committee of Revision. National Formulary Board. (April 29, 1975)-. Periodical. English. sa. $480.00 Maryland; $458.00 other. U. S. Pharmacopeial Convention, 12601 Twinbrook Parkway, Rockville MD 20852. **Tel** (301)881-0666, (800)227-8772, telex 710 8289787. **NLM** QV 738 AA1 P51.

US/0042-0441
**UNLISTED DRUGS.** [Unlisted drugs]. **Added/Corp** Special Libraries Association. Unlisted Drugs Committee. Specal Libraries Association. Pharmaceutical Section. Special Libraries Association. Pharmaceutical Division. Vol. 1, No. 1 (Jan. 1949)-. Periodical. English. Twelve times a year (includes semiannual indexes). $480.00. Pharmaco Medical Documentation, PO Box 429, Chatham NJ 07928. **Tel** (201)822-9200, FAX (201)765-0722. **ED** Boris R. Anzlowar. **LC** RS1; .U55. **DD** 615. **NLM** W1 UN975. Index available. cum. index. **Bk Rev. Ad Acc.** available on Cards (monthly sets - $720.00).
**Desc:** Each issue contains 200 descriptive abstracts of new investigational and marketed drugs worldwide.

US/8755-7142
**UNLISTED DRUGS. INDEX-GUIDE.** [Unlisted drugs index-guide]. **VFOAT** Index-Guide; Index Guide. 1st Ed. (1969)-. English. te. $630.00. Pharmaco Medical Documentation, PO Box 429, Chatham NJ 07928. **Tel** (201)822-9200, FAX (201)765-0722. **LC** RS1; .U552. **DD** 615.
**Desc:** Containing alphabetical listing of some 90,000 drug entries, thoroughly cross-referenced, also coded to two manufacturer address directories; other information of pharmaceutical interest.

US/0740-6916
**USP DI. ADVICE FOR THE PATIENT.** [USP DI, Advice patient]. **Added/Corp** United States Pharmacopeial Convention. **VFOAT** Advice for the Patient; U.S.P. D.I. Advice for the Patient; USP DI. Advice for the Patient. **VAT** United States Pharmacopeia Dispensing Information. Advice for the Patient. (1983)-. English. an (published in December). $61.60 (sales tax included) Maryland residents; $59.00 other (subscription includes updates). U. S. Pharmacopeial Convention, 12601 Twinbrook Parkway, Rockville MD 20852. **Tel** (301)881-0666, (800)227-8772, telex 710 8289787. **ED** A. V. Precup. **LC** RM300; .U83. **DD** 615/.1. **NLM** QV 740; AA1 U601A. **Bk Rev.** available on diskette. ***Continues in part*** *United States Pharmacopeia Dispensing Information, 0276-5373.*

**Desc:** Drug information prepared specifically for the consumer, written in an easy-to-understand form that is uncluttered by technical data and terminology.

US/1045-8298
**USP DI. APPROVED DRUG PRODUCTS AND LEGAL REQUIREMENTS.** (USP DI. VOL. III, APPROVED DRUG PRODUCTS AND LEGAL REQUIREMENTS.). [USP DI, Approv. drug prod. leg. requir.]. **Added/Corp** United States Pharmacopeial Convention. **VFOAT** Approved Drug Products and Legal Requirements; USP DI. Vol. III, Approved Drug Products and Legal Requirements. **VAT** United States Pharmacopeia Dispensing Information. Approved Drug Products and Legal Requirements. 9th Ed. (1989)-. English. Thirteen times a year (1 annual book published in Dec. and 12 monthly updates). $108.75 (includes sales tax) Maryland residents; $104.00 other; includes selected state laws pertaining to the practice of pharmacy). U. S. Pharmacopeial Convention, 12601 Twinbrook Parkway, Rockville MD 20852. **Tel** (301)881-0666, (800)227-8772, telex 710 8289787. **LC** RS131.2; .U86. **DD** 615/.1173. **NLM** QV 740; AA1 U487. ***Continues in part*** *United States Pharmacopeia Dispensing Information, 0276-5373.*

US/0740-4174
**USP DI. DRUG INFORMATION FOR THE HEALTH CARE PROVIDER. Added/Corp** United States Pharmacopeial Convention. **VFOAT** U.S.P.D.I. Drug Information for the Health Care Provider; Drug Information for the Health Care Provider; USP DI. Vol. I, Drug Information for the Health Care Provider; USP DI. Drug Information for the Health Care Professional; Drug Information for the Health Care Professional. **VAT** United States Pharmacopeia Dispensing Information. Drug Information for the Health Care Provider. (1983)-. English. an. $124.25 (includes sales tax) Maryland residents; $119.00 other (subscription includes updates). U. S. Pharmacopeial Convention, 12601 Twinbrook Parkway, Rockville MD 20852. **Tel** (301)881-0666, (800)227-8772, telex 710 8289787. **ED** A. V. Precup. **LC** RM300; .U833. **DD** 615/.1. **NLM** QV 740; AA1 U601. **Bk Rev.** ***Continues in part*** *United States Pharmacopeia Dispensing Information, 0276-5373.*
**Desc:** National consensus drug information system specifically written for health professionals. Provides clinically relevant, current information on virtually all drugs.

US
**USP DI; UNITED STATES PHARMACOPOEIA DISPENSING INFORMATION. Added/Corp** United States Pharmacopoeial Convention. (1980)-. English. an. U. S. Pharmacopeial Convention, 12601 Twinbrook Parkway, Rockville MD 20852. **Tel** (301)881-0666, (800)227-8772, telex 710 8289787.

US/0730-1324
**USP DI/UPDATE.** ***Ceased.*** (USP DI UPDATE / U.S. PHARMACOPEIAL CONVENTION.). [USP DI/Update]. **Added/Corp** United States Pharmacopeial Convention. **VAT** United States Pharmacopeia Dispensing Information Update. Vol. 1, No. 1 (Jan./Feb. 1980)-Ceased (May 1991). Periodical. English. bm. US Pharmacopeial Convention, 12601 Twinbrook Parkway, Rockville MD 20852. **DD** 615. **NLM** QV 740 AA1 U601A. ***Absorbed*** *USP DI Review, 1045-8301.*

GW/0074-9729
**VEROEFFENTLICHUNGEN DER INTERNATIONALEN GESELLSCHAFT FUER GESCHICHTE DER PHARMAZIE. NEUE FOLGE, DIE. Main/Corp** International Society for the History of Pharmacy. Vol. 1 (1953)-. Academic Scholarly Publication. German. ir. Price varies per volume. Wissenschaftliche Verlagsgesellschaft mbH, Postfach 101061, D 70009 Stuttgart Germany. **Tel** 011 49 711 258200, FAX 011 49 711 2582290, telex 723636 DAZ D. **ED** Wolfgang - Hagen Hein. **NLM** W1 VE784I. **CODEN** ISHPAO. Documents available from CASDDS. ***Supersedes*** *Gesellschaft fuer Geschichte der Pharmazie. Veroeffentlichungen der (Internationalen) Gesellschaft fuer Geschichte der Pharmazie.*
**Ind/Abst** Chem. Abstr. (1953-1983).

GW
**VERZEICHNIS WISSENSCHAFTLICHER PUBLIKATIONEN. Main/Corp** Akademie der Wissenschaften der DDR. Institut fur Wirkstofforschung. German. an. Akademie der Wissenschaften Zentinst, Permoserstrasse 15, O-7010 Leipzig Germany. **LC** QP901; .A42A. **DD** 615/.1/05.

US/0042-6717
**VIRGINIA PHARMACIST, THE. Added/Corp** Virginia. Board of Pharmacy. Virginia Pharmaceutical Association. Vol. 1 (Sept. 1916)-. English. mo. $30.00. Virginia Pharmaceutical Association, 3119 West Clay Street, Richmond VA 23219. **Tel** (804)355-7941. **ED** Paul E Galanti, Ilene B Stiff. **DD** 615.1. **NLM** W1 VI823H. **Bk Rev. Ad Acc. Circ:** 2,000.
**Desc:** A journal for the professional pharmacists in Virginia. Content includes healthcare supplied by pharmacists, general news, meetings, continuing education and convention news.
**Ind/Abst** Int. Pharm. Abstr.

US/0739-9588
**VITAL SIGNS PHARMACY SERVICES NEWSLETTER.** (19??)-. Newsletter. English. mo. $75.00. RX Data Pac Service, PO Box 42020, Cincinnati OH 45242. **Tel** (513)489-0943. **ED** I. H. Goodman. **Circ:** 2,000.
**Desc:** A pharmacy-nursing newsletter service to assist in meeting JCAHO requirements.

US/0507-2379
**VOICE OF THE PHARMACIST.** [Voice pharm.]. **Added/Corp** American College of Apothecaries. Vol. 1 Sept. (1957)-. Periodical. English. qt (Jan., April, July, Oct.). $40.00. American College of Apothecaries, 205 Daingerfield Road, Alexandria VA 22314. **Tel** (703)684-8603, FAX (703)683-3619. **ED** D C Huffman. **DD** 615. **NLM** W1 VO335. **Circ:** 1,000 (ctrl).
**Desc:** This newsletter consists of articles of interest on timely topics for independent pharmacy practitioners.
**Ind/Abst** Int. Pharm. Abstr.

JA/0289-730X
**WAKAN IYAKU GAKKAISHI. See** Medical Science and Technology.

JA
**WAKAN-YAKU KENKYUJO NEMPO. Main/Corp** Toyama Daigaku. Wakan-Yaku Kenkyujo. **VFOAT** Annual Report. Vol. 1 (1974)-. Academic Scholarly Publication. Japanese. Toyama Ika Yakka Daigaku Wakan'yaku Kenkyujo, (Research Institute for Wakan-Yaku, Toyama Medical and Pharmaceutical University), 2630 Sugitani Toyamashi Toyamaken 930-01 Japan. **LC** RS180.J3; T68A. **CODEN** WKNDDH. Documents available from CASDDS.
**Ind/Abst** Chem. Abstr.

TH/0125-1570
**WARASAN PHESATCHESAT MAHA WITTHAYALAI MAHIDON.** (MAHIDOL UNIVERSITY JOURNAL OF PHARMACEUTICAL SCIENCES / MAHAWITTHAYALAI MAHIDON.). [Warasan Phesatchesat Maha Witthayalai Mahidon]. **Added/Corp** Mahawitthayalai Mahidon. **VFOAT** Mahidol University Journal of Pharmaceutical Sciences. (19??)-. Periodical. Thai (English and Thai). **CODEN** VPSADN. Documents available from CASDDS.
**Ind/Abst** Chem. Abstr.; Int. Pharm. Abstr.

●US/1069-4218
**WARNING LETTER BULLETIN.** (WARNING LETTER BULLETIN : BIWEEKLY ALERT TO FDA ENFORCEMENT ACTIVITIES, INSPECTIONS & COMPLIANCE PROGRAMS.). [Warn. lett. bull.]. **Added/Corp** Washington Information Source. Vol. 1, No. 1 (June 7, 1993)-. Bulletin. English. bw (26 issues per year). $359.00 non-subscribers; $295.00 subscribers of Medical Device Approval Letter. Washington Information Source Company, 6506 Old Stage Road, Suite 700, Rockville MD 20852. **DD** 344. **[CCC].**
**Desc:** Summaries of FDA warning letters on human drugs, animal drugs, medical devices, blood and biologics.

US/0194-1291
**WASHINGTON DRUG LETTER (WASHINGTON. 1979).** (WASHINGTON DRUG LETTER.). [Wash. drug lett.]. (Oct. 22, 1979)-. Periodical. English. Fifty-one times per year (published Mondays). $747.00 US, Canada and Mexico; $822.00 other. Washington Business Information Inc., 1117 North 19th Street, Suite 200, Arlington VA 22209. **Tel** (703)247-3433, (800)426-0416, FAX (703)247-3421. **ED** John Briley. **LC** KF3885.A15; W37. **DD** 344.73/04233/05; 347.304423305. **NLM** W1 WA598B; W1 WA598B. **[CCC].** available on an online database (file 158/Full-Text) from DIALOG. ***Continues*** *Washington Drug & Device Letter, 0162-2994;* ***Absorbed*** *Pharmaceutical & Biotech Daily.*
**Desc:** Focuses on regulation and legislation affecting prescription and proprietary drugs. Offers news about FDA actions on new drug applications, manufacturing procedures, advertising and labeling, compliance cases, research and testing rules.

US/0745-7413
**WASHINGTON PHARMACIST, THE. Added/Corp** Washington State Pharmaceutical Association. (19??)-. Periodical. English. bm. $20.00 (included in membership dues). Washington State Pharmaceutical Association, 1415 Seneca SW, Renton WA 98055.
**Ind/Abst** Int. Pharm. Abstr. (199?-).

US/0043-1893
**WEEKLY PHARMACY REPORTS.** [Wkly. pharm. rep.]. **VFOAT** Green Sheet. (1952)-. Government Publication. English. wk. $65.00. FDC Reports Inc., 5550 Friendship Boulevard/Suite 1, Chevy Chase MD 20815. **Tel** (301)657-9830. **ED** Louis LaMarca. **NLM** W1 W171. **CODEN** WPHRAR. **[CCC].** Documents available from UMI Article Clearinghouse. ***Absorbed*** *Drug News Weekly.*
**Desc:** Introduction and pricing of new pharmaceuticals, government regulatory activity (federal as well as state), coverage of national and state pharmacy association meetings.
**Ind/Abst** Pharm. News Index (Dec. 1977-).

GW
**WEHRMEDIZIN UND WEHRPHARMAZIE. Added/Corp** Gesellschaft fËur Wehrmedizin und Wehrpharmazie (Germany). Vol. 7 (Jan./Feb. 1969)-. German. qt. DM68.00, $49.22 Europe; DM76.00, $55.02 other. Beta Verlag Marketinggesellsch, Celsiusstrasse 43, D 53125 Bonn 1 Germany. **Tel** 011 49 228 252061, FAX 011 49 228 252067, telex 8869 536 BETA D. **LC** RC970; .W42. **NLM** W1 WE226A. **Bk Rev. Ad Acc.** ctrl circ. ***Continues*** *Wehrmedizin.*
**Desc:** A journal providing information on medical and health services in the bundeswehr.

GW/0379-7031
**WELEDA KORRESPONDENZBLATTER FUR ARZTE. Added/Corp** Weleda AG. 1900-. Periodical. German. **NLM** W1 WE255.

NR/0303-691X
**WEST AFRICAN JOURNAL OF PHARMACOLOGY AND DRUG RESEARCH. Added/Corp** West African Society for Pharmacology. **VFOAT** Africaine Ouest Journal de Pharmacologie et Recherche Drogue. Vol. 1 (Jan. 1974)-. Academic Scholarly Publication. English (summaries and/or abstracts in French). sa. University of Nigeria, Department of Pharmacology and Therapeutics, PMB 01129 Enugu Nigeria. **NLM** W1 WE329K. **CODEN** WAJPAS. Documents available from BIOSIS Document Express, CASDDS.
**Ind/Abst** Biol. Abstr. (19??-); Chem. Abstr. (19??-); EMBASE (19??-).

US/0043-3292
**WEST VIRGINIA PHARMACIST, THE.** (THE WEST VIRGINIA PHARMACIST : OFFICIAL PUBLICATION OF THE WEST VIRGINIA PHARMACIST ASSOCIATION.). **Added/Corp** West Virginia Pharmacist Association. Vol. 1, No. 1 (1976)-. Periodical. English. qt. West Virginia Association, 4004 MacCorkle Avenue SE, Charleston WV 25304. **NLM** W1 WE457. ***Continues*** *West Virginia Pharmacist.*
**Ind/Abst** Int. Pharm. Abstr.

SZ/1010-9609
**WHO DRUG INFORMATION.** [WHO drug inf.]. **Added/Corp** World Health Organization. **VAT** World Health Organization Drug Information. Vol. 1, No. 1 (1987)-. Periodical. English. qt. $53.00 (surface Mail), $63.00 (airmail). World Health Organization, Distribution and Sales, 20 Avenue Appia, CH-1211 Geneva 27 Switzerland. **Tel** 011 41 22 7912111, FAX 011 41 22 7880401. **NLM** W1; WH46. **CODEN** WDINE8.
**Desc:** Communicates drug information that is either developed and issued by or transmitted to WHO by research and regulatory agencies throughout the world. Most information comes from sources that would not otherwise be available in published form. Information includes regular presentation of proposed and recommended International Nonproprietary Names for Pharmaceutical substances.
**Ind/Abst** Trop. Dis. Bull.

SW
**WHO DRUG REFERENCE LIST.** English. ir. $290.00 (paper print); $3,880.00 (magnet tape or diskette). Who Collaborating Ctr Intl, Drug Monitoring, PO Box 26, 575103 Uppsala Sweden. available on magnetic tape; available on diskette.

US/0743-3778
**WHOLESALE DRUGS MAGAZINE.** [Wholes. drugs mag.]. **VFOAT** Wholesale Drugs. Vol. 16, No. 2, (Apr/May 1964)-. Periodical. English. Ten times a year (Oct/Nov. and Dec/Jan. issues combined). $15.00 US; $60.00 other. Western Communications, 333 West Hampden Avenue, Suite 1050, Englewood CO 80110-2340. **Tel** (303)761-8818, FAX (303)761-2440. **ED** ElRoy Fitzsenry. **LC** HD9666.1; .W46. **DD** 615.1/068/8. **Ad Acc. Circ:** 4,000. ***Continues*** *Wholesale Drug Salesman.*
**Desc:** This magazine exclusively devoted to the wholesale drugs marketing.
**Ind/Abst** Int. Pharm. Abstr.

FR
**WHO'S WHO DANS L'INDUSTRIE PHARMACEUTIQUE.** French. an. 290.00F. MVF, 15 Bis rue Raspail, 92300 Levallois Perret France. **Tel** 011 33 1 47393702.

US
**WINDHOVER'S HEALTH CARE STRATEGIST. See** Medical Science and Technology.

US/0043-6585
**WISCONSIN PHARMACIST, THE.** (THE WISCONSIN PHARMACIST: OFFICIAL PUBLICATION OF THE WISCONSIN PHARMACIST ASSOCIATION.). **Added/Corp** Wisconsin Pharmacists Association. (19??)-. Periodical. English. mo. $60.00. Wisconsin Pharmacists Association, 202 Price Place, Madison WI 53705. **Tel** (608)238-5515. **ED** Anna Hahm and Robert E.

Henry. **NLM** W1 WI8025. **Bk Rev. Ad Acc. Circ:** 1,800 (ctrl). ***Continues** Wisconsin Druggist.*
**Desc:** Articles and features about the practice of pharmacy (especially professional and socioeconomic aspects), Wisconsin Pharmacists, and the Wisconsin Pharmacists Association.
**Ind/Abst** Int. Pharm. Abstr.

UK
**WORLD DRUG MARKET ANNUAL.** (19??)-. Trade Publication. English. qt. £5,100.00. IMS World Publications Ltd, 7 Harwood Avenue, london NW1 6JB England. **Tel** 011 44 71 393 5000, FAX 011 44 393 5900. available on CD-ROM.

UK/0961-1118
**WORLD PHARMACEUTICAL STANDARDS REVIEW.** ***Title Change.*** Vol. 1, No. 1 (Oct. 1990)-(19??). Periodical. English. mo. BNA International Inc., Herron, HSE Dean 10 Farrar Street, 6th Floor, London SW1H 0DL England. **Tel** (44) 71 222 8831, FAX (44) 71 222 0294, telex 262570 BNA LONG. **ED** Joel Kolko. **NLM** W1; WO8977PH. ***Continued by** World Pharmaceuticals Report.*
**Desc:** Twice monthly journal provides timely news on the development, production, use and promotion of pharmaceuticals. Safety and quality standard, clinical trials, product authorization, integration of the European community, patents, biotechnology, packaging, advertising and labeling, product and environmental liability, provision of patient information, reporting requirements, environmental concerns, pricing and reinbursement systems, import/export issues and national and international government actions.

US/0276-2277
**WORLD PHARMACEUTICALS DIRECTORY.** [World pharm. dir.]. **VFOAT** WPD. (1980)-. Directory. English. te. $620.00. Pharmaco Medical Documentation, PO Box 429, Chatham NJ 07928. **Tel** (201)822-9200, FAX (201)765-0722. **LC** RM39; .W67. **DD** 615/.19/0025. **NLM** QV 22.1 W928.
**Desc:** Lists some 200,000 drug entries under some 8,200 worldwide pharmaceutical research and marketing organizations, in two major sections.

●UK/0966-7687
**WORLD PHARMACEUTICALS REPORT.** [World pharm. rep.]. (1992)-. Periodical. English. bw. £348.00 UK; $595.00 other. BNA International Inc., Herron, HSE Dean 10 Farrar Street, 6th Floor, London SW1H 0DL England. **Tel** (44) 71 222 8831, FAX (44) 71 222 0294, telex 262570 BNA LONG. **DD** 338.476151. ***Continues** World Pharmaceutical Standards Review, 0961-1118.*

KO/0377-9556
**YAGHAG-HOI-JI.** (YAKHAKHOE CHI.). **Main/Corp** Taehan Yakhakhoe. **VFOAT** Yakhak Hoeji; Journal of the Pharmaceutical Society of Korea. (195?)-. Academic Scholarly Publication. Korean (summaries and/or abstracts in English; table of contents in English). bm. $90.00. College of Pharmacy / South Korea, Seoul National University, Seoul South Korea. **Tel** 02-762-8320. **ED** Eun Bang Lee. **LC** RS1. **NLM** W1 YA435. **CODEN** YAHOA3. cum. index. Documents available from CASDDS.
**Ind/Abst** Chem. Abstr.; EMBASE; Int. Pharm. Abstr.; NAPRALERT.

KO
**YAKCHE HAKHOE CHI. JOURNAL OF KOREAN PHARMACEUTICAL SCIENCES.** **Main/Corp** Han'guk Yakche Hakhoe. **VFOAT** Journal of Korean Pharmaceutical Sciences. (19??)-. Periodical. Korean (summaries and/or abstracts in English). **LC** RS1; .H35. **NLM** W1; YA434. Documents available from CASDDS.
**Ind/Abst** Chem. Abstr.; Int. Pharm. Abstr. (199?).

JA/0044-0035
**YAKKYOKU.** [Yakkyoku]. **VFOAT** Journal of Practical Pharmacy. (1950)-. Japanese. Twelve times a year. $346.00 (surface mail); $270.00 (airmail). Nanzando, 1-11, Yushima 4 Chome, Bunkyoku, Tokyoto 113, Japan. **(Subscription address:** Kyowa Book Company Inc., 1 38 Kanda Jinbocho Chiyoda-ku, Tokyo 101 Japan.**)** **CODEN** YKYUA6.
**Ind/Abst** Int. Pharm. Abstr.

JA/0285-5313
**YAKUBUTSU, SEISHIN, KODO. See** Psychology.

JA/0386-2062
**YAKUGAKU TOSHOKAN. PHARMACEUTICAL LIBRARY BULLETIN. See** Library and Information Sciences.

JA/0031-6903
**YAKUGAKU ZASSHI.** (YAKUGAKU ZASSHI. JOURNAL OF THE PHARMACEUTICAL SOCIETY OF JAPAN.). **Main/Corp** Nippon Yakugakkai. **Added/Corp** Nihon Yakugakkai. **VFOAT** Journal of the Pharmaceutical Society of Japan. No. 1 (1881)-. Academic Scholarly Publication. Japanese (summaries and/or abstracts in English). mo. $370.00. Nihon Yakugakkai, (Pharmaceutical Soc. of Japan), 12-15, Shibuya 2 Chome, Shibuyaku, Tokyoto 150, Japan. **(Subscription address:** Kyowa Book Company Inc., 1 38 Kanda Jinbocho Chiyoda-ku, Tokyo 101 Japan.**)** **NLM** W1 YA4493. **CODEN** YKKZAJ. **[CCC].** Index available in last issue of volume--attached. cum. index. **Pr Rev.** Documents available from The Genuine Article, BIOSIS Document Express, CASDDS.
**Ind/Abst** AGRICOLA; Anal. Abstr.; Anim. Breed. Abstr.; Bibliogr. Mission.; Biol. Abstr.; Chem. Abstr.; Chem. Titles; Crop Physiol. Abstr.; CSA Neuro. Abstr. (?-?); Curr. Chem. React.; Curr. Contents Life Sci.; EMBASE; Food Sci. Technol. Abstr.; Hortic. Abstr.; Index Chem.; Index Med.; Int. Pharm. Abstr.; Methods Organ. Synth.; NAPRALERT; Nat. Prod. Updates; Ornamental Hort. (1991-); Life Sci. Collect.; PESTDOC; Res. Alert [Full Cov.]; Rev. Med. Vet. Entomol.; Rev. Med. Vet. Mycology; Rice Abstr.; Sci. Cit. Index; SCISEARCH.

JA
**YAKUJI KOGYO SEISAN DOTAI TOKEI NEMPO.** **Main/Corp** Japan. Koseisho. **Added/Corp** Japan. Koseisho. Yakumukyoku. **VFOAT** Koseisho Yakuji Kogyo Seisan Dotai Tokei Nempo. (1952)-. Periodical. Japanese. an. ¥9,000. Yakugyo Keizai Kenkyujo, (Research Institute of Economic on Pharmaceutical Industry), 2-6 Kasumigaseki 3-chome, Chiyoda-ku Tokyoto 100 Japan. **LC** HD9672.J28; J34a.

JA/0386-3603
**YAKURI TO CHIRYO.** (YAKURI TO CHIRYO. / BASIC PHARMACOLOGY & THERAPEUTICS.). [Yakuri to chiryo]. **VFOAT** Basic Pharmacology & Therapeutics. Vol. 1 (August 1973)-. Academic Scholarly Publication. Japanese. mo. $308.00. Raifu Saiensu Shuppan K.K, (Life Science Publishing Co., Ltd.), 5-10, Kyobashi 2 Chome, Chuoku, Tokyoto, 103 Japan. **(Subscription address:** Kyowa Book Company Inc., 1 38 Kanda Jinbocho Chiyoda-ku, Tokyo 101 Japan.**)** **NLM** W1 YA451N. **CODEN** YACHDS. Documents available from CASDDS.
**Ind/Abst** Chem. Abstr.; EMBASE.

JA/0372-7629
**YAKUZAIGAKU.** (YAKUZAIGAKU / JOURNAL OF PHARMACEUTICAL SCIENCE AND TECHNOLOGY.). [Yakuzaigaku]. **Added/Corp** Nihon Yakuzaishi Kyokai. Chozai Gijutsu Iinkai. Nihon Yakugakkai. **VFOAT** Archives of Practical Pharmacy. (1941)-. Academic Scholarly Publication. Japanese (summaries and/or abstracts in English). qt. $55.00. Nihon Yakuzai Gakkai, (Academy of Pharmaceutical Science & Technology, Japan), c/o Nihon Gakkai Jimu Senta, 4-16, Yayoi 2 Chome, Bunkyoku, Tokyoto 113, Japan. **(Subscription address:** Japan Publications Trading Company, Ltd., PO Box 5030, Tokyo International, Tokyo 100-31 Japan.**)** **CODEN** YAKUA2. **[CCC].** Documents available from CASDDS.
**Ind/Abst** Bibliogr. Mission.; Chem. Abstr.; EMBASE; Int. Pharm. Abstr.

CC
**YANG YAO WU, HAI.** **Added/Corp** Chung-Kuo Yao Hsueh Hui. Shan-Tung Sheng Hai Yang Yao wu ko Hsueh yen Chiu so. **VFOAT** Journal of Marine Drugs; Hai Yang Yao Wu tsa Chih. (19??)-. Periodical. Chinese (summaries and/or abstracts in English). qt. **LC** RS160.7; .H35.
**Ind/Abst** Aquat. Sci. Fish. Abstr. (Computer File).

CC/0513-4870
**YAO HSUEH HSUEH PAO.** [Yao hsueh hsueh pao]. **VFOAT** Acta Pharmaceutica Sinica. (1953)-. Academic Scholarly Publication. Chinese (summaries and/or abstracts in English). mo. RMBY340.80. Science Press, 16 Donghuangchenggen North Street, Beijing 100707, People's Republic of China. **Tel** 011 86 1 4019821, 011 86 1 4010642, FAX 011 86 1 4012180, 011 86 1 4019810, telex 210147. **ED** Song Zhen-Yu. **LC** RS1; .Y35. **DD** 615.1/05. **CODEN** YHHPAL. **Ad Acc. Circ:** 10,000. available on microfilm from University Microfilms International (UMI). Documents available from BIOSIS Document Express, CASDDS. ***Continues** Chung-Kuo Yao Hsueh Tsa Chih.*
**Desc:** Original research articles on pharmaceutical sciences including medicinal chemistry, pharmaceutical analysis, chemistry of natural products, antibiotics, pharmacology, toxicology, pharmacy and pharmacognosy.
**Ind/Abst** Biol. Abstr. (1986-); Chem. Abstr.; Crop Physiol. Abstr.; For. Abstr.; Helminthol. Abstr.; Hortic. Abstr.; Index Med.; Int. Pharm. Abstr.; NAPRALERT; Ornamental Hort. (1991-); Seed Abstr.

CC/0254-1793
**YAOWU FENXI ZAZHI.** (YAO WU FEN HSI TSA CHIH.). [Yaowu fenxi zazhi]. **VFOAT** Chinese Journal of Pharmaceutical Analysis. Vol. 1, (Jan. 1981)-. Academic Scholarly Publication. Chinese. bm. $21.00. **(Subscription address:** China International Book Trading Corporation, PO Box 399, Library Service Department, Beijing 100044 People's Republic of China.**)** **ED** Tu Guo-Shi. **LC** RS189. **DD** 615.1/05. **NLM** W1 YA701S. **CODEN** YFZADL. **Bk Rev. Ad Acc. Circ:** 90,000. Documents available from CASDDS.
**Desc:** Research on the methods of drug analysis and control of qualities of pharmaceutical products.
**Ind/Abst** Anal. Abstr.; Chem. Abstr.; Int. Pharm. Abstr.; NAPRALERT.

US/0271-7956
**YEAR BOOK OF CLINICAL PHARMACY, THE.** [Year book clin. pharm.]. **VAT** Yearbook of Clinical Pharmacy. 1981-. English. an. $29.95. Mosby Year Book Inc., 11830 Westline Industrial Drive, St Louis MO 63146. **Tel** (800)325-4177, (314)872-8370, FAX (314)432-1380, telex 44-2402. **LC** RM300; .Y42. **DD** 615/.7/05. **NLM** W1 YE114B.

US/0084-3733
**YEAR BOOK OF DRUG THERAPY, THE.** [Year book drug ther.]. (1949)-. English. an. $64.95. Mosby Year Book Inc., 11830 Westline Industrial Drive, St Louis MO 63146. **Tel** (800)325-4177, (314)872-8370, FAX (314)432-1380, telex 44-2402. **ED** Leo E. Hollister and Louis Lasagna. **DD** 615. **NLM** W1 YE126. ***Continues** Year Book of General Therapeutics, 0270-0638.*

AT/0817-2455
**YOUR PHARMACY.** [Your pharm.]. (1987)-. Periodical. English. Twelve times a year. 36.00Aus$ Australia; 60.00Aus$ others. Reed Business Publishing Pty Ltd. / Australia, 1 5 Railway Street, Level 12 North Tower, Chatswood W 2067 NSW Australia. **Tel** 011 61 2 3725222, FAX 011 61 2 4197533. **DD** 615.40994.

CZ/0231-7834
**ZBORNIK PRAC USTAVU EXPERIMENTALNEJ FARMAKOLOGIE SAV.** [Zb. pr. Ust. exp. farmakol. SAV]. **Added/Corp** Ustav Experimentaalnej Farmakologie (Slovenska Akademia Vied). (1978)-. Periodical. Czech. **CODEN** ZPUSDT. Documents available from CASDDS.
**Ind/Abst** Chem. Abstr.

SZ/0049-8696
**ZENTRALBLATT FUER PHARMAZIE, PHARMAKOTHERAPIE UND LABORATORIUMSDIAGNOSTIK.** ***Ceased.*** [Zentralbl. Pharm., Pharmakother. Laboratoriumsdiagn.]. Academic Scholarly Publication. German (summaries and/or abstracts in English and Russian). mo. VCH Publishers Inc, 220 East 23rd Street, New York NY 10010. **Tel** (212)683-8333, , FAX (212)481-0897. **(Subscription address:** 303 NW 12th Avenue, Deerfield Beach FL 33442; telephone: (305)428-5566**)** **LC** RM1. **NLM** W1 ZE784. **CODEN** ZPPLBF. **[CCC].** Documents available from BIOSIS Document Express, CASDDS. ***Formed by the union of** Pharmazeutische Zentralhalle fur Deutschland **and** Arzneimittelstandardisierung.*
**Ind/Abst** Anal. Abstr.; Biol. Abstr.; Chem. Abstr.; EMBASE; Int. Pharm. Abstr. (19??-199?); PESTDOC (?-?); Rev. Med. Vet. Mycology.

CC/0253-2670
**ZHONGCAOYAO.** (CHUNG TSAO YAO.). [Zhongcaoyao]. **Added/Corp** Honan i Yao Kung Yeh Yen Chiu So. **VFOAT** Zhongcaoyao; Chinese Traditional and Herbal Drugs. (1980)-. Academic Scholarly Publication. Chinese (English). mo. $21.13. **(Subscription address:** China International Book Trading Corporation, PO Box 399, Library Service Department, Beijing 100044 People's Republic of China.**)** **NLM** W1; ZH33. **CODEN** CTYAD8. Documents available from CASDDS. ***Continues** Chung Tsao Yao Tung Hsun.*
**Ind/Abst** Chem. Abstr.; Int. Pharm. Abstr.

CC/1001-8689
**ZHONGGUO KANGSHENGSU ZAZHI.** (ZHONGGUO KANGSHENGSU ZAZHI.). **VFOAT** Chinese Journal of Antibiotics. (1985)-. Academic Scholarly Publication. Chinese (English). bm. RMBY27.00, $100.00. Sichuan Ind Inst Antibiotics, Editorial Office C J A, 9 Sha-Ban-Qiao Road, Chengdu Sichuan 610051, People's Republic of China. **Tel** 011 86 4444641, FAX 011 86 028 4443218, telex 60111 SIIA CN. **ED** Huang Le-yi. **DD** 615.329. Index available. cum. index. **Bk Rev. Ad Acc.** Full Page (B&W) $1,100.00. Half Page (B&W) $600.00. **Pr Rev. Circ:** 6,500. ***Continues** Kangshengsu, 0254-6116.*
**Ind/Abst** EMBASE.

CH/1001-0408
**ZHONGGUO YAOFANG.** **VFOAT** Journal of China Pharmacy. (1990)-. Periodical. Chinese. bm. **DD** 615.1.
**Ind/Abst** Int. Pharm. Abstr.

CC/1000-5048
**ZHONGGUO YAOKE DAXUE XUEBAO.** **VFOAT** Journal of China Pharmaceutical University. (1979)-. Academic Scholarly Publication. Chinese. qt. China Pharmaceutical University, 24 Tongjia Xiang, 210009 Nanjing, Jiangsu, People's Repubic of China. **DD** 615.1. Documents available from CASDDS.
**Ind/Abst** Chem. Abstr.; EMBASE; Int. Pharm. Abstr.

CC/0253-9756
**ZHONGGUO YAOLI XUEBAO.** (CHUNG-KUO YAO LI HSUEH PAO.). [Zhongguo yaoli xuebao]. **VFOAT** Acta Pharmacologica Sinica. Vol. 1 (Sept. 1980)-. Academic Scholarly Publication. Chinese. bm. $72.00. Science Press, 16 Donghuangchenggen North Street, Beijing 100707, People's Republic of China. **Tel** 011 86 1 4019821, 011 86 1 4010642, FAX 011 86 1 4012180, 011 86 1 4019810, telex 210147. **(Subscription address:** China International Book Trading Corporation, PO Box 399, Library Service Department, Beijing 100044

People's Republic of China.) **LC** RM1. **DD** 615.1/05. **NLM** W1 CH991C. **CODEN** CYLPDN. **Pr Rev.** Documents available from The Genuine Article, BIOSIS Document Express, CASDDS.
**Desc:** Contains information on pharmacology.
**Ind/Abst** Biol. Abstr.; Chem. Abstr.; Chem. Titles; EMBASE; Health Plan. Adminis.; Helminthol. Abstr.; Hortic. Abstr.; Index Med. (1980-); NAPRALERT; Nutr. Abstr. Rev., Ser. A, Hum. Exp.; PESTDOC; Protozoolog. Abstr.; Res. Alert [Full Cov.]; Rev. Med. Vet. Mycology; Sci. Cit. Index; SCISEARCH; Seed Abstr.; Soc. Sci. Cit. Index [Select. Cov.]; Trop. Dis. Bull.

CC/1000-3002
**ZHONGGUO YAOLIXUE YU DULIXUE ZAZHI.** **See** Medical Science and Technology-Toxicology.

CC/1001-2494
**ZHONGGUO YAOXUE ZAZHI (1989).** (CHUNG-KUO YAO HSUEH TSA CHIH.). [Zhongguo yaoxue zazhi]. **Added/Corp** Chung-kuo Yao Hsueh Hui. **VFOAT** Chinese Pharmaceutical Journal; Zhongguo Yaoxue Zazhi. (Jan. 1989)-. Periodical. Chinese (summaries and/or abstracts in English). mo. $37.51. Chung-Kuo Yao Hsueh Hui, Beijing, China. **(Subscription address:** China National Publishers / Industry & Trade, PO Box 782, Beijing, China.) **LC** RS1; .C564. **DD** 615/.1/05. **CODEN** ZYZAEU. Documents available from BIOSIS Document Express, CASDDS. ***Continues*** *Yao Hsueh Tung Pao.*
**Ind/Abst** Biol. Abstr. (1990-); Chem. Abstr.; Int. Pharm. Abstr.

CC/1001-8255
**ZHONGGUO YIYAO GONGYE ZAZHI.** (CHUNG-KUO I YAO KUNG YEH TSA CHIH.). [Zhongguo yiyao gongye zazhi]. **Added/Corp** Kuo Chia i Yao Kuan Li Chu i Yao Kung Yeh Ching Pao Chung Hsin Chan. Shang-Hai i Yao Kung Yeh Yen Chiu Yuan. **VFOAT** Chinese Journal of Pharmaceuticals. (198?)-. Academic Scholarly Publication. Chinese. mo. $36.00. Shanghai Yiyao Gongye Yanjiuyuan / Shanghai Institute of Pharmaceutical Industry, 1320 Beijing Xilu, Shanghai 200040, People's Republic of China. **Tel** 2479808. **ED** Wang Qizhuo. **CODEN** ZYGZEA. **Bk Rev. Circ:** 6,500. Documents available from CASDDS, BLDSC, CASDDS. ***Continues*** *Ti Yao Kung Yeh, 0255-7223.*
**Ind/Abst** Chem. Abstr.

NE/0169-2720
**ZIEKENHUISFARMACIE.** (ZIEKENHUISFARMACIE : TIJDSCHRIFT VAN DE NEDERLANDSE VERENIGING VAN ZIEKENHUISAPOTHEKERS.). [Ziekenhuisfarmacie]. **Added/Corp** Nederlandse Vereniging van Ziekenhuisapothekers. **VFOAT** Ziekenhuis Farmacie. (1985)-. Academic Scholarly Publication. Dutch. Four times a year. Fl50.00. KNMP Secretariaat NVZA, Postbus 30460, 2500 GL Den Haag Netherlands. **Tel** 11 31 70 3624111. **CODEN** ZIFAEM. Documents available from CASDDS.
**Ind/Abst** Chem. Abstr. (1986-); Curr. Biotechnol.

## ABSTRACTING, BIBLIOGRAPHIES AND STATISTICS

US/0898-4654
**AMERICAN STATISTICAL ASSOCIATION PROCEEDINGS OF THE BIOPHARMACEUTICAL SECTION.** [Proc. Biopharm. Sect.]. **Main/Corp** American Statistical Association. Meeting. **Added/Corp** American Statistical Association. Biopharmaceutical Section. **VFOAT** Proceedings of the Biopharmaceutical Section. (1983)-. Statistical Publication. English. an. $53.50. American Statistical Association, 1429 Duke Street, Alexandria VA 22314. **Tel** (703)684-1221, (202)393-3253, FAX (703)684-2037 (orders). **DD** 615. **NLM** W1; AM8127.
**Ind/Abst** Curr. Index Stat.; Int. Bibliogr. Sociol.

US
**IDIS SYSTEM / CD-ROM.** (19??)-. English. mo. $2610.00 US, Canada, and Mexico; $2870.00 other. Iowa Drug Information Service, The University of Iowa, 100 Oakdale Campus, N330 OH, Iowa City IA 52242-5000. **Tel** (319)335-4800, (800)525-4347, FAX (319)335-4077. available on microfiche; available on an online database.
**Desc:** Database of index records to drug therapy articles with full text from leading medical and pharmaceutical journals.

UK/0019-3925
**INDEX OF NEW PRODUCTS.** (19??)-. Periodical. English. Twenty-four times a year. $1,300.00. IMS World Publications Ltd, 7 Harwood Avenue, london NW1 6JB England. **Tel** 011 44 71 393 5000, FAX 011 44 393 5900.

US/0020-8264
**INTERNATIONAL PHARMACEUTICAL ABSTRACTS.** [Int. pharm. abstr.]. **Added/Corp** American Society of Hospital Pharmacists. Vol. 1, No. 1 (Jan. 15, 1964)-. Abstracting/Indexing Service. English. sm. $100.00 (ASHP members), $425.00 (non-member) US. American Society of Hospital Pharmacists, 7272 Wisconsin Avenue, Bethesda MD 20814. **Tel** (301)657-3000, (301)657-4383, FAX (301)652-8278. **ED** Dwight R Tousignaut. **LC** RS1; .I63. **DD** 615. **NLM** ZQV 704 I61. **CODEN** IPMAAH. **[CCC].** cum. index. **Bk Rev. Ad Acc. Circ:** 1,500 (ctrl). available on an online database from UTOPIA; DATA-STAR; DIMDI; NLM; BRS; DIALOG; and European Space Agency; available on CD-ROM from Cambridge Scientific Abstracts; available on microfilm and microfiche from University Microfilms International (UMI); available on microfiche; available on magnetic tape.
**Desc:** Provides abstracts on a variety of topics ranging from drug interactions, new drugs, and investigational drugs to educational, management and reimbursement issues.
**Ind/Abst** Anal. Abstr.

US
**IOWA DRUG INFORMATION SERVICE.** (1972)-. Abstracting/Indexing Service. English. CD-ROM/$3,700 plus shipping & handling; MICROFICHE/$1,590 plus shipping & handling. Iowa Drug Information Service, The University of Iowa, 100 Oakdale Campus, N330 OH, Iowa City IA 52242-5000. **Tel** (319)335-4800, (800)525-4347, FAX (319)335-4077. available on microfiche and CD-ROM; available on an online database.

US
**NAPRALERT [ONLINE DATABASE].** Abstracting/Indexing Service. English. $100.00-$10,000.00. University of Illinois at Chicago, Program for Collaborative Research in the Pharmaceutical Sciences (M/C 877), College of Pharmacy, Box 6998, Chicago IL 60680. **Tel** (312)996-7253, telex 206243. available on an online database (electronic mail) from Compuserve; Prodigy; Internet; and BITNET.
**Desc:** An acronym for NAtural PRoducts ALERT, it is a unique data base of world literature on the chemical constituents and pharmacology of plant, microbial and animal (primarily marine) extracts. Contains considerable data on the chemistry and pharmacology (including human studies) of secondary metabolites on known structure, derived from natural sources.

NZ/0110-9510
**NEW ETHICALS CATALOGUE.** [New ethicals cat.]. (1973)-. Periodical. English. Three times a year (Apr., Aug., Dec.). 120.00NZ$ New Zealand; 124.00NZ$ Pacific Region; 143.00NZ$ US, Canada and Asia; 147.00NZ$ UK, Europe & other. ADIS International Ltd, 41 Centorian Drive, Private Bag 65901, Mairangi Bay, Auckland 10 New Zealand. **Tel** 011 64 9 4798100, FAX 011 64 9 4791418. **(Subscription address:** US/ 582 Middletown Boulevard B-30, Langhorne, PA 19047-1822; HK/ 18/F Tung Sun Commercial Centre, 194-200 Lockhard Road, Wanchai Hong Kong) **ED** J. Sutherland. **NLM** QV 772 N531. **[CCC].** Each issue contains an index to its own contents (no volume index)--loose. **Ad Acc. Circ:** 9,000 (ctrl). ***Continues in part*** *New Ethicals and Medical Progress.*
**Desc:** Listing of all prescription medicine drugs available in New Zealand by brand with all prescribing data, adverse reactions etc. Extensive cross references to medical journal articles and New Ethicals Compendium.

CN/0829-741X
**OPERATING RESULTS. RETAIL DRUG STORES.** (OPERATING RESULTS, RETAIL DRUG STORES / STATISTICS CANADA, MERCHANDISING AND SERVICES DIVISION, RETAIL TRADE SECTION.). [Oper. results, Retail drug stores]. **Added/Corp** Statistics Canada. Merchandising and Services Division. Analysis and Development Section. Statistics Canada. Retail Trade Section. **VFOAT** Retail Drug Stores; Pharmacies au Retail; Resultants de l'Exploitation, Pharmacies au Retail. (1978)-. English (French). an. 15.00Can$ Canada; $16.00 other. Statistics Canada, Publications Sales & Services, Main Building Room 1710, Ottawa Ontario K1A 0T6 Canada. **Tel** (613)951-5078, (800)267-6677, FAX (613)951-1584, telex 053-3585. **LC** HD9670.C2; O63. **DD** 381/.456151/0971021.
**Desc:** Presents data on retail drug stores: operating results, gross profit, detailed expense items and net profit as a percentage of net sales for incorporated and unincorporated firms. These ratios are stratified by sales size and by province or region whenever possible. Includes data analysis, methodology and bibliography.

US/0362-4439
**PHARMACEUTICAL NEWS INDEX.** [Pharm. news index]. Vol. 1 (Jan. 1976)-. Abstracting/Indexing Service. English. mo. Price varies per vendor (Vendors: BRS, DIALOG Information Services, ORBIT Search Service, OCLC). University Microfilms International, 300 North Zeeb Road, Ann Arbor MI 48106-1346. **Tel** (313)761-4700, (800)521-0600 Exts. 2490, 2491, FAX (313)973-1540. **NLM** ZQV 4 P5355. cum. index. available on magnetic tape.
**Desc:** Online service containing indexing of articles published in over twenty major pharmaceutical publications. Coverage dates from 1974. The complete database contains more than 438,000 records; more than 720 are added every week.

US
**PMA STATISTICAL FACTBOOK.** **See** Pharmacy and Pharmacology.

UK
**RINGDOC.** Vol. 1, No. 1 (Nov. 1964)-. Abstracting/Indexing Service. English. wk. £293.00 (except North America). Derwent Publications Ltd., Derwent House 14, Great Queen Street, London WC2B 5DF England. **Tel** 011 44 71 3442800.
**Desc:** Aims to meet the scientific documentation needs of the pharmaceutical industry, which includes all important articles relating to drug development, manufacture, evaluation and use. All articles giving significant information on one or more drugs (including vaccines) are selected whether the subject of the paper is chemistry, biochemistry, pharmaceutics, pharmacology, medicine, etc. All papers describing isolation, synthesis, formulation, pharmacology, toxicology, metabolism, clinical trials, etc. of novel or established drugs are included. Papers which do not mention drugs, contain relatively trivial references to drugs, site purely incidental drug therapy unrelated to the subject of study, site routine use of anesthetics and diagnostic agents, discuss generic drug groups (unless these are the main subject of the paper), or contain items of purely Vetdoc (veterinary), Pestdoc (pesticides, plant protection and related subjects) or biotechnological interest are not included. Papers discussing drug legislation, regulatory affairs, documentation, sales, abuse, alcoholism, or tobacco smoking are not included.

# PHILANTHROPY

SP/0532-8500
**ANALES DE LA FUNDACION JUAN MARCH.** **Main/Corp** Fundacion Juan March. (1956-1962)-. Spanish. an. Free. Fundacion Juan March, Castello 77, 28006 Madrid Spain. **Tel** 11 34 1 435 4240. **ED** Andres Berlanga. **LC** AS911.F816; A15. **DD** 011.4/4. **Bk Rev.** ctrl circ.
**Desc:** Collects information on the activities developed by the Juan March Foundation in the corresponding year.

US
**ANNUAL INDEX OF FOUNDATION REPORTS / OFFICES OF THE ATTORNEY GENERAL.** English. an. $35.00. Maryland Office of Attorney General, 1 South Calvert Street, Baltimore MD 21202. **Tel** (301)576-6300. **ED** Sharon Sullivan. **LC** HV98.M3; A6. **DD** 361.7/632/025752. **Ad Acc.** ctrl circ.
**Desc:** Information on private foundations contributions given, etc.

US/0069-0635
**ANNUAL REPORT - CARNEGIE CORPORATION OF NEW YORK.** **Main/Corp** Carnegie Corporation of New York. (1953)-. English. an (Spring). Free. Carnegie Corporation of New York, 437 Madison Avenue, New York NY 10022. **Tel** (212)371-3200. **NLM** W1 CA84. cum. index. **Circ:** 17,000. ***Continues*** *Carnegie Corporation of New York. Reports of Officers for the Fiscal Year Ended September 30 ... .*

US
**ANNUAL REPORT OF THE DUKE ENDOWMENT.** **Main/Corp** Duke Endowment. 1962/63-. English. an. **LC** HV97.D8; D82A. **DD** 001.4/4/0973. **NLM** W1 DU648P. ***Formed by the union of*** *Duke Endowment. Financial Statement* ***and*** *Annual Reports of the Hospital and Orphan Sections.*

US/0066-8168
**ARTS PATRONAGE SERIES.** **See** The Arts.

US/0272-0825
**BARNES ASSOCIATES NATIONAL FUND RAISER.** **Main/Corp** Barnes Associates. **VFOAT** National Fund Raiser. (1974)-. Periodical. English. Twelve times a year. $95.00. Barnes Associates, 603 Douglas Boulevard, Roseville CA 95678-3244. **Tel** (916)786-7471, (800)231-4157, FAX (916)782-2145. **ED** W. David Barnes. Index available. cum. index. **Bk Rev.** (Qty: 2-3). **Circ:** 1,900. Documents available from the publisher. ***Continues*** *Barnes Fund Raiser.*
**Desc:** "How-to" instructions for organizing and implementing fund-raising programs successfully.

●US/1065-7282
**CALIFORNIA PHILANTHROPY REPORT.** (1992)-. Periodical. English. qt. $47.00. California Philanthropy Report, PO Box 4098, Newport Beach CA 92661.

GW/0008-6614
**CARITAS (FREIBURG IM BREISGAU).** (CARITAS.). [Caritas]. **Added/Corp** Deutscher Caritasverband. (1910)-. Periodical. German. mo. DM70.00. Lambertus-Verlag GmbH, Postfach 1026, 79010 Freiburg, Germany. **Tel** 011 49 761 3 68 25 0, FAX

011 49 761 3 70 64. Index available. cum. index. **Bk Rev. Ad Acc. Circ:** 2,000. ***Continues*** *Charitas.*
**Ind/Abst** Bibliogr. Mission.

US/0278-0593
**CHARITABLE GIVING AND SOLICITATION.** No. 1 (1981)-. English. mo. Warren Gorham & Lamont Inc., Park Square Building, 31 St. James Avenue, Boston MA 02116-4112. **Tel** (617)423-2020, (800)950-1207, FAX (617)423-2026.

●US/1052-3979
**CHARITABLE ORGANIZATIONS OF THE U.S.** [Charit. organ. U.S.]. **Added/Corp** Gale Research Inc. **VFOAT** Charitable Organizations of the US. **VAT** Charitable Organizations of the United States. 1st Edition (1991-1992)-. English. be. $150.00. Gale Research Inc., 835 Penobscot Building, Detroit MI 48226. **Tel** (800)877-GALE, (313)961-2242, FAX (313)961-6083, telex TWX 810-221-7086. **LC** HV89; .C48. **DD** 361.7/025/73.

UK/0265-5209
**CHARITY LONDON. 1983.** [Charity Lond. 1983]. (1983)-. Periodical. English. mo. £38.00 UK; £54.80 other. Charities Aid Foundation, 48 Penbury Road, Tonbridge Kent TN9 2JD England. **Tel** 011 44 732 771333, FAX 011 44 732 350570. **ED** Stewart Laurie. **Bk Rev. Ad Acc. Circ:** 2,500 (ctrl).
**Desc:** View on the charitable world, with news of campaigns, investments, fundraising, finance, and appeals. Information on appointments, legislation and government involvement.

US/1040-676X
**CHRONICLE OF PHILANTHROPY, THE.** [Chron. philanthr.]. Vol. 1, No. 1 (Oct. 25, 1988)-. Periodical. English. Twenty-four times a year. $67.50. Chronicle of Higher Education, 1255 23rd Street Northwest, Washington DC 20037. **Tel** (202)466-1200. **(Subscription address:** Chronicle of Philanthropy, PO Box 1989, Marion OH 43305.**) ED** Philip W. Semas. **DD** 361. **Bk Rev. Ad Acc. Circ:** 20,000. available on microfilm and microfiche from University Microfilms International (UMI).
**Desc:** Provides news and information for fund raisers, professional employees of foundation, corporate grant makers, and people who work for non-profit, tax exempt organizations in health, education, religion, the arts, and social services. It offers service features as lists of grants, fund raising ideas, statistics, updates on regulations, and an extensive job advertising section.

US/1070-7840
**COMPLETE GUIDE TO FLORIDA FOUNDATIONS, THE.** [Complete guide Fla. found.]. **Added/Corp** Florida. Dept. of Community Affairs. (1986)-. English. an (Dec). $90.00. Florida Funding Publications Inc, 9350 South Dixie Hwy, Suite 1560, Miami FL 33156. **Tel** (305)670-2203, FAX (305)670-2208. **ED** Alice Culbreath, Ivett Perez. **LC** HV98.F5; C66. **DD** 361.7/632/025759. Index available. **Circ:** 1,000.
**Desc:** Directory of over 1,450 Florida private foundations which make grants to charitable causes. Appendices include distribution by city, corporate and community foundations and by giving priority.

US/0734-4694
**CONNECTICUT FOUNDATION DIRECTORY.** **Added/Corp** United Way of Greater New Haven. (1979)-. English. ir. $90.00 (latest edition). Data Inc., 70 Audubon Street, New Haven CT 06510-1206. **Tel** (203)772-1345. **LC** AS911.A2; C67. **DD** 001.4/4.

CN/1195-6925
**CONTACT - ASSOCIATION DE SPINA-BIFIDA ET D'HYDROCEPHALIE DU QUEBEC.** (CONTACT.). [Contact - Assoc. spina-bifida hydroc,eph. Qu,e.]. **Added/Corp** Spina Bifida and Hydrocephalus Association of Quebec. Vol. 1, No. 1 (Sept. 1988)-. Periodical. English (French). Three times a year. 10.00Can$ (individuals), 15.00Can$ (institutions) Comes with Spinda-Bifida Association of Quebec membership. Spinda-Bifida Association of Quebec, 5757 Avenue of Decelles, Suite 425, Montreal Quebec H3S 2C3 Canada. **Tel** (514)340-9019, FAX (514)340-9109. **DD** 616.7. Index available. cum. index. **Ad Acc, Adv Mgr:** S. Beliale, **Tel** (514)340-9019. available on an online database from the publisher.
**Desc:** A newsletter for giving information to our members who have spina-bifida, to different schools, hospitals and CLSC.

US/0197-937X
**CORPORATE 500. THE DIRECTORY OF CORPORATE PHILANTHROPY.** [Corp. 500, Dir. corp. philanthr.]. **Added/Corp** Public Management Institute. **VFOAT** Corporate Five Hundred. The Directory of Corporate Philanthropy; Directory of Corporate Philanthropy. **VAT** Corporate Five-Hundred. The Directory of Corporate Philanthropy. (1980)-. Directory. English. an. $360.00. Gale Research Inc., 835 Penobscot Building, Detroit MI 48226. **Tel** (800)877-GALE, (313)961-2242, FAX (313)961-6083, telex TWX 810-221-7086. **ED** Kenneth Gilman. **LC** HV97.A3; C63. **DD** 361.7/65/02573. **Circ:** 3,000.
**Desc:** Source of factual information on the funding programs of the 580 American corporations with the most active programs. This edition adds profiles of 70 corporations responsible for gifts of $95 million to nonprofit organizations.

US
**CORPORATE FOUNDATION PROFILES.** **Added/Corp** Foundation Center. 1st (1980)-. English. be. $149.50. Foundation Center, 79 Fifth Avenue, Department EN, New York NY 10003. **Tel** (212)620-4230, (800)424-9836, FAX (212)807-3677. **LC** HV89; .C68. **DD** 361.7/632/02573.
**Ind/Abst** Curr. Lit. Fam. Plan. (19??-19??).

US/1055-0623
**CORPORATE GIVING DIRECTORY.** [Corp. giv. dir.]. **Added/Corp** Taft Group (Rockville, Md.). 12th Ed. (1991)-. Directory. English. an (published in Sept. of prior year). $365.00 (also comes in combination with Taft Foundation Reporter). Taft Group, 835 Penobscott Building, Customer Service, Detroit MI 48226. **Tel** (800)877-8238, FAX (313)961-6083. **(Subscription address:** Taft Group, PO Box 71701, Chicago, IL 60694; telephone: (800)877-8238 ext. 1716**) LC** HV97.A3; T29. **DD** 361.7/65/097305. **NLM** HV 97.A3; T1243. ***Continues*** *Taft Corporate Giving Directory, 0882-7176.*

US
**CORPORATE PHILANTHROPY IN NEW ENGLAND. VOLUME 3, MAINE.** **Added/Corp** D.A.T.A., Inc. (1985)-. Directory. English. ir. $14.95. Development and Technical Assistance Center (DATA), 30 Arbor Street North, Hartford CT 06106. **Tel** (203)786-5225. **ED** Mike Burns. **LC** HV98.M2; C58. **DD** 361.7/65/09741. Index available. **Circ:** 500.
**Desc:** Directory of 300 Maine corporate philanthropic policies, practices and procedures.

US
**CORPORATE PHILANTHROPY IN NEW ENGLAND. VOLUME 4, VERMONT.** Began in 1985. English. ir. $14.95. The Development and Technical Assistance Center, 25 Science Park/Suite 502, New Haven CT 06511. **Tel** (203)786-5225. **ED** Mike Burns. **LC** HV98.V5; C67. **DD** 361.7/65/09743. Index available. **Circ:** 500.
**Desc:** A directory of 50 corporate philanthropic policies and priorities.

US/1051-6514
**CORPORATE PHILANTHROPY IN RHODE ISLAND.** [Corp. philanthr. R. I.]. English. ir. The Development and Technical Assistance Center, 25 Science Park/Suite 502, New Haven CT 06511. **Tel** (203)786-5225. **ED** Mike Burns. **DD** 361. Index available. **Circ:** 500.
**Desc:** Directory of over 200 Rhode Island corporate philanthropic policies, priorities and procedures.

US/0885-8365
**CORPORATE PHILANTHROPY REPORT.** **Added/Corp** Public Management Institute. Vol. 1, No. 2 (Aug. 1985)-. Periodical. English. mo (10 issues). $200.00. Capitol Publications, 1101 King Street, Suite 444, Alexandria VA 22314. **Tel** (703)683-4100, (800)655-5597. **(Subscription address:** Capitol Publications, PO Box 1453, Alexandria, VA 22313**) ED** Craig Smith. **DD** 361. **Circ:** 2,000. ***Continues*** *Corporate Philanthropy.*
**Desc:** Publication on trends and analysis for corporate support of nonprofit organizations. Details new ways to get corporate grants.

US
**COUNCIL COLUMNS / COUNCIL ON FOUNDATIONS.** **Added/Corp** Council on Foundations. Vol. 8, No. 4 (April 7, 1989)-. Periodical. English. Nineteen times a year. free to members; $45.00 (one year), $80.00 (two year) nonmembers. Council on Foundations, 1828 L Street Northwest, Washington DC 20036. **Tel** (202)466-6512, FAX (202)785-3926. **ED** Robin Hettleman and Margaret Schmid Odell. **Bk Rev**, (Qty: 15). **Circ:** 8,000 (ctrl). ***Continues*** *Newsletter (Council on Foundations).*
**Desc:** Features updates on legislative regulatory activities of Congress, and coverage of key events and activities of the Council on Foundations and its members.

US
**D.C. DIRECTORY OF NATIVE AMERICAN FEDERAL AND PRIVATE PROGRAMS / NATIVE AMERICAN-PHILANTHROPIC NEWS SERVICE.** ***Title Change.*** Directory. English. an. Native American Directory, PO Box 39003, Washington DC 20016. **Tel** (312)380-2700. ***Continued by*** *Robinson's Redbook : A Native American Guide to Washington, DC.*

US/0884-9056
**DIRECTORY OF FOUNDATIONS OF THE GREATER WASHINGTON AREA.** [Dir. found. gt. Wash. area]. **Added/Corp** Community Foundation of Greater Washington. (1984)-. Periodical. English. an (Published in odd years). $13.50 (two years). Community Foundation of Greater Washington Inc, 1002 Wisconson Avenue Northwest, Washington DC 20007. **Tel** (202)338-8993. **LC** HV99.W29; D44. **DD** 361.7/632/025753.
**Desc:** Contains detailed descriptions of more than 500 private foundations in the Washington Metropolitan area. More than 4,000 names of foundation directors, board members, and trustees and the most current information available on each foundation.

US/0736-7759
**DIRECTORY OF FREE PROGRAMS, PERFORMING TALENT AND ATTRACTIONS, THE.** **See** The Arts-Performing Arts.

UK
**DIRECTORY OF GRANT-MAKING TRUSTS.** **Added/Corp** Charities Aid Fund. Charities Aid Foundation. (1968)-. Directory. English. be. £50.00. CAF Publications, 48 Pembury Road, Tonbridge Kent TN9 2JD England. **ED** Anne Villemur. **LC** AS911.A2; D57. **DD** 001.4/4/02541. **Circ:** 7,000.
**Desc:** Detailed, cross-referenced entries for 2,500 Trusts and Foundations.

US/1046-4263
**DIRECTORY OF INTERNATIONAL CORPORATE GIVING IN AMERICA.** [Dir. int. corp. giv. Am.]. **Added/Corp** Taft Group (Rockville, Md.). **VFOAT** International Corporate Giving in America; Directory of International Corporate Giving in America and Abroad. 1st Ed. (1989)-. Directory. English. an. $160.00. Taft Group, 835 Penobscott Building, Customer Service, Detroit MI 48226. **Tel** (800)877-8238, FAX (313)961-6083. **LC** PAR; HG4028.C6; D57. **DD** 361.
**Desc:** Gives in-depth, double-checked profiles of corporate charitable giving programs of hundreds of internationally-owned, U.S.-based companies. Includes non-monetary support-donated goods and services.

US
**DIRECTORY OF NEW AND EMERGING FOUNDATIONS.** **Added/Corp** Foundation Center. (1988)-. English. be (every two years). $99.50. Foundation Center, 79 Fifth Avenue, Department EN, New York NY 10003. **Tel** (212)620-4230, (800)424-9836, FAX (212)807-3677.
**Desc:** Provides access to information on the new foundations making grants in specific geographic locations and subject areas.

US
**DIRECTORY OF TEXAS FOUNDATIONS.** **VFOAT** Texas Foundations. (1975)-. Directory. English. an. $115.00. Funding Information Center of Texas, PO Box 15070, 530 McCollough #600, San Antonio TX 78212. **Tel** (210)227-4333, FAX (210)227-0310. **ED** Mary W. Walters. **Bk Rev. Circ:** 1,500.
**Desc:** Lists all 2,257 private and community foundations in Texas and includes full descriptions of over 1,700.

●US
**DIRECTORY OF THE MAJOR INDIANA FOUNDATIONS, THE.** **Added/Corp** Logos Associates. (1992)-. Directory. English. Logos Associates, 7 Park Street, Room 212, Attleboro MA 02703. **LC** HV98.I6; D58.

US/0014-6137
**F R I MONTHLY PORTFOLIO.** **Main/Corp** Fund Raising Institute. (1962)-. Periodical. English. mo (12 issues). $75.00 (includes Fund Raising Institute Letter and Fund Raising Institute Bulletin). Taft Group, 835 Penobscott Building, Customer Service, Detroit MI 48226. **Tel** (800)877-8238, FAX (313)961-6083. **(Subscription address:** Taft Group, PO Box 71701, Chicago, IL 60694; telephone: (800)877-8238 ext. 1716**)** Index available (bound in Dec. issue).

●US/1066-8896
**FEDERAL SUPPORT FOR NONPROFITS.** [Fed. support nonprofits]. (1993)-. English. an. $150.00. Taft Group, 835 Penobscott Building, Customer Service, Detroit MI 48226. **Tel** (800)877-8238, FAX (313)961-6083. **DD** 361.
**Desc:** Focuses specifically on the approximately 800 federal programs that give grants to nonprofit organizations.

●US
**FISCAL YEAR ESTIMATED TAX ON UNRELATED BUSINESS TAXABLE INCOME FOR TAX-EXEMPT ORGANIZATIONS (WORKSHEET).** **See** Public Administration-Public Finance and Taxation.

US/0071-7274
**FORD FOUNDATION ANNUAL REPORT.** **Main/Corp** Ford Foundation. **Added/Corp** Ford Foundation. Annual Report. Ford Foundation. Report. (1951)-. English. an. Free. Ford Foundation, 320 East 43rd Street, New York NY 10017. **Tel** (212)573-5169. **ED** Robert Tolles. **LC** AS911.F6; A442. **DD** 061. **NLM** W1 FO558C. **Circ:** 14,000. ***Continues***

*Ford Foundation. Preliminary Report.*
**Desc:** A complete review of grants and finances of the Ford Foundation.

●US/1067-7828
**FOUNDATION 1000, THE.** (THE FOUNDATION 1000 / COMPILED BY THE FOUNDATION CENTER.). [Found. 1000]. **Added/Corp** Foundation Center. **VFOAT** Foundation One Thousand. (1992/1993)-. English. an. $265.00. Foundation Center, 79 Fifth Avenue, Department EN, New York NY 10003. **Tel** (212)620-4230, (800)424-9836, FAX (212)807-3677. **LC** HV97.F65; F67a. **DD** 361.7/6/3202573. ***Continues*** *Source Book Profiles, 1067-7925.*
**Desc:** A thorough analyses of the 1,000 largest US foundations and their extensive grant-making programs.

●US/1062-4686
**FOUNDATION & CORPORATE GRANTS ALERT.** [Found. corp. grants alert]. **VFOAT** Foundation and Corporate Grants Alert. Vol. 1, No. 1 (Jan. 1992)-. Periodical. English. mo. $227.00. Capitol Publications, 1101 King Street, Suite 444, Alexandria VA 22314. **Tel** (703)683-4100, (800)655-5597. **(Subscription address:** Capitol Publications, PO Box 1453, Alexandria, VA 22313**)** **DD** 361.

US/0071-8092
**FOUNDATION DIRECTORY, THE.** [Found. dir.]. **Added/Corp** Foundation Center. Foundation Library Center. Russell Sage Foundation. 1st Ed. (1960)-. Directory. English. an. $199.50 (hard bound), $174.50 (paperbound). Foundation Center, 79 Fifth Avenue, Department EN, New York NY 10003. **Tel** (212)620-4230, (800)424-9836, FAX (212)807-3677. **ED** Loren Renz. **LC** AS911.A2; F65. **DD** 061; 060. **NLM** AS 911 F771. Index available. available on an online database from DIALOG. ***Supersedes*** *American Foundations and their Fields.*
**Desc:** Provides detailed descriptions of over 4,400 of the largest US foundations, including address, contact person, and complete financial data. Subject, personnel geographic, and type of support indexes are also included.
**Ind/Abst** Curr. Lit. Fam. Plan. (19??-199?).

●US/1058-6210
**FOUNDATION DIRECTORY. PART 2, A GUIDE TO GRANT PROGRAMS, $25,000-$100,000, THE.** (THE FOUNDATION DIRECTORY. PART 2, A GUIDE TO GRANT PROGRAMS, $25,000-$100,000/ COMPILED BY THE FOUNDATION CENTER.). [Found. dir., Pt. 2 Guide grant prog. $25,000-$100,000]. **Added/Corp** Foundation Center. **VFOAT** Guide to Grant Programs, $25,000-$100,000. (1992)-. Directory. English. be. $174.50. Foundation Center, 79 Fifth Avenue, Department EN, New York NY 10003. **Tel** (212)620-4230, (800)424-9836, FAX (212)807-3677. **LC** AS911.A2; F652. **DD** 061.
**Desc:** Designed specifically for nonprofit organizations that want to broaden their funding base to include mid-sized foundations, those with annual grant programs from $50,000 to $200,000.

US/1066-0445
**FOUNDATION GIVING.** (FOUNDATION GIVING : YEARBOOK OF FACTS AND FIGURES ON PRIVATE, CORPORATE AND COMMUNITY FOUNDATIONS.). [Found. giv.]. **Added/Corp** Foundation Center. (1991)-. English. ir. $24.45 (per copy). Foundation Center, 79 Fifth Avenue, Department EN, New York NY 10003. **Tel** (212)620-4230, (800)424-9836, FAX (212)807-3677. **LC** HV85; .F68. **DD** 361.7/632/097305. ***Continues*** *Foundations Today.*

US/0741-7004
**FOUNDATION GIVING WATCH.** [Found. giv. watch]. **Added/Corp** Taft Corporation. Vol. 1, Issue 1 (June 1981)-. Periodical. English. mo (12 issues). $149.00, includes Foundation updates (comes also with Taft Foundation Information System). Taft Group, 835 Penobscott Building, Customer Service, Detroit MI 48226. **Tel** (800)877-8238, FAX (313)961-6083. **(Subscription address:** Taft Group, PO Box 71701, Chicago, IL 60694; telephone: (800)877-8238 ext. 1716**)** **DD** 361.
**Ind/Abst** Curr. Lit. Fam. Plan. (19??-199?).

US/0090-1601
**FOUNDATION GRANTS INDEX, THE.** [Found. grants index]. **Added/Corp** Foundation Center. Vol. 1 (1970/1971)-. English. an. $150.00. Foundation Center, 79 Fifth Avenue, Department EN, New York NY 10003. **Tel** (212)620-4230, (800)424-9836, FAX (212)807-3677. **LC** AS911.A2; F66. **DD** 001.4/4. **NLM** AS 911; F773. Index available.
**Desc:** Lists grants of $5000 and more awarded by approximately 450 major foundations annually with indexes by recipient name and type, subject, population served, and geographic focus.
**Ind/Abst** Curr. Lit. Fam. Plan. (19??-199?).

US
**FOUNDATION GRANTS INDEX QUARTERLY, THE.** **Added/Corp** Foundation Center. (March 1990)-. Periodical. English. qt. $85.00. Foundation Center, 79 Fifth Avenue, Department EN, New York NY 10003. **Tel** (212)620-4230, (800)424-9836, FAX (212)807-3677. Each issue contains an index to its own contents (no volume index)--loose. ***Continues*** *Foundation Grants Index Bimonthly, 0735-2522.*
**Desc:** Brings you the latest series of grants awarded by some of the country's most influential funders, keeping you abreast of potential funding sources and current trends in your field.

US
**FOUNDATION GRANTS TO INDIVIDUALS / COMPILED BY THE FOUNDATION CENTER.** **Added/Corp** Foundation Center. 1st Ed. (1977)-. English. be. $59.50. Foundation Center, 79 Fifth Avenue, Department EN, New York NY 10003. **Tel** (212)620-4230, (800)424-9836, FAX (212)807-3677. **ED** Loren Renz. **LC** LB2336; .F599. Index available.
**Desc:** Directory describing over 1000 foundations that have programs for or make grants to individual applicants. Includes address and telephone, contact person, application procedures, limitations on giving, etc.

US/0015-8976
**FOUNDATION NEWS.** ***Title Change.*** [Found. news]. **Added/Corp** Council on Foundations. Foundation Library Center. Foundation Center. **VFOAT** FoundatioNews. (1960)-(1994). Periodical. English. bm. Foundation News, 1828 L Street NW, Washington DC 20036. **Tel** (202)466-6512. **ED** Arlie Schardt. **LC** AS911.A2; F68. **DD** 001.4/4/05. **NLM** AS 1 F746. **Bk Rev. Ad Acc. Circ:** 13,000 (ctrl). available on microfilm and microfiche from University Microfilms International (UMI). ***Continued by*** *Foundation News & Commentary, 1076-3961;* ***Continued in part by*** *Foundation Grants Index Bimonthly, 0735-2522.*
**Desc:** Magazine for both grantmakers and grantseekers. Covers how-to's of reviewing proposals and evaluating programs; spotlights innovations in philanthropy; and much more. Includes corporate, research and international columns.
**Ind/Abst** Curr. Lit. Fam. Plan. (19??-199?); Health Plan. Adminis. (?-?); Hospit. Health Admin. Index (?-?); Urban Aff. Abstr. (?-?).

●US/1076-3961
**FOUNDATION NEWS & COMMENTARY.** [Found. news comment.]. **Added/Corp** Council on Foundations. **VFOAT** Foundation News and Commentary; Foundation News. Vol. 35, No. 2 (Mar./Apr. 1994)-. Periodical. English. bm. $35.50 US, Canada & Puerto Rico; $72.00 other. Foundation News, 1828 L Street NW, Washington DC 20036. **Tel** (202)466-6512. **(Subscription address:** KCMS Fulfillment, 3401 East West Highway, Hyattsville MD 20785.**)** **LC** AS911.A2; F68. **DD** 001. Index available in last issue of volume--attached. ***Continues*** *Foundation News, 0015-8976.*
**Desc:** Magazine for both grantmakers and grantseekers. Covers how-to's of reviewing proposals and evaluating programs; spotlights innovations in philanthropy; and much more. Includes corporate, research and international columns.
**Ind/Abst** Hospit. Lit. Index; Ref. Sources.

US/0360-8042
**FOUNDATIONS IN WISCONSIN.** (FOUNDATIONS IN WISCONSIN: A DIRECTORY.). **Added/Corp** Marquette University. Memorial Library. (1975)-. Directory. English. an. $18.00. Foundation Collection, Marquette University Library, Milwaukee WI 53233. **Tel** (414)224-1515. **ED** Susan Hopwood. **LC** AS911.A2; F69. **DD** 001.4/4/025775. **Circ:** 900.
**Desc:** Lists 610 active grantmaking foundations.

US/1045-1951
**FUND RAISER'S GUIDE TO HUMAN SERVICE FUNDING.** [Fund rais. guide human serv. funding]. **Added/Corp** Taft Group (Rockville, Md.). **VFOAT** Guide to Human Service Funding. 1st Ed. (1988)-. English. ir. $120.00. Taft Group, 835 Penobscott Building, Customer Service, Detroit MI 48226. **Tel** (800)877-8238, FAX (313)961-6083. **(Subscription address:** Taft Group, PO Box 71701, Chicago, IL 60694; phone 800 877-8238 ext. 1716**)** **LC** HV89; .F848. **DD** 361.7/068/1.
**Desc:** Identifies and describes approximately 1,770 donors, providing access to more than $4.5 billion in annual aid.

US/1042-0053
**FUND RAISER'S GUIDE TO RELIGIOUS PHILANTHROPY.** [Fund raiser's guide relig. philanthr.]. **Added/Corp** Taft Group (Rockville, Md.). **VFOAT** Guide to Religious Philanthropy; Religious Philanthropy. (1987)-. English. an (published in Oct. of prior year). $145.00. Taft Group, 835 Penobscott Building, Customer Service, Detroit MI 48226. **Tel** (800)877-8238, FAX (313)961-6083. **(Subscription address:** Taft Group, PO Box 71701, Chicago, IL 60694; telephone: (800)877-8238 ext.1716**)** **LC** HV89; .F85. **DD** 361.7/5/02573.
**Desc:** Accurate, detailed profiles of hundreds of private foundations providing grant support to religious organizations and charities, each contributing at least $50,000 annually.

US
**GIVE BUT GIVE WISELY / PHILANTHROPIC ADVISORY SERVICE, COUNCIL OF BETTER BUSINESS BUREAUS.** **Added/Corp** Council of Better Business Bureaus. Philanthropic Advisory Service. (19??)-. Periodical. English. Six times a year. $12.00. Council of Better Business Bureaus, 4200 Wilson Boulevard, Suite 800, Arlington VA 22203. **Tel** (703)276-0100, FAX (703)525-8277.
**Desc:** Collects and distributes information on thousands of nonprofit organization that solicit nationally or have national or international program services. It routinely asks such organizations for information about their programs, governance, fund raising practices, and finances when they have been the subject of inquiries.

US/0436-0257
**GIVING USA.** [Giv. USA]. **Added/Corp** American Association of Fund-Raising Counsel. **VAT** Giving United States of America. 1 (1956)-. Periodical. English. an. $45.00. American Association Fund Raising Counsel, 25 West 43rd Street, New York NY 10036. **Tel** (212)354-5799, FAX (212)768-1795. **ED** Nathan Weber. **LC** HV89; .G5. **DD** 361.705873. **Circ:** 8,500.
**Desc:** A compilation of facts and trends on American philanthropy annually.
**Ind/Abst** Stat. Ref. Index.

US/0899-3793
**GIVING USA UPDATE.** [Giv. USA update]. **VAT** Giving United States of America Update. (Jan./Feb. 1988)-. Periodical. English. bm. $35.00. American Association Fund Raising Counsel, 25 West 43rd Street, New York NY 10036. **Tel** (212)354-5799, FAX (212)768-1795. **ED** Nathan Weber. **LC** HV41; .F9415. **DD** 361.7/0973. **Bk Rev. Circ:** 3,200. ***Continues*** *Fund Raising Review, 0735-8873.*
**Desc:** A summary of articles, speeches, and trends on philanthropy.

●US
**GRANT$ FOR ALCOHOL AND DRUG ABUSE.** **Added/Corp** Foundation Center. **VFOAT** Grants for Alcohol and Drug Abuse; Alcohol and Drug Abuse. (1991/1992)-. English. an. $70.00. Foundation Center, 79 Fifth Avenue, Department EN, New York NY 10003. **Tel** (212)620-4230, (800)424-9836, FAX (212)807-3677. ***Continues*** *Alcohol & Drug Abuse.*
**Desc:** Grants for counseling, education, treatment, medical research, residential care and half-way houses; and projects on alcohol and drug abuse prevention.

US
**GRANT$ FOR ARTS, CULTURE & THE HUMANITIES.** **Added/Corp** Foundation Center. **VFOAT** Grants for Arts, Culture, and the Humanities; Arts, Culture & the Humanities. (1991)-. English. an. $70.00. Foundation Center, 79 Fifth Avenue, Department EN, New York NY 10003. **Tel** (212)620-4230, (800)424-9836, FAX (212)807-3677. **LC** AZ188.U5; G68. ***Continues*** *Grant$ for Arts and Cultural Programs.*
**Desc:** Grants to arts and cultural organizations, historical societies and historic preservation, media visual arts, performing arts, music and museums.

US
**GRANT$ FOR CRIME, LAW ENFORCEMENT, & ABUSE PREVENTION.** **Added/Corp** Foundation Center. **VFOAT** Grants for Crime, Law Enforcement, and Abuse Prevention; Crime, Law Enforcement & Abuse Prevention. (1991)-. English. an. $70.00. Foundation Center, 79 Fifth Avenue, Department EN, New York NY 10003. **Tel** (212)620-4230, (800)424-9836, FAX (212)807-3677. ***Continues*** *Grants for Crime & Law Enforcement.*
**Desc:** Grants for crime prevention, rehabilitation services for offenders, courts and the administration of justice, law enforcement agencies, and protection against and prevention of neglect, abuse, or exploitation.

US
**GRANT$ FOR ENVIRONMENTAL PROTECTION AND ANIMAL WELFARE.** **Added/Corp** Foundation Center. **VFOAT** Grants for Environmental Protection and Animal Welfare. (1991)-. English. an. $70.00. Foundation Center, 79 Fifth Avenue, Department EN, New York NY 10003. **Tel** (212)620-4230, (800)424-9836, FAX (212)807-3677. ***Continues*** *Grants for Environmental Law, Protection and Education.*
**Desc:** Grants to environmental protection and legal agencies; for pollution abatement and control, conservation, and environmental education; and for animal protection and welfare, wildlife preservation, zoos, botanical gardens and aquariums.

US/1045-2761
**GRANT$ FOR HIGHER EDUCATION.** (GRANTS FOR HIGHER EDUCATION / THE FOUNDATION CENTER.). [Grant$ high. educ.]. **Added/Corp** Foundation Center. **VFOAT** Grant$ for Higher Education; Higher Education. (1982)-. English. an. $70.00. Foundation Center, 79 Fifth Avenue, Department EN, New York NY 10003. **Tel** (212)620-4230, (800)424-9836, FAX (212)807-3677. **LC** LB2337.2; .G7. **DD** 378.3/3/02573.

**Desc:** Grants to higher education and graduate/professional schools for programs in all disciplines, as well as to academic libraries and student services and organizations.

US
**GRANT$ FOR HOSPITALS, MEDICAL CARE, & RESEARCH.** **Added/Corp** Foundation Center. **VFOAT** Grants for Hospitals, Medical Care, and Research; Hospitals, Medical Care & Research. (1990/1991)-. English. an (Sept.). $70.00. Foundation Center, 79 Fifth Avenue, Department EN, New York NY 10003. **Tel** (212)620-4230, (800)424-9836, FAX (212)807-3677. ***Continues*** *Foundation Center. Grants for Hospitals and Medical Care Programs.*
**Desc:** Grants for hospitals, clinics, nursing homes, health care facilities, health support services, public health programs, reproductive health care, and medical research.

US
**GRANT$ FOR LIBRARIES AND INFORMATION SERVICES.** **Added/Corp** Foundation Center. **VFOAT** Grants for Libraries and Information Services; Libraries and Information Services. (19??)-. English. an. $70.00. Foundation Center, 79 Fifth Avenue, Department EN, New York NY 10003. **Tel** (212)620-4230, (800)424-9836, FAX (212)807-3677.
**Desc:** Grants for public, academic, research, special and school libraries; for archives and information centers; and for consumer information and philanthropy information centers.

●US
**GRANT$ FOR MENTAL HEALTH, ADDICTIONS & CRISIS SERVICES.** **Added/Corp** Foundation Center. **VFOAT** Grants for Mental Health, Addictions and Crisis Services; Mental Health, Addictions & Crisis Services. (1991/1992)-. English. an. $70.00. Foundation Center, 79 Fifth Avenue, Department EN, New York NY 10003. **Tel** (212)620-4230, (800)424-9836, FAX (212)807-3677. ***Continues*** *Mental Health.*
**Desc:** Grants to hospitals, health centers, residential treatment facilities, group homes and mental health associations; for addiction prevention and treatment; for hotline/crisis intervention services; and for public education and research.

US
**GRANT$ FOR MUSEUMS, ZOOS, & BOTANICAL GARDENS.** **Added/Corp** Foundation Center. **VFOAT** Grants for Museums, Zoos, and Botanical Gardens; Museums, Zoos & Botanical Gardens. (1990/1991)-. English. an. $70.00. Foundation Center, 79 Fifth Avenue, Department EN, New York NY 10003. **Tel** (212)620-4230, (800)424-9836, FAX (212)807-3677. ***Continues*** *Grants for Museums.*

US
**GRANT$ FOR PUBLIC HEALTH AND DISEASES.** **Added/Corp** Foundation Center. **VFOAT** Grants for Public Health and Diseases; Public Health and Diseases. (1990/1991)-. English. an. $70.00. Foundation Center, 79 Fifth Avenue, Department EN, New York NY 10003. **Tel** (212)620-4230, (800)424-9836, FAX (212)807-3677. ***Continues*** *Grants for Public Health.*
**Desc:** Grants for public health programs and diseases, including genetic diseases, birth defects, cancer, AIDS, diseases of specific organs, nerve, muscle, and bone diseases, allergies, and other specific named diseases; for prevention of sexually transmitted diseases and for epidemiology.

US
**GRANT$ FOR PUBLIC POLICY AND PUBLIC AFFAIRS.** **Added/Corp** Foundation Center. **VFOAT** Grants for Public Policy and Public Affairs; Public Policy and Public Affairs. (1991)-. English. an. $70.00. Foundation Center, 79 Fifth Avenue, Department EN, New York NY 10003. **Tel** (212)620-4230, (800)424-9836, FAX (212)807-3677. ***Continues*** *Grants for Public Policy and Political Science.*
**Desc:** Grants for government and public administration, public affairs, leadership development, foreign policy, international peace and security, and a wide range of public policy studies.

US
**GRANT$ FOR RECREATION, SPORTS, & ATHLETICS.** **Added/Corp** Foundation Center. **VFOAT** Grants for Recreation, Sports, and Athletics; Recreation, Sports & Athletics. (1990/1991)-. English. an. $70.00. Foundation Center, 79 Fifth Avenue, Department EN, New York NY 10003. **Tel** (212)620-4230, (800)424-9836, FAX (212)807-3677. ***Continues*** *Grants for Recreation.*
**Desc:** Grants to clubs, leagues, camps, parks, scouting, social service agencies, community organizations, and secondary educational institutions for recreation, athletics and physical fitness.

US
**GRANT$ FOR RELIGION, RELIGIOUS WELFARE, & RELIGIOUS EDUCATION.** **Added/Corp** Foundation Center. **VFOAT** Grants for Religion, Religious Welfare, and Religious Education; Religion, Religious Welfare & Religious Education. (1991)-. English. an. $70.00. Foundation Center, 79 Fifth Avenue, Department EN, New York NY 10003. **Tel** (212)620-4230, (800)424-9836, FAX (212)807-3677. ***Continues*** *Foundation Center. Grants for Religion and Religious Education.*
**Desc:** Includes grants to churches, synagogues, missionary societies and religious orders; and to associations and organizations concerned with religious welfare and education.

●US
**GRANT$ FOR SCHOLARSHIPS, STUDENT AID & LOANS.** **Added/Corp** Foundation Center. **VFOAT** Grants for Scholarships, Student Aid and Loans; Scholarships, Student Aid & Loans. (1991/1992)-. English. an. $70.00. Foundation Center, 79 Fifth Avenue, Department EN, New York NY 10003. **Tel** (212)620-4230, (800)424-9836, FAX (212)807-3677. ***Continues*** *Scholarships, Student Aid & Loans.*
**Desc:** Grants to organizations that provide scholarships and student aid, including undergraduate colleges and universities, medical and dental schools, law schools, nursing schools, music and art schools, cultural organizations, vocational and technical schools, and social service organizations.

US
**GRANT$ FOR SOCIAL AND POLITICAL SCIENCE PROGRAMS.** **Added/Corp** Foundation Center. **VFOAT** Grants for Social and Political Science Programs; Social and Political Science Programs. (1990/91)-. English. an. $70.00. Foundation Center, 79 Fifth Avenue, Department EN, New York NY 10003. **Tel** (212)620-4230, (800)424-9836, FAX (212)807-3677. ***Continues*** *Foundation Center. Grants for Social Science Programs.*
**Desc:** Grants for research and education in political science, anthropology, sociology, psychology, economics, behavioral science, population studies, international studies, ethnic studies, women's studies, urban and rural studies, poverty studies and law.

●US
**GRANT$ FOR SOCIAL SERVICES.** **Added/Corp** Foundation Center. **VFOAT** Grants for Social Services; Social Services. (1992)-. English. an. $70.00. Foundation Center, 79 Fifth Avenue, Department EN, New York NY 10003. **Tel** (212)620-4230, (800)424-9836, FAX (212)807-3677. ***Continues*** *Grant$ for Human Services, Multipurpose Agencies.*
**Desc:** Grants to human service organizations for a broad range of services, including children's and youth services, family services, personal social services, emergency assistance, residential/custodial care; and services to promote the independence of specific population groups such as the homeless and developmentally disabled.

US
**GRANT$ FOR THE AGED / THE FOUNDATION CENTER.** **Added/Corp** Foundation Center. **VFOAT** Grants for the Aged; Grants for the Aging; Aged. (1985)-. English. an. $70.00. Foundation Center, 79 Fifth Avenue, Department EN, New York NY 10003. **Tel** (212)620-4230, (800)424-9836, FAX (212)807-3677.
**Desc:** Grants for advocacy and legal rights, housing, education and community services, employment, health and medical care, recreation, arts and culture, volunteer services and social research.

●US
**GRANT$ FOR THE HOMELESS.** **Added/Corp** Foundation Center. **VFOAT** Grants for the Homeless; Homeless. (1991/1992)-. English. an. $70.00. Foundation Center, 79 Fifth Avenue, Department EN, New York NY 10003. **Tel** (212)620-4230, (800)424-9836, FAX (212)807-3677. ***Continues*** *Homeless.*
**Desc:** Grants to shelters and temporary housing services, legal rights and advocacy programs, food services and health care; and to services for homeless families, children and youth.

US
**GRANTS FOR ELEMENTARY AND SECONDARY EDUCATION / THE FOUNDATION CENTER.** **Added/Corp** Foundation Center. (1984)-. English. an. $70.00. Foundation Center, 79 Fifth Avenue, Department EN, New York NY 10003. **Tel** (212)620-4230, (800)424-9836, FAX (212)807-3677.
**Desc:** Grants to elementary and secondary schools for academic programs, scholarships, counseling, educational testing, drop-out prevention, teacher training and education, salary support, student activities and school libraries.

US
**GRANTS FOR FILM, MEDIA & COMMUNICATIONS / THE FOUNDATION CENTER.** **Added/Corp** Foundation Center. **VAT** Grants for Film, Media and Communications. (1985)-. English. an. $70.00. Foundation Center, 79 Fifth Avenue, Department EN, New York NY 10003. **Tel** (212)620-4230, (800)424-9836, FAX (212)807-3677.
**Desc:** Grants for film, video, documentaries, radio, television, printing, publishing and censorship issues.

US/1056-649X
**GRANTS FOR FOREIGN AND INTERNATIONAL PROGRAMS.** [Grants foreign int. prog.]. **Added/Corp** Foundation Center. **VFOAT** Foreign and International Programs. (1991)-. English. an. $70.00. Foundation Center, 79 Fifth Avenue, Department EN, New York NY 10003. **Tel** (212)620-4230, (800)424-9836, FAX (212)807-3677. **LC** HC59.8; .G73. **DD** 361.7/632/025. ***Continues*** *Grants for International and Foreign Programs.*
**Desc:** Grants for broad purposes to institutions and organizations in foreign countries, to domestic recipients for international activities, development and relief, peace and security, arms control, policy research, human rights and conferences and research.

US
**GRANTS FOR MEDICAL AND PROFESSIONAL HEALTH EDUCATION.** **Added/Corp** Foundation Center. **VFOAT** Medical and Professional Health Education; Medical & Professional Health Education. (19??)-. English. an. $70.00. Foundation Center, 79 Fifth Avenue, Department EN, New York NY 10003. **Tel** (212)620-4230, (800)424-9836, FAX (212)807-3677.
**Desc:** Grants to graduate/professional schools of medicine, dentistry, nursing and public health for general support, faculty development, scholarships and fellowships, student loans, and symposiums and conferences.

US
**GRANTS FOR MINORITIES / FOUNDATION CENTER.** **Added/Corp** Foundation Center. **VFOAT** Minorities. (1982)-. English. an. $70.00. Foundation Center, 79 Fifth Avenue, Department EN, New York NY 10003. **Tel** (212)620-4230, (800)424-9836, FAX (212)807-3677.
**Desc:** Grants for ethnic groups and minority populations, including African Americans, Hispanics, Asian Americans, Native Americans, gays and lesbians, and immigrants and refugees.

US
**GRANTS FOR PHYSICALLY AND MENTALLY DISABLED.** **Added/Corp** Foundation Center. **VFOAT** Grants for the Physically and Mentally Disabled; Physically and Mentally Disabled. (19??)-. English. an. $70.00. Foundation Center, 79 Fifth Avenue, Department EN, New York NY 10003. **Tel** (212)620-4230, (800)424-9836, FAX (212)807-3677. **LC** IN PROCESS. **NLM** W 22; AA1 G7.
**Desc:** Grants to hospitals, schools, and primary care facilities for research, medical and dental care, employment and vocational training, education, diagnosis and evaluation, recreation and rehabilitation, legal aid and scholarships.

US
**GRANTS FOR SCIENCE AND TECHNOLOGY PROGRAMS.** **Added/Corp** Foundation Center. (1988)-. Periodical. English. an. $70.00. Foundation Center, 79 Fifth Avenue, Department EN, New York NY 10003. **Tel** (212)620-4230, (800)424-9836, FAX (212)807-3677. ***Continues*** *Grants for Science Programs.*
**Desc:** Grants for education and research in computer science and technology, scientific societies, associations and institutes, science museums, planetariums, and libraries.

US/1064-4377
**GRANTS FOR WOMEN AND GIRLS.** (GRANT$ FOR WOMEN AND GIRLS / THE FOUNDATION CENTER.). [Grants women girls]. **Added/Corp** Foundation Center. **VFOAT** Grants for Women and Girls; Women and Girls. (1982)-. English. an. $70.00. Foundation Center, 79 Fifth Avenue, Department EN, New York NY 10003. **Tel** (212)620-4230, (800)424-9836, FAX (212)807-3677. **LC** AS911.A2; G64. **DD** 001.4/4.
**Desc:** Includes grants for education, career guidance, vocational training, equal rights, rape prevention, shelter programs for victims of domestic violence, health programs, abortion rights, pregnancy programs, athletics and recreation, arts programs, and social research.

US/0741-2487
**GRANTSMANSHIP NEWS.** ***Ceased.*** 1971-?. Periodical. English. mo. Grantsmanship News Inc, 81 Barrow Street, New York NY 10014. **Tel** (415)675-4264. **ED** William J Lavelle, Robert D Oliver. **Circ:** 1,000 (ctrl).
**Desc:** Information on available grants and contracts for the educational and health-related institutions from government sources and private and public foundations.

US/0740-4832
**GRASSROOTS FUNDRAISING JOURNAL.** [Grassroots fundrais. j.]. (1982)-. Periodical. English. Six times a year. $25.00 US; $32.00 (includes postage) other. Grassroots Fundraising, PO Box 11607, Berkeley CA 94701. **Tel** (415)663-8562. **ED** Kim Klein and Nancy Aders. cum. index (first 9 years). **Bk Rev**, (Qty: 4). **Ad Acc. Circ:** 1,100.

**Desc:** Provides practical, hands-on fundraising techniques and strategies for community based organizations.
**Ind/Abst** Altern. Press Index (199?-).

US/1070-7832
**GUIDE TO FLORIDA STATE PROGRAMS, A.** [Guide Fla. state programs]. **Added/Corp** John L. Adams & Co. **VFOAT** Florida State Programs. (1988)-. English. an (July). $80.00. Florida Funding Publications Inc, 9350 South Dixie Hwy, Suite 1560, Miami FL 33156. **Tel** (305)670-2203, FAX (305)670-2208. **ED** Alice Culbreath, Ivett Perez. **LC** HJ11; .F618. **DD** 353.9759008/025. Index available. **Circ:** 500.
**Desc:** Only directory of Florida state and federally administered grant programs for Florida entitles including government, education, and nonprofit. Contains profiles of over 140 grant and loan programs.

US/0163-383X
**GUIDE TO GIFTS AND BEQUESTS, CALIFORNIA, THE.** 1978/79-. English. be. 440 Park Avenue South, New York NY 10016. **LC** AS28.C2; G84. **DD** 001.4/4/025.

●US/1071-202X
**GUIDE TO U.S. FOUNDATIONS, THEIR TRUSTEES, OFFICERS, AND DONORS.** (GUIDE TO U.S. FOUNDATIONS, THEIR TRUSTEES, OFFICERS, AND DONORS / COMPILED BY THE FOUNDATION CENTER.). [Guide U.S. found. trust. off. donors]. **Added/Corp** Foundation Center. **VFOAT** Guide to United States Foundations, Their Trustees, Officers, and Donors. (1993)-. Periodical. English. The Foundation Center, 79 Fifth Avenue, New York NY 10003. **LC** HV97.A3; G84. **DD** 361.7/632/02573. ***Continues*** *National Data Book of Foundations, 1045-151X.*

CN/0319-0323
**INSIDE OXFAM.** No. 23- Fall 1971-. English. Oxfam-Canada Ontario Region, 175 Carlton Street, Toronto Ontario M5A 2K3 Canada. **Tel** (416)961-3935. **ED** Stephen Allen. **DD** 361/.006/271. ctrl circ. ***Continues*** *Oxfam-Canada News, 0319-0331.*

UK/0143-3474
**INTERNATIONAL DIRECTORY OF VOLUNTARY WORK.** [Int. dir. volunt. work]. (1979)-. Directory. English. be. $15.95. Peterson's Guides, 202 Carnegie Center, Department 2342, Princeton NJ 08543. **Tel** (800)338-3282, FAX (609)452-0966.
**Desc:** Lists and describes over 500 organizations that need short- and long-term volunteers with varied skills.

US
**INTERNATIONAL FOUNDATION DIRECTORY, THE.** **Added/Corp** Gale Research Company. 1st Ed. (1974)-. Directory. English. an. Price varies per volume; 1994 edition--$170.00. Europa Publications Ltd, 18 Bedford Square, London WC1B 3JN England. **Tel** 011 44 71 5808236, telex 21540 EUROPA G. **(Subscription address:** Gale Research Co., 835 Penobscot Building, Detroit MI 48226.**)** **LC** HV7; .I56. **DD** 361.7/632/025. **NLM** HV 7; I613.
**Desc:** Provides a comprehensive picture of foundation activity on a world scale for international foundations, trusts, and other similar international nonprofit institutions. Also covers selected national foundations located throughout the world. Includes foundations or institutions that either operate internationally, offer fellowships or similar awards to applicants from outside its own country, or operate within its own national territory on a scale large enough to establish its international importance.

●US/1061-1266
**MAJOR DONORS.** [Major donors]. **Added/Corp** Taft Group (Rockville, Md.). 1st Ed. (1993)-. English. an. $180.00. Taft Group, 835 Penobscott Building, Customer Service, Detroit MI 48226. **Tel** (800)877-8238, FAX (313)961-6083. **LC** HV91; .M27. **DD** 361.7/4/02573.
**Desc:** Tracks the gifts made by the major supporters of the largest non-profits and charities in the US.

UK
**MANAGEMENT OF VOLUNTARY ORGANISATIONS.** (19??)-. Periodical. English. £118.05. Croner Publ Ltd, Croner House, London Road, Kingston upon Thames, Surrey KT2 6SR England. **Tel** 011 44 81 5473333, FAX 081 547-2637.

US/1052-9098
**MATCHING GIFT DETAILS.** **VFOAT** CASE Matching Gift Details. (1986)-. English. an. $93.00 (nonmembers), $67.00 (members). Council for Advancement and Support of Education, PO Box 90386, Washington DC 20090. **Tel** (800)554-8536. **(Subscription address:** Council for Advancement and Support of Education, 2700 Prosperity Avenue, Fairfax, VA 22031 (800-336-4776)**)** **LC** HG4028.C6; C37. **DD** 361.7/65/0973. ***Continues*** *CASE Matching Gift Details.*

US/0362-1561
**MICHIGAN FOUNDATION DIRECTORY.** **Added/Corp** Council of Michigan Foundations. Michigan League for Human Services. (1976)-. Directory. English. be. $30.00. Michigan League Human Services, 300 North Washington Square, Suite 401, Lansing MI 48933. **Tel** (517)487-5436. **ED** Jeri Fischer. **LC** HV98.M5; M53. **DD** 361.7/6/025774. Index available. **Bk Rev. Circ:** 100,000 (ctrl).
**Desc:** Detailed listing of Michigan foundations with assets of $200,000 and or grant making of $25,000. Lists of smaller foundations as well. Survey of foundation grant making patterns and listing of corporate-giving programs.

US
**MITCHELL GUIDE TO FOUNDATIONS, CORPORATIONS, AND THEIR MANAGERS : NEW JERSEY, THE.** **VFOAT** Mitchell Guide. (198?)-. Periodical. English. be. Mitchell Guide, 195 Nassau Street, PO Box 413, Princeton NJ 08540. ***Continues*** *New Jersey Mitchell Guide.*

US/1070-5228
**MONEY MARKET DIRECTORY OF TAX-EXEMPT ORGANIZATIONS, THE.** (DIRECTORY OF TAX-EXEMPT ORGANIZATIONS.). [Money mark. dir. tax-exempt organ.]. **Added/Corp** Money Market Directories, Inc. **VFOAT** Directory of Tax Exempt Organizations; Money Market Directory of Tax-Exempt Organizations; TEO. (1993)-. Directory. English. an. $395.00. Money Market Directories Inc, 320 East Main Street, PO Box 1608, Charlottesville VA 22902. **Tel** (800)446-2810, (804)977-1450. **LC** HJ2337.U6; D57.

US/1050-9852
**NATIONAL DIRECTORY OF CORPORATE GIVING.** (NATIONAL DIRECTORY OF CORPORATE GIVING / COMPILED BY THE FOUNDATION CENTER.). [Natl. dir. corp. giving]. **Added/Corp** Foundation Center. 1st Ed. (1989)-. Directory. English. be. $199.50. Foundation Center, 79 Fifth Avenue, Department EN, New York NY 10003. **Tel** (212)620-4230, (800)424-9836, FAX (212)807-3677. **LC** HV89; .N26. **DD** 361.7/65/02573.
**Desc:** A guide to over 2,300 corporate philanthropies and grants.

US/1048-8154
**NATIONAL DIRECTORY OF NONPROFIT ORGANIZATIONS.** [Natl. dir. nonprofit organ.]. **Added/Corp** Taft Group (Rockville, Md.). 1st Ed. (1990)-. English. an (published in March). $450.00. Taft Group, 835 Penobscott Building, Customer Service, Detroit MI 48226. **Tel** (800)877-8238, FAX (313)961-6083. **(Subscription address:** Taft Group, PO Box 71701, Chicago, IL 60694; telephone: (800)877-8238 ext. 1716**)** **LC** AS29.5; .N38. **DD** 061. ***Continues*** *Taft Directory of Nonprofit Organizations.*
**Desc:** Provides contact information to hospitals, universities, museums, charities and every non-profit group in the United States with revenues exceeding $100,000.

US
**NEW DIMENSIONS IN GIVING.** Three times a year. Assemblies of God Archives, 1445 Boonville Avenue, Springfield MO 65802-1894. **Tel** (417)862-2781, (417)862-1447, FAX (417)862-8558. **ED** Mel J. DeVries and Freda L. Jackson. **Pr Rev. Circ:** 35,000 (ctrl).
**Desc:** Articles on current tax, financial, and estate planning topics, and how they relate to out right and deferred charitable gifts. Designed to encourage donors to make significant gifts to A/G ministries.

US/0742-3497
**NONPROFIT COUNSEL, THE.** (198?)-. Periodical. English. mo. $108.00. John Wiley & Sons, Inc., 605 Third Avenue, New York NY 10158-0012. **Tel** (212)850-6000, (212)850-6645, FAX (212)850-6088, telex 12-7063. **(Subscription address:** John Wiley & Sons Inc / New Jersey, PO Box 2575, Secaucus NJ 07096-2575.**)**

US/0882-5769
**ORGANIZATION TRENDS.** [Organ. trends]. Vol. 1, No. 1 (July 1984)-. Periodical. English. mo. $125.00. Organization Trends, 1612 K Street NW/Suite 704, Washington DC 20006. **Tel** (202)822-8666, FAX (202)785-5634. **ED** William T Poole. **DD** 060. Index available. **Bk Rev. Circ:** 3,500 (ctrl).
**Desc:** Organization trends focuses on critical issues in philanthropy and public policy and advocacy organizations, and the funding sources that sustain them, and the points at which they intersect.

US/0884-996X
**OUA/DATA'S ... GUIDE TO CORPORATE & FOUNDATION GIVING IN VERMONT.** ***Title Change.*** [OUA/DATA's guide corp. & found. giv. Vt.]. **VFOAT** OUADATA'S ... Guide to Corporate & Foundation Giving in Vermont; Guide to Corporate & Foundation Giving in Vermont; Guide to Corporate and Foundation Giving. 1984-1985-?. English. be. The Development and Technical Assistance Center, 25 Science Park/Suite 502, New Haven CT 06511. **Tel** (203)786-5225. **ED** Mike Burns. **LC** HV98.V5; O9. **DD** 361.7/6/025743. **Circ:** 500. ***Continued by*** *Corporate Philanthropy in New England. Volume 4, Vermont.*
**Desc:** A directory of 100 foundations and 50 corporate philanthropic policies, and priorities.

US/0883-2730
**OUA/DATA'S ... GUIDE TO CORPORATE GIVING IN MAINE.** ***Title Change.*** [OUA/DATA's guide corp. giv. Maine]. **VFOAT** OUADATA'S ... Guide to Corporate Giving in Maine; Guide to Corporate Giving in Maine. **VAT** Office of Urban Affairs/Development and Technical Assistance Research and Resource Center's Guide to Corporate Giving in Maine. 1984-?. English. be. Data Inc., 70 Audubon Street, New Haven CT 06510-1206. **Tel** (203)772-1345. **LC** HV98.M2; O92. **DD** 001.4/4/025741. **Bk Rev. Ad Acc. Circ:** 500 (ctrl). ***Continued by*** *Corporate Philanthropy in New England. Volume 3, Maine.*
**Desc:** A directory of 300 Maine corporation philanthropic policies, practices and procedures.

US
**OUA/DATA'S ... GUIDE TO CORPORATE GIVING IN RHODE ISLAND.** **Added/Corp** OUA/DATA (Organization). **VFOAT** Guide to Corporate Giving in Rhode Island. (1985)-. English. be. $7.50. Data Inc., 70 Audubon Street, New Haven CT 06510-1206. **Tel** (203)772-1345. **ED** Mike Burns. **LC** HG4057.R5; O92. **DD** 361.7/65/025745. **Circ:** 500 (ctrl).
**Desc:** A directory of 300 Rhode Island philanthropy corporation policies, priorities and procedures.

US/0480-2853
**PHILANTHROPIC DIGEST.** (19??)-. Periodical. English. Twelve times a year. $89.95 nonmembers; $69.95 members. Philanthropic Digest Inc., 414 Plaza Drive Suite 209, Westmont IL 60559. **Tel** (708)655-0177. **ED** Aline F. Anderson. **Circ:** 600 (ctrl). available on diskette.
**Desc:** Summary of philanthropic news - giving to education, health and hospitals, social services, the arts and museums, libraries, religion and related philanthropy.

US/1058-6946
**PHILANTHROPIC STUDIES INDEX.** [Philanthr. stud. index]. **Added/Corp** Indiana University Center on Philanthropy. **VFOAT** PSI. Vol. 1, No. 1 (Sept. 1991)-. English. Four times a year. $75.00. Indiana University Press, 601 North Morton Street, Bloomington IN 47404. **Tel** (812)855-3830, (800)842-6796. **LC** HV85; .P47. **DD** 361.7/63/097305. ***Continues in part*** *Research-in-Progress (Washington, D.C. : 1983).*

US/1065-1659
**PHILANTHROPIC TRENDS DIGEST, THE.** [Philanthr. trends dig.]. **Added/Corp** Douglas M. Lawson Associates. (19??)-. Periodical. English. mo. $48.00. Douglas M Lawson Associates, 545 Madison Avenue, New York NY 10022. **Tel** (212)759-5660, (800)238-0004, FAX (212)759-1893. **ED** Joyce Rosen. **DD** 361. ctrl circ.

CN/0316-3849
**PHILANTHROPIST, THE.** [Philanthr.]. **Added/Corp** Canadian Bar Association. Special Committee on Charitable Organizations. **VFOAT** Philanthrope. Vol. 1 (Fall 1972)-. Periodical. English. ir. 40.00Can$. Canadian Centre Philanthropy, 36 Bessemer Court, Unit 3, Concord Ontario L4K 3C9 Canada. **Tel** (416)669-5373. available on microfilm from University Microfilms International (UMI).
**Ind/Abst** Can. Legal Lit.; Index Can. Leg. Period. Lit.; Leg. Resour. Index; LegalTrac (1988-).

US/1071-6661
**PHILANTHROPY MONTHLY, THE.** [Philanthr. mon.]. **VFOAT** Nonprofit Report; Non-Profit Report; NP Report. (1968)-. Periodical. English. mo (except combined July/Aug.). $84.00 profit making institutions; $65.00 other. The Philanthropy Monthly, PO Box 989, New Milford CT 06776. **Tel** (203)354-7132. **ED** Henry C. Suhrke. **LC** HV85; .P48. **DD** 361.7/63/0973. Index available. **Ad Acc. Circ:** 4,000. ***Continues*** *Non-Profit Report, 0029-1064.*
**Desc:** Issues concerning nonprofits including fund raising, postal rates, accounting, corporate and foundation giving practices, and new legislation.

AT
**PHILANTHROPY. THE QUARTERLY NEWSLETTER OF THE AUSTRALIAN ASSOCIATION OF PHILANTHROPY.** (19??)-. Newsletter. English. Four times a year (Jan., Apr., July, Oct.). 30.00Aus$. Australian Association of Philanthropy, 8th Floor 20 Queen Street, Melbourne Victoria 3000 Australia. **Tel** 011 61 3 6144191, FAX 011 61 3 6148471. **ED** Max Dumais. Index available ($40.00). **Ad Acc.** ctrl circ.

US/1052-4770
**PLANNED GIVING TODAY.** [Planned giv. today]. **VFOAT** PGT. Vol. 1, No. 1 (Sept. 1990)-. Periodical. English. mo. $149.00 (1 year), $280.00 (2 year) US; $153.90 (1 year), $308.00 (2 year) other. Planned Giving Today, 2315 Northwest 198th Street, Seattle WA 98177. **Tel** (206)546-8505, FAX (206)546-6268. **ED** G. Roger Schoenhals. **DD** 361. cum. index. **Bk Rev**, (Qty: 6).
**Desc:** The practical newsletter for gift-giving professionals.

US
**PRACTICAL GUIDE TO PLANNED GIVING.** (1991)-. English. an (published in Nov. of prior year). $120.00 (also comes in combination with Planned Gifts Counselor). Taft Group, 835 Penobscott Building, Customer Service, Detroit MI 48226. **Tel** (800)877-8238, FAX (313)961-6083. **(Subscription address:** Taft Group, PO Box 71701, Chicago, IL 60694; telephone: (800)877-8238 ext. 1716**)**

US
**PRESENTING THE SEASON.** See Societies and Clubs.

US
**PROCEEDINGS - NOTRE DAME INSTITUTE ON CHARITABLE GIVING, FOUNDATIONS, AND TRUSTS.** **Main/Conf** Notre Dame Institute on Charitable Giving, Foundations, and Trusts. V. 1- 1976-. Proceedings. English. Notre Dame Law School, PO Box 486, Notre Dame IN 46556. **Tel** (219)239-5918, (219)255-2938. **ED** R W Campfield. Each issue contains an index to its own contents (no volume index)--loose.

UK
**PROFESSIONAL FUNDRAISING.** (19??)-. English. bm (6 issues). £40.00 UK; £75.00 other. Greenhouse Publishing, 56 Portland Road, Bishops Stort CM23 3SJ United Kingdom.

US/0749-9701
**REPORT ON ACTIVITIES / JOHN D. AND CATHERINE T. MACARTHUR FOUNDATION.** **Main/Corp** John D. and Catherine T. MacArthur Foundation. (1980/81)-. English. an. Free upon request. Macarthur Foundation, 140 S Dearborn Street, Chicago IL 60603. **Tel** (312)726-8000. **LC** AS911.J48; A43.
**Desc:** Information on research support, charities and foundations.

CN/0833-1677
**RESEARCH MONEY.** [Res. money]. **VFOAT** Research. Vol. 1, No. 1 (Jan. 21, 1987)-. Periodical. English. Twenty times a year. $375.00 (one year), $565.00 (two year), $695.00 (three year), add $100.00 for each additional issue. Evert Communications Ltd, 1296 Carling Avenue, Ottawa, Ontario, K1Z 7K8 Canada. **Tel** (613)728-4621, FAX (613)728-0385. **(Subscription address:** PO Box 3158, Ottawa Ontario K1Y 4J4 Canada**)** **ED** Vincent Wright. **DD** 001.4/4/0971. Index available.
**Desc:** Contains reports, interpretation and commentary on issues relating to funding of commercial research and development activities in the public and private sectors, and in universities, in Canada. Examines public policy including government programs, tax and other incentives, and the programs of R&D performers.

US/1056-2214
**RESPONSE! (ROCKVILLE, MD.).** ***Ceased.*** (RESPONSE : MAL WARWICK'S MONTHLY WORKSHOP FOR DIRECT MAIL AND TELEPHONE FUNDRAISERS.). [Response!]. **Added/Corp** Taft Group (Rockville, Md.). Vol. 1, No. 1 (June 1991)-(1992). Periodical. English. mo. Taft Group, 835 Penobscott Building, Customer Service, Detroit MI 48226. **Tel** (800)877-8238, FAX (313)961-6083. **DD** 361.

US/1065-0008
**RESPONSIVE PHILANTHROPY.** [Respon. philanthr.]. **Added/Corp** National Committee for Responsive Philanthropy (U.S.). (19??)-. Periodical. English. qt. $25.00 US; $30.00 Canada and Mexico; $35.00 other. National Committee for Responsive Philanthropy, 2001 S Street NW #620, Washington DC 20009. **Tel** (202)387-9177, FAX (202)332-5084. **ED** Robert O. Bothwell. **DD** 361. **Bk Rev**, (Qty: 4/yr). **Ad Acc**, **Adv Mgr:** Beth Daley. **Circ:** 5,000 (ctrl).
**Desc:** Covers changes and trends in philanthropy and fund raising, with emphasis on "social justice" and non-traditional nonprofit organizations.

US/0739-2184
**SMITH FUNDING REPORT.** See Education-Higher Education.

US/0882-5750
**STUDIES IN PHILANTHROPY (WASHINGTON, D.C.).** (STUDIES IN PHILANTHROPY.). [Stud. philanthr.]. **Added/Corp** Capital Research Center (Washington, D.C.). (1985)-. Monographic series. English. Price varies per volume. Capital Research Center, 1612 K Street NW, Washington DC 20006. **LC** UNC. **DD** 361.

●US/1070-9061
**SUCCESSFUL FUND RAISING.** [Success. fund rais.]. **Added/Corp** Stevenson Consultants. Vol. 1, No. 1 (Jan. 1993)-. Periodical. English. Twelve times a year. $92.00. Stevenson Consultants, PO Box 4528, Souix City IA 51104. **Tel** (712)239-3010, FAX (713)239-3010. **ED** Scott C. Stevenson. **DD** 361. **Bk Rev**, (Qty: 1-5).
**Desc:** Designed to provide concise articles on successful fund raising ideas, stategies, and management issues.

US
**TEXAS CONNECTION.** Newsletter. English. qt (Mar., June, Sept., Dec.). $49.00. Funding Information Center of Texas, PO Box 15070, 530 McCollough #600, San Antonio TX 78212. **Tel** (210)227-4333, FAX (210)227-0310. **ED** Laura Jones.
**Desc:** Features articles by experts on fundraising tips, money-saving ideas, news of Texas foundations, and items of interest to non-profit organizations.

US/0192-477X
**TRANSATLANTIC PERSPECTIVES.** (TRANSATLANTIC PERSPECTIVES : A PUBLICATION OF THE GERMAN MARSHALL FUND OF THE UNITED STATES.). **Added/Corp** German Marshall Fund of the United States. **VFOAT** Perspectives. No. 1 (June 1979)-. Periodical. English. Three times a year. Free. The German Marshall Fund of the United States, 11 Dupont Circle NW, Washington DC 20036. **Tel** (202)745-3950. **ED** E. Jane Beckwith. **LC** HC101; .T69. **DD** 905. **Bk Rev. Circ:** 5,000 (ctrl).
**Desc:** Articles of about 2,000 words in which grantees report on their German Marshall Fund-supported work. Topics include technology, jobs, international economics, trade, environment, immigration, and the media.
**Ind/Abst** Index Free Period.; Urban Aff. Abstr.

UK/0957-8765
**VOLUNTAS : INTERNATIONAL JOURNAL OF VOLUNTARY AND NON-PROFIT ORGANISATIONS.** **Added/Corp** Charities Aid Foundation. **VFOAT** International Journal of Voluntary and Non-Profit Organisations. Vol. 1, No. 1 (May 1990)-. Periodical. English (French and German; summaries and/or abstracts in French and German). sa. $120.00 (institution), $60.00 (individual). Manchester University Press, Journals Dept, Oxford Road, Manchester M13 9PL England. **Tel** 011 44 061 2735539, FAX 011 44 061 2743346, telex 668932. **ED** Martin Knapp and Helmut Anheier. **LC** HD62.6; .V64. **CODEN** VOLUE8. **Bk Rev. Ad Acc. Pr Rev. Circ:** 350.
**Desc:** Publishes the very latest international research into the voluntary, or non-profit sector, as well as notes, comments on research and book review essays.
**Ind/Abst** Soc. Plann. Policy Dev. Abstr. (19??-); Soc. Work Abstr. (19??-) [Select. Cov.]; Sociol. Abstr. (1990-) [Full Cov.].

US/0889-7956
**W.K. KELLOGG FOUNDATION ANNUAL REPORT.** (ANNUAL REPORT FOR ... / W.K. KELLOGG FOUNDATION.). [W.K. Kellogg Found. annu. rep.]. **Main/Corp** W. K. Kellogg Foundation. **Added/Corp** W.K. Kellogg Foundation. **VFOAT** Annual Report; W.K. Kellogg Foundation Annual Report. (1962)-. English. an. Free on request. W K Kellogg Foundation, 400 North Avenue, Battle Creek MI 49016. **Tel** (616)965-1221. **LC** HV97.K4; A3. **DD** 361.7/63/097305. ***Continues*** *W. K. Kellogg Foundation. Report for ... .*

US/0043-0609
**WASHINGTON INTERNATIONAL ARTS LETTER.** See Humanities.

US/0275-0031
**WISE GIVING GUIDE.** [Wise giv. guide]. **Added/Corp** National Information Bureau (U.S.). (197?)-. Periodical. English. Three times a year. $25.00. National Charities Information Bureau, 19 Union Square West, New York NY 10003. **Tel** (212)929-6300. **Circ:** 5,000.
**Desc:** Contains list of national non-profit organizations which solicit from the public coded summary of findings using eight standards in philanthropy.

## PHILOSOPHY

●US/1065-3112
**1650-1850 (NEW YORK, N.Y.).** (1650-1850 : IDEAS, AESTHETICS, AND INQUIRIES IN THE EARLY MODERN ERA.). **VFOAT** Ideas, Aesthetics, and Inquiries in the Early Modern Era. (1993)-. Periodical. English. an. $52.50. AMS Press Inc., 56 East 13th Street, New York NY 10003. **Tel** (212)777-4700, FAX (212)995-5413, telex 710 581 2302.

US
**AAH EXAMINER : THE NEWSLETTER OF AFRICAN AMERICANS FOR HUMANISM.** **Added/Corp** African Americans for Humanism. **VFOAT** Newsletter of African Americans for Humanism. (1991)-. Newsletter. English. qt.

GW/0017-9574
**ABHANDLUNGEN DER HEIDELBERGER AKADEMIE DER WISSENSCHAFTEN, PHILOSOPHISCH-HISTORISCHE KLASSE.** **Main/Corp** Heidelberger Akademie der Wissenschaften. Philosophisch-Historische Klasse. **Added/Corp** Heidelberger Akademie der Wissenschaften. Philosophisch-Historische Klasse. (1913)-. Monographic series. German. ir. Price varies per volume. Universitatsverlag Carl Winter, POB 106140, D 69051 Heidelberg Germany. **Tel** 011 49 6221 770260. **LC** AS182; .H435. **Circ:** 1,000 (ctrl).
**Desc:** Monograph series on philosophy, history, philology and the classics.

NE/0001-5342
**ACTA BIOTHEORETICA.** See Biology.

FI/0355-1792
**ACTA PHILOSOPHICA FENNICA.** [Acta philos. fenn.]. **Added/Corp** Filosofinen Yhdistys. Suomen Filosofinen Yhdistys. Vol. 1 (1935)-. Monographic series. English (German). ir. Price varies per volume. Akademische Buchhandlung, Postbox 128, SF 00101 Helsinki 10 Finland. **Tel** 011 358 012141. **LC** B28.F5; A3. **CODEN** APFEDB. **[CCC].**
**Ind/Abst** Math. Rev.; Philos. Index; Zentralbl. Math. Ihre Grenzgeb.

SW/0283-2380
**ACTA PHILOSOPHICA GOTHOBURGENSIA.** [Acta philos. Gothobg.]. Vol. 1 (1986)-. Monographic series. English. ir. Price varies per volume. Acta Universitatis Gothoburgensis, PO Box 5096, S-402 22 Goteborg Sweden. **Tel** 011 46 31 7731000. **ED** Claes Aberg.

●IT/1121-2179
**ACTA PHILOSOPHICA ROMA.** [Acta philos.Roma]. (1992)-. Periodical. Multiple languages. sa. L40000. Armando Editore SRL, Viale Trastevere 236, 00153 Rome Italy. **Tel** 011 39 6 580-6420. **ED** Angel Rodriguez Luno. **UDC** 1.

XR/0567-8293
**ACTA UNIVERSITATIS CAROLINAE. PHILOSOPHICA ET HISTORICA.** [Acta Univ. Carol., Philos. hist.]. **Added/Corp** Universita Karlova. **VFOAT** Philosophica et Historica. (1958)-. Monographic series. Czech (summaries and/or abstracts in English, French, German and Russian). ir. Price varies per volume. Carolinum Press, Ovochny TRH 5, 11636 Prague 1 Czech Republic. **Tel** 011 42 2 228441. **LC** AS141; .A52. ***Continues in part*** *Acta Universitatis Carolinae.*
**Ind/Abst** Am. Hist. Life (1963-); BHA : Biblio. Hist. Art.

XR/0567-8307
**ACTA UNIVERSITATIS CAROLINAE. PHILOSOPHICA ET HISTORICA. MONOGRAPHIA.** See History(General).

SP/0211-4143
**ACTUALIDAD BIBLIOGRAFICA DE FILOSOFIA Y TEOLOGIA.** [Actual. bibliogr. filos. teol.]. **Added/Corp** Facultades de Filosofia y Teologia San Francisco de Borja. Vol. 7, No. 13 (Jan./June 1970)-. Periodical. Spanish. Twice a year (June & Dec.). $30.00. Selecciones de Teologia, Roger de Lluria 13, 08010 Barcelona Spain. **Tel** 011 34 3 3012350, FAX 011 34 3 3178704. **ED** Josep Boada. Index available. **Bk Rev. Pr Rev. Circ:** 700. ***Continues*** *Selecciones de Libros, 0037-1181.*
**Desc:** Contains recensions and critical judgements of books.
**Ind/Abst** Am. Hist. Life (1973).

CG
**AFRIQUE ET PHILOSOPHIE.** No. 1 (Jan./July 1977)-. Periodical. French. $20.00. Departement de Philosophie et Religions Africaines, Faculte de Theologie Catholique de Kinshasa, B P 1534, Kinshasa/Limete Congo. **LC** B5300; .A37. **DD** 199/.6/05.

II
**AGE OF ATHEISM, THE.** English. The Atheist Society of India, Thompson Street, Visakhapathnam 53001 India. **LC** BL2747.3; .A33. **DD** 211/.8/05.

SP
**AGORA, PAPELES DE FILOSOFIA.** an. 2.200ptas Spain, 2.300ptas other. Universidad de Santiago / Publicaciones, Servicio de Publicaciones e Intercambio Cientifico, Campus Universitario, Santiago de Compostela, E-15706 Santiago Spain. **Tel** 011 34 59-35-00. **ED** Esperanza Guisan and Jose L Barreiro. Index available. **Bk Rev. Pr Rev. Circ:** 600 (ctrl).
**Desc:** Articles of Spanish and international authors on the next subjects: social anthropology, social philosophy, logic and philosophy of science, philosophy of law, moral and political philosophy.

US/0731-5880
**AITIA.** [Aitia]. (1972)-. Periodical. English. Three times a year (Spring, Fall, & Winter). $14.00 (individuals), $16.00 (institutions). Aitia Friel, Knapp Hall 15, Suny Farmingdale, Farmingdale NY 11735. **Tel** (516)420-2047, (516)420-2050. **ED** James P. Friel. **LC** B1; .A43. **DD** 105. **Bk Rev. Ad Acc. Circ:** 2,000.
**Desc:** Educational and philosophical problems combined with contemporary problems. Cross cultural emphasis and poetry. Concerned with cultural development, with an interdisciplinary emphasis.
**Ind/Abst** Philos. Index.

FI/0355-1725
**AJATUS; SUOMEN FILOSOFISEN YHDISTYKSEN VUOSIKIRJA.** (AJATUS.). [Ajatus]. **Added/Corp** Suomen Filosofinen Yhdistys. Filosofinen Yhdistys. Vol. 1 (1926)-. English (Finnish and German). an. Fmk108.00. Academic Bookstore Akateeminen, Postilokero 23, FIN-00371 Helsinki Finland. **Tel** 011 358 0 12141. **LC** B31; .A55. **DD** 105.
**Ind/Abst** Math. Rev.; Philos. Index.

RU
**AKTUALNYE PROBLEMY ISTORII FILOSOFII NARODOV SSSR. Added/Corp** Moskovskii Gosudarstvennyi Universitet Im. M.V. Lomonosova. Kafedra Istorii Filosofii Narodov SSSR. (1972)-. Periodical. Russian. Izdatelstvo Moskovskogo Universiteta, K-9 Ulitsa Gertsena 5/7, Moscow Russia. **Tel** (301)881-5973. **LC** B4231; .A47.

LY
**AL-HIKMAH.** V. 1- October 1976-. Periodical. Arabic. Jamiat Al-Fatih Kulliyat Al-Tarbiyah, Qism Al-Falsafah Wa-Al-Ijtima, PO Box 2558, Tarabulus Libya. **LC** B740; .H54.

CK/0120-0216
**ALEPH (MANIZALES, COLOMBIA). See** Literature.

NE/0002-5275
**ALGEMEEN NEDERLANDS TIJDSCHRIFT VOOR WIJSBEGEERTE.** [Alg. Ned. tijdschr. wijsb.]. Vol. 62E, No. 1 (Jan. 1970)-. Periodical. Dutch. qt. Fl70.00 (members and students), Fl85.00 (regular) Netherlands; Fl97.50 (members and students), Fl112.50 (regular) other. Van Gorcum & Company BV, PO Box 43, NL 9400 AA Assen Netherlands. **Tel** 011 31 5920 46846, FAX 011 31 5920 72064. **ED** F Jacobs. **LC** B8.D8; A4. Index available. cum. index. **Bk Rev. Ad Acc. Circ:** 800 (ctrl). ***Continues*** *Algemeen Nederlands Tijdschrift voor Wijsbegeerte en Psychologie.*
**Ind/Abst** Linguist. Lang. Behav. Abstr.; Philos. Index; Soc. Plann. Policy Dev. Abstr.; Sociol. Abstr.

GW
**ALLGEMEINE ZEITSCHRIFT FUER PHILOSOPHIE. Added/Corp** Allgemeine Gesellschaft fuer Philosophie in Deutschland. (1976)-. Periodical. German. Three times a year. DM32.00 (single issue). Friedrich Frommann Verlag, Koenig Karlstrasse 27, D 70372 Stuttgart 50 Germany. **Tel** 011 49 711 9559690. **ED** Werner Stegmaier and Josef Simon. **LC** B3; .A47. **Bk Rev. Ad Acc. Circ:** 1,200 (ctrl).

US/0516-9623
**AMERICAN ATHEIST, THE. *Suspended.* See** Religion and Theology.

US/1051-3558
**AMERICAN CATHOLIC PHILOSOPHICAL QUARTERLY.** (AMERICAN CATHOLIC PHILOSOPHICAL QUARTERLY : JOURNAL OF THE AMERICAN CATHOLIC PHILOSOPHICAL ASSOCIATION.). [Am. Cathol. philos. q.]. **Added/Corp** American Catholic Philosophical Association. **VFOAT** ACPQ. Vol. 64, No. 1 (Winter 1990)-. Periodical. English. qt. $30.00 US; $34.50 other. American Catholic Philosophy Association, Catholic University, 403 Administration Building, Washington DC 20064. **Tel** (202)635-5518, FAX (202)635-5518. **ED** Robert Wood (editor's address: 1843 East Northgate Drive, Irving TX 75062). **LC** IN PROCESS. **DD** 105. cum. index. **Bk Rev**, (Qty: Varies). **Ad Acc. Circ:** 1,600. available on microfilm and microfiche from University Microfilms International (UMI). Documents available from The Genuine Article. ***Continues*** *New Scholasticism, 0028-6621.*
**Desc:** Philosophical research and scholarship.
**Ind/Abst** Annu. Bibliogr. Engl. Lang. Lit.; Arts Humanit. Citation Index [Full Cov.]; Curr. Contents Arts Humanit.; Index Book Rev. Humanit.; Philos. Index; Res. Alert [Full Cov.]; Soc. Sci. Cit. Index [Select. Cov.]; Abr. Cathol. Period. Lit. Index; Cathol. Period. Lit. Index.

US/0194-3448
**AMERICAN JOURNAL OF THEOLOGY & PHILOSOPHY.** [Am. j. theol. philos.]. **Added/Corp** American Society for Social Philosophy and Philosophical Theology. **VAT** American Journal of Theology and Philosophy. Vol. 1 (Jan. 1980)-. Periodical. English. Three times a year (Jan., Mar., Nov.). $18.00 (individuals); $30.00 (institutions. American Journal of Theology & Philosophy, PO Box 2009, Highlands NC 28741. **Tel** (704)526-4038. **ED** Tyron Inbody, (editor's address: United Theological Seminary, phone: (513)278-5817). **LC** BR1; .A42. **DD** 230/.05. Index available. cum. index. **Ad Acc. Pr Rev. Circ:** 550 (ctrl). available on microfilm and microfiche from University Microfilms International (UMI).
**Desc:** American theology and its dialogue with philosophy.
**Ind/Abst** Index Book Rev. Relig.; Philos. Index; Relig. Index One Period. (1980-); Relig. Theol. Abstr.

UK/0003-0481
**AMERICAN PHILOSOPHICAL QUARTERLY (OXFORD).** (AMERICAN PHILOSOPHICAL QUARTERLY.). [Am. philos. q.]. Vol. 1 (Jan. 1964)-. Periodical. English. qt. $148.00 (institutions), $38.00 (individuals). Philosophy Documentation Center, Bowling Green State University, Bowling Green OH 43403-0189. **Tel** (419)372-2419, (800)444-2419, FAX (419)372-6987. **ED** Nicholas Rescher. **Circ:** 1,520. Documents available from The Genuine Article, UMI Article Clearinghouse.
**Desc:** The scope of the journal is the entire range of philosophical inquiry. Publishes articles of high quality regardless of the school of thought from which it derives.
**Ind/Abst** Acad. Search (July 1993-); Annu. Bibliogr. Engl. Lang. Lit.; Arts Humanit. Citation Index [Full Cov.]; Curr. Contents Arts Humanit.; Expand. Acad. Index (1989-); Humanit. Index; Humanit. Source (Jul. 1993-); INFO-SOUTH Abstr.; Int. Bibliogr. Sociol.; Linguist. Lang. Behav. Abstr.; Mag. Search; Newsp. Period. Abstr. (1991-); Philos. Index; Res. Alert [Full Cov.]; Soc. Plann. Policy Dev. Abstr.; Soc. Sci. Cit. Index [Select. Cov.]; Sociol. Abstr.

US/0003-0708
**AMERICAN RATIONALIST, THE.** [Am. ration.]. Vol. 1 (May 1956)-. Periodical. English. bm. $6.00. American Rationalist, PO Box 994, St Louis MO 63188. **Tel** (314)846-8105. **ED** Gordan Stein. **LC** BL2700; .A69. **DD** 149.7. available on microfilm and microfiche from University Microfilms International (UMI).
**Desc:** For skeptics, humanists, atheists, agnostics and thinking non-conformists. Promoter of American Rationalism, a natural and scientific philosophy , religious, liberty and intellectual freedom. Critically examines myths, dogmas and claims of all theologies and scrutinizes mysticism, blind faith and irrationality.

US/0883-105X
**AMERICAN STUDIES INTERNATIONAL. See** History(General)-History of North, South, and Central America.

RM
**ANALELE UNIVERSITATII BUCURESTI : FILOSOFIE. Main/Corp** Universitatea Din Bucuresti. Vol. 26 (1977)-. Periodical. English (French and Romanian). an. DM164.00. **(Subscription address:** Kubon & Sagner, ABT Zeitschriftenimport, D 80328 Munich Germany.**) LC** B8.R8; B83b. **DD** 105. ***Continues in part*** *Analele Universitatii Bucuresti. Filosofie, Istorie, Drept.*
**Ind/Abst** Am. Hist. Life (1959-1974, 1977-); Linguist. Lang. Behav. Abstr.; Soc. Plann. Policy Dev. Abstr.; Sociol. Abstr.

SP/0008-7750
**ANALES DE LA CATEDRA FRANCISCO SUAREZ.** [An. Catedr. Francisco Suarez]. **Added/Corp** Catedra Francisco Suarez. Universidad de Granada. Departamento de Filosofia del Derecho. (1961)-. Periodical. Spanish (English, German and Italian). an. **LC** B5; .A514. **DD** 105.
**Ind/Abst** Am. Hist. Life.

SP
**ANALES DEL SEMINARIO DE HISTORIA DE LA FILOSOFIA. Main/Conf** Seminario de Historia de la Filosofia (Spain). **Added/Corp** Universidad Complutense de Madrid. Departamento de Historia de la Filosofia. (1980)-. Spanish. Editorial Complutense, Donoso Cortes 65 1RA Planta, 28003 Madrid Spain. **Tel** 011 34 1 3946372. **LC** B5; .S45a. **DD** 109.

SP/0580-8650
**ANALES DEL SEMINARIO DE METAFISICA.** [An. Semin. Metafis.]. Periodical. Spanish. an. Editorial Complutense, Donoso Cortes 65 1RA Planta, 28003 Madrid Spain. **Tel** 011 34 1 3946372. **LC** BD115; .M28A. **DD** 105.
**Ind/Abst** Philos. Index.

AG/0326-1301
**ANALISIS FILOSOFICO. Added/Corp** SADAF (Organization). (1981)-. Periodical. Spanish (English). Twice a year (May & Nov.). $10.00 Argentina; $18.00 others. SADAF, Bulnes 642, 1176 Buenos Aires Argentina. **ED** E. Rabossi. **LC** B808.5; .A48. **DD** 146. **Bk Rev. Ad Acc. Pr Rev. Circ:** 500 (ctrl).
**Desc:** Various topics concerning philosophy.

US/0003-2638
**ANALYSIS (NEW YORK (N.Y.).** (ANALYSIS.). Vol. 1, No. 1 (Nov. 1933)-. Academic Scholarly Publication. English. Four times a year. $44.00 North America; £22.00 other. Basil Blackwell Publishers Ltd, 108 Cowley Road, Oxford 0X4 1JF England. **Tel** 011 44 865 791100, FAX 011 44 865 791347, telex 837022 OXBOOK G. **(Subscription address:** Blackwell Publishers / UK, Marston Book Services, PO Box 87, Oxford OX2 0DT England.**) ED** Christopher Kirwan. **LC** B1; .A112. **DD** 105. cum. index. **Bk Rev. Ad Acc. Circ:** 600 (ctrl). available on microfilm and microfiche from University Microfilms International (UMI). Documents available from The Genuine Article.
**Desc:** Publishes short discussions of questions of detail in philosophy. These range over topics in philosophical logic, philosophy of mind, moral and political philosophy.
**Ind/Abst** Arts Humanit. Citation Index [Full Cov.]; Int. Bibliogr. Sociol.; Linguist. Lang. Behav. Abstr.; Philos. Index; Res. Alert [Full Cov.]; Soc. Plann. Policy Dev. Abstr.; Sociol. Abstr.

US/0890-5118
**ANALYTIC TEACHING.** [Anal. teach.]. **Added/Corp** Texas Wesleyan College. (198?)-. Periodical. English. sa (May, November). $15.00. Analytic Teaching / Viterbo College, 815 South 9th Street, Sa Cross WI 54601. **Tel** (608)791-0280. **ED** Richard Morehouse, David Kennedy. **DD** 370. Index available. cum. index. **Bk Rev**, (Qty: 6). **Ad Acc. Pr Rev. Circ:** 300 (ctrl).
**Desc:** Contains articles regarding philosophy for children.

GW
**ANALYTICA.** (19??)-. English. ir. $160.00 (latest issue). Philosophia Verlag GmbH, Oettingenstr 25, D-80538 Munich Germany. **Tel** 011 49 89 299350. **(Subscription address:** Philosophia, PO Box 4194, Hamden, CT 06514; telephone: (203)785-8688**)**

BE
**ANCIENT AND MEDIEVAL PHILOSOPHY. SERIES 2. Added/Corp** Centre de Wulf-Mansion. (1979)-. Monographic series. Latin. ir. Price varies per volume. Universitaire Pers Leuven, Leuven University Press, Krakenstraat 3, B-3000 Leuven, Belgium. **Tel** 32 16 28 41 75, FAX 32 16 28 41 76. **ED** R. Macken, G. Wilson, J. Decorte, L. Hodl, M. Haverals and R. Wielockx. **LC** UNC.

US/0740-2007
**ANCIENT PHILOSOPHY (PITTSBURGH, PA.).** (ANCIENT PHILOSOPHY.). [Anc. philos.]. Vol. 1, No. 1 (Fall 1980)-. Periodical. English (French, German and Italian). Twice a year (May and Nov.). $20.00 (individuals); $45.00 (institutions). Duquesne University Department of Philosophy, c/o Ronald Polansky, Department of Philosophy, Pittsburgh PA 15282. **Tel** (412)396-6500. **ED** Ronald Polansky. **Bk Rev**, (Qty: 50). **Ad Acc. Pr Rev. Circ:** 600.
**Desc:** Articles, discussions, and reviews in the field of ancient Greek and Roman philosophy and science.
**Ind/Abst** Philos. Index.

US/1060-8052
**ANCIENT WISDOM FOR MODERN LIVING. *Ceased.*** [Anc. wisdom mod. living]. Charter Issue (Spring 1991)-(Summer 1993). English. Philosophical Research Society, 3910 Los Feliz Boulevard, Los Angeles CA 90027-2399. **Tel** (310)663-2167. **DD** 140.

IT/0003-3081
**ANGELICUM.** [Angelicum]. **Added/Corp** Pontificio Ateneo "Angelicum". Pontificia Studiorum Universitas a Sancto Thoma Aquinate in Urbe. Vol. 2 (Feb./March 1925)-. Periodical. Italian (French, English, German and Spanish). qt. $50.00. Amministrazine Rivista Angelicum, Largo Angelicum 1, 00184 Rome Italy. **Tel** 011 39 6 67021. **ED** Dr. St. Krasic. **LC** BX800.A1; A5. **DD** 230/.2/05. Index available in last issue of volume--attached. cum. index. **Bk Rev. Circ:** 800. ***Continues*** *Unio Thomistica.*
**Desc:** A review of theology, philosophy, and canon law published by Pontifical University St Thomas in Rome, Italy.
**Ind/Abst** Bibliogr. Mission.; MLA Int. Bibl. Books Artic. Mod. Lang. Lit.; New Testam. Abstr.; Old Testam. Abstr.; Relig. Theol. Abstr.; Abr. Cathol. Period. Lit. Index; Cathol. Period. Lit. Index.

FR
**ANNALES.** (19??)-. Periodical. French. an. Bruxelles Universite Institut Philosophy, 50 Avenue Franklin Roosevelt, 1050 Brussels, Belgium. **Tel** 011 32 02 642 21 11.

BE
**ANNALES DE L'INSTITUT DE PHILOSOPHIE ET DE PHILOSOPHIE ET DE SCIENCES MORALES.** (1979)-. Monographic series. French. ir. Price varies per volume. Editions University de Bruxelles, Avenue Paul Heger 26, B-1050 Bruxelles Belgium. **Tel** 32 2 642 3789, 3799, FAX 32 2 642 3794, telex 23069 UNILIB. **(Subscription address:** Centre Export Livre Francais, 9 rue de Toul, 75012 Paris France, telephone: 011 33 1 43473003**) LC** B2; .A48. **DD** 105. ***Continues*** *Annales de l'Institut de Philosophie.*
**Ind/Abst** Linguist. Lang. Behav. Abstr.; Soc. Plann. Policy Dev. Abstr.; Sociol. Abstr.

LE/0250-8036
**ANNALES DE PHILOSOPHIE. Added/Corp** Universite Saint-Joseph (Beirut, Lebanon). Faculte des Lettres et des Sciences Humaines. Vol. 1 (1980)-. French. an. 70.00F. Universite Saint-Joseph, Faculty Lettres Science Humaines, BP 175, 208 Gemayze Lebanon. **(Subscription address:** Bureau Administratif de l'Universite St. Joseph, 42 rue Grenelle, 75343 Paris Cedex 07 France.**) LC** B2; .A56.

PL/0066-2240
**ANNALES UNIVERSITATIS MARIAE CURIE-SKLODOWSKA. SECTION I: PHILOSOPHIA-SOCIOLOGIA.** **Main/Corp** Uniwersytet Marii Curie-Skodowskiej. Miedzyuczelniany Instytut Filozofii i Sociologii. Vol. 1 (1976)-. Periodical. Polish (summaries and/or abstracts in English and Russian). Uniwersytet Marii Curie-Skodowskiej / Krakowskie, Krakowskie Przedmiescie 7, 00068 Warsaw Poland. **Tel** 375304. **LC** B6; .L83A.
**Ind/Abst** Philos. Index; Pig News Inf.

HU/0524-9023
**ANNALES UNIVERSITATIS SCIENTIARUM BUDAPESTINENSIS DE ROLANDO EOTVOS NOMINATAE. SECTIO PHILOSOPHICA ET SOCIOLOGICA.** **Main/Corp** Eotvos Lorand Tudomanyegyetem. V. 1- 1962-. Periodical. Multiple languages (English, French, German and Russian). an. $40.00. Eotvos Lorand Tudomanyegyetem, Bolcseszettudomanyi Kar, Pesti BUL, H-1052 Budapest Hungary. **Tel** 36 11 180 966. Index available. **Ad Acc. Circ:** 550 (ctrl).
**Ind/Abst** Am. Hist. Life (1979-).

IT
**ANNALI DEL DIPARTIMENTO DI FILOSOFIA / UNIVERSITA DE FIRENZE.** **Added/Corp** Universita di Firenze. Dipartimento di Filosofia. (1985)-. Italian. an. L41000. Casa Editrice Leo S. Olschki, Viuzzo del Pozzetto, Casella Postale 66, 50126 Florence Italy. **Tel** 011 39 55 6530684, FAX 011 39 55 6530214. Index available. **Pr Rev. Circ:** 500. ***Continues*** *Universita de Firenze. Istituto di Filosofia. Annali Dell'Instituto di Filosofia.*
**Desc:** Studies in the history of philosophy.

IT
**ANNALI DELLA FACOLTA DI LETTERE E FILOSOFIA.** **Main/Corp** Universita di Bari. Facolta di Littere e Filosofia. (1954)-. Italian. an. L50000. Adriatica Bari Editrice, Libreria Dell Universita, Via Andrea da Bari 122 Italy. **Tel** 080-235640. **LC** AS222.B3.
**Ind/Abst** Numis. Lit.; Philos. Index.

IT/0076-1818
**ANNALI DELLA FACOLTA DI LETTERE E FILOSOFIA, UNIVERSITA DI MACERATA.** (ANNALI DELLA FACOLTA DI LETTERE E FILOSOFIA.). [Ann. Fac. Lett. Filos., Univ. Macerata]. **Main/Corp** Universita di Macerata. Facolta di Lettere e Filosofia. (1968)-. Italian. L120000. Editrice Antenore, Via G Rusca 15, 35100 Padua Italy. **Tel** 011 39 49 686566.
**Ind/Abst** BHA : Biblio. Hist. Art; MLA Int. Bibl. Books Artic. Mod. Lang. Lit.

IT/0392-095X
**ANNALI DELLA SCUOLA NORMALE SUPERIORE DI PISA, CLASSE DI LETTERE E FILOSOFIA.** **See** Literature.

IT/0394-1809
**ANNUARIO FILOSOFICO.** [Annu. filos.]. Vol. 1 (1985)-. Periodical. Italian. an (Feb.). L70000 (latest volume). Gruppo Mursia, via Tadino 29, 20124 Milan Italy. **Tel** 011 39 2 9566983, FAX 011 39 2 2041557, telex 325294. **LC** B4; .A65. **DD** 105. ctrl circ.

XV/0587-5161
**ANTHROPOS (LJUBLJANA).** **See** Psychology.

IT/0003-6064
**ANTONIANUM.** **See** Religion and Theology.

SP/0066-5215
**ANUARIO FILOSOFICO.** [Anu. filos.]. **Added/Corp** Universidad de Navarra. Facultad de Filosofia y Letras. Vol. 1 (1968)-. Spanish. Three times a year. $40.00. Anuario Filsosfico / Edificio de Bibliotecas / Universidad de Navarra, 31080 Pamplona Spain. **Tel** 011 34 948 252700 Ext 2490, FAX 011 34 948 173650. **LC** B25; .A56. **DD** 105. **CODEN** ANFIEA. cum. index.
**Ind/Abst** Bibliogr. Mission.; Linguist. Lang. Behav. Abstr. (1992-); Philos. Index; Soc. Plann. Policy Dev. Abstr. (1992-); Sociol. Abstr. (1992-).

AU/0378-8652
**ANZEIGER / OSTERREICHISCHE AKADEMIE DER WISSENSCHAFTEN, PHILOSOPHISCH-HISTORISCHE KLASSE.** **See** History(General)-History of Europe.

●US/1067-9464
**APA NEWSLETTERS ON THE BLACK EXPERIENCE, COMPUTER USE, FEMINISM, LAW, MEDICINE, TEACHING.** (APA NEWSLETTERS ON THE BLACK EXPERIENCE, COMPUTER USE, FEMINISM, LAW, MEDICINE, TEACHING : A PUBLICATION OF THE AMERICAN PHILOSOPHICAL ASSOCIATION.). [APA newsl. black exp. comput. use fem. law med. teach.]. **Added/Corp** American Philosophical Association. **VFOAT** Newsletters on the Black Experience, Computer Use, Feminism, Law, Medicine, Teaching; American Philosophical Association Newsletters on Philosophy and the Black Experience, Computer Use in Philosophy, Feminism and Philosophy, Philosophy and Law, Philosophy and Medicine, Teaching Philosophy. Vol. 91, No. 1 (Spring 1992)-. Periodical. English. Twice a year (Spring & Fall). $10.00. American Philosophical Association, University of Delaware, Newark DE 19716. **Tel** (302)831-1112, FAX (302)831-8690. **ED** Leonard Harris, Diana T. Meyers, G. J. Mattey, II., Hilde Hein, Professor Jesse Yoder, Rex Martin, Rosamond Rhodes and Professor Tziporah Kasachkoff. **LC** B63; .N49. **DD** 105. **Bk Rev**, (Qty: varies). **Ad Acc, Adv Mgr:** Diana Walls, **Tel** (302)831-1112. ctrl circ. ***Continues*** *Newsletters on the Black Experience, Computer Use, Feminism, Law, Medicine, Teaching, 1067-9456.*

CN/0003-6390
**APEIRON (CLAYTON).** **See** Classical Studies.

IT/0003-7362
**AQUINAS.** [Aquinas]. **Added/Corp** Pontificia Universita Lateranense. Facolta di Filosofia. Vol. 1 (1958)-. Periodical. English (French, German, Italian, Latin and Spanish). Three times a year (Apr., Aug., Dec.). L65000 Italy; L90000 others. Pontificia Universita Lateranense, Piazza S Giovanni Laterano 4, 00120 Citta del Vaticano. **Tel** 011 39 6 69886401, FAX 011 39 6 69886103. **LC** B765.T54; A12. Index available. **Bk Rev.**
**Ind/Abst** Bibliogr. Mission.; MLA Int. Bibl. Books Artic. Mod. Lang. Lit.; Philos. Index.

US/0066-5614
**AQUINAS LECTURE.** [Aquinas lect.]. **Added/Corp** Marquette University. Marquette University. Aristotelian Society. Phi Sigma Tau. Wisconsin Alpha Chapter (Marquette University). (19??)-. Monographic series. English. ir. Price varies per volume. Marquette University Publications, 1131 West Wisconsin Avenue, Milwaukee WI 53233. **Tel** (414)288-7000, (414)288-7190. **ED** Paul McInerny. **LC** UNC.
**Desc:** For classroom use, library additions, or private collections.

GW/0003-8946
**ARCHIV FUER BEGRIFFSGESCHICHTE.** **Added/Corp** Akademie der Wissenschaften und Literatur, Mainz. Kommission fur Philosophie und Begriffsgeschichte. Akademie der Wissenschaften und Literatur, Mainz. Kommission fur Philosophie. Vol. 1 (1955)-. German. sa. DuMont Buchverlag GmbH & Co. KG, Postfach 100468, D 50441 Cologne Germany. **Tel** 011 49 221 20530.
**Ind/Abst** Philos. Index.

GW/0003-9101
**ARCHIV FUER GESCHICHTE DER PHILOSOPHIE.** [Arch. Gesch. Philos.]. Vol. 40, No. 1 (1931)-. Periodical. German (English and French). tq. $148.10. Walter de Gruyter Inc., PO Box 303421, D 10728 Berlin Germany. **Tel** 011 49 30 260050, FAX 011 49 30 26005251. **LC** B3; .A69. **[CCC].** ***Continues*** *Archiv fuer Geschichte der Philosophie und Soziologie.*
**Ind/Abst** MLA Int. Bibl. Books Artic. Mod. Lang. Lit.; Philos. Index; Soc. Sci. Cit. Index [Select. Cov.].

GW/0003-9101
**ARCHIV FUER GESCHICHTE DER PHILOSOPHIE.** **VFOAT** Archiv fur Philosophie; Archiv fur Philosophie und Soziologie. Vol. 1 (1888)-. Periodical. English (French, German and Italian). Three times a year. $142.60 North America. Walter de Gruyter Inc., PO Box 303421, D 10728 Berlin Germany. **Tel** 011 49 30 260050, FAX 011 49 30 26005251. **(Subscription address:** US and Canada/ 200 Saw Mill River Road, Hawthorne, NY 10532**) [CCC].** cum. index. Documents available from The Genuine Article. ***Absorbed in part*** *Philosophische Monatshefte.*
**Ind/Abst** Arts Humanit. Citation Index [Full Cov.]; Curr. Contents Arts Humanit.; MLA Int. Bibl. Books Artic. Mod. Lang. Lit.; Philos. Index; Res. Alert [Full Cov.].

FR/0003-9632
**ARCHIVES DE PHILOSOPHIE.** [Arch. philos.]. (1923)-. Periodical. French. qt. 375.00F (France); 450.00F (other). Beauchesne Editeur, 72 rue des Saints Peres, 75007 Paris France. **Tel** 011 33 1 45488028. **ED** M Regnier. **LC** B1; .A12. **DD** 105. cum. index. **Bk Rev. Ad Acc. Circ:** 1,200 (ctrl). Documents available from The Genuine Article.
**Desc:** Mostly philosophy, history of philosophy, philosophy of science. Yearly bulletins: Cartesian studies, Spinoza, Hegel, etc. About 120 reviews yearly.
**Ind/Abst** Arts Humanit. Citation Index [Full Cov.]; Bibliogr. Mission.; Curr. Contents Arts Humanit.; Int. Polit. Sci. Abstr.; Philos. Index; Res. Alert [Full Cov.]; Romant. Move.

FR/0373-5478
**ARCHIVES D'HISTOIRE DOCTRINALE ET LITTERAIRE DU MOYEN AGE.** [Arch. hist. doctrin. litt. m.-age]. (1926/1927)-. French (English). an (Jan. or Feb.). 498.00F. Librarie Philosophique J Vrin, 6 Place de la Sorbonne, F-75005 Paris France. **Tel** 011 33 1 43540347. **ED** Mrs. Hudry. **LC** B720; .A7. **DD** 189/.05. Index available. **Circ:** 850.
**Desc:** Each volume presents unpublished medieval texts (3 or 4) and studies about medieval texts, either philosophical or literary.
**Ind/Abst** MLA Int. Bibl. Books Artic. Mod. Lang. Lit.

US/0160-7081
**ARCHIVES OF THE FOUNDATION OF THANATOLOGY (1976).** (ARCHIVES OF THE FOUNDATION OF THANATOLOGY.). **Main/Corp** Foundation of Thanatology. Vol. 6, No. 1 (1976)-. Periodical. English. Four times a year. $71.00. Foundation Book & Periodical, 391 Atlantic Avenue, Brooklyn NY 11217. **Tel** (718)270-3725. **ED** Austin H. Kutscher. **NLM** W1 AR489C. **Ad Acc. Circ:** 200. ***Continues*** *Foundation of Thanatology. Proceedings, 0160-4384.*
**Desc:** Abstracts of conference papers on themes relating to aging, dying, death and grief.

IT/0004-0088
**ARCHIVIO DI FILOSOFIA.** [Arch. filos.]. **Added/Corp** Istituto di Studi Filosofici. Associazione Filosofica Italiana. (1931)-. Periodical. Italian. an. L85000 Italy; L120000 other. Cedam Spa, Via Jappelli 5 6, 35121 Padua Italy. **Tel** 011 39 49 65667. **LC** B4; .A7. **DD** 105.
**Ind/Abst** Bibliogr. Mission.; Philos. Index.

GW/0004-1157
**ARGUMENT, DAS.** (DAS ARGUMENT; BERLINER HEFTE FUER PROBLEME DER GESELLSCHAFT.). [Argument]. **VFOAT** Berliner Hefte fuer Probleme der Gesellschaft. Vol. 1, No. 1 (1959)-. Periodical. German. Six times a year (Jan., Mar., May, July, Sept., Nov.). Price varies. Argument Verlag GmbH, Rentzelstr 1, D 21046 Hamburg Germany. **Tel** 011 49 40 453680, 011 49 40 456018. **ED** Wolfgang Fritz Haug and Frigga Haug. **Bk Rev. Ad Acc. Pr Rev. Circ:** 5,000. Documents available from The Genuine Article.
**Desc:** Marxist debates in the field of Marxist socialist theory, politics, and feminism. Reviews in philosophy, linguistics, literary criticism, sociology, pedogogics, medicine, political science, and economics.
**Ind/Abst** Arts Humanit. Citation Index [Select. Cov.]; Energy Res. Abstr. (Oct. 1978-); Linguist. Lang. Behav. Abstr.; Res. Alert [Full Cov.]; Soc. Plann. Policy Dev. Abstr.; Soc. Sci. Cit. Index [Full Cov.]; Sociol. Abstr.

NE/0920-427X
**ARGUMENTATION.** [Argumentation]. Vol. 1, No. 1 (1987)-. Periodical. English (French). qt. $350.00. Kluwer Academic Publishers, Postbus 322, 3300 AH Dordrecht, The Netherlands. **Tel** 011 (31) 78 524400, FAX 011 31 78 183273, telex 20083. **ED** Michel Meyer (University of Brussels). **LC** BC1. **DD** 168/.05. **CODEN** ARGMEL. **[CCC]. Pr Rev.** available on microfilm and microfiche from University Microfilms International (UMI).
**Desc:** Contributions from all schools of thought, ranging from literary rhetoric to linguists, from history to logic, from theological argument to legal reasoning, from natural inference to the argumentative structures of science. Of interest to specialists in speech and communication, philosophers, literary critics and linguists, and those interested in argumentation and reasoning as branches of natural and artificial intelligence.
**Ind/Abst** Annu. Bibliogr. Engl. Lang. Lit.; Commun. Abstr. (?-?); Int. Bibliogr. Sociol.; Linguist. Lang. Behav. Abstr.; Soc. Plann. Policy Dev. Abstr.; Sociol. Abstr.

GW
**ARISTOTELES WERKE.** (19??)-. Monographic series. German. ir. Price varies per volume. Akademie-Verlag GmbH, Muehlenstrasse 33 34, D 13162 Berlin Germany. **Tel** 011 49 30 47889300, FAX 011 49 30 47889357. **(Subscription address:** VCH Publishers Inc., 303 Northwest 12th Avenue, Journals Department, Deerfield FL 33442.**) ED** Hellmud Floshar. **Ad Acc.**
**Desc:** Presents the most important philosophical, ethical, political and scientific works of Aristotle in a new German translation with commentaries.

CC
**ASIAN JOURNAL OF PHILOSOPHY, THE.** **VFOAT** AJP. (1987)-. Periodical. Chinese (French and German). an. $14.00 (individuals), $16.00 (institutions). National Taiwan University Department of Philosophy, 106 Taipei Taiwan. **Tel** 886 35 323022, 886 2 3630231 ext. 2639, FAX 886 2 3630544. **ED** Tran Van Doan. Index available. cum. index. **Bk Rev**, (Qty: 10). **Ad Acc.** Full Page (B&W) $200.00. Half Page (B&W) $100.00. **Pr Rev. Circ:** 800.
**Desc:** Publishes contributions which may be of help in the development of philosophy in Asia.
**Ind/Abst** Philos. Index.

US/0066-8443
**ASIAN PHILOSOPHICAL STUDIES.** No. 1-. Monographic series. English. ir. Price varies per volume. St Johns University, Law Review Association, Grand Central & Utopia Parkways, Jamaica NY 11432. **Tel** (718)990-6654, FAX (718)990-6649.

UK/0955-2367
**ASIAN PHILOSOPY.** Vol. 1, No. 1 (1991)-. Periodical. English. sa (Mar. and Oct.). £84.00. Carfax Publishing Company, PO Box 25 Abingdon, Oxfordshire OX14 3UE England. **Tel** 011 44 235 555335, FAX (0279)31067, telex 817484. **(Subscription address:** US and Canada/ PO Box 2025, Dunnellon, FL 34430-2025; telephone:(904)489-6996**) ED** Indira Mahalingham &

Brian Carr. **LC** B5000; .A33. **[CCC].** Index available. available on microfiche.
**Desc:** Publishes articles in the central philosophical areas of metaphysics, philosophy of mind, epistemology, logic, moral and social philosophy as well as applied philosophical areas such as aesthetics and jurisprudence.

XO
**ATEIZMUS. Added/Corp** Ustav Vedeckeho Ateizmu (Slovenska Akademia Vied). (19??)-. Periodical. Slovak. bm (6 issues). $36.00. **(Subscription address:** Slovart GTG Ltd., Krupinska 4, 852 99 Bratislava Slovakia.**) LC** BL2700; .A684.

IT/0004-8011
**AUGUSTINIANUM.** [Augustinianum]. **Added/Corp** Collegium Internationale Augustinianum. Vol. 1 (Apr. 1961)-. Periodical. Italian (English, French, German, Spanish, Greek and Modern, Latin). ir (May & Oct.). L50000 Italy; L60000 other. Curia Gen Agostiniana, Via Paolo VI 25, 00193 Rome Italy. **Tel** 011 39 6 680061. cum. index. **Bk Rev. Circ:** 1,000.
**Desc:** Research in the area of the literature of Christian antiquity and the thought of the fathers of the Church.
**Ind/Abst** Bibliogr. Mission.; BHA : Biblio. Hist. Art; MLA Int. Bibl. Books Artic. Mod. Lang. Lit.; New Testam. Abstr.; Old Testam. Abstr.

US/0733-4311
**AUSLEGUNG.** [Auslegung]. **Added/Corp** University of Kansas. Dept. of Philosophy. (197?)-. English. sa. $15.00 (institutions), $10.00 (individuals). Auslegung, Department of Philosophy, University of Kansas, Lawrence KS 66045. **Tel** (913)864-3976. **ED** David Larson. **LC** B1; .A78. **DD** 105. **Bk Rev. Ad Acc. Circ:** 200.
**Desc:** A forum of expression for any and all philosophical perspectives; publishes primarily the work of students pursuing the doctorate and non-tenured Ph.D's.
**Ind/Abst** Philos. Index.

AT/0004-8402
**AUSTRALASIAN JOURNAL OF PHILOSOPHY.** [Australas. j. philos.]. **Added/Corp** Australasian Association of Psychology and Philosophy. Australasian Association of Philosophy. Vol. 25, No. 1-2 (Aug. 1947)-. Periodical. English. Four times a year (Mar., June, Sept., Dec.). 65.00Aus$. Australasian Association of Philosophy, La Trobe University, Philosophy Department, Bundoora Victoria 3083 Australia. **Tel** 011 61 3 4792424, FAX 011 61 3 4785814. **ED** Robert Young. **LC** B1; .A8. **DD** 105. **Bk Rev. Ad Acc. Circ:** 1,200 (ctrl). Documents available from The Genuine Article. ***Continues*** *Australasian Journal of Psychology and Philosophy.*
**Desc:** The journal publishes articles, discussions, critical notices, and book reviews mainly on contemporary issues in Anglo-American and Australian philosophy.
**Ind/Abst** Am. Hist. Life (1963-1974); Annu. Bibliogr. Engl. Lang. Lit.; APAIS, Aust. Public Aff. Inf. Ser. (1963-); Arts Humanit. Citation Index [Full Cov.]; Curr. Contents Arts Humanit.; Linguist. Lang. Behav. Abstr.; Philos. Index; Res. Alert [Full Cov.]; Soc. Plann. Policy Dev. Abstr.; Soc. Sci. Cit. Index [Select. Cov.]; Sociol. Abstr.

AT
**AUSTRALIAN RATIONALIST.** (19??)-. English. Four times a year (Mar., June, Sept., Dec.). 20.00Aus$. Australian Rationalist Society, 42 Ruskin Avenue, Croydon Victoria 3136 Australia. **Tel** 011 61 3 7232792, FAX 011 61 3 7232792.

IT/0005-0601
**AUT AUT.** [Aut aut]. (Jan. 1951)-. Periodical. Italian. Six times a year. L70000 Italy; L90000 other. La Nuova Italia Editrice Spa, Via Ernesto Codignola, 50018 Scandicci Florence Italy. **Tel** 011 39 55 75901, FAX 011 39 55 7590208. **ED** William Hanaway. **LC** B4; .A88. Index available (free). **Bk Rev. Circ:** 300. Documents available from The Genuine Article.
**Desc:** Journal of Middle Eastern and comparative literature, including philosophy.
**Ind/Abst** Arts Humanit. Citation Index [Full Cov.]; Curr. Contents Arts Humanit.; MLA Int. Bibl. Books Artic. Mod. Lang. Lit.; Res. Alert [Full Cov.]; Soc. Sci. Cit. Index [Select. Cov.].

US/0005-3643
**BACK TO GODHEAD.** (BACK TO GODHEAD; THE MAGAZINE OF THE HARE KRISHNA MOVEMENT.). [Back godhead]. 1- 1966-. Periodical. English. mo (except March). $16.00 US; $20.00 other. Back to Godhead, PO Box 18928, Philadelphia PA 19119. **Tel** (215)822-0787. **Circ:** 240,000. available on microfilm and microfiche from University Microfilms International (UMI).
**Desc:** The magazine of the Hare Krishna movement, concerned with the philosophy of Bhakt, Yoga, vegetarianism, Karma, reincarnation and the activities of Iskcon.

SP/0210-0088
**BASILISCO (OVIEDO, SPAIN).** (EL BASILISCO.). No. 1 (March-April 1978)-. Periodical. Spanish. Four times a year. 4.000ptas. El Basilisco, Apartado 360, 33080 Oviedo Spain. **Tel** 011 34 8 5293334. **ED** Carlos Raimundo Iglesias Fueyo. **LC** AS302.O84; A17. **DD** 056/.1. Index available. cum. index. **Bk Rev. Pr Rev. Circ:** 3,000.
**Desc:** Articles on philosophy, general humanities, theory of science and culture.

UK/0005-7339
**BEACON (LONDON, ENGLAND).** (THE BEACON.). (1922)-. Periodical. English. Six times a year (Jan., Mar., May, July, Sept., Nov.). $17.00 (one year); $32.00 (two years); $48.00 (three years). Lucis Publishing Company, PO Box 722 Cooper Station, New York NY 10276. **Tel** (212)982-8770. **ED** Sarah McKechnie. **Bk Rev. Circ:** 1,800.
**Desc:** A magazine of esoteric philosophy, presenting the principles of the Ageless Wisdom as a contemporary way of life.

CN/0832-9966
**BEFFROI. See** Literature.

CC/1000-5919
**BEIJING DAXUE XUEBAO ZHEXUE SHEHUI KEXUE BAN.** (BEIJING DAXUE XUEBAO.). **VFOAT** Journal of Peking University (Philosophy and Social Sciences). (1978)-. Periodical. Chinese. bm (6 issues). $60.00 surface mail, $88.50 airmail. Beijing Daxue Chubanshe, Beijing, Peoples Republic of China. **(Subscription address:** China Books & Periodicals Inc., 2929 24th Street, San Francisco CA 94110.**) DD** 505.
**Ind/Abst** Am. Hist. Life (1990-).

GW
**BEITRAEGE ZUR GESCHICHTE DER PHILOSOPHIE UND THEOLOGIE DES MITTELALTERS. SUPPLEMENTBAND.** (1935)-. Monographic series. German. ir. Price varies per volume. Aschendorffsche Verlagsbuchhan, Postfach 1124, D 48135 Muenster Germany. **Tel** 011 49 251 690132. ***Continues*** *Beitrage zur Geschichte der Philosophie des Mittelalters. Supplementband.*

GW/0067-5024
**BEITRAEGE ZUR GESCHICHTE DER PHILOSOPHIE UND THEOLOGIE DES MITTELALTERS. TEXTE UND UNTERSUCHUNGEN. VFOAT** Beitraege zur Geschichte der Philosophie des MA. Vol. 1 (1891)-. Monographic series. German. ir. Price varies per volume. Aschendorffsche Verlagsbuchhandlung, Postfach 1124, D-48135 Muenster Germany. **Tel** 011 49 251 690132, telex 08-92 830 WN MS D. **ED** Ludwig Hoedl and Wolfgang Kluxen.
**Desc:** Contributions to the history of philosophy and theology in the middle ages; texts and research.
**Ind/Abst** MLA Int. Bibl. Books Artic. Mod. Lang. Lit.

IE/0332-026X
**BERKELEY NEWSLETTER.** [Berkeley newsl.]. **Added/Corp** Trinity College (Dublin, Ireland). Philosophy Dept. Royal Irish Academy. International Berkeley Society. No. 1 (Oct. 1977)-. Newsletter. English. an. Free on request. Trinity College / Philosophy Department, Dublin Ireland. **Tel** 011 353 1 6772941.

GW
**BERNARD BOLZANO GESAMTAUSGABE.** (19??)-. German. ir. Price varies per volume. Friedrich Frommann Verlag, Koenig Karlstrasse 27, D 70372 Stuttgart 50 Germany. **Tel** 011 49 711 9559690.

II/0006-0518
**BHAVAN'S JOURNAL.** V. 1- 1954-. Periodical. English. Rs48.00. Bharatiya Vidya Bhavan, Munshi Sadan, Kulapati KM Munshi Marg, Bombay 400 007 India. **Tel** 011 91 22 3634463. **ED** S Ramakrishman. **LC** AP8. **Bk Rev. Ad Acc. Circ:** 2,500.
**Desc:** Devoted to life, literature, and culture and fostering higher values of life and living.

IT
**BIBLIOGRAFIA FILOSOFICA ITALIANA. Added/Corp** Centro di Studi Filosofici di Gallarate. (1977)-. Periodical. Italian. ir. Casa Editrice Leo S. Olschki, Viuzzo del Pozzetto, Casella Postale 66, 50126 Florence Italy. **Tel** 011 39 55 6530684, FAX 011 39 55 6530214.

IT/0084-7836
**BIBLIOGRAPHIA INTERNATIONALIS SPIRITUALITATIS / A PONTIFICIO INSTITUTO SPIRITUALITATIS O.C.D. EDITA. Added/Corp** Pontificio Istituto di Spiritualita del Teresianum. **VFOAT** BIS. Vol. 1 (1966)-. Latin (English, French, German, Italian and Spanish). an (Aug.). L100000. Edizioni de Teresianum, Piazza San Pancrazio 5A, Rome 00152 Italy. **Tel** 011 39 6 582362, 011 39 6 5810140.

GW/0173-1831
**BIBLIOGRAPHIEN ZUR PHILOSOPHIE.** (1979)-. Monographic series. German. ir. Price varies per volume. Edition Gemini, Juelichstr 7, D 50354 Hurth Germany. **Tel** 011 49 2233 63550.

FR/0523-5057
**BIBLIOTHEQUE DES ARCHIVES DE PHILOSOPHIE.** Monographic series. French. ir. Price varies per volume. Beauchesne Editeur, 72 rue des Saints Peres, 75007 Paris France. **Tel** 011 33 1 45488028.

BE
**BIBLIOTHEQUE PHILOSOPHIQUE. Main/Corp** Louvain. Universite Catholique. Institut Superieur de Philosophie. (194?)-. Monographic series. French. ir. Price varies per volume. Universite Catholique de Louvain Core, 34 Voie du Roman Pays, B 1348 Louvain Belgium. **Tel** 011 32 10 474321.

JA/0520-0962
**BIGAKU / BIGAKKAI HEN. Added/Corp** Bigakkai (Japan). **VFOAT** Aesthetics. (1950)-. Periodical. Japanese. qt. $48.00. **(Subscription address:** Kyowa Book Company Inc., 1 38 Kanda Jinbocho Chiyoda-ku, Tokyo 101 Japan.**) LC** BH8.J3; B53. **DD** 100; 700.
**Ind/Abst** Philos. Index; RILM Abstr.

NE
**BIJDRAGEN TIJDSCHRIFT VOOR FILOSOFIE EN THEOLOGIE. VFOAT** International Journal of Philosophy and Theology. Vol. 4 (1953)-. Academic Scholarly Publication. Dutch (English, French and German). qt. Fl175.00 (institutions), Fl95.00 (individuals). Krips Repro BV, PO Box 1106, 7940 KC Meppel Netherlands. **Tel** 011 31 5220 65900, FAX 011 31 5220 60008. Index available. **Bk Rev,** (Qty: 26). **Pr Rev. Circ:** 600 (ctrl). ***Continues*** *Bijdragen Uitgegeven voor de Philosophische en Theologische Faculteiten der Noord- en Zuid-Nederlandse Jezuieten.*
**Desc:** A scholarly review which aims to reflect the research done at theological facilities today. Publishes articles in the fields of philosophy, theology, exegesis, canon law, and others.
**Ind/Abst** Index Book Rev. Relig.; Int. Zeitschriftenschau Bibelwissenschaft Grenzgeb.; Philos. Index; Relig. Index One Period.

NE/0169-3867
**BIOLOGY & PHILOSOPHY. See** Biology.

GW/0721-3743
**BLOCH-ALMANACH.** (BLOCH-ALMANACH / HERAUSGEGEBEN VOM ERNST-BLOCH-ARCHIV DER STADTBIBLIOTHEK LUDWIGSHAFEN.). [Bloch-Alm.]. **Added/Corp** Stadtbibliothek Ludwigshafen. Ernst-Bloch-Archiv. **VFOAT** Bloch Almanach. Vol. 1 (1981)-. Periodical. German (English and French). an. DM17.00. E Bloch Archiv, Bismarckstr 44, D 67012 Ludwigshafen Germany. **Tel** 11 49 621 5042592, FAX 11 49 621 5043784. **ED** Karl Weigand. **LC** B3209.B754; A35. **DD** 193. Index available. **Pr Rev. Circ:** 700.
**Desc:** Unpublished texts of Bloch, his life and work.
**Ind/Abst** MLA Int. Bibl. Books Artic. Mod. Lang. Lit.

BL
**BOLETIN - ASOC. LATINO-AMERICANA DE FILOSOFOS CAT. Main/Corp** Asociacion Latino-Americana de Filosofos Catolicos. No. 1- 1974-. Multiple languages (Portuguese and Spanish). Directoria Central de la Asociacion, Via Anhanguera, Km 26 Caixa Postal 11 587, Sao Paulo Brazil. **LC** B1001; .A8A.

IT/0392-7334
**BOLLETTINO DEL CENTRO DI STUDI VICHIANI.** [Boll. Centr. Studi Vichiani]. **Main/Corp** Centro di Studi Vichiani. Vol. 1 (1971)-. Periodical. Italian. an. L40000. Bibliopolis, Via Arangio Ruiz 83, 80122 Naples Italy. **Tel** 011 39 81 664606. **LC** B3583; .C4A. **DD** 195.
**Ind/Abst** Linguist. Lang. Behav. Abstr.; MLA Int. Bibl. Books Artic. Mod. Lang. Lit.; Philos. Index; Soc. Plann. Policy Dev. Abstr.; Sociol. Abstr.

US/0524-112X
**BOSTON COLLEGE STUDIES IN PHILOSOPHY.** ***Ceased.*** **Added/Corp** Boston College. (1966)-Series complete. English. ir. Boston College Studies in Philosophy, Carney Hall 216, Boston College, Department of Philosophy, Chestnut Hill MA 02167. **Tel** (617)552-3547. **ED** James Bernauer. **DD** 100.
**Ind/Abst** Philos. Index.

US
**BOSTON UNIVERSITY STUDIES IN PHILOSOPHY AND RELIGION.** (1980)-. Monographic series. English. ir. Price varies per volume. University of Notre Dame Press, PO Box 635, South Bend IN 46624. **Tel** (219)239-6349, (800)677-3232, FAX (219)239-8148. **ED** Leroy S Rouner.

●UK/0960-8788
**BRITISH JOURNAL FOR THE HISTORY OF PHILOSOPHY.** (1993)-. Academic Scholarly Publication. English. sa (2 issues). £36.00 (institutions), £28.00 (individuals). Thoemmes Press, 85 Park Street, Bristol BS1 5PJ England. **Tel** 011 44 272 291377, FAX 011 44 272 221918. **ED** Dr. G.A.J Rogers. **Bk Rev,** (Qty: 16). **Ad Acc, Adv Mgr:** Deborah Mann, **Tel** same as publisher. **Acid Free.**
**Desc:** Includes articles and reviews on the history of philosophy and related intellectual history from the

ancient world through to the early decades of the twentieth century. The journal's primary objective is to foster understanding of the history of philosophy through a deeper appreciation of the argument of past philosophers by a study of their texts, and through a proper awareness of the context - intellectual, political, social - in which the text was created.

UK/0007-0882
**BRITISH JOURNAL FOR THE PHILOSOPHY OF SCIENCE, THE. See** Science and Technology.

II
**BULLETIN. Main/Corp** SRI Aurobindo International Centre of Education, Pondicherry, India. Bulletin. English (French and Hindi). qt. $25.00. Sri Aurobindo Ashram, International Centre of Education, Pondicherry S 605002 India. **(Subscription address:** Prints India, 11 Darya Ganj, New Delhi, 110002 India, (Phone: 011 91 11 3268645)) **ED** Harikant C Patel. **Ad Acc. Circ:** 2,200.
**Desc:** Main subjects contains Yoga philosophy and psychology, teachings of Sri Aurobindo and the Mother, activities of the Education Centre.

GR/0007-4217
**BULLETIN DE CORRESPONDANCE HELLENIQUE.** [Bull. corresp. hell.]. **Added/Corp** Ecole Francaise d'Athenes. **VFOAT** Deltion HellenikÂes Allelographias. (1877)-. Bulletin. French (Greek, Modern). Twice a year. Diffusion de Boccard, 11 rue de Medicis, 75006 Paris France. **Tel** 011 33 1 43260037. **LC** DF10; .B9. Documents available from The Genuine Article.
**Ind/Abst** Arts Humanit. Citation Index [Full Cov.]; BHA : Biblio. Hist. Art; Curr. Contents Arts Humanit.; MLA Int. Bibl. Books Artic. Mod. Lang. Lit.; Res. Alert [Full Cov.].

US/1042-6833
**BULLETIN DE LA SOCIETE AMERICAINE DE PHILOSOPHIE DE LANGUE FRANCAISE.** [Bull. Soc. Am. philos. lang. Fr.]. **Added/Corp** Societe Americaine de Philosophie de Langue Francaise. Vol. 1, No. 1 (Winter 1989)-. Periodical. French (English). Twice a year. $20.00. Societe Americaine Philosophie Langue Francaise, 5 Moraine Terrace, Dekalb IL 60115. **Tel** (815)756-4156. **DD** 190.
**Ind/Abst** MLA Int. Bibl. Books Artic. Mod. Lang. Lit.

CN/0701-1385
**BULLETIN DE LA SOCIETE DE PHILOSOPHIE DU QUEBEC.** ***Ceased.*** **Main/Corp** Societe de Philosophie du Quebec. Vol. 1 (Oct. 1974)-(19??). Bulletin. French. ir. Societe de Philosophie du Quebec, Case Postale 1370, Place Bonaventure, Montreal Quebec H5A 1H2 Canada. **DD** 105.

FR/0037-9352
**BULLETIN DE LA SOCIETE FRANCAISE DE PHILOSOPHIE.** [Bull. Soc. fr. philos.]. **Main/Corp** Societe Francaise de Philosophie. Vol. 1 (1901)-. Periodical. French. qt. $43.00. Librairie Armand Colin, BP 22, 41354 Vineuil Cedex France. **Tel** 011 33 54 438994. **(Subscription address:** Librarie Armand Colin, 7A Boulevard de Perolles,, CH-1701 Fribourg Switzerland.**) LC** B12; .S6. **DD** 106.2.
**Ind/Abst** Philos. Index.

BE/0068-4023
**BULLETIN DE PHILOSOPHIE MEDIEVALE. Added/Corp** International Society for the Study of Medieval Philosophy. Vol. 6 (1964)-. Periodical. French (English, German, Spanish and Italian). an (Dec.). 1000F. SIEPM, College Thomas More, Chemin d'Aristote 1, B1348 Louvain-La-Neuve Belgium. **Tel** 011 32 10 474807, FAX 011 31 10 474819. **ED** Jacqueline Hamesse. **LC** B721; .I57a. **DD** 189/.05. Index available. **Circ:** 1,000 (ctrl). ***Continues*** *International Society for the Study of Medieval Philosophy. Bulletin de la Societe Internationale pour l'Etude de la Philosophie Medievale.*
**Desc:** Prospecting bibliography materials for the study of medieval Latin, Arabic, and Jewish philosophy.
**Ind/Abst** Bibliogr. Mission.

US
**BULLETIN OF THE EVANGELICAL PHILOSOPHICAL SOCIETY. Main/Corp** Evangelical Philosophical Society. **Added/Corp** Evangelical Philosophical Society. Vol. 1, (1978)-. Periodical. English. Twice a year (Spring & Fall). $20.00. Bulletin of the Evangelical Philosophical Society, Bethel Seminary, 3949 Bethel Drive, St Paul MN 55112. **Tel** (612)638-6167, FAX (612-638-6002. **ED** Dr. Steve Clinton, (phone: (407)826-2072). **Bk Rev. Pr Rev. Circ:** 250.
**Desc:** Discusses philosophy of religion, ethics, and philosophical theology from an orthodox Protestant viewpoint.

UK/0263-5232
**BULLETIN OF THE HEGEL SOCIETY OF GREAT BRITAIN, THE.** [Bull. Hegel Soc. G.B.]. **Added/Corp** Hegel Society of Great Britain. No. 1 (Spring/Summer 1980)-. Bulletin. English. Twice a year. £12.00 (institutions), £8.00 (individuals) Europe; $24.00 (institutions), $17.00 (individuals) other. University of Sheffield / Department of Philosophy, Sheffield S10 2TN England. **Tel** 44 742 824604, FAX 44 742 824604. **ED** Dr. Robert Stern (editor's phone: 44 742 824901). **LC** B2900; .B84. **DD** 193. **Bk Rev**, (Qty: 20). **Ad Acc, Adv Mgr:** Dr. Robert Stern. **Circ:** 300.
**Desc:** Articles, reviews and information on Hegel, German idealism and related topics.
**Ind/Abst** Philos. Index.

JA/0286-2190
**BYOTAI SEIRI (OSAKA. 1982).** (BYOTAI SEIRI.). [Byotai seiri]. **VFOAT** Medicina Philosophica. Vol. 1, No. 1 (1982)-. Periodical. Japanese. mo. Nagai Shoten Company Ltd, 21-15 8-Chome Fukushima, Fukushima Osaka 553 Japan. **Tel** 06-452-1881, FAX 06-452-1882. **NLM** W1; BY998J. **CODEN** MDPHDG. Documents available from CASDDS.
**Ind/Abst** Chem. Abstr.

SZ/0250-6971
**CAHIERS DE LA REVUE DE THEOLOGIE ET DE PHILOSOPHIE. See** Religion and Theology.

FR/0241-2799
**CAHIERS PHILOSOPHIQUES.** [Cah. philos.]. (1979)-. Periodical. French. qt. 142.00F France; 160.00F other. Centre National Documentation Pedagogique, 21 Square St. Charles, BP 7, 75012 Paris, France. **Tel** 011 33 1 40020333, 011 33 1 46349425. **UDC** 1.

CG
**CAHIERS PHILOSOPHIQUES AFRICAINS. VFOAT** African Philosophical Journal. No. 1 (Jan. 1972)-. Periodical. English (French). $5.00. University Nationale du Zaire, Box 257, Kinshasa 11 Zaire. **LC** B5300; .C33.

FR/0181-1126
**CAHIERS SIMONE WEIL.** (CAHIERS SIMONE WEIL : REVUE TRIMESTRIELLE PUBLIEE PAR L'ASSOCIATION POUR L'ETUDE DE LA PENSEE DE SIMONE WEIL.). [Cah. Simone Weil]. Vol. 1, No. 1 (June 1978)-. Periodical. French. qt. 160.00F France; 170.00F, 220.00F (airmail) other. Michel Narcy, 198 Allee du Lavoir, 91190 Gif-Sur Yvette France. **Tel** 60 12 01 51. **(Subscription address:** Association pour l'Etude de la Pensee de Simone Weil, Tresoriere Mme Colette Charot, les Buis B 38, Avenue Philippe Solari, 13090 Aix en Provence France**) ED** Michel Narcy. **LC** B2430.W474; C25. **DD** 194. Index available. **Bk Rev. Circ:** 600 (ctrl).
**Desc:** Original essays on various aspects of the writings of Simone Weil (1909-1943), French mystic and philosopher.
**Ind/Abst** MLA Int. Bibl. Books Artic. Mod. Lang. Lit.

FR/0152-593X
**CAHIERS SPINOZA.** No. 1 (Summer 1977)-. Monographic series. French. ir. Prices varies per volume. Editions Eres, 11 rue des Alouettes, Ramonville St. Agne France. **Tel** 011 33 61 751576. **LC** B3951; .C33. **DD** 199/.492.

UK/0950-6322
**CAMBRIDGE STUDIES IN FRENCH.** [Camb. stud. Fr.]. (19??)-. Monographic series. English. ir. Price varies per volume. Cambridge University Press, The Edinburgh Building, Shaftesbury Road, Cambridge CB2 2RU United Kingdom. **Tel** 011 44 223 312393, FAX 011 44 223 325959. **(Subscription address:** Cambridge University Press / North America, 110 Midland Avenue, Port Chester NY 10573.**)**
**Desc:** Series covering French literary and cultural theory and thought.
**Ind/Abst** MLA Int. Bibl. Books Artic. Mod. Lang. Lit.

CN/0045-5091
**CANADIAN JOURNAL OF PHILOSOPHY.** [Can. j. philos.]. **Added/Corp** Canadian Association for Publishing in Philosophy. Vol. 1 (Sept. 1971)-. Periodical. English (French). qt. $40.00 (institutions), $25.00 (individuals). University of Calgary Press, 2500 University Drive Northwest, Calgary Alberta T2N 1N4 Canada. **Tel** (403)220-7578. **ED** David Copp, Marsha P. Hanen, Philip Hanson, John King-Farlow, Bernard Linsky, Mohan Matten, Kai Nielsen, Robert Ware. **LC** B1; .C36. **DD** 105. **[CCC]. Bk Rev. Ad Acc. Circ:** 1,000 (ctrl). Documents available from The Genuine Article, UMI Article Clearinghouse.
**Desc:** Sponsored by the Canadian Association for Publishing in Philosophy. Its purpose is the publication of philosophical work of high quality in any field of philosophy.
**Ind/Abst** Acad. Abstr. Full Text Elite (Jan. 1992-); Acad. Abstr. (Jan. 1992-); Acad. Search (Jan. 1992-); Arts Humanit. Citation Index [Full Cov.]; Can. Index; Can. Period. Index (19??-); Curr. Contents Arts Humanit.; Expand. Acad. Index (1989-); Humanit. Index; Humanit. Source (Jan. 1992-); INFO-SOUTH Abstr.; Int. Bibliogr. Sociol.; Mag. Search; MLA Int. Bibl. Books Artic. Mod. Lang. Lit.; Newsp. Period. Abstr. (1991-); Philos. Index; Res. Alert [Full Cov.]; Soc. Sci. Cit. Index [Select. Cov.].

CN/0228-491X
**CANADIAN PHILOSOPHICAL REVIEWS.** [Can. philos. rev.]. **VFOAT** Revue Canadienne de Comptes Rendus en Philosophie. Vol. 1, No. 1 (Spring 1981)-. Periodical. English (French). mo. $25.00 (institutions, Canada), $28.00 (institutions, U.S.), $10.00 (individual, Canada), $12.00 (individual, U.S.), $7.00 (students). Academic Printing and Publishing, PO Box 4218, South Edmonton, Alberta T6E 4T2 Canada. **Tel** (403)435-5898. **ED** Roger A Shiner. **LC** B1; .C365. **DD** 105. **Ad Acc. Circ:** 350 (ctrl).
**Desc:** New books in various areas of philosophical interest reviewed quickly by scholars in the field. Valuable aid in choosing books for personal and classroom use.
**Ind/Abst** Book Rev. Index; Philos. Index.

CN/0045-544X
**CANADIAN THEOSOPHIST, THE. See** Religion and Theology.

CN/0317-073X
**CARLETON UNIVERSITY STUDENT JOURNAL OF PHILOSOPHY, THE.** Began with March 1974 issue. Periodical. English. sa. Free. The Carleton University Student Journal of Philosophy, Carleton University, Department of Philosophy, Colonel by Drive, Ottawa Ontario K1S 5B6 Canada. **Tel** 613-564-3868. **ED** Bruce Collins, Julie Maybee, Rob DaVidi and Andrew Hunter. **DD** 105. **Bk Rev. Ad Acc. Circ:** 150.
**Desc:** Publishes papers of philosophical interest written by students.

CN/0706-1250
**CARREFOUR. Added/Corp** Societe de Philosophie de l'Outaouais. (1979)-. Periodical. French. Twice a year. 40.00Can$. Carrefour / Societe Philosophie Outaouais, 65 rue Universite, Ottawa Ontario K1N 6N5 Canada. **Tel** (613)564-9025. **ED** Roberto Miguelez. **LC** AS42.S64; A24. **DD** 061/.1384. **Ad Acc, Adv Mgr:** C. Campeau. **Pr Rev. Circ:** 560 (ctrl).
**Desc:** Forum for the discussion of problems that beset modernity.

CC
**CHE HSUEH YEN CHIU. ZHEXUE YANJIU. VFOAT** Zhexue Yanjiu. (19??)-. Periodical. Chinese. mo. Science Press, 16 Donghuangchenggen North Street, Beijing 100707, People's Republic of China. **Tel** 011 86 1 4019821, 011 86 1 4010642, FAX 011 86 1 4012180, 011 86 1 4019810, telex 210147. **LC** B8.C5; C42.

US/0023-8627
**CHINESE STUDIES IN PHILOSOPHY.** [Chin. stud. philos.]. **Added/Corp** M.E. Sharpe, Inc. International Arts and Sciences Press. (1969)-. Periodical. English (Chinese). qt. $381.00 US; $421.00 other. M. E. Sharpe Inc., 80 Business Park Drive, Armonk NY 10504. **Tel** (914)273-1800, (800)541-6563, FAX (914)273-2106. **ED** Chung-Ying Cheng. **LC** B1; .C55. **DD** 105. **Bk Rev. Ad Acc. Circ:** 200 (ctrl). available on microfilm from University Microfilms International (UMI). Documents available from The Genuine Article. ***Supersedes in part*** *Chinese Studies in History and Philosophy.*
**Desc:** The journal contains unabridged translations of articles from Chinese sources. The aim is to present the more important Chinese studies in this field.
**Ind/Abst** Arts Humanit. Citation Index [Full Cov.]; Curr. Contents Arts Humanit.; Philos. Index; Res. Alert [Full Cov.].

US/0888-9384
**CHRYSALIS (NEW YORK, N.Y.).** (CHRYSALIS : JOURNAL OF THE SWEDENBORG FOUNDATION.). [Chrysalis]. **Added/Corp** Swedenborg Foundation. Vol. 1, Issue 1, Spring (1986)-. Periodical. English. Three times a year. $20.00 (one year); $35.00 (two year); $48.00 (three year). Swendenborg Foundation, PO Box 549, West Chester PA 19381. **Tel** (800)355-3222, FAX (215)430-7982. **ED** Carol S. Lawson (Editor's Address: Route 1 Box 184, Dillwyn, VA 23936). **DD** 230. **Bk Rev**, (Qty: 12 or more). **Ad Acc, Adv Mgr:** Susanna Lawson, **Tel** (804)983-3021. **Pr Rev. Circ:** 3,000.
**Desc:** Journal of ideas challenging readers to find new perspectives on contemporary life, the arts, and religion. Articles, fiction, poetry, and film reviews focus on a different theme in each issue, placing Swedenborgien thought alongside other traditions in an ecumenical, though not religious, tradition.

CC
**CHUNG-KUO CHE HSUEH.** V. 1 (Aug. 1979)-. Periodical. Chinese. RMBY1.20. San Lien Shu Tien, Beijing China, People's Republic of China. **LC** B8.C5; C48. **DD** 181/.11.

CC
**CHUNG-KUO CHE HSUEH SHIH YEN CHIU. VFOAT** Research in History of Chinese Philosophy. Periodical. Chinese. qt. RMBY0.70. Science Press, 16 Donghuangchenggen North Street, Beijing 100707, People's Republic of China. **Tel** 011 86 1 4019821, 011 86 1 4010642, FAX 011 86 1 4012180, 011 86 1 4019810, telex 210147. **LC** B8.C5; C47. **DD** 181/.11/09.

CH/1017-6462
**CHUNG-KUO WEN CHE YEN CHIU CHI KAN. See** Literature.

# Philosophy

**BL**
**CIENCIA E FILOSOFIA.** No. 1-. Periodical. Portuguese. an. $15.00. Faculdade de Filosofia / Sao Paulo, Letras e Ciencias Humanas - USP, Secao de Publicacoes, Caixa Postal 8105, 05508 Butanta Sao Paulo SP Brazil. **Tel** (011)211-2431. **LC** B67; .C5.

UK/0950-8864
**COGITO (BRISTOL, ENGLAND).** (COGITO.). **Added/Corp** Cogito Society. University of Bristol. Vol. 1, No. 1 (Jan. 1987)-. Periodical. English. Three times a year (Feb., Jun., Oct.). £96.00. Carfax Publishing Company, PO Box 25 Abingdon, Oxfordshire OX14 3UE England. **Tel** 011 44 235 555335, FAX (0279)31067, telex 817484. **(Subscription address:** US and Canada/ PO Box 2025, Dunnellon, FL 34430-2025; telephone:(904)489-6996**) ED** Gordon Reddiford (editor's address: University of Bristol, Department of Philosophy, 9 Woodland Road, Bristol BS8 1TB United Kingdom). **LC** B1; .C65. **[CCC]**. **Circ:** 800. available on microfiche.
**Desc:** Seeks to promote an interest in philosophy both in the general public and among young people in particular.

VE/0505-1827
**COLECCION TESIS DOCTORALES.** **Main/Corp** Venezuela. Universidad Central, Caracas. Instituto de Filosofia. Spanish. Universidad Central de Venezuela / Instituto de Filosofia, Caracas Venezuela. **DD** 080.

US/0164-1522
**COLLABORATION (HIGH FALLS).** (COLLABORATION.). Periodical. English. qt. $12.00 US; $22.00 other. Sri Aurobindo Association, PO Box 372, High Falls NY 12440. **Tel** (914)687-9222. **ED** Jeanne Korstange. **Bk Rev. Circ:** 1,500 (ctrl).
**Desc:** Devoted to the spiritual, evolutionary vision of Sri Aurobindo and the mother and containing excerpts of their writings, news and photographs from Auroville, an international community.

FR/0530-8089
**COLLECTION IDEES.** Periodical. French. Editions Gallimard, 5 rue Sebastien Bottin, 75007 Paris France.

US/0098-9436
**COLUMBIA STUDIES IN PHILOSOPHY.** No. 1- 1941-. Monographic series. English. ir. Price varies per volume. Columbia University Press, 136 South Broadway, Irvington NY 10533. **Tel** (914)591-9111.

AU/0010-5155
**CONCEPTUS.** (May 1967)-. Periodical. German. Six times a year. DM55.00. Institut Philosophie, Johann Kepler University, A 4040 Linz Auhof Austria.
**Ind/Abst** Math. Rev.; Philos. Index.

DM/0377-6824
**CONSEQUENCE (COTONOU).** (CONSEQUENCE.). No. 1- Jan./June 1974-. Periodical. Multiple languages (English and French). 1.400. Inter-African Council for Philosophy, PO Box 1268, Cotonou Dahomey. **LC** B5300; .C65. **DD** 199/.6.

CN/0709-6461
**CONSIDERATIONS.** V. 1- June 1977-. Periodical. French. Three times a year. $3.50 students. Faculte de Philosophie Secretariat, Bureau 644/Tour des Arts, Universite Laval, Quebec Quebec G1K 7P4 Canada. **DD** 105.

UK
**CONTEMPORARY BRITISH PHILOSOPHY : PERSONAL STATEMENTS.** 1st- Series. English. **ED** J H Muirhead. **LC** B1615. **DD** 192.

US/0740-719X
**CONTEMPORARY GERMAN PHILOSOPHY.** *Ceased.* [Contemp. Ger. philos.]. Vol. 1 (1982)-Vol 4 ?. English. an. Pennsylvania State University Press, 820 North University Drive, Suite C, University Park PA 16802-1003. **Tel** (814)865-1327, (800)326-9180, FAX (814)863-1408. **ED** Darrel E Christensen. **LC** B3181; .C66. **DD** 105.
**Desc:** A yearbook which makes originally German contributions to philosophical comprehension available in English. Varied articles and book reviews in each volume.

NE
**CONTEMPORARY PHILOSOPHY.** (19??)-. Monographic series. English. ir. Price varies per volume. Kluwer Academic Publishers, Postbus 322, 3300 AH Dordrecht, The Netherlands. **Tel** 011 (31) 78 524400, FAX 011 31 78 183273, telex 20083.

US/0732-4944
**CONTEMPORARY PHILOSOPHY (BOULDER, COLO.).** (CONTEMPORARY PHILOSOPHY.). [Contemp. philos.]. **Added/Corp** Institute for Advanced Philosophic Research (U.S.). Vol. 7, No. 5 (Late Fall 1978)-. Periodical. English. bm. $30.00 (one year), $55.00 (two year), $75.00 (three year), $250.00 (life-time membership), $20.00 (student). Institute of Advanced Philosophic Research, PO Box 1373, Boulder CO 80306. **Tel** (313)444-0071. **ED** Alfred E. Koenig. **Bk Rev. Circ:** 1,500. *Continues* Philosophic Research and Analysis.
**Desc:** Covers philosophy and philosophy of science.

US
**CONTEMPORARY STUDIES IN PHILOSOPHY AND THE HUMAN SCIENCES.** English. an. $15.00. Humanities Press, 165 1st Avenue, Atlantic Highlands NJ 07716. **Tel** (908)872-1441, (800)221-3845, FAX (908)872-0717, telex 752233. **ED** John Sallis. Index available.
**Desc:** Explores recent developments in philosophy, stressing fundamental issues and current styles in philosophical thought.

US/0889-468X
**CONTINUING THE CONVERSATION.** *Ceased.* [Contin. conversat.]. (19??)-(1992). Periodical. English. qt. Hort Ideas, Rt. 1 Box 302, Gravel Switch KY 40328. **DD** 100.

US/0084-926X
**CONTRIBUTIONS IN PHILOSOPHY.** (19??)-. Monographic series. English. ir. Price varies per volume. Greenwood Press Inc., PO Box 5007, Westport CT 06881-5007. **Tel** (203)226-3571, FAX (203)222-1502. **LC** UNC.
**Desc:** This series combines the far-reaching work of original thinkers with important new monographs on the history of philosophy.

DK/0589-8080
**CORPUS PHILOSOPHORUM DANICORUM MEDII AEVI.** **Added/Corp** Danske Sprog- Og Litteraturselskab. (1955)-. Monographic series. Latin (French and English). ir. Price varies per volume. Danish Society of Language and Literature, Frederiksholms Kanal 18A, 1220 Copenhagen K Denmark. **Tel** 011 45 1 130660. **(Subscription address:** GEC GADS Forlag, Vimmelskaftet 32, 1161 Copenhagen K Denmark.**) ED** Sten Ebbesen. **Circ:** 600 (ctrl).
**Desc:** Medieval Danish writers in philosophy, linguistics and natural science are edited with apparatus, introduction, and glossary, normally for the first time after manuscript sources only.

UK
**CORRESPONDENCE OF JOHN LOCKE.** (19??)-. Monographic series. English. ir. Price varies per volume. Oxford University Press / New York, 200 Madison Avenue, New York NY 10016. **Tel** (212)679-7300, (919)677-0977, (800)451-7556, (800)445-9714, FAX (919)677-1303.

MX/0011-1503
**CRITICA; REVISTA HISPANOAMERICANA DE FILOSOFIA.** **Added/Corp** Universidad Nacional Autonoma de Mexico. Instituto de Investigaciones Filosoficas. Vol.1 (Jan. 1967). Periodical. Spanish (English and Portuguese). Three times a year. $30.00 (individuals); $36.00 (institutions). Universidad Nacional Autonoma de Mexico, Instituto de Investigaciones Filosoficas, Apartado Postal 70 447, 04510 Mexico DF Mexico. **Tel** 52 5 5505215, FAX 52 5 5507014. **ED** Antonio Zirion. **LC** B1; .A14. Index available (bound in Dec. issue). cum. index. **Bk Rev**, (Qty: 8). **Ad Acc, Adv Mgr:** F Maxinoz, **Tel** 52 5 6227434. **Circ:** 1,000 (ctrl). Documents available from The Genuine Article.
**Desc:** Publishes quality essays, brief discussions and critical reviews of books regardless of the author's philosophical school or point of view.
**Ind/Abst** Arts Humanit. Citation Index [Full Cov.]; Curr. Contents Arts Humanit.; HAPI Hisp. Am. Period. Index; Philos. Index; Res. Alert [Full Cov.]; Soc. Sci. Cit. Index [Select. Cov.].

US/0097-7209
**CRYSTAL MIRROR. See** Religion and Theology-Buddhism.

CL
**CUADERNOS DE FILOSOFIA.** **Added/Corp** Concepcion, Chile (City). Universidad. Instituto de Filosofia. (19??)-. Spanish (Portuguese and English). an. $5.00. Miguel da Costa Leiva, Depto Filosofia y Cs de la Educacion, Universidad de Concepcion Chile. **Tel** 234985, telex ANEXD 2104. **LC** B5; .C783. Index available. **Bk Rev. Circ:** 500 (ctrl).
**Desc:** History of philosophy, logic, philosophy of science, axiology, ethics, deontology, and aesthetics.
**Ind/Abst** HAPI Hisp. Am. Period. Index; Philos. Index.

CK/0120-8462
**CUADERNOS DE FILOSOFIA LATINOAMERICANA / ORGANO DE DIVULGACION DE LA FACULTAD DE FILOSOFIA Y EL CENTRO DE ENSENANZA DESESCOLARIZADA DE LA UNIVERSIDAD SANTO TOMAS.** **Added/Corp** Universidad de Santo Tomas (Bogota, Colombia). Centro de Ensenanza Desescolarizada. Universidad de Santo Tomas (Bogota, Colombia). Facultad de Filosofia. (19??)-. Periodical. Spanish. qt. $4.50. Cuadernos de Filosofia, Latinoamericana Universidad Santo Tomas, Carrera 9A. No. 51-23, Bogota 2 Colombia. **LC** B1001; .C8. **DD** 199/.8/05.

CK/0120-0992
**CUADERNOS DE FILOSOFIA Y LETRAS.** (CUADERNOS DE FILOSOFIA Y LETRAS : [PUBLICACION DE LA FACULTAD DE FILOSOFIA Y LETRAS DE LA UNIVERSIDAD DE LOS ANDES].). [Cuad. filos. let.]. **Added/Corp** Universidad de los Andes (Bogota, Colombia). Facultad de Filosofia y Letras. (1978)-. Periodical. Spanish. ir. Universidad de Los Andes / Facultad de Humanidades y Ciencias, Comite de Publicaciones, Bogota Colombia.
**Ind/Abst** Am. Hist. Life (1980).

UY
**CUADERNOS DE SEMIOTICA.** No. 1- 1978-. Periodical. Spanish (summaries and/or abstracts in English). Garibaldi 2844, Montevideo Uruguay.

SP
**CUADERNOS SALMANTINOS DE FILOSOFIA.** **Added/Corp** Universidad Pontificia de Salamanca. Vol. 1 (1974)-. Spanish. an. $52.00. Universidad Pontificia de Salamanca, Apartado de Correos 541, 37080 Salamanca Spain. **Tel** 011 34 23 215140. **LC** B5; .C82. **DD** 105.

NE/0921-3740
**CULTURAL DYNAMICS.** *Ceased.* **See** Sociology.

AG
**CUYO : ANUARIO DE FILOSOFIA ARGENTINA Y AMERICANA.** **Added/Corp** Universidad Nacional de Cuyo. Instituto de Filosofia Argentina y Americana. (1984)-. Spanish. *Continues* Cuyo (Mendoza, Argentina : 1965), 0590-4595.
**Ind/Abst** Am. Hist. Life (1965-1969).

IS/0334-2336
**DAAT.** **See** Religion and Theology-Judaism.

DK/0070-2749
**DANISH YEARBOOK OF PHILOSOPHY.** [Dan. yearb. philos.]. **Added/Corp** Selskabet for Filosofi og Psykologi (Denmark). Vol. 1 (1964)-. Danish (German). an. kr175.00. Museum Tusculanum Press, University of Copenhagen, Njalsgade 94, DK-2300 Copenhagen D Denmark. **Tel** 011 45 31542211. **LC** B1; .A16. available on CD-ROM.
**Desc:** Includes articles mainly relating to Danish philosophy or by authors with ties to Danish philosophy.
**Ind/Abst** Philos. Index.

II
**DARSHAN-MANJARI: THE BURDWAN UNIVERSITY JOURNAL OF PHILOSOPHY.** **Added/Corp** University of Burdwan. **VFOAT** Burdwan University Journal of Philosophy; Journal of Philosophy. Vol. 1, No. 1 (1984)-. Periodical. English (Bengali). an. Rs10.00. University of Budwan, Department of Philosophy, Golabag Burdwan 713104 India. **ED** Aminul Haque and Gopal Ch Khan. **LC** B1; .D28. **DD** 105.
**Ind/Abst** Philos. Index.

II/0011-6734
**DARSHANA INTERNATIONAL.** [Darshana int.]. Vol. 3 (Jan. 1963)-. Periodical. English. qt (January, April, July and October). $40.00. Darshana International, JP Atreya, Diwan Bazar, Moradabad 244 001 India. **Tel** 23370/28712. **(Subscription address:** Prints India, 11 Darya Ganj, New Delhi, 110002 India, (Phone: 011 91 11 3268645)**) DD** 100. **Bk Rev. Ad Acc. Circ:** 1,000 (ctrl). *Continues* Darshana.
**Ind/Abst** Philos. Index.

US/0273-2483
**DEATH & DYING (BOCA RATON, FLA.).** [Death dying]. **VFOAT** Death and Dying. **VAT** Death and Dying (Boca Raton). V. 1, Article 1-. Periodical. English. an. Social Issues Resources Series Inc, PO Box 2348, Boca Raton FL 33427. **Tel** (800)327-0513, (407)994-0079. **ED** Eleanor C Goldstein. **LC** HQ1073.5.U6; D4. **DD** 306/.9/05.
**Desc:** Interdisciplinary resource material consisting of reprinted articles from popular and professional journals, newspapers, magazines and government documents.

GR
**DEUKALION : PERIODIKE EKDOSE TOU KENTROU PHILOSOPHIKON EREUNON.** Periodical. Greek, Modern (English, French and German). qt. $50.00. Charitos 3, Athens 139 Greece. **LC** B8.G7; D48.

GW/0012-1045
**DEUTSCHE ZEITSCHRIFT FUER PHILOSOPHIE.** [Dtsch. Z. Philos.]. Vol. 1 (1953)-. Periodical. German. bm. $150.00. Akademie-Verlag GmbH, Muehlenstrasse 33 34, D 13162 Berlin Germany. **Tel** 011 49 30 47889300, FAX 011 49 30 47889357. **(Subscription address:** VCH Publishers Inc., 303 Northwest 12th Avenue, Journals Department, Deerfield

FL 33442.) **ED** A. Honneth, H.P. Krueger, H. Hagl-Docekal, H.J. Schneider. **LC** B3; .D4. **DD** 100. cum. index. **Pr Rev.** Documents available from The Genuine Article.
**Desc:** Promotes open dialogue between philosophers of differing schools of thought and the communications between representatives of different philosophical cultures.
**Ind/Abst** Arts Humanit. Citation Index [Full Cov.]; Curr. Contents Arts Humanit.; Int. Polit. Sci. Abstr.; Linguist. Lang. Behav. Abstr.; Philos. Index; Res. Alert [Full Cov.]; Soc. Plann. Policy Dev. Abstr.; Soc. Sci. Cit. Index [Full Cov.]; Sociol. Abstr.

SZ/0012-2017
**DIALECTICA.** (DIALECTICA : INTERNATIONAL REVIEW OF PHILOSOPHY OF KNOWLEDGE.). [Dialectica]. Vol. 1, No. 1 (Feb. 15, 1947)-. Periodical. English (French and German). Four times a year (Mar., June, Sept., Dec.). 108.00F. Geiger AG Bern, Habsburgstrasse 19, CH 3000 Bern 16 Switzerland. **Tel** 011-41-31-3524344, FAX 011-41-31-448050. **ED** Henri Lauener. **LC** B1; .A15. **DD** 105. Index available (Bound in last issue). cum. index. **Bk Rev**. **Ad Acc**. **Circ:** 700. Documents available from The Genuine Article.
**Desc:** Review of philosophy and dialectic of knowledge.
**Ind/Abst** Arts Humanit. Citation Index (19??-19??) [Full Cov.]; Curr. Contents Arts Humanit.; Linguist. Lang. Behav. Abstr.; Math. Rev.; Philos. Index; Res. Alert [Full Cov.]; Soc. Plann. Policy Dev. Abstr.; Soc. Sci. Cit. Index [Select. Cov.]; Sociol. Abstr.; Zentralbl. Math. Ihre Grenzgeb.

GW/0939-5512
**DIALEKTIK.** **VFOAT** Enzyklopadische Zeitschrift Fur Philosophie und Wissenschaften. (1991)-. Periodical. German. tq. DM98.00. Felix Meiner Verlag, Postfach 760742, D 22057 Hamburg Germany. **Tel** 011 49 40 294870, FAX 011 49 40 2993614. ***Continues** Dialektik.*

US
**DIALOG ONDISC. PHILOSOPHER'S INDEX [COMPUTER FILE].** **Added/Corp** DIALOG Information Services. Bowling Green State University. Philosophy Documentation Center. **VFOAT** Dialog On Disc. Philosopher's Index; Philosopher's Index. (Dec. 1990)-. Periodical. English. qt. Dialog Information Services, 3460 Hillview Avenue, Palo Alto CA 94304. **Tel** (415)858-4240, (800)334-2564. **LC** Z7127; .P474.
**Desc:** Provides indexing and abstracts from books and over 270 journals on philosophy and related interdisciplinary fields published in the US and the Western World. Coverage is from 1940 to the present for US materials and 1967 to the present for non-US materials.

SP/0213-1196
**DIALOGO FILOSOFICO.** [Dialogo filos.]. (1985)-. Periodical. Spanish. Three times a year. 3000ptas Spain; 3700ptas other. Dialogo Filosofico, Apartado Correos 721, 28770 Colmenar Viejo Spain. **Tel** 011 34 1 8462973, FAX 011 34 1 8462973. **UDC** 1. Index available. **Bk Rev**. **Ad Acc**. **Circ:** 1,000 (ctrl).

PR/0012-2122
**DIALOGOS.** [Dialogos]. **Added/Corp** University of Puerto Rico (Rio Piedras Campus). Departamento de Filosofia. Vol. 1, No. 1, Sept. (1964)-. Periodical. Spanish (English). sa. $16.00 institutions; $12.00 individuals. University de Puerto Rico / Oficina de Publicaciones, Apartado 23322 Estacion UPR, San Juan Puerto Rica 00931-1787. **Tel** (809)250-0615, (809)250-0725, (809)250-0725, FAX (809)753-9116. **ED** Roberto Torretti. **LC** B5; .D5. **DD** 105. Index available. **Bk Rev**. **Ad Acc**. **Circ:** 800.
**Desc:** A professional journal open to all currents of philosophy and philosophical scholarship.
**Ind/Abst** HAPI Hisp. Am. Period. Index; Philos. Index.

PL
**DIALOGUE AND HUMANISM.** **Added/Corp** International Society for Universalism. Vol. 1, No. 1 (Spring 1991)-. Periodical. English. qt. $24.00 (individuals), $32.00 (institutions). Institute of Philosophy, Warsaw University, Krakowskie Prezedmiescie 3, 00-047 Warsaw Poland. **LC** B809.7; .D523. ***Continues** Dialectics and Humanism, 0324-8275.*
**Ind/Abst** BHA : Biblio. Hist. Art.

CN/0012-2173
**DIALOGUE - CANADIAN PHILOSOPHICAL ASSOCIATION.** (DIALOGUE.). [Dialogue - Can. Philos. Assoc.]. **Added/Corp** Canadian Philosophical Association. Canada Council. Social Sciences and Humanities Research Council of Canada. **VFOAT** Canadian Philosophical Review; Revue Canadienne de Philosophie. Vol. 1 (June 1962)-. Periodical. English (French). qt. 75.00Can$ Canada; $80.00 other. Wilfrid Laurier University Press, 75 University Avenue West, Waterloo Ontario N2L 3C5 Canada. **Tel** (519)884-1970, FAX (519)725-1399. **ED** Michael McDonald. **LC** B1; .D5. **DD** 105. **Bk Rev**. **Ad Acc**. **Circ:** 1,350. Documents available from The Genuine Article.
**Desc:** Represents most of the main areas of philosophy, such as the history of philosophy, metaphysics, logic, ethics, etc.
**Ind/Abst** Arts Humanit. Citation Index [Full Cov.]; Book Rev. Index; Curr. Contents Arts Humanit.; Linguist. Lang. Behav. Abstr.; Math. Rev.; MLA Int. Bibl. Books Artic. Mod. Lang. Lit.; Philos. Index; Res. Alert [Full Cov.]; Soc. Plann. Policy Dev. Abstr.; Soc. Sci. Cit. Index [Select. Cov.]; Sociol. Abstr.

US/0012-2246
**DIALOGUE (MILWAUKEE, WIS.).** (DIALOGUE.). [Dialogue]. **Added/Corp** Phi Sigma Tau. (April 1956)-. Periodical. English. Twice a year. $5.00 (one year), $10.00 (two year), $13.50 (three year) US; $5.50 (one year), $11.00 (two year), $15.00 (three year) other. Marquette University / Phi Sigma Tau, c/o Department of Philosophy, Milwaukee WI 53233. **Tel** (414)288-6857, FAX (414)288-3300. **ED** Thomas Prendergast. **LC** B1; .D53. **Bk Rev**. **Ad Acc**. **Circ:** 2,000.
**Desc:** The official journal of Phi Sigma Tau, the national honor society in philosophy. Provides a vehicle for exchange of philosophical ideas among graduates and undergraduate students.
**Ind/Abst** Philos. Index.

MX
**DIANOIA, ANUARIO DE FILOSOFIA.** **Added/Corp** Fondo de Cultura Economica, Mexico. Mexico (City). Universidad Nacional. Centro de Estudios Filosoficos. Vol. 1 (1955)-. Monographic series. Spanish. ir. price varies per volume. Fondo de Cultura Economica, Av Picacho Ajusco 227 / Pedregal, 14200 Mexico DF Mexico. **Tel** 011 52 5 2274670 71, FAX 011 52 5 2274683, telex 01775866. **LC** B31; .D28.
**Ind/Abst** HAPI Hisp. Am. Period. Index; Philos. Index.

US/0890-4294
**DIFFERENTIA (FLUSHING, N.Y.).** (DIFFERENTIA.). [Differentia]. No. 1 (Autumn 1986)-. Periodical. English. ir. $30.00 US and Canada; $35.00 other. Differentia Ltd., Queens College, 65 30 Kissina Kiely Hall 706, Flushing NY 11367. **Tel** (718)997-5660. **LC** AC40; .D54. **DD** 052.
**Ind/Abst** MLA Int. Bibl. Books Artic. Mod. Lang. Lit.

FR/0419-1633
**DIOGENE (EDITION FRANCAISE).** **See** Humanities.

IT/0392-1921
**DIOGENES (ENGLISH ED.).** (DIOGENES.). [Diogenes]. **Added/Corp** International Council for Philosophy and Humanistic Studies. No. 1 (1953)-. Periodical. English (French and Spanish). qt (Mar., Jun., Sep., Dec.). £80.00. Carfax Publishing Company, PO Box 25 Abingdon, Oxfordshire OX14 3UE England. **Tel** 011 44 235 555335, FAX (0279)31067, telex 817484. **(Subscription address:** US and Canada/ PO Box 2025, Dunnellon, FL 34430-2025; telephone:(904)489-6996) **ED** Jean D'Ormesson. **LC** AS4; .D5. **DD** 051; 100; 301. cum. index. **Ad Acc**. **Circ:** 600. available on microfilm and microfiche from University Microfilms International (UMI); available on an online database from DIALOG. Documents available from The Genuine Article, UMI Article Clearinghouse.
**Desc:** Offers an internal assessment of each country including the Chicano/Latino experience.
**Ind/Abst** Acad. Search (Jan. 1994-); Am. Hist. Life (1955-1977, 1987-89); Arts Humanit. Citation Index [Full Cov.]; Curr. Contents Arts Humanit.; Expand. Acad. Index (1989-); Humanit. Index; Humanit. Source (Jul. 1993-); INFO-SOUTH Abstr.; Linguist. Lang. Behav. Abstr.; Mag. Search; Middle East Abstr. Index; Newsp. Period. Abstr. (1991-); Philos. Index; Res. Alert [Full Cov.]; Soc. Plann. Policy Dev. Abstr.; Soc. Sci. Cit. Index [Select. Cov.]; Sociol. Abstr.

CN/0705-1085
**DIONYSIUS.** **See** Classical Studies.

GR/1010-7363
**DIOTIMA.** [Diotima]. **Added/Corp** Hellenike Hetaireia Philosophikon Meleton. (1973)-. English (French). an. $40.00. Hellenic Society for Philosophical Studies, 40 Hypsilantou Street, 140 Athens Greece. **Tel** 7217797. **ED** Evanghelos A Moutsopoulos. **LC** B1; .A165. **DD** 105. Index available. cum. index. **Bk Rev**. **Ad Acc**. **Circ:** 1,000 (ctrl).
**Desc:** Articles centered each year on one particular subject dealing with ontology, aesthetics, etc. Also a particular philosophical school.
**Ind/Abst** Philos. Index.

US/0070-508X
**DIRECTORY OF AMERICAN PHILOSOPHERS.** **Added/Corp** Bowling Green State University. Philosophy Documentation Center. Vol. 1 (1962/1963)-. Directory. English. be. $109.00. Philosophy Documentation Center, Bowling Green State University, Bowling Green OH 43403-0189. **Tel** (419)372-2419, (800)444-2419, FAX (419)372-6987. **LC** B935; .D5. **Circ:** 1,000.
**Desc:** Handbook of philosophy covering the US and Canada. Information on faculties of philosophy, names, addresses, and specialties of philosophers, journals, societies, institutions, publishers, etc.

US
**DIRECTORY OF SUICIDE PREVENTION/CRISIS INTERVENTION AGENCIES IN THE UNITED STATES : SUPPLEMENT.** Directory. English. $15.00 US; $20.00 other. American Association of Suicidology, 2459 South Ash, Denver CO 80222. **Tel** 303 692-0985, FAX 303 756-3299.

IT/0012-4257
**DIVUS THOMAS; COMMENTARIUM DE PHILOSOPHIA ET THEOLOGIA.** **See** Religion and Theology.

IO
**DRIJARKARA.** ***Title Change.*** **Added/Corp** Sekolah Tinggi Filsafat Driyarkara. Dewan Mahasiswa. (19??-?. Periodical. Indonesian. qt. Seksi Majalah, Publikasi Dewan Mahasiswa Sekolah, Tinggi Filsafat Driyarkara, Jakarta Indonesia. **LC** B8.I55; D75. ***Continued by** Driyarkara.*

UK/0266-2671
**ECONOMICS AND PHILOSOPHY.** **See** Economics.

CN/0707-2287
**EDIOS.** **Added/Corp** University of Waterloo Philosophy Graduate Student Association. Vol. 1 (July 1978)-. Periodical. English (French). Twice a year (June & Dec.). 18.00Can$ Canada; 35.00Can$ others. Edios / The Canadian Graduate, Department of Philosophy, University of Waterloo, Waterloo Ontario N2L 3G1 Canada. **Tel** (519)885-1211 ext. 3809. **ED** Mano Daniel and Susan Dawn Wake. **DD** 105. Index available. cum. index. **Bk Rev**. **Ad Acc**. **Circ:** 150.
**Desc:** Articles are primarily by graduate students, but also by professional philosophers.
**Ind/Abst** Philos. Index.

UK
**EFRYDIAU ATHRONYDDOL.** (1938)-. Welsh. an. £1.50. University of Wales Press, 6 Gwennyth Street, Cathays Cardiff CF2 4YD Wales United Kingdom. **Tel** 011 44 222 231919. **(Subscription address:** University of Wales Press, Freepost, Cardiff CF1 1YZ United Kingdom**)** **ED** J I Daniel and W L Gealy. **LC** B8.W45; E35. **Bk Rev**. **Ad Acc**. **Circ:** 200.

SW/0013-5933
**ELEMENTA.** [Elementa]. (1938)-. Swedish (German and English). qt. Humanities Press, 165 1st Avenue, Atlantic Highlands NJ 07716. **Tel** (908)872-1441, (800)221-3845, FAX (908)872-0717, telex 752233. **CODEN** EMNTAE. Index available. ***Continues** Tidskrift foer Elementaer Matematik, Fysik och Kemi.*
**Desc:** Monographs on philosophy, aesthetics and ethics.

IT/0392-7342
**ELENCHOS.** (ELENCHOS : RIVISTA DI STUDI SUL PENSIERO ANTICO.). [Elenchos]. **Added/Corp** Centro di Studio del Pensiero Antico (Italy). Vol. 1, No. 1 (1980)-. Periodical. Italian (English, French and German). Twice a year. L40000 Italy; L50000 other. Bibliopolis, Via Arangio Ruiz 83, 80122 Naples Italy. **Tel** 011 39 81 664606. **LC** B175.I7; E54. **DD** 180/.5.

CN/0843-8064
**ELEUTHERIA (OTTAWA).** (ELEUTHERIA.). [Eleutheria (Ott.)]. **Added/Corp** Institute of Speculative Philosophy. Vol. 1, No. 1 (Spring 1989)-. Periodical. English. sa. 20.00Can$. Institute of Speculative Philosophy, P.O.Box 913 Station B, Ottawa ONT K1P 5P9 Canada. **Tel** (613)594-5881, FAX (613)594-5881. **ED** Francis K. Peddle. **DD** 110/.5. **Bk Rev**, (Qty: 2-3). **Circ:** 50.
**Desc:** Publishes articles, book reviews, and serialized monographs on speculative philosophy and philosophy in general.

US/0883-6000
**EMORY VICO STUDIES.** [Emory Vico stud.]. Vol. 1 (1986)-. English. Peter Lang Publishing, 62 West 45th Street, 4th Floor, New York NY 10036. **Tel** (212)764-1471, (800)770-5264, telex 6973364 PLNY. **ED** Donald Verene. **DD** 195. **Pr Rev.**
**Desc:** Covers different aspects of Emory Vico's works.

SP/0211-402X
**ENRAHONAR.** 1 (First issue in 1981)-. Periodical. Catalan (French, Italian and Spanish). sa. Servei de Publicacions de la Universitat Autonoma de Barcelona, Bellaterra, Barcelona Spain. **LC** B5; .E48.

VE
**EPISTEME NS : REVISTA DEL INSTITUTE DE FILOSOFIA.** 1 (Jan./Dec. 1981)-. Periodical. Spanish. Three times a year. $15.00. Instituto de Filosofia, Apartado 47342, Caracas 1041 Venezuela. **Tel** 662-47-63. **LC** B5; .E54. **DD** 105. **Bk Rev**. **Ad Acc**.
**Desc:** Theoretical analysis of the main problems of philosophy, contemporary discussions on logics and philosophy of language, methodology and epistemological problems of natural and social sciences, etc.

GR
**EPOPTEIA.** (197?)-. Periodical. Greek, Modern. tq (Feb, June, Oct). $100.00. Pan Drakopoulos, 6 Averof Street, Chalandri 15232, Athens Greece. **Tel** 011 30 1 6831972, FAX 011 30 1 6826084. **ED** Pan Drakopoulos. Index available. **Bk Rev**, (Qty: 20). **Ad Acc. Circ:** 2,500 (ctrl).
**Desc:** Magazine of philosophy, culture and current affairs. Emphasis on the history of consciousness.

US/1043-0687
**EQUATOR (SAN FRANCISCO, CALIF. 1991), THE.** (THE EQUATOR : MAGAZINE OF NUCLEAR THINKING.). [Equator]. Vol. 1, No. 1 (Jan.-Apr. 1991)-. Periodical. English. mo. $6.00. Nuclear Thinking, 509 Cultural Center, 509 Ellis Street, San Francisci CA 94109. **DD** 105.

CN/0071-1063
**ERASMUS IN ENGLISH.** ***Ceased.*** [Erasmus Engl.]. English. an. University of Toronto Press, 5201 Dufferin Street, Downsview Ontario M3H 5T8 Canada. **Tel** (416)667-7781, (416)667-7782, FAX (416)667-7803. **ED** R M Schoeffel. **LC** B785.E65; E72. **DD** 199/.492. **Bk Rev. Ad Acc. Circ:** 3,500.
**Desc:** A newsletter which provides information about progress of the collected works of Erasmus and about Erasmus studies in general.
**Ind/Abst** Am. Hist. Life; MLA Int. Bibl. Books Artic. Mod. Lang. Lit.

NE/0165-0106
**ERKENNTNIS.** [Erkenntnis]. Vol. 9 (May 1975)-. English. bm. $714.00. Kluwer Academic Publishers, Postbus 322, 3300 AH Dordrecht, The Netherlands. **Tel** 011 (31) 78 524400, FAX 011 31 78 183273, telex 20083. **ED** Carl G Hempel, Wolfgang Spohn, and Wilhelm K Essler. **LC** B1; .J77. **DD** 105. **CODEN** ERKEDQ. **[CCC]. Bk Rev. Ad Acc. Pr Rev. Circ:** 750. available on microfilm and microfiche from University Microfilms International (UMI). ***Continues*** *Journal of Unified Science (Erkenntnis).*
**Desc:** A philosophical journal publishing papers which are committed in one way or another to philosophical attitude which is signified by the label analytic philosophy. It concentrates on those philosophical fields which are particularly inspired by this attitude, though other topics are welcome as well.
**Ind/Abst** Math. Rev.; Philos. Index; Soc. Plann. Policy Dev. Abstr.; Sociol. Abstr.

US/1059-3551
**ERNEST BECKER. See** Medical Science and Technology-Psychiatry.

AG/0325-4933
**ESCRITOS DE FILOSOFIA / C.ACADEMIA NACIONAL DE CIENCIAS, CENTRO DE ESTUDIOS FILOSOFICOS. Added/Corp** Academia Nacional de Ciencias Buenos Aires, Argentina). Centro de Estudios Filosoficos. (1978)-. Periodical. Spanish. sa. $15.00. Academia Nacional de Ciencias, Avenida Alvera 1711 3rd Floor, CP 1114, 1014 Buenos Aires Argentina. **LC** B5; .E58. **DD** 105.

SP/0014-0716
**ESPIRITU.** (ESPIRITU : CUADERNOS DEL INSTITUTO FILOSOFICO DE BALMESIANA.). [Espiritu]. **Added/Corp** Instituto Filosofico de Balmesiana. (1952)-. Periodical. Spanish (Catalan). sa. 600ptas Spain; $10.00 other. Espiritu, Duran y Bas 9, 08002 Barcelona Spain. **Tel** (93)302 68 40. **ED** Juan Pegueroles. Index available. cum. index (1952-1976). **Bk Rev. Circ:** 500 (ctrl).
**Desc:** Philosophical investigation and information based on the Christian faith.
**Ind/Abst** Am. Hist. Life (1955-1957); Philos. Index.

UY
**ESTUDIOS DE CIENCIAS Y LETRAS : REVISTA DEL INSTITUTO DE FILOSOFIA, CIENCIAS Y LETRAS. Added/Corp** Instituto de Filosofia, Ciencias y Letras (Montevideo, Uruguay). No. 1 (1981)-. Periodical. Spanish. Avda 8 de Octubre, 2738 Montevideo Uruguay. **LC** AS89.A1; E85. **DD** 068/.895/13.

AG
**ESTUDIOS DE FILOSOFIA Y RELIGIONES DEL ORIENTE.** V. 1- 1971-. Sanskrit (Spanish). Universidad de Buenos Aires / Filosofia Oriental, Centro de Estudios de Estudios de Filosofia Oriental, 25 de Mayo 217 20 Piso, Buenos Aires Argentina. **LC** B121; .E85.

VE
**ESTUDIOS FILOSOFICOS. Added/Corp** Sociedad Venezolana de Filosofia. (1974)-. Periodical. Spanish. Three times a year. 2,850ptas Spain; $32.00 US. Instituto Superior D Filosofia, Plaza San Pablo, 4 Apartado 586, 47080 Valladolid Spain. **Tel** 011 34 83 356700. Index available. cum. index. **Bk Rev. Ad Acc. Circ:** 900.
**Desc:** All topics of philosophical interest; history of ideas, contemporary problems on philosophy, theoretic aspects of scientific research, etc.
**Ind/Abst** Philos. Index; Soc. Plann. Policy Dev. Abstr.; Sociol. Abstr.

SP/0210-6086
**ESTUDIOS FILOSOFICOS (VALLADOLID).** (ESTUDIOS FILOSOFICOS : MEMORIA DE LOS CURSOS ACADEMICOS DEL ESTUDIO GENERAL DE FILOSOFIA DE LAS CALDAS DE BESAYA (SANTANDER-ESPANA).). [Estud. filos.]. **Added/Corp** Estudio General de Filosofia de Las Caldas de Besaya. Instituto Superior de Filosofia de Valladolid. (1952)-. Periodical. Spanish. Three times a year. 4000ptas (Spain); 5500ptas (other). Instituto Superior d Filosofia, Plaza san Pablo 4 Apartado 586, 47080 Valladolid Spain. **Tel** 11 34 83 356700. **LC** B5; .E7.
**Ind/Abst** Sociol. Abstr.

SP/0504-9806
**ESTUDIOS Y DOCUMENTOS. Main/Corp** Universidad de Valladolid. Facultad de Filosofia y Letras. **Added/Corp** Valladolid. Universidad. Departamento de Historia Moderna. Valladolid. Universidad. Departamento de Historia Medieval. Universidad de Valladolid. Facultad de Filosofia y Letras. No. 1 (1954)-. Monographic series. Spanish. ir. Price varies per volume. Universidad de Valladolid / Filosofia, Facultad de Filosofia y Letras, Valladolid Spain. **LC** WMLC 91/5504. **DD** 940.

CN/0708-319X
**ETIENNE GILSON SERIES, THE. Added/Corp** Pontifical Institute of Mediaeval Studies. (1979)-. Monographic series. English. ir. Price varies per volume. Pontifical Institute of Mediaeval Studies, 59 Queens Park Crescent East, Toronto Ontario M5S 2C4 Canada. **Tel** (416)926-7144, FAX (416)926-7276.
**Desc:** Monographs on medieval philosophy with an emphasis on thomistic philosophy.

FR/0249-7921
**ETUDES DE PHILOSOPHIE MEDIEVALE.** [Etud. philos. mediev.]. (1922)-. Monographic series. French (English). ir. Price varies per volume. Librairie Philosophique J Vrin, 6 Place de la Sorbonne, 75005 Paris France. **Tel** 011 33 1 43540347. **ED** Etienne Gilson.
**Ind/Abst** MLA Int. Bibl. Books Artic. Mod. Lang. Lit.

FR
**ETUDES DE PSYCHOLOGIE ET DE PHILOSOPHIE.** 1-. Monographic series. French. ir. Price varies per volume. Librairie Philosophique J Vrin, 6 Place de la Sorbonne, 75005 Paris France. **Tel** 011 33 1 43540347. **ED** J P Vernant.
**Desc:** Different from one book to another, but always concerning these areas: philosophy and psychology.

FR/0531-1888
**ETUDES MUSULMANES. See** Religion and Theology-Islam, Bahaism, Theosophy.

BE
**ETUDES PHENOMENOLOGIQUES. Added/Corp** Universite Catholique de Louvain (1970- ). Centre d'Etudes Phenomenologiques. Vol. 1, No. 1 (1985)-. Periodical. French. Twice a year. $18.00. OUISA SC, Avenue Maurice 23, B 1050 Brussels Belgium. **Tel** 6470184.

FR/0395-7632
**ETUDES PHILOSOPHIQUES.** (LES ETUDES PHILOSOPHIQUES : ORGANE OFFICIEL DE LA SOCIETE D'ETUDES PHILOSOPHIQUES.). [Etud. philos.]. **Added/Corp** Societe d'Etudes Philosophiques (Marseille, France) Centre National de la Recherche Sscientifique (France). (1928)-. Periodical. French. ir (4 issues per year). 370.00F France; 425.00F other. Presses Universitaires de France, Department des Revues, 14 Avenue du Bois de l'Epine, BP 90, 91003 Evry Cedex France. **Tel** (1)60 77 82 05, FAX (1) 60 79 20 45, telex PUF 600 474 F. **ED** Pierre Aubenque, J. Brun and L. Millet. **LC** B2; .E86. **DD** 105. Documents available from The Genuine Article. ***Continues*** *Bulletin de la Societe d'Etudes Philosophiques du Sud-Est.*
**Desc:** Philosophers explains the central ideas of their work. Also covered are aesthetics, teaching and practical philosophy.
**Ind/Abst** Arts Humanit. Citation Index [Full Cov.]; Bibliogr. Mission.; Curr. Contents Arts Humanit.; MLA Int. Bibl. Books Artic. Mod. Lang. Lit.; Philos. Index; Res. Alert [Full Cov.]; Romant. Move.; Soc. Sci. Cit. Index [Select. Cov.].

UK/0966-8373
**EUROPEAN JOURNAL OF PHILOSOPHY.** Academic Scholarly Publication. English. Three times a year. £85.00 UK and Europe; $125.00 North America; £90.00 other. Basil Blackwell Publishers Ltd, 108 Cowley Road, Oxford 0X4 1JF England. **Tel** 011 44 865 791100, FAX 011 44 865 791347, telex 837022 OXBOOK G. **(Subscription address:** Blackwell Publishers / UK, Marston Book Services, PO Box 87, Oxford OX2 0DT England.**)**

UK/0261-1376
**EXPLORATIONS IN KNOWLEDGE.** Vol. 1, No. 1/2 (1984)-. Periodical. English. Twice a year (January and June). £13.00. Sombourne Press, 294 Leigh Road, Chandlers Ford, Eastleigh Hants SO5 3AU England. **ED** Dr. David Lamb (editor's telephone: 0703-269687). **Bk Rev**, (Qty: 20+). **Ad Acc, Adv Mgr:** same as editor. **Pr Rev. Circ:** 300 (ctrl).
**Ind/Abst** Philos. Index.

US/0739-7046
**FAITH AND PHILOSOPHY : JOURNAL OF THE SOCIETY OF CHRISTIAN PHILOSOPHERS.** [Faith philos.]. **Added/Corp** Society of Christian Philosophers. Vol. 1, No. 1 (Jan. 1984)-. Periodical. English. qt. $40.00 (institution), $25.00 (individuals), US; $44.00 (institution ), $29.00 (individuals), Canada; $46.00 (institution) $31.00 (individuals), other. Asbury College / Department of Philosophy, Asbury College, c/o Michael L Peterson, Wilmore KY 40390. **Tel** (606)858-3511 ext 212. **ED** Philip L. Quinn. **DD** 200. Index available (October). **Bk Rev. Ad Acc. Circ:** 2,000. available on microfilm from University Microfilms International (UMI).
**Desc:** Philosophical discussion of issues pertaining to Christian faith.
**Ind/Abst** Christ. Period. Index (19??-); Index Book Rev. Relig.; Philos. Index; Relig. Index One Period.; Relig. Theol. Abstr.

IT
**FENOMENOLOGIA E SOCIETA. Added/Corp** Comunita di Ricerca. Istituto Italiano di Fenomenologia. Vol. 1, No. 1 (Dec. 1977)-. Periodical. Italian. Three times a year. L72000 Italy; L90000 other. Communita di Ricerca, Via Corregio 36, 20149 Milan Italy. **Tel** 011 39 2 4814213. **LC** B829.5; .F449.

IT/0015-1823
**FILOSOFIA.** [Filosofia]. Vol. 1, Issue 1 (Jan. 1950)-. Periodical. Italian. Three times a year. L30000. Edizioni Ape, Via Tadino 29, 20124 Milan Italy. **Tel** 02 2041557. **ED** Augusto Guzzo. **LC** B4; .F5. cum. index. **Bk Rev.** Documents available from The Genuine Article.
**Desc:** Everything that has to do with philosophy and with history of philosophy.
**Ind/Abst** Arts Humanit. Citation Index [Full Cov.]; Curr. Contents Arts Humanit.; Philos. Index; Res. Alert [Full Cov.]; Soc. Sci. Cit. Index [Select. Cov.].

GR/1105-2120
**FILOSOFIA (ATHENAI).** (PHILOSOPHIA.). [Filosofia]. **Added/Corp** Kentron Ereunes Tes Hellenikes Philosophias. (1971)-. Greek, Modern (English, French and German; summaries and/or abstracts in English, French and German). an (Jan.). $47.00 Western Hemisphere; $20.00 Greece; $22.00 other. Kentron Ereunes Tes Hellenikes Philosophias, Academy of Athens, 14 Anagnostopoulou Street, 10673 Athens Greece. **Tel** 011 30 1 3600140. **ED** Anna Kelesidou. **LC** B31; .P48. **DD** 105. **Bk Rev. Circ:** 1,000.
**Desc:** Theory, history, reviews and news.
**Ind/Abst** Philos. Index.

IT
**FILOSOFIA OGGI.** Vol. 1, No. 1 (Jan.-March 1978)-. Periodical. English (French, German, Italian, Spanish and Portuguese). qt. $70.00. Arcipelago Sociedad Internationale Unita. Scienze, Casella Postale 997, 16100 Genova Italy. **ED** M.A. Raschini and P.P. Ottonello. **LC** B1; .A19. **DD** 105. Index available (Bound in last issue). cum. index. **Bk Rev. Circ:** 600.
**Desc:** Review of classical and contemporary philosophy with theoretical articles and original contributions in the principal languages.
**Ind/Abst** Bibliogr. Mission.

BL
**FILOSOFIA POLITICA.** Vol. 1 (1984)-. Periodical. Portuguese. tq. L80000.00 Italy; L120000.00. Societa Editrice il Mulino, Strada Maggiore 37, 40125 Bologna Italy. **Tel** 011 39 51 256011, FAX 011 39 51 256034.

NE
**FILOSOFIE EN PRAKTIJK.** (19??)-. Dutch. qt (4 issues). Fl39.50 Netherlands; Fl55.00 other. Daedalus Uitgekj, Postbus 115, 1120 AC Landsmeer Netherlands. **Tel** 011 31 2908 24122.

LI/0235-7186
**FILOSOFIJA, SOCIOLOGIJA / LIETUVOS MOKSLU AKADEMIJA. Added/Corp** Lietuvos Mokslu Akademija. **VFOAT** Filosofiia, Sotsiologiia; Philosophy, Sociology; Filosofija ir Sociologija. No. 1 (1990)-. Periodical. Lithuanian (summaries and/or abstracts in English and Russian). tq. **LC** B8.L6; F535. ***Continues in part*** *Lietuvos TSR Mokslu Akademijos Darbai. Serija A, 0131-3843.*

BU/0015-184X
**FILOSOFSKA MISUL.** ***Title Change.*** **Added/Corp** Institut po Filosofiia (Bulgarska Akademiia na Naukite). Aug. (1945)-(199?). Periodical. Bulgarian. mo. **(Subscription address:** Hemus Foreign Trade Organization, 1 B Raiko Daskalov Square, 1000 Sofia Bulgaria**) LC** HX8; .F5. ***Continued by*** *Filosofski Alternative, 0861-7899.*
**Ind/Abst** Annu. Bibliogr. Engl. Lang. Lit.

●BU/0861-7899
**FILOSOFSKI ALTERNATIVI. Added/Corp** Institut za Filosofski Nauki (Bulgarska Akademiia na Naukite). (Jan./Febr. 1992)-. Periodical. Bulgarian. bm (6 issues). DM215.00. **(Subscription address:** Kubon & Sagner, ABT Zeitschriftenimport, D 80328 Munich Germany.) ***Continues*** *Filosofska Misul, 0015-184X.*

RU/0235-1188
**FILOSOFSKIE NAUKI. Added/Corp** Soviet Union. Ministerstvo Vysshego i Srednego Spetsialnogo Obrazovaniia. (1987)-. Periodical. Russian. mo. available on microfilm from University Microfilms International (UMI). ***Continues*** *Nauchnye Doklady Vysshei Shkoly. Filosofskie Nauki, 0130-9749.*
**Ind/Abst** Math. Rev.

KZ/0320-5452
**FILOSOFSKIE NAUKI (ALMA-ATA).** (FILOSOFSKIE NAUKI.). [Filos. nauki]. **Added/Corp** Alma-Ata, Kazakhstan. Universitet. No. 1 (1971)-. Russian. bm. $31.00. **(Subscription address:** Victor Kamkin, 4956 Boiling Brook Parkway, Rockville MD 20852.) **LC** B809.8; .F4828.
**Desc:** Information on dialectical materialism, philosophy and communism.
**Ind/Abst** Soc. Plann. Policy Dev. Abstr.; Sociol. Abstr.

XO/0046-385X
**FILOZOFIA (BRATISLAVA).** (FILOZOFIA.). [Filozofia]. **Added/Corp** Slovenska Akademia vied. Filozoficky ustav. Ustav Filozofie a Sociologie Slovenska Akademia Vied). (1966)-. Periodical. Slovak (summaries and/or abstracts in Russian and English). bm. DM252.75. Veda, Publishing House of the Slovak Academy of Sciences, Klemensova 19, 814 30 Bratislava Slovakia. **Tel** (7)583-15. **(Subscription address:** Kubon & Sagner, ABT Zeitschriftenimport, D 80328 Munich Germany.) **ED** Vladimir Cirbes. **Bk Rev. Ad Acc. Circ:** 1,450 (ctrl). ***Continues*** *Otazky Marxistickej Filozofie.*
**Desc:** Original works by Slovak authors about basic questions of Marxist philosophy, theoretical problems of the building of socialism, and communism, philosophical questions of natural and social sciences, as well as on the subjects of historical philosophy and scientific atheism.
**Ind/Abst** Soc. Plann. Policy Dev. Abstr.; Sociol. Abstr.

XR/0015-1831
**FILOZOFICKY CASOPIS (USTAV PRO FILOZOFII A SOCIOLOGII CSAV).** (FILOSOFICKY CASOPIS.). [Filoz. cas.]. **Added/Corp** Kabinet Pro Filosofii Pri Cs. Akademii Ved. Ceskoslovenska Akademie Ved. Filosoficky Ustav. Ceskoslovenska Akademie Ved. Vedecke Kolegium Filosofie a Sociologie CSAV. Ustav Pro Filozofii a Sociologii CSAV. Filozoficky Ustav CSAV. **VFOAT** Filozoficky Casopis. Vol. 1, No. 1 (1953)-. Periodical. Czech (table of contents in English, French, German and Russian). bm (6 issues). DM250.00. **(Subscription address:** Kubon & Sagner, ABT Zeitschriftenimport, D 80328 Munich Germany.) **LC** B8.C9; F48. Index available. **Bk Rev. Pr Rev.** Documents available from The Genuine Article. ***Continues*** *Filosoficky Casopis.*
**Desc:** Publishes papers devoted to discussing the basic problems of Marxist philosophy, such as questions concerning dialectics, ontology, gnoseology and historical materialism.
**Ind/Abst** Arts Humanit. Citation Index [Full Cov.]; Curr. Contents Arts Humanit.; Curr. Contents Soc. Behav. Sci.; Philos. Index; Res. Alert [Full Cov.]; Soc. Sci. Cit. Index [Full Cov.].

CI/0351-4706
**FILOZOFSKA ISTRAZIVANJA.** Periodical. Serbo-Croatian (Roman) (summaries and/or abstracts in English, French and German). qt. Filozofski Fakultet, D Salaja 3, 41000 Zagreb Croatia. **Tel** 513-155-304. **LC** B6; .F53.
**Ind/Abst** Philos. Index.

XV/0353-4510
**FILOZOFSKI VESTNIK / SLOVENSKA AKADEMIJA ZNANOSTI IN UMETNOSTI, ZNANSTVENORAZISKOVALNI CENTER SAZU, FILOZOFSKI INSTITUT. VFOAT** FV. Vol. 10, (1989)-. Periodical. Slovenian. sa. ***Continues*** *Vestnik (Institut za Marksisticne Studije (Slovenska Akademija Znanosti in Umetnosti), 0351-6881.*
**Ind/Abst** Arts Humanit. Citation Index [Full Cov.].

CN/0709-5201
**FLORILEGIUM. See** History(General).

US/0890-3379
**FOCUSING FOLIO, THE. Added/Corp** Focusing Institute (Chicago, Ill.). (198?)-. Periodical. English. tq. $50.00. The Focusing Institute, 29 South La Salle Street 1195, Chicago IL 60603. **Tel** (312)922-9277. **DD** 128.

CN/0711-3897
**FOURTHOUGHT NEWSLETTER.** [Fourthought newsl.]. No. 1 (Apr. 1, 1981)-. Newsletter. English. ir. $8.00. Fourthought Media, Apt 708/50 Hillsboro Avenue, Toronto Ontario M5R 1S8 Canada. **DD** 105.

FR/1157-3694
**FRANCIS BULLETIN SIGNALETIQUE. 519, PHILOSOPHIE. Added/Corp** Institut de l'Information Scientifique et Technique (France). **VFOAT** Philosophie; Philosophy; Francis Bulletin Signaletique. 519, Philosophy. Vol. 45, No. 1 (1991)-. Bulletin. French. qt (4 issues). 540.00F France; 570.00F other. CNRS / Institut d'Information Scientifique et Technique, (Centre National de la Recherche Scientifique), 15 Quai Anatole France, Paris 75700 France. **Tel** 011 33 1 47531515, telex 299 356 F. **(Subscription address:** Institut d'Information Scientifique et Technique Diffusion, 2 Allee du Parc de Brabois, 54514 Vandoeuvre Nancy France.) **LC** Z7127; .F7118; B77. **DD** 016.1. Index available (free). available on CD-ROM. ***Continues*** *Bulletin Signaletique. 519, Philosophie, 0007-554X.*

CK/0120-1468
**FRANCISCANUM.** [Franciscanum]. **Added/Corp** Colegio Mayor de San Buenaventura. Universidad de San Buenaventura. (1959)-. Periodical. Spanish (Latin). Three times a year. $20.00. Franciscanum, Transversal 26, No. 172-08, Santafe de Bogota-Colombia. **Tel** 011 571 1 2354942. **ED** P. Adolfo Galeano. **LC** BR7; .F7. Index available. cum. index. **Ad Acc. Circ:** 1,000 (ctrl).

GW/0016-0067
**FRANZISKANISCHE STUDIEN. See** Religion and Theology-Catholicism.

US/0272-0701
**FREE INQUIRY (BUFFALO).** (FREE INQUIRY.). [Free inq.]. **Added/Corp** Council for Democratic and Secular Humanism (Buffalo, N.Y.). Vol. 1, No. 1 (Winter 1980/1981)-. Periodical. English. qt. $25.00 (one year), $43.00 (two year), $59.00 (three year) US. Council for Democratic and Secular Humanism Inc, PO Box 664, Buffalo NY 14226-0664. **Tel** (716)636-7571, FAX (716)636-1733. **ED** Paul Kurtz. **LC** BL2700; .F57a. **DD** 210. Index available. **Bk Rev. Circ:** 20,000 (ctrl). available on microfilm and microfiche from University Microfilms International (UMI). Documents available from UMI Article Clearinghouse.
**Desc:** Countering religious fundamentalists, the humanist scholars who write this controversial magazine are dedicated to defending freedom and secularism in the contemporary world.
**Ind/Abst** Curr. Lit. Fam. Plan.; Expand. Acad. Index (1992-); Newsp. Period. Abstr. (1992-); PAIS Int. Print (1991-?); Philos. Index.

US/0742-3748
**FREE PHILOSOPHER QUARTERLY, THE.** (THE FREE PHILOSOPHER QUARTERLY : FPQ.). [Free philos. q.]. **VFOAT** FPQ; F.P.Q. Vol. 1 No. 1 (Summer 1983)-. Periodical. English. qt. $16.00 US and Canada. Printing Works, PO Box 6145, Bellevue WA 98007. **LC** B1; .F74. **DD** 190/.5.

UK/0016-0687
**FREETHINKER, THE.** Vol. 1 (May 1881)-. Periodical. English. mo. £7.20 UK; £12.81 other. G. W. Foote & Company LTD, 702 Holloway Road, London N19 3NL England. **Tel** 011 44 1 2721266. **ED** William McIlroy. **LC** BL2700; .F6. **Bk Rev. Circ:** 1,500.
**Desc:** A secular-humanist monthly dealing mainly with religion, from a critical viewpoint.

●US/1071-7269
**FREETHOUGHT HISTORY.** (Jan. 1992)-. Periodical. English. qt. $10.00. Peoples Culture, PO Box 5224, Kansas City KS 66119. **Tel** (913)588-1996. **ED** Fred Whitehead. **DD** 211. **Bk Rev. Ad Acc. Circ:** 200. available in Loose-leaf.
**Desc:** Collecting information on the history of agnosticism, atheism, and kindred aspects of the freethought movement; includes bibliographies, scholarly articles, poetry, news and notes.

SZ/0016-0725
**FREIBURGER ZEITSCHRIFT FUER PHILOSOPHIE UND THEOLOGIE.** [Freibg. Z. Philos. Theol.]. Vol. 1 (1954)-. Periodical. German (French and English). Twice a year (Spring & Autumn). 67.00F Switzerland; 70.00F Europe; 75.00F others. Editions Saint Paul Paulus Verlag, Boulevard de Perolles 42, CH-1700 Fribourg Switzerland. **Tel** 011 41 37 864331, FAX 011 41 37 864330. **LC** BR45; .F7. Index available (Bound in last issue). cum. index. **Bk Rev. Ad Acc. Circ:** 500 (ctrl). ***Supersedes*** *Divus Thomas.*
**Ind/Abst** Bibliogr. Mission.; Index Book Rev. Relig.; MLA Int. Bibl. Books Artic. Mod. Lang. Lit.; New Testam. Abstr.; Philos. Index; Relig. Index One Period.

SP
**GADES. See** Education-Higher Education.

SZ/0016-5867
**GEGENWART. See** Religion and Theology.

GW
**GESAMMELTE WERKE GEORG WILHELM FRIEDRICH HEGEL.** (19??)-. Monographic series. German. ir. Price varies per volume. Felix Meiner Verlag, Postfach 760742, D 22057 Hamburg Germany. **Tel** 011 49 40 294870, FAX 011 49 40 2993614. ctrl circ.

GW
**GESTALT; ABHANDLUNGEN ZU EINER ALLGEMEINEN MORPHOLOGIE, DIE.** (19??)-. Monographic series. German. Price varies per volume. Max Niemeyer Verlag, Postfach 2140, D 72011 Tuebingen Germany. **Tel** 011 49 7071 989494, FAX 011 49 7071 87419.

IT
**GIORNALE DI METAFISICA.** (Jan./Apr. 1979)-. Periodical. Italian (French and German). tq. L51000 Italy; $62.00 other. Tilgher Genova SAS, Via Assarotti 52, 16122 Genova Italy. **Tel** 011 39 10 870653, 8391140. **Bk Rev. Ad Acc. Circ:** 1,000. ***Supersedes*** *Giornale di Metafisica.*
**Desc:** A journal of philosophical studies reproposing the primacy of the speculative philosophy and the research of the meaning and of the value of man throughout the history of civilization.
**Ind/Abst** Bibliogr. Mission.; Philos. Index.

US/0732-7781
**GIST (CAMPO, CALIF.).** (GIST.). **Added/Corp** God Unlimited/University of Healing. (19??)-. Periodical. English (German). Twelve times a year. $15.00. God Unlimited, University of Healing, 1101 Far Valley Road, Campo CA 92006. **Tel** (619)478-5111. **ED** Herbert L. Beierle. **Circ:** 2,500 (ctrl).
**Ind/Abst** Curr. Biotechnol.

US/0748-884X
**GNOSIS ANTHOLOGY.** [Gnosis anthol.]. Vol. 1-. Periodical. English (Russian). be. Gnosis Press, PO Box 42, Prince Street Station, New York NY 10012.

CN/0316-618X
**GNOSIS (MONTREAL).** (GNOSIS.). [Gnosis]. **Added/Corp** Sir George Williams University. Dept. of Philosophy. Vol. 1 (1973)-. Periodical. English (French). an. 3.00Can$ (individuals), 5.00Can$ (institutions). Sir George Williams University, 1455 de Maisonneuve Boulevard West, Montreal Quebec H3G 1M8 Canada. **Tel** (514)848-3636 2500, FAX (514)848-3494. **ED** Kenneth Todd. **DD** 105. **Bk Rev**, (Qty: varies). **Ad Acc. Circ:** 150. Documents available.
**Ind/Abst** Philos. Index.

US/0017-1425
**GNOZIS.** [Gnozis]. **VFOAT** Gnosis. 1968-. Periodical. English (Russian). qt. $12.00 (individuals), $20.00 (institutions). Gnosis Press, PO Box 42, Prince Street Station, New York NY 10012. **LC** B1; .G56. **DD** 001.3/05.

XN/0350-1892
**GODISEN ZBORNIK - FILOZOFSKI FAKULTET NA UNIVERZITETOT, SKOPJE. VFOAT** Annuaire - Faculte de Philosophie de l'Universite de Skopje. (1948)-. Periodical. Macedonian. an. **UDC** 1.
**Ind/Abst** BHA : Biblio. Hist. Art.

US/0093-4240
**GRADUATE FACULTY PHILOSOPHY JOURNAL.** [Grad. fac. philos. j.]. **Added/Corp** New School for Social Research (New York, N.Y.). Philosophy Dept. Vol. 1, (1971)-. Periodical. English. sa. $20.00 (institutions), $13.00 (individuals). Graduate Faculty of Philosophy, 65 5th Avenue, New York NY 10003. **Tel** (212)229-5735, (212)741-5707. **LC** B1; .G7. **DD** 105. **Bk Rev. Ad Acc. Circ:** 4,000 (ctrl).
**Desc:** A journal of continental philosophy which treats political, historical, literary and scientific issues.
**Ind/Abst** Philos. Index.

NE/0165-9227
**GRAZER PHILOSOPHISCHE STUDIEN.** [Grazer philos. Stud.]. Vol. 1, (1975)-. Monographic series. Multiple languages (English, French and German). ir. Price varies per volume. Editions Rodopi BV, Keizersgracht 302-304, 1016 Ex Amsterdam Netherlands. **Tel** 011 31 20 6227507, FAX 011 31 20 380948. **ED** Rudolf Haller. **LC** B20.6; .G73. **DD** 105.
**Desc:** Aims at developing different traditions of analytic philosophy. Journal attracts contributors from all over the world.
**Ind/Abst** Philos. Index.

FR
**GUIDE DES RELATIONS PRESSE, LE.** 1984-. French. an. 180F. Edinove, 135 Avenue de Wagram, 75017 Paris France. **LC** HD59; .G84. **DD** 659.2/025/44.

US
**HAMMARSKJOLD FORUMS.** Periodical. English. ir. Oceana Publications, Inc., 75 Main Street, Dobbs Ferry NY 10522. **Tel** (914)693-1320, FAX (914)693-0402.

US/1062-6239
**HARVARD REVIEW OF PHILOSOPHY, THE.** [Harv. rev. philos.]. **Added/Corp** Harvard Review of Philosophy (Organization). **VFOAT** Philosophy. Vol. 1, No. 1 (Spring 1991)-. Periodical. English. sa. Harvard Review of Philosophy, Emerson Hall, Harvard University, Cambridge MA 02138. **DD** 100; 100.

GW/0073-1587
**HEGEL-STUDIEN.** Vol. 1 (1961)-. German. an. $30.44. Bouvier GMBH & Company KG ABT Verlag, Am HOF 28, D53113 Bonn Germany. **Tel** 011 49 228 7290141. **ED** F Nicolin and O Poggeler. **LC** B2900. Documents available from The Genuine Article.
**Ind/Abst** Arts Humanit. Citation Index [Full Cov.]; Curr. Contents Arts Humanit.; Res. Alert [Full Cov.]; Soc. Sci. Cit. Index [Select. Cov.].

GW/0440-5927
**HEGEL-STUDIEN. BEIHEFT,. Added/Corp** Deutsche Forschungsgemeinschaft. Hegel-Kommission. (1964)-. Monographic series. English. an. Price varies per volume. Bouvier GMBH & Company KG ABT Verlag, Am HOF 28, D53113 Bonn Germany. **Tel** 011 49 228 7290141. **(Subscription address:** VVA Bertelsmann Distributors GmbH, Postfach 7777, D-33310 Guetersloh Germany.**)**

GW/0885-4580
**HEIDEGGER STUDIES.** [Heidegger stud.]. Vol. 1 (1985)-. English (French and German). an. DM69.60 Germany; DM71.00 other. Duncker und Humblot Verlag, Postfach 410329, D-12113 Berlin Germany. **Tel** 011 49 30 79000612, 011 49 30 79000613. **LC** B3279.H49; H3523. **DD** 193.
**Ind/Abst** Philos. Index.

IE/0018-0750
**HERMATHENA.** [Hermathena]. **Added/Corp** Trinity College (Dublin, Ireland). (1873)-. English (French and German). sa. $40.00. Hermathena, Trinity College, Dublin 2 Ireland. **Tel** 011 353 1 772941, FAX 011 353 1 772646. **ED** B. C. McGing. **LC** AS121; .H5. **DD** 052. Index available. **Bk Rev. Ad Acc. Pr Rev. Circ:** 500. available on microfilm and microfiche from University Microfilms International (UMI). Documents available from The Genuine Article.
**Desc:** Articles by members of Trinity College Dublin. Wide range of disciplines - philosophy, classics, history of Trinity College and religion.
**Ind/Abst** Abstr. Engl. Stud.; Am. Hist. Life (1955-); Arts Humanit. Citation Index [Full Cov.]; Br. Humanit. Index; Curr. Contents Arts Humanit.; MLA Int. Bibl. Books Artic. Mod. Lang. Lit.; Old Testam. Abstr.; Philos. Index; Res. Alert [Full Cov.].

FR/0440-7237
**HERNE, L'.** (CAHIERS DE L'HERNE.). (1961)-. Monographic series. French. ir. 1137.44F France; 1350.00F other. Editions de l' Herne, 41 rue de Verneuil, F 75007 Paris France. **Tel** 011 33 1 42612506, FAX 42 60 10 00. Index available. cum. index. **Circ:** 3,000 (ctrl).

GW/0440-7563
**HESTIA.** 1960/61-. Periodical. German. Bouvier GmbH & Co. KG ABT Verlag, AM Hof 28, D 53113 Bonn Germany. **Tel** 011 49 228 7290141. **LC** WMLC L 83/754.

UK/0018-1196
**HEYTHROP JOURNAL. See** Religion and Theology-Catholicism.

US/0891-6144
**HIMALAYAN INSTITUTE QUARTERLY GUIDE TO PROGRAMS AND OTHER OFFERINGS.** [Himal. Inst. q. guide programs other offer.]. **Added/Corp** Himalayan International Institute of Yoga Science & Philosophy. **VFOAT** Himalayan Institute Quarterly; Himalayan Institute. (Winter 1987)-. Periodical. English. Four times a year. Free. Himalayan International Institute, Rural Route 1 Box 400, Honesdale PA 18431. **Tel** (717)253-4929. **ED** Larry Clarke. **DD** 181. **Bk Rev. Circ:** 37,000 (ctrl). ***Continues*** *Himalayan News, 0275-9802.*
**Desc:** A publication of course offerings devoted to yoga, meditation, philosophy, psychology and holistic living.

DK/0106-0481
**HISTORISK-FILOSOFISKE MEDDELELSER. See** History(General).

UK/0144-5340
**HISTORY AND PHILOSOPHY OF LOGIC.** [Hist. philos. logic]. Vol. 1 (1980)-. English (French and German). sa (2 issues). £102.00 UK; $169.00 other. Taylor & Francis Ltd., Rankine Road, Basingstoke Hampshire, RG24 8PR United Kingdom. **Tel** 011 44 256 840366, FAX 011 44 256 479438, telex 858540. **(Subscription address:** Taylor & Francis Inc., 1900 Frost Road, Suite 101, Bristol PA 19007-1598.**) ED** I. Grattan-Guinness (editor's address: Middlesex Polytechnic at Enfield, Middlesex EN3 4SF United Kingdom). **LC** BC1; .H57. **DD** 160/.5. **[CCC]. Bk Rev.** available on microfilm from University Microfilms International (UMI). Documents available from The Genuine Article.
**Desc:** Devoted to the study of the historical development of logic and its broader philosophical concerns. Primarily concerned with general philosophical questions in logic-existential and ontological aspects, the relationship between classical and non-classical logics, including their historical development. In addition, it treats the relationships between logic and other fields of knowledge, such as mathematics, physics, philosophy of science, epistemology, linguistics, psychology and, latterly, computing.
**Ind/Abst** Acad. Search (July 1993-); Am. Hist. Life (1985-); Arts Humanit. Citation Index [Full Cov.]; Curr. Contents Arts Humanit.; Curr. Contents Soc. Behav. Sci.; Hist. Source (July 1993-); Humanit. Source (Jul. 1993-); INFO-SOUTH Abstr.; Mag. Search; Math. Rev.; Philos. Index; Res. Alert [Full Cov.]; Soc. Sci. Cit. Index [Full Cov.]; Zentralbl. Math. Ihre Grenzgeb.

IT
**HISTORY OF LOGIC.** (1982)-. Monographic series. English. an. Price varies per volume. Humanities Press, 165 1st Avenue, Atlantic Highlands NJ 07716. **Tel** (908)872-1441, (800)221-3845, FAX (908)872-0717, telex 752233. **ED** C. Celluci. Index available.
**Desc:** Monographs on the history of logic, ranging from twelfth-century scholasticism to twentieth-century Godel.
**Ind/Abst** Math. Rev.; Zentralbl. Math. Ihre Grenzgeb.

US/0740-0675
**HISTORY OF PHILOSOPHY QUARTERLY.** (HISTORY OF PHILOSOPHY QUARTERLY : HPQ.). [Hist. philos. q.]. **Added/Corp** Bowling Green State University. Philosophy Documentation Center. **VFOAT** HPQ. Vol. 1, No. 1 (Jan. 1984)-. Periodical. English. qt. $148.00 (institutions), $38.00 (individuals). Philosophy Documentation Center, Bowling Green State University, Bowling Green OH 43403-0189. **Tel** (419)372-2419, (800)444-2419, FAX (419)372-6987. **Bk Rev. Circ:** 400 (ctrl).
**Desc:** Ideally, the journal's contributions regard work in the history of philosophy and in philosophy itself as parts of a seamless whole.
**Ind/Abst** Philos. Index.

NE/0921-5891
**HOBBES STUDIES. Added/Corp** International Hobbes Association. Vol. 1 (1988)-. English (French). an. Fl50.00 (members of the International Hobbes Association), Fl75.00 (institutions and libraries), Fl60.00 (regular) Netherlands; Fl60.00 (members of the International Hobbes Association), Fl85.00 (institutions and libraries), Fl70.00 (regular) other. Van Gorcum & Company BV, PO Box 43, NL 9400 AA Assen Netherlands. **Tel** 011 31 5920 46846, FAX 011 31 5920 72064. **ED** Martin A Bertman. Index available. **Bk Rev. Ad Acc. Circ:** 400 (ctrl).
**Ind/Abst** Philos. Index.

GW
**HOLDERLIN FRIEDRICH SAMTLICHE WERKE.** W Kohlhammer Verlag GMBH, Postfach 800430, D70549 Stuttgart Germany. **Tel** 011 49 711 78631.

CN/0709-4469
**HORIZONS PHILOSOPHIQUES.**
**Added/Corp** College Edouard-Montpetit. Vol. 1, No 1 (1990)-. Periodical. French. sa. US; 27.00Can$ other. College Edouard Montpetit, 945 Chemin de Chambly, Longueuil Quebec J4H 3M6 Canada. **Tel** (514)679-2630 ext. 467, FAX (514)679-4170, telex 05-560592. **LC** B2; .H67. **DD** 105. ***Continues*** *Petite Revue de Philosophie.*
**Ind/Abst** Philos. Index (1990-).

CC
**HSIA-MEN TA HSUEH HSUEH PAO. CHE HSUEH SHE HUI KO HSUEH PAN.**
**Added/Corp** Hsia-men Ta Hsueh. **VFOAT** Xiamendaxue Xuebao; Universitatis Amoiensis Acta Scientiarum Socialium. (19??)-. Periodical. Chinese. ir. $6.00. China National Publishing Company, 380 Bei Su Zhou Lu, Shanghai, People's Republic of China. **LC** H8.C47; H85. **DD** 300/.5.

NE/0163-8548
**HUMAN STUDIES.** [Hum. stud.]. **Added/Corp** Society for Phenomenology and the Human Sciences. Vol. 1 (Jan. 1978)-. Periodical. English. qt. $376.00. Kluwer Academic Publishers, Postbus 322, 3300 AH Dordrecht, The Netherlands. **Tel** 011 (31) 78 524400, FAX 011 31 78 183273, telex 20083. **ED** George Psathas. **LC** B1; .H79. **DD** 105. **CODEN** HUSTDT. **[CCC]. Pr Rev.** available on microfilm and microfiche from University Microfilms International (UMI). Documents available from The Genuine Article.
**Desc:** Dedicated primarily to advancing the dialogue between phenomenological and existential philosophy, on the one hand, and phenomenological, existential and ethnomethodological approaches in the social sciences, on the other.
**Ind/Abst** Acad. Search (July 1993-); Arts Humanit. Citation Index [Select. Cov.]; Curr. Contents Soc. Behav. Sci.; INFO-SOUTH Abstr.; Int. Bibliogr. Sociol.; Mag. Search; MLA Int. Bibl. Books Artic. Mod. Lang. Lit.; Philos. Index; Res. Alert [Full Cov.]; Soc. Plann. Policy Dev. Abstr.; Soc. Sci. Source (Jul. 1993-); Soc. Sci. Cit. Index [Full Cov.]; Sociol. Abstr. [Full Cov.]; Stud. Women Abstr.

US/1052-5203
**HUMANIST ALMANAC AND DATEBOOK, A.** [Humanist alm. dateb.]. **VFOAT** AHA and D; AHA&D. (1991)-. English. $9.00. Bandanna Books, 319 Anacapa Street, Santa Barbara CA 93101. **DD** 144.

US/0018-7399
**HUMANIST (BUFFALO, N.Y.), THE.** (THE HUMANIST.). [Humanist]. **Added/Corp** American Humanist Association. American Ethical Union. (Spring 1941)-. Periodical. English. bm (6 issues). $24.95 (one year), $46.95 (two years), $67.95 (three years). American Humanist Association, 7 Harwood Drive, PO Box 1188, Amherst NY 14226. **Tel** (716)839-5080, (800)743-6646. **ED** Don Page. **LC** B821.A1; H8. **DD** 144. **Bk Rev. Ad Acc. Circ:** 20,000 (ctrl). available on microfilm and microfiche from University Microfilms International (UMI). Documents available from UMI Article Clearinghouse, Magazine Collection. ***Continues*** *Humanist Bulletin;* ***Absorbed*** *Ethical Forum, 0425-4201.*
**Desc:** The oldest periodical in North America devoted to the philosophy of humanism. Since 1941, it has presented a nontheistic, secular, and naturalistic approach to philosophy, science, and broad areas of personal and social concern.
**Ind/Abst** Acad. Abstr. Full Text Elite (Jan. 1984-); Acad. Abstr. (Jan. 1984-); Acad. Ind. [Computer File] (1984-); Acad. Search (Jan. 1984-); Book Rev. Index; Curr. Index J. Educ.; Curr. Lit. Fam. Plan.; Expand. Acad. Index (1984-); Film Lit. Index; Gen. Period. Index (1985-); Humanit. Index; Index Am. Period. Verse; Index Period. Artic. Relat. Law; INFO-SOUTH Abstr.; Mag. Artic. Summar. Elite (Jan. 1984-); Mag. Artic. Summar. Select (Jan. 1984-); Mag. Artic. Summar. CD-ROM (Jan. 1984-); Mag. Express (1988-) [Full Txt.]; Mag. Index Plus (1989-); Mag. Index. Sel. (1986-); Mag. Search; Med. Rev. Dig.; Middle East Abstr. Index; Newsp. Period. Abstr. (1988-); PAIS Int. Print (1991-); Peace Res. Abstr. J. (1964-1973, 1977-1979); Philos. Index; Read. Guide Abstr. Select Ed.; Read. Guide Period. Lit.; Resource/One Ondisc; Soc. Plann. Policy Dev. Abstr.; Soc. Sci. Source (Jan. 1984-); Sociol. Abstr.; Mag. Index (1977-); Vocat. Search (Jan. 1984-); Women Stud. Abstr.

CN
**HUMANIST IN CANADA.** [Humanist Can.]. No. 18 (Fall 1967)-. English. Four times a year. 15.00Can$ Canada; 19.00Can$ other. Canadian Humanist Publications, Box 3769 Station C, Ottawa Ontario K1Y 4J8 Canada. **Tel** (613)749-8929, FAX (613)825-8226. **ED** J.E. Piercy. Index available (Bound in March issue). **Bk Rev**, (Qty: 20-25). **Ad Acc, Adv Mgr:** Dan Morrison, **Tel** (613)225-7216. **Circ:** 1,200 (ctrl). available on microfilm and microfiche from University Microfilms International (UMI). ***Formed by the union of*** *Victoria Humanist, 0506-8657* ***and*** *Montreal Humanist.*
**Desc:** Divergent views and topics cover a wise spectrum of human interest topics from a non-religious perspective. An "alternative" periodical for those who believe it possible to lead a moral life without dogma.
**Ind/Abst** Altern. Press Index (-199?); Can. Index (?-?); Can. Period. Index (19??-).

II/0018-7429
**HUMANIST OUTLOOK.** (1966)-. Periodical. English. Indian Humanist Union, Naini Tal, India. **(Subscription address:** Prints India, 11 Darya Ganj, New Delhi, 110002 India, (Phone: 011 91 11 3268645)**)**

US/0441-4195
**HUMANISTIC JUDAISM. See** Religion and Theology-Judaism.

IT
**HUMANITAS (BRESCIA, ITALY).** (HUMANITAS.). (Jan. 1946)-. Periodical. Italian. Six times a year. L45000 Italy; L70000 other. Edizioni Morcelliana Spa, Via Gabrielle Rosa 71, 25121 Brescia Italy. **Tel** 011 39 030-46451, 030-57522. **ED** Stefano Minelli. **LC** AP37; .H85. Index available in last issue of volume--attached. cum. index. **Bk Rev. Ad Acc. Circ:** 2,000 (ctrl).
**Desc:** Philosophy, religion, history, sociology, and literature. Problems of the Catholic Church today, ecumenical problems, reviews of national conferences, and sometimes monographic issues.
**Ind/Abst** HAPI Hisp. Am. Period. Index; MLA Int. Bibl. Books Artic. Mod. Lang. Lit.

US/0319-7336
**HUME STUDIES.** [Hume stud.]. Vol. 1 (Apr. 1975)-. Periodical. English. Twice a year (Apr. & Nov.). $15.00 (individual); $30.00 (institution). University of Utah / 338 Orson Spencer Hall, D. Garrett, Salt City UT 84112. **Tel** (801)581-8161, FAX (801)585-5195. **ED** Don Garrett. **DD** 192. **Bk Rev. Pr Rev. Circ:** 400.
**Desc:** Study of David Hume.
**Ind/Abst** Am. Hist. Life (1976-1981); Philos. Index.

NE/0167-9848
**HUSSERL STUDIES.** Vol. 1, No. 1 (1984)-. Periodical. English (German). Three times a year. $300.00. Kluwer Academic Publishers, Postbus 322, 3300 AH Dordrecht, The Netherlands. **Tel** 011 (31) 78 524400, FAX 011 31 78 183273, telex 20083. **ED** William McKenna, Karl Schuhmann, Wojciech Zelaniec. **LC** B3279.H94; A15. **DD** 193. **CODEN** HUSTEU. **[CCC]. Bk Rev. Ad Acc. Pr Rev.** available on microfilm and microfiche from University Microfilms International (UMI). Documents available from The Genuine Article.
**Desc:** An international journal which underlines the relevance of Husserl's phenomenology, both for contemporary philosophy and the wider academic field. Intercultural and interdisciplinary contributions are particularly welcomed by the journal. Includes critical reviews of current Husserl literature, as well as reviews of

other philosophical works which have a direct bearing on Husserl research.
**Ind/Abst** Arts Humanit. Citation Index (19??-19??) [Full Cov.]; Curr. Contents Soc. Behav. Sci.; Philos. Index; Res. Alert [Full Cov.]; Soc. Sci. Cit. Index [Select. Cov.].

NE/0923-4128
**HUSSERLIANA DEN HAAG.**
(HUSSERLIANA.). [Husserliana Den Haag]. (1977)-. Periodical. German. ir. Price varies per volume. Kluwer Academic Publishers / Massachusetts, PO Box 358, Accord Station, Hingham MA 02018. **Tel** (617)871-6600. **UDC** 165.62. **Pr Rev.**

US/0046-8541
**IDEALISTIC STUDIES.** [Ideal. stud.]. Vol. 1 (Jan. 1971)-. Periodical. English. Three times a year. $39.95 (institutions), $25.00 (individuals) US; $44.50 (institutions), $29.95 (individuals) other. Clark University, C/O M. J. Beckett, 950 Main Street, Economics Geography Department, Worcester MA 01610. **Tel** (617)793-7311, FAX (508)793-8881. **LC** B823; .I33. **DD** 105. Documents available from The Genuine Article.
**Ind/Abst** Arts Humanit. Citation Index [Full Cov.]; Curr. Contents Arts Humanit.; Philos. Index; Res. Alert [Full Cov.]; Romant. Move.; Soc. Sci. Cit. Index [Select. Cov.].

US/0741-6180
**IN CONTEXT (SEQUIM, WASH.).** (IN CONTEXT.). [In context]. **Added/Corp** Context Foundation (Sequim, Wash.) North Olympic Living Lightly Association. Context Institute (Bainbridge Island, Wash.). (Winter 1983)-. Periodical. English. qt. $24.00 (one year), $42.00 (two year), $56.00 (three year) US; $31.00 (one year), $56.00 (two year), $77.00 (three year) other. Context Institute, PO Box 11470, Bainbridge WA 98110. **Tel** (206)842-0216, FAX (206)842-5208. **ED** Robert Gilman. **Bk Rev. Circ:** 11,000.
**Ind/Abst** Altern. Press Index (199?-).

II/0376-415X
**INDIAN PHILOSOPHICAL QUARTERLY.**
[Indian philos. q.]. **Added/Corp** Pratap Centre of Philosophy (Amalner, India) University of Poona. Dept. of Philosophy. Vol. 1 (Oct. 1973)-. Periodical. English. qt. $50.00. Indian Philosophical Quarterly University of Poona, Pune 411 007 India. **Tel** 336061. **(Subscription address:** Prints India, 11 Darya Ganj, New Delhi, 110002 India, (Phone: 011 91 11 3268645)) **ED** S S Barlingay, Rajendra Prasad, M P Marathe, R Sundara Rajan, Mrinal Miri, S S Deshpande. **LC** B130; .I59. **DD** 105. Index available. **Bk Rev. Ad Acc. Circ:** 1,000. ***Continues*** *Philosophical Quarterly.*
**Desc:** All areas of philosophy; history of philosophy, philosophy of Indian origin.
**Ind/Abst** Bibliogr. Mission.; Philos. Index.

US
**INDICES - MONOGRAPHS IN PHILOSOPHICAL LOGIC & FORMAL LINGUISTICS.** **See** Linguistics.

NE/0019-7246
**INDO-IRANIAN JOURNAL.** [Indo-Iran. j.]. Vol. 1, No. 1 (1957)-. Periodical. English. qt. $398.00. Kluwer Academic Publishers, Postbus 322, 3300 AH Dordrecht, The Netherlands. **Tel** 011 (31) 78 524400, FAX 011 31 78 183273, telex 20083. **ED** J. W. De Jong, M. Witzel, H. W. Bodewitz. **LC** PK1; .I5. **[CCC].** cum. index. **Bk Rev. Ad Acc. Pr Rev. Acid Free. Circ:** 500. available on microfilm and microfiche from University Microfilms International (UMI). Documents available from The Genuine Article.
**Desc:** Papers on ancient and medieval Indian languages, literature, philosophy, and religion, ancient and medieval Iran, and Tibet. Recent issues have contained linguistic articles on Sanskrit, Middle Indian (Pakrit), New-Indo-Aryan, on Munda linguistics (including the results of fieldwork), old and modern Dravidian languages (including new material on little known Central Dravidian languages).
**Ind/Abst** Arts Humanit. Citation Index [Full Cov.]; Curr. Contents Arts Humanit.; Index Book Rev. Relig.; Linguist. Lang. Behav. Abstr.; Middle East Abstr. Index; MLA Int. Bibl. Books Artic. Mod. Lang. Lit.; Relig. Index One Period.; Res. Alert [Full Cov.]; Soc. Plann. Policy Dev. Abstr.; Sociol. Abstr.

CN/0824-2577
**INFORMAL LOGIC (WINDSOR, ONT.).**
(INFORMAL LOGIC.). [Informal logic]. Vol. 6, No. 1 (Jan. 1984)-. Periodical. English. Three times a year (Jan., May, Sept.). 46.73Can$ (institutions), 28.04Can$ (individuals) Canada; $50.00 (institutions), $30.00 (individuals) US; $55.00 (institutions), $33.00 (individuals) other. Informal Logic, Department of Philosophy, University of Windsor, Windsor Ontario N9B 3P4 Canada. **Tel** (519)253-4232 Ext.2332, FAX (519)973-7050. **ED** Ralph H. Johnson and J. Anthony Blair. **DD** 160/.5. **CODEN** INLOEA. **[CCC]. Bk Rev. Pr Rev. Circ:** 350. ***Continues*** *Informal Logic Newsletter, 0226-1448.*
**Desc:** Journal of informal logic and critical thinking.
**Ind/Abst** Philos. Index; Soc. Plann. Policy Dev. Abstr.

SZ
**INFORMATION PHILOSOPHIE.** (1970)-. German. qt. DM54.50 Germany; DM58.00 other. Claudia Moser Verlag & Buchhdl, Hauptstrasse 42, D 79540 Loerrach Germany. **Tel** 011 49 7621 87125.

RU/0207-6861
**INFORMATSIONNYE MATERIALY / AKADEMIIA NAUK SSSR, FILOSOFSKOE OBSHCHESTVO SSSR.**
**Added/Corp** Filosofskoe Obshchestvo SSSR. (197?)-. Academic Scholarly Publication. Russian. bm. Izdatelstvo Nauka / Akademiia Nauk, Publishing House of the Russian Academy of Sciences, Leninskii Porspekt 14, 117901 Moscow Russia. **Tel** 011 95 954-21-53, FAX 011 95 938-21-44, telex 411964. **LC** B4201; .I53.

IT
**INFORMAZIONE FILOSOFICA.** (19??)-. Italian. Five times a year. L45000 Italy; L70000 Europe; L160000 other. Ediform, Viale Monte Nero 68, 20135 Milan Italy. **Tel** 011 39 2 55190714.

NO/0020-174X
**INQUIRY (OSLO).** (INQUIRY : AN INTERDISCIPLINARY JOURNAL OF PHILOSOPHY.). [Inquiry]. Vol. 1, (Spring 1958)-. Academic Scholarly Publication. English. Four times a year (Mar., June, Sept., Dec.). Kr650.00, $112.00. Scandinavian University Press, PO Box 2959 Toeyen, N 0608 Oslo 6 Norway. **Tel** 011 47 2 2575400, FAX 011 47 2 2575353, telex 71896 UROR N. **(Subscription address:** Scandinavian University Press, 200 Meacham Ave., Elmont NY 11003.**) ED** Alastair Hannay. **[CCC]. Bk Rev. Ad Acc. Pr Rev. Circ:** 1,000. available on microfilm and microfiche from University Microfilms International (UMI). Documents available from The Genuine Article, UMI Article Clearinghouse.
**Desc:** Scholarly articles, discussions, and review discussions in all areas of philosophy. It is a general aim to which specialists from various academic fields, as well as non-specialists, may have critical access.
**Ind/Abst** ABC POL SCI (19??-19??); Acad. Ind. [Computer File] (1984-); Am. Hist. Life (1972-); Arts Humanit. Citation Index [Full Cov.]; Curr. Contents Arts Humanit.; Expand. Acad. Index (1984-); Humanit. Index; Int. Polit. Sci. Abstr.; Newsp. Period. Abstr. (1991-); Philos. Index; Res. Alert [Full Cov.]; Soc. Plann. Policy Dev. Abstr.; Soc. Sci. Cit. Index [Select. Cov.]; Soc. Work Abstr. [Select. Cov.]; Sociol. Abstr.

NR/0794-7968
**INSIGHT LAGOS. 1987.** **See** Religion and Theology.

US/0161-1380
**INTEGRAL YOGA.** **Added/Corp** Satchidananda Ashram-Yogaville, Inc. Vol. 1 (Dec. 1969)-. Periodical. English. bm. $15.00. Satchidananda Ashram, Route 1 Box 1720, Buckingham VA 23921. **Tel** (804)969-3121. **ED** Swami Prakashananda. **Bk Rev. Ad Acc. Circ:** 1,600 (ctrl).
**Desc:** The ecumenical yoga teachings of Swami Satchidananda, articles about all religions, health and diet.

US/0074-4603
**INTERNATIONAL DIRECTORY OF PHILOSOPHY AND PHILOSOPHERS.**
**Added/Corp** Bowling Green State University. Philosophy Documentation Center. **VFOAT** Repertoire International de la Philosophie et des Philosophes. 1st Ed. (1965)-. Directory. English. ir. $99.00. Philosophy Documentation Center, Bowling Green State University, Bowling Green OH 43403-0189. **Tel** (419)372-2419, (800)444-2419, FAX (419)372-6987. **ED** Ramona Cormier and Richard H. Lineback. **LC** B35; .I55. **DD** 102.5. **Circ:** 600.
**Desc:** Handbook of philosophy covering Europe, Central and South America, Asia, Africa, and Australia. Provides data on universities, societies, institutes, journals, and publishers of philosophy.

US/0191-3379
**INTERNATIONAL FORUM FOR LOGOTHERAPY, THE.** [Internation. forum logother.]. **Added/Corp** Institute of Logotherapy (U.S.). **VFOAT** Logotherapy. Vol. 1, No. 1 (Winter 1978-Spring 1979)-. Periodical. English. sa. $36.00. International Forum of Logotherapy, PO Box 2852, Saratoga CA 95070. **Tel** (915)692-9597. **ED** Joseph Fabry. **LC** RC489.L6; I58. **DD** 616.89/14. **NLM** W1; IN7628. **CODEN** IFLODL. **[CCC].** Index available. cum. index. **Bk Rev. Ad Acc. Circ:** 800. available on microfilm from University Microfilms International (UMI). ***Continues*** *Uniquest, 0360-8182.*
**Desc:** Philosophy and methods of Viktor Frankl's Logotherapy helping people find meaning and direction in their lives.
**Ind/Abst** Psychol. Abstr. (1981-); PsycINFO; PsycLit.

NE
**INTERNATIONAL HUMANIST.** 1981, No. 1-. Periodical. English. qt. F30.00. Intl Humanist and Ethical Union, Oudkerkhof 11, 3512 GH Utrecht Netherlands. **Tel** 30-31 21 55, telex 70104 HUMAN NL. **ED** Don Page. **LC** B821.A1; I54. **DD** 144/.05. **Bk Rev. Circ:** 1,500 (ctrl). ***Continues*** *International Humanism.*
**Desc:** Covers humanist issues, representative of the humanist philosophy or life stance.

NE/0020-7047
**INTERNATIONAL JOURNAL FOR PHILOSOPHY OF RELIGION.** **See** Religion and Theology.

UK/0967-2559
**INTERNATIONAL JOURNAL OF PHILOSOPHICAL STUDIES, THE.** English. Twice a year. $85.00 (US & Canada); £55.00 (UK); £60.00 (other). Routledge, 11 New Fetter Lane, London EC4P 4EE England. **Tel** 071 583 9855, FAX 071 842 2298. **(Subscription address:** Kinokuniya Company Ltd., 38-1 Sakuragaoka 5, chome Setagaya-ku, Tokyo 156 Japan.**) ED** Prof Dermot Moran.

●US/1061-530X
**INTERNATIONAL JOURNAL OF PHILOSOPHY, PSYCHOLOGY, AND SPIRITUALITY.** (1992)-. Periodical. English. qt. $12.00. Shanti Publishing House, 2245 Fulton Street, San Francisco CA 94117.

UK/0951-5429
**INTERNATIONAL JOURNAL OF THEOLOGY AND PHILOSOPHY IN AFRICA : TPA, THE.** **See** Religion and Theology.

US/0019-0365
**INTERNATIONAL PHILOSOPHICAL QUARTERLY.** (INTERNATIONAL PHILOSOPHICAL QUARTERLY : IPQ.). [Int. philos. q.]. **Added/Corp** Fordham University. Fordham University. Dept. of Philosophy. Berchmans Philosophicum. Facultes Universitaires Notre-Dame de la Paix, Namur. Foundation for International Philosophical Exchange. **VFOAT** IPQ. Vol. 1, No. 1 (Feb. 1961)-. Periodical. English. Four times a year (Mar., June, Sept., Dec.). $35.00 (institutions), $22.00 (individuals) US & Canada; $40.00 (institutions), $27.00 (individuals) other. International Philosophical Quarterly, Fordham University, Bronx NY 10458. **Tel** (718)817-4776, FAX (718)817-4785. **ED** Vincent G. Potter. **LC** B1; .I2. **DD** 105. Index available (Bound in Dec. iss.). **Bk Rev**, (Qty: 40). **Ad Acc, Adv Mgr:** Sara Penella. **Pr Rev. Circ:** 1,600. available on microfilm, microfiche, and CD-ROM from University Microfilms International (UMI). Documents available from The Genuine Article, UMI Article Clearinghouse.
**Desc:** Aims to provide an international forum for interchange of basic philosophical ideas between the Americas and Europe and between East and West.
**Ind/Abst** Acad. Search (July 1993-); Annu. Bibliogr. Engl. Lang. Lit.; Arts Humanit. Citation Index [Full Cov.]; Bibliogr. Mission.; Book Rev. Index; Curr. Contents Arts Humanit.; Expand. Acad. Index (1989-); Humanit. Index; Humanit. Source (July 1993-); Index Book Rev. Relig.; Index Book Rev. Humanit.; INFO-SOUTH Abstr.; Middle East Abstr. Index; Newsp. Period. Abstr. (1991-); Philos. Index; Ref. Sources; Res. Alert [Full Cov.]; Romant. Move.; Soc. Sci. Cit. Index [Select. Cov.]; Abr. Cathol. Period. Lit. Index; Cathol. Period. Lit. Index.

CN/0825-0456
**INTERNATIONAL SEMIOTIC SPECTRUM.** **See** Humanities.

US/0270-5664
**INTERNATIONAL STUDIES IN PHILOSOPHY.** [Int. stud. philos.]. **Added/Corp** State University of New York at Binghamton. **VFOAT** Studi Internazionali di Filosofia. (Fall 1974)-. Academic Scholarly Publication. English (French, German and Italian). tq. $35.00 individuals, $55.00 institutions. Scholars Press / Georgia, PO Box 15399, Atlanta GA 30333-0399. **Tel** (404)636-4757, (404)727-2320, FAX (404)727-2348. **LC** B1; .A255. **DD** 105. **Circ:** 180. Documents available from The Genuine Article. ***Continues*** *Studi Internazionali di Filosofia.*
**Desc:** Publishes articles, discussions, and book reviews in all areas of philosophy for a scholarly international audience. The summer issue consists entirely of papers read at the North American Nietzsche Society meetings.
**Ind/Abst** Arts Humanit. Citation Index [Full Cov.]; Curr. Contents Arts Humanit.; Philos. Index; Res. Alert [Full Cov.]; Soc. Sci. Cit. Index [Select. Cov.].

UK/0269-8595
**INTERNATIONAL STUDIES IN THE PHILOSOPHY OF SCIENCE : I.S.P.S.** **See** Science and Technology.

US/0277-092X
**INTERNATIONAL YOGA GUIDE.** **See** Health and Personal Fitness.

GW/0942-3028
**INTERNATIONALE ZEITSCHRIFT FUER PHILOSOPHIE.** [Int. Z. Philos.]. (1992)-. Periodical. Multiple languages. sa. DM68.00. Metzler Poeschel Verlag Veroeffen, Statist Bundesamt Kernerstr 43, D 70182 Stuttgart Germany. **Tel** 011 49 7071 935350. **ED** Petra Waegenbaur. **UDC** 01. **Ad Acc.** Full Page (B&W) DM800.00. Half Page (B&W) DM500.00.
**Desc:** Journal of philosophy and related subjects. Specific objective is to bridge the gaps still existing between the different continental and Anglo-American traditions of thought.

JA/0910-4607
**INTERSECT.** **Added/Corp** PHP Kenkyujo. **VFOAT** Intersect PHP. (1989)-. Periodical. English. mo. $115.50. **(Subscription address:** Japan Publications Trading

Company, Ltd., PO Box 5030, Tokyo International, Tokyo 100-31 Japan.) **LC** BJ1545; .P15. **DD** 952.04/05. ***Continues*** *PHP Intersect, 0910-4607.*

US/0075-0395
**IOWA PUBLICATIONS IN PHILOSOPHY.** 1963-. English. ir. Martinus Nijhoff Publishers, Subsidiary of Kluwer Academic Publishers, Koraalrood 50, 2718 SC Zoetermeer Netherlands. **Tel** 011 31 79 684400.

IT
**IRIDE (LUCCA, ITALY).** (IRIDE : FILOSOFIA E DISCUSSIONE PUBBLICA.). **Added/Corp** Istituto Gramsci Toscano (Florence, Italy). (July/Dec. 1988)-. Periodical. Italian. Three times a year. L100000 Italy; L60000 other. Societa Editrice il Mulino, Strada Maggiore 37, 40125 Bologna Italy. **Tel** 011 39 51 256011, FAX 011 39 51 256034. **LC** WMLC 93/2310.

UK/0266-9080
**IRISH PHILOSOPHICAL JOURNAL.** **Added/Corp** Queen's University of Belfast. Dept. of Scholastic Philosophy. Vol. 1, No. 1 (Spring 1984)-. Periodical. English. an. £5.00 (individuals); £18.00 (institutions). Queen's University of Belfast, Department of Scholastic Philosophy, Belfast BT7 1NN N Ireland. **Tel** 011 44 232245133. **LC** WMLC 93/2289.
**Ind/Abst** Philos. Index.

SP/1130-2097
**ISEGORIA : REVISTA DE FILOSOFIA MORAL Y POLITICA / INSTITUTO DE FILOSOFIA.** **Added/Corp** Instituto de Filosofia (Consejo Superior de Investigaciones Cientificas). No. 1 (May 1990)-. Periodical. Spanish. sa. $18.18 (Spain); $28.18 (other). Consejo Superior de Investigaciones Cientificas CSIC, Insituto Filosofia C Pinar 25, 28006 Madrid Spain. **Tel** 34 1 4111098. **(Subscription address:** Editorial Anthropos SA, Apartado 387, 08190 S Cugat Vlles BCN Spain, Tel. 34 3 5894884**)** **LC** B5; .I85. **DD** 105.

II/0021-4043
**JAIN JOURNAL.** (1966)-. Periodical. English. qt (Jan., Apr., July, Oct.). Rs10.00 India; Rs90.00 other. Jain Bhawan, P-25 Kalakar Street, Calcutta 7 India. **Tel** 011 91 11 2382655. **(Subscription address:** Prints India, 11 Darya Ganj, New Delhi 110002 India.**)** **ED** Satya Ranjan Banerjee. **LC** B162.5; .J33. Index available. cum. index. **Bk Rev.** (Qty: 10). **Ad Acc. Circ:** 600.
**Desc:** Quarterly on Jainology and Jaina philosophy.

UK/0007-1773
**JBSP. JOURNAL OF THE BRITISH SOCIETY FOR PHENOMENOLOGY.** (JBSP; THE JOURNAL OF THE BRITISH SOCIETY FOR PHENOMENOLOGY.). [JBSP. J. Br. Soc. Phenomenol.]. **Main/Corp** British Society for Phenomenology. **VAT** Journal of the British Society for Phenomenology. Vol.1 (Jan. 1970). Periodical. English. tq (Jan., May, Oct.). $47.50 members; $60.00 (institutions), $54.00 (individuals) other. Haigh & Hochland Ltd, The Precinct Centre, Oxford Road, Manchester M13 9QA England. **Tel** 011 44 61 273 4156, FAX 011 44 61 273 4340. **ED** Dr. Wolfe Mays (editor's address: Institute of Advanced Studies, Manchester Metropolitan University, All Saints Manchester M156BH United Kingdom. **LC** B829.5; .B69. **DD** 142/.7/05. **Bk Rev. Ad Acc. Circ:** 425. Documents available from The Genuine Article.
**Desc:** Papers on phenomenology and existential philosophy as well as contributions from other fields of philosophy.
**Ind/Abst** Arts Humanit. Citation Index [Full Cov.]; Curr. Contents Arts Humanit.; Philos. Index; Res. Alert [Full Cov.].

US/1044-5757
**JOHN MACMURRAY STUDIES.** [John Macmurray stud.]. (1990)-. Monographic series. English. ir. Price varies per volume. Peter Lang Publishing, 62 West 45th Street, 4th Floor, New York NY 10036. **Tel** (212)764-1471, (800)770-5264, telex 6973364 PLNY. **DD** 192.

NE/0925-4560
**JOURNAL FOR GENERAL PHILOSOPHY OF SCIENCE.** [J. gen. philos. sci.]. **VFOAT** Zeitschrift Fur Allgemeine Wissenschaftstheorie. Vol. 21, No. 1 (1990)-. Periodical. English (German). sa. $284.00. Kluwer Academic Publishers, Postbus 322, 3300 AH Dordrecht, The Netherlands. **Tel** 011 (31) 78 524400, FAX 011 31 78 183273, telex 20083. **ED** Lutz Geldsetzer and Gert Konig. **LC** Q3; .Z32. **CODEN** JGPSE4. **[CCC]. Pr Rev. Acid Free.** available on microfilm and microfiche from University Microfilms International (UMI). Documents available from Ask*IEEE. ***Continues*** *Zeitschrift Fur Allgemeine Wissenschaftstheorie, 0044-2216.*
**Desc:** A forum for the discussion of a variety of attitudes concerning the philosophy of science. It has as its subject matter the philosophical, especially methodological, ontological, epistemological, anthropological, and ethical foundations of the individual sciences. Particular emphasis is laid on bringing both the natural, the cultural, and the technical sciences into a philosophical context, within which the historical presuppositions and conditions of the current problems of the philosophy of science are also included in the discussion.
**Ind/Abst** INSPEC (1990-); Math. Rev.; Philos. Index.

UG/1018-8592
**JOURNAL OF AFRICAN RELIGION AND PHILOSOPHY.** Vol. 1, No. 2 (1990)-. Periodical. English (summaries and/or abstracts in French). sa. £25.00. Serendip, PO Box 16144, Wandegeya, Kampala Uganda. **LC** BL2400; .A2. **DD** 199/.6/05. ***Continues*** *African Mind.*

UK/0264-3758
**JOURNAL OF APPLIED PHILOSOPHY.** Vol. 1, No. 1 (1984)-. Academic Scholarly Publication. English. Three times a year. $198.00 North America; £114.00 other. Basil Blackwell Publishers Ltd, 108 Cowley Road, Oxford 0X4 1JF England. **Tel** 011 44 865 791100, FAX 011 44 865 791347, telex 837022 OXBOOK G. **(Subscription address:** Blackwell Publishers / UK, Marston Book Services, PO Box 87, Oxford OX2 0DT England.**)** **LC** B1; .J59. **DD** 105. **[CCC].** available on microfiche.
**Ind/Abst** Ergon. Abstr.; Philos. Index; School Organ. Manage. Abstr.; Sociol. Educ. Abstr.; Stud. Women Abstr.

NE/0167-4544
**JOURNAL OF BUSINESS ETHICS. See** Ethics.

US/0301-8121
**JOURNAL OF CHINESE PHILOSOPHY.** [J. Chin. philos.]. V. 1- Dec. 1973-. Periodical. English. qt. $199.00 (one year), $370.00 (two year) institution, $69.74 (one year), $125.00 (two year), individual. Dialogue Publishing Company, PO Box 11071, Honolulu HI 96828. **Tel** (808)956-6081. **ED** Chung-Ying Cheng. **LC** B5230.A1; J67. **DD** 181/.111/05. **Bk Rev. Ad Acc. Circ:** 500 (ctrl). Documents available from The Genuine Article.
**Desc:** Devoted to the study of Chinese philosophy and Chinese thought in all phases and stages of development.
**Ind/Abst** Arts Humanit. Citation Index [Full Cov.]; Curr. Contents Arts Humanit.; MLA Int. Bibl. Books Artic. Mod. Lang. Lit.; Philos. Index; Res. Alert [Full Cov.]; Soc. Sci. Cit. Index [Select. Cov.].

II/0253-7222
**JOURNAL OF DHARMA. See** Religion and Theology.

II
**JOURNAL OF INDIAN COUNCIL OF PHILOSOPHICAL RESEARCH.** **Added/Corp** Indian Council of Philosophical Research. **VFOAT** J.I.C.P.R.; JICPR. Vol. 1, No. 1 (Autumn 1983)-. Periodical. English. Three times a year. $35.00. Motila Banarsidass, Bungalow Road, Jawahar Nagar, New Delhi 110007 India. **Tel** 2911985, FAX 2926803, telex (0)31-65367 KKRC IN. **(Subscription address:** Prints India, 11 Darya Ganj, New Delhi 110002 India, (Phone: 011 91 11 3268645)**)** **ED** D P Chattopadhyaya. **LC** B130; .J66. **CODEN** JICPEC. **Bk Rev. Ad Acc. Circ:** 700.
**Desc:** Devoted to publications of original papers of high standard on any branch of philosophy, specially inter-disciplinary research with direct philosophical relevance.
**Ind/Abst** Philos. Index.

NE/0022-1791
**JOURNAL OF INDIAN PHILOSOPHY.** [J. Indian philos.]. Vol. 1 (Oct. 1970)-. Periodical. English. qt. $453.00. Kluwer Academic Publishers, Postbus 322, 3300 AH Dordrecht, The Netherlands. **Tel** 011 (31) 78 524400, FAX 011 31 78 183273, telex 20083. **ED** Bimal K Matilal. **LC** B130; .J67. **[CCC]. Bk Rev. Ad Acc. Pr Rev. Circ:** 500. available on microfilm and microfiche from University Microfilms International (UMI). Documents available from The Genuine Article.
**Desc:** Encourages creative activities among orientalists and philosophers along with the various combinations that two classes can form. Contributions to the journal are bounded by the limits of rational enquiry and avoid questions that lie in the fields of speculative sociology and parapsychology. In a very general sense, the method is analytical and comparative, aiming at a rigorous precision in the translation of terms and statements. Space is devoted to the works of philosophers of the past as well as to the creative researchers of contemporary scholars on such philosophic problems as were addressed by past philosophers.
**Ind/Abst** Arts Humanit. Citation Index [Full Cov.]; Curr. Contents Arts Humanit.; Index Book Rev. Relig.; Int. Bibliogr. Sociol.; MLA Int. Bibl. Books Artic. Mod. Lang. Lit.; Philos. Index; Relig. Index One Period.; Res. Alert [Full Cov.].

●NE/0925-8531
**JOURNAL OF LOGIC, LANGUAGE, AND INFORMATION.** **Added/Corp** European Foundation for Logic, Language, and Information. Vol. 1, No. 1 (1992)-. Periodical. English. qt. $435.00. Kluwer Academic Publishers, Postbus 322, 3300 AH Dordrecht, The Netherlands. **Tel** 011 (31) 78 524400, FAX 011 31 78 183273, telex 20083. **ED** Peter Gardenfors. **LC** P39; .J68. **DD** 410/.285. **CODEN** JLLIEN. **Pr Rev. Acid Free.** available on microfilm and microfiche from University Microfilms International (UMI).
**Desc:** The scope of this journal is the logical and computational foundations of natural, formal, and programming languages, as well as the different forms of human and mechanized inference. Examples of main subareas are Intensional Logics including Dynamic Logic; Nonmonotonic Logic and Belief Revision; Constructive Logics; Complexity Issues in Logic and Linguistics Theoretical problems of Logic Programming and Resolution; Categorial Grammar and Type Theory; Generalized Quantification; Information-Oriented Theories of Semantic Structure like Situation Semantics, Discourse Representation Theory, and Dynamic Semantics; Connectionist models of logical and linguistic structures. The emphasis will be on the theoretical aspects of these areas. The purpose of the journal is to act as a forum for researchers interested in the theoretical foundations of the above subjects and their interdisciplinary connections, with an emphasis on general ideas increasing coherence.
**Ind/Abst** Soc. Plann. Policy Dev. Abstr.; Sociol. Abstr.

NE/0360-5310
**JOURNAL OF MEDICINE AND PHILOSOPHY, THE. See** Medical Science and Technology.

US/0271-0137
**JOURNAL OF MIND AND BEHAVIOR, THE. See** Psychology.

●US/1065-5840
**JOURNAL OF NEOPLATONIC STUDIES, THE.** (THE JOURNAL OF NEOPLATONIC STUDIES : JOURNAL OF THE INTERNATIONAL SOCIETY FOR NEOPLATONIC STUDIES.). [J. neoplatonic stud.]. **Added/Corp** Institute of Global Cultural Studies. International Society for Neoplatonic Studies. Vol. 1, No. 1 (Fall 1992)-. Periodical. English. sa. $25.00 (institutions), $15.00 (individuals). Journal of Neoplatonic Studies, Anthony Preus, Binghamton University, Binghamton NY 13902. **Tel** (607)777-2886. **DD** 141.

NE/0022-3611
**JOURNAL OF PHILOSOPHICAL LOGIC. See** Linguistics.

US/1053-8364
**JOURNAL OF PHILOSOPHICAL RESEARCH.** (JOURNAL OF PHILOSOPHICAL RESEARCH : JPR.). [J. philos. res.]. **Added/Corp** Bowling Green State University. Philosophy Documentation Center. American Philosophical Association. Canadian Philosophical Association. University of Nebraska--Lincoln. **VFOAT** JPR. Vol. 15 (1990)-. English. an. $60.00 (institutions), $25.00 (individuals). Philosophy Documentation Center, Bowling Green State University, Bowling Green OH 43403-0189. **Tel** (419)372-2419, (800)444-2419, FAX (419)372-6987. **ED** Robert Audi. **LC** B1; .P575. **DD** 105. ***Continues*** *Philosophy Research Archives (Bowling Green, Ohio : 1982), 0164-0771.*
**Desc:** Sponsored by the American Philosophical Association, the Canadian Philosophical Association, and the Philosophy Documentation Center. The journal has no restrictions on articles' size or scope.
**Ind/Abst** Philos. Index.

US/0022-362X
**JOURNAL OF PHILOSOPHY, THE.** [J. philos.]. Vol. 18, No. 1 (Jan. 6, 1921)-. Periodical. English. mo. $65.00 (institutions), $35.00 (individuals). Journal of Philosophy, 709 Philos Hall, Columbia University, New York NY 10027. **Tel** (212)666-4419. **ED** Michael Kelly. **LC** B1; .J6. **DD** 100. **[CCC].** Index available. cum. index. **Bk Rev. Ad Acc. Circ:** 4,664. available on microfilm. Documents available from The Genuine Article, UMI Article Clearinghouse. ***Continues*** *Journal of Philosophy, Psychology and Scientific Methods, 0160-9335.*
**Desc:** Contains philosophical articles of current interest and encourages the interchange of ideas, especially between philosophy and the special disciplines.
**Ind/Abst** Acad. Ind. [Computer File] (1992-); Acad. Search (July 1993-); Am. Hist. Life (1955-1958, 1962-1965); Annu. Bibliogr. Engl. Lang. Lit.; Arts Humanit. Citation Index [Full Cov.]; BHA : Biblio. Hist. Art; Book Rev. Index; Expand. Acad. Index (1989-); Humanit. Index; Humanit. Source (Jul. 1993-); INFO-SOUTH Abstr.; Int. Bibliogr. Sociol.; Mag. Search; Math. Rev.; MLA Int. Bibl. Books Artic. Mod. Lang. Lit.; Newsp. Period. Abstr. (1988-); Philos. Index; Res. Alert [Full Cov.]; Soc. Sci. Cit. Index [Select. Cov.].

UK/0956-2834
**JOURNAL OF PHILOSOPHY AND THE VISUAL ARTS.** [J. philos. vis. arts]. (1989)-. Periodical. English. ir (4 issues). Academy Editions, 42 Leinster Gardens, London W2 3AN England. **Tel** 011 44 71 402 2141, FAX 01-723-9540, telex 896928 ACADEM G.
**Ind/Abst** BHA : Biblio. Hist. Art.

US/0963-8016
**JOURNAL OF POLITICAL PHILOSOPHY.** (1993)-. Academic Scholarly Publication. English. Three times a year. $291.00 North America; £92.00 other. Basil Blackwell Publishers Ltd, 108 Cowley Road, Oxford 0X4 1JF England. **Tel** 011 44 865 791100, FAX 011 44 865 791347, telex 837022

OXBOOK G. **(Subscription address:** Blackwell Publishers / UK, Marston Book Services, PO Box 87, Oxford OX2 0DT England.) **[CCC].**

US/0162-9662
**JOURNAL OF PRE-COLLEGE PHILOSOPHY, THE. VFOAT** Pre-College Philosophy. Vol. 1- Jan. 1975-. Periodical. English. qt. $6.00. Jersey City State College / Department of Philosophy, 2039 Kennedy Boulevard, Jersey City NJ 07305. **LC** B52; .J68. **DD** 107/.12/73.

II/0379-8194
**JOURNAL OF SIKH STUDIES. See** Religion and Theology.

US/0047-2786
**JOURNAL OF SOCIAL PHILOSOPHY. See** Social Sciences.

US/0891-625X
**JOURNAL OF SPECULATIVE PHILOSOPHY, THE.** [J. specul. philos.]. Vol. 1, No. 1 (1867)-Vol. 22, No. 4 (Dec. 1893); New Series Vol. 1, No. 1-. Periodical. English. qt. $40.00 (institutions), $27.50 (individuals) US; $45.00 (institutions), $32.50 (individuals) other. Pennsylvania State University Press, 820 North University Drive, Suite C, University Park PA 16802-1003. **Tel** (814)865-1327, (800)326-9180, FAX (814)863-1408. **ED** Carl Hausman. **LC** B1; .J7. **DD** 105. **[CCC].** Index available. cum. index. **Bk Rev. Ad Acc. Circ:** 350 (ctrl). available on microfilm and microfiche from University Microfilms International (UMI).
**Ind/Abst** Philos. Index.

II
**JOURNAL OF THE DEPARTMENT OF PHILOSOPHY. Main/Corp** Calcutta. University. Dept. of Philosophy. V. 1- 1975-. English. Rs5.00 single copy. University of Calcutta / Philosophy, Department of Philosophy, Calcutta University, Publications Sales Counter, Asutosh Building, Calcutta India. **LC** B21; .C24A. **DD** 105.

NE/0022-5010
**JOURNAL OF THE HISTORY OF BIOLOGY. See** Biology.

US/0022-5037
**JOURNAL OF THE HISTORY OF IDEAS.** [J. hist. ideas]. Vol. 1, (Jan. 1940)-. Periodical. English. Four times a year. $45.00 US; $49.40 Canada and Mexico; $56.00 other. Johns Hopkins University Press, 2715 North Charles Street, Baltimore MD 21218-4319. **Tel** (410)516-6987, FAX (410)516-6968. **(Subscription address:** John Hopkins University Press, Journals Publishing Division, PO Box 19966, Baltimore MD 21211.) **ED** Donald R. Kelley. **LC** B1; .J75. **DD** 105. **NLM** B 1 J86. **[CCC].** cum. index. **Bk Rev. Ad Acc. Pr Rev. Circ:** 3,700 (ctrl). available on microfilm and microfiche from University Microfilms International (UMI). Documents available from The Genuine Article, UMI Article Clearinghouse.
**Desc:** Published studies on the history of philosophy, literature and the arts, natural and social sciences, religion, political and social movements.
**Ind/Abst** Abstr. Engl. Stud.; Acad. Abstr. Full Text Elite (Jan. 1991-); Acad. Abstr. (Jan. 1991-); Acad. Ind. [Computer File] (1987-); Acad. Search (Jan. 1991-); Am. Hist. Life (1954-); Annu. Bibliogr. Engl. Lang. Lit.; ARTbibliogr. Mod.; Arts Humanit. Citation Index [Full Cov.]; BHA : Biblio. Hist. Art; Book Rev. Index; Curr. Contents Arts Humanit.; Curr. Contents Soc. Behav. Sci.; Expand. Acad. Index (1987-); Hist. Source (July 1990-); Humanit. Index; Humanit. Source (Jul. 1990-); Index Book Rev. Relig.; INFO-SOUTH Abstr.; Int. Bibliogr. Sociol.; Int. Polit. Sci. Abstr.; Mag. Search; Middle East Abstr. Index; MLA Int. Bibl. Books Artic. Mod. Lang. Lit.; Newsp. Period. Abstr. (1990-); Philos. Index; Relig. Index One Period.; Res. Alert [Full Cov.]; Romant. Move.; Soc. Sci. Cit. Index [Full Cov.]; U.S. Polit. Sci. Doc.; West. Hist. Q.; Women Stud. Abstr.

US/0022-5053
**JOURNAL OF THE HISTORY OF PHILOSOPHY.** [J. hist. philos.]. Vol. 1, No. 1 (Oct. 1963)-. Periodical. English (French and German). qt. $25.00 (individual), $65.00 (institution). Journal of the History of Philosophy, Department of Philosophy, Washington University, Campus Box 1073, St Louis MO 63130-4899. **Tel** (314)432-8089. **ED** Rudolf A Makkreel. **LC** B1; .A214. **DD** 105. **Bk Rev. Ad Acc. Circ:** 1,600. available on microfilm and microfiche from University Microfilms International (UMI). Documents available from The Genuine Article, UMI Article Clearinghouse.
**Desc:** Scope is international consisting of articles, notes discussions and book reviews on the history of philosophy, history of ideas and intellectual history.
**Ind/Abst** Acad. Search (July 1993-); Am. Hist. Life (1963-); Annu. Bibliogr. Engl. Lang. Lit.; Arts Humanit. Citation Index [Full Cov.]; Curr. Contents Arts Humanit.; Expand. Acad. Index (1989-); Hist. Source (July 1993-); Humanit. Index; Humanit. Source (Jul. 1993-); INFO-SOUTH Abstr.; Int. Bibliogr. Sociol.; Mag. Search; Middle East Abstr. Index; Newsp. Period. Abstr. (1991-); Philos. Index; Res. Alert [Full Cov.]; Romant. Move.; Soc. Sci. Cit. Index [Select. Cov.].

II/0019-4271
**JOURNAL OF THE INDIAN ACADEMY OF PHILOSOPHY, THE. Main/Corp** Indian Academy of Philosophy. Vol. 1 (July 1961/Feb. 1962)-. Periodical. English. sa. $20.00. Indian Academy of Philosophy, Belgachia Villa, Block F Flat 8, Calcutta 37 India. **Tel** 56-5086. **(Subscription address:** Prints India, 11 Darya Ganj, New Delhi, 110002 India, (Phone: 011 91 11 3268645)) **ED** C Bhattacharya. **LC** B1; .I55. **Bk Rev. Ad Acc. Circ:** 200.

SA
**JOURNAL OF THE PHILOSOPHICAL SOCIETY. Main/Corp** Philosophical Society (Fourah Bay College). V. 1- 1977-. English. an. University of Sierra Leone Philosophical Society, Freetown South Africa. **LC** B1; .F75A. **DD** 105.

NE/0022-5363
**JOURNAL OF VALUE INQUIRY, THE.** [J. value inq.]. **Added/Corp** University of Akron. Vol. 1 (Spring 1967)-. Periodical. English. qt. $422.00. Kluwer Academic Publishers, Postbus 322, 3300 AH Dordrecht, The Netherlands. **Tel** 011 (31) 78 524400, FAX 011 31 78 183273, telex 20083. **LC** BD232; .J68. **CODEN** JVINEP. **[CCC]. Pr Rev.** available on microfilm and microfiche from University Microfilms International (UMI). Documents available from The Genuine Article.
**Desc:** Devoted to the stimulation and communication of current research in value studies. Papers published in the journal address themselves to questions concerning the nature, origin, experience and scope of value in general, as well as to problems, of value in such fields as culture, aesthetics, religion, social and legal theory or practice, ethics, education, and methodology, technology and the sciences. The journal is a forum for presentation of the rich diversity of approaches available to value inquiry. It is committed to openness, cosmopolitanism, and the sharing of insights about humanity.
**Ind/Abst** Arts Humanit. Citation Index (19??-19??) [Full Cov.]; Philos. Index; Res. Alert [Full Cov.]; Soc. Sci. Cit. Index [Select. Cov.].

US/0741-627X
**JOURNAL - SOCIETY FOR THE STUDY OF BLACK PHILOSOPHY (U.S.), THE.** (THE JOURNAL.). [J. - Soc. Study Black Philos. (U.S.)]. **VFOAT** Journal for the Study of Black Philosophy. Vol. 1, No. 1 (Winter-Spring 1984)-. Periodical. English. sa. $15.00. M B P I, 215 West 98th Street/Suite 12B, New York NY 10025. **DD** 191.

IO/0853-4454
**JURNAL FILSAFAT. Added/Corp** Lembaga Studi Filsafat. Institute for Philosophy and the Future of Humanity (Universitas Nasional (Indonesia)). (1991)-. Periodical. Indonesian. qt.

FR/1148-9227
**KAIROS. Added/Corp** Universite de Toulouse-Le Mirail. Faculte de Philosophie. No. 1 (1990)-. French. an. 100.00F. Universite de Toulouse--Le Mirail, 56 Rue du Taur, 31000 Toulouse France. **Tel** 011 33 61 225831, FAX 011 33 61 218420. **LC** B2; .K35. **DD** 105. ***Continues*** *Philosophie (Toulouse, France), 0182-7103.*

GW/0022-8877
**KANT-STUDIEN.** (KANT-STUDIEN; PHILOSOPHISCHE ZEITSCHRIFT.). [Kant-Stud.]. **Added/Corp** Kant-Gesellschaft. Vol. 1 (1897)-. Periodical. German (English, French and German). qt. $123.10. Walter de Gruyter Inc., PO Box 303421, D 10728 Berlin Germany. **Tel** 011 49 30 260050, FAX 011 49 30 26005251. **ED** G. Funke and R. Malter. **LC** B2750; .K3. **[CCC].** cum. index. **Bk Rev. Ad Acc. Circ:** 1,000. Documents available from The Genuine Article.
**Desc:** Publishes papers, reports, and book reviews on the investigation and interpretation of Kantian philosophy.
**Ind/Abst** Arts Humanit. Citation Index [Full Cov.]; Curr. Contents Arts Humanit.; Philos. Index; Res. Alert [Full Cov.]; Romant. Move.

RU/0207-6918
**KANTOVSKII SBORNIK / MINISTERSTVO VYSSHEGO I SREDNEGO SPETSIALNOGO OBRAZOVANIIA RSFSR, KALININGRADSKII GOSUDARSTVENNYI UNIVERSITET. Added/Corp** Kaliningradskii Gosudarstvennyi Universitet. Vol. 6 (1981)-. Russian. 1.10rub. Kaliningradskii Gosudarstvennyi Universitet / Kaliningrad State University, Ulitsa A Nevskogo 14, 236041 Kaliningrad Russia. **Tel** 46-59-17, FAX 46-58-13, telex 262116. **LC** B2798; .V58. **DD** 142/.3/05. ***Continues*** *Voprosy Teoreticheskogo Naslediia Immanuila Kanta.*

GW
**KANTSTUDIEN. ERGANZUNGSHEFTE / IM AUFTRAGE DER KANT-GESELLSCHAFT. Added/Corp** Kant-Gesellschaft. **VFOAT** Kant-Studien. Erganzungshefte. (1906)-. Monographic series. German. ir. Price varies per volume. Walter de Gruyter Inc. / Hawthorne, 200 Saw Mill River Road, Hawthorne NY 10532. **Tel** (914)747-0110, GERMANY: 011/49/30/260050, FAX (914)747-1326, telex 646677.

PH
**KARUNUNGAN. VFOAT** Sophia. 1984-. English (English). an. **LC** B5221; .K37. **DD** 181/.17/05.

NE/0165-1773
**KENNIS EN METHODE.** [Kennis methode]. **VFOAT** K & M. Vol. 1 (1977)-. Periodical. Dutch. qt (4 issues). Fl141.50 (individuals), Fl172.00 (institutions). Uitgeverij Boom, Postbus 400, 7940 AK Meppel Netherlands. **Tel** 011 31 20 5220 57012, FAX 011 31 20 5220 54452, telex 42829. **ED** L. Boon. **Bk Rev. Ad Acc. Circ:** 600 (ctrl).
**Desc:** Published for those interested in philosophy of science and methodology.
**Ind/Abst** Philos. Index; Soc. Res. Methodol. Abstr. (1978-).

DK/0075-6032
**KIERKEGAARDIANA. Added/Corp** Sren Kierkegaard Selskabet. (1955)-. Danish (English, French and German). be. CA Reitzels Forlag AS, Norregade 20, DK-1165 Copenhagen K Denmark. **Tel** 011 45 3 3122400. **LC** B4377; .K5. ***Supersedes*** *Meddelelser - Sren Kierkegaard Selskabet.*

US/0023-1568
**KINESIS (CARBONDALE, ILL.).** (KINESIS.). **Added/Corp** Southern Illinois University at Carbondale. Dept. of Philosophy. Vol. 1 (Fall 1968)-. Periodical. English. Twice a year. $15.00. Southern Illinois University / Carbondale - Philosophy, Department of Philosophy, Carbondale IL 62901. **Tel** (618)453-7447. **ED** Stephen A. Kennett. **LC** B1; .K5. **DD** 105. Index available. **Bk Rev. Ad Acc. Pr Rev. Circ:** 200. available on microfilm and microfiche from University Microfilms International (UMI).
**Desc:** The journal believes that the philosophical work of graduate students constitutes a substantial contribution to the debate on contemporary philosophical and socio-political issues.
**Ind/Abst** Philos. Index.

US/0886-4063
**KNOWLEDGE MATTERS. Added/Corp** Knowledge Matters Publishing Company. **VFOAT** Knowledge Matters. (1985)-. Periodical. English. Four times a year. $49.00 US; $69.00 Canada and Mexico; $89.00 other. Knowledge Matters Publishing Company, PO Box 4337, Walnut Creek CA 94596. **Tel** (510)947-4878. **ED** Michael D. Nelson and Earl C. Ruby. **DD** 005. Index available. cum. index. **Bk Rev. Ad Acc.** available on diskette (and on BBS download).

SA/0023-270X
**KOERS.** Vol. 1 (Aug. 1933)-. Periodical. Afrikaans (English and Dutch). Four times a year (Mar., June, Sept., Dec.). R36.00 South Africa; R46.00 other. Bureau for Scholarly Journals, Private Bag X6001, Potchefstroom 2520 South Africa. **Tel** 011 27 148 991769, FAX 011 27 148 991562, telex 346019. **ED** Prof. A.L. Combrink (phone: 11 27 148 991552) and M. Venter (phone: 011 27 148 991769). Index available in last issue of volume--attached. cum. index. **Bk Rev**, (Qty: 4). **Ad Acc. Pr Rev. Circ:** 280. ***Continues Wagtoring.***
**Desc:** Interdisciplinary studies with a foundation in world views and principles. Research articles from all fields of research are published.

GW/0454-448X
**KOSMOSOPHIE.** [Kosmosophie]. (1962)-. Monographic series. German. ir. Price varies per volume. Franz Steiner Verlag GmbH, Postfach 101061, D 70009 Stuttgart Germany. **Tel** 011 49 0711 2582372, FAX 011 49 0711 2582290, telex 723636 daz d. **(Subscription address:** Brockhaus Commission, Kreidlerstrasse 9, D 70803 Kornwestheim Germany.) **UDC** 141.33 :248.2.

US/0894-5233
**KRISIS (INTERNATIONAL CIRCLE FOR RESEARCH IN PHILOSOPHY).** (KRISIS.). [Krisis]. **Added/Corp** International Circle for Research in Philosophy. Vol. 1, No. 1 (Summer 1983)-. Periodical. English (French, German, Italian and Spanish). Twice a year. $17.50. International Circle for Research in Philosophy, 1421 Branard, Houston TX 77006. **Tel** (713)529-1440. **LC** AS30; .K74. **DD** 105. **Bk Rev. Ad Acc. Circ:** 780 (ctrl). available on diskette.

BL/0100-512X
**KRITERION.** [Kriterion]. **Added/Corp** Universidade Federal de Minas Gerais. Universidade de Minas Gerais. Faculdade de Filosofia. (July/Sept. 1947)-. Academic Scholarly Publication. Portuguese (English and French). Six times a year. $60.00. Faculdade de Filsofia e Ciencias Humanas, Revista Kriterion, Depto de Filosofia-Sala 4043, AV Antonio Carlos 6027, CP 253, Belo Horizonte-MG Brazil CEP 31270. **ED** Newton Bignotts. **LC** AS80.A1; K7. **Bk Rev**, (Qty: 10). **Pr Rev. Circ:** 500 (ctrl). available on diskette.
**Ind/Abst** MLA Int. Bibl. Books Artic. Mod. Lang. Lit.; Philos. Index.

SI
**KRITIK.** English. an. Philosophical Society, c/o Philosophy Department, University of Singapore, Singapore. **LC** B1; .K75. **DD** 105.

# Philosophy

GW/0023-5466
**KUNST + UNTERRICHT.** *Title Change.* (KUNST + I.E. UND UNTERRICHT.). [Kunst. Unterr.]. **VFOAT** Kunst und Unterricht. Vol. 1- Sept. 1968-. Periodical. German. ir. Bouvier GMBH & Company KG ABT Verlag, Am HOF 28, D53113 Bonn Germany. **Tel** 011 49 228 7290141. **LC** BH61; .K85. *Continued by* K. + U. Kunst + Unterricht, 0170-6225.

CN/0023-9054
**LAVAL THEOLOGIQUE ET PHILOSOPHIQUE. See** Religion and Theology.

CN/0023-9054
**LAVAL THEOLOGIQUE ET PHILOSOPHIQUE. See** Religion and Theology.

NE/0167-5249
**LAW AND PHILOSOPHY. See** Law.

GW
**LEIBNIZ : SAEMTLICHE SCHRIFTEN UND BRIEFE.** (19??)-. Monographic series. German. ir. Price varies per volume. Akademie-Verlag GmbH, Muehlenstrasse 33 34, D 13162 Berlin Germany. **Tel** 011 49 30 47889300, **FAX** 011 49 30 47889357. **(Subscription address:** VCH Publishers Inc., 303 Northwest 12th Avenue, Journals Department, Deerfield FL 33442.**)**

US/0272-5959
**LIBERTARIAN DIGEST, THE. See** Political Science.

US/0075-9139
**LIBRARY OF LIVING PHILOSOPHERS, THE.** [Libr. living philos.]. Vol. 1 (1939)-. Monographic series. English. ir. Price varies per volume. Open Court Publishing Company, 315 Fifth Street, PO Box 300, Peru IL 61354. **Tel** (800)435-6850, (815)223-1500, **FAX** (815)224-6675. **DD** 105.

US
**LIBRARY OF RELIGIOUS PHILOSOPHY.** (1989)-. English. ir. University of Notre Dame Press, PO Box 635, South Bend IN 46624. **Tel** (219)239-6349, (800)677-3232, **FAX** (219)239-8148.

SW
**LIBRARY OF THEORIA.** Monographic series. English. ir. Price varies per volume. Liber International, S-205 10 Malmo Sweden. **Tel** 46-40-70650. **ED** Liber. **Ind/Abst** Math. Rev.

NE/0165-0157
**LINGUISTICS AND PHILOSOPHY. See** Linguistics.

US/0024-4414
**LISTENING (RIVER FOREST). See** Religion and Theology.

US/0460-1297
**LITTLE LAMP, THE. See** Religion and Theology.

UK/0307-2606
**LOCKE NEWSLETTER, THE.** [Locke newsl.]. No. 1 (Autumn 1970)-. Periodical. English. an. £8.00. Locke Newsletter, c/o Roland Hall, Summerfields, The Glade, Escrick, York YO4 6LH England. **Tel** 011 44 0904 728408, telex 57933. **ED** Roland Hall. **LC** B1250; .L6. **DD** 192. Index available. cum. index. **Bk Rev**, (Qty: 4/year). **Ad Acc. Pr Rev. Circ:** 600 (ctrl). **Ind/Abst** Philos. Index.

IT/0024-5887
**LOGOS.** [Logos]. Periodical. Italian. L8.000. Libreria Scientifica, Corso Umberto I 38 40, 80138 Naples Italy. **LC** B4; .L58. **DD** 105. **Ind/Abst** Philos. Index.

AG
**LOGOS (BUENOS AIRES).** (LOGOS; REVISTA DE LA FACULTAD DE FILOSOFIA Y LETRAS.). **Added/Corp** Buenos Aires. Universidad. Facultad de Filosofia y Letras. Vol. 1, No. 1 (1941)-. Periodical. Spanish. ir. Universidad de Buenos Aires / Argentina, Facultdad Filosofia Letras Puan 470, Buenos Aires 1406, Argentina. **Tel** 011 54 1 4320537, 011 54 1 4328696. **LC** AP63; .L77. **DD** 056.

MX/0185-6375
**LOGOS (MEXICO).** (LOGOS.). [Logos]. **Added/Corp** Universidad La Salle. Escuela de Filosofia. Vol. 1, No. 1 (Enero/Abr. 1973)-. Periodical. Spanish. Three times a year. Apartado Postal 18-907, Colonia Tacubaya, Delegacion Miguel Hildago, 11870 Mexico DF Mexico. **Ind/Abst** HAPI Hisp. Am. Period. Index; Philos. Index.

GW/0941-9683
**LOGOS, NEUE FOLGE.** (19??)-. German. qt. DM98.00. JCB Mohr / Paul Siebeck, Postfach 2040, D 72010 Tuebingen Germany. **Tel** 011 49 7071 9230, **FAX** 011 49 7071 51104, telex 7/262872 mohr d. **ED** Michael Sukale, Hans Jurgen Wendel.

US/0276-5667
**LOGOS (SANTA CLARA, CALIF.).** *Ceased.* (LOGOS : PHILOSOPHIC ISSUES IN CHRISTIAN PERSPECTIVE.). [Logos]. Vol. 1 (1980)-Ceased Vol. 12, 1991. Periodical. English. an. Santa Clara University Department of Philosophy, Santa Clara CA 95053. **Tel** (408)554-4093. **ED** Elizabeth Radcliffe. **LC** BR100; .L63. **DD** 190/.5. **Ad Acc. Pr Rev. Circ:** 100.
**Desc:** Refereed philosophic essays focusing in each issue on a single topic of particular interest to those concerned with philosophy's contribution to Christian humanism.
**Ind/Abst** Philos. Index.

BL
**LUA NOVA.** Vol. 1, No. 1 (April/June 1984)-. Portuguese. qt. $40.00. CEDEC, Rua Airosa Galvao 64, C 05002 Sao Paulo SP Brazil. **Tel** 011 55 11 8712966, **FAX** 011 55 11 8712123. **ED** Gabriel Cohn. Index available. **Ad Acc. Pr Rev.**
**Desc:** The main concerns are the theoretical and political dimensions of controversial issues in the contemporary world.

IR
**MAARIF.** (July 1984)-. Academic Scholarly Publication. Persian. tq. £24.00 Middle East; £25.00 Europe & Asia; £30.00 American & Far East. Iran University Press, 85 Park Avenue, PO Box 15875/4748, Tehran Iran. **Tel** 623232, **FAX** (008921)4661749, telex 213636-8-D5300. **ED** Nasrollah Pourjavady. **Circ:** 3,000.
**Desc:** Includes articles and comparative studies related to philosophy, theology, mysticism, history and literature, especially by Islamic and Iranian scholars.

JA
**MACHIKANEYAMA RONSO : BIGAKUHEN.** **VFOAT** Machikaneyama Ronso: Aesthetics. No. 9-; 1975- summaries and/or abstracts in Japanese, French, English, French and German. Osaka Daigaku Bungakubu, 1-1 Machikaneyamacho, Toyonaka Osaka Japan. **Tel** (06)844-1151. **LC** BH8.J3; M33. **UDC** 809.451.1. *Continues in part* Machikaneyama Ronso: Tetsugakuhen.

JA/0387-4818
**MACHIKANEYAMA RONSO : TETSUGAKUHEN. See** Humanities.

HU/0025-0090
**MAGYAR FILOZOFIAI SZEMLE.** [M. filoz. sz.]. **Added/Corp** Magyar Tudomanyos Akademia, Budapest. Filozofiai Intezet. Magyar Tudommayos Akademia. Filozofiai Bizottsag. (1957)-. Academic Scholarly Publication. Hungarian. Six times a year. $35.00. Akademiai Kiado, Publishing House of the Hungarian Academy of Sciences, Prielle Kornelia u. 19-35, H-1117 Budapest Hungary. **Tel** 011 36 1 1811991, **FAX** 011 36 1 1811991, telex 22-6228 AKNYO H. **(Subscription address:** Kultura, Hungarian Foreign Trading Company, PO Box 149, H-1389 Budapest 62 Hungary**)** **ED** F Landvai. Index available in last issue of volume--attached. **Circ:** 1,950 (ctrl).
**Desc:** Philosophical aspects of contemporary social and natural sciences as well as "traditional" philosophical issues. Results of new investigations. Critical studies.
**Ind/Abst** Philos. Index; Soc. Plann. Policy Dev. Abstr.

US/0150-1630
**MAIMONIDEAN STUDIES.** [Maimonidean stud.]. Vol. 1 (1990)-. Periodical. English (Hebrew). an (September). $35.00. KTAV Publishing House, Inc., 900 Jefferson Street, PO Box 6249, Hoboken NJ 07030-7205. **Tel** (201)963-9524, **FAX** (201)963-0102. **LC** B759.M34; A16. **DD** 296.1/72/05.

GW/0076-2776
**MAINZER PHILOSOPHISCHE FORSCHUNGEN.** Vol. 1 (1966)-. Monographic series. German. ir. Price varies per volume. Bouvier GMBH & Company KG ABT Verlag, Am HOF 28, D53113 Bonn Germany. **Tel** 011 49 228 7290141. **(Subscription address:** VVA Bertelsmann Distributors GmbH, Postfach 7777, D-33310 Guetersloh Germany.**)**

NE/0025-1534
**MAN AND WORLD.** [Man world]. **Added/Corp** I. P. R. Associates. Vol. 1 (Feb. 1968)-. Periodical. English (French and German; summaries and/or abstracts in French and German). qt. $326.00. Kluwer Academic Publishers, Postbus 322, 3300 AH Dordrecht, The Netherlands. **Tel** 011 (31) 78 524400, **FAX** 011 31 78 183273, telex 20083. **ED** John M Anderson, Joseph J Kockelmans and Calvin O Schrag. **LC** B1; .A218. **CODEN** MWORE5. **(CCC). Pr Rev.** available on microfilm and microfiche from University Microfilms International (UMI). Documents available from The Genuine Article.
**Desc:** The journal seeks to elicit, within this international dialogue space, discussions of fundamental philosophical problems and original approaches towards their solution. It encourages explorations in the domain of art, morality, science and religion as they relate to specific philosophical concerns. Although not an advocate of any one trend or school in philosophy, the journal has a commitment to keep abreast of developments within phenomenology and contemporary continental philosophy and is interested in investigations that probe possible points of intersection between the continental and the Anglo-American tradition.
**Ind/Abst** Arts Humanit. Citation Index [Full Cov.]; Int. Polit. Sci. Abstr.; Philos. Index; Res. Alert [Full Cov.]; Soc. Sci. Cit. Index [Select. Cov.].

BL/0100-6045
**MANUSCRITO.** **Added/Corp** Universidade Estadual de Campinas. Centro de Logica, Epistemologia e Historia de Ciencia. Vol. 1 (Oct. 1977)-. Periodical. English (French, Portuguese and Spanish). Twice a year (Apr., Oct.). $12.00 (Latin America), $20.00 (other) institution; $8.00 (Latin America), $15.00 (other) individual. Centro de Logica Unicamp, Caixa Postal 6133, 13081 970 Campinas, SP Brazil. **Tel** 11 55 192 393269. **LC** B1; .A219. **DD** 105. **Circ:** 700.
**Desc:** Articles of the original Brazilian and other foreign researches in the history of philosophy of science language.
**Ind/Abst** Philos. Index.

US
**MASTER THOUGHTS. See** Religion and Theology-Bible.

AU
**MATERIALIEN ZUR GESCHICHTE DER RAMANUJA-SCHULE.** 1-. Monographic series. German. Price varies per volume. **LC** AS142; .V31 subser; B133.R366.

KO
**MAUM.** **VFOAT** Journal of the Korea Philosophical Minds. V. 1-. Periodical. English (Korean). W900. EWHA Women's University / Philosophy, Department of Philosophy, Seoul 120 South Korea. **LC** B8.K6; M37.

US/1071-328X
**MEANING OF LIFE, THE.** [Mean. life]. Vol. I, No. 1 (Jan. 1988)-. Periodical. English. qt. $15.00. Meaning of Life, 1823 West Barry Avenue, Chicago IL 60657. **ED** Bob Lichtenber. **DD** 100. Index available. cum. index. **Ad Acc. Circ:** 300.
**Desc:** Features three articles on the meaning of life. Explores meaning in art, meaning in religion, and also has aphorisms on the meaning of life.

PL/0076-5880
**MEDIAEVALIA PHILOSOPHICA POLONORUM.** [Mediaev. philos. pol.]. **Added/Corp** Instytut Filozofii i Socjologii (Polska Akademia Nauk). No. 1 (1958)-. Periodical. French (German and Latin).
**Ind/Abst** MLA Int. Bibl. Books Artic. Mod. Lang. Lit.

US/1057-0608
**MEDIEVAL PHILOSOPHY AND THEOLOGY.** (MEDIEVAL PHILOSOPHY & THEOLOGY.). [Mediev. philos. theol.]. Vol. 1 (1991)-. English. an. $31.95 hardcover; $16.95 paperback. University of Notre Dame Press, PO Box 635, South Bend IN 46624. **Tel** (219)239-6349, (800)677-3232, **FAX** (219)239-8148. **(Subscription address:** University of Chicago Press, Book Division, 11030 South Langley Avenue, Chicago IL 60628.**)** **ED** Mark D. Jordan. **LC** B721; .M454. **DD** 189/.05.

IT/0391-2566
**MEDIOEVO.** [Medioevo]. (1975)-. Periodical. English (Italian). ir. L55000. Editrice Antenore, Via G Rusca 15, 35100 Padua Italy. **Tel** 011 39 49 686566. **LC** B720; .M44. **DD** 189/.05.

CC
**MEI HSUEH SHU LIN / LIU KANG-CHI, WU YUEH PIEN.** V. 1 (June 1983)-. Periodical. Chinese. RMBY1.55. Hsin Hua Shu Tien / Hu-Pei Sheng China, People's Republic of China. **LC** BH8.C4; M45. **DD** 111/.85.

CC
**MEI TI YEN CHIU YU HSIN SHANG / HSI NAN SHIH FAN HSUEH YUAN CHUNG WEN HSI, CHUNG-CHING SHIH WEN HSUEH I SHU CHIEH LIEN HO HUI, CHUNG-CHING CHU PAN SHE PIEN CHI PU, CHU PAN.** V. 1, 1982-. Periodical. Chinese. RMBY1.28. Ssu-Chuan Sheng Hsin Hua Shu Tien / Chung-Ching Fa Hsing So, People's Republic of China. **LC** BH8.C4; M47. **DD** 111/.85.

US/0065-9738
**MEMOIRS OF THE AMERICAN PHILOSOPHICAL SOCIETY HELD AT PHILADELPHIA FOR PROMOTING USEFUL KNOWLEDGE.** (MEMOIRS OF THE AMERICAN PHILOSOPHICAL SOCIETY, PHILADELPHIA.). [Mem. Am. Philos. Soc. held Phila. promot. useful knowl.]. **Main/Corp** American Philosophical Society. **Added/Corp** American Philosophical Society. Vol. 1 (1935)-. Monographic series. English. ir. Price varies per volume. American Philosophical Society, PO Box 40098, Philadelphia PA 19106. **Tel** (215)440-3427, **FAX** (215)440-3436. **DD** 506.272. **CODEN** MAPSAP. Documents available from BIOSIS Document Express.
**Ind/Abst** Biol. Abstr.; GeoRef; Math. Rev.; MLA Int. Bibl. Books Artic. Mod. Lang. Lit.

UK/0026-1068
**METAPHILOSOPHY.** [Metaphilosophy]. Vol. 1 (Jan. 1970)-. Academic Scholarly Publication. English. Four times a year. £82.00 UK and Europe; $169.00 North America; £82.00 other. Basil Blackwell Publishers Ltd, 108 Cowley Road, Oxford 0X4 1JF England. **Tel** 011 44 865 791100, FAX 011 44 865 791347, telex 837022 OXBOOK G. **(Subscription address:** Blackwell Publishers / UK, Marston Book Services, PO Box 87, Oxford OX2 0DT England.**) ED** Terrell Ward Bynum. **LC** B1; .M46. **DD** 105. **[CCC]. Bk Rev. Ad Acc. Circ:** 600 (ctrl). available on microfilm and microfiche from University Microfilms International (UMI). Documents available from The Genuine Article.
**Desc:** Publishes articles and book reviews in a wide range of philosophical topics including the foundations, scope and function of philosophy.
**Ind/Abst** Arts Humanit. Citation Index [Full Cov.]; Curr. Contents Arts Humanit.; Philos. Index; Res. Alert [Full Cov.]; Soc. Plann. Policy Dev. Abstr.; Sociol. Abstr.

US/0736-7392
**METHOD (LOS ANGELES, CALIF.).** (METHOD.). [Method]. **Added/Corp** Loyola Marymount University. Boston College. Lonergan Institute. Institute for Integrative Studies (Los Angeles, Calif.). Vol. 1, No. 1 (Spring 1983)-. Periodical. English. Twice a year. $25.00 (institutions), $14.00 (individuals). Boston College Studies in Philosophy, Carney Hall 216, Boston College, Department of Philosophy, Chestnut Hill MA 02167. **Tel** (617)552-3547. **ED** Mark D. Morelli, Patrick H. Byrne, and Charles C. Hefling, Jr. **LC** BD241; .M357. **DD** 101/.8. **Bk Rev. Ad Acc. Pr Rev. Circ:** 320 (ctrl).
**Desc:** It aims, first, at furthering interpretive, historical, and critical study of the philosophical,; theological, economic, and methodological writings of Bernard Lonergan. Secondly, it aims at promoting original research into the methodological foundations of the sciences and disciplines.
**Ind/Abst** Philos. Index.

US/0363-6550
**MIDWEST STUDIES IN PHILOSOPHY.** [Midwest stud. philos.]. **Added/Corp** University of Minnesota, Morris. Vol. 1 (1976)-. Monographic series. English. ir. Price varies per volume. Midwest Studies in Philosophy, University Notre Dame Press, Notre Dame IN 46556. **Tel** (219)631-6346. **ED** Peter French, Theodore E. Uehling Jr. and Howard K. Wehstein. Documents available from The Genuine Article.
**Desc:** Each volume in the series is a collection of papers focusing on a single topic in philosophy.
**Ind/Abst** Arts Humanit. Citation Index (19??-19??) [Full Cov.]; Philos. Index; Res. Alert [Full Cov.].

UK/0026-4423
**MIND.** [Mind]. **Added/Corp** Mind Association. Vol. 1 (Jan. 1876)-. Periodical. English. qt. £35.00 UK and Europe; $62.00 other. Oxford University Press, Walton Street, Oxford OX2 6DP England. **Tel** 011 44 865 56767, FAX 011 44 865 267773, telex 837330 OXPRES G. **(Subscription address:** Oxford University Press / USA, Journals Marketing Department, Oxford University Press, 2001 Evans Road, Cary NC 27513.**) ED** Simon Blackburn. **LC** B1; .M65. **DD** 190/.5. **NLM** W1 MI619H. **[CCC].** Index available. cum. index. **Bk Rev. Ad Acc. Circ:** 3,200 (ctrl). available on microfilm and microfiche from University Microfilms International (UMI). Documents available from The Genuine Article, UMI Article Clearinghouse.
**Desc:** Leading philosophical ideas of the times. Expresses and gives direction to currents of thought in epistemology, the philosophy of language, metaphysics and philosophical psychology.
**Ind/Abst** Acad. Ind. [Computer File] (1992-); Acad. Search (July 1993-); Am. Hist. Life (1955-1966); Arts Humanit. Citation Index [Full Cov.]; Br. Humanit. Index; Curr. Contents Arts Humanit.; Expand. Acad. Index (1989-); Humanit. Index; Humanit. Source (Jul. 1993-); INFO-SOUTH Abstr.; Int. Bibliogr. Sociol.; Mag. Search; Math. Rev.; MLA Int. Bibl. Books Artic. Mod. Lang. Lit.; Newsp. Period. Abstr. (1991-); Philos. Index; Res. Alert [Full Cov.]; Soc. Plann. Policy Dev. Abstr.; Soc. Sci. Cit. Index [Select. Cov.]; Sociol. Abstr.

GW/0590-451X
**MITTEILUNGEN UND FORSCHUNGSBEITRAGE DER CUSANUS-GESELLSCHAFT.** [Mitt. Forsch.beitr. Cusanus-Ges.]. **Main/Corp** Cusanus Gesellschaft, Vereinigung zur Forderung der Cusanusforschun. **Added/Corp** Cusanus-Gesellschaft. Vol. 1 (1961)-. Periodical. German. an. DM98.00. Paulinus Verlag, Postfach 3040 65, D 54220 Trier Germany. **Tel** 011 49 651 4604162, FAX 011 49 651 4604153, telex 472735. **ED** Rudolf Haubst. **LC** B765.N54; A13. **DD** 060. Index available. **Bk Rev.**
**Desc:** Articles and research on Nicholas of Cusa (1401-64), chief philosopher and theologist of the 15th Century, German cardinal, humanist and early empiricist.
**Ind/Abst** MLA Int. Bibl. Books Artic. Mod. Lang. Lit.

US/0026-8402
**MODERN SCHOOLMAN, THE.** [Mod. sch.man]. 1925. Periodical. English. qt. $26.00. St Louis University / Philosophy, Department of Philosophy, 221 North Grand Avenue, St Louis MO 63103. **Tel** (314)658-3149. **ED** William C Charron. **LC** B1; .M675. Index available. cum. index. **Bk Rev. Ad Acc. Pr Rev. Circ:** 650 (ctrl). Documents available from The Genuine Article.
**Desc:** Promotes historical research and critical analysis in all periods of philosophy: ancient, medieval, renaissance and modern.
**Ind/Abst** Arts Humanit. Citation Index [Full Cov.]; Curr. Contents Phys. Chem. Earth Sci.; Middle East Abstr. Index; Philos. Index; Res. Alert [Full Cov.]; Abr. Cathol. Period. Lit. Index; Cathol. Period. Lit. Index.

US/0026-9662
**MONIST, THE.** [Monist]. **Added/Corp** Hegeler Institute. Vol. 1, (Oct. 1890)-. Periodical. English. qt. $48.00 (1 year), $85.00 (2 year) institutional; $25.00 (1 year), $45.00 (2 year) individual. Hegeler Institute, Box 600, Lasalle IL 61301. **Tel** (815)223-1500 Ext 325, FAX (815)223-4486. **ED** Barry Smith. **LC** B1; .M7. **DD** 105. Index available. **Bk Rev. Ad Acc. Circ:** 1,600. available on microfilm from University Microfilms International (UMI). Documents available from The Genuine Article, UMI Article Clearinghouse.
**Desc:** Journal of general philosophic inquiry, chiefly concerned with matters of epistemology, metaphysics, aesthetics, and ethics.
**Ind/Abst** Acad. Search (July 1993-); Annu. Bibliogr. Engl. Lang. Lit.; Arts Humanit. Citation Index [Full Cov.]; Curr. Contents Arts Humanit.; Expand. Acad. Index (1989-); Humanit. Index; Humanit. Source (Jul. 1993-); INFO-SOUTH Abstr.; Mag. Search; Middle East Abstr. Index; Newsp. Period. Abstr. (1990-); Philos. Index; Res. Alert [Full Cov.]; Soc. Plann. Policy Dev. Abstr.

FR/0339-7203
**MONITOIRES DU CYMBALUM PATAPHYSICUM.** (1986)-. Periodical. French. ir. P Gayot, Courtaumont Par Sermiers, 51500 Rilly La Montagne France. ***Continues*** *Organographes du Cymbalum Pataphysicum.*

US
**MONOGRAPH ... OF THE SOCIETY FOR ASIAN AND COMPARATIVE PHILOSOPHY.** **Main/Corp** Society for Asian and Comparative Philosophy. **Added/Corp** Society for Asian and Comparative Philosophy. **VFOAT** Monographs of the Society for Asian and Comparative Philosophy. No. 1 (1974)-. Monographic series. English. ir. Price varies per volume. University of Hawaii Press, 2840 Kolowalu Street, Honolulu HI 96822. **Tel** (808)956-8833, (808)948-8697, FAX (808)988-6052. **ED** Eliot Deutsch.
**Desc:** A monograph series on specialized topics in Asian and comparative philosophy. The monographs are more detailed than journal articles, more specialized, and of shorter length than standard books.

GW
**MONOGRAPHIEN ZUR PHILOSOPHISCHEN FORSCHUNG.** Vol. 1 (1947)-. Monographic series. German. ir. Price varies per volume. VVA Bertelsmann Dist GmbH, Postfach 7600, D 33310 Gutersloh Germany. **Tel** 011 49 5241 803294. **Bk Rev. Ad Acc.**
**Desc:** An analysis of a wide range of philosophical themes.

GW/0254-9948
**MONUMENTA SERICA.** **See** History(General).

US/0890-6130
**NATURE, SOCIETY, AND THOUGHT.** **See** Social Sciences.

RU
**NAUCHNYI ATEIZM / MINISTERSTVO PROSVESCHENIIA RSFSR, PERMSKII GOSUDARSTVENNYI PEDAGOGISCHESKII INSTITUT, KAFEDRA MARKSISTSKO-LENINSKOI FILOSOFII.** **Added/Corp** Permskii Gosudarstvennyi Pedagogicheskii Institut. Kafedra Marksistsko-Leninskoi Filosofii. (1971)-. Russian. mo. $9.00. **(Subscription address:** Victor Kamkin, 4956 Boiling Brook Parkway, Rockville MD 20852.**) LC** BL2747.3; .N34. **DD** 211/.8.

RU/0301-5386
**NEKOTORYE FILOSOFSKIE VOPROSY SOVREMENNOGO ESTESTVOZNANIJA.** (NEKOTORYE FILOSOFSKIE VOPROSY SOVREMENNOGO ESTESTVOZNANIIA.). **Added/Corp** Leningradskii Gosudarstvennyi Universitet, Imeni A.A. Zhdanova. No. 1 (1973)-. Russian. 0.66rub single issue. St Petersburg State University / Izdatelstvo Leningradskogo Universiteta, Universitetskaia Nab 7/9, 199034 St Petersburg Russia. **Tel** 011 95 218-97-88, FAX 011 95 218-51-52, telex 121481. **LC** B67; .N39. **NLM** W1 NE196C.

GW
**NEUE HEFTE FUER PHILOSOPHIE.** [Neue Hefte Philos.]. Issue 1 (1971)-. Periodical. Multiple languages (English and German). an. DM43.00. Vandenhoeck & Ruprecht, Robert Bosch Breite 6, D-37079 Goettingen Germany. **Tel** 011 49 551 695911, FAX 011 49 551 695917, telex 965226 VAN d. **ED** R. Bubner, K. Cramer, and R. Wiehl.
**Ind/Abst** Philos. Index.

UK/0306-512x
**NEW HUMANIST (LONDON, ENGLAND).** (NEW HUMANIST : THE BIMONTHLY JOURNAL OF THE RATIONALIST PRESS ASSOCIATION.). **Added/Corp** Rationalist Press Association. Vol. 1, No. 1 (May 1972)-. Periodical. English. Four times a year (Mar., June, Sept., Dec.). £15.00 (institutions), £12.00 (individuals). Rationalist Press Association Ltd., 15 Lambs Conduit Passage, London WC1R 4RH England. **Tel** 011 44 71 4301371, FAX 011 44 71 4301271. **ED** Jim Henick. **LC** AP4; .N38. **DD** 052. **Bk Rev. Ad Acc. Circ:** 2,000. available on microfilm and microfiche from University Microfilms International (UMI). ***Continues*** *Humanist (London, England).*
**Ind/Abst** Br. Humanit. Index.

US/0028-6443
**NEW PHILOSOPHY, THE.** [New philos.]. **Added/Corp** Swedenborg Scientific Association. Vol. 1 (Mar. 1898)-. Periodical. English. Four times a year. $8.00. Swedenborg Scientific Association, Box 757, Bryn Athyn PA 19009. **Tel** (215)947-2577. **ED** E. J. Brock. **LC** BX8701; .N8. **DD** 289.4/05. Index available. cum. index. **Bk Rev. Circ:** 300.
**Desc:** Studies of the philosophy of Emanuel Swedenborg and related subjects.

US/0893-6005
**NEW STUDIES IN AESTHETICS.** **See** The Arts-Art.

US/0733-9542
**NEW VICO STUDIES.** [New Vico stud.]. **Added/Corp** Institute for Vico Studies. (1983)-. Periodical. English. an. $39.95. Humanities Press, 165 1st Avenue, Atlantic Highlands NJ 07716. **Tel** (908)872-1441, (800)221-3845, FAX (908)872-0717, telex 752233. **ED** Giorgio Tagliacozzo and Donald Phillip Verene. **LC** B3580.A1; N48. **DD** 195. **Bk Rev. Ad Acc, Adv Mgr:** G. Tagliacozzo, **Tel** (212)989-2909. **Circ:** 300.
**Desc:** Includes Vico's works as well as other ideas that are Vichian in nature involved in Vico's thoughts.
**Ind/Abst** Int. Bibliogr. Sociol.; MLA Int. Bibl. Books Artic. Mod. Lang. Lit.; Philos. Index.

US
**NEWSLETTERS ON THE BLACK EXPERIENCE, COMPUTER USE, FEMINISM, LAW, MEDICINE, TEACHING : A PUBLICATION OF THE AMERICAN PHILOSOPHICAL ASSOCIATION.** **Added/Corp** American Philosophical Association. Vol. 90:3 (Fall 1991)-. Periodical. English. sa. **LC** B63; .N49. **DD** 105. ***Continues*** *Newsletters on Computer Use, Feminism, Law, Medicine, Teaching, 1049-8788.*

GW
**NIETZSCHE BRIEFWECHSEL.** (19??)-. German. ir. DM360.00. Walter de Gruyter Inc., PO Box 303421, D 10728 Berlin Germany. **Tel** 011 49 30 260050, FAX 011 49 30 26005251.

GW/0342-1422
**NIETZSCHE-STUDIEN.** [Nietzsche-Stud.]. **VFOAT** Nietzsche Studien. Vol. 1 (1972)-. German (English and German). an. Price and postage varies according to size. Walter de Gruyter Inc., PO Box 303421, D 10728 Berlin Germany. **Tel** 011 49 30 260050, FAX 011 49 30 26005251.
**Ind/Abst** MLA Int. Bibl. Books Artic. Mod. Lang. Lit.

GW
**NIETZSCHE WERKE.** (19??)-. Monographic series. German. ir. Price varies per volume. Walter de Gruyter Inc., PO Box 303421, D 10728 Berlin Germany. **Tel** 011 49 30 260050, FAX 011 49 30 26005251. **(Subscription address:** North America: Walter de Gruyter Inc., 200 Saw Mill River Road, Hawthorne, NY 10532**)**

SZ/0078-0936
**NOCTES ROMANAE.** Vol. 1 (1949)-. Monographic series. German. ir. Price varies per volume. Verlag Paul Haupt, Falkenplatz 11, CH-3001 Bern Switzerland. **Tel** 011 41 31 3012435, FAX 011 41 30 243023, telex 912 906 HAUP CH. **ED** Georg Luck. **[CCC].**
**Desc:** Edition of books on Roman and Greek philosophy and philology (thesis, inaugural dissertations etc.).

NO/0029-1943
**NORSK FILOSOFISK TIDSSKRIFT.** [Nor. filos. tidsskr.]. (1966)-. Periodical. Norwegian. qt. Kr340.00, $57.00. Scandinavian University Press, PO Box 2959 Toeyen, N 0608 Oslo 6 Norway. **Tel** 011 47 2 2575400, FAX 011 47 2 2575353, telex 71896 UROR N. **(Subscription address:** Scandinavian University Press, 200 Meacham Ave., Elmont NY 11003.**) ED** Audun Oefsti. **DD** 105. **UDC** 378.4. **Bk Rev. Ad Acc. Circ:** 350.
**Desc:** Norwegian journal of philosophy.

US/1058-062X
**NORTHROP FRYE NEWSLETTER.** [Northrop Frye newsl.]. Vol. 1, No. 1 (Fall 1988)-. Newsletter. English. Twice a year (May & Dec.). Free.

Roanoke College / English Department, Robert Denham, Salem VA 24153. **Tel** (703)375-2365. **LC** WMLC 93/2088; PN75.F7; N67. **DD** 801/.95/05; 920.

IT
**NOTES ET DOCUMENTS (INSTITUT INTERNATIONAL JACQUES MARITAIN).** (NOTES ET DOCUMENTS / INSTITUT INTERNATIONAL J MARITAIN.). **VFOAT** Notes et Documents de l'Institut International Jacques Maritain. Yearly V. 1, No. 1 (Dec. 1975)-. Periodical. French (English). qt. L30000 Italy; $30.00 US. Institut International, Jacques Maritain, Via Quintino Sella 33, 00187 Rome Italy. **Tel** 4743719/4755188. **LC** B2430.M34; A16. **DD** 194. **Bk Rev. Ad Acc. Circ:** 3,000 (ctrl).
**Ind/Abst** Bibliogr. Mission.

US/0029-4527
**NOTRE DAME JOURNAL OF FORMAL LOGIC.** [Notre Dame j. form. log.]. **Added/Corp** University of Notre Dame. Vol. 1, (Jan. 1960)-. Periodical. English. qt. $45.00 (institutions), $25.00 (individuals). Notre Dame Journal of Formal Logic, The University of Notre Dame, PO Box 5, Notre Dame IN 46556. **Tel** (219)239-6157, FAX (219)239-8609. **ED** M. Detlefsen and Anand Pillay. **LC** BC1; .N6. **CODEN** NDJFAM. Index available. cum. index. **Bk Rev. Ad Acc. Circ:** 850. Documents available from Ask*IEEE.
**Desc:** Publishes work in areas of philosophical and mathematical logic, philosophy of language, formal semantics for natural languages, philosophy, history and foundations of logic and mathematics.
**Ind/Abst** INSPEC (July 1971-); Math. Rev.; Philos. Index; Pollut. Abstr. Indexes; Zentralbl. Math. Ihre Grenzgeb.

US/0029-4624
**NOUS (BLOOMINGTON).** (NOUS.). [Nous]. **Added/Corp** Wayne State University. Dept. of Philosophy. Wayne State University. Indiana University. Vol. 1 (March 1967)-. Periodical. English. qt. $81.50 North America; $96.00 other. Blackwell Publishers, 238 Main Street, Cambridge MA 02142. **Tel** (617)547-7110, (800)835-6770, FAX (617)547-0789. **ED** Hector-Neri Castaneda. **LC** B1; .N62. **DD** 105. **[CCC].** Index available. cum. index. **Bk Rev. Ad Acc. Circ:** 1,100 (ctrl). available on microfilm and microfiche from University Microfilms International (UMI). Documents available from The Genuine Article.
**Desc:** Publishes outstanding essays that extend the frontiers of philosophical research, emphasizing positive theoretical work that takes full account of current philosophical developments.
**Ind/Abst** Arts Humanit. Citation Index (19??-19??) [Full Cov.]; Curr. Contents Arts Humanit.; Math. Rev.; Philos. Index; Res. Alert [Full Cov.]; Soc. Plann. Policy Dev. Abstr.; Soc. Sci. Cit. Index [Select. Cov.]; Sociol. Abstr.

CN/0317-1442
**NOUVEAU DIALOGUE.** ***Title Change.*** **Added/Corp** Conference Catholique Canadienne. Service Incroyance et Foi. No. 10 (Jan. 1975)-?. French. qt. Service Incroyance et Foi, 7400 Blvd. Saint Laurent, Suite 226, Montreal Quebec, H2R 2Y1 Canada. **Tel** (514)948-3186. **DD** 200.1. ***Continued by*** *Dialogue, 0317-3747.*

CN/1183-3637
**NOUVELLE ACROPOLE (MONTREAL).** (NOUVELLE ACROPOLE.). [Nouv. acropole]. **Added/Corp** Centre Nouvelle Acropole Canada. No 1 (Mar/April 1991)-. Periodical. French. bm. 3.85Can$ per issue. Centre Nouvelle Acropole Canada, 1631 St.-Denis, Montreal Quebec H2X 3K3 Canada. **DD** 128.

NE
**NOUVELLES CARTESIENNES. VFOAT** Cartesian Newsletter. 1 (Sept. 1980)-. French (English). Quadratures, Boite Postale 6463, NL-1005 El Amsterdam Netherlands.

RU
**NOVAIA INOSTRANNAIA LITERATURA PO OBSHCHESTVENNYM NAUKAM: FILOSOFIIA I SOTSIOLOGIIA. Added/Corp** Institut Nauchnoi Informatsii po Obshchestvennym Naukam (Akademiia Nauk SSSR). (1976)-. Multiple languages (Russian and Multiple languages). mo. 0.40rub (single issue). Izdatelstvo Nauka / Akademiia Nauk, Publishing House of the Russian Academy of Sciences, Leninskii Porspekt 14, 117901 Moscow Russia. **Tel** 011 95 954-21-53, FAX 011 95 938-21-44, telex 411964. **ED** A Daukaev and A Korz. **LC** Z7127; .N65; B53. ***Continues*** *Novaia Inostrannaia Literatura Po Filosofii.*

RU/0134-2932
**NOVAIA OTECHESTVENNAIA I INOSTRANNAIA LITERATURA PO OBSHCHESTVENNYM NAUKAM. RELIGIOVEDENIE / ROSSIISKAIA AKADEMIIA NAUK, INSTITUT NAUCHNOI INFORMATSII PO OBSHCHESTVENNYM NAUKAM.** ***Title Change.*** **See** Religion and Theology.

RU
**NOVAIA OTECHESTVENNAIA LITERATURA PO OBSHCHESTVENNYM NAUKAM. FILOSOFIIA I SOTSIOLOGIIA / ROSSIISKAIA AKADEMIIA NAUK, INSTITUT NAUCHNOI INFORMATSII PO OBSHCHESTVENNYM NAUKAM.** ***Title Change.*** **Added/Corp** Institut Nauchnoi Informatsii po Obshchestvennym Naukam (Rossiiskaia Akademiia Nauk). **VFOAT** Filosofiia i Sotsiologiia. (1992)-(1992). Periodical. Russian. mo. Inion An SSSR, Ulitsa Krasikova D 28/45, Moscow Russia. **Tel** 128.89.71. **(Subscription address:** East View Publications Inc., 3020 Harbor Lane North, Suite 110, Minneapolis MN 55447.) **LC** Z7129.R9; N65; B4201. ***Continues*** *Novaia Sovetskaia Literatura po Obshchestvennym Naukam. Filosofskie Nauki, 0134-2789.* ***Continued by*** *Novaia Literatura po Sotsialnym i Gumanitarnym Naukam. Filosofiia i Sotsiologiia.*

BL/0101-3300
**NOVOS ESTUDOS CEBRAP. See** Political Science.

IT
**NUOVA CIVILTA DELLE MACCHINE.** Vol. 1, No. 1 (1983)-. Periodical. Italian (summaries and/or abstracts in English). qt. Nuova Eri, Edizioni Rai, Via Arsenale 41, 10121 Turin Italy. **Tel** 011 39 11 8102238.

IT/0029-6155
**NUOVA CORRENTE.** [Nuova corrente]. Vol. 1 (1954)-. Periodical. Italian. Twice a year. $29.76 Italy; $62.50 others. Tilgher Genova SAS, Via Assarotti 52, 16122 Genova Italy. **Tel** 011 39 10 870653, 8391140. **ED** M. Boselli, G. Franck, G. Sertoli and S. Verdino. **Bk Rev. Ad Acc. Circ:** 1,000.
**Desc:** Particularly careful to the modern theories of textual criticism and to the relation between literature and philosophy.
**Ind/Abst** Abstr. Engl. Stud.; MLA Int. Bibl. Books Artic. Mod. Lang. Lit.

RU
**OBSHCHESTVENNYE NAUKI V ROSSII. SERIIA 3, FILOSOFIIA / ROSSIISKAIA AKADEMIIA NAUK, INSTITUT NAUCHNOI INFORMATSII PO OBSHCHESTVENNYM NAUKAM.** ***Title Change.*** **Added/Corp** Institut Nauchnoi Informatsii po Obshchestvennym Naukam (Rossiiskaia Akademiia Nauk). **VFOAT** Filosofiia. (1992)-(1992). Academic Scholarly Publication. Russian (table of contents in English). bm. Izdatelstvo Nauka / Akademiia Nauk, Publishing House of the Russian Academy of Sciences, Leninskii Porspekt 14, 117901 Moscow Russia. **Tel** 011 95 954-21-53, FAX 011 95 938-21-44, telex 411964. **LC** Z7128.D5; O27; B809.8. ***Continues*** *Obshchestvennye Nauki v SSSR. Seriia 3, Filosofskie Nauki, 0202-2052.* ***Merged with*** *Obshchestvennye Nauki za Rubezhom. Seriia 3, Filosofiia* ***to form*** *Sotsialnye i Gumanitarnye Nauki, Seriia 3, Filosofskie Nauki.*

SA
**OCCASIONAL RESEARCH PAPERS - DEPARTMENT OF RELIGIOUS STUDIES AND PHILOSOPHY, MAKERERE UNIVERSITY. See** Religion and Theology.

US/0748-9919
**ORIGINS RESEARCH.** [Orig. res.]. **Added/Corp** Students for Origins Research (U.S.). Vol. 5, No. 1 (Winter-Spring 1982)-. Periodical. English. Twice a year. $10.00. Access Research Network, PO Box 38069, Colorado Springs CO 80937. **Tel** (719)633-1772. **ED** Dennis A. Wagner and Mark Hartwig. **DD** 113. **Bk Rev. Circ:** 5,500. available on an online database from CREVO/BBS. ***Continues*** *Students for Origins Research.*
**Desc:** Newspaper journal that examines scientific and philosophical evidence related to creation and evolution. Often features debates and reviews of current literature.

US/0030-7580
**OWL OF MINERVA, THE.** [Owl Minerva]. **Added/Corp** Hegel Society of America. Villanova University. Philosophy Dept. Florida State University. Vol. 1, (Summer 1969)-. Periodical. English. sa (Apr. and Sept.). $25.00. Hegel Society of America, LS Stepelevich, Department of Philosophy, Villanova PA 19085. **Tel** (610)519-4747. **ED** Lawrence S. Stepelevich. **LC** B2900; .O85. **DD** 193. Index available. cum. index. **Bk Rev**, (Qty: 12 yr). **Ad Acc. Pr Rev. Circ:** 600. available on microfilm.
**Desc:** Official journal of Hegel Society of America features articles, book reviews and notes on Hegel and contemporaries, Hegelianism today and idealistic philosophy in general.
**Ind/Abst** Philos. Index.

UK/0265-7651
**OXFORD STUDIES IN ANCIENT PHILOSOPHY.** [Oxf. stud. anc. philos.]. Vol. 1 (1983)-. English. ir. Price varies per volume. Oxford University Press, Walton Street, Oxford OX2 6DP England. **Tel** 011 44 865 56767, FAX 011 44 865 267773, telex 837330 OXPRES G. **(Subscription address:** Oxford University Press / USA, Journals Marketing Department, Oxford University Press, 2001 Evans Road, Cary NC 27513.) **LC** B1; .O9. **DD** 180/.5.
**Ind/Abst** Br. Humanit. Index.

UK/0279-0750
**PACIFIC PHILOSOPHICAL QUARTERLY.** [Pac. philos. q.]. **Added/Corp** University of Southern California. School of Philosophy. Vol. 61, No. 1/2 (Jan./Apr. 1980)-. Academic Scholarly Publication. English. Four times a year. £49.00 UK & Europe; $63.50 North America; £54.50 other. Basil Blackwell Publishers Ltd, 108 Cowley Road, Oxford 0X4 1JF England. **Tel** 011 44 865 791100, FAX 011 44 865 791347, telex 837022 OXBOOK G. **(Subscription address:** Blackwell Publishers / UK, Marston Book Services, PO Box 87, Oxford OX2 0DT England.) **ED** Hartry Field, Barbara Herman, Brian Loar and Miles Morgan. **LC** AP2; .P46. **DD** 105. **CODEN** PPHQEJ. **[CCC].** Index available. **Ad Acc. Circ:** 1,000 (ctrl). available on microfilm and microfiche from University Microfilms International (UMI). Documents available from The Genuine Article, UMI Article Clearinghouse. ***Continues*** *Personalist, 0031-5621.*
**Ind/Abst** Acad. Search (July 1993-); Annu. Bibliogr. Engl. Lang. Lit.; Arts Humanit. Citation Index [Full Cov.]; Curr. Contents Arts Humanit.; Expand. Acad. Index (1992-); Humanit. Index; Humanit. Source (Jul. 1993-); INFO-SOUTH Abstr.; Mag. Search; Newsp. Period. Abstr. (1991-); Philos. Index; Res. Alert [Full Cov.]; Romant. Move.; Soc. Plann. Policy Dev. Abstr.

US/0190-1176
**PAIDEIA (BUFFALO).** ***Ceased.*** (PAIDEIA.). [Paideia]. **Added/Corp** State University College at Buffalo. State University College, Brockport, N.Y. Vol. 1 (1972)-(19??). Periodical. English. an. Paideia Journal Fund, Faculty-Student Association, State University College of Buffalo, 1300 Elmwood Avenue, Buffalo NY 14222. **Tel** (716)878-5302. **LC** B1; .P27.
**Ind/Abst** MLA Int. Bibl. Books Artic. Mod. Lang. Lit.

US/0742-5368
**PANTHEIST VISION.** (PANTHEIST VISION : THE NEWSLETTER OF THE UNIVERSAL PANTHEIST SOCIETY.). Newsletter. English. qt. $8.00. Universal Pantheist Society, PO Box 265, Big Pine CA 93513. **Tel** (209)739-8527. **ED** Harold Wood. **Bk Rev.** ctrl circ.
**Desc:** Philosophical works regarding the place of people within the universe, and the value of nature as the ultimate context for human experience.

IT
**PARADIGMI.** Vol. 1, No. 1 (Jan./April 1983)-. Periodical. Italian. Three times a year. Grafischena, Viale Stazione 177, 72015 Fasano Italy.
**Ind/Abst** Bibliogr. Mission.

●US/1055-761X
**PARADOXIST MOVEMENT, THE.** (1991)-. Periodical. English. ir. Xiquan Publishing House, PO Box 42561L, Phoenix AZ 85080. ***Continues*** *Le Sens du Non-Sens.*

BE/0773-9532
**PART DE L'IL, LA. See** The Arts-Art.

AG/0325-2280
**PATRISTICA ET MEDIAEVALIA.** **Added/Corp** Universidad de Buenos Aires. Centro de Estudios de Filosofia Medieval. Vol. 1 (1975)-. Periodical. Latin (Spanish). ir. $35.00. Universidad de Buenos Aires / Argentina, Facultdad Filosofia Letras Puan 470, Buenos Aires 1406, Argentina. **Tel** 011 54 1 4320537, 011 54 1 4328696. **LC** B5; .P37.
**Ind/Abst** Philos. Index.

II
**PAURNAMASI. VFOAT** Pournamasi. Periodical. English (Hindi, Oriya and Sanskrit). ir. 15.00. Shree Sadasiva Kendriya, Sanskrit Vidyapeetham, Puri Orissa 752001 India. **LC** PK401; .P38.

SP/0031-4749
**PENSAMIENTO (MADRID).** (PENSAMIENTO; REVISTA TRIMESTRAL DE INVESTIGACION E INFORMACION FILOSOFICA.). [Pensamiento]. (1945)-. Periodical. Spanish. qt. $52.00. Centro Loyola, Pablo Aranda 3, 28006 Madrid Spain. **Tel** 011 34 1 565-4930, 562-6604, FAX 011 34 1 563-4073. **LC** B5; .P42. **Bk Rev.** Documents available from The Genuine Article.
**Ind/Abst** Arts Humanit. Citation Index [Full Cov.]; Curr. Contents Arts Humanit.; Philos. Index; Res. Alert [Full Cov.]; Soc. Sci. Cit. Index [Select. Cov.].

FR/0031-4781
**PENSEE CATHOLIQUE, LA. See** Religion and Theology-Catholicism.

IT
**PER LA FILOSOFIA. Added/Corp** Associazione dei Docenti Italiani di Filosofia di Ispirazioni Cristiana. No. 1 (1984)-. Periodical. Italian. Three times a year (Apr., July, Dec.). L40000 Italy; L55000 other Italy; L80000 other. Casa Editrice Massimo SAS, V Le Bacchiglione 20

A, 20139 Milan Italy. **Tel** 011 39 2 55211220, FAX 011 39 2 55211315. **Bk Rev**, (Qty: 25). **Ad Acc**, **Adv Mgr:** Cesare Crespi, **Tel** 5521-1220. **Circ:** 1,000 (ctrl).

US/0889-065X
**PERSONALIST FORUM, THE.** [Pers. forum]. Vol. 1, No. 1 (Spring 1985)-. Periodical. English. sa. Personalist Forum, Furman University Deparment of Philosophy, Greenville SC 29613. **Tel** (800)294-2083, (800)294-2024. **(Subscription address:** Mercer Press, 1400 Coleman Avenue, Macon, GA 31207**) LC** B828.5.A1; P47. **DD** 141. **[CCC].**
**Ind/Abst** Philos. Index.

US/0733-6217
**PERSPECTIVES ON DEATH AND DYING SERIES.** [Perspect. death dying ser.]. Vol. 1, (1980)-. Monographic series. English. ir. Price varies per volume. Foundation Book & Periodical, 391 Atlantic Avenue, Brooklyn NY 11217. **Tel** (718)270-3725. **ED** Richard A. Kalish. **LC** UNC.
**Desc:** Provides in-depth, specialized discussions of the vital issues of death and dying. Each volume is a carefully selected collection of significant scholarly articles targeted to a specific area of thanatological concern. Important original research case histories and conceptual papers are presented with a minimum of technical jargon, making these books perfect for undergraduates as well as researchers and professionals.

NE/0171-1288
**PERSPEKTIVEN DER PHILOSOPHIE.** [Perspekt. Philos.]. Vol. 1 (1975)-. German. an. $50.00. Editions Rodopi BV, Keizersgracht 302-304, 1016 Ex Amsterdam Netherlands. **Tel** 011 31 20 6227507, FAX 011 31 20 380948. **LC** B3; .P47. ***Supersedes*** *Philosophische Perspektiven.*
**Ind/Abst** Philos. Index.

NE/0079-1350
**PHAENOMENOLOGICA.** (1958)-. Monographic series. English (French and German). ir. Price varies per volume. Kluwer Academic Publishers, Postbus 322, 3300 AH Dordrecht, The Netherlands. **Tel** 011 (31) 78 524400, FAX 011 31 78 183273, telex 20083. **(Subscription address:** Kluwer Academic Publishers / US Subscriptions, PO Box 253, Accord Station, Hingham MA 02018.**)**

GW
**PHANOMENOLOGISCHE FORSCHUNGEN. PHENOMENOLOGICAL STUDIES. RECHERCHES PHENOMENOLOGIQUES. VFOAT** Phenomenological Studies; Recherches Phenomenologiques. Vol. 1 (1975)-. Monographic series. German (English, French and German). sa. $68.00. Verlag Karl Alber GmbH, Hermann Herder Strasse 4, D 79104 Freiburg Germany. **Tel** 011 49 761 273495.

US/0885-3886
**PHENOMENOLOGICAL INQUIRY.** [Phenomenol. inq.]. **Added/Corp** World Institute for Advanced Phenomenological Research and Learning. Vol. 9 (Oct. 1985)-. Periodical. English (Japanese and Chinese). an (Oct.). $30.00 (institutions), $25.00 (individuals) US; $35.00 (institutions), $30.00 (individuals) other. World Phenomenology Institute, 348 Payson Road, Belmont MA 02178. **Tel** (617)489-3696, (802)295-3487, telex 988722. **ED** Anna-Teresa Tymieniecka. **LC** B829.5; .P476. **DD** 142/.7/05. **Bk Rev**, (Qty: 5-8). **Circ:** 800. ***Continues*** *Phenomenology Information Bulletin, 0278-8322.*
**Desc:** Dedicated to the development of phenomenological philosophy and its interaction with human sciences, literature and fine arts.

CN/0820-9189
**PHENOMENOLOGY AND PEDAGOGY.** ***Ceased.*** (PHENOMENOLOGY + PEDAGOGY.). [Phenomenol. pedagogy]. **Added/Corp** University of Alberta. Faculty of Education. **VAT** Phenomenology Plus Pedagogy. Vol. 1 No. 1 (1983)-Vol. 10 (1992). Periodical. English. Three times a year. University of Alberta Publishing Service, 4-116 Education North, Edmonton Alberta T6G 2G5 Canada. **Tel** (403)492-4204, FAX (403)492-0236. **ED** Margaret Haughey. **DD** 370.15. **[CCC]. Bk Rev. Circ:** 300.
**Desc:** A human science journal dedicated to interpretive and critical studies of a broad range of pedagogic relations and situations.

CN/0318-4412
**PHI ZERO.** ***Ceased.*** [Phi zero]. Vol. 1 (Jan./Feb. 1973)-?. French. ir. University of Montreal Department de Philosophie, CP 6128, Montreal Quebec H3C 3J7 Canada. **Tel** (514)343-6321. **DD** 105.
**Ind/Abst** Point Repere (1983-).

PH/0554-0577
**PHILIPPINIANA SACRA. See** History(General).

CN/0820-7313
**PHILOCRITIQUE.** [Philocritique]. No. 1 (Winter 81)-. Periodical. French. sa. $3.00 per no., $6.00 per year individuals; $10.00 per year institutions. Philocritique, c/o Module de Philosophie Universite du Quebec A, Montreal C P 8888 Succursale A, Montreal Quebec H3C 3P8 Canada. **DD** 105.

UK
**PHILOSOPHER, THE. Added/Corp** Philosophical Society of England. (April/June 1923)-(Dec. 1948); New Series (Mar. 1949)-. Periodical. English. Twice a year (Spring and Autumn). £16.00 UK; £21.00 other. Philosophical Society of England, BM Box 1129, London WC1N 3XX England. **Tel** 11 44 923 229784, FAX 11 44 923 229784. **ED** Keith Seddon. **LC** B1; .P45. **Bk Rev**, (Qty: 20). **Ad Acc. Pr Rev. Circ:** 200 (ctrl).
**Desc:** Philosophy studies by professionals and amateurs. The society conducts study courses for its diplomas of associate and fellow.

CN/0827-1887
**PHILOSOPHER (MONTREAL, QUEBEC).** (PHILOSOPHER.). [Philosopher]. **Added/Corp** Philosophie au College (Association de Professeurs). No. 1 (1985)-. Periodical. French. sa (2 issues). 45.00Can$ (institutions), 25.00Cans (individuals) Canada; 50.00Can$ (institutions), 30.00Can$ (individuals) other. Periodica Inc, PO Box 444, Outremont Quebec H2V 4R6 Canada. **Tel** (514)274-5468, FAX (514)274-0201. **ED** Cohen-Bacrie Pierre. **DD** 107/.11714. **Bk Rev. Ad Acc. Circ:** 700.
**Desc:** Covers philosophy, teaching, culture, and book reviews.
**Ind/Abst** Point Repere.

US/0031-7993
**PHILOSOPHER'S INDEX. See** Philosophy-Abstracting, Bibliographies and Statistics.

BE/0079-1679
**PHILOSOPHES MEDIEVAUX. Added/Corp** Louvain. Universite Catholique. Institut Superieur de Philosophie. Vol. 1 (1948)-. Monographic series. French (Latin). ir. Price varies per volume. Editions Peeters SA, Bondgenotenlaan 153, BP 41, B-3000 Leuven Belgium. **Tel** 32 16 235170, FAX 32 16 228500, telex 65987 PUL B. ***Supersedes*** *Les Philosophes Belges.*

DK
**PHILOSOPHIA. Added/Corp** Filosofisk Forening i Arhus. (December 1977)-. Periodical. Danish. Four times a year. $275.00. Forlaget Philosophia/Dept Phil, Aarhus University, Institute for Filosofi, DK-8000 Aarhus C Denmark. **Tel** 011 45 86 136711 Ext. 386. ***Continues*** *Philosophia Arhusiensis.*

FR
**PHILOSOPHIA. VFOAT** Collection "Philosophia". No. 1 (1976)-. Monographic series. French. ir. Price varies per volume. Editions Klincksieck, 8 rue de la Sorbonne, 75005 Paris France. **Tel** 11 33 1 43545953, FAX 11 33 1 432252553.

NE/0079-1687
**PHILOSOPHIA ANTIQUA.** Vol. 1 (1946)-. Monographic series. English (French and German). ir. Price varies per volume. E. J. Brill, Postbus 9000, 2300 PA Leiden Netherlands. **Tel** 011 31 71 312624, FAX 011 31 71 317532, telex 39296 BRILL NL.
**Desc:** A series of monographs on ancient philosophy.
**Ind/Abst** Math. Rev.

GW/0031-8027
**PHILOSOPHIA NATURALIS.** [Philos. nat.]. Vol. 1 (1950)-. Monographic series. English (German). Twice a year. Price varies per volume. Vittorio Klostermann, Frauenlobstrasse 22, D 60487 Frankfurt Germany. **Tel** 011 49 69 9708160. **ED** Joseph Meurers. **LC** B3; .P62. **DD** 105. **Bk Rev. Ad Acc. Circ:** 600 (ctrl).
**Desc:** Covers natural philosophy research.
**Ind/Abst** Energy Res. Abstr. (March 1982-); Math. Rev.; Philos. Index.

SZ
**PHILOSOPHIA PERENNIS.** (1988)-. French. an. Editions l'Age d'Homme / Switzerland, Case Postale 67, CH 1211 Geneva 25 Switzerland. **Tel** 011 41 21 220095.

IS/0048-3893
**PHILOSOPHIA (RAMAT GAN).** (PHILOSOPHIA.). [Philosophia (Ramat Gan)]. **Added/Corp** Universitat Bar-Ilan. Mahlakah le-Ilosofyah. Vol. 1 (Jan. 1971)-. Periodical. English. qt. $28.00. Universitat Bar-Ilan, Department of Philosophy, Ramat Gan 52900 Israel. **Tel** 11 972 3 5318575, 11 972 3 5318401, telex 342290 BARIL IL. **ED** Asa Kasher. Index available. **Bk Rev. Ad Acc. Pr Rev. Circ:** 700 (ctrl).
**Desc:** Covers all subjects of philosophy.
**Ind/Abst** Arts Humanit. Citation Index [Full Cov.]; Curr. Contents Arts Humanit.; Philos. Index.

NE/0031-8035
**PHILOSOPHIA REFORMATA.** (PHILOSOPHIA REFORMATA : ORGAAN VAN DE VERENIGING VOOR CALVINISTISCHE WIJSBEGEERTE.). [Philos. reform.]. **Added/Corp** Vereniging voor Calvinistische Wijsbegeerte. (1936)-. English (Dutch). sa. F60.00. Stichting Reform Wijsbegeerte, Postbus 368, 3500 AJ Utrecht Netherlands. **Tel** 011 31 30 342030. **LC** BX9401; .P48. **Bk Rev. Ad Acc. Circ:** 700 (ctrl).
**Desc:** Scientific articles on all sorts of subjects from a reformational-philosophical point of view.
**Ind/Abst** Philos. Index.

US/0193-5046
**PHILOSOPHIC EXCHANGE.** [Philos. exch.]. **Added/Corp** State University College, Brockport, N.Y. Center for Philosophic Exchange. State University College, Brockport, N.Y. Center for Philosophic Exchange. Proceedings. Vol. 1 (1970)-. English. an. $30.00. Center for Philosophic Exchange, State of New York College at Brockport, Department of Philosophy, Brockport NY 14420. **Tel** (716)395-2493. **ED** Jack Glickman. **LC** B21; .P4. **DD** 105.
**Ind/Abst** Philos. Index.

II
**PHILOSOPHICA.** Periodical. English (Bengali). qt. Shankar Basu, 38A/10 Belgachia Road, Calcutta 700037 India. **LC** B1; .P473. **DD** 105.
**Ind/Abst** Philos. Index.

BE/0379-8402
**PHILOSOPHICA.** [Philosophica]. **Added/Corp** Rijksuniversiteit te Gent. Vol. 13 (1974)-. Periodical. Dutch (French, German and English). sa. 600F Belgium. Rijksuniversiteit Ghent, Rozier 44, B-9000 Gent Belgium. **Tel** 011 32 91 643754. **ED** Diderik Batens. **LC** B63; .P46. **Bk Rev. Ad Acc. Circ:** 350. ***Continues*** *Philosophica Gandensia.*
**Desc:** A journal of philosophical inquiry devoted to current epistemological, axiological and social political issues.
**Ind/Abst** Philos. Index.

XR/0474-1021
**PHILOSOPHICA, AESTHETICA. Main/Corp** Olomouc, Moravia. Palackejp Universita. Filosoficka Fakulta. 1 (1964)-. Monographic series. Multiple languages (Czech, English and German; summaries and/or abstracts in Russian and German). Price varies per volume. **LC** B26; .O55.

UK/0031-8051
**PHILOSOPHICAL BOOKS.** [Philos. books]. Vol. 1 (Jan. 1960)-. Academic Scholarly Publication. English. Four times a year. £69.00 UK and Europe; $137.00 North America; £88.50 other. Basil Blackwell Publishers Ltd, 108 Cowley Road, Oxford 0X4 1JF England. **Tel** 011 44 865 791100, FAX 011 44 865 791347, telex 837022 OXBOOK G. **(Subscription address:** Blackwell Publishers / UK, Marston Book Services, PO Box 87, Oxford OX2 0DT England.**) ED** Anthony Ellis. **LC** Z7127; .P48. **DD** 105. **[CCC]. Bk Rev. Ad Acc. Circ:** 700 (ctrl). available on microfilm and microfiche from University Microfilms International (UMI).
**Desc:** Publishes scholarly reviews to assist both librarians and individuals in the choice of professional works of philosophy.
**Ind/Abst** Philos. Index; Soc. Plann. Policy Dev. Abstr.

NE
**PHILOSOPHICAL CURRENTS.** (1971)-. Periodical. English. ir. BR Gruner BV, Nieuwe Herengracht 31, 1011 RM Amsterdam Netherlands. **Tel** 20-264371. **ED** David H DeGrood. **Circ:** 400.
**Desc:** Series dedicated to bringing philosophy back into mainstream of intellectual and political life and presenting works involved with important issues of our revolutionary age.

US/0031-806X
**PHILOSOPHICAL FORUM, THE.** [Philos. forum]. **Added/Corp** Boston University. Dept. of Philosophy. Boston University. Philosophical Club. Vol. 1-23, (1943-65) Vol. 1 (Fall 1968). Periodical. English. qt. $15.00 (1 year), $25.00 (2 year), $35.00 (3 year) individuals, $60.00 (1 year), $115.00 ( 2 years), $170.00 (3 year) institutions US; $19.00 (1 year), $33.00 (2 year), $47.00 (3 year) individuals; $64.00 (1 year), $123.00 (2 year), $182.00 (3 year) institutions other. Philosophical Forum, Baruch College CUNY, Box 239, New York NY 10010. **Tel** (212)387-1682. **ED** Marx Wartofsky. **LC** B1; .P475. **DD** 105. **Bk Rev. Ad Acc. Circ:** 2,000. Documents available from The Genuine Article.
**Desc:** Provides open-minded discussions which aim not so much at agreement as at lively response.
**Ind/Abst** Arts Humanit. Citation Index [Full Cov.]; Curr. Contents Arts Humanit.; Int. Polit. Sci. Abstr.; Math. Rev.; Philos. Index; Res. Alert [Full Cov.]; Soc. Sci. Cit. Index [Select. Cov.].

US/1054-2884
**PHILOSOPHICAL INQUIRIES.** [Philos. inq.]. No. 1 (1991)-. Monographic series. English. Price varies per volume. Texas Tech University Press, Administrative Education Room 43, West Basement, Lubbock TX 79409-1037. **Tel** (800)832-4042, (806)742-2982. **DD** 501. ***Continues*** *Graduate Studies (Texas Tech University), 0082-3198.*
**Ind/Abst** Math. Rev.

GR/1105-235X
**PHILOSOPHICAL INQUIRY.** [Philos. inq.]. **Added/Corp** Aristoteleio Panepistemio Thessalonikes. Vol. 1, No. 1 (Fall 1978)-. Periodical. English (French and German). qt. $35.00. Arist Univ Thessa Dep Philos, PO Box 84, Thessaloniki Greece. **Tel** 30 31 942485.
**Ind/Abst** Philos. Index.

US/0190-0536
**PHILOSOPHICAL INVESTIGATIONS.** [Philos. invest.]. Vol. 1 (Winter 1978)-. Academic Scholarly Publication. English. Four times a year. £77.50 UK and Europe; $160.00 North America; £103.00 other. Basil Blackwell Publishers Ltd, 108 Cowley Road, Oxford 0X4 1JF England. **Tel** 011 44 865 791100, FAX 011 44 865 791347, telex 837022 OXBOOK G. **(Subscription address:** Blackwell Publishers / UK, Marston Book Services, PO Box 87, Oxford OX2 0DT England.**) ED** D Z Phillips. **LC** B1; .P477. **DD** 149/.94/05. **[CCC]. Bk Rev.** available on microfilm and microfiche from University Microfilms International (UMI). Documents available from The Genuine Article.
**Desc:** Articles in every branch of philosophy.
**Ind/Abst** Arts Humanit. Citation Index [Full Cov.]; Curr. Contents Arts Humanit.; Philos. Index; Res. Alert [Full Cov.]; Soc. Plann. Policy Dev. Abstr

SA/0556-8641
**PHILOSOPHICAL PAPERS (GRAHAMSTOWN).** (PHILOSOPHICAL PAPERS.). [Philos. pap.]. **Added/Corp** Rhodes University. Library. Publication Dept. Rhodes University. Library. Rhodes University. Dept. of Philosophy. Vol. 1 (1972)-. Periodical. English. Three times a year. $18.00 individuals; $54.00 institutions. Philosophical Papers, Rhodes University, Philosophy Department, PO Box 94, 6140 Grahamstown South Africa. **Tel** 011 27 461 22023, FAX 011 27 461 25049. **ED** Michael Pendlebury. **Bk Rev. Ad Acc. Circ:** 350.
**Desc:** Publishes submitted and invited articles, notes, and critical studies in all branches of philosophy within the analytical tradition.
**Ind/Abst** Philos. Index.

UK/0951-5089
**PHILOSOPHICAL PSYCHOLOGY. See** Psychology.

UK/0031-8094
**PHILOSOPHICAL QUARTERLY, THE.** [Philos. q.]. **Added/Corp** University of St. Andrews. Scots Philosophical Club. Vol. 1 (Oct. 1950)-. Academic Scholarly Publication. English. Four times a year (Jan., Apr., July, Oct.). £57.00 UK & Europe; $117.00 North America; £76.00 other. Basil Blackwell Publishers Ltd, 108 Cowley Road, Oxford 0X4 1JF England. **Tel** 011 44 865 791100, FAX 011 44 865 791347, telex 837022 OXBOOK G. **(Subscription address:** Blackwell Publishers / UK, Marston Book Services, PO Box 87, Oxford OX2 0DT England.**) ED** Leslie Stevenson. **LC** B1; .P49. **DD** 105. **[CCC]. Bk Rev. Ad Acc. Circ:** 1,500. available on microfilm and microfiche from University Microfilms International (UMI). Documents available from The Genuine Article, UMI Article Clearinghouse.
**Desc:** Aims to foster and publish significant contributions in every branch of the subject, promoting discussion of recent philosophical work.
**Ind/Abst** Acad. Abstr. Full Text Elite (July 1990); Acad. Abstr. (July 1990); Acad. Search (July 1990-); Arts Humanit. Citation Index [Full Cov.]; Br. Humanit. Index; Curr. Contents Arts Humanit.; Expand. Acad. Index (1989-); Humanit. Index; Humanit. Source (Jul. 1990-); INFO-SOUTH Abstr.; Mag. Search; Math. Rev.; MLA Int. Bibl. Books Artic. Mod. Lang. Lit.; Newsp. Period. Abstr. (1990-); Philos. Index; Res. Alert [Full Cov.]; Romant. Move.; Soc. Plann. Policy Dev. Abstr.; Soc. Sci. Cit. Index [Select. Cov.].

US/0031-8108
**PHILOSOPHICAL REVIEW, THE.** [Philos. rev.]. **Added/Corp** Sage School of Philosophy. Vol. 1, No. 1 (Jan. 1892)-. Periodical. English. qt (4 issues). $50.00 institution; $30.00 individual. Philosophical Review, 327 Goldwin Smith Hall, Cornell University, Ithaca NY 14853. **Tel** (607)255-6817. **ED** Helen Taylor-Way. **LC** B1; .P5. **DD** 105. Index available (bound in last issue). cum. index. **Bk Rev. Ad Acc. Circ:** 3,200 (ctrl). available on microfilm and microfiche from University Microfilms International (UMI). Documents available from The Genuine Article, UMI Article Clearinghouse.
**Desc:** Topics of contemporary philosophy discussed, ranging from logic to philosophy of science, mathematics, language and history of philosophy.
**Ind/Abst** Acad. Search (Jan. 1994-); Am. Hist. Life (1955-1958); Annu. Bibliogr. Engl. Lang. Lit.; Arts Humanit. Citation Index [Full Cov.]; Book Rev. Index; Curr. Contents Arts Humanit.; Expand. Acad. Index (1989-); Humanit. Index; Humanit. Source (Jul. 1993-); INFO-SOUTH Abstr.; Mag. Search; MLA Int. Bibl. Books Artic. Mod. Lang. Lit.; Newsp. Period. Abstr. (1991-); Philos. Index; Res. Alert [Full Cov.]; Romant. Move.; Soc. Plann. Policy Dev. Abstr.; Soc. Sci. Cit. Index [Select. Cov.]; Sociol. Abstr.

NE/0031-8116
**PHILOSOPHICAL STUDIES.** [Philos. stud.]. Vol. 1 (Jan. 1950)-. Periodical. English. mo. $1,128.00. Kluwer Academic Publishers, Postbus 322, 3300 AH Dordrecht, The Netherlands. **Tel** 011 (31) 78 524400, FAX 011 31 78 183273, telex 20083. **ED** Stewart Cohen. **LC** B21; .P53. **DD** 108.2. **[CCC]. Ad Acc. Pr Rev. Circ:** 900. available on microfilm and microfiche from University Microfilms International (UMI). Documents available from The Genuine Article.
**Desc:** Devoted to the rapid publication of analytical contributions, particularly (but not exclusively) in epistemology, philosophical logic, the philosophy of language, and ethics. A diligent reader of the journal will be kept informed of the major problems and contributions of contemporary analytic philosophy.
**Ind/Abst** Annu. Bibliogr. Engl. Lang. Lit.; Arts Humanit. Citation Index [Full Cov.]; Curr. Contents Arts Humanit.; Linguist. Lang. Behav. Abstr.; Math. Rev.; MLA Int. Bibl. Books Artic. Mod. Lang. Lit.; Philos. Index; Res. Alert [Full Cov.]; Soc. Plann. Policy Dev. Abstr.; Soc. Sci. Cit. Index [Select. Cov.]; Sociol. Abstr.

IE/0554-0739
**PHILOSOPHICAL STUDIES (DUBLIN, IRELAND).** ***Ceased.*** (PHILOSOPHICAL STUDIES.). (June 1951)-Vol. 32, (April 1991). Periodical. English. an. Philosophical Studies, 58 Trimleston Gardens, Booterstown County, Dublin Ireland. **Tel** 692693. **ED** James Bastable. **LC** WMLC L 82/255. **Bk Rev.**
**Desc:** Contemporary philosophy with references to theological, social and scientific reflection.
**Ind/Abst** Curr. Contents Arts Humanit.; Philos. Index; Abr. Cathol. Period. Lit. Index; Cathol. Period. Lit. Index.

US/0160-7561
**PHILOSOPHICAL STUDIES IN EDUCATION.** [Philos. stud. educ.]. **Main/Corp** Ohio Valley Philosophy of Education Society. (1976)-. English. an (Fall). $15.00. Terence O'Connor, School of Education, Indiana State University, Terre Haute IN 47809. **Tel** (812)237-2880, FAX (812)237-4348. **ED** Richard Brosio and Terence O'Connor. **LC** L107; .O37A. **DD** 370.1. cum. index. **Pr Rev. Circ:** 200 (ctrl). available on microfilm and microfiche from University Microfilms International (UMI). ***Continues Proceedings of the Annual Meeting of the Ohio Valley Philosophy of Education Society, 0092-8178.***
**Desc:** An annual proceeding of refereed essays dealing with issues and topics in philosophy of education.
**Ind/Abst** Philos. Index.

NE
**PHILOSOPHICAL STUDIES SERIES.** **VFOAT** PSS. Vol. 37 (1987)-. Monographic series. English. ir. Price varies per volume. Kluwer Academic Publishers, Postbus 322, 3300 AH Dordrecht, The Netherlands. **Tel** 011 (31) 78 524400, FAX 011 31 78 183273, telex 20083. **(Subscription address:** Kluwer Academic Publishers / US Subscriptions, PO Box 253, Accord Station, Hingham MA 02018.**)** ***Continues Philosophical Studies Series in Philosophy.***

US/0276-2080
**PHILOSOPHICAL TOPICS.** [Philos. top.]. **Added/Corp** Southwestern Philosophical Society. Vol. 12, No. 1 (Spring 1981)-. Periodical. English. Twice a year. $45.00 institutions, $25.00 individuals US and Canada; $50.00 institutions, $30.00 individuals other. University of Arkansas Press / Philosophical Topics, 201 Ozark, Fayetteville AR 72701. **Tel** (501)575-3551. **ED** Christopher Hill. **LC** B1; .S58. **DD** 105. Index available. **Ad Acc. Circ:** 600. ***Continues Southwestern Journal of Philosophy, 0038-481X.***
**Desc:** Issues on designated topics: epistemology, value theory and history of philosophy.
**Ind/Abst** Philos. Index.

FR/0294-1805
**PHILOSOPHIE (PARIS, FRANCE : 1984).** (PHILOSOPHIE.). No. 1 (Jan. 1984)-. Periodical. French. qt. 178.20F France; 226.00F other. Les Editions de Minuit, 7 rue Bernard-Palissy, 75006 Paris France. **Tel** 011 33 1 44393920, FAX 011 33 1 45448236.

CN/0316-2923
**PHILOSOPHIQUES.** [Philosophiques]. Vol. 1 (April 1974)-. Periodical. French (English; summaries and/or abstracts in English). Twice a year (Apr., Nov.). 40.00Can$ (individual), 60.00Can$ (institutions) Canada; 45.00Can$ (individual), 65.00 (institutions) others. Editions Bellarmin, 165 rue Deslauriers, St. Laurent Que H4N 2S4 Canada. **Tel** (514)745-4290, FAX (514)745-4299. **ED** Mrs. Josiane Boulad-Ayoub. **LC** B2; .P5. **DD** 105. **Bk Rev. Pr Rev. Circ:** 500.
**Ind/Abst** Philos. Index; Point Repere (1983-).

GW/0175-6508
**PHILOSOPHISCHE ABHANDLUNGEN.** [Philos. Abh.]. (1935)-. Monographic series. German. ir. Price varies per volume. Vittorio Klostermann, Frauenlobstrasse 22, D 60487 Frankfurt Germany. **Tel** 011 49 69 9708160.
**Ind/Abst** Math. Rev.

GW/0031-8159
**PHILOSOPHISCHE RUNDSCHAU.** [Philos. Rundsch.]. Vol. 1 (1953)-. Periodical. German (English and French). qt. DM132.00. JCB Mohr / Paul Siebeck, Postfach 2040, D 72010 Tuebingen Germany. **Tel** 011 49 7071 9230, FAX 011 49 7071 51104, telex 7/262872 mohr d. **ED** Rudiger Bubner and Bernhard Waldenfels. **LC** B3; .P67. **DD** 105. **[CCC].** cum. index. **Bk Rev. Ad Acc. Circ:** 1,250. Documents available from The Genuine Article.
**Desc:** Has a general outlook on trends, schools and research programs. Fulfills an important function in an age where the unity of philosophy yields to ever growing specialization in isolated disciplines as well as national traditions.
**Ind/Abst** Arts Humanit. Citation Index [Full Cov.]; Curr. Contents Arts Humanit.; Philos. Index; Res. Alert [Full Cov.]; Soc. Sci. Cit. Index [Select. Cov.].

GW/0554-0828
**PHILOSOPHISCHE RUNDSCHAU. BEIHEFT.** (1957)-. Monographic series. German. ir. Price varies per volume. JCB Mohr / Paul Siebeck, Postfach 2040, D 72010 Tuebingen Germany. **Tel** 011 49 7071 9230, FAX 011 49 7071 51104, telex 7/262872 mohr d. **ED** Christin Waldenfels. cum. index. **Bk Rev. Ad Acc. Circ:** 1,250.
**Desc:** Follows the international publications in philosophy with general outlook in trends, schools and research programs.

GW/0031-8175
**PHILOSOPHISCHER LITERATURANZEIGER.** Vol. 1- 1949-. Periodical. German. qt. DM138.00. Vittorio Klostermann, Frauenlobstrasse 22, D 60487 Frankfurt Germany. **Tel** 011 49 69 9708160. **ED** R Luthe, S Nachtsheim and G Wolandt. Index available. **Bk Rev. Ad Acc. Circ:** 800 (ctrl).
**Desc:** Reviews of philosophical books only for philosophers, students of philosophy, university libraries, etc.
**Ind/Abst** Romant. Move.

GW/0031-8183
**PHILOSOPHISCHES JAHRBUCH (FREIBURG).** (PHILOSOPHISCHES JAHRBUCH.). [Philos. Jahrb.]. **Added/Corp** Goerres-Gesellschaft. Vol. 1 (1888)-. Periodical. German. Twice a year (Mar., Oct.). DM104.00. Verlag Herder Freiburg, Postfach 79080, Frieburg, Germany. **Tel** (0761)27-17-0, FAX (0761)27 17-520, telex 761489. **ED** Hermann Krings. **LC** B3; .P75. **[CCC].** Index available (Free). cum. index. **Bk Rev. Circ:** 800. Documents available from The Genuine Article.
**Ind/Abst** Arts Humanit. Citation Index (19??-19??) [Full Cov.]; Bibliogr. Mission.; Curr. Contents Arts Humanit.; Math. Rev.; MLA Int. Bibl. Books Artic. Mod. Lang. Lit.; Philos. Index; Res. Alert [Full Cov.]; Romant. Move.; Soc. Sci. Cit. Index [Select. Cov.].

UK
**PHILOSOPHY.** Vol. 1 (Jan. 1926)-. Academic Scholarly Publication. English. bm. $150.00 US and Canada; £72.00 UK; £79.00 other. Cambridge University Press, The Edinburgh Building, Shaftesbury Road, Cambridge CB2 2RU United Kingdom. **Tel** 011 44 223 312393, FAX 011 44 223 325959. **(Subscription address:** US/ 110 Midland Avenue, Port Chester, NY 10573**) ED** Renford Barnbrough. **LC** B1. **Bk Rev.** available on microfilm. Documents available from The Genuine Article.
**Desc:** Concerned with the study of logic, metaphysics, aesthetics, social and political philosophy and the philosophies of religion, science, history, language, mind and education.
**Ind/Abst** Am. Hist. Life; Br. Humanit. Index; Expand. Acad. Index (1989-); Humanit. Index; Middle East Abstr. Index; Res. Alert [Full Cov.]; Soc. Plann. Policy Dev. Abstr.; Sociol. Abstr. (?-?).

US
**PHILOSOPHY AND COMPUTING.** ***Ceased.*** (19??)-(1993). English. qt. Ablex Publishing Corporation, 355 Chestnut Street, Norwood NJ 07648. **Tel** (201)767-8450, (201)767-8455 (Customer Service), FAX (201)767-6717.

US/0190-0013
**PHILOSOPHY AND LITERATURE.** [Philos. lit.]. **Added/Corp** University of Michigan--Dearborn. Whitman College. Vol. 1 (Fall 1976)-. Periodical. English. Twice a year (Apr., & Oct.). $43.00 US; $46.00 Canada & Mexico; $48.50 other. Johns Hopkins University Press, 2715 North Charles Street, Baltimore MD 21218-4319. **Tel** (410)516-6987, FAX (410)516-6968. **(Subscription address:** John Hopkins University Press, Journals Publishing Division, PO Box 19966, Baltimore MD 21211.**) ED** Denis Dutton and Patrick Henry. **LC** PN2; .P5. **DD** 809. **CODEN** PHILEL. **[CCC].** Index available. **Bk Rev. Ad Acc. Circ:** 1,000. available on microfilm and microfiche from University Microfilms International (UMI). Documents available from The Genuine Article.
**Desc:** Publishes philosophical interpretations of literature and literary investigations of classic works in philosophy.
**Ind/Abst** Abstr. Engl. Stud.; Am. Bibliogr. Slavic East Europ. Stud.; Am. Humanit. Index; Annu. Bibliogr. Engl. Lang. Lit.; Arts Humanit. Citation Index [Full Cov.]; Curr. Contents Arts Humanit.; Lit. Crit. Regist.; MLA Int. Bibl. Books Artic. Mod. Lang. Lit.; Philos. Index; Res. Alert [Full Cov.]; Romant. Move.; Soc. Plann. Policy Dev. Abstr.; Soc. Sci. Cit. Index [Select. Cov.].

NE/0376-7418
**PHILOSOPHY AND MEDICINE.** [Philos. med.]. Vol. 1 (1975)-. Monographic series. English. ir. Price varies per volume. Kluwer Academic Publishers, Postbus 322, 3300 AH Dordrecht, The Netherlands. **Tel** 011 (31) 78 524400, FAX 011 31 78 183273, telex 20083. **(Subscription address:** Kluwer Academic Publishers / US Subscriptions, PO Box 253, Accord Station, Hingham MA 02018.**) ED** H. T. Engelhardt Jr and S. F. Spicker. **LC** UNC. **NLM** W3 PH609. **CODEN** PHIMDN. Documents available from BIOSIS Document Express.
**Ind/Abst** Biol. Abstr.

US/0031-8205
**PHILOSOPHY AND PHENOMENOLOGICAL RESEARCH.** [Philos. phenomenol. res.]. **Added/Corp** International Phenomenological Society. Vol. 1, (Sept. 1940)-. Periodical. English. Four times a year (Mar., June, Sept., Dec.). $19.00 (individuals); $53.00 (institutions) US. Philosophy & Phenomenological Research, Box 1947, Brown University, Providence RI 02912-1947. **Tel** (401)863-3215, FAX (401)863-2719. **ED** Ernest Sosa. **LC** B1; .P57. **DD** 105. **CODEN** PPHRAI. **Bk Rev**, (Qty: 25-30). **Ad Acc, Adv Mgr:** S. Berwnad, **Tel** (401)863-3215. **Pr Rev. Circ:** 1,800. available on microfiche from Johnson Associates; available on microfilm from Xerox; available on microfilm and microfiche from University Microfilms International (UMI). Documents available from The Genuine Article.
**Desc:** Publishes a wide range of areas including philosophy of mind, epistemology, ethics, metaphysics, and the philosophical history of philosophy.
**Ind/Abst** Am. Bibliogr. Slavic East Europ. Stud.; Annu. Bibliogr. Engl. Lang. Lit.; Arts Humanit. Citation Index [Full Cov.]; Crim. Penol. Police Sci. Abstr.; Curr. Contents Arts Humanit.; Expand. Acad. Index (March 1990-June 1990); Index Book Rev. Humanit.; Middle East Abstr. Index; MLA Int. Bibl. Books Artic. Mod. Lang. Lit.; Philos. Index; Psychol. Abstr. (1965-); Res. Alert [Full Cov.]; Soc. Plann. Policy Dev. Abstr.; Soc. Sci. Cit. Index [Select. Cov.]; Sociol. Abstr.

US/0031-8213
**PHILOSOPHY & RHETORIC.** [Philos. rhetor.]. **VAT** Philosophy and Rhetoric. Vol. 1 (Jan. 1968)-. Periodical. English. qt. $40.00 (institutions), $27.50 (individuals) US; $48.00 (institutions), $35.00 (individuals) other. Pennsylvania State University Press, 820 North University Drive, Suite C, University Park PA 16802-1003. **Tel** (814)865-1327, (800)326-9180, FAX (814)863-1408. **ED** Donald Phillip Verene. **LC** B1; .P572. **DD** 105. **UDC** 105. **[CCC]. Circ:** 950. available on microfilm and microfiche from University Microfilms International (UMI). Documents available from The Genuine Article.
**Ind/Abst** Abstr. Engl. Stud.; Annu. Bibliogr. Engl. Lang. Lit.; Arts Humanit. Citation Index [Full Cov.]; Curr. Contents Arts Humanit.; Lit. Crit. Regist.; MLA Int. Bibl. Books Artic. Mod. Lang. Lit.; Philos. Index; Res. Alert [Full Cov.]; Romant. Move.; Soc. Plann. Policy Dev. Abstr.; Soc. Sci. Cit. Index [Select. Cov.].

US/0191-4537
**PHILOSOPHY & SOCIAL CRITICISM.** [Philos. soc. crit.]. **VFOAT** Philosophy and Social Criticism. Vol. 5 (Jan. 1978)-. Periodical. English. Six times a year. $160.00. Sage Publications Ltd., 6 Bonhill Street, London EC2A 4PU, UK. **Tel** 071 374 0645, FAX 071 374 8741, telex 296207 SAGE G. **LC** AS30; .C84. **DD** 301. **Bk Rev. Ad Acc. Acid Free. Circ:** 700 (ctrl). ***Continues*** *Cultural Hermeneutics.*
**Desc:** Strives to foster a critical attitude in politics and social theory, socio-economic thought, critique of science, theory and praxis.
**Ind/Abst** Am. Bibliogr. Slavic East Europ. Stud.; BHA : Biblio. Hist. Art; Left Index; Philos. Index; Soc. Plann. Policy Dev. Abstr.; Sociol. Abstr.

US/0031-8221
**PHILOSOPHY EAST & WEST.** [Philos. east west]. **VAT** Philosophy East and West. Vol. 1 (April 1951)-. Periodical. English. qt (January, April, July and October). $33.00 (one year), $59.00 (two year) institution, $26.00 (one year), $47.00 (two year) individual, $13.00 (student). University of Hawaii Press, 2840 Kolowalu Street, Honolulu HI 96822. **Tel** (808)956-8833, (808)948-8697, FAX (808)988-6052. **ED** Roger T. Ames. **LC** B1; .P573. **DD** 105. **Bk Rev. Ad Acc. Circ:** 1,400. available on microfilm and microfiche from University Microfilms International (UMI). Documents available from The Genuine Article, UMI Article Clearinghouse.
**Desc:** Journal of Asian and comparative thought, with specialized articles that relate philosophy to the arts, literature, science, and social practice of Asian civilizations.
**Ind/Abst** Acad. Search (July 1993-); Annu. Bibliogr. Engl. Lang. Lit.; Arts Humanit. Citation Index [Full Cov.]; Curr. Contents Arts Humanit.; Expand. Acad. Index (1989-); Humanit. Index; Humanit. Source (Jul. 1993-); INFO-SOUTH Abstr.; Int. Bibliogr. Sociol.; Mag. Search; Middle East Abstr. Index; MLA Int. Bibl. Books Artic. Mod. Lang. Lit.; Newsp. Period. Abstr. (1991-); Philos. Index; Relig. Theol. Abstr.; Res. Alert [Full Cov.]; Soc. Plann. Policy Dev. Abstr.; Soc. Sci. Cit. Index [Select. Cov.]; Sociol. Abstr.

US/0742-2733
**PHILOSOPHY IN CONTEXT.** ***Suspended.*** [Philos. context]. Vol. 1- 1972-?. Periodical. English. an. $10.00. Cleveland State University / Philosophy Department, Philosophy Department, Euclid Avenue at East 24th Street, Cleveland OH 44115. **Tel** (216)687-3900. **ED** Richard M Fox and Joseph P DeMarco. **LC** B1; .P574. **DD** 105. **Bk Rev. Ad Acc. Circ:** 200.
**Desc:** Original philosophical essays about the theory and practice of applied philosophy.
**Ind/Abst** Philos. Index.

UK/0031-8191
**PHILOSOPHY (LONDON).** (PHILOSOPHY : THE JOURNAL OF THE BRITISH INSTITUTE OF PHILOSOPHICAL STUDIES.). [Philosophy]. **Added/Corp** British Institute of Philosophical Studies. British Institute of Philosophy. Royal Institute of Philosophy. Vol. 6, No. 22 (April 1931)-. Academic Scholarly Publication. English. Four times a year (plus 2 supplements). $195.00 US, Canada and Mexico; £108.00 other. Cambridge University Press, The Edinburgh Building, Shaftesbury Road, Cambridge CB2 2RU United Kingdom. **Tel** 011 44 223 312393, FAX 011 44 223 325959. **(Subscription address:** Cambridge University Press / North America, 110 Midland Avenue, Port Chester NY 10573.**) ED** Renford Bambrough. **LC** B1; .P55. **Bk Rev. Ad Acc. Circ:** 2,200. available on microfilm and microfiche from University Microfilms International (UMI). Documents available from UMI Article Clearinghouse. ***Continues*** *Journal of Philosophical Studies.*
**Desc:** The journal of the Royal Institute of Philosophy. Founded to build bridges between specialist philosophers and a wider educated public. Contributors are required to avoid needless technicality of language and presentation. Each issue contains an editorial on a topic of philosophical or public interest, and a "New Books" section.
**Ind/Abst** Acad. Search (Jan. 1994-); Am. Hist. Life (1955-1973); Arts Humanit. Citation Index [Full Cov.]; Humanit. Index; Humanit. Source (Jul. 1993-); INFO-SOUTH Abstr.; Mag. Search; Newsp. Period. Abstr. (1991-); Philos. Index; Soc. Sci. Cit. Index [Select. Cov.].

US
**PHILOSOPHY, PSYCHIATRY, & PSYCHOLOGY.** (1993)-. Periodical. English. Four times a year. $85.00 US; $89.50 Canada & Mexico; $94.00 other. Johns Hopkins University Press, 2715 North Charles Street, Baltimore MD 21218-4319. **Tel** (410)516-6987, FAX (410)516-6968. **(Subscription address:** John Hopkins University Press, Journals Publishing Division, PO Box 19966, Baltimore MD 21211.**)**

US/0890-2461
**PHILOSOPHY, THEOLOGY.** [Philos. theol.]. **Added/Corp** Marquette University. Dept. of Philosophy. Marquette University. Theology Dept. **VFOAT** Philosophy and Theology; Philosophy & Theology. Vol. 1, No. 1 (Fall 1986)-. Periodical. English. Four times a year (Mar., June, Sept., Dec.). $25.00 US & Canada; $35.00 other. Philosophy and Theology / Marquette University Press, Cudahy Hall, 1313 West Wisconsin Avenue, Milwaukee WI 53233. **Tel** (414)288-6857, (414)288-7170, FAX (414)288-3300. **ED** Reverend Phillip Rossi, S. J. (editor's address: Department of Theology, Marquette University, Milwaukee, WI 53233). **DD** 100. **Circ:** 175. available on diskette.
**Ind/Abst** Index Book Rev. Relig.; Philos. Index; Relig. Index One Period.

US/0031-8256
**PHILOSOPHY TODAY (CELINA).** (PHILOSOPHY TODAY.). [Philos. today]. **Added/Corp** Priests of the Most Precious Blood. Vol. 1, (Mar. 1957)-. Periodical. English. Four times a year. $21.00 (one year), $40.00 (two year), $58.00 (three year). Philosophy Today, DePaul University, 2320 North Kenmore Avenue, Chicago IL 60614-3214. **Tel** (312)362-8767, FAX (312)341-5324. **ED** David Pellauer. **LC** B1; .P576. **DD** 150/.5. Index available. cum. index. **Bk Rev. Ad Acc. Pr Rev. Circ:** 1,150. available on microfilm and microfiche from University Microfilms International (UMI). Documents available from The Genuine Article, UMI Article Clearinghouse.
**Desc:** Trends and interest of contemporary philosophy: existentialism, phenomenology, hermeneutics, post-structuralism, philosophy of language.
**Ind/Abst** Acad. Abstr. Full Text Elite (Jan. 1990-); Acad. Abstr. (July 1990-); Acad. Search (Jan. 1990-); Annu. Bibliogr. Engl. Lang. Lit.; Arts Humanit. Citation Index [Full Cov.]; Curr. Contents Arts Humanit.; Expand. Acad. Index (1989-); Humanit. Index; Humanit. Source (Jul. 1990-); INFO-SOUTH Abstr.; Mag. Search; Newsp. Period. Abstr. (1988-); Philos. Index; Res. Alert [Full Cov.]; Abr. Cathol. Period. Lit. Index; Cathol. Period. Lit. Index.

NE/0031-8868
**PHRONESIS.** [Phronesis]. Vol. 1 (Nov. 1955)-. Periodical. English (French, German and Latin). Three times a year. Fl70.00 (students), Fl105.00 (regular) Netherlands; Fl95.00 (students), Fl130.00 (regular) other. Van Gorcum & Company BV, PO Box 43, NL 9400 AA Assen Netherlands. **Tel** 011 31 5920 46846, FAX 011 31 5920 72064. **ED** D J Allan and J B Skemp. **LC** B1; .P59. **DD** 180. Index available in last issue of volume--attached. cum. index. **Bk Rev. Ad Acc. Circ:** 1,100 (ctrl). Documents available from The Genuine Article.
**Desc:** An international journal focused on the study of philosophy from its very beginning to the sixth century after Christ.
**Ind/Abst** Arts Humanit. Citation Index [Full Cov.]; Index Book Rev. Humanit.; Philos. Index; Res. Alert [Full Cov.].

NE/0031-8868
**PHRONESIS (HEIDELBERG, GERMANY).** (PHRONESIS.). (19??)-. Academic Scholarly Publication. English (French, German and Italian). Three times a year. Fl105.00 Netherlands; Fl130.00 other. Van Gorcum & Company BV, PO Box 43, NL 9400 AA Assen Netherlands. **Tel** 011 31 5920 46846, FAX 011 31 5920 72064. **ED** Bob Sharples. Index available. **Bk Rev. Ad Acc. Circ:** 1,100. Documents available from FAXON Xpress, The UnCover Company.
**Ind/Abst** Arts Humanit. Citation Index; Curr. Contents; Index Book Rev. Humanit.; Philos. Index.

US/1056-8522
**PLANETARY CITIZEN : HONORING THE EARTH, HUMANITY, AND THE SACRED IN ALL LIFE.** ***Ceased.*** (1991)-(1993). Periodical. English. qt. Planetary Citizen, Meetinghouse Road, PO Box 640, Walpole NH 03608. ***Continues*** *Intentions, 1053-5446.*

NE/0303-8157
**POZNAN STUDIES IN THE PHILOSOPHY OF THE SCIENCES AND THE HUMANITIES.** **VFOAT** Studies in the Philosophy of the Sciences and the Humanities; Poznan Studies. (1975)-. Monographic series. English. ir. Price varies per volume. Editions Rodopi BV, Keizersgracht 302-304, 1016 Ex Amsterdam Netherlands. **Tel** 011 31 20 6227507, FAX 011 31 20 380948. **CODEN** PSSHEY. Index available.
**Desc:** Covers philosophical issues relating to history, law, and society.
**Ind/Abst** Philos. Index.

II
**PRAJNALOKA (NAGPUR, INDIA).** (PRAJNALOKA.). Periodical. Marathi (Marathi). qt. Rs10.00. Bharatiya Dharana Samiti, Ruikar Road, Nagpur 440002 India. **LC** DS423; .P74.

BL
**PRESENCA FILOSOFICA.** No. 1/3- 1974-. Portuguese. $25.00. Sociedade Brasileira de Filosofos Catolicos, Via Anhanguera KM 26, Caixa Postal 11.587, Sao Paulo Brazil. **LC** B5; .P7. **DD** 105.

RU
**PROBLEMY DIALEKTIKI.** **Added/Corp** Problemnyi Sovet po Materialisticheskoi Dialektike. Vol. 1 (1972)-. Russian. an. St Petersburg State University / Izdatelstvo Leningradskogo Universiteta, Universitetskaia Nab 7/9, 199034 St Petersburg Russia. **Tel** 011 95 218-97-88, FAX 011 95 218-51-52, telex 121481. **LC** B809.8; .P718.

US/0065-972X
**PROCEEDINGS AND ADDRESSES OF THE AMERICAN PHILOSOPHICAL ASSOCIATION.** [Proc. addresses Am. Philos. Assoc.]. **Main/Corp** American Philosophical Association. Vol. 1 (1927)-. Periodical. English. Five times a year. $50.00. American Philosophical Association, University of Delaware, Newark DE 19716. **Tel** (302)831-1112, FAX (302)831-8690. **LC** B11; .A52. **DD** 106/.073. Index available. cum. index. **Ad Acc, Adv Mgr:** Donna Benedetti, **Tel** (302)831-2012. **Circ:** 9,200 (ctrl). available on microfilm and microfiche from University Microfilms International (UMI). ***Supersedes*** *American Philosophical Association. Proceedings of the Annual Meeting.*
**Desc:** Contains the presidential addresses delivered to each of its divisions, the minutes of the meetings of the divisions and of the board of officers. Reports of APA committees, contributed articles on "Issues in the Profession," notices of conferences and publications.
**Ind/Abst** Philos. Index.

US/0065-7638
**PROCEEDINGS OF THE AMERICAN CATHOLIC PHILOSOPHICAL ASSOCIATION.** [Proc. Am. Cathol. Philos. Assoc.]. **Main/Corp** American Catholic Philosophical Association. Vol. 11 (1935)-. Proceedings. English. an. $20.00 US; $23.00 other. American Catholic Philosophy Association, Catholic University, 403 Administration Building, Washington DC 20064. **Tel** (202)635-5518, FAX (202)635-5518. **ED** Robert Wood (editor's address: 1845 East Northgate Drive, Irving TX 75062). **LC** B11; .A4. **DD** 105. Index available. cum. index. **Pr Rev. Circ:** 1,600. available on microfilm and microfiche from University Microfilms International (UMI). ***Continues*** *Proceedings of the Annual Meeting of the American Catholic Philosophical Association.*
**Desc:** Philosophical research and scholarship.
**Ind/Abst** Philos. Index; Abr. Cathol. Period. Lit. Index; Cathol. Period. Lit. Index.

US/0003-049X
**PROCEEDINGS OF THE AMERICAN PHILOSOPHICAL SOCIETY.** (PROCEEDINGS OF THE AMERICAN PHILOSOPHICAL SOCIETY HELD AT PHILADELPHIA FOR PROMOTING USEFUL KNOWLEDGE.). [Proc. Am. Phil. Soc.]. **Added/Corp** American Philosophical Society. Vol. 1, No. 1 (Jan./March 1838)-. Monographic series. English. ir. Price varies per volume. American Philosophical Society, PO Box 40098, Philadelphia PA 19106. **Tel** (215)440-3427, FAX (215)440-3436. **LC** Q11; .P5. **NLM** W1 PR584KV. **CODEN** PAPCAA. cum. index. available on microfilm and microfiche from University Microfilms International (UMI). Documents available from Article Express International, The Genuine Article, BIOSIS Document Express, Ask*IEEE, CASDDS.
**Desc:** Contains papers which have been read at the Spring and Autumn meetings of the Society and others

that have been accepted by the Committee on Publications. Several important symposia held at the Society have been published in the Proceedings, notably those on Copernicus, Milton, Computers and American Society, Animal Communities, Ecology of Child Development, and more recently, Penological Practices and Reforms.
**Ind/Abst** ABC POL SCI; Am. Hist. Life (1955-); Am. Bibliogr. Slavic East Europ. Stud.; Annu. Bibliogr. Engl. Lang. Lit.; ARTbibliogr. Mod.; Arts Humanit. Citation Index [Full Cov.]; Biol. Abstr.; Chem. Abstr.; Curr. Contents Arts Humanit.; Ei Page One; Eng. Index Annu.; Geogr. Abstr. Human Geogr.; GeoRef; Index Period. Artic. Relat. Law; INSPEC; Int. Aerosp. Abstr.; MLA Int. Bibl. Books Artic. Mod. Lang. Lit.; PAIS Int. Print (1991-); Life Sci. Collect.; Res. Alert [Full Cov.]; Romant. Move.; Soc. Plann. Policy Dev. Abstr.; Sociol. Abstr.

UK/0066-7374
**PROCEEDINGS OF THE ARISTOTELIAN SOCIETY.** [Proc. Aristot. Soc.]. **Main/Corp** Aristotelian Society (Great Britain). Vol. 1-3, No. 2 (1887/1888)-. Proceedings. English. an. £32.00 UK & Europe; $56.00 North America; £37.50 other. Basil Blackwell Publishers Ltd, 108 Cowley Road, Oxford 0X4 1JF England. **Tel** 011 44 865 791100, FAX 011 44 865 791347, telex 837022 OXBOOK G. **(Subscription address:** Blackwell Publishers / UK, Marston Book Services, PO Box 87, Oxford OX2 0DT England.**) DD** 104. cum. index. **Ad Acc.**
**Desc:** Includes report of the executive committee and more.
**Ind/Abst** Philos. Index; Soc. Plann. Policy Dev. Abstr.

US
**PROCEEDINGS OF THE BOSTON AREA COLLOQUIUM IN ANCIENT PHILOSOPHY.** Proceedings. English. an. $20.00 (paper), $35.00 (cloth). University Press of America, 4720 A Boston Way, Lanham MD 20706. **Tel** (301)459-3366, (800)462-6420.
**Ind/Abst** Philos. Index.

UK/0078-0251
**PROCEEDINGS OF THE UNIVERSITY OF NEWCASTLE-UPON-TYNE PHILOSOPHICAL SOCIETY.** [Proc. Univ. N.castle. Tyne Philos. Soc.]. **Main/Corp** Newcastle-Upon-Tyne. University. Philosophical Society. Vol. 1 (1964)-. Proceedings. English. **CODEN** PUNSAI. Documents available from Ask*IEEE. ***Continues*** *Durham, England. University. Philosophical Society. Proceedings of the University of Durham Philosophical Society. Series A. Science; Durham, England. University. Philosophical Society. Proceedings of the University of Durham Philosophical Society. Series B. Art.*
**Ind/Abst** INSPEC (1968-).

US/0360-6503
**PROCESS STUDIES.** [Process stud.]. Vol. 1 (Spring 1971)-. Academic Scholarly Publication. English. Four times a year (Jan., Apr., July, Oct.,). $50.00 (one year) membership; $30.00 (institutions); $20.00 (individuals);. Center for Process Studies, 1325 North College Avenue, Claremont CA 91711. **Tel** (909)626-3521 Ext. 224. **ED** Lewis Ford. **LC** BD372; .P75. **DD** 230. Index available. **Bk Rev. Ad Acc. Circ:** 1,150 (ctrl). available on microfilm and microfiche from University Microfilms International (UMI). Documents available from The Genuine Article.
**Desc:** Scholarly articles and book reviews exploring the wide range of applications of process philosophy from theology to natural sciences.
**Ind/Abst** Arts Humanit. Citation Index [Full Cov.]; Curr. Contents Arts Humanit.; Index Book Rev. Relig.; Old Testam. Abstr.; Philos. Index; Relig. Index One Period. (1975-); Relig. Theol. Abstr.; Res. Alert [Full Cov.].

US/0734-3027
**PROPHETIC VOICES (NOVATO, CALIF.).** **See** Literature.

US/0030-8250
**PRS JOURNAL.** **VAT** Philosophy, Religion, Science Journal; Philosophical Research Society Journal. V. 1- Aug. 1941-. Periodical. English. qt. $11.00 domestic; $12.00 other. Philosophical Research Society, 3910 Los Feliz Boulevard, Los Angeles CA 90027-2399. **Tel** (310)663-2167. **ED** Manly P Hall and Edith Waldron. **LC** BF1995. **Circ:** 1,600 (ctrl). available on microfilm and microfiche from University Microfilms International (UMI). ***Continues*** *Horizon.*
**Desc:** Useful knowledge in the fields of philosophy, comparative religions and psychology.

US/0270-8647
**PSA (EAST LANSING, MICH.).** **See** Science and Technology.

IT/0076-8677
**PUBBLICAZIONI DELL'UNIVERSITA CATTOLICA DEL SACRO CUORE. CONTRIBUTI, SERIE III. SCIENZE FILOSOFICHE.** ***Ceased.*** **Main/Corp** Universita Cattolica del Sacro Cuore. **Added/Corp** Universita Cattolica del Sacro Cuore Pubblicazioni Dell'Universita Cattolica del Sacro Cuore. Serie III. Scienze Filosofiche. (1960)-(19??). Monographic series. Italian. **LC** B29; .M52.

US/0887-0373
**PUBLIC AFFAIRS QUARTERLY.** [Public aff. q.]. **Added/Corp** Bowling Green State University. Philosophy Documentation Center. Vol. 1, No. 1 (Jan. 1987)-. Academic Scholarly Publication. English. qt. $132.00 (institutions), $38.00 (individuals). Philosophy Documentation Center, Bowling Green State University, Bowling Green OH 43403-0189. **Tel** (419)372-2419, (800)444-2419, FAX (419)372-6987. **LC** H96; .P83. **DD** 361.6/7/05. **Circ:** 300.
**Desc:** Scholarly journal devoted to the philosophical study of public policy issues; seeks to enhance the quality of our understanding of public issues by publishing essays that bring philosophical depth and sophistication to the consideration of matters on the agenda of public debate that would otherwise be left to the tender mercies of political rhetoric and journalistic oversimplication.
**Ind/Abst** Int. Bibliogr. Sociol.; PAIS Int. Print; Philos. Index.

GW
**QUELLEN UND STUDIEN ZUR PHILOSOPHIE.** Vol. 1 (1971)-. Monographic series. German. ir. Price varies per volume. Walter de Gruyter Inc., PO Box 303421, D 10728 Berlin Germany. **Tel** 011 49 30 260050, FAX 011 49 30 26005251. **(Subscription address:** US and Canada/ 200 Saw Mill River Road, Hawthorne, NY 10532**) LC** B23; .Q45. ***Continues*** *Quellen und Studien zur Geschichte der Philosophie.*
**Ind/Abst** Math. Rev.

ZA/1011-226X
**QUEST (LUSAKA, ZAMBIA).** (QUEST.). **Added/Corp** University of Zambia. Dept. of Philosophy. **VFOAT** Quest, Philosophical Discussions; Philosophical Discussions. Vol. 1, No. 1 (June 1987)-. Periodical. English (French; summaries and/or abstracts in Multiple languages). Twice a year (June and December). $20.00 (institutions), $15.00 (individuals) Africa; $35.00 (institutions), $25.00 (individuals) other. Quest/Zambia, PO Box 9114, 9703 LC Croningen Netherlands. **Tel** 31 (0)50-418862, FAX 31(0)50-636160. **ED** P. Boele van Hensbroek. **LC** B1; .A235. **DD** 199/.6/05. Index available (Bound in 2nd issues every 3rd year.). cum. index. **Bk Rev**, (Qty: 10). **Ad Acc. Circ:** 150.
**Desc:** An African Journal of Philosophy.
**Ind/Abst** Int. Bibliogr. Sociol.

US/1040-533X
**QUEST (WHEATON, ILL.), THE.** (THE QUEST.). [Quest]. **Added/Corp** Theosophical Society in America. Vol. 1, No. 1 (Autumn 1988)-. Periodical. English. Four times a year (Feb., May, Aug., Nov.). $13.97 one year; $25.97 two years. Theosophical Society in America, Box 270, Wheaton IL 60189-0270. **Tel** (708)668-1571, FAX (708)665-8791. **(Subscription address:** Quest, PO Box 3000, Denville, N.J. 07834**) ED** William Metzger. **DD** 291. **Bk Rev**, (Qty: 24). **Ad Acc, Adv Mgr:** Ray. **Circ:** 25,000. ***Separated from*** *American Theosophist, 0003-1402.*
**Desc:** An journal about philosophy science, religion, and the arts.

UK/0300-211X
**RADICAL PHILOSOPHY.** **Added/Corp** Radical Philosophy Group (Great Britain). (Jan. 1972)-. Periodical. English. Three times a year. £18.00 (institutions), £8.50 (individuals, one year) £16.00 (two year) UK; £29.00/$60.00 (institutions, one year), £11.00/$20.00 (individuals, one year) £21.00 (two year) (surface mail), £15.00/$30.00 (individuals, one year), £35.00/$80.00 (institutions, one year), £28.00/$56.00 (two year) (air mail) other. Radical Philosophy, Open Univ. Milton, Keynes MK7 6AA England. **LC** B1; .R25. cum. index. **Bk Rev. Ad Acc. Circ:** 2,000.
**Desc:** Aims to criticize the current state of academic philosophy and to encourage philosophical discussion on the left.
**Ind/Abst** Arts Humanit. Citation Index [Select. Cov.]; Br. Humanit. Index; Left Index; Philos. Index; Soc. Sci. Cit. Index [Full Cov.].

YU/0352-6798
**RADOVI. RAZDIO FILOZOFIJE, PSIHOLOGIJE, SOCIOLOGIJE I PEDAGOGIJE / SVEUCILISTE U SPLITU, FILOZOFSKI FAKULTET--ZADAR.** **Added/Corp** Sveuciliste u Splitu. Filozofski Fakultet Zadar. **VFOAT** Razdio Filozofije, Psihologije, Sociologije i Pedagogije. (1984/1985)-. Serbo-Croatian (Roman) (English). an. **LC** B1; .A237.
**Ind/Abst** Soc. Plann. Policy Dev. Abstr.

CI/0350-3623
**RADOVI - SVEUCILISTE U SPLITU, FILOZOFSKI FAKULTET, RAZDIO FILOLOS-KIH ZNANOSTI.** (RADOVI. RAZDIO DRUSTVENIH ZNANOSTI / SVEUCILISTE U ZAGREBU, FILOZOFSKI FAKULTET, ZADAR.). [Rad. - Sveuc. Splitu, Filoz. fak., Razdio filol. znan.]. **Added/Corp** Sveuciliste u Zagrebu. Filozofski Fakultet u Zadru. Sveuciliste u Splitu. Filozofski Fakultet Zadar. **VFOAT** Razdio Drustvenih Znanosti. (19??)-. Serbo-Croatian (Roman) (summaries and/or abstracts in English, French, German and Italian). an. **LC** DR1202; .R33. **CODEN** RFFZEM.
**Ind/Abst** Art Archaeol. Tech. Abstr.; Soc. Plann. Policy Dev. Abstr.

FR/0033-9075
**RAISON PRESENTE.** [Raison presente]. No. 1 (1966)-. Periodical. French. Four times a year. 250.00F France; 260.00F other. Nouvelles ED Rationalistes, 14 rue de l'Ecole Polytechnique, 75005 Paris France. **Tel** 33 1 46330350. **ED** Gabriel Gohan. **Circ:** 2,000.
**Desc:** Essays on various subjects such as education, physics, psychology, history, politics, etc.
**Ind/Abst** PAIS Int. Print; Soc. Plann. Policy Dev. Abstr.; Sociol. Abstr.

IT/0557-6857
**RASSEGNA DI LETTERATURA TOMISTICA.** **See** Literature.

UK/0034-0006
**RATIO (OXFORD).** (RATIO.). [Ratio]. Vol. 1 (Dec. 1957)-. Academic Scholarly Publication. English. Three times a year. £77.00 UK and Europe; $153.00 North America; £99.00 other. Basil Blackwell Publishers Ltd, 108 Cowley Road, Oxford 0X4 1JF England. **Tel** 011 44 865 791100, FAX 011 44 865 791347, telex 837022 OXBOOK G. **(Subscription address:** Blackwell Publishers / UK, Marston Book Services, PO Box 87, Oxford OX2 0DT England.**) ED** Martin Hollis. **LC** B1; .R27. **[CCC]. Bk Rev. Ad Acc.** available on microfilm and microfiche from University Microfilms International (UMI). Documents available from The Genuine Article. ***Supersedes*** *Abhandlungen der Frieschen Schule.*
**Desc:** Deals with all branches of pure and applied philosophy.
**Ind/Abst** Arts Humanit. Citation Index [Full Cov.]; Br. Humanit. Index; Curr. Contents Arts Humanit.; Math. Rev.; Philos. Index; Res. Alert [Full Cov.]; Soc. Plann. Policy Dev. Abstr.; Sociol. Abstr.

FR/0180-0345
**RECHERCHES SUR LE XVIIEME SIECLE / CENTRE D'HISTORIE DES SCIENCES ET DES DOCTRINES.** **VFOAT** Recherches sur le XVIIE Siecle; Recherches sur le 17E Siecle; Recherches sur le Dix-Septieme Siecle. Began in 1976. Periodical. French (Italian). sa. Editions du CNRS, 22 rue Saint Armand, F 75015 Paris France. **Tel** 011 33 1 45075050. **LC** CB401; .R43. **DD** 909/.6/05. **Circ:** 1,500.
**Desc:** French-Italian accounts dedicated to the philosophy of the 17th Century.

US
**REPORTS OF INVESTIGATIONS - INSTITUTE FOR THE STUDY OF EARTH AND MAN.** **Main/Corp** Southern Methodist University, Dallas, Texas. Institute for the Study of Earth and Man. 1-. English. ir. Southern Methodist University / English, Department of English, c/o Theresa Enos, Dallas TX 75275. **Tel** (214)692-2945.

PL/0324-8712
**REPORTS ON PHILOSOPHY.** [Rep. philos.]. Periodical. English. Z20.00 per copy. Polish Scientific Publishers, Nosy Swiat 69, Warszawa Poland. **Tel** 26-07-46, 26-84-78, telex IPNIS PL WARSZAWA 812285. **LC** B1; .R3. **DD** 105. ***Supersedes*** *Prace Filozoficzne.*
**Ind/Abst** Philos. Index.

CN/0383-6150
**RES BUREAUX BULLETIN.** **Main/Corp** Res Bureaux. No. 1- July 15, 1974-. Bulletin. English. ir. Free. Res Bureaux, PO Box 1598, Kingston Ontario K7L 5C8 Canada. **DD** 001.9/4/05.

US/0085-5553
**RESEARCH IN PHENOMENOLOGY.** [Res. phenomenol.]. **VFOAT** RP. Vol. 1, (1971)-. English. an. $49.95 (institutions); $39.95 (individuals); $29.95 (Back Issues). Humanities Press, 165 1st Avenue, Atlantic Highlands NJ 07716. **Tel** (908)872-1441, (800)221-3845, FAX (908)872-0717, telex 752233. **ED** John Sallis, Vanderbilt University, Nashville, TN. **LC** B829.5; .R47. **DD** 142/.7. **Bk Rev. Ad Acc, Adv Mgr:** J. Camlin, **Tel** (908)872-1441. **Circ:** 400. available on microfilm and microfiche from University Microfilms International (UMI). Documents available from The Genuine Article, UMI Article Clearinghouse.
**Desc:** Dedicated to encouraging original, creative phenomenological research, to furthering the interpretative and critical study of the writings of major phenomenological philosophers, and to providing in-depth reviews of the most important current work in phenomenology.
**Ind/Abst** Acad. Search (Jan. 1994-); Arts Humanit. Citation Index (19??-19??) [Full Cov.]; Curr. Contents Arts Humanit.; Expand. Acad. Index (1989-); Humanit. Index; Humanit. Source (Jul. 1993-); INFO-SOUTH Abstr.; Mag. Search; Newsp. Period. Abstr. (1991-); Philos. Index; Res. Alert [Full Cov.].

II/0048-7325
**RESEARCH JOURNAL OF PHILOSOPHY & SOCIAL SCIENCES.** Vol. 1, (1963)-. Monographic series. English. Twice a year (Mar., Sept.,). Price varies per volume. Anu Books,

Shivaji Road, Meerut 250001 India. **Tel** 011 91 75346. **(Subscription address:** Prints India, 11 Darya Ganj, New Delhi, 110002 India, (Phone: 011 91 11 3268645)) **ED** Dr. Ram Nath Sharma. **LC** B1; .R335.

BE
**RESEAUX.** **Added/Corp** Universite de Mons. Centre Interdisciplinaire d'Etudes Philosophiques. No. 18/19 (1972)-. French (English). Three times a year. 1200F (institutions), 600F (individuals) Belgium; 1500F (institutions), 900F (individuals) other. Ciephum, 20 Place du Parc, B 7000 Mons Belgium. **Tel** 011 32 65 373736. **LC** AS161; .R28. ***Continues** Revue Universitaire de Science Morale.*
**Desc:** Interdisciplinary journal about moral and political philosophy, focusing on the constant confrontation of human experiences acquired in every work of life.
**Ind/Abst** Int. Polit. Sci. Abstr.; Soc. Plann. Policy Dev. Abstr.; Sociol. Abstr.

US/0743-1244
**RETURN TO THE SOURCE.** **See** Religion and Theology.

II/0258-1701
**REVIEW JOURNAL OF PHILOSOPHY & SOCIAL SCIENCE.** [Rev. j. philos. soc. sci.]. **VFOAT** Review Journal of Philosophy and Social Science. Vol. 1 (1977)-. Periodical. English. Twice a year (Mar., & Sept.). $10.00. Anu Books, Shivaji Road, Meerut 250001 India. **Tel** 011 91 75346. **(Subscription address:** Prints India, 11 Darya Ganj, New Delhi 110002 India.**)** **ED** Michael Belok. **LC** H1; .R43. **DD** 300/.5. Index available. cum. index. **Bk Rev**, (Qty: 1-2). **Circ:** 250 (ctrl).
**Desc:** Concerned with the history of education, such as educational policy studies, the philosophy of education, and education and the social sciences.
**Ind/Abst** Philos. Index.

US/0034-6632
**REVIEW OF METAPHYSICS, THE.** [Rev. metaphys.]. **Added/Corp** Philosophy Education Society. Vol. 1 No. 1 (Sept. 1947)-. Periodical. English. Four times a year. $42.00 institutions; $25.00 individuals; $75.00 sustaining institutions. Catholic University of America / School of Philosophy, Washington DC 20064. **Tel** (202)635-8778, FAX (202)319-4731. **ED** Jude P. Dougherty. **LC** B1; .R34. **DD** 110.5. Index available (Bound in June issue, for $11.00). **Bk Rev**, (Qty: 120). **Ad Acc. Circ:** 2,500. available on microfilm and microfiche from University Microfilms International (UMI). Documents available from The Genuine Article, UMI Article Clearinghouse.
**Desc:** Devoted to the promotion of definitive contributions to philosophical knowledge, regardless of the writers' affiliations.
**Ind/Abst** Acad. Search (Jan. 1994-); Am. Hist. Life (1954-1974); Arts Humanit. Citation Index [Full Cov.]; Bibliogr. Mission.; Book Rev. Index; Curr. Contents Arts Humanit.; Expand. Acad. Index (1989-); Humanit. Index; Humanit. Source (Jul. 1993-); INFO-SOUTH Abstr.; Newsp. Period. Abstr. (1991-); Philos. Index; Res. Alert [Full Cov.]; Soc. Plann. Policy Dev. Abstr.; Soc. Sci. Cit. Index [Select. Cov.]; Sociol. Abstr.

US/0275-6935
**REVISION (CAMBRIDGE, MASS.).** **See** Literature.

US/0899-9937
**REVISIONING PHILOSOPHY.** [Revis. philos.]. English. an. Peter Lang Publishing, 62 West 45th Street, 4th Floor, New York NY 10036. **Tel** (212)764-1471, (800)770-5264, telex 6973364 PLNY. **DD** 101.

US
**REVISIONS (UNIVERSITY OF NOTRE DAME PRESS).** (REVISIONS.). Began publication with V. 1 in 1981. Monographic series. English. Price varies per volume. University of Notre Dame Press, PO Box 635, South Bend IN 46624. **Tel** (219)239-6349, (800)677-3232, FAX (219)239-8148.

BL/0034-7205
**REVISTA BRASILEIRA DE FILOSOFIA.** V. 1- (No. 1- ). Periodical. Portuguese. qt. $20.00. Instituto Brasileiro Filosofia, Rua Barao Itapetininga 88 7, Sao Paulo Brazil. **Tel** 011 55 11 2552149. **LC** B1041; .I553. **DD** 190/.5. available on microfilm and microfiche from University Microfilms International (UMI).

VE
**REVISTA DE FILOSOFIA.** **Added/Corp** Zulia, Venezuela. Universidad. Centro de Estudios Filosoficos. Zulia, Venezuela. Universidad. Centro de Estudios Filosoficos. Revista. **VFOAT** Revista Centro de Estudios Filosoficos. No. 1 (1974)-. Periodical. Spanish. Centro de Estudios Filosoficos de la Facultad de Humanidades y Educacion de la Universidad del Zulia, Edificio Viyaluz, Piso 8 / 8th Floor, Apartado Postal 526, Maracaibo Venezuela. **ED** Angel Munoz Garcia. **LC** B5; .R4113. ***Supersedes** Universidad del Zulia. Centro de Estudios Filosoficos. Boletin del Centro de Estudios Filosoficos.*
**Ind/Abst** Philos. Index.

CL
**REVISTA DE FILOSOFIA.** **Added/Corp** Chile. Universidad, Santiago. Departamento de Filosofia. (1???)-. Periodical. Spanish. mo. $9.60. Universidad de Chile / Linguistica, Deptamento de Literatura, Casilla Postal 10136, Santiago Chile. **Tel** 011 52 2 2725978 Ext 42, FAX 011 52 2 2716823. **LC** B5; .R412.

MX/0185-3481
**REVISTA DE FILOSOFIA.** [Rev. filos.]. 1968-. Periodical. Spanish (English). Three times a year. $35,000 Mexico; $20.00 other. Universidad Iberoamericana / Filosofia, Departamento de Filosofia, Paseo de la Reforma No 880, Lormas de Santa Fe, CP 01210 DF Mexico. **Tel** 011 52 5 570-2074, FAX 011 52 5 570-7070. **ED** Jorge Aguirre Sala. **LC** B5; .R3967. Index available. cum. index. **Bk Rev. Ad Acc. Pr Rev. Circ:** 5,000.
**Desc:** International articles on subjects of philosophy, theology, religion and humanities on a Christian and Catholic vision. (Book reviews and some advertising of titles on the same subject).
**Ind/Abst** Philos. Index.

CR/0034-8252
**REVISTA DE FILOSOFIA DE LA UNIVERSIDAD DE COSTA RICA.** [Rev. filos. Univ. Costa Rica]. **Added/Corp** Universidad de Costa Rica. Departamento de Filosofia. Universidad de Costa Rica. Escuela de Filosofia. Vol. 1, No. 1 (Jan./June 1957)-. Periodical. Spanish (English). Twice a year. $20.00. Universidad de Costa Rica / Editorial, Apartado 75, 2060 Ciudad Universitaria, San Jose Costa Rica. **Tel** 011 506 2247051, 2253133. **ED** Rafael Angel Herra. **LC** B5; .R413. cum. index. **Bk Rev. Pr Rev. Circ:** 750 (ctrl).
**Desc:** Covers philosophy and similar subjects. Specialty and theoretical viewpoints welcome.
**Ind/Abst** Am. Hist. Life (1970-1985); HAPI Hisp. Am. Period. Index; Philos. Index.

VE/0798-1171
**REVISTA DE FILOSOFIA MARACAIBO.** (REVISTA DE FILOSOFIA). [Rev. filos. Maracaibo]. **VFOAT** Revista - Centro de Estudios Filosoficos. (1974)-. Periodical. Spanish. Revista de Filosofia, Edificio Viyaluz, Piso 8, Apartado 526, Maracaibo Venezuela. **ED** Angel Bustillos Pena. **DD** 105. ***Continues** Boletin del Centro de Estudios Filosoficos.*

EC/0556-5987
**REVISTA DE HISTORIA DE LAS IDEAS.** No. 1-2 (1959-60)-. Periodical. Spanish. sa. Casa de la Cultura Ecuatoriana, Nucleo del Azuay, Aptdo. 01-01-4907, Cuenca, Ecuador. **Tel** 593 2 565808, 565721. **LC** B5.
**Ind/Abst** HAPI Hisp. Am. Period. Index.

AG/0325-0725
**REVISTA LATINOAMERICANA DE FILOSOFIA.** [Rev. latinoam. filos.]. **Added/Corp** Centro de Investigaciones Filosoficas. Vol.1 (March 1975)-. Periodical. Portuguese (Spanish; summaries and/or abstracts in English). sa. $36.00 (individuals), $46.00 (institutions). Centro de Investigaciones Filosoficas, Casilla 5379, 1000 Buenos Aires Argentina. **Tel** 011 54 1 7870533. **ED** Osvaldo Guariglia. **LC** B5; .R45. **Bk Rev. Pr Rev. Circ:** 500 (ctrl).
**Desc:** Latin American philosophical journal.
**Ind/Abst** Philos. Index.

PO/0870-5283
**REVISTA PORTUGUESA DE FILOSOFIA.** [Rev. port. filos.]. **Added/Corp** Faculdade de Filosofia (Braga, Portugal). (1945)-. Periodical. Portuguese (Spanish, French, English and German). qt (4 issues). $60.00. Faculdade de Filosofia Braga, Braga Portugal. **Tel** 011 351 53 616200. **DD** 105. Index available (bound in issue). cum. index. **Bk Rev. Ad Acc. Circ:** 1,100.
**Desc:** Studies philosophy.
**Ind/Abst** MLA Int. Bibl. Books Artic. Mod. Lang. Lit.; Philos. Index.

VE/1013-2368
**REVISTA VENEZOLANA DE FILOSOFIA.** [Rev. venez. filos.]. **Added/Corp** Universidad Simon Bolivar. Departamento de Filosofia. Sciedad Venezolana de Filosofia. (1973)-. Spanish. sa. Bs8.00. University Simon Bolivar, Department of Philosophy, Caracas Venezuela. **ED** Angel J Cappelletti. **LC** B5; .R47. **Bk Rev. Circ:** 1,000.
**Desc:** Articles and notes on philosophy and history of philosophy in an open and pluralist direction.
**Ind/Abst** Philos. Index.

FR/0035-1571
**REVUE DE METAPHYSIQUE ET DE MORALE (PARIS, FRANCE : 1945).** (REVUE DE METAPHYSIQUE ET DE MORALE.). [Rev. metaphys. morale]. **Added/Corp** Societe Francaise de Philosophie. (1945)-. Periodical. French. qt. $76.00. Librairie Armand Colin, BP 22, 41354 Vineuil Cedex France. **Tel** 011 33 54 438994. **(Subscription address:** 7A Boulevard de Perolles, CH-1701 Fribourg Switzerland**)** **LC** B2; .R2. **DD** 105. Documents available from The Genuine Article. ***Continues** Etudes de Metaphysique et de Morale.*
**Ind/Abst** Arts Humanit. Citation Index [Full Cov.]; Bibliogr. Mission.; Curr. Contents Arts Humanit.; MLA Int. Bibl. Books Artic. Mod. Lang. Lit.; Philos. Index; Res. Alert [Full Cov.]; Romant. Move.

SZ/0035-1784
**REVUE DE THEOLOGIE ET DE PHILOSOPHIE.** [Rev. theol. philos.]. **Added/Corp** Schweizerische Geisteswissenschaftliche Gesellschaft. (1913-1950); New Series (1951)-. Periodical. French (English and German). Four times a year (Mar., June, Sept., Dec.). 75.00F (institutions), 59.00F (individuals) Switzerland; 80.00F (institutions), 63.00F (individuals) other. Atar S A, 11 Rue de la Dole, CH 1211 Geneva 13 Switzerland. **Tel** 011 41 22 3446400, FAX 011 41 22 3446865. cum. index. **Bk Rev. Ad Acc. Circ:** 1,000 (ctrl). ***Continues** Revue de Theologie et Philosophie et Compte-Rendu des Principales Publications Scientifiques.*
**Desc:** Religion, church history, theology, philosophy, ministry of philosophy and science of religion.
**Ind/Abst** Bibliogr. Mission.; Index Book Rev. Relig.; New Testam. Abstr.; Old Testam. Abstr.; Philos. Index; Relig. Index One Period. (1955-); Romant. Move.

FR/0035-2195
**REVUE DES SCIENCES HUMAINES.** [Rev. sci. hum.]. **Added/Corp** Universite de Lille. Faculte des Lettres. New Series, Issue 45 (Jan./Mar. 1947)-. Periodical. French. qt. 300.00F France; 340.00F other. Universite de Lille III, Duljva BP 149, 59653 Villnve Dascq Cedex France. **Tel** 011 33 20 336044. Documents available from The Genuine Article. ***Continues** Revue d'Histoire de la Philosophie et d'Historie Generale de la Civilisation.*
**Ind/Abst** Arts Humanit. Citation Index [Full Cov.]; Curr. Contents Arts Humanit.; MLA Int. Bibl. Books Artic. Mod. Lang. Lit.; Res. Alert [Full Cov.]; Romant. Move.; Soc. Sci. Cit. Index [Select. Cov.].

FR/0035-2209
**REVUE DES SCIENCES PHILOSOPHIQUES ET THEOLOGIQUES (PARIS : 1947).** (REVUE DES SCIENCES PHILOSOPHIQUES ET THEOLOGIQUES.). [Rev. Sci. Philos. Theol.]. Vol. 31 (1947)-. Periodical. French. qt. $118.00. Librairie Philosophique J Vrin, 6 Place de la Sorbonne, 75005 Paris France. **Tel** 011 33 1 43540347. Index available. **Bk Rev. Circ:** 1,100 (ctrl). Documents available from The Genuine Article. ***Continues** Sciences Philosophiques et Theologiques.*
**Desc:** In addition to recension of specialized reviews, also includes original thematic recensions in the shape of ecclesiology, philosophy or patrology bulletins. Contains several philosophical and purely theological articles.
**Ind/Abst** Arts Humanit. Citation Index [Full Cov.]; Curr. Contents Arts Humanit.; Index Book Rev. Relig.; MLA Int. Bibl. Books Artic. Mod. Lang. Lit.; New Testam. Abstr.; Old Testam. Abstr.; Philos. Index; Relig. Index One Period. (1969-); Relig. Theol. Abstr.; Res. Alert [Full Cov.]; Romant. Move.; Soc. Sci. Cit. Index [Select. Cov.].

FR
**REVUE D'ESTHETIQUE.** (1974)-. Monographic series. French. sa. 550.00F (institutions) Europe; 620.00F (institutions) other. Les Editions Jean Michel Place, 12 rue Pierre et Marie Curie, 75005 Paris France. **Tel** 011 33 1 46330511, 011 33 1 42390045, FAX 46 34 52 65. Documents available from The Genuine Article. ***Supersedes** Revue d'Esthetique.*
**Ind/Abst** ARTbibliogr. Mod. (1984-); ARTbibliogr. Curr. Titles; Arts Humanit. Citation Index [Full Cov.]; BHA : Biblio. Hist. Art; Curr. Contents Arts Humanit.; MLA Int. Bibl. Books Artic. Mod. Lang. Lit.; Music Index; Philos. Index; Res. Alert [Full Cov.]; Romant. Move.

BE/0048-8143
**REVUE INTERNATIONALE DE PHILOSOPHIE.** [Rev. int. philos.]. Vol. 1, No. 1 (Oct. 15, 1938)-. Periodical. Multiple languages (French, English, Spanish, Italian and German). Four times a year. 2480.00F Belgium; $76.30 US. Universite Libre de Bruxelles, 50 Avenue F D Roosevelt CP 188, 1050 Brussels Belgium. **Tel** 011 32 2 6423611. **LC** B1; .A24. **Bk Rev. Ad Acc.** ctrl circ. Documents available from The Genuine Article.
**Desc:** Information pertaining to philosophy and sciences.
**Ind/Abst** Annu. Bibliogr. Engl. Lang. Lit.; Arts Humanit. Citation Index [Full Cov.]; Curr. Contents Arts Humanit.; Math. Rev.; MLA Int. Bibl. Books Artic. Mod. Lang. Lit.; Philos. Index; Res. Alert [Full Cov.]; Soc. Plann. Policy Dev. Abstr.; Sociol. Abstr.

FR
**REVUE PHILOSOPHIQUE.** 390.00F France; 450.00F other. Presses Universitaires de France, Department des Revues, 14 Avenue du Bois de l'Epine, BP 90, 91003 Evry Cedex France. **Tel** (1)60 77 82 05, FAX (1) 60 79 20 45, telex PUF 600 474 F.

FR/0035-3833
**REVUE PHILOSOPHIQUE DE LA FRANCE ET DE L'ETRANGER.** [Rev. philos. Fr. etrang.]. Vol. 1, No. 1 (Jan. 1876)-. Periodical. French. qt. 410.00F France; 470.00F other. Presses Universitaires de France, Department des Revues, 14 Avenue du Bois de l'Epine, BP 90, 91003 Evry Cedex France. **Tel** (1)60 77 82 05, FAX (1) 60 79 20 45, telex PUF 600 474 F. **LC** B2; .R4. **DD** 105. **NLM** W1 RE96H. **[CCC].** cum. index. **Bk Rev.** Documents available from The Genuine Article.
**Desc:** Covers a fundamental notion or a certain period in history or a certain philosopher or a celebration. Each

issue contains a list of books published on the same subject.
**Ind/Abst** Arts Humanit. Citation Index [Full Cov.]; Curr. Contents Arts Humanit.; Int. Polit. Sci. Abstr.; Philos. Index; Res. Alert [Full Cov.]; Romant. Move.; Soc. Plann. Policy Dev. Abstr.; Soc. Sci. Cit. Index [Select. Cov.].

BE/0035-3841
**REVUE PHILOSOPHIQUE DE LOUVAIN.** [Rev. philos. Louv.]. **Added/Corp** Universite Catholique de Louvain (1835-1969). Institut Superieur de Philosophie. Societe Philosophique de Louvain. Vol. 44 (1946)-. Periodical. French. qt. 2000F; 3200F (combination with Repertoire Bibliographique de la Philosophie). Editions Peeters SA, Bondgenotenlaan 153, BP 41, B-3000 Leuven Belgium. **Tel** 32 16 235170, FAX 32 16 228500, telex 65987 PUL B. **ED** Cl. Troisfontaines. Index available. **Bk Rev. Ad Acc.** ctrl circ. Documents available from The Genuine Article. ***Continues** Revue Neoscolastique de Philosophie.*
**Ind/Abst** Arts Humanit. Citation Index [Full Cov.]; Bibliogr. Mission.; Curr. Contents Arts Humanit.; MLA Int. Bibl. Books Artic. Mod. Lang. Lit.; Philos. Index; Res. Alert [Full Cov.]; Soc. Sci. Cit. Index [Select. Cov.]; Abr. Cathol. Period. Lit. Index; Cathol. Period. Lit. Index.

RM
**REVUE ROUMAINE DE PHILOSOPHIE / ACADEMIA ROMANA.** **Added/Corp** Academia Romana. Vol. 35, No. 1/2 (Jan./June 1991)-. Periodical. French. qt. DM260.00. **(Subscription address:** Kubon & Sagner, ABT Zeitschriftenimport, D 80328 Munich Germany.) ***Continues** Revue Roumaine de Philosophie et Logique.*

FR/0035-4295
**REVUE THOMISTE. See** Religion and Theology.

US/0882-3731
**RIGHT OF AESTHETIC REALISM TO BE KNOWN, THE.** **Added/Corp** Aesthetic Realism Foundation (New York, N.Y.). (1973)-. Periodical. English. wk. $18.00 US; $28.00 Canada and Mexico; $40.00 other. Aesthetic Realism Foundation, 141 Greene Street, New York NY 10012. **Tel** (212)777-4490, FAX (212)777-4426. **ED** Ellen Reiss. **DD** 149. **Bk Rev.**
**Desc:** Lectures, articles and commentary showing that personally and internationally "contempt is the great failure of man" and "man's deepest desire...is to like the world". Strives to interpret world events and the inner self on an aesthetic basis.

IT/0035-6212
**RIVISTA DI ESTETICA.** [Riv. estet.]. **Added/Corp** Universita di Padova. Istituto di Filosofia. Universita di Turin. Istituto di Estetica. Vol. 1 (Jan./April l956)-. Periodical. Italian (English and French). Three times a year. L72000 Italy; L92000 Europe; L115000 other. Rosenberg & Sellier, Via Andrea Doria 14, 10123 Turin Italy. **Tel** 011 39 11 8127808, telex 224202 ROSSELI. **ED** Vattimo Gianni. **Bk Rev. Ad Acc. Circ:** 1,200.
**Desc:** One of the most useful presences of the Italian philosophical culture and has given outstanding help to aesthetics as an interdisciplinary science.
**Ind/Abst** Annu. Bibliogr. Engl. Lang. Lit.; ARTbibliogr. Mod. (1981-); BHA : Biblio. Hist. Art; MLA Int. Bibl. Books Artic. Mod. Lang. Lit.

IT/0035-6239
**RIVISTA DI FILOSOFIA.** [Riv. filos.]. **Added/Corp** Societa Filosofica Italiana. Vol. 1 (1909)-. Periodical. Italian. tq. L70000.00 Italy; L120000.00 (surface mail), L140000.00 (airmail) other. Societa Editrice il Mulino, Strada Maggiore 37, 40125 Bologna Italy. **Tel** 011 39 51 256011, FAX 011 39 51 256034. ***Supersedes** Rivista Filosofica.*
**Ind/Abst** Philos. Index.

IT/0035-6247
**RIVISTA DI FILOSOFIA NEO-SCOLASTICA.** [Riv. filos. neo-scolast.]. **Added/Corp** Universita Cattolica del Sacro Cuore. Societa Italiana per Gli Studi Filosofici e Psicologici. Universita Cattolica del Sacro Cuore. Facolta di Lettere e Filosofia. Vol. 1 (Jan. 1909)-. Periodical. Italian. Four times a year. L50.02 Italy; L110.00 others. Vita e Pensiero, Pubblic University, Largo Gemelli 1, 20123 Milan Italy. **Tel** 011 39 2 72342310, 011 39 2 72342370. **LC** B4; .R5. **DD** 149. Documents available from The Genuine Article.
**Ind/Abst** Arts Humanit. Citation Index [Full Cov.]; Bibliogr. Mission.; Curr. Contents Arts Humanit.; MLA Int. Bibl. Books Artic. Mod. Lang. Lit.; Philos. Index; Res. Alert [Full Cov.]; Soc. Sci. Cit. Index [Select. Cov.].

IT
**RIVISTA DI STORIA DELLA FILOSOFIA (MILAN, ITALY : 1984).** (RIVISTA DI STORIA DELLA FILOSOFIA.). Vol. 39, No. 1 (1984)-. Periodical. Italian. qt. L110000 Italy; L140000 other. Franco Angeli Riviste SRL, Viale Monza 106, 20127 Milan Italy. **Tel** 011 39 2 2827651, 011 39 2 289562. Documents available from The Genuine Article. ***Continues** Rivista Critica di Storia della Filosofia, 0035-581x.*
**Ind/Abst** Bibliogr. Mission.; Curr. Contents Arts Humanit.; Res. Alert [Full Cov.]; Soc. Sci. Cit. Index [Select. Cov.].

IT/0035-6727
**RIVISTA INTERNAZIONALE DI FILOSOFIA DEL DIRITTO. See** Law.

PL/0035-7685
**ROCZNIKI FILOSOFICZNE.** [Rocz. filoz.]. **Added/Corp** Katolicki Uniwersytet Lubelski. Towarzystwo Naukowe. **VFOAT** Annales de Philosophie. Vol. 1 (1948)-. Periodical. Polish. qt. Price on Request. **(Subscription address:** ARS Polona, PO Box 1001, 00068 Warsaw Poland.) **LC** B31; .R6. **CODEN** RFLZBF.
**Ind/Abst** Psychol. Abstr. (1960-).

UK/0080-4436
**ROYAL INSTITUTE OF PHILOSOPHY LECTURES.** ***Ceased.*** **Added/Corp** Royal Institute of Philosophy. **VFOAT** Royal Institute of Philosophy Lecture Series. Vol. 1 (1966/67)-(19??). Monographic series. English. an. St. Martin's Press, 175 Fifth Avenue, New York NY 10010. **Tel** (800)221-7945, (212)982-3900, FAX (212)777-6359.

PL/0035-9599
**RUCH FILOZOFICZNY.** **Added/Corp** Polskie Towarzystwo Filozoficzne. Vol. 1 (Jan. 1911)-. Periodical. Polish. qt. Price on Request. **(Subscription address:** ARS Polona, PO Box 1001, 00068 Warsaw Poland.)

FR
**RUE DESCARTES.** **Added/Corp** College International de Philosophie. (April 1991)-. Periodical. French. ir. 341.23F. Editions Albin Michel, 22 rue Huyghens, 75014 Paris, France. **Tel** 011 33 1 42791000, FAX 011 33 1 43272158, telex 203379.

CN/0036-0163
**RUSSELL.** [Russell]. **Added/Corp** Bertrand Russell Archives. (Spring 1971)-. Periodical. English. sa (June and December). 28.00Can$ universities in Montreal and Ontario Canada; 32.00Can$ other. McMaster University Library Press, 1280 Main Street West, Hamilton Ontario L8S 4L6 Canada. **Tel** (905)525-9140 ext.24737, FAX (905)546-0625. **ED** Kenneth Blackwell. **LC** B1649 .R94; A17. **DD** 192 [B]. **Bk Rev. Circ:** 650. Documents available from The Genuine Article.
**Desc:** Articles and reviews relating to Russell's work.
**Ind/Abst** Arts Humanit. Citation Index (19??-19??) [Full Cov.]; Philos. Index; Res. Alert [Full Cov.].

●US/1065-9374
**RUSSIAN AND EAST EUROPEAN STUDIES IN AESTHETICS AND THE PHILOSOPHY OF CULTURE. See** The Arts-Art.

●US/1061-1967
**RUSSIAN STUDIES IN PHILOSOPHY.** [Russ. stud. philos.]. Vol. 31, No. 1 (Summer 1992)-. Periodical. English (translations available in Russian). qt. $381.00 US; $421.00 other. M. E. Sharpe Inc., 80 Business Park Drive, Armonk NY 10504. **Tel** (914)273-1800, (800)541-6563, FAX (914)273-2106. **LC** B1; .S6. **DD** 105. Documents available from The Genuine Article. ***Continues** Soviet Studies in Philosophy, 0038-5883.*
**Ind/Abst** Arts Humanit. Citation Index [Full Cov.]; Curr. Contents Arts Humanit.; Curr. Contents Soc. Behav. Sci.; Philos. Index; Res. Alert [Full Cov.]; Soc. Sci. Cit. Index [Full Cov.].

AU/0080-5696
**SALZBURGER JAHRBUCH FUER PHILOSOPHIE.** Vol. 1 (1957)-. German. an. S390.00. Universitatsverlag Anton Pustet, Postfach 144, A-5021 Salzburg Austria. **Tel** 066276392. **ED** Paus, Koehler, Neidl. **Bk Rev. Ad Acc. Circ:** 250.
**Ind/Abst** Philos. Index.

II
**SAMBODHI.** **Added/Corp** Lalbhai Dalpatbhai Institute of Indology. Vol. 1 (Apr. 1972)-. Periodical. English (Gujarati, Hindi and Sanskrit). qt. $15.00. LD Institute of Indology, Ahmedabad-9 India. **Tel** 44 24 63. **(Subscription address:** Prints India, 11 Darya Ganj, New Delhi, 110002 India, (Phone: 011 91 11 3268645)) **ED** R S Betai. **LC** B130; .S27. **DD** 181/.4/05. Index available. **Bk Rev.** ctrl circ.

AG/0036-4703
**SAPIENTIA.** [Sapientia]. **Added/Corp** Pontificia Universidad Catolica Argentina Santa Maria de Los Buenos Aires. Facultad de Filosofia. Vol.1 (1946)-. Periodical. Spanish. qt. $60.00. Fundacion Universidad Catolica Argentina, Bartolome Mitre 1869, CP 1039 Buenos Aires, Argentina. available on microfilm and microfiche from University Microfilms International (UMI).
**Ind/Abst** Bibliogr. Mission.; HAPI Hisp. Am. Period. Index; Philos. Index.

IT/0036-4711
**SAPIENZA.** [Sapienza]. **Added/Corp** Dominicans. Vol. 1 (1948)-. Periodical. Italian (French). qt (4 issues). L40000 Italy; L45000 other. Edizione Domenicane Italiane, Via Luigi Palmieri 19, 80133 Naples Italy. **Tel** 011 39 81 459003. **ED** Michele Miele. Index available (bound in Oct. issue). cum. index. **Bk Rev.**
**Desc:** Research and discussions of problems in philosophy and theology especially those of San Tommaso and the school of Tomisthe.
**Ind/Abst** Bibliogr. Mission.; MLA Int. Bibl. Books Artic. Mod. Lang. Lit.; New Testam. Abstr.; Old Testam. Abstr.; Philos. Index.

US/0161-7729
**SCHOLARS' FACSIMILES AND REPRINTS (SERIES). See** Linguistics.

GW/0170-3609
**SCHRIFTEN DER MAINZER PHILOSOPHISCHEN FAKULTATSGESELLSCHAFT E. V.** [Schr. Mainz. Philos. Fak.ges. e. V.]. **VFOAT** Mainzer Philosophische-Fakultatsgesellschaft : Schriften der Mainzer Philosophischen Fakult...atsgesellschaft e. V. (1973)-. Monographic series. German. ir. Price varies per volume. Franz Steiner Verlag GmbH, Postfach 101061, D 70009 Stuttgart Germany. **Tel** 011 49 0711 2582372, FAX 011 49 0711 2582290, telex 723636 daz d. **UDC** 009.

NE/0926-7220
**SCIENCE & EDUCATION. See** Education-Teaching and Curriculum.

CN/0316-5345
**SCIENCE ET ESPRIT.** (SCIENCE ET ESPRIT / LES FACULTES DE THEOLOGIE ET DE PHILOSOPHIE DE LA COMPAGNIE DE JESUS DE MONTREAL ET DES TROIS-RIVIERES.). [Sci. esprit]. **Added/Corp** Jesuits. Province du Canada Francais. Faculte de Philosophie. Jesuits. Province du Canada Francais. Faculte de Theologie. (1968)-. Periodical. English (French and Italian). Three times a year (Jan., May, Oct.). 20.00Can$. Editions Bellarmin, 165 rue Deslauriers, St. Laurent Que H4N 2S4 Canada. **Tel** (514)745-4290, FAX (514)745-4299. **ED** Gilles Langevin. **LC** BR3; .S39. **DD** 230/.05. ***Continues** Sciences Ecclesiastiques, 0316-5337.*
**Ind/Abst** Bibliogr. Mission.; Index Book Rev. Relig.; MLA Int. Bibl. Books Artic. Mod. Lang. Lit.; New Testam. Abstr.; Old Testam. Abstr.; Point Repere (1983-); Relig. Index One Period. (1973-).

US/0036-8458
**SCIENCE OF MIND.** (19??)-. Periodical. English. Twelve times a year. $18.00. Science of Mind, PO Box 75127, Los Angeles CA 90075. **Tel** (800)247-6463, (213)388-2181. **ED** Kathy Juline, Cliff Johnson and Deanna Brady. **Ad Acc. Circ:** 100,000 (ctrl).
**Desc:** Expresses the science of mind, a philosophy of successful living. Teaches how to use spiritual understanding to experience happiness, health, prosperity and greater self-awareness.

NR/0331-3379
**SECOND ORDER.** [Second order]. Vol. 1, No. 1 (Jan. 1972)-. Periodical. English. Twice a year. $17.00. Obafemi Awolowo University, PO Box 1044, Ile Ife Oshun State Nigeria. **Tel** 011 234 36 230290. **LC** B5300; .S43. **DD** 199/.6/05.
**Ind/Abst** Philos. Index; Soc. Plann. Policy Dev. Abstr.; Sociol. Abstr.

IT
**SEGNI E COMPRENSIONE.** **Added/Corp** Universita Degli Studi di Lecce. Dipartimento di Filosofia. Centro Italiano di Ricerche Fenomenologiche. Comunita di Ricerca. Vol. 1, No. 1 (1987)-. Periodical. Italian. Three times a year. L34000.00 Italy; L68000.00 other. Capone Editore, Via Provinciale Lecce Cavallino, 73020 Cavallino Italy. **Tel** 011 39 832 612618, FAX 011 39 832 611877.

US/0037-1564
**SELF-REALIZATION.** **Added/Corp** Self-Realization Fellowship. Vol. 43 (Winter 1971)-. Periodical. English. Four times a year (Feb., May, Aug., Nov.). $3.00 US; $4.00 others. Self-Realization Fellowship, 3880 San Rafael Avenue, Los Angeles CA 90065. **Tel** (213)342-0336 ext. 718, FAX (213)225-2471. **ED** Jane Brush. **LC** B132.Y6; S4. Index available. **Bk Rev. Circ:** 30,000. ***Continues** Self-Realization Magazine.*
**Desc:** Practical application of spiritual principles for healing of body, removing mental inharmonies by concentration and positive thinking, freeing the soul from ignorance by yoga meditation.

BL
**SEMANA NACIONAL DE FILOSOFIA NO BRASIL: ANAIS.** 1A.-. Portuguese. Editora Universitaria, Campus Universitario, 58.000 Joao Pessoa Paraiba Brazil. **LC** B1041; .S45A. **DD** 199/.81.

●RU
**SERIIA 6, FILOSOFIIA, POLITOLOGIIA, SOTSIOLOGIIA, PSIKHOLOGIIA, PRAVO.** **Added/Corp** Leningradskii Gosudarstvennyi Universitet Imeni A.A. Zhdanova. **VFOAT** Filosofiia, Politologiia, Sotsiologiia, Psikhologiia, Pravo. No. 3 (Sept. 1991)-. Periodical. Russian (summaries and/or abstracts in English). ir. $119.95. St Petersburg State University / Izdatelstvo Leningradskogo Universiteta, Universitetskaia Nab 7/9, 199034 St Petersburg Russia. **Tel** 011 95 218-97-88, FAX 011 95 218-51-52, telex 121481. **(Subscription address:** East View Publications

Inc., 3020 Harbor Lane North, Suite 110, Minneapolis MN 55447.) **LC** AS262; .L463 subser. ***Continues*** *Seriia 6, Filosofiia, Politologiia, Teoriia i Istoriia Sotsializma, Sotsiologiia, Psikhologiia, Pravo, 0233-7541.*

XR
**SESITY / USTAV PRO FILOSOFII A SOCIOLOGII CSAV.** **Added/Corp** Ustav pro Filosofii a Sociologii CSAV. **VFOAT** Sesity Ustavu Pro Filosofii A Sociologii CSAV. (1971)-. Monographic series. Czech. ir. Price varies per volume. **LC** B8.C9; S47.

JA
**SHIKIHAKU DAYORI.** Periodical. Japanese. qt. Matsuyama Shiritsu Shiki Kinen Hakubutsukan 1-30, Dogo Koen Matsuyama-shi, Ehime-ken 790 Japan. **LC** PL811.A83; Z934.

JA
**SHISO (TOKYO, JAPAN : 1921).** (SHISO.). (Oct. 1921)-. Periodical. Japanese. mo. $230.50. Iwanami Shoten Publishers, 2-5-5 Hitotsubashi, Chiyoda-ku, Tokyo 101-02, Japan. **Tel** 03 3265 4111, FAX 03 3221 8998, telex 39495. **(Subscription address:** Japan Publications Trading Company, Ltd., PO Box 5030, Tokyo International, Tokyo 100-31 Japan.) **LC** UNC.

US/0049-0385
**SH'MA (PORT WASHINGTON, N.Y.).** (SH'MA.). [Sh'ma]. (Nov. 9, 1970)-. Periodical. English. Twenty times a year (Sept. - May). $18.00. SH'MA Inc, 99 Park Avenue, Suite S -300, New York NY 10016. **Tel** (212)867-8888, FAX (212)867-8853. **ED** Nina Beth Cardin. Index available. **Bk Rev. Circ:** 8,500 (ctrl). available on microfilm from University Microfilms International (UMI); available on an online database from Internet.
**Desc:** A forum for discussion of topics of interest to the Jewish community, free of any organizational censorship or restraint.
**Ind/Abst** Index Jew. Period. (199?-).

IT/0037-5888
**SISTEMATICA.** ***Suspended.*** (SISTEMATICA; RIVISTA DI FILOSOFIA.). Vol. 1 (1968)-. Periodical. Italian. Four times a year. L30000. Pergamena, Viale Ezio 7, 20149 Milan Italy. **Tel** 011 39 2 228119. **LC** B4; .S57.

GW/0138-3957
**SITZUNGSBERICHTE DER SACHSISCHEN AKADEMIE DER WISSENSCHAFTEN ZU LEIPZIG, PHILOLOGISCH-HISTORISCHE KLASSE.** [Sitz.ber. Sachs. Akad. Wiss. Leipz., Philol.-Hist. Kl.]. **Added/Corp** Sachsische Akademie der Wissenschaften zu Leipzig. Philologisch-Historische Klasse. Vol. 107, No. 1 (1962)-. Monographic series. German. ir. Price varies per volume. Akademie-Verlag GmbH, Muehlenstrasse 33 34, D 13162 Berlin Germany. **Tel** 011 49 30 47889300, FAX 011 49 30 47889357. **(Subscription address:** VCH Publishers Inc., 303 Northwest 12th Avenue, Journals Department, Deerfield FL 33442.) **LC** AS182; .S213. ***Continues*** *Berichte Uber die Verhandlungen der Sachsischen Akademie der Wissenschaften zu Leipzig. Philologisch-Historische Klasse, 0138-5151.*
**Ind/Abst** MLA Int. Bibl. Books Artic. Mod. Lang. Lit.

UK/0269-1728
**SOCIAL EPISTEMOLOGY.** [Soc. epistemol.]. Vol. 1, No. 1 (Jan.-March 1987)-. Periodical. English. qt. £118.00 UK; $195.00 other. Taylor & Francis Ltd., Rankine Road, Basingstoke Hampshire, RG24 8PR United Kingdom. **Tel** 011 44 256 840366, FAX 011 44 256 479438, telex 858540. **(Subscription address:** Taylor & Francis Inc., 1900 Frost Road, Suite 101, Bristol PA 19007-1598.) **ED** Steve Fuller. **LC** BD175; .S62. **[CCC]. Pr Rev.** available on microfilm from University Microfilms International (UMI).
**Desc:** Provides a forum for philosophical and sociological enquiry that incorporates the work of scholars from a variety of disciplines who share a concern with the production, assessment and validation of knowledge. The journal covers both empirical research into the origination and transmission of knowledge and normative considerations which arise as such research is implemented, serving as a guide for directing contemporary knowledge enterprises.
**Ind/Abst** Appl. Soc. Sci. Index Abstr.; Philos. Index; Soc. Plann. Policy Dev. Abstr.

US/0147-5231
**SOMATICS.** **Added/Corp** Novato Institute for Somatic Research and Training. Vol. 1 (Autumn 1976)-. Periodical. English. Twice a year. $25.00 (institutions), $20.00 (individuals) US; $29.00 (institutions), $24.00 (individuals) Canada & Mexico & Central America; $33.00 (institutions), $28.00 (individuals) Europe & South America; $35.00 (institutions), $30.00 (individuals) other. The Novato Institute for Somatic Research & Training, 1516 Grant Avenue, Suite 220, Novato CA 94945. **Tel** (415)897-0336. **ED** Eleanor Criswell Hanna. **NLM** W1 SO887L. Index available. cum. index. **Bk Rev. Ad Acc. Circ:** 1,200 (ctrl).
**Desc:** Research articles for professionals and laypersons in the body-mind field.
**Ind/Abst** Except. Hum. Exp.; Soc. Plann. Policy Dev. Abstr.; Sociol. Abstr.; SportSearch.

AT/0038-1527
**SOPHIA.** **See** Religion and Theology.

RU
**SOTSIALNYE I GUMANITARNYE NAUKI. SERIIA 3, FILOSOFSKIE NAUKI : OTECHESTVENNAIA I ZARUBEZHNAIA LITERATURA / ROSSIISKAIA AKADEMIIA NAUK, INSTITUT NAUCHNOI INFORMATSII PO OBSHCHESTVENNYM NAUKAM.** **Added/Corp** Institut Nauchnoi Informatsii po Obshchestvennym Naukam (Rossiiskaia Akademiia Nauk). (1993)-. Academic Scholarly Publication. Russian. qt. Izdatelstvo Nauka / Akademiia Nauk, Publishing House of the Russian Academy of Sciences, Leninskii Porspekt 14, 117901 Moscow Russia. **Tel** 011 95 954-21-53, FAX 011 95 938-21-44, telex 411964. **LC** B6; .O273. ***Formed by the union of*** *Obshchestvennye Nauki za Rubezhom. Seriia 3, Filosofiia* ***and*** *Obshchestvennye Nauki v Rossii. Seriia 3, Filosofiia.*

SA/0258-0136
**SOUTH AFRICAN JOURNAL OF PHILOSOPHY.** [S. Afr. j. philos.]. **Added/Corp** Foundation for Education, Science, and Technology (South Africa). Bureau for Scientific Publications. Philosophical Society of Southern Africa. **VFOAT** Suid-Afrikaanse Tydskrif vir Wyseegeerte; Philosophy; Wysbegeerte. Vol. 1, No. 1 (1982)-. Periodical. English (Afrikaans). qt. R87.00 South Africa; R90.00 other. Foundation for Education Science & Technology, PO Box 1758, Pretoria 0001 South Africa. **Tel** 011 27 12 3226404, FAX 011 27 12 3207803. **CODEN** SAJPEM. **[CCC].** Documents available from The Genuine Article.
**Ind/Abst** Arts Humanit. Citation Index [Full Cov.]; Curr. Contents Arts Humanit.; Philos. Index; Res. Alert [Full Cov.]; Soc. Sci. Cit. Index [Select. Cov.].

US/0038-4283
**SOUTHERN JOURNAL OF PHILOSOPHY, THE.** [South. j. philos.]. **Added/Corp** Memphis State University. Dept. of Philosophy. Vol. 1 (Spring 1963)-. Periodical. English. qt (Mar., June, Sept., Dec.). $25.00 (institutions); $15.00 (individuals). Memphis State University / Department of Philosophy, Department of Philosophy, Southern Journal of Philosophy, Memphis TN 38152. **Tel** (901)678-2669, FAX (901)678-4365. **ED** Nancy D. Simco. **LC** B1; .S57. **DD** 105. Index available. cum. index. **Ad Acc, Adv Mgr:** Leigh Tanner. **Pr Rev. Circ:** 900. available on microfilm and microfiche from University Microfilms International (UMI). Documents available from The Genuine Article.
**Desc:** Articles from all perspectives in all areas of philosophy.
**Ind/Abst** Annu. Bibliogr. Engl. Lang. Lit.; Arts Humanit. Citation Index [Full Cov.]; Curr. Contents Arts Humanit.; Philos. Index; Res. Alert [Full Cov.]; Soc. Sci. Cit. Index [Select. Cov.].

US/0885-9310
**SOUTHWEST PHILOSOPHICAL STUDIES.** [Southwest philos. stud.]. Vol. 1 (Apr. 1976)-. Periodical. English. an. $30.00. Southwest Texas State University / Philosophy, Department of Philosophy, V Luizz, San Marcos TX 78666. **DD** 105. ***Continues*** *New Mexico-West Texas Philosophical Society. Proceedings;* ***Formed by the union of*** *Proceedings of the ... Annual Meeting of the Southwestern Philosophical Society, 0882-1607.*
**Ind/Abst** Philos. Index.

US/0897-2346
**SOUTHWEST PHILOSOPHY REVIEW.** (SOUTHWEST PHILOSOPHY REVIEW : PAPERS PRESENTED AT THE ... ANNUAL MEETING OF THE SOUTHWESTERN PHILOSOPHICAL SOCIETY.). [Southwest philos. rev.]. **Added/Corp** Southwestern Philosophical Society. (1987)-. Periodical. English. sa (Jan., July). $30.00 institutions US and Canada; $45.00 institutions other; $20.00 individuals US and Canada; $35.00 individuals other. Westminster College / Department of Philosophy, 501 Westminster Avenue, Fulton MO 65251-1299. **Tel** (314)592-1277, FAX (314)642-2176. **ED** J.K. Swindler. **LC** B1; .S577. **DD** 105. Index available (included occasionally). **Bk Rev,** (Qty: 5-10/year). **Ad Acc. Pr Rev. Circ:** 350.
**Desc:** Journal of the Southwestern Philosophical Society. January issue is dedicated to papers from the Society's annual meeting; July issue is open to submissions on any topic in philosophy from any philosophical perspective.
**Ind/Abst** Philos. Index.

US/0038-5883
**SOVIET STUDIES IN PHILOSOPHY.** ***Title Change.*** [Sov. Stud. Philos.]. **Added/Corp** International Arts and Sciences Press. Vol. 1 (Summer 1962)-(1991). Periodical. English (translations available in Russian). qt. M. E. Sharpe Inc., 80 Business Park Drive, Armonk NY 10504. **Tel** (914)273-1800, (800)541-6563, FAX (914)273-2106. **ED** John Somerville. **LC** B1; .S6. **DD** 105. **Bk Rev. Ad Acc. Pr Rev. Circ:** 300 (ctrl). available on microfilm from University Microfilms International (UMI). ***Continued by*** *Russian Studies in Philosophy, 1061-1967.*
**Desc:** A source for complete and unabridged translations of current articles by Soviet philosophers, taken from Soviet journals covering the entire range of philosophy.
**Ind/Abst** Arts Humanit. Citation Index (19??-19??) [Full Cov.]; Philos. Index.

RU
**SOVREMENNAIA ZARUBEZHNAIA FILOSOFIIA I SOTSIOLOGIIA.** **Added/Corp** Institut Nauchnoi Informatsii po Obshchestvennym Naukam (Akademiia Nauk SSSR). (19??)-. Academic Scholarly Publication. Multiple languages (Russian and Multiple languages). 0.28rub (single issue). Izdatelstvo Nauka / Akademiia Nauk, Publishing House of the Russian Academy of Sciences, Leninskii Porspekt 14, 117901 Moscow Russia. **Tel** 011 95 954-21-53, FAX 011 95 938-21-44, telex 411964. **ED** G G Kritchevskij. **LC** Z7125; .S72; B53.

XR
**SPISY UNIVERZITY J.E. PURKYNE V BRNE, FILOZOFICKA FAKULTA.** **Added/Corp** Univerzita J.E. Purkyne v Brne. Filozoficka Fakulta. **VFOAT** Spisy University J.E. Purkyne v Brne, Filosoficka Fakulta; Opera Universitatis Purkynianae Brunensis, Facultas Philosophica. (1923)-. Monographic series. Czech. Price varies per volume.
**Ind/Abst** Soc. Plann. Policy Dev. Abstr.

US/0271-1192
**SPRINGER SERIES ON DEATH AND SUICIDE, THE.** (THE SPRINGER SERIES ON DEATH AND SUICIDE.). [Springer ser. death suicide]. **VFOAT** Springer Series on Death and Suicide. (1979)-. Monographic series. English. ir. Price varies per volume. Springer-Verlag New York Inc., 175 5th Avenue, New York NY 10010. **Tel** (212)460-1500, telex 232 235 SPB UR. **(Subscription address:** Springer Verlag New York Inc. / for North America, 44 Hartz Way, Secaucus NJ 07096.) **ED** R. Kastenbaum. **NLM** W1 SP685P.
**Desc:** A series that addresses a most important contemporary psychosocial topic. The experience of death for the dying and the living.

GW/0081-3877
**SPRINGER TRACTS IN NATURAL PHILOSOPHY.** (SPRINGER TRACTS IN NATURAL PHILOSOPHY : ERGEBNISSE DER ANGEWANDTEN MATHEMATIK.). [Springer tracts nat. philos.]. Vol. 1 (1964)-. Monographic series. English (German). ir. Price varies per volume. Springer-Verlag New York Inc., 175 5th Avenue, New York NY 10010. **Tel** (212)460-1500, telex 232 235 SPB UR. **(Subscription address:** Springer Verlag New York Inc. / for North America, 44 Hartz Way, Secaucus NJ 07096.) **[CCC].** ***Continues*** *Ergebnisse der Angewandten Mathematik.*
**Desc:** Contains articles on theory, methods, analysis, and functions of philosophy.
**Ind/Abst** Math. Rev.; Zentralbl. Math. Ihre Grenzgeb.

KO
**SSIAL UI SORI.** **VFOAT** Voice of the People. Began with Apr. 1970 issue. Periodical. Korean (Korean). W3,000. Ssial Ui Sori Sa, 70 4-ka Wonhyo Ro, Yongsan-ku 140, Seoul South Korea. **LC** B8.K6; S75.

US/1059-8375
**ST. WILLIBRORD STUDIES IN PHILOSOPHY AND RELIGION.** **See** Religion and Theology.

IT
**STUDI DI SCIENZE RELIGIOSE.** **See** Religion and Theology.

IT
**STUDI FILOSOFICI.** 1-. Periodical. French (Italian; summaries and/or abstracts in English). L4.000 each issue. Istituto Universitario Orientale di Napoli, Piazza S Giovanni, Maggiore 30, 80134 Naples Italy. **LC** B4; .S77. **DD** 105.

IT
**STUDIA ANSELMIANA; PHILOSOPHICA, THEOLOGICA.** (1933)-. Monographic series. Multiple languages (English, French, German and Latin). ir. Price varies per volume. Herder Editrice e Libreria SRL, Piazza Montecitorio 117-120, 00186 Rome Italy. **Tel** 011 39 6 679 4628, FAX 011 39 6 678 4751.
**Desc:** Monographic series on the Benedictines of St. Anselmo in Rome.

PN/0323-2220
**STUDIA COMENIANA ET HISTORICA.** **See** Education.

PL/0039-3142
**STUDIA FILOZOFICZNE.** ***Ceased.*** [Stud. filoz.]. 1957, No. 1-?. Periodical. Polish (English). mo. **(Subscription address:** ARS Polona, PO Box 1001, 00068 Warsaw Poland.) **LC** B6; .S75. ***Continues in part*** *MYSL Filozoficzna.*
**Ind/Abst** Am. Hist. Life (1955-1956, 1965-); ARTbibliogr. Mod.; Romant. Move.

GW/0039-3185
**STUDIA LEIBNITIANA.** [Stud. Leibnitiana]. (1969)-. Periodical. German (French and English). sa. DM128.00. Franz Steiner Verlag GmbH, Postfach 101061, D 70009 Stuttgart Germany. **Tel** 011 49 0711 2582372, FAX 011 49 0711 2582290, telex 723636 daz d. **ED** G. H. R. Parkinson, Heinrich Schepers, and Wilhelm Totok. **LC** B2550; .S8. **CODEN** STLBBI. **[CCC]. Bk Rev. Ad Acc. Circ:** 450. Documents available from The Genuine Article.
**Desc:** Dedicated to Leibniz' philosophy and to the history of philosophy as well as the history of science.
**Ind/Abst** Arts Humanit. Citation Index [Full Cov.]; Curr. Contents Arts Humanit.; Math. Rev.; Philos. Index; Res. Alert [Full Cov.].

GW
**STUDIA LEIBNITIANA. SONDERHEFT.** (19??)-. Monographic series. German. ir. Price varies per volume. Franz Steiner Verlag GmbH, Postfach 101061, D 70009 Stuttgart Germany. **Tel** 011 49 0711 2582372, FAX 011 49 0711 2582290, telex 723636 daz d. **(Subscription address:** Brockhaus Commission, Kreidlerstrasse 9, D 70803 Kornwestheim Germany.**) ED** G.H.R. Parkinson, Heinrich Schepers, Wilhelm Totok.

GW/0303-5980
**STUDIA LEIBNITIANA. SUPPLEMENTA.** (STUDIA LEIBNITIANA. SUPPLEMENTA : IM AUFTRAGE DER GOTTFRIED-WILHELM-LEIBNIZ-GESELLSCHAFT E.V.). [Stud. Leibnit., Suppl.]. **Added/Corp** Gottfried-Wilhelm-Leibniz-Gesellschaft. (1968)-. Monographic series. German (French). ir. Price varies per volume. Franz Steiner Verlag GmbH, Postfach 101061, D 70009 Stuttgart Germany. **Tel** 011 49 0711 2582372, FAX 011 49 0711 2582290, telex 723636 daz d. **(Subscription address:** Brockhaus Commission, Kreidlerstrasse 9, D 70803 Kornwestheim Germany.**) ED** G.H.R. Parkinson, Heinrich Schepers, Wilhelm Totok. **LC** B2550; .S931.
**Ind/Abst** Math. Rev.

PL/0039-3215
**STUDIA LOGICA.** [Stud. logica]. **Added/Corp** Instytut Filozofii i Socjologii (Polska Akademia Nauk). Polska Akademia Nauk. Komitet Filozoficzny. Vol. 1 (1953)-. Periodical. English (Polish). qt. $552.00. Kluwer Academic Publishers, Postbus 322, 3300 AH Dordrecht, The Netherlands. **Tel** 011 (31) 78 524400, FAX 011 31 78 183273, telex 20083. **ED** Ryszard Wojcicki. **CODEN** SLOGAP. **[CCC].** Index available. **Bk Rev. Ad Acc. Pr Rev. Circ:** 400. available on microfilm and microfiche from University Microfilms International (UMI).
**Desc:** Publishes original papers on various logical systems, which utilize methods of contemporary formal logic (those of algebra, model theory, proof theory, etc). The distinctive feature is its series of monothematic issues edited by outstanding scholars and devoted to important topics of contemporary logic or covering significant conferences.
**Ind/Abst** Linguist. Lang. Behav. Abstr.; Math. Rev.; MLA Int. Bibl. Books Artic. Mod. Lang. Lit.; Philos. Index; Soc. Plann. Policy Dev. Abstr.; Zentralbl. Math. Ihre Grenzgeb.

PL/0039-3231
**STUDIA MEDIEWISTYCZNE. Added/Corp** Polska Akademia Nauk. Instytut Filozofii i Socjologii. Polska Akademia Nauk. Zakad Historii Filozofii Starozytnej i Sredniowiecznej. (1958)-. Polish (Latin; summaries and/or abstracts in French). sa. $14.30. **(Subscription address:** ARS Polona, PO Box 1001, 00068 Warsaw Poland.**)**
**Ind/Abst** MLA Int. Bibl. Books Artic. Mod. Lang. Lit.

IT/0039-3304
**STUDIA PATAVINA. See** Religion and Theology.

US/1052-4533
**STUDIA PHILONICA ANNUAL, THE.** [Stud. Philon. annu.]. **VFOAT** Studies in Hellenistic Judaism. Vol. 1 (1989)-. English (French and German). an. Scholars Press / Georgia, PO Box 15399, Atlanta GA 30333-0399. **Tel** (404)636-4757, (404)727-2320, FAX (404)727-2348. **LC** B689.Z7; A16. **DD** 181/.06. ***Continues** Studia Philonica, 0093-5808.*

PL/0585-5470
**STUDIA PHILOSOPHIAE CHRISTIANAE.** [Stud. philos. christ.]. Vol. 1-. Periodical. Polish (summaries and/or abstracts in English, French and German). sa. **(Subscription address:** ARS Polona, PO Box 1001, 00068 Warsaw Poland.**) LC** BR9.P6; S76.
**Ind/Abst** Bibliogr. Mission.; Philos. Index.

SZ
**STUDIA PHILOSOPHICA. Added/Corp** Schweizerische Philosophische Gesellschaft. Vol. 6 (1946)-. German (French). an. price varies per volume. Verlag Paul Haupt, Falkenplatz 11, CH-3001 Bern Switzerland. **Tel** 011 41 31 3012435, FAX 011 41 30 243023, telex 912 906 HAUP CH. cum. index. ***Continues** Jahrbuch der Schweizerischen Philosophischen Gesellschaft.*
**Ind/Abst** Philos. Index.

GW
**STUDIA SPINOZANA.** Vol. 1 (1985)-. English (French, German and Italian). an. DM63.00. Verlag Koenigshausen & Neumann, Postfach 6007, W 8700 Wuerzburg Germany. **Tel** 011 49 931 76401, FAX 011 49 931 83620. **ED** Dr Walther. **LC** B3950; .S78. **DD** 199/.492. **Bk Rev. Ad Acc. Circ:** 600.
**Ind/Abst** Philos. Index.

US/0361-6045
**STUDIA SWEDENBORGIANA. Added/Corp** Swedenborg School of Religion. Vol. 1 (Jan. 1974)-. Periodical. English. Twice a year. $6.50. Studia Swedenborgiana, 48 Sargent Street, Newton MA 02158. **Tel** (617)244-0504. available on microfilm from University Microfilms International (UMI).
**Ind/Abst** Index Book Rev. Relig.; Relig. Index One Period.

NE
**STUDIEN ZUR OSTERREICHISCHEN PHILOSOPHIE.** Vol. 1 (1979)-. Monographic series. German. ir. Price varies per volume. Humanities Press, 165 1st Avenue, Atlantic Highlands NJ 07716. **Tel** (908)872-1441, (800)221-3845, FAX (908)872-0717, telex 752233. **ED** Rudolf Haller. Index available.
**Desc:** Monographs on issues and leading figures in European philosophy.

GW/0081-735X
**STUDIEN ZUR PHILOSOPHIE UND LITERATUR DES NEUNZEHNTEN JAHRHUNDERTS.** Vol. 1 (1968)-. Monographic series. German. ir. Price varies per volume. Vittorio Klostermann, Frauenlobstrasse 22, D 60487 Frankfurt Germany. **Tel** 011 49 69 9708160.

NE
**STUDIEN ZUR PROBLEMGESCHICHTE DER ANTIKEN UND MITTELALTERLICHEN PHILOSOPHIE.** (1966)-. Monographic series. German. ir. Price varies per volume. E. J. Brill, Postbus 9000, 2300 PA Leiden Netherlands. **Tel** 011 31 71 312624, FAX 011 31 71 317532, telex 39296 BRILL NL.

UK
**STUDIES IN APPLIED PHILOSOPHY.** 1985-. Monographic series. English. Price varies per volume. Humanities Press, 165 1st Avenue, Atlantic Highlands NJ 07716. **Tel** (908)872-1441, (800)221-3845, FAX (908)872-0717, telex 752233. **ED** Brenda Almond and Anthony O'Hear. Index available.
**Desc:** Aims to make constructive contribution to ethical problems in such areas as law, politics, economics, science policy, medicine and education.

NE/0925-9392
**STUDIES IN EAST EUROPEAN THOUGHT.** English (German and French). qt. $345.00. Kluwer Academic Publishers, Postbus 322, 3300 AH Dordrecht, The Netherlands. **Tel** 011 (31) 78 524400, FAX 011 31 78 183273, telex 20083. **ED** Edward M. Swiderski, Guido Kung, and Nikolaus Lobkowicz. **Pr Rev. *Continues*** *Studies in Soviet Thought, 0039-3797.*
**Desc:** It is intended to provide a forum for Western language (English and German) writings on philosophy and philosophers who identify with the history and cultures of East and Central Europe, including Russia, Ukraine, and the Baltic States. The editors welcome descriptive, critical, comparative, and historical studies of individuals, schools, currents, and institutions whose works and influence are widely regared in their own environments to be philosophical or provide insight into the socio-cultural conditions of philosophical life in Eastern Europe.
**Ind/Abst** Arts Humanit. Citation Index [Full Cov.]; Soc. Sci. Cit. Index [Full Cov.].

US
**STUDIES IN HUME AND SCOTTISH PHILOSOPHY.** 1-. Monographic series. English. Price varies per volume. Austin Hill Press Inc, 2955 Renault Place, San Diego CA 92122.

NE/0924-4662
**STUDIES IN LINGUISTICS AND PHILOSOPHY. See** Linguistics.

UK/0081-8399
**STUDIES IN PHILOSOPHY.** 1 (1963)-. Monographic series. English. ir. Price varies per volume. Walter de Gruyter Inc. / Hawthorne, 200 Saw Mill River Road, Hawthorne NY 10532. **Tel** (914)747-0110, GERMANY: 011/49/30/260050, FAX (914)747-1326, telex 646677.

US/0039-3746
**STUDIES IN PHILOSOPHY AND EDUCATION.** [Stud. philos. educ.]. Vol. 1 (1960)-. Periodical. English. qt. $300.00. Kluwer Academic Publishers, Postbus 322, 3300 AH Dordrecht, The Netherlands. **Tel** 011 (31) 78 524400, FAX 011 31 78 183273, telex 20083. **ED** David P.Ericson. **LC** L11; .S92. **CODEN** SPYEAT. **[CCC].** Index available. cum. index. **Bk Rev. Ad Acc. Pr Rev. Acid Free.** available on microfilm and microfiche from University Microfilms International (UMI).
**Desc:** Internationally focuses on the philosophical, normative, and conceptual problems and issues in educational research policy and practice. Promotes exchange and collaboration among philosophers, philosophers of education, educational and social science researchers, and education policy-makers throughout the world. Welcomes contributions of philosophical interest from non-philosophers in the educational and social science community.
**Ind/Abst** Acad. Search (Jan. 1993-); Aust. Educ. Index (-199?); Educ. Index; Humanit. Source (Jul. 1993-); INFO-SOUTH Abstr.; Int. Bibliogr. Sociol.; Mag. Search; Philos. Index; Soc. Plann. Policy Dev. Abstr.; Sociol. Abstr.; Sociol. Educ. Abstr.

US/0585-6965
**STUDIES IN PHILOSOPHY AND THE HISTORY OF PHILOSOPHY.** [Stud. philos. hist. philos.]. Vol. 1 (1961)-. Monographic series. English. ir. Price varies per volume. Catholic University of America Press, 620 Michigan Avenue Northeast, Administration Building/Room 303, Washington DC 20064. **Tel** (202)319-5052, FAX (202)319-5802. **LC** B21; .S78. **DD** 108.2.
**Ind/Abst** Philos. Index.

NE/0039-3797
**STUDIES IN SOVIET THOUGHT. *Title Change.*** [Stud. Sov. thought]. **Added/Corp** Universite de Fribourg. Ost-Europa Institut. Boston College. Russian Philosophical Studies Program. Boston College. Center for East Europe, Russia and Asia. Universitat Munchen. Seminar fur Politische Theorie und Philosophie. Vol. 1 (1961)-. Periodical. English (German and French). qt. Kluwer Academic Publishers, Postbus 322, 3300 AH Dordrecht, The Netherlands. **Tel** 011 (31) 78 524400, FAX 011 31 78 183273, telex 20083. **ED** Thomas J Blakeley. **LC** B809.8; .S853. **DD** 197/.2. **CODEN** SSVTBD. **[CCC]. Bk Rev. Ad Acc. Pr Rev. Circ:** 600. available on microfilm and microfiche from University Microfilms International (UMI). Documents available from The Genuine Article. ***Continued by** Studies in East European Thought, 0925-9392.*
**Desc:** Modern and recent Soviet thought, and pre-revolutionary developments.
**Ind/Abst** ABC POL SCI; Am. Hist. Life (1969-); Am. Bibliogr. Slavic East Europ. Stud. (1969-); ARTbibliogr. Mod.; Arts Humanit. Citation Index (19??-19??) [Full Cov.]; Curr. Contents Arts Humanit.; Curr. Contents Soc. Behav. Sci.; Index Period. Artic. Relat. Law (19??-19??); Int. Polit. Sci. Abstr.; Philos. Index; Res. Alert [Full Cov.]; Soc. Sci. Cit. Index (19??-19??) [Full Cov.].

FR
**STUDIES ON TEACHING AND RESEARCH IN PHILOSOPHY THROUGHOUT THE WORLD. Added/Corp** Unesco. (1984)-. Monographic series. English. ir. Price varies per volume. UNESCO / France, 31 rue Francois Bonvin, 75732 Paris Cedex 15 France. **Tel** 011 33 1 45684564, 011 33 1 45684565, FAX 011 33 1 42733007, telex 204461 Paris.

BE
**STUDIES VAN HET CENTRUM VOOR LOGICA, WETENSCHAPSFILOSOFIE EN FILOSOFIE VAN DE TAAL, HOGER INSTITUUT VOOR WIJSBEGEERTE, K.U. LEUVEN.** No. 1- 1984-. Monographic series. English. Price varies per volume. Uitgeverij Acco, Tiensestraat 134-136, 3000 Leuven Belgium.

RM
**STUDII DE ISTORIE A FILOZOFIEI UNIVERSALE (BUCHAREST, ROMANIA : 1974).** (STUDII DE ISTORIE A FILOZOFIEI UNIVERSALE / ACADEMIA DE STIINTE SOCIALE SI POLITICE A REPUBLICII SOCIALISTE ROMANIA, INSTITUTUL DE FILOZOFIE.). **Added/Corp** Institutul de Filozofie (Academia de Stiinte Sociale si Politice a Republicii Socialiste Romania). **VFOAT** Studies on the History of World Philosophy. (1974)-. Periodical. Romanian. Editura Academia Republicii Socialiste Romania, Calea Victoriei Nr 125, R-79717 Bucuresti Romania. **Tel** telex 10376 PRSFI R. **LC** B8.R8; S77. ***Continues** Filozofie Moderna Si Contemporana.*

IT/0394-4360
**SUBSIDIA AL CORPUS PHILOSOPHORUM MEDII AEVI.** Vol. 1- 1980-. Monographic series. Italian. Price varies per volume. Casa Edtrice Leo S Olschki, Casella Postale PO Box 50100, Firenze Italy.

US/0562-6048
**SUNRISE (ALTADENA, CALIF.).** (SUNRISE THEOSOPHIC PERSPECTIVES.). [Sunrise]. Vol. 1, (Oct. 1951)-. Periodical. English (Dutch, German and Swedish). Six times a year (Feb., Apr., June, Aug., Oct., Dec.). $9.00 US; $12.00 other. Theosophical University Press, PO Box C, Pasadena CA 91109-7107. **Tel** (818)798-3378, FAX (818)798-4749. **ED** Grace F. Knoche. **LC** BP500; .S8. **DD** 212.05. Index available (Aug/Sept. iss.). cum. index. **Bk Rev**, (Qty: 6-20). available on audiocassette; available on microfilm and

microfiche from University Microfilms International (UMI). *Supersedes Theosophical Forum.*
**Desc:** Presents a wide range of philosophic and scientific themes in the light of ancient and modern theosophy and its application to daily experience; reviews of significant books and trends; commentary on the apiritual principles spiritual the core of the world's sacred traditions; and insights into the nature of man and the universe.

UK/0309-7013
**SUPPLEMENTARY VOLUME - ARISTOTELIAN SOCIETY.**
(SUPPLEMENTARY VOLUME.). [Suppl. vol. - Aristot. Soc.]. **Main/Conf** Aristotelian Society (Great Britain). Vol. 1 (1918)-. Academic Scholarly Publication. English. an. £33.00 UK and Europe; $57.00 North America; £38.50 other. Basil Blackwell Publishers Ltd, 108 Cowley Road, Oxford 0X4 1JF England. **Tel** 011 44 865 791100, FAX 011 44 865 791347, telex 837022 OXBOOK G. **(Subscription address:** Blackwell Publishers / UK, Marston Book Services, PO Box 87, Oxford OX2 0DT England.) cum. index. **Ad Acc.**
**Ind/Abst** Philos. Index.

US/1044-0011
**S'VARA (NEW YORK, N.Y.).** ***Suspended.***
(S'VARA : A JOURNAL OF PHILOSOPHY AND JUDAISM.). [S'vara]. **Added/Corp** Columbia University. School of Law. Mekhon Shalom Hartman (Jerusalem). Vol. 1, No. 1 (Winter 1990)-Suspended with Vol. 3, No. 1 (1992). Periodical. English. sa. Columbia University School of Law, 435 West 116th Street, New York NY 10027. **Tel** (212)854-4398, (212)854-3742. **LC** BM1; .S88. **DD** 181/.06/05.
**Desc:** Covers Jewish law and philosophy and Judaism.

GW/0082-0660
**SYMBOLON.** ***Ceased.*** **See** Religion and Theology.

GW
**SYMPOSION; PHILOSOPHISCHE SCHRIFTENREIHE.** 1-. Monographic series. German. ir. Price varies per volume. Verlag Karl Alber GmbH, Hermann Herder Strasse 4, D 79104 Freiburg Germany. **Tel** 011 49 761 273495. ***Supersedes*** *Symposium; Jahrbuch fuer Philosophie.*

GW/0930-3472
**SYMPTOME.** **Added/Corp** Ruhr-Universitat Bochum. Fachschaft Philosophie. (1986)-. Periodical. German.

CN/0823-1435
**SYNAPSE (REGINA).** (SYNAPSE : THE MENSA PHILOSOPHY SIG NEWSLETTER.). [Synapse]. **Added/Corp** Mensa Philosophy SIG. (1976)-. Periodical. English. bm. Free to members, $1.00 each number to others. MENSA Philosophy Sig, PO Box 212, Regina Saskatchewan S4P 2ZP Canada. **DD** 105.

NE/0039-7857
**SYNTHESE (DORDRECHT).** (SYNTHESE.). [Synthese]. (1936)-. Periodical. Dutch (English, French and German). mo. $1,428.00. Kluwer Academic Publishers, Postbus 322, 3300 AH Dordrecht, The Netherlands. **Tel** 011 (31) 78 524400, FAX 011 31 78 183273, telex 20083. **ED** Jaakko Hinrikka. **LC** AP1; .S9. **DD** 050. **CODEN** SYNTAE. **[CCC].** cum. index. **Bk Rev. Pr Rev. Circ:** 1,100. available on microfilm and microfiche from University Microfilms International (UMI). Documents available from The Genuine Article, BIOSIS Document Express.
**Desc:** Theory of knowledge, scientific discovery, induction, probability, causation, and role of mathematics. Statistics and logic, symbolic logic, foundations of mathematics, and sociology. Most of the issues are organized into thematic issues, taking the character of symposia dealing with described themes.
**Ind/Abst** Arts Humanit. Citation Index [Full Cov.]; Biol. Abstr. (1989-); Curr. Contents Arts Humanit.; Curr. Contents Soc. Behav. Sci.; Math. Rev.; MLA Int. Bibl. Books Artic. Mod. Lang. Lit.; Peace Res. Abstr. J. (1971); Philos. Index; Res. Alert [Full Cov.]; Soc. Plann. Policy Dev. Abstr.; Soc. Sci. Cit. Index [Full Cov.]; Sociol. Abstr.; Stat. Theory Method Abstr. (1970); Zentralbl. Math. Ihre Grenzgeb.

NE/0166-6991
**SYNTHESE LIBRARY.** [Synth. libr.]. (1959)-. Monographic series. English. ir. Price varies per volume. Kluwer Academic Publishers, Postbus 322, 3300 AH Dordrecht, The Netherlands. **Tel** 011 (31) 78 524400, FAX 011 31 78 183273, telex 20083.
**Ind/Abst** Math. Rev.; Zentralbl. Math. Ihre Grenzgeb.

US/1064-0584
**TANTRA (TORREON, N.M.).** (TANTRA.). [Tantra]. (1991)-. Periodical. English. qt (Feb., May, Aug., Nov.). $18.00 US; $22.00 Canada & Mexico; $24.00 other. Tantra, PO Box 79, Torreon NM 87061. **Tel** (505)384-2292. **ED** Susana Andrews (editor's telephone: (505)898-8246). **DD** 181. **Bk Rev**, (Qty: 12-24). **Ad Acc. Circ:** 11,500.

US/0145-5788
**TEACHING PHILOSOPHY.** [Teach. philos.]. Vol. 1 (Summer 1975)-. Periodical. English. qt. $63.00 (institutions), $26.00 (individuals). Philosophy Documentation Center, Bowling Green State University, Bowling Green OH 43403-0189. **Tel** (419)372-2419, (800)444-2419, FAX (419)372-6987. **ED** Arnold Wilson. **LC** B52; .T37. **DD** 107. **[CCC]. Bk Rev. Ad Acc. Circ:** 900.
**Desc:** Publishes articles, discussions, reports, and reviews on theoretical issues in philosophy, innovative methods and courses, new texts and audiovisual materials.
**Ind/Abst** Contents Pages Educ.; Med. Rev. Dig.; Philos. Index.

UK/0040-2184
**TEILHARD REVIEW, THE.** **See** Anthropology.

US/0739-2303
**TEILHARD STUDIES.** [Teilhard stud.]. **Added/Corp** American Teilhard Association for the Future of Man. No. 1 (Winter 1978)-. Monographic series. English. sa. Price varies per volume. Anima Publications, 1053 Wilson Avenue, Chambersburg PA 17201. **Tel** (717)267-0087, FAX (717)267-0087. **LC** B2430.T374; A18. **DD** 194.
**Ind/Abst** Relig. Index One Period. (1978-).

BL
**TEMPO E PRESENCA.** **See** Political Science.

SP/0210-1602
**TEOREMA.** ***Suspended.*** [Teorema]. **Added/Corp** Universidad de Valencia. Departamento de Logica y Filosofia de la Ciencia. Universidad de Valencia. Departamento de Historia de la Filosofia. (March 1971)-(19??). Periodical. Spanish. qt. 3000ptas. Universidad Complutense de Madrid / Logica, APDO Correos 61159, 28080 Madrid Spain. **LC** B5; .T36.
**Ind/Abst** Math. Rev.; Philos. Index.

JA
**TETSUGAKU.** **Added/Corp** Tokyo Daigaku. Kyoyo Gakubu. Tetsugaku Kenkyu-Shitsu. **VFOAT** Series of Philosophy. 1 (1953)-. Periodical. Japanese. be. Tokyo Daigaku Shuppankai, Todai Konai Hongo Bunkyo-ku, Tokyo 113 Japan. **LC** B8.J3; T44.

JA
**TETSUGAKU RONSO.** No. 1- July, 1977-. German (Japanese). Osaka Daigaku Bungakubu, 1-1 Machikaneyamacho, Toyonaka Osaka Japan. **Tel** (06)844-1151. **LC** B8.J3; T48.

JA
**TETSUGAKU SHISO RONSHU.** **VFOAT** Studies in Philosophy. No. 7- (1981)-. Japanese (summaries and/or abstracts in French and English). Tsukuba Daigaku Tetsugaku Shiso Gakukei, 1-1 Tennodai 1-chome Sakura-Mura Niihari-gun, Ibaraki-ken 305 Japan. **LC** B8.J3; T78A . ***Continues*** *Tsukuba Daigaku Tetsugaku Shiso Gakukei Ronshu.*

FR/1157-0466
**THANATOLOGIE (PARIS).** (THANATOLOGIE). (1990)-. Periodical. French. Siege Social / Wagram, 58 Avenue de Wagram, 75017 Paris France. **Tel** 33-1-45 30 22 28, FAX 33-1-45 30 22 69.

US/0160-8681
**THANATOS.** [Thanatos]. **Added/Corp** Florida Consumer Information Bureau. Vol. 1 (Sept. 1975)-. Periodical. English. qt (Mar., June, Sept., Dec.). $16.00. Florida Funeral Directors Services Inc, PO Box 6009, Tallahassee FL 32314. **Tel** (904)224-1969, FAX (904)224-7965. **ED** Jan Scheff. **LC** BD444; .T53. **DD** 128/.5. **Bk Rev**, (Qty: 12-15). **Circ:** 6,000. available on microfiche (University Microfilms International) from University Microfilms International (UMI).
**Desc:** Realistic journal concerning death, dying, and bereavement. It offers a humanistic approach to the issues of death and dying. Created by professionals and individuals it represents no particular philisophical viewpoint. Written with insight and compassion, the articles relate triumph and pain, provide understanding, and promote growth and healing.

GW/0040-5655
**THEOLOGIE UND PHILOSOPHIE.** **See** Religion and Theology.

NE/0167-9902
**THEORETICAL MEDICINE.** **See** Medical Science and Technology.

SP/0495-4548
**THEORIA.** **Added/Corp** Universidad del Pais Vasco. Centro de Analisis, Logica, e Informatica Juridica. Vol. 1, No. 1 (1985)-. Periodical. Spanish. irtq. $30.00 South America, the Caribbean & Portugal; $45.00 other. Servicio de Publications, Universidas Pais Vasco, Leioa 48940 Vizcaya Spain. **Tel** 34 4 4648800 ext. 2153, FAX 34 4 4801314. ***Continues*** *Theoria (Madrid, Spain).*
**Ind/Abst** Math. Rev. (1985-).

SW/0040-5825
**THEORIA.** [Theoria]. Vol. 1 (1935)-. Periodical. English (Norwegian, Danish, English, French and German). Three times a year. $30.00. Theoria Bengt Hansson, Filosofiska Institutionen, S-222 22 Lund Sweden. **Tel** 011 46 46 107593. **ED** Bengt Hansson, Krister Segerberg, and Ingemar Persson. **LC** B1; .A27. **DD** 105. **CODEN** THRAA5. cum. index. **Bk Rev. Ad Acc.** Documents available from The Genuine Article.
**Desc:** Publishes articles in all fields of philosophy, with no preference for any particular school or subject area and with academic excellence as the only criterion for acceptance.
**Ind/Abst** Arts Humanit. Citation Index (19??-19??) [Full Cov.]; Curr. Contents Arts Humanit.; Math. Rev.; Philos. Index; Res. Alert [Full Cov.]; Soc. Plann. Policy Dev. Abstr.; Zentralbl. Math. Ihre Grenzgeb.

CN
**THEORIA/PRAXIS: A GRADUATE JOURNAL OF THEORY AND CRITICISM.**
**See** Social Sciences.

NE/0040-5833
**THEORY AND DECISION.** [Theory decis.]. Vol. 1, No. 1 (Oct. 1970)-. Periodical. English (French). bm. $658.00. Kluwer Academic Publishers, Postbus 322, 3300 AH Dordrecht, The Netherlands. **Tel** 011 (31) 78 524400, FAX 011 31 78 183273, telex 20083. **ED** Bertrand Munier. **LC** H61; .T465. **DD** 300/.1. **CODEN** THDCBA. **[CCC].** Index available in last issue of volume--attached. **Bk Rev. Ad Acc. Pr Rev. Acid Free. Circ:** 850. available on microfilm and microfiche from University Microfilms International (UMI). Documents available from The Genuine Article.
**Desc:** Philosophy and methodology of the social sciences: application of advanced methodology of philosophy of science, logic, and mathematics, discussion of empirical models, etc. The purpose of the journal is to let the engineering of decision making (i.e. of intelligence, choicem choice out, ranking, uncertainty and conflict resolution) gradually emerge.
**Ind/Abst** Acad. Search (July 1993-); Commun. Abstr. (?-?); Curr. Contents Soc. Behav. Sci.; Econ. Lit. Index; Humanit. Source (Jul. 1993-); Int. Abstr. Oper. Res. [Full Cov.]; Int. Bibliogr. Sociol.; Int. Polit. Sci. Abstr.; Mag. Search; Math. Rev.; Philos. Index; Psychol. Abstr. (1973-); PsycINFO (1973-); PsycLit; Res. Alert [Full Cov.]; Sage Public Adm. Abstr. (?-?); Soc. Plann. Policy Dev. Abstr.; Soc. Sci. Cit. Index [Full Cov.]; Sociol. Abstr.; Soc. Res. Methodol. Abstr. (1975-); Zentralbl. Math. Ihre Grenzgeb.

NE/0304-2421
**THEORY AND SOCIETY.** **See** Sociology.

US/0040-5906
**THEOSOPHY.** [Theosophy]. **Added/Corp** Theosophy Company. Vol. 1 (1912)-. Periodical. English. Twelve times a year. $10.00. The Theosophy Company, 245 West 33rd Street, Los Angeles CA 90007-4194. **Tel** (310)748-7244. **ED** Adella Bivins. Index available. **Bk Rev. Circ:** 800 (ctrl).
**Desc:** General articles contributed by present-day students bring the light to bear on contemporary problems and suggest applications of the philosophy in terms of daily life.

US/0190-3330
**THINKING.** **See** Education-Teaching and Curriculum.

●UK/1354-6783
**THINKING AND REASONING.** (1995)-. English. qt. £50.00 EC; $90.00 US; £55.00 other. Lawrence Erlbaum Associates Ltd., 27 Palmeira Mansions, Church Road, Hove East Sussex BN3 2FA England. **Tel** 011 44 273 207411. **(Subscription address:** Turpin Distribution Services Limited, Blackhorse Road, Letchworth, Hertfordshire SG6 1HN, United Kingdom.) **ED** Jonathan St.B.T. Evans.
**Desc:** Dedicated to the understanding of human thought processes, with particular emphasis on studies on reasoning. The primary focus is on psychological studies of thinking; however, contributions are welcomed from philosophers, artificial intelligence researchers and other cognitive scientists.

US/0040-6325
**THOMIST, THE.** [Thomist]. **Added/Corp** Dominicans. Province of St. Joseph. Vol. 1 (April 1939)-. Periodical. English. qt. $25.00 individuals; $45.00 institutions US; $35.00 individuals, $45.00 institutions other. Thomist Press, 487 Michigan Avenue NE, Washington DC 20017. **Tel** (202)529-5300. **ED** Joseph A Dinoia. **LC** BX801; .T5. **DD** 230.05. Index available. cum. index. **Bk Rev. Ad Acc. Circ:** 1,000 (ctrl). available on microfilm and microfiche from University Microfilms International (UMI). Documents available from The Genuine Article.
**Desc:** In the tradition and spirit of Thomas Aquinas, seeks to promote original and penetrating inquiry into the full range of contemporary philosophical and theological questions.
**Ind/Abst** Annu. Bibliogr. Engl. Lang. Lit.; Arts Humanit. Citation Index [Full Cov.]; Curr. Contents Arts Humanit.; Index Book Rev. Relig.; New Testam. Abstr.; Philos. Index; Relig. Theol. Abstr.; Res. Alert [Full Cov.]; Soc. Sci. Cit. Index [Select. Cov.]; Abr. Cathol. Period. Lit. Index; Cathol. Period. Lit. Index.

US/1055-7326
**THOREAU RESEARCH NEWSLETTER.**
[Thoreau res. newsl.]. Vol. 1, No. 1 (Jan. 1990)-. Newsletter. English. qt. $10.00 US; $12.00 other. Transpacific Communications, Route 2, Box 36, Ayden NC 28513. **DD** 141.

II/0254-9808
**TIBETAN BULLETIN.** See Religion and Theology.

BE/0040-750X
**TIJDSCHRIFT VOOR FILOSOFIE.** (Feb. 1939)-. Periodical. Dutch. qt. Redaktie en Administratie, Ravenstraat 112, B3000 Louvain Belgium. cum. index. Documents available from The Genuine Article.
**Ind/Abst** Arts Humanit. Citation Index [Full Cov.]; Res. Alert [Full Cov.]; Soc. Plann. Policy Dev. Abstr.; Soc. Sci. Cit. Index [Select. Cov.].

BE
**TIJDSCHRIFT VOOR PHILOSOPHIE.** **VFOAT** Tijdschrift voor Filosofie. Vol. 1, No. 1 (Feb. 1939)-. Periodical. Dutch (English, French and German). qt. Redaktie en Administratie, Ravenstraat 112, B3000 Louvain Belgium. cum. index.
**Ind/Abst** Philos. Index.

●UK/0961-463X
**TIME & SOCIETY.** **VFOAT** Time and Society. Vol. 1, No. 1 (Jan. 1992)-. Periodical. English. tq. £72.00. Sage Publications Ltd., 6 Bonhill Street, London EC2A 4PU, UK. **Tel** 071 374 0645, FAX 071 374 8741, telex 296207 SAGE G. **CODEN** TIMSEB. **Acid Free.**

NE/0167-7411
**TOPOI.** [Topoi]. **Added/Corp** D. Reidel Publishing Company. Vol. 1, No. 1 & 2 (Dec. 1982)-. Periodical. English (French). sa. $314.00. Kluwer Academic Publishers, Postbus 322, 3300 AH Dordrecht, The Netherlands. **Tel** 011 (31) 78 524400, FAX 011 31 78 183273, telex 20083. **ED** Ermanno Bencivenga and Enrico M Forni. **LC** B1; .T66. **DD** 105. **[CCC].** Index available. **Bk Rev. Ad Acc. Circ:** 400. available on microfilm and microfiche from University Microfilms International (UMI). Documents available from The Genuine Article.
**Desc:** Philosophical studies and the history of philosophy, the most important topics that have emerged, the growth of discussing these topics and the tendencies that developed. This journal does not adhere to expression of any one philosophical school or tradition, but rather promotes the exchange between philosophers from a variety of linguistic and cultural backgrounds.'
**Ind/Abst** Arts Humanit. Citation Index (19??-19??) [Full Cov.]; Math. Rev.; Philos. Index; Res. Alert [Full Cov.]; Soc. Sci. Cit. Index [Select. Cov.].

US/0065-9746
**TRANSACTIONS OF THE AMERICAN PHILOSOPHICAL SOCIETY.** [Trans. Am. Philos. Soc.]. **Added/Corp** American Philosophical Society. (1771)-. Monographic series. English. ir. $90.00. American Philosophical Society, PO Box 40098, Philadelphia PA 19106. **Tel** (215)440-3427, FAX (215)440-3436. **LC** Q11; .P6. **CODEN** TAPSAY. Index available in last issue of volume--attached. available on microfilm and microfiche from University Microfilms International (UMI). Documents available from The Genuine Article.
**Ind/Abst** Annu. Bibliogr. Engl. Lang. Lit.; Arts Humanit. Citation Index [Full Cov.]; Curr. Contents Arts Humanit.; GeoRef; Math. Rev.; Res. Alert [Full Cov.]; Romant. Move.; Soc. Plann. Policy Dev. Abstr.; Soc. Sci. Cit. Index [Select. Cov.].

US/0009-1774
**TRANSACTIONS OF THE CHARLES S. PIERCE SOCIETY.** [Trans. Charles S. Pierce Soc.]. **Main/Corp** Charles S. Pierce Society. (Spring 1965)-. Periodical. English. qt (Feb., May, Aug., Nov.). $60.00 US (1 year); $65.00 others (1 year). Hare State University of New York, Philosophy Dept., Baldy Hall, Buffalo NY 14260. **Tel** (716)645-2444, FAX (716)645-3825. **ED** Peter H Hare. **LC** B945.P44; A13. **DD** 191. Index available. **Bk Rev. Ad Acc. Pr Rev. Circ:** 500 (ctrl). Documents available from The Genuine Article.
**Desc:** History of American philosophy.
**Ind/Abst** Arts Humanit. Citation Index [Full Cov.]; Curr. Contents Arts Humanit.; Philos. Index; Res. Alert [Full Cov.].

BL/0101-3173
**TRANSFORMACAO.** **Added/Corp** Faculdade de Filosofia, Ciencias e Letras de Assis. Departamento de Filosofia. Universidade Estadual Paulista. **VFOAT** Trans/Form/Acao. No. 1 (1974)-. Abstracting/Indexing Service. Multiple languages (Portuguese and French). an. Universidade Estadual Paulista, Coordenadoria Geral de Bibliotecas, Av. Vicente Ferreira 1 2 7 8, CP 603, CEP 17526-901 Marilia SP Brazil. **LC** B5; .T7. **DD** 105. **Circ:** 500.
**Desc:** Publishes interviews and original articles. Papers deal with philosophical subjects or subjects related to philosophy.
**Ind/Abst** HAPI Hisp. Am. Period. Index; Philos. Index.

CC
**TUNG-PEI SHIH TA HSUEH PAO. CHE HSUEH SHE HUI KO HSUEH PAN.** **VFOAT** Dongbei Shida Xuebao; Journal of Northeastern Normal University. Philosophy and Social Sciences. Periodical. Chinese. bm. RMBY0.40. Science Press, 16 Donghuangchenggen North Street, Beijing 100707, People's Republic of China. **Tel** 011 86 1 4019821, 011 86 1 4010642, FAX 011 86 1 4012180, 011 86 1 4019810, telex 210147. **LC** AS451; .T87. **DD** 089/.951.

●CH/1010-0725
**TUNG WU CHE HSUEH CHUAN HSI LU / TUNG WU TA HSUEH.** **Added/Corp** Tung wu ta Hsueh (Taipei, Taiwan). Che Hsueh Hsi. **VFOAT** Philosophical Research. (Mar. 1992)-. Periodical. Chinese. Tung Wu Ta Hsueh, 56 Kueiyang Street/Section 1, Taipei 100 Taiwan. **Tel** (02)8819471. **LC** B8.C5; C46. **DD** 105. ***Continues*** *Chuan Hsi Lu.*

RU/0502-9988
**UCHENYE ZAPISKI KAFEDR MARKSISTSKO-LENINSKOI FILOSOFII VYSSHEI PARTIINOI SHKOLY PRI TSK KPSS I MESTNYKH VYSSHIKH PARTIINYKH SHKOL.** **Added/Corp** TSK KPSS. Vysshaia Partiinaia Shkola. (1958)-. Russian. ir. MYSL, 117071 B-71 Leninskii Prospekt 15, Moscow Russia. **(Subscription address:** Victor Kamkin, 4956 Boiling Brook Parkway, Rockville MD 20852.**)** **LC** B6; .U3.

CN/0709-549X
**ULTIMATE REALITY AND MEANING.** [Ultim. real. mean.]. **Added/Corp** Institute for Encyclopedia of Human Ideas on Ultimate Reality and Meaning. Vol. 1, No. 1 (1978)-. Periodical. English (French). qt (Jan., Apr., July, Oct.). $43.00. University of Toronto Press, 5201 Dufferin Street, Downsview Ontario M3H 5T8 Canada. **Tel** (416)667-7781, (416)667-7782, FAX (416)667-7803. **ED** Tibor Horvath. **LC** BD331; .U43. **DD** 110/.5. Index available. cum. index. **Circ:** 450. Documents available from The Genuine Article.
**Desc:** Publishes studies dealing with axiomatic presuppositions operating in various sciences, philosophies, religions, and value systems as well as in individuals' personal life. Offers an opportunity to participate in an ongoing dialogue in which scholars and interested readers from all parts of the world explore past and present human effort to conceptualize reality and to find meaning in our world.
**Ind/Abst** Arts Humanit. Citation Index [Full Cov.]; Curr. Contents Arts Humanit.; Guide Soc. Sci. Relig.; Index Book Rev. Relig.; Philos. Index; Relig. Index One Period. (1978-); Relig. Theol. Abstr.; Res. Alert [Full Cov.]; Soc. Plann. Policy Dev. Abstr.; Sociol. Abstr.

CK/0120-5323
**UNIVERSITAS PHILOSOPHICA.** (Sept. 1983)-. Periodical. Spanish. sa. Facultad de Filosofia, Univeridad Javeriana, Carrera 7 No 39-08, Bogota DE 2 Colombia.

BE
**UNIVERSITE LIBRE DE BRUXELLS, FACULTE DE PHILOSOPHIE ET LETTRES.** Universite Libre de Bruxelles, 50 Avenue F D Roosevelt CP 188, 1050 Brussels Belgium. **Tel** 011 32 2 6423611.

II
**UNIVERSITY OF MADRAS. CENTRE OF ADVANCED STUDY IN PHILOSOPHY. YEAR BOOK.** (YEAR BOOK / THE DR. S. RADHAKRISHNAN INSTITUTE FOR ADVANCED STUDY IN PHILOSOPHY.). **Main/Corp** Dr. S. Radhakrishnan Institute for Advanced Study in Philosophy. 1976/77-. English. Free. University of Madras Institute for Advanced Study in Philosophy, Madras 600 005 India. **LC** B130; .M27A. **DD** 181/.4/05.

US
**UNIVERSITY OF NOTRE DAME STUDIES IN THE PHILOSOPHY OF RELIGION.** See Religion and Theology.

GW/0233-2957
**UNTERSUCHUNGEN ZUR LOGIK UND ZUR METHODOLOGIE : BEITRAEGE DES KOOPERATIONSRATES LOGIK AN DER KARL-MARX-UNIVERSITAT / HERAUSGEGEBEN IM AUFTRAG DES REKTORS DER KARL-MARX-UNIVERSITAT LEIPZIG VOM KOOPERATIONSRAT LOGIK AN DER KARL-MARX-UNIVERSITAT LEIPZIG.** **Added/Corp** Karl-Marx-Universitat Leipzig. Kooperationsrat Logik. (1984)-. German. an. **LC** BC1; .U58. **DD** 160/.5.
**Desc:** Concerned with logic and methodology.
**Ind/Abst** Zentralbl. Math. Ihre Grenzgeb.

II/0042-2983
**VEDANTA KESARI, THE.** **Added/Corp** Sri Ramakrishna Math, Madras. Vol. 1 (1914)-. Periodical. English. mo. $20.00. Sri Ramakrishna Math, 16 Ramakrishna Math Road, Madras 600004 India. **Tel** 71231. **(Subscription address:** Prints India, 11 Darya Ganj, New Delhi, 110002 India, (Phone: 011 91 11 3268645)**)** **ED** Swami Tyagananda. Index available. **Bk Rev. Ad Acc. Circ:** 5,000.
**Desc:** Ideas in the areas of philosophy, religion and culture.

IT/0391-4186
**VERIFICHE.** [Verifiche]. (Sept. 1972)-. Italian (summaries and/or abstracts in German). qt. L60000 Italy; L70000 other. Verifiche Assoc. Trentina, Scienze Umane CP 269, 38100 Trento Italy. **Tel** 011 39 461 987264. **ED** Giuliano Rigoni and Mario Rigoni. **LC** B4; .V47. **Circ:** 2,000. Documents available from The Genuine Article.
**Ind/Abst** Am. Hist. Life (1977-); Arts Humanit. Citation Index (19??-) [Full Cov.]; Bibliogr. Mission. (19??-); Curr. Contents Arts Humanit. (19??-); Res. Alert (19??-) [Full Cov.].

RU
**VESTNIK MOSKOVSKOGO UNIVERSITETA. SERIIA VII : FILOSOFIIA.** **Main/Corp** Moskovskii Gosudarstvennyi Universitet Im. M.V. Lomonosova. **VFOAT** Filosofiia. (Jan./Feb. 1977)-. Periodical. Russian. bm. $79.95. Izdatelstvo Moskovskogo Universiteta, K-9 Ulitsa Gertsena 5/7, 103009 Moscow Russia. **Tel** (301)881-5973. **(Subscription address:** East View Publications Inc., 3020 Harbor Lane North, Suite 110, Minneapolis MN 55447.**)** **LC** B6; .M68b. ***Supersedes*** *Vestnik Moskovskogo Universiteta. Seriia VIII: Filosofiia.*
**Ind/Abst** Soc. Plann. Policy Dev. Abstr.; Sociol. Abstr. (?-?).

BL
**VINCULO.** Yearly V. 1- March 1973-. Multiple languages (French and Portuguese). Faculdade de Filosofia / Montes Clares, rua Coronel Celestino 75, 39400 Montes Clares M G Brazil. **LC** AS80.F85; A37.

II/0042-7187
**VISVA-BHARATI JOURNAL OF PHILOSOPHY, THE.** **Added/Corp** Visva Bharati. Centre of Advanced Studies in Philosophy. Vol. 1 (Aug. 1964)-. Periodical. English. Twice a year. Visva-Bharati, 6 Acharya Jagadish Bose Road, Calcutta 700017 India. **Tel** 011 91 33 449868.

IT/0042-725X
**VITA E PENSIERO.** [Vita pensiero]. Vol. 1 (1915)-. Periodical. Italian. Eleven times a year (Aug.). L38000. Vita e Pensiero, Pubblic University, Largo Gemelli 1, 20123 Milan Italy. **Tel** 011 39 2 72342310, 011 39 2 72342370. **ED** Adriano Bausola. **Bk Rev. Ad Acc. Circ:** 35,000 (ctrl).
**Ind/Abst** Bibliogr. Mission.; MLA Int. Bibl. Books Artic. Mod. Lang. Lit.

NE/0042-7543
**VIVARIUM.** [Vivarium]. Vol. 1 (May 1963)-. Periodical. English (French and German). sa (2 issues). Fl114.00 (institutions) Netherlands; $65.25 (institutions) other. E. J. Brill, Postbus 9000, 2300 PA Leiden Netherlands. **Tel** 011 31 71 312624, FAX 011 31 71 317532, telex 39296 BRILL NL. **ED** L. M. de Rijk. **LC** B1; .A3. **DD** 189/.05. **[CCC]. Bk Rev. Ad Acc. Circ:** 288. Documents available from The Genuine Article.
**Desc:** Includes extended examinations of fundamental philosophical problems and of the history of ideas, first editions of smaller texts with introduction and notes, studies on manuscript tradition and on the history of texts, review articles and reviews. Special attention is paid to the profane side of philosophy and to its relationship to other domains of thought and learning of the period.
**Ind/Abst** Arts Humanit. Citation Index [Full Cov.]; Middle East Abstr. Index; MLA Int. Bibl. Books Artic. Mod. Lang. Lit.; Philos. Index; Res. Alert [Full Cov.].

II
**VOICE OF SANKARA, THE.** **VFOAT** Sankara-Bharati. Began with issue for May 1976. Periodical. English (Hindi and Sanskrit). qt. $10.00. Adi Sankara Advaita Research Centre, 26 College Road, Nungambakkam Madras 600006 India. **LC** B132.A3; V64. **DD** 181/.482/05.

RU/0042-8744
**VOPROSY FILOSOFII.** (VOPROSY FILOSOFII / AKADEMIIA NAUK SSSR, INSTITUT FILOSOFII.). [Vopr. filos.]. **Added/Corp** Institut Filosofii (Akademiia Nauk SSSR). Vol. 1 (1947)-. Academic Scholarly Publication. Russian (English, French, German and Spanish). mo. $138.00. Izdatelstvo Nauka / Akademiia Nauk, Publishing House of the Russian Academy of Sciences, Leninskii Porspekt 14, 117901 Moscow Russia. **Tel** 011 95 954-21-53, FAX 011 95 938-21-44, telex 411964. **(Subscription address:** East View Publications Inc., 3020 Harbor Lane North, Suite 110, Minneapolis MN 55447.**)** **[CCC].** available on microfilm from University Microfilms International (UMI). Documents available from The Genuine Article.
**Ind/Abst** Am. Hist. Life (1954-1957, 1971-); Arts Humanit. Citation Index [Full Cov.]; Curr. Contents Arts Humanit.; Int. Aerosp. Abstr.; Int. Bibliogr. Sociol.; Int. Polit. Sci. Abstr.; Math. Rev.; Res. Alert [Full Cov.]; Soc. Plann. Policy Dev. Abstr.; Soc. Sci. Cit. Index [Select. Cov.]; Sociol. Abstr.; Curr. Dig. Post Sov. Press.

RU
**VOPROSY METODOLOGII.** **Added/Corp** Soiuz Nauchnykh i Inzhenernykh Obshchestv SSSR.

Komitet po Sistemo-DeiatenostnoÊi Metodologii i Organizatsionno-Deiatelnostnym Igram. (1991)-. Russian.

RU/0321-0847
**VOPROSY NAUCNOGO ATEIZMA (MOSKVA).** (VOPROSY NAUCHNOGO ATEIZMA / AKADEMIIA OBSHCHESTVENNYKH NAUK PRI TSK KPSS, INSTITUT NAU CHNOGO ATEIZMA.). [Vopr. naucn. ateizma]. **Added/Corp** Institut Nauchnogo Ateizma (Akademiia Obshchestvennykh Nauk). (1966)-. Russian. ir. MYSL, 117071 B-71 Leninskii Prospekt 15, Moscow Russia. **LC** BL2700; .V64.
**Ind/Abst** Int. Bibliogr. Sociol.

CC
**WAI KUO CHE HSUEH SHIH YEN CHIU CHI KAN - CHUNG-KUO SHE HUI KO HSUEH YUAN CHE HSUEH YEN CHIU SO, HSI FANG CHE HSUEH SHIH YEN CHIU SHIH PIEN.** **VFOAT** Research on Empiricism and Rationalism in the History of Modern European Philosophy. Began with Dec. 1978 issue. Chinese. RMBY0.86. Hsin Hua Shu Tien / Shang-Hai Fa Hsing So, Shanghai, People's Republic of China. **LC** B816; .W3. **DD** 109.

AU/0083-999X
**WIENER JAHRBUCH FUR PHILOSOPHIE.** V. 1- 1968-. German. an. Wilhelm Braumueller, Servitengasse 5, A 1092 Vienna, Austria. **Tel** 011 43 1 3191482, 3191159. **ED** Wilhelm Braumuller. **LC** B31; .W47. **DD** 105. **Bk Rev. Ad Acc. Circ:** 500 (ctrl). ***Continues in part*** *Wiener Zeitschrift fur Philosophie, Psychologie, Padagogik.*
**Desc:** Yearbook of the Institute of Philosophy of the University of Vienna.

NE/0084-0084
**WIENER ZEITSCHRIFT FUR DIE KUNDE SUDASIENS UND ARCHIV FUR INDISCHE PHILOSOPHIE.** **Added/Corp** Osterreichische Akademie der Wissenschaften. Osterreichisches Akademie der Wissenschaften. Kommission fur Sprachen und Kulturen Sudasiens. Universitat Wien. Indologisches Institut. **VFOAT** Archiv fur Indische Philosophie. Vol. 14 (1970)-. German (English, French and Italian; summaries and/or abstracts in English). an. S570.00. Oesterreichischen Akademie Wissenschaften, Dr. Ignaz Seipel Platz 2, A-1010 Vienna Austria. **Tel** 011 43 1 51581. **LC** DS2; .W54. ***Continues*** *Wiener Zeitschrift fur die Kunde Sud- und Ostasiens und Archiv fur Indische Philosophie.*
**Ind/Abst** MLA Int. Bibl. Books Artic. Mod. Lang. Lit.

NE
**WIJSGERIG PERSPECTIEF OP MAATSCHAPPIJ EN WETENSCHAP.** Vol. 1, No. 1 (Sept. 1960)-. Dutch. bm. Fl60.00 (individuals). Uitgeverij Boom, Postbus 400, 7940 AK Meppel Netherlands. **Tel** 011 31 20 5220 57012, FAX 011 31 20 5220 54452, telex 42829.

AU/0043-6798
**WISSENSCHAFT UND WELTBILD; ZEITSCHRIFT FUER GRUNDFRAGEN DER FORSCHUNG UND WELTANSCHAUUNG.** (1948)-. Periodical. German. qt. S250.00. Arthur Werner Verlag, Sandwirtgasse 21, Vienna A-1060 Austria. Index available. **Bk Rev.**
**Ind/Abst** Am. Hist. Life (1954-); Philos. Index.

GW/0179-0080
**WISSENSCHAFTLICHER BUCH BESPRECHUNGSDIENST : WIBB.** **See** Religion and Theology.

US
**WITNESS FOR PEACE NEWSLETTER.** **See** Political Science.

GW/0342-5940
**WOLFENBUETTELER STUDIEN ZUR AUFKLAERUNG.** [Wolfenb. Stud. Aufklaer.]. **Added/Corp** Lessing-Akademie. Vol. 1 (1974)-. Monographic series. German. ir. Price varies per volume. Max Niemeyer Verlag, Postfach 2140, D 72011 Tuebingen Germany. **Tel** 011 49 7071 989494, FAX 011 49 7071 87419. **LC** B802; .W64.
**Ind/Abst** MLA Int. Bibl. Books Artic. Mod. Lang. Lit.

US/0260-4027
**WORLD FUTURES.** [World futures]. Vol. 17, No. 1/2 (Jan. 1981)-. Periodical. English. ir. Price varies. Gordon & Breach Science Publishers, Inc., PO Box 786, Cooper Station, New York NY 10276. **Tel** (212)206-8900, FAX (212)645-2459. **(Subscription address:** Gordon & Breach Science Publishers / England, PO Box 90, Reading RG1 8JL England.**) ED** Ervin Laszlo. **LC** B1; .P25. **DD** 303.4. **CODEN** WOFUDM. **[CCC]. Bk Rev. Ad Acc.** Documents available from UMI Article Clearinghouse. ***Continues*** *Philosophy Forum, 0031-823X.*
**Ind/Abst** Acad. Search (July 1993-); Expand. Acad. Index (1989-); Humanit. Index; Humanit. Source (Jul. 1993-); INFO-SOUTH Abstr.; Int. Bibliogr. Sociol.; Mag. Search; Math. Rev.; Newsp. Period. Abstr. (1991-); Philos. Index; Soc. Plann. Policy Dev. Abstr.; Sociol. Abstr. (?-?).

US/0043-8804
**WORLD ORDER.** **See** Religion and Theology.

GW/0512-6614
**XEROGRAMMATA; HOCHSCHULSCHRIFTEN ZUR PHILOSOPHIE.** Vol. 1 (1967)-. German. Bouvier GmbH & Co. KG ABT Verlag, AM Hof 28, D 53113 Bonn Germany. **Tel** 011 49 228 7290141. **DD** 100.

II
**YEAR BOOK - BANARAS HINDU UNIVERSITY. CENTRE OF ADVANCED STUDY IN PHILOSOPHY.** **Main/Corp** Banaras Hindu University. Centre of Advanced Study in Philosophy. (19??)-. English. Banaras Hindu University Centre of Advanced Study in Philosophy, Varanasi 5 India. **LC** B130; .B34a. **DD** 107/.11/542.

US/0065-9762
**YEAR BOOK - THE AMERICAN PHILOSOPHICAL SOCIETY.** [Year book - Am. Philos. Soc.]. **Main/Corp** American Philosophical Society. **VAT** Yearbook - American Philosophical Society. (1937)-. English. an (Summer). $20.00 US; $24.00 others. American Philosophical Society, PO Box 40098, Philadelphia PA 19106. **Tel** (215)440-3427, FAX (215)440-3436. **LC** Q11; .P613. **DD** 506.273. **NLM** W1 YE102D. **CODEN** YAPSAL. available on microfilm from University Microfilms International (UMI). ***Continued in part by*** *Grantees' Reports, 0893-7346.*
**Desc:** Bring together in one place reports, notices, accounts of the present state of the society and its activities which have heretofore been published in separate pamphlet.
**Ind/Abst** Am. Hist. Life (1961-1972); GeoRef.

UK/0953-2161
**YOGA AND HEALTH.** English. mo. £17.00 UK; £19.00, £30.00 (air mail) other. Yoga & Health, 21 Caburn Crescent Lewes East, Sussex BN7 1NR England. **ED** J Sill. **Bk Rev. Ad Acc. Circ:** 14,000. ***Continues*** *Yoga Today.*
**Desc:** All aspects of yoga both practical and classical and all aspects of health and healthy living.

CN/0824-2526
**YOGA LIFE (1982).** (YOGA LIFE.). [Yoga life]. Vol. 1, No. 1 (Winter 1982/83)-. Periodical. English. sa. Free. Sivananda Ashram Yoga Camp, 243 West 24th Street, New York NY 10011. **Tel** (212)255-4560. **DD** 613.7/046/0601. **Bk Rev. Circ:** 100,000 (ctrl). ***Continues*** *Sivananda Yoga Life, 0227-4930.*
**Desc:** Presents articles on yoga science, holistic health, biology, biophysics, preventive medicine, nutrition and diet, meditation, science of mind, world peace and general news of Sivananda Yoga Vedanta Centers International.

IS/0021-3306
**YWN.** (IYYUN.). [Ywn]. **Added/Corp** Jerusalem Philosophical Society. Merkaz S. H. Bergman le-iyun Filosofi. **VFOAT** Eyoon; Iyyun. Vol.1 (Nov. 1946)-. Periodical. Hebrew (English). qt. $27.00. Jerusalem Philosophical Society, Hebrew University, Department of Philosophy, Jerusalem 91905 Israel. **Tel** 11 972 2 883879, FAX 972-2-322545, telex 26458. **ED** Eddy M Zemach. cum. index. **Bk Rev. Circ:** 700.
**Desc:** Publishes articles, critical studies and reviews on philosophy, irrespective of the author's philosophical school or method of inquiry.
**Ind/Abst** Philos. Index.

XO
**ZBORNIK FILOZOFICKEJ FAKULTY. PHILOSOPHICA.** **VFOAT** Philosophica; Zbornik Univerzity Komensskeho; Zbornik Filozofickej Fakulty Univerzity Komenskeho. Philosophica. Vol. 17-18 (1976/77)-. Periodical. Slovak (Czech). ir. Slovenske Pedagogicke Nakladetelstvo, Sasinkova 5, 891 12 Bratislava, Slovakia. **ED** Milan Zigo. **LC** B26; .B72. **Circ:** 500. ***Continues*** *Sbornik Filozofickej Fakulty Univerzity Komenskeho. Philosophica, 0083-4181.*
**Ind/Abst** Philos. Index.

GW/0044-3301
**ZEITSCHRIFT FUER PHILOSOPHISCHE FORSCHUNG.** [Z. philos. Forsch.]. **Added/Corp** Allgemeine Gesellschaft fuer Philosophie in Deutschland. Vol. 1 (1946)-. Periodical. German (English and French). Four times a year. Vittorio Klostermann, Frauenlobstrasse 22, D 60487 Frankfurt Germany. **Tel** 011 49 69 9708160. **ED** Hans Michael Baumgartner and Otfried Hoffe. **LC** B3; .Z33. **DD** 015. Index available. cum. index. **Bk Rev. Ad Acc. Circ:** 1,400 (ctrl). Documents available from The Genuine Article.
**Desc:** Research in all branches of philosophy. Written for philosophers, students of philosophy, university libraries, and institutes.
**Ind/Abst** Arts Humanit. Citation Index [Full Cov.]; Curr. Contents Arts Humanit.; Philos. Index; Res. Alert [Full Cov.]; Romant. Move.; Soc. Sci. Cit. Index [Select. Cov.].

AU
**ZEITSCHRIFT FUR GANZHEITSFORSCHUNG.** **Added/Corp** Gesellschaft fur Ganzheitsforschung. (19??)-. Periodical. German. qt. S200.00 Austria; $19.00 US. Wirtschaftsuniversitaet, Augasse 2-6, A-1090 Vienna Austria. **Tel** 011 31336 4527 26, FAX 011 31336 4727. **ED** J Hanns Pichler. **LC** AS141; .Z44. Index available. **Bk Rev**, (Qty: 20-30). **Ad Acc, Adv Mgr:** M. Stueckler. **Pr Rev. Circ:** 500.

IT
**ZETA (BOLOGNA, ITALY).** (ZETA.). Periodical. Italian. qt. Vica Castiglione 27, 40124 Bologna Italy. **LC** R724; .Z48. **DD** 362.9/05.

## ABSTRACTING, BIBLIOGRAPHIES AND STATISTICS

MX/0185-240X
**BIBLIOGRAFIA FILOSOFICA MEXICANA.** Vol. 1 (1968)- No. 1-. Spanish. an. $10,000.00 Mexico; $4.00 US and other. Instituto de Investigaciones Filosoficas-UNAM, Circuito Mtro. Mario De La Cueva., Ciudad Universitaria, CP 04510 DF Mexico. **(Subscription address:** Apartado Postal 70-447, Ciudad Universitaria, 04510 Mexico DF**) LC** Z7125; .B554; B92. **DD** 105. **Bk Rev. Ad Acc. Circ:** 1,000. available on diskette.
**Desc:** Works published in Mexico on philosophy and related areas.

FR/0006-1352
**BIBLIOGRAPHIE DE LA PHILOSOPHIE.** (BIBLIOGRAPHIE DE LA PHILOSOPHIE. BIBLIOGRAPHY OF PHILOSOPHY.). [Bibliogr. philos.]. **Added/Corp** International Institute of Philosophy. International Federation of Philosophical Societies. **VFOAT** Bibliography of Philosophy. (1954)-. Bibliography. French (German and English). ir. $131.00. Librarie Philosophique, J Vrin, 6 Place de la Sorbonne, 75005 Paris, France. **Tel** 11 33 1 43540347. **LC** Z7127; .B5; B77. **DD** 016.1. Index available in last issue of volume--attached. **Bk Rev. Ad Acc.** ***Supersedes*** *Bibliographie de la Philosophie, 0006-1352.*
**Desc:** It is the only journal in the world devoted exclusively to providing up-to-date information and abstracts of books published in philosophy and related fields.

GW/0034-2262
**BIBLIOGRAPHIE PHILOSOPHIE.** ***Ceased.*** (1967)-Ceased (Jan. 1989). Periodical. German. qt. Deutscher Judo Verband, Redaktion Ippon Segewaldweg 40, D 12557 Berlin Germany. **Tel** 011 49 711 210770, telex 051 678. **LC** Z7127; .B6; B53. **DD** 016.1.

US
**BIBLIOGRAPHIES OF FAMOUS PHILOSOPHERS.** **Added/Corp** Ohio. State University, Bowling Green. Philosophy Documentation Center. (1974)-. Monographic series. English. ir. Price varies per volume. Philosophy Documentation Center, Bowling Green State University, Bowling Green OH 43403-0189. **Tel** (419)372-2419, (800)444-2419, FAX (419)372-6987. **ED** Richard H. Lineback.
**Desc:** A series of bibliographies of famous philosophers. Includes works on Heidegger, Husserl, Santayana, Hobbes, Sartre, Bergson, Ortega and Whitehead.

FR/0986-1653
**ENSEIGNEMENT PHILOSOPHIQUE, L'.** (1987)-. Periodical. French. bm. 208.53F European Union; 250.00F other. Association Professuers Philosophie, Claude Brochard les Bertons, 17350 St Savinien France. **Tel** 011 33 46901773. **UDC** 37. **Bk Rev. Ad Acc. Circ:** 1,500 (ctrl).

IT/0393-7380
**FOGLIO TORINO.** [Foglio Torino]. (1971)-. Periodical. Italian. mo (9 issues per year.). L25000. Associazione Amici Foglio, via Boston 60, 10137 Turin Italy. **Tel** 011 39 11 357522. **UDC** 2. **Bk Rev. Circ:** 900-1,000.
**Desc:** Social, political, cultural and religious themes.

GW/0420-0985
**KLEINE PHILOSOPHISCHE BIBLIOGRAPHIEN.** Vol. 1- 1968-. German. ir. $40.00. K.G. Saur Verlag KG, A Reed Reference Publishing Company, Part of Reed International PLC, Ortlerstrasse 8, D 81373 Munich Germany. **Tel** 011 49 89 769020, FAX 011 49 89 76902150, telex 5212067-SAUR-D. **(Subscription address:** 175 Fifth Avenue, New York, NY 10010**) ED** Alwin Diener.

US/0031-7993
**PHILOSOPHER'S INDEX.** **Added/Corp** Bowling Green State University. Bowling Green State University. Philosophy Documentation Center. Vol. 1 (Spring 1967)-. Abstracting/Indexing Service. English (French, German, Italian and Spanish). qt. $174.00 (institutions), $52.00 (individuals). Philosophy

Documentation Center, Bowling Green State University, Bowling Green OH 43403-0189. **Tel** (419)372-2419, (800)444-2419, FAX (419)372-6987. **ED** Richard H. Lineback. cum. index. **Bk Rev. Ad Acc. Circ:** 1,500. available on CD-ROM.
**Desc:** An up-to-date index of articles from more than 380 international philosophy and interdisciplinary journals and philosophy books.

BE/0034-4567
**REPERTOIRE BIBLIOGRAPHIQUE DE LA PHILOSOPHIE. Added/Corp** Societe Philosophique de Louvain. Vol. 1 (Feb. 1949)-. Bibliography. French (Multiple languages). qt. 1750F; 3200F (combination with Revue Philosophique de Louvain). Editions Peeters SA, Bondgenotenlaan 153, BP 41, B-3000 Leuven Belgium. **Tel** 32 16 235170, FAX 32 16 228500, telex 65987 PUL B. **ED** Cl. Troisfontaines. **LC** Z7127; .R42. **DD** 016.1. Index available. cum. index. **Circ:** 1,800 (ctrl). ***Supersedes** Repertoire Bibliographique.*
**Desc:** Bibliographical repeorium of studies, monographs and articles on philosophy.
**Ind/Abst** Bibliogr. Mission.

## PHOTOGRAPHY AND VIDEO

US/0746-9837
**4SIGHT.** (4SIGHT : MAGAZINE / NATIONAL PRESS PHOTOGRAPHERS ASSN OF REGION 4.). **Added/Corp** National Press Photographers Association (U.S.). Region 4. **VFOAT** 4 Sight; Four Sight; Forsight. (198?)-. Periodical. English. bm. 4Sight, PO Box 1146, Durham NC 27702.

CN/0822-4331
**596.** (596 / CANADIAN CENTRE OF PHOTOGRAPHY AND FILM.). [596]. **Added/Corp** Canadian Centre of Photography and Film. **VFOAT** Five Ninety-Six. Vol. 1, No. 3 (June/July 1983)-. Periodical. English. bm. $15.00. Canadian Centre of Photography and Film, 596 Markham Street, Toronto Ontario M6G 2L8 Canada. **Tel** (416)367-1305. **DD** 779/.092/2. ***Continues** Focus (Canadian Centre of Photography and Film), 0822-4323.*

AG
**ACAFO.** free. Camara de Comerciantes de Articulos Fotograficos, Florida 1 - P10, 1005 Buenos Aires Argentina. **ED** Jose Quiroga. **Ad Acc. Pr Rev. Circ:** 10,000 (ctrl).
**Desc:** Covers photography in all aspects: artistic, scienctific, commercial and industrial.

SP
**ACTAS DE CULTURA Y ENSAYOS FOTOGRAFICOS F/8. Added/Corp** Grupo Fotografico de Libre Expresion (Spain). (19??)-. Periodical. Spanish (English). qt. 2,500ptas each issue. Grupo Fotografico de Libre Expresion, Apartado de Correos 459, Seville Spain. **Tel** 954-217086. **LC** TR1; .A23. **DD** 770/.5. Index available. cum. index. **Bk Rev. Ad Acc. Circ:** 110. available in paper back.
**Desc:** Contains studies, essays, original portfolios signed by the author (if alive), and everything about actual and historical photography.

SP
**ACTIVIDADES. Added/Corp** Real Sociedad Fotografica. (19??)-. Periodical. Spanish.

US/0883-7090
**ADULT VIDEO NEWS.** [Adult video news]. (198?)-. Periodical. English. mo (12 issues). $44.95. Adult Video News Publications, 8600 West Chester Park/Suite 300, Upper Darby PA 19082. **Tel** (215)789-2085, FAX (215)446-0237. **ED** Paul Fishbein. **DD** 791. **Bk Rev. Ad Acc. Circ:** 27,000 (ctrl).
**Desc:** Complete coverage of the field of adult video reviews of every video release, interviews, feature stories, profiles and industry news.

SP/0514-9193
**AF, ARTE FOTOGRAFICO. VFOAT** Arte Fotografico. No. 1- 1952-. Periodical. Spanish. 5.300ptas Spain; $79.00 North America. Ediarte SA, Santo Angel 76, 28043 Madrid Spain. **ED** Virginia Massegosa. Index available. cum. index. **Bk Rev. Ad Acc.**
**Ind/Abst** ARTbibliogr. Mod. (1985-).

IT
**AFT : SEMESTRALE DELL'ARCHIVIO FOTOGRAFICO TOSCANO. Added/Corp** Archivio Fotografico Toscano. Vol. 1, No. 1 (May 1985)-. Periodical. Italian. sa (Jun. & Dec.). L20000 Italy; L45000 other. Opus Libri Srl, Via della Torretta 16, 50137 Florence Italy. **Tel** 011 39 55 660833.
**Desc:** History of photography.
**Ind/Abst** BHA : Biblio. Hist. Art.

US/0300-7472
**AFTERIMAGE.** [Afterimage]. **Added/Corp** Visual Studies Workshop. (1972)-. Academic Scholarly Publication. English. Ten times a year (Except July & Aug.). $30.00 (individuals); $40.00 (institutions) Comes with Visual Studies Workshop membership. Visual Studies Workshop, 31 Prince Street, Rochester NY 14607. **Tel** (716)442-8676. **ED** Grant Kester and Nadine McGann. **LC** TR640; .A2. **DD** 770/.5. Index available. cum. index. **Bk Rev. Circ:** 2,500. available on microfilm (16mm and 35mm) from University Microfilms International (UMI). Documents available from UMI Article Clearinghouse.
**Desc:** Features issues on the work of emerging artists and the latest developments in cultural theory, and groundbreaking scholarly essays. It listed films, video, photography, and alternative publishing, bringing our readers interviews with leading artistic and critical figures.
**Ind/Abst** Art Index; ARTbibliogr. Mod.; BHA : Biblio. Hist. Art; Book Rev. Index (1984-); Expand. Acad. Index (1992-); Film Lit. Index; Newsp. Period. Abstr. (1989-).

UK
**AL-VIDYU AL-ARABI. VFOAT** Videoarab; Video Arab; Majallat Al-Vidyu Al-Arabi. Periodical. Arabic. mo. $2.50. Trytel International Publications Ltd, 26/28 Agnes Road, London W3 7YF England. **LC** PN1992.95; .V56 . **UDC** 892.7.

IT/0393-9758
**ALMANACCO DI FOTOGRAFARE.** [Alm. fotogr.]. (1967)-. Periodical. Italian. Four times a year. L30000 Italy; L60000 other. Cesco Ciapanna Editore Spa, Via Lipari 8, 00141 Rome Italy. **Tel** 011 39 6 87183441, FAX 011 39 6 87183995. **ED** Francesco Ciapanna. **UDC** 77. **Ad Acc. Circ:** 55,000.
**Desc:** Articles, descriptions and prices of all photographic and video items sold in Italy.

UK/0002-6840
**AMATEUR PHOTOGRAPHER.** [Amat. photogr.]. Vol. 95, No. 2954, June (1945)-. Periodical. English. Fifty-two times a year. $140.00. Reed Business Publishing / West Sussex, England, Perrymount Road, Haywards Heath, West Sussex RH16 3DH England. **Tel** 011 44 81 6523500. **DD** 770. **[CCC].** available on microfiche from University Microfilms International (UMI). ***Continues** Amateur Photographer & Cinematographer.*

US
**AMERICAN FILM AND VIDEO FESTIVAL. Main/Conf** American Film and Video Festival (New York, N.Y.). **VFOAT** Film and Video Festival. 28th (May 27-June 1, 1986)-. English. an. $12.00. American Film and Video Association, 85 Van Reypen Street, Jersey City NJ 07306. **ED** Ray Rolff. ***Continues** American Film Festival.*

US/1046-8986
**AMERICAN PHOTO.** [Am. photo]. **VFOAT** Photo. Vol. 1, No. 1 (Jan./Feb. 1990)-. Periodical. English. bm (6 issues). $20.00. Hachette Magazines Inc., 1633 Broadway, New York NY 10019. **Tel** (212)767-6000. **(Subscription address:** Neodata / Colorado, PO Box 2606, Boulder Boulder CO 80322.**) ED** David Schonauer. **LC** TR1; .A563. **DD** 770/.5. **Ad Acc, Adv Mgr:** Arlene Weinberg. **Circ:** 250,000. available on microfilm and microfiche from University Microfilms International (UMI). Documents available from UMI Article Clearinghouse, Magazine Collection. ***Continues** American Photographer, 0161-6854.*
**Desc:** All about creative photography for people who want to get the most out of their own picture taking. Contains profiles, personalities and their contributions to art, history, fashion, journalism and advertising. Features include book and exhibition reviews, professional working methods, reader's photos and picture portfolios.
**Ind/Abst** Acad. Ind. [Computer File] (1992-); Access (1980-); Art Index; Expand. Acad. Index (1992-); Gen. Period. Index (1990-); Mag. Artic. Summar. Elite (July 1994-); Mag. Index Plus (1990-); Newsp. Period. Abstr. (1990-); Mag. Index.

US
**AMERICAN PHOTOGRAPHY.** English. an. $65.00. American Illustration, 49 East 21st Street 8th Floor, New York NY 10010. **Tel** (212)979-4500. Index available ($60.00).

US/0278-8314
**AMERICAN PHOTOGRAPHY SHOWCASE. *Title Change.*** [Am. photogr. showc.]. **VFOAT** American Showcase Photography. Vol. 5 (1982)-Vol. 16 (Oct. 1993). Periodical. English. an. American Showcase, 915 Broadway, 14th Floor, New York NY 10010. **Tel** (212)673-6600, FAX (212)673-9795, telex 880356 AMSHOW P. **(Subscription address:** Watson Guptill Publications, PO Box 2014, Lakewood NJ 08101.**) ED** Ira Shapiro. **LC** TR690.4; .A4. **DD** 770/.25/73. **Bk Rev. Circ:** 33,600 (ctrl). ***Continues in part** American Showcase, 0742-6100. **Continued by** Klik Photo Showcase.*
**Desc:** Superbly printed professional sourcebook representing the latest work from America's most outstanding commercial advertising photographers.

US/0278-8683
**AMERICAN SHOWCASE OF ILLUSTRATION AND PHOTOGRAPHY.** [Am. showc. illus. photogr.]. **VFOAT** American Showcase of Illustration & Photography. 1982-. English. an. $67.50. American Showcase, 915 Broadway, 14th Floor, New York NY 10010. **Tel** (212)673-6600, FAX (212)673-9795, telex 880356 AMSHOW P. **LC** TR690; .A453. **DD** 770/.25/73. **Bk Rev. Circ:** 35,000 (ctrl). ***Continues in part** American Showcase, 0742-6100.*
**Desc:** Oversized, full-color, two-volume set highlighting latest work from this country's illustrators, photographers and graphic designers.

US
**ANNUAL REPORT / INTERNATIONAL CENTER OF PHOTOGRAPHY. Main/Corp** International Center of Photography. (198?)-. English. an. International Center of Photography, 1130 Fifth Avenue, New York NY 10128. **Tel** (212)860-1781. ***Continues** International Center of Photography. International Center of Photography, a ... Year Report.*
**Desc:** Comes with International Center of Photography membership.

US
**ANNUAL REPORT / TENNESSEE FILM, TAPE, AND MUSIC COMMISSION. See** Motion Picture.

FR/0767-2055
**ANTIGONE.** (198?)-. Periodical. French. Twice a year. 200.00F (two years) France; 250.00F (two years) other. Antigone Editions, Aigremont, 30360 Ledogmam France. **Tel** 33 66 834434. **ED** Sylvie Nayral. **Circ:** 600.

SP
**ANUARIO DE LA FOTOGRAFIA ESPANOLA.** Began in 1958. Spanish. Editorial Everest, Carretera Leon-Astorga KM 4 500/Apartado 339, Leon Spain. **LC** TR640; .A4.

US/1046-4522
**APA MAGAZINE.** [APA mag.]. **VAT** Advertising Photographers of America Magazine. Premiere Issue (Winter 1989)-. Periodical. English. qt. Advertising Photographers of America, 27 West 20th Street/Suite 601, New York NY 10011. **DD** 778.

US/0003-6420
**APERTURE (MILLERTON, N.Y.).** (APERTURE.). [Aperture]. No. 1 (1952)-. Periodical. English. qt. $47.00 US; $50.47 Canada; $57.00 other (institution). Aperture Inc., PO Box 6678, Syracuse NY 13217. **Tel** (800)825-0061, (212)505-5555. **ED** Lawrence Frascella. **LC** TR1; .A62. **DD** 770/.5. **Bk Rev. Ad Acc. Circ:** 10,000. available on microfilm and microfiche from University Microfilms International (UMI). Documents available from The Genuine Article, UMI Article Clearinghouse.
**Desc:** A forum for fine art photography.
**Ind/Abst** Acad. Ind. [Computer File] (1992-); Acad. Search (Jan. 1993-); Art Index; ARTbibliogr. Mod.; Arts Humanit. Citation Index [Full Cov.]; BHA : Biblio. Hist. Art; Curr. Contents Arts Humanit.; Expand. Acad. Index (1989-); Humanit. Index; Humanit. Source (Jan. 1993-); INFO-SOUTH Abstr.; Mag. Search; Newsp. Period. Abstr. (1991-); Res. Alert [Full Cov.]; Vocat. Search (Jan. 1993-).

US/0735-5572
**ARCHIVE (TUCSON, ARIZ.), THE.** (ARCHIVE / CENTER FOR CREATIVE PHOTOGRAPHY, UNIVERSITY OF ARIZONA.). [Archive]. **Added/Corp** University of Arizona. Center for Creative Photography. No. 14 (Dec. 1981)-. Periodical. English. sa. $25.00. Center Creative Photography, The University of Arizona, Tucson AZ 85721. **Tel** (602)621-7968, FAX (602)621-9444. **LC** TR640; .A73. **DD** 770/.74/019177. **Circ:** 2,000 (ctrl). ***Continues** Center for Creative Photography (Series).*
**Desc:** A research series devoted to twentieth century photographers and photographic movements; issues usually include reproductions from the Center's archives and collections.
**Ind/Abst** ARTbibliogr. Mod.; BHA : Biblio. Hist. Art.

US/0882-4932
**ARIZONA PORTFOLIO, THE. See** The Arts-Art.

SZ
**ART DIRECTORS' INDEX TO ILLUSTRATORS.** No. 7 (1987)-. Periodical. English (French and German). an. Watson Guptill Publications, PO Box 2014, Lakewood NJ 08701. **Tel** (800)451-1741, (908)363-5679. ***Continues** Art Director's Index to Illustration, Graphics & Design.*
**Desc:** Contains a large number of photos by top-ranking international photographers, making this index to international photographers a reference and learning text for all who wish to be informed in the field of photography today. The book offers illustrations of the latest trends and inspires creative ideas. The quality of the reproductions and layout are excellent.

UK/0587-3576
**ART DIRECTORS' INDEX TO PHOTOGRAPHERS.** No. 1 (1970)-. Multiple languages (English, French, German and Italian). an. DM162.00. Rotovision SA, Route Suisse 9, CH1295 Mies Switzerland. **Tel** 011 41 22 7553055, FAX 011 41 22 7554072, telex 419246. **LC** TR12. **DD** 779.

# Photography and Video

US/1047-5427
**AS PICTURE PROFESSIONAL.** [AS pict. prof.]. Added/Corp American Society of Picture Professionals. VFOAT Picture Professional. VAT American Society Picture Professional. Vol. 16, No. 1 (Fall 1986)-. Periodical. English. qt. $12.50 (nonmember, single issue). American Society for Picture Professionals, PO Box 5283, Grand Central Station, New York NY 10017. **LC** PAR. **DD** 770. *Continues* ASPP Newsletter (New York, N.Y.), 0740-4115.

US/0094-1417
**ASTROGRAPH (ARLINGTON), THE.** *See* Astronomy.

US/0147-4855
**AURA (BUFFALO).** (AURA.). V. 1- Feb. 1976-. Periodical. English. qt. $10.00. Andromeda Gallery, 493 Franklin Street, Buffalo NY 14203. **LC** TR640; .A97. **DD** 779/.05.

AT/1035-641X
**AUSTRALIAN CAMERA CRAFT AND SHOOTING VIDEO.** (1987)-. Periodical. English. mo. 47.00Aus$ Australia; 57.00Aus$. Horwitz Grahame Pty Ltd, 506 Miller Street, Cammeray New South Wales, 2062 Australia. **Tel** 011 61 2 9296144, FAX 011 61 2 9571814. *Continues* Australian Camera Craft Magazine, 0158-2658.

AT/0158-2658
**AUSTRALIAN CAMERA CRAFT MAGAZINE.** *Title Change.* (1979)-(1987). Periodical. English. mo. Horwitz Grahame Pty Ltd, 506 Miller Street, Cammeray New South Wales, 2062 Australia. **Tel** 011 61 2 9296144, FAX 011 61 2 9571814. **[CCC].** *Continued by* Australian Camera Craft and Shooting Video, 1035-641X.

AT/1031-5462
**AUSTRALIAN FILM DATA.** *See* Motion Picture.

AT/0159-0030
**AUSTRALIAN HI-FI.** [Aust. hi-fi]. (1970)-. Periodical. English. mo. 86.70Aus$ Australia; 97.00Aus$ other. Horwitz Grahame Pty Ltd, 506 Miller Street, Cammeray New South Wales, 2062 Australia. **Tel** 011 61 2 9296144, FAX 011 61 2 9571814. **DD** 621.38933205. Index available.

AT/0004-9964
**AUSTRALIAN PHOTOGRAPHY.** (1950)-. Periodical. English. mo. 47.00Aus$ Australia; 127.00Aus$ other. Yaffa Publishing Group Pty Ltd., GPO Box 606, Sydney NSW 2001 Australia. **Tel** 011 61 2 2812333, FAX 011 61 2 2812750.

AT/0816-3669
**AUSTRALIAN PHOTOGRAPHY DIRECTORY.** (1964)-. English. an. 6.95Aus$. Yaffa Publishing Group Pty Ltd., GPO Box 606, Sydney NSW 2001 Australia. **Tel** 011 61 2 2812333, FAX 011 61 2 2812750.

US/1075-0363
**BE-HOLD (BINGHAMTON, N.Y.).** (BE-HOLD.). [Be-hold]. VFOAT Behold. (1982)-. Periodical. English. sa (Published in May & October). $25.00. Larry Gottheim, 33 Orton Avenue, Binghamton NY 13905. **Tel** (607)797-1685, FAX (607)797-4775. **DD** 779. **Circ:** 500. *Continues* Photographic Brochure.

US/0161-4762
**BEST OF PHOTOJOURNALISM, THE.** Added/Corp National Press Photographers Association (U.S.) University of Missouri--Columbia. School of Journalism. (1977)-. Periodical. English. an (Aug.). $24.45. Running Press, 125 South 22nd Street, Philadelphia PA 19103. **Tel** (800)428-1111, (215)567-5080, telex 90 2633. **LC** TR820; .B48. **DD** 779/.0973. *Continues* Photojournalism, 0363-5996.
**Desc:** Award-winning 'pictures of the year' as selected by NPPA.

US/0739-4845
**BIBLIOGRAPHY SERIES / CENTER FOR CREATIVE PHOTOGRAPHY, UNIVERSITY OF ARIZONA.** [Bibliogr. ser. - Univ. Ariz., Cent. Creat. Photogr.]. Added/Corp University of Arizona. Center for Creative Photography. No. 1 (1980)-. Monographic series. English. ir. University of Arizona Press, 1230 North Park Avenue, Suite 102, Tucson AZ 85719. **Tel** (602)882-3065, (800)426-3797.

GW/0006-2383
**BILD UND TON (BERLIN, DDR).** *Ceased.* *See* Motion Picture.

SW/1100-5203
**BILDTIDNINGEN.** [Bildtidningen]. **VFOAT** Fotograficentrums Bildtidning. (1989)-. Periodical. Swedish. ir. **UDC** 77. *Continues* Bild (Stockholm. 1985), 0283-6041.
**Ind/Abst** BHA : Biblio. Hist. Art.

US/0145-8000
**BIZARRE CLASSIX.** V. 1-. English. $7.00 plus postage. Belier Press, PO Box 1234 Old Chelsea Station, New York NY 10113. **Tel** (212)620-4276. **LC** TR676; .B58. **DD** 760.

US/1054-464X
**BLACK BOOK STOCK.** [Black book stock]. (1991)-. English. $34.95. Creative Black Book, 115 Fifth Avenue, Third Floor, New York NY 10003. **LC** TR12; .B58. **DD** 026/.779/02573.

US/0090-7197
**BLACK PHOTOGRAPHERS ANNUAL, THE.** 1973-. English. an. Another View Inc, PO Box 1921, Brooklyn NY 11202. **LC** TR640; .B53. **DD** 779/.05.

US/0882-7532
**BLACK VIDEO GUIDE, THE.** *See* Motion Picture.

CN/0826-3922
**BLACKFLASH.** [Blackflash]. Added/Corp Photographers Gallery (Saskatoon, Sask.). VFOAT Black Flash. V. 1, No. 1 (Spring 1984)-. Periodical. English. qt. 8.00Can$ (one year), 12.00Can$ (two year). Photographers Gallery, 12 23rd Street East, 2nd Floor, Saskatoon, Saskatchewan S7K 0H5 Canada. **Tel** (306)244-8018. **DD** 779/.0971/074011242. *Continues* Photographers Gallery (Saskatoon, Sask.). Photographers Gallery, 0823-2326.
**Ind/Abst** Can. Period. Index (19??-).

●US/1068-1647
**BLIND SPOT PHOTOGRAPHY.** [Blind spot photogr.]. (1993)-. Periodical. English. Twice a year (Spring & Fall). $24.00. Blind Spot Inc, 49 West 23rd Street, New York NY 10010. **Tel** (212)633-1317, FAX (212)691-5465. **DD** 790. **Ad Acc, Adv Mgr:** Micheal C., **Tel** (212)633-1317. **Circ:** 10,000.

US/0147-0663
**BLUE BOOK ILLUSTRATED PRICE GUIDE TO COLLECTABLE CAMERAS.** VFOAT Illustrated Price Guide to Collectable Cameras. English. an. $8.95. Photographic Memorabilia, PO Box 351, Lexington MA 02173. **LC** TR6.5; .B48. **DD** 771.3/1/075.

US/0738-8322
**BLUE BOOK OF PHOTOGRAPHY PRICES.** *Ceased.* [Blue book photogr. prices]. (May 1972)-Ceased (1991). English. mo. Photography Research Inst, 21237 South Moneta Avenue, Carson CA 90745. **Tel** (310) 328-9272. **DD** 770. **Bk Rev. Circ:** 10,000 (ctrl).

UK
**BODY BEAUTIFUL.** Periodical. English. bm.

UK/0007-1196
**BRITISH JOURNAL OF PHOTOGRAPHY.** [Br. j. photogr.]. Periodical. English. wk. £45.50 UK; $181.22 Middle East and North Africa; $199.34 Southeast Asia and Oceania; $190.28 (airmail), $102.39 (surface mail) other. Henry Greenwood & Company Ltd, 58 Fleet Street, London EC4U 1JU England. **Tel** 011-44-71-583-0175. **ED** Chris Dickie. **CODEN** BRJFAM. **Bk Rev. Ad Acc. Circ:** 11,000. Documents available from Ask*IEEE. *Continues* Photographic Journal.
**Desc:** Photography of technology and science.
**Ind/Abst** Art Index; ARTbibliogr. Mod.; Curr. Technol. Index; Imaging Abstr.; INSPEC (Sept. 1971-); Print. Abstr.

●UK
**BRITISH JOURNAL OF PHOTOGRAPHY. PHOTO.** VFOAT Photo; Annual of the British Journal of Photography; BJP Annual. (1992)-. Periodical. English. Henry Greenwood & Company Ltd, 58 Fleet Street, London EC4U 1JU England. **Tel** 011-44-71-583-0175. **LC** TR1; .B83. *Continues* British Journal of Photography Annual.

US/0361-9168
**BULLETIN - ASMP--THE SOCIETY OF PHOTOGRAPHERS IN COMMUNICATIONS.** Main/Corp ASMP--The Society of Photographers in Communications. VAT Bulletin - American Society of Magazine Photographers--The Society of Photographers in Communications. Bulletin. English. mo. American Society of Medical Photography, 14 Washington Road, Suite 502, Princeton Junction NJ 08550-1033. **Tel** (609)799-8300, FAX (609)799-2233. **LC** TR820; .A18A. **DD** 770/.6/273.

UK
**BULLETIN (ROYAL PHOTOGRAPHIC SOCIETY OF GREAT BRITAIN. COLOUR GROUP).** (BULLETIN / THE ROYAL PHOTOGRAPHIC SOCIETY COLOUR GROUP.). VFOAT Royal Photographic Society Colour Group Bulletin. Bulletin. English. Royal Photographic Society, The Octagon, Milsom Street, Bath BA1 1DN England. **Tel** (0225)462821, FAX (0225)448688.

FR/0244-6014
**BULLETIN - SOCIETE FRANCAISE DE PHOTOGRAMMETRIE ET DE TELEDETECTION.** [Bull. - Soc. fr. phtogramm. teledetect.]. Main/Corp Societe Francaise de Photogrammetrie et de Teledetection. (19??)-. Bulletin. French (summaries and/or abstracts in English). qt. 562.50F France. Societe Francaise de Photogrammetrie et de Teledetection, 2 Avenue Pasteur BP 68, 94160 Sainte Mande France. **Tel** 011 33 43 988073, FAX 011 33 43 742104. **ED** Guy Ducher, **Tel** TR693; .S6a. **DD** 621.36/78/05. **CODEN** BSFTDK. Index available. cum. index. **Bk Rev. Ad Acc. Circ:** 650 (ctrl) Documents available from Ask*IEEE. *Continues* Bulletin / Societe Francaise de Photogrammetrie, 0049-108X.
**Ind/Abst** Art Archaeol. Tech. Abstr.; Bioeng. Abstr.; Ei Page One; Geogr. Abstr. Phys. Geogr.; Geogr. Abstr. Human Geogr.; GeoRef; INSPEC (1980-); Int. Aerosp. Abstr.

BE
**BULLETIN TRIMESTRIEL DE LA SOCIETE BELGE DE PHOTOGRAMMETRIE-TELEDETECTION ET CARTOGRAPHIE.** Added/Corp Societe Belge de Photogrammetrie-Teledetection et Cartographie. VFOAT Driemaandelijks Tijdschrift van de Belgische Vereniging voor Fotogrammetrie-Teledetectie en Kartografie. (19??)-. Periodical. Dutch (English and French). Twice a year (Aug. & Feb.). 450F. Societe Belge Photogrammetrie Teledetection & Cartographie, BD Jardin Botanique 50, BTE 38, 1010 Brussels Belgium. **Tel** 011 32 2 2103598. **ED** A. Verdin. **LC** TR693.A1; S6. **DD** 526.9/8/05. **Bk Rev,** (Qty: 2). **Ad Acc, Adv Mgr:** J. Van Hemelrijck, **Tel** 011 32 2 2103598. **Circ:** 375. *Continues* Bulletin Trimestriel de la Societe Belge de photogramm,etrie et de t,el,edetection, 0771-7873.

US/0362-0131
**BUYER'S GUIDE TO MICROGRAPHIC EQUIPMENT, PRODUCTS AND SERVICES.** Added/Corp National Micrographics Association. (19??)-. English. 8728 Colesville Road, Silver Spring MD 20910. **LC** TR835; .B88. **DD** 338.4/7/68.

CN
**C V PHOTO.** (19??)-. English. Four times a year. 35.00Can$ (institutions), 28.00Can$ (individuals) Canada; 45.00Can$ (institutions), 35.00Can$ (individuals) other. Les Productions Ciel Variable, 4060 Boulevard St. Laurent #301, Montreal Quebec H2W 1Y9 Canada. **ED** Robert Legendre, Marcel Blouin. **Bk Rev,** (Qty: 4). **Ad Acc. Circ:** 800. *Continues* Ciel Variable.
**Desc:** Covers contemporary photography.

FR
**CAHIERS DE CHROMOTOGRAPHIE.** French. an. Free. Lab Merck Cleveneau la Guerand, Montee de la Transhumance, 13300 Sal de Provenance France. **Tel** 011 33 16 90566387.

FR
**CAHIERS DE LA PHOTOGRAPHIE, LES.** Added/Corp Association de Critique Contemporaine en Photographie (France). (1981)-. Periodical. French. ir. 385.00F France; 450.00F other. Association Critique Contemporaine en Photographie, 32 rue Saint Marc, 75002 Paris France. **Tel** 011 33 1 42606151.
**Ind/Abst** ARTbibliogr. Mod.; BHA : Biblio. Hist. Art.

JA
**CAMCORDER.** *Ceased.* (19??)-(1992). English. an. Dempa Publications Inc., 1 11 15 Higashi Gotanda, Shinagawa Ku Tokyo 141 Japan. **Tel** 011 81 3 34456111. **(Subscription address:** Dempa Publications, 400 Madison Avenue, New York, NY 10017) **LC** TR882; .C35. **DD** 778.59/9.

UK
**CAMCORDER USER.** (1988)-. English. mo. £24.00 UK; £40.00 Europe; £65.00 other. WV Publications, 57-59 Rochester Place, London NW1 9JU England. **Tel** 011 44 71 485-0011. **(Subscription address:** WV Publications, Unit 5 Billet, LN Berkhamsted, Herts HP4 1HL England)

US/1048-8804
**CAMCORDER (VENTURA, CALIF.).** (CAMCORDER.). [Camcorder]. (Dec. 1989)-. Periodical. English. bm. $23.00 (one year), $36.00 (two year), $49.00 (three year). Miller Magazines Inc, 4880 Market Street, Ventura CA 93003. **Tel** (805)664-3824, FAX (805)664-3875. **LC** TR882; .C36. **DD** 778.59/9. *Continues* Camcorder Report, 1047-8787.

US/1056-8484
**CAMERA & DARKROOM.** [Camera darkroom]. VFOAT Camera and Darkroom. Vol. 13, No. 5 (May 1991)-. Periodical. English. mo. $24.95. LFP Inc., 9171 Wilshire Boulevard/Suite 300, Beverly Hills CA 90210. **Tel** (310)858-7100, FAX (310)274-7985. **(Subscription address:** Kable Publishers Aide, 308 East Hitt Street, Subscription Department, Mt. Morris IL 61054-1473.) **LC** TR287; .D37. **DD** 771. *Continues* Camera & Darkroom Photography, 1056-8484.

AU/1015-1915
**CAMERA AUSTRIA.** ***Title Change.*** No. 1 (1980)-No. 35 (199?). Periodical. English (German). qt. Forum Stadtpark Graz, Stadtpark 1, Camera Austria, A-8010 Graz Austria. **Tel** 011 43 316 827734, 825369, FAX 011 43 316 8253696. **LC** TR1; .C117. **DD** 770/.5. ***Continued by*** *Camera Austria International.*
**Desc:** Expressly dedicated to international contemporary photography with no commitment to a narrow programme of "photography as art" but with the intention to be a platform for artistic and theoretical work in and about photography.
**Ind/Abst** ARTbibliogr. Mod.

AU
**CAMERA AUSTRIA INTERNATIONAL.** **VFOAT** Camera Austria. (1991)-. Periodical. English (German). qt. S520.00. Forum Stadtpark Graz, Stadtpark 1, Camera Austria, A-8010 Graz Austria. **Tel** 011 43 316 827734, 825369, FAX 011 43 316 8253696. **ED** Manfred Willmann. Index available. **Ad Acc. Circ:** 3,000 (ctrl). ***Continues*** *Camera Austria, 1015-1915.*

CN/0008-2090
**CAMERA CANADA.** [Camera Can.]. **Added/Corp** National Association for Photographic Art. Association for Photographic Art. **VFOAT** APA Camera Canada; National APA Camera Canada. No. 1 (March 1969)-. Periodical. English (French). Four times a year (Seasonally). 16.00Can$. National Association for Photographic Art, 31858 Hopedale Avenue, Clearbrook British Colombia, V2T 2G7 Canada. **Tel** (604)855-4848. **(Subscription address:** 22 Abbeville Road, Scarborough Ontario M1H 1Y3 Canada**) ED** Marilyn McEwen (editor's address: 1140 South Dyke Road, New Westminister, B. C. V3M 5A2 Canada). **Ad Acc. Circ:** 2,500 (ctrl).
**Desc:** The aims of the association and of the magazine are to promote good Canadian photography and to provide useful information for photographers. It tries to showcase the work of as many different photographers as possible through their portfolios, including a short bibliography of how they started, their philosophy and their method of working.
**Ind/Abst** ARTbibliogr. Mod.; Can. Index (?-?); Can. Period. Index (19??-).

US/0883-489X
**CAMERA (DURANGO, COLO.).** (CAMERA.). **Added/Corp** Orion Research Corporation. **VFOAT** Orion Camera Blue Book. (198?)-. English. an (Dec.). Price varies. Orion Research Corporation, 14555 North Scottsdale Road, Suite 330, Scottsdale AZ 85260. **Tel** (800)844-0759, (602)951-1114, FAX (602)951-1117. **(Subscription address:** Oryx Press, 4041 North Central Indian School Road, Phoenix AZ 85012.**) ED** Roger Rohrs. **LC** TR197; .C35. **DD** 771/.075. **Bk Rev.** ***Continues*** *Camera Reference Guide, 0740-1647.*
**Desc:** Lists more than 14,000 products, including lenses, cameras of all types, enlargers, projectors and screens.

FR/0765-9849
**CAMERA INTERNATIONAL.** **VFOAT** Camera. No. 1, (Nov. 1984)-. Periodical. French (English). qt. 320.00F (1 year), 600.00F (2 year) France; 400.00F (1 year), 700.00F (2 year) other. Camera International, 99 rue d Amsterdam, 75008 Paris France. **Tel** 011 33 1 42806855, FAX 011 33 1 45262480. **LC** TR1; .C118. **DD** 770/.5.
**Ind/Abst** ARTbibliogr. Mod.

JA/0008-2082
**CAMERART.** Vol. 1 (Spring 1958)-. Periodical. English. mo. $76.67. Camerart Inc, Hinode Building, 5-4/2-chome, Kyobashi Chuo-ku Tokyo Japan. **Tel** 011 81 3 3563 4871, FAX 011 81 3 5646996. **ED** Todoriki Kunika. **DD** 770. **Bk Rev. Ad Acc. Circ:** 19,000.
**Desc:** English camera magazine.
**Ind/Abst** ARTbibliogr. Mod.

JA
**CAMERART PHOTO TRADE DIRECTORY.** (19??)-. Directory. English. an (December). price varies per volume. Camerart Inc, Hinode Building, 5-4/2-chome, Kyobashi Chuo-ku Tokyo Japan. **Tel** 011 81 3 3563 4871, FAX 011 81 3 5646996. **ED** Kunika Todoriki. **LC** HD9708.A1; C36. **DD** 681/.481/029473. **Bk Rev. Ad Acc. Circ:** 13,000.
**Desc:** The source of information on the Japanese photography trade and industry for importers, exporters and dealers.

●US
**CAMERAWORK.** **Added/Corp** San Francisco Camerawork. Vol. 19, No. 1 (Spring 1992)-. Periodical. English. sa. $35.00. SF Camerawork, 70 12th Street, San Francisco CA 94103. **Tel** (415)621-1001. **LC** TR640; .N48. **Bk Rev. Ad Acc.** ctrl circ. ***Continues*** *SF Camerawork Quarterly.*

CN
**CANADIAN PHOTOGRAPHY. BUYING GUIDE.** **VFOAT** Guide d'Achat. Began with 1970 issue. Consumer Publication. English (French). an. $9.28. Maclean Hunter Canada / Montreal, 1001 bvd. de Maisonneuve W., Montreal, Quebec H3A 3E1 Canada. **Tel** 514-845-5141, FAX 514-845-4302, telex 055-60604. **DD** 338.4/7/68141802571.

US/0146-2199
**CAPE ROCK, THE.** **See** Literature-Poetry.

US
**CATALOG OF FINE ANTIQUE CAMERAS & PHOTOGRAPHIC IMAGES.** **See** Antiques.

US/0890-4634
**CENTER QUARTERLY.** [Cent. q.]. **Added/Corp** Catskill Center for Photography (Woodstock, N.Y.) Center for Photography at Woodstock (Woodstock, N.Y.). **VFOAT** CQ. (197?)-. Periodical. English. Four times a year. $25.00 US; $40.00 Canada & Mexico; $45.00 other. Center Photography Woodstock, 59 Tinker Street, Woodstock NY 12498. **Tel** (914)679-9957, FAX (914)679-6337. **ED** Kathleen Kenyon. **DD** 770. Index available. cum. index. **Bk Rev**, (Qty: Varies). **Ad Acc**, **Adv Mgr:** Larry Lewis. **Circ:** 8,000.
**Desc:** Presents an alternative vision of creative photography. Read what the mainstream photography magazines leave out. This critical journal, published four times a year since 1979, covers new concepts, critiques old ones, presents new visual artists and writers, and explores contemporary ideas from across the national and international field. Each issue investigates a timely theme in photography and related arts (including film and video). Recent topics include: New Relations; Revisiting the Family of Man, and The Surrogate Figue; Intersepted Figure in Intercepted Photography.

FR/0396-8235
**CHASSEUR D'IMAGES.** (1976)-. Periodical. French. Eleven times a year. 260.00F France; 300.00F other. Editions Jibena GH Publication, La Petite Monte Senille, 86100 Chatellerault France. **Tel** 011 33 49 854985. **UDC** 7.

CN/0831-3091
**CIEL VARIABLE :LE MANIFESTE DU TEMPS.** ***Title Change.*** **See** The Arts-Art.

SI
**CINE NEWS.** Periodical. English. ir. Singapore Cine Club, 293-A Selegie Complex, Singapore 7 Singapore. **LC** TR845; .C535. **DD** 778.5/3/05.

US/0895-805X
**CINEVUE.** (CINEVUE : A PUBLICATION OF ASIAN CINEVISION.). [CineVue]. **Added/Corp** Asian CineVision (Organization). **VFOAT** Cine Vue. Vol. 1, No. 1 (April 1986)-. Periodical. English. Four times a year. $20.00 (institutions), $10.00 (individuals). Asian Cinevision Inc, 32 East Broadway, New York NY 10002. **Tel** (212)925-8685. **ED** Bill J. Gee. **DD** 791. **Bk Rev. Ad Acc. Circ:** 16,000.
**Desc:** The first national publication focusing solely on Asian American media arts. Each issue contains news reports, features on filmmakers and video artists, reviews of new and important works.

FR
**CLICHES.** (1983)-. Periodical. French. mo. Editions du Stratege, 36 rue du Houblon, B-1000 Bruxelles Belgium. **LC** TR640; .C58. **DD** 770/.5.
**Ind/Abst** BHA : Biblio. Hist. Art.

US/0896-9043
**COLLECTORS PHOTOGRAPHY.** [Collect. photogr.]. (1???)-. Periodical. English. bm (6 issues). Melrose Publishing Group, 9021 Melrose Avenue, Suite 301, Los Angeles CA 90069. **DD** 770. ***Continues*** *Collector's Editions Review.*

US/0145-899X
**COMBINATIONS.** [Combinations]. Vol. 1, No. 1 (Spring 1977)-. Periodical. English. $14.00. Mary Ann Lynch, Greenfield Center, New York NY 12833. **ED** M A Lynch. **LC** TR640; .C65. **DD** 770/.5.

JA
**COMMERCIAL PHOTO.** Japanese. mo. $239.00 California; $245.00 other US. **(Subscription address:** Kinokuniya Company Ltd., 38-1 Sakuragaoka 5, chome Setagaya-ku, Tokyo 156 Japan.**)**

AT/1037-6992
**COMMERCIAL PHOTOGRAPHY IN AUSTRALIA.** [Commer. photogr. Aust.]. **VFOAT** Commercial Photography. (1991)-. Periodical. English. Six times a year. 26.40Aus$ Australia; 76.00Aus$ other. Yaffa Publishing Group Pty Ltd., GPO Box 606, Sydney NSW 2001 Australia. **Tel** 011 61 2 2812333, FAX 011 61 2 2812750. **DD** 770.23. ***Continues*** *Industrial and Commerical Photography., 0313-4393.*

CN/0709-6771
**COMMERCIAL PRICE LIST FOR STILL PHOTOGRAPHS.** ***Title Change.*** [Commer. price list still photogr.]. **Main/Corp** National Film Board of Canada. Periodical. English. National Film Board of Canada, PO Box 6100 Station A, Montreal Quebec H3C 3H5 Canada. **Tel** (514)283-9427, FAX (514)283-7564. ***Continued by*** *Canada. Information Canada. Phototheque. Commercial Price List, 0706-1684.*

US/1061-4850
**COMPLETE GUIDE TO SPECIAL INTEREST VIDEOS, THE.** [Complete guide spec. interest videos]. (1991)-. English. James-Robert Publishing, Ontario Commerce Center, 3535 East Inland Empire Boulevard, Ontario CA 91764. **DD** 011.

US/0091-4576
**CONSUMER GUIDE PHOTOGRAPHIC EQUIPMENT TEST REPORTS.** (CONSUMER GUIDE PHOTOGRAPHIC EQUIPMENT TEST REPORTS : BEST BUYS & DISCOUNT PRICES.). **VFOAT** Photographic Equipment Test Reports. English. an. $1.95. Consumer Guide, 3841 West Oakton Street, Skokie IL 60076. **Tel** (312)676-3470, telex 280084. **LC** TR196; .C65. **DD** 771.

US/0742-9975
**CORPORATE SHOWCASE.** **See** The Arts-Graphic Arts.

SP/0376-7590
**COTECFLASH.** 1973-. Periodical. Spanish. Co Tec, Rocafort 41 Entlo, Barcelona Spain. **LC** TR640; .C67. **DD** 779/.05.

UK/0011-0876
**CREATIVE CAMERA.** [Creat. camera]. No. 44, (Feb. 1968)-. Periodical. English. bm. $50.00 (individuals), $70.00 (institutions) US; £24.00 (individuals), £35.00 (institutions) UK; £30.00 (individuals), £40.00 (institutions) other. Cornerhouse Publications, 70 Oxford Street, Manchester M15 NH England. **Tel** 011 44 61 2379662, FAX 011 44 61 2379664. **ED** Peter Turner. **LC** TR640; .C74. **DD** 770/.5. **Bk Rev. Ad Acc. Circ:** 6,000. ***Continues*** *Creative Camera Owner.*
**Desc:** Portfolios, news and reviews of photography as a visual art.
**Ind/Abst** Art Index; ARTbibliogr. Mod.

AT/0726-3589
**CREATIVE SOURCE AUSTRALIA.** **VFOAT** Wizards of Oz. 2nd Book (1982)-. Monographic series. English. an. Price varies per volume. Armadillo Publishers Pty Ltd., 205-207 Scotchmer Street/Fitzroy, North Melbourne Victoria 3068 Australia. **Tel** 011 61 03 489-9559, FAX 011 61 03 489-5576. **ED** David Lyons and Elaine Howell. **Ad Acc. Circ:** 3,500. ***Continues*** *Art Directors Guide to Photographers in Australia.*
**Desc:** Pictorial reference book of creative work in Australia. Contains photography, illustration, design, SFX food, styling, etc.

●GW
**CVA NEWSLETTER / COMMISSION ON VISUAL ANTHROPOLOGY.** **See** Anthropology.

US
**DARKROOM & CREATIVE CAMERA TECHNIQUES.** **VFOAT** Darkroom Techniques and Creative Camera; Darkroom and Creative Camera Techniques; Darkroom Techniques & Creative Camera. Vol. 5, No. 1 (Jan./Feb. 1984)-. Periodical. English. Six times a year. $17.95 US; $22.95 other. Preston Publications Inc., 7800 Merrimac Avenue, PO Box 48312, Niles IL 60714. **Tel** (708)965-0566, FAX (708)965-7639, telex 910-223-1780 PRESTON NILE. **(Subscription address:** Darkroom & Creative Camera Techniques, PO Box 585, Mt. Morris IL 61054.**) LC** TR287; .D375. **DD** 770/.28. ***Continues*** *Darkroom Techniques, 0195-3850.*
**Ind/Abst** Index Inf. (1980-).

JA/0387-916X
**DENSHI SHASHIN GAKKAISHI.** **Added/Corp** Denshi Shashin Gakkai. **VFOAT** Electrophotography. (1979)-. Academic Scholarly Publication. Japanese (summaries and/or abstracts in English). Four times a year. $150.00. Denshi Shashin Gakkai (Society of Electrophotography of Japan), c/o Tokyo Institute of Polytechnics, 2-9-5 Honcho, Nakano-ku, Tokyo 164, Japan. **(Subscription address:** Kyowa Book Company Inc., 1-38 Kanda Jinbo-Cho, Chiyoda-Ku, Tokyo 101, Japan) **CODEN** DSHGDD. Documents available from Ask*IEEE, CASDDS. ***Continues*** *Denshi Shashin.*
**Ind/Abst** Chem. Abstr.; INSPEC (1972-).

BE
**DIFFUSION DES PROGRAMMES AUDIOVISUELS, LA.** (19??)-. French. 1100F Belgium & Luxembourg; 320F France; 2200F other. Edimedia ASBL, rue de la Constitution 22, 1030 Brussels Belgium. **Tel** 011 32 2 2180031. **Bk Rev. Ad Acc.**

CN/1181-7917
**DIGITAL EVOLUTION MAGAZINE.** ***Title Change.*** **See** Communication-Broadcasting.

FR/0419-5361
**DOCUMENTATION PHOTOGRAPHIQUE, LA.** **Added/Corp** France. Direction de la Documentation. France. Institut Pedagogique National. (19??)-. Periodical. French. bm (6 issues). 256.42F. Documentation Francaise, 29 Quai Voltaire, 75344 Paris Cedex 7 France. **Tel** 011 33 1 40157000, FAX 011 33 1

## Photography and Video

40157230, telex 204 826 DOCFRAN. **(Subscription address:** Documentation Francaise, 124 rue Henri Barbusse, 93308 Aubervilliers Cdx France; Phone: 011 33 1 48395600**)**

FR/0240-8392
**DOUBLE PAGE.** VFOAT Photos Double Page. No. 1-. Periodical. French. mo. 525.00F France; 555.00F other. Nathan Abonnements, 75640 Paris Cedex 13 France. **Tel** 011 33 1 44085000, 011 33 1 44085070, **FAX** 011 33 1 43375300.
**Ind/Abst** ARTbibliogr. Mod.

US/1055-3878
**DRYDEN THEATRE, CURTIS THEATRE AT THE INTERNATIONAL MUSEUM OF PHOTOGRAPHY AT GEORGE EASTMAN HOUSE : [SCHEDULE OF EVENTS].** [Dryden Theatre, Curtis Theatre Int. Mus. Photogr. George Eastman House]. **Added/Corp** International Museum of Photography at George Eastman House. Winter Schedule (1991)-. English. qt. Free. International Museum of Photography at George Eastman House, 900 East Avenue, Rochester NY 14607. **DD** 790.

GW
**DUMONT FOTO.** (1978)-. German. an. DuMont Buchverlag GmbH & Co. KG, Postfach 100468, D 50441 Cologne Germany. **Tel** 011 49 221 20530. **LC** TR640; .D85. **DD** 770/.5.
**Ind/Abst** ARTbibliogr. Mod.

US/0896-0976
**ELECTRONIC PHOTOGRAPHY NEWS.** [Electron. photogr. news]. VFOAT EPN. (Sept. 1987)-. Periodical. English. Twelve times a year. $81.00 one year; $90.00 other. Photofinishing News Inc, 10915 Bonita Beach Road, Suite 1091, Bonita Springs FL 33923. **Tel** (813)992-4421, FAX (813)992-6328. **ED** Don Franz. **DD** 621. **Bk Rev**, (Qty: 5-6). **Circ:** 300.
**Desc:** Records and analyzes the development of electronic photography.

US/0886-845X
**ENTRY (ANN ARBOR, MICH.).** (ENTRY). [Entry]. (198?)-. Periodical. English. Ten times a year. $22.00. Entry, PO Box 7648, Ann Arbor MI 48107-7648. **Tel** (313)663-4686. **ED** Jennifer Hill. **DD** 770. **Ad Acc**.
**Desc:** Lists current photographic competitions and juried exhibitions. Also includes information on photo workshops, grants, exhibition screenings and film/video competitions.

GW/0172-7028
**EUROPEAN PHOTOGRAPHY (GOTTINGEN, GERMANY).** (EUROPEAN PHOTOGRAPHY.). [Eur. photogr.]. Vol. 1 (Jan./Feb./March 1980)-. Periodical. English (German). sa. $32.00. European Photography, PO Box 3043, D-37020 Goettingen Germany. **Tel** 011 49 551 24820. **LC** TR640; .E78. **DD** 770/.5. *Absorbed* Print Letter.
**Ind/Abst** ARTbibliogr. Mod. (1985-); ARTbibliogr. Curr. Titles.

SP
**EVERFOTO.** Spanish (Spanish). Espana Editorial Everest, Carretera Leon-Astorga KM 4 500, Leon Spain. **LC** TR640; .E83.

US/0098-8863
**EXPOSURE (NEW YORK, N.Y.).** (EXPOSURE.). [Exposure]. **Added/Corp** Society for Photographic Education. (19??)-. Periodical. English. Three times a year. $35.00. Society for Photographic Education, PO Box 222116, Dallas TX 75222. **Tel** (817)273-2845. **LC** TR1; .E93. **DD** 770/.5.
**Ind/Abst** BHA : Biblio. Hist. Art.

UK/0950-737X
**EYEPIECE.** (EYEPIECE : JOURNAL OF THE GUILD OF BRITISH CAMERA TECHNICIANS.). [Eyepiece]. (1978)-. Trade Publication. English. bm. £26.50 UK and Europe; £37.50 other. Guild of British Camera Technicians, 5-11 Taunton Road/Metro Centre, Greenford Middlesex UB6 8UQ England. **Tel** 011 44 081 578 9243, FAX 011 44 081 575 5972. **ED** Charles Hewitt and Kerry Anne Burrows. **DD** 778.53. Index available. cum. index. **Ad Acc, Adv Mgr:** Ron Bowyer, **Tel** 081 464 6738. **Pr Rev.** Acid Free. **Circ:** 3,500-5,000 (ctrl). *Continues* Eyepiece/GBCT News.
**Desc:** Movies and cinefilm and video making films, commercials, pop promotions, etc.
**Ind/Abst** Film Lit. Index (19??-).

CN/0836-1002
**FILM/VIDEO CANADIANA.** *See* Motion Picture.

US/0147-1686
**FLOATING ISLAND.** *See* Literature-Poetry.

CN/1183-4757
**FOCUS ON EDUCATION (TORONTO).** (FOCUS ON EDUCATION.). [Focus educ.]. **Added/Corp** Kodak Canada Inc. Vol. 1, Issue 1 (Apr. 1991)-. Periodical. English. sa. Limited free distribution. Kodak Canada, Inc., 3500 Eglinton Avenue West, Toronto Ontario K6M 1V3 Canada. **DD** 770.

UK
**FORENSIC PHOTOGRAPHY.** (1972)-. Periodical. English. qt. $2.21. Forensic Photography, PO Box 18, Bognor Regis PO2 27AA England.

NE/0015-8682
**FOTO.** [Foto]. **Added/Corp** Bond van Nederlandse Amateur Fotografen Verenigingen. Nederlandse Fotografen Kunstkring. (1946)-. Academic Scholarly Publication. Dutch. mo. Foto Fotohandel, PO Box 3, 3830 AA Leusden Netherlands. available on microfilm from University Microfilms International (UMI).
**Ind/Abst** EMBASE.

NE/0165-5531
**FOTO & DOKA.** [Foto doka]. (1979)-. Periodical. Dutch. mo (12 issues). Fl87.50. PVO Abonnementservices, Postbus 77, 5126 ZH Gilze Netherlands. **Tel** 011 31 1615 7450. **UDC** 77.

GW/0721-7730
**FOTO CREATIV.** **Ceased.** (19??)-(Jan. 1993). Periodical. German. bm. Vereinigte Motor Verlag GmbH, Motor Presse, POB 106036, D 70049 Stuttgart Germany. **Tel** 011 49 711 1821506, 011 49 711 1821545. **UDC** 77:379.825. **CODEN** 77:689.

US/0272-1252
**FOTO FINDER.** English. $10.00. The Photoletter, Pine Lake Farm, Osceola WI 54020. **Tel** (715)248-3800, telex 6501892053. **LC** TR12; .F65. **DD** 770/.25/73.

SP
**FOTO GALAXIS.** Multiple languages. Galaxis, Zamora 46-48, Barcelona Spain. **LC** TR690; .F56.

GW/0340-6660
**FOTO MAGAZIN.** (April 1949)-. Periodical. German. mo. $85.00. Ringier Verlag GmbH, Gustav Heinemann Ring 212, D 81739 Munich Germany. **Tel** 011 49 89 638180. **LC** TR1. **Ad Acc. Circ:** 134,000 (ctrl). *Supersedes* Foto-Spiegel.

SP/0211-9552
**FOTO PROFESIONAL.** **Title Change.** [Foto prof.]. (1982)-(19??). Periodical. Spanish. mo. Grupo Foto, Tortolas 7, Apartado 264, 28230 Las Rozas Spain. **Tel** 011 34 1 636-0909. **UDC** 77. *Continued by* Revista Foto SL.

SW/0345-3626
**FOTO (STOCKHOLM, SWEDEN : 1983).** (FOTO.). Vol. 45, No. 1 (Jan. 1983)-. Periodical. Swedish. mo. Kr19.75. Specialtidningsforlaget, Sveavagen 53, 113 59 Stockholm Sweden. **LC** TR1; .F593. *Continues* Foto Och Filmteknik.
**Ind/Abst** ARTbibliogr. Mod.

PL/0324-8453
**FOTO (WARSAW, POLAND).** (FOTO : MAGAZYN FOTOGRAFICZNY.). Vol. 1 (Jan. 1975)-. Periodical. Polish. Twelve times a year. $27.50. **(Subscription address:** ARS Polona, PO Box 1001, 00068 Warsaw Poland.**) ED** Z. Szargut.

GW/0720-5260
**FOTOGESCHICHTE.** [Fotogeschichte]. Vol. 1, No. 1 (1981)-. Periodical. German. qt (Mar., June, Sep., Dec.). DM110.00 Germany; DM122.00 other. Jonas Verlag Kunst & Literatur, Weidenhauser Str 88, D 35037 Marburg Germany. **Tel** 011 49 6421 17880. **ED** Timm Starl. **LC** TR15; .F67. **DD** 770/.9. Index available. cum. index. **Bk Rev. Ad Acc. Circ:** 1,000.
**Desc:** Essays on the history and aesthetics of photography.
**Ind/Abst** ARTbibliogr. Mod.; BHA : Biblio. Hist. Art.

IT
**FOTOGRAFARE.** (196?)-. Periodical. Italian. Twelve times a year. L50000 Italy; L75000 other. Cesco Ciapanna Editore Spa, Via Lipari 8, 00141 Rome Italy. **Tel** 011 39 6 87183441, FAX 011 39 6 87183995.

PL/0015-8801
**FOTOGRAFIA (WARSAW, POLAND).** (FOTOGRAFIA.). No. 1 (July 1953)-. Periodical. Polish. **(Subscription address:** ARS Polona, PO Box 1001, 00068 Warsaw Poland.**)**

XR/0009-0549
**FOTOGRAFIE.** (Jan. 1991)-. Periodical. Czech (summaries and/or abstracts in English, German and Russian). mo. kcs60.00 Czech Republic; $61.70 US. Fotografie, Mrstikova 23, 101 00 Prague 10, Czech Republic. **Tel** 011 2-781553. **Circ:** 57,000. available with illustrations. *Continues* Ceskoslovenska Fotografie (1946).

SZ/0015-8836
**FOTOGRAFIE.** **Ceased. Added/Corp** Deutsches Kulturbund. Germany (Democratic Republic, 1949- ). Zentrale Kommission Fotografie. (1947)-(19??). Periodical. German (summaries and/or abstracts in English, French and Russian). mo. Deutscher Judo Verband, Redaktion Ippon Segewaldweg 40, D 12557 Berlin Germany. **Tel** 011 49 711 210770, telex 501 678. *Formed by the union of* Gebrauchsgrafik; Fotografische Rundschau; Kleinbild and Farben-Fotografie.
**Ind/Abst** ARTbibliogr. Mod.

SW
**FOTOGRAFISKA MUSEET / STATENS KONSTMUSEER.** Vol. 1 (1976)-. Periodical. Swedish.
**Ind/Abst** ARTbibliogr. Mod.

MX
**FOTOGRAMETRIA, FOTOINTERPRETACION Y GEODESIA.** Spanish. Tacuba No 5, Corredores Entrada No 4, Salon No 39, Mexico 1 Mexico. **LC** TA593; .F67.

IT
**FOTOGUIDE, LE.** Italian. sa. Editrice Progress SRL, Viale Piceno 14, 20129 Milan Italy. **Tel** 02/715939, FAX 02/71 30 30. **Circ:** 15,000.
**Desc:** Covers all you need to know about cameras.

NE
**FOTOHANDEL.** Dutch. Eleven times a year. Fl60.00 Netherlands; Fl74.00 other. Foto Fotohandel, PO Box 3, 3830 AA Leusden Netherlands. **ED** Fre Withoff and Peter Noorland. **Bk Rev. Ad Acc. Circ:** 3,500 (ctrl).
**Desc:** Product and other news for camera shops, minilabs, importers and manufacturers of photographic products; interviews, marketing information and comments.

IT
**FOTOLOGIA.** Vol. 1 (1984)-. Periodical. Italian. Fratelli Alinari IDEA SPA, Largo Fratelli Alinari 15, 50123 Florence Italy. **Tel** 011 39 55 210202, 011 39 55 218950. **LC** TR1; .F749. **DD** 770/.5.
**Ind/Abst** BHA : Biblio. Hist. Art.

GW/0340-6660
**FOTOMAGAZIN.** [Fotomagazin]. VFOAT Foto Magazin. (19??)-. Periodical. German. DM86.40 Germany; DM96.00 other. Ringier Verlag GmbH, Gustav Heinemann Ring 212, D 81739 Munich Germany. **Tel** 011 49 89 638180. Index available. *Continues* Foto Magazin; *Absorbed* Camera (Lucerne, Switzerland), 0366-7073.
**Ind/Abst** ARTbibliogr. Mod. (1982-).

HU/0532-3010
**FOTOMUVESZET.** [Fotomuveszet]. (1969)-. Periodical. Hungarian. qt. **LC** TR640; .F675.
**Ind/Abst** Soc. Plann. Policy Dev. Abstr.; Sociol. Abstr.

CU
**FOTOTECNICA.** Periodical. Spanish. Secretariado Ejecutivo Union de Periodistas de Cuba, Calle 23 No 452, Esq A I Vedado, La Habana Cuba. **LC** TR820; .F64.

GW/0340-6644
**FOTOWIRTSCHAFT, DIE.** (1975)-. Periodical. German. Twelve times a year. DM132.00. Ringier Verlag GmbH, Gustav Heinemann Ring 212, D 81739 Munich Germany. **Tel** 011 49 89 638180. **UDC** 771.3/.4-681.77 :339.3. **CODEN** 778.

US/0895-6030
**FRAME/WORK (LOS ANGELES, CALIF.).** (FRAME/WORK.). [Frame/work]. **Added/Corp** Los Angeles Center for Photographic Studies. **VAT** Frame Work. Vol. 1, No. 1 (1987)-. Periodical. English. Three times a year. $28.00 (institutions), $18.00 (individuals) US; $34.00 (institutions), $24.00 (individuals) other. Los Angeles Ctr Photo Studies, 1048 West Sixth Street, Los Angeles CA 90017. **Tel** (213)482-3566. **DD** 770. **Ad Acc. Circ:** 2500. *Formed by the union of* Camera Lucida, 0740-8641 *and* Obscura, 0273-0235.

UK
**FREE-LANCE WRITING & PHOTOGRAPHY.** Victoria House / United Kingdom, Victoria Road, Halecheshire WA19 2BP United Kingdom.

US/0190-1567
**FREE STOCK PHOTOGRAPHY DIRECTORY, THE.** Directory. English. an. $10.00. Infosource Business Publications, 1600 Lehigh Parkway East, Allentown PA 18103. **LC** TR12; .F73. **DD** 779/.074/013.

JA/0915-1478
**FUJI FIRUMU KENKYU HOKOKU.** **Added/Corp** Fuji Shashin Firumu Kabushiki Kaisha. Fuji Shashin Firumu Kabushiki Kaisha. Ashigara Kenkyujo. Gijutsu Shiryoshitsu. VFOAT Fuji Film Research and Development; Fuji Film Research & Development. **VAT** Fuji Shashin Firumu Kabushiki Kaisha Kenkyu Hokoku. No. 34 (1989)-. Japanese (English). Fuji Photo Film Co Ltd, Ashigara Research Laboratories, Minami-Ashigara, Kanagaw 250-01 Japan. **LC** TR196.5.F85; F85. Documents available from Article Express International. *Continues* Fuji Shashin Firumu Kenkyu Hokoku, 0367-3189.
**Ind/Abst** Ei Page One; Eng. Index Annu.

SP/0214-2244
**FV. FOTO-VIDEO ACTUALIDAD.** [FV, Foto-video actual.]. VFOAT Foto-Video Actualidad. (1988)-. Periodical. Spanish. mo. 5812.50ptas.

Ommnicon SV, Hierro 9 3A 7, 28045 Madrid Spain. **Tel** 011 34 1 5278249. **ED** Juan Varela. **UDC** 77. **Bk Rev. Ad Acc. Circ:** 12,500.

CC/1000-3231
**GANGUANG KEXUE YU GUANGHUAXUE.** (KAN KUANG KO HSUEH YU KUANG HUA HSUEH.). [Ganguang kexue yu guanghuaxue]. **Added/Corp** Chung-Kuo Kan Kuang Yen Chiu Hui. Chung-Kuo Ko Hsueh Yuan. Kan Kuang Hua Hsueh Yen Chiu So. **VFOAT** Photographic Science and Photochemistry. (19??)-. Periodical. Chinese (summaries and/or abstracts in English). qt. $80.40. Science Press, 16 Donghuangchenggen North Street, Beijing 100707, People's Republic of China. **Tel** 011 86 1 4019821, 011 86 1 4010642, FAX 011 86 1 4012180, 011 86 1 4019810, telex 210147. **LC** TR692; .K36. **CODEN** GKKHE9. Documents available from CASDDS.
**Ind/Abst** Chem. Abstr.

US/0435-5806
**GERMAN PHOTOGRAPHIC ANNUAL, THE.** 1956-. English. an. Kampmann & Company, 226 West 26 Street/8th Floor, New York NY 10001. **Tel** (800)526-7626. **ED** W Strache and O Steinert.

US/0894-6663
**GOLD BOOK OF PHOTOGRAPHY PRICES.** [Gold book photogr. prices]. **Added/Corp** Photography Research Institute Carson Endowment. (1984)-. English. an. $39.95 (one year). Masspirg, Publications Department, 29 Temple Place, Boston MA 02111. **Tel** (617)292-4800. **LC** TR690; .G58. **DD** 770/.68/8.

SZ
**GRAPHIS PHOTO.** (1988)-. English (French and German). an. $69.00. Graphis Press Corporation NY, 141 Lexington Avenue, New York NY 10016. **Tel** (212)532-9387. ***Continues*** *Photographis, 0079-1830.*

US/0360-8654
**GUIDE TO MICROGRAPHIC EQUIPMENT.** 6th Ed. (1975)-. English. an. Association for Information & Image Management, Business Office, 1100 Wayne Avenue/Suite 1100, Silver Spring MD 20910. **Tel** (301)587-8202, FAX (301)587-2711. **LC** TR835; .N29. **DD** 380.1/45/68165. **Ad Acc.** ***Continues*** *Guide to Microreproduction Equipment.*

US/1054-8904
**GUIDE TO PHOTOGRAPHY WORKSHOPS & SCHOOLS.** [Guide photogr. workshops sch.]. 2nd Ed. (1991)-. English. $16.95. Shaw Associates, 625 Biltmore Way, Suite 1406, Coral Gables FL 33134. **Tel** (305)446-8888, FAX (305)446-1837. **DD** 770. ***Continues*** *Guide to Photography Workshops, 1044-9108.*

SW/0282-5449
**HASSELBLAD FORUM. Added/Corp** Victor Hasselblad Aktiebolag. Vol. 21, No. 1 (March 1985)-. Periodical. English (Swedish and German). qt. $22.00. Victor Hasselblad, Box 220, S-40123 Goteborg 1 Sweden. **Tel** 011 61 31 102400, FAX 4631 135074, telex 2279. **(Subscription address:** Victor Hasselblad Inc., 10 Madison Road, Fairfield, NJ 07006**) ED** Odd Tommelstad. Index available. **Bk Rev. Circ:** 30,000. ***Continues*** *Hasselblad Magazine.*
**Desc:** Publishes the works of photographers using Hasselblad.

US/1050-8996
**HBO'S GUIDE TO MOVIES ON VIDEOCASSETTE AND CABLE TV.** [HBO's guide movies videocass. cable TV]. **Added/Corp** Home Box Office (Firm). **VFOAT** Guide to Movies on Videocassette and Cable TV; Movies on Videocassette and Cable TV. **VAT** Home Box Office's Guide to Movies on Videocassette and Cable Television. 1st Ed. (1990)-. English. an. $12.95. Harper & Row Publishers Inc, 10 East 53rd Street, New York NY 10022. **Tel** (717)343-4761. **DD** 791.
**Desc:** Lists more than 7,000 movies.

US
**HEALTHCARE VIDEODISC DIRECTORY. VFOAT** Videodisc; Interactive Healthcare Directory. Videodisc; Videodisc Directory. (1991)-. Directory. English. Stewart Publishing Inc., 6471 Merritt Court, Alexandria VA 22312. **Tel** (703)354-8155. **NLM** ZW 18; H4344. ***Continues in part*** *Interactive Healthcare Directory.*

US/0092-5365
**HERE'S HOW (NEW YORK).** (THE HERE'S HOW.). [Here's how]. **Main/Corp** Eastman Kodak Company. English. $1.25. Eastman Kodak Company, 343 State Street, Department 412 L, Rochester NY 14650. **Tel** (716)724-4000, (800)242-2424. **LC** TR147; .E235A. **DD** 770/.28.

UK/0308-7298
**HISTORY OF PHOTOGRAPHY.** [Hist. photogr.]. Vol. 1 (Jan. 1977)-. Periodical. English. qt. £97.00 UK; $160.00 other. Taylor & Francis Ltd., Rankine Road, Basingstoke Hampshire, RG24 8PR United Kingdom. **Tel** 011 44 256 840366, FAX 011 44 256 479438, telex 858540. **(Subscription address:** Taylor & Francis Inc., 1900 Frost Road, Suite 101, Bristol PA 19007-1598.**) ED** Dr. Mike Weaver (editor's address: Linacre College, Oxford OX1 1SY United Kingdom) and Anne Hammond, associate editor. **LC** TR15; .H57. **DD** 770/.9. **[CCC]. Ad Acc. Circ:** 550 (ctrl). available on microfilm from University Microfilms International (UMI). Documents available from The Genuine Article.
**Desc:** Devoted exclusively to the history and early development of the graphic art form of photography. Covers the early uses of photography in painting and sculpture, the history of photo-journalism, and the preservation and restoration of old photographs. It is designed to supply the needs of curators, scholars, and critics, and to support the work of graduate students entering this field of study. It is also an repository of documentary texts, indexes, and bibliographies of all periods.
**Ind/Abst** Art Archaeol. Tech. Abstr.; Art Index; ARTbibliogr. Mod.; ARTbibliogr. Curr. Titles; Arts Humanit. Citation Index [Full Cov.]; Avery Index Archit. Period. Suppl. Colum. Univ. (Apr.-June 1989); BHA : Biblio. Hist. Art; Curr. Contents Arts Humanit.; Res. Alert [Full Cov.]; RILA, Int. Rep. Lit. Art; Soc. Sci. Cit. Index [Select. Cov.]; West. Hist. Q.

JA
**HODO SHASHIN.** (19??)-. Periodical. Japanese. ¥1500. Chunichi Shimbun Honsha, 6-1 Sannomatu 1-chome, Naka-ku 460, Nagoya Japan. **LC** TR820; .H58.

US/0739-120X
**HOLOSPHERE.** ***Suspended.*** [Holosphere]. -Suspended with Vol. 18. No. 1. Periodical. English. qt. $30.00 US; $45.00 other. Museum of Holography, 11 Mercer Street, New York NY 10013. **DD** 774.

●US/1061-3765
**HOME STUDIO FORUM.** (HOME STUDIO FORUM: THE COMMUNICATIONS CONNECTION FOR HOME-BASED PHOTOGRAPHERS.). **VFOAT** Home Studio. (1992)-. Periodical. English. mo. $59.00. Endless Possiblities Publications, 1031 Old Tannery Creek Trail, Petoskey MI 49770-9358.

US/0161-9055
**HOME VIDEO REPORT, THE.** (1978)-. Periodical. English. sm. $95.00. Knowledge Industry Publications Inc, 701 Westchester Avenue, White Plains NY 10604. **Tel** (914)328-9157, (800)800-5474, FAX (914)328-9093. ***Continues*** *Video Publisher, 0300-7057.*

UK/0959-6933
**HOT SHOE INTERNATIONAL.** [Hotshoe int.]. (198?)-. Periodical. English. Four times a year. £15.00 UK; £21.00 Europe; £35.00 other. Creative Magazines Ltd., 35 Britannia Row, London N1 8QH England. **Tel** 011 44 071 226 1739, FAX 011 44 071 226 1540. **DD** 770.5. **Bk Rev. Ad Acc. Circ:** 12,000. ***Continues*** *Hot Shoe, 0260-5783.*
**Desc:** A showcase for the work of leading advertising photographers with interviews about their work.

US/1059-2660
**ILLUSTRATED LIGHT.** [Illus. light]. Vol. 1, No. 1 (Feb. 1991)-. Periodical. English. qt. $25.00. Don Eddy, 2201 Stanford Road, Ft. Collins CO 80525. **DD** 770.

US/0536-5465
**IMAGE (ROCHESTER).** (IMAGE.). [Image]. **Added/Corp** International Museum of Photography at George Eastman House. George Eastman House. Vol. 1, (Jan. 1952)-. Academic Scholarly Publication. English. Twice a year. $40.00 US; $50.00 other (membersship). International Museum of Photography, 900 East Avenue, George Eastman House, Rochester NY 14607. **Tel** (716)271-3361, FAX (716)271-3970. **ED** James L Enyeart. **LC** TR1; .I47. **DD** 770.974789. Index available. cum. index. **Circ:** 3,000 (ctrl). available on microfilm from University Microfilms International (UMI). Documents available from The Genuine Article.
**Desc:** International journal of scholarly essays and fine reporductions covering the science, history, and art of photography and film.
**Ind/Abst** Art Index; ARTbibliogr. Mod.; Arts Humanit. Citation Index [Full Cov.]; BHA : Biblio. Hist. Art; Curr. Contents Arts Humanit.; Energy Res. Abstr. (Aug. 1982-); Film Lit. Index; Res. Alert [Full Cov.]; RILA, Int. Rep. Lit. Art.

PE
**IMAGEN.** Yearly V. 1- August 1973-. Spanish. Direccion General de Aerofotografia, Apartado Barranco-38, Lima Peru. **LC** TR810; .I48.

FR/0995-1121
**IMAGES DOC PARIS.** (IMAGES DOC.). (1989)-. Periodical. French. mo. 45.53Can$. Bayard Presse, Svc Client, 3 rue Bayard/Dept 2, 75393 Paris Cedex 08 France. **Tel** 011 33 1 44356060, 011 33 1 44356262. **(Subscription address:** Bayard Presse Notre Temps, BP2, 99505 Paris Enterprises France.**) UDC** 001-053.5.

US/0896-100X
**IMAGING ABSTRACTS. See** Photography and Video-Abstracting, Bibliographies and Statistics.

US/0019-0012
**IMC JOURNAL. See** Office Equipment and Services.

CN
**IMPRESSIONS MONOGRAPH.** Began publication in 1974?. Monographic series. English. Price varies per volume. Impressions, PO Box 5 Station B, Toronto Ontario M5T 2T2 Canada. **ED** S Sugino and J Pendergrast. **DD** 779.

US/0889-6208
**IN MOTION FILM & VIDEO PRODUCTION MAGAZINE.** [In motion film video prod. mag.]. **VFOAT** In Motion Film and Video Production Magazine; In Motion. (198?)-. Periodical. English. Twelve times a year. Available to qualified subscribers only. Phillips Business Information, Inc., 1201 Seven Locks Road, Potomac MD 20854. **Tel** (301)424-3338, (800)777-5006, FAX (301)309-3847. **LC** HD9697.M68; I5. **DD** 778. ctrl circ. ***Continues*** *Maryland In Motion Film & Video Production Directory.*
**Desc:** Covers film and video production techniques.

US
**INCIDENTS OF THE WAR.** Vol. 1, No. 1 (Spring 1986)-. Academic Scholarly Publication. English. qt. $12.00 US; $17.00, $22.00 (first class) other. D Mark Katz, PO Box 4776, Gettysburg PA 17325-0765. **Tel** (717)334-0751. **ED** D Mark Katz. **Bk Rev. Ad Acc. Circ:** 1,500 (ctrl).
**Desc:** Devoted to the study and interpretation of the relationship between photography and the Civil War, highlighted by scholarly articles and text.

US/0019-8595
**INDUSTRIAL PHOTOGRAPHY.** [Ind. photogr.]. Vol. 1 (Fall 1952)-. Periodical. English. Twelve times a year. $60.00 US; $85.00 other. PTN Publishing Company, 445 Broad Hollow Road, Melville NY 11747. **Tel** (516)845-2700, FAX (516)845-7109. **CODEN** INPHA5. available on microfilm and microfiche from University Microfilms International (UMI). Documents available from Article Express International, Ask*IEEE, CASDDS.
**Ind/Abst** Abstr. Graphic Arts Tech. Found. (1984); Appl. Sci. Technol. Index; Bus. Source (Jan. 1993-); Chem. Abstr.; Ei Page One; Eng. Index Annu.; Graph. Arts Bull. Inst. Pap. Sci. Technol. (Sept. 1989); Index Inf. (1970-); INSPEC (March 1972-); Mag. Search; Vocat. Search (July 1993-).

US
**INDUSTRY STANDARD. Added/Corp** National Microfilm Association. **VFOAT** NMA Standard. No. 1 (1971)-. Monographic series. English. Price varies per volume.

US/0892-3876
**INFORM (SILVER SPRING, MD.).** (INFORM.). [Inform]. **Added/Corp** Association for Information and Image Management (U.S.). Vol. 1, No. 1 (Jan. 1987)-. Periodical. English. mo. $85.00. Association for Information & Image Management, Business Office, 1100 Wayne Avenue/Suite 1100, Silver Spring MD 20910. **Tel** (301)587-8202, FAX (301)587-2711. **ED** Gregory E. Kaebnick. **LC** TR835; .J67. **DD** 686. **CODEN** INFREN. **[CCC].** Index available. cum. index. **Bk Rev. Ad Acc. Circ:** 8,000. available on microfilm and microfiche from University Microfilms International (UMI). Documents available from UMI Article Clearinghouse, Ask*IEEE. ***Continues*** *Journal of Information and Image Management, 0745-9963.*
**Desc:** Journal for document image management.
**Ind/Abst** ABI/INFORM Glob. Ed.; ABI Inform Ondisc (Jan. 1987-); Abstr. Bull. Inst. Pap. Sci. Tech.; AESIS Q.; Anbar Account. Finan. Abstr. [Full Txt.]; Anbar Mark. Distr. Abstr. [Full Txt.]; Anbar Top Manage. Abstr. [Full Txt.]; Comput. Lit. Index; Health Plan. Adminis.; Hospit. Health Admin. Index (Jan. 1987-); Inf. Instruc. Technol.; Inf. Manage. Technol.; Inf. Sci. Abstr. [Full Cov.]; INSPEC (Jan. 1987-); Libr. Inf. Sci. Abstr. (Jan. 1987-); Libr. Lit. (Jan. 1987-); Manage. Bibliogr. Rev.; Oper. Prod. Manage. Abstr. [Full Txt.]; Person. Train. Abstr. [Full Txt.]; Print. Abstr. (Jan. 1987-); Women Manage. Rev. [Full Txt.].

UK/0256-1840
**INTERNATIONAL ARCHIVES OF PHOTOGRAMMETRY AND REMOTE SENSING. See** Engineering.

US/1063-7478
**INTERNATIONAL ASSOCIATION OF PANORAMIC PHOTOGRAPHERS :.** [Int. Assoc. Panor. Photogr.]. **Added/Corp** International Association of Panoramic Photographers. **VFOAT** IAPP. (19??)-. Periodical. English. Five times a year. $30.00 (membership). International Association Panormaic Photograph, 1739 Limewood Lane, Orlando FL 32818. **Tel** (407)293-8003, FAX (407)293-8003. **ED** Warren & Patty Wight (phone: (407)339-3756). **LC** TR661; .I54. **DD** 778.3/6/05. **Bk Rev. Ad Acc. Circ:** 500.

US/0148-5121
**INTERNATIONAL FILE OF MICROGRAPHICS EQUIPMENT & ACCESSORIES.** [Int. file microgr. equip. accessories]. **Added/Corp** Microform Review Inc. **VAT** International File of Micrographics Equipment and Accessories. (19??)-. Periodical. English. be. $250.00. Microform Review Inc, 520 Riverside Avenue, Box 405, Westport CT 06880. **Tel** (203)226-6967. **LC** TR835; .I52. **DD** 338.4/7/681418.

US
**INTERNATIONAL FIRE PHOTOGRAPHERS ASSOCIATION : NEWSLETTER : IFPA.** **VFOAT** Newsletter; IFPA. Newsletter. English. qt. $6.00. PO Box 201, Elmhurst IL 60126. **Tel** (312)530-3097. **ED** Robert Trivalos. **Bk Rev. Ad Acc. Circ:** 750 (ctrl).
**Desc:** Uses of fire photography to educate public and fire service. Promotion of proper uses of fire photography as evidence. Tools and techniques for fire photographers, uses for public education programs and video tape uses.

US/0020-8299
**INTERNATIONAL PHOTOGRAPHER.** **Added/Corp** International Alliance of Theatrical Stage Employees and Moving Picture Operators of the United States and Canada. Local 659. (19??)-. Periodical. English. mo. $24.00 US; $50.00 (surface mail), $70.00 (air mail) other. International Photographer, 7715 Sunset Boulevard, Suite 300, Hollywood CA 90046. **Tel** (213)876-0160, FAX (213)876-6383. **ED** George Toscas. **Ad Acc. Circ:** 10,000.
**Desc:** Covers professional cinematography.

US/0895-2213
**INTERNATIONAL TELEVISION & VIDEO ALMANAC.** **See** Communication-Broadcasting.

JA
**JAPAN CAMERA TRADE NEWS.** (19??)-. Periodical. English. mo. $95.40. **(Subscription address:** Maruzen Company Ltd., PO Box 5050, Import & Export Department, Tokyo 100 31 Japan.**)**

US/0273-9917
**JOURNAL FOR EDUCATION IN PHOTOJOURNALISM, THE.** **VAT** Journal for Education in Photo Journalism. Vol. 1, No. 1 (Winter 1981)-. Periodical. English. qt. The Journal for Education in Photojournalism, Box 1393, Garden Grove CA 92642. **LC** TR820; .J68. **DD** 778.9/907.

GW/0863-0453
**JOURNAL OF INFORMATION RECORDING MATERIALS (1985).** (JOURNAL OF INFORMATION RECORDING MATERIALS / EDITED BY VEB FOTOCHEMISCHES KOMBINAT WOLFEN.). [J. inf. rec. mater.]. **Added/Corp** Fotochemisches Kombinat Wolfen, VEB. (198?)-. Periodical. English (German; summaries and/or abstracts in Russian). bm (1 volume). $239.00 (academic institutions), $373.00 (corporate institutions). Gordon & Breach Science Publishers, PO Box 90, Reading RG1 8JL England. **Tel** 011 44 734 560080, FAX 011 44 734 568211. **(Subscription address:** International Publishers Distributor at one of the following addresses: 820 Town Center Drive, Langhorne, PA 19047; or PO Box 90, Reading Berkshire RG1 8JL UK; or Kent Ridge PO Box 1180, Singapore 9111, Republic of Singapore**) LC** TR280; .J68. **DD** 661/.808. **CODEN** JIRMEA. **[CCC]. Pr Rev.** Documents available from The Genuine Article, Ask*IEEE, CASDDS. ***Continues*** *Journal fur Signalaufzeichnungsmaterialen, 0323-598X.*
**Ind/Abst** Chem. Abstr.; Curr. Contents Eng. Tech. Appl. Sci.; Graph. Arts Bull. Inst. Pap. Sci. Technol. (Jan. 1989, Aug. 1989); INIS Atomindex [Micro.]; INSPEC (1987-); Res. Alert [Full Cov.]; SCISEARCH.

UK/0022-3638
**JOURNAL OF PHOTOGRAPHIC SCIENCE, THE.** [J. photogr. sci.]. **Added/Corp** Royal Photographic Society of Great Britain Photographic Alliance (Great Britain). Vol. 1, (Jan./Feb. 1953)-. Periodical. English. Six times a year. £89.00 UK; £99.00 other. Royal Photographic Society, The Octagon, Milsom Street, Bath BA1 1DN England. **Tel** (0225)462841, FAX (0225)448688. **ED** R. B. Collins. **LC** TR1; .J84. **DD** 770.5. **CODEN** JPTSAF. Index available (published in each issue). **Bk Rev. Ad Acc. Pr Rev. Circ:** 3,000. Documents available from The Genuine Article, Ask*IEEE, CASDDS. ***Continues*** *Photographic Journal. Section B, Scientific and Technical Photography.*
**Desc:** All aspects of photographic scientific and technological research and its applications.
**Ind/Abst** Art Archaeol. Tech. Abstr. (1968-); Chem. Abstr.; Curr. Contents Eng. Tech. Appl. Sci.; Curr. Technol. Index; INSPEC (1968-); Int. Aerosp. Abstr.; Leadscan; Print. Abstr.; Res. Alert [Full Cov.]; Sci. Cit. Index; SCISEARCH.

US
**JOURNAL OF SCIENTIFIC AND APPLIED PHOTOGRAPHY AND CINEMATOGRAPHY.** Began with: V. 3, No. 4, 1958. Periodical. English. ir. $712.00 (corporations), $438.00 (academic libraries). Gordon & Breach Science Publishers, Inc., PO Box 786, Cooper Station, New York NY 10276. **Tel** (212)206-8900, FAX (212)645-2459. **(Subscription address:** International Publishers Distributor at one of the following addresses: 820 Town Center Drive, Langhorne, PA 19047; or PO Box 90, Reading Berkshire RG1 8JL UK; or Kent Ridge PO Box 1180, Singapore 9111, Republic of Singapore**) ED** K V Chibison. **LC** TR1. **DD** 778.0822. **Bk Rev. Ad Acc.**

US
**JOURNAL OF THE DAGUERREIAN SOCIETY.** (19??)-. English. Six times a year (Jan., Mar., May, July, Sept., Nov.). $35.00 Comes with Daguerreian Society membership. Daguerreian Society, PO Box 2129, Green Bay WI 54306. **Tel** (414)498-2580, FAX (414)498-2580. Index available (Bound in issues). **Bk Rev**, (Qty: 4-5). **Ad Acc, Adv Mgr:** John Grat, **Tel** (414)339-9389. **Pr Rev. Circ:** 500.
**Desc:** A non-profit organization dedicated to the history, art, and science of the world's first form of photography - the daguerrotype.

GW/0022-8109
**KAMERA UND SCHULE.** Began with: April/June 1962. Periodical. German. qt. DM17.80. Junger Verlag GmbH, Postfach 100962, W-6050 Offenbach Germany. **Tel** (069)840003-37, telex 4 152 889 JUE D. **Bk Rev. Ad Acc. Circ:** 4,000 (ctrl).
**Desc:** Used in photography classes in school, gives suggestions for the teacher. The subscription is read by students, teachers, and photo amateurs.

DK/0904-2334
**KATALOG.** **Added/Corp** Museet for Fotokunst (Odense, Denmark) Forlaget Brandts Kldefabrik. Vol. 1 No. 1 (1988)-. Periodical. Danish (English, French, Norwegian and Swedish). qt.
**Ind/Abst** BHA : Biblio. Hist. Art.

US/0162-3702
**KELLNER'S MONEYGRAM.** Periodical. English. mo. Kellner's Photo Services, 1768 Rockville Drive, Baldwin NY 11510.

US
**KLIK PHOTO SHOWCASE.** (19??)-. English. an. $45.00 (latest edition). American Showcase, 915 Broadway, 14th Floor, New York NY 10010. **Tel** (212)673-6600, FAX (212)673-9795, telex 880356 AMSHOW P. **(Subscription address:** Watson Guptill Publications, PO Box 2014, Lakewood NJ 08101.**)** ***Continues*** *American Photography Showcase.*

US
**KODAK HIGHLIGHTS.** (19??)-. Periodical. English. Four times a year. Free. Eastman Kodak Company, 343 State Street, Department 412 L, Rochester NY 14650. **Tel** (716)724-4000, (800)242-2424.

US/0094-8926
**KODAK STUDIO LIGHT.** **Main/Corp** Eastman Kodak Company. **VFOAT** Studio Light. (19??)-. English. ir. Eastman Kodak Company, 343 State Street, Department 412 L, Rochester NY 14650. **Tel** (716)724-4000, (800)242-2424. **LC** TR1; .E255a. **DD** 770/.5. ***Continues*** *New Kodak Studio Light.*

US/0452-2591
**KODAK TECH BITS.** (TECH BITS / EASTMAN KODAK COMPANY.). [Kodak tech bits]. **Added/Corp** Eastman Kodak Company. Professional, Commercial, and Industrial Markets Division. (1963)-. Periodical. English. Three times a year. Free on request. Eastman Kodak Company, 343 State Street, Department 412 L, Rochester NY 14650. **Tel** (716)724-4000, (800)242-2424. ctrl circ.

GW/0024-0621
**LEICA-FOTOGRAFIE.** ***Title Change.*** (Aug.-Sept. 1949)-?. Periodical. English (German and French). ir (8 times a year). PDQ Distribution Inc, PO Box 2013, River Vale NJ 07675. **Tel** (201)767-5717. **ED** Edmund Bugdoll. **LC** TR1; .L415. **[CCC]. Bk Rev. Ad Acc. Circ:** 5,000. ***Continued by*** *Leica Fotografie International.*
**Desc:** International magazine of 35mm photography. Contains photo essays, profiles of leading photographers, how-to articles, equipment news. Excellent reproductions in color and black and white.

GW/0937-3977
**LEICA FOTOGRAFIE INTERNATIONAL.** Vol. 1 (1989)-. Periodical. English (French and German). ir (8 issues per year). Umschau Verlag, Postfach 110262, D-60037 Frankfurt Germany. **Tel** 011 49 69 2600692, FAX 011 49 69 2600223, telex 411964. **(Subscription address:** German Language Publications Inc., 153 South Deanstreet, Englewood NJ 07631.**) ED** Dr. Martina Mettner, DGPh. **LC** TR1; .L416. **DD** 770/.5. **Bk Rev. Ad Acc.** ***Continues*** *Leica Fotografie (English Ed.), 0174-0253.*
**Desc:** Contains information on Leica cameras and equipment, and the artistic aspects of photography. Includes reproductions in color and black and white.

US/0093-9374
**LEICA MANUAL.** English. Morgan & Morgan Inc, 145 Palisade Street, Dobbs Ferry NY 10522. **Tel** (914)693-0023, FAX (914)693-1572. **LC** TR146; .M77. **DD** 771.3/1. ***Continues*** *Leica Manual.*

●US/1064-0452
**LEONARD'S ANNUAL PRICE INDEX OF PRINTS, POSTERS & PHOTOGRAPHS.** [Leonard's annu. price index prints posters photogr.]. **VFOAT** Annual Price Index of Prints, Posters & Photographs; Prints, Pposters & Photographs; Prints, Posters and Photographs. Vol. 1 (July 1, 1991)-(June 30, 1992)-. English. an. $195.00. Auction Index Inc, 30 Valentine Park, Newton MA 02165. **Tel** (617)964-2876, FAX (617)969-9912. **LC** NE85; .L46. **DD** 760/.075.

US/0161-4223
**LIGHTWORKS.** **See** The Arts-Art.

BE
**MARCHE MONDIAL DE L'AUDIOVISUEL, LE.** (19??)-. French. 60000F Belgium & Luxembourg; 9500F France; 62000F other. Edimedia ASBL, rue de la Constitution 22, 1030 Brussels Belgium. **Tel** 011 32 2 2180031. **Bk Rev. Ad Acc.**

US/1073-8924
**MARKEE (SANFORD, FLA.).** **See** Motion Picture.

UK
**MASTER PHOTOGRAPHER.** English. bm. Master Photographers Association, 1 W Ruislip Station, IC Kesham, Ruislip Middlesex HA4 7DW England.

GW/0024-8142
**MFM. MODERNE FOTOTECHNIK.** [MFM, Mod. Fototech.]. **VFOAT** Moderne Fototechnik. (1965)-. Periodical. German. mo. DM125.04. A G T Verlag Thum GMBH, Postfach 109, D 71601 Ludwigsburg Germany. **Tel** 011 49 7141 223156. **UDC** 77.

US
**MICHIGAN PHOTOGRAPHY JOURNAL : A PUBLICATION OF THE MICHIGAN FRIENDS OF PHOTOGRAPHY.** **Added/Corp** Michigan Friends of Photography. (1987)-. Periodical. English. an. Michigan Friends Photography, PO Box 3048, Trolley Station, Detroit MI 48231.

US/0149-8975
**MICROGRAPHICS INDEX, THE.** **Added/Corp** National Micrographics Association. National Microfilm Association. (1974)-. English. National Micrographics Association, 8728 Colesville Road, Silver Spring MD 20910. **ED** R Tatis. **LC** TR835; .M499. **DD** 001.55/23/016.

US/0149-9882
**MICROGRAPHICS INDEX. SUPPLEMENT, THE.** **Added/Corp** National Micrographics Association. (1976)-. Periodical. English. be. Association for Information & Image Management, Business Office, 1100 Wayne Avenue/Suite 1100, Silver Spring MD 20910. **Tel** (301)587-8202, FAX (301)587-2711. **LC** TR835; .M499 suppl. **DD** 001.55/23/016.

US/0149-9300
**MICROGRAPHICS TODAY.** **Added/Corp** National Micrographics Association. Vol. 10 (Aug. 1975)-. Periodical. English. mo. Association for Information & Image Management, Business Office, 1100 Wayne Avenue/Suite 1100, Silver Spring MD 20910. **Tel** (301)587-8202, FAX (301)587-2711. ***Continues*** *Micro-News Bulletin, 0026-2544.*

US
**MINI LAB FOCUS.** Newsletter. English. mo (12 issues per year). Photo Marketing Association International, 3000 Picture Place, Jackson MI 49201. **Tel** (517)788-8100, FAX (517)788-8371. **ED** Gary Pageau. **Circ:** 2,400 (ctrl).
**Desc:** Newsletter for retail minilab owners. Provides the latest advertising and marketing techniques, financial management tips and customer relations strategies.

JA
**MINOLTA MIRROR.** **Added/Corp** Minoruta Kamera Kabushiku Kaisha. (19??)-. English. an. $6.95. Minolta Corporation, 101 Williams Drive, Ramsey NJ 07446. **Tel** (201)825-4000. ctrl circ.
**Desc:** An international magazine for people interested in outstanding photography. Provides beautifully produced photographs and informative articles.

US/0580-8162
**MODERN PHOTOGRAPHY ANNUAL.** [Mod. photogr. annu.]. 1970-. Multiple languages (English, French and German). an. $1.50. Billboard Publ Co, 165 W 46th Street, New York NY 10036. **LC** TR640; .M63. **DD** 779/.05.

US/0197-5986
**MODERN PHOTOGRAPHY'S GUIDE TO THE WORLD'S BEST CAMERAS.** [Mod. photogr. guide world's best cameras]. **VFOAT** World's Best Cameras. (197?)-. Periodical. English. an. $3.95. ABC Consumer Magazine, 825 7th Avenue, New York NY 10019. **Tel** (212)887-8469. **LC** TR250; .M6. **DD** 771.3.

US
**MOTION PICTURE ANNUAL, THE. See** Motion Picture.

US/1051-5488
**MOVIE MARKETPLACE.** [Movie marketpl.]. **VFOAT** Movie Market Place; Video Marketplace. Vol. 3, No. 6 (Aug. 1990)-. Periodical. English. bm. $19.94 US; $24.00 other. Century Publishing Company, 990 Grove Street, Evanston IL 60201-4370. **Tel** (708)491-6440, (800)321-3333, FAX (708)491-0459. **LC** PN1992.95; .V4945. **DD** 016.79143/75. ***Continues** Video Marketplace, 0895-2892.*
**Desc:** Features articles, plus 5,000 videos for sale.

US/1053-5314
**MOVIES ON TV AND VIDEOCASSETTE. See** Communication-Broadcasting.

US
**NATURAL IMAGE, THE.** Newsletter. English. Four times a year. $18.00. Lepp & Associates, PO Box 6240, Los Osos CA 93412. **Tel** (805)528-7385.
**Desc:** Newsletter for enthusiasts of nature photography.

US/1049-6602
**NATURE PHOTOGRAPHER.** [Nat. photogr.]. Vol. 1, No. 1 (July/Aug. 1990)-. Periodical. English. bm. $11.95 (U.S.), $14.95 (Can.). **DD** 770.

JA
**NENKAN NIHON NO KOKOKU SHASHIN. VFOAT** Nihon No Kokoku Shashin; Advertising Photography in Japan. '82-. English (Japanese). an. ¥7800. Kodansha Ltd / Japan, 12-21 Otowa 2-chome, 112 Bunkyo-ku, Tokyo Japan. **Tel** 03 5395 3517, FAX 03 9466200, telex 22570. **(Subscription address:** Nippon Shuppan Hanbai USA Inc 1115 West 57th Street, New York NY 10019**) LC** TR690.4; .N43. **DD** 779/.974167/095205. **Circ:** 1,500 (ctrl).
**Desc:** Publication displays commercial photography from Japan over the past two years.

US/1058-6970
**NEW ENGLAND BIENNIAL : [CATALOG] : A JURIED EXHIBITION OF NEW ENGLAND PHOTOGRAPHERS / ORGANIZED BY THE PHOTOGRAPHIC RESOURCE CENTER. Added/Corp** Photographic Resource Center (Boston, Mass.). (1991)-. English. be. Photographic Resource Center at Boston University, 602 Commonwealth Avenue, Boston MA 02215.

US/0199-2422
**NEWS PHOTOGRAPHER.** [News photogr.]. **Added/Corp** National Press Photographers Association (U.S.). (1974)-. Periodical. English. mo. $72.00 US; $86.50 Canada; $116.00 other. National Press Photographers Assn., 3200 Croasdaile Dr., Suite 306, Durham NC 27705. **Tel** (919)383-7246, FAX (919)383-7261. **ED** James Gordon, 1446 Conneaut Avenue, Bowling Green, OH 43402; Tel: (419)352-8175. **LC** TR820; .N272. Index available. **Bk Rev**, (Qty: (varies)). **Ad Acc. Pr Rev. Circ:** 12,000 (ctrl). Documents available from UMI Article Clearinghouse. ***Continues** National Press Photographer, 0027-9935.*
**Ind/Abst** Expand. Acad. Index (1992-); Newsp. Period. Abstr. (1989-).

US/0272-7994
**NEWSLETTER / INTERNATIONAL CONGRESS ON HIGH SPEED PHOTOGRAPHY AND PHOTONICS. VFOAT** HSSP Newsletter. Vol. 1, No. 1 (Winter 1981)-. Newsletter. English. Three times a year. Society of Photo-Optical Instrumentation Engineers, PO Box 10, Bellingham WA 98227. **Tel** (206)676-3290, telex 46-7053.

US/1055-3886
**NEWSLETTER (INTERNATIONAL MUSEUM OF PHOTOGRAPHY AT GEORGE EASTMAN HOUSE).** [Newsl. - Int. Mus. Photogr. George Eastman House]. **Added/Corp** International Museum of Photography at George Eastman House. Vol. 8, No. 1 (Spring 1986)-. Newsletter. English. Six times a year. comes with membership. International Museum of Photography, 900 East Avenue, George Eastman House, Rochester NY 14607. **Tel** (716)271-3361, FAX (716)271-3970. **LC** TR1; .G46. **DD** 770. ***Continues** George Eastman House Newsletter.*

NE/0927-8311
**NIEUWSBRIEF / NEDERLANDS FOTOARCHIEF.** [Nieuwsbr. - Ned. Fotoarch.]. (1991)-. Periodical. Dutch. Three times a year. Nederlands Fotoarchief, Sint-Jobsweg 30, 3024 EJ Rotterdam, Netherlands. **Tel** 011 31 10 425-9019, FAX 011 31 10 477-2072. **UDC** 77.
**Desc:** Covers current news and information as it relates to the history of Dutch photography.

JA/0369-5662
**NIHON SHASHIN GAKKAISHI.** [Nihon Shashin Gakkaishi]. **Added/Corp** Nihon Shashin Gakkai. **VFOAT** Journal of the Society of Photographic Science and Technology of Japan. (1937)-. Academic Scholarly Publication. Japanese (summaries and/or abstracts in English). bm (6 issues). $168.00. Nihon Shashin Gakkai, (Soc. of Photographic Science & Technology of Japan), Tokyo Kogei Daigaku, 9-5, Honcho 2 Chome, Nakanoku, Tokyoto 164, Japan. **(Subscription address:** Kyowa Book Company Inc., 1-38 Kanda Jinbo-Cho, Chiyoda-Ku Tokyo 101, Japan**) CODEN** NSGKAP. cum. index. Documents available from Ask*IEEE, CASDDS.
**Ind/Abst** Chem. Abstr.; INSPEC (1937-).

US
**NIKON WORLD. Added/Corp** Nikon, Inc. Vol. 1 (1967)-. Periodical. English. qt (4 issues). $9.95. Nikon Inc., 230 Hilton Avenue, Hempstead NY 11550. **Tel** (516)486-4200. **ED** Nancy Stevens. **LC** TR1; .N47. **Bk Rev. Circ:** 45,000.
**Desc:** Portfolios of Nikon photographers and new product information.

US/0277-8076
**NORTHLIGHT (TEMPE, ARIZ.).** ***Suspended.*** (NORTHLIGHT.). [Northlight]. Periodical. English. ir. $6.50. Friends of Photography at ASU, Art Department, Arizona State University, Tempe AZ 85281. **Tel** (602)965-6517. **LC** TR1; .N83. **DD** 770/.5.
**Ind/Abst** ARTbibliogr. Mod.

US
**NTIS ALERT. PHOTOGRAPHY & RECORDING DEVICES. Added/Corp** United States. National Technical Information Service. (19??)-. Periodical. English. Twenty-four times a year. $140.00 US; $195.00 other. National Technical Information Service - NTIS, Room 2027S, 5285 Port Royal Road, Springfield VA 22161. **Tel** (703)487-4630, (703)487-4660, (703)487-4650, FAX (703)321-8547, telex 89-9405.

US/0887-5855
**NUEVA LUZ.** (NUEVA LUZ : A PHOTOGRAPHIC JOURNAL.). [Nueva luz]. **Added/Corp** En Foco, Inc. Vol. 1, No. 1 (Winter Issue 1985)-. Periodical. English (Spanish). Three times a year. $25.00 (individuals), $40.00 (institutions). En Foco Inc., 32 E Kingsbridge Road, Bronx NY 10468. **Tel** (718)584-7718. **ED** Charles Biasiny-Rivera. **DD** 770. cum. index. **Ad Acc, Adv Mgr:** M. Romais. **Circ:** 5,000.
**Desc:** A photographic journal published by "En Foco Inc.", a non-profit visual arts organization. Each issue features three American photographers of color, a critical essay and editorials.

CN/0712-6107
**OBJECTIF - A.L.P.A.** (L'OBJECTIF : LE JOURNAL DE L'A.L.P.A.). [Object. - A.L.P.A.]. **VFOAT** Journal de l'A.L.P.A. **VAT** Objectif - Association Longueuilloise des Photographes Amateurs. April 81-. Periodical. French. qt. Free to members. Objectif, c/o Association Longueuilloise des Photographes Amateurs, 100 rue St-Laurent, Longueuil Quebec J4H 1M1 Canada. **DD** 770/.23/305.

DK/0107-6329
**OBJEKTIV HELLERUP.** (OBJEKTIV.). [Objektiv Hellerup]. **VFOAT** Medlemsinformation - Dansk Fotohistorisk Selskab. (1976)-. Periodical. Danish. Four times a year. $40.00. Dansk Fotohistorisk Selskab, c/o Flemming Berendt,, Teglgaardsvej 308,, 3050 Humlebaek, Denmark. **DD** 770.9. **Bk Rev. Ad Acc. Circ:** 400. available with illustrations.
**Ind/Abst** BHA : Biblio. Hist. Art.

GW/0030-0594
**OFFSETPRAXIS.** (1965)-. Periodical. German. mo (with July-Aug. issue combined). DM90.00 Germany; DM102.00 other. Fachschriften Verlag GmbH, Hoehenstrasse 17, D 70736 Fellbach Germany. **Tel** 011 49 711 5206256. **UDC** 655.2.
**Ind/Abst** Infomat Int. Bus.

US/0146-4183
**OUI ALBUM.** English. mo. Oui Magazine, 300 West 43rd Street, New York NY 10036. **Tel** (914)469-2102. **LC** TR676; .O93. **DD** 779/.28.

US/1058-7756
**OUTDOOR & TRAVEL PHOTOGRAPHY.** ***Ceased.*** [Outdoor travel photogr.]. **VFOAT** Outdoor and Travel Photography. (1988)-(19??). Periodical. English. Six times a year. Harris Publications, 1115 Broadway/8th Floor, New York NY 10010. **Tel** (212)807-7100. **LC** TR659.5; .O87. **DD** 778.7/1.

US/0890-5304
**OUTDOOR PHOTOGRAPHER.** [Outdoor photogr.]. (1985)-. Periodical. English. Ten times a year. $21.95. Werner Publishing Corporation, 12121 Wilshire Boulevard, Suite 1220, Los Angeles CA 90025. **Tel** (213)820-1500. **(Subscription address:** Neodata / Colorado, PO Box 2606, Boulder Boulder CO 80322.**) LC** WMLC 93/1764. **DD** 778.

CN/0704-9153
**OVO MAGAZINE (1978).** ***Ceased.*** (OVO MAGAZINE.). (1978)-(August 1987). Periodical. English. qt. OVO Magazine, 307 rue Ste-Catherine Ouest/Local 300, Montreal Quebec H2X 2A3 Canada. **LC** TR640; .O18. **DD** 770/.5.

IT
**PATALOGO. CINEMA + TELEVISIONE + VIDEO, IL. See** Motion Picture.

US/0363-003X
**PENTHOUSE PHOTO WORLD.** V. 1- April/May 1976-. Periodical. English. bm. $12.00. Penthouse Inc, 1965 Broadway, New York NY 10023. **Tel** (212)496-6100. **LC** TR1; .P44. **DD** 770/.5.

NE/0167-9104
**PERSPEKTIEF. Added/Corp** Perspektief (Association). **VFOAT** P. (1980)-. Periodical. Dutch (English). qt. $35.29 Netherlands; $40.72 other. Perspektief, Sint Jobsweg 30, 3024 EJ Rotterdam Netherlands. **Tel** 011 31 10 4765208. **ED** Bas Vroege. Index available. cum. index. **Bk Rev. Ad Acc. Circ:** 3,500 (ctrl).
**Ind/Abst** ARTbibliogr. Mod.

US/0199-4913
**PETERSEN'S PHOTOGRAPHIC.** [Petersen's photogr.]. **VFOAT** Photographic. Vol. 8, No. 7, (Nov. 1979)-. Periodical. English. mo. $19.94 US; $28.83 Canada; $30.94 other. Petersen Publishing Company, 6420 Wilshire Bouldevard, Los Angeles CA 90048. **Tel** (213)782-2485. **(Subscription address:** Neodata / Colorado, PO Box 2606, Boulder Boulder CO 80322.**) ED** Bill Hurter. Index available. cum. index. **Bk Rev. Ad Acc. Circ:** 285,530. available on microfilm and microfiche from University Microfilms International (UMI); available on an online database (file 647/Full-Text) from DIALOG. Documents available from UMI Article Clearinghouse. ***Continues** Petersen's Photographic Magazine, 0048-3583.*
**Desc:** "How-to" magazine written for every photographer -- amateur and professional alike. Each issue offers insights into increasing photographic knowledge, skill and enjoyment. Readers get advice on buying camera equipment and accessories, and recieve updates on workshops, schools, seminars, contests, books, photo travel, and more.
**Ind/Abst** Abr. Read. Guide Period. Lit.; Acad. Abstr. Full Text Elite (Jan. 1984-); Acad. Abstr. (Jan. 1984-); Acad. Search (Jan. 1984-); Book Rev. Index; Consum. Index Prod. Eval. Inf. Source; Index Inf.; INFO-SOUTH Abstr.; Mag. Artic. Summar. Elite (Jan. 1984-); Mag. Artic. Summar. Select (Jan. 1984-); Mag. Artic. Summar. CD-ROM (Jan. 1984-); Mag. Index Plus (1989-); Mag. Index. Sel. (1986-); Mag. Search; Newsp. Period. Abstr. (1988-); Read. Guide Abstr. Select Ed.; Read. Guide Period. Lit.; Mag. Index (Nov. 1979-); Vocat. Search (Jan. 1984-).

US
**PFA NEWSLETTER.** Newsletter. English. qt. $7.50. PFA / Photography in the Fine Arts Newsletter, 1309 Bannock Street, Denver CO 80204. **Tel** (303)623-4059.

●US/1076-4526
**PHILLIPS BUSINESS INFORMATION'S INTERACTIVE VIDEO NEWS.** [Phillips Bus. Inf. interact. video news]. **Added/Corp** Phillips Business Information, Inc. **VFOAT** Interactive Video News. Vol. 2, No. 11 (May 31, 1994)-. Periodical. English. bw (25 issues). $597.00 US; $630.00 other. Phillips Business Information, Inc., 1201 Seven Locks Road, Potomac MD 20854. **Tel** (301)424-3338, (800)777-5006, FAX (301)309-3847. **DD** 384. ***Formed by the union of** Video Services News, 1067-3849 **and** Video Marketing News, 0196-4429; **Absorbed** PayPerViews; On-Demand Video; CableSports.*

FR/0151-7848
**PHOT ARGUS EDITION GENERALE.** (1973)-. Periodical. French. bm. 220.00F France; 279.00F other. Editions V M, 1160 Boulevard Malesherbes, F-75017 Paris France. **Tel** 011 33 1 42272544. **UDC** 73. **[CCC].**

AT/1036-384X
**PHOTO & VIDEO RETAILER.** [Photo video retail.]. **VFOAT** Photo and Video Retailer. (1991)-. Periodical. English. Twelve times a year. 38.00Aus$ Australia; 105.00Aus$ other. Yaffa Publishing Group Pty Ltd., GPO Box 606, Sydney NSW 2001 Australia. **Tel** 011 61 2 2812333, FAX 011 61 2 2812750. **DD** 380.1457710994. ***Continues** Photo Retailer, 0816-1909.*

UK/0956-8719
**PHOTO ANSWERS.** No. 1 (April 1989)-. English. Twelve times a year. £21.00 UK; £33.50 others. EMAP National Publications Ltd, Farndon Road, Market Harborough, Leicestershire, LE16 9NR England. **Tel** 011 44 733 555161. ***Continues** SLR Photography.*

US/0890-8753
**PHOTO BUSINESS.** ***Title Change.*** [Photo bus.]. Vol. 1, No. 1 (Sept. 1986)-(19??). Periodical. English. mo (12 issues). Billboard Publications Inc., 1515 Broadway Billboard, New York NY 10036. **Tel** (212)764-7300, FAX (305)755-7048, telex WU TWX 710-581-6279. **(Subscription address:** Fulco, 30 Broad Street, Denville, NJ 07834**) DD** 381. available on microfiche from University Microfilms International (UMI); available on an online database (file 16/Full-Text) from DIALOG. ***Continues*** *Photo Weekly, 0031-8647.* ***Merged into*** *Photographic Trade News.*
**Desc:** Complete coverage of camera, film and photo accessory retailing, video camera/camcorder and blank tape retailing and photo finishing retailing. Delivers all of the vital information necessary to help both the professional and semi-pro photographer.

CN/0708-5435
**PHOTO COMMUNIQUE.** V. 1- Mar./Apr. 1979-. Periodical. English. qt. 14.00Can$ (individuals), 19.00Can$ (institutions) Canada; $14.00 (individuals), $19.00 (institutions) US; $17.00 (individuals), $34.50 (institutions) other. Photo Communique, PO Box 155 Station B, Toronto Ontario M5T 2T3 Canada. **Tel** (416)868-1443. **ED** Gail Fisher-Taylor. **LC** TR640; .P465. **DD** 770/.5. **Bk Rev. Ad Acc. Circ:** 11,000.
**Desc:** Explores the ways in which photography has come to touch every aspect of our lives and culture with diverse articles, sensitively reproduced photos and insightful interviews and book reviews. Offers interesting reading to anyone who likes to delve beneath the surface of visual imagery. Includes current news, opinions and a calendar listing of photographic events.
**Ind/Abst** ARTbibliogr. Mod.

US/0194-1348
**PHOTO CRAFT NEWS.** [Photo craft news]. V. 1- Sept./Oct. 1979. Periodical. English. qt. $18.00 US; $20.00 Canada. Embee Press, 82 Pine Grove Avenue, Kingston NY 12401. **Tel** (914)338-2226. **ED** Mark Baczynsky. **Circ:** 5,000.
**Desc:** A newsletter covering various practical aspects of the photographic craft: equipment construction, innovative processes and easy-to-follow how-to articles.

US/0888-5680
**PHOTO/DESIGN.** ***Ceased.*** [Photo/des.]. **VFOAT** P/D. **VAT** Photo Design. Vol. 1, No. 1 (Aug./Sept. 1984)-(19??). Periodical. English. bm. Billboard Publications Inc., 1515 Broadway Billboard, New York NY 10036. **Tel** (212)764-7300, FAX (305)755-7048, telex WU TWX 710-581-6279. **LC** TR640; .P466. **DD** 770/.5.
**Desc:** Addresses the information and inspirational needs of creative professionals who commission and produce photography for advertising, editorial and corporate communications. Promotes graphic excellence and the promotion of photography as the most versatile art option.

CN/0843-6029
**PHOTO DIGEST.** [Photo dig.]. (June/July/Aug. 1990)-. Periodical. English. Eight times a year. 23.00Can$ (one year), 43.00Can$ (two years) Canada; 33.00Can$ US; 38.00Can$ other. Carni Publishers Ltd, 850 Pierre-Bertrand Boulevard, Suite 440, Vanier Quebec G1M 3K8 Canada. **Tel** (418)687-3550, FAX (418)687-1679. **ED** Carni (editor's address: 2550 TD Center, PO Box 77, Toronto Ontrio M5K 1E7 Canada; editor's phone: (406)287-6357). **DD** 770/.5. **Bk Rev. Ad Acc, Adv Mgr:** J Dumont.
**Desc:** Photo magazines targeted to the amateur/intermediate and professional photographers.

US/1045-8158
**PHOTO DISTRICT NEWS (EASTERN ED.).** (PHOTO DISTRICT NEWS.). [Photo dist. news]. (198?)-. Periodical. English. mo. $36.00 one year; $60.00 two year. Billboard Publications Inc., 1515 Broadway Billboard, New York NY 10036. **Tel** (212)764-7300, FAX (305)755-7048, telex WU TWX 710-581-6279. **DD** 650. ***Continues in part*** *Photo District News, 0883-766X.*
**Desc:** Designed to help commercial photographers manage their businesses better. Packed with national and local news and information from copyright and tax laws to new camera and lighting equipment, business trends, sources and suppliers.

US/1048-0161
**PHOTO DISTRICT NEWS (MIDWESTERN ED.).** (PHOTO DISTRICT (MIDWESTERN ED.)). [Photo dist. news]. Periodical. English. mo. $36.00 one year; $60.00 two year. Billboard Publications Inc., 1515 Broadway Billboard, New York NY 10036. **Tel** (212)764-7300, FAX (305)755-7048, telex WU TWX 710-581-6279. **DD** 650. ***Continues in part*** *Photo District News, 0883-766X.*
**Desc:** Designed to help commercial photographers manage their businesses better. Packed with national and local news and information from copyright and tax laws to new camera and lighting equipment, business trends, sources and suppliers.

US/1048-0153
**PHOTO DISTRICT NEWS (SOUTHERN ED.).** (PHOTO DISTRICT NEWS.). [Photo dist. news]. (198?)-. Periodical. English. mo. $36.00 one year; $60.00 two year. Billboard Publications Inc., 1515 Broadway Billboard, New York NY 10036. **Tel** (212)764-7300, FAX (305)755-7048, telex WU TWX 710-581-6279. **DD** 650. ***Continues in part*** *Photo District News, 0883-766X.*
**Desc:** Designed to help commercial photographers manage their businesses better. Packed with national and local news and information from copyright and tax laws to new camera and lighting equipment, business trends, sources and suppliers.

US/1048-0145
**PHOTO DISTRICT NEWS. (WESTERN ED.).** [Photo dist. news]. (198?)-. Periodical. English. mo. $36.00 one year; $60.00 two year. Billboard Publications Inc., 1515 Broadway Billboard, New York NY 10036. **Tel** (212)764-7300, FAX (305)755-7048, telex WU TWX 710-581-6279. **DD** 650. ***Continues in part*** *Photo District News, 0883-766X.*
**Desc:** Designed to help commercial photographers manage their businesses better. Packed with national and local news and information from copyright and tax laws to new camera and lighting equipment, business trends, sources and suppliers.

US/1060-4936
**PHOTO ELECTRONIC IMAGING.** [Photo electron. imaging]. **VFOAT** PhotoElectronic Imaging. Vol. 34, No. 11 (Nov. 1991)-. Periodical. English. mo. $18.00 US; $28.00 Canada; $45.00 other. Professional Photographers of America, 1090 Executive Way, Des Plaines IL 60018. **Tel** (708)299-8161, FAX (708)299-2685. **ED** Kim Brady. **LC** TR1; .P2. **DD** 770. **Ad Acc, Adv Mgr:** Donna McMahan. **Circ:** 50,000 (ctrl). available on microfilm and microfiche from University Microfilms International (UMI). ***Continues*** *Photomethods, 0146-0153.*
**Ind/Abst** Art Archaeol. Tech. Abstr.

AT
**PHOTO - FORUM.** ***Ceased.*** **VFOAT** Photo Forum. (197?)-(Oct. 1993). Periodical. English. mo. Horwitz Grahame Pty Ltd, 506 Miller Street, Cammeray New South Wales, 2062 Australia. **Tel** 011 61 2 9296144, FAX 011 61 2 9571814. **ED** Margaret Brown. **Bk Rev. Ad Acc. Circ:** 1,200 (ctrl). ***Continues*** *New Zealand Photography.*
**Desc:** Sent to 1,200 people who comprise a large part of the amateur photo market in Australia. Information for photo shops, mini labs, etc.

US/0093-1365
**PHOTO INFORMATION ALMANAC.** ***Ceased.*** [Photo inf. alm.]. English. an. ABC Leisure Magazine Inc, 825 7th Avenue, New York NY 10019. **Tel** (212)265-8360. **LC** TR150; .P53. **DD** 770/.5. **Ad Acc. Circ:** 125,000.
**Desc:** Compilation of photographic reference tables, data, hints, and tips, lighting and exposure information, listings of all films, developers and batteries for photography.

JA/0289-0143
**PHOTO INTERNATIONAL TOKYO. 1969.** [Photo int. Tokyo, 1969]. (1969)-. Periodical. English. mo. $100.00. **(Subscription address:** Maruzen Company Ltd., PO Box 5050, Import & Export Department, Tokyo 100 31 Japan.**) DD** 771.

FR/0031-8523
**PHOTO INTERPRETATION.** [Photo interpret.]. Vol. 1, (March 1962)-. Periodical. French (English and Spanish). Four times a year. 1018.61F France; 1202.00F others. Editions Eska, 27 rue Dunois, 75013 Paris France. **Tel** 011 33 1 44068042. **ED** M. Guy and F. Verger. **LC** TR810; .P47. **DD** 778.3/5. **CODEN** POITAM. **Circ:** 1,000 (ctrl).
**Desc:** Devoted to the methodology of interpreting images of the earth for geologists, hydrologists, botanists, oceanographers, geographers, town-planners and regional developers.
**Ind/Abst** Ecol. Abstr.; For. Abstr.; Geogr. Abstr. Phys. Geogr.; Geogr. Abstr. Human Geogr.; Geol. Abstr.; Int. Dev. Abstr.; Life Sci. Collect.; Soils Fert.

IT
**PHOTO ITALIA.** ***Ceased.*** (19??)-(Oct. 1992). Italian. Publimedia Editrice SRL, Corso Venezia 18, 20121 Milan Italy. **Tel** 011 39 2 77521.

FR
**PHOTO JEUNESSE.** French. bm. 52.00F. Ligue Francaise l'Enseignement Education Permanente, BP 313, 75989 Paris Cedex 20 France. **Tel** 011 33 1 43589642.

US/0884-9528
**PHOTO-LAB-INDEX.** [Photo lab index]. **VFOAT** Photo Lab Index. Began in June 1939. English. Four times a year. $30.00 US; $33.00 other. Morgan & Morgan Inc, 145 Palisade Street, Dobbs Ferry NY 10522. **Tel** (914)693-0023, FAX (914)693-1572. **ED** Liliane DeCock. **DD** 770. **Bk Rev. Ad Acc. Circ:** 6,000 (ctrl).
**Desc:** An up-to-date encyclopedia of photographic methods, procedures, and materials available.

US/0164-4769
**PHOTO LAB MANAGEMENT.** [Photo lab manage.]. Vol. 1 (Mar./Apr. 1979)-. Periodical. English. Twelve times a year. $15.00. PLM Publishing Company Inc, 1312 Lincoln Boulevard, Santa Monica CA 90406. **Tel** (310)451-1344. **ED** Carolyn Ryan. **LC** TR287; .P46. **DD** 771/.1. **Ad Acc. Circ:** 12,292 (ctrl).
**Desc:** Directed to photo lab management personnel including lab owners, managers and production and quality control supervisors. Includes columns directed to prime areas of process chemistries, control, equipment, etc.
**Ind/Abst** Graph. Arts Bull. Inst. Pap. Sci. Technol. (June 1989, Sept. 1989).

CN/0700-3021
**PHOTO LIFE.** [Photo life]. **VFOAT** Photo Dealer News. Vol. 1 (Oct. 1976)-. Periodical. English. Eight times a year. 19.95Can$. Camar Publications Ltd., 130 Spy Court, Markham Ontario L3R 5H6 Canada. **Tel** (416)475-8440, FAX (416)475-9246. **ED** Chris Knowles. **DD** 770/.5. **Ad Acc. Circ:** 80,000.
**Desc:** Caters to the interests of the Canadian photographer, from the avid amateur to the seasoned professional. Each issue contains nature photography, landscapes, exotic travel images, special effects, techniques to suit each season, darkroom tips, plus all the latest in equipment and accessories, Canadian photographic news and upcoming events.
**Ind/Abst** Can. Index.

US/0031-8531
**PHOTO MARKETING.** **Added/Corp** Photo Marketing Association International. Master Photo Dealers and Finishers Association. (June 1924)-. Trade Publication. English. Twelve times a year. $50.00 (with Newsline Newsletter), $30.00 (without Newsline) US; $55.00 (with Newsline), $35.00 (without Newsline) Canada; $70.00 (with Newsline), $50.00 (without Newsline) other. Photo Marketing Association International, 3000 Picture Place, Jackson MI 49201. **Tel** (517)788-8100, FAX (517)788-8371. **ED** Margaret Hooks. Index available in last issue of volume--attached. **Ad Acc. Circ:** 19,800 (ctrl).
**Desc:** Trade association magazine for photo/video retailers, photo processors, finishers, manufacturers and distributors in the photographic industry.
**Ind/Abst** Mark. Advert. Ref. Serv.; Predicasts F&S Index, U. S. Annu. Ed.

US/0888-1138
**PHOTO METRO.** [Photo metro]. (198?)-. Periodical. English. Ten times a year. $20.00 (1 year), $35.00 (2 year) US; $65.00 (1 year), $115.00 (2 year) other. Photo Metro, 17 Tehama, San Francisco CA 94105. **Tel** (415)243-9917, FAX (415)243-9919. **ED** Jo Leggett. **DD** 770. **Bk Rev. Ad Acc, Adv Mgr:** E.Muller. **Circ:** 15,000.
**Desc:** Interviews and portfolios of photographers, photobook and exhibition reviews and articles on photographic issues.

US/0899-4587
**PHOTO OPPORTUNITY.** **See** Business-General Management.

FR/0399-8568
**PHOTO PARIS.** (PHOTO.). [Photo Paris]. (1967)-. Periodical. French. mo (10 issues). 195.89F France; 285.00F other. Publications Filipacchi, 63-65 Champs Elysees, 75008 Paris France. **Tel** 011 33 1 40747000, telex 651-294. **UDC** 77.

CN/0826-5712
**PHOTO PIPELINE.** (THE PHOTO PIPELINE : NEWS FROM THE PHOTOGRAPHERS' UNION.). [Photo pipeline]. Periodical. English. ir. $15.00 per year membership, $10.00 per year for students. Photographers' Union, 210 Napier Street, Hamilton Ontario L8R 1S7 Canada. **DD** 770/.5.

SZ
**PHOTO PORTFOLIO ANNUAL.** French (German). an. Editions Jean Spinatsch, CH-1246 Corsier Geneve Switzerland. **LC** TR640; .P475. **DD** 779/.09494.

US/0736-671X
**PHOTO RESOURCES.** Vol. 1, No. 1 (Feb. 1983)-. Periodical. English. mo. Free. AMR Company, 156 5th Avenue, New York NY 10010.

US/0363-6488
**PHOTO REVIEW, THE.** Vol. 7, No. 4 (Summer 1984)-. Periodical. English. qt. $25.00 (one year), $43.00 (two year) US. Photo Review, 301 Hill Avenue, Langhorne PA 19047. **ED** S Perloff. ***Continues*** *Philadelphia Photo Review.*

CN/1187-1725
**PHOTO SELECTION (1991).** (PHOTO SELECTION.). [Photo sel.]. (1991)-. Periodical. French. Eight times a year. 28.00Can$ Canada; 38.00Can$ others; 43.00Can$ US. Carni Publications, 850 Boulevard

Pierre-Bertrand, Suite 440, Ville-de Vanier Quebec G1M 3K8 Canada. **Tel** (418)687-3550, FAX (418)682-3253. **DD** 770. ***Continues*** *Le Nouveau Photo Selection., 0848-9807.*

UK
**PHOTO TECHNIQUE.** (19??)-. Periodical. English. bm. £15.00 UK; £20.00 other. IPC Business Press, Oakfield HS, Perrymount Road, Hayward Heath, West Sussex RH16 3DH England. **Tel** 011 44 444 440421, FAX 011 44 444 440619, telex 892084 REEDBP G.

GW
**PHOTO TECHNIQUE INTERNATIONAL.** Vol. 1 (1984)-. Periodical. English. qt. DM68.00. Verlag Photo Technik Intl GmbH, Rupert Mayer Str 45, D 81379 Munich Germany. **Tel** 011 49 89 7231992. **LC** TR1; .I64. **DD** 770/.5. ***Continues*** *International Photo Technique.*

UK
**PHOTO TECHNIQUE (LONDON, ENGLAND).** ***Ceased.*** (PHOTO TECHNIQUE.). Periodical. English. mo. Penblade Publishing, 93 Sirdar Road, London W11 4EQ England.

US/0889-2393
**PHOTOFINISHING NEWS LETTER. VFOAT** Photofinishing Newsletter. (198?)-. Periodical. English. Twenty-six times a year. $100.00 US; $125.00 other. Photofinishing News Inc, 10915 Bonita Beach Road, Suite 1091, Bonita Springs FL 33923. **Tel** (813)992-4421, FAX (813)992-6328. **ED** Don Franz. **DD** 338. **Bk Rev**, (Qty: 2-3). **Circ:** 500.

FR
**PHOTOGENIES.** No 1, (April 1983)-. Periodical. French. 10F. 42 Avenue des Gobelins, 75013 Paris France. **LC** TR1; .P6887. **DD** 770/.5.

US/0099-1112
**PHOTOGRAMMETRIC ENGINEERING AND REMOTE SENSING. See** Engineering.

FI
**PHOTOGRAMMETRIC JOURNAL OF FINLAND. Added/Corp** Finnish Society of Photogrammetry. Teknillinen Korkeakoulu. Institute of Photogrammetry. (1967)-. Periodical. English (German). an. Free on request. Tekninen Korkeakoulu, Fotogramm Kaudokart Laboratori, Otakari 1 02150 Espoo Finland. **Tel** 011 358 0 4513901. **LC** TR693; .P5.
**Ind/Abst** Geogr. Abstr. Phys. Geogr.; Geogr. Abstr. Human Geogr.; Int. Dev. Abstr.

US/0271-0838
**PHOTOGRAPH COLLECTOR, THE.** [Photogr. collect.]. Vol. 1 (Oct. 1980)-. Periodical. English. mo. $125.00 US; $149.00 other. Consultant Press, 163 Amsterdam Avenue #201, New York NY 10023. **Tel** (212)838-8640, FAX (212)873-7065. **ED** Robert S. Persky. **Bk Rev. Ad Acc. Circ:** 1,000.
**Desc:** For collectors of and dealers in fine art photography. Gallery, museum, and university exhibitions, dealer news, auction coverage, and conservation news.

US
**PHOTOGRAPH COLLECTORS' RESOURCE DIRECTORY / THE PHOTOGRAPHIC ARTS CENTER, THE. Added/Corp** Photographic Arts Center. (1983)-. English. an. $27.95. The Photographic Arts Center, 163 Amsterdam Avenue, Suite 201, New York NY 10023. **Tel** (212)838-8640, FAX (212)873-7065. **ED** Robert S. Persky. **LC** TR12; .P492. **Bk Rev. Ad Acc. Circ:** 2,500.
**Desc:** A directory of galleries, dealers and museums dealing and/or showing photography.

UK/0031-8698
**PHOTOGRAPHER, THE.** ***Ceased.*** Vol. 1 (Jan. 1966)-(1989). Periodical. English. mo. Penblade Publishers Ltd, Aspen House, 1 Gayford Road, London W12 9BY England. **Tel** 01-743-8618, FAX 01-740-9333, telex 25221. **ED** C Wordsworth. **LC** TR1; .P698. **Ad Acc. Circ:** 10,880 (ctrl). ***Absorbed*** *Record.*
**Desc:** Articles for the professional photographer.

CN/0701-1326
**PHOTOGRAPHER (VANCOUVER).** (PHOTOGRAPHER.). Vol. 3 (Summer 1976)-. Periodical. English. qt. $5.00. Photographer, PO Box 24954 Station C, Vancouver British Columbia V5T 4G3 Canada. **LC** TR1; .P699. **DD** 770/.5. ***Continues*** *B C Photographer, 0315-0755.*

US
**PHOTOGRAPHER'S ALMANAC, THE.** English. an. $15.00 US; $18.25 other. Astronomical Data Service, 3922 Leisure Lane, Colorado Springs CO 80917. **Tel** (719)597-4068. **ED** Roger L Mansfield. **LC** TR690 .M54. **DD** 770/.68.
**Desc:** Custom prepared, astronomical almanac for photographers who wish to image the rising/setting sun/moon from a particular location.

US/0194-5467
**PHOTOGRAPHER'S FORUM.** [Photogr. forum]. Vol. 1, No. 2 (Feb. 1979)-. Periodical. English. Four times a year (Feb., May, Sept., Nov.). $12.00 one year; $18.95 two years; $25.00 three years. Serbin Communications Inc., 511 Olive, Santa Barbara CA 93101. **Tel** (805)963-0439, FAX (805)965-0496. **ED** Glen Serbin. **LC** TR1; .P718. **Bk Rev. Ad Acc. Circ:** 28,000. ***Continues*** *Student Forum, 0148-589X.*
**Desc:** Dedicated to college photography. Interviews of the shortest works and either articles of interest to college photographs.

US/0147-247X
**PHOTOGRAPHER'S MARKET.** (1978)-. English. an (published in Sept. of the prior year). $22.95. Writer's Digest Books, 1507 Dana Avenue, Cincinnati OH 45207. **Tel** (513)531-2222, (800)289-0963, FAX (513)531-4744. **ED** Sam Marshall. **LC** TR12; .P515. **DD** 381/.45/7702573. Each issue contains an index to its own contents (no volume index)--loose. **Circ:** 35,000. ***Continues in part*** *Artists & Photographer's Market, 0146-8294.*
**Desc:** Contains 2,500 up-to-date listings of U.S. and international buyers of freelance photos. Each listing contains the contact name and address, submission requirements, photo specifications, pay rates and tips from the buyer on how to "break in." Everything photographers need to increase their sales and success.

US/1053-7031
**PHOTOGRAPHIC ART MARKET.** [Photogr. art mark.]. **Added/Corp** Photographic Arts Center. (1981)-. English. an. $49.95. Photographic Arts Center Ltd, 163 Amsterdam Avenue, Suite 201, New York NY 10023. **Tel** (212)838-8640, FAX (212)873-7065. **ED** Robert S. Persky. **LC** TR6.5; .P52. **DD** 779/.075/0973. **Ad Acc. Circ:** 500.
**Desc:** A compilation of auction prices in the photographic art market.

●US/1066-0704
**PHOTOGRAPHIC BUYERS GUIDE. Added/Corp** Petersen Publishing Company. (1993)-. English. $3.95. Petersen Publishing Company, 6420 Wilshire Bouldevard, Los Angeles CA 90048. **Tel** (213)782-2485.

CN/0704-0024
**PHOTOGRAPHIC CANADIANA. Added/Corp** Photographic Historical Society of Canada. Vol. 1 (March 1975)-. Periodical. English. ir (Jan., Mar., May, Sept., Nov.). Free to members, 20.00Can$ membership. Photographic Historical Society of Canada, 1712 Avenue Road Box 54620, Toronto Ontario M5M 4N5 Canada. **Tel** (416)232-1199 or, 622-0433. **ED** Everett Roseborough. **DD** 770/.9. Index available. cum. index. **Bk Rev. Circ:** 270.
**Desc:** Deals with historic photographic equipment, images and people with emphasis on the history of photography in Canada.

US/0898-7572
**PHOTOGRAPHIC INSIGHT.** ***Ceased.*** [Photogr. INsight]. **Added/Corp** Bristol Workshops in Photography. **VFOAT** Photographic In Sight; IN Sight. Journal 1, No. 1 (Fall 1987)-Vol. 3, No. 1 (March 1993). Periodical. English. qt. Photographic Insight Foundation, 474 Thames Street, Bristol RI 02809. **Tel** (401)253-2351. **ED** Stephen Brigidi, Sandra Feeney and Patrick Garner. **DD** 770. **Bk Rev. Circ:** 1,200.
**Desc:** A journal on historical and contemporary photography and related visual arts.

UK/0031-8736
**PHOTOGRAPHIC JOURNAL (1956).** (THE PHOTOGRAPHIC JOURNAL.). [Photogr. j.]. **Added/Corp** Royal Photographic Society of Great Britain. Photographic Alliance (Great Britain). Jan. 1956-. Periodical. English. mo. £55.00 UK; £60.00 other. Royal Photographic Society, The Octagon, Milsom Street, Bath BA1 1DN England. **Tel** (0225)462841, FAX (0225)448688. **ED** Roy Green. **LC** TR1; .P778. **DD** 770/.5. Index available (published in each issue). **Bk Rev. Ad Acc. Circ:** 10,000 (ctrl). ***Continues*** *Photographic Journal. Section A, Pictorial & General Photography.*
**Desc:** Published continuously for 133 years covering all aspects of photography plus details of the activities of the Royal Photographic Society.
**Ind/Abst** Abstr. Graphic Arts Tech. Found. (1979); Art Index; ARTbibliogr. Mod.; Curr. Technol. Index; Graph. Arts Bull. Inst. Pap. Sci. Technol. (Jan. 1989); Print. Abstr.; World Surf. Coat. Abstr.

US/0031-8744
**PHOTOGRAPHIC PROCESSING.** [Photogr. process.]. (1964)-. Periodical. English. Twelve times a year. $40.00 US; $65.00 other. PTN Publishing Company, 445 Broad Hollow Road, Melville NY 11747. **Tel** (516)845-2700, FAX (516)845-7109. **LC** WMLC L 83/3986.

UK/0302-4210
**PHOTOGRAPHIC TECHNIQUES IN SCIENTIFIC RESEARCH.** [Photogr. tech. sci. res.]. Vol. 1 (1973)-. Monographic series. English. ir. Price varies per volume. Academic Press, Inc., 6277 Sea Harbor Drive, Orlando FL 32887. **Tel** (800)543-9534, (407)345-4100, FAX (407)363-9661. **ED** A. A. Newman. **LC** TR692; .P52. **DD** 778.3/08. **NLM** W1 PH67. **CODEN** PTSRD2. Documents available from CASDDS.
**Ind/Abst** Chem. Abstr.; GeoRef.

US/0092-4709
**PHOTOGRAPHIC TECHNOLOGY USSR.** [Photogr. technol. U.S.S.R.]. **VAT** Photographic Technology Union of Soviet Socialist Republics. V. 1-1973-. Periodical. English. bm. $50.00. Foreign Resources Associates, PO Box 2353, Fort Collins CO 80052. **LC** TR692; .P53. **DD** 770/.1/5.

US
**PHOTOGRAPHIC TRADE NEWS MASTER BUYING GUIDE.** (MASTER BUYING GUIDE.). **Main/Corp** Photographic Trade News. **VFOAT** New Product Review. (1977)-. Consumer Publication. English. an. $25.00. PTN Publishing Company, 445 Broad Hollow Road, Melville NY 11747. **Tel** (516)845-2700, FAX (516)845-7109.

US
**PHOTOGRAPHICA. Added/Corp** American Photographic Historical Society. Vol. 17, No. 1 (June 1988)-. Periodical. English. Four times a year (Jan., Apr., July, Oct.). $25.00. American Photographic Historical Society Inc., 1150 Avenue of the Americas, New York NY 10036. **Tel** (212)575-0483. **ED** George Gilbert. Index available. cum. index. **Bk Rev. Ad Acc. Circ:** 500 (ctrl). available on microfilm from University Microfilms International (UMI). ***Continues in part*** *Photographica Journal.*
**Desc:** News and features of interest to print and cameras collection.

SZ
**PHOTOGRAPHIE.** Vol. 1 (Jan. 1977)-. Periodical. German. Twelve times a year. 93.00F Switzerland; 108.50F Mediterranean Countries and Europe except Switzerland and Germany; $120.00 other. Novapress AG, Zaehringerstrasse 26, CH 8001 Zurich Switzerland. **Tel** 011 41 1 2526970, telex 896040. **LC** TR1; .P642. Index available. **Bk Rev. Ad Acc.** ctrl circ.

FR/0988-7679
**PHOTOGRAPHIES MAGAZINE.** (19??)-. Periodical. French. Ten times a year. 205.00F France; 300.00F others. Photographies Magazine Edition, 51 rue de l'Amiral Mouchez, 75013 Paris France. **Tel** 011 33 1 45654600. **(Subscription address:** Photographies Magazine, Service Abonnements, 99 rue d'Amsterdam, 75008 Paris France.**) ED** Jacques Aschen. **Bk Rev**, (Qty: 9/yr). **Ad Acc, Adv Mgr:** P. Hevllant. **Circ:** 76,000 (ctrl).

US/0740-4158
**PHOTOGRAPHS (NEW YORK, N.Y. : 1982).** (PHOTOGRAPHS.). [Photographs]. Vol. 1, No. 1 (Nov. 18, 1981)-. Periodical. English. ir. $65.00 for 12 issues. Photographs, 450 Broome Street/#4E, New York NY 10013. **Tel** (212)925-7597. **ED** Allen G Arpadi and Matthew F Witchell. **DD** 770. **Bk Rev. Circ:** 1,000 (ctrl).
**Desc:** Provides informative articles for collectors of photography.

US/0079-1849
**PHOTOGRAPHY ANNUAL.** ***Ceased.*** (1951)-?. English. an. Ziff-Davis, One Park Avenue, 5th Floor, New York NY 10016. **Tel** (212)503-3500, (609)786-8230. **LC** TR1; .P8813. **DD** 770.58.

US/1040-0346
**PHOTOGRAPHY IN NEW YORK.** [Photogr. N. Y.]. Vol. 1, No. 1 (Nov./Dec. 1988)-. Periodical. English. Six times a year. $18.00 US; $25.00 Canada; $30.00 other. Photography in New York, 64 West 89th Street, Suit 3-F, New York NY 10024. **Tel** (212)787-0401, FAX (212)799-3054. **ED** Bill Mindlin. **DD** 770. **Bk Rev. Ad Acc. Circ:** 8,000 (ctrl).
**Desc:** Guide to photography exhibitions, prints, dealers, bookstores and classes.

US/0193-2810
**PHOTOGRAPHY INDEX.** [Photogr. index]. Vol. 1 (1977)-. English. an. $16.95 (add $2.00 for postage) US, (add $3.00 for postage) other. Photographic Research Publications, PO Box 333 Seven Oaks Station, Detroit MI 48235. **Tel** (313)569-2268, FAX (313)569-2298. **ED** Damon B Flowers. **LC** Z7134; .P47. **DD** 016.77. Index available. cum. index.
**Desc:** Subject index to domestic and international photography periodicals.

UK/0950-2009
**PHOTOGRAPHY (LONDON, ENGLAND : 1986).** ***Suspended.*** (PHOTOGRAPHY.). [Photography]. No. 1 (Oct. 1986)-Suspended April 1992. Periodical. English. mo. Artus Specialist Publications Ltd, 10-13 Times House, Hemel Hempstead HP1 1BB England. **Tel** 0442-41221. **DD** 770. ***Continues*** *35MM Photography (London, England : 1983), 0265-7198.*

US/0095-439X
**PHOTOGRAPHY MARKET PLACE.** ***Suspended.*** (1975/76)-Suspended with (1977/78) Edition. English. R R Bowker, A Reed Reference Publishing Company, Part of Reed International PLC, PO

Box 31, 121 Chanlon Drive, New Providence NJ 07974. **Tel** (908)464-6800, (800)521-8110, FAX (908)665-6688, telex 138-755. **LC** TR12; .P52. **DD** 380.1/45/7702573.

UK
**PHOTOGRAPHY YEAR BOOK. VFOAT** Photography Yearbook; Internationales Jahrbuch der Fotografie. (1935)-. English. an. Fountain Press, Queensborough House, 2 Clermont Road, Surbotin, Surrey KT6, 4QU England. **LC** TR1; .P88213. **DD** 770.58. ***Continues*** *Photography Today.*

BE
**PHOTOHISTORICA.** Periodical. English. sa. £20.00 (individual members), £30.00 (collective members). European Society for the History of Photography, 74 94 Cherry Orchard Road Acorn, Croydon Cro 6BA England. **Tel** 011 44 81 6818339. **ED** K Van Deuren. cum. index. **Circ:** 350.

US
**PHOTO*LETTER. Added/Corp** Texas Photographic Society. **VFOAT** Photoletter. Vol. 4, No. 3 (Fall 1983)-. Periodical. English. qt. ***Continues*** *Austin Photographic Cooperative Newsletter, 0735-5580.*

US/0190-1400
**PHOTOLETTER, THE.** (19??)-. Periodical. English. Twelve times a year. $90.00. The Photoletter, Pine Lake Farm, Osceola WI 54020. **Tel** (715)248-3800, telex 6501892053. **ED** Lori Johnson. **[CCC].** Index available. **Bk Rev.** available on microfilm.

CN/0226-7411
**PHOTOMAG (VILLE LEMOYNE).** (PHOTOMAG.). [Photomag]. V. 1- Jan. 1980-. Periodical. French. mo. $2.00 per no. Editions du Gemeau, Photomag, 88 rue St-Louis, Ville Lemoyne Quebec J4R 2L4 Canada. **DD** 770/.5.

US/1049-8974
**PHOTOPRO (TITUSVILLE, FLA.).** (PHOTOPRO.). [PhotoPro]. **VFOAT** Photo Pro; Photograph Professional. Vol. 1, No. 1 (Spring 1990)-. Periodical. English. Six times a year. $16.95. Patch Publishing, 5211 South Washington Avenue, Titusville FL 32780. **Tel** (407)268-5010, FAX (407)267-7216. **DD** 770.
**Desc:** Concentrates on practical solutions to photographic problems.

UK/0958-2606
**PHOTORESEARCHER / EUROPEAN SOCIETY FOR THE HISTORY OF PHOTOGRAPHY. Added/Corp** European Society for the History of Photography. **VFOAT** Photo Researcher. No. 1 (Oct. 1990)-. Periodical. English. Twice a year. £35.00 (individuals), £40.00 (institutions) Europe; £45.00 (individuals), £50.00 (institutions) others Comes with European Society for the History of Photography membership. European Society for the History of Photography, 74 94 Cherry Orchard Road Acorn, Croydon Cro 6BA England. **Tel** 011 44 81 6818339.
**Ind/Abst** BHA : Biblio. Hist. Art.

BE
**PHOTOSCOOP / PICTORIAL MAGAZINE.** (19??)-. French. qt. Free. Paul Nemerlin, Vautierstraat 48, 1050 Brussels Belgium. **Tel** (02)648 8070, FAX (02)646 6243. **ED** Raymond Naumann. **Ad Acc.** Full Page (B&W) 2372F. Half Page (B&W) 1200F. **Circ:** 13,000. ***Continues*** *Pictorial New Vautier Magazine.*

CN/0834-227X
**PHOTOVIDEO.** ***Title Change.*** [Photovideo]. Vol. 3, No. 8 Oct. (1986)-. Periodical. English. Maclean Hunter Canada / Montreal, 1001 bvd. de Maisonneuve W., Montreal, Quebec H3A 3E1 Canada. **Tel** 514-845-5141, FAX 514-845-4302, telex 055-60604. **DD** 381/.45621388332. available on microfilm and microfiche from University Microfilms International (UMI). ***Merged with*** *Photovideo Retailer, 0828-9611* ***to form*** *Photovideo Professional, 0828-962X.*

SP/0211-7029
**PHOTOVISION. VFOAT** Photo Vision. No. 1 (July/Aug. 1981)-. Periodical. Spanish. qt (Mar., June, Sept., Dec.). $46.00 (Americas); $40.00 (Europe except Spain); $55.00 (others). Arte y Proyectos, PO Box 164, 41710 Utrera Seville Spain. **Tel** 34 95 4862895. Index available (extra $12.00).

UK/0956-2281
**PIC : PEOPLE IN CAMERA.** [PIC, People camera]. **VFOAT** People in Camera. (1989)-. Periodical. English. Twelve times a year. £30.00 UK; £36.00 others. PIC Subscriptions Dept, Lingley House, Commissioners Road, Rochester Kent ME2 4EU England. **Tel** 011 44 634 291115.

BE
**PICTORIAL NEW VAUTIER MAGAZINE.** ***Title Change.*** (19??)-(19??). French (Dutch). qt. Paul Nemerlin, Vautierstraat 48, 1050 Brussels Belgium. **Tel** (02)648 8070, FAX (02)646 6243. **ED** Paul Nemerlin. **Ad Acc. Circ:** 11,000. ***Continues*** *Vautier.* ***Continued by*** *Photoscoop / Pictorial Magazine.*
**Desc:** Information about photography and video.

US/1045-0629
**PICTURE PERFECT.** English (Spanish). bm. $30.00 US; $54.00 other. Aquino Productions, Box 15760, Stamford CT 06901. **Tel** (203)967-2512, FAX (203)323-8362. **ED** Andres Aquino. Index available. cum. index. **Bk Rev. Ad Acc. Circ:** 170,000 (ctrl). available on microfilm; available on microfiche; available on videocassette.
**Desc:** Edited for professionals in the photography field. It also covers fashion, travel, beauty and entertainment.

US/0732-1511
**PICTURE (SANTA FE SPRINGS, CALIF.).** (PICTURE.). [Picture]. Issue 18 (Sept. 1981)-. Periodical. English. qt. $45.00 US; $52.50 other. Picture Magazine, 348 North Norton Avenue, Los Angeles CA 90004. **LC** TR640; .P54. **DD** 770/.5. ***Continues*** *Picture Magazine (Los Angeles, Calif.), 0279-0432.*

CN/0382-9286
**PIN UPS.** V. 6, No. 5- May/June 1975-. Periodical. English. bm. $5.00. Galaxy Press, 489 Krug Street, Kitchener Ontario, N2B 1L2 Canada. **DD** 779/.24/05. ***Continues*** *Quest, 0382-926X.*

US/0885-1476
**PINHOLE JOURNAL. Added/Corp** Pinhole Resource (Organization). Vol. 1, No. 1, (Dec. 1985)-. Periodical. English. Three times a year. $32.50 US; $37.50 other. Pinhole Journal, Star Route 15, PO Box 1655, San Lorenzo NM 88057. **Tel** (505)536-9942. **ED** Eric Renner and Nancy Spencer. **DD** 770. **Bk Rev. Ad Acc. Circ:** 500.
**Desc:** Definitive periodical on the art and science of pinhole photography and optics.

●US/1061-2505
**PIQUE (NEW YORK, N.Y.).** (PIQUE.). [Pique]. No. 1 (1992)-. Periodical. English. bm. $9.95 (single issue). Black Book Marketing Group, 866 3rd Avenue, 29th Floor, New York NY 10022. **Tel** (212)702-9700, FAX (212)605-4808. **DD** 770.

CN/0227-115X
**PLEIN CADRE.** [Plein cadre]. **Added/Corp** Association Pour le Jeune Cinema Quebecois. (1979)-. Periodical. French. mo. $7.74. Plein Cadre, 1415 Rue Jarry Est, Montreal Quebec H2Z 2Z7 Canada. **Tel** (514)374-4700. **DD** 778.5/349/060714. ***Supersedes*** *Debobinons, 0319-5899.*

KO
**PODO SAJIN YONGAM / NEWS PHOTOGRAPHY ANNUAL. Added/Corp** Hanguk Sajin Kijadan. **VFOAT** News Photography Annual. (19??)-. Korean (Korean). an. W10,000. Hanguk Sajin Kijadan Sinmun Goegwan, 213-Hosil 31 Taepyongno, 1-ka Chung-ku, Seoul Korea. **LC** DS922; .P63.

US/0032-4582
**POPULAR PHOTOGRAPHY (1955).** (POPULAR PHOTOGRAPHY.). [Pop. photogr.]. Vol. 1 (May 1937)-. Periodical. English. mo. $20.00. Hachette Magazines Inc., 1633 Broadway, New York NY 10019. **Tel** (212)767-6000. **(Subscription address:** Neodata / Colorado, PO Box 2606, Boulder Boulder CO 80322.**) ED** Sean Callahan and Steve Pollock. **LC** TR1; .P8845. **DD** 770/.5. **Ad Acc.** available on microfilm and microfiche from University Microfilms International (UMI); available on an online database (file 647/Full-Text) from DIALOG. Documents available from UMI Article Clearinghouse, Magazine Collection. ***Absorbed*** *Prize Photography; Photo Arts, 0026-8240; Camera Magazine and American Photography.*
**Desc:** Provides extensive analysis of new cameras and equipment, articles on techniques, and more.
**Ind/Abst** Acad. Abstr. Full Text Elite (Jan. 1984-) [Full Txt.]; Acad. Abstr. (Jan. 1984-); Acad. Ind. [Computer File] (1984-); Acad. Search (Jan. 1984-); ARTbibliogr. Mod.; Book Rev. Index; Expand. Acad. Index (1984-); Film Lit. Index; Gen. Period. Index (1985-); Index Inf.; INFO-SOUTH Abstr.; Mag. Artic. Summar. Elite (Jan. 1984-) [Full Txt.]; Mag. Artic. Summar. Select (Jan. 1984-); Mag. Artic. Summar. CD-ROM (Jan. 1984-); Mag. Index Plus (1989-); Mag. Index Sel. Microfiche (1986-) [Full Txt.]; Mag. Index. Sel. (1989-); Mag. Search; Newsp. Period. Abstr. (1988-); Read. Guide Abstr. Select Ed.; Read. Guide Period. Lit.; Resource/One Ondisc (1988-); Mag. Index; TOM Gen. Index (1985-) [Full Txt.]; Vocat. Search (Jan. 1984-) [Full Txt.].

US/0075-0301
**POPULAR PHOTOGRAPHY'S INVITATION TO PHOTOGRAPHY.** ***Ceased.*** [Pop. photogr. invit. photogr.]. **VFOAT** Invitation to Photography. (1966)-(19??). English. Ziff-Davis, One Park Avenue, 5th Floor, New York NY 10016. **Tel** (212)503-3500, (609)786-8230. **LC** TR1; .P8858. **DD** 770/.28.

UK/0747-8798
**POPULAR PHOTOGRAPHY'S SLR PHOTOGRAPHY.** ***Title Change.*** **VFOAT** S.L.R. Photography; SLR Photography. (19??)-(19??). Periodical. English. an. Tower Publishing, Tower House, Sovereign Park, Market Harborough, Leicester LE16 9EF England. **Tel** 011 44 858 468888. **LC** TR1; .P8859. **DD** 770/.28/22. ***Continues*** *SLR Camera.* ***Continued by*** *Photo Answers.*

IT
**PORTFOLIO ILLUSTRATORI E FOTOGRAFI.** ***Suspended.*** (19??)-(Dec. 1992). Maclean Hunter SRL / Italy, P LE A Cantore 12, 20123 Milan Italy. **Tel** 02 89401365, FAX 02 8378590. ***Continues*** *Portfolio Illustratori.*

UK/0960-3913
**PORTFOLIO MAGAZINE EDINBURGH.** (PORTFOLIO MAGAZINE.). [Portf. mag. Edinb.]. (1988)-. Periodical. English. qt. £18.00 (institutions), £12.00 (individuals) UK; £22.00 (institutions), £16.00 (individuals) other. Photography Workshop Edinburgh Ltd., 43 Candlemaker Row, Edinburgh EH11 2QB Scotland. **Tel** 011 44 31 2201911. **DD** 770.9411.

US/1053-3869
**PORTFOLIO (ZEPHYRHILLS, FLA.).** (PORTFOLIO : A PUBLICATION FOR THE VISUAL ARTIST.). **Added/Corp** Institute for Photographic Excellence. Vol. 1, Issue 1 (Jan. 1991)-. Periodical. English. mo. $59.00 (includes membership). Institute for Photographic Excellence, PO Box 1506, Zephyrhills FL 33539. **DD** 770.

US/1062-9661
**PORTRAITS (NEW YORK, N.Y.).** (PORTRAITS.). [Portraits]. Jan. (1991). Periodical. English. mo. $46.50. Holland & Edwards Publishing, 155 Spring Street, 4th Floor, New York NY 10012. **DD** 757.

UK
**PRACTICAL PHOTOGRAPHY.** English. mo. EMAP National Publications Ltd, Farndon Road, Market Harborough, Leicestershire, LE16 9NR England. **Tel** 011 44 733 555161.

US/8755-3902
**PRC NEWSLETTER.** [PRC newsl.]. **Added/Corp** Photographic Resource Center (Boston, Mass.). **VFOAT** P.R.C. Newsletter. **VAT** Photographic Resource Center Newsletter. Vol. 7, No. 1 (Jan. 1983)-. Periodical. English. Ten times a year. $45.00 Comes with Photographic Resource Center membership. Photographic Resource Center, 602 Commonwealth Avenue, Boston MA 02215. **Tel** (617)353-0700, FAX (617)353-1662. **ED** Darsie Alexander. **LC** TR1; .P467. **DD** 770. Index available. **Bk Rev. Ad Acc. Circ:** 3,500 (ctrl). ***Continues*** *Newsletter (Photographic Resource Center (Boston, Mass.)).*
**Desc:** Lists photographic exhibitions, lectures, workshops, contests and other events in the New England area.

US
**PRICE GUIDE TO ANTIQUE AND CLASSIC CAMERAS. VFOAT** Price Guide to Antique & Classic Cameras; Price Guide to Cameras. (1985)-. English. be. $59.95 or $69.95 (hardbound). Centennial Photo Service, 11595 State Road 70, Grantsburg WI 54840. **Tel** (715)689-2153. **ED** J.M. McKeown and J.C. McKeown. **LC** TR6.5; .P74. ***Continues*** *Price Guide to Antique and Classic Still Cameras.*

US/0748-9099
**PRO REVIEW, THE.** [Pro rev.]. **VFOAT** Proreview. Vol. 1, No. 1 (June 1985)-. Periodical. English. mo. Free (first 6 issues, professional). Dynamic Publications Inc, 901 Bonifant Road, Silver Spring MD 20904. **DD** 770.

US/1018-9181
**PROCEEDINGS OF THE INTERNATIONAL CONGRESS ON HIGH SPEED PHOTOGRAPHY AND PHOTONICS. Main/Conf** International Congress on High Speed Photography and Photonics. 13th- (1978)-. Proceedings. English. be. Society for Photo-Optical Instrumentation Engineers, PO Box 10, Bellingham WA 98227. **Tel** (206)676-3290. ***Continues*** *International Congress on High Speed Photography. Proceedings.*

UK/0019-784X
**PROFESSIONAL PHOTOGRAPHER.** Vol. 20, No. 3 (Mar. 1980)-. Periodical. English. mo. £26.00 UK; £38.00 other. EMAP Readerlink, Audit House, 260 Field End Road, Ruislip Middlesex HA4 9LT England. **Tel** 011 44 081 868 4499, FAX 011 44 081 429 3117. **ED** David Warr. **LC** TR690.A1; I5. **DD** 770/.5. **[CCC]. Ad Acc.** available on microfilm and microfiche from University Microfilms International (UMI). ***Continues*** *Industrial and Commercial Photographer.*
**Desc:** A magazine for UK professional photography market.
**Ind/Abst** Graph. Arts Bull. Inst. Pap. Sci. Technol. (March 1989); Index Inf.

US/0033-0167
**PROFESSIONAL PHOTOGRAPHER (1964), THE.** (THE PROFESSIONAL PHOTOGRAPHER.). **Added/Corp** Professional Photographers of America. (Jan. 1964)-. Periodical. English. mo. $24.50 (one year), $42.00 (two year), $63.00 (three year) US; $40.00 (one year), $70.00 (two year), $105.00 (three year) Canada. Professional

Photographers of America, 1090 Executive Way, Des Plaines IL 60018. **Tel** (708)299-8161, FAX (708)299-2685. **ED** Alfred DeBat. **LC** TR690; .N3. **DD** 770. Index available. cum. index. **Bk Rev**, (Qty: 12 per year). **Ad Acc, Adv Mgr:** Donna McMahon, **Tel** (708)299-8161. **Circ:** 30,000 (ctrl). available on microfilm and microfiche from University Microfilms International (UMI). ***Continues*** *National Professional Photographer, 0734-7529.*

AT
**PROFESSIONAL PHOTOGRAPHY.** English. mo. 78.00Aus$ Australia; 77.00Aus$ (surface mail) 100.00Aus$ (air mail) other. Horwitz Grahame Pty Ltd, 506 Miller Street, Cammeray New South Wales, 2062 Australia. **Tel** 011 61 2 9296144, FAX 011 61 2 9571814.

SA/0033-0329
**PROFOTO.** [Profoto]. (1964)-. Periodical. English. mo. $54.00. Professional Photographers South Africa, PO Box 47044, Parklands 2121 South Africa. **Tel** 011 27 11 7833107, FAX 011 27 11 8801648. **DD** 770.

SP
**PROGRESSO FOTOGRAFICO, EL.** (1920)-. Periodical. Spanish. Ten times a year. L72000 Italy; L90000 other. Progresso Fotografico & Csas, Viale Piceno 14, 20129 Milan Italy. **Tel** 011 39 2 7490866, 011 39 2 715939. **LC** TR1; .P96.

US/0030-8277
**PSA JOURNAL.** [P.S.A. j.]. **Added/Corp** Photographic Society of America. (1947)-. Periodical. English. mo. Free to members of the Photographic Society of America. Photographic Society of America, 3000 United Founders Boulevard, Suite 103, Oklahoma City OK 73112. **Tel** (405)843-1437, FAX (405)843-1438. **ED** Dennis Ramsey. **DD** 770. Index available. **Bk Rev**, (Qty: varies). **Ad Acc, Adv Mgr:** T Dresser, **Tel** (405)843-1437. **Circ:** 10,000 (ctrl). available on microfilm and microfiche from University Microfilms International (UMI); available on an online database (files 647,648/Full-Text) from DIALOG. Documents available from UMI Article Clearinghouse. ***Continues*** *Photographic Society of America. Journal of the Photographic Society of America, 0096-5812.*
**Ind/Abst** Acad. Search (July 1993-); Bus. ASAP (1990-) [Full Txt.]; Bus. Index (1985-); Gen. BusinessFile (1985-); Gen. Period. Index (1985-); INFO-SOUTH Abstr.; Int. Aerosp. Abstr.; Mag. ASAP Plus [Full Txt.]; Mag. Index Plus (1989-); Mag. Search; Newsp. Period. Abstr. (1988-); Mag. Index (1977-); Trade Ind. ASAP [Full Txt.]; Trade Ind. Index [Full Txt.].

US/1053-8968
**PTN (MELVILLE, N.Y.).** (PTN : THE MARKETING MAGAZINE FOR PHOTO VIDEO AND PHOTOFINISHING RETAILERS.). [PTN]. **VAT** Photographic Trade News. Vol. 53, No. 7 (Apr. 3, 1989)-. Periodical. English. Twelve times a year. $25.00 US and Canada; $50.00 other. PTN Publishing Company, 445 Broad Hollow Road, Melville NY 11747. **Tel** (516)845-2700, FAX (516)845-7109. **DD** 381. ***Continues*** *Photographic Video Trade News, 1054-0601.*

US/0194-9055
**QUICK FOOT.** Periodical. English. mo. $2.20. Kidsport Photo, 2761 North Haven/Suite 4141, Dallas TX 75229.

US/0033-9202
**RANGEFINDER (SANTA MONICA), THE.** (THE RANGEFINDER.). Vol. 1 (June 1952)-. Periodical. English. Twelve times a year. $18.00 (one year), $24.00 (two year), $28.00 (three year). Rangefinder Publishing Company Inc, PO Box 1703, Santa Monica CA 90406. **Tel** (213)451-8506, FAX (213)395-9058. **ED** Arthur Stern. **Ad Acc, Adv Mgr:** Jerry Goldstein, **Tel** (310)451-8506. **Circ:** 50,000 (ctrl). ***Absorbed*** *School Photographers Digest.*
**Desc:** Dedicated to the advancement of the field of professional photography. Editorial material covers improving products and services and increasing sales potential.
**Ind/Abst** Index Inf.

FR
**RECHERCHE PHOTOGRAPHIQUE, LA.** **Added/Corp** Paris Audiovisuel (Firm) Presses Universitaires de Vincennes. **VFOAT** Recherche, Histoireesthetique, Photographique; Recherche Photographique, Histoireesthetique. No. 1 (Oct. 1986)-. Periodical. French. sa. 190.00F France; 350.00F North Africa & Europe; 390.00F other. Paris Audiovisuel, 35 rue de la Boetie, 75008 Paris France. **Tel** 011 33 1 43593361.

IT/0393-473X
**REFLEX ROMA.** (REFLEX.). [Reflex Roma]. (1980)-. Periodical. Italian. mo. L55000.00 Italy; L120000.00 other. Editrice Reflex, Via Villa Severini 54, 00191 Rome Italy. **Tel** 011 39 6 3276756. **UDC** 77.

JA
**RENZU. / LENS.** **VFOAT** Lens. (19??)-. Periodical. Japanese. Yomiuri Shimbun Publication Department, 1-7-1 Otemachi Chiyoda-ku, Tokyo 100-55 Japan. **Tel** 03 242 1111, telex 22228. **LC** TR820; .R39.

UK/1350-4010
**REPORTAGE; THE INTERNATIONAL MAGAZINE OF PHOTOJOURNALISM.** **See** Journalism.

FR
**REPRODUIRE.** French. Ten times a year. 650.00F France; 980.00F other. Reproduire, 40 rue St Anne, 75002 Paris France. **Tel** 011 33 1 40150261, FAX 011 33 1 42963708.

GW
**REPROGRAF, DER.** **Added/Corp** Fachverband Reprografie. (19??)-. Periodical. German. Five times a year. DM100.00. Fachverband Reporgrafie e v, An den Drei Steinen 23, 6000 Frankfurt 50 Germany. **Tel** (069)541073, FAX (069)541016. **LC** TR920; .R45. **DD** 686.4/05. **Bk Rev**, (Qty: 10). **Ad Acc. Circ:** 1,500. ***Continues*** *Reprograf und Lichtpauser.*

US/0891-5326
**RE:VIEW - FRIENDS OF PHOTOGRAPHY.** (RE:VIEW : NEWSLETTER OF THE FRIENDS OF PHOTOGRAPHY.). [Re:v. - Friends Photogr.]. **Added/Corp** Friends of Photography. **VFOAT** Re:View. Vol. 10 No. 1 (Jan. 1987)-. Newsletter. English. bm. Free to members. Friends of Photography, 250 4th Street, San Francisco CA 94103. **Tel** (415)495-7000. **ED** David Featherstone. **DD** 770. **Bk Rev. Circ:** 14,200 (ctrl). ***Continues*** *Friends of Photography. Newsletter of the Friends of Photography, 0163-9552.*
**Desc:** Contains in-depth reviews of photography books and a book rating section. Also includes essays, interviews and news relating to photography.

SP
**REVISTA DE LA IMAGEN Y EL SONIDO: EIKONOS.** **VFOAT** Eikonos. (19??)-. Spanish. Eleven times a year. $16.00. Editoral ECO SA, Calle de la Cruz 44, Barcelona 17 Spain. **LC** TR1; .R474. **Bk Rev. Ad Acc. Circ:** 12,000 (ctrl). available with illustrations.

SP
**REVISTA FOTO SL.** (19??)-. Spanish. mo. 6000ptas Spain; 13000ptas other Europe; 17500ptas other. Revista Foto, Calle Real 22, 28230 Las Rozas Spain. **Tel** 011 34 1 637-7948. ***Continues*** *Foto Profesional, 0211-9552.*

IT
**RIVISTA DI STORIA E CRITICA DELLA FOTOGRAFIA.** Yearly V. 1, No. 1, (Oct. 1980)-. Italian (summaries and/or abstracts in English). Three times a year. $24.00. **LC** TR1; .R56. **DD** 770/.9.
**Ind/Abst** ARTbibliogr. Mod.

US
**ROGER EBERT'S MOVIE HOME COMPANION / BY ROGER EBERT.** ***Title Change.*** **See** Motion Picture.

US/0883-735X
**ROTKIN REVIEW, THE.** ***Suspended.*** [Rotkin rev.]. Vol. 1, Issue 1 (Summer 1985)-(19??). Periodical. English. qt. Free to acquisition libraries, $25.00 other. Photography for Industry Books, 1697 Broadway, New York NY 10019. **Tel** (212)757-9255. **ED** Charles E Rotkin. **DD** 770. **Bk Rev. Ad Acc. Circ:** 8,500 (ctrl).
**Desc:** Reviews fine photographic, art, and communications books. The reviews are written by working professionals in their fields and books are directed and marketed at discounts.

KO
**SADAN.** Periodical. Korean. mo. Taehan Chigop Sajinga, Hyophoe 121 Myo-dong Chongno-ku, Seoul Korea. **LC** TR1; .S23.

IO
**SALONFOTO INDONESIA.** Indonesian. **LC** TR646.I52; B37.

JA
**SANGAKU SHASHIN NENKAN.** (1974)-. Periodical. Japanese. Yama-Kei Publishers Co. Ltd., 1-1-33 Shibadaimon, Minatoku Tokyo 105 Japan. **Tel** 03 4364021, FAX 03 4334057. **LC** TR787; .S23.

GW
**SCHRIFTENREIHE DER DEUTSCHEN GESELLSCHAFT FUER PHOTOGRAPHIE.** **Added/Corp** Deutsche Gesellschaft fur Photographie. (1980)-. Monographic series. German. Price varies per volume. K.G. Saur Verlag KG, A Reed Reference Publishing Company, Part of Reed International PLC, Ortlerstrasse 8, D 81373 Munich Germany. **Tel** 011 49 89 769020, FAX 011 49 89 76902150, telex 5212067-SAUR-D.

GW
**SCHRIFTENREIHE - INSTITUT FUER PHOTOGRAMMETRIE DER UNIVERSITAT STUTTGART.** **Main/Corp** Stuttgart. Universitat. Institut fur Photogrammetrie. No. 1-. Periodical. German. DM50.00. Direktor Institut fur Photogrammetrie, Universitat Stuttgart, Keplerstrasse 11, Postfach 560, W-7000 Stuttgart 1 Germany.
**Ind/Abst** GeoRef.

US/1063-4088
**SCIENTIFIC & APPLIED PHOTOGRAPHY.** [Sci. appl. photogr.]. **VFOAT** Scientific and Applied Photography. (19??)-. Periodical. English (translations available in Russian). bm. Gordon & Breach Science Publishers, Inc., PO Box 786, Cooper Station, New York NY 10276. **Tel** (212)206-8900, FAX (212)645-2459. **(Subscription address:** International Publishers Distributor at one of the following addresses: 820 Town Center Drive, Langhorne, PA 19047; or PO Box 90, Reading Berkshire RG1 8JL UK; or Kent Ridge PO Box 1180, Singapore 9111, Republic of Singapore**)** **LC** TR1; .Z5135. **DD** 770/.5. ***Continues*** *Zhurnal Nauchnoi i Prikladnoi Fotografii i Kinematografii. English. Scientific & Applied Photography & Cinematography, 0734-1504.*

US/0424-2017
**SCIENTIFIC PUBLICATIONS FROM EASTMAN KODAK LABORATORIES.** **Main/Corp** Eastman Kodak Company. Research Laboratories. 1965/66-. English. an. Eastman Kodak Company, 343 State Street, Department 412 L, Rochester NY 14650. **Tel** (716)724-4000, (800)242-2424. **LC** TR7; .E32. ***Supersedes*** *Abridged Scientific Publication from the Kodak Research Laboratories, 0097-5761.*

UK/0269-1787
**SCOTTISH PHOTOGRAPHY BULLETIN.** Bulletin. English. sa. £27.00 UK; £32.00 other. Scottish Society for the History of Photography, 1 Queen Street, c/o Scottish National Portrait Gallery, Edinburgh EH2 1JD England. **ED** Sara Stevenson and Alison Morrison-Low. **Bk Rev. Ad Acc. Circ:** 200 (ctrl).
**Desc:** The house journal of the Scottish Society for the History of Photography, and principal forum for critical discussion of photographic history in Scotland.

GW
**SELECT : THE PHOTOGRAPHIC SHOWCASE.** English. Three times a year. $80.00 (two year). Moser & Colby GMBH, Duisburger Str 44, 40477 Dusseldorf Germany. **Tel** 011 49 211 4982068. **(Subscription address:** The Manipulator, 241 West 13th Street, Studio B, New York, NY 10011**)** **ED** Wilhem Moser, David Colby and Johno Du Plessis. Index available. cum. index. **Bk Rev. Circ:** 26,000.
**Desc:** A city profile through photography.

JA/0371-0106
**SHASHIN KOGYO.** [Shashin Kogyo]. **VFOAT** Photographic Industries. (1952)-. Japanese. mo. Shashin Kogyo Shuppansha, (Shashin Kogyo Publishing Co., Ltd.), 1-65, Kanda Jinbocho, Chiyodaku, Tokyo 101, Japan. **CODEN** SHKOAZSHKOAZ. Documents available from CASDDS.
**Ind/Abst** Chem. Abstr.

HK
**SHE YING CHIA TSO HSIN SHANG.** **VFOAT** Photos Annual. V. 2-; 1975-. Chinese. $16.00. She Ying Hua Pao She, Lee Yuen Subscription Agencies, 1 On Ning Lane, Sai Ying Pun, Hsiang-Kang Hong Kong. **LC** TR1; .S42. ***Continues*** *She Ying Chia Tso Chi.*

HK
**SHE YING SHIH CHIEH.** **VFOAT** Photography Publishers. V. 1- July; 1972? Year 11 Month-. Periodical. Chinese. $20.00. 802 Shih Hung Chi Ta Hsia Yu-to-li, Huang Hou Chien, Hong Kong Hong Kong. **LC** TR1; .S43.

CC
**SHE YING TSUNG KAN.** **VFOAT** Sheyingcongkan. 1-. Periodical. Chinese. RMBY0.78. Hsin Hua Shu Tien / Shang-Hai Fa Hsing So, Shanghai, People's Republic of China. **LC** TR1; .S445.

●US/1058-2789
**SHOOTER'S RAG.** [Shoot. rag]. Vol. 1, No. 1 (Winter 1992)-. Periodical. English. Four times a year. $12.00 North America; $16.00 other. Havelin Communications, PO Box 8509, Asheville NC 28814. **Tel** (704)254-6700. **DD** 771.

US/1048-793X
**SHOTS (DANVILLE, KY.).** (SHOTS.). [Shots]. **VFOAT** Shots Magazine. (198?)-. English. bm (6 issues). $15.00 (1 year), $25.00 (2 year) US; $50.00 other. Shots, Box 109, Joseph OR 97846. **ED** Daniel Price. **LC** TR640; .S5. **DD** 779. **Ad Acc. Circ:** 1700.
**Desc:** A journal about the fine art of photography.

US/0895-321X
**SHUTTERBUG.** [Shutterbug]. **VFOAT** Shutter Bug. (19??)-. Periodical. English. mo. $19.95. Patch Publishing, 5211 South Washington Avenue, Titusville FL 32780. **Tel** (407)268-5010, FAX (407)267-7216. **ED** Christi Ashby. **LC** TR197; .S58. **DD** 771. Index available. cum. index. **Bk Rev. Ad Acc.** Full Page (B&W) $1895.00. **Circ:** 120,000. ***Continues*** *Shutterbug Ads Photographic News.*

**Desc:** Information and buying source for serious photographers today. Each jumbo issue is filled with useful articles on photo equipment and techniques.

FR/1148-4322
**SON, MUSIQUE, VIDEO MAG. VFOAT** Son Mag; Son, Musique, Video. (19??)-. Periodical. French. mo. Editions Frequences, 1 Boulevard Ney, 75018 Paris France. **Tel** 011 33 1 40360197, FAX 011 33 1 40361196. **LC** TK6655.V5; S67. **DD** 621.389/3. ***Continues*** *Son, Video Magazine, 0765-3530.*

SP
**SPAFOTO.** Began with Vol. for 1972. Spanish. 1650. Cotec, Rocafort 39-41 Edificio Avenida, 15 Barcelona Spain. **LC** TR690.4; .S66.

US
**SPECIALTY LAB UPDATE.** Newsletter. English. mo (12 issues per year). Photo Marketing Association International, 3000 Picture Place, Jackson MI 49201. **Tel** (517)788-8100, FAX (517)788-8371. **ED** Gary Pageau. **Circ:** 1,500 (ctrl).
**Desc:** Newsletter for commercial and people labs, featuring industry innovations, member profiles, business updates and news.

CI
**SPOT.** 1972-. Periodical. Serbo-Croatian (Roman). $16.00. Galereje Grada Zagreba, Katerenin Trg 2, Zagreb 41000 Croatia. **LC** TR1; .S83.

US/1049-0450
**SPOT (HOUSTON, TEX.).** (SPOT.). [Spot]. **Added/Corp** Houston Center for Photography. Vol. 2, No. 3 (Fall 1984)-. Periodical. English. Three times a year (May, July, Sept.). $15.00. Houston Center for Photography, 1441 West Alabama, Houston TX 77006. **Tel** (713)529-4755, FAX (713)529-9248. **ED** Karen Gillen Allen. **DD** 770. **Bk Rev**, (Qty: 12). **Ad Acc. Circ:** 12,000. ***Continues*** *Image (Houston Center for Photography).*
**Desc:** Publishes articles on photography theory, critical studies of photographers and photographic books and reviews of regional exhibitions and events of interest to the photographic community.

UK
**SSHOP NEWSLETTER. Added/Corp** Scottish Society for the History of Photography. **VAT** Scottish Society for the History of Photography Newsletter. No. 1 (June 1984)-. Newsletter. English. Scottish Society for the History of Photography, 1 Queen Street, c/o Scottish National Portrait Gallery, Edinburgh EH2 1JD England.

US/0191-4030
**STEREO WORLD.** [Stereo world]. **Added/Corp** National Stereoscopic Association (U.S.). (19??)-. Periodical. English. Six times a year. $22.00 with membership. National Stereoscopic Association, PO Box 14801, Columbus OH 43214. **Tel** (614)263-4296. **LC** TR780; .S78. **DD** 778.4/05.
**Desc:** Magazine of stereo (3-D) photography, its history, publishers, photographers; information for collectors, photohistorians, 3-D photographers and enthusiasts.
**Ind/Abst** GeoRef.

US
**STILL.** 1- 1970-. English. ir. Graphic Design Office, Box 2004 Yale Station, 212 York Street, New Haven CT 06520. **LC** TR640. **DD** 779/.05.

US/0897-6287
**STOCK PHOTO DESKBOOK, THE.** [Stock photo deskb.]. **Added/Corp** Photographic Arts Center. (1989)-. Periodical. English. an. $32.95. Photographic Arts Center Ltd, 163 Amsterdam Avenue, Suite 201, New York NY 10023. **Tel** (212)838-8640, FAX (212)873-7065. **DD** 779. ***Continues*** *Stock Photo and Assignment Source Book, 0146-5961.*

US/1058-997X
**STUDIES IN MODERN ART. See** The Arts.

US/0746-0996
**STUDIO PHOTOGRAPHY.** [Stud. photogr.]. **Added/Corp** Professional School Photographers of America. (July 1985)-. Periodical. English. Twelve times a year. $40.00 US; $65.00 other. PTN Publishing Company, 445 Broad Hollow Road, Melville NY 11747. **Tel** (516)845-2700, FAX (516)845-7109. ***Continues*** *Photographic Business and Product News.*
**Ind/Abst** Abstr. Bull. Inst. Pap. Sci. Tech.

US
**TAPE/DISC DIRECTORY / BILLBOARD. See** Sound Recordings and Systems.

UK
**TELEVISUAL. See** Communication-Broadcasting.

UK/0142-9663
**TEN.8. VFOAT** Ten 8; Ten Eight; 10 8. No. 1 (Feb. 1979)-No. 36 (Spring 1990); New Ser., Vol . 2, No 1 (Spring 1991)-. Periodical. English. qt. £39.95 UK; £44.45 other (institutions); £29.95 UK; £34.45 other (individuals). Ten 8 Ltd, 9 Key Hill Drive, Hockley, Birmingham B18 5NY England. **Tel** 021-554-2237. **ED** John Taylor, Derek Bishion, Rhonda Wilson, Roshini Kempaduo, David A Bailey and Karen Hope. **Bk Rev. Ad Acc. Circ:** 4,000.
**Desc:** Internationally acclaimed as the most radical photographic magazine in the United Kingdom. The magazine has presented photographs and ideas across a broad spectrum of contemporary theory and practice, from high street portraiture to photography and fine arts. Includes such diverse issues as the representation of the miner's strike and black cultural politics both in the United Kingdom and the USA.
**Ind/Abst** BHA : Biblio. Hist. Art.

US
**TEXAS PROFESSIONAL PHOTOGRAPHER.** English. bm (6 issues). $20.00 non-members; Free to members. Texas Professional, PO Box 828, Temple TX 76501. **Tel** (817)778-3232, FAX (817)778-3232. **ED** Walt Hawkins. **Ad Acc, Adv Mgr:** same as editor. **Circ:** 925 (ctrl).
**Desc:** Photographic Association news and related articles about professional photography.

SW/1100-6323
**TIDSKRIFT FOR MEDICINSK OCH TEKNISK FOTOGRAFI.** [Tidskr. med. tek. fotogr.]. (1989)-. Periodical. Swedish. qt. Kr175.00. Jan Ulof Yxell, Uddevallatplatsen 9, S-41670 Goteborg Sweden. **Tel** 011 46 31 7721717. **ED** Jan - Olof Yxell. **UDC** 77. **Bk Rev. Ad Acc. Circ:** 750. ***Continues*** *SIFF-Media, 0349-8948.*
**Desc:** Articles about methods and techniques in medical and technical science/photography.

IT/0041-4395
**TUTTI FOTOGRAFI.** [Tutti fotogr.]. (1969)-. Periodical. Italian. Eleven times a year. L57000.00 Italy; L75000.00 other. Progresso Fotografico & Csas, Viale Piceno 14, 20129 Milan Italy. **Tel** 011 39 2 7490866, 011 39 2 715939. **UDC** 77.

US
**U.S. CAMERA.** (1935)-. English. US Camera Publishing Corporation, PO Box 562, Des Moines IA 50302. **LC** TR1; .U5. **DD** 770.5.

US/1018-7928
**ULTRAHIGH- AND HIGH-SPEED PHOTOGRAPHY, VIDEOGRAPHY, AND PHOTONICS.** [Ultrah.- high-speed photogr. videogr. photonics]. **Added/Corp** Society of Photo-Optical Instrumentation Engineers. 9th (1991)-. English. $62.00. International Society for Optical Engineering, PO Box 10, Bellingham WA 98227-0010. **Tel** (206)676-3290, FAX (206)647-1445, telex 46-7053. **LC** TR593; .H534. **DD** 621. ***Continues*** *Ultrahigh- and High-Speed Photography, Videography, Photonics, and Velocimetry, 1053-4334.*

US/0163-7916
**UNTITLED (CARMEL).** ***Ceased.*** (UNTITLED.). No. 1 (3rd Quarter 1972)-(June 1994). Monographic series. English. Three times a year. Friends of Photography, 250 4th Street, San Francisco CA 94103. **Tel** (415)495-7000. **ED** James Alinder. Index available. **Circ:** 14,000 (ctrl).
**Desc:** Usually photographic monographs, sometimes books of critical essays on photography.
**Ind/Abst** ARTbibliogr. Mod.

RU
**USPEKHI NAUCHNOI FOTOGRAFII. Added/Corp** Akademiia Nauk SSSR. Komissiia po Nauchnoi Fotografii i Kinematografii. (1951)-. Academic Scholarly Publication. Russian. Izdatelstvo Nauka / Akademiia Nauk, Publishing House of the Russian Academy of Sciences, Leninskii Porspekt 14, 117901 Moscow Russia. **Tel** 011 95 954-21-53, FAX 011 95 938-21-44, telex 411964. Documents available from CASDDS.
**Ind/Abst** Chem. Abstr.

SW
**UTBLICK LANDSKAP. See** Architecture.

US/1066-8810
**VARIETY'S VIDEO DIRECTORY PLUS.** (VARIETY'S VIDEO DIRECTORY PLUS [COMPUTER FILE].). [Var. video dir. plus]. **Added/Corp** R.R. Bowker Company. **VFOAT** Video Directory Plus; Video Directory. (1986)-. Directory. English. qt. $395.00. R R Bowker Electronic Publishing, A Reed Reference Publishing Company, Part of Reed International PLC, 121 Chanlon Drive, New Providence NJ 07974. **Tel** (800)323-3288. **LC** PN1992.95. **DD** 384.
**Desc:** Includes over 88,000 citations with complete, current and reliable video information.

CN
**VIDEO AND FILM CATALOGUE. See** Motion Picture.

US/1055-0267
**VIDEO ANNUAL, THE. See** Library and Information Sciences.

FR
**VIDEO BROADCAST. See** Communication-Broadcasting.

US/0279-571X
**VIDEO BUSINESS.** [Video bus.]. Vol. 1, No. 1 (Jan. 1981)-. Periodical. English. wk. $70.00 US; $150.00 Canada & Mexico; $190.00 other. Chilton, 825 7th Avenue, New York NY 10019. **Tel** (212)887-8560. **LC** HD9697.V543; U546. **DD** 621.388/33.
**Ind/Abst** Trade Ind. ASAP [Full Txt.]; Trade Ind. Index [Full Txt.].

US/1042-7694
**VIDEO INVESTOR.** [Video investor]. **Added/Corp** Paul Kagan Associates. No. 54 (Jan. 31, 1989)-. Periodical. English. mo. $525.00. Kagan World Media Inc., 126 Clock Tower Place, Carmel CA 93923-8734. **Tel** (408)624-1536, FAX (408)625-3225. **DD** 384. ***Continues*** *VCR Letter, 8755-9927.*

US/0887-6851
**VIDEO LIBRARIAN, THE.** [Video libr.]. Vol. 1, No. 1 (Mar. 1, 1986)-. Newsletter. English. Six times a year. $47.00 US; $52.00 Canada; $69.00 other. Video Librarian, PO Box 2725, Bremerton WA 98310. **Tel** (206)377-2231, FAX (206)692-7608. **ED** Randy Pitman. **LC** Z692.V52; V52. **DD** 025. Index available. **Bk Rev**, (Qty: 10 or less). **Circ:** 750.
**Desc:** Articles and news on the subject of video in public schools and libraries. Reviews approximately 100 videos per issue.

US
**VIDEO MARKETING NEWS.** ***Title Change.*** Vol. 11, No. 19 (Oct. 15, 1990)-(1994). Periodical. English. bw (25 issues). Phillips Business Information, Inc., 1201 Seven Locks Road, Potomac MD 20854. **Tel** (301)424-3338, (800)777-5006, FAX (301)309-3847. **LC** TK6655.V5; V53. available on an online database (files 570,636,648/Full-Text) from DIALOG. ***Continues*** *Video Marketing Newsletter, 0196-4429;* ***Absorbed*** *VideoNews International; Home Video Publisher.* ***Merged with*** *Video Services News, 1067-3849* ***to form*** *Phillips Business Information's Interactive Video News, 1076-4526.*
**Ind/Abst** Mark. Advert. Ref. Serv. [Full Txt.]; PTS Newsl. Database [Full Txt.]; Trade Ind. ASAP [Full Txt.]; Trade Ind. Index [Full Txt.].

US/0272-1236
**VIDEO PROGRAMS INDEX, THE.** [Video programs index]. 1st- Ed.; 1976-. English. an. Video Programs Index, 15 Madison Avenue, Summit NJ 07901. **LC** PN1992.95; .V5. **DD** 381/.4579143/029573.

UK
**VIDEO RETAILER.** (19??)-. Periodical. English. mo. £24.00 UK; £31.00 other. Link House Magazines Ltd., Link House, Dingwall Avenue, Croydon, Surrey CR9 2TA England. **Tel** 011 44 81 686 2599, FAX 011 44 81 760 0973, telex 947709. **(Subscription address:** Link House Magazines Ltd., 120 126 Lavendar Avenue, Mitcham Surrey CR4 3HP England.**)**

US/0196-8793
**VIDEO REVIEW (NEW YORK, N.Y.).** (VIDEO REVIEW.). [Video rev.]. Vol. 1 (April 1980)-. Periodical. English. Eight times a year. $15.97 US; $27.80 Canada; $37.80 other. Media Works Group, 271 North Avenue, Suite 318, New Rochelle NY 10801. **Tel** (914)576-8800, (914)576-8815. **(Subscription address:** Neodata / Colorado, PO Box 2606, Boulder Boulder CO 80322.**)** available on microfilm and microfiche from University Microfilms International (UMI). Documents available from UMI Article Clearinghouse.
**Ind/Abst** Acad. Abstr. Full Text Elite (Sept. 1987-May 1992); Acad. Abstr. (Sept. 1987-May 1992); Acad. Search (Sept. 1987-May 1992); Gen. Period. Index (1989-); INFO-SOUTH Abstr.; Mag. Artic. Summar. Elite (Jan. 1989-May 1992, Jan. 1993-); Mag. Artic. Summar. Select (Jan. 1989-May 1992); Mag. Artic. Summar. CD-ROM (Sept. 1987-May 1992); Mag. Index Plus (1989-); Mag. Index. Sel. (1989-); Mag. Search; Newsp. Period. Abstr. (1988-); Pop. Period. Index; Read. Guide Period. Lit.; Resource/One Ondisc (1988-); Mag. Index (1989-).

US/1067-3849
**VIDEO SERVICES NEWS / PHILLIPS BUSINESS INFORMATION, INC.** ***Title Change.*** [Video serv. news]. **Added/Corp** Phillips Business Information, Inc. (1993)-(June 1994). Periodical. English. bw (25 issues). Phillips Business Information, Inc., 1201 Seven Locks Road, Potomac MD 20854. **Tel** (301)424-3338, (800)777-5006, FAX (301)309-3847. **DD** 384. **[CCC].** ***Merged with*** *Video Marketing News, 0196-4429* ***to form*** *Phillips Business Information's Interactive Video News, 1076-4526.*

US/1046-607X
**VIDEO SOFTWARE MAGAZINE.** [Video softw. mag.]. **VFOAT** VSM. (198?)-. Periodical. English. mo. $60.00 US; $90.00 Canada; $120.00 other. Chilton, 825 7th Avenue, New York NY 10019. **Tel** (212)887-8560. **DD** 791. ***Continues*** *Video Software Dealer, 0894-3001.*

US/0748-0881
**VIDEO SOURCE BOOK, THE.** [Video source book]. **Added/Corp** National Video Clearinghouse. 1st. Ed. (1979)-. English. an. $260.00. Gale Research Inc., 835 Penobscot Building, Detroit MI 48226. **Tel** (800)877-GALE, (313)961-2242, FAX (313)961-6083, telex TWX 810-221-7086. **ED** Julia C. Furtaw. **LC** PN1992.95; .V52. **DD** 011/.37. **NLM** LB 1044.7; V652. **Ad Acc.** available on magnetic tape; available on diskette.
**Desc:** Over 91,000 entries describe 130,000 currently

available video programs in all areas of entertainment, education, culture, medicine, and business. Up to twenty points of information given for each video in an easy-to-read entry and page format. Listings indicate how the title may be acquired and the name, address, and phone number of the distributor is given for each video. A separate section of the directory provides a complete listing of the name, address, and telephone numbers for 2,500 distributors.

GW
**VIDEO (STUTTGART, GERMANY).**
(VIDEO.). (19??)-. Periodical. German. mo. $70.00. Vereinigte Motor Verlag GmbH, Motor Presse, POB 106036, D 70049 Stuttgart Germany. **Tel** 011 49 711 1821506, 011 49 711 1821545. **(Subscription address:** German Language Publ, Inc., 153 South Deanstreet, Englewood, NJ 07631**)** **LC** PN1992.95; .V48. **DD** 791.43/75/0953.

US/1040-2772
**VIDEO TECHNOLOGY NEWSLETTER.**
[Video technol. newsl.]. Vol. 1, No. 1 (Sept. 26, 1988)-. Newsletter. English. bw (25 issues). $595.00 US; $630.00 other. Phillips Business Information, Inc., 1201 Seven Locks Road, Potomac MD 20854. **Tel** (301)424-3338, (800)777-5006, FAX (301)309-3847. **DD** 384. **[CCC].** available on an online database (file 636/Full-Text) from DIALOG. ***Absorbed in part*** *Home Media Technology News.*

US/0742-8111
**VIDEO TIMES (SKOKIE, ILL.).** ***Ceased.***
(VIDEO TIMES : FOR HOME VIEWING ON TAPE & DISC.). Vol. 1, No. 1 (Jan. 1985)-Ceased Vol. 4, No. 4. Periodical. English. mo. Publications International Ltd., 7373 North Cicero Avenue, Lincolnwood IL 60646. **Tel** (708)676-3470. **ED** Estelle Weber. **LC** PN1992.95; .V495. **DD** 791.45/05. **Bk Rev**. **Ad Acc**. **Circ:** 150,000. ***Continues*** *Video Movies, 0742-8111.*
**Desc:** Reviews from 200 to 300 video tape and disk releases. Reviews include movies, documentaries and alternative programming.

US/1070-9991
**VIDEO WATCHDOG.** **See** Motion Picture.

US/1066-6958
**VIEWCAMERA (SACRAMENTO, CALIF.).**
(VIEW CAMERA.). [Viewcamera]. (198?)-. Periodical. English. bm. $25.00 (1 year), $46.00 (2 year), $62.00 (3 year) US; $40.00 (1 year), $75.00 (2 year) Canada and Mexico; $65.00 (1 year), $115.00 (2 year) other. View Camera, PO Box 8166, Sacramento CA 95818. **Tel** (916)441-2557, FAX (916)441-7407. **DD** 770. **Bk Rev**. **Ad Acc**.
**Desc:** The journal of large format photography.

US/0743-8044
**VIEWS (BOSTON, MASS.).** (VIEWS.). [Views]. **Added/Corp** Photographic Resource Center (Boston, Mass.). Vol. 1, No. 1 (May 1979)-. Periodical. English. Three times a year. $45.00 (1 year), $80.00 (2 year), $115.00 (3 year) US; $53.00 (1 year), $96.00 (2 year), $139.00 (3 year) Canada; $62.00 (1 year), $114.00 (2 year), $166.00 (3 year) other; includes Photographic Resource Center membership and newsletter. Photographic Resource Center, 602 Commonwealth Avenue, Boston MA 02215. **Tel** (617)353-0700, FAX (617)353-1662. **ED** Daniel P Younger. **Bk Rev**. **Ad Acc**, **Adv Mgr:** Darsie Alexander. **Circ:** 2,000.
**Desc:** Feature articles, interviews, news items, book and exhibition reviews related to the photographic arts.
**Ind/Abst** ARTbibliogr. Mod.

US/1064-8658
**VISIONS MAGAZINE (BOSTON, MASS.).**
(VISIONS MAGAZINE : FILM/TELEVISION ARTS.). [Vis. mag.]. (1991)-. Periodical. English. Four times a year (Spring, Summer, Fall, Winter). $45.00 (institutions), $20.00 (individual). Boston Center for the Arts, 551 Tremont Street, Studio 212, Boston MA 02116. **Tel** (617)695-1360, FAX (617)695-1277. **ED** Marie-France Alderman. **DD** 791. **Bk Rev**, (Qty: 4). **Ad Acc**. **Circ:** 25,000.

US/1058-7187
**VISUAL ANTHROPOLOGY REVIEW.** **See** Anthropology.

US/1046-9001
**VISUAL RESOURCES ASSOCIATION BULLETIN.** **See** The Arts-Art.

FI
**VUODEN LUONNONKUVAT ... .** **VFOAT** Nature Photographs of the Year ... . English. **LC** TR721; .V86. **DD** 779/.3.

US/0738-8039
**WESTERN PHOTOGRAPHER.** (19??)-. Periodical. English. Twelve times a year. $22.00 (one year); $36.00 (two years). Western Photographer, 8708 Lake Ashmere Drive, San Diego CA 92119. **Tel** (619)463-1711.

AT
**WHAT'S ON VIDEO AND CINEMA.**
***Suspended.*** Vol. 5, No. 51 (March 1986)-?. Periodical. English. mo. $20.00. Video & Cinema Subscriptions, PO Box 1024, Richmond North 3121 Australia. **Tel** (03)429-5599. **LC** PN1992.95; .A9. **DD** 791.43/05. **Bk Rev**. **Ad Acc**. **Circ:** 135,000. ***Continues*** *Australian Video and Cinema.*

UK/0263-9106
**WHICH CAMERA?.** [Which camera?]. (1981)-. Periodical. English. bm (6 issues). £10.00 UK; £16.00 Eire & Europe; £26.00 America, Middle East, India & Africa; £27.00 Australia, New Zealand & Japan; £16.00 other. Haymarket Publishing Ltd., 12 14 Ansdell Street, London W8 5TR England. **Tel** 011 44 483 733800, FAX 011 44 483 776573. **(Subscription address:** Haymarket Publishing Ltd, PO Box 219, Subscriptions Department, Woking Surrey GU21 1ZW, United Kingdom.**)** **DD** 771.3029.

US/0163-3430
**WHITE HOUSE NEWS PHOTOGRAPHERS ANNUAL AWARDS.**
**Added/Corp** White House News Photographers Association. (19??)-. Periodical. English. an (May). $10.00. Ultimate Consultant, 101 1 2 South Union Street, Alexandria VA 22314. **Tel** (703)683-2557. **LC** TR820; .W43. **DD** 770/.7/9. **Ad Acc**. **Circ:** 4,000.
**Desc:** Award winning works from White House News Photographers Association, annual competition. Also, editorial contributions by well known individuals.

●US/1062-0427
**WHODUZZIT? (NEW YORK, N.Y.).**
(WHODUZZIT?.). [Whoduzzit?]. **VFOAT** Who Does It?. (1992)-. English. sa. $17.95. American Showcase, 915 Broadway, 14th Floor, New York NY 10010. **Tel** (212)673-6600, FAX (212)673-9795, telex 880356 AMSHOW P. **ED** Jon Saddlebrook. **DD** 659. Index available (bound in each issue). **Circ:** 10,000 (ctrl).
**Desc:** A directory of commercial photographers and directors categorized by specialty (i.e. automotive, people, location, food, still life, and architecture.

●US/1052-4037
**WHO'S WHO IN PHOTOGRAPHY (PLYMOUTH, VT.).** (WHO'S WHO IN PHOTOGRAPHY.). [Who's who photogr.]. (1992)-. English. be. $89.95 (single issue). Five Corners Publications, Ltd., Rt 100, HCR 70, Box 7A, Plymouth VT 05056. **LC** TR139; .W488. **DD** 770/.92/273; B.

US/1048-2563
**WHO,S WHO IN PROFESSIONAL PHOTOGRAPHY.** [Who's who prof. photogr.]. **Added/Corp** Professional Photographers of America. **VFOAT** Professional Photography. (1988-89). English. PPA Publications Inc, 1090 Executive Way, Des Plaines IL 60018-1587. **Tel** (312)299-8161. **LC** TR12; .D49. **DD** 770/.25/73. ***Continues*** *Directory of Professional Photography, 0070-6132.*

AU/0084-0998
**WISSENSCHAFTLICHE UND ANGEWANDTE PHOTAGRAPHIE, DIE.**
(1955)-. Monographic series. German. ir. Price varies per volume. Springer-Verlag Wien, Sachsenplatz 4 6, PO Box 89, A-1201 Vienna Austria. **Tel** 011 43 1 3302415. **(Subscription address:** Springer Verlag New York Inc. / for North America, 44 Hartz Way, Secaucus NJ 07096.**)**

US/0897-5132
**WOLFMAN REPORT ON THE PHOTOGRAPHIC & IMAGING INDUSTRY IN THE UNITED STATES.**
[Wolfman rep. photogr. imaging ind. U.S.]. (1985)-. English. an (July). $175.00 one year. Wolfman Report Popular Photos, 1633 Broadway 43rd Street, New York NY 10019. **Tel** (212)767-6048. **ED** Harold Martin. **LC** TR1; .W6. **DD** 338.4/7/77. **Circ:** 10,000 (ctrl). ***Continues*** *Wolfman Report on the Photographic Industry in the United States.*
**Desc:** Many articles and information on the photography and videos around the world.
**Ind/Abst** F&S Index Plus Text, Int. [Select. Cov.]; PROMT.

US/0049-8165
**WORLD TRIBUNE.** (19??)-. Periodical. English (Spanish, Japanese, Korean and Chinese). Fifty-two times a year. $44.00. World Tribune Press, PO Box 1427, Santa Monica CA 90406. **Tel** (310)451-8811. **ED** Mr. Ted Mouno. cum. index. **Bk Rev**, (Qty: 10). **Circ:** 120,000 (ctrl). available on an online database.
**Desc:** The organ publication of the Nichiren Shoshu Soka Gakkai of America. An non-profit Buddhist organization.

US/0277-6162
**WRITER'S & PHOTOGRAPHER'S GUIDE TO NEWSPAPER MARKETS.** [Writ. photogr. guide newsp. mark.]. **VAT** Writer's and Photographer's Guide to Newspaper Markets. English. an. $9.95. Helm Publishing, Box 10512, Costa Mesa CA 92627.

US/0734-1504
**ZHURNAL NAUCHNOI I PRIKLADNOI FOTOGRAFII I KINEMATOGRAFII.** ***Title Change.*** (SCIENTIFIC & APPLIED PHOTOGRAPHY & CINEMATOGRAPHY.). [Sci. appl. photogr. cinematogr.]. **VFOAT** Scientific and Applied Photography and Cinematography. Vol. 28, No. 1 (1984)-(19??). Periodical. English (summaries and/or abstracts in Russian; translations available in Russian). Six times a year. Gordon & Breach Science Publishers, Inc., PO Box 786, Cooper Station, New York NY 10276. **Tel** (212)206-8900, FAX (212)645-2459. **(Subscription address:** International Publishers Distributor at one of the following addresses: 820 Town Center Drive, Langhorne, PA 19047; or PO Box 90, Reading Berkshire RG1 8JL UK; or Kent Ridge PO Box 1180, Singapore 9111, Republic of Singapore**)** **ED** K V Chibisov. **LC** TR1; .Z5135. **DD** 770/.5. **CODEN** SAPHES. **[CCC].** Index available. **Bk Rev**. **Ad Acc**. ***Continued by*** *Zhurnal Nauchnoi i Prikladnoi Fotografii. English. Scientific & Applied Photography, 1063-4088.*
**Desc:** Cover-to-cover translation of the latest research, technical developments and applications to emerge from the Soviet Union.

●RU
**ZHURNAL NAUCHNOI I PRIKLADNOI FOTOGRAFII / ROSSIISKAIA AKADEMIIA NAUK.** **Added/Corp** Rossiiskaia Akademiia Nauk. (1992)-. Academic Scholarly Publication. Russian (table of contents in English). Six times a year. $89.95. Izdatelstvo Nauka / Akademiia Nauk, Publishing House of the Russian Academy of Sciences, Leninskii Porspekt 14, 117901 Moscow Russia. **Tel** 011 95 954-21-53, FAX 011 95 938-21-44, telex 411964. **(Subscription address:** East View Publications Inc., 3020 Harbor Lane North, Suite 110, Minneapolis MN 55447.**)** **LC** TR1; .Z5. ***Continues*** *Zhurnal Nauchnoi i Prikladnoi Fotografii i Kinematografii.*

US
**ZOOM.** ***Ceased.*** (19??)-(19??). Periodical. English (French). Seven times a year. Zoom, PO Box 2000, Long Island NY 11101. **Tel** (718)937-4606. **LC** TR640; .Z66. **DD** 770/.5.
**Ind/Abst** ARTbibliogr. Mod.

IT
**ZOOM (MILAN, ITALY).** (ZOOM.). No. 1 (1972)-. Periodical. Italian. mo. Progresso Fotografico & Csas, Viale Piceno 14, 20129 Milan Italy. **Tel** 011 39 2 7490866, 011 39 2 715939.

## ABSTRACTING, BIBLIOGRAPHIES AND STATISTICS

US/1051-290X
**BOWKER'S COMPLETE VIDEO DIRECTORY.** [Bowker's complete video dir.]. **VFOAT** Complete Video Directory. (1990)-. Directory. English. ir. $219.95 (3 volume set). R R Bowker, A Reed Reference Publishing Company, Part of Reed International PLC, PO Box 31, 121 Chanlon Drive, New Providence NJ 07974. **Tel** (908)464-6800, (800)521-8110, FAX (908)665-6688, telex 138-755. **LC** PN1992.95; .V29. **DD** 016.29143/75. available on CD-ROM. ***Continues*** *Variety's Complete Home Video Directory, 0000-1015.*
**Desc:** Covers over 85,000 videos especially for libraries, schools, and video resource centers.

US/0896-100X
**IMAGING ABSTRACTS.** **Added/Corp** Royal Photographic Society of Great Britain. Imaging Science and Technology Group. Vol. 1 (1988)-. Abstracting/Indexing Service. English. bm. £330.00 UK; $528.00 US. Pira International, Randalls Road, Leatherhead, Surrey KT22 7RU England. **Tel** 011 44 372 376161, FAX 011 44 372 377526. **LC** TR1; .P727. **DD** 770/.5. **[CCC].** available on microfilm and microfiche from University Microfilms International (UMI); available on an online database (through Pergamon ORBIT InfoLine). ***Continues*** *Photographic Abstracts, 0031-8701.*
**Desc:** Provides a strong central source of references to bibliographic information on all types of adhesives and sealants.

US/0164-4769
**PHOTO LAB MANAGEMENT.** **See** Photography and Video.

# PHYSICAL THERAPY

NR/0331-9113
**ABUH PHYSIO : THE JOURNAL OF THE PHYSIOTHERAPY DEPT. OF THE INSTITUTE OF HEALTH, AHMADU BELLO UNIVERSITY, ZARIA.** [Abuh physio]. Began with: No. 1 (Dec. 1979). Periodical. English. qt. Ahmadu Bello University / Department of the Institute of Health, Department of the Institute of Health, Zaria. **NLM** W1; A113F.

TI
**AFAQ SIHHIYAH / AL-MUNAZZAMAH AL-RIYADIYAH WA-AL-THAQAFIYAH LIL-MUAQIN.** **Added/Corp** Munazzamah Al-Riyadiyah Wa-al-Thaqafiyah Lil-Muaqin (Tunisia). **VFOAT** Horizon Sante. No. 1, (1980)-. Periodical. Arabic (French). **LC** RM930.A1; A36.

US/0194-6536
**AMERICAN CHIROPRACTOR, THE.** [Am. chiropr.]. (197?)-. Periodical. English. Twelve times a year. $84.00 (one year), $168.00 (three years) libraries US; $56.00 (one year), $112.00 (three years) individuals US; add $20.00 postage per year other. American Chiropractor, 5005 Rivera Court/Mr Rose, Fort Wayne IN 46825. **Tel** (219)484-9600, FAX (219)484-9604. **ED** Laura A Allen. **DD** 615. **NLM** W1; AM314L. **Bk Rev. Ad Acc. Circ:** 32,000 (ctrl). available on microfilm from University Microfilms International (UMI).
**Desc:** Editorial emphasis on clinical and research articles, legal and financial articles specifically for the chiropractic doctor, and interviews with leaders in their fields.

US/0894-9115
**AMERICAN JOURNAL OF PHYSICAL MEDICINE & REHABILITATION.** [Am. j. phys. med. rehabil.]. **Added/Corp** Association of Academic Physiatrists. **VFOAT** Physical Medicine & Rehabilitation; Physical Medicine and Rehabilitation; American Journal of PM & R. Vol. 67, No. 1 (Feb. 1988)-. Periodical. English. bm. $125.00 (institution) $75.00 (two year) US; $100.00 (individual), $150.00 (institution) other. Williams & Wilkins Company, 428 East Preston Street, Baltimore MD 21202-3993. **Tel** (410)528-4000, (800)638-6423, FAX (410)528-8596, telex 87669. **(Subscription address:** Williams & Wilkins, PO Box 64380, Baltimore MD 21264.**)** **LC** RM735.A1; O3. **DD** 615.8/515/05. **NLM** W1; AM501K. **CODEN** AJPREP. **[CCC]. Pr Rev.** Documents available from Article Express International, The Genuine Article, BIOSIS Document Express, Ask*IEEE, Quick Copies. ***Continues*** *American Journal of Physical Medicine, 0002-9491.*
**Desc:** The official journal of The Association of Academic Physiatrists. Examines acute problems and their treatment by the latest methods and equipment.
**Ind/Abst** Annals Behav. Med.; Bioeng. Abstr.; Biol. Abstr.; CSA Neuro. Abstr. (?-?); Cumul. Index Nurs. Allied Health Lit.; Curr. Contents Clin. Med.; Ei Page One; EMBASE; Energy Res. Abstr.; Eng. Index Annu.; Ergon. Abstr.; Health Plan. Adminis.; Index Med. (Feb. 1988-); INIS Atomindex [Micro.]; INSPEC (Feb. 1988-); Life Sci. Collect.; Res. Alert [Full Cov.]; Sci. Cit. Index; SCISEARCH; Soc. Sci. Cit. Index [Select. Cov.]; SPORT Discus.

FR/0309-427X
**ANNALES DE KINESITHERAPIE.** **Added/Corp** Societe de Kinesitherapie. Vol. 1 (Jan./Feb. 1974)-. Periodical. French. Eight times a year. $148.00. Masson Editeur, Box Postale 22, 41353 Vineuil 16 France. **Tel** 011 33 54 438994. **(Subscription address:** 7A Boulevard de Perolles, CH-1701 Fribourg Switzerland**)** **NLM** W1 AN336K. ***Formed by the union of*** *Journal de Kinesitherapie, 0021-7751* ***and*** *Revue de Kinesitherapie, 0035-1172.*
**Ind/Abst** SPORT Discus; SportSearch (May 1987-).

FR/0402-4621
**ANNALES DE READAPTATION ET DE MEDECINE PHYSIQUE : REVUE SCIENTIFIQUE DE LA SOCIETE FRANCAISE DE REEDUCATION FONCTIONNELLE DE READAPTATION ET DE MEDECINE PHYSIQUE.** **Added/Corp** Societe Francaise de Reeducation Fonctionnelle de Readaptation et de Medecine Physique. Vol. 25, No 1 (1982)-. Academic Scholarly Publication. French (summaries and/or abstracts in English). Eight times a year. 1350.00F France; 1500.00F other. Editions Scientifique Elsevier, 141 rue de Javel, 75747 Paris Cedex 15 France. **Tel** 011 33 1 47 07 11 22, FAX 011 33 1 43 36 80 93. **(Subscription address:** Editions Scientifiques Elsevier / for North America, PO Box 7247-7576, Philadelphia PA 19170-7576.**)** **NLM** W1; AN377F. available on microfilm and microfiche from University Microfilms International (UMI). ***Continues*** *Annales de Medecine Physique (Lille, France).*
**Ind/Abst** EMBASE.

US
**ANNUAL IN THERAPEUTIC RECREATION.** **Added/Corp** American Alliance for Health, Physical Education, Recreation, and Dance. American Association for Leisure and Recreation. American Therapeutic Recreation Association. University of Missouri--Columbia. Dept. of Parks, Recreation, and Tourism. Vol. 1 (1990)-. English. an (June). ATRA, PO Box 15215, Hattiesburg MS 39404. **Tel** (800)553-0304, or (601)264-3168. **LC** RC489.R4; A56. **DD** 615.8/5153. **NLM** W1; AN753AT.
**Ind/Abst** Leis. Recreat. Tour. Abstr.; SPORT Discus.

CN/0713-4436
**ARBRE DE VIE (LOUISEVILLE).** (L'ARBRE DE VIE.). [Arbre de vie]. V. 1, No. 1 (Feb. 15, 1982)-. Periodical. French. mo. Free. L'Arbre de Vie, 21 rue St-Laurent, Louiseville Quebec J5V 1J5 Canada. **DD** 615.5/34/05.

US/0003-9993
**ARCHIVES OF PHYSICAL MEDICINE AND REHABILITATION.** [Arch. phys. med. rehabil.]. Vol. 34 (Jan. 1953)-. Academic Scholarly Publication. English. mo (12 issues plus study guide published in May). $168.00 (institution), $139.00 (individual), US; $189.00 (institution), $165.00 (individual) other. W.B. Saunders Company, A Subsidiary of Harcourt Brace Jovanovich, Inc., The Curtis Center/Suite 300, Independence Square West, Philadelphia PA 19106-3399. **Tel** (215)238-7800 or, 5587, FAX (215)238-7883, telex 173146. **(Subscription address:** W. B. Saunders Company / North America Subscriptions, c/o Periodicals, 6277 Sea Harbour Drive, 4th Floor, Orlando FL 32887.**)** **ED** Marvin A. Schroder. **LC** RM845. **DD** 615.8/2/05. **NLM** W1 AR475. **CODEN** APMHAI. **[CCC].** Index available. cum. index. **Bk Rev. Ad Acc. Pr Rev. Circ:** 8,300 (ctrl). available on microfilm and microfiche from University Microfilms International (UMI). Documents available from The Genuine Article, BIOSIS Document Express, CASDDS. ***Continues*** *Archives of Physical Medicine, 0096-6622.*
**Desc:** A scientific journal including articles written by professionals in the related fields of rehabilitation medicine.
**Ind/Abst** Abr. Index Med.; Annals Behav. Med.; Biol. Abstr.; Chem. Abstr.; CSA Neuro. Abstr. (?-?); Cumul. Index Nurs. Allied Health Lit.; Curr. Contents Clin. Med.; EMBASE; Energy Res. Abstr. (Nov. 1976-); Health Saf. Sci. Abstr.; Health Plan. Adminis.; Index Med.; INIS Atomindex [Micro.]; Life Sci. Collect.; Phys. Educ. Index; Physic. Medline Plus; Res. Alert [Full Cov.]; Saf. Health Work; Sci. Cit. Index; SCISEARCH; Soc. Plann. Policy Dev. Abstr.; Soc. Sci. Cit. Index [Select. Cov.]; Sociol. Abstr. (?-?); SPORT Discus; SportSearch.

US
**AUDIT REPORT, TEXAS BOARD OF CHIROPRACTIC EXAMINERS.** **Main/Corp** Texas Board of Chiropractic Examiners. **VFOAT** Texas Board of Chiropractic Examiners. English. State Auditor, John H Reagan, State Office Building, PO Box 12067, Austin TX 78711. **LC** RZ205.U52; T47A. **DD** 353.97640084/1.

AT/0004-9514
**AUSTRALIAN JOURNAL OF PHYSIOTHERAPY, THE.** [Aust. j. physiother.]. **Added/Corp** Australian Physiotherapy Association. Vol. 1 (Oct. 1954)-. Periodical. English. qt. 62.00Aus$ Australia; 90.00Aus$ other. Australian Physiotherapy Association, PO Box 7028, Melbourne VIC 3004 Australia. **Tel** 011 61 3 8668366, FAX (03)482 2348. **ED** Stephen Downes. **NLM** W1 AU615. Index available. **Bk Rev. Ad Acc. Circ:** 6,995 (ctrl).
**Desc:** For physiotherapists in all areas of the profession in Australia and overseas, and other health professionals and researchers in related fields. Features include clinical research papers, letters to the editor, topical therapy, coming events, etc.
**Ind/Abst** Br. Humanit. Index; EMBASE.

XR/0302-8070
**BALNEOLOGIA BOHEMICA.** [Balneol. Bohem.]. **Added/Corp** Vyzkumny Ustav Balneologicky. Vol. 1 (1972)-. Periodical. German (summaries and/or abstracts in Czech, English, French and Russian). qt. Balnea, Ladova 1, 128 00 Prague 2 Czech Republic. **Tel** 294948, telex PRAGUE 122215. **ED** Jaroslav Benda (editor's address: Research Institute of Balneology, Ruska 28, 353 57 Marianske Lazne, Czechoslovakia). **LC** RM801; .B17. **NLM** W1 BA496G. **CODEN** BLBHAE. Index available. cum. index. **Circ:** 1,500 (ctrl). Documents available from BIOSIS Document Express.
**Desc:** Studies on effects of various methods of balneotherapy on human organisms and health; analyses of natural healing resources, and introduction of Czechoslovakian spas and their indications.
**Ind/Abst** Biol. Abstr.

NE/0168-9711
**BEWEGEN & HULPVERLENING.** [Beweg. hulpverlen.]. **VFOAT** Multidisciplinair Tijdschrift Bewegen & Hulpverlening. (1984)-. Periodical. Dutch. qt. Fl105.00. Bohn Stafleu Van Loghum BV, Postbus 246, 3990 GA Houten Netherlands. **Tel** 011 31 3403 95782. **(Subscription address:** Intermedia BV, Postbus 4, 2400 MA Alphen Rijn Netherlands.**)** **UDC** 615.85.

US
**BIENNIAL REPORT OF EXAMINING AND LICENSING BOARDS.** ***Title Change.*** **Main/Corp** Minnesota State Board of Chiropractic Examiners. English. be. Board of Chiropractic Examiners, 717 Delaware Street SE, Department of Health, Minneapolis MN 55414. **LC** RZ205.U52; M63. **DD** 353.9/776/008243. ***Continued by*** *Biennial Report of Examining and Licensing Boards.*

US
**BIENNIAL REPORT OF EXAMINING AND LICENSING BOARDS.** **See** Medical Science and Technology-Musculoskeletal System.

IT/0393-3423
**BOLLETTINO S.I.A.M.E.** (BOLLETTINO S.I.A.M.E. / SOCIETA ITALIANA PER L'ASSISTENZA MEDICO-PSICO-PEDAGOGICA ALLETA EVOLUTIVA.). [Boll. S.I.A.M.E.]. **VAT** Bollettino Societa Italiana per l'Assistenza Medico-Psico-Pedagogica Alleta Evolutiva. (1979)-. Periodical. Italian. Three times a year. **NLM** W1 BO646.

UK
**BRITISH JOURNAL OF THERAPY & REHABILITATION.** (19??)-. Periodical. English. Twelve times a year. £80.00 (institutions), £40.00 (individuals) UK and EIRE; £100.00 (institutions), £70.00 (individuals) other. Mark Allen Publishing Ltd., Croxped Mews, 288 Croxped Road, London SE24 9DA England. **Tel** 011 44 1 671 7521.

CN/0828-0827
**CANADIAN JOURNAL OF REHABILITATION.** [Can. j. rehabil.]. **VFOAT** Revue Canadienne de Readaptation; CJR; RCR. Vol. 1, No. 1 (Fall 1987)-. Periodical. English (French). Four times a year (Mar., June, Sept., Dec.). 54.00Can$ Canada; 64.00Can$ other. Canadian Association of Research Rehabilitation, 13325 St Albert Trail, Edmonton Alberta T5L 4R3 Canada. **Tel** (403)454-9656, FAX (403)451-0168. **(Subscription address:** CJR RCR, Faculty of Rehabilitation Medicine, 3 48 Corbett Hall, University of Alberta, Edmonton Alberta T6G 2G4 Canada; telephone: (403)492-1734**)** **ED** J. W. Vargo PhD, H. H. Mueller PhD, S. S. Dennis, D. Bevan and J. E. Semple. **NLM** W1; CA6060. **CODEN** CJREEI. Index available. cum. index. **Bk Rev. Ad Acc. Pr Rev.**
**Desc:** A scholarly vehicle for the promotion and communication of research, theory and best practice in habilitation and rehabilitation.
**Ind/Abst** Can. Index; Cumul. Index Nurs. Allied Health Lit.; EMBASE; Psychol. Abstr. (1987-); PsycINFO (1990-); PsycLit.

US
**CARDIOPULMONARY PHYSICAL THERAPY JOURNAL.** (19??)-. English. Three times a year. $20.00. American Physical Therapy Association, 1111 North Fairfax Street, Suite 200, Alexandria VA 22314-1488. **Tel** (703)684-2782, FAX (703)684-7343. **ED** William Temer. **Bk Rev. Ad Acc. Pr Rev. Circ:** 1,000 (ctrl).
**Desc:** Publishes articles related to cardiac and pulmonary medicine and rehabilitation, particularly as it pertains to the clinician involved in treating cardiopulmonary patients. Reports written on clinical and basic research, case and clinical reports, and abstracts of current literature.

US/1059-3896
**CAREER PLANNING GUIDE FOR PHYSICAL AND OCCUPATIONAL THERAPISTS.** [Career plan. guide phys. occup. ther.]. **VFOAT** Career Planning Guide. Vol. 1, No. 1 Nov. (1991)-. Periodical. English. sa. Free to licensed physical and occupational therapists. **DD** 615.

US
**CARF WORK HARDENING STANDARDS.** English. Catholic Spirit, Box 13327, Austin TX 78711. **Tel** (512) 476-4888.

US/0897-6058
**CHIROPRACTIC (FORT WAYNE, IND.).** (CHIROPRACTIC.). [Chiropractic]. **VFOAT** Chiropractic, The Journal of Chiropractic Research; Chiropractic, Study and Clinical Investigation. Vol. 1, No. 1 (Apr. 1988)-. Periodical. English. Four times a year. $76.00 (one year), $152.00 (three years) libraries US; $60.00 (one year), $120.00 (three years) individuals US; add $15.00 postage per year other. American Chiropractor, 5005 Rivera Court/Mr Rose, Fort Wayne IN 46825. **Tel** (219)484-9600, FAX (219)484-9604. **DD** 615. **NLM** W1; CH811X. ***Absorbed*** *Journal of Chiropractic Research, 1044-1050.*

US/0736-4377
**CHIROPRACTIC HISTORY.** (CHIROPRACTIC HISTORY : THE ARCHIVES AND JOURNAL OF THE ASSOCIATION FOR THE HISTORY OF CHIROPRACTIC.). [Chiropr. hist.]. **Added/Corp** Association for the History of Chiropractic. Vol. 1, No. 1 (1981)-. Periodical. English. Twice a year. $50.00 (state & provincial association & regular voting members & libraries) US; $57.00 (regular voting members) others; $60.00 (libraries) others; $100.00 (corporate members & national association) except Canada and colleges Comes with Association for the History of Chiropractic membership. Association for the History of Chiropractic, 1000 Brady Street, Davenport IA 52803. **Tel** (319)326-9190, FAX (319)326-5826. **ED** Russ Gibbons, (editor's address: 207 Grandview Drive South, Pittsburgh, PA 15215, phone: (412)237-4554). **LC** RZ221; .C45. **DD** 615. **NLM** W1 CH8129. cum. index.

AT/1036-0913
**CHIROPRACTIC JOURNAL OF AUSTRALIA.** [Chiropr. j. Aust.]. (1991)-. Periodical. English. Four times a year (Mar., June, Sept., Dec.). 60.00Aus$ Australia; 75.00Aus$ other. Australian Chiropractors Association, PO Box 748, Wagga Wagga,

New South Wales, 2650 Australia. **Tel** 11 61 69 213238, FAX 011 61 69 218869. **ED** Dr. Mary Ann Chance and Dr. Rolf E. Peters. **DD** 615.53405. **Bk Rev**. **Ad Acc**. **Pr Rev.** ctrl circ. available in microform from University Microfilms International (UMI). ***Continues*** *The Journal of the Australian Chiropractors' Association, 0045-0359.*
**Desc:** Contains research, professional and papers relevant to the practice of chiropractic. News briefs on interest to chiropractors and allied professionals that includes history, commentary and abstracts.

CN/0836-1444
**CHIROPRACTIC REPORT, THE.** [Chiropr. rep.]. (Nov. 1986)-. Periodical. English. bm. $110.00 Quebec; $76.00 other Canada, US; $80.00. The Chiropractic Report, 3080 Yonge Street #3002, Toronto Ontario M4N 3N1 Canada. **Tel** (416)484-9601, FAX (416)484-9665. **ED** David Chapman-Smith. **DD** 615.5/34/05. **Bk Rev**, (Qty: 1-2). **Circ:** 8,000.

US/0899-6938
**CHIROPRACTIC RESEARCH JOURNAL.** **See** Medical Science and Technology-Musculoskeletal System.

JA/0386-8109
**CHIRYOGAKU.** **See** Medical Science and Technology.

CC/1000-4610
**CHUNG-HUA CHI KUNG / CHUAN KUO CHUNG I HSUEH HUI CHI KUNG KO YEN HUI CHU PAN.** [Zhonghua qigong]. Periodical. Chinese. RMBY0.35. Post Office Beijing, Beijing, People's Republic of China. **LC** RM727.C54; C47. **DD** 613.7/1.

US/1053-072X
**CLINICAL CHIROPRACTIC REPORT.** ***Ceased.*** (1991)-(199?). Periodical. English. qt. Mosby Year Book Inc., 11830 Westline Industrial Drive, St Louis MO 63146. **Tel** (800)325-4177, (314)872-8370, FAX (314)432-1380, telex 44-2402. **[CCC].**
**Desc:** Concentrates on a single clinical topic in each issue. For example, early issues will comprehensively cover lumbar disc disease, headache, and the cervical spine.

US/0896-9620
**CLINICAL KINESIOLOGY.** (CLINICAL KINESIOLOGY : JOURNAL OF THE AMERICAN KINESIOTHERAPY ASSOCIATION.). [Clin. kinesiol.]. **Added/Corp** American Kinesiotherapy Association. Vol. 42 No. 1 (Jan./Feb./Mar 1988)-. Periodical. English. Four times a year (Mar., June, Sept., Dec.). $45.00 (libraries and institutions), US; $25.00 (non-member individuals). American Kinesiotherapy Association, University of Toledo, 2801 W Bancroft, Toledo OH 43606. **Tel** (419)537-2743, FAX (419)537-4759. **ED** Evelyn Scott. **LC** RD795; .A75. **DD** 615.8/2/05. **NLM** W1; CL724P. **CODEN** CLKIE9. Index available. cum. index. **Pr Rev.** available on microfilm and microfiche from University Microfilms International (UMI). Documents available from BIOSIS Document Express. ***Continues*** *American Corrective Therapy Journal, 0002-8088.*
**Desc:** Research and programs in physical activity for handicapping conditions.
**Ind/Abst** Biol. Abstr. (1988-); Cumul. Index Nurs. Allied Health Lit.; EMBASE; Highw. Res. Abstr.; Phys. Educ. Index; Psychol. Abstr. (1970-); SPORT Discus.

US
**CLINICAL MANAGEMENT : THE MAGAZINE OF THE AMERICAN PHYSICAL THERAPY ASSOCIATION.** ***Title Change.*** Vol. 10, No. 1 (Jan./Feb. 1990)-(1993). Periodical. English. bm. American Physical Therapy Association, 1111 North Fairfax Street, Suite 200, Alexandria VA 22314-1488. **Tel** (703)684-2782, FAX (703)684-7343. **ED** Michelle P B Ferrier. **NLM** W1; CL726G. Index available. **Ad Acc**. **Circ:** 51,000 (ctrl). available on microfilm; available on microfiche. ***Continues*** *Clinical Management in Physical Therapy, 0276-8038.* ***Merged into*** *PT: Magazine of Physical Therapy, 1065-5077.*
**Desc:** Based on individual experience and observations, articles share hands-on advice, opinions, and new ideas about physical therapy that relate to patient care and clinical management.
**Ind/Abst** Cumul. Index Nurs. Allied Health Lit.; Except. Child Educ. Resour. (19??-19??).

US/0269-2155
**CLINICAL REHABILITATION.** [Clin. rehabil.]. **Added/Corp** Society for Research in Rehabilitation. Vol. 1, No. 1 (1987)-. Periodical. English. qt (February, May, August and November). $220.00 North America; £137.50 Europe; £149.50 Other. Edward Arnold, 338 Euston Road, London NW1 3BH England. **Tel** 011 44 71 873 6000, FAX 011 44 071 873 6325. **(Subscription address:** Edward Arnold, PO Box 386, Avenel NJ 07001-0386.**) ED** K. Andrews. **NLM** W1; CL768Q. **CODEN** CEHAEN.
**Desc:** Provides a forum for the exchange of ideas and information by all those concerned with rehabilitation, publishing articles on practical approaches to problems encountered in rehabilitation. Original scientific papers, review articles, reports on equipment, aids and appliances, and case studies are included. Since rehabilitation is still in the relatively early stages of scientific and research development, description of new approaches and ideas will be considered for publication to encourage further research.
**Ind/Abst** Cumul. Index Nurs. Allied Health Lit.; EMBASE; Psychol. Abstr.; PsycINFO; PsycLit; Ref. Z.

KO/0379-752X
**DAIHAN JAIHWAR NUIHAG HOIJI.** (TAEHAN CHAEHWAL UIHAKHOE CHI.). **VFOAT** The Journal of Korean Academy of Rehabilitation Medicine. Began with Mar. 1977 issue. Periodical. Korean (summaries and/or abstracts in English). sa. Taehan Chaehwal Uihakhoe, 1 2-ka Myong-dong Chung-ku, Seoul Korea. **LC** RM695. **NLM** W1 TA392BJ.

DK/0105-0648
**DANSKE FYSIOTERAPEUTER.** [Dan. fysioter.]. **Added/Corp** Danske Fysioterapeuter. Vol. 56 (1974)-. Periodical. Danish. ir. $93.00 (1994 edition). Danske Fysioterapeuter, Norre Voldgade 90, 1358 Copenhagen K Denmark. **Tel** 011 45 33 138211. **NLM** W1 DA697. ***Continues*** *Tidsskrift for Fysioterapeuter, 0040-7054.*

US
**DIRECTORY OF LICENSES.** Directory. English. an. North Carolina Board of Physical Therapy Examiners, 2426 Tryon Road, Durham NC 27705-5512. **LC** RM697.U5; D57. **DD** 615.8/2/025756. ctrl circ.

US/0162-5543
**DIRECTORY OF PHYSICAL THERAPISTS AND PHYSICAL THERAPISTS ASSISTANTS LICENSED AND REGISTERED IN TENNESSEE.** Directory. English. State Licensing Board for the Healing Arts, TDPH State Office Building, Ben Allen Road, Nashville TN 37216. **LC** RM697.T4; A3. **DD** 615/.8/025768. **NLM** WB 22 AT2 D55. ***Continues*** *Directory of Physical Therapists Registered in Tennessee.*

AU/1017-6721
**EUROPEAN JOURNAL OF PHYSICAL MEDICINE & REHABILITATION.** **Added/Corp** Societt Royale Belge de Medecine Physique et de Rehabilitation. **VFOAT** PMR. Vol. 1, No. 1 (Feb. 1991)-. Periodical. English. bm. S1680.00 Austria; S1850.00 other. Medizinische Verlagsgesellschaft mbH, Feldgasse 13, A-1238 Vienna Austria. **Tel** 011 43 1 8893646, FAX 011 43 1 889364724, telex 8893647. **NLM** W1; EU72EAL. Documents available from ADONIS. ***Continues*** *Acta Belgica. Medica Physica, 0771-5684.*
**Ind/Abst** ADONIS.

NE/0014-4231
**EXCERPTA MEDICA. SECTION 19. REHABILITATION AND PHYSICAL MEDICINE.** **See** Medical Science and Technology-Abstracting, Bibliographies and Statistics.

SP/0211-5638
**FISIOTERAPIA.** [Fisioterapia]. (1979)-. Periodical. Spanish. Four times a year. 4500.00ptas. Editorial Garsi SA, Juan Bravo 46, 28006 Madrid, Spain. **Tel** 011 34 1 4021212, telex 98358 GARSI E. **UDC** 615.8.
**Ind/Abst** Indice Med. Esp.

FR/0249-6550
**JOURNAL D'ERGOTHERAPIE PARIS.** [J. ergother. Paris]. **Added/Corp** Sociation Nationale Francaise des Ergotherapeutes. (1965)-. Periodical. French. qt. $100.00. Masson Editeur, Box Postale 22, 41353 Vineuil 16 France. **Tel** 011 33 54 438994. **UDC** 615.85. **[CCC].**

US/1062-9920
**JOURNAL OF CHIROPRACTIC TECHNIQUE.** ***Title Change.*** **See** Medical Science and Technology-Musculoskeletal System.

US/0271-4817
**JOURNAL OF CLINICAL CHIROPRACTIC.** [J. clin. chiropr.]. **VFOAT** JCC. V. 3-. Periodical. English. $17.95. JCC Publishing Company, 259 Robby Lane, New Hyde Park NY 11040. **NLM** W1 JO587C. ***Continues*** *J.C.C. Journal of Clinical Chiropractic, 0097-4706.*

US/0894-1130
**JOURNAL OF HAND THERAPY.** (JOURNAL OF HAND THERAPY : OFFICIAL JOURNAL OF THE AMERICAN SOCIETY OF HAND THERAPISTS.). [J. hand ther.]. **Added/Corp** American Society of Hand Therapists. Vol. 1, No. 1 (Oct./Dec. 1987)-. Periodical. English. qt. $52.00 (US & possessions), $62.00 (other) individual; $62.00 (US & possessions), $72.00 (other) institution. Hanley & Belfus Inc., 210 South 13th Street, Philadelphia PA 19107. **Tel** (215)546-7293, FAX (215)790-9330. **ED** Evelyn Macken. **DD** 617. **NLM** W1; JO669RH. **[CCC]. Bk Rev. Ad Acc. Pr Rev. Circ:** 3,000.
**Desc:** A peer-reviewed journal focused on rehabilitation therapy of hand problems. Official publication of American Society of Hand Therapists.

US/0885-9701
**JOURNAL OF HEAD TRAUMA REHABILITATION, THE.** [J. head trauma rehabil.]. **VFOAT** JHTR; Head Trauma Rehabilitation. Vol. 1, No. 1 (March 1986)-. Periodical. English. bm (6 issues). $99.00 US. Aspen Publishers Inc., 7201 McKinney Circle, Frederick MD 21701. **Tel** (800)234-1660, (301)698-7100, FAX (301)251-5784, telex 5106014543. **(Subscription address:** Aspen Publishers Inc., PO Box 990, Frederick MD 21701.**) ED** Mitchell Rosenthal, PhD and Nathaniel H. Mayer, MD. **DD** 616. **NLM** W1; JO669RU. **[CCC]. Bk Rev. Pr Rev. Circ:** 4,700. available on microfilm and microfiche from University Microfilms International (UMI).
**Desc:** Provides information on clinical management and rehabilitation of persons with head injuries for the practicing professional. Topical in format, each issue offers timely information on a specific topic of importance to rehabilitation professionals.
**Ind/Abst** Cumul. Index Nurs. Allied Health Lit.; EMBASE; Except. Child Educ. Resour.; Psychol. Abstr. (1986-); PsycINFO; PsycLit.

US/0161-4754
**JOURNAL OF MANIPULATIVE AND PHYSIOLOGICAL THERAPEUTICS.** [J. manip. physiol. ther.]. **Added/Corp** National College of Chiropractic. **VFOAT** Manipulative and Physiological Therapeutics; JMPT. Vol. 1 (March 1978)-. Periodical. English. Nine times a year. $82.00 (individual), $110.00 (institution) US; $112.00 (individual), $140.00 (institutionsa) other. Williams & Wilkins Company, 428 East Preston Street, Baltimore MD 21202-3993. **Tel** (410)528-4000, (800)638-6423, FAX (410)528-8596, telex 87669. **(Subscription address:** Williams & Wilkins, PO Box 64380, Baltimore MD 21264.**) LC** RM724; .J68. **DD** 615/.534/05. **NLM** W1 JO748F. **[CCC]. Ad Acc. Pr Rev.** Documents available from The Genuine Article, Quick Copies.
**Desc:** Original scientific and clinical articles relating to chiropractic medicine; i.e., the diagnosis and treatment of human ailments by manipulation, physiological therapeutics and other conservative methods on a primary-care-physician basis.
**Ind/Abst** Curr. Contents Clin. Med.; EMBASE; Index Med.; Res. Alert [Select. Cov.]; SCISEARCH; Soc. Sci. Cit. Index [Select. Cov.].

II/0022-4162
**JOURNAL OF REHABILITATION IN ASIA, THE.** ***Ceased.*** [J. rehabil. Asia]. **VFOAT** Rehabilitation in Asia. Vol. 1 (1959)-(1989). Periodical. English. Three times a year. Indian Society of Rehabilitation Handicapped, c/o P C Hansotia Company, Simg Road, Bombay 400032 India. **ED** W G Rama Rao. **LC** RM930.A1. **NLM** W1 JO867. **Bk Rev. Ad Acc.**
**Desc:** Concerns rehabilitation and the handicapped.
**Ind/Abst** EMBASE.

US/0748-7711
**JOURNAL OF REHABILITATION RESEARCH AND DEVELOPMENT.** (JOURNAL OF REHABILITATION RESEARCH AND DEVELOPMENT / VETERANS ADMINISTRATION, DEPARTMENT OF MEDICINE AND SURGERY, REHABILITATION R & D SERVICE.). [J. rehabil. res. dev.]. **Added/Corp** United States. Veterans Administration. Rehabilitation R & D Service. United States. Veterans Health Services and Research Administration. Rehabilitation Research and Development Service. United States. Veterans Health Administration. Rehabilitation Research and Development Service. Vol. 21, No. 1 (May 1984)-. Periodical. English. Four times a year (Jan., Apr., July, Oct.). VA Prosthetics R & D Center, 103 South Gay Street, Office of Technology Transfer, Baltimore MD 21202. **Tel** (410)962-1800. **LC** RD130; .B8. **DD** 617/.58. **NLM** W1; JO867RA. **CODEN** JRRDDB. available on microfilm and microfiche from University Microfilms International (UMI). Documents available from Article Express International, The Genuine Article, BIOSIS Document Express, UMI Article Clearinghouse. ***Continues*** *Journal of Rehabilitation R & D, 0742-3241.*
**Ind/Abst** Acad. Search (Jan. 1993-); Bioeng. Abstr.; Biol. Abstr.; Curr. Contents Clin. Med.; Curr. Contents Soc. Behav. Sci.; Ei Page One; EMBASE; Eng. Index Annu.; Highw. Res. Abstr.; Mag. Search; Newsp. Period. Abstr. (1991-); Res. Alert [Full Cov.]; Soc. Sci. Cit. Index [Full Cov.]; SPORT Discus.

US/1052-2263
**JOURNAL OF VOCATIONAL REHABILITATION.** [J. vocat. rehabil.]. **VFOAT** Vocational Rehabilitation. Vol. 1, No. 1 (Jan. 1991)-. Periodical. English. qt. $95.00 (institution), $60.00 (individual) US and Canada; $110.00 (institution), $75.00 (individual) other. Andover Medical Publishers Inc., A Subsidiary of Butterworth-Heinemann, 80 Montvale Avenue, Stoneham MA 02180. **Tel** (800)366-2665, (617)438-8464, FAX (617)279-4851. **DD** 362. **NLM** W1; JO971L. **[CCC].**
**Ind/Abst** Except. Child Educ. Resour.

US/0899-1855
**JOURNAL, PHYSICAL THERAPY EDUCATION.** [J. phys. ther. educ.]. **Added/Corp** American Physical Therapy Association (1921- ). Section

for Education. **VFOAT** Journal of Physical Therapy Education. Vol. 1, No. 1 (Winter 1987)-. Periodical. English. sa (2 issues). $30.00 (institution), $15.00 (individual). American Physical Therapy Association, 1111 North Fairfax Street, Suite 200, Alexandria VA 22314-1488. **Tel** (703)684-2782, FAX (703)684-7343. **(Subscription address:** Section for Education, PO Box 327, c/o Sharon Craven, Alexandria VA 22313.**)** **DD** 615. **NLM** W1; JO836PE.
**Ind/Abst** Cumul. Index Nurs. Allied Health Lit.

FR/0023-1576
**KINESITHERAPIE SCIENTIFIQUE.** [Kinesither. sci.]. **Added/Corp** Federation Francaise des Masseurs Kinesitherapeutes Reeducateurs. Confederation Europeenne pour la Therapie Physique. Federation Europeenne des Kinesitherapeutes, Praticiens en Physiotherapie. (1965)-. Periodical. French. Eleven times a year. 607.25F France; 630.00F other. Spek, 24 rue des Petits Hotels, 75010 Paris France. **Tel** 011 33 1 42468007. **NLM** W1 KI648S. **CODEN** KNTSAC. **[CCC].** Documents available from BIOSIS Document Express.
**Ind/Abst** Biol. Abstr.

GW/0023-4494
**KRANKENGYMNASTIK.** [Krankengymnastik]. **Added/Corp** Zentralverband Krankengymnastik. Vol. 1 (1949)-. Academic Scholarly Publication. German. mo. DM144.00 Germany; DM168.00 other. Richard Pflaum Verlag Gmbh, Postfach 190737, D 80607 Munich Germany. **Tel** 011 49 89 126070, FAX 011 49 89 12607200, telex 5216075. **NLM** W1 KR241. **[CCC].**
**Ind/Abst** EMBASE.

RU
**KURORTOLOGIIA I FIZIOTERAPIIA.** Vol. 10 (1977)-. Monographic series. Russian. qt. Price varies per volume. **NLM** W1 KU708S. ***Continues*** *Fizicheskie I Kurortnye Faktory I Ikh Lechebnoe Primenenie.*

FR
**LOISIRS SANTE.** **Added/Corp** Federation francaise d'education physique et de gymnastique volontaire. **VFOAT** Sante Loisirs. No. 1 (Sept. 1982)-. Periodical. French. Five times a year. 64.00F France; 130.00F other. FFEPGV, 41-43 rue de Reuilly, 75012 Paris France. **Tel** 011 33 1 43418610, FAX 011 33 1 43403435. ***Continues*** *Gymnastique Volontaire.*
**Ind/Abst** SportSearch (May 1987-).

SP/0214-8714
**MEDICINA DE REHABILITACION.** ***Suspended.*** [Med. rehabil.]. (1988)-(1993). Periodical. Spanish. qt. Editores Medicos SA, Calle Gabriela Mistral 2, 28035 Madrid Spain. **Tel** 011 34 1 3860033, 34 1 3860366, FAX 34 1 3739907. **ED** A. Orolina Monno. **UDC** 615. Index available. **Bk Rev. Ad Acc. Pr Rev.** ctrl circ.

US/0738-128X
**MONOGRAPH / [WORLD REHABILITATION FUND].** [Monogr. - World Rehabil. Fund]. **Added/Corp** World Rehabilitation Fund. National Institute of Handicapped Research (U.S.). No. 1, (1979)-. Monographic series. English. ir. Price varies per volume. World Rehabilitation Fund Inc, 400 East 34th Street, New York NY 10016. **ED** Diane E Woods. **LC** UNC. **NLM** W1 MO5559. **Circ:** 4,000 (ctrl).
**Desc:** International rehabilitation.

●US
**NATIONAL DIRECTORY OF CHIROPRACTIC, THE.** **See** Medical Science and Technology-Musculoskeletal System.

NE
**NEDERLANDS TIJDSCHRIFT VOOR FYSIOTHERAPIE.** Dutch. mo. Ned Genootschap Fysiotherapy, PO Box 248, 3800 AE Amersfoort Netherlands. **Tel** 011 31 033 622400.

GW/0933-2715
**NEUROLINGUISTIK : ZEITSCHRIFT FUER APHASIEFORSCHUNG UND -THERAPIE.** (1987)-. Periodical. German (summaries and/or abstracts in English). sa (Mar. & Sept.). DM80.00. Hochschulverlag GmbH, Postfach 5426, D-79021 Freiburg Germany. **Tel** 011 49 761 26255. **NLM** W1; NE328KE.
**Ind/Abst** MLA Int. Bibl. Books Artic. Mod. Lang. Lit.

NZ/0303-7193
**NEW ZEALAND JOURNAL OF PHYSIOTHERAPY.** [N. Z. j. physiother.]. **Added/Corp** New Zealand Society of Physiotherapists. Vol. 1, (Sept. 1938)-. Periodical. English. Three times a year (Apr., Aug., Dec.). 45.00NZ$ (except New Zealand); 50.00NZ$ (New Zealand); 59.00NZ$ (US); 53.00NZ$ (Australia); 64.00NZ$ (other). New Zealand Society of Physiotherapists, Level 3 Wang House, 195-201 Willis Street, PO Box 27 386, Wellington. New Zealand. **Tel** 04 801 6500, FAX 04 801 5571. **ED** Bryan Paynter. **NLM** W1 NE9732E. Index available. **Bk Rev. Ad Acc. Circ:** 1,500 (ctrl).
**Desc:** Professional material pertaining to physiotherapy.
**Ind/Abst** Cumul. Index Nurs. Allied Health Lit.

US/0279-5507
**NRA NEWSLETTER (ALEXANDRIA, VA.).** ***Title Change.*** (NRA NEWSLETTER / NATIONAL REHABILITATION ASSOCIATION.). **Added/Corp** National Rehabilitation Association. **VAT** National Rehabilitation Association Newsletter. (19??)-(198?). Newsletter. English. bm. National Rehabilitation Association, 633 South Washington Street, Alexandria VA 22314. **Tel** (703)836-0850, , FAX (703)836-0850. **NLM** W1 N255. ***Continues*** *News Letter / National Rehabilitation Association.* ***Continued by*** *National Rehabilitation Association Newsletter.*

●UK/0966-7903
**OCCUPATIONAL THERAPY INTERNATIONAL.** (1993)-. English. qt. £40.00 (individual), £80.00 (institution). Whurr Publishers Ltd, 19B Compton Terrace, London N1 2UN England. **Tel** 011 44 71 359 5979, FAX 011 44 71 226 5290. **(Subscription address:** Turpin Distribution Services Limited, Blackhorse Road, Letchworth, Hertfordshire SG6 1HN, United Kingdom.**)** **ED** Frank Stein. **Ad Acc.** Full Page (B&W) £250.00. Half Page (B&W) £150.00. **Pr Rev. Acid Free.**
**Desc:** In response to the increasingly prominent role of rehabilitation and occupational therapy in health care. Publishes papers on clinical research, current practices, technology, professional issues, education, trends in health care, industrial health and other areas of interest to the growing number of occupational therapists throughout the world.

●US/1059-1516
**ORTHOPAEDIC PHYSICAL THERAPY CLINICS OF NORTH AMERICA.** (1992)-. Periodical. English. qt. $55.00 (individual), $73.00 (institution) US; $70.00 (individual), $88.00 (institution) other. W.B. Saunders Company, A Subsidiary of Harcourt Brace Jovanovich, Inc., The Curtis Center/Suite 300, Independence Square West, Philadelphia PA 19106-3399. **Tel** (215)238-7800 or, 5587, FAX (215)238-7883, telex 173146. **(Subscription address:** W. B. Saunders Company / North America Subscriptions, c/o Periodicals, 6277 Sea Harbour Drive, 4th Floor, Orlando FL 32887.**)** **NLM** W1; OR796N.
**Ind/Abst** Physic. Medline Plus.

US/0898-5669
**PEDIATRIC PHYSICAL THERAPY.** **See** Medical Science and Technology-Pediatrics.

US/0270-3181
**PHYSICAL & OCCUPATIONAL THERAPY IN GERIATRICS.** [Phys. occup. ther. geriatr.]. **VAT** Physical and Occupational Therapy in Geriatrics. Vol. 1, No. 1 (Fall 1980)-. Periodical. English. qt. $180.00 US; $252.00 other. The Haworth Press Inc, 10 Alice Street, Binghamton NY 13904-1580. **Tel** (607)722-5857, (800)3-HAWORTH, FAX (607)722-1424. **ED** Ellen Taira (editor's address: POB 182, Roosevelt Island, New York, NY 10044). **LC** RC952.A1; P48. **DD** 615.8/2. **NLM** W1 PH683M. **Bk Rev. Ad Acc. Pr Rev. Acid Free. Circ:** 523. available on microfilm and microfiche from University Microfilms International (UMI). Documents available from Haworth Document Delivery Service.
**Desc:** The forum for allied health professionals to share information, clinical experience, research and therapeutic practice in geriatrics, current practice and emerging issues in the health care of the older client.
**Ind/Abst** Abstr. Soc. Gerontol.; Abstr. Res. Pastor. Care Couns. (19??-); Commun. Abstr. (?-?); Cumul. Index Nurs. Allied Health Lit.; EMBASE; Index Period. Lit. Aging; Int. Nurs. Index; Pollut. Abstr. Indexes; Psychol. Abstr. (1982-); PsycINFO; PsycLit; Soc. Work Abstr. [Select. Cov.].

US/0194-2638
**PHYSICAL & OCCUPATIONAL THERAPY IN PEDIATRICS.** [Phys. occup. ther. pediatr.]. **VFOAT** Physical and Occupational Therapy in Pediatrics. **VAT** Physical and Occupational Therapy in Pediatrics. Vol. 1, No. 1 (Fall 1980)-. Periodical. English. qt. $200.00 US; $280.00 other. The Haworth Press Inc, 10 Alice Street, Binghamton NY 13904-1580. **Tel** (607)722-5857, (800)3-HAWORTH, FAX (607)722-1424. **ED** Suzann K. Campbell (editor's address: 151 Le Moyne Parkway, Oak Park, IL 60302-1158). **LC** RJ53.P5; P49. **DD** 615.8/2. **NLM** W1 PH683P. **CODEN** POTPDY. **Bk Rev. Ad Acc. Pr Rev. Acid Free. Circ:** 1,345. available on microfilm and microfiche from University Microfilms International (UMI). Documents available from BIOSIS Document Express, Haworth Document Delivery Service.
**Desc:** Designed for physical therapy and occupational therapy pediatric professionals in hospitals, rehabilitation centers, schools, communities, and health and human service agencies. Provides the latest clinical research and practical applications.
**Ind/Abst** Biol. Abstr.; Cumul. Index Nurs. Allied Health Lit.; EMBASE; Except. Child Educ. Resour.; Psychol. Abstr. (1980-); PsycINFO; PsycLit; Soc. Work Abstr. [Select. Cov.].

US/1047-9651
**PHYSICAL MEDICINE AND REHABILITATION CLINICS OF NORTH AMERICA.** **See** Physically Impaired.

US/0031-9023
**PHYSICAL THERAPY.** [Phys. ther.]. **Added/Corp** American Physical Therapy Association (1921- ). Vol. 44 (Jan. 1964)-. Academic Scholarly Publication. English. mo. $95.00 (institution), $70.00 (individual) US; $120.00 (institution), $90.00 (individual) other. American Physical Therapy Association, 1111 North Fairfax Street, Suite 200, Alexandria VA 22314-1488. **Tel** (703)684-2782, FAX (703)684-7343. **ED** Jules Rothstein. **LC** RM695; .A53. **DD** 615/.82/05. **NLM** W1 PH749J. **CODEN** PTHEA. Index available (bound in Dec. issue). cum. index. **Bk Rev. Ad Acc. Pr Rev. Circ:** 53,200 (ctrl). available on microfilm and microfiche from University Microfilms International (UMI); available on an online database (file 149/Full-Text) from DIALOG. Documents available from The Genuine Article. ***Continues*** *American Physical Therapy Association (Founded 1921). Journal.*
**Desc:** The official journal of the American Physical Therapy Association. Includes scientific and professional articles on clinical and testing procedures, basic science, philosophy, and history of P.T., as well as book reviews, abstracts, continuing education and classified advertising.
**Ind/Abst** Abr. Index Med.; Cumul. Index Nurs. Allied Health Lit.; Curr. Contents Clin. Med.; Dev. Med. Child Neurol.; EMBASE; Except. Child Educ. Resour.; Health Devices Alerts; Health Index (1989-); Health Period. Database [Full Txt.]; Index Med.; Life Sci. Collect.; Phys. Educ. Index; Physic. Medline Plus; Res. Alert [Full Cov.]; Sci. Cit. Index; SCISEARCH; Soc. Sci. Cit. Index [Select. Cov.]; SPORT Discus; SportSearch.

●US/1075-4342
**PHYSICAL THERAPY FORUM (KING OF PRUSSIA, PA. 1994).** (PHYSICAL THERAPY FORUM.). [Phys. ther. forum]. (1994)-. Periodical. English. bw. Free on request to licensed physical therapists. Physical Therapy Forum Inc., 251 West DeKalb Pike / Suite A-115, King of Prussia PA 19406. **Tel** (215)337-0381. **DD** 615. ctrl circ. ***Formed by the union of*** *Physical Therapy Forum (Middle Atlantic Ed.), 8750-2119* ***and*** *Physical Therapy Forum (Northeast Ed.), 8750-0968 Physical Therapy Forum (Western Ed.), 1064-6590 Physical Therapy Forum (Midwest/Southern Ed.), 1064-6582.*

US/8750-2119
**PHYSICAL THERAPY FORUM (MIDDLE ATLANTIC ED.).** ***Title Change.*** (PHYSICAL THERAPY FORUM.). [Phys. ther. forum]. **Added/Corp** Physical Therapy Forum, Inc. (198?)-(1994). Periodical. English. wk. Physical Therapy Forum Inc., 251 West DeKalb Pike / Suite A-115, King of Prussia PA 19406. **Tel** (215)337-0381. **DD** 615. ***Merged with*** *Physical Therapy Forum (Northeast Ed.), 8756-0968; Physical Therapy Forum (Midwest/Southern Ed.), 1064-6582; Physical Therapy Forum (Western Ed.), 1064-6590* ***to form*** *Physical Therapy Forum (King of Prussia, Pa. : 1994), 1075-4342.*

US/1054-8513
**PHYSICAL THERAPY PRACTICE.** ***Ceased.*** [Phys. ther. pract.]. **VFOAT** PTP. Vol. 1, No. 1 (Winter 1992)-Vol. 3 (1994). Periodical. English. qt. Andover Medical Publishers Inc., A Subsidiary of Butterworth-Heinemann, 80 Montvale Avenue, Stoneham MA 02180. **Tel** (800)366-2665, (617)438-8464, FAX (617)279-4851. **DD** 615. **NLM** W1; PH749JH. **[CCC].**

●US/1073-9483
**PHYSICAL THERAPY REIMBURSEMENT NEWS.** (1993)-. English. bm (6 issues). $110.00 US. American Physical Therapy Association, 1111 North Fairfax Street, Suite 200, Alexandria VA 22314-1488. **Tel** (703)684-2782, FAX (703)684-7343.

US/1042-2579
**PHYSICAL THERAPY TODAY.** (PHYSICAL THERAPY TODAY : OFFICIAL PUBLICATION OF THE PRIVATE PRACTIVE SECTION, AMERICAN PHYSICAL THERAPY ASSOCIATION.). [Phys. ther. today]. **Added/Corp** American Physical Therapy Association. Private Practice Section. (1988)-. Periodical. English. qt (4 issues). $80.00 (institution), $60.00 (individual) US. American Physical Therapy Association, 1111 North Fairfax Street, Suite 200, Alexandria VA 22314-1488. **Tel** (703)684-2782, FAX (703)684-7343. **DD** 615. **[CCC].** ***Continues*** *Whirlpool.*
**Desc:** Addresses the day-to-day business as well as clinical concerns of private practice physical therapists.

GW/0940-6689
**PHYSIKALISCHE MEDIZIN.** **Added/Corp** Deutsche Gesellschaft fuer Physikalische Medizin und Rehabilitation. (199?)-. Periodical. German. bm. $103.00. Georg Thieme Verlag Stuttgart, Postfach 301120, D 70451 Stuttgart Germany. **Tel** 011 49 711 89310, FAX 011 49 711 8931298, telex 7 252 275 GTVD. **(Subscription address:** Thieme Medical Publishers Inc., 381 Park Avenue South, New York NY 10016.**)** **CODEN** PMRKEU. ***Formed by the union of*** *Zeitschrift fuer Physiotherapie* ***and*** *Zeitschrift fuer Physikalische Medizin, Balneologie, Med. Klimatologie, 0720-9762.*
**Ind/Abst** EMBASE.

CN/0708-1006
**PHYSIOQUEBEC.** Vol. 1 (Sept. 1975)-. Periodical. English (French). Free to members. Professional Corporation of Physiotherapists of Quebec, #816, 1440 West St. Catherine Street, Montreal Quebec H3G 1R8 Canada. **DD** 615/.8/05.

UK/0031-9406
**PHYSIOTHERAPY.** [Physiotherapy]. **Added/Corp** Chartered Society of Physiotherapy (Great Britain). Vol. 34 (Jan. 1948)-. Academic Scholarly Publication. English. mo. £50.00. Chartered Society of Physiotherapy, 14 Bedford Row, London WC1R 4ED England. **Tel** 011 44 71 242 1941, FAX 011 44 71 831 4509. **NLM** W1 PH966. Index available. **Bk Rev. Ad Acc. Pr Rev. Circ:** 30,000 (ctrl). available on microfilm and microfiche from University Microfilms International (UMI). ***Continues*** *Journal of the Chartered Society of Physiotherapy.*
**Ind/Abst** Cumul. Index Nurs. Allied Health Lit.; Dev. Med. Child Neurol.; EMBASE; Health Serv. Abstr.; SportSearch.

UK/0950-6659
**PHYSIOTHERAPY INDEX : CURRENT AWARENESS TOPICS SERVICES.** **Added/Corp** British Library. Medical Information Service. **VFOAT** Current Awareness Topics Services. Vol. 1, (1986)-. Periodical. English. Twelve times a year. £50.00 UK & ECC; £65.00 other. British Library / Publications Sale Unit, Boston Spa, Wetherby, West Yorkshire LS23 7BQ England. **Tel** 011 44 937 546546 546543, FAX 011 44 937 546333, telex 557381. **NLM** ZWB 460; P578. **Pr Rev.**

UK/0959-3985
**PHYSIOTHERAPY THEORY AND PRACTICE.** [Physiother. theory pract.]. Vol. 6, No. 1 (March 1990)-. Periodical. English. qt. $160.00 US; £87.00 Europe; £92.00 other. Lawrence Erlbaum Associates Ltd., 27 Palmeira Mansions, Church Road, Hove East Sussex BN3 2FA England. **Tel** 011 44 273 207411. **(Subscription address:** Turpin Distribution Services Limited, Blackhorse Road Letchworth, Hertfordshire SG6 1HN, United Kingdom.**) ED** Hilary Baddeley. **NLM** W1; PH969. **CODEN** PTHPEA. **Pr Rev.** Documents available from BIOSIS Document Express. ***Continues*** *Physiotherapy Practice, 0266-6154.*
**Desc:** Aims to provide a peer-reviewed forum for recent developments and research in all aspects of physiotherapy/physical therapy.
**Ind/Abst** Biol. Abstr. (1991-); EMBASE.

PL/0860-6161
**POSTEPY REHABILITACJI / AKADEMIA WYCHOWANIA FIZYCZNEGO.** **Added/Corp** Akademia Wychowania Fizycznego m. gen. Karola Swierczewskiego w Warszawie. (198?)-. Periodical. Polish (summaries and/or abstracts in English and Russian; table of contents in English and Russian). qt. **NLM** W1; PO944.
**Ind/Abst** SPORT Discus.

US/0162-3907
**PROGRESS REPORT - AMERICAN PHYSICAL THERAPY ASSOCIATION.** ***Title Change.*** **Main/Corp** American Physical Therapy Association (1921- ). (19??)-(19??). Periodical. English. mo (except combined July/Aug. issue). American Physical Therapy Association, 1111 North Fairfax Street, Suite 200, Alexandria VA 22314-1488. **Tel** (703)684-2782, FAX (703)684-7343. **ED** Tommye Morton. **Ad Acc. Circ:** 48,700 (ctrl). ***Merged into*** *PT: Magazine of the American Physical Therapy Association.*
**Desc:** A newsletter on APTA activities, physical therapy practice, and legislative updates and coming events.

●US/1065-5077
**PT (ALEXANDRIA, VA.).** (PT : MAGAZINE OF PHYSICAL THERAPY.). [PT]. **Added/Corp** American Physical Therapy Association (1921- ). **VFOAT** PT Magazine. **VAT** Physical Therapy. Vol 1, No. 1 (Jan. 1993)-. Periodical. English. mo. $80.00 (institutions), $60.00 (individuals) US; $95.00 (institutions), $75.00 (individuals) other. American Physical Therapy Association, 1111 North Fairfax Street Suite 200, Alexandria VA 22314-1488. **Tel** (703)684-2782, FAX (703)684-7343. **DD** 615. **NLM** W1; PT72. ***Continues*** *Clinical Management: The Magazine of the American Physical Therapy Association, 0276-8038* ***and*** *Progress Report - American Physical Therapy Association.*

CN/0227-7611
**RAPPORT ANNUEL / LA CORPORATION PROFESSIONNELLE DES PHYSIOTHERAPEUTES DU QUEBEC.** [Rapp. annu. - Corp. prof. physiother. Que.]. **Main/Corp** Corporation Professionnelle des Physiotherapeutes du Quebec. French. an. Corporation Professionnelle des Physiotherapeutes du Quebec, 1440 Ouest rue Ste-Catherine/Bureau 816, Montreal Quebec H3G 1R8 Canada. **LC** RM695; .C65A. **DD** 615.8/2/060714.

US/0899-6237
**REHAB MANAGEMENT.** [Rehab manage.]. Vol. 1, No. 1 (Nov./Dec. 1988)-. Periodical. English. Six times a year. Free. Curant Communications, 4676 Admiralty Way, Suite 202, Marina Del Ray CA 90292. **Tel** (310)479-1769. **ED** Tony Ramos. **DD** 615. **NLM** W1; RE173JU. **Ad Acc. Circ:** 20,000.
**Desc:** A combination of clinical and business/management articles for physical therapists, directors of rehabilitation hospitals and occupational therapists.

SP/0048-7120
**REHABILITACION (MADRID).** (REHABILITACION.). [Rehabilitacion]. **Added/Corp** Sociedad Espanola de Rehabilitacion. Vol. 1 (1967)-. Academic Scholarly Publication. Spanish. Six times a year. 58ptas Spain; $87.00 Europe; $99.00 other. Sociedad Espanola de Rehabilitacion, Villanueva 11, 28001 Madrid Spain. **(Subscription address:** Editorial Garsi, C Juan Bravo, 28006 Madrid Spain.**) NLM** W1 RE173LK. **Pr Rev.**
**Ind/Abst** EMBASE; Indice Med. Esp.

UK/0955-0984
**REHABILITATION INDEX / THE BRITISH LIBRARY, MEDICAL INFORMATION SERVICE.** **Added/Corp** British Library. Medical Information Service. (198?)-. Periodical. English. Twelve times a year. £50.00 UK & ECC; £65.00 other. British Library / Publications Sale Unit, Boston Spa, Wetherby, West Yorkshire LS23 7BQ England. **Tel** 011 44 937 546546 546543, FAX 011 44 937 546333, telex 557381. **(Subscription address:** Medical Information Service, Bldsc Boston Spa West Yorkshire, Wetherby LS23 7BQ United Kingdom.**) NLM** ZW 1; R3445. Index available. cum. index. **Pr Rev.** available on an online database from DATA-STAR.
**Desc:** Monthly bibliography of articles in rehabilitation medicine.

●US/1070-5767
**REHABILITATION NURSING RESEARCH.** **See** Medical Science and Technology-Nursing.

US/0090-5550
**REHABILITATION PSYCHOLOGY.** **See** Psychology.

US/0882-7753
**REHABILITATION R&D PROGRESS REPORTS.** (REHABILITATION R & D PROGRESS REPORTS / VETERANS ADMINISTRATION, DEPARTMENT OF MEDICINE AND SURGERY.). [Rehabil. R D prog. rep.]. **Added/Corp** United States. Veterans Administration. Rehabilitation R & D Service. United States. Veterans Administration. Rehabilitation R & D Service. Office of Technology Transfer. United States. Veterans Health Services and Research Administration. Rehabilitation Research and Development Service. Office of Technology Transfer. United States. Veterans Health Services and Research Administration. Scientific and Technical Publications Section. **VFOAT** Rehabilitation R and D Progress Reports; R&D Progress Reports; Progress Reports. **VAT** Rehabilitation Research and Development Progress Reports. (1983)-. English. an. Free on request. VA Prosthetics R & D Center, 103 South Gay Street, Office of Technology Transfer, Baltimore MD 21202. **Tel** (410)962-1800. **LC** UB363; .R44. **DD** 355.1/156/072073. **NLM** WB 22.1; R345. **CODEN** RRPREU.

US/0096-1531
**RESEARCH DIRECTORY OF THE REHABILITATION RESEARCH AND TRAINING CENTERS.** (RESEARCH DIRECTORY OF THE REHABILITATION RESEARCH AND TRAINING CENTERS / REHABILITATION SERVICES ADMINISTRATION, OFFICE OF THE ASSISTANT SECRETARY FOR HUMAN DEVELOPMENT SERVICES.). **Added/Corp** United States. Rehabilitation Services Administration. Arkansas Rehabilitation Research and Training Center. Information Exchage Program. Arkansas. Division of Rehabilitation Services. George Washington University. Medical Center. Science Communication Division. George Washington University. Medical Center. Rehabilitation Research and Training Center. United States. Social and Rehabilitation Service. National Institute of Handicapped Research (U.S.). (1968/1969)-. English. an. National Institute of Handicapped Research, Department of Education, 330 C Street SW, Washington DC 20202. **LC** RM930.5.U6; R47. **DD** 362.1/786/072073. **NLM** HD 7256.U5 R432.

CN/1192-0238
**REVUE QUEBECOISE D'ERGOTHERAPIE.** [Rev. que. ergother.]. (1992)-. Periodical. French. qt (Mar., June, Spet., Dec.). 40.00Can$ (individuals) Canada; 55.00Can$ (individuals) other. Corporation Professionnelle des Ergotherapeutes, 1259 Rue Berri Bureau 710, Montreal Quebec H2L 4C7 Canada. **Tel** (514)844-5778, FAX (514)844-7462. **DD** 615.85150971405. **Pr Rev. Circ:** 2,300. ***Continues*** *Transfert (Montreal. 1979), 0713-4355.*

IT
**RIABILITAZIONE, LA.** Italian. qt. $91.00. Masson SA, Avenue Beauregard 12, CH-1701 Fribourg Switzerland. **Tel** 011 41 37 249585, FAX 011 41 37 247559, telex 942658 SEMI CH.
**Ind/Abst** EMBASE.

IT/0393-7518
**RIABILITAZIONE E APPRENDIMENTO.** [Riabil. apprendimento]. (1980)-. Periodical. Multiple languages. Four times a year. L90000.00. Liviana Medicina SRL, Via A de Gasperi 55, 80133 Naples Italy. **Tel** 011 39 81 5524733, FAX 011 39 81 5518295. **UDC** 376. **Bk Rev**, (Qty: 20). **Ad Acc. Circ:** 3,000 (ctrl).

IT
**RIABILITAZIONE OGGI.** (19??)-. Italian. mo. Free on request. Editrice Spec Riabilitazione, Via Saint Denis 100, 20099 Sestos S Giovanni Italy. **Tel** 011 39 2 2423066.

US/8756-0364
**STROKING TIMES, THE.** [Stroking times]. **Added/Corp** Stroking Community. Naturist Society. Massage Special Interest Group. (19??)-. Periodical. English. mo. $8.00. The Stroking Times, PO Box 12980, Philadelphia PA 19108-0980. **Tel** (215)543-9080. **ED** David Linton. **DD** 615. **Bk Rev. Circ:** 500.
**Desc:** Newsletter about massage and other hands-on healing, articles, news, reviews, and opinion plus a calendar of learning opportunities nationwide for "people who knead people".

US/1053-5926
**TEAMREHAB REPORT.** [TeamRehab rep.]. **VFOAT** Team Rehab Report. (1990)-. Periodical. English. Six times a year. $24.00 (one year), $60.00 (three year). Miramar Publishing Company, 6133 Bristol Parkway, PO Box 3640, Culver City CA 90231. **Tel** (800)543-4116, (310)337-9717. **LC** HD9995.P54; T43. **DD** 338.4/7681761. **NLM** W1; TE129T.
**Desc:** Targets rehabilitation professionals, and provides them with information on new equipment and technologies, as well as therapy techniques.

●US/1074-9357
**TOPICS IN STROKE REHABILITATION.** (1994)-. Periodical. English. qt. $68.00. Aspen Publishers Inc., 7201 McKinney Circle, Frederick MD 21701. **Tel** (800)234-1660, (301)698-7100, FAX (301)251-5784, telex 5106014543. **(Subscription address:** Aspen Publishers Inc., PO Box 990, Frederick MD 21701.**)**

US/0364-1953
**UPPER CERVICAL MONOGRAPH, THE.** V. 1- Mar. 1973-. Periodical. English. qt. NUCCA Monograph Editor, 221 West Second Street, Monroe MI 48161. **NLM** W1 UP65.

GW/0003-9357
**ZEITSCHRIFT FUER PHYSIOTHERAPIE.** ***Title Change.*** **Added/Corp** Gesellschaft fuer Physiotherapie der D D R. (Jan./Feb. 1971)-(19??). Academic Scholarly Publication. German. bm. VCH Publishers Inc, 220 East 23rd Street, New York NY 10010. **Tel** (212)683-8333, , FAX (212)481-0897. **(Subscription address:** 303 NW 12th Avenue, Deerfield Beach FL 33442; telephone: (305)428-5566**) NLM** W1 ZE54. **CODEN** ZPYTAF. ***Continues*** *Archiv fur Physikalische Therapie, Balneologie und Klimatologie.* ***Merged with*** *Zeitschrift feur Physikalishe Medizin, Balneologie, Med. Klimatologie, 0720-9762* ***to form*** *Physikalische Medizin, Rehabilitationsmedizin, Kurortmedizin.*
**Ind/Abst** EMBASE; SportSearch.

CC/0254-1408
**ZHONGHUA LILIAO ZAZHI.** (CHUNG-HUA LI LIAO TSA CHIH.). [Zhonghua liliao zazhi]. **Added/Corp** An-shan Shih Tang-kang-tzu li Liao I Yuan. Chung-hua I Hsueh Hui. **VFOAT** Zhonghua Liliao Zazhi; Chinese Journal of Physical Therapy. (Aug. 1978)-. Periodical. Chinese (table of contents in English). qt. $3.00. Chinese Society of Medical Sciences / Zhonghua Yixuehui, Tang Gang Zi, Anshan, Liaoning 114048, People's Republic of China. **LC** RM695; .C585. **DD** 615.8/2/05. **NLM** W1 CH982KH. **Bk Rev. Ad Acc. Circ:** 17,097.
**Desc:** Contains original articles, clinicopathologica conferences, basic sciences, lecturers and reviews, short reports, case reports, questions and answers, etc.

## PHYSICALLY IMPAIRED

US/0095-3474
**A.C.A. INDUSTRY GUIDE TO HEARING AIDS. INTERNATIONAL EDITION.** (A.C.A. INDUSTRY GUIDE TO HEARING AIDS.). **Main/Corp** Acoustic Corporation of America. **VFOAT** Industry Guide to Hearing Aids. 1973/75-. English. an. Acoustic Corporation of America, 145 Tremont Street, Boston MA 02111. **LC** RF310; .A27A. **DD** 617.8/9.

CN/1183-3149
**ACCESS (GLOUCESTER).** (ACCESS / ACTIVE LIVING ALLIANCE FOR CANADIANS WITH A DISABILITY.). [Access]. **Added/Corp** Active Living Alliance for Canadians with a Disability. **VFOAT** Acces. Vol. 1, No. 1 (Winter 1991)-. Periodical. English (French). Three times a year. Free, Comes with Active Living Alliance for Canadians with a Disability membership. Active Living Alliance for Canadians with a Disability, 1600 James Naismith Drive, Suite 312, Gloucester Ontario K1B 5N4 Canada. **Tel** (613)748-5772. **DD** 362.4.

CN/0227-1435
**ACCESS (HALIFAX).** (ACCESS.). [Access]. Dec. 1979-. Periodical. English. qt. 2.00Can$. Coordinating Council on Deafness of Nova Scotia, 5185 Prince Street, Halifax Nova Scotia B3J 1L6 Canada. **DD** 362.4/2/09716. ***Continues** Coordinating Council on Deafness of Nova Scotia. Newsletter, 0227-1427.*

US/1069-6784
**ACCESS USA NEWS.** [Access USA news]. (19??)-. Periodical. English. Six times a year (Jan., Mar., May, July, Sept., Nov.). $15.00 one year; $27.00 two years; $39.00 three years. Roadrunner Publishing Inc., PO Box 1134, Crystal Lake IL 60039-1134. **Tel** (815)363-0900 or (815)363-0922, FAX (815)363-0923. **ED** Kim Lucatorto. **DD** 362. **Bk Rev. Ad Acc, Adv Mgr:** Dan Ramage, **Tel** (708)679-1100. **Circ:** 30,000 (ctrl).
**Desc:** An lifestyle magazine about the people with disabilities. Regular columnists and features cover a wide variety of topics and including employment, education, travel, legislation and people and many more.

AT/0729-8463
**ACROD NEWSLETTER.** [ACROD newsl.]. **VFOAT** Australian Council for Rehabilitation of Disabled Newsletter. (1981)-. Periodical. English. Ten times a year (Jan./Feb. & Nov./Dec. issues combined). 65.00Aus$ Australia; 75.00Aus$ others. Australian Council Rehab of Disabled, PO Box 60, Curtin ACT 2605 Australia. **Tel** 011 61 6 2824333, FAX 011 61 6 2813488. **DD** 362.4048. ***Continues** Rehabilitation in Australia, 0157-6658.*

AT/0725-3249
**ACTIVITIES DIGEST.** ***Ceased.*** **See** Medical Science and Technology-Geriatrics.

AG
**AD VERBUM.** Periodical. Spanish. Confederacion Argentina de Sordomudos, Av Pedro Medrano 1352 Of 12, Buenos Aires Argentina. **LC** HV2350; .A3. **NLM** W1 AD1125.

US/1054-5948
**ADA COMPLIANCE GUIDE.** **Added/Corp** Thompson Publishing Group. **VAT** Americans with Disabilities Act Compliance Guide. (1990)-. Periodical. English. mo. $287.00. Thompson Publishing Group, 7711 Anderson Road, Tampa FL 33634. **Tel** (800)677-3789, (813)282-8607.

US/1067-4713
**ADA POLICY & LAW.** ***Ceased.*** **See** Law.

●US/1062-0176
**ADA WATCH.** ***Suspended.*** (ADA WATCH : REPORT ON THE AMERICANS WITH DISABILITIES ACT.). **Added/Corp** Federal News Service. **VFOAT** Americans with Disabilities Act Watch. (1992)-(199?). English. sm. $157.00. Federal News Service, PO Box 13460, Silver Spring MD 20911-3460.

●US/1065-7037
**ADAC REPORT.** **Added/Corp** Association for Disability Act Compliance. **VAT** Association for Disability Act Compliance Report. (1992)-. Periodical. English. qt. ADAC Inc., PO Box 23, Wynnewood PA 19096.

US/0163-3805
**ADDRESS LIST, REGIONAL AND SUBREGIONAL LIBRARIES FOR THE BLIND AND PHYSICALLY HANDICAPPED.** **See** Library and Information Sciences.

SZ/0254-8747
**ADVANCES IN AUDIOLOGY.** [Adv. audiol.]. Vol. 1 (1984)-. Monographic series. English. an. 200.00F (approx. per volume). S. Karger AG, Allschwilerstrasse 10, PO Box - Postfach - Case Postale, CH-4009 Basel Switzerland. **Tel** 011 41 61 306-1111, FAX 011 41 61 306-1234, telex CH 962 652. **ED** M. Hoke. **NLM** W1; AD436D. **[CCC].** Documents available from BIOSIS Document Express.
**Desc:** Contributions are selected to cover and update important aspects relating to the structure, function, and pathology of the audiovestibular system, developments in the surgical or medical management of hearing disorders, as well as evaluative and rehabilitative procedures still in the experimental stage. Progress reports on newly applied methods for measuring hearing, records of test results and their interpretation, and statements on new possibilities, objectives, and procedures for therapy provide practical information.
**Ind/Abst** Biol. Abstr.; Ref. Upd. Deluxe Ed.

CN/0229-5407
**ADVOCATE (TORONTO. 1976).** ***Ceased.*** (ADVOCATE / ONTARIO MARCH OF DIMES.). [Advocate]. (July 1976)-ceased (July 90). Periodical. English. qt. Ontario March of Dimes, 60 Overlea Boulevard, Toronto Ontario M4H 1B6 Canada. **Tel** (416)425-0501. **ED** Gillian Kearney. **DD** 362.4/3/060713. Index available. **Bk Rev. Ad Acc. Circ:** 7,000. ***Continues** Ability Advocate, 0710-1899.*
**Desc:** A tabloid newspaper for disabled adults and those interested in issues concerning disabled people.

CN/0227-0897
**ALPHA ACTION REPORTER.** [ALPHA action report.]. **Added/Corp** ALPHA. **VAT** Action League of Physically Handicapped Adults Action Reporter. (Winter 1977)-. Periodical. English. ir. Free to members, $5.00 membership. Alpha, 627 Maitland Street, London Ontario N5Y 2V7 Canada. **Tel** 433-7221. **DD** 362.4/09713/26. **Ad Acc. Circ:** 100 (ctrl).
**Desc:** Serves as a forum to distribute community news, update activities and discuss various issues which impact the disabled consumer.

US/0002-726X
**AMERICAN ANNALS OF THE DEAF (WASHINGTON, D.C. 1886).** (AMERICAN ANNALS OF THE DEAF.). [Am. ann. deaf]. **Added/Corp** Convention of American Instructors of the Deaf. Conference of Superintendents and Principals of American Schools for the Deaf. Conference of Executives of American Schools for the Deaf. Conference of Educational Administrators Serving the Deaf. **VFOAT** A.A.D.; AAD. Vol. 31, No. 4 (Oct. 1886)-. Academic Scholarly Publication. English. Five times a year. $50.00. American Annals of the Deaf, 800 Florida Avenue Northeast, Washington DC 20002. **Tel** (202)651-5340, FAX (202)651-5708. **LC** HV2510; .A5. **DD** 371. **NLM** W1 AM149H. **CODEN** ANDFAL. **[CCC].** Index available ($10.00 (single issue)). **Bk Rev. Ad Acc, Adv Mgr:** Susan Flanagan, **Tel** (202)651-5340. **Pr Rev. Circ:** 3,500. available on microfilm and microfiche from University Microfilms International (UMI). Documents available from The Genuine Article, UMI Article Clearinghouse. ***Continues** American Annals of the Deaf and the Dumb, 0093-1284.*
**Ind/Abst** Curr. Contents Soc. Behav. Sci.; Curr. Index J. Educ.; Educ. Index; EMBASE; Except. Child Educ. Resour.; Expand. Acad. Index (1992-); Health Plan. Adminis.; Index Med.; Linguist. Lang. Behav. Abstr.; Newsp. Period. Abstr. (1992-); PAIS Int. Print (1991-); Psychol. Abstr. (1928-); PsycINFO; PsycLit; Public Aff. Inf. Serv. Bull.; Res. Alert [Full Cov.]; Soc. Plann. Policy Dev. Abstr.; Soc. Sci. Cit. Index [Full Cov.]; Sociol. Abstr.; Spec. Educ. Needs Abstr.

US/1059-0889
**AMERICAN JOURNAL OF AUDIOLOGY.** [Am. j. audiol.]. **Added/Corp** American Speech-Language-Hearing Association. **VFOAT** AJA. Vol. 1, No. 1 (Nov. 1991)-. Periodical. English. Three times a year. $32.00. American Speech Language and Hearing Association, 10801 Rockville Pike, Rockville MD 20852. **Tel** (301)897-5700. **LC** RF286; .A44. **DD** 617.8/005. **NLM** W1; AM4485. **[CCC].**
**Desc:** Addresses all aspects of clinical practice in audiology. Topics include screening, assessment and treatment techniques, prevention, professional issues, supervision and administration.

US/0895-8017
**AMERICAN JOURNAL OF MENTAL RETARDATION.** [Am. j. ment. retard.]. **Added/Corp** American Association on Mental Retardation. **VFOAT** AJMR; American Journal on Mental Retardation. Vol. 92, No. 3 (Nov. 1987)-. Periodical. English. bm (6 issues). $100.00 (1 year), $180.00 (2 year), $265.00 (3 year). American Association on Mental Retardation, 444 North Capitol Street Northwest, Suite 846, Washington DC 20001. **Tel** (202)387-1968, (800)424-3688. **ED** Stephen R. Schroeder. **LC** RC326; .A415. **DD** 616.85/88. **NLM** W1; AM494C. **CODEN** AJMREA. **[CCC].** Index available (bound in May issue). available on microfilm and microfiche from University Microfilms International (UMI). Documents available from The Genuine Article, BIOSIS Document Express. ***Continues** American Journal of Mental Deficiency, 0002-9351.*
**Desc:** Presenting original contributions in the biological, behavioral, and educational sciences that extend knowledge of mental retardation. Includes empirical research, theory papers, and systematic reviews of literature, emphasizing an objective, experimental, and theoretical approach.
**Ind/Abst** Annals Behav. Med.; Biol. Abstr. (1988-); Book Rev. Index; Curr. Contents Soc. Behav. Sci.; Curr. Index J. Educ. (March 1990); Dev. Med. Child Neurol.; Educ. Index; EMBASE; Except. Child Educ. Resour.; Health Plan. Adminis.; Index Med. (1987-); Linguist. Lang. Behav. Abstr.; Nutr. Res. Newsl.; Psychol. Abstr. (1940-); PsycINFO (1990-); PsycScan: Develop. Psych.; Res. Alert [Full Cov.]; Soc. Plann. Policy Dev. Abstr.; Soc. Sci. Cit. Index [Full Cov.]; Soc. Work Abstr. [Select. Cov.]; Sociol. Abstr.; Spec. Educ. Needs Abstr.

US/1058-0360
**AMERICAN JOURNAL OF SPEECH-LANGUAGE PATHOLOGY.** [Am. j. speech-lang. pathol.]. **Added/Corp** American Speech-Language-Hearing Association. **VFOAT** American Journal of Speech Language Pathology; AJSLP. Vol. 1, No. 1 (Sept. 1991)-. Periodical. English. Three times a year. $32.00. American Speech Language and Hearing Association, 10801 Rockville Pike, Rockville MD 20852. **Tel** (301)897-5700. **LC** RC423.A1; A43. **DD** 616. **NLM** W1; AM522L.
**Ind/Abst** Except. Child Educ. Resour.

US
**ANNUAL PROGRESS REPORT TO THE GOVERNOR AND TO THE JOINT COMMITTEE ON HUMAN SERVICES OF THE ... CONNECTICUT GENERAL ASSEMBLY FROM OFFICE AND BOARD OF PROTECTION AND ADVOCACY FOR HANDICAPPED AND DEVELOPMENTALLY DISABLED PERSONS.** **Main/Corp** Connecticut. Office of Protection and Advocacy for Handicapped and Developmentally Disabled Persons. **Added/Corp** Connecticut. P & A Advocacy Board. **VFOAT** Annual Report. English. 401 Trumbull Street, Hartford CT 06103. **LC** HV1555.C8; C65a. **DD** 353.97460084/4/06. ***Continues** Report to the Governor and to the Joint Committee on Human Services of the ... Connecticut General Assembly from the Office and Board of Protection and Advocacy for Handicapped and Developmentally Disabled Persons.*

US
**ANNUAL REPORT ... / ARIZONA COUNCIL FOR THE DEAF.** **Main/Corp** Arizona Council for the Deaf. (19??)-. English. an. Arizona Council for the Hearing Impaired, 1300 West Washington/Room 105, Phoenix AZ 85007. **Tel** (602)542-3323. **ED** Stuart Brackney. **LC** HV2561.A6; A74a. **DD** 353.97910084/4. **Pr Rev. Circ:** 500 (ctrl).
**Desc:** Informs governor and legislature of findings and makes recommendations on how to meet the needs of deaf and hearing impaired in Arizona. Includes the goals and missions of the agency along with program descriptions.

US/0732-8826
**ANNUAL REPORT / INTERNATIONAL CENTER FOR THE DISABLED.** [Annu. rep. - Int. Cent. Disabl.]. **Main/Corp** International Center for the Disabled. 1980-. English. an. International Center for the Disabled, 340 East 24th Street, New York NY 10010. **LC** RD701.N8; A33. **DD** 362.4/048/097471. ***Continues** ICD Rehabilitation and Research Center. Annual Report, 0163-0806.*

US
**ANNUAL REPORT - IOWA DEPARTMENT FOR THE BLIND.** **Main/Corp** Iowa. Dept. for the Blind. 1988-. English. an. Iowa Department for the Blind, 524-4th Street, Des Moines IA 50309-2364. **LC** HV1796.I88; A2. **DD** 362.4/1/0977705. ***Continues** Annual Report / Iowa Commission for the Blind.*

US
**ANNUAL REPORT / MISSISSIPPI SCHOOL FOR THE BLIND.** **Main/Corp** Mississippi School for the Blind. English. Mississippi School for the Blind, 1252 Eastover Drive, Jackson MS 39211. **LC** HV1796.M72; M57a. **DD** 371.91/1/09762. ***Continues** Annual Report to the Governor, Legislature, and General Public.*

CN/0707-963X
**ANNUAL REPORT - SASKATCHEWAN HEALTH, HEARING AID PLAN.** (ANNUAL REPORT - HEARING AID PLAN.). **Main/Corp** Saskatchewan. Hearing Aid Plan. 1974/75-. English. an. Saskatchewan Health, T C Douglas Building, 3475 Albert Street, Regina Saskatchewan S4S 6X6 Canada. **LC** RF300; .S28A. **DD** 354.71240084/4.
**Desc:** Report for 1973/74 included with the Annual report of the Dept. of Health.

CN/0712-1873
**ARCHTYPE (TORONTO).** (ARCHTYPE : PROMOTING AWARENESS OF LEGAL ISSUES AFFECTING THE DISABLED.). [ARCHtype]. **Added/Corp** Advocacy Resource Centre for the Handicapped. **VFOAT** Arch Type. **VAT** Advocacy Resource Centre for the Handicapped Type. Vol. 1, No. 1 (Jan. 1981)-. Periodical. English. Six times a year. $25.00 Can$, professionals & organizations in Canada, (one year); $15.00 Can$, individuals Canada (one year); $30.00 Can$ , others (one year). Advocacy Resource Center, 40 Orchard View Boulevard, Suite 255, Toronto Ontario M4R 1B9 Canada. **Tel** (416)482-8255, FAX (416)482-2981. **ED** Lynda Nancoo. **DD** 344.71/0324/05. **Bk Rev. Ad Acc, Adv Mgr:** Lynda Nancoo, **Tel** (416)482-8255. **Circ:** 2,000. available on magnetic tape. ***Absorbed** ARCH Alert, 0832-0373.*
**Desc:** Published by a legal clinic for the disabled. Legal, consumer, advocacy issues relating to spectrum of disabilities. Special interest in charter of rights and disability.

US
**ASHA MEMBERSHIP DIRECTORY. See** Medical Science and Technology-Otorhinolaryngology.

US/0066-071X
**ASHA MONOGRAPHS.** [ASHA monogr.]. **Added/Corp** American Speech-Language-Hearing Association. American Speech and Hearing Association. **VAT** American Speech-Language-Hearing Association Monograph. No. 12 (1965)-. Monographic series. English. ir. Price varies per volume. American Speech Language and Hearing Association, 10801 Rockville Pike, Rockville MD 20852. **Tel** (301)897-5700. **ED** Robin Chapman. **NLM** W1 A152B. **Circ:** 5,000 (ctrl). ***Continues*** *Journal of Speech and Hearing Disorders. Monograph Supplement.*
**Desc:** Reports of integrated series of experiments or of complex and extensive projects in speech, hearing, and language sciences.
**Ind/Abst** Index Med.

US/0001-2475
**ASHA (ROCKVILLE, MD.). See** Education-Special Education and Rehabilitation.

US/1040-0435
**ASSISTIVE TECHNOLOGY.** (ASSISTIVE TECHNOLOGY : THE OFFICIAL JOURNAL OF RESNA, ...). [Assist. technol.]. (1989)-. Periodical. English. Twice a year. $62.00 (institution), $49.95 (individual) US and Canada; $75.00 (institution), $59.95 (individual) other. RESNA, 1700 North Moore Street, Suite 1540, Arlington VA 22209. **Tel** (703)524-6686, FAX (703)524-6630. **ED** Lawrence Trachtman (editor's telephone: (919)850-2787). **LC** RM698; .A86. **DD** 617.1/03. **NLM** W1; AS364J. Index available in last issue of volume--attached. **Bk Rev. Pr Rev. Circ:** 1,800.
**Desc:** Directed at practitioners involved in the application of assistive and rehabilitation technologies and the delivery of related services. Technological developments are covered in occupational and physical therapy, nursing, orthopedics, physiatry, neurology, clinical engineering, prosthetics and orthotics, speech and language pathology, special education, vocational rehabilitation, and health policy and management.

FR/0985-0120
**ATHAREP. See** Sociology-Social Services and Welfare.

CN/1184-115X
**ATLANTIC SILENT NEWS.** [Atl. silent news]. **Added/Corp** Coordinating Council on Deafness of Nova Scotia. Ecumenical Ministry of the Deaf (Halifax, N.S.) Society of Deaf and Hard of Hearing Nova Scotians. Vol. 3, No. 4 (Oct. 1990)-. Periodical. English. ir. Atlantic Silent News, Suite 101, Roy Building, 1657 Barrington Street, Halifax, Nova Scotia B3J 2A1 Canada. **DD** 362.4/2/0971505. ***Continues*** *News (Society of Deaf and Hard of Hearing Nova Scotians)., 0849-536X.*

US/0004-7473
**AUDECIBEL.** [Audecibel]. **Added/Corp** National Hearing Aid Society (U.S.) Society of Hearing Aid Audiologists. Vol. 1, No. 2 (1952)-. Periodical. English. qt. $25.00 US; $35.00 other. National Hearing Aid Society, 20361 Middlebelt Road, Livonia MI 48152. **Tel** (313)478-2610, FAX (313)478-4520. **ED** Lois M White. **DD** 617. **NLM** W1 AU201. Index available. **Bk Rev**, (Qty: 10). **Ad Acc. Circ:** 21,000 (ctrl). available on microfilm and microfiche from University Microfilms International (UMI). ***Continues*** *Decibel (Chicago, Ill.).*
**Desc:** Information on hearing loss, hearing instrumentation, education, training, and related articles of this field.

GW/0172-8261
**AUDIOLOGISCHE AKUSTIK. AUDIOLOGICAL ACOUSTICS.** [Audiol. Akust.]. **VFOAT** Audiological Acoustics. Volume 19 (January 1980)-. Academic Scholarly Publication. German (English and German). bm. DM48.00 Germany; DM63.00 other Europe; DM71.40 other. Median-Verlag, Postfach 103964 Haupstrasse 64, D 69029 Heidelberg 1 Germany. **Tel** 011 49 6221 25731, FAX 011 49 6221 25030. **NLM** W1 AU201FM. **CODEN** AUKADP. Index available. **Bk Rev. Ad Acc. Circ:** 2,900. Documents available from BIOSIS Document Express, Ask*IEEE. ***Continues*** *Zeitschrift fur Horgeate-Akustik, 0044-2860.*
**Desc:** Concerns hearing and speech impairments and hearing loss. The latest surgical and technological advancements in hearing and speech.
**Ind/Abst** Biol. Abstr. (1986-); EMBASE; INSPEC (Sept.-Oct. 1982-).

FR/0222-3856
**AUDITION & PAROLE.** [Aud. parole]. **VFOAT** Audition et Parole. Vol. 1, 1-. Periodical. French. qt. $45.38. Deutscher Judo Verband, Redaktion Ippon Segewaldweg 40, D 12557 Berlin Germany. **Tel** 011 49 711 210770, telex 051 678. **NLM** W1 AU202F.

US
**AURICLE.** English. Four times a year. $20.00. Auditory Verbal International, 305 Merchants Bank Building, Easton PA 18042. **Tel** (215)253-6616, FAX (215)253-6709.

AT/0726-3864
**AUSTRALIA AND NEW ZEALAND JOURNAL OF DEVELOPMENTAL DISABILITIES.** [Aust. N.Z. j. dev. disabil.]. **Added/Corp** Australian Group for the Scientific Study of Mental Deficiency. New Zealand Association for the Scientific Study of Mental Deficiency. Victoria College (Vic.). Vol. 8, No. 1 (Mar. 1982)-. Academic Scholarly Publication. English. Four times a year. 60.00Aus$ (individuals), 100.00Aus$ (institutions) Australia; 80.00Aus$ (individuals), 120.00Aus$ (institutions) other. Australian Society Study of Intellectual Disability / Macquarie University, New South Wales 2109 Australia. **Tel** 011 61 02 805 8706, FAX 011 61 02 805 8674. **ED** Trevor R. Parmenter. **NLM** W1 AU388. **CODEN** ANZDDQ. Index available. cum. index. **Bk Rev. Ad Acc. Pr Rev. Circ:** 1,500 (ctrl). available on microfilm and microfiche from University Microfilms International (UMI). Documents available from BIOSIS Document Express. ***Continues*** *Australian Journal of Developmental Disabilities, 0159-9011.*
**Desc:** Scholarly reports of the scientific study of the causes, prevention and intervention programs for persons with developmental disabilities.
**Ind/Abst** APAIS, Aust. Public Aff. Inf. Ser. (1982-); Aust. Educ. Index (1982-); Biol. Abstr.; Child Dev. Abstr. Bibliogr.; Curr. Index J. Educ.; EMBASE; Except. Child Educ. Resour.; Multicult. Educ. Abstr.; Psychol. Abstr. (1982-); PsycINFO; PsycLit; Soc. Sci. Index; Spec. Educ. Needs Abstr.

AT/0813-4537
**AUSTRALIAN DISABILITY REVIEW.** (AUSTRALIAN DISABILITY REVIEW : JOURNAL OF THE DISABILITY ADVISORY COUNCIL OF AUSTRALIA / DACA.). [Aust. disabil. rev.]. **Added/Corp** Disability Advisory Council of Australia. Vol. 1, (1987)-. English. Four times a year (Mar., June, Sept., Dec.). Free. Disability Advisory Council Australia, GPO Box 0848, Canberra ACT 2601 Australia. **Tel** 011 61 6 2891555. **NLM** W1; AU524E. **[CCC]. *Continues*** *Australian Rehabilitation Review.*
**Ind/Abst** APAIS, Aust. Public Aff. Inf. Ser.

AT/0310-6853
**AUSTRALIAN JOURNAL OF HUMAN COMMUNICATION DISORDERS.** **Added/Corp** Australian Association of Speech and Hearing. Australian College of Speech Therapists. **VFOAT** Human Communication Disorders. Vol. 1, June (1973)-. Periodical. English. sa. 60.00Aus$ (institutions), 50.00Aus$ (individuals) Australia; 75.00Aus$ (institutions), 65.00Aus$ (individuals) other. Australian Association of Speech & Hearing, 212 Clarendon, Melbourne Victoria 3002 Australia. **Tel** 03 419-0422. **ED** Carl Parsons. **NLM** W1 AU6122. **Bk Rev. Ad Acc. Circ:** 2,500 (ctrl). ***Continues*** *Journal of the Australian College of Speech Therapists.*
**Desc:** Communication disorders, language, phonology, voice, stuttering, autism, mental retardation, deafness, speech pathology.
**Ind/Abst** Aust. Educ. Index (1983-); Linguist. Lang. Behav. Abstr. (1988-) [Full Cov.]; Soc. Plann. Policy Dev. Abstr.; Sociol. Abstr.

AT/0005-0334
**AUSTRALIAN TEACHER OF THE DEAF.** **See** Education-Special Education and Rehabilitation.

US
**AWARENESS / NATIONAL ASSOCIATION FOR PARENTS OF THE VISUALLY IMPAIRED. Added/Corp** National Association for Parents of the Visually Impaired. Periodical. English. qt. $25.00 (professional associates), $50.00 (community groups and agencies). National Association Parent Visual Impairs, 2180 Linway Drive, Beloit WI 53511. **Tel** (800)562-6265.

CN/0228-7161
**B.C. DEAF ADVOCATE, THE.** [B.C. deaf advocate]. **VFOAT** BC Deaf Advocate; Deaf Advocate. **VAT** British Columbia Deaf Advocate. Vol. 1, No. 1 (July 1976)-. Periodical. English. sa. Deaf Advocate, 1959 East 1st Avenue, Vancouver BC V5N 1B3. **DD** 362.4/2/09711.

US/8756-4661
**BALLOON (IRVINE, CALIF.).** (BALLOON.). Periodical. English. mo. $12.00. Balloon, 4521 Campus Drive/Suite 282, PO Box 19553, Irvine CA 92715. **ED** Jeff Colburn and Hedy Colburn.
**Desc:** A publication listing current events for the hearing impaired in the following categories: leisure activities, entertainment events, and general information.

GW
**BERUFLICHE REHABILITATION, ARBEITS- UND BERUFSFORDERUNG BEHINDERTER IN DEN JAHREN.** **Added/Corp** Bundesanstalt fuer Arbeit (Germany). **VFOAT** Arbeits- und Berufsforderung Behinderter (Berufliche Rehabilitation) in den Jahren ... . (19??)-. German. DM44.00. Lambertus-Verlag GmbH, Postfach 1026, 79010 Freiburg, Germany. **Tel** 011 49 761 3 68 25 0, FAX 011 49 761 3 70 64. **LC** HD7256.G3; B48. **DD** 331.5/9/0943.

AT
**BETTER HEARING. Added/Corp** Australian Association for Better Hearing. (19??)-. Periodical. English. Four times a year (Mar., June, Sept., Dec.). 20.00Aus$. The Better Hearing / Australia, PO Box 164, Kangaroo Ground Victoria 3097 Australia. **Tel** 011 49 68 8050. **ED** Wendy Bradley (Editor's address: 51 Skyline Road, Kangaroo Ground Victoria, 3097 Australia). **Bk Rev**, (Qty: 6). **Ad Acc, Adv Mgr:** Trevor Kingston. **Circ:** 3,000.
**Desc:** Provides directly or indirectly assistance, advice, information, training, and services to many thousands of people, those with hearing disabilities and disorders of the ear, their partners, family and those who work with people with hearing disabilities.

AT/0815-8398
**BIENNIAL CONFERENCE - AUSTRALIAN & NEW ZEALAND ASSOCIATION OF EDUCATORS OF THE VISUALLY HANDICAPPED. See** Education-Teaching and Curriculum.

US/0363-7689
**BLINDNESS, VISUAL IMPAIRMENT, DEAF-BLINDNESS.** (Summer 1976)-. English. sa. $5.00. Nevil Interagency Referral Service, Room 400/919 Walnut Street, Philadelphia PA 19107. **LC** Z5346.A2; B54. **DD** 011. **NLM** W1; YE41T; Z 5346; B347BA.
**Desc:** Consists of abstracts of literarure not indexed in Index Medicus.

●US/1063-3111
**BNA'S AMERICANS WITH DISABILITIES ACT MANUAL. NEWSLETTER.** [BNA's Am. Disabil. Act man., Newsl.]. **Added/Corp** Bureau of National Affairs (Washington, D.C.). **VFOAT** Americans with Disabilities Act Manual. Newsletter. **VAT** Bureau of National Affairs' Americans with Disabilities Act Manual. (Jan 1992)-. Newsletter. English. mo. $390.00. Bureau of National Affairs Inc., 9435 Key West Avenue, Rockville MD 20850. **Tel** (800)372-1033, (301)258-1033, FAX (301)948-5823. **DD** 346. **[CCC].**

US/0006-873X
**BRAILLE BOOK REVIEW.** [Braille book rev.]. **Added/Corp** Library of Congress. National Library Service for the Blind and Physically Handicapped. American Foundation for the Blind. Library of Congress. Division for the Blind and Physically Handicapped. (1932)-. Periodical. English. bm. American Foundation for the Blind, 15 West 16th Street, New York NY 10011. **Tel** (212)620-2000, (800)829-0500. **ED** Ruth Nicland. **LC** Z5346.Z9; B73. **DD** 011/.63. **Circ:** 5,000 (ctrl). available in braille.
**Desc:** Lists braille magazines and books available to blind and physically handicapped readers.

US/0277-5247
**BRAILLE BOOKS. See** Publishing-Books and Bookmaking.

US/0006-8829
**BRAILLE MONITOR, THE. Added/Corp** National Federation of the Blind. **VFOAT** Voice of the National Federation of the Blind. (195?)-. Periodical. English. Twelve times a year. $25.00. National Federation of the Blind, 1800 Johnson Street, Baltimore MD 21230. **Tel** (410)659-9314, FAX (410)685-5653. **NLM** W1 BR107. Index available. cum. index. **Bk Rev. Circ:** 25,000. available on audiocassette (and talking book discs); available in braille.
**Desc:** This magazine is called "the voice of the blind". It reports on action by the NFB on current legislative issues, legal cases, and social concerns affecting the blind, gives news of aids and appliances and how-to information features on blind persons.

UK
**BRAILLE SCIENCE JOURNAL.** mo. $5.00. Scottish Braille Press, Craigmillar Park, Edinburgh EH16 5NB Scotland. **Tel** 011 44 31 667 6230.
**Desc:** Contains informative articles on many aspects of scientific development. Eminently suitable for the reader with a general interest in scientific progress and achievement.

US/0145-3165
**BRAILLE SCORES CATALOG. INSTRUMENTAL. See** Music.

US/0145-3149
**BRAILLE SCORES CATALOG. ORGAN. See** Music.

US/1051-1016
**BRAILLE SCORES CATALOG. VOCAL. See** Music.

US/0006-8918
**BRAILLE STAR THEOSOPHIST, THE.** Periodical. English. bm. Free. Theosophical Book Association for the Blind Inc, Krotona 54, Ojai CA 93023. **Tel** (805)646-2121. **ED** Dennis Gottschalk. available in braille.

US/0738-498X
**BRANDING IRON OF THE BILL RICE RANCH, THE.** **VFOAT** Branding Iron. Periodical. English. mo. Bill Rice Ranch, Route 2 Franklin Road, Murfreesboro TN 37130.

US
**BREAKING NEW GROUND.** **Added/Corp** Purdue University. Dept. of Agricultural Engineering. Vol. 1, No. 1 (Fall 1982)-. Periodical. English. qt. Free upon request. Purdue University / Agriculture, 1146 Agricultural Engineering Building, West Lafayette IN 47907. **Tel** (317)494-5088, FAX (317)496-1115. **ED** Melissa Deason. **Circ:** 13,000.
**Ind/Abst** Agric. Eng. Abstr. (1991-).

UK/0007-0602
**BRITISH DEAF NEWS.** **Added/Corp** British Deaf and Dumb Association. (Jan./Feb. 1955/56)-. Periodical. English. mo. £8.00 UK; £13.00 other Europe; £26.00 other. The British Deaf Association, 38 Victoria Place, Carlisle CA1 1HU England. **Tel** 011 44 228 48844, FAX 011 44 228 41420. **ED** Irene Hall. **DD** 362. Index available. **Bk Rev.** **Ad Acc. Circ:** 6,000 (ctrl). ***Absorbed*** *Deaf Quarterly; Deaf News; British Deaf Times.*
**Desc:** News, articles and other items of interest to the deaf community of the UK.
**Ind/Abst** Appl. Soc. Sci. Index Abstr.

UK
**BRITISH JOURNAL OF DISORDERS OF COMMUNICATION. MONOGRAPH.** **VFOAT** Monograph. Monographic series. English. Three times a year. Price varies per volume. College of Speech Therapists, Harold Poster House, 6 Lechmere Road, London NW2 5BU England. **Tel** 459-8521. **ED** Ruth Lessor. **NLM** W1 BR526LM. **Bk Rev.** **Ad Acc. Circ:** 5,000. available in microform.
**Desc:** Monographs of technical import for all people involved at any level with speech therapy.

UK/0264-6196
**BRITISH JOURNAL OF VISUAL IMPAIRMENT, THE.** **Added/Corp** Association for the Education and Welfare of the Visually Handicapped (Great Britain). No. 1 (Summer 1983)-. Periodical. English. Three times a year (Mar., July, & Dec.). £25.00 associate membership; £75.00 corporate membership. Association Education and Welfare of Visually Handicapped, 12 The Bank Stoneleigh, Coventry CV8 3DA England. **ED** Monique Raffray. **LC** HV1571; .B83. **DD** 362.4/1/05. **NLM** W1; BR648T. Index available. **Bk Rev.** **Ad Acc. Circ:** 2,500 (ctrl). available in braille; available on audiocassette. ***Formed by the union of*** *Insight (Birmingham, West Midlands, England)* ***and*** *Inter-Regional Review.*
**Desc:** Academic journal addressed to those professionally concerned with children and adults with a visual impairment. With articles and correspondence on related research, education and welfare.
**Ind/Abst** Br. Educ. Index; Except. Child Educ. Resour.; Spec. Educ. Needs Abstr.

DK/0106-3308
**BRNEKLINIKENS VEJLEDNINGER.** [Brneklin. vejl.]. Danish. **NLM** W1 BO135; B34210000.

US/0550-5666
**BULLETIN OF THE NATIONAL BRAILLE ASSOCIATION, INC.** **See** Education-Special Education and Rehabilitation.

US/0162-0150
**BUREAU MEMORANDUM.** (BUREAU MEMORANDUM - WISCONSIN. DIVISION FOR HANDICAPPED CHILDREN.). **Main/Corp** Wisconsin. Division for Handicapped Children. Periodical. English. qt. Department of Public Instruction / Wisconsin, PO Box 7841, Madison WI 53707. **Tel** (608)266-2188. available on microfilm and microfiche from University Microfilms International (UMI).

CN/0380-9129
**CALGARY CORD, THE.** **Added/Corp** Society for Hearing Handicapped. Society for Hearing Handicapped Children. (1965)-. English. mo. $12.00. Society for the Hearing Handicapped, 120 13th Avenue Southeast, Calgary Alberta T2G 1B3 Canada. **Tel** (403)240-3111, (403)282-1204. **(Subscription address:** Deaf & Hard of Hearing, 63 Carnell Road Northwest, Calgary Alberta I2L 0L4 Canada.**)** **DD** 362.4/2/0627123.

US
**CALIFORNIA CONNECTIONS / DEPARTMENT OF DEVELOPMENTAL SERVICES.** Vol. 1, No. 1 (May 1991)-. English. **LC** HV1570.5.U62; C35. ***Continues*** *DDS Insight.*

CN/0045-4001
**CALIPER (TORONTO).** (CALIPER.). **VFOAT** Caliper Registered. Began publication in 194?. Periodical. English (French). qt. 10.00Can$ (individuals), 13.00Can$ (institutions) Canada; $12.00 (individuals), $15.00 (institutions). Canadian Paraplegic Association National Office, 1500 Don Mills Road/Suite 201, Toronto Ontario M3B 3H4 Canada. **Tel** (416)391-0203. **ED** Gregory J Pyc. **NLM** W1 CA444. **Bk Rev.** **Ad Acc. Circ:** 4,500 (ctrl).
**Desc:** The official journal of the Canadian Paraplegic Association. Features include a variety of items and commentaries of interest to physically disabled persons.

CN/0823-6674
**CANADIAN AMPUTEE SPORTS ASSOCIATION.** **See** Recreation, Leisure-Sports.

US/1071-0418
**CAREERISM NEWSLETTER.** (1970)-. Newsletter. English. Twelve times a year. $95.00 (one year); $155.00 (two years). WWWWW / Information Services Inc, Box 10046, Rochester NY 14610. **Tel** (716)482-2022. **ED** Mark Jones. **DD** 331.
**Desc:** Pinpoints opportunities and product aids for the physically and emotionally challenged.

US/1056-277X
**CAREERS & THE DISABLED.** **See** Occupations and Careers.

UK/0968-8838
**CARERS WORLD.** (1982)-. Trade Publication. English. bm. £9.00. A E Morgan Publications Ltd, Stanley House, 9 West Street, Epsom Surrey KT18 7RL England. **Tel** 011 44 3727 41411, FAX 0372 744493, telex 291561 VIA SOS G. **ED** Charles Lloyd. **Circ:** 3,300. ***Continues*** *Caring: for the Disabled Carers and the Elderly.*
**Desc:** Directed at caretakers of the elderly and disabled.

US
**CARING CONNECTION.** (19??). Periodical. English. mo. $13.50. Phyllis Burns, 3060 East Bridge Street/Suite 342, Brighton CO 80601. **Tel** (303)659-4463. ***Continues*** *Handicap News.*

UK
**CARING : FOR THE DISABLED CARERS AND THE ELDERLY.** ***Title Change.*** (19??)-(1993). English. Six times a year. A E Morgan Publications Ltd, Stanley House, 9 West Street, Epsom Surrey KT18 7RL England. **Tel** 011 44 3727 41411, FAX 0372 744493, telex 291561 VIA SOS G. ***Continues*** *Handicapped Living.* ***Continued by*** *Carers World.*

US/0363-9029
**CASSETTE BOOKS.** **See** Publishing-Books and Bookmaking.

US
**CATALOG OF CAPTIONED FILMS/VIDEOS FOR THE DEAF.** **Added/Corp** Modern Talking Picture Service, Inc. Special Education Programs (U.S.). Captioning and Adaptation Branch. **VFOAT** Catalog of Captioned Films Videos for the Deaf; Catalog of Captioned Entertainment, Short Subject, and Continuing Education Materials for the Hearing Impaired; Catalog of Captioned Feature and Special Interest Films and Videos for the Hearing Impaired; Captioned Films/Videos for the Deaf. (1989-1990)-. Catalog. English. Captioned Films for the Deaf, 5000 Park Street North, St Petersburg FL 33709. **Tel** (800)237-6213. **LC** HV2395; .U48a. ***Continues*** *Catalog of Captioned Films for the Deaf.*

US
**CATALOG OF TAPE RECORDED BOOKS / RECORDINGS FOR THE BLIND.** **Main/Corp** Recording for the Blind. **VFOAT** Catalog / Recording for the Blind. Catalog. English. ir. $14.00. Recording for the Blind, 20 Roszel Road, Princeton NJ 08540. **Tel** (609)452-0606. **ED** John Kelly. Index available. **Circ:** 7,000.
**Desc:** Catalogue of recorded textbooks available free to blind and reading impaired students at elementary, high school, college and postgraduate levels.

CN/0824-3042
**CCB NATIONAL NEWSLETTER.** (CCB NATIONAL NEWSLETTER / CANADIAN COUNCIL OF THE BLIND.). [CCB natl. newsl.]. **VAT** Canadian Council of the Blind National Newsletter. (March 1983)-. Newsletter. English. Free to members. Canadian Council of the Blind, 220 Dundas Street, Suite 510, London Ontario N6A 1H3 Canada. **Tel** (519)433-3946. **DD** 362.4/1/06071. ***Continues*** *CCB Newsletter, 0824-6173.*

KO
**CHAEHWAL YONGU.** **VFOAT** Rehabilitation Studies; Journal of Rehabilitation. Periodical. Korean. an. Samyuk Adong Chaehwarwon, 722-3 Pongchon-dong Kwanak-ku, Seoul Korea. **LC** HV3024.K6; C47.

US
**CHILDRENS BRAILLE BOOK CLUB.** English. Twelve times a year. $100.00. National Braille Press Inc., 88 St. Stephen Street, Boston MA 02115. **Tel** (617)266-6160.

JA
**CHOFUKU SHOGAI KYOIKU KANKEI BUNKEN MOKUROKU.** **See** Education-Special Education and Rehabilitation.

CN/0843-0578
**CLAIRVOYANT (MONTREAL).** (LE CLAIRVOYANT / L'ASSOCIATION QUEBECOISE DES PARENTS D'ENFANTS HANDICAPES VISUELS.). [Clairvoyant]. **Added/Corp** Association Quebecoise des Parents d'Enfants Handicapes Visuels. Vol. 8, No. 5 (Dec. 1987)-. Periodical. French. Six times a year (Feb., May, June, Sept., Oct., Nov.). 10.00Can$. Association Quebecoise des Parents d'Enfants Handicapes Visuels, 3700 rue Berri, Suite 448, Montreal Quebec H2L 4G9 Canada. **Tel** (514)849-8729. **DD** 362.4/1/060714. ***Continues*** *AQPEHV, 0228-4758.*

US/0890-409X
**CLINICAL CONNECTION, THE.** [Clin. connect.]. Vol. 1, No. 1 (Fall 1986)-. Periodical. English. qt. $39.00 US; $59.00 other. The Clinical Connection, 708 Pendleton Street, Alexandria VA 22314. **Tel** (703)683-0991, FAX (703)548-5563. **ED** Marilyn Newhoff and Georgina Ruley-Parks. **LC** RJ496.C67; C54. **DD** 616. **NLM** W1; CL69D. Index available. cum. index. **Bk Rev**, (Qty: 4). ctrl circ.
**Desc:** For the speech and language pathologist working with the young communicator.

US/0896-9620
**CLINICAL KINESIOLOGY.** **See** Physical Therapy.

FR
**COMME LES AUTRES.** French. qt. 80.00F. Assoc Natl Parents d'Enfants, Avenugles 74 rue de Sevres, Paris 75007 France.

●US
**COMMUNICATION AND LANGUAGE INTERVENTION SERIES.** Vol. 1 (1992)-. Monographic series. English. Price varies per volume. **NLM** W1; CO4272C.

CN/0228-5401
**COMMUNICATION - CANADIAN CO-ORDINATING COUNCIL ON DEAFNESS.** ***Ceased.*** (COMMUNICATION : THE NEWSLETTER OF THE CANADIAN CO-ORDINATING COUNCIL ON DEAFNESS.). [Commun. - Can. Coord. Counc. Deafness]. **VFOAT** Communication. **VAT** Communication - Conseil Canadien de Coordination de la Deficience Auditive. Newsletter. English (French). qt. Canadian Co-Ordinating Council on Deafness, 116 Lisgar Street/Suite 203, Ottawa Ontario K2P OC2 Canada. **Tel** (613)232-2611. **ED** Laurie Haig. **DD** 362.4/2/0971. **Bk Rev.** **Ad Acc. Circ:** 1,500.
**Desc:** Contains news articles and features of interest to deaf and hard of hearing consumers, parents, professionals, agencies and government. Communication is Canada's only national magazine for the deaf and hard of hearing.

US/0161-4126
**COMMUNICATION OUTLOOK.** **See** Communication.

US
**COMMUNIQUE / CALIFORNIA GOVERNOR'S COMMITTEE FOR EMPLOYMENT OF DISABLED PERSONS.** **Main/Corp** California Governor's Committee for Employment of Disabled Persons. Vol. 1, No. 1 (Apr. 1990)-. English. **LC** HD7256.U6; C241. ***Continues*** *California Governor's Committee for Employment of the Handicapped. Communique.*

UK
**COMMUNITY BASED REHABILITATION NEWS : CBR.** English. Three times a year. Free to developing countries; £10.00 other. Ahtag, 1 London Bridge Street, London SE1 9SG England. **Tel** 011 44 71 486 4175. **ED** Ann Darnbrough. **Pr Rev.**
**Desc:** Information on community based rehabilitation in developing countries and the rights of disabled people.
**Ind/Abst** Trop. Dis. Bull.

●NZ/1171-8587
**COMMUNITY MOVES.** [Community moves]. **VFOAT** IHC Community Moves. (1992)-. Periodical. English. Four times a year. 18.00NZ$ Comes with Intellectually Handicapped Community membership. New Zealand Society for the Intellectually Handicapped Inc., PO Box 4155, Wellington New Zealand. **Tel** 011 64 4 722247. **DD** _a362.3099305. ***Continues*** *IH Review, 0110-7747.*
**Desc:** News and information for the handicapped.

US
**COMPANION.** **Main/Corp** Minnesota. School for the Deaf, Faribault. Periodical. English. Seven times a year. $3.00. Minnesota State Academy for the Deaf, PO Box 308, Faribault MN 55021. **ED** Douglas D. Bahl. **Circ:** 1,000.

●US/1063-0023
**COMPLETE DIRECTORY FOR PEOPLE WITH DISABILITIES, THE.** (THE COMPLETE DIRECTORY FOR PEOPLE WITH DISABILITIES: PRODUCTS, RESOURCES, BOOKS, SERVICES.). [Complete dir. people disabil.]. (1992)-. Directory. English. $125.00. Grey House Publishing, Inc., Pocket Knife Square, Lakeville CT 06039. **(Subscription address:** US & Canada: Gale Research Co., 835 Penobscot Building, Detroit, MI 48226**)** **LC** HV1553; .C58. **DD**

362.4/048/02573. **NLM** WB 22; AA1 C7.
**Desc:** Large type directory that provides more than 6,000 descriptions and contact information for associations, government agencies, research centers, and more.

US
**COMPUTER-DISABILITY NEWS.** ***Ceased.*** **Added/Corp** National Easter Seal Society (U.S.). **VFOAT** Computer Disability News. (198?)- Vol. 11, No. 3 (19??). Periodical. English. qt. National Easter Seal Society, 230 West Monroe, Suite 1800, Chicago IL 60606. **Tel** (312)726-6200.

US/1070-8154
**CONNECTIONS (MINNEAPOLIS, MINN. 1993).** (CONNECTIONS : THE NEWSLETTER OF THE NATIONAL CENTER FOR YOUTH WITH DISABILITIES.). [Connections]. **Added/Corp** National Center for Youth with Disabilities (Minneapolis, Minn.). (19??)-. Newsletter. English. tq. Free. National Center for Youth with Disabilities, University of Minnesota, Box 721-UMHC, Harvard Street at East River Road, Minneapolis MN 55455. **Tel** (612)626-2825, (800)333-6293, (612)624-3939 (TDD). **ED** Peggy Mann Rinehart. **DD** 362. **Bk Rev. Circ:** 9,000.
**Desc:** Addresses key issues of youth with disabilities, current research, new programs, and training materials.

UK
**CONTACT.** English. qt. £6.00 UK; £9.00 other. Royal Assn Disability & Rehabilitation, 25 Mortimer Street, London W1N 8AB England. **Tel** 071 637 5700, FAX 071 637 1827. **Bk Rev. Ad Acc.** ctrl circ.
**Desc:** Articles that will be of interest to disabled people or who work with disabled people.

CN/0319-7379
**CONTACT (TORONTO. 1972).** ***Ceased.*** (CONTACT.). [Contact]. **Added/Corp** Canadian Cerebral Palsy Association. **VFOAT** Contact. (Jan. 1972)-(19??). Periodical. English (French). qt. Canadian Cerebral Palsy Association, 40 Dundas Street West/Suite 222, PO Box 111, Toronto Ontario M5G 2C2 Canada. **Tel** (416)923-2932. **ED** Arthur M Timms. **Bk Rev. Ad Acc. Circ:** 1,800 (ctrl). ***Supersedes*** *Cerebral Palsy Contact, 0319-7395.*
**Desc:** News and views of interest to the physically disabled community. Specific information about this association's policy development, events and action.

CN/0824-7226
**CPA FREEWHEELER.** (THE CPA FREEWHEELER : NEWSLETTER OF THE CANADIAN PARAPLEGIC ASSOCIATION, ONTARIO DIVISION.). Winter 1982/83-. Newsletter. English. qt. $10.00 membership fee. Canadian Paraplegic Association Ontario Division, 520 Sutherland Drive, Toronto Ontario M4G 3V9 Canada. **Tel** (416)422-5644, FAX (416)422-5943. **ED** Gillian Kearny. **DD** 362.4/3. **Ad Acc.** ctrl circ. ***Continues*** *Freewheeler, 0225-5618.*
**Desc:** A magazine published by the Ontario Division of the Canadian Paraplegic Association. Features include articles which deal with informing and addressing the issues and concerns of physically disabled persons.

US/0749-3177
**CRD NEWS / COMMITTEE FOR THE RIGHTS OF THE DISABLED.** **See** Political Science-Civil Rights.

US/1041-6196
**CUED SPEECH CENTER LINES.** [Cued Speech Cent. lines]. **Added/Corp** Cued Speech Center. Vol. 1, No. 1 (July 1984)-. Periodical. English. qt. $10.00. Cued Speech Center Inc, PO Box 31345, Raleigh NC 27622. **Tel** (919)828-1218. **ED** Mary Elsie Daisey. **DD** 369. **Bk Rev. Circ:** 1,000 (ctrl).

US/1059-8243
**CUED SPEECH JOURNAL.** [Cued speech j.]. **Added/Corp** National Cued Speech Association. Vol. 4 (1990)-. Periodical. English. ir. $7.00. National Cued Speech Association, PO Box 31345, Raleigh NC 27622. **Tel** (919)828-1218. **DD** 419. ***Continues*** *Cued Speech Annual, 1041-6226.*

US/0888-9112
**CUED SPEECH NEWS.** [Cued speech news]. **Added/Corp** Gallaudet College. Cued Speech Program. Gallaudet College. Cued Speech Programs. Gallaudet College. Cued Speech Office. **VFOAT** Cued Speech; CS News. Vol. 1, No. 1 (Nov. 1967)-. Periodical. English. Four times a year (Jan., Apr., Aug., Oct.). $10.00 US; $15.00 others. Audiology, Gallaudet University, Cued Speech, 800 Florida Avenue Northeast, Washington DC 20002. **Tel** (202)651-5330. **LC** HV2500; .C83. **DD** 419. **Circ:** 500.

FR
**DANS LE VENT.** (19??)-. French. mo (11 issues). 115.00F. Association Valentin Hauy, 5 rue Duroc, 75343 Paris Cedex 07 France. **Tel** 011 33 1 47340790.

US/0737-6235
**DBPH NEWSLETTER.** **See** Library and Information Sciences.

●CN/1195-3349
**DEAF CANADA.** **Main/Corp** Canadian Association of the Deaf. (1992)-. Periodical. English (French). mo (12 issues per year). 25.00Can$. Canadian Association of Deaf, 205 2435 Holly Lane, Ottawa Ontario K1V 7P2 Canada. **Tel** (613)526-4785, FAX (613)526-4718. **ED** Michael Ryan. **Ad Acc.** ***Continues*** *Deaf Canadian Advocate, 0841-9116.*

CN/0841-9116
**DEAF CANADIAN ADVOCATE.** ***Title Change.*** (THE DEAF CANADIAN ADVOCATE / THE CANADIAN ASSOCIATION OF THE DEAF.). [Deaf Can. advocate]. **Added/Corp** Canadian Association of the Deaf. **VFOAT** Defenseur des Sourds Canadiens. Vol. 1, No. 1 (Feb./March 1985)-(19??). Periodical. English (French). mo (12 issues per year). Canadian Association of Deaf, 205 2435 Holly Lane, Ottawa Ontario K1V 7P2 Canada. **Tel** (613)526-4785, FAX (613)526-4718. **ED** Michael Ryan. **DD** 362.4/2/06071. **Ad Acc.** ***Absorbed*** *Defenseur des Sourds Canadiens, 0841-9124.* ***Continued by*** *Deaf Canada.*

US/0898-719X
**DEAF LIFE.** [Deaf life]. **VFOAT** Deaf Life Magazine. **VAT** DeafLife. Vol. 1, No. 1 (July 1988)-. Periodical. English. Twelve times a year. $30.00. MSM Productions, PO Box 63083, Marketplace Mall, Rochester NY 14623-6383. **Tel** (716)328-6700, FAX (716)328-6720. **ED** Matthew Moore. **DD** 362. Index available. cum. index. **Bk Rev**, (Qty: 6-12). **Ad Acc. Circ:** 35,000 (ctrl).
**Desc:** Full of exciting features of photo-essays, profiles and interviews of newsmakers. Coverage of controversial issues like the arts, politics, technology, media reviews from a deaf perspective and more. Educational, informative, entertaining, and enlightening.

US/0898-5480
**DEAF USA.** [Deaf U. S. A.]. **Added/Corp** Eye Festival Communications. **VAT** Deaf United States of America. (1987)-. Periodical. English. mo. $20.00 US; $40.00 other. Eye Festival Communications Inc, 4717 Laurel Canyon Boulevard, #210, North Hollywood CA 91607-3944. **Tel** 800 735-2922 ask for (818)760-3292, FAX (818)760-3391. **ED** David Rosenbaum. **DD** 362. **Bk Rev**, (Qty: 12/yr). **Ad Acc. Circ:** 7,700.
**Desc:** Publication covers issues and activities of interests to deaf, hard of hearing, hearing impaired persons, professionals and associates.

RU/0130-3074
**DEFEKTOLOGIJA.** **See** Education-Special Education and Rehabilitation.

CN/0709-2148
**DEFI.** (LE DEFI / SERVCOM COTE-NORD.). [Defi]. Vol. 1, No. 1 (Sept. 1979)-. Periodical. French. bm. **DD** 362.4/09714/17.

CN/1184-0412
**DEVELOPMENTAL DISABILITIES BULLETIN.** [Dev. disabil. bull.]. **Added/Corp** University of Alberta. Developmental Disabilities Centre. (1990)-. Bulletin. English. Twice a year (Apr., and Oct.). 19.25Can$ (individual), 32.10Can$ (institutions) Canada; $15.00 (individual), $25.00 (institutions) other. University of Alberta Developmental Disabilities Centre, 6-123 D Education North, Edmonton Alberta T6G 2G5 Canada. **Tel** (403)492-4439, FAX (403)492-1318. **ED** Jack Goldberg. **DD** 362.1/968. **Bk Rev. Ad Acc, Adv Mgr:** H. Groot, **Tel** (403)492-4505. **Circ:** 350-400 (ctrl). ***Continues*** *Mental Retardation and Learning Disability Bulletin, 0822-4277.*
**Desc:** Articles which have both research and direct application to the education of, and provision of services for, persons with mental retardation, learning disability, and multiple handicaps.
**Ind/Abst** Except. Child Educ. Resour.; Psychol. Abstr. (1972-); PsycLit.

CN/0842-8336
**DIALOG (EDMONTON).** (DIALOG.). [Dialog]. **Added/Corp** Dialog with Disabled Persons Society of Alberta. Vol. 1, Issue 1 (May 1988)-. Periodical. English. bm. 20.00Can$. Dialog / Canada, 502 10136-100 Street, Edmonton ALTA T5J 0P1 Canada. **Tel** (403)428-9342. **ED** Blanche Martin. **DD** 362.4/097123. **Bk Rev**, (Qty: 2). **Ad Acc, Adv Mgr:** Kim Harrold. **Circ:** 10,000.
**Desc:** A networking vehicle between disabled and abled individuals, and the organizations that seek to serve them, through the dissemination of information and opinions, with the goal to initiate positive change.

US/1069-6865
**DIALOGUE (BRAILLE ED.).** (DIALOGUE.). [Dialogue]. (19??)-. Periodical. English. Four times a year (Jan., Apr., July, Oct.). $25.00. Blindskills Inc., c/o Carol McCall, PO Box 5181, Salem OR 97304. **Tel** (503)581-4224. **ED** Carol McCarl. **DD** 305. **Bk Rev**, (Qty: 2). **Circ:** 10,000 (ctrl). available in large print; available on audiocassette.
**Desc:** Written for blind and newly blind persons by blind and visually impaired writers. Articles cover a wide range of subject matter, including mobility, employment, independence, guide dogs, arts and crafts, health, technology, cuisine and gardening.

US/1069-6873
**DIALOGUE (CASSETTE ED.).** (DIALOGUE. THE MAGAZINE FOR THE VISUALLY IMPAIRED SOUND RECORDING.). [Dialogue]. (19??)-. Periodical. English. Four times a year (Jan., Mar., July, Oct.). $25.00. Blindskills Inc., c/o Carol McCall, PO Box 5181, Salem OR 97304. **Tel** (503)581-4224. **ED** Carol McCarl. **DD** 305. **Bk Rev**, (Qty: 2). **Circ:** 10,000 (ctrl). available in braille; available in large print.

US/1069-6857
**DIALOGUE (LARGE PRINT ED.).** (DIALOGUE.). [Dialogue]. (196?)-. Periodical. English. Four times a year (Jan., Apr., July, Oct.). $25.00. Blindskills Inc., c/o Carol McCall, PO Box 5181, Salem OR 97304. **Tel** (503)581-4224. **ED** Carol M. McCarl. **DD** 305. **Bk Rev**, (Qty: 2). **Circ:** 10,000. available in braille; available on audiocassette; available in large print. ***Continues*** *Talking Lion.*
**Desc:** Written for blind and newly blind persons by blind and visually impaired writers. Articles cover a wide range of subject matter, including mobility, employment, independence, guide dogs, arts and crafts, health, technology, cuisine and gardening.

US/0363-5414
**DIKTA.** **See** Library and Information Sciences.

CN/0843-5979
**DIRECT ACCESS (CALGARY).** (DIRECT ACCESS : TECHNICAL RESOURCE CENTRE BI-MONTHLY NEWSLETTER.). [Dir. access]. **Added/Corp** Technical Resource Centre (Calgary, Alta.). (Sept. 1988)-. Newsletter. English. bm. 30.00Can$. Technical Research Center, 1201 5th Street SW, Suite 200, Calgary Alberta T2R 0V6 Canada. **Tel** (403)262-9445, FAX (403)262-4539. **DD** 362.4/0483. **Circ:** 350 (ctrl). available on an online database. ***Continues*** *Newsletter (Technical Resource Centre (Calgary, Alta.)), 1194-2606.*

US
**DIRECT LOAN PROGRAM FOR THE ELDERLY OR HANDICAPPED.** **See** Sociology-Social Services and Welfare.

CN/1182-4441
**DIRECTIONS - BRITISH COLUMBIA PREMIER'S ADVISORY COUNCIL FOR PERSONS WITH DISABILITIES.** (DIRECTIONS : NEWSLETTER OF THE BRITISH COLUMBIA PREMIER'S ADVISORY COUNCIL FOR PERSONS WITH DISABILITIES.). [Dir. - B.C. Prem. Advis. Counc. Pers. Disabil.]. **Main/Corp** British Columbia. Premier's Advisory Council for Persons with Disabilities. Vol. 1, No. 1 (Summer 1990)-. Newsletter. English. **DD** 362.4/06/0711.

CN/0836-6160
**DIRECTIONS - ONTARIO ASSOCIATION FOR COMMUNITY LIVING.** (DIRECTIONS : NEWSLETTER OF THE ONTARIO ASSOCIATION FOR COMMUNITY LIVING.). [Dir. - Ont. Assoc. Community Living]. **Added/Corp** Ontario Association for Community Living. Vol. 5, No. 2 (1987)-. Newsletter. English. Four times a year. Free to libraries; 5.00Can$ others. Hamilton Association for the Mentally Retarded, 191 York Avenue, Hamilton Ontario L8R 1Y6 Canada. **Tel** (905)528-0281. **DD** 362.3/09713. ***Continues*** *Directions (Ontario Association for the Mentally Retarded)., 0823-2512.*

CN/0848-8134
**DIRECTORY OF BARRIER-FREE BUILDING PRODUCTS.** **See** Architecture.

US/0743-5096
**DIRECTORY OF BILINGUAL SPEECH-LANGUAGE PATHOLOGISTS AND AUDIOLOGISTS.** [Dir. biling. speech-lang. pathol. audiol.]. **Main/Corp** American Speech-Language-Hearing Association. (1983)-. English. ir (every two years). $3.70 Maryland; $3.80 others. American Speech Language and Hearing Association, 10801 Rockville Pike, Rockville MD 20852. **Tel** (301)897-5700. **NLM** WV 22 AA1 A55. ctrl circ.
**Desc:** Directory of bilingual speech-language pathologists and audiologists for thirty-four languages.

●CN/1191-1514
**DIRECTORY OF CANADIAN REHABILITATION SERVICES.** (DIRECTORY OF CANADIAN REHABILITATION SERVICES/ CANADIAN REHABILITATION COUNCIL FOR THE DISABLED.). [Dir. Can. rehabil. serv.]. **Added/Corp** Canadian Rehabilitation Council for the Disabled. **VFOAT** Repertoire des Services de Readaptation Canadiens. (1992)-. Directory. English (summaries and/or abstracts in French). $22.95 per v. Canadian Rehabilitation Council for the Disabled, 45 Sheppard Avenue East/Suite 801, Toronto Ontario M2N 5W9 Canada. **Tel** (416)250-7490, FAX (416)229-1371. **DD** 362.4/048/02571.

CN/1187-7219
**DIRECTORY OF DISABILITY MEDIA IN CANADA.** [Dir. disabil. media Can.]. **Added/Corp** Katz Communications. (1991)-. English. an (Feb.). 48.50Can$ Canada; 57.50Can$ US & Mexico; 65.00Can$ others. Katz Communications, 5977 A Park Avenue, Montreal Quebec H2V 4H4 Canada. **DD** 362.4/0971/05.

US
**DIRECTORY OF GRANTS FOR ORGANIZATIONS SERVING PEOPLE WITH DISABILITIES.** (1993)-. Directory. English. an. $51.50. Research Grant Guides, PO Box 1214, Loxahatchee FL 33470. **Tel** (407)795-6129, FAX (407)795-7794. Index available (Free). ***Continues*** *Handicapped Funding Directory, 0733-4753.*

US
**DIRECTORY OF ORGANIZATIONS INTERESTED IN THE HANDICAPPED.** **Added/Corp** People-to-People Committee for the Handicapped. (197?)-. Periodical. English. ir (approx. every three years). $3.00. People-to-People Program, 1522 K Street NW/1130, Washington DC 20005. **Tel** (202)638-2487.

US/0899-2533
**DIRECTORY OF SERVICES FOR BLIND AND VISUALLY IMPAIRED PERSONS IN THE UNITED STATES.** [Dir. serv. blind vis. impair pers U. S.]. **VFOAT** American Foundation for the Blind Directory of Services for Blind and Visually Impaired Persons in the United States. 23rd Ed.(1988)-. Directory. English. sa. $39.95. American Foundation for the Blind, 15 West 16th Street, New York NY 10011. **Tel** (212)620-2000, (800)829-0500. **DD** 362. **NLM** HV 1791; D598. ***Continues*** *American Foundation for the Blind Directory of Agencies Serving the Visually Handicapped in the U.S., 0732-1341.*

US/0092-2455
**DIRECTORY OF SPECIFIC LEARNING DISABILITY SERVICES.** **See** Education-Special Education and Rehabilitation.

II/0970-356X
**DISABILITIES AND IMPAIRMENTS.** [Disabil. Impair.]. (1987)-. Periodical. English. sa. $60.00. **(Subscription address:** Prints India, 11 Darya Ganj, New Delhi, 110002 India, (Phone: 011 91 11 3268645)) **UDC** 616.

●UK/0963-8288
**DISABILITY AND REHABILITATION.** Vol. 14, No. 1 (Jan.-Mar. 1992)-. Periodical. English. Eight times a year. £149.00 UK; $249.00 other. Taylor & Francis Ltd., Rankine Road, Basingstoke Hampshire, RG24 8PR United Kingdom. **Tel** 011 44 256 840366, FAX 011 44 256 479438, telex 858540. **(Subscription address:** Taylor & Francis Inc., 1900 Frost Road, Suite 101, Bristol PA 19007-1598.**)** **ED** Dave Muller. **NLM** W1; DI7255H. **CODEN** DREHET. ***Continues*** *International Disability Studies, 0259-9147.*
**Desc:** An international, multidisciplinary journal which seeks to encourage a better understanding of all aspects of disability, and to promote the rehabilitation process. The journal publishes review articles, experimental and clinical research papers, case studies, short reports of work in progress, clinical and educational commentaries and major book reviews, spanning a range of issues including the severity and magnitude of disability, clinical medicine including gerontology, psychosocial adjustment, social policy issues, vocational and educational training, and rehabilitation engineering.
**Ind/Abst** EMBASE; Ergon. Abstr.; Index Med. (1992-).

UK
**DISABILITY & SOCIETY.** English. qt. £134.00. Carfax Publishing Company, PO Box 25 Abingdon, Oxfordshire OX14 3UE England. **Tel** 011 44 235 555335, FAX (0279)31067, telex 817484. **(Subscription address:** US and Canada/ PO Box 2025, Dunnellon, FL 34430-2025; telephone:(904)489-6996**)** available on microfiche. ***Continues*** *Disability, Handicap & Society.*

US
**DISABILITY COMPLIANCE BULLETIN.** (1991)-. Bulletin. English. Twenty-four times a year. $150.00. LRP Publications, 747 Dresher Road, PO Box 980, Horsham PA 19044-0980. **Tel** (800)341-7874, (215)784-0860, FAX (215)784-9639, (215)784-0870.
**Desc:** Covers developments and happenings regarding disability law and rights. Provides case summaries of the decisions reported in the National Disability Law Reporter, articles from experts in the field and news.

UK/0267-4645
**DISABILITY, HANDICAP & SOCIETY.** ***Title Change.*** **See** Sociology-Social Services and Welfare.

US/1063-9373
**DISABILITY ISSUES.** [Disabil. issues]. **Added/Corp** Information Center for Individuals with Disabilities (Boston, Mass.) Massachusetts Rehabilitation Commission. (19??)-. Periodical. English. mo. Free to the disabled; $25.00 other. Information Center for Individuals with Disabilities, 27-43 Wormwood Street, Fort Point, Boston MA 02210. **Tel** (617)727-5540, FAX (617)345-9743. **ED** Linda Hillyer. **DD** 362. **Bk Rev**, (Qty: 10). **Ad Acc. Circ:** 5,000. available on audiocassette; available in large print. ***Continues Together*** *(Information Center for Individuals with Disabilities (Boston, Mass.)).*
**Desc:** Publication of the Information Center for Individuals with Disabilities, a nonprofit agency that provides information, referral, and problem-solving assistance on disability issues in Massachusetts.

UK/0964-010X
**DISABILITY NEWS.** [Disabl. news]. (1990)-. English. qt (Feb., May, Aug., Nov.). £8.00. Disability Scotland, Princes House, 5 Shandwick Place, Edinburgh EH24RG Scotland. **Tel** 011 44 31229-8632, FAX 011 44 31 229-5168. **DD** 305.9081609411. ***Continues*** *News - Scottish Council on Disability, 0264-5475.*

UK/0049-1840
**DISABILITY NOW.** English. mo. £10.00 (individual), £15.00 (institution- UK), £20.00 (institution-other). Spastics Society, 12 Park Crescent, London W1N 4EQ England. ***Continues*** *Spastics News.*
**Ind/Abst** Spec. Educ. Needs Abstr.

US/0749-8586
**DISABILITY RAG, THE.** (198?)-. Periodical. English. Six times a year (Jan., Mar., May, July, Sept., Nov.). $17.50 (individual); $35.00 (institution) US; $42.00 other. Disability Rag, PO Box 145, Louisville, KY 40201. **Tel** (502)459-5343. **ED** Sharon Kute Mellem, Managing Editor. **LC** HV1553; .D57. **Ad Acc, Adv Mgr:** Sharon Kute Mellem, **Tel** (502)459-5343. available on microfiche from University Microfilms International (UMI).
**Desc:** Covers disability rights and societal response.
**Ind/Abst** Altern. Press Index (199?-).

US
**DISABILITY STATISTICS REPORT / NATIONAL INSTITUTE ON DISABILITY AND REHABILITATION RESEARCH.** **Added/Corp** National Institute on Disability and Rehabilitation Research (U.S.) United States. Office of Special Education and Rehabilitative Services. (1991)-. English. US Department of Education Rehabilitation Services Administration, Office of Special Education & Rehabilitative Services, Washington DC 20202. **NLM** W2; A N2055d.

US/1041-5718
**DISABILITY STUDIES QUARTERLY : DSQ.** [Disabil. stud. q.]. **Added/Corp** Brandeis University. Dept. of Sociology. **VFOAT** DSQ. (19??)-. Periodical. English. Four times a year. $40.00 (institutions), $30.00 (individuals), $15.00 (students) US; $35.00 Canada; $45.00 other. Disability Studies Quarterly, Brandeis University, Dept of Sociology, PO Box 9110, Waltham MA 02254-9110. **Tel** (617)736-2644, FAX (617)736-4724 Sociology, telex 7607715. **(Subscription address:** Taped version (for visually impaired): Irving Kenneth Zola, Sociology, Brandeis University, PO Box 9110, Waltham, MA 02254-9110**)** **ED** Irving Kenneth Zola. **DD** 362. ***Continues*** *Disability and Chronic Disease Quarterly.*
**Desc:** Digest for and by those concerned with policy research aspects of disability.

CN/1186-9666
**DISABILITY TODAY (ST. CATHARINES).** (DISABILITY TODAY.). [Diabil. today]. Vol. 1, Issue 1 (Summer 1991)-. Periodical. English. qt (Feb., May, Aug., Nov.). 16.82Can$ Canada; 24.00Can$ US & Mexico; 28.00Can$ other. Disability Today Publishing Group, PO Box 237, Grimsby, Ontario, L3M 4G3 Canada. **Tel** (416) 945-5577. **ED** Hilda Hoch & Jeff Tiessen. **DD** 362.4/0971/05. **Ad Acc. Circ:** 25,000.

AT/1032-2396
**DISABLED AND AGED PERSONS AUSTRALIA ... PRELIMINARY RESULTS.** **See** Physically Impaired-Abstracting, Bibliographies and Statistics.

US
**DISABLED OUTDOORS.** English. qt. $10.00 (one year) $19.00 (two year) $27.00 (three year) US; $16.00 (one year) $30.00 (two year) Canada. Disabled Outdoors, 2052 West 23rd Street, Chicago IL 60608. **Tel** (708)358-4160, FAX (708)358-4160. Index available. **Bk Rev. Ad Acc. Pr Rev.** ctrl circ.
**Desc:** Covers all types of outdoor recreational activities for persons with disabilities, including hunting, camping, how-to, new products and services for disabled sportspersons throughout the US and Canada.

US/1067-098X
**DISABLED OUTDOORS MAGAZINE.** [Disabl. Outdoors Mag.]. **VFOAT** Disabled Outdoors. (1987)-. Periodical. English. qt. $10.00 US; $16.00 Canada; $30.00 other. Disabled Outdoors, 2052 West 23rd Street, Chicago IL 60608. **Tel** (708)358-4160, FAX (708)358-4160. **ED** Carolyn Dohme. **DD** 362. **Bk Rev. Ad Acc. Circ:** 6,000 (ctrl).
**Desc:** For sportspersons with disabilities. Covers all types of outdoor recreation, accesssible travel, services, adaptive products and instructions.

AU/0173-170X
**DISORDERS OF HUMAN COMMUNICATION.** ***Ceased.*** **See** Medical Science and Technology-Otorhinolaryngology.

GW/0177-8293
**DMSG AKTIV.** [DMSG akt.]. **VFOAT** Deutsche Multiple-Sklerose-Gesellschaft Aktiv. (1984)-. Periodical. German. qt. Deutsche Multiple Sklerose Gesellschaft, Bundesverband e. V., Vahrenwalder Strasse 205-207, 30165 Hannover Germany. **Tel** 05 11 63 30 23, FAX 05 11 63 38 87. **ED** Dorothea Pitschnau. **UDC** 616.832-004.2. ***Continues*** *Mitteilungsblatt - Deutsche Multiple-Sklerose-Gesellschaft e.V., 0175-7334.*

US
**DORS OPENERS.** **Added/Corp** Illinois. Dept. of Rehabilitation Services. Vol. 1, No. 1 (Spring 1986)-. Periodical. English. qt. Department of Rehabilitation Services, PO Box 1587, Springfield IL 62705. **Tel** (216)785-3893. ***Continues*** *DORS Openers.*

US
**DOWN SYNDROME TODAY.** Winter (1992)-. English. $16.00. Down Syndrome Today, PO Box 212, Holtsville NY 11742. **Tel** (516)654-3242. **DD** 616.85. **Ad Acc.**
**Desc:** Features cover all aspects of Down Syndrome, and standing columns are written by medical experts.

AT
**DOWNS SYNDROME ASSOCIATION OF NEW SOUTH WALES NEWSLETTER.** (19??)-. Newsletter. English. Six times a year (Feb., Apr., June, Aug., Oct., Dec.). 20.00Aus$ (individuals); 30.00Aus$ (institutions) Comes with Downs Syndrome Association of New South Wales membership. Downs Syndrome Association of New South Wales, PO Box 2356, Parramatta NSW 2151 Australia. **Tel** 011 61 02 6834333, FAX 011 61 02 6834020. **ED** C. J. Baker. **Bk Rev**, (Qty: 4). **Circ:** 1,300 (ctrl).
**Desc:** News and information about the people with Downs Syndrome.

CN/0843-2716
**DPWT TIMES, THE.** [DPWT times]. **Added/Corp** Disabled Persons Working Together. **VAT** Disabled Persons Working Together Times. Vol. 1, No. 3 (Sept. 1988)-. Periodical. English. Twelve times a year. $30.00 schools, hospitals, and non-profit organizations; $18.00 individuals; $38.00 other. Disabled Persons Working Together, 517 College Street Suite 410, Toronto Ontario M6G 4A2 Canada. **Tel** (416)966-0100. **DD** 362.4/05. ***Continues*** *DPWT Newsletter, 0843-2708.*

US/0893-6633
**DYSMORPHOLOGY AND CLINICAL GENETICS.** ***Ceased.*** [Dysmorphol. clin. genet.]. Vol. 1, No. 1 (1987)-(19??). Academic Scholarly Publication. English. qt. Blackwell Scientific Publishers, 238 Main Street, Cambridge MA 02142. **Tel** (617)547-7110, (800)835-6770, FAX (617)547-0789. **DD** 616. **NLM** W1; DY994. **[CCC]**. available on microfilm and microfiche from University Microfilms International (UMI). ***Continues*** *Journal of Clinical Dysmorphology, 0736-4407;* ***Absorbed*** *Tielines.*
**Ind/Abst** EMBASE (19??-19??).

FR
**ECHOS DU MONDE / COSMOS EN BRAILLE.** (19??)-. French. ir (10 issues). 120.00F. Assn Valentin Hay pur le Bien des Aveugles, 97 Boul des Belges, 69006 Lyon France.

FR
**ECHOS DU MONDE / ETOILE EN BRAILLE.** French. ir (10 issues). 110.00F. Assn Valentin Hay pur le Bien des Aveugles, 97 Boul des Belges, 69006 Lyon France.

CN
**EDMONTON AUTISM SOCIETY UPDATE.** **See** Medical Science and Technology-Neurology.

UK/0141-7282
**EDUCARE LONDON.** **See** Education-Special Education and Rehabilitation.

US
**EDUCATIONAL OPPORTUNITIES THROUGH FEDERAL ASSISTANCE PROGRAMS - (OHIO).** **See** Education.

CN/0318-9139
**ENTENDRE.** **Added/Corp** Association du Quebec Pour Enfants Avec Problemes Auditifs. Vol. 2, No. 4 (Summer 1974)-. French. Six times a year (Feb., Apr., June, Aug., Oct., Dec.). 30.00Can$ (individual), 50.00Can$ (institutions), Canada; 40.00Can$ (individual), 60.00Can$ (institutions), other. Association of Quebec Enfants Problemes Auditifs, 3700 Berri/Suite 440, Montreal Quebec H2L 4G9 Canada. **Tel** (514)842-3926, FAX 9514)842-8706. **DD** 362.4/2/05. cum. index. **Ad Acc. Circ:** 1,000 (ctrl). ***Continues*** *Association du Quebec Pour Enfants Avec Problemes Auditifs. Bulletin, 0318-9120.*

# Physically Impaired

**Desc:** Information about contacts with the specialists, speech therapists and audiology-ORL and others, who deals with deaf children.

CN/1183-2738
**ENTRE-NOUS - ASSOCIATION CANADIENNE DE LA DYSTROPHIE MUSCULAIRE.** (ENTRE-NOUS.). [Entre-nous - Assoc. can. dystrophie musculaire]. **Added/Corp** Association Canadienne de la Dystrophie Musculaire. Section u Quebec. **VFOAT** Bulletin d'Information. **VAT** Bulletin d'Information - Association Canadienne de la Dystrophie Musculaire; Bulletin d'Information Entre-Nous. Vol. 1, No 1 (Mar. 1991)-. Periodical. French. Limited free distribution. Association Canadienne de la Dystrophie Musculaire, Section du Quebec, Bureau 782, 1265 Rue Berri, Montreal Quebec H2L 4X4 Canada. **DD** 616.7/48/006071.

CN/1181-974X
**EQUITY NEWSLETTER (TORONTO).** (EQUITY NEWSLETTER.). [Equity newsl.]. **Added/Corp** Disabled People for Employment Equity. Vol. 1, No. 1 (July 1990)-. Newsletter. English. Three times a year. $6.00. Disabled People for Employment Equity, Suite B-5, 597 Parliament Street, Toronto, Ontario M4X 1W3 Canada. **DD** 305.9.

FR
**ET LA LUMIERE FUT.** (19??)-. Periodical. French. Eleven times a year. 146.00F. Association Valentin Hauy, 5 rue Duroc, 75343 Paris Cedex 07 France. **Tel** 011 33 1 47340790.

US/0098-0986
**EUROPEAN REGISTER OF RESEARCH ON VISUAL IMPAIRMENT.** (1974)-. Periodical. English. American Foundation for the Blind, 15 West 16th Street, New York NY 10011. **Tel** (212)620-2000, (800)829-0500. **ED** J M Gill and M J Tobin. **NLM** WW 22 GA1 E8.

US/1044-8217
**FAMILIES AND DISABILITY NEWSLETTER.** (FAMILIES AND DISABILITY NEWSLETTER / THE UNIVERSITY OF KANSAS, BEACH CENTER ON FAMILIES AND DISABILITY.). [Fam. disabil. newsl.]. **Added/Corp** University of Kansas. Beach Center on Families and Disability. **VFOAT** Families and Disability. Vol. 1, No. 1 (Spring 1989)-. Periodical. English. Three times a year (Mar., July, Oct.). Free to US; $5.00 Canada & Mexico; $10.00 others. Beach Center on Families & Disability, 3111 Haworth Hall, University of Kansas, Lawrence KS 66045. **Tel** (913)864-7600, FAX (913)864-7605. **ED** Cindy Higgins. **DD** 362. **Pr Rev. Circ:** 13,000.
**Desc:** Contain research findings and programs information of use to families who have a member with a disability. It lists the service providers, policy makers and other related topics.

SP
**FARO DEL SILENCIO.** Spanish. mo. 2.968ptas Spain, $38.00 other. Federation Nacional Sordos Esp, Calle Acala 160 1 F, 28028 Madrid Spain. **Tel** 011 34 1 3565610, FAX 3554336. **Ad Acc. Circ:** 2,500 (ctrl).
**Desc:** Specialized publication for people related with the deaf world.

US
**FINANCIAL AND STATISTICAL REPORT: SPECIAL EDUCATION (ILLINOIS).** See Education-Special Education and Rehabilitation.

US/0099-2135
**FLORIDA STATE PLAN FOR THE EDUCATION OF EXCEPTIONAL STUDENTS.** See Education-Special Education and Rehabilitation.

US/0740-4956
**FOCUS, LIBRARY SERVICE TO OLDER ADULTS, PEOPLE WITH DISABILITIES.** See Library and Information Sciences.

CN/1182-1353
**FOCUS / SOCIETY FOR MANITOBANS WITH DISABILITIES.** [Focus - Soc. Manit. Disabil.]. **Added/Corp** Society for Manitobans with Disabilities. (1984)-. Periodical. English. qt. Limited free distribution. **DD** 362.4/097127.

US/0093-2825
**FOR YOUNGER READERS.** (FOR YOUNGER READERS : BRAILLE AND TALKING BOOKS.). Began with 1964/65. Irregular. be. National Library Service for the Blind and Physically Handicapped, Library of Congress, 1291 Taylor Street Northwest, Washington DC 20542. **Tel** (800)424-8567, (202)707-5100, (800)424-9100. **LC** Z5345.A2; F6. **DD** 028.52/05. available in braille; available on audiocassette.

US/0748-4615
**FOREIGN LANGUAGE BOOKS.** [Foreign lang. books]. **VFOAT** Libros en Espanol; Livres en Francais; Livros em Portugues; Libri in Italiano; Bucher Auf Deutsch. 1984-. English (French, German, Italian, Portuguese and Spanish). ir (biennial or triennial). Free. National Library Service for the Blind and Physically Handicapped, Library of Congress, 1291 Taylor Street Northwest, Washington DC 20542. **Tel** (800)424-8567, (202)707-5100, (800)424-9100. **LC** Z5347; .L54; HV1731. **DD** 011. cum. index. **Circ:** 2,000. available on diskette (8 RPM). **Continues** Libros Parlantes.
**Desc:** Catalog of recorded and braille books in foreign languages produced by the Library of Congress for blind and physically handicapped persons.

US/0149-967X
**FORUM (DEVON).** See Education.

●US/1062-8134
**FREE SPIRIT (MIAMI, FLA.).** (FREE SPIRIT.). [Free spirit]. **VFOAT** Free Spirit USA. Vol. 1, No. 1 (June 1992)-. Periodical. English. mo. $15.00. Free Spirit Publishing Co., Inc., PO Box 2000, Coconut Grove FL 33233-2000. **Tel** (305)569-9990, FAX (305)461-3094. **ED** Noel Leon. **DD** 362. **Bk Rev**, (Qty: 12-15). **Ad Acc, Adv Mgr:** Dee Johns. Full Page (B&W) $3150.00. Half Page (B&W) $1575.00. Full Page (Color) $3845.00. Half Page (Color) $1923.00. **Pr Rev. Acid Free. Circ:** 55,000.
**Desc:** Offers news, features and information to persons with physical or developmental disabilities, their supporters (family, friends) and to the health care providers who serve the disability community.

US/0883-3419
**FUTURE REFLECTIONS.** (FUTURE REFLECTIONS : THE NATIONAL FEDERATION OF THE BLIND MAGAZINE FOR PARENTS OF BLIND CHILDREN.). [Future reflect.]. **Added/Corp** National Federation of the Blind. Vol. 1, No. 5 (Oct./Nov. 1982)-. Periodical. English. Four times a year. $8.00 (members); $15.00 (non-members). National Federation of the Blind, 1800 Johnson Street, Baltimore MD 21230. **Tel** (410)659-9314, FAX (410)685-5653. **DD** 362. **Bk Rev. Circ:** 10,000. available on audiocassette (2-track). **Continues** NFB Newsletter for Parents of Blind Children.
**Desc:** Features articles written by parents, blind adults, and educators about all aspects of blindness and raising a blind or visually impaired child.

US/0016-4089
**GALLAUDET TODAY.** See Education-Special Education and Rehabilitation.

US/0739-7453
**GLAD NEWS, THE.** (THE GLAD NEWS : OFFICIAL ORGAN OF THE GREATER LOS ANGELES COUNCIL ON DEAFNESS, INC.). **Added/Corp** Greater Los Angeles Council on Deafness. **VFOAT** G.L.A.D. News. **VAT** Greater Los Angeles Council on Deafness News. (19??)-. Periodical. English. qt. $13.50 (members), $18.50 (non-members). Greater Los Angeles Council on Deafness, 2222 Laverna Avenue, Los Angeles CA 90041. **Tel** (213)478-8000, FAX (213)383-3803.

SZ
**GLANEUSE.** French. ir. 25.00F. Asile des Aveugles, Av de France 15, 1004 Lausanne Switzerland. **Tel** 011 41 21 250211.

CN/0820-7518
**GOELAND (MONTREAL).** See Sociology-Social Services and Welfare.

US/0731-0730
**GOVERNMENTAL AFFAIRS REVIEW.** Ceased. (GOVERNMENTAL AFFAIRS REVIEW : REPORT ON ISSUES AFFECTING THE COMMUNICATIVELY IMPAIRED.). [Gov. aff. rev.]. **Added/Corp** American Speech-Language-Hearing Association. (198?)-(19??). Periodical. English. qt. American Speech Language and Hearing Association, 10801 Rockville Pike, Rockville MD 20852. **Tel** (301)897-5700.

US
**GRANTS FOR PHYSICALLY AND MENTALLY DISABLED.** See Philanthropy.

US/0196-9870
**GREEN PAGES REHAB SOURCEBOOK, THE.** See Sociology-Social Services and Welfare.

US/0884-7347
**GUIDE TO GRADUATE EDUCATION IN SPEECH-LANGUAGE PATHOLOGY AND AUDIOLOGY.** See Education-Higher Education.

CN/0821-7815
**HABILITES LOISIRS.** (HABILITES LOISIRS : BULLETIN D'INFORMATION DE L'ASSOCIATION QUEBECOISE DE LOISIR POUR PERSONNES HANDICAPEES.). V. 1, No 1 (Feb. 1983)-. Bulletin. French. qt. Free. Association Quebecoise de Loisir pour Personnes Handicapees, 4545 Ave Pierre-de-Coubertin, CP 1000, Succursale M, Montreal Quebec H1V 3R2 Canada. **Tel** (514)252-3144. **DD** 790.1/96/09714.

NE
**HANDICAP MAGAZINE.** English. mo. Wegener Tijl Tijdschriften Group, Postbus 9943, 1006 AP Amsterdam Netherlands. **Tel** 011 31 20 5182828.

US/0194-7818
**HANDICAPPED REQUIREMENTS HANDBOOK. SUPPLEMENT.** Title Change. **Added/Corp** Federal Programs Advisory Service. (197?)-(199?). English. mo. Thompson Publishing Group, 7711 Anderson Road, Tampa FL 33634. **Tel** (800)677-3789, (813)282-8607. **[CCC]. Continued by** Section 504 Compliance Handbook. Supplement, 1068-6533.

FR/0180-9040
**HANDICAPS ET INADAPTATIONS PARIS.** (HANDICAPS ET INADAPTATIONS LES CAHIERS DU CTNERHI.). (1978)-. Periodical. French. qt. 333.01F France; 360.00F other. CTNERHI, 236 Bis rue de Tolbiac, 75013 Paris France. **Tel** 011 33 1 45655900. **UDC** 36. Index available.

KO
**HANGUK CHONGSONYON SONDO KYOYUK YONGAM.** **Added/Corp** Taehan Chongsonyon Sondo Hyophoe. **VFOAT** Chongsonyon Sondo Kyoyuk Yongam. (1990/1991)-. Korean. Taehan Chongsonyon Sondo Hyophoe, 72-29-Ho Sungin-Dong, Chongno-ku Seoul Korea. **LC** LC4097.K6; H36.

JA
**HATARAKU HIROBA.** **Added/Corp** Shintai Shogaisha Koyo Sokushin Kyokai (Japan). (1977)-. Japanese. ¥180. Shintai Shogaisha Koyo Sokushin Kyokai, c/o Toranomon Toso Building, 9-2 Shiba Kotohirachoi, Minato-ku 105, Tokyo Japan. **LC** HD7256.J3; H37.

US/0162-5667
**HEARING & SPEECH ACTION.** [Hear. speech action]. **Added/Corp** National Association for Hearing and Speech Action. **VAT** Hearing and Speech Action. Vol. 45, No. 6/Vol. 46, No. 1 (Nov./Dec. 1977/Jan./Feb. 1978)-. Periodical. English. bm. $6.00. NAHSA, 814 Thayer Avenue, Silver Springs MD 20910. **DD** 362. available on microfilm and microfiche from University Microfilms International (UMI). **Continues** H & S, Hearing & Speech Action, 0162-5667.

US/0360-9278
**HEARING REHABILITATION QUARTERLY.** [Hear. rehabil. q.]. **Added/Corp** New York League for the Hard of Hearing. Vol. 1 (Fall 1975)-. Periodical. English. qt. $25.00 US; $35.00 other. New York League for the Hard of Hearing, 71 West 23rd Street, New York NY 10010. **Tel** (212)741-7650. **ED** John McKendry. **LC** HV2350; .H4. **DD** 362.4/2. **NLM** W1 HE6418. cum. index. **Bk Rev. Ad Acc. Circ:** 3,000 (ctrl). **Supersedes** Highlights / New York (1960), 0360-9286.
**Desc:** A benefit of membership in the New York League for the Hard of Hearing; invites previously unpublished articles concerning otology, audiology, communication therapies, education, psychological factors, prosthetics-technology, and personal experiences.
**Ind/Abst** Psychol. Abstr. (1975-); PsycINFO; PsycLit.

US
**HEARSAY.** Spring 1986-. Periodical. English. sa. $40.00. Ohio Speech and Hearing Association, 9331 Union Road South, Miamisburg OH 45342. **Tel** (513)886-4972. **ED** Wayne Secord, Jean Blosser and Bob Glaser. **Ad Acc. Pr Rev. Circ:** 4,000. **Continues** Ohio Journal of Speech and Hearing, 0736-5381.

US
**HERALD (FLORIDA SCHOOL FOR THE DEAF AND BLIND).** See College and School Publications.

US/1065-1918
**HIP REPORT, THE.** (THE HIP REPORT / HELP FOR INCONTINENT PEOPLE.). [HIP rep.]. **Added/Corp** Help for Incontinent People (Organization). (19??)-. Periodical. English. qt. Free to members; $15.00 membership. HIP Inc., PO Box 544, Union SC 29379. **Tel** (803)579-7900. **DD** 616.

GW/0342-4898
**HORGESCHADIGTEN PADAGOGIK.** **Added/Corp** Bund Deutscher Taubstummenlehrer. (1972)-. Periodical. German. Six times a year (Feb., Apr., June, Aug., Oct., Dec.). DM49.00. Julius Groos Verlag, Postfach 102423 Hertzstrasse 6, D 69104 Heidelberg Germany. **Tel** 011 49 6221 303621, FAX 011 49 6221 301993. **ED** Manfred Breitinger. **NLM** W1 HO459L. **[CCC].** Index available. **Ad Acc. Circ:** 2,000. **Continues** Neue Blatter fuer Taubstummenbildung, 0028-310X.

US/1064-6434
**HORIZONS (GAMBRILLS, MD.).** (HORIZONS : NEWS BY AND FOR PEOPLE WITH DISABILITIES.). [Horizons]. Vol. 1, No. 1 (1986)-. Periodical. English. mo. $15.00. Haras and Terbor Inc., PO Box 985, Gambrills MD 21054. **Tel** (301)621-9332. **ED** J M Storrs. **DD** 362. **Bk Rev. Ad Acc.**

Physically Impaired

US/0091-4584
**HOW FEDERAL AGENCIES HAVE SERVED THE HANDICAPPED.** **Main/Corp** United States. President's Committee on Employment of the Handicapped. English. Presidents Committee on Employment of the Handicapped, 1111 20th Street NW, Washington DC 20210. **LC** HV1553; .U5A. **DD** 362.4/0973. **NLM** W2 A P7HA.

CN/1198-3795
**ICIDH AND ENVIRONMENTAL FACTORS INTERNATIONAL NETWORK.** **See** Sociology-Social Services and Welfare.

CN/1182-5049
**ICIDH INTERNATIONAL NETWORK.** ***Title Change.*** **See** Sociology-Social Services and Welfare.

US/1053-6035
**ILLUSTRATED DIRECTORY OF HANDICAPPED PRODUCTS, THE.** [Illus. dir. handicap. prod.]. **VFOAT** Illustrated Directory. (1989/90)-. Directory. English. an. $32.95. Illustrated Directory of Handicapped Products, 2102 Rexford Road, Suite 172, Charlotte NC 28211. **Tel** (704)364-0719, FAX (704)362-1733. **ED** Monte Mace. **LC** HV1569.5; .I43. **DD** 681/.761. **NLM** W 26; I295. **Ad Acc. Circ:** 7,000.
**Desc:** Lists products for the physically challenged including wheelchairs, adapted vehicles, exercise equipment, eating/drinking aids, bathroom/hygiene aids, and respiratory products.

US/0732-1953
**ILRU INSIGHTS.** (ILRU INSIGHTS : A PUBLICATION OF THE ILRU PROJECT.). [ILRU insights]. **Added/Corp** ILRU Project. **VFOAT** I.L.R.U. Insights. Vol. 1, No. 1 (Mar. 1982)-. Periodical. English. Six times a year (Jan., Mar., May, July, Sept., Nov.). Free. ILRU Research & Training Center, 2323 South Shepherd, Suite 1000, Houston TX 77019. **Tel** (713)520-0232. **ED** Laurel Richards. **Circ:** 2,000 (ctrl).
**Desc:** Addresses issues concerning programs assisting disabled people to live more independently. Includes updates on research and training activities, publications, and federal/state trends affecting independent living.

CN/0383-9710
**IMAGE (VANCOUVER).** **See** Medical Science and Technology.

SA/0019-2724
**IMFAMA.** [Imfama]. (1961)-. Periodical. English (Afrikaans). Six times a year (Feb., Apr., June, Aug., Oct., Dec.). R40.00. South Africa National Council for the Blind, PO Box 11149 Brooklyn, Pretoria 0011 South Africa. **Tel** 011 27 12 346 1171, FAX 011 27 12 346 1177. **ED** Dr. William Rowland. **DD** _a362.41. **Bk Rev**, (Qty: 6). **Ad Acc, Adv Mgr:** same as editor. **Circ:** 1350. available in braille from Tape Aids for the Blind.
**Desc:** Covers visual disability.

US/0888-9724
**IN THE MAINSTREAM (WASHINGTON, D.C.).** (IN THE MAINSTREAM.). [In mainstream]. **Added/Corp** Mainstream, Inc. (Washington, D.C.). **VFOAT** Mainstream. Vol. 1 (Jan/Feb. 1975)-. Periodical. English. Six times a year (Jan., Mar., May, July, Sept., Nov.). $60.00 (mainstream); $135.00 (mainstream information network); $149.95 (mainstream manager). Mainstream Inc., 3 Bethesda Metro Center, Suite 830, Bethesda MD 20814. **Tel** (301)654-2400, FAX (301)654-2403. **ED** Fritz Rumpel. **DD** 331. cum. index. **Bk Rev**, (Qty: 2). **Circ:** 1,300. available on audiocassette.
**Desc:** Covers issues affecting the employers and persons with disabilities.

AT/0815-2276
**INDEPENDENT LIVING.** [Indep. living]. (1984)-. Periodical. English. Four times a year. 23.00Aus$ Australia; 29.00Aus$ New Zealand; 35.00Aus$ others. Rala Publications, PO Box 134, 203-205 Darling Street, Balmain NSW 2041 Australia. **Tel** 011 61 2 5551944, FAX 011 61 2 5551496. **(Subscription address:** Independent Living Centre NSW, 600 Victoria Road, PO Box 706, Ryde NSW 2112 Australia, telephone: 011 61 2 808-2233**) ED** Charlotte Smedley. **DD** 362.404830994. **Bk Rev. Ad Acc, Adv Mgr:** Maria Hermanson, **Tel** (07)341-0461.
**Desc:** Disseminates and exchanges information on commercially available products and equipment for people with a disability.

US/1048-3772
**INDEPENDENT LIVING (1989).** (INDEPENDENT LIVING.). [Indep. living]. Vol. 4, No. 1 (1989)-. Periodical. English. qt. $15.00 (1 year), $27.00 (2 year), $40.00 (3 year). Equal Opportunity Publications Inc, 150 Motor Parkway Suite 420, Hauppage NY 11788. **Tel** (516)273-0066, FAX (516)273-8936. **LC** RA645.35; .I58. **DD** 362.1/0973/05. **NLM** W1; IN116VD. available on an online database (file 149/Full-Text) from DIALOG. ***Continues*** *Independent Living & Health Care Today, 1040-6417.*
**Ind/Abst** Acad. Abstr. Full Text Elite (Jan. 1992-); Acad. Abstr. (Jan. 1992-); Acad. Search (Jan. 1992-); Health Index (1989-); Health Period. Database [Full Txt.]; Health Ref. Cent. (Jan. 1989-) [Full Txt.] [Full Cov.]; Health Source (Jan. 1992-); INFO-SOUTH Abstr.; Mag. Search.

US/1055-520X
**INDIVIDUAL WITH DISABILITIES EDUCATION LAW REPORT.** **See** Law.

UK
**INFORMATION BULLETIN : SPOD.** (19??)-. Bulletin. English. qt. £6.00. SPOD, 86 Camden Road, London N7 0BJ England. **Tel** 011 44 71 607 8851.
**Desc:** Association to aid the sexual and personal relationships of people with a disability.

US
**INFORMATION FOR PERSONS WITH HANDICAPS OR DISABILITIES : FOR USE IN PREPARING ... RETURNS.** ***Title Change.*** **Added/Corp** United States. Internal Revenue Service. (1992)-(1992). English. Eastern Area Distribution Center, PO Box 85074, Richmond VA 23261-5074. ***Continues*** *Tax Information for Persons with Handicaps or Disabilities.* ***Continued by*** *Information for Persons with Disabilities.*

UK
**INFORMATION SERVICE FOR THE DISABLED.** (19??)-. Periodical. English. ir. £95.00. Information Service for the Disabled Living Foundation, 380-384 Harrow Road, London W9 2HU England. **Tel** 011 44 71 289 6111.

CN/0713-8474
**INFORMATION UPDATE - HUB, INFORMATION SERVICES.** (INFORMATION UPDATE.). [Inf. update - Hub, Inf. Serv.]. **Added/Corp** HUB (Physically Handicapped Service Centre). **VFOAT** Hub Information Update. **VAT** Hub Information Update. (1978)-. Periodical. English. ir. Free on request. Information Services / Canada, PO Box 13788, St John's Newfoundland, A1B 4G3 Canada. **Tel** (709)754-0352. **DD** 016.3624/048. **Circ:** 1,000 (ctrl).

IT/0393-8859
**INSEGNARE ALL' HANDICAPPATO.** **See** Education-Special Education and Rehabilitation.

US/0145-2525
**INSTRUCTIONAL CASSETTE RECORDINGS CATALOG.** **See** Music.

US/0145-2517
**INSTRUCTIONAL DISC RECORDINGS CATALOG.** **See** Music.

US/0196-5743
**INTERCHANGE (SACRAMENTO).** (INTERCHANGE.). Periodical. English. Three times a year. Free. Southwestern Region Deaf and Blind Center, 721 Capitol Mall, Sacramento CA 95814.

US/0735-0112
**INTERNATIONAL DIRECTORY OF ACCESS GUIDES, THE.** (THE INTERNATIONAL DIRECTORY OF ACCESS GUIDES / PREPARED BY THE STAFF OF REHABILITATION WORLD.). [Int. dir. access guides]. **VFOAT** Access Guides. Began with 1978-79. Directory. English. an. Rehabilitation International, 25 East 21st Street/4th Floor, New York NY 10010. **Tel** (212)420-1500, FAX (212)505-0871, telex 446-412. **NLM** HV 3022 I61.

GW/0342-5282
**INTERNATIONAL JOURNAL OF REHABILITATION RESEARCH.** [Int. j. rehabil. res.]. **Added/Corp** Rehabilitation International. **VFOAT** Internationale Zeitschrift fur Rehabilitationsforschung; Revue Internationale de Recherches de Readaptation; IJRR. Vol. 1 (Jan. 1978)-. Periodical. English (French and German). qt. $120.00 US and Canada; £70.00 Europe; £75.00 other. Chapman & Hall, 2-6 Boundary Row, London SE1 8HN England. **Tel** 011 44 71 865 0066, FAX 011 44 71 522 9623, telex 290164 Chapmag. **(Subscription address:** Chapman & Hall, Cheriton House, North Way, Andover, Hampshire, SP10 5BE England.**) ED** P. Cornes. **LC** RM695; .I58. **DD** 617.1/03/05. **NLM** W1 IN785T. **CODEN** IJRRDK. Index available. **Bk Rev. Ad Acc. Pr Rev. Circ:** 500. Documents available from BIOSIS Document Express, ADONIS.
**Desc:** Forum for the publication of research into disability and handicap experienced by people of all ages in both developed and developing societies. Areas of interest include disability and age, psychiatric rehabilitation, mental health of the physically disabled, testing of disability, vocational development, and the physical, practical, social and educational aspects of disability and rehabilitation.
**Ind/Abst** ADONIS; Biol. Abstr.; Cumul. Index Nurs. Allied Health Lit.; Curr. Index J. Educ.; EMBASE; Ergon. Abstr. (?-?); Except. Child Educ. Resour.; HILITES; Index Med.; Psychol. Abstr. (1977-); PsycINFO; PsycLit; Soc. Plann. Policy Dev. Abstr.; Soc. Work Abstr. (?-?); Sociol. Abstr.; SportSearch.

UK/0959-6402
**INTERNATIONAL JOURNAL OF SIGN LINGUISTICS.** **See** Linguistics.

US/0020-8477
**INTERNATIONAL REHABILITATION REVIEW.** [Int. rehabil. rev.]. **Added/Corp** International Society for Rehabilitation of the Disabled. International Society for Rehabilitation of the Disabled. (Jan. 1962)-. Academic Scholarly Publication. English. Three times a year. $30.00. Rehabilitation International, 25 East 21st Street/4th Floor, New York NY 10010. **Tel** (212)420-1500, FAX (212)505-0871, telex 446-412. **ED** Barbara Duncan. **NLM** W1 IN828D. **CODEN** IRERB. **Bk Rev. Circ:** 10,000 (ctrl). available on microfilm and microfiche from University Microfilms International (UMI). ***Supersedes*** *International Society for Rehabilitation of the Disabled. Bulletin.*
**Desc:** Reports on trends concerning disability prevention and rehabilitation of people with disabilities from an international perspective.
**Ind/Abst** EMBASE; Soc. Work Abstr. [Select. Cov.].

US/0160-7472
**INTERNATIONAL TELEPHONE DIRECTORY OF THE DEAF.** ***Title Change.*** **See** Communication-Telecommunications.

FR/0249-6550
**JOURNAL D'ERGOTHERAPIE PARIS.** **See** Physical Therapy.

US/8756-7342
**JOURNAL FOR COMPUTER USERS IN SPEECH AND HEARING.** ***Ceased.*** [J. comput. users speech hear.]. **Added/Corp** Computer Users in Speech and Hearing (Organization). **VFOAT** CUSH Journal. Vol. 1, No. 1 (May 1985)-Vol. 9 (1993). Periodical. English. sa (2 issues per year). CUSH Busines Office, PO Box 2160, William Seaton, Hudson OH 44230. **Tel** (216)655-2392. **LC** RC429; .J68. **DD** 616.85/506. **NLM** W1; JO379L.

US/1056-263X
**JOURNAL OF DEVELOPMENTAL AND PHYSICAL DISABILITIES.** [J. dev. phys. disabil.]. Vol. 3, No. 1 (Mar. 1991)-. Periodical. English. Four times a year. $160.00 institutions, $42.00 individuals US; $185.00 institutions, $49.00 individuals other. Plenum Press, 233 Spring Street, New York NY 10013-1578. **Tel** (212)620-8000, (800)221-9369, FAX (212)463-0742, (212)807-1047, telex 23/421139. **LC** HV1551; .J68. **DD** 362.4/05. **NLM** W1; JO619TK. **CODEN** JDPDE6. **[CCC].** available on microfilm and microfiche from University Microfilms International (UMI). ***Continues*** *Journal of the Multihandicapped Person, 0892-7561.*
**Ind/Abst** Psychol. Abstr. (1989-); PsycINFO.

US/0097-8892
**JOURNAL OF DEVELOPMENTAL DISABILITIES, THE.** ***Suspended.*** Vol. 1 (1974)-?. Periodical. English. qt. $10.50. Journal of Developmental Disabilities, PO Box 8470 Gentilly Station, New Orleans LA 70182. **LC** HV3000; .J68. **DD** 362.4/05.

US/1047-1448
**JOURNAL OF DISABILITY.** [J. disabil.]. **Added/Corp** American Academy of Disability Evaluating Physicians. (1990)-. Periodical. English. qt (Jan., Apr., July, Oct.). $100.00 (institutions), $80.00 (individuals) US; $170.00 (institutions), $150.00 (individuals) other. American Academy of Disability, 2045 South Arlington Heights Road, Suite 104, Arlington Heights IL 60005. **Tel** (708)228-6095. **DD** 362. **NLM** W1; JO622W.

US/1044-2073
**JOURNAL OF DISABILITY POLICY STUDIES, THE.** [J. disabil. policy stud.]. **Added/Corp** University of Arkansas, Fayetteville. Dept. of Rehabilitation Education and Research. **VFOAT** DP. Vol. 1, No. 1 (Spring 1990)-. Periodical. English. sa. $22.00 (institutions), $14.00 (individuals). University of Arkansas Department of Rehabilitation Education, 346 North West Avenue, Fayetteville AR 72701. **Tel** (501)575-3656. **ED** Kay Fletcher Schriner. **LC** HV1551; .J67. **DD** 362.4/0973/05. **NLM** W1; JO622K. cum. index. **Bk Rev. Ad Acc. Pr Rev.**
**Desc:** Topics on disability policy from the perspectives of a variety of academic disciplines and publishes articles pertaining to both macro-policy and micro-policy issues.

CN/0711-222X
**JOURNAL OF LEISURABILITY (1980).** (JOURNAL OF LEISURABILITY.). [J. leis.]. Vol. 7, No. 3 (July 1973)-. Periodical. English. an. 40.00Can$ (institutions), 30.00Can$ (individuals). Leisurability Publications, 36 Bessemer Court, Unit 3, Concord Ontario L4K 3C9 Canada. **Tel** (416)669-5373, FAX (416)669-1927. **ED** Judith McGill. **DD** 362.4/05. **NLM** W1 JO745E. **[CCC].** Index available. **Pr Rev. Acid Free. Circ:** 500. available on microfilm and microfiche from University Microfilms International (UMI). ***Continues*** *Leisurability, 0317-2317.*
**Desc:** Focuses on a specific theme with general application to a wide range of people and areas of life. The central topic is further developed through a series of support articles examining current and future trends.

**Ind/Abst** Leis. Recreat. Tour. Abstr.; Phys. Educ. Index; Rural Dev. Abstr.; SPORT Discus; SportSearch; World Agric. Econ.

●US/1065-1438
**JOURNAL OF MEDICAL SPEECH-LANGUAGE PATHOLOGY.** [J. med. speech-lang. pathol.]. **VFOAT** Journal of Medical Speech Language Pathology. (1993)-. Periodical. English. Four times a year (Mar, June, Sept, Dec). $96.00. Singular Publishing Group, 4284 41st Street, San Diego CA 92105. **Tel** (800)521-8545, (619)521-8000, FAX (619)563-9008. **ED** Leonard L. LaPointe Ph.D., (phone: (602)965-2905). **DD** 616. **CODEN** JSLPEP. Index available (Bound in 4th iss., in (Dec).). **Pr Rev. Circ:** 850.

CN/0707-7807
**JOURNAL OF PRACTICAL APPROACHES TO DEVELOPMENTAL HANDICAP.** [J. pract. approaches dev. handicap]. **Added/Corp** Vocational and Rehabilitation Research Institute. Vol. 1 (Feb. 1977)-. Periodical. English (French; summaries and/or abstracts in French). sa. 14.00Can$ (institutions), 11.00Can$ (individuals) Canada; 16.00Can$ other. University of Calgary Press, 2500 University Drive Northwest, Calgary Alberta T2N 1N4 Canada. **Tel** (403)220-7578. **DD** 362.4'05. **NLM** W1 JO84. **Bk Rev. Pr Rev. Circ:** 400 (ctrl).
**Desc:** Publication concerning disability, practice and applied research in the field of rehabilitation.
**Ind/Abst** Appl. Soc. Sci. Index Abstr.; Spec. Educ. Needs Abstr.

US/0148-3846
**JOURNAL OF REHABILITATION ADMINISTRATION.** [J. rehabil. adm.]. Vol. 1 (Jan. 1977)-. Periodical. English. qt. $48.00 (institutions), $24.00 (individuals). Journal of Rehabilitation Administration, P.O.Box 19891, San Diego CA 92159. **ED** John F Newman. **LC** HD7255.A2; J67. **NLM** W1 JO866RE. Index available. cum. index. **Bk Rev. Ad Acc. Circ:** 1,900 (ctrl).
**Desc:** Theoretical papers, applied research studies, and practice reports designed to improve the practice of administration, management, and supervision in a wide variety of rehabilitation settings.
**Ind/Abst** Psychol. Abstr. (1980-); PsycINFO; PsycLit.

NE/0923-0211
**JOURNAL OF REHABILITATION SCIENCES.** **Added/Corp** Nederlandse Vereniging van Artsen voor Revalidatie en Physische Geneeskunde. Scientific Society for Research into Rehabilitation in the Netherlands. **VFOAT** Tijdschrift Voor Revalidatie Wetenschappen. (198?)-. Periodical. English (summaries and/or abstracts in Dutch). qt. Fl45.00 (members VRA/WGR), Fl65.00 Netherlands; Fl95.00 other. Van Gorcum & Company BV, PO Box 43, NL 9400 AA Assen Netherlands. **Tel** 011 31 5920 46846, FAX 011 31 5920 72064. **NLM** W1; JO8675J.
**Ind/Abst** EMBASE.

●US/1059-9258
**JOURNAL OF RELIGION IN DISABILITY & REHABILITATION.** **See** Religion and Theology.

US/0022-4669
**JOURNAL OF SPECIAL EDUCATION, THE.** **See** Education-Special Education and Rehabilitation.

US/0022-4685
**JOURNAL OF SPEECH AND HEARING RESEARCH.** [J. speech hear. res.]. **Added/Corp** American Speech and Hearing Association. American Speech-Language-Hearing Association. **VFOAT** JSHR. Vol. 1 (March 1958)-. Academic Scholarly Publication. English. bm (6 issues). $114.00. American Speech Language and Hearing Association, 10801 Rockville Pike, Rockville MD 20852. **Tel** (301)897-5700. **ED** Theodore J. Glattke and Tanya M. Gallagher. **LC** RC423; .J7. **NLM** W1 JO902N. **CODEN** JSPHAH. **[CCC].** Index available. cum. index. **Ad Acc. Pr Rev. Circ:** 51,700. available on microfilm and microfiche from University Microfilms International (UMI). Documents available from BIOSIS Document Express, Ask*IEEE, UMI Article Clearinghouse, CASDDS. ***Absorbed** Journal of Speech and Hearing Disorders, 0022-4677.*
**Desc:** An archival research publication that includes papers pertaining to the processes and disorders of hearing, language and speech and to their diagnosis and treatment.
**Ind/Abst** Acad. Abstr. Full Text Elite (Jan. 1991-); Acad. Abstr. (Jan. 1991-); Acad. Ind. [Computer File] (1991-); Acad. Search (Jan. 1991-); Annu. Bibliogr. Engl. Lang. Lit.; Appl. Soc. Sci. Index Abstr.; Biol. Abstr.; Chem. Abstr.; Curr. Index J. Educ.; Dev. Med. Child Neurol. (March 1972-); Educ. Index; EMBASE; Energy Res. Abstr. (Aug. 1982-); Except. Child Educ. Resour.; Expand. Acad. Index (1991-); Health Source (Jul. 1990-); Index Med.; INFO-SOUTH Abstr.; INSPEC (March 1972-); Mag. Search; MLA Int. Bibl. Books Artic. Mod. Lang. Lit.; Newsp. Period. Abstr. (1992-); Psychol. Abstr. (1958-); PsycINFO; PsycLit; Soc. Sci. Cit. Index [Full Cov.]; Soc. Work Abstr. (?-?); Spec. Educ. Needs Abstr.

CN/0848-1970
**JOURNAL OF SPEECH-LANGUAGE PATHOLOGY AND AUDIOLOGY.** [J. speech-lang. pathol. audiol.]. **Added/Corp** Canadian Association of Speech-Language Pathologists and Audiologists. **VFOAT** Revue d'Orthophonie et d'Audiologie; JSLPA/ROA. Vol. 13, No. 1 (Mar. 1989)-. Periodical. English (French). Four times a year (Mar., June, Sept., Dec.). 45.00Can$ (individuals), $55.00 (institutions) Canada; 55.00Can$ (individuals), 65.00 (institutions) others. Canada Association of Speech Language Pathologists Audiologists, PO Box 2097, 340 Laurier West Street D, Ottawa ONT K1P 5W3 Canada. **Tel** (902)532-5104, FAX (902)532-7190. **ED** Christine Sloan. **DD** 616.85/5/005. **NLM** W1; JO902NM. **CODEN** JSLAEE. **Bk Rev. Ad Acc, Adv Mgr:** J. Sweeny, **Tel** (902)532-5104. **Pr Rev. Circ:** 4,000 (ctrl). ***Continues** Human Communication Canada, 0822-5486.*
**Desc:** It's purpose is to disseminate knowledge pertaining to human communication and human communication disorders. It is of particular interest to speech-language pathologists, audiologists, and other professionals from disciplines that impact on the broad areas of human communication and its disorders. JSLPA / ROA publishes clinical and research articles, reviews of professional resources, practice and technical notes, and professional commentaries and debates, all of which reflect the broad interests of these professionals.
**Ind/Abst** Linguist. Lang. Behav. Abstr. (1991-) [Full Cov.]; Soc. Plann. Policy Dev. Abstr.

US/0899-9228
**JOURNAL OF THE AMERICAN DEAFNESS AND REHABILITATION ASSOCIATION : JADARA.** [J. Am. Deaf. Rehabil. Assoc.]. **Added/Corp** American Deafness and Rehabilitation Association. **VFOAT** JADARA. Vol. 21, No. 4 (April 1988)-. Periodical. English. qt. $46.00 US; $56.00 other. American Deafness and Rehabilitation Association, PO Box 251554, Little Rock AR 72225. **Tel** (501)868-8850, FAX (501)868-8812. **LC** HV2350; .J68. **DD** 362.4/28/05. **NLM** W1; JO908VK. ***Continues** Journal of Rehabilitation of the Deaf, 0730-1626.*
**Ind/Abst** Except. Child Educ. Resour.; Psychol. Abstr. (1972-); PsycINFO; PsycLit; Soc. Plann. Policy Dev. Abstr.

UK/0266-4062
**JOURNAL OF THE BRITISH ASSOCIATION OF TEACHERS OF THE DEAF, THE.** **See** Education-Special Education and Rehabilitation.

US/0028-5935
**JOURNAL OF THE NEW JERSEY SPEECH AND HEARING ASSOCIATION.** ***Ceased.*** **Main/Corp** New Jersey Speech and Hearing Association. Periodical. English. an. New Jersey Speech Language and Hearing Association, 120 Finderne Avenue, Bridgewater NJ 08807. **NLM** W1 JO942Q.

US
**JOURNAL OF THE PENNSYLVANIA SPEECH-LANGUAGE-HEARING ASSOCIATION, THE.** **Added/Corp** Pennsylvania Speech-Language-Hearing Association. Vol. 15, No. 1 (March 1982)-. Periodical. English. sa. $5.00. Pennsylvania Speech and Hearing Association, PO Box 1385, North Wales PA 19454-1385. **Tel** (215)368-2153. **NLM** W1; JO946DE. ***Continues** Journal of the Pennsylvania Speech and Hearing Association, 0555-9596.*

US/0145-482X
**JOURNAL OF VISUAL IMPAIRMENT & BLINDNESS.** [J. vis. impair. blind.]. **Added/Corp** American Foundation for the Blind. **VFOAT** Visual Impairment & Blindness. **VAT** Journal of Visual Impairment and Blindness. Vol. 71 (Jan. 1977)-. Periodical. English. bm. $45.00 (1 year), $65.00 (2 year), $85.00 (3 year) individual; $75.00 (1 year), $100.00 (2 year), $125.00 (3 year) institutions US; $70.00 (1 year), $115.00 (2 year), $160.00 (3 year) individual; $100.00 (1 year), $150.00 (2 year), $200.00 (3 year) institutions other. American Foundation for the Blind, 15 West 16th Street, New York NY 10011. **Tel** (212)620-2000, (800)829-0500. **ED** Mary Ellen Hulholland and Griffin Smith. **LC** HV1571; .O85. **DD** 362.4/1/05. **NLM** W1 JO9704. Index available. cum. index. **Bk Rev. Ad Acc. Pr Rev. Circ:** 5,000. available in braille; available on audiocassette; available on microfilm and microfiche from University Microfilms International (UMI). Documents available from The Genuine Article. ***Formed by the union of** New Outlook for the Blind, 0028-6435 **and** Research Bulletin - American Foundation for the Blind, 0065-8367.*
**Desc:** The interdisciplinary journal of record for practitioners and researchers professionally concerned with blind and visually impaired persons.
**Ind/Abst** Abstr. Soc. Work.; Acad. Search (July 1993-); Arts Humanit. Citation Index [Select. Cov.]; Curr. Contents Soc. Behav. Sci.; Curr. Index J. Educ.; Educ. Index; EMBASE; Except. Child. Educ. Abstr.; Except. Child Educ. Resour.; INFO-SOUTH Abstr.; Lang. Lang. Behav. Abstr.; Mag. Search; Psychol. Abstr. (1977-); PsycINFO; PsycLit; Ref. Sources; Res. Alert [Full Cov.]; Soc. Plann. Policy Dev. Abstr.; Soc. Sci. Cit. Index [Full Cov.]; Soc. Work Abstr. [Select. Cov.]; Spec. Educ. Needs Abstr.; SportSearch.

CN/0824-281X
**JUST CAUSE.** **See** Law.

BE
**KATHOLIEKE VERENIGING GEHANDICAPTEN.** (19??)-. Dutch. Twelve times a year. KVG Huize Mathieu Van Gorp, Arthur Goemaerlei 66, B-2018 Antwerp Belgium. **Tel** 03 216 2590, FAX 03 248 14 42. **ED** Vanbael Lief. **Ad Acc.**

JA
**KENKYU HOKOKU SHU - TOKYO-TO SHINSHIN SHOGAISHA FUKUSHI SENTA.** **See** Sociology-Social Services and Welfare.

US/0190-1656
**KURZWEIL REPORT, THE.** V. 1- Spring 1978-. Periodical. English. Free. Kurzweil Computer Products, 264 Third Street, Cambridge MA 02142. **NLM** W1 KU723.

US/0161-1461
**LANGUAGE, SPEECH & HEARING SERVICES IN SCHOOLS.** **See** Education-Special Education and Rehabilitation.

US/0363-8472
**LARGE-PRINT SCORES AND BOOKS CATALOG.** **See** Music.

US/0733-6233
**LAW OF THE HANDICAPPED : REPORTER AND COMMENTATOR, THE.** **See** Law.

US/0149-547X
**LIBRARIES FOR COLLEGE STUDENTS WITH HANDICAPS.** **See** Library and Information Sciences.

US
**LIBRARY ACCESS : SERVICES FOR PEOPLE WITH DISABILITIES.** ***Ceased.*** **See** Library and Information Sciences.

US/0364-1236
**LIBRARY RESOURCES FOR THE BLIND & PHYSICALLY HANDICAPPED.** **See** Library and Information Sciences.

US
**LIFEPRINTS.** (19??)-. English. Four times a year (Jan., Mar., July, Oct.). $25.00. Blindskills Inc., c/o Carol McCall, PO Box 5181, Salem OR 97304. **Tel** (503)581-4224. **ED** Carol McCarl. **Bk Rev,** (Qty: 2). **Circ:** 2,000 (ctrl). available in braille; available on videocassette; available in large print.
**Desc:** This magazine is for the visually impaired youth and adults which features information about career opportunities, educational skills and recreation activities. Its primary purpose is to give readers an opportunity to learn about interesting and successful people who happen to be blind.

US
**LIGHT.** **See** Sociology-Social Services and Welfare.

AT/0158-5460
**LINK-UP.** **See** Library and Information Sciences.

CN/1183-1820
**LISTEN (ENGLISH EDITION, OTTAWA).** (LISTEN : OFFICIAL JOURNAL OF THE CANADIAN HARD OF HEARING ASSOCIATION). [Listen]. **Added/Corp** Canadian Hard of Hearing Association. **VFOAT** Ecoute. Vol. 1, No. 1 (Summer 1991)-. Periodical. English (French). qt. 15.21Can$ institutions; 11.42Can$ individuals. Canadian Hard of Hearing Association, 2435 Holly Lane, Suite 205, Ottawa, Ontario, K1V 7P2 Canada. **Tel** (613)526-1584. **DD** 617.8/0971/05. ***Absorbed** CHHA Communique, 0834-1486.*

CN/1183-1820
**LISTEN (FRENCH EDITION, OTTAWA).** (LISTEN : OFFICIAL JOURNAL OF THE CANADIAN HARD OF HEARING ASSOCIATION.). [Listen]. **Added/Corp** Association des Malentendants Canadiens. **VFOAT** Ecoute. Vol. 1, No. 1 (Summer 1991)-. Periodical. French (English). Four times a year. 15.00Can$ (individuals); 20.00Can$ (institutions). Canadian Hard of Hearing Association, 2435 Holly Lane, Suite 205, Ottawa, Ontario, K1V 7P2 Canada. **Tel** (613)526-1584. **ED** Jan Fraser and Carole Theberge. **DD** 617.8/0971/05. **Ad Acc, Adv Mgr:** Ian Fraser. ctrl circ.

US/0196-7258
**LISTENING (WASHINGTON).** ***Title Change.*** (LISTENING.). [Listening]. **Added/Corp** National Catholic Office for the Deaf. Vol. 1 (Sept./Oct. 1977)-(19??). Periodical. English. bm. National Catholic Office for the Deaf, 814 Thayer Avenue, Silver Spring MD 20910. **Tel** (301)587-7992. **ED** Nora Letourneau. Index available. **Bk Rev. Ad Acc. Circ:** 2,700 (ctrl). available in braille.

***Continued by*** *Vision.*
**Desc:** Provides pastoral service to persons who are deaf or hard of hearing.
**Ind/Abst** Middle East Abstr. Index; Relig. Theol. Abstr.; Abr. Cathol. Period. Lit. Index; Cathol. Period. Lit. Index.

NE/0166-252X
**LOGOPEDIE EN FONIATRIE.** [Logop. foniatr.]. **VFOAT** Logopaedie en Phoniatrie. (1929)-. Periodical. Dutch (English). Eleven times a year. Fl100.00 Netherlands; Fl120.00 others. Nederlandse Vereninging voor Logopedie enFoniatrie, Postbus 3022, 2800 CD Gouda. **Tel** 011 31 01820 24266, FAX 011 31 01820 17655. **UDC** 376.3. Index available (April issue). cum. index. **Bk Rev. Ad Acc. Circ:** 5,000.
**Desc:** Aimed to provide specialist information for speech therapists in Holland.

US/0362-4889
**LOW VISION ABSTRACTS.** (1971)-. English. sa. $5.00. **LC** RE1; .L68. **DD** 617.7/5.

US/1046-6355
**MAINSTREAM NEWS.** (MAINSTREAM NEWS / CLARKE SCHOOL.). [Mainstream news]. **Added/Corp** Clarke School for the Deaf. Mainstream Center (Clarke School for the Deaf). (1981)-. Periodical. English. Eight times a year. $15.00. Mainstream Center Clarke, 48 Round Hill Road, Northhampton MA 01060. **Tel** (413)582-1121, FAX (413)586-6654. **ED** Dr. David Manning. **DD** 371. available on an online database from Compuserve.
**Desc:** This magazine is designed to help readers understand how students, parents, and professionals in the area of deafness can work together more effectively.

US/0278-8225
**MAINSTREAM (SAN DIEGO, CALIF.).** (MAINSTREAM.). [Mainstream]. **Added/Corp** Los Conquistadores, Inc. Able-Disabled Advocacy, Inc. Vol. 1, No. 1 (Apr. 1976)-. Periodical. English. mo (except Jan. and July). $24.00 (one year), $44.00 (two year), $60.00 (three year) US; $44.00 (one year), $84.00 (two year) Canada; $52.00 (one year), $100.00 (two year) other. Mainstream, 2973 Beech Street, San Diego CA 92102. **Tel** (619)234-3138. **ED** William Stothers. **LC** HV3023.C3; M34. **DD** 362.4/09794/98. Index available. **Bk Rev**, (Qty: 6). **Ad Acc**, **Adv Mgr Tel** (617)444-0600. **Circ:** 18,000 (ctrl). available on diskette.
**Desc:** An upbeat perspective on issues affecting disabled individuals: sports, travel, civil rights, education accessibility, personal relations and employment.
**Ind/Abst** Acad. Abstr. Full Text Elite (Jan. 1992-); Acad. Abstr. (Jan. 1992-); Acad. Search (Jan. 1992-); Comput. Lit. Index; Health Index (1989-); Health Period. Database [Full Txt.]; Health Ref. Cent. (Jan. 1989-) [Full Txt.] [Full Cov.]; Health Source (Jan. 1992-); INFO-SOUTH Abstr.; Mag. Search.

CN/0704-0652
**MARITIMER (AMHERST).** ***Title Change.*** (THE MARITIMER.). V. 1- Spring 1977-. Periodical. English. qt. Atlantic Provinces Resource Centre for the Hearing Handicapped, PO Box 308, Amherst Nova Scotia B4H 3Z6 Canada. **Tel** (902)667-3808, FAX (902)667-0893. **ED** Phyllis A Cameron and Bette Matheson. **DD** 371.9'12'09715. **Circ:** 1,100 (ctrl). ***Continues*** *New Scotian, 0028-6672.* ***Continued by*** *New Scotian, 0028-6672.*
**Desc:** An eight page publication sent to parents, staff, Departments of Education, School Boards, schools etc. to inform them programs and important events in the education of hearing impaired children in APRCHH programs.

CN/0229-8066
**MASTER TAPE LIST OF EDUCATIONAL TEXTS FOR THE VISUALLY AND PHYSICALLY HANDICAPPED ... .** **See** Education-Special Education and Rehabilitation.

US/0025-5955
**MATILDA ZIEGLER MAGAZINE FOR THE BLIND.** Began publication in 1907?. Periodical. English. ir (10 times a year). Free. 20 West 17th Street, New York NY 10011. **Tel** (212)242-0263. **ED** Michael Mellor. **Bk Rev. Circ:** 10,000. available in braille (and flexible disc (which requires Library of Congress player)).
**Desc:** Reprints, articles, short stories, humor, and poetry in braille and recorded disc and gives news and information of special interest to blind/visually impaired.

●US/1068-5405
**MEALEY'S LITIGATION REPORTS. AMERICANS WITH DISABILITIES ACT.** **See** Law.

US/0883-7902
**MENTAL AND PHYSICAL DISABILITY LAW REPORTER.** **See** Law.

US/0742-3284
**MICHIGAN SPEECH-LANGUAGE-HEARING ASSOCIATION JOURNAL / MSHA.** ***Suspended.*** [Michigan Speech-Lang.-Hear. Assoc. j.]. **VFOAT** Michigan Speech Language Hearing Association Journal; M.S.H.A. Journal; MSHA Journal. Vol. 17, No. 1 (Fall 1981)-?. Periodical. English. an. $15.00. Michigan Speech-Language-Hearing Association, 855 Grove Street, East Lansing MI 48823. **Tel** (517)332-5691. **ED** Ralph R Rupp. **LC** RJ496.S7. **DD** 616.85/5/005. **NLM** W1; MI228. **Ad Acc. Circ:** 1,200 (ctrl). ***Continues*** *MSHA: Journal of the Michigan Speech and Hearing Association, 0224-8398.*

CN/0847-5636
**MINORITE INVISIBLE.** ***Ceased.*** (MINORITE INVISIBLE / INVISIBLE MINORITY / ASSOCIATION MULTI-ETHNIQUE POUR L'INTEGRATION DES PERSONNES HANDICAPEES U QUEBEC / QUEBEC MULTI-ETHNIC ASSOCIATION FOR INTEGRATION OF HANDICAPPED PEOPLE.). [Minor. invis.]. **Added/Corp** Quebec Multi-Ethnic Association for the Integration of Handicapped People. **VFOAT** Invisible Minority. Vol. 1 No. 1 (1990)-(19??). Periodical. English (French). an (February). Ameiphq, 6462 Boul Street Laurent, Montreal QUE H2S 3C4 Canada. **Tel** (514)272-0680, FAX (514)272-8530. **DD** 362.84/009714.

US
**MONITORING & REPORTING PROJECT / GOVERNOR'S TASK FORCE FOR HANDICAPPED CITIZENS.** **Added/Corp** Texas. Governor's Task Force for Handicapped Citizens. Texas Governor's Committee on Employment of the Handicapped. **VFOAT** Monitoring and Reporting Project. (19??)-. English. an. Texas Governor's Committee on Employment of the Handicapped, 118 East Riverside Drive, Austin TX 78704. **LC** HV1555.T4; M65. **DD** 353.97640084/4.

US/0738-128X
**MONOGRAPH / [WORLD REHABILITATION FUND].** **See** Physical Therapy.

US/1071-5657
**MOUTH.** No. 1 (May 1972)-. Periodical. English. bm. $16.00 persons with disabilities; $32.00 non-disabled individuls; $48.00 institutions and agencies. Free Hand Press, Inc., 61 Brighton Street, Rochester NY 14607. **Tel** (716)473-6764, FAX (716)442-2916. **ED** Lucy Gwin. **Bk Rev. Circ:** 4,500. available on an online database; available on audiocassette.
**Desc:** The voice of disability rights. An irreverent, hard hitting antidote to do-gooderism, humor, anger and news.

US/1056-7240
**MOVING FORWARD : THE NATIONAL NEWSPAPER FOR PEOPLE WITH DISABILITIES.** [Mov. forw.]. Vol. 7, No. 1 (Sept./Oct. 1991)-. Periodical. English. bm. $11.50 (one year), $19.50 (two year) US and possessions; $36.00 (one year) other. Aziz Unlimited, 1689 East Del Amo, Carson CA 90746. **Tel** (310)603-9923, FAX (310)603-9932. **ED** Paul R Aziz. **DD** 362. **Bk Rev. Ad Acc, Adv Mgr:** WG Holdsworth, **Tel** (714)544-2555 (West), (708)934-0084 (Midwest). **Circ:** 25,000. ***Continues*** *Challenged American, 0892-290X.*

CN/1187-466X
**MS TORONTO (1991).** ***Title Change.*** (MS TORONTO / MULTIPLE SCLEROSIS SOCIETY OF CANADA, METROPOLITAN TORONTO CHAPTER.). [MS Tor.]. **Added/Corp** Multiple Sclerosis Society of Canada. Metropolitan Toronto Chapter. **VAT** Multiple Sclerosis Toronto (1991). (199?)-(1992). Periodical. English. qt. Metropolitan Toronto Chapter of the Multiple Sclerosis Society of Canada, 250 Bloor Street East, Suite 820, Toronto Ontario M4W 3P9 Canada. **DD** 362.1. ***Continues*** *Multiple Sclerosis Society Report., 0838-7818.* ***Continued by*** *Metro Scope, 1197-4613.*

US/0278-9051
**MUSIC CIRCULAR.** **See** Music.

US/0364-7501
**MUSICAL MAINSTREAM, THE.** **See** Music.

US
**NAD BROADCASTER, THE.** **Added/Corp** National Association of the Deaf. **VFOAT** Broadcaster. (1979)-. Periodical. English. mo. $20.00. National Association of the Deaf, 814 Thayer Avenue, Silver Spring MD 20910. **Tel** (301)587-1788.

JA
**NAIGAI TOKUSHU KYOIKU KANKYU KIKAN TO ICHIRAN.** **Added/Corp** Kokuritsu Tokushu Kyoiku Sogo Kenkyujo. (19??)-. Japanese. Kokuritsu Tokushu Kyoiku Sogo Kenkyujo, 5-1-1 Nobi, Yokosuka 239 Japan. **Tel** 011 81 469 48 4121. **LC** L900; .N34.

US/0743-4081
**NATIONAL DIRECTORY OF BLIND TEACHERS.** **See** Education.

US/1053-1084
**NATIONAL DISABILITY LAW REPORTER.** **See** Law.

US/0194-4754
**NATIONAL HOOKUP.** **Added/Corp** Indoor Sports Club. (19??)-. Periodical. English. bm. $6.00. Indoor Sports Club Inc, PO Box 26603, Tuscon AZ 85726. **Tel** (602)328-1857. **ED** Larry Lucas (Editor's Phone: (602)795-3383). **Ad Acc. Pr Rev. Circ:** 1,300 (ctrl).
**Desc:** News from chapters and districts, articles pertaining to the problems of the disabled, national and state laws for the disabled and poetry.

US/0891-3064
**NATIONAL NEWSPATCH, THE.** **See** Education-Special Education and Rehabilitation.

US/0739-9278
**NATIONAL TECHNICAL INSTITUTIE FOR THE DEAF FOCUS.** **Added/Corp** National Technical Institute for the Deaf. Rochester Institute of Technology. **VFOAT** N.T.I.D. Focus; Focus. **VAT** National Technical Institute for the Deaf Focus. (197?)-. Periodical. English. Three times a year (Mar., July, Nov.). Free on request. National Technical Institute for the Deaf, One Lomb Memorial Drive, PO Box 9887, Rochester NY 14623-0887. **Tel** (716)475-6753, telex V TDD. **ED** Lynne Bohlman Dewilde, (phone: (716)475-6312). **Bk Rev**, (Qty: 2). **Circ:** 20,000 (ctrl).
**Desc:** Articles on deafness research, education of deaf persons, successful deaf professionals.

US/0470-570X
**NEBRASKA SPEECH AND HEARING JOURNAL.** ***Ceased.*** Vol. 1 (March 1962)-Vol. 25 (1987). Periodical. English. an. Nebraska Speech & Hearing, PO Box 4516, Lincoln NE 68504. **Tel** (402)330-3858. **ED** Kathy L Coufal. **Bk Rev. Ad Acc. Circ:** 400 (ctrl).
**Desc:** Data based research articles, clinical concerns and professional affairs for speech-language pathologists and audiologists.

US/1053-8135
**NEUROREHABILITATION (READING, MASS.).** **See** Medical Science and Technology-Neurology.

UK/0028-4270
**NEW BEACON.** [New beacon]. (1993)-. Periodical. English. mo (11 issues per year). £13.75. Royal National Institute for the Blind, PO Box 173, Peterborough PE2 6WS England. **Tel** 011 44 733 730777. ***Continues*** *Beacon (London. 1917).*
**Desc:** Features in-depth articles relating to visual impairment, the magazine contains classified ads, leisure notes and reviews, and a calendar of events and announcements.
**Ind/Abst** Spec. Educ. Needs Abstr.

US
**NEW DIRECTIONS.** **Added/Corp** National Association of Coordinators of State Programs for the Mentally Retarded, Incorporated. (Jan. 1992)-. Periodical. English. mo. $55.00. National Association of State Directors of Developmental, Disabilities Services, 113 Oronoco Street, Alexandria VA 22314. **Tel** (703)683-4202, FAX (703)684-1395. **ED** Sally A. Carson. **Ad Acc.** ctrl circ.

NZ
**NEW ZEALAND DISABLED.** (19??)-. English. ir (Mar., May, July, Sep., Oct., Dec.). 13.50NZ$ (individuals), 16.90NZ$ (institutions) New Zealand; 22.00NZ$ (individuals), 25.00NZ$ (institutions) other. New Zealand Disabled, PO Box 90-366, Auckland New Zealand. **Tel** 011 64 9 762100, FAX 011 64 9 784527. **ED** Pat McCarthy. **Bk Rev**, (Qty: at least 6). **Ad Acc, Adv Mgr:** Patricia Zimmerman, **Tel** (04)818-9329. **Circ:** 1,800 (ctrl).

US
**NEWS DIGEST / NICHCY.** **Added/Corp** National Information Center for Children and Youth with Disabilities (U.S.). **VFOAT** NICHCY News Digest. **VAT** National Information Center for Children and Youth with Disabilities News Digest. Vol. 1, No. 1 (1991)-. Periodical. English. Three times a year. Free on request. National Information Center for Children and Youth with Disabilities, PO Box 1492, Washington DC 20013. **Tel** (703)893-6061. ***Continues*** *News Digest (National Information Center for Children and Youth with Handicaps (U.S.)).*

US/1046-1663
**NEWS - LIBRARY OF CONGRESS. NATIONAL LIBRARY SERVICE FOR THE BLIND AND PHYSICALLY HANDICAPPED.** (NEWS / NATIONAL LIBRARY SERVICE FOR THE BLIND AND PHYSICALLY HANDICAPPED, LIBRARY OF CONGRESS.). [News - Libr. Congr., Natl. Libr. Serv. Blind Phys. Handicap.]. **Added/Corp** Library of Congress. National Library Service for the Blind and Physically Handicapped. Vol. 9, No. 3, (May/June 1978)-. Periodical. English. Four times a year. Free on request. National Library Service for the Blind and Physically Handicapped, Library of Congress, 1291 Taylor Street Northwest, Washington DC 20542. **Tel** (800)424-8567, (202)707-5100, (800)424-9100. **ED** Vicki

Fitzpatrick. **LC** HV1783; .U54a. **DD** 362.4/1/05. ***Continues*** *Library of Congress. Division for the Blind and Physically Handicapped. News, 0160-9211.*

US
**NEWSBRIEF : EMPLOYMENT, OPPORTUNITY, EMPOWERMENT.** **Added/Corp** United States. President's Committee on Employment of People with Disabilities. **VFOAT** President's Committee on Employment of People with Disabilities Newsbrief. Vol. 1, No. 1 (1991)-. Periodical. English. mo. President's Committee on Employment of People with Disabilities, 1331 F Street NW, Washington DC 20004-1107. ***Continues*** *Tips and Trends.*

AT/0810-0926
**NEWSLETTER - SOUTH AUSTRALIAN ADVISORY COMMITTEE ON LIBRARY SERVICES TO THE DISABLED.** **See** Library and Information Sciences.

SW/0029-1471
**NORDISK TIDSKRIFT FOR DOVUNDERVISNINGEN.** **See** Education-Special Education and Rehabilitation.

US
**NORTH CAROLINA ANNUAL PROGRAM PLAN AMENDMENT.** **See** Education-Special Education and Rehabilitation.

CN/0848-8770
**NOUVEAU PARAQUAD.** (LE NOUVEAU PARAQUAD / ASSOCIATION DES PARAPLEGIQUES DU QUEBEC.). [Nouv. paraquad]. **Added/Corp** Association des Paraplegiques du Quebec. **VFOAT** Paraquad. No. 49 (Autumn 1989)-. Periodical. English (French). qt. Free to members. Association des Paraplegiques du Quebec, 4545 Chemin Queen Mary, Montreal Quebec H3W 1W4 Canada. **Tel** (514)340-2053, FAX (514)283-2102. **DD** 362.4/3/09714.

US
**OHIO CHRONICLE, THE.** **See** College and School Publications.

US/0740-218X
**ON THE BEAM.** (ON THE BEAM : NEWSLETTER OF THE LOWE'S SYNDROME ASSOCIATION.). [On the beam]. **Added/Corp** Lowe's Syndrome Association. Vol. 2, No. 2 (Summer 1983)-. Newsletter. English. Three times a year (Feb., June, Oct.). $15.00. Lowe's Syndrome Association, 222 Lincoln Street, West Lafayette IN 47906. **Tel** (317)743-3634. **ED** Jane Gallery Phone: (312)525-4669. **Circ:** 300 (ctrl). ***Continues*** *Lowe's Syndrome Family Newsletter.*
**Desc:** Letters from families affected by Lowe's syndrome and pictures of their children, medical and educational articles, organizational news.

CN/0821-6258
**OUTFRONT (OTTAWA).** (OUTFRONT.). [Outfront]. Summer 1983-. Periodical. English. qt. Free to members. Council of the Disabled of Ottawa-Carleton, Room 1200/505 Smyth Road, Ottawa Ontario K1H 8M2 Canada. **DD** 362.4/09713/84.

US/0161-1828
**OVERSEAS OUTLOOK.** (OVERSEAS OUTLOOK / NATIONAL LIBRARY SERVICE FOR THE BLIND AND PHYSICALLY HANDICAPPED.). [Overseas outlook]. Began with Fall 1977. Periodical. English. sa. National Library Service for the Blind and Physically Handicapped, Library of Congress, 1291 Taylor Street Northwest, Washington DC 20542. **Tel** (800)424-8567, (202)707-5100, (800)424-9100. **LC** HV1571; .O87. **DD** 362.4/1/05.

US/8756-5811
**PALAESTRA (MACOMB, ILL.).** (PALAESTRA.). [Palaestra]. **Added/Corp** United States Olympic Committee. Committee on Sports for the Disabled. Vol. 1, No. 1 (Fall 1984)-. Periodical. English. Four times a year (Feb., May, Aug., Nov.). $18.00 (individuals); $24.00 (institutions). Challenge Publications Ltd, PO Box 508, Macomb IL 61455. **Tel** (309)833-1902. **ED** David P. Beaver. **DD** 796. **NLM** W1; PA361UD. Index available. **Bk Rev. Ad Acc. Pr Rev. Circ:** 6,000 (ctrl). available on audiocassette; available on an online database (file 149/Full-Text) from DIALOG.
**Desc:** Offers well balanced feature content dealing with all aspects of sport and physical education and recreation for the disabled. Focus is on special competitive events, training techniques, biomechanics, and teaching methods. Published in cooperation with the USOC's Committee on Sport for the Disabled.
**Ind/Abst** Health Index (1989-); Health Period. Database [Full Txt.]; Health Ref. Cent. (Jan. 1989-) [Full Cov.]; Phys. Educ. Index; SPORT Discus; SportSearch.

CN/0048-2935
**PARAGRAPHIC.** **See** Education-Special Education and Rehabilitation.

UK/0031-1758
**PARAPLEGIA.** [Paraplegia]. **Added/Corp** International Medical Society of Paraplegia. Vol. 1 (1963)-. Academic Scholarly Publication. English (summaries and/or abstracts in French and German). mo. £180.00 UK and EEC; £200.00 (surface mail), £240.00 (airmail) other. Macmillan Magazines Ltd., Houndmills, Basingstoke, Hampshire RG21 2XS England. **Tel** 011 44 256 29242, FAX 011 44 256 812358, telex 858493. **ED** Philip Harris. **NLM** W1 PA629. **CODEN** PRPLBL. **[CCC].** Index available in last issue of volume--attached. **Pr Rev.** available on microfilm and microfiche from University Microfilms International (UMI). Documents available from The Genuine Article, BIOSIS Document Express.
**Desc:** Provides an international forum for the exchange of experiences with the intricate problems concerned with injuries and diseases of the spinal cord, the manifold aspects of paraplegia and tetraplegia and the rehabilitation of the paralyzed.
**Ind/Abst** Biol. Abstr. (1986-); Curr. Contents Clin. Med.; EMBASE; Helminthol. Abstr. (19??-19??); Index Med.; Med. Abstr. Newsl.; Life Sci. Collect.; Res. Alert [Select. Cov.]; SCISEARCH; Soc. Sci. Cit. Index [Select. Cov.].

US/0031-1766
**PARAPLEGIA NEWS.** Vol. 1 (1946)-. Periodical. English. Twelve times a year. $21.00. Paralyzed Veterans of America Publications, 2111 East Highland, Suite 180 B, Phoenix AZ 85016. **Tel** (602)246-9426, FAX (602)224-0507. **ED** Cliff Crase. **NLM** W1 PA631. Index available. cum. index. **Bk Rev. Ad Acc. Circ:** 25,000. available on an online database (file 149/Full-Text) from DIALOG. ***Absorbed*** *Journal of Paraplegia.*
**Desc:** Research, legislation, news and general interest articles to particular interest and applicability to the wheelchair user.
**Ind/Abst** Consum. Health Nutr. Index (?-?); Health Index (1989-); Health Period. Database [Full Txt.]; Health Ref. Cent. (Jan. 1989-) [Full Cov.]; SPORT Discus.

CN/0832-0543
**PARATRACKS / CANADIAN PARAPLEGIC ASSOCIATION-MANITOBA DIVISION.** [ParaTracks]. (Aug. 1985)-. Periodical. English. Three times a year. Free. Manitoba Division, Canadian Paraplegic Association, 825 Sherbrooke Street, Winnipeg Manitoba R3A 1M5 Canada. **DD** 362.4/3/097127. ***Continues*** *Son of Paratracks, 0227-339X.*

GW/0173-301X
**PATHOLINGUISTICA.** **See** Medical Science and Technology-Otorhinolaryngology.

US/0031-4609
**PENNSYLVANIA MESSAGE.** **Added/Corp** Pennsylvania Association of Retarded Persons. Association for Retarded Citizens, Pennsylvania. Periodical. English. qt. Association for Retarded Citizens, 718 West Burnside, Suite 316, Portland OR 97209.

US/1051-6204
**PERSPECTIVES IN EDUCATION AND DEAFNESS.** [Perspect. educ. deaf.]. **Added/Corp** Gallaudet University. Pre-College Programs. **VFOAT** Perspectives. Vol. 8, No. 2 (Nov./Dec. 1989)-. Periodical. English. Five times a year (Jan., Mar., May, Sept., Nov.). $15.00. Perspectives in Education & Deafness, 800 Florida Avenue Northeast, KDES PAS 6, Washington DC 20002. **Tel** (202)651-5340, FAX (202)651-5708. **LC** HV2510; .P47. **DD** 371.91/2/097305. Index available (Bound in 5th iss., in (May/June).). **Bk Rev. Ad Acc. Pr Rev. Circ:** 3,000. ***Continues*** *Perspectives for Teachers of the Hearing Impaired, 0735-6315.*
**Desc:** Focused toward professionals and families involved with the education of deaf and hard of hearing students. Provides a forum for exchange of creative approaches to classroom teaching, as well as broad, well-informed view of current issues in deafness and education.
**Ind/Abst** Comput. Lit. Index; Curr. Index J. Educ.; Except. Child Educ. Resour.

US/0279-411X
**PHYSICAL DISABILITIES SPECIAL INTEREST SECTION NEWSLETTER.** **See** Education-Special Education and Rehabilitation.

US/1047-9651
**PHYSICAL MEDICINE AND REHABILITATION CLINICS OF NORTH AMERICA.** [Phys. med. rehabil. clin. North Am.]. Vol. 1, No. 1 (Nov. 1990)-. Periodical. English. qt. $82.00 (individual), $100.00 (institution), US; $116.00 (individual), $123.00 (institution) other. W.B. Saunders Company, A Subsidiary of Harcourt Brace Jovanovich, Inc., The Curtis Center/Suite 300, Independence Square West, Philadelphia PA 19106-3399. **Tel** (215)238-7800 or, 5587, FAX (215)238-7883, telex 173146. **(Subscription address:** W. B. Saunders Company / North America Subscriptions, c/o Periodicals, 6277 Sea Harbour Drive, 4th Floor, Orlando FL 32887.**)** **LC** IN PROCESS. **DD** 617.
**Ind/Abst** Cumul. Index Nurs. Allied Health Lit.

US/0554-4246
**POINTER, THE.** ***Title Change.*** **See** Education-Special Education and Rehabilitation.

US/0891-8791
**POSITIVE APPROACH, A.** [Posit. approach]. (1986)-. Periodical. English. qt (Mar., June, Sept., Dec.). $15.00 US: $23.00 (includes postage) other. Positive Approach Inc., PO Box 910, Millville NJ 08332. **Tel** (609)451-4777, FAX (609)451-6678. **ED** Patricia Johnson. **DD** 362. **NLM** W1; PO886. **Bk Rev**, (Qty: 40). **Ad Acc, Adv Mgr:** Pat Swart, **Tel** (609)451-4777 ext. 3. **Circ:** 40,000 (ctrl).
**Desc:** Designed to encourage and inform persons with a physical disability or handicap. The purpose of publication is to help the physically challenged individual develop a wholeness approach to life that includes physiological, emotional, mental and spiritual involvement.

RU
**PREODOLENIE.** **Added/Corp** Rossiiskoe Informatsionnoe Agentstvo "Novosti.". (Nov. 1991)-. Periodical. Russian. mo. $79.95. Novosti Press Agency Publishing House, 4 Zubovski Boulevard, Moscow Russia. **Tel** 095-201-2424, FAX 095-201-2119, telex 411321. **(Subscription address:** East View Publications Inc., 3020 Harbor Lane North, Suite 110, Minneapolis MN 55447.**)** **LC** IN PROCESS.

US
**PREVENT BLINDNESS NEWS.** (Summer 1975)-. Periodical. English. Three times a year. Free on request. National Society to Prevent Blindness, 500 East Remington Road, Schaumburg IL 60173. **Tel** (212)684-3505. ***Formed by the union of*** *Prevention of Blindness News, 0032-8014* ***and*** *Wise Owl News, 0043-6755.*

US/0436-2438
**PROCEEDINGS, ANNUAL GOVERNOR'S CONFERENCE ON THE HANDICAPPED.** (PROCEEDINGS ... ANNUAL GOVERNOR'S CONFERENCE ON THE HANDICAPPED / SPONSORED BY THE INDIANA STATE COMMISSION FOR THE HANDICAPPED.). **Main/Conf** Governor's Conference on the Handicapped. Began with 1st (1961). Proceedings. English. an. Indiana State Commission for the Handicapped, 1330 West Michigan Street, Indianapolis IN 46206. **LC** HV1555.I6; G6. **DD** 362.4/09772. **NLM** W3 GO536.

CN/0824-0493
**PROCEEDINGS OF THE ... ANNUAL CONFERENCE / INSTITUT DE READAPTATION DE MONTREAL.** [Actes ... colloq. annu. - Inst. readapt. Montr.]. **Main/Corp** Rehabilitation Institute of Montreal. Meeting. **VFOAT** Actes du ... Colloque Annuel. 2E (1/2 Dec. 1983)-. Proceedings. French (English). ir. Institut de Readaptation de Montreal, 6300 Darlington Avenue, Montreal Quebec H3S 2J4 Canada. **Tel** 340-2085. **LC** RM930.A1; I53A. **DD** 362.4/05.

US/0148-5342
**PROGRESS IN COMMUNICATION.** (PROGRESS IN COMMUNICATION : VIRGINIA COUNCIL FOR THE DEAF REPORT.). [Prog. commun.]. **Main/Corp** Virginia. Council for the Deaf. 1974/76-. English. Virginia Council for the Deaf, 4615 West Street/Suite 210, Richmond VA 23230. **LC** HV2561.V8; V57A. **DD** 353.9/755/008442.

DK/0309-3646
**PROSTHETICS AND ORTHOTICS INTERNATIONAL.** [Prosthet. orthot. int.]. **Added/Corp** International Society for Prosthetics and Orthotics. National Centre for Training and Education in Prosthetics and Orthotics. Vol. 1 (Apr. 1977)-. Periodical. English. Three times a year. £75.00. ISPO, Borgervaenget 5, 2100 Copenhagen Denmark. **Tel** 011 45 31 207260. **ED** J Hughes, N Jacobs and R Donovan. **NLM** W1 PR778. **CODEN** POIND7. Index available. **Bk Rev. Ad Acc. Pr Rev. Circ:** 2,700 (ctrl). Documents available from The Genuine Article, BIOSIS Document Express, Ask*IEEE. ***Supersedes*** *Prosthetics International.*
**Desc:** Covers prosthetics, orthotics, amputation surgery, neuromuscular and skeletal disorders, rehabilitation engineering, and related topics.
**Ind/Abst** Biol. Abstr.; Curr. Contents Clin. Med.; Dev. Med. Child Neurol. (-1990); EMBASE; Index Med.; INSPEC (April 1979-); Life Sci. Collect.; Res. Alert [Full Cov.]; Soc. Sci. Cit. Index [Select. Cov.].

●UK/0962-9343
**QUALITY OF LIFE RESEARCH.** (1992)-. Periodical. English. bm. $450.00 US; £265.00 other. Rapid Communications of Oxford Ltd, The Old Malthouse, Paradise Street, Oxford OX1 1LD England. **Tel** 011 44 0865 790447, FAX 011 44 0865 244012, telex 9403712. **NLM** W1; QU158LG. **CODEN** QLREEG. **[CCC]. Ad Acc. Acid Free.**
**Desc:** Aimed specifically for researchers involved with any aspect of quality of life research in theory, methodology and clinical practice. Educational issues are also included. Maintaining a multidisciplinary perspective, the journal will cover the following fields: oncology, cardiovascular diseases, pediatrics, adolescence, rheumatology, chronic respiratory diseases, diabetes, organ transplantation, neurology and psychiatry, AIDS, pain management, palliative care, addiction, rehabilitation, home and ambulatory care, treatment of the elderly, biostatistics, and psychopharmacology.
**Ind/Abst** Soc. Sci. Cit. Index [Full Cov.].

CN/0822-9279
**R.A.P.H.A.T. REGROUPEMENT DES ASSOCIATIONS DE PERSONNES HANDICAPEES DE L'ABITIBI-TEMISCAMINGUE.** See Sociology-Social Services and Welfare.

UK/0954-237X
**RADAR BULLETIN.** [RADAR bull.]. **VFOAT** Royal Association for Disability and Rehabilitation Bulletin. (1986)-. English. mo. Royal Association for Disability & Rehabilitation, 25 Mortimer Street, London W1N 8AB England. **Tel** 011 44 71 637-5400, FAX 011 44 71 637-1827. **DD** 362.40941. ***Continues*** *Bulletin - Royal Association for Disability and Rehabilitation, 0140-2692.*

CN/0841-9507
**REACH.** (RESEARCH / ASSOCIATION FOR THE HEARING HANDICAPPED.). [Reach]. Vol. 1, Issue 3 (Nov. 1987)-. Periodical. English. qt. Free to members (membership $10.00 per year). Association for the Hearing Handicapped, 11342-127 Street, Edmonton Alberta T5M 0T8 Canada. **Tel** (403)454-9581. **DD** 362.4/2/0971233. ***Continues*** *Edmon-tone, 0823-6895.*

US
**RED NOTEBOOK. COMMUNICATING WITH HEARING PEOPLE, THE.** English. an. $36.00. Library for Deaf Action, 2930 Craiglawn Road, Silver Springs MD 20904-1816. **Tel** (301)572-5168 TTY, FAX (301)572-4134. **Bk Rev.** ctrl circ.
**Desc:** News and information of national interest to deaf culture, hearing health care, and auxiliary aids and service.

CN/0048-7139
**REHABILITATION DIGEST.** [Rehabil. dig.]. **Added/Corp** Canadian Rehabilitation Council for the Disabled. Vol. 1 (Summer 1969)-. Periodical. English (French; summaries and/or abstracts in French). qt. 24.00Can$. Canadian Rehabilitation Council for the Disabled, 45 Sheppard Avenue East/Suite 801, Toronto Ontario M2N 5W9 Canada. **Tel** (416)250-7490, FAX (416)229-1371. **ED** Heather Ney. **Bk Rev.** **Ad Acc.** **Circ:** 2,000 (ctrl). ***Absorbed*** *Access, 0226-2657.*
**Desc:** Offers news, views and in-depth articles on physical rehabilitation for professionals and disabled people. Published by the Canadian Rehabilitation Council for the Disabled, it illuminates key issues such as the economics of disability, employment, sexuality, housing, technology and transportation. Provides a forum where professionals can share knowledge and experience.
**Ind/Abst** Can. Index; Can. Period. Index (19??-); Except. Child Educ. Resour.

US/0361-4166
**REHABILITATION GAZETTE.** [Rehabil. gaz.]. Vol. 13 (1970)-. English. sa (January, June). $20.00 US; $22.00 other. Gazette International Networking Institute, 5100 Oakland Avenue, Number 206, St Louis MO 63110. **Tel** (314)534-0475, FAX (314)534-5070. **ED** Joan Headley. **LC** HV1553; .R45. **DD** 362.4/0483/05. **NLM** W1 RE174R. **CODEN** RHGZA. **Ad Acc.** **Circ:** 12,000 (ctrl). ***Continues*** *Toomey J. Gazette.*
**Desc:** Journal on independent living by disabled individuals. For polio survivors, spinal cord injured, ventilator users, and others with neuromuscular diseases and disabilities. This international journal is written by individuals with a disability, and seeks to motivate its readers to attain full and independent lives by relating practical responses and creative solutions to life with a disability.
**Ind/Abst** EMBASE.

US/0360-0726
**REHABILITATION WORLD.** ***Ceased.*** [Rehabil. world]. V. 1- July 1975-?. Periodical. English. qt. Rehabilitation International USA, 1123 Broadway, New York NY 10010. **LC** HD7255.A2; R45. **DD** 362.8/5. **NLM** W1 RE1769.
**Ind/Abst** EMBASE; Except. Child Educ. Resour.

US
**REPORT - FLORIDA COUNCIL FOR THE BLIND.** **Main/Corp** Florida. Council for the Blind. English. an. Florida Council for the Blind, Tampa FL 33679. **LC** HV1796; .F67. **DD** 362.4.

US/1043-1209
**REPORT ON DISABILITY PROGRAMS.** [Rep. disabil. programs]. Vol. 12, No. 1 (Jan. 12, 1989)-. Periodical. English. bw (26 issues). $286.00 (includes Handicapped Rights & Regulations). Business Publishers Inc., 951 Pershing Drive, Silver Spring MD 20910-4464. **Tel** (301)587-6300, (800)274-0122, FAX (301)585-9075. **LC** KF480.A15; H36. **DD** 353.0084/4/05. **[CCC].** ***Continues*** *Handicapped Americans Report Including Handicapped Rights & Regulations.*
**Desc:** Features the latest reports on legislation, regulations, court cases and state news affecting disabled Americans.

US/0093-741X
**REPORT ON VISUAL IMPAIRMENT SERVICES TEAMS.** **Main/Corp** United States. Veterans Administration. Dept. of Medicine and Surgery. English. US Veterans Administration / Washington DC, 810 Vermont Avenue Southwest, Washington DC 20420. **Tel** (202)393-2124. **LC** UB369; .U57A. **DD** 362.8. **NLM** W2 A V54RA.

UK/0958-9775
**RESIDENTIAL ACCOMMODATION FOR ELDERLY PEOPLE WITH PHYSICAL OR VISUAL DISABILITIES / WELSH OFFICE.** **VFOAT** Llety Preswyl i Bobl Oedrannus a Phobl Ag Anabledd Corfforol Neu Weledol. (19??)-. Statistical Publication. English (Welsh). an. Welsh Office Publications Unit, Crown Building, Cathay's Park, Cardiff CF1 3NQ Wales. **Tel** 011 44 222 825111. **LC** HV3020.2.G72; W347. **DD** 362.4/085/0942905. ***Continues*** *Residential Accomodation for the Elderly, Blind, and Physically Disabled.*

US/0899-1510
**RE:VIEW (WASHINGTON, D.C.).** (RE:VIEW.). [RE:view]. **Added/Corp** Association for Education and Rehabilitation of the Blind and Visually Impaired (U.S.). **VFOAT** Re : View; View. **VAT** Rehabilitation, Education : View. Vol. 21, No. 1 (Spring 1989)-. Periodical. English. qt. $29.00 (individual), $57.00 (institutional), add $12.00 (foreign postage). Heldref Publications, 1319 Eighteenth Street Northwest, Washington DC 20036-1802. **Tel** (202)296-6267, (800)365-9753, FAX (202)296-5149. **ED** Michael J Bina, Jane N Erin, and Richard L Welsh. **LC** HV1571; .I523. **DD** 371.91/1/05. **NLM** W1; RE252EH. available on microfilm and microfiche from University Microfilms International (UMI). ***Continues*** *Education of the Visually Handicapped, 0013-1458.*
**Desc:** Interests all persons concerned with services for visually handicapped children, youth, and adults, including those who are multihandicapped and/or deaf-blind. Articles deal with useful practices, research findings, investigations, professional experiences, and controversial issues in education, rehabilitation teaching and counseling, orientation and mobility, and other services for the visually handicapped.
**Ind/Abst** Acad. Abstr. Full Text Elite (July 1993-) [Full Txt.]; Acad. Abstr. (July 1993-); Acad. Search (July 1993-); Contents Pages Educ.; Curr. Index J. Educ. (March 1990); Educ. Index; Except. Child Educ. Resour.; INFO-SOUTH Abstr.; Mag. Artic. Summar. Elite (July 1993-) [Full Txt.]; Mag. Artic. Summar. CD-ROM (July 1993-); Mag. Search; Psychol. Abstr. (1969-); PsycINFO (1990-); PsycLit; Spec. Educ. Needs Abstr.

UK/0307-238X
**REVIEWS OF RESEARCH AND PRACTICE OF THE INSTITUTE FOR RESEARCH INTO MENTAL AND MULTIPLE HANDICAP.** See Medical Science and Technology-Psychiatry.

CN/0382-7976
**REVUE ACEDA.** See Education-Special Education and Rehabilitation.

FR/0397-7900
**REVUE DE L'INFIRMIERE ET DE L'ASSISTANTE SOCIALE.** [Rev. infirm. assist. soc.]. **VFOAT** Revue de l'Infirmiere. (1951)-. Periodical. French. Twenty times a year. 390.00F (France); 615.00 (other). Expansion Scientifique Francaise, 31 Boulevard de la Tour-Maubourg, 75007 Paris France. **Tel** 011 33 1 40 62 64 00, 011 33 1 40626439. **[CCC].**
**Ind/Abst** Point Repere (1979-).

IT/0557-9430
**RIABILITAZIONE.** [Riabilitazione]. (1968)-. Periodical. Italian. qt (4 issues). L88200 Italy. Masson S.P.A, Via Statuto 2/4, 20121 Milan Italy. **Tel** 011 39 2 63671, FAX 011 39 2 6367211. **UDC** 61.

●US/1068-6533
**SECTION 504 COMPLIANCE HANDBOOK. SUPPLEMENT.** [Sect. 504 compliance handb., Suppl.]. **Added/Corp** Thompson Publishing Group. No. 170 (Jan. 1993)-. English. mo. $218.00. Thompson Publishing Group, 7711 Anderson Road, Tampa FL 33634. **Tel** (800)677-3789, (813)282-8607. **DD** 346. Index available (free). ***Continues*** *Handicapped Requirements Handbook. Supplement, 0194-7818.*

US
**SEE WHAT'S HAPPENING.** ***Suspended.*** (198?)-Suspended. Periodical. English. qt. $6.00. Modern Signs Press Inc, PO Box 1181, Los Alamitos CA 90720. **Tel** 3103)596-8548.
**Desc:** Newsletter for deaf children.

US/0037-0819
**SEEING EYE GUIDE.** **Added/Corp** Seeing Eye, Inc. (19??)-. Periodical. English. Four times a year (Mar., June, Sept., Dec.). Free on request. The Seeing Eye Inc, PO Box 375, Morristown NJ 07963-0375. **Tel** (201)539-4425, FAX (201)539-0922. **ED** Carol Gray, (editor's address: The Seeing Eye, PO Box 375, Morrison, NJ 07963, phone: (201)539-4425). **Circ:** 25,000 (ctrl).

US/0730-9880
**SENSORY WORLD.** No. 30 (Mar. 1978)-. Periodical. English. qt. $16.00 institutions and libraries, $14.00 individuals, $18.00 overseas. PO Box 270, Lusby MD 20657. **ED** Robert M Harmon. **LC** HV1551; .R48. **DD** 362.4/05. ***Continues*** *Review of Sensory Disability, 0146-9185.*

US
**SERVICES FOR STUDENTS WITH DISABILITIES IN CALIFORNIA PUBLIC HIGHER EDUCATION.** See Education-Higher Education.

US/0146-1044
**SEXUALITY AND DISABILITY.** [Sex. disabil.]. Vol. 1 (Spring 1978)-. Periodical. English. qt. $160.00 US; $185.00 other. Human Sciences Press, PO Box 735, 233 Spring Street, New York NY 10013. **Tel** (212)620-8000, FAX (212)807-1047, telex 23421139. **(Subscription address:** Eurospan Ltd., Journals and Serials Division, 3 Henrietta Street, Covent Garden, London WC2E 8LU England.**)** **ED** Stanley Ducharme. **LC** HQ30.5; .S483. **DD** 613.9/5. **NLM** W1 SE99J. **CODEN** SDISDC. **[CCC].** available on microfilm and microfiche from University Microfilms International (UMI). Documents available from BIOSIS Document Express.
**Desc:** The purpose of this journal is to provide an ongoing and contemporary forum for clinical and research progress developments in the area of sexuality as it relates to a wide range of physical and mental illness and disabling conditions.
**Ind/Abst** Abstr. Res. Pastor. Care Couns. (19??-); Biol. Abstr. (1978-); Cumul. Index Nurs. Allied Health Lit.; Curr. Lit. Fam. Plan.; EMBASE; Health Saf. Sci. Abstr.; Pollut. Abstr. Indexes; Psychol. Abstr. (1978-); PsycINFO; PsycLit; Soc. Plann. Policy Dev. Abstr.; Sociol. Abstr.; Stud. Women Abstr. (?-1987).

US/0743-4189
**SHAA.** (SHAA : A JOURNAL OF THE SPEECH AND HEARING ASSOCIATION OF ALABAMA.). [SHAA]. **Added/Corp** Speech and Hearing Association of Alabama. **VFOAT** SHAA Journal. **VAT** Speech and Hearing Association of Alabama. (1970)-. Periodical. English. Twice a year. University of Montevallo, Station 240, Montevallo AL 35115. **Tel** (205)665-2521.

US/0883-1688
**SHHH.** (SHHH / SELF HELP FOR HARD OF HEARING PEOPLE, INC.). [Shhh]. **Added/Corp** Self Help for Hard of Hearing People. **VAT** Self Help for Hard of Hearing. (19??)-. Periodical. English. Six times a year. $20.00 US; $30.00 Canada and Mexico; $40.00 other. Self Help for Hard of Hearing People, Inc., 7910 Woodmont Avenue Suite 1200, Bethesda MD 20814. **Tel** (301)657-2248, 657-2249. **ED** Barbara Harris. **DD** 371. Index available. cum. index. **Bk Rev.** **Ad Acc.** **Circ:** 48,000 (ctrl).
**Desc:** Reaches hearing-impaired families and health professionals. Gives information on conditions, remedies and coping.
**Ind/Abst** Except. Child Educ. Resour.

AT/1033-792X
**SHHH NEWS.** (19??)-. English. qt. 25.00Aus$ Australia. SHHH Australia, 1334 Pacific Highway, Turramurra NSW 2074 Australia. **Tel** 011 61 2 44 7586, 011 61 2 449 9144, FAX (02)449 2381. **ED** Shirley Neil (phone: (02)419-7297). Index available (contents only). cum. index (Payment on postage and photocopies done May each year). **Bk Rev**, (Qty: 6). **Ad Acc.** **Circ:** 900 (ctrl).
**Desc:** Contains articles on issues and current events geared toward helping hearing impaired adults cope better with their hearing loss.

US/0163-5727
**SIGCAPH NEWSLETTER.** See Computers-Computer Assisted Instruction.

US/0037-5187
**SILENT ADVOCATE, THE.** Periodical. English. St Rita School for the Deaf and Hard of Hearing, 1720 Glendale-Milford Road, Cincinnati OH 45215.

CN/0840-8386
**SMDI INTERNATIONAL NEWSLETTER.** See Medical Science and Technology-Musculoskeletal System.

GW
**SONDERPADAGOGIK.** See Education-Special Education and Rehabilitation.

FI
**SOTILASAVUSTUS.** See Military and Defense.

●CN/1195-3349
**SOURDS DU CANADA.** [Deaf Can.]. **Main/Corp** Canadian Association of the Deaf. **Added/Corp** Association des Sourds du Canada. Association Canadienne de Sports pour les Sourds. Societe Culturelle Canadienne des Sourds. **VFOAT** Deaf Canada. Vol. 1, Issue 2 (Jan./Feb. 1993)-. Periodical. French (English). qt. 10.00Can$. Canadian Association of Deaf, 205 2435 Holly Lane, Ottawa Ontario K1V 7P2 Canada. **Tel**

# Physically Impaired

(613)526-4785, FAX (613)526-4718. **ED** Michael Ryan. **DD** 362.4/2/0971. **Ad Acc**. *Continues Deaf Canadian Advocate, 1195-3349.*

SA/0379-8046
**SOUTH AFRICAN JOURNAL OF COMMUNICATION DISORDERS.** See Medical Science and Technology-Neurology.

US/0147-474X
**SOUTH DAKOTA GOVERNOR'S ADVISORY COMMITTEE ON EMPLOYMENT OF THE HANDICAPPED.** **Main/Corp** South Dakota. Governor's Advisory Committee on Employment of the Handicapped. English. South Dakota Governor's Advisory Committee, Employment of the Handicapped, 222 East Capital, Pierre SD 57501. **LC** HD7256.U6; S69. **DD** 331.5/9/09783.

GW
**SOZIALLEISTUNGEN. REIHE 5.1, SCHWERBEHINDERTE / HERAUSGEBER, STATISTISCHES BUNDESAMT WIESBADEN.** **VFOAT** Schwerbehinderte Fachserie 13. (1985)-. German. be. DM9.00. Verlag W Kohlhammer GmbH, Abt Veroffentlichungen des Statistischen Bundesamtes, Philipp-Reis-Strasse 3, W-6500 Mainz 42 Germany. **LC** HHD7256.G3; S69. *Continues Sozialleistungen. Reihe 5.1, Behinderte.*

●US
**SPECIAL EDUCATION REPORT: THE INDEPENDENT BI-WEEKLY NEWS SERVICE ON LEGISLATION, REGULATION AND FUNDING OF PROGRAMS FOR CHILDREN AND YOUTHS WITH DISABILITIES.** Vol. 18, No. 12, (June 17, 1992)-. Periodical. English. bw. $278.00 North America; $313.00 other. Capitol Publications, 1101 King Street, Suite 444, Alexandria VA 22314. **Tel** (703)683-4100, (800)655-5597. *Continues Education of the Handicapped, 0194-2255.*

US/0747-0185
**SPECIAL RECREATION DIGEST.** **Suspended.** See Recreation, Leisure.

CN/0226-9228
**SPECTRUM (TORONTO. 1981).** See Sociology-Social Services and Welfare.

CN/1195-5767
**SPINAL COLUMNS.** English. Three times a year. $20.00. Canadian Paraplegic Association, 1110 101st Street, Suite 305, Edmonton Alberta P5H 4B9 Canada. **Tel** (403)438-5046. **Ad Acc.**

CN/0700-5229
**SPOKESMAN (EDMONTON). Suspended.** (THE SPOKESMAN.). Vol. 5, No. 6 (Aug./Sept. 1976)-Suspended with (Oct. 1990). Periodical. English. mo. 10.00Can$ (one year), 18.00Can$ (two years) Canada and U.S. Spokesman, #219 10136-100 Street, Edmonton Alberta T5J 0P1 Canada. **Tel** (403)429-1639. **ED** Vivian Carson. **DD** 362.4/097123. **Bk Rev. Ad Acc. Circ:** 7,000 (ctrl). *Continues A H C S News, 0700-5210.*
**Desc:** Articles pertaining to or of interest to Alberta's disabled community.

US/0161-6706
**SPORTS 'N SPOKES.** See Recreation, Leisure-Sports.

GW/0342-0477
**SPRACHE-STIMME-GEHOR.** [Sprache Stimme Gehor]. **Added/Corp** Zentralverband fuer Logopaedie (Germany). Vol. 1, (March 1977)-. Academic Scholarly Publication. German (summaries and/or abstracts in English). qt. $59.00. Georg Thieme Verlag Stuttgart, Postfach 301120, D 70451 Stuttgart Germany. **Tel** 011 49 711 89310, FAX 011 49 711 8931298, telex 7 252 275 GTVD. **(Subscription address:** Thieme Medical Publishers Inc., 381 Park Avenue South, New York NY 10016.) **NLM** W1 SP675. **[CCC].**
**Ind/Abst** EMBASE.

AU/0586-660X
**SPRACHHEILPADAGOGE, DER.** **Added/Corp** Oesterreichische Gesellschaft fuer Sprachheilpadagogik. (Feb. 1969)-. Periodical. German. qt. **NLM** W1 SP675N. **Supersedes** *Mitteilungen der Arbeitsgemeinschaft der Sprachheilpadagogen in Oesterreich.*

US/0038-9447
**STANDARD BEARER (SACRAMENTO), THE.** (STANDARD BEARER.). Periodical. English. bm. Northwestern Publishing Association, PO Box 20234, Sacramento CA 95820.

US/0098-7468
**STATE OF ILLINOIS REPORT ON TITLE I, PUBLIC LAW 89-313.** See Education-Special Education and Rehabilitation.

US/0149-9505
**STATE OF OREGON COMPREHENSIVE DEVELOPMENTAL DISABILITIES PLAN.** **Main/Corp** Oregon. State Council on Developmental Disabilities. **VFOAT** Oregon Developmental Disabilities State Plan. English. State Council on Developmental Disabilities, PO Box 25191, Portland OR 97225. **LC** HV3006.O7; O77A. **DD** 353.9/795/00843.

US
**STATE SERVICES FOR THE VISUALLY HANDICAPPED: RECOMMENDATIONS.** **Main/Corp** Texas. Governor's Coordinating Office for the Visually Handicapped. (1979)-. English. be. Governor's Coordinating Office for the Visually Handicapped, Stokes Building/Suite 105, Austin TX 78701. **LC** HV1796.T5; T49a. **DD** 362.4/18/09764. *Continues Recommendations Regarding State Services to the Visually Handicapped.*

CN/0844-8671
**STATUS REPORT / THE PREMIER'S COUNCIL ON THE STATUS OF PERSONS WITH DISABILITIES, ALBERTA, THE.** [Status rep. - Alta., Prem. Counc. Status Pers. Dis.]. March 1989)-. Periodical. English. qt. Premiers Council, 11044 82nd Avenue Suite 250, Edmonton Alta T6G 0TZ Canada. **Tel** (403)422-1095. **DD** 354.71230084/4.

US/0148-625X
**SUMMARY OF SELECTED LEGISLATION RELATED TO THE HANDICAPPED, A.** See Law.

CN/0848-5771
**SUMMARY OF THE ACTIVITY REPORT - CENTRE DE RECHERCHES MINERALES SAINTE-FOY.** (SUMMARY OF THE ... ACTIVITY REPORT). [Summ. act. rep. - Cent. rech. miner.St.-Foy]. (198?)-. French. Six times a year. free. OFC Personnes Handicapees QUE, PO Box 820, Drummondville QU J2B6X2 Canada. **Tel** (819)477-7100. **DD** 549.0971405. **Circ:** 15,000. *Continues Summary of the Annual Report - Centre de Recherches Minerales (Sainte-Foy), 0848-5763.*
**Desc:** An educational magazine on the handicaps.

PL/0238-9746
**SWIAT CISZY.** (1983)-. Periodical. Polish. mo. $15.00. **(Subscription address:** ARS Polona, PO Box 1001, 00068 Warsaw Poland.) **UDC** 362.4-056.263.

US/0039-9183
**TALKING BOOK TOPICS.** **Added/Corp** Library of Congress. National Library Service for the Blind and Physically Handicapped. American Foundation for the Blind. Library of Congress. American Printing House for the Blind (Louisville, Ky.) Royal National Institute for the Blind. Library of Congress. Division for the Blind and Physically Handicapped. (1935)-. Periodical. English. ir. Free. National Library Service for the Blind and Physically Handicapped, Library of Congress, 1291 Taylor Street Northwest, Washington DC 20542. **Tel** (800)424-8567, (202)707-5100, (800)424-9100. **ED** George Thuronyi. **LC** HV1708; .T3. **Circ:** 380,000 (ctrl). available on diskette. *Continues Research Bulletin. American Foundation for the Blind.*
**Desc:** An annotated list of books recently added to the national recorded books collection of the Library of Congress, National Library Service for the Blind and Physically Handicapped.

CN/0229-4028
**TALKING BOOKS CATALOGUE SUPPLEMENT.** See Publishing-Books and Bookmaking.

US/1046-8927
**TBC NEWS.** [TBC news]. **Added/Corp** Bicultural Center. (March 1988)-. Periodical. English. Six times a year. $25.00 (institutions), $20.00 (individuals). Bicultural Center, 5506 Kenilworth Avenue, Suite 105, Riverdale MD 20737. **Tel** (301)277-3945, FAX (301)699-5226. **LC** HV2510; .T33. **DD** 362.4/2/05. **Bk Rev**, (Qty: 3-4). **Pr Rev. Circ:** 3,000 (ctrl).

AT/0725-2919
**TECHNICAL AID TO THE DISABLED JOURNAL.** [Tech. Aid Disabl. j.]. **VFOAT** TAD Journal. (1981)-. Periodical. English. Four times a year (Mar., June, Sept., Dec.). 10.00Aus$ Australia; 30.00Aus$ other. Technical Aid to the Disabled, PO Box 108, Ryde NSW 2112 Australia. **Tel** 011 61 2 8082022, FAX 011 61 2 8097670. **ED** P. M. Manning. **DD** 362.4028. cum. index. **Bk Rev**, (Qty: 6-10). **Ad Acc. Circ:** 3,500. *Continues TAD News, 0157-2261.*

US/1055-4181
**TECHNOLOGY AND DISABILITY.** (1991)-. Periodical. English. qt. $95.00 (institution) $60.00 (individual) US and Canada; $110.00 (institution), $75.00 (individual) other. Butterworth Heinemann / Woburn, MA, 225 Wildwood Avenue, Unit B, Woburn MA 01801. **Tel** (800)366-2665, FAX (617)928-2620, telex 880052. **NLM** W1; TE211BG. **[CCC].** Documents available from The Genuine Article.
**Ind/Abst** Except. Child Educ. Resour.; Res. Alert [Full Cov.]; Soc. Sci. Cit. Index [Select. Cov.].

US/0896-8586
**TECHNOLOGY UPDATE (PALO ALTO, CALIF.).** (TECHNOLOGY UPDATE / SENSORY AIDS FOUNDATION.). [Technol. update (Palo Alto, Calif.)]. **Added/Corp** Sensory Aids Foundation. (Mar. 1985)-. Periodical. English. Six times a year (Feb., Apr., June, Aug., Oct. and Dec.). $37.00 (individuals), $47.00 (institutions) US & Canada; $57.00 (individuals), $67.00 (institutions), other; $30.00 (individuals), US & Canada & Mexico, visually impaired; $47.00 (individuals), others, visually impaired. Sensory Access Foundation, 385 Sherman Avenue, Suite 2, Palo Alto CA 94306. **Tel** (415)329-0430, FAX (415)323-1062. **ED** Margy Kahn (phone: (415)329-0430). **DD** 362. Index available. cum. index. **Bk Rev. Ad Acc. Circ:** 500 (ctrl). available in print ((large)); available on audiocassette. *Continues Sensory Aids Technology Update, 0743-8001.*
**Desc:** Consumers' guide to technology for blind and visually impaired persons.

US/0040-5914
**THERAPEUTIC RECREATION JOURNAL.** [Ther. recreat. j.]. **Added/Corp** National Therapeutic Recreation Society (U.S.). Vol. 2, No. 3 (1968)-. Periodical. English. qt. $28.00 (members), $46.00 (nonmembers). National Recreation and Park Association, 2775 South Quincy Street, Suite 300, Arlington VA 22206. **Tel** (703)820-4940, (703)578-5564, FAX (703)671-6772. **ED** Peter A. Witt. **NLM** W1 TH158T. ctrl circ. available on microfilm and microfiche from University Microfilms International (UMI). **Supersedes** *TR, Therapeutic Recreation.*
**Desc:** Devoted to the advancement of therapeutic recreation services for the ill, disabled, and other groups with special needs.
**Ind/Abst** Curr. Index J. Educ.; Hospit. Health Admin. Index (1967-1988); Leis. Recreat. Tour. Abstr.; Phys. Educ. Index; SPORT Discus; SportSearch.

CN/0229-0715
**THIRD EYE (TORONTO).** (THE THIRD EYE.). [Third eye]. **Added/Corp** BOOST. (1975)-. Periodical. English. Four times a year. Free. Blind Organ Ontario Selfhelp Tact - BOOST, 597 Parlament Street, Suite B3, Toronto Ontario M4X 1W3 Canada. **Tel** (416)964-6838. **DD** 362.4/1/09713.

JA
**TOKUSHU KYOIKU KANKEI KIKAN DANTAI NI YORU SHUPPANBUTSU ZASSHI TO MOKUROKU.** See Education-Special Education and Rehabilitation.

JA/0387-3374
**TOKUSHU KYOKUGAKU KENKYU.** See Education-Special Education and Rehabilitation.

US/0271-8294
**TOPICS IN LANGUAGE DISORDERS.** See Linguistics.

CN/0824-2801
**TOUTE JUSTICE (OTTAWA, ONT.), EN.** See Law.

US/1052-1615
**TRAVELIN TALK NEWSLETTER, THE.** See Travel and Tourism.

CN/0845-1338
**UPDATE (EASTER SEAL SOCIETY (ONTARIO).** (UPDATE / THE EASTER SEAL SOCIETY.). [Update - Easter Seal Soc.]. Vol. 1, No. 1 (July 1988)-. Periodical. English. bm. Free. The Easter Seal Society, 250 Ferrand Drive/Suite 200, Don Mills Ontario M3C 3P2 Canada. **Tel** (416)421-8377. **DD** 362.4/383/088054.

CN/0227-6755
**VIBRATIONS (TORONTO).** (VIBRATIONS.). [Vibrations]. **Added/Corp** Canadian Hearing Society. (1974)-. Periodical. English. qt. 15.00Can$ (comes with Canadian Hearing Society membership). Canadian Hearing Society / Toronto, 271 Spadina Road, Toronto Ontario M5R 2V3 Canada. **Tel** (416)964-9595, FAX (416)323-4750. **ED** Liz Brady. **DD** 362.4/2/0971. **Ad Acc, Adv Mgr:** Bob Hickey. **Circ:** 7,000.
**Desc:** Publishes material of interest to deaf and hard of hearing people, advocates their interests, and promotes services of the Canadian Hearing Society.

US/0738-7091
**VIP NEWSLETTER.** [VIP newsl.]. **Added/Corp** International Institute for Visually Impaired, 0-7. **VFOAT** V.I.P. Newsletter. **VAT** Visually Impaired Newsletter. (19??)-. Newsletter. English. qt. $10.00. International Institute of the Visually Impaired, 8500 West Capital Street, Milwaukee WI 53222. **Tel** (414)464-3000. **ED** Sherry Raynor and Yale Cohen. cum. index. **Bk Rev**.

US
**VISION RESOURCE UPDATE.** English. $20.00. Vision Foundation Inc, Vision Resource Inc, 818

Mt Auburn Street, Watertown MA 02171. **Tel** (617)926-4232. **ED** Fran Weisse. **Bk Rev.** ctrl circ. available on audiocassette; available in large print.
**Desc:** Information and resources of interest to individuals coping with sight loss.

US/0160-8312
**VOCATIONAL EVALUATION AND WORK ADJUSTMENT BULLETIN.** [Vocat. eval. work adjust. bull.]. **Added/Corp** Vocational Evaluation and Work Adjustment Association. **VFOAT** Evaluation and Work Adjustment Bulletin. Vol. 1 (1968)-. Bulletin. English. qt. $25.00 (individuals), $30.00 (institutions) US; $35.00 (individuals), $40.00 (institutions) other. VEWAA Office, Research and Training Center, University of Wisconsin-Stout, Menomonie WI 54751. **Tel** (715)232-1370. **ED** Darrell Coffey. **LC** HD7256.U5; V58. **DD** 362/.0425. **NLM** W1; VO161L. **CODEN** VEWBD3. Index available (bound in 4 issues). cum. index. **Bk Rev. Ad Acc. Pr Rev. Circ:** 2,000 (ctrl).
**Desc:** Research on vocational evaluation and work adjustment of people with disabilities. Innovations in vocational evaluation and work adjustment techniques.
**Ind/Abst** Psychol. Abstr. (1971-); PsycINFO; PsycLit.

US/0888-2517
**VOICE (DALLAS, TEX.), THE.** ***Title Change.*** (THE VOICE.). [Voice]. (1985)-(19??). Periodical. English. Ten times a year. The Voice, PO Box 2663, Corpus Christie TX 78403. **Tel** (512)884-8388, (800)327-7347, FAX (512)884-3314. **DD** 362. ***Continues*** *Texas Voice.* ***Continued by*** *Hearing Health, 0888-2517.*
**Desc:** For, of, by and about hearing impaired people and professionals.

CN/0826-4503
**VOIR DIRE (MONTREAL).** (VOIR DIRE.). [Voir dire]. **Added/Corp** Association des Sourds du Montreal-Metropolitain. Vol. 1, No 1 (Sept./Oct. 1983)-. Periodical. French. Six times a year. 20.00Can$ Canada; 25.00Can$ other. Les Publications Voir Dire, 65 Decastelnali Ouest, Montreal Que H2R 2W3 Canada. **Tel** (5140279-7609, FAX 9514)279-5373. **ED** Arthur LeBlanc. **DD** 362.4/2/09714. Index Available Received separately--bound from publisher ($4.00). cum. index. **Bk Rev**, (Qty: 6). **Ad Acc. Circ:** 1,000 (ctrl).

US/0042-8639
**VOLTA REVIEW, THE.** [Volta rev.]. **Added/Corp** Volta Bureau (U.S.) Volta Speech Association for the Deaf (U.S). Alexander Graham Bell Association for the Deaf. Vol. 12, No. 1 (Apr. 1910)-. Monographic series. English. Five times a year. $42.00. Alexander Graham Bell Association for the Deaf, 3417 Volta Place Northwest, Washington DC 20007. **Tel** (202)337-5220. **ED** Richard Stoker. **LC** HV2350; .V7. **DD** 362. **NLM** W1 VO594. **CODEN** VOLRAT. **[CCC].** Index available. **Bk Rev. Ad Acc. Pr Rev. Circ:** 5,400 (ctrl). available on microfilm and microfiche from University Microfilms International (UMI). Documents available from The Genuine Article. ***Absorbed*** *Auditory Outlook;* ***Continues*** *Association Review.*
**Desc:** Professional journal dealing with deafness and the oral approach to communication. Articles deal with speech, hearing and language development.
**Ind/Abst** Acad. Search (July 1993-); Appl. Soc. Sci. Index Abstr.; Curr. Contents Soc. Behav. Sci.; Curr. Index J. Educ.; Educ. Index; Except. Child Educ. Resour.; INFO-SOUTH Abstr.; Mag. Search; Psychol. Abstr. (1935-); PsycINFO; PsycLit; Res. Alert [Full Cov.]; Soc. Plann. Policy Dev. Abstr.; Soc. Sci. Cit. Index [Full Cov.].

US/0193-113X
**VOLUNTEERS WHO PRODUCE BOOKS.** (VOLUNTEERS WHO PRODUCE BOOKS / NATIONAL LIBRARY SERVICE FOR THE BLIND AND PHYSICALLY HANDICAPPED, THE LIBRARY OF CONGRESS.). English. an. Free. National Library Service for the Blind and Physically Handicapped, Library of Congress, 1291 Taylor Street Northwest, Washington DC 20542. **Tel** (800)424-8567, (202)707-5100, (800)424-9100. **LC** HV1790. **DD** 362.4/1/02573. **NLM** HV 1790; V943.
**Desc:** Listing by state of special reading services for the blind and deaf.

US/0043-0757
**WASHINGTON SOUNDS.** 1966-. Periodical. English. mo. $15.00. National Association of Hearing and Speech, 814 Thayer Avenue/Suite 202, Silver Spring MD 20910. **Tel** (301)588-5242.

US/0882-472X
**WHAT'S LINE.** **See** Library and Information Sciences.

US
**WORKLIFE : A PUBLICATION ON EMPLOYMENT AND PERSONS WITH DISABILITIES.** **Added/Corp** United States. President's Committee on Employment of the Handicapped. United States. President's Committee on Employment of People with Disabilities. Vol. 1, No. 1 (Jan./Feb./Mar. 1988)-. Periodical. English. qt. President's Committee on Employment of People with Disabilities, 1331 F Street NW, Washington DC 20004-1107. ***Continues*** *Disabled USA, 0148-5407.*
**Ind/Abst** Health Index (1989-); Health Period. Database [Full Txt.]; Health Ref. Cent. (Jan. 1989-) [Full Txt.] [Full Cov.].

US/0199-8293
**WORLD AROUND YOU, THE.** [World around you]. Periodical. English. mo (September through May). $7.00 (regular edition), $10.00 (teacher's edition) US; $12.00 (regular edition), $15.00 (teacher's edition) other. Gallaudet University Department of English, 800 Florida Avenue Northeast, Washington DC 20002. **Tel** (202)651-5580. **(Subscription address:** World Around You, KDES PAS 6 800 Florida Avenue Northeast, Washington DC 20002**)** **ED** Cathryn Carroll. **Bk Rev. Ad Acc. Circ:** 12,000 (ctrl).
**Desc:** Publication for young, deaf people; focuses on hearing impairment and hearing impaired people.

US/0738-8101
**YOUNG AND ALIVE.** **Added/Corp** Christian Record Braille Foundation (U.S.). (19??)-. Periodical. English. Four times a year. Free. Christian Record Services, Box 6097, 4444 South 52nd Street, Lincoln NE 68506. **Tel** (402)488-0981. **ED** Richard Kaiser. **Circ:** 26,000 (ctrl). available in braille. ***Continues*** *Youth Happiness.*
**Desc:** Stories and articles which challenge the thinking of today's young people. It includes such topics as nature, sports, hobbies, travel, health and Christianity.

## ABSTRACTING, BIBLIOGRAPHIES AND STATISTICS

US/1069-6865
**DIALOGUE (BRAILLE ED.).** **See** Physically Impaired.

AT/1032-2396
**DISABLED AND AGED PERSONS AUSTRALIA ... PRELIMINARY RESULTS.** [Disabl. aged persons Aust., Prelim. results]. **Added/Corp** Australian Bureau of Statistics. (1988)-. English. ir. 12.50Aus$. Australian Bureau of Statistics, PO Box 10, Belconnen Australian Capital Territory, 2616 Australia. **Tel** 011 61 6 2527911, FAX 011 61 6 2516009. **DD** 305.9080994021.
**Desc:** Contains summary tables of number of disabled people and number of handicapped by type and severity of handicap and requirements for care by activities of daily living.

## PHYSICS

GW/0341-9843
**ABHANDLUNGEN DER AKADEMIE DER WISSENSCHAFTEN IN GOTTINGEN. MATHEMATISCH-PHYSIKALISCHE KLASSE.** **See** Mathematics.

FI/0001-5105
**ACTA ACADEMIAE ABOENSIS. SERIES: B, MATHEMATICA ET PHYSICA.** **See** Mathematics.

FR
**ACTA ACUSTICA.** (19??)-. Periodical. English (French). bm. 2450.00F. European Acoustics Association, PO Box 34 Mr Dancer Isl, 68301 St. Louis Cedex France. **Tel** 011 33 1 89695094. **(Subscription address:** Les Editions de Physique, Avenue du Hoggar BP 112, 91944 Les Ulis Cedex A France.**)** ***Absorbed*** *Journal d Acoutique.*

II/0253-732X
**ACTA CIENCIA INDICA. PHYSICS.** [Acta cienc. indica, Phys.]. **Added/Corp** Society for the Progress of Science (India). **VFOAT** Physics. Vol. 5, No. 1 (1979)-. Academic Scholarly Publication. English. qt. $50.00. Pragati Prakashan, PO Box 62, Begum Bridge, 250001 Meerut India. **Tel** 73022. **(Subscription address:** Prints India, 11 Darya Ganj, New Delhi 110002 India.**)** **ED** V.P. Kudasiya and K.K. Mittal. **LC** QC1; .A337. **DD** 530/.5. **CODEN** ACIPD2. **Bk Rev. Ad Acc. Circ:** 1,000. Documents available from Ask*IEEE, CASDDS. ***Continues in part*** *Acta Ciencia Indica, 0379-5411.*
**Ind/Abst** Chem. Abstr.; INSPEC (1979-).

HU/0567-7947
**ACTA PHYSICA ET CHIMICA DEBRECINA.** [Acta phys. chim. Debrecina]. **Added/Corp** Kossuth Lajos Tudomanyegyetem. (1962)-. Periodical. Latin. an. **CODEN** APDBAN. Documents available from CASDDS. ***Supersedes in part*** *Acta Universitatis Debreceniensis de Ludovico Kossuth Nominatae.*
**Ind/Abst** Chem. Abstr.

HU/0231-4428
**ACTA PHYSICA HUNGARICA.** [Acta phys. hung.]. **Added/Corp** Magyar Tudomanyos Akademia. Vol. 54, No. 1-2 (1983)-. Academic Scholarly Publication. English (French, German and Russian). Four times a year. $96.00. Akademiai Kiado, Publishing House of the Hungarian Academy of Sciences, Prielle Kornelia u. 19-35, H-1117 Budapest Hungary. **Tel** 011 36 1 1811991, FAX 011 36 1 1811991, telex 22-6228 AKNYO H. **ED** Istvan Kovacs (editor's address: Department of Atomic Physics, Technical University, Budafoki ut 8, 1521 Budapest Hungary). **LC** QC3; .A255. **DD** 530/.05. **NLM** W1; AC9189. **CODEN** APHUE2. **[CCC].** Documents available from Ask*IEEE, CASDDS. ***Continues*** *Acta Physica Academiae Scientiarum Hungaricae, 0001-6705.*
**Desc:** Publishes original papers (articles with abstracts and short communications) in the sphere of theoretical and experimental physics, including the fundamental problems and applications of classical and quantum physics, elementary particles and fields, nuclear physics, atomic and molecular physics, optics, acoustics, thermodynamics, fluids and plasmas, the properties of condensed matter, etc.
**Ind/Abst** Chem. Abstr. (1983-); INSPEC (1983-); Int. Aerosp. Abstr. (1984-); Leadscan; Math. Rev.

PL/0587-4246
**ACTA PHYSICA POLONICA, A.** [Acta phys. Pol., A]. **Added/Corp** Instytut Fizyki (Polska Akademia Nauk) Polskie Towarzystwo Fizyczne. Vol. 37 (Jan. 1970)-. Periodical. English. mo. $189.00. **(Subscription address:** ARS Polona, PO Box 1001, 00068 Warsaw Poland.**)** **LC** QC1; .A345. **NLM** W1 AC919A. **CODEN** ATPLB6. **[CCC]. Pr Rev.** Documents available from The Genuine Article, Ask*IEEE, CASDDS. ***Supersedes in part*** *Acta Physica Polonica, 0001-673X.*
**Ind/Abst** Acoust. Abstr.; Alum. Ind. Abstr.; Ceram. Abstr.; Chem. Abstr.; Chem. Titles; Curr. Contents Phys. Chem. Earth Sci.; Energy Res. Abstr.; Eng. Mater. Abstr.; INSPEC (Jan. 1970-); Leadscan; Math. Rev.; Met. Abstr.; Res. Alert [Full Cov.]; Sci. Cit. Index.

US/1044-8357
**ACTA PHYSICA SINICA.** ***Ceased.*** (JOURNAL OF CHINESE PHYSICS.). [Acta phys. Sin.]. **Added/Corp** Chung-kuo wu li Hsueh Hui. **VFOAT** Acta Physica Sinica. (1989)-(19??). Periodical. English (translations available in Chinese). bm. Allerton Press, Inc., 150 Fifth Avenue, New York NY 10011. **Tel** (212)924-3950, FAX (212)463-9684, telex 427441 ALPRES. **LC** QC1; .W8133. **DD** 530/.05.

XO/0323-0465
**ACTA PHYSICA SLOVACA.** [Acta phys. Slovaca]. **Added/Corp** Fyzikalny Ustav SAV. Vol. 23 (1973)-. Academic Scholarly Publication. English (summaries and/or abstracts in English and Russian). Six times a year. $100.00. Slovenska Akademia Vied / Slovak Academy of Sciences, PO Box 57, 81005 Bratislava Slovakia. **Tel** 011 42 7 3782715, 011 42 7 3782925, FAX 011 42 7 496849, telex 93261. **LC** QC1; .F54. **DD** 530/.05. **CODEN** APSVCO. Documents available from Ask*IEEE, CASDDS. ***Continues*** *Fyzikalny Casopis, 0532-9132.*
**Ind/Abst** Chem. Abstr.; Energy Res. Abstr. (Feb. 1974-); Eng. Mater. Abstr.; INSPEC (Feb. 1974-); Int. Aerosp. Abstr.; Leadscan; Math. Rev.

XO/0231-889X
**ACTA PHYSICA UNIVERSITATIS COMENIANAE.** (ACTA PHYSICA UNIVERSITATIS COMENIANAE / UNIVERSITAS COMENIANA.). [Acta phys. Univ. Comen.]. **Added/Corp** Univerzita Komenskeho v Bratislave. (1983)-. English (Russian; summaries and/or abstracts in Russian and Slovak). an. **LC** QC1; .B64. **CODEN** APUCED. Documents available from Ask*IEEE, CASDDS. ***Continues*** *Acta Facultatis Rerum Naturalium Universitatis Comenianae. Physica, 0524-2355.*
**Ind/Abst** Chem. Abstr.; INSPEC (1983-).

FI/0355-2721
**ACTA POLYTECHNICA SCANDINAVICA. APPLIED PHYSICS SERIES PH.** (ACTA POLYTECHNICA SCANDINAVICA. APPLIED PHYSICS SERIES.). [Acta polytech. scand. Appl. phys. ser.]. **Added/Corp** Teknillisten Tieteiden Akatemia. **VFOAT** Applied Physics Series. (1976)-. Academic Scholarly Publication. English. ir. Price varies per volume. The Finnish Academy of Technology, Tekniikantie 12, Fin 02150 Espoo Finland. **Tel** 011 358 0 4554565, FAX 011 358 0 6945041. **LC** QC1; .A35. **DD** 530/.05. **CODEN** APSSDG. Index available. **Circ:** 600. available on microfilm from University Microfilms International (UMI). Documents available from Article Express International, The Genuine Article, Ask*IEEE, CASDDS. ***Continues*** *Acta Polytechnica Scandinavica. Physics Including Nuvlronics Series.*
**Desc:** Scientific research report series consisting of monographs.
**Ind/Abst** Bioeng. Abstr.; Chem. Abstr.; Curr. Contents Eng. Tech. Appl. Sci.; Ei Page One; Energy Res. Abstr. (April 1978-); Eng. Index Annu.; GeoRef; INSPEC (1981-); Int. Aerosp. Abstr.; Leadscan; Res. Alert [Full Cov.]; SCISEARCH; Soc. Sci. Cit. Index [Select. Cov.].

XR/0001-7140
**ACTA UNIVERSITATIS CAROLINAE. MATHEMATICA ET PHYSICA.** **See** Mathematics.

PL/0084-2966
**ACTA UNIVERSITATIS WRATISLAVIENSIS. MATEMATYKA, FIZYKA, ASTRONOMIA.** See Mathematics.

UN/0320-7218
**ADSORBCIJA I ADSORBENTY.** (ADSORBTSIIA I ADSORBENTY.). [Adsorbcija adsorbenty]. **Added/Corp** Instytut Fizychnoi Khimii im. L.V. Pysarzhevskoho. (1972)-. Periodical. Russian. Documents available from CASDDS.
**Ind/Abst** Chem. Abstr.

SI
**ADVANCED SERIES IN MATHEMATICAL PHYSICS.** Vol. 1 (1987)-. Monographic series. English. World Scientific Publishing Company, PO Box 128, Farrer Road, Singapore 9128 Singapore. **Tel** 011 65 3825663, FAX 011 65 3825919, telex RS 28561 WSPC.
**Ind/Abst** Math. Rev. (1988-); Zentralbl. Math. Ihre Grenzgeb.

NE
**ADVANCES IN EXPLORATION IN GEOPHYSICS.** See Earth Sciences-Geology.

●US/1075-1629
**ADVANCES IN METAL AND SEMICONDUCTOR CLUSTERS.** See Chemistry-Inorganic Chemistry.

UK/0001-8732
**ADVANCES IN PHYSICS.** [Adv. phys.]. Vol. 1 (Jan. 1952)-. Periodical. English. Six times a year. $536.00 US; £325.00 other. Taylor & Francis Ltd., Rankine Road, Basingstoke Hampshire, RG24 8PR United Kingdom. **Tel** 011 44 256 840366, FAX 011 44 256 479438, telex 858540. **(Subscription address:** Taylor & Francis Inc., 1900 Frost Road, Suite 101, Bristol PA 19007-1598.**) ED** D. Sherrington (editor's address: Department of Physics, University of Oxford, 1 Keble Road, Oxford OX1 3NP United Kingdom). **LC** QC1. **DD** 530.5. **UDC** 53. **NLM** W1 AD783. **CODEN** ADPHAH. **[CCC]. Pr Rev.** available on microfilm and microfiche from University Microfilms International (UMI). Documents available from Article Express International, The Genuine Article, Ask*IEEE, CASDDS.
**Desc:** Provides definitive reviews of recent advances centering around condensed matter physics. Physicists of international repute who have made important contributions present their work in perspective against the general background of the field and discuss the wider implications of their own and other significant developments in the subject.
**Ind/Abst** Alum. Ind. Abstr.; Bioeng. Abstr.; Ceram. Abstr.; Chem. Abstr.; Curr. Contents Phys. Chem. Earth Sci.; Curr. Technol. Index; Ei Page One; Eng. Mater. Abstr.; Eng. Index Annu. [Select. Cov.]; GeoRef; Index Sci. Rev. [Full Cov.]; INSPEC (1968-); Int. Aerosp. Abstr.; Mass Spect. Bull.; Math. Rev.; Met. Abstr.; Pollut. Abstr. Indexes; Res. Alert [Full Cov.]; Sci. Cit. Index; SCISEARCH.

UK/0309-2534
**ADVANCES IN RAMAN SPECTROSCOPY.** [Adv. raman spectrosc.]. **Added/Corp** International Conference on Raman Spectroscopy. Proceedings. (1973)-. Monographic series. English. ir. Price varies per volume. Vieweg Publishing, PO Box 5829, D 65048 Wiesbaden Germany. **Tel** 011 49 611 160230, FAX 011 49 611 160229. **CODEN** AVRSAG. Documents available from CASDDS.
**Ind/Abst** Chem. Abstr.

US/1040-5852
**ADVANCES IN VLSI SERIES.** [Adv. VLSI ser.]. **VAT** Advances in Very Large Scale Integration Series. Vol. 1 (1989)-. Monographic series. English. Price varies per volume. Computer Science Press Inc, 9125 Fall River Lane, Potomac MD 20854. **Tel** (301)251-9050. **DD** 621. **CODEN** AVSEEH. Documents available from Ask*IEEE. ***Continues*** *Journal of VLSI and Computer Systems, 0733-5644.*
**Ind/Abst** INSPEC; Zentralbl. Math. Ihre Grenzgeb.

US/0094-243X
**AIP CONFERENCE PROCEEDINGS.** [AIP conf. proc.]. **Added/Corp** American Institute of Physics. **VFOAT** A.I.P. Conference Proceedings. No. 1 (1970)-. Monographic series. English. ir. Price varies per volume. American Institute of Physics, 500 Sunnyside Boulevard, Woodbury NY 11797-2999. **Tel** (516)576-2200, FAX (516)349-7669, telex 960983. **(Subscription address:** AIP / Vermont, c/o AIDC, PO Box 20, Williston VT 05495.**) CODEN** APCPCS. **[CCC].** Documents available from Article Express International, BIOSIS Document Express, Ask*IEEE, CASDDS. ***Continues*** *Quarterly Bulletin - American Association of Physicists in Medicine, 0001-0162.*
**Ind/Abst** Biol. Abstr.; Chem. Abstr.; Coal Abstr.; Curr. Phys. Index; Energy Res. Abstr. (Sept. 1972-); Eng. Index Annu. [Select. Cov.]; GeoRef; INIS Atomindex [Micro.]; INSPEC (1970-); Mass Spect. Bull. (?-?); Math. Rev.; SPIN (1972-).

US/0002-9505
**AMERICAN JOURNAL OF PHYSICS.** [Am. j. phys.]. **Added/Corp** American Association of Physics Teachers. American Institute of Physics. Vol. 8 (Feb. 1940)-. Academic Scholarly Publication. English. mo. $236.00 US; $246.00 other. American Association of Physics Teachers, One Physics Ellipse, College Park MD 20740-3845. **Tel** (301)209-3333, FAX (301)209-0845. **ED** Robert H. Romer. **NLM** W1 AM505. **CODEN** AJPIAS. **[CCC].** (bound in last issue). cum. index. **Bk Rev. Ad Acc. Pr Rev. Circ:** 7,700 (ctrl). Documents available from The Genuine Article, Ask*IEEE, UMI Article Clearinghouse, CASDDS. ***Continues*** *American Physics Teacher, 0096-0322.*
**Desc:** Focuses upon the instructional and cultural aspects of the physical sciences, including novel approaches to laboratory and classroom instruction, apparatus notes, book and film reviews.
**Ind/Abst** Abstr. Bull. Inst. Paper Chem.; Abstr. Bull. Inst. Pap. Sci. Tech.; Acad. Ind. [Computer File] (1992-); Acad. Search (July 1993-); Acoust. Abstr.; Appl. Sci. Technol. Index; Arts Humanit. Citation Index [Select. Cov.]; Ceram. Abstr.; Chem. Abstr.; Curr. Contents Phys. Chem. Earth Sci.; Curr. Index J. Educ.; Curr. Phys. Index; Energy Res. Abstr.; Expand. Acad. Index (1989-); Gen. Sci. Index; Gen. Sci. Source (Jul. 1993-); HTFS Dig.; INFO-SOUTH Abstr.; INIS Atomindex [Micro.]; INSPEC (1968-); Int. Aerosp. Abstr.; Leadscan; Mass Spect. Bull.; Math. Rev.; Newsp. Period. Abstr. (1992-); Res. Alert [Full Cov.]; Res. High. Educ. Abstr.; Sci. Cit. Index; SCISEARCH; Soc. Sci. Cit. Index [Select. Cov.]; SPIN (1970-); Surf. Treat. Technol. Abstr.

II/0250-5002
**AMPI MEDICAL PHYSICS BULLETIN.** [AMPI med. phys. bull.]. **Added/Corp** Association of Medical Physicists of India. **VFOAT** Medical Physics Bulletin. **VAT** Association of Medical Physicists of India Medical Physics Bulletin. (1976)-. Bulletin. English. qt. $50.00. Association of Medical Physicists of India, Trombay, Bombay, India. **(Subscription address:** Prints India, 11 Darya Ganj, New Delhi 110002 India.**) NLM** W1; AM9017. **CODEN** AMPBDV.

RM
**ANALELE UNIVERSITATI DIN GALATI. FASCICULA II - MATEMATICA, FIZICA, MECANICA TEORETICA.** See Mathematics.

RM/0254-8895
**ANALELE UNIVERSITATII BUCURESTI. FIZICA (1977).** (ANALELE UNIVERSITATII BUCURESTI. FIZICA.). [An. Univ. Bucur., Fiz.]. **Added/Corp** Universitatea din Bucuresti. **VFOAT** Fizica. Vol. 26 (1977)-. Romanian (English and French). an. DM164.00. **(Subscription address:** Kubon & Sagner, ABT Zeitschriftenimport, D 80328 Munich Germany.**) LC** QC1; .A596. **CODEN** ABFZA7. Documents available from Ask*IEEE, CASDDS. ***Continues in part*** *Universitatea din Bucuresti. Analele Universitatii Bucuresti. Stiintele Naturii, 0254-8887.*
**Ind/Abst** Ceram. Abstr. (19??-); Chem. Abstr.; INSPEC (1978-); Math. Rev.

RM/0253-1860
**ANALELE UNIVERSITATII DIN CRAIOVA. MATHEMATICA, FIZICA-CHIMIE.** See Mathematics.

RM/0082-4453
**ANALELE UNIVERSITATII DIN TIMISOARA. SERIA STINTE FIZICE-CHIMICE.** [An. Univ. Timis., Ser. stiinte fiz.-chim.]. **Main/Corp** Universitatea din Timisoara. (1969)-. Academic Scholarly Publication. English (French, German and Romanian). sa. **(Subscription address:** Ilexim Press Department, PO Box 1, 136-1-137, Bucharest, Romania.**) LC** QA1; .T55. **CODEN** ATFCBV. Documents available from CASDDS. ***Continues in part*** *Universitatea din Timisoara. Analele Universitatii din Timisoara. Seria Stiinte Matematice-Fizice, 0563-5608.*
**Ind/Abst** Chem. Abstr. (1969-1981); Math. Rev.

●SP/1133-0376
**ANALES DE FISICA.** **Added/Corp** Real Sociedad Espanola de Fisica. Vol. 88, (1992)-. Periodical. Spanish (English). Real Sociedad Espanola de Fisica, Facultad de Ciencias, Ciudad Universitaria, Madrid Spain. **LC** QC1; .A5995. **DD** 530/.05. ***Formed by the union of*** *Anales de Fisica. Serie A: Fenomenos e Interacciones, 0211-6243* ***and*** *Anales de Fisica. Serie B: Aplicaciones, Metodos e Instrumentos, 0211-6251.*
**Ind/Abst** Anal. Abstr.; Chem. Abstr.; GeoRef; INSPEC.

SP/0211-6243
**ANALES DE FISICA. SERIE A, FENOMENOS E INTERACCIONES.** ***Title Change.*** (ANALES DE FISICA. SERIE A, FENOMENOS E INTERACCIONES : PUBLICACION DE LA REAL SOCIEDAD ESPANOLA DE FISICA.). [An. fis., Ser. A, Fenom interacciones]. **Added/Corp** Real Sociedad Espanola de Fisica. **VFOAT** Fenomenos e Interacciones. Vol. 77, No. 1 (Jan./Apr. 1981)-(199?). Periodical. English (Spanish). Three times a year. Real Sociedad Espanola de Fisica, Facultad de Ciencias, Ciudad Universitaria, Madrid Spain. **LC** QC1; .A598. **DD** 530/.05. **CODEN** AFAIDU. Documents available from Ask*IEEE, CASDDS. ***Continues in part*** *Anales de Fisica, 0365-4818.* ***Merged with*** *Anales de Fisica. Serie B, Aplicaciones, Metodos e Intrumentos, 0211-6251* ***to form*** *Anales de Fisica (Madrid, Spain : 1992), 1133-0376.*
**Ind/Abst** Ceram. Abstr. (19??-); Chem. Abstr.; INSPEC (Jan./April 1981-).

SP
**ANALES DE QUIMICA. SERIE A, QUIMICA FISICA Y QUIMICA TECNICA.** Spanish. Facultad de Fisica y Quimica, Ciudad Universitaria, 28040 Madrid Spain.
**Ind/Abst** Ceram. Abstr. (19??-); Mass Spect. Bull.

US/0195-7236
**ANL-HEP-CP (ARGONNE NATIONAL LABORATORY, HIGH ENERGY PHYSICS DIVISION).** (ANL-HEP-CP.). **Main/Corp** Argonne National Laboratory. High Energy Physics Division. (19??)-. Monographic series. English. Argonne National Laboratory, 9700 South Cass Aveue, Argonne IL 60439. **Tel** (708)972-2000, FAX (708)972-5510. **CODEN** ANLRDW. Documents available from CASDDS.
**Ind/Abst** Chem. Abstr.

GW/0003-3804
**ANNALEN DER PHYSIK.** [Ann. phys.]. Vol. 1, No. 4 (1900)-. Academic Scholarly Publication. German. Eight times a year. DM632.00. Johann Ambrosius Barth, Prager Strasse 16 B, D 04103 Leipzig Germany. **Tel** 011 49 341 7137570. **(Subscription address:** Huethig Publishing Inc., 29 Macintosh Drive, Oxford CT 06478.**) NLM** W1 AN295. **CODEN** ANPYA2. **Pr Rev.** available on microfilm and microfiche from University Microfilms International (UMI). Documents available from The Genuine Article, Ask*IEEE, CASDDS. ***Continues*** *Annalen der Physik und Chemie.*
**Ind/Abst** Ceram. Abstr.; Chem. Abstr.; Curr. Contents Phys. Chem. Earth Sci.; Ei Page One; Energy Res. Abstr.; INSPEC (1968-); Leadscan; Math. Rev.; Res. Alert [Full Cov.]; Sci. Cit. Index; SCISEARCH; Zentralbl. Math. Ihre Grenzgeb.

FI/0066-2003
**ANNALES ACADEMIAE SCIENTIARUM FENNICAE. SERIES A. VI: PHYSICA.** ***Ceased.*** **Main/Corp** Suomalainen Tiedeakatemia. **Added/Corp** Suomalainen Tiedeakatemia. Toimituksia. Annales. Sarja/Series A. VI: Physica. (1957)-(1992). Monographic series. English (French). ir. **(Subscription address:** Academic Bookstore Akateeminen Kirjakauppa, PO Box 128, SF 00101 Helsinki 10 Finland.**) LC** QC1; .S87. ***Supersedes in part*** *Suomalainen Tiedeakatemia. Toimituksia. Annales. Sarja/Series A. I: Mathematica-Physica.*
**Ind/Abst** Ceram. Abstr. (19??-); Energy Res. Abstr.; GeoRef; INSPEC (1968-); Int. Aerosp. Abstr.; Math. Rev.

CG
**ANNALES DE LA FACULTE DES SCIENCES: SECTION MATHEMATIQUE-PHYSIQUE.** See Mathematics.

FR/0182-4295
**ANNALES DE LA FONDATION LOUIS DE BROGLIE.** [Ann. fond. Louis Broglie]. **Main/Corp** Fondation Louis de Broglie. Vol. 1 (1975)-. Periodical. French (English, German and Latin; summaries and/or abstracts in English, German, Italian and French). qt. 500.00F (institutions), 400.00F (individuals) France; $600.00 (institutions), $500.00 (individuals) US. Fondation Louis de Broglie, 23 Quai de Conti, 75006 Paris France. **Tel** 011 33 1 40460554. **CODEN** AFLBDU. Documents available from Article Express International, Ask*IEEE.
**Ind/Abst** Ei Page One; Energy Res. Abstr. (Sept. 1980-); Eng. Index Annu.; INSPEC (1981-).

FR/0246-0211
**ANNALES DE L'I.H.P. PHYSIQUE THEORIQUE.** [Ann. I.H.P. Phys. theor.]. **Added/Corp** Institut Henri Poincare. **VFOAT** Annales de l'I.H.P. Theoretical Physics; Annales Institut Henri Poincare. Section A. Physique Theorique; Physique Theorique. **VAT** Annales de l'Institut Henri Poincare. Physique Theorique. Vol. 38 No. 1 (1983)-. Academic Scholarly Publication. English (French and German). Eight times a year. 1790.00F France; 2230.00F other. Gauthier-Villars, 15 rue Gossin, 92543 Montrouge Cedex France. **Tel** 33 1 40 92 65 00, FAX 33 1 40 92 65 97. **(Subscription address:** Centrale des Revues, 11 rue Gossin, 92543 Montrouge Cedex France.**) ED** J. Ginibre. **LC** QC19.2; .A56. **CODEN** AIPTEO. **[CCC]. Bk Rev. Ad Acc. Pr Rev. Circ:** 700. Documents available from

Ask*IEEE, CASDDS. ***Continues*** *Annales de l'Institut Henri Poincare. Section A. Physique Theorique, 0020-2339.*
**Desc:** Welcomes manuscripts from all areas of theoretical and mathematical physics.
**Ind/Abst** Chem. Abstr. (1983-1985); Ei Page One; INSPEC (1984-); Math. Rev.; Sci. Cit. Index.

FR
## ANNALES DE PHYSIQUE. COLLOQUE.
**Added/Corp** Societe Francaise de Physique. (1986)-. Monographic series. French (French; summaries and/or abstracts in English). ir. Editions de Physique, 7 Avenue du Hoggar BP 112, 91944 Les Ulis Cedex France. **Tel** 011 33 1 69073688, FAX 011 33 1 69288491, telex 602321 F.

FR/0003-4169
## ANNALES DE PHYSIQUE (PARIS).
(ANNALES DE PHYSIQUE.). [Ann. phys.]. (1914)-. Periodical. French (English; summaries and/or abstracts in English; table of contents in English). Nine times a year. 2100.00F France; $432.34 US. Les Editions de Physique, 7 Avenue du Hoggar, Z.I. de Courtaboeuf - BP 112, 91944 les Ulis Cedex A France. **Tel** 011 33 1 69 07 36 88, FAX 011 33 1 69 28 84 91, telex EDITPHY 692321F. **ED** C. Boisson. **LC** QC1; .A65. **DD** 530.5. **NLM** W1 AN375. **CODEN** ANPHAJ. **[CCC].** Index available. cum. index. **Bk Rev. Ad Acc. Pr Rev. Circ:** 1,000. Documents available from The Genuine Article, Ask*IEEE, CASDDS. ***Supersedes in part*** *Annales de Chimie et de Physique, 0365-1444.*
**Desc:** Covers the basics of atomic and molecular physics, condensed matter, nuclear physics and astrophysics.
**Ind/Abst** Alum. Ind. Abstr. (19??-); Chem. Abstr. (19??-); Curr. Contents Phys. Chem. Earth Sci. (19??-); Energy Res. Abstr. (19??-); Eng. Mater. Abstr. (19??-); GeoRef (19??-); INSPEC (1968-); Int. Aerosp. Abstr. (19??-); Leadscan (19??-); Met. Abstr. (19??-); Res. Alert (19??-) [Full Cov.]; Sci. Cit. Index; SCISEARCH (19??-); Surf. Treat. Technol. Abstr. (19??-).

FR/0294-1228
## ANNALES FRANCAISES DES MICROTECHNIQUES ET DE CHRONOMETRIE.
[Ann. fr. microtech. chronom.]. (1982)-. Periodical. French. an. 47.90F. Annales Francaises des Microtechniques et de Chronometrie, 41 bis Avenue de l'Observatoire, F 25000 Besancon France. **Tel** 011 33 81 666930. **CODEN** AFMCE5. **Circ:** 400. Documents available from Ask*IEEE. ***Continues*** *Annales Francaises de Chronometrie et de Micromecanique, 0221-0665.*
**Desc:** Physics, engineering, time, frequency, domain, frequency standards, precision measurement, time scales, time dissemination, quartz resonators, displays, systems and circuits, industrial realizations and quality control listing.
**Ind/Abst** INSPEC (1982-).

PL/0137-6861
## ANNALES UNIVERSITATIS MARIAE CURIE-SKODOWSKA. SECTIO AAA: PHYSICA.
[Ann. Univ. Mariae Curie-Skodowska, Sect. AAA]. **Main/Corp** Uniwersytet Marii Curie-Skodowskiej. Vol. 31/32 (1977)-. Polish (summaries and/or abstracts in English and Russian). Uniwersytet Marii Curie-Sklodowskiej, Pl Marii Curie-Sklodowskiej 5, 20-031 Lublin Poland. **Tel** 37-53-04, telex 0643223. **LC** QC1; .L7932a. **DD** 530/.05. **CODEN** AUMADZ. Documents available from CASDDS. ***Continues in part*** *Annales. Sectio AA. Physica et Chemia.*
**Ind/Abst** Chem. Abstr.

US/0003-4916
## ANNALS OF PHYSICS.
[Ann. phys.]. Vol. 1 (April 1957)-. Academic Scholarly Publication. English. Sixteen times a year. $1628.00 US and Canada; $1886.00 other. Academic Press, Inc., 6277 Sea Harbor Drive, Orlando FL 32887. **Tel** (800)543-9534, (407)345-4100, FAX (407)363-9661. **ED** Herman Feshbach. **LC** QC1; .A72. **DD** 530.5. **NLM** W1 AN62G. **CODEN** APNYA6. **[CCC].** cum. index. **Pr Rev.** Documents available from The Genuine Article, Ask*IEEE, CASDDS.
**Desc:** Presents original work in all areas of basic physics research. Publishes papers on particular topics spanning theory, methodology, and applications. Ideas are developed and fully explored, and thorough treatment is given to first principles and ultimate applications. Emphasizes clarity and intelligibility in the articles it publishes, thus making them as accessible as possible. Readers familiar with recent developments in the field are provided with sufficient detail and background to follow the arguments and understand their significance.
**Ind/Abst** Alum. Ind. Abstr.; Chem. Abstr.; Chem. Titles; Curr. Contents Phys. Chem. Earth Sci.; Ei Page One; Energy Res. Abstr.; INIS Atomindex [Micro.]; INSPEC (1968-); Int. Aerosp. Abstr.; Leadscan; Math. Rev.; Met. Abstr.; Pollut. Abstr. Indexes; Res. Alert [Full Cov.]; Sci. Cit. Index; SCISEARCH; SPIN (1970-); Surf. Treat. Technol. Abstr.; Zentralbl. Math. Ihre Grenzgeb.

US/1042-0851
## ANNOUNCER (COLLEGE PARK, MD.).
(ANNOUNCER / AMERICAN ASSOCIATION OF PHYSICS TEACHERS.). [Announcer]. **Main/Corp** American Association of Physics Teachers. (198?)-. Periodical. English. qt. $26.00 US; $36.00 other. American Association of Physics Teachers, One Physics Ellipse, College Park MD 20740-3845. **Tel** (301)209-3333, FAX (301)209-0845. **LC** WMLC 93/1317. **DD** 530. ***Continues*** *American Association of Physics Teachers. AAPT Announcer, 0275-5696.*
**Desc:** Information on national meetings, section meetings, happenings in physics and science education. Serves as meeting program for national meetings.

FR
## ANNUAIRE INFORMATIQUE-PHYSIQUE.
1975/76-. French. 80.00. CNRS / Institut d'Information Scientifique et Technique, (Centre National de la Recherche Scientifique), 15 Quai Anatole France, Paris 75700 France. **Tel** 011 33 1 47531515, telex 299 356 F. **LC** Q180.F7; A68. **DD** 530/.07/2044.

US/0099-9512
## ANNUAL PROCEEDINGS, RELIABILITY PHYSICS SYMPOSIUM.
[Annu. Proc. Reliab. Phys. symp.]. **VFOAT** Annual Reliability Physics Symposium, Proceedings; Reliability Physics Symposium, Annual Proceedings. (1967)-. English. an. Institution of Electrical Engineers / IEE, Michael Faraday House, Six Hills Way, Stevenage Herts SG1 2AY UK. **Tel** 011 44 438 313311, FAX 011 44 438 742840, telex 825578 IEESTV G. **(Subscription address:** IEE / UK, Publications Sales Department, PO Box 96, Stevenage, Herts, SG1 2SD England.**) CODEN** ARLPBI. Documents available from CASDDS. ***Continues*** *Physics of Failure in Electronics, 0097-2088.*
**Ind/Abst** Chem. Abstr.

AT/0158-7439
## ANNUAL REPORT (INSTITUTE OF PHYSICAL SCIENCES (COMMONWEALTH SCIENTIFIC AND INDUSTRIAL RESEARCH ORGANIZATION)).
(ANNUAL REPORT / CSIRO, INSTITUTE OF PHYSICAL SCIENCES.). **Added/Corp** Institute of Physical Sciences (Commonwealth Scientific and Industrial Research Organization). (19??)-. Periodical. English. an. CSIRO Publications, PO Box 89, 314 Albert Street, East Melborne Victoria 3002 Australia. **Tel** 011 61 3 4187333, 4187217, FAX 011 61 3 4190459, telex AA 30236. **LC** QC51.A82; C653. **DD** 500.2/05. **Circ:** 2,000.

DK
## ANNUAL REPORT / INSTITUTE OF PHYSICS, AARHUS UNIVERSITY.
**Main/Corp** Aarhus Universitet. Fysisk Institut. (1990)-. English. Aarhus University Press, Aarhus University, Building 170, DK-8000 Aarhus C Denmark. **Tel** 011 45 86 197033, FAX 011 45 86 198433, telex 16600. **LC** QC1; .A15a. **DD** 530/.5. ***Continues*** *Aarhus Universitet. Fysisk Institut. Aarsrapport - Det Fysiske Institut.*

IT/0304-7091
## ANNUAL REPORT - INTERNATIONAL CENTRE FOR THEORETICAL PHYSICS.
(ANNUAL REPORT.). **Main/Corp** International Centre for Theoretical Physics. **Added/Corp** International Atomic Energy Agency. 1st (1964/1965)-. English. an. Free. International Centre for Theoretical Physics, PO Box 586, I-34100 Trieste Italy. **Tel** (40)22.401, FAX (40)22.41.63, telex 460390 ICTP I. **ED** A.M. Hamende. **LC** QC1.I6285; A28. **DD** 530. **Circ:** 2,000 (ctrl).
**Desc:** Review of courses held in previous solar year, with listing of lectures and statistics on participation.

CH/0304-5293
## ANNUAL REPORT OF THE INSTITUTE OF PHYSICS, ACADEMIA SINICA.
[Annu. rep. Inst. Phys., Acad. Sin.]. **Main/Corp** Chung Yang Yen Chiu Yuan. Wu Li Yen Chiu So. **Added/Corp** Chung Yang Yen Chiu Yuan. Wu Li Yen Chiu So. Chung Yang Yen Chiu Yuan Wu Li Yen Chiu So Chi Kan. **VFOAT** Chung Yang Yen Chiu Yuan Wu Li Yen Chiu So Chi Kan. (1971)-. Multiple languages (English and Chinese). an. Institute of Physics, Academia Sinica, Nankang, Taipei, Taiwan. **LC** QC1; .C525a. **CODEN** RIPSD3. Documents available from Ask*IEEE, CASDDS.
**Ind/Abst** Chem. Abstr.; INSPEC (Dec. 1978-).

NE/0304-8292
## ANNUAL REPORT - TECHNISCH-PHYSISCHE DIENST TNO-TH.
**Main/Corp** Technisch-Physische Dienst TNO-TH. (19??)-. Dutch (English). Technisch Physische Dienst Tno-th, Stieltjesweg 1, PO Box 155, 2600 AD Delft Netherlands. **Tel** (015)788020, telex 38091 TPD DT NL. **ED** A. Verbreack. **LC** QC1; .N433. **DD** 530/.07/20492. **Circ:** 2,500 (ctrl).
**Desc:** Report of activities.

IT/0567-6738
## ANNUARIO DELLA ACCADEMIA DELLE SCIENZE DELL'INSTITUTO DI BOLOGNA : CLASSE DI SCIENZE FISICHE.
**Main/Corp** Accademia delle Scienze dell'Istituto di Bologna. Italian. an. Palazzo Universitario, Via Zamboni 31, Bologna Italy. **LC** QC1; .A3213.
**Ind/Abst** Numis. Lit. (?-?).

RU/0937-9347
## APPLIED MAGNETIC RESONANCE.
[Appl. magn. reson.]. **Added/Corp** Akademiia Nauk SSSR. Otdelenie Obshchei Fiziki i Astronomii. Kazanskii Fiziko-Tekhnicheskii Institut. **VFOAT** AMR. Vol. 1, No. 1 (June 1990)-. Periodical. English. Eight times a year. DM1050.00. Springer-Verlag Wien, Sachsenplatz 4 6, PO Box 89, A-1201 Vienna Austria. **Tel** 011 43 1 3302415. **(Subscription address:** Springer Verlag New York Inc. / for North America, 44 Hartz Way, Secaucus NJ 07096.**) ED** K M Salikhov. **LC** QC762; .A48. **NLM** W1; AP525M. **CODEN** APMREI. **[CCC]. Bk Rev. Ad Acc. Pr Rev.** available on microfilm. Documents available from Ask*IEEE, CASDDS.
**Desc:** Provides an international forum for the application of magnetic resonance in physics, chemistry, biology, medicine, geochemistry, ecology, engineering, and related fields. AMR also publishes original articles with a strong emphasis on new applications of the technique and on new experimental methods.
**Ind/Abst** Chem. Abstr.; Curr. Aware. Biol. Sci., CABS; INSPEC (1992-).

GW/0721-7250
## APPLIED PHYSICS. A, SOLIDS AND SURFACES.
[Appl. phys., A]. **VFOAT** Solids and Surfaces. Vol. A26, No. 1 (Sept. 1981)-. Academic Scholarly Publication. English. Twelve times a year. DM2068.00; DM3521.00 combination subscription with Section B. Springer-Verlag GmbH & Company KG, Heidelberger Platz 3, D 14197 Berlin Germany. **Tel** 011 49 30 8207223, FAX 011 49 30 8214091, telex 183 319 SPBLN D. **(Subscription address:** Springer Verlag New York Inc. / for North America, 44 Hartz Way, Secaucus NJ 07096.**) ED** H K V Lotsch. **LC** QC1; .A733. **DD** 530.4/1. **CODEN** APSFDB. **[CCC]. Ad Acc. Pr Rev. Circ:** 65. available on microfilm and microfiche from University Microfilms International (UMI). Documents available from Article Express International, The Genuine Article, Ask*IEEE, CASDDS. ***Continues in part*** *Applied Physics, 0340-3793.*
**Desc:** Covers primarily the condensed state, including surface science and engineering.
**Ind/Abst** Alum. Ind. Abstr.; Bioeng. Abstr.; Chem. Abstr.; Chem. Titles; Curr. Contents Phys. Chem. Earth Sci.; Ei Page One; Energy Res. Abstr. (Feb. 1982-); Eng. Index Annu.; HTFS Dig.; INSPEC (Sept. 1981-); Int. Aerosp. Abstr.; Leadscan; Mass Spect. Bull.; Met. Abstr.; Phys. Briefs; Res. Alert [Full Cov.]; Sci. Cit. Index; SCISEARCH.

US/0277-9374
## APPLIED PHYSICS COMMUNICATIONS.
***Ceased.*** [Appl. phys. commun.]. Vol. 1, No. 1 (1981)-Vol. 13. Academic Scholarly Publication. English. qt. Marcel Dekker Inc., 270 Madison Avenue, New York NY 10016. **Tel** (212)696-9000, (800)228-1160, FAX (212)685-4540, telex 421419. **(Subscription address:** Marcel Dekker Inc, PO Box 5017, Monticello NY 12701.**) ED** Allen M. Hermann, John A. Woollam, Sy-Hwang Liou. **LC** TA1; .A658. **DD** 620/.005. **CODEN** APCODQ. **[CCC]. Bk Rev. Ad Acc.** ctrl circ. available on microfiche. Documents available from Article Express International, Ask*IEEE, CASDDS.
**Desc:** Offers rapid publication of topical material in a broad range of disciplines of applied physics. Some of the subject areas covered are: inorganic and organic insulators, photoconductors and conductors, solid state devices including solar cells, semiconductor physics, polymer physics, medical and biological physics and instrumentation, applied optics, plasmas, superconducting materials and devices, carbon, graphite, coal, and applied electrochemistry.
**Ind/Abst** Alum. Ind. Abstr.; Bioeng. Abstr.; Chem. Abstr.; Ei Page One; Energy Res. Abstr. (Nov. 1981-); Eng. Mater. Abstr.; Eng. Index Annu.; INIS Atomindex [Micro.]; INSPEC (1981-); Met. Abstr.

US/0003-6951
## APPLIED PHYSICS LETTERS.
[Appl. phys. lett.]. **Added/Corp** American Institute of Physics. Vol. 1 (Sept. 1962)-. Periodical. English. wk. $1195.00 US. American Institute of Physics, 500 Sunnyside Boulevard, Woodbury NY 11797-2999. **Tel** (516)576-2200, FAX (516)349-7669, telex 960983. **LC** QC1; .A74. **CODEN** APPLAB. **[CCC].** Index Available, published separately, free-automatically sent. **Pr Rev.** available on microfilm and microfiche (16mm or 35mm). Documents available from Article Express International, The Genuine Article, Ask*IEEE, CASDDS.
**Ind/Abst** Acoust. Abstr.; Alum. Ind. Abstr.; Ceram. Abstr.; Chem. Abstr.; Chem. Titles; Curr. Contents Phys. Chem. Earth Sci.; Curr. Phys. Index; Curr. Titles Electrochem.; Energy Res. Abstr.; Eng. Mater. Abstr.; Eng. Index Annu. [Select. Cov.]; GeoRef; INIS Atomindex [Micro.]; INSPEC (1968-); Int. Aerosp. Abstr. (1991-); Leadscan; Mass Spect. Bull.; Met. Abstr.; Pollut. Abstr. Indexes; Res. Alert [Full Cov.]; Sci. Cit. Index; SCISEARCH; SPIN (1970-); World Ceram. Abstr.

NE/0169-4332
**APPLIED SURFACE SCIENCE.** [Appl. surf. sci.]. Vol. 24, No. 1 (June/July 1985)-. Academic Scholarly Publication. English. Forty-Four times a year (11 vols.). Fl4521.00. Elsevier Science Publishers BV, PO Box 211, 1000 AE Amsterdam Netherlands. **Tel** 011 31 20 5803642, FAX 011 31 20 5862696, telex 15682. **ED** L.C. Feldman and W.F. van der Weg, J. Nishizawa. **LC** TA418.7; .A66. **DD** 620.4. **CODEN** ASUSEE. **[CCC]. Pr Rev.** available on microfilm and microfiche from University Microfilms International (UMI). Documents available from Article Express International, The Genuine Article, Ask*IEEE, CASDDS. ***Continues*** *Applications of Surface Science, 0378-5963.*
**Desc:** Concerned with the tools and knowledge of surface science. Strives to study the microscopic phenomena which determine the synthesis and behaviour of surfaces and interfaces.
**Ind/Abst** Anal. Abstr.; Ceram. Abstr. (1985-); Chem. Abstr. (1985-); Chem. Titles; Civ. Struct. Eng. Abstr.; Curr. Contents Eng. Tech. Appl. Sci.; Curr. Contents Phys. Chem. Earth Sci.; Curr. Titles Electrochem.; Ei Page One; Elect. Comm. Abstr.; Eng. Mater. Abstr.; Eng. Index Annu.; INSPEC (1985-); Leadscan; Manuf. Process Eng. Abstr.; Mass Spect. Bull.; Mater. Sci. Eng. Abstr.; Mech. Eng. Abstr.; Met. Abstr.; Phys. Briefs; Res. Alert [Full Cov.]; Sci. Cit. Index; SCISEARCH; Solid State Supercond. Abstr.

AT/0518-1623
**APPROACH TO PHYSICAL SCIENCES.** **Added/Corp** University of New South Wales New South Wales. University, Kensington. Summer School for Senior Science Teachers. (1970)-. Periodical. English. an. University of New South Wales / School of Physics, PO Box 1, Kensington New South Wales 2003 Australia. ***Continues*** *Approach to Chemistry.*

●US/1058-8132
**APSNEWS.** (APS NEWS.). [APSnews]. **Main/Corp** American Physical Society. **VFOAT** American Physical Society News; APS News. Vol. 1, No. 1 (Jan. 1992)-. Periodical. English. mo. $130.00 US. American Institute of Physics, 500 Sunnyside Boulevard, Woodbury NY 11797-2999. **Tel** (516)576-2200, FAX (516)349-7669, telex 960983. **LC** QC1; .A59a. **DD** 530/.06073. **CODEN** ANWSEN. **[CCC]. *Continues in part*** *American Physical Society. Bulletin of the American Physical Society, 0003-0503.*

CL
**AREA FISICA.** **Added/Corp** Universidad de Santiago (Chile) Universidad Tecnica del Estado (Chile). **VFOAT** Area de Fisica; Physics. (1974)-. Monographic series. Spanish (English). Price varies per volume. Universidad Tecnica del Estado, Chile. ***Continues*** *Fisica (Santiago, Chile).*

NO/0365-2459
**ARKIV FOR DET FYSISKE SEMINAR I TRONDHEIM.** [Ark. Fys. semin. Trondheim]. **Main/Corp** Trondheim. Norges Tekniske Hgskole. Det Fysiske Seminar. (1963)-. Periodical. Norwegian. **CODEN** AFYTAA. Documents available from Ask*IEEE, CASDDS.
**Ind/Abst** Chem. Abstr.; INSPEC (1991-).

●US/1067-9804
**ASIC & EDA.** (ASIC & EDA : TECHNOLOGIES FOR SYSTEM DESIGN.). [ASIC EDA]. **Added/Corp** Verecom Group. **VFOAT** ASIC and EDA. (1992)-. Periodical. English. mo. $48.00. The Verecom Group, 5150 el Camino Real, Suite C20, Los Altos CA 94022. **DD** 621. ***Continues*** *ASIC Technology & News, 1043-9617.*

AI/0571-7132
**ASTROFIZIKA.** **See** Astronomy.

TU/1015-5295
**ASTRONOMI VE FIZIK DERGISI / ISTANBUL UNIVERSITESI, FEN FAKULTESI.** **See** Astronomy.

●NE/0927-6505
**ASTROPARTICLE PHYSICS.** (1993)-. Academic Scholarly Publication. English. qt (1 volume). Fl363.00. Elsevier Science Publishers BV, PO Box 211, 1000 AE Amsterdam Netherlands. **Tel** 011 31 20 5803642, FAX 011 31 20 5862696, telex 15682. **ED** V.S. Berezinsky, J. Ellis, T.K. Gaisser, G. Giacomelli, M. Koshiba, G. Raffelt, A.A. Watson. Documents available from Ask*IEEE.
**Desc:** Publishes experimental and theoretical research papers in the interacting fields of cosmic ray physics, astrophysics, cosmology and particle physics.
**Ind/Abst** INSPEC; Phys. Briefs.

US/0067-0049
**ASTROPHYSICAL JOURNAL. SUPPLEMENT SERIES, THE.** **See** Astronomy.

US/0571-7256
**ASTROPHYSICS.** [Astrophysics]. **Added/Corp** Consultants Bureau. Vol. 1 (Jan./Mar. 1965)-. Periodical. English (Russian). Four times a year. $920.00 US; $1075.00 other. Consultants Bureau, A Division of Plenum Publishing Corporation, 233 Spring Street, New York NY 10013. **Tel** (212)620-8000, (212)620-8466, FAX (212)463-0742, telex 23/421139. **ED** L. V. Mirzoyan. **LC** QB461; .A77. **DD** 523. **CODEN** ATPYAA. **[CCC].** Index available. available on microfilm and microfiche from University Microfilms International (UMI). Documents available from Ask*IEEE, CASDDS.
**Ind/Abst** Appl. Mech. Rev.; Chem. Abstr.; INSPEC (1968-); Int. Aerosp. Abstr.; Math. Rev.; Life Sci. Collect.

●US/1067-5221
**ATM NEWSLETTER.** (ATM NEWSLETTER: ASYNCHRONOUS TRANSFER MODE.). [ATM newsl.]. **Added/Corp** Information Gatekeepers, Inc. **VFOAT** Asynchronous Transfer Mode. **VAT** Asynchronous Transfer Mode Newsletter. Vol. 1, No. 1 (Nov. 1992)-. Newsletter. English. mo. $545.00 US & Canada; $595.00 other. Information Gatekeepers Inc., 214 Harvard Avenue, Boston MA 02134. **Tel** (617)232-3111, (800)323-1088, FAX (617)734-8562. **DD** 621.

IT
**ATTI DELLA ACCADEMIA PELORITANA DEI PERICOLANTI. CLASSE I DI SCIENZE FIS., MAT. E NATURALI.** Periodical. Italian (summaries and/or abstracts in English). **LC** QC1; .A785. **DD** 505. ***Continues in part*** *Atti Della. Accademia Peloritana.*
**Ind/Abst** Math. Rev.; Zentralbl. Math. Ihre Grenzgeb.

AT/1036-3831
**AUSTRALIAN & NEW ZEALAND PHYSICIST : A PUBLICATION OF THE AUSTRALIAN INSTITUTE OF PHYSICS & THE NEW ZEALAND INSTITUTE OF PHYSICS, THE.** [Aust. N. Z. phys.]. **Added/Corp** Australian Institute of Physics. New Zealand Institute of Physics. **VFOAT** Australian and New Zealand Physicist. Vol. 28, No. 1/2 (Jan./Feb. 1991)-. Academic Scholarly Publication. English. mo (Jan. & Feb. issues combined). 50.00Aus$ Australia; 62.00Aus$ (surface mail), 74.00Aus$ (air mail) other. Impress Studios, 14 Ridley Street, Turner ACT 2601 Australia. **Tel** 011 61 49 613319, FAX 011 61 62491563. **ED** Jak Kelly. **CODEN** ANZPET. **Bk Rev**, (Qty: 170). **Ad Acc. Pr Rev. Circ:** 2,900 (ctrl). Documents available from Ask*IEEE, CASDDS. ***Continues*** *Australian Physicist, 0004-9972.*
**Ind/Abst** Aust. Educ. Index (199?-); Chem. Abstr. (1991-); Ei Page One; INSPEC (Jan./Feb. 1991-); Int. Aerosp. Abstr. (1991-).

AT/0004-9506
**AUSTRALIAN JOURNAL OF PHYSICS.** [Aust. j. phys.]. **Added/Corp** Commonwealth Scientific and Industrial Research Organization (Australia) Australian National Research Council. Institute of Physics (Great Britain). Australian Branch. Vol. 6, (March 1953)-. Periodical. English. bm. 290.00Aus$ Australia & New Zealand; $290.00 other. CSIRO Publications, PO Box 89, 314 Albert Street, East Melborne Victoria 3002 Australia. **Tel** 011 61 3 4187333, 4187217, FAX 011 61 3 4190459, telex AA 30236. **ED** R. Peter Robertson. **LC** QC1; .A85. **DD** 530/.05. **NLM** W1 AU614. **CODEN** AUJPAS. **[CCC].** Index available. **Ad Acc. Pr Rev. Acid Free. Circ:** 750. available on microfilm and microfiche from University Microfilms International (UMI). Documents available from Article Express International, The Genuine Article, Ask*IEEE, CASDDS. ***Continues in part*** *Australian Journal of Scientific Research. Series A: Physical Science.*
**Desc:** All aspects of physics are covered, ranging from elementary particles and fields to astronomy and astrophysics. Publishes research papers and review articles. Publishes papers that make a new and significant contribution to any field of physics. Review articles, especially those that survey developments in physics that have taken place largely in Australia, are included.
**Ind/Abst** ACM Guide Comput. Lit.; Alum. Ind. Abstr.; Bioeng. Abstr.; Ceram. Abstr.; Chem. Abstr.; Comput. Rev.; Curr. Contents Phys. Chem. Earth Sci.; Ei Page One; Electron. Commun. Abstr. J.; Eng. Mater. Abstr.; Eng. Index Annu.; GeoRef; INSPEC (1968-); Int. Aerosp. Abstr. (1991-); ISMEC Bull.; Leadscan; Mass Spect. Bull.; Math. Rev.; Met. Abstr.; Meteorol. Geoastrophys. Abstr. (-199?); Nucl. Sci. Abstr.; Pollut. Abstr. Indexes; Res. Alert [Full Cov.]; Saf. Sci. Abstr. J.; Sci. Cit. Index; SCISEARCH; Stat. Theory Method Abstr. (1959-1963); Surf. Treat. Technol. Abstr.; World Alum. Abstr.; World Text. Abstr.; Zentralbl. Math. Ihre Grenzgeb.

US/0146-3969
**BATTERIES (NEW YORK).** (BATTERIES.). [Batteries]. Vol. 1 (1974)-. Monographic series. English. Price varies per volume. Marcel Dekker Inc., 270 Madison Avenue, New York NY 10016. **Tel** (212)696-9000, (800)228-1160, FAX (212)685-4540, telex 421419. **(Subscription address:** Marcel Dekker Inc, PO Box 5017, Monticello NY 12701.**)** **DD** 621. **CODEN** BATTDW. Documents available from CASDDS.
**Ind/Abst** Chem. Abstr.

US/0277-4747
**BENCHMARK PAPERS IN PHYSICAL CHEMISTRY AND CHEMICAL PHYSICS.** **See** Chemistry-Physical and Theoretical Chemistry.

GW/0072-9280
**BERICHT / HAHN-MEITNER-INSTITUT BERLIN GMBH.** **See** Chemistry.

BL/0067-6640
**BIBLIOGRAFIA BRASILEIRA DE FISICA.** V. 1, (1967)-. Portuguese. ir. Instituto Nacional de Estudos e Pesquisas Educacionais Coordenadoria de Editoracao e Divulgacao, Via N 2 Anexo I do MEC, Subsolo 70047, Brasilia D F Brazil. **Tel** 242-2915. **LC** Z7143. ***Supersedes in part*** *Bibliografia Brasileira de Matematica e Fisica.*

AT/0812-339X
**BIENNIAL REPORT / CSIRO, DIVISION OF RADIOPHYSICS.** **Main/Corp** Commonwealth Scientific and Industrial Research Organization (Australia). Division of Radiophysics. (July 1981 to June 1983)-. English. be. CSIRO Publications, PO Box 89, 314 Albert Street, East Melborne Victoria 3002 Australia. **Tel** 011 61 3 4187333, 4187217, FAX 011 61 3 4190459, telex AA 30236. **LC** QB475.A1; C65a.

US/0889-4191
**BIOELECTROMAGNETICS SOCIETY NEWSLETTER.** [Bioelectromagn. Soc. newsl.]. **Added/Corp** Bioelectromagnetics Society (Gaithersburg, Md.). (19??)-. Newsletter. English. qt. $55.00 US; $60.00 other. Bioelectromagnetics Society, 120 West Church, Frederick MD 21701. **Tel** (301)663-4252, FAX (301)663-1915. **ED** Dr. Ben Greenebaum. **DD** 621. **Circ:** 700.

PL/0460-2366
**BIULETYN LUBELSKIE TOWARZYSTWA NAUKOWEGO. MATEMATYKA, FIZYKA-CHEMIA.** **See** Mathematics.

TA/0321-4885
**BJULLETEN INSTITUTA ASTROFIZIKI.** (BIULLETENI INSTITUTI ASTROFIZIKA.). [Bjull. Inst. astrofiz.]. **Added/Corp** Instituti Astrofizika (Akademiiai Fanhoi RSS Tojikiston). **VFOAT** Biulleten Instituta Astrofiziki; Biulleten Instituta Astrofiziki Akademii Nauk Tadzhikskoi SSR. (1958)-. Periodical. Russian (summaries and/or abstracts in English). **LC** QB4; .S822. ***Continues*** *Biulleten Stalinabadskoi Astronomicheskoi Observatorii, 0568-6865.*
**Desc:** Information on astrophysics.
**Ind/Abst** Energy Res. Abstr. (Jan. 1972-); Int. Aerosp. Abstr.

●BL/0103-9733
**BRAZILIAN JOURNAL OF PHYSICS.** [Braz. j. phys.]. **Added/Corp** Sociedade Brasileira de Fisica. Vol. 22, No. 1 (Mar. 1992)-. Periodical. English. Four times a year (Mar., June, Sept., Dec.). $50.00. Soc Brasil Fisica Inst Fisica, Univ Sao Paulo, CX Postal 20553, 01498 970 Sao Paulo SP Brazil. **Tel** 55 11 815 5599 Ext 222, telex 001379220. **ED** Cid Bartolomeu de Araujo. **CODEN** BJPHE6. Documents available from CASDDS. ***Continues*** *Revista Brasileira de Fisica, 0374-4922.*
**Ind/Abst** Chem. Abstr.

US/0899-6725
**BROADCAST TECHNICAL DATA AND APPLICATION INFORMATION MANUAL.** [Broadcast tech. data appl. inf. man.]. **VFOAT** Technical Data and Application Information; Technical Data & Application Information; Broadcast Technical Data & Application Information. 1989-. English. an. $80.00. Bill Daniels Company, PO Box 2056, Shawnee Mission KS 66201. **Tel** (913)492-9900. **LC** TK6540; .B846. **DD** 621.384.

BU/0323-9217
**BULGARIAN JOURNAL OF PHYSICS.** [Bulg. j. phys.]. **Added/Corp** Bulgarska Akademiia na Naukite. **VFOAT** Bolgarskii Fizicheskii Zhurnal. Vol. 1 (1974)-. Periodical. English (Russian; summaries and/or abstracts in Russian and English). bm (6 issues). DM215.00. Izdatelstvo na Bulgarskata Akademiia Na Naukite, 6 Rouski Boulevard, Sofia Bulgaria. **Tel** FAX 80 13 41, telex 22267 HEMKIK. **(Subscription address:** Kubon & Sagner, ABT Zeitschriftenimport, D 80328 Munich Germany.**)** **LC** QC1; .B79. **CODEN** BJPHD5. **[CCC]. Bk Rev. Ad Acc.** Documents available from Ask*IEEE, CASDDS. ***Formed by the union of*** *Izvestiia na Fizicheskiia Institut S Aneb* ***and*** *Institut po Elektronika (Bulgarska Akademiia na Naukite). Izvestiia, 0525-079X.*
**Desc:** The magazine covers unique scientific results from theoretical and experimental investigations in the main branches of physics/atom physics, electronics, optics, etc.
**Ind/Abst** Alum. Ind. Abstr.; Ceram. Abstr.; Chem. Abstr.; Energy Res. Abstr. (July 1975-); Eng. Mater. Abstr.; INSPEC (1974-); Int. Aerosp. Abstr.; Math. Rev.; Met. Abstr.; Pollut. Abstr. Indexes; Zentralbl. Math. Ihre Grenzgeb.

FR/0037-9360
**BULLETIN DE LA SOCIETE FRANCAISE DE PHYSIQUE.** (BULLETIN DE LA SOCIETE FRANCAISE DE PHYSIQUE / SOCIETE FRANCAISE DE PHYSIQUE (SFP).). [Bull. Soc. fr. phys.].

**Added/Corp** Societe Francaise de Physique. (1961)-. Bulletin. French. Five times a year. 265.46F (France); 280.00F (other). Societe Francaise de Physique, 33 Rue Croulebarbe, 75013 Paris France. **Tel** telex 33 1 17073298. **CODEN** BFPYAP. Documents available from CASDDS. ***Continues in part*** *Journal de Physique et le Radium.*
**Ind/Abst** Chem. Abstr.

FR/0366-3876
**BULLETIN DE L'UNION DES PHYSICIENS.** [Bull. Union phys.]. **Added/Corp** Union des Physiciens (France). (19??)-. Academic Scholarly Publication. French. mo (with combined July/Aug./Sept.). 630.00F. Union des Physiciens, 44 Boulevard Saint-Michel, 75270 Paris Cedex 06 France. **Tel** 011 33 1 43256153. **ED** Andre Boussie. **CODEN** BTUPAJ. Index available. cum. index. **Bk Rev. Ad Acc. Circ:** 9,500 (ctrl). Documents available from CASDDS.
**Desc:** A journal in education devoted to the strengthening of the teaching of physics and chemistry.
**Ind/Abst** Chem. Abstr.; Energy Res. Abstr.

FR/0373-9023
**BULLETIN D'INFORMATION - BUREAU GRAVIMETRIQUE INTERNATIONAL.** (BULLETIN D'INFORMATION.). [Bull. inf. - Bur. gravim. int.]. **Main/Corp** International Gravimetric Bureau. (19??)-. Bulletin. Multiple languages (English and French). Twice a year (June & Dec.). 140.00F. Bureau Gravimetrique International, 18 Ave Edouard Belin, 31055 Toulouse Cedex France. **Tel** 011 33 61 332980, FAX 011 33 61 253098, telex 530776F. **LC** QB330; .I55a. **DD** 531/.14. ctrl circ.
**Desc:** The main task of this publication is to collect on a worldwide basis, all gravity measurements and pertinent information about the gravity field of the Earth, to compile and store them in a computerized database in order to redistribute them on request to a large variety of users for scientific purposes.
**Ind/Abst** GeoRef; Plant Breed. Abstr.

SZ/0434-6971
**BULLETIN DU GROUPEMENT D'INFORMATIONS MUTUELLES AMPERE.** **Main/Corp** Group for the Study of Atoms and Molecules from Radio-Electric Research. **VFOAT** Bulletin AMPERE. (July 1956)-. Periodical. French (English). Four times a year. 35.00F Switzerland; $22.05 US. Centre Comptable Faculte des Sciences, 32 Boulevard d'Yvoy, 1211 Geneve 4 Switzerland. **Tel** 41 22 219355, telex 421 159 SIAD CM. **ED** Georges J. Bene. **DD** 621.38. **Bk Rev. Ad Acc. Circ:** 300 (ctrl).
**Desc:** Information about works done in university labs on magnetic resonance and meetings of the Ampere Group.

II
**BULLETIN OF PURE & APPLIED SCIENCES. SEC. D, PHYSICS.** **VFOAT** Bulletin of Pure and Applied Sciences. Sec. D, Physics; Physics. (1985)-. Bulletin. English. an. $24.00. Dr Ajay Kumar Sharma, PO Box 38, Modinagar 201204 India. **(Subscription address:** Prints India, 11 Darya Ganj, New Delhi 110002 India.**) ED** A K Sharma. **LC** QC1; .B855. **DD** 530. **Bk Rev. Ad Acc. Pr Rev. Circ:** 500. ***Continues in part*** *Bulletin of Pure & Applied Sciences.*

II/0253-6897
**BULLETIN OF RADIATION PROTECTION.** [Bull. radiat. protect.]. **Added/Corp** Indian Association for Radiation Protection. (1978)-. Bulletin. English. qt. $50.00. Indian Association for Radiation Protection, Bombay, India. **(Subscription address:** Prints India, 11 Darya Ganj, New Delhi, 110002 India, (Phone: 011 91 11 3268645)**) CODEN** BRPRDN.

US/0003-0503
**BULLETIN OF THE AMERICAN PHYSICAL SOCIETY.** [Bull. Am. Phys. Soc.]. **Main/Corp** American Physical Society. **Added/Corp** American Physical Society. Membership Directory. American Physical Society. APS Membership Directory. (1925)-. Bulletin. English. ir (14 issues). $350.00 US. American Institute of Physics, 500 Sunnyside Boulevard, Woodbury NY 11797-2999. **Tel** (516)576-2200, FAX (516)349-7669, telex 960983. **LC** QC1; .A56. **DD** 530/.05. **NLM** W1 BU842. **CODEN** BAPSA6. **[CCC].** Documents available from CASDDS. ***Continues*** *Directory of Physics and Astronomy Staff Members.* ***Continued in part by*** *APSnews, 1058-8132.*
**Ind/Abst** Chem. Abstr.; Mass Spect. Bull.

II/0304-9523
**BULLETIN OF THE ASTRONOMICAL SOCIETY OF INDIA.** **See** Astronomy.

II/0970-2334
**BULLETIN OF THE INDIAN VACUUM SOCIETY.** [Bull. Indian Vac. Soc.]. **Added/Corp** Indian Vacuum Society. (1986)-. Bulletin. English. qt. $100.00. Indian Vacuum Society, Bombay, India. **(Subscription address:** Prints India, 11 Darya Ganj, New Delhi, 110002 India, (Phone: 011 91 11 3268645)**) CODEN** BIVSES. ***Continues*** *Vac News, 0254-7848.*

●US/1068-3356
**BULLETIN OF THE LEBEDEV PHYSICS INSTITUTE.** (BULLETIN OF THE LEBEDEV PHYSICS INSTITUTE.). [Bull. Lebedev Phys. Inst.]. **Added/Corp** Fizicheskii Institut Imeni P.N. Lebedeva. No. 1 (1992)-. Bulletin. English (translations available in Russian). mo (12 issues). $780.00. Allerton Press, Inc., 150 Fifth Avenue, New York NY 10011. **Tel** (212)924-3950, FAX (212)463-9684, telex 427441 ALPRES. **LC** QC1; .S79522. **DD** 530. **CODEN** BLPIEN. **[CCC].** ***Continues*** *Soviet Physics -- Lebedev Institute Reports, 0364-2321.*

●US/1062-8738
**BULLETIN OF THE RUSSIAN ACADEMY OF SCIENCES. PHYSICS.** [Bull. Russ. Acad. Sci., Phys.]. **Added/Corp** Rossiiskaia Akademiia Nauk. **VFOAT** Physics BRAS.; Izvestiya Rossiiskoi Akademii Nauk. Seriya Fizicheskaya; B.R.A.S. Physics. Vol. 56, No. 1 (Jan. 1992)-. Bulletin. English (translations available in Russian). mo (12 issues). $1445.00; Physics of Vibrations quarterly supplement $200.00. Allerton Press, Inc., 150 Fifth Avenue, New York NY 10011. **Tel** (212)924-3950, FAX (212)463-9684, telex 427441 ALPRES. **LC** QC1; .A392. **DD** 530/.05. **CODEN** BRSPEX. **[CCC].** Documents available from Ask*IEEE. ***Continues*** *Bulletin of the Academy of Sciences of the USSR. Physical Series, 0001-432X.*
**Ind/Abst** INSPEC (1992-).

FR
**BULLETIN SIGNALETIQUE. 165: ATOMES ET MOLECULES, FLUIDES ET PLASMAS.** **Added/Corp** Centre National de la Recherche Scientifique (France). Centre de Documentation. Vol. 36 (1975)-. Bulletin. French. mo. 250.00F. Editions du CNRS, 22 rue Saint Armand, F 75015 Paris France. **Tel** 011 33 1 45075050. **LC** QC170; .B84. ***Continues*** *Bulletin Signaletique. 165: Physique Atomique et Moleculaire.*

SP/1130-4758
**BUTLLETI DE LES SOCIETATS CATALANES DE FISICA, QUIMICA, MATEMATIQUES I TECNOLOGIA.** [Butll. Soc. Catalanes Fis. Quim. Mat. Tecnol.]. (1989)-. Periodical. Catalan. qt. **UDC** 5. ***Continues*** *Butlleti de la Societat Catalana de Ciencies Fisiques, Quimiques i Matematiques, 0211-4305.*
**Ind/Abst** Zentralbl. Math. Ihre Grenzgeb.

CN/0318-1634
**C R E S S SPECTROSCOPIC REPORT.** **Main/Corp** York University (Toronto, Ont.). Centre for Research in Experimental Space Science. No. 1- Mar. 1970-. Monographic series. English. Price varies per volume. York University Centre for Research in Experimental Space Science, 4700 Keele Street/Suite 701, Downsview Ontario M3J 2R5 Canada. **DD** 539/.12.

CN/0226-8442
**C. W. E. A. NEWS.** [C.W.E.A. news]. **Main/Corp** Canadian Wind Engineering Association. **VFOAT** Canadian Wind Engineering Association Newsletter. **VAT** Canadian Wind Engineering Association News. No. 1- 1977-. English. an. Free to members. University of British Columbia / Department of Mechanical Engineering, Vancouver British Columbia V6T 1W5 Canada. **DD** 621.4/5.

CN/0008-4204
**CANADIAN JOURNAL OF PHYSICS.** [Can. j. phys.]. **Added/Corp** National Research Council of Canada. National Research Council Canada. **VFOAT** Journal Canadien de Physique. Vol. 29, No. 1 (Jan. 1951)-. Periodical. English (French). mo. 296.00Can$ (institutions), 94.00Can$ (individuals) Canada; $296.00 (institutions), $96.00 (individuals) other. National Research Council of Canada, Receiver General for Canada, Ottawa Ontario K1A 0R6 Canada. **Tel** (613)993-0362, FAX (613)952-7656. **ED** R. W. Nicholls. **LC** QC1; .N332. **DD** 530.5. **NLM** W1 CA599. **CODEN** CJPHAD. **[CCC].** Index available. **Ad Acc. Pr Rev. Circ:** 1,516. available on microfilm and microfiche from University Microfilms International (UMI). Documents available from Article Express International, The Genuine Article, Ask*IEEE, CASDDS. ***Continues*** *Canadian Journal of Research. Section A, Physical Sciences.*
**Desc:** Publishes research papers in all areas of physics, as well as in cross-disciplinary areas.
**Ind/Abst** Abstr. Bull. Inst. Pap. Sci. Tech.; Acoust. Abstr.; Ceram. Abstr.; Chem. Abstr.; Chem. Titles; Curr. Contents Phys. Chem. Earth Sci.; Curr. Titles Electrochem.; Dairy Sci. Abstr. (1968-); Eng. Mater. Abstr.; Eng. Index Annu. [Select. Cov.]; GeoRef; HTFS Dig.; INIS Atomindex [Micro.]; INSPEC (1968-); Int. Aerosp. Abstr.; Leadscan; Mass Spect. Bull.; Math. Rev.; Meteorol. Geoastrophys. Abstr.; Res. Alert [Full Cov.]; Sci. Cit. Index; SCISEARCH; Soc. Sci. Cit. Index [Select. Cov.]; Surf. Treat. Technol. Abstr.

XR/0009-0700
**CESKOSLOVENSKY CASOPIS PRO FYSIKU.** [Cesk. cas. fyz.]. **Added/Corp** Ceskoslovenska Akademie ved. Fyzikalni Ustav Akademie ved Ceske Republiky. **VFOAT** Ceskoslovensky Casopis pro Fyziku; Czechoslovak Journal of Physics. Vol. 4 (1954)-. Academic Scholarly Publication. Czech (Slovak and English; summaries and/or abstracts in English). bm (6 issues). DM287.00 Germany; DM327.00 other. **(Subscription address:** Kubon & Sagner, ABT Zeitschriftenimport, D 80328 Munich Germany.**) ED** Ivan Gregora. **LC** QC1; .C43. **CODEN** CKCFAH. Index available. cum. index. **Bk Rev. Circ:** 1,300. Documents available from Ask*IEEE, CASDDS. ***Continues*** *Casopis pro Pestovani Fysiki.*
**Desc:** Contains papers, short communications, reviews, articles and reports on events in the physics community.
**Ind/Abst** Chem. Abstr.; GeoRef; INSPEC (1968-); Int. Aerosp. Abstr.

US/0270-0492
**CGCR. COMPRESSED GASES AND CRYOGENICS REPORT.** [CGCR, Compress. gases cryog. rep.]. **VFOAT** Compressed Gases and Cryogenics Report. V. 1- Aug. 1980-. Periodical. English. mo. $144.00 US; $168.00 other. Van Nostrand Reinhold Company Inc., 115 5th Avenue, New York NY 10003. **Tel** (212)254-3232, FAX (212)673-1239, telex 272562.

US/1054-1500
**CHAOS (WOODBURY, N.Y.).** (CHAOS.). [Chaos]. **Added/Corp** American Institute of Physics. Vol. 1, No. 1 (1991)-. Periodical. English. qt. $265.00 US. American Institute of Physics, 500 Sunnyside Boulevard, Woodbury NY 11797-2999. **Tel** (516)576-2200, FAX (516)349-7669, telex 960983. **LC** Q172.5.C45; C427. **DD** 003/.7. **UDC** 108. **CODEN** CHAOEH. **[CCC].** Documents available from Ask*IEEE.
**Desc:** Examines theories and behavior in systems of nonlinear (chaotic) phenomena in diverse fields within the physical, biological and social sciences as well as engineering.
**Ind/Abst** INSPEC (1991-).

UK/0142-3401
**CHEMICAL PHYSICS OF SOLIDS AND THEIR SURFACES.** [Chem. phys. solids their surf.]. **Added/Corp** Chemical Society. Vol. 7 (1978)-. Academic Scholarly Publication. English. ir. Price varies per volume. Royal Society of Chemistry, Thomas Graham House, Science Park, Cambridge CB4 4WF England. **Tel** 011 44 223 420066, FAX 011 44 223 423429, telex 818293 ROYAL. **(Subscription address:** Royal Society of Chemistry, Distribution Center, Blackhorse Road, Letchworth, SG6 1HN England.**) LC** QC176.8.E4; S87. **DD** 530.4/1/05. **CODEN** CPSSD4. Documents available from CASDDS. ***Continues*** *Surface and Defect Properties of Solids.*
**Ind/Abst** Chem. Abstr.

US/0890-9903
**CHINESE JOURNAL OF INFRARED AND MILLIMETER WAVES.** (CHINESE JOURNAL OF INFRARED AND MILLIMETER WAVES : A PUBLICATION OF THE OPTICAL SOCIETY OF CHINA.). [Chin. j. infrared millim. waves]. **Added/Corp** Chung-Kuo Kuang Hsueh Hsueh Hui. **VFOAT** Hung Wai Yen Chiu; Hongwai Yianjiu, Series A. Vol. 6, No. 1 (1987)-. Periodical. English (translations available in Chinese). Six times a year. $450.00. Allerton Press, Inc., 150 Fifth Avenue, New York NY 10011. **Tel** (212)924-3950, FAX (212)463-9684, telex 427441 ALPRES. **LC** TA1570; .H843. **DD** 621.36/2/05. **CODEN** CJIWER. **[CCC].** Documents available from Article Express International.
**Ind/Abst** Ei Page One; Eng. Index Annu.

CH/0577-9073
**CHINESE JOURNAL OF PHYSICS (TAIPEI).** (CHINESE JOURNAL OF PHYSICS.). [Chin. j. phys. (Taipei)]. **Added/Corp** Physical Society of the Republic of China. **VFOAT** Chung-kuo Wu Li Hsueh Kan. Vol. 1, No. 1 (Apr. 1963)-. Periodical. English. Four times a year. Physical Society of the Republic of China, Physics Department, National Taiwan University, Taipei, Taiwan. **DD** 530. **CODEN** CJOPAW. Documents available from The Genuine Article, Ask*IEEE, CASDDS.
**Ind/Abst** Chem. Abstr.; INSPEC (1968-); Res. Alert; Sci. Cit. Index.

US/0899-9988
**CHINESE JOURNAL OF SEMICONDUCTORS.** ***Ceased.*** [Chin. j. semicond.]. **VFOAT** Pan Tao Ti Hsueh Pao. (1988)-?. Periodical. English. qt. Allerton Press, Inc., 150 Fifth Avenue, New York NY 10011. **Tel** (212)924-3950, FAX (212)463-9684, telex 427441 ALPRES. **LC** TK7871.85; .P3477. **DD** 621.381/52/05. **[CCC].**
**Ind/Abst** Curr. Titles Electrochem.

US/0273-429X
**CHINESE PHYSICS.** ***Ceased.*** (CHINESE PHYSICS : A PUBLICATION OF THE AMERICAN INSTITUTE OF PHYSICS.). [Chin. phys.]. **VFOAT** Chung Kuo Wu Li. Vol. 1, No. 1 (Jan./March 1981)-Vol 12 (1992). Academic Scholarly Publication. English (Chinese). qt. American Institute of Physics, 500 Sunnyside Boulevard, Woodbury NY 11797-2999. **Tel** (516)576-2200, FAX (516)349-7669, telex 960983. **(Subscription address:** UK/ Institute of Physics, Techno House, Redcliffe Way, Bristol BS1 6NX England**) LC** QC1. **DD** 530/.05. **CODEN** CHPHD2. **[CCC]. Pr Rev.** Documents available from The Genuine Article, Ask*IEEE.

**Ind/Abst** Acoust. Abstr.; Curr. Phys. Index; EMBASE; Energy Res. Abstr. (Aug. 1981-); INIS Atomindex [Micro.]; INSPEC (1981-); Int. Aerosp. Abstr.; Leadscan; Math. Rev.; Res. Alert [Full Cov.]; Sci. Cit. Index (19??-19??); SCISEARCH; SPIN (1981-).

US/0256-307X
**CHINESE PHYSICS LETTERS.** [Chin. phys. lett.]. **Added/Corp** Chung-Kuo Wu Li Hsueh Hui. **VFOAT** Chung-Kuo wu li K'uai Pao; CPL. Vol. 1, No. 1 (Aug. 1984)-. Academic Scholarly Publication. English. mo (12 issues). $370.00. Allerton Press, Inc., 150 Fifth Avenue, New York NY 10011. **Tel** (212)924-3950, FAX (212)463-9684, telex 427441 ALPRES. **ED** Hao Bailin. **CODEN** CPLEEU. **[CCC]. Ad Acc. Pr Rev. Circ:** 3,000. Documents available from The Genuine Article, Ask*IEEE, CASDDS. ***Continues in part*** *Wu Li Hsueh Pao, 0372-736X.*
**Desc:** Devoted to the rapid publication of short reports of important research in all fields of physics.
**Ind/Abst** Ceram. Abstr. (19??-); Chem. Abstr. (1984-); Curr. Contents Phys. Chem. Earth Sci.; INIS Atomindex [Micro.]; INSPEC (Aug. 1984-); Math. Rev. (1984-); Res. Alert [Full Cov.]; Sci. Cit. Index; SCISEARCH.

RU
**CHTENIIA PAMIATI A.F. IOFFE / AKADEMIIA NAUK SSSR, ORDENA LENINA FIZIKO-TEKHNICHESKII INSTITUT IMENI A.F. IOFFE. Added/Corp** Fiziko-Tekhnicheskii Institut Im. A.F. Ioffe. (19??)-. Russian. ir.

CN/0822-5516
**CIRCUIT FERME (INSTITUT TECCART).** (LE CIRCUIT FERME / TECCART.). [Circuit ferme - Inst. Teccart]. Periodical. French. ir. Institut Teccart, 3155 rue Hochelaga, Montreal Quebec H1W 1G4 Canada. **DD** 621.381/05.

UK/0264-9381
**CLASSICAL AND QUANTUM GRAVITY.** [Classical quantum gravity]. **Added/Corp** Institute of Physics (Great Britain) American Institute of Physics. Vol. 1, No. 1 (Jan. 11, 1984)-. Academic Scholarly Publication. English. mo (12 issues per volume). $1,074.00. Institute of Physics, Techno House, Redcliffe Way, Bristol BS1 6NX England. **Tel** 011 44 272 297481, FAX 011 44 272 294318, telex 449149 INSTP G. **(Subscription address:** American Institute of Physics, Publishing Sales, 500 Sunnyside Blvd., Woodbury NY 11797.**) ED** K S Stelle. **LC** QC178; .C45. **DD** 530.1. **CODEN** CQGRDG. **[CCC].** available on microfilm and microfiche. Documents available from The Genuine Article, Ask*IEEE, CASDDS. ***Continues in part*** *Journal of Physics A. Mathematical and General, 0305-4470.*
**Desc:** Devoted to the publication of papers and letters on classical general relativity, quantum gravity, generally-covariant systems, supergravity and superstrings, and cosmology and the early universe.
**Ind/Abst** Chem. Abstr. (1984-); Curr. Contents Phys. Chem. Earth Sci.; INSPEC (Jan. 1984-); Math. Rev.; Res. Alert [Full Cov.]; Sci. Cit. Index; SCISEARCH; Zentralbl. Math. Ihre Grenzgeb.

UK/0143-0815
**CLINICAL PHYSICS AND PHYSIOLOGICAL MEASUREMENT.** ***Title Change.*** [Clin. phys. physiol. meas.]. Vol. 1, No. 1 (Feb. 1980)-(199?). Periodical. English (summaries and/or abstracts in French and German). qt (supplements). Institute of Physics, Techno House, Redcliffe Way, Bristol BS1 6NX England. **Tel** 011 44 272 297481, FAX 011 44 272 294318, telex 449149 INSTP G. **(Subscription address:** US, Canada and Mexico/ American Institute of Physics, 500 Sunnyside Boulevard, Woodbury, NY 11797**) ED** A Murray and D J Wheatley. **NLM** W1; CL766. **CODEN** CPPMD5. **[CCC]. Pr Rev.** available on microfiche. Documents available from Article Express International, The Genuine Article, BIOSIS Document Express, Ask*IEEE. ***Continued by*** *Physiological Measurement, 0967-3334.*
**Desc:** Reports the applications of physics and physical measurement to clinical practice and investigation, and serving the collaborative interests of medical physicists, biomedical engineers and medical specialists. Emphasis is on the quantitative measurement of structure and function in clinical research and practice and on the development of new methods of measurement and the validation of their use.
**Ind/Abst** Biol. Abstr.; CSA Neuro. Abstr. (?-?); Curr. Contents Clin. Med.; Ei Page One; EMBASE; Eng. Index Annu.; Health Plan. Adminis.; Index Med.; INSPEC (Feb. 1980-); Life Sci. Collect.; Phys. Med. Biol. (19??-19??); Pollut. Abstr. Indexes; Res. Alert [Full Cov.]; Sci. Cit. Index; SCISEARCH.

US/0883-5985
**COGENERATION JOURNAL, THE.** ***Title Change.*** [Cogener. j.]. **Added/Corp** AEE Cogeneration Institute (U.S.). Vol. 1, No. 1 (Sept. 1985)-(1992). Periodical. English. qt. Multi Science Publishing Company Ltd., 107 High Street, Brentwood, Essex CM14 4RX England. **Tel** 011 44 277 224632, FAX 011 44 277 223453, telex 89-8452. **ED** F William Payne. **LC** TK1041; .C64. **DD** 621. **Bk Rev. Circ:** 2,200. ***Continued by*** *Cogeneration and Competitive Power Journal, 1066-8683.*
**Desc:** Concentrates its editorial on more substantial issues and developments, probing the reasons why and what lies ahead in cogeneration.
**Ind/Abst** Coal Abstr.; Ei Page One; Energy Inf. Abstr.; Gas Abstr.

US
**COLLECTED REPRINTS - ATMOSPHERIC PHYSICS AND CHEMISTRY LABORATORY. Main/Corp** Atmospheric Physics and Chemistry Laboratory. **Added/Corp** Environmental Research Laboratories. United States. National Oceanic and Atmospheric Administration. **VFOAT** Atmospheric Physics and Chemistry Laboratory Collected Reprints. (197?)-. Periodical. English. US Department of Commerce / National Oceanic & Atmospheric Administration NOAA, 6010 Executive Boulevard, Washington Science Center, Building 5, Rockville MD 20852. **Tel** (202)482-6090, FAX (202)482-3154.

CN/0843-3607
**COLOURIST (OTTAWA).** (THE COLOURIST / CANADIAN SOCIETY FOR COLOR IN ART, INDUSTRY AND SCIENCE.). [Colourist]. **Added/Corp** Canadian Society for Color. Vol. 15, No. 4 (Nov. 1988)-. Periodical. English. ir. Free (members). Canadian Society for Color, c/o Division of Physics, National Research Council, Ottawa Ontario K1A 0R6 Canada. **DD** 535.6/06/071. ***Continues*** *Newsletter - Canadian Society for Colour in Art, Industry and Science, 0317-1825.*

FI/0788-5717
**COMMENTATIONES PHYSICO-MATHEMATICAE ET CHEMICO-MEDICAE.** [Comment. phys.-math. chem.-med.]. **Added/Corp** Suomen Tiedeseura. **VFOAT** Commentationes Physico Mathematicae et Chemico Medicae. (1991)-. Monographic series. English. ir. Academic Bookstore Akateeminen, Postilokero 23, FIN-00371 Helsinki Finland. **Tel** 011 358 0 12141. **LC** Q60; .F555; Q60.2. **DD** 505. **CODEN** CPMCET. Documents available from Ask*IEEE. ***Continues*** *Commentationes Physico-Mathematicae, 0069-6609.*
**Ind/Abst** INSPEC (1992-).

US/0146-2970
**COMMENTS ON ASTROPHYSICS. See** Astronomy.

UK/0885-4483
**COMMENTS ON MODERN PHYSICS. PART B, COMMENTS ON CONDENSED MATTER PHYSICS.** [Comments on mod. phys., Part B Comments condens. matter phys.]. **VFOAT** Comments on Condensed Matter Physics. Vol. 12, No. 3 (March 1986)-. Academic Scholarly Publication. English. bm (2 volumes). $425.00 (academic institutions), $662.00 (corporate institutions). Gordon & Breach Science Publishers, PO Box 90, Reading RG1 8JL England. **Tel** 011 44 734 560080, FAX 011 44 734 568211. **LC** QC176.A1; C6. **DD** 530.4/1/05. **CODEN** CCMPEB. **[CCC].** Documents available from Ask*IEEE, CASDDS. ***Continues*** *Comments on Solid State Physics, 0308-1206.*
**Ind/Abst** Chem. Abstr. (1986-); INSPEC (1985-).

US/0374-2806
**COMMENTS ON PLASMA PHYSICS AND CONTROLLED FUSION.** [Comments plasma phys. contr. fusion]. Vol. 1 (Jan./Feb. 1972)-. Academic Scholarly Publication. English. bm (1 volume). $425.00 (academic institutions), $662.00 (corporate institutions). Gordon & Breach Science Publishers, Inc., PO Box 786, Cooper Station, New York NY 10276. **Tel** (212)206-8900, FAX (212)645-2459. **ED** B.D. Fried. **LC** QC717.6; .C63. **DD** 530.4/4/05. **CODEN** CPCFBJ. **[CCC]. Bk Rev. Ad Acc.** Documents available from Ask*IEEE, CASDDS.
**Ind/Abst** Chem. Abstr.; Energy Res. Abstr. (June 1972-); INIS Atomindex [Micro.]; INSPEC (Jan./Feb. 1972-).

TU
**COMMUNICATIONS DE LA FACULTE DES SCIENCES DE L'UNIVERSITE D'ANKARA. SERIES AB2S, AB3S, PHYSICS, ENGINEERING PHYSICS AND ASTRONOMY. Added/Corp** Ankara Universitesi. Fen Fakultesi. **VFOAT** Physics, Engineering Physics and Astronomy. (198?)-. Periodical. French. sa. Faculty of Sciences, University of Ankara, 06 100, Ankara, Turkey. **Tel** (4)212-6720. **ED** Aral Olcay. Documents available from CASDDS. ***Formed by the union of*** *Communications de la Faculte des Sciences de l'Universite d'Ankara. Serie Ab2s. Physique* ***and*** *Communications de la Faculte des Sciences de l'Universite d'Ankara. Serie Ab3s. Astronomie.*
**Ind/Abst** Chem. Abstr.; Zentralbl. Math. Ihre Grenzgeb.

NE
**COMMUNICATIONS FROM THE KAMERLINGH ONNES LABORATORY OF THE UNIVERSITY OF LEIDEN.** No. 217 (November 1931)-. Periodical. English (French and German). an. Free. Kamerlingh Onnes Laboratorium, Rijksuniversiteit Leiden, Ellie van Rijsewijk, Postbus 9506, 2300 RA Leiden The Netherlands. **Tel** 071-275400, telex 39058/ASTRO NL. **ED** M Durieux. ctrl circ. ***Continues*** *Communications from the Physical Laboratory at the University of Leiden.*
**Desc:** The abstracts of the articles published in one year from the Kamerlingh Onnes Laboratory.

GW/0010-3616
**COMMUNICATIONS IN MATHEMATICAL PHYSICS.** [Commun. math. phys.]. Vol. 1 (1965/1966)-. Periodical. English (French and German). Twenty-four times a year. DM5920.00. Springer-Verlag GmbH & Company KG, Heidelberger Platz 3, D 14197 Berlin Germany. **Tel** 011 49 30 8207223, FAX 011 49 30 8214091, telex 183 319 SPBLN D. **(Subscription address:** Springer Verlag New York Inc. / for North America, 44 Hartz Way, Secaucus NJ 07096.**) ED** A Jaffe. **LC** QC20; .C68. **CODEN** CMPHAY. **[CCC]. Pr Rev.** available on microfilm and microfiche from University Microfilms International (UMI). Documents available from The Genuine Article, Ask*IEEE.
**Desc:** Journal devoted to physics papers with mathematical content. Covers a broad spectrum from classical to quantum physics, individual editorial sections illustrate this scope.
**Ind/Abst** Compumath Citation Index [Full Cov.]; Curr. Contents Phys. Chem. Earth Sci.; Energy Res. Abstr.; INSPEC (1968-); Int. Aerosp. Abstr.; Math. Rev.; Phys. Briefs; Res. Alert [Full Cov.]; Sci. Cit. Index; SCISEARCH; Zentralbl. Math. Ihre Grenzgeb. (1968-).

CC/0253-6102
**COMMUNICATIONS IN THEORETICAL PHYSICS.** [Commun. theor. phys.]. **Added/Corp** Hua Chung Kung Hsueh Yuan. Vol. 1, No. 1 (1982)-. Academic Scholarly Publication. English. Eight times a year. 955.00F (includes distribution costs). Huazhong University Science & Technology Press, Editorial Department, Wuhan Hubei, People's Republic of China. **(Subscription address:** Baltzer Science Publishers, Asterweg 1A, 1031 HL Amsterdam Netherlands**) LC** QC19.2; .C64. **DD** 530.1/05. **CODEN** CTPHDI. **Pr Rev.** Documents available from The Genuine Article, Ask*IEEE, CASDDS.
**Desc:** Published by the Allahabad Mathematical Society, founded November, 1958. Publishes original research papers in theoretical physics.
**Ind/Abst** Chem. Abstr.; Curr. Contents Phys. Chem. Earth Sci.; INSPEC (1982-); Math. Rev.; Res. Alert [Full Cov.]; Sci. Cit. Index; SCISEARCH.

IE/0070-7414
**COMMUNICATIONS OF THE DUBLIN INSTITUTE FOR ADVANCED STUDIES. SERIES A. See** Mathematics.

●FR
**COMPTES RENDUS DE L'ACADEMIE DES SCIENCES. SERIE II, MECANIQUE, PHYSIQUE, CHIMIE, ASTRONOMIE. Added/Corp** Academie des Sciences (France). **VFOAT** Mecanique, Physique, Chimie, Astronomie. T. 318, No. 1 (Jan. 6, 1994)-. Periodical. French (English). Twenty-six times a year. Dunod Gauthier Villars, 15 rue Gossin, 92543 Montrouge cedex France. **Tel** 011 33 1 46 56 52 66, FAX 011 33 1 46 57 40 69. **(Subscription address:** Centrale des Revues, 11 rue Gossin, 92543 Montrouge Cedex France.**) LC** Q46; .C7. **DD** 500.2. **CODEN** CRAMED. ***Continues in part*** *Comptes Rendus de l'Academie des Sciences. Serie II, Mecanique, Physique, Chimie, Sciences de l'Univers, Sciences de la Terre, 0764-4450.*
**Ind/Abst** Sci. Cit. Index.

●FR
**COMPTES RENDUS DE L'ACADEMIE DES SCIENCES. SERIE II, SCIENCES DE LA TERRE ET DES PLANETES / EARTH & PLANETARY SCIENCES. Added/Corp** Academie des Sciences (France). **VFOAT** Sciences de la Terre et des Planetes; Earth & Planetary Sciences; Earth and Planetary Sciences. (1994)-. Periodical. French (English). sm. Dunod Gauthier Villars, 15 rue Gossin, 92543 Montrouge cedex France. **Tel** 011 33 1 46 56 52 66, FAX 011 33 1 46 57 40 69. **LC** QE1; .C7724. **DD** 550/.5. ***Continues in part*** *Comptes Rendus de l'Academie des Sciences. Serie II, Mecanique, Physique, Chimie, Sciences de l'Univers, Sciences de la Terre, 0764-4450.*

FR/0223-6335
**COMPTES RENDUS DES TRAVAUX DES COLLOQUES.** English. Societe Francaise du Vide, 19 rue du Renard, 75004 Paris France. **Tel** 011 33 1 42781582. Index available. **Ad Acc.**

NE/0010-4655
**COMPUTER PHYSICS COMMUNICATIONS.** [Comput. phys. commun.]. Vol. 1 (July 1969)-. Academic Scholarly Publication. English. Twenty-one times a year (7 volumes). Fl4368.00. Elsevier Science Publishers BV, PO Box 211, 1000 AE Amsterdam Netherlands. **Tel** 011 31 20 5803642, FAX 011 31 20 5862696, telex 15682. **ED** P. G. Burke, G. H. F. Diercksen, J. W. Eastwood, J. E. Inglesfield, F James,

and D. G. Truhlar. **LC** QC52; .C65. **DD** 530/.028/5. **CODEN** CPHCBZ. **[CCC].** cum. index. **Pr Rev.** available on microfilm and microfiche from University Microfilms International (UMI). Documents available from Article Express International, The Genuine Article, Ask*IEEE, CASDDS.
**Desc:** Publishes descriptions of computer programs in physics and chemical physics. It also publishes papers and letters on computational methods and the application of computers to physics.
**Ind/Abst** Bioeng. Abstr.; Chem. Abstr.; Compumath Citation Index [Full Cov.]; Comput. Rev.; Curr. Contents Phys. Chem. Earth Sci.; Ei Page One; Eng. Index Annu.; GeoRef; INSPEC (July 1969-); Math. Rev.; Pollut. Abstr. Indexes; Res. Alert [Full Cov.]; Sci. Cit. Index; SCISEARCH; Zentralbl. Math. Ihre Grenzgeb.

US/0894-1866
**COMPUTERS IN PHYSICS.** [Comput. phys.]. **Added/Corp** American Institute of Physics. (1987)-. Periodical. English. bm. $265.00 US; $275.00 Canada, Mexico, Central and South America, and the Caribbean; $285.00 other. American Institute of Physics, 500 Sunnyside Boulevard, Woodbury NY 11797-2999. **Tel** (516)576-2200, FAX (516)349-7669, telex 960983. **LC** QC52; .C66. **DD** 530/.028/5. **CODEN** CPHYE2. **[CCC].** Documents available from Article Express International, Ask*IEEE.
**Ind/Abst** ACM Guide Comput. Lit.; Comput. Rev.; Ei Page One; Eng. Index Annu. [Select. Cov.]; INIS Atomindex [Micro.]; INSPEC (Nov./Dec. 1987-); Int. Aerosp. Abstr.

US/1056-7046
**CONDENSED MATTER NEWS.** [Condens. matter news]. Vol. 1, Issue 1 (1991)-. Periodical. English. bm. $441.00 (academic institutions), $688.00 (corporate institutions). Gordon & Breach Science Publishers, Inc., PO Box 786, Cooper Station, New York NY 10276. **Tel** (212)206-8900, FAX (212)645-2459. **LC** QC173.4.C65; C657. **DD** 530.4/1. **CODEN** CMAWE8. **[CCC].** ***Absorbed*** *Ferroelectrics Bulletin, 0887-6622* ***and*** *Molecular Crystals & Liquid Crystals Bulletin (New York, N.Y. : 1991).*

US/0893-861X
**CONDENSED MATTER THEORIES.** [Condens. matter theor.]. Vol. 2 (1987)-. Monographic series. English. an. $98.00. Nova Science Publishers Inc., 6080 Jericho Turnpike, Suite 207, Commack NY 11725-2808. **Tel** (516)499-3103, (516)499-3106, FAX (516)499-3146. **LC** QC173.4.C65; I48a. **DD** 530.4/1/05. Documents available from CASDDS. ***Continues*** *International Workshop on Condensed Matter Physics. Condensed Matter Theories, 0893-861X.*
**Ind/Abst** Chem. Abstr.

US
**CONFERENCE ON PRECISION ELECTROMAGNETIC MEASUREMENT.** (19??)-. Periodical. English. ir. IEEE, Institution of Electrical and Electronics Engineers, Inc., 345 East 47th Street, New York NY 10017-2394. **Tel** (908)981-1393, FAX (908)981-9667.

US/0272-2488
**CONTEMPORARY CONCEPTS IN PHYSICS.** [Contemp. concepts phys.]. Vol. 1 (1981)-. Monographic series. English. ir. Price varies per volume. Harwood Academic Publishers / New York, PO Box 786, Cooper Station, New York NY 10276. **Tel** (212)206-8900, (201)643-7500. **ED** H. Feshbach. **DD** 539.
**Ind/Abst** Math. Rev.

UK/0010-7514
**CONTEMPORARY PHYSICS.** [Contemp. phys.]. Vol. 1, No. 1 (Oct. 1959)-. Periodical. English. bm. £199.00 UK; $329.00 other. Taylor & Francis Ltd., Rankine Road, Basingstoke Hampshire, RG24 8PR United Kingdom. **Tel** 011 44 256 840366, FAX 011 44 256 479438, telex 858540. **(Subscription address:** Taylor & Francis Inc., 1900 Frost Road, Suite 101, Bristol PA 19007-1598.**) ED** J. S. Dugdale (editor's address: Department of Physics, University of Leeds, Leeds LS2 9JT United Kingdom). **LC** QC1; .C76. **DD** 530. **NLM** W1 CO769P. **CODEN** CTPHAF. **[CCC].** cum. index. **Pr Rev.** available on microfilm and microfiche from University Microfilms International (UMI). Documents available from The Genuine Article, Ask*IEEE, UMI Article Clearinghouse, CASDDS.
**Desc:** Provides authoritative articles on important developments in physics. The articles are written by leading scientists, and place specialist topics in a broad context. The journal is of value to academic and industrial scientists, teachers and students, indeed all who need to keep abreast of progress in pure and applied physics. References are provided at the end of each article for those who wish to explore further.
**Ind/Abst** Acad. Search (July 1993-); Acoust. Abstr.; Alum. Ind. Abstr.; Ceram. Abstr.; Chem. Abstr.; Curr. Contents Phys. Chem. Earth Sci.; EMBASE; Eng. Mater. Abstr.; Expand. Acad. Index (1989-); Gen. Sci. Index; Gen. Sci. Source (Jul. 1993-); GeoRef; HTFS Dig.; Index Sci. Rev. [Full Cov.]; INFO-SOUTH Abstr.; INSPEC (1968-); Int. Aerosp. Abstr.; Mag. Search; Mass Spect. Bull.; Met. Abstr.; Newsp. Period. Abstr. (1989-); Res. Alert [Full Cov.]; Sci. Cit. Index; SCISEARCH.

GW/0863-1042
**CONTRIBUTIONS TO PLASMA PHYSICS (1988).** (CONTRIBUTIONS TO PLASMA PHYSICS.). [Contrib. plasma phys.]. Vol. 28 No. 1 (1988)-. Periodical. English. bm. $620.00. Akademie-Verlag GmbH, Muehlenstrasse 33 34, D 13162 Berlin Germany. **Tel** 011 49 30 47889300, FAX 011 49 30 47889357. **(Subscription address:** VCH Publishers Inc., 303 Northwest 12th Avenue, Journals Department, Deerfield FL 33442.**) LC** QC717.6; .C68. **DD** 530.4/4 /2 19. **CODEN** CPPHEP. **[CCC].** Documents available from The Genuine Article, Ask*IEEE, CASDDS. ***Continues*** *Beitrage aus der Plasmaphysik, 0005-8025.*
**Ind/Abst** Chem. Abstr.; Curr. Contents Phys. Chem. Earth Sci.; INSPEC (1988-); Res. Alert [Full Cov.]; Sci. Cit. Index; SCISEARCH.

UK/0143-926X
**COSMATOM.** [Cosmatom]. (1973)-. Periodical. English. ir. £18.00. Cosmatom, PO Box 12, Worthing Sussex BN14 7HB England. **DD** 523.101.

SW/0348-9329
**COSMIC AND SUBATOMIC PHYSICS REPORT.** [Cosm. subat. phys. rep.]. Academic Scholarly Publication. English. ir (ten issues per year). Price varies per volume. Cosmic and Subatomic Physics, Solvegatan 14, S-223 62 Lund Sweden. **Tel** +046 46 107706, FAX +046 46 104709, telex 33533 LUNIVER S. **CODEN** CSPLDN. **Circ:** 200. Documents available from CASDDS.
**Desc:** Reports on results of basic scientific research on the properties of nuclear matter performed by physicists at the Division of Cosmic and Subatomic Physics at the University of Lund, Sweden.
**Ind/Abst** Chem. Abstr.

US/0147-6262
**CRC HANDBOOK OF CHEMISTRY AND PHYSICS.** **See** Chemistry.

US/1040-8436
**CRITICAL REVIEWS IN SOLID STATE AND MATERIALS SCIENCES.** [Crit. rev. solid state mater. sci.]. **VFOAT** CRC Critical Reviews in Solid State and Materials Sciences. **VAT** Chemical Rubber Company Critical Reviews in Solid State and Materials Sciences. Vol. 9, Issue 1 (1980)-. Academic Scholarly Publication. English. Four times a year. $285.00 institution. CRC Press Inc., 2000 Corporate Boulevard Northwest, Boca Raton FL 33431. **Tel** (407)994-0555, (800)272-7737, FAX (407)998-9784, telex 568689. **(Subscription address:** CRC Press Inc., PO Box 750, Pearl River NY 10965.**) ED** Joseph E. Greene. **LC** QC176.A1; C453. **DD** 530.4/1/05. **CODEN** CCRSDA. **[CCC]. Pr Rev.** Documents available from Article Express International, The Genuine Article, BIOSIS Document Express, Ask*IEEE, CASDDS. ***Continues*** *CRC Critical Reviews in Solid State and Materials Sciences, 0161-1593.*
**Desc:** Provides a comprehensive, critical assessment of theoretical and experimental solid state materials science.
**Ind/Abst** Biol. Abstr. (?-1990); Ceram. Abstr. (19??-); Chem. Abstr.; Curr. Contents Phys. Chem. Earth Sci.; Energy Res. Abstr. (1981-); Eng. Index Annu.; Index Sci. Rev. [Full Cov.]; INIS Atomindex [Micro.]; INSPEC (1990-); Res. Alert [Full Cov.]; Sci. Cit. Index; SCISEARCH; SPIN (1980-).

US/1052-0139
**CRYOGAS INTERNATIONAL.** **See** Engineering-Mechanical Engineering and Machinery.

UK/0011-2275
**CRYOGENICS (GUILFORD).** (CRYOGENICS.). [Cryogenics]. Vol. 1, No. 1 (Sept. 1960)-. Periodical. English (summaries and/or abstracts in French, German, Italian and Russian). Twelve times a year. $880.00 The Americas; £590.00 other. Butterworth Heinemann Publishers, Linacre House, Jordan Hill, Oxford OX2 8DP England. **Tel** 011 44 865 310366. **(Subscription address:** Elsevier Science Ltd. Oxford Fulfillment Centre, PO Box 800, Kidlington, Oxford OX5 1DX United Kingdom.**) ED** Marija Vukovojac. **LC** TP480; .C75. **NLM** W1 CR999. **CODEN** CRYOAX. **[CCC].** Index available. **Bk Rev. Ad Acc. Pr Rev.** available on microfilm and microfiche from University Microfilms International (UMI). Documents available from Article Express International, The Genuine Article, Ask*IEEE, CASDDS.
**Desc:** Provides a forum for papers concerned with cryoengineering and cryophysics. Covers a wide variety of subjects in low temperature engineering and research.
**Ind/Abst** Acoust. Abstr.; Alum. Ind. Abstr.; Appl. Sci. Technol. Index; Bioeng. Abstr.; Chem. Abstr.; Chem. Titles; Curr. Contents Eng. Tech. Appl. Sci.; Curr. Contents Phys. Chem. Earth Sci.; Curr. Technol. Index; Ei Page One; Eng. Mater. Abstr.; Eng. Index Annu.; Gas Abstr. (?-?); HTFS Dig.; INSPEC (1968-); Int. Aerosp. Abstr. (19??-19??); Met. Abstr.; Proc. Chem. Eng.; Res. Alert [Full Cov.]; Sci. Cit. Index; SCISEARCH; Theoret. Chem. Eng.

UK/0011-3786
**CURRENT PAPERS IN PHYSICS.** **See** Physics-Abstracting, Bibliographies and Statistics.

US/0098-9819
**CURRENT PHYSICS INDEX.** **See** Physics-Abstracting, Bibliographies and Statistics.

US/0732-4383
**CURRENT TOPICS IN CHINESE SCIENCE. SECTION A, PHYSICS.** [Curr. top. Chin. sci., Sect. A, Phys.]. **VFOAT** Physics. Vol. 1 (1982)-. Periodical. English. an. Gordon & Breach Science Publishers, Inc., PO Box 786, Cooper Station, New York NY 10276. **Tel** (212)206-8900, FAX (212)645-2459. **(Subscription address:** International Publishers Distributor at one of the following addresses: 820 Town Center Drive, Langhorne, PA 19047; or PO Box 90, Reading Berkshire RG1 8JL UK; or Kent Ridge PO Box 1180, Singapore 9111, Republic of Singapore**) LC** QC1; .C88. **DD** 530/.05.

UK/1053-122X
**CURRENT TOPICS IN PHOTOVOLTAICS.** (1985)-. Monographic series. English. ir. Price varies per volume. Academic Press, Inc., 6277 Sea Harbor Drive, Orlando FL 32887. **Tel** (800)543-9534, (407)345-4100, FAX (407)363-9661. **LC** TK2960; .C88. **DD** 621.31/244. **CODEN** CTPHEJ. Documents available from CASDDS.
**Ind/Abst** Chem. Abstr.

XR/0011-4626
**CZECHOSLOVAK JOURNAL OF PHYSICS.** [Czech. j. phys.]. **Added/Corp** Ceskoslovenska Akademie Ved. Vol. B16 (1966)-. Academic Scholarly Publication. English (German and Russian). Twelve times a year. $745.00 US; $870.00 other. Plenum Press, 233 Spring Street, New York NY 10013-1578. **Tel** (212)620-8000, (800)221-9369, FAX (212)463-0742, (212)807-1047, telex 23/421139. **ED** J. Kvasnica. **LC** QC1; .C435. **CODEN** CZYPAO. cum. index. **Pr Rev.** available on microfilm and microfiche from University Microfilms International (UMI). Documents available from The Genuine Article, Ask*IEEE, CASDDS. ***Continues*** *Chekhoslovatskii Fizicheskii Zhurnal, 0011-4626.*
**Ind/Abst** Alum. Ind. Abstr.; Ceram. Abstr.; Chem. Abstr.; Curr. Contents Phys. Chem. Earth Sci.; Eng. Mater. Abstr.; GeoRef; INIS Atomindex [Micro.]; INSPEC (1968-); Int. Aerosp. Abstr.; Math. Rev.; Met. Abstr.; Res. Alert [Full Cov.]; Sci. Cit. Index; SCISEARCH; Surf. Treat. Technol. Abstr.

PL
**DELTA.** **See** Mathematics.

US
**DEVELOPMENTS IN THE QUARK THEORY OF HADRONS.** Vol. 1 (1964/1978)-. English. an. $70.00 (latest volume). Hadronic Press Inc, PO Box 1577, Palm Harbor FL 34682. **Tel** (813)934-9593.

GW/0720-485X
**DIFFERENTIAL GEOMETRICAL METHODS IN MATHEMATICAL PHYSICS.** English. ir. Springer-Verlag New York Inc., 175 5th Avenue, New York NY 10010. **Tel** (212)460-1500, telex 232 235 SPB UR. **(Subscription address:** Springer Verlag New York Inc. / for North America, 44 Hartz Way, Secaucus NJ 07096.**)**
**Desc:** Proceedings of symposia held at various places ...

SI
**DIRECTIONS IN CONDENSED MATTER PHYSICS.** (1989)-. Monographic series. English. Price varies per volume. World Scientific Publishing Company, PO Box 128, Farrer Road, Singapore 9128 Singapore. **Tel** 011 65 3825663, FAX 011 65 3825919, telex RS 28561 WSPC. ***Continues*** *World Scientific Series on Directions in Condensed Matter Physics, 0218-0332.*
**Ind/Abst** Math. Rev.; Zentralbl. Math. Ihre Grenzgeb.

US/0882-6056
**DIRECTORY OF CONSULTANTS IN LASERS AND PHYSICS, THE.** [Dir. consult. lasers phys.]. **VFOAT** Directory of Consultants in Lasers & Physics. 1st. Edition (1985)-. English. ir. $85.00 (per copy). Gale Research Inc., 835 Penobscot Building, Detroit MI 48226. **Tel** (800)877-GALE, (313)961-2242, FAX (313)961-6083, telex TWX 810-221-7086. **LC** QC16.2; .D57. **DD** 530/.025/73.

CN/0709-8448
**DIRECTORY / SPECTROSCOPY SOCIETY OF CANADA.** [Dir. - Spectrosc. Soc. Can.]. **Main/Corp** Spectroscopy Society of Canada. **VFOAT** Annuaire. Began with V. for 1979. Directory. English. ir (six issues per year). $80.00. Spectroscopy Society of Canada, PO Box 332, Station A, Ottawa Ontario K1N 8V3 Canada. **Tel** 011 613 990 8396. **ED** I S Butler and T Theophanides. **LC** QC450; .S64A. **DD** 535.8/4/06071. **Bk Rev. Ad Acc. Circ:** 1,200 (ctrl).
**Desc:** An international bilingual journal published for all branches of fundamental and applied spectroscopy.

US/1040-0214
**DISCRETE SEMICONDUCTORS. POWER SEMICONDUCTORS.** [Discrete semicond. Power semicond.]. **Added/Corp** D.A.T.A. Business Publishing. **VFOAT** Power Semiconductors; Power Semiconductors Digest. (1988)-. English. sa. $205.00. DATA Business Publishing, PO Box 6510, 15 Inverness Way East, Englewood CO 80155. **Tel** (800)447-4666, (303)799-0381, FAX (303)799-4082. **ED** Bill Dennison, Paul Magin, and James Mastt. **LC** TK7871.85; .P67. **DD** 621.381/52/0294. Index available. cum. index. ***Continues*** *Power Semiconductors (1982), 0738-324X.*

US/1040-0222
**DISCRETE SEMICONDUCTORS. THYRISTORS. Added/Corp** D.A.T.A. Business Publishing. **VFOAT** Thyristors; Discrete Semiconductors Digest. Thyristors. (1988)-. English. sa (March & September). $235.00 US; $275.00 other. DATA Business Publishing, PO Box 6510, 15 Inverness Way East, Englewood CO 80155. **Tel** (800)447-4666, (303)799-0381, FAX (303)799-4082. **LC** TK7871.99.T5; T53. **DD** 621.381/528/0294. ***Continues*** *Thyristor, 0732-6092.*
**Desc:** Information on thyristors.

US/1040-0230
**DISCRETE SEMICONDUCTORS. TRANSISTORS.** [Discrete semicond., Transistors]. **Added/Corp** D.A.T.A. Business Publishing. **VFOAT** Transistors. (1988)-. English. sa. $235.00 US; $275.00 other. DATA Business Publishing, PO Box 6510, 15 Inverness Way East, Englewood CO 80155. **Tel** (800)447-4666, (303)799-0381, FAX (303)799-4082. **ED** Bill Dennison, Paul Magin, and James Mastt. **LC** TK7871.9; .D57. **DD** 621.381/528/0294. Index available. cum. index. ***Continues*** *Transistor, 0732-6203.*

CC/1000-3258
**DIWEN WULI XUEBAO.** (TI WEN WU LI HSUEH PAO.). [Diwen wuli xuebao]. **Added/Corp** Chung-Kuo Ko Hsueh Chi Shu Ta Hsueh. **VFOAT** Chinese Journal of Low Temperature Physics. (1986)-. Academic Scholarly Publication. Chinese. bm. $88.20. Science Press, 16 Donghuangchenggen North Street, Beijing 100707, People's Republic of China. **Tel** 011 86 1 4019821, 011 86 1 4010642, FAX 011 86 1 4012180, 011 86 1 4019810, telex 210147. **ED** Y. Xixian. **CODEN** DWXUES. **Ad Acc. Pr Rev. Circ:** 5,950. Documents available from CASDDS, BLDSC, Ask*IEEE, CASDDS. ***Continues*** *Ti Wen Wu Li, 0253-3634.*
**Ind/Abst** Chem. Abstr.; INSPEC (Dec. 1987-).

TU/1010-7630
**DOGA. TURKISH JOURNAL OF PHYSICS. Added/Corp** Turkiye Bilimsel ve Teknik Arastrma Kurumu. **VFOAT** Turkish Journal of Physics; Doga. Turk Fizik Dergisi; Turk Fizik Dergisi. (198?)-. Periodical. English (Turkish). Three times a year. Scientific and Technical Research Council of Turkey, Ataturk Bulvari 221, Kavaklidere Ankara Turkey. **Tel** 3420845, FAX 1175902, telex BTAK TR 43186. Documents available from Ask*IEEE, CASDDS. ***Continues*** *Doga. Turk Fizik Astrofizik Dergisi.*
**Ind/Abst** Chem. Abstr.; Fluid Abstr., Civil Eng.; Fluid Abstr. Proc. Eng.; FLUIDEX; Geogr. Abstr. Phys. Geogr.; INSPEC (1991-).

TA/0002-3469
**DOKLADHOI AKADEMIAI FANHOI RSS TOCIKISTON.** ***Title Change.*** **See** Mathematics.

UN
**DOKLADY AKADEMII NAUK UKRAINSKOI SSR. SERIIA A, FIZIKO-MATEMATICHESKIE I TEKHNICHESKIE NAUKI.** ***Title Change.*** **See** Mathematics.

FR
**DYMAT JOURNAL.** (19??)-. Periodical. English (French). qt. 900.00F. Les Editions de Physique, 7 Avenue du Hoggar, Z.I. de Courtaboeuf - BP 112, 91944 les Ulis Cedex A France. **Tel** 011 33 1 69 07 36 88, FAX 011 33 1 69 28 84 91, telex EDITPHY 692321F.

ER
**EESTI TEADUSTE AKADEEMIA TOIMETISED. FUUSIKA, MATEMAATIKA. Added/Corp** Eesti Teaduste Akadeemia. **VFOAT** Fuusika, Matemaatika; Fizika, Matematika; Physics, Mathematics; Izvestiia Akademii Nauk Estonii. Fizika, Matematika; Proceedings of the Estonian Academy of Sciences. Physics, Mathematics. (1990)-. Periodical. Russian (English, Estonian, French and German). qt. $132.95. Kirjastus Perioodika, Pk 107, Parnu Mnt 8, Tallinn EE0090 Estonia. **Tel** 0142 441 262, FAX 0142 442 484. **(Subscription address:** East View Publications Inc., 3020 Harbor Lane North, Suite 110, Minneapolis MN 55447.**) CODEN** ETAMEF. Documents available from CASDDS. ***Continues*** *Eesti NSV Teaduste Akadeemia Toimetised. Fuusika, Matemaatika, 0367-1429.*
**Ind/Abst** Chem. Abstr.; Int. Aerosp. Abstr.

UA/0376-8724
**EGYPTIAN JOURNAL OF PHYSICS. VFOAT** Majallah Al-Misriyah Lil-Fiziqa. Academic Scholarly Publication. English (summaries and/or abstracts in Arabic). sa. $15.00 US. National Information & Documentation Center, A1-Tahrir St Dokki AGWAF, Cairo Egypt. **Tel** 011 20 2 701696, telex 93069. **ED** M El Nadi. **LC** QC1. **DD** 530/.05. **CODEN** EJPHB2. **Pr Rev. Circ:** 700 (ctrl). Documents available from CASDDS. ***Continues*** *United Arab Republic Journal of Physics.*
**Desc:** Publishes original scientific research papers on all branches of physics. Submitted papers are refereed by internal and external authorities.
**Ind/Abst** Acoust. Abstr.; Chem. Abstr.

US/1051-5690
**ELEKTOR ELECTRONICS USA.** ***Ceased.*** [Elektor electron. USA]. Vol. 1, No. 1 (Oct. 1990)-(1992). Periodical. English. mo (July/Aug issue combined). Audio Amateur Publications, PO Box 576, Peterborough NH 03458. **Tel** (603)924-9464, FAX (603)924-9467. **DD** 621.

UK/1042-1939
**ENERGY AND ENGINEERING SCIENCE SERIES.** [Energy eng. sci. ser.]. Monographic series. English. ir. Price varies per volume. Gordon & Breach Science Publishers, PO Box 90, Reading RG1 8JL England. **Tel** 011 44 734 560080, FAX 011 44 734 568211. **(Subscription address:** International Publishers Distributor at one of the following addresses: 820 Town Center Drive, Langhorne, PA 19047; or PO Box 90, Reading Berkshire RG1 8JL UK; or Kent Ridge PO Box 1180, Singapore 9111, Republic of Singapore**) DD** 621.

FR/0997-7546
**EUROPEAN JOURNAL OF MECHANICS. B. FLUIDS.** [Eur. j. mech. B, Fluids]. **VFOAT** Fluids; EJM B/Fluids; E.J.M. B/Fluids; B/Fluids. Vol. 8, No. 1 (1989)-. Periodical. English. Six times a year. 1950.00F EEC; 2170.00F other. Gauthier-Villars, 15 rue Gossin, 92543 Montrouge Cedex France. **Tel** 33 1 40 92 65 00, FAX 33 1 40 92 65 97. **(Subscription address:** Centrale des Revues, 11 rue Gossin, 92543 Montrouge Cedex France.**) LC** QA901; .E97. **DD** 620.1/06/05. **CODEN** EJBFEV. **[CCC].** Documents available from Article Express International, The Genuine Article, Ask*IEEE. ***Continues in part*** *Journal de Mecanique Theorique et Appliquee, 0750-7240.*
**Desc:** Provides a forum published in English for discussion of research topics in the field of fluids mechanics.
**Ind/Abst** Appl. Mech. Rev.; Curr. Contents Eng. Tech. Appl. Sci.; Curr. Contents Phys. Chem. Earth Sci.; Ei Page One; Eng. Index Annu.; INSPEC (1988-); Int. Aerosp. Abstr.; Math. Rev.; Res. Alert; Sci. Cit. Index; SCISEARCH; Shock Vibr. Dig.; Zentralbl. Math. Ihre Grenzgeb.

UK/0143-0807
**EUROPEAN JOURNAL OF PHYSICS.** (EUROPEAN JOURNAL OF PHYSICS : A JOURNAL OF THE EUROPEAN PHYSICAL SOCIETY.). [Eur. j. phys.]. **Added/Corp** European Physical Society. Institute of Physics (Great Britain) American Institute of Physics. (1980)-. Academic Scholarly Publication. English (summaries and/or abstracts in French and German). bm. $286.00. Institute of Physics, Techno House, Redcliffe Way, Bristol BS1 6NX England. **Tel** 011 44 272 297481, FAX 011 44 272 294318, telex 449149 INSTP G. **(Subscription address:** American Institute of Physics, Publishing Sales, 500 Sunnyside Blvd., Woodbury NY 11797.**) ED** Sir Brian Pippard. **LC** QC1; .E84. **DD** 530/.05. **CODEN** EJPHD4. Index available. available on microfiche; available on microfilm. Documents available from Ask*IEEE, CASDDS.
**Desc:** Deals with education and scholarly studies in physics and closely related sciences at university level. Welcomes letters and comments on any aspect of university physics teaching and also includes brief coverage of news, events and books, focusing, in particular, on Europe.
**Ind/Abst** Acoust. Abstr.; Chem. Abstr.; Ei Page One; INSPEC (1980-); Int. Aerosp. Abstr.; Math. Rev.; Phys. Briefs.

SZ/0378-2271
**EUROPHYSICS CONFERENCE ABSTRACTS.** [Europhys. conf. abstr.]. **Main/Corp** European Physical Society. Vol. 1 (1975)-. Academic Scholarly Publication. English. ir. 320.00F (previous subscribers); 360.00F (regular subscribers). European Physical Society, PO Box 39, 1213 Petit-Lancy 2 Switzerland. **Tel** 011 41 22 7931130, FAX 011 41 22 7931317. **ED** K. Bethge and G. Thomas. **CODEN** ECABDW. Documents available from CASDDS.
**Ind/Abst** Chem. Abstr.; Energy Res. Abstr. (Feb. 1982-).

FR/0295-5075
**EUROPHYSICS LETTERS.** [Europhys. lett.]. **Added/Corp** European Physical Society. Vol. 1, No. 1 (Jan. 1, 1986)-. Academic Scholarly Publication. English (French, Russian and German). Thirty-six times a year. 7470.00F. Les Editions de Physique, 7 Avenue du Hoggar, Z.I. de Courtaboeuf - BP 112, 91944 les Ulis Cedex A France. **Tel** 011 33 1 69 07 36 88, FAX 011 33 1 69 28 84 91, telex EDITPHY 692321F. **ED** W. Buckel. **LC** QC1; .E88. **DD** 530/.05. **CODEN** EULEEJ. cum. index. **Pr Rev. Circ:** 1,500. Documents available from The Genuine Article, Ask*IEEE, CASDDS. ***Formed by the union of*** ***Lettere Al Nuovo Cimento, 0375-930X and Journal de Physique. Lettres, 0302-072X.***
**Desc:** Covers all domains of physics; articles submitted should contain non-trivial new results, ideas, concepts, experimental methods, theoretical treatments, etc., and be of interest and importance to one or several sections of the community.
**Ind/Abst** Acoust. Abstr. (19??-); Ceram. Abstr. (19??-); Chem. Abstr. (1986-); Chem. Titles (19??-); Curr. Contents Phys. Chem. Earth Sci. (19??-); Eng. Mater. Abstr. (1972-); INSPEC (1986-); Math. Rev. (19??-); Res. Alert (19??-) [Full Cov.]; Sci. Cit. Index (19??-); SCISEARCH (19??-).

SZ/0531-7479
**EUROPHYSICS NEWS.** [Europhys. news]. Academic Scholarly Publication. English. mo. 120.00F. European Physical Society, PO Box 39, 1213 Petit-Lancy 2 Switzerland. **Tel** 011 41 22 7931130, FAX 011 41 22 7931317. **ED** P Boswell. **CODEN** EUPNAS. **Ad Acc.** Documents available from Ask*IEEE, CASDDS.
**Ind/Abst** Chem. Abstr.; Energy Res. Abstr. (Aug. 1981-); INSPEC (Oct. 1980-).

GW/0014-4924
**EXPERIMENTELLE TECHNIK DER PHYSIK.** [Exp. Tech. Phys.]. Vol. 1, (1953)-. Academic Scholarly Publication. German. Six times a year. DM440.00. Heldermann Verlag Berlin, Nassauische Str 26, D 10717 Berlin Germany. **Tel** 011 49 30 870446. **CODEN** EXPPAL. Documents available from Ask*IEEE, CASDDS.
**Ind/Abst** Acoust. Abstr.; Chem. Abstr.; Ei Page One; Energy Res. Abstr. (Sept. 1979-); INSPEC (1968-); Math. Rev.

AT/0812-3985
**EXPLORATION GEOPHYSICS (MELBOURNE).** (EXPLORATION GEOPHYSICS.). [Explor. geophys.]. **Added/Corp** Australian Society of Exploration Geophysicists. **VFOAT** Bulletin of the Australian Society of Exploration Geophysicists. Vol. 15, No. 1 (Mar. 1984)-. Academic Scholarly Publication. English. Four times a year (Mar., June, Sept., Dec.). 100.00Aus$ Australia; 160.00 others. Australia Society Exploration Geophysicists, 672B Glenferrie Road, Suite 5, Hawthorn Victoria 3122 Australia. **Tel** 011 61 3 8181272, FAX 011 61 3 8181286. **ED** John Denham (editor's address: 61 Bursaria Avenue, Ferntree Victoria 3156 Australia (phone: 011 61 3 7582750). **LC** TN269; .A845a. **DD** 622/.15/05. **CODEN** EXGEEF. **[CCC].** Index available. cum. index. **Bk Rev**, (Qty: 1-2). **Ad Acc, Adv Mgr:** G. Dickson, **Tel** 011 61 3 8892522. **Pr Rev. Circ:** 2,020 (ctrl). available on microfiche from the publisher. Documents available from Ask*IEEE, CASDDS. ***Continues*** *Australian Society of Exploration Geophysicists. Bulletin -Australian Society of Exploration Geophysicists, 0314-2876.*
**Desc:** Papers which reports the results of significant case histories, reviews, and relevant research in geophysics, with emphasis on application to Australian and similar to environments.
**Ind/Abst** Chem. Abstr. (-1986); INSPEC (1986-).

US/0889-8197
**EXPLORATORIUM QUARTERLY.** ***Title Change.*** **See** Museums and Galleries.

●US
**EXPLORING MAGAZINE. See** Museums and Galleries.

US/0015-0193
**FERROELECTRICS.** [Ferroelectrics]. Vol. 1, No. 1 (March 1970)-. Periodical. English. Four times a year. Price varies. Gordon & Breach Science Publishers, Inc., PO Box 786, Cooper Station, New York NY 10276. **Tel** (212)206-8900, FAX (212)645-2459. **(Subscription address:** Gordon & Breach Science Publishers / US, 820 Town Center Drive, Langhorne PA 19047.**) ED** George W. Taylor. **LC** QC595; .F4. **DD** 537.2/44. **CODEN** FEROA8. **[CCC]. Bk Rev. Ad Acc. Pr Rev.** available in microform. Documents available from Article Express International, The Genuine Article, Ask*IEEE, CASDDS.
**Ind/Abst** Alum. Ind. Abstr.; Bioeng. Abstr.; Chem. Abstr.; Chem. Titles; Coal Abstr.; Curr. Contents Phys. Chem. Earth Sci.; Ei Page One; Eng. Index Annu.; INSPEC (March 1970-); Int. Aerosp. Abstr.; Leadscan; Met. Abstr.; Res. Alert [Full Cov.]; Sci. Cit. Index; SCISEARCH; Soils Fert.

UK/0883-8283
**FERROELECTRICS AND POLAR MATERIAL.** 1989-. English. ir. Gordon & Breach Science Publishers, PO Box 90, Reading RG1 8JL England. **Tel** 011 44 734 560080, FAX 011 44 734 568211. **(Subscription address:** International Publishers Distributor at one of the following addresses: 820 Town Center Drive, Langhorne, PA 19047; or PO Box 90, Reading Berkshire RG1 8JL UK; or Kent Ridge PO Box 1180, Singapore 9111, Republic of Singapore**)**

GW/0430-3393
**FESTKORPERPROBLEME.** [Festkorperprobleme]. **VFOAT** Advances in Solid State Physics. (1962)-. Monographic series. Multiple languages (German and English). ir. Price varies per volume.

Vieweg Publishing, PO Box 5829, D 65048 Wiesbaden Germany. **Tel** 011 49 611 160230, FAX 011 49 611 160229. **(Subscription address:** VVA Bertelsmann Distributors GmbH, Postfach 7777, D-33310 Guetersloh Germany.**) LC** TK7871.85; .F47. **DD** 621.381/52/08. **CODEN** FSTKA2. **[CCC].** Documents available from Article Express International, The Genuine Article, Ask*IEEE, CASDDS. ***Supersedes** Halbleiterprobleme.*
**Ind/Abst** Bioeng. Abstr.; Chem. Abstr.; Ei Page One; Eng. Index Annu.; INSPEC; Res. Alert [Full Cov.]; Sci. Cit. Index; SCISEARCH.

US/1051-1946
**FIBER OPTIC SENSORS AND SYSTEMS.** (FIBER OPTIC SENSORS AND SYSTEMS : FOSP2S.). [Fiber opt. sens. syst.]. **VFOAT** FOSp2s; FOSp2s Newsletter. (1987)-. Newsletter. English. mo. $545.00 US & Canada; $595.00 other. Information Gatekeepers Inc., 214 Harvard Avenue, Boston MA 02134. **Tel** (617)232-3111, (800)323-1088, FAX (617)734-8562. **DD** 621. **[CCC].**

RU
**FILOSOFIIA I FIZIKA.** (1972)-. Periodical. Russian. Izdatelstvo Voronezhskogo Universiteta / Voronezh State University, Universitetskaia Pl 1, Voronezh 294693 Russia. **Tel** 5-29-83. **LC** QC5.56; .F54.

●CI/1330-0016
**FIZIKA B : A JOURNAL OF EXPERIMENTAL AND THEORETICAL PHYSICS. Added/Corp** Physical Society of the Republic of Croatia. Vol. 1, No. 1 (Jan.-Apr. 1992)-. Periodical. English. tq. **LC** QC1; .F4974. ***Continues in part** Fizika, 0015-3206.*

RU
**FIZIKA ELEMENTARNYKH CHASTITS I ATOMNOGO IADRA. Added/Corp** Dubna, Russia (Moscow Province) Obedinennyi Institut Iadernykh Issledovanii. **VFOAT** Problems of Elementary Particle and Atomic Nucleus Physics; Physics of Elementary Particles and Atomic Nuclei. (1970)-. Academic Scholarly Publication. Russian (summaries and/or abstracts in English). bm. $176.00. **(Subscription address:** East View Publications Inc., 3020 Harbor Lane North, Suite 110, Minneapolis MN 55447.**)** available in microform. Documents available from Ask*IEEE, CASDDS.
**Ind/Abst** Chem. Abstr.; INSPEC (1973-); Math. Rev.

RU/0430-6228
**FIZIKA GORENIIA I VZRYVA.** [Fiz. goren. vzryva]. **VFOAT** The Physics of Combustion and Explosion. (1965)-. Periodical. Russian (table of contents in English). Six times a year. $136.00. **(Subscription address:** East View Publications Inc., 3020 Harbor Lane North, Suite 110, Minneapolis MN 55447.**) CODEN** FGVZA7. **[CCC].** Documents available from Article Express International, Ask*IEEE, CASDDS. ***Continues** Nauchno-Tekhnicheskie Problemy Goreniia i Vzryva.*
**Ind/Abst** Chem. Abstr.; Coal Abstr.; Ei Page One; Energy Res. Abstr.; Eng. Index Annu.; INSPEC (1968-); Int. Aerosp. Abstr.

UK/0264-729X
**FIZIKA I KHIMIIA OBRABOTKI MATERIALOV.** (PHYSICS AND CHEMISTRY OF MATERIALS TREATMENT.). Periodical. English (summaries and/or abstracts in Russian). bm. £220.00 EC; $350.00 other. Riecansky Science Publishing Company, 7 Meadow Walk, Great Abington, Cambridge CB1 6AZ England. **Tel** 011 44 223 893295, FAX 011 44 462 480947, telex 825372 TURPIN G. **CODEN** PCMTEU. Documents available from Ask*IEEE.
**Ind/Abst** Chem. Titles; Civ. Struct. Eng. Abstr.; Comput. Inf. Syst. Abstr. J. [Full Cov.]; Elect. Comm. Abstr.; Eng. Mater. Abstr.; INSPEC (1983-); Manuf. Process Eng. Abstr.; Mater. Sci. Eng. Abstr.; Mech. Eng. Abstr.; Solid State Supercond. Abstr.

RU/0203-4654
**FIZIKA I TEHNIKA VYSOKIH DAVLENIJ.** [Fiz. teh. vysok. davl.]. (1980)-. Periodical. Russian. **UDC** 53.
**Desc:** Information on high pressure physics.
**Ind/Abst** Int. Aerosp. Abstr.

UN
**FIZIKA MNOGOCHASTICHNYKH SISTEM.** No. 1-. Academic Scholarly Publication. Russian. 1.60rub. Izdatelstvo Naukova Dumka / Ukrainian Academy of Sciences, Vladimirskaia Ulitsa 54, 252601 Kiev Ukraine. **Tel** 225-63-66, telex 131376. **LC** QC173; .F57. **DD** 539/.6/05. Documents available from CASDDS.
**Ind/Abst** Chem. Abstr.

RU/0134-5052
**FIZIKA PLAZMY (MOSKVA. 1975).** (FIZIKA PLAZMY.). [Fiz. plazmy]. **Added/Corp** Akademiia Nauk SSSR. (1975)-. Academic Scholarly Publication. Russian. mo. $269.00. Izdatelstvo Nauka / Akademiia Nauk, Publishing House of the Russian Academy of Sciences, Leninskii Porspekt 14, 117901 Moscow Russia. **Tel** 011 95 954-21-53, FAX 011 95 938-21-44, telex 411964. **(Subscription address:** East View Publications Inc., 3020 Harbor Lane North, Suite 110, Minneapolis MN 55447.**) LC** QC7176; .F57. **CODEN** FIPLDK. Documents available from Ask*IEEE, CASDDS.
**Ind/Abst** Chem. Abstr.; INSPEC (March/April 1975-); Int. Aerosp. Abstr.

BU/0204-6946
**FIZIKA (SOFIA).** (FIZIKA.). [Fizika]. **Added/Corp** Bulgaria. Ministerstvo na Narodnata Prosveta. Suiuz na Bulgarskite Uchiteli. TSentralen Komitet. (1976)-. Academic Scholarly Publication. Bulgarian. bm (6 issues). DM120.00. **(Subscription address:** Kubon & Sagner, ABT Zeitschriftenimport, D 80328 Munich Germany.**) LC** QC1; .F493. **CODEN** FZKADD. Documents available from CASDDS. ***Continues in part** Matematika i Fizika.*
**Ind/Abst** Chem. Abstr.

RU/0130-5522
**FIZIKA V SHKOLE : NAUCHNO-METODICHESKII ZHURNAL MINISTERSTVO PROSVESHCHENIIA SSSR. Added/Corp** Soviet Union. Ministerstvo Prosveshcheniia. Russian S.F.S.R. Ministerstvo Prosveshcheniia. (1937)-. Academic Scholarly Publication. Russian (Russian). Six times a year. $49.95. **(Subscription address:** East View Publications Inc., 3020 Harbor Lane North, Suite 110, Minneapolis MN 55447.**) LC** QC1; .F5. **CODEN** FIZSAK. Documents available from CASDDS. ***Continues in part** Matematika i Fizika v Shkole.*
**Ind/Abst** Chem. Abstr.

UN/0302-5470
**FIZIKA ZHIDKOGO SOSTOIANIIA.** (1973)-. Russian (summaries and/or abstracts in English). 0.77 rub. **LC** QC138; .F58. **CODEN** FZSSA2. Documents available from CASDDS.
**Ind/Abst** Chem. Abstr.

HU/0015-3257
**FIZIKAI SZEMLE.** [Fiz. szle.]. **Added/Corp** Eotvos Lorand Fizikai Tarsulat. Vol. 1 (1951)-. Academic Scholarly Publication. Hungarian. mo. **(Subscription address:** Kultura, PO Box 149, H 1389 Budapest 62 Hungary**) CODEN** FISZA6. Documents available from Ask*IEEE, CASDDS. ***Continues in part** Mathematikai es Physikai Lapok, 0302-7317.*
**Ind/Abst** Chem. Abstr.; INSPEC (Dec. 1969-).

BU/0204-5958
**FIZIKO-HIMICESKA MEHANIKA. See** Chemistry-Physical and Theoretical Chemistry.

BU/0015-3265
**FIZIKO-MATEMATICHESKO SPISANIE.** Vol. 1 (1958)-. Academic Scholarly Publication. Bulgarian. qt. DM125.00. Bulgarian Academy of Sciences, 1 rue 15 Noemvri, 1040 Sofia Bulgaria. **Tel** 011 359 2 803127. **(Subscription address:** Kubon & Sagner, ABT Zeitschriftenimport, D 80328 Munich Germany.**) ED** L. Ieiev. **CODEN** FMBMAC. **Bk Rev.** Documents available from CASDDS. ***Supersedes** Spisanie.*
**Desc:** Articles in physics and mathematics, history and biography, personalia, problems and solutions, news, new books in physics and mathematics.
**Ind/Abst** Chem. Abstr.; Math. Rev.

XR/0323-0287
**FOLIA FACULTATIS SCIENTIARUM NATURALIUM UNIVERSITATIS PURKYNIANAE BRUNENSIS. PHYSICA.** [Folia Fac. Sci. Nat. Univ. Purkynianae Brunensis, Phys.]. **Added/Corp** Univerzita J.E. Purkyne v Brne. Prirodovedecka Fakulta. **VFOAT** Physica. (1960)-. Monographic series. English (summaries and/or abstracts in Czech and Russian). Univ J E Purkyne V Brne, Janackovo Nam 2A, Brno Czech Republic. **CODEN** FFSPER. Documents available from Ask*IEEE, CASDDS.
**Ind/Abst** Chem. Abstr.; INSPEC (1973-); Math. Rev.

GW
**FORSCHUNGSBERICHT / INSTITUT FUER PLASMAFORSCHUNG DER UNIVERSITAT STUTTGART. See** Medical Science and Technology-Hematology.

GW/0015-8208
**FORTSCHRITTE DER PHYSIK (BERLIN : 1953).** (FORTSCHRITTE DER PHYSIK.). [Fortschr. Phys.]. **Added/Corp** Physikalische Gesellschaft in der Deutschen Demokratischen Republik. Vol. 1 (1953)-. Academic Scholarly Publication. German. Eight times a year. $530.00. Akademie-Verlag GmbH, Muehlenstrasse 33 34, D 13162 Berlin Germany. **Tel** 011 49 30 47889300, FAX 011 49 30 47889357. **(Subscription address:** VCH Publishers Inc., 303 Northwest 12th Avenue, Journals Department, Deerfield FL 33442.**) LC** QC1; .F69. **CODEN** FPYKA6. **[CCC].** cum. index. **Pr Rev.** Documents available from The Genuine Article, Ask*IEEE, CASDDS.
**Ind/Abst** Chem. Abstr.; Energy Res. Abstr.; INSPEC (1968-); Int. Aerosp. Abstr.; Math. Rev.; Res. Alert [Full Cov.]; Sci. Cit. Index; SCISEARCH.

US/0015-9018
**FOUNDATIONS OF PHYSICS.** [Found. phys.]. Vol. 1 (1970)-. Periodical. English. Twelve times a year. $865.00 US; $1,010.00 other. Plenum Press, 233 Spring Street, New York NY 10013-1578. **Tel** (212)620-8000, (800)221-9369, FAX (212)463-0742, (212)807-1047, telex 23/421139. **ED** Alwyn van der Merwe. **LC** QC1; .F75. **DD** 530/.05. **CODEN** FNDPA4. **[CCC].** Index available. **Pr Rev.** available on microfilm and microfiche from University Microfilms International (UMI). Documents available from The Genuine Article, Ask*IEEE.
**Desc:** An international journal devoted to the conceptual bases and fundamental theories of modern physics, biophysics and cosmology.
**Ind/Abst** Curr. Contents Phys. Chem. Earth Sci.; Energy Res. Abstr. (Aug. 1972-); INIS Atomindex [Micro.]; INSPEC (March 1973-); Int. Aerosp. Abstr.; Leadscan; Math. Rev.; Pollut. Abstr. Indexes; Res. Alert [Full Cov.]; Sci. Cit. Index; SCISEARCH; SPIN (1977-).

US/0894-9875
**FOUNDATIONS OF PHYSICS LETTERS.** [Found. phys. lett.]. Vol. 1, No. 1 (Mar. 1988)-. Periodical. English. Six times a year. $295.00 institutions, $92.00 individuals US; $345.00 institutions, $108.00 individuals other. Plenum Press, 233 Spring Street, New York NY 10013-1578. **Tel** (212)620-8000, (800)221-9369, FAX (212)463-0742, (212)807-1047, telex 23/421139. **ED** Alwyn Van der Merwe. **LC** QC1; .F76. **DD** 530/.05. **CODEN** FPLEET. **[CCC].** available on microfilm and microfiche from University Microfilms International (UMI). Documents available from The Genuine Article, Ask*IEEE.
**Desc:** Devoted to the rapid dissemination of short research communications of immediate relevance to the international physics community.
**Ind/Abst** Curr. Contents Phys. Chem. Earth Sci.; INSPEC (Mar. 1988-); Math. Rev. (1988-); Res. Alert [Select. Cov.]; SCISEARCH.

JA
**FP: FUSION PLANNING. *Ceased.*** (19??)-(1993). Japanese. mo. **(Subscription address:** Maruzen Company Ltd., PO Box 5050, Import & Export Department, Tokyo 100 31 Japan.**)**

NO/0015-9247
**FRA FYSIKKENS VERDEN.** [Fra fys. verden]. Began 1939. Academic Scholarly Publication. Norwegian. qt. Kr90.00. University of Oslo Department of Physics, Box 1048, Blindern, 0316 Oslo 3 Norway. **Tel** 011 47 2 456428, FAX 47-2-456422. **ED** Divin Holter and Finn Ingebretsen. **LC** WMLC L 83/2338. **CODEN** FYVDAX. Index available. **Bk Rev. Ad Acc. Circ:** 1,400 (ctrl). Documents available from Ask*IEEE, CASDDS.
**Ind/Abst** Chem. Abstr.; Energy Res. Abstr.; INSPEC (1972-).

US/0429-7725
**FRONTIERS IN PHYSICS.** [Front. phys.]. (1961)-. Monographic series. English. ir. Price varies per volume. Addison Wesley Publishing Company, 350 Bridge Parkway, Suite 208, Redwood City CA 94065. **Tel** (415)594-4423, (800)447-2226. **DD** 530. **CODEN** FRPHAY. Documents available from Ask*IEEE.
**Ind/Abst** INSPEC; Math. Rev.; Zentralbl. Math. Ihre Grenzgeb.

NE/0168-1222
**FUNDAMENTAL THEORIES OF PHYSICS.** [Fundam. theor. phys.]. (1982)-. Monographic series. English. ir. **UDC** 530.1.
**Ind/Abst** Zentralbl. Math. Ihre Grenzgeb.

US/0094-5846
**FUNDAMENTALS OF COSMIC PHYSICS. See** Astronomy.

DK
**FYSIK-KEMI.** Periodical. Danish. ir. 44.00. Danmarks Fysik Og Kemilrerforening, Dyrl Jurgensensgade 11, 3740 Svaneke Denmark. **LC** QC30; .F95.

DK/0016-3392
**FYSISK TIDSSKRIFT.** [Fys. tidsskr.]. Vol. 1- ; 1902-. Periodical. Danish. qt. Harck and Gjellerups Booksellers, Fiolstraede 31, 1171 Copenhagen K Denmark. **LC** QC1; .F9. **CODEN** FYTIA4. cum. index. Documents available from Ask*IEEE, CASDDS.
**Ind/Abst** Chem. Abstr.; Energy Res. Abstr.; INSPEC (1971-).

US/0749-4823
**GENERAL PHYSICS ADVANCE ABSTRACTS.** [Gen. phys. adv. abstr.]. **Added/Corp** American Institute of Physics. Vol. 1, No. 1 (Jan. 10, 1985)-. Periodical. English. sm. $570.00 US; $590.00 Canada, Mexico, Central and South America, and the Caribbean; $605.00 other. American Institute of Physics, 500 Sunnyside Boulevard, Woodbury NY 11797-2999. **Tel** (516)576-2200, FAX (516)349-7669, telex 960983. **DD** 530. **CODEN** GPAAE7. **[CCC].**

US/0001-7701
**GENERAL RELATIVITY AND GRAVITATION.** [Gen. relativ. gravit.]. **Added/Corp** International Committee on General Relativity and Gravitation. **VFOAT** GRG Journal. Vol. 1 (1970)-. Periodical. English. Twelve times a year. $675.00 institutions, $165.00 individuals US; $790.00 institutions, $193.00 individuals other. Plenum Press, 233 Spring Street, New York NY 10013-1578. **Tel** (212)620-8000,

(800)221-9369, FAX (212)463-0742, (212)807-1047, telex 23/421139. **ED** A. Held. **LC** QC173.6; .G45. **DD** 530.1/1. **CODEN** GRGVA8. **[CCC].** Index available. **Pr Rev.** available on microfilm and microfiche from University Microfilms International (UMI). Documents available from The Genuine Article, Ask*IEEE.
**Desc:** Publishes research papers on general relativity and related topics.
**Ind/Abst** Astron. Astrophys. Abstr.; Curr. Contents Phys. Chem. Earth Sci.; INSPEC (June 1972-); Int. Aerosp. Abstr.; Math. Rev.; Pollut. Abstr. Indexes; Ref. Z.; Res. Alert [Full Cov.]; Sci. Cit. Index; SCISEARCH; Zentralbl. Math. Ihre Grenzgeb.

MX/0016-7169
**GEOFISICA INTERNACIONAL : REVISTA DE LA UNION GEOFISICA MEXICANA AUSPICIADA POR EL INSTITUTO DE GEOFISICA DE LA UNIVERSIDAD NACIONAL AUTONOMA DE MEXICO.** [Geofis. int.]. Vol. 1, No. 1 (Jan. 10, 1961)-. Periodical. Spanish (French and English). qt. $70.00 institute; $40.00 individual. Universidad Nacional Autonoma de Mexico (UNAM) / Instituto de Geofisica, Postal 22 188 Seccion Ed, 14000 Mexico DF Mexico. **Tel** 011 52 5 5505215 Ext. 4363. **ED** Ismael Herrera Revilla. **LC** QC801; .G35. **DD** 551. **CODEN** GFINAC. **Bk Rev. Circ:** 1,200 (ctrl). Documents available from CASDDS.
**Desc:** Physics of the earth's interior: seismology, vulcanology, chemistry of the earth's interior, tectonics, geomagnetism aeronomy, meteorology, physics of the earth, hydrology and geophysical exploration.
**Ind/Abst** Chem. Abstr.; Ecol. Abstr.; Geogr. Abstr. Phys. Geogr.; Geogr. Abstr. Human Geogr.; Geol. Abstr.; GeoRef; Int. Aerosp. Abstr.; Meteorol. Geoastrophys. Abstr. (199?-).

IT
**GIORNALE DI FISICA.** Italian. qt. $50.00 (nonmembers), $45.00 (members). Editrice Compositori SRL, Viale Stalingrado 97 2, 40128 Bologna Italy. **Tel** 011 39 51 327811. Documents available from Ask*IEEE, CASDDS.
**Ind/Abst** Chem. Abstr.; INSPEC (Jan./March 1983-).

US/1045-5027
**GLASS AUDIO.** [Glass audio]. Vol. 1, No. 1 (1989)-. Periodical. English. Four times a year. $20.00 (individuals), $25.00 (institutions) US & Canada; $35.00 (individuals), $40.00 (institutions) others. Audio Amateur Publications, PO Box 576, Peterborough NH 03458. **Tel** (603)924-9464, FAX (603)924-9467. **LC** IN PROCESS. **DD** 621.
**Ind/Abst** Index Inf.

●US
**GLASS, PHYSICS & CHEMISTRY.** Vol. 18 (1993)-. English. bm (6 issues). $785.00 US and Canada; $920.00 other. Plenum Press, 233 Spring Street, New York NY 10013-1578. **Tel** (212)620-8000, (800)221-9369, FAX (212)463-0742, (212)807-1047, telex 23/421139. **(Subscription address:** Plenum Press Subscription Department, PO Box 730, Canal Street Station NY 10013-1578.**)** ***Continues*** *Soviet Journal Glass, Physics and Chemistry.*
**Desc:** Devoted to theoretical and applied research in glass technology.

BU
**GODISHNIK NA SOFIISKIIA UNIVERSITET "SV. KLIMENT OKHRIDSKI", FIZICHESKI FAKULTET.** **Added/Corp** Sofiiski Universitet "Sv. Kliment Okhridski". Fizicheski Fakultet. **VFOAT** Annuaire de l'Universite de Sofia "St. Kliment Ohridski", Faculte de Physique. (19??)-. Bulgarian (summaries and/or abstracts in English). an. Izdatelstvo na Bulgarskata Akademiia Na Naukite, 6 Rouski Boulevard, Sofia Bulgaria. **Tel** FAX 80 13 41, telex 22267 HEMKIK. **LC** QC1; .G567. Documents available from CASDDS. ***Continues*** *Godishnik na Sofiiskiia Universitet "Kliment Okhridski", Fizicheski Fakultet.*
**Ind/Abst** Chem. Abstr.

US/0147-1821
**GRADUATE PROGRAMS IN PHYSICS, ASTRONOMY AND RELATED FIELDS.** **Added/Corp** American Institute of Physics. (1978)-. Monographic series. English. an. $45.00. American Institute of Physics, 500 Sunnyside Boulevard, Woodbury NY 11797-2999. **Tel** (516)576-2200, FAX (516)349-7669, telex 960983. **(Subscription address:** AIP / Vermont, c/o AIDC, PO Box 20, Williston VT 05495.**)** ***Continues*** *Graduate Programs: Physics, Astronomy, and Related Fields, 0147-1821.*
**Desc:** Provides valuable information on over 300 departments in the United States, Canada, and Mexico.

JA
**GRAPHS OF NEUTRON INTENSITIES.** **Main/Corp** Japan. Nihon Gakujutsu Kaigi. Kokusai Chikyu Kansoku Tokubetsu Iinkai. Taiyo Chikyukan Butsurigaku Bunkakai. English. Science Council of Japan, 7-22-34 Roppongi Minato-ku, Tokyo 106 Japan. **LC** QC485.8.V3; J36A. **DD** 551.5/276.

BL
**GUIA DAS INSTITUICOES EM FISICA NO BRASIL / CENTRO BRASILEIRO DE PESQUISAS FISICAS, COORDENACAO DE DOCUMENTACAO E INFORMACAO CIENTIFICA, DIVISAO DE INFORMACAO CIENTIFICA.** **Added/Corp** Centro Brasileiro de Pesquisas Fisicas. Divisao de Informacao Cientifica. Centro Brasileiro de Pesquisas Fisicas. Area de Informacao Cientifica. (1982)-. Portuguese. an. Centro Brasileiro de Pesquisas Fisicas-CBPF, Coordenacao de Documenta Cao e Informacao Cientifica-CDI, Area de Informacao Cientifica, rua Dr Xavier Sigaud, 150 5O. Andar, 22 290 Rio de Janeiro RJ Brasil. **LC** QC47.B6; G85. **DD** 530/.07/1181.

US/0882-5394
**HADRONIC JOURNAL SUPPLEMENT.** [Hadronic j. suppl.]. Vol. 1, No. 1 (Mar. 1985)-. Periodical. English. Four times a year. $160.00. Hadronic Press Inc, PO Box 1577, Palm Harbor FL 34682. **Tel** (813)934-9593. **LC** QC793.5.H32; H335. **DD** 539.7/216/05. **CODEN** HJSUEO. Documents available from Ask*IEEE, CASDDS.
**Ind/Abst** Chem. Abstr.; INIS Atomindex [Micro.]; INSPEC (March 1985-); Math. Rev.; Zentralbl. Math. Ihre Grenzgeb.

US
**HADRONIC PRESS MONOGRAPHS IN THEORETICAL PHYSICS.** No. 1 (1978)-. Monographic series. English. Hadronic Press Inc, PO Box 1577, Palm Harbor FL 34682. **Tel** (813)934-9593.
**Ind/Abst** Zentralbl. Math. Ihre Grenzgeb.

CN/0824-7773
**HAGALO USTED MISMO - BRACE RESEARCH INSTITUTE.** (HAGALO USTED MISMO-HOJA / MCGILL UNIVERSITY, FACULTY OF ENGINEERING, BRACE RESEARCH INSTITUTE.). **VFOAT** Hagalo Usted Mismo. Monographic series. Spanish. Price varies per volume. Brace Research Institute, PO Box 900, Ste-Anne-de-Bellevue Quebec H9X 1C0 Canada. **DD** 621.

US/0196-9366
**HANDBOOK OF CYCLICAL INDICATORS.** **Added/Corp** United States. Bureau of Economic Analysis. (May 1977)-. Government Publication. English. ir. $5.30. US Department of Commerce, 14th Street & Constitution Avenue NW, Washington DC 20230. **Tel** (202)482-2000, FAX (202)482-3772.

US/0017-9078
**HEALTH PHYSICS (1958).** (HEALTH PHYSICS : OFFICIAL JOURNAL OF THE HEALTH PHYSICS SOCIETY.). [Health phys.]. **Added/Corp** Health Physics Society. Vol. 1, No. 1 (June 1958)-. Academic Scholarly Publication. English. mo. $169.00 (individual), $633.00 (institution) US; $643.00 (institutions) other. Williams & Wilkins Company, 428 East Preston Street, Baltimore MD 21202-3993. **Tel** (410)528-4000, (800)638-6423, FAX (410)528-8596, telex 87669. **(Subscription address:** Williams & Wilkins, PO Box 64380, Baltimore MD 21264.**)** **ED** Genevieve Roessler. **LC** QH505.A1; H4. **DD** 612.01448. **NLM** W1 HE4705. **CODEN** HLTPAO. **[CCC].** cum. index. **Pr Rev.** available on microfilm and microfiche from University Microfilms International (UMI). Documents available from The Genuine Article, BIOSIS Document Express, Ask*IEEE, CASDDS, Documents on Demand, ADONIS, Quick Copies.
**Desc:** The official journal of the Health Physics Society. Provides nuclear chemists and health physicists a practical and effective means for communicating with radiation professionals around the globe.
**Ind/Abst** ADONIS; AGRICOLA; Biol. Abstr.; Chem. Abstr.; Chem. Titles; CIS Abstr.; Coal Abstr.; Cumul. Index Nurs. Allied Health Lit.; Curr. Aware. Biol. Sci., CABS; Curr. Biotechnol.; Curr. Contents Life Sci.; Dairy Sci. Abstr.; EMBASE; Energy Inf. Abstr.; Energy Res. Abstr.; Environ. Abstr.; Environ. Period. Bibliogr.; Field Crop Abstr.; Food Sci. Technol. Abstr.; GeoRef; Grasslands For. Abstr.; Health Saf. Sci. Abstr.; Health Devices Alerts; Health Plan. Adminis.; Index Med.; Index Vet.; Ind. Hyg. Dig. (19??-19??); INIS Atomindex [Micro.]; INSPEC (Jan. 1972-); Int. Aerosp. Abstr.; Maize Abstr.; MINPROC; Mintec, Min. Technol. Abstr.; Nucl. Sci. Abstr.; Nutr. Abstr. Rev., Ser. B, Live Feeds and Feed.; Nutr. Abstr. Rev., Ser. A, Hum. Exp.; Life Sci. Collect.; Phys. Med. Biol. (19??-19??); Pollut. Abstr. Indexes; Poult. Abstr.; Res. Alert [Full Cov.]; Risk Abstr.; Saf. Health Work; Sci. Cit. Index; SCISEARCH; Sel. Water Resour. Abstr.; Soc. Sci. Cit. Index [Select. Cov.]; Soils Fert.; Soyabean Abstr.; Vet. Bull.; Toxicol. Abstr.; Trop. Dis. Bull.; Wheat Barley Trit. Abstr.

US/8756-1964
**HEAVY-ION REACTIONS.** ***Ceased.*** [Heavy-ion react.]. **VFOAT** Heavy Ion Reactions. (Jan. 15, 1985)-Ceased (Dec. 1987). English. sm. National Technical Information Service - NTIS, Room 2027S, 5285 Port Royal Road, Springfield VA 22161. **Tel** (703)487-4630, (703)487-4660, (703)487-4650, FAX (703)321-8547, telex 89-9405. **DD** 539.

SZ/0018-0238
**HELVETICA PHYSICA ACTA.** [Helv. phys. acta]. **Added/Corp** Schweizerische Physikalische Gesellschaft. Vol. 1 (1928)-. Periodical. Multiple languages (French, German and Italian). Eight times a year. 730.90F Switzerland; 747.00F other. Birkhaeuser Verlag Ag, Klosterberg 23, PO Box 133, CH-4010 Basel Switzerland. **Tel** 011 41 61 2717400, FAX 011 41 0 61 2717666, telex 963475 birk ch. **(Subscription address:** Birkhauser Verlag AG, PO Box 151, CH 4106 Therwil Switzerland; Phone: 011 41 61 7217740**)** **ED** O. Piguet. **LC** QC1; .H4. **CODEN** HPACAK. **[CCC]. Pr Rev.** available on microfilm and microfiche from University Microfilms International (UMI). Documents available from The Genuine Article, Ask*IEEE, CASDDS.
**Desc:** Publishes articles in theoretical and mathematical physics.
**Ind/Abst** Acoust. Abstr.; Ceram. Abstr.; Chem. Abstr.; Curr. Contents Phys. Chem. Earth Sci.; Energy Res. Abstr.; GeoRef; INSPEC (1968-); Int. Aerosp. Abstr.; Mass Spect. Bull.; Math. Rev.; Pollut. Abstr. Indexes; Res. Alert [Full Cov.]; Sci. Cit. Index; SCISEARCH; Stat. Theory Method Abstr. (1959-1963); Surf. Treat. Technol. Abstr.

GW/0018-1447
**HIGH ENERGY PHYSICS INDEX / HOCHENERGIEPHYSIK-INDEX.** **Added/Corp** Zentralstelle fuer Atomkernenergie-Dokumentation. Deutsches Elektronen-Synchrotron (Center). **VFOAT** Hochenergiephysik-Index. Vol. 1 (1962)-. Periodical. English (German). Twenty-six times a year. DM460.00 Germany; DM522.40 others. Fachinformationszentrum Karlsruhe, Physics & Math, D 76344 Eggenstein Germany. **Tel** 011 49 7247 808149. Index available. cum. index. **Ad Acc. Circ:** 160 (ctrl).
**Desc:** The world's most comprehensive collection of bibliographic information on experimental and theoretical particle physics, high energy instrumentation, accelerator technology, quantum field theory and other closely related topics.
**Ind/Abst** Energy Res. Abstr.

US/0895-7959
**HIGH PRESSURE RESEARCH.** [High press. res.]. **Added/Corp** International Association for the Advancement of High Pressure Science and Technology. Vol. 1, No. 1 (1988)-. Periodical. English. $425.00 (academic institutions), $662.00 (corporate institutions). Gordon & Breach Science Publishers, Inc., PO Box 786, Cooper Station, New York NY 10276. **Tel** (212)206-8900, FAX (212)645-2459. **(Subscription address:** International Publishers Distributor at one of the following addresses: 820 Town Center Drive, Langhorne, PA 19047; or PO Box 90, Reading Berkshire RG1 8JL UK; or Kent Ridge PO Box 1180, Singapore 9111, Republic of Singapore**)** **ED** M. Ross. **LC** QC280; .H54. **DD** 531/.1. **CODEN** HPRSEL. **[CCC].** Documents available from Article Express International.
**Ind/Abst** Comput. Inf. Syst. Abstr. J. [Full Cov.]; Ei Page One; Elect. Comm. Abstr.; Eng. Index Annu.; Fluid Abstr., Civil Eng.; Fluid Abstr. Proc. Eng.; FLUIDEX (19??-); Mech. Eng. Abstr.

IS/0334-6455
**HIGH TEMPERATURE MATERIALS AND PROCESSES.** [High temp. mater. processes]. Vol. 6, No. 1 & 2 (1984)-. Academic Scholarly Publication. English. qt. $220.00. Freund Publishing House Ltd, PO Box 35010, 61 Nachmani Street, Tel Aviv 61350 Israel. **Tel** 011 972 3 5662925, FAX 011 972 3 5605335. **(Subscription address:** Freund Publishing House Ltd., Suite 500 Chesham House, 150 Regent Street, London W1R 5FA England.**)** **ED** A. Rosen, Y. Waseda. **CODEN** HTMPEF. Documents available from Article Express International, CASDDS. ***Continues*** *Reviews on High-Temperature Materials, 0370-5331.*
**Ind/Abst** Chem. Abstr. (1984-); Ei Page One; Eng. Index Annu.

US/0890-9997
**HISTORICAL STUDIES IN THE PHYSICAL AND BIOLOGICAL SCIENCES.** (HISTORICAL STUDIES IN THE PHYSICAL AND BIOLOGICAL SCIENCES : HSPS.). [Hist. stud. phys. biol. sci.]. **Added/Corp** University of California, Berkeley. Office for History of Science and Technology. **VFOAT** HSPS; H.S.P.S. Vol. 16, Part 1 (1986)-. Academic Scholarly Publication. English. sa (Mar. and Sept.). $22.00 (individuals), $38.00 (institutions). University of California Press, 2120 Berkeley Way, Berkeley CA 94720. **Tel** (510)642-4191, (510)642-3907, FAX (510)642-9917. **ED** J. L. Heilbron. **LC** QC7; .H69. **DD** 509. **NLM** W1; HI799H. **CODEN** HSPSEW. **[CCC]. Bk Rev. Ad Acc. Pr Rev. Circ:** 800 (ctrl). available on microfilm from University Microfilms International (UMI). Documents available from The Genuine Article, CASDDS. ***Continues*** *Historical Studies in the Physical Sciences, 0073-2672.*
**Desc:** Articles on the history of the physical sciences.
**Ind/Abst** Am. Hist. Life (1969-); Chem. Abstr. (1986-); Curr. Contents Phys. Chem. Earth Sci.; Res. Alert [Select. Cov.]; SCISEARCH.

CC/1001-0610
**HSIEN TAI WU LI CHIH SHIH / MODERN PHYSICS.** **Added/Corp** Kao Neng Wu Li Yen Chiu So (China). **VFOAT** Modern Physics. (1989)-. Periodical. Chinese. bm. $18.60. Science Press, 16 Donghuangchenggen North Street, Beijing 100707, People's Republic of China. **Tel** 011 86 1 4019821, 011 86 1 4010642, FAX 011 86 1 4012180, 011 86 1 4019810, telex 210147. **LC** QC1; .H75. **DD** 530/.05. **CODEN** XWZHEF. **Ad Acc. Circ:** 10,000. ***Continues*** *Gaoneng Wuli / High Energy Physics, 0253-4266.*

SI
**ICTP SERIES IN THEORETICAL PHYSICS, THE.** **Added/Corp** International Centre for Theoretical Physics. Vol. 1 (1984)-. Monographic series. English. World Scientific Publishing Company, PO Box 128, Farrer Road, Singapore 9128 Singapore. **Tel** 011 65 3825663, FAX 011 65 3825919, telex RS 28561 WSPC. **CODEN** ISTPEK. Documents available from CASDDS.
**Ind/Abst** Chem. Abstr.; Math. Rev.

II/0379-0479
**INDIAN JOURNAL OF CRYOGENICS.** [Indian j. cryog.]. **Added/Corp** Indian Cryogenics Council. Vol. 1, No. 1 (1976)-. Academic Scholarly Publication. English. qt. $50.00. Indian Cryogenics Council, Jadavpur University, Calcutta 700032 India. **Tel** 722847. **(Subscription address:** Prints India, 11 Darya Ganj, New Delhi, 110002 India, (Phone: 011 91 11 3268645)) **ED** A Bose, A K Dutta. **CODEN** IJCRDD. Index available. **Bk Rev. Ad Acc. Circ:** 300. Documents available from Ask*IEEE, CASDDS.
**Ind/Abst** Alum. Ind. Abstr.; Chem. Abstr.; INSPEC (1977-); Met. Abstr.

II/0252-9262
**INDIAN JOURNAL OF PHYSICS A AND PROCEEDINGS OF THE INDIAN ASSOCIATION FOR THE CULTIVATION OF SCIENCE A.** (THE INDIAN JOURNAL OF PHYSICS. PART A.). [Indian j. phys. A proc. Indian Assoc. Cultiv. Sci. A]. **VFOAT** Proceedings of the Indian Association for the Cultivation of Science. Vol. 51A, No. 1 (Jan. 1977)-. Periodical. English. bm. Indian Association of Cultivation of Science, 2-3 Raja Subadh Mullick Road, Jadavpur, Calcutta 700032 India. **Tel** 46-9371-5, FAX 91 33 4732805, telex 021-5501 IACS IN. **LC** QC1; .I526. **DD** 530/.05. **CODEN** IJPYAS. Documents available from Ask*IEEE, CASDDS. ***Continues in part*** *Indian Journal of Physics and Proceedings of the Indian Association for the Cultivation of Science, 0019-5480.*
**Ind/Abst** Alum. Ind. Abstr.; Ceram. Abstr. (19??-); Chem. Abstr.; Chem. Titles; INSPEC (Jan. 1977-); Met. Abstr.

II/0019-5480
**INDIAN JOURNAL OF PHYSICS AND PROCEEDINGS OF THE INDIAN ASSOCIATION FOR THE CULTIVATION OF SCIENCE.** **See** Science and Technology.

II/0252-9254
**INDIAN JOURNAL OF PHYSICS B AND PROCEEDINGS OF THE INDIAN ASSOCIATION FOR THE CULTIVATION OF SCIENCE B.** (THE INDIAN JOURNAL OF PHYSICS. PART B.). [Indian j. phys. B proc. Indian Assoc. Cultiv. Sci. B]. **VFOAT** Proceedings of the Indian Association for the Cultivation of Science. Vol. 51B, No. 1 (Feb. 1977)-. Periodical. English. bm. Indian Association of Cultivation of Science, 2-3 Raja Subadh Mullick Road, Jadavpur, Calcutta 700032 India. **Tel** 46-9371-5, FAX 91 33 4732805, telex 021-5501 IACS IN. **LC** QC1; .I527. **DD** 530/.05. **CODEN** IJPYAS. Documents available from Ask*IEEE, CASDDS. ***Continues in part*** *Indian Journal of Physics and Proceedings of the Indian Association for the Cultivation of Science, 0019-5480.*
**Ind/Abst** Alum. Ind. Abstr.; Ceram. Abstr. (19??-); Chem. Abstr.; Chem. Titles; INSPEC (1977-); Met. Abstr.

II/0019-5596
**INDIAN JOURNAL OF PURE & APPLIED PHYSICS.** [Indian j. pure appl. phys.]. **Added/Corp** Council of Scientific & Industrial Research (India). **VFOAT** Indian Journal of Pure and Applied Physics. **VAT** Indian Journal of Pure and Applied Physics. Vol. 1, No. 1 (Jan. 1963)-. Periodical. English. mo. $160.00. Council of Scientific & Industrial Research, Publications & Information Director, Hillside Road, New Delhi 110012 India. **Tel** FAX 011 91 11 5731353. **(Subscription address:** Prints India, 11 Darya Ganj, New Delhi 110002 India.**)** **ED** D.S. Sastry. **LC** QC1; .I53. **DD** 530/.05. **CODEN** IJOPAU. **Ad Acc. Pr Rev. Circ:** 1,000. Documents available from Article Express International, The Genuine Article, BIOSIS Document Express, Ask*IEEE, CASDDS. ***Continues in part*** *Journal of Scientific and Industrial Research. Section B. Physical Sciences, 0368-4210.*
**Desc:** Condensed matter physics, chemical physics, mathematical physics, nuclear physics, atomic and molecular physics, electronics, electrical engineering, elementary particles, and fields classical areas of phenomenology.
**Ind/Abst** Acoust. Abstr.; Alum. Ind. Abstr.; Anal. Abstr.; Art Archaeol. Tech. Abstr.; Bioeng. Abstr.; Biol. Abstr.; Ceram. Abstr. (19??-); Chem. Abstr.; Chem. Titles; Coal Abstr.; Curr. Contents Phys. Chem. Earth Sci.; Curr. Titles Electrochem.; Ei Page One; Eng. Mater. Abstr.; Eng. Index Annu.; GeoRef; Indian Geosci. Abstr.; INSPEC (1968-); Int. Aerosp. Abstr.; Leadscan; Mass Spect. Bull.; Math. Rev.; Met. Abstr.; Pollut. Abstr. Indexes; Res. Alert [Select. Cov.]; SCISEARCH; World Text. Abstr.

II/0367-8393
**INDIAN JOURNAL OF RADIO & SPACE PHYSICS.** [Indian j. radio space phys.]. **Added/Corp** Council of Scientific & Industrial Research (India) Indian National Science Academy. **VAT** Indian Journal of Radio and Space Physics. Vol. 1 (Mar. 1972)-. Periodical. English. bm. $100.00. Council of Scientific & Industrial Research, Publications & Information Director, Hillside Road, New Delhi 110012 India. **Tel** FAX 011 91 11 5731353. **(Subscription address:** Prints India, 11 Darya Ganj, New Delhi, 110002 India, (Phone: 011 91 11 3268645)) **LC** QC801; .I42. **DD** 523.01/05. **CODEN** IJRSAK. **Pr Rev.** Documents available from The Genuine Article, Ask*IEEE, CASDDS.
**Ind/Abst** Chem. Abstr.; Curr. Contents Phys. Chem. Earth Sci.; INSPEC (March 1972-); Int. Aerosp. Abstr.; Res. Alert [Select. Cov.]; SCISEARCH.

II/0019-5693
**INDIAN JOURNAL OF THEORETICAL PHYSICS.** [Indian j. theor. phys.]. **Added/Corp** Institute of Theoretical Physics (India). Vol. 1 (June 1953)-. Periodical. English. qt. $50.00. Institute of Theoretical Physics, Secretary B Kutie, 4 1 Mohan Began Lane, Calcutta 700004 India. **Tel** 55-5726. **(Subscription address:** Prints India, 11 Darya Ganj, New Delhi, 110002 India, (Phone: 011 91 11 3268645)) **ED** P R Ghosh, M Ghosh, S D Chatterjee, J Biswas, A Roy Chowdhury, S Sen Gupta, P P Chatterjee, D K Sinha, Mrs C Dutta, J G Chakravorty, Mrs A Basu, and A K Bhattacharyya. **LC** QC1; .I533. **CODEN** IJTPAL. **Bk Rev. Circ:** 250. Documents available from Ask*IEEE, CASDDS.
**Ind/Abst** Acoust. Abstr.; Chem. Abstr.; INSPEC (1968-); Int. Aerosp. Abstr.

UK/0020-0891
**INFRARED PHYSICS.** ***Title Change.*** [Infrared phys.]. Vol. 1 (Mar. 1961)-(1993). Periodical. English (English). bm. Pergamon Press, An Imprint of Elsevier Science Ltd., The Boulevard, Langford Lane, Kidlington, Oxford OX5 1GB United Kingdom. **Tel** 011 44 865 843000, 011 44 865 843699, FAX 011 44 865 843010. **(Subscription address:** US/ 395 Saw Mill River Road, Elmsford, NY 10523; Can/ 150 Consumers Road/Suite 104, Willowdale Ontario M2J 1P9; Aus-NZ/ POB 544, Potts Point NSW 2011**)** **ED** T Moss. **LC** QC457; .I5. **CODEN** INFPAD. cum. index. **Pr Rev.** available on microfilm and microfiche from University Microfilms International (UMI). Documents available from Article Express International, The Genuine Article, Ask*IEEE, CASDDS. ***Continued by*** *Infrared Physics and Engineering.*
**Ind/Abst** Acoust. Abstr.; Alum. Ind. Abstr.; Bioeng. Abstr.; Ceram. Abstr.; Chem. Abstr.; Curr. Biotechnol.; Curr. Contents Phys. Chem. Earth Sci.; Ei Page One; Eng. Mater. Abstr.; Eng. Index Annu.; GeoRef; INIS Atomindex [Micro.]; INSPEC (1968-); Int. Aerosp. Abstr.; Leadscan; Met. Abstr.; Pollut. Abstr. Indexes; Res. Alert [Full Cov.]; Sci. Cit. Index; SCISEARCH.

UK
**INFRARED PHYSICS AND ENGINEERING.** ***Title Change.*** (19??)-(19??). English. Seven times a year (1 volume). Pergamon Press, An Imprint of Elsevier Science Ltd., The Boulevard, Langford Lane, Kidlington, Oxford OX5 1GB United Kingdom. **Tel** 011 44 865 843000, 011 44 865 843699, FAX 011 44 865 843010. ***Continued by*** *Infrared Physics and Technology, 1350-4495.*

●UK/1350-4495
**INFRARED PHYSICS & TECHNOLOGY.** **VFOAT** Infrared Physics and Technology; Infrared Phys. Technol. Vol. 35, No. 1 (Feb. 1994)-. Academic Scholarly Publication. English. Seven times a year. $820.00 The Americas; £550.00 other. Pergamon Press, An Imprint of Elsevier Science Ltd., The Boulevard, Langford Lane, Kidlington, Oxford OX5 1GB United Kingdom. **Tel** 011 44 865 843000, 011 44 865 843699, FAX 011 44 865 843010. **(Subscription address:** Elsevier Science Ltd. Oxford Fulfillment Centre, PO Box 800, Kidlington, Oxford OX5 1DX United Kingdom.**)** **ED** F.K. Kneubuhl, W.L. Wolfe. **LC** QC457; .I5. **CODEN** IPTEEY. **[CCC].** Documents available from Ask*IEEE, CASDDS. ***Continues*** *Infrared Physics, 0020-0891.*
**Desc:** Covers the whole field of infrared physics and its applications.
**Ind/Abst** Chem. Abstr.; Curr. Contents Phys. Chem. Earth Sci.; INSPEC; Sci. Cit. Index (19??-19??); SCISEARCH.

UK/0951-3248
**INSTITUTE OF PHYSICS CONFERENCE SERIES.** [Inst. Phys. conf ser.]. (1985)-. Academic Scholarly Publication. English. ir. Price varies per volume. IOP Publishing Limited, Unit 1 & 2, Audie House 260 Field End Road, Ruislip Middlesex HA4 9LG England. **Tel** 011 44 81 8684499. **CODEN** IPCSEP. **[CCC].** Documents available from Article Express International, The Genuine Article, Ask*IEEE, CASDDS. ***Continues*** *Conference Series (Institute of Physics (Great Britain)), 0305-2346.*
**Ind/Abst** Bioeng. Abstr.; Chem. Abstr. (1985-); Civ. Struct. Eng. Abstr.; Comput. Inf. Syst. Abstr. J. [Full Cov.]; Ei Page One; Elect. Comm. Abstr.; Eng. Index Annu.; GeoRef; INSPEC; Manuf. Process Eng. Abstr.; Mater. Sci. Eng. Abstr.; Mech. Eng. Abstr.; Res. Alert [Full Cov.]; Sci. Cit. Index; SCISEARCH; Solid State Supercond. Abstr.

US/0020-4412
**INSTRUMENTS AND EXPERIMENTAL TECHNIQUES (NEW YORK).** (INSTRUMENTS AND EXPERIMENTAL TECHNIQUES.). [Instrum. exp. tech.]. **Added/Corp** Consultants Bureau. Instrument Society of America. Consultants Bureau Enterprises. (Apr. 1959)-. Academic Scholarly Publication. English (Russian). Twelve times a year. $1375.00 US; $1610.00 other. Consultants Bureau, A Division of Plenum Publishing Corporation, 233 Spring Street, New York NY 10013. **Tel** (212)620-8000, (212)620-8466, FAX (212)463-0742, telex 23/421139. **ED** M. S. Khaikin. **LC** QC53; .P213. **DD** 530.78. **CODEN** INETAK. **[CCC]. Pr Rev.** available on microfilm and microfiche from University Microfilms International (UMI). Documents available from Article Express International, The Genuine Article, Ask*IEEE, CASDDS.
**Desc:** Provides articles and research on physical measurement techniques and applications of various laboratory instruments, new materials used in the instrumentation industry.
**Ind/Abst** Appl. Mech. Rev.; Bioeng. Abstr.; Chem. Abstr.; Comput. Abstr.; Curr. Contents Eng. Tech. Appl. Sci.; Ei Page One; Eng. Index Annu.; Fluid Abstr., Civil Eng.; Fluid Abstr. Proc. Eng.; FLUIDEX (1973-1990); INIS Atomindex [Micro.]; INSPEC (1968-); Leadscan; Mass Spect. Bull.; Res. Alert [Full Cov.]; Sci. Cit. Index; SCISEARCH.

SI
**INTERNATIONAL CONFERENCE ON THE PHYSICS OF SEMICONDUCTORS : PROCEEDINGS.** **Added/Corp** International Union of Pure and Applied Physics. **VFOAT** Physics of Semiconductors. 18th (Aug. 11-15, 1986)-. English. be. World Scientific Publishing Company, PO Box 128, Farrer Road, Singapore 9128 Singapore. **Tel** 011 65 3825663, FAX 011 65 3825919, telex RS 28561 WSPC. **ED** John D. Joannopoulos and E. Anastassakis. **Bk Rev. Circ:** 2,000. ***Continues*** *International Conference on the Physics of Semiconductors. Proceedings of the ... International Conference on the Physics of Semiconductors (1980).*

NE/0168-1176
**INTERNATIONAL JOURNAL OF MASS SPECTROMETRY AND ION PROCESSES.** [Int. j. mass spectrom. ion process.]. Vol. 54, Nos. 1/2 (Oct. 1, 1983)-. Academic Scholarly Publication. English. Thirty-three times a year (11 volumes). Fl4620.00. Elsevier Science Publishers BV, PO Box 211, 1000 AE Amsterdam Netherlands. **Tel** 011 31 20 5803642, FAX 011 31 20 5862696, telex 15682. **ED** M T Bowers, H Schwarz and J F J Todd. **LC** QC454; .I66. **DD** 539. **CODEN** IJMPDN. **[CCC]. Pr Rev.** available on microfilm and microfiche from University Microfilms International (UMI). Documents available from The Genuine Article, Ask*IEEE, CASDDS, ADONIS. ***Continues*** *International Journal of Mass Spectrometry and Ion Physics, 0020-7381.*
**Desc:** Contains papers dealing with fundamental aspects of mass spectrometry and ion processes, and the study of the application of mass spectrometric techniques to specific problems.
**Ind/Abst** ADONIS; Anal. Abstr.; Chem. Abstr.; Chem. Titles; Curr. Contents Phys. Chem. Earth Sci.; EMBASE; GeoRef; INSPEC (1983-); Int. Aerosp. Abstr. (1984-); Mass Spect. Bull.; Res. Alert [Full Cov.]; Sci. Cit. Index; SCISEARCH.

SI/0217-751X
**INTERNATIONAL JOURNAL OF MODERN PHYSICS A.** (INTERNATIONAL JOURNAL OF MODERN PHYSICS. A, PARTICLES AND FIELDS, GRAVITATION, COSMOLOGY.). [Int. j. mod. phys. A]. **VFOAT** Journal of Modern Physics A; Particles and Fields, Gravitation, Cosmology; Particles and Fields, Gravitation and Cosmology. Vol. 1, No. 1 (April 1986)-. Academic Scholarly Publication. English. Thirty-two times a year. $920.00 individual, $1,840.00 institution. World Scientific Publishing Company, PO Box 128, Farrer Road, Singapore 9128 Singapore. **Tel** 011 65 3825663, FAX 011 65 3825919, telex RS 28561 WSPC. **(Subscription address:** US: World Scientific Publishing Co., Inc., 1060 Main Street, River Edge, NJ 07661 Telephone: (201)487-9655, Fax: (201)487-9656; Europe: World Scientific Publishing Co Ltd, 73 Lynton Mead, Totteridge, London N20 8DH United Kingdom Telephone: 011 44 81 4462461, Fax: 011 44 81 4463356; India: World Scientific Publishing Co Pte Ltd, 4911 9th Floor, High Point IV, 45 Palace Road, Bangalore 560 001 India Telephone: (80) 2205972, Fax: (80) 3344593, Telex: 0845-2900 PCO IN; Hong Kong: World Scientific Publishing (HK) Co, PO Box 72482, Kowloon Central Post Office, Hong Kong Telephone: 852-7718791, Fax: 852-7718155**)** **LC** QC793; .I5545. **DD** 539.7/21. **CODEN** IMPAEF. **[CCC].** cum. index. **Pr Rev. Circ:** 500. Documents available from The Genuine Article, Ask*IEEE, CASDDS.

Desc: The journal consists of in-depth reviews and original papers covering the latest developments in particles and fields, gravitation and cosmology.
**Ind/Abst** Chem. Abstr. (1986-); Curr. Contents Phys. Chem. Earth Sci.; INSPEC (1987-); Math. Rev.; Res. Alert [Select. Cov.]; SCISEARCH; Zentralbl. Math. Ihre Grenzgeb.

SI/0217-9792
**INTERNATIONAL JOURNAL OF MODERN PHYSICS B.** (INTERNATIONAL JOURNAL OF MODERN PHYSICS. B, CONDENSED MATTER PHYSICS, STATISTICAL PHYSICS, APPLIED PHYSICS.). [Int. j. mod. phys. b]. **VFOAT** Condensed Matter Physics, Statistical Physics, Applied Physics. Vol. 1, No. 1 (April 1987)-. Statistical Publication. English. Twenty-eight times a year. $625.00 individuals, $1,290.00 institutions. World Scientific Publishing Company, PO Box 128, Farrer Road, Singapore 9128 Singapore. **Tel** 011 65 3825663, FAX 011 65 3825919, telex RS 28561 WSPC. **(Subscription address:** US: World Scientific Publishing Co., Inc., 1060 Main Street, River Edge, NJ 07661 Telephone: (201)487-9655, Fax: (201)487-9656; Europe: World Scientific Publishing Co Ltd, 73 Lynton Mead, Totteridge, London N20 8DH United Kingdom Telephone: 011 44 81 4462461, Fax: 011 44 81 4463356; India: World Scientific Publishing Co Pte Ltd, 4911 9th Floor, High Point IV, 45 Palace Road, Bangalore 560 001 India Telephone: (80) 2205972, Fax: (80) 3344593, Telex: 0845-2900 PCO IN; Hong Kong: World Scientific Publishing (HK) Co, PO Box 72482, Kowloon Central Post Office, Hong Kong Telephone: 852-7718791, Fax: 852-7718155) **LC** QC173.4.C65; I44. **DD** 530. **CODEN** IJPBEV. **[CCC]. Pr Rev.** Documents available from The Genuine Article, Ask*IEEE.
**Desc:** Publishes high quality research papers and extensive review articles in condensed matter physics, statistical physics and applied physics.
**Ind/Abst** Ceram. Abstr. (19??-); Curr. Contents Phys. Chem. Earth Sci.; INSPEC (1987-); Math. Rev.; Res. Alert [Select. Cov.]; Sci. Cit. Index; SCISEARCH; Zentralbl. Math. Ihre Grenzgeb.

SI/0129-1831
**INTERNATIONAL JOURNAL OF MODERN PHYSICS. C.** (INTERNATIONAL JOURNAL OF MODERN PHYSICS. C, PHYSICS AND COMPUTERS.). [Int. j. mod. phys., C]. **VFOAT** Physics and Computers. Vol. 1, No. 1 (April 1990)-. Periodical. English. bm. $180.00 individuals, $380.00 institutions. World Scientific Publishing Company, PO Box 128, Farrer Road, Singapore 9128 Singapore. **Tel** 011 65 3825663, FAX 011 65 3825919, telex RS 28561 WSPC. **(Subscription address:** US: World Scientific Publishing Co., Inc., 1060 Main Street, River Edge, NJ 07661 Telephone: (201)487-9655, Fax: (201)487-9656; Europe: World Scientific Publishing Co Ltd, 73 Lynton Mead, Totteridge, London N20 8DH United Kingdom Telephone: 011 44 81 4462461, Fax: 011 44 81 4463356; India: World Scientific Publishing Co Pte Ltd, 4911 9th Floor, High Point IV, 45 Palace Road, Bangalore 560 001 India Telephone: (80) 2205972, Fax: (80) 3344593, Telex: 0845-2900 PCO IN; Hong Kong: World Scientific Publishing (HK) Co, PO Box 72482, Kowloon Central Post Office, Hong Kong Telephone: 852-7718791, Fax: 852-7718155) **LC** QC52; .I58. **DD** 530/.0285. **CODEN** IJMPEO. Documents available from Ask*IEEE.
**Ind/Abst** INSPEC (1990-); Math. Rev.

●SI/0218-2718
**INTERNATIONAL JOURNAL OF MODERN PHYSICS. D, GRAVITATION, ASTROPHYSICS, COSMOLOGY. VFOAT** Gravitation, Astrophysics, Cosmology. Vol. 1, No. 1 (1992)-. Periodical. English. Six times a year. $120.00 individuals, $235.00 institutions. World Scientific Publishing Company, PO Box 128, Farrer Road, Singapore 9128 Singapore. **Tel** 011 65 3825663, FAX 011 65 3825919, telex RS 28561 WSPC. **(Subscription address:** US: World Scientific Publishing Co., Inc., 1060 Main Street, River Edge, NJ 07661 Telephone: (201)487-9655, Fax: (201)487-9656; Europe: World Scientific Publishing Co Ltd, 73 Lynton Mead, Totteridge, London N20 8DH United Kingdom Telephone: 011 44 81 4462461, Fax: 011 44 81 4463356; India: World Scientific Publishing Co Pte Ltd, 4911 9th Floor, High Point IV, 45 Palace Road, Bangalore 560 001 India Telephone: (80) 2205972, Fax: (80) 3344593, Telex: 0845-2900 PCO IN; Hong Kong: World Scientific Publishing (HK) Co, PO Box 72482, Kowloon Central Post Office, Hong Kong Telephone: 852-7718791, Fax: 852-7718155) **LC** QB460; .I579. **DD** 523.01/05.

UK/0883-2889
**INTERNATIONAL JOURNAL OF RADIATION APPLICATIONS AND INSTRUMENTATION. PART A, APPLIED RADIATION AND ISOTOPES.** ***Title Change.*** [Int. j. radiat. appl. instrum., A, Appl. radiat. isot.]. **VFOAT** Applied Radiation and Isotopes. Vol. 37 No. 1-Vol. 43 No. 12 (Dec. 1992). Academic Scholarly Publication. English. mo. Pergamon Press, An Imprint of Elsevier Science Ltd., The Boulevard, Langford Lane, Kidlington, Oxford OX5 1GB United Kingdom. **Tel** 011 44 865 843000, 011 44 865 843699, FAX 011 44 865 843010. **(Subscription address:** US/ 395 Saw Mill River Road, Elmsford, NY 10523; Can/ 150 Consumers Road/Suite 104, Willowdale Ontario M2J 1P9; Aus-NZ/ POB 544, Potts Point NSW 2011) **LC** QC770; .I6. **DD** 621.48/37/05. **NLM** W1; IN778E. **CODEN** ARISEF. **[CCC]. Pr Rev.** available on microfilm and microfiche from University Microfilms International (UMI). Documents available from Article Express International, The Genuine Article, BIOSIS Document Express, Ask*IEEE, CASDDS. ***Continues*** *International Journal of Applied Radiation and Isotopes, 0020-708X.* ***Continued by*** *Applied Radiation and Isotopes.*
**Desc:** Publishes papers describing methods, techniques and instrumentation relating to the production, measurement and application of radionuclides and radiation in any branch of science and technology.
**Ind/Abst** AGRICOLA [Select. Cov.]; Anal. Abstr.; Biol. Abstr. (1986-); Chem. Abstr. (1986-); Coal Abstr. (1986-); CSA Neuro. Abstr. (?-?); Curr. Aware. Biol. Sci., CABS; Curr. Contents Life Sci.; Curr. Contents Phys. Chem. Earth Sci.; Ei Page One; EMBASE; Energy Inf. Abstr. (1986-); Energy Res. Abstr. (1986-); Eng. Index Annu.; GeoRef (1986-); Health Saf. Sci. Abstr.; Health Plan. Adminis.; Index Med. (1986-); INSPEC (1986-); Int. Aerosp. Abstr. (1986-); Mass Spect. Bull. (?-?); Life Sci. Collect. (1986-); PESTDOC (1986-?); Phys. Med. Biol. (19??-19??); Pollut. Abstr. Indexes; Postharvest News Inf.; Res. Alert [Full Cov.]; Rev. Agric. Entomol.; Sci. Cit. Index (19??-19??); SCISEARCH; Soils Fert.; Toxicol. Abstr.; Wheat Barley Trit. Abstr.

US/0020-7748
**INTERNATIONAL JOURNAL OF THEORETICAL PHYSICS.** [Int. j. theor. phys.]. Vol. 1 (May 1968)-. Periodical. English (French and German). Twelve times a year. $695.00 US; $815.00 other. Plenum Press, 233 Spring Street, New York NY 10013-1578. **Tel** (212)620-8000, (800)221-9369, FAX (212)463-0742, (212)807-1047, telex 23/421139. **ED** David Finkelstein. **LC** QC1; .I64. **DD** 530/.05. **CODEN** IJTPBM. **[CCC].** Index available. **Pr Rev.** available on microfilm and microfiche from University Microfilms International (UMI). Documents available from The Genuine Article, Ask*IEEE, CASDDS.
**Desc:** A journal of original research and reviews in theoretical physics and related mathematics; dedicated to the unification of physics.
**Ind/Abst** Chem. Abstr.; Curr. Contents Phys. Chem. Earth Sci.; INIS Atomindex [Micro.]; INSPEC (Oct. 1969-); Int. Aerosp. Abstr.; Math. Rev.; Pollut. Abstr. Indexes; Ref. Z.; Res. Alert [Full Cov.]; Sci. Cit. Index; SCISEARCH; Zentralbl. Math. Ihre Grenzgeb.

US/0195-928X
**INTERNATIONAL JOURNAL OF THERMOPHYSICS.** [Int. j. thermophys.]. Vol. 1, No. 1 (Mar. 1980)-. Academic Scholarly Publication. English. Six times a year. $595.00 US: $695.00 other. Plenum Press, 233 Spring Street, New York NY 10013-1578. **Tel** (212)620-8000, (800)221-9369, FAX (212)463-0742, (212)807-1047, telex 23/421139. **ED** Ared Cezairliyan. **LC** QC192; .I57. **DD** 536/.7. **CODEN** IJTHDY. **[CCC].** Index available. **Pr Rev.** available on microfilm and microfiche from University Microfilms International (UMI). Documents available from Article Express International, The Genuine Article, Ask*IEEE, CASDDS.
**Desc:** International medium for the publication of papers in the thermophysics field with the intent to serve both the generations and the users of thermophysical properties data.
**Ind/Abst** Alum. Ind. Abstr.; Bioeng. Abstr.; Chem. Abstr.; Chem. Titles; Curr. Contents Phys. Chem. Earth Sci.; Ei Page One; Eng. Mater. Abstr.; Eng. Index Annu.; HTFS Dig.; INIS Atomindex [Micro.]; INSPEC (March 1980-); Met. Abstr.; Ref. Z.; Res. Alert [Full Cov.]; Sci. Cit. Index; SCISEARCH; World Ceram. Abstr.

IT/0392-3967
**INTERNATIONAL PHYSICS SERIES.** [Int. phys. ser.]. (1971)-. English. ir. Editrice Compositori SRL, Viale Stalingrado 97 2, 40128 Bologna Italy. **Tel** 011 39 51 327811. Documents available from CASDDS.
**Ind/Abst** Chem. Abstr.

UK/0950-5563
**INTERNATIONAL SERIES OF MONOGRAPHS ON PHYSICS (UK).** (INTERNATIONAL SERIES OF MONOGRAPHS ON PHYSICS.). [Int. ser. monogr. phys.]. (19??)-. Monographic series. English. ir. Price varies per volume. Oxford University Press, Walton Street, Oxford OX2 6DP England. **Tel** 011 44 865 56767, FAX 011 44 865 267773, telex 837330 OXPRES G. **(Subscription address:** Oxford University Press / USA, Journals Marketing Department, Oxford University Press, 2001 Evans Road, Cary NC 27513.) **ED** J. Birman, S.F. Edwards, C.H. Llewellyn Smith and M. Rees. **CODEN** IMPHAW. Documents available from Ask*IEEE.
**Ind/Abst** INSPEC; Math. Rev.

US/0074-9931
**INTERSCIENCE MONOGRAPHS AND TEXTS IN PHYSICS AND ASTRONOMY.** [Interscience monogr. texts phys. astron.]. **VFOAT** Monographs and Texts in Physics and Astronomy. (1957)-. Academic Scholarly Publication. English. ir. Price varies per volume. John Wiley & Sons, Inc., 605 Third Avenue, New York NY 10158-0012. **Tel** (212)850-6000, (212)850-6645, FAX (212)850-6088, telex 12-7063. **(Subscription address:** John Wiley & Sons / England, Baffins Lane, Chichester, West Sussex PO19 1UD England.) **LC** UNC. **CODEN** IMTPA8. Documents available from CASDDS.
**Ind/Abst** Chem. Abstr.

US/0074-9958
**INTERSCIENCE TRACTS ON PHYSICS AND ASTRONOMY.** ***Ceased.*** [Intersci. tracts phys. astron.]. (195?)-Ceased (19??). Monographic series. English. ir. John Wiley & Sons, Inc., 605 Third Avenue, New York NY 10158-0012. **Tel** (212)850-6000, (212)850-6645, FAX (212)850-6088, telex 12-7063. **(Subscription address:** John Wiley & Sons / England, Baffins Lane, Chichester, West Sussex PO19 1UD England.)

BW/0021-0285
**INZENERNO-FIZICESKIJ ZURNAL.** **See** Engineering.

UN/0234-4483
**IONNYE RASPLAVY I TVERDYE ELEKTROLITY.** (IONNYE RASPLAVY I TVERDYE ELEKTROLITY / AKADEMIIA NAUK USSR, INSTITUT OBSHCHEI I NEORGANICHESKOI KHIMII.). [Ion. rasplavy tverd. elektrolity]. **Added/Corp** Instytut Zahalnoi ta Neorhanichnoi Khimii (Akademiia Nauk Ukrainskoi RSR). Vol. 1 (1986)-. Russian. an. Izdatelstvo Naukova Dumka / Ukrainian Academy of Sciences, Vladimirskaia Ulitsa 54, 252601 Kiev Ukraine. **Tel** 225-63-66, telex 131376. **LC** QD189; .I63. **CODEN** IRTEEE. Documents available from CASDDS.
**Ind/Abst** Chem. Abstr.

RU
**IONNYI OBMEN I IONOMETRIIA / LENINGRADSKII GOSUDARSTVENNYI UNIVERSITET IMENI A.A. ZHDANOVA.** **Added/Corp** Leningradskii Gosudarstvennyi Universitet Imeni A.A. Zhdanova. Vol. 1 (1976)-. Periodical. Russian. St Petersburg State University / Izdatelstvo Leningradskogo Universiteta, Universitetskaia Nab 7/9, 199034 St Petersburg Russia. **Tel** 011 95 218-97-88, FAX 011 95 218-51-52, telex 121481. **LC** QD561; .I68. **DD** 541.3/723/05. **CODEN** IOIODZ. Documents available from CASDDS.
**Ind/Abst** Chem. Abstr.

RU
**IONOSFERNYE ISSLEDOVANIIA. IONOSPHERIC RESEARCHES. Added/Corp** Akademiia Nauk SSSR. Mezhduvedomstvennyi Komitet po Provedeniiu Mezhdunarodnogo Geofizicheskogo Goda. Akademiia Nauk SSSR. Mezhduvedomstvennyi Geofizicheskii Komitet. **VFOAT** Ionosfera.; Ionospheric Researches. No.1 (1959)-. Academic Scholarly Publication. Russian (summaries and/or abstracts in English). Izdatelstvo Nauka / Akademiia Nauk, Publishing House of the Russian Academy of Sciences, Leninskii Porspekt 14, 117901 Moscow Russia. **Tel** 011 95 954-21-53, FAX 011 95 938-21-44, telex 411964. Documents available from CASDDS.
**Ind/Abst** Chem. Abstr.

UK/0269-8986
**IOP SHORT MEETINGS SERIES.** [IOP short meet. ser.]. **Added/Corp** Institute of Physics (Great Britain). **VFOAT** IOP Short Meetings. **VAT** Institute of Physics Short Meetings Series. No. 1 (1986)-. Monographic series. English. Institute of Physics, Techno House, Redcliffe Way, Bristol BS1 6NX England. **Tel** 011 44 272 297481, FAX 011 44 272 294318, telex 449149 INSTP G. **(Subscription address:** American Institute of Physics, Publishing Sales, 500 Sunnyside Blvd., Woodbury NY 11797.) **CODEN** IPSSE3. Documents available from Ask*IEEE, CASDDS.
**Ind/Abst** Chem. Abstr.; INSPEC; Zentralbl. Math. Ihre Grenzgeb.

SW/0021-1915
**ISOTOPENPRAXIS.** [Isotopenpraxis]. Vol. 1 (1965)-. Academic Scholarly Publication. English. qt (2 volumes). $202.00 (academic institutions), $314.00 (corporate institutions). Gordon & Breach Science Publishers, PO Box 90, Reading RG1 8JL England. **Tel** 011 44 734 560080, FAX 011 44 734 568211. **(Subscription address:** International Publishers Distributor at one of the following addresses: 820 Town Center Drive, Langhorne, PA 19047; or PO Box 90, Reading Berkshire RG1 8JL UK; or Kent Ridge PO Box 1180, Singapore 9111, Republic of Singapore) **DD** 621. **NLM** W1 IS579. **CODEN** IPRXA9. **[CCC]. Pr Rev.** Documents available from The Genuine Article, CASDDS.
**Ind/Abst** Anal. Abstr.; Art Archaeol. Tech. Abstr.; Chem. Abstr.; Chem. Titles; Coal Abstr.; Curr. Contents Phys. Chem. Earth Sci.; EMBASE; INIS Atomindex [Micro.]; Mass Spect. Bull.; Res. Alert [Full Cov.]; Sci. Cit. Index; SCISEARCH.

RU/0202-7933
**ITOGI NAUKI I TEHNIKI - VSESOJUZNYJ INSTITUT NA UCNOJ I TEHNICESKOJ INFORMACII, SERIJA FIZIKA PLAZMY.** (ITOGI NAUKI I TEKHNIKI. SERIIA FIZIKA PLAZMY / GOSUDARSTVENNYI KOMITET SSSR PO NAUKE I

TEKHNIKE, AKADEMIIA NAUK SSSR, VSESOIUZNYI INSTITUT NAUCHNOI I TEKHNICHESKOI INFORMATSII.). [Itogi nauki teh. - Vses. inst. naucn. teh. inf., Ser. fiz. plazmy]. **Added/Corp** Vsesoiuznyi Institut Nauchnoi i Tekhnicheskoi Informatsii (Soviet Union). **VFOAT** Seriia Fizika Plazmy; Fizika Plazmy; Itogi Nauki i Tekhniki. Fizika Plazmy. Vol. 1, Ch. 1 (1980)-. Periodical. Russian. VINITI - Vsesoyuznyi Institut Nauchno-Tekhnicheskoi Informatsii, All-Union Scientific and Technical Information Institute, Baltiiskaia Ulitsa 14, 125219 Moscow Russia. **Tel** 238-46-00, FAX 9430060, telex 411160. **(Subscription address:** V/O Mezhdunarodnaya Kniga, 113095 Dimitrova Ul 39, Moscow USSR**)** **LC** QC717.6; .I87.
**Ind/Abst** Int. Aerosp. Abstr.

AI
**IZVESTIIA AKADEMII NAUK ARMENII. FIZIKA.** **Added/Corp** Hayastani Gitutyunneri Akademia. **VFOAT** Fizika; Gitutyunner Erkri Masin; Hayastani Gitutyunneri Akademiayi Teghekagir. Gitutyunner Erkri Masin. (19??)-. Periodical. Russian (summaries and/or abstracts in Armenian and English). bm. **LC** IN PROCESS. **CODEN** IAAFE7. ***Continues*** *Izvestiia Akademii Nauk Armianskoi SSR. Fizika, 0002-3035.*

●RU
**IZVESTIIA AKADEMII NAUK. FIZIKA ATMOSFERY I OKEANA / ROSSIISKAIA AKADEMIIA NAUK.** **Added/Corp** Rossiiskaia Akademiia Nauk. **VFOAT** Fizika Atmosfery i Okeana; Atmospheric and Oceanic Physics; Izvestiya of Academy of Sciences. Atmospheric and Oceanic Physics. (1992)-. Academic Scholarly Publication. Russian (summaries and/or abstracts in English; table of contents in English). Six times a year. $216.00. Izdatelstvo Nauka / Akademiia Nauk, Publishing House of the Russian Academy of Sciences, Leninskii Porspekt 14, 117901 Moscow Russia. **Tel** 011 95 954-21-53, FAX 011 95 938-21-44, telex 411964. **(Subscription address:** East View Publications Inc., 3020 Harbor Lane North, Suite 110, Minneapolis MN 55447.**)** **CODEN** IAKOEG. Documents available from The Genuine Article. ***Continues*** *Izvestiia Akademii Nauk SSSR. Fizika Atmosfery i Okeana, 0002-3515.*
**Ind/Abst** Aquat. Sci. Fish. Abstr. (Computer File); Ocean. Abstr.; Res. Alert [Full Cov.]; Sci. Cit. Index; SCISEARCH.

KG
**IZVESTIIA AKADEMII NAUK RESPUBLIKI KYRGYZSTAN. FIZIKO-TEKHNICHESKIE, MATEMATICHESKIE I GORNO-GEOLOGICHESKIE NAUKI.**
**Added/Corp** Kyrgyz Respublikasy Ilimder Akademiiasy. **VFOAT** Fiziko-Tekhnicheskie, Matematicheskie i Gorno-Geologicheskie Nauki; Fizika-Tekhnikalyk, Matematika Zhana Too-Geologiia Ilimderi; Physics-Technical Sciences, Mathematics and Geology; Kyrgyz Respublikasy Ilimder Akademiiasynyn Kabarlary. Fizika-Tekhnikalyk, Matematika Zhana Too-Geologiia Ilimderi; Proceedings of the Kyrghyzstan Academy of Sciences. Physics-Technical Sciences, Mathematics and Geology. No. 1 (1991)-. Periodical. Russian (table of contents in English and Kirghiz). qt. ***Continues*** *Izvestiia Akademii Nauk Kirgizskoi SSR. Fiziko-Tekhnicheskie i Matematicheskie Nauki, 0235-0076.*

●RU
**IZVESTIIA AKADEMII NAUK. SERIIA FIZICHESKAIA / ROSSIISKAIA AKADEMIIA NAUK.** **Added/Corp** Rossiiskaia Akademiia Nauk. **VFOAT** Seriia Fizicheskaia; Izvestiia Rossiiskoi Akademii Nauk. Seriia Fizicheskaia; Izvestiia RAN. Seriia Fizicheskaia. Vol. 56 (Feb. 1992)-. Academic Scholarly Publication. Russian (table of contents in English). mo. $375.00. Izdatelstvo Nauka / Akademiia Nauk, Publishing House of the Russian Academy of Sciences, Leninskii Porspekt 14, 117901 Moscow Russia. **Tel** 011 95 954-21-53, FAX 011 95 938-21-44, telex 411964. **(Subscription address:** East View Publications Inc., 3020 Harbor Lane North, Suite 110, Minneapolis MN 55447.**)** **LC** AS262; .A62455. **CODEN** IRAFEO. Documents available from Ask*IEEE, CASDDS. ***Continues*** *Izvestiia Akademii Nauk SSSR. Seriia Fizicheskaia, 0367-6765.*
**Ind/Abst** Chem. Abstr. (1992-); Energy Res. Abstr. (1992-); GeoRef (1992-); INSPEC (1992-); Int. Aerosp. Abstr. (1992-); Met. Abstr. (1992-).

RU/0002-3337
**IZVESTIIA AKADEMII NAUK SSSR. FIZIKA ZEMLI.** ***Title Change.*** [Izv. Akad. nauk SSSR, Fiz. zemli]. **Added/Corp** Akademiia Nauk SSSR. **VFOAT** Fizika Zemli. (1965-1992). Academic Scholarly Publication. Russian (table of contents in English). mo. **(Subscription address:** Victor Kamkin, 4956 Boiling Brook Parkway, Rockville MD 20852.**)** **LC** QC801; .A357. **CODEN** IAFZAK. **[CCC]. Pr Rev.** Documents available from The Genuine Article, Ask*IEEE, Petroleum Abstracts Document Delivery Service, CASDDS. ***Continues in part*** *Izvestiia Akademii Nauk SSSR. Seriia Geofizicheskaia, 0568-5311.* ***Continued by*** *Izvestiia Akademii Nauk. Fizika Zemli.*
**Ind/Abst** Chem. Abstr.; Ei Page One; Energy Res. Abstr.; INSPEC (1968-); Int. Aerosp. Abstr.; Math. Rev.; Pet. Abstr.; Res. Alert [Full Cov.]; Sci. Cit. Index (19??-19??); SCISEARCH.

TK
**IZVESTIIA AKADEMII NAUK TURKMENISTANA. SERIIA FIZIKO-MATEMATICHESKIKH, TEKHNICHESKIKH, KHIMICHESKIKH I GEOLOGICHESKIKH NAUK.** **Added/Corp** Turkmenistan Ylymlar Akademiiasy. **VFOAT** Seriia Fiziko-Matematicheskikh, Tekhnicheskikh, Khimicheskikh i Geologicheskikh Nauk; Fizika-Matematiki, Tekhniki, Khimiki ve Geologik Ylymlaryng Seriiasy; Turkmenistan Ylymlar Akademiiasynyng Khabarlary. Fizika-Matematiki, Tekhniki, Khimiki ve Geologik Ylymlaryng Seriiasy. (199?)-. Periodical. Russian (summaries and/or abstracts in English). Four times a year. $119.95. **(Subscription address:** East View Publications Inc., 3020 Harbor Lane North, Suite 110, Minneapolis MN 55447.**)** **LC** QC1; .A42823. ***Continues*** *Izvestiia Akademii Nauk Turkmenskoi SSR. Seriia Fiziko-Matematicheskikh, Tekhnicheskikh, Khimicheskikh i Geologicheskikh Nauk.*

TK
**IZVESTIIA AKADEMII NAUK TURKMENSKOI SSR. SERIIA FIZIKO-MATEMATICHESKIKH, TEKHNICHESKIKH, KHIMICHESKIKH I GEOLOGICHESKIKH NAUK.** ***Title Change.*** **Added/Corp** Turkmenistan SSR Ylymlar Akademiiasy. **VFOAT** Fizika-Matematika, Tekhnika, Khimiia ve Geologiia Ylymlarynyng seriiasy; Seriia Fiziko-Matematicheskikh, Tekhnicheskikh, Khimicheskikh i Geologicheskikh nauk; Turkmenistan SSR Ylymlar Akademiiasynyng Khabarlary. Fiziko-Matematika, Tekhnika, Khimiia ve Geologiia Ylymlarynyng Seriiasy. (1991)-(199?). Periodical. Russian. bm. ***Continues*** *Izvestiia Akademii Nauk Turkmenskoi SSR. Seriia Fiziko-Tekhnicheskikh, Khimicheskikh i Geologicheskikh Nauk, 0002-3507.* ***Continued by*** *Izvestiia Akademii Nauk Turkmenistana. Seriia Fiziko-Matematicheskikh, Tekhnicheskikh, Khimicheskikh i Geologicheskikh Nauk.*

UZ/0131-8012
**IZVESTIIA AKADEMII NAUK UZSSR. SERIIA FIZIKO-MATEMATICHESKIKH NAUK.** **Added/Corp** Uzbekiston SSR Fanlar Akademiiasi. **VFOAT** Seriia Fiziko-Matematicheskikh Nauk; UzSSR Fanlar Akademiiasining Akhboroti; Fizika-Matematika Fanlari Seriiasi; UzSSR Fanlar Akademiiasining Akhboroti. Fizika-Matematika Fanlari Seriiasi. (1957)-. Periodical. Russian (summaries and/or abstracts in Uzbek; table of contents in Uzbek). bm. **(Subscription address:** Victor Kamkin, 4956 Boiling Brook Parkway, Rockville MD 20852.**)** **LC** QC1.A449; A2. **CODEN** IUZFAU. Documents available from CASDDS. ***Continues in part*** *Izvestiia Akademii Nauk UzSSR.*
**Ind/Abst** Chem. Abstr.

RU
**IZVESTIIA. SERIIA FIZICHESKAIA.**
**Main/Corp** Akademiia Nauk SSSR. Vol. 1 (1936)-. Periodical. Multiple languages (Russian, English, French and German). mo. $139.00. **(Subscription address:** Victor Kamkin, 4956 Boiling Brook Parkway, Rockville, MD 20852**)** **LC** AS262; .A62455. Documents available from Ask*IEEE.
**Ind/Abst** Index Med.; INSPEC (1968-).

●RU
**IZVESTIIA SORAN. SIBIRSKII FIZIKO-TEKHNICHESKII ZHURNAL.**
**Added/Corp** Rossiiskaia Akademiia Nauk. Sibirskoe Otdelenie. **VFOAT** Sibirskii Fiziko-Tekhnicheskii Zhurnal; Izvestiia Sibirskogo Otdeleniia Rossiiskoi Akademii Nauk. Sibirskii Fiziko-Tekhnicheskii Zhurnal. (1992)-. Periodical. Russian. bm. ***Continues*** *Izvestiia So An SSSR. Sibirskii Fiziko-Tekhnicheskii Zhurnal.*

RU/0021-3411
**IZVESTIIA VYSSHIKH UCHEBNYKH ZAVEDENII. FIZIKA / MINISTERSTVO VYSSHEGO OBRAZOVANIIA SSSR.**
**Added/Corp** Soviet Union. Ministerstvo Vysshego Obrazovaniia. Soviet Union. Ministerstvo Vysshego i Srednego Spetsialnogo Obrazovaniia. **VFOAT** Fizika; Izvestiia Vuzov. Fizika; Izvestiia Vysshikh Uchebnykh Zavedenii Mv i SSO SSSR; ZIKA. (1957)-. Academic Scholarly Publication. Russian (Russian; table of contents in English). mo. $179.95. Izdatelstvo Tomskogo Universiteta / Tomsk State University, Prospekt Lenina 36, 634050 Tomsk Russia. **Tel** 23-44-65, FAX 22-24-66, telex 128258. **(Subscription address:** East View Publications Inc., 3020 Harbor Lane North, Suite 110, Minneapolis MN 55447.**)** **[CCC]. Pr Rev.** Documents available from The Genuine Article, Ask*IEEE, CASDDS. ***Absorbed in part*** *Nauchnye Doklady Vyssehi Shkoly. Fiziko-Matematicheskie Nauki.*
**Ind/Abst** Chem. Abstr.; INSPEC (1968-); Leadscan; Math. Rev.; Res. Alert [Full Cov.]; Sci. Cit. Index (19??-19??); SCISEARCH.

AI/0002-3035
**IZVESTIJA AKADEMII NAUK ARMJANSKOJ SSR. FIZIKA.** ***Title Change.*** (IZVESTIIA AKADEMII NAUK ARMIANSKOI SSR. FIZIKA.). [Izv. Akad. nauk Arm. SSR, Fiz.]. **Added/Corp** Haykakan SSR Gitutyunneri Akademia. Haykakan SSH Gitutyunneri Akademia. **VFOAT** Fizika; Haykakan SSR Gitutyunneri Akademiayi Teghekagir. Fizika; Haykakan SSH Gitutyunneri Akademiayi Teghekagir. Fizika. Vol. 1 (1966)-(19??). Periodical. Russian (summaries and/or abstracts in Armenian and English; table of contents in Armenian). bm. **CODEN** IAAFA3. Documents available from Ask*IEEE, CASDDS. ***Continues in part*** *Izvestiia Akademii Nauk Armianskoi SSR. Seriia Fiziko-Matematicheskikh Nauk.* ***Continued by*** *Izvestiia Akademii Nauk Armenii. Fizika.*
**Ind/Abst** Chem. Abstr. (?-?); INSPEC (1985-).

AJ/0002-3108
**IZVESTIJA AKADEMII NAUK AZERBAJDZANSKOJ SSR. SERIJA FIZIKO-TEHNICESKIH I MATEMATICESKIH NAUK.** ***Title Change.*** (IZVESTIIA AKADEMII NAUK AZERBAIDZHANSKOI SSR. SERIIA FIZIKO-TEKHNICHESKIKH I MATEMATICHESKIKH NAUK.). [Izv. Akad. nauk Azerb. SSR, Ser. fiz.-teh. mat. nauk]. **Added/Corp** Azarbaijan SSR Elmlar Akademiiasy. **VFOAT** Seriia Fiziko-Tekhnicheskikh i Matematicheskikh Nauk; Fizika-Tekhnika va Riiaziiiat Elmlari Seriiasy; Matematika, Fizika, Tekhnika; Riiaziiat, Fizika, Tekhnika; Azarbaijan SSR Elmlar Akademiiasynyn Khabarlari. Fizika-Tekhnika va Riiaziiiat Elmlari Seriiasy; Izvestiia. Matematika, Fizika, Tekhnika; Khabarlari. Riiaziiiat, Fizika, Tekhnika. (1964)-(19??). Periodical. Russian (summaries and/or abstracts in Azerbaijani and English; table of contents in Azerbaijani). bm. **CODEN** IAFMAF. **[CCC].** Documents available from Ask*IEEE, CASDDS. ***Continues*** *Izvestiia Akademii Nauk Azerbaidzhanskoi SSR. Seriia Fiziko-Matematicheskikh i Tekhnicheskikh Nauk.* ***Continued by*** *Izvestiia Akademii Nauk Azerbaidzhna. Seriia Fiziko-Tekhnicheskikh i Matematicheskikh Nauk.*
**Ind/Abst** Chem. Abstr. (?-?); INSPEC (1973-).

RU/0367-6765
**IZVESTIJA AKADEMII NAUK SSSR. SERIJA FIZICESKAJA.** ***Title Change.*** (IZVESTIIA AKADEMII NAUK SSSR. SERIIA FIZICHESKAIA.). [Izv. Akad. nauk SSSR. Ser. fiz.]. **Added/Corp** Akademiia Nauk SSSR. **VFOAT** Seriia Fizicheskaia. (1939)-Vol. 56, No. 1 (1992). Periodical. Russian (table of contents in English). mo. **(Subscription address:** Victor Kamkin, 4956 Boiling Brook Parkway, Rockville MD 20852.**)** **CODEN** IANFAY. **[CCC].** Documents available from The Genuine Article, Ask*IEEE, CASDDS. ***Continues*** *Izvestiia Akademii Nauk SSSR. Otdelenie Matematicheskikh i Estestvennykh Nauk. Seriia Fizicheskaia.* ***Continued by*** *Izvestiia Akademii nauk. Seriia Fizicheskaia.*
**Ind/Abst** Alum. Ind. Abstr. (?-1992); Ceram. Abstr. (19??-19??); Chem. Abstr. (-1992); Energy Res. Abstr. (July 1981-1992); GeoRef (?-1992); INSPEC (1968-1992); Int. Aerosp. Abstr. (-1992); Met. Abstr. (-1992); Res. Alert [Full Cov.]; Sci. Cit. Index (19??-19??); SCISEARCH.

NE
**JAARVERSLAG - TECHNISCH PHYSISCHE DIENST TNO-TH.** **Main/Corp** Nederlandse Centrale Organisatie voor. Dutch (English). an. Free. Technisch Physische Dienst Tno-th, Stieltjesweg 1, PO Box 155, 2600 AD Delft Netherlands. **Tel** (015)788020, telex 38091 TPD DT NL. **ED** A Verbraeck. **LC** QC1; .N44. **Circ:** 2,500 (ctrl). ***Continues*** *Nederlandse Centrale Organisatie voor Toegepast-Natuurwetenschappelijk Onderzoek. Technisch-Physische Dienst. Verslag.*
**Desc:** Report of activities.

GW
**JAHRESBERICHT / MAX-PLANCK-INSTITUT FUER PHYSIK UND ASTROPHYSIK, WERNER-HEISENBERG-INSTITUT FUER PHYSIK.** ***Title Change.*** **Main/Corp** Werner-Heisenberg-Institut fuer Physik. (19??)-(19??). German. an. Werner-Heisenberg-Institut fuer Physik, Fohringer Ring 6, W-8000 Munchen 40 Germany. **Tel** 011 89 323081, FAX 011 89 3225704. **LC** QC1; .W43a. **DD** 530/.05. ***Continued by*** *Jahresbericht / Max-Planck-Institut fuer Physik, Werner-Heisenberg-institut.*

GW
**JAHRESBERICHT / MAX-PLANCK-INSTITUT FUER PHYSIK, WERNER-HEISENBERG-INSTITUT.** (19??)-. German. an. Free. Werner-Heisenberg-Institut fuer Physik, Fohringer Ring 6, W-8000 Munchen 40 Germany. **Tel** 011 89 323081, FAX 011 89 3225704. **Circ:** 750. ***Continues*** *Jahresbericht / Max-Planck-Institut fuer Physik und Astrophysik, Werner-Heisenberg-institut fuer Physik.*

JA
**JAPANESE JOURNAL OF APPLIED PHYSICS. PART 1, REGULAR PAPERS & SHORT NOTES.** **Added/Corp** Nihon Butsuri Gakkai. Oyo Butsuri Gakkai. **VFOAT** Japanese Journal of Applied Physics. Part 1, P.Regular Papers, Short Notes, Review papers; Regular Papers & Short Notes; Regular Papers and Short Notes; Regular Papers, Short Notes & Review Papers; Regular Papers, Short Notes, and Review Papers. Vol. 21, No. 1 (Jan. 1982)-. Academic Scholarly Publication. English (French and German). mo. ¥85000 (part 1 only); ¥110000 (combined with part 2). Japanese Journal of Applied Physics, 24-8 Shinbashi 4-chome, Minato Tokyo 105 Japan. **Tel** FAX 81-3-3432-0728. **LC** QC1; .J28. **DD** 620/.005. **CODEN** JAPNDE. available on microfilm. Documents available from Article Express International, The Genuine Article, Ask*IEEE, CASDDS. ***Continues in part*** *Japanese Journal of Applied Physics, 0021-4922.*
**Desc:** Presents research information in the field of applied physics.
**Ind/Abst** Acoust. Abstr.; Alum. Ind. Abstr.; Bioeng. Abstr.; Ceram. Abstr. (19??-); Chem. Abstr.; Chem. Titles; Curr. Contents Phys. Chem. Earth Sci.; Ei Page One; Eng. Index Annu.; INSPEC (Jan. 1982-); Int. Aerosp. Abstr.; Mass Spect. Bull.; Met. Abstr.; Res. Alert [Full Cov.]; Sci. Cit. Index; SCISEARCH.

JA
**JAPANESE JOURNAL OF APPLIED PHYSICS. PART 2, LETTERS.** **Added/Corp** Nihon Butsuri Gakkai. Oyo Butsuri Gakkai. **VFOAT** JJAP Letters; J.J.A.P. Letters. Vol. 21, No. 1 (Jan. 1982)-. Academic Scholarly Publication. English (French and German). sm. ¥55000 (part 2 only); ¥110000 (combined with part 1). Japanese Journal of Applied Physics, 24-8 Shinbashi 4-chome, Minato Tokyo 105 Japan. **Tel** FAX 81-3-3432-0728. **LC** QC1; .J283. **DD** 620/.005. **CODEN** JAPLD8. available on microfilm (and microjacket). Documents available from Article Express International, The Genuine Article, Ask*IEEE, CASDDS. ***Continues*** *JJAP Letters, 0021-4922; J.J.A.P. Letters;* ***Continues in part*** *Japanese Journal of Applied Physics.*
**Desc:** Presents information in the field of applied physics.
**Ind/Abst** Acoust. Abstr.; Alum. Ind. Abstr.; Bioeng. Abstr.; Ceram. Abstr. (19??-); Chem. Abstr.; Chem. Titles; Curr. Contents Clin. Med.; Ei Page One; Eng. Mater. Abstr.; Eng. Index Annu.; INSPEC (Jan. 1982-); Int. Aerosp. Abstr.; Met. Abstr.; Res. Alert [Full Cov.]; Sci. Cit. Index; SCISEARCH.

JA
**JAPANESE JOURNAL OF APPLIED PHYSICS. SUPPLEMENT.** (197?)-. Monographic series. English. ir. Price varies per volume. Japanese Journal of Applied Physics, 24-8 Shinbashi 4-chome, Minato Tokyo 105 Japan. **Tel** FAX 81-3-3432-0728. **LC** UNC. Documents available from Ask*IEEE.
**Desc:** Presents the proceedings from international conferences in the field of applied physics and other features.
**Ind/Abst** INSPEC (1982-).

US/0021-3640
**JETP LETTERS.** [JETP lett.]. **Added/Corp** American Institute of Physics. **VFOAT** Soviet Physics. JETP. Letters to the Editor. Vol. 1 (April 1, 1965)-. Periodical. English (translations available in Russian). sm (24 issues). $1165.00 US; $1185.00 Canada, Mexico, Central and South America, and the Caribbean; $1200.00 other. American Institute of Physics, 500 Sunnyside Boulevard, Woodbury NY 11797-2999. **Tel** (516)576-2200, FAX (516)349-7669, telex 960983. **CODEN** JTPLA2. **[CCC].** Index available (bound in last issue). cum. index. **Pr Rev.** Documents available from Article Express International, The Genuine Article, Ask*IEEE, CASDDS.
**Ind/Abst** Acoust. Abstr.; Alum. Ind. Abstr.; Chem. Abstr.; Curr. Contents Phys. Chem. Earth Sci.; Ei Page One; Energy Res. Abstr.; Eng. Mater. Abstr.; Eng. Index Annu. [Select. Cov.]; INIS Atomindex [Micro.]; INSPEC (1968-); Int. Aerosp. Abstr.; Leadscan; Mass Spect. Bull.; Math. Rev.; Met. Abstr.; Res. Alert [Full Cov.]; Sci. Cit. Index; SCISEARCH; SPIN (1970-).

JA
**JJAP SERIES.** [JJAP ser.]. **VFOAT** Japanese Journal of Applied Physics Series. (1988)-. Monographic series. Multiple languages. ir. Price varies per volume. Japanese Journal of Applied Physics, 24-8 Shinbashi 4-chome, Minato Tokyo 105 Japan. **Tel** FAX 81-3-3432-0728.
**Desc:** Covers conferences, research group findings and other important academic documents.

FR/1155-4304
**JOURNAL DE PHYSIQUE. I (LES ULIS).** (JOURNAL DE PHYSIQUE. I : JP.). [J. phys., I]. **Added/Corp** Societe Francaise de Physique. Centre National de la Recherche Scientifique (France). **VFOAT** JP; Journal de Physique. 1; Journal de Physique. Un; General Physics, Statistical Physics, Condensed Matter, Cross-Disciplinary physics; Physique Generale, Physique Statistique, Matiere Condensee, Domaines Interdisciplinaires; Journal de Physique. I, General Physics, Statistical Physics, Condensed Matter, Cross-Disciplinary Physics; Journal de Physique. I, Physique Generale, Physique Statistique, Matiere Condensee, Domaines Interdisciplinaires. Vol. 1, No 1 (Jan. 1991)-. Periodical. English (French). mo. 3450.00F. Les Editions de Physique, 7 Avenue du Hoggar, Z.I. de Courtaboeuf - BP 112, 91944 les Ulis Cedex A France. **Tel** 011 33 1 69 07 36 88, FAX 011 33 1 69 28 84 91, telex EDITPHY 692321F. **LC** QC1; .J82. **DD** 530/.05. **CODEN** JPGCE8. Documents available from The Genuine Article, Ask*IEEE, CASDDS. ***Continues in part*** *Journal de Physique (Societe Francaise de Physique), 0302-0738.*
**Ind/Abst** Chem. Abstr. (19??-); Curr. Contents Phys. Chem. Earth Sci. (19??-); INSPEC (Jan. 1991-); Leadscan (19??-); Res. Alert (19??-) [Full Cov.]; Sci. Cit. Index (19??-); SCISEARCH.

FR/1155-4312
**JOURNAL DE PHYSIQUE. II (LES ULIS).** (JOURNAL DE PHYSIQUE. II : JP.). [J. phys., II]. **Added/Corp** Societe Francaise de Physique. Centre National de la Recherche Scientifique (France). **VFOAT** JP; Journal de Physique. 2; Journal de Physique. Deux; Atomic, Molecular, and Cluster Physics, Chemical Physics, Mechanics, and Hydrodynamics; Physique Aatomique et Moleculaire, Physico-Chimie, Mecanique et Hydrodynamique; Journal de Physique. II, Atomic, Molecular and Cluster Physics, Chemical Physics, Mechanics and Hydrodynamics; Journal de Physique. N.II, Physique Atomique et Moleculaire, Physico-Chimie, Mecanique et Hydrodynamique. Vol. 1 No 1 (Jan. 1991)-. Periodical. English (French and German; summaries and/or abstracts in French). mo. 3450.00F. Les Editions de Physique, 7 Avenue du Hoggar, Z.I. de Courtaboeuf - BP 112, 91944 les Ulis Cedex A France. **Tel** 011 33 1 69 07 36 88, FAX 011 33 1 69 28 84 91, telex EDITPHY 692321F. **LC** QC1; .J822. **DD** 530/.05. **CODEN** JPAHER. **[CCC].** Documents available from The Genuine Article, Ask*IEEE, CASDDS. ***Continues in part*** *Journal de Physique (Societe Francaise de Physique), 0302-0738.*
**Ind/Abst** Ceram. Abstr. (19??-); Chem. Abstr. (19??-); Curr. Contents Phys. Chem. Earth Sci. (19??-); INSPEC (Jan. 1991-); Res. Alert (19??-) [Full Cov.]; Sci. Cit. Index (19??-); SCISEARCH.

FR/1155-4320
**JOURNAL DE PHYSIQUE. III (LES ULIS).** (JOURNAL DE PHYSIQUE. III). [J. phys., III]. **Added/Corp** Centre National de la Recherche Scientifique (France) Societe Francais de Physique. **VFOAT** Journal de Physique N.III, Applied Physics, Materials Science, Fluids, Plasma and instrumentation; Applied Physics, Materials Science, Fluids, Plasma and Instrumentation.; Journal de Physique N.III, Physique Appliquee, Science des Materiaux, Fluides, Plasmas et Instrumentation; Physique Appliquee, Science des Materiaux, Fluides, Plasmas et Instrumentation. Vol. 1 No 1 (1991)-. Periodical. English (French). mo. 3650.00F. Les Editions de Physique, 7 Avenue du Hoggar, Z.I. de Courtaboeuf - BP 112, 91944 les Ulis Cedex A France. **Tel** 011 33 1 69 07 36 88, FAX 011 33 1 69 28 84 91, telex EDITPHY 692321F. **LC** QC1; .J823. **DD** 530/.05. **CODEN** JPAIEU. **[CCC].** Documents available from The Genuine Article, Ask*IEEE, CASDDS. ***Continues in part*** *Journal de Physique, 0302-0738;* ***Continues*** *Revue de Physique Appliquee, 0035-1687.*
**Ind/Abst** Ceram. Abstr. (19??-); Chem. Abstr. (19??-); Curr. Contents Phys. Chem. Earth Sci. (19??-); INSPEC (Jan. 1991-); Leadscan (19??-); Res. Alert (19??-) [Full Cov.]; Sci. Cit. Index (19??-); SCISEARCH (19??-).

FR/1155-4339
**JOURNAL DE PHYSIQUE. IV (LES ULIS).** (JOURNAL DE PHYSIQUE. IV : JP.). [J. phys., IV]. **Added/Corp** Societe Francaise de Physique. Centre National de la Recherche Scientifique (France). **VFOAT** JP; Journal de Physique. Quatre; JP IV; Journal de Physique IV. Vol. 1 (1991)-. Academic Scholarly Publication. English (summaries and/or abstracts in French). ir (8 to 10 issues/year). 5300.00F. Les Editions de Physique, 7 Avenue du Hoggar, Z.I. de Courtaboeuf - BP 112, 91944 les Ulis Cedex A France. **Tel** 011 33 1 69 07 36 88, FAX 011 33 1 69 28 84 91, telex EDITPHY 692321F. **LC** QC1; .J834. **CODEN** JPICEI. **[CCC].** Documents available from Article Express International, The Genuine Article, Ask*IEEE, CASDDS. ***Continues*** *Colloque de Physique, 0449-1947.*
**Ind/Abst** Bioeng. Abstr. (1991-); Chem. Abstr. (1991-); Curr. Contents Phys. Chem. Earth Sci. (19??-); Ei Page One (1991-); Energy Res. Abstr. (1991-); Eng. Index Annu. (1991-); Eng. Index Energy Abstr. (1991-); GeoRef (1991-); INSPEC (March 1991-); Nucl. Sci. Abstr. (1991-); Res. Alert (19??-) [Full Cov.]; Sci. Cit. Index (19??-); SCISEARCH (19??-).

US/0021-8944
**JOURNAL OF APPLIED MECHANICS AND TECHNICAL PHYSICS.** **See** Engineering-Mechanical Engineering and Machinery.

US/0021-8979
**JOURNAL OF APPLIED PHYSICS.** [J. appl. physi.]. **Added/Corp** American Institute of Physics. American Physical Society. Vol. 8 (Jan. 1937)-. Periodical. English. Twenty-four times a year. $1860.00 US; $1940.00 Canada, Mexico, Central and South America, and the Caribbean; $2050.00 other. American Institute of Physics, 500 Sunnyside Boulevard, Woodbury NY 11797-2999. **Tel** (516)576-2200, FAX (516)349-7669, telex 960983. **DD** 530. **NLM** W1 JO542E. **CODEN** JAPIAU. **[CCC].** Index available (free). available on microfiche. Documents available from Article Express International, The Genuine Article, Ask*IEEE, UMI Article Clearinghouse, CASDDS. ***Continues*** *Physics, 0148-6349.*
**Desc:** Devoted to general physics and its application to sciences and technology.
**Ind/Abst** Abstr. Bull. Inst. Pap. Sci. Tech.; Acoust. Abstr.; Alum. Ind. Abstr. (1970-); Appl. Sci. Technol. Index; Bioeng. Abstr.; Ceram. Abstr.; Chem. Abstr.; Chem. Titles; Coal Abstr. (1968-); Curr. Contents Phys. Chem. Earth Sci.; Curr. Phys. Index; Ei Page One (1973-); Energy Res. Abstr.; Eng. Mater. Abstr.; Eng. Index Annu. [Select. Cov.]; Fluid Abstr., Civil Eng.; Fluid Abstr. Proc. Eng.; FLUIDEX; GeoRef; HTFS Dig.; INIS Atomindex [Micro.]; INSPEC (1968-); Int. Aerosp. Abstr.; Leadscan; Mass Spect. Bull.; Met. Abstr.; Newsp. Period. Abstr. (1992-); Polymer Contents; Res. Alert [Full Cov.]; Sci. Cit. Index; SCISEARCH; SPIN; Surf. Treat. Technol. Abstr.; World Ceram. Abstr.; World Text. Abstr. (1968-).

US
**JOURNAL OF APPLIED PHYSICS. [MICROFICHE].** [J. appl. physi.]. **Added/Corp** American Institute of Physics. American Physical Society. Vol. 8 (Jan. 1937)-. Periodical. English. sm. $1860.00 (microfiche). American Institute of Physics, 500 Sunnyside Boulevard, Woodbury NY 11797-2999. **Tel** (516)576-2200, FAX (516)349-7669, telex 960983. **LC** Microfiche (o) 90/6082. available in print. ***Continues*** *Physics, 0148-6349.*
**Ind/Abst** Expand. Acad. Index (1992-).

US/0021-9606
**JOURNAL OF CHEMICAL PHYSICS, THE.** [J. chem. phys.]. **Added/Corp** American Institute of Physics. **VFOAT** Chemical Physics. Vol. 1 (Jan. 1933)-. Periodical. English. ir (48 issues). $2740.00 US; $2840.00 Canada, Mexico, Central and South America, and the Caribbean; $2990.00 other. American Institute of Physics, 500 Sunnyside Boulevard, Woodbury NY 11797-2999. **Tel** (516)576-2200, FAX (516)349-7669, telex 960983. **LC** QD1; .J94. **DD** 541.05. **NLM** W1 JO581J. **CODEN** JCPSA6. **[CCC].** Index available (free). **Pr Rev.** available on microfilm and microfiche (16mm or 35mm). Documents available from Article Express International, The Genuine Article, Ask*IEEE, Petroleum Abstracts Document Delivery Service, CASDDS.
**Ind/Abst** Abstr. Bull. Inst. Pap. Sci. Tech.; Acoust. Abstr.; AQUAREF; Ceram. Abstr.; Chem Inform; Chem. Abstr.; Chem. Titles; Curr. Contents Phys. Chem. Earth Sci.; Curr. Phys. Index; Ei Page One; Energy Res. Abstr.; Eng. Index Annu. [Select. Cov.]; GeoRef; HTFS Dig.; INIS Atomindex [Micro.]; INSPEC (1968-); Int. Aerosp. Abstr.; Mass Spect. Bull.; Math. Rev.; Pet. Abstr.; Proc. Chem. Eng.; Ref. Upd. Deluxe Ed.; Res. Alert [Full Cov.]; Sci. Cit. Index; SCISEARCH; Soils Fert.; SPIN (1968-); Surf. Treat. Technol. Abstr.; Theoret. Chem. Eng.; World Ceram. Abstr.

US/0730-2886
**JOURNAL OF CLASSICAL PHYSICS, THE.** [J. cl. phys.]. **Added/Corp** Institute of Classical Physics. Vol. 1, Pt. 1 (Jan. 1982)-. Periodical. English. Twice a year (Jan., June). $25.00 membership. Institute of Classical Physics, 48 31 45th Street, Room 5, New York NY 11377. **LC** QC1; .J84. **DD** 530/.05.

US/0021-9991
**JOURNAL OF COMPUTATIONAL PHYSICS.** [J. comput. phys.]. Vol. 1 (Aug. 1966)-. Academic Scholarly Publication. English. Fourteen times a year. $1530.00 US and Canada; $1828.00 other. Academic Press, Inc., 6277 Sea Harbor Drive, Orlando FL 32887. **Tel** (800)543-9534, (407)345-4100, FAX (407)363-9661. **ED** Berni J. Alder, John B. Bell, Gerald W. Hedstrom, Kenneth D. Marx and Arthur A. Mirin. **LC** QC20; .J64. **DD** 530.15. **CODEN** JCTPAH. **[CCC].** **Pr Rev.** Documents available from The Genuine Article, Ask*IEEE, CASDDS.
**Desc:** Treats the computational aspects of physical problems, emphasizing techniques involved in the numerical solution of mathematical equations and in automated data reduction over the physical significance of the solutions to these problems.
**Ind/Abst** ACM Guide Comput. Lit.; Chem. Abstr.; Compumath Citation Index [Full Cov.]; Comput. Rev.; Curr. Contents Phys. Chem. Earth Sci.; Energy Res. Abstr.; GeoRef; HTFS Dig.; INIS Atomindex [Micro.]; INSPEC (1968-); Int. Aerosp. Abstr.; Math. Rev.; Res. Alert [Full Cov.]; Sci. Cit. Index; SCISEARCH; SPIN (1977-); Zentralbl. Math. Ihre Grenzgeb.

US/1068-3372
**JOURNAL OF CONTEMPORARY PHYSICS.** (JOURNAL OF CONTEMPORARY PHYSICS / ARMENIAN ACADEMY OF SCIENCES.). [J. contemp. phys.]. **Added/Corp** Hayastani Gitutyunneri Akademia. Vol. 26, No. 1 (1991)-. Periodical. English (translations available in Russian). Six times a year. $660.00. Allerton Press, Inc., 150 Fifth Avenue, New York NY 10011. **Tel** (212)924-3950, FAX (212)463-9684, telex 427441 ALPRES. **LC** QC1; .I97. **DD** 530/.05. **[CCC].** ***Continues*** *Izvestiia Akademii Nauk Armianskoi SSR. Fizika. English. Soviet Journal of Contemporary Physics, 8755-4585.*

●US/1062-0125
**JOURNAL OF ENGINEERING PHYSICS AND THERMOPHYSICS.** [J. eng. phys. thermophys.]. **Added/Corp** Consultants Bureau. Vol. 62, No. 1 (Jan. 1992)-. Academic Scholarly Publication. English (translations available in Russian). mo. $1330.00 US; $1555.00 other. Consultants Bureau, A Division of Plenum Publishing Corporation, 233 Spring Street, New York NY 10013. **Tel** (212)620-8000, (212)620-8466, FAX (212)463-0742, telex 23/421139. **DD** 536. **CODEN** JEPTER. **[CCC].** Documents available from Article Express International, Ask*IEEE, CASDDS. ***Continues*** *Journal of Engineering Physics, 0022-0841.*
**Ind/Abst** Appl. Mech. Rev.; Bioeng. Abstr.; Chem. Abstr.; Ei Page One; Eng. Index Annu.; Eng. Index Energy Abstr.; Fluid Abstr., Civil Eng.; Fluid Abstr. Proc. Eng.; FLUIDEX; INIS Atomindex [Micro.]; INSPEC; Int. Aerosp. Abstr.; ISMEC Mech. Eng. Abstr.; Math. Rev.

●US/1063-7761
**JOURNAL OF EXPERIMENTAL AND THEORETICAL PHYSICS.** [J. exp. theor. phys.]. **Added/Corp** American Institute of Physics. **VFOAT** JETP. Vol. 76, No. 1 (Jan. 1993)-. Periodical. English (translations available in Russian). mo. $2375.00 US; $2395.00 Canada, Mexico, Central and South America, and the Caribbean; $2430.00 other. American Institute of Physics, 500 Sunnyside Boulevard, Woodbury NY 11797-2999. **Tel** (516)576-2200, FAX (516)349-7669, telex 960983. **LC** QC1; .Z472. **DD** 530.5. **CODEN** JTPHES. **[CCC].** Index available (bound in last issue). Documents available from Ask*IEEE. ***Continues*** *Soviet Physics, JETP, 0038-5646.*
**Ind/Abst** Alum. Ind. Abstr.; Curr. Phys. Index; Energy Res. Abstr.; INSPEC; Int. Aerosp. Abstr.; Math. Rev.; Met. Abstr.; Pollut. Abstr. Indexes; SPIN.

NE/0393-0440
**JOURNAL OF GEOMETRY AND PHYSICS.** **VFOAT** Geometry and Physics; JGP. Vol. 1, No. 1 (1984)-. Academic Scholarly Publication. English (French). Twelve times a year (3 volumes). Fl1053.00. Elsevier Science Publishers BV, PO Box 211, 1000 AE Amsterdam Netherlands. **Tel** 011 31 20 5803642, FAX 011 31 20 5862696, telex 15682. **ED** M. Modugno. **CODEN** JGPHE5. **[CCC].** Documents available from Ask*IEEE.
**Desc:** Strives to stimulate the interaction between geometry and physics by publishing primary research, feature and review articles which are of common interest to practitioners in both fields.
**Ind/Abst** INSPEC (Feb. 1992-); Math. Rev. (1984-); Zentralbl. Math. Ihre Grenzgeb.

●US/1070-2458
**JOURNAL OF GROUP THEORY IN PHYSICS.** (JOURNAL OF GROUP THEORY IN PHYSICS : JGTP.). **VFOAT** JGTP. (1993)-. Periodical. English. Four times a year. $315.00. Nova Science Publishers Inc., 6080 Jericho Turnpike, Suite 207, Commack NY 11725-2808. **Tel** (516)499-3103, (516)499-3106, FAX (516)499-3146.

US/0022-1481
**JOURNAL OF HEAT TRANSFER.** **See** Engineering.

FR
**JOURNAL OF HIGH TEMPERATURE CHEMICAL PROCESSES.** (19??)-. Periodical. English (French). bm. 1250.00F. Les Editions de Physique, 7 Avenue du Hoggar, Z.I. de Courtaboeuf - BP 112, 91944 les Ulis Cedex A France. **Tel** 011 33 1 69 07 36 88, FAX 011 33 1 69 28 84 91, telex EDITPHY 692321F.

NE/0928-0219
**JOURNAL OF INVERSE AND ILL-POSED PROBLEMS.** **See** Mathematics.

US/0022-2291
**JOURNAL OF LOW TEMPERATURE PHYSICS.** [J. low temp. phys.]. Vol. 1 (Feb. 1969)-. Periodical. English. Twenty-four times a year. $955.00 US; $1,165.00 other. Plenum Press, 233 Spring Street, New York NY 10013-1578. **Tel** (212)620-8000, (800)221-9369, FAX (212)463-0742, (212)807-1047, telex 23/421139. **ED** John G. Daunt and John P. Harrison. **LC** QC278; .J68. **DD** 536/.56/05. **CODEN** JLTPAC. **[CCC].** Index available. **Pr Rev.** available on microfilm and microfiche from University Microfilms International (UMI). Documents available from Article Express International, The Genuine Article, Ask*IEEE, CASDDS.
**Desc:** An international medium for the publication of original papers on fundamental, theoretical and experimental research in ion temperature physics.
**Ind/Abst** Alum. Ind. Abstr.; Appl. Mech. Rev.; Bioeng. Abstr.; Chem. Abstr.; Chem. Titles; Curr. Contents Phys. Chem. Earth Sci.; Ei Page One; Energy Res. Abstr.; Eng. Mater. Abstr.; Eng. Index Annu.; INIS Atomindex [Micro.]; INSPEC (Oct. 1969-); Int. Aerosp. Abstr.; Leadscan; Met. Abstr.; Pollut. Abstr. Indexes; Res. Alert [Full Cov.]; Sci. Cit. Index; SCISEARCH; SPIN (1977-).

US/0022-2348
**JOURNAL OF MACROMOLECULAR SCIENCE. PHYSICS.** [J. macromol sci., Phys.]. Vol. B1, No. 2 (Aug. 1967)-. Academic Scholarly Publication. English. qt. $635.00 US; $649.00 other. Marcel Dekker Inc., 270 Madison Avenue, New York NY 10016. **Tel** (212)696-9000, (800)228-1160, FAX (212)685-4540, telex 421419. **(Subscription address:** Marcel Dekker Inc, PO Box 5017, Monticello NY 12701.**) ED** Phillip H. Geil, R. Bonart, M. Takayanagi and I. M. Ward. **LC** QD380; .J68. **DD** 547.7. **CODEN** JMAPBR. **[CCC].** Index available. **Ad Acc. Pr Rev.** available in microform. Documents available from Article Express International, The Genuine Article, BIOSIS Document Express, Ask*IEEE, CASDDS. ***Continues*** *Journal of Macromolecular Science. Part B, Physics, 0022-2348.*
**Desc:** An international journal devoted to the publication of significant fundamental contributions to the physics of macromolecular solids and liquids. Besides all of the areas generally included in polymer solid state physics, this authoritative journal contains papers reporting research in transition mechanisms and structure property relationships, the physics of polymer solutions and melts, of glassy and rubbery amorphous solids, and the physics of individual polymer molecules and natural polymers. In addition, new instruments and techniques appropriate to polymer physics and short descriptions of new data are critically noted.
**Ind/Abst** Bioeng. Abstr. (1967-); Biol. Abstr. (1967-); Chem. Abstr. (1967-); Curr. Contents Phys. Chem. Earth Sci.; Ei Page One (1967-); Eng. Index Annu.; Eng. Index Energy Abstr. (1967-); INIS Atomindex [Micro.]; INSPEC (1967-); Int. Aerosp. Abstr. (1967-); Nucl. Sci. Abstr.; Res. Alert [Full Cov.]; Sci. Cit. Index; SCISEARCH.

Il/0047-2557
**JOURNAL OF MATHEMATICAL AND PHYSICAL SCIENCES.** **See** Mathematics.

US/0022-2488
**JOURNAL OF MATHEMATICAL PHYSICS.** [J. math. phys.]. **Added/Corp** American Institute of Physics. Vol. 1 (Jan./Feb. 1960)-. Academic Scholarly Publication. English. mo. $1310.00 US; $1340.00 Canada, Mexico, Central and South America and the Caribbean; $1385.00 other. American Institute of Physics, 500 Sunnyside Boulevard, Woodbury NY 11797-2999. **Tel** (516)576-2200, FAX (516)349-7669, telex 960983. **LC** QC20; .J65. **CODEN** JMAPAQ. **[CCC].** Index available (free). **Pr Rev.** available on microfilm. Documents available from The Genuine Article, BIOSIS Document Express, Ask*IEEE, CASDDS.
**Desc:** Provides a unique link for specialists.
**Ind/Abst** Biol. Abstr.; Chem. Abstr.; Compumath Citation Index [Full Cov.]; Curr. Contents Phys. Chem. Earth Sci.; Curr. Phys. Index; Energy Res. Abstr.; INIS Atomindex [Micro.]; INSPEC (1968-); Int. Aerosp. Abstr.; Math. Rev.; Pollut. Abstr. Indexes; Res. Alert [Full Cov.]; Sci. Cit. Index; SCISEARCH; SPIN (1970-); Zentralbl. Math. Ihre Grenzgeb.

UK/0960-1317
**JOURNAL OF MICROMECHANICS AND MICROENGINEERING : STRUCTURES, DEVICES, AND SYSTEMS.** **See** Engineering-Electricity, Electrical Engineering, Electronics.

US/0047-2689
**JOURNAL OF PHYSICAL AND CHEMICAL REFERENCE DATA.** [J. phys. chem. ref. data]. **Added/Corp** American Chemical Society. American Institute of Physics. United States. National Bureau of Standards. Vol. 1 (1972)-. English. Six times a year. $510.00 (institution) US. American Chemical Society, 1155 Sixteenth Street Northwest, Washington DC 20036. **Tel** (800)333-9511, (800)227-5558, (614)447-3776, FAX (202)833-7736. **(Subscription address:** American Chemical Society / Ohio, Department L 0011, Columbus OH 43268-0011.**) ED** David R. Lide, Jr. **LC** Q199; .J68. **DD** 530/.021/2. **NLM** W1 JO832K. **CODEN** JPCRBU. **[CCC].** (free). cum. index. **Pr Rev. Acid Free. Circ:** 1,000. available on microfiche. Documents available from The Genuine Article, Ask*IEEE, CASDDS.
**Desc:** Compilations and reviews produced under NSRDS at the NBS. Covers chemical kinetics, thermodynamics, physical properties, molecular structure, spectroscopy, etc. Bound reprints of each compilation.
**Ind/Abst** Appl. Sci. Technol. Index (?-1990); Ceram. Abstr.; Chem. Abstr.; Curr. Contents Phys. Chem. Earth Sci.; Curr. Phys. Index; Energy Res. Abstr. (Aug. 1972-); Eng. Mater. Abstr.; HTFS Dig.; INSPEC (1973-); Mass Spect. Bull.; Res. Alert [Select. Cov.]; SCISEARCH; Soils Fert.; SPIN (1974-).

UK/0305-4470
**JOURNAL OF PHYSICS. A : MATHEMATICAL AND GENERAL.** [J. phys. A]. **Added/Corp** Institute of Physics (Great Britain). Vol. 8 (Jan. 1975)-. Periodical. English. Twenty-four times a year. $1,975.00. Institute of Physics, Techno House, Redcliffe Way, Bristol BS1 6NX England. **Tel** 011 44 272 297481, FAX 011 44 272 294318, telex 449149 INSTP G. **(Subscription address:** American Institute of Physics, Publishing Sales, 500 Sunnyside Blvd., Woodbury NY 11797.**) ED** D Sherrington. **LC** QC1; .J8474. **DD** 530/.05. **NLM** W1 JO836RB. **CODEN** JPHAC5. **[CCC].** Index available (bound in last issue). available on microfiche; available on microfilm. Documents available from Article Express International, The Genuine Article, Ask*IEEE, CASDDS. ***Supersedes in part*** *Journal of Physics A. Mathematical, Nuclear and General, 0301-0015.* ***Continued in part by*** *Classical and Quantum Gravity.*
**Desc:** Concerned with the development of mathematical and computational methods in physics and with their fundamental applications, particularly in classical mechanics, chaotic and complex systems, quantum mechanics of particles and fields, statistical physics and random systems.
**Ind/Abst** Acoust. Abstr.; Ceram. Abstr.; Chem. Abstr.; Ei Page One; Eng. Index Annu.; GeoRef; HTFS Dig.; INSPEC (1975-); Int. Aerosp. Abstr.; Math. Rev.; Res. Alert [Full Cov.]; Sci. Cit. Index; SCISEARCH; World Ceram. Abstr.; Zentralbl. Math. Ihre Grenzgeb.

UK/0022-3697
**JOURNAL OF PHYSICS AND CHEMISTRY OF SOLIDS, THE.** [J. phys. chem. solids]. Vol. 24 (1963)-. Periodical. English (French and German). mo. $1796.00 The Americas; £1205.00 other. Pergamon Press, An Imprint of Elsevier Science Ltd., The Boulevard, Langford Lane, Kidlington, Oxford OX5 1GB United Kingdom. **Tel** 011 44 865 843000, 011 44 865 843699, FAX 011 44 865 843010. **(Subscription address:** Elsevier Science Ltd. Oxford Fulfillment Centre, PO Box 800, Kidlington, Oxford OX5 1DX United Kingdom.**) ED** David E. Cox, George Sawatzky, Robert Shelton, Yasuhiko Fujii. **LC** QC176.A1; J6. **NLM** W1 JO836S. **CODEN** JPCSAW. **[CCC].** available on microfilm from Microfilms International Marketing Corp.; available on microfilm and microfiche from University Microfilms International (UMI); available on microfiche from the publisher. Documents available from Article Express International, The Genuine Article, Ask*IEEE, CASDDS. ***Continues*** *Physics and Chemistry of Solids.* ***Superseded in part by*** *Solid State Communications, 0038-1098.*
**Desc:** International medium for publication of research in condensed matter and materials science. Emphasis is placed on experimental and theoretical work which contributes to a basic understanding of and new insight into the properties and behavior of condensed matter.
**Ind/Abst** Alum. Ind. Abstr.; Bioeng. Abstr.; Ceram. Abstr.; Chem. Abstr.; Curr. Contents Phys. Chem. Earth Sci.; Ei Page One; Energy Res. Abstr.; Eng. Mater. Abstr.; Eng. Index Annu. [Select. Cov.]; GeoRef; INIS Atomindex [Micro.]; INSPEC (1968-); Int. Aerosp. Abstr.; Mass Spect. Bull.; Met. Abstr.; Res. Alert [Full Cov.]; Sci. Cit. Index; SCISEARCH; Soc. Sci. Cit. Index [Select. Cov.]; World Ceram. Abstr.

UK/0953-4075
**JOURNAL OF PHYSICS. B : ATOMIC, MOLECULAR, AND OPTICAL PHYSICS.** **Added/Corp** Institute of Physics (Great Britain) American Institute of Physics. **VFOAT** Atomic, Molecular, and Optical Physics. Vol. 21, No. 1 (Jan. 14, 1988)-. Periodical. English. sm. $1,607.00. Institute of Physics, Techno House, Redcliffe Way, Bristol BS1 6NX England. **Tel** 011 44 272 297481, FAX 011 44 272 294318, telex 449149 INSTP G. **(Subscription address:** American Institute of Physics, Publishing Sales, 500 Sunnyside Blvd., Woodbury NY 11797.**) ED** J P Connerade. **LC** QC770; .J67. **DD** 539/.05. **NLM** W1; JO836UD. **[CCC].** Index available (bound in last issue). **Pr Rev.** available on microfilm and microfiche. Documents available from Article Express International, The Genuine Article, Ask*IEEE. ***Continues*** *Journal of Physics. B: Atomic and Molecular Physics, 0022-3700.*
**Desc:** The study of atoms, ions, molecules or clusters, their structure and their interactions with particles, photons or fields; also those aspects of spectroscopy, quantum optics and non-linear optics, maser and laser physics, astrophysics, plasma physics, surface physics and other investigations where the objects of study are the elementary atomic, ionic or molecular properties or processes.
**Ind/Abst** Ei Page One; Eng. Index Annu. [Select. Cov.]; INSPEC (Jan. 1988-); Leadscan; Mass Spect. Bull.; Res. Alert [Full Cov.]; Sci. Cit. Index; SCISEARCH; World Ceram. Abstr.

UK/0953-8984
**JOURNAL OF PHYSICS. CONDENSED MATTER : AN INSTITUTE OF PHYSICS JOURNAL.** [J. phys., Condens. matter]. **Added/Corp** Institute of Physics (Great Britain) American Institute of Physics. **VFOAT** Condensed Matter. Vol. 1, No. 1 (Jan. 9, 1989)-. Academic Scholarly Publication. English (French and German). Fifty times a year. $3,212.00. Institute of Physics, Techno House, Redcliffe Way, Bristol BS1 6NX England. **Tel** 011 44 272 297481, FAX 011 44 272 294318, telex 449149 INSTP G. **(Subscription address:** American Institute of Physics, Publishing Sales, 500 Sunnyside Blvd., Woodbury NY 11797.**) ED** R A Cowley. **LC** QC173.4.C65; J68. **CODEN** JCOMEL. **[CCC].** Index available (bound in last issue). **Pr Rev.** available on microfiche (16mm or 35mm); available on microfilm (16mm or 35mm). Documents available from The Genuine Article, Ask*IEEE, CASDDS. ***Formed by the union of*** *Journal of Physics. C: Solid State Physics, 0305-4608* ***and*** *Journal of Physics. F: Metal Physics, 0022-3719.*
**Desc:** Reports experimental and theoretical studies of

the structural, thermal, mechanical, electrical, magnetic and optical properties of condensed matter, including crystals, quasicrystals and liquid crystals; amorphous and polymeric materials; alloys and metallic materials; liquids.
**Ind/Abst** Ceram. Abstr. (19??-); Chem. Abstr. (1989-); GeoRef; INSPEC (Jan. 1989-); Leadscan; Res. Alert [Full Cov.]; Sci. Cit. Index; SCISEARCH; World Ceram. Abstr.

UK/0022-3727
**JOURNAL OF PHYSICS. D : APPLIED PHYSICS.** [J. phys. D.]. **Added/Corp** Institute of Physics (Great Britain) Institute of Physics and the Physical Society. **VFOAT** Applied Physics. Vol. 3 (Jan. 1970)-. Periodical. English. mo. $900.00. Institute of Physics, Techno House, Redcliffe Way, Bristol BS1 6NX England. **Tel** 011 44 272 297481, FAX 011 44 272 294318, telex 449149 INSTP G. **(Subscription address:** American Institute of Physics, Publishing Sales, 500 Sunnyside Blvd., Woodbury NY 11797.**) ED** S B Palmer. **LC** QC1; .J848. **DD** 530/.05. **NLM** W1 JO836V. **CODEN** JPAPBE. **[CCC]. Pr Rev.** available on microfilm and microfiche. Documents available from Article Express International, The Genuine Article, Ask*IEEE, CASDDS. ***Continues*** *British Journal of Applied Physics. Series 2. Journal of Physics D.*
**Desc:** Novel theoretical and experimental aspects of physics as applied to interdisciplinary science, engineering or industry. The journal provides an international forum for original research papers, rapid communications and review articles. Its broad coverage includes: properties of novel materials, opto-electronic and molecular electronic phenomena, electrical, electronic, magnetic and superconductive properties of materials, dielectrics and insulators, etc.
**Ind/Abst** Abstr. Bull. Inst. Pap. Sci. Tech.; Acoust. Abstr.; Alum. Ind. Abstr.; Appl. Sci. Technol. Index; Bioeng. Abstr.; Ceram. Abstr.; Chem. Abstr.; Chem. Titles; Coal Abstr.; Curr. Technol. Index; Curr. Titles Electrochem.; Dairy Sci. Abstr.; Ei Page One; Eng. Mater. Abstr.; Eng. Index Annu.; Fluid Abstr., Civil Eng.; Fluid Abstr. Proc. Eng.; FLUIDEX (1973-); GeoRef; HTFS Dig.; INSPEC (Jan. 1970-); Int. Aerosp. Abstr.; Leadscan; Mass Spect. Bull.; Met. Abstr.; Res. Alert [Full Cov.]; Saf. Health Work; Sci. Cit. Index; SCISEARCH; World Ceram. Abstr.; World Text. Abstr.

UK/0022-3778
**JOURNAL OF PLASMA PHYSICS.** [J. plasma phys.]. Vol. 1 (Feb. 1967)-. Academic Scholarly Publication. English. bm (6 issues). $578.00 US, Canada and Mexico; £298.00 other. Cambridge University Press, The Edinburgh Building, Shaftesbury Road, Cambridge CB2 2RU United Kingdom. **Tel** 011 44 223 312393, FAX 011 44 223 325959. **(Subscription address:** Cambridge University Press / North America, 110 Midland Avenue, Port Chester NY 10573.**) ED** J. P. Dougherty. **LC** QC718; .J6. **DD** 537.1/6/05. **CODEN** JPLPBZ. **[CCC]. Bk Rev. Pr Rev.** available on microfilm and microfiche from University Microfilms International (UMI). Documents available from Article Express International, The Genuine Article, Ask*IEEE, CASDDS.
**Desc:** Publishes primary research articles in plasma physics, both theoretical and experimental, and its applications. Basic topics include the fundamental physics of plasmas, ionization, kinetic theory, particle orbits, stochastic dynamics, wave propagation, solutions, stability, shock waves, transport, heating and diagnostics. Applications include fusion, laboratory plasmas and communications devices, laser plasmas, space physics and astrophysics.
**Ind/Abst** Bioeng. Abstr.; Chem. Abstr.; Curr. Contents Phys. Chem. Earth Sci.; Ei Page One; Energy Res. Abstr.; Eng. Index Annu.; INSPEC (1968-); Int. Aerosp. Abstr.; Pollut. Abstr. Indexes; Res. Alert [Full Cov.]; Sci. Cit. Index; SCISEARCH.

●US/1062-7944
**JOURNAL OF QUANTUM NONLINEAR PHENOMENA.** [J. quantum nonlinear phenom.]. (1992)-. Periodical. English. Four times a year. $325.00. Nova Science Publishers Inc., 6080 Jericho Turnpike, Suite 207, Commack NY 11725-2808. **Tel** (516)499-3103, (516)499-3106, FAX (516)499-3146. **LC** QC20.7.N6; J7. **DD** 530.1/2.

JA/0386-3034
**JOURNAL OF SCIENCE OF THE HIROSHIMA UNIVERSITY. SERIES A. PHYSICS AND CHEMISTRY (1971).** (JOURNAL OF SCIENCE OF THE HIROSHIMA UNIVERSITY. SERIES A. PHYSICS AND CHEMISTRY.). [J. sci. Hiroshima Univ. Ser. A.]. **Main/Corp** Hiroshima Daigaku. (June 1971)-. Periodical. English. tq. (Free upon request). Hiroshima University Faculty of Science, 1 89 Higashisenda Machi 1Chome, Naka Ku Hiroshima 730 Japan. **Tel** 81 82 241 1221. **LC** QC1; .H56. **DD** 530/.05. **CODEN** JHPCAR. Documents available from Ask*IEEE, CASDDS. ***Continues*** *Hiroshima Daigaku. Journal of Science of the Hiroshima University. Series A-II, Physics and Chemistry, 0439-173X.*
**Ind/Abst** Chem. Abstr.; INSPEC (1968-).

US/0022-4715
**JOURNAL OF STATISTICAL PHYSICS.** [J. stat. phys.]. Vol. 1 (1969)-. Statistical Publication. English. Twenty-four times a year. $1,495.00 US; $1,750.00 other. Plenum Press, 233 Spring Street, New York NY 10013-1578. **Tel** (212)620-8000, (800)221-9369, FAX (212)463-0742, (212)807-1047, telex 23/421139. **ED** Joel L. Lebowitz. **LC** QC175; .J6. **DD** 530.13/2/05. **CODEN** JSTPSB. **[CCC].** Index available. **Pr Rev.** available on microfilm and microfiche from University Microfilms International (UMI). Documents available from Article Express International, The Genuine Article, Ask*IEEE.
**Desc:** This journal accepts original and review papers in the fields of statistical mechanics and thermodynamics of equilibrium and non-equilibrium processes; also plasma physics and non-linear dynamics.
**Ind/Abst** Appl. Mech. Rev.; Compumath Citation Index [Full Cov.]; Curr. Contents Phys. Chem. Earth Sci.; Ei Page One; Energy Res. Abstr.; Eng. Index Annu.; INSPEC (1969-); Int. Aerosp. Abstr.; Math. Rev.; Ref. Z.; Res. Alert [Full Cov.]; Sci. Cit. Index; SCISEARCH; Soc. Sci. Cit. Index [Select. Cov.]; SPIN (1977-); Zentralbl. Math. Ihre Grenzgeb.

PL/0324-8313
**JOURNAL OF TECHNICAL PHYSICS.** [J. tech. phys.]. Vol. 16- (1975)-. Periodical. English (summaries and/or abstracts in Polish and Russian). qt. $14.00. VCH Publishers Inc, 220 East 23rd Street, New York NY 10010. **Tel** (212)683-8333, , FAX (212)481-0897. **(Subscription address:** VCH Publishers Inc., 303 Northwest 12th Avenue, Journals Department, Deerfield FL 33442.**) LC** TA355; .P75. **DD** 620.1/005. **CODEN** JTPHDR. **[CCC].** Documents available from Article Express International, Ask*IEEE, CASDDS. ***Continues*** *Proceedings of Vibration Problems.*
**Ind/Abst** Bioeng. Abstr.; Chem. Abstr.; Ei Page One; Eng. Index Annu.; GeoRef; INSPEC (1975-); Int. Aerosp. Abstr.; Math. Rev.; Soc. Plann. Policy Dev. Abstr.; Zentralbl. Math. Ihre Grenzgeb.

II/0253-7257
**JOURNAL OF THE ACOUSTICAL SOCIETY OF INDIA.** (JOURNAL OF THE ACOUSTICAL SOCIETY OF INDIA / ACOUSTICAL SOCIETY OF INDIA.). [J. Acoust. Soc. India]. **Added/Corp** Acoustical Society of India. Vol. 1, No. 1 (Jan. 1973)-. Periodical. English. qt. $40.00. Acoustical Society of India, Hyderabad, India. **(Subscription address:** Prints India, 11 Darya Ganj, New Delhi, 110002 India, (Phone: 011 91 11 3268645)**) CODEN** JSOIDI.

IR/0378-1046
**JOURNAL OF THE EARTH AND SPACE PHYSICS.** [J. earth space phys.]. **VFOAT** Journal of Earth and Space Physics. V. 1- 1972-. Periodical. English (French, German and Persian). qt. University of Tehran-Institute Geophysics, Shahreza Avenue, Tehran Iran. **CODEN** JESPCS.
**Ind/Abst** Abstr. J. Earthq. Eng. (?-?); GeoRef.

KO/0374-4884
**JOURNAL OF THE KOREAN PHYSICAL SOCIETY.** (JOURNAL.). [J. Korean Phys. Soc.]. **Main/Corp** Hanguk Mullia Hakhoe. Vol. 1 (Mar. 1968)-. Periodical. English. sa. **CODEN** JKPSDV. Documents available from Ask*IEEE, CASDDS.
**Ind/Abst** Chem. Abstr.; INSPEC (March 1968-); Sci. Cit. Index.

UK/0960-0175
**JOURNAL OF THE MOSCOW PHYSICAL SOCIETY : JMPS. Added/Corp** Moscow Physical Society. Institute of Physics (Great Britain) American Institute of Physics. **VFOAT** JMPS. Vol. 1 (1991)-. Academic Scholarly Publication. English. Four times a year. $325.00. Institute of Physics, Techno House, Redcliffe Way, Bristol BS1 6NX England. **Tel** 011 44 272 297481, FAX 011 44 272 294318, telex 449149 INSTP G. **(Subscription address:** American Institute of Physics, Publishing Sales, 500 Sunnyside Blvd., Woodbury NY 11797.**) ED** L V Keldysh. **CODEN** JMPSEC. Index available in last issue of volume--attached. available on microfiche. Documents available from Ask*IEEE, CASDDS.
**Desc:** Publishes original research papers and brief reviews on current developments in fundamental physics. An international editorial board ensures worldwide coverage, including the full spectrum of fundamental physics: mathematical and general physics; classical phenomenology, nonlinear phenomena; plasma physics; optics and spectroscopy; condensed matter; high energy physics; field theory; general relativity.
**Ind/Abst** Chem. Abstr. (Feb. 1991-); INSPEC (Feb. 1991-); Math. Rev.

JA/0031-9015
**JOURNAL OF THE PHYSICAL SOCIETY OF JAPAN.** [J. Phys. Soc. Jpn.]. **Main/Corp** Nippon Butsuri Gakkai. **Added/Corp** Nihon Butsuri Gakkai. Vol. 1 (July/Dec. 1946)-. Periodical. English. mo. $750.00. Physical Society of Japan, Rm 211 3-5-8 Shiba-Koen, Minato-ku, Tokyo 105 Japan. **Tel** (292)3751-9. **(Subscription address:** Japan Publications Trading Company, Ltd., PO Box 5030, Tokyo International, Tokyo 100-31 Japan.**) LC** QC1; .P47. **DD** 530.5. **CODEN** JUPSAU. Index available. cum. index. **Pr Rev.** available on microfiche. Documents available from Article Express International, The Genuine Article, Ask*IEEE, CASDDS. ***Continues in part*** *Nihon Sugaku Butsuri Gakkai. Proceedings of the Physico-Mathematical Society of Japan.*
**Desc:** Contains full papers, letters, short notes, comments. The letters section is intended to secure prompt publication of discoveries in physics.
**Ind/Abst** Acoust. Abstr.; Alum. Ind. Abstr.; Bioeng. Abstr.; Ceram. Abstr.; Chem. Abstr.; Chem. Titles; Curr. Contents Phys. Chem. Earth Sci.; Ei Page One; Eng. Index Annu.; INSPEC (1968-); Int. Aerosp. Abstr.; Math. Rev.; Met. Abstr.; Life Sci. Collect.; Pollut. Abstr. Indexes (1968-); Res. Alert [Full Cov.]; Sci. Cit. Index; SCISEARCH; SEA Abstr.; Soils Fert.; Surf. Treat. Technol. Abstr.

US/0731-3764
**JOURNAL OF UNDERGRADUATE RESEARCH IN PHYSICS, THE.** [J. undergrad. res. phys.]. **Added/Corp** American Institute of Physics. Society of Physics Students (American Institute of Physics). Vol. 1, No. 1 (April 1982)-. Periodical. English. sa (Apr., Oct.). $10.00 institution, $5.00 individual (US); $12.00 institution, $7.00 individual (other) surface; $20.00 institution, $15.00 individual (other) air freight. Guilford College / Department of Physics, c/o R Adelberger, Greensboro NC 27410. **Tel** (919)316-2279, FAX (919) 316-2951. **ED** Rexford E Adelberger. **Bk Rev**, (Qty: 2). **Circ:** 7,000.
**Desc:** Devoted to research done by undergraduate students in physics and physics related fields.

US/0734-2101
**JOURNAL OF VACUUM SCIENCE & TECHNOLOGY. A: VACUUM, SURFACES, AND FILMS.** [J. vac. sci. technol., A, Vac. surf. films]. **Added/Corp** American Vacuum Society. American Institute of Physics. **VFOAT** Journal of Vacuum Science and Technology. A, Vacuum, Surfaces, and Films. 2nd Ser., Vol. 1, No. 1 (Jan./Mar. 1983)-. Academic Scholarly Publication. English. bm. $530.00 US; $550.00 Canada & Mexico & Central and South America & Caribbean; $574.00 others. Slack Inc., 6900 Grove Road, Thorofare NJ 08086. **Tel** (609)848-1000, (800)257-8290, FAX (609)853-5991, telex 517108 SLACK INC VD. **(Subscription address:** AVS, c/o SLACK Inc., 6900 Grove Road, Thorofare NJ 08086.**) LC** TJ940; .J668. **DD** 621.5/5/05. **CODEN** JVTAD6. **[CCC]. Pr Rev.** available on microfilm. Documents available from Article Express International, The Genuine Article, Ask*IEEE, CASDDS. ***Continues in part*** *Journal of Vacuum Science and Technology, 0022-5355.*
**Ind/Abst** Alum. Ind. Abstr.; Ceram. Abstr. (19??-); Chem. Abstr.; Chem. Titles; Coal Abstr.; Curr. Contents Eng. Tech. Appl. Sci.; Curr. Contents Phys. Chem. Earth Sci.; Curr. Phys. Index; Ei Page One; Eng. Mater. Abstr.; Eng. Index Annu. [Select. Cov.]; INIS Atomindex [Micro.]; INSPEC (Jan.-March 1983-); Leadscan; Mass Spect. Bull.; Met. Abstr.; Res. Alert [Full Cov.]; Sci. Cit. Index; SCISEARCH; SPIN (1983-).

US/1071-1023
**JOURNAL OF VACUUM SCIENCE & TECHNOLOGY. B, MICROELECTRONICS AND NANOMETER STRUCTURES PROCESSING, MEASUREMENT AND PHENOMENA.** (JOURNAL OF VACUUM SCIENCE & TECHNOLOGY. B, MICROELECTRONICS AND NANOMETER STRUCTURES PROCESSING, MEASUREMENT AND PHENOMENA : AN OFFICIAL PUBLICATION OF THE AMERICAN VACUUM SOCIETY.). [J. vac. sci. technol., B, Microelectron. nanometer struct. process. meas. phenom.]. **Added/Corp** American Vacuum Society. American Institute of Physics. **VFOAT** Microelectronics and Nanometer Structures Processing, Measurement and Phenomena; Journal of Vacuum Science and Technology. B, Microelectronics and Nanometer Structures Processing, Measurement and Phenomena. Vol. 9, No. 1 (Jan./Feb. 1991)-. Periodical. English. bm. $430.00 US; $455.00 Canada, Mexico, Central and South America, and the Caribbean; $474.00 other. Slack Inc., 6900 Grove Road, Thorofare NJ 08086. **Tel** (609)848-1000, (800)257-8290, FAX (609)853-5991, telex 517108 SLACK INC VD. **(Subscription address:** AVS, c/o SLACK Inc., 6900 Grove Road, Thorofare NJ 08086.**) LC** TJ940; .J669. **DD** 621. ***Continues*** *Journal of Vacuum Science & Technology. Microelectronics and Processing and Phenomena, 0734-211X.*

MY
**JURNAL FIZIK MALAYSIA.** Vol. 5, No. 1 (March 1984)-. Academic Scholarly Publication. English (Malay). qt. $40.00, $80.00 (institutions) US; $20.00, $40.00 (institutions) developing countries. Business Manager Jurnal Fizik Malaysia, c/o Jabatan Fizik, Universiti Malaysia, 59100 Kuala Lumpur Malaysia. **Tel** 7555466, FAX 006037573661, telex MA 39845 UNIMAL. **ED** S Lee. **LC** QC1; .B788. **DD** 530/.05. **CODEN** JFMAEU. **Pr Rev. Circ:** 500. Documents available from Ask*IEEE, CASDDS. ***Continues*** *Buletin Fizik, 0126-9674.*
**Desc:** Original research papers and notes in theoretical and experimental physics.
**Ind/Abst** Chem. Abstr. (1984-); INSPEC (June 1984-).

JA/0011-3336
**KAGAKU GIJUTSU BUNKEN SOKUHO. BUTSURI, OYO BUTSURI-HEN.** See Physics-Abstracting, Bibliographies and Statistics.

UK/0950-4818
**KEY ABSTRACTS. MEASUREMENTS IN PHYSICS.** See Physics-Abstracting, Bibliographies and Statistics.

HU/0368-5330
**KFKI.** [KFKI]. **Added/Corp** Magyar Tudomanyos Akademia. Kozponti Fizikai Kutato Intezet. (1965)-. Academic Scholarly Publication. English (summaries and/or abstracts in Hungarian and Russian). Price varies per volume. Central Research Institute for Physics, Hungarian Academy of Sciences, Budapest Hungary. **LC** QC1; .M23. **DD** 530/.05. **CODEN** KFKRAA. Documents available from Ask*IEEE, CASDDS.
**Ind/Abst** Chem. Abstr.; INSPEC.

UN/0233-7665
**KINEMATIKA I FIZIKA NEBESNYH TEL.** (KINEMATIKA I FIZIKA NEBESNYKH TEL.). [Kinemat. fiz. nebesnyh tel]. **Added/Corp** Akademiia Nauk Ukrainskoi RSR. Viddilennia Fizyky i Astronomii. Vol. 1 (1985)-. Academic Scholarly Publication. Russian (Russian; summaries and/or abstracts in English). Six times a year. $119.95. Izdatelstvo Naukova Dumka / Ukrainian Academy of Sciences, Vladimirskaia Ulitsa 54, 252601 Kiev Ukraine. **Tel** 225-63-66, telex 131376. **(Subscription address:** East View Publications Inc., 3020 Harbor Lane North, Suite 110, Minneapolis MN 55447.**)** **LC** QB461; .K52. **CODEN** KFNTEZ. Documents available from Ask*IEEE, CASDDS. ***Formed by the union of*** *Astrometriia i Astrofizika, 0582-3198; Vrashchenie i Prilivnye Deformatsii Zemli; Problemy Kosmicheskoi Fiziki, 0555-2796; Vestnik l'Vovskogo Universiteta. Seriia Astronomicheskaia Astronomiia Solnechnoi Sistemy* ***and*** *Astronomiia Solnechnoi Sistemy.*
**Ind/Abst** Astron. Astrophys. Abstr.; Chem. Abstr. (1985-); GeoRef; INSPEC (Jan./Feb. 1985-); Int. Aerosp. Abstr.; Math. Rev.

JA
**KINKI DAIGAKU GENSHIRYOKU KENKYUJO NENPO.** [Kinki Daigaku Genshiryoku Kenkyujo nenpo]. **Added/Corp** Kinki Daigaku Genshiryoku Kenkyujo. **VFOAT** Annual Report of Kinki University Atomic Energy Research Institute. (1963)-. Japanese. an. Kinki University Atomic Energy Research Institute, 3-4-1 Kowakae, Higashiosaka-shi 577, Osaka Japan. **CODEN** KDGNBX. Documents available from CASDDS.
**Ind/Abst** Chem. Abstr.

DK/0023-3323
**KONGELIGE DANSKE VIDENSKABERNES SELSKAB. MATEMATISK-FYSISKE MEDDELELSER.** See Mathematics.

DK
**KONGELIGE DANSKE VIDENSKABERNES SELSKAB MATHEMATISK FYSISKE MEDDELESER.** See Mathematics.

JA
**KOTAI BUTSURI. A SHIRIZU.** [Kotai butsuri, A]. **Added/Corp** Agne Gijutsu Center. **VFOAT** Solid State Physics. A Series. (1976)-. Academic Scholarly Publication. Japanese. mo. $386.00. Agune Gijutsu Senta, (Agune Gijutsu Center), 1-25, Minamiaoyama 5 Chome, Minatoku, Tokyoto 107, Japan. **(Subscription address:** Kyowa Book Company Inc., 1-38 Kanda Jinbo-Cho, Chiyoda-Ku Tokyo 101, Japan**)** **ED** Seizo Nagasaki. **CODEN** KBUADI. **Ad Acc. Circ:** 6,000 (ctrl). Documents available from CASDDS. ***Continues in part*** *Kotai Butsuri.*
**Desc:** Introduces experimentation and theory of solid state physics.
**Ind/Abst** Chem. Abstr.

RU/0455-0595
**KRATKIE SOOBSCENIA PO FIZIKE.** (KRATKIE SOOBSHCHENIIA PO FIZIKE / AKADEMIIA NAUK SSSR, ORDENA LENINA I ORDENA OKTIABRSKOI REVOLIUTSII FIZICHESKII INSTITUT IMENI P.N. LEBEDEVA.). [Kratkie soobsc. fiz.]. **Added/Corp** Fizicheskii Institut Imeni P.N. Lebedeva. (1970)-. Periodical. Russian. mo. **LC** QC1; .K73. **CODEN** KRSFAU. Documents available from CASDDS.
**Ind/Abst** Chem. Abstr.

CC/0258-1825
**KUNG CHI TUNG LI HSUEH HSUEH PAO.** **Added/Corp** Chung-kuo Kung Chi Tung li Hsueh Yen Chiu Hui. **VFOAT** Kung Chi Tung li Hsueh; Acta Aerodynamica Sinica; Kongqidonglixue Xuebao. (19??)-. Periodical. Chinese (summaries and/or abstracts in English). qt. Zhongguo Kongqi Dongli Yanjiu yu Fazhan Zhongxin, PO Box 211, Mianyang, Sichuan 621000, People's Republic of China. **Tel** 0816-22490. **ED** Z. Fenggan. **LC** QA930; .K76. **DD** 533/.62/05. **Pr Rev.**
**Ind/Abst** Int. Aerosp. Abstr.

US/0148-0987
**LASER INTERACTION AND RELATED PLASMA PHENOMENA.** [Laser interact. relat. plasma phenom.]. **Main/Conf** Workshop on Laser Interaction and Related Plasma Phenomena, Rensselaer Polytechnic Institute. **Added/Corp** Rensselaer Polytechnic Institute. Naval Postgraduate School (U.S.). (1969)-. Academic Scholarly Publication. English. ir. Price varies per volume. Plenum Press, 233 Spring Street, New York NY 10013-1578. **Tel** (212)620-8000, (800)221-9369, FAX (212)463-0742, (212)807-1047, telex 23/421139. **LC** QC718.5.P5; L37. **DD** 530.4/4. **CODEN** LIPPAR. Documents available from Ask*IEEE, CASDDS.
**Ind/Abst** Chem. Abstr. (1969-1984)(19??-); INSPEC (1984-).

RU/1054-660X
**LASER PHYSICS.** **Added/Corp** Akademiia Nauk SSSR. Rossiiskaia Akademiia Nauk. **VFOAT** Laser Physics, Soviet. Vol. 1, No. 1 (Jan.-Feb. 1991)-. Periodical. English. bm (6 issues). $542.00 US and Canada; $601.00 other. MAIK Nauka / Interperiodica, Ulitsa Profsoyuznaya 90, Moscow 117864 Russia. **(Subscription address:** Interperiodica Publishing, Subscription Office, PO Box 1831, Birmingham AL 35201-1831.**)** **ED** Alexander M. Prokhorov. **LC** QC685; .L29. **DD** 621.36/6. **CODEN** LAPHEJ.
**Desc:** Offers a comprehensive view of theoretical and experimental laser research and applications by top Soviet and international authors.

GW/0722-9003
**LASER UND OPTOELEKTRONIK.** [Laser Optoelektron.]. **VFOAT** Laser und Elektro-Optik. Vol. 14, No. 1 (April 1982)-. Academic Scholarly Publication. English (German). Six times a year. DM170. At-Fachverlag GMBH, Postfach 50 01 80, 7000 Stuttgart 50 Germany. **Tel** 011 49 711 9529510, FAX 1 528 1539, telex 7 254 879. **ED** Gabriele Rausch. **LC** TA1671; .L37. **DD** 621.36/6/05. **NLM** W1; LA78TH. **CODEN** LAOPD3. **[CCC].** Index available. cum. index. **Bk Rev. Ad Acc. Circ:** 5,075. Documents available from Ask*IEEE. ***Continues*** *Laser + Elektro-Optik, 0344-5186.*
**Desc:** Active in research, applications, development and manufacturing in the field of lasers and optoelectronics in technology, communications, physics, chemistry, analysis, biology and medicine.
**Ind/Abst** EMBASE (April 1982-); Energy Res. Abstr. (Aug. 1982-); INSPEC (April 1982-).

LV/0868-8257
**LATVIAN JOURNAL OF PHYSICS AND TECHNICAL SCIENCES.** **VFOAT** Latvijas Fizikas un Tehnisko Zinatnu Zurnals; Latviiskii Fiziko-Tekhnicheskii Zhurnal. (1991)-. Periodical. English (Latvian and Russian). bm. Zinatne / Science Publishing House, Turgeneva Iela 19, Riga Latvia 1530. **Tel** 3712 212 797. Documents available from Ask*IEEE, CASDDS. ***Continues*** *Izvestiia Latviiskoi Akademii Nauk. Seriia Fizicheskikh i Tekhnicheskikh Nauk.*
**Ind/Abst** Chem. Abstr.; INSPEC (1991-); Math. Rev.

GW/0075-8450
**LECTURE NOTES IN PHYSICS.** [Lect. notes phys.]. (1969)-. Monographic series. English (French and German). ir. Price varies per volume. Springer-Verlag GmbH & Company KG, Heidelberger Platz 3, D 14197 Berlin Germany. **Tel** 011 49 30 8207223, FAX 011 49 30 8214091, telex 183 319 SPBLN D. **(Subscription address:** Springer Verlag New York Inc. / for North America, 44 Hartz Way, Secaucus NJ 07096.**)** **CODEN** LNPHA4. **[CCC].** Documents available from BIOSIS Document Express, Ask*IEEE, CASDDS.
**Desc:** Contains articles on solutions of Einstein's equations, phase transitions in equilibrium nonequilibrium systems and nuclear physics.
**Ind/Abst** Biol. Abstr. (1985-); Chem. Abstr.; Ei Page One; Energy Res. Abstr. (March 1982-); GeoRef; INSPEC; Math. Rev.; Zentralbl. Math. Ihre Grenzgeb.

GW
**LECTURE NOTES IN PHYSICS. NEW SERIES M, MONOGRAPHS.** **VFOAT** Monographs. (1991)-. Monographic series. English. Springer-Verlag GmbH & Company KG, Heidelberger Platz 3, D 14197 Berlin Germany. **Tel** 011 49 30 8207223, FAX 011 49 30 8214091, telex 183 319 SPBLN D. **(Subscription address:** Springer Verlag New York Inc. / for North America, 44 Hartz Way, Secaucus NJ 07096.**)**
**Ind/Abst** Math. Rev.

II/0970-6313
**LECTURES ON MATHEMATICS AND PHYSICS.** See Mathematics.

NE/0377-9017
**LETTERS IN MATHEMATICAL PHYSICS.** [Lett. math. phys.]. Vol. 1 (Dec. 1975)-. Academic Scholarly Publication. English. mo. $1,143.00. Kluwer Academic Publishers, Postbus 322, 3300 AH Dordrecht, The Netherlands. **Tel** 011 (31) 78 524400, FAX 011 31 78 183273, telex 20083. **ED** G. Dell'Antonio, M. Flato, E.H. Lieb, S.T. Yau, and J.C. Cortet. **LC** QC19.2; .L47. **DD** 530.1/5/05. **CODEN** LMPHDY. **[CCC]. Ad Acc. Pr Rev. Acid Free. Circ:** 600. available on microfilm and microfiche from University Microfilms International (UMI). Documents available from The Genuine Article, Ask*IEEE, CASDDS.

**Desc:** Group theory and applications to physics; quantum-field theory; mathematical models for particle, nuclear, plasma, and solid-state physics; classical, quantum, and statistical mechanics.
**Ind/Abst** Chem. Abstr.; Compumath Citation Index [Full Cov.]; Curr. Contents Phys. Chem. Earth Sci.; INSPEC (1975-); Math. Rev.; Pollut. Abstr. Indexes; Res. Alert [Full Cov.]; Sci. Cit. Index; SCISEARCH; Zentralbl. Math. Ihre Grenzgeb. (-1991).

●LI
**LIETUVOS FIZIKOS ZURNALAS / LITHUANIAN JOURNAL OF PHYSICS / LITOVSKII FIZICHESKII ZHURNAL / LIETUVOS FIZIKU DRAUGIJA.** **Added/Corp** Lietuvos Fiziku Draugija. **VFOAT** Lithuanian Journal of Physics; Litovskii Fizicheskii Zhurnal. (1993)-. Periodical. Russian (English; summaries and/or abstracts in Lithuanian; table of contents in Lithuanian). qt. **(Subscription address:** Victor Kamkin, 4956 Boiling Brook Parkway, Rockville MD 20852.**)** ***Continues*** *Litovskii Fizicheskii Sbornik, 0024-2969.*
**Ind/Abst** Acoust. Abstr.; Alum. Ind. Abstr.; Ceram. Abstr.; Chem. Abstr.; INSPEC; Int. Aerosp. Abstr.; Math. Rev.; Met. Abstr.; Pollut. Abstr. Indexes.

US/1047-4064
**LITOVSKII FIZICHESKII SBORNIK.** (LITHUANIAN PHYSICS JOURNAL.). [Lith. phys. j.]. Vol. 29, No. 1 (1989)-. Periodical. English (translations available in Russian). Six times a year. $800.00. Allerton Press, Inc., 150 Fifth Avenue, New York NY 10011. **Tel** (212)924-3950, FAX (212)463-9684, telex 427441 ALPRES. **LC** QC1; .L731. **DD** 530. **CODEN** LPJOED. **[CCC].** Documents available from Ask*IEEE. ***Continues*** *Litovskii Fizicheskii Sbornik. English. Soviet Physics-Collection, 0363-7891.*
**Ind/Abst** INSPEC (1989-); Math. Rev.

LI/0024-2969
**LITOVSKIJ FIZICESKIJ SBORNIK.** ***Title Change.*** (LITOVSKII FIZICHESKII SBORNIK / AKADEMIIA NAUK LITOVSKOI SSR, VYSSHIE UCHEBNYE ZAVEDENIIA LITOVSKOI SSR.). [Litov. fiz. sb.]. **Added/Corp** Lietuvos TSR Mokslu Akademija. Lietuvos Mokslu Akademija. Lietuvos TSR Fiziku Draugija. Lietuvos Fiziku Draugija. **VFOAT** Lietuvos Fizikos Rinkinys. (1961)-(1992). Periodical. Russian (Lithuanian and English; summaries and/or abstracts in English, French, German and Lithuanian). qt. **(Subscription address:** Victor Kamkin, 4956 Boiling Brook Parkway, Rockville MD 20852.**)** **LC** QC1; .L73. **CODEN** LFRMA7. Documents available from Ask*IEEE, CASDDS. ***Continued by*** *Lietuvos Fizikos Zurnalas.*
**Ind/Abst** Acoust. Abstr.; Alum. Ind. Abstr.; Ceram. Abstr. (19??-); Chem. Abstr.; INSPEC (1968-); Int. Aerosp. Abstr.; Math. Rev.; Met. Abstr.; Pollut. Abstr. Indexes.

US/0893-8067
**LIVING PHYSICS.** (LIVING PHYSICS [VIDEORECORDING].). [Living phys.]. **Added/Corp** Tesla Foundation. Vol. 1 No. 1 (1988)-. Periodical. English. Four times a year. Tesla Foundation, PO Box 3037, Princeton NJ 08543. **DD** 530. ***Continues*** *Adventures in Experimental Physics, 0044-6386.*

UK
**LOW TEMPERATURE DIRECTORY : THE NEWSLETTER OF THE BRITISH CRYOGENICS COUNCIL.** (1973)-. Directory. English. qt. $45.00. University of Southampton Institute of Cryogenics, Southampton SO9 5NH England. **Tel** 011 44 0703 593348. **ED** John Harris. **Ad Acc. Circ:** 300.

●US/1063-777X
**LOW TEMPERATURE PHYSICS.** [Low temp. phys.]. **Added/Corp** American Institute of Physics. Vol. 19, No. 1 (Jan. 1993)-. Academic Scholarly Publication. English (translations available in Russian). mo. $1835.00 US; $1850.00 Canada, Mexico, Central and South America and the Caribbean; $1865.00 other. American Institute of Physics, 500 Sunnyside Boulevard, Woodbury NY 11797-2999. **Tel** (516)576-2200, FAX (516)349-7669, telex 960983. **LC** QC278; .S62. **DD** 536/.56/05. **CODEN** LTPHEG. **[CCC].** Index available (bound in last issue). Documents available from Ask*IEEE, CASDDS. ***Continues*** *Soviet Journal of Low Temperature Physics, 0360-0335.*
**Ind/Abst** Chem. Abstr.; Curr. Phys. Index; Energy Res. Abstr.; INSPEC; Int. Aerosp. Abstr.; SPIN.

RM
**LUCRARILE SEMINARULUI DE MATEMATICA SI FIZICA AL INSTITUTULUI POLITEHNIC "TRAIAN VUIA" TIMISOARA.** See Mathematics.

●SZ/1022-1352
**MACROMOLECULAR CHEMISTRY AND PHYSICS.** See Chemistry.

IR
**MAJALLAH-I FIZIK.** **Added/Corp** Markaz-i Nashr-i Danishgahi (Iran). Guruh-i Fizik. **VFOAT** Iranian Journal of Physics. Vol. 1, No. 1, (Winter 1983)-. Academic Scholarly Publication. Persian. qt. £24.00

Middle East; £25.00 Europe & Asia; £30.00 America & Far East. Iran University Press, 85 Park Avenue, PO Box 15875/4748, Tehran Iran. **Tel** 623232, FAX (008921)4661749, telex 213636-8-D5300. **ED** R. Mansourit. **LC** QC1; .M25. **Bk Rev. Circ:** 4,000.
**Desc:** Contains original research and instructional papers, review articles, translation of articles from international journals, book reviews, new books, problems, news, and news of Iranian Physical Society.

UN/0233-7568
**MATEMATICHESKAIA FIZIKA I NELINEINAIA MEKHANIKA.** **Added/Corp** Instytut Matematyky (Akademiia Nauk Ukrainskoi RSR). (1984)-. Periodical. Russian. Izdatelstvo Naukova Dumka / Ukrainian Academy of Sciences, Vladimirskaia Ulitsa 54, 252601 Kiev Ukraine. **Tel** 225-63-66, telex 131376. **LC** QC19.2; .M36. Documents available from Ask*IEEE. ***Continues*** *Matematicheskaia Fizika, 0542-9986.*
**Ind/Abst** INSPEC (1984-1989); Int. Aerosp. Abstr.; Math. Rev. (1984-); Zentralbl. Math. Ihre Grenzgeb.

US/0272-9172
**MATERIALS RESEARCH SOCIETY SYMPOSIA PROCEEDINGS.** **See** Engineering-Electricity, Electrical Engineering, Electronics.

NE/0165-2419
**MATHEMATICAL PHYSICS AND APPLIED MATHEMATICS.** **See** Mathematics.

NE/0921-3767
**MATHEMATICAL PHYSICS STUDIES.** [Math. phys. stud.]. **VFOAT** Mathematical Physics Studies Book Series. Vol. 1 (1979)-. Monographic series. English. ir. Price varies. Kluwer Academic Publishers, Postbus 322, 3300 AH Dordrecht, The Netherlands. **Tel** 011 (31) 78 524400, FAX 011 31 78 183273, telex 20083. **(Subscription address:** Kluwer Academic Publishers / US Subscriptions, PO Box 253, Accord Station, Hingham MA 02018.**)**
**Ind/Abst** Math. Rev.; Zentralbl. Math. Ihre Grenzgeb.

GW/0340-8914
**MAX-PLANCK-INSTITUT FUER PLASMAPHYSIK GARCHING BEI MUNCHEN.** (MAX-PLANCK-INSTITUT FUER PLASMAPHYSIK GARCHING BEI MUNCHEN : [BERICHT].). [Max-Planck-Inst. Plasmaphys. Garch. Munch.]. **Added/Corp** Max-Planck-Institut fur Plasmaphysik. **VFOAT** Max Planck Institut fur Plasmaphysik Garching bei Munchen. (1972)-. Monographic series. German (summaries and/or abstracts in English). **CODEN** MPIPDL. Documents available from CASDDS.
**Ind/Abst** Chem. Abstr.

UK/0957-0233
**MEASUREMENT SCIENCE & TECHNOLOGY.** [Meas. sci. technol.]. **Added/Corp** Institute of Physics (Great Britain) American Institute of Physics. **VFOAT** Measurement Science and Technology. Vol. 1, No. 1 (Jan. 1990)-. Academic Scholarly Publication. English. mo. $602.00. Institute of Physics, Techno House, Redcliffe Way, Bristol BS1 6NX England. **Tel** 011 44 272 297481, FAX 011 44 272 294318, telex 449149 INSTP G. **(Subscription address:** American Institute of Physics, Publishing Sales, 500 Sunnyside Blvd., Woodbury NY 11797.**) ED** Julian D C Jones. **LC** QC39; .M397. **DD** 681.2. **NLM** W1; ME104M. **CODEN** MSTCEP. **[CCC].** available on microfiche. Documents available from Article Express International, The Genuine Article, Ask*IEEE, CASDDS, ADONIS. ***Continues*** *Journal of Physics. E: Scientific Instruments, 0022-3735.*
**Desc:** The theory and practice of measurement and the apparatus involved in the pursuit of physics, chemistry and the life sciences from discovery to commercial exploitation. The apparatus includes the instruments, sensors, techniques, hardware, software and informatic systems involved, including automatic data acquisition, reduction and analysis and their incorporation for control purposes. Regular reviews on aspects of instrument physics and measurement, articles on measurement science and technology, authoritative viewpoint articles and company profiles are included as well as book reviews and conference reports.
**Ind/Abst** Abstr. Bull. Inst. Pap. Sci. Tech.; ADONIS; Appl. Sci. Technol. Index; Art Archaeol. Tech. Abstr.; Chem. Abstr.; Curr. Contents Eng. Tech. Appl. Sci.; Curr. Contents Phys. Chem. Earth Sci.; Ei Page One; EMBASE; Eng. Index Annu.; Fluid Abstr., Civil Eng.; Fluid Abstr. Proc. Eng.; FLUIDEX (1973-); GeoRef; HTFS Dig.; INSPEC (1990-); Int. Aerosp. Abstr.; Met. Abstr.; Res. Alert [Full Cov.]; Sci. Cit. Index; SCISEARCH; World Ceram. Abstr.

US/0025-6544
**MECHANICS OF SOLIDS.** [Mech. solids]. **Main/Corp** Akademiiâ Nauk SSSR. (19??)-. Academic Scholarly Publication. English (Russian). bm. $925.00. Allerton Press, Inc., 150 Fifth Avenue, New York NY 10011. **Tel** (212)924-3950, FAX (212)463-9684, telex 427441 ALPRES. **LC** QC176.A1; A482a. **DD** 530.4/1. **CODEN** MESOBN. **[CCC].** Documents available from Article Express International, Ask*IEEE, CASDDS. ***Continues*** *Mechanics of Solids, 0025-6544.*
**Ind/Abst** Acoust. Abstr.; Bioeng. Abstr.; Chem. Abstr. (-1983); Ei Page One; Eng. Index Annu.; INSPEC (1979-); Int. Aerosp. Abstr.; Math. Rev.; Pollut. Abstr. Indexes.

UK/0143-0203
**MEDICAL PHYSICS HANDBOOKS.** [Med. phys. handb.]. **Added/Corp** Hospital Physicists' Association. (1979)-. Monographic series. English. ir. Price varies per volume. **LC** UNC. **NLM** W1 ME409V. **CODEN** MPHAE6. Documents available from BIOSIS Document Express, Ask*IEEE.
**Ind/Abst** Biol. Abstr. (1985-); INSPEC.

US/0094-2405
**MEDICAL PHYSICS (LANCASTER).** (MEDICAL PHYSICS.). [Med. phys.]. **Added/Corp** American Association of Physicists in Medicine. American Institute of Physics. Vol. 1 (1974)-. Academic Scholarly Publication. English. Twelve times a year. $430.00 US; $450.00 Canada, Mexico, Central & South America and the Caribbean; $470.00 other. American Institute of Physics, 500 Sunnyside Boulevard, Woodbury NY 11797-2999. **Tel** (516)576-2200, FAX (516)349-7669, telex 960983. **LC** R895.A1; M44. **DD** 610/1/53. **NLM** W1 ME409R. **CODEN** MPHYA6. **[CCC]. Pr Rev.** available on microfiche; available on microfilm. Documents available from The Genuine Article, BIOSIS Document Express, Ask*IEEE, CASDDS. ***Continues*** *Quarterly Bulletin - American Association of Physicists in Medicine, 0001-0162.*
**Desc:** Covers medical physics and biophysics.
**Ind/Abst** Acoust. Abstr.; Biol. Abstr.; Chem. Abstr.; Curr. Contents Clin. Med.; Curr. Contents Life Sci.; Curr. Phys. Index; EMBASE; Energy Res. Abstr. (Sept. 1974-); Health Devices Alerts; Index Med.; INIS Atomindex [Micro.]; INSPEC (1974-); Int. Aerosp. Abstr.; Life Sci. Collect.; Phys. Med. Biol. (19??-19??); Pollut. Abstr. Indexes; Res. Alert [Full Cov.]; Sci. Cit. Index; SCISEARCH; SPIN (1974-).

US/0163-1802
**MEDICAL PHYSICS MONOGRAPH.** **Added/Corp** American Association of Physicists in Medicine. American Institute of Physics. (1978)-. Monographic series. English. ir. Price varies per volume. American Institute of Physics, 500 Sunnyside Boulevard, Woodbury NY 11797-2999. **Tel** (516)576-2200, FAX (516)349-7669, telex 960983. **LC** UNC. **DD** 610/.1/53. **NLM** W1 ME409W. ***Continues*** *AAPM Monograph.*

US/0895-7738
**MELTS.** ***Ceased.*** [Melts]. **Added/Corp** Consultants Bureau. **VFOAT** Rasplavy. (May 1988)-Vol. 7 (1993). Academic Scholarly Publication. English (translations available in Russian). Six times a year. Consultants Bureau, A Division of Plenum Publishing Corporation, 233 Spring Street, New York NY 10013. **Tel** (212)620-8000, (212)620-8466, FAX (212)463-0742, telex 23/421139. **ED** N A Vatolin. **LC** TN689; .R372. **DD** 669/.94. **CODEN** MLTSEO. **[CCC].** available in microform from University Microfilms International (UMI). Documents available from CASDDS.
**Desc:** Concerned with the physical chemistry of oxide, salt, and metal melts.
**Ind/Abst** Chem. Abstr.

JA/0368-9689
**MEMOIRS OF THE FACULTY OF SCIENCE, KYOTO UNIVERSITY. SERIES OF PHYSICS, ASTROPHYSICS, GEOPHYSICS AND CHEMISTRY.** [Mem. Fac. Sci., Kyoto Univ., Ser. phys. astrophys. geophys. chem.]. **Main/Corp** Kyoto Daigaku. Rigakubu. Vol. 32 (Sept. 1967)-. English. ir. Kyoto University / Faculty of Science, Yoshida Honmachi Sakyo Ku, Kyotoshi Kyotofu 606 Japan. **Tel** (075)751-2111, telex 5422693 LIBKYU J. **LC** Q77; .K7. **DD** 500.2/08. **CODEN** MFKPAQ. **Circ:** 750 (ctrl). Documents available from Ask*IEEE, CASDDS. ***Continues*** *Memoirs of the College of Science, University of Kyoto. Series A.*
**Ind/Abst** Chem. Abstr.; INSPEC (1968-); Int. Aerosp. Abstr.

JA/0388-4112
**MEMOIRS OF THE NATIONAL DEFENSE ACADEMY. MATHEMATICS, PHYSICS, CHEMISTRY, AND ENGINEERING.** **See** Mathematics.

GW/0170-9321
**METHODEN UND VERFAHREN DER MATHEMATISCHEN PHYSIK.** **See** Mathematics.

US/0076-695X
**METHODS OF EXPERIMENTAL PHYSICS.** [Methods exp. phys.]. Vol. 1 (1959)-. Monographic series. English. ir. Price varies per volume. Academic Press, Inc., 6277 Sea Harbor Drive, Orlando FL 32887. **Tel** (800)543-9534, (407)345-4100, FAX (407)363-9661. **ED** Robert Celotta and Judah Levine. **LC** UNC. **CODEN** MEEPAN. **[CCC].** Documents available from Ask*IEEE, CASDDS.
**Ind/Abst** Chem. Abstr.; GeoRef; INSPEC.

ER
**METODOLOGICHESKIE VOPROSY FIZIKI.** **Added/Corp** Tartu Riiklik Ulikool. (1975)-. Periodical. Russian (summaries and/or abstracts in Estonian, English and German). 0.47rub (single issue). Tartu Riiklik Ulikool, Ulitsa Uilikooli 18, 202400 Tartu Estonia. **Tel** 30851. **LC** AS262.T22; A25 subser; QC6. ***Continues*** *Filosofskie Voprosy Fiziki.*

UK/0958-5036
**MICROGRAVITY QUARTERLY.** (MICROGRAVITY QUARTERLY : MGQ.). [Microgravity q.]. **VFOAT** MGQ. Vol. 1, No. 1 (1990)-. Periodical. English. bm (6 issues). $200.00. Editoriale Scientifica SRL, Via Generale Orsini 42, 80132 Naples Italy. **Tel** 011 39 81 7646084. **LC** TL1489; .M53. **DD** 620/.4. **CODEN** MGQUEE. **[CCC].** available on microfilm and microfiche from University Microfilms International (UMI). Documents available from Ask*IEEE.
**Ind/Abst** INSPEC (1990-); Int. Aerosp. Abstr.

GW/0938-0108
**MICROGRAVITY SCIENCE AND TECHNOLOGY.** [Microgravity sci. technol.]. **VFOAT** Micro Gravity Science and Technology. Vol. 3 Issue 1 (May 1990)-. Periodical. English. qt. DM482.00. Carl Hanser Verlag, Postfach 860420, D 81631 Munich Germany. **Tel** 011 49 89 998300, FAX 011 49 89 984809. **ED** Hans J. Rath, Gottfried Greger. **LC** TL1489; .A65. **DD** 620/.4. **CODEN** MSTYEN. **[CCC]. Ad Acc. Circ:** 1,500. Documents available from BIOSIS Document Express. ***Continues*** *Applied Microgravity Technology, 0931-9530.*
**Desc:** Presents research on the use of microgravity, developments in experimental technique and instrumentation, and articles on application-oriented research in space and on earth.
**Ind/Abst** Biol. Abstr. (1990-); Int. Aerosp. Abstr.

US/0192-6225
**MICROWAVE JOURNAL (INTERNATIONAL ED.).** (MICROWAVE JOURNAL.). [Microw. j.]. **VFOAT** Microwave Journal International. Vol. 7, No. 7- (July 1964)-. Periodical. English. mo. $75.00 US; $135.00 other. Horizon House, 685 Canton Street, Norwood MA 02062. **Tel** (617)365-4595. **DD** 621. **CODEN** MJIEEF. available on microfilm from University Microfilms International (UMI). ***Continues in part*** *Microwave Journal, 0026-2897.*
**Ind/Abst** Int. Aerosp. Abstr.

US/0885-9434
**MIT PRESS SERIES IN SIGNAL PROCESSING, OPTIMIZATION, AND CONTROL, THE.** [MIT Press ser. signal process. optim. control]. **VFOAT** Series in Signal Processing, Optimization, and Control. **VAT** Massachusetts Institute of Technology Press Series in Signal Processing, Optimization, and Control. (1979)-. Monographic series. English. ir. Price varies per volume. Massachusetts Institute of Technology (MIT) Press, 55 Hayward Street, Cambridge MA 02142-1399. **Tel** (617)253-2889, (617)625-8481, FAX (617)258-6779. **ED** Alan S. Willsky. **LC** UNC. **DD** 621.
**Ind/Abst** Math. Rev.; Zentralbl. Math. Ihre Grenzgeb.

GW/0030-834X
**MITTEILUNGEN - PTB.** **See** Science and Technology.

SI/0217-9849
**MODERN PHYSICS LETTERS. B, CONDENSED MATTER PHYSICS, STATISTICAL PHYSICS, APPLIED PHYSICS.** **VFOAT** Condensed Matter Physics, Statistical Physics, Applied Physics. Vol. 1, No. 1 & 2 (May 1987)-. Academic Scholarly Publication. English. Thirty times a year. $1,020.00 institutions, $510.00 individuals. World Scientific Publishing Company, PO Box 128, Farrer Road, Singapore 9128 Singapore. **Tel** 011 65 3825663, FAX 011 65 3825919, telex RS 28561 WSPC. **(Subscription address:** US: World Scientific Publishing Co., Inc., 1060 Main Street, River Edge, NJ 07661 Telephone: (201)487-9655, Fax: (201)487-9656; Europe: World Scientific Publishing Co Ltd, 73 Lynton Mead, Totteridge, London N20 8DH United Kingdom Telephone: 011 44 81 4462461, Fax: 011 44 81 4463356; India: World Scientific Publishing Co Pte Ltd, 4911 9th Floor, High Point IV, 45 Palace Road, Bangalore 560 001 India Telephone: (80) 2205972, Fax: (80) 3344593, Telex: 0845-2900 PCO IN; Hong Kong: World Scientific Publishing (HK) Co, PO Box 72482, Kowloon Central Post Office, Hong Kong Telephone: 852-7718791, Fax: 852-7718155**) LC** QC173.4.C65; M63. **DD** 530.4/1. **[CCC].** Documents available from Ask*IEEE, CASDDS.
**Desc:** Published in response to the widely-felt need for a rapid dissemination of new and important findings in statistical physics, condensed matter physics and applied physics. It aims at maintaining a high international standard and is made accessible to physicists all over the world.
**Ind/Abst** Chem. Abstr.; INSPEC (May 1987-); Math. Rev.

US/0027-1349
**MOSCOW UNIVERSITY PHYSICS BULLETIN.** [Moscow Univ. phys. bull.]. **Main/Corp** Moskovskii gosudarstvennyi universitet im. M.V. Lomonosova. Vol. 21 (1966)-. Bulletin. English (Russian). Six times a year. $785.00. Allerton Press, Inc., 150 Fifth Avenue, New York NY 10011. **Tel** (212)924-3950, FAX (212)463-9684, telex 427441 ALPRES. **LC** Q4; .M68323a. **DD** 530/.05. **CODEN** MUPBAC. **[CCC].** Documents available from Ask*IEEE.
**Ind/Abst** INSPEC (Sept./Oct. 1966-); Int. Aerosp. Abstr.; Math. Rev.; Zentralbl. Math. Ihre Grenzgeb.

●US/1061-1606
**MULTIVAC UPDATE.** [Multivac update]. **Added/Corp** Multivac, Inc. **VFOAT** Multivac Update. Vol. 1, No. 1 (Apr. 1992)-. Periodical. English. qt. Multivac, Inc., 11021 NW Pomona Avenue, Kansas City MO 64153. **DD** 621.

US/0083-1832
**NATIONAL BUREAU OF STANDARDS MONOGRAPH.** (NBS MONOGRAPH.). [Natl. Bur. Stand. monogr.]. **VFOAT** N.B.S Monograph; Monograph. No. 1 (1959)-. Monographic series. English. ir. Price varies per volume. National Bureau of Standards, Room 120, Voice of Z39, Washington DC 20234. **LC** QC100; .U556. **DD** 602/.18. **CODEN** NBSMA6. Documents available from CASDDS. ***Continues** National Bureau of Standards Circular, 0096-9648.*
**Ind/Abst** Ceram. Abstr.; Chem. Abstr. (1959-1982); Ei Page One; Eng. Mater. Abstr.; GeoRef.

NE/0925-5338
**NEDERLANDS TIJDSCHRIFT VOOR FOTONICA.** [Ned. tijdschr. foton.]. (1981)-. Periodical. Dutch. bm. Fl65.00. Nederlandse Ver Voor Fotonica, Populierendreef 514, c/o G J Kunz, 2272 HH Voorburg Netherlands. **UDC** 530.145. Index available. cum. index. **Bk Rev. Ad Acc.** ***Continues** Fotonica Mededelingen, 0925-5346.*
**Desc:** Articles on photons which carry information or energy in the most general way.

NE/0926-4264
**NEDERLANDS TIJDSCHRIFT VOOR NATUURKUNDE (AMSTERDAM. 1991).** **See** Science and Technology.

JA/0386-2615
**NETSUSOKUTEI.** **See** Chemistry.

●US/1069-126X
**NETWORK ECONOMICS LETTER.** [Netw. econ. lett.]. Vol. 1 No. 1 (June 1993)-. Periodical. English. mo. $395.00. Computer Economics Inc., 5841 Edison Place, Carlsbad CA 92008. **Tel** (800)326-8100, (619)438-8100, FAX (619)431-1126. **DD** 621.

FR
**NEW TRENDS IN PHYSICS TEACHING. TENDANCES NOUVELLES DE L'ENSEIGNEMENT DE LA PHYSIQUE.** **Added/Corp** Unesco. **VFOAT** Tendances Nouvelles de l'Enseignement de la Physique. Vol. 1 (1965/66)-. Monographic series. English (French). ir. Price varies per volume. UNIPUB, 4611-F Assembly Drive, Lanham MD 20706-4391. **Tel** (800)274-4888, FAX (301)459-0056, telex 28787 GATT CH. **LC** QC30; .N48. **DD** 530/.07/1.

IT
**NEWS FROM ICTP / INTERNATIONAL CENTRE FOR THEORETICAL PHYSICS.** **VFOAT** News from the ICTP. No. 1 (Dec. 1984)-. Periodical. English. International Centre for Theoretical Physics, PO Box 586, I-34100 Trieste Italy. **Tel** (40)22.401, FAX (40)22.41.63, telex 460390 ICTP I.

JA
**NIIGATA RIKAGAKU : THE JOURNAL OF PHYSICS AND CHEMISTRY OF NIIGATA.** [Niigata rikagaku]. **Added/Corp** Niigata-ken Rikagaku Gijutsu Shokuin Kyokai. **VFOAT** Journal of Physics and Chemistry of Niigata. (1975)-. Academic Scholarly Publication. Japanese. Niigataken Rikagaku Gijutsu Shokuin Kyogikai, (Assoc. of Physical & Chemical Staff, Niigata Prefecture), Nigataken Eisei Kogai Kenkyujo, 314-1, Sowa, Niigatashi, Niigataken 950-21 Japan. **CODEN** NIRID7. Documents available from CASDDS.
**Ind/Abst** Chem. Abstr.

JA/0029-0181
**NIPPON BUTSURIGAKKAI SHI.** **Added/Corp** Nippon Butsugakkai. Nippon Butsurigakkai. Proceedings. **VFOAT** Butsuri; Proceedings of the Physical Society of Japan. Vol. 1 (December 1946)-. Academic Scholarly Publication. Japanese. mo. $350.00. Physical Society of Japan, Rm 211 3-5-8 Shiba-Koen, Minato-ku, Tokyo 105 Japan. **Tel** (292)3751-9. **(Subscription address:** Maruzen Company Ltd., PO Box 5050, Import & Export Department, Tokyo 100 31 Japan.) **CODEN** NBGSAW. Documents available from CASDDS.
**Ind/Abst** Chem. Abstr.; GeoRef.

UK/0960-3360
**NIR NEWS.** [NIR news]. (1990)-. Periodical. English. bm. $105.00. NIR Publications, 6 Charlton Mill, Charlton Chichester PO18 0HY England. **Tel** 011 44 243 811334, FAX 011 44 243 811711. **ED** A.M.C. Davies. **DD** 621.3612. **Bk Rev. Ad Acc. Pr Rev. Circ:** 220.
**Desc:** Each issue contains two pages of abstracts and summaries of NIR research papers, feature articles, reviews, application articles, plus news and views from around the world and regular columns on history, reader's problems and forthcoming events.

US/1048-776X
**NIST SPECIAL PUBLICATION.** (NIST SPECIAL PUBLICATION / U.S. DEPARTMENT OF COMMERCE, NATIONAL INSTITUTE OF STANDARDS AND TECHNOLOGY.). [NIST spec. publ.]. **Added/Corp** United States. National Institute of Standards and Technology. **VFOAT** NIST SP. **VAT** National Institute of Standards and Technology Special Publication. (1988)-. Academic Scholarly Publication. English. Price varies per volume. US Department of Commerce / National Bureau of Standards / Maryland, Gaithersburg MD 20899. **LC** QC100; .U57. **DD** 353.0082/1. Documents available from Article Express International, CASDDS. ***Continues** NBS Special Publication, 0083-1883.*
**Ind/Abst** Bioeng. Abstr. (1988-); Chem. Abstr.; Coal Abstr. (1988-); Ei Page One (1988-); Eng. Index Annu.; Eng. Index Energy Abstr. (1988-); GeoRef (1988-); Nucl. Sci. Abstr. (1988-); World Surf. Coat. Abstr. (1988-).

PL/0044-1597
**NONLINEAR VIBRATION PROBLEMS.** (ZAGADNIENIA DRGAN NIELINIOWYCH.). [Nonlinear vib. probl.]. 1-. Periodical. Polish (summaries and/or abstracts in English and Russian). Panstwowe Wydawn Naukowe, Miodowa 10, PO Box 391, 00251 Warsaw Poland. **LC** QA935; .Z28. **CODEN** NLVBAO. Documents available from Article Express International, Ask*IEEE.
**Desc:** Vol. 5 consists of proceedings in English or Russian of the 2d conference on Nonlinear Vibrations, Warsaw, Sept., 1962.
**Ind/Abst** Bioeng. Abstr.; Ei Page One; Eng. Index Annu. [Select. Cov.]; INSPEC (1977-); Int. Aerosp. Abstr.; Zentralbl. Math. Ihre Grenzgeb.

BL
**NOTAS DE FISICA.** V. 1- 1978-. Monographic series. English (French, Italian and Portuguese). ir. Price varies per volume. Cent Brasil de Pesquisas Fisic, 22290 Rio de Janeiro RJ Brazil. **Tel** (021)541-0337, telex 21-22563 CBPQ. ctrl circ.
**Ind/Abst** Energy Res. Abstr. (Oct. 1981-).

CN/0826-2799
**NOUVELLES DE L'A.Q.T.** (NOUVELLES DE L'A.Q.T. / L'ASSOCIATION QUEBECOISE DE TELEDETECTION.). [Nouv. A.Q.T.]. **Main/Corp** Association Quebecoise de Teledetection. **VAT** Nouvelles de l'Association Quebecoise de Teledetection. Vol. 1, No. 1 (Sept. 1983)-. Periodical. French. sa. 15.00Can$ (membership), 5.00Can$ (students). Association Quebecoise de Teledetection, C P 10047, Ste Foy Quebec G1V 4C6 Canada. **Tel** (819)821-7180. **ED** Paul Gagnon. **DD** 621.36/78/060714. **Bk Rev. Ad Acc. Circ:** 500.
**Desc:** Newsletter-type publication provided to members of the Association Quebecoise de Teledetection (Quebec Remote Sensing Association). Contains articles pertaining to remote sensing activities in Quebec and Canada.

UK/0959-2423
**NPL REPORT DMM (A).** [NPL rep. DMM (A)]. (1989)-. Academic Scholarly Publication. English. ir. Price varies per volume. National Physical Laboratory, Teddington Middlesex TW11 0LW England. **DD** 620.1108. Documents available from CASDDS. ***Continues** National Physical Laboratory. Division of Materials Applications. DMA, 0143-7313.*
**Ind/Abst** Chem. Abstr.

SA
**NU SCIENCE.** V. 1- Mar. 1968-. Periodical. English. University of Natal Science Council, King George 5th Avenue, Durban South Africa. **LC** QC1; .N79. **DD** 505.

IT/0369-4100
**NUOVO CIMENTO DELLA SOCIETA ITALIANA DI FISICA. SEZIONE B.** (IL NUOVO CIMENTO DELLA SOCIETA ITALIANA DI FISICA. B.). [Nuovo cimento Soc. ital. fis. B]. **Added/Corp** Societa Italiana di Fisica. **VFOAT** Relativity, Classical and Statistical Physics; General Physics, Relativity, Astronomy and Plasmas. Vol. 1B (Jan. 11, 1971)-. Academic Scholarly Publication. Italian (English; summaries and/or abstracts in Russian). mo. $620.00 (nonmembers), $510.00 (members). Editrice Compositori SRL, Viale Stalingrado 97 2, 40128 Bologna Italy. **Tel** 011 39 51 327811. **CODEN** NIFBAP. **[CCC]. Bk Rev. Ad Acc. Circ:** 1,000 (ctrl). Documents available from The Genuine Article, Ask*IEEE, CASDDS. ***Continues** Nuovo Cimento. B, 0369-3554.*
**Desc:** Covers mathematical methods in physics, classical and quantum physics, mechanics and fields, relativity and gravitation, electricity and magnetism, optics, acoustics, fluid, plasmas and electric discharges, fundamental astronomy and astrophysics, instrumentation, techniques, and astronomical observations.
**Ind/Abst** Chem. Abstr.; Curr. Contents Phys. Chem. Earth Sci.; EMBASE; Energy Res. Abstr. (Feb. 1981-); INSPEC (1971-); Math. Rev.; Life Sci. Collect.; Res. Alert [Full Cov.]; Sci. Cit. Index; SCISEARCH.

IT/0390-5551
**NUOVO CIMENTO DELLA SOCIETA ITALIANA DI FISICA [SEZIONE] C, IL.** (IL NUOVO CIMENTO DELLA SOCIETA ITALIANA DI FISICA. C.). [Nuovo cimento Soc. ital. fis. c]. **Added/Corp** Societa Italiana di Fisica. Vol. 1C (Jan./Feb. 1978)-. Periodical. Italian (English, French, Italian and German). bm. $310.00 (nonmembers), $245.00 (members). Editrice Compositori SRL, Viale Stalingrado 97 2, 40128 Bologna Italy. **Tel** 011 39 51 327811. **CODEN** NIFCAS. **[CCC]. Pr Rev.** Documents available from The Genuine Article, Ask*IEEE, CASDDS.
**Ind/Abst** Chem. Abstr.; Curr. Contents Phys. Chem. Earth Sci.; GeoRef; INSPEC (Jan./Feb. 1978-); Int. Aerosp. Abstr.; Math. Rev.; Meteorol. Geoastrophys. Abstr. (19??-); Res. Alert [Select. Cov.]; SCISEARCH.

IT
**NUOVO SAGGIATORE : BOLLETTINO DELLA SOCIETA ITALIANA DI FISICA, IL.** **Added/Corp** Societa Italiana di Fisica. Vol. 1 No. 1 (Jan./Feb. 1985)-. Periodical. Italian. bm. $60.00. Editrice Compositori SRL, Viale Stalingrado 97 2, 40128 Bologna Italy. **Tel** 011 39 51 327811. **LC** QC1; .N95. **Bk Rev. Ad Acc. Circ:** 1,000 (ctrl). ***Continues in part** Bollettino della Societa Italiana di Fisica, 0037-8801.*
**Desc:** Covers data and proceedings of the conferences of physics, as well as articles of physics in general.

US/1065-2035
**NUTS & VOLTS MAGAZINE.** [Nuts volts mag.]. **VFOAT** Nuts & Volts; Nuts and Volts Magazine. (19??)-. Periodical. English. mo. $34.00 (first class), $17.00 (1 year, third class), $31.00 (2 year, third class) U.S.; $35.00 (first class) Canada & Mexico. T and L Publications Incorporated, 430 Princeland Court, Corona CA 91719. **Tel** (714)371-8497, FAX (714)371-3052. **DD** 621.

XV/0473-7466
**OBZORNIK ZA MATEMATIKO IN FIZIKO.** **See** Mathematics.

UK
**OXFORD PHYSICS SERIES.** No. 1 (1973)-. Monographic series. English. ir. Price varies per volume. Oxford University Press, Walton Street, Oxford OX2 6DP England. **Tel** 011 44 865 56767, FAX 011 44 865 267773, telex 837330 OXPRES G. **(Subscription address:** Oxford University Press / USA, Journals Marketing Department, Oxford University Press, 2001 Evans Road, Cary NC 27513.) **CODEN** OXPSD7. Documents available from Ask*IEEE.
**Ind/Abst** INSPEC.

JA/0369-8009
**OYO BUTSURI.** [Oyo butsuri]. **Added/Corp** Oyo Butsuri Danwakai. Oyo Butsuri Gakkai. **VFOAT** Oyo Buturi; Journal of Applied Physics, Japan; Japanese Journal of Applied Physics. (1932)-. Academic Scholarly Publication. Japanese (summaries and/or abstracts in English). mo. $302.00. Oyo Butsuri Gakkai, (Japan Soc. of Applied Physics), Kunimatsu Biru, 2-6, Kudan Kita 1 Chome, Chiyodaku, Tokyoto 102, Japan. **(Subscription address:** Kyowa Book Company Inc., 1-38 Kanda Jinbo-Cho, Chiyoda-Ku Tokyo 101, Japan) **LC** QC1; .O93. **CODEN** OYBSA9. Documents available from Ask*IEEE, CASDDS.
**Ind/Abst** Chem. Abstr.; INSPEC (Aug. 1968-).

US/1063-9136
**P-A-M BULLETIN.** **See** Mathematics.

US/0272-4723
**PAPER SUMMARIES - AMERICAN SOCIETY FOR NONDESTRUCTIVE TESTING.** **See** Engineering.

US/0031-2460
**PARTICLE ACCELERATORS.** [Part. accel.]. Vol. 1 (March 1970)-. Periodical. English. bm. $746.00 (academic institutions), $1164.00 (corporate institutions). Gordon & Breach Science Publishers, Inc., PO Box 786, Cooper Station, New York NY 10276. **Tel** (212)206-8900, FAX (212)645-2459. **(Subscription address:** International Publishers Distributor at one of the following addresses: 820 Town Center Drive, Langhorne, PA 19047; or PO Box 90, Reading Berkshire RG1 8JL UK; or Kent Ridge PO Box 1180, Singapore 9111, Republic of Singapore) **ED** F. T. Cole. **LC** QC787.P3; P35. **DD** 539.7/3/05. **CODEN** PLACBD. **[CCC]. Bk Rev. Ad Acc.** Documents available from Article Express International, Ask*IEEE, CASDDS.
**Ind/Abst** Bioeng. Abstr.; Chem. Abstr.; Ei Page One; Eng. Index Annu.; INSPEC (March 1970-).

GW/0934-0866
**PARTICLE & PARTICLE SYSTEMS CHARACTERIZATION.** **See** Chemistry.

UK/0260-4280
**PERSPECTIVE OF PHYSICS.** (A PERSPECTIVE OF PHYSICS.). [Perspect. phys.]. Vol. 1 (1976)-. Monographic series. English. ir. Price varies per volume. Gordon & Breach Science Publishers, Inc., PO Box 786, Cooper Station, New York NY 10276. **Tel** (212)206-8900, FAX (212)645-2459. **(Subscription address:** Gordon & Breach Science Publishers, 820 Town Center Drive, Langhorne, PA 19047; Telephone: (217)750-2642**)** **LC** QC1; .P35. **DD** 530/.05.

US/0141-1594
**PHASE TRANSITIONS.** [Phase transit.]. Vol. 1 (Sept. 1979)-. Academic Scholarly Publication. English. qt. $508.00 (academic institutions), $792.00 (corporate institutions). Gordon & Breach Science Publishers, Inc., PO Box 786, Cooper Station, New York NY 10276. **Tel** (212)206-8900, FAX (212)645-2459. **(Subscription address:** International Publishers Distributor at one of the following addresses: 820 Town Center Drive, Langhorne, PA 19047; or PO Box 90, Reading Berkshire RG1 8JL UK; or Kent Ridge PO Box 1180, Singapore 9111, Republic of Singapore**)** **ED** A. M. Glazer. **LC** QC176.8.P45; P45. **DD** 536/.401/05. **CODEN** PHTRDP. **[CCC]. Bk Rev. Ad Acc. Pr Rev.** Documents available from Article Express International, The Genuine Article, Ask*IEEE, CASDDS.
**Ind/Abst** Acoust. Abstr.; Alum. Ind. Abstr. (Sept. 1979-); Bioeng. Abstr.; Chem. Abstr. (Sept. 1979-); Curr. Contents Phys. Chem. Earth Sci.; Ei Page One; Eng. Mater. Abstr.; Eng. Index Annu.; INSPEC (Sept. 1979-); Leadscan; Met. Abstr. (Sept. 1979-); Res. Alert [Full Cov.]; Sci. Cit. Index; SCISEARCH.

UK/1062-7901
**PHASE TRANSITIONS AND CRITICAL PHENOMENA.** [Phase transit. crit. phenom.]. Vol. 1 (1972)-. Academic Scholarly Publication. English. ir. Price varies per volume. Academic Press, Inc., 6277 Sea Harbor Drive, Orlando FL 32887. **Tel** (800)543-9534, (407)345-4100, FAX (407)363-9661. **ED** C. Domb and M. S. Green. **LC** QC175.16.P5; P48. **DD** 530.1/3. **CODEN** PTCPEJ. Documents available from CASDDS.
**Ind/Abst** Chem. Abstr.

UK/0141-8610
**PHILOSOPHICAL MAGAZINE. A, PHYSICS OF CONDENSED MATTER, DEFECTS AND MECHANICAL PROPERTIES.** [Philos. mag., A. Phys. condens. matter. Defects mech. prop.]. **VFOAT** Physics of Condensed Matter, Defects and Mechanical Properties. **VAT** Philosophical Magazine A. Vol. 37, No. 1 (Jan. 1978)-. Academic Scholarly Publication. English (French and German; summaries and/or abstracts in French, German and English). mo. £745.00 UK; $1230.00 other (parts A and B). Taylor & Francis Ltd., Rankine Road, Basingstoke Hampshire, RG24 8PR United Kingdom. **Tel** 011 44 256 840366, FAX 011 44 256 479438, telex 858540. **(Subscription address:** Taylor & Francis Inc., 1900 Frost Road, Suite 101, Bristol PA 19007-1598.**)** **ED** E. A. Davis (editor's address: University of Leicester, Department of Physics, University Road, Leicester LE1 7RH United Kingdom); J. L. Smith (editor's address: Los Alamos National Laboratory, Los Alamos, NM 87545). **LC** QC173.4.C65; P444. **DD** 530.4/1. **CODEN** PMAADG. **[CCC].** Index available in last issue of volume--attached. **Pr Rev.** available on microfilm and microfiche from University Microfilms International (UMI). Documents available from Article Express International, The Genuine Article, Ask*IEEE, CASDDS. ***Continues in part*** *Philosophical Magazine (London, England : 1945), 0031-8086.*
**Desc:** A primary journal of experimental, theoretical and applied physics of condensed matter. Part A covers defects and mechanical properties; Part B covers structural, electronic, optical and magnetic properties.
**Ind/Abst** Acoust. Abstr.; Alum. Ind. Abstr.; Bioeng. Abstr.; Ceram. Abstr. (19??-); Chem. Abstr.; Chem. Titles; Curr. Contents Phys. Chem. Earth Sci.; Curr. Technol. Index; Electron. Commun. Abstr. J.; Eng. Index Annu.; GeoRef; INSPEC (Jan. 1978-); ISMEC Bull.; Met. Abstr.; Pollut. Abstr. Indexes; Res. Alert [Full Cov.]; Saf. Sci. Abstr. J.; Sci. Cit. Index; SCISEARCH; World Alum. Abstr.

UK/0958-6644
**PHILOSOPHICAL MAGAZINE. B, PHYSICS OF CONDENSED MATTER, STRUCTURAL, ELECTRONIC, OPTICAL, AND MAGNETIC PROPERTIES.** [Philos. mag., B Phys. condens. matter, Struct. electron. opt. magn. prop.]. **VFOAT** Philosophical Magazine B; Physics of Condensed Matter, Structural, Electronic, Optical, and Magnetic Properties; Philosophical Magazine. **VAT** Philosophical Magazine B. Vol. 53, No. 5 (May 1986)-. Periodical. English. mo. £745.00 UK; $1230.00 other (combined price for parts A & B). Taylor & Francis Ltd., Rankine Road, Basingstoke Hampshire, RG24 8PR United Kingdom. **Tel** 011 44 256 840366, FAX 011 44 256 479438, telex 858540. **(Subscription address:** Taylor & Francis Inc., 1900 Frost Road, Suite 101, Bristol PA 19007-1598.**)** **LC** QC173.4.C65; P445. **DD** 530.4/1. **[CCC]. Pr Rev.** Documents available from Article Express International, The Genuine Article, Ask*IEEE, CASDDS. ***Continues*** *Philosophical Magazine. B, Physics of Condensed Matter, Electronic, Optical, and Magnetic Properties, 0141-8637.*
**Ind/Abst** Acoust. Abstr.; Alum. Ind. Abstr.; Bioeng. Abstr.; Ceram. Abstr. (19??-); Chem. Abstr.; Ei Page One; Eng. Index Annu.; Geol. Abstr.; GeoRef; INSPEC (May 1986-); Met. Abstr.; Res. Alert [Full Cov.]; Sci. Cit. Index; SCISEARCH.

UK/0950-0839
**PHILOSOPHICAL MAGAZINE LETTERS.** [Philos. mag. lett.]. Vol. 55, No. 1 (Jan. 1987)-. Academic Scholarly Publication. English (French and German; summaries and/or abstracts in English). mo. £203.00 UK; $335.00 other. Taylor & Francis Ltd., Rankine Road, Basingstoke Hampshire, RG24 8PR United Kingdom. **Tel** 011 44 256 840366, FAX 011 44 256 479438, telex 858540. **(Subscription address:** Taylor & Francis Inc., 1900 Frost Road, Suite 101, Bristol PA 19007-1598.**)** **ED** E. A. Davis, J. L. Smith and S. R. Elliot. **LC** QC173.4.C65; P446. **DD** 530.4/1. **CODEN** PMLEEG. **[CCC]. Pr Rev.** Documents available from The Genuine Article, Ask*IEEE, CASDDS.
**Desc:** A rapid communications part of the highly respected Philosophical Magazine. Short contributions are published covering original research in the broad field of condensed matter physics. Defects and mechanical properties are dealt with, as well as structural electronics, optical and magnetic properties.
**Ind/Abst** Ceram. Abstr.; Chem. Abstr. (1987-); Curr. Contents Phys. Chem. Earth Sci.; Ei Page One; INSPEC (1987-); Res. Alert [Full Cov.]; Sci. Cit. Index; SCISEARCH.

UK/0962-8428
**PHILOSOPHICAL TRANSACTIONS - ROYAL SOCIETY OF LONDON. PHYSICAL SCIENCES AND ENGINEERING.** (PHILOSOPHICAL TRANSACTIONS OF THE ROYAL SOCIETY OF LONDON. SERIES A, PHYSICAL SCIENCES AND ENGINEERING.). [Philos. trans. - R. Soc. Lond., Phys. sci. eng.]. **Added/Corp** Royal Society (Great Britain). **VFOAT** Physical Sciences and Engineering; Philosophical Transactions of the Royal Society of London. Vol. 332, No. 1623 (1990)-. Periodical. English. mo. $891.00 North America; £490.00 UK; £539.00 other. Royal Society, 6 Carlton House Terrace, London SW1Y 5AG England. **Tel** 011 44 71 839 5561, FAX 071-976 1837, telex 917876 ROYAL G. **ED** F. T. Smith. **LC** Q41; .L849617b. **DD** 500.2. Index available. **Pr Rev. Circ:** 980. Documents available from The Genuine Article, Ask*IEEE. ***Continues*** *Philosophical Transactions of the Royal Society of London. Series A, Mathematical and Physical Sciences, 0080-4614.*
**Desc:** Original papers on mathematical, physical, engineering and earth science subjects from Royal Society Discussion Meetings.
**Ind/Abst** Curr. Contents Phys. Chem. Earth Sci.; Ecology Abstr.; Fluid Abstr., Civil Eng.; Fluid Abstr. Proc. Eng.; FLUIDEX (199?-); GeoRef; INSPEC (July 1990-); Math. Rev.; Res. Alert [Full Cov.]; Sci. Cit. Index; SCISEARCH.

CN/0824-3794
**PHOTOVOLTAICS TECHNIQUE.** ***Ceased.*** Vol. 1, No. 1 (Dec. 1982)-?. Periodical. English. bm. Spectral Engineering Ltd, 29 Popular Plains Crescent, Toronto Ontario M4E 1E9 Canada. **DD** 621.3815/42.

CN/0710-0140
**PHYS 13 NEWS.** [Phys 13 news]. **Added/Corp** University of Waterloo. Dept. of Physics. No. 1 (Oct. 1971)-. Periodical. English. ir. $6.00 US; 5.00Can$ Canada; 8.00Can$ other. University of Waterloo/Phil Eastman ED, PHYS 13 News, Department of Physics, Waterloo, Ontario N2L 3G1 Canada. **Tel** (519)885-1211. **DD** 530/.0712.

NE/0378-4371
**PHYSICA A.** [Physica A]. **VFOAT** Theoretical and Statistical Physics; Statistical and Theoretical Physics. (Jan. 1975)-. Academic Scholarly Publication. English (French and German; summaries and/or abstracts in French, German and English). Forty-Four times a year (11 vols.). Fl4851.00. Elsevier Science Publishers BV, PO Box 211, 1000 AE Amsterdam Netherlands. **Tel** 011 31 20 5803642, FAX 011 31 20 5862696, telex 15682. **ED** H. W. Capel, H. J. Hilhorst, C. M. Knobler, H.N.W. Lekkerkerker, H. E. Stanley. **LC** QC1; .P383. **DD** 530.1/5. **CODEN** PHYADX. **[CCC].** cum. index. **Pr Rev.** available on microfilm and microfiche from University Microfilms International (UMI). Documents available from The Genuine Article, Ask*IEEE, CASDDS. ***Continues in part*** *Physica, 0031-8914.*
**Desc:** Contains papers on theoretical physics, with the emphasis on statistical mechanics.
**Ind/Abst** Acoust. Abstr. (1975-); Chem. Abstr.; Curr. Contents Phys. Chem. Earth Sci.; Ei Page One; Energy Res. Abstr. (June 1975-); HTFS Dig.; INSPEC (1975-); Leadscan; Math. Rev. (1975-); Phys. Briefs; Res. Alert [Full Cov.]; Sci. Cit. Index; SCISEARCH; Soc. Sci. Cit. Index [Select. Cov.]; Zentralbl. Math. Ihre Grenzgeb. (1975-).

NE/0921-4526
**PHYSICA B. CONDENSED MATTER.** [Physica, B, Condens. matter]. **VFOAT** Condensed Matter. Vol. 152, Nos. 1 & 2 (Aug. 2, 1988)-. Academic Scholarly Publication. English (French and German). Forty-eight times a year (12 vols.). Fl5292.00. Elsevier Science Publishers BV, PO Box 211, 1000 AE Amsterdam Netherlands. **Tel** 011 31 20 5803642, FAX 011 31 20 5862696, telex 15682. **ED** F.R. de Boer, Z. Fisk, R. Jochemsen, G.H. Lander. **LC** QC1; .P3823. **DD** 530.4/1. **CODEN** PHYBE3. **[CCC]. Pr Rev.** available on microfilm and microfiche from University Microfilms International (UMI). Documents available from Article Express International, The Genuine Article, Ask*IEEE, CASDDS. ***Continues in part*** *Physica B + C, 0378-4363.*
**Desc:** Contains papers, both experimental and theoretical, in the realm of the physics of condensed matter.
**Ind/Abst** Chem. Abstr. (Aug. 1988-); Curr. Contents Phys. Chem. Earth Sci.; Eng. Index Annu.; INSPEC (Aug. 1988-); Phys. Briefs; Res. Alert [Full Cov.]; Sci. Cit. Index; SCISEARCH.

NE/0921-4534
**PHYSICA C. SUPERCONDUCTIVITY.** [Phys. C, Supercond.]. **VFOAT** Superconductivity. Vol. 152, No. 1 (March 1, 1988)-. Academic Scholarly Publication. English. ir (76 issues per year). Fl8379.00. Elsevier Science Publishers BV, PO Box 211, 1000 AE Amsterdam Netherlands. **Tel** 011 31 20 5803642, FAX 011 31 20 5862696, telex 15682. **ED** M.B. Brodsky, G.W. Crabtree, B.D. Dunlap, R.P. Griessen, S. Maekawa, Yu.A. Osipyan, H.R. Ott, S. Tanaka. **LC** QC611.9; .P49. **DD** 537.6/23. **CODEN** PHYCE6. **[CCC]. Pr Rev.** available on microfilm and microfiche from University Microfilms International (UMI). Documents available from Article Express International, The Genuine Article, Ask*IEEE, CASDDS. ***Continues in part*** *Physica B + C, 0378-4363.*
**Desc:** Serves as an exclusive, rapid channel for publications on superconductivity and related subjects.
**Ind/Abst** Chem. Abstr. (Mar. 1988-); Curr. Contents Phys. Chem. Earth Sci.; Eng. Index Annu.; INSPEC (Mar. 1988-); Res. Alert [Full Cov.]; Sci. Cit. Index; SCISEARCH; Soc. Sci. Cit. Index [Select. Cov.].

NE/0167-2789
**PHYSICA. D.** (PHYSICA D. NONLINEAR PHENOMENA.). [Physica, D]. (Apr. 1980)-. Academic Scholarly Publication. English. Forty times a year (10 vols.). Fl4410.00. Elsevier Science Publishers BV, PO Box 211, 1000 AE Amsterdam Netherlands. **Tel** 011 31 20 5803642, FAX 011 31 20 5862696, telex 15682. **ED** H. Flaschka, F. Busse. **LC** QC1; .P3834. **DD** 530/.05. **CODEN** PDNPDT. **[CCC]. Pr Rev.** available on microfilm and microfiche from University Microfilms International (UMI). Documents available from The Genuine Article, Ask*IEEE, CASDDS. ***Continues in part*** *Physica, 0031-8914.*
**Desc:** Publishes reports of experiments, techniques and ideas which, although they may be derived and explained in the context of a particular field, advance the understanding of nonlinear phenomena in general.
**Ind/Abst** ACM Guide Comput. Lit.; Acoust. Abstr. (April 1980-); Chem. Abstr. (April 1980-); Compumath Citation Index [Full Cov.]; Comput. Rev. (April 1980-); Curr. Contents Phys. Chem. Earth Sci.; Ei Page One; HTFS Dig.; INSPEC (April 1980-); Int. Aerosp. Abstr.; Math. Rev.; Res. Alert [Full Cov.]; Sci. Cit. Index; SCISEARCH; Zentralbl. Math. Ihre Grenzgeb.

SW/0031-8949
**PHYSICA SCRIPTA.** [Phys. scr.]. **Added/Corp** Kungl. Svenska Vetenskapsakademien. Vol. 1 (1970)-. Periodical. English (French and German). mo. $900.00 US, Canada & Mexico; Kr4725.00 Nordic countries; DM1575.00 other. Royal Swedish Academy of Sciences, Publications Department, Box 50005, S-104 05 Stockholm Sweden. **Tel** 011 46 8 150430, FAX 011 46 8 155670, telex 17073 ROYACOD S. **ED** Anders Barany. **LC** QC1; .P392. **NLM** W1 PH683. **CODEN** PHSTBO. **[CCC].** Index available in last issue of volume--attached. **Pr Rev. Circ:** 800. Documents available from The Genuine Article, Ask*IEEE, CASDDS. ***Supersedes*** *Arkiv for Fysik;* ***Absorbed*** *Physica Fennica, 0031-8922.*
**Desc:** General physics journal with special emphasis on cross-disciplinary fields of physics; also, topical issues included in the subscription.
**Ind/Abst** Acoust. Abstr.; Alum. Ind. Abstr.; Chem. Abstr.; Curr. Contents Phys. Chem. Earth Sci.; Ei Page One; Energy Res. Abstr.; Eng. Mater. Abstr.; GeoRef; INSPEC (1970-); Int. Aerosp. Abstr. (19??-19??); Leadscan; Mass Spect. Bull.; Math. Rev.; Met. Abstr.; Res. Alert [Full Cov.]; Sci. Cit. Index; SCISEARCH.

GW/0031-8965
**PHYSICA STATUS SOLIDI. A: APPLIED RESEARCH.** [Phys. status solidi. A, Appl. res.]. Vol. 1 (Jan. 1970)-. Periodical. English (French, German and Russian; summaries and/or abstracts in French, German and Russian). mo. $1765.00. Akademie-Verlag GmbH, Muehlenstrasse 33 34, D 13162 Berlin Germany. **Tel** 011 49 30 47889300, FAX 011 49 30 47889357. **(Subscription address:** VCH Publishers Inc., 303 Northwest 12th Avenue, Journals Department, Deerfield FL 33442.**)** **NLM** W1 PH683F. **CODEN** PSSABA. **[CCC].** Index Available, published separately, free-automatically sent. cum. index. **Pr Rev.** Documents available from Article Express International, The Genuine Article, Ask*IEEE, CASDDS. ***Continues in part*** *Physica Status Solidi, 0031-8957.*
**Ind/Abst** Alum. Ind. Abstr.; Bioeng. Abstr.; Ceram. Abstr.; Chem. Abstr.; Curr. Contents Phys. Chem. Earth Sci.; Curr. Titles Electrochem.; Ei Page One; Energy Res.

Abstr.; Eng. Index Annu.; GeoRef; INSPEC (1970-); Int. Aerosp. Abstr.; Leadscan; Mass Spect. Bull.; Met. Abstr.; Pollut. Abstr. Indexes; Res. Alert [Full Cov.]; Sci. Cit. Index; SCISEARCH; Soils Fert.

GW/0370-1972
**PHYSICA STATUS SOLIDI. B : BASIC RESEARCH.** [Phys. status solidi, b Basic res.]. Vol. 43, (Jan. 1971)-. Periodical. English (German, French and Russian; summaries and/or abstracts in German, French and Russian). mo. $1765.00. Akademie-Verlag GmbH, Muehlenstrasse 33 34, D 13162 Berlin Germany. **Tel** 011 49 30 47889300, FAX 011 49 30 47889357. **(Subscription address:** VCH Publishers Inc., 303 Northwest 12th Avenue, Journals Department, Deerfield FL 33442.**) CODEN** PSSBBD. **[CCC].** Index available in last issue of volume--attached. **Pr Rev.** Documents available from Article Express International, The Genuine Article, Ask*IEEE, CASDDS. ***Continues in part*** *Physica Status Solidi, 0031-8957.*
**Ind/Abst** Alum. Ind. Abstr.; Bioeng. Abstr.; Chem. Abstr.; Curr. Contents Phys. Chem. Earth Sci.; Ei Page One; Energy Res. Abstr. (Sept. 1971-); Eng. Mater. Abstr.; Eng. Index Annu.; INSPEC (1971-); Int. Aerosp. Abstr.; Leadscan; Mass Spect. Bull.; Math. Rev.; Met. Abstr.; Pollut. Abstr. Indexes; Res. Alert [Full Cov.]; Sci. Cit. Index; SCISEARCH.

US/1050-2947
**PHYSICAL REVIEW. A.** [Phys. rev., A]. **Added/Corp** American Physical Society. American Institute of Physics. **VFOAT** Atomic, Molecular, and Optical Physics; Statistical Physics, Plasmas, Fluids, and Related Interdisciplinary Topics. Third Series, Vol. 41, No. 1 (Jan. 1, 1990)-. Periodical. English. mo. $1120.00 US. American Institute of Physics, 500 Sunnyside Boulevard, Woodbury NY 11797-2999. **Tel** (516)576-2200, FAX (516)349-7669, telex 960983. **LC** QC1; .P42. **DD** 530/.05. **[CCC]. Pr Rev.** Documents available from Article Express International, Ask*IEEE. ***Continues*** *Physical Review. A, General Physics, 0556-2791.* ***Continued in part by*** *Physical Review. E, Statistical Physics, Plasmas, Fluids, and Related Interdisciplinary Topics, 1063-651X.*
**Ind/Abst** Curr. Contents Phys. Chem. Earth Sci.; Eng. Index Annu. [Select. Cov.]; INSPEC (Jan. 1990-); Leadscan; Sci. Cit. Index.

US/0048-4024
**PHYSICAL REVIEW ABSTRACTS.** **Added/Corp** American Physical Society. American Institute of Physics. Vol. 1 (1970)-. English. sm. $350.00 US; $370.00 Canada, Mexico, Central & South America and the Caribbean; $380.00 other. American Institute of Physics, 500 Sunnyside Boulevard, Woodbury NY 11797-2999. **Tel** (516)576-2200, FAX (516)349-7669, telex 960983. **CODEN** PRVABI. **[CCC].**
**Ind/Abst** Abstr. Bull. Inst. Pap. Sci. Tech.

US/0094-0003
**PHYSICAL REVIEW AND PHYSICAL REVIEW LETTERS INDEX.** [Phys. rev. Phys. rev. lett. index]. **Added/Corp** American Institute of Physics. American Physical Society. 3rd Ser., Vol. 2 (July/Dec. 1970)-. English. an (May). $90.00 US; $95.00 Canada, Mexico, Central & South America and the Caribbean; $105.00 other. American Institute of Physics, 500 Sunnyside Boulevard, Woodbury NY 11797-2999. **Tel** (516)576-2200, FAX (516)349-7669, telex 960983. **LC** Z7143; .P5; QC1. **DD** 530/.05. **NLM** W1 PH737E. **CODEN** PRPIEF. ***Continues*** *Physical Review Index.*

US
**PHYSICAL REVIEW. A[15], STATISTICAL PHYSICS, PLASMAS, FLUIDS, AND RELATED INTERDISCIPLINARY TOPICS.** **Added/Corp** American Physical Society. American Institute of Physics. **VFOAT** Statistical Physics, Plasmas, Fluids, and Related Interdisciplinary Topics. Ser. 3, Vol. 41, No. 2 (Jan. 15, 1990)-. Statistical Publication. English. mo. $100.00 (members), $900.00 (non-members). American Physical Society, One Physics Ellipse, College Park MD 20740. **Tel** (301)209-3248. ***Continues in part*** *Physical Review. A, General Physics, 0556-2791.*

US/0163-1829
**PHYSICAL REVIEW B : CONDENSED MATTER.** [Phys. rev., B, Condens. matter]. **Added/Corp** American Physical Society. American Institute of Physics. **VFOAT** Condensed Matter. Vol. 18, No. 1 (July 1978)-. Academic Scholarly Publication. English. Forty-eight times a year. $3510.00 US; $3670.00 Canada, Mexico, Central and South America, and Caribbean; $3935.00 other. American Institute of Physics, 500 Sunnyside Boulevard, Woodbury NY 11797-2999. **Tel** (516)576-2200, FAX (516)349-7669, telex 960983. **LC** QC176.A1; P513. **DD** 530.4/1. **CODEN** PRBMDO. **[CCC]. Pr Rev.** available on microfilm and microfiche. Documents available from The Genuine Article, Ask*IEEE, CASDDS. ***Continues*** *Physical Review. B. Solid State, 0556-2805.*
**Desc:** Deals with all aspects of condensed matter phenomena. Mainly deals with electronic structure, semiconductors, and chemical physics.
**Ind/Abst** Abstr. Bull. Inst. Pap. Sci. Tech.; Acoust. Abstr.; Alum. Ind. Abstr.; Ceram. Abstr.; Chem. Abstr. (1970-); Chem. Titles; Curr. Contents Phys. Chem. Earth Sci.; Curr. Phys. Index; Energy Res. Abstr. (May 1979-); Eng. Mater. Abstr.; GeoRef; INSPEC (Jan. 1979-); Int. Aerosp. Abstr.; Leadscan; Mass Spect. Bull.; Math. Rev. (?-199?); Met. Abstr.; Res. Alert [Full Cov.]; Sci. Cit. Index; SCISEARCH; SPIN (1970-).

US/0556-2821
**PHYSICAL REVIEW D : PARTICLES AND FIELDS.** ***Title Change.*** [Phys. rev. D]. Vol. 1 No. 1 (Jan. 1970)-(19??). Periodical. English. sm. American Institute of Physics, 500 Sunnyside Boulevard, Woodbury NY 11797-2999. **Tel** (516)576-2200, FAX (516)349-7669, telex 960983. **(Subscription address:** UK/ Institute of Physics, Techno House, Redcliffe Way, Bristol BS1 6NX England**) LC** QC721. **DD** 539.7/05. **NLM** W1 PH737D. **CODEN** PRVDAQ. **[CCC]. Pr Rev.** available on microfilm and microfiche. Documents available from The Genuine Article, Ask*IEEE, CASDDS. ***Continues*** *Physical Review, 0031-899X.* ***Continued by*** *Physical Review. D.*
**Desc:** Articles report on general quantum mechanics, scattering theory, general relativity and gravitation, cosmology, astrophysics, and cosmic ray physics.
**Ind/Abst** Chem. Abstr.; Chem. Titles; Curr. Contents Clin. Med.; Curr. Phys. Index; Energy Res. Abstr.; INSPEC (Jan. 1970-); Int. Aerosp. Abstr.; Math. Rev.; Res. Alert [Full Cov.]; Sci. Cit. Index; SCISEARCH; SPIN (1970-).

●US/1063-651X
**PHYSICAL REVIEW E. STATISTICAL PHYSICS, PLASMAS, FLUIDS, AND RELATED INTERDISCIPLINARY TOPICS.** [Phys. rev., E Stat. phys. plasmas fluids relat. interdiscip. topics]. **Added/Corp** American Physical Society. American Institute of Physics. **VFOAT** Statistical Physics, Plasmas, Fluids, and Related Interdisciplinary Topics. 3rd Ser., Vol. 47, No. 1 (Jan. 1993)-. Statistical Publication. English. mo. $950.00 US; $990.00 Canada, Mexico, Central & South America and the Caribbean; $1065.00 other. American Institute of Physics, 500 Sunnyside Boulevard, Woodbury NY 11797-2999. **Tel** (516)576-2200, FAX (516)349-7669, telex 960983. **LC** QC174.7; .P48. **DD** 530.1/3. **CODEN** PLEEE8. ***Continues in part*** *Physical Review. A, 1050-2947.*
**Desc:** Deals primarily with extranuclear "many body" phenomena, except for solid state. Sections are devoted to general methods in statistical physics, kinetic and transport theory and fluid structure and more.
**Ind/Abst** Sci. Cit. Index; Soc. Sci. Cit. Index [Select. Cov.].

US/0031-9007
**PHYSICAL REVIEW LETTERS.** [Phys. rev. lett.]. **Added/Corp** American Physical Society. Vol. 1 (July 1958)-. Periodical. English. Fifty times a year. $1580.00 US; $1640.00 Canada, Mexico, Central & South America and the Caribbean; $1720.00 other. American Institute of Physics, 500 Sunnyside Boulevard, Woodbury NY 11797-2999. **Tel** (516)576-2200, FAX (516)349-7669, telex 960983. **LC** QC1; .P43. **DD** 530.5. **NLM** W1 PH739. **CODEN** PRLTAO. **[CCC]. Pr Rev.** available on microfilm and microfiche (16mm or 35mm). Documents available from Article Express International, The Genuine Article, Ask*IEEE, CASDDS. ***Supersedes in part*** *Physical Review, 0031-899X.*
**Desc:** Covers major advances in all fields of physics and of developments with significant consequences across sub-disciplines.
**Ind/Abst** Acoust. Abstr.; Alum. Ind. Abstr.; Ceram. Abstr.; Chem. Abstr.; Chem. Titles; Curr. Contents Phys. Chem. Earth Sci.; Curr. Phys. Index; Energy Res. Abstr.; Eng. Mater. Abstr.; Eng. Index Annu. [Select. Cov.]; GeoRef; INSPEC (1968-); Int. Aerosp. Abstr.; Leadscan; Mass Spect. Bull.; Math. Rev.; Met. Abstr.; Res. Alert [Full Cov.]; Sci. Cit. Index; SCISEARCH; SPIN (1970-).

UK/0162-2528
**PHYSICAL TECHNIQUES IN MEDICINE.** **See** Medical Science and Technology-Biotechnology.

UK/0036-8091
**PHYSICS ABSTRACTS. See** Physics-Abstracting, Bibliographies and Statistics.

UK
**PHYSICS ABSTRACTS. AUTHOR INDEX.** **Added/Corp** Institution of Electrical Engineers. **VFOAT** Author Index; Science Abstracts. Series A, Physics Abstracts. Author Index. (19??)-. Periodical. English. sa. $1,395. Institution of Electrical Engineers / IEE, Michael Faraday House, Six Hills Way, Stevenage Herts SG1 2AY UK. **Tel** 011 44 438 313311, FAX 011 44 438 742840, telex 825578 IEESTV G. **(Subscription address:** IEE / UK, Publications Sales Department, PO Box 96, Stevenage, Herts, SG1 2SD England.**)**

UK
**PHYSICS ABSTRACTS. SUBJECT INDEX.** **Added/Corp** Institution of Electrical Engineers. **VFOAT** Subject Index; Science Abstracts. Series A, Physics Abstracts. Subject Index. (19??)-. Periodical. English. sa. $2,330. Institution of Electrical Engineers / IEE, Michael Faraday House, Six Hills Way, Stevenage Herts SG1 2AY UK. **Tel** 011 44 438 313311, FAX 011 44 438 742840, telex 825578 IEESTV G. **(Subscription address:** IEE / UK, Publications Sales Department, PO Box 96, Stevenage, Herts, SG1 2SD England.**)**

GW/0079-1938
**PHYSICS AND CHEMISTRY IN SPACE.** [Phys. chem. space]. Vol. 1 (1970)-. Monographic series. German. ir. Price varies per volume. Springer-Verlag GmbH & Company KG, Heidelberger Platz 3, D 14197 Berlin Germany. **Tel** 011 49 30 8207223, FAX 011 49 30 8214091, telex 183 319 SPBLN D. **(Subscription address:** Springer Verlag New York Inc. / for North America, 44 Hartz Way, Secaucus NJ 07096.**) ED** J. G. Roederer and J. Zahringer. **LC** QC801; .P46. **CODEN** PCSPDD. Documents available from Ask*IEEE.
**Ind/Abst** INSPEC.

NE/0378-1917
**PHYSICS AND CHEMISTRY OF MATERIALS WITH LAYERED STRUCTURES.** [Phys. chem. mater. layered struct.]. Academic Scholarly Publication. English. ir. Reidel Publishing, 101 Philip Drive, Norwell MA 02061-1677. **Tel** (617)871-6600, telex 200190. **LC** QD478; .P47. **DD** 530.4/1. **CODEN** PCMSDQ. Documents available from CASDDS.
**Ind/Abst** Chem. Abstr.

IT
**PHYSICS AND DEVELOPMENT / INTERNATIONAL ATOMIC ENERGY AGENCY AND UNITED NATIONS EDUCATIONAL, SCIENTIFIC, AND CULTURAL ORGANIZATION, INTERNATIONAL CENTRE FOR THEORETICAL PHYSICS.** **Added/Corp** International Centre for Theoretical Physics. (19??)-. Periodical. English. International Centre for Theoretical Physics, PO Box 586, I-34100 Trieste Italy. **Tel** (40)22.401, FAX (40)22.41.63, telex 460390 ICTP I. **LC** QC9.D44; P485. **DD** 338.9/26.

UK/0170-7434
**PHYSICS BRIEFS. See** Physics-Abstracting, Bibliographies and Statistics.

●US/1063-7753
**PHYSICS-DOKLADY.** [Physics-Doklady]. **Added/Corp** American Institute of Physics. **VFOAT** Physics. Vol. 38 (Jan./Dec. 1993)-. Periodical. English (translations available in Russian). mo. $1465.00 US; $1480.00 Canada, Mexico, Central & South America and the Caribbean; $1500.00 other. American Institute of Physics, 500 Sunnyside Boulevard, Woodbury NY 11797-2999. **Tel** (516)576-2200, FAX (516)349-7669, telex 960983. **LC** QC1; .A386. **DD** 530.5. **CODEN** PHDOE5. **[CCC].** Index available (bound in last issue). Documents available from Ask*IEEE. ***Continues*** *Soviet Physics, Doklady, 0038-5689.*
**Ind/Abst** Curr. Phys. Index; Energy Res. Abstr.; GeoRef; INSPEC; Int. Aerosp. Abstr.; Math. Rev.; Pollut. Abstr. Indexes; SPIN.

UK/0031-9120
**PHYSICS EDUCATION.** [Phys. educ.]. **Added/Corp** Institute of Physics and the Physical Society. Institute of Physics (Great Britain). Vol. 1 (May 1966)-. Periodical. English. bm (supplement). $143.00. Institute of Physics, Techno House, Redcliffe Way, Bristol BS1 6NX England. **Tel** 011 44 272 297481, FAX 011 44 272 294318, telex 449149 INSTP G. **(Subscription address:** American Institute of Physics, Publishing Sales, 500 Sunnyside Blvd., Woodbury NY 11797.**) ED** John Avison. **LC** QC30; .P46. **CODEN** PHEDA7. **[CCC].** Index available (bound in last issue). available on microfiche from the publisher. Documents available from Ask*IEEE, CASDDS.
**Desc:** For teachers and lecturers in schools, colleges, polytechnics and universities. Intended for all concerned with the teaching of physics in school and up to first-year undergraduate level. Provides reliable treatments of difficult concepts in physics, and is regarded as a major medium for the exchange of ideas on physics teaching.
**Ind/Abst** Br. Educ. Index (1968-); Chem. Abstr. (1966-1983); Curr. Index J. Educ.; Educ. Technol. Abstr.; INSPEC (1968-); Med. Rev. Dig.; Res. High. Educ. Abstr.; Stud. Women Abstr. (1968-); Tech. Educ. Train. Abstr. (1966-1983).

II/0970-5953
**PHYSICS EDUCATION (MADRAS). See** Education-Higher Education.

CN/0836-1398
**PHYSICS ESSAYS.** [Phys. essays]. Vol. 1 No. 1 (Apr 1988)-. Periodical. English (summaries and/or abstracts in French). qt (Mar., June, Sept., Dec.). $240.00 Canada; $195.00 US. Physics Essays Publishing, 189 7 Deveault Street, Hull Quebec J8Z 1S7 Canada. **Tel** (819)777-0548, FAX (819)770-3862. **ED** Emilio Panarella. **DD** 530/.05. **CODEN** PHESEM. **[CCC].** cum. index. **Ad Acc, Adv Mgr:** Ken Charbobbeau, **Tel** (819)777-0548. **Pr Rev. Circ:** 300. available on microfilm. Documents available from The Genuine Article, Ask*IEEE.
**Desc:** Dedicated to theoretical and experimental aspects of fundamental problems in physics.
**Ind/Abst** Curr. Contents Phys. Chem. Earth Sci.; INSPEC (Dec. 1990-); Res. Alert [Select. Cov.]; SCISEARCH.

CN/0031-9147
**PHYSICS IN CANADA.** **Added/Corp** Canadian Association of Physicists. **VFOAT** Physique au Canada. Vol. 8, No. 1 (Autumn 1952)-. Periodical. English (French). bm. 35.00Can$. Canadian Association of Physicists, 151 Slater Suite 903, Ottawa Ontario K1P 5H3 Canada. **Tel** (613)237-3392, FAX (613)238-1677. **ED** J S C McKee. **Bk Rev**, (Qty: 6). **Ad Acc, Adv Mgr:** F Brule. available on microfilm and microfiche from University Microfilms International (UMI). ***Absorbed** Canadian Association of Physicists. Bulletin., 0380-6669.*
**Desc:** Reaches the majority of canadian physicists in academic institutions, industry and government research laboratories. Six issues are published annually, every two months, including the special Congress issue published in May.

NE/0375-9601
**PHYSICS LETTERS : PART A.** [Phys. lett., Sect. A]. Vol. 24A (Jan. 2, 1967)-. Academic Scholarly Publication. English (French and German). Seventy-eight issues per year (13 volumes). FI5005.00; FI16807.00 combination subscription with Physics Letters B. Elsevier Science Publishers BV, PO Box 211, 1000 AE Amsterdam Netherlands. **Tel** 011 31 20 5803642, FAX 011 31 20 5862696, telex 15682. **ED** V. M. Agranovich, A. R. Bishop, J. Flouquet, A. P. Fordy, B. Fricke, D. D. Holm, A. Lagendijk, M. Porkolab, L.J. Sham, J.P. Vigier, P.R. Holland. **LC** QC1; .P45. **DD** 530/.05. **CODEN** PYLAAG. **[CCC].** Index available in last issue of volume--attached. cum. index. **Pr Rev.** available on microfilm and microfiche from University Microfilms International (UMI). Documents available from The Genuine Article, Ask*IEEE, CASDDS. ***Supersedes in part** Physics Letters, 0031-9163.*
**Desc:** Devoted to the rapid publication of short communications in all fields of physics excluding nuclear physics and particle physics.
**Ind/Abst** Acoust. Abstr.; Alum. Ind. Abstr.; Ceram. Abstr.; Chem. Abstr. (1968-); Chem. Titles; Curr. Contents Phys. Chem. Earth Sci.; Energy Res. Abstr.; Eng. Mater. Abstr.; GeoRef; INSPEC (1968-); Leadscan; Mass Spect. Bull.; Math. Rev.; Met. Abstr. (1968-); Phys. Briefs; Res. Alert [Full Cov.]; Sci. Cit. Index; SCISEARCH.

US/0569-5716
**PHYSICS MANPOWER, EDUCATION AND EMPLOYMENT STUDIES.** **See** Physics-Abstracting, Bibliographies and Statistics.

II
**PHYSICS NEWS (BOMBAY).** (PHYSICS NEWS.). [Phys. news]. **Added/Corp** Indian Physics Association. (Sept. 1970)-. English. qt. $25.00. Indian Physics Association, Bombay, India. **(Subscription address:** Prints India, 11 Darya Ganj, New Delhi 110002 India.**)** **LC** QC1; .P65625. **DD** 530/.05. **CODEN** PNEWD7.

US/0160-3353
**PHYSICS NEWS (NEW YORK).** (PHYSICS NEWS.). **Added/Corp** American Institute of Physics. (1975)-. English. an (Nov.). $5.00. American Institute of Physics, 500 Sunnyside Boulevard, Woodbury NY 11797-2999. **Tel** (516)576-2200, FAX (516)349-7669, telex 960983. **LC** QC1; .P65626. **DD** 530/.05. ***Continues** Physics, 0092-8437.*

●US/1070-6631
**PHYSICS OF FLUIDS (1994).** (PHYSICS OF FLUIDS.). [Phys. fluids]. **Added/Corp** American Institute of Physics. Vol. 6, No. 1 (Jan. 1994)-. Periodical. English. mo. $1180.00 US; $1205.00 Canada, Mexico, Central & South America, and the Caribbean; $1235.00 other. American Institute of Physics, 500 Sunnyside Boulevard, Woodbury NY 11797-2999. **Tel** (516)576-2200, FAX (516)349-7669, telex 960983. **LC** QC150; .P475. **DD** 532/.05. **CODEN** PHFLE6. ***Continues** Physics of Fluids. A, Fluid Dynamics, 0899-8213.*

US/0899-8213
**PHYSICS OF FLUIDS. A, FLUID DYNAMICS.** ***Title Change.*** (PHYSICS OF FLUIDS. A, FLUID DYNAMICS : A PUBLICATION OF THE AMERICAN INSTITUTE OF PHYSICS.). [Phys. fluids, A Fluid dyn.]. **Added/Corp** American Institute of Physics. **VFOAT** Fluid Dynamics. Vol. 1, No. 1 (Jan. 1989)-Vol. 5, No. 12 (Dec. 1993). Academic Scholarly Publication. English. mo. American Institute of Physics, 500 Sunnyside Boulevard, Woodbury NY 11797-2999. **Tel** (516)576-2200, FAX (516)349-7669, telex 960983. **(Subscription address:** AIP Subscription Fulfillment Division, 335 East 45th Street, New York NY 10017.**)** **ED** Andreas Acrivas. **LC** QC150; .P475. **DD** 532/.05. **CODEN** PFADEB. Index available. cum. index. **Pr Rev.** ctrl circ. available on microfiche; available on microfilm; available in microform. Documents available from Article Express International, The Genuine Article, Ask*IEEE, CASDDS. ***Continues in part** Physics of Fluids, 0031-9171.* ***Continued by** Physics of Fluids (Woodbury, N.Y. : 1994), 1070-6631.*
**Ind/Abst** Abstr. Bull. Inst. Pap. Sci. Tech.; Chem. Abstr. (1989-); Curr. Contents Phys. Chem. Earth Sci.; Eng. Index Annu. [Select. Cov.]; Fluid Abstr., Civil Eng.; Fluid Abstr. Proc. Eng.; FLUIDEX; INSPEC (Jan. 1989-); Int. Aerosp. Abstr.; Math. Rev.; Res. Alert [Full Cov.]; Sci. Cit. Index; SCISEARCH.

US/0899-8221
**PHYSICS OF FLUIDS. B, PLASMA PHYSICS.** ***Title Change.*** (PHYSICS OF FLUIDS. B, PLASMA PHYSICS : A PUBLICATION OF THE AMERICAN INSTITUTE OF PHYSICS.). [Phys. fluids, B Plasma phys.]. **Added/Corp** American Institute of Physics. **VFOAT** Plasma Physics. Vol. 1, No. 1 (Jan. 1989)-Vol. 5, No. 12 (Dec. 1993). Academic Scholarly Publication. English. mo. American Institute of Physics, 500 Sunnyside Boulevard, Woodbury NY 11797-2999. **Tel** (516)576-2200, FAX (516)349-7669, telex 960983. **(Subscription address:** AIP Subscription Fulfillment Division, 335 East 45th Street, New York NY 10017.**)** **ED** Fred L. Ribe. **LC** QC717.6; .P46. **DD** 530.4/4. **CODEN** PFBPEI. Index available. cum. index. ctrl circ. available on microfiche; available on microfilm; available in microform. Documents available from Article Express International, The Genuine Article, Ask*IEEE, CASDDS. ***Continues in part** Physics of Fluids, 0031-9171.* ***Continued by** Physics of Plasmas, 1070-664X.*
**Ind/Abst** Abstr. Bull. Inst. Pap. Sci. Tech.; Chem. Abstr. (1989-?); Curr. Contents Phys. Chem. Earth Sci.; Eng. Index Annu. [Select. Cov.]; Fluid Abstr., Civil Eng.; Fluid Abstr. Proc. Eng.; FLUIDEX; INSPEC (Jan. 1989-?); Int. Aerosp. Abstr.; Math. Rev.; Res. Alert [Full Cov.]; Sci. Cit. Index; SCISEARCH.

●RU/1061-7582
**PHYSICS OF HIGH ENERGY DENSITY.** (1992)-. Periodical. English. qt. John Wiley & Sons Ltd., Baffins Lane, Chichester West Sussex PO19 1UD England. **Tel** 0243 779777, FAX 0243 776128 BTG:JWP001, telex 86290 WIBOOKG. **(Subscription address:** North, South and Central America/ John Wiley & Sons, Inc., Subscription Department, 605 Third Avenue, New York, NY 10158-0012, USA; telephone: (212)850-6645; FAX: (212)850-6021**)** **CODEN** PEDEEM.

●US/1070-664X
**PHYSICS OF PLASMAS.** [Phys. plasmas]. **Added/Corp** American Institute of Physics. Vol. 1, No. 1 (Jan. 1994)-. Periodical. English. mo. $1410.00 US. American Institute of Physics, 500 Sunnyside Boulevard, Woodbury NY 11797-2999. **Tel** (516)576-2200, FAX (516)349-7669, telex 960983. **LC** IN PROCESS; QC717.6; .P462. **DD** 530. **CODEN** PHPAEN. ***Continues** Physics of Fluids. B, Plasma Physics, 0899-8221.*

●US/1063-7834
**PHYSICS OF THE SOLID STATE.** [Phys. solid state]. **Added/Corp** American Institute of Physics. Vol. 35, No. 1 (Jan. 1993)-. Periodical. English (translations available in Russian). mo. $2480.00 US; $2500.00 Canada, Mexico, Central & South America and the Caribbean; $2530.00 other. American Institute of Physics, 500 Sunnyside Boulevard, Woodbury NY 11797-2999. **Tel** (516)576-2200, FAX (516)349-7669, telex 960983. **LC** QC176; .A413. **DD** 531.705. **CODEN** PSOSED. **[CCC].** Documents available from Article Express International, Ask*IEEE. ***Continues** Soviet Physics, Solid State, 0038-5654.*
**Ind/Abst** Alum. Ind. Abstr.; Bioeng. Abstr.; Curr. Phys. Index; Ei Page One; Energy Res. Abstr.; Eng. Index Annu.; INSPEC; Int. Aerosp. Abstr.; Met. Abstr.; Pollut. Abstr. Indexes.

NE/0370-1573
**PHYSICS REPORTS.** [Phys. rep.]. **VFOAT** Physics Letters. Part C. Vol. 1C (March 1971)-. Academic Scholarly Publication. English. Seventy-two issues per year (12 volumes). FI4620.00. Elsevier Science Publishers BV, PO Box 211, 1000 AE Amsterdam Netherlands. **Tel** 011 31 20 5803642, FAX 011 31 20 5862696, telex 15682. **ED** D.F. Brewer, G.E. Brown, J.I. Budnick, D.K. Campbell, G.H.F. Diercksen, J. Eichler, M.L. Klein, A.A. Maradudin, E.W. McDaniel, D.L. Mills, R. Petronzio, I. Procaccia, D.N. Schramm, A. Schwimmer, R. Slansky, R.N. Sudan, W. Weise. **LC** QC1; .P6563. **DD** 530/.05. **CODEN** PRPLCM. **[CCC].** **Pr Rev.** available on microfilm and microfiche from University Microfilms International (UMI). Documents available from The Genuine Article, Ask*IEEE, CASDDS. ***Absorbed** Case Studies in Atomic Physics.*
**Desc:** Provides physicists with timely reviews of specific fields of physics which have witnessed recent and important developments.
**Ind/Abst** Chem. Abstr.; Curr. Contents Phys. Chem. Earth Sci.; Index Sci. Rev. [Full Cov.]; INSPEC (1978-); Math. Rev.; Phys. Briefs; Res. Alert [Full Cov.]; Sci. Cit. Index; SCISEARCH.

UK/0959-8472
**PHYSICS REVIEW DEDDINGTON.** (PHYSICS REVIEW.). [Phys. rev. Deddington]. (1991)-. Periodical. English. Five times a year. £19.50 UK; £29.00 Europe; £34.00 other. Philip Allan Publishers Ltd, Market Place, Deddington Oxford, OX15 0SE England. **Tel** 011 44 869 38652, FAX 011 44 869 38803. **DD** 530.05.

US/0031-921X
**PHYSICS TEACHER, THE.** **See** Education-Teaching and Curriculum.

US/0031-9228
**PHYSICS TODAY.** [Phys. today]. **Added/Corp** American Institute of Physics. Vol. 1 (May 1948)-. Periodical. English. mo. $147.00 US; $162.00 Canada, Mexico, Central & South America and the Caribbean; $177.00 other. American Institute of Physics, 500 Sunnyside Boulevard, Woodbury NY 11797-2999. **Tel** (516)576-2200, FAX (516)349-7669, telex 960983. **ED** Gloria Lubkin. **LC** QC1; .P658. **DD** 530.5. **NLM** W1 PH847. **CODEN** PHTOAD. **[CCC].** Index available (bound in last issue). **Bk Rev. Pr Rev.** available on microfilm and microfiche. Documents available from Article Express International, The Genuine Article, Ask*IEEE, UMI Article Clearinghouse, CASDDS.
**Desc:** Magazine of physics research and information accessible to both professionals and laymen. Technical and non-technical coverage of the latest advances, along with government and institutional activities that affect physics. Includes articles, news, editorial opinion, letters to the editors, and a calendar of meetings.
**Ind/Abst** Acad. Abstr. Full Text Elite (Jan. 1984-); Acad. Abstr. (Jan. 1984-); Acad. Ind. [Computer File] (1984-); Acad. Search (Jan. 1984-); Acoust. Abstr.; Appl. Sci. Technol. Index; Art Archaeol. Tech. Abstr.; Ceram. Abstr. (19??-); Chem. Abstr.; Coal Abstr.; Curr. Contents Phys. Chem. Earth Sci.; Curr. Index J. Educ.; Curr. Phys. Index; EMBASE; Energy Res. Abstr.; Eng. Index Annu. [Select. Cov.]; Expand. Acad. Index (1984-); Gen. Period. Index (1985-); Gen. Sci. Index; Gen. Sci. Source (Jan. 1988-); Geogr. Abstr. Phys. Geogr.; Geol. Abstr.; GeoRef; HTFS Dig.; INFO-SOUTH Abstr.; INSPEC (1968-); Int. Aerosp. Abstr.; Leadscan; Mag. Artic. Summar. Elite (Jan. 1984-); Mag. Artic. Summar. Select (Jan. 1984-); Mag. Artic. Summar. CD-ROM (Jan. 1984-); Mag. Index Plus (1989-); Mag. Index. Sel. (1986-); Mag. Search; Mass Spect. Bull.; Math. Rev.; Newsp. Period. Abstr. (1988-); Peace Res. Abstr. J. (1959-1970); Read. Guide Abstr. Select Ed.; Read. Guide Period. Lit.; Res. Alert [Full Cov.]; Sci. Cit. Index; SCISEARCH; Shock Vibr. Dig.; Soc. Sci. Cit. Index [Select. Cov.]; SPIN (1974-); SportSearch; Surf. Treat. Technol. Abstr.; Mag. Index (1977-); TOM Gen. Index (1985-); Vocat. Search (Jan. 1984-).

●US/1063-7869
**PHYSICS, USPEKHI.** [Phys. Uspekhi]. **Added/Corp** Rossiiskaia Akademiia Nauk. American Institute of Physics. Vol. 36, No. 1 (Jan. 1993)-. Periodical. English (translations available in Russian). mo. $950.00. **(Subscription address:** Turpin Distribution Services Limited, Blackhorse Road, Letchworth, Hertfordshire SG6 1HN, United Kingdom.**)** **LC** QC1; .U812. **DD** 530.5. **CODEN** PHUSEY. **[CCC].** Documents available from Ask*IEEE. ***Continues** Soviet Physics, Uspekhi, 0038-5670.*
**Ind/Abst** Coal Abstr.; Curr. Phys. Index; Energy Res. Abstr.; GeoRef; INSPEC; Int. Aerosp. Abstr.; Math. Rev.; SPIN.

UK/0953-8585
**PHYSICS WORLD.** [Physics world]. **Added/Corp** Institute of Physics (Great Britain) American Institute of Physics. **VFOAT** Physics. (Oct. 1988)-. Academic Scholarly Publication. English. mo (buyer's guide). $112.00. Institute of Physics, Techno House, Redcliffe Way, Bristol BS1 6NX England. **Tel** 011 44 272 297481, FAX 011 44 272 294318, telex 449149 INSTP G. **(Subscription address:** American Institute of Physics, Publishing Sales, 500 Sunnyside Blvd., Woodbury NY 11797.**)** **ED** P Campbell. **LC** QC1; .P66. **DD** 530. **CODEN** PHWOEW. **[CCC].** Index available (loose in last issue of volume). available on microfilm and microfiche. Documents available from The Genuine Article, Ask*IEEE, CASDDS. ***Formed by the union of** Physics in Technology, 0305-4624 **and** Physics Bulletin, 0031-9112.*
**Desc:** For physicists in industry, government, education or academia, 'pure' or applied physics, engineering or business. A mix of editorial features, news and current affairs, and scientific and technological updates from scientists and journalists worldwide.
**Ind/Abst** Chem. Abstr. (Oct. 1988-); Curr. Contents Phys. Chem. Earth Sci.; Curr. Technol. Index; Ei Page One; INSPEC (Oct. 1988-); Res. Alert [Select. Cov.]; SCISEARCH; Soc. Sci. Cit. Index [Select. Cov.].

GW/0344-8401
**PHYSIK DATEN.** [Phys. Daten]. **VFOAT** Physics Data. V. 1-. Academic Scholarly Publication. English (German). ir. Fachinformationszentrum Karlsruhe, Physics & Math, D 76344 Eggenstein Germany. **Tel** 011 49 7247 808149. **ED** H Behrens and P Luksch. **CODEN** PHDADU. **Bk Rev. Ad Acc. Circ:** 250-300 (ctrl). Documents available from Ask*IEEE, CASDDS.
**Desc:** The ever increasing number of publications makes it more difficult for scientists and engineers to extract, evaluate and finally select the physical data relevant to their work from the original literature. The present series was created with the aim to relieve this shortcoming by regularly publishing data compilations for special topics. These compilations are constantly brought up to date.
**Ind/Abst** Alum. Ind. Abstr.; Chem. Abstr.; Energy Res. Abstr. (March 1982-); Eng. Mater. Abstr.; INSPEC (1981-); Met. Abstr.; Phys. Briefs (1979-).

GW/0031-9252
**PHYSIK IN UNSERER ZEIT.** [Phys. unserer Zeit]. Vol. 1, (1970)-. Academic Scholarly Publication. German. bm. $75.00. VCH Gesellschaft GmbH, Postfach 101161, D 69451 Weinheim Germany. **Tel** 011 49 6201 606459, FAX 011 49 6201 606184. **(Subscription address:** VCH Publishers Inc., 303 Northwest 12th Avenue, Journals Department, Deerfield FL 33442.**)** **LC** QC1; .P674. **DD** 530/.05. **CODEN** PHUZAH. **[CCC].**

Documents available from CASDDS.
**Ind/Abst** Art Archaeol. Tech. Abstr.; Chem. Abstr.; Energy Res. Abstr. (Sept. 1971-); Int. Aerosp. Abstr.

GW/0340-8515
**PHYSIK UND DIDAKTIK.** ***Title Change.* See** Education-Teaching and Curriculum.

GW/0031-9279
**PHYSIKALISCHE BLATTER.** [Phys. bl.]. **Added/Corp** Deutsche Physikalische Gesellschaft (1963-). (1947)-. Academic Scholarly Publication. German. mo. $200.00. VCH Gesellschaft GmbH, Postfach 101161, D 69451 Weinheim Germany. **Tel** 011 49 6201 606459, FAX 011 49 6201 606184. **(Subscription address:** VCH Publishers Inc., 303 Northwest 12th Avenue, Journals Department, Deerfield FL 33442.**)** **CODEN** PHBLAG. **[CCC].** Index Available, published separately, free-automatically sent. cum. index. Documents available from Ask*IEEE, CASDDS. ***Continues*** *Neue Physikalische Blatter.*
**Ind/Abst** Chem. Abstr.; EMBASE; Energy Res. Abstr.; INSPEC (1968-); Int. Aerosp. Abstr.

●UK/0967-3334
**PHYSIOLOGICAL MEASUREMENT. See** Medical Science and Technology-Biotechnology.

RU/0370-274X
**PISMA V ZHURNAL EKSPERIMENTALNOI I TEORETICHESKOI FIZIKI. Added/Corp** Akademiia Nauk SSSR. **VFOAT** Pisma v ZHETF; Zhurnal Eksperimentalnoi i Teoreticheskoi Fiziki. Vol. 9 (Jan. 1969)-. Academic Scholarly Publication. Russian. mo. $248.00. Izdatelstvo Nauka / Akademiia Nauk, Publishing House of the Russian Academy of Sciences, Leninskii Porspekt 14, 117901 Moscow Russia. **Tel** 011 95 954-21-53, FAX 011 95 938-21-44, telex 411964. **(Subscription address:** East View Publications Inc., 3020 Harbor Lane North, Suite 110, Minneapolis MN 55447.**)** **LC** QC1; .Z46. **CODEN** PZETAB. Documents available from Ask*IEEE, CASDDS. ***Continues*** *ZHETF. Pisma v Redaktsiiu.*
**Ind/Abst** Alum. Ind. Abstr.; Ceram. Abstr.; Chem. Abstr.; Chem. Titles; GeoRef; INSPEC (April 1977-); Int. Aerosp. Abstr.; Math. Rev.; Met. Abstr.

RU/0320-0116
**PISMA V ZURNAL TEHNICESKOJ FIZIKI.** (PISMA V ZHURNAL TEKHNICHESKOI FIZIKI.). [Pisma Z. teh. fiz.]. **Added/Corp** Akademiia Nauk SSSR. (1975)-. Academic Scholarly Publication. Russian. Six times a year. $242.00. **(Subscription address:** East View Publications Inc., 3020 Harbor Lane North, Suite 110, Minneapolis MN 55447.**)** **LC** QC1; .P815. **CODEN** PZTFDD. **[CCC]. Pr Rev.** Documents available from The Genuine Article, Ask*IEEE, CASDDS.
**Ind/Abst** Chem. Abstr.; Chem. Titles; Curr. Contents, Agric. Biol. Environ. Sci.; INSPEC (Feb. 1975-); Int. Aerosp. Abstr.; Res. Alert [Full Cov.]; Sci. Cit. Index; SCISEARCH.

AU/0589-1469
**PLASMA PHYSICS AND CONTROLLED NUCLEAR FUSION RESEARCH.** (PLASMA PHYSICS AND CONTROLLED NUCLEAR FUSION RESEARCH : PROCEEDINGS OF THE ...). [Plasma phys. control. nucl. fusion res.]. **Main/Conf** International Conference on Plasma Physics and Controlled Nuclear Fusion Research. **Added/Corp** International Atomic Energy Agency. 3rd Edition (1968)-. English. an. Price varies. International Atomic Energy Agency / IAEA, Wagramerstrasse 5, PO Box 100, A-1400 Vienna Austria. **Tel** 011 43 1 2360 ext. 2530, FAX 011 43 1 234564. **(Subscription address:** UNIPUB, 4611 F Assembly Drive, Lanham MD 20706.**)** **LC** QC717.6; .C67a. **DD** 621.48/4. **CODEN** PPCRDU. Documents available from Article Express International. ***Continues*** *Conference on Plasma Physics and Controlled Nuclear Fusion Research. Plasma Physics and Controlled Nuclear Fusion Research, 0589-1469.*
**Ind/Abst** Bioeng. Abstr.; Ei Page One; Eng. Index Annu.

●US/1063-780X
**PLASMA PHYSICS REPORTS.** [Plasma phys. rep.]. **Added/Corp** American Institute of Physics. Vol. 19, No. 1 (Jan. 1993)-. Academic Scholarly Publication. English (translations available in Russian). mo. $1710.00 US; $1720.00 Canada, Mexico, Central & South America and the Caribbean; $1740.00 other. American Institute of Physics, 500 Sunnyside Boulevard, Woodbury NY 11797-2999. **Tel** (516)576-2200, FAX (516)349-7669, telex 960983. **LC** QC717.6; .S66. **DD** 530.4/4/05. Index available (bound in last issue). Documents available from Article Express International, Ask*IEEE, CASDDS. ***Continues*** *Soviet Journal of Plasma Physics, 0360-0343.*
**Ind/Abst** Bioeng. Abstr.; Chem. Abstr.; Curr. Phys. Index; Ei Page One; Energy Res. Abstr.; Eng. Index Annu.; Eng. Index Energy Abstr.; INSPEC; Int. Aerosp. Abstr.; SPIN.

UK/0963-0252
**PLASMA SOURCES SCIENCE AND TECHNOLOGY.** Vol. 1 (1992)-. English. qt. $231.00. Institute of Physics, Techno House, Redcliffe Way, Bristol BS1 6NX England. **Tel** 011 44 272 297481, FAX 011 44 272 294318, telex 449149 INSTP G. **(Subscription address:** American Institute of Physics, Publishing Sales, 500 Sunnyside Blvd., Woodbury NY 11797.**)** **ED** Noah Hershkowitz. **CODEN** PSTEEU. Index available in last issue of volume--attached. available on microfiche.
**Desc:** Publishes papers on non-fusion plasma sources which operate at all ranges of pressure and density: low pressure plasma sources; low to medium pressure sources-plasma surface interactions; high pressure sources, thermal plasmas; plasma diagnostic techniques.
**Ind/Abst** Ei Page One.

●US
**PLASMAS AND POLYMERS : AN INTERNATIONAL JOURNAL.** (1994)-. Periodical. English. Four times a year. $150.00 institutions, $50.00 individuals US; $175.00 institutions, $59.00 individuals other. Plenum Press, 233 Spring Street, New York NY 10013-1578. **Tel** (212)620-8000, (800)221-9369, FAX (212)463-0742, (212)807-1047, telex 23/421139.

RU/0044-4626
**PMTF.** [PMTF]. **Added/Corp** Akademiia Nauk SSSR. Sibirskoe Otdelenie. **VFOAT** Zhurnal Prikladnoi Mekhaniki i Tekhnicheskoi Fiziki. **VAT** Prikladnaia Mekhanika i Tekhnicheskaia Fizika. (May/June 1960)-. Academic Scholarly Publication. Russian. Six times a year. $185.95. **(Subscription address:** East View Publications Inc., 3020 Harbor Lane North, Suite 110, Minneapolis MN 55447.**)** **LC** QC1; .P15. **DD** 530/.05. **CODEN** ZPMFAF. **[CCC].** Documents available from Ask*IEEE, CASDDS.
**Ind/Abst** Alum. Ind. Abstr.; Chem. Abstr.; Ei Page One; Energy Res. Abstr.; GeoRef; INSPEC (1968-); Int. Aerosp. Abstr.; Math. Rev.; Met. Abstr.

PO/0048-4903
**PORTUGALIAE PHYSICA.** [Port. phys.]. **Added/Corp** Instituto para a Alta Cultura (Portugal) Faculdade de Ciencias de Lisboa. Instituto de Alta Cultura (Portugal) Sociedade Portuguesa de Fisica. Centro de Estudos de Fisica (Portugal). Vol. 1 (1943)-. Academic Scholarly Publication. French (English). an. $60.00 (institution); $24.00 (individual). Faculdade de Ciencias de Lisbon, Laboratorid de Fisica, rua da Escola Politecnia 58, Lisbon 2 Portugal. **CODEN** POPYA4. Documents available from Ask*IEEE, CASDDS.
**Ind/Abst** Acoust. Abstr.; Chem. Abstr.; INSPEC (1968-); Math. Rev. (?-199?).

PL/0032-5430
**POSTEPY FIZYKI.** [Postepy fiz.]. **Added/Corp** Polskie Towarzystwo Fizyczne. Vol. 1 (1949)-. Academic Scholarly Publication. Polish. bm. $42.00. **(Subscription address:** ARS Polona, PO Box 1001, 00068 Warsaw Poland.**)** **LC** QC1; .P853. **CODEN** PSTFAT. Documents available from Ask*IEEE, CASDDS.
**Ind/Abst** Chem. Abstr.; INSPEC (1968-).

US/0734-1520
**POVERKHNOST.** (PHYSICS, CHEMISTRY AND MECHANICS OF SURFACES.). [Phys., chem. mech. surf.]. No. 1 (1982)-. Periodical. English (Russian). mo. Gordon & Breach Science Publishers, Inc., PO Box 786, Cooper Station, New York NY 10276. **Tel** (212)206-8900, FAX (212)645-2459. **(Subscription address:** Gordon & Breach Science Publishers / Singapore, PO Box 1180, Kent Ridge PO, Singapore 9111 Singapore.**)** **ED** E. P. Velikhov. **LC** QC173.4.S94; P48. **DD** 530.4. **CODEN** PCMSER. **[CCC]. Bk Rev. Ad Acc.** Documents available from Article Express International, Ask*IEEE.
**Ind/Abst** Ei Page One; Eng. Index Annu.; Fluid Abstr., Civil Eng.; Fluid Abstr. Proc. Eng.; FLUIDEX (19??-); INSPEC (1984-).

US/0882-7419
**POWERTECHNICS MAGAZINE.** [Powertech. mag.]. **VFOAT** Powertechnics; Power Technics Magazine; Power Technics. Vol. 1, No. 1 (June 1985)-. Periodical. English. Twelve times a year. $75.00. Darnell Research Inc., PO Box 223, Norco CA 91760-0223. **Tel** (714)283-1123, FAX (714)2823-4022. **ED** Jeffrey Shepard and Robert Margolin. **DD** 621. **CODEN** PTMAEO. **[CCC]. Ad Acc. Circ:** 24,000 (ctrl). Documents available from Ask*IEEE.
**Desc:** Primarily deals with power system design and specifier information.
**Ind/Abst** INSPEC (March 1990-).

II/0304-4289
**PRAMANA.** [Pramana]. **Added/Corp** Indian Academy of Sciences. Indian Physics Association. Indian National Science Academy. (July 1973)-. Academic Scholarly Publication. English. mo. $175.00. Indian Academy of Sciences Circulation, PO Box 8005, Department of Sadashivanagar, Bangalore 560 080 India. **Tel** 011 91 812 342546, 342310, telex 0845-2178 ACAD IN. **(Subscription address:** Prints India, 11 Darya Ganj, New Delhi 110002 India.**)** **ED** E S Raja Gopal. **LC** QC1; .P8835. **DD** 530. **CODEN** PRAMCI. Index available. **Pr Rev. Circ:** 700. Documents available from The Genuine Article, Ask*IEEE, CASDDS.
**Desc:** A journal covering a wide spectrum of topics. Includes statistical mechanics and quantum physics, nuclear and particle physics, atomic and molecular physics, optics, plasma physics and solid state physics.
**Ind/Abst** Alum. Ind. Abstr.; Ceram. Abstr. (19??-); Chem. Abstr.; Curr. Titles Electrochem.; Eng. Mater. Abstr.; GeoRef; INSPEC (July 1973-); Int. Aerosp. Abstr.; Math. Rev.; Met. Abstr.; Ref. Z.; Res. Alert [Full Cov.]; Sci. Cit. Index; SCISEARCH.

GW/0177-8374
**PRAXIS DER NATURWISSENSCHAFTEN PHYSIK.** [Prax. Nat.wiss., Phys.]. (1980)-. Periodical. German. mo. DM107.20 Germany; DM115.20 other. Aulis Verlag Deubner & Company, Antwerpenerstrasse 6 12, 50672 Koln Germany. **Tel** 011 49 221 518051, FAX 011 49 221 518443. **UDC** 53. ***Continues*** *Praxis der Naturwissenschaften. Physik im Unterricht der Schulen, 0342-8729;* ***Absorbed*** *Der Physikunterricht, 0031-9295* ***and*** *Physik und Didaktik, 0340-8515.*

RU
**PREPRINT / AKADEMIIA NAUK SSSR, INSTITUT OBSHCHEI FIZIKI. Added/Corp** Institut Obshchei Fiziki (Akademiia nauk SSSR). (19??)-. Monographic series. Russian (English). Price varies per volume.
**Ind/Abst** Int. Aerosp. Abstr.

RU
**PREPRINT (FIZICHESKII INSTITUT IMENI P.N. LEBEDEVA).** (PREPRINT.). **Added/Corp** Fizicheskii Institut Imeni P.N. Lebedeva. (19??)-. Monographic series. Russian (English). ir. Price varies per volume.

RU
**PREPRINT (INSTITUT FIZIKI METALLOV (AKADEMIIA NAUK SSSR).** (PREPRINT / AKADEMIIA NAUK SSSR, URALSKOE OTDELENIE, ORDENA TRUDOVOGO KRASNOGO ZNAMENI INSTITUT FIZIKI METALLOV.). **Added/Corp** Akademiia Nauk SSSR. Uralskoe Otdelenie. Institut Fiziki Metallov (Akademiia Nauk SSSR). (19??)-. Monographic series. Russian. ir. Price varies per volume.

RU/0552-2056
**PROBLEMY FIZIKI ATMOSFERY.** [Probl. fiz. atmos.]. **Added/Corp** Leningradskii Gosudarsvennyi Universitet Imeni A.A. Zhdanova. (1963)-. Academic Scholarly Publication. Russian. ir. $199.95. Izdatelstvo Moskovskogo Universiteta, K-9 Ulitsa Gertsena 5/7, Moscow Russia. **Tel** (301)881-5973. **(Subscription address:** East View Publications Inc., 3020 Harbor Lane North, Suite 110, Minneapolis MN 55447.**)** **LC** QC880; .P75. **CODEN** PFATAL. Documents available from CASDDS.
**Ind/Abst** Chem. Abstr.; GeoRef; Int. Aerosp. Abstr.

RU/0370-0305
**PROBLEMY KINETIKI I KATALIZA.** (PROBLEMY KINETIKI I KATALIZA / ADADEMIIA NAUK SSSR, ORDENA LENINA INSTITUT KHIMICHESKOI FIZIKI.). [Probl. kinet. katal.]. **Added/Corp** Institut Khimicheskoi Fiziki (Akademiia Nauk SSSR). (1935)-. Academic Scholarly Publication. Russian. Price varies per volume. Izdatelstvo Nauka / Akademiia Nauk, Publishing House of the Russian Academy of Sciences, Leninskii Porspekt 14, 117901 Moscow Russia. **Tel** 011 95 954-21-53, FAX 011 95 938-21-44, telex 411964. **CODEN** PKKAAF. Documents available from CASDDS.
**Ind/Abst** Chem. Abstr.

RU/0555-2818
**PROBLEMY MATEMATICESKOJ FIZIKI.** (PROBLEMY MATEMATICHESKOI FIZIKI.). [Probl. mat. fiz.]. **Added/Corp** Leningradskii Gosudarstvenni Universitet Imeni A.A. Zhdanova. Vol. 1 (1966)-. Periodical. Russian. **LC** QC20; .P75.
**Ind/Abst** Int. Aerosp. Abstr.; Math. Rev.; Zentralbl. Math. Ihre Grenzgeb.

SZ/0534-8706
**PROCEEDINGS. Main/Conf** International Conference on High Energy Physics. **Added/Corp** European Organization for Nuclear Research. (1950)-. Proceedings. French. ir. World Scientific Publishing Company, PO Box 128, Farrer Road, Singapore 9128 Singapore. **Tel** 011 65 3825663, FAX 011 65 3825919, telex RS 28561 WSPC. **(Subscription address:** World Scientific Publishing Company, Inc., 1060 Main Street, Suite 1B River Edge, NJ 07661; Telephone: (800)227-7562 or (201)487-9655**)**

UK/0962-8444
**PROCEEDINGS. MATHEMATICAL AND PHYSICAL SCIENCES / THE ROYAL SOCIETY. Main/Corp** Royal Society (Great Britain). **VFOAT** Mathematical and Physical Sciences; Proceedings of the Royal Society of London. Series A. Began with: Vol. 430, No. 1878 (July 1990)-. Proceedings. English. mo. Royal Society, 6 Carlton House Terrace, London SW1Y 5AG England. **Tel** 011 44 71 839 5561, FAX 071-976 1837, telex 917876 ROYAL G. Documents available from Ask*IEEE. ***Continues*** *Royal Society (Great Britain). Proceedings of the Royal Society of London. Series A, Mathematical and Physical Sciences, 0080-4630.*
**Ind/Abst** INSPEC (1968-); Int. Aerosp. Abstr.

UK/0962-8444
**PROCEEDINGS. MATHEMATICAL AND PHYSICAL SCIENCES / THE ROYAL SOCIETY.** See Mathematics.

US/0146-1273
**PROCEEDINGS OF SUMMER INSTITUTE ON PARTICLE PHYSICS.** [Proc. Summer Inst. Part. Phys.]. **Main/Conf** Summer Institute on Particle Physics. **VFOAT** Proceedings of the SLAC Summer Institute on Particle Physics. Began in 1973. Academic Scholarly Publication. English. an. $12.75. National Technical Information Service - NTIS, Room 2027S, 5285 Port Royal Road, Springfield VA 22161. **Tel** (703)487-4630, (703)487-4660, (703)487-4650, FAX (703)321-8547, telex 89-9405. **CODEN** PSIPD7. available on microfiche. Documents available from CASDDS.
**Ind/Abst** Chem. Abstr.

US
**PROCEEDINGS OF THE ACADEMY OF SCIENCES OF THE USSR. APPLIED PHYSICS SECTIONS.** **Main/Corp** Akademiia Nauk SSSR. **Added/Corp** Consultants Bureau. **VFOAT** Applied Physics Sections. Vol. 112, Issues 1/6 (Jan./Feb. 1957)-. Periodical. English. mo. Plenum Press, 233 Spring Street, New York NY 10013-1578. **Tel** (212)620-8000, (800)221-9369, FAX (212)463-0742, (212)807-1047, telex 23/421139.

US/1068-7491
**PROCEEDINGS OF THE ... IEEE FREQUENCY CONTROL SYMPOSIUM.** ***Title Change.*** [Proc. IEEE Freq. Control Symp.]. **Added/Corp** Institute of Electrical and Electronics Engineers. IEEE Ultrasonics, Ferroelectrics, and Frequency Control Society. Army Research Laboratory (St. Monmouth, N.J.). (1992)-(1992). Academic Scholarly Publication. English. an. IEEE, Institution of Electrical and Electronics Engineers, Inc., 345 East 47th Street, New York NY 10017-2394. **Tel** (908)981-1393, FAX (908)981-9667. **DD** 621. **CODEN** PFCSEW. Documents available from CASDDS. ***Continues*** *Frequency Control Symposium. Proceedings of the ... Annual Frequency Control Symposium, 0161-6404.* ***Continued by*** *Proceedings of the IEEE International Frequency Control Symposium.*
**Ind/Abst** Bioeng. Abstr.; Chem. Abstr.; Index IEEE Publ.

US
**PROCEEDINGS OF THE IEEE INTERNATIONAL FREQUENCY CONTROL SYMPOSIUM.** Proceedings. English. IEEE, Institution of Electrical and Electronics Engineers, Inc., 345 East 47th Street, New York NY 10017-2394. **Tel** (908)981-1393, FAX (908)981-9667. ***Continues*** *Proceedings of the Annual Frequency Control Symposium.*

US/0272-880X
**PROCEEDINGS OF THE INTERNATIONAL CENTRE FOR HEAT AND MASS TRANSFER.** ***Ceased.*** [Proc. Int. Cent. Heat Mass Transf.]. **Added/Corp** International Center for Heat and Mass Transfer. (19??)-(19??). Academic Scholarly Publication. English. ir. Taylor & Francis Ltd., Rankine Road, Basingstoke Hampshire, RG24 8PR United Kingdom. **Tel** 011 44 256 840366, FAX 011 44 256 479438, telex 858540. **(Subscription address:** Taylor & Francis Inc., 1900 Frost Road, Suite 101, Bristol PA 19007-1598.**) CODEN** PCHTD4. **[CCC].** Documents available from CASDDS.
**Ind/Abst** Chem. Abstr. (19??)-(19??).

US/0197-453X
**PROCEEDINGS OF THE INTERNATIONAL CONFERENCE ON FLUIDIZED BED COMBUSTION.** (THE PROCEEDINGS OF THE ... INTERNATIONAL CONFERENCE ON FLUIDIZED-BED COMBUSTION / SPONSORED BY U.S. ENERGY RESEARCH AND DEVELOPMENT ADMINISTRATION ; COORDINATED BY THE MITRE CORPORATION.). [Proc. Int. Conf. Fluid. Bed Combust.]. **Added/Corp** United States. Energy Research and Development Administration. Mitre Corporation. American Society of Mechanical Engineers. Advanced Energy Systems Division. Electric Power Research Institute. Tennessee Valley Authority. **VFOAT** Fluidized-Bed Combustion. (19??)-. Academic Scholarly Publication. English. The American Society of Mechanical Engineers, United Engineering Center, 345 East 47th Street, New York NY 10017. **LC** TJ254.5; .I55a. **DD** 621.402/3. **CODEN** PCFCDB. Documents available from CASDDS.
**Ind/Abst** Bioeng. Abstr.; Chem. Abstr.

US/0190-4132
**PROCEEDINGS OF THE INTERNATIONAL CONFERENCE ON LASERS.** See Science and Technology.

US
**PROCEEDINGS OF THE ... INTERNATIONAL CONGRESS ON RHEOLOGY.** **Main/Corp** International Congress on Rheology. Began publication with 1st in 1948?. Proceedings. English (French and German). ir. University Park Press, PO Box 4034, New York NY 10163. **LC** QC189; .I52.

NE/0074-784X
**PROCEEDINGS OF THE INTERNATIONAL SCHOOL OF PHYSICS "ENRICO FERMI".** [Proc. Int. Sch. Phys. Enrico Fermi]. **Added/Corp** Societa Italiana di Fisica. **VFOAT** Rendiconti della Scuola Internazionale di Fisica "Enrico Fermi". (196?)-. Academic Scholarly Publication. Italian. **CODEN** PIPFA7. Documents available from CASDDS. ***Continues*** *International School of Physics "Enrico Fermi." Rendiconti della Scuola Internazionale di Fisica "Enrico Fermi", 0505-0189.*
**Ind/Abst** Chem. Abstr.; Math. Rev.

JA/0386-2208
**PROCEEDINGS OF THE JAPAN ACADEMY. SERIES B: PHYSICAL AND BIOLOGICAL SCIENCES.** See Biology.

US/0275-617X
**PROCEEDINGS OF THE JOHNS HOPKINS WORKSHOP ON CURRENT PROBLEMS IN PARTICLE THEORY.** (PROCEEDINGS OF THE JOHNS HOPKINS WORKSHOP ON CURRENT PROBLEMS IN PARTICLE THEORY / UNIVERSITY OF BONN, UNIVERSITY OF FLORENCE, THE JOHNS HOPKINS UNIVERSITY.). [Proc. Johns Hopkins Workshop Curr. Probl. Part. Theory]. (19??)-. Academic Scholarly Publication. English. ir. Taylor & Francis Ltd., Rankine Road, Basingstoke Hampshire, RG24 8PR United Kingdom. **Tel** 011 44 256 840366, FAX 011 44 256 479438, telex 858540. **(Subscription address:** Taylor & Francis Inc., 1900 Frost Road, Suite 101, Bristol PA 19007-1598.**) LC** UNC. **CODEN** PJHTDJ. Documents available from CASDDS.
**Ind/Abst** Chem. Abstr.

US/0896-8462
**PROCEEDINGS OF THE LEBEDEV PHYSICS INSTITUTE OF THE ACADEMY OF SCIENCES OF RUSSIA.** [Proc. Lebedev Phys. Inst. Acad. Sci. USSR]. **Added/Corp** Fizicheskii Institut Imeni P.N. Lebedeva. **VFOAT** Proceedings of the Lebedev Physics Institute. Vol. 165 (1987)-. Proceedings. English (translations available in Russian). ir. Price varies per volume. Nova Science Publishers Inc., 6080 Jericho Turnpike, Suite 207, Commack NY 11725-2808. **Tel** (516)499-3103, (516)499-3106, FAX (516)499-3146. **LC** QC1; .A4114. **DD** 530. Documents available from Ask*IEEE. ***Continues*** *Trudy Fizicheskogo Instituta. English. Proceedings (Trudy) of the P.N. Lebedev Physics Institute, 0568-5508.*
**Ind/Abst** INSPEC (1987-).

UA
**PROCEEDINGS OF THE MATHEMATICAL AND PHYSICAL SOCIETY OF EGYPT.** See Mathematics.

II/0369-8203
**PROCEEDINGS OF THE NATIONAL ACADEMY OF SCIENCES, INDIA. SECTION A : PHYSICAL SCIENCES.** (PROCEEDINGS OF THE NATIONAL ACADEMY OF SCIENCES, INDIA. SECTION A.). [Proc. Natl. Acad. Sci., India, Sect. A]. **Added/Corp** National Academy of Sciences, India. **VFOAT** Section A. Vol. 12, Pt. 4 (Nov. 1942)-. Academic Scholarly Publication. English. Four times a year. $50.00 (surface mail); Rs90.00 (members); Rs120.00 (non-members). National Academy of Sciences India, 5 Lajpatrai Road, Allahabad 211002 India. **Tel** 55224. **LC** Q73; .P75. **CODEN** PAIAA3. Documents available from BIOSIS Document Express, CASDDS. ***Continues in part*** *Proceedings of the National Academy of Sciences, India, 0369-3236.*
**Ind/Abst** Biol. Abstr. (-1990); Chem. Abstr.; Math. Rev.; Zentralbl. Math. Ihre Grenzgeb.

NE/0079-6417
**PROGRESS IN LOW TEMPERATURE PHYSICS.** [Prog. low temp. phys.]. Vol. 1 (1955)-. Academic Scholarly Publication. English. ir. Price varies per volume. Elsevier Science Publishers BV, PO Box 211, 1000 AE Amsterdam Netherlands. **Tel** 011 31 20 5803642, FAX 011 31 20 5862696, telex 15682. **ED** D.F. Brewer. **LC** QC277.9; .P76. **CODEN** PLTPAA. Documents available from CASDDS.
**Ind/Abst** Chem. Abstr.

UK/0265-9697
**PROGRESS IN MEDICAL AND ENVIRONMENTAL PHYSICS.** [Prog. med. environ. phys.]. Vol. 1 (1982)-. Monographic series. English. ir. Price varies per volume. Blackie Academic & Prof, Bishopbriggs, Glasgow G64 2NZ Scotland. **Tel** 041 762-2332, FAX 041 772-7521. **ED** Daphne F. Jackson. **NLM** W1 PR67088. Documents available from Ask*IEEE.
**Desc:** A series of two books covering the state of the art for medical physicist in imaging techniques.
**Ind/Abst** INSPEC (1982-).

US/0033-0671
**PROGRESS OF PHYSICS.** **VFOAT** Fortschritte der Physik. (19??)-. Monographic series. English (English). ir. Price varies per volume. Birkhauser Boston, Inc., c/o Springer Publishers New York Inc., Customer Service Department, 333 Meadowlands Parkway, Secaucus NJ 07096-2491. **Tel** (201)348-4033, (800)777-4643. **(Subscription address:** Birkhauser Boston Books, c/o Springer Verlag, PO Box 19386, Newark, NJ 07195; Phone: (201)348-4033**) LC** QC1; .P8848. **DD** 530/.05.
**Ind/Abst** Math. Rev.

JA/0375-9687
**PROGRESS OF THEORETICAL PHYSICS. SUPPLEMENT.** [Prog. theor. phys. Suppl.]. No. 1 (1955)-. Academic Scholarly Publication. English. qt. Price varies per volume. Progress of Theoretical Physics, c/o Yukawa Hall, Kyoto University, Kyoto 606 Japan. **Tel** (075)722-3540. **CODEN** PTPSAL. Index available. cum. index. Documents available from The Genuine Article, Ask*IEEE, CASDDS.
**Desc:** Surveys the developments in various fields of fundamental physics.
**Ind/Abst** Chem. Abstr. (1955-1983); Curr. Contents Phys. Chem. Earth Sci.; INSPEC (1968-); Int. Aerosp. Abstr.; Math. Rev.; Res. Alert [Full Cov.]; Sci. Cit. Index; SCISEARCH.

US/0888-6903
**PROPERTY DATA UPDATE.** ***Ceased.*** [Prop. data update]. **Added/Corp** Soviet Union. Gosudarstvennaia sluzhba standartnykh i spravochnykh dannykh. Vol. 1, No. 1 (1988)-Vol. 2 (?). Periodical. English (translations available in Russian). Four times a year. Taylor & Francis Ltd., Rankine Road, Basingstoke Hampshire, RG24 8PR United Kingdom. **Tel** 011 44 256 840366, FAX 011 44 256 479438, telex 858540. **(Subscription address:** Taylor & Francis Inc., 1900 Frost Road, Suite 101, Bristol PA 19007-1598.**) ED** A D Kozlov. **LC** QD65; .P75. **DD** 541.3/0212. **CODEN** PDUPEV. **[CCC].** available on microfilm from University Microfilms International (UMI).
**Desc:** Reports officially approved and correlated property data for a variety of important substances. Includes such fields as physics of atoms, nuclei, and molecules, thermodynamic and transport properties of liquids and gases, electrophysical properties, mechanical, thermophysical, electrical magnetic properties of substances and optical properties of solids and materials.

US
**PROQUEST. INSPEC. PHYSICS. [COMPUTER FILE].** **Added/Corp** Institution of Electrical Engineers. **VFOAT** Inspec. Physics. (19??)-. English. qt. University Microfilms International, 300 North Zeeb Road, Ann Arbor MI 48106-1346. **Tel** (313)761-4700, (800)521-0600 Exts. 2490, 2491, FAX (313)973-1540. **(Subscription address:** IEE / UK, Publications Sales Department, PO Box 96, Stevenage, Herts, SG1 2SD England.**)**

BL/0101-3084
**PUBLICACAO IPEN.** **Added/Corp** Instituto de Pesquisas Energeticas e Nucleares (Brazil). **VFOAT** Publicacao I.P.E.N. (1979)-. Academic Scholarly Publication. English (Portuguese). ir. Instituto de Pesquisas Energeticas e Nucleares-CNEN SP, Caixa Postal 11049-Pinheiros, CEP 05508, Sao Paulo 01000 Brazil. **Tel** 11 55 11 2116011, telex (011)23592. **LC** QC791.9; .P83. **DD** 621.48/05. **CODEN** PUIPDL. Documents available from CASDDS.
**Ind/Abst** Chem. Abstr.

US/0079-8193
**PURE AND APPLIED PHYSICS.** ***Ceased.*** [Pure appl. phys.]. ( )-Vol. 43 (1985). Academic Scholarly Publication. English. ir. Academic Press, Inc., 6277 Sea Harbor Drive, Orlando FL 32887. **Tel** (800)543-9534, (407)345-4100, FAX (407)363-9661. **CODEN** PAPHAP. Documents available from Ask*IEEE, CASDDS.
**Ind/Abst** Chem. Abstr.; Ei Page One; INSPEC.

UK
**QUANTUM AND SEMICLASSICAL OPTICS: JOURNAL OF THE EUROPEAN OPTICAL SOCIETY - B.** (19??)-. Periodical. English. mo. $265.00. Institute of Physics, Techno House, Redcliffe Way, Bristol BS1 6NX England. **Tel** 011 44 272 297481, FAX 011 44 272 294318, telex 449149 INSTP G. **(Subscription address:** American Institute of Physics, Publishing Sales, 500 Sunnyside Blvd., Woodbury NY 11797.**)**

US/0481-1275
**QUANTUM PHYSICS AND ITS APPLICATIONS.** Vol. 1 (1964)-. English. Gordon & Breach Science Publishers, Inc., PO Box 786, Cooper Station, New York NY 10276. **Tel** (212)206-8900, FAX (212)645-2459. **(Subscription address:** International Publishers Distributor at one of the following addresses: 820 Town Center Drive, Langhorne, PA 19047; or PO

Box 90, Reading Berkshire RG1 8JL UK; or Kent Ridge PO Box 1180, Singapore 9111, Republic of Singapore) **DD** 539.

US/1048-8820
**QUANTUM (WASHINGTON, D.C.).** See Mathematics.

●UK/0969-806X
**RADIATION PHYSICS AND CHEMISTRY.** Vol. 41, No. 1/2 (Jan./Feb. 1993)-. Periodical. English. mo. $991.00 The Americas; £665.00 other. Pergamon Press, An Imprint of Elsevier Science Ltd., The Boulevard, Langford Lane, Kidlington, Oxford OX5 1GB United Kingdom. **Tel** 011 44 865 843000, 011 44 865 843699, FAX 011 44 865 843010. **(Subscription address:** Elsevier Science Ltd. Oxford Fulfillment Centre, PO Box 800, Kidlington, Oxford OX5 1DX United Kingdom.) **ED** J. Hubbell, A. Charlesby. **LC** QD601.A1; I54. Documents available from Ask*IEEE, CASDDS, ADONIS. ***Continues*** *International Journal of Radiation Applications and Instrumentation. Part C, Radiation Physics and Chemistry.*
**Desc:** Provides a medium to assist the growth in knowledge of radiation reactions and processes and of their application in technological and other fields.
**Ind/Abst** ADONIS; Chem. Abstr.; Curr. Contents Phys. Chem. Earth Sci.; Health Saf. Sci. Abstr.; INSPEC; Res. Alert; Sci. Cit. Index; SCISEARCH; Toxicol. Abstr.

XR/0322-8657
**RADIOISOTOPY.** (RADIOISOTOPY / USTAV PRO VYZKUM, VYROBU A VYUZITI RADIOISOTOPU.). [Radioisotopy]. **Added/Corp** Ustav pro Vyzkkum, Vyrobu a Vyuziti Radioisotopu (Prague, Czechoslovakia). (19??)-. Academic Scholarly Publication. Czech (summaries and/or abstracts in English). bm. 77.90. **(Subscription address:** Artia Pegas Press Ltd., Palac Metro Narodni Trida 25, 11210 Prague 1 Czech Republic.) **CODEN** RAISBC. Documents available from CASDDS.
**Ind/Abst** Chem. Abstr.; Energy Res. Abstr.

UK/0308-4272
**RADIOLOGICAL PROTECTION BULLETIN.** [Radiol. prot. bull.]. (1972)-. Periodical. English. mo. £24.00 UK; £30.00 other. National Radiological Protection Board, Information Services, Chilton Oxon OX11 0RQ England. **Tel** 011 44 235 831600.
**Ind/Abst** AESIS Q.; Geogr. Abstr. Human Geogr.

US/1056-0793
**RADTECH REPORT.** [RadTech rep.]. **Added/Corp** RadTech International North America. (198?)-. Academic Scholarly Publication. English. bm. RadTech International North America, 60 Revere Drive, Suite 500, Northbrook IL 60062. **DD** 621. Documents available from CASDDS.
**Ind/Abst** Chem. Abstr.

FR
**RAPPORT NATIONAL DE CONJONCTURE SCIENTIFIQUE : PHYSIQUE.** **Main/Corp** France. Centre National de la Recherche Scientifique. Comite National de la Recherche Scientifique. French. CNRS / Institut d'Information Scientifique et Technique, (Centre National de la Recherche Scientifique), 15 Quai Anatole France, Paris 75700 France. **Tel** 011 33 1 47531515, telex 299 356 F. **LC** QC1; .F77A. **DD** 530/.05.

RU/0034-2343
**REFERATIVNYI ZHURNAL. FIZIKA.** **Added/Corp** Vsesoiuznyi Institut Nauchnoi I Tekhnicheskoi Informatsii (Soviet Union). Akademiia Nauk SSSR. Institut Nauchnoi Informatsii. No. 1 (1954)-. Periodical. Russian. mo. $1,024.50. VINITI - Vsesoyuznyi Institut Nauchno-Tekhnicheskoi Informatsii, All-Union Scientific and Technical Information Institute, Baltiiskaia Ulitsa 14, 125219 Moscow Russia. **Tel** 238-46-00, FAX 9430060, telex 411160. **LC** QC1; .A419633. cum. index. Documents available from CASDDS.
**Ind/Abst** Chem. Abstr.

BL
**RELATORIO DA PRESIDENCIA.** **Main/Corp** Centro Brasileiro de Pesquisas Fisicas. (19??)-. Portuguese. ir. Av Venceslau Braz, 71 Fundos Casa 27, Rio de Janeiro RJ CEP 222 Brazil. **Tel** (021)295-4846, 295-4442, FAX (021)541-5342, telex (21)36952. **LC** QC47.B6; C45a.

BL
**RELATORIO DAS ATIVIDADES ADMINISTRATIVAS.** **Main/Corp** Centro Brasileiro de Pesquisas Fisicas. Portuguese. Av Venceslau Braz, 71 Fundos Casa 27, Rio de Janeiro RJ CEP 222 Brazil. **Tel** (021)295-4846, 295-4442, FAX (021)541-5342, telex (21)36952. **LC** QC47.B6; C45B.

US/0894-5217
**REMOTE SENSING NEWSLETTER IN ANTHROPOLOGY AND ARCHAEOLOGY.** [Remote sens. newsl. anthropol. archaeol.]. **Added/Corp** American Association for the Advancement of Science. Section H--Anthropology. Vol. 1, Issue 1 (Jan. 1987)-. Newsletter. English. qt. Remote Sensing Newsletter in Anthropology and Archaeology, 113 North Randall Road, Slidell LA 70458. **DD** 621.

US/1055-9922
**REMOTE SENSING OF EARTH RESOURCES (ALBUQUERQUE, N.M.), THE.** ***Ceased.*** (THE REMOTE SENSING OF EARTH RESOURCES.). [Remote sensing earth resour.]. **Added/Corp** University of New Mexico. Technology Application Center. Vol. 20 No. 1 (Jan.-March 1991)-Vol. 23 (1994). Periodical. English. qt. Earth Data Analysis Center, University of New Mexico, 2500 Yale Boulevard Southeast, Suite 100, Albuquerque NM 87131-6031. **Tel** (505)277-3622, FAX (505)277-3614, telex 660461 ASBKS UNM ABQ. **LC** G70.4; .Q37. **DD** 621.36/78. ***Continues*** *Remote Sensing of Natural Resources.*

NO/0078-6780
**REPORT - INSTITUTE OF THEORETICAL ASTROPHYSICS.** (REPORT / INSTITUTE OF THEORETICAL ASTROPHYSICS, BLINDERN, OSLO.). [Rep. - Inst. heor. astrophysics]. Began with No. 1 in 1952. English. **LC** QB461; .O8. **DD** 523.01. **CODEN** OTARAY. Documents available from CASDDS.
**Ind/Abst** Chem. Abstr.

US/0732-7935
**REPORT (JOINT INSTITUTE FOR LABORATORY ASTROPHYSICS).** (REPORT / JOINT INSTITUTE FOR LABORATORY ASTROPHYSICS.). [Rep. - Jt. Inst. Lab. Astrophys.]. **VFOAT** JILA Report. Academic Scholarly Publication. English. University of Colorado Joint Institute for Laboratory Astrophysics, Boulder CO 80309. **Tel** (303)492-7801. **DD** 523. **CODEN** JILRAP. Documents available from CASDDS.
**Desc:** Bibliographies and evaluated compilations of data on electron and photon collisions with atoms and ions and low-energy heavy particle collisions.
**Ind/Abst** Chem. Abstr. (1962-1981).

JA
**REPORT OF RESEARCH CENTER OF ION BEAM TECHNOLOGY, HOSEI UNIVERSITY. SUPPLEMENT.** **VFOAT** Hosei Daigaku Ion Bimu Kogaku Kenkyujo Kokoku. Bessatsu. No. 1 (Dec. 1980)-. Academic Scholarly Publication. English (English). Hosei Diagaku Ion Bimu Kogaku Kenkyujo, (Research Center of Ion Beam Technology, Hosei University), 7-2, Kajinocho 3 Chome, Koganeishi, Tokyoto 184, Japan. **LC** QC702.7.B65; R46. **DD** 537.5/6. **CODEN** RCISDS. Documents available from CASDDS.
**Ind/Abst** Chem. Abstr.

NO/0332-5571
**REPORT SERIES / UNIVERSITY OF OSLO, DEPARTMENT OF PHYSICS.** [Rep. ser. - Univ. Oslo, Inst. Phys.]. Academic Scholarly Publication. English (Norwegian). ir (30 to 40 issues per year). Price varies per volume. University of Oslo Department of Physics, Box 1048, Blindern, 0316 Oslo 3 Norway. **Tel** 011 47 2 456428, FAX 47-2-456422. **ED** Ole Lonsjo. **CODEN** RUSPDP. **Circ:** 200 (ctrl). Documents available from CASDDS.
**Desc:** The report series contains scientific and technical reports of work from the department of physics.
**Ind/Abst** Chem. Abstr.

PL/0034-4877
**REPORTS ON MATHEMATICAL PHYSICS.** [Rep. math. phys.]. Vol. 1 (Aug. 1970)-. Periodical. English. bm. $515.00 The Americas; £345.00 other. Pergamon Press, An Imprint of Elsevier Science Ltd., The Boulevard, Langford Lane, Kidlington, Oxford OX5 1GB United Kingdom. **Tel** 011 44 865 843000, 011 44 865 843699, FAX 011 44 865 843010. **(Subscription address:** Elsevier Science Ltd. Oxford Fulfillment Centre, PO Box 800, Kidlington, Oxford OX5 1DX United Kingdom.) **ED** A. Jamiolkowski. **LC** QC19.2; .R4. **DD** 530.1/5/05. **CODEN** RMHPBE. **[CCC]. Bk Rev. Ad Acc.** available on microfilm and microfiche from University Microfilms International (UMI). Documents available from Ask*IEEE, CASDDS.
**Desc:** Publishes papers in theoretical physics which present a rigorous mathematical approach to problems of quantum and classical mechanics and field theories, relativity and gravitation statistical physics, mathematical foundations of physical theories, etc.
**Ind/Abst** Chem. Abstr.; INSPEC (Aug. 1970-); Math. Rev.; Pollut. Abstr. Indexes; Zentralbl. Math. Ihre Grenzgeb.

UK/0034-4885
**REPORTS ON PROGRESS IN PHYSICS.** [Rep. prog. phys.]. **Added/Corp** Institute of Physics (Great Britain) Physical Society (Great Britain) Institute of Physics and the Physical Society. Vol. 1 (1934)-. Periodical. English. mo. $871.00. Institute of Physics, Techno House, Redcliffe Way, Bristol BS1 6NX England. **Tel** 011 44 272 297481, FAX 011 44 272 294318, telex 449149 INSTP G. **(Subscription address:** American Institute of Physics, Publishing Sales, 500 Sunnyside Blvd., Woodbury NY 11797.) **ED** M. Hart. **LC** QC3; .P47. **NLM** W1 PH747. **CODEN** RPPHAG. **[CCC].** Index available (Bound into last issue of monthly edition, and included in each hardcover part of quarterly edition.). cum. index. **Pr Rev.** available on microfilm and microfiche. Documents available from The Genuine Article, Ask*IEEE, CASDDS.
**Desc:** Publishes reviews covering all branches of physics. Articles survey the development of selected topics, typically over the previous decade, within the wider context of physics. Authors combine a critical evaluation of their field for established workers with a reliable and accessible introduction for newcomers and specialists in other fields. Reviews are commissioned and are refereed to the same high standards as research papers. Provides a basic foundation of reviews for all research libraries and a broad overview of physics for other libraries.
**Ind/Abst** Alum. Ind. Abstr.; Appl. Mech. Rev.; Ceram. Abstr. (19??-); Chem. Abstr.; Curr. Contents Phys. Chem. Earth Sci.; Eng. Mater. Abstr.; GeoRef; Index Sci. Rev. [Full Cov.]; INSPEC (1968-); Int. Aerosp. Abstr.; Leadscan; Math. Rev.; Met. Abstr.; Res. Alert [Full Cov.]; Sci. Cit. Index; SCISEARCH; Surf. Treat. Technol. Abstr.; World Ceram. Abstr.

UK/0308-9290
**RESEARCH FIELDS IN PHYSICS AT UNITED KINGDOM UNIVERSITIES AND POLYTECHNICS.** [Res. fields phys. U.K. univ. polytech.]. **VFOAT** Research Field in Physics. (1970)-. English. ir. £72.00. IOP Publishing Limited, Unit 1 & 2, Audie House 260 Field End Road, Ruislip Middlesex HA4 9LG England. **Tel** 011 44 81 8684499.

UK
**RESEARCH FIELDS IN PHYSICS AT UNITED KINGDOM UNIVERSITIES AND POLYTECHNICS.** English. IOP Publishing Limited, Unit 1 & 2, Audie House 260 Field End Road, Ruislip Middlesex HA4 9LG England. **Tel** 011 44 81 8684499.

US
**RESEARCH IN SURFACE FORCES / KONFERENTSIIA PO POVERKHNOSTYM SILAM.** **Main/Conf** Konferentrsia po Poverkhnostym Silam. **Added/Corp** Institut Fizicheskoi Khimii (Akademiia Nauk SSSR) Consultants Bureau. (1960)-. English (translations available in Russian). ir. Plenum Press, 233 Spring Street, New York NY 10013-1578. **Tel** (212)620-8000, (800)221-9369, FAX (212)463-0742, (212)807-1047, telex 23/421139.

SI/0129-055X
**REVIEWS IN MATHEMATICAL PHYSICS.** Vol. 1, No. 1 (1989)-. Periodical. English. Eight times a year. $220.00 individuals, $445.00 institutions. World Scientific Publishing Company, PO Box 128, Farrer Road, Singapore 9128 Singapore. **Tel** 011 65 3825663, FAX 011 65 3825919, telex RS 28561 WSPC. **(Subscription address:** US: World Scientific Publishing Co., Inc., 1060 Main Street, River Edge, NJ 07661 Telephone: (201)487-9655, Fax: (201)487-9656; Europe: World Scientific Publishing Co Ltd, 73 Lynton Mead, Totteridge, London N20 8DH United Kingdom Telephone: 011 44 81 4462461, Fax: 011 44 81 4463356; India: World Scientific Publishing Co Pte Ltd, 4911 9th Floor, High Point IV, 45 Palace Road, Bangalore 560 001 India Telephone: (80) 2205972, Fax: (80) 3344593, Telex: 0845-2900 PCO IN; Hong Kong: World Scientific Publishing (HK) Co, PO Box 72482, Kowloon Central Post Office, Hong Kong Telephone: 852-7718791, Fax: 852-7718155) **ED** H. Araki. **LC** QC19.2; .R43. **DD** 530.1/5. **CODEN** RMPHEX. **[CCC].** cum. index. **Circ:** 180. Documents available from Ask*IEEE.
**Desc:** Covers gauge fields, quantum field theory, statistical mechanics, dynamical systems, and functional analysis.
**Ind/Abst** INSPEC (1989-); Sci. Cit. Index; Zentralbl. Math. Ihre Grenzgeb.

US/0034-6861
**REVIEWS OF MODERN PHYSICS.** [Rev. mod. phys.]. **Added/Corp** American Institute of Physics. American Physical Society. Vol. 2, No. 1 (Jan. 1930)-. Academic Scholarly Publication. English. qt. $300.00 US; $310.00 Canada, Mexico, Central & South America, and the Caribbean; $325.00 other. American Institute of Physics, 500 Sunnyside Boulevard, Woodbury NY 11797-2999. **Tel** (516)576-2200, FAX (516)349-7669, telex 960983. **LC** QC1; .R4. **DD** 530. **NLM** W1 RE257E. **CODEN** RMPHAT. **[CCC].** Index available (bound in last issue). **Pr Rev.** available on microfilm; available on microfiche. Documents available from The Genuine Article, Ask*IEEE, CASDDS. ***Continues*** *Physical Review Supplement.*
**Desc:** Provides information and enhances communication among physicists.
**Ind/Abst** Chem. Abstr.; Curr. Contents Phys. Chem. Earth Sci.; Curr. Phys. Index; EMBASE; Energy Res. Abstr.; GeoRef; INSPEC (1968-); Int. Aerosp. Abstr.; Mass Spect. Bull.; Math. Rev.; Res. Alert [Full Cov.]; Sci. Cit. Index; SCISEARCH; SPIN (1970-); Surf. Treat. Technol. Abstr.

SI/0218-1029
**REVIEWS OF THE SOLID STATE SCIENCE.** ***Ceased.*** [Rev. solid state sci.]. **Added/Corp** International Council of Scientific Unions. Committee on Science and Technology in Developing

Countries. Vol. 1, No. 1 (Aug. 1987)-(1992). Periodical. English. qt. World Scientific Publishing Company, PO Box 128, Farrer Road, Singapore 9128 Singapore. **Tel** 011 65 3825663, FAX 011 65 3825919, telex RS 28561 WSPC. **LC** QC176.A1; R48. **DD** 530.4/1/05. **CODEN** RVSSE8. **[CCC].** Documents available from Ask*IEEE, CASDDS.
**Ind/Abst** Chem. Abstr.; INSPEC (Aug. 1988-).

BL/0374-4922
**REVISTA BRASILEIRA DE FISICA.** ***Title Change.*** [Rev. bras. fis.]. **Added/Corp** Sociedade Brasileira de Fisica. Vol. 1 (April 1971)-(19??). Periodical. Portuguese (Portuguese, English, Spanish and French; summaries and/or abstracts in English). qt. Soc Brasil Fisica Inst Fisica, Univ Sao Paulo, CX Postal 20553, 01498 970 Sao Paulo SP Brazil. **Tel** 55 11 815 5599 Ext 222, telex 001379220. **ED** Nicin Fagury. **CODEN** RBFSA3. **Ad Acc.** Documents available from Ask*IEEE, CASDDS. ***Continued by*** *Brazilian Journal of Physics.*
**Desc:** General physics.
**Ind/Abst** Chem. Abstr.; Coal Abstr.; INSPEC (April 1971-); Int. Aerosp. Abstr.

CU/0253-9268
**REVISTA CUBANA DE FISICA.** [Rev. Cub. fis.]. 1-. Academic Scholarly Publication. Spanish (summaries and/or abstracts in English). Three times a year. 35.93Can$ North America; 37.13Can$ South America; 39.52Can$ other. Ediciones Cubanas, Obispo 527, Altos ESQ Bernaza, CP 10100 Havana Cuba. **Tel** 011 632980, 631942, FAX 011 631011, telex 512337, 6540. **CODEN** RECFD7. Documents available from CASDDS.
**Ind/Abst** Chem. Abstr.; Energy Res. Abstr. (Aug. 1982-).

AG
**REVISTA DE BIOLOGIA Y MEDICINA NUCLEAR.** **See** Medical Science and Technology-Nuclear Medicine.

RM
**REVISTA DE FIZICA SI CHIMIE.**
**Added/Corp** Societatea de Stiinte Fizice si Chimice din Republica Socialista Romania. (19??)-. Periodical. Romanian. mo. **(Subscription address:** Ilexim Press Department, PO Box 1, 136-1-137, Bucharest, Romania.**)** **LC** QC1; .R417. available with illustrations. ***Formed by the union of*** *Revista de Fizica Si Chimie. Seria A* ***and*** *Revista de Fizica Si Chimie. Seria B.*
**Desc:** Scientific publication on physics and chemistry, for youth.

MX/0185-1101
**REVISTA MEXICANA DE ASTRONOMIA Y ASTROFISICA.** **See** Astronomy.

MX/0035-001X
**REVISTA MEXICANA DE FISICA.** [Rev. mex. fis.]. **Added/Corp** Sociedad Mexicana de Fisica. Vol. 1, (Apr. 1952)-. Academic Scholarly Publication. Spanish (English). Six times a year (Feb., Apr., June, Aug., Oct., Dec.). $110.00 The Americas; $112.00 Europe and Africa; $115.00 other. Sociedad Mexicana de Fisica AC Ciudad Universidad, ADPO Postal 70 348 Coyoacan, 04511 Mexico D. F. Mexico. **Tel** 011 52 5 5505910. **ED** Matias Moreno. **LC** QC1; .R42. **CODEN** RMXFAT. Index available. **Circ:** 1,600 (ctrl). Documents available from The Genuine Article, Ask*IEEE, CASDDS.
**Desc:** Original research papers on theoretical and experimental physics, scientific instrumentation history and philosophy of physics, teaching and educational policy and scientific policy.
**Ind/Abst** Chem. Abstr.; Curr. Contents Phys. Chem. Earth Sci.; INSPEC (1968-); Math. Rev.; Res. Alert [Full Cov.]; Sci. Cit. Index.

RM/0035-4090
**REVUE ROUMAINE DE PHYSIQUE.** ***Title Change.*** **Added/Corp** Academia Republicii Populare Romine. Academia Republicii Socialiste Romania. Vol. 1 (1956)-(19??). Periodical. English (French, German and Russian). Ten times a year. **(Subscription address:** Orion Press SRL, SPL Independentei 202-A, Bucharest 6 Romania.**)** **LC** QC1; .R43. Documents available from Ask*IEEE, CASDDS. ***Continued by*** *Romanian Journal of Physics.*
**Desc:** Publishes studies on physics.
**Ind/Abst** ACM Guide Comput. Lit.; Ceram. Abstr.; Chem. Abstr.; Chem. Titles; Comput. Rev.; Ei Page One; INSPEC (1968-); Leadscan; Math. Rev.; Zentralbl. Math. Ihre Grenzgeb.

RM/0035-4066
**REVUE ROUMAINE DES SCIENCES TECHNIQUES. SERIE ELECTROTECHNIQUE ET ENERGETIQUE.** ***Title Change.*** [Rev. roum. sci. tech., Ser. electrotech. energ.]. **Added/Corp** Academia Republicii Socialiste Romania. (1964)-(19??). Academic Scholarly Publication. Multiple languages (English, German, Russian, French and Spanish). qt. **(Subscription address:** Rompresfilatelia, PO Box 12 201, Bucharest Romania.**)** **CODEN** RTEEAE. Documents available from Article Express International, Ask*IEEE, CASDDS. ***Continues in part*** *Revue d'Electrotechnique et d'Energetique, Serie A: Electrotechnique, Electroenergetique et Energetique Generale* ***and*** *Revue d'Electrotechnique et d'Energetique, Serie B: Thermoenergetique et Utilisation Energetique des Combustibles.* ***Continued by*** *Revue Roumaine Electrotechnique et Energetique.*
**Desc:** Publishes studies on electrical engineering and energetics.
**Ind/Abst** Bioeng. Abstr.; Ceram. Abstr.; Chem. Abstr.; Coal Abstr.; Ei Page One; Energy Res. Abstr.; Eng. Index Annu.; INSPEC (1968-); Int. Aerosp. Abstr.; Math. Rev.

RM
**REVUE ROUMAINE ELECTROTECHNIQUE ET ENERGETIQUE.** (19??)-. Multiple languages (English, Russian, German, French and Spanish). $137.00. **(Subscription address:** Orion Press SRL, SPL Independentei 202-A, Bucharest 6 Romania.**)** ***Continues*** *Revue Roumaine des Sciences Techniques Serie Electrotechnique et Energetique, 0035-4066.*

GW/0035-4511
**RHEOLOGICA ACTA.** [Rheol. acta]. Vol. 1 (May 1958)-. Periodical. English (French and German; summaries and/or abstracts in French and German). Six times a year. DM1178.00. Dr Dietrich Steinkopff Verlag, PO Box 111442, D 64229 Darmstadt Germany. **Tel** 011 49 6151 17450. **(Subscription address:** Springer Verlag New York Inc. / for North America, 44 Hartz Way, Secaucus NJ 07096.**)** **ED** H. Giesekus. **LC** QC189; .R45. **DD** 531/.11. **CODEN** RHEAAK. **[CCC].** **Pr Rev.** Documents available from The Genuine Article, Ask*IEEE, Petroleum Abstracts Document Delivery Service, CASDDS.
**Desc:** Publishes theoretical and experimental contributions covering phenomenological rheology and structural rheology, electro- and magnetorheology, rheooptics, rheometry and applied rheology.
**Ind/Abst** Acoust. Abstr.; Chem. Abstr.; Coal Abstr.; Curr. Contents Phys. Chem. Earth Sci.; Dairy Sci. Abstr.; Energy Res. Abstr.; Food Sci. Technol. Abstr.; INSPEC (1968-); Int. Aerosp. Abstr.; Math. Rev.; Pet. Abstr.; Proc. Chem. Eng.; Res. Alert [Full Cov.]; Sci. Cit. Index; SCISEARCH; Theoret. Chem. Eng.; World Surf. Coat. Abstr.; Zentralbl. Math. Ihre Grenzgeb.

NE
**RHEOLOGY SERIES.** (1984)-. Monographic series. English. Price varies per volume. Elsevier Science Publishers BV, PO Box 211, 1000 AE Amsterdam Netherlands. **Tel** 011 31 20 5803642, FAX 011 31 20 5862696, telex 15682.
**Ind/Abst** Math. Rev.; Zentralbl. Math. Ihre Grenzgeb.

JA/0020-3084
**RIKA GAKU KENKYUSHO HOKOKU.** ***Ceased.*** (RIKAGAKU KENKYUJO HOKOKU.). [Rika gaku Kenkyusho hokoku]. **Added/Corp** Rikagaku Kenkyujo (Japan). **VFOAT** Reports of the Institute of Physical and Chemical Research. Vol. 34, No. 6 (Nov. 1958)-(1992). Periodical. Japanese. bm. Rikagaku Kenkyujo, (Inst. of Physical & Chemical Research), 2-1, Hirosawa, Wakoshi, Saitamaken 351-01 Japan. **CODEN** RKKHAO. Documents available from CASDDS. ***Continues*** *Kagaku Kenkyujo Hokoku.*
**Ind/Abst** Chem. Abstr.

IT/0035-5917
**RIVISTA DEL NUOVO CIMENTO.** (LA RIVISTA DEL NUOVO CIMENTO / A CURA DELLA SOCIETA ITALIANA DI FISICA.). [Riv. Nuovo cimento]. **Added/Corp** Societa Italiana di Fisica. **VFOAT** Rivista del Nuovo Cimento della Societa Italiana di Fisica. Ser. 1, Vol. 7, No. 1 (Jan./March 1969)-Vol. 2, No. 4 (Oct./Dec. 1970)-. Periodical. Italian. mo. $340.00 (nonmembers), $265.00 (members). Editrice Compositori SRL, Viale Stalingrado 97 2, 40128 Bologna Italy. **Tel** 011 39 51 327811. **LC** QC1; .N852. **NLM** W1 RI351E. **CODEN** RNUCAC. **[CCC].** **Bk Rev.** **Ad Acc.** **Pr Rev.** **Circ:** 1,000 (ctrl). Documents available from The Genuine Article, Ask*IEEE, CASDDS. ***Continues in part*** *Supplemento Al Nuovo Cimento.*
**Desc:** Provides coverage of stellar grains, absorption and emission by minor atmospheric gases in the radiation balance of the earth, conformal quantum electrodynamics and nondecomposable representations, photoreactions above the giant-dipole resonance, etc.
**Ind/Abst** Chem. Abstr.; Curr. Contents Phys. Chem. Earth Sci.; Energy Res. Abstr.; GeoRef; INSPEC (Jan./March 1969-); Math. Rev.; Res. Alert [Full Cov.]; Sci. Cit. Index; SCISEARCH.

RM
**ROMANIAN JOURNAL OF PHYSICS / ROMANIAN ACADEMY.** **Added/Corp** Academia Romana. (19??)-. Periodical. English. Ten times a year. DM524.00. **(Subscription address:** Kubon & Sagner, ABT Zeitschriftenimport, D 80328 Munich Germany.**)** **LC** QC1; .R43. **DD** 530/.05. **CODEN** RJPHEC. ***Continues*** *Revue Roumaine de Physique.*
**Ind/Abst** Chem. Abstr.

●RM/1221-1451
**ROMANIAN REPORTS IN PHYSICS.** **Added/Corp** Academia Romana. (1992)-. Periodical. Romanian. Ten times a year. DM384.00. **(Subscription address:** Kubon & Sagner, ABT Zeitschriftenimport, D 80328 Munich Germany.**)** **LC** QC1; .A28. ***Continues*** *Studii si Cercetari de Fizica, 0039-3940.*

GW/0138-3140
**ROSTOCKER PHYSIKALISCHE MANUSKRIPTE.** [Rostocker phys. Manuskr.]. **Added/Corp** Wilhelm-Pieck-Universitat Rostock. Sektion Physik. (1977)-. Monographic series. German. Wilhelm-Pieck-Universitat Rostock, Abt Wissenschaftspublizistik, Vogelsang 13/14, Rostock O-2500 Germany. **Tel** GDR 81/369 577. **CODEN** RPMADH. Documents available from CASDDS.
**Ind/Abst** Chem. Abstr.

US/1051-8053
**RUSSIAN JOURNAL OF ENGINEERING THERMOPHYSICS.** ***Ceased.*** **See** Engineering.

●RU/1061-9208
**RUSSIAN JOURNAL OF MATHEMATICAL PHYSICS.** [Russ. j. math. phys.]. **VFOAT** Mathematical Physics. (1992)-. Periodical. English. Four times a year. $340.00 US; $380.00 Canada & Mexico; $395.00 other. John Wiley & Sons, Inc., 605 Third Avenue, New York NY 10158-0012. **Tel** (212)850-6000, (212)850-6645, FAX (212)850-6088, telex 12-7063. **(Subscription address:** John Wiley & Sons / England, Baffins Lane, Chichester, West Sussex PO19 1UD England.**)** **ED** Victor P. Maslov. **LC** IN PROCESS. **DD** 530. **CODEN** RJMPEL.
**Desc:** Publishes original papers with complete proofs, short communications on recent achievements and reviews on topics of modern mathematical physics, regarded at present as the foundation of mathematical models of natural science, amalgamating a vast number of mathematical disciplines that were developing independently in the past.

●US/1064-8887
**RUSSIAN PHYSICS JOURNAL.** **Added/Corp** Consultants Bureau. **VFOAT** Izvestiya VUZ. Fizika. (1992)-. Academic Scholarly Publication. English (translations available in Russian). mo. $1295.00 US; $1515.00 other. Consultants Bureau, A Division of Plenum Publishing Corporation, 233 Spring Street, New York NY 10013. **Tel** (212)620-8000, (212)620-8466, FAX (212)463-0742, telex 23/421139. **[CCC].** Documents available from Article Express International, Ask*IEEE, CASDDS. ***Continues*** *Soviet Physics Journal, 0038-5697.*
**Ind/Abst** Appl. Mech. Rev.; Bioeng. Abstr.; Chem. Abstr.; Ei Page One; Electron. Commun. Abstr. J.; Eng. Index Annu.; Eng. Index Energy Abstr.; INSPEC (Nov./Dec. 1965-); Int. Aerosp. Abstr.; ISMEC Bull.; Math. Rev.; Pollut. Abstr. Indexes; Saf. Sci. Abstr. J.

KO/0374-4914
**SAE MULLI.** **VFOAT** New Physics. Academic Scholarly Publication. Korean (summaries and/or abstracts in English). Hanguk Mulli Hakhoe, San 76-561 Yoksam-dong Kangnam-ku, Seoul Korea. **LC** QC1; .S22. **CODEN** NWPYA4. Documents available from Ask*IEEE, CASDDS.
**Ind/Abst** Chem. Abstr.; INSPEC (March 1971-).

JA/0388-5607
**SCIENCE REPORTS OF THE TOHOKU UNIVERSITY. EIGHTH SERIES. PHYSICS AND ASTRONOMY, THE.** **Added/Corp** Tohoku Daigaku. Rigakubu. Tohoku Daigaku. Butsurigakka. Annual Report. Tohoku Daigaku. Temmongaku Kyoshitsu. Annual Report. **VFOAT** Physics and Astronomy; Science Reports. Eighth Series. Vol. 1 No. 1 (June 1980)-. Academic Scholarly Publication. English (Japanese). ir (one to three issues per year). Free. Professor S Yoshida, Faculty of Science, Tohoku University, Sendai Japan. **Tel** 022 222 1800, FAX 81 22 2251891, telex 852246 THUCOMJ. **ED** Akio Kotani and Keiya Takakubo. **LC** Q77; .S34. **DD** 530/.05. **CODEN** SRTAD9. **Circ:** 450. Documents available from Ask*IEEE, CASDDS. ***Continues in part*** *Science Reports of the Tohoku University. Series 1, Physics, Chemistry, Astronomy.*
**Desc:** Includes annual reports for the physics and astronomy departments.
**Ind/Abst** Chem. Abstr. (1980-1982); Eng. Mater. Abstr.; INSPEC (June 1980-).

IR
**SCIENTIFIC BULLETIN OF THE ATOMIC ENERGY ORGANIZATION OF IRAN.** **Added/Corp** Atomic Energy Organization of Iran. (1983)-. Bulletin. English. **CODEN** SBAIEV. Documents available from CASDDS. ***Continues*** *Technical Bulletin (Atomic Energy Organization of Iran).*
**Ind/Abst** Chem. Abstr.

US/0737-0164
**SEG ABSTRACTS.** **See** Earth Sciences-Geology.

JA/0582-4052
**SEIBUTSU BUTSURI.** [Seibutsu butsuri]. **Added/Corp** Nihon Seibutsu Gakkai. **VFOAT** Biophysics. (1961)-. Periodical. Japanese. bm. Nihon Seibutsu Butsuri Gakkai, (Biophysical Soc. of Japan), Yoshioka Shoten, 87, Tanaka Monzencho, Sakyoku, Kyotoshi, Kyotofu 606 Japan. **NLM** W1 SE249N. **CODEN** SEBUAL. Documents available from CASDDS.
**Ind/Abst** Chem. Abstr.

UK/0268-1242
**SEMICONDUCTOR SCIENCE AND TECHNOLOGY.** [Semicond. sci. technol.]. **Added/Corp** Institute of Physics (Great Britain) American Institute of Physics. Vol. 1, No. 1 (July 1986)-. Periodical. English. mo (2 supplements per volume). $889.00. Institute of Physics, Techno House, Redcliffe Way, Bristol BS1 6NX England. **Tel** 011 44 272 297481, FAX 011 44 272 294318, telex 449149 INSTP G. **(Subscription address:** American Institute of Physics, Publishing Sales, 500 Sunnyside Blvd., Woodbury NY 11797.**) ED** R A Stradling. **LC** QC610.9; .S45. **DD** 621.381/52/05. **CODEN** SSTEET. **[CCC].** Index available in last issue of volume--attached. **Pr Rev.** available on microfilm and microfiche. Documents available from Article Express International, The Genuine Article, Ask*IEEE, CASDDS.
**Desc:** Experimental and theoretical studies of the structural, electrical, optical and acoustic properties and the doping of bulk, low-dimensional and amorphous semiconductors; computational semiconductor physics; interface properties; including the physics and chemistry of heterojunctions, metal-semiconductor junctions; all multilayered structures involving semiconductor components.
**Ind/Abst** Acoust. Abstr.; Appl. Sci. Technol. Index; Chem. Abstr.; Curr. Contents Eng. Tech. Appl. Sci.; Curr. Contents Phys. Chem. Earth Sci.; Eng. Index Annu.; INSPEC (1986-); Mass Spect. Bull.; Res. Alert [Full Cov.]; Sci. Cit. Index.

US/0309-5991
**SEMICONDUCTORS AND INSULATORS.** ***Ceased.*** [Semicond. insul.]. Vol. 2, No. 4 (May 1977)-Vol. 5, No. 3 (Jan. 1993). Academic Scholarly Publication. English. Gordon & Breach Science Publishers, Inc., PO Box 786, Cooper Station, New York NY 10276. **Tel** (212)206-8900, FAX (212)645-2459. **(Subscription address:** International Publishers Distributor at one of the following addresses: 820 Town Center Drive, Langhorne, PA 19047; or PO Box 90, Reading Berkshire RG1 8JL UK; or Kent Ridge PO Box 1180, Singapore 9111, Republic of Singapore**) ED** A C Damask. **LC** QC610.9; .S46. **DD** 537.6/22. **CODEN** SINSD4. **[CCC]. Bk Rev. Ad Acc.** Documents available from Ask*IEEE, CASDDS. ***Continues*** *Journal of Nonmetals and Semiconductors, 0140-1653.*
**Ind/Abst** Ceram. Abstr. (-1983); Chem. Abstr.; INSPEC (1977-).

●US/1063-7826
**SEMICONDUCTORS (NEW YORK, N.Y.).** (SEMICONDUCTORS.). [Semiconductors]. **Added/Corp** American Institute of Physics. Vol. 27, No. 1 (Jan. 1993)-. Academic Scholarly Publication. English (translations available in Russian). mo. $2240.00 US; $2255.00 Canada, Mexico, Central & South America, and the Caribbean; $2285.00 other. American Institute of Physics, 500 Sunnyside Boulevard, Woodbury NY 11797-2999. **Tel** (516)576-2200, FAX (516)349-7669, telex 960983. **LC** QC612.S4; F557. **DD** 537. **CODEN** SMICES. **[CCC].** Index available (bound in last issue). Documents available from Article Express International, Ask*IEEE, CASDDS. ***Continues*** *Soviet Physics. Semiconductors, 0038-5700.*
**Ind/Abst** Alum. Ind. Abstr.; Bioeng. Abstr.; Chem. Abstr.; Curr. Phys. Index; Ei Page One; Electron. Commun. Abstr. J.; Energy Res. Abstr.; Eng. Index Annu.; Eng. Index Energy Abstr.; INSPEC (Feb. 1976-); Int. Aerosp. Abstr.; ISMEC Bull.; Met. Abstr.; Nucl. Sci. Abstr.; Pollut. Abstr. Indexes; Saf. Sci. Abstr. J.; Sci. Cit. Index; SPIN.

JA
**SENSOR GIJUTSU: SENSOR TECHNOLOGY.** **See** Computers-Cybernetics.

PL
**SERIA FIZYKA / UNIWERSYTET IM. ADAMA MICKIEWICZA W POZNANIU, WYDZIA MATEMAYKI, FIZYKI, CHEMII.** **Added/Corp** Uniwersytet im. Adama Mickiewicza w Poznaniu. Uniwersytet im. Adama Mickiewicza w Poznaniu. Wydzia Matemayki, Fizyki i Chemii. No. 5 (1970)-. Monographic series. Polish (English). Documents available from CASDDS. ***Continues*** *Uniwersytet im. Adama Mickiewicza w Poznaniu. Wydzia Matematyki, Fizyki i Chemii. Prace Wydziau Matematyka, Fizyka, Chemia. Seria Fizyka.*
**Ind/Abst** Chem. Abstr.

NE
**SERIES OF MONOGRAPHS ON SELECTED TOPICS IN SOLID STATE PHYSICS.** (1962)-. Monographic series. English. ir. Price varies per volume. Elsevier Science Publishers BV, PO Box 211, 1000 AE Amsterdam Netherlands. **Tel** 011 31 20 5803642, FAX 011 31 20 5862696, telex 15682. Documents available from Ask*IEEE.
**Ind/Abst** INSPEC.

SI
**SERIES ON PROGRESS IN HIGH TEMPERATURE SUPERCONDUCTIVITY.** **VFOAT** Progress in High Temperature Superconductivity. Vol. 1 (1987)-. Academic Scholarly Publication. English. ir. Price varies per volume. World Scientific Publishing Company, PO Box 128, Farrer Road, Singapore 9128 Singapore. **Tel** 011 65 3825663, FAX 011 65 3825919, telex RS 28561 WSPC. **CODEN** SPHSEQ. Documents available from Ask*IEEE, CASDDS.
**Ind/Abst** Chem. Abstr.; INSPEC.

CC
**SHU HSUEH WU LI HSUEH PAO. VFOAT** Acta Mathematica Scientia. Vol. 1, No. 1 (1981)-. Periodical. Chinese (English). qt. RMBY1.25. Acta Mathematica Scientia, PO Box 30, Wuhan 43007, People's Republic of China. **LC** QC19.2; .S55. **DD** 530.1/5/05. Documents available from The Genuine Article.
**Ind/Abst** Compumath Citation Index [Full Cov.]; Math. Rev.; Res. Alert [Full Cov.]; SCISEARCH; Soc. Sci. Cit. Index [Select. Cov.]; Zentralbl. Math. Ihre Grenzgeb.

SI/0217-4251
**SINGAPORE JOURNAL OF PHYSICS.** [Singap. j. phys.]. **Added/Corp** Institute of Physics, Singapore. (1984)-. Periodical. English. **CODEN** SJPHEN.

NE/0038-0938
**SOLAR PHYSICS.** **See** Astronomy.

US/0038-1098
**SOLID STATE COMMUNICATIONS.** [Solid state commun.]. Vol. 1 (June 1963)-. Periodical. English (French, German and Russian). Forty-eight times a year. $1945.00 The Americas; £1305.00 other. Pergamon Press, An Imprint of Elsevier Science Ltd., The Boulevard, Langford Lane, Kidlington, Oxford OX5 1GB United Kingdom. **Tel** 011 44 865 843000, 011 44 865 843699, FAX 011 44 865 843010. **(Subscription address:** Elsevier Science Ltd. Oxford Fulfillment Centre, PO Box 800, Kidlington, Oxford OX5 1DX United Kingdom.**) ED** Manuel Cardona. **LC** QC176.A1; S6. **DD** 530.4/1/05. **CODEN** SSCOA4. **[CCC]. Bk Rev. Ad Acc. Pr Rev.** available on microfilm from Microfilms International Marketing Corp.; available on microfilm and microfiche from University Microfilms International (UMI); available on microfiche from the publisher. Documents available from Article Express International, The Genuine Article, Ask*IEEE, CASDDS.
**Desc:** Contains abstracts of important papers published in Soviet solid-state physics.
**Ind/Abst** Acoust. Abstr.; Bioeng. Abstr.; Ceram. Abstr.; Chem. Abstr.; Chem. Titles; Civ. Struct. Eng. Abstr.; Coal Abstr.; Curr. Contents Phys. Chem. Earth Sci.; Ei Page One; Elect. Comm. Abstr.; Eng. Mater. Abstr.; Eng. Index Annu.; GeoRef; INSPEC (1968-); Int. Aerosp. Abstr.; Manuf. Process Eng. Abstr.; Mass Spect. Bull.; Mater. Sci. Eng. Abstr.; Mech. Eng. Abstr.; Met. Abstr.; Pollut. Abstr. Indexes; Res. Alert [Full Cov.]; Sci. Cit. Index; SCISEARCH; Solid State Supercond. Abstr.

NE/0167-2738
**SOLID STATE IONICS.** [Solid state ion.]. Vol. 1/2 (April 1980)-. Academic Scholarly Publication. English. Thirty-six times a year (9 volumes). Fl3564.00. Elsevier Science Publishers BV, PO Box 211, 1000 AE Amsterdam Netherlands. **Tel** 011 31 20 5803642, FAX 011 31 20 5862696, telex 15682. **ED** M. S. Whittingham. **LC** QC176.A1; S615. **DD** 530.4/1. **CODEN** SSIOD3. **[CCC]. Pr Rev.** available on microfilm and microfiche from University Microfilms International (UMI). Documents available from Article Express International, The Genuine Article, Ask*IEEE, CASDDS. ***Absorbed*** *Reactivity of Solids (Amsterdam, Netherlands : 1985).*
**Desc:** Devoted to the physics, chemistry and materials science of diffusion in and reactivity of solids.
**Ind/Abst** Alum. Ind. Abstr.; Bioeng. Abstr.; Ceram. Abstr (19??-); Chem. Abstr.; Chem. Titles; Curr. Contents Phys. Chem. Earth Sci.; Curr. Titles Electrochem.; Ei Page One; Elect. Comm. Abstr.; Eng. Mater. Abstr. (April 1980-); Eng. Index Annu.; INSPEC (April 1980-); Mater. Sci. Eng. Abstr.; Mech. Eng. Abstr.; Met. Abstr.; Phys. Briefs (April 1980-); Res. Alert [Full Cov.]; Sci. Cit. Index; SCISEARCH; Soc. Sci. Cit. Index [Select. Cov.]; Solid State Supercond. Abstr.

●NE/0926-2040
**SOLID STATE NUCLEAR MAGNETIC RESONANCE.** Vol. 1, No. 1 (Feb. 1992)-. Academic Scholarly Publication. English. Six times a year (1 volume). Fl485.00. Elsevier Science Publishers BV, PO Box 211, 1000 AE Amsterdam Netherlands. **Tel** 011 31 20 5803642, FAX 011 31 20 5862696, telex 15682. **ED** J. Klinowski. **NLM** W1; SO887DP. **CODEN** SSNRE4. **[CCC].** Documents available from Ask*IEEE, CASDDS.
**Desc:** Publishes original manuscripts dealing with all experimental and theoretical aspects of solid state NMR.
**Ind/Abst** Chem. Abstr.; INSPEC (1992-); Sci. Cit. Index.

US/0081-1955
**SOLID STATE PHYSICS : ADVANCES IN RESEARCH AND APPLICATIONS. SUPPLEMENT.** [Solid state phys., Suppl.]. **VFOAT** Supplement. (1958)-. Academic Scholarly Publication. English. ir. Price varies per volume. Academic Press, Inc., 6277 Sea Harbor Drive, Orlando FL 32887. **Tel** (800)543-9534, (407)345-4100, FAX (407)363-9661. **ED** H. Ehrenreich, Frederick Seitz and David Turnbull. **DD** 539. **CODEN** SSPSAD. Documents available from The Genuine Article, CASDDS.
**Ind/Abst** Chem. Abstr. (1958-1983); Res. Alert [Full Cov.]; Sci. Cit. Index; SCISEARCH.

US/0081-1947
**SOLID STATE PHYSICS (NEW YORK. 1955).** (SOLID STATE PHYSICS.). [Solid state phys.]. Vol. 1 (1955)-. Academic Scholarly Publication. English. ir. Price varies per volume. Academic Press, Inc., 6277 Sea Harbor Drive, Orlando FL 32887. **Tel** (800)543-9534, (407)345-4100, FAX (407)363-9661. **ED** F. Seitz and D. Turnbull. **LC** QC173; .S477. **DD** 539.2. **CODEN** SSPHAE. **[CCC].** cum. index. Documents available from CASDDS.
**Ind/Abst** Chem. Abstr.; Ei Page One; GeoRef; Index Sci. Rev. [Full Cov.].

SA/0379-4377
**SOUTH AFRICAN JOURNAL OF PHYSICS.** ***Ceased.*** [S. Afr. j. phys.]. **Added/Corp** South African Institute of Physics. Foundation for Education, Science, and Technology (South Africa). Bureau for Scientific Publications. **VFOAT** Suid-Afrikaanse Tydskrif vir Fisika. Vol. 1 (1978)-Vol. 15 (1992). Academic Scholarly Publication. English (Afrikaans). qt. Foundation for Education Science & Technology, PO Box 1758, Pretoria 0001 South Africa. **Tel** 011 27 12 3226404, FAX 011 27 12 3207803. **ED** C A Engelbrecht. **CODEN** SAPHDR. **[CCC]. Bk Rev. Ad Acc. Circ:** 750. Documents available from Ask*IEEE, CASDDS.
**Desc:** Original research in any branch of physics.
**Ind/Abst** Alum. Ind. Abstr.; Chem. Abstr.; Eng. Mater. Abstr.; INSPEC (1978-); Int. Aerosp. Abstr.; Met. Abstr.; Pollut. Abstr. Indexes.

US/8755-4585
**SOVIET JOURNAL OF CONTEMPORARY PHYSICS.** ***Title Change.*** (SOVIET JOURNAL OF CONTEMPORARY PHYSICS / ARMENIAN ACADEMY OF SCIENCES.). [Sov. j. contemp. phys.]. **Added/Corp** Haykakan SSH Gitutyunneri Akademia. **VFOAT** Izvestiia Akademii Nauk Armianskoi SSR. Vol. 19, No. 1 (1984)-(1993). Periodical. English (translations available in Russian). bm. Allerton Press, Inc., 150 Fifth Avenue, New York NY 10011. **Tel** (212)924-3950, FAX (212)463-9684, telex 427441 ALPRES. **LC** QC1; .I97. **DD** 530/.05. **[CCC].** Documents available from Ask*IEEE. ***Continued by*** *Journal of Contemporary Physics / Armenian Academy of Sciences.*
**Ind/Abst** INSPEC (1985-).

US/0360-0343
**SOVIET JOURNAL OF PLASMA PHYSICS.** ***Title Change.*** [Sov. j. plasma phys.]. **Added/Corp** American Institute of Physics. Vol. 1 (Jan./Feb. 1975)-(1993). Academic Scholarly Publication. English (Russian). bm. American Institute of Physics, 500 Sunnyside Boulevard, Woodbury NY 11797-2999. **Tel** (516)576-2200, FAX (516)349-7669, telex 960983. **(Subscription address:** UK/ Institute of Physics, Techno House, Redcliffe Way, Bristol BS1 6NX England**) LC** QC717.6; .S66. **DD** 530.4/4/05. **CODEN** SJPPDC. **[CCC].** Documents available from Article Express International, Ask*IEEE, CASDDS. ***Continued by*** *Plasma Physics Report.*
**Ind/Abst** Bioeng. Abstr.; Chem. Abstr.; Curr. Phys. Index; Ei Page One; Energy Res. Abstr. (Sept. 1976-); Eng. Index Annu.; INSPEC (July/Aug. 1975-); Int. Aerosp. Abstr.; SPIN (1975-).

US/0038-5689
**SOVIET PHYSICS-DOKLADY.** ***Title Change.*** [Sov. phys. dokl.]. **Added/Corp** American Institute of Physics. Vol. 1 (Aug. 1956)-(1993). Periodical. English (Russian). mo. American Institute of Physics, 500 Sunnyside Boulevard, Woodbury NY 11797-2999. **Tel** (516)576-2200, FAX (516)349-7669, telex 960983. **(Subscription address:** UK/ Institute of Physics, Techno House, Redcliffe Way, Bristol BS1 6NX England**) LC** QC1; .A386. **DD** 530.5. **CODEN** SPHDA9. **[CCC].** available on microfilm. Documents available from Ask*IEEE. ***Continued by*** *Physics - Doklady.*
**Ind/Abst** Acoust. Abstr.; Curr. Phys. Index; Energy Res. Abstr. (Sept. 1974-); GeoRef; HTFS Dig.; INSPEC (1968-); Int. Aerosp. Abstr.; Mass Spect. Bull.; Math. Rev.; Pollut. Abstr. Indexes; Soils Fert.; SPIN (1970-); Zentralbl. Math. Ihre Grenzgeb.

US/0038-5646
**SOVIET PHYSICS-JETP.** ***Title Change.*** [Sov. phys. JETP]. **Added/Corp** American Institute of Physics. **VFOAT** JETP. **VAT** Soviet Physics, Journal of Experimental and Theoretical Physics. Vol. 1 (July 1955)-(1993). Periodical. English (Russian). mo. American Institute of Physics, 500 Sunnyside Boulevard, Woodbury NY 11797-2999. **Tel** (516)576-2200, FAX (516)349-7669, telex 960983. **(Subscription address:** UK/ Institute of Physics, Techno House, Redcliffe Way, Bristol BS1 6NX England**) LC** QC1; .Z472. **DD** 530.5. **CODEN** SPHJAR. **[CCC].** cum. index. available on microfilm. Documents available from Ask*IEEE. ***Continued by*** *Journal of Experimental and Theoretical Physics.*
**Ind/Abst** Acoust. Abstr.; Alum. Ind. Abstr.; Ceram. Abstr (199?-199?); Curr. Phys. Index; Energy Res. Abstr.; Eng. Mater. Abstr.; INSPEC (1968-); Int. Aerosp. Abstr.; Mass Spect. Bull.; Math. Rev.; Met. Abstr.; Pollut. Abstr. Indexes; SPIN (1970-).

US/0038-5697
**SOVIET PHYSICS JOURNAL.** ***Title Change.*** [Sov. phys. j.]. **Added/Corp** Consultants Bureau. **VFOAT**

Fizika; Izvestiya VUZ. Fizika. (Jan./Feb. 1965)-(Sept. 1992). Periodical. English (translations available in Russian). mo. Plenum Press, 233 Spring Street, New York NY 10013-1578. **Tel** (212)620-8000, (800)221-9369, FAX (212)463-0742, (212)807-1047, telex 23/421139. **ED** V N Detinko. **LC** QC1; .S7952. **DD** 530. **CODEN** SOPJAQ. **[CCC].** Index available. available on microfilm and microfiche from University Microfilms International (UMI). Documents available from Article Express International, Ask*IEEE, CASDDS. ***Continued by*** *Izvestiia Vysshikh Uchebnykh Zavedenii. Fizika. English. Russian Physics Journal, 1064-8887.*
**Desc:** Publishes English translations of original Russian research by the Academy of Science of the USSR in physics.
**Ind/Abst** Acoust. Abstr.; Appl. Mech. Rev.; Bioeng. Abstr.; Chem. Abstr.; Ei Page One; Eng. Index Annu.; INSPEC (Nov./Dec. 1965-); Int. Aerosp. Abstr.; Math. Rev.; Pollut. Abstr. Indexes.

US/0364-2321
**SOVIET PHYSICS-LEBEDEV INSTITUTE REPORTS.** ***Title Change.*** [Sov. phys., Lebedev Inst. rep.]. No. 1 (1974)-(1993). Periodical. English (Russian). mo. Allerton Press, Inc., 150 Fifth Avenue, New York NY 10011. **Tel** (212)924-3950, FAX (212)463-9684, telex 427441 ALPRES. **LC** QC1; .S79522. **DD** 530/.05. **CODEN** SPLRD6. **[CCC].** Documents available from Article Express International, Ask*IEEE. ***Continued by*** *Bulletin of the Lebedev Physics Institute.*
**Ind/Abst** Bioeng. Abstr.; Ei Page One; Eng. Index Annu.; INSPEC (1974-).

US/0038-5700
**SOVIET PHYSICS-SEMICONDUCTORS.** ***Title Change.*** [Sov. phys. Semiconduct.]. **Added/Corp** American Institute of Physics. Consultants Bureau. **VFOAT** Semiconductors. Vol. 1 (July 1967)-(1993). Periodical. English (Russian). mo. American Institute of Physics, 500 Sunnyside Boulevard, Woodbury NY 11797-2999. **Tel** (516)576-2200, FAX (516)349-7669, telex 960983. **(Subscription address:** UK/ Institute of Physics, Techno House, Redcliffe Way, Bristol BS1 6NX England**) ED** A Tybulewicz. **LC** QC612.S4; F557. **DD** 537.6/22/05. **CODEN** SPSEBY. **[CCC]. Pr Rev.** Documents available from Article Express International, The Genuine Article, Ask*IEEE, CASDDS. ***Continued by*** *Semiconductors.*
**Desc:** Reports of Soviet research in the USSR Journal of Physics and Technics of Semiconductors.
**Ind/Abst** Acoust. Abstr.; Alum. Ind. Abstr.; Bioeng. Abstr.; Ceram. Abstr.; Chem. Abstr.; Curr. Contents Phys. Chem. Earth Sci.; Curr. Phys. Index; Ei Page One; Energy Res. Abstr. (Feb. 1976-); Eng. Mater. Abstr.; Eng. Index Annu.; INSPEC (1968-); Int. Aerosp. Abstr.; Met. Abstr.; Pollut. Abstr. Indexes; Res. Alert [Full Cov.]; Sci. Cit. Index; SCISEARCH; SPIN (1970-).

US/0038-5654
**SOVIET PHYSICS-SOLID STATE.** ***Title Change.*** [Sov. phys., Solid state]. **Added/Corp** American Institute of Physics. Vol. 1 (Jan. 1959)-(1993). Periodical. English (Russian). mo. American Institute of Physics, 500 Sunnyside Boulevard, Woodbury NY 11797-2999. **Tel** (516)576-2200, FAX (516)349-7669, telex 960983. **(Subscription address:** UK/ Institute of Physics, Techno House, Redcliffe Way, Bristol BS1 6NX England**) LC** QC176; .A413. **DD** 531.705. **CODEN** SPSSA7. **[CCC].** available on microfilm. Documents available from Article Express International, Ask*IEEE. ***Continued by*** *Physics of the Solid State.*
**Ind/Abst** Acoust. Abstr. (1968-); Alum. Ind. Abstr.; Bioeng. Abstr.; Curr. Phys. Index; Ei Page One; Energy Res. Abstr.; Eng. Mater. Abstr. (1968-); Eng. Index Annu.; INSPEC (1968-); Int. Aerosp. Abstr.; Met. Abstr.; MINPROC; Pollut. Abstr. Indexes; SPIN (1970-).

US/0038-5662
**SOVIET PHYSICS-TECHNICAL PHYSICS.** ***Title Change.*** [Sov. phys. Tech. phys.]. **Added/Corp** American Institute of Physics. Vol. 1 (Oct. 1956)-(1993). Periodical. English (Russian). mo. American Institute of Physics, 500 Sunnyside Boulevard, Woodbury NY 11797-2999. **Tel** (516)576-2200, FAX (516)349-7669, telex 960983. **(Subscription address:** UK/ Institute of Physics, Techno House, Redcliffe Way, Bristol BS1 6NX England**) LC** QC1; .S795. **DD** 530.947. **CODEN** SPTPA3. **[CCC].** Documents available from Article Express International, Ask*IEEE. ***Continued by*** *Technical Physics.*
**Ind/Abst** Acoust. Abstr.; Bioeng. Abstr.; Ceram. Abstr. (199?-199?); Curr. Phys. Index; Ei Page One; Energy Res. Abstr.; Eng. Index Annu.; INSPEC (1968-); Int. Aerosp. Abstr.; Mass Spect. Bull.; SPIN (1970-).

US/0038-5670
**SOVIET PHYSICS-USPEKHI.** ***Title Change.*** [Sov. phys., Usp.]. **Added/Corp** American Institute of Physics. Vol. 1 (Sept./Oct. 1958)-(1993). Periodical. English (Russian). mo. American Institute of Physics, 500 Sunnyside Boulevard, Woodbury NY 11797-2999. **Tel** (516)576-2200, FAX (516)349-7669, telex 960983. **(Subscription address:** UK/ Institute of Physics, Techno House, Redcliffe Way, Bristol BS1 6NX England**) LC** QC1; .U812. **DD** 530.5. **CODEN** SOPUAPSPUSB1. **[CCC].** available on microfilm. Documents available from Ask*IEEE. ***Continued by*** *Physics - Uspekhi.*
**Ind/Abst** Acoust. Abstr. (1970-); Coal Abstr.; Curr. Phys. Index; Energy Res. Abstr.; GeoRef; INSPEC (1968-); Int. Aerosp. Abstr.; Mass Spect. Bull.; Math. Rev. (?-1993); SPIN (1970-).

SZ/0143-0394
**SOVIET SCIENTIFIC REVIEWS. SECTION A, PHYSICS REVIEWS.** [Sov. sci. rev., A, Phys. rev.]. **Added/Corp** Akademiia Nauk SSSR. **VFOAT** Physics Reviews. Vol. 1 (1979)-. Academic Scholarly Publication. English (translations available in Russian). an. $441.00 (academic institutions), $688.00 (corporate institutions). Harwood Academic Publishers, PO Box 90, Reading RG1 8JL England. **Tel** 011 44 734 560080. **(Subscription address:** International Publishers Distributor at one of the following addresses: 820 Town Center Drive, Langhorne, PA 19047; or PO Box 90, Reading Berkshire RG1 8JL UK; or Kent Ridge PO Box 1180, Singapore 9111, Republic of Singapore**) LC** QC1; .S79527. **DD** 530/.05. **CODEN** SSRPDH. **[CCC].** Documents available from Ask*IEEE, CASDDS.
**Ind/Abst** Chem. Abstr.; INSPEC.

SZ/0143-0416
**SOVIET SCIENTIFIC REVIEWS. SECTION C, MATHEMATICAL PHYSICS REVIEWS.** [Sov. sci. rev., C, Math. phys. rev.]. **VFOAT** Mathematical Physics Reviews. Vol. 1 (1980)-. English (translations available in Russian). an. Price varies. Harwood Academic Publishers, PO Box 90, Reading RG1 8JL England. **Tel** 011 44 734 560080. **(Subscription address:** Harwood Academic Publishers, PO Box 786, Cooper Station, New York NY 10276.**) LC** QC19.2; .S65. **DD** 530.1/5. **CODEN** SRCREA. **[CCC].** Documents available from Ask*IEEE.
**Ind/Abst** INSPEC; Zentralbl. Math. Ihre Grenzgeb.

US/0360-120X
**SOVIET TECHNICAL PHYSICS LETTERS.** ***Title Change.*** [Sov. tech. phys. lett.]. **Added/Corp** American Institute of Physics. Consultants Bureau. Vol. 1 (Jan. 1975)-(1993). Periodical. English (Russian). mo. American Institute of Physics, 500 Sunnyside Boulevard, Woodbury NY 11797-2999. **Tel** (516)576-2200, FAX (516)349-7669, telex 960983. **(Subscription address:** UK/ Institute of Physics, Techno House, Redcliffe Way, Bristol BS1 6NX England**) LC** QC1; .S7953. **DD** 530/.05. **CODEN** STPLD2. **[CCC].** Documents available from Ask*IEEE. ***Continued by*** *Technical Physics Letters.*
**Ind/Abst** Acoust. Abstr.; Curr. Phys. Index; Energy Res. Abstr. (Sept. 1976-); INSPEC (Sept. 1975-); Int. Aerosp. Abstr.; Mass Spect. Bull.; SPIN (1975-).

GW
**SPECIAL BIBLIOGRAPHY. PLASMA PHYSICS.** ***Ceased.*** **Added/Corp** Fachinformationszentrum Energie, Physik, Mathematik. **VFOAT** Plasma Physics. Vol. 1 (1984)-(1993). Periodical. English. mo. Fachinformationszentrum Karlsruhe, Physics & Math, D 76344 Eggenstein Germany. **Tel** 011 49 7247 808149. **LC** Z7144.P5; F32; QC718. **DD** 016.621044. ***Continues*** *Fachbibliographie Plasmaphysik.*

UK/0584-8547
**SPECTROCHIMICA ACTA. PART B : ATOMIC SPECTROSCOPY.** [Spectrochim. acta, Part B: At. spectrosc.]. **VFOAT** Spectrochimica Acta Electronica. Vol. 23B (March 1967)-. Academic Scholarly Publication. English (French and German; summaries and/or abstracts in English). Fourteen times a year. $1535.00 The Americas; £1030.00 other. Pergamon Press, An Imprint of Elsevier Science Ltd., The Boulevard, Langford Lane, Kidlington, Oxford OX5 1GB United Kingdom. **Tel** 011 44 865 843000, 011 44 865 843699, FAX 011 44 865 843010. **(Subscription address:** Elsevier Science Ltd. Oxford Fulfillment Centre, PO Box 800, Kidlington, Oxford OX5 1DX United Kingdom.**) ED** P.W.J.M. Boumans. **LC** QD95; .S634. **DD** 539.7. **NLM** W1; SP315B; 0101102. **CODEN** SAASBH. **[CCC]. Pr Rev.** available on microfilm and microfiche from University Microfilms International (UMI); available on microfiche from the publisher. Documents available from Article Express International, The Genuine Article, BIOSIS Document Express, Ask*IEEE, CASDDS, ADONIS. ***Continues in part*** *Spectrochemica Acta.*
**Desc:** Covers topics from rapidly expanding areas in atomic spectroscopy.
**Ind/Abst** ADONIS; Alum. Ind. Abstr.; Anal. Abstr.; Aqualine Abstr.; Biol. Abstr.; Chem. Abstr.; Chem. Titles; Civ. Struct. Eng. Abstr.; Comput. Inf. Syst. Abstr. J. [Full Cov.]; Curr. Contents Phys. Chem. Earth Sci.; Ei Page One; Elect. Comm. Abstr.; EMBASE; Eng. Mater. Abstr.; Eng. Index Annu.; GeoRef; INSPEC (1968-); Manuf. Process Eng. Abstr.; Mass Spect. Bull.; Mater. Sci. Eng. Abstr.; Mech. Eng. Abstr.; Met. Abstr.; Pollut. Abstr. Indexes; Res. Alert [Full Cov.]; Sci. Cit. Index; SCISEARCH; Solid State Supercond. Abstr.

US
**SPIN.** **See** Physics-Abstracting, Bibliographies and Statistics.

GW/0930-8989
**SPRINGER PROCEEDINGS IN PHYSICS.** [Springer proc. phys.]. Vol. 1 (1984)-. Academic Scholarly Publication. English. Price varies per volume. Springer-Verlag GmbH & Company KG, Heidelberger Platz 3, D 14197 Berlin Germany. **Tel** 011 49 30 8207223, FAX 011 49 30 8214091, telex 183 319 SPBLN D. **(Subscription address:** Springer Verlag New York Inc. / for North America, 44 Hartz Way, Secaucus NJ 07096.**) CODEN** SPPPEL. Documents available from BIOSIS Document Express, CASDDS.
**Ind/Abst** Biol. Abstr. (1986-); Chem. Abstr. (1984-); Zentralbl. Math. Ihre Grenzgeb.

GW/0172-5726
**SPRINGER SERIES IN COMPUTATIONAL PHYSICS.** [Springer ser. comput. phys.]. (1977)-. Monographic series. German. ir. Price varies per volume. Springer-Verlag New York Inc., 175 5th Avenue, New York NY 10010. **Tel** (212)460-1500, telex 232 235 SPB UR. **(Subscription address:** Springer Verlag New York Inc. / for North America, 44 Hartz Way, Secaucus NJ 07096.**)**
**Desc:** Contains topics on computational Galerkin methods, computer studies of phase transitions and critical phenomena, methods for fluid flow, optimal shape design for elliptic systems.
**Ind/Abst** Math. Rev.

GW/0171-1873
**SPRINGER SERIES IN SOLID-STATE SCIENCES.** **See** Chemistry.

GW/0931-5195
**SPRINGER SERIES IN SURFACE SCIENCES.** [Springer ser. surf. sci.]. (1986)-. Academic Scholarly Publication. English. ir. Price varies per volume. Springer-Verlag GmbH & Company KG, Heidelberger Platz 3, D 14197 Berlin Germany. **Tel** 011 49 30 8207223, FAX 011 49 30 8214091, telex 183 319 SPBLN D. **(Subscription address:** Springer Verlag New York Inc. / for North America, 44 Hartz Way, Secaucus NJ 07096.**) LC** UNC. **CODEN** SSSSEW. Documents available from Ask*IEEE, CASDDS.
**Ind/Abst** Chem. Abstr. (1985-); INSPEC (1985-).

GW/0177-6495
**SPRINGER SERIES ON ATOMS + PLASMAS.** [Springer ser. atoms plasmas]. **VFOAT** Springer Series on Atoms and Plasmas. (1985)-. Monographic series. English. ir. Price varies per volume. Springer-Verlag New York Inc., 175 5th Avenue, New York NY 10010. **Tel** (212)460-1500, telex 232 235 SPB UR. **(Subscription address:** Springer Verlag New York Inc. / for North America, 44 Hartz Way, Secaucus NJ 07096.**) LC** UNC.

GW/0081-3869
**SPRINGER TRACTS IN MODERN PHYSICS.** Vol. 1 (1922)-. Monographic series. English (German). ir. Price varies per volume. Springer-Verlag GmbH & Company KG, Heidelberger Platz 3, D 14197 Berlin Germany. **Tel** 011 49 30 8207223, FAX 011 49 30 8214091, telex 183 319 SPBLN D. **(Subscription address:** Springer Verlag New York Inc. / for North America, 44 Hartz Way, Secaucus NJ 07096.**) ED** G. Hoehler. **LC** QC1. cum. index. **Circ:** 300. Documents available from The Genuine Article, Ask*IEEE.
**Desc:** Devoted to reviews of a tutorial nature in which the literature is sifted by experts. Organized around a certain theme in the areas of atomic, elementary-particle, nuclear, and solid-state physics.
**Ind/Abst** Index Sci. Rev. [Full Cov.]; INSPEC; Res. Alert [Full Cov.]; Sci. Cit. Index; SCISEARCH.

US/0197-6761
**SPS CHAPTER LIST.** ***Title Change.*** [SPS Chapter list]. **Main/Corp** Society of Physics Students. **VAT** Society of Physics Students Chapter List. English. an. American Institute of Physics, 500 Sunnyside Boulevard, Woodbury NY 11797-2999. **Tel** (516)576-2200, FAX (516)349-7669, telex 960983. **(Subscription address:** UK/ Institute of Physics, Techno House, Redcliffe Way, Bristol BS1 6NX England**)** ***Absorbed by*** *SPS Information Book (Society of Physics Students (American Institute of Physics)), 1043-9870.*

UK/0372-4255
**SRD REPORT. UNITED KINGDOM ATOMIC ENERGY AUTHORITY, SAFETY AND RELIABILITY DIRECTORATE.** [SRD Rep., U. K. At. Energy Auth., Saf. Reliab. Dir.]. **VFOAT** United Kingdom Atomic Energy Authority, SRD Report. (1971)-. Academic Scholarly Publication. English. **CODEN** UKSRAP. Documents available from CASDDS.
**Ind/Abst** Chem. Abstr.

IT/1120-4222
**STABILITY & APPLIED ANALYSIS OF CONTINUOUS MEDIA.** **See** Mathematics.

US/0891-5490
**STOPPING AND RANGES OF IONS IN MATTER, THE.** Vol. 1 (1977)-. Monographic series. English. ir. Price varies per volume. Pergamon Press, An Imprint of Elsevier Science Ltd., The Boulevard, Langford Lane, Kidlington, Oxford OX5 1GB United Kingdom. **Tel** 011 44 865 843000, 011 44 865 843699, FAX 011 44 865 843010. **DD** 539. **CODEN** SRIMEP. Documents available from Ask*IEEE.
**Ind/Abst** INSPEC (1985-).

FR
## STP NEWSLETTER / INTERNATIONAL COUNCIL OF SCIENTIFIC UNIONS, SCIENTIFIC COMMITTEE ON SOLAR-TERRESTRIAL PHYSICS.
**Added/Corp** International Council of Scientific Unions. Scientific Committee on Solar-Terrestrial Physics. **VFOAT** S.T.P. Newsletter. **VAT** Solar Terrestrial Physics Newsletter. (19??)-. English. qt. Free. ICSTI, 51 Boulevard de Montmorency, 75016 Paris France. **Tel** 33 (1) 45250329. **(Subscription address:** SCOSTEP Secretariat / STP NL, c/o NOAA/ NGDC, 325 Broadway, Boulder CO 80303.**)** **LC** QB520; .S77. **DD** 550.
**Desc:** Contains minutes, results and resolutions form SCOSTEP meeting and those of its supporting elements. Summaries are included of scientific meetings and some technical papers may be published.

RM/0258-8730
## STUDIA UNIVERSITATIS BABES-BOLYAI. PHYSICA.
[Stud. Univ. Babes-Bolyai, Phys.]. **Main/Corp** Universitatea Babes-Bolyai. **Added/Corp** Universitatea "Babes-Bolyai.". (1975)-. Academic Scholarly Publication. English (French and Romanian). an. Universitatis Babes-Bolyai, Biblioteca Centrala Universitara, Str. Clinicilor 2, Cluj Napoca 3400 Romania. **Tel** 95 117092, FAX 95 117633. **(Subscription address:** Rompresfilatelia, PO Box 12 201, Bucharest Romania.**)** **LC** QC1; .C58a. **DD** 530/.05. **CODEN** SBBPAJ. Documents available from CASDDS. ***Continues** Studia Universitatis Babes-Bolyai. Series Physica, 0370-8578.*
**Ind/Abst** Ceram. Abstr. (19??-); Chem. Abstr.; Int. Aerosp. Abstr.; Math. Rev.

SZ/0270-4730
## STUDIES IN HIGH ENERGY PHYSICS.
[Stud. high energy physics]. (1979)-. Academic Scholarly Publication. English. ir. Price varies per volume. Harwood Academic Publishers, PO Box 90, Reading RG1 8JL England. **Tel** 011 44 734 560080. **(Subscription address:** Harwood Academic Publishers, PO Box 786, Cooper Station, New York NY 10276.**)** **ED** M. Charap. **DD** 539. **CODEN** SEPHDL. Documents available from CASDDS.
**Ind/Abst** Chem. Abstr.

UK/1355-2198
## STUDIES IN HISTORY AND PHILOSOPHY OF SCIENCE. PART B : MODERN PHYSICS.
(19??)-. English. Three times a year. $203.00 The Americas; £136.00 other. Pergamon Press, An Imprint of Elsevier Science Ltd., The Boulevard, Langford Lane, Kidlington, Oxford OX5 1GB United Kingdom. **Tel** 011 44 865 843000, 011 44 865 843699, FAX 011 44 865 843010. **(Subscription address:** Elsevier Science Ltd. Oxford Fulfillment Centre, PO Box 800, Kidlington, Oxford OX5 1DX United Kingdom.**)**

NE/0166-6061
## STUDIES IN MODERN THERMODYNAMICS.
**See** Chemistry-Physical and Theoretical Chemistry.

RM/0039-3940
## STUDII SI CERCETARI DE FIZICA. *Title Change.*
[Stud. cercet. fiz.]. **Added/Corp** Institutul de Fizica Atomica. Institutul de Fizica (Academia Republicii Populare Romine) Academia Republicii Socialiste Romania. Academia Romana. **VFOAT** Etudes et Recherches de Physique; Trudy i Issledovaniia Po Fizike. (1950)-(1992). Periodical. Romanian (English; summaries and/or abstracts in English; table of contents in French and Russian). mo. **(Subscription address:** Rompresfilatelia, PO Box 12 201, Bucharest Romania.**)** **LC** QC1; .A28. **CODEN** SCEFAB. Documents available from Ask*IEEE, CASDDS. ***Continues** Studii Si Cercetari de Fizica.* ***Continued by** Romanian Reports in Physics, 1221-1451.*
**Desc:** Contains original research on physics.
**Ind/Abst** Alum. Ind. Abstr. (?-?); Ceram. Abstr. (?-?); Chem. Abstr. (?-?); Eng. Mater. Abstr. (?-?); INSPEC (1968-); Int. Aerosp. Abstr. (?-?); Math. Rev. (?-?); Met. Abstr. (?-?); Pollut. Abstr. Indexes (?-?); Zentralbl. Math. Ihre Grenzgeb. (?-?).

US/0235-8964
## SUPERCONDUCTIVITY: PHYSICS, CHEMISTRY, TECHNIQUE.
(SUPERCONDUCTIVITY.). [Supercond. phys. chem. tech.]. **Added/Corp** American Institute of Physics. Institut Atomnoi Energii im I.V. Kurchatova. **VFOAT** Sverkhprovodimost. (198?)-. Periodical. English (translations available in Russian). mo. $800.00 institution, $500.00 individual. Kurchatov Institute of Atomic Energy, Kurchatov Square, 123182 Moscow Russia. **Tel** 011 7 0951969496. **ED** Dr. V. I. Ozhogin. **LC** QC611.9; .S885. **DD** 537.6/23. **CODEN** SPCUE5. **[CCC].** Documents available from Ask*IEEE.
**Desc:** Dedicated to the rapid dissemination of the latest research, this interdisciplinary journal focuses on superconductivity as a grand unification of physics and chemistry.
**Ind/Abst** INSPEC (Jan. 1990-).

UK
## SUPERCONDUCTOR PATENT PROFILE.
English. £1410.00 (standard), £1060.00 (subscription). Derwent Publications Ltd., Derwent House 14, Great Queen Street, London WC2B 5DF England. **Tel** 011 44 71 3442800.
**Desc:** Publication includes, novel compositions, fabrication by sintering, sputtering, extrusion, vapour deposition,ect.

US/0886-618X
## SURFACE MOUNT TECHNOLOGY TODAY.
(SURFACE MOUNT TECHNOLOGY TODAY : SMTT.). **VFOAT** SMTT. (Oct. 1985)-. Periodical. English. mo. $395.00 US; $445.00 other. Micro Process Technology, 2431 Quantico Court, San Jose CA 95128. **DD** 621.

NE/0167-5729
## SURFACE SCIENCE REPORTS.
**See** Engineering-Electricity, Electrical Engineering, Electronics.

●US/1063-7842
## TECHNICAL PHYSICS.
[Tech. phys.]. **Added/Corp** American Institute of Physics. (Jan. 1993)-. Periodical. English (translations available in Russian). mo. $2190.00 US; $2205.00 Canada, Mexico, Central & South America and the Caribbean; $2230.00 other. American Institute of Physics, 500 Sunnyside Boulevard, Woodbury NY 11797-2999. **Tel** (516)576-2200, FAX (516)349-7669, telex 960983. **LC** QC1; .S795. **DD** 530.947. **CODEN** TEPHEX. **[CCC].** Index available (bound in last issue). Documents available from Article Express International, Ask*IEEE. ***Continues** Soviet Physics. Technical Physics, 0038-5662.*
**Ind/Abst** Bioeng. Abstr.; Curr. Phys. Index; Ei Page One; Energy Res. Abstr.; Eng. Index Annu.; INSPEC; Int. Aerosp. Abstr.

●US/1063-7850
## TECHNICAL PHYSICS LETTERS.
[Tech. phys. lett.]. **Added/Corp** American Institute of Physics. Vol. 19, No. 1 (Jan. 1993)-. Periodical. English (translations available in Russian). mo. $1375.00 US; $1390.00 Canada, Mexico, Central & South America and the Caribbean; $1410.00 other. American Institute of Physics, 500 Sunnyside Boulevard, Woodbury NY 11797-2999. **Tel** (516)576-2200, FAX (516)349-7669, telex 960983. **LC** QC1; .S7953. **DD** 530. **[CCC].** Index available (bound in last issue). Documents available from Ask*IEEE. ***Continues** Soviet Technical Physics Letters, 0360-120X.*
**Ind/Abst** Curr. Phys. Index; Energy Res. Abstr.; INSPEC; Int. Aerosp. Abstr.; SPIN.

UK/0308-5392
## TECHNIQUES OF PHYSICS.
[Tech. phys.]. (1973)-. Monographic series. English. ir. Price varies per volume. Academic Press, Inc., 6277 Sea Harbor Drive, Orlando FL 32887. **Tel** (800)543-9534, (407)345-4100, FAX (407)363-9661. **ED** John F. Cornwell. **CODEN** TEPHDW. Documents available from Ask*IEEE.
**Ind/Abst** INSPEC; Zentralbl. Math. Ihre Grenzgeb.

GW/0082-2590
## TECHNISCHE PHYSIK IN EINZELDARSTELLUNGEN.
(19??)-. Monographic series. English (German). ir. Price varies per volume. Springer-Verlag New York Inc., 175 5th Avenue, New York NY 10010. **Tel** (212)460-1500, telex 232 235 SPB UR. **(Subscription address:** Springer Verlag New York Inc. / for North America, 44 Hartz Way, Secaucus NJ 07096.**)**

RU/0564-6162
## TEORETICESKAJA I MATEMATICESKAJA FIZIKA.
(TEORETICHESKAIA I MATEMATICHESKAIA FIZIKA.). [Teor. mat. fiz.]. **Added/Corp** Akademiia Nauk SSSR. Vol. 1 (1969)-. Periodical. Russian (summaries and/or abstracts in English). mo. $269.95. **(Subscription address:** East View Publications Inc., 3020 Harbor Lane North, Suite 110, Minneapolis MN 55447.**)** **LC** QC20; .T4. **CODEN** TMFZAL. Documents available from Ask*IEEE, CASDDS.
**Ind/Abst** Chem. Abstr.; Energy Res. Abstr.; INSPEC (Jan. 1972-); Int. Aerosp. Abstr.; Math. Rev.

RU/0040-3644
## TEPLOFIZIKA VYSOKIKH TEMPERATUR.
[Teplofiz. vys. temp.]. **Added/Corp** Akademiia Nauk SSSR. Vol. 1, (1963)-. Academic Scholarly Publication. Russian. bm. $192.00. Izdatelstvo Nauka / Akademiia Nauk, Publishing House of the Russian Academy of Sciences, Leninskii Porspekt 14, 117901 Moscow Russia. **Tel** 011 95 954-21-53, FAX 011 95 938-21-44, telex 411964. **(Subscription address:** East View Publications Inc., 3020 Harbor Lane North, Suite 110, Minneapolis MN 55447.**)** **CODEN** TVYTAP. **[CCC].** Index available. **Bk Rev**. Documents available from Article Express International, Ask*IEEE, CASDDS.
**Ind/Abst** Alum. Ind. Abstr.; Ceram. Abstr. (19??-); Chem. Abstr.; Ei Page One; Eng. Mater. Abstr.; Eng. Index Annu.; INSPEC (1968-); Int. Aerosp. Abstr.; Met. Abstr.; World Alum. Abstr.

US/0172-5998
## TEXTS AND MONOGRAPHS IN PHYSICS.
[Texts monogr. phys.]. (1976)-. Monographic series. English. ir. Price varies per volume. Springer-Verlag New York Inc., 175 5th Avenue, New York NY 10010. **Tel** (212)460-1500, telex 232 235 SPB UR. **(Subscription address:** Springer Verlag New York Inc. / for North America, 44 Hartz Way, Secaucus NJ 07096.**)** Documents available from Ask*IEEE.
**Desc:** Contains articles on quantum dynamics and foundations of quantum mechanics.
**Ind/Abst** INSPEC; Math. Rev.

US/0935-4964
## THEORETICAL AND COMPUTATIONAL FLUID DYNAMICS.
[Theor. comput. fluid dyn.]. Vol. 1, No. 1 (1989)-. Periodical. English. Six times a year. DM735.00. Springer-Verlag GmbH & Company KG, Heidelberger Platz 3, D 14197 Berlin Germany. **Tel** 011 49 30 8207223, FAX 011 49 30 8214091, telex 183 319 SPBLN D. **(Subscription address:** Springer Verlag New York Inc. / for North America, 44 Hartz Way, Secaucus NJ 07096.**)** **ED** M Y Hussaini. **LC** QA911; .T45. **DD** 532/.05. **CODEN** TCFDEP. **[CCC].** available on microfilm and microfiche from University Microfilms International (UMI). Documents available from Ask*IEEE.
**Desc:** Reports original research of scholarly value in theoretical and computational fluid dynamics aimed at elucidating flow physics.
**Ind/Abst** Fluid Abstr., Civil Eng.; Fluid Abstr. Proc. Eng.; FLUIDEX (19??-); INSPEC (1990-); Int. Aerosp. Abstr.; Zentralbl. Math. Ihre Grenzgeb.

US/0040-5779
## THEORETICAL AND MATHEMATICAL PHYSICS.
[Theor. math. phys.]. **Added/Corp** Consultants Bureau. Vol. 1 (Oct. 1969)-. Periodical. English (translations available in Russian). mo. $1195.00 US; $1400.00 other. Consultants Bureau, A Division of Plenum Publishing Corporation, 233 Spring Street, New York NY 10013. **Tel** (212)620-8000, (212)620-8466, FAX (212)463-0742, telex 23/421139. **ED** A. A. Logunov. **LC** QC20; .T413. **DD** 530/.01/51. **CODEN** TMPHAH. **[CCC].** Index available. **Pr Rev.** available on microfilm and microfiche from University Microfilms International (UMI). Documents available from The Genuine Article, Ask*IEEE, CASDDS.
**Desc:** Reports on current developments in theoretical physics as well as mathematical problems related to theoretical physics.
**Ind/Abst** Appl. Mech. Rev.; Chem. Abstr.; Compumath Citation Index [Full Cov.]; Curr. Contents Phys. Chem. Earth Sci.; INSPEC (Jan. 1972-); Math. Rev.; Phys. Briefs; Pollut. Abstr. Indexes; Res. Alert [Full Cov.]; Sci. Cit. Index; SCISEARCH; Zentralbl. Math. Ihre Grenzgeb.

UK
## THESAURUS.
**See** Engineering-Electricity, Electrical Engineering, Electronics.

CC/0253-2379
## TIANTI WULI XUEBAO.
(TIEN TI WU LI HSUEH PAO.). [Tianti wuli xuebao]. **Added/Corp** Pei-ching Tien Wen Hsueh Hui. Chung-kuo Tien Wen Hsueh Hui. **VFOAT** Acta Astrophysica Sinica. Vol. 1 (1981)-. Academic Scholarly Publication. Chinese (summaries and/or abstracts in English). qt. $39.08. **(Subscription address:** China International Book Trading Corporation, PO Box 399, Library Service Department, Beijing 100044 People's Republic of China.**)** **LC** QB461; .T54. **DD** 523.01. **CODEN** TWXUDX. Documents available from Ask*IEEE, CASDDS.
**Desc:** Contains information on astrophysics.
**Ind/Abst** Astron. Astrophys. Abstr.; Chem. Abstr.; Ei Page One; Energy Res. Abstr. (Oct. 1982-); INSPEC (April 1984-); Math. Rev.; SPIN (1982-).

GW/0303-4216
## TOPICS IN APPLIED PHYSICS.
[Top. appl. phys.]. Vol. 1 (1973)-. Monographic series. English. Three times a year. Price varies per volume. Springer-Verlag GmbH & Company KG, Heidelberger Platz 3, D 14197 Berlin Germany. **Tel** 011 49 30 8207223, FAX 011 49 30 8214091, telex 183 319 SPBLN D. **(Subscription address:** Springer Verlag New York Inc. / for North America, 44 Hartz Way, Secaucus NJ 07096.**)** **NLM** W1 TO539E. **CODEN** TAPHD4. available on microfilm; available on microfiche. Documents available from The Genuine Article, BIOSIS Document Express, Ask*IEEE, CASDDS.
**Ind/Abst** Biol. Abstr. (-1977); Chem. Abstr.; Energy Res. Abstr. (March 1982-); Index Sci. Rev. [Full Cov.]; INSPEC; Res. Alert [Full Cov.]; Sci. Cit. Index; SCISEARCH; Zentralbl. Math. Ihre Grenzgeb.

GW/0342-6793
## TOPICS IN CURRENT PHYSICS.
[Top. curr. phys.]. (1976)-. Academic Scholarly Publication. English. ir. Price varies per volume. Springer-Verlag GmbH & Company KG, Heidelberger Platz 3, D 14197 Berlin Germany. **Tel** 011 49 30 8207223, FAX 011 49 30 8214091, telex 183 319 SPBLN D. **(Subscription address:** Springer Verlag New York Inc. / for North America, 44 Hartz Way, Secaucus NJ 07096.**)** **CODEN** TCPHDI. Documents available from Ask*IEEE, CASDDS.
**Desc:** Contains articles on physics.
**Ind/Abst** Chem. Abstr.; Energy Res. Abstr. (June 1978-); INSPEC; Zentralbl. Math. Ihre Grenzgeb.

UK/0372-3666
**TRANSLATION - UNITED KINGDOM ATOMIC ENERGY AUTHORITY, RESEARCH GROUP, CULHAM LABORATORY.** [Transl. - U. K. At. Energy Auth., Res. Group, Culham Lab.]. (19??)-. Academic Scholarly Publication. English. **CODEN** UACTAH. Documents available from CASDDS.
**Ind/Abst** Chem. Abstr.

US/1063-9195
**TRIBOMATERIALS NEWS.** (TRIBOMATERIALS NEWS : A QUARTERLY PUBLICATION FROM TRIBOMATERIALS INFORMATION SERVICES,). [TriboMat. news]. **Added/Corp** Tribomaterials Information Services. **VFOAT** Tribo Materials News. (1991)-. Periodical. English. Four times a year (Mar., June, Oct., Dec.). $18.00 (one year), $30.00 (two years). Tribomaterials Information Services, PO Box 4427, Oak Ridge TN 37831. **Tel** (615)483-7675, FAX (615)483-6813. **ED** Peter J. Blau, Ph.D. **DD** 621. Index available. cum. index. **Bk Rev**, (Qty: 2-4). **Ad Acc**, **Adv Mgr Tel** (615)574-5377. **Circ:** 100.
**Desc:** Current activities in friction and wear testing labs and equipment.

RU/0131-3940
**TRUDY ASTROFIZICESKOGO INSTITUTA.** **See** Aeronautics, Astronautics.

RU/0132-0114
**TRUDY FIZICHESKOGO INSTITUTA / AKADEMIIA NAUK SSSR, FIZICHESKII INSTITUT IM. P.N. LEBEDEVA.** [Tr. ordena Lenina fiz. inst. im. P.N. Lebedeva]. **Added/Corp** Fizicheskii Iinstitut Imeni P.N. Lebedeva. **VFOAT** Trudy Fizicheskogo Iinstituta im. P.N. Lebedeva; Trudy Ordena Lenina Fizicheskogo Instituta im. P.N. Lebedeva; Trudy Ordena Lenina i Ordena Oktiabrskoi Revoliutsii Fizicheskogo Instituta im. P.N. Lebedeva; Trudy FIAN; Trudy Fizicheskogo Instituta im. P.N. Lebedeva Akademii nauk SSSR. (1936)-. Monographic series. Russian. Price varies per volume. Izdatelstvo Nauka / Akademiia Nauk, Publishing House of the Russian Academy of Sciences, Leninskii Porspekt 14, 117901 Moscow Russia. **Tel** 011 95 954-21-53, FAX 011 95 938-21-44, telex 411964. **LC** QC1; .A4. **DD** 530/.05. **CODEN** TFILAD. Documents available from Ask*IEEE, CASDDS. ***Continues in part*** *Trudy Fiziko-Matematicheskogo Instituta Imeni V.A. Steklova.*
**Ind/Abst** Chem. Abstr.; Energy Res. Abstr. (1981-1985); INSPEC (1977-1985); Int. Aerosp. Abstr.; Math. Rev.

RU/0371-9685
**TRUDY ORDENA LENINA MATEMATICESKOGO INSTITUTA IM. V.A. STEKLOVA.** **See** Mathematics.

UN/0503-1265
**UKRAINSKIJ FIZICESKIJ ZURNAL (KIEV, 1967).** (UKRAINSKII FIZICHESKII ZHURNAL.). [Ukr. fiz. z.]. **Added/Corp** Akademiia Nauk Ukrainskoi RSR. Viddil Fizyky. Vol. 1 (1967)-. Academic Scholarly Publication. Russian (Ukrainian; summaries and/or abstracts in English). mo. $139.00. **(Subscription address:** East View Publications Inc., 3020 Harbor Lane North, Suite 110, Minneapolis MN 55447.**) CODEN** UFIZAW. **[CCC]. Pr Rev.** Documents available from The Genuine Article, Ask*IEEE, CASDDS.
**Ind/Abst** Acoust. Abstr.; Alum. Ind. Abstr.; Chem. Abstr.; Chem. Titles; Curr. Contents Phys. Chem. Earth Sci.; Eng. Mater. Abstr.; INSPEC (1968-); Int. Aerosp. Abstr.; Met. Abstr.; Res. Alert [Full Cov.]; Sci. Cit. Index; SCISEARCH.

UK/0041-624X
**ULTRASONICS.** [Ultrasonics]. Vol. 1 (Jan./March 1963)-. Periodical. English. bm. $492.00 (with Ultrasonics Sonochemistry) The Americas; £330.00 (with Ultrasonics Sonochemistry) other. Butterworth Heinemann Publishers, Linacre House, Jordan Hill, Oxford OX2 8DP England. **Tel** 011 44 865 310366. **(Subscription address:** Elsevier Science Ltd. Oxford Fulfillment Centre, PO Box 800, Kidlington, Oxford OX5 1DX United Kingdom.**) ED** Marija Vukovojac. **LC** TA367; .U42. **NLM** W1 UL748. **CODEN** ULTRA3. **[CCC].** Index available. **Bk Rev. Ad Acc. Pr Rev.** available on microfilm and microfiche from University Microfilms International (UMI). Documents available from Article Express International, The Genuine Article, Ask*IEEE, CASDDS.
**Desc:** Covers the whole field of ultrasound and all its many applications, transducers, non-destructive testing, cleaning, signal processing, welding, sonochemistry, cavitation, underwater ultrasonics, medical applications, surface acoustic waves, etc. The journal is always ready to welcome papers on new applications of ultrasound technology.
**Ind/Abst** Abstr. Bull. Inst. Pap. Sci. Tech.; Acoust. Abstr.; Alum. Ind. Abstr.; Appl. Sci. Technol. Index; Bioeng. Abstr.; Chem. Abstr.; Curr. Contents Eng. Tech. Appl. Sci.; Curr. Technol. Index (1973-); Ei Page One; EMBASE; Eng. Mater. Abstr.; Eng. Index Annu.; Fluid Abstr., Civil Eng.; Fluid Abstr. Proc. Eng.; FLUIDEX (1973-1990); For. Prod. Abstr.; GeoRef; Highw. Res. Abstr.; Index Med.; INSPEC (1968-); Int. Aerosp. Abstr.; Met. Abstr.; Life Sci. Collect.; Res. Alert [Full Cov.]; Saf. Health Work; Sci. Cit. Index; SCISEARCH.

●UK/1350-4177
**ULTRASONICS SONOCHEMISTRY.** Vol. 1, No. 1 (Mar. 1994)-. Periodical. English. sa. $120.00 (regular subscription), $492.00 (combination subscription with Ultrasonics) The Americas; £80.00 (regular subscription), £330.00 (combination subscription with Ultrasonics) other. Butterworth Heinemann Publishers, Linacre House, Jordan Hill, Oxford OX2 8DP England. **Tel** 011 44 865 310366. **(Subscription address:** Elsevier Science Ltd. Oxford Fulfillment Centre, PO Box 800, Kidlington, Oxford OX5 1DX United Kingdom.**) LC** IN PROCESS. **NLM** W1; UL748AK.

KO/1013-7009
**UNGYONG MULLI.** **VFOAT** Korean Applied Physics. (1988)-. Academic Scholarly Publication. Multiple languages. qt. Documents available from CASDDS.
**Ind/Abst** Chem. Abstr.

GW/0172-8741
**UNIVERSITAT BONN, PHYSIKALISCHES INSTITUT. IR.** [aUniv. Bonn Phys. Inst., IR]. **VFOAT** Universitat Bonn, Physikalisches Institut. Internal Report; Bonn-IR. (1975)-. Academic Scholarly Publication. German. ir. **UDC** 53. Documents available from CASDDS.
**Ind/Abst** Chem. Abstr.

SW/0348-677X
**UPPSALA UNIVERSITY, INSTITUTE OF PHYSICS.** [Upps. Univ. Inst. Phys.]. **VFOAT** UUIP. (1966)-. Academic Scholarly Publication. English. ir. **UDC** 53. Documents available from CASDDS.
**Ind/Abst** Chem. Abstr.

RU/0042-1294
**USPEHI FIZICESKIH NAUK.** (USPEKHI FIZICHESKIKH NAUK / AKADEMIIA NAUK SSSR.). [Uspehi fiz. nauk]. **Added/Corp** Akademiia Nauk SSSR. Rossiiskiia Akademiia Nauk. **VFOAT** Fizicheskii Zhurnal. Seriia D, Uspekhi Fizicheskikh Nauk. Vol. 1 (1918)-. Academic Scholarly Publication. Russian (summaries and/or abstracts in English; table of contents in English). Six times a year. $283.00. Izdatelstvo Nauka / Akademiia Nauk, Publishing House of the Russian Academy of Sciences, Leninskii Porspekt 14, 117901 Moscow Russia. **Tel** 011 95 954-21-53, FAX 011 95 938-21-44, telex 411964. **(Subscription address:** East View Publications Inc., 3020 Harbor Lane North, Suite 110, Minneapolis MN 55447.**) LC** QC1; .U8. **CODEN** UFNAAG. **[CCC].** Index available. cum. index. **Bk Rev. Circ:** 5,000. Documents available from The Genuine Article, Ask*IEEE, CASDDS.
**Ind/Abst** Alum. Ind. Abstr.; Chem. Abstr.; Curr. Contents Phys. Chem. Earth Sci.; GeoRef; Index Sci. Rev. [Full Cov.]; INSPEC (1968-); Int. Aerosp. Abstr.; Math. Rev. (?-199?); Met. Abstr.; Res. Alert [Full Cov.]; Sci. Cit. Index; SCISEARCH; SportSearch; World Alum. Abstr.

US
**USSR AND EASTERN EUROPE SCIENTIFIC ABSTRACTS. PHYSICS.** **VFOAT** Physics. No. 41- Apr. 3, 1978-. Periodical. English. National Technical Information Service - NTIS, Room 2027S, 5285 Port Royal Road, Springfield VA 22161. **Tel** (703)487-4630, (703)487-4660, (703)487-4650, FAX (703)321-8547, telex 89-9405. ***Continues*** *USSR and Eastern Europe Scientific Abstracts. Physics and Mathematics.*

US/1069-4579
**VACUUM PHYSICS AND TECHNOLOGY.** [Vac. phys. technol.]. (1993)-. Periodical. English. Four times a year. $325.00. Nova Science Publishers Inc., 6080 Jericho Turnpike, Suite 207, Commack NY 11725-2808. **Tel** (516)499-3103, (516)499-3106, FAX (516)499-3146. **LC** IN PROCESS. **DD** 621.

GW/0934-9758
**VAKUUM IN DER PRAXIS.** [Vak. Prax.]. (1989)-. Academic Scholarly Publication. German. qt. $140.00. VCH Gesellschaft GmbH, Postfach 101161, D 69451 Weinheim Germany. **Tel** 011 49 6201 606459, FAX 011 49 6201 606184. **(Subscription address:** VCH Publishers Inc., 303 Northwest 12th Avenue, Journals Department, Deerfield FL 33442.**) UDC** 62. **[CCC].** Documents available from CASDDS. ***Absorbed*** *Vakuum-Technik, 0042-2266.*
**Ind/Abst** Chem. Abstr.; Ei Page One.

US/0893-3537
**VERSATILITY.** Vol. 1, No. 1 (May 1987)-. Periodical. English. bm. $29.95 US; $39.95 other. Ariel Communications Inc, PO Box 203550, Austin TX 78720-3550. **Tel** (512)250-1700, FAX (512)250-1016. **DD** 621.

●BW
**VESCI AKADEMII NAVUK BELARUSI. SERYA HIMICNYH NAVUK.** **See** Chemistry.

UN/0372-607X
**VESTNIK KIEVSKOGO UNIVERSITETA. FIZIKA / MINISTERSTVO VYSSHEGO I SREDNEGO SPETSIALNOGO OBRAZOVANIIA USSR.** **Added/Corp** Kyivskyi Derzhavnyi Universytet im. T.H. Shevchenka. **VFOAT** Fizika. (1982)-. Russian. Tarasivska 11, Kiev Ukraine. **LC** QC1; .K52a. ***Continues*** *Kyivskyi Derzhavnyi Universytet im. T.H. Shevchenka.* ***and*** *Visnyk Kyivskoho Universytetu. Seriia Fizyky.*

RU/0579-9392
**VESTNIK MOSKOVSKOGO UNIVERSITETA. SERIIA III, FIZIKA, ASTRONOMIIA.** [Vestn. Mosk. univ. Ser. III]. **Added/Corp** Moskovskii Gosudarstvennyi Universitet im. M.V. Lomonosova. (1960)-. Academic Scholarly Publication. Russian. Six times a year. $79.95. Izdatelstvo Moskovskogo Universiteta, K-9 Ulitsa Gertsena 5/7, Moscow Russia. **Tel** (301)881-5973. **(Subscription address:** East View Publications Inc., 3020 Harbor Lane North, Suite 110, Minneapolis MN 55447.**) CODEN** VMUFAO. **[CCC].** Documents available from The Genuine Article, Ask*IEEE, CASDDS. ***Continues in part*** *Vestnik Moskovskogo Universiteta. Seriia Matematiki, Mekhaniki, Astronomii, Fiziki, Khimii.*
**Ind/Abst** AGRICOLA; Alum. Ind. Abstr.; Chem. Abstr.; Energy Res. Abstr.; Eng. Mater. Abstr.; GeoRef; INSPEC (1979-); Int. Aerosp. Abstr.; Math. Rev.; Met. Abstr.; Meteorol. Geoastrophys. Abstr.; Res. Alert [Full Cov.]; Sci. Cit. Index; SCISEARCH; Zentralbl. Math. Ihre Grenzgeb.

US/1066-8268
**VIBRATIONS (CLARENDON HILLS, ILL.).** (VIBRATIONS.). [Vibrations]. **Added/Corp** Vibration Institute. Vol. 1, No. 1 (June 1985)-. Periodical. English. qt. $55.00 (US); $60.00 (other). The Vibration Institute, 6262 South Kingery Highway, Suite 212, Willowbrook IL 60514. **Tel** (708)654-2254, FAX (708)654-2271, telex (708)654-2271. **DD** 620.
**Desc:** Provides information about the activities of the Institute and its chapters and contains articles on applications of vibration technology to practical problems, case histories, book reviews, and standard updates.
**Ind/Abst** Shock Vibr. Dig.

FR/0223-4335
**VIDE, LES COUCHES MINCES, LE.** [Vide, couches minces]. **Added/Corp** Societe Francaise du Vide. (1974)-. Academic Scholarly Publication. French (summaries and/or abstracts in English). Five times a year. 822.72F France, 975.00F other. Societe Francaise du Vide, 19 rue du Renard, 75004 Paris France. **Tel** 011 33 1 42781582. **LC** QC166; .S6. **DD** 533/.5/05. **CODEN** VCMIDS. Index available. **Bk Rev. Ad Acc. Pr Rev. Circ:** 2,000 (ctrl). Documents available from Article Express International, The Genuine Article, Ask*IEEE, CASDDS. ***Continues*** *Vide, 0042-5281.*
**Desc:** Articles about: thin films, vacuum metallurgy, vacuum science, surfaces, industrial vacuum, plasma, dry etching, and leak detection.
**Ind/Abst** Alum. Ind. Abstr.; Bioeng. Abstr.; Chem. Abstr.; Curr. Contents Eng. Tech. Appl. Sci.; Ei Page One; Energy Res. Abstr. (Sept. 1980-); Eng. Mater. Abstr.; Eng. Index Annu.; INSPEC (Jan./March 1979-); Met. Abstr.; Res. Alert [Select. Cov.]; Soc. Sci. Cit. Index [Select. Cov.].

UN
**VISNYK KYIVSKOHO UNIVERSYTETU. SERIIA FIZYKY.** ***Title Change.*** **Main/Corp** Kiev. Universytet. **VFOAT** Seriia Fizyky. No. 8 (1967)-(19??). Ukrainian (summaries and/or abstracts in English). Tarasivska 11, Kiev Ukraine. **LC** QC1; .K52a. ***Supersedes in part*** *Visnyk Kyivskoho Universytetu. Seriia Fizyky ta Khimii.* ***Continued by*** *Vestnik Kievskogo Universiteta. Fizika.*

US/0080-2050
**VOPROSY TEORII PLAZMY.** (REVIEWS OF PLASMA PHYSICS.). [Rev. plasma phys.]. (1965)-. Monographic series. English (Russian). ir. Price varies per volume. Plenum Press, 233 Spring Street, New York NY 10013-1578. **Tel** (212)620-8000, (800)221-9369, FAX (212)463-0742, (212)807-1047, telex 23/421139. **LC** QC718; .V63. **DD** 530. **CODEN** RPLPAK. Documents available from Ask*IEEE.
**Ind/Abst** INSPEC.

UK/0959-7174
**WAVES IN RANDOM MEDIA.** (WAVES IN RANDOM MEDIA : AN INSTITUTE OF PHYSICS JOURNAL.). [Waves random media]. **Added/Corp** Institute of Physics (Great Britain) American Institute of Physics. Vol. 1, No. 1 (Jan. 1991)-. Periodical. English (French and German). qt (January, April, July and October). $235.00. Institute of Physics, Techno House, Redcliffe Way, Bristol BS1 6NX England. **Tel** 011 44 272 297481, FAX 011 44 272 294318, telex 449149 INSTP G. **(Subscription address:** American Institute of Physics, Publishing Sales, 500 Sunnyside Blvd., Woodbury NY 11797.**) ED** A Ishimaru (editor's address: Department of Electrical Engineering, University of Washington, Seattle WA). **LC** QC669; .W38. **DD** 539.2. **CODEN** WRMEEV. Index available. **Pr Rev.** available on microfiche; available on microfilm. Documents available from The

Genuine Article, Ask*IEEE.
**Desc:** New and original theoretical developments in wave propagation and scattering and scattering in random media, and new experimental or numerical studies demonstrating basic principles and theories.
**Ind/Abst** Curr. Contents Phys. Chem. Earth Sci.; INSPEC (Jan. 1991-); Res. Alert [Select. Cov.]; Zentralbl. Math. Ihre Grenzgeb.

US/0277-2477
**WILEY MONOGRAPHS IN CHEMICAL PHYSICS.** [Wiley monogr. chem. phys.]. (19??)-. Monographic series. English. ir. Price varies per volume. John Wiley & Sons, Inc., 605 Third Avenue, New York NY 10158-0012. **Tel** (212)850-6000, (212)850-6645, FAX (212)850-6088, telex 12-7063.

US/0271-602X
**WILEY SERIES IN PLASMA PHYSICS.** [Wiley ser. plasma phys.]. (19??)-. Monographic series. English. ir. Price varies per volume. John Wiley & Sons, Inc., 605 Third Avenue, New York NY 10158-0012. **Tel** (212)850-6000, (212)850-6645, FAX (212)850-6088, telex 12-7063. **(Subscription address:** John Wiley & Sons / England, Baffins Lane, Chichester, West Sussex PO19 1UD England.**)**

GW/0138-2179
**WISSENSCHAFTLICHE BERICHTE - ZENTRALINSTITUT FUER FESTKORPERPHYSIK UND WERKSTOFFORSCHUNG.** [Wiss. Ber. - Zentralinst. Festkorperphys. Werkstofforsch.]. **Main/Corp** Zentralinstitut fur Festkorperphysik und Werkstofforschung. (19??)-. Academic Scholarly Publication. German. **CODEN** WBAWDE. Documents available from CASDDS.
**Ind/Abst** Chem. Abstr.

SI
**WORLD SCIENTIFIC LECTURE NOTES IN PHYSICS.** No. 1 (1985)-. Monographic series. English. ir. Price varies per volume. World Scientific Publishing Company, PO Box 128, Farrer Road, Singapore 9128 Singapore. **Tel** 011 65 3825663, FAX 011 65 3825919, telex RS 28561 WSPC.
**Ind/Abst** Math. Rev.; Zentralbl. Math. Ihre Grenzgeb.

CC
**WU LI.** **VFOAT** Wuli. (1972)-. Academic Scholarly Publication. Chinese. mo. $53.16. **(Subscription address:** China International Book Trading Corporation, PO Box 399, Library Service Department, Beijing 100044 People's Republic of China.**) LC** QC1; .W79. **CODEN** WULIAL. Documents available from CASDDS.
**Ind/Abst** Art Archaeol. Tech. Abstr.; Chem. Abstr.; Energy Res. Abstr. (Aug. 1973-).

CC
**WU LI HSUEH CHIN CHAN / CHUNG-KUO WU LI HSUEH HUI CHU PAN.** **VFOAT** Progress in Physics. Periodical. Chinese (summaries and/or abstracts in English). qt. 1.20. Science Press, 16 Donghuangchenggen North Street, Beijing 100707, People's Republic of China. **Tel** 011 86 1 4019821, 011 86 1 4010642, FAX 011 86 1 4012180, 011 86 1 4019810, telex 210147. **LC** QC1; .W797. **DD** 530/.05.

CC/1000-6818
**WULI HUAXUE XUEBAO.** **See** Chemistry.

CC/1000-3290
**WULI XUEBAO.** (WU LI HSUEH PAO.). **Added/Corp** Chung-Kuo wu li Hsueh Hui. **VFOAT** Acta Physica Sinica. Vol. 9, No. 1 (Jan. 1953)-. Academic Scholarly Publication. Chinese (summaries and/or abstracts in English and Russian). mo. $188.40. Science Press, 16 Donghuangchenggen North Street, Beijing 100707, People's Republic of China. **Tel** 011 86 1 4019821, 011 86 1 4010642, FAX 011 86 1 4012180, 011 86 1 4019810, telex 210147. **(Subscription address:** China International Book Trading Corporation, PO Box 399, Library Service Department, Beijing 100044 People's Republic of China.**) LC** QC1; .W813. **DD** 530/.05. **CODEN** WLHPAR. available on microfilm from University Microfilms International (UMI). Documents available from Ask*IEEE, CASDDS. ***Continues*** *Chinese Journal of Physics, 0366-6158.* ***Continued in part by*** *Chinese Physics Letters, 0256-307X.*
**Ind/Abst** Alum. Ind. Abstr.; Chem. Abstr.; Energy Res. Abstr.; INIS Atomindex [Micro.]; INSPEC; Int. Aerosp. Abstr. (1991-); Math. Rev.; Met. Abstr.; NAPRALERT; SPIN (1982-); Zentralbl. Math. Ihre Grenzgeb.

KO
**YONGU NONMUNJIP.** **Added/Corp** Chungnam Taehakkyo. Mulli, Hwahak Yonguso. **VFOAT** Reports of the Research Institute of Physics and Chemistry; Mulli, Hwahak Yonguso Yonguso Yongu Nonmunjip. (1984)-. Periodical. Korean (summaries and/or abstracts in English). Eleanor Smeal Report, PO Box 19995, Washington DC 20036. **LC** QD95; .Y66. ***Continues*** *Yongu Nonmunjip (Chungnam Taehakkyo. Hwahak Pungwanghak Yonguso).*

GW/0075-7918
**ZAHLENWERTE UND FUNKTIONEN AUS NATURWISSENSCHAFTEN UND TECHNIK GRUPPE 2. ATOM- UND MOLEKULARPHYSIK.** **VFOAT** Numerical Data and Functional Relationships in Science and Technology. Group 2. Atomic and Molecular Physics. **VAT** Zahlenwerte und Funktionen aus Naturwissenschaften und Technik. Gruppe Zwei, Atom- und Molekularphysik. English. Springer-Verlag New York Inc., 175 5th Avenue, New York NY 10010. **Tel** (212)460-1500, telex 232 235 SPB UR. **(Subscription address:** Springer Verlag New York Inc. / for North America, 44 Hartz Way, Secaucus NJ 07096.**)**

GW/0075-787X
**ZAHLENWERTE UND FUNKTIONEN AUS NATURWISSENSCHAFTEN UND TECHNIK GRUPPE 3. KRISTALL- UND FESTKORPERPHYSIK.** **VFOAT** Numerical Data and Functional Relationships in Science and Technology. Group 3. Crystal and Solid State Physics. **VAT** Zahlenwerte und Funktionen aus Naturwissenschaften und Technik. Gruppe Drei, Kristall- und Festkorperphysik. German. Springer-Verlag GmbH & Company KG, Heidelberger Platz 3, D 14197 Berlin Germany. **Tel** 011 49 30 8207223, FAX 011 49 30 8214091, telex 183 319 SPBLN D. **(Subscription address:** Springer Verlag New York Inc. / for North America, 44 Hartz Way, Secaucus NJ 07096.**)**

GW
**ZAHLENWERTE UND FUNKTIONEN AUS NATURWISSENSCHAFTEN UND TECHNIK, NEUE SERIE.** **VFOAT** Landolt - Bornstein; Numerical Data Functional Relationships in Science and Technology. (1961)-. Monographic series. English (German). ir. Price varies per volume. Springer-Verlag GmbH & Company KG, Heidelberger Platz 3, D 14197 Berlin Germany. **Tel** 011 49 30 8207223, FAX 011 49 30 8214091, telex 183 319 SPBLN D. **(Subscription address:** Springer Verlag New York Inc. / for North America, 44 Hartz Way, Secaucus NJ 07096.**) LC** QC61; .Z3. ***Supersedes*** *Zahlenwerte und Funktionen aus Physik, Chemie, Astronomie, Geophysik und Technik.*

GW
**ZAHLENWERTE UND FUNKTIONEN AUS NATURWISSENSCHAFTEN UND TECHNIK NEUE SERIE, GRUPPE VII, BIOPHYSIK.** **VFOAT** Numerical Data and Functional Relationships in Science and Technology; Biophysik; Biophysics; Landolt-Bornstein. Vol. 1 (1989)-. Monographic series. English (English). Price varies per volume. Springer-Verlag GmbH & Company KG, Heidelberger Platz 3, D 14197 Berlin Germany. **Tel** 011 49 30 8207223, FAX 011 49 30 8214091, telex 183 319 SPBLN D. **(Subscription address:** Springer Verlag New York Inc. / for North America, 44 Hartz Way, Secaucus NJ 07096.**)**

YU/0352-0889
**ZBORNIK RADOVA PRIRODNO-MATEMATICKOG FAKULTETA. SERIJA ZA FIZIKU.** **VFOAT** Physics Series; Serija Za Fiziku; Review of Research. Physics Series. Began in 1981 with V. 11. Periodical. English (Serbo-Croatian (Roman)). an. $15.00. Prirodno-Matematickog Fakultet U Novom Sadu, Ul Dr Ilije Djuricica 4, 21000 Novi Sad Yugoslavia. **ED** Mario Skrinjar. **LC** QC1; .Z38. **Circ:** 250. Documents available from Ask*IEEE. ***Continues in part*** *Univerzitet u Novom Sadu. Prirodno-Matematicki Fakultet. Zbornik Radova.*
**Desc:** Review of research of the Institute of Physics. Publishes papers in condensed matter physics, nuclear physics, physics of atoms, molecules and ionized gases and applied physics.
**Ind/Abst** INSPEC (1979-); Ref. Z.

SZ/0044-2275
**ZEITSCHRIFT FUER ANGEWANDTE MATHEMATIK UND PHYSIK : ZAMP.** **See** Mathematics.

GW/0932-0784
**ZEITSCHRIFT FUER NATURFORSCHUNG.** (ZEITSCHRIFT FUER NATURFORSCHUNG. A, A JOURNAL OF PHYSICAL SCIENCES.). [Z. Nat.forsch., A j. phys. sci.]. **Added/Corp** Max-Planck-Gesellschaft zur Foerderung der Wissenschaften. **VFOAT** Journal of Physical Sciences; Physical Sciences. Vol. 42, No. 1 (Jan. 1987)-. Academic Scholarly Publication. English (German). Twelve times a year. DM510.00. Verlag der Zeitschrift fuer Naturforschung Tubingen, PO Box 2645, D 72016 Tuebingen Germany. **Tel** 011 49 7071 31555, FAX 07032/75465. **ED** S. Grossmann, A. Klemm, and D. Pfirsch. **LC** QC1; .Z42. **DD** 530. **CODEN** ZNASEI. **[CCC].** Index available. **Ad Acc. Circ:** 1,000 (ctrl). Documents available from The Genuine Article, Ask*IEEE, CASDDS. ***Continues*** *Zeitschrift fuer Naturforschung. Teil A, Physik, Physikalische Chemie, Kosmophysik, 0340-4811.*

**Ind/Abst** Chem Inform; Chem. Abstr. (1987-); Curr. Contents Phys. Chem. Earth Sci.; INSPEC (Aug. 1983-); Mass Spect. Bull.; Math. Rev.; NAPRALERT; Res. Alert [Full Cov.]; Sci. Cit. Index; SCISEARCH; Zentralbl. Math. Ihre Grenzgeb.

GW/0722-3277
**ZEITSCHRIFT FUER PHYSIK. B, CONDENSED MATTER.** [Z. Phys., B, Condens. matter]. **Added/Corp** Deutsche Physikalische Gesellschaft. **VFOAT** Condensed Matter. Vol. 38, No. 1 (1980)-. Academic Scholarly Publication. English (German). Twelve times a year. DM2388.00. Springer-Verlag GmbH & Company KG, Heidelberger Platz 3, D 14197 Berlin Germany. **Tel** 011 49 30 8207223, FAX 011 49 30 8214091, telex 183 319 SPBLN D. **(Subscription address:** Springer Verlag New York Inc. / for North America, 44 Hartz Way, Secaucus NJ 07096.**) ED** H Horner and F Steglich. **CODEN** ZPCMDN. **[CCC]. Pr Rev.** available on microfilm and microfiche from University Microfilms International (UMI). Documents available from The Genuine Article, Ask*IEEE, CASDDS. ***Continues*** *Zeitschrift fur Physik. B, Condensed Matter and Quanta, 0340-224X.*
**Desc:** Covers the physics of condensed matter and general physics. Emphasis is also put on quantum optics and statistical physics, especially in the area of nonequilibrium processes and cooperative phenomena.
**Ind/Abst** Alum. Ind. Abstr.; Ceram. Abstr. (19??-); Chem. Abstr.; Curr. Contents Phys. Chem. Earth Sci.; Energy Res. Abstr. (1980-); INSPEC (1981-); Math. Rev.; Met. Abstr.; Phys. Briefs; Res. Alert [Full Cov.]; Sci. Cit. Index; SCISEARCH.

GW/0170-9739
**ZEITSCHRIFT FUER PHYSIK. C, PARTICLES AND FIELDS.** (ZEITSCHRIFT FUER PHYSIK. C, PARTICLES AND FIELDS / UNTER MITWIRKUNG DER DEUTSCHEN PHYSIKALISCHEN GESELLSCHAFT.). [Z. Phys. C, Part. fields]. **Added/Corp** Deutsche Physikalische Gesellschaft (1963- ). **VFOAT** Particles and Fields. (1979)-. Academic Scholarly Publication. English. Sixteen times a year. DM4080.00. Springer-Verlag GmbH & Company KG, Heidelberger Platz 3, D 14197 Berlin Germany. **Tel** 011 49 30 8207223, FAX 011 49 30 8214091, telex 183 319 SPBLN D. **(Subscription address:** Springer Verlag New York Inc. / for North America, 44 Hartz Way, Secaucus NJ 07096.**) ED** G Kramer. **LC** QC1; .Z43. **DD** 539.7/21. **CODEN** ZPCFD2. **[CCC]. Pr Rev.** available on microfilm and microfiche from University Microfilms International (UMI). Documents available from The Genuine Article, Ask*IEEE, CASDDS. ***Continues in part*** *Zeitschrift fur Physik, 0044-3328.*
**Desc:** Devoted to the experimental and theoretical investigation of elementary particles.
**Ind/Abst** Chem. Abstr.; Curr. Contents Phys. Chem. Earth Sci.; Energy Res. Abstr. (Aug. 1979-); INSPEC (1979-); Math. Rev.; Phys. Briefs; Res. Alert [Full Cov.]; Sci. Cit. Index; SCISEARCH.

GW/0178-7683
**ZEITSCHRIFT FUER PHYSIK. D, ATOMS, MOLECULES AND CLUSTERS.** [Z. Phys. D : At., mol. clusters]. **Added/Corp** Deutsche Physikalische Gesellschaft (1963- ). **VFOAT** Atoms, Molecules and Clusters. Vol. 1, No. 1 (Jan. 1986)-. Academic Scholarly Publication. English. Sixteen times a year. DM2280.00. Springer-Verlag GmbH & Company KG, Heidelberger Platz 3, D 14197 Berlin Germany. **Tel** 011 49 30 8207223, FAX 011 49 30 8214091, telex 183 319 SPBLN D. **(Subscription address:** Springer Verlag New York Inc. / for North America, 44 Hartz Way, Secaucus NJ 07096.**) ED** I V Hertel. **LC** QC170; .Z45. **DD** 539/.05. **CODEN** ZDACE2. **[CCC]. Pr Rev.** available on microfilm and microfiche from University Microfilms International (UMI). Documents available from The Genuine Article, Ask*IEEE, CASDDS. ***Continues in part*** *Zeitschrift fur Physik. A: Atoms and Nuclei, 0340-2193.*
**Desc:** Brings together in one journal reports of research on free atoms, molecules and clusters, and their properties and interactions as individual entities in gaseous, liquid, and solid environments.
**Ind/Abst** Chem. Abstr. (1986); Curr. Contents Phys. Chem. Earth Sci.; INSPEC (1986); Mass Spect. Bull.; Res. Alert [Full Cov.]; Sci. Cit. Index; SCISEARCH.

PL/0072-470X
**ZESZYTY NAUKOWE - POLITECHNIKA SLASKA. MATEMATYKA. FIZYKA.** **See** Mathematics.

PL
**ZESZYTY NAUKOWE UNIWERSYTETU JAGIELLONSKIEGO. UNIVERSITATIS IAGELLONICAE FOLIA PHYSICA.** **Added/Corp** Uniwersytet Jagiellonski. **VFOAT** Universitatis Iagellonicae Folia Physica; Acta Scientiarum Litterarumque. Universitatis Iagellonicae Folia Physica. (1991)-. Monographic series. English. Uniwersytet Jagiellonski, Ul. Golebia 24, 31-007 Krakow Poland. **LC** QC1; .K7. ***Continues*** *Zeszyty Naukowe Uniwersytetu Jagiellonskiego. Prace Fizyczne.*
**Ind/Abst** Math. Rev.

PL
**ZESZYTY NAUKOWE WYDZIAU MATEMATYKI, FIZYKI I CHEMII. PROBLEMY DYDAKTYKI FIZYKI.**
**Main/Corp** Uniwersytet Gdanski. Wydzia Matematyki, Fizyki i Chemii. **VFOAT** Problemy Dydaktyki Fizyki. No. 1 (19??)-. Academic Scholarly Publication. Polish (summaries and/or abstracts in English and Russian). z8.00 (single issue). **LC** QC30; .U57a. Documents available from CASDDS.
**Ind/Abst** Chem. Abstr.

RU/0044-4510
**ZURNAL EKSPERIMENTALNOJ I TEORETICESKOJ FIZIKI.** (ZHURNAL EKSPERIMENTALNOI I TEORETICHESKOI FIZIKI / AKADEMIIA NAUK SSSR.). [Z. eksp. teor. fiz.]. **Added/Corp** Akademiia Nauk SSSR. **VFOAT** Fizicheskii Zhurnal. Seriia A, Zhurnal Eksperimentalnoi i Teoreticheskoi Fiziki. (1936)-. Academic Scholarly Publication. Russian (summaries and/or abstracts in English; table of contents in English). mo. $605.00. Izdatelstvo Nauka / Akademiia Nauk, Publishing House of the Russian Academy of Sciences, Leninskii Porspekt 14, 117901 Moscow Russia. **Tel** 011 95 954-21-53, FAX 011 95 938-21-44, telex 411964. **(Subscription address:** East View Publications Inc., 3020 Harbor Lane North, Suite 110, Minneapolis MN 55447.**)** **CODEN** ZETFA7. **[CCC].** Documents available from The Genuine Article, Ask*IEEE, CASDDS. ***Continues** Fizicheskii Zhurnal. Seriia A, Zhurnal Eksperimentalnoii I Teoreticheskoi Fiziki.*
**Ind/Abst** Alum. Ind. Abstr.; Ceram. Abstr. (19??-); Chem. Abstr.; Curr. Contents Phys. Chem. Earth Sci.; INSPEC (1968-); Int. Aerosp. Abstr.; Math. Rev.; Met. Abstr.; Res. Alert [Full Cov.]; Sci. Cit. Index; SCISEARCH.

RU/0044-4642
**ZURNAL TEHNICESKOJ FIZIKI.** (ZHURNAL TEKHNICHESKOI FIZIKI.). [Z. teh. fiz.]. **Added/Corp** Akademiia Nauk SSSR. **VFOAT** Fizicheskii Zhurnal. Vol. 1, (1931)-. Academic Scholarly Publication. Russian. mo. $348.00. Izdatelstvo Nauka / Akademiia Nauk, Publishing House of the Russian Academy of Sciences, Leninskii Porspekt 14, 117901 Moscow Russia. **Tel** 011 95 954-21-53, FAX 011 95 938-21-44, telex 411964. **(Subscription address:** East View Publications Inc., 3020 Harbor Lane North, Suite 110, Minneapolis MN 55447.**)** **LC** QC1; .Z48. **CODEN** ZTEFA3. **[CCC].** Index available. **Pr Rev.** Documents available from The Genuine Article, Ask*IEEE, CASDDS. ***Formed by the union of** Zhurnal Prikladnoi Fiziki **and** Fizika I Proizvodstvo.*
**Ind/Abst** Alum. Ind. Abstr.; Ceram. Abstr. (19??-); Chem. Abstr.; Curr. Contents Phys. Chem. Earth Sci.; GeoRef; INSPEC (1968-); Int. Aerosp. Abstr.; Met. Abstr.; Res. Alert [Full Cov.]; Sci. Cit. Index; SCISEARCH; World Alum. Abstr.

RU/0044-4669
**ZURNAL VYCISLITELNOJ MATEMATIKI I MATEMATICESKOJ FIZIKI.** (ZHURNAL VYCHISLITELNOI MATEMATIKI I MATEMATICHESKOI FIZIKI.). [Z. vycisl. mat. mat. fiz.]. **Added/Corp** Akademiia Nauk SSSR. (1961)-. Academic Scholarly Publication. Russian. Twelve times a year. $288.00. Izdatelstvo Nauka / Akademiia Nauk, Publishing House of the Russian Academy of Sciences, Leninskii Porspekt 14, 117901 Moscow Russia. **Tel** 011 95 954-21-53, FAX 011 95 938-21-44, telex 411964. **(Subscription address:** East View Publications Inc., 3020 Harbor Lane North, Suite 110, Minneapolis MN 55447.**)** **LC** QA297; .Z5. **CODEN** ZVMFAN. **[CCC].** cum. index. Documents available from Ask*IEEE, CASDDS.
**Ind/Abst** Chem. Abstr. (?-1973); INSPEC (1968-); Int. Aerosp. Abstr.; Math. Rev.

## ABSTRACTING, BIBLIOGRAPHIES AND STATISTICS

UK/0001-4974
**ACOUSTICS ABSTRACTS.** [Acoust. abstr.]. Vol. 1, No. 1 (March/April 1967)-. Abstracting/Indexing Service. English. mo. £202.00 UK and Europe; £206.00 other (plus £23 airmail). Multi Science Publishing Company Ltd., 107 High Street, Brentwood, Essex CM14 4RX England. **Tel** 011 44 277 224632, FAX 011 44 277 223453, telex 89-8452. **NLM** Z 7144.S6 A185. **CODEN** ACOABJ. **[CCC].** Index Available, published separately, free-automatically sent.
**Desc:** Provides information on all aspects of acoustics. The abstracts of recently published papers cover areas such as: solid, liquid and gaseous state acoustics; acoustic diagnostic techniques; acoustic measurements; ultrasonic applications; underwater acoustics; audio frequencies; architectural acoustics; and vibration and shock.
**Ind/Abst** Fluid Abstr., Civil Eng.; Fluid Abstr. Proc. Eng.; FLUIDEX (1973-1989).

AU
**CINDA.** **Added/Corp** International Atomic Energy Agency. **VFOAT** Computer Index of Neutron Data. **VAT** C I N D A. (1976)-. English. an. Price varies per volume. International Atomic Energy Agency / IAEA, Wagramerstrasse 5, PO Box 100, A-1400 Vienna Austria. **Tel** 011 43 1 2360 ext. 2530, FAX 011 43 1 234564. **(Subscription address:** UNIPUB, 4611 F Assembly Drive, Lanham MD 20706.**)** **LC** Z7144.N8; C55; QC793.5.N4628. **DD** 016.5397/213.
**Desc:** Index to literature and computer files on microscopic neutron data. Worldwide bibliography of the literature on microscopic neutron data resulting from experiments, theory and evaluations.

UK/0011-3786
**CURRENT PAPERS IN PHYSICS.** [Curr. pap. phys.]. **Added/Corp** Institution of Electrical Engineers, London. American Institute of Physics. No. 1 (Jan. 10, 1966)-. Abstracting/Indexing Service. English. sm. £275.00. Institution of Electrical Engineers / IEE, Michael Faraday House, Six Hills Way, Stevenage Herts SG1 2AY UK. **Tel** 011 44 438 313311, FAX 011 44 438 742840, telex 825578 IEESTV G. **(Subscription address:** IEE / UK, Publications Sales Department, PO Box 96, Stevenage, Herts, SG1 2SD England.**)** **LC** QC5.5; .C87x. **CODEN** CPPHAL. **[CCC].**
**Desc:** Gives the title and full details of the bibliographic reference of each article selected from the world's scientific and technical literature.
**Ind/Abst** FLUIDEX (1973-).

US/0098-9819
**CURRENT PHYSICS INDEX.** [Curr. phys. index]. **Added/Corp** American Institute of Physics. Vol. 1 (1975)-. Abstracting/Indexing Service. English. Four times a year. $1190.00 US; $1210.00 Canada, Mexico, Central and South America, and the Caribbean; $1250.00 other (includes cumulative index). American Institute of Physics, 500 Sunnyside Boulevard, Woodbury NY 11797-2999. **Tel** (516)576-2200, FAX (516)349-7669, telex 960983. **LC** Z7143; .C87; QC1. **DD** 530/.08. **NLM** Z 7143 C977. **[CCC].** Index available. cum. index.

AU/0004-7139
**INIS ATOMINDEX.** ***Title Change.*** (INIS ATOMINDEX. INIS ATOMINDEKS.). [INIS atomindex]. **Added/Corp** International Atomic Energy Agency. **VFOAT** Atomindex; INIS Atomindeks. **VAT** International Nuclear Information System Atomindex. Vol. 1 (May 1970)-(19??). Abstracting/Indexing Service. English (Multiple languages). sm. UNIPUB, 4611-F Assembly Drive, Lanham MD 20706-4391. **Tel** (800)274-4888, FAX (301)459-0056, telex 28787 GATT CH. **LC** Z7144.N8; I18. **DD** 016.5397. **NLM** Z 7144.N8 I105. **CODEN** INAXAC. cum. index. Documents available from CASDDS. ***Supersedes** Atomindex. **Continued by** INIS Atomindex.*
**Desc:** Contains bibliographic descriptions and abstracts and/or descriptors for all items recorded in the International Nuclear Information System; includes books, research reports, patents, journal articles, conference papers and other items. The approximately 80,000 references are grouped by subject category.
**Ind/Abst** Chem. Abstr.; Energy Res. Abstr. (Sept. 1980-); Mass Spect. Bull.

AU
**INIS ATOMINDEX [MICROFORM].**
**Added/Corp** International Atomic Energy Agency. **VAT** International Nuclear Information System Atomindex. Vol. 19, No. 1 (Jan. 1, 1988)-. Abstracting/Indexing Service. English. Twenty-four times a year. S6900.00 Subscription A; S5500.00 Subscription B. International Atomic Energy Agency / IAEA, Wagramerstrasse 5, PO Box 100, A-1400 Vienna Austria. **Tel** 011 43 1 2360 ext. 2530, FAX 011 43 1 234564. **(Subscription address:** UNIPUB, 4611 F Assembly Drive, Lanham MD 20706.**)** **LC** Microfiche (o) 89/2525 . cum. index. available on CD-ROM (INIS) from SilverPlatter (US). ***Continues** INIS Atomindex, 0004-7139.*
**Desc:** Contains bibliographic descriptions and abstracts and/or descriptors for all items recorded in the International Nuclear Information System; includes books, research reports, patents, journal articles, conference papers and other items. The approximately 80,000 references are grouped by subject category.

AU/1014-1561
**INIS. AUTHORITY LIST FOR CORPORATE ENTRIES AND REPORT NUMBER PREFIXES.** **Main/Corp** International Atomic Energy Agency. **Added/Corp** International Nuclear Information System. International Atomic Energy Agency. **VFOAT** International Nuclear Information System, Authority List for Corporate Entries and Report Number Prefixes. (19??)-. English. S780.00. International Atomic Energy Agency / IAEA, Wagramerstrasse 5, PO Box 100, A-1400 Vienna Austria. **Tel** 011 43 1 2360 ext. 2530, FAX 011 43 1 234564. **(Subscription address:** UNIPUB, 4611 F Assembly Drive, Lanham MD 20706.**)** **LC** Z699.5.A85; I2 subser.; Z695.8. **DD** 025.04S 025.06/333792/4. ***Continues** INIS, Authority List for Corporate Entries.*
**Desc:** Contains the standard INIS entries of the names of corporate bodies. Contains the names of 29,682 organizations reported to INIS as corporate authors and issuing bodies.

AU
**INIS : AUTHORITY LIST FOR JOURNAL TITLES.** (19??)-. English. an. S440.00. International Atomic Energy Agency / IAEA, Wagramerstrasse 5, PO Box 100, A-1400 Vienna Austria. **Tel** 011 43 1 2360 ext. 2530, FAX 011 43 1 234564. **(Subscription address:** UNIPUB, 4611 F Assembly Drive, Lanham MD 20706.**)**
**Desc:** Contains the names of 10,797 journal titles covered by INIS. Titles are grouped by country or international organization responsible for the processing of the journal for INIS.

AU
**INIS, DESCRIPTIVE CATALOGUING SAMPLES.** **Main/Corp** International Atomic Energy Agency. **VFOAT** Descriptive Cataloging Samples. (19??)-. English. S80.00. International Atomic Energy Agency / IAEA, Wagramerstrasse 5, PO Box 100, A-1400 Vienna Austria. **Tel** 011 43 1 2360 ext. 2530, FAX 011 43 1 234564. **(Subscription address:** UNIPUB, 4611 F Assembly Drive, Lanham MD 20706.**)**
**Desc:** Contains cataloging samples for each of the pieces of literature described in Rev. 7 (1988) of IAEA-INIS-1.

AU
**INIS : THESAURUS.** **Added/Corp** International Atomic Energy Agency. **VFOAT** I.N.I.S. : Thesaurus. (1970)-. English. S1320.00. International Atomic Energy Agency / IAEA, Wagramerstrasse 5, PO Box 100, A-1400 Vienna Austria. **Tel** 011 43 1 2360 ext. 2530, FAX 011 43 1 234564. **(Subscription address:** UNIPUB, 4611 F Assembly Drive, Lanham MD 20706.**)**
**Desc:** Gives the controlled vocabulary to be used by INIS members to index the literature they report to INIS.

CN/0022-0264
**JOURNAL OF CURRENT LASER ABSTRACTS.** **Added/Corp** Institute for Laser Documentation. (1967)-. Periodical. English. Twelve times a year. $455.00 US and Canada; $475.00 other. PennWell Publishing Company, Ten Tara Boulevard 5th Floor, Nashua NH 03062-2801. **Tel** (603)891-0123, (603)891-9177, FAX (603)891-0624, (603)891-0574. **ED** Richard Feinberg. Index available. cum. index (annual). **Bk Rev.** **Ad Acc.** ***Continues** Laser/Maser International.*
**Desc:** Abstract journal covering more than 1,000 publications. Over 100 laser subject classifications from applications to theory: scientific, industrial, medical, surgical, dental, ophthalmic, communications. Includes author/corporate indexes.

JA/0011-3336
**KAGAKU GIJUTSU BUNKEN SOKUHO. BUTSURI, OYO BUTSURI-HEN.** **VFOAT** Current Bibliography on Science and Technology. Pure and Applied Physics; Bunsoku. Butsuri, oyo Butsuri-Hen. (1959)-. Bibliography. Multiple languages. sm. $1830.00. Japan Information Center of Science and Technology, 5-2 Nagatacho 2 chome, Chiyodaku, Tokyo 100 Japan. **DD** 016.53 061.62. **Circ:** 500.

UK/0950-4818
**KEY ABSTRACTS. MEASUREMENTS IN PHYSICS.** [Key abstr., Meas. phys.]. **Added/Corp** INSPEC (Information Service) Institute of Electrical and Electronics Engineers. **VFOAT** Measurements in Physics. (Jan. 1987)-. Abstracting/Indexing Service. English. mo. $178.00. Institution of Electrical Engineers / IEE, Michael Faraday House, Six Hills Way, Stevenage Herts SG1 2AY UK. **Tel** 011 44 438 313311, FAX 011 44 438 742840, telex 825578 IEESTV G. **(Subscription address:** IEEE / Institute of Electrical and Electronics Engineers, 445 Hoes Lane, PO Box 1331, Piscataway NJ 08855-1331.**)** **LC** QC39; .K45. **DD** 530.8. ***Continues** Key Abstracts. Physical Measurements and Instrumentation, 0307-7969.*
**Desc:** Covers radiation detectors and measurements, mass spectrometry, plasma diagnostics, measurements and instrumentation in mechanics, heat, optics, fluid dynamics and the environment.

US/0163-9587
**MOSSBAUER EFFECT REFERENCE AND DATA JOURNAL.** [Mossbauer eff. ref. data j.]. **Added/Corp** Mossbauer Effect Data Center. Vol. 1, (Jan. 1978)-. Academic Scholarly Publication. English. Ten times a year (Except July/Aug.). $530.00 (surface mail), $565.00 (airmail) without index; $440.00 (airmail) index only; $740.00 (surface mail) index only. Mossbauer Effect Data Center / North Carolina, University of North Carolina, Asheville NC 28804-3299. **Tel** (704)251-6617, FAX (704)251-6002. **ED** John G. Stevens. **DD** 537. **CODEN** MERJD5. Index available. **Bk Rev.** **Ad Acc,** **Adv Mgr:** Christine R. Boss, **Tel** (704)251-6617. **Circ:** 200 (ctrl). Documents available from CASDDS.
**Desc:** Bibliographical listing and abstracted data from articles on Mossbauer spectroscopy, also subject, isotope indexes and name and address listing of selected authors. Other information including news.
**Ind/Abst** Chem. Abstr.

FR/1146-5360
**PASCAL. E 27, METHODES DE FORMATION ET TRAITEMENT DES IMAGES.** **VFOAT** PASCAL. E 27, Imaging and Image Processing; PASCAL. E Vingt-sept, Methodes de Formation et Traitement des Images. (1990)-. Periodical. Multiple languages. Ten times a year. 760.00F France; 800.00F other. CNRS / Institut d'Information Scientifique et Technique, (Centre National de la Recherche

Scientifique), 15 Quai Anatole France, Paris 75700 France. **Tel** 011 33 1 47531515, telex 299 356 F. **UDC** 011. ***Continues*** *Pascal Explore. E27 : Methodes de Formation et Traitement des Images.*

UK/0036-8091
**PHYSICS ABSTRACTS.** (SCIENCE ABSTRACTS. SERIES A, PHYSICS ABSTRACTS.). [Phys. abstr.]. **Added/Corp** Institution of Electrical Engineers. American Institute of Physics. Institute of Electrical and Electronics Engineers. INSPEC (Information Service). **VFOAT** Physics Abstracts. Vol. 70, No. 829 (Jan. 1967)-Vol. 94, No. 1414 (Dec. 1991) No. 1-(1st Jan. 1992)-. Abstracting/Indexing Service. English. sm. £1,780. Institution of Electrical Engineers / IEE, Michael Faraday House, Six Hills Way, Stevenage Herts SG1 2AY UK. **Tel** 011 44 438 313311, FAX 011 44 438 742840, telex 825578 IEESTV G. **(Subscription address:** IEE / UK, Publications Sales Department, PO Box 96, Stevenage, Herts, SG1 2SD England.**)** **LC** QC1; .P46. **DD** 530/.05. **NLM** Z 7141 S416. **CODEN** PYASAF. **[CCC].** cum. index. ***Continues*** *Science Abstracts. Physics Abstracts.*
**Desc:** Guide to recently published research in all areas of physics, including particle, nuclear, atomic, molecular, fluid, plasma and solid-state physics, biophysics, geophysics, astrophysics, measurement and instrumentation.

UK/0170-7434
**PHYSICS BRIEFS.** [Phys. briefs]. **Added/Corp** Deutsche Physikalische Gesellschaft. Fachinformationszentrum Energie, Physik, Mathematik (Eggenstein-Leopoldshafen, Germany) American Institute of Physics. **VFOAT** Physikalische Berichte. Vol. 1 (Jan. 15, 1979)-. Abstracting/Indexing Service. English. sm. $3250.00 US; $3300.00 Canada and Mexico. Institute of Physics, Techno House, Redcliffe Way, Bristol BS1 6NX England. **Tel** 011 44 272 297481, FAX 011 44 272 294318, telex 449149 INSTP G. **(Subscription address:** American Institute of Physics, Publishing Sales, 500 Sunnyside Blvd., Woodbury NY 11797.**)** **LC** QC1; .P6535. **DD** 016.53. **NLM** Z 7141 P578. **CODEN** PHBRD3. Each issue contains an index to its own contents (no volume index)--loose. **Circ:** 350. Documents available from CASDDS. ***Supersedes*** *Physikalische Berichte.*
**Desc:** Covers physics, astronomy and other related fields.
**Ind/Abst** Chem. Abstr.; Energy Res. Abstr. (March 1982-).

US/0569-5716
**PHYSICS MANPOWER, EDUCATION AND EMPLOYMENT STUDIES.** **Main/Corp** American Institute of Physics. (19??)-. English. ir (every three years). $15.00. American Institute of Physics, 500 Sunnyside Boulevard, Woodbury NY 11797-2999. **Tel** (516)576-2200, FAX (516)349-7669, telex 960983. **LC** QC29; .A42. **DD** 530/.023. ***Continues*** *American Institute of Physics. Physics: Education, Employment, Financial Support; A Statistical Handbook.*
**Desc:** Education and employment statistics concerning physicists in the United States.

US/0896-5900
**SOLID STATE AND SUPERCONDUCTIVITY ABSTRACTS.** [Solid state supercond. abstr.]. **Added/Corp** Cambridge Scientific Abstracts, Inc. Vol. 28, No. 1 (Jan. 1988)-. Abstracting/Indexing Service. English. bm (plus annual index). $995.00 US; $1195.00 other. Cambridge Scientific Abstracts, 7200 Wisconsin Avenue, #601, Bethesda MD 20814-4823. **Tel** (301)961-6750, (800)843-7751, FAX (301)961-6720. **ED** Evelyn Beck. **LC** TK7800; .S6. **DD** 530.4/1/05. Index available. cum. index. **Bk Rev.** available on magnetic tape; available on an online database; available via Internet (to the current year's abstracts and five-year backfiles) from Cambridge Scientific Abstracts. ***Continues*** *Solid State Abstracts Journal, 0038-108X.*
**Desc:** Covers solid state physics, chemistry, crystal growth; superconductivity theory, materials, applications and problem areas.

US
**SPIN.** Abstracting/Indexing Service. English. American Institute of Physics, 500 Sunnyside Boulevard, Woodbury NY 11797-2999. **Tel** (516)576-2200, FAX (516)349-7669, telex 960983. **(Subscription address:** Institute of Physics, Techno House, Redcliffe Way, Bristol BS1 6NX England.**)** available on magnetic tape; available on an online database from DIALOG.
**Desc:** A computer-readable service. Dates from 1970 to the present and contains approximately 350,000 records.

## ANALYTIC AND EXPERIMENTAL MECHANICS

CC/0567-7718
**ACTA MECHANICA SINICA.** **Added/Corp** Chung-Kuo Li Hsueh Hsueh Hui. **VFOAT** Li Hsueh Hsueh Pao; Chinese Journal of Mechanics. Vol. 1 (Mar. 1985)-. Periodical. English. Four times a year. $395.00. (Chinese Society of Theoretical and Applied Mechanics), Science Press, 16 Donghuangchenggen North Street, Beijing 100707, People's Republic of China. **Tel** 011 86 1 4019821, FAX 011 86 4012180, telex 210147. **(Subscription address:** Allerton Press Inc., 150 Fifth Avenue, New York NY 10011.**)** **ED** Hwang Kehchih. **LC** QA801; .L5. **DD** 531/.05. **[CCC].** **Ad Acc.** **Pr Rev. Circ:** 6,000. Documents available from Ask*IEEE.
**Desc:** Includes information on all aspects of mechanics.
**Ind/Abst** INSPEC (1978-); Math. Rev.; Zentralbl. Math. Ihre Grenzgeb.

US/1049-0787
**ANNUAL REVIEW OF HEAT TRANSFER.** ***Ceased.*** [Annu. rev. heat transf.]. Vol. 3 (1990)-Vol. 4 (1992). Academic Scholarly Publication. English. Taylor & Francis Ltd., Rankine Road, Basingstoke Hampshire, RG24 8PR United Kingdom. **Tel** 011 44 256 840366, FAX 011 44 256 479438, telex 858540. **(Subscription address:** Taylor & Francis Inc., 1900 Frost Road, Suite 101, Bristol PA 19007-1598.**)** **LC** QA901; .A56. **DD** 621.402/2. **CODEN** ARHTED. Documents available from CASDDS. ***Continues*** *Annual Review of Numerical Fluid Mechanics and Heat Transfer, 0892-6883.*
**Ind/Abst** Chem. Abstr. (19??)-(19??).

GW/0003-9527
**ARCHIVE FOR RATIONAL MECHANICS AND ANALYSIS.** [Arch. ration. mech. anal.]. Vol. 1 (1957)-. English (French, German, Italian and Latin). Sixteen times a year. DM2224.00. Springer-Verlag GmbH & Company KG, Heidelberger Platz 3, D 14197 Berlin Germany. **Tel** 011 49 30 8207223, FAX 011 49 30 8214091, telex 183 319 SPBLN D. **(Subscription address:** Springer Verlag New York Inc. / for North America, 44 Hartz Way, Secaucus NJ 07096.**)** **ED** S S Antman. **LC** QA801.A7. **DD** 531.017. **CODEN** AVRMAW. **[CCC].** cum. index. **Pr Rev.** available on microfilm and microfiche from University Microfilms International (UMI). Documents available from Article Express International, The Genuine Article, Ask*IEEE, CASDDS.
**Desc:** Nourishes the disciplines of mechanics as a deductive, mathematical science in the classical tradition and promotes pure analysis, particularly in contexts of application.
**Ind/Abst** Appl. Mech. Rev. (1973-); Bioeng. Abstr.; Chem. Abstr.; Compumath Citation Index [Full Cov.]; Curr. Contents Eng. Tech. Appl. Sci.; Curr. Contents Phys. Chem. Earth Sci.; Ei Page One; Energy Res. Abstr.; Eng. Index Annu. [Select. Cov.]; Fluid Abstr., Civil Eng.; Fluid Abstr. Proc. Eng.; FLUIDEX (1973-1988); INSPEC (Sept. 1973-); Int. Aerosp. Abstr.; Math. Rev.; Phys. Briefs; Res. Alert [Full Cov.]; Sci. Cit. Index; SCISEARCH; Stat. Theory Method Abstr. (1966, 1970, 1972, 1974-1975, 1979); Zentralbl. Math. Ihre Grenzgeb.

FR
**BULLETIN SIGNALETIQUE. 160: PHYSIQUE DE L'ETAT CONDENSE.** **Added/Corp** Centre National de la Recherche Scientifique (France). Centre de Documentation. (19??)-. Bulletin. French. Centre de Documentation Scientifique et Technique, Centre National de la Recherche Scientifique, 26 rue Boyer, 75971 Paris Cedex 20 France. **Tel** (1) 43 58 35 59, telex CNRSDOC 220880F. **LC** QC176.A1; B84. ***Supersedes*** *Bulletin Signaletique. 160: Structure de la Matiere I-Physique de l'Etat Condense, Physique Atomique et Moleculaire, Spectroscopie.*

JA/0385-9843
**BUSSEIKEN DAYORI (TOKYO).** [Busseiken dayori]. **Main/Corp** Tokyo Daigaku. Bussei Kenkyujo. (1957)-. Academic Scholarly Publication. Japanese. bm. Tokyo Daigaku Bussei Kenkyujo, (Institute of Solid State Physics), University of Tokyo, 22-1 Roppongi 7-chome, Minatoku Tokyo 106 Japan. **Tel** 03-478-6811, FAX 03-401-5169, telex ISSPUT J32469. **LC** QC176.A1; T58A. **CODEN** BUDADZ. **Circ:** 630 (ctrl). Documents available from CASDDS.
**Desc:** Bulletin of the Institute for Solid State Physics, University of Tokyo. Contains contributed articles, abstracts of scientific meetings and announcements.
**Ind/Abst** Chem. Abstr. (1961-1983).

CN/0826-9343
**C.S.N.D.T. JOURNAL.** [C.S.N.D.T. j.]. **Added/Corp** Canadian Society for Nondestructive Testing. **VAT** Canadian Society for Nondestructive Testing Journal; CSNDT Journal. Vol. 1, No. 1 (Oct. 1979)-. Periodical. English. Six times a year (Jan., Mar., May, July, Sept., Nov.). 75.00Can$ Canada; 100.00Can$ US; 125.00Can$ other. Canadian Society Nondestructive Testing Inc., National Office, Unit 47, 2400 Lucknow Drive,, Mississauga ONT, Canada L5S 1T9. **Tel** (416)676-0785, FAX (416)673-9255. **ED** Susan Mercer. **DD** 620.1/127/05.
**Desc:** A vehicle for news, chapter reports, technical articles, and new products.

RU/0302-6086
**CISLENNYE METODY V DINAMIKE RAZREZENNYH GAZOV.** (CHISLENNYE METODY V DINAMIKE RAZREZHENNYKH GAZOV.). [Cisl. metody din. razrez. gazov]. **Main/Corp** Akademiia Nauk SSSR. Laboratoriia Teorii Protsessov Perenosa. No. 1, (1973)-. Academic Scholarly Publication. Russian. **LC** QA930; .A433a. **CODEN** CMRGA7. Documents available from CASDDS.
**Ind/Abst** Chem. Abstr. (1973-1979); Int. Aerosp. Abstr.

FR/0997-7538
**EUROPEAN JOURNAL OF MECHANICS. A. SOLIDS.** [Eur. j. mech. A. Solids]. **VFOAT** Solids; A/Solids; E.J.M. A, Solids; E.J.M. A/Solids; Eur. J. Mech. A, Solids. Vol. 8, No 1 (1989)-. Periodical. English. Six times a year. 2150.00F EEC countries; 2380.00F other. Gauthier-Villars, 15 rue Gossin, 92543 Montrouge Cedex France. **Tel** 33 1 40 92 65 00, FAX 33 1 40 92 65 97. **(Subscription address:** Centrale des Revues, 11 rue Gossin, 92543 Montrouge Cedex France.**)** **LC** QA801; .E97. **DD** 620.1/005. **CODEN** EJASEV. **[CCC].** Documents available from Article Express International, The Genuine Article, Ask*IEEE. ***Continues in part*** *Journal de Mecanique Theorique et Appliquee, 0750-7240.*
**Desc:** Provides a forum published in English for discussion of the widest possible range of research topics in the field of solids mechanics.
**Ind/Abst** Appl. Mech. Rev.; Curr. Contents Eng. Tech. Appl. Sci.; Curr. Contents Phys. Chem. Earth Sci.; Ei Page One; Eng. Index Annu.; GeoRef; INSPEC (1989-); Int. Aerosp. Abstr.; Math. Rev.; Res. Alert; Sci. Cit. Index; SCISEARCH; Shock Vibr. Dig.; Zentralbl. Math. Ihre Grenzgeb.

US/0014-4851
**EXPERIMENTAL MECHANICS.** [Exp. mech.]. **Added/Corp** Society for Experimental Mechanics. Society for Experimental Stress Analysis. Vol. 1 (Jan. 1961)-. Periodical. English. qt (Mar., June, Sept., Dec.). $79.00 (comes with Society for Experimental Mechanics membership). Society for Experimental Mechanics, 7 School Street, Bethel CT 06801-1405. **Tel** (203)790-6373, FAX (203)790-4472. **ED** Kenneth A. Galione and Meg E. Yergin. **LC** TA401; .E9. **DD** 620.1/1/0287. **CODEN** EXMCAZ. **[CCC].** Index available. cum. index. **Pr Rev. Circ:** 4,000 (ctrl). available on microfilm and microfiche from University Microfilms International (UMI). Documents available from Article Express International, The Genuine Article, Ask*IEEE, CASDDS.
**Desc:** Contains original investigations in experimental mechanics.
**Ind/Abst** Abstr. Bull. Inst. Paper Chem.; Abstr. Bull. Inst. Pap. Sci. Tech.; Abstr. J. Earthq. Eng.; Acoust. Abstr.; Alum. Ind. Abstr.; Appl. Sci. Technol. Index; Bioeng. Abstr.; Chem. Abstr.; Coal Abstr.; Curr. Contents Eng. Tech. Appl. Sci.; Ei Page One; Eng. Mater. Abstr.; Eng. Index Annu.; INSPEC (Sept. 1973-); Int. Aerosp. Abstr.; Met. Abstr.; Nucl. Sci. Abstr.; Res. Alert [Full Cov.]; Sci. Cit. Index; SCISEARCH; Shock Vibr. Dig.; World Alum. Abstr.; World Ceram. Abstr.

US/0894-1777
**EXPERIMENTAL THERMAL AND FLUID SCIENCE.** (EXPERIMENTAL THERMAL AND FLUID SCIENCE : ETF SCIENCE.). [Exp. therm. fluid sci.]. **VFOAT** ETF Science; ETFS. Vol. 1, No. 1 (Jan. 1988)-. Academic Scholarly Publication. English. Eight times a year (2 volumes). $542.00 US; $587.00 other. Elsevier Science Publishing Company Inc, Madison Square Station, PO Box 882, New York NY 10159-0882. **Tel** (212)633-3950, FAX (212)633-3990. **ED** R H Shah, E N Ganic. **LC** TJ260; .E96. **DD** 621.402/2. **CODEN** ETFSEO. **[CCC].** **Bk Rev.** **Ad Acc.** **Pr Rev.** Documents available from Article Express International, The Genuine Article, CASDDS.
**Desc:** Provides a forum for research emphasizing experimental work that enhances basic understanding of heat transfer, thermodynamics and fluid mechanics, and their applications. Publishes papers reporting experimental work together with theory, analysis and numerical studies, and papers analyzing original or existing experimental data, together with theory or numerical results.
**Ind/Abst** Chem. Abstr.; Curr. Contents Eng. Tech. Appl. Sci.; Ei Page One; Eng. Index Annu.; Fluid Abstr., Civil Eng.; Fluid Abstr. Proc. Eng.; FLUIDEX (199?-); HTFS Dig.; Int. Aerosp. Abstr.; Res. Alert [Full Cov.]; SCISEARCH.

RU
**FIZIKA I TEKHNIKA VYSOKIKH DAVLENII / AKADEMIIA NAUK UKRAINSOI SSR, DONETSKII FIZIKO-TEKHNICHESKII INSTITUT.** [Fiz. teh. vys. davlenii]. **Added/Corp** Donetskyi Fizyko-Tekhnichnyi Instytut. (1980)-. Academic Scholarly Publication. Russian (summaries and/or abstracts in English). 1.40rub. Izdatelstvo Naukova Dumka / Ukrainian Academy of Sciences, Vladimirskaia Ulitsa 54, 252601 Kiev Ukraine. **Tel** 225-63-66, telex 131376. **LC** QC281; .F59. **DD** 531/.11. **CODEN** FTVDDZ. Documents available from CASDDS.
**Ind/Abst** Chem. Abstr.

UN/0202-2915
**FIZIKA TVERDOGO TELA (DONETSKII GOSUDARSTRENNYI UNIVERSITET).** (FIZIKA TVERDOGO TELA.). [Fiz. tverd. tela]. **Added/Corp** Soviet Union. Gosudarstvennyi Komitet po Narodnomu Obrazovaniiu. Donetskyi Derzhavnyi Universytet. Kharkivskyi Derzhavnyi Universytet Imeni O.M. Horkoho. **VFOAT** Fizyka Tverdoho Tila. No. 1 (1970)-. Academic Scholarly Publication. Russian (Ukrainian). mo. $359.95. **(Subscription address:** East View Publications Inc., 3020 Harbor Lane North, Suite

110, Minneapolis MN 55447.) LC QC176; .A1F49. CODEN FZTTAA. Documents available from The Genuine Article, Ask*IEEE, CASDDS.
**Ind/Abst** Ceram. Abstr. (19??-); Chem. Abstr. (-1982); Chem. Titles; Curr. Contents Phys. Chem. Earth Sci.; INSPEC (1968-); Res. Alert [Full Cov.]; Sci. Cit. Index; SCISEARCH.

FR/0018-4357
**HOMMES ET FONDERIE.** [Hommes et fonderie]. (1970)-. Academic Scholarly Publication. French. ir. 432.00F France; 565.00F other. PYC Edition, 5 Avenue de Verdun, BP 105, 94208 Ivry S Seine Cedex France. **Tel** 011 33 1 49608636. **CODEN** HFONDM. **[CCC].** Documents available from CASDDS. ***Continues*** *Association Technique de Fonderie. Revue Mensuelle d'Information.*
**Ind/Abst** Alum. Ind. Abstr.; Chem. Abstr.; Eng. Mater. Abstr.; Met. Abstr.

GW/0340-0743
**IFF BULLETIN.** [IFF-Bull.]. **Main/Corp** Kernforschungsanlage Julich. Institut fur Festkorperforschung. **VAT** Institut fur Festkorperforschung Bulletin. Bulletin. German (English). **LC** QC176.A1; K46A.
**Ind/Abst** Energy Res. Abstr. (Oct. 1974-).

US/0927-7056
**INTERFACE SCIENCE.** English. qt. $456.00. Kluwer Academic Publishers / Massachusetts, PO Box 358, Accord Station, Hingham MA 02018. **Tel** (617)871-6600. **ED** David Srolovitz. **Pr Rev. Acid Free.**
**Desc:** A major focus of the journal is on the interfaces between dissimilar materials, such as the composite materials and films on substrates.

US/0020-7462
**INTERNATIONAL JOURNAL OF NON-LINEAR MECHANICS.** [Int. j. non-linear mech.]. Vol. 1 (Apr. 1966)-. Periodical. English. bm. $805.00 The Americas; £540.00 other. Pergamon Press, An Imprint of Elsevier Science Ltd., The Boulevard, Langford Lane, Kidlington, Oxford OX5 1GB United Kingdom. **Tel** 011 44 865 843000, 011 44 865 843699, FAX 011 44 865 843010. **(Subscription address:** Elsevier Science Ltd. Oxford Fulfillment Centre, PO Box 800, Kidlington, Oxford OX5 1DX United Kingdom.**) ED** William A. Nash. **LC** QA427; .I48. **DD** 531. **CODEN** IJNMAG. **[CCC]. Pr Rev.** available on microfilm and microfiche from University Microfilms International (UMI). Documents available from Article Express International, The Genuine Article, Ask*IEEE.
**Ind/Abst** Abstr. J. Earthq. Eng.; Acoust. Abstr.; Appl. Mech. Rev.; Bioeng. Abstr.; Civ. Struct. Eng. Abstr.; Comput. Inf. Syst. Abstr. J. [Full Cov.]; Curr. Contents Eng. Tech. Appl. Sci.; Ei Page One; Elect. Comm. Abstr.; Energy Res. Abstr.; Eng. Index Annu.; INSPEC (1968-); Int. Aerosp. Abstr.; Leadscan; Mater. Sci. Eng. Abstr.; Math. Rev.; Mech. Eng. Abstr.; Pollut. Abstr. Indexes; Res. Alert [Full Cov.]; Sci. Cit. Index; SCISEARCH; Zentralbl. Math. Ihre Grenzgeb.

RU/0578-9583
**ISSLEDOVANIIA PO UPRUGOSTI I PLASTICHNOSTI.** [Issl. uprug. plast.]. **Added/Corp** Leningrad. Universitet. Matematiko-Mekhanicheskii Fakultet. Vol. 1 (1961)-. Academic Scholarly Publication. Russian. St Petersburg State University / Izdatelstvo Leningradskogo Universiteta, Universitetskaia Nab 7/9, 199034 St Petersburg Russia. **Tel** 011 95 218-97-88, FAX 011 95 218-51-52, telex 121481. **LC** QA931 .I77. **CODEN** IDUPAI. Documents available from CASDDS.
**Ind/Abst** Chem. Abstr. (1961-1980) Int. Aerosp. Abstr.; Zentralbl. Math. Ihre Grenzgeb.

RU
**ITOGI NAUKI I TEKHNIKI : MEKHANIKA DEFORMIRUEMOGO TVERDOGO TELA.** **Added/Corp** Vsesoiuznyi Institut Nauchnoi Tekhnicheskoiinformatsii (Soviet Union). **VFOAT** Mekhanika Deformiruemogo Tverdogo Tela; Itogi Nauki I Tekhniki: Seriia Mekhanika Deformiruemogo Tverdogo Tela. Vol. 10, (1977)-. Periodical. Russian. 1.31rub. VINITI - Vsesoiuznyi Institut Nauchno-Tekhnicheskoi Informatsii, All-Union Scientific and Technical Information Institute, Baltiiskaia Ulitsa 14, 125219 Moscow Russia. **Tel** 238-46-00, FAX 9430060, telex 411160. **LC** QA801; .I765. ***Continues*** *Itogi Nauki I Tekhniki: Mekhanika Tverdykh Deformiruemykh Tel.*
**Ind/Abst** Zentralbl. Math. Ihre Grenzgeb.

RU
**ITOGI NAUKI I TEKHNIKI : OBSHCHAIA MEKHANIKA.** **Added/Corp** Vsesoiuznyi Institut Nauchnoi i Tekhnicheskoi Informatsii (Soviet Union). **VFOAT** Obshchaia Mekhanika; Itogi Nauki I Tekhniki: Seriia Obshchaia Mekhanika. Vol. 2, (1975)-. Periodical. Russian. 0.90rub. VINITI - Vsesoiuznyi Institut Nauchno-Tekhnicheskoi Informatsii, All-Union Scientific and Technical Information Institute, Baltiiskaia Ulitsa 14, 125219 Moscow Russia. **Tel** 238-46-00, FAX 9430060, telex 411160. **LC** QA801; .I77. ***Continues*** *Itogi Nauki: Obshchaia Mekhanika.*
**Ind/Abst** Zentralbl. Math. Ihre Grenzgeb.

SA/0254-1912
**JAARLIKSE SEMINAAR OOR TEORETIESE FISIKA.** (ANNUAL SEMINAR ON THEORETICAL PHYSICS : [PROCEEDINGS].). [Jaarl. Semin. Teor. Fis.]. **Added/Corp** South African Institute of Physics. Theoretical Physics. **VFOAT** Jaarlikse Seminaar oor Teoretiese Fisika B.[Verslag]. (19??)-. Afrikaans (English). an. Organization of Theoretical Physicists, Do Physics Division, Atomic Energy Board, Private Bag X256, Pretoria South Africa 0001. **CODEN** ASTPDX. Documents available from CASDDS.
**Ind/Abst** Chem. Abstr.

XR/0447-6441
**JEMNA MECHANIKA A OPTIKA.** [Jemna mech. opt.]. Began publication in 1956. Czech. mo. $101.20. **(Subscription address:** Artia Pegas Press Ltd., Palac Metro Narodni Trida 25, 11210 Prague 1 Czech Republic.**) LC** TS500; .J4. **CODEN** JMKOA5. Documents available from Ask*IEEE.
**Ind/Abst** INSPEC (1968-); Int. Aerosp. Abstr.; Saf. Health Work.

UK/0021-8928
**JOURNAL OF APPLIED MATHEMATICS AND MECHANICS.** [J. appl. math. mech.]. **Added/Corp** American Society of Mechanical Engineers. Pergamon Institute. **VFOAT** Applied Mathematics and Mechanics. Vol. 22 (1958)-. Periodical. English (Russian). Six times a year. $1230.00 The Americas; £825.00 other. Pergamon Press, An Imprint of Elsevier Science Ltd., The Boulevard, Langford Lane, Kidlington, Oxford OX5 1GB United Kingdom. **Tel** 011 44 865 843000, 011 44 865 843699, FAX 011 44 865 843010. **(Subscription address:** Elsevier Science Ltd. Oxford Fulfillment Centre, PO Box 800, Kidlington, Oxford OX5 1DX United Kingdom.**) ED** VV Rumyantsev and Iu P. Gupalo. **LC** QA801; .P713. **DD** 531.017. **CODEN** JAMMAR. **[CCC].** cum. index. available on microfilm and microfiche from University Microfilms International (UMI). Documents available from Article Express International, The Genuine Article, Ask*IEEE, CASDDS.
**Desc:** Concerned with high-level mathematical investigations of modern physical and mechanical problems and reports current progress in this field.
**Ind/Abst** Acoust. Abstr.; Bioeng. Abstr.; Chem. Abstr.; Compumath Citation Index [Full Cov.]; Ei Page One; Eng. Index Annu.; INSPEC (1968-); Int. Aerosp. Abstr.; Math. Rev.; Res. Alert [Full Cov.]; Sci. Cit. Index (19??-19??); SCISEARCH; Zentralbl. Math. Ihre Grenzgeb.

US/0193-2691
**JOURNAL OF DISPERSION SCIENCE AND TECHNOLOGY.** [J. dispers. sci. technol.]. Vol. 1 (1980)-. Academic Scholarly Publication. English. Six times a year. $445.00 US; $466.00 other. Marcel Dekker Inc., 270 Madison Avenue, New York NY 10016. **Tel** (212)696-9000, (800)228-1160, FAX (212)685-4540, telex 421419. **(Subscription address:** Marcel Dekker Inc, PO Box 5017, Monticello NY 12701.**) ED** Stig E. Friberg and Paul Becher. **LC** QD549; .J68. **DD** 541.3/451. **CODEN** JDTEDS. **[CCC]. Bk Rev. Ad Acc. Pr Rev.** ctrl circ. available on microfiche; available on microfilm; available in microform. Documents available from Article Express International, The Genuine Article, CASDDS.
**Desc:** This is the only journal dealing with dispersions on the technological level. It demonstrates the power of colloid sciences in solving real-world dispersion problems, and serves as the definitive source for researchers, educators, and all industry personnel working in this area. The journal emphasizes discussion and application of theoretical aspects, and includes both reviews of the latest findings and original research papers.
**Ind/Abst** Acoust. Abstr.; Bioeng. Abstr.; Chem. Abstr.; Chem. Titles; Curr. Contents Phys. Chem. Earth Sci.; Dairy Sci. Abstr.; Ei Page One; Eng. Index Annu.; Food Sci. Technol. Abstr.; Int. Pharm. Abstr.; Lit. Pat. Abstr., Oilfield Chem. (1982-1990); Lit. Abstr., Catal. Catal.; Lit. Abstr., Health Environ.; Lit. Abstr., Pet. Refin. Petrochem.; Lit. Abstr., Pet. Substit.; Lit. Abstr., Transp. Storage; Proc. Chem. Eng.; Res. Alert [Full Cov.]; Sci. Cit. Index; SCISEARCH; Theoret. Chem. Eng.; World Surf. Coat. Abstr.

NE/0374-3535
**JOURNAL OF ELASTICITY.** [J. elast.]. Vol. 1 (Sept. 1971)-. Periodical. English (summaries and/or abstracts in English, French and German). mo. $1,716.00. Kluwer Academic Publishers, Postbus 322, 3300 AH Dordrecht, The Netherlands. **Tel** 011 (31) 78 524400, FAX 011 31 78 183273, telex 20083. **ED** D E Carlson. **LC** QA931; .J68. **DD** 531/.3823/05. **CODEN** JELSAY. **[CCC]. Ad Acc. Pr Rev. Acid Free. Circ:** 400 (ctrl). available on microfilm and microfiche from University Microfilms International (UMI). Documents available from Article Express International, The Genuine Article, Ask*IEEE.
**Desc:** Aims to report, via full papers or research notes, original and significant discoveries in elasticity; well-documented historical essays are acceptable.
**Ind/Abst** Bioeng. Abstr.; Curr. Contents Eng. Tech. Appl. Sci.; Ei Page One; Eng. Index Annu.; GeoRef; INSPEC (Sept. 1971-); Int. Aerosp. Abstr.; Math. Rev.; Pollut. Abstr. Indexes; Res. Alert [Full Cov.]; Sci. Cit. Index; SCISEARCH; Zentralbl. Math. Ihre Grenzgeb.

US/0148-6055
**JOURNAL OF RHEOLOGY (NEW YORK, N.Y.).** (JOURNAL OF RHEOLOGY.). [J. rheol.]. **Added/Corp** Society of Rheology (U.S.). Vol. 22 (Feb. 1978)-. Academic Scholarly Publication. English. bm. $375.00 US; $385.00 Canada, Mexico, Central and South America, and the Caribbean; $395.00 other. American Institute of Physics, 500 Sunnyside Boulevard, Woodbury NY 11797-2999. **Tel** (516)576-2200, FAX (516)349-7669, telex 960983. **LC** QC189; .S6. **DD** 531/.11/05. **CODEN** JORHD2. **[CCC]. Ad Acc. Pr Rev. Circ:** 1,900. Documents available from Article Express International, The Genuine Article, Ask*IEEE, CASDDS. ***Continues*** *Transactions of the Society of Rheology, 0038-0032.*
**Desc:** Contains detailed articles on the science of the deformation and flow of matter. Serving especially those in plastics, rubbers, paint coatings, fibers and structural materials. It also covers dispersions and includes salient abstracts from the Journal of the Society of Rheology, Japan.
**Ind/Abst** Abstr. Bull. Inst. Pap. Sci. Tech.; Abstr. Graphic Arts Tech. Found. (1984); Art Archaeol. Tech. Abstr.; Bioeng. Abstr.; Ceram. Abstr.; Chem. Abstr.; Crop Physiol. Abstr.; Curr. Contents Phys. Chem. Earth Sci.; Ei Page One; Energy Res. Abstr. (Oct. 1979-); Eng. Mater. Abstr.; Eng. Index Annu.; Field Crop Abstr.; Food Sci. Technol. Abstr.; Hortic. Abstr.; INIS Atomindex [Micro.]; INSPEC (Feb. 1978-); Int. Aerosp. Abstr.; Math. Rev.; Polymer Contents; Postharvest News Inf.; Potato Abstr.; Res. Alert [Full Cov.]; Sci. Cit. Index; SCISEARCH; SPIN (1980-); Zentralbl. Math. Ihre Grenzgeb.

JA
**KENKYU ROMBUN SHOROKU SHU.** **Main/Corp** Kyushu Daigaki, Fukuoka Japan. Tokyo Rikigaku Kenkyujo. **VFOAT** Abstracts of Papers. Multiple languages (English and Japanese). Kyushu Daigaku Oyo Rikigaku Kenkyujo, 10-1 Hakozaki 6, Higashi-ku 812 Fukuoka Japan. **LC** TA349; .K97A.

BE/0377-8312
**LECTURE SERIES - VON KARMAN INSTITUTE FOR FLUID DYNAMICS.** **See** Engineering-Hydraulic Engineering.

CC
**LI HSUEH CHIN CHAN.** **VFOAT** Advances in Mechanics. Periodical. Chinese. qt. RMBY0.80. Hsin Hua Shu Tien, Beijing, People's Republic of China. **Tel** 551253. **LC** QC120; .L5. **DD** 531/.05.

CC/1000-0879
**LIXUE YU SHIJIAN.** (LI HSUEH YU SHIH CHIEN / MECHANICS AND PRACTICE.). [Lixue yu shijian]. **Added/Corp** Chung-kuo Li Hsueh Hsueh Hui. **VFOAT** Mechanics and Practice. (19??)-. Academic Scholarly Publication. Chinese. bm. $76.80. Science Press, 16 Donghuangchenggen North Street, Beijing 100707, People's Republic of China. **Tel** 011 86 1 4019821, 011 86 1 4010642, FAX 011 86 1 4012180, 011 86 1 4019810, telex 210147. **(Subscription address:** China International Book Trading Corporation, PO Box 399, Library Service Department, Beijing 100044 People's Republic of China.**) ED** Ben Lan-Gui. **LC** TA349; .L5. **DD** 620.1. **Ad Acc. Circ:** 16,000.
**Ind/Abst** Math. Rev.

NE/0025-6455
**MECCANICA (MILAN).** (MECCANICA.). [Meccanica]. **Added/Corp** Associazione Italiana di Meccanica Teorica e Applicata. Vol. 1 (1966)-. Periodical. English (Italian; summaries and/or abstracts in Italian). qt. $578.00. Kluwer Academic Publishers, Postbus 322, 3300 AH Dordrecht, The Netherlands. **Tel** 011 (31) 78 524400, FAX 011 31 78 183273, telex 20083. **ED** G. Augusti. **LC** QA801; .M395. **CODEN** MECCB9. Index available. **Bk Rev. Ad Acc. Pr Rev. Acid Free. Circ:** 1,000. available on microfilm and microfiche from University Microfilms International (UMI). Documents available from Ask*IEEE, CASDDS.
**Desc:** Encompasses theoretical and applied mechanics, and all their branches: mechanics of fluids, mechanics of solids, mechanics of structures, mechanics of machines, computational mechanics, stochastic mechanics, etc.
**Ind/Abst** Acoust. Abstr.; Chem. Abstr.; Ei Page One; Fluid Abstr., Civil Eng. March 1968-; Fluid Abstr. Proc. Eng.; FLUIDEX (1973-1990); INSPEC (1968-); Int. Aerosp. Abstr.; Math. Rev.; Pollut. Abstr. Indexes; Shock Vibr. Dig.; Zentralbl. Math. Ihre Grenzgeb.

NE/0921-9749
**MECHANICS AND MATHEMATICAL METHODS SECOND SERIES, THERMAL STRESSERS.** (1986)-. Monographic series. English. ir. Price varies per volume. Elsevier Science Publishers BV, PO Box 211, 1000 AE Amsterdam Netherlands. **Tel** 011 31 20 5803642, FAX 011 31 20 5862696, telex 15682. **UDC** 531.
**Ind/Abst** Zentralbl. Math. Ihre Grenzgeb.

NE/0921-9331
**MECHANICS AND MATHEMATICAL METHODS. THIRD SERIES, ACOUSTIC, ELECTROMAGNETIC, AND ELASTIC WAVE SCATTERING.** [Mech. math. methods, Third ser. Acoust. electromagn. elast. wave scatt.]. **VFOAT** Handbook on Acoustic, Electromagnetic, and

Elastic Wave Scattering. (198?)-. Monographic series. English. Price varies per volume. Elsevier Science Publishers BV, PO Box 211, 1000 AE Amsterdam Netherlands. **Tel** 011 31 20 5803642, FAX 011 31 20 5862696, telex 15682. **CODEN** MMMEEM.
**Ind/Abst** Math. Rev.; Zentralbl. Math. Ihre Grenzgeb.

NE/0926-9282
**MECHANICS AND PHYSICS OF DISCRETE SYSTEMS.** [Mech. phys. discrete syst.]. (1988)-. Monographic series. English. ir. Price varies per volume. Elsevier Science Publishers BV, PO Box 211, 1000 AE Amsterdam Netherlands. **Tel** 011 31 20 5803642, FAX 011 31 20 5862696, telex 15682. **UDC** 531.
**Ind/Abst** Math. Rev.; Zentralbl. Math. Ihre Grenzgeb.

NE/0924-2139
**MECHANICS OF STRUCTURAL SYSTEMS.** [Mech. struct. syst.]. (1973)-. Monographic series. English. ir. Price varies per volume. Sijthoff & Noordhoff International Publications, 20010 Century Boulevard, Germantown MD 20767. **UDC** 531.
**Ind/Abst** Zentralbl. Math. Ihre Grenzgeb.

US/0093-6413
**MECHANICS RESEARCH COMMUNICATIONS.** [Mech. res. commun.]. **Added/Corp** International Centre for Mechanical Sciences. Vol. 1 (1974)-. Periodical. English. bm. $523.00 The Americas; £351.00 other. Pergamon Press, An Imprint of Elsevier Science Ltd., The Boulevard, Langford Lane, Kidlington, Oxford OX5 1GB United Kingdom. **Tel** 011 44 865 843000, 011 44 865 843699, FAX 011 44 865 843010. **(Subscription address:** Elsevier Science Ltd. Oxford Fulfillment Centre, PO Box 800, Kidlington, Oxford OX5 1DX United Kingdom.**) ED** Bruno A. Boley. **LC** TA349; .M425. **DD** 620.1/005. **CODEN** MRCOD2. **[CCC]. Pr Rev.** available on microfilm and microfiche from University Microfilms International (UMI). Documents available from Article Express International, The Genuine Article, Ask*IEEE.
**Ind/Abst** Acoust. Abstr.; Appl. Mech. Rev.; Curr. Contents Eng. Tech. Appl. Sci.; Ei Page One; Eng. Index Annu. [Select. Cov.]; INSPEC (1974-); Int. Aerosp. Abstr.; Math. Rev.; Res. Alert [Full Cov.]; Sci. Cit. Index; SCISEARCH; Shock Vibr. Dig.; Zentralbl. Math. Ihre Grenzgeb.

PL/0079-3701
**MECHANIKA TEORETYCZNA I STOSOWANA.** (MECHANIKA TEORETYCZNA I STOSOWANA / POLSKIE TOWARZYSTWO MECHANIKI TEORETYCZNEJ I STOSOWANEJ.). [Mech. teor. stosow.]. **Added/Corp** Polskie Towarzystwo Mechaniki Teoretycznej i Stosowanej. (1963)-. Periodical. Polish (summaries and/or abstracts in English and Russian). qt. $80.00. **(Subscription address:** ARS Polona, PO Box 1001, 00068 Warsaw Poland.**) LC** QA801; .M36. **CODEN** MTYSAX. Documents available from Article Express International, Ask*IEEE.
**Ind/Abst** Bioeng. Abstr.; Ei Page One; Eng. Index Annu.; INSPEC (1968-); Int. Aerosp. Abstr.; Math. Rev.; Zentralbl. Math. Ihre Grenzgeb.

UN/0321-1975
**MEHANIKA TVERDOGO TELA (KIEV).** (MEKHANIKA TVERDOGO TELA.). [Meh. tverd. tela]. **Added/Corp** Instytut Prykladnoi Matematyky i Mekhaniky (Akademiia Nauk Ukrainskoi RSR). (1969)-. Periodical. Russian. Six times a year. Price varies. **(Subscription address:** East View Publications Inc., 3020 Harbor Lane North, Suite 110, Minneapolis MN 55447.**) [CCC].** Documents available from Ask*IEEE.
**Ind/Abst** INSPEC (1972-1989); Int. Aerosp. Abstr. (1983-); Math. Rev.; Zentralbl. Math. Ihre Grenzgeb.

GW
**MITTEILUNGEN / GESELLSCHAFT FUER ANGEWANDTE MATHEMATIK UND MECHANIK.** **See** Mathematics.

RU/0201-8268
**MODELIROVANIE V MEKHANIKE / AKADEMIIA NAUK SSSR, SIBIRSKOE OTDELENIE, VYCHISLITELNYI TSENTR [I] INSTITUT TEORETICHESKOI I PRIKLADNOI MEKHANIKI.** **Added/Corp** Akademiia Nauk SSSR. Sibirskoe Otdelenie. Vychislitelnyi Tsentr. Institut Teoreticheskoi i Prikladnoi Mekhaniki (Akademiia Nauk SSSR). Vol. 1, No. 1 (1987)-. Monographic series. Russian. Price varies per volume. **LC** QA808.2; .C5. ***Continues*** *Chislennye Metody Mekhaniki Sploshnoi Sredy, 1010-5581.*
**Ind/Abst** Math. Rev.; Zentralbl. Math. Ihre Grenzgeb.

US/0892-7022
**MOLECULAR SIMULATION.** [Mol. simul.]. Vol. 1, No. 1 and 2 (1987)-. Academic Scholarly Publication. English. $543.00 (academic institutions), $847.00 (corporate institutions). Gordon & Breach Science Publishers, Inc., PO Box 786, Cooper Station, New York NY 10276. **Tel** (212)206-8900, FAX (212)645-2459. **LC** QC167.5; .M64. **DD** 539/.6. **CODEN** MOSIEA. **[CCC].** Documents available from The Genuine Article, CASDDS.
**Ind/Abst** Chem. Abstr.; Curr. Contents Phys. Chem. Earth Sci.; Res. Alert [Full Cov.]; Sci. Cit. Index.

US/0027-1330
**MOSCOW UNIVERSITY MECHANICS BULLETIN.** [Moscow Univ. mech. bull.]. **Main/Corp** Moskovskii Gosudarstvennyi Universitet IM. M. V. Lomonosova. **VFOAT** Mechanics Bulletin. (1969)-. Bulletin. English (Russian). Six times a year. $745.00. Allerton Press, Inc., 150 Fifth Avenue, New York NY 10011. **Tel** (212)924-3950, FAX (212)463-9684, telex 427441 ALPRES. **CODEN** MUVMB8. **[CCC].** Documents available from Article Express International, CASDDS.
**Ind/Abst** Bioeng. Abstr.; Chem. Abstr.; Ei Page One; Eng. Index Annu.; Int. Aerosp. Abstr.; Zentralbl. Math. Ihre Grenzgeb.

GW
**NOTES ON NUMERICAL FLUID MECHANICS.** Vol. 1 (1978)-. Monographic series. English. ir. Price varies per volume. Vieweg Publishing, PO Box 5829, D 65048 Wiesbaden Germany. **Tel** 011 49 611 160230, FAX 011 49 611 160229. **LC** UNC.
**Ind/Abst** Math. Rev.; Zentralbl. Math. Ihre Grenzgeb.

US/1046-6789
**PROCEEDINGS OF THE SOCIETY FOR EXPERIMENTAL MECHANICS.** [Proc. Soc. Exp. Mech.]. **Main/Corp** Society for Experimental Mechanics (U.S.). **VFOAT** Experimental Mechanics. Vol. 41 (1984)-. Proceedings. English. an. $106.00 Connecticut (includes sales tax); $100.00 other. Society for Experimental Mechanics, 7 School Street, Bethel CT 06801-1405. **Tel** (203)790-6373, FAX (203)790-4472. **DD** 620. **[CCC]. Pr Rev.** available on microfilm from University Microfilms International (UMI). ***Continues*** *Society for Experimental Stress Analysis. Proceedings of the Society for Experimental Stress Analysis.*
**Ind/Abst** BMT Abstr. (-199?).

JA/0033-068X
**PROGRESS OF THEORETICAL PHYSICS.** [Prog. theor. phys.]. **Added/Corp** Kyoto Daigaku. Kiso Butsurigaku Kenkyujo. Nihon Butsuri Gakkai. Vol. 1 (July 1946)-. Periodical. English. Sixteen times a year. $750.00. Progress of Theoretical Physics, c/o Yukawa Hall, Kyoto University, Kyoto 606 Japan. **Tel** (075)722-3540. **(Subscription address:** Maruzen Company Ltd., PO Box 5050, Import & Export Department, Tokyo 100 31 Japan.**) ED** Y. Abe, T. Inami, T. Kawasaki, T. Kugo, Y. Kuramoto, Z. Maki, T. Maskawa, H. Sato, M. Yamamura, T. Tsuzuki, M. Yoshimura, K. Fujikawa, K. Yazaki and Y. Nagaoka. **LC** QC1; .P885. **DD** 530.1/5. **CODEN** PTPKAV. **[CCC].** Index available. cum. index. **Pr Rev.** available on microfiche; available on microfilm. Documents available from The Genuine Article, Ask*IEEE, CASDDS.
**Desc:** Publishes original theoretical papers in particles and fields, nuclear physics, solid state physics, statistical physics, astrophysics and cosmology. There is also a section which is devoted to the rapid dissemination of works in short communication; this section also includes reports on experimental results connected with theoretical developments.
**Ind/Abst** Chem. Abstr.; Curr. Contents Phys. Chem. Earth Sci.; GeoRef; INSPEC (1968-); Int. Aerosp. Abstr.; Math. Rev.; Res. Alert [Full Cov.]; Sci. Cit. Index; SCISEARCH.

UK
**RECENT ADVANCES IN NUMERICAL METHODS IN FLUIDS / EDITED BY TAYLOR AND K. MORGAN.** Vol. 1 (1980)-. English. ir. £50.00. Pineridge Press Ltd, Journals Division, 54 Newton Road, Mumbles Swansea SA3 4BQ Wales. **Tel** 011 44 792 361557, FAX 011 44 792 295532.
**Ind/Abst** Zentralbl. Math. Ihre Grenzgeb.

GW
**RHEOLOGY.** English (German). qt. Curt R. Vincentz Verlag, Postfach 6247, D 30062 Hannover Germany. **Tel** 011 49 511 990980, FAX 011 49 511 9909899, telex 923846. Documents available from The Genuine Article.
**Ind/Abst** Fluid Abstr., Civil Eng.; Fluid Abstr. Proc. Eng.; FLUIDEX (19??-); Res. Alert [Full Cov.].

UK/0035-452X
**RHEOLOGY ABSTRACTS.** [Rheol. abstr.]. **Added/Corp** British Society of Rheology. Vol. 1 (1958)-. English. qt. $380.00 The Americas; £255.00 other. Pergamon Press, An Imprint of Elsevier Science Ltd., The Boulevard, Langford Lane, Kidlington, Oxford OX5 1GB United Kingdom. **Tel** 011 44 865 843000, 011 44 865 843699, FAX 011 44 865 843010. **(Subscription address:** Elsevier Science Ltd. Oxford Fulfillment Centre, PO Box 800, Kidlington, Oxford OX5 1DX United Kingdom.**) ED** G. Brownsey. **LC** QC189; .R53. **DD** 531/.11. **NLM** ZQC 189 R471. **CODEN** RHABA3. **[CCC].** Index available. available on microfilm and microfiche from University Microfilms International (UMI). ***Supersedes in part*** *British Society of Rheology. Bulletin - British Society of Rheology.*
**Desc:** Aims at covering any paper which describes work within the science and practice of rheology, the study of deformation and flow. Comprehensive sources of abstracts from many disciplines are used to help increase the area of knowledge available to researchers in this field.

JA/0559-8516
**SHINKU.** [Shinku]. **Added/Corp** Nihon Shinku Kyokai. **VFOAT** Journal of the Vacuum Society of Japan. (1958)-. Academic Scholarly Publication. Japanese (Japanese; summaries and/or abstracts in English). Twelve times a year. $192.00. Nihon Shinku Kyokai, (Vacuum Society of Japan), 5-8, Shiba Koen 3 Chome, Minatoku, Tokyoto 105, Japan. **(Subscription address:** Kyowa Book Company Inc., 1 38 Kanda Jinbocho Chiyoda-ku, Tokyo 101 Japan.**) CODEN** SHINAM. ctrl circ. Documents available from Ask*IEEE, CASDDS. ***Formed by the union of*** *Shinku Kogyo* ***and*** *Shinku Gijutsu.*
**Ind/Abst** Chem. Abstr.; Eng. Mater. Abstr.; INSPEC (1972-).

GW/0938-1287
**SHOCK WAVES.** [Shock waves]. Vol. 1, No. 1 (Mar. 1991)-. Periodical. English. Six times a year. DM368.00. Springer-Verlag GmbH & Company KG, Heidelberger Platz 3, D 14197 Berlin Germany. **Tel** 011 49 30 8207223, FAX 011 49 30 8214091, telex 183 319 SPBLN D. **(Subscription address:** Springer Verlag New York Inc. / for North America, 44 Hartz Way, Secaucus NJ 07096.**) ED** I I Glass. **CODEN** SHWAEN. **[CCC]. Pr Rev. Circ:** 400 (ctrl). available on microfilm and microfiche from University Microfilms International (UMI). Documents available from Ask*IEEE.
**Desc:** Aimed at publishing theoretical and experimental results on shock-wave phenomena in gases, liquids, solids, and two-phase media from both the fundamental research and the applications point of view.
**Ind/Abst** INSPEC (March 1991-); Int. Aerosp. Abstr.

US/0896-5900
**SOLID STATE AND SUPERCONDUCTIVITY ABSTRACTS.** **See** Physics-Abstracting, Bibliographies and Statistics.

UK
**SPON'S MECHANICAL ELECTRICAL SERVICES PRICE BOOK.** English. an (includes three updates). £45.00. International Thompson Publishing Services Ltd, North Way, Cheriton House, Andover Hampshire SP10 5BE England. **Tel** 011 44 264 342840.

NE/0081-8542
**STUDIES IN STATISTICAL MECHANICS.** [Stud. stat. mech.]. Vol. 1, (1962)-. Statistical Publication. English. ir. Price varies. Elsevier Science Publishers BV, PO Box 211, 1000 AE Amsterdam Netherlands. **Tel** 011 31 20 5803642, FAX 011 31 20 5862696, telex 15682. **ED** E.W. Montroll and J.L. Lebowitz. **LC** QC175; .S77. **CODEN** SSTMBG. Documents available from Ask*IEEE, CASDDS.
**Ind/Abst** Chem. Abstr.; INSPEC; Zentralbl. Math. Ihre Grenzgeb.

RM/0039-4017
**STUDII SI CERCETARI DE MECANICA APLICATA.** (STUDII SI CERCETARI DE MECANICA APLICATA / ACADEMIA REPUBLICII POPULARE ROMINE, INSTITUTUL DE MECANICA APLICATA.). [Stud. cercet. mec. apl.]. **Added/Corp** Institutul de Mecanica Aplicata. Institutul de Mecanica Aplicata "Traian Vuia." Academia Romana. Vol. 5, (1954)-. Periodical. Romanian. bm (6 issues). DM321.00. **(Subscription address:** Kubon & Sagner, ABT Zeitschriftenimport, D 80328 Munich Germany.**) LC** TA350; .A3. **CODEN** SCMAA2. Documents available from CASDDS. ***Continues in part*** *Studii si Cercetari de Mecanica si Metalurgie, 0039-4017.*
**Desc:** Publishes studies on applied mechanics.
**Ind/Abst** Alum. Ind. Abstr.; Chem. Abstr. (1955-1983); Eng. Mater. Abstr.; Int. Aerosp. Abstr.; Math. Rev.; Met. Abstr.; Surf. Treat. Technol. Abstr.

BU
**TEORETICHNA I PRILOZHNA MEKHANIKA / BULGARSKA AKADEMIIA NA NAUKITE, NATSIONALEN KOMITET PO TEORETICHNA I PRILOZHNA MEKHANIKA.** **Added/Corp** Bulgarska Akademiia na Naukite. Natsionalen Komitet po Teoretichna i Prilozhna Mekhanika. **VFOAT** Theoretical and Applied Mechanics. (1969)-. Bulgarian (English, German and Russian). Four times a year. DM162.00. **(Subscription address:** Kubon & Sagner, ABT Zeitschriftenimport, D 80328 Munich Germany.**) LC** QA801; .N28a.
**Ind/Abst** Zentralbl. Math. Ihre Grenzgeb.

YU/0353-8249
**TEORIJSKA I PRIMENJENA MEHANIKA.** [Teor. primenj. meh.]. **VFOAT** Theoretical and Applied Mechanics; Teoreticeskaja i Prikladnaja Mehanika. (1975)-. Periodical. Multiple languages. ir.

US/0939-2475
**TEXTS IN APPLIED MATHEMATICS.** [Texts appl. math.]. **VFOAT** TAM. (1988)-. Monographic series. English. ir. Price varies per volume. Springer

Verlag New York Inc., PO Box 19386 Books, Newark NJ 07195. **Tel** (201)348-4033.
**Ind/Abst** Zentralbl. Math. Ihre Grenzgeb.

NE/0167-8442
**THEORETICAL AND APPLIED FRACTURE MECHANICS.** [Theor. appl. fract. mech.]. Vol. 1, No. 1 (March 1984)-. Academic Scholarly Publication. English. Six times a year (2 vols.). Fl902.00. Elsevier Science Publishers BV, PO Box 211, 1000 AE Amsterdam Netherlands. **Tel** 011 31 20 5803642, FAX 011 31 20 5862696, telex 15682. **ED** G C Sih. **[CCC]. Pr Rev.** available on microfilm and microfiche from University Microfilms International (UMI). Documents available from Article Express International, The Genuine Article, Ask*IEEE.
**Desc:** Devoted to research in the theoretical and experimental aspects of material damage.
**Ind/Abst** Curr. Contents Eng. Tech. Appl. Sci.; Curr. Titles Electrochem.; Ei Page One; Eng. Mater. Abstr.; Eng. Index Annu.; GeoRef; Health Saf. Sci. Abstr.; INSPEC (1985-); Int. Aerosp. Abstr. (1984-); Math. Rev. (1985-); Pollut. Abstr. Indexes; Res. Alert [Full Cov.]; Sci. Cit. Index; SCISEARCH; Shock Vibr. Dig.

YU/0350-2708
**THEORETICAL AND APPLIED MECHANICS.** (THEORETICAL AND APPLIED MECHANICS / YUGOSLAV SOCIETY OF MECHANICS.). [Theor. appl. mech.]. **VFOAT** Teoreticheskaia I Prikladnaia Mekhanika; Teorijska I Primenjena Mehanika. 1 (1975)-. Periodical. English (Russian, French and German). an. Prirodno-Matematicki Fakultet Institut za Mehaniku, Postanski Pregradak 550, 11000 Belgrad Yugoslavia.
**Ind/Abst** Abstr. J. Earthq. Eng. (?-?); Math. Rev.

US/0041-1450
**TRANSPORT THEORY AND STATISTICAL PHYSICS.** [Transp. theory stat. phys.]. Vol. 1 (Jan. 1971)-. Statistical Publication. English. Nine times a year. $895.00 US; $926.50 other. Marcel Dekker Inc., 270 Madison Avenue, New York NY 10016. **Tel** (212)696-9000, (800)228-1160, FAX (212)685-4540, telex 421419. **(Subscription address:** Marcel Dekker Inc, PO Box 5017, Monticello NY 12701.**) ED** Paul Nelson, G. D. Allen, Chia-Ren Hu, George W. Kattawar. **LC** QC175.2; .T73. **DD** 531/.1137/05. **CODEN** TTSPB4. **[CCC]. Bk Rev. Ad Acc.** ctrl circ. available on microfiche. Documents available from Article Express International, Ask*IEEE, CASDDS.
**Desc:** With emphasis on fundamental studies, this unique journal covers such diverse areas as neutral-particle transport, kinetic theory, radiative transfer, charged-particle transport, macroscopic transport phenomena, and articles devoted to topics such as novel computational methods, convergence theorems, and mathematical existence and uniqueness results. Offering a range of information and research methodologies unavailable elsewhere, 'Transport Theory and Statistical Physics' brings together closely related mathematical concepts and techniques used in many areas of study to encourage a productive, interdisciplinary exchange of ideas.
**Ind/Abst** Bioeng. Abstr.; Chem. Abstr.; Ei Page One; Energy Res. Abstr. (Nov. 1971-); Eng. Index Annu.; INSPEC (Jan. 1971-); Int. Aerosp. Abstr.; Math. Rev.; SPIN (1981-); Zentralbl. Math. Ihre Grenzgeb.

PL/0137-3722
**USPEKHI MEKHANIKI.** [Usp. meh.]. **Added/Corp** Institut po Mekhaniki i BNiomekhanika (Bulgarska Akademiia na Naukite). **VFOAT** Advances in Mechanics. (1978)-. Periodical. Russian (summaries and/or abstracts in English). qt. Z720.00 Poland; $80.00 US. Wydawnictwa Ippt Pan, Swietokrzyska 21, 00-049 Warszawa Poland. **Tel** 26 60 22, telex 815 638. **LC** QA801; .U86. **Circ:** 650.
**Ind/Abst** Int. Aerosp. Abstr. (1982-); Math. Rev.; Zentralbl. Math. Ihre Grenzgeb.

UK/0042-207X
**VACUUM.** [Vacuum]. Vol. 1 (Jan. 1951)-. Academic Scholarly Publication. English. mo. $924.00 The Americas; £620.00 other. Pergamon Press, An Imprint of Elsevier Science Ltd., The Boulevard, Langford Lane, Kidlington, Oxford OX5 1GB United Kingdom. **Tel** 011 44 865 843000, 011 44 865 843699, FAX 011 44 865 843010. **(Subscription address:** Elsevier Science Ltd. Oxford Fulfillment Centre, PO Box 800, Kidlington, Oxford OX5 1DX United Kingdom.**) ED** T.L. Barr, L. Holland, L.G. Hultman. **LC** QC166; .V33. **DD** 533.12*. **NLM** W1 VA244. **CODEN** VACUAV. **[CCC]. Pr Rev.** available on microfilm and microfiche from University Microfilms International (UMI). Documents available from Article Express International, The Genuine Article, Ask*IEEE, CASDDS.
**Desc:** International forum for the publication of original papers dealing with all aspects of vacuum research and technology concerned with an environment in which the total gas pressure is below that of the atmosphere.
**Ind/Abst** Alum. Ind. Abstr.; Anal. Abstr.; Appl. Sci. Technol. Index; Bioeng. Abstr.; Chem. Abstr.; Curr. Contents Eng. Tech. Appl. Sci.; Curr. Contents Phys. Chem. Earth Sci.; Curr. Technol. Index; Ei Page One; Eng. Mater. Abstr.; Eng. Index Annu.; Fluid Abstr., Civil Eng.; Fluid Abstr. Proc. Eng.; FLUIDEX (1973-1989); INSPEC (1968-); Int. Aerosp. Abstr.; Mass Spect. Bull.; Met. Abstr.; Res. Alert [Full Cov.]; Sci. Cit. Index; SCISEARCH; Surf. Treat. Technol. Abstr.

RU
**VOPROSY KVANTOVOI TEORII ATOMOV I MOLEKUL.** **Added/Corp** Leningradskii Gosudarstvennyi Universitet Imeni A.A. Zhdanova. Vol. 1 (1978)-. Periodical. Russian. 2.25rub single issue. St Petersburg State University / Izdatelstvo Leningradskogo Universiteta, Universitetskaia Nab 7/9, 199034 St Petersburg Russia. **Tel** 011 95 218-97-88, FAX 011 95 218-51-52, telex 121481. **LC** QC173.96; .V36.

KO
**YONGU NONMUNJIP (PUSAN TAEHAKKYO. MULSONG YONGUSO).** (YONGU NONMUNJIP.). **Added/Corp** Pusan Taehakkyo. Mulsong Yonguso. (19??)-. Periodical. English (Korean). an. Pusan Taehakkyo Mulsong Yonguso, San 30 Tongnae-ku, Pusan Korea. **LC** QC172; .Y66.

---

## HEAT

---

US/0065-2482
**ADVANCES IN CRYOGENIC ENGINEERING.** **See** Engineering.

US/0886-1587
**ADVANCES IN CRYOGENIC ENGINEERING MATERIALS.** **See** Engineering.

US/0065-2717
**ADVANCES IN HEAT TRANSFER.** [Adv. heat transf.]. Vol. 1 (1964)-. Academic Scholarly Publication. English. ir. $129.00 (Vol. 25). Academic Press, Inc., 6277 Sea Harbor Drive, Orlando FL 32887. **Tel** (800)543-9534, (407)345-4100, FAX (407)363-9661. **ED** Thomas F. Irvine Jr. and James P. Hartnett. **LC** QC320.A1; A3. **DD** 536.2082. **UDC** 536.24. **CODEN** AHTRAR. **[CCC].** Documents available from Ask*IEEE.
**Ind/Abst** Energy Res. Abstr.; GeoRef; HTFS Dig.; INIS Atomindex [Micro.]; INSPEC.

US/0271-2334
**ADVANCES IN TRANSPORT PROCESSES.** ***Ceased.*** [Adv. transp. processes]. Vol. 1-?. Academic Scholarly Publication. English. ir. John Wiley & Sons, Inc., 605 Third Avenue, New York NY 10158-0012. **Tel** (212)850-6000, (212)850-6645, FAX (212)850-6088, telex 12-7063. **(Subscription address:** John Wiley & Sons / England, Baffins Lane, Chichester, West Sussex PO19 1UD England.**) LC** QC319.8; .A35. **DD** 531/.1137. **CODEN** ATRPDU. Documents available from CASDDS.
**Ind/Abst** Chem. Abstr.; Ei Page One.

US/1049-0787
**ANNUAL REVIEW OF HEAT TRANSFER.** ***Ceased.*** **See** Physics-Analytic and Experimental Mechanics.

PL/0208-4198
**ARCHIVUM COMBUSTIONIS.** (ARCHIVUM COMBUSTIONIS / POLSKA AKADEMIA NAUK, KOMITET TERMODYNAMIKI I SPALANIA.). [Arch. combust.]. **Added/Corp** Polska Akademia Nauk. Komitet Termodynamiki i Spalania. Akademiia Nauk. Komitet Ssgoraniia. Vol. 1, No. 1/2 (1981)-. Academic Scholarly Publication. English (Russian). qt. $52.00. **(Subscription address:** ARS Polona, PO Box 1001, 00068 Warsaw Poland.**) CODEN** ACOMEO. Documents available from CASDDS. ***Continues in part*** *Archiwum Termodynamiki i Spalania.*
**Ind/Abst** Chem. Abstr.; Ei Page One; Int. Aerosp. Abstr.

PL/0208-418X
**ARCHIWUM TERMODYNAMIKI.** (ARCHIWUM TERMODYNAMIKI / POLSKA AKADEMIA NAUK, KOMITET TERMODYNAMIKI I SPALANIA.). [Arch. termodyn.]. **Added/Corp** Polska Akademia Nauk. Komitet Termodynamiki i Spalania. **VFOAT** Archives of Thermodynamics. Vol. 1, No. 1 (1980)-. Academic Scholarly Publication. English (Polish; summaries and/or abstracts in Russian). qt. $52.00. **(Subscription address:** ARS Polona, PO Box 1001, 00068 Warsaw Poland.**) LC** TJ265; .A63. **CODEN** ATERD5. Documents available from CASDDS. ***Continues in part*** *Archiwum Termodynamiki i Spalania.*
**Ind/Abst** Chem. Abstr.; Coal Abstr.

FR/0013-9084
**ENTROPIE.** **See** Engineering.

UK/0891-6152
**EXPERIMENTAL HEAT TRANSFER.** [Exp. heat transf.]. Vol. 1, No. 1 (1987)-. Periodical. English. qt. £124.00 UK; $205.00 other. Taylor & Francis Ltd., Rankine Road, Basingstoke Hampshire, RG24 8PR United Kingdom. **Tel** 011 44 256 840366, FAX 011 44 256 479438, telex 858540. **(Subscription address:** Taylor & Francis Inc., 1900 Frost Road, Suite 101, Bristol PA 19007-1598.**) ED** G. F. Hewitt (editor's address: Department of Chemical Engineering and Chemical Technology, Imperial College, London SW7 2BY United Kingdom); C. L. Tien (editor's address: Office of the Chancellor, University of California, Berkeley, CA 94720). **LC** TJ260; .E95. **DD** 621.402/2/05. **CODEN** EXHTEV. **[CCC].** Index available. **Bk Rev. Ad Acc. Circ:** 300. available on microfilm and microfiche from University Microfilms International (UMI). Documents available from Article Express International, Ask*IEEE, CASDDS.
**Desc:** Provides an important forum for research on measurement techniques, and results of experimental studies in heat and mass transfer as well as related fluid flows. Contributions to this journal establish an important foundation for understanding the phenomena of heat and mass transfer. The journal publishes original experimental information which enhances the basic understanding of heat and mass transfer and fluid flow problems and their applications; papers on experiments with theory, analysis and numerical studies are welcome.
**Ind/Abst** Abstr. Bull. Inst. Pap. Sci. Tech.; Chem. Abstr.; Ei Page One; Eng. Index Annu.; HTFS Dig.; INSPEC (1990-).

US/0894-1777
**EXPERIMENTAL THERMAL AND FLUID SCIENCE.** **See** Physics-Analytic and Experimental Mechanics.

UN/0132-6414
**FIZIKA NIZKIH TEMPERATUR (KIEV).** (FIZIKA NIZKIKH TEMPERATUR.). [Fiz. nizk. temp.]. **Added/Corp** Akademiia Nauk Ukrainskoi RSR. Viddil Fizyky. **VFOAT** Low Temperature Physics. (1975)-. Academic Scholarly Publication. Russian (summaries and/or abstracts in English; table of contents in English). mo. $249.95. Izdatelstvo Naukova Dumka / Ukrainian Academy of Sciences, Vladimirskaia Ulitsa 54, 252601 Kiev Ukraine. **Tel** 225-63-66, telex 131376. **(Subscription address:** East View Publications Inc., 3020 Harbor Lane North, Suite 110, Minneapolis MN 55447.**) LC** QC278; .F59. **CODEN** FNTEDK. Documents available from The Genuine Article, Ask*IEEE, CASDDS.
**Ind/Abst** Chem. Abstr.; Curr. Contents Phys. Chem. Earth Sci.; Ei Page One; INSPEC (1975-); Int. Aerosp. Abstr.; Leadscan; Res. Alert [Full Cov.]; Sci. Cit. Index; SCISEARCH.

CC/0253-231X
**GONGCHENG REWULI XUEBAO.** (KUNG CHENG JE WU LI HSUEH PAO.). [Gongcheng rewuli xuebao]. **Added/Corp** Chung-Kuo Kung Cheng je wu li Hsueh Hui. **VFOAT** Journal of Engineering Thermodynamics; Journal of Engineering Thermophysics. Vol. 1 (Feb. 1980)-. Academic Scholarly Publication. Chinese (summaries and/or abstracts in English). qt. $71.60. Science Press, 16 Donghuangchenggen North Street, Beijing 100707, People's Republic of China. **Tel** 011 86 1 4019821, 011 86 1 4010642, FAX 011 86 1 4012180, 011 86 1 4019810, telex 210147. **LC** QC310.15; .K86. **DD** 621.402/1/05. **CODEN** KCJPDF. Documents available from CASDDS.
**Ind/Abst** Chem. Abstr.; Coal Abstr.; Fluid Abstr., Civil Eng.; Fluid Abstr. Proc. Eng.; FLUIDEX (1980-); Int. Aerosp. Abstr.

GW
**HEAT AND MASS TRANSFER.** (19??)-. English. Six times a year. DM988.00. Springer-Verlag GmbH & Company KG, Heidelberger Platz 3, D 14197 Berlin Germany. **Tel** 011 49 30 8207223, FAX 011 49 30 8214091, telex 183 319 SPBLN D. **(Subscription address:** Springer Verlag New York Inc. / for North America, 44 Hartz Way, Secaucus NJ 07096.**)** ***Continues*** *Waerme- und Stoffuebertragung.*

IT/0392-8764
**HEAT AND TECHNOLOGY.** [Heat Technol.]. **VFOAT** Calore e Tecnologia; International Journal of Heat and Technology. (Aug. 1983)-. Academic Scholarly Publication. English. sa. $150.00. ETS Editrice, P ZA Torricelli 2, 56126 Pisa Italy. **Tel** 011 39 50 29544. **CODEN** HETEEE. Documents available from Article Express International, Ask*IEEE, CASDDS.
**Ind/Abst** Chem. Abstr. (1983-); Ei Page One; Eng. Index Annu.; INSPEC (March 1984-); Int. Aerosp. Abstr. (1984-); Zentralbl. Math. Ihre Grenzgeb.

US/0741-2533
**HEAT EXCHANGER DESIGN HANDBOOK : HEDH.** ***Ceased.*** [Heat exch. des. handb.]. **VFOAT** HEDH; H.E.D.H. (19??)-(19??). English. sa. Taylor & Francis Ltd., Rankine Road, Basingstoke Hampshire, RG24 8PR United Kingdom. **Tel** 011 44 256 840366, FAX 011 44 256 479438, telex 858540. **(Subscription address:** Taylor & Francis Inc., 1900 Frost Road, Suite 101, Bristol PA 19007-1598.**) ED** Ernst U Schlunder.
**Desc:** The standard reference in the field is divided into seven looseleaf volumes providing correlations, design procedures, plans, diagrams, tables, and property lists.

UK/0890-4332
**HEAT RECOVERY SYSTEMS & CHP.** [Heat recovery syst. CHP]. **VFOAT** Heat Recovery Systems and CHP. **VAT** Heat Recovery Systems and Combined Heat and Power. Vol. 7, No. 1 (1987)-. Academic Scholarly Publication. English. Eight times a year. $537.00 The Americas; £360.00 other. Pergamon Press, An Imprint of Elsevier Science Ltd., The Boulevard, Langford Lane, Kidlington, Oxford OX5 1GB United Kingdom. **Tel** 011 44 865 843000, 011 44 865

843699, FAX 011 44 865 843010. **(Subscription address:** Elsevier Science Ltd. Oxford Fulfillment Centre, PO Box 800, Kidlington, Oxford OX5 1DX United Kingdom.**)** **ED** David Reay. **LC** TJ260; .J58. **DD** 621.402. **CODEN** HRSCEQ. **[CCC]. Pr Rev.** available on microfiche; available on microfilm. Documents available from Article Express International, The Genuine Article, Ask*IEEE, CASDDS, Documents on Demand. ***Continues*** *Journal of Heat Recovery Systems, 0198-7593.*
**Ind/Abst** Abstr. AIT Rep. Publ. Energy; Alum. Ind. Abstr. (1987-); Appl. Mech. Rev.; Bioeng. Abstr. (1987-); Chem. Abstr. (1987-); Curr. Contents Eng. Tech. Appl. Sci.; Curr. Technol. Index; Ei Page One (1987-); Energy Inf. Abstr. (1987-); Energy Res. Abstr. (1987-); Eng. Index Annu.; Environ. Abstr. (1987-?); Fluid Abstr., Civil Eng.; Fluid Abstr. Proc. Eng.; FLUIDEX (1987-); HTFS Dig.; INIS Atomindex [Micro.]; INSPEC (1988-); Int. Build. Serv. Abstr.; Met. Abstr. (1987-); Res. Alert [Select. Cov.]; SCISEARCH.

US/0017-9337
**HEAT TECHNOLOGY.** [Heat technol.]. **Added/Corp** Selas Corporation of America. (1970)-. Academic Scholarly Publication. English. ir. Free. Selas Corporation of America, PO Box 200, Dresher PA 19025. **Tel** (215)646-6600. **CODEN** HTTCA7. Documents available from CASDDS.
**Ind/Abst** Chem. Abstr.

US
**HEAT TRANSFER AND FLUID FLOW DATA BOOK. Main/Corp** General Electric Company. Research and Development Center. (1943)-. English. ir. $405.00. Genium Publishing Corporation, One Genium Plaza, Schenectady NY 12304. **Tel** (518)377-8854, FAX (518)377-1891.

US/0096-0802
**HEAT TRANSFER. JAPANESE RESEARCH.** (HEAT TRANSFER: JAPANESE RESEARCH.). [Heat transfer, Jpn. res.]. **Added/Corp** Kagaku Kogaku Kyokai. American Society of Mechanical Engineers. Heat Transfer Division. Scripta Technica, Inc. **VFOAT** Heat Transfer--Japanese Research. Vol. 1 (Jan./March 1972)-. Periodical. English (translations available in Japanese). Eight times a year. $1,152.00 US; $1,232.00 Canada and Mexico; $1,262.00 other. Scripta Technica, A Subsidiary of John Wiley & Sons, Inc., 7961 Eastern Avenue, Silver Spring MD 20910. **Tel** (301)588-0484, FAX (301)588-5278. **(Subscription address:** John Wiley & Sons / England, Baffins Lane, Chichester, West Sussex PO19 1UD England.**) ED** Thomas F. Irvine, K. Suzuki, and J. P. Hartnett. **LC** QC320; .H374. **DD** 621.4/022/05. **CODEN** HTJPAU. **[CCC]. Ad Acc. Circ:** 400. available on microfilm and microfiche from University Microfilms International (UMI). Documents available from Article Express International, Ask*IEEE, CASDDS.
**Desc:** Deals with the entire field of heat transfer and pertinent areas of fluid dynamics. Topics covered include heat exchanger design and optimization, convective, conductive, radiative heat transfer, computer modeling techniques, and heat transfer with non-Newtonian fluids.
**Ind/Abst** Appl. Mech. Rev.; Bioeng. Abstr.; Chem. Abstr.; Ei Page One; Energy Res. Abstr. (Aug. 1972-); Eng. Index Annu.; Fluid Abstr., Civil Eng.; Fluid Abstr. Proc. Eng.; FLUIDEX (1973-); HTFS Dig.; INIS Atomindex [Micro.]; INSPEC (Jan./March 1972-);; Int. Aerosp. Abstr.; Nucl. Sci. Abstr.; Proc. Chem. Eng.; Theoret. Chem. Eng.

US/0018-151X
**HIGH TEMPERATURE.** [High temp.]. **Added/Corp** Consultants Bureau. Consultants Bureau Enterprises. American Institute of Physics. Vol. 1 (July/Aug. 1963)-. Periodical. English (translations available in Russian). bm. $1245.00 US; $1455.00 other. Plenum Press, 233 Spring Street, New York NY 10013-1578. **Tel** (212)620-8000, (800)221-9369, FAX (212)463-0742, (212)807-1047, telex 23/421139. **(Subscription address:** Plenum Press Subscription Department, PO Box 730, Canal Street Station NY 10013-1578.**) ED** V. M. Batenin. **LC** QC276; .H5. **DD** 536/.57/05. **CODEN** HITEA4. **[CCC].** Index available. **Pr Rev.** available on CD-ROM; available on microfilm and microfiche from University Microfilms International (UMI). Documents available from Article Express International, The Genuine Article, Ask*IEEE, CASDDS.
**Desc:** Presents the results of the latest investigations in the numerical simulation of complex thermal gas dynamics and heat and mass exchange processes. Also highlights new achievements in high-temperature theory.
**Ind/Abst** Appl. Mech. Rev.; Bioeng. Abstr.; Ceram. Abstr. (19??-); Chem. Abstr.; Coal Abstr.; Curr. Contents Phys. Chem. Earth Sci.; Ei Page One; Energy Res. Abstr.; Eng. Index Annu.; Fluid Abstr., Civil Eng.; Fluid Abstr. Proc. Eng.; FLUIDEX (1973-); HTFS Dig.; INSPEC (1968-); Int. Aerosp. Abstr.; Pollut. Abstr. Indexes; Proc. Chem. Eng.; Res. Alert [Full Cov.]; Sci. Cit. Index; SCISEARCH; SPIN (1972-); Theoret. Chem. Eng.

UK/0018-1544
**HIGH TEMPERATURES - HIGH PRESSURES.** [High temp. High press.]. **VFOAT** High Pressures. Vol. 1 (1969)-. Periodical. English (French and German). Six times a year. £260.00 UK; $420.00 US. Pion Ltd., 207 Brondesbury Park, London NW2 5JN England. **Tel** 011 44 81 459 0066, FAX 011 44 81 451 6454, telex 94016265 PION G. **ED** Erich Fitzer and Roy Taylor. **LC** QC276; .H54. **CODEN** HTHPAK. Index available. **Bk Rev. Ad Acc. Circ:** 500. Documents available from Article Express International, Ask*IEEE, CASDDS.
**Desc:** Experimental and theoretical study of matter under extreme thermal and mechanical conditions. Applications to chemical and mechanical engineering, materials science and metallurgy.
**Ind/Abst** Alum. Ind. Abstr.; Bioeng. Abstr.; Ceram. Abstr.; Chem. Abstr.; Coal Abstr.; Ei Page One; Eng. Mater. Abstr.; Eng. Index Annu.; Geol. Abstr.; GeoRef; HTFS Dig.; INSPEC (1969-); Int. Aerosp. Abstr.; Met. Abstr.; Mineral. Abstr.; Text. Technol. Dig. (19??-199?).

UK/0952-2654
**HTFS DIGEST (1987). See** Engineering-Abstracting, Bibliographies and Statistics.

US/0019-8374
**INDUSTRIAL HEATING.** [Ind. heat.]. **VFOAT** Journal of Heat Technology. Vol. 1 (Oct. 1934)-. Academic Scholarly Publication. English. mo. $49.00 US; $61.00 Canada; $89.00 other. Business News Publishing Company, 755 West Big Beaver Road, Suite 1000, Troy MI 48084. **Tel** (810)362-3700, FAX (810)362-0317, telex 230295. **ED** S B Lasday. **LC** TH7201; .I5. **DD** 697.05. **CODEN** INHTAZ. **Bk Rev. Ad Acc. Circ:** 23,500 (ctrl). available on microfilm from University Microfilms International (UMI). Documents available from Article Express International, CASDDS, Documents on Demand.
**Desc:** Brings you the latest changes in high temperature heat treating as they apply to metals, ceramics and composites.
**Ind/Abst** Alum. Ind. Abstr.; Bioeng. Abstr.; Ceram. Abstr; Chem. Abstr.; Coal Abstr.; Ei Page One; EMBASE; Energy Inf. Abstr.; Eng. Mater. Abstr.; Eng. Index Annu.; Environ. Abstr.; Gas Abstr.; Health Saf. Sci. Abstr.; Ind. Hyg. Dig.; INIS Atomindex [Micro.]; Leadscan; Met. Abstr.; Nucl. Sci. Abstr.; Surf. Treat. Technol. Abstr.; World Ceram. Abstr.

US/0735-1933
**INTERNATIONAL COMMUNICATIONS IN HEAT AND MASS TRANSFER.** [Int. commun. heat mass transf.]. Vol. 10, No. 1 (Jan./Feb. 1983)-. Academic Scholarly Publication. English. bm. $450.00 (regular subscription), $2176.00 (combination subscription with International Journal of Heat & Mass Transfer) The Americas; £302.00 (regular subscription), £1460.00 (combination subscription with International Journal of Hear & Mass Transfer) other. Pergamon Press, An Imprint of Elsevier Science Ltd., The Boulevard, Langford Lane, Kidlington, Oxford OX5 1GB United Kingdom. **Tel** 011 44 865 843000, 011 44 865 843699, FAX 011 44 865 843010. **(Subscription address:** Elsevier Science Ltd. Oxford Fulfillment Centre, PO Box 800 Kidlington, Oxford OX5 1DX United Kingdom.**) ED** J. P. Hartnett and W. J. Minkowycz. **LC** QC319.8; .L47. **DD** 536/.2/005. **CODEN** IHMTDL. **[CCC]. Pr Rev.** available on microfilm and microfiche from University Microfilms International (UMI). Documents available from Article Express International, The Genuine Article, Ask*IEEE, CASDDS. ***Continues*** *Letters in Heat and Mass Transfer, 0094-4548.*
**Desc:** Serves as a world forum for the rapid dissemination of new ideas, new measurement techniques and preliminary findings of current investigations, discussions and criticisms in the field of heat and mass transfer.
**Ind/Abst** Abstr. Bull. Inst. Pap. Sci. Tech.; Chem. Abstr. (1983-); Civ. Struct. Eng. Abstr.; Coal Abstr.; Comput. Inf. Syst. Abstr. J. [Full Cov.]; Curr. Contents Eng. Tech. Appl. Sci.; Ei Page One; Elect. Comm. Abstr.; Energy Res. Abstr. (Jan. 1983-); Eng. Index Annu.; Environ. Eng. Abstr.; Fluid Abstr., Civil Eng.; Fluid Abstr. Proc. Eng.; FLUIDEX (1983-); HTFS Dig.; INIS Atomindex [Micro.]; INSPEC (Jan.-Feb. 1983-); Int. Aerosp. Abstr.; Manuf. Process Eng. Abstr.; Mater. Sci. Eng. Abstr.; Mech. Eng. Abstr.; Proc. Chem. Eng.; Res. Alert [Full Cov.]; SCISEARCH; Solid State Supercond. Abstr.; Theoret. Chem. Eng.

UK/0017-9310
**INTERNATIONAL JOURNAL OF HEAT AND MASS TRANSFER.** [Int. j. heat mass transfer]. **VFOAT** Heat and Mass Transfer. Vol. 1 (June 1960)-. Academic Scholarly Publication. Multiple languages (English and Multiple languages; summaries and/or abstracts in French, German and Russian). Eighteen times a year. $1841.00 (regular subscription), $2176.00 (combination subscription with International Communications in Heat & Mass Transfer) The Americas; £1235.00 (regular subscription), £1460.00 (combination subscription with International Communications in Heat & Mass Transfer) other. Pergamon Press, An Imprint of Elsevier Science Ltd., The Boulevard, Langford Lane, Kidlington, Oxford OX5 1GB United Kingdom. **Tel** 011 44 865 843000, 011 44 865 843699, FAX 011 44 865 843010. **(Subscription address:** Elsevier Science Ltd. Oxford Fulfillment Centre, PO Box 800, Kidlington, Oxford OX5 1DX United Kingdom.**) ED** J.P. Hartnett. **LC** QC320; .I55. **DD** 536.205. **CODEN** IJHMAK. **[CCC]. Pr Rev.** available in microform from Microforms International; available on microfilm and microfiche from University Microfilms International (UMI); available on microfiche from the publisher. Documents available from Article Express International, The Genuine Article, Ask*IEEE, Petroleum Abstracts Document Delivery Service, CASDDS, Documents on Demand.
**Desc:** Provides a central vehicle for exchange of basic ideas in heat and mass transfer between research workers and engineers throughout the world.
**Ind/Abst** Abstr. Bull. Inst. Pap. Sci. Tech.; Acoust. Abstr.; Appl. Mech. Rev.; Appl. Sci. Technol. Index (1991-); Bioeng. Abstr.; Ceram. Abstr.; Chem. Abstr. (1960-1985); Coal Abstr.; Curr. Contents Eng. Tech. Appl. Sci.; Curr. Technol. Index; Ei Page One; EMBASE; Energy Inf. Abstr.; Energy Res. Abstr.; Eng. Index Annu.; Environ. Abstr.; Fluid Abstr., Civil Eng.; Fluid Abstr. Proc. Eng.; FLUIDEX (1973-); Gas Abstr.; GeoRef; HTFS Dig.; INIS Atomindex [Micro.]; INSPEC (1968-); Int. Aerosp. Abstr.; Lit. Pat. Abstr., Oilfield Chem. (1969-); Lit. Abstr., Catal. Catal.; Lit. Abstr., Health Environ.; Lit. Abstr., Pet. Refin. Petrochem.; Lit. Abstr., Pet. Substit.; Lit. Abstr., Transp. Storage; Pet. Abstr.; Pollut. Abstr. Indexes; Proc. Chem. Eng.; Res. Alert [Full Cov.]; Sci. Cit. Index; SCISEARCH; Theoret. Chem. Eng.; Zentralbl. Math. Ihre Grenzgeb.

US/0737-0652
**JOURNAL OF ENERGETIC MATERIALS (JOEM).** (JOURNAL OF ENERGETIC MATERIALS.). [J. energ. mater.]. **VFOAT** Energetic Materials. Vol. 1, No. 1 (1983)-. Academic Scholarly Publication. English. Five times a year. $250.00. Dowden Broden & Devine Inc., PO Box 188, Stroudsburg PA 18360. **Tel** (717)629-3422. **LC** IN PROCESS. **DD** 536. **CODEN** JOEMDK. Index available. Documents available from CASDDS.
**Ind/Abst** Chem. Abstr. (1985-).

●US/1051-3248
**JOURNAL OF ENERGETICS AND FLUIDS ENGINEERING.** ***Suspended.*** **See** Engineering-Hydraulic Engineering.

II/0970-9991
**JOURNAL OF ENERGY, HEAT AND MASS TRANSFER. See** Energy.

●US/1065-5131
**JOURNAL OF ENHANCED HEAT TRANSFER: AN INTERNATIONAL JOURNAL OF THEORY AND APPLICATION IN HIGH-PERFORMANCE HEAT AND MASS TRANSFER.** (1993)-. English. Gordon & Breach Science Publishers, Inc., PO Box 786, Cooper Station, New York NY 10276. **Tel** (212)206-8900, FAX (212)645-2459. **(Subscription address:** International Publishers Distributor at one of the following addresses: 820 Town Center Drive, Langhorne, PA 19047; or PO Box 90, Reading Berkshire RG1 8JL UK; or Kent Ridge PO Box 1180, Singapore 9111, Republic of Singapore**)**
**Desc:** Publishes papers related to enhanced heat transfer in natural and forced convection of liquids and gases, boiling, condensation, and radiative heat transfer.

GW/0340-0204
**JOURNAL OF NON-EQUILIBRIUM THERMODYNAMICS.** [J. non-equilib. thermodyn.]. **VFOAT** Non-Equilibrium Thermodynamics. Vol. 1 (1976)-. Academic Scholarly Publication. English. Four times a year. $509.90. Walter de Gruyter Inc., PO Box 303421, D 10728 Berlin Germany. **Tel** 011 49 30 260050, FAX 011 49 30 26005251. **ED** J. U. Keller. **LC** QC318.I7; J68. **DD** 536/.7. **CODEN** JNETDY. **[CCC]. Bk Rev. Ad Acc. Pr Rev. Circ:** 400. Documents available from Article Express International, The Genuine Article, Ask*IEEE, CASDDS.
**Desc:** The journal deals with the physical foundations and the engineering applications of non-equilibrium thermodynamics.
**Ind/Abst** Bioeng. Abstr.; Chem. Abstr.; Coal Abstr.; Curr. Contents Phys. Chem. Earth Sci.; Ei Page One; Energy Res. Abstr. (Jan. 1977-); Eng. Index Annu.; HTFS Dig.; INSPEC (1979-); Int. Aerosp. Abstr.; Res. Alert [Full Cov.]; Sci. Cit. Index; SCISEARCH; Zentralbl. Math. Ihre Grenzgeb.

US/0887-8722
**JOURNAL OF THERMOPHYSICS AND HEAT TRANSFER.** [J. thermophys. heat transf.]. **Added/Corp** American Institute of Aeronautics and Astronautics. **VFOAT** J. Thermophysics. Vol. 1, No. 1 (Jan. 1987)-. Academic Scholarly Publication. English. qt (4 issues). $220.00 North America; $260.00 other. American Institute of Aeronautics & Astronautics, 370 l'Enfant Promenade Southwest, Washington DC 20024-2518. **Tel** (202)646-7400, FAX (202)646-7508, telex 204792 AIAA UR. **ED** Alfred L. Crosbie. **LC** TL900; .J68. **DD** 629.1/1. **CODEN** JTHTEO. **[CCC].** Index available. **Pr Rev. Circ:** 2,000. available on microfilm and microfiche from University Microfilms International (UMI). Documents available from Article Express International, The Genuine Article, Ask*IEEE, CASDDS.
**Desc:** Covers thermal energy transfer and storage in gases, liquids, and solids or combinations thereof, including conductive, convective, and radiative modes alone or in combination and the effects of the environment.
**Ind/Abst** Chem. Abstr. (1987-); Ei Page One; Eng. Mater. Abstr.; Eng. Index Annu.; Fluid Abstr., Civil Eng.; Fluid Abstr. Proc. Eng.; FLUIDEX (19??-); INSPEC (1987-); Int. Aerosp. Abstr.; Res. Alert [Full Cov.].

UK/0265-2994
**MONOGRAPHS ON CRYOGENICS.** [Monogr. cryog.]. (1981)-. Monographic series. English. ir. Price varies per volume. Oxford University Press, Walton Street, Oxford OX2 6DP England. **Tel** 011 44 865 56767, FAX 011 44 865 267773, telex 837330 OXPRES G. **(Subscription address:** Oxford University Press / USA, Journals Marketing Department, Oxford University Press, 2001 Evans Road, Cary NC 27513.**) LC** UNC. Documents available from Ask*IEEE.
**Ind/Abst** INSPEC.

US/1040-7782
**NUMERICAL HEAT TRANSFER. PART A, APPLICATIONS.** [Numer. heat transf., A Appl.]. **VFOAT** Applications. Vol. 15, No. 1 (Feb. 1989)-. Periodical. English. mo. £558.00 UK; $965.00 other. Taylor & Francis Ltd., Rankine Road, Basingstoke Hampshire, RG24 8PR United Kingdom. **Tel** 011 44 256 840366, FAX 011 44 256 479438, telex 858540. **(Subscription address:** Taylor & Francis Inc., 1900 Frost Road, Suite 101, Bristol PA 19007-1598.**) ED** W. J. Minkowycz (editor's address: Department of Mechanical Engineering, University of Illinois at Chicago, Chicago, IL 60680). **LC** QC319.8; .N832. **DD** 621.402/2. **CODEN** NHAAESNUHTD6. **[CCC]. Bk Rev. Ad Acc. Pr Rev. Circ:** 580. available on microfilm and microfiche from University Microfilms International (UMI). Documents available from Article Express International, The Genuine Article, Ask*IEEE. ***Continues in part*** *Numerical Heat Transfer, 0149-5720.*
**Desc:** Covers numerically based, results-oriented papers addressing problems in heat transfer, mass transfer, and fluid flow. Features experimental results that serve as a foundation for numerical solutions.
**Ind/Abst** Alum. Ind. Abstr.; Bioeng. Abstr.; Curr. Contents Eng. Tech. Appl. Sci.; Ei Page One; Eng. Index Annu.; Fluid Abstr., Civil Eng.; Fluid Abstr. Proc. Eng.; FLUIDEX (1978-); HTFS Dig.; INSPEC (Jan./March 1978-); Int. Aerosp. Abstr.; Met. Abstr.; Res. Alert [Full Cov.]; Sci. Cit. Index; SCISEARCH; World Alum. Abstr.

US/1040-7790
**NUMERICAL HEAT TRANSFER. PART B, FUNDAMENTALS.** [Numer. heat transf., B Fundam.]. **VFOAT** Fundamentals. Vol. 15, No. 1 (March 1989)-. Periodical. English. Eight times a year. £242.00 UK; $400.00 other. Taylor & Francis Ltd., Rankine Road, Basingstoke Hampshire, RG24 8PR United Kingdom. **Tel** 011 44 256 840366, FAX 011 44 256 479438, telex 858540. **(Subscription address:** Taylor & Francis Inc., 1900 Frost Road, Suite 101, Bristol PA 19007-1598.**) ED** W. J. Minkowycz (editor's address: Department of Mechanical Engineering, University of Illinois at Chicago, Chicago, IL 60680). **LC** QC319.8.N833. **DD** 621.402/2. **CODEN** NHBFEE. **[CCC].** Index available. cum. index. **Bk Rev. Ad Acc. Pr Rev. Circ:** 292. available on microfilm and microfiche from University Microfilms International (UMI). Documents available from Article Express International, The Genuine Article, Ask*IEEE. ***Continues in part*** *Numerical Heat Transfer, 0149-5720.*
**Desc:** An international journal addressing all aspects of the methodology for the numerical solution of problems in heat and mass transfer, as well as fluid flow. Also encompasses modeling of complex physical phenomena that serves as a foundation for attaining numerical solutions and includes numerical or experimental results that support methodology development.
**Ind/Abst** Alum. Ind. Abstr.; Bioeng. Abstr.; Curr. Contents Eng. Tech. Appl. Sci.; Ei Page One; Eng. Index Annu.; Fluid Abstr., Civil Eng.; Fluid Abstr. Proc. Eng.; FLUIDEX (1978-); HTFS Dig.; INSPEC (Jan./March 1978-); Int. Aerosp. Abstr.; Met. Abstr.; Res. Alert [Full Cov.]; Sci. Cit. Index; SCISEARCH; World Alum. Abstr.

FR/1146-5107
**PASCAL. F 10, MECANIQUE, ACOUSTIQUE ET TRANSFERT DE CHALEUR.** See Physics-Sound.

US/0094-9477
**PREVIEWS OF HEAT AND MASS TRANSFER. Added/Corp** International Center for Heat and Mass Transfer. Vol. 1 (Sept. 1974)-. Periodical. English. bm. $278.00 The Americas; £187.00 other. Pergamon Press, An Imprint of Elsevier Science Ltd., The Boulevard, Langford Lane, Kidlington, Oxford OX5 1GB United Kingdom. **Tel** 011 44 865 843000, 011 44 865 843699, FAX 011 44 865 843010. **(Subscription address:** Elsevier Science Ltd. Oxford Fulfillment Centre, PO Box 800, Kidlington, Oxford OX5 1DX United Kingdom.**) ED** T. F. Irvine, Jr, J.P. Hartnett. **LC** QC319.8; .P73. **DD** 536/.2. **[CCC].** available on microfilm and microfiche from University Microfilms International (UMI).
**Desc:** Provides abstracts of recently published papers in heat and mass transfer from over 100 journals around the world. Includes up-to-date information on research reports from industrial and university laboratories, recently published technical books, and university dissertations.
**Ind/Abst** Ei Page One.

●US/1077-5870
**PROCESS HEATING.** (1994)-. Trade Publication. English. bm (6 issues). $27.00. Business News Publishing Company, 755 West Big Beaver Road, Suite 1000, Troy MI 48084. **Tel** (810)362-3700, FAX (810)362-0317, telex 230295.
**Desc:** Serves individuals involved in heat transfer processes such as curing, drying, baking and purifying. Provides comprehensive coverage of technology, troubleshooting, trends, case histories and practical applications of thermal processing operations at temperatures up to 1000F.

US
**QUARTERLY PROGRESS REPORT ON BLOWDOWN HEAT TRANSFER SEPARATE-EFFECTS PROGRAM FOR ... / ENGINEERING TECHNOLOGY DIVISION.** English. qt. Government Printing Office Sales Program, Division of Technical Information and Document Control, US Nuclear Regulatory Commission, Washington DC 20555.

US/0035-3434
**REVUE INTERNATIONALE DES HAUTES TEMPERATURES ET DES REFRACTAIRES.** See Chemistry-Physical and Theoretical Chemistry.

US/0360-0335
**SOVIET JOURNAL OF LOW TEMPERATURE PHYSICS.** ***Title Change.*** [Sov. j. low temp. phys.]. **Added/Corp** American Institute of Physics. Consultants Bureau. Vol. 1 (Jan. 1975)-(1993). Academic Scholarly Publication. English (Russian). mo. American Institute of Physics, 500 Sunnyside Boulevard, Woodbury NY 11797-2999. **Tel** (516)576-2200, FAX (516)349-7669, telex 960983. **(Subscription address:** UK/ Institute of Physics, Techno House, Redcliffe Way, Bristol BS1 6NX England**) LC** QC278; .S62. **DD** 536/.56/05. **CODEN** SJLPDQ. **[CCC].** Documents available from Ask*IEEE, CASDDS. ***Continued by*** *Low Temperature Physics.*
**Ind/Abst** Acoust. Abstr.; Ceram. Abstr. (199?-199?); Chem. Abstr.; Curr. Phys. Index; Energy Res. Abstr. (Sept. 1976-); INSPEC (Sept. 1975-); Int. Aerosp. Abstr.; SPIN (1975-).

UK/0892-6808
**SOVIET TECHNOLOGY REVIEWS. SECTION B, THERMAL PHYSICS REVIEWS.** [Sov. technol. rev., B Therm. phys. rev.]. **VFOAT** Thermal Physics Reviews; Sovetskie Tekhnologicheskie Obzory. Section B, Thermal; SICS Reviews. Vol. 1 (1987)-. Periodical. English (translations available in Russian). an. $441.00 university and hospital libraries; $688.00 other. Harwood Academic Publishers, PO Box 90, Reading RG1 8JL England. **Tel** 011 44 734 560080. **LC** QC192; .S68. **DD** 530.4. **CODEN** STBREJ. **[CCC].**

US/1050-3943
**STUDIES OF HIGH TEMPERATURE SUPERCONDUCTORS.** See Engineering-Electricity, Electrical Engineering, Electronics.

UK/0953-2048
**SUPERCONDUCTOR SCIENCE & TECHNOLOGY.** See Physics-Magnetism.

US
**TEMPERATURE DEVELOPMENTS.** (198?)-. Periodical. English. Four times a year. $50.00. Omega Press, One Omega Drive, Box 4047, Stamford CT 06907. **Tel** (203)322-1666. ctrl circ.
**Desc:** Measurement and control handbooks for temperature, pressure flow, hand tools and ph. All books are in full color and all include prices and complete descriptions.

LV
**TEPLOPROVODNOST' I DIFFUZIIA. Main/Corp** Riga. Politehniskais Instituts. Kafedra Promyshlennoi Teploenergetiki. Began in 1969. Russian. 0.54rub each issue. Rigas Politehniskais Instituts, Riga Latvia. **LC** QC319.8; .R54A.

US/0163-9005
**THERMAL CONDUCTIVITY (1975).** (THERMAL CONDUCTIVITY.). [Therm. conduct.]. (1975)-. Monographic series. English. an. Price varies per volume. Plenum Press, 233 Spring Street, New York NY 10013-1578. **Tel** (212)620-8000, (800)221-9369, FAX (212)463-0742, (212)807-1047, telex 23/421139. **DD** 536. **CODEN** THCOD9. Documents available from CASDDS. ***Continues*** *Advances in Thermal Conductivity : Papers Presented at the International Conference on Thermal Conductivity.*
**Ind/Abst** Chem. Abstr.

US
**TRC THERMODYMANIC TABLES NON-HYDROCARBONS.** English. an (Supplements published in June & Dec.). $3,200 (industries), $1,500 (universities) US; $2,050 (universities) other - ten volumes looseleaf includes binder. TRC - Thermodynamics Research Center Data Distribution, Texas A&M University, Tees Business Office, College Station TX 77843-3124. **Tel** (409)845-5981, FAX (409)862-2352, telex 510-892-7689 TXINTLPRO COSN. **ED** Kenneth N. Marsh. cum. index. available on an online database from STN International.

US
**TRC THERMODYNAMIC TABLES - HYDROCARBONS.** English. an (Supplements published in April & Oct.). $3,800.00 (industries), $1,750.00 (universities) US; $2,400 (universities) other - thirteen volumes includes binder. TRC - Thermodynamics Research Center Data Distribution, Texas A&M University, Tees Business Office, College Station TX 77843-3124. **Tel** (409)845-5981, FAX (409)862-2352, telex 510-892-7689 TXINTLPRO COSN. **ED** Kenneth N. Marsh (telephone 409-845-4940). cum. index. available on an online database from STN International.

RU
**VYSOKOTEMPERATURNAIA SVERKHPROVODIMOST / LENINGRADSKII GOSUDARSTVENNYI UNIVERSITET. Added/Corp** Leningradskii Gosudarstvennyi Universitet. **VFOAT** Vysoko-Temperaturnaia Sverkh-Provodimost. (1989)-. Periodical. Russian. St Petersburg State University / Izdatelstvo Leningradskogo Universiteta, Universitetskaia Nab 7/9, 199034 St Petersburg Russia. **Tel** 011 95 218-97-88, FAX 011 95 218-51-52, telex 121481. **LC** QC611.98.H54; V9. **CODEN** VSAPEY.
**Ind/Abst** Int. Aerosp. Abstr.

---

## LIGHT, OPTICS, RADIATION

---

●US
**AAVSO PHOTOELECTRIC PHOTOMETRY NEWSLETTER.** (1992)-. Newsletter. English. ir (3-4 times per year). Free (individuals) members; $10.00 (individuals) non-members; $15.00 others. American Association of Variable Star Observers (AAVSO), 25 Birch Street, Cambridge MA 02138-1205. **Tel** (617)354-0484, FAX (617)354-0665.

UK
**ABSORPTION SPECTRA IN THE INFRARED REGION.** V. 1- 1974-. English. sa. Butterworth Heinemann Publishers, Linacre House, Jordan Hill, Oxford OX2 8DP England. **Tel** 011 44 865 310366. **LC** QC457; .A33. **DD** 547/.308/5.

US/0192-5652
**ABSTRACTS - SYMPOSIUM ON MOLECULAR SPECTROSCOPY. Main/Conf** Symposium on Molecular Spectroscopy. **Added/Corp** Ohio State University. Dept. of Physics. (1976)-. English. an. Molecular Spectroscopy Symposium, 174 West 19th Avenue, Columbus OH 43210. **LC** QC451; .S93a. **DD** 539/.12. ***Continues*** *Abstracts - Symposium on Molecular Structure and Spectroscopy, 0362-7624.*

JA/0065-1621
**ACTA RADIOBOTANICA ET GENETICA. BULLETIN OF THE INSTITUTE OF RADIATION BREEDING. Added/Corp** Hoshasen Ikushujo. Hoshasen Ikushujo. Kenkyu Hokoku - Hoshasen Ikushujo. Bulletin of the Institute of Radiation Breeding. **VFOAT** Bulletin of the Institute of Radiation Breeding. No. 1 (Aug. 1967)-. Bulletin. Japanese (English). Norin Suisansho Nogyo Seibutsu Shigen Kenkyujo Hoshasen Ikushujo, (Institution of Radiation Breeding, National Institution of Agrobiological Resources, Ministry of Agriculture, Forestry and Fisheries), Omiyamachi, Nakagun, Ibarakiken 319-22 Japan. **CODEN** ARBGB9. Documents available from BIOSIS Document Express.
**Ind/Abst** AGRICOLA [Select. Cov.]; Biol. Abstr. (1985-); Energy Res. Abstr. (Apr. 1972-).

UK/0264-8423
**ADVANCES IN LASER SPECTROSCOPY (LONDON, ENG.).** (ADVANCES IN LASER SPECTROSCOPY.). [Adv. laser spectrosc.]. Vol. 1, (1982)-. Academic Scholarly Publication. English. ir. Price varies per volume. John Wiley & Sons Ltd., Baffins Lane, Chichester West Sussex PO19 1UD England. **Tel** 0243 779777, FAX 0243 776128 BTG:JWP001, telex 86290 WIBOOKG. **(Subscription address:** John Wiley & Sons Inc / New Jersey, PO Box 2575, Secaucus NJ 07096-2575.**) LC** QD96.L3; A34. **DD** 535.8/4. **CODEN** ALSPDD. Documents available from CASDDS.
**Ind/Abst** Chem. Abstr.

UK/0887-2430
**ADVANCES IN MASS SPECTROMETRY (1985).** ***Title Change.*** (ADVANCES IN MASS SPECTROMETRY.). [Adv. mass spectrom.]. (1985)-(19??). Academic Scholarly Publication. English. te. Elsevier Science Publishers BV, PO Box 211, 1000 AE Amsterdam Netherlands. **Tel** 011 31 20 5803642, FAX

011 31 20 5862696, telex 15682. **DD** 545. Documents available from CASDDS. ***Continues*** *Mass Spectrometry Advances.* ***Continued by*** *Mass Spectrometery Advances.*
**Ind/Abst** Art Archaeol. Tech. Abstr.; Chem. Abstr.; Mass Spect. Bull. (?-?).

UK/0065-3012
**ADVANCES IN OPTICAL AND ELECTRON MICROSCOPY. See** Biology-Microscopy.

UK/0892-2888
**ADVANCES IN SPECTROSCOPY (1986).** (ADVANCES IN SPECTROSCOPY.). [Adv. spectrosc.]. Vol. 13 (1986)-. Academic Scholarly Publication. English. ir. Price varies per volume. John Wiley & Sons Ltd., Baffins Lane, Chichester West Sussex PO19 1UD England. **Tel** 0243 779777, FAX 0243 776128 BTG:JWP001, telex 86290 WIBOOKG. **(Subscription address:** John Wiley & Sons Inc / New Jersey, PO Box 2575, Secaucus NJ 07096-2575.**) DD** 543. **NLM** W1; AD873G. **[CCC].** Documents available from CASDDS. ***Continues*** *Advances in Infrared and Raman Spectroscopy, 0309-426X.*
**Ind/Abst** Chem. Abstr.; Energy Res. Abstr.; GeoRef.

NE/0926-4345
**ANALYTICAL SPECTROSCOPY LIBRARY.** [Anal. spectrosc. libr.]. (198?)-. Monographic series. English. Price varies per volume. Elsevier Science Publishers BV, PO Box 211, 1000 AE Amsterdam Netherlands. **Tel** 011 31 20 5803642, FAX 011 31 20 5862696, telex 15682. **CODEN** ASLIE7. Documents available from BIOSIS Document Express, CASDDS.
**Ind/Abst** Biol. Abstr.; Chem. Abstr.

BE/0250-5010
**ANNALEN VAN DE BELGISCHE VERENIGING VOOR STRALINGSBESCHERMING.** (ANNALEN VAN DE BELGISCHE VERENIGING VOOR STRALINGSBESCHERMING. ANNALES DE L'ASSOCIATION BELGE DE RADIOPROTECTION.). [Ann. Belg. Ver. Stralingsbescherming]. **Main/Corp** Association Belge de Radioprotection. **Added/Corp** Association Belge de Radioprotection. Annales de l'Association Belge de Radioprotection. (19??)-. Periodical. Dutch (French and Dutch). qt. **LC** QC795.32.S3; A77a. **CODEN** ABVSDZ. Documents available from CASDDS.
**Ind/Abst** Chem. Abstr.

JA
**ANNUAL REPORT OF OSAKA PREFECTURAL RADIATION RESEARCH INSTITUTE. Added/Corp** Osaka Furitsu Hoshasen Chuo Kenkyujo. (1989?)-. Academic Scholarly Publication. English (summaries and/or abstracts in Japanese). **CODEN** AROIEF. Documents available from BIOSIS Document Express, CASDDS. ***Continues*** *Annual Report of the Radiation Center of Osaka Prefecture, 0474-7879.*
**Ind/Abst** Biol. Abstr. (1990-); Chem. Abstr.; Trop. Dis. Bull.

AU/1018-6247
**APPLIED FLUORESCENCE TECHNOLOGY.** (1989)-. Periodical. English. bm (6 issues). Lambda Fluoreszenztechnologie, Grottenhofstr 3, A 8053 Graz Austria. **Tel** 011 43 316 278300352. **UDC** 535.7.

UK/0305-7615
**APPLIED HEALTH PHYSICS ABSTRACTS AND NOTES.** Vol. 1 (1975)-. Periodical. English. qt. £160.00 UK; $330.00 other. Nuclear Technology Publishing, PO Box 7, Ashford Kent TN23 1YW England. **Tel** 0233 641683, FAX 0233 610021, telex 966119 NTPUK G. **ED** E P Goldfinch. **LC** RA569; .A66. **DD** 363.1/79. **NLM** ZWN 110 A652. Index available. **Bk Rev. Ad Acc. Circ:** 1,000 (ctrl).
**Desc:** An international abstracts journal in applied health physics covering radiation protection, radiation dosimetry, measurement techniques, radiation effects and radiation accidents.

•US/1075-0207
**APPLIED MICROWAVE & WIRELESS.** [Appl. microw. wirel.]. **VFOAT** Applied Microwave and Wireless; Microwave & Wireless; Microwave and Wireless. Vol. 5, No. 4 (Fall 1993)-. Periodical. English. ir. $30.00 (6 issues). J. F. White Publications, Box 1504, East Orleans MA 02643-1504. **Tel** (617)863-9603, FAX (617)861-2995. **ED** Joseph F. White. **DD** 621.381/3. Index available. **Ad Acc. Circ:** 25,000. Documents available from Article Express International, Ask*IEEE. ***Continues*** *Applied Microwave Magazine, 1061-3528.*
**Desc:** Written for professionals in the RF, microwave and optical fields.
**Ind/Abst** Eng. Index Annu. [Select. Cov.]; INSPEC.

US/1061-3528
**APPLIED MICROWAVE MAGAZINE. *Title Change.*** [Appl. microw. mag.]. **VFOAT** Applied Microwave. Vol. 1, No. 1 (May 1989)-(1993). Periodical. English. qt. J. F. White Publications, Box 1504, East Orleans MA 02643-1504. **Tel** (617)863-9603, FAX (617)861-2995. **ED** Joseph F. White. **LC** TK7876; .A66. **DD** 621.381/3. **CODEN** AMIMEU. Index available. **Ad Acc. Circ:** 25,000. Documents available from Article Express International, Ask*IEEE. ***Continued by*** *Applied Microwave & Wireless, 1075-0207.*
**Desc:** Written for professionals in the RF, microwave and optical fields.
**Ind/Abst** Eng. Index Annu. [Select. Cov.]; INSPEC (Aug./Sep. 1989-19??).

US/0003-6935
**APPLIED OPTICS.** [Appl. opt.]. **Added/Corp** Optical Society of America. American Institute of Physics. Vol. 1 (Jan. 1962)-. Periodical. English. Thirty-six times a year. $1220.00 US; $1274.00 Canada; $1381.00 Europe & Asia. Optical Society of America, 2010 Massachusetts Avenue Northwest, Washington DC 20036. **Tel** (202)223-8130, (800)762-6960, (800)582-0416, FAX (202)223-1096, telex 510 600 3965. **ED** William Rhodes, Duncan Moore, Alexander Sawchuk and John Murray. **LC** QC350; .O62. **DD** 535.05. **NLM** W1 AP528J. **CODEN** APOPAI. **[CCC].** Index available (bound in last issue.). cum. index. **Pr Rev.** available on microfiche; available on microfilm. Documents available from Article Express International, The Genuine Article, Ask*IEEE, UMI Article Clearinghouse, CASDDS.
**Desc:** Reports all significant optics applications and patents.
**Ind/Abst** Abstr. Bull. Inst. Pap. Sci. Tech.; Acoust. Abstr.; Appl. Sci. Technol. Index; Art Archaeol. Tech. Abstr.; Bioeng. Abstr.; Ceram. Abstr. (1970-); Chem. Abstr.; Coal Abstr.; Comput. Abstr.; Curr. Contents Eng. Tech. Appl. Sci.; Curr. Contents Phys. Chem. Earth Sci.; Curr. Phys. Index; Ei Page One; EMBASE; Energy Res. Abstr.; Eng. Index Annu.; Expand. Acad. Index (1992-); Fluid Abstr., Civil Eng.; Fluid Abstr. Proc. Eng.; FLUIDEX (1973-1990); GeoRef; HTFS Dig.; INIS Atomindex [Micro.]; INSPEC (1968-); Int. Aerosp. Abstr. (1991-); Leadscan; Meteorol. Geoastrophys. Abstr.; Newsp. Period. Abstr. (1992-); Life Sci. Collect.; Res. Alert [Full Cov.]; Sci. Cit. Index; SCISEARCH; Soc. Sci. Cit. Index [Select. Cov.]; SPIN (1970-); Sug. Indus. Abstr.

US/0197-8535
**APPLIED OPTICS AND OPTICAL ENGINEERING.** [Appl. opt. opt. eng.]. (1965)-. Academic Scholarly Publication. English. ir. $89.00 (latest volume). Academic Press, Inc., 6277 Sea Harbor Drive, Orlando FL 32887. **Tel** (800)543-9534, (407)345-4100, FAX (407)363-9661. **ED** Robert R. Shannon and James C. Wyant. **LC** TA1501; .A66. **DD** 621.36. **CODEN** AOOEDF. Documents available from Ask*IEEE, CASDDS.
**Ind/Abst** Chem. Abstr.; INSPEC.

•GW
**APPLIED PHYSICS. B, LASERS AND OPTICS. VFOAT** Lasers and Optics. Vol. B58, No. 1 (Jan. 1994)-. Periodical. English. mo. Springer-Verlag GmbH & Company KG, Heidelberger Platz 3, D 14197 Berlin Germany. **Tel** 011 49 30 8207223, FAX 011 49 30 8214091, telex 183 319 SPBLN D. **LC** QC1; .A734. ***Continues*** *Applied Physics. B, Photophysics and Laser Chemistry, 0721-7269.*
**Ind/Abst** Bioeng. Abstr.; Chem. Abstr.; Chem. Titles; Curr. Contents Phys. Chem. Earth Sci.; Ei Page One; Energy Res. Abstr.; Eng. Index Annu.; HTFS Dig.; INSPEC; Int. Aerosp. Abstr.; Mass Spect. Bull.; Phys. Briefs; Res. Alert; Sci. Cit. Index; SCISEARCH.

GW/0721-7269
**APPLIED PHYSICS. B, PHOTOPHYSICS AND LASER CHEMISTRY.** [Appl. phys., B,]. **VFOAT** Photophysics and Laser Chemistry. Vol. B26, No. 1 (Sept. 1981)-(1993). Academic Scholarly Publication. English. Twelve times a year. Springer-Verlag GmbH & Company KG, Heidelberger Platz 3, D 14197 Berlin Germany. **Tel** 011 49 30 8207223, FAX 011 49 30 8214091, telex 183 319 SPBLN D. **(Subscription address:** Springer Verlag New York Inc. / for North America, 44 Hartz Way, Secaucus NJ 07096.**) ED** H. K. V. Lotsch. **LC** QC1; .A734. **DD** 535/.05. **CODEN** APPCDL. **[CCC]. Ad Acc. Pr Rev. Circ:** 70. available on microfilm and microfiche from University Microfilms International (UMI). Documents available from Article Express International, The Genuine Article, Ask*IEEE, CASDDS. ***Continues in part*** *Applied Physics, 0340-3793.* ***Continued by*** *Applied Physics. B, Lasers and Optics.*
**Desc:** Journal for the rapid publication of experimental and theoretical investigations of applied research. Covers primarily the gaseous state, including the application of laser radiation in chemistry.
**Ind/Abst** Bioeng. Abstr.; Chem. Abstr.; Chem. Titles; Curr. Contents Phys. Chem. Earth Sci.; Ei Page One; Energy Res. Abstr. (Feb. 1982-); Eng. Index Annu.; HTFS Dig.; INSPEC (Sept. 1981-); Int. Aerosp. Abstr. (19??-19??); Mass Spect. Bull.; Phys. Briefs; Res. Alert [Full Cov.]; Sci. Cit. Index; SCISEARCH.

•UK/0969-8043
**APPLIED RADIATION AND ISOTOPES : INCLUDING DATA, INSTRUMENTATION AND METHODS FOR USE IN AGRICULTURE, INDUSTRY AND MEDICINE.** Vol. 44, No. 1/2 (Jan./Feb. 1993)-. Periodical. English. Twelve times a year. $1021.00 The Americas; £685.00 other. Pergamon Press, An Imprint of Elsevier Science Ltd., The Boulevard, Langford Lane, Kidlington, Oxford OX5 1GB United Kingdom. **Tel** 011 44 865 843000, 011 44 865 843699, FAX 011 44 865 843010. **(Subscription address:** Elsevier Science Ltd. Oxford Fulfillment Centre, PO Box 800, Kidlington, Oxford OX5 1DX United Kingdom.**) ED** W.L. McLaughlin, D.M. Taylor. **LC** QC770; .I6. **DD** 621.48/37/05. **NLM** W1; AP528P. Documents available from CASDDS, ADONIS. ***Continues*** *International Journal of Radiation Applications and Instrumentation. Part A, Applied Radiation and Isotopes, 0883-2889.*
**Desc:** Provides a medium for the publication of substantial original papers and short articles which describe methods, techniques and instrumentation relating to the production, measurement and application of radionuclides and radiation in any branch of science and technology.
**Ind/Abst** ADONIS; Chem. Abstr.; PESTDOC; Sci. Cit. Index; Soc. Sci. Cit. Index [Select. Cov.].

US/0003-7028
**APPLIED SPECTROSCOPY.** [Appl. spectrosc.]. **Added/Corp** Society for Applied Spectroscopy. Vol. 6 (Nov. 1951)-. Periodical. English. mo (12 issues). $180.00 US; $240.00 Canada and Mexico; $270.00 (air freight), $300.00 (air mail) other. Society for Applied Spectroscopy, 198 Thomas Johnson Drive, Suite S-2, PO Box 1438, Frederick MD 21702. **Tel** (301)694-8122, FAX (301)694-6860. **ED** William G. Fateley. **LC** QD71; .A6. **DD** 544.605. **NLM** W1 AP529. **CODEN** APSPA4. **[CCC].** Index available (bound in last issue). cum. index. **Bk Rev. Ad Acc. Pr Rev. Acid Free. Circ:** 6,500. available on microfilm. Documents available from Article Express International, The Genuine Article, BIOSIS Document Express, Ask*IEEE, CASDDS, Documents on Demand. ***Continues*** *Society for Applied Spectroscopy. Bulletin - Society for Applied Spectroscopy, 0096-8706.*
**Desc:** Original contributions covering the theory and practice of atomic, molecular and surface spectroscopy. Includes all forms of optical spectroscopy, x-ray, NMR and mass spectroscopy.
**Ind/Abst** Abstr. Bull. Inst. Paper Chem.; Abstr. Bull. Inst. Pap. Sci. Tech.; AGRICOLA; Alum. Ind. Abstr.; Anal. Abstr.; Biol. Abstr.; Ceram. Abstr.; Chem. Abstr.; Chem. Titles; Coal Abstr.; Curr. Contents Eng. Tech. Appl. Sci.; Curr. Contents Phys. Chem. Earth Sci.; Ei Page One; EMBASE; Energy Inf. Abstr.; Energy Res. Abstr.; Eng. Mater. Abstr.; Eng. Index Annu. [Select. Cov.]; Environ. Abstr.; GeoRef; HTFS Dig.; INIS Atomindex [Micro.]; INSPEC (1968-); Int. Aerosp. Abstr. (1983-); Leadscan; Mass Spect. Bull.; Met. Abstr.; Numis. Lit.; Ref. Sources; Res. Alert [Full Cov.]; Sci. Cit. Index; SCISEARCH; Sel. Water Resour. Abstr.; Soc. Sci. Cit. Index [Select. Cov.]; SPIN (1970-); Sug. Indus. Abstr.; World Alum. Abstr.; World Ceram. Abstr.; World Surf. Coat. Abstr.

PL/0138-0184
**ATMOSPHERIC OZONE ... SOLAR RADIATION.** 1982-. English (summaries and/or abstracts in Polish). an. Panstwowe Wydawn Naukowe, Miodowa 10, PO Box 391, 00251 Warsaw Poland. **LC** QC879.73.P7; P64A. ***Continues*** *Atmospheric Ozone, Optics of Atmosphere, Solar Radiation.*
**Ind/Abst** Int. Aerosp. Abstr. (1983-).

IT/0391-2051
**ATTI DELLA FONDAZIONE GIORGIO RONCHI (1976).** (ATTI DELLA FONDAZIONE GIORGIO RONCHI.). [Atti fond. Giorgio Ronchi]. **Added/Corp** Fondazione "Giorgio Ronchi.". Vol. 31 (Jan./Feb. 1976). Academic Scholarly Publication. Italian (English and French). bm. L240000.00 Italy; L250000.00 other. Fondazione Giorgio Ronchi, Via San Felice a Ema 20, 50125 Florence Italy. **Tel** 011 39 55 2320844. **LC** QC350; .F59. **DD** 535/.05. **NLM** W1 AT775Q. **CODEN** AFDGA2. **Bk Rev. Pr Rev. Circ:** 500 (ctrl). Documents available from Ask*IEEE, CASDDS. ***Continues*** *Atti della Fondazione Giorgio Ronchi e Contributi dell'Istituto Nazionale de Ottica, 0365-236X.*
**Desc:** Topics of pure and applied optics; history and philosophy of science.
**Ind/Abst** Chem. Abstr. (1976-1982); EMBASE; INSPEC (Jan./Feb. 1976-); Psychol. Abstr. (1979-); PsycINFO; PsycLit.

NE/0921-8637
**BEAM MODIFICATION OF MATERIALS.** [Beam modif. mater.]. (1984)-. Monographic series. English. ir. Elsevier Science Publishers BV, PO Box 211, 1000 AE Amsterdam Netherlands. **Tel** 011 31 20 5803642, FAX 011 31 20 5862696, telex 15682. **UDC** 54. Documents available from CASDDS.
**Ind/Abst** Chem. Abstr.

●UK/0966-9051
**BIOIMAGING.** **Added/Corp** American Institute of Physics. Vol. 1, No. 1 (Mar. 1993)-. Periodical. English. qt. $169.00. Institute of Physics, Techno House, Redcliffe Way, Bristol BS1 6NX England. **Tel** 011 44 272 297481, FAX 011 44 272 294318, telex 449149 INSTP G. **(Subscription address:** American Institute of Physics, Publishing Sales, 500 Sunnyside Blvd., Woodbury NY 11797.**)** **NLM** W1; BI666D.
**Desc:** Serves as a forum for the report of original research and innovative developments in the field of biological imaging. Publishes work on novel experimental and theoretical techniques and important applications in all biology and medicine. Quantitative digital approaches to imaging are emphasized.

CC/1000-4556
**BOPUXUE ZAZHI.** (PO PU HSUEH TSA CHIH.). [Bopuxue zazhi]. **Added/Corp** Chung-Kuo Wu Li Hsueh Hui. Po Pu Hsueh Chuan Yeh Wei Yuan Hui. Chung-Kuo Ko Hsueh Yuan. Wu-Han Wu Li Yen Chiu So. **VFOAT** Chinese Journal of Microwave & Radio-Frequency Spectroscopy. (198?)-. Academic Scholarly Publication. Chinese (English). qt. $60.00 institution, $30.00 individual. Zhongguo Kexueyuan / Wuhan Wuli Yanjiusuo, Chinese Academy of Sciences, Wuhan Institute of Physics, PO Box 71010, Xiaohongshan, Wuchang-qu, Wuhan, Hubei 430071 People's Republic of China. **Tel** 86 27 722544, FAX 86 27 725291. **ED** Ye Chaohui. **CODEN** BOZAE2. **Ad Acc, Adv Mgr:** Qianmai Sun. **Circ:** 600 (paid), 200 (controlled). Documents available from CASDDS, CASDDS.
**Ind/Abst** Chem. Abstr.

FR/0376-5954
**BULLETIN INTERIEUR - ASSOCIATION POUR LA PROTECTION CONTRE LES RAYONNEMENTS IONISANTS.** **Added/Corp** Association pour la Protection Contre les Rayonnements Ionisants. (196?)-. Bulletin. French. **NLM** W1 BU663.

JA/0038-7002
**BUNKO KENKYU.** [Bunko kenkyu]. **VFOAT** Journal of the Spectroscopical Society of Japan. (June 1951)-. Academic Scholarly Publication. Japanese. bm (6 issues). $208.00. Tokyo International, PO Box 5030, Tokyo 100 31 Japan. **Tel** 03 811 7238. **(Subscription address:** Kyowa Book Company Inc., 1 38 Kanda Jinbocho Chiyoda-ku, Tokyo 101 Japan.**)** **DD** 535. **NLM** W1 BU944G. **CODEN** BUKKAT. Documents available from Ask*IEEE, CASDDS.
**Ind/Abst** Anal. Abstr.; Chem. Abstr.; INSPEC (1975-).

US
**BUYING GUIDE.** **VFOAT** Fiberoptic Product News ... Buying Guide. 1986/87-. Consumer Publication. English. an. $55.00 book rate, $60.00 first class. High Tech Publications Inc, PO Box 1952, Dover NJ 07801-0952. **Tel** (213)378-0261, telex 703003 LASAPP. **LC** TA1800; .B89. **DD** 621.36/92/029.

UK
**CAMBRIDGE STUDIES IN MODERN OPTICS.** **VFOAT** Studies in Modern Optics. (198?)-. Monographic series. English. ir. Price varies per volume. Cambridge University Press, The Edinburgh Building, Shaftesbury Road, Cambridge CB2 2RU United Kingdom. **Tel** 011 44 223 312393, FAX 011 44 223 325959. **(Subscription address:** Cambridge University Press / North America, 110 Midland Avenue, Port Chester NY 10573.**)** Documents available from CASDDS.
**Ind/Abst** Chem. Abstr.

CN/1183-7306
**CANADIAN JOURNAL OF APPLIED SPECTROSCOPY.** [Can. j. appl. spectrosc.]. **Added/Corp** Spectroscopy Society of Canada. **VFOAT** Applied Spectroscopy. Vol. 35, No. 4 (Aug. 1990)-. Academic Scholarly Publication. English (French). Six times a year. 165.00Can$ Canada; 175.00Can$ other; Also comes with membership. Polyscience Publications Inc., PO Box 148, Morin Heights, Quebec J0R 1H0 Canada. **Tel** (514)226-5870, FAX (514)226-5866. **ED** Ian Butler; Telephone: (514)398-6910. **LC** QC451; .C29. **DD** 543/.0858/05. **CODEN** CJSPEM. Index available in last issue of volume--attached. cum. index. **Bk Rev.** **Ad Acc.** **Pr Rev.** **Circ:** 1,000. Documents available from The Genuine Article, BIOSIS Document Express, Ask*IEEE, CASDDS. ***Continues*** *Canadian Journal of Spectroscopy, 0045-5105.*
**Desc:** An international bilingual journal for all branches of fundamental and applied spectroscopy. The official publication of the Spectroscopy Society of Canada. Supported in part by the Natural Sciences and Engineering Research Council of Canada.
**Ind/Abst** Biol. Abstr. (1991-); Chem. Abstr. (1990-); Curr. Contents Phys. Chem. Earth Sci.; INIS Atomindex [Micro.]; INSPEC (Dec. 1990-); Leadscan; Res. Alert [Full Cov.]; Sci. Cit. Index; SCISEARCH.

CN/0381-5447
**CANADIAN SPECTROSCOPIC NEWS (1972).** (CANADIAN SPECTROSCOPIC NEWS.). V. 1 (March 1972)-. Periodical. English. ir (3 times a year). $5.00. Spectroscopy Society of Canada, PO Box 332, Station A, Ottawa Ontario K1N 8V3 Canada. **Tel** 011 613 990 8396. **ED** H F Shurvell. **Bk Rev.** ***Supersedes in part*** *Canadian Spectroscopy, 0008-5057.*

CC
**CHI KUANG CHI SHU.** **Added/Corp** China. Kuo Chia ko Wei. **VFOAT** Laser Technology. (19??)-. Periodical. Chinese (summaries and/or abstracts in English). bm. **LC** QC976.L36; C46. **DD** 621.36/6/05. Documents available from Article Express International.
**Ind/Abst** Ei Page One; Eng. Index Annu.

CC/1001-5078
**CHI KUANG YU HUNG WAI.** **Added/Corp** Hua Pei Kuang Tien Chi Shu Yen Chiu So. **VFOAT** Laser and Infrared; Laser & Infrared. (1971)-. Periodical. Chinese (summaries and/or abstracts in English). bm. **LC** TA1671; .C485. Documents available from Article Express International.
**Ind/Abst** Ei Page One; Eng. Index Annu.

US
**DMSP SSM/I BRIGHTNESS TEMPERATURE GRIDS. POLAR REGIONS [COMPUTER FILE] / NATIONAL SNOW AND ICE DATA CENTER.** **Added/Corp** Defense Meteorological Satellite Program (U.S.) National Snow and Ice Data Center (U.S.). **VFOAT** Brightness Temperature Grids. Polar Regions. **VAT** Defense Meteorological Satellite Program Special Sensor Microwave Imager Brightness Temperature Grids. (1987)-. English. National Snow and Ice Data Center, Cooperative Institute for Research in Environmental Sciences, University of Colorado, Boulder CO 80309-0449. **LC** QC484; .D57.

UK/0013-4589
**ELECTRO OPTICS.** [Electro Opt.]. Vol. 1, No. 1 (March 1971)-. Periodical. English. Five times a year. £90.00 UK; £100.00 other. Milton Publishing Company, 5 Tranquil Passage, Blackheath London SE3 0BY England. **Tel** 011 44 81 2971097. **CODEN** EOPTA4. Documents available from Ask*IEEE.
**Ind/Abst** INSPEC (Sept. 1987-).

US/1057-4956
**EUROPEAN ELECTRO-OPTICS.** ***Ceased.*** [Eur. electro-opt.]. **VFOAT** Laser Focus World European Electro-Optics. (Spring 1991)-(199?). Periodical. English. qt. PennWell Publishing Company, 1421 South Sheridan, PO Box 1260, Tulsa OK 74101. **Tel** (918)835-3161, (800)331-4463, FAX (918)831-9497. **LC** TA1501; .L375. **DD** 621.36/6. **CODEN** EEOPEN. Documents available from Ask*IEEE. ***Continues*** *Laser Focus World. European Supplement.*
**Ind/Abst** INSPEC (Autumn 1991-).

FR
**EUROPEAN SYNCHROTON RADIATION FACILITY.** English. BP 220, 38043 Grenoble Cedex France.

US/0146-8030
**FIBER AND INTEGRATED OPTICS.** [Fiber integr. opt.]. Vol. 1 (1977)-. Academic Scholarly Publication. English. qt. £121.00 UK; $200.00 other. Taylor & Francis Ltd., Rankine Road, Basingstoke Hampshire, RG24 8PR United Kingdom. **Tel** 011 44 256 840366, FAX 011 44 256 479438, telex 858540. **(Subscription address:** Taylor & Francis Inc., 1900 Frost Road, Suite 101, Bristol PA 19007-1598.**)** **ED** Henri Hodara (editor's address: Tetra Tech Inc., 9645 Scranton Road, Suite 200, San Diego CA 92121). **LC** TA1800; .F49. **DD** 621.36/92/05. **CODEN** FOIOD2. **[CCC].** **Bk Rev.** **Ad Acc.** **Pr Rev.** **Circ:** 800 (ctrl). available on microfilm and microfiche from University Microfilms International (UMI). Documents available from Article Express International, The Genuine Article, BIOSIS Document Express, Ask*IEEE, Petroleum Abstracts Document Delivery Service, CASDDS.
**Desc:** International journal that focuses on fiberoptic developments and in-depth surveys. Also serves as a forum for valuable information exchange between scientists, engineers, manufacturers and business people. The journal is a powerful vehicle to report significant progress in this field by bridging various disciplines scattered through a variety of journals such as optics, electronics, materials, manufacturing techniques and business economics.
**Ind/Abst** Acoust. Abstr.; Bioeng. Abstr.; Biol. Abstr.; Ceram. Abstr.; Chem. Abstr.; Curr. Contents Eng. Tech. Appl. Sci.; Ei Page One; Eng. Index Annu.; INSPEC (1977-); Int. Aerosp. Abstr.; Mar. Sci. Contents Tables; Ocean. Abstr.; Pet. Abstr.; Pollut. Abstr. Indexes; Res. Alert [Full Cov.]; SCISEARCH.

UK
**FIBER OPTICS DEVELOPMENTS.** English. mo. £150.00 UK; £165.00 Europe. Evison Enterprises, 65 Ashey Road, Ryde, Isle of Wight, England. **Tel** 011 44 983 566541.

US/8756-2049
**FIBER OPTICS NEWS.** Vol. 5, No. 1 (Jan. 14, 1985)-. Periodical. English. wk (50 issues). $697.00 US; $760.00 other. Phillips Business Information, Inc., 1201 Seven Locks Road, Potomac MD 20854. **Tel** (301)424-3338, (800)777-5006, FAX (301)309-3847. **ED** Dave Chaffee. **DD** 535. **[CCC].** available on an online database (files 636,648/Full-Text) from DIALOG. ***Continues*** *Fiber Laser/News, 0275-6099;* ***Absorbed*** *Military & Commercial Fiber Business.*
**Desc:** Covers military applications, routes, marker share, contracts and joint ventures, regulation, and international competition.
**Ind/Abst** PROMT [Full Txt.]; PTS Newsl. Database [Full Txt.]; Trade Ind. ASAP [Full Txt.]; Trade Ind. Index [Full Txt.].

US/1057-9362
**FIBEROPTIC APPLICATIONS ... .** Vol. 1, No. 1 (Feb. 1991)-. Periodical. English. Gordon Publications Inc, A Subsidiary of Cahners Publishing Company, 301 Gibraltar Drive, Box 650, Morris Plains NJ 07950. **Tel** (201)292-5100. **DD** 621.

UK
**FIBRE OPTIC SENSORS.** English. bw. $290.00. Institution of Electrical Engineers / IEE, Michael Faraday House, Six Hills Way, Stevenage Herts SG1 2AY UK. **Tel** 011 44 438 313311, FAX 011 44 438 742840, telex 825578 IEESTV G. **(Subscription address:** IEE / UK, Publications Sales Department, PO Box 96, Stevenage, Herts, SG1 2SD England.**)**

US/0161-2220
**FINNIGAN SPECTRA.** [Finnigan spectra]. Academic Scholarly Publication. English. Three times a year. **CODEN** FISPDD. Documents available from CASDDS.
**Ind/Abst** Chem. Abstr.

GW/0176-7984
**FORTSCHRITTE IN DER ATOMSPEKTROMETRISCHEN SPURENANALYTIK.** [Fortschr. atomspektrom. Spurenanal.]. (1984)-. Monographic series. German (English). **CODEN** FOASE9. Documents available from CASDDS.
**Ind/Abst** Chem. Abstr.

DK/0108-0954
**GAMMA (KBENHAVN).** (GAMMA.). [Gamma]. **Added/Corp** Niels Bohr Institutet. (1971)-. Periodical. Danish. Niehls Bohr Institutet, Blegdamsvej 17, 2100 Kbenhavn Denmark. **CODEN** GMMADB. Documents available from CASDDS.
**Ind/Abst** Chem. Abstr.

CC/0253-2239
**GUANGXUE XUEBAO.** (KUANG HSUEH HSUEH PAO.). [Guangxue xuebeo]. **Added/Corp** Chung-kuo Kuang Hsueh Hsueh Hui. **VFOAT** Acta Optica Sinica. (1981)-. Academic Scholarly Publication. Chinese (summaries and/or abstracts in English). mo. $72.84. **(Subscription address:** China International Book Trading Corporation, PO Box 399, Library Service Department, Beijing 100044 People's Republic of China.**)** **LC** QC350; .K8. **DD** 621..388/13/05. **CODEN** GUXUDC. Documents available from Article Express International, Article Express International, CASDDS.
**Ind/Abst** Chem. Abstr.; Ei Page One; Energy Res. Abstr. (Aug. 1982-); Eng. Index Annu.; SPIN (1982-).

SZ/0899-2711
**HANDBOOK OF LASER SCIENCE AND TECHNOLOGY.** [Handb. laser sci. technol.]. (1988)-. Monographic series. English. ir. Price varies per volume. Harwood Academic Publishers, PO Box 90, Reading RG1 8JL England. **Tel** 011 44 734 560080. **(Subscription address:** International Publishers Distributor at one of the following addresses: 820 Town Center Drive, Langhorne, PA 19047; or PO Box 90, Reading Berkshire RG1 8JL UK; or Kent Ridge PO Box 1180, Singapore 9111, Republic of Singapore**)** **DD** 621.

UK/0951-3914
**HOLOGRAPHICS INTERNATIONAL.** ***Suspended.*** [Hologr. int.]. 1987-?. Periodical. English. qt. £15.00 UK; $25.00 US. Holographics International, BCM-Holographics, London WC1N 3XX United Kingdom. **Tel** +44 816642 8381. **ED** Sunny Bains. **Bk Rev.** **Ad Acc.** **Circ:** 2,500.
**Desc:** International magazine covering artistic, scientific and commercial uses of holograms. Printed in full colour.

JA/0285-3604
**HOSHASEN.** [Hoshasen]. **VFOAT** Ionizing Radiation. Academic Scholarly Publication. Japanese. Three times a year. Oyo Butsuri Gakkai, (Japan Soc. of Applied Physics), Kunimatsu Biru, 2-6, Kudan Kita 1 Chome, Chiyodaku, Tokyoto 102, Japan. **CODEN** HOSHDJ. Documents available from CASDDS.
**Ind/Abst** Chem. Abstr.; Energy Res. Abstr. (May 1979-).

US/1055-6877
**IEEE LTS : THE MAGAZINE OF LIGHTWAVE TELECOMMUNICATIONS SYSTEMS.** ***Ceased.*** [IEEE LTS]. **Added/Corp** IEEE Communications Society. Lasers and Electro-Optics Society (Institute of Electrical and Electronics Engineers). **VFOAT** LTS. **VAT** Institute of Electrical and Electronics Engineers Lightwave Telecommunication Systems. Vol. 2, No. 2 (May 1991)-(1992). Periodical. English. qt. IEEE, Institution of Electrical and Electronics Engineers, Inc., 345 East 47th Street, New York NY 10017-2394. **Tel** (908)981-1393, FAX (908)981-9667. **LC** TA1800; .I33. **DD** 621.382/75. **CODEN** IELTEU. **[CCC].** Documents available from Ask*IEEE. ***Continues*** *IEEE LCS,*

1045-9235.
**Ind/Abst** Appl. Sci. Technol. Index; Index IEEE Publ.; INSPEC (May 1991-).

US/1041-1135
**IEEE PHOTONICS TECHNOLOGY LETTERS.** (IEEE PHOTONICS TECHNOLOGY LETTERS : A PUBLICATION OF THE IEEE LASER AND ELECTRO-OPTICS SOCIETY.). [IEEE photonics technol. lett.]. **Added/Corp** Lasers and Electro-Optics Society (Institute of Electrical and Electronics Engineers) Institute of Electrical and Electronics Engineers. **VFOAT** Photonics Technology Letters. **VAT** Institute of Electrical and Electronics Engineers Photonics Technology Letters. Vol. 1, No. 1 (Jan. 1989)-. Periodical. English. mo. $290.00. IEEE, Institution of Electrical and Electronics Engineers, Inc., 345 East 47th Street, New York NY 10017-2394. **Tel** (908)981-1393, FAX (908)981-9667. **(Subscription address:** IEEE / Institute of Electrical and Electronics Engineers, 445 Hoes Lane, PO Box 1331, Piscataway NJ 08855-1331.) **LC** WMLC 93/2133. **DD** 539. **[CCC]. Pr Rev.** Documents available from Article Express International, The Genuine Article, Ask*IEEE.
**Desc:** Covers original research relevant to photonics technology. This field emphasizes laser and electro-optic technology, laser physics and systems, applications and photonic/lightwave components and applications.
**Ind/Abst** Curr. Contents Phys. Chem. Earth Sci.; Ei Page One; Eng. Index Annu.; Index IEEE Publ.; INSPEC (Jan. 1989-); Int. Aerosp. Abstr.; Res. Alert [Full Cov.]; Sci. Cit. Index; SCISEARCH.

US/1059-4043
**IMAGING TECHNOLOGY NEWS : THE NEWSLETTER FOR IMAGING END USERS.** [Imaging technol. news]. (1991)-. Newsletter. English. mo. $55.00. Imaging Technology News, 108 River Holly Drive, Mechanicsville VA 23111. **DD** 621.

●US/0941-4185
**INDUSTRIAL LASER HANDBOOK, THE.** (1992-1993) Ed.-. English. be. Springer-Verlag New York Inc., 175 5th Avenue, New York NY 10010. **Tel** (212)460-1500, telex 232 235 SPB UR. **(Subscription address:** Springer Verlag New York Inc. / for North America, 44 Hartz Way, Secaucus NJ 07096.) **LC** TA1671; .I53. **DD** 621.366/05. **Continues** The Industrial Laser Annual Handbook., 0886-0106.

US/0888-935X
**INDUSTRIAL LASER REVIEW.** [Ind. laser rev.]. **VFOAT** ILR. Vol. 1, No. 1 (June 1986)-. Periodical. English. Twelve times a year. $240.00 US and Canada; $280.00 other. PennWell Publishing Company, Ten Tara Boulevard 5th Floor, Nashua NH 03062-2801. **Tel** (603)891-0123, (603)891-9177, FAX (603)891-0624, (603)891-0574. **DD** 621. **[CCC]**.
**Desc:** Link between users, manufacturers, and suppliers of industrial lasers. Coverage includes news of lasers on the production line, reports on actual applications, new systems and other products, technical and economic analyses, market trends, and exclusive conference reports.

CN/0822-8493
**INFORMATION COULEUR (MONTREAL).** (INFORMATION COULEUR / CENTRE QUEBECOIS DE LA COULEUR.). [Inf. coul.]. Vol. 1, No. 1 (Jan. 1984)-. Periodical. French. Three times a year. Centre Quebecois de la Couleur, Universite du Quebec A Montreal CP 888, Succursale A, Montreal Quebec H3C 3P8 Canada. **DD** 535.6/05.

US/0195-9271
**INTERNATIONAL JOURNAL OF INFRARED AND MILLIMETER WAVES.** [Int. j. infrared millim. waves]. Vol. 1, No. 1 (Mar. 1980)-. Academic Scholarly Publication. English. Twelve times a year. $495.00 US; $580.00 other. Plenum Press, 233 Spring Street, New York NY 10013-1578. **Tel** (212)620-8000, (800)221-9369, FAX (212)463-0742, (212)807-1047, telex 23/421139. **ED** Kenneth J. Button. **LC** TA1570; .I6. **DD** 621.36/12/05. **CODEN** IJIWDO. **[CCC].** Index available. **Pr Rev.** available on microfilm and microfiche from University Microfilms International (UMI). Documents available from Article Express International, The Genuine Article, Ask*IEEE, CASDDS.
**Desc:** This journal provides a common forum for rapid dissemination of the results of original research in millimeter, submillimeter and far, infra red theory techniques, devices, systems, spectroscopy and applications.
**Ind/Abst** Bioeng. Abstr.; Chem. Abstr.; Curr. Contents Eng. Tech. Appl. Sci.; Ei Page One; Eng. Index Annu.; INIS Atomindex [Micro.]; INSPEC (March 1980-); Int. Aerosp. Abstr.; Pollut. Abstr. Indexes; Ref. Z.; Res. Alert [Full Cov.]; Sci. Cit. Index; SCISEARCH.

●SI/0218-1991
**INTERNATIONAL JOURNAL OF NONLINEAR OPTICAL PHYSICS. VFOAT** Nonlinear Optical Physics. Vol. 1, No. 1 (Jan. 1992)-. Periodical. English. Four times a year. $180.00 individuals, $365.00 institutions. World Scientific Publishing Company, PO Box 128, Farrer Road, Singapore 9128 Singapore. **Tel** 011 65 3825663, FAX 011 65 3825919, telex RS 28561 WSPC. **(Subscription address:** US: World Scientific Publishing Co., Inc., 1060 Main Street, River Edge, NJ 07661 Telephone: (201)487-9655, Fax: (201)487-9656; Europe: World Scientific Publishing Co Ltd, 73 Lynton Mead, Totteridge, London N20 8DH United Kingdom Telephone: 011 44 81 4462461, Fax: 011 44 81 4463356; India: World Scientific Publishing Co Pte Ltd, 4911 9th Floor, High Point IV, 45 Palace Road, Bangalore 560 001 India Telephone: (80) 2205972, Fax: (80) 3344593, telex: 0845-2900 PCO IN; Hong Kong: World Scientific Publishing (HK) Co, PO Box 72482, Kowloon Central Post Office, Hong Kong Telephone: 852-7718791, Fax: 852-7718155) **LC** QC446.15; .I62. **DD** 535.2. **CODEN** IJNOEQ. Documents available from Ask*IEEE.
**Ind/Abst** INSPEC (1992-).

UK/0952-5432
**INTERNATIONAL JOURNAL OF OPTOELECTRONICS.** [Int. j. optoelectron.]. **VFOAT** IJO. Vol. 3, No. 1 (Jan./Feb. 1988)-. Periodical. English. bm. £224.00 UK; $370.00 other. Taylor & Francis Ltd., Rankine Road, Basingstoke Hampshire, RG24 8PR United Kingdom. **Tel** 011 44 256 840366, FAX 011 44 256 479438, telex 858540. **(Subscription address:** Taylor & Francis Inc., 1900 Frost Road, Suite 101, Bristol PA 19007-1598.) **ED** B. Culshaw and A. Rogers. **LC** TA1750; .I594. **DD** 621.381/045. **CODEN** IJOOEV. **[CCC].** Index available. **Bk Rev. Ad Acc. Pr Rev. Circ:** 200. available on microfilm from University Microfilms International (UMI). Documents available from Ask*IEEE. **Continues** International Journal of Optical Sensors, 0951-5992; **Absorbed** Optical Computing & Processing.
**Desc:** Meets the need for a single publication covering the whole field of optoelectronics, from optical sensors, fibres and waveguides, to materials, devices, detectors, processors, networks and systems. Presents applications, developments and implementations.
**Ind/Abst** Ei Page One; HTFS Dig.; INSPEC (1988-).

UK
**INTERNATIONAL JOURNAL OF RADIATION APPLICATIONS AND INSTRUMENTATION. PART D, NUCLEAR TRACKS AND RADIATION MEASUREMENTS. Title Change. See** Physics-Nuclear Physics.

●US/1066-7016
**INTERNATIONAL JOURNAL OF RADIATION HYGIENE.** [Int. j. radiat. hygiene]. (1993)-. Periodical. English. Four times a year. $285.00. Nova Science Publishers Inc., 6080 Jericho Turnpike, Suite 207, Commack NY 11725-2808. **Tel** (516)499-3103, (516)499-3106, FAX (516)499-3146. **DD** 612.

UK/0957-476X
**INTERNATIONAL JOURNAL OF RADIOACTIVE MATERIALS TRANSPORT.** [Int. j. radioact. mater. transp.]. **VFOAT** RAMTRANS; Radioactive Materials Transport. Vol. 1, No. 1 (1990)-. Periodical. English. qt. £96.00 UK; $195.00 other. Nuclear Technology Publishing, PO Box 7, Ashford Kent TN23 1YW England. **Tel** 0233 641683, FAX 0233 610021, telex 966119 NTPUK G. **CODEN** IJRTER.
**Desc:** Covers all aspects of the transport of radioactive materials including regulations, package design, safety assessments, testing, accidents and experience in the transport of all forms of radioactive materials.

UA/0021-1907
**ISOTOPE AND RADIATION RESEARCH.** (ISTOPE AND RADIATION RESEARCH / BULLETIN ISSUED BY THE MIDDLE EASTERN REGIONAL RADIOISOTOPE CENTRE FOR THE ARAB COUNTRIES.). [Isot. radiat. res.]. **Added/Corp** Middle Eastern Regional Radioisotope Centre for the Arab Countries. **VFOAT** Buhuth al-Nazair wa-al-Isaaa. (196?)-. Academic Scholarly Publication. English. Twice a year. $25.00. Middle Eastern Regional Radioisotope Centre for the Arab Countries - MERRCAC, SH Malaeb el Gamaa Dokki, 11321 Cario Egypt. **Tel** 011 20 2 700569 or 700588. **CODEN** ISRRAC. Documents available from Ask*IEEE, CASDDS.
**Ind/Abst** AGRICOLA; Agric. Eng. Abstr.; Biodeter. Abstr.; Chem. Abstr.; EMBASE; Energy Res. Abstr.; Helminthol. Abstr. (1991-); INSPEC (July 1987-); Nutr. Abstr. Rev., Ser. B, Live Feeds and Feed.; Postharvest News Inf.; Rev. Agric. Entomol.; Rev. Med. Vet. Mycology; Rice Abstr.; Soils Fert.

RU
**ISSLEDOVANIIA PO NELINEINOI OPTIKE I SPEKTROSKOPII.** Vol. 1 (1973)-. Academic Scholarly Publication. Russian. 1.00rub (single issue). Saratov N.G. Chernyshevskii State University, Astrakhanskaya Ulitsa 83, 410071 Saratov Russia. **Tel** 24-16-96, FAX 24-04-46, telex 241125. **LC** QC446.15; .I87. **CODEN** INOSD2. Documents available from CASDDS.
**Ind/Abst** Chem. Abstr. (?-1973);(-1973).

SA/0377-0311
**JAARLIKSE STRALINGSVERSLAG.**
**Main/Corp** South Africa. Weather Bureau. **VFOAT** Annual Radiation Report. English. R3.75. Government Printer / South Africa, Bosman Street, Private Bag X85, Pretoria 0001 South Africa. **Tel** 011 27 12 3239731 Ext. 262. **LC** QC911; .S68. **DD** 551.5/271/0968.

GW/0075-272X
**JAHRBUCH FUER OPTIK UND FEINMECHANIK.** (19??)-. German. an. DM44.00. Fachverlag Schiele & Schoen, Markgrafenstrasse 11, W-1000 Berlin 61 Germany. **Tel** 011/49/30/2516029, FAX 011/49/30/2517248, telex 841/181470. **LC** Q185; .J25. **[CCC].**

GW
**JAHRESBERICHT / MAX-PLANCK-INSTITUT FUER QUANTENOPTIK. VFOAT** MPQ Jahresbericht. (1981)-. Periodical. German (English). an. Free. Max-Planck-Institut fur Quantenoptik, W-8046 Garching Bei Munchen Germany. **Tel** 089/329050, telex 529206 MPQD. **ED** T Haensch, K Kompa, H Walther and S Witkowski. **LC** TA1671; .M39a. **DD** 621.36/6/05. **Circ:** 1,000 (ctrl). Documents available from CASDDS. **Continues** Max-Planck-Gesellschaft zur Forderung der Wissenschaften. Projektgruppe fur Laserforschung. PLF Jahresbericht.
**Desc:** Review of the annual scientific work of the Max-Planck Institut for quantum optics.
**Ind/Abst** Chem. Abstr.

US/0887-9362
**JAPAN LASER REPORT. Title Change.** [Japan laser rep.]. Vol. 1, No. 1 (Apr. 1986)-(1993). Periodical. English. mo. PennWell Publishing Company, 1421 South Sheridan, PO Box 1260, Tulsa OK 74101. **Tel** (918)835-3161, (800)331-4463, FAX (918)831-9497. **(Subscription address:** Laser Report, PO Box 989, 1 Technology Park Drive, Westford, MA 01886) **DD** 621. **Absorbed by** Laser Report.
**Desc:** Covers the laser industry timely and invaluable information needed to manage in a global marketplace. Learn about the latest trends, find out about the latest technological developments, and keep abreast of new products, competitive strategies, government policies and proposals.

XR/0447-6441
**JEMNA MECHANIKA A OPTIKA. See** Physics-Analytic and Experimental Mechanics.

CN/0022-0264
**JOURNAL OF CURRENT LASER ABSTRACTS. See** Physics-Abstracting, Bibliographies and Statistics.

NE/0368-2048
**JOURNAL OF ELECTRON SPECTROSCOPY AND RELATED PHENOMENA.** [J. electron spectros. relat. phenomena]. Vol. 1 (Oct. 1972)-. Academic Scholarly Publication. English. Eighteen times a year (6 vols.). Fl2400.00. Elsevier Science Publishers BV, PO Box 211, 1000 AE Amsterdam Netherlands. **Tel** 011 31 20 5803642, FAX 011 31 20 5862696, telex 15682. **ED** C.R. Brundle, G.E. McGuire, J.J. Pireaux. **LC** QC454.E4; J67. **DD** 543/.0858. **CODEN** JESRAW. **[CCC].** Index available in last issue of volume-attached. **Pr Rev.** available on microfilm and microfiche from University Microfilms International (UMI). Documents available from The Genuine Article, Ask*IEEE, CASDDS.
**Desc:** Publishes experimental and theoretical work in the field of electron spectroscopy and all subjects relevant to it.
**Ind/Abst** Anal. Abstr.; Ceram. Abstr.; Chem. Abstr.; Chem. Titles; Curr. Contents Phys. Chem. Earth Sci.; Ei Page One; INSPEC (Oct. 1972-); Int. Aerosp. Abstr.; Mass Spect. Bull.; Res. Alert [Full Cov.]; Sci. Cit. Index; SCISEARCH.

US/1053-0509
**JOURNAL OF FLUORESCENCE.** [J. fluoresc.]. Vol. 1, No. 1 (Mar. 1991)-. Academic Scholarly Publication. English. Four times a year. $195.00 institutions, $43.00 individuals US; $230.00 institutions, $50.00 individuals other. Plenum Press, 233 Spring Street, New York NY 10013-1578. **Tel** (212)620-8000, (800)221-9369, FAX (212)463-0742, (212)807-1047, telex 23/421139. **ED** Joseph Lakowicz. **LC** QC477; .J68. **DD** 535/.35. **NLM** W1; JO65N. **CODEN** JOFLEN. **[CCC]. Pr Rev.** Documents available from CASDDS.
**Desc:** An international forum for the publication of high-quality, peer-reviewed, original papers, review articles, and short communications covering advances in the understanding of fluorescence.
**Ind/Abst** Chem. Abstr.; Ei Page One.

US/1042-346X
**JOURNAL OF LASER APPLICATIONS.** [J. laser appl.]. **Added/Corp** Laser Institute of America. Vol. 1, No. 1 (Oct. 1988)-. Periodical. English. qt. $159.00 US and Canada; £110.00 Europe; £125.00 Other. Chapman & Hall, 2-6 Boundary Row, London SE1 8HN England. **Tel** 011 44 71 865 0066, FAX 011 44 71 522 9623, telex 290164 Chapmag. **(Subscription address:** Chapman & Hall, Cheriton House, North Way, Andover, Hampshire, SP10 5BE England.) **LC** TA1671; .J68. **DD** 621.36/6/05.

**NLM** W1; JO736E. **CODEN** JLAPEN. **[CCC].** Documents available from Article Express International.
**Ind/Abst** Ei Page One; Eng. Index Annu.

JA/0387-8805
**JOURNAL OF LIGHT & VISUAL ENVIRONMENT.** (JOURNAL OF LIGHT & VISUAL ENVIRONMENT / ILLUMINATING ENGINEERING INSTITUTE OF JAPAN). [J. light visual environ.]. **Added/Corp** Illuminating Engineering Institute of Japan. **VFOAT** Journal of Light and Visual Environment. Vol. 1 (1977)-. Academic Scholarly Publication. English. sa. $76.00. Illuminating Engineering Institute of Japan, 7-1 Yurakucho 1-chome Chiyoda-ku, Tokyo 100 Japan. **(Subscription address:** Kyowa Book Company Inc., 1-38 Kanda Jinbo-Cho, Chiyoda-Ku, Tokyo 101, Japan**)** **CODEN** JLEVDQ. **[CCC].** Documents available from Ask*IEEE, CASDDS.
**Ind/Abst** Chem. Abstr.; INSPEC (1984-).

US/0733-8724
**JOURNAL OF LIGHTWAVE TECHNOLOGY.** (JOURNAL OF LIGHTWAVE TECHNOLOGY : A JOINT IEEE/OSA PUBLICATION.). [J. lightwave technol.]. **Added/Corp** Institute of Electrical and Electronics Engineers. Optical Society of America. Vol. LT-1, No. 1 (Mar. 1983)-. Academic Scholarly Publication. English. mo. $495.00. IEEE, Institution of Electrical and Electronics Engineers, Inc., 345 East 47th Street, New York NY 10017-2394. **Tel** (908)981-1393, FAX (908)981-9667. **(Subscription address:** IEEE / Institute of Electrical and Electronics Engineers, 445 Hoes Lane, PO Box 1331, Piscataway NJ 08855-1331.**)** **ED** Donald B. Keck. **LC** TA1501; .J678. **DD** 621.36/92/05. **CODEN** JLTEDG. **[CCC].** cum. index. **Pr Rev.** available in microform (16mm or 35mm); available on microfiche. Documents available from Article Express International, The Genuine Article, Ask*IEEE, CASDDS.
**Desc:** Co-published by the Optical Society of America, contains original contributions of theoretical and experimental papers. Presents advances in the science, technology, and engineering of optical guided waves.
**Ind/Abst** Acoust. Abstr.; Chem. Abstr. (1983-); Curr. Contents Eng. Tech. Appl. Sci.; Ei Page One; Eng. Index Annu.; Index IEEE Publ.; INIS Atomindex [Micro.]; INSPEC (March 1983-); Int. Aerosp. Abstr. (1983-); Pollut. Abstr. Indexes; Res. Alert [Full Cov.]; Sci. Cit. Index; SCISEARCH.

NE/0022-2313
**JOURNAL OF LUMINESCENCE.** [J. lumin.]. Vol. 1/2 (1970)-. Academic Scholarly Publication. English. Twenty-four times a year (4 vols.). Fl2120.00. Elsevier Science Publishers BV, PO Box 211, 1000 AE Amsterdam Netherlands. **Tel** 011 31 20 5803642, FAX 011 31 20 5862696, telex 15682. **ED** R.S. Meltzer. **LC** QC476.4; .J67. **DD** 535/.35/05. **CODEN** JLUMA8. **[CCC]. Pr Rev.** available on microfilm and microfiche from University Microfilms International (UMI). Documents available from Article Express International, The Genuine Article, BIOSIS Document Express, Ask*IEEE, CASDDS.
**Desc:** Provides a means of communication between scientists in different disciplines who share a common interest in the electronic excited state of molecular, ionic and covalent systems, whether crystalline, amorphous, or liquid.
**Ind/Abst** Acoust. Abstr.; Bioeng. Abstr.; Biol. Abstr.; Ceram. Abstr.; Chem. Abstr.; Chem. Titles; Curr. Aware. Biol. Sci., CABS; Curr. Contents Phys. Chem. Earth Sci.; Curr. Titles Electrochem.; Ei Page One; Eng. Index Annu.; GeoRef; INSPEC (April 1970-); Leadscan; Phys. Briefs; Res. Alert [Full Cov.]; Sci. Cit. Index; SCISEARCH.

UK/0950-0340
**JOURNAL OF MODERN OPTICS.** [J. mod. opt.]. **Added/Corp** European Physical Society. Institute of Physics (Great Britain). **VFOAT** Modern Optics. Vol. 34, No. 1 (Jan. 1987)-. Academic Scholarly Publication. English (French and German). mo. £770.00 UK; $1,270.00 other. Taylor & Francis Ltd., Rankine Road, Basingstoke Hampshire, RG24 8PR United Kingdom. **Tel** 011 44 256 840366, FAX 011 44 256 479438, telex 858540. **(Subscription address:** Taylor & Francis Inc., 1900 Frost Road, Suite 101, Bristol PA 19007-1598.**)** **ED** P. L. Knight (editor's address: Optics Section, Blackett Laboratory, Imperial College, Prince Consort Road, London SW7 2BZ UK); H. A. Macleod (editor's address: Optical Sciences Center, University of Arizona, Tuscon, AR 85721). **LC** QC350; .053. **DD** 535. **NLM** W1; JO77S. **CODEN** JMOPEW. **[CCC]. Bk Rev. Pr Rev.** available on microfilm and microfiche from University Microfilms International (UMI). Documents available from The Genuine Article, Ask*IEEE, CASDDS. ***Continues** Optica Acta, 0030-3909.*
**Desc:** Covers both the fundamental and applied aspects of contemporary research world-wide on such topics as nonlinear and quantum optics; laser physics, coherence and speckle; optical fibres and thin films; integrated optics and electro-optics; optical design and testing. The journal carries a rapid-publication letters section and book reviews.
**Ind/Abst** Acoust. Abstr.; Chem. Abstr. (1987-); Curr. Contents Eng. Tech. Appl. Sci.; Curr. Contents Phys. Chem. Earth Sci.; Ei Page One; EMBASE (1987-); INSPEC (1987-); Int. Aerosp. Abstr. (1987-); ISMEC Bull. (1987-); Math. Rev. (1988-); Pollut. Abstr. Indexes (1987-); Res. Alert [Full Cov.]; Saf. Sci. Abstr. J. (1987-); Sci. Cit. Index; SCISEARCH.

US/0022-2852
**JOURNAL OF MOLECULAR SPECTROSCOPY.** [J. mol. spectrosc.]. Vol. 1 (July 1957)-. Academic Scholarly Publication. English. mo. $1398.00 US and Canada; $1600.00 other. Academic Press, Inc., 6277 Sea Harbor Drive, Orlando FL 32887. **Tel** (800)543-9534, (407)345-4100, FAX (407)363-9661. **ED** K. Narahari Rao, Frank C. De Lucia, Jon T. Hougen and James K. G. Watson. **LC** QC451; .J65. **DD** 539.105. **NLM** W1 JO774. **CODEN** JMOSA3. **[CCC]. Pr Rev.** Documents available from Article Express International, The Genuine Article, BIOSIS Document Express, Ask*IEEE, CASDDS.
**Desc:** Presents experimental and theoretical articles on all subjects relevant to molecular spectroscopy and its modern applications. A medium for the publication of works by the most significant researchers in the field. An invaluable resource for chemists, physicists, and others involved in molecular spectroscopy research and practice.
**Ind/Abst** Abstr. Bull. Inst. Pap. Sci. Tech.; AGRICOLA; Biol. Abstr.; Chem Inform; Chem. Abstr.; Chem. Titles; Curr. Contents Phys. Chem. Earth Sci.; Ei Page One; Eng. Index Annu. [Select. Cov.]; INIS Atomindex [Micro.]; INSPEC (1968-); Int. Aerosp. Abstr.; Life Sci. Collect.; Res. Alert [Full Cov.]; Sci. Cit. Index; SCISEARCH.

UK
**JOURNAL OF NEAR INFRARED SPECTROSCOPY.** (19??)-. English. Four times a year. $205.00. NIR Publications, 6 Charlton Mill, Charlton Chichester PO18 0HY England. **Tel** 011 44 243 811334, FAX 011 44 243 811711. **ED** A.M.C. Davis. **Bk Rev. Ad Acc, Adv Mgr:** Ian Michael. **Pr Rev. Circ:** 150.

GW/0173-4911
**JOURNAL OF OPTICAL COMMUNICATIONS.** [J. opt. commun.]. Vol. 1, No. 1 (Sept. 1980)-. Academic Scholarly Publication. English. bm. DM362.00 Europe; DM357.00 Germany; DM372.00 other. Fachverlag Schiele & Schoen, Markgrafenstrasse 11, W-1000 Berlin 61 Germany. **Tel** 011/49/30/2516029, FAX 011/49/30/2517248, telex 841/181470. **CODEN** JOCODG. **[CCC].** Documents available from Article Express International, Ask*IEEE, CASDDS.
**Ind/Abst** Acoust. Abstr.; Chem. Abstr.; Ei Page One; Eng. Index Annu.; INSPEC (Sept. 1981-); Int. Aerosp. Abstr.

●US/1070-9762
**JOURNAL OF OPTICAL TECHNOLOGY.** **Added/Corp** Optical Society of America. (1994)-. Periodical. English. mo. $1345,00 US; $1358.00 Canada; $1370.00 Europe and Asia. Optical Society of America, 2010 Massachusetts Avenue Northwest, Washington DC 20036. **Tel** (202)223-8130, (800)762-6960, (800)582-0416, FAX (202)223-1096, telex 510 600 3965. ***Continues** Soviet Journal of Optical Technology.*

US/0150-536X
**JOURNAL OF OPTICS.** [J. opt.]. **VFOAT** J. Optics (Paris). Vol. 8 (Jan./Feb. 1977)-. Academic Scholarly Publication. English (French). bm. $330.00. Masson Editeur, Box Postale 22, 41353 Vineuil 16 France. **Tel** 011 33 54 438994. **(Subscription address:** 7A Boulevard de Perolles, CH-1701 Fribourg Switzerland**)** **LC** QC350; .N68. **DD** 535/.05. **NLM** W1 JO803RE. **CODEN** JOOPDB. **[CCC]. Pr Rev.** available on microfilm and microfiche from University Microfilms International (UMI). Documents available from Article Express International, The Genuine Article, Ask*IEEE, CASDDS. ***Continues** Nouvelle Revue d'Optique, 0335-7368.*
**Ind/Abst** Bioeng. Abstr.; Ceram. Abstr.; Chem. Abstr.; Curr. Contents Eng. Tech. Appl. Sci.; Ei Page One; EMBASE; Energy Res. Abstr. (Feb. 1979-); Eng. Index Annu.; GeoRef; INSPEC (Jan./Feb. 1977-); Int. Aerosp. Abstr.; Res. Alert [Full Cov.]; Sci. Cit. Index; SCISEARCH.

US
**JOURNAL OF OPTICS RESEARCH.** (19??)-. English. Four times a year. $295.00. Nova Science Publishers Inc., 6080 Jericho Turnpike, Suite 207, Commack NY 11725-2808. **Tel** (516)499-3103, (516)499-3106, FAX (516)499-3146.

UK/0022-4073
**JOURNAL OF QUANTITATIVE SPECTROSCOPY & RADIATIVE TRANSFER.** [J. quant. spectrosc. radiat. transfer]. **VFOAT** Journal of Quantitative Spectroscopy and Radiative Transfer. Vol. 1 (Sept. 1961)-. English. mo. $1885.00 The Americas; £1265.00 other. Pergamon Press, An Imprint of Elsevier Science Ltd., The Boulevard, Langford Lane, Kidlington, Oxford OX5 1GB United Kingdom. **Tel** 011 44 865 843000, 011 44 865 843699, FAX 011 44 865 843010. **(Subscription address:** Elsevier Science Ltd. Oxford Fulfillment Centre, PO Box 800, Kidlington, Oxford OX5 1DX United Kingdom.**)** **ED** P. Varanasi. **LC** QC451; .J67. **CODEN** JQSRAE. **[CCC]. Pr Rev.** available on microfilm and microfiche from University Microfilms International (UMI). Documents available from The Genuine Article, BIOSIS Document Express, Ask*IEEE, CASDDS, Documents on Demand.
**Desc:** International outlet for papers dealing with studies of radiative transfer, laser spectroscopy, and other related topics.
**Ind/Abst** Biol. Abstr.; Chem. Abstr.; Curr. Contents Phys. Chem. Earth Sci.; Energy Inf. Abstr.; Energy Res. Abstr.; Environ. Abstr.; INSPEC (1968-); Int. Aerosp. Abstr.; Res. Alert [Full Cov.]; Sci. Cit. Index; SCISEARCH.

US/1057-5715
**JOURNAL OF RADIATION CURING AND RADIATION CURING.** [J. radiat. curing radiat. curing]. **VFOAT** Journal of Radiation Curing, Radiation Curing; Journal of Radiation Curing/Radiation Curing. Vol. 17 (Fall 1990)-. Periodical. English. qt. $98.00 (US); $113.00 (other). Technology Marketing Corporation, One Technology Plaza, Norwalk CT 06854. **Tel** (203)852-6800, FAX (203)853-2845. **LC** TP156.C8; J683. **DD** 664/.0288. **CODEN** JRCCE2. Documents available from Article Express International. ***Formed by the union of** Journal of Radiation Curing, 0361-6428 **and** Radiation Curing, 0146-4604.*
**Ind/Abst** Bioeng. Abstr.; Ei Page One; Energy Res. Abstr.; Eng. Index Annu.; Print. Abstr.

JA/0449-3060
**JOURNAL OF RADIATION RESEARCH.** [J. radiat. res.]. **Added/Corp** Nihon Hoshasen Eikyo Gakkai. Vol. 1 (June 1960)-. Periodical. English. qt. $110.00. Nihon Hoshasen Eikyo Gakkai, (Japan Radiation Research Soc.), Hoshasen Igaku Sogo Kenkyujo, 9-1, Anagawa 4 Chome, Chibashi, Chibaken 280 Japan. **(Subscription address:** Maruzen Company Ltd., PO Box 5050, Import & Export Department, Tokyo 100 31 Japan.**)** **LC** QH652.A1; J66. **NLM** W1 JO864. **CODEN** JRARAX. **Pr Rev.** ctrl circ. Documents available from The Genuine Article, BIOSIS Document Express, Ask*IEEE, CASDDS.
**Desc:** Papers of radiation, biology, medicine and agriculture.
**Ind/Abst** AGRICOLA; Biol. Abstr.; Chem. Abstr.; Coal Abstr.; Curr. Contents Life Sci.; EMBASE; Energy Res. Abstr.; Health Saf. Sci. Abstr.; Index Med.; INSPEC (March 1972-); Life Sci. Collect.; Phys. Med. Biol. (19??-19??); Pollut. Abstr. Indexes; Res. Alert [Full Cov.]; Risk Abstr.; Sci. Cit. Index; SCISEARCH.

UK/0952-4746
**JOURNAL OF RADIOLOGICAL PROTECTION.** (JOURNAL OF RADIOLOGICAL PROTECTION : OFFICIAL JOURNAL OF THE SOCIETY FOR RADIOLOGICAL PROTECTION.). [J. radiol. prot.]. **Added/Corp** Society for Radiological Protection. American Institute of Physics. Vol. 8, No. 1, (March 1988)-. Academic Scholarly Publication. English. Four times a year (Mar., June, Sept., Dec.). $182.00. Institute of Physics, Techno House, Redcliffe Way, Bristol BS1 6NX England. **Tel** 011 44 272 297481, FAX 011 44 272 294318, telex 449149 INSTP G. **(Subscription address:** American Institute of Physics, Publishing Sales, 500 Sunnyside Blvd., Woodbury NY 11797.**)** **ED** G. Meggitt. **NLM** W1; JO8642R. **CODEN** JRPREA. **[CCC].** Index available in last issue of volume--attached. **Pr Rev.** available on microfiche. Documents available from BIOSIS Document Express, Ask*IEEE, CASDDS. ***Continues** Journal of the Society for Radiological Protection, 0260-2814.*
**Desc:** All aspects of radiological protection are covered, including ionizing as well as non-ionizing radiations. Incorporates the Society for Radiological Protection newsletter, and news, information, book reviews and meetings reports of international interest. Contributions can be as scientific or technical papers, notes and letters. Has established itself as an important addition to the international literature, has worldwide contributors and subscribers, and is widely abstracted. A continuing aim of the journal is to provide rapid publication of quality refereed papers.
**Ind/Abst** Biol. Abstr. (1988-); Chem. Abstr.; Ei Page One; EMBASE; INSPEC (Mar. 1988-); Phys. Med. Biol. (19??-19??).

UK/0377-0486
**JOURNAL OF RAMAN SPECTROSCOPY.** [J. Raman spectrosc.]. **VFOAT** JRS. Vol. 1 (April 1973)-. Periodical. English. mo. $1,795.00. John Wiley & Sons Ltd., Baffins Lane, Chichester West Sussex PO19 1UD England. **Tel** 0243 779777, FAX 0243 776128 BTG:JWP001, telex 86290 WIBOOKG. **(Subscription address:** John Wiley / Philadelphia, PO Box 7247, Philadelphia PA 19170.**)** **ED** D. A. Long and J. R. Durig. **LC** QC454.R36; J67. **DD** 544/.64. **CODEN** JRSPAFJRSPAN. **[CCC]. Pr Rev. Circ:** 800. available on microfilm and microfiche from University Microfilms International (UMI). Documents available from The Genuine Article, Ask*IEEE, CASDDS.
**Desc:** Provides readers with original work in all aspects of Raman spectroscopy including higher order processes and Brillouin and Rayleigh scattering.
**Ind/Abst** Abstr. Bull. Inst. Pap. Sci. Tech.; Ceram. Abstr. (19??-); Chem. Abstr.; Chem. Titles; CSA Neuro. Abstr. (?-?); Curr. Contents Phys. Chem. Earth Sci.; EMBASE; Energy Res. Abstr. (Aug. 1976-); INSPEC (April 1973-); Int. Aerosp. Abstr.; Res. Alert [Full Cov.]; Sci. Cit. Index; SCISEARCH.

●US/1071-2836
**JOURNAL OF RUSSIAN LASER RESEARCH.** [J. Russ. laser res.]. **Added/Corp** Consultants Bureau. Vol. 15, No. 1 (Jan.-Feb. 1994)-.

Periodical. English (translations available in Russian). bm **(6 issues)**. $595.00 US; $695.00 other. Consultants Bureau, A Division of Plenum Publishing Corporation, 233 Spring Street, New York NY 10013. **Tel** (212)620-8000, (212)620-8466, FAX (212)463-0742, telex 23/421139. **LC** TA1501; .T68. **DD** 621.36/6/0947. **CODEN** JRLREO. **[CCC].** ***Continues*** *Journal of Soviet Laser Research, 0270-2010.*

US/0270-2010
**JOURNAL OF SOVIET LASER RESEARCH.** ***Title Change.*** [J. Sov. laser res.]. Vol. 1, No. 1 (Jan.-Mar. 1980)-(199?). Periodical. English (Russian). bm. Plenum Press, 233 Spring Street, New York NY 10013-1578. **Tel** (212)620-8000, (800)221-9369, FAX (212)463-0742, (212)807-1047, telex 23/421139. **ED** N G Basov. **LC** TA1501. **DD** 621.36/6/0947. **NLM** W1 JO901VH. **CODEN** JSLRDU. **[CCC].** available on microfilm and microfiche from University Microfilms International (UMI). Documents available from Article Express International, BIOSIS Document Express, Ask*IEEE. ***Continued by*** *Journal of Russian Laser Research.*
**Ind/Abst** Bioeng. Abstr.; Biol. Abstr.; Ei Page One; Energy Res. Abstr. (May 1982-); Eng. Index Annu.; INIS Atomindex [Micro.]; INSPEC (Jan.-March 1980-); Int. Aerosp. Abstr.; Pollut. Abstr. Indexes.

TU
**JOURNAL OF SPECTROSCOPY.**
**Added/Corp** Spectroscopy Society (Turkey). (198?)-. Periodical. English. Spectroscopy Society, Izmir Turkey. **NLM** W1; JO902GD. **CODEN** JOSPEW. Documents available from CASDDS. ***Continues*** *Spektroskopi Dergisi.*
**Ind/Abst** Chem. Abstr.

●UK
**JOURNAL OF THE EUROPEAN OPTICAL SOCIETY, PART B, QUANTUM OPTICS.** **Added/Corp** European Optical Society. Institute of Physics (Great Britain) American Institute of Physics. **VFOAT** Quantum Optics. Vol. 4, No. 1 (Feb. 1992)-. Periodical. English (French and German). bm. $343.00. Institute of Physics, Techno House, Redcliffe Way, Bristol BS1 6NX England. **Tel** 011 44 272 297481, FAX 011 44 272 294318, telex 449149 INSTP G. **(Subscription address:** American Institute of Physics, Publishing Sales, 500 Sunnyside Blvd., Woodbury NY 11797.**)** ***Continues*** *Quantum Optics, 0954-8998.*
**Ind/Abst** Math. Rev.

US/0039-3941
**JOURNAL OF THE OPTICAL SOCIETY OF AMERICA.** **Main/Corp** Optical Society of America. **Added/Corp** American Institute of Physics. Vol. 1 (Jan. 1917)-. Periodical. English. Twenty-four times a year. $1220.00 US; $1328.00 Europe and Asia; $1258.00 other. Optical Society of America, 2010 Massachusetts Avenue Northwest, Washington DC 20036. **Tel** (202)223-8130, (800)762-6960, (800)582-0416, FAX (202)223-1096, telex 510 600 3965. Index available (bound in last issue.). cum. index. Documents available from The Genuine Article, Ask*IEEE, CASDDS.
**Ind/Abst** Abstr. Graphic Arts Tech. Found.; Appl. Mech. Rev.; Appl. Sci. Technol. Index; Chem. Abstr.; Graph. Arts Bull. Inst. Pap. Sci. Technol. (Feb. 1989, April 1989); Index Med.; INSPEC (1968-Dec. 1983); Int. Aerosp. Abstr.; Math. Rev.; Psychol. Abstr.; Res. Alert [Full Cov.]; Sci. Cit. Index (19??-19??); SCISEARCH; Surf. Treat. Technol. Abstr.

US/0740-3232
**JOURNAL OF THE OPTICAL SOCIETY OF AMERICA. A, OPTICS AND IMAGE SCIENCE.** ***Title Change.*** [J. Opt. Soc. Am., A, Opt. image sci.]. **Added/Corp** Optical Society of America. **VFOAT** Optics and Image Science; JOSA A. Vol. 1, No. 1 (Jan. 1984)-Vol. 10, No. 7 (July 1993). Academic Scholarly Publication. English. mo. Optical Society of America, 2010 Massachusetts Avenue Northwest, Washington DC 20036. **Tel** (202)223-8130, (800)762-6960, (800)582-0416, FAX (202)223-1096, telex 510 600 3965. **ED** Bahaa E A Saleh. **LC** QC350; .J68. **DD** 535/.05. **NLM** W1; JO944GD. **CODEN** JOAOD6. **[CCC].** Index available (bound in last issue.). cum. index. **Pr Rev. Circ:** 5,300. available on microfilm and microfiche. Documents available from Article Express International, Ask*IEEE, CASDDS. ***Continues in part*** *Journal of the Optical Society of America (1930), 0030-3941.* ***Continued by*** *Journal of the Optical Society of America. A, Optics, Image Science, and Vision.*
**Desc:** Presents accounts of experimental and theoretical investigations contributing new knowledge and understanding of principles and methods of optical phenomena. Includes topics such as: atmospheric optics; color vision, design, and diffraction; image processing; scattering and coherence theory; machine vision; physiological optics; and statistical optics.
**Ind/Abst** Abstr. Bull. Inst. Pap. Sci. Tech.; Acoust. Abstr.; Appl. Sci. Technol. Index; Ceram. Abstr.; Chem. Abstr. (1984-); Curr. Contents Eng. Tech. Appl. Sci.; Curr. Contents Phys. Chem. Earth Sci.; Curr. Phys. Index; Ei Page One; Eng. Index Annu.; Ergon. Abstr.; HTFS Dig.; Index Med.; INSPEC (Jan. 1984-); Mass Spect. Bull.; Math. Rev.; Phys. Briefs; Psychol. Abstr. (1984-); PsycINFO (1990-); PsycLit; Soc. Sci. Cit. Index [Select. Cov.]; SPIN (1984-); World Ceram. Abstr.

●US
**JOURNAL OF THE OPTICAL SOCIETY OF AMERICA. A, OPTICS, IMAGE SCIENCE, AND VISION.** **Added/Corp** Optical Society of America. **VFOAT** Optics, Image Science, and Vision; JOSA A. Vol. 10, No. 8 (Aug. 1993)-. Periodical. English. mo. $685.00 US; $706.00 Canada; $742.00 Europe & Asia. Optical Society of America, 2010 Massachusetts Avenue Northwest, Washington DC 20036. **Tel** (202)223-8130, (800)762-6960, (800)582-0416, FAX (202)223-1096, telex 510 600 3965. **LC** QC350; .J68. ***Continues*** *Journal of the Optical Society of America. A, Optics and Image Science, 0740-3232.*
**Ind/Abst** Sci. Cit. Index.

US/0740-3224
**JOURNAL OF THE OPTICAL SOCIETY OF AMERICA. B, OPTICAL PHYSICS.** [J. Opt. Soc. Am., B, Opt. phys.]. **Added/Corp** Optical Society of America. **VFOAT** Optical Physics; JOSA B. Vol. 1, No. 1 (Mar. 1984)-. Academic Scholarly Publication. English. mo. $685.00 US; $706.00 Canada; $742.00 Europe and Asia. Optical Society of America, 2010 Massachusetts Avenue Northwest, Washington DC 20036. **Tel** (202)223-8130, (800)762-6960, (800)582-0416, FAX (202)223-1096, telex 510 600 3965. **ED** Paul F. Liao. **LC** QC392; .J68. **DD** 535/.05. **CODEN** JOBPDE. **[CCC].** Index available (bound in last issue.). cum. index. **Pr Rev.** available on microfilm and microfiche. Documents available from Article Express International, The Genuine Article, Ask*IEEE, CASDDS. ***Continues in part*** *Journal of the Optical Society of America (1930), 0030-3941.*
**Desc:** Topics include: lasers, nonlinear optics, optical coherent transients, multiphoton processes, effects of laser radiation, spectroscopy, and advances in nonlinear optical materials, science and technology.
**Ind/Abst** Abstr. Bull. Inst. Pap. Sci. Tech.; Acoust. Abstr.; Appl. Sci. Technol. Index; Ceram. Abstr.; Chem. Abstr. (1984-); Chem. Titles; Curr. Contents Eng. Tech. Appl. Sci.; Curr. Contents Phys. Chem. Earth Sci.; Curr. Phys. Index; Ei Page One; Eng. Index Annu.; INSPEC (March 1984-); Mass Spect. Bull.; Psychol. Abstr. (1984-); Res. Alert [Full Cov.]; Sci. Cit. Index; SCISEARCH; SPIN (1984-).

HU/0023-0480
**KEP ES HANGTECHNIKA.** [Kep es hangtech.]. **Added/Corp** Optikai es Kinotechnikai Tudomanyos Egyesuelet. (1955)-. Periodical. Hungarian (summaries and/or abstracts in English, German and Russian). bm. $26.00. Lapkiado Vallalat, Lenin Korut 9-11, 1073 Budapest 7, Hungary. **Tel** 222-408. **(Subscription address:** Kultura, PO Box 149, H 1389 Budapest 62 Hungary.**)** **LC** TR845; .K4. **CODEN** KEHTAS. **Ad Acc. Circ:** 950. Documents available from CASDDS, Ask*IEEE, CASDDS.
**Ind/Abst** Chem. Abstr.; INSPEC (Dec. 1979-).

JA/0389-6625
**KOGAKU.** [KÂogaku]. **Added/Corp** Oyo Butsuri Gakkai. Kogaku Konwakai. **VFOAT** Japanese Journal of Optics. (1972)-. Periodical. Japanese. bm. $270.00. **(Subscription address:** Kyowa Book Company Inc., 1-38 Kanda Jinbo-Cho, Chiyoda-Ku Tokyo 101, Japan**)** **CODEN** KOGAD5.

RU/0368-6485
**KOSMICHESKIE LUCHI. COSMIC RAYS.** **Added/Corp** Akademiia Nauk SSSR. Mezhduvedomstvennyi Komitet po Provedeniiu Mezhdunarodnogo Geofizicheskogo Goda. Akademiia Nauk SSSR. Mezhduvedomstvennyi Geofizicheskii Komitet. **VFOAT** Cosmic Rays. No. 1 (1959)-. Academic Scholarly Publication. Russian (summaries and/or abstracts in English). Izdatelstvo Nauka / Akademiia Nauk, Publishing House of the Russian Academy of Sciences, Leninskii Porspekt 14, 117901 Moscow Russia. **Tel** 011 95 954-21-53, FAX 011 95 938-21-44, telex 411964. **LC** QC485; .A45. **CODEN** KOLUAJ. Documents available from CASDDS.
**Ind/Abst** Chem. Abstr.

UK/0263-0346
**LASER AND PARTICLE BEAMS.** [Laser part. beams]. Vol. 1, Pt. 1 (Feb. 1983)-. Academic Scholarly Publication. English. qt. $333.00 US, Canada and Mexico; £175.00 other. Cambridge University Press, The Edinburgh Building, Shaftesbury Road, Cambridge CB2 2RU United Kingdom. **Tel** 011 44 223 312393, FAX 011 44 223 325959. **(Subscription address:** Cambridge University Press / North America, 110 Midland Avenue, Port Chester NY 10573.**)** **ED** G. H. Miley. **LC** QC689.5.L37; L38. **DD** 535.5/8. **CODEN** LPBEDA. **[CCC]. Bk Rev. Ad Acc. Pr Rev. Circ:** 250. available on microfilm from University Microfilms International (UMI). Documents available from Article Express International, The Genuine Article, Ask*IEEE, CASDDS.
**Desc:** An international journal which deals with generation of intense laser and particle beams, the interaction of these beams with matter, and their applications. Its aims are to promote this field, to understand and to model its phenomena, in particular non-linear and non-LTE phenomena. Subjects covered include intense sources of coherent radiation from the microwave to the X-ray region and high current particle accelerators; physics of high energy densities; hot dense matter and related atomic, plasma and hydrodynamic physics; and beam-wave interaction.
**Ind/Abst** Chem. Abstr. (1983-); Curr. Contents Phys. Chem. Earth Sci.; Ei Page One; Eng. Index Annu.; INSPEC (Feb. 1983-); Res. Alert [Full Cov.]; Sci. Cit. Index; SCISEARCH.

IT
**LASER & TECHNOLOGY.** **Added/Corp** Societa Internazionale di Laserterapia Medico-Chirurgica. **VFOAT** Laser and Technology. Vol. 1, No. 1 (Jan.-Apr. 1991)-. Periodical. English (Italian). Three times a year. Wichtig Editore, Via Friuli 72 74, 20135 Milan Italy. **Tel** 011 39 2 55195443. **NLM** W1; LA78EL.

US/1043-8092
**LASER FOCUS WORLD.** [Laser focus world]. Vol. 25, No. 1 (Jan. 1989)-. Periodical. English. mo. $149.00 US; $219.00 other. PennWell Publishing Company, 1421 South Sheridan, PO Box 1260, Tulsa OK 74101. **Tel** (918)835-3161, (800)331-4463, FAX (918)831-9497. **(Subscription address:** Laser Focus World, Publishing Services, PO Box 3004, Tulsa OK 74101.**)** **LC** TA1501; .L37. **DD** 621.36/6. **NLM** W1; LA78M. **CODEN** LFWOE8. **[CCC].** available on microfilm and microfiche from University Microfilms International (UMI); available on an online database (file 648/Full-Text) from DIALOG. Documents available from The Genuine Article, CASDDS. ***Continues*** *Laser Focus (Littleton, Mass.), 0740-2511.*
**Desc:** Editorial content covering the entire spectrum of electro-optic technologies. Subjects covered include: lasers, optoelectronics, fiberoptics, optics, materials, components, sub-systems, systems, instrumentation, and imaging and display equipment.
**Ind/Abst** Appl. Sci. Technol. Index; Ceram. Abstr. (199?-); Chem. Abstr.; Curr. Contents Eng. Tech. Appl. Sci.; Ei Page One; F&S Index Plus Text, Int. [Select. Cov.]; Graph. Arts Bull. Inst. Pap. Sci. Technol. (May 1989); INIS Atomindex [Micro.]; PROMT; Res. Alert [Full Cov.]; Sci. Cit. Index; SCISEARCH.

US
**LASER FOCUS WORLD BUYERS' GUIDE.** 24th Ed. (1989)-. Consumer Publication. English. an. $109.00 US; $127.00 Canada; $127.00 (seamail), $167.00 (airmail) other. PennWell Publishing Company, 1421 South Sheridan, PO Box 1260, Tulsa OK 74101. **Tel** (918)835-3161, (800)331-4463, FAX (918)831-9497. **(Subscription address:** Laser Focus World Buyers Guide, PennWell Books, PO Box 21288, Tulsa OK 74101.**)** Index available. **Ad Acc. Circ:** 45,000 (ctrl). ***Continues*** *Laser Focus. Buyers' Guide.*
**Desc:** An international sourcebook of suppliers of products and services necessary in the technologies of lasers, optics, fiberoptics, detectors and imaging.
**Ind/Abst** Appl. Sci. Technol. Index.

GW/0937-7069
**LASER-PRAXIS.** [Laser-Prax.]. **VFOAT** Laser Praxis. (1988)-. Periodical. German. sa. Carl Hanser Verlag, Postfach 860420, D 81631 Munich Germany. **Tel** 011 49 89 998300, FAX 011 49 89 984809. **LC** TA1671; .L3747. **DD** 621.36/6. **CODEN** LASPEO. Documents available from Ask*IEEE.
**Ind/Abst** INSPEC (June 1990-); Shock Vibr. Dig.

UK
**LASER-RAMAN & INFRARED SPECTROSCOPY ABSTRACTS.** **VAT** Laser-Raman and Infrared Spectroscopy Abstracts. Vol. 5 (1976)-. Periodical. English. qt. PRM Science & Technology Agency Ltd, 261A Finchley Road Hampstead, London NW3 6LV England. **Tel** 011 44 71 431 0372. **LC** QC454.L3; L34. **DD** 016.535/84. ***Formed by the union of*** *Infrared Spectroscopy Abstracts* ***and*** *Laser-Raman Spectroscopy Abstracts.*

US/0023-8600
**LASER REPORT.** [Laser rep.]. (19??)-. Newsletter. English. Twenty-four times a year. $340.00 US and Canada; $350.00 other. PennWell Publishing Company, Ten Tara Boulevard 5th Floor, Nashua NH 03062-2801. **Tel** (603)891-0123, (603)891-9177, FAX (603)891-0624, (603)891-0574. **ED** Barbara Akerley. **LC** CURRENT ISSUES ONLY. **DD** 621. **[CCC]. Circ:** 400. available on an online database (file 648/Full-Text) from DIALOG; available via fax ($450.00 US; $485.00 other). ***Continues*** *Laser Focus Mid-Month Report.*
**Desc:** Focuses on global laser news including the latest from the US, Europe and Asia.
**Ind/Abst** F&S Index Plus Text, Int. [Select. Cov.].

UK/0898-5901
**LASER THERAPY.** [Laser ther.]. Vol. 1, No. 1 (Jan.-Mar. 1989)-. Periodical. English. qt. $175.00. University of Hokkaido Press, Nisha 5 Kita 8 Kita Ku, Sapporo 060 Japan. **Tel** 011 81 11 71624111. **(Subscription address:** Laser Therapy, Royal Oldham Hospital, Rochdale Road, Oldham OL1 2JH United Kingdom.**)** **DD** 615. **NLM** W1; LA78TG. **CODEN** LATHE5. **[CCC].** available on microfilm and microfiche from University Microfilms International (UMI). Documents available from BIOSIS Document Express, Ask*IEEE.
**Desc:** The first journal to link an international outlook in

the field of laser therapy with high standards of academic contents. It will contain clinical and basic scientific studies in the use of low level laser therapy.
**Ind/Abst** Biol. Abstr. (1991-); EMBASE; INSPEC (1989-).

US/0892-9947
**LASERS & OPTRONICS.** [Lasers optron.]. **VFOAT** Lasers and Optronics. Vol. 6, No. 5 (May 1987)-. Periodical. English. mo (13 issues). $55.00 US, Canada & Mexico; $70.00 (surface mail), $115.00 (airmail) other; Includes "Technology and Industry Reference Manual". Cahners Publishing Company, 249 West 17th Street, New York NY 10011. **Tel** (212)645-0067, FAX (212)242-6987. **(Subscription address:** Gordon Publications, Inc., Paid Circulation Department, 301 Gibralter Drive, Box 650, Morris Plains NJ 07950-0650.**)** **ED** Thomas V. Higgins. **LC** TA1671; .L376. **DD** 621.36/6. **CODEN** LAOPE4. **[CCC].** Index available. **Bk Rev. Ad Acc. Circ:** 40,000 (ctrl). available on microfilm and microfiche from University Microfilms International (UMI); available on an online database (files 648,675/Full-Text) from DIALOG. Documents available from Ask*IEEE. ***Continues*** *Lasers & Applications, 0733-303X.*
**Desc:** Covers laser and optoelectronic application, design and technology. News, features, product reviews, technological advances and the latest in laser and optoelectronic applications are covered in each issue.
**Ind/Abst** Comput. ASAP [Full Txt.]; Comput. Database [Full Txt.]; F&S Index Plus Text, Int. [Select. Cov.]; INSPEC (1987-); PROMT; Trade Ind. ASAP [Full Txt.]; Trade Ind. Index [Full Txt.].

SZ/0886-0467
**LASERS IN THE LIFE SCIENCES.** [Lasers life sci.]. Vol. 1, No. 1 (Oct. 1986)-. Periodical. English. ir. Price varies. Harwood Academic Publishers, PO Box 90, Reading RG1 8JL England. **Tel** 011 44 734 560080. **(Subscription address:** Harwood Academic Publishers, PO Box 786, Cooper Station, New York NY 10276.**) ED** Ashley J. Welch. **DD** 610. **NLM** W1; LA784H. **CODEN** LLSCES. **[CCC].** Documents available from Ask*IEEE.
**Ind/Abst** EMBASE; INSPEC (1986-).

GW/0172-3286
**LICHT-FORSCHUNG.** (LICHT FORSCHUNG : ORGAN DER LICHTTECHNISCHEN GESELLSCHAFT E.V.). [Licht-Forsch.]. Began publication in 1979. Periodical. German (summaries and/or abstracts in English). sa. DM80.00. Richard Pflaum Verlag Gmbh, Postfach 190737, D 80607 Munich Germany. **Tel** 011 49 89 126070, FAX 011 49 89 12607200, telex 5216075. **LC** TH7700; .L48. **DD** 621.32/05. **CODEN** LIFODB. Documents available from Article Express International. ***Continues in part*** *Lichttechnik, 0024-2861.*
**Ind/Abst** Bioeng. Abstr.; Coal Abstr.; Ei Page One; Eng. Index Annu.

IT
**LIGHTING DESIGN.** Italian. bm. L60000 Italy; L120000 other. Stammer Spa, Via della Liberazione 1, 20068 Peschiera Borromeo, Italy. **Tel** 011 39 2 55302606, FAX 011 39 2 55302700, telex 321083.

US/0741-5834
**LIGHTWAVE.** [Lightwave]. **VFOAT** Light Wave. (Jan. 1984)-. Trade Publication. English. Thirteen times a year (annual with annual product listing). $86.00 (institutions), $59.00 (individuals) US; $81.00 Canada; $99.00 other. PennWell Publishing Company, 1421 South Sheridan, PO Box 1260, Tulsa OK 74101. **Tel** (918)835-3161, (800)331-4463, FAX (918)831-9497. **(Subscription address:** Lightwave Magazine, PO Box 2139, Tulsa OK 74101.**) ED** Sharon Scully. **LC** TA1800; .L55. **DD** 621.36/92/05. **[CCC].** Index available. **Bk Rev. Ad Acc. Circ:** 15,000 (ctrl). available on microfilm and microfiche from University Microfilms International (UMI).
**Desc:** Serves a concentrated audience of fiber optics market including telecommunications, data communications, lightwave systems and components, sensing, process control, and military applications on all levels and job functions. Provides comprehensive coverage of fiber optics technology in all its applications including telecommunications, data communications, local area networks, and cable television distribution.
**Ind/Abst** Energy Inf. Abstr.; Infomat Int. Bus.

US
**LIGHTWAVE BUYERS GUIDE.** (19??)-. Consumer Publication. English. an. $65.00 US; $75.00 other. PennWell Publishing Company, 1421 South Sheridan, PO Box 1260, Tulsa OK 74101. **Tel** (918)835-3161, (800)331-4463, FAX (918)831-9497. **(Subscription address:** Lightwave Buyers Guide, Publishing Services, PO Box 2750, Tulsa OK 74101.**)**
**Desc:** Provides the key manufactures and distributors of hundreds of fiber optic products.

RU
**LIUMINESTSENTNYE MATERIALY I OSOBO CHISTYE VSHCHESTVA.** **Main/Corp** Vsesoiuznyi Nauchno-Issledovatelskii Institut Liuminoforov i Osobo Chistykh Veshchestv. (19??)-. Russian (summaries and/or abstracts in English). 1.00rub single issue. Pr Khimikov 1, Stavropol Russia. **Tel** 6-33-48, telex NIT 223171. **ED** E G Morozov. **LC** QC477.8; .V8a. **Circ:** 500.
**Desc:** Covers phosphors, high purity substances, research, synthesis, qualities, technology and economics.

IT/0024-7189
**LUCE.** Tecniche Nuove SPA, Via Ciro Menotti 14, 20129 Milan Italy. **Tel** 011 39 2 75701, FAX 011 39 2 7610351, telex 334647 TECHS I.

●US/1061-3420
**MICROBEAM ANALYSIS (NEW YORK, N.Y.).** (MICROBEAM ANALYSIS: THE OFFICIAL JOURNAL OF THE MICROBEAM ANALYSIS SOCIETY.). **Added/Corp** Microbeam Analysis Society. Vol. 1, No. 1 (1992)-. Periodical. English. bm. $195.00. VCH Publishers Inc, 220 East 23rd Street, New York NY 10010. **Tel** (212)683-8333, , FAX (212)481-0897. **(Subscription address:** VCH Publishers Inc., 303 Northwest 12th Avenue, Journals Department, Deerfield FL 33442.**) DD** 502.

US/0745-2993
**MICROWAVES & RF.** [Microw. RF]. **VFOAT** Microwaves and RF; Microwaves and Radio Frequency. **VAT** Microwaves & Radio Frequency. Vol. 21, No. 12 (Nov. 1982)-. Periodical. English. Thirteen times a year (includes Data Directory). $60.00 US; $100.00 Canada; $120.00 Mexico; $140.00 other. Penton Publishing, 1100 Superior Avenue, Cleveland OH 44114-2543. **Tel** (216)696-7000, FAX (216)696-0836. **(Subscription address:** Penton Publishing, PO Box 96732, Chicago IL 60693.**) LC** TK7800; .M54. **DD** 621.381/3/05. **CODEN** MIRFDL. **[CCC]. Pr Rev.** available on microfilm and microfiche from University Microfilms International (UMI); available on an online database (file 648/Full-Text) from DIALOG. Documents available from Article Express International, The Genuine Article, Ask*IEEE. ***Continues*** *Microwaves (New York, N.Y.), 0026-2919.*
**Desc:** Serves the microwave and radio frequency fields, defined as plants, laboratories, government and military installations and other facilities concerned with the research, design development, application, and use of devices, components, systems techniques involving frequencies from 10 KHZ through light.
**Ind/Abst** Appl. Sci. Technol. Index; Curr. Contents Eng. Tech. Appl. Sci.; Ei Page One; Eng. Index Annu.; F&S Index Plus Text, Int. [Select. Cov.]; Infomat Int. Bus.; INSPEC (Nov. 1982-); Int. Aerosp. Abstr.; Int. Packag. Abstr.; PROMT; Res. Alert [Select. Cov.]; SCISEARCH; Soc. Sci. Cit. Index [Select. Cov.].

US
**MICROWAVES & RF PRODUCT DATA DIRECTORY.** **See** Engineering-Electricity, Electrical Engineering, Electronics.

US
**MICROWAVES & RF PRODUCT EXTRA.** **See** Engineering-Electricity, Electrical Engineering, Electronics.

US/1051-2470
**MILITARY & COMMERCIAL FIBER BUSINESS.** ***Title Change.*** (MILITARY & COMMERCIAL FIBER BUSINESS / PHILLIPS PUBLISHING, INC.). [Mil. commer. fiber bus.]. **Added/Corp** Phillips Publishing. **VFOAT** Military and Commercial Fiber Business. (1990)-(Nov. 1992). Periodical. English. bw. Phillips Business Information, Inc., 1201 Seven Locks Road, Potomac MD 20854. **Tel** (301)424-3338, (800)777-5006, FAX (301)309-3847. **DD** 623. **[CCC].** available on an online database (file 636/Full-Text) from DIALOG. ***Continues*** *Military Fiber Optics News, 0887-2465.* ***Merged into*** *Fiber Optics News.*
**Ind/Abst** PTS Newsl. Database [Full Txt.].

●US/1058-7268
**MOLECULAR CRYSTALS AND LIQUID CRYSTALS SCIENCE AND TECHNOLOGY SECTION B, NONLINEAR OPTICS.** [Mol. cryst. liq. cryst. sci. technol., B, Nonlinear opt.]. **VFOAT** Nonlinear Optics. Vol. 2, No. 1 (1992)-. Periodical. English. qt (3 volumes). $375.00 (academic institutions), $588.00 (corporate institutions). Gordon & Breach Science Publishers, Inc., PO Box 786, Cooper Station, New York NY 10276. **Tel** (212)206-8900, FAX (212)645-2459. **(Subscription address:** International Publishers Distributor at one of the following addresses: 820 Town Center Drive, Langhorne, PA 19047; or PO Box 90, Reading Berkshire RG1 8JL UK; or Kent Ridge PO Box 1180, Singapore 9111, Republic of Singapore**) LC** QC446.15; .N68. **DD** 535.2/05. **CODEN** MCLOEB. **[CCC].** ***Continues*** *Nonlinear Optics, 1053-3729.*

●US/1058-7284
**MOLECULAR CRYSTALS AND LIQUID CRYSTALS SCIENCE AND TECHNOLOGY SECTION D, DISPLAY AND IMAGING.** **VFOAT** Display and Imaging. (1994)-. Periodical. English. Six times a year (1 volume). $457.00 (academic institutions), $713.00 (corporate institutions). Gordon & Breach Science Publishers, Inc., PO Box 786, Cooper Station, New York NY 10276. **Tel** (212)206-8900, FAX (212)645-2459. **(Subscription address:** International Publishers Distributor at one of the following addresses: 820 Town Center Drive, Langhorne, PA 19047; or PO Box 90, Reading Berkshire RG1 8JL UK; or Kent Ridge PO Box 1180, Singapore 9111, Republic of Singapore**) [CCC].** ***Continues in part*** *Molecular Crystals and Liquid Crystals (New York, N.Y. : 1991), 1056-8816; Nonlinear Optics.*

RU
**MOLEKULIARNAIA SPEKTROSKOPIIA.** **Added/Corp** Leningradskii Gosudarstvennyi Universitet, Imeni A. A. Zhdanova. Vol. 1 (1960)-. Academic Scholarly Publication. Russian. be. 2.00rub. St Petersburg State University / Izdatelstvo Leningradskogo Universiteta, Universitetskaia Nab 7/9, 199034 St Petersburg Russia. **Tel** 011 95 218-97-88, FAX 011 95 218-51-52, telex 121481. **ED** M O Bulanin. **LC** QC454.M6; M654. **DD** 535/.84/05. **CODEN** MLKSA9. **Bk Rev. Ad Acc. Circ:** 1,000. Documents available from CASDDS.
**Desc:** Collection of original and review papers on spectroscopic studies of molecular dynamics and intermolecular interactions including hydrogen bonding in various phases.
**Ind/Abst** Chem. Abstr. (?-1981);(-1981).

US/0077-0973
**MONOGRAPHS ON APPLIED OPTICS.** No. 1-. Monographic series. English. ir. Price varies per volume. Elsevier Science Publishing Company Inc, Madison Square Station, PO Box 882, New York NY 10159-0882. **Tel** (212)633-3950, FAX (212)633-3990. **NLM** W1 MO569S.

UK/0141-9064
**MOSSBAUER SPECTROSCOPY ABSTRACTS.** [Mossbauer spectrosc. abstr.]. Vol. 1 (Jan./Mar. 1978)-. Periodical. English. qt. PRM Science & Technology Agency Ltd, 261A Finchley Road Hampstead, London NW3 6LV England. **Tel** 011 44 71 431 0372. **NLM** Z 5524.S75 M694.

US/0160-2136
**NATIONAL CONFERENCE ON RADIATION CONTROL.** 1st- 1969-. English. an. Free. BRH Technical Information Staff, 5600 Fishers Lane, Rockville MD 20857. **NLM** W3 NA454E.
**Desc:** Contains proceedings of the annual National Conference on Radiation Control.

US
**NCRP NEWS.** (1966)-. Periodical. English. ir. free. National Council on Radiation Protection and Measurements Report, 7910 Woodmont Avenue, Suite 800, Bethesda MD 20814. **Tel** (301)657-2652, (800)229-2652. **Circ:** 1,000.
**Desc:** News of new NCRP publications and significant NCRP activity.

US/0883-3311
**NRC TLD DIRECT RADIATION MONITORING NETWORK.** [NRC TLD direct radiat. monit. netw.]. **VAT** Nuclear Regulatory Commission's Thermoluminescent Dosimeter (TLD) Direct Radiation Monitoring Network. Vol. 1, Nos. 1, 2 (Jan.-June 1981)-. Periodical. English. qt. $17.00; $13.00 (single issues) US; $21.25; $16.25 (single issues) other. Nuclear Regulatory Commission, 1717 H Street NW, Washington DC 20555. **Tel** (301)492-7000. **LC** TD195.E4; N7. **DD** 363.1/79.
**Desc:** Provides the status and results of the NRC thermoluminescent dosimeter (TLD) direct radiation monitoring. It presents the radiation levels measured in the vicinity of NRC licensed facility sites throughout the country.

US/1048-6879
**OE REPORTS.** [OE rep.]. **Added/Corp** Society of Photo-Optical Instrumentation Engineers. No. 49 (January 1988)-. Periodical. English. mo. $25.00 North America; $35.00 other. International Society for Optical Engineering, PO Box 10, Bellingham WA 98227-0010. **Tel** (206)676-3290, FAX (206)647-1445, telex 46-7053. **LC** TA1501; .O4. **DD** 621.36. **[CCC].** ***Formed by the union of*** *Optical Engineering Reports (U.S. ed.), 0741-5931* ***and*** *Optical Engineering Reports (European ed.), 0933-8551.*
**Ind/Abst** Meteorol. Geoastrophys. Abstr.

●UK/0966-9809
**OLE. OPTO & LASER EUROPE.** [OLE, Opto laser Eur.]. **VFOAT** Opto & Laser Europe; OLE. (1992)-. Periodical. English. bm. $70.00 (paper), $42.00 (microfiche) US, Canada and Mexico; £35.00 (paper), £21.00 (microfiche) other. Institute of Physics, Techno House, Redcliffe Way, Bristol BS1 6NX England. **Tel** 011 44 272 297481, FAX 011 44 272 294318, telex 449149 INSTP G. **(Subscription address:** American Institute of Physics, Publishing Sales, 500 Sunnyside Blvd., Woodbury NY 11797.**) ED** J. Bell. **DD** 338.47621381045094. available on microfiche.
**Desc:** For all scientists, engineers and managers in the laser and electro-optics industries. Features a topical mixture of industrial and scientific news and comment, articles covering technology and applications, software reviews and new product information.

PL/0078-5466
**OPTICA APPLICATA.** [Opt. appl.]. **Added/Corp** Breslau. Politechnika. Vol. 1 (1971)-. Academic Scholarly Publication. Polish. qt. $122.00. **(Subscription address:** ARS Polona, PO Box 1001, 00068 Warsaw Poland.**) LC** QC350; .O64. **CODEN** OPAPBZ. **Pr Rev.** Documents

available from The Genuine Article, Ask*IEEE, CASDDS. **Ind/Abst** Chem. Abstr.; Curr. Contents Eng. Tech. Appl. Sci.; Ei Page One; INSPEC (1980-); Leadscan; Res. Alert [Select. Cov.]; SCISEARCH.

SP/0030-3917
**OPTICA PURA Y APLICADA.** [Opt. pura apl.]. **Added/Corp** Instituto de Optica Daza de Valdes. Vol. 1 (1968)-. Academic Scholarly Publication. English (French and Spanish; summaries and/or abstracts in Spanish). Three times a year. 4500ptas Spain; $45.00 US. Instituto de Optica, Serrano 121, Madrid 6 Spain. **Tel** 011 34 1 2616800, FAX 011 34 1 4113077, telex 42182. **ED** A. Corrons. **LC** QC350; .O54. **DD** 535/.05. **CODEN** OPAPAY. **[CCC].** Index available. cum. index. **Bk Rev.** ctrl circ. Documents available from Ask*IEEE, CASDDS.
**Desc:** Ideas in the areas of color, solar energy, spectroscopy, luminescence, image formation, photography, vision, physical and theoretical optics, instruments.
**Ind/Abst** Chem. Abstr.; INSPEC (1968-); Int. Aerosp. Abstr.

UK/0306-8919
**OPTICAL AND QUANTUM ELECTRONICS.** [Opt. quantum electron.]. Vol. 7 (1975)-. Periodical. English. mo. $695.00 US and Canada; £395.00 Europe; £425.00 other. Chapman & Hall, 2-6 Boundary Row, London SE1 8HN England. **Tel** 011 44 71 865 0066, FAX 011 44 71 522 9623, telex 290164 Chapmag. **(Subscription address:** Chapman & Hall, Cheriton House, North Way, Andover, Hampshire, SP10 5BE England.**)** **ED** G. Parry, A. Miller, I. White. **LC** TA1671; .O68. **DD** 621.36/05. **CODEN** OQELDI. **[CCC].** Index available. **Bk Rev. Ad Acc. Pr Rev. Circ:** 800. available on microfilm and microfiche from University Microfilms International (UMI). Documents available from Article Express International, The Genuine Article, Ask*IEEE, CASDDS. ***Continues** Opto-Electronics, 0030-4077.*
**Desc:** Papers on optical physics, optical engineering and optoelectronics with the emphasis on fibres, nonlinear and coherent optics.
**Ind/Abst** Acoust. Abstr.; Bioeng. Abstr.; Chem. Abstr.; Coal Abstr.; Curr. Contents Eng. Tech. Appl. Sci.; Ei Page One; Eng. Index Annu.; INSPEC (Jan. 1975-); Int. Aerosp. Abstr.; Res. Alert [Full Cov.]; Sci. Cit. Index; SCISEARCH.

US
**OPTICAL & REPROGRAPHIC EQUIPMENT.** (19??)-. English. mo. $225.00. Predicasts Inc., A Ziff Communications Company, 11001 Cedar Avenue, Cleveland OH 44106. **Tel** (800)321-6388, (216)795-3000, FAX (216)229-9944, telex 985 604. **(Subscription address:** Information Access Company, PO Box 61000, Department 1851, San Francisco, CA 94161; Phone: (800)321-6388**)**

US/0091-3286
**OPTICAL ENGINEERING.** (OPTICAL ENGINEERING : THE JOURNAL OF THE SOCIETY OF PHOTO-OPTICAL INSTRUMENTATION ENGINEERS.). [Opt. eng.]. **Added/Corp** Society of Photo-Optical Instrumentation Engineers. Vol. 11, No. 1 (Jan./Feb. 1972)-. Periodical. English. mo. $255.00 North America; $315.00 other. International Society for Optical Engineering, PO Box 10, Bellingham WA 98227-0010. **Tel** (206)676-3290, FAX (206)647-1445, telex 46-7053. **ED** Jack Gaskill. **LC** TR692.5; .S65. **DD** 621.36/05. **CODEN** OPEGAR. **[CCC].** Index available. cum. index. **Bk Rev. Ad Acc. Pr Rev. Circ:** 9,000. available on microfilm and microfiche from University Microfilms International (UMI). Documents available from Article Express International, The Genuine Article, Ask*IEEE, CASDDS. ***Continues** Journal (Society of Photo-Optical Instrumentation Engineers).*
**Desc:** Publishes technical papers relating to the engineering, design, production, and application of optical and optoelectronic applied science and technology.
**Ind/Abst** Acoust. Abstr.; Appl. Sci. Technol. Index; Bioeng. Abstr.; Ceram. Abstr.; Chem. Abstr.; Coal Abstr.; Curr. Contents Eng. Tech. Appl. Sci.; Curr. Contents Phys. Chem. Earth Sci.; Ei Page One; EMBASE; Eng. Index Annu.; HTFS Dig.; INSPEC; Int. Aerosp. Abstr.; Pollut. Abstr. Indexes; Res. Alert [Full Cov.]; Sci. Cit. Index; SCISEARCH; Soc. Sci. Cit. Index [Select. Cov.].

US/0892-354X
**OPTICAL ENGINEERING (NEW YORK, N.Y.).** **See** Engineering.

●US/1068-5200
**OPTICAL FIBER TECHNOLOGY.** (1994)-. Academic Scholarly Publication. English. qt (4 issues). $184.00 US and Canada; $221.00 other. Academic Press, Inc., 6277 Sea Harbor Drive, Orlando FL 32887. **Tel** (800)543-9534, (407)345-4100, FAX (407)363-9661. **[CCC].**

UK
**OPTICAL FIBRES.** English. bw. $290.00. Institution of Electrical Engineers / IEE, Michael Faraday House, Six Hills Way, Stevenage Herts SG1 2AY UK. **Tel** 011 44 438 313311, FAX 011 44 438 742840, telex 825578 IEESTV G. **(Subscription address:** IEE / UK, Publications Sales Department, PO Box 96, Stevenage, Herts, SG1 2SD England.**)**

US/0191-0639
**OPTICAL INDUSTRY & SYSTEMS ENCYCLOPEDIA & DICTIONARY, THE.** **VAT** The Optical Industry and Systems Encyclopedia and Dictionary. 25th- Ed.; 1979-. English. $50.00 US; $60.00 other. The Optical Publishing Company Inc, PO Box 1146, Berkshire Common, Pittsfield MA 01201. **Tel** (413)499-0514. **ED** Teddi C Laurin. **LC** TA1509; .O64. **DD** 621.36/05. **Bk Rev. Ad Acc. Circ:** 52,000 (ctrl). ***Supersedes in part** Optical Industry & Systems Directory, 0078-5474.*
**Desc:** The voice of photonics technology, optics, electro-optics, lasers, fiber optics and imaging.

US/0162-7643
**OPTICAL INFORMATION PROCESSING.** **Main/Conf** US-USSR Science Cooperation Seminar on Optical Information Processing. (1975)-. English. Plenum Press, 233 Spring Street, New York NY 10013-1578. **Tel** (212)620-8000, (800)221-9369, FAX (212)463-0742, (212)807-1047, telex 23/421139. **LC** TA1630; .U54a. **DD** 621.3819/59.

●NE/0925-3467
**OPTICAL MATERIALS.** Vol. 1, No. 1 (Jan. 1992)-. Academic Scholarly Publication. English. Six times a year (1 volume). Fl580.00. Elsevier Science Publishers BV, PO Box 211, 1000 AE Amsterdam Netherlands. **Tel** 011 31 20 5803642, FAX 011 31 20 5862696, telex 15682. **ED** R.C. Powell. **CODEN** OMATET. **[CCC].** Documents available from Article Express International, Ask*IEEE, CASDDS.
**Desc:** Strives to provide a means of communication and technology transfer between researchers who are interested in materials for potential device applications.
**Ind/Abst** Chem. Abstr.; Ei Page One; Elect. Comm. Abstr.; Eng. Index Annu.; INSPEC; Manuf. Process Eng. Abstr.; Mater. Sci. Eng. Abstr.; Solid State Supercond. Abstr.

US
**OPTICAL MATERIALS AND ENGINEERING NEWS.** (19??)-. English. mo. $350.00. Business Communications Inc., 25 Van Zant Street, Suite 13, Norwalk CT 06855. **Tel** (203)853-4266. available on an online database (file 636/Full-Text) from DIALOG.
**Ind/Abst** PTS Newsl. Database [Full Txt.].

JA
**OPTICAL REVIEW.** (19??)-. Periodical. Japanese. bm. $300.00. **(Subscription address:** Maruzen Company Ltd., PO Box 5050, Import & Export Department, Tokyo 100 31 Japan.**)**

RU
**OPTICHESKII ZHURNAL. Added/Corp** Vserossiiskii Nauchnyi Tsentr "Gosudarstvennyi Opticheskii Institut Imeni S.I. Vavilova". **VFOAT** Soviet Journal of Optical Technology. (Sept. 1990)-. Periodical. Russian. mo. $119.95. **(Subscription address:** East View Publications Inc., 3020 Harbor Lane North, Suite 110, Minneapolis MN 55447.**)** **LC** QC350; .O686. ***Continues** Optiko-Mekhanicheskaia Promyshlennost.*

UK/0030-3992
**OPTICS AND LASER TECHNOLOGY.** [Opt. laser technol.]. (Aug. 1970)-. Academic Scholarly Publication. English. bm. $403.00 The Americas; £270.00 other. Butterworth Heinemann Publishers, Linacre House, Jordan Hill, Oxford OX2 8DP England. **Tel** 011 44 865 310366. **(Subscription address:** Elsevier Science Ltd. Oxford Fulfillment Centre, PO Box 800, Kidlington, Oxford OX5 1DX United Kingdom.**)** **ED** Stephen Bailey. **LC** QC350; .O66. **DD** 535/.05. **CODEN** OLTCAS. **[CCC].** Index available. **Bk Rev. Ad Acc. Pr Rev. Circ:** 1,200. available on microfilm and microfiche from University Microfilms International (UMI). Documents available from Article Express International, The Genuine Article, Ask*IEEE, CASDDS. ***Continues** Optics Technology.*
**Desc:** An international journal bridging the research/applications gap. Review articles, original research papers and news are published.
**Ind/Abst** Acoust. Abstr.; Bioeng. Abstr.; Ceram. Abstr.; Chem. Abstr.; Curr. Contents Eng. Tech. Appl. Sci.; Curr. Contents Phys. Chem. Earth Sci.; Curr. Technol. Index; Ei Page One; Eng. Index Annu.; Fluid Abstr., Civil Eng.; Fluid Abstr. Proc. Eng.; FLUIDEX (1973-); HTFS Dig.; INSPEC (Nov. 1970-); Int. Aerosp. Abstr.; Pollut. Abstr. Indexes; Res. Alert [Full Cov.]; Sci. Cit. Index; SCISEARCH; World Publ. Monit.

UK/0143-8166
**OPTICS AND LASERS IN ENGINEERING.** [Opt. lasers eng.]. Vol. 1, No. 1 (July/Sept. 1980)-. Academic Scholarly Publication. English. Ten times a year. $559.00 The Americas; £375.00 other. Elsevier Applied Science, An Imprint of Elsevier Science Ltd., The Boulevard, Langford Lane, Kidlington, Oxford OX5 1GB United Kingdom. **Tel** 011 44 865 843000, 011 44 865 843699, FAX 011 44 865 843010. **(Subscription address:** Elsevier Science Ltd. Oxford Fulfillment Centre, PO Box 800, Kidlington, Oxford OX5 1DX United Kingdom.**)** **ED** G. T. Reid and F. P. Chiang. **CODEN** OLENDN. **[CCC]. Pr Rev.** available on microfilm and microfiche from University Microfilms International (UMI). Documents available from Article Express International, The Genuine Article, Ask*IEEE.

**Desc:** Covers all aspects relating to the development and application of non-ionising radiation in engineering.
**Ind/Abst** Alum. Ind. Abstr.; Bioeng. Abstr.; Curr. Contents Eng. Tech. Appl. Sci.; Ei Page One; Eng. Mater. Abstr.; Eng. Index Annu.; INSPEC (July-Sept. 1980-); Int. Aerosp. Abstr.; Met. Abstr.; Res. Alert [Full Cov.]; Sci. Cit. Index; SCISEARCH.

US/1047-6938
**OPTICS AND PHOTONICS NEWS.** [Optics photonics news]. **Added/Corp** Optical Society of America. **VFOAT** Optics & Photonics News. Vol. 1, No. 1 (Jan. 1990)-. Periodical. English. mo. $99.00 US; $111.00 Canada; $119.00 Europe and Asia. Optical Society of America, 2010 Massachusetts Avenue Northwest, Washington DC 20036. **Tel** (202)223-8130, (800)762-6960, (800)582-0416, FAX (202)223-1096, telex 510 600 3965. **ED** Andrea Pendleton. **LC** TA1501; .O664. **DD** 621.36. **NLM** W1; OP8634. **CODEN** OPPHEL. **[CCC].** Index available (bound in last issue.). Documents available from Ask*IEEE. ***Continues** Optics News, 0098-907X.*
**Desc:** Articles of interest to the entire optics industry. Blends timely papers on research and industry trends with news and features covering a broad range of topical areas. Regular contents include a comprehensive optics meeting calendar, book reviews, and reports of recent research, plus industry and OSA advertising.
**Ind/Abst** Abstr. Bull. Inst. Pap. Sci. Tech.; INSPEC (June 1990-).

US/0030-400X
**OPTICS AND SPECTROSCOPY.** [Opt. spectrosc.]. **Added/Corp** American Institute of Physics. Optical Society of America. Vol. 6 (Jan. 1959)-. Periodical. English (Russian). mo. $1425.00 US; $1445.00 Canada; $1467.00 Europe and Asia. Optical Society of America, 2010 Massachusetts Avenue Northwest, Washington DC 20036. **Tel** (202)223-8130, (800)762-6960, (800)582-0416, FAX (202)223-1096, telex 510 600 3965. **ED** Scott B. Elliott. **LC** QC350; .O6813. **DD** 535.05. **NLM** W1 OP864. **CODEN** OPSUA3. **[CCC].** Index available (bound in last issue.). cum. index. Documents available from Article Express International, Ask*IEEE, CASDDS.
**Desc:** A translation of "Optika y Spektroskopiya", a major spectroscopic journal published in the former Soviet Union by the Academy of Sciences. Recent issues included papers on such topics as Cherenkov radiation, nonlinear Qeeman effects, ring gas lasers, LC devices, and digital holographic filters for pattern recognition.
**Ind/Abst** Abstr. Bull. Inst. Pap. Sci. Tech.; Ceram. Abstr.; Chem. Abstr.; Curr. Phys. Index; Ei Page One; Energy Res. Abstr.; Eng. Index Annu.; GeoRef; INSPEC (1968-); Int. Aerosp. Abstr.; Mass Spect. Bull.; Pollut. Abstr. Indexes; SPIN (1970-); World Ceram. Abstr.

NE/0030-4018
**OPTICS COMMUNICATIONS.** [Opt. commun.]. Vol. 1 (Apr. 1969)-. Academic Scholarly Publication. English (French and German). Sixty times a year (10 volumes). Fl4530.00. Elsevier Science Publishers BV, PO Box 211, 1000 AE Amsterdam Netherlands. **Tel** 011 31 20 5803642, FAX 011 31 20 5862696, telex 15682. **ED** F. Abeles, N.B. Abraham, L.M. Narducci, H. Walther. **LC** QC350; .O684. **DD** 535/.05. **CODEN** OPCOB8. **[CCC].** cum. index. **Pr Rev.** available on microfilm and microfiche from University Microfilms International (UMI). Documents available from Article Express International, The Genuine Article, Ask*IEEE, CASDDS.
**Desc:** Publishes short papers on instrumental and physical optics and on spectroscopy, i.e. on the interaction of light with matter.
**Ind/Abst** Bioeng. Abstr.; Ceram. Abstr.; Chem. Abstr.; Civ. Struct. Eng. Abstr.; Comput. Inf. Syst. Abstr. J. [Full Cov.]; Curr. Contents Eng. Tech. Appl. Sci.; Curr. Contents Phys. Chem. Earth Sci.; Ei Page One; Elect. Comm. Abstr.; Eng. Index Annu.; GeoRef; HTFS Dig.; INSPEC (April 1969-); Int. Aerosp. Abstr.; Mass Spect. Bull. (?-?); Mater. Sci. Eng. Abstr.; Mech. Eng. Abstr.; Phys. Briefs; Pollut. Abstr. Indexes; Res. Alert [Full Cov.]; Sci. Cit. Index; SCISEARCH; Solid State Supercond. Abstr.

US/1071-8842
**OPTICS INDEX (PRINT).** (OPTICS INDEX.). [Opt. index]. **Added/Corp** Optical Society of America. (1974-1979)-. English. ir (every five years). $45.00 US and US Possessions; $50.00 Canada, Mexico, South America; $60.00 other. Optical Society of America, 2010 Massachusetts Avenue Northwest, Washington DC 20036. **Tel** (202)223-8130, (800)762-6960, (800)582-0416, FAX (202)223-1096, telex 510 600 3965. **(Subscription address:** Optical Society of America, 335 East 45th Street, New York NY 10017.**)** **LC** QC350; .O6624. **DD** 535/.05.

US/0146-9592
**OPTICS LETTERS.** [Opt. lett.]. **Added/Corp** Optical Society of America. Vol. 1 (July 1977)-. Academic Scholarly Publication. English. Twenty-four times a year. $700.00 US; $724.00 Canada; $755.00 Europe and Asia. Optical Society of America, 2010 Massachusetts Avenue Northwest, Washington DC 20036. **Tel** (202)223-8130, (800)762-6960, (800)582-0416, FAX (202)223-1096, telex 510 600 3965. **ED** Peter W. E. Smith. **LC** QC350; .O663. **DD** 535/.05. **NLM** W1 OP864D. **CODEN** OPLEDP. **[CCC].** Index available (bound in last issue.).

cum. index. **Pr Rev.** available on microfilm and microfiche. Documents available from Article Express International, The Genuine Article, Ask*IEEE, CASDDS.
**Desc:** Coverage emphasizes optical sciences including atmospheric optics, quantum electronics, fourier optics, integrated optics and fiber optics. Newsworthiness to a substantial part of the optics community and the effect of rapid publication of the research of others are among the criteria used in determining acceptability of contributions.
**Ind/Abst** Acoust. Abstr.; Chem. Abstr.; Curr. Contents Eng. Tech. Appl. Sci.; Curr. Contents Phys. Chem. Earth Sci.; Curr. Phys. Index; Ei Page One; EMBASE; Energy Res. Abstr. (1977-); Eng. Index Annu.; Graph. Arts Bull. Inst. Pap. Sci. Technol. (April 1989); HTFS Dig.; INSPEC (July 1977-); Int. Aerosp. Abstr.; Leadscan; Res. Alert [Full Cov.]; Sci. Cit. Index; SCISEARCH; SPIN (1977-).

GW/0030-4026
**OPTIK (STUTTGART).** (OPTIK.). [Optik]. **Added/Corp** Deutsche Gesellschaft fuer Elektronenmikroskopie. Deutsche Gesellschaft fuer Angewandte Optik. Vol. 1 (July 1946)-. Periodical. German (English). mo. DM432.00. Wissenschaftliche Verlagsgesellschaft mbH, Postfach 101061, D 70009 Stuttgart Germany. **Tel** 011 49 711 258200, FAX 011 49 711 2582290, telex 723636 DAZ D. **ED** Theo Tschudi. **LC** QC350; .O67. **DD** 535.05. **NLM** W1 OP865. **CODEN** OTIKAJ. **[CCC].** **Pr Rev.** Documents available from Article Express International, The Genuine Article, Ask*IEEE, CASDDS.
**Desc:** Journal for light and electron optics.
**Ind/Abst** Bioeng. Abstr.; Chem. Abstr.; Curr. Contents Eng. Tech. Appl. Sci.; Curr. Contents Phys. Chem. Earth Sci.; Ei Page One; Energy Res. Abstr.; Eng. Index Annu.; INSPEC (1968-); Phys. Briefs; Res. Alert [Full Cov.]; Sci. Cit. Index; SCISEARCH.

GW
**OPTIK; ZEITSCHRIFT FUER LICHT- UND ELEKTRONENOPTIK.** **Added/Corp** Deutsche Gesellschaft fur Elektronenmikroskopie. Deutsche Gesellschaft fur Angewandte Optik. **VFOAT** Zeitschrift fur Licht- und Elektronenoptik. Vol. 25, (1967)-. Periodical. German (English). mo. DM328.00 (add DM4.49 postage) Germany; (add DM4.40 postage) other. Wissenschaftliche Verlagsgesellschaft mbH, Postfach 101061, D 70009 Stuttgart Germany. **Tel** 011 49 711 258200, FAX 011 49 711 2582290, telex 723636 DAZ D. **ED** Theo Tschudi. **Bk Rev**. **Ad Acc. Circ:** 600 (ctrl). Documents available from Ask*IEEE. ***Continues** Optik; Zeitschrift fur das Gesamte Gebiet der Licht- und Elektronenoptik,, 0030-4026,.*
**Desc:** Unpublished articles on subjects for light and electron optics.
**Ind/Abst** Curr. Contents Eng. Tech. Appl. Sci.; Curr. Contents Phys. Chem. Earth Sci.; INSPEC (1968-); Phys. Briefs.

●RU
**OPTIKA ATMOSFERY I OKEANA.**
**Added/Corp** Institut Optiki Atmosfery SO RAN. (1992)-. Periodical. Russian (summaries and/or abstracts in English; table of contents in English). mo. $199.95. **(Subscription address:** East View Publications Inc., 3020 Harbor Lane North, Suite 110, Minneapolis MN 55447.**)** **CODEN** OAOKEM. ***Continues** Optika Atmosfery, 0235-277X.*
**Ind/Abst** Int. Aerosp. Abstr.

RU/0030-4034
**OPTIKA I SPEKTROSKOPIJA.** (OPTIKA I SPEKTROSKOPIIA; SBORNIK STATEI.). [Opt. spektrosk.]. **Added/Corp** Akademiia Nauk SSSR. Otdelenie Fiziko-Matematicheskikh Nauk. (1956)-. Academic Scholarly Publication. Russian. mo. $372.00. **(Subscription address:** East View Publications Inc., 3020 Harbor Lane North, Suite 110, Minneapolis MN 55447.**)** **LC** QC476.5; .O6. **CODEN** OPSPAM. **[CCC].** Index available in last issue of volume--attached. cum. index. **Pr Rev.** Documents available from The Genuine Article, Ask*IEEE, CASDDS.
**Ind/Abst** Chem. Abstr.; INSPEC (1968-); Int. Aerosp. Abstr.; Res. Alert [Full Cov.]; Sci. Cit. Index; SCISEARCH.

US/8756-6990
**OPTOELECTRONICS, INSTRUMENTATION, AND DATA PROCESSING.** (OPTOELECTRONICS INSTRUMENTATION & DATA PROCESSING.). [Optoelectron. instrum. data process.]. **Added/Corp** Akademiia Nauk SSSR. Sibirskoe Otdelenie. No. 1 (1984)-. Periodical. English (Russian). Six times a year. $980.00. Allerton Press, Inc., 150 Fifth Avenue, New York NY 10011. **Tel** (212)924-3950, FAX (212)463-9684, telex 427441 ALPRES. **LC** TK7878; .A87. **DD** 621.38/0414. **CODEN** OIDPE4. **[CCC].** Documents available from Ask*IEEE. ***Continues** Automatic Monitoring and Measuring, 0005-1292.*
**Ind/Abst** INSPEC (1984-); Int. Aerosp. Abstr.

JA/0286-9659
**OPUTORONIKUSU.** (OPUTORONIKUSU / OPTRONICS.). [Oputoronikusu]. **VFOAT** Optronics. (1982)-. Academic Scholarly Publication. Japanese. Twelve times a year. $211.00. **(Subscription address:** Japan Publications Trading Company, Ltd., PO Box 5030, Tokyo International, Tokyo 100-31 Japan.**)** **CODEN** OPUTDD. Documents available from CASDDS.
**Ind/Abst** Chem. Abstr.

FR/1146-5360
**PASCAL. E 27, METHODES DE FORMATION ET TRAITEMENT DES IMAGES.** **See** Physics-Abstracting, Bibliographies and Statistics.

US/1067-5345
**PHOTONICS AND OPTOELECTRONICS.** [Photon. optoelectron.]. Vol. 1, No. 1 (1993)-. Academic Scholarly Publication. English. qt. $245.00. Allerton Press, Inc., 150 Fifth Avenue, New York NY 10011. **Tel** (212)924-3950, FAX (212)463-9684, telex 427441 ALPRES. **LC** TA1501; .P43. **DD** 621.381/045/05. **CODEN** PHOPET. **[CCC].** Documents available from CASDDS.
**Ind/Abst** Chem. Abstr.

US/1044-1425
**PHOTONICS DIRECTORY, THE.** **VFOAT** Photonics Corporate Guide to Profiles & Addresses; Photonics Buyers' Guide to Products & Manufactures; Photonics Design & Applications Handbook; Photonics Design and Applications Handbook; Photonics Dictionary. 35th Ed. (1989)-. Directory. English. an. $108.00 US; $114.00 other. Laurin Publishing Company Inc, PO Box 4949, Pittsfield MA 01202. **Tel** (413)499-0514, FAX (413)442-3180, telex 232-055 ASAS. **ED** Patricia L. Trotti, Deborah L. Monahan, Teresa F. Fields, Kathleen A. Zappula, and Holly B. Moriarty. **LC** TS511.U6; O67. **DD** 621.36/029/473. **Pr Rev.** ***Continues** Optical Industry & Systems Purchasing Directory, 0191-0647.*
**Desc:** The voice of photonics technology, optics, electro-optics, lasers, fiber optics and imaging. Design and graph information, dictionary.

US/0731-1230
**PHOTONICS SPECTRA (PITTSFIELD, MASS. 1982).** (PHOTONICS SPECTRA.). [Photonics spectra]. **VFOAT** Photonics. Vol. 16, Issue 1 (Jan. 1982)-. Academic Scholarly Publication. English. mo. $98.00 (one year), $176.00 (two year), $218.00 (three year) US; $123.00 (one year), $226.00 (two year), $293.00 (three year) surface mail other; $173.00 (one year), $321.00 (two year), $428.00 (three year) airmail other. Laurin Publishing Company Inc, PO Box 4949, Pittsfield MA 01202. **Tel** (413)499-0514, FAX (413)442-3180, telex 232-055 ASAS. **ED** Diane L. Morgenstein. **LC** TS510; .O6. **DD** 681/.4/05. **NLM** W1 PH671H. **CODEN** PHSAD3. Index available. cum. index. **Bk Rev**. **Ad Acc. Circ:** 75,000 (ctrl). available on microfilm and microfiche from University Microfilms International (UMI); available on an online database (file 648/Full-Text) from DIALOG. Documents available from Article Express International, The Genuine Article, Ask*IEEE, CASDDS. ***Continues** Optical Spectra, 0030-395X. **Continued in part by** Photonics European Directory, 1056-9324.*
**Desc:** International journal of optics, electro-optics, lasers, fiber optics and imaging technology. Directed to scientists, engineers, technicians and management personnel of the photonics industry.
**Ind/Abst** Alum. Ind. Abstr.; Chem. Abstr. (1982-1984); Curr. Contents Eng. Tech. Appl. Sci.; Ei Page One; Eng. Mater. Abstr.; Eng. Index Annu.; F&S Index Plus Text, Int. [Select. Cov.]; GeoRef; Graph. Arts Bull. Inst. Pap. Sci. Technol. (July 1989); INSPEC (Jan. 1982-); Met. Abstr.; PROMT; Res. Alert [Select. Cov.]; SCISEARCH; Soc. Sci. Cit. Index [Select. Cov.]; Trade Ind. ASAP [Full Txt.]; Trade Ind. Index [Full Txt.].

●US/1064-1068
**POF NEWSLETTER.** [POF newsl.]. **Added/Corp** Information Gatekeepers, Inc. **VAT** Plastic Optical Fibers Newsletter. Vol. 1, No. 1 (July 1992)-. Newsletter. English. Six times a year. $250.00 US & Canada; $300.00 other. Information Gatekeepers Inc., 214 Harvard Avenue, Boston MA 02134. **Tel** (617)232-3111, (800)323-1088, FAX (617)734-8562. **DD** 621.

RU/0370-2715
**PRIKLADNAIA IADERNAIA SPEKTROSKOPIIA.** [Prikl. jad. spektrosk.]. (1970)-. Academic Scholarly Publication. Russian. **CODEN** PYSPAS. Documents available from CASDDS.
**Ind/Abst** Chem. Abstr.

●US
**PROCEEDINGS / IAPR INTERNATIONAL CONFERENCE ON PATTERN RECOGNITION.** **Added/Corp** International Association for Pattern Recognition. 11th (Aug. 30-Sept. 3, 1992)-. Proceedings. English. be. $300.00 (4 volume set). IEEE Computer Society, 10662 Los Vaqueros Circle, PO Box 3014, Los Alamitos CA 90720-1264. **Tel** (714)821-8380, (800)272-6657, FAX (714)821-4641. **LC** Q327; .I62a. **DD** 001. ***Continues** International Conference on Pattern Recognition. International Conference on Pattern Recognition [Proceedings].*

US
**PROCEEDINGS OF THE ... ANNUAL TRI-SERVICE CONFERENCE ON THE BIOLOGICAL EFFECTS OF MICROWAVE RADIATION.** **Main/Conf** Tri-Service Conference on the Biological Effects of Microwave Radiation. **Added/Corp** Rome Air Development Center. (1960)-. Proceedings. English. ir. Price varies per volume. Plenum Press, 233 Spring Street, New York NY 10013-1578. **Tel** (212)620-8000, (800)221-9369, FAX (212)463-0742, (212)807-1047, telex 23/421139. **LC** QH652; .T75. **DD** 574.19.

NE/0079-6638
**PROGRESS IN OPTICS.** [Prog. opt.]. Vol. 1 (1961)-. Monographic series. English. ir. Price varies per volume. Elsevier Science Publishers BV, PO Box 211, 1000 AE Amsterdam Netherlands. **Tel** 011 31 20 5803642, FAX 011 31 20 5862696, telex 15682. **ED** E. Wolf. **LC** QC351; .P7. **DD** 535/.05. **NLM** W1 PR676K. **CODEN** POPTAN. **[CCC].** Documents available from Article Express International, The Genuine Article, Ask*IEEE, CASDDS.
**Desc:** Deals with theoretical and applied optics and related subjects.
**Ind/Abst** Bioeng. Abstr.; Chem. Abstr. (1961-1984); Ei Page One; Eng. Index Annu.; Index Sci. Rev. [Full Cov.]; INSPEC; Res. Alert [Full Cov.]; Sci. Cit. Index.

UK/0963-9659
**PURE AND APPLIED OPTICS: JOURNAL OF THE EUROPEAN OPTICAL SOCIETY PART A.** Vol. 1 (1992)-. English. bm. $231.00. Institute of Physics, Techno House, Redcliffe Way, Bristol BS1 6NX England. **Tel** 011 44 272 297481, FAX 011 44 272 294318, telex 449149 INSTP G. **(Subscription address:** American Institute of Physics, Publishing Sales, 500 Sunnyside Blvd., Woodbury NY 11797.**)** **ED** M Bertolotti. **CODEN** PAOAE3. Index available in last issue of volume--attached. available on microfiche. Documents available from Article Express International.
**Desc:** Covers all aspects of modern and classical optics: experimental and theoretical studies, applications and instrumentation, including (but not restricted to): propagation, scattering, diffraction; linear and nonlinear phenomena; spectroscopy, interferometry, instrumentation; thin films, optical materials; interaction of radiation with matter; design, fabrication and testing, integrated optics; optoelectronics, electro-optics, optical communication, modulation, computing, switching; ultrafast phenomena, high-field phenomena; applications in space, aeronautics, life sciences, industry.
**Ind/Abst** Eng. Index Annu.

US/1040-3078
**RADIATION EMBRITTLEMENT.** English. ASTM - American Society fo Testing and Materials, 1916 Race Street, Philadelphia PA 19103. **Tel** (215)299-5585.

UK/1350-4487
**RADIATION MEASUREMENTS.** (19??)-. English. Eight times a year. $611.00 The Americas; £410.00 other. Pergamon Press, An Imprint of Elsevier Science Ltd., The Boulevard, Langford Lane, Kidlington, Oxford OX5 1GB United Kingdom. **Tel** 011 44 865 843000, 011 44 865 843699, FAX 011 44 865 843010. **(Subscription address:** Elsevier Science Ltd. Oxford Fulfillment Centre, PO Box 800, Kidlington, Oxford OX5 1DX United Kingdom.**)** **ED** S.W.S. McKeever. Documents available from ADONIS.
**Desc:** Provides a forum for the exposition of the latest developments in the broad field of radiation measurements.
**Ind/Abst** ADONIS; Biol. Abstr.; Curr. Contents Phys. Chem. Earth Sci.; Eng. Index Annu.; Health Saf. Sci. Abstr.; Sci. Cit. Index (19??-19??); SCISEARCH; Toxicol. Abstr.

US
**RADIATION PHYSICS, BIOPHYSICS AND RADIATION BIOLOGY.** **Main/Corp** Columbia University. Radiological Research Laboratory. Government Publication. English. US Department of Energy, 1000 Independence Avenue SW, Washington DC 20585. **Tel** (202)586-5000, FAX (202)586-4073.

UK/0144-8420
**RADIATION PROTECTION DOSIMETRY.** [Radiat. prot. dosim.]. Vol. 1, No. 1 (1981)-. Academic Scholarly Publication. English. Twenty times a year. £550.00 UK; $1190.00 other. Nuclear Technology Publishing, PO Box 7, Ashford Kent TN23 1YW England. **Tel** 0233 641683, FAX 0233 610021, telex 966119 NTPUK G. **ED** J A Dennis. **LC** R905; .R33. **DD** 363.1/79. **NLM** W1 RA164R. **CODEN** RPDODE. Index available. cum. index. **Bk Rev**. **Ad Acc. Pr Rev. Circ:** 1,000 (ctrl). Documents available from The Genuine Article, Ask*IEEE, CASDDS, Documents on Demand.
**Desc:** Covers all aspects of personnel and environmental dosimetry and monitoring for ionising and non-ionising radiations including biological aspects, physical concepts, external and internal dosimetry and monitoring, environmental and workplace monitoring and dosimetry related to the protection of patients.
**Ind/Abst** Calcium Calcif. Tissue Abstr.; Chem. Abstr.; Coal Abstr.; Curr. Contents Eng. Tech. Appl. Sci.;

EMBASE; Energy Inf. Abstr.; Energy Res. Abstr. (Oct. 1981-); Environ. Abstr.; Health Saf. Sci. Abstr.; INSPEC (1981-); Pollut. Abstr. Indexes; Res. Alert [Select. Cov.]; Risk Abstr.; Toxicol. Abstr.

US/0033-7587
**RADIATION RESEARCH.** [Radiat. res.]. **Added/Corp** Radiation Research Society (U.S.). Vol. 1 (Feb. 1954)-. Academic Scholarly Publication. English. mo. $560.00 US and Canada; $648.00 other. Kluge, Carden & Jennings, 853 West Main Street, Charlottesville VA 22903. **Tel** (804)979-4913, FAX (804)979-4025. **ED** R.J.M. Fry. **LC** QC770; .R3. **DD** 539.705. **NLM** W1 RA166. **CODEN** RAREAE. **[CCC].** cum. index. **Pr Rev.** Documents available from The Genuine Article, BIOSIS Document Express, Ask*IEEE, CASDDS.
**Desc:** Includes original articles on the physical, chemical, and biological effects of radiation and related subjects in the area of physics, chemistry, biology, and medicine.
**Ind/Abst** AGRICOLA; Biol. Abstr.; Chem. Abstr.; Chem. Titles; Coal Abstr.; Curr. Aware. Biol. Sci., CABS; Curr. Contents Life Sci.; EMBASE; Energy Res. Abstr.; Environ. Period. Bibliogr.; Genet. Abstr.; Index Med.; INSPEC (1968-); Int. Aerosp. Abstr.; Oncog. Growth Factors Abstr.; Life Sci. Collect.; Pig News Inf.; Pollut. Abstr. Indexes; Ref. Upd. Basic Ed.; Ref. Upd. Deluxe Ed.; Res. Alert [Full Cov.]; Risk Abstr.; Sci. Cit. Index; SCISEARCH; Toxicol. Abstr. (19??-).

●RU
**RADIATSIONNAIA BIOLOGIIA, RADIOECOLOGIIA / ROSSIISKAIA AKADEMIIA NAUK.** **Added/Corp** Rossiiskaia Akademiia Nauk. **VFOAT** Radiation Biology, Radioecology. (1993)-. Academic Scholarly Publication. Russian (summaries and/or abstracts in English; table of contents in English). Six times a year. $99.95. Izdatelstvo Nauka / Akademiia Nauk, Publishing House of the Russian Academy of Sciences, Leninskii Porspekt 14, 117901 Moscow Russia. **Tel** 011 95 954-21-53, FAX 011 95 938-21-44, telex 411964. **(Subscription address:** East View Publications Inc., 3020 Harbor Lane North, Suite 110, Minneapolis MN 55447.**)** **NLM** W1; RA176. ***Continues*** *Radiobiologiia, 0033-8192.*
**Desc:** Contains information on radiation effects, radioactive pollutants, and radiobiology.

UK/0954-8211
**RADIOGRAPHY TODAY.** [Radiogr. today]. **Added/Corp** College of Radiographers (Great Britain). Vol. 54, No. 617 (Oct. 1988)-. Periodical. English. mo. £60.00. College of Radiographers, 14 Upper Wimpole Street, London W1M 8BN England. **Tel** 011 44 71 935 5726. **NLM** W1; RA264BH. **CODEN** RATOEO. Documents available from BIOSIS Document Express. ***Formed by the union of*** *Radiography, 0033-8281* ***and*** *Radiography News.*
**Ind/Abst** Biol. Abstr.; Health Plan. Adminis.; Index Med.

US/0033-8443
**RADIOPHYSICS AND QUANTUM ELECTRONICS.** [Radiophys. quantum electron.]. **Main/Corp** Soviet Union. Ministerstvo Vysshego I Spednego Spetsialnogo Obrazovaniia. Obrazovaniia. **Added/Corp** Consultants Bureau. (1967)-. Academic Scholarly Publication. English (translations available in Russian). mo. $1295.00 US; $1515.00 other. Consultants Bureau, A Division of Plenum Publishing Corporation, 233 Spring Street, New York NY 10013. **Tel** (212)620-8000, (212)620-8466, FAX (212)463-0742, telex 23/421139. **ED** V. L. Ginzburg. **LC** QC661; .R813. **DD** 539.2/05. **CODEN** RPQEAC. **[CCC].** Index available. available on microfilm and microfiche from University Microfilms International (UMI). Documents available from Article Express International, Ask*IEEE, CASDDS. ***Continues*** *Izvestiia Vysshikh Uchebnykh Zavedenii. Radiofizika. English Soviet Radiophysics, 0097-1545.*
**Desc:** This journal reports on the properties and applications of electromagnetic radiation in the radio and optical bands. Covers radio astronomy, plasma theory, millimeter and submillimeter waves, antenna and wave guide technology.
**Ind/Abst** Appl. Mech. Rev.; Bioeng. Abstr.; Chem. Abstr.; Ei Page One (1984); Eng. Index Annu.; INSPEC (Jan. 1970-); Math. Rev.; Pollut. Abstr. Indexes.

RU/0131-8098
**RADIOSPEKTROSKOPIIA.** **Added/Corp** Permskii Gosudarstvennyi Universitet Imeni A.M. Gorkogo. (1962)-. Academic Scholarly Publication. Russian. 1.20rub. **LC** QD96.M5; R34. **CODEN** RDSPD8. Documents available from CASDDS.
**Ind/Abst** Chem. Abstr.

FR/0245-3827
**RAPPORT D'ACTIVITE / MINISTERE DE LA SANTE, MINISTERE DU TRAVAIL, INSERM, SERVICE CENTRAL DE PROTECTION CONTRE LES RAYONNEMENTS IONISANTS.** **Added/Corp** Institut National de la Sante et de la Recherche Medicale (France). Service Central de Protection Contre les Rayonnements Ionisants. (19??)-. French. **NLM** W1; RA487UK.

FR/0397-9210
**RAYONNEMENTS IONISANTS.** [Rayonnem. ionis.]. (1971)-. Periodical. French. Four times a year. 130.00F France; 150.00F other. Association Tech. Sci. Radioprotection, 28 Residence de la Madeleine, 78460 Cheuvreuse France. **Tel** 011 33 30 521431. **UDC** 614.876.
**Ind/Abst** Ei Page One.

US/0161-0406
**REFRACTORIES (BUREAU OF THE CENSUS).** ***Ceased.*** (CURRENT INDUSTRIAL REPORTS. MQ-32C, REFRACTORIES.). [Refractories]. **Added/Corp** United States. Bureau of the Census. **VFOAT** Refractories. Government Publication. English. qt. US Department of Commerce, 14th Street & Constitution Avenue NW, Washington DC 20230. **Tel** (202)482-2000, FAX (202)482-3772. **LC** HD9600.R43; U64. **DD** 380.1/4566672/0973. **CODEN** CIRRDF. Documents available from CASDDS, Documents on Demand.
**Desc:** Presents timely data on the production, inventories, and orders of approximately 5,000 products, which represents 40 percent of all US manufacturing.
**Ind/Abst** Am. Stat. Index (1961-1984); Chem. Abstr. (1961-1984).

US/0147-2887
**REPORT ON ENVIRONMENTAL RADIATION SURVEILLANCE IN NORTH CAROLINA.** **See** Environmental Issues-Pollution and Waste Management.

UK
**REPORT ON RADIOLOGICAL PROTECTION AND OCCUPATIONAL HEALTH FOR THE YEAR ... / UNITED KINGDOM ATOMIC ENERGY AUTHORITY.** **Added/Corp** United Kingdom Atomic Energy Authority. (19??)-. Academic Scholarly Publication. English. **LC** RA569; .R437. **DD** 363.17/997/0941. Documents available from CASDDS.
**Ind/Abst** Chem. Abstr.

US/0743-0752
**REVIEWS OF INFRARED AND MILLIMETER WAVES.** (1983)-. Academic Scholarly Publication. English. Plenum Press, 233 Spring Street, New York NY 10013-1578. **Tel** (212)620-8000, (800)221-9369, FAX (212)463-0742, (212)807-1047, telex 23/421139. **ED** Kenneth J. Button. **LC** TK7876; .R482. **DD** 621.381/3. **CODEN** RIMVDV. Documents available from CASDDS.
**Ind/Abst** Chem. Abstr. (1983-).

JA
**REZA KAGAKU KENKYU.** [Reza kagaku kenkyu]. **VFOAT** Laser Science Progress Report of IPCR; Laser Science Progress Report of I.P.C.R. Began in 1979. Academic Scholarly Publication. Japanese (summaries and/or abstracts in English). an. Laser Science Research Group, Rikigaku Kenkyusho, Wako-shi, Saitama 351-01 Japan. **Tel** 0484(62)1111, FAX 0484(62)1554, telex 02962818 RIKEN J. **LC** TA1671; .R49. **CODEN** RKAKDK. **Circ:** 900 (ctrl). Documents available from CASDDS.
**Ind/Abst** Chem. Abstr.

JA/0387-0200
**REZA KENKYU.** [Reza kenkyu]. **Added/Corp** Reza Gakkai (Japan). **VFOAT** Review of Laser Engineering. (1973)-. Periodical. Japanese (summaries and/or abstracts in English). bm. $280.00. Reza Gakkai, (Laser Soc. of Japan), 2-6, Yamadaoka, Suitashi, Osakafu 565 Japan. **(Subscription address:** Kyowa Book Co., Inc., 1 38 Kanda Jinbocho Chiyoda Ku, Tokyo 101 Japan, Tel. 81 3 3293 0727**)** **CODEN** REKEDA. Documents available from CASDDS.
**Ind/Abst** Chem. Abstr.

RU/0371-1722
**SBORNIK NAUCHNYKH TRUDOV / VSESOIUZNYI NAUCHNO-ISSLEDOVATELSKII INSTITUT LIUMINOFOROV I OSOBO CHISTYKH VESHCHESTV, VNIILIUMINOFOROV.** [Sb. naucn. tr. - Vses. naucno-issled. inst. ljuminoforov osobo cist. vescestv]. **Added/Corp** Vsesoiuznyi Nauchno-Issledovatelskii Institut liuminoforov i Osobo Chistykh Veshchestv (Soviet Union). (1969)-. Monographic series. Russian (summaries and/or abstracts in English). Price varies per volume. **CODEN** SNVNAR. Documents available from CASDDS.
**Ind/Abst** Chem. Abstr.

JA/0386-8044
**SEKIGAISEN GIJUTSU.** [Sekigaisen gijutsu]. **Added/Corp** Sekigaisen Gijutsu Kenkyukai. **VFOAT** Proceeding of the Infrared Society of Japan. (1976)-. Periodical. Japanese. Infrared Society of Japan, Kyoto Japan. **CODEN** SEGIEE. Documents available from CASDDS.
**Ind/Abst** Chem. Abstr.

US
**SOVIET JOURNAL OF OPTICAL TECHNOLOGY.** ***Title Change.*** **Added/Corp** Optical Society of America. American Institute of Physics. Vol. 57, No. 9 (Sept. 1990)-. Academic Scholarly Publication. English. mo. Optical Society of America, 2010 Massachusetts Avenue Northwest, Washington DC 20036. **Tel** (202)223-8130, (800)762-6960, (800)582-0416, FAX (202)223-1096, telex 510 600 3965. **LC** TS510; .S65. Documents available from CASDDS. ***Continued by*** *Journal of Optical Technology, 1070-9762.*
**Ind/Abst** Chem. Abstr.; Curr. Phys. Index; Energy Res. Abstr. (Feb. 1973-); Int. Aerosp. Abstr.; Pollut. Abstr. Indexes.

UK/0960-0884
**SOVIET LIGHTWAVE COMMUNICATIONS.** ***Ceased.*** **Added/Corp** Institute of Physics (Great Britain) Akademiia nauk SSSR. American Institute of Physics. Vol. 1 (1991)-Vol. 3 No. 4 (1993). Periodical. English. qt. Institute of Physics, Techno House, Redcliffe Way, Bristol BS1 6NX England. **Tel** 011 44 272 297481, FAX 011 44 272 294318, telex 449149 INSTP G. **ED** A M Prokhorov. **LC** TK5103.59; .S68. **DD** 621.382/75. **CODEN** SLCOER. Index available in last issue of volume--attached. available on microfiche. Documents available from Article Express International, Ask*IEEE.
**Desc:** Reflects changes and developments in a rapidly developing and changing field. Initial coverage includes: linear and non-linear propagation in conventional and special fibres, including rare-earth doped, birefringent, etc. fibres, fibre technology, fibre sensors, optical fibres as waveguides for telecommunications, and physics and chemistry of various kinds of materials for fibre optics.
**Ind/Abst** Ei Page One; Eng. Index Annu.; INSPEC (Feb. 1991-).

UK/0584-8539
**SPECTROCHIMICA ACTA. PART A : MOLECULAR SPECTROSCOPY.** [Spectrochim. acta, Part A: Mol. spectrosc.]. Vol. 23A (Jan. 1967)-. Periodical. English (French and German). Fourteen times a year. $1416.00 The Americas; £950.00 other. Pergamon Press, An Imprint of Elsevier Science Ltd., The Boulevard, Langford Lane, Kidlington, Oxford OX5 1GB United Kingdom. **Tel** 011 44 865 843000, 011 44 865 843699, FAX 011 44 865 843010. **(Subscription address:** Elsevier Science Ltd. Oxford Fulfillment Centre, PO Box 800, Kidlington, Oxford OX5 1DX United Kingdom.**)** **ED** Sidney Kettle and Jeffrey Steinfeld. **LC** QD95; .S633. **DD** 543/.085. **NLM** W1 SP315A. **CODEN** SAMCASSAMCS. **[CCC].** **Pr Rev.** available on microfilm from Microfilms International Marketing Corp.; available on microfilm and microfiche from University Microfilms International (UMI); available on microfiche from the publisher. Documents available from The Genuine Article, BIOSIS Document Express, Ask*IEEE, CASDDS, ADONIS. ***Continues in part*** *Spectrochimica Acta.*
**Desc:** Intended for the rapid publication of original work dealing with molecular spectroscopy, and its application in chemical problems.
**Ind/Abst** Abstr. Bull. Inst. Pap. Sci. Tech.; ADONIS; Anal. Abstr.; Biol. Abstr.; Ceram. Abstr. (19??-); Chem. Abstr.; Chem. Titles; Curr. Contents Phys. Chem. Earth Sci.; Ei Page One; GeoRef; INSPEC (1968-); Nat. Prod. Updates; Life Sci. Collect.; Pollut. Abstr. Indexes; Res. Alert [Full Cov.]; Sci. Cit. Index; SCISEARCH; World Ceram. Abstr.

UK/0958-319X
**SPECTROCHIMICA ACTA REVIEWS.** ***Ceased.*** Vol. 13, No. 1 (1990)-Vol. 15 (1993). Academic Scholarly Publication. English. bm. Pergamon Press, An Imprint of Elsevier Science Ltd., The Boulevard, Langford Lane, Kidlington, Oxford OX5 1GB United Kingdom. **Tel** 011 44 865 843000, 011 44 865 843699, FAX 011 44 865 843010. **(Subscription address:** US/ 395 Saw Mill River Road, Elmsford, NY 10523; Can/ 150 Consumers Road/Suite 104, Willowdale Ontario M2J 1P9; Aus-NZ/ POB 544, Potts Point NSW 2011**)** **ED** J-M Mermet and R Sturgeon. **LC** QD96.A8; P76. **DD** 543/.0858. **[CCC].** available on microfilm and microfiche from University Microfilms International (UMI). Documents available from Article Express International, The Genuine Article, CASDDS. ***Continues*** *Progress in Analytical Spectroscopy, 0884-1837.*
**Ind/Abst** Anal. Abstr.; Chem. Abstr.; Curr. Contents Phys. Chem. Earth Sci.; Ei Page One; Eng. Index Annu.; Res. Alert [Full Cov.]; Sci. Cit. Index; SCISEARCH.

US/0958-319X
**SPECTROCHIMICA ACTA REVIEWS [MICROFORM].** Vol. 13, No. 1 (1990)-. Periodical. English. Pergamon Press, An Imprint of Elsevier Science Ltd., The Boulevard, Langford Lane, Kidlington, Oxford OX5 1GB United Kingdom. **Tel** 011 44 865 843000, 011 44 865 843699, FAX 011 44 865 843010. **LC** QD96.A8; P75. **[CCC].** ***Continues*** *Progress in Analytical Spectroscopy.*

US/0038-6995
**SPECTROSCOPIA MOLECULAR.** [Spectrosc. mol.]. Vol. 1, No. 1 (May 1952)-. Academic Scholarly Publication. mo. F Cleveland, Spectroscopia Laboratory, University of Kentucky, Lexington KY 40506. **LC** QC451; .S62. **DD** 535/.84/05. **CODEN** SPMOAX. available on microfilm and microfiche from University

Microfilms International (UMI). Documents available from CASDDS.
**Ind/Abst** Chem. Abstr.

●GW/0966-0941
**SPECTROSCOPY EUROPE. VFOAT** Spectroscopy Europe. Vol. 4, No. 2 (Mar./Apr. 1992)-. Academic Scholarly Publication. English. bm. $78.00. VCH Gesellschaft GmbH, Postfach 101161, D 69451 Weinheim Germany. **Tel** 011 49 6201 606459, FAX 011 49 6201 606184. **(Subscription address:** VCH Publishers Inc., 303 Northwest 12th Avenue, Journals Department, Deerfield FL 33442.) **LC** QC450; .S639. **NLM** W1; SP318. **CODEN** SPEUEF. Documents available from CASDDS. ***Formed by the union of*** *Spectroscopy International, 1040-7669* ***and*** *Spectroscopy World.*
**Ind/Abst** Chem. Abstr.

US/0038-7010
**SPECTROSCOPY LETTERS.** [Spectrosc. lett.]. Vol. 1 (Jan. 1968)-. Academic Scholarly Publication. English (summaries and/or abstracts in French and Spanish; table of contents in French and Spanish). Eight times a year. $795.00 US; $823.00 other. Marcel Dekker Inc., 270 Madison Avenue, New York NY 10016. **Tel** (212)696-9000, (800)228-1160, FAX (212)685-4540, telex 421419. **(Subscription address:** Marcel Dekker Inc, PO Box 5017, Monticello NY 12701.) **ED** James W. Robinson. **LC** QD95; .S6367. **NLM** W1 SP317. **CODEN** SPLEBX. **[CCC]. Bk Rev. Ad Acc. Pr Rev.** ctrl circ. available on microfiche. Documents available from The Genuine Article, Ask*IEEE, CASDDS.
**Desc:** This rapid publication journal provides vital coverage of fundamental developments in spectroscopy. Offering communications of original, experimental, and theoretical work, this international journal reports such methods as NMR, ESR, microwave, IR, Raman, and UV spectroscopy. In addition, atomic emission and absorption, X-ray spectroscopy, mass spectrometry, lasers, electron microscopy, molecular fluorescence, and molecular phosphorescence are discussed.
**Ind/Abst** AGRICOLA; Air Pollut. Titles; Anal. Abstr.; Ceram. Abstr.; Chem. Abstr.; Chem. Titles; Coal Abstr.; Curr. Contents Phys. Chem. Earth Sci.; EMBASE; Energy Res. Abstr.; GeoRef; INSPEC (Sept. 1969-); Int. Aerosp. Abstr.; Mass Spect. Bull.; Nat. Prod. Updates; Phys. Briefs; Res. Alert [Full Cov.]; Sci. Cit. Index; SCISEARCH; Soils Fert.; SPIN (1981-).

●US/1058-045X
**SPIE HOLOGRAPHICS INTERNATIONAL DIRECTORY & RESOURCE GUIDE.** [SPIE hologr. int. dir. resour. guide]. **Added/Corp** Society of Photo-Optical Instrumentation Engineers. **VFOAT** Society of Photo-Optical Instrumentation Engineers Holographics International Directory and Resource guide; SPIE Holographics International Directory and Resource Guide; Holographics International; Holographics. (1992)-. Directory. English. an. $52.00 (non-members), $37.00 (members). International Society for Optical Engineering, PO Box 10, Bellingham WA 98227-0010. **Tel** (206)676-3290, FAX (206)647-1445, telex 46-7053. **LC** TA1542; .S68. **DD** 621.36/75.

GW/0172-6218
**SPRINGER SERIES IN CHEMICAL PHYSICS.** [Springer ser. chem. phys.]. V. 1-. Academic Scholarly Publication. English. Price varies per volume. Springer-Verlag GmbH & Company KG, Heidelberger Platz 3, D 14197 Berlin Germany. **Tel** 011 49 30 8207223, FAX 011 49 30 8214091, telex 183 319 SPBLN D. **(Subscription address:** Springer Verlag New York Inc. / for North America, 44 Hartz Way, Secaucus NJ 07096.) **CODEN** SSCPDA. Documents available from Article Express International, BIOSIS Document Express, Ask*IEEE, CASDDS.
**Desc:** Contains articles on laser processing, chemistry of solid surfaces, atoms in strong light fields, and formations of organic solids.
**Ind/Abst** Biol. Abstr. (-1979); Chem. Abstr.; Ei Page One; Eng. Index Annu.; INSPEC.

US/0342-4111
**SPRINGER SERIES IN OPTICAL SCIENCES.** [Springer ser. opt. sci.]. Vol. 1 (1976)-. Academic Scholarly Publication. English. ir. Price varies per volume. Springer-Verlag GmbH & Company KG, Heidelberger Platz 3, D 14197 Berlin Germany. **Tel** 011 49 30 8207223, FAX 011 49 30 8214091, telex 183 319 SPBLN D. **(Subscription address:** Springer Verlag New York Inc. / for North America, 44 Hartz Way, Secaucus NJ 07096.) **LC** UNC. **CODEN** SSOSDB. **[CCC].** Documents available from Article Express International, Ask*IEEE, CASDDS.
**Desc:** Contains articles on optical phase conjugation, laser physics, scanning electron microscopy, and holography and deformation analysis.
**Ind/Abst** Bioeng. Abstr.; Chem. Abstr.; Ei Page One; Energy Res. Abstr. (March 1982-); Eng. Index Annu.; INSPEC.

US
**STUDIES IN RADIATION EFFECTS : SERIES A, PHYSICAL AND CHEMICAL.** ***Title Change.*** Vol. 1, 1966-?. Periodical. English. ir. Gordon & Breach Science Publishers, Inc., PO Box 786, Cooper Station, New York NY 10276. **Tel** (212)206-8900, FAX (212)645-2459. **(Subscription address:** International Publishers Distributor at one of the following addresses: 820 Town Center Drive, Langhorne, PA 19047; or PO Box 90, Reading Berkshire RG1 8JL UK; or Kent Ridge PO Box 1180, Singapore 9111, Republic of Singapore) **LC** QC475; .S78. ***Continued by*** *Studies in Radiation Effects on Solids.*

●US/1065-7665
**STUDIES OF VACUUM ULTRAVIOLET AND X-RAY PROCESSES.** (1992)-. English. AMS Press Inc., 56 East 13th Street, New York NY 10003. **Tel** (212)777-4700, FAX (212)995-5413, telex 710 581 2302.

●US/1055-5269
**SURFACE SCIENCE SPECTRA.** [Surf. sci. spectra]. **Added/Corp** American Vacuum Society. American Institute of Physics. Vol. 1, No. 1 (1992)-. Periodical. English. qt. $987.00 US; $997.00 Canada, Mexico, Central & South America and the Caribbean; $1007.00 other. American Institute of Physics, 500 Sunnyside Boulevard, Woodbury NY 11797-2999. **Tel** (516)576-2200, FAX (516)349-7669, telex 960983. **LC** QC173.4.S94; S9645. **DD** 543/.0858/05. **CODEN** SSSPEN.
**Ind/Abst** Curr. Phys. Index.

US/0894-0886
**SYNCHROTRON RADIATION NEWS.** [Synchrotron radiat. news]. Vol. 1, No. 1 (Jan./Feb. 1988)-. Periodical. English. bm. $508.00 (academic institutions), $792.00 (corporate institutions). Gordon & Breach Science Publishers, Inc., PO Box 786, Cooper Station, New York NY 10276. **Tel** (212)206-8900, FAX (212)645-2459. **(Subscription address:** International Publishers Distributor at one of the following addresses: 820 Town Center Drive, Langhorne, PA 19047; or PO Box 90, Reading Berkshire RG1 8JL UK; or Kent Ridge PO Box 1180, Singapore 9111, Republic of Singapore) **DD** 539. **[CCC].**

FR/1143-3760
**TRANSFIL EUROPE PARIS. See** Communication-Telecommunications.

GW/0177-7513
**UKW-BERICHTE.** [UKW-Ber.]. **VFOAT** Ultrakurzwellen-Berichte. (1962)-. Periodical. German. Four times a year. DM36.00 Germany; DM40.00 other. Verlag UKW Berichte, Postfach 80, D 91081 Baiersdorf Germany. **Tel** 011 49 9133 77980. **UDC** 621.396.24.

US/0275-3901
**UV/EB NEWS.** [UV/EB news]. **VAT** Ultraviolet, Electron Beam News. Vol. 1, No. 1 (Jan. 1981)-. Periodical. English. bm. $111.00. Technology Marketing Corporation, One Technology Plaza, Norwalk CT 06854. **Tel** (203)852-6800, FAX (203)853-2845. **ED** Kathleen Delaney. **Ad Acc. Circ:** 5,000.
**Desc:** Newsletter featuring general industry news as they relate to ultraviolet, electron beam and infrared technologies.

UN
**VESTNIK KIEVSKOGO POLITEKHNICHESKOGO INSTITUTA. SERIIA RADIOELEKTRONIKA. Main/Corp** Kyivskyi Politekhnichnyi Instytut. **VFOAT** Seriia Radioelektronika. No. 5 (1968)-. Academic Scholarly Publication. Russian (summaries and/or abstracts in English). **CODEN** VKPRBM. Documents available from CASDDS. ***Continues*** *Visnyk Kyivskoho Politekhnichnoho Instytuta. Seriia Radioelektroniky.*
**Ind/Abst** Chem. Abstr.

NE/0090-1911
**VIBRATIONAL SPECTRA AND STRUCTURE.** [Vib. spectra struct.]. Vol. 1 (1972)-. Academic Scholarly Publication. English. ir. Price varies per volume. Elsevier Science Publishing Company Inc, Madison Square Station, PO Box 882, New York NY 10159-0882. **Tel** (212)633-3950, FAX (212)633-3990. **(Subscription address:** Elsevier Science Inc. / New York Books, 655 Avenue of the Americas, New York NY 10010.) **ED** J. Durig. **LC** QC454.V5; V53. **DD** 537.53/52. **NLM** W1 VI169E. **CODEN** VBSSBB. **Pr Rev.** Documents available from Ask*IEEE, CASDDS.
**Desc:** This is an ongoing series. Each title has a different subject.
**Ind/Abst** Chem. Abstr.; INSPEC.

RU/0134-5400
**VOPROSY ATOMNOJ NAUKI I TEHNIKI. FIZIKA RADIACIONNYH POVREZDENIJ I RADIACIONNOE MATERIALOVEDENIE.** (VOPROSY ATOMNOI NAUKI I TEKHNIKI. SERIIA FIZIKA RADIATSIONNYKH POVREZHDENII I RADIATSIONNOE MATERIALOVEDENIE.). [Vopr. at. nauki teh., Fiz. radiac. povr. radiac. materialoved.]. **Added/Corp** Fizyko-Tekhnichnyi Instytut (Akademiia Nauk Ukrainskoi RSR) TSentralnyi Nauchno-Issledovatelskii Institut Informatsii i Tekhniko-Ekonomicheskikh IssledovaniÊi po Atomnoi Nauke i Tekhnike. **VFOAT** Seriia Fizika Radiatsionnykh Povrezhdenii i Radiatsionnoe Materialovedenie; Fizika Radiatsionnykh Povrezhdenii i Radiatsionnoe Materialovedenie. (1974)-. Academic Scholarly Publication. Russian (summaries and/or abstracts in English). **LC** PAR. Documents available from CASDDS.
**Ind/Abst** Chem. Abstr.

RU
**VOPROSY ATOMNOJ NAUKI I TEHNIKI. RADIACIONNAJA TEHNIKA.** (VOPROSY ATOMNOI NAUKI I TEKHNIKI. RADIATSIONNAIA TEKHNIKA / GOSUDARSTVENNYI KOMITET PO ISPOLZOVANIIU ATOMNOI ENERGII SSSR, VSESOIUZNYI NAUCHNO-ISSLEDOVATELSKII INSTITUT RADIATSIONNOI TEKHNIKI.). [Vopr. at. nauki teh., Radiac. teh.]. **Added/Corp** Vsesoiuznyi Nauchno-Issledovatelskii Institut Radiatsionnoi Tekhniki (Soviet Union). **VFOAT** Radiatsionnaia Tekhnika. (19??)-. Academic Scholarly Publication. Russian. **CODEN** VANTDI. Documents available from CASDDS.
**Ind/Abst** Chem. Abstr.

RU
**VOPROSY OPTOELEKTRONIKI I SPEKTROSKOPII.** [Vopr. optoelektron. spektrosk.]. **Added/Corp** Ulianovskii Gosudarstvennyi Pedagogicheskii Institut. (1976)-. Academic Scholarly Publication. Russian. **LC** TA1750; .V66. **CODEN** VOSPDR. Documents available from CASDDS.
**Ind/Abst** Chem. Abstr.

US/0277-2493
**WILEY SERIES IN PURE AND APPLIED OPTICS.** [Wiley ser. pure appl. optics]. (19??)-. Monographic series. English. ir. Price varies per volume. John Wiley & Sons, Inc., 605 Third Avenue, New York NY 10158-0012. **Tel** (212)850-6000, (212)850-6645, FAX (212)850-6088, telex 12-7063. **(Subscription address:** John Wiley & Sons / England, Baffins Lane, Chichester, West Sussex PO19 1UD England.) **[CCC].**
**Ind/Abst** Math. Rev.

UK
**X-RAY DIFFRACTION ABSTRACTS. Added/Corp** Science & Technology Agency. (19??)-. Periodical. English. qt. $78.00. PRM Science & Technology Agency Ltd, 261A Finchley Road Hampstead, London NW3 6LV England. **Tel** 011 44 71 431 0372. **LC** QC482.D5; X73. **DD** 543/.085.

JA/0911-7806
**X-SEN BUNSEKI NO SHINPO.** [X-sen bunseki no shinpo]. **Added/Corp** Nihon Bunseki Kagakkai. X-Sen Bunseki Kenkyu Konwakai. **VFOAT** Advances in X-Ray Chemical Analysis. (1970)-. Academic Scholarly Publication. Japanese. Nihon Bunseki Kagakkai, (Japan Soc. for Analytical Chemistry), 26-2 Nishigotanda 1 chome, Shinagawaku Tokyoto 114 Japan. **NLM** W1; XS266. **CODEN** XBNSDA. Documents available from CASDDS.
**Ind/Abst** Chem. Abstr. (1986-).

●GW/0941-7567
**ZEISS INFORMATION WITH JENA REVIEW. Added/Corp** Carl Zeiss (Firm : 1946) Carl Zeiss Jena GmbH. No. 1 (1992)-. Periodical. English (summaries and/or abstracts in French and Spanish; translations available in German). ir. Free. Carl Zeiss Ltd., Zeiss Information, W 7085 Oberkochen Germany. **Tel** 011 49 7364 203408. **LC** IN PROCESS. **CODEN** ZIJREP. ***Formed by the union of*** *Zeiss Information (English Ed.), 0044-2054* ***and*** *Jenaer Rundschau. English. Jena Review, 0448-9497.*
**Ind/Abst** Chem. Abstr.

CC/0258-7025
**ZHONGGUO JIGUANG.** (CHUNG-KUO CHI KUANG / CHUNG-KUO KUANG HSUEH HSUEH HUI, CHUNG-KUO CHI KUANG PIEN CHI YUAN HUI CHU PIEN.). [Zhongguo jiguang]. **Added/Corp** Chung-Kuo Kuang Hsueh Hsueh Hui. Chung-Kuo Chi Kuang Pien Chi Yuan Hui. **VFOAT** Chinese Journal of Lasers. (1983)-. Academic Scholarly Publication. Chinese (summaries and/or abstracts in English). bm. $100.80. Science Press, 16 Donghuangchenggen North Street, Beijing 100707, People's Republic of China. **Tel** 011 86 1 4019821, 011 86 1 4010642, FAX 011 86 1 4012180, 011 86 1 4019810, telex 210147. **ED** Tang Xingli. **CODEN** ZHJIDO. Documents available from Article Express International, Ask*IEEE. ***Continues*** *Chi Kuang Tsa Chih, 0253-2743.*
**Desc:** Represents contributions from China's laser physicists, optical scientists, materials researchers, and medical physicists. Co-published by the Optical Society of America.
**Ind/Abst** Ei Page One; Eng. Index Annu.; INSPEC (Jan. 1983-).

RU/0514-7506
**ZURNAL PRIKLADNOI SPEKTROSKOPII (MINSK).** (ZHURNAL PRIKLADNOI SPEKTROSKOPII.). [Z. prikl. spektrosk.]. **Added/Corp** Instytut Fiziki (Akademiia Navuk Belaruskai SSR). **VFOAT** Vsesoiuznyi Zhurnal Prikladnoi Spektroskopii. Vol. 1 (Sept. 1964)-. Periodical. Russian. Six times a year. $179.95. **(Subscription address:** East View Publications Inc., 3020 Harbor Lane North, Suite 110, Minneapolis MN 55447.) **CODEN** ZPSBAX. cum. index. Documents available from Ask*IEEE, CASDDS.

**Ind/Abst** Abstr. Bull. Inst. Pap. Sci. Tech.; Chem. Abstr.; Coal Abstr.; Curr. Biotechnol.; Energy Res. Abstr. (Sept. 1976-); INSPEC (1968-); Int. Aerosp. Abstr.; Mass Spect. Bull.

## MAGNETISM

US/1057-2732
**ADVANCES IN MAGNETIC AND OPTICAL RESONANCE.** [Adv. magn. opt. reson.]. Vol. 15 (1990)-. Academic Scholarly Publication. English. ir. $95.00 (Vol. 18). Academic Press, Inc., 6277 Sea Harbor Drive, Orlando FL 32887. **Tel** (800)543-9534, (407)345-4100, FAX (407)363-9661. **DD** 538. **NLM** W1; AD675E. **CODEN** AMORE7. **[CCC].** Documents available from BIOSIS Document Express, Ask*IEEE, CASDDS. ***Continues*** *Advances in Magnetic Resonance, 0065-2873.*
**Ind/Abst** Biol. Abstr. (1991-); Chem. Abstr.; INSPEC.

US/1043-707X
**ADVANCES IN MAGNETIC RESONANCE. SUPPLEMENT.** ***Title Change.*** [Adv. magn. reson., Suppl.]. No. 1 (1976)-(19??). Monographic series. English. ir. Academic Press, Inc., 6277 Sea Harbor Drive, Orlando FL 32887. **Tel** (800)543-9534, (407)345-4100, FAX (407)363-9661. **DD** 538. ***Continued by*** *Advances in Magnetic and Optical Resonance. Supplement.*

BE
**ANNUAIRE: MAGNETISME TERRESTRE. JAARBOEK: AARDMAGNETISME.** **Added/Corp** Institut Royal Meteorologique de Belgique. **VFOAT** Jaarboek : Aardmagnetisme. (19??)-. French (Flemish). an. Institut Royal Meteorologique de Belgique, Avenue Circulaire 3, B 1180 Bruxelles Belgium. **Tel** 32-2-3730502, FAX 32-2-3751259. **LC** QC830.D68; A55.

CN
**ANNUAL REPORT FOR MAGNETIC OBSERVATORIES AND REPEAT STATIONS.** **Added/Corp** Canada. Energy, Mines and Resources Canada. Geological Survey of Canada. **VFOAT** Rapport Annuel des Observatoires Magnetiques et des Stations de Repetition. (198?)-. English (French). an. Energy Mines and Resources, One Observatory Crescent, Ottawa Ontario K1A OY3 Canada. **Tel** (613)994-5891. **LC** QE185; .A42 subser.; QC825.1. **DD** 538/.78/71. ***Continues*** *Annual Report for Magnetic Observatories, 0704-3023.*

UK/0066-4103
**ANNUAL REPORTS ON NMR SPECTROSCOPY.** [Annu. rep. NMR spectrosc.]. **VAT** Annual Reports on Nuclear Magnetic Resonance Spectroscopy. Vol. 3 (1970)-. Academic Scholarly Publication. English. ir. $125.00 (Vol. 28). Academic Press, Inc., 6277 Sea Harbor Drive, Orlando FL 32887. **Tel** (800)543-9534, (407)345-4100, FAX (407)363-9661. **ED** G. Webb. **LC** QC490; .A5. **DD** 538/.3. **NLM** W1 AN769GP. **CODEN** NMRPAJ. Documents available from Ask*IEEE, CASDDS. ***Continues*** *Annual Review of NMR Spectroscopy.*
**Ind/Abst** AGRICOLA [Select. Cov.]; Chem. Abstr.; INSPEC.

US/1054-4887
**APPLIED COMPUTATIONAL ELECTROMAGNETICS SOCIETY JOURNAL.** [Appl. Comput. Electromagn. Soc. j.]. **Added/Corp** Applied Computational Electromagnetics Society. **VFOAT** Journal; ACES Journal. Vol. 4, No. 1 (Spring 1989)-. Periodical. English. sa (July and Nov.). Comes with ACES membership. Applied Computational Electromagnetics Society (ACES), Naval Postgraduate School, ECAB, Monterey CA 93943. **Tel** (408)646-2352. **LC** IN PROCESS. **DD** 621. **CODEN** JCSOED. Documents available from Article Express International, Ask*IEEE. ***Continues in part*** *Applied Computational Electromagnetics Society Journal and Newsletter.*
**Ind/Abst** Ei Page One; Eng. Index Annu.; INSPEC (Summer 1990-).

US/0192-6020
**BIOLOGICAL MAGNETIC RESONANCE.** [Biol. magn. reson.]. (1978)-. Academic Scholarly Publication. English. ir. Price varies per volume. Plenum Press, 233 Spring Street, New York NY 10013-1578. **Tel** (212)620-8000, (800)221-9369, FAX (212)463-0742, (212)807-1047, telex 23/421139. **ED** Lawrence J. Berliner and Jacques Reuben. **NLM** W1 BI75R; W1 BI75R. **CODEN** BMGRDB. Each issue contains an index to its own contents (no volume index)--loose. Documents available from CASDDS.
**Ind/Abst** Chem. Abstr.

PO
**BOLETIM GEOMAGNETICO PRELIMINAR.** **Main/Corp** Instituto Nacional de Meteorologia e Geofisica. Bulletin. Portuguese. Instituto Nacionel de Meteorologia e Geofisica, rua Saraiva de Carvalho 2, Lisbon Portugal. **LC** QC825.4; .P67A. **DD** 538/.78/469.

US/0163-559X
**BULLETIN OF MAGNETIC RESONANCE.** [Bull. magn. reson.]. **Added/Corp** International Society of Magnetic Resonance. Vol. 1, No. 1 (Winter 1979)-. Academic Scholarly Publication. English. qt. $80.00. International Society of Magnetic Resonance, Purdue Department of Chemistry, c/o D Gorenstein, W Layfayette IN 47907. **Tel** (317)494-7851, FAX (317)494-0239. **ED** David Gorenstein. **LC** QC762; .B8. **DD** 538/.36/05. **CODEN** BUMRDT. **Pr Rev.** Documents available from CASDDS.
**Ind/Abst** Chem. Abstr.

US/0895-5824
**CA SELECTS: SOLID STATE NMR.** **See** Chemistry-Abstracting, Bibliographies and Statistics.

●CN/1191-2707
**CMM : CANADIAN MEDIA MAG.** [CMM, Can. media mag]. **Added/Corp** 3M Canada Inc. **VFOAT** Canadian Media Mag. (Spring 1992)-. Periodical. English. qt. Limited free distribution. 3M Canada, PO Box 5757, London Ontario N6A 4T1 Canada. **Tel** (519)451-2500, telex 0645886. **DD** 621.382. ***Continues*** *CVQ., 0828-5772.*

US/1043-7347
**CONCEPTS IN MAGNETIC RESONANCE.** [Concepts magn. reson.]. Vol. 1, No. 1 (July 1989)-. Academic Scholarly Publication. English. qt. $198.00 (institutions), $99.00 (individuals) US; $230.00 (institutions), $112.00 (individuals) Canada; $258.00 (institutions), $125.00 (individuals) other. NMR Concepts, PO Box 1577, Kingston RI 02881. **Tel** (401)792-5091, FAX (401)792-2104. **ED** Daniel D Traficante. **LC** QC762; .C588. **DD** 538/.362/05. **NLM** W1; CO459RHH. **CODEN** CMAEEM. **[CCC].** Index available (bound in fourth issue). cum. index. **Bk Rev**, (Qty: 1-4). **Ad Acc, Adv Mgr:** L O'Neill. **Pr Rev. Circ:** 725. Documents available from The Genuine Article, CASDDS.
**Ind/Abst** Chem. Abstr.; Res. Alert [Full Cov.].

JA
**DATA CATALOGUE - WORLD DATA CENTER C2 FOR GEOMAGNETISM.** **Main/Corp** World Data Center C2 for Geomagnetism. 1978-. English. be. Free. World Data Center C2, Faculty of Science, Kyoto University, Kyoto 606 Japan. **Tel** (075)722-0865, telex 5422693 LIBKYU. **ED** T Araki. **LC** QC811; .W67. **DD** 538/.7. **Circ:** 400. ***Continues*** *World Data Center C2 for Geomagnetism. Catalogue of Data.*
**Desc:** Catalogue of geomagnetic data collected by World Data Center for Geomagnetism which is operated by Kyoto University and guided by the panel on the World Data Centers of the International Council of Scientific Unions.

UN
**DIELEKTRIKI I POLUPROVODNIKI.** (1973)-. Russian (summaries and/or abstracts in English). **LC** QC585; .D53. **CODEN** DLPLAG. Documents available from CASDDS. ***Continues*** *Dielektriki.*
**Ind/Abst** Chem. Abstr.

●US/1061-9526
**ELECTRO- AND MAGNETOBIOLOGY.** **See** Biology.

US/0046-1709
**ELECTROMAGNETIC METROLOGY CURRENT AWARENESS SERVICE.** (ELECTROMAGNETIC METROLOGY.). **Added/Corp** United States. National Bureau of Standards. (19??)-. English. mo. $100.00. National Bureau of Standards Electromagnetic Metrology Info. Center, 325 Broadway Street, Boulder CO 80303-3328. **LC** QC535; .E43. **DD** 016.537.

UK
**ELECTROMAGNETICS NEWS.** (19??)-. English. bm (6 issues). £18.00 (individuals), £44.00 (institutions). Electromagnetics News, PO Box 25, Liphook Hants GU30 7SE England.
**Desc:** Covers the health hazards of electromagnetic fields from powerless, radio frequency, microwave and other frequencies. Also covers the positive uses of EMF'S in orthodox and alternative medicine.

●US/1069-4595
**ELECTROMAGNETOEFFECT (COMMACK, N.Y.).** **See** Engineering-Electricity, Electrical Engineering, Electronics.

UK/0301-7575
**ELECTRON SPIN RESONANCE SPECTROSCOPY ABSTRACTS.** [Electron spin reson. spectrosc. abstr.]. **Added/Corp** Science & Technology Agency. V. 1- July/Sept. 1973-. Periodical. English. qt. $78.00. Science & Technology Agency, 261A Finchley Road Hampstead, London NW3 6LU England. **LC** QD95; .E55. **DD** 538/.3.

GW/0343-7493
**ERGEBNISSE DER BEOBACHTUNGEN AM ERDMAGNETISCHEN OBSERVATORIUM FURSTENFELDBRUCK IM JAHRE.** **Added/Corp** Erdmagnetisches Observatorium Furstenfeldbruck. Universitat Munchen. Geophysikalisches Observatorium Furstenfeldbruck. (1940)-. German. an. Geophysikalisches Observatorium, Ludwigshoehe 8, 82256 Fuerstenfeldbruck, Bundesrepublik Deutschland Germany. **Tel** 011 49 8141 32470, FAX 011 49 8141 4704. **ED** Dr. Beblo. **LC** QC830.F8; E74. **DD** 538/.78431. ***Continues*** *Ergebnisse der Erdmagnetischen Beobachtungen im Jahre ... .*

UK/0271-1869
**EXPERIMENTAL MAGNETISM.** [Exp. magn.]. (1979)-. Academic Scholarly Publication. English. John Wiley & Sons Ltd., Baffins Lane, Chichester West Sussex PO19 1UD England. **Tel** 0243 779777, FAX 0243 776128 BTG:JWP001, telex 86290 WIBOOKG. **(Subscription address:** North, South and Central America/ John Wiley & Sons, Inc., Subscription Department, 605 Third Avenue, New York, NY 10158-0012, USA; telephone: (212)850-6645; FAX: (212)850-6021**)** **CODEN** EXPMDF. Documents available from CASDDS.
**Ind/Abst** Chem. Abstr.

RU
**FIZIKA MAGNITNYKH MATERIALOV.** **Added/Corp** Kalininskii Gosudarstvennyi Universitet. No. 1 (1973)-. Academic Scholarly Publication. Russian. 0.97rub (single issue). Gosudarstvennaia Biblioteka, Informatsionnyi Tsentr, Imeni V. I. Lenina, Prospekt Kalinina 3, 121019 Moscow Russia. **LC** QC750; .F58. Documents available from CASDDS.
**Ind/Abst** Chem. Abstr.

PL/0137-8996
**FIZYKA DIELEKTRYKOW I RADIOSPEKTROSKOPIA.** [Fiz. dielektr. radiospektrosk.]. (1966)-. Polish (summaries and/or abstracts in English and French). **LC** QC584; .F58; Q111; .P67. **CODEN** FDRSBE. Documents available from CASDDS. ***Continues*** *Fizyka Dielektrykow.*
**Ind/Abst** Chem. Abstr.

US/0163-4402
**GEOMAGNETIC DATA.** English. World Data Center A for Solar-Terrestrial Physics, United States Department of Commerce, NOAA/NGSDC, Boulder CO 80302. **LC** QC811; .A56. **DD** 538/.7.

US/0016-7932
**GEOMAGNETISM AND AERONOMY.** **See** Aeronautics, Astronautics.

RU/0016-7940
**GEOMAGNETIZM I AERONOMIJA.** (GEOMAGNETIZM I AERONOMII.). [Geomagn. aeron.]. **Added/Corp** Akademiia Nauk SSSR. Vol. 1, (1961)-. Academic Scholarly Publication. Russian. bm. $159.95. Izdatelstvo Nauka / Akademiia Nauk, Publishing House of the Russian Academy of Sciences, Leninskii Porspekt 14, 117901 Moscow Russia. **Tel** 011 95 954-21-53, FAX 011 95 938-21-44, telex 411964. **(Subscription address:** East View Publications Inc., 3020 Harbor Lane North, Suite 110, Minneapolis MN 55447.**)** **CODEN** GEAEA6. **[CCC].** Index available. **Bk Rev. Pr Rev.** Documents available from The Genuine Article, Ask*IEEE, CASDDS.
**Ind/Abst** Chem. Abstr.; Energy Res. Abstr.; GeoRef; INSPEC (1968-); Int. Aerosp. Abstr. (1984-); Meteorol. Geoastrophys. Abstr.; Res. Alert [Full Cov.]; Sci. Cit. Index; SCISEARCH.

●US/1076-8408
**HIGH SPEED TRANSPORT NEWS.** (1994)-. Periodical. English. sm. $495.00. Waters Information Services, PO Box 2248, Binghamton NY 13902-2248. **Tel** (607)770-8535, FAX (607)798-1692. ***Continues*** *Maglev News, 1065-6561.*

NE/0304-3843
**HYPERFINE INTERACTIONS.** [Hyperfine interact.]. Vol. 1 (1975)-. Academic Scholarly Publication. English. Twenty-eight times a year. 2334.50F (includes distribution costs). Baltzer Science Publishers BV, Asterweg 1A, 1031 HL Amsterdam Netherlands. **Tel** 011 31 20 6370061, FAX 011 31 20 6323651. **LC** QC762; .H89. **DD** 538/.3. **CODEN** HYINDN. **Pr Rev.** Documents available from The Genuine Article, Ask*IEEE, CASDDS. ***Continues*** *Muon Catalyzed Fusion.*
**Ind/Abst** Art Archaeol. Tech. Abstr.; Chem. Abstr.; Chem. Titles; Coal Abstr.; Curr. Contents Phys. Chem. Earth Sci.; INSPEC (June 1975-); Leadscan; Res. Alert [Full Cov.]; Sci. Cit. Index; SCISEARCH; Soils Fert.

US/0018-9464
**IEEE TRANSACTIONS ON MAGNETICS.** [IEEE trans. magn.]. **Added/Corp** Institute of Electrical and Electronics Engineers. Magnetics Group. IEEE Magnetics Society. **VAT** Institute of Electrical and Electronics Engineers Transactions on Magnetics. Vol. 1, No. 1 (Mar. 1965)-. Academic Scholarly Publication. English. bm. $280.00. IEEE, Institution of Electrical and Electronics Engineers, Inc., 345 East 47th Street, New York NY 10017-2394. **Tel** (908)981-1393, FAX (908)981-9667. **(Subscription address:** IEEE / Institute

of Electrical and Electronics Engineers, 445 Hoes Lane, PO Box 1331, Piscataway NJ 08855-1331.) **LC** TK454.4.M3; I48. **DD** 621.34/05. **CODEN** IEMGAQ. **[CCC].** cum. index. **Pr Rev.** Documents available from Article Express International, The Genuine Article, Ask*IEEE, CASDDS. ***Absorbed*** *Intermag Conference. Proceedings of the Intermag Conference.*
**Desc:** Covers the fundamental development, design, and application of magnetic devices as well as magnetic materials and phenomena as relevant to engineering purposes.
**Ind/Abst** Acoust. Abstr.; Bioeng. Abstr.; Chem. Abstr.; Coal Abstr.; Comput. Abstr.; Curr. Contents Eng. Tech. Appl. Sci.; Curr. Contents Phys. Chem. Earth Sci.; Ei Page One; Energy Inf. Abstr.; Energy Res. Abstr.; Eng. Index Annu.; Expand. Acad. Index (1992-); Index IEEE Publ.; INSPEC (1968-); Int. Aerosp. Abstr.; Res. Alert [Full Cov.]; Sci. Cit. Index; SCISEARCH.

US/0882-4959
**IEEE TRANSLATION JOURNAL ON MAGNETICS IN JAPAN.** ***Ceased.*** (IEEE TRANSLATION JOURNAL ON MAGNETICS IN JAPAN : A PUBLICATION OF THE IEEE MAGNETICS SOCIETY.). [IEEE transl. j. magn. Jpn.]. **Added/Corp** IEEE Magnetics Society. **VFOAT** Translation Journal on Magnetics in Japan; Oyo Jiki Honyaku Janaru. Vol. TJMJ-1, No. 1 (April 1985)-(19??). Periodical. English (English). mo. IEEE, Institution of Electrical and Electronics Engineers, Inc., 345 East 47th Street, New York NY 10017-2394. **Tel** (908)981-1393, FAX (908)981-9667. **(Subscription address:** IEEE / Institute of Electrical and Electronics Engineers, 445 Hoes Lane, PO Box 1331, Piscataway NJ 08855-1331.) **LC** TK454.4.M3; I34. **DD** 621.34/05. **CODEN** ITJJER. **[CCC].** Documents available from Article Express International, Ask*IEEE.
**Desc:** Presents translations of selected highly technical, quality papers originally published in the field of magnetics by the Magnetics Society of Japan and the Institute of Electronics and Communications Engineers in Japan.
**Ind/Abst** Acoust. Abstr.; Ei Page One; Elect. Comm. Abstr.; Eng. Index Annu.; Index IEEE Publ. (April 1985-); INIS Atomindex [Micro.]; INSPEC (1985-); Mech. Eng. Abstr.; Solid State Supercond. Abstr.

NE/0925-2096
**INTERNATIONAL JOURNAL OF APPLIED ELECTROMAGNETICS IN MATERIALS.** [Int. j. appl. electromagn. mater.]. **VFOAT** Journal of Applied Electromagnetics in Materials; Applied Electromagnetics in Materials. Vol. 1, No. 1 (July 1990)-. Periodical. English. Four times a year. Fl376.00. IOS Press, Van Diemenstraat 94, 1013 CN Amsterdam Netherlands. **Tel** 011 31 20 6382189, FAX 011 31 20 620 3419. **ED** K Miya. **CODEN** IAMTE7. **[CCC].** **Ad Acc.** **Pr Rev.** available on microfilm and microfiche from University Microfilms International (UMI). Documents available from Article Express International, Ask*IEEE.
**Desc:** Physics and mechanics of electromagnetics in materials and devices. Computational applications magnetic levitation, the forming of metals, and information storage.
**Ind/Abst** Civ. Struct. Eng. Abstr.; Comput. Inf. Syst. Abstr. J. [Full Cov.]; Ei Page One; Eng. Index Annu.; Environ. Eng. Abstr.; INSPEC (July 1990-); Mech. Eng. Abstr.; Met. Abstr.; Solid State Supercond. Abstr.

US/0022-2364
**JOURNAL OF MAGNETIC RESONANCE.** ***Title Change.*** [J. magn. reson.]. Vol. 1-100 (Jan. 1969)-(Dec. 1992). Academic Scholarly Publication. English. mo (including an annual subject index). Academic Press, Inc., 6277 Sea Harbor Drive, Orlando FL 32887. **Tel** (800)543-9534, (407)345-4100, FAX (407)363-9661. **ED** Wallace S Brey Jr. **LC** QC762; .J68. **DD** 538/.3. **CODEN** JOMRA4. **Pr Rev.** Documents available from The Genuine Article, Ask*IEEE, CASDDS. ***Split into*** *Journal of Magnetic Resonance. Series A* ***and*** *Journal of Magnetic Resonance. Series B.*
**Desc:** A leading source of up-to-date authoritative information on theory, techniques, methods of spectral analysis and interpretation, spectral correlations, and results of magnetic resonance spectroscopy. Presents notes, complete accounts of work of limited scope, and communications, preliminary accounts of work of special novelty or general interest. Featuring original research in both nuclear and electron magnetic resonance as well as related fields, the 'Journal of Magnetic Resonance' is a valuable tool for all those interested in this important methodology.
**Ind/Abst** Abstr. Bull. Inst. Pap. Sci. Tech.; Ceram. Abstr.; Chem. Abstr.; Chem. Titles; Coal Abstr.; Curr. Contents Phys. Chem. Earth Sci.; INSPEC (March 1970-); Int. Aerosp. Abstr.; Life Sci. Collect.; Pollut. Abstr. Indexes; Ref. Upd. Deluxe Ed.; Res. Alert [Full Cov.]; Sci. Cit. Index (19??-19??); SCISEARCH.

●US/1064-1858
**JOURNAL OF MAGNETIC RESONANCE. SERIES A.** [J. magn. reson., Ser. A]. Vol. 101, No. 1 (Jan. 1993)-. Academic Scholarly Publication. English. mo. $1024.00 (Series A), $1361.50 (Series A and B) US and Canada; $1221.00 (Series A), $1633.50 (Series A and B) other. Academic Press, Inc., 6277 Sea Harbor Drive, Orlando FL 32887. **Tel** (800)543-9534, (407)345-4100, FAX (407)363-9661. **LC** QC762; .J682. **DD** 538. **CODEN** JMRAE2. **[CCC].** Documents available from CASDDS. ***Continues in part*** *Journal of Magnetic Resonance, 0022-2364.*
**Ind/Abst** Chem. Abstr.; INIS Atomindex [Micro.]; Int. Aerosp. Abstr.; Leadscan; Life Sci. Collect.; Pollut. Abstr. Indexes; Sci. Cit. Index.

●US/1064-1866
**JOURNAL OF MAGNETIC RESONANCE. SERIES B.** [J. magn. reson., Ser. B]. Vol. 101, No. 1 (Feb. 1993)-. Academic Scholarly Publication. English. mo. $448.00 (Series B), $1361.50 (Series A and B) US and Canada; $539.00 (Series B), $1633.50 (Series A and B) other. Academic Press, Inc., 6277 Sea Harbor Drive, Orlando FL 32887. **Tel** (800)543-9534, (407)345-4100, FAX (407)363-9661. **LC** QH324.9.M28; J68. **DD** 538. **NLM** W1; JO748DC. **CODEN** JMRBE5. **[CCC].** Documents available from CASDDS. ***Continues in part*** *Journal of Magnetic Resonance, 0022-2364.*
**Ind/Abst** Chem. Abstr.; Int. Aerosp. Abstr.; Life Sci. Collect.; Pollut. Abstr. Indexes; Sci. Cit. Index.

NE/0304-8853
**JOURNAL OF MAGNETISM AND MAGNETIC MATERIALS.** [J. magn. magn. mater.]. Vol. 1 (Oct. 1975)-. Academic Scholarly Publication. English. Thirty-six times a year (12 volumes). Fl6564.00. Elsevier Science Publishers BV, PO Box 211, 1000 AE Amsterdam Netherlands. **Tel** 011 31 20 5803642, FAX 011 31 20 5862696, telex 15682. **ED** A.J. Freeman. **LC** QC750; .J68. **DD** 538/.05. **CODEN** JMMMDC. **[CCC].** **Pr Rev.** available on microfilm and microfiche from University Microfilms International (UMI). Documents available from Article Express International, The Genuine Article, Ask*IEEE, CASDDS.
**Desc:** Provides an important forum for the disclosure and contributions covering the whole spectrum of topics from basic magnetism to the technology and applications of magnetic materials and magnetic recording.
**Ind/Abst** Alum. Ind. Abstr.; Bioeng. Abstr.; Ceram. Abstr. (19??-); Chem. Abstr.; Chem. Titles; Civ. Struct. Eng. Abstr.; Comput. Inf. Syst. Abstr. J. [Full Cov.]; Curr. Contents Phys. Chem. Earth Sci.; Ei Page One; Elect. Comm. Abstr.; Eng. Mater. Abstr.; Eng. Index Annu.; GeoRef; INSPEC (Nov. 1975-); Int. Aerosp. Abstr.; Leadscan; Manuf. Process Eng. Abstr.; Mater. Sci. Eng. Abstr.; Mech. Eng. Abstr.; Met. Abstr.; Res. Alert [Full Cov.]; Sci. Cit. Index; SCISEARCH; Solid State Supercond. Abstr.

US
**JOURNAL OF MAGNETOHYDRODYNAMICS & PLASMA RESEARCH. See** Engineering-Electricity, Electrical Engineering, Electronics.

US/1065-6561
**MAGLEV NEWS.** ***Title Change.*** (MAGLEV NEWS : MAGNETIC LEVITATION & STEEL-WHEEL SYSTEMS.). [Maglev news]. (1992)-(1994). Periodical. English. Twenty-six times a year. Waters Information Services, PO Box 2248, Binghamton NY 13902-2248. **Tel** (607)770-8535, FAX (607)798-1692. **DD** 625. ***Continued by*** *High Speed Transport News, 1076-8408.*

US/1055-6915
**MAGNETIC AND ELECTRICAL SEPARATION.** [Magn. electr. sep.]. Vol. 3, No. 1 (Sept. 1991)-. Periodical. English. Four times a year. $339.00 (academic institutions), $529.00 (corporate institutions). Gordon & Breach Science Publishers, Inc., PO Box 786, Cooper Station, New York NY 10276. **Tel** (212)206-8900, FAX (212)645-2459. **(Subscription address:** International Publishers Distributor at one of the following addresses: 820 Town Center Drive, Langhorne, PA 19047; or PO Box 90, Reading Berkshire RG1 8JL UK; or Kent Ridge PO Box 1180, Singapore 9111, Republic of Singapore) **LC** TP156.M26; M34. **DD** 660.2/842. **CODEN** MELSE3. Documents available from Article Express International. ***Continues*** *Magnetic Separation News, 0731-3632.*
**Ind/Abst** Ei Page One; Eng. Index Annu.

US
**MAGNETIC FUSION PROGRAM SUMMARY DOCUMENT. Main/Corp** United States. Dept. of Energy. Office of Fusion Energy. English. an. US Department of Energy Office of Energy Technology, 1000 Independence Avenue SW, Washington DC 20585.

US/0739-6481
**MAGNETIC NORTH.** ***Ceased.*** **VFOAT** Magnetic North Magazine. Vol. 1, No. 1 (Summer 1983)-Ceased (1990). Periodical. English. qt. Thorn Books, PO Box 230, Littleton NH 03561.

US/0097-7330
**MAGNETIC RESONANCE REVIEW.** [Magn. reson. rev.]. Vol. 1 (Jan. 1972)-. Academic Scholarly Publication. English. qt (1 volume). $764.00 (academic institutions), $1191.00 (corporate institutions). Gordon & Breach Science Publishers, PO Box 90, Reading RG1 8JL England. **Tel** 011 44 734 560080, FAX 011 44 734 568211. **(Subscription address:** Gordon & Breach Science Publishers / US, 820 Town Center Drive, Langhorne PA 19047.) **ED** Charles P. Poole. **LC** QC762; .M245. **DD** 538/.3. **CODEN** MRSRBL. **[CCC].** **Bk Rev. Ad Acc.** Documents available from Ask*IEEE, CASDDS.
**Desc:** Surveys magnetic resonance literature on a calendar year basis.
**Ind/Abst** Alum. Ind. Abstr.; Chem. Abstr.; Eng. Mater. Abstr.; INSPEC (Oct. 1972-); Met. Abstr.

US/0731-3632
**MAGNETIC SEPARATION NEWS.** ***Title Change.*** [Magn. sep. news]. Vol. 1, No. 1 (Dec. 1983)-(19??). Periodical. English. qt. Gordon & Breach Science Publishers, Inc., PO Box 786, Cooper Station, New York NY 10276. **Tel** (212)206-8900, FAX (212)645-2459. **(Subscription address:** International Publishers Distributor at one of the following addresses: 820 Town Center Drive, Langhorne, PA 19047; or PO Box 90, Reading Berkshire RG1 8JL UK; or Kent Ridge PO Box 1180, Singapore 9111, Republic of Singapore) **ED** Martin Parker. **LC** TP156.M26; M34. **DD** 660.2/842. **CODEN** MSNWDK. **[CCC].** **Bk Rev. Ad Acc.** ***Continued by*** *Magnetic and Electrical Separation, 1055-6915.*
**Ind/Abst** Eng. Mater. Abstr.

US/0464-4387
**MAGNETISM.** [Magnetism]. (19??)-. Academic Scholarly Publication. English. ir. Price varies per volume. Academic Press, Inc., 6277 Sea Harbor Drive, Orlando FL 32887. **Tel** (800)543-9534, (407)345-4100, FAX (407)363-9661. **CODEN** MAGNAX. Documents available from CASDDS.
**Ind/Abst** Chem. Abstr.

US/0024-998X
**MAGNETOHYDRODYNAMICS (NEW YORK, N.Y. 1965).** (MAGNETOHYDRODYNAMICS.). [Magnetohydrodynamics]. **Added/Corp** Latvijas Padomju Socialistiskas Republikas Zinatnu Adakemija. Consultants Bureau. Vol. 1 (Jan./Mar. 1965)-. Periodical. English (Russian; translations available in Russian). qt (4 issues). $945.00 US; $1105.00 other. Consultants Bureau, A Division of Plenum Publishing Corporation, 233 Spring Street, New York NY 10013. **Tel** (212)620-8000, (212)620-8466, FAX (212)463-0742, telex 23/421139. **ED** J. Lielpeteris. **LC** QC717.6; .M3. **DD** 538. **CODEN** MGHDAG. **[CCC].** Index available. available on microfilm and microfiche from University Microfilms International (UMI). Documents available from Article Express International, Ask*IEEE, CASDDS.
**Desc:** The scope of this journal embraces not only magnetohydrodynamic, but also plasma, physics, magnetoaerodynamics, and magnetogasdynamics.
**Ind/Abst** Appl. Mech. Rev.; Bioeng. Abstr.; Chem. Abstr.; Ei Page One; Energy Res. Abstr.; Eng. Index Annu.; INSPEC (Fall 1967-); Int. Aerosp. Abstr.; Math. Rev.; SPIN (1980-); Zentralbl. Math. Ihre Grenzgeb.

LV/0025-0015
**MAGNITNAJA GIDRODINAMIKA.** (MAGNITNAIA GIDRODINAMIKA.). [Magn. gidrodin.]. **Added/Corp** Latvijas PSR Zinatnu Akademija. (1965)-. Academic Scholarly Publication. Russian. qt. $99.95. **(Subscription address:** East View Publications Inc., 3020 Harbor Lane North, Suite 110, Minneapolis MN 55447.) **LC** QC718; .M28. **DD** 538/.6/05. **CODEN** MAGIAI. **[CCC].** Documents available from Article Express International, Ask*IEEE, CASDDS.
**Ind/Abst** Chem. Abstr.; Ei Page One; Eng. Index Annu.; INSPEC (1968-); Int. Aerosp. Abstr. (19??-19??); Math. Rev.; Pollut. Abstr. Indexes; Zentralbl. Math. Ihre Grenzgeb.

RU
**MAGNITO-POLUPROVODNIKOVYE I ELEKTROMASHINNYE ELEMENTY AVTOMATIKI. See** Engineering-Electricity, Electrical Engineering, Electronics.

●CN/1191-2693
**MMC : MEDIAS MAGNETIQUES CANADA.** [MMC, Medias magn. Can.]. **Added/Corp** 3M Canada Inc. **VFOAT** Medias Magnetiques Canada. (Spring 1992)-. Periodical. French. qt. Limited free distribution. 3M Canada, PO Box 5757, London Ontario N6A 4T1 Canada. **Tel** (519)451-2500, telex 0645886. **DD** 621.382. ***Continues*** *VCT., 0844-0069.*

JA/0285-0192
**NIHON OYO JIKI GAKKAISHI.** [Nihon Oyo Jiki Gakkaishi]. **Added/Corp** Nihon Oyo Jiki Gakkai. **VFOAT** Journal of the Magnetics Society of Japan; Journal of Magnetics Society of Japan. (1977)-. Academic Scholarly Publication. Japanese. bm. $240.00. Nihon Oyo Jiki Gakkai, (Magnetics Soc. of Japan), 2-8, Toranomon 1 Chome, Minatoku, Tokyoto 105, Japan. **(Subscription address:** Maruzen Company Ltd., PO Box 5050, Import & Export Department, Tokyo 100 31 Japan.) **LC** QC750; .N54. **CODEN** NOJGD3. Documents available from CASDDS.
**Ind/Abst** Chem. Abstr.; Coal Abstr.

UK/0305-9804
**NUCLEAR MAGNETIC RESONANCE.** [Nucl. magn. reson.]. **Added/Corp** Chemical Society (Great Britain) Royal Society of Chemistry (Great Britain). Vol. 1, (1971)-. English. an. £155.00. Royal Society of Chemistry, Thomas Graham House, Science Park,

Cambridge CB4 4WF England. **Tel** 011 44 223 420066, FAX 011 44 223 423429, telex 818293 ROYAL. **(Subscription address:** Royal Society of Chemistry, Distribution Center, Blackhorse Road, Letchworth, SG6 1HN England.) **ED** G. A. Webb. **LC** QC762; .N88. **DD** 538/.3. **CODEN** NMRNBE. **[CCC]. Pr Rev.** Documents available from CASDDS.
**Desc:** Helpful to individuals who want to become quickly familiar with a specific subfield of NMR spectroscopy.
**Ind/Abst** Chem. Abstr.; GeoRef.

UK/0048-1033
**NUCLEAR MAGNETIC RESONANCE SPECTROMETRY ABSTRACTS.**
**Added/Corp** Science & Technology Agency. Vol. 1 (Jan./Feb. 1971)-. Periodical. English. bm (6 issues). PRM Science & Technology Agency Ltd, 261A Finchley Road Hampstead, London NW3 6LV England. **Tel** 011 44 71 431 0372. **LC** QC762; .N93. **DD** 538/.3.

GW
**NUMERISCHE ERGEBNISSE UND MAGNETOGRAMME WINGST / DEUTSCHES HYDROGRAPHISCHES INSTITUT. Added/Corp** Deutsches Hydrographisches Institut. (1973)-. Periodical. German. an. **LC** QC830.W56; E73. **DD** 538/.79/4359. ***Continues*** *Ergebnisse der Erdmagnetischen Beobachtungen im Observatorium Wingst im Jahre ... .*

RU/0370-0704
**PARAMAGNITNYI REZONANS. Added/Corp** Kazanskii Gosudarstvennyi Universitet Im. V.I. Ulianova-Lenina. (19??)-. Academic Scholarly Publication. Russian. 0.58rub single issue. Izdatelstvo Kazanskogo Universiteta SFSR. **LC** QC762; .P338. **CODEN** PMRZA3. Documents available from CASDDS.
**Ind/Abst** Chem. Abstr.

JA
**PROCEEDINGS OF THE NIPR SYMPOSIUM ON UPPER ATMOSPHERE PHYSICS. Main/Conf** NIPR Symposium on Upper Atmosphere Physics. No. 1 (Feb. 1988)-. Proceedings. English. ir. National Institute of Polar Research, Kokuritsu Kyokuchi Kenkyujo, 9-10 Kaga 1-Chome, Itabashi-ku Tokyo 173 Japan. **Tel** 81 3 962 4711, FAX 83 3 962-25 29. **ED** Takao Hoshiai. **LC** QC878.5; .N56A. **DD** 551.5/14/05. **Circ:** 850 (ctrl).

●US/1065-9889
**PROCEEDINGS OF THE SOCIETY OF MAGNETIC RESONANCE IN MEDICINE.**
**Added/Corp** Society of Magnetic Resonance in Medicine (U.S.). (1993)-. Proceedings. English. mo. $65.00. Society of Magnetic Resonance in Medicine, 1918 University Avenue, Suite 3C, Berkeley CA 94704. **Tel** (510)841-1899. ***Continues*** *Society of Magnetic Resonance in Medicine (U.S.) Meeting Book of Abstracts, 0891-7612.*

US/1043-626X
**PROGRESS IN ELECTROMAGNETICS RESEARCH.** (PROGRESS IN ELECTROMAGNETICS RESEARCH : PIER.). [Prog. electromagn. res.]. **VFOAT** PIER. (1989)-. Academic Scholarly Publication. English. Twice a year. $148.00. EMW Publishing, One Kendall Square, Suite 2200, Cambridge MA 02142. **Tel** (617)621-7108. **ED** J. A. Kong. **LC** QC759.6; .P76. **DD** 537/.05. **CODEN** PELREX. **Pr Rev.** Documents available from CASDDS.
**Desc:** Devoted to reporting on advances and applications in the modern development of electromagnetics. Serves as an international forum for state-of-the-art articles on a vast range of important topics in the field, and keeps the reader up to date and informed on new theories, methodologies and computational techniques, as well as offering interpretations of both theoretical and experimental results.
**Ind/Abst** Chem. Abstr.

US
**PROTON NMR COLLECTION. CUMULATIVE CHEMICAL CLASS INDEX. See** Physics-Nuclear Physics.

AU/0370-3657
**RADEX RUNDSCHAU.** [Radex Rundsch.].
**Added/Corp** Osterreichisch-Amerikanische Magnesit Aktiengesellschaft (Radenthein, Austria). (May 1946)-. Academic Scholarly Publication. German. **LC** TN948.M2; R33. **CODEN** RAXRAF. Documents available from Article Express International, CASDDS.
**Ind/Abst** Alum. Ind. Abstr.; Ceram. Abstr. (19??-); Chem. Abstr.; Coal Abstr.; Ei Page One; Eng. Index Annu.; GeoRef; Met. Abstr.

JA
**REPORT OF THE GEOMAGNETIC AND GEOELECTRIC OBSERVATIONS.**
**Main/Corp** Chijike Kansokujo, Kakioka, Japan. **VFOAT** Geomagnetic and Geoelectric Observations. Began publication with issue for 1957/58. English. Kishocho Chijiki Kansokujo, (Kakioka Magentic Observatory, Japan Meteorological Agency), 595, Kakioka, Yasatocho, Niiharigun, Ibarakiken 315-01, Japan. **LC** QC830.
**Ind/Abst** GeoRef.

PL
**RESULTS OF GEOMAGNETIC OBSERVATIONS, BELSK. Main/Corp** Instytut Geofizyki (Polska Akademia Nauk). (19??)-. Periodical. English. an. Z200.00. Instytut Geofizyki, Polskiej Akademii Nauk, Ul Ksiecia Janusza 64, 01-452 Warszawa Poland. **Tel** 364440, telex 817582 PL. **ED** Jerzy Jankowski. **LC** QC830.B46; P64a. **DD** 538/.79/4383. **Circ:** 400.
**Desc:** Results of geomagnetic observations. Tables of mean hourly values of inclination, horizontal and vertical intensity of geomagnetic field.

JA
**SEIDENKI GAKKAI KOEN RONBUNSHU : SEIDENKI GAKKAI ZENKOKU TAIKAI.**
**VFOAT** Seidenki Gakkai Zenkoku Taikai; Proceedings of ... Annual Meeting of the Institute of Electrostatics Japan. Issue No. 1 (1977)-. Japanese (English). an. Seidenki Gakkai / c/o Sharumu, 80 5A 1-3 Hongo 4, Bunkyo-ku Tokyo 113 Japan. **LC** QC570; .S44a . Index available. **Bk Rev. Ad Acc. Circ:** 500.

JA/0386-2550
**SEIDENKI GAKKAI SHI. Added/Corp** Seidenki Gakkai (Japan). **VFOAT** Proceedings of the Institute of Electrostatics Japan. (1977)-. English (Japanese). bm. 18,000. Seidenki Gakkai / c/o Gakkaishi Kanko Senta, 4-16 Yayoi 2, Bunkyo-ku Tokyo-to 113 Japan. **Tel** 03-815-4171. **ED** Akira Watanabe. **LC** QC570; .S45. **DD** 537/.2/05. **Ad Acc. Circ:** 2,000 (ctrl).
**Desc:** Main fields of this journal are theory and application of electrostatics. Applications induce electrostatic precipitator, electrostatic imaging, electrostatic coatings, electrostatic separations and electrets.
**Ind/Abst** Coal Abstr.

RU/0134-9007
**SPEKTROSKOPIJA GAZORAZRJADNOJ PLAZMY.**
(SPEKTROSKOPIIA GAZORAZRIADNOI PLASMY.). [Spektrosk. gazorazrjadnoj plazmy]. **Added/Corp** Leningradskii Gosudarstvennyi Universitet Imeni A.A. Zhdanova. Vol. 1 (1976)-. Academic Scholarly Publication. Russian. be. 0.2rub. St Petersburg State University / Izdatelstvo Leningradskogo Universiteta, Universitetskaia Nab 7/9, 199034 St Petersburg Russia. **Tel** 011 95 218-97-88, FAX 011 95 218-51-52, telex 121481. **ED** N P Penkin. **LC** QC718.5.S6; S67. **CODEN** SGPLDD. **Ad Acc.** Documents available from CASDDS.
**Desc:** Original studies in atomic and ion collisions in pure gases and mixtures. Processes of plasma properties formation at low density plasma are studied also. Optical methods and probe method are used either in stationary or in decay plasma.
**Ind/Abst** Chem. Abstr. (1976-1980).

UK/0953-2048
**SUPERCONDUCTOR SCIENCE & TECHNOLOGY.** [Supercond. sci. technol.].
**Added/Corp** Institute of Physics (Great Britain) American Institute of Physics. **VFOAT** Superconductor Science and Technology. Vol. 1, No. 1 (1988)-. Academic Scholarly Publication. English. mo. $396.00. Institute of Physics, Techno House, Redcliffe Way, Bristol BS1 6NX England. **Tel** 011 44 272 297481, FAX 011 44 272 294318, telex 449149 INSTP G. **(Subscription address:** American Institute of Physics, Publishing Sales, 500 Sunnyside Blvd., Woodbury NY 11797.) **ED** D. Dew-Hughes. **LC** QC611.9; .S86. **DD** 537.6/23. **CODEN** SUSTEF. **[CCC].** Index available in last issue of volume--attached. **Pr Rev.** available on microfiche. Documents available from Article Express International, The Genuine Article, Ask*IEEE, CASDDS.
**Desc:** Publishes original research papers, review articles and research Letters on all aspects of superconductivity. Provides a forum for chemists, physicists, materials scientists, and electronics and electrical engineers involved in any aspect of the science and technology of superconductors, both conventional and the new ceramic materials.
**Ind/Abst** Chem. Abstr.; Curr. Contents Phys. Chem. Earth Sci.; Ei Page One; Energy Inf. Abstr.; Eng. Index Annu.; INSPEC (1988-); Res. Alert [Full Cov.]; Sci. Cit. Index; SCISEARCH.

US
**SYMPOSIUM RECORD / IEEE ... INTERNATIONAL SYMPOSIUM ON ELECTROMAGNETIC COMPATIBILITY.**
**See** Engineering-Electricity, Electrical Engineering, Electronics.

CC
**TI TZU KUAN TSE PAO KAO. VFOAT** Report of Geomagnetic Observation; Wu-Lu-Mu-Chi Ti Tzu Kuan Tse Pao Kao. Vol. 1-2 (1978-1979)-. Periodical. Chinese (English). Ti Chen Chu Pan She, 63 Fu Hsing Road, Beijing, People's Republic of China. **LC** QC830.U78; T5. **DD** 538/.78/516.

CH
**TI TZU KUAN TSE PAO KAO (KUANG-CHOU TI TZU TAI).** (TI TZU KUAN TSE PAO KAO.). **VFOAT** Report of Geomagnetic Observation; Kuanu-Chou Ti Tzu Kuan Tse Pao Kao. Periodical. Chinese (English). Ti Chen Chu Pan She, 63 Fu Hsing Road, Beijing, People's Republic of China. **LC** QC830.C27; T5. **DD** 538/79/5129.

LV
**VOPROSY ELEKTRODINAMIKI I MEKHANIKI SPLOSHNYKH SRED.**
**Added/Corp** Latvia. Augstakas un Videjas Specialas Izglitibas Ministrija. Petera Stuckas Latvijas Valsts Universitate. Kafedra Elektrodinamiki i Mekhaniki Sploshnykh Sred. (19??)-. Periodical. Russian. 0.66rub (Single issue). Latviiskii Gosudarstvennyi Universitet / University of Latvia, Bulvar Raina 19, 1586 Riga Latvia. **Tel** 22-90-76, FAX 22-50-39, telex 116172. **LC** QC630; .V66.

RU/0507-4045
**VOPROSY TEORII PLAZMY.** [Vopr. teor. plazmy]. (1963)-. Academic Scholarly Publication. Russian. **LC** QC501; .V65. **CODEN** VTPLAW. Documents available from CASDDS.
**Ind/Abst** Chem. Abstr.; Energy Res. Abstr. (May 1973-); Int. Aerosp. Abstr.

---

## NUCLEAR PHYSICS

---

PL/0587-4254
**ACTA PHYSICA POLONICA, B.** [Acta phys. Pol., B]. **Added/Corp** Instytut Fizyki (Polska Akademia Nauk) Polskie Towarzystwo Fizyczne. Vol. B1 (Jan./March 1970)-. Periodical. English. mo. $135.00. **(Subscription address:** ARS Polona, PO Box 1001, 00068 Warsaw Poland.) **LC** QC770; .A28. **NLM** W1 AC919B. **CODEN** APOBBB. **[CCC]. Pr Rev.** Documents available from The Genuine Article, Ask*IEEE, CASDDS. ***Supersedes in part*** *Acta Physica Polonica, 0001-673X.*
**Ind/Abst** Acoust. Abstr.; Alum. Ind. Abstr.; Ceram. Abstr.; Chem. Abstr.; Chem. Titles; Curr. Contents Phys. Chem. Earth Sci.; Ei Page One; Energy Res. Abstr.; Eng. Mater. Abstr.; INSPEC (1970-); Leadscan; Math. Rev.; Met. Abstr.; Res. Alert [Full Cov.]; Sci. Cit. Index; SCISEARCH.

US/0065-2970
**ADVANCES IN NUCLEAR PHYSICS.** [Adv. nucl. phys.]. Vol. 1 (1968)-. Monographic series. English. ir. Price varies per volume. Plenum Press, 233 Spring Street, New York NY 10013-1578. **Tel** (212)620-8000, (800)221-9369, FAX (212)463-0742, (212)807-1047, telex 23/421139. **ED** M. Baranger and E. Vogt. **LC** QC173; .A2545. **DD** 539.7/05. **CODEN** ANUPBZ. **[CCC]. Pr Rev.** Documents available from The Genuine Article, Ask*IEEE, CASDDS.
**Ind/Abst** Chem. Abstr.; Energy Res. Abstr.; Index Sci. Rev. [Full Cov.]; INIS Atomindex [Micro.]; INSPEC; Res. Alert [Full Cov.]; Sci. Cit. Index; SCISEARCH; SPIN (1977-).

UK/0143-7178
**ADVANCES IN NUCLEAR QUADRUPOLE RESONANCE. *Ceased.*** [Adv. nucl. quadrup. reson.]. Began publication with Vol. 1 in 1974, ceased with Vol.5 1991. Academic Scholarly Publication. English. ir. John Wiley & Sons Ltd., Baffins Lane, Chichester West Sussex PO19 1UD England. **Tel** 0243 779777, FAX 0243 776128 BTG:JWP001, telex 86290 WIBOOKG. **(Subscription address:** North, South and Central America/ John Wiley & Sons, Inc., PO Box 7247-8491, Philadelphia, PA 19170-8491) **ED** J A S Smith. Documents available from CASDDS.
**Ind/Abst** Chem. Abstr.; Energy Res. Abstr. (Jan. 1982-).

US/0065-2989
**ADVANCES IN NUCLEAR SCIENCE AND TECHNOLOGY. See** Engineering-Nuclear Engineering.

FR
**ANNUAIRE. Main/Corp** Universite Paris-Sud. Institut de Physique Nucleaire. (19??)-. French (summaries and/or abstracts in English). an. Free. Orsay, Institut de Physique Nucleaire, Orsay 91406 France. **Tel** 69417305, FAX 69416470, telex IPNORS 692 006 F. **ED** Ipn Orsay. **LC** QC789.4.F73; U513. **DD** 539.7. ctrl circ. available on CD-ROM; available on an online database. Documents available from BLDSC.
**Desc:** Review of the experimental and theoretical work done during the year in the different departments and in technical services.

JA
**ANNUAL REPORT. Main/Corp** Koenerugi Butsurigaku Kenkyujo (Japan). **VFOAT** K.E.K. Annual Report; KEK Annual Report. (19??)-. English. an. Technical Information Office, National Laboratory for High Energy Physics, Ibaraki-ken 305 Japan. **LC** QC789.2.J32; K64a. **DD** 539.7/072052/13. Documents available from CASDDS.
**Ind/Abst** Chem. Abstr.

JA
**ANNUAL REPORT - INSTITUTE FOR NUCLEAR STUDY, UNIVERSITY OF TOKYO.** **Main/Corp** Tokyo Daigaku. Genshikaku Kenkyujo. (19??)-. Academic Scholarly Publication. English. Tokyo Daigaku Genshikaku Kenkyujo, (Inst. for Nuclear Study, University of Tokyo), 2-1 Midoricho, 3 Chome, Tanashishi, Tokyoto 188 Japan. Documents available from CASDDS.
**Ind/Abst** Chem. Abstr.

US/0078-2904
**ANNUAL REPORT / OAK RIDGE ASSOCIATED UNIVERSITIES.** [Annu. rep. - Oak Ridge Assoc. Univ.]. **Main/Corp** Oak Ridge Associated Universities. **Added/Corp** U.S. Atomic Energy Commission. (1967)-. English. an. Free. Oak Ridge Associated Universities, PO Box 117, Oak Ridge TN 37831. **Tel** (615)576-3000, telex TWX 810-572-1076. **LC** QC789.O3; A4. **DD** 621.48/072073. **Circ:** 2,000 (ctrl). ***Continues*** *Oak Ridge Institute of Nuclear Studies. Annual Report, 0742-4760.*
**Desc:** Describe programs and services of Oak Ridge Associated Universities, a consortium of colleges and management and operating contractor to the U.S. Department of Energy.

SZ/0071-2973
**ANNUAL REPORT OF THE EUROPEAN ORGANIZATION FOR NUCLEAR RESEARCH.** **Main/Corp** European Organization for Nuclear Research. **Added/Corp** European Laboratory for Particle Physics. **VFOAT** Annual Report; Rapport Annuel; CERN Annual Report. (1955)-. English (French). an. Cern Courier, Cern Publications, 1211 Geneva 23 Switzerland. **Tel** 41 022 767-4103, FAX 41 022 782-1906. **LC** QC770; .E83a. **DD** 539.7/07204. Documents available from CASDDS.
**Ind/Abst** Chem. Abstr.

SW
**ANNUAL REPORT - STUDSVIK ENERGITEKNIK AB.** **Main/Corp** Studsvik Energiteknik AB. English (Swedish). Studsvik AB, S-61182, Nykoping Sweden. **LC** QC792.8.S82; A852A. **DD** 338.7/62148/094857. ***Continues*** *Studsvik Energiteknik AB. Studsvik Energiteknik AB.*

JA/0454-9244
**ANNUAL REPORTS OF THE RESEARCH REACTOR INSTITUTE, KYOTO UNIVERSITY.** [Annu. rep. Res. React. Inst., Kyoto Univ.]. **Main/Corp** Kyoto Daigaku. Genshiro Jikkenjo. Vol. 1 (1968)-. English. Kyoto University / Research Reactor Institute, Kumatori-cho Sonnan-gun, Osaka 590-04 Japan. **LC** QC770; .K95. **NLM** W1 KY9828. **CODEN** KURAAV. Documents available from Article Express International, BIOSIS Document Express, Ask*IEEE, CASDDS.
**Ind/Abst** Alum. Ind. Abstr.; Bioeng. Abstr.; Biol. Abstr.; Chem. Abstr.; Ei Page One; Eng. Index Annu.; INSPEC (Oct. 1968-); Met. Abstr.

US/0163-8998
**ANNUAL REVIEW OF NUCLEAR AND PARTICLE SCIENCE.** [Annu. rev. nucl. part. sci.]. Vol. 28 (1978)-. Academic Scholarly Publication. English. an (December). $62.00 US; $67.00 other. Annual Reviews Inc., 4139 El Camino Way, PO Box 10139, Palo Alto CA 94303-0139. **Tel** (415)493-4400, (800)523-8635, FAX (415)855-9815. **ED** J. D. Jackson. **LC** QC770; .A5. **DD** 539.7/05. **NLM** W1 AN778BN. **CODEN** ARPSDF. **[CCC].** Index available. cum. index. **Pr Rev.** ctrl circ. available on microfilm from University Microfilms International (UMI). Documents available from Article Express International, The Genuine Article, BIOSIS Document Express, Ask*IEEE, CASDDS, Documents on Demand. ***Continues*** *Annual Review of Nuclear Science, 0066-4243.*
**Desc:** Comprehensive, thorough coverage of latest advances in nuclear and particles science, written by acknowledged experts in the field. Extensive literature citations included.
**Ind/Abst** Biol. Abstr.; Chem. Abstr.; Curr. Contents Phys. Chem. Earth Sci.; Energy Inf. Abstr.; Energy Res. Abstr. (Jan. 1982-); Eng. Index Annu.; Environ. Abstr.; GeoRef; Index Sci. Rev. [Full Cov.]; INIS Atomindex [Micro.]; INSPEC; Leadscan; Res. Alert [Full Cov.]; Sci. Cit. Index (19??-19??); SCISEARCH; SPIN (1978-).

LU
**ANNUAL STATUS REPORT. NUCLEAR MEASUREMENTS / COMMISSION OF THE EUROPEAN COMMUNITIES.**
**Added/Corp** Commission of the European Communities. Joint Research Centre. Commission of the European Communities. Joint Research Centre. Multiannual Programme of the Joint Research Centre, 1980-1983. **VFOAT** Nuclear Measurements. (19??)-. English. an. **LC** QC784.5; .A56. **DD** 539.7/028/7.

AT/1031-8216
**ANSTO TECHNOLOGY.** [Ansto technol.]. **Added/Corp** Australian Nuclear Science and Technology Organisation. **VFOAT** Australian Nuclear Science and Technology Organisation Technology. (1988)-. English. ir. Australian Nuclear Science and Technology Organisation, Private Mailbag 1, Menai 2234 New South Wales Australia. **DD** 539.705.
**Ind/Abst** AESIS Q.

IO/0126-1568
**ATOM INDONESIA.** [At. Indones.]. Vol. 1, No. 1-2 (July 1975)-. Academic Scholarly Publication. English. sa. Free. Atom Indonesia, PO Box 85 KBY, Jakarta Selatan Indonesia. **Tel** telex 46354. **LC** QC791.9; .A87. **DD** 539.7/05. **CODEN** ATINDD. **Circ:** 500. Documents available from CASDDS.
**Ind/Abst** Chem. Abstr. (1975-1982); Energy Res. Abstr. (Aug. 1976-).

UK/0004-7015
**ATOM (LONDON, ENGLAND).** (ATOM.). [Atom]. **Added/Corp** United Kingdom Atomic Energy Authority. No. 1 (Nov. 1956)-. Periodical. English. mo (10 issues per year). Free on request. AEA Technology Communication, Dir 11 Charles II Street, London SW1Y 4QP England. **Tel** 011 44 71 3896565. **LC** HD9698.G7; A85. **DD** 333.79/24/0941. **CODEN** ATMMAR. Documents available from Article Express International, Ask*IEEE.
**Ind/Abst** AESIS Q.; BMT Abstr.; Coal Abstr.; Ei Page One; EMBASE; Energy Res. Abstr.; Eng. Index Annu. [Select. Cov.]; Fluid Abstr., Civil Eng.; Fluid Abstr. Proc. Eng.; FLUIDEX (1973-1990); INSPEC (Aug. 1968-); Int. Aerosp. Abstr.; World Text. Abstr.

US/0092-640X
**ATOMIC DATA AND NUCLEAR DATA TABLES.** [At. data nucl. data tables]. Vol. 12 (1973)-. Academic Scholarly Publication. English. bm (6 issues). $448.00 US and Canada; $524.00 other. Academic Press, Inc., 6277 Sea Harbor Drive, Orlando FL 32887. **Tel** (800)543-9534, (407)345-4100, FAX (407)363-9661. **ED** Angela Li-Scholz. **LC** QC173; .A824. **DD** 539.7/021/2. **CODEN** ADNDAT. **[CCC]. Pr Rev.** Documents available from The Genuine Article, Ask*IEEE, CASDDS. ***Formed by the union of*** *Atomic Data, 0004-7082* ***and*** *Nuclear Data Tables (New York), 0090-0214.*
**Desc:** Presents compilations of experimental and theoretical information in atomic physics and in nuclear physics as well as in closely related fields. Extensive and comprehensive compilations of experimental and theoretical results are featured.
**Ind/Abst** Chem. Abstr.; Curr. Contents Phys. Chem. Earth Sci.; Ei Page One; Energy Res. Abstr. (Feb. 1974-); INIS Atomindex [Micro.]; INSPEC (Aug. 1973-); Int. Aerosp. Abstr.; Res. Alert [Full Cov.]; Sci. Cit. Index; SCISEARCH; SPIN (1977-).

RU/0004-7163
**ATOMNAIA ENERGIIA.** **See** Energy.

GW/0341-4213
**ATW NEWS.** ***Ceased.*** [Atw news]. **VFOAT** Atomwirtschaft, Atomtechnik News. (1975)-(1994). Periodical. English. mo. Handelsblatt GmbH, Postfach 102716, D-40018 Duesseldorf Germany. **Tel** 011 49 211 8871730. **UDC** 621.039. **[CCC].** ***Continues*** *ATW News of the Month, 0340-9252.*

GW/0366-0885
**BERICHTE DER KERNFORSCHUNGSANLAGE JULICH.** (BERICHTE / FORSCHUNGSZENTRUM JULICH.). [Ber. Kernforsch.anl. Jul.]. **Added/Corp** Forschungszentrum Julich. Forschungszentrum Julich. Zentralbibliothek. **VFOAT** Berichte der Kernforschungsanlage Julich; Berichte des Forschungszentrum Julich; Jul. No. 2327 (1989)-. Monographic series. German (English). Forschungszentrum Julich GmbH, Offentlichkeitsarbeit, Postfach 1913, W-5170 Julich 1 Germany. **Tel** (02461)61-4661, FAX 02461-61466. **CODEN** FJBEE5. Documents available from Ask*IEEE, CASDDS. ***Continues*** *Berichte der Kernforschungsanlage Julich, 0366-0885.*
**Ind/Abst** Chem. Abstr.; INSPEC; Math. Rev.

CN/0709-082X
**BIRCH BARK ALLIANCE, THE.** **Main/Corp** Birch Bank Alliance. V. 1- Oct. 1978-. Periodical. English. qt. 8.00Can$ (for 2 years). Opirg-Peterborough, c/o Trent University, Peterborough Ontario K9J 7B8 Canada. **DD** 338.4/7/621480971.

US/0092-1548
**BROOKHAVEN HIGHLIGHTS.** Began with 1970/71. English. an. National Technical Information Service - NTIS, Room 2027S, 5285 Port Royal Road, Springfield VA 22161. **Tel** (703)487-4630, (703)487-4660, (703)487-4650, FAX (703)321-8547, telex 89-9405. **LC** QC789.U62; U628A. **DD** 539.7/07/2074725. ***Continues*** *Annual Report (Brookhaven National Laboratory), 0498-6520.*

CN/0714-7074
**BULLETIN - CANADIAN NUCLEAR SOCIETY.** (CANADIAN NUCLEAR SOCIETY BULLETIN.). [Bull. - Can. Nucl. Soc.]. **VFOAT** Bulletin de la Societe Nucleaire Canadienne. Vol. 8 I.E. 9 No. 5 (Sept./Oct. 1988)-. Bulletin. English (French). bm. Free to members. Canadian Nuclear Association, 144 Front Street West, Suite 725, Toronto Ontario M5J 2L7 Canada. **Tel** (416)977-6152, (416)977-7620, FAX (416)979-8356, telex 06-23741. **LC** QC770; .C22. **DD** 621.48. ***Continues*** *CNS Bulletin, 0714-7074.*

SZ/0304-288X
**CERN COURIER.** [CERN cour.]. **Added/Corp** European Organization for Nuclear Research. **VAT** Conseil Europeen pour la Recherche Nucleaire Courier. No. 1 (Aug. 1959)-. Periodical. English (French). Ten times a year (monthly with Jan./Feb. & July/Aug. issues combined). Free. Cern Courier, Cern Publications, 1211 Geneva 23 Switzerland. **Tel** 41 022 767-4103, FAX 41 022 782-1906. **ED** Gordon Fraser. **LC** QC770; .C25. **CODEN** CECOA2. Index available. **Bk Rev. Ad Acc, Adv Mgr:** Micheline Falciola. ctrl circ. Documents available from Ask*IEEE.
**Ind/Abst** Energy Res. Abstr.; INSPEC (Sept. 1981-).

AU
**CINDA.** **See** Physics-Abstracting, Bibliographies and Statistics.

FR/0298-6248
**CLEFS C.E.A.** (CLEFS CEA : REVUE SCIENTIFIQUE ET TECHNIQUE DU COMISSARIAT A L'ENERGIE ATOMIQUE.). [Clefs C.E.A.]. **Added/Corp** France. Commissariat a l'Energie Atomique. Departement des Relations Publiques et de la Communication. No 1 (Apr. 1986)-. Periodical. French (table of contents in English). qt. CEA Department des Relations Publiques et de la Communication, 31-33 rue de la Federation, 75752 Paris Cedex 15 France. **LC** QC791.9; .C56. **DD** 621.48. **CODEN** CEACES. Documents available from Ask*IEEE, CASDDS.
**Ind/Abst** Chem. Abstr.; INSPEC (Jan. 1987-).

AG/0325-1403
**CNEA / REPUBLICA ARGENTINA, COMISION NACIONAL DE ENERGIA ATOMICA.** **Added/Corp** Argentina. Comision Nacional de Energia Atomica. **VFOAT** CNEA Informe. (1965)-. Monographic series. Spanish. **LC** UNC. Documents available from CASDDS. ***Continues*** *Informe (Argentina. Comision Nacional de Energia Atomica).*
**Ind/Abst** Chem. Abstr.

UK/0010-2687
**COMMENTS ON ATOMIC AND MOLECULAR PHYSICS.** [Comments at. mol. phys.]. Vol. 1 (April/May 1969)-. Periodical. English. bm (1 volume). $425.00 (academic institutions), $662.00 (corporate institutions). Gordon & Breach Science Publishers, PO Box 90, Reading RG1 8JL England. **Tel** 011 44 734 560080, FAX 011 44 734 568211. **ED** H.H. Stroke. **LC** QC770; .C5. **DD** 539/.05. **CODEN** CAMPBS. **[CCC]. Bk Rev. Ad Acc.** Documents available from Ask*IEEE, CASDDS.
**Ind/Abst** Chem. Abstr. (?-1988); INIS Atomindex [Micro.]; INSPEC (April/May 1969-); Mass Spect. Bull. (April/May 1969-).

US/0010-2709
**COMMENTS ON NUCLEAR AND PARTICLE PHYSICS.** [Comments nucl. part. phys.]. Vol. 1 (Jan. 1967)-. Periodical. English. bm (2 volumes). $425.00 (academic institutions), $662.00 (corporate institutions). Gordon & Breach Science Publishers, Inc., PO Box 786, Cooper Station, New York NY 10276. **Tel** (212)206-8900, FAX (212)645-2459. **DD** 539. **CODEN** CNPPAV. **[CCC].** Documents available from Ask*IEEE, CASDDS.
**Desc:** Devoted to critical commentaries on significant current developments appearing in scientific literature, featuring columns in the fields of particle physics, nuclear physics and astrophysics.
**Ind/Abst** Chem. Abstr.; Energy Res. Abstr.; INIS Atomindex [Micro.]; INSPEC (1968-).

SZ
**COURRIER CERN.** **Added/Corp** European Organization of Nuclear Research. (19??)-. French. ir. Free. Public Information Office / Switzerland, 1211 Geneva 23 Switzerland. **ED** Gordon Fraser. **LC** QC788; C68. **DD** 539.7/05. **Ad Acc. Circ:** 18,000 (ctrl).
**Desc:** International journal of high energy physics and related topics.

CC/0258-0934
**DIANZIXUE YU TANCE JISHU, HE.** **See** Engineering-Electricity, Electrical Engineering, Electronics.

US/0277-8203
**DNA - UNITED STATES. DEFENSE NUCLEAR AGENCY.** (DNA.). [DNA - U.S., Def. Nucl. Agency]. **Added/Corp** United States. Defense Nuclear Agency. (19??)-. English. **CODEN** DNASDD. Documents available from CASDDS.
**Ind/Abst** Chem. Abstr.

UK
**ENERGY & NUCLEAR SCIENCES INTERNATIONAL WHO'S WHO.** **Added/Corp** Longman (Firm). **VFOAT** Energy and Nuclear Sciences International Who's Who. 2nd Ed. (1987)-. English. ir. $396.00. Longman Group Ltd., Fourth Avenue, Longman House, Harlow Essex CM19 5SR England. **Tel** 011 44 279 429655, FAX 011 44 279 431059, telex 81259. **(Subscription address:** Gale Research Co., 835 Penobscot Building, Detroit, MI 48226) **LC** TJ163.45; .I58. **DD** 621.042/092; B.

*Continues International Who's Who in Energy and Nuclear Sciences, 0952-1100.*
**Desc:** Provides personal, career, and professional data on more than 3,000 energy and nuclear scientists and engineers.

US/0897-5566
**FERMILAB REPORT.** [Fermilab rep.]. **Added/Corp** Fermi National Accelerator Laboratory. **VFOAT** Fermi National Accelerator Laboratory Monthly Report. (19??)-. Periodical. English. Twelve times a year. Free. Fermi National Accelerator Laboratory, PO Box 500, Batavia IL 60510. **DD** 539.

AU/0177-7963
**FEW-BODY SYSTEMS.** [Few-body syst.]. **VFOAT** Few Body Systems. Vol. 1, No. 1 (1986)-. Academic Scholarly Publication. English. Eight times a year. DM832.00. Springer-Verlag GmbH & Company KG, Heidelberger Platz 3, D 14197 Berlin Germany. **Tel** 011 49 30 8207223, FAX 011 49 30 8214091, telex 183 319 SPBLN D. **(Subscription address:** Springer Verlag New York Inc. / for North America, 44 Hartz Way, Secaucus NJ 07096.**)** **ED** H Mitter. **CODEN** FBSYEQ. **[CCC]. Pr Rev.** available on microfilm and microfiche from University Microfilms International (UMI). Documents available from The Genuine Article, Ask*IEEE, CASDDS. ***Continues*** *Acta Physica Austriaca, 0001-6713.*
**Desc:** Devoted to the publication of original research work, both theoretical and experimental, in the field of few-body systems.
**Ind/Abst** Chem. Abstr. (1986-); Curr. Contents Phys. Chem. Earth Sci.; INSPEC (1986-); Leadscan; Res. Alert [Full Cov.]; Sci. Cit. Index; SCISEARCH.

AU/0177-8811
**FEW-BODY SYSTEMS. SUPPLEMENTUM.** [Few-body syst., Suppl.]. (1986)-. Monographic series. English. ir. Price varies per volume. Springer-Verlag Wien, Sachsenplatz 4 6, PO Box 89, A-1201 Vienna Austria. **Tel** 011 43 1 3302415. **(Subscription address:** Springer Verlag New York Inc. / for North America, 44 Hartz Way, Secaucus NJ 07096.**)** **ED** H. Mitter. **CODEN** FBSSE8. available on microfilm and microfiche from University Microfilms International (UMI). Documents available from Ask*IEEE, CASDDS. ***Continues*** *Acta Physica Austriaca. Supplementum, 0065-1559.*
**Ind/Abst** Chem. Abstr.; INSPEC (1986-).

AU
**FILM CATALOGUE ... / VIENNA INTERNATIONAL CENTRE LIBRARY.** ***Title Change.*** **Main/Corp** Vic Library. **Added/Corp** International Atomic Energy Agency. (19??)-(19??). English. **LC** QC792.72.Z9; I56a. **DD** 016.62148. **NLM** WN 18; I13. ***Continues*** *Vic Library Film Catalogue.* ***Continued by*** *Film and Video Catalogue.*

RU
**FIZIKA ATOMNOGO IADRA / AKADEMIIA NAUK SSSR, LENINGRADSKII INSTITUT IADERNOI FIZIKI IM. B.P. KONSTANTINOVA.** **Added/Corp** Leningradskii Institut Iadernoi Fiziki im. B.P. Konstantinova. **VFOAT** Materialy ... Zimnei Shkoly LIIAF. (197?)-. Periodical. Russian. an. **LC** QC770; .Z53a. **CODEN** FAYADA. Documents available from CASDDS. ***Continues in part*** *Zimniaia Shkola LIIAF Po Fizike Iadra i Elementarnykh Chastits. Materialy ... Zimnei Shkoly LIIAF Po Fizike Iadra i Elementarnykh Chastits.*
**Ind/Abst** Chem. Abstr.

RU
**FIZIKA ELEMENTARNYKH CHASTITS / AKADEMIIA NAUK SSSR, LENINGRADSKII INSTITUT IADERNOI FIZIKI IM. B.P. KONSTANTINOVA.** **Added/Corp** Leningradskii Institut Iadernoi Fiziki im. B.P. Konstantinova. **VFOAT** Materialy ... Zimnei Shkoly LIIAF. (197?)-. Periodical. Russian. an. **(Subscription address:** Victor Kamkin, 4956 Boiling Brook Parkway, Rockville MD 20852.**)** **LC** QC793; .Z553b. **CODEN** FECHDH. Documents available from CASDDS. ***Continues in part*** *Zimniaia Shkola LIIAF Po Fizike Iadra i Elementarnykh Chastits. Materialy ... Zimnei Shkoly LIIAF Po Fizike Iadra i Elementarnykh Chastits.*
**Ind/Abst** Chem. Abstr.

RU
**FIZIKA VYSOKIKH ENERGII / AKADEMIIA NAUK SSSR, LENINGRADSKII INSTITUT IADERNOI FIZIKI IM. B.P. KONSTANTINOVA.** **Added/Corp** Leningradskii Institut Iadernoi Fiziki im. B.P. Konstantinova. **VFOAT** Materialy ... Zimnei Shkoly LIIAF. (197?)-. Periodical. Russian. an. **(Subscription address:** Victor Kamkin, 4956 Boiling Brook Parkway, Rockville MD 20852.**)** **LC** QC793; .Z553a. **CODEN** FVENDS. Documents available from CASDDS. ***Continues in part*** *Zimniaia Shkola LIIAF Po Fizike Iadra i Elementarnykh Chastits. Materialy ... Zimnei Shkoly LIIAF Po Fizike Iadra i Elementarnykh Chastits.*
**Ind/Abst** Chem. Abstr.

JA
**GAIKOKU GENSHIRYOKU KIKAN KANKO SHIRYO GEPPO. / MONTHLY LIST OF SELECTED ATOMIC ENERGY PUBLICATIONS.** **Added/Corp** Kokuritsu Kokkai Toshokan (Japan). Sanko Shoshibu. **VFOAT** Monthly List of Selected Atomic Energy Publications. Vol. 18 (1972)-. Periodical. Multiple languages (English, French, German, Italian, Spanish and Russian). mo. Kokuritsu Kokkai Toshokan, (National Diet Library), 1-10-1 Nagatacho Chiyoda-ku, Tokyo 100 Japan. **Tel** 03 3581-2331, FAX 03 3597-9104. **LC** Z5160; .G34; QC792. ***Continues*** *Genshiryoku Kankei Shiryo Mokuroku.*

CC/0254-3052
**GAONENG WULI YU HE WULI.** (KAO NENG WU LI YU HO WU LI.). [Gaoneng wuli yu he wuli]. **Added/Corp** "Kao Neng Wu Li Yu Ho Wu Li" Pien Wei Hui. **VFOAT** Physica Energiae Fortis et Physica Nuclearis. Vol. 1 (Nov. 1977)-. Academic Scholarly Publication. Chinese (summaries and/or abstracts in English). mo. $103.08. Chinese Society of High Energy Physics, Science Press, 16 Donghuangchenggen North Street, Beijing 100707, People's Republic of China. **Tel** 011 86 1 4019821, FAX 011 86 4012180, telex 210147. **(Subscription address:** China International Book Trading Corporation, PO Box 399, Library Service Department, Beijing 100044 People's Republic of China.**)** **LC** QC793; .K36. **CODEN** KNWLD9. **Ad Acc. Circ:** 6,000. Documents available from Ask*IEEE, CASDDS.
**Desc:** Covers information on physics research in China.
**Ind/Abst** Chem. Abstr.; Energy Res. Abstr. (March 1979-); INSPEC (Jan. 1987-); Math. Rev.; SPIN (1982-).

US/0162-5519
**HADRONIC JOURNAL.** [Hadron. j.]. Vol. 1 (April 1978)-. Academic Scholarly Publication. English. bm. $260.00. Hadronic Press Inc, PO Box 1577, Palm Harbor FL 34682. **Tel** (813)934-9593. **LC** QC793.5.H322; H3. **DD** 539.7/216. **CODEN** HAJODX. Documents available from Ask*IEEE, CASDDS.
**Ind/Abst** Chem. Abstr.; Energy Res. Abstr. (April 1982-); INIS Atomindex [Micro.]; INSPEC (April 1978-); Math. Rev.; Zentralbl. Math. Ihre Grenzgeb.

CC/0253-9950
**HE HUAXUE YU FANGSHE HUAXUE.** **See** Chemistry.

CC/0254-6086
**HE JUBIAN YU DENGLIZITI WULI.** (HO CHU PIEN YU TENG LI TZU TI WU LI.). [He jubian yu dengliziti wuli]. **VFOAT** Nuclear Fusion and Plasma Physics. (1981)-. Academic Scholarly Publication. Chinese (summaries and/or abstracts in English). qt. Post Office / China, People's Republic of China. **LC** QC790.95; .H6. **DD** 539.7/64/05. **CODEN** HYDWDP. Documents available from Ask*IEEE, CASDDS.
**Ind/Abst** Chem. Abstr.; Energy Res. Abstr. (Oct. 1982-); INSPEC (1984-); SPIN (1982-).

CH/0029-5647
**HE ZI KE XUE.** (HO TZU K'O HSUEH.). [He zi ke xue]. **VFOAT** Nuclear Science Journal. (1964)-. Academic Scholarly Publication. English (Chinese). bm. 67 Lane 144, Keelung Road, Section 4, Taipei 107 Taiwan. **CODEN** HTKHAB. Documents available from Ask*IEEE, CASDDS.
**Ind/Abst** Chem. Abstr.; Energy Res. Abstr.; Environ. Period. Bibliogr. (?-?); INSPEC (Dec. 1982-); SEA Abstr.

US/0899-9996
**HIGH ENERGY PHYSICS & NUCLEAR PHYSICS.** [High energy phys. nucl. phys.]. **VFOAT** High Energy Physics and Nuclear Physics. Vol. 12, No. 1 (1988)-. Periodical. English (translations available in Chinese). qt (4 issues). $410.00. Allerton Press, Inc., 150 Fifth Avenue, New York NY 10011. **Tel** (212)924-3950, FAX (212)463-9684, telex 427441 ALPRES. **LC** QC793; .K37. **DD** 539.7. **[CCC].** Documents available from The Genuine Article.
**Ind/Abst** Curr. Contents Phys. Chem. Earth Sci.; Res. Alert [Select. Cov.].

JA/0917-1746
**HOBUNSHU / KYOTO DAIGAKU GENSHIRO JIKKENJO GAKUJUTSU KOENKAI.** **See** Chemistry-Physical and Theoretical Chemistry.

JA
**HOSEI DAIGAKU ION BIMU KOGAKU KENKYUJO HOKOKU.** [Hosei Daigaku Ion Bimu Kogaku Kenkyujo hokoku]. **Added/Corp** Hosei Daigaku. Ion Bimu Kogaku Kenkyujo. **VFOAT** Report of Research Center of Ion Beam Technology, Hosei University. (1980)-. Periodical. Japanese. Hosei Daigaku Ion Bimu Kogaku Kenkyujo, (Research Center of Ion Beam Technology, Hosei University), 7-2, Kajinocho 3 Chome, Koganeishi, Tokyoto 184 Japan. **CODEN** HDIHDS. Documents available from CASDDS.
**Ind/Abst** Chem. Abstr.

US
**I N I S REFERENCE SERIES.** English. ir. UNIPUB, 4611-F Assembly Drive, Lanham MD 20706-4391. **Tel** (800)274-4888, FAX (301)459-0056, telex 28787 GATT CH. Documents available from CASDDS.
**Ind/Abst** Chem. Abstr.

AU
**IAEA NEWSBRIEFS : INTERNATIONAL ATOMIC ENERGY AGENCY.** **See** Energy.

AU
**IAEA YEARBOOK.** **Added/Corp** International Atomic Energy Agency. **VFOAT** IAEA Year Book; International Atomic Energy Agency Yearbook. **VAT** International Atomic Energy Agency Yearbook. (1989)-. English. an. S500.00. International Atomic Energy Agency / IAEA, Wagramerstrasse 5, PO Box 100, A-1400 Vienna Austria. **Tel** 011 43 1 2360 ext. 2530, FAX 011 43 1 234564. **(Subscription address:** UNIPUB, 4611 F Assembly Drive, Lanham MD 20706.**)** **LC** QC791.9; .I23. **DD** 333.792/4/0601.
**Desc:** Provides a comprehensive global coverage of progress in the fields of nuclear power, the nuclear fuel cycle, radioactive waste management, nuclear safety and radiation protection, and highlights developments in particular areas of research involving the application of nuclear techniques, as well as describing aspects of the IAEA safeguards system and technology transfer activities in various parts of the world.

AU/0004-7139
**INIS ATOMINDEX.** ***Title Change.*** **See** Physics-Abstracting, Bibliographies and Statistics.

AU
**INIS ATOMINDEX [MICROFORM].** **See** Physics-Abstracting, Bibliographies and Statistics.

AU/1014-1561
**INIS. AUTHORITY LIST FOR CORPORATE ENTRIES AND REPORT NUMBER PREFIXES.** **See** Physics-Abstracting, Bibliographies and Statistics.

AU
**INIS : AUTHORITY LIST FOR JOURNAL TITLES.** **See** Physics-Abstracting, Bibliographies and Statistics.

AU
**INIS, DESCRIPTIVE CATALOGUING SAMPLES.** **See** Physics-Abstracting, Bibliographies and Statistics.

AU
**INIS MANUAL FOR ONLINE RETRIEVAL.** (19??)-. English. S170.00. International Atomic Energy Agency / IAEA, Wagramerstrasse 5, PO Box 100, A-1400 Vienna Austria. **Tel** 011 43 1 2360 ext. 2530, FAX 011 43 1 234564. **(Subscription address:** UNIPUB, 4611 F Assembly Drive, Lanham MD 20706.**)**
**Desc:** Describes the INISSTAIRS database installed on the IAEA mainframe computer and the IAEA/STAIRS retrieval language.

AU
**INIS SPECIFICATIONS FOR MACHINE READABLE DATA EXCHANGE.** (19??)-. English. S60.00. International Atomic Energy Agency / IAEA, Wagramerstrasse 5, PO Box 100, A-1400 Vienna Austria. **Tel** 011 43 1 2360 ext. 2530, FAX 011 43 1 234564. **(Subscription address:** UNIPUB, 4611 F Assembly Drive, Lanham MD 20706.**)**
**Desc:** Contains instructions on how to encode symbols occuring in scientific and technical texts.

AU
**INIS : THESAURUS.** **See** Physics-Abstracting, Bibliographies and Statistics.

●SI/0218-3013
**INTERNATIONAL JOURNAL OF MODERN PHYSICS. E, NUCLEAR PHYSICS.** **VFOAT** Nuclear Physics. Vol. 1, No. 1 (1992)-. Periodical. English. qt. $105.00 individuals, $205.00 institutions. World Scientific Publishing Company, PO Box 128, Farrer Road, Singapore 9128 Singapore. **Tel** 011 65 3825663, FAX 011 65 3825919, telex RS 28561 WSPC. **(Subscription address:** US: World Scientific Publishing Co., Inc., 1060 Main Street, River Edge, NJ 07661 Telephone: (201)487-9655, Fax: (201)487-9656; Europe: World Scientific Publishing Co Ltd, 73 Lynton Mead, Totteridge, London N20 8DH United Kingdom Telephone: 011 44 81 4462461, Fax: 011 44 81 4463356; India: World Scientific Publishing Co Pte Ltd, 4911 9th Floor, High Point IV, 45 Palace Road, Bangalore 560 001 India Telephone: (80) 2205972, Fax: (80) 3344593, Telex: 0845-2900 PCO IN; Hong Kong: World Scientific Publishing (HK) Co, PO Box 72482, Kowloon Central Post Office, Hong Kong Telephone: 852-7718791, Fax: 852-7718155**)** **LC** QC770; .I615. **DD** 539.7/05. **CODEN** IMPEER.

UK
**INTERNATIONAL JOURNAL OF RADIATION APPLICATIONS AND INSTRUMENTATION. PART D, NUCLEAR TRACKS AND RADIATION MEASUREMENTS.** ***Title Change.*** **VFOAT** Nuclear Tracks and Radiation Measurements. Vol. 11 No.

1/2 (1986)-(1993). Academic Scholarly Publication. English. Eight times a year. Pergamon Press, An Imprint of Elsevier Science Ltd., The Boulevard, Langford Lane, Kidlington, Oxford OX5 1GB United Kingdom. **Tel** 011 44 865 843000, 011 44 865 843699, FAX 011 44 865 843010. **(Subscription address:** US/ 395 Saw Mill River Road, Elmsford, NY 10523; Can/ 150 Consumers Road/Suite 104, Willowdale Ontario M2J 1P9; Aus-NZ/ POB 544, Potts Point NSW 2011**) ED** S Durrani and E Benton. **CODEN** NTRMDS. available on microfilm and microfiche from University Microfilms International (UMI). Documents available from CASDDS. ***Continues*** *Nuclear Tracks and Radiation Measurements, 0735-245X.* ***Continued by*** *Radiation Measurements.*
**Ind/Abst** Chem. Abstr.; Crop Physiol. Abstr.; Curr. Contents Phys. Chem. Earth Sci.; Hortic. Abstr.; Soils Fert.

SI
**INTERNATIONAL REVIEW OF NUCLEAR PHYSICS.** Vol. 1 (1984)-. Academic Scholarly Publication. English. an. Price varies per volume. World Scientific Publishing Company, PO Box 128, Farrer Road, Singapore 9128 Singapore. **Tel** 011 65 3825663, FAX 011 65 3825919, telex RS 28561 WSPC. **CODEN** IRNPEH. Documents available from Ask*IEEE, CASDDS.
**Ind/Abst** Chem. Abstr. (1984-); INSPEC.

NE
**JAARVERSLAG / UNIVERSITAIR REACTOR INSTITUUT. Main/Corp** Interuniversitair Reactor Instituut. Dutch. an. **LC** QC789.2.N42; I584A.

GW
**JAHRESBERICHT. Main/Corp** Forschungszentrum Julich. **VFOAT** Annual Report. (1990)-. German (summaries and/or abstracts in English). an. Free. Forschungszentrum Julich GmbH, Offentlichkeitsarbeit, Postfach 1913, W-5170 Julich 1 Germany. **Tel** (02461)61-4661, FAX 02461-61466. **ED** Siegfried A Weinhold. Index available. **Circ:** 6,000 (ctrl). ***Continues*** *Jahresbericht, 0341-8790.*
**Desc:** Report of the Julich Research Centre.

GW
**JAHRESBERICHT - DYNAMITRON-TANDEM-LABORATORIUM, BOCHUM. Main/Corp** Dynamitron-Tandem- Laboratorium (Bochum, Germany). German. an. Dynamitron-Tandem-Laboratorium, Universitatsstr 150 Gebaude NT, 4630 Bochum 1 Germany. **LC** QC789.G32; D95A. **DD** 539.7/05.

GW
**JAHRESBERICHT (JOHANNES GUTENBERG-UNIVERSITAT. INSTITUT FUR KERNPHYSIK).** (JAHRESBERICHT / INSTITUT FUER KERNPHYSIK, JOHANNES GUTENBERG-UNIVERSITAT.). (1984/85)-. German. be. **LC** QC789.2.G32; J64. **DD** 539.7/072043/43. ***Continues*** *Tatigkeitsbericht / Johannes Gutenberg-Universitat. Institut fur Kernphysik.*

GW
**JAHRESBERICHT / MAX-PLANCK-INSTITUT FUER KERNPHYSIK. Main/Corp** Max-Planck-Institut fur Kernphysik. (19??)-. German. an. **LC** WMLC L 83/2058. Documents available from CASDDS.
**Ind/Abst** Chem. Abstr.

AU
**JAHRESBERICHT / OSTERREICHISCHES FORSCHUNGSZENTRUM SEIBERSDORF. Main/Corp** Osterreichisches Forschungszentrum Seibersdorf. (1979)-. German. an. Osterreichisches Forschungszentrum Seibersdorf Ges M B H, Lenaugasse 10, 1082 Vienna Austria. **LC** QC792.78.A9; O37a. ***Continues*** *Osterreichische Studiengesellschaft fur Atomenergie. Jahresbericht.*

UK/0954-3899
**JOURNAL OF PHYSICS. G: NUCLEAR AND PARTICLE PHYSICS.** [J. phys. G Nucl. part. phys.]. **Added/Corp** Institute of Physics (Great Britain) American Institute of Physics. **VFOAT** Nuclear and Particle Physics. Vol. 15, No. 1 (Jan. 1989)-. Academic Scholarly Publication. English. Twelve times a year. $1,085.00. Institute of Physics, Techno House, Redcliffe Way, Bristol BS1 6NX England. **Tel** 011 44 272 297481, FAX 011 44 272 294318, telex 449149 INSTP G. **(Subscription address:** American Institute of Physics, Publishing Sales, 500 Sunnyside Blvd., Woodbury NY 11797.**) ED** A. Faessler. **LC** QC770; .J673. **DD** 539.7. **CODEN** JPGPED. Index available (bound in last issue). **Pr Rev.** available on microfiche. Documents available from The Genuine Article, Ask*IEEE, CASDDS. ***Continues*** *Journal of Physics. G, Nuclear Physics, 0305-4616.*
**Desc:** Theoretical and experimental topics in the physics of elementary particles and fields, intermediate-energy physics and nuclear physics. Also, all aspects of cosmic ray particle physics and cosmic ray astrophysics together with related areas of radioastronomy and gamma ray astronomy. The scope covers experimental techniques within all the above topics, including instrumental and data analysis.
**Ind/Abst** Chem. Abstr. (1989-); GeoRef; INSPEC (Jan. 1989-); Int. Aerosp. Abstr.; Leadscan; Pollut. Abstr. Indexes; Res. Alert [Full Cov.]; Sci. Cit. Index; SCISEARCH.

KO/0372-7327
**JOURNAL OF THE KOREAN NUCLEAR SOCIETY.** (WONJARYOK HAKHOE CHI.). [J. Korean Nucl. Soc.]. **Added/Corp** Hanguk Wonjaryok Hakhoe. **VFOAT** Journal of the Korean Nuclear Society. Vol. 1, No. 1 (Sept. 1969)-. Periodical. Korean (English; summaries and/or abstracts in English). qt. Korean Nuclear Society, PO Box 7, Cheong Ryang, Seoul Korea. **CODEN** WJHKAW. Documents available from Ask*IEEE, CASDDS.
**Ind/Abst** Chem. Abstr.; INSPEC (Dec. 1976-).

MY
**JURNAL SAINS NUKLEAR MALAYSIA. Added/Corp** Malaysia. Unit Tenaga Nuklear. **VFOAT** Nuclear Science Journal of Malaysia; JSNM. (1985)-. Periodical. English (Malay). sa. Unit Tenaga Nuklear, Kajung Malaysia. **CODEN** JSNMEQ. Documents available from CASDDS. ***Continues*** *Jurnal Sains Nukleus.*
**Ind/Abst** Chem. Abstr.

JA/0385-2105
**KAKURIKEN KEDKYU HOKOKU.** [Kakuriken kenkyu hokoku]. **Main/Corp** Tohoku Daigaku, Sendai, Japan. Genshikaku Rigaku Kenkyu Shisetsu. **VFOAT** Research Report of Laboratory of Nuclear Science, Tohoku University. Began in 1968. Academic Scholarly Publication. Japanese (English). Tohoku Daigaku, (Tohoku University), 1-1, Katahira 2 Chome, Sendaishi, Miyagiken 980, Japan. **LC** QC770; .T58A. **DD** 539.7/05. **CODEN** TLNRBV. Documents available from CASDDS.
**Ind/Abst** Chem. Abstr.; Energy Res. Abstr.

JA/0387-1029
**KARYOKU GENSHIRYOKU HATSUDEN.** [Karyoku genshiryoku hatsuden]. **VFOAT** The Thermal and Nuclear Power; Thermal and Nuclear Power. (1973)-. Periodical. Japanese (Japanese). mo. $122.00. Karyoku Genshiryoku Hatsuden Gijutsu Kyokai, (Thermal Power Engineering Soc. of Japan), 7-25, Kitaaoyama 2 Chome, Minatoku, Tokyoto 107 Japan. **(Subscription address:** Kyowa Book Company Inc., 1-38 Kanda Jinbo-Cho, Chiyoda-Ku, Tokyo 101, Japan (Phone: 03-3293-0727)**) LC** TK1001; .K33.
**Ind/Abst** Coal Abstr.

JA
**KOENERUGIKEN GEPPO. Main/Corp** Koenerugi Butsurigaku Kenkyujo. (1972)-. Periodical. Japanese. mo. Koenerugi Butsurigaku Kenkyujo, (National Laboratory for High Energy Physics), 1-1 Oho Tsukuba-shi, Ibaraki-ken 305 Japan. **LC** QC770; .K64.

US/0882-1305
**LBL RESEARCH REVIEW.** [LBL res. rev.]. **Added/Corp** Lawrence Berkeley Laboratory. **VAT** Lawrence Berkeley Laboratory Research Review. Vol. 10 No. 1 (Spring 1985)-. Periodical. English. tq. Free. LBL Research Review, Lawrence Berkeley Laboratory, Building 50C, Berkeley CA 94720. **Tel** (510)486-6598, telex FTS 451-6598. **ED** Barbara Storms. **LC** QC789.U62; L34b. **DD** 539/.0720794/67. **NLM** W1; LB432. **Bk Rev. Circ:** 9,000 (ctrl). ***Continues*** *LBL Newsmagazine, 0146-2725.*
**Desc:** A review of accomplishments in scientific research at Lawrence Berkeley Laboratory.
**Ind/Abst** Environ. Period. Bibliogr.; Int. Aerosp. Abstr.

US/0097-1065
**METHODS IN SUBNUCLEAR PHYSICS.** [Methods subnucl. phys.]. Monographic series. English. ir. Price varies per volume. Gordon & Breach Science Publishers, Inc., PO Box 786, Cooper Station, New York NY 10276. **Tel** (212)206-8900, FAX (212)645-2459. **(Subscription address:** International Publishers Distributor at one of the following addresses: 820 Town Center Drive, Langhorne, PA 19047; or PO Box 90, Reading Berkshire RG1 8JL UK; or Kent Ridge PO Box 1180, Singapore 9111, Republic of Singapore**) CODEN** MSNPBV. Documents available from Ask*IEEE, CASDDS.
**Desc:** Proceedings of the International School of Elementary Particle Physics, Herceg-Novi (Yugoslavia).
**Ind/Abst** Chem. Abstr.; INSPEC.

SI/0217-7323
**MODERN PHYSICS LETTERS A.** [Mod. phys. lett. A]. Vol. 1, No. 1 (April 1986)-. Academic Scholarly Publication. English. Forty times a year. $585.00 individuals, $1,170.00 institutions. World Scientific Publishing Company, PO Box 128, Farrer Road, Singapore 9128 Singapore. **Tel** 011 65 3825663, FAX 011 65 3825919, telex RS 28561 WSPC. **(Subscription address:** US: World Scientific Publishing Co., Inc., 1060 Main Street, River Edge, NJ 07661 Telephone: (201)487-9655, Fax: (201)487-9656; Europe: World Scientific Publishing Co Ltd, 73 Lynton Mead, Totteridge, London N20 8DH United Kingdom Telephone: 011 44 81 4462461, Fax: 011 44 81 4463356; India: World Scientific Publishing Co Pte Ltd, 4911 9th Floor, High Point IV, 45 Palace Road, Bangalore 560 001 India Telephone: (80) 2205972, Fax: (80) 3344593, Telex: 0845-2900 PCO IN; Hong Kong: World Scientific Publishing (HK) Co, PO Box 72482, Kowloon Central Post Office, Hong Kong Telephone: 852-7718791, Fax: 852-7718155**) LC** QC770; .M63. **DD** 539.7/05. **CODEN** MPLAEQ. **[CCC].** cum. index. **Pr Rev. Circ:** 500. Documents available from The Genuine Article, Ask*IEEE, CASDDS.
**Desc:** Gathers important and meaningful research findings in particles and fields, gravitation, cosmology and nuclear physics. Thus ties between theoretical and experimental groups are made closer through easy access to work done by each.
**Ind/Abst** Chem. Abstr. (1987-); Curr. Contents Phys. Chem. Earth Sci.; INSPEC (Dec. 1987-); Res. Alert [Select. Cov.]; SCISEARCH.

BE/0534-1299
**MONOGRAPHIE - INSTITUT INTERUNIVERSITAIRE DES SCIENCES NUCLEAIRES. Main/Corp** Institut Interuniversitaire des Sciences Nucleaires. No. 1- 1957-. Multiple languages (French, Dutch and English). **CODEN** IINMA9.

SZ/0259-9805
**MUON CATALYZED FUSION.** ***Title Change.*** [Muon catal. fusion]. Vol. 1 (1987)-Vol.8 (1993). Academic Scholarly Publication. English. qt. Baltzer Science Publishers BV, Asterweg 1A, 1031 HL Amsterdam Netherlands. **Tel** 011 31 20 6370061, FAX 011 31 20 6323651. **CODEN** MCFUEX. Documents available from Ask*IEEE, CASDDS. ***Merged into*** *Hyperfine Interactions.*
**Ind/Abst** Chem. Abstr.; INSPEC (1987-).

US/0148-4192
**NBS. REACTOR. SUMMARY OF ACTIVITIES.** ***Title Change.*** (NBS REACTOR, SUMMARY OF ACTIVITIES / REACTOR RADIATION DIVISION, NATIONAL MEASUREMENT LABORATORY, NATIONAL BUREAU OF STANDARDS.). **Main/Corp** National Measurement Laboratory (U.S.). Reactor Radiation Division. **VFOAT** N.B.S. Reactor, Summary of Activities. **VAT** National Bureau of Standards Reactor. Summary of Activities. (1971/1972)-(19??). English. an. Reactor Radiation Division, National Measurement Laboratory, Route 270, Gaithersburg MD 20234. **LC** QC100; .U5753 subser; QC786.4. **DD** 602/.15; 530. **CODEN** NBTNAE. available on microfiche (Vols. for (1981-1982-) distributed to depository libraries). ***Continued by*** *NBS Reactor, Summary of Activities.*

FR
**NOUVELLES NUCLEAIRES, LES.** French. Groupement Interet Economique, 31/33 rue de la Federation, F-75752 Paris Cedex France.

US/0090-3752
**NUCLEAR DATA SHEETS (NEW YORK).** (NUCLEAR DATA SHEETS.). [Nucl. data sheets]. Vol. 6 (July 1971)-. Academic Scholarly Publication. English. mo. $623.00 US and Canada; $735.00 other. Academic Press, Inc., 6277 Sea Harbor Drive, Orlando FL 32887. **Tel** (800)543-9534, (407)345-4100, FAX (407)363-9661. **ED** M. J. Martin and J. K. Tuli. **LC** QC783; .N844. **DD** 539.7/021/2. **CODEN** NDTSBA. **[CCC].** Documents available from Ask*IEEE, CASDDS. ***Continues*** *Nuclear Data Current Sheets. Section B, 0090-550X.*
**Desc:** Devoted to nuclear structure data evaluations and to nuclear structure bibliographies.
**Ind/Abst** Chem. Abstr.; Energy Res. Abstr. (Oct. 1977-); INSPEC (Dec. 1974-); SPIN (1977-).

AU/0029-5515
**NUCLEAR FUSION.** (NUCLEAR FUSION. FUSION NUCLEAIRE. IADERNYI SINTEZ. FUSION NUCLEAR.). [Nucl. fus.]. **Added/Corp** International Atomic Energy Agency. **VFOAT** Fusion Nucleaire; Iadernyi Sintez; Fusion Nuclear. Vol. 1 (Sept. 1960)-. Periodical. English. mo. $900.00 US; $1000.00 other. International Atomic Energy Agency / IAEA, Wagramerstrasse 5, PO Box 100, A-1400 Vienna Austria. **Tel** 011 43 1 2360 ext. 2530, FAX 011 43 1 234564. **(Subscription address:** UNIPUB, 4611 F Assembly Drive, Lanham MD 20706.**) LC** QC791; .N8. **DD** 621.48/4/05. **CODEN** NUFUAU. Index available in last issue of volume--attached. **Pr Rev.** available on microfilm from University Microfilms International (UMI). Documents available from Article Express International, The Genuine Article, Ask*IEEE, CASDDS, Documents on Demand.
**Desc:** Presents original articles, letters, review papers, comments and conference reports in the field of controlled nuclear fusion. Contents cover the following areas: plasma effects; processes and phenomena relating to fusion research; plasma production and heating; plasma confinement including magnetic and inertial systems; and application of experimental and diagnostic techniques.
**Ind/Abst** Bioeng. Abstr.; Chem. Abstr.; Chem. Titles; Curr. Contents Phys. Chem. Earth Sci.; Ei Page One; Electron. Commun. Abstr. J.; Energy Inf. Abstr.; Energy Res. Abstr. (Oct. 1976-); Eng. Index Annu.; Environ.

Abstr.; INSPEC (1968-); Int. Aerosp. Abstr.; ISMEC Bull.; Pollut. Abstr. Indexes; Res. Alert [Full Cov.]; Saf. Sci. Abstr. J.; Sci. Cit. Index; SCISEARCH.

US/0271-0706
**NUCLEAR INDEX, THE.** [Nucl. index]. Began with V. 1, No. 1 in Jan. 1980. English. mo. $195.00. McGraw Hill Publishing Company, Inc., 1221 Avenue of the Americas, New York NY 10020. **Tel** (212)512-6410, (800)525-5003, FAX (212)512-6111.

NE/0168-9002
**NUCLEAR INSTRUMENTS & METHODS IN PHYSICS RESEARCH. SECTION A, ACCELERATORS, SPECTROMETERS, DETECTORS AND ASSOCIATED EQUIPMENT.** [Nucl. instrum. & methods phys. res., A, Accel., spectrom., detect. ass. equip.]. **VFOAT** Accelerators, Spectrometers, Detectors and Associated Equipment; Nuclear Instruments and Methods in Physics Research. Section A. Vol. 219, No. 1 (Jan. 1, 1984)-. Academic Scholarly Publication. English. Forty-Five times a year (15 volumes). Fl10740.00; Fl18536.00 combined subscription with Nuclear Instruments and Methods in Physics Research Section B: Beam Interaction with Materials and Atoms. Elsevier Science Publishers BV, PO Box 211, 1000 AE Amsterdam Netherlands. **Tel** 011 31 20 5803642, FAX 011 31 20 5862696, telex 15682. **ED** K. Siegbahn and E. Karlsson. **LC** QC785.5; .N82. **DD** 539.7/028. **CODEN** NIMAER. **[CCC]. Pr Rev.** available on microfilm and microfiche from University Microfilms International (UMI). Documents available from Article Express International, The Genuine Article, Ask*IEEE, CASDDS. ***Continues in part*** *Nuclear Instruments & Methods in Physics Research, 0167-5087.*
**Desc:** Covers all technical aspects of research in nuclear physics, high energy physics and related fields such as synchrotron radiation.
**Ind/Abst** Anal. Abstr.; Bioeng. Abstr.; Chem. Abstr. (1984-); Chem. Titles; Comput. Abstr.; Comput. Inf. Syst. Abstr. J. [Full Cov.]; Curr. Contents Eng. Tech. Appl. Sci.; Curr. Contents Phys. Chem. Earth Sci.; Ei Page One; Elect. Comm. Abstr.; Eng. Index Annu.; INSPEC (Jan. 1984-); Leadscan; Manuf. Process Eng. Abstr.; Mass Spect. Bull.; Mater. Sci. Eng. Abstr.; Mech. Eng. Abstr.; Life Sci. Collect.; Phys. Briefs; Res. Alert [Full Cov.]; Sci. Cit. Index; SCISEARCH; Solid State Supercond. Abstr.

NE/0168-583X
**NUCLEAR INSTRUMENTS & METHODS IN PHYSICS RESEARCH. SECTION B, BEAM INTERACTIONS WITH MATERIALS AND ATOMS.** [Nucl. instrum. methods phys. res., B, Beam interact. mater. atoms]. **VFOAT** Beam Interactions with Materials and Atoms; Nuclear Instruments and Methods in Physics Research. Vol. B1, No. 1 (Jan. 1984)-. Academic Scholarly Publication. English. Fifty-two times a year (13 volumes). Fl9308.00; Fl18536.00 combined subscription with Nuclear Instruments and Methods on Physics Research Section A: Accelerators, Spectrometers, Detectors and Associated Equipment. Elsevier Science Publishers BV, PO Box 211, 1000 AE Amsterdam Netherlands. **Tel** 011 31 20 5803642, FAX 011 31 20 5862696, telex 15682. **ED** K. Siegbahn. **LC** QC785.5; .N83. **DD** 539.7/028. **CODEN** NIMBEU. **[CCC]. Pr Rev.** available on microfilm and microfiche from University Microfilms International (UMI). Documents available from Article Express International, The Genuine Article, Ask*IEEE, CASDDS. ***Continues in part*** *Nuclear Instruments & Methods in Physics Research, 0167-5087.*
**Desc:** Topics of general interest include: atomic collisions in solids, particle channeling, all aspects of collision cascades, the modification of materials by energetic beams, ion implantation, irradiation-induced changes in materials by all forms of energetic radiation.
**Ind/Abst** Anal. Abstr.; Bibliogr. Mission.; Bioeng. Abstr.; Chem. Abstr. (1984-); Chem. Titles; Comput. Abstr.; Curr. Contents Eng. Tech. Appl. Sci.; Curr. Contents Phys. Chem. Earth Sci.; Ei Page One; Eng. Index Annu.; GeoRef; INSPEC (Jan. 1984-); Mass Spect. Bull.; Life Sci. Collect.; Res. Alert [Full Cov.]; Sci. Cit. Index; SCISEARCH; Soc. Sci. Cit. Index [Select. Cov.].

US/0893-3774
**NUCLEAR LICENSING REPORTS. See** Engineering-Nuclear Engineering.

US/0889-3411
**NUCLEAR MONITOR, THE.** [Nucl. monitor]. **Added/Corp** Nuclear Information and Resource Service (Washington, D.C.). (Sept. 1985)-. Periodical. English. Twenty-five times a year. $250.00 (one year), $400.00 (two years) profit organizations; $150.00 non profit orgazinations. Nuclear Information Monitor, 1424 16th Street Northwest, Suite 601, Washington DC 20036. **Tel** (202)328-0002, FAX (202)462-2183. **ED** Michael Mariette. **LC** HD9698.A1; N83. **DD** 363. **Bk Rev**, (Qty: 1-5). **Circ:** 1,000. available on an online database. ***Continues*** *The Monitor (Washington, D.C.).*
**Desc:** News and analysis on nuclear power, radiation, waste and sustainable energy issues.

NE/0375-9474
**NUCLEAR PHYSICS. A.** [Nucl. phys., A]. Vol. A90 (Jan. 1967)-. Academic Scholarly Publication. English. Sixty times a year (15 volumes). Fl9435.00; Fl23046.00 combined subscription with Nuclear Physics B and Proceedings Supplements. Elsevier Science Publishers BV, PO Box 211, 1000 AE Amsterdam Netherlands. **Tel** 011 31 20 5803642, FAX 011 31 20 5862696, telex 15682. **ED** G.E. Brown, C.L. Schwarz. **LC** QC173; .N8838. **DD** 539.7/05. **CODEN** NUPABL. **[CCC].** cum. index. **Pr Rev.** available on microfilm and microfiche from University Microfilms International (UMI). Documents available from The Genuine Article, Ask*IEEE, CASDDS. ***Continues in part*** *Nuclear Physics.*
**Desc:** Covers the domain of general nuclear physics together with intermediate energy and heavy-ion physics, and astrophysics.
**Ind/Abst** Chem. Abstr.; Chem. Titles (1968-); Curr. Contents Phys. Chem. Earth Sci.; Energy Res. Abstr.; INSPEC (1968-); Leadscan; Math. Rev. (?-199?); Phys. Briefs; Res. Alert [Full Cov.]; Sci. Cit. Index; SCISEARCH.

NE/0550-3213
**NUCLEAR PHYSICS. B.** [Nucl. phys., B]. Vol. B1 (Jan. 1967)-. Academic Scholarly Publication. English. ir (75 issues per year). Fl15400.00; Fl23046.00 combined subscription with Nuclear Physics A and Proceedings Supplements. Elsevier Science Publishers BV, PO Box 211, 1000 AE Amsterdam Netherlands. **Tel** 011 31 20 5803642, FAX 011 31 20 5862696, telex 15682. **ED** G. Altarelli, W. Bartel, C. Becchi, J.L. Cardy, M. Derrick, L. DiLella, R.H. Dijkgraaf, L. Maiani, H.R. Rubinstein. **LC** QC173; .N8839. **DD** 539.7/05. **CODEN** NUPBBO. **[CCC]. Pr Rev.** available on microfilm and microfiche from University Microfilms International (UMI). Documents available from The Genuine Article, Ask*IEEE, CASDDS. ***Continues in part*** *Nuclear Physics.*
**Desc:** Focuses on the domain of high energy physics and quantum field theory.
**Ind/Abst** Chem. Abstr.; Chem. Titles; Curr. Contents Phys. Chem. Earth Sci.; Energy Res. Abstr.; INSPEC (1968-); Math. Rev.; Phys. Briefs; Res. Alert [Full Cov.]; Sci. Cit. Index; SCISEARCH.

US/1061-9127
**NUCLEAR PHYSICS NEWS.** (NUCLEAR PHYSICS NEWS : A PUBLICATION OF NUPECC AND EPS-NPB.). [Nucl. phys. news]. **Added/Corp** NuPECC (Organization) EPS-NPB (Organization). (1991)-. Periodical. English. Six times a year. $373.00 (academic institutions), $582.00 (corporate institutions). Gordon & Breach Science Publishers, Inc., PO Box 786, Cooper Station, New York NY 10276. **Tel** (212)206-8900, FAX (212)645-2459. **(Subscription address:** International Publishers Distributor at one of the following addresses: 820 Town Center Drive, Langhorne, PA 19047; or PO Box 90, Reading Berkshire RG1 8JL UK; or Kent Ridge PO Box 1180, Singapore 9111, Republic of Singapore**) LC** IN PROCESS. **DD** 539. ***Continues*** *European Nuclear Physics News, 1050-6896.*

NE/0920-5632
**NUCLEAR PHYSICS. SECTION B, PROCEEDINGS SUPPLEMENT.** (NUCLEAR PHYSICS. B, PROCEEDINGS, SUPPLEMENTS.). [Nucl. phys., Sect. B Proc. suppl.]. **VFOAT** Proceedings, Supplements; Nuclear Physics B (Proc. Suppl.). Vol. 1A (Sept. 1987)-. Academic Scholarly Publication. English. Eighteen times a year (6 volumes). Fl2082.00; Fl23046.00 combined subscription with Nuclear Physics A and Nuclear Physics B. Elsevier Science Publishers BV, PO Box 211, 1000 AE Amsterdam Netherlands. **Tel** 011 31 20 5803642, FAX 011 31 20 5862696, telex 15682. **ED** K. Jones. **LC** QC173; .N884. **CODEN** NPBSE7SPBSE7B. **[CCC].** Documents available from Ask*IEEE, CASDDS.
**Desc:** Offers a representative collection of proceedings of large international conferences as well as more specialized meetings, all of genuine interest to the high-energy physics community.
**Ind/Abst** Chem. Abstr.; INSPEC (Sept. 1987-); Math. Rev.

PL
**NUCLEAR SCIENCE ABSTRACTS OF POLAND. Added/Corp** Osrodek Informacji o Energii Jadrowej (Poland). Vol. 1 (July 1, 1965)-. English (Polish). qt. Nuclear Energy Information Center of the Polish Government, Commissioner for Use of Nuclear Energy, Palace of Culture and Science, Warsaw Poland. **LC** QC173; .N8845.

US/0029-5639
**NUCLEAR SCIENCE AND ENGINEERING. See** Engineering-Nuclear Engineering.

CC/1001-8042
**NUCLEAR SCIENCE AND TECHNIQUES.** [Nucl. Sci. Tech.]. (1990)-. Academic Scholarly Publication. English. qt. $138.00 US; $158.00 other (institution). Science Press, 16 Donghuangchenggen North Street, Beijing 100707, People's Republic of China. **Tel** 011 86 1 4019821, 011 86 1 4010642, FAX 011 86 1 4012180, 011 86 1 4019810, telex 210147. **DD** 621.48. Documents available from CASDDS.
**Ind/Abst** Chem. Abstr.

SZ/0191-1686
**NUCLEAR SCIENCE APPLICATIONS.** (NUCLEAR SCIENCE APPLICATIONS. SECTION B.). [Nucl. sci. appl.]. Vol. 1, No. 2 (Aug. 1981)-. Academic Scholarly Publication. English. £167.00. Harwood Academic Publishers, PO Box 90, Reading RG1 8JL England. **Tel** 011 44 734 560080. **(Subscription address:** International Publishers Distributor at one of the following addresses: 820 Town Center Drive, Langhorne, PA 19047; or PO Box 90, Reading Berkshire RG1 8JL UK; or Kent Ridge PO Box 1180, Singapore 9111, Republic of Singapore**) ED** R Klapisch and A Zucker. **LC** QC770; .N822. **DD** 539.7/05. **NLM** W1; NU127H. **CODEN** NSAPDD. **[CCC]. Bk Rev. Ad Acc.** available in microform. Documents available from Ask*IEEE, CASDDS.
**Desc:** Nuclear and particle science, single-topic issues.
**Ind/Abst** Chem. Abstr.; INSPEC (1982-).

SZ/0191-1686
**NUCLEAR SCIENCE APPLICATIONS.** (NUCLEAR SCIENCE APPLICATIONS. SECTION A, SHORT REVIEWS, RESEARCH PAPERS, AND COMMENTS.). [Nucl. sci. appl.]. Vol. 1, No. 1 (July 1980)-. Periodical. English. ir. Price varies. Harwood Academic Publishers, PO Box 90, Reading RG1 8JL England. **Tel** 011 44 734 560080. **(Subscription address:** Harwood Academic Publishers, PO Box 786, Cooper Station, New York NY 10276.**) ED** R. Klapisch and A. Zucker. **LC** QC770; .N82. **DD** 539.7. **CODEN** NSAPDD. **[CCC]. Bk Rev. Ad Acc.** available in microform. Documents available from Ask*IEEE.
**Desc:** Nuclear and particle science, single-topic issues.
**Ind/Abst** Energy Res. Abstr. (Dec. 1980-); INSPEC (1981-).

JA/0029-5620
**NUCLEAR SCIENCE INFORMATION OF JAPAN. Added/Corp** Nihon Genshiryoku Kenkyujo. (May 1970)-. Periodical. English. Three times a year. Tokai Research Establishment, Tokai-mura Naka-gun, Ibaraki Ken Japan. **LC** Z7144.N8; N79; Q776. **DD** 016.5397. **NLM** Z 7144.N8 N969. **Circ:** 600 (ctrl). ***Continues*** *Nuclear Science Abstracts of Japan.*

US/0250-4375
**NUCLEAR SCIENCE RESEARCH CONFERENCE SERIES.** [Nucl. sci. res. conf. ser.]. Vol. 1 (1980)-. Academic Scholarly Publication. English. ir. Price varies per volume. Harwood Academic Publishers / New York, PO Box 786, Cooper Station, New York NY 10276. **Tel** (212)206-8900, (201)643-7500. **(Subscription address:** International Publishers Distributor at one of the following addresses: 820 Town Center Drive, Langhorne, PA 19047; or PO Box 90, Reading Berkshire RG1 8JL UK; or Kent Ridge PO Box 1180, Singapore 9111, Republic of Singapore**) ED** A. Zucker. **DD** 539. **CODEN** NSRSD5. Documents available from Ask*IEEE, CASDDS.
**Ind/Abst** Chem. Abstr.; INSPEC; Math. Rev.

US/0048-105X
**NUCLEONICS WEEK. See** Energy.

CL/0716-0054
**NUCLEOTECNICA. See** Engineering-Nuclear Engineering.

IT/0392-6737
**NUOVO CIMENTO DELLA SOCIETA ITALIANA DI FISICA, [SEZIONE] D.** (IL NUOVO CIMENTO DELLA SOCIETA ITALIANA DI FISICA. D, CONDENSED MATTER, ATOMIC, MOLECULAR AND CHEMICAL PHYSICS, BIOPHYSICS.). [Nuovo Cimento Soc. ital. fis., D]. **Added/Corp** Societa Italiana di Fisica. **VFOAT** Condensed Matter, Atomic, Molecular and Chemical Physics, Biophysics; D, Condensed Matter, Atomic, Molecular and Chemical Physics, Biophysics. Vol. 1, No. 1 (Jan./Feb. 1982)-. Academic Scholarly Publication. Italian (English, French, German, Italian and Spanish). mo. $530.00 (nonmembers), $420.00 (members). Editrice Compositori SRL, Viale Stalingrado 97 2, 40128 Bologna Italy. **Tel** 011 39 51 327811. **CODEN** NCSDDN. **[CCC]. Pr Rev. Circ:** 500 (ctrl). Documents available from The Genuine Article, Ask*IEEE, CASDDS.
**Desc:** Covers atomic and molecular physics.
**Ind/Abst** Alum. Ind. Abstr.; Chem. Abstr.; Curr. Contents Phys. Chem. Earth Sci.; INSPEC (Jan.-Feb. 1982-); Math. Rev.; Met. Abstr.; Res. Alert [Full Cov.]; Sci. Cit. Index; SCISEARCH.

IT/0369-4097
**NUOVO CIMENTO DELLA SOCIETA ITALIANA DI FIZICA. SEZIONE A.** (IL NUOVO CIMENTO DELLA SOCIETA ITALIANA DI FISICA. A.). [Nuovo cimento Soc. ital. fiz. A]. **Added/Corp** Societa Italiana di Fisica. Vol. 1A, No. 1 (Jan. 1971)-. Academic Scholarly Publication. Italian (English; summaries and/or abstracts in Russian). Twelve times a year. $880.00 (nonmembers), $710.00 (members). Editrice Compositori SRL, Viale Stalingrado 97 2, 40128 Bologna Italy. **Tel** 011 39 51 327811. **CODEN** NIFAAM. **[CCC].** cum. index. **Bk Rev. Ad Acc. Pr Rev. Circ:** 1,500 (ctrl). Documents available from The Genuine Article, Ask*IEEE, CASDDS. ***Continues*** *Nuovo Cimento. A, 0369-3546.*
**Desc:** The physics of elementary particles and fields and nuclear physics.
**Ind/Abst** Chem. Abstr.; Chem. Titles; Curr. Contents Phys. Chem. Earth Sci.; EMBASE; Energy Res. Abstr.

(Feb. 1981-); INSPEC (1971-); Math. Rev.; Life Sci. Collect.; Res. Alert [Full Cov.]; Sci. Cit. Index; SCISEARCH.

US/0278-1670
**NUREG/CR (UNITED STATES. NUCLEAR REGULATORY COMMISSION).** See Engineering-Nuclear Engineering.

UK/1043-6790
**PARTICLE WORLD.** [Part. world]. **Added/Corp** Association "Diffusion de la Connaissance". Vol. 1, No. 1 (Sept. 1989)-. Periodical. English. Six times a year. $441.00 (academic institutions), $688.00 (corporate institutions). Gordon & Breach Science Publishers, PO Box 90, Reading RG1 8JL England. **Tel** 011 44 734 560080, FAX 011 44 734 568211. **(Subscription address:** International Publishers Distributor at one of the following addresses: 820 Town Center Drive, Langhorne, PA 19047; or PO Box 90, Reading Berkshire RG1 8JL UK; or Kent Ridge PO Box 1180, Singapore 9111, Republic of Singapore) **LC** QC793; .P363. **DD** 539.7/2. **CODEN** PARWEG. **[CCC].** Documents available from Ask*IEEE.
**Ind/Abst** INSPEC (Sept. 1989-).

UK
**PARTICLE WORLD COMMUNICATIONS : THE INTERNATIONAL JOURNAL OF SUBNUCLEAR PHYSICS.** English. Gordon & Breach Science Publishers, PO Box 90, Reading RG1 8JL England. **Tel** 011 44 734 560080, FAX 011 44 734 568211. **(Subscription address:** International Publishers Distributor at one of the following addresses: 820 Town Center Drive, Langhorne, PA 19047; or PO Box 90, Reading Berkshire RG1 8JL UK; or Kent Ridge PO Box 1180, Singapore 9111, Republic of Singapore)

US/0556-2813
**PHYSICAL REVIEW C : NUCLEAR PHYSICS.** [Phys. rev. C. Nucl. phys.]. **Added/Corp** American Institute of Physics. American Physical Society. **VFOAT** Nuclear Physics. Vol. 1, No. 1 (Jan. 1970)-. Periodical. English. mo. $920.00 US; $950.00 Canada, Mexico, Central and South America, and the Caribbean; $1000.00 other. American Institute of Physics, 500 Sunnyside Boulevard, Woodbury NY 11797-2999. **Tel** (516)576-2200, FAX (516)349-7669, telex 960983. **ED** Henry H. Barschall. **LC** QC770; .P45. **DD** 539.7/05. **NLM** W1 PH737C. **CODEN** PRVCAN. **[CCC].** **Pr Rev.** available on microfiche. Documents available from The Genuine Article, Ask*IEEE, CASDDS. ***Continues in part*** *Physical Review, 0031-899X.*
**Desc:** Contains research articles reporting experimental and theoretical results in all aspects of nuclear physics, including nucleon-nucleon interactions, nuclear decay and radioactivity, as well as in applied areas such as nuclear energy and nuclear medicine.
**Ind/Abst** Chem. Abstr.; Chem. Titles (1970-); Curr. Contents Phys. Chem. Earth Sci.; Curr. Phys. Index; Energy Res. Abstr.; INSPEC (Jan. 1970-); Int. Aerosp. Abstr.; Leadscan; Math. Rev. (?-199?); Res. Alert [Full Cov.]; Sci. Cit. Index; SCISEARCH; SPIN (1970-).

US
**PHYSICAL REVIEW. D.** **Added/Corp** American Physical Society. American Institute of Physics. **VFOAT** Particles and Fields; Particles, Fields, Gravitation, and Cosmology. Vol. 44, No. 1 (July 1, 1991)-. Periodical. English. Twenty-four times a year. $1470.00 US; $1525.00 Canada, Mexico, Central & South America and the Caribbean; $1615.00 other. American Institute of Physics, 500 Sunnyside Boulevard, Woodbury NY 11797-2999. **Tel** (516)576-2200, FAX (516)349-7669, telex 960983. **CODEN** PRVDAQ. ***Continues*** *Physical Review. D. Particles and Fields, 0556-2821.*
**Ind/Abst** Curr. Contents Phys. Chem. Earth Sci.; Math. Rev.

US
**PHYSICAL REVIEW. D[15], PARTICLES, FIELDS, GRAVITATION, AND COSMOLOGY.** **Added/Corp** American Physical Society. American Institute of Physics. **VFOAT** Particles, Fields, Gravitation, and Cosmology. Vol. 44, No. 2 (July 1991)-. Periodical. English. mo. American Physical Society, One Physics Ellipse, College Park MD 20740. **Tel** (301)209-3248. ***Continues*** *Physical Review. D. Particles and Fields, 0556-2821.*

NE/0370-2693
**PHYSICS LETTERS : PART B.** [Phys. lett., Sect. B]. Vol. 24B (Jan. 9, 1967)-. Academic Scholarly Publication. English (French and German). ir (96 issues per year; 24 volumes). Fl9240.00; Fl16807.00 combined subscription with Section A. Elsevier Science Publishers BV, PO Box 211, 1000 AE Amsterdam Netherlands. **Tel** 011 31 20 5803642, FAX 011 31 20 5862696, telex 15682. **ED** G.F. Bertsch, M. Dine, R. Gatto, H. Georgi, P.V. Landshoff, C. Mahaux, L. Montanet, J.P. Schiffer, R.H. Siemssen, K. Winter. **LC** QC1; .P6562. **DD** 530/.05. **NLM** W1; PH844LB. **CODEN** PYLBAJ. **[CCC].** cum. index. **Pr Rev.** available on microfilm and microfiche from University Microfilms International (UMI). Documents available from The Genuine Article, Ask*IEEE, CASDDS. ***Supersedes in part*** *Physics Letters, 0031-9163.*
**Desc:** Devoted to the rapid publication of important new results in nuclear physics.
**Ind/Abst** Chem. Abstr.; Chem. Titles (1968-); Curr. Contents Phys. Chem. Earth Sci.; Energy Res. Abstr. (Feb. 1981-); INSPEC (1968-); Leadscan; Mass Spect. Bull.; Math. Rev.; Phys. Briefs; Res. Alert [Full Cov.]; Sci. Cit. Index; SCISEARCH.

●US/1063-7788
**PHYSICS OF ATOMIC NUCLEI.** [Phys. at. nucl.]. **Added/Corp** American Institute of Physics. Vol. 56, No 1 (Jan. 1993)-. Periodical. English (translations available in Russian). mo. $2485.00 US; $2505.00 Canada, Mexico, Central & South America and the Caribbean; $2535.00 other. American Institute of Physics, 500 Sunnyside Boulevard, Woodbury NY 11797-2999. **Tel** (516)576-2200, FAX (516)349-7669, telex 960983. **LC** QC770; .S64. **DD** 539. **CODEN** PANUEO. **[CCC].** Index available (bound in last issue). available on microfilm. Documents available from Ask*IEEE. ***Continues*** *Soviet Journal of Nuclear Physics, 0038-5506.*
**Ind/Abst** Curr. Phys. Index; Energy Res. Abstr.; INSPEC; Math. Rev.; Sci. Cit. Index; SPIN.

●US/1063-7796
**PHYSICS OF PARTICLES AND NUCLEI.** [Physics part. nucl.]. **Added/Corp** American Institute of Physics. (1993)-. Periodical. English (translations available in Russian). bm (6 issues). $1385.00 US; $1395.00 Canada, Mexico, Central & South America and the Caribbean; $1410.00 other. American Institute of Physics, 500 Sunnyside Boulevard, Woodbury NY 11797-2999. **Tel** (516)576-2200, FAX (516)349-7669, telex 960983. **DD** 539. **[CCC].** Index available (bound in last issue). Documents available from Ask*IEEE. ***Continues*** *Soviet Journal of Particles and Nuclei, 0090-4759.*
**Ind/Abst** Curr. Phys. Index; Energy Res. Abstr.; INSPEC; Math. Rev.; SPIN.

FR
**PHYSIQUE, ATOMIQUE ET MOLECULAIRE PLASMAS.** French. ir. 1199.68F France; 1250.00F other. CNRS / Institut d'Information Scientifique et Technique, (Centre National de la Recherche Scientifique), 15 Quai Anatole France, Paris 75700 France. **Tel** 011 33 1 47531515, telex 299 356 F. ***Continues*** *Pascal Explore E11, Physique Atomique et Moleculaire Plasmas.*

UK/0741-3335
**PLASMA PHYSICS AND CONTROLLED FUSION.** [Plasma phys. control. fusion]. **Added/Corp** Institute of Physics (Great Britain). **VFOAT** Plasma Physics. Vol. 26, No. 1A (Jan. 1984)-. Academic Scholarly Publication. English. mo. $965.00. Institute of Physics, Techno House, Redcliffe Way, Bristol BS1 6NX England. **Tel** 011 44 272 297481, FAX 011 44 272 294318, telex 449149 INSTP G. **(Subscription address:** American Institute of Physics, Publishing Sales, 500 Sunnyside Blvd., Woodbury NY 11797.) **ED** Peter Stott. **LC** QC770; .P5. **DD** 530.4/4/05. **CODEN** PPCFET. **[CCC].** Index available in last issue of volume--attached. **Pr Rev.** available on microfilm and microfiche from University Microfilms International (UMI). Documents available from The Genuine Article, Ask*IEEE, CASDDS. ***Continues*** *Plasma Physics, 0032-1028.*
**Desc:** Leading international journal publishing research papers on all aspects of plasma physics and controlled nuclear fusion, together with the plasma physics of highly ionized gases and high-temperature collective processes.
**Ind/Abst** Appl. Sci. Technol. Index; Chem. Abstr. (1984-); Curr. Contents Phys. Chem. Earth Sci.; INSPEC (1984-); Math. Rev.; Pollut. Abstr. Indexes; Res. Alert [Full Cov.]; Sci. Cit. Index; SCISEARCH.

JA
**PNC REVIEW.** **Added/Corp** Doryokuro Kakunenryo Kaihatsu Jigyodan. No. 1 (Nov. 1984)-. Periodical. English. sa. Tokai Works, Power Reactor & Nuclear Fuel Development Corporation, Tokai Japan. ***Continues in part*** *Tokai Works Annual Progress Report; PNC News and Reports.*
**Ind/Abst** AESIS Q.

UN/0131-3142
**PROBLEMY JADERNOJ FIZIKI I KOSMICESKIH LUCHEJ.** (PROBLEMY IADERNOI FIZIKI I KOSMICHESKIKH LUCHEI.). [Probl. jad. fiz. kosm. luchej]. No. 1 (1974)-. Academic Scholarly Publication. Russian (summaries and/or abstracts in English). Izdatelskoe Obedinenie Vyshcha Shkola / Russia, Universitetskaia 16, Kharkov Ukraine. **Tel** 22 46 47. **LC** QC770; .P74. **CODEN** PIFLDC. **Circ:** 700. Documents available from CASDDS.
**Desc:** Information on nuclear physics and cosmic rays.
**Ind/Abst** Chem. Abstr.; Int. Aerosp. Abstr.; Math. Rev.

RU/0370-2189
**PROBLEMY TEORII GRAVITATSII I ELEMENTARNYKH CHASTITS.** (1966)-. Academic Scholarly Publication. Russian. an. 1.90rub. Energoizdat 113114, Shliuzova Nab 10, Moscow M 114 Russia. **LC** QC178; .P765. **DD** 531/.14/05. **CODEN** PTGEA2. Documents available from CASDDS.
**Ind/Abst** Chem. Abstr.; Int. Aerosp. Abstr.; Math. Rev.

IT
**PROCEEDINGS - INTERNATIONAL CONFERENCE ON INSTRUMENTATION FOR HIGH- ENERGY PHYSICS.** **Main/Conf** International Conference on Instrumentation for High-Energy Physics. **Added/Corp** United States. Atomic Energy Commission. International Union of Pure and Applied Physics. Lawrence Radiation Laboratory. (19??)-. Proceedings. English. **LC** QC786; .I57.

GW/0720-8715
**PROCEEDINGS OF THE INTERNATIONAL WORKSHOP ON GROSS PROPERTIES OF NUCLEI AND NUCLEAR EXCITATIONS.** [Proc. Int. Workshop Gross Prop. Nucl. Nucl. Excitations]. **Main/Conf** International Workshop on Gross Properties of Nuclei and Nuclear Excitations. Began in 1973-. Academic Scholarly Publication. English. **LC** QC793.3.S8; I59A. **DD** 539.7/23/05. **CODEN** IWGEDH. Documents available from CASDDS.
**Ind/Abst** Chem. Abstr.

UK/0079-6565
**PROGRESS IN NUCLEAR MAGNETIC RESONANCE SPECTROSCOPY.** [Prog. nucl. magn. reson. spectrosc.]. Vol. 1 (1966)-. English. Six times a year. $395.00 The Americas; £265.00 other. Pergamon Press, An Imprint of Elsevier Science Ltd., The Boulevard, Langford Lane, Kidlington, Oxford OX5 1GB United Kingdom. **Tel** 011 44 865 843000, 011 44 865 843699, FAX 011 44 865 843010. **(Subscription address:** Elsevier Science Ltd. Oxford Fulfillment Centre, PO Box 800, Kidlington, Oxford OX5 1DX United Kingdom.) **ED** J. Emsley, J. Feeney. **LC** QC762; .P75. **DD** 539.1. **CODEN** PNMRAT. **[CCC].** **Pr Rev.** available on microfilm from Pergamon Press; available on microfilm and microfiche from University Microfilms International (UMI). Documents available from Article Express International, The Genuine Article, Ask*IEEE, CASDDS, ADONIS.
**Desc:** Publishes review articles covering applications, as well as in-depth treatments of the fundamental theory and instrumental developments of NMR spectroscopy.
**Ind/Abst** ADONIS; Alum. Ind. Abstr.; Chem. Abstr.; Curr. Contents Phys. Chem. Earth Sci.; Eng. Mater. Abstr.; Eng. Index Annu. [Select. Cov.]; Index Sci. Rev. [Full Cov.]; INSPEC (1975-); Met. Abstr.; Res. Alert [Full Cov.]; Sci. Cit. Index; SCISEARCH.

UK/0146-6410
**PROGRESS IN PARTICLE AND NUCLEAR PHYSICS.** [Prog. part. nucl. phys.]. **Added/Corp** International School of Nuclear Physics. Proceedings of the International School of Nuclear Physics. **VFOAT** Particle and Nuclear Physics. Vol. 1 (1978)-. Academic Scholarly Publication. English. Twice a year. $686.00 The Americas; £460.00 other. Pergamon Press, An Imprint of Elsevier Science Ltd., The Boulevard, Langford Lane, Kidlington, Oxford OX5 1GB United Kingdom. **Tel** 011 44 865 843000, 011 44 865 843699, FAX 011 44 865 843010. **(Subscription address:** Elsevier Science Ltd. Oxford Fulfillment Centre, PO Box 800, Kidlington, Oxford OX5 1DX United Kingdom.) **ED** Amand Faessler. **LC** QC770; .P76. **DD** 539.7/21. **CODEN** PPNPDB. **[CCC].** **Pr Rev.** available on microfilm and microfiche from University Microfilms International (UMI). Documents available from The Genuine Article, Ask*IEEE, CASDDS. ***Continues*** *Progress in Nuclear Physics, 0079-659X.*
**Ind/Abst** Chem. Abstr.; Curr. Contents Phys. Chem. Earth Sci.; INSPEC (1978-); Res. Alert [Full Cov.]; Sci. Cit. Index; SCISEARCH.

US
**PROTON NMR COLLECTION. CUMULATIVE CHEMICAL CLASS INDEX.** **Main/Corp** Sadtler Research Laboratories. **VFOAT** Standard Proton NMR Spectra Collection. Cumulative Chemical Class Index. 1980-. Monographic series. English. Price varies per volume. Sadtler Research Laboratories Inc., 3316 Spring Garden Street, Philadelphia PA 19104. **Tel** (215)382-7800.

PL/0302-9034
**RAPORT - INSTYTUT FIZYKI I TECHNIKI JADROWEJ AGH.** [Rap., Inst. Fiz. Tech. Jad. AGH]. **Main/Corp** Instytut Fizyki i Techniki Jadrowej AGH. **VFOAT** Report - Institute of Nuclear Physics and Techniques. **VAT** Raport - Instytut Fizyki i Techniki Jadrowej Akademia Gorniczo-Hutnicza. (1973)-. Academic Scholarly Publication. Multiple languages (Polish and English). **CODEN** IFTJA9. Documents available from CASDDS. ***Continues*** *Instytut Techniki Jadrowej AGH. Raport.*
**Ind/Abst** Chem. Abstr.

LV/0302-8453
**RASCETY ATOMNYH I JADERNYH KONSTANT.** (RASCHETY ATOMNYKH I IADERNYKH KONSTANT.). [Rasc. at. jad. konstant]. **Main/Corp** Petera Stuckas Latvijas Valsts Universitate. Skaitlosanas Centrs. (1970)-. Russian. 1.72rub single issue. Redaktsionno-Izdatelskii Otdel Lgu Im Petra Stuchki, 50 Ulitsa Veidenbauma 5, Riga Latvia. **LC** QC770; .R57a.

AU
**REFERENCE DATA SERIES.** **Added/Corp** International Atomic Energy Agency. **VFOAT** Nuclear Power and Its Fuel Cycle. No. 1 (1982)-. Monographic series. English. ir. Price varies per volume. International Atomic Energy Agency / IAEA, Wagramerstrasse 5, PO Box 100, A-1400 Vienna Austria. **Tel** 011 43 1 2360 ext. 2530, FAX 011 43 1 234564. **(Subscription address:** UNIPUB, 4611 F Assembly Drive, Lanham MD 20706.**)** **LC** UNC.

BL
**RELATORIO ANUAL.** **Main/Corp** Minas Gerais, Brazil. Universidade Federal. Instituto de Pesquisas Radioativas. (19??)-. Portuguese. an. Universidad Federal de Minas Gerais, Instituto de Pesquisas Radioativas, Caixa Postal 1941, Cidade Universitaria, Belo Horizonte Brazil. **LC** QC770; .M54a.

IS/0367-6617
**REPORT - ISRAEL ATOMIC ENERGY COMMISSION.** [Rep. - Isr. A. E. C.]. (19??)-. English. ir. Israel Atomic Energy Commission, Tel Aviv Technical Information Dep, Tel Aviv Israel. **CODEN** IAERAP. Documents available from CASDDS.
**Ind/Abst** Chem. Abstr.

CN/0825-0162
**RESEARCH REPORT / ATOMIC ENERGY CONTROL BOARD.** **See** Energy.

FR/0379-5640
**REUNION - COMITE INTERNATIONAL DES POIDS ET MESURES, COMITE CONSULTATIF POUR LES ETALONS DE MESURE DES RAYONNEMENTS IONISANTS, SECTION II.** [Com. int. poids mes., Com. consult. etal. mes. rayonnem. ionis., Sect. 2 : mes. radionucl.]. **Main/Corp** Comite International des Poids et Mesures. Comite Consultatif pour les Etalons de Mesure des Rayonnements Ionisants. Section II. 1st- 1970-. French. Bureau International des Poids et Mesures, Pavillon de Breteuil, 12 Bis Gde. Rue, 92312 Sevres France. **Tel** 011 33 1 45077070, FAX 011 33 1 65342121, telex 531351 BIPM F. **LC** QC795.42; .C64B. **DD** 539.7/7. **CODEN** CIMRBM. **Circ:** 350. ***Absorbed*** *Comite International des Poids et Mesures. Comite Consultatif pour les Etalons.*
**Desc:** Contains the proceedings of the meetings of the relevant committee whose attendees are representatives of national laboratories engaged in standardization and related researches.

●US/1061-6411
**REVIEW - INSTITUTE OF NUCLEAR POWER OPERATIONS (U.S.).** (REVIEW.). [Rev. - Inst. Nucl. Power Oper. (U.S.)]. **Added/Corp** Institute of Nuclear Power Operations (U.S.). Vol. 1, No.1 Jan.-Feb. (1992)-. Periodical. English. bm. Institute of Nuclear Power Operations, Suite 1500, 1100 Circle, 75 Parkway, Atlanta GA 30339. **DD** 621. ***Formed by the union of*** *Review (Institute of Nuclear Power Operations (U.S.): 1981), 1051-5941* ***and*** *Impact.*
**Ind/Abst** Energy Res. Abstr. (Dec. 1981-).

US/0362-0751
**REVIEW / OAK RIDGE NATIONAL LABORATORY.** [Rev., Oak Ridge Natl. Lab.]. **Main/Corp** Oak Ridge National Laboratory. **VFOAT** Oak Ridge National Laboratory Review. Vol. 1 (Summer 1967)-. Academic Scholarly Publication. English. qt. Free. Oak Ridge National Library, PO Box 2008, Oak Ridge TN 37831. **Tel** (615)574-6755, (615)574-5845. **LC** QC789.3.T43; U516. **DD** 0505. **CODEN** ORNRAH. Documents available from CASDDS.
**Ind/Abst** Chem. Abstr.; Coal Abstr.; Pollut. Abstr. Indexes.

CG/0252-1091
**REVUE ZAIROISE DES SCIENCES NUCLEAIRES.** [Rev. zair. sci. nucl.]. **VFOAT** Zairian Journal of Nuclear Sciences. Vol. 1, No. 1 (June 1980)-. Periodical. English (French). $20.00. Commissariat Generale a l'Energie Atomique, Boite Postale 868, Kinshasa XI Republic du Zaire. **LC** QC770; .R49. **DD** 539.7/05.
**Ind/Abst** Energy Res. Abstr. (Dec. 1981-).

FR/1149-0276
**SESSION D'ETUDES BIENNALE DE PHYSIQUE NUCLEAIRE.** (197?)-. Monographic series. French. **UDC** 539. Documents available from CASDDS.
**Ind/Abst** Chem. Abstr.

US/0038-5506
**SOVIET JOURNAL OF NUCLEAR PHYSICS.** ***Title Change.*** [Sov. j. nucl. phys.]. **Added/Corp** American Institute of Physics. **VFOAT** Yadernaya Fizika. Vol. 1 (July 1965)-(1992). Periodical. English (Russian). mo. American Institute of Physics, 500 Sunnyside Boulevard, Woodbury NY 11797-2999. **Tel** (516)576-2200, FAX (516)349-7669, telex 960983. **(Subscription address:** UK/ Institute of Physics, Techno House, Redcliffe Way, Bristol BS1 6NX England**)** **LC** QC770; .S64. **DD** 539. **CODEN** SJNCAS. **[CCC].** cum. index. **Pr Rev.** available on microfilm. Documents available from The Genuine Article, Ask*IEEE, CASDDS. ***Continued by*** *Physics of Atomic Nuclei.*
**Ind/Abst** Chem. Abstr. (?-?); Curr. Contents Phys. Chem. Earth Sci.; Curr. Phys. Index; Energy Res. Abstr.; INSPEC (1968-); Math. Rev.; Res. Alert [Full Cov.]; Sci. Cit. Index; SCISEARCH; SPIN (1970-); Zentralbl. Math. Ihre Grenzgeb.

US/0090-4759
**SOVIET JOURNAL OF PARTICLES AND NUCLEI.** ***Title Change.*** [Sov. j. part. nucl.]. **Added/Corp** American Institute of Physics. Consultants Bureau. (19??)-(1993). Periodical. English (Russian). bm. American Institute of Physics, 500 Sunnyside Boulevard, Woodbury NY 11797-2999. **Tel** (516)576-2200, FAX (516)349-7669, telex 960983. **(Subscription address:** UK/ Institute of Physics, Techno House, Redcliffe Way, Bristol BS1 6NX England**)** **LC** QC793; .F5913. **DD** 539.7/21/05. **CODEN** SJPNA3. **[CCC].** available on microfilm. Documents available from Ask*IEEE. ***Continued by*** *Physics of Particles and Nuclei.*
**Ind/Abst** Curr. Phys. Index; Energy Res. Abstr. (Feb. 1973-); INSPEC (Jan.-March 1973-); Math. Rev.; SPIN (1975-).

US/8756-4475
**SUBNUCLEAR SERIES, THE.** [Subnucl. ser.]. **Added/Corp** International School of Subnuclear Physics. Vol. 1 (1963)-. Academic Scholarly Publication. English. ir. Price varies per volume. Plenum Press, 233 Spring Street, New York NY 10013-1578. **Tel** (212)620-8000, (800)221-9369, FAX (212)463-0742, (212)807-1047, telex 23/421139. **ED** Antonio Zichichi. **DD** 539. **CODEN** SUSEE4. Documents available from CASDDS.
**Ind/Abst** Chem. Abstr. (1984-).

US
**SUMMARIES OF RESEARCH IN NUCLEAR PHYSICS.** **Main/Corp** United States. Dept. of Energy. Division of Nuclear Physics. English. an. US Department of Energy Office of Energy Research, 1000 Independence Avenue SW, Room 7B-058, Washington DC 20585. **Tel** (202)586-5430, FAX (202)586-4120.

SZ/0142-2413
**SURVEYS IN HIGH ENERGY PHYSICS.** [Surv. high energy phys.]. Vol. 1, No. 1 (Oct. 1979)-. Academic Scholarly Publication. English. qt. $441.00 (academic institutions), $688.00 (corporate institutions). Harwood Academic Publishers, PO Box 90, Reading RG1 8JL England. **Tel** 011 44 734 560080. **(Subscription address:** International Publishers Distributor at one of the following addresses: 820 Town Center Drive, Langhorne, PA 19047; or PO Box 90, Reading Berkshire RG1 8JL UK; or Kent Ridge PO Box 1180, Singapore 9111, Republic of Singapore**)** **ED** J. M. Charap. **LC** QC793; .S88. **DD** 539.7/21/05. **CODEN** SHEPDB. **[CCC]. Bk Rev. Ad Acc.** Documents available from Article Express International, Ask*IEEE, CASDDS.
**Ind/Abst** Chem. Abstr. (1979-1986); Ei Page One; Eng. Index Annu.; INSPEC (1980-).

SZ/0036-777X
**SVA BULLETIN : OFFIZIELLES ORGAN DER SVA UND DESOAF.** **Added/Corp** Schweizerische Vereinigung fur Atomenergie. Osterreichisches Atomforum. (19??)-. Bulletin. German (French). Twenty-one times a year. 370.00F. Schweizerische Vereinigung fur Atomenergie, Postfach 5032, CH-3001 Bern Switzerland. **Tel** 011 41 312 25882, FAX 011 41 312 16972, telex 912 110. **ED** Dr. Peter Zuhlke. **LC** QC770; .S3. **DD** 539.7/05. Index available. **Bk Rev. Ad Acc. Circ:** 1,800. ***Continues*** *Bulletin (Schweizerische Vereinigung for Atomenergie).*

IS
**TRANSACTIONS - THE ISRAEL NUCLEAR SOCIETY, THE ISRAEL HEALTH PHYSICS SOCIETY, RADIATION RESEARCH SOCIETY OF ISRAEL, THE ISRAEL SOCIETY OF MEDICAL PHYSICS, THE ISRAEL SOCIETY OF NUCLEAR MEDICINE.** **Main/Corp** Agudah Ha-Yisreelit Le-Madae Ha-GArin. English. Israel Institute of Technology, Haifa, Technion City, Israel. **LC** QC770; .A37A. **DD** 539.7/05.

TU/0254-5446
**TURKISH JOURNAL OF NUCLEAR SCIENCES.** (TURKISH JOURNAL OF NUCLEAR SCIENCES / TURKISH ATOMIC ENERGY COMMISSION.). [Turk. j. nucl. sci.]. **Added/Corp** Atom Energisi Komisyonu (Turkey). (1981)-. Academic Scholarly Publication. English. Twice a year (June, Dec.). Free. Turkish Atomic Energy Commission, Alacam Sokak 9, 11 Cankaya Ankara Turkey. **Tel** 011 910 41 1273071, FAX 1181938, telex 44455. **ED** Atilla Ozmen. **CODEN** TJNSDM. **Ad Acc.** ctrl circ. available on microfilm; available on videocassette; available on diskette. Documents available from CASDDS. ***Continues*** *Technical Journal (Atom Enerjisi Komisyonu (Turkey)).*
**Ind/Abst** Chem. Abstr.; Coal Abstr.; Energy Inf. Abstr.; Energy Res. Abstr. (Jan. 1982-).

RU/0207-0472
**VOPROSY ATOMNOI NAUKI I TEKHNIKI. SERIIA OBSHCHAIA I IADERNAIA FIZIKA.** [Vopr. at. nauki teh., Ser., Obsc. jad. fiz.]. **Added/Corp** Fizyko-Tekhnichnyi Instytut (Akademiia Nauk Ukrainskoi RSR) TSentralnyi Nauchno-Issledovatelskii Institut Informatsii i Tekhniko-Ekonomicheskikh Issledovanii po Atomnoi Nauke i Tekhnike. **VFOAT** Seriia Obshchaia i Iadernaia Fizika.; Obshchaia i Iadernaia Fizika. (197?)-. Academic Scholarly Publication. Russian. **CODEN** VANFDA. Documents available from CASDDS.
**Ind/Abst** Chem. Abstr.; Int. Aerosp. Abstr.

RU/0207-0480
**VOPROSY ATOMNOI NAUKI I TEKHNIKI. SERIIA TEKHNIKA FIZICHESKOGO EKSPERIMENTA.** **Added/Corp** Fizyko-Tekhnichnyi Instytut (Akademiia Nauk Ukrainskoi RSR) TSentralnyi Nauchno-Issledovatelskii Institut Informatsii i Tekhniko-Ekonomicheskikh Issledovanii po Atomnoi Nauke i Tekhnike. **VFOAT** Seriia Tekhnika Fizicheskogo Eksperimenta; Tekhnika Fizicheskogo Eksperimenta. (19??)-. Academic Scholarly Publication. Russian. **LC** PAR. **CODEN** VASEDW. Documents available from CASDDS.
**Ind/Abst** Chem. Abstr. (1982-).

RU
**VOPROSY TEORETICHESKOI I IADERNOI FIZIKI.** **Added/Corp** Saratovskii Gosudarstvennyi Universitet Im. N.G. Chernyshevskogo. Kafedra Teoreticheskoi i Iadernoi Fiziki. Saratovskii Gosudarstvennyi Universitet im. N.G. Chernyshevskogo. Kafedra Elektroniki. Saratovskii Gosudarstvennyi Universitet im. N.G. Chernyshevskogo. Problemnaia Laboratoriia Iadernoi Fiziki. Vol. 4 (1973)-. Academic Scholarly Publication. Russian. 1.05rub (single issue). Saratov N.G. Chernyshevskii State University, Astrakhanskaya Ulitsa 83, 410071 Saratov Russia. **Tel** 24-16-96, FAX 24-04-46, telex 241125. **LC** QC770; .N42. **CODEN** VTYFDS. Documents available from CASDDS. ***Continues*** *Kvantovo-Polevye Metody i Ikh Premenenie.*
**Ind/Abst** Chem. Abstr. (?-1973);(-1973).

KO
**WONJARYOK KISUL CHONGBO.** Periodical. Korean. Hanguk Wonjaryok Yonguso, PO Box 7 Chongyangni, Seoul South Korea. **LC** QC770; .W63. ctrl circ.

CC/0253-3790
**YUANZIHE WULI.** ***Ceased.*** (YUAN TZU HO WU LI.). [Yuanzihe wuli]. **VFOAT** Chinese Journal of Nuclear Physics. Vol. 1 ( )-(1989). Academic Scholarly Publication. Chinese (summaries and/or abstracts in English). qt. Science Press, 16 Donghuangchenggen North Street, Beijing 100707, People's Republic of China. **Tel** 011 86 1 4019821, 011 86 1 4010642, FAX 011 86 1 4012180, 011 86 1 4019810, telex 210147. **ED** Yuan Zhi-Shang. **LC** QC770; .Y83. **DD** 539.7/05. **CODEN** YTHLDS. **Bk Rev. Ad Acc. Circ:** 2,000. Documents available from Ask*IEEE, CASDDS.
**Desc:** Covers academic theses in theoretical nuclear physics and experimental nuclear physics.
**Ind/Abst** Chem. Abstr. (?-?); Chem. Titles (?-?); Energy Res. Abstr. (Oct. 1982-); INIS Atomindex [Micro.]; INSPEC (1982-).

GW/0939-7922
**ZEITSCHRIFT FUER PHYSIK. A, HADRONS AND NUCLEI.** [Z. Physik., A Hadrons nuclei]. **Added/Corp** Deutsche Physikalische Gesellschaft (1963- ). **VFOAT** Hadrons and Nuclei. Vol. 338, No. 1 (Jan. 1991)-. Academic Scholarly Publication. English. Twelve times a year. DM2094.00. Springer-Verlag GmbH & Company KG, Heidelberger Platz 3, D 14197 Berlin Germany. **Tel** 011 49 30 8207223, FAX 011 49 30 8214091, telex 183 319 SPBLN D. **(Subscription address:** Springer Verlag New York Inc. / for North America, 44 Hartz Way, Secaucus NJ 07096.**)** **LC** QC1; .Z428. **DD** 539.7/216/05. **CODEN** ZPAHEX. available on microfilm and microfiche from University Microfilms International (UMI). Documents available from The Genuine Article, Ask*IEEE, CASDDS. ***Continues*** *Zeitschrift fur Physik. A, Atomic Nuclei, 0930-1151.*
**Ind/Abst** Chem. Abstr.; Curr. Contents Phys. Chem. Earth Sci.; INSPEC (1991-); Res. Alert [Full Cov.]; Sci. Cit. Index; SCISEARCH.

## SOUND

US/0270-5117
**ACOUSTICAL IMAGING.** (ACOUSTICAL IMAGING : PROCEEDINGS.). [Acoust. imag.]. **Main/Conf** International Symposium on Acoustical Imaging. (1979)-. Academic Scholarly Publication. English. ir. Price varies per volume. Plenum Press, 233 Spring Street, New York NY 10013-1578. **Tel** (212)620-8000, (800)221-9369, FAX (212)463-0742, (212)807-1047, telex 23/421139. **LC** QC244.5; .I53A. **DD** 621.36/75. **CODEN** ACIGD9. **[CCC].** Documents available from Article Express International, Ask*IEEE,

CASDDS. ***Continues*** *Acoustical Imaging, 0270-5117.*
**Ind/Abst** Bioeng. Abstr.; Chem. Abstr.; Ei Page One; Eng. Index Annu.; GeoRef; INSPEC.

●US/1063-7710
**ACOUSTICAL PHYSICS.** [Acoust. phys.]. **Added/Corp** American Institute of Physics. **VFOAT** Acoustics. Vol. 39, No. 1 (Jan./Feb. 1993)-. Academic Scholarly Publication. English (translations available in Russian). bm. $970.00 US. American Institute of Physics, 500 Sunnyside Boulevard, Woodbury NY 11797-2999. **Tel** (516)576-2200, FAX (516)349-7669, telex 960983. **LC** QC221; .S6. **DD** 534. **CODEN** AOUSEK. **[CCC].** Index available (bound in last issue). Documents available from Article Express International, Ask*IEEE, CASDDS. ***Continues*** *Soviet Physics. Acoustics, 0038-562X.*
**Ind/Abst** Chem. Abstr.; Curr. Phys. Index; Ei Page One; EMBASE; Energy Res. Abstr.; Eng. Index Annu.; INSPEC; Int. Aerosp. Abstr.; Math. Rev.; Nucl. Sci. Abstr.; Life Sci. Collect.; Sci. Cit. Index; SPIN.

UK/0001-4974
**ACOUSTICS ABSTRACTS. See** Physics-Abstracting, Bibliographies and Statistics.

AT/0814-6039
**ACOUSTICS AUSTRALIA / AUSTRALIAN ACOUSTICAL SOCIETY.** **Added/Corp** Australian Acoustical Society. Began with Vol. 13 No. 1, Apr. (1985)-. Periodical. English. Three times a year. 28.00Aus$ (one year), 56.00 Aus$ (two year), $84.00 (three year) Australia; 40.00Aus$ (one year), 80.00Aus$ (two year), 120.00Aus$ (three year) other. Acoustics Australia, PO Box 579, Cronulla 2230 NSW Australia. **Tel** 011 61 2 5284362, FAX 011 61 2 5239637. Documents available from Ask*IEEE. ***Continues*** *Bulletin (Australian Acoustical Society), 0310-1029.*
**Ind/Abst** Ei Page One; Highw. Res. Abstr.; INSPEC (Vol. 13, No. 1 April 1985-); Shock Vibr. Dig.

UK/0308-437X
**ACOUSTICS BULLETIN.** [Acoust. bull.]. (1976)-. Bulletin. English. bm. £33.00. Institute of Acoustics, PO Box 320 St. Albans, Herts AL1 1PZ England. **Tel** 011 44 727 48195, FAX 011 44 727 50553. **ED** J.W.Tyler. **Circ:** 2,500. ***Continues*** *Newsletter - Institute of Acoustics.*

UK/0140-1599
**ACOUSTICS LETTERS.** [Acoust. lett.]. Vol. 1 (1977)-. Academic Scholarly Publication. English. mo. $166.00. Parjon Information Services, PO Box 144, Haywards Heath, West Sussex RH16 2YX England. **ED** J.C. Scott. **CODEN** ACLEDI. Index available. **Bk Rev. Pr Rev.** Documents available from Ask*IEEE, CASDDS.
**Desc:** Short papers on all aspects of acoustics.
**Ind/Abst** Chem. Abstr.; Ei Page One; INSPEC (July 1979-); Int. Aerosp. Abstr.

GW/0001-7884
**ACUSTICA.** [Acustica]. Vol. 1 (1951)-. Periodical. English (French and German). Six times a year. DM672.00. S. Hirzel Verlag Stuttgart, Postfach 101061, D 70009 Stuttgart Germany. **Tel** 011 49 711 25820, FAX 0711/2582 290, telex 723636 daz d. **ED** G. Canevet, R. C. Chivers, H. Kuttruff. **LC** QC221; .A5. **DD** 534.05. **CODEN** ACUSAY. **[CCC].** Index available. **Bk Rev. Ad Acc. Pr Rev. Circ:** 1,500. Documents available from Article Express International, The Genuine Article, BIOSIS Document Express, Ask*IEEE, CASDDS, Documents on Demand.
**Desc:** Original research and books concerning acoustics.
**Ind/Abst** Acoust. Abstr.; Appl. Mech. Rev.; Bioeng. Abstr.; Biol. Abstr.; Chem. Abstr.; CIS Abstr.; Curr. Contents Eng. Tech. Appl. Sci.; Curr. Contents Phys. Chem. Earth Sci.; Ei Page One; EMBASE; Energy Inf. Abstr.; Energy Res. Abstr.; Eng. Index Annu.; Environ. Abstr.; INSPEC (1968-); Int. Aerosp. Abstr.; Int. Civil Eng. Abstr.; Linguist. Lang. Behav. Abstr.; Math. Rev.; Nucl. Sci. Abstr.; Life Sci. Collect.; Pollut. Abstr. Indexes; Res. Alert [Full Cov.]; Saf. Health Work; Sci. Cit. Index; SCISEARCH; Shock Vibr. Dig.; Soc. Plann. Policy Dev. Abstr.; Sociol. Abstr.; Soft. Abstr. Eng.; Zentralbl. Math. Ihre Grenzgeb.

US
**AES : JOURNAL OF THE AUDIO ENGINEERING SOCIETY, AUDIO/ACOUSTICS/APPLICATIONS.** **See** Sound Recordings and Systems.

RU/0320-7919
**AKUSTICESKIJ ZURNAL.** (AKUSTICHESKII ZHURNAL.). [Akust. z.]. **Added/Corp** Akademiia Nauk SSSR. Vol. 1, (1955)-. Academic Scholarly Publication. Russian. bm. $192.00. Izdatelstvo Nauka / Akademiia Nauk, Publishing House of the Russian Academy of Sciences, Leninskii Porspekt 14, 117901 Moscow Russia. **Tel** 011 95 954-21-53, FAX 011 95 938-21-44, telex 411964. **(Subscription address:** East View Publications Inc., 3020 Harbor Lane North, Suite 110, Minneapolis MN 55447.**)** **LC** QC221; .A53. **CODEN** AKZHAE. **[CCC].** Index available. **Bk Rev.** Documents available from Article Express International, Ask*IEEE, CASDDS.
**Ind/Abst** Acoust. Abstr.; Chem. Abstr.; Eng. Index Annu.; INSPEC (1968-); Int. Aerosp. Abstr. (19??-19??); Math. Rev.

PL/0137-5075
**ARCHIVES OF ACOUSTICS.** (ARCHIVES OF ACOUSTICS QUARTERLY.). [Arch. acoust.]. **Added/Corp** Polska Akademia Nauk. Komitet Akustyki. Polskie Towarzystwo Akustyczne. Vol. 1 (1976)-. Academic Scholarly Publication. English (Polish). qt. $120.00. **(Subscription address:** ARS Polona, PO Box 1001, 00068 Warsaw Poland.**)** **LC** QC221; .A72. **DD** 534/.05. **CODEN** AACODN. Documents available from Article Express International, Ask*IEEE, CASDDS.
**Ind/Abst** Acoust. Abstr.; Bioeng. Abstr.; Chem. Abstr.; Ei Page One; Eng. Index Annu.; INSPEC (1978-).

CC/1001-1455
**BAOZHA YU CHONGJI.** (PAO CHA YU CHUNG CHI.). [Baozha yu chongji]. **Added/Corp** Chung-Kuo Li Hsueh Hsueh Hui. **VFOAT** Explosion and Shock Waves. (19??)-. Periodical. Chinese (summaries and/or abstracts in English). qt. **LC** QD516; .P26. **CODEN** BAYCE7. Documents available from CASDDS.
**Ind/Abst** Chem. Abstr.

US/0882-5432
**BILL DANIELS' ILLUSTRATED TRADE REFERENCES. PROFESSIONAL AUDIO AND COMMERCIAL/INDUSTRIAL SOUND EQUIPMENT BUYERS' GUIDE.** (PROFESSIONAL AUDIO AND COMMERCIAL/INDUSTRIAL SOUND EQUIPMENT BUYERS' GUIDE.). [Bill Daniels' illus. trade ref., Prof. audio commer./ind. sound equip. buy. guide]. **Added/Corp** Bill Daniels Co. **VFOAT** Professional Audio and Commercial, Industrial Sound Equipment Buyers' guide; Audio; Audio Equipment Buyers' Guide. (1988)-. Consumer Publication. English. $195.00. Bill Daniels Company, PO Box 2056, Shawnee Mission KS 66201. **Tel** (913)492-9900. **LC** TS2301.A7; I47. **DD** 621.389/3/029473. ***Continues*** *Illustrated Audio Buyers Guide, 0749-355X.*

CC
**CHINESE JOURNAL OF ACOUSTICS.** (CHINESE JOURNAL OF ACOUSTICS / EDITED BY THE ACOUSTICAL SOCIETY OF CHINA.). **Added/Corp** Chung-Kuo Sheng Hsueh Hsueh Hui. Vol. 1, No. 1 (July/Sept. 1982)-. Periodical. English. qt. $325.00. Allerton Press, Inc., 150 Fifth Avenue, New York NY 10011. **Tel** (212)924-3950, FAX (212)463-9684, telex 427441 ALPRES. **Bk Rev. Ad Acc.**
**Desc:** Publishes original research papers and technical notes on all aspects of acoustics, covering both theoretical and experimental aspects.

US
**DB THE SOUND ENGINEERING MAGAZINE.** Vol. 23, No. 3 (May/June 1989)-. Periodical. English. Six times a year (Jan., Mar., May, July, Sept., Nov.). $18.00 US; $21.00 Canada & Mexico; $28.00 other. ELAR, 203 Commack Road, Suite 1010, Commack NY 11725. **Tel** (516)433-6530. ***Continues*** *DB (Plainville, N.Y.).*

US
**DIRECTORY OF EDUCATIONAL PROGRAMS (NEW YORK, N.Y. : 1984).** (DIRECTORY OF EDUCATIONAL PROGRAMS / [PREPARED BY THE EDUCATION COMMITTEE OF THE AUDIO ENGINEERING SOCIETY].). **Added/Corp** Audio Engineering Society. Education Committee. (1984)-. English. ir. $6.00 per copy. Audio Engineering Society Inc, 60 East 42nd Street, Room 2520, New York NY 10165. **Tel** (212)661-8528, (800)541-7299, FAX (212)682-0477. **LC** TK5981; .D53. **DD** 621.389/3/071.

BE/0422-888X
**ELECTROACOUSTIQUE.** [Electroacoustique]. No. 1- July 1959-. Periodical. French. ir. 400F Belgium; 480F other. Monte Fiore Institute, University of Liege, 33 rue St Gilles, Liege Belgium. **CODEN** ELACBS. Documents available from Ask*IEEE.
**Ind/Abst** INSPEC (Aug. 1969-).

KO
**HANGUK UMHYANG HAKHOE CHI. See** Engineering.

US/0885-3010
**IEEE TRANSACTIONS ON ULTRASONICS, FERROELECTRICS, AND FREQUENCY CONTROL.** [IEEE trans. ultrason. ferroelectr. freq. control]. **Added/Corp** IEEE Ultrasonics, Ferroelectrics, and Frequency Control Society. **VFOAT** Transactions on Ultrasonics, Ferroelectrics, and Frequency Control; Ultrasonics, Ferroelectrics, and Frequency Control. Vol. UFFC-33, No. 1 (Jan. 1986)-. Academic Scholarly Publication. English. bm. $230.00. IEEE, Institution of Electrical and Electronics Engineers, Inc., 345 East 47th Street, New York NY 10017-2394. **Tel** (908)981-1393, FAX (908)981-9667. **(Subscription address:** IEEE / Institute of Electrical and Electronics Engineers, 445 Hoes Lane, PO Box 1331, Piscataway NJ 08855-1331.**)** **LC** QC244; .I53. **DD** 620.2/8. **CODEN** ITUCER. **[CCC]. Pr Rev.** Documents available from Article Express International, The Genuine Article, Ask*IEEE, CASDDS. ***Continues*** *IEEE Transactions on Sonics and Ultrasonics, 0018-9537.*
**Desc:** Covers the theory, design, and application on generation, transmission, and detection of bulk and surface mechanical waves; fundamental studies in physical acoustics; design of sonic and ultrasonic devices and their applications in industry, biomedicine, and signal processing.
**Ind/Abst** Acoust. Abstr.; Bioeng. Abstr. (1986-); Chem. Abstr. (1986-); Comput. Lit. Index; Curr. Contents Eng. Tech. Appl. Sci.; Ei Page One (1986-); EMBASE (1986-); Energy Res. Abstr. (1986-); Eng. Index Annu.; Expand. Acad. Index (1992-); HTFS Dig.; Index IEEE Publ. (Jan. 1986-); INIS Atomindex [Micro.]; INSPEC (Jan. 1986-); Int. Aerosp. Abstr. (1986-); Phys. Med. Biol. (19??-19??); Res. Alert [Full Cov.]; Sci. Cit. Index; SCISEARCH.

FR/0988-4319
**JOURNAL D'ACOUSTIQUE.** ***Title Change.*** Vol. 1, No. 1 (Mar.-June 1988)-(19??). Periodical. French (English, German and Russian). Six times a year. CNET SFA Secretariat, Route de Tregastel, 22300 Lannion France. **Tel** 011 33 96 052029. **(Subscription address:** Editions de Physique, Zi de Courtaboeuf, BP 112, 91944 Les Ulis Cedex France.**)** **[CCC].** Documents available from Ask*IEEE. ***Merged into*** *Acta Acustica.*
**Ind/Abst** INSPEC (1988-).

SI/0218-396X
**JOURNAL OF COMPUTATIONAL ACOUSTICS.** English. Four times a year. $105.00 individuals, $205.00 institutions. World Scientific Publishing Company, PO Box 128, Farrer Road, Singapore 9128 Singapore. **Tel** 011 65 3825663, FAX 011 65 3825919, telex RS 28561 WSPC. **(Subscription address:** US: World Scientific Publishing Co., Inc., 1060 Main Street, River Edge, NJ 07661 Telephone: (201)487-9655, Fax: (201)487-9656; Europe: World Scientific Publishing Co Ltd, 73 Lynton Mead, Totteridge, London N20 8DH United Kingdom Telephone: 011 44 81 4462461, Fax: 011 44 81 4463356; India: World Scientific Publishing Co Pte Ltd, 4911 9th Floor, High Point IV, 45 Palace Road, Bangalore 560 001 India Telephone: (80) 2205972, Fax: (80) 3344593, Telex: 0845-2900 PCO IN; Hong Kong: World Scientific Publishing (HK) Co, PO Box 72482, Kowloon Central Post Office, Hong Kong Telephone: 852-7718791, Fax: 852-7718155**)**

UK/0022-460X
**JOURNAL OF SOUND AND VIBRATION.** [J. sound vib.]. Vol. 1 (Jan. 1964)-. Academic Scholarly Publication. English. Fifty times a year. $3225.00. Academic Press Ltd., A Division of Harcourt Brace & Company Ltd., 24-28 Oval Road, London NW1 7DX England. **Tel** 071 267 4466, FAX 071 482 2293, 071 485 4752, telex 25775 ACPRES G. **(Subscription address:** Harcourt Brace & Company, Ltd., Foots Cray, High Street, Sidcup Kent DA14 5HP England.**)** **ED** P. E. Doak and W. Soedel. **LC** QC221; .J6. **NLM** W1 JO901N. **CODEN** JSVIAG. **[CCC]. Pr Rev.** Documents available from Article Express International, The Genuine Article, BIOSIS Document Express, Ask*IEEE.
**Desc:** Devoted to the prompt publication of original papers on experimental and theoretical work on any aspect of sound and vibration, and serves as an official medium of publication for the Institute of Acoustics.
**Ind/Abst** Abstr. J. Earthq. Eng.; Acoust. Abstr.; Bioeng. Abstr.; Biol. Abstr.; Curr. Contents Eng. Tech. Appl. Sci.; Curr. Technol. Index (1973-); Ei Page One; EMBASE; Eng. Index Annu.; Ergon. Abstr.; Fluid Abstr., Civil Eng.; Fluid Abstr. Proc. Eng.; FLUIDEX (1973-1990); Health Saf. Sci. Abstr.; Highw. Res. Abstr.; HTFS Dig.; INSPEC (1968-); Int. Aerosp. Abstr.; Math. Rev.; Life Sci. Collect.; Pollut. Abstr. Indexes; Res. Alert [Full Cov.]; Saf. Health Work; Sci. Cit. Index; SCISEARCH; Shock Vibr. Dig.; Zentralbl. Math. Ihre Grenzgeb.

US/0001-4966
**JOURNAL OF THE ACOUSTICAL SOCIETY OF AMERICA, THE.** [J. Acoust. Soc. Am.]. **Added/Corp** Acoustical Society of America. Vol. 1 (Oct. 1929)-. Academic Scholarly Publication. English. mo (plus three supplements). $855.00 US; $895.00 Canada, Mexico, Central and South America, and the Caribbean; $955.00 other. American Institute of Physics, 500 Sunnyside Boulevard, Woodbury NY 11797-2999. **Tel** (516)576-2200, FAX (516)349-7669, telex 960983. **ED** Dr. Daniel W. Martin. **NLM** W1 JO907D. **CODEN** JASMAN. **[CCC].** Index available (free). cum. index. **Pr Rev.** available on microfilm; available on microfiche. Documents available from Article Express International, The Genuine Article, BIOSIS Document Express, Ask*IEEE, Petroleum Abstracts Document Delivery Service, CASDDS, Documents on Demand.
**Desc:** Emphasis on both the theory and applications in acoustics.
**Ind/Abst** Abstr. Bull. Inst. Pap. Sci. Tech.; Abstr. J. Earthq. Eng.; Acoust. Abstr.; Annu. Bibliogr. Engl. Lang. Lit.; Appl. Sci. Technol. Index; Aquat. Sci. Fish. Abstr. (Computer File); Biol. Abstr.; Ceram. Abstr.; Chem. Abstr.; Curr. Aware. Biol. Sci., CABS; Curr. Contents Eng. Tech. Appl. Sci.; Curr. Contents Life Sci.; Curr. Phys. Index; Ei Page One; EMBASE; Energy Res. Abstr.; Eng. Index Annu. [Select. Cov.]; Environ. Abstr.; Ergon. Abstr.; Fish Rev.; Fluid Abstr., Civil Eng.; Fluid Abstr. Proc. Eng.; FLUIDEX; Geol. Abstr.; GeoRef; Highw. Res. Abstr.; Index Med.; INIS Atomindex [Micro.]; INSPEC (1968-);

Int. Aerosp. Abstr.; Key Word Index Wildl. Res.; Leadscan; Math. Rev.; Meteorol. Geoastrophys. Abstr.; MLA Int. Bibl. Books Artic. Mod. Lang. Lit.; Ocean. Abstr.; Pet. Abstr.; Psychol. Abstr. (1930-); PsycINFO (1990-); PsycLit; Ref. Upd. Deluxe Ed.; Res. Alert [Full Cov.]; Saf. Health Work; Sci. Cit. Index; SCISEARCH; Shock Vibr. Dig.; Soc. Sci. Cit. Index [Select. Cov.]; SPIN (1970-); Wildl. Rev.; Zentralbl. Math. Ihre Grenzgeb.

JA/0388-2861
**JOURNAL OF THE ACOUSTICAL SOCIETY OF JAPAN (E), THE.** [J. Acoust. Soc. Jpn., E]. **Added/Corp** Nihon Onkyo Gakkai. Vol. 1, No. 1 (Jan. 1980)-. Academic Scholarly Publication. English. Six times a year. $90.00. Nihon Onkyo Gakkai, (Acoustical Society of Japan), Ikeda Biru, 7-7, Yoyogi 2 Chome, Shibuyaku, Tokyoto 151, Japan. **(Subscription address:** Maruzen Company Ltd., PO Box 5050, Import & Export Department, Tokyo 100 31 Japan.**) NLM** W1 JO907E. **CODEN** JASED2. Documents available from Ask*IEEE, Petroleum Abstracts Document Delivery Service.
**Desc:** Contains original papers, technical reports, notes in the areas of architectural acoustics, noise, speech, ultrasonics, etc.
**Ind/Abst** Acoust. Abstr.; Ei Page One; EMBASE; INSPEC (Jan. 1980-); Pet. Abstr.

US/1048-9002
**JOURNAL OF VIBRATION AND ACOUSTICS.** [J. vib. acoust.]. **VFOAT** Vibration and Acoustics. Vol. 112, No. 1 (Jan. 1990)-. Academic Scholarly Publication. English. qt. $140.00 (nonmember), $40.00 (member) US and Canada. American Society of Mechanical Engineers, 22 Law Drive, Fairfield NJ 07007. **Tel** (201)882-1167, (212)705-7722 (editorial). **LC** TA174; .T72. **DD** 620.3. **[CCC].** available on microfilm and microfiche from University Microfilms International (UMI). Documents available from Article Express International, The Genuine Article. ***Continues*** *Journal of Vibration, Acoustics, Stress, and Reliability in Design, 0739-3717.*
**Ind/Abst** Abstr. J. Earthq. Eng.; Alum. Ind. Abstr.; Curr. Contents Eng. Tech. Appl. Sci.; Ei Page One; EMBASE; Eng. Index Annu.; Fluid Abstr., Civil Eng.; Fluid Abstr. Proc. Eng.; FLUIDEX; Int. Aerosp. Abstr.; Met. Abstr.; Res. Alert [Select. Cov.]; Shock Vibr. Dig.

FR
**MECANIQUE ET ACOUSTIC.** French. CNRS / Institut d'Information Scientifique et Technique, (Centre National de la Recherche Scientifique), 15 Quai Anatole France, Paris 75700 France. **Tel** 011 33 1 47531515, telex 299 356 F.

JA/0474-1528
**ONSEI NO KENKYU. THE STUDY OF SOUNDS. Added/Corp** Nihon Onseigakkai. World Congress of Phoneticians. Papers. **VFOAT** Study of Sounds. Vol. 1 (1927)-. English (French, German and Japanese). **(Subscription address:** Japan Publications Trading Company, Ltd., PO Box 5030, Tokyo International, Tokyo 100-31 Japan.**) LC** P215; .O54.

FR/1146-5107
**PASCAL. F 10, MECANIQUE, ACOUSTIQUE ET TRANSFERT DE CHALEUR. VFOAT** PASCAL. F 10, Mechanics, Acoustic and Heat Transfer; PASCAL. F DIX, Mecanique, Acoustique et Transfert de Chaleur. (1990)-. Bibliography. French (English and Spanish). ir (10 issues). 1530.00F France; 1625.00F other. Institut de l'Information Scientique et Technique (INIST), 2 Allee du Parc de Brabois, 54514 Vandoeuvre Nancy Cedex France. **Tel** 011 33 83 504600, FAX 011 33 83 504650. **ED** Mr. Claude Patou. **UDC** 011. **CODEN** 536. Index available. cum. index. **Ad Acc, Adv Mgr:** Ms. Guinuarc. available on microfiche and CD-ROM; available on magnetic tape.

US/0893-388X
**PHYSICAL ACOUSTICS.** (PHYSICAL ACOUSTICS : PRINCIPLES AND METHODS.). [Phys. acoust.]. Vol. 1, Pt. A (1964)-. Academic Scholarly Publication. English. ir. Price varies per volume. Academic Press, Inc., 6277 Sea Harbor Drive, Orlando FL 32887. **Tel** (800)543-9534, (407)345-4100, FAX (407)363-9661. **ED** Warren P. Mason. **LC** QC242.8; .P49. **DD** 534. **CODEN** PHACEM. **[CCC].** Documents available from The Genuine Article, CASDDS.
**Ind/Abst** Chem. Abstr.; Index Sci. Rev. [Full Cov.]; Res. Alert [Full Cov.]; Sci. Cit. Index; SCISEARCH.

UK/0309-8117
**PROCEEDINGS OF THE INSTITUTE OF ACOUSTICS.** [Proc. Inst. Acoust.]. **VFOAT** Proceedings - Institute of Acoustics. (1976)-. English. an. Institute of Acoustics, PO Box 320 St. Albans, Herts AL1 1PZ England. **Tel** 011 44 727 48195, FAX 011 44 727 50553. ***Continues*** *Proceedings - British Acoustical Society, 0309-6742.*

US/1044-4793
**PROFESSIONAL SOUND (DURANGO, COLO. : 1989).** (PROFESSIONAL SOUND.). **Added/Corp** Orion Research Corporation. **VFOAT** Orion Professional Sound Blue Book. (1989)-. English. $114.00. Orion Research Corporation, 14555 North Scottsdale Road, Suite 330, Scottsdale AZ 85260. **Tel** (800)844-0759, (602)951-1114, FAX (602)951-1117. **LC** TK7881.4; .P76. **DD** 621.389/3/0297. ***Continues in part*** *Professional Sound & Musical Instruments.*

CN/1186-1797
**PROFESSIONAL SOUND (TORONTO).** (PROFESSIONAL SOUND.). [Prof. sound]. Vol. 1, No. 1 (Fall 1990)-. Periodical. English. qt. $10.00 Canada; $12.50 other. Norris-Whitney Communications Inc., 23 Hannover Drive Unit 7, St. Catharine Ontario L2W 1A3 Canada. **Tel** (905)641-3471, FAX (905)641-1648. **DD** 621.382/8.

US/0163-0970
**REFERENCES TO CONTEMPORARY PAPERS ON ACOUSTICS.** [Ref. contemp. pap. acoust.]. **Added/Corp** Acoustical Society of America. (1975)-. English. an. Comes with Journal of the Acoustical Society of America; $855.00 US (journal). American Institute of Physics, 500 Sunnyside Boulevard, Woodbury NY 11797-2999. **Tel** (516)576-2200, FAX (516)349-7669, telex 960983. **CODEN** RCACD8. ***Supersedes in part*** *Journal of the Acoustical Society of America, 0001-4966.*
**Ind/Abst** Ocean. Abstr.

UK
**RUSSIAN ULTRASONICS.** Vol. 1, No. 1 (Jan./Mar. 1971)-. Periodical. English. bm. £200.00 UK and Europe; £210.00 (add £15.00 for airmail) other. Multi Science Publishing Company Ltd., 107 High Street, Brentwood, Essex CM14 4RX England. **Tel** 011 44 277 224632, FAX 011 44 277 223453, telex 89-8452. **ED** B. R. V. Hughes, J. M. D. G. Parry. Documents available from Article Express International.
**Desc:** For those with a research or professional interest in ultrasonics.
**Ind/Abst** Eng. Index Annu.

CC/0371-0025
**SHENG HSUEH HSUEH PAO.** [Sheng xue xue bao]. **VFOAT** Acta Acustica. No. 1 (1978)-. Academic Scholarly Publication. Chinese (summaries and/or abstracts in English). bm. $103.20. Science Press, 16 Donghuangchenggen North Street, Beijing 100707, People's Republic of China. **Tel** 011 86 1 4019821, 011 86 1 4010642, FAX 011 86 1 4012180, 011 86 1 4019810, telex 210147. **(Subscription address:** China International Book Trading Corporation, PO Box 399, Library Service Department, Beijing 100044 People's Republic of China.**) LC** QC221; .S53. **DD** 534/.05. **CODEN** SHGHAS. Documents available from Ask*IEEE, CASDDS.
**Ind/Abst** Chem. Abstr. (1978-1983); Energy Res. Abstr. (Oct. 1982-); INSPEC (Oct. 1982-); Math. Rev.; SPIN (1982-).

GW/0938-1287
**SHOCK WAVES. See** Physics-Analytic and Experimental Mechanics.

FR/0243-4938
**SONO PARIS.** (SONO.). (1978)-. Periodical. French. mo (July/Aug. issue combined). 262.00F France; 367.00F other. Publ Georges Ventillard, 2 A 12 rue d Bellevue, 75019 Paris Cedex 19 France. **Tel** 011 33 1 42003305. **UDC** 621.395.6. ***Continues*** *Le Haut-Parleur. Sono, 0243-492X.*

US/0038-562X
**SOVIET PHYSICS-ACOUSTICS. *Title Change.*** [Sov. phys. Acoust.]. **Added/Corp** American Institute of Physics. **VFOAT** Acoustics. Vol. 1 (Jan./June 1955)-(19??). Academic Scholarly Publication. English (Russian). bm. American Institute of Physics, 500 Sunnyside Boulevard, Woodbury NY 11797-2999. **Tel** (516)576-2200, FAX (516)349-7669, telex 960983. **(Subscription address:** UK/ Institute of Physics, Techno House, Redcliffe Way, Bristol BS1 6NX England**) LC** QC221; .S6. **DD** 534.05. **CODEN** SOPAAX. **[CCC]. Pr Rev.** available on microfilm. Documents available from Article Express International, The Genuine Article, Ask*IEEE, CASDDS. ***Continued by*** *Acoustical Physics.*
**Ind/Abst** Acoust. Abstr.; Chem. Abstr.; Curr. Contents Eng. Tech. Appl. Sci.; Curr. Contents Phys. Chem. Earth Sci.; Curr. Phys. Index; Ei Page One; EMBASE; Energy Res. Abstr.; Eng. Index Annu.; INSPEC (1968-); Int. Aerosp. Abstr.; Math. Rev.; Life Sci. Collect.; Res. Alert [Full Cov.]; Sci. Cit. Index; SCISEARCH; SPIN (1970-).

US/0887-6703
**SPECTROSCOPY.** [Spectroscopy]. Vol. 1, No. 1 (Jan. 1986)-. Academic Scholarly Publication. English. Nine times a year. $59.00 US and possessions; $79.00 Canada; $117.00 other. Advanstar Communications Inc., 131 West First Street, Duluth MN 55802. **Tel** (218)723-9477, (800)346-0085. **ED** Michael MacRae. **LC** QC450. **DD** 543/.0858. **NLM** W1; SP3169. **CODEN** SPECET. **[CCC]. Circ:** 30,000. available on microfilm from University Microfilms International (UMI). Documents available from CASDDS.
**Desc:** Publishes concise research and applications articles of immediate interest to users and buyers of all types of spectroscopic equipment and related accessories. The editorial combines practical information with principles of modern science for analysts in industrial, academic, and governement laboratories. Topics include UV/VIS, IR, FT-IR, Laser, NMR, Mass, AA, ICP, Fluorescence, X-ray, Raman spectroscopies, etc.
**Ind/Abst** Abstr. Bull. Inst. Pap. Sci. Tech.; Anal. Abstr.; Chem. Abstr. (1986-); Mass Spect. Bull.

UK/0049-2639
**SURFACE WAVE ABSTRACTS.** Vol. 1, No. 1 (Jan./Mar. 1971)-. Periodical. English. qt. £128.00 UK & Europe; £137.00 other (surface mail), £149.00 (airmail). Multi Science Publishing Company Ltd., 107 High Street, Brentwood, Essex CM14 4RX England. **Tel** 011 44 277 224632, FAX 011 44 277 223453, telex 89-8452. **LC** QC157; .S9. **DD** 531/.1133. **[CCC].** Index available (free). **Bk Rev.**
**Desc:** Covers the world's major periodical literature, conference proceedings and unpublished reports. Represents an invaluable store of knowledge and offers ways of keeping abreast of what is happening in acoustic surface waves.

US/0038-1810
**SV. SOUND AND VIBRATION.** [S.V. Sound vib.]. **VFOAT** Sound and Vibration. Vol. 1 (Jan. 1967)-. Periodical. English. mo. $20.00 US; $25.00 Canada; $60.00 other. Acoustical Publications, 27101 E Oviatt Rd, PO Box 40416, Bay Village OH 44140. **Tel** (216)835-0101, FAX (216)835-9303. **ED** Jack Mowry. **LC** TA365; .S18. **DD** 620.2/05. **CODEN** SOVIAJ. **[CCC].** cum. index. **Ad Acc, Adv Mgr:** Lisa King. **Circ:** 22,000 (ctrl). available on microfilm and microfiche from University Microfilms International (UMI). Documents available from Article Express International, Ask*IEEE, Documents on Demand.
**Desc:** Noise and vibration control, machinery monitoring, structural analysis, dynamic measurements and dynamic testing.
**Ind/Abst** Appl. Sci. Technol. Index; Bioeng. Abstr.; BMT Abstr. (-199?); Ei Page One; Eng. Index Annu.; Environ. Abstr.; Health Saf. Sci. Abstr.; Ind. Hyg. Dig.; INSPEC (June 1971-); Int. Aerosp. Abstr.; Pollut. Abstr. Indexes; Saf. Health Work; Shock Vibr. Dig.; Soc. Plann. Policy Dev. Abstr.

US/1050-4443
**YEAR BOOK OF ULTRASOUND, THE.** [Year book ultrasound]. **VFOAT** Yearbook of Ultrasound; Ultrasound. (1991)-. Periodical. English. an (Sept.). $75.00. Mosby Year Book Inc., 11830 Westline Industrial Drive, St Louis MO 63146. **Tel** (800)325-4177, (314)872-8370, FAX (314)432-1380, telex 44-2402. **LC** RC78.7.U4; Y4. **DD** 616.07/543/05. **NLM** W1; YE344.

CC
**YING YUNG SHENG HSUEH. See** Engineering.

## PLASTICS

UK
**ADVANCED COMPOSITES BULLETIN.** (1987)-. Bulletin. English. Twelve times a year (1 volume). $397.00 The Americas; £266.00 other. Elsevier Advanced Technology, An Imprint of Elsevier Science Ltd., The Boulevard, Langford Lane, Kidlington, Oxford OX5 1GB United Kingdom. **Tel** 011 44 865 843000, 011 44 865 843699, FAX 011 44 865 843010. **(Subscription address:** Elsevier Science Ltd. Oxford Fulfillment Centre, PO Box 800, Kidlington, Oxford OX5 1DX United Kingdom.**) ED** Dr. Paul Hogg. available on microfilm from University Microfilms International (UMI); available on an online database (file 636/Full-Text) from DIALOG.
**Desc:** Reports on all forms of advanced composites and the development of manufacturing techniques: including organic and inorganic fibres and fillers, polymer, metal and ceramic matrices, hybrid and macrocomposite systems, pultrusion, resin transfer and injection moulding, and sheet moulding and bulk moulding compounds.
**Ind/Abst** PTS Newsl. Database [Full Txt.].

US/1058-7489
**ADVANCES IN POLYMER BLENDS AND ALLOYS TECHNOLOGY.** [Adv. polym. blends alloys technol.]. Vol. 1 (1988)-. Periodical. English. an. $55.00 (vol. 5), $175.00 (vol. 1-5). Technomic Publishing Company, Inc., 851 New Holland Avenue, Box 3535, Lancaster PA 17604. **Tel** (717)291-5609, (800)233-9936, FAX (717)295-4538. **LC** TP1080; .A38. **DD** 668.9/05. **CODEN** APBTE3. Documents available from CASDDS.
**Ind/Abst** Chem. Abstr.

US/0730-6679
**ADVANCES IN POLYMER TECHNOLOGY.** [Adv. polym. technol.]. Vol. 2, No. 1 (Winter 1982)-. Academic Scholarly Publication. English. qt. $412.00 US; $452.00 Canada and Mexico; $467.00 other. John Wiley & Sons, Inc., 605 Third Avenue, New York NY 10158-0012. **Tel** (212)850-6000, (212)850-6645, FAX (212)850-6088, telex 12-7063. **(Subscription address:** John Wiley & Sons / England, Baffins Lane, Chichester, West Sussex PO19 1UD England.**) ED** Marino Xanthos. **LC** TP1101; .A38. **DD** 668.9/05. **CODEN** APTYD5. **[CCC]. Ad Acc. Circ:** 500. available on CD-ROM; available on microfilm and microfiche from University Microfilms International (UMI).

Documents available from Article Express International, CASDDS. ***Continues*** *Advances in Plastics Technology, 0272-9504.*
**Desc:** Presents important developments in polymeric materials, production and processing methods, and equipment and product design. In addition to original articles on trends and advances in polymer technology, the journal welcomes review articles, technico-economic studies, and patent reviews, as well as short communications on new processing and product technologies for plastics, elastomers, and other polymers.
**Ind/Abst** Bioeng. Abstr.; Chem. Abstr.; Ei Page One; Eng. Mater. Abstr.; Eng. Index Annu.; FLUIDEX (19??-); Pollut. Abstr. Indexes; Polymer Contents.

US/1073-1776
**AGRI-PLASTICS REPORT, THE. See** Agriculture.

SZ/0003-3146
**ANGEWANDTE MAKROMOLEKULARE CHEMIE.** (DIE ANGEWANDTE MAKROMOLEKULARE CHEMIE. APPLIED MACROMOLECULAR CHEMISTRY AND PHYSICS.). [Angew. makromol. chem.]. **VFOAT** Applied Macromolecular Chemistry and Physics. Vol. 1 (Dec. 1967)-. Periodical. German (English and French). Ten times a year. $98.00. Huethig & Wepf Verlag, Auf Dem Wolf 4, CH 4018 Basel Switzerland. **Tel** 011 41 61 3115125. **ED** D. Braun. **LC** TP1101; .A5. **DD** 668/.4/05. **NLM** W1 AN223L. **CODEN** ANMCBO. **[CCC].** cum. index. **Ad Acc. Pr Rev.** Documents available from The Genuine Article, CASDDS.
**Ind/Abst** AGRICOLA; Chem. Abstr.; Chem. Titles; Coal Abstr.; Curr. Biotechnol.; Curr. Contents Phys. Chem. Earth Sci.; Energy Res. Abstr.; Int. Aerosp. Abstr.; Leadscan; Polymer Contents; Res. Alert [Full Cov.]; Sci. Cit. Index; SCISEARCH; World Surf. Coat. Abstr.; World Text. Abstr.

UK/0307-6164
**BP&R BRITISH PLASTICS AND RUBBER.** (BRITISH PLASTICS AND RUBBER.). [BP&R Br. plast. rubber]. **VFOAT** BP&R. (Oct. 1975)-. Periodical. English. Twelve times a year. £65.00 UK; £90.00 other. MCM Publishing Ltd, 37 Nelson Road, Caterham, Surrey CR3 5PP England. **Tel** 011 44 883 347059, FAX 011 44 81 675 8046. **ED** Peter Taylor. **LC** HD9661.G7; B73. **DD** 338.4/7/66840941. **[CCC]. Ad Acc. Circ:** 14,380 (ctrl). available on an online database (file 648/Full-Text) from DIALOG. Documents available from Article Express International. ***Continues*** *Polymer Age.*
**Desc:** Technical magazine for UK plastics and rubber processors. Detailing developments in materials processing machinery and ancillary equipment.
**Ind/Abst** Curr. Technol. Index; Ei Page One; EMBASE; Eng. Index Annu. [Select. Cov.]; Int. Packag. Abstr.; Leadscan; Text. Technol. Dig.; Trade Ind. ASAP [Full Txt.]; Trade Ind. Index [Full Txt.].

CN/1187-127X
**BULLETIN SUR LES COMPOSITES.** (BULLETIN SUR LES COMPOSITES / FIBERGLAS CANADA, INC.). [Bull. compos.]. **Added/Corp** Fiberglas Canada Ltee. **VFOAT** Nouvelles Realisations en Plastique Renforce de Fibres de Verre (PRF). Vol. 30, No. 1 (Spring 1991)-. Bulletin. French. qt. Limited free distribution. Fiberglass Canada, 334 Est Rue Dundas, Toronto Ontario H5A 2A1 Canada. **DD** 338.4. ***Continues*** *RP Report. Francais., 0842-1110.*

US/1049-1341
**C2C ABSTRACTS JAPAN. PLASTICS. See** Plastics-Abstracting, Bibliographies and Statistics.

CN/0008-4778
**CANADIAN PLASTICS.** [Can. plast.]. Vol. 1, (Aug. 1943)-. Trade Publication. English. Eight times a year. 47.00Can$ (one year), 59.00Can$ (two year), 73.00Can$ (three year) Canada; 58.00Can$ (one year), 80.00Can$ (two year) US; 89.00Can$ other. Southam Information and Technology Group Inc., 1450 Don Mills Road, Don Mills Ontario M3B 2X7 Canada. **Tel** (416)445-6641, (800)668-2374, FAX (416)442-2261. **ED** Judith Nancekivell. **CODEN** CNPLAJ. **[CCC]. Ad Acc. Circ:** 11,000 (ctrl). available on microfilm and microfiche from University Microfilms International (UMI); available on an online database (file 16/Full-Text) from DIALOG. Documents available from CASDDS. ***Absorbed*** *Progressive Plastics, 0033-0809.*
**Desc:** Trade magazine covering plastics markets and technology in Canada.
**Ind/Abst** Chem. Abstr. (1943-1983); Eng. Mater. Abstr.; F&S Index Plus Text, Int. [Select. Cov.]; PROMT (1943-1983, 19??-).

CN/0843-2392
**CANADIAN PLASTICS AUTOMOTIVE DIRECTORY. See** Transportation-Automobiles.

CN/0068-9459
**CANADIAN PLASTICS DIRECTORY & BUYER'S GUIDE. VFOAT** Plastics Directory. (1971/1972)-. Directory. English. an. 65.00Can$. Southam Information and Technology Group Inc., 1450 Don Mills Road, Don Mills Ontario M3B 2X7 Canada. **Tel** (416)445-6641, (800)668-2374, FAX (416)442-2261. **ED** Judith Nancekivell. **DD** 338.4/7/668402571. **Ad Acc. Circ:** 11,500 (ctrl). ***Supersedes*** *Plastics Directory of Canada, 0554-2944.*
**Desc:** Published to provide information about products, materials, machinery and mold makers in Canada for people that have an interest in the industry.

CN/0828-5810
**CANADIAN PLASTICS STATISTICAL YEAR BOOK. See** Plastics-Abstracting, Bibliographies and Statistics.

UK/0262-4893
**CELLULAR POLYMERS.** [Cell. polym.]. Vol. 1, No. 1 (1982)-. Academic Scholarly Publication. English. bm (6 issues). £220.00 UK; $400.00 US; £240.00 other. RAPRA Technology Ltd., Shawbury Shrewsbury, Shropshire SY4 4NR England. **Tel** 011 44 939 250383, FAX 011 44 939 251118, telex 35134 RAPRA G. **ED** Jack Buist. **LC** TP1183.F6; C29. **DD** 668.9. **CODEN** CELPDJ. **Bk Rev. Ad Acc. Circ:** 200 (ctrl). Documents available from Article Express International, The Genuine Article, CASDDS. ***Continues*** *European Journal of Cellular Plastics, 0162-7600.*
**Desc:** An international journal covering properties, processing and applications of cellular polymers from clastomeric foams to rigid, structural plastics.
**Ind/Abst** Chem. Abstr.; Curr. Contents Eng. Tech. Appl. Sci.; EMBASE; Eng. Index Annu.; Life Sci. Collect.; Polymer Contents; Res. Alert [Full Cov.]; SCISEARCH.

AU/0251-1126
**CHEMIE, KUNSTSTOFFE AKTUELL. See** Chemistry-Chemical Technology.

HK
**CHINA PLASTIC & RUBBER JOURNAL.** Chinese. qt. HK$156.00 Hong Kong; $44.00 other. Adsale Publishing Company, 14/F Devon House Taikoo Place, 979 King's Road, Quarry Bay, Hong Kong. **Tel** 011 852 811 8897, FAX 011 852 516 5119. **ED** Josephine Cheng. **Ad Acc. Pr Rev. Circ:** 15,000 (ctrl).
**Desc:** A specilized industrial magazine designed to introduce to China advanced technology, market trends and products of the plastic and rubber industry.

CN/1186-2300
**COMPONENT ACCEPTANCE DIRECTORY, PLASTICS PROGRAM.** [Compon. accept. dir. plast. program]. **Added/Corp** Canadian Standards Association. **VFOAT** CSA Component Acceptance, Plastics Program. (1987)-. Periodical. English. sa. 30.00Can$. Canadian Standards Association, 178 Rexdale Boulevard, Rexdale Ontario M9W 1R3 Canada. **Tel** (416)747-4000, (416)747-4044, telex 06-989344. **DD** 668.4/9/029671.
**Desc:** Provides information on components already approved for use in products. Describes how the components acceptance program works, and also provides a summary of the tests involved, charts of polymer and color descriptions, and a list of participating firms.

UK/0952-6919
**COMPOSITE POLYMERS.** ***Title Change.*** Vol. 1, No. 1 (1988)-(19??). Academic Scholarly Publication. English. Six times a year. RAPRA Technology Ltd., Shawbury Shrewsbury, Shropshire SY4 4NR England. **Tel** 011 44 939 250383, FAX 011 44 939 251118, telex 35134 RAPRA G. **ED** G Pritchard. **LC** TA418.9.C6; C615. **DD** 620.1/92. **CODEN** COPOE5. **Bk Rev. Ad Acc. Circ:** 200 (ctrl). Documents available from Article Express International, CASDDS. ***Merged into*** *Polymers & Polymer Composites.*
**Desc:** Covers properties, processing and applications of polymer-based composites, particularly in automotive, aerospace and engineering industries.
**Ind/Abst** Chem. Abstr.; Ei Page One; Eng. Index Annu.

US/0888-1227
**COMPOSITES & ADHESIVES NEWSLETTER, THE. See** Chemistry-Chemical Technology.

FR/0763-0018
**COMPOSITES ET NOUVEAUX MATERIAUX.** [Compos. nouv. mater.]. (1984)-. Periodical. French. Eighteen times a year. 2350.64F France; 2500.00F other. A Jour, 11 rue du Marche St Honore, 75001 Paris France. **Tel** 011 33 1 44553849. **UDC** 62.

FR/0754-0876
**COMPOSITES PARIS.** [Composites Paris]. (1983)-. Periodical. French. bm (6 issues). 2791.38F France; 2850.00F other. Centre de Promotion Composites, 65 rue de Prony, 75854 Paris Cedex 17 France. **Tel** 011 33 1 47631259. **UDC** 666. ***Continues*** *Plastiques Renforces, Fibres de Verre Textile, 0240-9917.*

CN/1187-1261
**COMPOSITES REPORT / FIBERGLAS CANADA INC.** [Compos. rep.]. **Added/Corp** Fiberglas Canada Ltd. **VFOAT** New Developments in Fiberglas-Reinforced Plastics (FRP). Vol. 30, No. 1 (Spring 1991)-. Periodical. English. qt. Limited free distribution. Fiberglas Canada Inc., 334 Dundas Street East, Toronto Ontario H5A 2A1 Canada. **DD** 338.4. ***Continues*** *RP Report. English., 0842-1129.*

US/1052-0643
**COMPUTATIONAL POLYMER SCIENCE.** [Comput. polym. sci.]. Vol. 1, No. 1 (Mar. 1991)-. Academic Scholarly Publication. English. Four times a year (Mar., June, Sept., Dec.). $190.00 (US & Canada); $205.00 (other). Polymer Research Association Inc., 9200 Montgomery Road, Suite 23 B, Cincinnati OH 45242. **Tel** (513)891-7030, FAX (513)891-5867. **ED** James Mark. **LC** QD381.9.M3; C66. **DD** 547.7/01/5118. **CODEN** CPOSEJ. **[CCC]. Pr Rev.** Documents available from The Genuine Article, CASDDS.
**Ind/Abst** Chem. Abstr.; Res. Alert [Full Cov.].

US
**CONFERENCE PROCEEDINGS / ANTEC. Main/Corp** Society of Plastics Engineers. Technical Conference. **VFOAT** ANTEC ..., Conference Proceedings; Society of Plastics Engineers, Technical Papers. 44th (1986)-. Proceedings. English. ir. Society of Plastics Engineers, 14 Fairfield Drive, Brookfield CT 06804. **Tel** (203)775-0471, FAX (203)775-8490, telex 643-712. Documents available from Article Express International. ***Continues*** *Conference Proceedings for the Society of Plastics Engineers, Inc., 0733-4192.*
**Ind/Abst** Ei Page One; Eng. Index Annu.

US
**CURRENT INDUSTRIAL REPORTS. MA-30D, SHIPMENTS OF SELECTED PLASTICS PRODUCTS / U.S. DEPARTMENT OF COMMERCE, BUREAU OF THE CENSUS. Added/Corp** United States. Bureau of the Census. **VFOAT** Shipments of Selected Plastics Products. (19??)-. English. an. Superintendent of Documents, US Government Printing Office, Washington DC 20402. **Tel** (202)275-3328, FAX (202)786-2377. **LC** HD9661.U6; S5. **DD** 381/.4566849/0973.
**Desc:** Presents data on the production, inventories, and orders of approximately 5,000 products, which represent 40 percent of all US manufacturing.

DK
**DANSK PLAST.** Periodical. Danish. ir. kr80.00. Tekinsk Forley, Skelbkgade 4, 1717 Copenhagen V Denmark. **LC** TP1101; .D35.

UK
**DEVELOPMENTS IN PLASTICS TECHNOLOGY.** Vol. 1 (1982)-. Academic Scholarly Publication. English. ir. Price varies per volume. Elsevier Science Publishers BV, PO Box 211, 1000 AE Amsterdam Netherlands. **Tel** 011 31 20 5803642, FAX 011 31 20 5862696, telex 15682. **LC** TP1101; .D48. **DD** 668.4/05. **CODEN** DPTEDC. **Pr Rev.** Documents available from CASDDS.
**Ind/Abst** Chem. Abstr.

UK/0262-155X
**DEVELOPMENTS IN POLYMER STABILISATION.** [Dev. polym. stab.]. (1979)-. Academic Scholarly Publication. English. ir. price varies per volume. Elsevier Science Publishers BV, PO Box 211, 1000 AE Amsterdam Netherlands. **Tel** 011 31 20 5803642, FAX 011 31 20 5862696, telex 15682. **ED** Gerald Scott. **LC** TP1122; .D482. **DD** 668.9. **CODEN** DPSTDI. **[CCC].** Documents available from Article Express International, CASDDS.
**Ind/Abst** Bioeng. Abstr.; Chem. Abstr.; Ei Page One; Eng. Index Annu.

UK/0260-9185
**DEVELOPMENTS IN REINFORCED PLASTICS.** [Dev. reinf. plast.]. (1980)-. Academic Scholarly Publication. English. Elsevier Science Publishers Ltd, Crown House, Linton Road, Barking Essex IG11 8JU England. **Tel** 011 44 81 5947272, FAX 081-594-5942, telex 896950. **LC** TP1177; .D48. **DD** 668.4/94/05. **CODEN** DRPLDR. Documents available from CASDDS.
**Ind/Abst** Chem. Abstr.; Ei Page One.

US
**DEWITT POLYMER SERVICE.** English. Twenty-six times a year (Every other Tues.). $2,500.00. Dewitt & Company Inc, 16800 Greenspoint Park, #120 N, Houston TX 77060. **Tel** (713)875-5525, (713)875-0296, FAX (713)875-0175, telex 762-854. **ED** Mark W. House, (phone: (713)875-0297). **Pr Rev.** ctrl circ.
**Desc:** Information on international market pricing review for PE, PP, PS, and PVC plastics resins.

US/0882-6021
**DIRECTORY OF CONSULTANTS IN PLASTICS AND CHEMICALS, THE.** [Dir. consult. plast. chem.]. **VFOAT** Directory of Consultants in Plastics & Chemicals (Including Chemical Engineering). (1985)-. Directory. English. ir. $85.00. Gale Research Inc., 835 Penobscot Building, Detroit MI 48226. **Tel** (800)877-GALE, (313)961-2242, FAX (313)961-6083, telex TWX 810-221-7086. **LC** TP1112; .D57. **DD** 668.4/025/73.

US/8756-4572
**DREXEL POLYMER NOTES.** ***Title Change.*** [Drexel polym. notes]. **Added/Corp** Drexel University. Materials Engineering Dept. Vol. 1, No. 1 (Jan. 1985)-(199?). Periodical. English. mo. Technomic Publishing Company, Inc., 851 New Holland Avenue, Box 3535, Lancaster PA 17604. **Tel** (717)291-5609, (800)233-9936, FAX (717)295-4538. **ED** Roger D Corneliussen. **DD** 668. **[CCC]. Circ:** 100. ***Continued by*** *Marco Polymer Notes, 1066-7717.*
**Desc:** Monthly overview of research and trends in specialty polymers. Emphasis on morphology, failure mechanisms, and blends and alloys.

US
**ELASTOMERS.** **Added/Corp** International Plastics Selector, Inc. Ed. 2 (1980)-. English. ir. $35.00. International Plastics Selector Inc & D A T A Inc, PO Box 26875, San Diego CA 92126. **Tel** (619)578-7600, telex 910 530 606. **ED** Steven d'Adolf. **Bk Rev. Ad Acc. Circ:** 100,000 (ctrl). ***Continues*** *Elastomeric Materials.*
**Desc:** Specific property data on 3,400 elastomers, 1,300 gum stocks, 350 liquid systems, 350 thermoplastic elastomers, 1,400 formulations and their additives, natural rubber and test data.

JA/0367-021X
**ENBI TO PORIMA.** [En bi to porima]. **VFOAT** Vinyl and Polymers. Vol. 12 (1972)-. Academic Scholarly Publication. Japanese. mo. ¥14,560. Inst of Polymer Industry Inc, Central PO Box 1176, Tokyo 100-91 Japan. **Tel** (03)211-7739, FAX (03)211-7730. **ED** SF Miyamoto. **CODEN** EBTPBO. **Bk Rev. Ad Acc. Circ:** 10,000. Documents available from The Genuine Article, CASDDS. ***Continues*** *Enka Biniiru to Porima.*
**Ind/Abst** Chem. Abstr.; Res. Alert [Full Cov.].

UK/0952-6900
**ENGINEERING PLASTICS.** Vol. 1 (1988)-. Periodical. English. bm (6 issues). £220.00 UK; $400.00 US; £240.00 other. RAPRA Technology Ltd., Shawbury Shrewsbury, Shropshire SY4 4NR England. **Tel** 011 44 939 250383, FAX 011 44 939 251118, telex 35134 RAPRA G. **ED** Keith Watkinson. **LC** TP1101; .E53. **DD** 668.4/05. **Bk Rev. Ad Acc. Circ:** 200 (ctrl).
**Desc:** An international journal covering processing properties and applications of high performance plastics.

UK
**ENGINEERING PLASTICS GUIDE.** 1976-. Periodical. English. £2.50 UK; $6.50 other. European Plastics News, 40 Bowling Green Lane, London EC1R 0NE England.

UK
**EUROPEAN PLASTICS DIRECTORY.** **Added/Corp** Rapra Technology Limited. (1989)-. English (French, German, Italian and Spanish). an. £80.00 UK; £90.00 other. RAPRA Technology Ltd., Shawbury Shrewsbury, Shropshire SY4 4NR England. **Tel** 011 44 939 250383, FAX 011 44 939 251118, telex 35134 RAPRA G. **LC** HD9661.A1; E97.
**Desc:** Information on the plastics industry and trade.

UK/0306-3534
**EUROPEAN PLASTICS NEWS.** [Eur. plast. news]. Vol. 1 (May 1974)-. Periodical. English. Twelve times a year. $170.00 US & Canada; $197.00 others; £99.00 UK; £99.00 Europe. EMAP Business Publishing Ltd, 258 Field End Road, Ferrari House, Ruislip Middlesex HA4 9UY England. **Tel** 44 81 8684499. **LC** TP1101; .E85. **DD** 668.4/05. **CODEN** EUPNBT. available on microfilm and microfiche from University Microfilms International (UMI). Documents available from CASDDS.
**Ind/Abst** BMT Abstr. (-199?); Chem. Abstr.; Chem. Bus. Bull.; Chem. Bus. NewsBase (1985-); Chem. Bus. Update; Chem. Ind. Notes; Curr. Technol. Index; Eng. Mater. Abstr.; F&S Index Plus Text, Int. [Select. Cov.]; Infomat Int. Bus.; Int. Packag. Abstr.; Leadscan; Nonwovens Abstr.; PROMT; Saf. Health Work; World Ceram. Abstr.

UK
**EUROPLASTICS YEARBOOK.** Multiple languages (English, French, German, Italian and Spanish). ir. Reed Business Publishing / West Sussex, England, Perrymount Road, Haywards Heath, West Sussex RH16 3DH England. **Tel** 011 44 81 6523500. **LC** TP1103; .E87. **DD** 338.4/7/6684094.

US/0276-0819
**EXTRUSION DIGEST.** [Extrus. dig.]. Vol. 1, No. 1 (June, 1981)-. Periodical. English. mo. $97.00. Tracom Inc, PO Box 533, Whelling IL 60090. **Tel** (219)769-4352.

US/0741-0859
**FACTS & FIGURES OF THE U.S. PLASTICS INDUSTRY.** (FACTS & FIGURES OF THE U.S. PLASTICS INDUSTRY / THE SOCIETY OF THE PLASTICS INDUSTRY, INC.). [Facts fig. U. S. plast. ind.]. **Added/Corp** Society of the Plastics Industry. **VFOAT** Facts and Figures of the U.S. Plastics Industry. (1982)-. English. an (Sept.). $200.00 (non-members) $103.00 (members) US; $135.00 (members), $240.00 (non-members). Society of Plastics Industry / Washington DC, 1275 K Street Northwest, Suite 400, Washington DC 20005. **Tel** (202)371-5256. **ED** Buzz Lippincott. **LC** HD9661.U6; F32. **DD** 338.4/76684/0973. **Circ:** 1,000. ***Continues*** *Facts & Figures of the Plastics Industry, 0740-8420.*
**Desc:** Statistical review of plastics industry including production, sales, capacities and markets, data on resins, machinery and finished products.
**Ind/Abst** F&S Index Plus Text, Int. [Select. Cov.].

JA
**FURASUCHIKKU GAIDO; GENTAIRYE FUKUZAIRYO HEN.** **VFOAT** Plastics Yearbook. Japanese (Japanese). Kogyo Chosakai, (Kogyo Chosakai Publishing Co., Ltd.), 14-7, Hongo 2 Chome, Bunkyoku, Tokyoto 113, Japan. **LC** TP1103; .P85.

CN/0835-1791
**GLOBAL PLASTICS REPORT.** ***Ceased.*** [Glob. plast. rep.]. Vol. 1, No. 1 (Jan. 1987)-(1991). Periodical. English. mo. Global Plastics Report, 233 Dupras Avenue, LaSalle Quebec H8R 3S4 Canada. **Tel** (514)366-8410, FAX (514)595-3772. **ED** Peter Stewart and Joy Carroll. **DD** 668.4/05. **Circ:** 1,000.
**Desc:** National and international news for executives in the plastics industry.

SP
**GUADALIMAR.** [Guadalimar]. (1975)-. Periodical. Spanish. bm. 7000ptas Europe; 15000ptas other. Miguel Fernandez-Braso, Villanueva 22, 28001 Madrid Spain. **Tel** 91 275 04 27.
**Ind/Abst** BHA : Biblio. Hist. Art.

SP
**GUIA CATALOGO PLASTICOS ESPANOLES.** Spanish. Agrupacion Nacional Autonoma de Industriales de Plasticos, Sindicato Nacional de Industrias Quimicas, San Bernardo 62, Madrid Spain. **LC** HD9661.S7; G85.
**Desc:** Vol. for 1974 covers period 1969-1973.

GW/0176-1625
**GUMMI, FASERN, KUNSTSTOFFE.** **See** Rubber.

UK/0264-7753
**HIGH PERFORMANCE PLASTICS.** [High perform. plast.]. Vol. 1, No. 1 (Nov. 1983)-. Periodical. English. Twelve times a year. $397.00 The Americas; £266.00 other. Elsevier Advanced Technology, An Imprint of Elsevier Science Ltd., The Boulevard, Langford Lane, Kidlington, Oxford OX5 1GB United Kingdom. **Tel** 011 44 865 843000, 011 44 865 843699, FAX 011 44 865 843010. **(Subscription address:** Elsevier Science Ltd. Oxford Fulfillment Centre, PO Box 800, Kidlington, Oxford OX5 1DX United Kingdom.**) ED** N. Brooks. **[CCC].** available on microfilm from University Microfilms International (UMI); available on an online database (file 636/Full-Text) from DIALOG.
**Desc:** Includes reinforced plastics, engineering plastics and other polymers produced for heavy-duty or other special applications.
**Ind/Abst** Int. Packag. Abstr.; Nonwovens Abstr.; Polymer Contents; PTS Newsl. Database [Full Txt.].

RU/0023-1118
**HIMICESKIE VOLOKNA.** (KHIMICHESKIE VOLOKNA.). [Him. volok.]. **Added/Corp** Soviet Union. Ministerstvo Khimicheskoi Promyshlennosti. (1959)-. Academic Scholarly Publication. Russian. bm. $69.95. Izdatelstvo Khimiia, Novaia Ploshchad. 10,, K-12, Moscow Russia. **(Subscription address:** East View Publications Inc., 3020 Harbor Lane North, Suite 110, Minneapolis MN 55447.**) CODEN** KVLKA4. Index available. **Bk Rev.** Documents available from Article Express International, CASDDS.
**Ind/Abst** Abstr. Bull. Inst. Paper Chem.; Abstr. Bull. Inst. Pap. Sci. Tech.; Anal. Abstr.; Chem. Abstr.; Curr. Biotechnol.; Ei Page One; Energy Res. Abstr.; Eng. Index Annu.; World Text. Abstr.

UK
**IAL PLASTICS YEARBOOK, THE.** English. an. £60.00. IAL Consultants Ltd, 14 Buckingham Palace Road, London SW1W 0QP United Kingdom. **Tel** 071 828 5036, FAX 071 828 9318, telex 918666 CRECON G.
**Desc:** Basic facts and statistics on the European plastics industry by selected countries.

US/0272-4685
**IEEE CONFERENCE RECORD OF ... ANNUAL CONFERENCE OF ELECTRICAL ENGINEERING PROBLEMS IN THE RUBBER AND PLASTICS INDUSTRIES.** **See** Engineering-Electricity, Electrical Engineering, Electronics.

CN/0835-5134
**INDUSTRIAL SPECIALTIES NEWS.** [Ind. spec. news]. Vol. 1, No. 1 (Apr. 1987)-. Periodical. English. Twenty-four times a year. 557.00Can$. Blendon Information Services, 126 Willowdale Avenue, Suite 1, Willowdale ONT M2N 442 Canada. **Tel** (416)223-5397, FAX (416)225-9297. **ED** Bob Orchard. **DD** 338.4/766/00971. available on an online database (files 16,636/Full-Text) from DIALOG.

NE/0922-4122
**INFORMATIEF NVR.** **VFOAT** Informatief Nederlandse Vereniging van Rubber- en Kunststoffabrikanten. (1988)-. Periodical. Dutch. Eleven times a year. Fl150.00. NVR, Postbus 418, 2266 AK Leidschendam Netherlands. **Tel** 011 31 70 3177243. **UDC** 678.4. ***Continues*** *NVR Informatief, 0165-7089.*

US/1045-1889
**INNOVATIONS IN POLYMER/ENGINEERING PLASTICS.** **See** Engineering-Materials Engineering and Mechanics.

US/0091-4037
**INTERNATIONAL JOURNAL OF POLYMERIC MATERIALS.** **See** Chemistry.

GW/0930-777X
**INTERNATIONAL POLYMER PROCESSING.** (INTERNATIONAL POLYMER PROCESSING : THE JOURNAL OF THE POLYMER PROCESSING SOCIETY.). [Int. polym. process.]. **Added/Corp** Polymer Processing Society. **VFOAT** Intern. Polymer Processing. (1986)-. Academic Scholarly Publication. English. qt. DM416.60. Carl Hanser Verlag, Postfach 860420, D 81631 Munich Germany. **Tel** 011 49 89 998300, FAX 011 49 89 984809. **ED** H.G. Fritz, T. Masuda and J.L. White. **LC** TP1080; .I58. **DD** 668.9. **CODEN** IPPREJ. **[CCC].** Index available. **Bk Rev. Ad Acc. Pr Rev. Circ:** 1,500. Documents available from The Genuine Article, CASDDS.
**Desc:** Goal is to foster scientific understanding and technical innovation in polymer processing by providing a discussion forum for the worldwide community of engineers and scientists in this field. Contains original research contributions, invited review papers and recent technological developments in processing of thermoplastics, thermosets, elastomers and fibers as well as polymer reaction engineering.
**Ind/Abst** Chem. Abstr. (1987-); Curr. Contents Eng. Tech. Appl. Sci.; Res. Alert [Full Cov.]; SCISEARCH.

IT/0392-3800
**INTERPLASTICS (MILANO).** (INTERPLASTICS : IP.). [Interplastics]. **VFOAT** IP; I.P. Began in 1978?. Academic Scholarly Publication. Italian. bm. L9000 (single issue); L48000 (one year), L80000 (two year) Italy; L100000 Europe; L140000 other. Tecniche Nuove SPA, Via Ciro Menotti 14, 20129 Milan Italy. **Tel** 011 39 2 75701, FAX 011 39 2 7610351, telex 334647 TECHS I. **CODEN** INPLDK. **Bk Rev. Ad Acc. Circ:** 4,697. Documents available from CASDDS.
**Ind/Abst** Chem. Abstr.

UK/0261-5487
**IRPI. INTERNATIONAL REINFORCED PLASTICS INDUSTRY.** [IRPI. Int. reinf. plast. ind.]. **VFOAT** International Reinforced Plastics Industry. (1981)-. Periodical. English. bm. £20.00 (non-trade), Free (trade), Europe; £30.00 other. Channel Publications Ltd, PO Box 1787 Gerrards Cross, Bucks, SL9 0TD England. **Tel** 011 44 753 890200, FAX 011 44 753 890200. **ED** D. Paminaton. **DD** 338.4766649405. **Bk Rev,** (Qty: 6). **Ad Acc. Circ:** 6,500 (ctrl).

JA/0021-4582
**JAPAN PLASTICS AGE.** ***Ceased.*** [Jpn. plast. age]. Ceased May 1987 with Issue 215. Academic Scholarly Publication. English. mo. Plastics Age Company Ltd., Okochi Building 1 10-6 Kajicho 1-chome, Chiyoda-ku Tokyo 101 Japan. **ED** Eiichi Asayama. **LC** TP986.A1; J27. **CODEN** JPLAAN. **Ad Acc. Circ:** 17,000. Documents available from CASDDS. ***Continues*** *Japan Plastics Age News.*
**Desc:** Review of plastics industries of Japan, with main interest in polymer technology, processing techniques, processing machine engineering and market developments.
**Ind/Abst** Chem. Abstr.; Eng. Mater. Abstr.; Int. Packag. Abstr.

JA/0448-8679
**JAPAN PLASTICS INDUSTRY ANNUAL.** (1958)-. Periodical. English. an. $40.00. Plastics Age Company Ltd., Okochi Building 1 10-6 Kajicho 1-chome, Chiyoda-ku Tokyo 101 Japan. **ED** Eiichi Asayama. **LC** TP1103; .J3. **Ad Acc. Circ:** 17,000. available on microfilm and microfiche from University Microfilms International (UMI).
**Desc:** Reviews the latest developments of the plastics industry of Japan. Directory section offers a source of material and equipment supplies.
**Ind/Abst** Eng. Mater. Abstr.

SP
**JAPANESE NEW MATERIALS IACA SERIES. ADVANCED PLASTICS.** (19??)-. English. qt. £215.00 UK; $370.00 US. Newmedia International Japan, AV Infanta Carlota 123 5 A, 08029 Barcelona Spain. **Tel** 011 34 3 4195690, FAX 414 42 13. available on an online database (files 16,636/Full-Text) from DIALOG.
**Ind/Abst** PROMT [Full Txt.]; PTS Newsl. Database [Full Txt.].

US/0021-955X
**JOURNAL OF CELLULAR PLASTICS.** [J. cell. plast.]. Vol. 1 (Jan. 1965)-. Periodical. English. bm (Jan., Mar., May, July, Sept., Nov.). $185.00 (one year), $360.00 (two year), $535.00 (three year). Technomic Publishing Company, Inc., 851 New Holland Avenue, Box

3535, Lancaster PA 17604. **Tel** (717)291-5609, (800)233-9936, FAX (717)295-4538. **ED** Sidney H. Metzger Jr. **LC** TP1183.F6; J6. **CODEN** JCUPAM. **[CCC]**. cum. index. **Ad Acc. Circ:** 1,000. available on microfilm and microfiche from University Microfilms International (UMI). Documents available from Article Express International, CASDDS.
**Desc:** The primary purpose is to provide a permanent record of international achievements in the science, technology, and economics of cellular plastics. Presents technical advances in chemistry, formulation, processing, testing, properties, performance, and applications.
**Ind/Abst** Chem. Abstr.; Civ. Struct. Eng. Abstr.; Ei Page One; Eng. Index Annu.; Int. Aerosp. Abstr.; Int. Packag. Abstr.; Mater. Sci. Eng. Abstr.; Polymer Contents.

US/0095-2443
**JOURNAL OF ELASTOMERS AND PLASTICS, THE.** [J. elastomers plast.]. Vol. 6 (Jan 1974)-. Periodical. English. qt (Jan., Apr., July, Oct.). $215.00 (one year), $420.00 (two year), $625.00 (three year). Technomic Publishing Company, Inc., 851 New Holland Avenue, Box 3535, Lancaster PA 17604. **Tel** (717)291-5609, (800)233-9936, FAX (717)295-4538. **ED** Melvyn A. Kohudic. **LC** TA455.P5; J6. **DD** 668.4/05. **CODEN** JEPLAX. **[CCC]**. cum. index. **Pr Rev. Circ:** 400. available on microfilm and microfiche from University Microfilms International (UMI). Documents available from Article Express International, The Genuine Article, CASDDS. ***Continues** Journal of Elastoplastics, 0022-071X.*
**Desc:** Reports the latest contributions to the technology and properties of elastomers and related polymeric products. Major emphasis is placed on specialty and high performance elastomers. Presents current information on the chemistry, processing, properties, and applications of recently developed and improved elastomeric materials. Articles offer in-depth marketing and technical analysis of the uses and profit opportunities for these materials. In addition to research reports, review articles and conference papers, industry news and a patent digest are included
**Ind/Abst** Bioeng. Abstr.; Chem. Abstr.; Curr. Contents Eng. Tech. Appl. Sci.; Ei Page One; EMBASE; Eng. Mater. Abstr.; Eng. Index Annu.; Polymer Contents; Res. Alert [Full Cov.]; SCISEARCH.

US/8756-0879
**JOURNAL OF PLASTIC FILM & SHEETING.** [J. plast. film sheeting]. **VFOAT** Journal of Plastic Film and Sheeting. Vol. 1, No. 1 (Jan. 1985)-. Academic Scholarly Publication. English. qt (Jan., Apr., July and Oct.). $280.00 (one year), $550.00 (two year), $820.00 (three year). Technomic Publishing Company, Inc., 851 New Holland Avenue, Box 3535, Lancaster PA 17604. **Tel** (717)291-5609, (800)233-9936, FAX (717)295-4538. **ED** James Harrington. **DD** 668. **CODEN** JPFSEH. **[CCC]**. cum. index. **Circ:** 400. available on microfilm from University Microfilms International (UMI). Documents available from Article Express International, The Genuine Article, CASDDS.
**Desc:** Reports on the wide variety of advances that are taking place in the technology of plastic film and sheeting.
**Ind/Abst** Chem. Abstr. (1985-); Ei Page One; Eng. Index Annu.; Food Sci. Technol. Abstr.; Foods Adlibra; Int. Packag. Abstr.; Polymer Contents; Res. Alert [Full Cov.].

US/0149-3108
**JOURNAL OF THE ADHESIVE AND SEALANT COUNCIL, THE. See** Chemistry-Chemical Technology.

US/0193-7197
**JOURNAL OF VINYL TECHNOLOGY.** [J. vinyl technol.]. **Added/Corp** Society of Plastics Engineers. **VFOAT** Vinyl Technology. Vol. 1 (March 1979)-. Academic Scholarly Publication. English. qt. $150.00 North America; $170.00 other. Society of Plastics Engineers, 14 Fairfield Drive, Brookfield CT 06804. **Tel** (203)775-0471, FAX (203)775-8490, telex 643-712. **ED** Robert P. Braddicks, Jr. **LC** TP1180.V48; J68. **DD** 668.4/236/05. **CODEN** JVTEDI. **[CCC]**. Index available (bound in Dec. issue). **Circ:** 600. available on microfilm from University Microfilms International (UMI). Documents available from Article Express International, The Genuine Article, CASDDS.
**Desc:** Technical articles aimed toward solving problems in the vinyl polymers area.
**Ind/Abst** Chem. Abstr.; Ei Page One; Eng. Mater. Abstr.; Eng. Index Annu.; Polymer Contents; Res. Alert [Full Cov.].

JA
**KOBUNSHI KAGAKU NO TEMBO.**
**Main/Corp** Kobunshi Gakkai. **VFOAT** Annual Review. (1970)-. Japanese (Japanese). ¥3400. Kobunshi Gakkai, Maruzen 2-6 Nihonbashitoori Chuo-ku, Tokyo Japan. **LC** TP1101; .K62A.

JA/0368-6426
**KOBUNSHI KAKO. VFOAT** Polymer Processing. V. 13, No. 4- (No. 147- ); 1964-. Academic Scholarly Publication. Japanese. mo. ¥8800. Kabuki Kankokai, Chiekoin Marutamachi Kudaru, Kamigyo-ku 60, Kyoto Japan. **LC** TP1080; .K59. **CODEN** KOKABN. Documents available from CASDDS.
**Ind/Abst** Chem. Abstr.

GW/0170-0693
**KUNSTHARZ NACHRICHTEN.**
[Kunstharz-Nachr.]. **Added/Corp** Hoechst AG. **VFOAT** Kunstharz-Nachrichten. (1972)-. Periodical. German. Hoechst Aktiengesellschaft, Frankfurt Germany. **CODEN** KUNADE. Documents available from CASDDS.
***Continues** Reichhold-Albert Nachrichten.*
**Ind/Abst** Chem. Abstr.

GW/0047-3766
**KUNSTSTOFF-JOURNAL.** [Kunststoffjournal]. **VAT** Kunststoff Journal. Academic Scholarly Publication. German. Ten times a year. Free. Europa-Fachpresse-Verlag GmbH, Thomas Dehler Str 27, 8000 Muenchen 83 Germany. **Tel** 089 67804 274, FAX 089 67804 108, telex 5216148 EFVD. **ED** Thomas Schwachulla. **LC** TP1101; .K87. **CODEN** KUNJD7. **Bk Rev. Ad Acc. Circ:** 13,500 (ctrl). Documents available from CASDDS.
**Desc:** A intermediary between the machine and raw material industry and plastics processor. Provides reports and information which are of direct use for practical application.
**Ind/Abst** Chem. Abstr.; Eng. Mater. Abstr.; Int. Packag. Abstr.

GW/0172-6374
**KUNSTSTOFFBERATER (1979).**
(KUNSTSTOFFBERATER.). [Kunststoffberater]. Vol. 24, No. 1/2 (Jan./Feb. 1979)-. Academic Scholarly Publication. German. Twelve times a year. DM180.00 Germany; DM182.40 others. Umschau Verlag, Postfach 110262, D-60037 Frankfurt Germany. **Tel** 011 49 69 2600692, FAX 011 49 69 2600223, telex 411964. **LC** TP1101; .K86. **CODEN** KUNSDY. **[CCC]**. Documents available from Ask*IEEE, CASDDS. ***Continues** Kunststoffberater Rundschau + Technik, 0340-8442.*
**Ind/Abst** Chem. Abstr.; Coal Abstr.; EMBASE; Energy Res. Abstr. (Jan. 1979-); INSPEC (Dec. 1968-); Int. Packag. Abstr.

GW/0023-5563
**KUNSTSTOFFE.** [Kunststoffe]. Vol. 1, No. 1 (Jan. 1911)-. Periodical. German (summaries and/or abstracts in English, French and Spanish). mo. DM276.00. Carl Hanser Verlag, Postfach 860420, D 81631 Munich Germany. **Tel** 011 49 89 998300, FAX 011 49 89 984809. **CODEN** KUNSAV. **[CCC]. Ad Acc. Circ:** 11,600. Documents available from The Genuine Article, CASDDS. ***Absorbed** Kunststoff-Technik und Kunststoff-Anwendung.*
**Desc:** Covers the whole field of plastics and rubber in a comprehensive, flexible manner. Information on new, expanding markets, the automotive industry, packaging, electrical/electronics are also included.
**Ind/Abst** Anal. Abstr.; Chem. Abstr.; F&S Index Plus Text, Int. [Select. Cov.]; Int. Civil Eng. Abstr.; PROMT; Res. Alert; SCISEARCH; Soc. Sci. Cit. Index [Select. Cov.]; World Surf. Coat. Abstr.

AU
**KUNSTSTOFFE IN OSTERREICH.**
**Added/Corp** Fachverband der Chemischen Industrie Osterreichs. Arbeitsgemeinschaft der Kunststoffverarbeitenden Gewerbebetriebe. (19??)-. German. ir. Julius Dressler Buch- und Aeitschriftenverlag, Schwindgasse 5, A-1041 Vienna, Austris. **LC** TP1112; .K83.

SZ/0023-5598
**KUNSTSTOFFE-PLASTICS (SOLOTHURN).** ***Title Change.***
(KUNSTSTOFFE-PLASTICS.). [Kunstst.-Plast.]. Vol. 1 (1954/1955)-(19??). Academic Scholarly Publication. German. ir. Vogt Schild AG, Druck Verlag, Postfach 748 Zuchwilserstr 21, CH 4501 Solothurn Switzerland. **Tel** 011 41 65 247247. **LC** TP986.A1; K83. **CODEN** KUPLAK. **[CCC]**. ctrl circ. Documents available from Article Express International, CASDDS. ***Continued by** Kunststoffe Synthetics.*
**Ind/Abst** Chem. Abstr.; Ei Page One; EMBASE; Eng. Index Annu.; Infomat Int. Bus.; Int. Packag. Abstr.

SZ/1021-0601
**KUNSTSTOFFE SYNTHETICS.** [Kunstst. synth.]. (1992)-. Periodical. German. Twelve times a year. F83.00 Switzerland; F103.00 others. Vogt Schild AG, Druck Verlag, Postfach 748 Zuchwilserstr 21, CH 4501 Solothurn Switzerland. **Tel** 011 41 65 247247. **UDC** 678. ***Continues** Kunststoffe Plastics (Monatlich Ausg.), 0023-5598.*

JA/0452-9685
**KYOKA PURASUCHIKKUSU.** [Kyoka purasuchikkusu]. **VFOAT** Reinforced Plastics. Began with Vol. 1, No. 1, 1955. Academic Scholarly Publication. Japanese. mo. Kyoka Purasuchikku Kyokai, (Japan Reinforced Plastics Soc.), 15-15, Ginza 3 Chome, Chuoku, Tokyoto 104, Japan. **(Subscription address:** Maruzen Company Ltd., PO Box 5050, Import & Export Department, Tokyo 100 31 Japan.**) ED** Takkaaki Toda. **CODEN** KYPUA7. **Ad Acc. Circ:** 1,800 (ctrl). Documents available from CASDDS.
**Desc:** Publishes dissertation and research materials of reinforced plastics.
**Ind/Abst** Chem. Abstr.

CN/0229-4567
**LABOUR SURVEY (SOCIETY OF THE PLASTICS INDUSTRY OF CANADA). See** Economics-Labor.

IT/0394-3453
**MACPLAS.** [Macplas]. (1976)-. Periodical. Italian. Ten times a year. L140000.00. Promaplast Srl, CP 24, 20090 Assago Milan Italy. **Tel** 011 39 2 57512700. **UDC** 678. Index available. cum. index. **Ad Acc. Pr Rev. Circ:** 11,000 (ctrl).
**Desc:** Technical information concerning the plastics and rubber field.

US
**MANUFACTURING HANDBOOK AND BUYERS' GUIDE / PLASTICS TECHNOLOGY.** (1984)-. Consumer Publication. English. an (July). $49.95. Bill Communications Inc., 355 Park Avenue South, New York NY 10010-1789. **Tel** (800)821-6897, (212)592-6262, FAX (212)592-6209. **(Subscription address:** Bill Communications, 200 South Route 130, Cinnaminson, NJ 08077**) *Continues** Plastics Manufacturing Handbook and Buyers' Guide (New York, N.Y. : 1980/81).*

US/0730-9120
**MAQUINARIA PARA PLASTICOS. See** Business-Marketing.

RM/0025-5289
**MATERIALE PLASTICE.** [Mater. plast.]. (1964)-. Academic Scholarly Publication. Romanian (summaries and/or abstracts in English, French, German and Russian; table of contents in English, French, German and Russian). Four times a year. $90.00. **(Subscription address:** Orion Press SRL, SPL Independentei 202-A, Bucharest 6 Romania.**) CODEN** MPLAAM. Documents available from Article Express International, The Genuine Article, CASDDS.
**Desc:** Publishes specialized articles on the plastic materials industry.
**Ind/Abst** Bioeng. Abstr.; Chem. Abstr.; Ei Page One; Eng. Mater. Abstr.; Eng. Index Annu.; Res. Alert [Full Cov.]; Saf. Health Work.

IT/0025-5459
**MATERIE PLASTICHE ED ELASTOMERI.** [Mater. plast. elastom.]. Vol. 29 (Jan. 1963)-. Periodical. Italian (Italian). ir. $35.64. Industria, Viale Monte Grappa 3, 20124 Milan Italy. **LC** TP1101; .M364. **CODEN** MPELAK. Documents available from Article Express International. ***Continues** Materie Plastiche.*
**Ind/Abst** Bioeng. Abstr.; Ei Page One; Eng. Index Annu.

IT
**MATERIE PLASTICHE : PRODOTTI PROCESSI MERCATI. SERVIZI DOCUMONT.** Italian. mo. Enichem, Cas Postale 10020, 20110 Milan Italy. **Tel** 011 39 2 62703388.

SP
**MEMORIA - INSTITUTO NACIONAL DE RACIONALIZACION Y NORMALIZACION. COMISION TECNICA DE TRABAJO NO. 53 INDUSTRIAS DE PLASTICS. Main/Corp** Instituto Nacional de Racionalizacion y Normalizacion. Comision Tecnica de Trabajo No. 53 Industrias de Plasticos y Caucho. Spanish. Instituto Nacional de Racionalizacion Y Normalizacion, Serrano 150, Madrid Spain. **LC** TP1122; .I56A.

US/0026-8275
**MODERN PLASTICS.** [Mod. plast.]. Vol. 12, No. 1 (Sept. 1934)-. Periodical. English. mo. $41.75 (one year), $62.70 (two year) US and possessions; $46.00 (one year), $69.00 (two year) Canada; $225.00 (one year), $450.00 (two year) other. McGraw Hill Publishing Company, Inc., 1221 Avenue of the Americas, New York NY 10020. **Tel** (212)512-6410, (800)525-5003, FAX (212)512-6111. **(Subscription address:** Modern Plastics, PO Box 601, Hightstown NJ 08520.**) ED** Robert J. Martino. **LC** TP986; .A1M6. **DD** 668. **CODEN** MOPLAY. **[CCC]**. Index Available, published separately, free-automatically sent. cum. index. **Bk Rev. Ad Acc. Circ:** 55,000. available on microfilm and microfiche from University Microfilms International (UMI); available on an online database (file 624/Full-Text) from DIALOG. Documents available from Article Express International, UMI Article Clearinghouse, UMI Article Clearinghouse, CASDDS. ***Continues** Plastic Products, 0096-9141.*
**Desc:** For personnel of companies that use or process plastics in the manufacture of products; provides analysis and assessment of significant developments in materials, processes, designs and markets. Circulation includes general management, production and engineering, research and development, design engineers, purchasing and marketing personnel.
**Ind/Abst** ABI/INFORM Glob. Ed.; ABI Inform Ondisc (Nov. 1987-); Abstr. Bull. Inst. Pap. Sci. Tech.; Acad. Search (July 1993-); Appl. Sci. Technol. Index; Bioeng. Abstr.; Bus. Index (1985-); Chem. Abstr.; Chem. Ind. Notes; Ei Page One; Eng. Mater. Abstr.; Eng. Index Annu. [Select. Cov.]; F&S Index Plus Text, Int. [Select. Cov.];

Foods Adlibra; Gen. BusinessFile (1985-); Gen. Period. Index (1985-); Mag. Search; PROMT; Soc. Sci. Cit. Index [Select. Cov.]; Stat. Ref. Index; Surf. Treat. Technol. Abstr.; Text. Technol. Dig.; Trade Ind. Index (1981-) [Full Txt.]; UMI ABI/Inform--Bus. Period. Ondisc (Nov. 1987-) [Full Txt.].

US/0085-3518
**MODERN PLASTICS ENCYCLOPEDIA (1954).** (MODERN PLASTICS ENCYCLOPEDIA.). (1954)-. English. an. $175.00 Austria, Belgium, Denmark, France, Japan, Luxembourg, The Netherlands, Switzerland, Germany; $139.00 Finland, Ireland, Italy, Norway, Portugal, Spain, Sweden & United Kingdom; $135.00 other. McGraw Hill Publishing Company, Inc., 1221 Avenue of the Americas, New York NY 10020. **Tel** (212)512-6410, (800)525-5003, FAX (212)512-6111. **(Subscription address:** Modern Plastics International, PO Box 605, Hightstown, NJ 08520**)** **[CCC].** ***Continues*** *Modern Plastics Encyclopedia and Engineers Handbook.*

SZ/0026-8283
**MODERN PLASTICS INTERNATIONAL.** [Mod. plast. int.]. (19??)-. Periodical. English. mo. $170.00 (subscription), $220.00 (including encyclopedia) (one year), $255.00 (subscription), $370.00 (including encyclopedia (two year). McGraw Hill Publishing Company, Inc., 1221 Avenue of the Americas, New York NY 10020. **Tel** (212)512-6410, (800)525-5003, FAX (212)512-6111. **(Subscription address:** Modern Plastics International, Box 605, Hightstown NJ 08520.**)** **[CCC].** available on microfilm and microfiche from University Microfilms International (UMI).
**Desc:** Covers research development, management, engineering, production and purchasing phases of the plastics industry. Each issue describes the current application of plastics to various industries, covers research and engineering developments, and reports on new materials, machinery and equipment.
**Ind/Abst** Chem. Bus. Bull.; Chem. Bus. NewsBase (1984-); Chem. Bus. Update; F&S Index Plus Text, Int. [Select. Cov.]; Infomat Int. Bus.; Int. Packag. Abstr.; Leadscan; Nonwovens Abstr.; PROMT; World Ceram. Abstr.

IT
**MPE JOURNAL.** Periodical. English. Industria, Viale Monte Grappa 3, 20124 Milan Italy. **LC** HD9661.A1; M17. **DD** 338.4/7/668405.

HU/0027-2914
**MUANYAG ES GUMI.** (MUANYAG ES GUMI. PLASTICS AND RUBBER.). [Muanyag es gumi]. **VFOAT** Plastics and Rubber. Vol. 3 (1966)-. Academic Scholarly Publication. Hungarian (summaries and/or abstracts in English, French, German and Russian). mo. 36.00ft. **(Subscription address:** Kultura, PO Box 149, H 1389 Budapest 62 Hungary.**)** **CODEN** MUGUAO. Documents available from CASDDS. ***Continues*** *Muanyag.*
**Ind/Abst** Chem. Abstr.; Int. Polym. Sci. Tech.

JA/0388-4384
**NETSU KOKASEI JUSHI.** [Netsu kokasei jushi]. **Added/Corp** Gosei Jushi Kogyo Kyokai (Japan). **VFOAT** Journal of Thermosetting Plastics, Japan. (1980)-. Academic Scholarly Publication. Japanese (summaries and/or abstracts in English; table of contents in English). qt. ¥4000. Gosei Jushi Kogyo Kyokai, 100 Tokyo-to Chiyoda-ku, Kasumigaseki 3-2-6 Japan. **CODEN** NKJUDH. Documents available from CASDDS.
**Ind/Abst** Chem. Abstr.

UK/0747-4954
**NEW TRADE NAMES IN THE RUBBER AND PLASTICS INDUSTRIES.** **See** Rubber.

JA/0029-0351
**NIHON PURASUCHIKKUSU SHINPO.** **VFOAT** Japan Plastics Journal. (1949)-. Japanese. Japan Plastics Progress Company.
**Ind/Abst** Int. Polym. Sci. Tech.

FR
**OFFICIEL DE LA DROGUERIE, ET SON COMPLEMENT "PLASTIQUES", L'.** ***Title Change.*** **VFOAT** Plastiques. (Nov. 1949)-Vol. 18, No. 190 (Nov. 1966). Periodical. French. mo. **LC** HD9653.1; .O35. ***Continued by*** *Officiel de la Droguerie.*

GW/0941-3596
**PE. PLAST EUROPE.** ***Title Change.*** [PE, Plast Eur.]. **VFOAT** Plast Europe; Kunststoffe. (1992)-(Jan. 1994). Periodical. Multiple languages. mo. Carl Hanser Verlag, Postfach 860420, D 81631 Munich Germany. **Tel** 011 49 89 998300, FAX 011 49 89 984809. **UDC** 678. ***Continues*** *Kunststoffe Europe, 0938-9849.* ***Merged into*** *Kunstoffe Plast Europe.*

●GW/0941-3596
**PLAST EUROPE : PE : KUNSTSTOFFE.** **VFOAT** PE. (1992)-. Periodical. English (French and German). mo. DM372.00. Carl Hanser Verlag, Postfach 860420, D 81631 Munich Germany. **Tel** 011 49 89 998300, FAX 011 49 89 984809. ***Continues*** *Kunststoffe Europe.*

IT
**PLAST RIVISTA DELLE MATERIE PLASTICHE.** Eris Spa, Via E Tellini 14, 20155 Milan Italy. **Tel** 011 39 2 33103305.

GW/0048-4350
**PLASTE UND KAUTSCHUK.** [Plaste Kautsch.]. **Added/Corp** Kammer der Technik. Vol. 1, (Jan. 1954)-. Academic Scholarly Publication. English. Six times a year. $175.00. Deutscher Verlag Grundstoffind, Karl Heine Strasse 27, D 04211 Leipzig Germany. **Tel** 011 49 341 4081011. **(Subscription address:** Thieme Medical Publishers Inc., 381 Park Avenue South, New York, NY 10016**)** **LC** TP986.A1; P4. **CODEN** PLKAAM. Documents available from Ask*IEEE, CASDDS.
**Ind/Abst** Alum. Ind. Abstr.; Chem. Abstr.; Chem. Titles; Ei Page One; Energy Res. Abstr.; Eng. Mater. Abstr.; INSPEC (1968-1985); Int. Packag. Abstr.; Met. Abstr.; Polymer Contents; Surf. Treat. Technol. Abstr.; World Surf. Coat. Abstr.

SW/0347-8262
**PLASTFORUM SCANDINAVIA.** [Plastforum Scand.]. (1977)-. Periodical. Swedish. Ten times a year. Kr425.00 Scandanavia; Kr545.00 (Europe); Kr675.00 (other). Indufa AB, Box 601, S 25106, Helsingborg, Sweden. **Tel** 011 46 42 173500, FAX 011 46 42 173600. **ED** Haus Widen (editors telephone 46/42/199911). **Ad Acc. Circ:** 5,000 (ctrl). ***Continues*** *Plastforum, 0048-4369.*

DK
**PLASTIC.** **Added/Corp** Plastic-Sammenslutningen. (1951)-. Periodical. Danish. mo (10 issues). Dansk Bladforlag K/S, 20 Holbergsgade, DK-1057 Copenhagen K Denmark. **LC** TP986.A1; P47.

US/0899-7519
**PLASTIC RAP.** (PLASTIC RAP / INTERNATIONAL PLASTICS SELECTOR.). [Plast. rap]. **Added/Corp** International Plastics Selector, Inc. Vol. 1, Issue 1 (June 1988)-. Periodical. English. sa. Free upon request. DATA Business Publishing, PO Box 6510, 15 Inverness Way East, Englewood CO 80155. **Tel** (800)447-4666, (303)799-0381, FAX (303)799-4082. **DD** 338.
**Desc:** A reference guide to thermoplastic and thermoset. It provides data on 13,000 commercial plastics including applications, the mechanical, thermal, electrical, and processing properties of the product, and its flammability.

RU/0554-2901
**PLASTICHESKIE MASSY.** [Plast. massy]. **Added/Corp** Russia (1923- U.S.S.R.). Gosudarstvennyi Komitet po Khimii. (1959)-. Periodical. Russian. bm. $159.95. **(Subscription address:** East View Publications Inc., 3020 Harbor Lane North, Suite 110, Minneapolis MN 55447.**)** **LC** TP986.A1; P516. Documents available from Article Express International.
**Ind/Abst** Abstr. Bull. Inst. Paper Chem.; Abstr. Bull. Inst. Pap. Sci. Tech.; Eng. Mater. Abstr.; Eng. Index Annu.; Food Sci. Technol. Abstr.; Int. Polym. Sci. Tech.

BL/0102-1931
**PLASTICO MODERNO.** [Plast. mod.]. (1982)-. Periodical. Portuguese. mo. **UDC** 678.06:621.798. ***Continues*** *Plasticos e Embalagem, 0102-1664.*
**Ind/Abst** PROMT.

BL
**PLASTICOS & I.E. E BORRACHA.** Periodical. Portuguese. 40.00. M & Z Representatives, 112 Ferry Street, Newark NJ 07105. **LC** TP1101; .P434.

SP/0303-4011
**PLASTICOS UNIVERSALES.** [Plast. univers.]. (1974)-. Academic Scholarly Publication. Spanish. bm. 7500ptas Spain; $86.00 other. Plastic Comunicacion S.L., Llacuna 162, Edificio Barcelona Act., 08018 Barcelona Spain. **Tel** 011 34 3 401-9833, FAX 011 34 3 401-9830. **ED** Wolfgang Glenz and Daniel Crespo. **CODEN** PLUVBY. **[CCC].** **Ad Acc. Circ:** 4,000 (ctrl). Documents available from CASDDS. ***Continues*** *Kunststoffe, Plasticos, 0023-558X.*
**Desc:** Every issue presents topics on new industrial developments, processing machinery, raw materials, devices, accessories, applications of plastics and company literature.
**Ind/Abst** Chem. Abstr.

JA/0551-0503
**PLASTICS AGE.** (PURASUCHIKKUSU EJI.). [Plast. age]. **VFOAT** Plastics Age. (1955)-. Academic Scholarly Publication. Japanese. mo. $323.00. Plastics Age Company Ltd., Okochi Building 1 10-6 Kajicho 1-chome, Chiyoda-ku Tokyo 101 Japan. **(Subscription address:** Maruzen Company Ltd., PO Box 5050, Import & Export Department, Tokyo 100 31 Japan.**)** **CODEN** PUEJDHPLAOAE. ctrl circ. Documents available from CASDDS.
**Desc:** Provides study of steps made in the industry.
**Ind/Abst** Chem. Abstr.

US/1051-0567
**PLASTICS & ENVIRONMENT.** ***Title Change.*** [Plast. environ.]. **VFOAT** Plastics and Environment. (June 29, 1990)-(19??). Periodical. English. bw. McGraw Hill Publishing Company, Inc., 1221 Avenue of the Americas, New York NY 10020. **Tel** (212)512-6410, (800)525-5003, FAX (212)512-6111. **DD** 658. ***Merged into*** *Plastics Week.*

UK/0309-4561
**PLASTICS AND RUBBER INTERNATIONAL.** ***Title Change.*** [Plast. rubber int.]. **Added/Corp** Plastics and Rubber Institute. Vol. 2 (Jan./Feb. 1977)-(199?). Academic Scholarly Publication. English. bm. Plastics & Rubber International, 11 Hobart Place London SW1W 0HL England. **Tel** 01 245 9555, telex 915719 PRIUK G. **ED** John Murphy. **LC** TP1101; .P47. **DD** 668.9/05. **CODEN** PRUID5. **[CCC].** Index available. cum. index. **Bk Rev. Ad Acc. Circ:** 11,000. available on microfilm and microfiche from University Microfilms International (UMI). Documents available from Ask*IEEE, CASDDS. ***Continues*** *Plastics and Rubber, 0308-311X.* ***Merged with*** *Metals and Materials (London, England : 1985), 0266-7185* ***and*** *British Ceramic, Transactions and Journal, 0266-7606* ***to form*** *Materials World, 0967-8638.*
**Desc:** Latest trends and developments related to plastics and rubber materials, products made from these materials and machinery and production processes for fabrication.
**Ind/Abst** Appl. Sci. Technol. Index (1991-); Chem. Abstr. (1977-1983); Chem. Bus. Bull.; Chem. Bus. NewsBase (1985-); Chem. Bus. Update; Curr. Technol. Index; Ei Page One; EMBASE; F&S Index Plus Text, Int. [Select. Cov.]; Infomat Int. Bus.; INSPEC (Jan./Feb. 1977-); Pollut. Abstr. Indexes; PROMT; Saf. Health Work; Text. Technol. Dig.; Trade Ind. Index.

UK/0032-1168
**PLASTICS & RUBBER WEEKLY.** [Plast. rubber wkly.]. **VFOAT** Plastics and Rubber Weekly; PRW. (19??)-. Periodical. English. wk (50 issues per year). £88.00 UK; £110.00 Europe; £120.00 other. EMAP Readerlink, Audit House, 260 Field End Road, Ruislip Middlesex HA4 9LT England. **Tel** 011 44 081 868 4499, FAX 011 44 081 429 3117. **LC** HD9661.A1; P53. **DD** 338.4/76782/05. **[CCC].** available on microfilm from University Microfilms International (UMI). ***Continues*** *Rubber & Plastics Weekly.*
**Ind/Abst** Chem. Bus. Bull.; Chem. Bus. NewsBase (1985-); Chem. Bus. Update; Coal Abstr.; F&S Index Plus Text, Int. [Select. Cov.]; Fluid Abstr., Civil Eng.; Fluid Abstr. Proc. Eng.; FLUIDEX (1973-); Infomat Int. Bus.; Int. Packag. Abstr.; Nonwovens Abstr.; PROMT; World Surf. Coat. Abstr.; World Text. Abstr.

US/1041-0821
**PLASTICS BRIEF/ DESIGN AND MATERIALS NEWSLETTER.** [Plast.Brief, Des. mater. newsl.]. **VFOAT** Plasticsbrief. Design and Materials Newsletter; Design and Materials Newsletter. Newsletter. English. wk. $249.00. Market Search Inc, 2727 Holland Sylvania Road/Suite A, Toledo OH 43615. **Tel** (419)535-7899, FAX (419)535-1243. **ED** Linda Best. **DD** 338. ***Continues*** *Plastics Brief (Design & Materials Edition), 0745-0133.*

US/1041-0813
**PLASTICS BRIEF/ EXTRUSION AND BLOW MOLDING NEWSLETTER.** [Plast.Brief, Extrus. blow molding newsl.]. **VFOAT** PlasticsBrief. Extrusion and Blow Molding Newsletter; Extrusion & Blow Molding Newsletter; Extrusion and Blow Molding Newsletter. (198?)-. Periodical. English. Fifty-two times a year. $124.00. Market Search Inc, 2727 Holland Sylvania Road/Suite A, Toledo OH 43615. **Tel** (419)535-7899, FAX (419)535-1243. **ED** Linda Best. **DD** 338. ***Continues*** *Plastics Brief (Extrusion & Blow Molding Edition), 0745-0141.*

US/1041-0805
**PLASTICS BRIEF/ REINFORCED PLASTICS NEWSLETTER.** [Plast.Brief, Reinf. plast. newsl.]. **VFOAT** Reinforced Plastics Newsletter. Newsletter. English. wk. $249.00. Market Search Inc, 2727 Holland Sylvania Road/Suite A, Toledo OH 43615. **Tel** (419)535-7899, FAX (419)535-1243. **ED** Linda Best. **DD** 338. ***Continues*** *Plastics Brief (Reinforced Plastics Edition), 0744-5296.*

US/1041-083X
**PLASTICS BRIEF/ THERMOPLASTIC MARKETING NEWSLETTER.** [Plast.Brief, Thermoplast. mark. newsl.]. **VFOAT** Thermoplastics Marketing Newsletter. Newsletter. English. wk. $249.00. Market Search Inc, 2727 Holland Sylvania Road/Suite A, Toledo OH 43615. **Tel** (419)535-7899, FAX (419)535-1243. **ED** Linda Best. **DD** 338. ***Continues*** *Plastics Brief (Marketing Edition), 0745-0168.*

BE
**PLASTICS BULLETIN.** (19??)-. Bulletin. English, French, Dutch and German. mo (except July and August). 1350F Belgium and Luxembourg; 2000F Europe; 2750F other (airmail). Rigi Media, Noordelaan 33, B-2030 Antwerpen Belgium. **Tel** 011 03 5417755, FAX 011 03 5418425. **ED** Jacques De Craene. Index available. **Bk Rev**, (Qty: 10). **Ad Acc, Adv Mgr:** Robert De Craene. **Circ:** 5,300.

CN/0229-0413
**PLASTICS BUSINESS.** [Plast. bus.]. Vol. 1, No. 1 (Sept./Oct. 1980)-. Periodical. English. Comes with subscription to Canadian Plastics. Southam Information and Technology Group Inc., 1450 Don Mills Road, Don Mills Ontario M3B 2X7 Canada. **Tel** (416)445-6641, (800)668-2374, FAX (416)442-2261. **DD** 338.4/76684/0971. available on microfilm and microfiche from University Microfilms International (UMI).

US/0734-1784
**PLASTICS BUSINESS NEWS.** [Plast. bus. news]. (1982)-. Periodical. English. wk. $327.00. Market Search Inc, 2727 Holland Sylvania Road/Suite A, Toledo OH 43615. **Tel** (419)535-7899, FAX (419)535-1243. ***Continues*** *Plastic Waste Strategies.*

US/1045-3806
**PLASTICS CANVAS CORNER.** [Plast. canvas corner]. **VFOAT** Plastic Canvas. 1989-. Periodical. English. bm. $15.00. Leisure Arts, PO Box 5595, Little Rock AR 72215. **Tel** (501)868-8800 ext. 338.

US/0148-9119
**PLASTICS COMPOUNDING.** [Plast. compd.]. (1977)-. Academic Scholarly Publication. English. bm (plus annual supplement). $48.00 US and possessions; $59.00 Canada; $75.00 other. Advanstar Communications Inc., 131 West First Street, Duluth MN 55802. **Tel** (218)723-9477, (800)346-0085. **ED** Mary C McMurrer. **LC** TP1101; .P49. **DD** 668.4/1/05. **CODEN** PLCODR. **[CCC]. Circ:** 13,071. available on microfilm and microfiche from University Microfilms International (UMI). Documents available from Article Express International, CASDDS.
**Desc:** Serves resin producers, formulators and compounders.
**Ind/Abst** Bioeng. Abstr.; Chem. Abstr.; Ei Page One; Eng. Index Annu.

US/0362-9376
**PLASTICS DESIGN FORUM.** [Plast. des. forum]. (March/April 1976)-. Periodical. English. bm. $48.00 US and possessions; $59.00 Canada; $75.00 other. Advanstar Communications Inc., 131 West First Street, Duluth MN 55802. **Tel** (218)723-9477, (800)346-0085. **ED** Mel Friedman. **LC** TP1101; .P5115. **DD** 668.4/05. **[CCC]. Ad Acc.** ctrl circ. available on microfilm and microfiche from University Microfilms International (UMI).
**Desc:** Serves engineers, design engineers, product designers and management personnel who evaluate and specify plastics for use in manufactured products or components.
**Ind/Abst** Eng. Mater. Abstr.; F&S Index Plus Text, Int. [Select. Cov.]; PROMT.

●US/1069-4358
**PLASTICS DIGEST.** [Plast. dig.]. Ed. 14 (1993)-. English. International Plastics Selector Inc & D A T A Inc, PO Box 26875, San Diego CA 92126. **Tel** (619)578-7600, telex 910 530 606. **LC** TA455.P5; P524. **DD** 668.4/0294. ***Continues*** *Plastics Materials. Plastics.*

US/0091-9578
**PLASTICS ENGINEERING.** [Plast. eng.]. **Added/Corp** Society of Plastics Engineers. Vol. 29, No. 8 (Aug. 1973)-. Academic Scholarly Publication. English. mo. $60.00 (one year), $90.00 (two year) North America; $80.00 (one year), $130.00 (two year) other. Society of Plastics Engineers, 14 Fairfield Drive, Brookfield CT 06804. **Tel** (203)775-0471, FAX (203)775-8490, telex 643-712. **ED** Roger M. Ferris. **LC** TP1101; .P513. **DD** 668.4/05. **CODEN** PLEGBB. **[CCC]. Bk Rev. Ad Acc. Circ:** 35,800. available on microfilm and microfiche from University Microfilms International (UMI). Documents available from Article Express International, Ask*IEEE, CASDDS, Documents on Demand. ***Continues*** *SPE Journal, 0036-1844.*
**Desc:** Coverage of the technical aspects of material use, equipment selection, product design and new product information.
**Ind/Abst** Abstr. Bull. Inst. Paper Chem.; Abstr. Bull. Inst. Pap. Sci. Tech.; Appl. Sci. Technol. Index; Bioeng. Abstr.; Chem. Abstr.; CIS Abstr.; Ei Page One; EMBASE; Energy Inf. Abstr.; Eng. Mater. Abstr.; Eng. Index Annu.; Environ. Abstr.; F&S Index Plus Text, Int. [Select. Cov.]; Infomat Int. Bus.; INSPEC (Aug. 1973-); Int. Packag. Abstr.; Polymer Contents; Predicasts; PROMT; Saf. Health Work; Trade Ind. Index [Full Txt.].

US/0554-2952
**PLASTICS FOCUS.** [Plast. focus]. Vol. 1 (1969)-. Periodical. English. bw. $265.00. The Plastics Connection Inc, PO Box 814, Amherst MA 01004. **Tel** (413)549-5020, FAX (413)549-9955. **ED** Michael L. Berins. **DD** 338.
**Desc:** Covers topics of major importance to the plastics industry - pricing, markets, technology, etc.

US/0147-2429
**PLASTICS IN BUILDING CONSTRUCTION. See** Building and Construction.

CN/0381-9620
**PLASTICS IN CONSTRUCTION. See** Building and Construction.

UK
**PLASTICS INDUSTRY DIRECTORY, THE.** (19??)-. Directory. English. an. £38.00. EMAP Readerlink, Audit House, 260 Field End Road, Ruislip Middlesex HA4 9LT England. **Tel** 011 44 081 868 4499, FAX 011 44 081 429 3117. **ED** Milary Jolmers. **Ad Acc. Circ:** 2,500.
**Desc:** Lists suppliers of machinery, materials services, molds, dyes and finished products.

UK/0268-8247
**PLASTICS INDUSTRY EUROPE.** [Plast. ind. Eur.]. (1977)-. Periodical. English. sm. Plastics Information Europe, 31 North Street, GB Carshalton SM5 2HW England. **Tel** 011 44 81 6479494.
**Ind/Abst** F&S Index Plus Text, Int. [Select. Cov.].

JA/0032-1206
**PLASTICS INDUSTRY NEWS.** [Plast. Ind. News]. **VFOAT** Chemicals, Polymers, Rubber & Plastics Industry News. (1955)-. English. mo. $148.00. Porima Kogyo Kenkyujo, (Inst. of Polymer Industry, Inc.), 7-3, Marunouchi 2 Chome, Chiyodaku, Tokyoto 100, Japan. **(Subscription address:** Maruzen Company Ltd., PO Box 5050, Import & Export Department, Tokyo 100 31 Japan.**) CODEN** PINWAE.

US/0886-9022
**PLASTICS INDUSTRY NEWS (DENVER, COLO.).** (PLASTICS INDUSTRY NEWS.). [Plast. ind. news]. Periodical. English. qt. Industry Media Inc, 1129 East 17th Avenue, Denver CO 80218. **DD** 338.
**Ind/Abst** Chem. Bus. Bull.; Chem. Bus. NewsBase (1985-); Chem. Bus. Update; F&S Index Plus Text, Int. [Select. Cov.]; Infomat Int. Bus.; PROMT.

US/0149-4899
**PLASTICS MACHINERY & EQUIPMENT.** [Plast. mach. equip.]. **VAT** Plastics Machinery and Equipment. (19??)-. Periodical. English. mo. $48.00 US and possessions; $59.00 Canada; $75.00 other. Advanstar Communications Inc., 131 West First Street, Duluth MN 55802. **Tel** (218)723-9477, (800)346-0085. **ED** Suzanne Witzler. **[CCC]. Circ:** 25,571. available on microfilm and microfiche from University Microfilms International (UMI).
**Desc:** Serves those who select and buy plastics processing machinery and equipment as well as those who manufacture plastics processing machinery, equipment and molds.

US/0099-0450
**PLASTICS MANUFACTURING CAPABILITIES IN MISSISSIPPI.** [Plast. manuf. capabil. Miss.]. English. be. Mississippi Research and Development Center, PO Drawer 2470, 3825 Ridgewood Road, Jackson MS 39205. **LC** TP1112; .P57. **DD** 338.4/7/6684025762.

US
**PLASTICS MANUFACTURING HANDBOOK AND BUYERS' GUIDE (NEW YORK, N.Y. : 1980/81).** ***Title Change.*** (THE PLASTICS MANUFACTURING HANDBOOK AND BUYERS' GUIDE.). **VFOAT** Manufacturing Handbook and Buyers' Guide. 1980/81-?. Consumer Publication. English. an. ***Continues*** *Plastics Technology. Special Plastics Manufacturing Handbook and Buyers' Guide Issue.* ***Continued by*** *Manufacturing Handbook & Buyers' Guide.*

US
**PLASTICS MATERIALS. ADHESIVES, SEALANTS, AND PRIMERS. See** Chemistry-Physical and Theoretical Chemistry.

US/1045-0769
**PLASTICS MATERIALS. PLASTICS.** ***Title Change.*** [Plast. mater., Plast.]. **VFOAT** Plastics; Plastic Materials. Plastics. Ed. 10 (1988)-Ed. 13 (1992). English. International Plastics Selector Inc & D A T A Inc, PO Box 26875, San Diego CA 92126. **Tel** (619)578-7600, telex 910 530 606. **LC** TA455.P5; P524. **DD** 668.4/0294. ***Continues*** *Plastics (San Diego, Calif.), 1041-0694.* ***Continued by*** *Plastics Digest.*

US/1042-802X
**PLASTICS NEWS (AKRON, OHIO).** (PLASTICS NEWS.). [Plast. news]. Vol. 1, No. 1 (Mar. 6, 1989)-. Periodical. English. Fifty-two times a year. $50.00 US and possessions; $84.00 other. Crain Communications Inc., 1400 Woodbridge, Detroit MI 48207. **Tel** (313)446-6000, (800)992-9970. **(Subscription address:** Crain Communications, 965 East Jefferson Avenue, Detroit MI 48207.**) ED** Robert Grace. **LC** HD 9661.A1; P55. **DD** 338.4/76684/05. **[CCC].** Index available. cum. index. **Bk Rev. Ad Acc. Circ:** 60,000. available on microfilm from University Microfilms International (UMI); available on an online database (file 16/Full-Text) from DIALOG.
**Desc:** Published for top North American executives in the plastics industry.
**Ind/Abst** F&S Index Plus Text, Int. [Full Txt.] [Select. Cov.]; PROMT [Full Txt.].

US
**PLASTICS PROCESSING & MACHINERY : TRENDS IN END-USE CONVERTING.** English. Twelve times a year. $650.00 (original), $120.00 (multiple) US and Canada. Springborn Laboratories Inc., 10 Springborn Center, Enfield CT 06082. **Tel** (203)749-8371 Ext. 295, FAX (203)749-8234, telex 4436041. **ED** Cherie P. Clark. Each issue contains an index to its own contents (no volume index)--loose. cum. index.
**Desc:** Provides an abstract service to keep industry professionals informed of new developments in the plastics industry.

US/1046-2201
**PLASTICS RECYCLING AS A FUTURE BUSINESS OPPORTUNITY : PROCEEDINGS, TECHNOLOGY EXCHANGE PROGRAM.** [Plast. recycl. future bus. oppor.]. **Main/Conf** Technology Exchange Program. **Added/Corp** Plastics Institute of America. **VFOAT** RecyclingPlas ... Conference. (June 20, 1986)-. Proceedings. English. an. $79.00. Technomic Publishing Company, Inc., 851 New Holland Avenue, Box 3535, Lancaster PA 17604. **Tel** (717)291-5609, (800)233-9936, FAX (717)295-4538. **LC** HD9661.U6; T43a. **DD** 338.4/76684.
**Desc:** Provides a valuable source of new information on the technology, management methods, and markets for practical plastics recycling.

UK/0959-8111
**PLASTICS, RUBBER AND COMPOSITES PROCESSING AND APPLICATIONS.** [Plast. rubber compos. process. appl.]. **Added/Corp** Plastics and Rubber Institute. Vol. 15, No. 1 (1991)-. Academic Scholarly Publication. English. Ten times a year. $611.00 The Americas; £410.00 other. Elsevier Applied Science, An Imprint of Elsevier Science Ltd., The Boulevard, Langford Lane, Kidlington, Oxford OX5 1GB United Kingdom. **Tel** 011 44 865 843000, 011 44 865 843699, FAX 011 44 865 843010. **(Subscription address:** Elsevier Science Ltd. Oxford Fulfillment Centre, PO Box 800, Kidlington, Oxford OX5 1DX United Kingdom.**) ED** N.G. McCrum. **LC** TP1101; .P485. **DD** 668.4/05. **CODEN** PRPAEP. **[CCC].** available on microfilm and microfiche from University Microfilms International (UMI). Documents available from Article Express International, The Genuine Article, Ask*IEEE, CASDDS. ***Continues*** *Plastics and Rubber Processing and Applications, 0144-6045.*
**Desc:** Provides an authoritative and truly international forum for the presentation of the science and technology involved in the plastics and rubber industries.
**Ind/Abst** Chem. Abstr.; Civ. Struct. Eng. Abstr.; Curr. Contents Eng. Tech. Appl. Sci.; Eng. Index Annu.; Highw. Res. Abstr.; INSPEC (1991-); Mater. Sci. Eng. Abstr.; Mech. Eng. Abstr.; Res. Alert [Full Cov.]; SCISEARCH.

US/0032-1257
**PLASTICS TECHNOLOGY.** [Plast. technol.]. **VFOAT** Plastics Technology Magazine. Vol. 1 (Feb. 1955)-. Academic Scholarly Publication. English. ir (13 issues per year). $65.00 US and Canada. Bill Communications Inc., 355 Park Avenue South, New York NY 10010-1789. **Tel** (800)821-6897, (212)592-6262, FAX (212)592-6209. **ED** Matthew Naitove. **LC** TP1101; .P557. **DD** 668.4/05. **CODEN** PLTEAB. **[CCC]. Bk Rev. Ad Acc. Circ:** 40,000. available on microfilm and microfiche from University Microfilms International (UMI); available on an online database (file 648/Full-Text) from DIALOG. Documents available from Article Express International.
**Desc:** Serves manufacturing managers in every plastics processing plant in the United States.
**Ind/Abst** Appl. Sci. Technol. Index; Bioeng. Abstr.; Chem. Ind. Notes; Ei Page One; EMBASE; Eng. Index Annu.; F&S Index Plus Text, Int. [Select. Cov.]; Infomat Int. Bus.; Int. Packag. Abstr.; Nonwovens Abstr.; PROMT; Trade Ind. ASAP [Full Txt.]; Trade Ind. Index [Full Txt.].

US/1044-9663
**PLASTICS WEEK (NEW YORK, N.Y.).** (PLASTICS WEEK.). [Plast. week]. (June 19, 1989)-. Periodical. English. wk. $440.00. McGraw Hill Publishing Company, Inc., 1221 Avenue of the Americas, New York NY 10020. **Tel** (212)512-6410, (800)525-5003, FAX (212)512-6111. **DD** 668.

US/0032-1273
**PLASTICS WORLD.** [Plast. world]. Vol. 1 (Apr. 1943)-. Periodical. English. Twelve times a year. $79.95 US; $104.95 Mexico; $112.30 Canada; $134.94 other. PTN Publishing Company, 445 Broad Hollow Road, Melville NY 11747. **Tel** (516)845-2700, FAX (516)845-7109. **ED** Bernard Miller. **LC** TP1101; .P562. **DD** 668.4/05. **CODEN** PLAWA4. **[CCC].** Index available (bound in all issues). **Ad Acc. Circ:** 60,000 (ctrl). available on microfilm and microfiche from University Microfilms International (UMI); available on an online database (file 648/Full-Text) from DIALOG. Documents available from Article Express International. ***Absorbed*** *Plastics Industry, 0096-9168.* ***Continued in part by*** *New Products News.*
**Desc:** Pertains to technical managers and engineers who buy plastics processing equipment and machinery, resins, and additives and services used in the manufacturing of plastics products. It provides practical

editorial for the entire buying team: general management, manufacturing and design.
**Ind/Abst** Acad. Search (July 1993-); Appl. Sci. Technol. Index; Bus. Index (1985-); Bus. Period. Index; Chem. Ind. Notes; Eng. Mater. Abstr.; Eng. Index Annu. [Select. Cov.]; F&S Index Plus Text, Int. [Select. Cov.]; Gen. BusinessFile (1985-); Gen. Period. Index (1985-); INFO-SOUTH Abstr.; Infomat Int. Bus.; Int. Packag. Abstr.; Mag. Search; Nonwovens Abstr.; PROMT; Text. Technol. Dig.; Trade Ind. ASAP [Full Txt.]; Trade Ind. Index [Full Txt.]; Wilson Bus. Abstr.

US/1041-0791
**PLASTICSBRIEF. INJECTION MOLDING NEWSLETTER.** [Plast.Brief, Inject. molding newsl.]. **VFOAT** Injection Molding Newsletter. (198?)-. Periodical. English. Fifty-two times a year. $124.00. Market Search Inc, 2727 Holland Sylvania Road/Suite A, Toledo OH 43615. **Tel** (419)535-7899, FAX (419)535-1243. **DD** 338. ***Continues*** *Plastics Briefs (Injection Molding Edition), 0745-015X.*

FR
**PLASTICULTURE. Added/Corp** Comite International des Plastiques en Agriculture. No.6 (June 1970)-. Periodical. French (English). qt. 400.00F. International Committee for Plastics in Agriculture, 65 rue de Prony, 75854 Paris Cedex 17 France. **Tel** 1 47 63 12 59, FAX 1 47 64 11 25, telex 641636 F. Index available. **Bk Rev. Ad Acc. Circ:** 1,000.
**Desc:** New plastics materials and products for application in agriculture and horticulture; agricultural techniques based partially or wholly on the use of plastics.
**Ind/Abst** AGRICOLA; Agric. Eng. Abstr. (1991-); Hortic. Abstr.; Irr. Drain. Abstr.; Maize Abstr.; Ornamental Hort. (19??-19??); Postharvest News Inf.; Rev. Agric. Entomol.; Rice Abstr.

FR/0180-9237
**PLASTIQUES FLASH.** [Plast. flash]. (1965)-. Periodical. French. mo (except Jan. & July). 324.62F France; 485.00F other. SPEI, 78 Route de la Reine, 92100 Boulogne France. **Tel** 011 33 1 46067826. **UDC** 678.5.

FR/0032-1303
**PLASTIQUES MODERNES ELASTOMERES.** [Plast. mod. elastom.]. English. 479.87F (one year), 898.48F (two year) France; 555.00F (one year), 1,050F (two year) other. Soc Publications Specialisees, 142 rue Montmartre, 75073 Paris Cedex 02 France. **Tel** 011 33 1 40268321 ext. 133. **LC** TP986.A1; I52. **CODEN** PMELAW. **[CCC].** Documents available from Article Express International.
**Desc:** Journal for the plastics and rubber industries. Articles on technological developments and economic changes in the industry with studies on processing and equipment, as well as notes on practical applications (cars and construction), and their environmental impact.
**Ind/Abst** Bioeng. Abstr.; Chem. Bus. Bull.; Chem. Bus. NewsBase (1985-); Chem. Bus. Update; Ei Page One; Energy Res. Abstr. (Nov. 1977-); Eng. Index Annu.; F&S Index Plus Text, Int. [Select. Cov.]; Infomat Int. Bus.; Point Repere (1979-1980); PROMT.

GW/0032-1338
**PLASTVERARBEITER, DER.** [Plastverarbeiter]. **VFOAT** Plast Verarbeiter. (April 1950)-. Academic Scholarly Publication. German. mo. $187.00. Dr. Alfred Huethig Verlag GmbH, Postfach 102869, D 69018 Heidelberg Germany. **Tel** 011 49 6221 489281. **(Subscription address:** Huethig Publishing Inc., 29 Macintosh Drive, Oxford CT 06478.**) ED** Fritz Vollmerand, Besulrard Liesh. **LC** TP986.A1; P718. **CODEN** PLARAN. **Bk Rev. Ad Acc. Circ:** 13,250. Documents available from Article Express International, CASDDS.
**Desc:** Covers processing and application of plastics, new procedures in the tool and machinery sector, further developments in the raw material sector.
**Ind/Abst** Bioeng. Abstr.; Chem. Abstr.; Ei Page One; EMBASE; Energy Res. Abstr. (July 1928-); Eng. Mater. Abstr.; Eng. Index Annu.; Int. Packag. Abstr.; Nonwovens Abstr.; Saf. Health Work.

CI/0351-1871
**POLIMERI (ZAGREB).** (POLIMERI.). [Polimeri]. **Added/Corp** Drustvo Plasticara i Gumaraca (Yugoslavia). (1980)-. Periodical. Serbo-Croatian (Roman) (summaries and/or abstracts in English). Six times a year. $100.00. Drustvo Plasticara i Gumaraca, Garicgradska 6, 41001 Zagreb, Croatia. **Tel** 011 385 41 388132, FAX 011 385 41 422936. **CODEN** PLMRDI. **Bk Rev. Ad Acc.** Documents available from CASDDS.
**Ind/Abst** Biodeter. Abstr.; Chem. Abstr.

IS/0370-2561
**POLIMERIM VE-HOMARIM PLASTIYIM. VFOAT** Polymers and Plastic Materials. Hebrew (summaries and/or abstracts in English). ir. 10.00. Center for Industrial Research, POB 311, Hefah Israel. **LC** TP1101. **CODEN** PVPLAE. Documents available from CASDDS.
**Ind/Abst** Chem. Abstr.

IT/0032-2768
**POLIPLASTI E PLASTICI RINFORZATI.** [Poliplasti plast. rinf.]. (1959)-. Academic Scholarly Publication. Italian. mo. Etas Kompass Periodici Tecnici, Via Mecenate 91, 20138 Milan Italy. **Tel** 011 39 2 50951. **CODEN** PPRFAW. Documents available from Article Express International, CASDDS. ***Continues*** *Poliplasti.*
**Ind/Abst** Bioeng. Abstr.; Chem. Abstr.; Ei Page One; Eng. Index Annu.; Int. Packag. Abstr.

US/0272-8397
**POLYMER COMPOSITES.** [Polym. compos.]. **Added/Corp** Society of Plastics Engineers. Vol. 1 (Sept. 1980)-. Academic Scholarly Publication. English. bm. $225.00 US; $250.00 other. Society of Plastics Engineers, 14 Fairfield Drive, Brookfield CT 06804. **Tel** (203)775-0471, FAX (203)775-8490, telex 643-712. **ED** Roger Porter. **LC** TA418.9.C6; P64. **DD** 668.4/94/05. **CODEN** PCOMDI. **[CCC]. Bk Rev. Ad Acc. Pr Rev. Circ:** 560. available on microfilm from University Microfilms International (UMI). Documents available from Article Express International, The Genuine Article, Ask*IEEE, CASDDS.
**Desc:** Contains abstracts, introductions, conclusions and references in technical articles.
**Ind/Abst** Bioeng. Abstr.; Chem. Abstr.; Curr. Contents Eng. Tech. Appl. Sci.; Ei Page One; Eng. Mater. Abstr.; Eng. Index Annu.; INSPEC (Jan. 1982-); Int. Aerosp. Abstr.; Leadscan; Polymer Contents; Res. Alert [Full Cov.]; Sci. Cit. Index; SCISEARCH.

UK/0883-153X
**POLYMER CONTENTS. See** Plastics-Abstracting, Bibliographies and Statistics.

UK/0141-3910
**POLYMER DEGRADATION AND STABILITY. See** Chemistry.

UK/0959-8103
**POLYMER INTERNATIONAL. Added/Corp** Society of Chemical Industry (Great Britain). Vol. 24, No. 1 (1991)-. Periodical. English. mo. $795.00. John Wiley & Sons Ltd., Baffins Lane, Chichester West Sussex PO19 1UD England. **Tel** 0243 779777, FAX 0243 776128 BTG:JWP001, telex 86290 WIBOOKG. **(Subscription address:** John Wiley / Philadelphia, PO Box 7247, Philadelphia PA 19170.**) LC** TP1101; .B73; TP1080; .P653. **DD** 668/.4/05. **CODEN** PLYIEI. **[CCC].** Documents available from Article Express International, The Genuine Article. ***Continues*** *British Polymer Journal.*
**Desc:** Publishes original papers and critical reviews from any branch of macromolecular science and technology.
**Ind/Abst** Civ. Struct. Eng. Abstr.; Comput. Inf. Syst. Abstr. J. [Full Cov.]; Curr. Contents Phys. Chem. Earth Sci.; Eng. Index Annu.; Environ. Eng. Abstr.; Mater. Sci. Eng. Abstr.; Mech. Eng. Abstr.; Res. Alert [Full Cov.]; Sci. Cit. Index; SCISEARCH; Solid State Supercond. Abstr.

US/0032-3918
**POLYMER NEWS.** [Polym. news]. Vol. 1 (Dec. 1970)-. Academic Scholarly Publication. English. ir. $533.00 (academic institutions), $831.00 (corporate institutions). Gordon & Breach Science Publishers, Inc., PO Box 786, Cooper Station, New York NY 10276. **Tel** (212)206-8900, FAX (212)645-2459. **(Subscription address:** Gordon & Breach Science Publishers / England, PO Box 90, Reading RG1 8JL England.**) ED** G. S. Kirshenbaum. **LC** TP1101; .P57. **DD** 668.4/05. **CODEN** PLYNBUPLYNBV. **[CCC].** Documents available from Ask*IEEE, CASDDS.
**Desc:** Source of information on polymer chemistry covering both academic and industrial research. It offers a comprehensive view of this fast-paced field for chemists, business people, marketing managers, product developers and others. Expanded coverage allows more information on polymer research, including elastomers, packaging, polymerization processes, etc.
**Ind/Abst** Chem. Abstr. (1971-); INSPEC (1971-); Polymer Contents (1971-).

US
**POLYMER PROCESSING AND RHEOLOGY.** (19??)-. Periodical. Six times a year. comes with Polymer Engineering and Science. Society of Plastics Engineers, 14 Fairfield Drive, Brookfield CT 06804. **Tel** (203)775-0471, FAX (203)775-8490, telex 643-712.

UK/0142-9418
**POLYMER TESTING.** [Polym. test.]. Vol. 1, No. 1 (Jan./March 1980)-. Academic Scholarly Publication. English. Five times a year. $400.00 The Americas; £268.00 other. Elsevier Applied Science, An Imprint of Elsevier Science Ltd., The Boulevard, Langford Lane, Kidlington, Oxford OX5 1GB United Kingdom. **Tel** 011 44 865 843000, 011 44 865 843699, FAX 011 44 865 843010. **(Subscription address:** Elsevier Science Ltd. Oxford Fulfillment Centre, PO Box 800, Kidlington, Oxford OX5 1DX United Kingdom.**) ED** Roger Brown. **LC** TA455.P58; P69. **DD** 620.1/92/0287. **CODEN** POTEDZ. **[CCC]. Bk Rev. Ad Acc. Pr Rev. Circ:** 300. available on microfilm and microfiche from University Microfilms International (UMI). Documents available from Article Express International, The Genuine Article, Ask*IEEE, CASDDS.
**Desc:** Forum for developments in testing of polymers and polymeric materials.
**Ind/Abst** Bioeng. Abstr.; Chem. Abstr.; Civ. Struct. Eng. Abstr.; Curr. Contents Eng. Tech. Appl. Sci.; Ei Page One; Elect. Comm. Abstr.; Eng. Mater. Abstr.; Eng. Index Annu.; INSPEC (1982-); Mater. Sci. Eng. Abstr.; Met. Abstr.; Polymer Contents; Res. Alert [Full Cov.]; Sci. Cit. Index; SCISEARCH.

US/0743-0515
**POLYMERIC MATERIALS SCIENCE AND ENGINEERING.** (POLYMERIC MATERIALS : SCIENCE AND ENGINEERING, PROCEEDINGS OF THE ACS DIVISION OF POLYMERIC MATERIALS, SCIENCE AND ENGINEERING.). [Polym. mater. sci. eng.]. Vol. 49 (Aug. 28-Sept. 2, 1983)-. Academic Scholarly Publication. English. Twice a year. $25.00. COJ Comstock Special Issues, 1155 16th Street Northwest, Washington DC 20036. **Tel** (800)227-5558. **(Subscription address:** American Chemical Society / Washington D.C., PO Box 57136, West End Station, Washington DC 20037.**) LC** TP935; .A515. **DD** 668.9/05. **CODEN** PMSEDG. Documents available from Article Express International, CASDDS. ***Continues*** *Organic Coatings and Applied Polymer Science Proceedings, 0732-7528.*
**Ind/Abst** Chem. Abstr. (1983-); Coal Abstr.; Curr. Biotechnol.; Ei Page One; Eng. Index Annu.; Int. Packag. Abstr.; Nonwovens Abstr.; Polymer Contents; Text. Technol. Dig.

UK/0967-3911
**POLYMERS & POLYMER COMPOSITES. VFOAT** Polymers and Polymer Composites. Vol. 1, No. 1 (1993)-. Periodical. English. bm (6 issues). £220.00 UK; $400.00 US; £240.00 other. RAPRA Technology Ltd., Shawbury Shrewsbury, Shropshire SY4 4NR England. **Tel** 011 44 939 250383, FAX 011 44 939 251118, telex 35134 RAPRA G. **LC** TA418.9.C6; P655. ***Continues*** *Composite Polymers.*

UK/0268-9812
**POLYMERS & RUBBER ASIA.** [Polym. rubber Asia]. (1985)-. Periodical. English. Six times a year. $108.00 (one year), $189.00 (two years), $270.00 (three years). SKC Communications Limited, Southfields, South View Road, Wadhurst East Sussex TN5 6TP England. **Tel** 011 44 892 784099, FAX 011 44 892 784089. **ED** Alessandro Vitelli. **Ad Acc. Circ:** 11,000 (ctrl).
**Desc:** News, information and comment on Asian and world plastics, rubber and processing machinery industries.
**Ind/Abst** Infomat Int. Bus.; PROMT [Full Txt.].

UK
**POLYMERS CERAMICS AND COMPOSITES ALERT.** English. mo. £165.00 UK; $275.00 other. The Institute of Materials, 1 Carlton House Terrace, London SW1Y 5DB England. **Tel** 011 44 71 839 4071, FAX (071)839 2078.

UK/0078-7817
**POLYMERS PAINT COLOUR YEAR BOOK. See** Paints and Painting.

II
**POPULAR PLASTICS & PACKAGING. VFOAT** Popular Plastics and Packaging. Vol. 34, No. 8 (Aug. 1989)-. Periodical. English. mo. $30.00. Colour Publications Private, 126A Dhuruwadi Off, c/o Dr. Nariman, Bombay 400025 India. **Tel** 011 91 22 4309318 6319, telex 71242 CEPE. **(Subscription address:** Prints India, 11 Darya Ganj, New Delhi 110002 India.**) ED** R V Raghavan. **CODEN** PPPAEB. **Bk Rev. Ad Acc. Circ:** 6,150 (ctrl). available on microfilm from University Microfilms International (UMI). ***Continues*** *Popular Plastics (Bombay, India : 1981), 0253-7303.*
**Desc:** Technical articles, special columns and news reports pertaining to the plastics industries.

US/0271-9312
**PROCEEDINGS OF THE CALIFORNIA CONFERENCE ON RUBBER-TOUGHENED PLASTICS.** [Proc. Calif. Conf. Rubber-Toughened Plast.]. **Main/Conf** California Conference on Rubber-Toughened Plastics. **Added/Corp** Carlhaven Corporation. Vol. 1 (1980)-. Academic Scholarly Publication. English. an. $80.00. Carlhaven Corporation, 1457 Firebird Way, Sunnyvale CA 94087. **Tel** (408)732-5325. **CODEN** PCCPDZ. Documents available from Article Express International, CASDDS.
**Ind/Abst** Bioeng. Abstr.; Chem. Abstr.; Ei Page One; Eng. Index Annu.

US/1073-1768
**PROCEEDINGS OF THE ... NATIONAL AGRICULTURAL PLASTICS CONGRESS. Main/Conf** National Agricultural Plastics Congress. **Added/Corp** National Agricultural Plastics Association (U.S.). (19??)-. English. ir. $68.00 US; $71.00 Canada & Mexico; $74.00 other. American Society Plasticulture, PO Box 860238, St Augustine FL 32086. **Tel** (904)797-0299, , FAX (904)829-1668. **Pr Rev. Circ:** 300 (ctrl). ***Continues*** *National Agricultural Plastics Conference. Proceedings ... National Agricultural Plastics Conference.*
**Desc:** News, information, and research papers on agriculture plastics presented at Congress.

US/0164-0402
**PROCEEDINGS OF THE WATER-BORNE AND HIGHER-SOLIDS COATINGS SYMPOSIUM.** [Proc. Water-borne High.-solids Coat. Symp.]. **Main/Conf** Water-Borne and

Higher-Solids Coatings Symposium. **Added/Corp** University of Southern Mississippi. Department of Polymer Science. Southern Society for Coatings Technology. (19??)-. Academic Scholarly Publication. English. an. $85.00. University of Southern Mississippi / Department of Polymer Science, South Street Box 10076, Hattiesburg MS 39406. **Tel** (601)266-4868. **ED** Shelby F. Thames. **CODEN** PWHSD5. **Circ:** 500. Documents available from Article Express International, CASDDS.
**Desc:** Copies of papers presented at the Water-Borne and Higher-Solids Coatings Symposiums.
**Ind/Abst** Bioeng. Abstr.; Chem. Abstr.; Ei Page One; Eng. Index Annu.

CN/0713-9098
**PRODUCTION AND SHIPMENTS OF BLOW-MOULDED PLASTIC BOTTLES.** (PRODUCTION AND SHIPMENTS OF BLOW - MOULDED PLASTIC BOTTLES / STATISTICS CANADA, INDUSTRY DIVISION.). [Prod. shipm. blow-mould. plast. bottles]. **Added/Corp** Statistics Canada. Manufacturing and Primary Industries Division. Statistics Canada. Industry Division. **VFOAT** Production et Livraisons de Bouteilles de Plastiques Formees par Soufflage. Vol. 1, No. 1 (March 31, 1982)-. Periodical. English (French). qt. 32.00Can$ Canada; $39.00 US; $45.00 other. Statistics Canada, Publications Sales & Services, Main Building Room 1710, Ottawa Ontario K1A 0T6 Canada. **Tel** (613)951-5078, (800)267-6677, FAX (613)951-1584, telex 053-3585. **ED** T. R. Schdeu. **LC** HD9662.B69; C226. **DD** 338.4/7668497. **Circ:** 200. ***Continues*** *Production and Shipments of Plastic Bottles, 0713-908X.*
**Desc:** Production and shipments of blow moulded plastic bottles by end use. Also materials used in production.

UK/0266-7320
**PROGRESS IN RUBBER AND PLASTICS TECHNOLOGY.** **See** Rubber.

JA/0555-7887
**PURASUCHIKKUSU.** [Purasuchikkusu]. **VFOAT** Japan Plastics (In Japanese); Plastics (Tokyo). (1950)-. Academic Scholarly Publication. Japanese. Twelve times a year. $233.00. Kogyo Chosakai, (Kogyo Chosakai Publishing Co., Ltd.), 14-7, Hongo 2 Chome, Bunkyoku, Tokyoto 113, Japan. **(Subscription address:** Maruzen Company Ltd., PO Box 5050, Import & Export Department, Tokyo 100 31 Japan.**)** **CODEN** PRSKAW. Documents available from CASDDS.
**Ind/Abst** Chem. Abstr.

US/0744-7493
**QUARTERLY - INTERNATIONAL PLASTIC MODELERS' SOCIETY. UNITED STATES BRANCH.** (QUARTERLY / INTERNATIONAL PLASTIC MODELERS' SOCIETY, U.S.A.). [Q. - Int. Plast. Model. Soc., U.S. Branch]. **Added/Corp** International Plastic Modeler's Society. United States Branch. (19??)-. Periodical. English. qt. IPMS, 4940 East Evans Avenue, Denver CO 80201. ***Continues*** *IPMS-USA Quarterly, 0096-3496.*
**Ind/Abst** Index Inf.

UK/0034-3617
**REINFORCED PLASTICS (LONDON).** (REINFORCED PLASTICS.). [Reinf. plast.]. (Sept. 1956)-. Academic Scholarly Publication. English. Eleven times a year. $127.00 The Americas; £85.00 other. Elsevier Advanced Technology, An Imprint of Elsevier Science Ltd., The Boulevard, Langford Lane, Kidlington, Oxford OX5 1GB United Kingdom. **Tel** 011 44 865 843000, 011 44 865 843699, FAX 011 44 865 843010. **(Subscription address:** Elsevier Science Ltd. Oxford Fulfillment Centre, PO Box 800, Kidlington, Oxford OX5 1DX United Kingdom.**)** **ED** A. Weaver. **LC** TA455.P55; R4. **DD** 668/.416/05. **[CCC].** Index available. **Bk Rev. Ad Acc. Circ:** 3,000. available on microfilm and microfiche from University Microfilms International (UMI). Documents available from CASDDS.
**Desc:** Descriptions and illustrations of new applications of reinforced plastics in all industries and trades, editorial on techniques of moulding, technical articles.
**Ind/Abst** Chem. Abstr.; Chem. Bus. Bull.; Chem. Bus. NewsBase (1985-); Chem. Bus. Update; Curr. Technol. Index; Ei Page One.

US/1052-4908
**RESOURCE RECYCLING'S PLASTICS RECYCLING UPDATE.** [Resour. recycl. plast. recycl. update]. **VFOAT** Plastics Recycling Update. (Dec. 1988)-. Periodical. English. Twelve times a year. $85.00 (one year); $146.00 (two years). Resource Recycling, PO Box 10540, Portland OR 97210. **Tel** (503)227-1319, (800)227-1424, FAX (503)227-6135. **ED** Chris Caffarella. **DD** 363. Index available. cum. index. **Ad Acc, Adv Mgr:** R. Downing, **Tel** (216)255-1454. **Circ:** 2,500. ***Continues*** *Plastics Recycling Update.*
**Desc:** Focusing on plastic scrap recovery and utilization.

SP/0034-8708
**REVISTA DE PLASTICOS MODERNOS.** **Added/Corp** Instituto de Plasticos y Caucho (Spain). (1963)-. Periodical. Spanish. mo. $60.00 surface mail; $160.00 air mail. Instituto Ciencia Tecnologia de Polimeros, Juan de la Cierva 3, 28006 Madrid Spain. **Tel** 011 34 561 3441, FAX 011 34 564 4853. **LC** TP986.A1; R46. **CODEN** RPMOAM. **[CCC].** Index available. **Circ:** 3,500. Documents available from CASDDS. ***Continues*** *Revista de Plasticos, 0370-4513.*
**Ind/Abst** Chem. Abstr.; Ei Page One; Nonwovens Abstr.; World Surf. Coat. Abstr.

CN/0835-0027
**RUBBER AND PLASTIC PRODUCTS INDUSTRIES.** **See** Rubber.

US/0300-6123
**RUBBER & PLASTICS NEWS.** **See** Rubber.

US/0197-2219
**RUBBER & PLASTICS NEWS II.** **See** Rubber.

UK
**RUBBICANA. EUROPE.** **See** Rubber.

CN/0229-4575
**SALARY SURVEY (SOCIETY OF THE PLASTICS INDUSTRY OF CANADA).** **See** Economics-Labor.

GW/0174-4003
**SCHRIFTENREIHE KUNSTOFF -FORSCHUNG.** [Schriftenr. Kunst. -Forsch.]. Academic Scholarly Publication. German. Price varies per volume. Universitatsbibliothek der Technischen Universitat, Berlin Abteilung Publikationen Strasse des 17 Juni 135, O-1000 Berlin Germany. **CODEN** SKFODY. Documents available from CASDDS.
**Ind/Abst** Chem. Abstr.

IT
**SELEPLAST.** (19??)-. Italian. mo (11 issues). L70000 Italy; L140000 other. Cida Editrice Srl, Viale Certosa 238, 20156 Milan Italy. **Tel** 011 39 2 3085141.

CN/0823-0900
**SHIPMENTS OF PLASTIC FILM AND BAGS MANUFACTURED FROM RESIN.** [Shipm. plast. film bass manuf. resin]. **Added/Corp** Statistics Canada. **VFOAT** Livraisons de Pellicules et Sacs en Matiere Plastique Fabriques de Resine; Livraisons de Pellicules et Sacs en Matiere Plastique Fabriques de Resines. Vol. 1, No. 1 (Mar. 31, 1983)-. English (French). qt. 32.00Can$ Canada; $39.00 US; $45.00 other. Statistics Canada, Publications Sales & Services, Main Building Room 1710, Ottawa Ontario K1A 0T6 Canada. **Tel** (613)951-5078, (800)267-6677, FAX (613)951-1584, telex 053-3585. **LC** HD9662.F543; C27. **DD** 381/.45668495/0971021.

JA/0038-1586
**SOSEI TO KAKO : NIHON SOSEI KAKO GAKKAI SHI.** [Sosei to kako]. **VFOAT** Journal of the Japan Society for Technology of Plasticity. (1960)-. Academic Scholarly Publication. Japanese. mo. $320.00. Nihon Sosei Kako Gakkai, (Japan Soc. for Techonology of Plasticity), 2-5, Roppongi 5 Chome, Minatoku, Tokyoto 106, Japan. **(Subscription address:** Japan Publications Trading Company, Ltd., PO Box 5030, Tokyo International, Tokyo 100-31 Japan.**)** **CODEN** SOKAB9. cum. index. Documents available from CASDDS.
**Ind/Abst** Alum. Ind. Abstr.; Chem. Abstr.; Met. Abstr.

CN/0714-346X
**SPI CANADA ... PROGRAM, ... ACCOMPLISHMENTS.** [SPI Can. program, accomp.]. **Main/Corp** Society of the Plastics Industry of Canada. **VAT** Society of the Plastics Industry of Canada Program, Accomplishments. 1981-. English. an. Society of the Plastics Industry of Canada, 1262 Don Mills Road, Suite 104, Don Mills Ontario, M3B 2W7 Canada. **Tel** (416)449-3444, FAX (416)449-5685, telex 06- 966739. **DD** 338.7/6684/0971. ctrl circ.

US
**SPI STATISTICAL REPORT ON THERMOPLASTIC AND THERMOSETTING RESINS.** (19??)-. Statistical Publication. English. mo. $75.00 summary data only; $550.00 internal use participants; $825.00 internal use non-participant. SPI / CRS, 1275 K Street NW, Suite 400, Washington DC 20005. **Tel** (202)371-5200.
**Desc:** Provides production, sales, and captive use data on major plastics resins, showing current month, same month a year earlier, and year-to-date comparisons with percent change.

●US/1065-7142
**STEPHENS' OHIO PLASTICS DIRECTORY.** (STEPHENS' OHIO PLASTICS DIRECTORY / COMPILED AND PUBLISHED BY INDUSTRY SERVICES.). [Stephens' Ohio plast. dir.]. **Added/Corp** Industry Services (Lansing, Mich.). **VFOAT** Ohio Plastics Directory. (1992/1993)-. Directory. English. Industry Services, PO Box 80315, Lansing MI 48908. **LC** IN PROCESS. **DD** 668.

US/8755-7371
**STRUCTURAL FOAM PLASTICS.** (STRUCTURAL FOAM PLASTICS : DIRECTORY & MARKETING GUIDE.). [Struct. foam plast.]. (1983)-. Directory. English. ir. Technomic Publishing Company, Inc., 851 New Holland Avenue, Box 3535, Lancaster PA 17604. **Tel** (717)291-5609, (800)233-9936, FAX (717)295-4538. **LC** HD9662.P53; U672. **DD** 381/.45668493/0973.

CC/1001-9456
**SULIAO (BEIJING).** (SU LIAO / PEI-CHING SU LIAO YEN CHIU SO PIEN.). [Suliao]. **Added/Corp** Pei-Ching su Liao Yen Chiu so (China). **VFOAT** Plastics. (1972)-. Academic Scholarly Publication. Chinese. bm. **LC** TP1101; .S8. **DD** 620.1/923/05. **CODEN** SULIEF. Documents available from CASDDS. ***Absorbed*** *Su Liao i Tsung.*
**Ind/Abst** Chem. Abstr. (1986-).

US
**SYNTHETIC ORGANIC CHEMICALS. UNITED STATES PRODUCTION AND SALES OF PLASTICIZERS.** (SYNTHETIC ORGANIC CHEMICALS.). **VFOAT** Plasticizers. Periodical. English. an. US International Trade Commission, 701 E Street NW, Washington DC 20436. **Tel** (202)523-0235.

US/0099-3492
**TECHNICAL PAPERS, REGIONAL TECHNICAL CONFERENCE.** **Added/Corp** Society of Plastics Engineers. Southern California Section. (19??)-. Academic Scholarly Publication. English. ir. Society of Plastics Engineers, 14 Fairfield Drive, Brookfield CT 06804. **Tel** (203)775-0471, FAX (203)775-8490, telex 643-712. **CODEN** TPRTAG. Documents available from CASDDS.
**Ind/Abst** Chem. Abstr.

FR/0245-9574
**TECHNIQUES DE L'INGENIEUR. PLASTIQUES.** [Tech. ing., Plast.]. (1980)-. French. qt. Editions Techniques, 141 rue de Javel, 75747 Paris Cedex 15 France. **Tel** 011 33 1 45589100. **UDC** 678.5. ***Continues*** *Techniques de l'Ingenieur. Generalites, 0399-4090.*

US/0013-7154
**TRENDS IN END-USE MARKETS FOR PLASTICS.** **Added/Corp** Debell and Richardson, Inc. **VFOAT** End-Use Markets for Plastics. (196?)-. English. mo. $520.00 (original); $120.00 (multiple). Springborn Laboratories Inc., 10 Springborn Center, Enfield CT 06082. **Tel** (203)749-8371 Ext. 295, FAX (203)749-8234, telex 4436041. **ED** Cherie P. Clark. **LC** HD9661.A1; T7. **DD** 338.4/5668/4. **CODEN** TEUMA. Each issue contains an index to its own contents (no volume index)--loose. cum. index. **Circ:** 350-400.
**Desc:** Provides an abstract service to keep industry professionals informed of new developments in the plastics industry.

US/0083-0968
**U.S. FOAMED PLASTICS MARKETS & DIRECTORY.** **VAT** United States Foamed Plastic Markets and Directory. Directory. English. an. $65.00. Technomic Publishing Company, Inc., 851 New Holland Avenue, Box 3535, Lancaster PA 17604. **Tel** (717)291-5609, (800)233-9936, FAX (717)295-4538. **LC** TP1183.F6; I55. **DD** 338.4/7/66849302573. **[CCC]. Ad Acc.** ***Continues*** *International Foamed Plastic Markets & Directory.*
**Desc:** Lists what companies provide what services and products related to foamed plastics. A description of each companies products or markets for rigid and flexible foamed plastics.

US/0149-1342
**URETHANE ABSTRACTS.** **Added/Corp** Franklin Institute (Philadelphia, Pa.). Science Information Service. Vol. 1 (Jan. 1972)-. English. mo. $205.00 (one year), $400.00 (two year), $595.00 (three year). Technomic Publishing Company, Inc., 851 New Holland Avenue, Box 3535, Lancaster PA 17604. **Tel** (717)291-5609, (800)233-9936, FAX (717)295-4538. **LC** TP1180.P8; U74. **DD** 668.4/23. **CODEN** URABB. **[CCC]. Circ:** 225. available on microfilm from University Microfilms International (UMI).
**Desc:** Digests of current international literature and U.S. patents on polyurethanes/polyisocyanurates. Summarizes articles from industry magazines, technical journals, newsletters, conference proceedings, and government and association reports. Market information includes statistics and projections. Provides a broad overview of new developments in urethane with sources for more detailed information in areas of specific interest.

UK/0265-637X
**URETHANES TECHNOLOGY.** Vol. 1, No. 1 (Feb. 1982)-. English. bm. £46.00 UK and Europe; $98.00 US and Canada. Crain Communications Ltd., 75-77 Cowcross Street, Cowcross Court, London EC1M 6BP England. **Tel** 011 44 71 6082774. **ED** David Reed. Index available. **Ad Acc. Circ:** 3,727. available on an online database (file 16/Full-Text) from DIALOG. Documents available from Article Express International.
**Desc:** Provides news and analysis of technical and commercial developments in the polyurethane and related end-user industries. Details new equipment, materials, processes and applications.
**Ind/Abst** Ei Page One (19??-); Eng. Index Annu. (19??-)

[Select. Cov.]; F&S Index Plus Text, Int. (19??-) [Full Txt.] [Select. Cov.]; Infomat Int. Bus. (19??-); PROMT (19??-) [Full Txt.].

CN/0382-0424
**VISION (MONTREAL).** (VISION.). **Added/Corp** Association des Professeurs d'Arts Plastiques du Quebec. (Spring 1969)-. Periodical. Multiple languages (French and English). an. Aquesap Vision, CP 567 Succ St Michel, Montreal Quebec H2A 3N2 Canada. **Tel** (514)641-3773, (514)658-1263.

US
**WHO'S WHO GUIDE OF PETROCHEMICAL & PLASTICS COMPANIES.** **VFOAT** Guide of Petrochemical & Plastics Companies; Guide of Petrochemical and Plastics Companies. (1990)-. English. Who's Who Information Services, 17 South Brian Hollow Lane, Suite 401, Houston TX 77027. **LC** IN PROCESS.

UK
**WORLD PLASTICS & RUBBER TECHNOLOGY.** English. an. £55.00. Cornhill Publications Ltd, 2 16 Goodge Street, London W1P 1SF England. **Tel** 011 44 71 240-1515. **Ad Acc.** ctrl circ.

US/0895-9099
**WORLD PLASTICS MONITOR.** [World plast. monit.]. **VFOAT** DRI World Plastics Monitor. Vol. 1, No. 1 (Oct. 1987)-. Periodical. English. bm. Free to clients of DRI World Plastics Service, $1000.00 others. McGraw Hill Publishing Company, Inc., 1221 Avenue of the Americas, New York NY 10020. **Tel** (212)512-6410, (800)525-5003, FAX (212)512-6111. **DD** 338.

US/1058-4358
**YEARBOOK OF BLOW MOLDED PACKAGING, THE.** [Yearb. blow molded packag.]. **VFOAT** Year Book Blow Molded Packaging. (1991)-. English. **LC** TP1150; .Y43. **DD** 668.4/97.

## ABSTRACTING, BIBLIOGRAPHIES AND STATISTICS

US/1049-1341
**C2C ABSTRACTS JAPAN. PLASTICS.** [C2C abstr. Jap., Plast.]. **VFOAT** Plastics. Vol. 1, No. 1 (Feb. 1990)-. English. mo. $200.00. SCAN C2C Inc, Attn Carol G Heffernan Marketing Director, 500 E Street Southwest, Suite 800, 8th Floor, Washington DC 20024. **Tel** (202)863-3850, (800)525-3865, FAX (202)863-3855. **DD** 668. Index available. cum. index. available on CD-ROM from DIALOG; available on an online database from ORBIT; DATA-STAR; and DIALOG.
**Desc:** English abstracts of over 500 Japanese science, technical and business journals in the field of plastics.

CN/0828-5810
**CANADIAN PLASTICS STATISTICAL YEAR BOOK.** [Can. plast. stat. year b.]. **Added/Corp** Society of the Plastics Institute Canada. **VFOAT** Canadian Plastics Industry. (1981)-. Statistical Publication. English. an. 35.00Can$. Society of the Plastics Industry of Canada, 1262 Don Mills Road, Suite 104, Don Mills Ontario, M3B 2W7 Canada. **Tel** (416)449-3444, FAX (416)449-5685, telex 06- 966739. **ED** F.R. Shammas. **DD** 338.4/76684/0971.

UK/0883-153X
**POLYMER CONTENTS.** **Added/Corp** Polymer Research Associates, Inc. (April 1985)-. Abstracting/Indexing Service. English. mo. $351.00 The Americas; £235.00 other. Elsevier Applied Science, An Imprint of Elsevier Science Ltd., The Boulevard, Langford Lane, Kidlington, Oxford OX5 1GB United Kingdom. **Tel** 011 44 865 843000, 011 44 865 843699, FAX 011 44 865 843010. (Subscription address: Elsevier Science Ltd. Oxford Fulfillment Centre, PO Box 800, Kidlington, Oxford OX5 1DX United Kingdom.) **ED** J. R. Richard. **DD** 668. **CODEN** PRPCEV. [CCC]. Index available. cum. index. **Ad Acc.** available on microfilm and microfiche from University Microfilms International (UMI). **Continues** PRA Report: Polymer Contents, 0749-534X.
**Desc:** The international current awareness publication for polymer science and engineering.

# POLITICAL SCIENCE

PO
**25 I.E. VINTE E CINCO DE SETEMBRO.** Periodical. Portuguese. $15.00. Comissariado Politico das FRLM 448, Maputo Portugal. **LC** DT463; .V54. **DD** 320.9/67/903.

US
**50-STATE LEGISLATIVE DIRECTORY.** **VFOAT** Fifty-State Legislative Directory. (1989-90)-. Directory. English. ir. $95.00. California Journal Press, 1714 Capitol Avenue, Sacramento CA 95814. **Tel** (916)444-2840, FAX (916)444-2339.

CN
**A.P.E.P. (ENGLISH EDITION).** (A.P.E.P. / PEOPLE'S SPAIN PRESS AGENCY.). No. 78 (Apr. 1, 1976)-. Periodical. English. ir. $4.00. National Publications Centre, PO Box 727 Adelaide Station, Toronto Ontario M5C 2J8 Canada. **Tel** (416)252-3658. **DD** 320.946.

IT
**A SINISTRA.** Italian. mo. L35000. Cooperativa Irene Arl, Via Farini 62, 00185 Rome Italy. **Tel** 6/4817342.

RU
**ABC OF SOCIAL AND POLITICAL KNOWLEDGE.** **See** Social Sciences.

US/0001-0456
**ABC POL SCI. ADVANCE BIBLIOGRAPHY OF CONTENTS: POLITICAL SCIENCE & GOVERNMENT.** **See** Political Science-Abstracting, Bibliographies and Statistics.

US/0736-5330
**ACARI INDEX, THE.** [ACARI index]. **VFOAT** A.C.A.R.I. Index. **VAT** Americans for Constitutional Action Research Institute Index. 1981-. English. an. 955 l'Enfant Plaza North SW, Suite 1000B, Washington DC 20024. **Continues** ACA Index.

US/0364-7625
**ACCESS REPORTS.** (ACCESS REPORTS / FREEDOM OF INFORMATION.). **VFOAT** Access Reports. (1981)-. English. sm. $325.00 North America; $375.00 other. Access Reports Inc, 1624 Dogwood Lane, Lynchburg VA 24503. **Tel** (804)384-5334, FAX (804)846-6928. **ED** Harry A Hammitt. **LC** JK468.S4; A64. **DD** 323.44/5/0973. Index available. available on an online database from NEWSNET. **Continues** Access Reports, 0364-7625.
**Desc:** The newsletter covers the Freedom of Information Act and also privacy issues as they relate to disclosure of government information. It deals with government information policy concerning the disclosure and protection of government information.

IT
**ACCIAIO.** **Ceased.** No. 1 Oct. (1976)-(19??). Periodical. Italian. mo. Siderservize S R L, Piazza Velasca 8, 20122 Milan Italy. **Tel** (02)865840, FAX 8052034, telex 311438. **ED** Giuseppe de Martino. **LC** JN5657.R5; A22. Index available. **Bk Rev.** **Ad Acc.** **Circ:** 3,500.
**Desc:** Examples of outstanding realizations of steel using projects, with schemes and pictures.

US
**ACCOMPLISHMENTS OF THE COMMITTEE ON INTERIOR AND INSULAR AFFAIRS OF THE HOUSE OF REPRESENTATIVES DURING THE ... CONGRESS.** **Main/Corp** United States. Congress. House. Committee on Interior and Insular Affairs. Government Publication. English. be. Superintendent of Documents, US Government Printing Office, Washington DC 20402. **Tel** (202)275-3328, FAX (202)786-2377. **LC** JK1430.I53; A35.

UK
**ACCOUNTS, TREASURER'S AND AUDITORS' REPORTS / AMNESTY INTERNATIONAL.** **Main/Corp** Amnesty International. **VFOAT** Amnesty International Accounts, Treasurer's and Auditor's Reports. English (Spanish and French). an. Amnesty International / International Secretariat, 1 Easton Street, London WC1X 8DJ England. **Tel** 011 44 71 413 5500, FAX 011 44 71 833 5100, telex 28502. **LC** JC571; .A44C. **DD** 323.4/9/0601.
**Desc:** This report documents Amnesty International's work and its concerns throughout the world.

NE/0001-6810
**ACTA POLITICA.** [Acta polit.]. **Added/Corp** Nederlandse Kring voor Wetenschap der Politiek. Vol. 1 (1966)-. Periodical. Dutch (English; summaries and/or abstracts in English). Four times a year (Jan., Apr., July, Oct.). Fl106.00 (individuals), Fl172.00 (institutions) Netherlands; Fl148.00 (individuals), Fl185.00 (institutions) others. Uitgeverij Boom, Postbus 400, 7940 AK Meppel Netherlands. **Tel** 011 31 20 5220 57012, FAX 011 31 20 5220 54452, telex 42829. **ED** K. Koch. Index available (Bound in issues). cum. index. **Bk Rev.** **Ad Acc.** **Circ:** 800. available on an online database.
**Desc:** Journal for political scientists, politicians, sociologists, and civil and federal administrators.
**Ind/Abst** ABC POL SCI; Am. Hist. Life (1971-); Int. Bibliogr. Sociol.; Int. Polit. Sci. Abstr. (1971-); Linguist. Lang. Behav. Abstr.; Middle East Abstr. Index; Soc. Plann. Policy Dev. Abstr.; Sociol. Abstr.

FR/1166-3286
**ACTION FRANCAISE HEBDO, L'.** **VFOAT** Action Francaise. (19??)-. Periodical. French. Forty-eight times a year (except 4 weeks in Aug.). 480.00F France; 900.00F French Overseas; 955.00F other. Aspects de la France, 10 rue Croix des Petits Champs, 75001 Paris France. **Tel** 011 33 1 40399206, FAX 011 33 1 40263163. **LC** HC271; .A63. **Bk Rev.** **Ad Acc.** **Circ:** 10,000 (ctrl).

PL
**ACTIVITY OF THE POLISH INSTITUTE OF INTERNATIONAL AFFAIRS.** **Title Change.** **Main/Corp** Polski Instytut Spraw Miedzynarodowych. English. Polish Institute of International Affairs, Ul Warecka 1A, POB 1000, 00-950 Warsaw Poland. **LC** JX38; .P6413. **DD** 327/.07/114384. **Continued by** International Affairs Studies, 0867-4493.

AG/0327-6058
**ACTUALIZACION POLITICA.** **Added/Corp** Fundacion Integracion Americana. No. 1 (Nov. 1991)-. Periodical. Spanish.

US/0896-3134
**ADA TODAY.** (ADA TODAY: A NEWSPAPER FOR LIBERAL ACTIVISTS FROM AMERICANS FOR DEMOCRATIC ACTION.). [ADA today]. **Added/Corp** Americans for Democratic Action. **VAT** Americans for Democratic Action Today. Vol. 40, No. 2 (Oct./Nov. 1985)-. Periodical. English. Four times a year (Feb., July, Sept., Dec.). $20.00. Americans for Democratic Action, 815 15th Street Northwest, Suite 210, Washington DC 20006. **Tel** (202)785-5980, FAX (202)785-5969. **ED** Valerie Dulk. **LC** E740; .A6. **DD** 973. **Circ:** 23,000. **Continues** ADA World, 0001-0871.
**Desc:** Covers recent events sponsored by ADA as well as announcing future activities, chapter work, legislation about which readers should contact their Representative and Senators and serves as a link between the national office and the community at large.

IT
**ADISTA : AGENZIA D'INFORMAZIONE STAMPA.** Italian. ir (90 issues per year). L100.000 (regular subscribers), L300.000 (sustaining subscribers). Adista, Agenzia Informazione Stampa, Vis Acciaioli 7, 00186 Rome Italy. **Tel** 39 6 6541924, FAX 39 6 6865898. Index available. cum. index. **Circ:** 12,000 (ctrl).

IE/0001-8325
**ADMINISTRATION (DUBLIN).** **See** Public Administration.

FR/0223-5439
**ADMINISTRATION PARIS. 1962.** (1962)-. Periodical. French. Four times a year. 170.00F France; 225.00F other. Assn Corps Prefect Hauts Fonct, 1 Bis Place des Saussaies, 75 Paris France. **Tel** 011 33 1 42603535 ext. 2349. **UDC** 353. **Bk Rev.** **Ad Acc.** **Circ:** 4,000.
**Desc:** Administrative, political and juridical sciences; specific points of history.

DK
**ADMINISTRATIONSDEPARTEMENTET : ARSBERETNING.** **Main/Corp** Denmark. Danish. an. Finansministeriet Administrationsdepartementet, Holmens Kanal 20 3, DK-1060 Kbenhavn K Denmark. **LC** JN7195; .D45A. **Continues** Beretning.

US
**ADMINISTRATIVE CODE COMMITTEE BIENNIAL REPORT TO THE ... LEGISLATURE.** **Main/Corp** Montana. Legislative Assembly. Administrative Code Committee. English. be. Montana Legislative Council, State Capitol/Room 138, Helena MT 59620-1706. **Tel** (406)444-3064, FAX (406)444-3036. **LC** KFM9011.6; .A35. **DD** 328.786/07658. **Continues** Montana. Legislative Assembly. Administrative Code Committee. Biennial Report to the Legislature.

SR
**ADVERTENTIEBLAD VAN DE REPUBLIEK SURINAME.** **Main/Corp** Surinam. Dutch. $40.00. Uitgeverij DAG, Gravenstraat 120, Paramaribo Surinam. **Tel** 73501. **ED** E D Findlay. **LC** J3; .D9A. **Ad Acc.** **Circ:** 1,000.
**Desc:** Government advertising and publication, commercial printing for government and private sector. Plans to print weekly newspaper. Also printing work for churches and other religious groups.

US
**ADVISORY COMMISSION ON INTERGOVERNMENTAL RELATIONS PUBLICATIONS.** English. $100.00. Advisory Commission on Intergovernmental Relations, 800 K Street NW, Suite 450 S Building, Washington DC 20575. **Tel** (202)653-5640, FAX (202)653-5429.

IT
**AESSE : AZIONE SOCIALE.** Italian. L40000 Italy; L55000 other. Idea 2000 Srl, V Portense 96B, 00153 Rome Italy. **Tel** 011 39 6 5809982.

SP/0212-1786
**AFERS INTERNACIONALS.** **Added/Corp** CIDOB (Center). **VFOAT** Revista CIDOB d'Afers Internacionals. (1983)-. Periodical. Spanish (French,

English and Catalan). Four times a year. $41.00. CIDOB, Elisabets 12, 08001 Barcelona Spain. **Tel** 011 34 3 3026495. **ED** Josep Ribera. **LC** WMLC 93/662. **Bk Rev. Ad Acc. Pr Rev. Circ:** 1,500.
**Desc:** Information on all aspects of political science.

FR/0244-9676
**AFGHANISTAN EN LUTTE. See** History(General)-History of Asia.

US/0748-4356
**AFRICA INSIDER.** (AFRICA-INSIDER.). [Afr. insid.]. **Added/Corp** Afritec, Inc. (198?)-. Periodical. English. Twenty-four times a year. $250.00 (corporate); $150.00 (Non-profit), $75.00 (individual). Matthews Associates, PO Box 53398, Temple Heights Station, Washington DC 20009. **Tel** (301)309-6632, FAX (301)309-6632. **ED** Dan Matthews. **LC** IN PROCESS. **DD** 327. **Bk Rev**, (Qty: 10).
**Desc:** A report on US-Africa relations, emphasizing vital intelligence rarely found by government agencies or members of the private sector. Includes foreign relations, human rights, military affairs, politics and policy, sanctions, environmental affairs and a forum.

●UK/0001-9844
**AFRICA RESEARCH BULLETIN. POLITICAL, SOCIAL, AND CULTURAL SERIES. See** Sociology.

UK
**AFRICA REVIEW. Added/Corp** World of Information (Firm). (1985)-. Periodical. English. an (Oct.). $109.00 North America. Kogan Page Ltd., 120 Pentonville Road, London N1 9BR England. **Tel** 011 44 71 2780433, FAX 011 44 71 8376348, telex 263088 KOGAN G. **(Subscription address:** Kogan Page / North America Subscriptions, PO Box 830430, Birmingham AL 35283-0430.**) ED** Richard Green. **LC** HC501; .A532. **DD** 330.96/005. ***Continues** Africa Guide, 0308-678X.*
**Desc:** Contains news on the year's political events and economic trends in Africa.

US/0001-9887
**AFRICA TODAY.** [Afr. today]. **Added/Corp** Africa Today Associates. American Committee on Africa. University of Denver. Center on International Race Relations. Vol. 1 (Jan./Feb. 1954)-. Periodical. English. Four times a year (Mar., June, Sept., Dec.). $48.00 US, $50.00 others (surface mail); $58.00 (airmail). Africa Today / Denver, c/o Graduate School of International StudiesStudies, University of Denver, Denver CO 80208. **Tel** (303)871-3678, FAX (303)871-2456. **ED** Jendayi Frazer. **LC** DT1; .A22. **DD** 960/.3/05. Index available. cum. index. **Bk Rev**, (Qty: 40). **Ad Acc, Adv Mgr:** Erik Hauser. **Pr Rev. Circ:** 2,300 (ctrl). available on microfilm and microfiche from University Microfilms International (UMI). Documents available from The Genuine Article, UMI Article Clearinghouse.
**Desc:** Provides in-depth analysis of African affairs. Appropriate for college libraries and courses, as well as for public, high school, and personal libraries, where there is an interest in contemporary Africa.
**Ind/Abst** ABC POL SCI; Abstr. Anthropol.; Acad. Abstr. Full Text Elite (July 1990-); Acad. Abstr. (July 1990-); Acad. Ind. [Computer File] (1987-); Acad. Search (July 1990-); Am. Hist. Life (1972-); Book Rev. Index; Curr. Contents Soc. Behav. Sci.; Curr. Geogr. Publ. (199?-); Expand. Acad. Index (1987-); Hist. Source (July 1990-); Hum. Rights Intern. Rep.; INFO-SOUTH Abstr.; Int. Bibliogr. Sociol.; Mag. Search; MLA Int. Bibl. Books Artic. Mod. Lang. Lit.; Newsp. Period. Abstr. (1986-); PAIS Int. Print; Public Aff. Inf. Serv. Bull.; Res. Alert [Full Cov.]; Soc. Sci. Source (Jul. 1990-); Soc. Sci. Cit. Index [Full Cov.]; Soc. Sci. Index; Soc. Sci. Index Fulltext (1988-) [Full Txt.].

●US/1062-8584
**AFRICA TODAY (NEW YORK, N.Y.).** (AFRICA TODAY.). **Added/Corp** African Developmnent Association. (1992)-. Periodical. English. qt. $9.00. Africa Today / New York, PO Box 1467, Tri-Borough Station, New York NY 10035.

UK/0001-9909
**AFRICAN AFFAIRS (LONDON).** (AFRICAN AFFAIRS.). [Afr. aff.]. **Added/Corp** Royal African Society. Vol. 43, No. 172 (July 1944)-. Periodical. English. qt. £58.00 UK and Europe; $110.00 other. Oxford University Press, Walton Street, Oxford OX2 6DP England. **Tel** 011 44 865 56767, FAX 011 44 865 267773, telex 837330 OXPRES G. **(Subscription address:** Oxford University Press / USA, Journals Marketing Department, Oxford University Press, 2001 Evans Road, Cary NC 27513.**) ED** Richard Hodder-Williams and Peter Woodward. **LC** DT1; .R62. **DD** 960/.05. **[CCC]**. Index available. **Bk Rev. Ad Acc. Pr Rev.** available on microfilm and microfiche from University Microfilms International (UMI). Documents available from The Genuine Article, UMI Article Clearinghouse. ***Continues** Journal of the Royal African Society.*
**Desc:** Contains original articles on current and recent social, economic and political developments, and a substantial section of book reviews, together with several other bibliographical aids to scholars and others interested in Africa.
**Ind/Abst** ABC POL SCI; Acad. Search (July 1993-); Agrofor. Abstr.; Am. Hist. Life (1959-); Anthropol. Index; Appl. Soc. Sci. Index Abstr.; Br. Humanit. Index; Curr. Contents Soc. Behav. Sci.; Curr. Geogr. Publ. (199?-); Expand. Acad. Index (1989-); Geogr. Abstr. Human Geogr.; Hist. Source (July 1993-); Humanit. Index; Humanit. Source (Jul. 1993-); Index Islam. Lit.; INFO-SOUTH Abstr.; Int. Dev. Abstr.; Int. Exec.; Int. Labour Doc.; Int. Polit. Sci. Abstr.; Leis. Recreat. Tour. Abstr.; Linguist. Lang. Behav. Abstr.; Mag. Search; Middle East Abstr. Index; Newsp. Period. Abstr. (1991-); Peace Res. Abstr. J. (1964-1984); Res. Alert [Full Cov.]; Rural Dev. Abstr.; Soc. Plann. Policy Dev. Abstr.; Soc. Sci. Source (Jul. 1993-); Soc. Sci. Cit. Index [Full Cov.]; Sociol. Abstr.; World Agric. Econ.

SA
**AFRICANUS. Added/Corp** University of South Africa. Department of Development Administration and Politics. University of South Africa. Dept. of Native Administration. (19??)-. English (Afrikaans). an. R7.00. University of South Africa, PO Box 392, Pretoria 0001 South Africa. **Tel** 011 27 12 4298468, FAX 011 (27)12 429 3321, telex (59)350068+. **ED** Richard Cornwell. **LC** DT763; .A66. **DD** 916.8/005. **Bk Rev. Circ:** 700.
**Desc:** Articles on development problems with special reference to the Third World and Southern Africa. Also politics and policy concerning inter-group relations.
**Ind/Abst** West. Hist. Q.

GW
**AFRIKA JAHRBUCH. VFOAT** Jahrbuch Afrika. (1987)-. German. an. DM39.00. Leske Verlag & Budrich GmbH, Postfach 300551, Gerhart Hauptmann Strasse 27, W-5090 Leverkusen 3 Opladen Germany. **Tel** 011 49 21712079. **(Subscription address:** Bertelsmann Distribution, VVA, Postfach 7777, 4830 Gutersloh West Germany**) ED** Rolf Hofmeier. **LC** DT348; A34. **DD** 967/.005. Index available. cum. index. **Bk Rev. Ad Acc. Pr Rev.** ctrl circ.
**Desc:** Covers political, economical and social relations in Africa.

US/0739-4853
**AGAINST THE CURRENT.** [Against curr.]. **Added/Corp** Center for Changes (Detroit, Mich.). Vol. 1 No. 1 (Fall 1980)-Vol. 3 No. 3 (Winter 1985); New Series, Vol. 1, No. 1 (Jan./Feb. 1986)-. Periodical. English. Six times a year (Jan., Mar., May, July, Sept., Nov.). $18.00 (individuals), $25.00 (institutions). Against the Current, 7012 Michigan Avenue, Detroit MI 48210. **Tel** (313)841-0161, FAX (313)841-8884. **ED** David Finkel. **LC** HX1; .A23. **DD** 335/.005. **Bk Rev**, (Qty: 10-15). **Circ:** 3,000. available on microfilm from University Microfilms International (UMI). ***Absorbed** Changes Socialist Journal, 0746-5335; Socialist Unity.*
**Desc:** A magazine of news, discussion and analysis of movements for social and political change. Special focus on union reform and rank and file activities. Also includes issues facing women - the energy crisis, American politics, major world events, the economy, socialist theory for today, and more.
**Ind/Abst** Altern. Press Index (1980-); Left Index.

FR/0983-737X
**AGENCE CAMBODGE - LAOS. VFOAT** Bulletin - Agence Cambodge-Laos; Bulletin - Droits de l'Homme et Solidarite. (1986)-. Periodical. French. bm. 100.00F France; 150.00F other. Agence Cambodge Laos, 127 rue Notre Dame des Champs, 75006 Paris France. **UDC** 363(596).
**Desc:** Studies of the political situation in Cambodia.

GW
**AGYPTEN, FORSCHUNGSPOLITIK UND FORSCHUNGSPRAXIS / BUNDESSTELLE FUER AUSSENHANDELSINFORMATION.** German. DM3.00. Bundesstelle fuer Aussenhandelsinformation, Agrippastr 87 93, D 50676 Cologne Germany. **Tel** 011 49 221 2057316, FAX 011 49 221 2057212. **LC** Q180.E3; A54. **DD** 338.96206.

CI
**AKTUELNI PROBLEMI PRIVREDNIH KRETANJA I EKONOMSKE POLITIKE JUGOSLAVIJE. See** Economics.

UA
**AL-DIBLUMASI. VFOAT** Diplomat. Arabic (Arabic). mo. **LC** D839; .D5.

SJ
**AL-HUKM AL-SHABI AL-MAHALLI. Added/Corp** Sudan. Wizarat al-Hukumah al-Mahalliyah. (19??)-. Periodical. Arabic (English). mo. 3.00. Wizarat Al-Hukumah Al-Mahalliyah, BP 597, Al-Khartum Sudan. **LC** JS7819.A1; H8.

UA
**AL-NAHAR. AL-KITAB AL-SANAWI.** (1974)-. Arabic. da. $300.00. Al Ahram, Al Ahram Building, Al Galaa Street, Cairo ARE Egypt. **Tel** 011 20 2 755500, 011 20 2 745666. **LC** D2; .N34.

US/0749-7415
**AL-NAZEER.** [Nazeer]. **Added/Corp** Jabhah al-IslamÂiyah fi Suriyah. (19??)-. Periodical. English (English). Islamic Front in Syria, c/o Mansour, PO Box 242, Clawson MI 48017. **LC** DS98; .N39. **DD** 323.

UA/0583-4597
**AL-SIYASAH AL-DAWLIYAH.** V. 1- (No. 1- ); 1965-. Periodical. Arabic. qt. Al Ahram, Al Ahram Building, Al Galaa Street, Cairo ARE Egypt. **Tel** 011 20 2 755500, 011 20 2 745666. **ED** Butrus Ghali. **LC** D839; .S55.

SJ
**AL-SIYASAH WA-AL-ISTRATIJIYAH. VFOAT** Majallat Assiyasa Walistratigia. Journal 1, No. 3, (May 1983)-. Periodical. Arabic. qt. 1.00 single issue. SB 1850, Khartoum Sudan. **LC** JA26; .M326. ***Continues** Majallat Al-Siyasah Wa-Al-Istratijiyah.*

IS
**AL-TALIAH; SIYASIYAH USBUIYAH. VFOAT** Attaliah Weekly. Periodical. Arabic. IL275.00, IL200.00 students. Shari Ibn Sina, PO Box 19372, Al-Quds Jerusalem Israel. **LC** DS127.6.O3; T34.

US
**ALASKA DATA INVENTORY CATALOG.** 1978-. Catalog. English. an. Alaska Library Association, PO Box 81084, Fairbanks AK 99708. **Tel** (907)479-4522. **LC** Z1223.5; .A4A4; J87.A4. **DD** 015.798.

US/0002-4651
**ALBANIA REPORT. *Ceased.*** Vol. 1 (Aug. 1970)-(19??). English. ir. Albania Report, PO Box 912, New York NY 10008. **Tel** (202)638-2256. **ED** Jack Shulman. **LC** DR901; .A58. **DD** 949.65/008. **Circ:** 3,000 (ctrl).
**Desc:** Reviews political, social developments in Albania.

AA/0044-7072
**ALBANIA TODAY. *Ceased.*** Vol. 1 (Nov./Dec. 1971)-(199?). Periodical. English. bm. Drejtoria Qendrore Perhapjes, Rruga Konferenca e Pezes, Tirana Albania. **DD** 320.9/4965/03.
**Ind/Abst** Int. Bibliogr. Sociol.

CN/1187-3396
**ALBERTA DEMOCRAT, THE.** [Alta. democr.]. **Added/Corp** Alberta New Democrats. Vol. 18, No. 1 (June 1991)-. Periodical. English. ir. Free with membership; $20.00, non-member individuals; $15.00, institutions. Alberta New Democratic Party, 5339-112 Avenue, Edmonton Alberta T5W 0N6 Canada. **DD** 324.27123/07. ***Continues** Alberta's New Democrat., 0837-0346.*

HU/0002-564X
**ALLAM- ES JOGTUDOMANY. See** Law.

GW
**ALLGEMEINES MINISTERIALBLATT DER BAYERISCHEN STAATSREGIERUNG, DES BAYERISCHEN MINISTERPRASIDENTEN, DER BAYERISCHEN STAATSKANZLEI, DES BAYERISCHEN STAATSMINISTERIUMS DER INNERN. Main/Corp** Bavaria (Germany). **Added/Corp** Bavaria (Germany). Ministerpraesident. Bavaria (Germany). Bayerische Staatskanzlei. Bavaria (Germany) Staatsministerium des Innern. Bavaria (Germany). Staatsministerium fuer Wirtschaft und Verkehr. Bavaria (Germany). Staatsministerium fuer Ernaehrung, Landwirtschaft und Forsten. Bavaria (Germany). Staatsministerium fuer Arbeit und Sozialordnung. Bavaria (Germany). Bayerisches Staatsministerium fuer Landesentwicklung und Umweltfragen. Bavaria (Germany). Bayerisches Staatsministerium fuer Bundes-und Europaangelegenheiten. Vol. 1, No. 1 (Jan. 11, 1988)-. Periodical. German. bw. DM120.00. Staatsministerium fur Arbeit und Sozialordnung, Winzererstrasse 9, W-8000 Munchen 40 Germany. **LC** J357.R1; B38a.

US/0362-076X
**ALMANAC OF AMERICAN POLITICS, THE.** [Alm. Am. polit.]. (1972)-. English. be (every two years). $65.95 hardcover edition; $53.85 softcover edition. National Journal Inc., 1501 M Street Northwest, Suite 300, Washington DC 20005. **Tel** (800)356-4838, (202)739-8541, (800)424-2921. **(Subscription address:** National Journal Inc. / Linn, MO, PO Box 920, Linn MO 65051.**) ED** M. Barone and G. Ujifusa. **LC** JK1012; .A44. **DD** 328.73/005. Index available. **Circ:** 40,000.
**Desc:** Presents a biography of every member of Congress and each governor.
**Ind/Abst** Curr. Lit. Fam. Plan. (19??-199?); NEXIS.

US/0886-2567
**ALMANAC OF FEDERAL PACS.** [Alm. fed. PACs]. (1986)-. English. ir (Published in Jan., of even years). $79.50 (two years). Amward Publications, 2000 National Press Building, Washington DC 20045. **Tel** (301)251-9009, FAX (301)251-9058. **ED** Edward Zuckerman. **LC** JK1991; .A744. **DD** 324/.4/0973. Index available.
**Desc:** For every federally registered political action committee (PAC) which contributes at least $50,000 to candidates, the almanac provides key financial data and information about the PACs' sponsoring organizations.

US/0276-9980
**ALMANAC OF VIRGINIA POLITICS, THE.** 1st Ed. (1977)-. English. be. Woman Activist Fund Inc, 2310 Barbour Road, Falls Church VA 22043. **ED** Flora Crater, Elizabeth Vantrease, Meg Williams. **LC** JK3968; .A74. **DD** 328.755/07345. **Circ:** 1,500.

US/0730-1766
**ALTERNATIVE MEDIA.** ***Ceased.*** [Altern. media]. (1975)-?. Periodical. English. qt. Alternative Media, 842 Broadway, New York NY 10003. **Tel** (212)974-1990. **ED** R J Smith. **Bk Rev. Ad Acc. Circ:** 5,000.
**Desc:** Media issues and criticism, frequently spotlighting journalists and artists outside the mainstream. Features and reviews with a commitment to progressive ideals.
**Ind/Abst** Altern. Press Index (-199?).

CN/0843-0586
**ALTERNATIVE (MONTREAL, QUEBEC).** ***Ceased.*** **See** Economics-Labor.

AG
**AMBITO FINANCIERO. See** Business.

US/0065-678X
**AMERICA VOTES.** [Am. votes]. **Added/Corp** Elections Research Center (Governmental Affairs Institute) Governmental Affairs Institute (U.S.). (1956)-. English. be. $132.00. Congressional Quarterly Inc., 1414 22nd Street Northwest, Washington DC 20037. **Tel** (202)887-8500, (800)432-2250 ext. 621, FAX (202)728-1863. **LC** JK1967; .A8. **DD** 324.973/092.
**Ind/Abst** Stat. Ref. Index.

US/1061-8570
**AMERICAN CAUCUS.** ***Ceased.*** Vol. 1, Issue 1 (Mar. 30-Apr. 12, 1992)-(Dec. 1992). Periodical. English. bw. Congressional Quarterly Inc., 1414 22nd Street Northwest, Washington DC 20037. **Tel** (202)887-8500, (800)432-2250 ext. 621, FAX (202)728-1863. **DD** 328. ***Continues*** *C-SPAN Update, 0746-3812.*

US/0891-3390
**AMERICAN GOVERNMENT.** [Am. gov.]. **VFOAT** Annual Editions. American Government. 10th Edition (1980/1981)-. English. an. $12.95. Dushkin Publishing Group Inc., Sluice Dock, Guilford CT 06437. **Tel** (203)453-4351, (800)243-6532, FAX (203)453-6000. **ED** Bruce Stinebrickner. **LC** JK1; .A74. **DD** 320.973/05. ***Continues*** *Readings in American Government.*
**Desc:** Presents over 50 timely selections covering the wide range of American government from the constitutional foundations through the current domestic and foreign policies of George Bush.

US/0090-547X
**AMERICAN GOVERNMENT : TEXT.** 1973/74-. English. Dushkin Publishing Group Inc., Sluice Dock, Guilford CT 06437. **Tel** (203)453-4351, (800)243-6532, FAX (203)453-6000. **LC** JK8; .A595. **DD** 320.4/73.

US/0092-5853
**AMERICAN JOURNAL OF POLITICAL SCIENCE.** [Am. j. polit. sci.]. **Added/Corp** Midwest Political Science Association (U.S.). Vol. 17, (Feb. 1973)-. Periodical. English. qt. $69.00 (one year), $136.00 (two year), $202.00 (three year), institutions; $30.00 (one year), $60.00 (two year), $90.00 (three year), individuals. University of Wisconsin Press, Journal Division, 114 North Murray Street, Madison WI 53715. **Tel** (608)262-4952, FAX (608)262-8909. **ED** David Rohde. **LC** JA1; .M5. **DD** 320/.05. **[CCC]. Ad Acc. Pr Rev. Circ:** 2,800 (ctrl). available on microfilm and microfiche from University Microfilms International (UMI). Documents available from The Genuine Article, UMI Article Clearinghouse. ***Continues*** *Midwest Journal of Political Science, 0026-3397.*
**Desc:** A journal of political science publishing articles in international, comparative, and American politics as well as political philosophy and methodology.
**Ind/Abst** ABC POL SCI; Acad. Abstr. Full Text Elite (July 1990-); Acad. Abstr. (July 1990-); Acad. Search (July 1990-); Am. Hist. Life (1957-); Annu. Bibliogr. Engl. Lang. Lit.; Crim. Justice Abstr.; Curr. Contents Soc. Behav. Sci.; Educ. Adm. Abstr.; Expand. Acad. Index (1989-); Index Period. Artic. Relat. Law; INFO-SOUTH Abstr.; Int. Bibliogr. Sociol.; Int. Polit. Sci. Abstr.; J. Plan. Lit.; Linguist. Lang. Behav. Abstr.; Mag. Search; Middle East Abstr. Index; Newsp. Period. Abstr. (1990-); PAIS Int. Print (1991-); Res. Alert [Full Cov.]; Sage Public Adm. Abstr. (?-?); Soc. Plann. Policy Dev. Abstr.; Soc. Sci. Source (Jul. 1990-); Soc. Sci. Cit. Index [Full Cov.]; Soc. Sci. Index; Soc. Sci. Index Fulltext (Nov. 1988-) [Full Txt.]; Sociol. Abstr.; Stud. Women Abstr.; U.S. Polit. Sci. Doc.

US/1045-3679
**AMERICAN LOBBYISTS DIRECTORY.** [Am. lobby. dir.]. (Sept. 1989)-. Directory. English. an. $175.00. Gale Research Inc., 835 Penobscot Building, Detroit MI 48226. **Tel** (800)877-GALE, (313)961-2242, FAX (313)961-6083, telex TWX 810-221-7086. **ED** Robert Wilson. **LC** JK1118; .A65.
**Desc:** Provides a unique, comprehensive source of information on registered lobbyists' activities at the federal and state government levels.

US/8755-562X
**AMERICAN POLITICAL REPORT, THE.** [Am. polit. rep.]. **Added/Corp** American Political Research Corporation. (Oct. 1971)-. Periodical. English. Twenty-six times a year. $195.00. American Political Research Company, 7316 Wisconsin Avenue, Bethesda MD 20814. **Tel** (301)654-4990, FAX (301)656-0822. **ED** Kevin P. Phillips. **LC** JK1; .A47. **DD** 320.973/005. **Circ:** 1,500. ***Absorbed*** *Business & Public Affairs Fortnightly.*
**Desc:** Nationwide monitor and analysis of U.S. elections, politics and political economics.

US/0003-0554
**AMERICAN POLITICAL SCIENCE REVIEW, THE.** [Am. Polit. Sci. Rev.]. **Added/Corp** American Political Science Association. Vol. 1 (Nov. 1906)-. Academic Scholarly Publication. English. Four times a year (Mar., June, Sept., Dec.). $154.00 US, $172.00 other (institution); Comes with American Political Science Association membership. American Political Science Association, 1527 New Hampshire Avenue Northwest, Washington DC 20036. **Tel** (202)483-2512, FAX (202)483-2657. **ED** Samuel C. Patterson. **LC** JA1; .A6. **DD** 320/.05. **Ad Acc. Pr Rev. Circ:** 12,600. available on microfilm and microfiche from University Microfilms International (UMI). Documents available from The Genuine Article, UMI Article Clearinghouse. ***Continued in part by*** *PS, 0030-8269.*
**Desc:** Scholarly journal covering the field of political science. Contains articles and review essays in all fields of political science.
**Ind/Abst** ABC POL SCI; Acad. Abstr. Full Text Elite (July 1990-); Acad. Abstr. (July 1990-); Acad. Ind. [Computer File] (1987-); Acad. Search (July 1990-); Am. Hist. Life (1954-); Am. Bibliogr. Slavic East Europ. Stud.; Annu. Bibliogr. Engl. Lang. Lit.; Arts Humanit. Citation Index [Select. Cov.]; Book Rev. Index; Commun. Abstr. (?-?); Crim. Penol. Police Sci. Abstr.; Curr. Contents Soc. Behav. Sci.; Econ. Lit. Index (-199?); Expand. Acad. Index (1987-); Index Period. Artic. Relat. Law (19??-19??); INFO-SOUTH Abstr.; Int. Bibliogr. Sociol.; Int. Polit. Sci. Abstr.; J. Econ. Lit.; J. Plan. Lit.; Mag. Artic. Summar. Elite (July 1990-); Mag. Artic. Summar. Select (July 1990-); Mag. Artic. Summar. CD-ROM (July 1990-); Mag. Search; Middle East Abstr. Index; Newsp. Period. Abstr. (1988-); PAIS Int. Print; Peace Res. Abstr. J. (1966-1969), (1976-1979); Res. Alert [Full Cov.]; Romant. Move.; Sage Public Adm. Abstr.; Soc. Sci. Source (Jul. 1990-); Soc. Sci. Cit. Index [Full Cov.]; Soc. Sci. Index; Soc. Sci. Index Fulltext (Dec. 1988-) [Full Txt.]; Soc. Work Abstr. [Select. Cov.]; U.S. Polit. Sci. Doc.; Vocat. Search (July 1990-); West. Hist. Q.

US/0044-7803
**AMERICAN POLITICS QUARTERLY.** [Am. polit. q.]. Vol. 1 (Jan. 1973)-. Periodical. English. qt. $155.00. SAGE Periodical Press, 2455 Teller Road, Thousand Oaks CA 91320. **Tel** (805)499-0721, FAX (805)499-0871, telex 100799. **ED** James C. Garand, Louisiana State University. **LC** JK1; .A48. **DD** 320.9/73/092. **[CCC]. Pr Rev. Acid Free.** available on microfilm and microfiche from University Microfilms International (UMI). Documents available from The Genuine Article, UMI Article Clearinghouse.
**Desc:** Promotes basic research in all areas of American political behavior, including urban, state and national policies, as well as pressing social problems requiring political solutions.
**Ind/Abst** ABC POL SCI; Am. Hist. Life (1973-); Commun. Abstr.; Curr. Contents Soc. Behav. Sci.; Educ. Adm. Abstr. (?-?); Expand. Acad. Index (1987-); Hum. Resour. Abstr. (?-?); Index Period. Artic. Relat. Law (19??-19??); Int. Polit. Sci. Abstr.; J. Plan. Lit.; Middle East Abstr. Index; Newsp. Period. Abstr. (1992-); PAIS Int. Print (1991-); Peace Res. Abstr. J. (1979-1981); Res. Alert [Full Cov.]; Sage Public Adm. Abstr.; Sage Race Relat. Abstr.; Soc. Sci. Cit. Index [Full Cov.]; U.S. Polit. Sci. Doc.

US/0741-1111
**AMERICAN POLITICS (WASHINGTON, D.C. : 1983).** (AMERICAN POLITICS.). [Am. polit.]. Vol. 1, No. 1 (Nov. 1983); Vol. 1, Issue 1 (Feb. 1986)-. Periodical. English. Eleven times a year. American Politics Inc, 810 18th Street, Suite 802, Washington DC 20006. **Tel** (202)347-1100. **LC** JK1; .A475. **DD** 973.92/05.

US/1049-7285
**AMERICAN PROSPECT, THE.** [Am. prospect]. No. 1 (Spring 1990)-. Periodical. English. Four times a year (Feb., Apr., July, Oct.). $25.00 (individuals); $40.00 (institutions); $60.00 (universities & libraries). New Prospect Inc, 146 Mt Auburn Street, Cambridge MA 02138. **Tel** (617)547-2950, FAX (617)547-3896. **ED** Paul Starr and Robert Kuttner. **LC** E838; .A54. **DD** 320.973. **CODEN** APROEY. **Bk Rev. Ad Acc. Circ:** 11,000.
**Desc:** Journal of liberal ideas, concerned with politics, public policy, and social and cultural trends.
**Ind/Abst** Econ. Lit. Index; Linguist. Lang. Behav. Abstr. (1992-); PAIS Int. Print (1991-); Sage Public Adm. Abstr.; Soc. Plann. Policy Dev. Abstr. (1992-); Sociol. Abstr. (1992-).

US
**AMERICAN REVIEW OF POLITICS.** English. qt (Mar., June, Sept., Dec.). $25.00 (institutions), $15.00 (individuals). University of Central Arkansas Department of Political Science, Conway AR 72035. **Tel** (501)450-5100. **ED** Gary D. Wekkin. Index available. cum. index (Typescript). **Bk Rev**, (Qty: 25-30). **Ad Acc, Adv Mgr:** M. LeDuc, **Tel** (501)450-3412. **Circ:** 300. ***Continues*** *Midsouth Political Science Journal, 1051-5054.*

US/0278-0585
**AMERICAN SENTINEL (WASHINGTON, D.C.), THE.** ***Title Change.*** (THE AMERICAN SENTINEL.). [Am. sentin.]. Issue #266 (Sept. 7, 1981)-(1993). Periodical. English. bw. Sentinel Communications Inc., 15113 Steele Creek Road, Charlotte NC 28273. **Tel** (704)587-0898. **LC** HN90.R3; P54. **DD** 322.4/0973. **[CCC].** Index available. ***Continues*** *Pink Sheet on the Left, 0048-4180.* ***Continued by*** *Pink Sheet on the Left (Annapolis, Md.: 1993).*

US/0003-1593
**AMERICA'S FUTURE (NEW ROCHELLE, N.Y.).** (AMERICA'S FUTURE.). [Am. future]. (1959)-. Periodical. English. Twelve times a year. Free. Americas Future, PO Box 1625, Milford PA 18337. **Tel** (717)296-2800, FAX (717)296-2811. **ED** Phillip C. Clark, (phone: (919)282-4860). **DD** 051. Index available (annually). **Bk Rev**, (Qty: 12). **Circ:** 10,000. available on microfilm from University Microfilms International (UMI).
**Desc:** A review of news and public affairs supporting the free enterprise system and constitutional form of government.

IT/0392-579X
**AMMINISTRAZIONE E POLITICA.** [Amm. polit.]. (1972)-. Periodical. Italian. bm. L50000.00. Amminist Provinciale Bari, Serv Tesoreria, Lungomare N Sauro, 70121 Bari Italy. **Tel** 011 39 80 5412314, FAX 011 39 80 558147. **UDC** 352(450.751). Index available. cum. index. **Bk Rev**, (Qty: 10). **Ad Acc.** ***Continues*** *Terra di Bari.*

JA
**AMPO.** [Ampo]. **Added/Corp** Beheiren. Gaikokujin Beheiren. Pacific-Asia Resources Center (Tokyo, Japan). **VFOAT** Japan-Asia Quarterly Review. (Nov. 1969)-. Periodical. English. Four times a year (Mar., June, Sept., Dec.). $28.00 (individuals), $40.00 (institutions). Ampo, Box 5250, Tokyo International Japan. **Tel** 011 81 3 3291 5901, , FAX 011 81 3 3291 2437. **ED** Koshida Kiyokazu. **LC** HQ799.J3; A65. **DD** 322/.42/05. Index available. cum. index. available on microfilm and microfiche from University Microfilms International (UMI).
**Desc:** A unique and important critical perspective on the dynamics of this region and of the people of the region. Includes a range of Japanese scholars and activists as well as representatives of movements throughout Asia, the Pacific, and from all over the world. Carries reports, anaylses, and interviews on politics, economics, society, culture, and on people's movements.
**Ind/Abst** Hum. Rights Intern. Rep.

SZ
**AMTLICHES BULLETIN DER BUNDESVERSAMMLUNG. Main/Corp** Switzerland. Bundesversammlung. Nationalrat. **VFOAT** Bulletin Officiel de l'Assemblee Federale. Bulletin. Multiple languages (French, German and Italian). 75.00F Switzerland; 85.00F other. Eidg Drucksachen- und Materialzentrale, 3000 Bern Switzerland. **Tel** 41 31 61 97 79, FAX 41 31 61 78 04, telex 33361 BRSLG CH. **ED** Ernst Frischknecht. **LC** J415; .H2. Index available. cum. index. **Circ:** 1,200. ***Continues*** *Amtliches Stenographisches Bulletin.*
**Desc:** Contains minutes of parliamentary debates in original language. Procedural form of demands or requests for action and for information (motions, postulates, interpellations, ordinary questions, question time).

IT
**ANDES (ROME, ITALY).** ***Suspended.*** (ANDES : QUADRIMESTRALE ISCOS DI POLITICA E CULTURA SULL'AMERICA LATINA.). **Added/Corp** Istituto Sindacale per la Cooperazione Con i Paesi in via di Sviluppo. Vol. 1, No. 1 (Dec. 1987)-(Dec. 1993). Periodical. Italian. Three times a year. Iscos, Via Boncompagni 19, 00187 Rome Italy. **Tel** 011 39 6 4885639. **LC** F1401; .A578. **DD** 980/.005.
**Ind/Abst** PAIS Int. Print.

BE
**ANNALES PARLEMENTAIRES. PARLEMENTAIRE HANDELINGEN.** **Main/Corp** Belgium. Parlement. Senat. **Added/Corp** Belgium. Parlement. Senat. Parlementaire Handelingen. **VFOAT** Parlementaire Handelingen. (18??)-. French (Dutch). ir. Moniteur Belge, rue de Louvain 40-42, 1000 Brussels Belgium. **Tel** 011 32 2 5120026. **LC** J393; .J2. ***Supersedes*** *Belgium. Parlement. Annales Parlementaires.*
**Desc:** Reproduces completely and verbatim discussions in the legislative houses.

US/0002-7162
**ANNALS OF THE AMERICAN ACADEMY OF POLITICAL AND SOCIAL SCIENCE. See** Social Sciences.

UK
**ANNUAL OF POWER AND CONFLICT.** **Added/Corp** Institute for the Study of Conflict. National

Strategy Infomation Center. (1971)-. English. an. $16.50. Research Institute for the Study of Conflict and Terrorism, 136 Baker Street, London W1M 1FH England. **Tel** 011 44 71 224 2659, FAX 011 44 71 486 3064. **LC** D839; .A397. **DD** 301.6/33/05.

II
**ANNUAL REGISTER OF INDIAN POLITICAL PARTIES, THE.** Vol. 1 (1973)-. English. an. Rs140.00. H S, 30 Kailash Colony Market, New Delhi 110048 India. **LC** JQ298.A1; A78. **DD** 329.9/54.

CN/0837-6425
**ANNUAL REPORT / MANITOBA RESEARCH COUNCIL.** ***Title Change.*** [Annu. rep. - Manit. Res. Counc.]. **Main/Corp** Manitoba Research Council. (1987)-(1992). English. **LC** IN PROCESS. **DD** 354.71270085/5. ***Separated from*** *Manitoba. Manitoba Industry, Trade and Technology. Annual Report, 0837-6409.* ***Continued by*** *Manitoba. Economic Innovation & Technology Council. Annual Report, 1199-3383.*

CN/0825-7361
**ANNUAL REPORT OF THE PRIVACY COMMISSIONER.** **See** Law.

US
**ANNUAL REPORT ... PROGRAM INSPECTOR GENERAL.** **Main/Corp** United States. Dept. of State. Office of the Program Inspector General. **VFOAT** Annual Report of the Program Inspector General. No. 6 (1985)-. English. US Department of State, 2201 C Street NW, Room 5819, Washington DC 20520. **Tel** (202)647-9859. **LC** JX1706; .A265a. **DD** 353.1. ***Continues*** *Annual Report, 0740-5774.*

US/0500-3970
**ANNUAL REPORT / SUBVERSIVE ACTIVITIES CONTROL BOARD.** **Main/Corp** United States. Subversive Activities Control Board. 1st (1950/1951)-. Government Publication. English. an. Superintendent of Documents, US Government Printing Office, Washington DC 20402. **Tel** (202)275-3328, FAX (202)786-2377.

US/0743-1287
**ANNUAL REPORT / THE AMERICAN COMMITTEE ON AFRICA.** [Annu. rep. - Am. Comm. Afr.]. **Main/Corp** American Committee on Africa. (19??)-. English. an. The Africa Fund, 198 Broadway, New York NY 10038. **Tel** (212)962-1210. **LC** DT1; .A66a. **DD** 320.96/006073.

US
**ANNUAL REPORT TO THE GOVERNOR.** **Main/Corp** Connecticut State Ethics Commission. English. Connecticut State Ethics Commission, 30 Trinity Street, Hartford CT 06115. **LC** JK3345; .C66a. **DD** 353.9746009. ***Continues*** *Annual Report / Connecticut State Ethics Commission.*

US/0748-8599
**ANNUAL REVIEW OF POLITICAL SCIENCE.** [Annu. rev. pol. sci.]. Vol. 1 (1986)-. English. an. Price varies. Ablex Publishing Corporation, 355 Chestnut Street, Norwood NJ 07648. **Tel** (201)767-8450, (201)767-8455 (Customer Service), FAX (201)767-6717. **ED** Samuel Long. **LC** JA1; .A7. **DD** 320/.05.
**Desc:** Annual book series of research and theory in areas of political science.

IT
**ANNUARIO POLITICO.** **Added/Corp** Italy. Parlamento. Camera de Deputati. Gruppo Democratico Cristiano. (19??)-. Italian. an. Unites SRL, Via Silvio Pellico 12, 20121 Milan Italy. **LC** JN5201; .A53.

AQ
**ANTIGUA AND BARBUDA FORUM : JOURNAL OF PUBLIC ISSUES FORUM.** **Added/Corp** Public Issues Forum. Vol. 1, No. 1 (Sept. 1982)-. Spanish. Public Issues Forum, St. John's Antigua and Barbuda. **LC** WMLC 93/228.

●BE/1370-009X
**ANTIPODES BRUXELLES.** (1993)-. French. qt. 600.00F Benelux; 700.00F Europe; 900.00F other. CID ITECO, 31 Rue du Boulet, 1000 Brussels Belgium. **Tel** 011 32 2 5114870. ***Continues*** *Peuples & Liberations (Bruxelles), 1370-0081.*

FR/0003-7176
**APRES-DEMAIN.** **Added/Corp** Ligue des Droits de L'Homme (Paris, France). (1957)-. Periodical. French. mo. 200.00F France; 300.00F other. Apres-Demain, 27 rue Jean-Dolent, 75014 Paris France. **Tel** 011 33 1 47051401. **ED** Francoise Seligmann. **LC** JA11; .A67. **DD** 320/.05. **Bk Rev.** **Ad Acc.**
**Desc:** Of interest to those who wish to understand or interpret the economic and social-political problems of the 20th century. Focuses on specific themes of youth, energy, law and the military and cultural institutions.
**Ind/Abst** PAIS Int. Print (1991-).

NR
**APRI JOURNAL.** **Added/Corp** African Peace Research Institute. Vol. 6, No. (Jan./Feb. 1991)-. Periodical. English. bm. ***Continues*** *APRI Newsletter.*

US
**APS REVIEW, THE.** **Main/Corp** Georgetown University, Washington, D.C. Graduate School. Academy in the Public Service. Vol. 1 (Spring 1978)-. English. Three times a year. $10.00. Georgetown University Academy in the Public Service, Graduate School, 2135 Wisconsin Avenue Northwest, Suite 403, Washington DC 20007. **LC** JS39; .G38a. **DD** 320.

US/0094-7954
**APSA DEPARTMENTAL SERVICES PROGRAM, SURVEY OF DEPARTMENTS.** **Main/Corp** American Political Science Association. (19??)-. English. an (May). $23.50; Comes also with American Political Science Association Departmental Services Program membership. American Political Science Association, 1527 New Hampshire Avenue Northwest, Washington DC 20036. **Tel** (202)483-2512, FAX (202)483-2657. **ED** Sheilah Mann. **LC** JA28; .A55918. **DD** 320/.07/1173. **Ad Acc. Circ:** 1,000.
**Desc:** Report of extensive questionnaire sent to departments of political science. Includes salary information, enrollment trends, etc.

US/0196-5255
**APSA DIRECTORY OF DEPARTMENT CHAIRPERSONS.** **Main/Corp** American Political Science Association. **Added/Corp** American Political Science Association. Directory of Department Chairpersons. **VAT** American Political Science Association Directory of Department Chairpersons. (19??)-. Directory. English. an (Nov.). $28.50 (non-members), $23.50 (members). American Political Science Association, 1527 New Hampshire Avenue Northwest, Washington DC 20036. **Tel** (202)483-2512, FAX (202)483-2657. **ED** Patricia Spellman. **LC** JA28; .A5592. **DD** 320/.07/1173. **Ad Acc. Circ:** 1,000 (ctrl). ***Continues*** *APSA Directory of Department Chairmen, 0092-8658.*
**Desc:** Names and addresses of chairpersons in departments offering political science at four-year institutions in United States with department, address and phone number.

US
**APSA DIRECTORY OF MEMBERS - AMERICAN POLITICAL SCIENCE ASSOCIATION.** ***Title Change.*** **Main/Corp** American Political Science Association. Directory. English. te. 1527 New Hampshire Avenue NW, Washington DC 20036. **Tel** (202)483-2512. **LC** JA28; .A562. **DD** 320/.06/273. **Ad Acc. Circ:** 3,500. ***Continued by*** *American Political Science Association Membership Directory, 0730-6385.*
**Desc:** Alphabetical listing of current APSA members, their training, affiliations and areas of specializations. Index for women, blacks, and Hispanics.

AT/0725-2390
**APSA NEWSLETTER.** [APSA newsl.]. (1980)-. Periodical. English. ir. Australasian Political Studies Association, c/o Department of Political Science, Australian National University, GPO Box 4, Canberra Australian Capital Territory 2601 Australia. **DD** 320.06094.

NE
**AR STAATKUNDE IN CHRISTEN-DEMOCRATISCH PERSPECTIEF.** Periodical. Dutch. mo (11 issues per year). Fl55.00, Fl35.00 (students and CDA members less than 30 years old). Het Wetenschappelijk Instituut voor het CDA, Dr Kuyperstraat 5, 2514 Ba Den Haag Netherlands. **Tel** 070-924021. **LC** JA26; .A5. ***Continues*** *Antirevolutionaire Staatkunde.*

UK/0196-3538
**ARAB-ASIAN AFFAIRS.** [Arab-Asian aff.]. **Added/Corp** World Reports Limited. **VAT** Arab Asian Affairs. No. 84 (Jan. 1980)-. Periodical. English. Ten times a year. £100.00 UK and Ireland; $175.00 other. World Reports Ltd., 108 Horse Ferry Road, Westminster, London SW1P 2EF United Kingdom. **Tel** 011 44 71 222 3836, FAX 11 44 71 233 0185. **LC** DS63.1; .A65. **DD** 956/.005. ***Continues*** *Afro-Asian Affairs, 0163-819X.*
**Desc:** Authoritative newsletter analysing intelligence from Washington and regional sources on developments in the Middle East, with specific focus on rivalries between the great powers in the region.

GW
**ARBEITSMAPPE SOZIAL- UND WIRTSCHAFTSKUNDE.** (19??)-. German. mo. DM219.85. Erich Schmidt Verlag GmbH, Postfach 304240, D 10724 Berlin Germany. **Tel** 011 49 30 25008525.

IT
**ARCO DI GIANO.** (19??)-. Italian. tq. L84000 Italy; L120000 other. Franco Angeli Riviste SRL, Viale Monza 106, 20127 Milan Italy. **Tel** 011 39 2 2827651, 011 39 2 289562.

AT/0004-0932
**ARENA.** ***Title Change.*** [Arena]. No. 1 (Sept. 1963)-(1992). Periodical. English. qt. Arena Publishing Association, PO Box 18, North Carlton Victoria 3054 Australia. **Tel** 011 61 3 4160232. **ED** Geoff Sharp, Doug White, Nonie Sharp, Gerry Gill, John Hinkson, Paul James, Alison Caddick. Index available. **Bk Rev. Ad Acc. Circ:** 3,000 (ctrl). ***Split into*** *Arena Magazine (Melbourne, Vic.); Arena Journal.*
**Desc:** Forum for social and cultural comment. Developed analyses in such areas as media and popular culture, intellectuals and society, technological change, nuclear politics, feminist theory, world economics, and regional and international politics including Southeast Asia, the Pacific and Australia.
**Ind/Abst** Altern. Press Index; APAIS, Aust. Public Aff. Inf. Ser. (1972-); Aust. Educ. Index.

UK
**ASIA & PACIFIC REVIEW.** **VFOAT** Asia and Pacific Review. (1985)-. English. an (Dec.). $109.00. Kogan Page Ltd., 120 Pentonville Road, London N1 9BR England. **Tel** 011 44 71 2780433, FAX 011 44 71 8376348, telex 263088 KOGAN G. **(Subscription address:** Kogan Page / North America Subscriptions, PO Box 830430, Birmingham AL 35283-0430.) **LC** HC411; .A73. **DD** 330.95/005. ***Continues*** *Asia & Pacific, 0262-5407.*
**Desc:** Accurate, comprehensive coverage of the region from Pakistan to the Pacific. Objective articles by experts on economics, politics, business, industry, and commerce. Includes a regional overview and country by country reviews essential for the businessman or traveller.

HK
**ASIAN INTELLIGENCE.** English. Two issues per month (fortnightly). $550.00. Political & Economic Risk Consultancy Ltd, GPO 1342, Hong Kong Hong Kong. **Tel** 011 852 5414088, FAX 011 852 8155032, telex 46926. **ED** Robert Broadfoot. ***Continues*** *Rundt's Asian Intelligence.*

FR
**ASPECTS DE LA FRANCE.** ***Title Change.*** **Added/Corp** Action Francais. (June 10, 1947)-(19??). Periodical. French. Forty-nine times a year. Aspects de la France, 10 rue Croix des Petits Champs, 75001 Paris France. **Tel** 011 33 1 40399206, FAX 011 33 1 40263163. **ED** Sniep. **LC** AP20; .A77. **DD** 054/.1. **Bk Rev. Ad Acc. Circ:** 30,000 (ctrl). ***Continued by*** *L Action Francaise Hebdo.*
**Desc:** Political analysis of politics, events and monarchy promotion.

US/1045-5930
**ASPEN INSTITUTE QUARTERLY (QUEENSTOWN, MD.), THE.** ***Ceased.*** **See** Social Sciences.

GR
**ATHENA MAGAZINE.** **Added/Corp** Institute for Political Research and Studies (Greece) International Studies Association. No. 1 (Jan. 1986)-. Periodical. English. Twelve times a year. $20.00. Athena Magazine, 24 Dimitriou Soutsou, 115 21 Athens Greece. **Tel** 6464835.
**Ind/Abst** Am. Hist. Life (1953-1958).

FR
**AUJOURD'HUI L'AFRIQUE.** **Added/Corp** Association Francaise d'Amitie et de Solidarite avec les Peuples d'Afrique. (1975)-. Periodical. French. Four times a year. 110.00F. Aujourd Hui l'Afrique, 21 rue Marceau, 93100 Montreuil France.

AT/1036-1146
**AUSTRALIAN JOURNAL OF POLITICAL SCIENCE.** **Added/Corp** Australasian Political Studies Association. Australian Defence Force Academy. Dept. of Politics. Vol. 25, No. 2 (Nov. 1990)-. Periodical. English. Three times a year (Mar., July, Nov.). 40.00Aus$ (individuals), $50.00 (institutions), Australia; 35.00Aus$ (individuals), $40.00Aus$ (institutions) other. APSA Politics Dept, Australian Defense Force Academy, Canberra ACT 2600 Australia. **Tel** 61 6 2688111, FAX (61)-60268-8852, telex 62694. **ED** Professor Ian McAllister. **LC** JQ3995.A1; P64. **DD** 320/.05. Index available. cum. index. **Bk Rev,** (Qty: 120). **Ad Acc. Pr Rev. Circ:** 1,000. Documents available from The Genuine Article. ***Continues*** *Politics (Kensington, N.S.W.).*
**Desc:** General political science, including political theory, international relations, Australian politics and comparative politics.
**Ind/Abst** ABC POL SCI; Am. Hist. Life (1971-); APAIS, Aust. Public Aff. Inf. Ser. (1990-); Arts Humanit. Citation Index [Select. Cov.]; Curr. Contents Soc. Behav. Sci.; Res. Alert [Full Cov.]; Sage Public Adm. Abstr.; Soc. Sci. Cit. Index [Full Cov.].

# Political Science

AT/0004-9522
**AUSTRALIAN JOURNAL OF POLITICS AND HISTORY, THE.** [Aust. j. polit. hist.]. Vol. 1, (Nov. 1955)-. Periodical. English. Three times a year. 60.00Aus$ (institution); 58.00Aus$ (individual) Australia; 88.00Aus$ (airmail) other. University of Queensland Press, PO Box 42, St Lucia Queensland 4067 Australia. **Tel** 011 61 7 3652127, **FAX** 011 61 7 3651988, telex UNIVQLD AA40315. **ED** John A. Moses. **LC** DU80; .A945. Index available. **Bk Rev. Ad Acc. Pr Rev. Circ:** 1,000. Documents available from The Genuine Article, BIOSIS Document Express.
**Desc:** Concerned with history and political theory in Australia and abroad, with regular articles on Australian foreign policy and a political chronicle of both state and federal Australian policy.
**Ind/Abst** ABC POL SCI; Am. Hist. Life (1955-); APAIS, Aust. Public Aff. Inf. Ser. (1963-); Arts Humanit. Citation Index [Full Cov.]; Biol. Abstr.; Curr. Contents Arts Humanit.; Curr. Contents Soc. Behav. Sci.; Int. Bibliogr. Sociol.; Int. Polit. Sci. Abstr.; Middle East Abstr. Index; Peace Res. Abstr. J. (1965, 1972-1975); Res. Alert [Full Cov.]; Soc. Sci. Cit. Index [Full Cov.]; Sociol. Abstr.; West. Hist. Q.

AT/0004-9638
**AUSTRALIAN LEFT REVIEW. Ceased.** [Aust. left rev.]. No. 1, (June/July 1966)-(1993). Periodical. English. mo. Communist Party of Australia, PO Box A247 Sydney South Post Office, Sydney New South Wales 2000 Australia. **Tel** 011 61 2 5651855, 5503831, **FAX** 011 61 2 5504460. **ED** David Burchell. **LC** HX9; .A8. **DD** 335.43/05. cum. index. **Bk Rev**, (Qty: 40). **Ad Acc, Adv Mgr Tel** 5651855. **Circ:** 3,000. **Supersedes** Communist Review.
**Ind/Abst** APAIS, Aust. Public Aff. Inf. Ser. (1974-).

AT
**AUSTRALIAN POLITICAL DIRECTORY.** (19??)-. Directory. English. ir. 395.00Aus$ Australia; 418.00Aus$ New Zealand, Papua New Guinea; 422.00Aus$ Indonesia, Malaysia, Singapore, 426.00Aus$ Japan, India; 432.00Aus$ US & Canada; 436.00Aus$ Europe. International Public Relations Pty Ltd., 33 Walsh Street, West Melbourne Victoria 3003 Australia. **Tel** 011 61 03 329 9333, FAX 011 61 03 329 7996.

GW
**AUSTRALIEN, FORSCHUNGSPOLITIK UND FORSCHUNGSPRAXIS / BUNDESSTELLE FUER AUSSENHANDELSINFORMATION.** German. an. DM3.00. Bundesstelle fuer Aussenhandelsinformation, Agrippastr 87 93, D 50676 Cologne Germany. **Tel** 011 49 221 2057316, FAX 011 49 221 2057212. **LC** Q180.A8; A877. **DD** 338.99406.

IT
**AVVENIMENTI.** Libera Informazione Editrice, Via Farini 62, 00185 Rome Italy.

NE/0166-7602
**AZANIA VRIJ.** [Azania vrij]. **Added/Corp** Azania Komitee. (1975)-. Periodical. Dutch. qt (4 issues). Fl12.50 Netherlands; Fl20.00 other. Azania Komitee, Postbus 5607, 3008 AP Rotterdam Netherlands. **Tel** 010 4193494. **UDC** 323.118.

US
**BACKGROUNDER (HERITAGE FOUNDATION (WASHINGTON, D.C.)).** (BACKGROUNDER / THE HERITAGE FOUNDATION.). Monographic series. English. ir. Price varies per volume. The Heritage Foundation, 214 Massachusetts Avenue NE, Washington DC 20002. **Tel** (202)546-4400. **ED** Burton Y Pines. **LC** WMLC L 83/252.
**Desc:** These are concise policy studies of long range issues which are unrelated to specific legislation.

IT
**BAILAMME. See** Religion and Theology.

US/1043-6898
**BALLOT ACCESS NEWS.** [Ballot access news]. **Added/Corp** Coalition for Free and Open Elections. Vol. 1, No. 12 (May 22, 1986)-. Periodical. English. Thirteen times a year. $8.00. Ballot Access News, PO Box 470296, San Francisco CA 94147. **Tel** (415)922-9779. **ED** Richard Winger. **LC** JK2446; .A25. **DD** 342. **Bk Rev**, (Qty: 1). **Circ:** 1,000. available via electronic mail from ECONET (Computer Bulletin Board). **Continues** HR 2320 News.
**Desc:** Covers developments in the law which affect political parties in the USA, especially "third" parties. Also covers major strategic decisions of USA "third" parties, and election returns.

US/1074-469X
**BEI-JING ZHI CHUN.** (PEI-CHING CHIH CHUN.). [Bei-jing zhi chun]. **VFOAT** Beijing Spring. (June 1993)-. Periodical. Chinese. mo $49.00 US & Canada; $65.00 Australia. Evergreen Publishing and Stationery, 136 South Atlantic Boulevard, Monterey Park CA 91754. **Tel** (818)284-9066, FAX (818)284-1571. **LC** DS779.26; .P453. **DD** 951.05/085. **Continues** Pei-Ching Chi Chun (Peking, China).

CC/0251-3137
**BEIJING INFORMATION.** (1978)-. Periodical. French. wk. 210.00F. Librairie le Phenix, 72 Boulevard de Sebastopol, 75003 Paris France. **Tel** 011 33 1 42727031, FAX 011 33 1 42722669. **UDC** 008:(510).

CC/1000-9140
**BEIJING REVIEW.** [Beijing Rev.]. **VFOAT** Pei-Ching Chou Pao. (Jan. 5, 1979)-. Periodical. English. wk. $50.80 (institution), $35.80 (individual). Beijing Review Publishing Company, 24 Baiwanzhuang lu, Beijing 100037, People's Republic of China. **(Subscription address:** China Books & Periodicals Inc., 2929 24th Street, San Francisco CA 94110.) **LC** DS701; .P42. **DD** 951/.005. **Bk Rev. Ad Acc. Circ:** 100,000. available in microform. **Continues** Peking Review. **Continued in part by** Beijing Review (North American Ed.).
**Desc:** News magazine which covers China's economic and social developments and carries important documents of the Chinese government and speeches made by state leaders.
**Ind/Abst** Acad. Search (July 1993-).

CC
**BEIJING REVIEW (NORTH AMERICAN EDITION).** (BEIJING REVIEW / PEI-CHING CHOU PAO.). **VFOAT** Pei-Ching Chou Pao. Vol. 30, No.43 (Oct. 26-Nov. 1, 1987)-. Periodical. English. wk. $50.80 (institution), $35.80 (individual). Beijing Review Publishing Company, 24 Baiwanzhuang lu, Beijing 100037, People's Republic of China. **(Subscription address:** China Books & Periodicals Inc., 2929 24th Street, San Francisco CA 94110.) **Bk Rev. Ad Acc. Circ:** 100,000. available in microform. **Separated from** Beijing Review.
**Desc:** News magazine which covers China's economic and social developments and carries important documents of the Chinese government and speeches made by state leaders.

GW/0522-6643
**BEITRAGE ZUR GESCHICHTE DES PARLAMENTARISMUS UND DER POLITISCHEN PARTEIEN / HERAUSGEGEBEN VON DER KOMMISSION FUER GESCHICHTE DES PARLAMENTARISMUS UND DER POLITISCHEN PARTEIEN. Added/Corp** Kommission fuer Geschichte des Parlamentarismus und der Politischen Parteien. No. 1 (1952)-. Monographic series. German. ir. Price varies per volume. Droste Verlag GmbH, Postfach 101135, D 40196 Dusseldorf Germany. **Tel** 011 49 211 505604.

GW/0582-0421
**BEITRAGE ZUR POLITISCHEN WISSENSCHAFT.** Vol. 1 (1967)-. Monographic series. German. ir (3-5 per year). Price varies per volume. Duncker and Humblot Verlag, Postfach 410329, D-12113 Berlin Germany. **Tel** 011 49 30 79000612, 011 49 30 79000613. **DD** 320.

NE
**BELEID & MAATSCHAPPIJ. JAARBOEK. See** Sociology.

GW
**BERICHTE AUS NAMIBIA.** (19??)-. German. sm (24 issues). Free on request. IPR Volker Stoltz GmbH, Venusbergweg 35, W 5300 Bonn 1 FR Germany. **Tel** 011 49 228 269020.

GW/0863-4564
**BERLINER DEBATTE INITIAL : ZEITSCHRIFT FUER SOCIALWISSENSCHAFTLICHEN DISKURS. See** Social Sciences.

US/1049-4421
**BETWEEN THE LINES (WASHINGTON, D.C.). Title Change.** (BETWEEN THE LINES : WATCHDOG ON POLITICS OF THE NEWS MEDIA AND HOLLYWOOD.). [Between lines]. Vol. 1, No. 1 (Feb. 1988)-(19??). Periodical. English. mo. Between the Lines, Box 43, Syracuse NY 13215. **Tel** (315)478-0351. **ED** Stephen N. Wolf. **DD** 302. Index available. cum. index. **Bk Rev. Ad Acc. Circ:** 400 (ctrl). **Continued by** American Sentinel, 1070-0285.

IT
**BIBLIOTECA DELLA LIBERTA. Ceased. Added/Corp** Centro di Ricerca e Documentazione Luigi Einaudi. **VFOAT** BDL. (19??)-(Dec. 1994). Periodical. Italian (English). qt. Franco Angeli Riviste SRL, Viale Monza 106, 20127 Milan Italy. **Tel** 011 39 2 2827651, 011 39 2 289562. **LC** JC571; .B5.

FR/0755-2238
**BILANS POLITIQUES ECONOMIQUES ET SOCIAUX HEBDOMADAIRES. See** Business.

US
**BIOGRAPHICAL DIRECTORY / AMERICAN POLITICAL SCIENCE ASSOCIATION. See** Biographies.

US/0272-1694
**BIPAC ACTION REPORT. Main/Corp** Business-Industry Political Action Committee, Political Action Division. **VFOAT** Action Report. Periodical. English. qt $25.00. Business-Industry Political Action Committee, Political Action Division, 1747 Pennsylvania Avenue NW, Washington DC 20006. **Tel** (202)833-1880. ctrl circ.

US/0032-3276
**BIPAC POLITICS.** (POLITICS; A DIGEST OF TRENDS AND DEVELOPMENTS.). [BIPAC polit.]. **Added/Corp** Business-Industry Political Action Committee, Political Education Division, New York. **VFOAT** BIPAC Politics. **VAT** Business-Industry Political Action Committee Politics. Vol. 1 (Nov./Dec. 1964)-. Periodical. English. Four times a year (Mar., June, Sept., Dec.). $30.00. Political Education Division, 1747 Pennsylvania Avenue Northwest, Washington DC 20006-4604. **Tel** (202)833-1880, FAX (202)833-2338. **Circ:** 30,000 (ctrl).
**Desc:** Political trends and developments of interest to the business community.

US/0882-1593
**BLACK ELECTED OFFICIALS.** (BLACK ELECTED OFFICIALS / JOINT CENTER FOR POLITICAL STUDIES.). [Black elect. off.]. **Added/Corp** Joint Center for Political Studies (U.S.) Joint Center for Political and Economic Studies (U.S.) (1984)-. English. an. $41.00. Joint Center for Political & Economic Studies, 1090 Vermont Avenue Northwest, Suite 1100, Washington DC 20005. **Tel** (202)789-3500. **(Subscription address:** University Press America, 4720 Boston Way, Lanham, MD 20706; Phone: (301)459-3366, (800)462-6420) **LC** E185.615; .N29. **DD** 353.002/22/08996073. **Continues** National Roster of Black Elected Officials, 0092-2935.
**Desc:** Gives complete, current information on each of the 6,056 black Americans holding elective office today.
**Ind/Abst** Stat. Ref. Index.

US/0891-9631
**BLACK POLITICAL STUDIES.** (1990)-. Monographic series. English. ir. Price varies per volume. Borgo Press, PO Box 2845, San Bernardino CA 92406. **Tel** (714)884-5813, (714)885-1161. **ED** Dr. Hanes Walton, Jr.
**Desc:** Monographs on Black politics and political figures, in North America and throughout the world.

US
**BLACK VIEW. Title Change. See** Ethnic Interests.

CV
**BOLETIM ANUAL DE ESTATISTICA (CAPE VERDE. DIRECCAO GERAL DE ESTATISTICA).** (BOLETIM ANUAL DE ESTATISTICA / CABO VERDE, DIRECCAO-GERAL DE ESTATISTICA.). (1987)-. Bulletin. Portuguese. an. **LC** HA2289; .A17. **DD** 316.658/05.

GT
**BOLETIN INTERNACIONAL / URNG, UNIDAD REVOLUCIONARIA NACIONAL GUATEMALTECA. Added/Corp** Unidad Revolucionaria Nacional Guatemalteca. No. 1 (Nov. 1986)-. Periodical. Spanish.
**Ind/Abst** Hum. Rights Intern. Rep.

IT
**BOLLETTINO UFFICIALE. Main/Corp** Abruzzi (Italy). (July 1970)-. Italian. Regione Abruzzo Bollettino Ufficiale, Via Aldo Moro, 67100 L Aquila Italy. **Tel** 011 39 862 647342. **LC** J7.I5; A25.

US/0278-9752
**BORGO POLITICAL SCENARIOS.** No. 1 (1981)-. Monographic series. English. ir. Price varies per volume. Borgo Press, PO Box 2845, San Bernardino CA 92406. **Tel** (714)884-5813, (714)885-1161.
**Desc:** Political speculations and proposals, and "what if?" scenarios by the major writers and politicians of our time.

US/0734-2306
**BOSTON REVIEW (CAMBRIDGE, MASS. : 1982). See** Literature.

BL
**BRASILINFORM. NEWS BRIEFS. See** Economics.

US
**BREAKTHROUGH (SAN FRANCISCO, CALIF.).** (BREAKTHROUGH : POLITICAL JOURNAL OF PFOC.). **Added/Corp** Prairie Fire Organizing Committee. Vol. 1, No. 1 (1977)-. Periodical. English. Three times a year. $10.00 (US), $15.00 (other) individuals; $15.00 institutions. John Brown Education Fund, PO Box 14422, San Francisco CA 94114. **Tel** (415)681-9040. **LC** IN PROCESS. **Bk Rev. Circ:** 5,000.
**Desc:** Political journal featuring interviews and analysis

concerning movements for social change around the world and inside the US.
**Ind/Abst** Altern. Press Index.

MX
## BRECHA (MEXICO CITY, MEXICO).
(BRECHA.). Vol. 1 (1986)-. Periodical. Spanish. qt. Roberto Iriarte, Apartado Postal 65-236, Mexico 8 DF Mexico. **LC** JL1281; .B74. **DD** 927.08/3/05. ***Formed by the union of*** *Coyoacan* ***and*** *Teoria y Politica (Mexico City, Mexico).*

TU
## BRIEFING.
**Added/Corp** Ekonomik Basin Ajansi. (1975)-. Periodical. English. wk. $310.00. Briefing, Ekonomik Basin Olgunlar Sokak, 2-1 Bakanlikar, Ankara Turkey. **Tel** 25 76 77-78. **ED** Yavuz Tolun. **Bk Rev. Ad Acc. Circ:** 2,000 (ctrl).
**Desc:** Inside perspective on Turkish political, economic and business affairs analysis, commentary, economic facts and figures.

NQ
## BRIGADA (MANAGUA, NICARAGUA).
**See** Economics.

FR
## BRISE-GLACE, LE.
No. 1 (1988)-. Periodical. French.

CN/0835-2925
## BRITISH COLUMBIA POLITICS & POLICY.
[B.C. polit. policy]. Vol. 1, No. 1 (Feb. 1987)-. Periodical. English. Twelve times a year. 258.00Can$. McMartin & Assoc Communic Ltd, PO Box 58236, Station L, Vancouver BC V6R 2E3 Canada. **Tel** (604)325-0030. **DD** 320.9711/05.

UK/0007-1234
## BRITISH JOURNAL OF POLITICAL SCIENCE.
[Br. j. polit. sci.]. Vol. 1 (Jan. 1971)-. Academic Scholarly Publication. English. qt (January, April, July and October). $152.00 US, Canada & Mexico; £83.00 other. Cambridge University Press, The Edinburgh Building, Shaftesbury Road, Cambridge CB2 2RU United Kingdom. **Tel** 011 44 223 312393, FAX 011 44 223 325959. **(Subscription address:** Cambridge University Press / North America, 110 Midland Avenue, Port Chester NY 10573.) **ED** Ivor Crewe, Anthony King and David Sanders. **DD** 320/.05. **[CCC]. Pr Rev.** available on microfilm and microfiche from University Microfilms International (UMI). Documents available from The Genuine Article, UMI Article Clearinghouse.
**Desc:** International in both subject matter and contributors. Contributions cover all branches of political science, and articles from scholars in related disciplines such as, sociology, social psychology, anthropology, economics and philosophy, appear frequently.
**Ind/Abst** ABC POL SCI; Acad. Abstr. Full Text Elite (Jan. 1992-); Acad. Abstr. (Jan. 1992-); Acad. Search (Jan. 1992-); Am. Hist. Life (1977-); Appl. Soc. Sci. Index Abstr.; Commun. Abstr.; Curr. Contents Soc. Behav. Sci.; Expand. Acad. Index (1989-); Hum. Resour. Abstr.; INFO-SOUTH Abstr.; Int. Bibliogr. Sociol.; Int. Polit. Sci. Abstr.; Leis. Recreat. Tour. Abstr.; Middle East Abstr. Index; Newsp. Period. Abstr. (1991-); PAIS Int. Print (1991-); Res. Alert [Full Cov.]; Rural Dev. Abstr.; Sage Public Adm. Abstr.; Sage Urban Stud. Abstr (?-?); Soc. Sci. Source (Jan. 1992-); Soc. Sci. Cit. Index [Full Cov.]; Soc. Sci. Index; Soc. Sci. Index Fulltext (Oct. 1988-) [Full Txt.]; Stud. Women Abstr.; World Agric. Econ.

UK/0144-1329
## BRITISH PUBLIC OPINION.
**See** Sociology.

US/1049-4065
## BROOKINGS DISCUSSION PAPERS IN GOVERNMENTAL STUDIES.
[Brook. discuss. pap. gov. stud.]. **Added/Corp** Brookings Institution. **VFOAT** Governmental Studies Discussion Papers. (19??)-. Monographic series. English. Price varies per volume. Brookings Institution, 1775 Massachusetts Avenue NW, Washington DC 20036. **Tel** (202)797-6112. **DD** 320.

SP
## BULGARSKI GLAS.
**VFOAT** Bulgarian Voice. Vol. 1- Nov. 1979-. Periodical. Bulgarian. bm. 3500ptas Spain; $30.00 North America; DM50.00 other. Bulgarski Glas, Apartado 99, E-29640 Fuengirola Spain. **Tel** 52-47 29 06, FAX 52-47 29 06. **ED** Emil Solemo. **LC** AP58.B8; B823. **Circ:** 1,200.

CN/0832-008X
## BULLETIN - CANADIAN POLITICAL SCIENCE ASSOCIATION (1979).
(BULLETIN / CANADIAN POLITICAL SCIENCE SOCIETY.). [Bull. - Can. Polit. Sci. Assoc.$b(1979)]. **Added/Corp** Canadian Political Science Association. Societe Quebecoise de Science Politique. **VAT** Bulletin - Association Canadienne de Science Politique; Bulletin - Societe Quebecoise de Science Politique. (Sept. 1979)-. Bulletin. French (English). Twice a year. 15.00Can$. Canadian Political Science Association, 1 Stewart Street, Suite 205, Ottawa Ontario K1N 6H7 Canada. **Tel** (613)564-4026. **DD** 320/.06271. ***Continues*** *Canadian Political Science Bulletin., 0705-341X.*

US
## BULLETIN / DEMOCRACY INTERNATIONAL COMMITTEE TO AID DEMOCRATIC DISSIDENTS IN YUGOSLAVIA.
**Added/Corp** Democracy International Committee to Aid Democratic Dissidents in Yugoslavia. (19??)-. Bulletin. English.
**Ind/Abst** Hum. Rights Intern. Rep.

●US
## BULLETIN OF ASIAN-PACIFIC ECONOMIC AND POLITICAL ISSUES.
**See** Economics-Economic History, Conditions.

US/0007-4810
## BULLETIN OF CONCERNED ASIAN SCHOLARS.
**See** History(General)-History of Asia.

●US
## BULLETIN OF EUROPEAN POLITICAL AND ECONOMIC ISSUES.
(1994)-. Periodical. English. Four times a year. $65.00. Nova Science Publishers Inc., 6080 Jericho Turnpike, Suite 207, Commack NY 11725-2808. **Tel** (516)499-3103, (516)499-3106, FAX (516)499-3146.

NO/0007-5035
## BULLETIN OF PEACE PROPOSALS.
***Title Change.*** [Bull. peace propos.]. **Added/Corp** International Peace Research Association. International Peace Research Institute. Vol. 1, No. 1 (1970)-(Sept. 1992). Bulletin. English (French and German). qt. Sage Publications Ltd., 6 Bonhill Street, London EC2A 4PU, UK. **Tel** 071 374 0645, FAX 071 374 8741, telex 296207 SAGE G. **ED** Magne Barth. **LC** JX1901; .B83. **DD** 327/.172/05. cum. index. **Bk Rev. Ad Acc. Pr Rev. Acid Free. Circ:** 800 (ctrl). available on microfilm and microfiche from University Microfilms International (UMI). Documents available. ***Continued by*** *Security Dialogue, 0967-0106.*
**Desc:** Discusses contemporary international and intergroup affairs, searching for solutions to conflict situations in the light of general peace research theory.
**Ind/Abst** Am. Hist. Life (1973-); Curr. Mil. Pol. Lit. (1973-); Energy Res. Abstr. (1980-); Hum. Rights Intern. Rep.; Int. Polit. Sci. Abstr. (1973-); J. Plan. Lit.; Linguist. Lang. Behav. Abstr. (?-?); Middle East Abstr. Index (1984-); PAIS Int. Print (1991-); Peace Res. Abstr. J. (1970-); Risk Abstr. (1973-); Soc. Plann. Policy Dev. Abstr.; Sociol. Abstr. (?-?).

UK
## BURKE'S PRESIDENTIAL FAMILIES OF THE UNITED STATES OF AMERICA.
English. ir. £35.00. Burkes Peerage, 12 Rickett Street, London SW6 1RU England. **Tel** 011 44 71 3854206. **LC** CS69. **DD** 973/.09/92.

UK
## C.P.C. : [PUBLICATIONS] / CONSERVATIVE POLITICAL CENTRE.
**Added/Corp** Conservative Political Centre (Great Britain). (1946)-. Monographic series. English. ir (Approx. 15 issues per year). Price varies per volume. Conservative Political Centre, 32 Smith Square, London SW1P 3HH England. **Tel** 011 44 71 222 7000, FAX 011 44 71 233 2065. **Circ:** 2,800.

SG
## CAAXAAN FAAXEE / JS.
**See** History(General)-History of Africa.

FR/0759-2736
## CABINETS MINISTERIELS.
[Cabinets minist.]. (1963)-. French. Four times a year. 168.83F France; 200.00F other. Les Cabinets Ministriels, 30 rue Saint Marc, 75002 Paris France. **Tel** 011 33 1 64334905. **UDC** 354(44).

BL
## CADERNOS DCP.
**Main/Corp** Universidade Federal de Minas Gerais. Departamento de Ciencia Politica. No. 1- March 1974-. Portuguese. Universidade Federal, Caixa Postal 1621, Belo Horizonte 30.000 Brazil. **LC** JA5; .M55A.

BL/0101-3211
## CADERNOS FUNDAP.
V. 1, No. 1, (June 1981)-. Periodical. Portuguese. ir. Cr$15,000 Brazil; $10.00 US. Fundacao do Desenvolvimento Administrativo, rua Cristiano Viana 428, CEP 05411 Sao Paulo SP Brazil. **Tel** 8815311, telex (011)30658 FDAD B. **LC** JA5; .C33. **DD** 350/.0005. Index available. cum. index. **Circ:** 2,500 (ctrl).
**Desc:** Articles, studies, research reports and essays in public administration and connected subjects.

FR/1145-5268
## CAHIERS DE L'IPAG NANCY.
(CAHIERS DE L'INSTITUT PANAFRICAIN DE GEOPOLITIQUE.). [Cah.IPAG Nancy]. **VFOAT** Cahiers de l'Institut Panafricain de Geopolitique (Nancy). (198?)-. Periodical. French. Three times a year. 146.91F. Inst Panafricain Geopolitique, 74 Place Saint Jacques, F 75014 Paris Cedex France. **Tel** 011 33 1 43315009. **UDC** 327.

FR/0339-3437
## CAHIERS D'ECONOMIE POLITIQUE.
**Added/Corp** Faculte d'Economie Appliquee d'Aix-Marseille. No. 1 (Oct. 1974)-. Periodical. French. ir. 220.00F (France); 280.00F (other). L' Harmattan, 7 rue de l'Ecole Polytechnique, 75005 Paris France. **Tel** 11 33 1 43547910, 43257651.

FR
## CAHIERS D'ETUDES ET DE RECHERCHES FRANCOPHONES SANTE ET DEVELOPPEMENT.
French. Six times a year. 650.00F (institutions), 380.00F (individuals), 250.00F (students) EEC; 325.00F (institutions), 190.00F (individuals), 125.00F (students) Latin America, Southeast Asia, Eastern Europe, Lebanon; 825.00F (institutions), 475.00 (individuals), 325.00 (students) Canada, US; 650.00F (institutions), 380.00F (individuals), 250.00F (students) other. John Libbey Eurotext Ltd, 6 rue Blanche, Isabelle Trope, 92120 Montrouge France. **Tel** 011 33 1 47358552. **(Subscription address:** ATEI John Libbey Eurotext, 23 25 rue Fernand Combette, 93100 Montreuil France.**)**

FR
## CAHIERS DU DOUBLE, LES.
(Fall 1977)-. French. Twice a year. Association des Cahiers du Double, Loi 1901, 12 rue Ganneron, 75018 Paris France.

CG
## CAHIERS ZAIROIS DE LA RECHERCHE ET DU DEVELOPPEMENT.
**VFOAT** Cahiers Zairois. 1971-. Periodical. French. $8.00. ONRD, BP 3119, Kinshasa Zaire. **LC** JQ3601.A1; C33. **DD** 320.9/675/103. ***Supersedes in part*** *Cahiers Congolais de la Recherche et du Developpement.*

II
## CALCUTTA JOURNAL OF POLITICAL STUDIES, THE.
Vol. 1, No. 1 (Winter 1980)-. Periodical. English. sa. Calcutta University / Publications Sales Counter, Asutosh Building, Calcutta 700073 India. **LC** JQ201; .C34. **DD** 320.954/05.
**Ind/Abst** Int. Polit. Sci. Abstr.

US/0279-0246
## CALIFORNIA EYE, THE.
(198?)-. Periodical. English. Twenty-four times a year. $150.00. Political Animal, 1000 W Sunset Blvd., Second Floor, Los Angeles CA 90012-2197. **Tel** (213)515-1300. **(Subscription address:** California Eye, PO Box 3249, Torrence CA 90510.**) ED** Bill Homer (phone: (213)481-3809). **Circ:** 250 (ctrl).
**Desc:** Political issues in the state of California.

US/0084-8271
## CALIFORNIA GOVERNMENT AND POLITICS ANNUAL.
**Added/Corp** California Center for Research and Education in Government. (19??)-. English. an. $10.70. California Journal Press, 1714 Capitol Avenue, Sacramento CA 95814. **Tel** (916)444-2840, FAX (916)444-2339. **ED** Hoeber and Price. **LC** JK8701; .C32. **DD** 320.4/794. **Circ:** 6,000.
**Desc:** Reprints of articles from California Journal regarding California government and politics.

US/0008-1205
## CALIFORNIA JOURNAL.
[Calif. j.]. **Added/Corp** California Center for Research and Education in Government. Vol. 1 (Jan. 1970)-. Periodical. English. mo (12 issues). $34.95, $59.00 (with index). California Journal Press, 1714 Capitol Avenue, Sacramento CA 95814. **Tel** (916)444-2840, FAX (916)444-2339. **ED** Rich Zeiger and A G Block. **LC** JK8701; .C33. **DD** 320.9/794. Index available. cum. index. **Bk Rev. Ad Acc. Circ:** 18,000. available on microfilm. Documents available from UMI Article Clearinghouse.
**Desc:** Analyses of the issues, personalities and politics of California.
**Ind/Abst** Calif. Period. Index (19??-); Expand. Acad. Index (1992-); Infobank (1970-); Newsp. Period. Abstr. (1989-); PAIS Int. Print (1991-); Urban Aff. Abstr.

●US
## CALIFORNIA JOURNAL'S ELECTION WEEKLY.
**VFOAT** Election Weekly. (Feb. 24, 1992)-. Periodical. English. wk. $225 for the 1992 election season. California Journal Press, 1714 Capitol Avenue, Sacramento CA 95814. **Tel** (916)444-2840, FAX (916)444-2339. **LC** JK8791.A1; E44.

US
## CALIFORNIA POLITICAL ALMANAC.
**VFOAT** Political Almanac. (1989-90)-. English. be. $34.95. California Journal Press, 1714 Capitol Avenue, Sacramento CA 95814. **Tel** (916)444-2840, FAX (916)444-2339. **LC** JK8701; .C333. ***Continues*** *Almanac of California Government and Politics.*
**Desc:** Almanac of political issues in California.

US
## CALIFORNIA VOTER.
**Added/Corp** League of Women Voters of California. Vol. 1 (Sept. 1949)-. Periodical. English. Three times a year. $4.00. League of Women Voters of California, 926 J Street, Suite 1000,

Sacramento CA 95814. **Tel** (916)442-7215, FAX (916)442-7362. **ED** Leslie Stewart. **Circ:** 15,000 (ctrl). available on diskette.

UK/0955-7571
**CAMBRIDGE REVIEW OF INTERNATIONAL AFFAIRS.** Periodical. English. Twice a year. £6.00 UK; $18.00 North America; £9.00 other. Centre of International Studies, England History Faculty Building, West Road, Cambridge CB3 9EF England. **Tel** (0223)335-333. **ED** Paul N Cornish. **LC** PAR. **Bk Rev. Ad Acc. Circ:** 300.
**Desc:** Contains articles and reviews from a wide range of authors, established academics and professionals. Written for students writing for the first time in the areas of international relations and modern and contemporary history.

US/0884-8351
**CAMPAIGN FINANCE LAW. See** Law.

US/0094-1921
**CAMPAIGN LAW REPORTER. Added/Corp** California Research (Firm). (Feb. 1974)-. English. Thirteen times a year. Pacific Communications Group, PO Box 162901, Sacramento CA 95816. **Tel** (916)343-1100. **LC** KFC710.A73; C35. **DD** 342/.794/0705.

US/0733-9771
**CAMPAIGN PEOPLE.** V. 1, No. 1 (March 8, 1982)-. Periodical. English. bw. $69.00. Campac Publications Inc, 306 A Street SE, Washington DC 20003. **Tel** (202)544-6300.

US/0361-056X
**CAMPAIGN PRACTICES REPORTS.** ***Ceased.* See** Law.

US/1061-964X
**CAMPAIGN (WASHINGTON, D.C. 1991).** (CAMPAIGN.). [Campaign]. **VFOAT** Campaign Magazine. Vol. 5, No. 6 (June 1991)-. Periodical. English. mo. Campaign Industry News, 205 Pennsylvania Avenue SE, Washington DC 20003-1164. **DD** 328. ***Continues*** *Campaign Magazine, 1054-0075.*

US/0899-7438
**CAMPAIGNETWORKS (LIBERTY, MO.).** (CAMPAIGNETWORKS.). **VFOAT** Campaign Networks. (1990)-. Periodical. English. bm. $24.95. Campaign Networks Inst Inc, 1200 East Hwy 210, Liberty MO 64068.

US/0197-0771
**CAMPAIGNS & ELECTIONS.** [Camp. elect.]. **VAT** Campaigns and Elections. Vol. 1, (Spring 1980)-. Periodical. English. Ten times a year (Oct/Nov. and Dec/Jan. issues combined). $41.17 Canada; $31.75 Washington DC add 6% tax; $29.95 US; $44.05 other. Campaigns and Elections, 1511 K Street NW, Suite 1020, Washington DC 20005. **Tel** (800)237-7842, (202)638-7788, FAX (202)638-4668. **ED** Ron Faueheux. **LC** JK1976; .C33. **DD** 324.7/0973. **[CCC]. Ad Acc. Circ:** 15,000. available on microfilm and microfiche from University Microfilms International (UMI). Documents available from UMI Article Clearinghouse.
**Desc:** Devoted to political campaign technology. Concentrates on the computer applications. Regular columns covers fund raising, election law, parties and campaign history.
**Ind/Abst** Expand. Acad. Index (1992-); Int. Polit. Sci. Abstr.; Newsp. Period. Abstr. (1992-); PAIS Int. Print (1991-).

CN/0315-1433
**CANADIAN ANNUAL REVIEW OF POLITICS AND PUBLIC AFFAIRS.** (1971)-. English (French; summaries and/or abstracts in French). an. $70.00. University of Toronto Press, 5201 Dufferin Street, Downsview Ontario M3H 5T8 Canada. **Tel** (416)667-7781, (416)667-7782, FAX (416)667-7803. **ED** David Leyton-Brown. **LC** F1001; .C215. **DD** 320.9/71/064. ***Continues*** *Canadian Annual Review, 0068-8215.*
**Desc:** Offers a concise record of the year's events and an appraisal of developments.
**Ind/Abst** Can. Index (?-?).

CN/0008-3402
**CANADIAN DIMENSION.** [Can. dimens.]. Vol. 1 (1963)-. Periodical. English. Six times a year. 35.00Can$ (institutions), 24.50Can$ (individuals) Canada; 41.00Can$ (institutions), 30.50Can$ (individuals) US; 45.00Can$ (institutions), 34.50Can$ (individuals) other. Canadian Dimension, 228 Notre Dame Avenue, Suite 707, Winnipeg Manitoba R3B 1N7 Canada. **Tel** (204)957-1519, FAX (204)943-4617. **ED** Yvonne Block. **LC** AP5; . C26. **Bk Rev**, (Qty: 5). **Ad Acc. Circ:** 3,000. available on microfilm from Information Access Company; and Micromedia Limited; available on microfiche from University Microfilms International (UMI); available on an online database (files 647,648/Full-Text) from DIALOG. Documents available from UMI Article Clearinghouse.
**Desc:** Covers the labor movement, women's lib, the fight for peace, native peoples, environmental issues and popular culture. Collectively-operated, non-profit, responsive network and forum for the ideas, work and hopes of people active in the movement for a better Canada.
**Ind/Abst** Acad. Abstr. Full Text Elite (Jan. 1992-); Acad. Abstr. (Jan. 1992-); Acad. Search (Jan. 1992-); Altern. Press Index; Am. Hist. Life (1972-1988); AQUAREF; Can. Index; Can. Period. Index; Gen. Period. Index (1983-); INFO-SOUTH Abstr.; Mag. Index Plus (1989-); Mag. Search; Middle East Abstr. Index; Newsp. Period. Abstr. (1988-); Peace Res. Abstr. J. (1970-1974); Mag. Index (1983-); Trade Ind. ASAP [Full Txt.]; Trade Ind. Index [Full Txt.].

CN/0008-4239
**CANADIAN JOURNAL OF POLITICAL SCIENCE.** [Can. j. polit. sci.]. **Added/Corp** Canadian Political Science Association. **VFOAT** Revue Canadienne de Science Politique. Vol. 1 (March 1968)-. Periodical. English (French). qt. 65.00Can$ (GST included) Canada; $65.00 non-OECD countries; $85.00 OECD countries. Wilfrid Laurier University Press, 75 University Avenue West, Waterloo Ontario N2L 3C5 Canada. **Tel** (519)884-1970, FAX (519)725-1399. **ED** John McMenemy. **[CCC].** Index available. cum. index. **Bk Rev. Ad Acc. Pr Rev. Circ:** 2,800. available on microfiche from University Microfilms International (UMI). Documents available from The Genuine Article, UMI Article Clearinghouse. ***Supersedes in part*** *Canadian Journal of Economics and Political Science, 0315-4890.*
**Desc:** Outlet for refereed scholarship in all fields of political science. Communication in the form of analytic articles, synthesizing essays, literature reviews (field analyses), comments and replies, and reviews of current publications.
**Ind/Abst** ABC POL SCI; Acad. Abstr. Full Text Elite (Jan. 1992-); Acad. Abstr. (Jan. 1992-); Acad. Search (Jan. 1992-); Am. Hist. Life (1954-); Am. Bibliogr. Slavic East Europ. Stud.; Appl. Soc. Sci. Index Abstr.; Can. Index; Can. Period. Index; Commun. Abstr. (?-?); Curr. Contents Arts Humanit.; Curr. Contents Soc. Behav. Sci.; Expand. Acad. Index (1989-); Index Can. Leg. Period. Lit.; Index Period. Artic. Relat. Law (19??-19??); INFO-SOUTH Abstr.; Int. Bibliogr. Sociol.; Int. Polit. Sci. Abstr.; Int. Bibliogr. Rezen. Wissen. Lit.; Linguist. Lang. Behav. Abstr.; Mag. Search; Middle East Abstr. Index; Newsp. Period. Abstr. (1991-); PAIS Int Print (1991-); Peace Res. Abstr. J. (1972-1973, 1975-); Point Repere (1983-); Res. Alert [Full Cov.]; Soc. Plann. Policy Dev. Abstr.; Soc. Sci. Source (Jan. 1992-); Soc. Sci. Cit. Index [Full Cov.]; Soc. Sci. Index; Soc. Sci. Index Fulltext (Dec. 1988-) [Full Txt.]; Sociol. Abstr.; U.S. Polit. Sci. Doc.; West. Hist. Q.

CN/0714-8143
**CANADIAN PARLIAMENTARY HANDBOOK.** (CANADIAN PARLIAMENTARY HANDBOOK / COMPILED BY JOHN BEJERMI.). [Can. parliam. handb.]. **VFOAT** Repertoire Parlementaire Canadien. **VAT** Repertoire Parliamentaire Canadien. (1982)-. English (French). an (May). 56.95Can$ Canada; 60.44Can$ US; 61.51Can$ other. Borealis Press, 9 Ashburn Drive, Ottawa Ontario K2E 6N4 Canada. **Tel** (613)224-6837, FAX (613)829-7783. **ED** John Bejermi. **DD** 328.71/002/02. Index available. **Circ:** 1,500.
**Desc:** Includes biographies, photographs and descriptions of members in the Governor General, Senate, House of Commons and Library of Parliament.

CN/0843-6940
**CANADIAN STRATEGIC FORECAST, THE.** [Can. strateg. forecast]. **Added/Corp** Canadian Institute of Strategic Studies. (1990)-. English. an (Dec. or Jan.). 20.00Can$. Canadian Institute of Strategic Studies, 76 St. Clair Avenue West, Suite 502, Toronto Ontario M4V 1N2 Canada. **Tel** (416)964-6632. **LC** UA10.5; .C36. **DD** 355/.033. ***Continues*** *Canadian Strategic Review, 0824-2216.*

FR/0008-5405
**CANARD ENCHAINE, LE.** Vol. 1 (1915)-. Periodical. French. wk. 321.00F France; 453.00F other. Le Canard Enchaine, 173 rue Saint Honore, 75051 Paris Cedex 01 France. **Tel** 011 33 1 42603136.
**Ind/Abst** Peace Res. Abstr. J. (1964-1969).

CN/0821-2643
**CAPITALISM (LONDON, ONT.).** (CAPITALISM.). [Capitalism]. 1st Issue Aug. (1982)-. Periodical. English. bm. $0.50 per no. Capitalism, c/o M Pettigrew, London Ontario N6A 4E3 Canada. **DD** 320.5/12.

UK/0966-1050
**CARF. CAMPAIGN AGAINST RACISM & FASCISM 1991.** (CARF). [CARF, Campaign Against Racism Fascism1991]. **VFOAT** Campaign Against Racism & Fascism (1991). (1991)-. Periodical. English. Searchlight / London, 37 B New Cavendish Street, London W1M 8JR England. **Tel** 011 44 71 6072646. **DD** 322.4. ***Continues in part*** *Searchlight (1977), 0262-4591.*

CN/0384-1464
**CARIBBEAN DIALOGUE.** Began with Aug./Sept. 1975 issue. Periodical. English. mo. $15.00 US and Canada. Caribbean Dialogue, PO Box 442 Station J, Toronto Ontario M4J 4Y8 Canada. **DD** 320.9/729/05.

US/0008-6525
**CARIBBEAN REVIEW.** [Caribb. rev.]. V. 1- Spring 1969-. Periodical. English. qt. $30.00 (one year), $78.00 (three year). Caribbean Review Inc, PO Box 1370, Miami FL 33265. **Tel** (305)284-8466, FAX (305)284-1019. **ED** Barry B. Levine. **LC** AP6; .C27. **DD** 079/.7295. **[CCC].** Index available. cum. index. **Bk Rev. Ad Acc. Circ:** 5,000. available on microfilm and microfiche from University Microfilms International (UMI).
**Desc:** Dedicated to Latin America, the Caribbean and their emigrant groups. Debate about the issues and personalities that concern this region.
**Ind/Abst** Abstr. Anthropol.; Am. Hist. Life (1979-); ARTbibliogr. Mod.; HAPI Hisp. Am. Period. Index; Hum. Rights Intern. Rep.; Int. Dev. Abstr.; Int. Polit. Sci. Abstr.; Leis. Recreat. Tour. Abstr.; Sage Race Relat. Abstr.; U.S. Polit. Sci. Doc.

CN/0824-2062
**CATALYST / CITIZENS FOR PUBLIC JUSTICE. Added/Corp** Committee for Justice and Liberty Foundation. Citizens for Public Justice. Vol. 5, No. 2 (Sept. 1982)-. Periodical. English. bm. 15.00Can$ Canada; 20.00Can$ other. Citizens for Public Justice, 229 College Street #311, Toronto Ontario M5T 1R4 Canada. **Tel** (416)979-2443. **ED** Andrew Brouwer. **Bk Rev**, (Qty: 10). **Circ:** 3,500 (ctrl). ***Continues*** *Catalyst for Public Justice, 0225-0772.*
**Desc:** A forum for discussion of varied political views from a Christian justice perspective.

AG
**CAUCES. Added/Corp** Fundacion Sergio Karakachoff (Buenos, Aires, Argentina). Vol. 1, No. 1 (Apr. 1989)-. Periodical. Spanish. Fundacion Sergio Karakachoff, Libertad 145, 1o Piso, 1012 Buenos Aires, Argentina. **LC** F2849.2; .C353. **DD** 982.06/4/05.
**Ind/Abst** PAIS Int. Print.

US/1060-3670
**CAWP NEWS & NOTES. See** Women's Interests.

US/0887-0594
**CENTRAL AMERICA NEWSPAK.** (CENTRAL AMERICA NEWSPAK / FROM THE CENTRAL AMERICA RESOURCE CENTER.). [Cent. Am. newspak]. **Added/Corp** Central America Resource Center (Austin, Tex.) Documentation Exchange (Organization). Vol. 1, No. 1 (Feb. 17-March 3, 1986)-. Periodical. English (Spanish). Twenty-six times a year. $38.00 US and Mexico; $42.00 Canada; $58.00 other. Documentation Exchange, PO Box 2327, Austin TX 78768. **Tel** (512)476-9841. **ED** Billy Pope. **DD** 972. **Circ:** 400.
**Desc:** A compilation of current news articles on Central America selected from eight major U.S. newspapers and translated from three Mexican newspapers.
**Ind/Abst** Hum. Rights Intern. Rep.

CN/0823-7689
**CENTRAL AMERICA UPDATE.** [Cent. Am. update]. **Added/Corp** Latin American Working Group. Jesuit Centre for Social Faith and Justice. Community Information Research Group (Vancouver, B.C.). (197?)-. Periodical. English. bm (6 issues). 40.00Can$ (institutions), 25.00Can$ (individuals). Latin American Working Group, 603 Parliament Street, Toronto Ontario M4X 1P9 Canada. **Tel** (416)966-4773, FAX (416)921-0071. **ED** Kathy Price. **DD** 972.8/052/05. **Ad Acc. Circ:** 1,200 (ctrl). available on an online database from DIALOG. ***Continues*** *Quarterly Report (Latin American Working Group), 0827-3928.*
**Desc:** Opens a vital window on the critical political changes occurring in the Americas. Provides facts and interpretations to understand the rapidly changing situations in Central America.
**Ind/Abst** Hum. Rights Intern. Rep.; PTS Newsl. Database [Full Txt.].

US
**CENTRAL AMERICA UPDATE (ALBUQUERQUE, N.M.).** ***Title Change.*** CENTRAL AMERICA UPDATE.). Periodical. English. sw. $300.00. Latin American Data Base, University of New Mexico, 801 Yale NE, Albuquerque NM 87131. **Tel** FAX (505)277-2961. **ED** Dr Nelson Valdex and Dr Barbara Kohl. **Circ:** 2,500 (ctrl). ***Continued by*** Noti Sur.

US/1054-8882
**CENTRAL AMERICA UPDATE (ALBUQUERQUE, N.M.).** ***Title Change.*** (CENTRAL AMERICA UPDATE [COMPUTER FILE].). [Cent. Am. update]. **Added/Corp** University of New Mexico. Latin America Database. (198?)-(19??). Periodical. English. sw. $300.00 (institutions). Latin American Data Base, University of New Mexico, 801 Yale NE, Albuquerque NM 87131. **Tel** FAX (505)277-2961. **ED** Nelson Valdex and Barbara Kohl. **DD** 320. **Circ:** 2,500 (ctrl). available on an online database (via commercial database services). ***Continued by*** Noti Sur.

BE/0771-3398
**CENTRE DE DOCUMENTATION PAYSANNE DU PARAGUAY. See** Economics-Economic History, Conditions.

IT
**CENTRO PRO UNIONE : [BOLLETTINO]. Added/Corp** Centro pro Unione (Rome, Italy). **VFOAT** Unione. No. 1 (1969)-. Periodical. Italian (English and French). sa. Free. Centro Pro Unione, Via S Maria dell'Anima 30, 00186 Rome Italy. **Tel** 06 687-9552. **ED** M P Froelicher. **Circ:** 1,000 (ctrl).
**Desc:** Ecumenical publication, chiefly interfaith dialogue

bibliographies.
**Ind/Abst** Index Book Rev. Relig.; Relig. Index One Period. (1989-).

UK/0962-3876
**CEPS PAPER.** [CEPS pap.]. **VFOAT** Centre for European Policy Studies Paper. (1982)-. Monographic series. English. ir. Price varies per volume. Brasseys UK Ltd., 33 John Street, London WC1N 2AT England. **Tel** 011 44 71 753 7777, FAX 011 44 71 753 7794. **(Subscription address:** Macmillan Publishing, Front and Brown Street, Riverside NJ 08075.**)**

US
**CHANGING CHINA : A PUBLICATION SPONSORED BY THE NORTH AMERICAN COALITION FOR CHINESE DEMOCRACY (NACCD), A.** ***Ceased.*** **Added/Corp** Foundation for Chinese Democracy. North American Coalition for Chinese Democracy. **VFOAT** Changing China, a North American Forum of the Democratic Movement. Vol. 1, No. 1 (Winter 1991)-(199?). Periodical. English. qt. Foundation for Chinese Democracy, 1118 Grant Avenue, Suite 101, San Francisco CA 94133. **LC** JQ1501.A1; C53.

UK/0084-8085
**CHECK LIST OF BRITISH OFFICIAL SERIAL PUBLICATIONS.** [Check list Br. off. ser. publ.]. 1967-. English. sm. £115.00 UK; £125.00 other. British Library / Publications Sale Unit, Boston Spa, Wetherby, West Yorkshire LS23 7BQ England. **Tel** 011 44 937 546546 546543, FAX 011 44 937 546333, telex 557381. **(Subscription address:** Publications Sales Unit, Boston Epa, Wetherby LS23 7BQ England**)** **ED** Hazel Finnie. **LC** Z2009; .B87; J301. **DD** 015/.41. **Circ:** 1,250.

CH
**CHENG CHIH CHIAO YU.** **VFOAT** Zheng Zhi Jiao Yu. Periodical. Chinese. bm. NT$0.26. Shang-Hai Shih Pao Kan Fa Hsing Chu, Shanghai, People's Republic of China. **LC** JA88.C45; C43. **DD** 320/.072051.

CC
**CHENG CHIH YU FA LU.** **VFOAT** Cheng Chih Yu Fa Lu Tsung Kan. Periodical. Chinese. RMBY0.55. Hsin Hua Shu Tien / Shang-Hai Fa Hsing So, Shanghai, People's Republic of China. **LC** JA26; .C53. **DD** 320/.05.

CC
**CHENG FA LUN TAN : CHUNG-KUO CHENG FA TA HSUEH HSUEH PAO.** **See** Law.

GW/0341-6631
**CHINA AKTUELL / INSTITUT FUER ASIENKUNDE.** **Added/Corp** Institut fuer Asienkunde (Hamburg, Germany). (1972)-. Periodical. German (English). mo. DM176.00 Europe, DM222.00 others (airmail); DM156.00 Germany, DM171.00 others (surface mail). Institute of Asian Affairs, Rothenbaumchaussee 32, D-20148 Hamburg Germany. **Tel** 011 49 40 443001, FAX 011 49 40 4107945. **ED** Gunter Hartmann. **LC** DS701; .C3553. **DD** 951/.005. Index available (free, published in May). **Ad Acc. Circ:** 1,200. available on microfiche from the publisher.
**Desc:** News from and on China; analyses, chronological presentation of events in the fields of domestic and foreign politics and economic development and relations.
**Ind/Abst** PAIS Int. Print (1991-).

NE/0920-203X
**CHINA INFORMATION.** [China inf.]. **Added/Corp** Rijksuniversiteit te Leiden. Documentatiecentrum Voor het Huidige China. **VFOAT** Chung-Kuo Ching Pao. Vol. 1, No. 1 (1986)-. Academic Scholarly Publication. English. qt. Fl75.00 Netherlands; Fl90.00 other (institution). Documentation and Research Centre for Contemporary China, PO Box 9515, 2300 RA Leiden Netherlands. **Tel** 011 33 71 272516. **ED** W. L. Chong. Index available (bound in last issue). **Bk Rev. Ad Acc. Circ:** 350 (ctrl). ***Continues*** *China Informatie, 0577-8832.*
**Desc:** An academic quarterly on contemporary China, published by the Documentation and Research Center for Contemporary China, Sinological Institute, Leiden University, the Netherlands. It provides articles on recent developments in politics, economics, social affairs, environmental issues, culture, art and literature, as well as on field work and sino-foreign cooperations projects.

●GW/0943-7533
**CHINA MONTHLY DATA / INSTITUTE OF ASIAN AFFAIRS.** **Added/Corp** Institut fuer Asienkunde (Hamburg, Germany). (Jan. 1993)-. Periodical. English. Twelve times a year. DM90.00 Germany; DM96.00 Europe; DM113.00 others. Institute of Asian Affairs, Rothenbaumchaussee 32, D-20148 Hamburg Germany. **Tel** 011 49 40 443001, FAX 011 49 40 4107945. ***Continues*** *PRC Official Activities and Monthly Bibliography.*
**Desc:** Political and economic data and bibliography on the PR China, Taiwan, Hong Kong and Macau.

HK
**CHINA REFORM.** **VFOAT** Kai Ko. Vol. 1, No. 1 (May 1988)-. Periodical. English. Four times a year. $58.00. China Reform Publishing Ltd, PO Box 20013 Hennessy Road, Hong Kong Hong Kong. **Tel** 544 2093.

US/0891-351X
**CHINA REPORT. POLITICAL, SOCIOLOGICAL AND MILITARY AFFAIRS.** [China rep., Polit. sociol. mil. aff.]. **VFOAT** Political, Sociological and Military Affairs. No. 1 (July 18, 1979)-. Periodical. English (Chinese). ir. **DD** 320. available on microfiche (Vols. for (Dec. 18, 1986-) distributed to depository libraries). ***Continues in part*** *Translations on People's Republic of China.*

US/0743-2291
**CHINESE FOR AFFIRMATIVE ACTION NEWSLETTER.** [Chin. Affirm. Action newsl.]. **Added/Corp** Chinese for Affirmative Action (Organization). (19??)-. Periodical. Chinese (English). mo. $10.00 (student or elderly); $25.00 (individual);, $600.00 (corporate). Chinese for Affirmative Action, 121 Waverly Place, San Francisco CA 94108-1301. **Tel** (415)398-8212. **LC** F868.S156; C47. **DD** 323.1/1951/079461.

HK
**CHIU SHIH NIEN TAI.** **VFOAT** 90 Nien Tai; The Nineties; Nineties. Vol. 172, (May 1984)-. Periodical. Chinese. mo. $53.00. **(Subscription address:** Chinese Periodical Distributors, 507 South Stoneman Avenue, Alhambra, CA 91801; Phone: (818)282-0387 or (818)282-0361**)** **LC** AP95.C4; C5467. ***Continues*** *Chi Shih Nien Tai.*

US
**CHRISTIC NEWS / THE CHRISTIC INSTITUTE OF LOS ANGELES, LA.** **Added/Corp** Christic Institute of Los Angeles. **VFOAT** Los Angeles Christic News. (Feb. 1991)-. English. **LC** JA3; .L33.

CH
**CHUAN MIN CHENG CHIH CHI KAN.** **VFOAT** Chuan Min Cheng Chih; Direct Democracy Quarterly. First published in May 1983. Periodical. Chinese. qt. 40 Lane, 269 Li San Street, Nei-Hu Taipei Taiwan. **LC** JQ1521.A1; C48. **DD** 951/.249057.

CC
**CHUNG HSUEH CHENG CHIH KO CHIAO HSUEH.** **VFOAT** Zhongxue Zheng Zhike Jiaoxue. (19??)-. Periodical. Chinese. mo. Post Office Beijing, Beijing, People's Republic of China. **LC** JA88.C45; C5. **DD** 320/.071/251.

KO
**CHUNGANG CHODAL.** Periodical. Korean. qt. Chodalchong, 48-26 Inui-dong 4-ka Chongno-ku, Seoul Korea. **LC** JQ1726.Z36; C48.

US/0009-6334
**CHURCH AND STATE.** **Added/Corp** Protestants and Other Americans United for Separation of Church and State. Americans United for Separation of Church and State. **VFOAT** Church & State. **VAT** Church and State. Vol. 5, No. 8 (Sept. 1952)-. Periodical. English. Eleven times a year (July/Aug. issues combined). $18.00. Church and State, 8120 Fenton Street, Silver Spring MD 20910. **Tel** (301)589-3707, FAX (301)495-9173. **ED** Joseph L. Conn. **LC** BR516; .C49. Index available (Dec. iss.). cum. index (Dec. iss. covers that year). **Bk Rev**, (Qty: varies). **Circ:** 30,000. available on microfilm and microfiche from University Microfilms International (UMI). Documents available from UMI Article Clearinghouse. ***Continues*** *Church and State Newsletter.*
**Desc:** News and analysis about church-state separation and religious liberty issues.
**Ind/Abst** Expand. Acad. Index (1992-); Index Book Rev. Relig.; Index Period. Artic. Relat. Law; Middle East Abstr. Index; Newsp. Period. Abstr. (1992-); PAIS Int. Print (1991-); Relig. Index One Period.; Sage Public Adm. Abstr. (?-?).

US
**CIA WORLD FACTBOOK. CD-ROM.** English. $57.95 Minnesota residents; $54.95 other. Quanta Press, Inc., 1313 Fifth Street Southeast, Suite 208C, Minneapolis MN 55414. **Tel** (612)379-3956, FAX (612)623-4570.
**Desc:** The government's own World Almanac of facts and figures for 249 countries and territories world-wide. Topics include: geography, government, economics, communications, military, the environment, illicit drugs, claims, treaties and other world affairs. Available in DOS and MAC formats.

FR/0181-4788
**CIMADE INFORMATION.** [CIMADE inf]. **VFOAT** CIMADE Informations; Comite Intermouvements Aupres des Evacues Information. (1972)-. Periodical. French. bm. **UDC** 32.
**Ind/Abst** Hum. Rights Intern. Rep.

US
**CITIZEN.** (19??)-. Periodical. English. mo. $20.00. Focus on the Family, Colorado Springs CO 80995. **Tel** (800)232-6459.
**Desc:** Focuses on current events issues surrounding the family and Christian family values.

US/0198-8468
**CITIZEN PARTICIPATION (MEDFORD).** ***Suspended.*** (CITIZEN PARTICIPATION.). [Citiz. particip.]. Vol. 1, No. 1 (Sept./Oct. 1979)-(Nov. 1988). Periodical. English. bm. $12.00 US; $14.00 other. Lincoln Filene Center for Citizenship & Public Affairs, Tufts University, Medford MA 02155. **Tel** (617)381-3456. **ED** Ken Thomson. **Bk Rev. Circ:** 5,000 (ctrl).
**Desc:** Useful models and careful analysis of citizen roles in government decisionmaking at local, state and federal levels. For citizen group leaders, government officials, and social scientists.
**Ind/Abst** Altern. Press Index (?-19??); Urban Aff. Abstr.

IT
**CITTA NUOVA, LA.** Vol. 1, No. 1 (1986)-. Periodical. Italian. bm. Gaetano Macchiaroli Editore, Via Michetti 11, 80127 Naples Italy. **Tel** 11 39 81 5783129, FAX 11 39 81 5780568.
**Ind/Abst** PAIS Int. Print.

●US/1060-8540
**CITY JOURNAL (NEW YORK, N.Y.), THE.** (THE CITY JOURNAL.). [City j.]. **Added/Corp** Manhattan Institute (New York, N.Y.). Vol. 2, No. 1 (Winter 1992)-. Periodical. English. qt. $24.00 (one year), $38.00 (two year). Manhattan Institute, 52 Vanderbilt Avenue, 2nd Floor, New York NY 10017. **Tel** (212)599-7000, FAX (212)599-3494. **ED** Fred Siegel. **LC** F128.55; .N52. **DD** 320.974.7/1. **Bk Rev**, (Qty: 4). **Ad Acc, Adv Mgr:** Margaret Laws. ***Continues*** *NY, 1057-3607.*
**Desc:** Public policy focusing on urban issues with particular emphasis on New York City.

IT/0009-8191
**CIVITAS.** [Civitas]. (1919)-. Periodical. Italian (summaries and/or abstracts in Spanish, French, English and German). bm (6 issues). L25000 Italy; L30000 Europe; L40000 other. Edizioni Civitas, Via Tirso 92, 00198 Rome Italy. **Tel** 011 39 6 8555651. **LC** H7; .C595. **Ad Acc. Circ:** 6,000.
**Desc:** Political and economic studies.
**Ind/Abst** Am. Hist. Life (1954-); Int. Bibliogr. Sociol.

US/0145-9686
**CLEMENTS' ENCYCLOPEDIA OF WORLD GOVERNMENTS.** [Clements' encycl. world gov.]. **VFOAT** Encyclopedia of World Governments. Vol. 1 (1974)-. Periodical. English. be. Political Research Inc., 16850 Dallas Parkway, Dallas TX 75248. **Tel** (214)931-8827. **LC** JF37; .C53. **DD** 320.4/03.

US/0733-0286
**CLEMENTS' ENCYCLOPEDIA OF WORLD GOVERNMENTS. BIANNUAL SUPPLEMENT.** [Clements' encycl. world gov., Biannu suppl.]. English. sa. $340.00. Political Research Inc., 16850 Dallas Parkway, Dallas TX 75248. **Tel** (214)931-8827. **ED** John Clements. **LC** JF37; .C54. **DD** 351/.0005. **Bk Rev**.
**Desc:** 170 countries of the world as they represent themselves. A 4-part service, directory, update, and monthly international events.

US/1075-1130
**CLINTON MONTHLY, THE.** ***Ceased.*** (1994)-(1994). English. mo. Politically Unique Publications, PO Box 5656, Buena Park CA 90622-5656. **Tel** (714)220-9415, FAX (714)220-9415. **ED** Mark S. Kennedy. **Ad Acc.**
**Desc:** Gives several conservative views and evaluations on how effectively or ineffectively the current Clinton Administration is handling foreign, domestic, congressional, military and economic policy. There will also be specialty sections in the newsletter allowing for certain free advertising of pro/anti Bill Clinton products, special quote sections provided by readers, letters to the editor and sections giving information about political clubs and organizations.

UK/0032-1370
**CO-OPERATORS' PLATFORM.** **VFOAT** Cooperators' Platform. Periodical. English. bm. Co-Operative Party, 158 Buckingham Palace Road, London SW1W 9UB England. **LC** JN1129.C8; P57. **DD** 324.241/097. ***Continues*** *Platform.*

US
**COIN INDEXED CHECKLIST TO COLORADO STATE PUBLICATIONS.** **VFOAT** Indexed Checklist to Colorado State Publications. V. 1- 1977-. Periodical. English. qt. $15.00; $4.00 microfiche. Colorado Index Project, 1362 Lincoln Street, Denver CO 80203. **LC** Z1223.5.C6; C25; J87.C6. **DD** 015/.788.

US/0277-3708
**COLORADO LEGISLATIVE ALMANAC.** 1981-. English. be. $25.00. Ackerman-Rorex Corporation, 2888 Bluff, Suite 208, Boulder CO 80301. **LC** JK7830; .C64. **DD** 328.788/072/0202.

US
**COMIC PRESS NEWS.** See Recreation, Leisure-Games and Amusements.

US/0884-6537
**COMMON CAUSE MAGAZINE.** [Common cause mag.]. **Added/Corp** Common Cause (U.S.). Vol. 9, No. 4 (July/Aug. 1983)-. Periodical. English. qt. Comes with Common Cause membership, $20.00 (regular membership), $30.00 (family membership). Common Cause, PO Box 220, Washington DC 20044. **Tel** (202)736-5790. **ED** Deborah Baldwin. **LC** JK1; .C636. **DD** 329.973/05. **Circ:** 260,000. available on microfilm and microfiche from University Microfilms International (UMI); available on an online database from NEXIS. Documents available from UMI Article Clearinghouse, Documents on Demand. ***Continues** Common Cause (Washington, D.C.), 0271-9592.*
**Desc:** Investigative reporting and features about national, state and local politics and people.
**Ind/Abst** Acad. Abstr. Full Text Elite (July 1989-) [Full Txt.]; Acad. Abstr. (July 1989-); Acad. Ind. [Computer File] (1989-); Acad. Search (July 1989-); Altern. Press Index; Environ. Abstr.; Expand. Acad. Index (1989-); Gen. Period. Index (1989-); INFO-SOUTH Abstr.; Mag. Artic. Summar. Elite (July 1989-) [Full Txt.]; Mag. Artic. Summar. Select (July 1989-); Mag. Artic. Summar. CD-ROM (July 1989-); Mag. Index Plus (1989-); Mag. Index. Sel. (1989-); Mag. Search; Newsp. Period. Abstr. (1988-); PAIS Int. Print; Read. Guide Abstr. Select Ed.; Read. Guide Period. Lit.; Mag. Index (1989-).

US/0197-7377
**COMMON SENSE (PORTSMOUTH).** (COMMON SENSE.). (19??)-. Periodical. English. Common Sense Upstart Publishing Company Inc, 366 Islington Street, Portsmouth NH 03801.

US/0010-4140
**COMPARATIVE POLITICAL STUDIES.** [Comp. polit. stud.]. **VFOAT** CPS. Vol. 1, No. 1 (April 1968)-. Periodical. English. qt (Jan., Apr., July, Oct.). $162.00. SAGE Periodical Press, 2455 Teller Road, Thousand Oaks CA 91320. **Tel** (805)499-0721, FAX (805)499-0871, telex 100799. **ED** James A. Caporaso (University of Washington). **LC** JA3; .C65. **DD** 320. **[CCC]. Bk Rev. Pr Rev. Acid Free.** available on microfilm and microfiche from University Microfilms International (UMI). Documents available from The Genuine Article, UMI Article Clearinghouse.
**Desc:** Publishes theoretical and empirical research articles by scholars engaged in cross-national study. Includes occasional review essays.
**Ind/Abst** ABC POL SCI; Acad. Abstr. Full Text Elite (Jan. 1992-); Acad. Abstr. (Jan. 1992-); Acad. Search (Jan. 1992-); Am. Hist. Life (1969-); Am. Bibliogr. Slavic East Europ. Stud.; Appl. Soc. Sci. Index Abstr.; Commun. Abstr.; Curr. Contents Soc. Behav. Sci.; Expand. Acad. Index (1989-); INFO-SOUTH Abstr.; Int. Bibliogr. Sociol.; Int. Polit. Sci. Abstr.; J. Plan. Lit.; Mag. Search; Middle East Abstr. Index; Newsp. Period. Abstr. (1991-); PAIS Int. Print (1991-); Res. Alert [Full Cov.]; Sage Public Adm. Abstr.; Sage Urban Stud. Abstr (?-?); Soc. Sci. Source (Jan. 1992-); Soc. Sci. Cit. Index [Full Cov.]; Soc. Sci. Index; Soc. Sci. Index Fulltext (Oct. 1988-) [Full Txt.]; Sociol. Educ. Abstr.; Stud. Women Abstr.; U.S. Polit. Sci. Doc.; West. Hist. Q.

US/0010-4159
**COMPARATIVE POLITICS.** [Comp. polit.]. Vol. 1 (Oct. 1968)-. Periodical. English. qt. $30.00 (individual), $50.00 (institution) US; $37.50 (individual), $57.50 (institution) other. Comparative Politics, 49 Sheridan Avenue, Albany NY 12210. **Tel** (518)436-9686. **LC** JA3; .C67. **DD** 320.5. **[CCC]. Pr Rev.** available on microfilm and microfiche from University Microfilms International (UMI). Documents available from The Genuine Article, UMI Article Clearinghouse.
**Ind/Abst** ABC POL SCI; Acad. Abstr. Full Text Elite (July 1990-); Acad. Abstr. (July 1990-); Acad. Ind. [Computer File] (1987-); Acad. Search (July 1990-); Am. Hist. Life (1968-); Am. Bibliogr. Slavic East Europ. Stud.; Curr. Contents Soc. Behav. Sci.; Expand. Acad. Index (1987-); Index Islam. Lit.; INFO-SOUTH Abstr.; Int. Bibliogr. Sociol.; Int. Polit. Sci. Abstr.; J. Plan. Lit.; Mag. Search; Maize Abstr.; Newsp. Period. Abstr. (1991-); PAIS Int. Print (1991-); Res. Alert [Full Cov.]; Soc. Sci. Source (Jul. 1990-); Soc. Sci. Cit. Index [Full Cov.]; Soc. Sci. Index; Soc. Sci. Index Fulltext (Oct. 1988-) [Full Txt.]; Sorghum Mill. Abstr.; U.S. Polit. Sci. Doc.; West. Hist. Q.

US/0741-7233
**COMPARATIVE POLITICS (GUILFORD, CONN.).** (COMPARATIVE POLITICS.). [Comp. polit.]. **VFOAT** Annual Editions. Comparative Politics. (1984)-. English. an. $12.95. Dushkin Publishing Group Inc., Sluice Dock, Guilford CT 06437. **Tel** (203)453-4351, (800)243-6532, FAX (203)453-6000. **ED** Christian Soe. **LC** JF37; .C65. **DD** 320.3/05.
**Desc:** Brings together recent articles to help bridge the gap between the theory and practice of politics in distant, foreign lands. Articles deal with topics of current interest and controversy in comparative politics. Written by informed and observant analysts and scholars, articles are selected for lucidity of expression, level, and analysis, and compatibility with a comparative approach.

US/1047-1006
**COMPARATIVE STATE POLITICS.** (COMPARATIVE STATE POLITICS : CSP / ILLINOIS LEGISLATIVE STUDIES CENTER, SANGAMON STATE UNIVERSITY.). [Comp. state polit.]. **Added/Corp** Illinois Legislative Studies Center. **VFOAT** CSP. Vol. 10, No. 4 (Aug. 1989)-. Periodical. English. bm (6 issues). $15.00 US; $17.50 Canada; $20.00 other. Illinois Legislative Studies Center, Sangamon State University, Springfield IL 62794. **Tel** (217)786-6574, FAX (217)786-6540. **ED** David H. Everson. **LC** JK2403; .C57. **DD** 320. Index available. **Bk Rev**, (Qty: 3). **Ad Acc, Adv Mgr:** Jackie Wright, **Tel** (218)786-6574. **Circ:** 400. ***Continues** Comparative State Politics Newsletter, 0273-1347.*
**Desc:** Articles on legislative developments in the United States.
**Ind/Abst** PAIS Int. Print.

UK
**COMPASS. Main/Corp** Communist League (Gt. Brit.). English. Four times a year. L5.00. Communist League, 26 Cambridge Road, Ilford Essex England. **ED** W Bland. **Bk Rev. Pr Rev. Circ:** 100 (ctrl).
**Desc:** A Marxist - Leninist analysis of current affairs.
**Ind/Abst** Soils Fert.

IT
**COMPENDIO DELLA LEGISLAZIONE ITALIAN SULL'AIUTO PUBBLICO ALLO SVILUPPO.** (19??)-. Italian. an. L150000. CEGI Soc Coop Arl, Via Virgilio 3, 00193 Rome Italy. **Tel** 011 39 6 68307376.

UK
**COMPLETE INTELLIGENCE DIGEST SERVICE.** (19??)-. English. ir. $425.00. Intelligence International Ltd., 17 Rodney Road, Cheltenham, Gloucestershire, GL50 1HX United Kingdom. **Tel** 0285-770451, FAX 0285-770088. **ED** Joseph de Gurcy. **Bk Rev. Circ:** 5,000.
**Desc:** A weekly review of political and strategic intelligence.

BL
**CONFIDENCIAL ECONOMICO NORDESTE.** See Economics.

US/1047-1324
**CONGRESS AND THE NATION.** [Congr. nation]. **Added/Corp** Congressional Quarterly, Inc. Vol. 1 (1964)-. English. ir. Congressional Quarterly Inc., 1414 22nd Street Northwest, Washington DC 20037. **Tel** (202)887-8500, (800)432-2250 ext. 621, FAX (202)728-1863. **LC** KF49; .C653. **DD** 328.73/005.

US/0734-3469
**CONGRESS & THE PRESIDENCY.** [Congr. pres.]. **Added/Corp** American University (Washington, D.C.). Center for Congressional and Presidential Studies. United States Capitol Historical Society. **VFOAT** Congress and the Presidency. Vol. 9, No. 1 (Winter, 1981/1982)-. Periodical. English. sa (fall and spring). $22.00 (institutions), $15.00 (individuals). American University, School of Public Affairs, Washington DC 20016. **Tel** (202)885-6226, FAX (202)885-2967. **ED** Jeff Fishel and Susan Webb Hammond. **LC** JK1041; .C36. **DD** 328.73/005. Index available. cum. index. **Bk Rev. Ad Acc. Pr Rev.** ctrl circ. Documents available from The Genuine Article, UMI Article Clearinghouse. ***Continues** Congressional Studies, 0194-4053.*
**Desc:** A journal of political science and history devoted to the publication of research on the Presidency, Congress, the interactions between them, and national policy making.
**Ind/Abst** ABC POL SCI; Acad. Search (July 1993-); Am. Hist. Life (1972-); Curr. Contents Soc. Behav. Sci.; Expand. Acad. Index (1992-); INFO-SOUTH Abstr.; Int. Polit. Sci. Abstr.; Mag. Search; Newsp. Period. Abstr. (1989-); PAIS Int. Print (1991-); Res. Alert [Full Cov.]; Sage Public Adm. Abstr. (?-?); Soc. Sci. Cit. Index [Full Cov.].

US/0010-5899
**CONGRESSIONAL DIGEST, THE.** (CONGRESSIONAL DIGEST.). [Congr. dig.]. Vol. 1, No. 5 (Feb. 1922)-. Periodical. English. Ten times a year. $35.95 (one year), $69.00 (two year), $101.00 (three year). Congressional Digest Corporation, 3231 P Street Northwest, Washington DC 20007. **Tel** (202)333-7332, FAX (202)625-6670. **ED** Page B Robinson. **LC** JK1; .C65. Index available in last issue of volume--attached. cum. index. available on microfilm and microfiche from University Microfilms International (UMI). Documents available from UMI Article Clearinghouse, Documents on Demand, Magazine Collection. ***Continues** Capitol Eye.*
**Ind/Abst** Abr. Read. Guide Period. Lit.; Acad. Abstr. Full Text Elite (Feb. 1984-); Acad. Abstr. (Feb. 1984-); Acad. Ind. [Computer File] (1984-); Acad. Search (Feb. 1984-); Energy Inf. Abstr.; Environ. Abstr.; Expand. Acad. Index (1984-); Gen. Period. Index (1985-); Guide Soc. Sci. Relig.; INFO-SOUTH Abstr.; Mag. Artic. Summar. Elite (Feb. 1984-); Mag. Artic. Summar. Select (Feb. 1984-); Mag. Artic. Summar. CD-ROM (Feb. 1984-); Mag. Index Plus (1989-); Mag. Index. Sel. (1986-); Mag. Search; Middle East Abstr. Index; Mid. Search (Feb. 1984-); Newsp. Period. Abstr. (1988-); PAIS Int. Print (1991-?); Read. Guide Abstr. Select Ed.; Read. Guide Period. Lit.; Resource/One Ondisc (1988-); Soc. Sci. Source (Feb. 1984-); Soc. Sci. Index; Soc. Sci. Index Fulltext (Nov. 1988-) [Full Txt.]; Mag. Index (1977-); TOM Gen. Index (1985-); Vocat. Search (Feb. 1984-).

US/0196-0784
**CONGRESSIONAL INSIGHT. *Ceased.*** [Congr. insight]. **Added/Corp** Congressional Quarterly, Inc. Vol. 1 (Dec. 31, 1976)-(Dec. 1994). Periodical. English. wk. Congressional Quarterly Inc., 1414 22nd Street Northwest, Washington DC 20037. **Tel** (202)887-8500, (800)432-2250 ext. 621, FAX (202)728-1863.

US/0095-6007
**CONGRESSIONAL QUARTERLY ALMANAC.** See Public Administration.

US/0010-5910
**CONGRESSIONAL QUARTERLY WEEKLY REPORT.** [Congr. q. wkly. rep.]. **VFOAT** CQ Congressional Quarterly Weekly Report; CQ Weekly Report. Vol. 14, No. 1 (Jan. 6, 1956)-. Periodical. English. wk. Comes with Congressional Quarterly Service. Congressional Quarterly Inc., 1414 22nd Street Northwest, Washington DC 20037. **Tel** (202)887-8500, (800)432-2250 ext. 621, FAX (202)728-1863. **LC** JK1. **DD** 328.73/005. **[CCC].** available on microfilm and microfiche from University Microfilms International (UMI). Documents available from UMI Article Clearinghouse. ***Continues** CQ Weekly Report.*
**Desc:** Provides thorough and objective coverage of the United States Congress in action: bills, resolutions, votes, elections and campaigns.
**Ind/Abst** Acad. Abstr. Full Text Elite (July 1990-) [Full Txt.]; Acad. Abstr. (July 1990-); Acad. Ind. [Computer File] (1987-); Acad. Search (July 1990-); Expand. Acad. Index (1987-); Gen. Period. Index (1987-); Index Period. Artic. Relat. Law; INFO-SOUTH Abstr.; Mag. Artic. Summar. Elite (July 1990-) [Full Txt.]; Mag. Artic. Summar. Select (July 1990-); Mag. Artic. Summar. CD-ROM (July 1990-); Mag. Index Plus (1992-); Mag. Search; Newsp. Period. Abstr. (1986-); NEXIS (Jan. 5, 1980-); PAIS Int. Print (1991-); Soc. Sci. Source (Jul. 1990-) [Full Txt.]; Soc. Sci. Index; Soc. Sci. Index Fulltext (Oct. 1988-) [Full Txt.]; TOM Gen. Index (1991-); Vocat. Search (July 1990-); Women Stud. Abstr.

US/1064-6809
**CONGRESSIONAL QUARTERLY'S POLITICS IN AMERICA.** [Congr. Q. polit. Am.]. **Added/Corp** Congressional Quarterly, Inc. **VFOAT** Politics in America. (1990)-. English. an (April). $84.95. Congressional Quarterly Inc., 1414 22nd Street Northwest, Washington DC 20037. **Tel** (202)887-8500, (800)432-2250 ext. 621, FAX (202)728-1863. **LC** JK1012; .C63. **DD** 328.73/073/025. ***Continues** Politics in America.*

FR
**CONJONCTURE IN FRANCE.** CNGP Insee, BP 2718, 1 rue V Auriol, F 80027 Amiens, Cedex 1 France. **Tel** 011 33 22 927322.

US/0277-5700
**CONNECTICUT DIGEST OF ADMINISTRATIVE REPORTS TO THE GOVERNOR.** (CONNECTICUT DIGEST OF ADMINISTRATIVE REPORTS TO THE GOVERNOR / STATE OF CONNECTICUT.). **Main/Corp** Connecticut. Dept. of Administrative Services. **VFOAT** Digest of Connecticut Administrative Reports to the Governor; Connecticut Administrative Reports. Vol. 32 (1977/78)-. English. an. free on request. State Publications, 165 Capitol Avenue/Room 225, Hartford CT 06106. **Tel** (203)566-8125. **LC** J87; .C8 date q. **DD** 353.9746/0006. ***Continues** Connecticut Digest of Administrative Reports to the Governor, 0277-5700.*

SZ
**CONSCIENCE ET LIBERTE.** See Religion and Theology.

UK
**CONSERVATIVE NEWSLINE. *Ceased.*** (Sept. 1982)-(1993). Periodical. English. mo. Conservative Central Office, 16 Stadium Way, Scours Lane, Reading Berks RG3 6BX England. **Tel** 734 413439. **ED** Joseph Tobin. **Bk Rev. Ad Acc. Circ:** 100,000. ***Continues** Conservative News.*
**Desc:** Provides up-to-date insight into what is happening at all levels of the conservative party and government.

CK
**CONSIGNA.** VFOAT Consigna Politica. Periodical. Spanish. sm. Diagonal, 34 No 5-11, Bogota Colombia.

UK/1351-0487
**CONSTELLATIONS : AN INTERNATIONAL JOURNAL OF CRITICAL AND DEMOCRATIC THEORY.** (19??)-. Academic Scholarly Publication. English. Three times a year. £97.00 UK & Europe; $189.00 North America; £120.00 other. Basil Blackwell Publishers Ltd, 108 Cowley Road, Oxford 0X4 1JF England. **Tel** 011 44 865 791100, FAX 011 44 865 791347, telex 837022 OXBOOK G. **(Subscription address:** Blackwell Publishers / UK, Marston Book Services, PO Box 87, Oxford OX2 0DT England.**)**

SZ/0010-6623
**CONSTITUTIONAL AND PARLIAMENTARY INFORMATION.** See Law-Constitutional Law.

US
**CONSTITUTIONS OF DEPENDENCIES AND SPECIAL SOVEREIGNTIES.** (1977)-. Periodical. English. ir. Oceana Publications, Inc., 75 Main Street, Dobbs Ferry NY 10522. **Tel** (914)693-1320, FAX (914)693-0402.

IT
**CONTRADDIZIONE, LA.** Italian. bm. L25,000. Associazione Cultura Marxista Contraddizione, CP 11-188 Montesacro, 00141 Rome Italy. Index available. cum. index. **Bk Rev. Circ:** 650 (ctrl).

BE/0770-8521
**CONTRADICTIONS BRUXELLES.** See Economics.

US
**CONTRAGATE ALERT / THE CHRISTIC INSTITUTE.** **Added/Corp** Christic Institute. (198?)-. English. Three times a year. Christic Institute, 1324 North Capitol Street Northwest, Washington DC 20002. **Tel** (310)287-1556.
**Ind/Abst** Hum. Rights Intern. Rep.

US/0147-1066
**CONTRIBUTIONS IN POLITICAL SCIENCE.** No. 1-. Monographic series. English. Price varies per volume. Greenwood Press Inc., PO Box 5007, Westport CT 06881-5007. **Tel** (203)226-3571, FAX (203)222-1502.

US
**COOK POLITICAL REPORT.** (19??)-. English. ir. $312.70 Washington; $295.00 others. Cook Political Report, 900 2nd Street Northeast, Suite 107, Washington DC 20002. **Tel** (202)333-7400. ***Absorbed*** *Baron Report, 363-549X.*

NO/0010-8367
**COOPERATION AND CONFLICT.** [Coop. confl.]. **Added/Corp** Nordic Committee for the Study of International Politics. Vol. 1 (1965)-. Periodical. English. qt. £75.00 (one year), £150.00 (two year). Sage Publications Ltd., 6 Bonhill Street, London EC2A 4PU, UK. **Tel** 071 374 0645, FAX 071 374 8741, telex 296207 SAGE G. **ED** Christian Thune. **LC** JX1; .C77. **[CCC]. Bk Rev. Ad Acc. Pr Rev. Acid Free. Circ:** 600 (ctrl). available on microfilm and microfiche from University Microfilms International (UMI).
**Desc:** Devoted to the studies of the foreign policies of the Nordic countries and to studies of international politics by Nordic scholars.
**Ind/Abst** ABC POL SCI; Am. Hist. Life (1968-); Chemorecept. Abstr. (1991-); Int. Polit. Sci. Abstr.; Middle East Abstr. Index; PAIS Int. Print.

DK
**COPENHAGEN POLITICAL STUDIES ABSTRACTS.** See Political Science-Abstracting, Bibliographies and Statistics.

NE/0169-7528
**CORRUPTION AND REFORM.** ***Title Change.*** Vol. 1, No. 1 (1986)-(19??). Periodical. English. Three times a year. Martinus Nijhoff Publishers, Subsidiary of Kluwer Academic Publishers, Koraalrood 50, 2718 SC Zoetermeer Netherlands. **Tel** 011 31 79 684400. **LC** JF1081; .C66. **DD** 350.9/94/05. **CODEN** CORFEM. **[CCC].** available on microfilm and microfiche from University Microfilms International (UMI). ***Merged into*** *Crime Law and Social Change.*
**Ind/Abst** Am. Hist. Life (1988-); Crim. Justice Abstr.; Crim. Penol. Police Sci. Abstr.; Int. Bibliogr. Sociol.; Int. Polit. Sci. Abstr.

US/0890-4952
**COUNTRY DATABASE.** ***Ceased.*** (COUNTRY DATABASE [COMPUTER FILE].). [Ctry. database]. **Added/Corp** Frost & Sullivan. (Aug. 1986)-(Aug. 1988). Periodical. English. qt. Frost & Sullivan Inc, 106 Fulton Street, Department W, New York NY 10036. **Tel** (315) 472-1224, FAX (315) 472-1235, telex 650 247-7174 (MCI). **DD** 330.
**Desc:** System requirements: IBM PC and compatibles; dBase III, LOTUS 1-2-3; or ASCII format.

US/1056-2036
**CQ RESEARCHER, THE.** [CQ res.]. **Added/Corp** Congressional Quarterly, Inc. EBSCO Publishing (Firm). **VAT** Congressional Quarterly Researcher. Vol. 1, No. 1 (May 10, 1991)-. Periodical. English. Forty-eight times a year. $309.00 (full service). Congressional Quarterly Inc., 1414 22nd Street Northwest, Washington DC 20037. **Tel** (202)887-8500, (800)432-2250 ext. 621, FAX (202)728-1863. **LC** H35; .E35. **DD** 300/.973/05; 300. **[CCC].** Index available. available on microfilm and microfiche from University Microfilms International (UMI). ***Continues*** *Congressional Quarterly's Editorial Research Reports, 1057-0926.*
**Desc:** Covers political planning and policy sciences.
**Ind/Abst** Acad. Abstr. Full Text Elite (May 1991-) [Full Txt.]; Acad. Abstr. (May 1991-); Acad. Ind. [Computer File] (1991-); Acad. Search (May 1991-); Expand. Acad. Index (1991-); Gen. Period. Index (1991-); INIS Atomindex [Micro.]; Mag. Artic. Summar. Elite (May 1991-) [Full Txt.]; Mag. Artic. Summar. Select (May 1991-) [Full Txt.]; Mag. Artic. Summar. CD-ROM (May 1991-); Mag. Index Plus (1992-); Mag. Search; PAIS Int. Print; Soc. Sci. Source (Jul. 1990-) [Full Txt.]; TOM Gen. Index (1991-); Vocat. Search (May 1991-) [Full Txt.].

US/0070-1459
**CREATIVE INTERFACE, THE.** V. 1-. Monographic series. English. Price varies per volume. American University, Massachusetts & Nebraska Avenues NW, Washington DC 20016. **Tel** (202)885-1414. **LC** HD3616.U46. **DD** 322/.3/0973.

CN/0705-3754
**CRESCENT INTERNATIONAL.** [Crescent int.]. **VFOAT** Crescent. **VAT** Crescent (Willowdale). Vol. 6, No. 1 (Mar. 15, 1977)-. Periodical. English (Urdu). Twenty-four times a year. $60.00 (institutions), $40.00 (individuals). Crescent International, 300 Steelcase Road West Unit #8, Markham Ontario L3R 2W2 Canada. **Tel** (416)474-9292, FAX (416)474-9293. **ED** Z Bangash. **LC** DS35.3; .C7. **DD** 954.9/105/05. cum. index. **Bk Rev. Circ:** 15,000 (ctrl). ***Continues*** *Fortnightly Crescent, 0700-6942.*
**Desc:** Reporting Islamic movement.

US/0891-3811
**CRITICAL REVIEW (NEW YORK, N.Y.).** (CRITICAL REVIEW.). [Crit. rev.]. **Added/Corp** Libertarian Review Foundation. Center for Independent Thought. Vol. 1, No. 1 (Winter 1987)-. Academic Scholarly Publication. English. qt. $62.00. Critical Review, 938 Howard Street, Suite 202, San Francisco CA 94103. **Tel** FAX (415)541-0597. **ED** Jefferey Friedman. **LC** JC599.U5; C75. **DD** 320.5/12. **CODEN** CTRVE3. Index available (bound in issue). **Bk Rev**, (Qty: 12). **Ad Acc, Adv Mgr:** David Brook, **Tel** (415)495-2157. **Pr Rev. Circ:** 2,000. available on microfilm and microfiche from University Microfilms International (UMI).
**Desc:** An international discussion on classical liberal thought, featuring research review essays, and scholarly articles developing and contesting libertarian economic, political and social theories.
**Ind/Abst** Econ. Lit. Index; Int. Bibliogr. Sociol.; Left Index; Linguist. Lang. Behav. Abstr.; PAIS Int. Print (1991-?); Soc. Plann. Policy Dev. Abstr.; Sociol. Abstr.; U.S. Polit. Sci. Doc. (199?-).

UK/0301-7605
**CRITIQUE (GLASGOW).** (CRITIQUE.). [Critique]. Vol. 1 (Spring 1973)-. Periodical. English. Twice a year (May & Sept.). Price varies. Glasgow College of Technology Department of Economics, Cowcaddens Road, Glasgow G4 0BA Scotland. **Tel** 011 44 41 3313312. **ED** Bob Arnot and H. Ticktin. **LC** DK246; .C73. **DD** 320.9/47/084. Index available. cum. index. **Circ:** 2,500. Documents available from The Genuine Article.
**Desc:** An independent journal which seeks to analyze both East and West from a critical Marxist perspective.
**Ind/Abst** Acad. Search (Jan. 1993-); Altern. Press Index; Am. Hist. Life (1973-); Arts Humanit. Citation Index [Full Cov.]; Linguist. Lang. Behav. Abstr.; Res. Alert [Full Cov.]; Soc. Plann. Policy Dev. Abstr.; Sociol. Abstr.

FR/0045-9089
**CRITIQUE SOCIALISTE.** (1???)-. Periodical. French. Five times a year. $13.30. Editions Syros, 1 rue de Varenne, 75006 Paris France.

CN/0704-6588
**CROSSCURRENTS (SASKATOON).** See The Arts.

US/1051-0575
**CROSSROADS (OAKLAND, CALIF.).** (CROSSROADS : CONTEMPORARY POLITICAL ANALYSIS & LEFT DIALOGUE.). [CrossRoads]. **Added/Corp** Institute for Social and Economic Studies (Oakland, Calif.). **VFOAT** Cross Roads. No. 1 (June 1990)- No. 28 (Feb. 1993)- No. 31 (May 1993)-. Periodical. English. Ten times a year (Jul/Aug issue combined). $40.00 (institution). Crossroads / Oakland, PO Box 2809, Oakland CA 94609. **Tel** (510)841-7495. **ED** May Elbaum. **LC** HN90.R3; C76. **DD** 335. **Bk Rev**, (Qty: 10). **Circ:** 2,500. ***Formed by the union of*** *Frontline (Oakland, Calif.), 0738-4769* ***and*** *North Star Review.*
**Desc:** This publication is intended to promote a candid appraisal of new realities; to foster dialogue on the U.S. left; to push forward the development of effective strategies for progressive and socialist activism. It aims to provide a forum for the re-examination of long-held Marxist tenets and the revitalization of Marxist thought.
**Ind/Abst** Altern. Press Index (199?-); Left Index (199?-).

US/1045-9170
**CRS REVIEW.** ***Ceased.*** [CRS rev.]. **Added/Corp** Library of Congress. Congressional Research Service. **VAT** Congressional Research Service Review. Vol. 10, No. 1 (Jan. 1989)-Vol. 13, No. 9 (Sept. 1992). Periodical. English. mo. Library of Congress, 101 Independence Avenue SE, Washington DC 20540. **Tel** (202)287-5000. **LC** JK1; .U54a. **DD** 300/.973. **NLM** W1; C89L. ***Continues*** *Congressional Research Service Review, 0193-8029.*
**Ind/Abst** PAIS Int. Print (1991-).

CU
**CUADERNOS DE NUESTRA AMERICA.** **Added/Corp** Centro de Estudios Sobre America. Vol. 1, No. 0 (Jul. 1983)-. Periodical. Spanish (summaries and/or abstracts in English). wk. $6.00. Ediciones Cubanas, Obispo 527, Altos ESQ Bernaza, CP 10100 Havana Cuba. **Tel** 011 632980, 631942, FAX 011 631011, telex 512337, 6540.

SP
**CUADERNOS REFORMA.** Spanish. Cuadernos Reforma, Apartado 48, 28080 Madrid Spain.

FR
**CULTURAL POLICY.** qt. Free. Council of Europe / Group Pact ED, Pharmacopoeia BP 907, 67029 Strasbourg Cedex 01 France. **Tel** 011 33 88 412036, FAX 011 33 88 41277181, telex 880388.

AT/0011-3182
**CURRENT AFFAIRS BULLETIN.** [Curr. aff. bull.]. **Added/Corp** University of Sydney. Dept. of Adult Education. Australia. Commonwealth Office of Education. Vol. 1 (Sept. 29, 1947)-. Bulletin. English. Eleven times a year. 40.00Aus$ (Australia); 57.00Aus$ (other). Current Affairs Bulletin, University of Sydney, Department of Adult Education, 72 Bathurst Street, Sydney New South Wales 2000 Australia. **Tel** 11 61 02 2645726, FAX 11 61 02 2677900. **ED** R Howard. **LC** D839; .C86. Index available (published in May issue). **Bk Rev. Ad Acc. Circ:** 4,500 (ctrl). available on microfilm and microfiche from University Microfilms International (UMI). ***Supersedes*** *Current Affairs Bulletin.*
**Ind/Abst** Annu. Bibliogr. Engl. Lang. Lit.; APAIS, Aust. Public Aff. Inf. Ser. (1963-); Peace Res. Abstr. J. (1964-1969).

●US/1067-7542
**CURRENT DIGEST OF THE POST-SOVIET PRESS, THE.** See Political Science-Abstracting, Bibliographies and Statistics.

US/0011-3425
**CURRENT DIGEST OF THE SOVIET PRESS, THE.** ***Title Change.*** [Curr. Dig. Sov. Press]. **Added/Corp** Joint Committee on Slavic Studies (U.S.) American Council of Learned Societies. Social Science Research Council (U.S.) American Association for the Advancement of Slavic Studies. **VFOAT** Digest of the Soviet Press. Vol. 1-43; Feb. 1, (1949)-Jan. 29, (1992). Periodical. English. wk. Current Digest of the Soviet Press, 3857 North High Street, Columbus OH 43214. **Tel** (614)292-4234, FAX (614)267-6310. **ED** Fred Schulze. **LC** D839; .C87. **DD** 057. Index available. cum. index. **Circ:** 1,200 (ctrl). available on microfilm from LEXIS; and NEXIS; available on an online database (file 645/Full-Text) from DIALOG. Documents available from UMI Article Clearinghouse. ***Absorbed*** *Current Abstracts of the Soviet Press, 0011-3166.* ***Continued by*** *Current Digest of the Post-Soviet Press.*
**Desc:** A journal of translations and abstracts in English of significant articles from 100 Soviet newspapers and periodicals. Quarterly indexes included; annual indexes sold separately.
**Ind/Abst** Expand. Acad. Index (1992-); Newsp. Period. Abstr. (1992-); NEXIS (June 1983-); PAIS Int. Print (1991-).

US/0161-6641
**CURRENT ISSUES (WASHINGTON).** (CURRENT ISSUES.). **Added/Corp** Close Up Foundation. (19??)-. English. an. $17.95. Close Up Foundation, 44 Canal Center Plaza, Alexandria VA 22314. **Tel** (800)765-3131, (703)706-3300, FAX (703)892-1118. **ED** Patricia Bandy. **LC** JK1; .C87. **DD** 309.1/73/092.
**Desc:** Handbook on 10 foreign and 10 domestic issues facing the nation and the world.

●US
**CURRENT POLITICS AND ECONOMICS OF CHINA.** (1994)-. Periodical. English. Four times a year. $95.00. Nova Science Publishers Inc., 6080 Jericho Turnpike, Suite 207, Commack NY 11725-2808. **Tel** (516)499-3103, (516)499-3106, FAX (516)499-3146.

US/1057-2309
**CURRENT POLITICS AND ECONOMICS OF EUROPE.** [Curr. polit. econ. Eur.]. Vol. 1, No. 1 (1991)-. Periodical. English. qt. $230.00. Nova Science Publishers Inc., 6080 Jericho Turnpike, Suite 207, Commack NY 11725-2808. **Tel** (516)499-3103, (516)499-3106, FAX (516)499-3146. **LC** D2009; .C87.

US/1056-7593
**CURRENT POLITICS AND ECONOMICS OF JAPAN.** [Curr. polit. econ. Jpn.]. Vol. 1, No. 1 (1991)-. Periodical. English. qt. $230.00. Nova Science Publishers Inc., 6080 Jericho Turnpike, Suite 207, Commack NY 11725-2808. **Tel** (516)499-3103, (516)499-3106, FAX (516)499-3146. **LC** HC462.9; .C87. **DD** 338.952/005.

US/1061-9186
**CURRENT POLITICS AND ECONOMICS OF RUSSIA.** [Curr. polit. econ. Russ.]. Vol. 2, No. 2 (1991)-. Periodical. English. qt. $115.00. Nova Science

Publishers Inc., 6080 Jericho Turnpike, Suite 207, Commack NY 11725-2808. **Tel** (516)499-3103, (516)499-3106, FAX (516)499-3146. **LC** DK510.763; .C87. ***Formed by the union of*** *Current Politics of the Soviet Union, 1048-7387* ***and*** *Political and Economic Spectrum of the Soviet Union, 1057-2295.*

●US
**CURRENT POLITICS AND ECONOMICS OF THE MIDDLE EAST.** (1994)-. Periodical. English. Four times a year. $95.00. Nova Science Publishers Inc., 6080 Jericho Turnpike, Suite 207, Commack NY 11725-2808. **Tel** (516)499-3103, (516)499-3106, FAX (516)499-3146.

US
**CURRENT POLITICS AND ECONOMICS OF THE UNITED STATES.** (19??)-. Periodical. English. Four times a year. $95.00. Nova Science Publishers Inc., 6080 Jericho Turnpike, Suite 207, Commack NY 11725-2808. **Tel** (516)499-3103, (516)499-3106, FAX (516)499-3146.

CN/0846-085X
**CURRENT STATUS OF LEGISLATION IN THE HOUSE OF COMMONS AND SENATE OF CANADA.** [Curr. status legis. House Commons Senate Can.]. Vol. 1, No. 1 (Jan. 21, 1991)-. Periodical. English. mo. Free with the Subscription of Ottawa Weekly Update. Publinet, 130 Slater Street, 11th Floor, Ottawa Ontario K1P 6E2 Canada. **DD** 348.71/01/05.

CN/0715-7045
**CURRENTS (TORONTO).** **See** Sociology.

CY/1015-2881
**CYPRUS REVIEW, THE.** [Cyprus rev.]. (1989)-. Periodical. English. sa. $25.00 individuals, $40.00 institutions. Intercollege, PO Box 4005, Nicosia, Cyprus. **Tel** 011-357-2-456892, 011-357-2-456813, 456208, FAX 011-357-2-456704, telex 4969 INTERCOL CY. **ED** Iacovos C. Iannou. **Bk Rev**, (Qty: 6-8). **Ad Acc**. available on an online database from DATA-STAR; and DIALOG.
**Desc:** This publication contains articles dealing with social, economic, and political issues.

BL
**D.O., DIARIO OFICIAL, ESTADO DO RIO DE JANEIRO. PARTE II.** **Main/Corp** Rio de Janeiro (Brazil : State). (19??)-. Portuguese. Cr$5.16. Caixa Postal N Po S 597, Niteroi Brazil. **LC** J6.B9; R522b. ***Continues*** *Diario Oficial do Estado do Rio de Janeiro. Parte II.*

US/1060-2240
**DAILY JAPAN DIGEST, THE.** [Dly. Jpn. dig.]. **VFOAT** Japan Digest. (May 14, 1990)-. Periodical. English. ir. $995.00 US & Canada; $2,700.00 others. KA Communications, 5510 Columbia Pike, Suite 207, Arlington VA 22204. **Tel** (703)528-7570, (800)669-7570, FAX (703)528-8123. **ED** Ayako Doi. **DD** 330. Index available. **Bk Rev**, (Qty: 20/yr). **Circ:** 150.
**Desc:** A concise summary of political, business, trade, technology and social issues news from Japan and Washington, D.C.

PE
**DEBATE (LIMA, PERU).** (DEBATE.). (Sept/Oct. 1979)-. Periodical. Spanish. Six times a year (Mar., May, July, Sept., Oct., Dec.). $40.00 one year. Apoyo SA, Apartado 671, Lima 100 Peru. **Tel** 011 51 14 445555, FAX 011 51 14 450536. **ED** Augusto Alvanef Rodrich. **LC** F3401; .D43. Index available. **Bk Rev. Ad Acc. Pr Rev. Circ:** 8,000 (ctrl).
**Desc:** Authoritative discussion of Peru's main problems and possibilities with to the economic and political development as well as a cultural heritage.
**Ind/Abst** HAPI Hisp. Am. Period. Index.

SA
**DEBATES OF THE NATIONAL ASSEMBLY.** **Main/Corp** Transkei. National Assembly. **VFOAT** N. A. Hansard; National Assembly Hansard. 1st- Assembly; Oct. 26/Nov. 18, 1976-. English. R1.00. Pretoria Duplicating Company, 10 van der Stel Buildings, Pretorius Street, Pretoria South Africa. **LC** J707.T3; T73A. **DD** 328.68/7. ***Supersedes*** *Transkei. Legislative Assembly. Debates.*

CN
**DEBATES OF THE SENATE.** **Main/Corp** Canada. Parliament. Senate. **VFOAT** Debats du Senat. (1868)-. Periodical. Multiple languages (English and French). da. 36.00Can$ Canada; 43.20Can$ other. Canada Communication Group Publishers, Order Processing, Ottawa Ontario K1A 0S9 Canada. **Tel** (819)956-4800, (819)956-4802.

PK/0376-8120
**DEBATES : OFFICIAL REPORT - PROVINCIAL ASSEMBLY OF SIND.** **Main/Corp** Sind, Pakistan. Provincial Assembly. Multiple languages (English, Sindhi and Urdu). Manager Sind Government Book Depot and Record Office, Abdullah Haroon Road, Karachi 4 Pakistan. **LC** J577.T3; S56A. **DD** 328.549/18/008.

SA
**DEBATTE VAN STAANDE KOMITEES / REPUBLIEK VAN SUID-AFRIKA, VOLKSRAAD.** **Main/Corp** South Africa. Parliament. House of Assembly. **VFOAT** Debates of Standing Committees. Afrikaans (English). Government Printer / South Africa, Bosman Street, Private Bag X85, Pretoria 0001 South Africa. **Tel** 011 27 12 3239731 Ext. 262. **LC** J705; .K22. **DD** 328.68/02. ***Continues*** *South African. Parliament. House of Assembly. Debates.*

SA/1017-0243
**DEMOCRACY IN ACTION.** (1990)-. Periodical. English. mo. Free on request. IDASA - Institute for a Democratic Alternative for South Africa, 1206 Sangro House 417 Smith Street, Durban 4001 South Africa. **Tel** 011 31 304 8893. **UDC** 32.
**Ind/Abst** Hum. Rights Intern. Rep.

UK/1011-1778
**DEMOCRACY INTERNATIONAL.** ***Ceased.*** No. 1 (Oct. 1987)-(19??). Periodical. English. ir. Democracy International, Suite 48, Westminister Place, London SW1P 1RR England. **LC** D839; .D4. **DD** 909.82.

CN/0070-3346
**DEMOCRAT (VANCOUVER).** (DEMOCRAT CANADA.). Vol. 1 (Nov. 1961)-. Periodical. English. Priorities, 3110 Boundary Road, Burnaby BC V5M 4A2 Canada. **Tel** (604)430-8600. ***Supersedes*** *CCF News for British Columbia and the Yukon.*

SG
**DEMOCRATE, LE.** No. 1- Nov. 1974-. Periodical. French. 4.500. Parti Democratique Senegalais, 7 rue de Thiong, Dakar Senegal. **LC** JQ3396.A98; D53. **DD** 329.9/66/3.

CN/0228-488X
**DEMOCRATE (PARTI NOUVEAU DEMOCRATIQUE DU QUEBEC).** (LE DEMOCRATE.). V. 1, No. 1, (Dec. 1963)-. Periodical. French (English). bw. Free. Nouveau Parti Democratique De Quebec, Suite 220, 180 Est, Boul. Dorchester, Montreal Quebec H2X 1N4. **DD** 324.2714/07/05. ctrl circ.

US/0094-7903
**DEMOCRATIC FOCUS, THE.** Periodical. English. bm. $10.00. 4024 North Stuart, Arlington VA 22207. **LC** HK2311; .D42. **DD** 329.3/005.

US/0164-3207
**DEMOCRATIC LEFT.** [Democr. left]. **Added/Corp** Democratic Socialists of America. Democratic Socialist Organizing Committee (U.S.). Vol. 7, No. 2 (Feb. 1979)-. Newsletter. English. bm (Jan., Mar., May, July, Sept., Nov.). $15.00 (institutions); $8.00 (individuals). Democratic Socialists of America, 180 Varick Street, New York NY 10014. **Tel** (212)727-8610. **ED** David Glenn. **Bk Rev**, (Qty: 1). **Ad Acc. Circ:** 9,000 (ctrl). ***Continues*** *Newsletter of the Democratic Left.*
**Desc:** Published by Democratic Socialists of America.
**Ind/Abst** Altern. Press Index.

US/0147-6769
**DEMOCRATIC PARTY. YEAR BOOK.** (DEMOCRATIC PARTY.). **Main/Corp** Illinois. State Board of Elections. English. an. State Board of Education / Illinois, 100 North First Street, Springfield IL 62777. **Tel** (217)782-4321. **LC** JK2311; .I44A. **DD** 329.3/0025/773.

US/0363-1834
**DEMOCRATIC REVIEW (WASHINGTON).** (DEMOCRATIC REVIEW.). Vol. 1 (Nov. 1974)-. Periodical. English. bm. $10.00. Democratic Forum, 1621 Connecticut Avenue NW, Washington DC 20009. **LC** JK2311; .D454. **DD** 329.3/005.

UK
**DEMOCRATIZATION.** English. Three times a year. $115.00. Frank Cass & Company Ltd, Newbury House, 890-900 Eastern Avenue, Newbury Park, Ilford, Essex IG2 7HH United Kingdom. **Tel** 011 44 81 599 8866, FAX 011 44 81 599 0984, telex 897719. **Ad Acc, Adv Mgr:** Anne Kidson.
**Desc:** The aim of this journal is to promote a better understanding of the process of democratization, of the many factors that influence the process and of its more far-reaching effects. While democratization is currently attracting large attention worldwide, and will provide the main focus, the journal will also build on the enduring interest in democracy itself and its analysis.

US/1051-1679
**DEMOCRATS (WASHINGTON, D.C.).** (DEMOCRATS.). [Democrats]. **Added/Corp** Democratic Party (U.S.) Democratic National Committee (U.S.). (198?)-. Periodical. English. Democratic National Committee, 430 South Capitol Street SE, Washington DC 20003. **DD** 324. ***Continues*** *Democrats Today, 0882-1615.*

IT
**DEMOCRAZIA DIRETTA.** **Added/Corp** Movimento Federativo Democratico. Vol. 1, No. 1 (Nov./Dec. 1986)-. Periodical. Italian. bm. L90000. Edizioni Scientifiche Italiane, Via Chiatamone 7, 80121 Naples Italy. **Tel** 011 39 81 7645768, 011 39 81 7645443, FAX 011 39 81 7646477.

DK/0011-8427
**DENMARK QUARTERLY REVIEW.** **See** Economics-Economic History, Conditions.

US/0740-882X
**DENUNCIA (WASHINGTON, D.C.).** (DENUNCIA / CONADE, COMITE NACIONAL DE DEFENSA DE LA DEMOCRACIA EN BOLIVIA.). [Denuncia]. **Added/Corp** Comite Nacional de Defensa de la Democracia en Bolivia (Washington, D.C.). (19??)-. Periodical. English (Spanish). mo. CONADE - Comite Nacional de Defensa de la Democracia en Bolivia, PO Box 32024, Washington DC 20007. **DD** 984.
**Ind/Abst** Hum. Rights Intern. Rep.

GW
**DEUTSCHER KURIER.** Periodical. German. DM1.20. Postfach 1580, 3 Hannover 1 Germany. **LC** DD259.4; .D4746. **DD** 320.9/43/087.

GW/0012-1428
**DEUTSCHLAND ARCHIV.** [Dtschl. Arch.]. Vol. 1 (Apr. 1968)-. Periodical. German. mo. Verlag Wissenschaft & Politik, Salierring 14 16, D 50677 Cologne Germany. **Tel** 011 49 221 312878. **LC** DD261; .D47. **DD** 320/.0943/1. Index available (Free). **Bk Rev. Ad Acc. Circ:** 6,000. ***Supersedes*** *SBZ-Archiv.*
**Desc:** Journal for questions of the German Democratic Republic and of German politics.
**Ind/Abst** Am. Hist. Life; Int. Bibliogr. Sociol.; PAIS Int. Print (1991-).

US/0160-8037
**DEVELOPING COUNTRY COURIER, THE.** V. 1- Feb. 1978-. Periodical. English. qt. $9.00. Developing Country Courier, PO Box 239, McLean VA 22101. **Tel** (703)356-7561. **ED** Allan F Matthews. **Bk Rev.**
**Desc:** Independent newsletter of the North-South issues. Covers political, economic, and social trends in news, statistics, and publications about interdependence toward a New International Order.

US/0276-4563
**DIALOGUE ON LIBERTY.** **Added/Corp** Young Americans for Freedom. (1971)-. Periodical. English. qt. $1.00. Young Americans for Freedom, PO Box 1002, Woodland Road, Sterling VA 22170. **Tel** (703)450-5162. **DD** 320.

NL
**DIARI DE SESSIONS DEL PARLAMENT DE CATALUNYA.** **Main/Corp** Catalonia (Spain). Parlament. 1A. Legislatura, No. 1-. Catalan. sw. 4620ptas. Servei de Publicacions del Parlament de Catalunya, Palau del Parlament Parc de la Ciutadella, Barcelona 08003 Catalonia Spain. **Tel** (93)300-6413, FAX (93)300-8962, telex 97-684. **LC** J409.T3; C43B. **DD** 328.46/7/01. Index available. cum. index. **Circ:** 1,000. available on CD-ROM; available on an online database.
**Desc:** Comprises a verbatim account of all interventions, agreements and events which take place in the Plenary Assembly or in the Committee meetings whenever such bodies, acting with full legislative authority, conclude parliamentary business or have an informative role with reports from Government representatives or other important people who have been summoned by the Committee.

GW
**DIENST FUER GESELLSCHAFTSPOLITIK.** (19??)-. German. wk (52 issues). DM651.63. Verlag Dienst fuer Gesellschaftspolitik, Decksteiner Str 43, 50935 Cologne FR Germany. **Tel** 011 49 221 431498 or 434823.

IT
**DIFESA DEL POPOLO.** Euganea Edit Comun SRL, UFF Abbonamenti Via Rome 82, 35122 Rome Italy.

FR/0247-9095
**DIFFERENCES PARIS. 1980.** [Differences Paris, 1980]. (1980)-. Periodical. French. mo.
**Ind/Abst** Hum. Rights Intern. Rep.

US/1052-0309
**DIPLOMATIC RECORD, THE.** [Dipl. rec.]. **Added/Corp** Georgetown University. Institute for the Study of Diplomacy. (1990)-. English. $55.00. Westview Press Inc, 5500 Central Avenue, Boulder CO 80301. **Tel** (303)444-3541, FAX (303)449-3356. **LC** JX1625; .D49. **DD** 327.2/09/048.

UK/0419-1714
**DIPLOMATIC SERVICE LIST (GREAT BRITAIN), THE.** **Main/Corp** Great Britain. Diplomatic Service Administration Office. (1966)-. English. an. Her Majesty's Stationery Office, 51 Nine Elms Lane, London SW8 5DR England. **Tel** 011 44 71 873 8459, 011 44 71 873 8499, FAX 011 44 71 873 8499, 011 44 71 873 8456, telex 297138. **(Subscription address:** Her Majesty's Stationery Office, PO Box 276, Publications Centre, London SW8 5DT England.**)** **LC** JX1783; .A22. **DD** 354.42061; 341.7. ***Continues*** *Great*

*Britain. Foreign Office. Foreign Office List and Diplomatic and Consular Year Book for ...; **Continues in part** Great Commonwealth Relations. Commonwealth Relations Office Year Book.*

UK/0070-4962
**DIPLOMAT'S ANNUAL, THE.** (1950)-. Periodical. English. an. Diplomatic Press & Publishing Company, 29 March Lane, London NW7 England. **DD** 341.

FR/1015-2512
**DIRE PARIS. 1988. VFOAT** Dire la Repression Contre les Palestiniens. (1988)-. Periodical. French. mo.
**Ind/Abst** Hum. Rights Intern. Rep.

AT/1030-391X
**DIRECTIONS IN GOVERNMENT.** [Dir. gov.]. (1987)-. Periodical. English. mo (except Dec.-Jan. combined issue). 65.00Aus$ (one year), 115.00Aus$ (two year); 85.00Aus$ (one year), 145.00Can$ (two year), combined with Comprehensive Index. Direction Publishing, 13 Weedon Road, Artamon NSW 2064 Australia. **Tel** 011 61 2 4112388, FAX 011 61 2 4116102. **ED** Fergan O'Sullivan. **DD** 354.940073.
**Ind/Abst** Aust. Educ. Index (199?-).

US/0731-7263
**DIRECTORY, CALIFORNIA CAMPAIGN CONTRIBUTORS. VFOAT** California Campaign Contributors; Directory of California Campaign Contributors. 1982-. Directory. English. an. ABC Clio Press, PO Box 1911, 130 Cremona, Santa Barbara CA 93117. **Tel** (805)968-1911, (800)422-2546, FAX (805)685-9685. **LC** JK1991.5.C2; D57. **DD** 324.7/8/09794.

●UK
**DIRECTORY OF BRITISH POLITICAL ORGANISATIONS UPDATING SERVICE.** (1994)-. Periodical. English. mo. £345.00 (Institutions). Longman Group Ltd., Fourth Avenue, Longman House, Harlow Essex CM19 5SR England. **Tel** 011 44 279 429655, FAX 011 44 279 431059, telex 81259.

US
**DIRECTORY OF MEMBERS / AMERICAN POLITICAL SCIENCE ASSOCIATION. Main/Corp** American Political Science Association. **VFOAT** Directory of Membership. (1991)-. Directory. English. ir (every three years). $41.00 members, $61.00 non-members; Also comes with American Political Science Association Departmental Services Program membership. American Political Science Association, 1527 New Hampshire Avenue Northwest, Washington DC 20036. **Tel** (202)483-2512, FAX (202)483-2657. **LC** JA28; .A562. ***Continues** American Political Science Association. American Political Science Association Membership Directory.*

US/0072-520X
**DIRECTORY OF ORGANIZATIONS AND INDIVIDUALS PROFESSIONALLY ENGAGED IN GOVERNMENTAL RESEARCH AND RELATED ACTIVITIES. Main/Corp** Governmental Research Association. **VFOAT** GRA Directory. (1935)-. English. ir. $30.00. Governmental Research Association, Samford University, 315 Samford Hall, Birmingham AL 35229. **Tel** (205)870-2482. **LC** JK3; .G627. **DD** 350.6273. **Circ:** 200.

●US/1071-796X
**DIRECTORY OF POLITICAL NEWSLETTERS (1994).** (DIRECTORY OF POLITICAL NEWSLETTERS.). **Added/Corp** Government Research Service. (1994)-. Directory. English. ir. $45.00. Government Research Service, 701 Jackson, Suite 304B, Topeka KS 66603. **Tel** (913)232-7720, (800)346-6898, FAX (913)232-1615. ***Continues** Directory of Political Periodicals, 1057-0578.*

US/0884-5859
**DIRECTORY OF UNDERGRADUATE POLITICAL SCIENCE FACULTY.** [Dir. undergrad. polit. sci. fac.]. **Added/Corp** American Political Science Association. (1984)-. Directory. English. te. $25.00 non-member; $15.00 member. American Political Science Association, 1527 New Hampshire Avenue Northwest, Washington DC 20036. **Tel** (202)483-2512, FAX (202)483-2657. **LC** JA28; .A564. **DD** 320/.07/1173. **Ad Acc. Circ:** 2,500 (ctrl).
**Desc:** Lists undergraduate departments of political science with names, and specializations of faculty members.

US/1043-2043
**DIRECTORY OF WORLD LEADERS & FACTBOOK. *Title Change.*** [Dir. world lead. factb.]. **VFOAT** Directory of World Leaders and Factbook. (1990)-(19??). English. an. Want Publishing Company, 1511 K Street Northwest, Suite 635, Washington DC 20005. **Tel** (202)783-1887, FAX (202)393-5106. **LC** D860; .D57. **DD** 909.82. **[CCC].**

IT
**DISEGNI E PROPOSTE DI LEGGE, RELAZIONI. Main/Corp** Italy. Parlamento. Camera dei Deputati. **VFOAT** Atti Parlamentari Disegni di Leggi, Relazioni. (1948/53)-. Periodical. Italian. ir. Libreria Camera Dei Depatati, Via Uffici del Vicario 17, 00186 Rome Italy. **LC** J388.
**Desc:** Includes special reports on the public finance of Italy.

US/0361-9508
**DISTRICT AND PRECINCT BOUNDARIES, STATE OF HAWAII. Main/Corp** Hawaii. Office of the Lieutenant Governor. (19??)-. English. Lieutenant Governor's Office, PO Box 2359, Honolulu HI 96804. **Tel** (808)548-2544. **LC** KFH420.85.A6; A85. **DD** 328.969/07/345.
**Desc:** Election district and precinct maps, polling place boundary for state of Hawaii.

US/1055-159X
**DIXON ARNETT'S CALIFORNIA COMMENT FROM WASHINGTON, DC.** [Dixon Arnett's Calif. comment Wash. D. C.]. **Added/Corp** Dixon Arnett Associates. **VFOAT** California Comment From Washington, DC. (1991)-. Periodical. English. ir. $83.00. Dixon Arnett Associates, 905-16th Street NW, #310, Washington DC 20006. **DD** 324.

US
**DOCUMENTARY HISTORY OF THE FIRST FEDERAL CONGRESS OF THE UNITED STATES OF AMERICA, MARCH 4, 1789-MARCH 3, 1791.** (1972)-. Monographic series. English. ir. Price varies per volume. Johns Hopkins University Press, 2715 North Charles Street, Baltimore MD 21218-4319. **Tel** (410)516-6987, FAX (410)516-6968. **ED** Linda Grant de Pauw. **LC** JK1059 1st; .D6. **DD** 328.73/01.

FR/0984-8541
**DOCUMENTATION-REFUGIES.** Periodical. French. bw. 850.00F France; 870.00FF (surface mail) Europe; 900.00F (airmail) other. Documentation Refugies, Svc Abonne 11 rue, Ferdinand-Gambon, F-75020 Paris France. **Tel** (1)43 48 15 66, FAX (1)43 48 17 22. **Bk Rev. Circ:** 400.

US/1060-0655
**DOMESTIC AFFAIRS.** [Domest. aff.]. (Summer 1991)-. Periodical. English. qt. $22.00 US; $30.00 other. Domestic Affairs, 555 13th Street Northwest, 1392 East Tower, Washington DC 20004. **Tel** (202)637-8518. **LC** IN PROCESS. **DD** 320.
**Ind/Abst** Acad. Search (Jan. 1994-).

IT
**DONNE PARLEMENTO E SOCIETA.** (19??)-. Italian. Partito Comunista Italiano, Via Delle Botteghe Oscure 4, 00186 Rome Italy.

MR
**DOSSIER SOCIO-POLITIQUE. VFOAT** Dossier Socio Politique. Periodical. French. Al Asas, B P 543, Sale Maroc. **LC** DT301; .D67. **DD** 964/.005. ***Continues** Dossier Economique (Sale, Morocco).*

FR/0292-5354
**DOSSIERS DU CANARD, LES.** [Doss. "Canard"]. No. 1, (April 1981)-. Periodical. French. 173 rue Saint-Honore, 75001 Paris France. **LC** DC411; .D67. **DD** 944/.005.

US
**DR. MCBIRNIE'S NEWSLETTER. VAT** Doctor McBirnie's Newsletter. Newsletter. English. bw. Free. Dr W S McBirnie, United Community Churches of America, Box 90, Glendale CA 91209. **Tel** (818)240-4871. **ED** McBirnie and MacCollam. **Circ:** 30,000 (ctrl).
**Desc:** Conservative news analysis from christian perspective.

KO/0011-5134
**DRP BULLETIN. Main/Corp** Minju Konghwadang. **VFOAT** Bulletin. **VAT** Democratic Republican Party Bulletin. V. 1- ; 1966-. Bulletin. English. Publicity Department, Democratic Republican Party, Central Office, Central Post Office Box 196, Seoul Korea.

GW/0720-2946
**DRUCKSACHE - BUNDESRAT.** [Drucks. - Bundesrat]. **Main/Corp** Germany (West). Bundesrat. 1958-. German. Verlag Dr Hans Heger, Postfach 200821, 5300 Bonn 2 Germany. cum. index.
**Ind/Abst** Coal Abstr.; Energy Res. Abstr. (Feb. 1975-).

US
**DUKE JOURNAL OF POLITICS. Added/Corp** Duke University. Vol. 3 (Spring 1985)-. English. Duke University Political Science Journal, Durham NC 27706. ***Continues** Duke Political Science Journal, 8755-3783.*

US/0741-0263
**DYNAMIC (NEW YORK, N.Y.).** (DYNAMIC : PUBLICATION OF THE YOUNG COMMUNIST LEAGUE OF THE U.S.A.). [Dynamic]. **Added/Corp** Young Communist League of the U.S. Vol. 1, No. 1 (August 1983)-. Newspaper. English. Four times a year. $10.00 (institutions), $4.00 (individuals) six issues US; $15.00 six issues other. Young Communist League/ Dynamic, 235 West 23rd Street/6th Floor, New York NY 10011. **Tel** (212)741-2016, FAX (212)645-5436. **ED** Jason Rabinowitz. **Bk Rev. Ad Acc. Circ:** 30,000 (ctrl).
**Desc:** A national youth magazine that covers a full range of issues of concern to youth--education, jobs, peace, racism, etc., from a left perspective.

●US
**EAST EUROPEAN CONSTITUTIONAL REVIEW. Added/Corp** Center for the Study of Constitutionalism in Eastern Europe. Central European University (Prague, Czechoslovakia). Vol. 1, No. 1 (Spring 1992)-. Periodical. English. qt. University of Chicago Law School, 1111 East 60th Street, Chicago IL 60637. **Tel** (312)962-9593.

US
**EAST EUROPEAN POLITICS AND SOCIETIES : EEPS. Added/Corp** Joint Committee on Eastern Europe. Social Science Research Council (U.S.). **VFOAT** EEPS. Vol. 4, No. 1 (Winter 1990)-. Periodical. English. Three times a year. $54.00 (institutions), $30.00 (individuals). University of California Press, 2120 Berkeley Way, Berkeley CA 94720. **Tel** (510)642-4191, (510)642-3907, FAX (510)642-9917. **ED** Ivo Banac. Documents available from The Genuine Article. ***Continues** Eastern European Politics and Societies.*
**Ind/Abst** ABC POL SCI; Curr. Contents Soc. Behav. Sci.; Expand. Acad. Index (1992-); Res. Alert [Full Cov.]; Soc. Sci. Cit. Index [Full Cov.].

FR/0150-3146
**ECHO DE L'AFRIQUE, L'.** [Echo Afr.]. (1971)-. Periodical. French. wk (except Aug. and Sept.). 832.50F France; 850.00F other. Segedo, 12 rue du Quatre Septembre, 75002 Paris France. **Tel** 011 33 1 42968607. **UDC** 32.

II/0012-9976
**ECONOMIC AND POLITICAL WEEKLY. See** Economics-Economic History, Conditions.

UK/0954-1985
**ECONOMICS & POLITICS (OXFORD, ENGLAND). See** Economics.

FR/0013-0710
**ECRITS DE PARIS.** (ECRITS DE PARIS; REVUE DES QUESTIONS ACTUELLES.). **Added/Corp** Centre d'Etudes des Questions Actuelles, Politiques, Economiques et Sociales. Bulletin Interieur - Centre d'Etudes des Questions Actuelles, Politiques, Economiques et Sociales. (1944)-. Periodical. French. mo. Societe Parisienne d'Edition, 9 Passage des Marais 9, 75010 Paris France. **Tel** 011 33 1 42089582.

US/0013-0966
**EDITORIALS ON FILE. Added/Corp** Facts on File, Inc. Vol. 1, Jan. 1/15, (1970)-. English. sm. $395.00. Facts on File Publications, 460 Park Avenue South, New York NY 10016. **Tel** (212)683-2244, (800)322-8755, FAX (212)683-3633, telex 238 552 FACTS UR. **ED** Carol C. Collins. **LC** D839; .E3. **DD** 081. **Acid Free. Circ:** 1,500.
**Desc:** Collection of editorials and political cartoons from US and Canadian newspapers (over 125) on current topics of interest in US world affairs.

CN/0226-6873
**EGALITE (MONCTON).** (EGALITE.). [Egalite]. **Added/Corp** Association des Ecrivains Acadiens. No. 1 (Fall 1980)-. Periodical. French. Twice a year. Price varies. Societe Acadienne D'Analyse Politique, PO Box 2815, Station A, Moncton New Brunswick E1C 8T8 Canada. **Tel** (506)858-4145. **ED** Rosella Melanson. **DD** 971.5/004114. Index available. cum. index. **Bk Rev. Ad Acc, Adv Mgr:** Jean-Claude Bellefeuille, **Tel** (506)383-5653. **Circ:** 300 (ctrl).
**Desc:** An independent journal of political studies established to promote understanding and discussion in respect to political, economic, social and cultural aspects of Acadian (French-Canadian) society.

UA/0752-4412
**EGYPTE/MONDE ARABE. Added/Corp** Markaz al-Dirasat wa-al-Wathaiq al-Iqtisadiyah wal-al-Qanuniyah wa-al-Ijtimaiyah (Cairo, Egypt). **VFOAT** Egypte, Monde Arabe. (1990)-. Periodical. French. qt. 400.00F France; 500.00F North America. CEDEJ, 14 rue Gameyet el-Nisr, Mohandessin- le Caire Egypt. **Tel** 361-1932, FAX 3493518, telex 93088 CEFEC UN. **LC** DT43; .E37. **DD** 962/.005. **Circ:** 1000. ***Formed by the union of** Bulletin du CEDEJ, 0255-755X **and** Revue de la Presse Egyptienne, 0752-4412.*
**Desc:** Social and human sciences publication about Egypt and Middle East.
**Ind/Abst** PAIS Int. Print.

US/0145-8124
**ELECTION ADMINISTRATION REPORTS. VFOAT** EA Reports. (Jan. 7, 1976)-. Periodical. English. bw. $127.00. Election Administration, 5620 33rd Street NW, c/o R Smolka, Washington DC

20015. **Tel** (202)244-5844. **ED** Richard G. Smolka. **LC** KF4886.A45; E4. **DD** 342/.73/07. **Bk Rev.** ***Continues*** *Electionews.*

US/1067-9774
**ELECTION CENTER REPORTS.** [Elect. cent. rep.]. **Added/Corp** Election Center (U.S.). (19??)-. Periodical. English. bm. $100.00. Election Center, 1312 Chetworth Court, Alexandria VA 22314. **Tel** (703)739-9579, FAX (703)739-9724. **DD** 324.

US/1062-5259
**EMPOWERMENT! (WASHINGTON, D.C.).** (EMPOWERMENT! / FREE CONGRESS FOUNDATION.). [Empowerment!]. **Added/Corp** Free Congress Research and Education Foundation. (Jan. 1991)-. Periodical. English. mo. $30.00. Free Congress Research and Education Foundation, 717 Second Street NE, Washington DC 20002. **Tel** (202)546-3000, (800)525-4992, FAX (202)546-7689. **DD** 320.

UK/0262-7922
**END PAPERS.** **Added/Corp** Bertrand Russell Peace Foundation. **VFOAT** Endpapers. (Winter 1981-1982)-. Periodical. English. Twice a year. £20.00 UK; $40.00 US. Bertrand Russell Peace Foundation Ltd, Bertrand Russell House, Gamble Street, Nottingham NG7 4ET England. **Tel** 011 44 602 784504. **ED** Ken Coates. **LC** JX1974.7; .E53. **DD** 327.1/74. **Bk Rev. Ad Acc. Circ:** 2,000. ***Continues*** *Spokesman.*
**Desc:** A regular medium for longer articles about European nuclear disarmament and associated issues.
**Ind/Abst** Hum. Rights Intern. Rep.; PAIS Int. Print (1991-?).

BL
**ENDERCOS DOS SENHORES SENADORES (BRAZIL).** **Main/Corp** Brazil. Congresso. Senado. Secao de Telex e Telefonia. Periodical. Portuguese. Senado Federal, Diretoria-Geral, Brasilia Brazil. **LC** J207; .J84C. **DD** 328.81/07/1025.

UK
**ENGLISH WHITE PAPER / SOCIAL & LIBERAL DEMOCRATS.** **Added/Corp** Social and Liberal Democrats (Great Britain). No. 1 (1988)-. Monographic series. English. Price varies per volume.

UK/0262-7612
**ENLIGHTENMENT AND DISSENT.** No. 1 (1982)-. Periodical. English. an. $32.00 (institutions), $9.00 (individuals). Martin Fitzpatrick, Department of History, University College of Wales, Aberystwyth Dyfed SY23 3DY, Great Britian. **Tel** 011 44 970 623111. **ED** D. O. Thomas and Martin Fitzpatrick. **LC** DA485; .E54. **DD** 320/.01. **Bk Rev. Ad Acc. Pr Rev. Circ:** 300 (ctrl). ***Continues*** *Price-Priestley Newsletter, 0140-8437.*
**Desc:** The study of the enlightenment, radicalism and religion especially, but not exclusively, in the Anglo-American world.

US
**EPRDF NEWS BULLETIN.** **Added/Corp** Ethiopian People's Revolutionary Democratic Party. Foreign Relations Bureau. **VFOAT** Ethiopian People's Revolutionary Democratic Party News Bulletin. Vol. 1 No. 1 (Jan. 31, 1991)-. Bulletin. English. **LC** IN PROCESS. ***Continues*** *People's Voice (Rome, Italy).*

FR/1168-1179
**ESPACES LATINO-AMERICAINS.** [Espaces latino-am.]. (1990)-. Periodical. French. Twelve times a year. 300.00F France; 350.00F other. Nouveaux Espaces Latino-Americains, 17 Bis rue Louis Adam, 69100 Villeurbanne France. **Tel** 011 33 1 78689377, FAX 011 33 1 78683408. **ED** Michel Sender. **UDC** 008(728+8). ***Continues*** *Chili Flash, 0765-4111.*

CN/1193-6886
**ESPOIR (LASALLE).** (L'ESPOIR.). [Espoir]. No. 1 (1991)-. Periodical. French. Four times a year. $20.00. L'Espoir, 522 ruw Trudeau, LaSalle Quebec H8R 3C4 Canada. **Tel** (514)367-1516. ***Continues*** *Revue Independantiste, 0702-8571.*

IT/0046-256X
**EST-OVEST.** **Added/Corp** Istituto di Studi e Documentazioni sull'Est Europeo. **VFOAT** Est Ovest. (1970)-. Periodical. Italian (English and French). Five times a year. L160.000 Italy; L200.000 other. Istituto di Studi e Documentazione sull'Europa Communitaria el'Europa Orientale, Corsa Italia 27, 34122 Trieste Italy. **Tel** 011 39 40639130, FAX 011 39 634248. Index available. **Bk Rev. Ad Acc. Circ:** 300 (ctrl).
**Desc:** Analysis and documentation, contributions, information about Eastern Europe and EEC's policies toward Eastern Europe.
**Ind/Abst** ABC POL SCI; Am. Hist. Life (1973-1989); Int. Labour Doc.; LABORDOC; PAIS Int. Print (1991-).

MX
**ESTRATEGIA.** ***Ceased.*** Vol. 1, No. 1 (1975)-(1993). Periodical. Spanish. bm. Revista Estrategia, Dr Vertiz 1295 202, 03650 Mexico DF Mexico. **Tel** (52)5-5439363. **LC** JA5; .E84. **DD** 320/.05.
**Ind/Abst** Hum. Rights Intern. Rep.

CL/0716-0240
**ESTUDIOS INTERNACIONALES.** (ESTUDIOS INTERNACIONALES : REVISTA DEL INSTITUTO DE ESTUDIOS INTERNACIONALES DE LA UNIVERSIDAD DE CHILE.). **Added/Corp** Universidad de Chile. Instituto de Estudios Internacionales. Yearly Vol. 1, No. 1 (April 1967)-. Periodical. Spanish. qt (Jan., Apr., July, Oct.). 6200.00Chil$ (1 year) individuals, 7400.00Chil$ (1 year) institutions Chile; $46.00 (1 year), $89.00 (2 year) individuals, $56.00 (1 year), $108.00 (2 year) institutions other. Instituto de Estudios Internacionales, Universidad de Chile, Casilla 14187, Sucursal 21, Santiago Chile. **Tel** (56-2)2745377, FAX (56-2)2740155, telex 443024 INTERC. **ED** Pilar Alamos. **LC** F1414.2; .E78. **Bk Rev. Circ:** 600.
**Ind/Abst** ABC POL SCI; Am. Hist. Life (1975-); Foreign Lang. Index; HAPI Hisp. Am. Period. Index; Int. Polit. Sci. Abstr.; PAIS Int. Print (1991-).

MX/0185-1616
**ESTUDIOS POLITICOS (MEXICO CITY, MEXICO).** (ESTUDIOS POLITICOS : REVISTA DEL CENTRE DE ESTUDIOS POLITICOS.). [Est. polit.]. V. 1, No. 1 (April/June 1975)-. Periodical. Spanish. qt. Facultad de Ciencias Politicas y Sociales, Universidad Nacional Autonoma de Mexico, Ciudad Universitaria, Mexico City Mexico. **LC** JA5; .E86.
**Ind/Abst** Am. Hist. Life (1977-1978, 1983-); Int. Polit. Sci. Abstr.

US/0279-2869
**ETHICS IN GOVERNMENT REPORTER.** **See** Ethics.

CN/0014-2123
**ETUDES INTERNATIONALES (QUEBEC).** (ETUDES INTERNATIONALES.). [Etud. int.]. **Added/Corp** Centre Quebecois de Relations Internationales. Canadian Institute of International Affairs. (1970)-. Periodical. French. qt. 55.00Can$ (institutions), 45.00Can$ (individuals) Canada; 60.00Can$ (institutions), 50.00Can$ (individuals) other. Centre Quebecois de Relations Internationales, Pavillon de Koninck/Bureau 5460, Universite Laval, Laval Quebec G1K 7P4 Canada. **Tel** (418)656-2462, FAX (418)656-3634. **LC** D849; .E88. **Ad Acc.** ctrl circ.
**Ind/Abst** ABC POL SCI; Am. Hist. Life (1970-); Foreign Lang. Index; Int. Labour Doc.; Point Repere (1983-).

IT
**EUI WORKING PAPER. SPS / DEPARTMENT OF POLITICAL AND SOCIAL SCIENCES, EUROPEAN UNIVERSITY INSTITUTE.** **See** Social Sciences.

US/0887-3100
**EURO-AMERICAN QUARTERLY.** [Euro-Am. q.]. **Added/Corp** Euro-American Alliance. (1980)-. Periodical. English. qt. $10.00. Euro - American Alliance, PO Box 2 1776, Milwaukee WI 53221. **Tel** (414)423-0565. **DD** 320. available on microfilm.

UK/0956-2273
**EUROPA WORLD YEAR BOOK, THE.** [Eur. world year b.]. **Added/Corp** Europa Publications Limited. 30th Ed. (1989)-. English. Twice a year (April and June). $610.00. Europa Publications Ltd, 18 Bedford Square, London WC1B 3JN England. **Tel** 011 44 71 5808236, telex 21540 EUROPA G. **(Subscription address:** Gale Research Co., 835 Penobscot Building, Detroit MI 48226.) **LC** JN1; .E85. **CODEN** EWYBEL. **[CCC].** ***Continues*** *Europa Year Book, 0071-2302.*
**Desc:** Contains background information, statistical data, and directories of businesses and institutions for every country. Each entry contains comprehensive data on the country's political, diplomatic, and judicial systems. A separate section provides full descriptions of 1,500 international organizations.

GW
**EUROPAISCHE INTEGRATION AUSWAHLBIBLIOGRAPHIE.** German. Ten times a year. Vertretung der Eg-Kommission, Zitelmannstrasse 22, 5300 Bonn 1 Germany. **Tel** (0228)53009-44. **ED** Armin Czysz. **LC** LAW. Index available. cum. index. **Bk Rev. Ad Acc. Circ:** 30,000 (ctrl).

GW
**EUROPAISCHE ZEITUNG.** Vol. 28, No. 6 (June 1977)-. Periodical. German. mo. DM32.00 Germany; DM32.50 other. Europa Union Verlag GmbH, Bachstrasse 32, Postfach 1529, D 53115 Bonn Germany. **Tel** 011 49 228 7290010, FAX 011 49 228 7290018, telex 8-86822. **Bk Rev. Ad Acc. Circ:** 40,000. ***Continues*** *Europa Union.*
**Desc:** Cardinal subject is 'European Intregration' in politics and economics.

GW
**EUROPAWAHL.** (19??)-. German. **LC** JN3971.A956; E95. **DD** 341.24/24.

UK/0269-3852
**EUROPE REVIEW.** [Eur. rev.]. **Added/Corp** World of Information (Firm). (1986)-. English. an (Dec.). $109.00. Kogan Page Ltd., 120 Pentonville Road, London N1 9BR England. **Tel** 011 44 71 2780433, FAX 011 44 71 8376348, telex 263088 KOGAN G. **(Subscription address:** Kogan Page / North America Subscriptions, PO Box 830430, Birmingham AL 35283-0430.) **ED** R. Green. **LC** HC240; .E819. **DD** 330.94/005. **Circ:** 6,172.
**Desc:** Accurate, comprehensive coverage of the continent. Articles by experts on economics, politics, business, industry, and commerce.
**Ind/Abst** AGRICOLA [Select. Cov.].

UK/0264-7362
**EUROPEAN ACCESS.** (1980)-. English. bm. $198.00. Chadwyck-Healey Limited, The Quorum Barnwell Road, Cambridge CB5 8SW England. **Tel** 011 44 223 215512, telex 9312102281 CH G. **(Subscription address:** Chadwyck Healey Inc. / US Subscriptions, 1101 King Street, Suite 380, Alexandria VA 22314.) **ED** Ian Thomson. **LC** Z7165.E8; E79; HC241.2. **DD** 016.34124/22. **Bk Rev. Ad Acc. Circ:** 500.
**Desc:** Current awareness bulletin on the developments, activities, and policies of the European community.
**Ind/Abst** World Agric. Econ. (19??-).

UK
**EUROPEAN CONSORTIUM FOR POLITICAL RESEARCH NEWS.** (19??)-. English. Three times a year. £12.00 UK, £13.50 other. University of Essex ECPR Central Service, Wivenhoe Park, Colchester CO4 3SQ England. **Tel** 011 44 206 873333, 872501, FAX 44 206872500. **ED** Kenneth Newton and Stephen Padgett. **Bk Rev. Ad Acc. Pr Rev.** ctrl circ.
**Desc:** News concerning European political science and social science and European political scientists.

IT/0394-6444
**EUROPEAN JOURNAL OF INTERNATIONAL AFFAIRS, THE.** ***Suspended.*** **VFOAT** European International. Vol. 1, No. 1 (Summer 1988)-Suspended. Periodical. English. qt. $45.00 US and Canada; $85.00 other. Erasmus Press / Italy, Via Dei Giubbonari 30, 00186 Rome Italy. **Tel** 011 39 6 6873196. **LC** D1050; .E88794. **DD** 940.55/05. **Bk Rev. Ad Acc. Circ:** 5,000.

NE/0304-4130
**EUROPEAN JOURNAL OF POLITICAL RESEARCH.** [Eur. j. polit. res.]. **Added/Corp** European Consortium for Political Research. Vol. 1 (April 1973)-. Periodical. English. Eight times a year (Eight times per year). $692.00. Kluwer Academic Publishers, Postbus 322, 3300 AH Dordrecht, The Netherlands. **Tel** 011 (31) 78 524400, FAX 011 31 78 183273, telex 20083. **ED** Mogens N Pederson and Michael Laver. **LC** JA88.E9; E93. **DD** 320/.05. **CODEN** EJPRDY. **[CCC].** Index available. **Bk Rev. Ad Acc. Pr Rev. Acid Free.** Documents available from The Genuine Article.
**Desc:** Publishes articles by political scientists and other scholars engaged in political research affiliated with European institutions of higher learning.
**Ind/Abst** ABC POL SCI; Am. Hist. Life; Appl. Soc. Sci. Index Abstr.; Commun. Abstr. (?-?); Curr. Contents Soc. Behav. Sci.; Int. Polit. Sci. Abstr.; Middle East Abstr. Index; Res. Alert [Full Cov.]; Soc. Plann. Policy Dev. Abstr.; Soc. Sci. Cit. Index [Full Cov.]; Sociol. Abstr.; Stud. Women Abstr.

FR/0070-105X
**EUROPEAN TREATY SERIES.** [Eur. treaty ser.]. **VFOAT** Serie des Traites et T Conventions Europeennes; Serie des Traites Europeennes. No. 1 (1949)-. Monographic series. English (French). Price varies per volume. Council of Europe / Group Pact ED, Pharmacopoeia BP 907, 67029 Strasbourg Cedex 01 France. **Tel** 011 33 88 412036, FAX 011 33 88 41277181, telex 880388. **(Subscription address:** Manhattan Publishing Company, PO Box 650, Croton-on-Hudson NY 10520) Index available.
**Desc:** Texts of each of the Council of Europe's convention and agreements concluded among countries which are members of the council.

US/0014-3650
**EVANS-NOVAK POLITICAL REPORT.** [Evans-Novak polit. rep.]. **VAT** Evans Novak Political Report. (1967)-. Periodical. English. bw (26 issues). $247.00 (one year), $447.00 (two year). Phillips Business Information, Inc., 1201 Seven Locks Road, Potomac MD 20854. **Tel** (301)424-3338, (800)777-5006, FAX (301)309-3847. **[CCC].** available on an online database (file 636/Full-Text) from DIALOG.
**Ind/Abst** PTS Newsl. Database [Full Txt.].

US/0738-4297
**EXECUTIVE'S HANDBOOK ON POLITICAL CONTRIBUTIONS.** [Exec. handb. polit. contrib.]. **Added/Corp** S & FA Reporting Services. State and Federal Associates. Publications Dept. (1977)-. Periodical. English. sa. $299.17 Ohio; $282.00 other. State and Federal Communications, 1799 Akron Peninsula Road, Akron OH 44313. **Tel** (216)940-3300. **(Subscription address:** State and Federal Communications, PO Box 25003, Alexandria VA 22313.) **LC** IN PROCESS. **DD** 324.

UK
**EXETER MIDDLE EAST POLITICS.** **VFOAT** Middle East Politics Series. (1986)-. Monographic series. English. Price varies per volume. Ithaca Press, 13 Southwark Street, London SE1 England.

US/0743-9849
**EXILE (PASADENA, CALIF.).** (EXILE.). [Exile]. Periodical. English. mo. $15.00. Exile, PO Box 67 Station B, Toronto Ont M5T 2CO Canada. **Tel** (416)736-5209. **ED** Bete Mariam. **LC** DT387.95; .E95. **DD** 963/.07/05. **Circ:** 500 (ctrl).
**Desc:** This newsletter deals with the life of Ethiopian political exiles and the problems in Ethiopia today.

AT/0949-138X
**FABIAN NEWSLETTER.** (19??)-. Newsletter. English. bm (6 issues). 40.00Aus$. Australian Fabian Society, Box 2707X, Melbourne Victoria 3001 Australia. ctrl circ.
**Desc:** Covers democratic socialist and social democratic policy development and promotion.

UK/0307-7535
**FABIAN TRACT.** **Main/Corp** Fabian Society (Great Britain). **Added/Corp** Fabian Society (Great Britain) Tract series. Fabian Society (Great Britain) Tract. No. 1 (1884)-. Monographic series. English. Eight times a year. £60.00 UK; £60.00 other. Fabian Society, 11 Dartmouth Street, London SW1H 9BN England. **Tel** 011 44 071 2228877, FAX 011 44 071 9767153. **ED** Stephen Tindale. **LC** HX11; .F25. **DD** 335.106242. Index available. cum. index. **Bk Rev**. **Ad Acc**, **Adv Mgr:** T. Upton. **Circ:** 4000 (ctrl).
**Desc:** Social policy and general political theory and practice.

US/0014-651X
**FACT FINDER (CHICAGO, ILL.), THE.** (THE FACT FINDER.). (19??)-. Periodical. English. Twenty-four times a year. $27.00 (one year), $50.00 (two year). Everingham Company, Box A, Scottsdale AZ 85252. **Tel** (602)947-4466.

US
**FACTS ON FILE. WORLD NEWS DIGEST WITH INDEX.** ***Ceased.*** (19??)-(19??). English. wk. Facts on File Publications, 460 Park Avenue South, New York NY 10016. **Tel** (212)683-2244, (800)322-8755, FAX (212)683-3633, telex 238 552 FACTS UR. **ED** Thomas G. Hitchings. Index available. cum. index.
**Desc:** Weekly indexed summary of national and international news used by librarians and other researchers to answer questions about the news.
**Ind/Abst** PTS Newsl. Database (?-?) [Full Txt.].

FR
**FAITS STRATEGIQUES.** French. an. **LC** U162; .F33. **DD** 355.02.

US
**FAMILY VOICE / CONCERNED WOMEN FOR AMERICA.** **Added/Corp** Concerned Women for America. Vol. 13, No. 10 (Oct. 1991)-. Periodical. English. Eleven times a year (monthly with Dec./Jan. issues combined). $15.00 Comes with Concerned Women for America membership. Concerned Women for America, 370 L Enfant Promenade, Suite 800, Washington DC 20024. **Tel** (202)488-7000. **LC** E838; .C66. ***Continues*** *Concerned Women for America: [News].*

●CN/1193-2821
**FEDERAL LOBBYISTS, THE.** [Fed. lobby.]. **Added/Corp** Advocacy Research Centre. (1992)-. English. $99.00 per volume. ARC Publications - Advocacy Research Centre Inc., 75 Sparks Street #600, Ottawa Ontario K1P 5A5 Canada. **Tel** (613)230-3029, FAX (613)237-9617. **DD** 328.71/078/025.

●US
**FEDERALISM REPORT, THE.** **Added/Corp** Temple University. Center for the Study of Federalism. International Association of Centers for Federal Studies. American Political Science Association. Section on Federalism and Intergovernmental Relations. Vol. 17, No. 2 (Winter 1992)-. Periodical. English. qt. Center for the Study of Federalism, Temple University, Gladfelter Hall, Philadelphia PA 19122. **Tel** (215)787-1482. ***Continues*** *CFS Notebook, 0194-2840.*

IT/0014-925X
**FEDERALISTE; REVUE DE POLITIQUE, LE.** Vol. 1- ;. Periodical. Italian.

CN/0828-6558
**FEMMES DEMOCRATIQUES.** (FEMMES DEMOCRATIQUES : ORGANE DE L'UNION DES FEMMES DEMOCRATIQUES DU CANADA.). [Femmes democr.]. Periodical. French. mo. $0.50 per no. Union des Femmes Democratiques du Canada, CP 382 Succursale U, Toronto Ontario M8Z 5P7 Canada. **DD** 335/.0088042.

UK/0143-5426
**FIGHT RACISM, FIGHT IMPERIALISM! : ANTI-IMPERIALIST BULLETIN OF THE REVOLUTIONARY COMMUNIST GROUP.** **Added/Corp** Revolutionary Communist Group (Great Britain). No. 1 (Nov./Dec. 1979)-. Periodical. English. Six times a year. £4.50 Britain; £6.00 Europe; £7.50 Africa, America, Middle East & South Asia; £8.50 other. Larkin Publications, BCM Box 5909, London WC1N 3XX England. **Tel** 011 44 71 8371688. **ED** D. Reed. **Bk Rev**, (Qty: 15). **Circ:** 2,000. ***Absorbed*** *Hands off Ireland.*
**Desc:** Communist analysis of contemporary events in Britain and internationally with specific emphasis on anti-racist and anti-imperialist causes.

US
**FLAMING CRESCENT, THE.** (1990)-. English. mo. $10.00. Flaming Crescent, PO Box 9103, Long Island City NY 11103. **Tel** (718)777-2427. **ED** Mickey Z. **Bk Rev. Ad Acc. Pr Rev. Acid Free. Circ:** 40,000 (ctrl).
**Desc:** A journal of opinion, satire and indifference.

AT/0726-7215
**FLINDERS JOURNAL OF HISTORY AND POLITICS.** [Flinders j. hist. polit.]. **Added/Corp** Flinders University History and Politics Society. Vol. 1 (July 1969)-. Academic Scholarly Publication. English. an. 5.00Aus$ Australia; 6.00Aus$ other. Flinders University University South Australia, PO Box 2100, Adelaide SA 5001 Australia. **Tel** 011 61 8 2013059, FAX 011 61 8 2013184. **ED** Terry O'Callaghan and Darryl Jarvis. **Bk Rev. Ad Acc. Circ:** 400.
**Desc:** Academic essays, some by students, reflecting range of scholarship in history and politics at this university. Covers Australia, China, political theory, and British public administration.
**Ind/Abst** Am. Hist. Life (1969, 1973-1974); APAIS, Aust. Public Aff. Inf. Ser. (1981-).

US/0426-6072
**FLORIDA VOTER, THE.** **Added/Corp** Florida League of Women Voters. League of Women Voters of Florida Education Fund. (1924)-. Periodical. English. bm (6 issues). $1.50 (non-members); free to members. League of Women Voters of Florida, 540 Beverly Court, Tallahassee FL 32301. **Tel** (904)224-2545.

DK/0903-6946
**FOLKETINGSTIDENDE. ARBOG OG REGISTRE.** **VFOAT** Arbog og Registre. 1986-87-. Danish. an. J H Schultz Boghandel, 19 Montergade, DK-1057 K Copenhagen Denmark. **LC** JN7269; .F6. ***Continues*** *Folketings Arbog, 0084-9707;* ***Continues in part*** *Folketingstidende.*

UK/0532-1328
**FOREIGN REPORT.** [Foreign rep.]. **Added/Corp** Economist Newspaper Limited. (19??)-. Periodical. English. Forty-eight times a year. $260.00. The Economist Intelligence Unit, 40 Duke Street, London W1A 1DW England. **Tel** 011 44 71 8301000. **(Subscription address:** Economist Intelligence Unit / North America Subscriptions, 111 West 57th Street, New York NY 10019.**)** **ED** Roland Dallas. **LC** D839; .F66. **[CCC]. Circ:** 5,000.
**Desc:** A confidential newsletter based on a continuous flow of information from high level sources in business and politics. Useful in political forecasting and business decisionmaking.

IT
**FORMULA.** Italian. bm. L60000.00 Italy; L120000.00 other. Societa Formula 80, Via Bolzano 16, 00198 Rome Italy. **Tel** 011 39 6 85565514, FAX 011 39 6 8414865. Index available. cum. index. **Bk Rev**, (Qty: 20). ctrl circ. ***Continues*** *Formula 80.*

IT
**FORMULA 80.** ***Title Change.*** (19??)-(1993. Italian. bm. Societa Formula 80, Via Bolzano 16, 00198 Rome Italy. **Tel** 011 39 6 85565514, FAX 011 39 6 8414865. ***Continued by*** *Formula.*

MX/0185-013X
**FORO INTERNACIONAL.** [Foro int.]. **Added/Corp** Colegio de Mexico. Vol. 1, No. 1 (July/Sept. 1960)-. Periodical. Spanish. Four times a year (Jan., Apr., July, Oct.). $50.00 (institutions), $32.00 (individuals) US & Canda; $34.00 (institutions), $26.00 (individuals) Latin America; $60.00 (institutions), $42.00 (individuals) other. Colegio de Mexico AC, Camino Al Ajusco No 20, 10740 Mexico DF Mexico. **Tel** 011 52 5 6455955 Ext. 3133, telex 1777585 COLME. **ED** Blanca Torres. **LC** D839; .F67. Index available. cum. index. **Bk Rev. Ad Acc. Pr Rev. Circ:** 1,500.
**Desc:** Foreign and domestic policies of Latin American countries, North-South relations, cooperation within the Third World superpowers and foreign policy toward Latin America.
**Ind/Abst** ABC POL SCI; Am. Hist. Life (1968-); Curr. Geogr. Publ. (199?-); Foreign Lang. Index; HAPI Hisp. Am. Period. Index; Int. Polit. Sci. Abstr. (1968-).

CN/0826-1458
**FORUM - FORUM FOR YOUNG CANADIANS.** (FORUM.). [Forum - Forum Young Can.]. 1984-. English (French). an. Free. Forum for Young Canadians, 800-77 Metcalfe Street, Ottawa Ontario K1P 5L6 Canada. **Tel** (613)233-4086. **DD** 320.971/06. ctrl circ. ***Continues*** *Forum for Young Canadians. Bulletin, 0705-1581.*
**Desc:** Designed to meet the objectives of the Foundation for the Study of Processes of Government in Canada. Gives young Canadians the opportunity of gaining a clearer understanding of the processes of government in Canada.

US/0015-9204
**FOURTH INTERNATIONAL (LONDON, ENGLAND).** (FOURTH INTERNATIONAL.). [Fourth Int.]. (1964)-. Periodical. English (German). sa. $30.00 North America; $40.00 Europe and Latin America; $45.00 India, Asia, Africa and Australia. Labor Publications, PO Box 33023, Detroit MI 48216. **Tel** (313)875-4745. **DD** 320. ***Supersedes*** *Labour Review (London, England).*
**Desc:** A journal of international Marxism.

FR/1146-0024
**FRANCE ITALIE.** (1977)-. Periodical. French. Six times a year. 270.00F France; 280.00F other. Camera Comm Ital Per Francia, 134 rue du FBG Saint Honore, 75008 Paris France. **Tel** 011 33 1 42254188, FAX 011 33 1 42891458. **ED** M. Raffano Alberico. **UDC** 334.788.2. **Ad Acc. Circ:** 16,000 (ctrl). available on microfilm.

GW/0429-6524
**FREIBURGER RECHTS- UND STAATSWISSENSCHAFTLICHE ABHANDLUNGEN.** **Added/Corp** Freiburg i.B. Universitat. Rechts- und Staatswissenschaftliche Fakultat. Vol. 1 (1955)-. Monographic series. German. ir. Price varies per volume. Verlag CF Mueller, Verlags GS, D-69018 Heidelberg Germany. **Tel** 011 49 6221 4890.

US/0882-1267
**FRENCH POLITICS AND SOCIETY.** [Fr. polit. soc.]. **Added/Corp** Conference Group on French Politics and Society. Harvard University. Center for European Studies. Issue 8 (Dec. 1984)-. Periodical. English (French). qt. $28.00 (individuals), $40.00 (institutions). Center for European Studies, Harvard University, 27 Kirkland Street at Cabot Way, Cambridge MA 02138. **Tel** (617)495-4303 ext. 203, FAX (617)495-8509. **ED** Gretchen R. Bouliane. **LC** DC417; .F73. **DD** 944.083/05. Index available. cum. index. **Bk Rev**, (Qty: 40-50). **Ad Acc. Circ:** 350. ***Continues*** *Newsletter (Conference Group on French Politics and Society).*
**Desc:** Contains articles on contemporary issues and debates in France. Of interest to political scientists, sociologists, historians, and general France-watchers.
**Ind/Abst** Romant. Move.

FR
**FUTUR ANTERIEUR.** No 1 (1990)-. Periodical. French. bm. 350.00F (France); 390.00F (other). L' Harmattan, 7 rue de l'Ecole Polytechnique, 75005 Paris France. **Tel** 11 33 1 43547910, 43257651. **LC** JA11; .F87. **DD** 320/.05.

UK
**GALLUP POLITICAL & ECONOMIC INDEX.** English. mo. £95.00 UK; £120.00 US; £106.00 other. Gallup Poll / London, 307 Finchley Road, London NW3 England. **(Subscription address:** 14 Soho Square, London W1V 5FB England; FAX: 071 734 7029**)** **ED** Bob Wybrow and Hilary Muggridge. **Circ:** 1,000 (ctrl). ***Continues*** *Gallup Political Index.*
**Desc:** Social surveys on a wide range of topical political and economic issues and events.

JA
**GENDAISHI KENKYU.** **Added/Corp** Gendaishi Kenkyukai (Japan). (19??)-. Periodical. Japanese. Kyokuto Shoten, 2 Kanda Jinbocho 2, Chiyoda-Ku, Japan. **LC** H51; .G46.
**Ind/Abst** Am. Hist. Life (1968-1970).

SZ/0016-6774
**GENEVE-AFRIQUE.** ***Ceased.*** **See** Sociology.

UY
**GEOPOLITICA (INSTITUTO URUGUAYO DE ESTUDIOS GEOPOLITICOS).** (GEOPOLITICA : ORGANO OFICIAL DEL INSTITUTO URUGUAYO DE ESTUDIOS GEOPOLITICOS.). V. 1, No. 1, (August 1976)-. Spanish. sa. $40.00 four issues. Revista Geopolitica, Soriano 1585 - 10 -6, Montevideo Uruguay. **LC** JC319; .G47. **DD** 327.1/01/105.

US/0739-9251
**GEORGIA VOTER.** **Added/Corp** League of Women Voters of Georgia. (19??)-. Periodical. English. qt. $10.00 US; $12.00 other. League of Women Voters of Georgia, 1776 Peachtree Street Northwest, Suite 233 North, Atlanta GA 30309. **Tel** (404)874-7352. **ED** Diane Bronson. **LC** WMLC L 83/9035. **Circ:** 2,000.

●UK/0964-4008
**GERMAN POLITICS.** **Added/Corp** Association for the Study of German Politics. (1992)-. Periodical. English. Three times a year. $98.00. Frank Cass & Company Ltd, Newbury House, 890-900 Eastern Avenue, Newbury Park, Ilford, Essex IG2 7HH United Kingdom. **Tel** 011 44 81 599 8866, FAX 011 44 81 599 0984, telex 897719. **ED** Gordon Smith, Eva Kolinsky, William Paterson, and Stephen Padgett. **LC** JN3201; .G47. **Ad Acc, Adv Mgr:** Anne Kidson.
**Desc:** Seeks to provide a balanced coverage of domestic politics aspects - together with a treatment of

international, European Community, and security issues from a German perspective. In addition to what should become a substantial review section of books appearing in English and German, the journal will publish articles on Austrian politics.

US/1056-4721
**GERMANY (SYRACUSE, N.Y.).** **See** Economics-Economic History, Conditions.

GW
**GESETZBLATT DER DEUTSCHEN DEMOKRATISCHEN REPUBLIK. TEIL 2.** **Main/Corp** Germany (Democratic Republic, 1949- ). German. ir. Deutscher Judo Verband, Redaktion Ippon Segewaldweg 40, D 12557 Berlin Germany. **Tel** 011 49 711 210770, telex 051 678.

NE
**GIDS (AMSTERDAM, NETHERLANDS).** (DE GIDS.). **Added/Corp** Christelijk Nationaal Vakverbond in Nederland. (19??)-. Periodical. Dutch. Ten times a year. Fl140.00. Meulenhoff BV, Postbus 100 Herengracht 507, 1017 KG Amsterdam Netherlands. **Tel** 011 31 30 6267555. **ED** G. van Benthem van den Bergh. **Ad Acc.**

IT
**GIUNTE E COMMISSIONI PARLAMENTARI.** **Main/Corp** Italy. Parlamento. Senato. (19??)-. Italian. Libreria Camera dei Deputati, Via Uffici del Vicario 17, 00186 Rome, Italy. **Tel** 011 39 6 67603715. **LC** J388; .J745a. **DD** 328.45/0765.

●US/1075-2846
**GLOBAL GOVERNANCE.** (GLOBAL GOVERNANCE : A REVIEW OF MULTILATERALISM AND INTERNATIONAL ORGANIZATIONS.). (1995)-. Periodical. English. qt. $65.00 (institutions), $32.00 (individuals) North America; $73.00 (institutions), $40.00 (individuals) other. Lynne Rienner Publishers, 1800 30th Street, Suite 314, Boulder CO 80301. **Tel** (303)444-6684, FAX (303)444-0824.

CN/0226-8205
**GLOBAL OUTLOOK.** [Global outlook]. V. 101 I.E. V. 1- March 22/April 5, 1980-. Periodical. English. bw. $300.00 Canada; $150.00 public libraries and other non-profit organizations. Global Outlook, 30 The Driveway, Ottawa Ontario K2P 1C9 Canada. **DD** 905.

US/0894-3842
**GOVERNING (WASHINGTON, D.C.).** (GOVERNING.). [Governing]. Vol. 1, No. 1 (Oct. 1987)-. Periodical. English. mo. $39.99. Congressional Quarterly Inc., 1414 22nd Street Northwest, Washington DC 20037. **Tel** (202)887-8500, (800)432-2250 ext. 621, FAX (202)728-1863. **(Subscription address:** Palm Coast Data, PO Box 420235, Agency Department, Palm Coast FL 32142.**)** **ED** Peter A. Harkness, Eileen Shanahan, Alan Ehrenhalt, John Martin and Diane Kittower. **LC** JK2403; .G68. **DD** 350/.000973. **[CCC]**. Index available. **Bk Rev. Ad Acc. Circ:** 85,000 (ctrl). available on microfilm. Documents available from UMI Article Clearinghouse. ***Absorbed*** *Public's Capital* ***and*** *City & State (Chicago, Ill.), 0885-940X.*
**Desc:** A magazine that tracks emerging trends and issues and analyzes the critical challenges shared by state and local officials from coast to coast.
**Ind/Abst** Gen. Period. Index (1989-); Mag. Index Plus (1989-); Newsp. Period. Abstr. (1988-); PAIS Int. Print (1991-); Read. Guide Period. Lit.; Mag. Index (1989-); Urban Aff. Abstr.

UK/0017-257X
**GOVERNMENT AND OPPOSITION (LONDON).** (GOVERNMENT AND OPPOSITION.). [Gov. & oppos.]. **Added/Corp** London School of Economics and Political Science. Vol. 1, No. 1 (Oct. 1965)-. Periodical. English. Four times a year. £70.00 (individuals); £90.00 (institutions). London School of Economics, Houghton Street, London WC2A 2AE England. **Tel** 011 44 71 9557438, FAX 011 44 71 9557446. **(Subscription address:** Government and Oppostions, Houghton Street, London WC2A 2AE England.**)** **ED** Ernest Gellner, Ghita Ionescu, and Isabel de Madariaga. **LC** JA8; .G6. Index available. cum. index. **Bk Rev. Ad Acc. Pr Rev. Circ:** 1,500. Documents available from The Genuine Article, UMI Article Clearinghouse.
**Desc:** A journal of comparative politics with worldwide coverage and an interest in modern political philosophy, political history and political sociology.
**Ind/Abst** ABC POL SCI; Acad. Abstr. Full Text Elite (Jan. 1992-); Acad. Abstr. (Jan. 1992-); Acad. Search (Jan. 1992-); Am. Hist. Life (1966-1979); Br. Humanit. Index; Curr. Contents Soc. Behav. Sci.; Expand. Acad. Index (1989-); INFO-SOUTH Abstr.; Int. Bibliogr. Sociol.; Int. Polit. Sci. Abstr.; Mag. Search; Middle East Abstr. Index; Newsp. Period. Abstr. (1991-); PAIS Int. Print; Res. Alert [Full Cov.]; Soc. Plann. Policy Dev. Abstr.; Soc. Sci. Source (Jan. 1992-); Soc. Sci. Cit. Index [Full Cov.]; Soc. Sci. Index; Soc. Sci. Index Fulltext (Autumn 1988-) [Full Txt.]; Sociol. Abstr.

PP
**GOVERNMENT GAZETTE.** **Main/Corp** Papua New Guinea. **VFOAT** Papua and New Guinea Gazette. (19??)-. English. Fifty-two times a year. k.30.00 Papua & New Guinea, k.52.00 Pan America & Asia, k.76.00 other (surface mail); k.90.00 Pan America & Asia, k.114.00 others (airmail). Papua New Guinea Government Printing Office, PO Box 1280, Port Moresby, Papua New Guinea. **Tel** 214211. **LC** J8; B942a. ***Supersedes*** *Territory of Papua Government Gazette.*

US
**GOVERNMENT INFORMATION INSIDER.** **See** Public Administration.

US
**GOVERNMENT SECURITIES MANUAL.** English. an. $245.00. Public Securities Association, 40 Broad St, 12th Floor, New York NY 10004. **Tel** (212)809-7000, (212)440-9430, FAX (212) 797-3895, (212) 742-1549.

IT
**GOVERNO.** ***Ceased.*** (19??)-(19??). Italian. mo. Rivista IL Governo, Via di Benci 4, 50122 Florence Italy.

●US/1065-6049
**GRADUATE FACULTY AND PROGRAMS IN POLITICAL SCIENCE.** (GRADUATE FACULTY AND PROGRAMS IN POLITICAL SCIENCE : A DIRECTORY TO THE FACULTY AND GRADUATE DEGREE PROGRAMS OF U.S. AND CANADIAN INSTITUTIONS.). [Grad. fac. programs polit. sci.]. **Added/Corp** American Political Science Association. Rev. 14th Ed. (1994)-. Directory. English. ir (published every 3 years). $49.50 non-members; $28.50 members; Comes also with American Political Science Association Departmental Services Program membership. American Political Science Association, 1527 New Hampshire Avenue Northwest, Washington DC 20036. **Tel** (202)483-2512, FAX (202)483-2657. **LC** JA88.U6; G8. **DD** 320/.071/173. ***Continues*** *Guide to Graduate Study In Political Science, 0091-9632.*

US
**GRASS ROOTS CAMPAIGNING.** Vol. 1, No. 1 (Jan. 1980)-. Periodical. English. mo. $36.00 US; $40.00 Canada; $50.00 other. Campaign Consultants Inc, PO Box 7281, Little Rock AR 72217. **Tel** (501)225-3996. **ED** Jerry L Russell. **Bk Rev. Circ:** 485.
**Desc:** Techniques, philosophy and psychology of political campaigning.

US/0017-3517
**GRASS ROOTS FORUM.** ***Suspended.*** -Suspended with Vol. 26 1981. Periodical. English. qt. $5.00. Grass Roots Publishing Company, PO Box 472, San Gabriel CA 91778. available on microfilm from University Microfilms International (UMI).

US/0017-4742
**GROUP RESEARCH REPORT.** **Main/Corp** Group Research, Inc. (Atlanta, Ga.). **Added/Corp** Group Research, Inc. (Atlanta, Ga.). Report. (1962)-. Periodical. English. Six times a year. $40.00. Group Research Inc, 2000 M Street NW, Suite 400, Washington DC 20036. **Tel** (202)546-2090. **ED** Wesley McCune and Gladys Segal. **LC** E838; .G7. **DD** 320.5/0973. Index available (published separately). **Bk Rev**, (Qty: 10-12).
**Desc:** Reports on movements, leaders and groups to the right of the center of the political, religious and social spectrum.

SP
**GUERRA CIVIL ESPANOLA.** (19??)-. Periodical. Spanish. ir. Historia 16, Hermanos Garcia Noblejas 41, 28037 Madrid Spain. **Tel** 011 34 1 4072700.

AT
**GUIDE TO THE AUSTRALIAN FEDERAL PARLIAMENT.** **Added/Corp** Australian Press Services. **VFOAT** Guide to the Federal Parliament. (19??)-. English. ir. Price varies. Australian Press Services, PO Box E160, Queen Victoria Terrace, ACT 2600 Australia. **Tel** 011 61 6 2731600. **ED** J. M. Hutchison.
**Desc:** Comprehensive detail of members of parliament, heads of government departments, industrial and business organisations, parliamentary press gallery and maps of electoral boundaries.

UK
**GUIDE TO THE HOUSE OF COMMONS.** **VFOAT** Times Guide to the House of Commons. (1970)-. English. ir. £20.00 (retail), £13.00 (trade), add £6.00 for postage. The Times / Printing House Square, London EC4P 4DE England. **ED** Alan Wood. **LC** JN956; .G9. **DD** 328.42/0922. **Bk Rev. Ad Acc. Circ:** 10,000. ***Supersedes*** *House of Commons.*
**Desc:** Complete guide to results of British general election including photos and biographies of all MPS. Published after each general election.

UK/0953-5411
**GULF STATES NEWSLETTER.** **See** Economics.

GY/0046-6654
**GUYANA JOURNAL.** V. 1- April 1968-. Periodical. English. ir. Ministry of External Affairs / Guyana, Georgetown Guyana.

KO
**HAEOE CHONGSE.** Periodical. Korean. mo. **LC** D839; .H26.

SW/0345-4789
**HAFTEN FOR KRITISKA STUDIER.** Periodical. Swedish. Four times a year. Kr165.00 (individuals), Kr250.00 (institutions), add Kr30.00 for postage. Haften for Kritiska Studier, Tomtebogatan 34, S-113 38 Stockholm Sweden. **Tel** 08/343689. **ED** Goran Fredriksson. Index available. cum. index. **Bk Rev. Ad Acc. Circ:** 2,100.
**Desc:** An independent socialist and feminist magazine providing an alternative in Sweden to bourgeois scholarship.
**Ind/Abst** Annu. Bibliogr. Engl. Lang. Lit.

FR/0296-807X
**HAITI INFORMATION LIBRE.** (1985)-. Periodical. French. mo. **UDC** 32(729.4).
**Ind/Abst** Hum. Rights Intern. Rep.

GW/0302-9247
**HAMBURG HANDBUCH.** [Hamb. Handb.]. German. Verlag P Hartung, Heidenkampsweg 82, 1 Hamburg Germany. **LC** JN4287; .H28.

UK
**HAMLYN LECTURES, THE.** **See** Law.

US/0095-2842
**HANDBOOK OF ILLINOIS GOVERNMENT.** **Main/Corp** Illinois. Office of Secretary of State. (19??)-. English. an (Mar.). Free. Secretary of State Administration, Code Unit, 288 Centennial Building, Springfield IL 62756. **Tel** (217)782-9786. **LC** JK5730; .I45a. **DD** 320.4/773.

US/0743-0728
**HANDBOOK OF STATE LEGISLATIVE LEADERS, THE.** ***Title Change.*** [Handb. state legis. lead.]. **Added/Corp** State Legislative Leaders Foundation (U.S.). **VFOAT** Handbook. (1984)-(1992). English. an. Ballinger Publishing Company, 10 E 53rd Street, New York NY 10022-5244. **LC** JK2484; .H27. **DD** 328/.362/02573. ***Continued by*** *Inside the Legislature.*

US/0194-3790
**HANDBOOK OF THE NATIONS.** (HANDBOOK OF THE NATIONS / COMPILED AND PUBLISHED BY DIRECTORATE OF INTELLIGENCE, U.S. CENTRAL INTELLIGENCE AGENCY.). [Handb. Nations]. **Added/Corp** United States. Central Intelligence Agency. Directorate of Intelligence. 1st Ed. (1979)-. English. ir. $110.00. Gale Research Inc., 835 Penobscot Building, Detroit MI 48226. **Tel** (800)877-GALE, (313)961-2242, FAX (313)961-6083, telex TWX 810-221-7086. **LC** G122; .W67. **DD** 910. ***Continues*** *National Basic Intelligence Factbook. Handbook of the Nations.*
**Desc:** Emphasizing up-to-date economic and governmental data, it also provides details on each political unit's land, people, communications, and defense forces.

US/0090-1032
**HARVARD POLITICAL REVIEW.** (19??)-. Periodical. English. qt. $15.00 (one year), $25.00 (two year), $30.00 (three year) US and Canada; $25.00 (one year), $35.00 (two year), $40.00 (three year) Europe; $30.00 (one year), $40.00 (two year), $45.00 (three year) other. Harvard Political Review, 79 John F. Kennedy Street, Cambridge MA 02138. **Tel** (617)495-1360. **ED** Maxwell Pouner. **LC** JK1; .H36. **DD** 320/.05. **Bk Rev. Ad Acc. Circ:** 3,000 (ctrl).
**Desc:** A non-partisan journal of political thought covering both domestic and international affairs.

FR
**HAWLIYAT SIYASIYAH.** **VFOAT** Annales Politiques; Political Quarterly. Vol. 1, No. 1, (Winter 1982)-. Periodical. Arabic (English). ir. $75.00. Hasad Editions, 2 rue Christine, Paris 75006 France. **LC** DS63.1; .H38.

US
**HEMISFILE: PERSPECTIVES ON POLITICAL AND ECONOMIC TRENDS IN THE AMERICAS.** **Added/Corp** Institute of the Americas. (Jan. 1990)-. Periodical. English. Six times a year. $45.00 US and Canada; $55.00 other. Institute of the Americas, 10111 North Torrey Pines Road, La Jolla CA 92037. **Tel** (619)534-6052. **ED** Jeff Carmel (phone: (619)453-5560).
**Desc:** Focuses on political and economic trends in the Western Hemisphere.

US/0898-3038
**HEMISPHERE (MIAMI, FLA.).** (HEMISPHERE.). [Hemisphere]. **Added/Corp** Florida International University. Latin American and Caribbean Center. Vol. 1, No. 1 (Fall 1988)-. Periodical. English. Three times a year. $20.00 US, Puerto Rico, Virgin Islands & Canada; $27.00 other. Latin American and Caribbean Center, Florida International University, Miami Campus, Miami FL 33199. **Tel** (305)348-2894, FAX (305)348-3593. **ED** Euuardo A. Gamarra. **LC** F1401; .H46. **DD** 980/.005. **Bk Rev. Ad Acc, Adv Mgr:** R.

Jurado. **Pr Rev. Circ:** 2,000 (ctrl).
**Desc:** A magazine of Latin American and Caribbean affairs. Provokes debate on the region's problems, initiatives, and achievements and provides an intellectual bridge between the concerned public of the Americas.
**Ind/Abst** HAPI Hisp. Am. Period. Index; Int. Dev. Abstr. (?-?).

FR/0767-9513
**HERMES (PARIS, FRANCE : 1988).** (HERMES.). (1988)-. Periodical. French. Three times a year. Editions du CNRS, 22 rue Saint Armand, F 75015 Paris France. **Tel** 011 33 1 45075050.

●US/1069-7268
**HETERODOXY (STUDIO CITY, LOS ANGELES, CALIF.).** (HETERODOXY : ARTICLES AND ANIMADIVERSIONS ON POLITICAL CORRECTNESS AND OTHER FOLLIES.). [Heterodoxy]. **Added/Corp** Center for the Study of Popular Culture. Vol. 1, No. 1 (Apr. 1992)-. Periodical. English. mo. $25.00. Center for the Study of Popular Culture, 12400 Ventura Boulevard, Suite 304, Studio City CA 91604. **Tel** (310)843-3699. **DD** 320.
**Desc:** The cultural equivalent of a drive-by shooting. Presents articles on topics such as the ten worst college administrators, the ten wackiest feminists on campus, multicultural mafia, womens studies imperialists, sensitivity police brutality and more.

SZ
**HISPO / ASSOCIATION D'HISTOIRE ET DE SCIENCE POLITIQUE.** **VFOAT** Historie et Science Politique. Journal 1 (Jan. 1983)-. Periodical. French. an. HISPO, Mrs. L Altermatt, Presidente, 96 Eichholzstr, 3084 Wabern/Bern Switzerland. **LC** DQ415; .H57. **DD** 949.4/5.

US/0892-080X
**HISTORIC DOCUMENTS.** [Hist. doc.]. **Added/Corp** Congressional Quarterly, Inc. **VFOAT** Historic Documents of ... . (1972)-. English. an (June). $112.00. Congressional Quarterly Inc., 1414 22nd Street Northwest, Washington DC 20037. **Tel** (202)887-8500, (800)432-2250 ext. 621, FAX (202)728-1863. **LC** E839.5; .H57. **DD** 917.3/03/9205. cum. index.

US/0196-4720
**HISTORICAL REPORT OF THE SECRETARY OF STATE, ARKANSAS.** **Main/Corp** Arkansas. Office of Secretary of State. (1958)-. English. ir. Secretary of State / Arkansas, Room 256, State Capitol, Little Rock AR 72201. **Tel** (501)682-3577. **LC** J87; .A84a. **DD** 320.9/767/05. ***Continues*** *Arkansas. Office of Secretary of State. Report.*

GW/0172-6404
**HISTORICAL SOCIAL RESEARCH (KOLN).** **See** Sociology.

UK/0143-781X
**HISTORY OF POLITICAL THOUGHT.** [Hist. polit. thought]. Vol. 1, Issue 1 (Spring 1980)-. Periodical. English. Four times a year. £52.00 (institutions), £26.50 (individuals) UK; £62.50 (institutions), £29.00 (individuals) other. Imprint Academic, 32 Haldon Road, Exeter Devon EX4 4D2 England. **Tel** 0392-438104, FAX 0392-425877. **ED** J Coleman and I P Hampsher-Monk. **LC** JA8; .H57. **DD** 320/.01/05. **Bk Rev**. **Ad Acc. Circ:** 600. Documents available from The Genuine Article.
**Desc:** The study of political thought in its international and historical context, from ancient Greece to the Modern period.
**Ind/Abst** ABC POL SCI; Acad. Search (July 1993-); Am. Hist. Life (1980-); Arts Humanit. Citation Index [Full Cov.]; Curr. Contents Arts Humanit.; Hist. Source (July 1993-); INFO-SOUTH Abstr.; Int. Polit. Sci. Abstr.; Mag. Search; Middle East Abstr. Index; Philos. Index; Res. Alert [Full Cov.]; Romant. Move.; Soc. Sci. Cit. Index [Select. Cov.].

JA/0073-2796
**HITOTSUBASHI JOURNAL OF LAW & POLITICS.** **Added/Corp** Hitotsubashi Daigaku. Hitotsubashi Gakkai. **VFOAT** Hitotsubashi Journal of Law and Politics. Vol. 1 (April 1960)-. Periodical. English (German). an. $29.00. **(Subscription address:** Japan Publications Trading Company, Ltd., PO Box 5030, Tokyo International, Tokyo 100-31 Japan.**)** **LC** LAW. **DD** 320/.05. ***Continues in part*** *Annals of the Hitotsubashi Academy, 0439-2841.*
**Ind/Abst** Int. Polit. Sci. Abstr.

JA
**HOGAKU.** **See** Law.

FR/0755-8074
**HOMMES ET FONCTIONS.** [Hommes fonct.]. (1972)-. Periodical. French. Fifty-two times a year. 2693.44F France; 3000.00F other. CEEPP, 120 Av des Champs Elysees, 75008 Paris France. **Tel** 011 33 1 45627642. **UDC** 323.

US/0748-4380
**HOOVER ESSAYS.** [Hoover essays]. **Added/Corp** Hoover Institution on War, Revolution, and Peace. (19??)-. Periodical. English. ir (4-6 issues). $5.00 per copy. Hoover Institution Press, Stanford University, HHMB Room 28, Stanford CA 94305. **Tel** (415)723-3373. **ED** Alvin Rabushka (editor's telephone: (415)723-2878). **LC** AS30; .H66. **DD** 081.

GW
**HORIZONT (BERLIN, GERMANY).** ***Ceased.*** (HORIZONT.). (1945/46)-Ceased ?. Periodical. German. sm. Deutscher Judo Verband, Redaktion Ippon Segewaldweg 40, D 12557 Berlin Germany. **Tel** 011 49 711 210770, telex 051 678.

US
**HOTLINE.** ***Ceased.*** **See** Business.

US
**HOTLINE, THE.** (1987)-. English. da (Mon.-Fri.). $950.00 (quarterly), $3600.00 (annual). The American Political Network, 282 North Washington Street, Falls Church VA 22046. **Tel** (703)237-5130, FAX (703)237-5142. **ED** Robert Balkin. Index available. cum. index. **Circ:** Not Disclosed. available via fax.
**Desc:** Daily briefing on American politics.

US
**HOUSE JOURNAL OF THE ... LEGISLATURE OF THE STATE OF MONTANA.** **Main/Corp** Montana. Legislature. House of Representatives. **VFOAT** House Journal. English. be. Montana Legislative Council, State Capitol/Room 138, Helena MT 59620-1706. **Tel** (406)444-3064, FAX (406)444-3036. **LC** J87; .M9 DATE C. **DD** 328.786/01. **Circ:** 350. ***Continues*** *Montana. Legislative Assembly. House of Representatives. House Journal.*
**Desc:** Official record of actions of the House of Representatives of the State of Montana.

UK/0309-0426
**HOUSE MAGAZINE.** [House mag.]. (1976)-. Periodical. English. ir (40 issues per year - Mondays when Parliament is in session). £137.00 UK; £217.00 other. Parliamentary Communications Ltd, 10 Little College Street, London SW1P 3SH England. **Tel** 011 44 71 2331388, FAX 011 44 71 976 0861. **ED** Patrick Cormack. Index available. **Bk Rev**. **Ad Acc.** ctrl circ.
**Desc:** Political and current events.

UK
**HOUSE OF COMMONS BOUND DEBATES.** (19??)-. English. ir. £75.00. Her Majesty's Stationery Office, 51 Nine Elms Lane, London SW8 5DR England. **Tel** 011 44 71 873 8459, 011 44 71 873 8499, FAX 011 44 71 873 8499, 011 44 71 873 8456, telex 297138. **(Subscription address:** Her Majesty's Stationery Office, PO Box 276, Publications Centre, London SW8 5DT England.**)**

NE
**HP-DE TIJD.** Dutch. wk. Medianet BV, Postbus 6298, 2001 LN Haarlem Netherlands. **Tel** 011 31 23 173311.

CH
**HSUEH HSI TSA CHIH.** **VFOAT** Xue Xi Za Zhi. Periodical. Chinese. mo. NT$0.20. Post Office Chung-tu Shih, Cheng-tu Shih, People's Republic of China. **LC** AP95.C4; H817. **DD** 320.5/323/0951.

US/0018-7194
**HUMAN EVENTS (WASHINGTON).** (HUMAN EVENTS.). [Hum. events]. **Added/Corp** National Foundation for Education in American Citizenship. (Feb. 2, 1944)-. Periodical. English. wk. $49.95 one year; $89.95 two years. Human Events, 422 1st Street SE, Washington DC 20003. **Tel** (202)546-0856. **ED** Thomas S. Winter. **LC** D410; .H8. **DD** 940.5305. **[CCC]**. Index available ($7.50). cum. index. **Bk Rev**. **Ad Acc. Circ:** 47,000 (ctrl). available on microfilm and microfiche from University Microfilms International (UMI).
**Desc:** Conservative political publication covering domestic and international politics with emphasis on developments in Washington. Particular attention is given to news stories of political importance which are underplayed in national news media.
**Ind/Abst** Acad. Search (July 1993-); Am. Hist. Life (1972-1973); Book Rev. Index; INFO-SOUTH Abstr.; Mag. Search; Pop. Period. Index.

US/0275-049X
**HUMAN RIGHTS INTERNET REPORTER.** **See** Political Science-Abstracting, Bibliographies and Statistics.

US
**HUNG CHI.** (CHINA REPORT. RED FLAG.). **VFOAT** Red Flag. Began with: May 4, 1979. Periodical. English (summaries and/or abstracts in Chinese). mo. National Technical Information Service - NTIS, Room 2027S, 5285 Port Royal Road, Springfield VA 22161. **Tel** (703)487-4630, (703)487-4660, (703)487-4650, FAX (703)321-8547, telex 89-9405. ***Continues*** *Translations from Red Flag.*

II/0250-9660
**ICSSR JOURNAL OF ABSTRACTS AND REVIEWS : POLITICAL SCIENCE.** **See** Political Science-Abstracting, Bibliographies and Statistics.

US
**ILLINI REVIEW.** Periodical. English. Michael Fumento, PO Box 2643, Station A, Champaign IL 61820-8643.

US/0738-9663
**ILLINOIS ISSUES.** [Ill. issues]. Vol. 1, (1975)-. Periodical. English. mo (except combined Aug./Sept.). $32.95 (1 year), $59.00 (2 year), $89.00 (3 year). Sangamon State University, Brookens 385, Springfield IL 62794. **Tel** (217)786-6084, (217)786-7435. **ED** Caroline Gheradini. Index available. **Bk Rev**. **Ad Acc. Circ:** 4,500 (ctrl).
**Desc:** A magazine providing in-depth coverage of the issues and people behind them in the Illinois political-governmental arena. Covers economics, education, business, environment, etc.
**Ind/Abst** PAIS Int. Print (1991-); Urban Aff. Abstr.

NE
**IN DE WAAGSCHAAL.** **See** Religion and Theology.

US/1055-9809
**IN DEPTH (WASHINGTON, D.C.).** (IN DEPTH : JOURNAL OF THE WASHINGTON INSTITUTE FOR VALUES IN PUBLIC POLICY.). [In depth]. **Added/Corp** Washington Institute for Values in Public Policy. Vol. 1, No. 1 (Spring 1991)-. Periodical. English. Three times a year (Apr., Aug., Dec.). $12.00 US; $15.00 other. Washington Institute, 1015 18th Street Northwest, Suite 300, Washington DC 20036-5204. **Tel** (202)293-7440, FAX (202)293-9393. **ED** Richard L. Rubenstein. **LC** D860; .I5. **DD** 909.82. Index Available Published separately--free--upon request. cum. index. **Ad Acc, Adv Mgr:** Larry Orman, **Tel** (202)293-7443. **Circ:** 1,000.
**Desc:** A scholarly journal committed to serious, non-partisan examination and analyses of important domestic and foreign policy issues confronting the American polity.

US/0275-8954
**IN POLITICS.** Vol. 1, No. 1 (Summer 1981)-. Periodical. English. ir. $1.25 single issue. In Politics, Connecticut College, Box 1322, New London CT 06320.

AT/1033-9957
**INDEPENDENT MONTHLY, THE.** [Indep. m.]. (1989)-. Periodical. English. mo (11 issues). 49.00Aus$. Independent Monthly, 4th Floor 64 Kippax Street, Surry Hills NSW 2010 Australia. **Tel** 011 61 02 211 3199, FAX 011 61 02 211 3490. **ED** Michael Duffy. **DD** 994.05. **Bk Rev**, (Qty: 30-40). **Ad Acc, Adv Mgr:** Steve Congerton. **Circ:** 30,000.

US/8750-2364
**INDEPENDENT REPUBLICAN.** Vol. 22 No. 1 (Aug. 1984)-. Periodical. English. wk. $22.00 Orange County New York; $20.00 other. Vail-Smith Company, 3301 Adams Avenue, San Diego CA 92116. **ED** Eugene Wright. **DD** 322. **Bk Rev**, (Qty: 4-5/yr). **Ad Acc. Circ:** 3800 (ctrl). available on microfilm from University Microfilms International (UMI). ***Continues*** *Republican, 0199-4549.*

II/0019-5510
**INDIAN JOURNAL OF POLITICAL SCIENCE, THE.** [Indian j. polit. sci.]. **Added/Corp** Indian Political Science Association. Vol. 1 (July/Sept. 1939)-. Periodical. English. qt. $65.00. Indian Political Science Association, New Delhi, India. **(Subscription address:** Prints India, 11 Darya Ganj, New Delhi, 110002 India, (Phone: 011 91 11 3268645)**)** **LC** JA26; .I5. **DD** 320.5.
**Ind/Abst** ABC POL SCI; Appl. Soc. Sci. Index Abstr.; Index Islam. Lit.; Int. Bibliogr. Sociol.; Int. Polit. Sci. Abstr.; Middle East Abstr. Index.

II/0251-303X
**INDIAN JOURNAL OF POLITICAL STUDIES, THE.** [Indian j. polit. stud.]. **Added/Corp** University of Jodphur. Dept. of Political Science. Vol. 1 (Jan. 1977)-. Periodical. English. an. $20.00. University of Jodhpur, PO Box 14, Jodhpur 342001 India. **Tel** 22606. **(Subscription address:** Prints India, 11 Darya Ganj, New Delhi, 110002 India, (Phone: 011 91 11 3268645)**)** **LC** JA26; .I514. **DD** 320/.05.
**Ind/Abst** Am. Hist. Life (1978-).

II/0303-9951
**INDIAN JOURNAL OF POLITICS.** [Indian j. polit.]. **Added/Corp** Aligarh Muslim University. Dept. of Political Science. Vol. 1 (Jan./June 1967)-. Periodical. English. qt. $25.00. Aligarh Muslim University Department of Political Science, Alegarh 202001 U P India. **Tel** 6720. **(Subscription address:** Prints India, 11 Darya Ganj, New Delhi, 110002 India, (Phone: 011 91 11 3268645)**)** **ED** S A H Bilgrami. **LC** JA26; .I52. **DD** 320/.05. **[CCC]**. **Bk Rev. Circ:** 300 (ctrl).
**Desc:** A nonprofit, unofficial, independent, academic journal dedicated to the advancement of research in all subfields of political science and their wider interdisciplinary nature.
**Ind/Abst** ABC POL SCI (19??-1984); Am. Hist. Life (1975-); Int. Polit. Sci. Abstr.

# Political Science

FR/0294-6475
**INDIAN OCEAN NEWSLETTER / LA LETTRE DE L'OCEAN INDIEN, THE.** See Economics.

II
**INDIAN REVIEW OF AFRICAN AFFAIRS : IRAA.** See Economics.

US/0737-7355
**INDIANA JOURNAL OF POLITICAL SCIENCE.** Suspended. [Indiana j. polit. sci.]. **Added/Corp** Indiana Political Science Association. Vol. 1 (1982)-Vol. 5 (1986). English. an. $15.00 North America; $25.00 other. Ball State University / Department of Political Science, Muncie IN 47304. **Tel** (317)285-8794, 289-1241. **ED** Fred A. Meyer Jr. **Ad Acc. Circ:** 100.

●US
**INDIANA LEGISLATIVE SOURCEBOOK.** **Added/Corp** Indiana Legislative Insight (Firm). **VFOAT** Indiana Legislative Source Book. (1992)-. English. $4.50. **LC** JK5630/ .I52.

US/0897-4519
**INDOCHINA CHRONOLOGY.** See History(General)-History of Asia.

CN/0826-2616
**INFO JEUNES PC.** [Info jeunes PC]. **Added/Corp** Federation des Jeunes Progressistes-Conservateurs du Canada. **VFOAT** Info PC. **VAT** Info Jeunes Progressistes-Conservateurs du Canada (1983); Info JPC (1983). Vol. 1, No. 1 (Oct. 1983)-. Periodical. French. Free. Federation des Jeunes Progressistes-Conservateurs du Canada, Bureau 200/161 Ouest Avenue Laurier, Ottawa Ontario K1P 5J2 Canada. **DD** 324.27104. **Continues** Info P.C., 0820-6279.

●US/1059-5910
**INFO-SOUTH ABSTRACTS.** See Economics-Abstracting, Bibliographies and Statistics.

US/0736-8666
**INFOBRAZIL / CENTER OF BRAZILIAN STUDIES.** See Economics-Economic History, Conditions.

GW
**INFORMATIONEN ZUR POLITISCHEN BILDUNG.** Monographic series. German. qt. Price varies per volume. Leske Verlag & Budrich GmbH, Postfach 300551, Gerhart Hauptmann Strasse 27, W-5090 Leverkusen 3 Opladen Germany. **Tel** 011 49 21712079. **LC** JA88.G3; A3. **DD** 320/.05. **Continues** Staatsbürgerliche Information.

GW/0721-5088
**INFORMATIONSDIENST SUDLICHES AFRIKA.** [Inf.dienst sudl. Afr.]. (1972)-. Periodical. German. Six times a year. DM70.00 (institutions), DM50.00 (individuals) Germany; DM85.00 (institutions), DM60.00 (individuals) other. ISSA, Informationsstelle Suedliches Afrika e.V., Koenigswinterer Str. 116, D 53227 Bonn Germany. **Tel** 011 49 221 464369, **FAX** 011 49 221 468177. **ED** Hein Mollers. **UDC** 323.12(=96)(6-13). Index Bound in First Issue. cum. index. **Bk Rev Ad Acc Circ:** 1,700.

US/0884-030X
**INSIDE ALABAMA POLITICS.** [Inside Ala. polit.]. Vol. 1, No. 1 July 26, (1985)-. English. Thirty-nine times a year. $65.00 (one year); $115.00 (two years); $150.00 (three years). Inside Alabama Politics, PO Box 3296, Montgomery AL 36109. **Tel** (800)624-5172 (205)264-6269. **ED** Bessie Ford. **DD** 320. **Circ:** 800.

CH
**INSIDE CHINA MAINLAND.** **Added/Corp** Institute of Current China Studies (Taiwan). (19??)-. Periodical. English. Twelve times a year. $17.00 Asia; $20.00 other. Institute of Current China Studies, PO Box 14-19, Taipei Taiwan. **Tel** 011 886 2 3517687. **ED** L. C. Chang. **LC** DS779.15; .I57. **DD** 951/.005. Index available. **Circ:** 4,100.
**Desc:** Presents translations of reprinted and original articles concerning issues of policy and politics in mainland China.

US/1059-2148
**INSIDE FLORIDA POLITICS.** Ceased. [Inside Fla. polit.]. Vol. 1, No. 1 (Oct. 14, 1991)-(1992). Periodical. English. sm. Spencer Publications Inc. / Florida, 2554 Garden Court, Hollywood FL 33026. **Tel** (305)433-7833. **ED** Norman S Gross. **DD** 320. ctrl circ.

US/1075-6752
**INSIDE THE LEGISLATURE.** Title Change. (INSIDE THE LEGISLATURE : THE GUIDE TO STATE POLICYMAKERS.). [Inside legis.]. **Added/Corp** State Legislative Leaders Foundation (1993)-(1993). English. an. State Legislative Leaders Foundation, PO Box 400, Centerville MA 02632. **Tel** (508)771-3821. **DD** 328. **Continues** Handbook of State Legislative Leaders, 0743-0728. **Continued by** Handbook of State Legislative Leaders (1994).

US/1051-4880
**INSIGHT ON THE NEWS (WASHINGTON, D.C.).** (INSIGHT ON THE NEWS.). [Insight news]. **VFOAT** Insight. Vol. 3, No. 52 (Dec. 28, 1987/Jan. 4, 1988)-. Periodical. English. wk. $34.84. Insight Magazine, PO Box 91022, Washington DC 20090. **Tel** (202)269-5365, **FAX** (202)526-3497. **ED** Kirk Oberfeld. **LC** IN PROCESS. **DD** 051. **[CCC].** Index available. cum. index. **Ad Acc, Adv Mgr:** Desiree DeLoatch, **Tel** (202) 636-8888. **Circ:** 100,000. available on microfilm and microfiche from University Microfilms International (UMI); available on CD-ROM. **Continues** Insight (Washington, D.C. : 1985), 0884-9285.
**Desc:** Concise, unbiased review of national events.
**Ind/Abst** Foods Adlibra (1988-).

US/0277-2302
**INSTAURATION.** [Instauration]. Vol. 1, No. 1 (Dec. 1975)-. Periodical. English. mo. $35.00. Howard Allen Enterprises, Box 76, Cape Canaveral FL 32920. **ED** Wilmot Robertson. **LC** AP2; .I625. **DD** 051. **Bk Rev,** (Qty: 5). available on microfiche.
**Desc:** Political and Social commentary on current events.

US
**INSTITUTE OF POLITICS NEWSLETTER.** **Added/Corp** John F. Kennedy School of Government. Institute of Politics. **VFOAT** Newsletter; IOP newsletter. Spring (1991)-. Newsletter. English. Harvard University Institute of Politics, 79 John F Kennedy Street, Cambridge MA 02138. **Continues** Report on Politics, 0896-9558.

US/0730-2355
**INTELLECTUAL ACTIVIST, THE.** (19??)-. Periodical. English. bm. $33.00 US; $45.00 other. Intellectual Activist, PO Box 582 Murray Hill Station, New York NY 10156. **Tel** (212)779-1027. **ED** Peter Schwartz. **Bk Rev.**
**Desc:** Political and economic analysis from a pro laissez-faire capitalism viewpoint.

UK
**INTELLIGENCE DIGEST (WEEKLY).** (INTELLIGENCE DIGEST : WEEKLY REVIEW.). No. 1182 (Feb. 19, 1975)-. Periodical. English. wk. $72.75 (9 month), $97.00 (one year), $291.00 (three year). **LC** D839; .I4548. **DD** 327/.05. **Bk Rev. Circ:** 15,000. **Continues** Weekly Review (Cirencester, Gloucestershire).
**Desc:** Provided with an unrivalled and complete source of inside trends throughout the world.

US/8755-9404
**INTERFAITH ACTION FOR ECONOMIC JUSTICE.** **VFOAT** Interfaith Action. Began with: issue for Sept. 1984. Periodical. English. ir (10 times a year). $10.00. Interfaith Action for Economic Justice, 110 Maryland Avenue Northeast, Washington DC 20002. **Tel** (202)543-2800. **ED** Stephen Clapp. **DD** 361. **Circ:** 4,000.
**Desc:** News and features on the religious community's response to issues of hunger and poverty in the U.S. and overseas.

CN
**INTERIM REPORT OF THE ELECTORAL BOUNDARIES COMMISSION OF THE PROVINCE OF ALBERTA.** Main/Corp Electoral Boundaries Commission for the Province of Alberta (Canada). **VFOAT** Interim Report. (19??)-. English. **LC** JL333; .E57a. **DD** 328.7123/07345.

US
**INTERNATIONAL BIBLIOGRAPHY OF SOCIAL SCIENCES: POLITICAL SCIENCE.** Bibliography. English. ir. $150.00 US; $187.50 Canada. Routledge Chapman & Hall Inc, 29 West 35th Street, New York NY 10001. **Tel** (212)244-3336, (212)244-6412.
**Desc:** Covers over 1,500 journals published throughout the world in 30 languages and stands as the long-term reference resource in the social sciences.

SZ/0259-3696
**INTERNATIONAL CHILDREN'S RIGHTS MONITOR.** Main/Corp Defence for Children International. Information and Documentation Service. Vol. 1, No. 1 (1983)-. Periodical. English (French and Spanish). qt. 30.00F (individuals), 50.00F (institutions). Defence for Children International, CP 88, CH-1211 Geneva 20 Switzerland. **Tel** 41 22 7340558, **FAX** 41 22 7401145, telex 414 128 DCI CH. **ED** M Paulo David. cum. index. **Bk Rev,** (Qty: 25). **Ad Acc, Adv Mgr:** same as editor. **Circ:** 6,500.
**Desc:** Concerning promotion, violation and monitoring of children's rights worldwide.
**Ind/Abst** Hum. Rights Intern. Rep.

US/0020-6652
**INTERNATIONAL EXECUTIVE.** See Political Science-Abstracting, Bibliographies and Statistics.

US/0891-1916
**INTERNATIONAL JOURNAL OF POLITICAL ECONOMY.** [Int. j. polit. econ.]. Vol. 17, No. 1 (Spring 1987)-. Periodical. English. qt. $450.00 US; $495.00 other. M. E. Sharpe Inc., 80 Business Park Drive, Armonk NY 10504. **Tel** (914)273-1800, (800)541-6563, **FAX** (914)273-2106. **ED** Arnold C. Tovell. **LC** JA1.A1; I59. **DD** 320/.05. **Bk Rev. Ad Acc:** 300 (ctrl). available on microfilm from University Microfilms International (UMI). **Continues** International Journal of Politics, 0012-8783.
**Desc:** A worldwide forum for the scholarship of the left, right and center on current political theory and practice.
**Ind/Abst** Am. Hist. Life (1987-); Int. Polit. Sci. Abstr.; PAIS Int. Print (1991-).

US/0891-4486
**INTERNATIONAL JOURNAL OF POLITICS, CULTURE, AND SOCIETY.** See Sociology.

UK
**INTERNATIONAL MARXIST REVIEW : IMR / ORGAN OF THE REVOLUTIONARY MARXIST TENDENCY OF THE FOURTH INTERNATIONAL.** Began with: No. 1 (June 1971). Periodical. English (French). Three times a year. £8.50 individuals, £15.00 institutions UK; $18.00 individuals, $25.00 institutions. IMR, 2 rue Richard Lenoir, 93108 Montreuil France. Index available. cum. index. **Bk Rev Ad Acc Circ:** 1,500.
**Desc:** English language theoretical and analytical journal of the Fourth International.

FR/0020-8345
**INTERNATIONAL POLITICAL SCIENCE ABSTRACTS.** See Political Science-Abstracting, Bibliographies and Statistics.

UK/0192-5121
**INTERNATIONAL POLITICAL SCIENCE REVIEW.** (INTERNATIONAL POLITICAL SCIENCE REVIEW : IPSR). [Int. polit. sci. rev.]. **Added/Corp** International Political Science Association. **VFOAT** IPSR; RISP; Revue Internationale de Science Politique; IPSR/RISP. Vol. 1 (Jan. 1980)-. Periodical. English (French). qt. $172.00 The Americas; £115.00 other. Butterworth Heinemann Publishers, Linacre House, Jordan Hill, Oxford OX2 8DP England. **Tel** 011 44 865 310366. **(Subscription address:** Elsevier Science Ltd. Oxford Fulfillment Centre, PO Box 800, Kidlington, Oxford OX5 1DX United Kingdom.) **ED** John Meisel and Jean Laponce. **LC** JA1.A1; R18. **DD** 320/.05. **[CCC]. Ad Acc.** available on microfilm and microfiche from University Microfilms International (UMI). Documents available from The Genuine Article.
**Desc:** Its content reflects the aims and intellectual tradition of the parent body: the creation and dissemination of rigorous political inquiry free of any subdisciplinary or other orthodoxy. This aim is to provide readers with work being done in political science on the central and currently controversial themes of the discipline and in the new areas of inquiry.
**Ind/Abst** ABC POL SCI; Curr. Contents Soc. Behav. Sci.; Int. Bibliogr. Sociol.; Int. Polit. Sci. Abstr.; Middle East Abstr. Index; Peace Res. Abstr. J. (1980-1986); Res. Alert [Full Cov.]; Soc. Sci. Cit. Index [Full Cov.]; U.S. Polit. Sci. Doc. (199?-).

US/0740-669X
**INTERNATIONAL REPORT (IRVINE, CALIF.).** (INTERNATIONAL REPORT.). [Int. rep.]. Vol. 1, No. 1 (March 1983)-. Periodical. English. Three times a year (Feb., July, Nov.). $6.00 (individuals), $50.00 (corporations and government agencies). International Report, PO Box 4882, Irvine CA 92716. **Tel** (714)856-7137, **FAX** (714)725-2436. **ED** Raul Fernandez. **LC** D839; .I538. **DD** 905. **Ad Acc. Circ:** 250. **Continues** Colombia Report, 0730-1073.
**Desc:** A political and economic analysis of international events, exposing actions of undemocratic governments and presenting popular resistance and organization against those governments.
**Ind/Abst** Hum. Rights Intern. Rep.

UK/0020-8736
**INTERNATIONAL SOCIALISM. SERIES 2.** **Added/Corp** Socialist Workers Party. (19??)-. Periodical. English. Four times a year. $19.12 (individuals); $31.86 (institutions). International Socialism, PO Box 82, 265 Seven Sisters Road, London N4 2DE England. **Tel** 011 44 81 802 6145. **Absorbed** International Discussion Bulletin.
**Ind/Abst** Int. Bibliogr. Sociol.

FR/0294-2925
**INTERNATIONAL VIEWPOINT.** **Added/Corp** Fourth International. United Secretariat. (March 1982)-. Periodical. English. sm. 280.00F. Presse Edition

Communication, 2 rue Richard Lenoir, 93108 Montreuil France. **Tel** 011 33 1 48590080.
**Ind/Abst** Altern. Press Index (199?-).

US/0074-9621
**INTERNATIONAL YEAR BOOK AND STATESMEN'S WHO'S WHO, THE. See** Biographies.

NE/0020-9317
**INTERNATIONALE SPECTATOR.** [Int. spect.]. **Added/Corp** Nederlandsch Genootschap voor Internationale Zaken. Nederlands Instituut voor Internationale Betrekkingen "Clingendael." Institut Royal des Relations Internationales (Brussels, Belgium). (1946)-. Periodical. Dutch (Dutch; summaries and/or abstracts in English). mo. Fl75.00 (students), Fl89.50 (regular) Netherlands; Fl107.50 (students), Fl122.50 (regular) Belgium; Fl117.50 (students), Fl132.50 (regular) other. Van Gorcum & Company BV, PO Box 43, NL 9400 AA Assen Netherlands. **Tel** 011 31 5920 46846, FAX 011 31 5920 72064. **LC** D839; .I6. **CODEN** ISPCET.
**Ind/Abst** Am. Hist. Life (1954-1970); Middle East J.; World Agric. Econ.

US/0020-9635
**INTERPRETATION (THE HAGUE).** (INTERPRETATION.). [Interpret.]. (Summer 1970)-. Periodical. English. Three times a year. $25.00 (individuals), $40.00 (institutions & libraries) US; $29.50 (individuals), $44.50 (institutions & libraries) Canada; $30.40 (individuals), $45.40 (institutions & libraries) other. Queens College / Interpretation, King Hall Room 101, 65-30 Kissena Boulevard, Flushing NY 11367. **Tel** (718)997-5000. **ED** Hilail Gildin. **LC** JA26; .I57. **DD** 320/.05. **Bk Rev. Pr Rev.** Documents available from The Genuine Article.
**Ind/Abst** Acad. Abstr. Full Text Elite (July 1990-); Acad. Abstr. (July 1990-); Acad. Search (July 1990-); Arts Humanit. Citation Index [Full Cov.]; Humanit. Source (Jul. 1990-); INFO-SOUTH Abstr.; Mag. Search; Middle East Abstr. Index; MLA Int. Bibl. Books Artic. Mod. Lang. Lit.; Philos. Index; Res. Alert [Full Cov.]; Soc. Sci. Cit. Index [Select. Cov.].

US/0163-0997
**INTERSEARCH.** [Intersearch]. Periodical. English. bw. $36.00. International Terrorist Research Center, PO Box 26804, El Paso TX 79926. ***Continues*** *Counterforce, 0146-812X.*

US/0360-7526
**IOWA ELECTION HANDBOOK WITH ELECTION LAWS OF IOWA. See** Law.

US/0199-4212
**IOWA VOTER.** Periodical. English. qt. Iowa Communications, PO Box 4826, Des Moines IA 50306-4826.

UK
**IRAN QUARTERLY. See** Economics-Economic History, Conditions.

IT
**ISIS.** ***Ceased.*** (19??)-Issue 17 (1993). Italian. Isis Informazione Stampa, Largo Arenula 26, 00186 Rome Italy.

US/8755-8912
**ISLAM INTERNATIONAL (DOVER, DEL.).** ***Suspended.*** (ISLAM INTERNATIONAL.). (1986)-(1993). Periodical. English. qt. $36.00. Dr. C. V. Ramastry Editor, PO Box 1755, Kantipath Kathmandu Nepal. **ED** Dr. C. V. Ramastry.

UK
**ISLAMIC AFFAIRS ANALYST.** (198?)-. Periodical. English. Twelve times a year. $297.00 US; £148.00 UK; £198.00 other. Intelligence International Ltd., 17 Rodney Road, Cheltenham, Gloucestershire, GL50 1HX United Kingdom. **Tel** 0285-770451, FAX 0285-770088. **ED** J.K.C. de Courcy.
**Desc:** An intelligence report on political, economic, and strategic developments throughout the Islamic world, from Indonesia to Senegal.

US/0021-2083
**ISRAEL HORIZONS. See** Religion and Theology-Judaism.

IS
**ISRAELI DEMOCRACY.** ***Ceased.*** **Added/Corp** Universitat Tel-Aviv. Makhon Le-heker Ha-tefutsot. **VFOAT** Democracy. Vol. 1, No. 1 (Feb. 1987)-(19??). Periodical. English. qt. IDI / Israeli Democracy Institute, PO Box 4702, 91040 Jerusalem Israel. **Tel** FAX 011 972 2 635319. **LC** DS101; .I69. **DD** 956.94/005.

IT
**ITALIAN POLITICS, A REVIEW.** (POLITICA IN ITALIA / CONFERENCE GROUP ON ITALIAN POLITICS AND SOCIETY E ISTITUTO CARLO CATTANEO.). Ed. 1986-. Italian. an. Societa Editrice il Mulino, Strada Maggiore 37, 40125 Bologna Italy. **Tel** 011 39 51 256011, FAX 011 39 51 256034. **LC** JN5201; .I875.

US/0899-4684
**JACK ANDERSON CONFIDENTIAL (1987).** ***Title Change.*** (JACK ANDERSON CONFIDENTIAL.). [Jack Anderson confid.]. **VFOAT** Behind the Scenes with Jack Anderson Confidential. (1987-1992). Periodical. English. sm. Jack Anderson's Washington Letter, 1401 16th Street NW, Washington DC 20036. **DD** 320. ***Continues*** *Jack Anderson's Washington Letter, 0743-0825.* ***Continued by*** *Jack Anderson First Alert, 1060-1147.*

●US/1064-4458
**JACK ANDERSON CONFIDENTIAL (1992).** (JACK ANDERSON CONFIDENTIAL.). [Jack Anderson confid.]. (1992)-. Periodical. English. sm. $89.00. Safe Money Institute, 2212 15th Avenue West, Seattle WA 98119. **Tel** (206)281-1615. **DD** 320. ***Continues*** *Jack Anderson First Alert, 1060-1147.*

IR
**JAHAN-I ZANAN.** Persian. 50.00IR (single issue). Khiyaban-I Mubarizan Kuchah-I Nik, Shumarah-I 18, Tabaqah-I 2, Tehran Iran. **LC** AP95.P3; J34.

GW/0075-2517
**JAHRBUCH DES OFFENTLICHEN RECHTS DER GEGENWART.** Vol. 1 (1907)-. German. an (Apr.). DM368.00. JCB Mohr / Paul Siebeck, Postfach 2040, D 72010 Tuebingen Germany. **Tel** 011 49 7071 9230, FAX 011 49 7071 51104, telex 7/262872 mohr d. **ED** Peter Haberle. **LC** JF13; .O31.
**Desc:** Contains articles, reports, and news on the latest legislation.
**Ind/Abst** Index Foreign Leg. Per.; Int. Polit. Sci. Abstr.

GW
**JAHRBUCH FUER POLITIK. VFOAT** Yearbook of Politics. (1991)-. Periodical. German (summaries and/or abstracts in English). sa. Nomos Verlagsgesellschaft, Postfach 610, D-76484 Baden Baden Germany. **Tel** 011 49 7221 21040.

GW
**JAHRBUCH ZUR STAATS- UND VERWALTUNGSWISSENSCHAFT. See** Public Administration.

US/0361-6169
**JAMES SPRUNT STUDIES IN HISTORY AND POLITICAL SCIENCE, THE. See** History(General).

II/0021-4221
**JANATA. Added/Corp** Socialist Party (India). **VFOAT** Janata Annual. Vol. 1 (Jan. 26, 1946)-. Periodical. English. Forty-six times a year. $8.00 (latest issues). GG Pskikh Publishing, National House, 6 Tulloch Road, Bombay 1 India. **LC** DS401; .J27. **DD** 329.954.

US/1051-1776
**JAPAN POLITICAL RESEARCH.** [Jpn. polit. res.]. **VFOAT** Nihon Seiji Kenkyu. Vol. 21 (March 1990)-. English. an. $7.00 US; $8.00 other. Brigham Young University / Department of Political Sciences, 740 SWKT, Provo UT 84602. **Tel** (801)378-3303. **DD** 320. ***Continues*** *Newsletter of Research on Japanese Politics, 0160-1164.*

GW
**JENAER BEITRAEGE ZUR PARTEIENGESCHICHTE.** Periodical. German. Friedrich-Schiller-Universitat, Goetheallee 1, O-6900 Jena FR Germany.
**Ind/Abst** Am. Hist. Life (1968-1981).

US/0075-3904
**JOHNS HOPKINS UNIVERSITY STUDIES IN HISTORICAL AND POLITICAL SCIENCE, THE. See** Social Sciences.

II
**JOURNAL - ANDHRA PRADESH, INDIA. LEGISLATURE. LEGISLATIVE COUNCIL. Main/Corp** Andhra Pradesh, India Legislature. Legislative Council. English. India Legislature, Legislative Council Hyderabad, Andhra Pradesh, Hyderabad India. **LC** J601.A4; J32. **DD** 328.54/81/01.

FR/0021-7794
**JOURNAL DE LA PAIX.** (1963)-. Periodical. French. Eight times a year. 135.00F France; 160.00F other. Sojapax, 18 rue Couste, BP 133, 94234 Cachan Cedex France. **Tel** 011 33 1 46631030, FAX 1 46 63 7088. **UDC** 172.4:282. **Circ:** 3,500.
**Desc:** News related to war and peace.

CN
**JOURNAL DES DEBATS : COMMISSIONS PARLEMENTAIRES. Main/Corp** Quebec (Province). National Assembly. French (English). ir. 150.00Can$. Assemblee Nationale Ministere Financiere, 5 Place Quebec Bureau 195, Quebec QUE G1R 5P3 Canada. **Tel** (418)643-2754. **LC** J107; .K74. **Circ:** 300. available on microfiche.

CN/0709-3632
**JOURNAL DES DEBATS (QUEBEC).** (JOURNAL DES DEBATS / ASSEMBLEE NATIONALE.). [J. debats]. **Main/Corp** Quebec (Province) Assemblee Nationale. **VFOAT** Debats de l'Assemblee Nationale. (1975)-. French (English). ir. 115.00Can$. Assemblee Nationale Ministere Financiere, 5 Place Quebec Bureau 195, Quebec QUE G1R 5P3 Canada. **Tel** (418)643-2754. **LC** J107; .K23. **DD** 328.714/02. **Bk Rev. Ad Acc. Circ:** 150 (ctrl). ***Continues*** *Quebec (Province). National Assembly. Journal des Debats.*
**Desc:** The content shows the debates of the National Assembly of our representatives elected in the Province of Quebec.

FR/0021-8103
**JOURNAL DES SAVANTS.** [J. Savants]. **Added/Corp** Academie des Inscriptions & Belles-Lettres (France) Institut de France. (Sept. 1816)-. Periodical. French. Twice a year. 350.00F. Diffusion de Boccard, 11 rue de Medicis, 75006 Paris France. **Tel** 011 33 1 43260037. **ED** Alfred Merlin. **LC** AS161; .J7. ***Continues*** *Journal des Scavans.*
**Ind/Abst** BHA : Biblio. Hist. Art; MLA Int. Bibl. Books Artic. Mod. Lang. Lit.

CN/0709-6003
**JOURNAL DU R C M, LE. Main/Corp** Rassemblement des Citoyens de Montreal. **VAT** Journal du Rassemblement des Citoyens de Montreal. June 1978-. Periodical. French (English). Rassemblement des Citoyens de Montreal, Bureau 101/1012 rue Mont-Royal, Montreal Quebec H2J 1X6 Canada. **DD** 329.9/714/281. ***Continues*** *Bulletin Info - R. C. M., 0703-9786.*

AU/0943-4011
**JOURNAL FUER RECHTSPOLITIK.** (19??)-. German. Four times a year. $105.00. Springer-Verlag Wien, Sachsenplatz 4 6, PO Box 89, A-1201 Vienna Austria. **Tel** 011 43 1 3302415. **(Subscription address:** Springer Verlag New York Inc. / for North America, 44 Hartz Way, Secaucus NJ 07096.**)**

US/0021-969X
**JOURNAL OF CHURCH AND STATE.** [J. church state]. **Added/Corp** Baylor University. J.M. Dawson Studies in Church and State. Vol. 1 (Nov. 1959)-. Academic Scholarly Publication. English. Three times a year. $20.00 (individuals), $35.00 (institutions). Journal of Church and State, PO Box 97308, Baylor University, Waco TX 76798. **Tel** (817)755-1510. **ED** James E. Wood. **LC** BV630.A1; J6. **DD** 322/.1/05. Index available. cum. index. **Bk Rev**, (Qty: 100-125). **Ad Acc, Adv Mgr Tel** (817)755-1510. Full Page (B&W) $200.00. Half Page (B&W) $125.00. **Circ:** 1,700. available on microfilm from Williams S Hein & Co. Documents available from The Genuine Article, UMI Article Clearinghouse.
**Desc:** Interfaith, international and interdisciplinary scholarly journal. Devoted to church-state relations.
**Ind/Abst** Acad. Search (July 1993-); Am. Hist. Life (1963-); Am. Bibliogr. Slavic East Europ. Stud.; Arts Humanit. Citation Index [Full Cov.]; Book Rev. Index; Christ. Period. Index; Curr. Contents Arts Humanit.; Curr. Law Index (1980-); Educ. Adm. Abstr. (?-?); Expand. Acad. Index (1984-); Humanit. Index; Humanit. Source (Jul. 1993-); Index Book Rev. Relig.; Index Period. Artic. Relat. Law (19??-19??); INFO-SOUTH Abstr.; Int. Bibliogr. Sociol.; Leg. Resour. Index (1980-); LegalTrac (1980-); Mag. Search; Middle East Abstr. Index; Newsp. Period. Abstr. (1991-); PAIS Int. Print (1991-); Relig. Index One Period. (1959-); Relig. Theol. Abstr.; Res. Alert [Full Cov.]; Soc. Sci. Cit. Index [Select. Cov.]; West. Hist. Q.

UK/0306-3631
**JOURNAL OF COMMONWEALTH & COMPARATIVE POLITICS, THE.** [J. commonw. comp. polit.]. **VAT** Journal of Commonwealth and Comparative Politics. Vol. 12 (March 1974)-. Periodical. English. Three times a year (MAR., JULY, NOV.). $145.00. Frank Cass & Company Ltd, Newbury House, 890-900 Eastern Avenue, Newbury Park, Ilford, Essex IG2 7HH United Kingdom. **Tel** 011 44 81 599 8866, FAX 011 44 81 599 0984, telex 897719. **ED** James Manor, Richard Crook and John Wiseman. **LC** JN248; .J65. **DD** 320.9/171/241. Index available (bound in last issue). **Bk Rev. Ad Acc, Adv Mgr:** Anne Kidson. **Pr Rev. Circ:** 1000. available on microfilm and microfiche from University Microfilms International (UMI). Documents available from The Genuine Article. ***Continues*** *Journal of Commonwealth Political Studies, 0021-9908.*
**Desc:** A leading production on the comparative politics of commonwealth countries, especially those in Asia, Africa and the Caribbean.
**Ind/Abst** ABC POL SCI; Am. Hist. Life (1961-); Br. Humanit. Index; Curr. Contents Soc. Behav. Sci.; Int. Dev. Abstr.; Int. Polit. Sci. Abstr.; Leis. Recreat. Tour. Abstr.; Middle East Abstr. Index; Res. Alert [Full Cov.]; Rural Dev. Abstr.; Soc. Plann. Policy Dev. Abstr.; Soc. Sci. Cit. Index [Full Cov.]; Sociol. Abstr.; World Agric. Econ.

II/0022-0043
**JOURNAL OF CONSTITUTIONAL AND PARLIAMENTARY STUDIES. See** Law.

US/1045-5736
**JOURNAL OF DEMOCRACY.** [J. democr.]. **Added/Corp** National Endowment for Democracy (U.S.). Vol. 1, No. 1 (Winter 1990)-. Periodical. English. Four times a year. $55.00 US; $58.80 Canada and Mexico; $62.70 other. Johns Hopkins University Press, 2715 North Charles Street, Baltimore MD 21218-4319. **Tel** (410)516-6987, FAX (410)516-6968. **ED** Marc F. Plattner and Larry Diamond. **LC** JF1051; .J68. **DD** 321.8/05. **[CCC].** Index available. **Bk Rev. Ad Acc. Circ:** 2,000.
**Desc:** Features articles concerning the problems and prospects of achieving and/or maintaining democratic governments abroad.
**Ind/Abst** ABC POL SCI; Am. Bibliogr. Slavic East Europ. Stud.; Hum. Rights Intern. Rep.; Middle East J.

KO
**JOURNAL OF EAST AND WEST STUDIES.** **Added/Corp** Yonse Taehakkyo. Tongso Munje Yonguwon. **VFOAT** Tongso Yongu. Vol. 1 (1973)-. Periodical. English. sa. $8.10 Korea; $19.10 Pan American countries; $17.10 other. Institute of East and West Studies, Yonsei University, Seodaemoon Gu Seoul S Korea. **Tel** (02) 392-0131, telex K29127. **ED** Dalchoong Kim, Hwang-Joe Kim, Euisoon Shin, and Nancy Undewood. **LC** CB251; .J68. cum. index. **Circ:** 900.
**Desc:** Welcomes articles in all disciplines pertinent to East-West relations, area studies and contemporary global issues.
**Ind/Abst** Econ. Lit. Index; Int. Bibliogr. Sociol.

II
**JOURNAL OF GOVERNMENT AND POLITICAL STUDIES.** V. 1- Sept. 1976-. Periodical. English. Rs10.00 India; $3.00 US. Punjabi University Department of Political Science, Editorial Office, Patiala 147002 India. **LC** JQ201; .J63. **DD** 320/.05.
**Ind/Abst** Int. Polit. Sci. Abstr.

US/0228-6939
**JOURNAL OF HISTORY AND POLITICS.** **See** History(General).

II
**JOURNAL OF INDIAN SCHOOL OF POLITICAL ECONOMY.** **See** Economics.

GW/0932-4569
**JOURNAL OF INSTITUTIONAL AND THEORETICAL ECONOMICS : JITE.** **See** Social Sciences.

US/0749-2227
**JOURNAL OF LAW & POLITICS.** **See** Law.

US/0738-7997
**JOURNAL OF NORTHEAST ASIAN STUDIES.** [J. northeast Asian stud.]. **VFOAT** Tung Pei Ya-Chou yen Chiu; Hokuto Ajia Kenkyu; Tongbuk Asea Yongu. Vol. 1, No. 1 (March 1982)-. Periodical. English. Four times a year. Fl153.00 (individual), Fl278.75 (institution). Transaction Publishers / Rutgers State University, New Brunswick NJ 08903. **Tel** (908)932-2280 Ext. 105, FAX (908)932-3138. **ED** Gaston J Sigur and Young C Kim. **LC** DS501; .J647. **DD** 951/.005. **UDC** 951/952. **[CCC]. Ad Acc. Circ:** 800. available on labels. Documents available from UMI Article Clearinghouse.
**Desc:** Analyses of social, political, economic, and military developments in post-World War Two Northeast Asia and of external factors likely to have a significant impact on China, Japan, and Korea.
**Ind/Abst** Am. Hist. Life (1982-); Am. Bibliogr. Slavic East Europ. Stud.; Asia.-Pac. Econ. Lit.; Expand. Acad. Index (1992-); Geogr. Abstr. Human Geogr.; Int. Dev. Abstr.; Int. Polit. Sci. Abstr.; Middle East Abstr. Index; Newsp. Period. Abstr. (1992-); PAIS Int. Print (1991-).

US/0276-8739
**JOURNAL OF POLICY ANALYSIS AND MANAGEMENT.** (JOURNAL OF POLICY ANALYSIS AND MANAGEMENT : THE JOURNAL OF THE ASSOCIATION FOR PUBLIC POLICY ANALYSIS AND MANAGEMENT.). [J. policy anal. manage.]. **Added/Corp** Association for Public Policy Analysis and Management (U.S.). Vol. 1, No. 1 (Fall 1981)-. Periodical. English. Six times a year. $260.00 US; $300.00 Canada and Mexico; $315.00 other. John Wiley & Sons, Inc., 605 Third Avenue, New York NY 10158-0012. **Tel** (212)850-6000, (212)850-6645, FAX (212)850-6088, telex 12-7063. **(Subscription address:** John Wiley & Sons / England, Baffins Lane, Chichester, West Sussex PO19 1UD England.**) ED** Lee S. Friedman. **LC** H97; .J68. **DD** 353.07/2/05. **NLM** W1 JO837I. **[CCC]. Pr Rev.** available on microfilm and microfiche from University Microfilms International (UMI). Documents available from The Genuine Article, UMI Article Clearinghouse. ***Formed by the union of*** *Policy Analysis, 0098-2067* ***and*** *Public Policy, 0033-3646.*
**Desc:** Encompasses issues and practices in policy analysis and public management. Listed among the contributors are economists, public managers and operations researchers. Features book reviews and discussing ideas and issues of importance to practitioners, researchers and academics.
**Ind/Abst** ABC POL SCI; Acad. Abstr. Full Text Elite (Jan. 1992-); Acad. Abstr. (Jan. 1992-); Acad. Search (Jan. 1992-); Am. Hist. Life (1986-); Bus. Index (1985-); Curr. Contents Soc. Behav. Sci.; Econ. Lit. Index; Energy Res. Abstr. (Dec. 1981-); Expand. Acad. Index (1984-); Gen. BusinessFile (1985-); Gen. Period. Index (1985-); Hospit. Health Admin. Index; Hum. Resour. Abstr.; INFO-SOUTH Abstr.; Int. Bibliogr. Sociol.; J. Econ. Lit.; J. Plan. Lit.; Mag. Search; Middle East Abstr. Index; Newsp. Period. Abstr. (1990-); PAIS Int. Print (1991-); Res. Alert [Full Cov.]; Risk Abstr.; Sage Public Adm. Abstr.; Soc. Plann. Policy Dev. Abstr.; Soc. Sci. Source (Jan. 1992-); Soc. Sci. Cit. Index [Full Cov.]; Soc. Sci. Index; Soc. Sci. Index Fulltext (Winter 1989-) [Full Txt.]; Soc. Work Abstr. (Summer 1987-?) [Select. Cov.]; Sociol. Abstr.; Urban Aff. Abstr.

US/0898-0306
**JOURNAL OF POLICY HISTORY.** (JOURNAL OF POLICY HISTORY : JPH.). [J. policy hist.]. **VFOAT** JPH. Vol. 1, No. 1 (1989)-. Periodical. English. qt. $40.00 (institutions), $27.50 (individuals) US; $45.00 (institutions), $32.50 (individuals) other. Pennsylvania State University Press, 820 North University Drive, Suite C, University Park PA 16802-1003. **Tel** (814)865-1327, (800)326-9180, FAX (814)863-1408. **LC** H96; .J66. **DD** 320.6/0973/05. **CODEN** JPHIEV. **[CCC].** available on microfilm and microfiche from University Microfilms International (UMI).
**Ind/Abst** Am. Hist. Life (1989-); Soc. Plann. Policy Dev. Abstr.

US/0098-4612
**JOURNAL OF POLITICAL SCIENCE (CLEMSON).** (JOURNAL OF POLITICAL SCIENCE.). [J. polit. sci.]. **Added/Corp** South Carolina Political Science Association. Vol. 1 (1973)-. Periodical. English. an. $16.00. Clemson University / Political Science, Department of Political Science, Clemson SC 29631. **Tel** (803)656-3233. **ED** Martin Slann. **LC** JA1; .J58. **DD** 320/.05. **Pr Rev. Circ:** 300. ***Continues*** *South Carolina Journal of Political Science.*
**Desc:** A publication that includes all the sub-discipline areas of political science and prefers brief articles that are written in readable and understandable prose.
**Ind/Abst** ABC POL SCI; Am. Hist. Life (1976-).

II/0047-2700
**JOURNAL OF POLITICAL STUDIES.** **Added/Corp** D.A.V. College, Jullundur, India. Post-Graduate Dept. of Political Science. (19??)-. Periodical. English. sa. $10.00. Post-Graduate Department of Political Science, D.A.V., Jullundur, India. **(Subscription address:** Prints India, 11 Darya Ganj, New Delhi, 110002 India, (Phone: 011 91 11 3268645)**) LC** JQ201; .J67. **DD** 320/.05.

US/0022-3816
**JOURNAL OF POLITICS, THE.** [J. polit.]. **Added/Corp** Southern Political Science Association. University of Florida. **VFOAT** JP. Vol. 1 (Feb. 1939)-. Periodical. English. qt (Feb., May, Aug. and Nov.). $50.00 (institutions), $25.00 (individuals) US; add $10.00 postage other. University of Texas Press, PO Box 7819, Austin TX 78713. **Tel** (512)471-4531, FAX (512)320-0668, telex 776453 UTEXPRES AUS. **ED** Cecil Eubanks and Ronald Weber. **LC** JA1; .J6. **DD** 320.5. **[CCC]. Bk Rev. Ad Acc. Pr Rev. Circ:** 3,723 (ctrl). available on microfilm and microfiche from University Microfilms International (UMI). Documents available from The Genuine Article, UMI Article Clearinghouse. ***Supersedes*** *Southern Political Science Association. Proceedings.*
**Desc:** The oldest regional Political Science journal including a broad range for approaches to American, comparative, and international political science. The journal of the Southern Political Science Association.
**Ind/Abst** ABC POL SCI; Acad. Abstr. Full Text Elite (July 1990-); Acad. Abstr. (July 1990-); Acad. Ind. [Computer File] (1987-); Acad. Search (July 1990-); Am. Hist. Life (1954-); Am. Bibliogr. Slavic East Europ. Stud.; Annu. Bibliogr. Engl. Lang. Lit. (1954-); Book Rev. Index (1954-); Commun. Abstr. (?-?); Expand. Acad. Index (1987-); Index Period. Artic. Relat. Law; INFO-SOUTH Abstr.; Int. Bibliogr. Sociol.; Int. Polit. Sci. Abstr.; J. Plan. Lit.; Mag. Search; Middle East Abstr. Index; Newsp. Period. Abstr. (1991-); PAIS Int. Print (1991-?); Res. Alert [Full Cov.]; Res. High. Educ. Abstr.; Soc. Plann. Policy Dev. Abstr.; Soc. Sci. Source (Jul. 1990-); Soc. Sci. Cit. Index [Full Cov.]; Soc. Sci. Index; Soc. Sci. Index Fulltext (Nov. 1988-) [Full Txt.]; Sociol. Abstr.; Sociol. Educ. Abstr.; U.S. Polit. Sci. Doc.; West. Hist. Q.

UK/0143-814X
**JOURNAL OF PUBLIC POLICY.** [J. public policy]. Vol. 1, Pt. 1 (Feb. 1981)-. Academic Scholarly Publication. English. Three times a year. $109.00 US, Canada and Mexico; £62.00 other. Cambridge University Press, The Edinburgh Building, Shaftesbury Road, Cambridge CB2 2RU United Kingdom. **Tel** 011 44 223 312393, FAX 011 44 223 325959. **(Subscription address:** Cambridge University Press / North America, 110 Midland Avenue, Port Chester NY 10573.**) ED** Richard Rose. **LC** H96; .J68. **DD** 361.6/1/05. **[CCC]. Bk Rev.** available on microfilm and microfiche from University Microfilms International (UMI).
**Desc:** Relates the world of social science ideas to the problems that face governments in advanced industrial societies. Publishes articles that meet the twin criteria of achieving a high standard of scholarship and making significant statements about major problems of contemporary societies. Articles deal with broad questions of relevance to social scientists and policy-makers in America, Europe, Japan and other advanced industrial nations. The journal also publishes critical analyses of ideas currently in vogue among academics or practitioners of public policy.
**Ind/Abst** ABC POL SCI; Appl. Soc. Sci. Index Abstr.; Geogr. Abstr. Human Geogr.; Hum. Resour. Abstr. (?-?); Int. Bibliogr. Sociol.; Int. Dev. Abstr.; Int. Polit. Sci. Abstr.; Middle East Abstr. Index; PAIS Int. Print (1991-); Res. High. Educ. Abstr.; Sage Public Adm. Abstr.; Soc. Plann. Policy Dev. Abstr.; Sociol. Abstr.; Sociol. Educ. Abstr.

US/0275-5327
**JOURNAL OF SOUTHERN AFRICAN AFFAIRS.** [J. South. Afr. aff.]. V. 1- Oct. 1976-. Periodical. English. qt. Kings Court Communications, PO Box 429, Brunswick OH 44212. **LC** DT727; .J67. **DD** 052.
**Ind/Abst** Am. Hist. Life (1976-1980); Annu. Bibliogr. Engl. Lang. Lit.

US/1043-2248
**JOURNAL OF STATE GOVERNMENT, THE.** ***Title Change.*** (THE JOURNAL OF STATE GOVERNMENT / NATIONAL CONFERENCE OF STATE LEGISLATURES [AND] THE COUNCIL OF STATE GOVERNMENTS.). [J. state gov.]. **Added/Corp** National Conference of State Legislatures. Council of State Governments. National Governors' Association. Vol. 59, No. 1 (Spring 1986)-(1992). Periodical. English. qt. Council of State Governments, PO Box 11910, Iron Works Pike, Lexington KY 40578-1910. **Tel** (800)800-1910, (606)231-1850. **ED** Dag Ryen and Elaine Knapp. **LC** JK2403; .S7. **DD** 328.73. **Ad Acc. Circ:** 5,500. available on microfilm and microfiche from University Microfilms International (UMI). Documents available from The Genuine Article, UMI Article Clearinghouse. ***Continues*** *State Government (Denver, Colo.), 0039-0097.* ***Continued by*** *Spectrum: The Journal of State Government.*
**Desc:** Provides a forum for discussion of state government. Highlights innovations, trends and issues of interest to public officials, community leaders, teachers, students, libraries and anyone concerned with governmental issues.
**Ind/Abst** ABC POL SCI; ABI/INFORM Glob. Ed.; ABI Inform Ondisc (Fall 1978-); Acad. Abstr. Full Text Elite (Jan. 1992-July 1992); Acad. Abstr. (Jan. 1992-Aug. 1992); Acad. Search (Jan. 1992-July 1992); Am. Hist. Life (1977-); Crim. Justice Abstr.; Curr. Contents Soc. Behav. Sci.; Expand. Acad. Index (1986-); Gen. Period. Index (1986-); Health Plan. Adminis.; INFO-SOUTH Abstr.; Int. Polit. Sci. Abstr.; Mag. Search; Newsp. Period. Abstr. (1991-); PAIS Int. Print; Res. Alert [Full Cov.]; Soc. Sci. Source (Jan. 1992-); Soc. Sci. Cit. Index (19??-19??) [Full Cov.]; Soc. Sci. Index; Soc. Sci. Index Fulltext (Sept. 1987-June 1992) [Full Txt.].

SI
**JOURNAL OF THE POLITICAL SCIENCE SOCIETY.** **Main/Corp** Singapore (City) University Political Science Society. (1970/71)-. English. ir. Singapore University / Department of Political Science, Bukit Timak Road, Singapore.

US
**JOURNAL OF THE SENATE OF THE UNITED STATES OF AMERICA.** **Main/Corp** United States. Congress. Senate. **VFOAT** Senate Journal. Began with 1st Congress, March 4/Sept. 1789. English. an. **LC** KF45; .A22. **DD** 328.73/01. available on microfiche (Vols. for 97th Congress, 2nd session, Jan. 25, 1982@ distributed to some depositories).

UK/0951-6298
**JOURNAL OF THEORETICAL POLITICS.** [J. theor. polit.]. Vol. 1, No. 1 (Jan. 1989)-. Periodical. English. qt. £105.00. Sage Publications Ltd., 6 Bonhill Street, London EC2A 4PU, UK. **Tel** 071 374 0645, FAX 071 374 8741, telex 296207 SAGE G. **ED** Richard Kimber. **LC** JA1.A1; J68. **DD** 320/.05. **CODEN** JTPOEF. **Acid Free.**
**Desc:** A new international journal which aims to foster the development of theory in the study of the political process. The journal publishes articles on theoretical topics, and presents new theoretical work in accessible form for social scientists.
**Ind/Abst** ABC POL SCI; Int. Bibliogr. Sociol.; Int. Polit. Sci. Abstr.; Soc. Plann. Policy Dev. Abstr.; Soc. Sci. Cit. Index [Full Cov.].

FR/0429-3088
**JOURNAL OFFICIEL DE LA REPUBLIQUE FRANCAISE. DEBATS PARLEMENTAIRES, ASSEMBLEE NATIONALE (CUMULATIF).** (DEBATS DE L'ASSEMBLEE NATIONALE.). [J. off. Repub. fr., Debats parlem., Assem. natl.]. **Main/Corp** France. Parlement (1946- ). Assemblee Nationale. Began in 1960. French. ir. Direction des Journaux Officiels, 26 rue Desaix, 75727 Paris Cedex 15 France. **Tel** 011 33 1 40587500. **LC** J341; .K25C. **DD** 328.44/02.

US/1062-6255
**JUST PEACE (WASHINGTON, D.C.).** **See** Women's Interests.

JA/0388-886X
**KANSAI UNIVERSITY REVIEW OF LAW AND POLITICS.** See Law.

US/0732-1074
**KAR INTERNATIONAL.** (KAR INTERNATIONAL / ORGANIZATION OF IRANIAN PEOPLE'S FEDAII GUERRILLAS, MAJORITY.). Fall 1980-. Periodical. Persian. bm. $10.00 for 10 issues. Kar International, PO Box 66156, Los Angeles CA 90066. **LC** DS318.8; .K37. **DD** 324.255/075.

NP
**KATHMANDU REVIEW.** See Economics.

UK
**KAYHAN.** Persian. wk. $110.00. Kayhan Publishing Ltd., 271-273 King Street, London House, London W6 9LZ England. **Tel** 11 44 81 748 5300. **ED** Mustapha Mesbahzadeh. **Ad Acc. Circ:** 25,000 per week (ctrl).
**Desc:** Quality London-based Persian language weekly newspaper aimed at three million Iranians who live outside Iran. An authoritative source for political, economic and cultural news and editorials on Iran and the Iranian community outside Iran. It is an effective advertising medium to reach Iranians world wide.

UK/0950-6128
**KEESING'S RECORD OF WORLD EVENTS.** (KEESING'S RECORD OF WORLD EVENTS / LONGMAN.). [Keesing's rec. world events]. **VFOAT** Record of World Events. Vol. 33, No. 1 (Jan. 1987)-. Periodical. English. mo. £146.00 Europe; $347.00 US; £169.00 other (institutions). Longman Group Ltd., Fourth Avenue, Longman House, Harlow Essex CM19 5SR England. **Tel** 011 44 279 429655, FAX 011 44 279 431059, telex 81259. **(Subscription address:** Longman Group Ltd., Subscription Office, PO Box 1584, Birmingham AL 35201-1584.**)** **LC** D410; .K4. **DD** 909.82. **[CCC].** Index available. available on microfilm from University Microfilms International (UMI). ***Continues*** *Keesing's Contemporary Archives, 0022-9679.*
**Desc:** Each monthly issue contains a comprehensive digest of the previous month's world news in which over 100 articles provide a full record of the month as a whole.

US/0095-6856
**KENTUCKY PRIMARY AND GENERAL ELECTION.** (KENTUCKY PRIMARY AND GENERAL ELECTION; REPORT.). **Main/Corp** Kentucky. Registry of Election Finance. 1969-. English. 310 West Liberty Street, Louisville KY 40202. **LC** JK1991; .K452A. **DD** 329/.025. ***Formed by the union of*** *Kentucky General Election* ***and*** *Kentucky Primary Election.*

US/0023-1770
**KIPLINGER WASHINGTON LETTER, THE.** **Added/Corp** Kiplinger Washington Agency, Inc. Kiplinger Washington Editors, Inc. No. 1 (Sept. 29, 1923)-. Newsletter. English. wk (52 issues). $68.00 (one year), $120.00 (two year). Kiplinger Washington Editors, 1729 H Street Northwest, Washington DC 20006. **Tel** (202)887-6400, (800)544-0155, FAX (202)331-1206. **(Subscription address:** Kiplinger Washington Editors, 3401 East West Highway, c/o Rick Topolski, Editors Park MD 20782.**)** **ED** Austin and Knight Kiplinger. **LC** HC101; .K5. **Circ:** 388,000.
**Desc:** Covers Washington politics and its impact on business.

●US/1075-6671
**KIPLINGER'S RETIREMENT REPORT.** [Kiplinger's retire. rep.]. Vol. 1, No. 1 (Feb. 1994)-. Periodical. English. mo. $59.95 (one year), $89.95 (two year). Kiplinger Washington Editors, 1729 H Street Northwest, Washington DC 20006. **Tel** (202)887-6400, (800)544-0155, FAX (202)331-1206. **DD** 332.

JA/0023-2793
**KOKKA GAKKAI ZASSHI.** **Added/Corp** Kokka Gakkai. **VFOAT** Zasshi; Journal of the Association of Political and Social Sciences. Vol. 1 (Mar. 1887)-. Periodical. Japanese (table of contents in English). bm. $270.00. **(Subscription address:** Kyowa Book Company Inc., 1 38 Kanda Jinbocho Chiyoda-ku, Tokyo 101 Japan.**)**
**Ind/Abst** Am. Hist. Life (1954-).

GW/0075-6539
**KOLNER SCHRIFTEN ZUR POLITISCHEN WISSENSCHAFT.** **Added/Corp** Cologne. Universitat. Forschungsinstitut fuer Politische Wissenschaft und Europaische Fragen. Vol. 1-5, (1964)-(1965); New Series, Vol. 1 (1969)-. Monographic series. German. ir. Price varies per volume. Duncker und Humblot Verlag, Postfach 410329, D-12113 Berlin Germany. **Tel** 011 49 30 79000612, 011 49 30 79000613.

DK
**KOMMUNAL HANDBOGEN.** See Public Administration.

DK/0904-339X
**KOMMUNALVALGENE I KOMMUNER OG AMTSKOMMUNER.** **Added/Corp** Danmarks Statistik. (19??)-. Danish. Danmarks Statistik, Sejrgade 11, DK-2100 Copenhagen Denmark. **Tel** 011 45 3 9173917, FAX 011 45 31 18 48 01, telex 1 62 36. **LC** JS6168.5; .K66.

GW
**KONSERVATIV HEUTE.** Periodical. German. 18.00. Verlag fur Konservative Publizistik, Gorresplatz 5-7, W-5400 Koblenz Germany. **LC** JA14; .K66.

GW/0176-4179
**KONTINENT (BERLIN, GERMANY).** (KONTINENT.). Periodical. German (Russian). qt. DM40.00 Germany; $36.00 (surface mail) US. Burg Verlag GmbH, Untere AU 41, D 74343 Sachsenheim Germany. **ED** Cornelia Gerstenmaier Djilas, A Rinsburg, E Kusnezow. **LC** DJK1; .K66. Index available. cum. index. **Bk Rev. Ad Acc. Circ:** 6,500 (ctrl).
**Desc:** A journal in which Soviet and other eastern European dissidents and regime critics can voice their views.

US/1048-2539
**KOREA REPORT.** [Korea rep.]. **Added/Corp** Korea Information & Resource Center. Vol. 1, No. 1 (Mar. 1987)-. Periodical. English. Four times a year (March, June, Sept., Dec.). $12.00 US; $18.00 other. Korea Information Resource Center, 1314 14th Street NW, Suite 5, Washington DC 20005. **Tel** (202) 387-2551, FAX (202)387-2984. **DD** 320.
**Ind/Abst** Hum. Rights Intern. Rep.

KO
**KOREAN SIGNAL.** Oct./Dec. 1975-. English. $13.80. Save-The-Nation National Council, IP Box 3385, Seoul Korea. **LC** DS901; .K85. **DD** 951.9/005.

KO
**KUKCHAEK YONGU.** First issue (Summer, 1984)-. Periodical. Korean. qt. W10.000. Minju Chonguidang Kukchaek Yonguso, 155-2 Kwanhun-dong Chongno-ku, Seoul Korea. **LC** DS922; .K838.

CN/0316-3393
**L. A. W. G. LETTER.** **Main/Corp** Latin American Working Group. V. 2, No. 1/2- Mar./Apr. 1974-. Periodical. English. Latin American Working Group, 603 Parliament Street, Toronto Ontario M4X 1P9 Canada. **Tel** (416)966-4773, FAX (416)921-0071. **DD** 320.9/8/03. ctrl circ. ***Continues*** *L. A. W. G. Newsletter, 0316-2850.*
**Ind/Abst** Hum. Rights Intern. Rep.

UK
**LABOUR PARTY ANNUAL REPORT.** English. an (Edition year publlished in following year). £40.00 UK; £60.00 other. Labour Party, 150 Walworth Road, London SE17 1JT England. **Tel** 011 44 701 1234, FAX 011 44 71 234 3416.

UK
**LAISSEZ-FAIRE.** ***Ceased.*** **Added/Corp** International Freedom Foundation. Vol. 1, No. 1 (Summer 1991)-(1992). Periodical. English. qt. IFF International Freedom Foundation, 150 Regent Street, Suite 500, Ches House, London W1R 5FA England. **Tel** 32 2 646 6561, FAX 32 2 646 6598, . ***Continues*** *European Freedom Review, 0954-979X.*

US/0895-8505
**LARKSPUR REPORT, THE.** Periodical. English. mo. $125.00. The Larkspur Report, c/o Bill Bradley, PO Box 221364, Sacramento CA 95822. **DD** 324.

US/0891-0650
**LAS AMERICAS JOURNAL.** [Am. j.]. **Added/Corp** Latin America Information Line. (19??)-. Periodical. English. Twelve times a year. $40.00. Latin America Information Line, 1219 Westlake Avenue North, Suite 104, Seattle WA 98109. **Tel** (206)283-0181. **DD** 327.

US/0090-9416
**LATIN AMERICAN INDEX.** **Main/Corp** Latin American Index, Ltd. Vol. 5, No. 14 (July 16/31, 1977)-. Periodical. English. sm (23 per year). $399.00 US; $409.00 Canada and Mexico; $429.00 other. Welt Publishing Company, 1413 K Street NW, Suite 1400, Washington DC 20005. **Tel** (202)371-0555, FAX (202)408-9369, telex 281409 TAOA UR. **LC** F1401; .L327. **DD** 980/.005. **Bk Rev**, (Qty: 5 per year). **Ad Acc, Adv Mgr:** Justin Ford. ***Continues*** *Latin American Index, 0090-9416.*
**Desc:** Features the latest economic and political developments in Mexico, the Caribbean, and Central and South America with information on the latest inter-American trends.

US/1062-7421
**LAW AND POLITICS BOOK REVIEW.** See Law.

GW/0341-6151
**LAW AND STATE.** ***Ceased.*** See Law-International Law.

US/8755-2620
**LEADER IN ACTION.** See Education-Higher Education.

US/0160-1857
**LEFT CURVE.** [Left curve]. (1974)-. Periodical. English. Three times a year. $30.00 (one year), $55.00 (two year), $75.00 (three year)*institution; $20.00 (one year), $35.00 (two year), $50.00*(three year) individual. Left Curve, PO Box 472, Oakland CA 94604. **Tel** (510)763-7193. **ED** C Polony (editor's address: 410 Webster Street, Oakland CA). **LC** NX180.R45; L43. **Bk Rev. Ad Acc, Adv Mgr:** same as editor. **Circ:** 1,200. available on microfilm from University Microfilms International (UMI).
**Desc:** An artist produced critical journal that addresses the problems of culture forms emerging from the crises of modernity that strive to be independent from the control of dominant institutions, and free from the shackles of instrumental rationality.
**Ind/Abst** Altern. Press Index; ARTbibliogr. Mod.; Left Index.

●CN/1192-1927
**LEFT HISTORY.** **Added/Corp** Queen's University (Kingston, Ont.). Dept. of History. Vol. 1, No. 1 (1993)-. Periodical. English. sa. 28.00Can$ institutions; 14.00Can$ individuals. Queens University Department of History, Kingston Ontario, K7L 3N6 Canada. **Tel** (613)531-8954, (613)545-2150, FAX (613)545-6298.

PO/0871-9497
**LEGISLACAO LISBOA. (1991).** [Legislacao Lisb., 1991]. **VFOAT** Cadernos de Ciencia de Legislacao. (1991)-. Periodical. Multiple languages. Three times a year. $20.00. Institute Nac. Admin/Centro Est, Palacio dos Marqueses Pombal, 2780 Oeiras Portugal. **Tel** 011 351 1 4432179, FAX 011 351 1 4432750. **UDC** 340.

US/0362-9805
**LEGISLATIVE STUDIES QUARTERLY.** [Legis. stud. q.]. **Added/Corp** University of Iowa. Comparative Legislative Research Center. Vol. 1, (Feb. 1976)-. Periodical. English. Four times a year (Feb., May, Aug., Nov.). $35.00 (individuals); $70.00 (institutions). Comparative Legislative Research, University of Iowa, 349 Schaeffer Hall, Iowa City IA 52242. **Tel** (319)335-2361. **LC** JF501; .L42. **DD** 328/.3/05. **[CCC].** Index available. cum. index. **Bk Rev. Pr Rev. Circ:** 1,000 (ctrl). available on microfilm and microfiche from University Microfilms International (UMI). Documents available from The Genuine Article.
**Desc:** International journal devoted to publication of research on representative assemblies.
**Ind/Abst** ABC POL SCI; Commun. Abstr.; Curr. Contents Soc. Behav. Sci.; Int. Polit. Sci. Abstr.; Middle East Abstr. Index; Res. Alert [Full Cov.]; Risk Abstr.; Sage Public Adm. Abstr.; Soc. Sci. Cit. Index [Full Cov.]; U.S. Polit. Sci. Doc.

FR/0996-9888
**LETTRE AFRIQUE EXPANSION, LA.** [Lett. Afr. expans.]. (1987)-. Newsletter. French. wk. 3800.00F. Le Moniteur, 17 rue d'Uzes, 75002 Paris France. **Tel** 011 33 1 40133381, FAX 011 33 1 40419495. **UDC** 338(6). **Bk Rev**, (Qty: 10). **Ad Acc. Circ:** 1,200 (ctrl). ***Continues*** *La Lettre des Marches Afrique Expansion, 1153-5954.*

FR/0298-3958
**LETTRE D'EUROPE AVENIR, LA.** [Lett. Eur. avenir]. (1986)-. Periodical. French. qt. 150.00F (members), 200.00F (nonmembers). Association Europe Avenir, 6 rue R Turquan, 75016 Paris France. **Tel** 011 33 1 45278976. **UDC** 32(4).

FR
**LETTRE DU CONTINENT : LC, LA.** See Economics.

US
**LIBERATION.** Periodical. English.

US/0047-4509
**LIBERTARIAN ANALYSIS.** **Added/Corp** Paul Avrich Collection (Library of Congress). Vol. 1 No. 1 (1970)-. Periodical. English. qt. $4.00. Libertarian Analysis, PO Box 210 Village Station, New York NY 10014. **LC** JC571; .L542. **DD** 320.5/05.

US/0272-5959
**LIBERTARIAN DIGEST, THE.** Vol. 1, No. 1 (Jan. 1981)-. Periodical. English. bm. $10.00. Libertarian Digest, 102 Mt Vernon Avenue, Alexandria VA 22301. **Tel** (703)680-9464. **ED** Fred Foldvary. **LC** JC571; .L5426. **DD** 320.5/12. **Bk Rev. Ad Acc. Circ:** 200 (ctrl). available on microfiche.
**Desc:** Summaries of articles in libertarian publications.

CN/0713-021X
**LIBERTARIAN VOICE.** [Libert. voice]. Vol. 1, No. 1 (Nov. 1981)-. Periodical. English. Libertarian Voice SLS, Suite 203/127 Yonge Street, Toronto Ontario M5C 2W4 Canada. **DD** 320.5/12.

GW/0341-9762
**LIBERTAS.** [Libertas]. (1976)-. Periodical. Multiple languages. Four times a year. DM60.00. Libertas Europlisches Institut GmBh, Hintere Gasse 35/1, D-71063 Sindelfingen, Germany. **Tel** 07031 81 1855, FAX 07031 81 3693. **ED** Hans Juergen Zahorka. **UDC** 327(4). **Bk Rev. Ad Acc, Adv Mgr:** Ute Hirschburger, **Tel** 07031 81 1855. **Acid Free. Circ:** 1,400.
**Desc:** A magazine on european and international politics,

# Political Science

economy, social and cultural trends, from a point of view in favor of European integration, transatlantic, partnership, and improved North and South relations. **Ind/Abst** PAIS Int. Print; Soc. Plann. Policy Dev. Abstr.

US/0145-7667
**LIBERTY BELL (REEDY, W. VA.).** (THE LIBERTY BELL.). (19??)-. Periodical. English. mo. $55.00 US; $65.00 other. Liberty Bell Publications, PO Box 21, Reedy WV 25270. **Tel** (304)927-4486. **ED** George P Dietz. **LC** PAR. **DD** 322. **Bk Rev**. available on microfilm from University Microfilms International (UMI).

US/0894-1408
**LIBERTY (PORT TOWNSEND, WASH.).** (LIBERTY.). [Liberty]. Vol. 1, No. 1 (Aug. 1987)-. Periodical. English. bm. $19.50 (one year), $35.00 (two year). Liberty, Circulation Department, PO Box 1167, Port Townsend WA 98368. **Tel** (206)385-5097. **ED** R. W. Bradford, Murray N. Rothbard, Karl Hess, Stephen Cox and David Ramsay Steele. **LC** WMLC 93/4369. **DD** 320. **Bk Rev**. **Ad Acc**. **Circ:** 4,200.
**Desc:** Review of ideas, culture and politics written mostly from a libertarian/classical liberal perspective.
**Ind/Abst** Index Period. Artic. Relat. Law.

US/1046-7912
**LIES OF OUR TIMES.** [Lies our times]. **Added/Corp** Institute for Media Analysis. **VFOAT** LOOT. Vol. 1 No. 1 (Jan. 1990)-. Periodical. English. mo (except Feb. and Aug.). $28.00 (1 year), $52.00 (2 year), $72.00 (3 year) US; $36.00 (1 year), $66.00 (2 year), $94.00 (3 year) Canada and Mexico; $40.00 (1 year), $74.00 (2 year), $106.00 (3 year). Sheridan Square Press Inc., 145 West 4th Street, New York NY 10012. **Tel** (212)254-1061, FAX (212)254-9598. **ED** Ellen Ray, Edward S. Herman, William H. Schaap. **LC** PN4888.P6; L54. **DD** 302. Index available. available on microfilm and microfiche from University Microfilms International (UMI).
**Desc:** Timely periodical devoted to the analysis of misinformation, disinformation, and propaganda in the major media of this country.
**Ind/Abst** Altern. Press Index (199?-).

●US/1065-0377
**LIMBAUGH LETTER, THE.** [Limbaugh lett.]. Vol. 1, No. 1 (Oct. 1992)-. Periodical. English. Twelve times a year. $29.95. Limbaugh Letter, PO Box 420058, Palm Coast FL 32142. **Tel** (800)829-5386. **DD** 320.

AU
**LISTY (BLATTER).** Periodical. German. 51.00. **LC** DB215.6; .L563. **DD** 320.9/437/04.

US/1068-7149
**LITIGATION UNDER THE FEDERAL OPEN GOVERNMENT LAWS.** (LITIGATION UNDER THE FEDERAL OPEN GOVERNMENT LAWS : THE FREEDOM OF INFORMATION ACT, THE PRIVACY ACT, THE GOVERNMENT IN THE SUNSHINE ACT, THE FEDERAL ADVISORY COMMITTEE ACT.). [Litig. fed. open gov. laws]. **Added/Corp** American Civil Liberties Union Foundation. 16th Edition (1991)-. English. an (June). $45.00. American Civil Liberties Union / Washington, 122 Maryland Avenue Northeast, Washington DC 20002. **Tel** (202)544-1681, FAX (202)546-0738. **LC** KF5753; .L572. **DD** 342.73/0853; 347.302853. **Continues** Litigation Under the Federal Freedom of Information Act and Privacy Act, 0748-8270.

US/1057-0853
**LOBBY MONITOR, THE.** [Lobby monit.]. **Added/Corp** ARC-Advocacy Research Corp. (1991)-. Periodical. English. bw. $249.00. Arc-Advocacy Research Corporation, PO Box 30435, Bethseda MD 20824. **DD** 324.

US/1058-2762
**LOBBYING & INFLUENCE ALERT.** [Lobby. influ. alert]. **VFOAT** Lobbying and Influence Alert. Vol. 1, No. 1 (Sept. 1991)-. Periodical. English. mo. $348.00. Global Success Corporation, 2400 Ninth Street North, Suite 450, Naples FL 33940. **Tel** (813)261-4335, FAX (813)261-6713. **DD** 328.

CN/1184-0471
**LOBBYISTS REGISTRATION ACT ANNUAL REPORT.** (LOBBYISTS REGISTRATION ACT ANNUAL REPORT FOR THE YEAR ENDED MARCH 31 ..). [Lobby. Regist. Act annu. rep.]. **Main/Corp** Canada. Consumer and Corporate Affairs. **VFOAT** Loi sur l'Enregistrement des Lobbyistes Rapport Annuel pour l'Exercice Termine le 31 Mars ... . (1990)-. English (French). **DD** 324.4/097105.

UK
**LOBSTER.** English. sa. $12.00. Lobster, 214 Westbourne Avenue, Hull HU5 3JB England.

UK
**LONDON BOROUGH COUNCIL ELECTIONS.** **Main/Corp** Greater London Council. Intelligence Unit. (19??)-. English. ir. Greater London Council, The County Hall, London SE1 7PB England. **Tel** (01)633-7139. **LC** JS3687; .A35. **DD** 329/.023/421. **Continues** Metropolitan Borough Council Elections.

●US
**LONG TERM VIEW, THE.** **Added/Corp** Massachusetts School of Law at Andover. **VFOAT** LTV. Vol. 1, No. 1 (Winter 1992)-. Periodical. English. qt. $10.00. Massachusetts School of Law at Andover, 500 Federal Street, Andover MA 01810. **Tel** (508)681-0800.

US
**LOYOLA LECTURE SERIES IN POLITICAL ANALYSIS.** (1977)-. English. ir. University of Notre Dame Press, PO Box 635, South Bend IN 46624. **Tel** (219)239-6349, (800)677-3232, FAX (219)239-8148. **ED** Richard Shelly Hartigan.

SW/0460-0037
**LUND POLITICAL STUDIES.** 1- 1960-. Monographic series. Multiple languages (English and Swedish). ir. Price varies per volume. Liber International, S-205 10 Malmo Sweden. **Tel** 46-40-70650.

US/1049-9776
**MACHIAVELLI STUDIES.** See Literature.

TZ
**MAELEXO BINAFSI YA WAGOMBEA UBUNGE WA TAIFA VITI MAALUM VYA WANAWAKE.** Swahili (Swahili). **LC** HQ1236.5.T34; M33.

FR/1150-4447
**MAGHREB CONFIDENTIEL PARIS.** (MAGHREB CONFIDENTIEL.). (1990)-. Periodical. French. bw. 2303.00F France; £230.00 UK; $426.00 US. Indigo Publications, 10 rue du Sentier, 75002 Paris France. **Tel** 011 33 1 45081480, FAX 011 33 1 45085983, telex 215405. **ED** Antoine Glaser. **UDC** 070.2(1-4).
**Desc:** Politics and economy in the countries of Maghreb, Algeria, Morocco, Tunisia and Libya.

UK/0961-9836
**MAGHREB QUARTERLY REPORT.** See Economics-Economic History, Conditions.

US/0749-2391
**MAINSTREAM AMERICA.** [Mainstream Am.]. **Added/Corp** Urban Improvement Corporation (Los Angeles, Calif.). Vol. 1, No. 1 (1982)-. Periodical. English. mo. Urban Improvement Corporation, 2714 West Vernon Avenue, Los Angeles CA 90008. **DD** 324.

SJ
**MAJALLAT AL-SIYASAH WA-AL-ISTIRATIJIYAH.** **Added/Corp** Mahad Al-Dirasat Al-Siyasiyah Wa-Al-Istiratijiyah (Sudan). **VFOAT** Majallat Assiyasa Walistratigia. (Oct. 1982)-. Periodical. Arabic. qt. 1.00 single issue. S B 1850, Khartoum Sudan. **LC** JA26; .M325.

●US/1059-3535
**MAJOR CONCEPTS IN POLITICS AND POLITICAL THEORY.** (1992)-. Periodical. English. Peter Lang Publishing, 62 West 45th Street, 4th Floor, New York NY 10036. **Tel** (212)764-1471, (800)770-5264, telex 6973364 PLNY.

CN/0706-3350
**MANITOBA GAZETTE, THE.** **VFOAT** Gazette de Manitoba. Periodical. English (French). wk. $32.50. Queens Printer Statutory Publishing, 200 Vaughn Street, Winnipeg Manitoba R3C 1T5 Canada. **Tel** (204)945-3102. **LC** J2. **DD** 354.71. cum. index. **Circ:** 1,600 (ctrl). available on microfilm and microfiche from University Microfilms International (UMI).
**Desc:** Public and private notices for permanent record and Manitoba regulations.

GW/0542-6758
**MARE BALTICUM.** **Added/Corp** Ostseegesellschaft. (1966)-. Monographic series. Multiple languages (German, English, Polish and Swedish). ir. Price varies per volume. Ostseegesellschaft EV, Europaweg 3, 23570 Luebeck Germany. **Tel** 04502-803203, FAX 04502-803200. **ED** Guenther Merr.

XR
**MARKSIZM-LENINIZM I NASHE VREMIA.** Vol. 1 (1974)-. Russian. kcs0.30 each issue. Mir I Sotsializm, 6 Tkhakurova 3, Prague Czech Republic. **LC** D839; .M33.

FR
**MAROC REPRESSION.** **Added/Corp** Association de Soutien aux Comites de Lutte Contre la Repression au Maroc (Paris, France). No. 69 (1985)-. Periodical. French. Six times a year. Association de Soutien aux Comites de Lutte Contre la Repression au Maroc, 14 rue Nanteuil, 75015 Paris France. **Tel** 011 33 1 45320189. **LC** IN PROCESS. **Continues** Comites de Lutte Contre la Repression au Maroc (Series).
**Ind/Abst** Hum. Rights Intern. Rep.

UK/0025-4118
**MARXISM TODAY.** **Ceased.** See General Interest-General Interest-Europe.

US
**MASSACHUSETTS VOTER / LEAGUE OF WOMEN VOTERS OF MASSACHUSETTS, THE.** **Added/Corp** League of Women Voters of Massachusetts. Vol. 67, No. 2 (Nov. 1990)-. Periodical. English. bm. $12.50. League of Women Voters of Massachusetts, 133 Portland Street, Boston MA 02114. **Tel** (617)523-2999, FAX (617)248-0881. **ED** Myrna Hewitt. **Ad Acc**. **Circ:** 8,000 (ctrl). **Continues** Voter (Boston, Mass.), 0899-4935.
**Desc:** Bi-monthly newsletter of the League of Women Voters of Massachusetts. It reports the League's position on issues and on happenings at the State House. Also reports on local League happenings.

GW/0340-0476
**MATERIALIEN ZUR POLITISCHEN BILDUNG.** (1973)-. German. qt. DM28.00. Leske Verlag & Budrich GmbH, Postfach 300551, Gerhart Hauptmann Strasse 27, W-5090 Leverkusen 3 Opladen Germany. **Tel** 011 49 21712079. **ED** R Engelland, K Hansen, Th Lang, A Pflinger, F W Rotherpieler, W Sauerhofer, J Tessmer, H Thum, G Walpuski, P L Weinacht. Index available. cum. index. **Bk Rev**. **Ad Acc**. ctrl circ.
**Desc:** Publishes the results of political sciences for the use of teachers focussed on political education.

TA
**MATERIALY PO ISTORII KOMMUNISTICHESKOI PARTII TADZHIKISTANA.** **Main/Corp** Dushanbe. Institut Istorii Partii. (1963)-. Russian. 0.63rub each issue. Ifrom / Light of Knowledge Publishing House, Kuchai Ayni 126, Dushanbe Tajikstan. **LC** JQ1089.A55; A44.

RU
**MATERIALY ... VERKHOVNOGO SOVETA SSSR.** **Main/Corp** Soviet Union. Verkhovnyi Sovet. (19??)-. Russian. 15 kop. 125811 GSP Moskva A-47, Miusskaia Pl 7, Moscow Russia. **LC** J397.H45; S69a.

US/0732-0205
**MCCARVILLE REPORT, THE.** No. 1 (Oct. 3, 1980)-. Periodical. English. wk. $95.00. Mike McCarville, 5805-B N. Grand Blvd., Oklahoma City OK 73118.

CI
**MEDJUNARODNA POLITIKA.** (19??)-. Serbo-Croatian (Roman). ir. Medjunarodna Politika, Nemanjina 34, PO Box 413, Belgrade Croatia.

AT/0085-3224
**MELBOURNE JOURNAL OF POLITICS.** [Melb. j. polit.]. **Added/Corp** Melbourne University Political Science Society. Vol. 1, (1968)-. English. an (Jan.). 10.00Aus$. University of Melbourne / Department of Political Science, Parkville Victoria 3052 Australia. **Tel** 011 61 3 344 4000, telex 35185. **ED** Vince Marotta. Index available (Bound in 20th iss. in Oct.). cum. index. **Bk Rev**, (Qty: 5). **Ad Acc**. **Pr Rev**. **Circ:** 600-1000.
**Desc:** Articles covering both political and social theory.
**Ind/Abst** APAIS, Aust. Public Aff. Inf. Ser. (1972-); PAIS Int. Print.

SZ
**MEMOPRESS.** **VFOAT** Memo Press. Periodical. German (German). sa.

CN/0229-7833
**MESSENGER (WASAGA BEACH).** (MESSENGER). [Messenger]. Vol. 2, No. 1 (Apr. 1977)-. Periodical. English. mo. $5.00. Huronia News Services, PO Box 345, Wasaga Beach, Ontario L0L 2P0 Canada. **DD** 324.2713/05/05. **Continues** Social Credit Messenger, 0229-7825.

●US/1069-3017
**MIAMI HERALD ALMANAC OF FLORIDA POLITICS, THE.** [Miami Herald alm. Fla. polit.]. **VFOAT** Almanac of Florida Politics. (1993)-. English. an. $100.00. Miami Herald Publishing Company, 1 Herald Plaza, Miami FL 33132. **Tel** (305)350-2111, (800)825-6245. **DD** 324.

CN/0317-8498
**MICHAEL (ROUGEMONT).** (MICHAEL.). **Added/Corp** Institute of Political Action. 14th Year No. 22 (Jan./Mar. 1974)-. Periodical. English. qt. 5.00Can$ Canada; 7.00Can$ other. Louis Even Institute of Social Justice, 1101 Rue Principale, Rougemont Quebec J0L 1M0 Canada. **Tel** (514)469-2209. **Supersedes** Vers Demain., 0317-848X.

US/0733-4486
**MICHIGAN JOURNAL OF POLITICAL SCIENCE.** (MICHIGAN JOURNAL OF POLITICAL SCIENCE : A UNIVERSITY OF MICHIGAN STUDENT JOURNAL OF POLITICAL STUDIES.). [Mich. j. polit. sci.]. **Added/Corp** University of Michigan. **VFOAT** University of Michigan Student Journal of Political Studies. Vol. 1, No. 1 (Winter 1981)-. Periodical. English. Twice a year (fall and winter). $12.00 one year; $18.00 two years; $24.00 three years. Michigan Journal of Political Science, University of Michigan, 5620 Haven Hall, Ann Arbor MI 48109-1045. **Tel** (313)764-6386. **ED** Mark C. Bishop. **LC**

JA1; .M48. **DD** 320/.05. **Bk Rev. Ad Acc. Circ:** 500.
**Desc:** Student journal of political studies.
**Ind/Abst** Am. Hist. Life (1981-).

US/0899-1545
**MICHIGAN VOTER, THE.** [Mich. voter]. **Added/Corp** League of Women Voters of Michigan. (19??)-. Periodical. English. Six times a year. Free to members; $10.00 nonmembers. League of Women Voters of Michigan, 200 Museum Drive, Suite 202, Lansing MI 48933. **DD** 324. **Pr Rev. Circ:** 2,700.
**Desc:** Provides non-partisan political information.

VI/0147-7935
**MICROSTATE STUDIES.** No. 1-. Periodical. English. $4.00 each issue. College of the Virgin Islands, Caribbean Research Institute, St Thomas Virgin Islands 00801. **LC** JC365; .M45. **DD** 321/.08.

US/0084-2311
**MIDDLE EAST AND SOUTH ASIA, THE.** **See** History(General)-History of the Middle East.

US/0731-9371
**MIDDLE EAST INSIGHT.** [Middle East insight]. Vol. 2, No. 2 (Jan./Feb. 1982)-. Periodical. English. Six times a year. $50.00. Middle East Insight, 1200 18th Street Northwest, Suite 305, Washington DC 20036. **Tel** (202)466-2146 or 2147. **ED** George A. Nader. **LC** D839; .I48. **DD** 909.82/05. Index available. **Bk Rev. Ad Acc. Circ:** 5,000. ***Continues*** *International Insight (Cleveland, Ohio), 0278-6710.*
**Desc:** Independent specialized publication on politics, economy history and diplomacy in the Middle East.
**Ind/Abst** PAIS Int. Print (1991-).

IS
**MIDDLE EAST MILITARY BALANCE / JAFFEE CENTER FOR STRATEGIC STUDIES, THE.** **See** Military and Defense.

US/0026-315X
**MIDDLE EAST MONITOR.** **Added/Corp** Middle East Institute (Washington, D.C.). **VFOAT** Monitor. Vol. 1, No. 1 (Feb. 1, 1971)-. Periodical. English. mo (12 issues). $100.00 US; $110.00 other. Middle East Monitor, PO Box 236, Ridgewood NJ 07451. **Tel** (201)670-9623, FAX (808)545-1058. **ED** Amir N Ghazaii. **Ad Acc. Circ:** 2,000. available on microfilm and microfiche from University Microfilms International (UMI). ***Absorbed*** *Middle East and African Economist, 0026-3087.*
**Desc:** Monitors and analyses politics and economic developments in Middle East.
**Ind/Abst** F&S Index Plus Text, Int. [Select. Cov.]; Predicasts Forecasts.

US/0276-5632
**MIDDLE EAST POLICY SURVEY.** **VFOAT** MEP Survey; M.E.P. Survey. No. 1 (Feb. 15, 1980)-. Periodical. English. Twenty-four times a year. $150.00 (one year), $240.00 (two year), $330.00 (three year). Middle East Policy Survey, 3405 Rodman Street NW, Washington DC 20008. **Tel** (202)363-3495, FAX (202)362-4513. **ED** Richard Straus. **LC** DS63.2.U5; M49. **DD** 327.56073. **Circ:** 450 (ctrl).
**Desc:** Insiders' political reporting and analysis of late breaking Middle East news not available in the general press or specialized periodicals.

UK
**MIDEAST MIRROR.** **See** Business.

US/1051-5054
**MIDSOUTH POLITICAL SCIENCE JOURNAL.** ***Title Change.*** [Midsouth polit. sci. j.]. **Added/Corp** Arkansas Political Science Association. Vol. 9, No. 1 (1988)-(19??). Periodical. English. University of Central Arkansas Department of Political Science, Conway AR 72035. **Tel** (501)450-5100. **LC** JK5101; .A73. **DD** 320/.05. ***Continues*** *Arkansas Political Science Journal.* ***Continued by*** *American Review of Politics.*
**Ind/Abst** PAIS Int. Print.

CC
**MIN TSU WEN HSUEH YEN CHIU.** First published in 1983. Periodical. Chinese. RMBY0.60. Hsin Hua Shu Tien, Beijing, People's Republic of China. **Tel** 551253. **LC** PL2278.5.M55; M56. **DD** 895.1/09.

US/1056-4667
**MINNESOTA POLITICAL ACTION REPORT.** (MINNESOTA POLITICAL ACTION REPORT / SUMMIT CAMPAIGN ASSOCIATES.). [Minn. polit. action rep.]. **Added/Corp** Summit Campaign Associates. **VFOAT** MN PAR. Vol. 1, No. 1 (Feb. 4, 1991)-. Periodical. English. bw. $84.00. Summit Campaign Associates, PO Box 10240, Minneapolis MN 55458-3240. **DD** 322.

US/0740-1191
**MINNESOTA VOTER, THE.** (THE MINNESOTA VOTER : A PUBLICATION OF THE LEAGUE OF WOMEN VOTERS OF MINNESOTA.). Periodical. English. qt. $5.00. League of Women Voters of Minnesota, 555 Wabasha Avenue, St Paul MN 55102. **Tel** (612)224-5445. **ED** Mary Santi. **Circ:** 3,600 (ctrl). ***Continues*** *Articulate Voter.*
**Desc:** Newsletter of the League of Women Voters of Minnesota.

●CN/1193-1043
**MINUTES OF PROCEEDINGS AND EVIDENCE OF THE SPECIAL COMMITTEE ON ELECTORAL REFORM.** [Minutes proc. evid. Spec. Comm. Elect. Reform]. **Main/Corp** Canada. Parliament. House of Commons. Special Committee on Electoral Reform. **VFOAT** Electoral Reform; Proces-Verbaux et Temoignages du Comite Special Charge de la Reforme Electorale. 34th Parliament, 3rd Session, Issue No. 1 (Feb. 26/Mar. 18. 1992)-. Proceedings. English (French). **DD** 354.710081/1/05.

●CN/1193-1043
**MINUTES OF PROCEEDINGS AND EVIDENCE OF THE SPECIAL COMMITTEE ON ELECTORAL REFORM (FRENCH EDITION).** [Minutes proc. evid. Spec. Comm. Elect. Reform]. **Main/Corp** Canada. Parliament. Chambre des communes. Comit,e sp,ecial charg,e de la r,eforme ,electorale. **VFOAT** Reforme Electorale; Proces-Verbaux et Temoignages du Comite Special Charge de la Reforme Electorale. 34th Parliament, 3rd Session, Issue No. 1 (Feb. 26/Mar. 18. 1992)-. Proceedings. French (English). **DD** 354.710081/1/05.

CN/1186-0375
**MINUTES OF PROCEEDINGS AND EVIDENCE OF THE SPECIAL JOINT COMMITTEE OF THE SENATE AND THE HOUSE OF COMMONS ON PROCESS FOR AMENDING THE CONSTITUTION OF CANADA.** [Minutes proc. evid. Spec. Jt. Comm. Senate House Commons Process Amend. Const. Can.]. **Main/Corp** Canada. Parliament. Special Joint Committee on the Process for Amending the Constitution of Canada. **VFOAT** Process for Amending the Constitution of Canada; Proces-Verbaux et Temoignages du Comite Mixte Special du Senat et de la Chambre des Ccommunes sur le Processus de Modification de la Constitution du Canada. Issue No. 1 (Feb. 5, 1991)-. Proceedings. English (French). Imprimeur de la Reine pour le Canada, c/o Receiver General for Canada, Ottawa Ontario K1A 0S9 Canada. **DD** 342.71/03.

NE/1381-2386
**MITIGATION AND ADAPTATION STRATEGIES FOR GLOBAL CHANGE.** (19??)-. English. qt. $396.00. Martinus Nijhoff Publishers, Subsidiary of Kluwer Academic Publishers, Koraalrood 50, 2718 SC Zoetermeer Netherlands. **Tel** 011 31 79 684400.

MV
**MOLDOVA I MIR.** (1991)-. Periodical. Russian. mo. $109.95. **LC** HX8; .K567. ***Continues*** *Politika (Kishinev, Moldavian S.S.R. : 1991), 0130-2396.*

CN/0319-4019
**MONARCHY CANADA.** **Added/Corp** Monarchist League of Canada. Vol. 3 (Spring 1973)-. Periodical. English (French). Four times a year. 23.00Can$ (libraries), 30.00Can$ (others) Canada; 25.00Can$ (libraries), 32.00Can$ (others) other. Monarchist League of Canada, PO Box 1057, Oakville Ontario L6J 5E9 Canada. **Tel** (416)338-3113. **ED** Arthur Bousfield (editor's address: 3050 Yonge Street, Suite 206, Toronto Ontario M4N 2K4 Canada; editor's phone: (416)482-4157). **Bk Rev**, (Qty: 25-30 per year). **Ad Acc, Adv Mgr:** same as editor. **Circ:** 8,000. ***Continues*** *Canadian Monarchist, 0319-4000.*
**Desc:** Looks at monarchy from a Canadian perspective and at Canada from a monarchist one. Offers current and historical articles (with Commonwealth and international coverage) on constitutional, social and political affairs, as well as personality profiles, interviews, comment and reviews of books and the arts.

FR/1241-5294
**MONDE ARABE PARIS.** (MONDE ARABE.). (1992)-. Periodical. French. qt. Librarie le Pont du Jour, 58 rue Gay Lassac, F 75005 Paris France. **Tel** 011 33 1 43262017. **UDC** 35.07(44).

US/0897-1153
**MONITOR (ATLANTA, GA.), THE.** (THE MONITOR.). [Monitor]. **Added/Corp** Center for Democratic Renewal. Vol. 1, No. 1 (Jan. 1986)-. Periodical. English. Center for Democratic Renewal CDR, PO Box 50469, Atlanta GA 30302. **Tel** (404) 221-0025. **DD** 305. ***Continues*** *National Anti-Klan Newsletter.*
**Ind/Abst** Hum. Rights Intern. Rep.

II
**MONTHLY PUBLIC OPINION SURVEYS.** [Mon. public opin. surv.]. **VFOAT** Monthly Public Opinion Surveys. Politics Social and Cultural Affairs. (1955)-. English. Twelve times a year. $90.00. Indian Institute of Public Opinion, PO Box 288, New Delhi 1 India. **Tel** 011 91 11 312846, 011 91 11 312742, FAX 011 91 11 310405, telex 31-65156 NEWS IN. **ED** E.P.W. da Costa. cum. index. **Bk Rev**, (Qty: 1-2). **Ad Acc.** ctrl circ.
**Desc:** Special articles on social, cultural, economics, and political affairs. Presents results of surveys conducted by the institute on current events by demographic variables of sex, age, income, occupation and education of the respondents broken in percentage terms.

FR/0243-6450
**MOTS.** No. 1 (Oct. 1980)-. Periodical. French. qt. 350.00F (France), 460.00F (other) institution; 265.00F (France), 315.00F (other) individual. Presses de la Fondation, Nationale des Sciences Politiques, 44 Rue du Four, 75006 Paris France. **Tel** 011 33 1 44393960, FAX 011 33 1 45480441. **ED** Maurice Tournier. **LC** JA11; .M68. **DD** 320/.014. **[CCC]**. Index available. **Bk Rev. Ad Acc.**
**Desc:** Articles on political and social discourse and vocabulary.
**Ind/Abst** Int. Polit. Sci. Abstr.

MZ
**MOZAMBIQUEFILE : A MOZAMBIQUE NEWS AGENCY MONTHLY / AIM.** **Added/Corp** Agencia de Informacao de Mocambique. **VFOAT** Mozambique File. No. 149 (Nov. 1988)-. Periodical. English. Twelve times a year. $14.00 Mozambique; $35.00 (institutions), $24.00 (individuals) other. Mozambique Information Agency, PO Box 896, Maputo Mozambique. **Tel** 430723, FAX 421906, telex 6446, 6430. **ED** Paul Fauvet. **LC** DT451; .A4. **DD** 967.905/05. **Ad Acc. Circ:** 2,000. ***Continues*** *AIM Information Bulletin (Maputo, Mozambique : 1977).*
**Desc:** Deals with political, economic, military and social developments in Mozambique.

US
**MULTIMEDIA WORLD FACTBOOK. CD-ROM.** (19??)-. English. $49.95. Bureau of Electronic Publishing Inc., 141 New Road, Parsippany NJ 07054. **Tel** (201)808-2700, FAX (201)808-2676.
**Desc:** Comprehensive country profiles are included, with details on geography, people, government, economy and much more.

PL/0867-0072
**MYSL NARODOWA POLSKA.** [Mysl Nar. Pol.]. (1990)-. Periodical. Polish. mo. Price on Request. **(Subscription address:** ARS Polona, PO Box 1001, 00068 Warsaw Poland.) **UDC** 323(438).

PO
**NACAO E DEFESA.** **Added/Corp** Portugal. Exercito. Estado Maior. Seccao de Estudos Politicos. Instituto da Defesa Nacional (Portugal). (1976)-. Periodical. Portuguese (English, French and Spanish). qt. $26.00. Instituto Nacional de Defesa, Calcada das Necessidades 5, 1300 Lisbon Portugal. **Tel** 011 351 1 601079, 011 35 1 601516. **LC** DP681; .N33.

FR
**NAMAH-I JIBHAH-I NAJAT-I IRAN.** **VFOAT** Front pour la Liberation de l'Iran. (1900)-. Periodical. Persian. wk. Namah-i Jibhah-i Najat-i Iran, BP 223 16, 75765 Paris Cedex 16 France.

ZA
**NAMIBIA ABSTRACTS.** **Added/Corp** United Nations Institute for Namibia. Information and Documentation Division. (19??)-. Periodical. English. qt. Free. Zambia Government Printer, POB 30136, Lusaka Zambia. **ED** S. Mkandla and C. C. Zulu. **LC** DT701; .N36. **DD** 016.9688. Index available. **Bk Rev. Ad Acc. Circ:** 1,200.
**Desc:** Guide to selected literature on Namibia in particular and Southern Africa in general.

AO
**NAMIBIA YOUTH : OFFICIAL BULLETIN OF THE SWAPO YOUTH LEAGUE.** **Added/Corp** SWAPO. Youth League. (19??)-. Periodical. English. qt (4 issues). $3.50 Europe and North America. SWAPO Department of Information and Publicity, PO Box 953, Luanda PR Angola.

●UZ/0869-0685
**NAROD I DEMOKRATIIA.** (Jan. 1992)-. Periodical. Russian. mo. ***Continues*** *Chelovek i Politika, 0130-2426.*

US/8755-9706
**NARODNO ZEMEDELSKO ZNAME.** (NARODNO ZEMEDELSKO ZNAME : ORGAN NA BULGARSKIIA ZEMEDELSKI NARODEN SUIUZ.). [Nar. zemed. znam.]. **VFOAT** Zemedelsko Zname; People's Agrarian Banner : Organ of the Bulgarian Agrarian National Union; People's Agrarian Banner. Began in 1982. Periodical. Bulgarian. ir. $12.00. Bulgarian Agrarian National Union (BANU), 109 Amherst Street, Highland Park NJ 08904. **Tel** (201)572-1137. **ED** Iskar Shumanov. **DD** 324. **Bk Rev. Ad Acc. Circ:** 2,840.
**Desc:** Covers history in the context of Bulgarian history, Agrarian ideology, and current affairs.

CN/0821-4964
**NASHARA AL-GHADA'ID AL-ALAMIYYAH (ARABIC ED.).** (NASHARAH AL-GHADA'ID AL-ALAMIYYAH.). **VFOAT** Scandalous International News. V. 1, No. 2 (1983)-. Periodical. Arabic. mo. 25.00Can$. Al-Dibabi, PO Box

4190, Station E, Ottawa Ontario K1N 8V2 Canada. **DD** 320/.0207. ***Continues in part*** *Scandalous International News. English, French & Arabic, 0820-7887.*

CY
**NASHRAH (NICOSIA, CYPRUS).** (AL-NASHRAH.). **VFOAT** Annashra. Periodical. Arabic. wk. $750.00. Pressrelay Middle East Ltd, 6 Naxos Street, PO Box 3994, Nicosia Cyprus. **LC** DS63.1; .N35.

FR
**NATION ROUMAINE B.-ORGANE DU CONSEIL DES PARTIS POLITIQUES ROUMAINS.** (19??)-. French.
**Ind/Abst** Am. Hist. Life (1954-1957).

US/0027-898X
**NATIONAL CHRONICLE (HAYDEN LAKE).** (NATIONAL CHRONICLE.). [Natl. chron.]. (19??)-. Periodical. English. ir. $15.00. National Chronicle, 1498 Bruce, c/o Hal W. Hunt, Anderson CA 96007.

II/0302-6973
**NATIONAL DEBATE, THE.** [Natl. debate]. V. 1 (Oct./Nov. 1973)-. Periodical. English. mo. Rs1.50 single issue. Surinder Singh, 175 Jeevan Nagar, New Delhi India. **LC** JQ201; .N37. **DD** 320.9/54/04.

US/0740-2813
**NATIONAL DIRECTORY OF WOMEN ELECTED OFFICIALS.** (NATIONAL DIRECTORY OF WOMEN ELECTED OFFICIALS / NATIONAL WOMEN'S POLITICAL CAUCUS.). [Natl. dir. women elect. off.]. **Added/Corp** National Women's Political Caucus (U.S.). (1981)-. Directory. English. be. Free on request. National Womens Political Caucus, 1275 K Street Northwest, Suite 750, Washington DC 20005-4051. **Tel** (202)898-1100. **LC** HQ1236; .N37. **DD** 320.973/088042.

US/0360-4217
**NATIONAL JOURNAL (1975).** (NATIONAL JOURNAL.). [Natl. j.]. **Added/Corp** Government Research Corporation. Vol. 7, No. 34 (Aug. 23, 1975)-. Periodical. English. Fifty-two times a year. $587.00 academic and public libraries; $935.98 other. National Journal Inc., 1501 M Street Northwest, Suite 300, Washington DC 20005. **Tel** (800)356-4838, (202)739-8541, (800)424-2921. **(Subscription address:** National Journal / Washington, DC, PO Box 96400, Washington DC 20077.) **ED** Richard S. Frank. **LC** JK1; .N28. **DD** 320.9/73/092. **[CCC].** Index available. cum. index. **Ad Acc. Circ:** 5,000. available on an online database from NEXIS; available on microfilm and microfiche from University Microfilms International (UMI). Documents available from UMI Article Clearinghouse, Documents on Demand. ***Continues*** *National Journal Reports, 0091-3685.*
**Desc:** A magazine on politics and government. Written for policy and decision makers who need to anticipate policy developments in Washington.
**Ind/Abst** Am. Bibliogr. Slavic East Europ. Stud.; Curr. Lit. Fam. Plan. (19??-199?); Energy Inf. Abstr.; Environ. Abstr.; Expand. Acad. Index (1992-); Health Plan. Adminis.; Hospit. Health Admin. Index; Index Period. Artic. Relat. Law; Infobank (1975-); Newsp. Period. Abstr. (1992-); NEXIS (Jan. 1, 1977-); PAIS Int. Print (1991-); Urban Aff. Abstr.

US/0049-044X
**NATIONAL NEWS REPORT.** ***Ceased.*** **See** Environmental Issues-Conservation and Natural Resources.

AT/0158-6270
**NATIONAL OUTLOOK SYDNEY. See** Sociology.

US/0896-629X
**NATIONAL POLITICAL SCIENCE REVIEW.** [Natl. polit. sci. rev.]. **Added/Corp** National Conference of Black Political Scientists. **VFOAT** NPSR. (1989)-. Periodical. English. an. $19.95 (paper). Transaction Publishers / Rutgers State University, New Brunswick NJ 08903. **Tel** (908)932-2280 Ext. 105, FAX (908)932-3138. **ED** Matthew Holden Jr. **LC** JK1; .N29. **DD** 323.1/73. **Bk Rev. Pr Rev.** available on microfiche; available on microfilm.
**Desc:** Examines the theoretical and empirical aspects of politics, and politics that aid disadvantaged groups by reasons of race, ethnicity, sex and other factors. A publication of the National Conference of Black Political Scientists.
**Ind/Abst** Am. Hist. Life (1989-).

US/0028-0038
**NATIONAL REVIEW (NEW YORK).** (NATIONAL REVIEW.). [Natl. rev.]. **VFOAT** National Review Bulletin. Vol. 1 (Nov. 19, 1955)-. Periodical. English. bw. $57.00. National Review Inc., 150 East 35th Street, New York NY 10016. **Tel** (212)679-7330. **(Subscription address:** Kable Publishers Aide, 308 East Hitt Street, Subscription Department, Mt. Morris IL 61054-1473.) **ED** William F. Buckley Jr. **LC** AP2; .N3545. **DD** 051. **Bk Rev. Ad Acc. Circ:** 100,000 (ctrl). available on microfilm and microfiche from University Microfilms International (UMI); available on an online database (files 647,648/Full-Text) from DIALOG. Documents available from UMI Article Clearinghouse.
**Desc:** Conservative magazine founded by William F. Buckley Jr. The biweekly offers reporting, editorials and analysis on domestic and international political, cultural, religious and economic trends, and reviews books, movies, music and TV.
**Ind/Abst** Abr. Read. Guide Period. Lit.; Acad. Abstr. Full Text Elite (Feb. 1984-) [Full Txt.]; Acad. Abstr. (Feb. 1984-); Acad. Ind. [Computer File] (1984-); Acad. Search (Feb. 1984-); Am. Bibliogr. Slavic East Europ. Stud.; Annu. Bibliogr. Engl. Lang. Lit.; Art Archaeol. Tech. Abstr.; Biogr. Index; Book Rev. Digest; Book Rev. Index; Expand. Acad. Index (1984-); Film Lit. Index; Gen. Period. Index (1985-); Index Period. Artic. Relat. Law; INFO-SOUTH Abstr.; Mag. Artic. Summar. Elite (Feb. 1984-) [Full Txt.]; Mag. Artic. Summar. Select (Feb. 1984-); Mag. Artic. Summar. CD-ROM (Feb. 1984-); Mag. ASAP Plus [Full Txt.]; Mag. ASAP Sel. [Full Txt.]; Mag. Express (1986-) [Full Txt.]; Mag. Index Plus (1989-); Mag. Index Sel. Microfiche (1986-) [Full Txt.]; Mag. Index. Sel. (1986-); Mag. Search; Med. Rev. Dig.; Middle East Abstr. Index; Newsp. Period. Abstr. (1986-); Peace Res. Abstr. J. (1964-1965); Read. Guide Abstr. Select Ed.; Read. Guide Period. Lit.; Resource/One Ondisc; Soc. Sci. Source (Feb. 1984-) [Full Txt.]; Mag. Index (1977-); TOM Gen. Index (1985-) [Full Txt.]; Vocat. Search (Feb. 1984-) [Full Txt.].

US/0028-0372
**NATIONAL VOTER, THE.** [Natl. voter]. **Added/Corp** League of Women Voters. (May 15, 1951)-. Periodical. English. qt. $15.00. League of Women Voters of the United States, 1730 M Street Northwest, 10th Floor, Washington DC 20036. **Tel** (202)429-1965, FAX (202)429-0854. **ED** William Woodwell. **LC** E740; .N36. **Ad Acc. Circ:** 130,000. available on microfilm and microfiche from University Microfilms International (UMI). ***Formed by the union of*** *Action* ***and*** *Trends in Government.*
**Desc:** In-depth coverage of selected national issues, interviews with political figures, accounts of citizen action on local issues throughout the country, current events.

UK
**NATIONALISM AND ETHNIC POLITICS.** Vol. 1 (199?)-. English. qt. $115.00. Frank Cass & Company Ltd, Newbury House, 890-900 Eastern Avenue, Newbury Park, Ilford, Essex IG2 7HH United Kingdom. **Tel** 011 44 81 599 8866, FAX 011 44 81 599 0984, telex 897719.

●UK/1354-5078
**NATIONS AND NATIONALISM.** Vol. 1 (1995)-. Academic Scholarly Publication. English. Three times a year. $89.00 US, Canada & Mexico; £59.00 other. Cambridge University Press, The Edinburgh Building, Shaftesbury Road, Cambridge CB2 2RU United Kingdom. **Tel** 011 44 223 312393, FAX 011 44 223 325959. **(Subscription address:** Cambridge University Press / North America, 110 Midland Avenue, Port Chester NY 10573.) **ED** Anthony D. Smith, Athena Leoussi, Obi Patience Igwara and Terry Mulhall. **Bk Rev.**
**Desc:** Includes articles on international relations, politics, sociology, political theory and anthropology, as well as social policy, social psychology, linguistics, area studies, international history, human geography, economics and archaeology.

NP/0749-0674
**NATO-WARSAW AND STRATEGIES.** **VFOAT** N.A.T.O. Warsaw and Strategies; NATO Warsaw and Strategies; N.A.T.O.-Warsaw and Strategies. Vol. 1 (1989)-. Periodical. English. bm. $100.00. Dr. C. V. Ramastry Editor, PO Box 1755, Kantipath Kathmandu Nepal. **Ad Acc.**
**Desc:** Aims to provide a forum and will examine the socio-economic, political and technological implications of NATO-Warsaw nations.

US
**NAZEER.** (AL-NADHIR.). Periodical. Arabic. mo. Mujahed, c/o Mansour, PO Box 242, Clawson MI 48017. **LC** DS98.2; .N39.

US
**NBC NEWS, RAND MCNALLY WORLD ATLAS & ALMANAC.** ***Ceased.*** **Added/Corp** NBC News. Rand McNally and Company. **VFOAT** World Atlas & Almanac; World Atlas and Almanac. (1991)-(1993). English. Rand McNally & Company, PO Box 32, Skokie IL 60076. **Tel** (708)673-0813, (800)444-4062. **LC** D440; .N32. ***Continues*** *NBC News, Rand McNally World News Atlas.*

PH/0116-4252
**NCCP NEWSLETTER.** **Added/Corp** National Council of Churches in the Philippines. (19??)-. Newsletter. English (Tagalog). bm.
**Ind/Abst** Hum. Rights Intern. Rep.

●US/1062-6867
**NED BACKGROUNDER: A FORUM FOR THE STUDY OF THE NATIONAL ENDOWMENT FOR DEMOCRACY AND OTHER U.S. GOVERNMENT DEMOCRATIZATION PROGRAMS, THE.** [NED backgr.]. **Added/Corp** Resource Center (Albuquerque, N.M.). **VAT** National Endowment for Democracy Backgrounder. (1992)-. Periodical. English. bm. Free. The Inter-Hemispheric Education Resource Center, PO Box 4506, Albuquerque NM 87196. **DD** 327.

US/0748-4526
**NEGOTIATION JOURNAL.** [Negot. j.]. Vol. 1, No. 1 (Jan. 1985)-. Periodical. English. Four times a year. $205.00 institutions, $44.00 individuals US; $240.00 institutions, $51.00 individuals other. Plenum Press, 233 Spring Street, New York NY 10013-1578. **Tel** (212)620-8000, (800)221-9369, FAX (212)463-0742, (212)807-1047, telex 23/421139. **ED** Jeffrey Z. Rubin. **LC** HD42; .N44. **DD** 302.3/05. **CODEN** NEJOEQ. **[CCC].** Index available. **Pr Rev.** available on microfilm and microfiche from University Microfilms International (UMI). Documents available from The Genuine Article.
**Desc:** International journal devoted to the publication of works that advance the theory analysis and practice of negotiation and dispute statement.
**Ind/Abst** Am. Hist. Life (1986-); Curr. Contents, Agric. Biol. Environ. Sci.; Curr. Contents Soc. Behav. Sci.; Index Period. Artic. Relat. Law; Int. Bibliogr. Sociol.; Int. Polit. Sci. Abstr.; PAIS Int. Print (1991-); Psychoanal. Abstr.; PsycScan: Appl. Exp. Eng. Psych.; PsycScan: LD/MR; PsycScan: Neuropsych.; Res. Alert [Full Cov.]; Sage Public Adm. Abstr.; Sage Urban Stud. Abstr; Soc. Plann. Policy Dev. Abstr.; Soc. Sci. Cit. Index [Full Cov.].

GW
**NEUSEELAND, FORSCHUNGSPOLITIK UND FORSCHUNGSPRAXIS / BUNDESSTELLE FUER AUSSENHANDELSINFORMATION.** German. DM3.00. Bundesstelle fuer Aussenhandelsinformation, Agrippastr 87 93, D 50676 Cologne Germany. **Tel** 011 49 221 2057316, FAX 011 49 221 2057212. **LC** Q180.N4; N46. **DD** 338.993106.

II/0047-9500
**NEW AGE WEEKLY.** **Added/Corp** Communist Party of India. Vol. 1 (Sept. 1952)-. Periodical. English. Fifty-two times a year. $3.25 India; $11.00 others (latest issues). Communist Party of India, 5 Randi Jhansi Road, New Delhi 1 Road. **Tel** 3310762, telex 3165982 CNSIN. **ED** Pauly V. Parakal. **Bk Rev. Ad Acc. Circ:** 25,000 (ctrl).
**Desc:** Interpretative journal of current events in India and abroad with particular reference to political science and economics analysed from Marxian view.

US/0885-6540
**NEW AMERICAN (BELMONT, MASS.), THE.** (THE NEW AMERICAN.). [New Am.]. Vol. 1, No. 1 (Sept. 30, 1985)-. Periodical. English. Twenty-six times a year. $39.00 (one year), $68.00 (two years), $89.00 (three years) US; $48.00 (one year), $86.00 (two years), $116.00 (three years) Canada and Hawaii; $66.00 (one year), $122.00 (two years), $170.00 (three years) other. New American, PO Box 8040, Appleton WI 54913. **Tel** (414)749-3784, FAX (414)749-3785. **ED** F R Duplantier. **LC** AP2; .N373. **DD** 051. **Bk Rev. Ad Acc. Circ:** 50,000 (ctrl). available on microfilm and microfiche from University Microfilms International (UMI). ***Formed by the union of*** *Review of the News, 0034-6802* ***and*** *American Opinion, 0003-0236.*
**Desc:** Edited from a free-market viewpoint. Thorough coverage of world and national current events. Features section on analysis of current world trends from a historical perspective.
**Ind/Abst** Guide Soc. Sci. Relig.

US
**NEW DEMOCRAT / DEMOCRATIC LEADERSHIP COUNCIL, THE.** **Added/Corp** Democratic Leadership Council (U.S.). Vol. 3, No. 2 (May 1991)-. Periodical. English. bm. Democratic Leadership Council, 316 Pennsylvania Avenue SE, Suite 500, Washington DC 20003. **LC** JK2311; .M35. **DD** 324.2736/05. ***Continues*** *Mainstream Democrat, 1045-8441.*

CN/1183-0247
**NEW DEMOCRATIC ALTERNATIVE.** [New Democr. altern.]. **Added/Corp** New Democratic Party. **VFOAT** Alternative Neo-Democrate. Vol. 1, No. 1 (Winter 1991)-. Periodical. English (French). qt. $20.00 per year. New Democratic Party of Canada, 600-280 Albert Street, Ottawa Onatrio K1P 5G8 Canada. **DD** 324.27107/05.

CN/1183-0247
**NEW DEMOCRATIC ALTERNATIVE.** [New Democr. altern.]. **Added/Corp** Nouveau Parti Democratique. **VFOAT** Alternative Neo-Democrate. Vol. 1, No. 1 (Winter 1991)-. Periodical. French (English). qt. $20.00 per yr. Nouveau Parti Democratique du Canada, Bureau 600, 280 Rue Albert, Ottawa Ontario K1P 5G8 Canada. **DD** 324.27107/05.

CN/0827-6153
**NEW DIRECTIONS (VANCOUVER. 1985).** ***Ceased.*** (NEW DIRECTIONS : LIFE AND POLITICS IN BC.). [New dir.]. **Added/Corp** Pacific New Directions Publishing Society. (June/July 1985)-(19??). Periodical. English. Six times a year. New Directions, PO Box 34279, Station D, Vancouver BC V6N 1H2 Canada. **Tel** (604)438-3149, FAX (604)438-3149. **ED** Bob Smith. **DD** 320.9711/05. **Bk Rev. Ad Acc. Circ:** 1,500. available on

microfiche from Micromedia Limited.
**Desc:** Covers life and politics from the left side of British Columbia's polarized social and political activity. The debates and actions of labor, the NDP and community groups are the focus of many articles, examined from alternative perspectives to those in the mainstream press. Writers include commentators such as Stan Persky, along with activists in the center of the political action.
**Ind/Abst** Can. Index.

US/1043-2264
**NEW FEDERALIST.** [New Fed.]. (1987)-. Newspaper. English. wk (except 1st full week after Christmas and Memorial Day). $35.00. KMW Publishing Company, PO Box 889, Leesburg VA 22075. **Tel** (703)777-9451, FAX (703)771-9492. **ED** Nancy Spannaus. **Bk Rev**, (Qty: 10). **Ad Acc**, **Adv Mgr:** Stanley Ezrol. **Circ:** 105,000.
**Desc:** Dedicated to reviving the American system of economics and politics, which defines the mission of the United States as: to foster economic and scientific progress, the republican form of government, and the inalienable right to life for all peoples, both at home and abroad.

US/0028-5137
**NEW GUARD.** ***Ceased.*** Vol. 1 (March 1961)-Vol. 25 (Dec. 1985). Periodical. English. qt. Young Americans for Freedom, PO Box 1002, Woodland Road, Sterling VA 22170. **Tel** (703)450-5162. **ED** Gerry O'Brien. **LC** AP2; .N6154. **DD** 320.9/73. **Bk Rev**. **Ad Acc**. **Circ:** 10,000 (ctrl). available on microfilm from University Microfilms International (UMI).
**Desc:** Politics and popular culture for today's youth with a conservative perspective. Now in our 25th year.

US/0276-9778
**NEW HAMPSHIRE POLITICAL ALMANAC, THE.** 1981-1982-. English. $15.00. Center for Leadership Studies, PO Box 400, Centreville MA 02632. **Tel** (508)775-4323, (800)833-7600, FAX (508)775-7310. **LC** JK2930; .N39. **DD** 328.742/073/025.

CN/0706-8409
**NEW INDIA BULLETIN.** (NEW INDIA BULLETIN. BULLETIN DE L'INDE NOUVELLE.). **Added/Corp** Indian People's Association in North America. **VFOAT** Bulletin de l'Inde Nouvelle. Vol. 1, (Sept. 1975)-. Bulletin. English. qt. New India Bulletin, c/o Ipana, Box 37 Westmont, Montreal Quebec Canada. **LC** DS480.84; .N47. **DD** 320.9/54/05.

US
**NEW JERSEY LEGISLATIVE MANUAL.** **Main/Corp** New Jersey. State Legislature. (1873)-. English. an. $27.25. New Jersey Legislative Manual, PO Box 2150, Trenton NJ 08607-2150. **Tel** (609)396-2669 ext. 2. **ED** Edward J Mullin.
**Desc:** The directory of government, politics, and public affairs in New Jersey. Over 1,000 pages fully indexed; cloth bound.

US/0893-7850
**NEW PERSPECTIVES QUARTERLY.** (NEW PERSPECTIVES QUARTERLY : NPQ.). [New perspect. q.]. **Added/Corp** Institute for National Strategy (U.S.) Center for the Study of Democratic Institutions. **VFOAT** NPQ. Vol. 3, No. 2 (Fall 1986)-. Periodical. English. qt (4 issues). $75.00 US; $80.00 Canada and Mexico; $90.00 other (institution). Center for the Study of Democratic Institutions, 10951 West Pico Boulevard, Suite 300, Los Angeles CA 90064. **Tel** (310)474-0011, (800)336-1007, FAX (310)474-8061. **ED** Nathan Gardels. **LC** E839.5; .N379. **DD** 973.92. Index available (free on request). cum. index. **Ad Acc**. **Circ:** 20,000 (ctrl). available on microfilm and microfiche from University Microfilms International (UMI). Documents available from UMI Article Clearinghouse. ***Continues*** *New Perspectives (Los Angeles, Calif.);* ***Absorbed*** *Center Magazine, 0008-9125.*
**Desc:** Engages world opinion-leaders in government, economics, the arts, and the media in discussions about some of the most important issues of our time.
**Ind/Abst** Acad. Abstr. Full Text Elite (Jan. 1988-); Acad. Abstr. (Jan. 1988-); Acad. Ind. [Computer File] (1989-); Acad. Search (Jan. 1988-); Expand. Acad. Index (1989-); Gen. Period. Index (1988-); Guide Soc. Sci. Relig.; INFO-SOUTH Abstr.; Mag. Artic. Summar. Elite (Jan. 1988-); Mag. Artic. Summar. Select (Jan. 1988-); Mag. Artic. Summar. CD-ROM (Jan. 1988-); Mag. Index Plus (1989-); Mag. Index. Sel. (1988-); Mag. Search; Newsp. Period. Abstr. (1988-); PAIS Int. Print (1991-?); Read. Guide Abstr. Select Ed.; Read. Guide Period. Lit.; Soc. Sci. Source (Jan. 1988-); Mag. Index (1989-); Vocat. Search (July 1984-).

US/0739-3148
**NEW POLITICAL SCIENCE.** [New polit. sci.]. **Added/Corp** Caucus for a New Political Science (U.S.). **VFOAT** N.P.S.; NPS. (1972)-. Academic Scholarly Publication. English. qt. $30.00 (individual), $60.00 (institution) US; $35.00 (individual), $65.00 (institution) other. New Political Science, c/o John C. Berg, Suffolk Univ., Dept. Gov't., Boston MA 02108-2770. **Tel** (617)573-8126, (617)436-1548. **ED** Meredith Reid Sarkees. **LC** JA1; .N46. **DD** 320/.05. **Bk Rev**, (Qty: 6-8 /yr). **Ad Acc**, **Adv Mgr:** John C. Berg. **Circ:** 250. ***Continues*** *New Political Science (Caucus for a New Political Science : 1972), 0739-3148.*
**Desc:** Official journal of the Caucus for a new Political Science. Publishes scholarly articles which reflect a commitment to progressive social change.
**Ind/Abst** Altern. Press Index (-199?); Left Index; PAIS Int. Print (1991-?); Soc. Plann. Policy Dev. Abstr.; Sociol. Abstr.

●RU
**NEW TIMES INTERNATIONAL.** **See** Political Science-International Relations.

US/1070-7727
**NEW UNIONIST (MINNEAPOLIS, MINN.).** **See** Economics-Labor.

US/0196-4623
**NEW YORK RED BOOK, THE.** (18??)-. English. an (Aug.). $60.00 (two years). New York Legal Publishing Corporation, 6 Charles Park, Guilderland NY 12084. **Tel** (518)456-2855, (800)541-2681. **LC** JK3430; .N5. **DD** 320.9/747. **Circ:** 13,000.
**Desc:** Lists facts concerning New York state, its political subdivisions and officials who administer its affairs. Bibliographies and photographs included.

US/0028-7873
**NEW YORK UNIVERSITY JOURNAL OF INTERNATIONAL LAW & POLITICS.** **See** Law-International Law.

NZ
**NEW ZEALAND GAZETTE, THE.** ***Ceased.*** **Main/Corp** New Zealand. (1???)-(19??). English. wk. Government Printing Office / New Zealand, 10 Mulgrave Street, Wellington New Zealand. **Tel** 011 64 4 4737211, FAX 011 64 4 734943, telex GOVPRINT NZ 31320. **(Subscription address:** Government Printing Office, PO Box 12052, Wellington New Zealand**)** **LC** J8; .B96. **Circ:** 1,300.
**Desc:** The official newspaper of the New Zealand Government.

US/0192-1142
**NEWMONTH.** ***Title Change.*** **VAT** New Month. (19??-19??). Periodical. English. bm. Phineas Corporation, 1043 South Clay Street, Green Bay WI 54301. **Tel** (414)433-0581. ***Continued by*** *Wisconsin Newmonth, 1059-0935.*

US/0028-8969
**NEWS & LETTERS.** **See** Economics.

US
**NEWS RELEASE FROM CONGRESSMAN AL BALDUS.** (19??)-. Periodical. English. Cannon House Office Building, Room 509, Washington DC 20515.

IS
**NEWSLETTER.** **Added/Corp** International Center for Peace in the Middle East. (198?)-. Newsletter. English.
**Ind/Abst** Hum. Rights Intern. Rep.

US/0882-6536
**NFF UPDATE.** [NFF update]. **VAT** National Foundation Forum Update. Periodical. English. bm. National Forum Foundation, 214 Massachusetts Avenue NE, Washington DC 20002. **DD** 322.

PL/0867-2237
**NIE WARSZAWA.** (NIE.). (1990)-. Periodical. Polish. wk. $104.00. **(Subscription address:** ARS Polona, PO Box 1001, 00068 Warsaw Poland.**)** **UDC** 327. **CODEN** 008(438).

NR/0189-5923
**NIGERIAN JOURNAL OF POLICY AND STRATEGY.** **Added/Corp** National Institute for Policy and Strategic Studies (Nigeria). **VFOAT** Nigerian Journal of Policy & Strategy. Vol. 1, No. 1 (June 1986)-. Periodical. English. sa. $16.00 (surface mail), $20.00 (air mail). National Institute for Policy and Strategic Studies, Kuru PMB 24, Bukuru, Plateau State, Nigeria. **LC** HC1055.A1; N56.
**Ind/Abst** PAIS Int. Print.

JA
**NIKKEI WEEKLY.** **See** Economics-International Economics.

AT/1031-6434
**NONVIOLENCE TODAY.** [Nonviol. today]. (1988)-. Periodical. English. bm. 25.00Aus$ Australia; 35.00Aus$ other. Editorial Collective, PO Box 5292, West End 4101 Australia. **Tel** 011 61 07 366-2660, FAX 011 61 07 366-3653. **DD** 303.6105. **Bk Rev**. ***Continues*** *Groundswell (Clifton Hill), 0812-0978.*
**Desc:** Nonviolence as a political theory. Covers the study and practice of non-violent action.

NO/0801-1745
**NORSK STATSVITENSKAPELIG TIDSSKRIFT.** [Nor. statsvitensk. tidsskr.]. Vol. 1, No. 1 (1985)-. Periodical. Norwegian. qt. Kr395.00, $66.00. Scandinavian University Press, PO Box 2959 Toeyen, N 0608 Oslo 6 Norway. **Tel** 011 47 2 2575400, FAX 011 47 2 2575353, telex 71896 UROR N. **(Subscription address:** Scandinavian University Press, 200 Meacham Ave., Elmont NY 11003.**)** **ED** Oddbjorn Knutsen and Bjorn-Erik Rasch. Index available. **Bk Rev**. **Ad Acc**. **Circ:** 800 (ctrl). ***Continues*** *Statsviteren, 0800-6245.*
**Desc:** Articles and analyses on politics, public administration, political behaviour and international politics.

GW/0340-014X
**NORTH KOREA QUARTERLY.** [North Korea q.]. (1974)-. Periodical. English. qt. DM97.00 Germany; DM105.00 other. Institute of Asian Affairs, Rothenbaumchaussee 32, D-20148 Hamburg Germany. **Tel** 011 49 40 443001, FAX 011 49 40 4107945. **ED** M. Y. Cho. **LC** DS930; .N57. **DD** 951.9/3. **Circ:** 300 (ctrl).
**Desc:** News and information topics on North Korea, chronology of events, documents, etc.

US/1058-3416
**NORTH SOUTH.** (NORTH-SOUTH : THE MAGAZINE OF THE AMERICAS.). [North South]. **Added/Corp** University of Miami. North-South Center. Vol. 1, No. 1 (June 1991)-. Periodical. English. Four times a year. Fl130.00 (individual), Fl255.50 (institution). Transaction Publishers / Rutgers State University, New Brunswick NJ 08903. **Tel** (908)932-2280 Ext. 105, FAX (908)932-3138. **ED** J. Suchlicki. **LC** E11; .N67; E11; .N6. **DD** 970.053/05. **[CCC]**. **Circ:** 2000.
**Desc:** Draws together writers representing a cross-section of schools of thought, from every country in the Western Hemisphere, to debate the principal questions confronting the region. Each issue includes information, interviews, and analysis of significant economic and political issues such as debt, economics, integration, democracy, education, public health and security.

FR/0298-7902
**NOTEBOOKS FOR STUDY AND RESEARCH - INTERNATIONAL INSTITUTE FOR RESEARCH AND EDUCATION.** (NOTEBOOKS FOR STUDY AND RESEARCH.). **VFOAT** NSR - International Institute for Research and Education. (1986)-. Periodical. English (French). Four times a year. 100.00F. Pierre Rousset, 2 rue Richard Lenoir, 93108 Montreuil France. **(Subscription address:** Pierre Rousset, Postbus 53290, 1007 RG Amsterdam Netherlands.**)** **ED** Pierre Rousset. **UDC** 323. **Bk Rev**. **Circ:** 2,000.
**Desc:** Analyzing both historical and contemporary, political, social and economical issues with a Marxist orientation.

CN/0713-8199
**NOTES DE RECHERCHE (UNIVERSITY OF OTTAWA. DEPT. OF POLITICAL SCIENCE).** (NOTES DE RECHERCHE / FACULTE DES SCIENCES SOCIALES, DEPARTEMENT DE SCIENCE POLITIQUE, UNIVERSITY D'OTTAWA.). [Notes rech. - Fac. sci. soc., Dep. sci. polit., Univ. Ottawa]. **VFOAT** Working Papers. **VAT** Working Papers - Faculty of Social Sciences. Department of Political Science. University of Ottawa. No. 1 (Nov. 1974)-. Monographic series. English (French). Price varies per volume. University of Ottawa / Department of Political Science, Faculty of Social Sciences, Ottawa Ontario K1N 6N5 Canada. **DD** 320.

IT/0392-7032
**NOTIZIE E DOCUMENTI.** [Not. doc.]. (1978)-. Periodical. Italian. tq. Instituto Nazionale per la Storia del Movimento di Liberazione in Italia, Piazza del Duomo, 14 20122 Milan Italy. **UDC** 945.094/095.

FR/1141-9946
**NOUVEL AFRIQUE ASIE, LE.** (Oct. 1989)-. Periodical. French. mo. $75.00 (1 year), $140.00 (2 year). Societe Des Editions Afrique Asie Amerique Latine, 3 rue de Metz, F 75010 Paris France. **Tel** 011 33 1 40220672. **LC** DT1; .N68. **DD** 950/.05. **Ad Acc**. **Circ:** 100,000 (ctrl). ***Continues*** *Afrique-Asie.*
**Desc:** Political, economic, social and cultural developments of the third world.

BE
**NOUVELLES ATLANTIQUES.** **VFOAT** Atlantic News. No. 633 (June 5, 1971)-. English (French). sw. 15000F. Agence Europe SA, 32 Rue Philippe II, BP 428, 2014 Luxembourg Luxembourg. **Tel** 011 352 20032.
**Desc:** Provides briefings on the political, military, technological and economic activities of Western and European security organizations.

CN/0703-1793
**NOVA SCOTIA LIBERAL, THE.** V. 1- Sept./Oct. 1976-. Periodical. English. bm. Free. Nova Scotia Liberal Association, PO Box 723, Halifax Nova Scotia B3J 2T3 Canada. **DD** 329.9/71. ctrl circ.

●RU
**NOVAIA LITERATURA PO SOTSIALNYM I GUMANITARNYM NAUKAM. GOSUDARSTVO I PRAVO / ROSSIISKAIA AKADEMIIA NAUK, INSTITUT NAUCHNOI INFORMATSII PO OBSHCHESTVENNYM NAUKAM.**
**Added/Corp** Institut Nauchnoi Informatsii po

Obshchestvennym Naukam (Rossiiskaia Akademiia Nauk). **VFOAT** Gosudarstvo i Pravo. (1993)-. Periodical. Russian. mo. Izdatelstvo Nauka / Akademiia Nauk, Publishing House of the Russian Academy of Sciences, Leninskii Porspekt 14, 117901 Moscow Russia. **Tel** 011 95 954-21-53, FAX 011 95 938-21-44, telex 411964. **(Subscription address:** Kubon & Sagner, ABT Zeitschriftenimport, D 80328 Munich Germany.**)** **LC** JA26.Z99; N68. ***Formed by the union of*** *Novaia Otechestvennaia Literatura po Obshchestvennym Naukam. Gosudarstvo i Pravo* ***and*** *Novaia Inostrannaia Literatura po Obshchestvennym Naukam. Gosudarstvo i Pravo.*

BL/0101-3300
**NOVOS ESTUDOS CEBRAP.** **Added/Corp** Centro Brasileiro de Analise e Planejamento. **VFOAT** Novos Estudos. Vol. 1, No. 1 (Dec. 1981)-. Periodical. Portuguese. Three times a year (March, July, November). $40.00 (individuals), $60.00 (institutions). Editora Brasileira de Ciencias, rua Morgado Mateus 615, 04015 Sao Paulo SP Brazil. **Tel** 55 11 5740399, FAX 55 11 5745928. **ED** Rodrigo Naves. **LC** F2501; .N68. **DD** 981/.005. Index available. cum. index. **Bk Rev**. **Circ:** 2,500. ***Continues*** *Centro Brasileiro de Analise e Planejamento. Estudos Cebrap.*
**Desc:** Covers politics, economy, sociology, and arts in general of Brazil and the world.
**Ind/Abst** Soc. Plann. Policy Dev. Abstr.

US/0734-5836
**NUCLEAR TIMES (NEW YORK, N.Y.).** ***Ceased.*** (NUCLEAR TIMES.). [Nucl. times]. Vol. 1, No. 1 (Oct. 1982)-Vol. 10 (Spring 1992). Academic Scholarly Publication. English. bm. Nuclear Times, 401 Commonwealth Avenue, Boston MA 02215. **Tel** (617)266-1193. **ED** Elliott Negin. **LC** JX1974.7; .N84. **DD** 327.1/74/05. **Bk Rev**. **Ad Acc**. **Circ:** 36,000 (ctrl). Documents available from UMI Article Clearinghouse, Documents on Demand.
**Desc:** Chronicles the antinuclear weapons movement in United States reports on legislative, scholarly, and grassroots efforts, new scientific and research information reviews, calendar of nationwide events.
**Ind/Abst** Altern. Press Index; Energy Inf. Abstr.; Environ. Abstr.; Expand. Acad. Index (1992-); Newsp. Period. Abstr. (1992-); PAIS Int. Print (1991-).

US/1056-8921
**NUEVA INTERNACIONAL.** [Nueva int.]. (1991)-. Periodical. Spanish. $12.95. 408 Printing and Publishing Inc, 410 West Street, New York NY 10014. **Tel** (212)243-6392, FAX (212)727-0150. **LC** HX9.S7; N85. **DD** 324.1/75/05.

VE
**NUEVA POLITICA.** (19??)-. Periodical. Spanish. qt. **LC** JA5; .N84.
**Ind/Abst** HAPI Hisp. Am. Period. Index (19??-).

IT
**NUOVI STUDI POLITICI.** Yearly V. 1- Jan./Feb. 1971-. Italian. qt. L25000 Italy; L37000 other. Bulzoni Editore Srl, Via dei Liburni 14, 00185 Rome Italy. **Tel** 011 39 6 445-5207, FAX 011 39 6 445-0355. **ED** Salvatore Valitutti. **LC** JN5201; .N86.

IT/0029-6376
**NUOVO MEZZOGIORNO.** **See** Economics.

NO/0800-336X
**NYTT NORSK TIDSSKRIFT.** No. 1 (1984)-. Periodical. Norwegian. qt. Kr470.00, $80.00. Scandinavian University Press, PO Box 2959 Toeyen, N 0608 Oslo 6 Norway. **Tel** 011 47 2 2575400, FAX 011 47 2 2575353, telex 71896 UROR N. **(Subscription address:** Scandinavian University Press, 200 Meacham Ave., Elmont NY 11003.**)** **ED** Rune Slagstad. **LC** JA26; .N97. Index available. **Bk Rev**. **Ad Acc**. **Circ:** 2,500.
**Desc:** A journal of science and politics, including contributions in fiction.
**Ind/Abst** Am. Hist. Life (1987-1990).

US/0360-1781
**OBF, OF THE PEOPLE, BY THE PEOPLE, FOR THE PEOPLE.** V. 1- Aug. 1975-. Periodical. English. mo. $12.00. OBF Inc, PO Box 10107, Eugene OR 97401. **LC** JK1; .O18. **DD** 320.9/73/0925.

RU
**OBSHCHESTVENNYE NAUKI V ROSSII. SERIIA 4, GOSUDARSTVO I PRAVO / ROSSIISKAIA AKADEMIIA NAUK, INSTITUT NAUCHNOI INFORMATSII PO OBSHCHESTVENNYM NAUKAM.** ***Title Change.*** **See** Law.

NZ/0113-1044
**OCCASIONAL PAPER / NEW ZEALAND INSTITUTE OF INTERNATIONAL AFFAIRS.** **Added/Corp** New Zealand Institute of International Affairs. (198?)-. Monographic series. English. ir. Price varies per volume. New Zealand Institute of International Affairs, Victoria University of Wellington, Private Bag, PO Box 600, Wellington New Zealand. **Tel** 11 64 4 4727430, FAX 11 64 4 4712070. **LC** UNC.

CN/0229-7000
**OCCASIONAL PAPERS - DEPARTMENT OF POLITICAL SCIENCE. CARLETON UNIVERSITY.** (OCCASIONAL PAPERS.). [Occas. pap. - Dep. Polit. Sci., Carleton Univ.]. Periodical. English. Gail Harmer, Graphic Services, 501 AB Carleton University, Ottawa Ontario K1S 5B6 Canada. **DD** 320/.05.

CN/0319-2733
**OCCIDENTE (TORONTO).** (OCCIDENTE.). V. 1- April 1975-. Periodical. Italian (English). mo. Occidente, 1756-A Ouest Av Eglinton, Toronto Ontario M6E 2H6 Canada. **DD** 320.5/32/05.
**Ind/Abst** Am. Hist. Life (1955-1956).

US/1068-5987
**OFARI'S BI-MONTHLY.** [Ofari's bi-mon.]. Vol. 1, No. 1 (Oct./Nov. 1984)-. Periodical. English. bm. $18.00 (one year), $36.00 (two year), $54.00 (three year) institutions; $10.00 (one year), $20.00 (two year), $30.00 (three year) individuals. Middle Passage Press, 5517 Secrest Drive, Los Angeles CA 90043-2029. **Tel** (213)298-0266. **ED** Barbara Bramwell. **LC** E185.5; .O33. **DD** 960. **Circ:** 300.
**Desc:** An opinion newsletter with an alternative look at social, political, and current events that affect the African American Community. Gives a historical perspective on current concerns.

US/0363-2938
**OFFICIAL ABSTRACT OF VOTES, GENERAL ELECTION.** (OFFICIAL ABSTRACT OF VOTES : GENERAL ELECTION - OREGON.). **Main/Corp** Oregon. Elections Division. English. Salem Secretary of State, Salem OR 97310. **LC** JK9092; .O74B. **DD** 329/.023/795.

US/0360-4373
**OFFICIAL ABSTRACT OF VOTES : PRIMARY ELECTION.** **Main/Corp** Oregon. Elections Division. English. Secretary of State Publishing Division, 300 North Salisbury Street, Raleigh NC 27603-5909. **Tel** (919)733-7355. **LC** JK9092; .O74A. **DD** 329/.0223/09795.

US/0091-0090
**OFFICIAL CANDIDATES PAMPHLET.** **Main/Corp** Washington (State). Office of the Secretary of State. English. Washington Office of The Secretary of State, State Capital, Seattle WA 98115. **LC** JK2023.W3; W37A. **DD** 329/.023/797.

US/0362-3556
**OFFICIAL JOURNAL OF THE PROCEEDINGS OF THE SENATE AND HOUSE OF REPRESENTATIVES OF THE STATE OF LOUISIANA AND THE LEGISLATIVE CALENDAR.** **Main/Corp** Louisiana. Legislature. Senate. Proceedings. English. 519 Fidelity Bank Building, Baton Rouge LA 70801. **LC** J87; .L8 DATE A. **DD** 328.763/01.

CN/1183-3580
**OFFICIAL REPORT OF DEBATES (HANSARD) - ONTARIO. LEGISLATIVE ASSEMBLY. SELECT COMMITTEE ON ONTARIO IN CONFEDERATION.** (OFFICIAL REPORT OF DEBATES (HANSARD) / JOURNAL DES DEBATS (HANSARD) / COMITE SPECIAL SUR LE ROLE DE L'ONTARIO AU SEIN DE LA CONFEDERATION. SELECT COMMITTEE ON ONTARIO IN CONFEDERATION). [Off. rep. debates (Hansard) - Ont., Legis. Assem., Sel. Comm. Ont. Confed.]. **Main/Corp** Ontario. Legislative Assembly. Select Committee on Ontario in Confederation. **VFOAT** Journal des Debats (Hansard). (1991)-. Periodical. English (French). **DD** 328.713/01/05.

US
**OFFICIAL RETURNS ... PRIMARY ELECTION.** **Added/Corp** Alaska. Division of Elections. (August 26, 1986)-. English. be. **LC** JK2075.A4; A25. **DD** 324.5/4/09798. ***Continues*** *Official Returns of Election Precincts. Primary Election.*

US
**OFFICIAL VOTERS PAMPHLET.** **Added/Corp** Washington (State). Office of the Secretary of State. **VFOAT** Voters Pamphlet. (198?)-. English. Secretary of State Publishing Division, 300 North Salisbury Street, Raleigh NC 27603-5909. **Tel** (919)733-7355. ***Continues*** *Washington (State). Office of the Secretary of State. Voters and Candidates Pamphlet.*

US/0164-6524
**OHIO REPUBLICAN NEWS.** Periodical. English. mo. Republican State Headquarters, 172 East State/Room 401, Columbus OH 43215.

US
**OKLAHOMA GOVERNMENT PUBLICATIONS.** Vol. 5, No. 1 (Jan. 1981)-. English. bm. Free. Oklahoma Publications Clearinghouse, Oklahoma Department of Libraries, Allen Wright Memorial Library Building, 200 Northeast 18th Street, Oklahoma City OK 73105. **Tel** (405)521-2502, FAX (405)525-7804. **ED** Steve Beleu. **LC** Z1223.5.O5; O38A; J87.O5. **DD** 015.766. Index available. **Circ:** 300 (ctrl). available on microfiche. ***Continues*** *Oklahoma Government Documents.*
**Desc:** An alphabetic listing by agency of publications issued by Oklahoma State Government and received by the Oklahoma Publications Clearinghouse.

US/0030-1795
**OKLAHOMA OBSERVER, THE.** (1969)-. Periodical. English. sm (22 issues per year). $25.00. Oklahoma Observer, Box 53371, Oklahoma City OK 73152. **Tel** (405)525-5582. **ED** Frosty Troy. **Bk Rev**. **Ad Acc**, **Adv Mgr:** Helen Troy. **Circ:** 7,500. available on microfilm and microfiche from University Microfilms International (UMI).
**Desc:** A journal of commentary on government, politics and social problems.
**Ind/Abst** Access (1975-).

●US/1065-0695
**OKLAHOMA POLITICS.** (OKLAHOMA POLITICS : YEARBOOK OF THE OKLAHOMA POLITICAL SCIENCE ASSOCATION.). **Added/Corp** Oklahoma Political Science Assocation. (1992)-. Periodical. English. $10.00. Oklahoma Political Science Association, Department of Political Science, Oklahoma State University, Stillwater OK 74087.

US/0887-9567
**ON BEYOND WAR.** ***Title Change.*** [On beyond war]. **Added/Corp** Beyond War (Group). (198?)-(19??). Periodical. English. mo. Foundation Global Community, 222 High Street, Palo Alto CA 94301. **Tel** (415)328-7756. ***Continued by*** *Timeline.*

CN/0384-5265
**ON HER MAJESTY'S SERVICE.** V. 1- July 1, 1976-. Periodical. English. $5.00. Vancouver and Greater Vancouver Monarchist Association, 1865 Barclay Street/Suite 402, Vancouver British Columbia V6G 1K7 Canada. **DD** 321.8/7.

CN/0380-5980
**ON TARGET (CANADIAN EDITION).** (ON TARGET.). (Aug. 1967)-. Periodical. English. Fifty times a year. 28.04Can$ US & Canada (surface mail); 35.00Can$ US & Canada, 50.00Can$ others (airmail). Canadian Intelligence Service, Bag 78, High River Alberta T0L 1B0 Canada. **Tel** (519)924-2848. **ED** Ron Gostick. **Circ:** 1,300 (ctrl).
**Desc:** Provides facts and documentation on current issues in a brief and concise form.

US/0147-4693
**ON THE LINE MAGAZINE.** **VFOAT** On the Line. V. 1- Winter 1977-. Periodical. English. qt. $8.00. K A Murray, 152 East 22nd Street, New York NY 10010.

CN/0827-2247
**ONTARIO DEMOCRAT, THE.** [Ont. democr.]. Vol. 22, No. 2 (Mar. 1984)-. Periodical. English (French). ir. 5.00Can$. Ontario New Democratic Party, 184 Main Street, Toronto Ontario M4E 2W1 Canada. **Tel** (416)391-5645. **ED** Marjorie Nichols. **DD** 324.2713/07/05. **Bk Rev**. **Ad Acc**. **Circ:** 26,000 (ctrl). ***Continues*** *New Democrat, 0028-4564.*
**Desc:** General interest democratic socialist material.

II
**OPINION.** (1960)-. Periodical. English. wk. A D Gorwala, 40 C Ridge Road, Bombay India. **LC** DS401; .O56. **DD** 320.9/54.

IQ
**OPINION DE BAGDAD, L'.** French. mo. $50.00 US. Matabi dar Al-Jamahir Lil-Sihafah, Al-Hurriya Press House, Karantina, Baghdad Iraq. **Tel** 5383171, telex 212984 MAMUN IK. **ED** Naji Al-Hadithi. **LC** DS79.65; .O65. **DD** 320.9/567/04. **Bk Rev**. **Ad Acc**. **Circ:** 5,000.
**Desc:** Political and cultural magazine covering affairs in Iraq.

US/0030-4387
**ORBIS (PHILADELPHIA).** (ORBIS.). [Orbis]. **Added/Corp** Foreign Policy Research Institute. University of Pennsylvania. International Relations Graduate Group. Vol. 1 (Apr. 1957)-. Periodical. English. qt. $160.00 (institutions), $60.00 (individuals) US; $180.00 (institutions), $80.00 (individuals) (surface mail), $200.00 (institutions), $100.00 (individuals) (air mail) other. JAI Press Inc., 55 Old Post Road, Suite 2, PO Box 1678, Greenwich CT 06836-1678. **Tel** (203)661-7602, FAX (203)661-0792. **ED** Patrick Clawson. **LC** D839; .O68. **DD** 909.82. **[CCC]**. Index available. cum. index. **Bk Rev**. **Ad Acc**. **Pr Rev**. **Circ:** 3,500 (ctrl). available on microfilm and microfiche from University Microfilms International (UMI). Documents available from The Genuine Article, UMI Article Clearinghouse.
**Desc:** Examines political, military, social and economic dimensions of contemporary international affairs; includes book reviews.
**Ind/Abst** ABC POL SCI; Acad. Abstr. Full Text Elite (July 1990-); Acad. Abstr. (July 1990-); Acad. Search (July 1990-); Am. Hist. Life (1962-); Arts Humanit. Citation Index [Select. Cov.]; Curr. Geogr. Publ. (199?-); Curr. Mil. Pol. Lit.; Expand. Acad. Index (1987-); Hum. Rights Intern. Rep.; INFO-SOUTH Abstr.; Int. Polit. Sci. Abstr.;

Newsp. Period. Abstr. (1991-); PAIS Int. Print (1991-); Peace Res. Abstr. J. (1965-1983); Res. Alert [Full Cov.]; Sage Public Adm. Abstr.; Soc. Sci. Source (Jul. 1990-); Soc. Sci. Cit. Index [Full Cov.]; Soc. Sci. Index; Soc. Sci. Index Fulltext (Fall 1988-) [Full Txt.]; Middle East J.; U.S. Polit. Sci. Doc.

GW
**ORDO POLITICUS. Main/Corp** Freiburg I.B. Arnold-Nergstraeser-Institut fur Kulturwissenschaftliche Forschung. Monographic series. English. ir. Price varies per volume. Duncker und Humblot Verlag, Postfach 410329, D-12113 Berlin Germany. **Tel** 011 49 30 79000612, 011 49 30 79000613. **ED** D. Oberndorfer.
**Desc:** Publishes works of the Arnold-Bergstraesser Institute of Freiburg West Germany. Studies in political science.
**Ind/Abst** Int. Polit. Sci. Abstr.

II
**ORGANISER. See** Sociology.

IT
**ORION.** Italian. mo. L70000.00 Italy; L110000.00 other. Orion Barbarossa, Via Plinio 32, 20129 Milan Italy. **Tel** 011 39 2 201310. **Bk Rev**, (Qty: 24-30). **Ad Acc**, **Adv Mgr:** M. Murelli, **Tel** same as publisher. **Circ:** 2000 (ctrl).

AU
**OST-DOKUMENTATION BILDUNGS- UND WISSENSCHAFTSPOLITIK.**
**Added/Corp** Oesterreichisches Ost- und Suedosteuropa-Institut. Abteilung fuer Bildung und Kultur. (1991)-. German. qt. Oesterreichisches Ost- und Suedosteuropa-Institut, Abteilung fuer Bildung und Kultur, Klosterneuburg Austria. **LC** IN PROCESS. ***Continues*** *Ost-Dokumentation Bildungswesen.*

AU/0378-5149
**OSTERREICHISCHE ZEITSCHRIFT FUER POLITIKWISSENSCHAFT.** [Osterr. Z. Polit.wiss.]. Vol. 1- 1972-. Periodical. German. qt. 370.00Aus$. Verlag fur Gesellschaftskritik, A-1070 Vienna Austria. **Tel** 011 43 222 526 3582. Index available. **Bk Rev**. **Ad Acc. Circ:** 1,300 (ctrl). Documents available from The Genuine Article.
**Ind/Abst** Arts Humanit. Citation Index [Select. Cov.]; Int. Bibliogr. Sociol.; Int. Polit. Sci. Abstr.; Res. Alert [Full Cov.]; Soc. Sci. Cit. Index [Full Cov.].

GW/0030-6428
**OSTEUROPA (STUTTGART).**
(OSTEUROPA.). [Osteuropa]. **Added/Corp** Deutsche Gesellschaft fuer Osteuropakunde. **VFOAT** Ost-Europa. Vol. 1 (Oct 1951)-. Periodical. German. Twelve times a year. DM114.00. DVA Deutsche Verlagsanstalt, Neckarstrasse 121, D-70190 Stuttgart Germany. **Tel** 011 49 711 26310. **(Subscription address:** Zenit Pressevertrieb Gmbh., Postfach 810640, D 70523 Stuttgart Germany, telephone: 011 49 711 7252191**) LC** DR1; .O8. **DD** 947/.0005. **[CCC].** Index available. cum. index. **Bk Rev. Ad Acc. Pr Rev. Circ:** 2,500 (ctrl). Documents available from The Genuine Article. ***Supersedes*** *Osteuropa.*
**Desc:** Reports, analysis and documentation regarding the Soviet Union, the Eastern European countries, other communist states and socialist regimes, and the international communist movement.
**Ind/Abst** ABC POL SCI; AGRICOLA; Am. Hist. Life (1954-); Arts Humanit. Citation Index [Select. Cov.]; Int. Bibliogr. Sociol.; Int. Polit. Sci. Abstr.; MLA Int. Bibl. Books Artic. Mod. Lang. Lit.; PAIS Int. Print (1991-); Res. Alert [Full Cov.]; Soc. Plann. Policy Dev. Abstr.; Soc. Sci. Cit. Index [Full Cov.]; Sociol. Abstr. (?-?); Middle East J.

MX
**OTHER SIDE OF MEXICO, THE.**
**Added/Corp** Equipo Pueblo (Mexico City, Mexico). No. 1 (April/June 1987)-. Periodical. English (Spanish; translations available in Spanish). Six times a year. $10.00 (individuals), $18.00 (institutions) Mexico; $15.00 (individuals), $20.00 (institutions) others. Equipo Pueblo, Apartado Postal 27-467, Mexico 06760 DF Mexico. **Tel** 011 52 5 5390015. **ED** Laura Carlsen, Carlos Heredia, and Ricardo Hernandez. **Circ:** 2,000.
**Desc:** News on and from Mexican grassroofs organizations.
**Ind/Abst** Hum. Rights Intern. Rep.

CN/0826-1113
**OTTAWA GREENS NEWSLETTER.**
[Ottawa Greens newsl.]. Vol. 1, No. 1 (Fall 1983)-. Newsletter. English. Free to members, $5.00 membership Green Party of Canada, $3.00 Green Party of Ontario. Ottawa Greens, PO Box 4089 Station E, Ottawa Ontario K1S 5B2 Canada. **DD** 324.271/09.

CN/0828-5713
**OTTAWA ON THE RECORD.** [Ottawa rec.]. Vol. 1, No. 1 (Sept. 13, 1984)-. Periodical. English. Forty-eight times a year. 190.00Can$. ECL Publishing, 155 Queen Street, Suite 1100, Ottawa ONT K1P 6L1 Canada. **Tel** (613)236-9522, FAX (613)234-5210. **DD** 320.971.

US/0886-9049
**OUR RIGHT TO KNOW.** (OUR RIGHT TO KNOW / FUND FOR OPEN INFORMATION AND ACCOUNTABILITY, INC.). [Our right know]. **Added/Corp** Fund for Open Information and Accountability, Inc. (New York, N.Y.). (19??)-. Periodical. English. qt. $10.00 (individuals), $25.00 (institutions). Fund for Open Information and Accountability Inc, PO Box 02 2397, Brooklyn NY 11202. **Tel** (212)477-3188. **ED** Adele Oltman. **DD** 323. **Circ:** 15,000. Documents available from UMI Article Clearinghouse.
**Desc:** News journal covering issues of government secrecy. Tracks FOIA developments in Congress and the courts. Also covers media distortion, and general information about the information industry.
**Ind/Abst** Altern. Press Index (-199?); Expand. Acad. Index (1992-); Hum. Rights Intern. Rep.; Newsp. Period. Abstr. (1992-).

CN/0700-3617
**OVERVIEW (TORONTO).** (OVERVIEW.). V. 1- Oct. 1976-. Periodical. English. bm. 90.00Can$. National Citizens Coalition, 100 Adelaide Street West, Suite 907, Toronto Ontario M5H 1S3 Canada. **Tel** (416)869-3838, FAX (416)869-1891. **ED** Alex Alvaro. **DD** 330.9/71/0644. **Bk Rev. Circ:** 8,000 (ctrl).
**Desc:** Journal dedicated to the promotion of freedom and free enterprise in Canada.

US
**P S R MONITOR. See** Medical Science and Technology.

CN/0030-851X
**PACIFIC AFFAIRS.** [Pac. aff.]. **Added/Corp** University of British Columbia. Institute of Pacific Relations. Vol. 1 (May 1928)-. Periodical. English. qt. 55.00Can$ (institutions), 40.00Can$ (individuals) Canada; 60.00Can$ (institution), 45.00Can$ (individuals) US; 65.00Can$ (institutions), 50.00Can$ (individuals) other. Pacific Affairs, University of British Columbia, 2029 West Mall, Vancouver British Columbia V6T 1Z2, Canada. **Tel** (604)822-6508, (604)822-4534. **ED** Ian D. Slater. **LC** DU1; .P13. **[CCC]. Bk Rev**, (Qty: 60). **Ad Acc. Pr Rev. Circ:** 3,000. available on microfilm and microfiche from University Microfilms International (UMI). Documents available from The Genuine Article, UMI Article Clearinghouse. ***Supersedes*** *Institute of Pacific Relations. News Bulletin.*
**Desc:** Insight into the social, cultural, political and economic issues of that region. Carries articles, review articles and research notes contributed by authors throughout the world.
**Ind/Abst** ABC POL SCI; Abstr. Anthropol.; Acad. Abstr. Full Text Elite (July 1990-); Acad. Abstr. (July 1990-); Acad. Ind. [Computer File] (1987-); Acad. Search (July 1990-); Am. Hist. Life (1954-); Am. Bibliogr. Slavic East Europ. Stud.; Arts Humanit. Citation Index [Select. Cov.]; Book Rev. Index; Can. Index; Can. Period. Index (19??-); Curr. Contents Soc. Behav. Sci.; Curr. Geogr. Publ. (199?-); Curr. Mil. Pol. Lit.; Educ. Adm. Abstr.; Expand. Acad. Index (1987-); Hum. Resour. Abstr.; Humanit. Index; Humanit. Source (Jul. 1990-); INFO-SOUTH Abstr.; Int. Bibliogr. Sociol.; Int. Labour Doc.; Int. Polit. Sci. Abstr.; LABORDOC; Mag. Search; Middle East Abstr. Index; Newsp. Period. Abstr. (1990-); Peace Res. Abstr. J. (1958-1964), (1968-1973); Res. Alert [Full Cov.]; Sage Public Adm. Abstr.; Soc. Sci. Source (Jul. 1990-); Soc. Sci. Cit. Index [Full Cov.]; Soc. Sci. Index; Soc. Sci. Index Fulltext (Fall 1988-) [Full Txt.].

AT/1031-6981
**PACIFIC REPORT (RED HILL). See** Business.

UK/0951-2748
**PACIFIC REVIEW (OXFORD, ENGLAND).** (THE PACIFIC REVIEW.). [Pac. rev.]. Vol. 1, No. 1 (1988)-. Periodical. English. Four times a year (Mar., Jun., Sep., Dec.). $115.00 (US & Canada); £84.00 (UK); £88.00 (other). Routledge, 11 New Fetter Lane, London EC4P 4EE England. **Tel** 071 583 9855, FAX 071 842 2298. **(Subscription address:** Kinokuniya Company Ltd., 38-1 Sakuragaoka 5, chome Setagaya-ku, Tokyo 156 Japan.**) ED** Gerald Segal. **LC** DU29; .P24. **DD** 990/.05. **[CCC].** cum. index. **Bk Rev. Ad Acc.** available on microfilm and microfiche from University Microfilms International (UMI).
**Desc:** Interdisciplinary forum for the exchange of ideas and trends in Pacific politics. Topics on history, domestic, foreign politics, military strategy, economics and culture are discussed.
**Ind/Abst** Int. Bibliogr. Sociol.; Int. Polit. Sci. Abstr.; PAIS Int. Print (1991-).

IS
**PANIM LE-KHAN ULE-KHAN. Added/Corp** Bet Berl. Mikhlalah. Makhon Le-Hinukh Le-Demokratyah. Israel. Misrad Ha-Hinukh Veha-Tarbut. Yehidah Le-Demokratyah Ule-Du-Kiyum. (Feb. 1988)-. Hebrew. bm. IL35.00 Israel; $20.00 other. Institute of Education in Democracy, Beit Berl College 44 905, Israel. **Tel** 052 454 662. **ED** Shlomo Zadikiya. **LC** DS101; .P453. **Ad Acc.**

GT
**PANORAMA CENTROAMERICANO. SERIE TEMAS Y DOCUMENTOS DE DEBATE. Added/Corp** Instituto Centroamericano de Estudios Politicos (Guatemala, Guatemala). **VFOAT** Serie Temas y Documentos de Debate; Temas y Documentos de Debate; Panorama Centroamericano. Temas y Documentos de Debate. (198?)-. Periodical. Spanish. bm. INCEP, 12 Calle 6 40 Zona 9 of 301, Guatemala Guatemala CA. **Tel** 011 502 2 345214. **LC** JL1416; .P36. **DD** 320.9728/005.
**Ind/Abst** PAIS Int. Print.

CW
**PAPERS AND ORDER PAPERS PRESENTED : OFFICIAL REPORT / PARLIAMENT OF THE COOK ISLANDS.**
**Main/Corp** Cook Islands. Parliament. (19??)-. English. **LC** J968.C6; H52. ***Continues*** *Cook Islands. Legislative Assembly.; Papers Presented and Order Papers.*

US
**PAPERS OF DWIGHT DAVID EISENHOWER.** (19??)-. Monographic series. English. ir. Price varies per volume. Johns Hopkins University Press, 2715 North Charles Street, Baltimore MD 21218-4319. **Tel** (410)516-6987, FAX (410)516-6968.

US
**PAPERS OF FREDERICK LAW OLMSTEAD.** (19??)-. Monographic series. English. ir. Price varies per volume. Johns Hopkins University Press, 2715 North Charles Street, Baltimore MD 21218-4319. **Tel** (410)516-6987, FAX (410)516-6968.

US
**PAPERS OF GEORGE CATLETT MARSHALL.** (19??)-. Monographic series. English. ir. Price varies per volume. Johns Hopkins University Press, 2715 North Charles Street, Baltimore MD 21218-4319. **Tel** (410)516-6987, FAX (410)516-6968.

US
**PAPERS OF THOMAS A. EDISON.** (19??)-. Monographic series. English. ir. Price varies per volume. Johns Hopkins University Press, 2715 North Charles Street, Baltimore MD 21218-4319. **Tel** (410)516-6987, FAX (410)516-6968.

CW
**PAPERS PRESENTED AND ORDER PAPERS - COOK ISLANDS. LEGISLATIVE ASSEMBLY.** ***Title Change.***
**Main/Corp** Cook Islands. Legislative Assembly. 13th Session, (1969)-(19??). English. T Kapi, Government Printer, Rarotonga Cook Islands. **LC** J968.C6; H52. **DD** 328.96/23/04. ***Continues*** *Cook Islands. Legislative Assembly. Papers and Bills Presented.* ***Continued by*** *Papers and Order Papers Presented.*

GW/0553-3139
**PARLAMENT, DAS. Added/Corp** Bundeszentrale fuer Politische Bildung (Germany) Bundeszentrale fuer Politische Bildung (Germany). Vol. 1 (Sept. 19, 1951)-. Periodical. German. wk. DM52.80. Bundeszentrale Polit Bildung, Berliner Freiheit 7, D-53111 Bonn Germany. **(Subscription address:** Paulinus Druckerei GmbH, Fleischstrasse 62 65, D 54290 Trier Germany.**) LC** D839; .P3.
**Ind/Abst** Energy Res. Abstr. (Feb. 1976-); Int. Labour Doc.

IT
**PARLAMENTO (ROME, ITALY).**
(PARLAMENTO.). Periodical. Italian. mo. Rivista Parlamento, Via dell Colonna Antonina 52, 00186 Rome Italy. **Tel** 011 39 6 6785814.

FR/0258-4751
**PARLEMENTS ET FRANCOPHONIE.**
(1985)-. Periodical. French. Four times a year (Apr., June, Sept., Dec.). 150.00F. Assemblee Internationale des Parlementaires de Langue Francaise AIPLF, 235 Blvd Saint Germain, 75007 Paris France. **Tel** 011 33 1 47052687, FAX 011 33 1 45511147. **ED** Alain Kremer. **UDC** 328. **Bk Rev**, (Qty: 2 or 4). **Ad Acc, Adv Mgr:** Frank Borotra. **Circ:** 1,700.

CN/0709-4582
**PARLIAMENTARY GOVERNMENT.**
[Parliam. gov.]. **Added/Corp** Institute for Research on Public Policy. Parliamentary Centre for Foreign Affairs and Foreign Trade. **VFOAT** Government Parliamentary. Vol. 1, (Oct. 1979)-. Periodical. English (French). Four times a year. $19.26. Parliamentary Centre, 275 Rue Slater Street, Suite 500, Ottawa Ontario K1P 5H9 Canada. **Tel** (613)237-0143, FAX (613)235-8237. **ED** Nicholas Swales. **DD** 328.71/005. **Circ:** 2,000-5,000 (ctrl).
**Desc:** Changing role of legislatures plus parliamentary and political reforms.
**Ind/Abst** Can. Index (?-?).

US/0048-2994
**PARLIAMENTARY JOURNAL.** Began in 1960. Periodical. English. qt. $10.00 (individuals), $9.00 (institutions). American Institute of Parliamentarians, PO Box 12452, Fort Wayne IN 46863. **Tel** (219)422-3680. **ED** Helen T McFadler(editor's address: PO Box 8, Cades, SC 29518). **LC** JF515; .P25. Index available. cum. index. **Circ:** 1,500. available on microfilm and microfiche from University Microfilms International (UMI).
**Desc:** A magazine for parliamentarians and students of

parliamentary procedure, to stimulate thought, discussion and action to improve the practice of parliamentary decision-making.

●CN/1188-2387
**PARLIAMENTARY WEEKLY QUARTERLY REPORT, THE.** [Parliam. wkly. q. rep.]. **Added/Corp** Bytown Research Group. Vol. 1, No. 1 (Mar. 1, 1992)-. Periodical. English. qt (March, June, Sep., Dec.). 28.00Can$ (one year), 52.00Can$ (two year) Canada; 33.00Can$ (one year), 57.00Can$ (two year) US; 38.00Can$ (one year), 62.00Can$ (two year) other. Bytown Research Group, 16-195 Cooper Street, Ottawa Ontario K2P 0E6 Canada. **Tel** (613)231-4573, FAX (613)231-4573. **ED** Larry Menard. **DD** 320.971/05. **Ad Acc**, **Adv Mgr:** Robert Renaud. **Pr Rev.** ctrl circ.
**Desc:** Provides news, digests, and a forum on diverse views of Canadian politics. Focuses on Canadian federate politics, policies and interest group concerns.

UK/0260-6755
**PARLIAMENTS, ESTATES & REPRESENTATION.** **Added/Corp** International Commission for the History of Representative and Parliamentary Institutions. **VFOAT** Parliaments, Estates and Representation; Parlements, Etats et Representation; Parlements, Etats & Representation. Vol. 1, Pt. 1 (June 1981)-. Periodical. English (French and German). sa. Pageant Publishing, 5 Turners Road, London NW11 6TD England. **Tel** 011 44 81 455 3703. **(Subscription address:** World-Wide Subscription Services, Unit 4, Gibbs Reed Farm Pashley Road, Ticehurst TN5 7HE England.**) LC** JF501; .P356. **DD** 328/.3/05. **[CCC].** Index available in last issue of volume--attached. **Bk Rev. Ad Acc. Pr Rev.**
**Ind/Abst** Am. Hist. Life (1981-).

CN/0709-6941
**PARTICIPATION (OTTAWA).** (PARTICIPATION : NEWSLETTER OF THE INTERNATIONAL POLITICAL SCIENCE ASSOCIATION.). [Particip.]. **Added/Corp** International Political Science Association. **VFOAT** Bulletin de l'Association Internationale de Science Politique. Vol. 1, No. 3 (1977)-. Newsletter. English (French). Three times a year. Free to members; $45.00 individual membership fee. Institute of Political Science / Oslo, University of Oslo, Box 1097 Blindern, 0317 Oslo 3 Norway. **Tel** 011 47 2 855168, 011 47 2 469256, FAX 011 47 2 854411. **ED** Francesco Kjellberg. **DD** 320/.06/01. **Circ:** 1,500 (ctrl). ***Continues*** *International Participation, 0822-6431.*

UZ
**PARTIINAIA ZHIZN.** **Added/Corp** TSK KP Uzbekistana. (1960)-. Periodical. Russian. mo. $18.00. **(Subscription address:** Victor Kamkin, 4956 Boiling Brook Parkway, Rockville MD 20852.**) LC** JN6598.K4; P3.

CN/0227-1745
**PC DISPATCH.** [PC dispatch]. Vol. 1, No. 1 (May 1980)-. Periodical. English. mo. Free. Pc Dispatch, 178 Queen Street, Ottawa K1P 5E1 Canada. **DD** 324.27104/005. ctrl circ. ***Continues in part*** *Progressive Conservative Party of Canada. Bulletin, 0316-814X.*

CN/0820-6260
**PC YOUTH TODAY.** [PC youth today]. **VAT** Progressive Conservative Youth Today. Periodical. English. Progressive Conservative Youth Federation, Suite 200/161 Laurier Avenue West, Ottawa Ontario K1P 5J3 Canada. **DD** 324.27104. ***Continues in part*** *Prospectus, 0707-7009.*

US/0015-9093
**PEACE AND FREEDOM.** **See** Women's Interests.

UK
**PEACE NEWS FOR NONVIOLENT REVOLUTION.** **VFOAT** Peace News. No. 2336 (Dec. 1990)-. Periodical. English. mo. **LC** JX1901; .P36. ***Continues*** *Peace News (London, England : 1988).*

US/1049-0779
**PEACE REPORTER.** **See** Education.

CN/0553-4283
**PEACE RESEARCH REVIEWS.** [Peace res. rev.]. **Added/Corp** Peace Research Institute-Dundas. Canadian Peace Research Institute. Vol. 1, No. 1 (1967)-. Monographic series. English. qt. 48.00Can$. Peace Research Institute, 25 Dundana Avenue, Dundas Ontario L9H 4E5 Canada. **Tel** (416)628-2356, FAX (416)628-1830. **LC** JX1901; .P395. **Circ:** 300.
**Desc:** Contains information on publications about economics of third world countries and nuclear disarmament.
**Ind/Abst** ABC POL SCI; Am. Hist. Life (1975-); Middle East Abstr. Index.

US/0031-3602
**PEACEMAKER, THE.** V. 1- June 1949-. Periodical. English. mo. $10.00. Peacemaker Movement, Box 627, Garberville CA 95440. **ED** Kathy Epling and Paul Encimer. **LC** JX1901; .P398. **Bk Rev. Ad Acc. Circ:** 1,000. available on microfilm and microfiche from University Microfilms International (UMI).
**Desc:** With nonviolence as a guide, stresses simple living, resisting government coercion through tax and the draft, nuclear war resistance, community building and feminism.

US/0895-9714
**PEACEMAKERS.** (1988)-. Periodical. English. mo. $18.00. Loiry Communications, 111 Smith Street, Tallahassee FL 32301. **Tel** (904)561-1393.

US/0748-0725
**PEACEWORK (CAMBRIDGE, MASS.).** (PEACEWORK.). [Peacework]. **Added/Corp** American Friends Service Committee. **VFOAT** Peace Work. No. 6 (Jan. 1973)-. Periodical. English. Eleven times a year. $10.00. American Friends Service Committee / Massachusetts, 2161 Massachusetts Avenue, Cambridge MA 02140. **Tel** (617)661-6130. **ED** Pat Farren. **DD** 321. Index available. cum. index. **Bk Rev. Circ:** 2,500. ***Continues*** *Final Draft/Only for Life.*
**Desc:** A New England peace and social justice journal published by The American Friends Service Committee with grassroots organizing news, listings, original articles, listings, etc.

CC
**PEKIN INFORMATION.** ***Title Change.*** **VFOAT** Pei-ching Chou Pao. No. 1 (1963)-(1994). Periodical. French. wk. Librairie le Phenix, 72 Boulevard de Sebastopol, 75003 Paris France. **Tel** 011 33 1 42727031, FAX 011 33 1 42722669. ***Continued by*** *Beijing Information, 0251-3137.*

IT
**PENSIERO MAZZINIANO, IL.** (1989)-. Periodical. Italian. Four times a year. L30000.00 Italy; L35000.00 other. Assn Mazziniana Italiana, Via Belle Arti 30, 40126 Bologna Italy. **Tel** 011 39 51 223195. **Bk Rev**, (Qty: 30-40). **Ad Acc, Adv Mgr:** Gian Franco Fontana, **Tel** 054220908. **Circ:** 3,500 (ctrl).

IT/0031-4846
**PENSIERO POLITICO, IL.** Vol. 1 (1968)-. Periodical. Italian. Three times a year. L75000 Italy; L95000 other. Casa Editrice Leo S. Olschki, Viuzzo del Pozzetto, Casella Postale 66, 50126 Florence Italy. **Tel** 011 39 55 6530684, FAX 011 39 55 6530214. **LC** JA18; .P45.
**Ind/Abst** ABC POL SCI; Am. Hist. Life (1973-); Int. Polit. Sci. Abstr.; MLA Int. Bibl. Books Artic. Mod. Lang. Lit.; Romant. Move.

SA
**PEOPLE IN POLITICS.** (19??)-. English. qt (4 issues). R342.00 (institution) South Africa. IDASA - Institute for a Democratic Alternative for South Africa, 1206 Sangro House 417 Smith Street, Durban 4001 South Africa. **Tel** 011 31 304 8893.
**Desc:** A review of political leadership.

UK
**PEOPLE'S VOICE (ROME, ITALY).** ***Title Change.*** (PEOPLE'S VOICE.). **Added/Corp** Tigre People's Liberation Front. Foreign Relations Bureau. **VFOAT** Sawt Al-Shab. (197?)-(19??). Periodical. English. bm. **LC** DT390.T5; P46. **DD** 963/.005. ***Continued by*** *EPRDF News Bulletin.*

UK/0958-3939
**PERESTROIKA ANNUAL.** ***Ceased.*** [Perestr. annu.]. (1988)-(19??). English. Little Brown & Company, 34 Beacon Street, Boston MA 02108. **Tel** (617)227-0730, (800)759-0190.

US/1045-7097
**PERSPECTIVES ON POLITICAL SCIENCE.** [Perspect. polit. sci.]. **Added/Corp** Helen Dwight Reid Educational Foundation. Vol. 19 No. 1 (Winter 1990)-. Periodical. English. qt. $45.00 (individual), $90.00 (institutions), add $12.00 (foreign postage). Heldref Publications, 1319 Eighteenth Street Northwest, Washington DC 20036-1802. **Tel** (202)296-6267, (800)365-9753, FAX (202)296-5149. **ED** Jerome J Hanus. **LC** JA1; .P48. **DD** 320. **Bk Rev.** available on microfilm and microfiche from University Microfilms International (UMI). ***Formed by the union of*** *Perspective, 0048-3494* ***and*** *Teaching Political Science, 0092-2013.*
**Desc:** Contains close to 100 reviews of new books in the ever changing fields of government, politics, international affairs, and political thought.
**Ind/Abst** ABC POL SCI; Am. Hist. Life (1990-); Book Rev. Index; Curr. Index J. Educ.; Educ. Index (1992-); Mag. Artic. Summar. Elite (July 1994-); U.S. Polit. Sci. Doc. (199?-).

US
**PERSPECTIVES ON SOUTHERN AFRICA.** (1971)-. Monographic series. English. ir. Price varies per volume. University of California Press, 2120 Berkeley Way, Berkeley CA 94720. **Tel** (510)642-4191, (510)642-3907, FAX (510)642-9917. **(Subscription address:** California Princeton Fullfilment Service 1445 Lower Ferry Road, Ewing, New Jersey 08618**) ED** William McClung.
**Desc:** Books on politics, economics and culture in Southern Africa.

PE
**PERU, CRONOLOGIA POLITICA.** **Added/Corp** Desco. Area de Estudios Politicos. (1973)-. Spanish. an. Desco Publications, Leon de la Fuente 110, Lima 17 Peru. **Tel** 011 51 14 627193. **LC** F3448.2; .P47.

US/0270-5516
**PETTIT REPORT ON THE POLITICS OF SAN FRANCISCO, THE.** **VFOAT** Pettit Report. V. 1- July 7, 1980-. Periodical. English. bw. $15.00. Pettit Report, 1715 Castro Street 2, San Francisco CA 94131-1838.

BE/1370-0081
**PEUPLES & LIBERATIONS BRUXELLES.** ***Title Change.*** **VFOAT** Peuples et Liberations (Bruxelles). (1978)-(1993). French. qt. CID ITECO, 31 Rue du Boulet, 1000 Brussels Belgium. **Tel** 011 32 2 5114870. ***Continued by*** *Antipodes (Bruxelles), 1370-009X.*

FR/1162-325X
**PHILOSOPHIE POLITIQUE PARIS. 1991.** (PHILOSOPHIE POLITIQUE.). [Philos. polit.Paris. 1991]. (1991)-. Periodical. French. sa. 305.00F France; 370.00F other. Presses Universitaires de France, Department des Revues, 14 Avenue du Bois de l'Epine, BP 90, 91003 Evry Cedex France. **Tel** (1)60 77 82 05, FAX (1) 60 79 20 45, telex PUF 600 474 F. **UDC** 32.001.

US/0556-0152
**PHYLLIS SCHLAFLY REPORT, THE.** [Phyllis Schlafly rep.]. Began with: Vol. 1 in 1957?. Periodical. English. mo. $20.00. Phyllis Schlafly Report, PO Box 618, Alton IL 62002. **Tel** (618)462-5415. **ED** Phyllis Schlafly. **LC** E839.5; .P45. **Circ:** 50,000.
**Desc:** Defense, family, politics, economics, education, culture, foreign policy, equal rights amendment.

●US/1070-0285
**PINK SHEET ON THE LEFT (1993), THE.** (THE PINK SHEET ON THE LEFT.). [Pink sheet left]. Issue #548 (Feb. 15, 1993)-. Periodical. English. ir (22 issues). $77.00. Sentinel Communications Inc., 15113 Steele Creek Road, Charlotte NC 28273. **Tel** (704)587-0898. **ED** Lee Bellinger. **DD** 322. **Circ:** 7,500. ***Continues*** *American Sentinel (Washington, D.C.), 0278-0585.*

US
**PINK SHEET ON THE NEW LEFT.** (1971)-. Periodical. English. bw. Phillips Publishing Inc, 7811 Montrose Road, Potomac MD 20854. **Tel** (800)722-9120, (301)340-2100.

BL
**PLURAL.** **VFOAT** Plural; Revista de Debates. (July/Sept. 1978)-. Periodical. Portuguese. qt. Rumo Grafica Editora Ltda, Praca Roosevelt, 200-12O. Andar CEP 01303, Sao Paulo Brazil.

US/1062-7456
**POINT OF VIEW.** [Point view]. (1991)-. Periodical. English. mo. $18.00. Pouler Communications, PO Box 456, College Park MD 20741. **DD** 320.

CN/0226-742X
**POINTS DE REPERE.** [Points repere]. **Added/Corp** Collectif d'Information et de Travail Anti-Imperialiste. **VFOAT** Points de Reperes. **VAT** Points de Reperes (Montreal). Vol. 1 (Fall 1979)-. Periodical. French. qt. 181.19F France; 185.00F French overseas departments & territories, EEC countries; 205.00F other. Bayard Presse, Svc Client, 3 rue Bayard/Dept 2, 75393 Paris Cedex 08 France. **Tel** 011 33 1 44356060, 011 33 1 44356262. **(Subscription address:** Novalis, PO Box 990, Outremont H2V 4S7 Canada.**) DD** 320.9172/4.

US/1069-8124
**POLICY ANALYSIS (CATO INSTITUTE).** (POLICY ANALYSIS.). [Policy anal.]. **Added/Corp** Cato Institute. (19??)-. Monographic series. English. $36.00. Cato Institute, 1000 Massachusetts Avenue NW, Washington DC 20001. **Tel** (202)842-0200, (800)767-1241, FAX (202)842-3490. **LC** H96; .P64. **DD** 320/.6/05. **Ad Acc.**

UK/0305-5736
**POLICY AND POLITICS.** [Policy polit.]. **Added/Corp** University of Bristol. School for Advanced Urban Studies. Vol. 1, No. 1 (Sept. 1972)-. Periodical. English. qt (4 issues). £66.00 (institutions), £26.00 (individuals) UK and Europe; £68.00 (institutions), £29.00 (individuals) other. University of Bristol, Rodney Lodge, Grange Road, Bristol BS8 4EA England. **Tel** 011 44 272 741117. **ED** Paul Burton. Index available. **Bk Rev. Ad Acc. Pr Rev. Circ:** 700. Documents available from The Genuine Article.
**Desc:** Covers the field of public policy studies. Focuses on domestic and local policies and policy-making in a British and European context.
**Ind/Abst** ABC POL SCI; Acad. Search (July 1993-); Am. Hist. Life (1973-1978); Appl. Soc. Sci. Index Abstr.; Br. Humanit. Index; Curr. Contents Soc. Behav. Sci.; Geogr. Abstr. Human Geogr.; INFO-SOUTH Abstr.; Int. Bibliogr. Sociol.; Int. Polit. Sci. Abstr.; J. Plan. Lit.; Mag. Search; Middle East Abstr. Index; PAIS Int. Print (1991-); Res. Alert [Full Cov.]; Soc. Sci. Cit. Index [Full Cov.]; Soc. Work Abstr. [Select. Cov.]; Soils Fert.; World Agric. Econ.

AT/1032-6634
**POLICY (CENTRE FOR INDEPENDENT STUDIES (N.S.W.)).** (POLICY.). Vol. 5, No. 1 (Autumn 1989)-. Periodical. English. Four times a year. 50.00Aus$ (Australia & South Pacific), 60.00Aus$ (other) institutions; 40.00Aus$ (Australia & South Pacific), 50.00Aus$ (other) individuals. Center for Independent Studies, PO Box 92, St Leonards New South Wales 2065 Australia. **Tel** 11 61 2 4384377, FAX 11 61 2 4397310, telex 71944. **ED** Dr. Michael James; Telephone: 11 61 3 4583175. **Bk Rev. Pr Rev. Circ:** 2,000 (ctrl). ***Continues*** *CIS Policy Report, 0814-9321.*
**Desc:** Journal of public policy and ideas.
**Ind/Abst** APAIS, Aust. Public Aff. Inf. Ser. (1989-).

US/8755-9412
**POLICY NOTES.** (POLICY NOTES / INTERFAITH ACTION FOR ECONOMIC JUSTICE.). [Policy notes]. Periodical. English. wk. $12.00. Interfaith Action for Economic Justice, 110 Maryland Avenue Northeast, Washington DC 20002. **Tel** (202)543-2800. **DD** 323.

CN/0226-5893
**POLICY OPTIONS.** [Policy options]. **VFOAT** Options Politiques. V. 1- March 1980-. Periodical. English (French). mo (10 times per year). 29.95Can$ (one year), 49.95Can$ (two year), 69.95Can$ (three year) Canada; 34.95Can$ (one year), 59.95Can$ (two year), 84.95Can$ (three year) US; 39.95Can$ (one year), 69.95Can$ (two year), 99.95Can$ (three year) other. Institute for Research on Public Policy, PO Box 3670, Halifax Nova Scotia B3T 3K6 Canada. **Tel** (902)424-3801. **ED** Walter Stewart. **LC** JL1; .P64. **DD** 320.971/05. **Bk Rev. Circ:** 4,400. available on microfiche.
**Desc:** Public affairs magazine launched by the Institute for Research on Public Policy in 1980. Its subject is the whole range of contemporary, national policy issues. Its approach is practical, its analysis informed and thoughtful without requiring specialist knowledge. Written by many of the people other people write about, contributors including leading academicians, politicians, businessmen, public servants.
**Ind/Abst** Can. Period. Index; PAIS Int. Print (1991-?); Sage Public Adm. Abstr. (?-?); Sage Urban Stud. Abstr (?-?).

NE/0032-2687
**POLICY SCIENCES.** [Policy sci.]. Vol. 1 (Spring 1970)-. Periodical. English. qt. $361.00. Kluwer Academic Publishers, Postbus 322, 3300 AH Dordrecht, The Netherlands. **Tel** 011 (31) 78 524400, FAX 011 31 78 183273, telex 20083. **ED** Douglas Torgerson, Eric Helleiner, and Peter Wylie. **LC** H1; .P7. **DD** 300/.5. **[CCC]. Pr Rev. Acid Free.** available on microfilm and microfiche from University Microfilms International (UMI). Documents available from The Genuine Article, UMI Article Clearinghouse.
**Desc:** Contains articles by authors from several disciplines, both for the different perspectives they offer and for the potential richness of comparative policy analysis. In detail this journal offers: articles which examine the normative aspects of policy sciences; conceptual articles which address concrete policy issues; special issues which analyze specific topics in some depth; articles on particularly controversial pieces of analysis; and opposing perspectives, such as critiques or rejoinders on articles already published, which open the journal to an exchange of views rather than restricting it to pure presentation.
**Ind/Abst** ABC POL SCI; Appl. Soc. Sci. Index Abstr.; Contents Pages Manage.; Curr. Contents Soc. Behav. Sci.; Econ. Lit. Index; Expand. Acad. Index (1992-); Hum. Resour. Abstr. (?-?); Int. Abstr. Oper. Res. [Select. Cov.]; Int. Polit. Sci. Abstr.; J. Econ. Lit.; J. Plan. Lit.; Middle East Abstr. Index; Newsp. Period. Abstr. (1992-); PAIS Int. Print (1991-); Res. Alert [Full Cov.]; Sage Public Adm. Abstr.; Sage Urban Stud. Abstr; Selec. Coop. Index Manage. Period; Soc. Plann. Policy Dev. Abstr.; Soc. Sci. Cit. Index [Full Cov.]; Sociol. Abstr.

UK/0144-2872
**POLICY STUDIES.** (POLICY STUDIES : THE JOURNAL OF THE POLICY STUDIES INSTITUTE.). [Policy stud.]. **Added/Corp** Policy Studies Institute. Vol. 1, Pt. 1 (July 1980)-. Periodical. English. qt. $108.00 (one year), $205.20 (two year), $297.00 (three year) (comes with Policy Studies Review). Policy Studies Institute, 100 Park Village East, London NW1 3SR England. **Tel** 011 44 71 387 2171. **(Subscription address:** Carfax Publishing Co., PO Box 25, Abingdon, Oxfordshire OX14 3UE United Kingdom.) **ED** Peter Willmott. **[CCC].** cum. index. **Bk Rev. Pr Rev. Circ:** 1,500.
**Desc:** Covers general policy related issues in sociology, political science and economics, from the work of PSI.
**Ind/Abst** Appl. Soc. Sci. Index Abstr.; Contents Pages Manage.; Int. Bibliogr. Sociol.; Int. Labour Doc.; LABORDOC; Middle East Abstr. Index; PAIS Int. Print (1991-).

US/0190-292X
**POLICY STUDIES JOURNAL.** (POLICY STUDIES JOURNAL : THE JOURNAL OF THE POLICY STUDIES ORGANIZATION.). [Policy stud. j.]. **Added/Corp** Policy Studies Organization. Vol. 1, No. 1 (Autumn 1972)-. Periodical. English. qt. $22.00 (individuals), $15.00 (students), $108.00 (libraries). Policy Studies Organization, 361 Lincoln Hall, University of Illinois, Urbana IL 61801. **Tel** (217)359-8541. **ED** David Rosenbloom and Mel Dubnick. **LC** H1; .P72. **DD** 361.6/1/05. **[CCC]. Bk Rev. Ad Acc. Pr Rev. Circ:** 2,500 (ctrl). available on microfilm and microfiche from University Microfilms International (UMI). Documents available from The Genuine Article, UMI Article Clearinghouse, Documents on Demand.
**Desc:** Covers the causes and effects of alternative public policies on such subjects as the economy, the environment, civil liberties, world peace, poverty, urban problems, education and governmental reform.
**Ind/Abst** ABC POL SCI; Acad. Search (July 1993-); Am. Hist. Life (1972-); Am. Bibliogr. Slavic East Europ. Stud.; Appl. Soc. Sci. Index Abstr.; Curr. Contents Soc. Behav. Sci.; Educ. Adm. Abstr.; Energy Inf. Abstr.; Energy Res. Abstr. (June 1977-); Environ. Abstr.; Expand. Acad. Index (1989-); Geogr. Abstr. Human Geogr.; High. Educ. Abstr. (1986-); INFO-SOUTH Abstr.; Inf. Sci. Abstr. (?-1991); Int. Dev. Abstr.; Int. Polit. Sci. Abstr.; J. Plan. Lit.; Mag. Search; Middle East Abstr. Index; Newsp. Period. Abstr. (1991-); PAIS Int. Print (1991-); Res. Alert [Full Cov.]; Sage Public Adm. Abstr.; Sage Urban Stud. Abstr (?-?); Soc. Plann. Policy Dev. Abstr.; Soc. Sci. Source (Jul. 1993-); Soc. Sci. Cit. Index [Full Cov.]; Soc. Sci. Index; Soc. Sci. Index Fulltext (Spring 1988-) [Full Txt.]; Sociol. Abstr.; U.S. Polit. Sci. Doc.

US/0278-4416
**POLICY STUDIES REVIEW.** [Policy stud. rev.]. **Added/Corp** Policy Studies Organization. University of Kansas. Center for Public Affairs. Morrison Institute for Public Policy. Arizona State University. School of Justice Studies. **VFOAT** P.S.R.; PSR. Vol. 1, No. 1 (Aug. 1981)-. Periodical. English. qt. Free to subscribers of Policy Studies Journal. Policy Studies Organization, 361 Lincoln Hall, University of Illinois, Urbana IL 61801. **Tel** (217)359-8541. **ED** Dennis Palumbo and Michael Musheno. **LC** H97; .P66. **DD** 361.6/1/05. **[CCC]. Bk Rev. Ad Acc. Circ:** 2,400 (ctrl). available on microfilm and microfiche from University Microfilms International (UMI); available on microfiche from KTO Microform. Documents available from Documents on Demand.
**Desc:** The nature, causes, and effects of alternative public policies including everything from agriculture to zoning.
**Ind/Abst** ABC POL SCI; Am. Hist. Life (1981-); Appl. Soc. Sci. Index Abstr.; Crim. Justice Abstr.; Curr. Contents Soc. Behav. Sci.; Educ. Adm. Abstr. (?-?); Energy Inf. Abstr.; Energy Res. Abstr.; Environ. Abstr.; Geogr. Abstr. Human Geogr.; Hum. Resour. Abstr. (?-?); Inf. Sci. Abstr. (?-1991); Int. Dev. Abstr.; Int. Polit. Sci. Abstr.; J. Plan. Lit.; Middle East Abstr. Index; PAIS Int. Print (1991-); Sage Fam. Stud. Abstr. (?-?); Sage Public Adm. Abstr. (?-?); Soc. Plann. Policy Dev. Abstr.; Sociol. Abstr.; U.S. Polit. Sci. Doc.

RU
**POLIS : POLITICHESKIE ISSLEDOVANIIA / AKADEMIIA NAUK SSSR.** **Added/Corp** Akademiia Nauk SSSR. **VFOAT** Politicheskie Issledovaniia. (Jan/Feb 1991)-. Periodical. Russian (summaries and/or abstracts in English; table of contents in English). Twelve times a year. $56.00. **LC** JA26; .P58. ***Continues*** *Rabochii Klass i Sovremennyi Mir, 0321-2017.*

UK
**POLISH AFFAIRS (LONDON, ENGLAND : 1974).** ***Ceased.*** (POLISH AFFAIRS.). No. 90 (May 1974)-Ceased (Jan. 1991). Periodical. English. qt. Polish Council of National Unity, 43 Eaton Place, London SW1K 8BX England. **LC** DK401; .P485. **DD** 943.8/05/05. ***Continues*** *Polish Affairs and Problems of Central & Eastern Europe.*

PL/0208-7375
**POLISH POLITICAL SCIENCE / POLISH ASSOCIATION OF POLITICAL SCIENCE.** **Added/Corp** Polskie Towarzystwo Nauk Politycznych. **VFOAT** Polish Political Science Yearbook. (1981)-. English. ir. price varies per volume. **(Subscription address:** ARS Polona, PO Box 1001, 00068 Warsaw Poland.) **ED** Longin Pastusiak, Wojciech Kostecki. **LC** HM7; .P65. **DD** 301/.05. **Bk Rev. Circ:** 400. ***Continues*** *Polish Round Table.*
**Desc:** Covers political science in Poland, theory of politics, and international relations, chronicle of scientific life.

PL/0032-3039
**POLISH WESTERN AFFAIRS.** [Pol. West. aff.]. **Added/Corp** Instytut Zachodni. Vol. 1 (1960)-. Periodical. English (French and German). sa. Price on Request. **(Subscription address:** ARS Polona, PO Box 1001, 00068 Warsaw Poland.) **LC** DK443; .P618. Index available in last issue of volume--attached. cum. index.
**Ind/Abst** Am. Hist. Life (1960-); Soc. Plann. Policy Dev. Abstr.

VE
**POLITEIA.** **Added/Corp** Universidad Central de Venezuela. Instituto de Estudios Politicos. (1972)-. Periodical. Spanish. ir. Universidad Central Venezuela / Facultad de Ciencias Juridicas, Caracas Venezuela. **Tel** 011 58 2 7523266. **LC** JA5; .P65.

DK/0105-0710
**POLITICA.** **Added/Corp** Aarhus Universitet. Institut for Statskundskab. Vol. 1 (1968)-. Monographic series. Danish (English, Swedish and Norwegian). qt. Price varies per volume. Tidsskriftet Politica, Institut for Statskundskab, Universitetsparken, 8000 Arhus C Denmark. **Tel** 89 42 12 53, FAX 504 51 93. **ED** Palle Suensson. **LC** JA26; .P6. Index available. **Bk Rev. Ad Acc. Pr Rev. Circ:** 1,000 (ctrl).
**Desc:** Analysis of politics and policies within specific areas. Each issue concentrates on one subject. International politics, sociology, comparative politics, public administration, policy analysis.
**Ind/Abst** Int. Bibliogr. Sociol.; Int. Polit. Sci. Abstr.

BL
**POLITICA.** No. 1- July/Sept. 1976-. Periodical. Portuguese. qt. $50.00. Fundacao Milton Campus, Caixa Postal 04/0341 CEP 70.000, Brasilia Brazil. **LC** JA5; .P652.

IT/0032-3063
**POLITICA DEL DIRITTO.** [Polit. dir.]. (July 1970)-. Periodical. Italian. qt. L80000.00 Italy; L120000.00 (surface mail), L150000.00 (airmail) other. Editrice Turistica SRL, Via Rasella 155, 00187 Rome Italy. **Tel** 011 39 6 4821539.
**Ind/Abst** PAIS Int. Print.

FR
**POLITICA HERMETICA.** **See** Religion and Theology.

VE/0798-1147
**POLITICA INTERNACIONAL CARACAS.** (POLITICA INTERNACIONAL : REVISTA VENEZOLANA DE ASUNTOS MUNDIALES Y POLITICA EXTERIOR.). [Pol. int. Caracas]. **VFOAT** Revista Venezolana de Asuntos Mundiales y Politica Exterior. (1986)-. Periodical. Spanish. qt. $30.00. Politica Internacional, Apartado 6475 Carmelitas, Caracas 1010 Venezuela. **Tel** 011 58 2 810639. **DD** _a327.1105.
**Ind/Abst** PAIS Int. Print.

IT
**POLITICA (SPERLING & KUPFER EDITORI).** (POLITICA.). (1982)-. Monographic series. Italian. Price varies per volume.

CL
**POLITICA (UNIVERSIDAD DE CHILE. INSTITUTO DE CIENCIA POLITICA).** (POLITICA.). **Added/Corp** Universidad de Chile. Instituto de Ciencia Politica. Vol. 1, No. 1 (Sept. 1982)-. Periodical. Spanish. Calle Belgrado, No 10 Santiago de Chile. **LC** JA5; .P654. **DD** 320/.05.
**Ind/Abst** PAIS Int. Print.

US/0032-3128
**POLITICAL AFFAIRS.** [Polit. aff.]. Vol. 24, No. 1 (Jan. 1945)-. Periodical. English. mo. $18.00 (individuals), $27.00 (institutions). Political Affairs Publishers, 235 West 23 Street, New York NY 10011. **Tel** (212)989-4994. **ED** Leonard Levenson. **LC** HX1; .P57. **DD** 335.43/05. Index available. **Bk Rev. Ad Acc. Circ:** 5,000 (ctrl). available on microfilm and microfiche from University Microfilms International (UMI). ***Continues*** *Communist.*
**Desc:** A journal of Marxist thought.
**Ind/Abst** Altern. Press Index; Middle East Abstr. Index; PAIS Int. Print (1991-).

CN/0712-4295
**POLITICAL ALERTS.** [Polit. alerts]. 4th Quarter, 1976-. Periodical. English. wk. $8000.00. F.H. Deacon, Hodgson, 105 Adelaide Street West, Toronto Ontario M5H 1R4 Canada. **DD** 338.971/005.

US/1047-1987
**POLITICAL ANALYSIS.** (POLITICAL ANALYSIS : AN ANNUAL PUBLICATION OF THE METHODOLOGY SECTION OF THE AMERICAN POLITICAL SCIENCE ASSOCIATION.). [Polit. anal.]. **Added/Corp** American Political Science Association. Methodology Section. Vol. 1 (1989)-. English. an. $42.50. University of Michigan Press, PO Box 1104, Ann Arbor MI 48106. **Tel** (313)764-4392. **LC** JA73; .P63. **DD** 320/.072. ctrl circ.

AT/0727-5994
**POLITICAL AND SOCIAL CHANGE MONOGRAPH.** **Added/Corp** Australian National University. Research School of Pacific Studies. Dept. of Political and Social Change. Vol. 1 (1982)-. Monographic series. English. ir. Price varies per volume. National Center for Development Studies, Australian National University, Canberra ACT 0200 Australia. **Tel** 011 61 6 2492760, FAX 011 61 6 2495525. **LC** CLASSED SEPARATELY.

US/1070-1753
**POLITICAL ANIMAL (1993), THE.** (THE POLITICAL ANIMAL.). [Polit. anim.]. (199?)-. Periodical. English. Twenty-four times a year. $150.00. Political Animal, 1000 W Sunset Blvd., Second Floor, Los Angeles CA 90012-2197. **Tel** (213)515-1300. **ED** Bill Homer (phone: (213)481-3809). **DD** 973. **Circ:** 230 (ctrl). ***Continues*** *Scott, Joe (Joseph III) Joe Scott's The Political Animal, 0747-5659.*

US/0190-9320
**POLITICAL BEHAVIOR.** [Polit. behav.]. Vol. 1 (Spring 1979)-. Periodical. English. Four times a year. $160.00 institutions, $42.00 individuals US; $185.00

institutions, $49.00 individuals other. Plenum Press, 233 Spring Street, New York NY 10013-1578. **Tel** (212)620-8000, (800)221-9369, FAX (212)463-0742, (212)807-1047, telex 23/421139. **ED** Richard A. Brody and Paul M. Sniderman. **LC** JA74.5; .P6. **DD** 306/.2. **[CCC].** available on microfilm and microfiche from University Microfilms International (UMI).
**Desc:** Provides a forum for the interdisciplinary study of groups and individuals as they interact in and with the political process. Drawing from the fields of economics, psychology, sociology, and political science. A unique and authoritative source for students of political behavior, featuring theoretical and empirical work at the forefront of this field.
**Ind/Abst** ABC POL SCI (1991-present); Int. Polit. Sci. Abstr.; Middle East Abstr. Index; Psychol. Abstr. (1981-); PsycINFO; PsycLit; Soc. Plann. Policy Dev. Abstr.; Sociol. Abstr.; U.S. Polit. Sci. Doc.

II
**POLITICAL CHANGE.** Periodical. English. sa. Rs15.00. Dr S L Verma, Institute of Correspondence Studies, University of Rajasthan, Jaipur 302004 Rajasthan India. **LC** JQ201; .P65. **DD** 320.954/005.

US/1042-3885
**POLITICAL CHRONICLE, THE.** (THE POLITICAL CHRONICLE : THE JOURNAL OF THE FLORIDA POLITICAL SCIENCE ASSOCIATION.). [Polit. chron.]. **Added/Corp** Florida Political Science Association. Vol. 1, No. 1 (1989)-. Periodical. English. sa. $15.00. Political Chronicle, Saint Leo College, PO Box 2127, Saint Leo FL 33574. **ED** Bernard Schechterman. **DD** 324. **Circ:** 300 (ctrl).
**Desc:** Covers American government, political theory, public law, international relations and comparative politics (area studies).

●US/1058-4609
**POLITICAL COMMUNICATION.** [Polit. commun.]. Vol. 9, No. 1 (Jan.-Mar. 1992)-. Periodical. English. qt (4 issues). £85.00 UK; $140.00 other. Taylor & Francis Ltd., Rankine Road, Basingstoke Hampshire, RG24 8PR United Kingdom. **Tel** 011 44 256 840366, FAX 011 44 256 479438, telex 858540. **(Subscription address:** Taylor & Francis Inc., 1900 Frost Road, Suite 101, Bristol PA 19007-1598.**) ED** Doris Graber. **LC** JF1525.P8; P64. **DD** 306/.2. **CODEN** PLCMEM. **[CCC].** Documents available from UMI Article Clearinghouse. ***Continues*** *Political Communication and Persuasion, 0195-7473.*
**Desc:** Encompasses all aspects of the field in the belief that political communication and political communicators are ultimately at the root of all political life. Covers the communication of political thought and ideology, political language and propaganda, political marketing and campaign communication, media relations with government and comparative and international political communications.
**Ind/Abst** ABC POL SCI; Commun. Abstr. (?-?); Curr. Mil. Pol. Lit.; Expand. Acad. Index (1992-); Int. Polit. Sci. Abstr.; Newsp. Period. Abstr. (1989-); PAIS Int. Print; Public Aff. Inf. Serv. Bull.; Soc. Plann. Policy Dev. Abstr.; Sociol. Abstr.

US/1056-6740
**POLITICAL CORRECTION.** [Polit. correct.]. **Added/Corp** Tahanga Research Association. (Apr 1 1991)-. Periodical. English. Free. Tahanga Research Association, PO Box 8714, La Jolla CA 92038-8714. **DD** 320 12.

NR
**POLITICAL DIGEST.** Vol. 1, No. 1 (June 1983)-. Periodical. English. mo. N1.00 Africa; $1.00 US. Spotlight Digest Ltd, PO Box 4490, Surulere Lagos Nigeria. **LC** JQ3081.A1; P64. **DD** 966.9/05/05.

●II/0971-2097
**POLITICAL ECONOMY JOURNAL OF INDIA : A QUARTERLY JOURNAL OF THE CENTRE FOR INDIAN DEVELOPMENT STUDIES.** **See** Economics.

●US/0270-353X
**POLITICAL FINANCE LOBBY REPORTER.** [Polit. finance lobby report.]. **VAT** Political Finance/Lobby Reporter. (1980)-(1982 as PACS & Lobbies)-Changed back to 0270-353X (199?)-. Periodical. English. Twenty-four times a year. $327.00. Amward Publications, 2000 National Press Building, Washington DC 20045. **Tel** (301)251-9009, FAX (301)251-9058. **ED** Edward Zuckerman. **DD** 322. **Bk Rev**. available on an online database from NEXIS; LEXIS; and NEWSNET.

●UK/0962-6298
**POLITICAL GEOGRAPHY.** **See** Geography.

US/0193-175X
**POLITICAL HANDBOOK OF THE WORLD (1975).** (POLITICAL HANDBOOK OF THE WORLD.). [Polit. handb. world]. **Added/Corp** State University of New York at Binghamton. Center for Comparative Political Research. Council on Foreign Relations. State University of New York at Binghamton. Center for Social Analysis. (1975)-. English. an (Dec.). $109.50 US; $113.00 other. State University of New York / CSA Publications, Box 6000, Binghamton NY 13902. **Tel** (607)777-2303, FAX (607)777-2675. **ED** Arthur S. Banks (phone: (607)777-2119). **LC** JF37; .P6. **DD** 320.9/047. Index available. **Bk Rev**, (Qty: 2). **Circ:** 3,500 (ctrl). ***Continues*** *Political Handbook and Atlas of the World.*
**Desc:** Authoritative standard for reference books in the political science field. Contains current, comprehensive information on the history and political activity of all countries, plus general economic and social trends.

US/0092-9735
**POLITICAL INQUIRY.** V. 1- Fall 1973-. Periodical. English. qt. $10.00. 2250 Pierce Road, Box 58, University Center MI 48710. **LC** JA1; .P57. **DD** 320/.05.

US/0895-4712
**POLITICAL PIX.** ***Ceased.*** **See** Journalism.

US/0198-8719
**POLITICAL POWER AND SOCIAL THEORY.** [Polit. power soc. theory]. Vol. 1 (1980)-. English. ir. $73.25. JAI Press Inc., 55 Old Post Road, Suite 2, PO Box 1678, Greenwich CT 06836-1678. **Tel** (203)661-7602, FAX (203)661-0792. **ED** Diane Davis and Howard Kimeldorf. **LC** JA1; .P585. **DD** 320/.05.
**Ind/Abst** Am. Bibliogr. Slavic East Europ. Stud.; Int. Polit. Sci. Abstr.; Soc. Plann. Policy Dev. Abstr.; Sociol. Abstr. [Full Cov.].

US/8756-9248
**POLITICAL PULSE.** [Polit. pulse]. **VFOAT** Bud Lembke's Newsletter of California Politics and Government. Vol. 1, No. 1 (Feb. 22, 1985)-. Periodical. English. Twenty-three times a year. $235.00. Political Pulse, 926 J Street, Suite 1218, Sacramento CA 95814. **Tel** (916)446-2048, FAX (916)446-5302. **ED** Bud Lembke. **LC** JK8701; .P65. **DD** 353. cum. index (beginning with 1993). **Circ:** 600.
**Desc:** Newsletter of California politics and government; includes news about campaigns, elected officials, issues, media and lobbyists.

UK/0032-3179
**POLITICAL QUARTERLY (LONDON. 1930).** (THE POLITICAL QUARTERLY.). [Polit. q.]. Vol. 1 (Jan. 1930)-. Academic Scholarly Publication. English. Five times a year. £62.00 UK & Europe; $115.00 North America; £74.00 other. Basil Blackwell Publishers Ltd, 108 Cowley Road, Oxford 0X4 1JF England. **Tel** 011 44 865 791100, FAX 011 44 865 791347, telex 837022 OXBOOK G. **(Subscription address:** Blackwell Publishers / UK, Marston Book Services, PO Box 87, Oxford OX2 0DT England.**) LC** JA8; .P72. **[CCC]. Pr Rev.** available on microfilm and microfiche from University Microfilms International (UMI). Documents available from UMI Article Clearinghouse.
**Ind/Abst** ABC POL SCI; Acad. Search (July 1993-); Am. Hist. Life (1955-1974, 1978); Appl. Soc. Sci. Index Abstr.; Br. Humanit. Index; Curr. Contents Soc. Behav. Sci.; Expand. Acad. Index (1992-); INFO-SOUTH Abstr.; Int. Bibliogr. Sociol.; Int. Labour Doc.; Int. Polit. Sci. Abstr.; Mag. Search; Middle East Abstr. Index; Newsp. Period. Abstr. (1991-); PAIS Int. Print (1991-); Peace Res. Abstr. J. (1971-1973); Soc. Sci. Source (Jul. 1993-); Soc. Sci. Cit. Index [Full Cov.]; Soc. Sci. Index; Soc. Sci. Index Fulltext (Oct. 1988-) [Full Txt.].

US
**POLITICAL QUOTATIONS : A COLLECTION OF NOTABLE SAYINGS ON POLITICS FROM ANTIQUITY THROUGH 1988.** (1990)-. English. $39.95. Gale Research Inc., 835 Penobscot Building, Detroit MI 48226. **Tel** (800)877-GALE, (313)961-2242, FAX (313)961-6083, telex TWX 810-221-7086. **ED** Daniel B Baker.
**Desc:** Collection of more than 4,000 notable, quotable sayings concerning politics from the dawn of civilization to the present day. Contains a diverse and extensive scope of sayings, presented by persons from a wide variety of backgrounds, that will help provide a focus when writing speeches or papers.

●US/1065-9129
**POLITICAL RESEARCH QUARTERLY.** [Polit. res. q.]. **Added/Corp** Western Political Science Association. (1993)-. Periodical. English. qt. $35.00 US; $37.50 Canada and Mexico; $39.00 other. University of Utah / 252 Orson Spencer Hall, Salt Lake City UT 84112. **Tel** (801)581-7031, (801)581-7137, FAX (801)581-6957. **ED** Walter J. Stone. **LC** JA1; .W4. **DD** 320.5. Index available (Once a year in Dec. issue). **Bk Rev. Ad Acc. Pr Rev. Circ:** 2,300. available on microfilm from University Microfilms International (UMI). ***Continues*** *Western Political Quarterly, 0043-4078.*
**Desc:** Journal of the Western Political Science Association. Offers articles based on research in the field of political science, aimed at the professional political scientist.
**Ind/Abst** ABC POL SCI; Acad. Abstr. (July 1993-); Acad. Search (July 1993-); Am. Hist. Life; Annu. Bibliogr. Engl. Lang. Lit.; Book Rev. Index; Public Aff. Inf. Serv. Bull.; Soc. Sci. Cit. Index [Select. Cov.]; Soc. Sci. Index; Soc. Work Abstr.

US
**POLITICAL RESOURCE DIRECTORY.** 1986/1987-. Directory. English. Planning Information Center, 65 Metro Square Building, St Paul MN 55101. **LC** JK2283; .P64. **DD** 320/.025/73.
**Desc:** Provides computer analysis, online information and mapping of data. Election totals, demographics and natural resources can be mapped by political district or Minor Civil Division.

US/0898-4271
**POLITICAL RESOURCE DIRECTORY (NATIONAL ED.).** (POLITICAL RESOURCE DIRECTORY.). [Polit. resour. dir.]. **Added/Corp** American Association of Political Consultants. (1988/1989)-. Directory. English. an. $95.00. Political Resource Inc., PO Box 3177, Burlington VT 05401. **Tel** (800)423-2677. **(Subscription address:** Gale Research Co., 835 Penobscot Building, Detroit MI 48226.**) ED** Carol Hess. **LC** JK2283; .P65. **DD** 324.7/025/73. Index available. **Bk Rev**. **Ad Acc.** ***Absorbed*** *American Association of Political Consultants. AAPC Directory, 0897-4284.*
**Desc:** Detailed information on 2,400+ organizations. Includes name, address, telephone and fax numbers, branch offices, geographic area served, specialization, a detailed description of the services offered, percentage of work that is politically oriented, party affiliation and 3,400 names of key executives.

US/0890-4928
**POLITICAL RISK DATABASE.** ***Ceased.*** (POLITICAL RISK DATABASE [COMPUTER FILE] / FROST & SULLIVAN, INC.). [Polit. risk database]. **Added/Corp** Frost & Sullivan. (Aug. 1986)-?. Periodical. English. qt. Frost & Sullivan Inc, 106 Fulton Street, Department W, New York NY 10036. **Tel** (315) 472-1224, FAX (315) 472-1235, telex 650 247-7174 (MCI). **DD** 332.
**Desc:** System requirements: IBM PC and compatibles; DOS; dBase III, LOTUS 1-2-3; or ASCII format.

US/0897-8530
**... POLITICAL RISK YEARBOOK. MIDDLE EAST & NORTH AFRICA, THE.** [Polit. risk yearb. Middle East North Afr.]. **Added/Corp** Frost & Sullivan. **VFOAT** Middle East & North Africa; Middle East and North Africa. (1987)-. English. an. $250.00 (per volume), $1000.00 (full set). Political Risk Services, 6320 Fly Road, Suite 102, PO Box 248, East Syracuse NY 13057-0248. **Tel** (315)431-0511, FAX (315)431-0200. **ED** William D. Coplin and Michael K. O'Leary. **LC** JQ1758.A1; P64. **DD** 320.9/048. available on CD-ROM.
**Desc:** Designed especially for research and archival purposes. Brings together pertinent economics, social, and political information of particular interest to those researching the answers to complex questions.

US/0897-8557
**POLITICAL RISK YEARBOOK. NORTH & CENTRAL AMERICA, THE.** [Polit. risk yearb. North Cent. Am.]. **Added/Corp** Frost & Sullivan. **VFOAT** Political Risk Yearbook. North and Central America; North & Central America; North and Central America. (1987)-. English. an. $250.00 (per volume), $1000.00 (full set). Political Risk Services, 6320 Fly Road, Suite 102, PO Box 248, East Syracuse NY 13057-0248. **Tel** (315)431-0511, FAX (315)431-0200. **ED** William D. Coplin and Michael K. O'Leary. **LC** JL1416; .P65. **DD** 970.053/7; 320. available on CD-ROM.
**Desc:** Designed especially for research and archival purposes. Brings together pertinent economic, social, and political information of particular interest to those researching the answers to complex questions.

US/0897-8549
**POLITICAL RISK YEARBOOK. SOUTH AMERICA, THE.** [Polit. risk yearb. South Am.]. **Added/Corp** Frost & Sullivan. **VFOAT** South America. (1987)-. English. an. $250.00 (per volume), $1000.00 (full set). Political Risk Services, 6320 Fly Road, Suite 102, PO Box 248, East Syracuse NY 13057-0248. **Tel** (315)431-0511, FAX (315)431-0200. **ED** William D. Coplin and Michael K. O'Leary. **LC** JL1866; .P65. **DD** 980/.037. available on CD-ROM.
**Desc:** Designed especially for research and archival purposes. Brings together pertinent economic, social, and political information of particular interest to those researching the answers to complex questions.

US/0889-2725
**POLITICAL RISK YEARBOOK. SUB-SAHARAN AFRICA, THE.** [Polit. risk yearb. Sub Saharan Afr.]. **Added/Corp** Frost & Sullivan. **VFOAT** Sub-Saharan Africa. **VAT** Political Risk Yearbook. Sub Saharan Africa; Sub Saharan Africa. (1987)-. English. an. $250.00 (per volume), $1000.00 (full set). Political Risk Services, 6320 Fly Road, Suite 102, PO Box 248, East Syracuse NY 13057-0248. **Tel** (315)431-0511, FAX (315)431-0200. **ED** William D. Coplin and Michael K. O'Leary. **LC** JQ1871.A1; P64. **DD** 967/.005. **[CCC].**
**Desc:** An annual publication designed especially for research and archival purposes. Brings together pertinent economic, social, and political information of particular interest to those researching the answers to complex questions.

US/0897-8565
**POLITICAL RISK YEARBOOK. VOL. 5, ASIA & THE PACIFIC.** **Added/Corp** Political Risk Services (IBC USA (Publications) Inc.). **VFOAT** Asia & the Pacific; Asia and the Pacific. (1991)-. English. an. $250.00 (per volume), $1000.00 (full set). Political Risk Services, 6320 Fly Road, Suite 102, PO Box 248, East Syracuse NY 13057-0248. **Tel** (315)431-0511, FAX (315)431-0200. **LC** JQ21.A1; P64. ***Continues*** *Political Risk Yearbook. Asia & The Pacific, 0897-8565.*
**Desc:** Designed especially for research and archival purposes. Brings together pertinent economic, social, and political information of particular interest to those researching the answers to complex questions.

US/1053-878X
**POLITICAL RISK YEARBOOK. VOL. 7, EUROPE. OUTSIDE THE EUROPEAN COMMUNITY.** [Polit. risk yearb., Vol. 7 Eur., Outs. Eur. Community]. **Added/Corp** Political Risk Services (IBC USA (Publications) Inc.). **VFOAT** Europe, Outside the European Community; Outside the European Community. (1991)-. English. an. $250.00 (per volume), $1000.00 (full set). Political Risk Services, 6320 Fly Road, Suite 102, PO Box 248, East Syracuse NY 13057-0248. **Tel** (315)431-0511, FAX (315)431-0200. **LC** JN12; .P645. **DD** 940. ***Continues*** *Political Risk Yearbook. Eastern Europe, 0897-8514.*

US
**POLITICAL SCIENCE.** **VFOAT** Publications in Political Science. Vol. 5 (1978)-. Monographic series. English. ir. Price varies per volume. Marcel Dekker Inc., 270 Madison Avenue, New York NY 10016. **Tel** (212)696-9000, (800)228-1160, FAX (212)685-4540, telex 421419. **(Subscription address:** Marcel Dekker Inc, PO Box 5017, Monticello NY 12701.**)** ***Continues*** *Political Science and Public Administration.*
**Desc:** Series covering topics such as liberalism and ethics.

NZ/0032-3187
**POLITICAL SCIENCE.** **Added/Corp** Victoria University College (Wellington, N.Z.). School of Political Science and Public Administration. Victoria University College, Wellington, N.Z. Political Science Society. Victoria University of Wellington. School of Political Science and Public Administration. Vol. 1, (Sept. 1948)-. Periodical. English. ir (2 issues per year (July, Dec.)). 30.00NZ$ New Zealand; 38.00NZ$ Australia; 44.00NZ$ other. Victoria University Press, PO Box 600, Wellington New Zealand. **Tel** 011 64 4 4955263, FAX 011 64 4 4955199, telex NZ 30882. **ED** Paul Harris and Elizabeth McLeary. **LC** JA1; .P6. **[CCC].** Index available. **Bk Rev. Ad Acc. Pr Rev. Circ:** 475. Documents available from The Genuine Article.
**Desc:** Broad field of political science with a focus on the Australasian and Pacific region research on any topic any field.
**Ind/Abst** ABC POL SCI; Am. Hist. Life (1954-); Br. Humanit. Index; Curr. Contents Soc. Behav. Sci.; Int. Polit. Sci. Abstr.; Middle East Abstr. Index; Res. Alert [Full Cov.]; Soc. Sci. Cit. Index [Full Cov.].

US/0731-8022
**POLITICAL SCIENCE ABSTRACTS. ANNUAL SUPPLEMENT.** [Polit. sci. abstr., Annu. suppl.]. (1980)-. Monographic series. English. an. Price varies per volume. Plenum Press, 233 Spring Street, New York NY 10013-1578. **Tel** (212)620-8000, (800)221-9369, FAX (212)463-0742, (212)807-1047, telex 23/421139. **LC** Z7161; .U643 Suppl. **DD** 016.3. ***Continues*** *Political Science, Government & Public Policy Series. Annual Supplement, 0364-5908.*

UK/0960-1538
**POLITICAL SCIENCE AND RELATED DISCIPLINES / INTERNATIONAL CURRENT AWARENESS SERVICES.** ***Ceased.*** **Added/Corp** International Current Awareness Services. British Library of Political and Economic Science. **VFOAT** Political Science. (1990)-(1994). Periodical. English. Twelve times a year. Routledge, 11 New Fetter Lane, London EC4P 4EE England. **Tel** 071 583 9855, FAX 071 842 2298. **(Subscription address:** Kinokuniya Company Ltd., 38-1 Sakuragaoka 5, chome Setagaya-ku, Tokyo 156 Japan.**) [CCC].**

US/0032-3195
**POLITICAL SCIENCE QUARTERLY.** [Polit. sci. q.]. **Added/Corp** Academy of Political Science (U.S.) Columbia University. Faculty of Political Science. Academy of Political Science in the City of New York. Vol. 1 (Mar. 1886)-. Academic Scholarly Publication. English. qt (within the seasons). $138.00 library and institution, $39.00 individual. Academy of Political Science, 475 Riverside Drive/Suite 1274, New York NY 10115-1274. **Tel** (212)870-2500, FAX (212)870-2202. **ED** Demetrios Caraley. **LC** H1; .P8. **DD** 320/.05. **Bk Rev. Ad Acc. Pr Rev. Circ:** 9,000 (ctrl). available on microfilm and microfiche from University Microfilms International (UMI); available on CD-ROM from University Microfilms International (UMI). Documents available from The Genuine Article, UMI Article Clearinghouse.
**Desc:** Scholarly journal of articles and essays on government, politics and policy. Each issue contains about 40 reviews of current books. Edited for readers with a serious interest in foreign and domestic public affairs.
**Ind/Abst** ABC POL SCI; Acad. Abstr. Full Text Elite (July 1990-); Acad. Abstr. (July 1990-); Acad. Ind. [Computer File] (1987-); Acad. Search (July 1990-); Am. Hist. Life (1955-); Am. Bibliogr. Slavic East Europ. Stud.; Annu. Bibliogr. Engl. Lang. Lit.; Arts Humanit. Citation Index [Select. Cov.]; Book Rev. Digest; Book Rev. Index; Curr. Contents Soc. Behav. Sci.; Expand. Acad. Index (1987-); Hum. Resour. Abstr. (?-?); Index Period. Artic. Relat. Law; INFO-SOUTH Abstr.; Int. Bibliogr. Sociol.; Int. Polit. Sci. Abstr.; J. Econ. Lit.; J. Plan. Lit.; Mag. Search; Middle East Abstr. Index; Newsp. Period. Abstr. (1988-); PAIS Int. Print (1991-); Peace Res. Abstr. J. (1969-1973); Read. Guide Period. Lit.; Res. Alert [Full Cov.]; Sage Public Adm. Abstr.; Soc. Sci. Source (Jul. 1990-); Soc. Sci. Cit. Index [Full Cov.]; Soc. Sci. Index; Soc. Sci. Index Fulltext (Winter 1988-) [Full Txt.]; Soc. Work Abstr. [Select. Cov.]; Sociol. Educ. Abstr.; U.S. Polit. Sci. Doc.; Urban Aff. Abstr.; West. Hist. Q.

II/0554-5196
**POLITICAL SCIENCE REVIEW.** [Polit. sci. rev.]. **Added/Corp** University of Rajasthan. Dept. of Political Science. Vol. 1 (Feb. 1962)-. English. qt. $50.00. University Rajasthan, Professor VR Mehta, Managing Editor, Department Political Science, Jaipur 302004 India. **(Subscription address:** Prints India, 11 Darya Ganj, New Delhi, 110002 India, (Phone: 011 91 11 3268645)**)** **LC** JA26; .P64.
**Ind/Abst** ABC POL SCI; Am. Hist. Life (1971-); Int. Polit. Sci. Abstr.

US/0091-3715
**POLITICAL SCIENCE REVIEWER, THE.** [Polit. sci. rev.]. Vol. 1 (1971)-. English. an. $10.00. Intercollegiate Studies Institute, #100 14 South Bryn Mawr Avenue, Bryn Mawr PA 19010. **Tel** (800)526-7022, (215)525-7501. **LC** JA1; .P62. **DD** 320/.05. Index available (free). **Bk Rev. Ad Acc.** available on microfilm and microfiche from University Microfilms International (UMI).
**Ind/Abst** Am. Hist. Life (1983-); Book Rev. Index; Int. Polit. Sci. Abstr.

US
**POLITICAL SCIENCE TEACHER.** **See** Education.

US/0362-4765
**POLITICAL SCIENCE UTILIZATION DIRECTORY, THE.** ***Ceased.*** (1975)-Ceased (1976). Directory. English. Policy Studies Organization, 361 Lincoln Hall, University of Illinois, Urbana IL 61801. **Tel** (217)359-8541. **LC** JA88.U6; P65. **DD** 353.

II/0032-3209
**POLITICAL SCIENTIST.** **Added/Corp** Ranchi, India (City). University. Dept. of Political Science. Vol. 1 (July/Dec. 1964)-. Periodical. English. Twice a year. Ranchi University / Political Science, Department of Political Science, Ranchi India. **LC** JA26; .P66.

UK/0032-3217
**POLITICAL STUDIES.** [Polit. stud.]. Vol. 1 (Feb. 1953)-. Academic Scholarly Publication. English. Five times a year. £78.00 UK and Europe; $150.00 North America; £90.00 other. Basil Blackwell Publishers Ltd, 108 Cowley Road, Oxford 0X4 1JF England. **Tel** 011 44 865 791100, FAX 011 44 865 791347, telex 837022 OXBOOK G. **(Subscription address:** Blackwell Publishers / UK, Marston Book Services, PO Box 87, Oxford OX2 0DT England.**) ED** Jack Hayward. **LC** JA1; .P63. **DD** +320.5. **[CCC].** Index available. cum. index. **Bk Rev. Ad Acc. Pr Rev. Circ:** 2,500. available on microfilm and microfiche from University Microfilms International (UMI). Documents available from The Genuine Article, UMI Article Clearinghouse.
**Desc:** Contains articles, research notes, review articles and book reviews of interest to scholars and students. The journal is attached to no political persuasion and is not bound to any area of political research. It covers the entire range of political and history of political thought, through empirical politics whether analytic or descriptive.
**Ind/Abst** ABC POL SCI; Acad. Search (July 1993-); Am. Hist. Life (1955-); Appl. Soc. Sci. Index Abstr.; Arts Humanit. Citation Index [Select. Cov.]; Br. Humanit. Index; Curr. Contents Soc. Behav. Sci.; Expand. Acad. Index (1989-); Index Period. Artic. Relat. Law; INFO-SOUTH Abstr.; Int. Polit. Sci. Abstr.; Mag. Search; Middle East Abstr. Index; Newsp. Period. Abstr. (1991-); PAIS Int. Print (1991-); Res. Alert [Full Cov.]; Sage Public Adm. Abstr.; Soc. Plann. Policy Dev. Abstr.; Soc. Sci. Source (Jul. 1993-); Soc. Sci. Cit. Index [Full Cov.]; Soc. Sci. Index; Soc. Sci. Index Fulltext (Sept. 1988-) [Full Txt.]; Soc. Work Abstr. (?-?); Sociol. Abstr.; Sociol. Educ. Abstr.

US/0090-5917
**POLITICAL THEORY.** [Polit. theory]. Vol. 1 (Feb. 1973)-. Periodical. English. qt (Feb., May, Aug., Nov.). $175.00. SAGE Periodical Press, 2455 Teller Road, Thousand Oaks CA 91320. **Tel** (805)499-0721, FAX (805)499-0871, telex 100799. **ED** Tracy B. Strong (University of California, San Diego). **LC** JA1.A1; P64. **[CCC].** Index available. **Ad Acc. Pr Rev. Acid Free. Circ:** 1,206. available on microfilm and microfiche from University Microfilms International (UMI). Documents available from The Genuine Article, UMI Article Clearinghouse.
**Desc:** Provides a forum for the diverse orientations in the study of political ideas, including the history of political thought, modern theory, conceptual analysis and polemic argumentation.
**Ind/Abst** ABC POL SCI; Acad. Abstr. Full Text Elite (Jan. 1992-); Acad. Abstr. (Jan. 1992-); Acad. Search (Jan. 1992-); Am. Hist. Life (1974-); Am. Bibliogr. Slavic East Europ. Stud.; Appl. Soc. Sci. Index Abstr.; Arts Humanit. Citation Index [Select. Cov.]; Curr. Contents Soc. Behav. Sci.; Expand. Acad. Index (1989-); INFO-SOUTH Abstr.; Int. Polit. Sci. Abstr.; Mag. Search; Middle East Abstr. Index; Newsp. Period. Abstr. (1991-); Philos. Index; Res. Alert [Full Cov.]; Sage Public Adm. Abstr. (?-?); Soc. Sci. Source (Jan. 1992-); Soc. Sci. Cit. Index [Full Cov.]; Soc. Sci. Index; Soc. Sci. Index Fulltext (Nov. 1988-) [Full Txt.]; U.S. Polit. Sci. Doc.

●US/1069-6652
**POLITICAL WOMAN (WHITE PLAINS, N.Y.).** (POLITICAL WOMAN.). [Polit. woman]. Vol. 1, No. 1 (Nov. 1992)-. Periodical. English. Eleven times a year (all except Sept.). $45.00. Political Woman, 276 Chatterton Parkway, White Plains NY 10606. **Tel** (914)285-9761, FAX (914)285-9763. **ED** Antonia Stolper & Robert Fertik. **DD** 363. **Circ:** 1,000.
**Desc:** Aimed at pro-choice office holders, policy leaders, activists, and anyone interested in the growth of women's political involvement. Reports on legislative action, political campaigns, media reporting, and the women's movement.

IT
**POLITICHE DEL LAVORO.** ***Ceased.*** No. 1 (1986)-(Dec. 1993). Periodical. Italian. qt. Franco Angeli Riviste SRL, Viale Monza 106, 20127 Milan Italy. **Tel** 011 39 2 2827651, 011 39 2 289562. **LC** HD8471; .P65.

RU/0202-2273
**POLITICHESKAIA ORGANIZATSIIA OBSHCHESTVA I UPRAVLENIE PRI SOTSIALIZME.** **Added/Corp** Leningradskii Gosudarastvennyi Universitet Imeni A.A. Zhdanova. (1979)-. Monographic series. Russian. Price varies per volume. St Petersburg State University / Izdatelstvo Leningradskogo Universiteta, Universitetskaia Nab 7/9, 199034 St Petersburg Russia. **Tel** 011 95 218-97-88, FAX 011 95 218-51-52, telex 121481.

BU/0861-4830
**POLITICHESKI IZSLEDVANIIA.** **Added/Corp** Institut za Politologichni Izsledvaniia (Bulgarska Akademiia na Naukite). Vol. 1 No. 1 (1991)-. Academic Scholarly Publication. Bulgarian. qt. 80lv. Bulgarska Assoziazsiia po Politiceski Izsledvaniia, 7 Noemvri St. 1, 1040 Sofia Bulgaria. **ED** Dobrin Kanev. **LC** H8; .I47a. ***Continues*** *Institut za Suvremenni Sotsialni Teorii. Suvremenni Sotsialni Teorii.*

CI/0032-3241
**POLITICKA MISAO.** [Polit. misao]. **Added/Corp** Sveuciliste u Zagrebu. Fakultet Politickih Nauka. (1964)-. Periodical. Serbo-Croatian (Roman) (summaries and/or abstracts in English and French). qt. cum. index.
**Ind/Abst** Am. Hist. Life (1971-1984).

IT/0032-325x
**POLITICO; RIVISTA ITALIANA DI SCIENZE POLITICHE, IL.** **Added/Corp** Universita di Pavia. Facolta di Scienze Politiche Pavia. Universita. Istituto di Scienze Politiche. Universita di Pavia. Vol. 1 (April 1928)-. Periodical. Italian. qt. L86000.00 Italy; L128000.00 other. Giuffre Editore SPA, Via Busto Arsizio 40, 20151 Milan Italy. **Tel** 011 398 2 38089200. **LC** JA18; .P65.
**Ind/Abst** Int. Bibliogr. Sociol.; PAIS Int. Print.

US/0749-4416
**POLITICS & MARKETS.** (POLITICS & MARKETS : A MONTHLY NEWSLETTER.). [Polit. mark.]. **VFOAT** Politics and Markets. Newsletter. English. mo. $115.00. Gallatin Institute, 1120 Connecticut Avenue/Suite 450, Washington DC 20063. **DD** 330.

US/0743-1082
**POLITICS AND POLICY.** ***Ceased.*** (POLITICS AND POLICY : JOURNAL OF THE NORTH CAROLINA POLITICAL SCIENCE ASSOCIATION.). [Polit. policy]. Vol. 4 (1984)-Ceased Vol. 9 (1989). Periodical. English. an. North Carolina Political Science Association, East Carolina University, Greenville NC 27834. **LC** JA1; .J69. **DD** 320/.05. ***Continues*** *Journal of the North Carolina Political Science Association, 0737-4801.*

US/0032-3292
**POLITICS & SOCIETY.** **See** Social Sciences.

GW/0939-6071
**POLITICS AND THE INDIVIDUAL.** (1991)-. Periodical. English. Twice a year. DM86.00 institutions; DM72.00 individuals. Verlag Dr. Reinhold Kraemer, Postfach 130584 / Rothenbaumchaussee, D - 20105 Hamburg Germany. **Tel** 11 49 40 4101429, FAX 11 49 40 455770. **ED** Verlag Dr. R. Kraemer. **UDC** 32. **Bk Rev. Ad Acc.**
**Desc:** Publishes original contributions in all area of political socialization and political psychology. Aims to achieve a better scientific understanding of the political beliefs and behaviors of individuals and groups.

US/0730-9384
**POLITICS AND THE LIFE SCIENCES.** (POLITICS AND THE LIFE SCIENCES : THE JOURNAL OF THE ASSOCIATION FOR POLITICS AND THE LIFE SCIENCES.). [Polit. life sci.]. **Added/Corp** Association for Politics and the Life Sciences (U.S.). Vol. 1, No. 1 (July 1982)-. Periodical. English. sa. £45.00. Beech Tree Publishing, 10 Waterford Close, Guildford Surrey GU1 2EP England. **Tel** +44 483 67497, FAX +44 0483 67497. **(Subscription address:** World-Wide Subscription Services, Unit 4, Gibbs Reed Farm Pashley Road, Ticehurst TN5 7HE England.**)** **LC** JA80; .P64. **DD** 320/.01. **NLM** W1; PO242H. **[CCC].** cum. index. **Bk Rev. Ad Acc. Pr Rev. Circ:** 500. Documents available from The Genuine Article.
**Desc:** Reports exclusively on important public policy, theoretical and methodological relationships between politics and the biological sciences. Publishes refereed articles, research notes, multiple reviews of books and bibliographic materials.
**Ind/Abst** ABC POL SCI; Asia.-Pac. Econ. Lit.; Biol. Dig.; Curr. Contents Soc. Behav. Sci.; Index Period. Artic. Relat. Law (19??-19??); Int. Bibliogr. Sociol.; Int. Polit. Sci. Abstr.; Res. Alert [Full Cov.]; Soc. Plann. Policy Dev. Abstr.; Soc. Sci. Cit. Index [Full Cov.].

US/0194-3669
**POLITICS (BATON ROUGE).** (POLITICS.). **Main/Corp** American Federation of Labor and Congress of Industrial Organizations. Louisiana. Political Information Committee. Periodical. English. mo. Free to members. Louisiana American Federation of Labor and Congress of Industrial Organizations (AFL-CIO), Political Information Committee, 429 Government Street, Baton Rouge LA 70821.

UK
**POLITICS BRIEFING.** No. 1- 1988-. Periodical. English. Four times a year. £8.00 UK; $25.00 (surface mail), $30.00 (airmail) other. Constitutional Reform Centre, 60 Chandos Place, London WC2N 4HG England. **Tel** (01)240 1719. **ED** Hilary Muggridge. **Circ:** 2,000 (ctrl).
**Desc:** Briefings on different aspects of politics mainly for students and teachers.

US
**POLITICS IN MINNESOTA. Added/Corp** Political Communications, Inc. (Saint Paul, Minn.). Vol. 1, No. 1 (July 2, 1982)-. Periodical. English. Twenty-two times a year. $48.00. Politics in Minnesota, 525 Park Street Suite 211, St. Paul MN 55103. **Tel** (612)293-3911. **ED** Wy Spano and D.J. Leary.

UK/0263-3957
**POLITICS (MANCHESTER (GREATER MANCHESTER)).** (POLITICS / POLITICAL STUDIES ASSOCIATION OF UNITED KINGDOM.). **Added/Corp** Political Studies Association of the United Kingdom. Vol. 1, No. 1 (April 1981)-. Academic Scholarly Publication. English. tq. £30.00 UK & Europe; $57.50 North America; £42.50 other. Basil Blackwell Publishers Ltd, 108 Cowley Road, Oxford 0X4 1JF England. **Tel** 011 44 865 791100, FAX 011 44 865 791347, telex 837022 OXBOOK G. **(Subscription address:** Blackwell Publishers / UK, Marston Book Services, PO Box 87, Oxford OX2 0DT England.**)** **ED** Vicky Randall. **[CCC]. Bk Rev. Pr Rev. Circ:** 1,000.
**Ind/Abst** Appl. Soc. Sci. Index Abstr.; Soc. Plann. Policy Dev. Abstr.

UK/0959-8480
**POLITICS REVIEW.** Vol. 1, No. 1 (Sept. 1991)-. Periodical. English. Four times a year. £16.95 UK; £23.00 Europe; £28.50 other. Philip Allan Publishers Ltd, Market Place, Deddington Oxford, OX15 0SE England. **Tel** 011 44 869 38652, FAX 011 44 869 38803. **LC** JA8; .P65. ***Continues** Social Studies Review.*
**Ind/Abst** Br. Humanit. Index.

UK
**POLITICS TODAY.** (Oct. 6, 1975)-. Periodical. English. bm. £17.00 UK; £23.00 other. Conservative Central Office, 16 Stadium Way, Scours Lane, Reading Berks RG3 6BX England. **Tel** 734 413439. **(Subscription address:** 16 Stadium Way, Reading Berks RG3 6BX England**)** **ED** A B Cooke. **LC** JN1129.C69; P64. **DD** 320.9/41/0857. Index available. cum. index. **Circ:** 3,000. ***Continues** Notes on Current Politics; **Formed by the union of** Old Queen Street Paper.*
**Desc:** Provides detailed explanations and analysis of all the main aspects of British politics.
**Ind/Abst** Mag. Index (1977-1980).

US/0160-4929
**POLITICS TODAY (SANTA BARBARA).** (POLITICS TODAY.). [Polit. today]. Vol. 5, No. 2 (March/April 1978)-. Periodical. English. bm. $9.00 US; $11.00 other. Skeptic Magazine Inc, Presidio Plaza, Santa Barbara CA 93101. **LC** AP2; .P753. **DD** 905. ***Continues** Skeptic, 0093-5050.*
**Ind/Abst** Mag. Index (March/April 1978-?).

FI/0032-3365
**POLITIIKKA.** [Politiikka]. **Added/Corp** Valtiotieteellinen Yhdistys. (1959)-. Periodical. English (Finnish and Swedish). qt. **LC** JN6701.A1; P64.
**Ind/Abst** ABC POL SCI; Am. Hist. Life (1954-); Int. Bibliogr. Sociol.; Selec. Coop. Index Manage. Period.

GW
**POLITIK UND KULTUR.** (19??)-. German. bm. DM30.00. Colloquium Verlag, Unter den Eichen 93, W-1000 Berlin 45 Germany. **Tel** 030-832 8085. **ED** Wilhelm Wolfgang Schuetz. **LC** AS181; .P64. Index available. **Bk Rev. Ad Acc. Circ:** 6,000.
**Desc:** Covers political, social and cultural developments in Germany.

SA/0258-9346
**POLITIKON.** [Politikon]. **Added/Corp** Political Science Association of South Africa. (June 1974)-. Periodical. Afrikaans (English). Twice a year (June, Dec.). $45.00. Political Science Association of South Africa, PO Box 1041, Florida 1710 South Africa. **Tel** 011 782 5500, FAX 011 782 5500. **ED** M. L. Frost. **LC** JA26; .P684. **Bk Rev. Pr Rev. Circ:** 850. available on microfilm from University Microfilms International (UMI).
**Ind/Abst** ABC POL SCI; Int. Polit. Sci. Abstr.

GW
**POLITIKWISSENSCHAFTLICHE PAPERBACKS. VFOAT** PWP; Politik Wissenschaftliche Paperbacks. 1981-. Monographic series. German. Price varies per volume. Studienverlag Dr N Brockmeyer, Querenburger Hohe 283, W-4630 Bochum Germany.

FR/0244-7827
**POLITIQUE AFRICAINE (PARIS, FRANCE : 1981).** (POLITIQUE AFRICAINE.). Vol. 1; Jan. 1981-. Monographic series. French. qt. 295.00F France; 370.00F French speaking Africa, Europe, Algeria, Morocco, Tunisia and French overseas departments and territories; 480.00F other. Editions Karthala, 22-24 Boulevard Arago, 75013 Paris France. **LC** JQ1872; .P65. **DD** 960.3/2/05.
**Ind/Abst** Int. Bibliogr. Sociol.; Int. Polit. Sci. Abstr.; PAIS Int. Print (1991-); Rice Abstr.; World Agric. Econ.

CN/1183-7993
**POLITIQUE ET ENVIRONNEMENT / GROUPE D'ETUDES ET DE RECHERCHES SUR LES POLITIQUES ENVIRONNEMENTALES.** [Polit. environ.]. **Added/Corp** Universite Laval. Groupe d'Etudes et de Recherches sur les Politiques Environnementales. **VFOAT** Bulletin de l'OCPEF. No. 1 (Jun 1991)-. Periodical. French. qt. Free Limited Distribution for Members. **DD** 363.7/056/05.

FR/0532-4092
**POLITIQUE ETRANGERE DE LA FRANCE, LA.** (LA POLITIQUE ETRANGERE DE LA FRANCE; TEXTES ET DOCUMENTS.). **Main/Corp** France. Direction de la Documentation. **Added/Corp** France. Documentation Francaise. France. Ministere des Affaires Etrangeres. Direction de la Presse, de l'Information et de la Communication. (1966)-. French. bm (6 issues). Documentation Francaise, 29 Quai Voltaire, 75344 Paris Cedex 7 France. **Tel** 011 33 1 40157000, FAX 011 33 1 40157230, telex 204 826 DOCFRAN. **(Subscription address:** Documentation Francaise, 124 rue Henri Barbusse, 93308 Aubervilliers Cedex France.**)**

FR/0766-6047
**POLITIQUE INDUSTRIELLE. See** Economics-Industry and Production.

FR
**POLITIQUE : REVUE INTERNATIONALE DES IDEES, DES INSTITUTIONS ET DE LA VIE POLITIQUE. Added/Corp** Academie Internationale de Science Politique et d'Histoire Constitutionelle. (195?)-. Periodical. French.
**Ind/Abst** Am. Hist. Life (1955-1970).

FR/0758-1726
**POLITIQUES ET MANAGEMENT PUBLIC.** [Polit. manage. public]. **VFOAT** Politiques & Management Public; P.M.P. Politiques et Management Public. (1983)-. Periodical. French. qt. 420.00F (individuals), 575.00F (institutions) France; 550.00F (individuals), 705.00F (institutions) other. Institute de Management Public, 23 rue de la Glaciere, 75013 Paris France. **Tel** 011 33 1 43311861, FAX 011 33 1 43318136. **ED** Patrick Gibert. **UDC** 336. cum. index. **Bk Rev**, (Qty: 3). **Ad Acc. Circ:** 800 (ctrl).

GW/0554-5455
**POLITISCHE BILDUNG (STUTTGART, GERMANY).** (POLITISCHE BILDUNG.). [Polit. Bild.]. (1967)-. Periodical. German. Three times a year. Ernst Klett Verlag, Postfach 106016, D 70049 Stuttgart Germany. **Tel** 011 49 711 667205. **(Subscription address:** Stuttgerter Verlagskontor, Postfatch 106016, D-70049 Stuttgart, Germany.**)**
**Ind/Abst** Foreign Lang. Index.

GW/0032-3462
**POLITISCHE STUDIEN.** Issue 1- 1950-. Periodical. German. bm. $19.47. Hanns Seidel Stiftung, Lazarettstrasse 19, W 8000 Munchen 19 Germany. **Tel** (089)293272. **LC** H35; .P66. available on microfilm from University Microfilms International (UMI).
**Ind/Abst** ABC POL SCI (19??-19??); Am. Hist. Life (1954-1957, 1962-1971); Int. Polit. Sci. Abstr.; PAIS Int. Print (1991-); Soc. Plann. Policy Dev. Abstr.; Sociol. Abstr. (?-?); World Agric. Econ.

GW/0578-0225
**POLITISCHES JAHRBUCH DER CHRISTLICH - DEMOKRATISCHEN UNION DEUTSCHLANDS. Main/Corp** Christlich-Demokratische Union Deutschlands (Germany : East). Vol. 1 (1967)-. Periodical. German. **LC** JN3971.5.A98; C4458. **DD** 324.2431/08.

FR/0295-2319
**POLITIX.** (1988)-. Periodical. French. qt. 375.00F (institution), 265.00F (individual) France; 460.00 (institution), 315.00F (individual) other. Presses de la Fondation, Nationale des Sciences Politiques, 44 Rue du Four, 75006 Paris France. **Tel** 011 33 1 44393960, FAX 011 33 1 45480441.

US/0032-3497
**POLITY.** [Polity]. **Added/Corp** Northeastern Political Science Association. (Fall 1968)-. Periodical. English. Four times a year. $35.00 (institutions), $20.00 (individuals) US; add $1.00 postage other. Polity, Political Science Department, 426 Thompson Hall, Amherst MA 01003. **Tel** (413)545-1354, FAX (413)545-4902. **LC** JA3; .P65. **DD** 320/.05. cum. index. **Bk Rev**, (Qty: 4). **Ad Acc. Pr Rev. Circ:** 1,200 (ctrl). available on microfilm and microfiche from University Microfilms International (UMI). Documents available from The Genuine Article.
**Desc:** A journal of political science covering all the topics in the discipline: American political thought, international relations, public policy, etc.
**Ind/Abst** ABC POL SCI; Am. Hist. Life (1968-); Am. Bibliogr. Slavic East Europ. Stud.; Arts Humanit. Citation Index [Select. Cov.]; Curr. Contents Soc. Behav. Sci.; Int. Polit. Sci. Abstr.; Middle East Abstr. Index; PAIS Int. Print (1991-); Res. Alert [Full Cov.]; Sage Public Adm. Abstr.; Soc. Sci. Cit. Index [Full Cov.]; U.S. Polit. Sci. Doc.; West. Hist. Q.

PL/0032-3500
**POLITYKA.** [Polityka]. (July 27, 1957)-. Periodical. Polish. wk. $91.00. **(Subscription address:** ARS Polona, PO Box 1001, 00068 Warsaw Poland.**)** **LC** AP54; .P59.
**Ind/Abst** MLA Int. Bibl. Books Artic. Mod. Lang. Lit.

US/0032-4515
**POPULAR GOVERNMENT.** [Pop. gov.]. **Added/Corp** Institute of Government (Chapel Hill, N.C.) University of North Carolina (1793-1962). Institute of Government. Vol. 1 (Jan. 1931)-. English. qt. $12.00. Institute of Government, University of North Carolina at Chapel Hill, CB #3300 Knapp Building, Chapel Hill NC 27599-3330. **Tel** (919)966-4119, FAX (919)962-2707. **ED** Robert P. Joyce. **LC** JK4101; .P6. Index available. **Circ:** 8,000 (ctrl). available on microfilm and microfiche from University Microfilms International (UMI).
**Desc:** Articles on North Carolina state and local government.
**Ind/Abst** Highw. Res. Abstr.; J. Plan. Lit.; PAIS Int. Print (1991-); Sage Public Adm. Abstr.; Sage Urban Stud. Abstr (?-?); Urban Aff. Abstr.

NE/0167-5923
**POPULATION RESEARCH AND POLICY REVIEW. See** Population Studies.

US/0748-2329
**PORTER'S GUIDE TO CONGRESSIONAL ROLL CALL VOTES. SENATE.** [Porter's guide Congr. roll call votes. Senate]. **VFOAT** Guide to Congressional Roll Call Votes. Senate; Porter's Guide. Senate; Porter's Guide. Senate. 98th Congress, 1st Session (1983)-. English. qt. $75.00. Legislative Information Group Press, 1718 Connecticut Avenue NW/Suite 410, Washington DC 20009. **Tel** (301)270-8939. **ED** Allison I Porter. **LC** JK1161; .P75. **DD** 328.73/071. Index available. **Bk Rev. Circ:** 100 (ctrl).
**Desc:** Reference books on congressional voting. Includes comprehensive indexes, vote descriptions, and member listings for 1983 and 1984 House and Senate sessions.

GW/0032-5201
**POSEV. VFOAT** Possev. Vol. 1 (1945)-. Periodical. Russian. Six times a year. DM80.00. Possev Verlag V Gorachek KG, Flurscheideweg 15, D 65936 Frankfurt Germany. **Tel** 011 49 69 341265. **ED** E Mirkovitch. **[CCC].** Index available. **Bk Rev. Ad Acc. Circ:** 2,000 (ctrl).
**Desc:** All about living in the Soviet Union and problems of opposition in the USSR.

GW/0938-555X
**POST-POLITISCHE INFORMATION.** [Post-Polit. Inf.]. **VFOAT** Post Politische Information. (1990)-. Periodical. German. mo. Free. Bundesministerium fur Post und Telekommunikation Referat fur Presse und Offentlichkeitsarbeit, Postfach 8001, W 5300 Bonn 1 Germany. **Tel** 011 49 228 149921, FAX 228-148975. **UDC** 656.

●US/1060-586X
**POST-SOVIET AFFAIRS. See** Economics.

US
**POST-SOVIET PROSPECTS.** **Added/Corp** Center for Strategic and International Studies (Washington, D.C.). No. 9 (Sept. 1991)-. Periodical. English. ir (7-8 per year). $24.00 US; $36.00 other. Post-Soviet Prospects, 1800 K Street NW Suite 400, Washington DC 20006. **Tel** (202)775-3240, FAX (202)775-3199. **ED** Gabriel Schoenfeld (editor's phone: (202)775-3185). **LC** DK1; .S5484. **Circ:** 4,000 (ctrl). ***Continues*** *Soviet Prospects, 1052-8601.*

●US/1062-0931
**PRAEGER SERIES IN PRESIDENTIAL STUDIES.** (1992)-. Monographic series. English. Price varies per volume. Greenwood Press Inc., PO Box 5007, Westport CT 06881-5007. **Tel** (203)226-3571, FAX (203)222-1502.

●US/1061-5261
**PRAEGER SERIES IN TRANSFORMATIONAL POLITICS AND POLITICAL SCIENCE.** (1992)-. Monographic series. English. Price varies per volume. Greenwood Press Inc., PO Box 5007, Westport CT 06881-5007. **Tel** (203)226-3571, FAX (203)222-1502.

PH/0116-709X
**PRAXIS: JOURNAL OF POLITICAL SCIENCE.** English (Tagalog). sa. P140.00 Philippines; $15.00 other. La Salle University Press, 2401 Taft Avenue, Manila Philippines. **Tel** (632)59-48-32, FAX (632) 5223661, telex RCA 23312 RHP-PH. **(Subscription address:** The Sales and Marketing Head, De La Salle University Press, 2401 Taft Avenue, Manila Philippines**) ED** Socorro Reyes. Index available. cum. index. **Bk Rev. Ad Acc. Circ:** 500.
**Desc:** The official publication of the Department of Political Science of DLSU. Articles published are scholary in nature, and reflect significant quantitative or qualitative research. They may be speeches, reports on research, book reviews and state of the art papers.

GW
**PRC OFFICIAL ACTIVITIES AND MONTHLY BIBLIOGRAPHY / INSTITUTE OF ASIAN AFFAIRS.** ***Title Change.*** **See** Political Science-Abstracting, Bibliographies and Statistics.

●US/1060-5088
**PRESIDENTS & PRIME MINISTERS.** [Pres. prime minist.]. **VAT** Presidents and Prime Ministers. Vol. 1, No. 1 (Sept./Oct. 1992)-. Periodical. English. Six times a year. $21.60. Equipment Engineering & Sales Inc., 799 Roosevelt Road Building 6, Suite 208, Glen Ellyn IL 60137. **Tel** (708)858-6161, FAX (708)858-8787. **LC** WMLC 93/409; JC362; .P74. **DD** 327. **CODEN** PPMIEK. **[CCC]. Bk Rev. Ad Acc, Adv Mgr:** Anu Agnihotci, **Tel** (208)858-6161.
**Desc:** Articles and news items are developed especially for readers interested in foreign affairs. Most of the articles and news items are statements by current presidents or prime ministers. Has departments on international trade, economy and finance, environment, health, food and agriculture, science and technology.
**Ind/Abst** Acad. Abstr. Full Text Elite (July 1993-) [Full Txt.]; Acad. Abstr. (July 1993-); Acad. Search (July 1993-); Mag. Artic. Summar. Elite (July 1993-) [Full Txt.]; Mag. Artic. Summar. CD-ROM (July 1993-).

CN/1181-7488
**PROBLEMATIQUE (DOWNSVIEW).** (PROBLEMATIQUE : JOURNAL OF POLITICAL STUDIES.). [Problematique]. **Added/Corp** York Political Science Graduate Students (Organization). **VFOAT** Journal of Political Studies; Revue d'Etudes Politiques. No. 1 (Spring 1991)-. English. $10.00. York Political Science Graduate Students, S655 Ross Building, York University, 4700 Keele Street, Downsview, Ontario M3J 1P3. **DD** 320/.05.

RU
**PROBLEMY PARTIINOGO I GOSUDARSTVENNOGO STROITELSTVA / AKADEMIIA OBSHCHESTVENNYKH NAUK PRI TSK KPSS.** **Added/Corp** Akademiia Obshchestvennykh Nauk (Moscow, R.S.F.S.R.). Vol. 1 (1981)-. Russian. an. **LC** JN6501; .P76. **DD** 320.947.

US/0739-7119
**PROBLEMY VOSTOCHNOI EVROPY.** **VFOAT** Problems of Eastern Europe. (1981)-. Periodical. Russian. Twice a year. $35.00. Problemy Vostochnoi Evropy, PO Box 6005, Washington DC 20005. **Tel** (202)387-4514. **LC** DJK50; .P77. **DD** 320.947.

US
**PROCEEDINGS OF THE ACADEMY OF POLITICAL SCIENCE.** ***Title Change.*** (PROCEEDINGS OF THE ACADEMY OF POLITICAL SCIENCE IN THE CITY OF NEW YORK.). [Proc. Acad. Politi. Sci.]. **Added/Corp** Academy of Political Science in the City of New York. **VFOAT** Proceedings of the Academy of Political Sciences. Vol. 1 (Oct. 1910)-(19??). Proceedings. English. sa. Academy of Political Science, 475 Riverside Drive/Suite 1274, New York NY 10115-1274. **Tel** (212)870-2500, FAX (212)870-2202. Index available. cum. index. **Bk Rev. Ad Acc. Circ:** 9,000 (ctrl). available on microfilm from University Microfilms International (UMI); available on an online database. ***Continued by*** *Proceedings of the Academy of Political Science, 0065-0684.*
**Desc:** Focuses on a single political, social, or economic issue.
**Ind/Abst** ABC POL SCI; Acad. Abstr. Full Text Elite (Jan. 1991-); Am. Hist. Life (1963-); Int. Polit. Sci. Abstr.; Middle East Abstr. Index; Soc. Sci. Index; Soc. Sci. Index Fulltext (1989-) [Full Txt.]; Soc. Work Abstr. [Select. Cov.]; Sociol. Educ. Abstr.; U.S. Polit. Sci. Doc. (?-19??).

US/0065-0684
**PROCEEDINGS OF THE ACADEMY OF POLITICAL SCIENCE.** ***Suspended.*** [Proc. Acad. Polit. Sci.]. **Added/Corp** Academy of Political Science (U.S.). Vol. 13, No. 1 (192?)-Suspended with Vol. 38, No. 2. Proceedings. English. ir. Academy of Political Science, 475 Riverside Drive/Suite 1274, New York NY 10115-1274. **Tel** (212)870-2500, FAX (212)870-2202. **DD** 324. available on microfilm and microfiche from University Microfilms International (UMI). Documents available from UMI Article Clearinghouse. ***Continues*** *Proceedings of the Academy of Political Science in the City of New York.*
**Desc:** Each issue focuses on a specific political topic.
**Ind/Abst** Acad. Abstr. (Jan. 1991-); Acad. Ind. [Computer File] (1987-); Acad. Search (Jan. 1991-); Expand. Acad. Index (1987-); INFO-SOUTH Abstr.; LABORDOC; Mag. Search; Newsp. Period. Abstr. (1988-); Soc. Sci. Source (Jul. 1990-).

US
**PROCEEDINGS OF THE GOVERNMENT STATISTICS SECTION / AMERICAN STATISTICAL ASSOCIATION.** **Main/Corp** American Statistical Association. Government Statistics Section. **Added/Corp** American Statistical Association. Meeting. (19??)-. Statistical Publication. English. $38.00. American Statistical Association, 1429 Duke Street, Alexandria VA 22314. **Tel** (703)684-1221, (202)393-3253, FAX (703)684-2037 (orders). **LC** HA37.U52; A44.
**Ind/Abst** Curr. Index Stat. (199?-).

FR/0992-5163
**PROFESSION POLITIQUE PARIS.** (PROFESSION POLITIQUE.). [Prof. polit. Paris]. **VFOAT** Profession Politique (Issy-les-Moulineaux). (1988)-. Periodical. French. bw (25 issues). 1469.15F. Profession Politique, 26 rue Marceau, 92130 Issy l'Moulineaux France. **Tel** 011 33 46292987. **UDC** 323 (44).

US
**PROGRAM & LEGISLATIVE ACTION BULLETIN.** Bulletin. English. Twelve times a year. $12.00. Women's International League for Peace and Freedom, 1213 Race Street, Philadelphia PA 19107-1691. **Tel** (215)563-7110, FAX (215)864-2022. **ED** Maren Gaughan.

FR
**PROGRAMMES ET ENGAGEMENTS ELECTORAUX.** **Main/Corp** France. Parlement (1946- ). Assemblee Nationale. **VFOAT** Barodet. 12/19 March 1978-. French. Impr de l'Assemblee Nationale, Parlement Secretariat General, Paris France. **LC** JN2957; .P37A. **DD** 324.2/3/0944. ***Continues*** *Recueil des Textes Authentiques des Programmes et Engagements Electoraux des Deputes Proclames Elus a la Suite des Elections Generales.*

CN/0829-1489
**PROJECT NORTH JOURNAL.** **See** Ethnic Interests.

GW
**PROTOKOLL - DEUTSCHER BUNDESTAG.** **Main/Corp** Germany (West). Bundestag. German. Verlag Dr H Hegen, Postfach 821, 53 Bonn-Bad Godesberg 1 Germany. **LC** J351; .K252A.

US/1049-0965
**PS, POLITICAL SCIENCE & POLITICS.** [PS polit. sci. polit.]. **Added/Corp** American Political Science Association. **VFOAT** PS, Political Science and Politics; Political Science & Politics; Political Science and Politics; PS. **VAT** Political Science. Vol. 21, No. 1 (Winter 1988)-. Periodical. English. qt. Free with membership. American Political Science Association, 1527 New Hampshire Avenue Northwest, Washington DC 20036. **Tel** (202)483-2512, FAX (202)483-2657. **LC** JA28; .P24. **DD** 320/.05. available on microfilm from University Microfilms International (UMI). Documents available from The Genuine Article, UMI Article Clearinghouse. ***Continues*** *PS, 0030-8269;* ***Absorbed*** *Political Science Teacher, 0896-0828.*
**Ind/Abst** ABC POL SCI (1988-); Acad. Abstr. Full Text Elite (Jan. 1992-); Acad. Abstr. (Jan. 1992-); Acad. Search (Jan. 1992-); Arts Humanit. Citation Index [Select. Cov.]; Curr. Contents Soc. Behav. Sci.; Curr. Index J. Educ.; Expand. Acad. Index (1989-); Index Period. Artic. Relat. Law (19??-); INFO-SOUTH Abstr.; J. Plan. Lit.; Mag. Search; Newsp. Period. Abstr. (1991-); Res. Alert [Full Cov.]; Soc. Sci. Source (Jan. 1992-); Soc. Sci. Cit. Index [Full Cov.]; Soc. Work Abstr. [Select. Cov.]; U.S. Polit. Sci. Doc. (199?-).

UK
**PSI RESEARCH RESULTS.** English. ir (4 issues). £40.00. Carfax Publishing Company, PO Box 25 Abingdon, Oxfordshire OX14 3UE England. **Tel** 011 44 235 555335, FAX (0279)31067, telex 817484. **(Subscription address:** US and Canada/ PO Box 2025, Dunnellon, FL 34430-2025; telephone:(904)489-6996**)**

NE/0048-5829
**PUBLIC CHOICE.** **See** Economics.

US/0742-5325
**PUBLIC JUSTICE REPORT.** **See** Public Administration.

US/0079-7790
**PUBLICATIONS ON RUSSIA AND EASTERN EUROPE.** **Main/Corp** Washington (State). University. Institute for Comparative and Foreign Area Studies. **Added/Corp** Washington (State) University. Far Eastern and Russian Institute. Publications on Russia and Eastern Europe. No. 1 (1969)-. Monographic series. English. ir. Price varies per volume. University of Washington Press, Box C-50096, Seattle WA 98145-0096. **Tel** (206)543-8870.

US/0048-5950
**PUBLIUS.** [Publius]. **Added/Corp** Temple University. Center for the Study of Federalism. Vol. 1 (1971)-. Periodical. English. qt. $25.00 (individuals), $35.00 (institutions) one year US; $30.00 (individuals), $40.00 (institutions) one year other; $48.00 (individuals), $70.00 (institutions) two years US; $58.00 (individuals), $80.00 (institutions) two years other. Publius, Department of Political Science, PO Box 5338, University of North Texas, Denton TX 76203. **Tel** (817)565-2313, FAX (817)565-2599. **ED** John Kincaid. **LC** JK1; .P88. **DD** 321/.02. Index available. **Bk Rev. Ad Acc. Pr Rev. Circ:** 1,100 (ctrl). available on microfilm and microfiche from University Microfilms International (UMI). Documents available from The Genuine Article, UMI Article Clearinghouse.
**Desc:** The premier journal devoted to studies and analyses of federalism and intergovernmental relations in the United States and around the world. Publius has earned worldwide respect for its consent articles by leading scholars on an exceptional range of timely and enduring issues of federalism, decentralization, and democratization on all continents.
**Ind/Abst** ABC POL SCI; Am. Hist. Life (1971-); Arts Humanit. Citation Index [Select. Cov.]; Energy Res. Abstr. (March 1979-); Expand. Acad. Index (1992-); Index Period. Artic. Relat. Law; Int. Polit. Sci. Abstr.; Middle East Abstr. Index; Newsp. Period. Abstr. (1992-); PAIS Int. Print (1991-); Res. Alert [Full Cov.]; Sage Public Adm. Abstr.; Sage Urban Stud. Abstr; Soc. Plann. Policy Dev. Abstr.; Soc. Sci. Cit. Index [Full Cov.]; Sociol. Abstr. (1971-); U.S. Polit. Sci. Doc.

US/0033-4030
**PUERTO RICO LIBRE!.** **Added/Corp** Puerto Rican Solidarity Committee. Committee for Puerto Rican Decolonization. Vol. 1 (Aug. 1973)-. Periodical. English. Six times a year. C O Solidarity Committee, Box 319 Cooper Station, New York NY 10003. **Tel** (212)741-3131.

II/0253-3960
**PUNJAB JOURNAL OF POLITICS.** **Added/Corp** Guru Nanak Dev University. Dept. of Political Science. Vol. 1 (1977)-. Periodical. English. an. $20.00. Guru Nanak Dev University / Department of Political Science, Amritsar, India. **(Subscription address:** Prints India, 11 Darya Ganj, New Delhi, 110002 India, (Phone: 011 91 11 3268645)**) LC** JA26; .P88. **DD** 320/.05.
**Ind/Abst** Am. Hist. Life (1986-).

MX
**PUNTO CRITICO.** **See** Economics.

US/1061-5636
**QIRAAT SIYASIYAH.** [Qiraat siyasiyah]. **Added/Corp** World & Islam Studies Enterprise (Tampa, Fla.). **VFOAT** Qira'at Siyasiyyah; Political Readings. Vol. 1 No. 1 (1991)-. Periodical. Arabic. qt (Jan., Apr., July, Oct.). $75.00 (one year), $140.00 (two year) institutions, $30.00 (one year), $50.00 (two year) institutions. World & Islam Studies Enterprise, PO Box 16648, Tampa FL 33687. **Tel** (813)985-4343. **LC** IN PROCESS. **DD** 320.

IT
**QUADERNI DI SCIENZA POLITICA.** (19??)-. Italian. ir. L60000 Italy; L90000 other. Giuffre Editore SPA, Via Busto Arsizio 40, 20151 Milan Italy. **Tel** 011 398 2 38089200.

IT
**QUADERNI DI STORIA DELL'ECONOMIA POLITICA.** ***Ceased.*** (1983)-(19??). Periodical. Italian. qt. Franco Angeli Editore Riviste, Via le Monza 106, 20127 Milan Italy. **Tel** 011 39 2 2827651 or, 289562, FAX 011 39 2 258004, telex 051-511650.

# Political Science

IT/0391-7312
**QUADERNI DI TERZO MONDO.** [Quad. Terzo Mondo]. **VFOAT** Terzo Mondo. (1973)-. Periodical. Italian. qt. $60.00 (institution); $30.00 (individual). Centro Studi Terzo Mondo, Via G Morgagni 39, 20129 Milan Italy. **Tel** 39 2 29409041. UDC 320.
**Ind/Abst** Soc. Plann. Policy Dev. Abstr.

SP/0210-7554
**QUADERNS D'ALLIBERAMENT. VFOAT** Quaderns Llil. 1 (1977)-. Periodical. Catalan. an. 900.00ptas. Edicions de la Magrana SA, Apartat de Correud 9487, 08023 Barcelona. **Tel** 210.36.96. **ED** Rafael Castellanos. **LC** DP302.C57; Q29. **DD** 946/.7/005. **Bk Rev. Circ:** 1,000.
**Desc:** Concerned with the problems of Catalonia: social linguistics, immigration, women and eurocommunism.

US/0738-9752
**QUARTERLY JOURNAL OF IDEOLOGY.**
See Sociology.

CN/0709-5643
**QUEBEC CANADA (MONTREAL).** (QUEBEC-CANADA.). **Main/Corp** Quebec-Canada (Movement). V. 1- Nov. 1977-. Periodical. English (French). mo. $3.00. Quebec-Canada, 1253 McGill College Avenue 470, Montreal Quebec H3B 2Y5 Canada. **DD** 329.9/714.

CN/0824-2348
**QUEBECER, THE.** [Quebecer]. Vol. 1, No. 1 (1983)-. Periodical. English. qt. Alliance Quebec / Montreal, 1411 rue Crescent/Suite 501, Montreal Quebec H3G 2B3 Canada. **DD** 323.1/12/0714.

CN/0703-4784
**QUEBECOIS DU COMTE DE VANIER, LE.** V. 1- Spring 1977-. Periodical. French. qt. Free. Association du Parti Quebecois du Comite Boulay, 33 rue de Gaspe, Quebec Quebec G1L 2A4 Canada. **DD** 329.9/714.

CN/0823-6321
**QUEBECOIS VAUDREUIL-SOULANGES, LE.** [Que. Vaudreuil-Soulanges]. Vol. 1, No. 1-. Periodical. French. Parti Quebecois De Vaudreuil-Soulanges, 208, Litbiniere, Vaudreuil Quebec Canada. **DD** 324.2714/093.

AG
**QUEHACER NACIONAL.** (Mar. 1982)-. Periodical. Spanish. mo. Hipolito Yrigoyen, 1394 Buenos Aires Argentina. **LC** F2849.2; .Q43. **DD** 982/.005.

SA
**RACE RELATIONS SURVEY / SOUTH AFRICAN INSTITUTE OF RACE RELATIONS. Added/Corp** South African Institute of Race Relations. Vol. 38 (1984)-. English. an. $22.00 (airmail) US; £15.00 (airmail) Europe; $325.00 (South African Institute of Race Relations subscription package--includes Fast Facts, Spotlight, Race Relations News, and Special Reports. South African Institute of Race Relations, PO Box 31044, Braamfontein 2017 South Africa. **Tel** 011 27 11 4033600, FAX 011 27 11 4033671. **LC** DT763; .S79. **DD** 968/.005. **Bk Rev. Circ:** 4,000. **Continues** Survey of Race Relations in South Africa, 0081-9778.
**Desc:** Annual monitor of the effects of apartheid on segregation, population, economy, business, employment, labor relations, urbanization, housing, transport, homeland affairs, education, welfare, politics and international research.

US/0033-7617
**RADICAL AMERICA.** [Radic. Am.]. Vol. 1 (1967)-. Periodical. English. Five times a year. $22.00 (1 year), $39.00 (2 year) individuals; $43.00 (1 year), $74.00 2 year), $105.00 (3 year) institutions. Radical America, One Summer Street, Somerville MA 02143. **Tel** (617)628-6585. **ED** John P Demeter. **LC** HD4802; .R33. **DD** 322/.2/0973. Index available. cum. index. **Bk Rev. Ad Acc. Circ:** 5,000. available on microfilm and microfiche from University Microfilms International (UMI).
**Desc:** Independent, left journal writing on politics, culture and world affairs since 1967. Published by an editorial collective in Boston.
**Ind/Abst** Altern. Press Index; Am. Hist. Life (1971-); Film Lit. Index (19??-); Left Index; Middle East Abstr. Index; Peace Res. Abstr. J. (1979); Sage Race Relat. Abstr.; Soc. Plann. Policy Dev. Abstr.; Sociol. Abstr.

BL
**RAG, REVISTA ADMINISTRATIVA DO GRANDE RIO.** Periodical. Portuguese. Visconde Rio Branco, 37 - 1 Andar, Rio de Janeiro Brazil. **LC** JL2499.R47; R14. **DD** 309.1/81/5.

FR/0767-4538
**RAPPORT AU PRESIDENT DE LA REPUBLIQUE ET AU PARLEMENT.** French. Journaux Officiels, 26 rue Desaix, 75727 Paris Cedex 15 France. **Tel** 40 58 77 27.

RU
**REABILITIROVAN POSMERTNO.** (1988)-. Periodical. Russian. ir.

AU/0080-0163
**RECHTS- UND STAATSWISSENSCHAFTEN.** (1947)-. Monographic series. German. ir. Price varies per volume. Springer-Verlag Wien, Sachsenplatz 4 6, PO Box 89, A-1201 Vienna Austria. **Tel** 011 43 1 3302415.
**(Subscription address:** Springer Verlag New York Inc. / for North America, 44 Hartz Way, Secaucus NJ 07096.)

US
**REFERENCE AID, CHIEFS OF STATE, AND CABINET MEMBERS OF FOREIGN GOVERNMENTS. Main/Corp** United States. Central Intelligence Agency. 1972. Periodical. English. ir. $300.00. Document Expediting Project, Exchange and Gift Division, Library of Congress, Photoduplication Service, Washington DC 20540. **Tel** (202)287-9527. **ED** CIA. **Circ:** 625 (ctrl).
**Desc:** Includes economic and energy statistics, directories of foreign Governments. Maps.

CN/0842-3148
**REFORMER (EDMONTON).** (THE REFORMER: THE OFFICIAL PUBLICATION OF THE REFORM PARTY OF CANADA.). [Reformer]. **Added/Corp** Reform Party of Canada. (April 1988)-. Periodical. English. qt. Free to members. Reform Party of Canada, Suite 501, 10053 11th Street, Edmonton, Alberta T5K 2H8 Canada. **ED** Laurie Watson. **DD** 324.271/093.
**Desc:** The official publication of the Reform Party of Canada.

CN/0384-9120
**REGARDS SUR ISRAEL (MONTREAL).** (REGARDS SUR ISRAEL.). V. 1- Dec. 1972-. French. mo. Comite Canada-Israel, 1310 Av Greene, Montreal Quebec H3Z 2B2 Canada.

UK
**REGIONAL POLITICS & POLICY. VFOAT** Regional Politics and Policy. Vol. 1, no. 1 (1991)-. Periodical. English. Three times a year. $135.00. Frank Cass & Company Ltd, Newbury House, 890-900 Eastern Avenue, Newbury Park, Ilford, Essex IG2 7HH United Kingdom. **Tel** 011 44 81 599 8866, FAX 011 44 81 599 0984, telex 897719. **Ad Acc, Adv Mgr:** Anne Kidson.

IT
**REGIONI / I.S.G.R.E., ISTITUTO DI STUDI GIURIDICI REGIONALI, LE. Added/Corp** Istituto di Studi Giuridici Regionali. **VFOAT** Rivista di Documentazione e Giurisprudenza. Vol. 1 (Jan./Feb. 1973)-. Italian. bm. L130000.00 Italy; L150000.00 (surface mail), L180000.00 (airmail) other. Societa Editrice il Mulino, Strada Maggiore 37, 40125 Bologna Italy. **Tel** 011 39 51 256011, FAX 011 39 51 256034. **LC** LAW.

US
**RELIGION & DEMOCRACY.** See Religion and Theology.

US/0279-0300
**RENEWAL (WINCHESTER, VA.).** (RENEWAL.). [Renewal]. Vol. 1, No. 1 (Jan. 26, 1981)-. Periodical. English. ir. $15.00. New World Alliance, 3129 Ninth Road, Arlington VA 22201. **Tel** (202)234-0747.

CN/0846-6351
**REPORT OF THE CHIEF ELECTORAL OFFICER OF CANADA.** [Rep. Chief Elect. Off. Can.]. **Main/Corp** Elections Canada. **VFOAT** Rapport du Directeur General des Elections du Canada. (1989)-. Periodical. English (French). Information Canada, 171 Slater Street, Ottawa Ontario K1A 0S9 Canada. **Tel** (819)997-1095. **DD** 354.710081/1. **Continues** Statutory Report of the Chief Electoral Officer of Canada., 0225-9486.

JM
**REPORT OF THE DIRECTOR OF ELECTIONS. Main/Corp** Jamaica. Electoral Office. (19??)-. English. Director of Elections, Electoral Office, Kingston Jamaica. **LC** JL639.A55; A32. **DD** 324.97292/0021. **Continues** General Election. Report.

US
**REPORT OF THE ELECTION LAW ENFORCEMENT COMMISSION. Main/Corp** New Jersey Election Law Enforcement Commission. English. an. New Jersey Election Law Enforcement Commission, 28 West State Street/Suite 1215, Trenton NJ 08608. **Continues** Annual Report of the New Jersey Election Law Enforcement Commission.

US
**REPORT ON FREEDOM. Added/Corp** Liberty Amendment Committee of the U.S.A. Periodical. English. mo. Liberty Amendment Committee, PO Box A, Prouo UT 84601. **Tel** (801)374-1800. **Continues** Report to America.

JA
**REPORT ON MEETING OF APU SECRETARIES-GENERAL IN TOKYO. Main/Corp** Asian Parliamentarians' Union. Central Secretariat. 1st (1972)-. English. TBR Building/Room No 807 10-2, 2-chome Nagata-cho, Chiyoda-ku Tokyo Japan. **LC** DS35; .A817a. **DD** 320.9/5.

US/0034-4931
**REPRINTS FROM THE SOVIET PRESS.** *Suspended.* See Economics.

US/0363-9290
**REPUBLICAN ALMANAC. Added/Corp** Republican National Committee (U.S.) Communications Division. Republican National Committee (U.S.) Political/Research Division. (19??)-. English. National Republican Committee, 310 First Street Northeast, Washington DC 20003. **LC** JK1967; .R36. **DD** 329/.00973.

US/1056-9278
**REPUBLICAN UPDATE.** [Repub. update]. **VFOAT** RCS Republican Update. (1991)-. Periodical. English. mo. $25.00. Republican Update, 4128 1/2 California Avenue, Suite 106, Seattle WA 98116. **DD** 324.

US/0092-671X
**RES PUBLICA (CLAREMONT).** (RES PUBLICA.). **Added/Corp** Claremont Men's College (Claremont, Calif.). (Spring 1973)-. Periodical. English. Four times a year. $51.00. Politologisch Instituut, Van Evenstraat 2B, B-3000 Louvain Belgium. **Tel** 011 32 16 283250, 283254. **LC** AP2; .R375. **Ad Acc.**
**Desc:** Concentrates on the analysis of Belgian politics (decision-making as well as policy) and on the general development of political science and the contribution of Belgium in this development.
**Ind/Abst** ABC POL SCI; Soc. Plann. Policy Dev. Abstr.; Sociol. Abstr.

UK
**RESEARCH AT LSE.** See Economics.

US
**RESEARCH IN BIOPOLITICS.** Vol. 1 (1991)-. English. an. $73.25. JAI Press Inc., 55 Old Post Road, Suite 2, PO Box 1678, Greenwich CT 06836-1678. **Tel** (203)661-7602, FAX (203)661-0792. **ED** Albert Somit. **LC** JA80; .R47. **DD** 320/.01/574.

US/1041-5858
**RESEARCH IN MICROPOLITICS.** [Res. micropolit.]. Vol. 1 (1986)-. English. ir. $73.25. JAI Press Inc., 55 Old Post Road, Suite 2, PO Box 1678, Greenwich CT 06836-1678. **Tel** (203)661-7602, FAX (203)661-0792. **ED** Michael X. Delli Carpini, Leonie Huddy, and Robert Y. Shapiro. **LC** JA1; .R37. **DD** 320/.05.
**Ind/Abst** Soc. Plann. Policy Dev. Abstr.

US/0895-9935
**RESEARCH IN POLITICAL SOCIOLOGY.**
See Sociology.

US/0885-212X
**RESEARCH IN POLITICS AND SOCIETY.** [Res. polit. soc.]. Vol. 1 (1985)-. English. ir. $73.25. JAI Press Inc., 55 Old Post Road, Suite 2, PO Box 1678, Greenwich CT 06836-1678. **Tel** (203)661-7602, FAX (203)661-0792. **ED** Gwen Moore. **LC** JA76; .R46. **DD** 306/.2.
**Ind/Abst** Am. Bibliogr. Slavic East Europ. Stud.; Soc. Plann. Policy Dev. Abstr.

US/0897-2613
**RESIST (SOMERVILLE, MASS.).** (RESIST.). [Resist]. **VFOAT** Resist Newsletter. (1967)-. Periodical. English. Ten times a year (June/July and Aug/Sept. combined). $15.00 one year; $25.00 two year. Resist, One Summer St., Somerville MA 02143. **Tel** (617)623-5110, FAX (617)628-2025. **ED** Tatiana Schreiber. **DD** 322. **Bk Rev,** (Qty: 1-2 per year). **Circ:** 10,000.
**Desc:** Carries informative, in-depth, readable articles on topics and issues of interest to all those concerned with peace and justice. Including articles on the women's gay and lesbian liberation, anti-racist, AIDS activist, and anti-intervention movements.

US
**RESISTANCE NEWS / NATIONAL RESISTANCE COMMITTEE. Added/Corp** National Resistance Committee (U.S.). Issue No. 1 (Mar. 3, 1980)-. Periodical. English. qt. $15.00 individual, $25.00 library. National Resistance Committee, PO Box 42488, San Francisco CA 94142. **Tel** (415)824-8562. **ED** Edward Hazbrouck and Liz Davidson. **Bk Rev. Circ:** 5,000.
**Desc:** The NRC works to resist current preparations for war and conscription by encouraging those of draft age to refuse registration.

CN/0824-586X
**RESISTANCE (VANCOUVER).** (RESISTANCE.). [Resistance]. Periodical. English. qt. $15.00. Resistance, c/o Friends of Durruti, PO Box 790 Station A, Vancouver British Columbia V6C 2N6 Canada. **DD** 322.4/05. **Bk Rev. Circ:** 7,000.
**Desc:** Covering militant autonomist, anti-imperialist, national liberation, feminist and anti-nuclear struggles in advanced capitalist countries, an important tool for revolutionary social change.

IT
**RESOCONTO SOMMARIO AULA E BOLLETTINO DELLE GIUNTE E COMMISSIONI PARLAMENTARI.** (19??)-. Italian. ir. L535000 Italy. Libreria Camera dei Deputati, Via Uffici del Vicario 17, 00186 Rome, Italy. **Tel** 011 39 6 67603715.

II
**RESUME OF BUSINESS TRANSACTED DURING SESSION OF THE MEGHALAYA LEGISLATIVE ASSEMBLY, ASSEMBLED UNDER THE DEMOCRATIC CONSTITUTION OF INDIA.** **Main/Corp** Meghalaya (India). Legislative Assembly. English. Meghalaya Legislative Assembly Secretariat, Legislative Assembly, Meghalaya Shillong India. **LC** J601.M43; H95A. **DD** 328.54/16.

UK/0034-5970
**RESURGENCE.** Vol. 1 (May/June 1966)-. Periodical. English. Six times a year. £22.00 (institutions), £16.00 (individuals) UK; £25.00 (institutions), £20.00 (individuals) other. Resurgence, Salem Cottage, Trelill Bodmin, Cornwall PL30 3HZ England. **Tel** 44 81 208 851304. **(Subscription address:** Salem Cottage, Trelill, Bodmin Cornwall PL30 3HZ England**) ED** Satish Kumar. **LC** JX1901; .R43. **Bk Rev. Ad Acc. Circ:** 10,000.
**Desc:** During the last several years the publication has been one of the poles, around which disciplined radical alternative thinking has taken shape.
**Ind/Abst** Environ. Period. Bibliogr.

RU
**RETROSPEKTIVNAIA I SRAVNITELNAIA POLITOLOGIIA.** **Added/Corp** Institut Vostokovedeniia (Akademiia Nauk SSSR). No. 1 (1991)-. Russian. Glav Red Vostochnoi, Lit-Ry Izd-Va Nauka Moscow K-31, Ulitsa Zhdanova 12/1 Russia. **LC** JA71; .R46.

UK/0305-6244
**REVIEW OF AFRICAN POLITICAL ECONOMY.** **See** Economics-Economic History, Conditions.

AT/0815-7251
**REVIEW OF INDONESIAN AND MALAYSIAN AFFAIRS.** [Rev. Indones. Malays. aff.]. **Added/Corp** University of Sydney. Dept. of Indonesian and Malayan Studies. Koninklijk Instituut voor Taal-, Land- en Volkenkunde (Netherlands). Afdeling Documentatie Modern Indonesie. **VFOAT** Indonesian and Malaysian Affairs; Rima. Vol. 17 (Winter/Summer 1983)-. Periodical. English. sa (Winter and Summer). 25.00Aus$ (Australia & New Zealand); 33.00Aus$ (surface mail) 45.00Aus$ (air mail) other. University of Sydney Department of Southeast Asian Studies, Broadway NSW 2006 Australia. **Tel** 011 61 2 6923121, FAX 011 61 2 6923173. ***Continues** Review of Indonesian and Malayan Affairs, 0034-6594.*
**Ind/Abst** APAIS, Aust. Public Aff. Inf. Ser. (1983-); MLA Int. Bibl. Books Artic. Mod. Lang. Lit.

UK/0953-8259
**REVIEW OF POLITICAL ECONOMY.** [Rev. polit. econ.]. Vol. 1, No. 1 (1989)-. Periodical. English. qt. $165.00 US, Canada and Mexico. Edward Arnold, 338 Euston Road, London NW1 3BH England. **Tel** 011 44 71 873 6000, FAX 011 44 071 873 6325. **(Subscription address:** Turpin Distribution Services Limited, Blackhorse Road, Letchworth, Hertfordshire SG6 1HN, United Kingdom.**) ED** John Pheby. **LC** HB1; .R46. **CODEN** RPECEI. **Bk Rev.**
**Desc:** Signifies a realistic approach which does not recognize narrow boundaries of the economic system and its analysis, but puts first priority on practical and policy issues, and tailors theoretical and empirical work accordingly. Devoted to encouraging creative and non-orthodox papers on a wide range of issues including institutionalist, subjectivist, and behavioral economists. Contains book reviews, review articles, and symposia. An occasional thematic issue is produced. A newletter section includes information on conferences, seminars, visiting scholars, and appointments.
**Ind/Abst** Appl. Soc. Sci. Index Abstr.; Br. Humanit. Index; Contents Recent Econ. J.; Econ. Lit. Index; J. Plan. Lit.; PAIS Bull.; Sociol. Abstr.

US/0034-6705
**REVIEW OF POLITICS, THE.** [Rev. polit.]. **Added/Corp** University of Notre Dame. Vol. 1, (Jan. 1939)-. Periodical. English. Four times a year (Jan., Apr., July, Oct.). $30.00 (institution); $25.00 (individual). Review of Politics, Box B, Notre Dame IN 46556. **Tel** (219)631-6623, FAX (212)631-8609. **ED** Donald P. Kommers. **LC** JA1; .R4. **DD** 320.5. Index available. **Bk Rev**, (Qty: 50). **Ad Acc. Pr Rev. Circ:** 1,700. available on microfilm and microfiche from University Microfilms International (UMI). Documents available from The Genuine Article, UMI Article Clearinghouse.
**Desc:** Devoted to the study of political realities and to political community. Articles and reviews present critical analyses of institutions and techniques. Distinctive emphasis is a concern with the philosophical and historical aspects of politics.
**Ind/Abst** ABC POL SCI; Acad. Abstr. Full Text Elite (July 1990-); Acad. Abstr. (July 1990-); Acad. Ind. [Computer File] (1987-); Acad. Search (July 1990-); Am. Hist. Life (1954-); Am. Bibliogr. Slavic East Europ. Stud.; Book Rev. Index; Curr. Contents Soc. Behav. Sci.; Expand. Acad. Index (1987-); Index Period. Artic. Relat. Law (19??-19??); INFO-SOUTH Abstr.; Mag. Search; Middle East Abstr. Index; Newsp. Period. Abstr. (1991-); PAIS Int. Print; Peace Res. Abstr. J. (1966-1967, 1973-1979); Res. Alert [Full Cov.]; Sage Public Adm. Abstr.; Soc. Sci. Source (Jul. 1990-); Soc. Sci. Cit. Index [Full Cov.]; Soc. Sci. Index; Soc. Sci. Index Fulltext (Fall 1988-) [Full Txt.]; Abr. Cathol. Period. Lit. Index; Cathol. Period. Lit. Index; U.S. Polit. Sci. Doc.; West. Hist. Q.

US/1050-2130
**REVIEW / OHIO COUNCIL FOR THE SOCIAL STUDIES, THE.** [Rev. - Ohio Counc. Soc. Stud.]. **Added/Corp** Ohio Council for the Social Studies. Cleveland State University. Dept. of History. **VFOAT** OCSS Review. **VAT** Ohio Council for the Social Studies Review. (196?)-. Periodical. English. $15.00 (includes membership). Ohio Council for the Social Studies, 24898 Fawn Drive, North Olmsted OH 44070. **LC** LB1584; .R47. **DD** 300/.71/2.
**Ind/Abst** Curr. Index J. Educ.

AG
**REVISTA ARGENTINA DE POLITICA Y TEORIA.** **VFOAT** Politica y Teoria. V. 1, No. 1- (April/July 1983)-. Periodical. Spanish. qt. $15.00. C C No 3521 C Central, 1000 Buenos Aires Argentina. **Tel** 27-2877. **LC** JL2001; .R48. **DD** 320.982/05. **Bk Rev. Circ:** 2,500.
**Desc:** A Marxist-Leninist, Maoist publication on historical, current and theoretical problems of revolution in Argentina, Latin America and world-wide.

BL/0034-7191
**REVISTA BRASILEIRA DE ESTUDOS POLITICOS.** [Rev. bras. estud. polit.]. **Added/Corp** Universidade de Minas Gerais. Universidade Federal de Minas Gerais. No. 1 (Dec. 1956)-. Periodical. Portuguese. Twice a year. $40.00. UFMG - Universidade Federal de Minas Gerais / Faculdade Direito, Av Alvares Cabral 211-1206, 30170-000 Belo Horizonte Brazil. **Tel** 011 55 31 2248507. **ED** Prof. Orlando M. Carvalho. **LC** JA5; .R46. Index available. **Bk Rev. Ad Acc. Circ:** 3,400.
**Desc:** Political science, constitutional law, political history.
**Ind/Abst** ABC POL SCI; Am. Hist. Life (1968-); Foreign Lang. Index; HAPI Hisp. Am. Period. Index; Int. Bibliogr. Sociol.; Int. Polit. Sci. Abstr.

CU/0864-4403
**REVISTA DE AFRICA Y MEDIO ORIENTE.** **Added/Corp** Centro de Estudios de Africa y Medio Oriente (Havana, Cuba). (198?)-. Periodical. Spanish. sa. 19.35Cub$ North America; 16.58Cub$ South America; 22.11Cub$ other. Ediciones Cubanas, Obispo 527, Altos ESQ Bernaza, CP 10100 Havana Cuba. **Tel** 011 632980, 631942, FAX 011 631011, telex 512337, 6540.
**Ind/Abst** Middle East J.

CL/0716-1417
**REVISTA DE CIENCIA POLITICA (SANTIAGO).** (REVISTA DE CIENCIA POLITICA.). [Rev. cienc. polit.]. **Added/Corp** Universidad Catolica de Chile. Instituto de Ciencia Politica. (1979)-. Periodical. Spanish (English). sa. Av Libertador Bernardo O Higgins, 340 of 14, Casilla 114-D, Santiago Chile. **Tel** 011 56 2 2224516. **LC** JA5; .R495. **DD** 320/.05. **Bk Rev**, (Qty: 3 per year). **Ad Acc, Adv Mgr Tel** 011 56 2 2224516 Ext. 2581. **Pr Rev. Circ:** 1,000.
**Ind/Abst** Int. Polit. Sci. Abstr.

PE/0034-7949
**REVISTA DE DERECHO Y CIENCIAS POLITICAS.** **See** Law.

SP/0048-7694
**REVISTA DE ESTUDIOS POLITICOS.** (REVISTA DE ESTUDIOS POLITICOS / INSTITUTO DE ESTUDIOS POLITICOS.). [Rev. estud. polit.]. **Added/Corp** Instituto de Estudios Politicos (Spain). Vol. 1, No. 1 (1941)-. Periodical. Spanish. Four times a year. $61.00. Center Estudios Constitucionales, C Fuencarial 45 6A, 28071 Madrid Spain. **Tel** 011 34 1 5325069. **(Subscription address:** Edisa, Lopez de Hoyos 141, 28002 Madrid Spain**) LC** H8; .R523.
**Ind/Abst** ABC POL SCI; Am. Hist. Life (1955-); PAIS Int. Print.

VE
**REVISTA DE LA FACULTAD DE CIENCIAS JURIDICAS Y POLITICAS.** **See** Law.

SP/0211-5581
**REVISTA DE POLITICA COMPARADA.** [Rev. polit. comp.]. No. 1 (Jan. 1980)-. Periodical. Spanish. qt. Universidad Internacional Menendez Pelayo y Departamento de Derecho Constitucional y Ciencia Politica de la Universidad de Alcala de Henares, Amador de los Rios 1 3O, Madrid-4 Spain. **LC** JA26; .R48. **DD** 320.3/05.

SP/0034-8716
**REVISTA DE POLITICA INTERNACIONAL.** **Added/Corp** Instituto de Estudios Politicos (Spain). (1950)-. Periodical. Spanish. bm. cum. index.
**Ind/Abst** Am. Hist. Life (1963-1967,1971-1979).

●BL
**REVISTA DO MERCOSUL.** **VFOAT** Revista del Mercosur. No. 1 (May 1992)-. Periodical. Portuguese (Spanish). mo. Cr$96000. Editora Terceiro Mundo, Rua da Gloria 122, 105-106, 20241 Rio de Janeiro RJ Brazil. **Tel** 011 21 242-0763, FAX 011 5521 252-8455. **LC** HC161; .R28. **DD** 337.1/805.

CR
**REVISTA FARABUNDO MARTI.** **VFOAT** Farabundo Marti. Periodical. Spanish. Editorial Farabundo Marti, Apartado 380, Curridabat Costa Rica. **LC** F1488.3; .R47. **DD** 320.9/7284.

CK/0120-3088
**REVISTA JAVERIANA (BOGOTA).** **See** General Interest-General Interest-South America.

VE
**REVISTA VENEZOLANA DE CIENCIA POLITICA.** **Added/Corp** Universidad de los Andes (Merida, Venezuela). Centro de Estudios Politicos y Sociales de America Latina. Vol. 1, No. 1 (Dec. 1987)-. Periodical. Spanish. sa. Bs560.00. Universidad de Los Andes / Publicaciones, Oficina de Publicaciones, Merida Venezuela. **Tel** 011 58 74 638814, 011 58 74 401111. **LC** JL3881; .R45. **DD** 987.06/33/05.

CN/0834-0366
**REVOLTES (MONTREAL, QUEBEC).** (REVOLTES.). [Revoltes]. No. 1 (March 1984)-. Periodical. French. sa. 16.00Can$. B P 973/Succ C, Montreal Quebec H2L 4V2 Canada. **DD** 322.4/4/05.

AE/0035-0621
**REVOLUTION AFRICAINE.** [Revolut. afr.]. **Added/Corp** Jabhat al-Tahrir al-Qawmi. No. 1, (Feb. 1963)-. Periodical. French. Fifty-two times a year. $42.63. Revolution Africaine, 7 rue du Stade a Hydra, Algiers Algeria.
**Ind/Abst** Int. Labour Doc.

US/0193-3612
**REVOLUTION (CHICAGO).** (REVOLUTION.). **Added/Corp** Revolutionary Communist Party, USA. Central Committee. (197?)-. Periodical. English. qt. $20.00. RCP Publications, PO Box 3486, Merchandise Mart, Chicago IL 60654. **Tel** (312)327-1689.
**Ind/Abst** Altern. Press Index.

UK
**REVOLUTIONARY ZIMBABWE.** Periodical. English. £1.50. Zimbawe Solidarity Front, 66A Etherley Road, London N15 England. **LC** DT962.62; .R48. **DD** 968.9/1/0405.

BE/0251-3722
**REVUE DE L'OTAN.** [Rev. Otan]. **VFOAT** Revue de l'Organisation du Traite de l'Atlantique Nord. (1975)-. Periodical. French. bm. ***Continues** Nouvelles de l'OTAN, 1010-2167.*
**Ind/Abst** Point Repere (1979-).

FR/0751-5804
**REVUE DES SCIENCES MORALES & POLITIQUES.** [Rev. sci. morales polit.]. **Added/Corp** Academie des Sciences Morales et Politiques (France). **VFOAT** Travaux de l'Academie des Sciences Morales et Politiques; Revue des Sciences Morales et Politiques. (1982)-. Periodical. French. Four times a year. 500.00F (institutions), 430.00F (individuals), 350.00 (students) France; 660.00F (institutions), 580.00F (individuals), 450.00 (students) other. Gauthier-Villars, 15 rue Gossin, 92543 Montrouge Cedex France. **Tel** 33 1 40 92 65 00, FAX 33 1 40 92 65 97. **(Subscription address:** Centrale des Revues, 11 rue Gossin, 92543 Montrouge Cedex France.**) LC** AS162; .P411. **DD** 054/.1. **[CCC].** ***Continues** Revue des Travaux de l'Academie des Sciences Morales & Politiques et Comptes Rendus de Ses Seances.*
**Ind/Abst** Am. Hist. Life (1954-); Int. Polit. Sci. Abstr.

CN/0703-6337
**REVUE D'INTEGRATION EUROPEENNE.** [Rev. integr. eur.]. **Added/Corp** Ecole des Hautes Etudes Commerciales (Montreal, Quebec). Centre d'Etudes et de Documentation Europeennes. **VFOAT** Journal of European Integration. Vol. 1 (Sept. 1977)-. Periodical. English (French). sa. 40.00Can$. Canadian Council for European Affairs, University of Saskatchewan, Department of Political Studies, Saskatoon Saskatchewan S7N 0W0 Canada. **Tel** (306)966-5231, FAX (306)966-8839, telex 074-2659. **ED** H J Michelmann. **DD** 341.24/2/05. Index available. **Bk Rev**, (Qty: 15). **Ad Acc. Pr Rev. Circ:** 400 (ctrl).
**Desc:** Articles on European political and economic integration, and politics of the European community, theory of regional, and especially European integration.
**Ind/Abst** Int. Polit. Sci. Abstr.; Point Repere (1983-).

# Political Science

FR/0035-2578
**REVUE DU DROIT PUBLIC ET DE LA SCIENCE POLITIQUE EN FRANCE ET A L'ETRANGER.** See Law-International Law.

●CN/1188-6161
**REVUE ELECTORALE, SYNTHESES ET DOCUMENTS, LA.** [Rev. elect.]. **Added/Corp** Directeur General des Elections du Quebec. (1992)-. Periodical. French. **DD** 324.2714/005.

FR/0035-2950
**REVUE FRANCAISE DE SCIENCE POLITIQUE.** [Rev. fr. sci. polit.]. **Added/Corp** Association Francaise de Science Politique. Fondation Nationale des Sciences Politiques. Vol. 1 (Jan./June 1951)-. Periodical. French (German, Italian and Latin; summaries and/or abstracts in English). bm. 660.00F (France), 380.00F (other) institution; 710.00F (France), 425.00F (other) individual. Presses de la Fondation, Nationale des Sciences Politiques, 44 Rue du Four, 75006 Paris France. **Tel** 011 33 1 44393960, FAX 011 33 1 45480441. **LC** JA11; .R6. **[CCC]**. Index available in last issue of volume--attached. cum. index. **Bk Rev. Ad Acc. Circ**: 2,500 (ctrl).
**Desc**: Major journal in political science, with an extensive book review section.
**Ind/Abst** ABC POL SCI; Am. Hist. Life (1974-); Int. Aerosp. Abstr.; Int. Bibliogr. Sociol.; Int. Labour Doc.; Int. Polit. Sci. Abstr.; PAIS Int. Print; Point Repere (1983-); Soc. Plann. Policy Dev. Abstr.; Sociol. Abstr. (?-?); World Agric. Econ.

CN/1189-9565
**REVUE QUEBECOISE DE SCIENCE POLITIQUE.** [Rev. que. sci. polit.]. **Added/Corp** Societe Quebecoise de Science Politique. **VFOAT** Politique. No. 17 (Winter 1990)-. Periodical. French. sa. 25.00Can$ (institutions), 16.00Can$ (individuals). Societe Quebecoise de Science Politique, Department de Science Politique, Universite du Quebec A Montreal, CP 8888, Succursale A, Montreal Quebec H3C 3P8 Canada. **Tel** (514)987-4582. **LC** JA4; .P65. **Continues** Politique (Montreal, Quebec : 1982), 0711-608X.

●US/1064-7414
**RIGHT GUIDE (ANN ARBOR, MICH.), THE.** (THE RIGHT GUIDE : A GUIDE TO CONSERVATIVE AND RIGHT-OF-CENTER ORGANIZATIONS.). [Right guide]. (1993)-. English. an. $74.95. Economics America, Inc, 612 Church Street, Ann Arbor MI 48104. **Tel** (313)995-0865, FAX (313)747-7258. **ED** Derk A Wilcox, Joshua Shackman and Penelope Naas. **DD** 324. Index available. **Circ**: 800.
**Desc**: An annual directory of conservative, libertarian, and right-of-center organizations; covering large, grassroots, domestic, international, publishing and newspaper organizations.

US/0035-5526
**RIPON FORUM. Added/Corp** Ripon Society. (1965)-. Periodical. English. bm. $20.00 federal government, $30.00 other US; $36.00 other. Ripon Society, 709 2nd Street NE, Suite 100, Washington DC 20002. **Tel** (202)546-1292. **ED** Mimi Canter. **LC** JK2351; .R55. cum. index. **Bk Rev. Ad Acc. Circ**: 5,000. available on microfilm. **Continues** Ripon Society Newsletter.
**Desc**: A Progressive Republican journal of opinion and political reporting.

US
**RISING SUN, THE. Title Change.** (19??)-(19??). English. Six times a year. Options Unlimited Inc., 617 Sunrise Lane, Green Bay WI 54301. **Tel** (414)339-0011, FAX (414)339-0012. **LC** DS840.84; .R55. **DD** 320.9/54/05. **Continued by** The Mannering Report.

RU
**RITM PERESTROIKI.** (1986)-. Russian. an. Izdatelstvo Ekonomika, Berezhkovskaia Nab., 6, 121864 Moscow Russia.

IT/0048-8402
**RIVISTA ITALIANA DI SCIENZA POLITICA.** [Riv. ital. sci. polit.]. Vol. 1 (April 1971)-. Periodical. Italian. tq. L65000.00 Italy; L120000.00 (surface mail), L140000.00 (airmail) other. Societa Editrice il Mulino, Strada Maggiore 37, 40125 Bologna Italy. **Tel** 011 39 51 256011, FAX 011 39 51 256034. **LC** JA18; .R52. **DD** 320/.05.
**Ind/Abst** ABC POL SCI; Am. Hist. Life (1971-); Int. Bibliogr. Sociol.; Soc. Plann. Policy Dev. Abstr.; Sociol. Abstr. (?-?).

US/0035-788X
**ROLL CALL (WASHINGTON, D.C.).** (ROLL CALL.). Vol. 1 (June 16, 1955)-. Periodical. English. sw. $210.00. Levitt Communications Inc, 900 Second Street NE, Suite 107, Washington DC 20002. **Tel** (202)289-4900, FAX (202)289-2205. **ED** Stacy Mason. **LC** JK1; .R6. **DD** 328.73/005. **Ad Acc. Circ**: 17,000 (ctrl).
**Desc**: Newspaper of the US Congress covering, in hometown paper style, the world's most important community.

US
**ROTHENBERG POLITICAL REPORT.** English. Twenty-six times a year. $197.00 (1 year), $345.00 (2 year). Rothenberg Political Report, 717 Second Street Northeast, Washington DC 20002. **Tel** (202)546-2822, FAX (202)546-7689. **Continues** Political Report, 1051-4287.

SA
**RSA WORLD.** Began in 1964. Periodical. English. ir (8 no. a year). $5.00. RSA World, Box 2660, Pretoria 0001 Republic of South Africa. **ED** Alexander Newman. **LC** DT779.9; .R18. **DD** 320.9/68/06. **Circ**: 3,500.
**Desc**: Southern African events in context of world trends.

US
**RUNDT'S WORLD BUSINESS INTELLIGENCE.** See Economics.

UK/0967-2265
**RUSSIA AND THE SUCCESSOR STATES BRIEFING SERVICE. VFOAT** Russia and the Successor States Briefing Service. Vol. 1, No. 1 (Feb. 1993)-. Periodical. English. bm. £153.00 Europe; $309.00 US; £160.00 other (institutions). Longman Group Ltd., Fourth Avenue, Longman House, Harlow Essex CM19 5SR England. **Tel** 011 44 279 429655, FAX 011 44 279 431059, telex 81259. **(Subscription address**: Longman Group Ltd., Subscription Office, PO Box 1584, Birmingham AL 35201-1584.) **LC** DK293; .R87.

US
**RUSSIAN AND EAST EUROPEAN STUDIES.** English. $73.25. JAI Press Inc., 55 Old Post Road, Suite 2, PO Box 1678, Greenwich CT 06836-1678. **Tel** (203)661-7602, FAX (203)661-0792. **ED** Steven K. Batalden and Thomas Noonan.

●US/1061-1940
**RUSSIAN POLITICS AND LAW.** See Law.

CN/0708-1960
**SAFRICAN NEWS.** 1st- Issue. Periodical. English. mo. $10.00 individuals, $5.00 institutions. Southern Africa Research Centre, Box 667 Station F, Toronto Ontario M4Y 2N6 Canada. **DD** 320.9/68/06. **Supersedes** Canadian Press and the Events in Southern Africa, 0381-8659.

US/0275-5297
**SAGE YEARBOOKS IN POLITICS AND PUBLIC POLICY.** [Sage yearb. polit. public policy]. V. 1- 1975-. Monographic series. English. an. Price varies per volume. SAGE Periodical Press, 2455 Teller Road, Thousand Oaks CA 91320. **Tel** (805)499-0721, FAX (805)499-0871, telex 100799. **Acid Free.**
**Ind/Abst** Int. Polit. Sci. Abstr.

FR
**SAHARA.** 1963- (No. 1- ). Periodical. French. sm. 1.125F France; 1.356F other. Agence France Presse, 13 Place de la Bourse, BP 20, 75061 Paris Cedex 02 France. **Tel** 011 33 1 40414646. **Circ**: 1,000.
**Ind/Abst** Anthropol. Lit.

FR/0150-262X
**SAHARA INFO.** [Sahara info]. (1976)-. Periodical. French. Association des Amis de la Republique Arabe Sahroule Democratique, Paris France. **UDC** 32.
**Ind/Abst** Hum. Rights Intern. Rep.

FR/0036-3650
**SALUT LES COPAINS.** Periodical. French. sm. Publications Filipacchi, 63-65 Champs Elysees, 75008 Paris France. **Tel** 011 33 1 40747000, telex 651-294.

UK
**SAUDI ARABIA QUARTERLY.** See Economics-Economic History, Conditions.

NO/0080-6757
**SCANDINAVIAN POLITICAL STUDIES.** [Scand. polit. stud.]. **VFOAT** SPS. Vol. 1 (1966)-. English. qt (4 issues a year). Kr525.00 , $95.00. Scandinavian University Press, PO Box 2959 Toeyen, N 0608 Oslo 6 Norway. **Tel** 011 47 2 2575400, FAX 011 47 2 2575353, telex 71896 UROR N. **(Subscription address:** Scandinavian University Press, 200 Meacham Ave., Elmont NY 11003.) **ED** Knut Heidar and Lawrence Rose. **LC** JN7001; .S3. **DD** 320.948. **[CCC]**. available on microfilm from University Microfilms International (UMI).
**Desc**: Editorially sponsored by the Nordic Political Science Association, presenting Scandinavian political studies to an international readership. Open to all Nordic scholars active in political research relevant to Scandinavia.
**Ind/Abst** ABC POL SCI; Am. Hist. Life (1978-).

GW
**SCHRIFTEN. Main/Corp** Deutsche Wahlergesellschaft. Vol. 1 (1947)-. Periodical. English. **LC** JN3971.A95; .D432.

GW/0582-0553
**SCHRIFTEN ZUR VERFASSUNGSGESCHICHTE.** Vol. 1 (1961)-. Monographic series. German. ir. Price varies per volume. Duncker und Humblot Verlag, Postfach 410329, D-12113 Berlin Germany. **Tel** 011 49 30 79000612, 011 49 30 79000613.

GW
**SCHRIFTENREIHE DER HOCHSCHULE FUER POLITIK MUNCHEN. Added/Corp** Hochschule fur Politik Munchen. Monographic series. German. Price varies per volume. **Continues** Schriftenreihe, N.F.

GW/0080-7168
**SCHRIFTENREIHE ZUR GESCHICHTE UND POLITISCHEN BILDUNG.** Vol. 1 (1965)-. Monographic series. German. ir. Price varies per volume. A Henn Verlag, Postfach 1180, 5448 Kastellaun Germany.

CN/1184-227X
**SCIENCE BULLETIN (OTTAWA).** (SCIENCE BULLETIN.). [Sci. bull.]. Oct. (1990)-. Bulletin. English. Twelve times a year. 374.50Can$. Science Bulletin, 41 Heney Street, Ottawa Ontario K1N 5V6 Canada. **Tel** (613)789-6239, (416)855-2840, FAX (416)822-8905. **ED** Wayne Kondro; Telephone: (613)789-6458. **DD** 332.9/26/097105. **Bk Rev. Continues** Science & Government Bulletin., 0845-8197.

UK
**SCOTTISH GOVERNMENT YEARBOOK, THE. Title Change. Added/Corp** University of Edinburg. Dept. of Politics. Unit for the Study of Government in Scotland. (1978)-(1992). English. an. USGS, Dept of Politics, 31 Bubcleuch Place, Edinburgh EN8 9JT Scotland. **LC** JN1187; .S38. **DD** 320.9/411/085. **Continues** Our Changing Scotland. **Continued by** Scottish Affairs.

●UK/0967-0106
**SECURITY DIALOGUE. Added/Corp** International Peace Research Institute. Vol. 23, No. 3 (Sept. 1992)-. Periodical. English. qt £89.00. Sage Publications Ltd., 6 Bonhill Street, London EC2A 4PU, UK. **Tel** 071 374 0645, FAX 071 374 8741, telex 296207 SAGE G. **LC** JX1901; .B83. **DD** 327/.05. **CODEN** SDIAER. **Acid Free. Continues** Bulletin of Peace Proposals, 0007-5035.
**Ind/Abst** Curr. Contents Soc. Behav. Sci.; Soc. Sci. Cit. Index [Full Cov.].

JA
**SEIJI HANDOBUKKU.** (1973)-. Japanese. ¥1360. Seiji Koho Seuta, 13-6 Akasaka 4-chome Minato-ku, Tokyo 107 Japan. **Tel** (03)582-2281. **ED** Miyakawa Takayoshi. **LC** JQ1621; .S44. **Bk Rev. Ad Acc. Circ**: 40 (ctrl).
**Desc**: Japanese government and all members of government, elections, agendas, results of elections analysis.

JA
**SEIJI KENKYU. Added/Corp** Kyushu Daigaku, Fukuoka, Japan. Seiji Kenkyushitsu. (19??)-. Periodical. Japanese. Kyushu Daigaku Seiji Kenkyushitsu, Kyudai Seiji Kenkyukai, Kyushu Daigaku Hogakubu, Hakozaki 6-chome, Fukuoka Japan. **LC** JA26; .S38.

JA
**SEIJIGAKU RONSHU. Added/Corp** Komazawa Daigaku, Tokyo. Hogakubu. Komazawa Daigaku, Tokyo. Political Science Review of Komazawa University. **VFOAT** Political Science Review of Komazawa University. (1974)-. Periodical. Japanese. Komazawa Daigaku Hogakubu Kenkyushitsu, 23-1 Komazawa 1-chome, Setagaya-ku, Tokyo Japan. **LC** JA26; .S44.

JA
**SEIRON.** (Oct. 1973)-. Periodical. Japanese. mo. ¥4800. Senkei Publishing Ltd, Sankei-Honsha Building, 1-7-2 Otemachi Chiyoda-ku Tokyo 100 Japan. **LC** AP95.J2; S45.

US
**SENATE AND HOUSE JOURNALS OF THE ... LEGISLATURE OF THE STATE OF MONTANA COMMENCING IN SPECIAL SESSION ... AND ENDING ... . Main/Corp** Montana. Legislature. **Added/Corp** Montana. Legislature. Legislative Council. **VFOAT** Senate and House Journals, Special Sessions. (19??)-. English. Montana Legislative Council, State Capitol/Room 138, Helena MT 59620-1706. **Tel** (406)444-3064, FAX (406)444-3036. **LC** J87; .M914a. **DD** 328.786/01.

US
**SENATE JOURNAL OF THE ... LEGISLATURE OF THE STATE OF MONTANA. Main/Corp** Montana. Legislature. Senate. English. Montana Legislative Council, State Capitol/Room 138, Helena MT 59620-1706. **Tel** (406)444-3064, FAX (406)444-3036. **LC** J87; .M9 DATE B. **DD** 328.786/01. **Continues** Montana. Legislative Assembly. Senate. Senate Journal.

●RU
**SERIIA 6, FILOSOFIIA, POLITOLOGIIA, SOTSIOLOGIIA, PSIKHOLOGIIA, PRAVO.** See Philosophy.

UK
**SEXUAL POLITICS IN BRITAIN; A BIBLIOGRAPHICAL GUIDE WITH HISTORICAL NOTES.** English. an. Harvester Wheatsheaf, Campus 400, Maylands Avenue, Hemel Hempstead, Hertfordshire HP2 7EZ England. **Tel** 011 44 442 881900.

VE/0049-0431
**SIC.** Vol. 1 (1938)-. Periodical. Spanish. Ten times a year. Bs200.00 Venezuela; $20.00 US. Edif Centro Valores Local 2, Esquina Luneta Apartado 4838, Caracas 1010-A Venezuela. **Tel** 5635096. Index available. **Bk Rev. Ad Acc. Circ:** 6,000 (ctrl).
**Desc:** Political and economic analysis of Venezuela; Latin America's theology of liberation.
**Ind/Abst** Int. Labour Doc.; LABORDOC.

US/0199-6177
**SIGNIFICANT SEC FILINGS REPORTER.** See Law.

BE
**SILLON BELGE, LE.** French. Le Sillon Belge, Avenue Leon Grosjean 92, 1140 Bruxelles Belgium.

PK
**SIND JOURNAL OF POLITICAL SCIENCE & MODERN HISTORY / SPONSORED BY THE DEPARTMENTS OF POLITICAL SCIENCE AND MODERN HISTORY, UNIVERSITY OF SIND.** **Added/Corp** University of Sind. Dept. of Political Science. University of Sind. Dept. of Modern History. **VFOAT** Sind Journal of Political Science and Modern History. (1976)-. Periodical. English. Twice a year. Rs25.00. University of Sind / Department of Political Science & Modern History, Jamshoro, Sind Pakistan. **(Subscription address:** Edinboro State University, PO Box 318, Edinboro PA 16412.**)** **LC** D839; .S516. **DD** 320/.05.

TU
**SIYASAL BILGILER FAKULTESI DERGISI.** **Main/Corp** Ankara. Universitesi. Siyasal Bilgiler Fakultesi. **VFOAT** Review of the Faculty of Political Science; Revue de la Faculte des Sciences Politiques; Zeitschrift de Staatswissenschaftlichen Fakultat. (1943)-. Periodical. Turkish (English, French and German). Four times a year. $50.00 Turkey; $58.00 Europe; $60.00 other. Siyasal Bilgiler Fakultesi, University of Ankara, Ankara Turkey. **Tel** 41 197720 ext. 29.

XR/0037-6922
**SLOVANSKY PREHLED.** [Slov. prehl.]. Vol. 1 (1898)-. Academic Scholarly Publication. Czech (summaries and/or abstracts in English, German and Russian). Four times a year. DM163.00 Germany; DM203.00 other. **(Subscription address:** Kubon & Sagner, ABT Zeitschriftenimport, D 80328 Munich Germany.**)** **LC** AP52; .S6. **Bk Rev.**
**Desc:** Scholarly articles on the history and culture of Central, Southeast and East European nations, their mutual relations and relations with the West. Deals also with the rise and development of the world Socialist system and with the problems of the history of the Slavic peoples.
**Ind/Abst** Am. Hist. Life (1955-1958, 1964-).

CN/0037-6957
**SLOVENSKA DRZAVA.** [Slov. drz.]. Vol. 1- July 1950-. Periodical. Slovenian (English). mo. $12.00 U.S. Slovenian National Federation Canada, 646 Euclid Avenue, Toronto Ontario Canada. **ED** V Mauko. **LC** MICROFILM 05321 E; E184.S65. Index available. **Bk Rev. Ad Acc. Circ:** 4,000 (ctrl). ***Supersedes*** *Slovenska Pravica.*
**Desc:** Preservation of Slovenian heritage.

UK/0954-6839
**SLOVO (LONDON, ENGLAND).** (SLOVO.). **Added/Corp** University of London. School of Slavonic and East European Studies. Vol. 1, No. 1 (May 1988)-. Periodical. English. sa. $15.00 institutions; $20.00 individuals. School of Slavonic and East European Studies, Attn: Alastair Brison, University of London / Senate House, Malet Street London WCIE 7HU. **Tel** 011 44 71 637-4934 ext 4110, FAX 011 44 71 436-8916.
**Ind/Abst** Int. Bibliogr. Sociol.

AT/0155-0306
**SOCIAL ALTERNATIVES.** See Sociology.

NE
**SOCIAL, ECONOMIC AND POLITICAL STUDIES OF THE MIDDLE EAST.** See History(General)-History of the Middle East.

●US/1072-4745
**SOCIAL POLITICS.** See Sociology.

US/0747-4237
**SOCIALIST ACTION (SAN FRANCISCO, CALIF.).** (SOCIALIST ACTION.). [Social. action]. (198?)-. Periodical. English. mo. $8.00 US; $12.00 Canada and Mexico; $15.00 other. Socialist Action, 3435 Army Street, Room 308, San Francisco CA 94110. **Tel** (415)821-0458.

PE
**SOCIEDAD Y POLITICA.** Year 1- June 1972-. Periodical. Spanish. $10.00. Apartado Postal 11154 Sta Beatriz, Lima Peru. **LC** F3401; .S64.

BU
**SOFIA NEWS.** ***Suspended.*** Suspended (August 1991). Periodical. English. wk. $57.95. **(Subscription address:** Hemus Foreign Trade Organization, 1 B Raiko Daskalov Square, 1000 Sofia Bulgaria**)**

PH
**SOLIDARIDAD.** **Added/Corp** Solidaridad Foundation. Resource Centre for Philippine Concerns (Hong Kong). Vol. 14, No. 1 (1991)-. Periodical. English. qt. Solidaridad Foundation, PO Box 10344 Broadway Centrum, 1112 Quezon City Philippines. **Tel** (632) 70 32 90. ***Continues*** *Solidaridad II.*

PH/0117-3138
**SOLIDARIDAD SAN JUAN, METRO MANILA.** [Solidaridad S. Juan Metro Manila]. (1978)-. Periodical. English. qt. P150.00 (Philippines); $35.00 (libraries), $25.00 (individuals), $5.00 (single copy) (US & Canada); $35.00 (libraries), $15.00 (individuals), $3.00 (single copy) (other). Solidaridad Foundation, PO Box 10344 Broadway Centrum, 1112 Quezon City Philippines. **Tel** (632) 70 32 90. **ED** Muriel Ordonez. **DD** 303.4. **Bk Rev,** (Qty: 40 / year). **Ad Acc. Circ:** 1000.
**Desc:** Contains news digest & analyses of the Philippine political economy. Expresses the views of the board - written for an international audience.

●RU
**SOTSIALNYE I GUMANITARNYE NAUKI. SERIIA 4, GOSUDARSTVO I PRAVO. OTECHESTVENNAIA LITERATURA / ROSSIISKAIA AKADEMIIA NAUK, INSTITUT NAUCHNOI INFORMATSII PO OBSHCHESTVENNYM NAUKAM.** See Law.

●RU
**SOTSIALNYE I GUMANITARNYE NAUKI. SERIIA 4, GOSUDARSTVO I PRAVO. ZARUBEZHNAIA LITERATURA / ROSSIISKAIA AKADEMIIA NAUK, INSTITUT NAUCHNOI INFORMATSII PO OBSHCHESTVENNYM NAUKAM.** See Law.

SA
**SOUTH AUSTRALIAN GOVERNMENT GAZETTE, THE.** **Main/Corp** South Australia. (1???)-. English. wk. 160.00Aus$. South Australian Government Printer, 282 Richmond Road, Netley SA 5037 Australia. **Tel** 011 61 8 2921311. **LC** J8; .B85.
**Ind/Abst** AESIS Q.

AT/1036-918X
**SOUTH AUSTRALIAN NEWSLETTER.** (1985)-. Periodical. English. Six times a year. 25.00Aus$ (individuals); 45.00Aus$ (institutions). Womens Electoral Lobby, 3 Lobelia Street, O'Connor ACT 2601 Australia. **Tel** 011 61 62 476679, FAX 011 61 62 474669. ***Continues*** *Newsletter - Women's Electoral Lobby-S.A., 0310-9062.*

KO
**SOUTH-NORTH DIALOGUE IN KOREA.** No. 1- July 1973-. Periodical. English. bm. Public Relations Association of Korea, I P O Box 2147, Seoul Korea. **LC** DS901; .S68. **DD** 320.9/519/043.

SI/0377-5437
**SOUTHEAST ASIAN AFFAIRS.** **Added/Corp** Institute of Southeast Asian Studies. (1974)-. English. an (Apr. or May). $14.00 (softcover), $26.00 (hardcover) US. Institute of Southeast Asian Studies / Singapore, Heng Mui Keng Terrace, Pasir Panjang Road, Singapore 0511 Republic of Singapore. **Tel** (11) 65 8702447, FAX 011 65 7781735, telex 37068. **LC** DS502; .S76. **DD** 915.9/03/05. **Pr Rev. Circ:** 2,000.
**Desc:** Review of significant developments and trends in the region, particular emphasis on the Asian countries. Analysis made of major political, economic, social and strategic developments with Southeast Asia.
**Ind/Abst** Int. Bibliogr. Sociol.; Int. Polit. Sci. Abstr.

US/0730-2177
**SOUTHEASTERN POLITICAL REVIEW.** [Southeast. polit. rev.]. **Added/Corp** Georgia Political Science Association. Vol. 9, No. 1 (Spring 1981)-. Periodical. English. Four times a year (Mar., June, Sept., Dec.). $35.00 (institutions); $18.00 (individuals). Southeastern Political Review, Box 8101, Georgia Southern University, Statesboro GA 30460. **Tel** (912)681-5698, FAX (912)681-5348. **ED** Roger Pajari (editor's phone: (912)681-5698). **LC** JA1; .G46a. **DD** 320/.05. **Bk Rev. Ad Acc, Adv Mgr Tel** (912)681-5698. **Pr Rev. Circ:** 400 (ctrl). ***Continues*** *GPSA Journal, 0092-9395.*
**Desc:** Publishes articles in all subfields of the discipline and utilizing a wide range of methodologies. It publishes papers on the politics and policies of governments in the South in its Southern Political Research section. It also publishes research notes.
**Ind/Abst** Int. Polit. Sci. Abstr.; PAIS Int. Print; U.S. Polit. Sci. Doc. (199?-).

US/0887-8706
**SOUTHERN AFRICA PROJECT ANNUAL REPORT.** ***Ceased.*** [South. Afr. Proj. annu. rep.]. **VFOAT** Annual Report. (1981)-(19??). English. an. Lawyers Committee for Civil Rights Under Law, 1450 G Street Northwest, Suite 400, Washington DC 20005. **Tel** (202)662-8600. **LC** LAW. **DD** 323.4/9/0968. ctrl circ. ***Continues*** *Annual Report of the Southern Africa Project.*

US
**SOUTHERN LIBERTARIAN MESSENGER, THE.** See Public Administration.

US/0739-1714
**SOUTHERN PARTISAN, THE.** **Added/Corp** Foundation for American Education. **VFOAT** Southern Partisan Magazine. Vol. 1, No. 3-4 (Spring/Summer 1981)-. Periodical. English. qt. $14.00 (1 year), $26.00 (2 year), $38.00 (3 year) US; $18.00 (1 year), $30.00 (2 year), $42.00 (3 year) Canada; $22.00 (1 year), $34.00 (2 year), $46.00 (3 year) other. Southern Partisan, PO Box 11708, Columbia SC 29201. **Tel** (803)254-3660, FAX (803)256-9220. **ED** Oran P Smith. **LC** F216.2; .S62. **DD** 975/.005. Index available. cum. index. **Bk Rev,** (Qty: 60). **Ad Acc, Adv Mgr:** Alicia LeJeune. **Pr Rev. Circ:** 10,000. ***Continues*** *Southern Partisan Quarterly Review.*
**Desc:** New voice of the Old South, in the spirit of the agrarian and conservative intellectual tradition.

US/0739-3938
**SOUTHERN POLITICAL REPORT.** (1978)-. Periodical. English. Twenty-four times a year (every other week with one issue in July and December). $157.00 US; $169.00 Canada; $181.00 other. Southern Political Report, PO Box 15507, Washington DC 20003-5507. **Tel** (202)547-8098. **ED** Hastings Wyman Jr. **Bk Rev,** (Qty: 1 or 2). **Circ:** 600.
**Desc:** Covers the politics and politicians of twelve Southern states: Alabama, Arkansas, Florida, Georgia, Kentucky, Louisiana, Mississippi, North Carolina, South Carolina, Tennessee, Texas, and Virginia.
**Ind/Abst** Curr. Lit. Fam. Plan. (19??-199?).

UK/0952-7524
**SOUTHSCAN.** **VFOAT** South Scan. Vol. 1, No. 1 (1986)-. Periodical. English. wk. Southscan Ltd, PO Box 724, London N16 5RZ England. **Tel** 011 44 11 71 359 2328.
**Desc:** Focuses on gathering pace of regionalisation in Southern Africa and on crucial economic relationship between the European community and the region. Presents in-depth analysis of major events of the month together with news reports from network of correspondents in South Africa, the regional capitals and abroad.
**Ind/Abst** Hum. Rights Intern. Rep.

UK/0049-1713
**SOVIET ANALYST.** [Sov. anal.]. Vol. 1 (Mar. 2, 1972)-. Periodical. English. Ten times a year. £175.00 UK and Ireland; $325.00 US. World Reports Ltd., 108 Horse Ferry Road, Westminster, London SW1P 2EF United Kingdom. **Tel** 011 44 71 222 3836, FAX 11 44 71 233 0185. **ED** Barry Holland. **LC** DK274; .S646. **DD** 320.9/47/085. **Bk Rev.**
**Desc:** Gives a detailed and accurate presentation of the nature of the Soviet system, and of the domestic and foreign policies of the CPSU, as well as the Eastern European satellites.

●US/1075-1262
**SOVIET AND POST-SOVIET REVIEW, THE.** [Sov. post-Sov. rev.]. **Added/Corp** University of Utah. College of Humanities. **VFOAT** Soviet and Post Soviet Review. Vol. 19, No. 1/3 (1992)-. Periodical. English (French, German and Russian). Three times a year. $17.25 (individuals); $32.25 (institutions). CMTS USC / Charles Schlacks Jr. Publisher, 734 West Adams Boulevard, Kerckhoff Hall, Los Angeles CA 90089. **Tel** (203)743-6510. **LC** DK266.A2; S753. **DD** 914.7/005. ***Continues*** *Soviet Union, 0094-2863.*

AT/1033-6257
**SOVIET REVIEW.** See Economics.

US/0584-9365
**SPOTLIGHT ON AFRICA.** **Added/Corp** American-African Affairs Association. Vol. 1 (Apr. 1966)-. Periodical. English. Six times a year (Jan., Mar., May, July, Sept., Nov.). $10.00. American African Affairs Association, 1001 Connecticut Avenue Northwest, Suite 1135, Washington DC 20036. **Tel** (202)223-5110. **ED** J. A. Parker. **LC** DT1; .S78. **Circ:** 1,800.

US/0891-608X
**SPSC LETTER.** [SPSC lett.]. **Added/Corp** Saharan Peoples Support Committee (Ada, Ohio). **VFOAT**

S.P.S.C. Letter. **VAT** Saharan Peoples Support Committee Letter. Vol. 1, No. 1 (June 1980)-. Periodical. English. qt. Saharan Peoples Support Committee, 217 East Lehr, Ada OH 45810. **DD** 320.
**Ind/Abst** Hum. Rights Intern. Rep.

UZ/0207-7280
**SSSR KHALQ DEPUTATLARI SEZDI VA SSSR OLII SOVETINING AKHBOROTNOMASI.** **Added/Corp** Soviet Union. Sezd Narodnykh Deputatov. Soviet Union. Verkhovnyi Sovet. **VFOAT** Akhborotnomasi. (1989)-. Uzbek (Russian). wk. Moskva 101000, Tsentr Prospekt Kalinina 3, Gosudarstvennaia Biblioteka SSR Imeni V I Lenina, Informatsionnyi Tsentr PO Problemam, Kultury I Iskusstva, Moscow Russia. **LC** J397.H45; V43.

US
**STAR NEWSLETTER / S.T.A.R. OF GUATEMALA, SOUTH TEXAS AID TO REFUGEES.** Newsletter. English. 521 East Quincy, San Antonio TX 78215.

US/0197-5668
**STATE PUBLICATIONS INDEX.** ***Ceased.*** (1980)-(19??). Periodical. English. qt. Information Handling Services, 15 Inverness Way East, Englewood CO 80150. **Tel** (800)525-7052, (303)790-0600, FAX (303)397-2599, telex 4322083. **LC** Z1223.5.A1; C38; J83. **DD** 015.73. ***Continues*** *Checklist of State Publications, 0164-1352.*

NR
**STATESMAN, THE.** V. 1- Apr. 1972-. Periodical. English. Political Science Association of Nigeria, c/o Okon 1 Udoh, Mellanby Hall, Ibadan Nigeria. **LC** JQ3081.A1; S73. **DD** 320.9/669/05.

US/0081-4601
**STATESMAN'S YEAR-BOOK, THE.** [Statesman's year-b.]. **VFOAT** Statesman's Yearbook. 1st Ed. (1864)-. English. an. $85.00. St. Martin's Press, 175 Fifth Avenue, New York NY 10010. **Tel** (800)221-7945, (212)982-3900, FAX (212)777-6359. **ED** Brian Hunter. **LC** JA51; .S7. **DD** 320. **NLM** JA 51 S797.
**Desc:** Listing of political, social and economic institutions and structures by country, covering every country of the present-day world.

SW/0039-0747
**STATSVETENSKAPLIG TIDSKRIFT.** Vol. 1 (Nov. 1897)-. Academic Scholarly Publication. Swedish (Norwegian, Danish and English). qt. Kr130.00. Department of Political Science / Lund Sweden, Box 52, S-22100 Lund Sweden. **Tel** (046)109776. **ED** Lennart Lundquist. cum. index. **Bk Rev. Ad Acc. Circ:** 1,000.
**Desc:** Contains articles, reviews of recent political and scholarly developments, and book reviews. Subscribers come mainly from the Nordic countries.
**Ind/Abst** ABC POL SCI; Am. Hist. Life (1954-); Int. Polit. Sci. Abstr.; Peace Res. Abstr. J. (1976-1979); Selec. Coop. Index Manage. Period.

US/0890-9776
**STEVE FORRESTER'S NORTHWEST LETTER FROM WASHINGTON, D.C.** [Steve Forrester's Northwest lett. Wash. Dist. Columb.]. **VFOAT** Northwest Letter from Washington, D.C. Vol. 1, No. 1 (Jan. 1981)-. Periodical. English. bw. $167.00. Northwest Letter, PO Box 210, Astoria OR 97103. **Tel** (503)325-3211. **DD** 320.

II
**STIR.** V. 1- Oct. 1, 1972-. Periodical. English. 1.00 each issue. 1005 Akashdeep Building Barakhamba Road, New Delhi 1 India. **LC** DS401; .S83. **DD** 320.9/54/05.

US/1040-2136
**STRATEGIES (LOS ANGELES, CALIF.).** ***Suspended.*** (STRATEGIES.). [Strategies]. No. 1 (Fall 1988)-?. Periodical. English. sa. $16.00. Univerity of California Los Angeles, Strategies Collective, 4289 Bunche Hall, Los Angeles CA 90024. **Tel** (310)871-0071. **DD** 306. **Ad Acc. Circ:** 250.
**Desc:** A journal of theory, culture and politics.
**Ind/Abst** Educ. Index; Film Lit. Index (19??-).

GW
**STREITBARBER MATERIALISMUS.** No. 10, (Jan. 1988)-. Periodical. German. ***Continues*** *Widerspruch (Berlin, Germany).*

IT
**STUDI PARLAMENTARI E DI POLITICA COSTITUZIONALE.** Studi Parlamentari e di Politica Costituzionale, Via Massa Fiscaglia 1, 00127 Rome Italy.

BE/0770-2965
**STUDIA DIPLOMATICA.** [Stud. dipl.]. Vol. 27, No. 5/6 (Sept./Nov. 1974)-. Periodical. Multiple languages (Dutch, English and French). bm. 2700F, 2400F (members), 4200F (airmail) Belgium; $100.00 US. Institut Royal des Relations Internationales, Avenue de la Couronne 88, B-1050 Bruxelles Belgium. **Tel** 02/648.20.00, telex 20.000 IRIKIB. **ED** E Coppeiters. **LC** D839; .C82. **DD** 320.9/04. Index available. cum. index. **Bk Rev. Ad Acc. Circ:** 2,000. ***Continues*** *Chronique de Politique Etrangere.*
**Desc:** Analyses of key political, legal and economic documents relating to international relations. Journal's objectivity is acknowledged worldwide in the diplomatic field.
**Ind/Abst** ABC POL SCI; Curr. Mil. Pol. Lit.; Int. Polit. Sci. Abstr.; PAIS Int. Print.

PL/0511-1765
**STUDIA NAUK POLITYCZNYCH.** [Stud. nauk polit.]. **Added/Corp** Centralny Osrodek Metodyczny Studiow Nauk Politycznych. (1968)-. Periodical. Polish (summaries and/or abstracts in English and Russian). bm. $42.00. **(Subscription address:** ARS Polona, PO Box 1001, 00068 Warsaw Poland.**)** **LC** JA26; .S78.
**Ind/Abst** Am. Hist. Life (1978-); Int. Polit. Sci. Abstr.

US/0898-588X
**STUDIES IN AMERICAN POLITICAL DEVELOPMENT.** [Stud. Am. polit. dev.]. Vol. 1 (1986)-. Academic Scholarly Publication. English. sa. $64.00 US, Canada & Mexico; £36.00 other. Cambridge University Press / New York, 40 West 20th Street, New York NY 10011-4211. **Tel** (212)924-3900, (800)221-4512. **(Subscription address:** Cambridge University Press / Outside of North America, Journal Fulfillment Department, The Edinburgh Building, Cambridge CB2 2RU United Kingdom.**)** **ED** Karen Orren and Stephen Skowronek. **LC** E183; .S795. **DD** 320.973.
**Desc:** Covers American political change and institutional development from a historical perspective. Articles focus on government institutions and their social, economic and cultural environment. The journal features in-depth original articles, which allow scholars to elaborate on the complex patterns of state-society relations. These longer articles also encourage an interdisciplinary approach, tying in relevant issues and related themes.
**Ind/Abst** Am. Hist. Life (1986-); Int. Bibliogr. Sociol.; Int. Polit. Sci. Abstr.

US
**STUDIES IN INTERNATIONAL AND COMPARATIVE POLITICS.** (1978)-. Monographic series. English. ir. ABC Clio Press, PO Box 1911, 130 Cremona, Santa Barbara CA 93117. **Tel** (805)968-1911, (800)422-2546, FAX (805)685-9685. ***Continues*** *Studies in Comparative Politics.*

US
**STUDIES IN MARXISM (MINNEAPOLIS, MINN.).** **See** Social Sciences.

CN/0707-8552
**STUDIES IN POLITICAL ECONOMY.** [Stud. polit. econ.]. No. 1 (Spring 1979)-. Academic Scholarly Publication. English. tq. $60.00 (institution), $110.00 (individual) US. Studies in Political Economy, PO Box 4729 Station E, Ottawa Ontario K1S 5H9, Canada. **Tel** (613)788-2600 ext 6625. **ED** E. Killean. **DD** 330/.05. Index available (bound in issues). **Bk Rev**, (Qty: varies). **Pr Rev. Circ:** 1,000.
**Desc:** A Canadian scholarly journal featuring original research from a socialist perspective on Canadian international and theoretical issues, with interdisciplinary approaches. It analyzes working class movements.
**Ind/Abst** Altern. Press Index (199?-); Am. Hist. Life (1986-); Can. Index (?-?); Can. Period. Index (19??-); Hum. Resour. Abstr.; Int. Bibliogr. Sociol.; Int. Polit. Sci. Abstr.; Left Index; PAIS Int. Print; Soc. Plann. Policy Dev. Abstr.; Sociol. Abstr.

GW/0585-7945
**STUTTGARTER BEITRAGE ZUR GESCHICHTE UND POLITIK.** Vol. 1 (1966)-. Monographic series. German. ir. Price varies per volume. Ernst Klett Verlag, Postfach 106016, D 70049 Stuttgart Germany. **Tel** 011 49 711 667205.

GW/0722-480X
**SUDOST EUROPA : [MONATSSCHRIFT DER ABTEILUNG GEGENWARTSFORSCHUNG DES SUDOST-INSTITUTS].** **See** Social Sciences.

GW
**SUDOSTEUROPA.** V. 1- 1959-. Periodical. German. mo. DM60.00. **Circ:** 1,000.
**Desc:** Bulletin of the Contemporary Studies Department of the Southeast Institute; reports on the socialist countries of Southeast Europe (Albania, Bulgaria, Yugoslavia, Romania and Hungary).
**Ind/Abst** PAIS Int. Print; World Agric. Econ.

SA/1011-7547
**SUID-AFRIKAAN, DIE.** **See** Economics.

US
**SULLIVAN COUNTY DEMOCRAT.** (18??)-. Newspaper. English. sw. $37.50 (one year), $66.00 (two years), $98.50 (three years) US; $107.50 (one year), $206.00 (two years), $308.50 (three years) other. Sullivan County Democrat, PO Box 308, Callicoon NY 12723. **Tel** (914)887-5200, FAX (914)887-5386. **ED** Frank Brownell (editor's adress: 101 Main Street, Callicoon NY 12723). **Bk Rev**, (Qty: 12). **Ad Acc, Adv Mgr:** J Price. **Circ:** 8,000 (ctrl).

CN/0830-9825
**SUMMARY REPORT ... CANADIAN REGIONAL CONFERENCE. COMMONWEALTH PARLIAMENTARY ASSOCIATION.** (SUMMARY REPORT / COMMONWEALTH PARLIAMENTARY ASSOCIATION, CANADIAN REGIONAL CONFERENCE.). [Summ. rep. Can. Reg. Conf. Commonw. Parliam. Assoc.]. **Main/Corp** Commonwealth Parliamentary Association. Canadian Regional Conference. **VFOAT** Compte Rendu. 24th (1984)-. English (French). an. Commonwealth Parliamentary Association, Canadian Region, PO Box 950, House of Parliament, Ottawa Ontario K1A 0A6 Canada. **DD** 328/.3/0601. ***Continues*** *Verbatim Report, ... Canadian Regional Conference, 0826-1970.*

US/0148-9399
**SUMMARY REPORT OF CAMPAIGN CONTRIBUTIONS AND EXPENDITURES, PRIMARY ELECTION.** **Main/Corp** Oregon. Elections Division. English. Elections Division, State Capitol/Room 122, Salem MA 97310. **LC** JK1991.5.O7; O73A. **DD** 329/.025/09795.

US/0164-2510
**SUPPLEMENT TO THE DIRECTORY OF THE AMERICAN RIGHT.** (DIRECTORY OF THE AMERICAN RIGHT. SUPPLEMENT.). Directory. English. be. $3.95. Laird Wilcox, PO Box 2047, Olathe KS 66061. **Tel** (913)829-0609.

UK/0039-6214
**SURVEY OF CURRENT AFFAIRS.** ***Title Change.*** **Added/Corp** British Information Services. Great Britain. Central Office of Information. Great Britain. Central Office of Information. Reference Division. Vol. 1-22 No. 6 (Jan. 1971)-(June 1992). Periodical. English. mo. Her Majesty's Stationery Office, 51 Nine Elms Lane, London SW8 5DR England. **Tel** 011 44 71 873 8459, 011 44 71 873 8499, FAX 011 44 71 873 8499, 011 44 71 873 8456, telex 297138. **(Subscription address:** PO Box 276, Public Centre, London SW8 5DT England**)** **LC** DA20; .S935. **DD** 320.9/42/085. available on microfilm and microfiche from University Microfilms International (UMI). ***Supersedes*** *Survey of British and Commonwealth Affairs.* ***Continued by*** *Current Affairs (London, England).*
**Desc:** A unique official journal of record. It deals primarily with British affairs but there is also coverage of developments elsewhere in which Britain may have a special interest.

US/0743-4324
**SURVEY OF PRESS FREEDOM IN LATIN AMERICA, A.** [Surv. press freedom Lat. Am.]. Vol. 1 (1982)-. English. an. $4.95. Council on Hemispheric Affairs, 1900 L Street NW, Suite 201, Washington DC 20036. **LC** PN4748.L29; S9. **DD** 323.44/5.

CN/0300-7944
**SURVIVAL (NORTH AMERICAN EDITION).** (SURVIVAL.). July 1970-. Periodical. English. $2.00 for 4 numbers. Gordon Edwards, 1300 Raimbault, St. Laurent Quebec H4L 4R9. **DD** 322.4/4/05.
**Desc:** An interrnatoinal and interprofessional movement for the survival of humanity.
**Ind/Abst** Peace Res. Abstr. J. (1964-1966, 1971).

RU
**SVOBODNAIA MYSL.** No. 14 (1991)-. Periodical. Russian (table of contents in French, German, Spanish and Chinese). mo. $139.95. **(Subscription address:** East View Publications Inc., 3020 Harbor Lane North, Suite 110, Minneapolis MN 55447.**)** **LC** IN PROCESS; JC421; .S863. **CODEN** SVMYE7. ***Continues*** *Kommunist (Moscow, R.S.F.S.R.), 0131-1212.*

SZ
**SVPW-JAHRBUCH = ANNUAIRE ASSP.** **Added/Corp** Association Suisse de Science Politique. **VFOAT** Annuaire ASSP; Schweizerisches Jahrbuch fur Politische Wissenschaft. **VAT** SVPW Jahrbuch. Vol. 26, (1986)-. French (German). ir. Verlag Paul Haupt, Falkenplatz 11, CH-3001 Bern Switzerland. **Tel** 011 41 31 3012435, FAX 011 41 30 243023, telex 912 906 HAUP CH. **LC** JA34; .A82. **DD** 320/.05. ***Continues*** *Annuaire Suisse de Science Politique, 0066-3727.*

TZ
**TAAMULI.** **Added/Corp** Chuo Kikuu cha Dar es Salaam. Dept. of Political Science. Vol. 1, No. 1 & 2 (1990)-. Periodical. English. sa (Jan., July). $25.00; $29.00 air mail. University of Dar es Salaam Department of Political Science, PO Box 35042, Dar es Salaam Tanzania. **Tel** 011 255 51 43130, FAX 011 255 051 48457, 011 255 051 43395, telex 41327 UNISCIE, 41561 UNIVIP. **ED** Prof. Samwel S. Mushi. **LC** JQ2945.A1; T22. **Bk Rev. Ad Acc. Circ:** 500 (ctrl). ***Continues*** *Taamuli, 0049-2817.*

UK/0955-8780
**TALKING POLITICS.** [Talking polit.]. **Added/Corp** Politics Association (Great Britain). Vol. 1, No. 1 (Autumn 1988)-. Periodical. English. Three times a year. £26.00 (institutions), £19.00 (individuals) UK; £26.00 (institutions), £22.00 (individuals) Europe; £30.00 (institutions), £29.00 (individuals) other. The Politics Association, 64 West Hill Drive, Dartford Kent DA1 3EA,

# Political Science

England. **Tel** 44 322 75145. **Continues** Teaching Politics (London, England), 0305-7771.
**Ind/Abst** ABC POL SCI (1988-); Br. Educ. Index.

UK
**TALKING POLITICS. Added/Corp** Conservative and Unionist Central Office (Great Britain) Conservative Party (Great Britain). Research Department. (19??)-. Periodical. English. bw. Conservative Central Office, 16 Stadium Way, Scours Lane, Reading Berks RG3 6BX England. **Tel** 734 413439.
**Desc:** A political briefing on events of the moment. It explains the government's case in a concise but highly readable style.

US/0887-6339
**TALON (MILWAUKEE, WIS.), THE.** (THE TALON / EURO-AMERICAN ALLIANCE.). [Talon]. **Added/Corp** Euro-American Alliance (Milwaukee, Wis.). Vol. 1, No. 1 (Nov. 1976)-. Periodical. English. mo. $15.00. Euro - American Alliance, PO Box 2 1776, Milwaukee WI 53221. **Tel** (414)423-0565. **DD** 320.

CN/0822-2762
**TAMIL EELAM DOCUMENTATION BULLETIN. See** Political Science-Civil Rights.

CC
**TANG TI CHIEN SHE / CHUNG-KUO KUNG CHAN TANG KAN-SU SHENG WEI YUAN HUI CHU PAN. VFOAT** Dangde Jianshe. Periodical. Chinese. RMBY0.15. Post Office, Lan-Chou Shih, People's Republic of China. **Tel** 26492. **LC** JQ1519.A5; T255935. **DD** 324.251/075/05.

US/0082-2183
**TAYLOR'S ENCYCLOPEDIA OF GOVERNMENT OFFICIALS, FEDERAL AND STATE.** Vol. 1 (1967/68)-. English. be. price varies per volume. Political Research Inc., 16850 Dallas Parkway, Dallas TX 75248. **Tel** (214)931-8827. **LC** JK6; .T36.

US/0733-0294
**TAYLOR'S ENCYCLOPEDIA OF GOVERNMENT OFFICIALS, FEDERAL AND STATE. SUPPLEMENT.** [Taylor's encycl. gov. off., fed. state, Suppl.]. **VFOAT** Encyclopedia of Government Officials, Federal and State. Supplement. Vol. 1 (1967/68)-. Periodical. English. qt. Political Research Inc., 16850 Dallas Parkway, Dallas TX 75248. **Tel** (214)931-8827.

II
**TEACHING POLITICS. Added/Corp** Delhi University Political Science Association. Vol. 1, (1975)-. Periodical. English. qt. Teaching Politics, Editor, c/o Department of Political Science, University of Delhi, Delhi 110007 India. **Tel** 2512266. **ED** Susheela Kaushik. **LC** DS445; .T4. **DD** 320/.05. **Bk Rev**. **Ad Acc. Circ:** 500.
**Desc:** Movement to make political science a dynamic discipline related to the concrete realities of the third world. To activate scholars to take stock of the trends in social sciences.
**Ind/Abst** Int. Polit. Sci. Abstr.

RU
**TELEFONNYI SPRAVOCHNIK : POLITICHESKIE PARTII I ORGANIZATSII. Added/Corp** Informatsionno-Ekspertnaia Gruppa "Panorama". **VFOAT** Political Parties and Organizations. (1991)-. Russian (English). **LC** DK288; .T44.

PK
**TEMPO.** Nov. 1974-. Periodical. English. $0.50 each issue. Anwer Jassan Mooraj, Golden Block Works Ltd, Golden Chambers Office I I, Chundrigar Road, Karachi Pakistan. **LC** JA8; .T44. **DD** 954.9/1/005.

BL
**TEMPO E PRESENCA. Added/Corp** Centro Ecumenico de Documentacao Informacao. No. 151 (1979)-. Periodical. Portuguese. mo. Centro Ecumenico de Documentacao e Informacao, Caixa Postal 16.082, 22241 Rio de Janeiro RJ Brazil. **LC** BL2540; .T46.
**Continues** CEI.
**Ind/Abst** Hum. Rights Intern. Rep.

IT
**TEMPO PRESENTE.** (19??)-. Italian. mo. L45000 Italy; L65000 other. Tempo Presente, Via Virgilio 1L, 00193 Rome, Italy. **Tel** 011 39 6 6873048. Index available (published separately). cum. index. **Bk Rev**. (Qty: 80). **Ad Acc. Circ:** 2,000.

CN/0703-5578
**TEMPS DE L'UNION NATIONALE, LE. Main/Corp** Union Nationale (Parti Politique). V. 1- March 1977-. Periodical. French. mo. Free to members, $2.00 others. Publications Unies, 130 Ouest Grande Allee, Quebec Quebec G1R 2G7 Canada. **DD** 329.9/714.

US/0194-1240
**TENNESSEE JOURNAL, THE.** (1974)-. Periodical. English. wk. $187.00. M. Lee Smith Publishers and Printers, 162 4th Avenue North, PO Box 198867, Nashville TN 37219. **Tel** (615)242-7395, (800)274-6774, **FAX** (615)256-6601. **ED** Brad Forrister. **Circ:** 1,400 (ctrl)
**Desc:** An insiders newsletter on Tennessee government, politics and business.

IT/0394-1248
**TEORIA POLITICA.** (1985)-. Periodical. Italian (summaries and/or abstracts in English). qt. L87000 Itaty; L110000 other. Franco Angeli Riviste SRL, Viale Monza 106, 20127 Milan Italy. **Tel** 011 39 2 2827651, 011 39 2 289562. **LC** JA18; .T46.

FR
**TERRITOIRES.** French. mo. 390.00F France; 450.00F other. Adels, 108 110 rue St. Maur, 75011 Paris France. **Tel** 011 33 1 43 554005. Index available. **Bk Rev**. **Ad Acc. Pr Rev. Circ:** 15,000.

US/1048-3276
**TERRORISM, AN INTERNATIONAL RESOURCE FILE. INDEX. See** Political Science-International Relations.

IT
**TERZAFASE. Ceased.** (19??)-(March 1993). Italian. mo. Centro Studi G Donati, Via Colonna Antonina 52, 00186 Rome Italy. **Tel** 011 39 6 6789848.

IT/0040-392X
**TERZO MONDO. See** Sociology.

US/0164-9221
**TEXAS GOVERNMENT NEWSLETTER.** (1973)-. Newsletter. English. ir (36 issues). $26.00. Texas Government Newsletter, PO Box 13274, Austin TX 78711. **Tel** (512)323-5051. **ED** Thomas L. Whatley. **Circ:** 2,000.
**Desc:** Review and analysis of Texas government and politics for a general audience. Current events summarized weekly along with in-depth analysis of a single topic.

US/0191-0930
**TEXAS JOURNAL OF POLITICAL STUDIES. Added/Corp** Sam Houston State University. Department of Government. (Fall 1978)-. Periodical. English. Twice a year (May & Dec.). $10.00 (one year); $20.00 (two years). Sam Houston State University / Department of Political Science, Huntsville TX 77341-2149. **Tel** (409)294-1462, **FAX** (409)294-3622. **ED** Jim Carter. **LC** JK4801; .T54. **DD** 320.9/764. Index available. cum. index. **Bk Rev**, (Qty: 20-25). **Ad Acc, Adv Mgr Tel** (409)294-1457. **Pr Rev. Circ:** 200 (ctrl).
**Desc:** Articles, research notes and book reviews containing political studies from local to world events. Political science, public administration, sociology, history and economics are represented.

US/0193-2322
**TEXAS LEGISLATIVE HANDBOOK.** English. $2.75. Legislative Handbook Inc, PO Box 10512, Dallas TX 75207. **LC** JK4830; .T38. **DD** 328.764/002/02.

FR
**THAI INFORMATION BULLETIN. Added/Corp** Comite de Solidarite avec le Peuple Thai. No. 1 (Oct. 1976)-. Bulletin. English.

TH/0125-6459
**THAILAND FOREIGN AFFAIRS NEWSLETTER / INFORMATION DEPARTMENT, MINISTRY OF FOREIGN AFFAIRS.** Newsletter. English. mo. Embassy of Thailand, 2300 Kalorama Road NW, Washington DC 20008. **LC** DS586; .T495. **Continues** News Bulletin / Thailand. Krasuang Kantangprathet. Krom Saranithet.

CN/0317-0659
**THIRD WORLD FORUM.** V. 1- Aug./Sept. 1974-. Periodical. English. bm. Free to prisoners, $15.00 US and Canada. Third World Forum/ Canada, PO Box 685, Station C, Montreal Quebec H2L 4K4 Canada. **DD** 320.9/172/4.
**Ind/Abst** Hum. Rights Intern. Rep.

UK/0143-6597
**THIRD WORLD QUARTERLY. See** Economics-Economic History, Conditions.

UK/0049-3740
**THIRD WORLD REPORTS.** Vol. 1 (March 1970)-. Periodical. English. bw (26 issues). £65.00 US. CSI Syndication Service, Wild Acre Plaw Hatch, West Sussex RH19 4JL England. **Tel** 011 44 342 810875, **FAX** 011 44 342 3905400, telex 305 892822. **ED** Colin Legum. Index available (free on request). cum. index. **Circ:** 200.
**Desc:** Two weekly reports on current affairs in Africa, Mid-East and other third world countries.

●US/1061-2734
**TIMELINE (PALO ALTO, CALIF.).** (TIMELINE : A BIMONTHLY PUBLICATION OF THE FOUNDATION FOR GLOBAL COMMUNITY.). [Timeline]. **Added/Corp** Foundation for Global Community (Palo Alto, Calif.). Issue No. 1 (Jan./Feb. 1992)-. Periodical. English. Six times a year. $25.00. Foundation Global Community, 222 High Street, Palo Alto CA 94301. **Tel** (415)328-7756. **DD** 172. **Continues** On Beyond War, 0887-9567.

IT
**TRACCE.** Vol. 1, No. 1 (Oct. 1980)-. Periodical. Italian. qt. Coop Tracce Arl, via Vittorio Veneto 47, 65100 Pescara Italy.

US
**TRANSITION.** Issue 51 (1991)-. Periodical. English. qt (4 issues). $56.00 institutions, $28.00 individuals US; $70.00 institutions, $42.00 individuals other. Oxford University Press / New York, 200 Madison Avenue, New York NY 10016. **Tel** (212)679-7300, (919)677-0977, (800)451-7556, (800)445-9714, **FAX** (919)677-1303. **(Subscription address:** Oxford University Press / USA, Journals Marketing Department, Oxford University Press, 2001 Evans Road, Cary NC 27513.) available on microfilm and microfiche from Micro-Graphic Corp. **Continues** Transition (Kampala, Uganda).

IT
**TRASGRESSIONI.** (1986)-. Periodical. Italian. Three times a year. L30000.00 Italy; L40000.00 other. La Roccia di Erec, Casella Postale 1292, 50122 Florence Italy. **Tel** 011 39 55 2340714, **FAX** 011 39 55 2340714. **Ad Acc. Pr Rev. Circ:** 1,000.

US/0275-5351
**TRIALOGUE. See** Economics-International Economics.

MX/0185-1039
**TRIMESTRE POLITICO.** [Trimest. polit.]. Vol. 1- July/Sept. 1975-. Periodical. Spanish. qt. $20.00. Fondo de Cultura Economica, Av Picacho Ajusco 227 / Pedregal, 14200 Mexico DF Mexico. **Tel** 011 52 5 2274670 71, **FAX** 011 52 5 2274683, telex 01775866. **LC** JL951.A1; T74.

US
**TRUTH AT LAST, THE.** No. 330 (1988)-. Periodical. English. mo. $15.00. Truth at Last, PO Box 1211, Marietta GA 30060. **Tel** (404)422-1180. **Bk Rev**. available on microfilm and microfiche from University Microfilms International (UMI). **Continues** Thunderbolt, 0040-6643.
**Desc:** Information on the American Segregation Party.

BE
**TU DO / TRIBUNE DES VIETNAMIENS LIBRE.** French (Vietnamese). mo. 1464.00F Belgium; 1666.00F other. Societe Cyber, 31 Ave de l'Europe, B-4020 Liege Belgium. **Tel** 011 32 4 1432550.

US/0082-6744
**TULANE STUDIES IN POLITICAL SCIENCE. Added/Corp** Tulane University. Dept. of Political Science. Vol. 1 (1954)-. Monographic series. English. ir. Price varies per volume. Tulane University / Political Science, Department of Political Science, Norman Mayer Building, New Orleans LA 70118. **Tel** (504)865-5800. **ED** Robert S. Robins. **Bk Rev. Circ:** 1,000 (ctrl).
**Desc:** Scholarly studies on political topics.

●CH
**TUNG WU CHENG CHIH HSUEH PAO. Added/Corp** Tung Wu ta Hsueh (Taipei, Taiwan). **VFOAT** Soochow Journal of Political Science. (1992)-. Periodical. Chinese (English). qt. Soochow University, Shin Lin, Taipei 11102 Taiwan. **LC** JA71; .T86. **Continues in part** Tung Wu Cheng Chih She Hui Hsueh Pao, 0259-3785.

CH
**TUNG WU CHENG CHIH SHE HUI HSUEH PAO. VFOAT** Soochow Journal of Political Science and Sociology. Vol. 7 (1977)-. Chinese (English). an. $240.00 Taiwan; $15.00 other. Soochow University Shih Lin Taipei, 111 Taipei Taiwan. **Tel** 002-886-2-8819, **FAX** 8829310. **ED** Ren-Fuw Kuo. **LC** H8.C47; T86. **Circ:** 400.

DK/0903-7845
**UDENRIGS. Added/Corp** Udenrigspolitike Selskab. **VFOAT** Udenrigspolitiske Magasin. (1988)-. Periodical. Danish. qt. Det Udenrigspolitiske Selskab, Amaliegade 40 A, 1256 Copenhagen K Denmark. **Tel** 1-148886. **Continues** Fremtiden (Copenhagen, Denmark : 1945), 0016-1020.

●US/1061-1304
**UKRAINE (SYRACUSE, N.Y.). See** Economics-Economic History, Conditions.

US/0041-6010
**UKRAINIAN QUARTERLY, THE.** [Ukr. q.]. **Added/Corp** Ukrainian Congress Committee of America. Vol. 1 (Oct. 1944)-. Periodical. English. qt. $25.00. Ukrainian Quarterly, 203 Second Avenue, New York NY 10003. **Tel** (212)228-6840, **FAX** (212)254-4721. **ED** Professor Volodymyr Stojko (Editor's phone: (212)228-6841). **LC** DK508.A2; U66. **DD** 947.7. Index available. cum. index. **Bk Rev**. **Ad Acc. Circ:** 1,500 (ctrl). available on microfilm and microfiche from University Microfilms International (UMI). **Absorbed**

*Ukrainian Bulletin, 0041-5987.*
**Desc:** Dedicated to providing information about Ukraine and neighboring countries, especially related to their national liberation movements.
**Ind/Abst** Am. Hist. Life (1954-); Am. Bibliogr. Slavic East Europ. Stud.; MLA Int. Bibl. Books Artic. Mod. Lang. Lit.

UK/0041-6029
**UKRAINIAN REVIEW (LONDON, ENGLAND).** (THE UKRAINIAN REVIEW.). [Ukr. rev.]. **Added/Corp** Association of Ukrainians in Great Britain. Organization for Defense of Four Freedoms for Ukraine. Canadian League for Ukraine's Liberation. Vol. 1 (Dec. 1954)-. Periodical. English. qt (Jan., Apr., July. Oct.). £20.00 UK; $40.00 US. Association Ukrainians in Great Britain Ltd, 49 Linden Gardens Notting Hill Gate, London W2 4HG England. **Tel** 011 44 71 229-8392, FAX 011 44 71 792-2499. **ED** Slava Sbecsko. **LC** DK508.A2; U664. **DD** 947.7. **Bk Rev. Ad Acc. Circ:** 1,100 (ctrl).
**Desc:** Political magazine devoted to the study of Ukraine, including the religion and history of Ukraine.
**Ind/Abst** Am. Hist. Life (1955-); MLA Int. Bibl. Books Artic. Mod. Lang. Lit.

US/0193-4783
**UNITED KINGDOM, THE COMMONWEALTH OF NATIONS, A DIRECTORY OF GOVERNMENTS, THE.** **VFOAT** United Kingdom, The Commonwealth of Nations. Vol. 1 (1979/1981)-. Directory. English. an. Political Research Inc., 16850 Dallas Parkway, Dallas TX 75248. **Tel** (214)931-8827. **ED** John Clements. **LC** JN248; .C48. **DD** 351/.00025/171241. **Bk Rev.**
**Desc:** Comprehensive resource of current facts on 49 member nations of the commonwealth and current governor of each.

US/0148-6063
**UNITED STATES POLITICAL SCIENCE DOCUMENTS.** **See** Political Science-Abstracting, Bibliographies and Statistics.

US
**UNIVERSITY REVIEW OF TEXAS.** **Added/Corp** Texas Review Society. **VFOAT** University Review. Vol. 1, No. 1 (Sept. 1990)-. Periodical. English. mo.

GW
**UNTERSUCHUNGEN UND MATERIALIEN ZUR VERFASSUNGS- UND LANDESGESCHICHTE.** 1- 1973-. Monographic series. German. ir. Price varies per volume. N G Elwert Verlag, Postfach 1128, Reitgasse 7+9, W-3550 Marburg Germany. **Tel** 06421 25023, FAX 06421 15487.

BE
**UP INFORMATION.** (19??)-. French. qt. 120.00F Belgium; $4.11 US. Universite de la Paix, 4 Boulevard du Nord, B-5000 Namur Belgium. **Tel** 011 32 81 226102, FAX 231882. **Ad Acc.** ctrl circ.
**Desc:** Covers conflict studies and peace.

US/0884-6227
**UPDATE USSR.** [Update USSR]. Vol. 53, No. 4 (July 1985)-. Periodical. English. ir (ten a year). $7.50 US; $8.50 other. N W R Publications, 239 West 23rd Street, New York NY 10011-2302. **Tel** (212)696-4765. **LC** DK266.A2; N46. **DD** 947/.005. **Bk Rev. Circ:** 5,000. available on microfilm and microfiche from University Microfilms International (UMI). ***Continues** New World Review, 0028-7067.*
**Desc:** Covers the Soviet Union and other socialist countries: economy, social programs, foreign policy, US/USSR relations, etc.
**Ind/Abst** Public Aff. Inf. Serv. Bull. (19??-).

US
**USA WARS: CIVIL WAR. CD-ROM.** English. $74.95. Quanta Press, Inc., 1313 Fifth Street Southeast, Suite 208C, Minneapolis MN 55414. **Tel** (612)379-3956, FAX (612)623-4570.
**Desc:** This text/image/sound database encompasses the war of the rebellion that tore the United States apart from 1860 to 1865. Available in DOS and MAC formats.

BU
**VEK 21 : IZDANIE NA RADIKALDEMOKRATICHESKATA PARTIIA.** **Added/Corp** Radikaldemokraticheska Partiia (Bulgaria). **VFOAT** Vek Dvadeset Purvii. (Mar. 17, 1990)-. Periodical. Bulgarian. wk. DM186.00. **(Subscription address:** Kubon & Sagner, ABT Zeitschriftenimport, D 80328 Munich Germany.**) LC** IN PROCESS; DR90; .V44.

GW
**VERHANDLUNGEN DES DEUTSCHEN BUNDESTAGES.** German. ir. DM183.79. Bundesanzeiger Verlagsges GmbH, Postfach 1320, D 53003 Bonn Germany. **Tel** 011 49 228 3820812.

NE
**VERTEGENWOORDIGINGEN VAN HET KONINKRIJK DER NEDERLANDEN IN HET BUITENLAND / MINISTERIE VAN BUITENLANDSE ZAKEN.** **Added/Corp** Netherlands. Ministerie van Buitenlandse Zaken. (19??)-. Dutch. sa. Staatsuitgeverij, Christoffel Plantijnstraat 1, 2515 TZ'S Gravenhage Netherlands. **Tel** 070/78-95-70. **LC** JX1806; .A23. ***Continues** Vertegenwoordigingen van Nederland in het Buitenland.*

AU
**VESTNIK.** English. mo. DM120.00 Europe; DM180.00 other. Radda & Dressler Verlag GmbH, Davidgasse 79, A-1100 Vienna Austria. **Tel** 011 43 222 60117.
**Desc:** Soviet magazine for politics, business science and culture.

●RU
**VICHE.** **Added/Corp** Ukraine. Verkhovna Rada. No. 1 (1992)-. Periodical. Ukrainian. mo.

US/1058-3831
**VIETNAM (SYRACUSE, N.Y.).** (VIETNAM : A POLITICAL AND ECONOMIC FORECAST.). [Vietnam]. **Added/Corp** Political Risk Services (IBC USA (Publications) Inc.). (1991)-. English. $295.00. Political Risk Services, 6320 Fly Road, Suite 102, PO Box 248, East Syracuse NY 13057-0248. **Tel** (315)431-0511, FAX (315)431-0200. **DD** 959.

CN/0042-5818
**VIEWPOINTS (MONTREAL).** (VIEWPOINTS.). **Added/Corp** Canadian Jewish Congress. Labor Zionist Movement of Canada. Vol. 1 (Fall 1965)-. Periodical. English. qt. $7.89. Canadian Labor Zionists Movement, 4770 Kent Avenue/Suite 300, Montreal Quebec H3W 1H2 Canada. **LC** DS101; .V53.

US/0042-6962
**VISION LETTER, THE.** ***Suspended.*** (19??)-(19??). English. Twelve times a year. $49.00. Vision Inc. / U.S., 310 Madison Avenue, Suite 1412, New York NY 10017. **Tel** (212)953-1308. **ED** Richard Schroeder. **LC** F1401; .V57. **DD** 320.9/8/003. **Bk Rev. Ad Acc.**
**Desc:** A political and economic report on Latin America.

US/0042-7004
**VISNYK.** [Visnyk]. **Added/Corp** Organization for Defense of Four Freedoms for Ukraine. **VFOAT** The Herald; Herald. (19??)-. Periodical. Ukrainian. qt. Organization for Defense of Four Freedoms for Ukraine Inc., 136 2nd Avenue, New York NY 10003. **Tel** (212)982-1170.

US/0749-8624
**VISNYK REPRESIJ V UKRAINI.** (VISNYK REPRESII V UKRAINI / ZAKORDONNE PREDSTAVNYTSTVO UKRAINSKOI HELSINSKOI HRUPY.). [Visn. represij Ukr.]. Vol. 1-. Periodical. Ukrainian. mo. $25.00. Ukrainian Helsinki Group, PO Box 770 Cooper Station, New York NY 10003. **LC** JC599.S582; U39. **DD** 323.

RU
**VOPROSY SOTSIALNO-POLITICHESKOGO RAZVITIIA SOVETSKOGO OBSHCHESTVA.** **Added/Corp** Kemerovskii Gosudarstvennyi Pedagogicheskii Institut. (1973)-. Russian. 0.50rub (single issue). 43 Sovetskii Prospekt, Kemerovo 117 Russia. **LC** JA49; .V66.

US
**VOTERS AND CANDIDATES PAMPHLET.** ***Title Change.*** **Main/Corp** Washington (State). Office of the Secretary of State. **Added/Corp** Washington (State). Office of the Secretary of State. State General Election. **VFOAT** State General Election. (19??)-(198?). English. Secretary of State Publishing Division, 300 North Salisbury Street, Raleigh NC 27603-5909. **Tel** (919)733-7355. **LC** JF495.W2; A3. **DD** 329/.023/797. ***Continues** Official Voters Pamphlet.* ***Continued by** Official Voters Pamphlet (1983).*

US
**VOTING INFORMATION NEWS : A MONTHLY ROUNDUP OF VOTING NEWS AND ISSUES FROM THE FEDERAL VOTING ASSISTANCE PROGRAM (FVAP).** **Added/Corp** Federal Voting Assistance Program (U.S.). Vol. 1, No. 1 (June 1991)-. Periodical. English. mo. Federal Voting Assistance Program, Pentagon, Washington DC 20301-1155.

US
**VOZ LAJERA : ORGANO OFICIAL DEL MUNICIPIO DE SAN JOSE DE LAS LAJAS EN EL EXILIO, LA.** **Added/Corp** San Jose de las Lajas (Cuba : Government in Exile, 1962-). Periodical. Spanish.

GW
**WAHL ZUM ... DEUTSCHEN BUNDESTAG AM ... IN NIEDERSACHSEN.** German. **LC** JN4945.L6865; W33. **DD** 324.943/59.

UK
**WAR CRY.** English. wk. £38.50. Salvationist Publishing and Supplies, 117-121 Judd St Kings Cross, London WC1H 9NN England. **Tel** 11 44 71 3871656, FAX 11 44 71 3873768.

GW/0043-0404
**WAS TUN.** (1968)-. Periodical. German. wk. DM39.00. Internationale Sozialistische Publikationen GmbH, Mainzer Landstr 147, Postfach 111107, 6000 Frankfurt M 1 Germany. **ED** Winfried Wolf. **LC** UNC. **Bk Rev. Ad Acc. Pub. Size:** Tabloid. **Circ:** 5,000. available with illustrations; available with charts.
**Desc:** Topics include politics, economics, trade union fights, international liberation movements, opposition in Eastern Europe, women's liberation, anti-racist movement, etc.

US/0083-7393
**WASHINGTON.** English. an. $79.50 Washington DC; $75.00 other. Columbia Books Inc, 1212 New York Avenue NW/Suite 330, Washington DC 20005. **Tel** (202)898-0662, FAX (202)898-0775.

US/0043-0633
**WASHINGTON MONTHLY, THE.** [Wash. mon.]. Vol. 1, (Feb. 1969)-. Periodical. English. Ten times a year. $39.00 (one year), $74.00 (two year), $99.00 (three year) US; $46.00 (one year), $80.00 (two year), $106.00 (three year) other. The Washington Monthly, 1611 Connecticut Avenue Northwest, Suite 7, Washington DC 20009. **Tel** (202)462-0128, FAX (202)332-8413. **(Subscription address:** The Washington Monthly, P.O.Box 587, Mt. Morris, IL 61054-7928**) ED** Charles Peters. **LC** E838; .W37. **DD** 320.9/73/092. **Bk Rev. Ad Acc. Circ:** 35,000. available on microfilm and microfiche from University Microfilms International (UMI); available on an online database (file 647/Full-Text) from DIALOG. Documents available from UMI Article Clearinghouse.
**Desc:** Original reporting about politics, media, and business, plus analysis of American institutions. Accepts traditional liberal values but not dogmatic liberal prejudices. Articles offer investigation and analysis of White House, Congress and federal government, as well as current issues. Includes reviews of forthcoming books on government and politics.
**Ind/Abst** Acad. Abstr. Full Text Elite (April 1984-); Acad. Abstr. (April 1984-); Acad. Ind. [Computer File] (1984-); Acad. Search (Apr. 1984-); Am. Hist. Life (1971-); Book Rev. Index; Energy Res. Abstr. (June 1980-); Expand. Acad. Index (1984-); Gen. Period. Index (1985-); Guide Soc. Sci. Relig.; INFO-SOUTH Abstr.; Infobank (Jan. 1969-); Int. Polit. Sci. Abstr.; Mag. Artic. Summar. Elite (April 1984-); Mag. Artic. Summar. Select (April 1984-); Mag. Artic. Summar. CD-ROM (April 1984-); Mag. Index Plus (1989-); Mag. Index. Sel. (1986-); Mag. Search; Middle East Abstr. Index; Newsp. Period. Abstr. (1988-); PAIS Int. Print; Read. Guide Abstr. Select Ed.; Read. Guide Period. Lit.; Soc. Sci. Index; Mag. Index (1977-); Vocat. Search (Apr. 1984-).

US/0748-6359
**WASHINGTON PACIFIC REPORT, THE.** [Wash. Pac. rep.]. Vol. 1, No. 1 (Oct. 1, 1982)-. Newsletter. English. Twenty-four times a year. $159.00 US; $184.00 other. Washington Pacific Publications Inc., c/o Fred Radewagen, 1615 New Hampshire Avenue NW, Suite 400, Washington DC 20009-2520. **Tel** (202)387-8100, FAX (202)332-9162. **ED** Fred Radewagen. **LC** DU30; .W37. **DD** 327.73095.
**Desc:** A current affairs newsletter concentrating on political, diplomatic and security issues and developments in the insular Pacific with special emphasis on U.S. activities and involvement with the region.

US/0733-8104
**WASHINGTON REPORT ON AFRICA.** [Washington rep. Afr.]. Vol. 1, Issue 1 (July 1, 1982)-. Periodical. English. sm (23 per year). $399.00 US; $409.00 Canada and Mexico; $429.00 other. Welt Publishing Company, 1413 K Street NW, Suite 1400, Washington DC 20005. **Tel** (202)371-0555, FAX (202)408-9369, telex 281409 TAOA UR. **ED** Rick Sherman. **LC** HC800.A1; W37. **DD** 330.96/005. **Bk Rev**, (Qty: 5 per year). **Ad Acc, Adv Mgr:** Justin Ford. ***Formed by the union of** African Business & Trade, 0732-670X **and** African Index, 0149-0796.*
**Desc:** Features political and economic developments in Africa, tapping into the most prominent trends and following events that impact bi/multi-lateral relations.

US/0192-060X
**WASHINGTON REPRESENTATIVES.** Vol. 3 (1979)-. English. an. $74.20 Washington, DC residents; $70.00 others. Columbia Books Inc, 1212 New York Avenue NW/Suite 330, Washington DC 20005. **Tel** (202)898-0662, FAX (202)898-0775. **ED** Arthur C Close. **LC** JK1118; .D58. **DD** 328.73/07/8025. Index available. **Circ:** 4,500. ***Continues** Directory of Washington Representatives of American Associations & Industry, 0147-216X.*
**Desc:** Directory of 14,500 lobbyists, lawyers and others

who represent American and foreign corporations, trade and professional association, labor unions and public interest and special issue groups in dealing with the federal government. Two main sections list representatives and organizations alphabetically. Two indices organized by subject of foreign country of interest. Also contains a special listing of over 300 federal government executive branch legislative affairs personnel.

US/0043-0846
**WASHINGTON STATE VOTER. Added/Corp** League of Women Voters of Washington. (19??)-. Periodical. English. qt (4 issues). $1.00. League of Woman Voters of Seattle, 1402 18th Avenue, Seattle WA 98122. **Tel** (206)329-4646.

US/0275-1216
**WASHINGTON WATCH (FOREST HILLS, NEW YORK, N.Y.).** (WASHINGTON WATCH.). Vol. 1, No. 1 (Aug. 1, 1981)-. Periodical. English. mo. $195.00. Card Research Inc., PO Box 514, Forest Hills NY 11375. **Tel** (212)263-2084.

JA
**WATASHITACHI NO SENKYO; SENKYO HAKUSHO UNDO NO TAIKEN KIROKU.** **Main/Corp** Akaruku Tadashii Senkyo Nagoya-Shi Suishin Kyogikai. Vol. 4- ; 1976-. Japanese. Nagoya Shiyakusho, 1-1 Sannomaru, 3-chome, Naka-ku 460, Nagoya Japan. **LC** JQ1693.N315; A7a. ***Continues*** *Watashitachi No Senkyo.*

US
**WATERBURY REPUBLICAN-AMERICAN. VFOAT** Waterbury Republican American; Waterbury American Republican; Sunday Republican; Republican-American. (Apr. 2, 1990)-. Newspaper. English. da. $88.00. Waterbury Republican American, PO Box 2090, Waterbury CT 06722. **Tel** (203)574-3636, FAX (203)596-9277. **ED** Bill Southerland. **Ad Acc. Circ:** 60,274. ***Formed by the union of*** *American (Waterbury, Conn. : 1986)* ***and*** *Waterbury Republican (Waterbury, Conn. : 1896).*

●US/1064-0568
**WE THE PEOPLE (NORTH READING, MASS.).** (WE THE PEOPLE : THE NEWSLETTER ABOUT THE BROWN FOR PRESIDENT CAMPAIGN.). [We people]. Vol. 1, No. 1 (May 1992)-. Newsletter. English. mo. $39.92 (8 months). We the People, 50 Main Street, Suite 32, North Reading MA 01864. **DD** 324.

EC/0252-2659
**WEEKLY ANALYSIS OF ECUADOREAN ISSUES. See** Economics.

US/1060-2259
**WEEKLY JAPAN DIGEST, THE.** (THE WEEKLY JAPAN DIGEST.). [Wkly. Jpn. dig.]. **VFOAT** Japan Digest. Vol. 1, No. 21 (Oct. 8, 1990)-. Periodical. English. Fifty-two times a year. $595.00 US, Canada and Mexico; $795 other. KA Communications, 5510 Columbia Pike, Suite 207, Arlington VA 22204. **Tel** (703)528-7570, (800)669-7570, FAX (703)528-8123. **ED** Ayako Doi. **DD** 330. **Bk Rev**, (Qty: 4-5). **Circ:** 150. available on an online database from NEWSNET.
**Desc:** A concise executive summary of political, foreign policy, defense, trade economic, business, science, technology and social issues news from and about Japan.
**Ind/Abst** Geogr. Abstr. Human Geogr.

UK
**WELSH POLITICAL ARCHIVE LECTURE, THE.** 1987-. Monographic series. English (Welsh). Price varies per volume.

UK/0140-2382
**WEST EUROPEAN POLITICS.** [West Eur. polit.]. (Feb. 1978)-. Periodical. English. qt. $195.00. Frank Cass & Company Ltd, Newbury House, 890-900 Eastern Avenue, Newbury Park, Ilford, Essex IG2 7HH United Kingdom. **Tel** 011 44 81 599 8866, FAX 011 44 81 599 0984, telex 897719. **ED** Gordon Smith and Vincent Wright. **LC** JN94.A1; W46. **DD** 320.94/5. Index available. **Bk Rev. Ad Acc, Adv Mgr:** Anne Kidson. **Circ:** 800. available on microfilm and microfiche from University Microfilms International (UMI). Documents available from UMI Article Clearinghouse.
**Desc:** Analyzes and discusses political and social issues relating to Western Europe.
**Ind/Abst** ABC POL SCI; Am. Hist. Life (1978-); Appl. Soc. Sci. Index Abstr.; Br. Humanit. Index; Expand. Acad. Index (1992-); Geogr. Abstr. Human Geogr.; Int. Bibliogr. Sociol.; Int. Polit. Sci. Abstr.; Newsp. Period. Abstr. (1992-); PAIS Int. Print; Sage Public Adm. Abstr.; Soc. Plann. Policy Dev. Abstr.; Sociol. Abstr.; Stud. Women Abstr.

CN/0824-3328
**WEST INDIAN (TORONTO).** (THE WEST INDIAN.). [West Indian]. Periodical. English. mo. $5.00. West Indian People's Organization, PO Box 37 Station P, Toronto Ontario M5S 2S6 Canada. **DD** 322.4/2.

AU
**WEST OST JOURNAL.** (19??)-. German (English and French). Six times a year. S510.00 Austria; S540.00 other. Jupiter Verlagsgesellschaft, Postfach 86, Robertgasse 2, A-1021 Vienna Austria. **Tel** 214-22-94. **ED** Hans Georg Zeiner. **Ad Acc. Circ:** 15,000.

US/0043-4078
**WESTERN POLITICAL QUARTERLY, THE.** ***Title Change.*** [West. polit. q.]. Vol. 1 (March 1948)-(1993). Periodical. English. qt. University of Utah / 252 Orson Spencer Hall, Salt Lake City UT 84112. **Tel** (801)581-7031, (801)581-7137, FAX (801)581-6957. **ED** Dean Mann. **LC** JA1; .W4. **DD** 320.5. Index available. cum. index. **Bk Rev. Ad Acc. Pr Rev.** ctrl circ. available on microfilm and microfiche from University Microfilms International (UMI). Documents available from The Genuine Article, UMI Article Clearinghouse. ***Continued by*** *Political Research Quarterly, 1065-9129.*
**Ind/Abst** ABC POL SCI; Acad. Abstr. Full Text Elite (July 1990-Dec. 1993); Acad. Abstr. (July 1990-Dec. 1993); Acad. Ind. [Computer File] (1987-); Acad. Search (July 1990-Dec. 1993); Am. Hist. Life (1955-1959, 1965-); Am. Bibliogr. Slavic East Europ. Stud.; Annu. Bibliogr. Engl. Lang. Lit. (19??-1993); Book Rev. Index; Chicano Index; Crim. Justice Abstr.; Curr. Contents Soc. Behav. Sci.; Expand. Acad. Index (1987-); Gen. Period. Index (1987-); Index Period. Artic. Relat. Law; INFO-SOUTH Abstr.; Int. Bibliogr. Sociol.; Int. Polit. Sci. Abstr.; Mag. Search; Middle East Abstr. Index; Newsp. Period. Abstr. (1991-); PAIS Int. Print; Peace Res. Abstr. J. (1974-1986); Res. Alert [Full Cov.]; Sage Public Adm. Abstr. (?-?); Soc. Sci. Source (Jul. 1990-); Soc. Sci. Index; Soc. Sci. Index Fulltext (Dec. 1988-) [Full Txt.]; Soc. Work Abstr. (?-?); U.S. Polit. Sci. Doc.; West. Hist. Q.

UK
**WHO'S WHO IN ASIAN AND AUSTRALASIAN POLITICS.** 1st Ed. (1991)-. English. Bowker Saur Ltd., A Reed Reference Publishing Company, Part of Reed International PLC, 59-60 Grosvenor Street, London WIX 9DA England. **Tel** 011 44 71 4935841, FAX 011 44 71 4991590.

●SZ
**WHO'S WHO IN EUROPEAN INSTITUTIONS AND ENTERPRISES.** (1993)-. English. ***Continues*** *Who's Who in European Institutions, Organizations, and Enterprises.*

IT
**WHO'S WHO IN EUROPEAN INSTITUTIONS, ORGANIZATIONS, AND ENTERPRISES.** ***Title Change.*** (1985)-(1992). English. te. Whos Who in Italy Srl, c/o Mr G Colombo, CP61, 20091 Bresso Milan Italy. **Tel** 011 39 2 6100237. **NLM** D 1070; W628. ***Continues*** *Who's Who in European Institutions and Organizations.* ***Continued by*** *Who's Who in European Institutions and Enterprises.*

US
**WHO'S WHO IN UNITED STATES POLITICS AND AMERICAN POLITICAL ALMANAC. See** Biographies.

US
**WILLIAM J. COOPER FOUNDATION LECTURES.** (19??)-. Monographic series. English. ir. Price varies per volume. Oxford University Press / New York, 200 Madison Avenue, New York NY 10016. **Tel** (212)679-7300, (919)677-0977, (800)451-7556, (800)445-9714, FAX (919)677-1303.

GW
**WIRTSCHAFT UND GESELLSCHAFT IM GETEILTEN DEUTSCHLAND. *Ceased.*** **Added/Corp** Forschungsstelle fuer Gesamtdeutsche Wirtschaftliche und Soziale Fragen. Vol. 1 (1988)-(19??). Monographic series. German. Verlag Arno Spitz, Pacelli Alle 5, W-1000 Berlin 33 Germany.

US
**WITNESS FOR PEACE NEWSLETTER.** **Added/Corp** Witness for Peace (Organization). (198?)-. Newsletter. English. qt. $30.00. Witness for Peace, 2201 P Street Northwest, Room 109, Washington DC 20037. **Tel** (202)797-1160. **LC** F1528; .W57.

US/0049-7770
**WOMAN ACTIVIST, THE.** (Jan. 14, 1971)-. Periodical. English. Ten times a year (Monthly with July/Aug. and Nov./Dec combined). $17.00 US; $22.00 other. Woman Activist Inc, 2310 Barbour Road, Falls Church VA 22043. **Tel** (703)573-8716. **ED** Flora Crater. **Bk Rev. Ad Acc. Circ:** 200 (ctrl).
**Desc:** Political, feminist call for actions. Congressional information, summaries and current feminist activity in relation to politics and equal rights amendment.

US/0195-7732
**WOMEN & POLITICS.** [Women polit.]. **VAT** Women and Politics. Vol. 1 (Spring 1980)-. Academic Scholarly Publication. English. qt. $175.00 US; $245.00 other. The Haworth Press Inc, 10 Alice Street, Binghamton NY 13904-1580. **Tel** (607)722-5857, (800)3-HAWORTH, FAX (607)722-1424. **ED** Rita Mae Kelly (editor's address: Professor of Public Affairs, Arizona State University, Social Science 103, Women's Studies Program, Tempe, AZ 85287). **LC** HQ1236; .W63. **DD** 305.4/2. **Bk Rev. Ad Acc. Pr Rev. Acid Free. Circ:** 469. available on microfilm and microfiche from University Microfilms International (UMI). Documents available from The Genuine Article, UMI Article Clearinghouse, Haworth Document Delivery Service.
**Desc:** Dedicated to uniting the field of women's studies with political science, sociology, and psychology. Interdisciplinary in scope, the journal draws articles from a wide spectrum of methodological approaches with a comparative perspective.
**Ind/Abst** ABC POL SCI; Acad. Search (July 1993-); Altern. Press Index (-199?); Am. Hist. Life (1982-); Am. Bibliogr. Slavic East Europ. Stud.; Curr. Contents Soc. Behav. Sci.; EMBASE; Expand. Acad. Index (1992-); INFO-SOUTH Abstr.; Int. Polit. Sci. Abstr.; Mag. Search; Middle East Abstr. Index; Multicult. Educ. Abstr.; Newsp. Period. Abstr. (1992-); PAIS Int. Print; Res. Alert [Full Cov.]; Soc. Plann. Policy Dev. Abstr.; Soc. Sci. Cit. Index [Full Cov.]; Soc. Work Abstr. [Select. Cov.]; Sociol. Abstr.; Stud. Women Abstr.; Urban Aff. Abstr.; Women Stud. Abstr.

US/0735-6927
**WOMEN'S POLITICAL REPORTER / GEORGIA WOMEN'S POLITICAL CAUCUS.** Periodical. English. PO Box 27519, Atlanta GA 30327.

US/0195-1688
**WOMEN'S POLITICAL TIMES. Added/Corp** National Women's Political Caucus (U.S.). (July 1976)-. Periodical. English. qt. $20.00. National Womens Political Caucus, 1275 K Street Northwest, Suite 750, Washington DC 20005-4051. **Tel** (202)898-1100. **ED** Pat Reilly. **LC** HQ1236.5.U6; W45. **DD** 320/.082. **Circ:** 20,000 (ctrl).
**Desc:** Publication of the National Women's Political Caucus, it contains information on issues affecting women and includes profiles and interviews on women legislators and policy makers.

SA
**WORK IN PROGRESS (JOHANNESBURG, SOUTH AFRICA).** ***Ceased.*** (WORK IN PROGRESS.). **Added/Corp** Southern African Research Service. **VFOAT** W.I.P.; WIP. No. 1 (Sept. 1977)-No. 95 (1994). Periodical. English. Eight times a year. South African Research Services, PO Box 32716, Braamfontein, South Africa 2017. **Tel** 011 27 11 4031912. **LC** DT1155 .W67. **DD** 968.06/3. **Circ:** 8,000. ***Absorbed*** *New Era (Cape Town, South Africa).*
**Desc:** Contemporary South African labour and politics; anti-apartheid oppositional, but independent in approach. Includes debates and information on resistance politics.
**Ind/Abst** Hum. Rights Intern. Rep.

US/0882-6366
**WORKERS' ADVOCATE SUPPLEMENT, THE.** (THE WORKERS' ADVOCATE SUPPLEMENT : VOICE OF THE MARXIST-LENINIST PARTY, USA.). [Work. advocate suppl.]. **Added/Corp** Marxist-Leninist Party, USA. Vol. 1, No. 1 (Jan. 15, 1985)-. Periodical. English. Eight times a year. $8.00 US, Canada & Mexico; $16.00 other. Marxist-Leninist Publications, Ontario Street Station, PO Box 11972, Chicago IL 60611. **ED** S T Simpson. **DD** 322. Index available. cum. index. **Bk Rev**, (Qty: 3-4).
**Desc:** Carries Marxist-Leninist analysis of US and world developments, and struggles for the cause of the workers and oppressed.

JM
**WORKERS TIME.** Periodical. English. Workers Time Ltd, 9 Central Avenue, Kingston 10 Jamaica.

US/1070-4205
**WORKERS WORLD WW. Added/Corp** Workers World Party. **VFOAT** Workers World Workers World. (199?)-. Periodical. English. wk. $30.00 (institutions), $20.00 (individuals). Workers World, 55 West 17th Street, 5th Floor, New York NY 10011. **Tel** (212)255-0352. ***Continues*** *Workers World, 0043-809X.*

US
**WORKING PAPERS / ANNUAL SEMINARS ON AFRICAN GOVERNANCE.** English. an (Mar.). $15.00 (individual); $22.50 (institution). Carter Center of Emory University, African Governance Program, 1 Copenhil, Atlanta GA 30307. **Tel** (404) 420-5151, FAX (404) 420-5196. **ED** editor telephone: (404) 420-5186. ctrl circ.
**Desc:** Conference papers submitted to the 2nd Annual Seminar of the African Governance Program.

US/1043-1535
**WORLD ALMANAC OF U.S. POLITICS, THE.** [World alm. U. S. polit.]. **VFOAT** World Almanac of US Politics. **VAT** World Almanac of United States Politics. (1991)-. English. ir. Price varies. Pharos Books, 200 Park Avenue, New York NY 10166. **Tel** (212)692-3700. **(Subscription address:** St. Martin's Press, 175 5th Avenue, New York NY 10010.**) LC** JK6; .W67. **DD** 320.973/02/02.
**Desc:** Designed to contain everything from every citizen that should know about who and what governs this

country.' This source covers topics such as the 1988 elections, political terminology, the legislative process, the budget process, how to contact government officials, the electoral college, political parties, voter registration, and campaign financing.

US/0749-4793
**WORLD FEDERALIST (ARLINGTON, VA.).** (WORLD FEDERALIST : NEWSMAGAZINE OF THE WORLD FEDERALISTS ASSOCIATION.). [World fed.]. **Added/Corp** World Federalists Association (U.S.) World Federalist Association (U.S.). Vol. 7, No. 1 (Mar. 1982)-. Periodical. English. qt. $15.00 US; $15.82 Canada; $16.44 other. World Federalist Association, 418 7th Street Southeast, Washington DC 20003-2796. **Tel** (202)546-3950, FAX (202)546-3749. **DD** 341. ***Continues*** *World Federalists Association (U.S.) World Federalist Newsletter, 0196-2574.*
**Desc:** Newsletter of the World Federatlist Movement; "working to transform the United Nations into a democratic world federation capable of ensuring peace, economic progress and environmental protection."

II
**WORLD FOCUS.** 1 (Jan. 1980)- = Vol. 1, No. 1-. Periodical. English. mo. Rs40.00 India; $12.00 US. Hari Sharan Chhabra, F-15 Bhagat Singh Market, New Delhi 110001 India. **LC** D839; .W555. **DD** 320.9/048.

US/0043-8618
**WORLD JURIST, THE.** **Added/Corp** World Peace Through Law Center. Vol. 7 No. 7/8 (July/Aug. 1970)-. English. bm. $75.00. World Peace Through Law Center, 1000 Connecticut Avenue NW, Suite 202, Washington DC 20036. **Tel** (202)466-5428, FAX (202)452-8540, telex 440456. **ED** Timothy Handy. **LC** K110.W67; A15. **DD** 340/.05. ***Continues*** *World Peace Through Law Center. Bulletin - World Peace Through Law Center.*
**Ind/Abst** Hum. Rights Intern. Rep.

UK
**WORLD MARXIST REVIEW.** ***Ceased.*** Vol. 1 (Sept. 1958)-(June 1990). Periodical. English. mo. Central Books Ltd, 14 Leathermarket, London SE1 3ER England.
**Ind/Abst** Am. Hist. Life; Middle East Abstr. Index.

US/0094-2316
**WORLD OF POLITICS.** (19??)-. English. ir. $15.00. Political Research Inc., 16850 Dallas Parkway, Dallas TX 75248. **Tel** (214)931-8827. **LC** JK1; .W67. **DD** 320.9/73/092.

●CH
**WORLD OUTLOOK / SHIH CHIEH CHAN WANG.** **Added/Corp** World League for Freedom and Democracy. **VFOAT** Shih Chieh Chan Wang. Vol. 1, No. 1 (Jan.-Feb. 1992)-. Periodical. English. Six times a year. $25.00 Asia; $30.00 others. World Outlook, 333 Tun Hua S Road Sec 2, 3rd Floor, Taipei 106 Taiwan. **Tel** 011 886 2 7387944. **LC** D860; .W66. ***Continues*** *Asian Outlook, 0004-4628.*
**Ind/Abst** PAIS Int. Print.

US/1058-1022
**WORLD PERSPECTIVES (MADISON, WIS.).** ***Suspended.*** (WORLD PERSPECTIVES : NEWS AND ANALYSIS FROM PEOPLES' NEWS SERVICE.). [World perspect.]. **Added/Corp** Peoples' News Service (Madison, Wis.). Vol. 1, No. 1 (Jan. 1990)-(1992). Periodical. English. mo. Peoples' News Service, PO Box 3074, Madison WI 53704-0074. **Tel** (608)241-4812. **ED** Esty Dinur. **DD** 327.

US/0198-0300
**WORLD POLITICS (GUILFORD).** (WORLD POLITICS.). [World polit.]. Periodical. English. an. $10.95. Dushkin Publishing Group Inc., Sluice Dock, Guilford CT 06437. **Tel** (203)453-4351, (800)243-6532, FAX (203)453-6000. **ED** Suzanne Ogden. **LC** D839; .W569. **DD** 327/.05.
**Desc:** Compilation of readings bringing together material addressing major, current problems concerning relations among nations in an easily understandable writing style and level. Designed to stimulate interest in learning about issues that often seem foreign, remote, and irrelevant, but which actually have profound consequences for economic well-being, security and survival. Publishes articles for those that are new to the study of world politics.
**Ind/Abst** Acad. Ind. [Computer File] (1987-); Expand. Acad. Index (1987-); Geogr. Abstr. Human Geogr.; Int. Dev. Abstr.

AT/0043-8960
**WORLD REVIEW.** ***Ceased.*** Vol. 1, (March 1962)-(Dec. 1993). Periodical. English. qt. The Business Manager World Review, PO Box 279, Indooroopilly 4068 QLD Australia. **Tel** 011 61 7 5841575, telex 40315. **ED** DR G St John Barclay. **LC** D839. **Ad Acc. Circ:** 700.
**Ind/Abst** APAIS, Aust. Public Aff. Inf. Ser. (1963-); Int. Bibliogr. Sociol.; Peace Res. Abstr. J. (1961-1964).

US/0364-8575
**WORLD THIS YEAR, THE.** 1971-. English. an. Simon & Schuster, 1230 Avenue of the Americas, New York NY 10020. **Tel** (212)698-7000. **LC** JF37; .W65. **DD** 320.9/046.

US/0894-1521
**WORLDWIDE GOVERNMENT DIRECTORY, WITH INTERNATIONAL ORGANIZATIONS.** See Public Administration.

US/0736-6175
**YALE POLITICAL MONTHLY.** [Yale polit. mon.]. Periodical. English. mo. Yale Political Monthly, 962 Yale Station, New Haven CT 06520. **LC** JA1; .Y34. **DD** 320/.05.

US/0084-3490
**YALE STUDIES IN POLITICAL SCIENCE.** **Added/Corp** Yale University. (1954)-. Monographic series. English. ir. Price varies per volume. Yale University Press, PO Box 209040, New Haven CT 06520. **Tel** (203)432-0940, (800)987-7323, FAX (203)432-0948. **LC** UNC. **DD** 320.

UK/0513-5982
**YOUNG FABIAN PAMPHLET.** **Added/Corp** Young Fabian Group. Fabian Society (Great Britain). (1961)-. Monographic series. English. ir. Price varies per volume. Fabian Society, 11 Dartmouth Street, London SW1H 9BN England. **Tel** 011 44 071 2228877, FAX 011 44 071 9767153. **ED** Stephen Pollard. **DD** 369.4. Index available. cum. index. **Circ:** 5,500 (ctrl).
**Desc:** Social policy and general political theory and practice.

II/0377-6727
**YOUNG MARCH, THE.** See Children and Youth Interests.

US/1056-5507
**Z MAGAZINE (BOSTON, MASS.).** (Z MAGAZINE.). [Z mag.]. **Added/Corp** Institute for Social and Cultural Communications. **VFOAT** Z. Vol. 2, No. 10 (Oct. 1989)-. Periodical. English. Eleven times a year (July/August is double issue). $25.00 (institutions), $26.00 (individuals) US; $40.00 Canada; $50.00 other. Z Magazine, 116 Saint Botolph Street, Boston MA 02115. **Tel** (617)787-4531, FAX (617)457-0626. **ED** Lydia Sargent (editor's phone: (508)548-9063). **LC** HN51; .Z15. **DD** 306/.0973. **Bk Rev**, (Qty: 20/year). **Circ:** 25,000. ***Continues*** *Zeta Magazine, 0896-1328.*
**Desc:** An independent political magazine of critical thinking on political, cultural, social and economic life in the U.S. It perceives race, sex, class and political dimensions of personal life as fundamental in understanding and trying to improve contemporary circumstances and works to assist activist efforts to attain a better future.

SZ
**ZAHLUNGSBILANZ DER SCHWEIZ IM JAHRE ... / KOMMISSION FUER KONJUNKTURFRAGEN, DIE.** German. an. Kommission fur Konjunkturfragen, Belpstrasse 53, 3003 Bern Switzerland. **LC** HC395; .Z34.

UK
**ZANZIBAR NEWSLETTER.** **Added/Corp** Zanzibar Organization. No. 1 (Jan. 1990)-. Newsletter. English. mo. **LC** DT435.62; .F74. **DD** 320.9678/1. ***Continues*** *Free Zanzibar Voice.*

GW/0044-3360
**ZEITSCHRIFT FUER POLITIK.** [Z. Polit.]. **Added/Corp** Hochschule fuer Politik Munchen. (Nov. 1907)-. Periodical. German. Four times a year. DM98.00. Carl Heymanns Verlag KG, Luxemburger Strasse 449, D 50939 Cologne Germany. **Tel** 011 49 221 460100, telex 8 881 888. **ED** R. Schmidt & A. Grabowsky. **LC** JA14; .Z4. **DD** 320/.05. Index available. **Bk Rev. Ad Acc. Circ:** 1,000 (ctrl).
**Ind/Abst** ABC POL SCI; Am. Hist. Life (1954-1957, 1961-); Int. Bibliogr. Sociol.; Int. Polit. Sci. Abstr.; Peace Res. Abstr. J. (1969-1972).

GW
**ZEITSCHRIFT FUER POLITISCHE, OEKONOMIE UND SOZIALISTISCHE POLITIK.** (19??)-. Periodical. German. Four times a year. Ed Westfaelisches Dampfboot, Dorotheenstrasse 26A Herr G. Thien, D 48145 Muenster Germany. **Tel** 011 49 251 6086080.

GW/0514-6496
**ZEITSCHRIFT FUER RECHTSPOLITIK.** [Z. Rechtspolit.]. Vol. 1 (Oct. 1968)-. Periodical. German. Twelve times a year. DM94.00. CH Beck Verlagsbuchhandlung, D 80791 Munich Germany. **Tel** 011 49 89 381891.
**Ind/Abst** Energy Res. Abstr. (Aug. 1978-); Index Foreign Leg. Per.; Int. Polit. Sci. Abstr.

PL/0137-2378
**ZESZYTY NAUKOWE UNIWERSYTETU JAGIELLONSKIEGO. PRACE Z NAUK POLITYCZNYCH.** **Added/Corp** Uniwersytet Jagiellonski. **VFOAT** Prace Z Nauk Politycznych; Schedae Politicae; Universitas Iagellonica Acta Scientiarum Litterarumque. P.Schedae Politicae. Began with No. 1 in (1971). Monographic series. Polish (summaries and/or abstracts in English and Russian; table of contents in English, French, German and Russian). Price varies per volume. **(Subscription address:** ARS Polona, PO Box 1001, 00068 Warsaw Poland.) **LC** JA49; .P73. **DD** 320.5/32.

XR
**ZPRAVA O SCHUZI SNEMOVNY NARODU / FEDERALNI SHROMAZDENI CESKOSLOVENSKE SOCIALISTICKE REPUBLIKY.** **Main/Corp** Czechoslovakia. Federalni Shromazdeni. **VFOAT** Zprava o Ustavujici Schuzi Snemovny Narodu. 1st electorial period, 1st session (Jan. 29, 1969). Czech. ir. Kancel AR Federalniho Shromazdeni, Vinohradska 1, 110 02 Prague Czech Republic. **LC** J338; .H453B. ***Continues in part*** *Zprava o Schuzich Narodniho Shromazdeni Ceskoslovenske Socialisticke Republiky.*

SZ/0167-9767
**ZUIDAFRIKAANSE KOERIER.** Periodical. Afrikaans. mo. Zuidafrikaanse Ambassade, Jungfraustrasse 1, 3003 Bern Switzerland. **LC** DT751; .Z86.

GW
**ZUM NACHDENKEN.** **Added/Corp** Hessische Landeszentrale fuer Politische Bildung. (19??)-. Periodical. German. DM28.00. Hessische Landeszentrale fuer Politische Bildung, Rheinbahnstr. 2, D 65185 Wiesbaden Germany. **LC** JA14; .Z77.

GW/0514-8294
**ZUR POLITIK UND ZEITGESCHICHTE.** **Added/Corp** Berlin. Freie Universitat. Otto-Suhr-Institut. Berlin. Landeszentrale fur Politische Bildungsarbeit. No. 1 (1960)-. German. Freie Universitaet, Otto-Suhr Institut, Altensteinstrasse 40, W-1000 Berlin 33 Germany. **DD** 909.

---

## ABSTRACTING, BIBLIOGRAPHIES AND STATISTICS

---

US/0001-0456
**ABC POL SCI. ADVANCE BIBLIOGRAPHY OF CONTENTS: POLITICAL SCIENCE & GOVERNMENT.** [ABC pol sci]. **VFOAT** Advance Bibliography of Contents: Political Science & Government. **VAT** Advance Bibliography of Contents Political Science; Advance Bibliography of Contents: Political Science and Government. Vol. 1 (March 1969)-. Abstracting/Indexing Service. English. Six times a year (including an annual index). Price varies. ABC Clio Press, PO Box 1911, 130 Cremona, Santa Barbara CA 93117. **Tel** (805)968-1911, (800)422-2546, FAX (805)685-9685. **ED** Lloyd W. Garrison. **LC** Z7161; .A214; JA71. **DD** 016.32. **CODEN** ABPSC. Index available (five year indexes available). cum. index. available on CD-ROM (as ABC POL SCI on Disc; available in portions in 1992).
**Desc:** A guide to current periodical literature in political science and government and related disciplines such as international affairs, law, sociology, and economics. Lists and indexes the tables of contents of more than 360 journals published worldwide.

US/0149-1962
**ANNUAL STATISTICAL REPORT OF EXPENDITURES MADE IN CONNECTION WITH ELECTIONS, THE.** **Main/Corp** Missouri. Office of the Secretary of State. (19??)-. Statistical Publication. English. an. Secretary of State / Jefferson City, PO Box 1370, Jefferson City MO 65101. **LC** JK1991.5.M8; M57a. **DD** 329/.025/09778.

SA
**BIBLIOGRAPHICAL SERIES / SOUTH AFRICAN INSTITUTE OF INTERNATIONAL AFFAIRS / BIBLIOGRAFIESE REEKS / SUID-AFRIKAANSE INSTITUUT VAN INTERNASIONALE AANGELEENTHEDE.** ***Ceased.*** **Main/Corp** South African Institute of International Affairs. **Added/Corp** South African Institute of International Affairs. **VFOAT** Bibliografiese Reeks. No. 1 (1976)-Vol. 16, No. 3 (Dec. 1992). Monographic series. English. ir. South African Institute of International Affairs, PO Box 31596, Braamfontein 2017 South Africa. **Tel** 011 27 11 3392021, telex 4-27291 SA. **ED** Jacqueline A. Kalley and Elna Schoeman. **Circ:** 300 (ctrl).

US/0742-6909
**BIBLIOGRAPHIES AND INDEXES IN LAW AND POLITICAL SCIENCE.** [Bibliogr. indexes law polit. sci.]. No. 1-. English. ir. Greenwood Press Inc., PO Box 5007, Westport CT 06881-5007. **Tel** (203)226-3571, FAX (203)222-1502. **DD** 016.

CN/0383-2848
**BIBLIOGRAPHY SERIES - NORMAN PATERSON SCHOOL OF INTERNATIONAL AFFAIRS (CARLETON UNIVERSITY).** (BIBLIOGRAPHY SERIES / THE NORMAN PATERSON SCHOOL OF

INTERNATIONAL AFFAIRS, CARLETON UNIVERSITY, OTTAWA, CANADA.). **Main/Corp** Norman Paterson School of International Affairs. **Added/Corp** Norman Paterson School of International Affairs. (1975)-. Monographic series. English (French). ir (1-2 per year). Price varies per volume. Norman Paterson School of International Affairs, Carleton University, Ottawa Ontario K1S 5B6 Canada. **Tel** (613)788-2600, FAX (613)788-2889, telex 053-4232. **ED** Vivian Cummins. **DD** 016.327. **Bk Rev. Circ:** 600.

DK
**COPENHAGEN POLITICAL STUDIES ABSTRACTS.** **Added/Corp** Kbenhavns Universitet. Institut for Samfundsfag. (19??)-. Periodical. English. Institute of Political Studies DK-1130 Rosenborggade 15, 2nd Floor, Copenhagen K Denmark. **Tel** (01)112626. **LC** JA88.D4; C66. **DD** 320/.0720489. **Circ:** 300.
**Desc:** Yearbook with abstracts of research papers from the Institute.

US/0740-1183
**COUNCIL SPOTLIGHT BOOKNOTES.** (COUNCIL SPOTLIGHT BOOKNOTES : A PUBLICATION OF THE WORLD AFFAIRS COUNCIL OF NORTHERN CALIFORNIA.). **VFOAT** Booknotes; Council Spotlight. Periodical. English. mo. $10.00. World Affairs Council of Northern California, World Affairs Center, 312 Sutter Street/Suite 200, San Francisco CA 94108. **Tel** (415)982-2541, FAX (415)982-5028. **ED** Lone Beeson. **Bk Rev. Circ:** 10,000 (ctrl).
**Desc:** A monthly review of new books on international relations, area studies, economics and development.

US/0041-7343
**CURRENT BIBLIOGRAPHICAL INFORMATION / DAG HAMMARSKJOLD LIBRARY.** ***Ceased.*** [Curr. bibliogr. inf. - U.N. Dag Hammarskjold Libr.]. **Main/Corp** Dag Hammarskjold Library. **VFOAT** Renseignements Bibliographiques d'Actualite; Information Bibliographique Courante. Vol. 1, No. 1 (Jan. 1, 1971)-Vol. 23, No. 6 (Dec. 1993). Government Publication. English (French). mo. United Nations Publications, 2 United Nations Plaza, Room DC2 0853, Department 007C, New York NY 10017. **Tel** (212)963-8303, (800)253-9646. **LC** Z733; .U392a. **DD** 016.34123. ***Formed by the union of*** *Dag Hammarskjold Library. New Publications in the Dag Hammarskjold Library* ***and*** *Dag Hammarskjold Library. Current Issues.*
**Desc:** Selectively analyzes books and articles from about 900 worldwide periodicals, UN systems and other, to provide a current awareness list of materials relevant to the work programmes of the United Nations.
**Ind/Abst** Popul. Index (?-?).

●US/1067-7542
**CURRENT DIGEST OF THE POST-SOVIET PRESS, THE.** [Curr. dig. post-Sov. press]. **Added/Corp** American Association for the Advancement of Slavic Studies. American Council of Learned Societies. Ohio State University. **VFOAT** Current Digest of the Soviet Press; Current Digest. Vol. 44, No. 1 (Feb. 5, 1992)-. Abstracting/Indexing Service. English. wk. $865.00 (first class mail) US; $845.00 Canada; $850.00 other. Current Digest of the Soviet Press, 3857 North High Street, Columbus OH 43214. **Tel** (614)292-4234, FAX (614)267-6310. **ED** Fred Schulze. **LC** D839; .C87. **DD** 057. Index available (published separately as). cum. index. **Circ:** 1,000 (ctrl). available on microfilm and microfiche from the publisher; available on an online database from NEXIS. ***Continues*** *Current Digest of the Soviet Press, 0011-3425.*
**Desc:** Translations from press materials of the states that made up the Soviet Union. Some publications not available outside Russia. Carefully selected by experienced editors and expertly translated. Published weekly since 1949.
**Ind/Abst** NEXIS; PAIS Int. Print.

SW
**CURRENT RESEARCH - THE SWEDISH INSTITUTE OF INTERNATIONAL AFFAIRS.** **Main/Corp** Utrikespolitiska Institutet (Sweden). English. Swedish Institute of International Affairs, Lilla Nygatan 23, S-111 28 Stockholm Sweden. **LC** Z6204; .U87A; D843. **DD** 016.327/09045.

GW
**DDR-PUBLIKATIONEN ZUR IMPERIALISMUSFORSCHUNG, AUSWAHLBIBLIOGRAPHIE.** German. sa. Free. Institut fur Internationale Politik und Wirtschaft, 1020 Breite/Strasse 11, Berlin Germany. **Tel** 2206215. **(Subscription address:** Leipziger Kommissions und Grobbuchhandel, Abt Exportversand, Arbeitsgruppe, Leninstr 16, O-7010 Leipzig Germany**) LC** Z7161; .D13. Index available. **Circ:** 450.
**Desc:** Covers political economy, world economy, foreign trade, politics, social structure, right class struggle, foreign policy, international relations, military arms race, and scientific technological progress.

US/0379-8127
**DOCUMENTS LIST.** **Main/Corp** United Nations Industrial Development Organization. English. ir. $120.00. United Nations Industrial Information Section, New York NY 10017. **Tel** (212)754-8302. **LC** JX1977; .A2 subser; Z6483.I5. **DD** 016.3389.

US
**ELECTION RESULTS AND STATISTICS / STATE OF OKLAHOMA.** **Main/Corp** Oklahoma. State Election Board. English. be. State Election Board, State Capitol, Oklahoma City OK 73105. **LC** JK7192; .O38A. **DD** 324.9766/053.

US/0894-4547
**GUIDE TO THE AMERICAN LEFT (KANSAS CITY, MO. 1984).** (GUIDE TO THE AMERICAN LEFT.). [Guide Am. left]. **Added/Corp** Editorial Research Service (Olathe, Kan.). **VFOAT** Directory of the American Left; Bibliography of the American Left. (198?)-. English. an. $19.95. Laird Wilcox, PO Box 2047, Olathe KS 66061. **Tel** (913)829-0609. **ED** Laird Wilcox. **LC** HX81; .D57. **DD** 320.5/3/06073. **Bk Rev. Circ:** 1,500 (ctrl). ***Continues*** *Directory of the American Left, 0733-9623.*
**Desc:** A current directory of over 1,300 organizations, publishers, book dealers, newsletters and journals identified with the American "left-wing," including liberal, socialist, radical, revolutionary, feminist, gay, anti-nuclear, environmental, ethnic (minority) nationalist, and other "left-wing" values.

US/8756-0216
**GUIDE TO THE AMERICAN RIGHT (KANSAS CITY, MO. 1984).** (GUIDE TO THE AMERICAN RIGHT.). [Guide Am. right]. **Added/Corp** Editorial Research Service (Olathe, Kan.). **VFOAT** Directory of the American Right; Bibliography of the American Right. (1984)-. English. an. $19.95. Laird Wilcox, PO Box 2047, Olathe KS 66061. **Tel** (913)829-0609. **ED** Laird Wilcox. **LC** HS2321; .D57. **DD** 320.5/2/06073. **Circ:** 2,000. ***Continues*** *Directory of the American Right, 0163-7541.*
**Desc:** A current directory of over 1,300 organizations, publishers, book dealers, newsletters and journals identified with the American "right wing," including conservative, patriotic, anti-communist, libertarian, pro-family, anti-abortion, free market and other "right-wing" values.

US/0275-049X
**HUMAN RIGHTS INTERNET REPORTER.** (HUMAN RIGHTS INTERNET REPORTER / HRI.). **Added/Corp** Human Rights Internet. Vol. 6 No. 1 (Sept./Oct. 1980)-. Abstracting/Indexing Service. English. Twice a year. $60.00 (Individuals), $80.00 (Institutions). Human Rights Internet / Human Rights Centre, University of Ottawa, 57 Louis Pasteur, Ottawa, Ontario K1N 6N5 Canada. **Tel** (613)564-3492, FAX (613)564-4054. **LC** JC571; .H7696a. **DD** 323.4/05. Index available. **Bk Rev. Circ:** 2,000. available on microfiche from InterDocumentation. ***Continues*** *Human Rights Internet Newsletter, 0163-9048.*
**Desc:** Abstracts and indexes hundreds of publication concerned with human rights violations and the work of non-governmental human rights organizations throughout the world.
**Ind/Abst** Altern. Press Index (199?-); Am. Bibliogr. Slavic East Europ. Stud.; Index Period. Artic. Relat. Law (19??-).

II/0250-9660
**ICSSR JOURNAL OF ABSTRACTS AND REVIEWS : POLITICAL SCIENCE.** **Main/Corp** Indian Council of Social Science Research. **Added/Corp** Indian Council of Social Science Research. Journal of Abstracts and Reviews: Political Science. **VFOAT** Journal of Abstracts and Reviews: Political Science. Vol. 4 (Jan./Dec. 1976)-. Periodical. English. Twice a year (Jan., July). $8.00. Indian Council of Social Science Research, 35 Ferozshah Road, New Delhi 110 001 India. **Tel** 011 91 11 38959, 011 91 11 381571. **ED** Kuldeep Mathur. **LC** JA26; .I48a. **DD** 320/.05. **Bk Rev. Ad Acc. Circ:** 550.
**Desc:** Publishes abstracts of researches and books reviews in political science.

US/0020-6652
**INTERNATIONAL EXECUTIVE.** [Int. exec.]. **Added/Corp** Foundation for the Advancement of International Business Administration (U.S.) American Management Association. American Graduate School of International Management. Vol. 1 (Winter 1959)-. Abstracting/Indexing Service. English. bm. $168.00 US; $228.00 Canada and Mexico; $250.50 other. John Wiley & Sons, Inc., 605 Third Avenue, New York NY 10158-0012. **Tel** (212)850-6000, (212)850-6645, FAX (212)850-6088, telex 12-7063. **(Subscription address:** John Wiley & Sons Inc / New Jersey, PO Box 2575, Secaucus NJ 07096-2575.**) ED** Beverly Springer. **LC** HF1; .I56. **DD** 658. **[CCC]. Bk Rev. Ad Acc. Circ:** 1,400. available on microfilm and microfiche from University Microfilms International (UMI). Documents available from UMI Article Clearinghouse.
**Desc:** Reports on trends and developments and serves as a forum for discussion of subjects of importance to international executives. Includes summaries of articles and books, plus special reference guide listing new articles and books by international management subject and country. Reflects new scholarship in international business, including human resource management, marketing, finance, accounting as well as economic, political, legal, cultural, technological and environmental issues.
**Ind/Abst** ABI/INFORM Glob. Ed.; ABI Inform Ondisc (Winter 1973-)(Winter 1973); Am. Bibliogr. Slavic East Europ. Stud.; Middle East Abstr. Index.

FR/0020-8345
**INTERNATIONAL POLITICAL SCIENCE ABSTRACTS.** (INTERNATIONAL POLITICAL SCIENCE ABSTRACTS / INTERNATIONAL POLITICAL SCIENCE ASSOCIATION [AND] INTERNATIONAL STUDIES CONFERENCE.). **Added/Corp** International Political Science Association. International Studies Conference. Unesco. Co-Ordinating Committee on Documentation in the Social Sciences. International Committee for Social Sciences Documentation. **VFOAT** Documentation Politique Internationale. Vol. 1, No. 1-2 (1951)-. Abstracting/Indexing Service. English (French). Six times a year. 1925.00F (institution); 550.00F (individual). International Political Science Abstracts - Documentation Politique Internationale, 27 rue St Guillaume, 75337 Paris Cedex 07 France. **Tel** 011 33 1 45495050, FAX 011 33 1 42223964, telex 201 022F SCIPOL. **ED** Serge Hurtig. **LC** JA36; .I5. **DD** 320.82. Index available. **Ad Acc. Circ:** 1,500 (ctrl).
**Desc:** Abstracts of articles in periodicals and yearbooks. Worldwide coverage of over 680 titles.

US/0733-2998
**LEFT INDEX.** [Left index]. No. 1 (Spring 1982)-. Abstracting/Indexing Service. English. qt (4 issues). $70.00 US. Reference and Research Services, 511 Lincoln Street, Santa Cruz CA 95060. **Tel** (408)426-4479. **ED** Joan Nordquist. **LC** Z7164.S67; L34; HX1. **DD** 016.33543.
**Desc:** Current author/subject index to the contents of periodical literature of the left perspective; includes book review index, and annual cumulated subject index.

US/0098-9509
**MARXISM AND THE MASS MEDIA.** (MARXISM AND THE MASS MEDIA : TOWARDS A BASIC BIBLIOGRAPHY.). Bibliography. English. ir. $10.00. International Mass Media Research Center, Box 350, New York NY 10013. **ED** Seth Siegelaub. **LC** Z7164.S67; M315; HX550.M35. **DD** 016.33543/8/301161. **Circ:** 2,000.
**Desc:** A continuing bibliography of Marxist, critical and progressive studies on all aspects of culture and communication.

US
**MASSACHUSETTS ELECTION STATISTICS / COMPILED IN THE ELECTIONS DIVISION, DEPARTMENT OF THE STATE SECRETARY.** **Added/Corp** Massachusetts. Elections Division. **VFOAT** Election Statistics. (1978)-. English. be. Free on request. Massachusetts Secretary of State, 1 Ashburton Place, Room 1705, Boston MA 02108. **Tel** (617)727-2828. **LC** J87; .M4 date p subser; JK3192. **DD** 300/.9744 S; 324.9744/043. ***Continues*** *Election Statistics, The Commonwealth of Massachusetts.*

CN/0823-9576
**NORTHERN POLITICS REVIEW.** (NORTHERN POLITICS REVIEW : AN ANNUAL PUBLICATION OF THE NORTHERN POLITICAL STUDIES PROGRAM.). [North. polit. rev.]. **Added/Corp** Northern Political Studies (Program). **VFOAT** NPR. **VAT** NRP. Northern Politics Review. (1984)-. Periodical. English. an. 30.00Can$. University of Calgary, 11th Floor, Calgary Alberta T2N 1N4 Canada. **Tel** (403)220-4038. **ED** W. Harriet Critchley and Frances Abele. **DD** 016.9719.

US/0031-3599
**PEACE RESEARCH ABSTRACTS JOURNAL.** **Added/Corp** Canadian Peace Research Institute. International Peace Research Association. Vol. 1 (June 1964)-. Abstracting/Indexing Service. English. bm (Feb., Apr., June, Aug., Oct., Dec.). $313.00. SAGE Periodical Press, 2455 Teller Road, Thousand Oaks CA 91320. **Tel** (805)499-0721, FAX (805)499-0871, telex 100799. **LC** JX1901; .P38. Index available. **Acid Free.**
**Desc:** Abstracts journal articles, books, conference proceedings and other materials from around the world on all aspects of peace studies and international relations.

GW
**PRC OFFICIAL ACTIVITIES AND MONTHLY BIBLIOGRAPHY / INSTITUTE OF ASIAN AFFAIRS.** ***Title Change.*** **Added/Corp** Institut fuer Asienkunde (Hamburg, Germany). **VFOAT** P.R.C. Official Activities and Monthly Bibliography. **VAT** People's Republic of China Official Activities and Monthly Bibliography. (1976)-(Dec. 1992). Periodical. English (German). Twelve times a year. Institute of Asian Affairs, Rothenbaumchaussee 32, D-20148 Hamburg Germany. **Tel** 011 49 40 443001, FAX 011 49 40 4107945. **ED** Gunter Hartmann. **LC** DS777.545; .P7. **DD** 951.05/05. **Ad Acc. Circ:** 100. ***Continued by*** *China Monthly Data, 0943-7533.*
**Desc:** Political and economic data and bibliography on the PR China, Taiwan, Hong Kong and Macau.

MX
**RELACIONES MEXICO-ESTADOS UNIDOS, BIBLIOGRAFIA ANUAL.** **Added/Corp** Colegio de Mexico. **VFOAT** Bibliografia Mexico-Estados Unidos. Vol. 1 (July 1980/June 1981)-. Spanish. an. $10,000 Mexico; $5.00 other. Colegio de Mexico AC, Camino Al Ajusco No 20, 10740 Mexico DF Mexico. **Tel** 011 52 5 6455955 Ext. 3133, telex 1777585 COLME. **ED** Marie Claire Fischer de Figueroa. **LC** Z6465.U5; R45; E183.8.M5. **DD** 016.3034/8273/072. Index available. **Ad Acc. Pr Rev. Circ:** 1,000.
**Desc:** References to monographs, journals, clippings, official documents and miscellanea on general relations, political economic, energy, border illegal aliens, Mexican, Americans, and cultural relations.

US/0883-282X
**SPECTRUM (WINTER HAVEN, FLA.).** (SPECTRUM.). [Spectrum]. **Added/Corp** Corbett, Bayliss. 15th Ed. (198?)-. English. ir. $19.95. Laird Wilcox, PO Box 2047, Olathe KS 66061. **Tel** (913)829-0609. **ED** Laird Wilcox. **LC** D839; .C46. **DD** 016.90982/8. **Circ:** 500. ***Continues*** *Censored, 0163-2280.*
**Desc:** A unique, general interest listing of little known sources of news and background information on current affairs, mostly U.S., scholarly to popular.

US/0250-5584
**UNDOC: CURRENT INDEX. UNITED NATIONS DOCUMENTS INDEX.** (UNDOC : CURRENT INDEX (UNITED NATIONS DOCUMENTS INDEX).). **Added/Corp** Dag Hammarskjold Library. **VFOAT** United Nations Documents Index. **VAT** United Nations Documents: Current Index. United Nations Documents Index. Vol. 1, No. 1 (Jan./Feb. 1979)-. Government Publication. English. qt. $150.00. United Nations Publications, 2 United Nations Plaza, Room DC2 0853, Department 007C, New York NY 10017. **Tel** (212)963-8303, (800)253-9646. **(Subscription address:** United Nations Publications, Subscription Office, PO Box 361, Birmingham AL 35201-0361.**) LC** Z6481; .U19; JX1977. **DD** 016.34123. ***Formed by the union of*** *UNDEX, United Nations Documents Index. Series A, Subject Index, 0303-7118; UNDEX, United Nations Documents Index. Series B, Country Index, 0303-7134* ***and*** *UNDEX, United Nations Documents Index. Series C, List of Documents Issued, 0303-7126.*
**Desc:** Gives comprehensive coverage of full bibliographic description, subject, author and title indexes, and a check-list of United Nations documents received at Headquarters.

US/0148-6063
**UNITED STATES POLITICAL SCIENCE DOCUMENTS.** (UNITED STATES POLITICAL SCIENCE DOCUMENTS (USPSD).). **Added/Corp** University of Pittsburgh. University Center for International Studies. American Political Science Association. **VFOAT** USPSD. Vol. 1 (1975)-. Abstracting/Indexing Service. English. an. $407.00 (including postage) US; $413.00 (including postage) other. Mid-Atlantic Technology Applications Center (MTAC), University of Pittsburgh, 823 William Pitt Union, Pittsburgh PA 15260. **Tel** (412)648-7010, FAX (412)648-7003. **ED** Maxine Heller, Tel. (412)648-7015. **LC** Z7163; .U58; H9. **DD** 016.3. Each issue contains an index to its own contents (no volume index)--loose. **Circ:** 300. available on an online database from DIALOG. ***Absorbed*** *Asian Studies Indexed Journal Reference Guide, 0149-1652.*
**Desc:** Contains comprehensive abstracts and indexes of articles from over 140 scholarly journals in the political and social sciences. Also included is a set of five indexes to the documents plus a rotated subject description display' and special features (maps, charts) section. Subject areas covered are foreign policy, international relations, behavioral sciences, public administration, economics, military science, law and contemporary problems, world politics, and all areas of political science, including theory methodology.

FI
**VALTIOLLISET VAALIT : KANSANEDUSTAJAIN VAALIT. Main/Corp** Finland. Tilastokeskus. **VFOAT** Statliga Val : Riksdagsmannavalen; National Elections : Parliamentary Elections. English (Finnish and Swedish). Tilastokeskus, PL 504, Annankatu 44, 00101 Helsinki Finland. **Tel** 358-0-17341, FAX 358-0-17342474, telex 1002111 TILASTO SF. **LC** HA1448; .F4 subser; JN6719.A15. **DD** 314.897 S; 324.94897/033.

GW
**WAHL ZUM NIEDERSACHSISCHEN LANDTAG DER ... .** German. Niedersachsisches Landesverwaltungsamt, Postfach 107, 3000 Hannover Germany. **Tel** (0511)108-9466. **LC** JN4945.L6865; W35. **DD** 324.943/59/005. **Bk Rev. Circ:** 500.
**Desc:** Results of the polling act for the Parliament of Niedersachsen (lower-Saxony).

GW
**ZU FRAGEN DES SOZIALISTISCHEN WELTSYSTEMS; AUSWAHLBIBLIOGRAPHIE.** German (Polish and Russian). an. DM3.00. Akademie fur Staats und Rechtswissenschaft der W, August-Bebel-Strasse 89, 1502 Potdam-Bebelsberg 2 Germany. **LC** Z7161; .Z8; HC701. **DD** 016.947.

## CIVIL RIGHTS

NE/0923-6198
**2E WERELD. Added/Corp** Stichting Tweede Wereld Centrum. **VFOAT** Tweede Wereld. (1990)-. Periodical. Dutch. bm. **LC** IN PROCESS. ***Continues*** *Boekovski Berichten.*
**Ind/Abst** Hum. Rights Intern. Rep.

US/0893-0724
**AAICJ NEWSLETTER.** [AAICJ newsl.]. **Added/Corp** American Association for the International Commission of Jurists. **VAT** American Association for the International Commission of Jurists Newsletter. No. 12 (1983)-. Newsletter. English. American Association for the International Commission of Jurists, 777 United Nations Plaza, New York NY 10017. **Tel** (212)972-0883. **DD** 341. ***Continues*** *Newsletter / American Association for the International Commission of Jurists, 0731-5295.*
**Ind/Abst** Hum. Rights Intern. Rep.

●CN/1192-1188
**ABILITY NETWORK. See** Physically Impaired.

US
**ACLU NEWS. Added/Corp** American Civil Liberties Union. Northern California Branch. **VAT** American Civil Liberties Union News. Vol. 36, No. 10 (Oct./Nov. 1971)-. Periodical. English. Six times a year (Jan., Mar., May, July, Sept., Nov.). $20.00 Comes with American Civil Liberties Union of Northern California membership. American Civil Liberties Union of Northern California - ACLU-NC, 1663 Mission Street, 4th Floor, San Francisco CA 94103. **Tel** (415)621-2493, FAX (415)255-1478. **ED** Elaine Elinson. Index available. **Bk Rev**, (Qty: 2-4). **Circ:** 30,000. ***Continues*** *American Civil Liberties Union-News.*
**Desc:** Covers civil liberties litigation, legislation and activities in California (and some national scope). This is the organ of the ACLU of Northern California.

US/0743-8834
**ACOA ACTION NEWS.** (ACOA ACTION NEWS / AMERICAN COMMITTEE ON AFRICA.). [ACOA action news]. **Added/Corp** American Committee on Africa. **VFOAT** A.C.O.A. Action News. **VAT** American Committee on Africa Action News. (19??)-. Periodical. English. sa. The Africa Fund, 198 Broadway, New York NY 10038. **Tel** (212)962-1210.
**Ind/Abst** Hum. Rights Intern. Rep.

AT/1032-2205
**ACSJC OCCASIONAL PAPERS.** [ACSJC occas. pap.]. **Added/Corp** Australian Catholic Social Justice Council. **VFOAT** Australian Catholic Social Justice Council Occasional Papers. (1988)-. Monographic series. English. ir. Price varies per volume. Australian Catholic Social Justice Council, Leo X11 HSE 19 MacKenzie Street, North Sydney New South Wales 2060 Australia. **Tel** 11 61 2 9565811, FAX 011 61 2 9565782. **DD** 261.805. Index Bound in First Issue. **Circ:** 2,000. ***Continues*** *CCJP Occasional Papers, 0813-5436.*
**Desc:** Covers social services and various social justice issues.

US
**ACTIVITIES REPORT - COLORADO. CIVIL RIGHTS COMMISSION. Main/Corp** Colorado. Civil Rights Commission. 1954/55-. Periodical. English. an. Colorado Civil Rights Commission, 1525 Sherman Street/Room 600 C, Denver CO 80203.

CN/0714-8828
**ACTUALITE VIE. See** Ethics.

NE
**ADVIESBRIEVEN EN- NOTA'S VAN DE EMANCIPATIERAAD. Main/Corp** Emancipatieraad (Netherlands). (198?)-. Dutch. an. Fl4.75. Distributiecentrum, Overheidspublikaties D O P, Postbus 20014, 2500 EA Den Haag The Netherlands. **LC** HQ1658; .E52a.

US
**ADVOCATE (INDIANAPOLIS, IND. : 1984).** (THE ADVOCATE / INDIANA CIVIL LIBERTIES UNION.). **Added/Corp** Indiana Civil Liberties Union. Vol. 1, No. 1 (Spring 1984)-. Periodical. English. qt. $15.00. Indiana Civil Liberties Union, 445 North Pennsylvania, Suite 911, Indianapolis IN 46204. **Tel** (317)635-4059. **ED** Susan Hopkins Milner. **Ad Acc. Circ:** 5,000. ***Continues*** *ICLU and You.*

US/0883-0029
**AEGIS (WASHINGTON, D.C.).** ***Suspended.*** (AEGIS : MAGAZINE ON ENDING VIOLENCE AGAINST WOMEN.). [Aegis]. **Added/Corp** Feminist Alliance Against Rape (U.S.) National Communications Network (U.S.) Alliance Against Sexual Coercion. (July/Aug. 1978)-(1986). Periodical. English (Spanish). qt. $10.50 individuals, $25.00 institutions. Feminist Alliance against Rape, Box 21033, Washington DC 20009. **ED** Diana Ouley/Campbell. **LC** HV6558; .F42. **DD** 305. Index available. **Bk Rev. Ad Acc. Circ:** 1,500 (ctrl). ***Continues*** *FAAR & NCN;* ***Formed by the union of*** *Feminist Alliance Against Rape. Newsltter - Feminist Alliance Against Rape* ***and*** *Newsletter (National Communications Network (U.S.)).*
**Desc:** Provides information on rape, battering, child sexual assault and other forms of violence against women. Directed primarily at grassroots activists and community groups.
**Ind/Abst** Altern. Press Index.

US
**AFFIRMATIVE ACTION PLAN - THOMAS JEFFERSON UNIVERSITY. Main/Corp** Thomas Jefferson University. 1976-. English.

CN/0849-987X
**AFFIRMATIVE ACTION/STATUS OF WOMEN.** [Affirm. action/Status women]. **Added/Corp** North York Board of Education (Ont.). Affirmative Action/Women's Studies Office. Periodical. English. sa. Limited free distribution. Affirmative Action, Womens Studies Department, North York Board of Education, Yonge Street, Willowdale Ontario M2N 5N8 Canada. **DD** 305.42/09713/54105. ***Continues*** *NY Affirmative Action Women's Studies News, 0712-595X.*

FR/0291-2708
**AFGHAN REALITIES.** [Afghan real.]. (1981)-. Periodical. English. mo. Association pour l'Information et la Documentation sur l'Afghanistan, Paris France. **UDC** 327.
**Ind/Abst** Hum. Rights Intern. Rep.

JA
**AITSUGU SABETSU JIKEN. Added/Corp** Buraku Kaiho Domei. Osaka-fu Rengokai. (19??)-. Japanese. an. ¥400. Buraku Kaiho Domei Osaka-Fu Rengokai, 1247 Kuboyoshicho Naniwa-ku, Osaka Japan. **LC** HT725.J3; A392.

EC
**ALDHU : BOLETIN INFORMATIVO DE LA ASOCIACION LATINOAMERICANA PARA LOS DERECHOS HUMANOS. Added/Corp** Asociacion Latinoamericana para los Derechos Humanos. **VFOAT** Boletin Informativo ALDHU. (1981)-. Periodical. Spanish.
**Ind/Abst** Hum. Rights Intern. Rep.

●CN/1188-875X
**ALERTA (TORONTO).** (ALERTA / COMITE INTER-EGLISES DES DROITS HUMAINS EN AMERIQUE LATINE. INTER-CHURCH COMMITTEE ON HUMAN RIGHTS IN LATIN AMERICA). [Alerta]. **Added/Corp** Inter-Church Committee on Human Rights in Latin America. No. 1 (1992)-. Periodical. English. bm. Inter-Church Committee on Human Rights in Latin America, Suite 201/40 Saint Clair Avenue East, Toronto Ontario M4T 1M9 Canada. **Tel** (416)921-4152. **DD** 323.4. ***Continues*** *Newsletter, 0226-661X.*

NE
**AMANDLA. Added/Corp** Boycot Outspan Aktie (Leiden, Netherlands) Komitee Zuidelijk Afrika (Amsterdam, Netherlands) Werkgroep Kiaros (Utrecht, Netherlands). (19??)-. Dutch. Ten times a year. F20.00 Netherlands; F33.00 Europe; F48.00 others. Kairos, PO Box 19218, 3500 de Utrecht Netherlands. **Tel** 011 31 30 319714. **LC** DT746; .A46.
**Ind/Abst** Hum. Rights Intern. Rep.

US/1068-8919
**AMERICAS WATCH.** ***Title Change.*** (AMERICAS WATCH : [NEWSLETTER].). [Am. Watch]. **Added/Corp** Americas Watch Committee (U.S.). **VFOAT** News from Americas Watch. (Feb. 25, 1991) -Vol. 6, No. 1 (1994). Periodical. English. ir. Human Rights Watch, 485 Fifth Avenue, New York NY 10017. **Tel** (212)972-8400, FAX (212)972-0905. **LC** JC599.L3; N49. **DD** 323. ***Continues*** *News from Americas Watch, 1061-9909.* ***Continued by*** *Human Rights Watch/Americas (Newsletter), 1077-6710.*
**Desc:** Monitors and promotes observance of internationally recognized human rights in Latin America and the Caribbean.

US
**AMNESTY ACTION / AI, USA. Added/Corp** Amnesty International USA. Vol. 1 (1966)-. English. bm. Free to members of Amnesty International USA. Amnesty International USA, 322 Eighth Avenue, New York NY 10001. **Tel** (212)807-8400, telex 666628. **ED** Ron Latole. **Bk Rev. Circ:** 300,000 (ctrl).
**Ind/Abst** Hum. Rights Intern. Rep.

UK/0308-6887
**AMNESTY INTERNATIONAL NEWSLETTER. Main/Corp** Amnesty International. (1971)-. Newsletter. English (French, Spanish and Arabic). Six times a year (Feb., Apr., June, Aug., Oct., Dec.). $40.00 Comes with Amnesty International membership. Amnesty International - New Zealand, New Zealand Section, Box 793, Wellington New Zealand. **Tel** 011 64 4 4993349, FAX 011 64 4 845949, telex 4993505. **ED** Colin Chiles. **Circ:** 60,000 (ctrl). ***Continues*** *AIR, Amnesty International Review.*
**Desc:** A report of major initiatives and exposes in the

## Political Science — Civil Rights

human rights field, covering the latest reports and appeals by Amnesty International.
**Ind/Abst** Hum. Rights Intern. Rep.

UK
**AMNESTY INTERNATIONAL REPORT, THE. Main/Corp** Amnesty International. **VFOAT** Report. Vol. 1, (1976)-. English (Spanish, French and Arabic). an (July). $22.00. Amnesty International / New York, 322 Eighth Avenue, New York NY 10001. **Tel** (212)807-8400. **ED** Adam Lloyd. **LC** JC571; .A44a. **DD** 323.4/9/05. *Continues* Amnesty International. Annual Report.
**Desc:** A country-by-country survey of human rights in over 125 countries throughout the world.
**Ind/Abst** Hum. Rights Intern. Rep.

PE
**ANDEAN NEWSLETTER / ANDEAN COMMISSION OF JURISTS. Added/Corp** Comision Andina de Juristas. No. 1 (Nov. 1986)-. Newsletter. English. mo. $15.00 (Peru); $25.00 (other). Andean Commission of Jurists, Los Sauces 285 San Isidro, Lima 27 Peru. **LC** KH54.C66; A225.
**Ind/Abst** Hum. Rights Intern. Rep.

US/0197-1239
**ANNUAL REPORT - AMERICAN CIVIL LIBERTIES UNION. Main/Corp** American Civil Liberties Union. (197?)-. English. an. American Civil Liberties Union, 132 West 43rd Street, New York NY 10036. **Tel** (212)944-9800 ext 422. *Continues* American Civil Liberties Union. ACLU Biennial Report, 0278-7741.

CN/0708-5516
**ANNUAL REPORT - CANADIAN HUMAN RIGHTS COMMISSION.** (RAPPORT ANNUEL - COMMISSION CANADIENNE DES DROITS DE LA PERSONNE.). **Main/Corp** Canada. Commission Canadienne des Droits de la Personne. **VFOAT** Annual Report. 1977/78-. French (English). an. Commission Canadienne des Droits de la Personne, 257 rue Slater, Ottawa Ontario K1A 1E1 Canada.

US
**ANNUAL REPORT - CITY OF DETROIT, HUMAN RIGHTS DEPT. Main/Corp** Detroit (Mich.) Human Rights Dept. (19??)-. English. an. City of Detroit / Human Rights Department, 150 Michigan Avenue, Detroit MI 48226. **LC** JC599.U52; M484. **DD** 352/.98/0977434.

UK
**ANNUAL REPORT / EQUAL OPPORTUNITIES COMMISSION.**
**Main/Corp** Great Britain. Equal Opportunities Commission. (19??)-. English. ir. Her Majesty's Stationery Office, 51 Nine Elms Lane, London SW8 5DR England. **Tel** 011 44 71 873 8459, 011 44 71 873 8499, 011 44 71 873 8499, 011 44 71 873 8456, telex 297138. (Subscription address: Her Majesty's Stationery Office, PO Box 276, Publications Centre, London SW8 5DT England.) **LC** HD4903.5.G7; G74a. **DD** 354.410083/3. *Continues* Great Britain. Equal Opportunities Commission. Annual Report of the Equal Opportunities Commission.
**Desc:** Covers sex discrimination in employment and against women.

US
**ANNUAL REPORT : INTER-AMERICAN COMMISSION ON HUMAN RIGHTS.**
**Main/Corp** Inter-American Commission on Human Rights. **VFOAT** Annual Report of the Inter-American Commission on Human Rights to the General Assembly. (19??)-. Periodical. English (Spanish; translations available in Spanish). an. $25.00. Organization of American States, 19th Street & Constitution Avenue NW, Suite 300, Washington DC 20006. **Tel** (202)458-6256. **LC** F1405.5 1959; .O7 subser.; JC599.A5. **DD** 341.24/5 S; 341.48/1.

US
**ANNUAL REPORT OF THE COMMUNITY RELATIONS SERVICE.** See Public Administration.

AT
**ANNUAL REPORT OF THE EQUAL OPPORTUNITY BOARD. Main/Corp** Victoria. Equal Opportunity Board. (1978)-. English. Government Printer / Victoria, PO Box 203, North Melbourne Victoria, 3051 Australia. **LC** JC599.A8; V52a. **DD** 354.945001/04.

US
**ANNUAL REPORT OF THE INTER-AMERICAN COMMISSION ON HUMAN RIGHTS / ORGANIZATION OF AMERICAN STATES. Main/Corp** Inter-American Commission on Human Rights. English (Spanish). an. *Continues* Annual Report / University of Rhodesia. Institute of Mining Research.

CN/0702-0538
**ANNUAL REPORT OF THE ONTARIO HUMAN RIGHTS COMMISSION. Main/Corp** Ontario Human Rights Commission. (19??)-. English. an. Ontario Human Rights Commission, 400 University Avenue, Toronto Ontario M5G 1R6 Canada. **LC** JC599.C2; O65a. **DD** 354.7130081/1.

CN/0825-7361
**ANNUAL REPORT OF THE PRIVACY COMMISSIONER.** See Law.

CN/0826-953X
**ANNUAL REPORT / SASKATCHEWAN HUMAN RIGHTS COMMISSION.** [Annu. rep. - Sask. Hum. Rights Comm.]. **Main/Corp** Saskatchewan Human Rights Commission. English. an. Free. Saskatchewan Human Rights Commission, 8th Floor Canterbury Towers, 224 4th Avenue South, Saskatoon Saskatchewan S7K 5M5 Canada. **Tel** 933-5952. **ED** Vera Marie Wolfe. **LC** KES458.A72; H852. **DD** 354.71240081/1. **Circ:** 500. available on audiocassette.
**Desc:** Report of the Saskatchewan Human Rights Commission which enforces human rights legislation in Saskatchewan.

US
**ANNUAL REPORTS / STATE OF ILLINOIS, DEPARTMENT OF HUMAN RIGHTS [AND] HUMAN RIGHTS COMMISSION. Main/Corp** Illinois. Dept. of Human Rights. **Added/Corp** Illinois. Human Rights Commission. **VFOAT** Annual Report. 1st (July 1, 1980)-(June 30, 1981)-. English. an. **LC** JC599.U52; I445a. **DD** 353.97730081/1.

FR
**ANNUAL REVIEW - EUROPEAN COMMISSION OF HUMAN RIGHTS.** *Title Change.* **Main/Corp** European Commission of Human Rights. **VFOAT** Compte Rendu Annuel. Multiple languages (English and French). an. Council of Europe / Group Pact ED, Pharmacopoeia BP 907, 67029 Strasbourg Cedex 01 France. **Tel** 011 33 88 412036, FAX 011 33 88 41277181, telex 880388. **LC** LAW. **DD** 342/.4/085. *Absorbed by* Stock-Talking on the European Convention on Human Rights.

US
**ANNUAL REVIEW - INTERNATIONAL LEAGUE FOR HUMAN RIGHTS. Main/Corp** International League For Human Rights. (19??)-. English. **LC** JC571; .I594. **DD** 323.4/062/1. *Continues* Annual Review - International League for the Rights of Man, 0363-9347.

UK
**ANTI-SLAVERY REPORTER (ANTI-SLAVERY SOCIETY FOR THE PROTECTION OF HUMAN RIGHTS).**
(ANTI-SLAVERY REPORTER / ANTI-SLAVERY SOCIETY FOR THE PROTECTION OF HUMAN RIGHTS.). **Added/Corp** Anti-Slavery Society for the Protection of Human Rights (Great Britain). Series 7, Vol. 13, No. 1 (Dec. 1981)-. Periodical. English. an. £5.50. Anti-Slavery International, Stable Yard, Broomgrove Road, London SW9 9TL England. **Tel** 011 44 71 924 9555, FAX 011 44 71 7384110. *Continues* Anti-Slavery Reporter and Aborigines' Friend.
**Ind/Abst** Hum. Rights Intern. Rep.

SP
**ANUARIO DE DERECHOS HUMANOS.** *Ceased.* Vol. 1 (1981)-(19??). Periodical. Spanish. an. Editorial Complutense, Donoso Cortes 65 1RA Planta, 28003 Madrid Spain. **Tel** 011 34 1 3946372. **LC** K1; .N9155. **DD** 342.46/085.
**Ind/Abst** Index Foreign Leg. Per.

NE/0920-7775
**ANUARIO INTERAMERICANO DE DERECHOS HUMANOS. Added/Corp** Organization of American States. General Secretariat. Inter-American Commission on Human Rights. Secretariat. Inter-American Commission on Human Rights. Inter-American Court of Human Rights. **VFOAT** Inter-American Yearbook on Human Rights. **VAT** Inter American Yearbook on Human Rights. (1968)-. Multiple languages (English and Spanish). ir. $325.00. Martinus Nijhoff Publishers, Subsidiary of Kluwer Academic Publishers, Koraalrood 50, 2718 SC Zoetermeer Netherlands. **Tel** 011 31 79 684400. **LC** LAW; KDZ574.A85; I68. **DD** 341.48/1/091812.

FR/0369-8262
**APARTHEID NON.** (19??)-. French. ir.
**Ind/Abst** Hum. Rights Intern. Rep.

US/0194-2832
**ARGENTINA OUTREACH. Added/Corp** Argentine Information and Service Center. (1976)-. Periodical. English. $6.00. Argentine Information Service Center, 2700 Bancroft, Berkeley CA 94704. **LC** JC599.A7; A7. **DD** 323.4/0982.

AT
**ASIA PACIFIC SOLIDARITY.** *Ceased.* qt.
**Ind/Abst** Hum. Rights Intern. Rep. (?-?).

AT/0312-0317
**BALTIC NEWS.** [Baltic news]. (1975)-. Periodical. English. mo. **DD** _a301.451 919 094.
**Ind/Abst** Hum. Rights Intern. Rep.

CN
**BEEDAUDJIMOWIN.** See Ethnic Interests.

US/0160-7731
**BILL OF RIGHTS IN ACTION.** [Bill rights action]. V. 10, No. 2- Sept. 1976-. Periodical. English. qt (during the school year). $4.00. Constitutional Rights Fdn, 1510 Cotner Avenue, Los Angeles CA 90025. **Tel** (310)473-5091. **LC** KF4742; .B54. **DD** 342/.73/085. available on microfilm and microfiche from University Microfilms International (UMI). *Continues* Bill of Rights Newsletter.

US/0006-2499
**BILL OF RIGHTS JOURNAL, THE.** See Law.

AG
**BOLETIN / CENTRO DE ESTUDIOS LEGALES Y SOCIALES. Added/Corp** Centro de Estudios Legales y Sociales (Argentina). No. 1 (Oct. 1984)-. Periodical. Spanish. Centro de Estudios Legales y Sociales, Rodriguez Pena 286, 10 Piso Buenos Aires, Republica Argentina. **LC** KHA3003.A15; B65.
**Ind/Abst** Hum. Rights Intern. Rep.

PE
**BOLETIN / COMISION ANDINA DE JURISTAS.** See Law.

NQ
**BOLETIN / COMISION NACIONAL DE PROMOCION Y PROTECCION DE LOS DERECHOS HUMANOS. Added/Corp** Comision Nacional de Promocion y Proteccion de los Derechos Humanos (Nicaragua). (198?)-. Periodical. Spanish. mo. **LC** JC599.N5; B66. **DD** 323.4/9/097285.
**Ind/Abst** Hum. Rights Intern. Rep.

BO
**BOLETIN DE DERECHOS HUMANOS.**
**Added/Corp** Asamblea Permanente de Derechos Humanos de Bolivia. No. 1 (Oct. 1978)-. Periodical. Spanish. mo. **LC** JC599.B6; B64. **DD** 323.4/0984.
**Ind/Abst** Hum. Rights Intern. Rep.

CK
**BOLETIN DE PRENSA / COMITE PERMANENTE POR LA DEFENSA DE LOS DERECHOS HUMANOS, COMISION COORDINADORA. Added/Corp** Comite Permanente por la Defensa de los Derechos Humanos (Colombia). Comision Coordinadora. (19??)-. Periodical. Spanish.
**Ind/Abst** Hum. Rights Intern. Rep.

MX
**BOLETIN INFORMATIVO / COMISION DE DERECHOS HUMANOS DE GUATEMALA. Added/Corp** Comision de Derechos Humanos de Guatemala (Mexico City, Mexico). (19??)-. Periodical. Spanish. Comision de Derechos Humano de Guatemala, Pitagoras 842, Mexico D. F. 03020.
**Ind/Abst** Hum. Rights Intern. Rep.

CR
**BRECHA : PUBLICACION MENSUAL DE LA COMISION PARA LA DEFENSA DE LOS DERECHOS HUMANOS EN CENTROAMERICA, CODEHUCA.**
**Added/Corp** Comision para la Defensa de los Derechos Humanos en Centroamerica. (1988)-. Periodical. Spanish. mo. *Continues* Informe Sobre la Situacion de los Derechos Humanos en Centroamerica.
**Ind/Abst** Hum. Rights Intern. Rep.

UK
**BRIEFING PAPER.** (19??)-. Periodical. English.
**Ind/Abst** Hum. Rights Intern. Rep.

CN/0831-9227
**BULLETIN (AMNESTY INTERNATIONAL. CANADIAN SECTION-ENGLISH-SPEAKING).**
(BULLETIN / AMNESTY INTERNATIONAL, CANADIAN SECTION (ENGLISH-SPEAKING).). [Bull. - Amnesty Int., Can. Sect. Engl.-Speak.]. **Added/Corp** Amnesty International. Canadian Section-English-Speaking. Vol. 8, No. 4 (April 1981)-. Bulletin. English. mo. 25.00Can$. Amnesty International Canadian Section, 130 Slater Street/Suite 900, Ottawa Ontario K1P 6E2 Canada. **Tel** (613)563-1891. **ED** Erika Rosenfeld and Patricia Acheson. **DD** 323.4/9/0601. **Bk Rev. Circ:** 12,000. *Continues* Bulletin (Amnesty International. Canadian Section), 0229-5539.
**Ind/Abst** Hum. Rights Intern. Rep.

UK/1011-3983
**BULLETIN (ARTICLE 19 ORGANIZATION).** (BULLETIN / ARTICLE 19.). **Added/Corp** Article 19 (Organization). Issue 1 (Aug./Sept. 1987)-. Bulletin. English. Three times a year (Varies). $25.00 (one year) Bulletin & comes with membership. International Centre on Censorship, 90 Borough High Street, London SE1 1LL England. **Tel** 011 44 71 403 4822. **Circ:** 8,500 (ctrl).
**Desc:** News and information on the international centre against censorship.

FR/0397-9717
**BULLETIN - C.R.I.D.E.V.** **VFOAT** Bulletin - Centre Rennais d'Information pour le Developpement et la Liberation des Peuples. (1975)-. Periodical. French. ir. 100.00F (all except Europe); 90.00F (Europe except France); 80.00F (France). Cridev, 41 Avenue Janvier, 35000 Rennes France. **Tel** 011 33 1 99302720.
**Ind/Abst** Hum. Rights Intern. Rep.

CN/0824-4448
**BULLETIN / CIVIL LIBERTIES ACTION SECURITY PROJECT.** [Bull. - Civ. Lib. Action Secur. Proj.]. **Added/Corp** Civil Liberties Action Security Project. **VFOAT** Bulletin of the Civil Liberties Action Security Project (CLASP); CLASP Bulletin. Vol. 1, No. 1/2 (Aug./Sept.)-. Bulletin. English. bm. $9.00. CLASP, PO Box 65369, Station F, Vancouver BC V5N 5P3 Canada. **DD** 323.4/0971.

SW
**BULLETIN FRANCOPHONE DE LIAISON ET DE DOCUMENTATION SUR LES DROITS DE L'HOMME.** No. 1 (1988)-. Bulletin. French. qt. Association Consult International Droits Homme, CID, Case Postale 529, CH-1211, Geneva Switzerland. **LC** Z7164.L6; B85; JC571. **DD** 016.323.

GW
**BULLETIN / GDR COMMITTEE FOR HUMAN RIGHTS.** **Added/Corp** DDR-Komitee fur Menschenrechte. (1975)-. Bulletin. English (German). Three times a year. Free. Sekreteriat of the GDR, Committee for Human Rights, Otto-Grotewohl Str 19, Berlin DDR 1080 Germany. **Tel** 22-51-24-74 OR 22-51-24-75. **LC** K4; .D17. **DD** 341.4/81/05. Index available. **Bk Rev.** ctrl circ. ***Continues*** *Information (DDR-Komitee fur Menschenrechte).*
**Desc:** Supports international cooperation in promoting human rights in the interest of securing peace, understanding among peoples and social progress.
**Ind/Abst** Hum. Rights Intern. Rep.

IE/0332-1584
**BULLETIN / IRISH COUNCIL FOR CIVIL LIBERTIES.** [Bull. - Ir. Counc. Civ. Lib.]. **Main/Corp** Irish Council for Civil Liberties. (1977)-. Bulletin. English. Irish Council for Civil Liberties, Liberty Hall, Room 2, Ground Floor, Dublin 1, Ireland.
**Ind/Abst** Hum. Rights Intern. Rep.

US/0897-1358
**BULLETIN / LAWYERS COMMITTEE FOR HUMAN RIGHTS.** [Bull. - Lawyers Comm. Hum. Rights (U. S.)]. **Added/Corp** Lawyers Committee for Human Rights (U.S.). **VFOAT** LCHR Bulletin. Vol. 5, No. 2 (Summer 1985)-. Bulletin. English. The Lawyers Committee for Human Rights, 330 7th Avenue/10th Floor, New York NY 10001-5010. **DD** 341. ***Continues*** *Bulletin (Lawyers Committee for International Human Rights).*
**Ind/Abst** Hum. Rights Intern. Rep.

HT
**BULLETIN - LIQUE HAITIENNE DES DROITS HUMAINS.** **Main/Corp** Ligue Haitienne des Droits Humains. No. 1- Mar. 1978-. Bulletin. French. Ligue Haitienne des Droits Humains, 11 rue Tertullien Guilbaud, Bourdon Port-Au-Prince Haiti. **LC** JC599.H2; L54. **DD** 323.4/097294.

SZ
**BULLETIN OF HUMAN RIGHTS.** **Added/Corp** United Nations. Division of Human Rights. **VFOAT** Bulletin des Droits de l'Homme. No. 19 (Jan./March 1978)-. Bulletin. English. qt. United Nations Division of Human Rights, Bureau 143/Palais des Nations, Geneve 1211 Switzerland. **Tel** 011 41 22 7346011. **LC** K3236.2; .H85. **DD** 323.4/05. ***Continues*** *Human Rights Bulletin.*

US/0741-5788
**BULWARK (CHICAGO, ILL.), THE.** (THE BULWARK : A PROJECT OF CITIZENS IN DEFENSE OF CIVIL LIBERTIES.). Vol. 1, No. 1 (Fall 1983)-. Periodical. English. qt. Political Research Associates, 678 Massachusetts Avenue, Suite 702, Cambridge MA 02139-3355. **Tel** (617)661-9313. **LC** KF4742; .B85. **DD** 342.73/085347.30285. ***Continues*** *National Lawyers Guild. Civil Liberties Committee. Newsletter.*

FR
**CAHIERS SLAVES.** **Added/Corp** Maison des Dciences de l'Homme d'Aquitaine. Centre d'Etudes et de Recherches sur les Civilisations Slaves. (19??)-. French. an. Institut d'Etudes Slaves, 9 rue Michelet, 75006 Paris France. **Tel** 011 33 1 43265089. **LC** DJK24; .C34. **DD** 947/.0005.

CH
**CAHR NEWSLETTER.** **Added/Corp** Chung-kuo jen Chuan Hsieh hui. **VFOAT** Chinese Association for Human Rights Newsletter. Vol. 1, No. 1 (May 1986)-. Newsletter. English. qt.
**Ind/Abst** Hum. Rights Intern. Rep.

UK
**CAMEROON MONITOR : BULLETIN OF THE COMMITTEE FOR HUMAN RIGHTS IN CAMEROON.** **Added/Corp** Committee for Human Rights in Cameroon. **VFOAT** Bulletin of the Committee for Human Rights in Cameroon. Vol. 1, No. 1 (Feb. 1986)-. Bulletin. English. qt. Committee for Human Rights in Cameroon, BM Box 551, London WC1N 3XX, United Kingdom. **LC** JC599.C17; C35. **DD** 323.4/9/096711.
**Ind/Abst** Hum. Rights Intern. Rep.

CN
**CAMINANDO!.** (19??)-. French. Four times a year. 20.00Can$ Canada; 23.00Can$ other. Comite Chretien pour les Droits Humaines en Amerique Latine, 25 rue Jarry Quest, Montreal Quebec H2P 1S6, Canada. **Tel** (514)387-2541.
**Ind/Abst** Hum. Rights Intern. Rep.

CN/0226-2177
**CANADIAN HUMAN RIGHT REPORTER.** [Can. hum. rights rep.]. Vol. 1, Decision 1(Jan. 1980)-. English (French). ir (ten issues a year). 375.00Can$ Canada; 395.00Can$ other. Canadian Human Rights Reporter, 1662 West 75th Avenue, Vancouver BC V6P 6G2 Canada. **Tel** (604)266-5322. **ED** Shelagh Day. **DD** 342.71/085. Index available. cum. index. **Bk Rev. Circ:** 800 (ctrl).
**Desc:** Full text case reports of all human rights decisions (federal and provincial) in Canada plus expert commentary on emerging issues.
**Ind/Abst** Can. Legal Lit.; Hum. Rights Intern. Rep.

CN/0824-5266
**CANADIAN HUMAN RIGHTS YEARBOOK.** [Can. hum. rights yearb.]. **VFOAT** Annuaire Canadien des Droits de la Personne. 1983-. English (French). an. 37.50Can$. Carswell / Canada, 2075 Kennedy Road, Scarborough Ontario M1T 3V4 Canada. **Tel** (416)609-3800, (800)387-5164. **ED** William Pentney and Daniel Proulx. **LC** K3; .A493. **DD** 342.71/085; 347.10285.
**Desc:** Highlights recent developments in the Canadian and international law of human rights.
**Ind/Abst** Can. Legal Lit.; Index Can. Leg. Period. Lit.; Index Foreign Leg. Per.

CN/0715-4860
**CANADIAN RIGHTS REPORTER. SECOND SERIES.** **Added/Corp** Butterworth & Co. (Canada). 2d (1991)-. Periodical. English. 120.00Can$. Butterworth & Company Ltd. / Canada, 75 Clegg Road, Markham Ontario L6G 1A1 Canada. **Tel** (905)479-2665, (800)668-6481.
**Desc:** Reports cases decided under the Canadian Charter of Rights and Freedoms.

AT
**CARPA BULLETIN.** **Main/Corp** Committee Against Repression in the Pacific and Asia. No. 1 (1978)-. Bulletin. English. qt. GOH Siong Hoe, PO Box K717, Haymarket New South Wales 2000 Australia.
**Ind/Abst** Hum. Rights Intern. Rep.

UY
**CARTA SERPAJ URUGUAY.** **Added/Corp** Servicio Paz y Justicia (Uruguay). **VFOAT** Carta SERPAJ. (198?)-. Periodical. Spanish. mo.
**Ind/Abst** Hum. Rights Intern. Rep.

US/0273-0642
**CASE DIGEST (LANSING).** (CASE DIGEST - MICHIGAN. CIVIL RIGHTS COMMISSION.). [Case dig.]. **Main/Corp** Michigan. Civil Rights Commission. Began with 1964/75 issue. English. $100.00. Michigan Department of Civil Rights, Leonard Plaza/Main Floor, 309 North Washington Square, Lansing MI 48933. **Tel** (916)443-2017. **LC** KFM4611.A59; M53. **DD** 344.774/01133.

US
**CASE ENFORCEMENT REPORT / DISTRICT OF COLUMBIA, OFFICE OF HUMAN RIGHTS.** **Main/Corp** District of Columbia. Office of Human Rights. **VFOAT** Annual Case Enforcement Report. (19??)-. English. an. Office of Human Rights / District of Columbia, 420 7th Street NW/2nd Floor, Washington DC 20004. **LC** JC599.U52; W332a. **DD** 352.94/11/09753.

US
**CATHOLIC LEAGUE FOR RELIGIOUS & CIVIL RIGHTS NEWSLETTER.** Newsletter. English. mo. $25.00. Catholic League for Religious & Civil Rights, 6324 W North Avenue, Wauwatosa WI 53213. **Tel** (414) 476-8911, 800 927-0056, FAX (414) 476-9511.

CN
**CCLA NEWS NOTES.** Canadian Civil Liberties Association, 229 Yonge Street; Suite 403, Toronto, Ontario M5B 1N9, Canada. **Tel** (416)363-0321.
**Ind/Abst** Hum. Rights Intern. Rep.

US
**CDHES / COMISION DE DERECHOS HUMANOS DE EL SALVADOR.** **Added/Corp** Comision de Derechos Humanos de El Salvador. **VAT** Comision de Derechos Humanos de El Salvador. (198?)-. Periodical. English. mo. ***Continues*** *Monthly Bulletin (Comision de Derechos Humanos de El Salvador).*
**Ind/Abst** Hum. Rights Intern. Rep.

UK/0267-4130
**CENTRAL AMERICA REPORT.** **Added/Corp** El Salvador Committee for Human Rights (London, England) Guatemala Committee for Human Rights (London, England). Issue 16 (Feb./Mar. 1984)-. Newsletter. English. bm. Central America Human Rights Committee / CAHRC, 83 Margaret Street, London W1N 7HB England. **Tel** 011 44 71 6314200, FAX 011 44 71 4361129. **ED** Andrew McEntee. Index available. cum. index. **Bk Rev**, (Qty: 12). **Circ:** 2,000. ***Continues*** *El Salvador Report (London, England), 0264-2263.*
**Ind/Abst** Hum. Rights Intern. Rep.

US/0893-8970
**CHAR-KOOSTA NEWS.** [Char-Koosta news]. **VFOAT** CSKT'S Char-Koosta News. Periodical. English. wk. Char-Koosta News, PO Box 278, Pablo MT 59855. **Tel** (406)675-2700. **DD** 323. ***Continues*** *Char-Koosta, 0528-8592.*

CN/0821-719X
**CHARTER OF RIGHTS DECISIONS.** (CHARTER OF RIGHTS DECISIONS : PROVIDING A DIGESTING SERVICE, BY SUBJECT, OF ALL DECISIONS RELATING TO CANADIAN BILL OF RIGHTS (1960) AND CANADIAN CHARTER OF RIGHTS AND FREEDOMS (1982).). [Chart. Rights decis.]. **Added/Corp** Canada. Canadian Bill of Rights. Canada. Canadian Charter of Rights and Freedoms. **VFOAT** Canadian Charter of Rights & Freedoms. Vol. 1 (1982)-. Periodical. English. ir. 400.00Can$. Western Legal Publications Ltd., 301 One Alexander Street, Vancouver BC V6A 1B2 Canada. **Tel** (800)663-0422, (604)687-5671. **DD** 342.71/085/02648.

CN/0838-4843
**CHARTER OF RIGHTS NEWSLETTER.** [Chart. rights newsl.]. **Added/Corp** Canada Law Book Inc. **VFOAT** Charter of Rights. Vol. 1, No. 1 (May 1988)-. Newsletter. English. Ten times a year. 107.00Can$. Canada Law Book Inc., 240 Edward Street, Aurora Ontario L4G 3S9 Canada. **Tel** (800)263-3269, (905)841-6472, FAX (905)841-5085. **ED** David J. Martin. **DD** 342.71/085.
**Desc:** Equips readers with an up-to-the-minute analysis of Charter issues and trends. Allows readers to quickly familiarize themselves with the most important recent Charter developments supported by the Supreme Court of Canada and Courts of Appeal rulings which contain new guidelines for the interpretation of individual Charter provisions or which signal new judicial trends in the application of the Charter.

US/0149-5372
**CHECKLIST OF HUMAN RIGHTS DOCUMENTS.** V. 1- Jan./May 1976-. English. mo. $75.00. Earl M Coleman Entp Inc, PO Box T, Crugers NY 10521. **Tel** (518)398-7193. **LC** K3236; .C54. **DD** 016.34208/5. ***Supersedes*** *Checklist of Human Rights Documents, 0149-5372.*

US/0300-6921
**CHICAGO REPORTER, THE.** **Added/Corp** Community Renewal Society (Chicago, Ill.). (1972)-. Periodical. English. mo (July/Aug. issues combined). $28.00 (one year), $50.00 (two year). Community Renewal Society, 332 South Michigan Avenue, Chicago IL 60604. **Tel** (312)236-4830, FAX (312)427-6130. **ED** Laura Washington. **LC** F548.9.N3; C54. **DD** 301.45/19/60730773. Index available. **Circ:** 4,500.
**Desc:** Investigates and identifies analyzes reports on the social, economic and political issues of metropolitan Chicago with a special focus on race and poverty.

UK
**CHILD LABOUR SERIES.** **Added/Corp** Anti-Slavery Society for the Protection of Human Rights (Great Britain). (1978)-. Monographic series. English. **LC** UNC.
**Ind/Abst** Hum. Rights Intern. Rep.

UK/0265-1459
**CHILDRIGHT.** **See** Children and Youth Interests.

US
**CHILE ACTION BULLETIN ON POLITICAL PRISONERS AND HUMAN RIGHTS.** **VFOAT** Chile Action Bulletin. Bulletin. English. bm. Bay Area Nich, 3105 Shattuck Avenue, Berkeley CA 94705.

## Political Science — Civil Rights

●US/1068-4166
**CHINA RIGHTS FORUM.** (CHINA RIGHTS FORUM. JEN YU JEN CHUAN.). [China rights forum]. **Added/Corp** Human Rights in China (Organization). **VFOAT** Jen Yu Jen Chuan; Human Rights in China. (Spring 1993)-. Periodical. English (Chinese). qt. $30.00 (institutions) $25.00 (individuals) US; $35.00 (institutions), $30.00 (individuals) other. Human Rights in China Inc, 485 5th Avenue, 3rd floor, New York NY 10017. **Tel** (212)661-2909, FAX (212)972-09005. **ED** Sophia Woodman. **LC** JC599.C6; H87. **DD** 323.4/9/0951. **Bk Rev**, (Qty: 4-10). *Continues Human Rights Tribune, 1057-0748.*

CL
**CHIP NEWS [COMPUTER FILE] / [COMPILED BY] STEVE ANDERSON.** **Added/Corp** Chile Information Project. Catholic Church. Archdiocese of Santiago (Chile). Vicaria de la Solidaridad. **VFOAT** Chile News. (19??)-. Periodical. English. da. Chile Information Project, Santiago Chile.
**Desc:** Summarizes articles from Chilean newspapers concerning human rights, political and environmental issues.

US
**CIVIL LIBERTIES ALERT : A LEGISLATIVE NEWSLETTER OF THE AMERICAN CIVIL LIBERTIES UNION/WASHINGTON OFFICE.** **Added/Corp** American Civil Liberties Union. Washington Office. Vol. 1, No. 1 (Jan. 1978)-. Periodical. English. an (Dec.). Free. American Civil Liberties Union / Washington, 122 Maryland Avenue Northeast, Washington DC 20002. **Tel** (202)544-1681, FAX (202)546-0738. **ED** Susan Hansen.
**Desc:** For those who actively participate in legislative lobbying. A national legislative report published at the end of each legislative year. Includes congressional voting records on selected votes and informs readers about important legislation in the Congress concerning civil liberties.

US/0749-3061
**CIVIL LIBERTIES IN TEXAS. Suspended.** (CIVIL LIBERTIES IN TEXAS / TEXAS CIVIL LIBERTIES UNION.). Suspended (Jan. 1992). Periodical. English. Texas Civil Liberties Union, 1611 East 1st Street, Austin TX 78702-4455. **DD** 323.

US/0009-790X
**CIVIL LIBERTIES (NEW YORK, N.Y.).** (CIVIL LIBERTIES.). [Civil lib.]. **Added/Corp** American Civil Liberties Union. No. 74 (Sept. 1949)-. English. sa. $20.00. American Civil Liberties Union, 132 West 43rd Street, New York NY 10036. **Tel** (212)944-9800 ext 422. **ED** Jean Carey Bond. **LC** JC599.U5; A45. **DD** 323.4/0973. **Circ**: 250,000. *Continues Civil Liberties Quarterly.*
**Desc:** Reports on the ACLU's litigation, legislative lobbying and public education efforts in defense of free speech, equal protection and other constitutional rights.
**Ind/Abst** Altern. Press Index; Chicano Index.

US
**CIVIL RIGHTS. Added/Corp** Civil Rights League (South Africa). (Jan. 1957)-. Periodical. English. **LC** Microfilm 89/2569. *Continues Civil Rights League (South Africa) News Letter.*
**Ind/Abst** Hum. Rights Intern. Rep.

US
**CIVIL RIGHTS & CIVIL LIBERTIES LITIGATION : A GUIDE TO [SECTION SYMBOL] 1983 / SHELDON H. NAHMOD.** English. ir. $170.00 (2 volumes). Shepards McGraw-Hill Inc, 555 Middle Creek Parkway, PO Box 35300, Colorado Springs CO 80935-3530. **Tel** (719)488-3000, FAX (800)525-0053. cum. index. **Bk Rev. Ad Acc.**
**Desc:** This dynamic text has been cited as an authority in many federal decisions and law reviews.

US/0360-1587
**CIVIL RIGHTS DIRECTORY.** (CIVIL RIGHTS DIRECTORY / U.S. COMMISSION ON CIVIL RIGHTS.). [Civ. rights dir.]. **Added/Corp** United States Commission on Civil Rights. (19??)-. Directory. English. US Commission on Civil Rights, 1121 Vermont Avenue/Room 700, Washington DC 20425. **Tel** (202)254-6600. **LC** KF4755; .A83 subser; JC599.U45. **DD** 323.4/0973 S.

US/0887-1191
**CIVIL RIGHTS LITIGATION AND ATTORNEY FEES ANNUAL HANDBOOK.** [Civ. rights litig. atty. fees annu. handb.]. **Added/Corp** Clark Boardman Company. Vol. 1 (1985)-. English. an. $85.00. Clark Boardman Callaghan, 155 Pfingsten Road, Deerfield IL 60015. **Tel** (800)323-8067. **LC** KF1325.C58; C58. **DD** 342.73/085; 347.30285.
**Desc:** Handbook featuring collection of original articles on articles on various aspects of civil rights actions; for lawyers.

US
**CIVIL RIGHTS MONITOR.** English. bm. $35.00. Leadership Conference Education Fund, 1629 K Street Northwest, Suite 1010, Washington DC 20006. **Tel** (202)466-3311, FAX (202)466-3435.

US/0893-0473
**CIVIL RIGHTS UPDATE.** (CIVIL RIGHTS UPDATE / UNITED STATES COMMISSION ON CIVIL RIGHTS.). [Civ. rights update]. **Added/Corp** United States Commission on Civil Rights. (Jan. 1978-June 1989; Jan./Feb 1991)-. Periodical. English. bm. US Commission on Civil Rights, 1121 Vermont Avenue/Room 700, Washington DC 20425. **Tel** (202)254-6600. **DD** 323.
**Ind/Abst** Hum. Rights Intern. Rep.

CN/0824-7552
**CIVIL RIGHTS (VANCOUVER).** (CIVIL RIGHTS.). [Civ. rights]. 7th Ed. (1984)-. English. $8.95 per no. International Self-Counsel Press, Head and Editorial Office, 1481 Charlotte Road, Vancouver British Columbia V7J 1H1 Canada. **Tel** (604)986-3947. **DD** 342.71/085. *Continues Civil Rights in Canada, 0824-7560.*

BL
**CLAMOR / COMMITTEE FOR THE DEFENSE OF HUMAN RIGHTS IN THE SOUTHERN CONE, SAO PAULO'S ARCHDIOCESAN PASTORAL COMMISSION FOR HUMAN RIGHTS AND THE MARGINALIZED. Added/Corp** Committee for the Defense of Human Rights in the Southern Cone. No. 1 (June 1978)-. Periodical. English. **LC** JC599.S57; C58. **DD** 323.4/9/098.
**Ind/Abst** Hum. Rights Intern. Rep.

NE
**CLS BULLETIN / PUBLISHED BY THE COUNCIL FOR THE LIBERATION OF SURINAME. Added/Corp** Council for the Liberation of Suriname (Netherlands). **VAT** Council for the Liberation of Suriname Bulletin. (1985)-. Bulletin. English. mo. CLS Council for the Liberation of Suriname, PO Box 5517, 3008 AM Rotterdam, Holland, Netherlands.
**Ind/Abst** Hum. Rights Intern. Rep.

HO
**CODEH : [BOLETIN] / COMITE PARA LA DEFENSA DE LOS DERECHOS HUMANOS EN HONDURAS. Added/Corp** Comite para la Defensa de los Derechos Humanos en Honduras. (19??)-. Periodical. Spanish. bm. **LC** JC599.H6; C63. **DD** 323.4/9/09283.
**Ind/Abst** Hum. Rights Intern. Rep.

US
**CODEPU FIFTH REGION BOLETIN.** (19??)-. Periodical. English. Ten times a year. $20.00 individuals; $35.00 institutions. Chile Information Network, Chile Center, Box 20179, Cathedral Finance Station, New York NY 10025. **Tel** (212)928-7600.

US/0413-7949
**COLORADO CIVIL LIBERTIES.** **Added/Corp** American Civil Liberties Union. Colorado. (1977)-. Periodical. English. bm (6 issues). $20.00. Colorado Civil Liberties, 1711 Pennsylvania Street, Denver CO 80302.

US/0090-7944
**COLUMBIA HUMAN RIGHTS LAW REVIEW.** [Columbia human rights law rev.]. **Added/Corp** Columbia University. School of Law. Vol. 4 (Winter 1972)-. English. Three times a year. $30.00. Columbia University School of Law, 435 West 116th Street, New York NY 10027. **Tel** (212)854-4398, (212)854-3742. **LC** K3; .O36. **DD** 344/.73/08505. **Bk Rev. Ad Acc. Circ:** 600 (ctrl). available on microfilm and microfiche from University Microfilms International (UMI). *Continues Columbia Survey of Human Rights Law, 0010-2008.*
**Desc:** Publishes professional and student articles on public interest themes arising from the interaction of human rights, the law and people's lives.
**Ind/Abst** Curr. Law Index (1980-); Hum. Rights Intern. Rep.; Index Leg. Period.; Leg. Resour. Index (1980-); LegalTrac (1980-].

US/0730-9988
**COMMITTEE REPORT / LAWYERS' COMMITTEE FOR CIVIL RIGHTS UNDER LAW.** [Comm. rep. - Lawyers' Comm. Civ. Rights Under Law]. **Added/Corp** Lawyers' Committee for Civil Rights Under Law. Vol. 1, No. 1 (Winter 1987)-. Periodical. English. qt. $20.00. Lawyers Committee for Civil Rights Under Law, 1450 G Street Northwest, Suite 400, Washington DC 20005. **Tel** (202)662-8600. **DD** 342. *Continues Lawyers' Committee for Civil Rights Under Law. Committee Report, 0730-9988.*
**Ind/Abst** Hum. Rights Intern. Rep.

TH/0857-491X
**CONTOURS BANGKOK.** [Contours Bangkok]. (1985)-. Periodical. English. qt. $12.00. Contours, PO Box 24 Chorakhebua, Bangkok 10230 Thailand. **Tel** 011 66 2 5107287. **DD** 910.41.
**Ind/Abst** Hum. Rights Intern. Rep.

US/1046-6231
**CONVERGENCE (WASHINGTON, D.C.). Suspended.** (CONVERGENCE / THE CHRISTIC INSTITUTE.). [Convergence]. **Added/Corp** Christic Institute. (1980)-(19??). Periodical. English. Twice a year. $25.00. Christic Institute, 1324 North Capitol Street Northwest, Washington DC 20002. **Tel** (310)287-1556. **DD** 353.
**Ind/Abst** Hum. Rights Intern. Rep.

US
**CONVERSION PLANNER, THE.** Vol. 1, (197?)-. Periodical. English. bm. Sane, 514 C Street Northeast, Washington DC 20002.

US
**COPRED PEACE CHRONICLE.** English. Consortium on Peace Research, Education and Development (COPRED), 4400 University Drive, Mason University, Fairfax VA 22030. **Tel** (703) 764-6515.
**Ind/Abst** Hum. Rights Intern. Rep.

US/0300-743X
**CORE. Main/Corp** Congress of Racial Equality. (19??)-. Periodical. English. qt. $10.00. Core, 30 Cooper Square, New York NY 10003. **Tel** (212)598-4000. **LC** E185.5; .C87. **DD** 322.4/4/0973. *Supersedes CORE-Lator, 0526-6769.*
**Ind/Abst** Br. Educ. Index.

US
**CORNELL STUDIES IN CIVIL LIBERTY. Main/Corp** Cornell University. (19??)-. Monographic series. English. ir. Price varies per volume. Cornell University Press, 124 Roberts Place, Ithaca NY 14853. **Tel** (607)277-2338.

US
**COUNCIL FOR HUMAN RIGHTS IN LATIN AMERICA NEWSLETTER, THE.** **Added/Corp** Council for Human Rights in Latin America (Eugene, Or.). **VFOAT** CHRLA Newsletter; Newsletter. (19??)-. Newsletter. English. Council for Human Rights in Latin America Newsletter, 1236 Kincaid Street, Eugene OR 97401.
**Ind/Abst** Hum. Rights Intern. Rep.

US/0198-9669
**COUNTRY REPORTS ON HUMAN RIGHTS PRACTICES.** (COUNTRY REPORTS ON HUMAN RIGHTS PRACTICES : REPORT SUBMITTED TO THE COMMITTEE ON FOREIGN RELATIONS, U.S. SENATE AND COMMITTEE ON FOREIGN AFFAIRS, U.S. HOUSE OF REPRESENTATIVES BY THE DEPARTMENT OF STATE IN ACCORDANCE WITH SECTIONS 116(D) AND 502B(B) OF THE FOREIGN ASSISTANCE ACT OF 1961, AS AMENDED.). [Ctry. rep. hum. rights pract.]. **Added/Corp** United States. Dept. of State. United States. Congress. House. Committee on Foreign Affairs. United States. Congress. Senate. Committee on Foreign Relations. (1979)-. Government Publication. English. an. Superintendent of Documents, US Government Printing Office, Washington DC 20402. **Tel** (202)275-3328, FAX (202)786-2377. **LC** JC571; .U48a. **DD** 323.4/05. available on microfiche (Vols. for (1986-) distributed to some depository libraries). *Continues Report on Human Rights Practices in Countries Receiving U.S. Aid.*

FR
**COURRIER DE L'A.C.A.T. / ACTION DES CHRETIENS POUR L'ABOLITION DE LA TORTURE. Added/Corp** Action des Chretiens pour l'Abolition de la Torture. **VFOAT** Courrier de l'ACAT. (197?)-. Periodical. French. mo.
**Ind/Abst** Hum. Rights Intern. Rep.

US/1056-8093
**CPJ UPDATE. Title Change.** (CPJ UPDATE / COMMITTEE TO PROTECT JOURNALISTS.). [CPJ update]. **Added/Corp** Committee to Protect Journalists. **VAT** Committee to Protect Journalists Update. (198?)-(199?). Periodical. English. qt. Committee to Protect Journalists, 330 Seventh Avenue 12th Floor, New York NY 10001. **Tel** (212)465-1004. **LC** PN4735; .C67. **DD** 302.44/5/05. *Continued by Dangerous Assignments, 1073-4741X.*
**Ind/Abst** Hum. Rights Intern. Rep.

US/0749-3177
**CRD NEWS / COMMITTEE FOR THE RIGHTS OF THE DISABLED.** [CRD news!]. **VFOAT** C.R.D. News. **VAT** Committee for the Rights of the Disabled News. Periodical. English. bm. Committee for the Disabled, 2487 W Washington Boulevard, Los Angeles CA 90018-1458. **DD** 344.

US
**CRIMINAL JUSTICE ISSUES. Added/Corp** United Church of Christ. Commission for Racial Justice. (1974)-. Periodical. English.
**Ind/Abst** Hum. Rights Intern. Rep.

JA/0911-7482
**CROWNED WITH THORNS.** [Crowned Thorns]. **VFOAT** Newsletter of Buraku Liberation Center, the Nihon Kirisuto Kyodan; Newsletter of the Nihon Kirisuto Kyodan Buraku Liberation Center. (1984)-. Periodical. English. tq (Feb., June and Oct.). $3.00. Buraku Liberation Center, 3 23 Minamino 5 Chome, Shijonawateshi Osaka, 575 Japan. **Tel** 011 81 720 79-6456. **DD** 301.45.
**Ind/Abst** Hum. Rights Intern. Rep.

CK
**CSPP BOLETIN. Added/Corp** Comite de Solidaridad con los Presos Politicos (Bogota, Colombia). (19??)-. Periodical. Spanish.
**Ind/Abst** Hum. Rights Intern. Rep.

US/0740-3291
**CULTURAL SURVIVAL QUARTERLY.** [Cult. surv. q.]. **Added/Corp** Cultural Survival Inc. Vol. 6, No. 3 (Summer 1982)-. Periodical. English. Four times a year. $60.00. Cultural Survival Inc., 215 First Street, Cambridge MA 02142. **Tel** (617)621-3818, FAX (617)621-3814. **ED** Amy Grunder. **LC** GN380; .N478. **DD** 306/.08/05. Index available. cum. index. **Ad Acc. Circ:** 8,000 (ctrl). **Continues** Quarterly (Cultural Survival Inc.).
 **Desc:** Addresses issues of immediate and long-term concern to indigenous peoples throughout the world. Serves to inform the general public and policy makers in the U.S. and abroad to stimulate action on behalf of tribal people and ethnic minorities.
**Ind/Abst** Altern. Press Index; Anthropol. Lit. (-Vol. 11, 1989); Environ. Period. Bibliogr.; Geogr. Abstr. Phys. Geogr. (?-?); Geogr. Abstr. Human Geogr.; Hum. Rights Intern. Rep.; Int. Bibliogr. Sociol.; Int. Dev. Abstr.

CN/0820-3296
**CURRENTS / CANADA-ASIA WORKING GROUP.** [Curr. - Can. Asia Work. Group]. **Added/Corp** Canada Asia Working Group. **VFOAT** Human Rights in Asia. (1986)-. Periodical. English. qt. 25.00Can$ (institutions), 15.00Can$ (individuals). Canadian-Asia Working Group, 11 Madison Avenue, Toronto Ontario M5R 2S2 Canada. **Tel** (416)921-5626. **DD** 950/.428. **Continues** Canada Asia Currents./, 0228-2402.
**Ind/Abst** Hum. Rights Intern. Rep.

US/1073-841X
**DANGEROUS ASSIGNMENTS.** (DANGEROUS ASSIGNMENTS / CPJ, COMMITTEE TO PROTECT JOURNALISTS.). (1993)-. English. qt. Committee to Protect Journalists, 330 Seventh Avenue 12th Floor, New York NY 10001. **Tel** (212)465-1004. **Continues** CPJ Update, 1056-8093.

DK
**DANIZDAT. Added/Corp** International Sakharov Committee. Sakharov Hoeringens Komite. No. 1 (1976)-. Periodical. Danish. bm. Sakharov Hoeringens Komite, Copenhagen Denmark.
**Ind/Abst** Hum. Rights Intern. Rep.

GW/0173-7767
**DATENSCHUTZ-NACHRICHTEN.** [Datenschutz-Nachr.]. **VFOAT** DANA. Datenschutz-Nachrichten. (1978)-. Periodical. German. tq. Dm33.00 Germany; DM45.00 other Europe; DM60.00 other. Deutsche Vereinigung fuer Datenschutz, Reuterstr 44, D-53118 Bonn Germany. **Tel** 011 49 228 222498. **UDC** 343.45:659.27:681.3.
 **Desc:** Civil rights and data protection news.

US
**DECENCY REPORTER / CHILDREN'S LEGAL FOUNDATION.** See Law.

FR/0379-8461
**DECISIONS AND REPORTS - EUROPEAN COMMISSION OF HUMAN RIGHTS.** (DECISIONS AND REPORTS / COUNCIL OF EUROPE [AND] EUROPEAN COMMISSION FOR HUMAN RIGHTS / DECISIONS ET RAPPORTS / CONSEIL DE L'EUROPE [ET] COMMISSION EUROPEENNE DES DROITS DE L'HOMME.). [Decis. rep. - Eur. Comm. Hum. Rights]. **Main/Corp** European Commission of Human Rights. **VFOAT** Decisions et Rapports. (1975)-. Multiple languages (English and French). ir. Manhattan Publishing Company, PO Box 650, Croton-on-Hudson NY 10520. **Tel** (914)271-5194. (**Subscription address:** Moniteur Belge Belg Staatsbald, rue de Louvain 40-42, 1000 Brussels Belgium.) Index available. cum. index. **Circ:** 10,000. **Continues** European Commission of Human Rights. Collection of Decisions of the European Commission of Human Rights, 0304-0127.

US/0744-186X
**DEFENDER (DES MOINES, IOWA), THE.** (THE DEFENDER : NEWSLETTER OF THE IOWA CIVIL LIBERTIES UNION.). Newsletter. English. qt. American Civil Liberties, 409 Shops Building, Des Moines IA 50309-3627.

EC
**DERECHOS DEL PUEBLO / COMISION ECUMENICA DE DERECHOS HUMANOS, LOS. Added/Corp** Comision Ecumenica de Derechos Humanos (Ecuador). (198?)-. Periodical. Spanish. bm. Comision Ecumenica de Derechos Humanos, Apartado 720-A 10 de Ahosto, 2730 Y Orellana, Quito, Ecuador.
**Ind/Abst** Hum. Rights Intern. Rep.

CL
**DERECHOS HUMANOS EN CHILE / ARZOBISPADO DE SANTIAGO, VICARIA DE LA SOLIDARIDAD. Added/Corp** Catholic Church. Archdiocese of Santiago (Chile). Vicaria de la Solidaridad. (19??)-. Spanish.
**Ind/Abst** Hum. Rights Intern. Rep.

NQ
**DERECHOS HUMANOS EN NICARAGUA. Added/Corp** Comision Nacional de Promocion y Proteccion de los Derechos Humanos (Nicaragua). **VFOAT** Human Rights in Nicaragua. (198?)-. Periodical. English (Spanish).
**Ind/Abst** Hum. Rights Intern. Rep.

SP
**DERECHOS HUMANOS : TRIBUNA INFORMATIVA / ASOCIACION PRO DERECHOS HUMANOS. Added/Corp** Asociacion Pro Derechos Humanos de Espana. (Mar. 1983)-. Periodical. Spanish.
**Ind/Abst** Hum. Rights Intern. Rep.

MX
**DERHECHOS HUMANOS / ACADEMIA MEXICANA DE DERECHOS HUMANOS. Added/Corp** Academia Mexicana de Derechos Humanos. **VFOAT** Derechos Humanos. (1990)-. Periodical. Spanish. bm. **LC** JC599.M4; D47. **DD** 323/.098. **Continues** Boletin (Academia Mexicana de Derechos Humanos).

CN/0229-0812
**DIGEST ON GAY RIGHTS.** (DIGEST ON GAY RIGHTS : I, HUMAN-CIVIL RIGHTS LEGISLATION / GAYS FOR EQUALITY.). [Dig. gay rights]. Periodical. English. an. Free. Gays for Equality, Box 1661, Winnipeg Manitoba R3C 2Z6 Canada. **Tel** (204)945-6660. **ED** Chris Vogel. **DD** 323.3. **Circ:** 2,000.
 **Desc:** Aggregated accumulation of historical and current status of human/civil rights laws, support, employment policies for homosexuals.

●US
**DOCKET : A JOURNAL OF THE INTERNATIONAL HUMAN RIGHTS LAW GROUP. Added/Corp** International Human Rights Law Group (Washington, D.C.). Vol. 8, No. 2 (Nov. 1993)-. Periodical. English. sa. $15.00 US and Canada; $20.00 other. International Human Rights Law Group, 733 15th Street NW, Suite 1000, Washington DC 20005. **Tel** (202) 639-8016. **LC** K3236.2; .L36. **DD** 323.4/05. **Continues** Law Group Docket.

PK/1018-1342
**DOSSIER - WOMEN LIVING UNDER MUSLIM LAWS.** See Women's Interests.

FR/0012-6411
**DROIT & LIBERTE : ORGANE MENSUEL DE MOUVEMENT CONTER LE RACISME, L'ANTISEMITISME, ET POUR LA PAIX.** Ceased. **VFOAT** Droit et Liberte. (1942)-?. Periodical. French. ir. Societe Droit et Liberte, 89 rue Oberkampf, 75011 Paris France. **Tel** 1 806 8800. **LC** WMLC L 83/1218.
**Ind/Abst** Hum. Rights Intern. Rep.

CN/0826-7766
**DROITS DE LA PERSONNE. BULLETIN D'INFORMATION SUR LA RECHERCHE ET L'ENSEIGNEMENT.** (HUMAN RIGHTS : RESEARCH AND EDUCATION BULLETIN.). [Droits pers., Bull inf. rech. enseign.]. **Added/Corp** University of Ottawa. Human Rights Research and Education Centre. **VFOAT** Droits de la Personne. No. 1 (Nov. 1984)-. Periodical. English (French). Four times a year. 24.30Can$ (institutions); 18.70Can$ (individuals). Human Rights Research Education Centre, University of Ottawa, 57 Copernicus, Ottawa Ontario K1N 6N5 Canada. **Tel** (613)564-4033. **ED** Ivana Caccia. **DD** 323.4/0971.
 **Desc:** Contains information on new publications, events and organizations related to human rights in Canada and abroad.
**Ind/Abst** Hum. Rights Intern. Rep.

BE/0776-0256
**DROITS DE L'HOMME SANS FRONTIERES.** [Droits homme sans front.]. (1988)-. Periodical. French. mo. **UDC** 342.7.
**Ind/Abst** Hum. Rights Intern. Rep.

SZ/0257-1676
**DROITS ET LIBERTES EN SYRIE.** [Droits lib. Syrie]. **VFOAT** Rights and Liberties in Syria. (1982)-. Periodical. French.
**Ind/Abst** Hum. Rights Intern. Rep.

CN
**EARTHBEAT.** See International Assistance and Development.

AT/0314-2825
**EAST TIMOR NEWS : BULLETIN OF THE EAST TIMOR NEWS AGENCY. Added/Corp** East Timor News Agency. Began with issue for Feb. 24, (1977)-. Bulletin. English. bw.

HK
**ECHOES FROM TIANANMEN. Added/Corp** Friends of Chinese Minzhu. **VFOAT** Tien-an men Chih hui Hsiang. No. 1 (June 1989)-. Periodical. English. (**Subscription address:** Friends of Chinese Minzhu c/o Hong Kong Trade Union Education Centre, 57 Peking Road 3/F Kowloon, Hong Kong)
**Ind/Abst** Hum. Rights Intern. Rep.

JA/0287-2145
**ECHOES OF PEACE.** See Ethics.

UY
**EDUCACION Y DERECHOS HUMANOS : CUADERNOS PARA DOCENTES : PUBLICACION DEL SERVICIO PAZ Y JUSTICIA (URUGUAY). Added/Corp** Servicio Paz y Justicia (Uruguay). **VFOAT** Cuadernos para Docentes. (198?)-. Periodical. Spanish. qt. **LC** LC213; .E36. **DD** 370.11.
**Ind/Abst** Hum. Rights Intern. Rep.

US
**EL SALVADOR CHRONOLOGY. Added/Corp** El Rescate Human Rights Department. Vol. 2, No. 1 (Jan. 1987)-. English (Spanish). mo. $45.00. El Rescate Human Rights Dep, 2675 West Olympic Boulevard, Los Angeles CA 90006. **Tel** (213)387-3284. **Continues** Chronology El Salvador.
**Ind/Abst** Hum. Rights Intern. Rep.

UK/0261-0159
**EQUAL OPPORTUNITIES INTERNATIONAL.** See Economics-Labor.

UK
**EQUAL OPPORTUNITIES REVIEW. Added/Corp** Industrial Relations Services. (198?)-. Periodical. English. bm. £160.00 UK; £176.00 other. Eclipse Publications Ltd, 18 20 Highbury Place, London N5 1QP England. **Tel** 011 44 71 354 5858. (**Subscription address:** Industrial Relations Services, 18 20 Highbury Place, London N5 1QP England.) **ED** Gary Bowker, Micheal Rubenstein. **LC** KD3102.A13; E68. **DD** 344.41/01133/05; 344.104113305. Index available. cum. index. **Circ:** 1,500 (ctrl). Documents available from UMI Article Clearinghouse.
 **Desc:** Central source of information and documentation on equal opportunities law and employment practice in terms of sex, race, disability, religion and age.
**Ind/Abst** ABI/INFORM Glob. Ed.; Manage. Market. Abstr.

CN/0832-9370
**EQUITY (TORONTO. 1986).** (EQUITY.). [Equity]. **Added/Corp** Ontario Association of Legal Clinics. Vol. 1 No. 1 (Oct./Nov. 1986)-. Periodical. English. bm. Free to members of Ontario Association of Legal Clinics, $10.00 other. Equity, 700 Bay Street/Suite 2303, Toronto Ontario M5G 1Z6 Canada. **Tel** (416)965-2324. **DD** 346.71301/3. **Continues** Newsletter (Ontario Association of Legal Clinics), 0827-2379.

CN
**ESTIMATES. PART III, CANADIAN HUMAN RIGHTS COMMISSION. Main/Corp** Canada. **VFOAT** Budget des Depenses. Partie III, Commission Canadienne des Droits de la Personne. (19??)-. English (French). $3.00 Canada; $3.60 other. Canada Communication Group Publishers, Order Processing, Ottawa Ontario K1A 0S9 Canada. **Tel** (819)956-4800, (819)956-4802. **LC** JC599.C2; C35a. **DD** 354.710081/1.

AU/0014-2492
**EUROPA ETHNICA.** See Ethnic Interests.

GW/0341-9800
**EUROPAEISCHE GRUNDRECHTE - ZEITSCHRIFT.** (EUROPAEISCHE GRUNDRECHTE.). [Eur. Grundr. - Z.]. **VFOAT** EuGRZ. (1977)-. Periodical. German. Twenty-four times a year. DM362.80. N P Engel Verlag, Gutenbergstrasse 29, D-77694 Kehl Germany. **Tel** 011 49 7851 2463, FAX 011 49 7851 4234, telex 753 560. **ED** Thomas Buergenthal. **LC** LAW. Index available. **Bk Rev. Ad Acc. Circ:** 1,300 (ctrl). **Continues** Grundrechte.
 **Desc:** Provides an up-to-date systematic service reporting and commenting on international, constitutional and supreme court decisions in the human rights field from all over Europe.
**Ind/Abst** Energy Res. Abstr. (Nov. 1981-); Index Foreign Leg. Per.; Int. Polit. Sci. Abstr.

FR
**EUROPEAN CONVENTION ON HUMAN RIGHTS; COLLECTION OF DECISIONS OF NATIONAL COURTS REFERRING TO THE CONVENTION. Main/Corp** Council of Europe. Directorate of Human Rights. (19??)-. Monographic series. English. an. Kluwer Academic Publishers, Postbus 322, 3300 AH Dordrecht, The Netherlands. **Tel** 011 (31) 78 524400, FAX 011 31 78 183273, telex 20083.

UK/0260-4868
**EUROPEAN HUMAN RIGHTS REPORTS.** [Eur. hum. rights rep.]. **Added/Corp** European Commission of Human Rights. European Court of Human Rights. (Jan. 1979)-. Periodical. English. mo. £265.00 Europe; £278.00 other. Sweet & Maxwell Ltd., South Quay Plaza, 183 Marsh Wall, London E14 9FT England. **Tel** 011 44 264 342899, FAX 011 44 264 342723, telex 929089 ITPINF G. **ED** Peter J. Duffy. **LC** LAW. **DD** 341.4/81/02684. Index available. cum. index. **Ad Acc. Circ:** 400 (ctrl).
**Desc:** Includes all judgments of European Court of Human Rights; also contains selected decisions of European Commission of Human Rights and summaries of other such decisions, resolutions and settlements.

US/0014-6919
**FAIR EMPLOYMENT REPORT. See** Economics-Labor.

US
**FBI NEWS. Added/Corp** National Committee Against Repressive Legislation (U.S.). **VFOAT** Federal Bureau of Investigation News. (19??)-. Periodical. English. **LC** KF4770.A15; F35. ***Absorbed** Right to Know & the Freedom to Act.*
**Desc:** Information concerning civil rights.

US/0734-2454
**FEDERAL CIVIL RIGHTS ENFORCEMENT BUDGET, THE.** [Fed. civ. rights enforc. budg.]. English. US Commission on Civil Rights, 1121 Vermont Avenue/Room 700, Washington DC 20425. **Tel** (202)254-6600. **LC** KF4755; .A83 subser; JC599.U5. **DD** 353.0072/236811.

US
**FIRST FREEDOM : A NEWSLETTER OF THE PUEBLA INSTITUTE, THE. Added/Corp** Puebla Institute. Vol. 1, No. 1 (June 1988)-. Newsletter. English. bm.
**Ind/Abst** Hum. Rights Intern. Rep.

US/0363-0447
**FIRST PRINCIPLES.** (FIRST PRINCIPLES : NATIONAL SECURITY AND CIVIL LIBERTIES.). **Added/Corp** Center for National Security Studies (Washington, D.C.) Project on National Security and Civil Liberties. Vol. 1 (Sept. 1975)-. English. ir (four-six issues per year). $15.00 US; $20.00 Canada; $25.00 other. Center for National Security Study, 122 Maryland Avenue Northeast, Washington DC 20002. **Tel** (202)544-1681, FAX (202)546-0738. **ED** Rachel Fischer and Gary Stern. **LC** KF4742; .F57. **DD** 323.4/0973. **Circ:** 4,000.
**Desc:** Carries articles and commentaries on the relationship between national security and civil liberties.
**Ind/Abst** Hum. Rights Intern. Rep.; Index Period. Artic. Relat. Law.

CN/0838-6595
**FOCUS ON EQUALITY.** [Focus equal.]. **Added/Corp** Toronto Board of Education. Vol. 1, No. 1 (Jan. 1987)-. Periodical. English. Free. Toronto Board of Education, 155 College Street, Toronto Ontario M5T 1P6 Canada. **DD** 370.19/34/09713541. ***Formed by the union of** Toronto Women & Education News, 0712-2675 **and** The Race Relations Newsletter, 0838-6587.*

US
**FOCUS ON HONDURAS. Added/Corp** HONDUNET (Organization). Bulletin No. 1 (Dec. 1991)-. Periodical. English.

GW/0071-7665
**FORSCHUNGEN ZUE ANTIKEN SKLAVEREI. Added/Corp** Akademie der Wissenschaften und der Literatur, Mainz. Kommission fuer Geschichte des Altertums. Vol. 1 (1967)-. Monographic series. German. ir. Price varies per volume. Franz Steiner Verlag GmbH, Postfach 101061, D 70009 Stuttgart Germany. **Tel** 011 49 0711 2582372, FAX 011 49 0711 2582290, telex 723636 daz d. **ED** Joseph Vogt and Heinz Bellen. **LC** HT857; .F6. **DD** 326/.08.
**Desc:** Monographs dedicated to the history of ancient slavery.

CN/1182-008X
**FREE SPEECH MONITOR.** [Free speech monit.]. **Added/Corp** Canadian Association for Free Expression. (Jan./Feb. 1990)-. Periodical. English. bm. Canadian Association for Free Expression, Box 278/Station K Canada. **DD** 323.44/3/0971. ***Continues** CAFE Quarterly., 0711-2408.*

US
**FREEDOM DAILY / THE FUTURE OF FREEDOM FOUNDATION. Added/Corp** Future of Freedom Foundation. (199?)-. Periodical. English. mo. $20.00 US; $25.00 other. Future of Freedom Foundation, PO Box 9752, Denver CO 80209. **Tel** (303)777-3588.

US/0732-6610
**FREEDOM IN THE WORLD.** [Freedom world]. (1978)-. English. an. $79.00 (hardback), $27.95 (paperback) US and Canada; $79.50 (hardback), $28.45 (paperback) other. Freedom House Inc, 120 Wall Street, New York NY 10005. **Tel** (212)514-8040. **ED** Raymond Gastil. **LC** JC571; .F66. **DD** 323.4/05.
**Ind/Abst** Hum. Rights Intern. Rep.

CN
**FREEDOM OF INFORMATION SERVICE. See** Law.

US/1054-3090
**FREEDOM REVIEW.** [Freedom rev.]. **Added/Corp** Freedom House (U.S.). Vol. 22, No. 1 (1989)-. Periodical. English. bm. $20.00. Freedom House Inc, 120 Wall Street, New York NY 10005. **Tel** (212)514-8040. **LC** JC571; .F67. **DD** 323/.05. **CODEN** FREVEP. available on microfilm and microfiche from University Microfilms International (UMI). ***Continues** Freedom at Issue, 0016-0520.*
**Desc:** Addresses the interaction and conflict of democracy and human rights in the realm of geopolitics.
**Ind/Abst** Acad. Search (July 1993-); Hum. Rights Intern. Rep.; INFO-SOUTH Abstr.; PAIS Int. Print (1991-).

US/0741-353X
**FROM THE STATE CAPITALS. CIVIL RIGHTS.** [From state cap., Civ. rights]. **VFOAT** Civil Rights. (1984)-. Periodical. English. wk. $211.50 (one year), $235.00 (two year) public and institutional library; $378.00 (one year), $420.00 (two year) other. Wakeman Walworth Inc., 300 North Washington Street #204, Alexandria VA 22314. **Tel** (703)549-8606. **ED** Emily Novick. **DD** 351. **[CCC]. *Continues** From the State Capitals. Racial Relations and Civil Rights, 0734-0893.*
**Desc:** Covers ethnic and sex discrimination, desegregation, affirmative action, discrimination compensation, civil rights of the disabled.

US/1049-4766
**GEORGE MASON UNIVERSITY CIVIL RIGHTS LAW JOURNAL. See** Law-Civil Law.

●US/1068-0187
**GUATEMALA BULLETIN.** (GUATEMALA BULLETIN / GUATEMALA HUMAN RIGHTS COMMISSION/USA.). [Guatem. bull.]. **Added/Corp** Guatemala Human Rights Commission/USA. Vol. 10, No. 2 (1992)-. Bulletin. English. qt. $10.00 US; $11.60 Canada; $14.00 other. Guatemala Human Rights Commission/USA, 1359 Monroe Street NE, Washington DC 20017. **Tel** (202)529-6599. **DD** 323. ***Continues** Information Bulletin (Guatemala Human Rights Commission/USA).*

NQ
**GUATEMALAN CHURCH IN EXILE : [NEWSLETTER]. Added/Corp** Iglesia Guatemalteca en el Exilio. (19??)-. Periodical. English. mo. **CODEN** 19.
**Ind/Abst** Hum. Rights Intern. Rep.

US/0148-0588
**GUILD NOTES.** [Guild notes]. **Added/Corp** National Lawyers Guild. National Office. (Apr./May 1972)-. Periodical. English. qt (4 issues). $50.00 institution. National Lawyers Guild / New York, 55 Avenue of the Americas, Suite 301, New York NY 10013. **Tel** (212)966-5000. **ED** Tim Ledwith. **LC** KF200; .G79. **DD** 340/.05. **Bk Rev. Circ:** 8,000. available on microfilm from University Microfilms International (UMI).
**Desc:** Articles of interest to progressive lawyers, legal workers, law students: international affairs, Central America, Native America, civil rights, economic rights, gay and women's rights, immigration, etc.
**Ind/Abst** Altern. Press Index; Music Artic. Guide (?-?).

US/0897-2761
**HARVARD BLACKLETTER JOURNAL, THE.** [Harv. blacklett. j.]. **Added/Corp** Harvard Law School. **VFOAT** Black Letter Journal; Harvard Black Letter Journal; Blackletter Journal. (Spring 1985)-. Periodical. English. an. $12.00 US; $14.00 other. Harvard Law School, Publications Center, Cambridge MA 02138. **Tel** (617)495-7984, (617)495-3694. **LC** K8; .A675. **DD** 342.73/0873; 347.302873. **Circ:** 300. ***Continues** Blackletter Journal.*
**Desc:** Journal committed to maintaining sophisticated legal dialogue on topics involving the minority community in general and African-Americans specifically.
**Ind/Abst** Index Leg. Period. (1992-).

US/0017-8039
**HARVARD CIVIL RIGHTS-CIVIL LIBERTIES LAW REVIEW.** [Harv. civ. rights-civil lib. law rev.]. **Added/Corp** Harvard Civil Rights Committee. Harvard Civil Liberties Research Service. Law Students Civil Rights Research Council. Harvard Civil Rights-Civil Liberties Research Committee. **VAT** Harvard Civil Rights Civil Liberties Law Review. Vol. 1 (Spring 1966)-. Periodical. English. sa (2 issues per year). $24.00 US; $28.00 other. Harvard Law School, Publications Center, Cambridge MA 02138. **Tel** (617)495-7984, (617)495-3694. **LC** K8; .A68. **DD** 342/.73/08505. Index available (Free). **Bk Rev. Circ:** 1,300 (ctrl). available on microfilm and microfiche from University Microfilms International (UMI). Documents available from The Genuine Article, UMI Article Clearinghouse.
**Desc:** A student edited journal focusing on civil rights: constitution theory, criminal law, property law and due process, equal protection.
**Ind/Abst** Crim. Justice Abstr.; Crim. Penol. Police Sci. Abstr.; Curr. Contents Soc. Behav. Sci.; Curr. Index J. Educ.; Curr. Law Index (1980-); Expand. Acad. Index (1992-); Index Leg. Period.; Leg. Resour. Index (1980-); LegalTrac (1980-); Newsp. Period. Abstr. (1992-); PAIS Int. Print; Res. Alert [Full Cov.]; Sage Public Adm. Abstr.; Soc. Sci. Cit. Index [Full Cov.]; Urban Aff. Abstr.

US/1057-5057
**HARVARD HUMAN RIGHTS JOURNAL.** [Harv. hum. rights j.]. **Added/Corp** Harvard Law School. Human Rights Program. Vol. 3 (Spring 1990)-. English. an (Summer). $15.00 US; $17.00 other. Harvard Law School, Publications Center, Cambridge MA 02138. **Tel** (617)495-7984, (617)495-3694. **ED** Paolo DiRosa. **LC** K8; .A6825. **DD** 323/.05. Index available (Free). **Bk Rev. Circ:** 400. ***Continues** Harvard Human Rights Yearbook, 1047-0174.*
**Desc:** Explores human rights issues, including notes on human rights issues in the United States foreign policy, book reviews, and student reports on overseas internships.
**Ind/Abst** Leg. Resour. Index; LegalTrac (1990-).

US/0749-8616
**HERALD OF REPRESSION IN UKRAINE.** (HERALD OF REPRESSION IN UKRAINE / EXTERNAL REPRESENTATION OF THE UKRAINIAN HELSINKI GROUP.). [Her. repress. Ukr.]. No. 1 (Jan. 1980)-. Periodical. English (Ukrainian). mo. $25.00. Ukrainian Helsinki Group, PO Box 770 Cooper Station, New York NY 10003. **LC** JC599.S582; U394. **DD** 323.4/9/094771.

FR/0180-8524
**HOMMES ET LIBERTES.** [Hommes lib.]. (1977)-. Periodical. French. Five times a year. 100.00F France; 150.00F other. Ligue des Droits de l'Homme, 27 rue Jean Dolent, 75014 Paris France. **Tel** 011 33 1 44088729. **UDC** 36. ***Continues** Bulletin National - Ligue des Droits de l'Homme, 0180-8516.*
**Ind/Abst** Hum. Rights Intern. Rep.

US/0273-2521
**HUMAN RIGHTS.** [Hum. rights]. V. 1, Article 1-. English. an. Social Issues Resources Series Inc, PO Box 2348, Boca Raton FL 33427. **Tel** (800)327-0513, (407)994-0079. **ED** Eleanor C Goldstein. **LC** JC571; .H7685. **DD** 323.4/05.
**Desc:** Interdisciplinary resource material consisting of reprinted articles from popular and professional journals, newspapers, magazines and government documents.
**Ind/Abst** Chicano Index; LegalTrac (1980-).

US
**HUMAN RIGHTS BULLETIN. Added/Corp** International League for Human Rights. (19??)-. Bulletin. English.
**Ind/Abst** Hum. Rights Intern. Rep.

US/1041-5866
**HUMAN RIGHTS BULLETIN (BERKELEY, CALIF.).** (HUMAN RIGHTS BULLETIN.). [Hum. rights bull.]. **Added/Corp** Casa Chile (Berkeley, Calif). Human Rights Committee. (Jan.-Feb. 1988)-. Bulletin. English. bm. Human Rights Committee of Casa Chile, PO Box 3620, Berkeley CA 94703. **DD** 323. ***Continues** Human Rights Leaflet.*
**Ind/Abst** Hum. Rights Intern. Rep.

AT/0729-2716
**HUMAN RIGHTS CANBERRA.** [Hum. rights Canberra]. (1982)-. Periodical. English. bm. **DD** 323.405. ***Continues** Community Relations News, 0727-2863.*
**Ind/Abst** Hum. Rights Intern. Rep.

UK
**HUMAN RIGHTS CASE DIGEST. Added/Corp** British Institute of Human Rights. European Court of Human Rights. European Commission of Human Rights. Vol. 1, Pt. 1 (Jan./Feb. 1990)-. English. bm (6 issues). £50.00 Europe; £54.00 other. Sweet & Maxwell Ltd., South Quay Plaza, 183 Marsh Wall, London E14 9FT England. **Tel** 011 44 264 342899, FAX 011 44 264 342723, telex 929089 ITPINF G.

US/0046-8185
**HUMAN RIGHTS (CHICAGO, ILL.). See** Law.

US/0732-0906
**HUMAN RIGHTS DIRECTORY WESTERN EUROPE.** (HUMAN RIGHTS DIRECTORY. WESTERN EUROPE / HRI.). [Human rights dir., West. Eur.]. **Added/Corp** Human Rights Internet. **VFOAT** Western Europe. No. 1 (1982)-. English.

be. Human Rights Internet Harvard, Law School, Pound Hall, Room 401, Cambridge MA 02138. **Tel** (617)495-9924. **LC** JC599.E9; H85. **DD** 323.4/06/04. ***Continues in part*** *Human Rights Directory, 0197-8101.*

US/1044-193X
**HUMAN RIGHTS IN SWEDEN.** (HUMAN RIGHTS IN SWEDEN : THE ANNUAL REPORTS.). [Hum. rights Swed.]. **Added/Corp** Institutet for Offentlig Och Internationell Ratt (Stockholm, Sweden). (1984)-. English. ir. $25.00. Fred B. Rothman & Company, 10368 West Centennial Road, Littleton CO 80127. **Tel** (800)457-1986, (303)979-5657, FAX (303)978-1457, telex 87669. **LC** KKV2460.A13; H86. **DD** 342.485/085; 344.850285.

FR
**HUMAN RIGHTS, INFORMATION SHEET.** **VFOAT** Information Sheet. Began with No. 1 in 1978?. Periodical. English (French). sa. Council of Europe / Group Pact ED, Pharmacopoeia BP 907, 67029 Strasbourg Cedex 01 France. **Tel** 011 33 88 412036, FAX 011 33 88 41277181, telex 880388. **(Subscription address:** Manhattan Publishing Company, PO Box 650, Croton-on-Hudson NY 10520**)**

US/0275-049X
**HUMAN RIGHTS INTERNET REPORTER.** **See** Political Science-Abstracting, Bibliographies and Statistics.

GW/0174-4704
**HUMAN RIGHTS LAW JOURNAL : HRLJ.** **See** Law-International Law.

CN/0711-2122
**HUMAN RIGHTS (MONTREAL, QUEBEC).** (HUMAN RIGHTS). [Hum. rights]. **Added/Corp** Canadian Human Rights Foundation. **VFOAT** Droits de l'Homme; Droits de la Personne. **VAT** Droits de l'Homme (Montreal). (1976)-. Periodical. English (French). qt. 27.12Can$. Canadian Human Rights Foundation, 3465 Cote des Neiges 301, Montreal Quebec H3H 1T7 Canada. **Tel** (514)932-7826. **ED** Daniel Turp. **DD** 323.4/06/071. **Bk Rev. Circ:** 2,000. ***Absorbed*** *Droits de la Personne (Montreal, Quebec), 0828-492X;* ***Continues*** *Newsletter (Canadian Human Rights Foundation)., 0711-2114.* ***Continued in part by*** *Droits de la Personne (Montreal, Quebec : 1984), 0828-492X.*
**Desc:** Activities of the Foundation. Reports of treaties, legislation and international and domestic cases involving human rights. Book reviews and bibliographies.

CN/0711-2122
**HUMAN RIGHTS (MONTREAL, QUEBEC: 1984).** (HUMAN RIGHTS.). [Hum. rights]. **VFOAT** Droits de la Personne. Vol. 2 (1984)-. Periodical. French (English). Fondation Canadienne des Droits de l'Homme, Bureau 340, 1980 Ouest rue Sherbrooke, Montreal Quebec H3H 1E8 Canada. **DD** 323.4/06/071. ***Absorbed*** *Droits de la Personne (Montreal, Quebec), 0828-492X.*

US/0098-0579
**HUMAN RIGHTS ORGANIZATIONS & PERIODICALS DIRECTORY.** ***Ceased.*** ( )-(1984). Directory. English. be. Legal Publications, PO Box 673, Berkeley CA 94701. **ED** David Christiano and Lisa Young. **LC** KF4741; .H84. **DD** 323.4/025/73.
**Desc:** A referral list of people needing information or assistance on innumerable issues.

US/0275-0392
**HUMAN RIGHTS QUARTERLY.** [Hum. rights q.]. Vol. 3, No. 1 (Feb. 1981)-. Periodical. English. Four times a year (February, May, August, November). $76.50 US; $80.20 Canada and Mexico; $86.50 other. Johns Hopkins University Press, 2715 North Charles Street, Baltimore MD 21218-4319. **Tel** (410)516-6987, FAX (410)516-6968. **ED** Bert B. Lockwood Jr. **LC** JC571; .U64. **DD** 323.4/05. **[CCC].** Index available. **Bk Rev. Ad Acc. Pr Rev. Circ:** 1,000. available on microfilm and microfiche from University Microfilms International (UMI). Documents available from The Genuine Article, UMI Article Clearinghouse. ***Continues*** *Universal Human Rights, 0163-2647.*
**Desc:** Presents current work in human rights research and policy analysis and philosophical essays probing the fundamental nature of human rights as defined by the Universal Declaration of Human Rights.
**Ind/Abst** ABC POL SCI; Acad. Abstr. Full Text Elite (Jan. 1992-); Acad. Abstr. (Jan. 1992-); Acad. Search (Jan. 1992-); Am. Hist. Life (1979-); Am. Bibliogr. Slavic East Europ. Stud.; Arts Humanit. Citation Index [Select. Cov.]; Curr. Contents Soc. Behav. Sci.; Curr. Law Index (1981-); Expand. Acad. Index (1983-); Gen. Period. Index (1985-); Hum. Rights Intern. Rep.; Index Book Rev. Relig.; Index Foreign Leg. Per.; INFO-SOUTH Abstr.; Int. Bibliogr. Sociol.; Int. Labour Doc.; Int. Polit. Sci. Abstr.; LABORDOC; Leg. Resour. Index (1981-); LegalTrac (1983-); Linguist. Lang. Behav. Abstr.; Mag. Search; Middle East Abstr. Index; Newsp. Period. Abstr. (1991-); PAIS Int. Print (1991); Relig. Index One Period.; Res. Alert [Full Cov.]; Sage Public Adm. Abstr.; Soc. Plann. Policy Dev. Abstr.; Soc. Sci. Source (Jan. 1992-); Soc. Sci. Cit. Index [Full Cov.]; Soc. Sci. Index; Soc. Sci. Index Fulltext (Nov. 1988-) [Full Txt.]; Sociol. Abstr.

FR
**HUMAN RIGHTS TEACHING / UNESCO.** **Added/Corp** Unesco. (19??)-. Periodical. English. sa. UNESCO / France, 31 rue Francois Bonvin, 75732 Paris Cedex 15 France. **Tel** 011 33 1 45684564, 011 33 1 45684565, FAX 011 33 1 42733007, telex 204461 Paris. **LC** JC571; .H779. **DD** 323.4/05.

●CN/1188-6226
**HUMAN RIGHTS TRIBUNE (OTTAWA).** (HUMAN RIGHTS TRIBUNE /TRIBUNE DES DROITS HUMAINS.). [Hum. rights trib.]. **Added/Corp** Human Rights Internet. University of Ottawa. Human Rights Research and Education Centre. International Centre for Human Rights and Democratic Development. **VFOAT** Tribune des Droits Humains. Vol. 1, No. 1 (Winter 1992)-. Periodical. English (French). Four times a year. $20.00 (individuals), $30.00 (institutions). Human Rights Internet / Human Rights Centre, University of Ottawa, 57 Louis Pasteur, Ottawa, Ontario K1N 6N5 Canada. **Tel** (613)564-3492, FAX (613)564-4054. **LC** JC571; .H7797; JC571; .H86. **DD** 323/.05.

US/0792-7797
**HUMAN RIGHTS UPDATE (CHICAGO, ILL.).** (HUMAN RIGHTS UPDATE / PALESTINE HUMAN RIGHTS INFORMATION CENTER.). [Hum. rights update]. **Added/Corp** Palestine Human Rights Information Center. Palestine Human Rights Information Center International. (Dec 1987)-. English. mo. Palestine Human Rights Information Center PHRIC International, 4201 Connecticut Avenue Northwest, #500, Washington DC 20008. **Tel** (202)686-5116, FAX (202)686-5140. **LC** JC599.I68; H85. **DD** 323.4/9/095694.
**Ind/Abst** Hum. Rights Intern. Rep.

JM
**HUMAN RIGHTS UPDATE / JAMAICA COUNCIL FOR HUMAN RIGHTS.** **Added/Corp** Jamaica Council for Human Rights. Vol. 1, No. 1 (Dec. 1984)-. Periodical. English. mo. Jamaica Council for Human Rights, 131 Tower Street, Kingston Jamaica.
**Ind/Abst** Hum. Rights Intern. Rep.

US
**HUMAN RIGHTS UPDATES & ALERTS.** Periodical. English. sm. $30.00 US; $32.40 Canada; $35.70 other. Guatemala Human Rights Commission/USA, 1359 Monroe Street NE, Washington DC 20017. **Tel** (202)529-6599.

●US/1077-6710
**HUMAN RIGHTS WATCH/AMERICAS.** (HUMAN RIGHTS WATCH/AMERICAS : [NEWSLETTER].). [Hum. Rights Watch/Am.]. **Added/Corp** Human Rights Watch/Americas. National Coalition for Haitian Refugees. **VFOAT** Human Rights Watch Americas; Americas Watch. Vol. 6, No. 2 (Feb. 1994)-. Periodical. English. mo. $40.00. Human Rights Watch, 485 Fifth Avenue, New York NY 10017. **Tel** (212)972-8400, FAX (212)972-0905. **LC** JC599.L3; N49. **DD** 323. ***Continues*** *Americas Watch (Newsletter), 1068-8919.*
**Desc:** Monitors and promotes observance of internationally recognized human rights in Latin America and the Caribbean.

US
**HUMAN RIGHTS WATCH QUARTERLY NEWSLETTER.** **Added/Corp** Human Rights Watch (Organization). **VFOAT** Quarterly Newsletter; Human Rights Watch Newsletter. (Fall 1991)-. Newsletter. English. qt. Human Rights Watch, 485 Fifth Avenue, New York NY 10017. **Tel** (212)972-8400, FAX (212)972-0905. **LC** JC571; .H86. ***Continues*** *Human Rights Watch : [Newsletter].*
**Desc:** Investigations of human rights abuses around the world.

US/1054-948X
**HUMAN RIGHTS WATCH WORLD REPORT.** [Human Rights Watch world rep.]. **Added/Corp** Human Rights Watch (Organization). **VFOAT** World Report. (1990)-. English. an. $24.00 US; $30.00 other. Human Rights Watch, 485 Fifth Avenue, New York NY 10017. **Tel** (212)972-8400, FAX (212)972-0905. **LC** JC571; .H785. **DD** 323.4/9/05. ***Formed by the union of*** *Administration's Record on Human Rights in ...* ***and*** *Human Rights Watch (Organization). Annual Report, 1041-8954.*
**Desc:** Analysis of human rights development, US policy, and review of work done by Human Rights Watch over the previous year in almost sixty countries worldwide.

CK
**HUMAN RIGHTS WORKING PAPER.** **Added/Corp** Instituto Latinoamericano de Servicios Legales Alternativos. **VFOAT** Working Paper. Vol. 1, No. 1 (Mar. 1991)-. Periodical. English (Spanish). Four times a year. $10.00. ILSA - Instituto Latinoamericano de Servicios Legales Alternativos, PO Box 077844, Bogota Colombia. **Tel** 011 57 1 2455995, 011 57 1 2884437, FAX 011 57 1 2884854. **LC** JC599.L3; H85. **DD** 323.4/9/098. Index Bound in First Issue. **Circ:** 3,000.
**Desc:** Focuses on human rights abuses in Latin America, especially in the Andean region. Looks at how US foreign policy affects human rights in Latin America.

SZ
**ICJ NEWSLETTER.** **Main/Corp** International Commission of Jurists (1952- ). (1979)-. Newsletter. English. qt. 25.00F surface mail; 28.00F airmail. International Commission of Jurists, 26 Chemin Joinville, PO Box 160, CH 1216 Geneva Switzerland. **Tel** 011 41 22 7884747. **LC** K3236.2; .I57. **DD** 341.4/81/05. **Circ:** 1,500.
**Desc:** Report on activities plus appendices on noteworthy current human rights information and documentation.
**Ind/Abst** Hum. Rights Intern. Rep.

PE
**IDEELE.** **Added/Corp** Instituto de Defensa Legal (Lima, Peru). No. 24 (Apr. 1991)-. Periodical. Spanish. mo. ***Continues*** *Informe Mensual (Instituto de Defensa Legal (Lima, Peru). Area de Informacion y Promocion de los Derechos Humanos).*

NE/0167-174X
**IFOR REPORT.** [Ifor rep.]. **VFOAT** International Fellowship of Reconciliation Report. (1977)-. Periodical. English. bm.
**Ind/Abst** Hum. Rights Intern. Rep.

UK/0306-4220
**INDEX ON CENSORSHIP.** **See** Literary and Political Reviews.

US
**INDOCHINA NEWSLETTER.** **Added/Corp** Indochina Aid and Friendship Project (U.S.) Asia Resource Center (U.S.). Issue 1 (Oct./Nov. 1979)-. Newsletter. English. bm. $14.00 US; $18.00 Canada and Pan American nations; $20.00 other. Asia Resource Center, PO Box 15275, Washington DC 20003. **Tel** (202)547-1114, FAX (202)543-7891.
**Desc:** Highlights current information on developments in Vietnam, Laos, and Cambodia.

AT
**INDONESIAN NEWS SELECTIONS : BULLETIN OF THE INDONESIA ACTION GROUP.** **Added/Corp** Indonesia Action Group. (19??)-. Bulletin. English. bm. $9.50. Indonesia Action Group, PO Box 137, Collingwood Victoria 3066 Australia. **LC** DS644.4; .I494. **DD** 959.8/03/05.

CR
**INFORMADOR, EL.** **Added/Corp** Asociacion Centroamericana de Familiares de Detenidos Desaparecidos. (19??)-. Spanish. **LC** HV6322.3.C35; I44.
**Ind/Abst** Hum. Rights Intern. Rep.

US
**INFORMATION BULLETIN / COMISION DE DERECHOS HUMANOS DE GUATEMALA, USA.** ***Title Change.*** **Added/Corp** Guatemala Human Rights Commission/USA. (198?)-(1992). Bulletin. English (Spanish). bm. Guatemala Human Rights Commission/USA, 1359 Monroe Street NE, Washington DC 20017. **Tel** (202)529-6599. Index available. cum. index. **Bk Rev. Circ:** 3,000. ***Continued by*** *Guatemala Bulletin, 1068-0187.*
**Desc:** Analysis of human rights situation in Guatemala.

UK/0268-3709
**INTERIGHTS BULLETIN.** [Interights bull.]. (1985)-. Periodical. English. Four times a year (Jan., Apr., July, Dec.). £28.00 (organizations), £18.00 (individuals). Interight, 5 15 Cromer Street, London WC1H 8LS England. **Tel** 011 44 71 2783230, FAX 011 44 71 2784334. **ED** Yvonne Terlingen. **Bk Rev**, (Qty: 8). **Circ:** 1,000 (ctrl).
**Ind/Abst** Hum. Rights Intern. Rep.

SZ/0259-3696
**INTERNATIONAL CHILDREN'S RIGHTS MONITOR.** **See** Political Science.

FI
**INTERNATIONAL MOBILISATION.** **Added/Corp** World Peace Council. United Nations Centre Against Apartheid. **VFOAT** International Mobilisation Against Apartheid and for the Liberation of South Africa. (Jan. 1980)-. Periodical. English. Information Centre of the World Peace Council, Lonnrotinkatu 25 A 5 KRS, PO Box 1811, 00180 Helsinki 18 Finland.
**Ind/Abst** Hum. Rights Intern. Rep.

US
**IOWA CIVIL RIGHTS COMMISSION, CASE REPORTS.** **Main/Corp** Iowa Civil Rights Commission. V. 1- 1965/77-. English. be. Iowa Civil Rights Commission, 211 East Maple Street/2nd Floor, Des Moines IA 50319. **Tel** (515)281-4121. **ED** Ione Shadduck. **LC** KFI4611; .A534. **DD** 342.777/085/0264; 347. 7702850264. **Circ:** 1,000.
**Desc:** Compilation of Civil Rights contested cases at Commission, State District and Appellate Courts and Federal District and Circuit Courts.

## Political Science — Civil Rights

US/1059-1729
**IR & R NEWS REPORT / SECTION OF INDIVIDUAL RIGHTS AND RESPONSIBILITIES.** See Law.

FR
**IRAN LIBERATION : BULLETIN D'INFORMATION DES MODJAHEDINES DU PEOPLE D'IRAN.** No. 1 (June 23, 1986)-. Bulletin. French (French). wk. *Continues* Iran Liberation (Paris, France).

US
**IRAN LIBERATION : NEWS BULLETIN OF THE PEOPLE'S MOJAHEDIN OF IRAN.** **Added/Corp** Sazman-i Mujahidin-i Khalq (Iran). No. 1 (July 7, 1986)-. Bulletin. English.
**Ind/Abst** Hum. Rights Intern. Rep.

US/0889-6291
**IRAN TODAY.** (IRAN TODAY : BIMONTHLY PUBLICATION OF THE COMMITTEE IN SOLIDARITY WITH THE PEOPLE OF IRAN (CISPI).). [Iran today]. **Added/Corp** Committee in Solidarity with the People of Iran (U.S.). (198?)-. Periodical. English. bm. $5.00 (individuals), $10.00 (institutions). Iran Today, PO Box 21233, Midtown Station, New York NY 10129. **DD** 322. *Continues* CISPI Newsletter.
**Ind/Abst** Hum. Rights Intern. Rep.

NE/0333-5925
**ISRAEL YEARBOOK OF HUMAN RIGHTS.** [Isr. yearb. hum. rights]. **Added/Corp** Universitat Tel-Aviv. Fakultah le-Mishpatim. Vol. 1 (1971)-. Periodical. English. an. Martinus Nijhoff Publishers, Subsidiary of Kluwer Academic Publishers, Koraalrood 50, 2718 SC Zoetermeer Netherlands. **Tel** 011 31 79 684400. (**Subscription address:** Kluwer Academic Publishers / US Subscriptions, PO Box 253, Accord Station, Hingham MA 02018.) **ED** Yoran Dinstein. **LC** LAW. **DD** 341.48/1. cum. index. **Ad Acc. Circ:** 1,000.
**Desc:** Devoted to studies on human rights in peace and war, with particular emphasis on problems relevant to the State of Israel and the Jewish people.
**Ind/Abst** ABC POL SCI; Hum. Rights Intern. Rep.; Index Foreign Leg. Per.; Int. Bibliogr. Sociol.; Int. Polit. Sci. Abstr.

IO
**JURNAL DEMOKRASI.** **Added/Corp** Yayasan Lembaga Bantuan Hukum Indonesia. No. 1 (Sep. 1991)-. Periodical. Indonesian. Yayasan Lembaga Bantuan Hukum, Jl. Diponegoro 74, Jakarta 13020 Indonesia.

PH/0116-6360
**JUSTICE & PEACE REVIEW.** **Added/Corp** Kilusan para sa Katarungan at Kapayapaan (Philippines). **VFOAT** Justice and Peace Review; JP Review. Vol. 1, No. 1 (1986)-. Periodical. English. qt. Ecumenical Movement for Justice and Peace, Room 502 Estuar Bldg., 41 Timog Avenue, Quezon City, Philippines. **LC** JC599.P5; J87. **DD** 323.4/9/09599. *Continues* Katarungan.
**Ind/Abst** Hum. Rights Intern. Rep.

AT/0157-6011
**JUSTICE TRENDS.** [Justice trends]. (1978)-. Periodical. English. Four times a year (Mar., June, Sept., Dec.). Free. Australian Catholic Social Justice Council, Leo X11 HSE 19 MacKenzie Street, North Sydney New South Wales 2060 Australia. **Tel** 11 61 2 9565811, FAX 011 61 2 9565782. **ED** Keith O'Neill. **DD** _a261.805. Index available. cum. index. **Ad Acc. Pr Rev. Circ:** 8,000.
**Desc:** Social justice issues within the Catholic and Australian communities.
**Ind/Abst** Hum. Rights Intern. Rep.

MX
**JUSTICIA Y PAZ.** **Added/Corp** Centro de Derechos Humanos "Fray Francisco de Vitoria, O.P.". No. 1 (Nov. 1985)-. Periodical. Spanish. qt. **LC** JC599.M4; J87. **DD** 323.4/9/0972.
**Ind/Abst** Hum. Rights Intern. Rep.

MX
**JUSTICIA Y PAZ / COMITE PRO JUSTICIA Y PAZ DE GUATEMALA.** **Added/Corp** Comite Pro Justicia y Paz de Guatemala. **VFOAT** Boletin Comite Pro Justicia y Paz de Guatemala. (198?)-. Periodical. Spanish (English).
**Ind/Abst** Hum. Rights Intern. Rep.

US/0892-9165
**KHRONIKA ZASHCHITY PRAV V SSSR.** [Hron. zasc. prav SSSR]. Vol. 1, No. 1- Nov. 1972/March 1973-. Periodical. Russian. Izdatelstvo Khronika, 505 8th Avenue, New York NY 10018. **LC** K11; .H76. **DD** 323.

US
**KLANWATCH INTELLIGENCE REPORT : A PROJECT OF THE SOUTHERN POVERTY LAW CENTER.** **Added/Corp** Southern Poverty Law Center. **VFOAT** Intelligence Report. (19??)-. Periodical. English. Six times a year. Free. Southern Poverty Law Center, 400 Washington Avenue, Montgomery AL 36104. **Tel** (205)264-0286.
**Ind/Abst** Hum. Rights Intern. Rep.

US
**KOREA/UPDATE.** **Added/Corp** North American Coalition for Human Rights in Korea. **VFOAT** Korea Update; Update; North American Coalition for Human Rights in Korea Update. No. 1 (Feb. 1980)-. Periodical. English. bm. $20.00. Korea Church Coalition, 475 Riverside Drive, Room 634, New York NY 10115. **Tel** (212)870-2123. **Bk Rev.**
**Desc:** Covers human rights, peace and social justice issues in the Korean peninsula.
**Ind/Abst** Hum. Rights Intern. Rep.

US
**LAW GROUP DOCKET, THE.** *Title Change.* **Added/Corp** International Human Rights Law Group (Washington, D.C.) Vol. 1, No. 1 (Spring 1981)-(1993). Periodical. English. qt. International Human Rights Law Group, 733 15th Street NW, Suite 1000, Washington DC 20005. **Tel** (202) 639-8016. **LC** K3236.2; .L36. **DD** 323.4/05. *Continued by* Docket (International Human Rights Law Group (Washington, D.C.).
**Ind/Abst** Hum. Rights Intern. Rep. (?-?).

CN/0824-4421
**LAW UNION NEWS (TORONTO).** See Law.

AT
**LAWASIA HUMAN RIGHTS BULLETIN.** **Added/Corp** Lawasia Human Rights Committee. **VFOAT** Human Rights Bulletin. **VAT** Law Association for Asia and the Western Pacific Human Rights Bulletin. Vol. 1, No. 1 (June 1982)-. Periodical. English. an. $12.00. Lawasia Human Rights Center, 130 HV Costa SJ St. Ateneo Law, Makati Metro Manila Philippines. **Tel** 011 63 2 8179701. **ED** Justice R.M. Hope. **LC** K3236.2; .L37. **DD** 342.5; 345.02. **Ad Acc. Circ:** 2,500 (ctrl).
**Desc:** Records and publishes material concerning the breaches of, and the promotion of awareness in, human rights issues in Asia and the Pacific.
**Ind/Abst** Hum. Rights Intern. Rep. (?-?).

CN/0848-1679
**LAWG REPORT.** (LAWG REPORT / LATIN AMERICAN WORKING GROUP.). [LAWG rep.]. **Added/Corp** Latin American Working Group. **VAT** Latin American Working Group Report. (Sept. 1988)-. Periodical. English. qt. Latin American Working Group, 603 Parliament Street, Toronto Ontario M4X 1P9 Canada. **Tel** (416)966-4773, FAX (416)921-0071. **DD** 980/.005. *Continues* Quarterly Report (Latin American Working Group)., 0827-3928.

US
**LEAGUE OF ACTION SERVICE.** See Women's Interests.

FR/0755-7876
**LETTRE DE LA F.I.D.H. / FEDERATION INTERNATIONALE DES DROITS DE L'HOMME, LA.** *Title Change.* **Main/Corp** Federation Internationale des Droits de l'Homme. **VAT** Lettre de la Federation Internationale des Droits de l'Homme. No. 1 (1983)-(199?). Periodical. French. Federation Internationale des Ligues des Droits de l'Homme, 14 Passage DuBail, 75010 Paris France. **Tel** 011 33 1 40375426. *Continued by* Lettre Hebdomadaire de la FIDH.
**Ind/Abst** Hum. Rights Intern. Rep. (?-?).

●FR
**LETTRE HEBDOMADAIRE DE LA FIDH / FEDERATION INTERNATIONALE DES LIGUES DES DROITS DE L'HOMME, LA.** **Added/Corp** Federation Internationale des Droits de l'Homme. **VFOAT** Lettre de la Federation Internationale des Droits de l'Homme. **VAT** Lettre Hebdomadaire de la Federation Internationale des Droits de l'Homme. (199?)-. Periodical. French. wk. Federation Internationale des Ligues des Droits de l'Homme, 14 Passage DuBail, 75010 Paris France. **Tel** 011 33 1 40375426. **LC** JC571; .L468. **DD** 323/.05. *Continues* Lettre de la F.I.D.H., 0755-7876.
**Ind/Abst** Hum. Rights Intern. Rep.

CN/1183-5249
**LIBERTAS (ENGLISH EDITION MONTREAL).** (LIBERTAS / CENTRE INTERNATIONAL DES DROITS DE LA PERSONNE ET DU DEVELOPPEMENT DEMOCRATIQUES.). [Libertas]. **Added/Corp** International Centre for Human Rights and Democratic Development. Vol. 1, No 2 (Mar. 1991)-. Periodical. English (French). qt. Free to members. International Centre for Human Rights and Democratic Development, 63 Rue de Bresoles, Montreal Quebec H2Y 1V7 Canada. **DD** 323/.05. *Continues* Centre International des Droits de la Personne et du Developpement Democratique (Newsletter)., 1187-001X.

GW
**LIST OF POLITICAL PRISONERS IN THE USSR.** (May 1982)-. Periodical. English. an. Cahiers du Samizdat, das Land und die Welt, Sendlingerstrasse 37, 8000 Munchen 2, BRD, Bruxelles (Belgium). **LC** HV8959.S65; S6532. *Continues in part* USSR News Brief.
**Ind/Abst** Hum. Rights Intern. Rep.

US/0199-5235
**MASSACHUSETTS DISCRIMINATION LAW REPORTER.** See Law.

NO/0800-0735
**MENNESKER OG RETTIGHETER.** **Added/Corp** Norske Menneskerettighetsprosjektet. Institutt for Menneskerettigheter. Norges Rde kors. Amnesty International. Norsk Avdeling. Redd Barna. **VFOAT** Nordic Journal on Human Rights. (1983)-. Periodical. Norwegian (English). qt. Kr310.00, $55.00. Scandinavian University Press, PO Box 2959 Toeyen, N 0608 Oslo 6 Norway. **Tel** 011 47 2 2575400, FAX 011 47 2 2575353, telex 71896 UROR N. (**Subscription address:** Scandinavian University Press, 200 Meacham Ave., Elmont NY 11003.) **ED** Bard-Anders Andreassen. **LC** JC585; .M567. Index available. cum. index. **Bk Rev. Ad Acc. Circ:** 900 (ctrl).

SZ
**MENSCH + RECHT : QUARTALSZEITSCHRIFT DER SCHWEIZERISCHEN GESELLSCHAFT FUR DIE EUROPAISCHE MENSCHENRECHTSKONVENTION (SGEMKO) / HERAUSGEBERIN SGEMKO.** **VFOAT** Mensch und Recht. No. 1 (May 1981)-. Periodical. German. qt. $12.50 US. SGEMKO, Postfach 10, CH-8127 Forch Switzerland. **Tel** (01)980-0454, telex 817 585 159 COM CH. **ED** Ludwig A Minelli. **LC** K13; .E363. **DD** 342.4/085; 344.0285. **Bk Rev. Ad Acc. Circ:** 13,000.
**Desc:** Covers European Convention of Human Rights. Also covers Swiss courts and the human rights policies of Switzerland.

US
**MINORITIES AND WOMEN IN HIGHER EDUCATION.** **Added/Corp** United States. Equal Employment Opportunity Commission. **VFOAT** Job Patterns for Minorities and Women in Higher Education. English. be. Equal Employment Opportunity Commission, 2401 E Street NW, Washington DC 20506. **Tel** (202)634-7062. **LC** LB2341; .E42. *Continues* EEOC ... Report. Minorities and Women in Institutions of Higher Education, 0731-8995.

US
**MINORITY TRENDSLETTER : A PUBLICATION FROM THE CENTER FOR THIRD WORLD ORGANIZING, THE.** *Title Change.* **Added/Corp** Center for Third World Organizing. Vol. 1 No. 1 (April 1987)-(1993). Periodical. English. qt. Center for Third World Organizing, 1218 East 21st Street, Oakland CA 94606. **Tel** (510)533-7583. **LC** E184.A1; M56. *Continues* Third force. *Continued by* Third Force (Oakland, Calif. : 1993), 1067-3237.
**Ind/Abst** Altern. Press Index (199?-?).

KO
**MINSA PALLYE YONGU / MINSA PALLYE YONGUHOE PYON.** Periodical. Korean. an. W8,500. Kyongmunsa 58-5 Kyonam-dong Chongno-ku, Seoul Korea. **LC** LAW.

CN/1187-4414
**MINUTES OF PROCEEDINGS AND EVIDENCE OF THE SUB-COMMITTEE ON DEVELOPMENT AND HUMAN RIGHTS OF THE STANDING COMMITTEE ON EXTERNAL AFFAIRS AND INTERNATIONAL TRADE.** [Minutes proc. evid. Sub-Comm. Dev. Hum. Rights Stand. Comm. Extern. Aff.Int. Trade]. **Main/Corp** Canada. Parliament. House of Commons. Sub-Committee on Development and Human Rights. **VFOAT** Development and Human Rights; Proces-Verbaux et Temoignages du Sous-Comite du Developpement et des Droits de la Personne du Comite Permanent des Affaires Etrangeres et du Commerce Exterieur. 34th Parliament, 3rd Session, Issue No. 1 (June 20/Sept. 30, 1991)-. Proceedings. English (French). **DD** 338.9/171/05.

CN/1187-4414
**MINUTES OF PROCEEDINGS AND EVIDENCE OF THE SUB-COMMITTEE ON DEVELOPMENT AND HUMAN RIGHTS OF THE STANDING COMMITTEE ON EXTERNAL AFFAIRS AND INTERNATIONAL TRADE.** [Minutes proc. evid. Sub-Comm. Dev. Hum. Rights Stand. Comm. Extern. Aff. Int. Trade]. **Main/Corp** Canada. Parlement. Chambre des communes. Sous-Comite du Developpement et Droits de la Personne. **VFOAT** Developpement et des Droits de la Personne; Proces-Verbaux et Temoignages du Sous-Comite du Developpement et des Droits de la Personne du Comite

## Political Science — Civil Rights

Permanent des Affaires Etrangeres et du Commerce Exterieur. No. 1 (June 20/Sept. 30, 1991)-. Proceedings. French (English). DD 338.9/171/05.

US/0746-0201
**N.Y. CIVIL LIBERTIES.** V. 23- Sept. 1974-. Periodical. English. qt. New York Civil Liberties Union York NY 10036-6503, 132 West 43rd Street, New York NY 10036. Tel (212)944-9800 ext.562. *Continues Civil Liberties in New York, 0009-7926.*

NE
**NETHERLANDS QUARTERLY OF HUMAN RIGHTS. Added/Corp** Studie- en Informatiecentrum Mensenrechten (Netherlands). **VFOAT** NHQR. Vol. 7, No. 1 (1989)-. Periodical. English. qt. $62.00. Kluwer Law and Taxation Publishers, Staverenstraat 32015, PO Box 23, 7400 GA Deventer Netherlands. Tel 011 31 5700 47261. **(Subscription address:** Kluwer Law & Taxation, 675 Massachusetts Avenue, Cambridge MA 02139.) LC IN PROCESS. *Continues Newsletter (Studie- en Informatiecentrum Mensenrechten (Netherlands)), 0169-3441.*

US/1046-4328
**NEW YORK LAW SCHOOL JOURNAL OF HUMAN RIGHTS.** [N. Y. Law Sch. j. hum. rights]. **Added/Corp** New York Law School. **VFOAT** Journal of Human Rights. Vol. 5, Pt. 1 (Fall 1987)-. Periodical. English. Twice a year. $22.00. New York Law School, 57 Worth Street, New York NY 10013. Tel (212)431-2109. LC K14; .E9348. DD 323.4/0973. *Continues New York Law School Human Rights Annual, 8756-8926.*
**Ind/Abst** Index Leg. Period.; Leg. Resour. Index; LegalTrac (1987-).

AT/1030-6110
**NEWSLETTER. Added/Corp** Cambodian Information Office (Canberra, A.C.T.). **VFOAT** CIO Newsletter. (19??)-. Newsletter. English. mo.
**Ind/Abst** Hum. Rights Intern. Rep.

CN/0226-2770
**NEWSLETTER - HUMAN RIGHTS COMMISSION OF BRITISH COLUMBIA.** [Newsl. - Hum. Rights Comm. Brit. Columbia]. **Main/Corp** Human Rights Commission of British Columbia. V. 1- Dec. 1979-. Newsletter. English. ir. Human Rights Commission of British Columbia, Parliament Buildings, Victoria British Columbia V8V 1X4 Canada. DD 345.7110081/1.

US
**NEWSLETTER - ILLINOIS STATE BAR ASSOCIATION.** See Law.

NE
**NJCM BULLETIN / NEDERLANDS JURISTEN COMITE VOOR DE MENSENRECHTEN. Added/Corp** Nederlands Juristen Comite voor de Mensenrechten. **VFOAT** N.J.C.M.-Bulletin. **VAT** NJCM-Bulletin. No 1 (Apr. 1976)-. Bulletin. Dutch. bm. Fl35.00. Nederlands Juristen Comite voor de Mensenrechten, Hugo de Grootstraat 27, 2311 XK Leiden Netherlands. LC K14; .J35. **Bk Rev. Circ:** 1,200.
**Ind/Abst** Hum. Rights Intern. Rep.

US/0270-2282
**NORTH AMERICAN HUMAN RIGHTS DIRECTORY. Ceased. Added/Corp** Human Rights Internet. **VFOAT** Human Rights Internet. (1980)-(19??). English. ir. Human Rights Internet / Human Rights Centre, University of Ottawa, 57 Louis Pasteur, Ottawa, Ontario K1N 6N5 Canada. Tel (613)564-3492, FAX (613)564-4054. **ED** Lori Wissboab. LC JC571; .H76944. DD 323.4/06/073. *Continues in part Human Rights Directory, 0197-8101.*
**Desc:** Lists organizations in North and South America concerned with human rights and social justice.

PY
**NOTAS TRIMESTRALES DEL COMITE DE IGLESIAS. Added/Corp** Comite de Iglesias (Asuncion, Paraguay). **VFOAT** Notas Trimestrales. (1987?)-. Spanish. qt. CIPAE Comite de Iglesias para Ayudas de Emergencia, General Diaz 429, Asuncion, Paraguay. LC JC599.P3N68. DD 323.4/9/09892.
**Ind/Abst** Hum. Rights Intern. Rep.

US/0251-7787
**NOTES AND DOCUMENTS - UNITED NATIONS, CENTRE AGAINST APARTHEID.** (1968)-. Periodical. English. tw.
**Ind/Abst** Hum. Rights Intern. Rep.

US
**NOTES FROM SURVIVAL INTERNATIONAL U.S.A.** Periodical. English. qt. Survival International USA, National Section, 2121 Decatur Place NW, Washington DC 20008. Tel (202)265-1077.

●US
**NOTICIAS DE OCR / OFFICINA DE DERECHOS CIVILES. Added/Corp** United States. Dept. of Health and Human Services. Office for Civil Rights. Vol. 1, No. 1 (1992)-. Spanish. Office Civil Rights, 330 Independence Avenue SW, Room 5400 Cohen Building, Washington DC 20201.

IT
**NOTIZIARIO DI AMNESTY INTERNATIONAL.** (19??)-. Italian. mo. L60000.00. Amnesty International / Italy, Viale Mazzini 146, 00195 Rome Italy. Tel 011 39 6 380898.

FR/0764-7565
**NOUVELLE ALTERNATIVE, LA.** [Nouv. alternative]. (April 1986)-. Periodical. French. qt. 250.00F (individuals), 350.00F (institutions). La Nouvelle Alternative, 14 16 rue des Petits Hotels, 75010 Paris France. Tel 011 33 1 45809046. LC JC599.E92; N68. *Continues Alternative (Paris, France : 1979), 0240-1568.*

US/0731-2512
**NUESTRA LUCHA (TOLEDO, OHIO).** (NUESTRA LUCHA.). Periodical. English (Spanish). ir. $10.00. F L O C, 507 South St Clair Street, Toledo OH 43602.

US/0029-7593
**OBJECTIVE : JUSTICE.** [Object.: justice]. **Added/Corp** United Nations. Office of Public Information. United Nations. Dept. of Public Information. Vol. 1 (1969)-. Government Publication. English. sa. $8.00. United Nations Publications, 2 United Nations Plaza, Room DC2 0853, Department 007C, New York NY 10017. Tel (212)963-8303, (800)253-9646. **(Subscription address:** PO Box 361, Birmingham, AL 35201-0361; telephone: (800)633-4931, FAX: (205)995-1588) LC HT1521; .O25. available on microfilm and microfiche from University Microfilms International (UMI).
**Desc:** A review dedicated to the promotion of justice through the self-determination of peoples, the elimination of apartheid and racial discrimination, and the advancement of human rights.
**Ind/Abst** PAIS Int. Print (1991-?).

US
**OCR REPORT / OFFICE FOR CIVIL RIGHTS. Added/Corp** United States. Dept. of Health and Human Services. Office for Civil Rights. **VFOAT** Office for Civil Rights Report. Vol. 1, No. 1 (Spring 1991)-. Periodical. English. qt. Office Civil Rights, 330 Independence Avenue SW, Room 5400 Cohen Building, Washington DC 20201.

US/0274-5615
**OHIO CIVIL LIBERTIES. Added/Corp** American Civil Liberties Union of Ohio. American Civil Liberties Union of Ohio & Foundation. (1969)-. Periodical. English. qt. $10.00. American Civil Liberties of Ohio, 360 South Third Street/Suite 450, Columbus OH 43215. Tel (614)228-8951. **ED** Mark B. Levy. **Ad Acc. Circ:** 5,500 (ctrl).
**Desc:** News regarding activities of ACLU in Ohio to defend and advance principles of free speech, press, religion; fundamental fairness; equality under the law; and the right to privacy.

CN/0706-9294
**OPERATION LIBERTE.** V. 1 (Feb. 1978)-. Periodical. English. 0.25Can$ each number. La Ligue des Droits de l'Homme, Montreal Quebec H2L 4A5 Canada. DD 323.4/0971.

US
**ORGANIZER : NEWSLETTER OF THE NATIONAL ALLIANCE AGAINST RACIST AND POLITICAL REPRESSION, THE. Added/Corp** National Alliance Against Racist and Political Repression (U.S.). **VFOAT** Newsletter of the National Alliance Against Racist and Political Repression. (1977?)-. Periodical. English. Five times a year. $7.00. National Alliance Against Racism and Pol Repress, 126 West 119 Street, Suite 101, New York NY 10026. Tel (212)866-8600.

US/0886-6457
**PACS & LOBBIES. Title Change.** [PACs lobbies]. **VFOAT** Political Action Committees & Lobbies; PACs and Lobbies; Political Action Committees and Lobbies. Vol. 3, No. 40 (Nov. 3, 1982)-(19??). Periodical. English. Twenty-four times a year. Amward Publications, 2000 National Press Building, Washington DC 20045. Tel (301)251-9009, FAX (301)251-9058. **ED** Edward Zuckerman. DD 322. **Bk Rev.** *Continues Political Finance Lobby Reporter, 0270-353X. Changed back to Political Finance Lobby Reporter, 0270-353X.*

US/0737-5549
**PALESTINE HUMAN RIGHTS BULLETIN.** [Palest. human rights bull.]. **Added/Corp** Palestine Human Rights Campaign. No. 1 (July 30, 1977)-. Bulletin. English. Palestine Human Rights Campaign, PO Box 3033, Washington DC 20010.
**Ind/Abst** Hum. Rights Intern. Rep.

US/0160-984X
**PALESTINE-ISRAEL BULLETIN.** (PALESTINE/ISRAEL BULLETIN.). **Added/Corp** Search for Justice and Equality in Palestine. Middle East Resource Center. Vol. 1 (Feb. 1978)-. Bulletin. English. mo. $6.00 (individual), $15.00 (institution).
**Ind/Abst** Hum. Rights Intern. Rep.

UK/0259-2878
**PAPER (INTERNATIONAL ORGANIZATION FOR THE ELIMINATION OF ALL FORMS OF RACIAL DISCRIMINATION).** (PAPER / THE INTERNATIONAL ORGANISATION FOR THE ELIMINATION OF ALL FORMS OF RACIAL DISCRIMINATION (EAFORD).). [Pap. - Int. Organ. Elimin. All Forms Racial Discrim.]. **Added/Corp** International Organization for the Elimination of All Forms of Racial Discrimination. (19??)-. Monographic series. English. ir. Price varies per volume. International Organization for the Elimination of All Forms of Racial Discrimination, 2025 I Street NW/Suite 1120, Washington DC 20006. LC HT1501; .P36. DD 305.8/005.
**Ind/Abst** Hum. Rights Intern. Rep.

UY
**PAZ & JUSTICIA. Added/Corp** Servicio Paz y Justicia (Uruguay). **VFOAT** Paz y Justicia. (Aug. 1985)-. Periodical. Spanish. mo. $120.00 (single issue). Servicio Paz y Justicia, Joaquin Requena 1642, Montevideo Uruguay. LC JC599.U7; P39. DD 323.4/9/09895. *Continues Sumario de Derechos Humanos.*
**Ind/Abst** Hum. Rights Intern. Rep.

US/1057-0624
**PERSECUTION OF HUMAN RIGHTS MONITORS. Ceased. Added/Corp** Human Rights Watch (Organization). (1987)-(19??). English. an. Human Rights Watch, 485 Fifth Avenue, New York NY 10017. Tel (212)972-8400, FAX (212)972-0905. LC JC571; .P422. DD 323/.044/05.

PE
**PERU SOLIDARITY FORUM.** (19??)-. Periodical. English.
**Ind/Abst** Hum. Rights Intern. Rep.

PH
**PHILIPPINE HUMAN RIGHTS UPDATE. Added/Corp** Task Force Detainees of the Philippines. Task Force Detainees of the Philippines. Documentation Desk. Vol. 1, No. 1 (Sept. 15, 1985)-. Periodical. English. mo. P72.00 (local), $24.00 (foreign). Task Force Detainees Philippines, 214 North Domingo Street, Quezon City 1111 Philippines. LC JC599.P5; P46. DD 323.4/9/09599. cum. index. *Continues Political Detainees Update (Philippines).*
**Ind/Abst** Hum. Rights Intern. Rep.

US
**PHILIPPINE WITNESS. Added/Corp** Church Coalition for Human Rights in the Philippines. No. 1 (May 1985)-. Periodical. English. bm. LC JC599.P6; P54.
**Ind/Abst** Hum. Rights Intern. Rep.

FR/0994-6993
**PHILIPPINES INFORMATION PARIS.** (PHILIPPINES INFORMATION.). (1982)-. Periodical. French. mo. Comite Solidarite Philippines, 68 rue de Babylone, 75007 Paris France. **UDC** 338 (914). *Continues in part Bulletin - Comite Solidarite Philippines, 0994-7329.*
**Ind/Abst** Hum. Rights Intern. Rep.

US
**PHILIPPINES UPDATE. Added/Corp** Church Coalition for Human Rights in the Philippines. (19??)-. Periodical. English. qt.
**Ind/Abst** Hum. Rights Intern. Rep.

CN/0710-1457
**PHOENIX RISING (TORONTO, ONT.). Ceased.** See Medical Science and Technology-Psychiatry.

US/0738-0623
**POLICE MISCONDUCT AND CIVIL RIGHTS LAW REPORT.** [Police misconduct civ. rights law rep.]. **Added/Corp** National Lawyers Guild. Civil Liberties Committee. Vol. 1, No. 1 (Apr. 1983)-. Periodical. English. bm (6 issues). $125.00. Clark Boardman Callaghan, 155 Pfingsten Road, Deerfield IL 60015. Tel (800)323-8067. LC KF4742; .P64. DD 342.73/085; 347.30285. Index available (Free). **Circ:** 3,200. *Continues tPolice Misconduct Litigation Report, 0275-9330.*
**Desc:** A report that covers the latest in police misconduct, civil rights litigation, and court-awarded attorney's fees.

US/0275-3170
**POLICY GUIDE OF THE AMERICAN CIVIL LIBERTIES UNION.** [Policy guide Am. Civil. Lib. Union]. **Main/Corp** American Civil Liberties Union. (1966)-. English. ir. $25.00. American Civil Liberties Union, 132 West 43rd Street, New York NY 10036. Tel (212)944-9800 ext 422. **ED** Ari Korpivaara. **Bk Rev. Circ:** 175,000 (ctrl).

**Desc:** Reports on ACLU's litigation, legislative lobbying and public education efforts in defense of free speech, equal protection and other constitutional rights.

CK
**PORTAVOZ. Added/Corp** Instituto Latinoamericano de Servicios Legales Alternativos. Asociaci,on Interamericana de Servicios Legales. (1986)-. Bulletin. Spanish. bm. Free (Latin America and the Caribbean); $10.00 other. ILSA - Instituto Latinoamericano de Servicios Legales Alternativos, PO Box 077844, Bogota Colombia. **Tel** 011 57 1 2455995, 011 57 1 2884437, FAX 011 57 1 2884854. **LC** KG574.A13; P67.
**Ind/Abst** Hum. Rights Intern. Rep.

FR
**PRESS COMMUNIQUE.** (PRESS COMMUNIQUE / COUNCIL OF EUROPE.). **Main/Corp** Council of Europe. **VFOAT** Human Rights News; Communique de Presse. English. ir. Service de Presse, Conseil de l'Europe, BP 431 R6, F-67006 Strasbourg France. ***Continues*** *Press Release / Council of Europe.*

NE
**PRIVACY EN REGISTRATIE.** Dutch. qt. F25.00 (individuals); F35.00 (organizations). St Waakzaamheid Persoonsregist, Postbus 711, 1000 AS Amsterdam Netherlands. **Tel** 020-627-1367, 011 31 20 6271367, FAX 020-6384310. Index available. **Bk Rev. Ad Acc. Pr Rev. Circ:** 2,000.
**Desc:** Contains information on privacy issues.

CN/0715-4356
**PRO-LIFE NEWS. See** Medical Science and Technology-Gynecology and Obstetrics.

FR
**PUBLICATIONS DE LA COUR EUROPEENNE DES DROITS DE L'HOMME SERIE B, MEMOIRES. VFOAT** Memoires, Plaidoiries et Documents; Pleadings, Oral Arguments, and Documents; Publications of the European Court of Human Rights. Series Pleadings, Oral Arguments and Documents. Vol. 1 (1965/1967)-. Monographic series. French (English). ir. Price varies per volume. Carl Heymanns Verlag KG, Luxemburger Strasse 449, D 50939 Cologne Germany. **Tel** 011 49 221 460100, telex 8 881 888. **(Subscription address:** Manhattan Publishing Company, PO Box 650, Croton-on-Hudson NY 10520**) LC** KJC5132.A52; E882. **DD** 341.4/84.
**Desc:** The official records of the 23 democratic countries in Western Europe.

II
**PUCL BULLETIN. Added/Corp** Makkal Civil Urimaik Kalakam (India). **VFOAT** P.U.C.L. Bulletin. (19??)-. Bulletin. English. Twelve times a year. $50.00 (latest issues). People's Union for Civil Liberties, A 11 Pushpanjali, New Delhi 110092 India. **LC** LAW. **DD** 323.4/0954.

CN/0229-1916
**QUAKER CONCERN. See** Religion and Theology-Protestantism.

US
**QUARTERLY REPORT / PEOPLE FOR THE AMERICAN WAY. Main/Corp** People for the American Way. (198?)-. Periodical. English. qt.
**Ind/Abst** Hum. Rights Intern. Rep.

RU
**RASY I NARODY.** (RASY I NARODY / AKADEMIIA NAUK SSSR, INSTITUT ETNOGRAFII IM. N.N. MIKLUKHO-MAKLAIA.). **Added/Corp** Institut Etnografii imeni N.N. Miklukho-Maklaia. (1971)-. Academic Scholarly Publication. Russian (summaries and/or abstracts in English; table of contents in French). an. $51.00. Izdatelstvo Nauka / Akademiia Nauk, Publishing House of the Russian Academy of Sciences, Leninskii Porspekt 14, 117901 Moscow Russia. **Tel** 011 95 954-21-53, FAX 011 95 938-21-44, telex 411964. **(Subscription address:** Victor Kamkin, 4956 Boiling Brook Parkway, Rockville MD 20852.**) LC** HT1521; .R425.
**Ind/Abst** Int. Bibliogr. Sociol.

US/1054-1675
**RECORD (SOMERVILLE, MASS.).** (RECORD / PHYSICIANS FOR HUMAN RIGHTS.). [Record]. **Added/Corp** Physicians for Human Rights (U.S.). **VFOAT** Physicians for Human Rights Record; PHR Record. Vol. 1, Issue 1 (Fall 1987)-. Periodical. English. Three times a year. Membership: $30.00 physicians; $60.00 individuals. Physicians for Human Rights / PHR Organization of Health Professionals, 100 Boylston Street, Suite 702, Boston MA 02116. **Tel** (617)695-0041. **LC** JC571; .R4397. **DD** 323.4/9/05.
**Ind/Abst** Hum. Rights Intern. Rep.

CN/0251-6500
**REFUGEE UPDATE ENGLISH ED.** [Refug. update Engl. ed.]. (1979)-. Periodical. English. Four times a year. 14.00Can$ (institutions), 10.00Can$ (individuals). Jesuit Centre, 947 Queen Street East, Toronto Ontario M4m 1J9 Canada. **Tel** (416)469-1123, FAX (416)469-3579. **ED** Colin MacAdam, Ezat Messullanejad. **UDC** 362.92. **Bk Rev. Pr Rev. Circ:** 1,500 (ctrl).
**Desc:** Strives to provide a regular critical analysis of the Canadian refugee policies and issues and to build a bridge among various refugee right groups all over Canada with information and analysis on policy and protections.

US
**REPORT - MISSOURI. COMMISSION ON HUMAN RIGHTS. *Title Change.* Main/Corp** Missouri. Commission on Human Rights. (19??)-(19??). English. an. **LC** JC599.U5; M63. ***Continued by*** *Annual Report - Missouri Commission on Human Rights.*

UK
**REPORT OF THE STANDING ADVISORY COMMISSION ON HUMAN RIGHTS.** **Main/Corp** Northern Ireland. Standing Advisory Commission on Human Rights. **Added/Corp** Northern Ireland. Standing Advisory Commission on Human Rights. Annual Report. **VFOAT** Annual Report - Standing Advisory Commission on Human Rights. (1975)-. English. **LC** KDE420; .A863. **DD** 323.4/09416.

US/0895-5999
**REPORT ON SCIENCE AND HUMAN RIGHTS.** (REPORT ON SCIENCE AND HUMAN RIGHTS / AAAS COMMITTEE ON SCIENTIFIC FREEDOM AND RESPONSIBILITY.). [Rep. sci. hum. rights]. **Added/Corp** AAAS Committee on Scientific Freedom and Responsibility. American Association for the Advancement of Science. Scientific and Human Rights Program. **VFOAT** AAAS Report on Science and Human Rights. Vol. 9, No. 2 (Summer 1987)-. Periodical. English. qt (4 issues). Free. American Association for the Advancement of Science, 1333 H Street Northwest, Washington DC 20005. **Tel** (202)326-6400, (203)326-6417, (202)326-6430, FAX (202)842-1065. **DD** 323. ***Continues*** *Clearinghouse Report on Science and Human Rights, 0734-4171.*
**Ind/Abst** Hum. Rights Intern. Rep.

UK/0305-6252
**REPORTS / MINORITY RIGHTS GROUP.** **Added/Corp** Minority Rights Group. **VFOAT** International Report; Minority Rights Group International Report. (1970)-. Monographic series. English (French). ir (at least six per year). £55.00. Minority Rights Group, 379 Brixton Road, London SW9 7DE England. **Tel** 044 071 978 9498, FAX 044 071 738 6265. **LC** UNC. **Bk Rev. Circ:** 1,500.
**Desc:** Each title examines a current minority rights issue, providing historical and background data, an objective analysis of present situations with recommendations for constructive change.
**Ind/Abst** Hum. Rights Intern. Rep.; Int. Labour Doc.; LABORDOC.

PE
**REPRESION. Added/Corp** Centro de Derechos Humanos Rupay. Vol. 2, No. 13 (June 1979)-. Periodical. Spanish. mo. Nuevo Mundo Jr, Camana 280 Of 305, Lima Peru. **LC** JC599.P4; R46. **DD** 323.4/9/0985. ***Continues*** *Represion en el Peru.*

US/0545-4158
**RESEARCH REPORT - NEW YORK CITY COMMISSION ON HUMAN RIGHTS.** (RESEARCH REPORT - CITY COMMISSION ON HUMAN RIGHTS.). **Main/Corp** New York (City). City Commission on Human Rights. (19??)-. Monographic series. English. Price varies per volume. **LC** JC599.U52; N56a. **DD** 323.4/09747/1.

CN/0713-0287
**REVIEW - SASKATCHEWAN ASSOCIATION ON HUMAN RIGHTS.** (REVIEW.). [Rev. - Sask. Assoc. Hum. Rights]. Periodical. English. bm. Free to members. Saskatchewan Association of Human Rights, 802 224 4th Avenue South, Saskatoon Saskatchewan S7K 2H6 Canada. **Tel** (306)665-7217. **DD** 323.4/097124. ***Continues*** *Saskatchewan Human Rights Review, 0713-0279.*

CL
**REVISTA CHILENA DE DERECHOS HUMANOS. Added/Corp** Programa de Derechos Humanos (Academia de Humanismo Cristiano). No. 1 (1985)-. Periodical. Spanish. qt. Academia de Humanismo Cristiano, Catedral 1063, Piso 5, Santiago Chile. **Tel** 011 56 2 6980864. **LC** K19; .C485. **DD** 342.83/085; 348.30285.
**Ind/Abst** Hum. Rights Intern. Rep.

CR
**REVISTA IIDH / INSTITUTO INTERAMERICANO DE DERECHOS HUMANOS. Added/Corp** Inter-American Institute of Human Rights. No. 1 (Jan./June 1985)-. Periodical. Spanish. qt. $30.00. Instituto Interamericano de Derechos Humanos, Apartado Postal 10-081-1000, San Jose Costa Rica. **Tel** 011 506 340404 340405.
**Ind/Abst** Hum. Rights Intern. Rep.; Int. Labour Doc.

FR
**REVUE QUART MONDE.** (1986)-. Periodical. French. qt. 150.00F. Science & Service Quart Monde, 15 rue Maitre Albert, 75005 Paris, France. **Tel** 011 33 1 46334977. **Bk Rev. *Continues*** *Igloos.*
**Desc:** Extreme poverty and human rights topics. How the poorest people have access to the human rights and can be functional citizens as other people do.

BE/0777-3579
**REVUE TRIMESTRIELLE DES DROITS DE L'HOMME.** Vol. 1, No. 1 (Jan. 1990)-. Periodical. French. qt. 435.00F France; 2900.00F Belgium; 2950.00F other. Editions Nemesis, Av du Manoir 3, B-1180 Brussels Belgium. **Tel** 011 32 2 3749170.
**Desc:** Covers human and civil rights.

GW/0937-714X
**REVUE UNIVERSELLE DES DROITS DE L'HOMME. VFOAT** RUDH. Vol. 1 (1989)-. French. Twelve times a year. $213.60 US; $224.60 other. N P Engel Verlag, Gutenbergstrasse 29, D-77694 Kehl Germany. **Tel** 011 49 7851 2463, FAX 011 49 7851 4234, telex 753 560.
**Ind/Abst** LABORDOC.

US
**RIGHT TO KNOW & THE FREEDOM TO ACT : NCARL'S FIRST AMENDMENT MONITORING SERVICE, THE. *Title Change.*** **Added/Corp** National Committee Against Repressive Legislation (U.S.). **VFOAT** Right to Know and the Freedom to Act. Vol. 1, No. 1 (Aug. 1987)-(199?). Periodical. English. bm. National Committee Against Repressive Legislation, 236 Massachusetts Avenue NE/Suite 406, Washington DC 20002. **LC** KF4770.A15; R54. ***Absorbed by*** *FBI News.*

UK/0950-8465
**RIGHTS AND HUMANITY.** [Rights humanity]. (1986)-. Periodical. English. tq.
**Ind/Abst** Hum. Rights Intern. Rep.

CN/1187-3272
**RIGHTS AND LIBERTIES.** [Rights liberties]. **Added/Corp** Manitoba Association for Rights and Liberties. Vol. 1, No. 1 (Spring 1991)-. Periodical. English. qt. Free to members. Manitoba Association for Rights and Liberties, 425 Elgin Avenue, Winnipeg Manitoba R3A 1P2 Canada. **DD** 323.4/06/07127. ***Continues*** *MARL Newsletter (1982)., 0821-5286.*

US/0035-5283
**RIGHTS (NEW YORK, N.Y. 1953).** (RIGHTS.). [Rights]. **Added/Corp** National Emergency Civil Liberties Committee (U.S.) Emergency Civil Liberties Committee. Vol. 1 (1953)-. Periodical. English. Twice a year (Semi-Annually). $15.00. National Emergency Civil Liberties Committee, 175 5th Avenue, New York NY 10010. **ED** Jeff Kesseloff. **LC** JC599.U5; R49. **DD** 323.4/0973. **Bk Rev**, (Qty: 1 per year). **Ad Acc, Adv Mgr:** Barbara Kross, **Tel** (212)673-2040. **Circ:** 8,500.
**Ind/Abst** Altern. Press Index; Hum. Rights Intern. Rep.

US/0364-7668
**RISING TIDE, THE. Added/Corp** Freedom Leadership Foundation (Washington, D.C.). (1971)-. English. mo. $7.50. Freedom Leadership Foundation, PO Box 7795, Ben Franklin, Washington DC 20044. **Tel** (202)347-8016. **LC** JC571; .R57. **DD** 323.4/05.

IT
**RIVISTA INTERNAZIONALE DEI DIRRITI DELL'UOMO.** Italian. qt. L122.000, $97.00. Vita e Pensiero, Pubblic University, Largo Gemelli 1, 20123 Milan Italy. **Tel** 011 39 2 72342310, 011 39 2 72342370.
**Desc:** Information about the activity of the organs which are put in charge of the defence of human rights.

SA/0036-4843
**SASH. Added/Corp** Black Sash. **VFOAT** Black Sash; Swart Serp. Vol. 13, No. 1 (May 1969)-. Periodical. English. qt. **LC** DT751; .B55. **DD** 305.8/00968. ***Continues*** *Black Sash.*
**Ind/Abst** Hum. Rights Intern. Rep.

●CN/1191-0933
**SASK RIGHTS.** (SASK RIGHTS : A SASKATCHEWAN HUMAN RIGHTS COMMISSION PUBLICATION.). [Sask rights]. **Main/Corp** Saskatchewan Human Rights Commission. **VFOAT** Saskrights. Vol. 21, No. 1 (Winter 1992)-. Periodical. English. Saskatchewan Human Rights Commission, 8th Floor Canterbury Towers, 224 4th Avenue South, Saskatoon Saskatchewan S7K 5M5 Canada. **Tel** 933-5952. **DD** 323/.097124/05. ***Continues*** *Newsletter - Saskatchewan Human Rights Commission., 0701-6336.*

IT
**SECRETARY GENERAL'S REPORT FOR THE YEAR ... / INTERNATIONAL INSTITUTE OF HUMANITARIAN LAW, THE. Main/Corp** International Institute of Humanitarian Law. Periodical. English. an.

TH
**SEEDS OF PEACE. Added/Corp** Thai Inter-Religious Commission for Development. Vol. 1, No. 1 (Apr. 1985)-. Periodical. English. sa. Thai

Inter-Religious Commission for Development, GPO Box 1960, Bangkok 10501, Thailand.
**Ind/Abst** Hum. Rights Intern. Rep.

AG
**SERVICIO EN LA INFORMACION / SERVICIO PAZ Y JUSTICIA EN AMERICA LATINA.** **Added/Corp** Servicio Paz y Justicia en America Latina. No. 1 (Nov. 1981)-. Periodical. Spanish.
**Ind/Abst** Hum. Rights Intern. Rep.

US/0097-9244
**SESQUIANNUAL REPORT - FLORIDA COMMISSION ON HUMAN RELATIONS.** **Main/Corp** Florida. Commission on Human Relations. July 1972/Dec. 1973-. English. ir. Florida Commission on Human Relations, 2571 Executive Center, Tallahassee FL 32301. **LC** JC599.U52; F63A. **DD** 353.9/759/00996.

US/0882-181X
**SIMON GREENLEAF LAW REVIEW : A PUBLICATION OF THE SIMON GREENLEAF SCHOOL OF LAW, THE.** **See** Law.

US
**SIUSA NEWS.** **Added/Corp** Survival International U.S.A. **VAT** Survival International U.S.A. News. Vol. 1, No. 1 (Spring 1981)-. Periodical. English. qt.
**Ind/Abst** Hum. Rights Intern. Rep.

UK/0144-039X
**SLAVERY & ABOLITION.** [Slavery abol.]. **VFOAT** Slavery and Abolition. Vol. 1, No. 1 (May 1980)-. Periodical. English. Three times a year. $155.00. Frank Cass & Company Ltd, Newbury House, 890-900 Eastern Avenue, Newbury Park, Ilford, Essex IG2 7HH United Kingdom. **Tel** 011 44 81 599 8866, FAX 011 44 81 599 0984, telex 897719. **ED** Gad Heuman, James Waluin, and John Ralph Willis. **LC** HT851; .S58. **DD** 326/.05. **Ad Acc, Adv Mgr:** Ann Kidson. available on microfilm and microfiche from University Microfilms International (UMI).
**Desc:** Devoted in its entirety to a discussion of the demographic, socio-economic, historical and psychological aspects of human bondage from ancient times to the present day.
**Ind/Abst** Am. Hist. Life (1983-); Br. Humanit. Index (1983-); Soc. Plann. Policy Dev. Abstr.; Sociol. Abstr. (1983-).

CL
**SOLIDARIDAD.** **See** Religion and Theology.

PH/0038-1160
**SOLIDARITY (MANILA).** (SOLIDARITY.). [Solidarity]. Vol. 1 (Jan./March 1966)-. Periodical. English. qt (4 issues). $16.00 Asia & Australia; $18.00 other. Solidaridad Publishing House, PO Box 3959, 531 P Faura Ermita, Manila Philippines. **Tel** 63 2 591241, 63 2 586581. **LC** AP8; .S58. **DD** 052. cum. index.
**Ind/Abst** Abstr. Engl. Stud.; Hum. Rights Intern. Rep.; Index Philip. Period.; MLA Int. Bibl. Books Artic. Mod. Lang. Lit.; Rural Dev. Abstr.; World Agric. Econ.

SA/0258-7203
**SOUTH AFRICAN JOURNAL ON HUMAN RIGHTS.** [S. Afr. j. hum. rights]. Vol. 1, Pt. 1 (May 1985)-. Periodical. English (Afrikaans). Three times a year. R130.50 South Africa; $39.74 US. Juta Subscription Services, PO Box 14373, Kenwyn 7790 South Africa. **Tel** 011 27 21 7975101, FAX (021)761-5010, telex 523072 SA. **ED** John Dugard, Laurel Angus, Geoffrey Budlender, Nicholas Haysom, Lydia Levin, Gilbert Marcus, Etienne Mureinik, Christina Murray, Joman Van Der Vyver. **LC** K23; .O68. **DD** 342.68/085; 346.80285. Index available (Free). cum. index. **Bk Rev**. **Ad Acc. Circ:** 900.
**Ind/Abst** Abstr. Anthropol.; Hum. Rights Intern. Rep.; Index Foreign Leg. Per.; Int. Bibliogr. Sociol.

US/0193-2446
**SOUTHERN CHANGES.** [South. chang.]. **Added/Corp** Southern Regional Council. Vol. 1 (Sept. 1978)-. Periodical. English. qt. $75.00 institutional membership; $30.00 other. Southern Regional Council, 134 Peachtree Street Northwest, Suite 1900, Atlanta GA 30303. **Tel** (404)522-8764, FAX (404)522-8791. **ED** Allen Tullos (editor's telephone: (404)727-6965). **LC** JC599.U5; S598. **DD** 323.4/0975. **Bk Rev**, (Qty: 20+). **Ad Acc. Circ:** 3,500. available on microfilm and microfiche from University Microfilms International (UMI).
**Desc:** Analysis and opinion on issues affecting the American South including civil rights, voting rights, politics and economics.
**Ind/Abst** Am. Hist. Life (1982-1985); Sage Race Relat. Abstr.

US
**SOUTHERN COMMUNITIES.** **See** Housing and Urban Development.

AT/0816-7095
**SRI LANKA HUMAN RIGHTS BULLETIN.** [Sri Lanka hum. rights bull.]. (1985)-. English. ir. **DD** 323.4095493.
**Ind/Abst** Hum. Rights Intern. Rep.

US/0741-224X
**STATE ADVISORY COMMITTEE HANDBOOK / UNITED STATES COMMISSION ON CIVIL RIGHTS.** [State Advis. Comm. handb.]. **Main/Corp** United States Commission on Civil Rights. **VFOAT** State Advisor Committee Hand Book. English. United States Commission on Civil Rights, Washington DC 20425. **LC** JC599.U5; U5A. **DD** 353.0081/1.

US/0161-9233
**STATE OF CIVIL RIGHTS, THE.** **Main/Corp** United States. Commission on Civil Rights. 1976-. English. an. US Commission on Civil Rights, 1121 Vermont Avenue/Room 700, Washington DC 20425. **Tel** (202)254-6600. **LC** KF4749; .A336. **DD** 323.4/0973.

US
**STEUBEN NEWS.** V. 1-. Periodical. English. ir (10 issues per year). $5.00. National Council Steuben Society of America, 67-05 Fresh Pond Road, Ridgewood NY 11385. **Tel** (718)381-0900. **ED** Henry Heinlein. **LC** MICROFILM 05487 NK; NK5100. **Bk Rev**. **Ad Acc. Circ:** 3,500 (ctrl).
**Desc:** A patriotic organization comprised of American citizens of German ancestry dedicated to the task of giving force and effect to the United States Constitution and to encourage citizen participation in government.

FR/0252-0613
**STOCK-TAKING ON THE EUROPEAN CONVENTION ON HUMAN RIGHTS.** (STOCK-TAKING ON THE EUROPEAN CONVENTION ON HUMAN RIGHTS / BY THE SECRETARY TO THE EUROPEAN COMMISSION OF HUMAN RIGHTS.). [Stock-tak. Eur. Conv. Hum. Rights]. **Added/Corp** European Commission of Human Rights. Council of Europe. **VFOAT** Stock Taking on the European Convention on Human Rights. (1960)-. English. ir. European Commission on Human Rights / Council of Eruope, BP431 R6 Publications Section, F 67075 Strasbourg Cedex France. **LC** KJC5132.A52; S76. **DD** 341.4/81/094. **Pr Rev. Circ:** 1,000. ***Absorbed*** *Annual Review / European Commission of Human Rights.*

US/0146-3586
**STUDIES IN HUMAN RIGHTS.** No. 1-. Monographic series. English. ir. Price varies per volume. Greenwood Press Inc., PO Box 5007, Westport CT 06881-5007. **Tel** (203)226-3571, FAX (203)222-1502. **ED** George W Shepherd. **Bk Rev**. **Ad Acc.**

JA
**SURVIVAL IN THE 21ST CENTURY.** **VFOAT** Survival. (1985)-. Periodical. English. mo. ¥5000 Japan; $21.00 US; £16.00 UK. Jei-Ai Publishing Company Ltd, PO Box 31, Musahino-shi Tokyo 180 Japan. **Tel** (202)785-4496. **(Subscription address:** 1377 Kay Street NW/Suite 59, Washington, DC 20005) **ED** Kotoko Tsutsumie and Takaya Urago.
**Desc:** Edited for individuals responsible for team involvement in the OR. Surgical procedures and equipment, aseptic technique and professional development.
**Ind/Abst** Energy Inf. Abstr.

UK
**SURVIVAL INTERNATIONAL ANNUAL REVIEW.** **Added/Corp** Survival International. (1988)-. English. an. Survival International, 310 Edgware Road, London W2 1DY England. **Tel** 011 44 71 723 5535, FAX 011 44 71 723 4059. ***Continues*** *Survival International Review, 0308-2857.*

UK
**SURVIVAL : THE INTERNATIONAL NEWSLETTER OF SURVIVAL INTERNATIONAL.** **Added/Corp** Survival International. **VFOAT** Survival International Newsletter. No. 27 (1990)-. Newsletter. English (French, Spanish and Italian). sa. £20.00 UK; £25.00 other. Survival International, 310 Edgware Road, London W2 1DY England. **Tel** 011 44 71 723 5535, FAX 011 44 71 723 4059. **Bk Rev. Circ:** 15,000. ***Continues*** *Survival International News, 0265-1327.*

US
**TAIWAN COMMUNIQUE.** **Added/Corp** International Committee for Human Rights in Taiwan. (Mar. 13, 1987)-. English. Six times a year (Feb., Apr., June, Aug., Oct., Dec.). $20.00. International Committee for Human Rights in Taiwan, PO Box 15182, Chevy Chase MD 20825. **Tel** (301)468-5932, FAX (301)468-5932. **ED** G. Van der Wees. **LC** JC599.T28; T36. **DD** 323.4/9/0951249. **Bk Rev. Circ:** 3,000.
**Desc:** Provides coverage of human rights developments in Taiwan.
**Ind/Abst** Hum. Rights Intern. Rep.

NE
**TAIWAN COMMUNIQUE (NORTH AMERICAN EDITION).** **Added/Corp** International Committee for Human Rights in Taiwan. (19??)-. Periodical. English. qt. ***Continues*** *Taiwan Communique (Seattle, Wash.).*
**Ind/Abst** Hum. Rights Intern. Rep.

CN/0822-2762
**TAMIL EELAM DOCUMENTATION BULLETIN.** [Tamil Eelam doc. bull.]. Vol. 1, No. 1 (Sept. 30, 1983)-. Bulletin. English (Tamil and French). qt. $25.00 Canada and US; £15.00 United Kingdom. Tamil Eelam International Research And Documentation Centre, PO Box 2426 Station D, Ottawa Ontario K1P 5W5 Canada. **Tel** (613)235-1688. **ED** Philip N Ratnapala, V Elagupillai. **DD** 909/.04948. **Bk Rev. Ad Acc. Circ:** 500.
**Desc:** Current problems facing the Tamils the world-over and especially in Sri Lanka, India. Articles relating to political solution to the Tamil question in Sri Lanka. Cultural and intellectual aspects of Tamil language and the spread of Tamil language throughout the world where Tamils live.

●US/1062-5887
**TEMPLE POLITICAL & CIVIL RIGHTS LAW REVIEW.** [Temple polit. civil rights law rev.]. **Added/Corp** Temple University. School of Law. **VFOAT** Temple Political and Civil Rights Law Review. (1992)-. Periodical. English. sa. $20.00 US; $24.00 other. Temple University School of Law, 1719 North Broad Street, Philadelphia PA 19122. **Tel** (215)204-1610. **ED** Susan E. Killam & Christopher C. Sharp. **LC** IN PROCESS. **DD** 342. **Bk Rev**, (Qty: 2). **Ad Acc.** ctrl circ. available on an online database from WESTLAW.
**Desc:** Forum for the discussion of contemporary political and civil rights issues. Articles reflect a spectrum of concerns ranging from immediate questions of law and policy to basic assumptions about the nature of individuals, groups, and institutions.

EC
**TESTIMONIO / COMISION POR LA DEFENSA DE LOS DERECHOS HUMANOS.** **Added/Corp** Comision por la Defensa de los Derechos Humanos (Ecuador). (19??)-. Periodical. Spanish.
**Ind/Abst** Hum. Rights Intern. Rep.

●US/1067-3237
**THIRD FORCE (1993).** (THIRD FORCE.). [Third force]. **Added/Corp** Center for Third World Organizing. Vol. 1, No. 1 (Mar./Apr. 1993)-. Periodical. English. bm. $22.00 (one year); $40.00 (two year); $60.00 (three year). Center for Third World Organizing, 1218 East 21st Street, Oakland CA 94606. **Tel** (510)533-7583. **LC** E184.A1; T55. **DD** 305. ***Continues*** *Minority Trendsletter.*

US
**TIERRA Y LIBERTAD.** **Added/Corp** Land Rights Council, Chama, Colo. (19??)-. Periodical. Spanish (English). mo. $10.00. Land Rights Council, PO Box 149, Chama CO 81126. **Tel** (303)672-3361.

CN/1184-0455
**TIMES FEMNIST.** **See** Women's Interests.

US
**TRIENNIAL REPORT / INDIANA CIVIL RIGHTS COMMISSION.** **Main/Corp** Indiana. Civil Rights Commission. 1977-1980-. English. te. The Indiana Civil Rights Commission, 32 East Washington/Suite 900, Indianapolis IN 46204-3526. **LC** KFI3411; .A84. **DD** 323.4/09772. ***Continues*** *Indiana. Civil Rights Commission. Annual Report, 0073-6856.*
**Desc:** Enforces Indiana Civil Rights Law, IC 22-9-1, stating that discrimination is illegal based on race, religion, color, sex, handicap, national origin or ancestry.

TH
**UCL NEWSLETTER.** **Added/Corp** Union for Civil Liberty (Thailand). **VFOAT** U.C.L. Newsletter. Vol. 1, No. 1 (July/Sept. 1984)-. Periodical. English. Twice a year (Jan. & July). $12.00 (the Americas), $11.00 (Europe & Australia), $10.00 (Asia)-institutions; $9.00 (the Americas), $8.00 (Europe & Australia), $7.00 (Asia)-individuals; $10.00 (America), $9.00 (Europe & Australia)-non-profit groups. Union for Civil Liberty, 109 Suthisaarnwinitchai Road, Bangkok 10310 Thailand. **Tel** 011 66 2 2754231 3. **LC** JC599.T5; U34.
**Ind/Abst** Hum. Rights Intern. Rep.

●US/1074-6250
**UNITY IN A MULTICULTURAL U.S.A.** [Unity multicult. U.S.A.]. **VFOAT** Unity; Unidad en los E.U. Multicultural; Unity/La Unidad Magazine. Vol. 16, No. 1 (Summer 1993)-. Periodical. English (Spanish). qt. $25.00. Unity Magazine, PO Box 29293, Oakland CA 94604. **Tel** (510)482-1432. **LC** IN PROCESS. **DD** 051. ***Continues*** *Unity (San Francisco, Calif. : English/Spanish edition), 0740-4603.*

UK
**URGENT ACTION BULLETIN.** (1982)-. Bulletin. English (French, Spanish, Italian, Portuguese, Hindi and Russian). ir (approximately every 2 months). Free to members. Survival International, 310 Edgware Road, London W2 1DY England. **Tel** 011 44 71 723 5535, FAX 011 44 71 723 4059. **ED** Alison Sanders.

US
**URGENT ACTION BULLETIN. ECUADOR.** **Added/Corp** Survival International. **VFOAT** Ecuador. (19??)-. Periodical. English. Survival International USA, National Section, 2121 Decatur Place NW, Washington DC 20008. **Tel** (202)265-1077.

## Political Science —Civil Rights

US
**URGENT ACTION BULLETIN. MALAYSIA.** VFOAT Malaysia. Bulletin. English. Survival International USA, National Section, 2121 Decatur Place NW, Washington DC 20008. **Tel** (202)265-1077.

BE
**USSR NEWS BRIEF.** VFOAT Vesti iz SSSR. No. 1 (1980)-. Periodical. English. bw. *Continues* Bulletin d'Information. *Continued in part by* List of Political Prisoners in the USSR.
**Ind/Abst** Hum. Rights Intern. Rep. (?-?).

US
**VETERANS' VOICE.** No. 1435 (June 20, 1984)-. Periodical. English. Research & Publicity Unit, Division of Veterans' Affairs, Executive Department, State of New York, 194 Washington Avenue, Albany NY 12210. **LC** UB358.N7; A32. **DD** 355.1/15/09747. *Continues* Newsletter (New York (State). Division of Veterans' Affairs).

GW
**VIERTE WELT AKTUELL.** Added/Corp Gesellschaft fur Bedrohte Volker. VFOAT 4. Welt Aktuell. (197?)-. Periodical. German.
**Ind/Abst** Hum. Rights Intern. Rep.

US/1061-7310
**VIETNAM INSIGHT.** [Vietnam insight]. Added/Corp Mat tran quoc gia thong nhat giai phong Viet Nam. General Directorate of Overseas Affairs. Vol. 1, No. 1 (July 1990)-. Newsletter. English. mo. $12.00 US; $24.00 other. National United Front for the Liberation of Vietnam, PO Box 7826, San Jose CA 95150-7826. **Tel** (408)226-2261. **ED** Angi John. **DD** 959. *Continues* Vietnamese Resistance, 1048-6577.
**Desc:** Articles concerned with the Vietnamese struggle for freedom and democracy.

●US
**VIETNAM JOURNAL : PROJECT OF THE VIETNAM HUMAN RIGHTS GROUP.** Added/Corp Vietnam Human Rights Group. Vol. 1, No. 1 (1992)-. Periodical. English. tq. $6.00 US; $10.00 other. Vietnam Journal, PO Box 1163, Burlingame CA 94010. *Continues* Indochina Journal, 0742-907X.

US/0360-7453
**VIOLATIONS OF HUMAN RIGHTS IN SOVIET OCCUPIED LITHUANIA, THE.** Main/Corp Lithuanian American Community. 1971-. English. an. $10.00. Lithuanian American Community, 9660 Pine Road, Philadelphia PA 19115. **Tel** (215)677-1684. **ED** Rasa Mazeika. **LC** LAW. **DD** 342/.475/085. **Circ:** 4,000.
**Desc:** Publication documenting the violations of human rights in Soviet occupied Lithuania.
**Ind/Abst** Hum. Rights Intern. Rep.

AT/1035-4859
**VIVA MT. LAWLEY.** *Ceased. See* Ethnic Interests.

●US/1065-8254
**WILLIAM AND MARY BILL OF RIGHTS JOURNAL, THE.** *See* Law.

US/0892-9408
**WITHOUT PREJUDICE.** *Ceased.* (WITHOUT PREJUDICE : THE EAFORD INTERNATIONAL REVIEW OF RACIAL DISCRIMINATION.). Vol. 1, No. 1 (Fall 1987)-Vol. 3, No. 1 ?. Periodical. English. sa. International Organization for the Elimination of all Forms of Racial Discrimination, 2025 I Street NW/Suite 1120, Washington DC 20006. **ED** Joseph Schechla and Virginia Tilley. **LC** HT1501; .W57. **DD** 305.8/005. **Bk Rev. Ad Acc. Circ:** 1,000.
**Desc:** International review of racial discrimination, focusing on racist ideologies and institutionalized discrimination in southern Africa, Palestine, the Americas, as well as issues related to indigenous peoples and minorities around the world.
**Ind/Abst** Hum. Rights Intern. Rep. (?-?); Int. Polit. Sci. Abstr.

US/0360-4780
**WOMEN'S PROGRAM.** *See* Women's Interests.

US/0892-3116
**WREE-VIEW OF WOMEN FOR RACIAL AND ECONOMIC EQUALITY, THE.** (THE WREE-VIEW OF WOMEN.). [WREE-view Women Racial Econ. Equal.]. Added/Corp Women for Racial and Economic Equality (Organization). VFOAT WREE-View. Vol. 8, No. 3 (May/June 1981)-. Periodical. English (Spanish). bm. $6.00. Women for Racial & Economic Equality, 130 East 16th Street, New York NY 10003. **Tel** (212)473-6111. **ED** Jan Jamshidi. **DD** 305. **Bk Rev. Ad Acc. Circ:** 5,000 (ctrl). *Continues* WREE-View.
**Desc:** News/information regarding women and peace (effects of military budget/militarization); economic equality (jobs, affirmative action, child care, etc); battle against racism; support for Women's Bill of Rights.
**Ind/Abst** Women Stud. Abstr.

US/1051-7022
**YALE JOURNAL OF LAW AND LIBERATION, THE.** *Suspended.* [Yale j. law lib.]. VFOAT Law and Liberation. Vol. 1, Issue 1 (Fall 1989)-Vol. 3. Periodical. English. $10.00 (institution), $8.00 (individual), $5.00 (student). Yale Journal of Law and Liberation, Box 401A, Yale Station, New Haven CT 06520. **Tel** (203)432-4037. **DD** 342.

DK/0902-6266
**YEARBOOK. (INTERNATIONAL WORK GROUP FOR INDIGENOUS AFFAIRS).** *Title Change.* Added/Corp International Work Group for Indigenous Affairs. VFOAT IWGIA Yearbook. (1987)-(1992). English. International Work Group for Indigenous Affairs, Fiolstraede 10, DK-1171 Copenhagen K Denmark. **Tel** 011 45 1 33124724. *Continues* IWGIA Yearbook, 1101-6087. *Continued by* Indigenous World.

NE
**YEARBOOK OF THE EUROPEAN CONVENTION ON HUMAN RIGHTS, THE EUROPEAN COMMISSION AND EUROPEAN COURT OF HUMAN RIGHTS.** Added/Corp European Commission of Human Rights. European Court of Human Rights. Council of Europe. Directorate of Human Rights. VFOAT Annuaire de la Convention Europeenne des Droits de l'Homme, Commission et Court Europeennes des Droits de l'Homme. (1959)-. Monographic series. English (French). ir. Price varies per volume. Kluwer Academic Publishers, Postbus 322, 3300 AH Dordrecht, The Netherlands. **Tel** 011 (31) 78 524400, **FAX** 011 31 78 183273, **telex** 20083. **(Subscription address:** Kluwer Academic Publishers / US Subscriptions, PO Box 253, Accord Station, Hingham MA 02018.**)** *Continues* Documents and/et Decisions.

US/0251-6519
**YEARBOOK ON HUMAN RIGHTS FOR ...** . (YEARBOOK ON HUMAN RIGHTS.). [Yearb. hum. rights]. Added/Corp United Nations. Secretariat. VFOAT Human Rights Yearbook. (1946)-. Government Publication. English. ir. price varies per volume. United Nations Publications, 2 United Nations Plaza, Room DC2 0853, Department 007C, New York NY 10017. **Tel** (212)963-8303, (800)253-9646. **LC** JC571; .U4. **DD** 323.4058.
**Desc:** Contains extracted texts and summaries of significant constitutional, legislative and judicial developments on personal, civil, political, economic, social and cultural rights throughout the world.

## INTERNATIONAL RELATIONS

GW/0002-0362
**3. WELT MAGAZIN.** VFOAT Dritte Welt Magazin; 3. i.e. Dritte WM; Dritte WM. No. 1/2 (May/June 1975)-. Periodical. German. mo. DM78.00. Progress Dritte Welt, Postfach 1528, W 5300 Bonn 1 Germany. **Tel** 011 49 228 215021. **LC** DT1; .A267. *Continues* Afrika Heute, III. Welt.

US
**AAUG MONOGRAPH SERIES.** Main/Corp Association of Arab-American University Graduates. (19??)-. Monographic series. English. ir. Price varies per volume. Association of Arab-American University Graduates, PO Box 408, Normal IL 61761. **Tel** (309)452-6588. **ED** Patricia M. Walsh.
**Desc:** Series focuses on US-Middle East relations, Arab world, Middle East and Palestinian-Israeli conflict.
**Ind/Abst** Hum. Rights Intern. Rep.

GW/0001-0545
**ABN CORRESPONDENCE.** Main/Corp Anti-Bolshevik Bloc of Nations. Added/Corp Anti-Bolshevik Bloc of Nations. Press Bureau. Anti-Bolshevik Bloc of Nations. Correspondence. VAT Anti-Bolshevik Bloc of Nations Correspondence. Vol. 1 (Feb. 1950)-. Periodical. English. bm. $27.46. AntiBolshevik Bloc of Nations, Zeppelinstrabe 67, W 8000 Munich 80 Germany. **Tel** 011 49 89 482532, **FAX** 011 49 89 486519. **ED** Slava Stetsko M A. **LC** DK272.5; .A2. **DD** 909/.09717082. **Bk Rev. Circ:** 6,000. available on an online database.
**Desc:** Articles regarding the national liberation movements of nations subjugated by Russian imperialism and communism, and its effect on the current political situation in the world today.
**Ind/Abst** Middle East Abstr. Index.

CN/0709-6895
**ABSTRACTS OF PAPERS PRESENTED AT THE ... WORLD CONGRESS OF THE INTERNATIONAL POLITICAL SCIENCE ASSOCIATION.** (ABSTRACTS OF PAPERS PRESENTED AT ... THE WORLD CONGRESS OF THE INTERNATIONAL POLITICAL SCIENCE ASSOCIATION / INTERNATIONAL POLITICAL SCIENCE ASSOCIATION WORLD CONGRESS.). Main/Corp International Political Science Association. Added/Corp International Political Science Association. Resumes des Communications Presentees au Congres Mondial de l'Association Internationale de Science Politique. VFOAT Resumes des Communications Presentee au Congres Mondial de l'Association Internationale de Science Politique. Vol. 1 (Aug. 1979)-. English (French; summaries and/or abstracts in French). ir (Published every three years). $10.00 (latest edition). International Political Science Association / Canada, University of Ottawa, Ottawa Ontario K1N 6N5 Canada. **Tel** (613)564-5818, **telex** 053-3338. **DD** 320. Index available. **Ad Acc.** available on microfiche.

AT/0811-4692
**ACFOA NEWS.** [ACFOA news]. Added/Corp Australian Council for Overseas Aid. VFOAT Australian Council for Overseas Aid News. (1983)-. Periodical. English. Five times a year. 5.00Aus$ Australia; 8.00Aus$ others. Australian Council for Overseas Aid, Private Bag 3, Deakin ACT 2600 Australia. **Tel** 011 61 62851816, **FAX** 011 61 1 62851720, **telex** 61643. **DD** 338.919401724. *Continues* Research and Information Service - Australian Council for Overseas Aid, 0813-0442.
**Ind/Abst** Hum. Rights Intern. Rep.

US/0745-5615
**ACTION AND REACTION.** [Action react.]. VFOAT Action. (197?)-. Newspaper. English. Forty-seven times a year. $30.00. Action Comm Arab-American Relations, PO Box 416, Grand Central Station, New York NY 10017. **Tel** (212)682-1154. *Continues* Action (New York, N.Y.).

CN/0382-8468
**ACTIVITES DU CQRI.** Main/Corp Centre Quebecois de Relations Internationales. No. 1- Spring 1972-. Periodical. French. sa. Centre Quebecois de Relations Internationales, Pavillon de Koninck/Bureau 5460, Universite Laval, Laval Quebec G1K 7P4 Canada. **Tel** (418)656-2462, **FAX** (418)656-3634.

PL
**ACTIVITY OF THE POLISH INSTITUTE OF INTERNATIONAL AFFAIRS.** *Title Change. See* Political Science.

UK/0567-932X
**ADELPHI PAPERS.** [Adelphi pap.]. Added/Corp International Institute for Strategic Studies. Institute for Strategic Studies (London, England). Vol. 1 (1963)-. Monographic series. English. Ten times a year. £87.00 UK and Europe; $139.00 other. Oxford University Press, Walton Street, Oxford OX2 6DP England. **Tel** 011 44 865 56767, **FAX** 011 44 865 267773, **telex** 837330 OXPRES G. **(Subscription address:** Oxford University Press / USA, Journals Marketing Department, Oxford University Press, 2001 Evans Road, Cary NC 27513.**)** **ED** John Cross. **LC** U162; .A3. cum. index. **Circ:** 7,500 (ctrl). available on microfilm and microfiche from University Microfilms International (UMI).
**Desc:** A series of scholarly monographs dealing with issues of international security.
**Ind/Abst** Curr. Mil. Pol. Lit.; Peace Res. Abstr. J. (1975-1977).

IT/0001-964x
**AFFARI ESTERI.** [Aff. esteri]. Added/Corp Associazione Italiana per gli Studi di Politica Estera. Vol. 1 (Jan. 1969)-. Periodical. Italian. qt. L45000 Italy; L48000 other. Affari Esteri, Largo Fontanella D Borghese 19, 00186 Rome Italy. **Tel** 011 39 6 6878926. **LC** D839; .E812. **DD** 327/.0904. *Supersedes* Esteri.
**Ind/Abst** Am. Hist. Life (1971-1978); Int. Polit. Sci. Abstr.; PAIS Int. Print.

PK
**AFGHANISTAN REPORT.** *Ceased.* (Aug. 1984)-. Periodical. English. mo. Institute of Strategic Studies Pakistan, PO Box 1173, Islamabad, Pakistan. **Tel** 011 92 51 824658 or 821340. **ED** Kamal Matinuddin. **LC** DS371.2; .A373. **DD** 958/.1044/05. **Bk Rev. Circ:** 300. *Continues* Report on Afghanistan.
**Desc:** The Crisis and Conflict Analysis Team of the Institute of Strategic Studies is comprised of leading academicians, strategists, researchers, and policy analysts interested in the study of international relations.

UK/0044-6483
**AFRICA CONFIDENTIAL.** [Afr. confid.]. (Jan. 6, 1967)-. Academic Scholarly Publication. English (French). bw. $430.00 North America; £165.00 UK; £214.00 Europe; ˜£220.00 other. Basil Blackwell Publishers Ltd, 108 Cowley Road, Oxford OX4 1JF England. **Tel** 011 44 865 791100, **FAX** 011 44 865 791347, **telex** 837022 OXBOOK G. **ED** Stephen Ellis. **LC** DT1; .A2125. **DD** 960/.05. Index available. **Circ:** 3,300. *Continues* Africa.
**Desc:** This newsletter provides recent information on the political situation in all African countries. Up-dates on political leaders and their movements. Brief biographies of African leaders, their affiliations and publications. Also describes current coalitions.

US/0748-4356
**AFRICA INSIDER.** *See* Political Science.

US/0191-6521
**AFRICA NEWS (DURHAM).** *Ceased.* (AFRICA NEWS.). [Afr. news]. (1973)-(1993). Periodical. English. bw. Africa News Service Inc, PO Box 3851, Durham NC

27702. **Tel** (919)286-0747, telex 3772229. **ED** Reed Kramer. **LC** DT1; .A2155. **DD** 960/.05. Index available. **Bk Rev**, (Qty: in every issue). **Ad Acc. Circ:** 3,200. available on microfilm and microfiche from University Microfilms International (UMI); available on an online database from NEWSNET. Documents available from UMI Article Clearinghouse.
**Desc:** Well-researched articles review the continent's leading stories, with emphasis on major political developments and US-Africa relations, both diplomatic and commercial.
**Ind/Abst** Altern. Press Index; Expand. Acad. Index (1992-); Hum. Rights Intern. Rep.; Newsp. Period. Abstr. (1992-).

SA
**AFRICANUS. See** Political Science.

GW/0340-5788
**AFRIKA. ENGLISH EDITION.** (AFRIKA.). [Afrika, Engl. ed.]. (1960)-. Periodical. English. Six times a year. DM21.42 Germany; DM21.60 others. Afrika Verlag, Postfach 1444, W 8068 Praffenhofen ILM Germany.

GW/0002-0389
**AFRIKA-POST.** (AFRIKA - POST / DEUTSCHE AFRIKA-STIFTUNG.). [Afr.-Post]. (1954)-. Periodical. German. Eleven times a year. DM 49.00; DM 24.50 students; DM 33.00 US; DM 27.00 airmail within Europe. Europa Union Verlag GmbH, Bachstrasse 32, Postfach 1529, D 53115 Bonn Germany. **Tel** 011 49 228 7290010, FAX 011 49 228 7290018, telex 8-86822. **ED** Gerhard Eickhorn. **LC** DT1; .A2159. **DD** 960/.05. **Bk Rev. Ad Acc. Circ:** 3,000 (ctrl).
**Desc:** Publication of information, reports and comments to convey knowledges and to rouse understanding for Africa; the importance of the African continent for the international cooperation.

FR/0002-0478
**AFRIQUE CONTEMPORAINE.** [Afr. contemp.]. **Added/Corp** France. Documentation Francaise. Centre d'tEudes et de Documentation sur l'Afrique et l'Outre Mer (France). No. 1 (Apr./May 1962)-. Periodical. French. Four times a year. 235.06F. Documentation Francaise, 29 Quai Voltaire, 75344 Paris Cedex 7 France. **Tel** 011 33 1 40157000, FAX 011 33 1 40157230, telex 204 826 DOCFRAN. **(Subscription address:** Documentation Francaise, 124 rue Henri Barbusse, 93308 Aubervilliers Cedex France.) **LC** DT348; .A36. cum. index.
**Ind/Abst** Bibliogr. Mission.; Curr. Geogr. Publ. (199?-); Geogr. Abstr. Human Geogr.; Int. Bibliogr. Sociol.; Int. Dev. Abstr. (No 161 Jan./Mar. 1992-); Int. Labour Doc.; Int. Polit. Sci. Abstr.; LABORDOC; Peace Res. Abstr. J. (1969-1975); Point Repere (1979-1980, 1992-).

BE/0002-080X
**AGENOR. Added/Corp** College d'Europe (Bruges, Belgium). Association des Anciens. No. 1 (1967)-. Periodical. English (French). Eight times a year. 1818.18F. Agenor-A European Review, 22 rue de Toulouse, 1040 Bruxelles Belgium. **Tel** 011 32 2 2304777. **ED** John Lambert. Index available (Free). ctrl circ.
**Desc:** Pamphlets reflect the critical thinking of the group on topical, political and economic issues arising in the European dimension.
**Ind/Abst** Middle East Abstr. Index.

SA
**AIDA PARKER NEWSLETTER.** (19??)-. Newsletter. English. Ten times a year (Jan./Feb. issues combined). $80.00. Aida Parker Newsletter, 17 Wargrave Avenue, Auckland Park 2006 South Africa. **Tel** 011 27 11 7266856, FAX 011 27 11 7265537. **ED** Aida Parker. **Bk Rev**, (Qty: varies). ctrl circ.
**Desc:** Focus mainly on geo-political of South Africa. Information on all aspects relevant to international events and activities.

LE
**AJME NEWS / AMERICANS FOR JUSTICE IN THE MIDDLE EAST. Added/Corp** Americans for Justice in the Middle East. (1975)-. Periodical. English. Six times a year. $15.00. AJME / America Justice in the Middle East, PO Box 113-5881, Beirut Lebanon. **(Subscription address:** AJME / America Justice in the Middle East, 226 Chambersburg Street, Gettysburg PA 17325.)
**Ind/Abst** Hum. Rights Intern. Rep.

UK
**AJR INFORMATION. Main/Corp** Association of Jewish Refugees in Great Britain. **VAT** Association of Jewish Refugees in Great Britain Information. V. 1- Jan. 1946-. Periodical. English (German). mo. £15.00. 8 Fairfax Mansions, London NW3 England. **Tel** 01-624 9096. **ED** M Stern. **LC** DS135.E5; A12. **Bk Rev. Ad Acc. Circ:** 5,000.
**Desc:** Everything concerning the history, background and personalia of German-Jewish refugees worldwide.

LE
**AL-ANBA.** Periodical. Arabic. £L1.50 per issue. Al-Hizb Al-Taqaddumi Al-Ishtiraki, PO Box 2893, Beirut Lebanon. **LC** DS87; .A663.

US
**AL-ARD. VFOAT** Al-Ard Magazine; Majallat Al-Ard. Periodical. Arabic (English). $10.00. 5503 North East Prescott, Portland OR 97218.

CY/0258-7947
**AL-MILAFF. VFOAT** Al-Malaf; Malaf. Journal 1, No. 1 (April 1984)-. Periodical. Arabic. sm. $750.00 public institutions, $500.00 private institutions. Manar Press & Publishing Agency Ltd, PO Box 4928, Nicosia Cyprus. **LC** DS119.7; .M4927.

NE
**ALAM AL-ISTITHMAR AL-ARABI. ARAB BUSINESS REPORT. See** Economics-Economic History, Conditions.

PH/0044-7439
**AMBASSADOR, THE.** [Ambassador]. Began with Aug. 1970 issue. Periodical. English. $10.00. The Ambassador Journal, 148 San Juan Street, Pasay City Philippines. **LC** JX18; .A4. **DD** 327/.2/05.

US/0731-6763
**AMERICAN-ARAB AFFAIRS.** ***Title Change.*** [Am.-Arab aff.]. **Added/Corp** American-Arab Affairs Council. Middle East Policy Council. **VFOAT** American Arab Affairs. No. 1 (Summer 1982)-(1992). Periodical. English. qt. American-Arab Affairs, 1730 M Street NW/Suite 512, Washington DC 20036. **Tel** (202)296-6767, FAX (202)296-5791, telex 440506 AMARA UI. **ED** Anne Joyce. **LC** DS63.1; .A43. **DD** 327.73017/4927/05. Index available. cum. index. **Bk Rev. Ad Acc. Circ:** 18,500 (ctrl). available on microfilm and microfiche from University Microfilms International (UMI). Documents available from UMI Article Clearinghouse. ***Continued by*** *Middle East Policy.*
**Desc:** Political and economic analysis, book reviews, documentation and bibliography dealing with U.S.-Arab relations and U.S. Middle East policies.
**Ind/Abst** ABC POL SCI; Book Rev. Index; Expand. Acad. Index (1992-); Hum. Rights Intern. Rep. (?-?); Index Islam.; Index Islam. Lit.; Index Period. Artic. Relat. Law; Int. Polit. Sci. Abstr.; Middle East Abstr. Index; Newsp. Period. Abstr. (1992-1992); PAIS Int. Print (1991-).

US/0501-9877
**AMERICAN FOREIGN POLICY CURRENT DOCUMENTS (WASHINGTON, D.C. : 1984).** (AMERICAN FOREIGN POLICY CURRENT DOCUMENTS.). [Am. foreign policy curr. doc.]. **Added/Corp** United States. Dept. of State. Office of the Historian. (1981)-. Government Publication. English. ir. Superintendent of Documents, US Government Printing Office, Washington DC 20402. **Tel** (202)275-3328, FAX (202)786-2377. **(Subscription address:** US Government Bookstore / O'Neil Building, 2023 3rd Avenue North, Birmingham AL 35203.) **LC** JX1417; .A33. **DD** 327.73. ***Continues*** *American Foreign Policy, Current Documents (Washington, D.C. : 1956), 0501-9877.*

US/0891-446X
**AMERICAN PURPOSE.** (AMERICAN PURPOSE : A REPORT AND COMMENTARY ON THE PEACE, FREEDOM, AND SECURITY DEBATE FROM THE JAMES MADISON FOUNDATION.). [Am. purp.]. **Added/Corp** James Madison Foundation. Vol. 1, No. 1 (Jan. 1987)-. Periodical. English. Ten times a year (May/June and July/Aug. issues combined). $50.00. Ethics and Public Policy Center, 1015 15th Street Northwest, Suite 900, Washington DC 20005. **Tel** (202)682-1200. **ED** George Weigel. **DD** 327. **Bk Rev. Circ:** 2,500 (ctrl). available on microfilm from University Microfilms International (UMI).
**Desc:** Brings its readers informed commentary on the peace, freedom, and security debate as it unfolds among US opinion leaders. Pays particular attention to the unfolding war/peace debate among religious, educational, and community world affairs leaders, and within the American peace movement.

IO/0126-222X
**ANALISIS CSIS. Added/Corp** Centre for Strategic and International Studies. (198?)-. Periodical. Indonesian. bm. Centre for Strategic and International Studies, Jalan Tanah Abang III 27 27, Jakarta 10160 Indonesia. **Tel** 011 62 21 356532. **LC** JX18; .A5. ***Continues*** *Analisa.*

US/0195-9328
**ANALISIS LATINOAMERICANO. VFOAT** Analisis; Latinoamericano Analisis. Yearly V. 1-. Periodical. Spanish. mo. $12.50. Associated Reporters, 130 West 42nd Street, Suite 1905, New York NY 10036.

US/1042-2471
**ANCIENT CONTROVERSY.** [Anc. controv.]. Vol. 1, No. 1 (Nov. 1988)-. Periodical. English. mo. $96.00. Spencer's International Enterprise Corporation, Box 43822, Los Angeles CA 90043-0822. **Tel** (310)937-3099. **DD** 327. **Bk Rev. Ad Acc.**
**Desc:** Prophecy about the world at large.

US
**ANNOUNCEMENT OF PROGRAMS / JAPAN-UNITED STATES FRIENDSHIP COMMISSION. Main/Corp** Japan-United States Friendship Commission. English (Japanese). an. Japan-United States Friendship Commission, 1200 Pennsylvania Avenue NW/3407, Washington DC 20004-2483.

BE/0771-7962
**ANNUAIRE DES COMMUNAUTES EUROPEENNES ET DES AUTRES ORGANISATIONS EUROPEENNES. VFOAT** European Communities Yearbook and Other European Organizations; Annuaire des Communautes Europeennes; European Communities Yearbook; Annuaire des Communautes Europeennes et d'Autres Organisations Europeennes; Yearbook of the European Communities and of the Other European Organizations. (1978)-. English (French and German). an (Sept.). 165.00F. Editions Delta / Scailquin, rue Scailquin 55, B-1030 Buxelles Belgium. **Tel** 011 32 7369060. **(Subscription address:** UNIPUB, 4611 F Assembly Drive, Lanham MD 20706.) **ED** Georges Francis Seingry. Index available. cum. index. **Bk Rev. Ad Acc. Circ:** 8,000 (ctrl). ***Continues*** *Annuaire des Communautes Europeennes.*
**Desc:** A working tool for those needing accurate information on the European communities and on the bodies, whether private or public, which contribute to European integration.

FR/0298-895X
**ANNUAIRE EUROPEEN DE DEFENSE. See** Military and Defense.

CN/0380-0768
**ANNUAL REPORT - COUNCIL OF MARITIME PREMIERS.** [Annu. rep. - Counc. Marit. Prem.]. **Main/Corp** Council of Maritime Premiers. **Added/Corp** Council of Maritime Premiers. Rapport Annuel. **VFOAT** Rapport Annuel. (1971/72)-. English (French). an. Free. Council of Maritime Premiers, Box 2044, Halifax Nova Scotia B3J 2Z1 Canada. **Tel** (902)424-7590, FAX (902)424-8976. **ED** Phil Hartling. **LC** HT395.C32; M374a. **DD** 309.2/5/09715. Index available. **Circ:** 2,100 (ctrl).
**Desc:** Includes cooperative activities among three governments in economic development, communications, transportation, energy, education, federal-provincial relations, environment, Canada-US relations.

US/0192-236X
**ANNUAL REPORT - COUNCIL ON FOREIGN RELATIONS, INC. Main/Corp** Council on Foreign Relations. (1953)-. English. an. Free. Council on Foreign Relations, 58 East 68th Street, New York NY 10021. **Tel** (212)734-0400 ext.225, telex 239852 CFR. **LC** JX27.C6; A15. **DD** 327.73/006. ***Continues*** *Report of the Executive Director. Council on Foreign Relations;* ***Absorbed*** *President's Report. Council on Foreign Relations, 0093-4615.*

CN/0848-4554
**ANNUAL REPORT / EXTERNAL AFFAIRS AND INTERNATIONAL TRADE CANADA.** [Annu. rep. - Extern. Aff. Int. Trade Can.]. **Main/Corp** Canada. External Affairs and International Trade Canada. **VFOAT** Rapport Annuel - Affaires Exterieures et Commerce Exterieur Canada. (1988/89)-. English (French). Information Canada, 171 Slater Street, Ottawa Ontario K1A 0S9 Canada. **Tel** (819)997-1095. **LC** JX1515.A2; C24b. ***Continues*** *Annual Report / Canada. Dept. of External Affairs, 0823-9185.*

IS
**ANNUAL REPORT OF ACTIVITIES / THE LEONARD DAVIS INSTITUTE FOR INTERNATIONAL RELATIONS. Main/Corp** Makhon Li-Yehasim Benleumiyim Al-Shem Leonard Daivis. English. Hebrew University of Jerusalem / Leonard Davis Institute for International Relations, Trumen Building, Mount Scopus 91 905 Jerusalem. **Tel** 820014 882312, FAX 826249, telex 26458. **LC** WMLC L 83/3397. ***Continues*** *Report of Activities.*

GR
**ANTI.** (1974)-. Periodical. Greek, Modern. Thirteen times a year. $54.00 Europe & Mediterranean countries; $60.00 others. Anti, Dimocharours 60, Athens 115 21 Greece. **Tel** 011 30 1 72 32 713, FAX 011 30 1 7226107. **ED** Christos G. Papoutsakis. **LC** DF854; .A57. cum. index. **Bk Rev. Ad Acc, Adv Mgr:** Roumpou, **Tel** 01 72 32 819. **Circ:** 18,000 (ctrl).

CN/0715-4054
**ARAB DAWN (1977).** (THE ARAB DAWN.). [Arab dawn]. **VFOAT** Al-Fajr Al-Arabiy; Fajr Al-Arabiy. **VAT** Faja Al-Arabiu (1977). Vol. 1, No. 1 (Oct. 1977)-. Periodical. Arabic (English). bm. $7.00. Canadian Arab Federation, PO Box 416 Station K, Toronto Ontario M4P 2G8 Canada. **DD** 327.5694017/4927. ***Continues*** *Arab Struggle, 0700-4079.*

SY
**ARAB PALESTINIAN RESISTANCE / PALESTINE LIBERATION ARMY--POPULAR LIBERATION FORCES. Added/Corp** Jaysh al-Tahrir al-Filastini. Popular Liberation Forces. Jaysh al-Tahrir al-Filastini. Idarat al-Tawjih al-Manawi. Jaysh al-Tahrir al-Filastini.

Information Dept. Jaysh al-Tahrir al-Filastini. Dept. of Moral and Political Guidance. **VFOAT** Resistance. (Sept. 1968)-. Periodical. English. mo. $100.00 Americas; $90.00 Europe. Arab Palestinian Resistance, PO Box 3577, Damascus Syria. **LC** DS119.7; .A674. **DD** 327.5694/017/427.

CN/0826-2667
**ARMENIAN CAUSE, THE. See** History(General)-History of Asia.

US/0886-3490
**ARMS CONTROL REPORTER, THE.** [Arms control report.]. **Added/Corp** Institute for Defense and Disarmament Studies (U.S.). No. 1 (Jan. 1982)-. Periodical. English. Eleven times a year (Aug./Sept issues combined). $375.00 institutions & universities with open access to the public; $625.00 business & government organizations. Institute for Defense and Disarmament Studies, 675 Massachusetts Avenue, 8th Floor, Cambridge MA 02139. **Tel** (617)354-4337, FAX (617)354-1450, telex 403618. **ED** Chalmers Hardenbegh. **DD** 327. ctrl circ. available on diskette.
**Desc:** Comprehensive developments in all international arms control negotiations and relevant weapons.

BG
**ASIAN AFFAIRS. Added/Corp** Study Group (Bangladesh). Vol. 1 (Jan./June 1980)-. Periodical. English. qt. $100.00 US. Centre for Development Research Bangladesh, 12 Eskaton Garden Road, GPO Box 4070, Dhaka Bangladesh. **Tel** 416910, 407591, telex 642881 AIRGO BJ. **ED** Mizanur Rahman Shelley. **LC** DS393; .A83. **DD** 950/.42/05. Index available. **Bk Rev. Ad Acc. Circ:** 5,500.
**Desc:** Articulates views of scholars and experts on matters related to development, regional and international cooperation, international affairs and other issues of topical significance.

US/0092-7678
**ASIAN AFFAIRS (NEW YORK).** (ASIAN AFFAIRS, AN AMERICAN REVIEW.). [Asian aff.]. **Added/Corp** American-Asian Educational Exchange. Vol. 1 (Sept./Oct. 1973)-. Periodical. English. qt. $36.00 (individual), $71.00 (institution). Heldref Publications, 1319 Eighteenth Street Northwest, Washington DC 20036-1802. **Tel** (202)296-6267, (800)365-9753, FAX (202)296-5149. **ED** Stephen P Cohen, James C Hsiung, and Donald E Weatherbee. **LC** DS33.4.U6; A85. **DD** 327.5/073. **[CCC]. Bk Rev. Ad Acc. Circ:** 450. available on microfilm and microfiche from University Microfilms International (UMI). Documents available from UMI Article Clearinghouse. ***Supersedes*** *Southeast Asian Perspectives, 0042-577X.*
**Desc:** Focuses on United States policy in Asia, as well as on domestic politics, economics and international relations of the Asian countries from Japan to Afghanistan. Resource for teachers, political analysts, and those involved in international business.
**Ind/Abst** ABC POL SCI; Acad. Abstr. (Jan. 1994-); Acad. Search (Jan. 1994-); Am. Hist. Life (1973-); Am. Bibliogr. Slavic East Europ. Stud.; Index Islam. Lit.; Mag. Artic. Summar. Elite (Jan. 1994-); Mag. Artic. Summar. CD-ROM (Jan. 1994-); Middle East Abstr. Index; Newsp. Period. Abstr. (1980-); PAIS Int. Print (1991-).

US/1062-1830
**ASIAN AMERICAN POLICY REVIEW. See** Ethnic Interests.

KO
**ASIAN PERSPECTIVE. Added/Corp** Kyongnam Taehak. Kuktong Munje Yonguso. Vol. 1 (Spring 1977)-. Periodical. English. sa. $21.00 Korea; $24.00 other. Institute for Far Eastern Studies, Kyungnam University, 28 42 Samchung dong, Chongro ku, Seoul Korea. **Tel** 011 82 2 735-3202/3, FAX 011 82 2 735-4359, telex KIFES K26834. **ED** Manwoo Lee. **LC** DS1; .A47459. **DD** 950/.05. **Bk Rev. Ad Acc, Adv Mgr:** J.M. You. **Circ:** 1,500 (ctrl).
**Desc:** Publishes distinguished articles on social sciences in general and particularly world/comparative politics and Asia's regional affairs.
**Ind/Abst** PAIS Int. Print.

JA
**ASIAN SECURITY. Added/Corp** Heiwa Anzen Hosho Kenkyujo (Tokyo, Japan). (1979)-. Periodical. English (Japanese). an. $44.00. Macmillan Publishing Company, 100 Front Street, Box 500, Riverside NJ 08075-7500. **Tel** (800)257-5755, (609)461-6500, FAX (609)461-7070. **LC** DS35; .A864. **DD** 327/.095. **Bk Rev.**
**Ind/Abst** Int. Polit. Sci. Abstr.

US/0749-0062
**ASIAN STUDIES CENTER BACKGROUNDER.** [Asian Stud. Cent. backgr.]. **VFOAT** Backgrounder. No. 1 (April 19, 1983)-. Periodical. English. $2.00. The Heritage Foundation, 214 Massachusetts Avenue NE, Washington DC 20002. **Tel** (202)546-4400. **ED** Burton Y Pines. **DD** 950.
**Desc:** Periodic studies 5,000 to 20,000 words addressing issues affecting U.S.-Asian relations.

US
**ATLANTIC PAPERS, THE.** (1970)-. English. Lexington Books, 125 Spring Street, Lexington MA 02173. **Tel** (800)235-3565, (617)862-6650.
**Ind/Abst** Middle East Abstr. Index.

NE/0571-7868
**ATLANTIC SERIES : A COLLECTION OF STUDIES ON SUBJECTS RELATED TO THE NORTH ATLANTIC TREATY ORGANIZATION. VFOAT** Serie Atlantique; Atlantische Reihe. Vol. 1 (1963)-. Monographic series. Multiple languages (English, French and German). ir. Price varies per volume. Academic Book Services, Netherlands.

GW/0004-8194
**AUSSENPOLITIK.** [Aussenpolitik]. (1950)-. Periodical. German. qt. DM63.75. Interpress Verlag GmbH, Hartwicusstrasse 3-4, D 22087 Hamburg Germany. **Tel** 011 49 40 228070, FAX 040-22 85 260, telex 2 14 733. **LC** D839; .A885. Index available. **Bk Rev. Ad Acc. Circ:** 2,300. available on microfiche.

GW/0587-3835
**AUSSENPOLITIK (ENGLISH EDITION).** (AUSSENPOLITIK.). [Aussenpolitik]. (1970)-. Periodical. English (German). Four times a year (Jan., Apr., July, Oct.). DM58.10 (surface mail) Germany; DM63.75 (surface mail), DM75.00 (air mail) other. Interpress Verlag GmbH, Hartwicusstrasse 3-4, D 22087 Hamburg Germany. **Tel** 011 49 40 228070, FAX 040-22 85 260, telex 2 14 733. **ED** Hans Apel, H. von Borch, K. Ritter, W. Scheel, H. Schmidt, R. V. Weizsacker, G. Wettig. **DD** 327.1/05. Index available. **Bk Rev. Ad Acc. Pr Rev. Circ:** 6,500. available on microfiche.
**Desc:** International news and information on the German foreign affairs of today.
**Ind/Abst** ABC POL SCI; Am. Hist. Life (1954-1972); Int. Polit. Sci. Abstr.; Leis. Recreat. Tour. Abstr.; PAIS Int. Print (1991-); Peace Res. Abstr. J. (1965-1967, 1980-1985); Rural Dev. Abstr.; Soc. Sci. Cit. Index [Full Cov.]; World Agric. Econ.

AU
**AUSSENPOLITISCHER BERICHT DES BUNDESMINISTERS FUER AUSWARTIGE ANGELEGENHEITEN. Main/Corp** Austria. Bundesministerium fuer Auswartige Angelegenheiten. (19??)-. German. an. **LC** JX1547; .A23a.

SZ/0004-8216
**AUSSENWIRTSCHAFT: ZEITSCHRIFT FUER INTERNATIONALE WIRTSCHAFTSBEZIEHUNGEN. Added/Corp** St. Gall, Switzerland. Handelshochschule. Schweizerisches Institut fur Aussenwirtschafts und Marktforschung. **VFOAT** Zeitschrift fur Internationale Wirtschaftsbeziehungen. Vol. 1 (Mar. 1946)-. Periodical. German (English and French). qt. 98.00F Switzerland; 130.00F other. Verlag Ruegger AG, Kasernenstrasse 1, CH 7007 Chur Switzerland. **Tel** 011 41 81 235111. Index available. **Bk Rev. Ad Acc. Circ:** 1,600 (ctrl).
**Desc:** For leading personalities in economy, law and politics, and for scientists in economy.
**Ind/Abst** Econ. Lit. Index (199?-); J. Econ. Lit.

AT/1033-6192
**AUSTRALIA AND WORLD AFFAIRS.** [Aust. world aff.]. (1989)-. Periodical. English. qt (Jan., Apr., July, Oct.). 70.00Aus$ (Australia); 75.00Aus$ (Europe); 70.00Aus$ (other). Council for National Interest, Natl Sec GPO Box 2347V, Melbourne VIC 3001 Australia. **Tel** 011 61 03 8661244. **DD** 327.94.
**Ind/Abst** APAIS, Aust. Public Aff. Inf. Ser. (1993-).

AT/1035-7718
**AUSTRALIAN JOURNAL OF INTERNATIONAL AFFAIRS.** (AUSTRALIAN JOURNAL OF INTERNATIONAL AFFAIRS : THE JOURNAL OF THE AUSTRALIAN INSTITUTE OF INTERNATIONAL AFFAIRS.). [Aust. j. int. aff.]. **Added/Corp** Australian Institute of International Affairs. Vol. 44 No. 1 (Apr. 1990)-. Periodical. English. sa (May & Nov.). 39.90Aus$ (Australia); 45.00Aus$ (other). Australian Institute of International Affairs, PO Box E 181, Queen Victoria Terrace, Canberra ACT 2600 Australia. **Tel** 61 6 2822133, or 822730. **LC** DU80; .A947. **DD** 327.94. **Bk Rev**, (Qty: 2). **Ad Acc. Circ:** 3,000 (ctrl). Documents available from The Genuine Article. ***Continues*** *Australian Outlook, 0004-9913.*
**Desc:** Authoritative on international relations. Articles by distinguished Australian and international scholars on foreign policy, trade, economies, diplomatic history, defense and strategic studies.
**Ind/Abst** ABC POL SCI; Am. Hist. Life (1954-); APAIS, Aust. Public Aff. Inf. Ser. (199?-); Curr. Contents Soc. Behav. Sci.; Curr. Geogr. Publ. (199?-); J. Plan. Lit.; Res. Alert [Full Cov.]; Soc. Sci. Cit. Index [Full Cov.].

CN/0708-0859
**B. C. PEACE NEWS. Added/Corp** B.C. Peace Council. **VAT** British Columbia Peace News. (Sept. 1978)-. English. qt. 5.00Can$ Canada; $5.00 US. British Columbia Peace Council, 712-207 West Hastings Road, Vancouver British Columbia V6B 1H7 Canada. **Tel** (604)685-9958. **ED** Rosaleen Ross and Dorothy Morrison. **DD** 327/174/05. **Bk Rev. Circ:** 500. ***Continues*** *B. C. News, 0708-0840.*
**Desc:** News and upcoming events on the peace movement in British Columbia.

SZ
**BACKGROUND INFORMATION / COMMISSION OF THE CHURCHES ON INTERNATIONAL AFFAIRS, WORLD COUNCIL OF CHURCHES. Added/Corp** Commission of the Churches on International Affairs. (1978)-. English. ir. 5.00F. World Council of Churches, PO Box 2100, CH 1211 Geneva 2 Switzerland. **Tel** 011 41 22 7906076, FAX 011 41 22 7910361, telex 23 423 OIK CH. **ED** Erich Weingartner. **LC** UNC. **DD** 261.8/7/05. **Circ:** 3,000. ***Continues*** *CCIA Background Information.*
**Desc:** Provides for church-related institutions, information and analyses on current issues in international relations, e.g. human rights, conflict-situations, militarism, disarmament, peace, etc.
**Ind/Abst** Hum. Rights Intern. Rep.

SP/0213-6945
**BCE. BOLETIN DE DERECHO DE LAS COMUNIDADES EUROPEAS.** ***Ceased.*** [BCE, Bol. Derecho Comunid. Eur.]. (1986)-Vol. 42 (Nov./Dec. 1992). Periodical. Spanish. bm. Office for Official Publications of the European Communities, 2 Rue Mercier, 2985 Luxembourg Luxembourg. **Tel** 011 352 499281, FAX 011 352 488573. **(Subscription address:** Mundi Prensa Libros SA, Castello 37, Apartado 1223, 28001 Madrid Spain; Telephone: 011 34 14313222) **UDC** 338.98. ***Continues*** *BCE.Boletin de las Comunidades Europeas, 0213-4438.*

GW
**BEFREIUNG.** (1973)-. Periodical. German. Four times a year. Redaktion Befreiung, Martin-Lutherstrasse 78, D 10825 Berlin Germany. **LC** JA14; .B38. **DD** 320/.05.

CN/0005-7983
**BEHIND THE HEADLINES.** [Behind headl.]. **Added/Corp** Canadian Institute of International Affairs. Canadian Association for Adult Education. Vol. 1 (Sept. 1940)-. English. Four times a year. 13.00Can$ Canada; 15.00Can$ other. Canadian Institute Intl Affair, 15 Kings College Circle, Toronto Ontario M5S 2V9 Canada. **Tel** (416)979-1851, (800)668-2442. **ED** David A T Stafford. **LC** F1034; .B4. **DD** 971.0082. **Circ:** 3,000. available on microfilm and microfiche from University Microfilms International (UMI); available on an online database.
**Desc:** International affairs with emphasis on economic, political, social, diplomatic and defense roles of Canada.
**Ind/Abst** Am. Hist. Life (1973-1977); Can. Index (?-?); Can. Period. Index (19??-).

LE/1019-0732
**BEIRUT REVIEW, THE.** [Beirut rev.]. (1991)-. Periodical. English. Twice a year (Fall & Spring). $48.00 (institutions), $24.00 (individuals) Lebanon; $60.00 (institutions), $36.00 (individuals) other. Lebanese Center Policy Studies, Tayyar Building, Mkalles Sin al-Fil, Beirut Lebanon. **Tel** 011 1 490561, FAX 011 1 490375, telex 40543. **ED** Michael Bacos Young. **UDC** 3(560). **Bk Rev**, (Qty: 6). **Ad Acc. Pr Rev. Circ:** 1,000 (ctrl).

US/1077-9043
**BIANNUAL NEWSLETTER OF THE CONFERENCE GROUP ON ITALIAN POLITICS & SOCIETY, THE.** [Biannu. newsl. Conf. Group Ital. Polit. Soc.]. **Added/Corp** Conference Group on Italian Politics and Society. **VFOAT** Italian Politics & Society; Italian Politics and Society. (19??)-. Newsletter. English (Italian). sa. University of Pittsburgh University Center for International Studies, A. Sbraggia, Pittsburgh PA 15260. **ED** K. Robert Nilsson (Editor's telephone: (717)245-1564). **LC** JN5201; .N48. **DD** 320.945/005. **Bk Rev. Ad Acc.** ctrl circ. ***Continues*** *Newsletter (Conference Group on Italian Politics and Society).*

CN/0383-2848
**BIBLIOGRAPHY SERIES - NORMAN PATERSON SCHOOL OF INTERNATIONAL AFFAIRS (CARLETON UNIVERSITY). See** Political Science-Abstracting, Bibliographies and Statistics.

US
**BIENNIAL REPORT / JAPAN-UNITED STATES FRIENDSHIP COMMISSION. Main/Corp** Japan-United States Friendship Commission. (1990)-. English. be. Japan-United States Friendship Commission, 1200 Pennsylvania Avenue NW/3407, Washington DC 20004-2483. ***Continues*** *Japan-United States Friendship Commission. Annual Report.*

BG
**BIISS JOURNAL. Added/Corp** Bangladesh Institute of International and Strategic Studies. **VFOAT** B.I.I.S.S. Journal. Vol. 1, No. 1 (1980)-. Periodical. English. Bangladesh Institute of International and Strategic Studies, 1/46 Elephant Road, Dacca Bangladesh. **LC** D839; .B49. **DD** 327/.09/048.

## Political Science — International Relations

GR
**BLUELINE : GREEK AND MEDITERRANEAN INTELLIGENCE.** VFOAT Greek and Mediterranean Intelligence. Vol. 1, No. 1 (June 1984)-. Periodical. English. mo.

CN/0833-9864
**BOUT DE PAPIER.** [Bout pap.]. **Added/Corp** Professional Association of Foreign Service Officers. (Sept. 1983)-. Periodical. English (French). qt. 16.00Can$. Bout de Papier, 45 Rideau Street/Suite 600, Ottawa Ontario K1N 5W8 Canada. **Tel** (613)234-1391. **ED** Kevin O'Shea. **DD** 354.710089/2/05. **Bk Rev.** (Qty: 15). **Ad Acc. Adv Mgr:** D. Hulley. **Circ:** 2,600 (ctrl).
**Desc:** Canada's magazine of foreign service and diplomacy. Examines all aspects of Canadian foreign policy with special emphasis on the conduct of diplomacy. Written with both the professional diplomat and the interested observer in mind. Includes regular and guest columnists, tales from abroad, interviews, a look at major issues and refugee policy, with book reviews and how the media covers Canadian diplomacy.

IT/0391-6723
**BOZZE.** **Ceased.** Vol. 1, No. 1 (Jan. 1978)-(1994). Periodical. Italian. bm. Edizioni Dedalo Spa, Casella Postale 362, Bari 70100 Italy. **Tel** 011 39 080 5311400, FAX 011 39 080 5311414. **Ad Acc. Circ:** 6,000.
**Desc:** Research of peace and war, arms race, love as political problem, USA-USSR, rights and liberation of peoples, Christianity, Roman Catholic Church, American bishops and deterrence in Latin America.

US/1041-3324
**BRANCH FOUR.** [Branch four]. VFOAT Branch Four Magazine. Vol. 1, Issue 1 (Aug. 1986)-. Periodical. English. qt. Branch Four Magazine, PO Box 65659, Washington DC 20035. **LC** D839; .B74. **DD** 909.82/8/05. **Ind/Abst** Hum. Rights Intern. Rep.

BL
**BRASIL, PERSPECTIVAS INTERNACIONAIS.** **Ceased.** Vol. 1 (June/July 1984)-Ceased Vol. 23 (1989). Periodical. Portuguese. qt. Instituto Relacoes Internacionais, Rua Marques S Vicente 225 #20 Gavea, Rio de Janeiro 22453 Brazil. **Tel** 021/2741296. **ED** Marie Cristina T Duarte. **LC** F2537; .B693. **DD** 327.81. **Circ:** 700.
**Ind/Abst** Int. Polit. Sci. Abstr.

US
**BREAKING THE SIEGE : THE NEWSLETTER OF THE MIDDLE EAST JUSTICE NETWORK.** **Added/Corp** Middle East Justice Network. (1989)-. Newsletter. English. bm (6 issues). $20.00 US; $30.00 other. Middle East Justice Network, PO Box 495, Boston MA 02112. **Tel** (617)542-5056, FAX (617)542-4947.

●US/1060-3093
**BRIDGEWATER-DAVIS PACIFIC INTELLIGENCE UPDATE.** (BRIDGEWATER-DAVIS PACIFIC INTELLIGENCE UPDATE : REPORT FROM THE BRIDGEWATER-DAVIS PACIFIC DESK.). **Added/Corp** Bridgewater-Davis Publishing Group. Pacific Desk. VFOAT Pacific Intelligence Update. 1992-. Periodical. English. bm. $300.00. Bridgewater-Davis Publishing Group, 4128-1/2 California Avenue SW, Suite 106, Seattle WA 98116.

US/1060-2941
**BRIEFING, THE COMPREHENSIVE SOURCE FOR INTERNATIONAL SECURITY INTELLIGENCE.** **Ceased.** (19??)-(June 1992). English. mo. Varro Press, 7130 Village Dr., PO Box 8413, Shawnee Mission KS 66208. **Tel** (913)432-5856.
**Desc:** A comprehensive report and analysis of incidents involving terrorism, low-intensity conflict, insurgency, civil war, guerilla war, civil disorder and protest. Every country in the world is covered.

FR
**BULLETIN D'INFORMATION ET DE DOCUMENTATION.** **Main/Corp** Association d'Amitie Franco-Vietnamienne. No. 1 (June 1972)-. Bulletin. French. **Continues** Association d'Amitie Franco-Vietnamienne. Bulletin Interieur.

US/0096-3402
**BULLETIN OF THE ATOMIC SCIENTISTS.** See Science and Technology.

US/0890-6165
**BULLETIN OF THE DEPARTMENT OF INTERNATIONAL AFFAIRS, AFL-CIO, THE.** [Bull. Dep. Int. Aff., AFL CIO]. **Added/Corp** AFL-CIO. Dept. of International Affairs. Vol. 1, No. 1 (Sept. 1986)-. Bulletin. English. mo (with July/Aug. combined). Free on request. Bulletin of Department of International Affairs, 815 16th Street Northwest, Room 705, Washington DC 20006. **Tel** (202)637-5372. **ED** Tom Kahn and Adrian Karatnycky. **DD** 331. **Bk Rev. Circ:** 8,500 (ctrl).
**Desc:** Covers international trade union and worker rights issues.

FR/0751-0772
**BULLETIN OFFICIEL (FRANCE. MINISTERE DES RELATIONS EXTERIEURES).** (BULLETIN OFFICIEL / MINISTERE DES RELATIONS EXTERIEURES.). [Bull. off. - Minist. relat. exter.]. Bulletin. French. Journaux Officiels, 26 rue Desaix, 75727 Paris Cedex 15 France. **Tel** 40 58 77 27. **LC** JX682; .B84. **DD** 354.440089.
**Continues** Bulletin Officiel (France. Ministere des Affaires Etrangeres).

●US/1065-0237
**BULLETIN - SEARCH FOR COMMON GROUND (ORGANIZATION). INITIATIVE FOR PEACE AND COOPERATION IN THE MIDDLE EAST.** (BULLETIN / SEARCH FOR COMMON GROUND, INITIATIVE FOR PEACE AND COOPERATION IN THE MIDDLE EAST.). [Bull. - Search Common Ground (Organ.), Initiat. Peace Coop. Middle East]. **Added/Corp** Search for Common Ground (Organization). Initiative for Peace and Cooperation in the Middle East. VFOAT Bulletin of Regional Cooperation in the Middle East. Vol. 1, No. 1 (Mar. 1, 1992)-. Bulletin. English. qt. $20.00. Search for Common Ground, 1601 Connecticut Avenue NW, Suite 200, Washington DC 20009. **DD** 327.

UK/0007-6724
**BUSINESS EUROPE.** See Business.

BE/0771-6435
**CAHIERS.** See History(General).

CN/0832-0683
**CANADA AMONG NATIONS.** [Can. nations]. **Added/Corp** Norman Paterson School of International Affairs. (1984)-. English. an. 32.95Can$ (cloth), 22.95Can$ (paper). Oxford University Press / Canada, 70 Wynford Drive, Don Mills, Toronto Ontario M3C 1J9 Canada. **Tel** (416)441-2941, FAX (416)441-3251. **LC** F1034.2; C279. **DD** 327.71.

CN/0045-4737
**CANADIAN FAR EASTERN NEWSLETTER, THE.** **Ceased.** (Jan. 1948)-(Dec. 1992). Newsletter. English. ir (ten issue per year). Canadian Far Eastern News, 232 Wychwood Avenue, Toronto Ontario M6C 2T3 Canada. **Tel** (416)651-5727. **ED** James G Endicott. **Ad Acc. Circ:** 1,500 (ctrl).
**Desc:** Interpretation of modern China, world peace, world revolutionary changes, and religious values.

CN/0838-5041
**CANADIAN PEACE REPORT.** (THE CANADIAN PEACE REPORT / THE CANADIAN PEACE ALLIANCE.). [Can. peace rep.]. **Added/Corp** Canadian Peace Alliance. VFOAT Peace Report. Vol. 1, No. 1 (Spring 1989)-. Periodical. English. qt (Apr., July, Sept., Dec.). 12.00Can$. Canadian Peace Alliace, 555 Bloor Street West, Suite 5, Toronto, Ontario M55 1Y6 Canada. **Tel** (416)588-5555. **DD** 327.1/72/0971. **Continues** Canadian Peace Alliance News., 0846-4650.
**Ind/Abst** Can. Period. Index (Vol. 2, No. 2, Fall 1990-).

CN
**CANADIAN REPRESENTATIVES ABROAD AND REPRESENTATIVES OF OTHER COUNTRIES IN CANADA.** **Main/Corp** Canada. Dept. of External Affairs. (19??)-. Periodical. English. an. 8.25Can$. Canada Communication Group Publishers, Order Processing, Ottawa Ontario K1A 0S9 Canada. **Tel** (819)956-4800, (819)956-4802. **LC** JX1729.A2; A3. **DD** 327.71.

CN/0382-8662
**CANADIAN WORLD FEDERALIST (1975).** See Law-International Law.

US/8756-324X
**CARIBBEAN UPDATE.** See Business.

NE
**CARIBBEAN YEARBOOK OF INTERNATIONAL RELATIONS, THE.** 1975-. English. Sijthoff & Noordhoff International Publishers BV, PO Box 4, Alphen aan der Rijn Leyden Netherlands. **ED** L F Manigat. **LC** F2155; .C37. **DD** 327/.09729.

CN/0702-8334
**CARLETON INTERNATIONAL STUDIES.** [Carleton int. stud.]. Vol. 1 (1977)-. Monographic series. English. ir. Price varies per volume. Norman Paterson School of International Affairs, Carleton University, Ottawa Ontario K1S 5B6 Canada. **Tel** (613)788-2600, FAX (613)788-2889, telex 053-4232. **Bk Rev.**

IE
**CARN.** **Added/Corp** Celtic League. No. 1 (Spring 1973)-. Periodical. Celtic languages (English). Four times a year. 9p UK & Ireland; 10p Europe; 11p others. Celtic League, Seana Gharrain, An Spideal, Co Na Gaillimhe Ireland. **Tel** 011 33 353 91 83423.

US/0891-1975
**CAUSA INTERNATIONAL SEMINAR SERIES (NEW YORK, N.Y. : 1986).** **Ceased.** (CAUSA INTERNATIONAL SEMINAR SERIES.). [CAUSA Int. semin. ser.]. (1986)-?. Monographic series. English. ir. International Security Council, 2000 L Street, NW, Suite 506, Washington DC 20036-2563. **Tel** (202)828-0802, FAX (202)429-2563, telex 229115 AUIS. **DD** 327. **Continues** Causa International, International Security Council Conference Series, 0892-3191.

US/0272-2429
**CENTER FOR STRATEGIC AND INTERNATIONAL STUDIES, GEORGETOWN UNIVERSITY, THE.** (THE CENTER FOR STRATEGIC AND INTERNATIONAL STUDIES, GEORGETOWN UNIVERSITY. [ANNUAL REPORT]). [Cent. Strateg. Int. Stud., Georgetown Univ.]. **Main/Corp** Georgetown University. Center for Strategic and International Studies. **Added/Corp** Georgetown University. Center for Strategic and International Studies. Annual Report. (19??)-. English. an. Center for Strategic and International Studies, 1800 K Street NW / Suite 520, Washington DC 20006. **Tel** (202)887-0200 Ext. 306. **ED** Susan Sojourner. **LC** UA10.5; .G46a. **DD** 327/.07/11753. Index available. cum. index. **Bk Rev. Pr Rev.**
**Desc:** The CSIS Significant Issues Series Monographs covers a diversity of topics of interest to the general reader as well as to the academic and policy-making communities.

US
**CENTRAL AMERICA REPORT.** (CENTRAL AMERICA REPORT / RELIGIOUS TASK FORCE OF CENTRAL AMERICA.). (19??)-. English. bm (6 issues). $15.00 (institutions), $10.00 (individuals). Religious Task Force on Central America, 1747 Connecticut Avenue NW, Washington DC 20009. **Tel** (202)387-7652. **ED** Margaret Swedish. **Bk Rev. Circ:** 3,000.
**Desc:** News and information on Latin America.

UK
**CENTREPIECES.** No. 1 (Spring 1982)-. Monographic series. English. ir. Price varies per volume. University of Aberdeen, Dunbar Street, Edward Wright Building, Aberdeen AB9 2TY Scotland. **Tel** 011 224 40241 ext. 5414.

BE
**CEPS PAPERS.** **Added/Corp** Centre for European Policy Studies (Louvain-la-Neuve, Belgium). VFOAT CEPS Paper. (1983)-. Monographic series. English. ir. Price varies per volume. Brasseys UK Ltd., 33 John Street, London WC1N 2AT England. **Tel** 011 44 71 753 7777, FAX 011 44 71 753 7794.
**Ind/Abst** World Agric. Econ.

UK/0143-5795
**CHATHAM HOUSE PAPERS.** [Chatham House pap.]. **Added/Corp** Royal Institute of International Affairs. (1979)-. Monographic series. English. ir. Price varies per volume. Council on Foreign Relations, 58 East 68th Street, New York NY 10021. **Tel** (212)734-0400 ext.225, telex 239852 CFR. **LC** UNC. **Bk Rev. Ad Acc. Circ:** 80.
**Desc:** Guides to policy debates on issues of foreign policy.

CC
**CHINA & THE WORLD.** VFOAT China and The World. (1982)-. English (German, Japanese and Spanish). $2.00 and up. Beijing Review, 24 Baiwanzhuang Road, Beijing 100037, People's Republic of China. **Tel** 8314318, FAX 8314318, telex 222374 FLPDA CN. **ED** Wany Youfen. **LC** DS779.27; .C487. **DD** 327.51. **Ad Acc.**
**Desc:** Publishes a selection on China's current political, economic, cultural and social developments.

CC/1002-4980
**CHIU SHIH.** **Added/Corp** Chung Kung Chung Yang Tang Hsiao. Chung-kuo Kung Chan Tang. Chung Yang wei Yuan hui. VFOAT Qiu Shi; Qiushi. (1988)-. Periodical. Chinese. sm. $28.82. (**Subscription address:** China International Book Trading Corporation, PO Box 399, Library Service Department, Beijing 100044 People's Republic of China.) **LC** AP95.C4; C54667. **DD** 324.251/075/05. **Continues** Hung Chi, 0441-4381.

NE
**CHRISTEN DEMOCRATISCHE VERKENNINGEN : MAANDBLAD VAN HET WETENSCHAPPELIJK INSTITUUT VOOR HET CDA.** 0/81-. Periodical. Dutch. mo. $16.17. Dr Kuyperstraat 5, 2415 Ba Den Haag Netherlands. **Tel** 070-924021. **LC** JN5981; .C463. cum. index. **Continues** Ar Staatkunde in Christian-Democratisch Perspectief; Christelijk Historisch

*Tijdschrift; Politiek Perspectief.*
**Ind/Abst** Maize Abstr.; Wheat Barley Trit. Abstr.; World Agric. Econ.

AT
**CHRISTIAN DEFENCE LEAGUE. See** History(General)-History of Australia and Oceania.

US
**CHRONICLE OF UNITED NATIONS DOCUMENT SERVICE, THE. Added/Corp** United Nations. **VFOAT** Chronicle of United Nations. No. 1 (May 1957)-. Government Publication. English. qt. $20.00. United Nations Publications, 2 United Nations Plaza, Room DC2 0853, Department 007C, New York NY 10017. **Tel** (212)963-8303, (800)253-9646. **(Subscription address:** Subscription Office, PO Box 361, Birmingham, AL 35201-0361, USA, Telephone: 800-633-4931**)**
**Desc:** Regular reports on the wide-ranging activities of the UN system from food and health to nuclear disarmament and the world economy. Each session of the Security Council and General Assembly are fully covered including their resolutions in the context of debates.

CN/0847-1304
**CHRONIQUE DES RELATIONS EXTERIEURES DU CANADA.** [Chron. relat. exter. Can.]. **Added/Corp** Centre Quebecois de Relations Internationales. Canada. Affaires Exterieures et Commerce Exterieur Canada. **VFOAT** Canadian International Relations Chronicle. (Jan./Mar. 1989)-. Periodical. French (English). qt. External Trade and International Affairs, 125 Promenade Sussex, Ottawa Ontario K1A 0G2 Canada. **Tel** (613)996-6137. **DD** 327.71.
**Ind/Abst** Can. Period. Index (19??-).

CN/0847-1304
**CHRONIQUE DES RELATIONS EXTERIEURES DU CANADA.** (CANADIAN INTERNATIONAL RELATIONS CHRONICLE.). [Chron. relat. exter. Can.]. **Added/Corp** Centre Quebecois de Relations Internationales. Canada. External Affairs and International Trade Canada. **VFOAT** Chronique des Relations Exterieures du Canada. (Jan./Mar. 1989)-. Periodical. English (French). qt. Free on request. External Trade and International Affairs, 125 Promenade Sussex, Ottawa Ontario K1A 0G2 Canada. **Tel** (613)996-6137. **DD** 327.71.
**Ind/Abst** Can. Period. Index (1989-).

US/0278-8365
**CHRONOLOGIES OF MAJOR DEVELOPMENTS IN SELECTED AREAS OF FOREIGN AFFAIRS (CUMULATIVE EDITION).** (CHRONOLOGIES OF MAJOR DEVELOPMENTS IN SELECTED AREAS OF FOREIGN AFFAIRS.). [Chronol. major dev. sel. areas foreign aff., Cumul. ed.]. **Added/Corp** United States. Congress. House. Committee on Foreign Affairs. Library of Congress. Foreign Affairs and National Defense Division. (1979)-. English. an. **LC** D839; .C823. **DD** 327/.09/047. ***Continues*** *Chronologies of Major Developments in Related Areas of International Relations (Cumulative Edition), 0278-8357.*

CH
**CHUNG-KUO TA LU YEN CHIU (KUO LI CHENG CHIH TA HSUEH. KUO CHI KUAN HSI YEN CHIU CHUNG HSIN).** (CHUNG-KUO TA LU YEN CHIU.). **VFOAT** Mainland China Studies. Periodical. Chinese. mo. $53.00 (surface mail), $79.00 (airmail). Institute of International Relations, Editorial and Publishing Section, 64 Wan Shou Road Mucha, Taipei Taiwan. **LC** DS779.15; .C54. **DD** 951.05/05. **Bk Rev. Ad Acc. Circ:** 4,000.
**Desc:** This journal is devoted to Mainland China Studies, and also provides a detailed monthly review of the general, personnel, transportation, communication and diplomatic activities of the Chinese Communists.

CK
**CIENCIA POLITICA.** (1985)-. Periodical. Spanish. qt. $34.00 North America; $24.00 Colombia; $36.00 other. Tierra Frime Editores, Carrera 9 A 99 02 406, Aereo 89299 Bogota Colombia. **Tel** 011 57 618 2372.
**Ind/Abst** PAIS Int. Print.

UK/1010-1845
**CIIR JUSTICE PAPERS.** [CIIR justice pap.]. **VFOAT** Catholic Institute for International Relations Justice Papers. (1981)-. Monographic series. English. an.
**Ind/Abst** Hum. Rights Intern. Rep.

UK/1010-1853
**CIIR NEWS.** [CIIR news]. **VFOAT** Catholic Institute for International Relations News. (1986)-. Periodical. English. qt. Catholic Institute for International Relations, 190A New N Road, Unit 3, Canonb Yd, London N1 7BJ United Kingdom. **Tel** 011 44 71 3540883, FAX 011 44 71 3590017, telex 21118 CIIR G.
**Ind/Abst** Hum. Rights Intern. Rep.

CN/0822-8418
**CIRCA. CONFLITS INTERNATIONAUX, LES REGIONS ET LE CANADA.** (CIRCA / SOUS LA DIRECTION DE ALBERT LEGAULT ET JOHN SIGLER.). [CIRCA, Confl. int. reg. Can.]. **VFOAT** Rapport Annuel sur les Conflits Regionaux et Intra-Regionaux; Conflits Internationaux, les Regions et le Canada. French (English). an. 12.00Can$ Canada and US. Centre Quebecois de Relations Internationales, Pavillon de Koninck/Bureau 5460, Universite Laval, Laval Quebec G1K 7P4 Canada. **Tel** (418)656-2462, FAX (418)656-3634. **DD** 327.1/1/05. **Ad Acc. Circ:** 400 (ctrl).
**Desc:** Report on international relations, specifically on conflicts in the world.

US/0897-4705
**CISA WORKING PAPER (LOS ANGELES, CALIF. : 1985).** (CISA WORKING PAPER.). [CISA work. pap.]. No. 47-. Monographic series. English. ir. Price varies per volume. Center for International and Strategic Affairs, UCLA, 11383 Bunche Hall, Los Angeles CA 90024-1486. **Tel** (310)825-0604. **ED** Ann M Florini. **DD** 327. Index available. **Circ:** 500. ***Continues*** *ACIS Working Paper (Los Angeles, Calif. : 1979).*

●US/1065-6391
**CISSM PAPERS. Added/Corp** University of Maryland, College Park. Center for International Security Studies at Maryland. **VAT** Center for International Security Studies at Maryland Papers. (1992)-. English. $5.00 (single issue). CISSM, University of Maryland, College Park MD 20742.

NE/0587-5994
**CO-EXISTENCE (DORDRECHT).** (CO-EXISTENCE.). [Co-existence]. **VFOAT** Coexistence. (1964)-. Periodical. English. qt. $352.00. Martinus Nijhoff Publishers, Subsidiary of Kluwer Academic Publishers, Koraalrood 50, 2718 SC Zoetermeer Netherlands. **Tel** 011 31 79 684400. **ED** Stephen White and Rene Beermann. **LC** H1; .C633. **DD** 300/.5. **[CCC]. Bk Rev. Ad Acc. Pr Rev. Acid Free.** available on microfilm and microfiche from University Microfilms International (UMI). Documents available.
**Desc:** Specializes in East-West relations, comparative studies of politics, institutions and structures of East and West, and issues of socio-economic development in a global context.
**Ind/Abst** ABC POL SCI; Am. Hist. Life (1973-1978); Index Period. Artic. Relat. Law; Int. Bibliogr. Sociol.; Int. Polit. Sci. Abstr. (1973-1978); Int. Bibliogr. Zeitschriftenliteratur Allen Gebieten Wissens; Linguist. Lang. Behav. Abstr.; Middle East Abstr. Index; Soc. Plann. Policy Dev. Abstr.; Sociol. Abstr. (1973-1978).

US/0730-1251
**COALITION CLOSE-UP.** (COALITION CLOSE-UP : NEWSLETTER OF THE COALITION FOR A NEW FOREIGN AND MILITARY POLICY.). **Added/Corp** Coalition for a New Foreign and Military Policy (U.S.). **VAT** Coalition Close Up. (19??)-. Periodical. English. qt. $20.00. Coalition New Foreign Policy, 712 G Street SE, Washington DC 20003-2852. **Tel** (202)546-8400. **ED** Cynthia Washington. **Bk Rev. Circ:** 15,000.
**Ind/Abst** Hum. Rights Intern. Rep.

US
**CODEPU FIFTH REGION BOLETIN. See** Political Science-Civil Rights.

NE
**COLLECTION DE RELATIONS INTERNATIONALES. Added/Corp** Graduate Institute of International Studies (Geneva, Switzerland). (1972)-. Monographic series. Multiple languages (English and French). ir. Price varies per volume. Rijksherbarium, PO Box 9514, 2300 RA Leiden Netherlands. **Tel** 011 31 71 273500. **DD** 327.

UK/0308-7093
**COMMENT LONDON. 1971.** [Comment Lond. 1971]. (1971)-. Monographic series. English. bm.
**Ind/Abst** Hum. Rights Intern. Rep.

US
**COMMENTS ON CURRENT WORLD AFFAIRS.** 1- (1962)-. Periodical. English. bw. 2372 Veteran Avenue, Los Angeles CA 90064.

●IS/0334-4142
**COMMONWEALTH OF INDEPENDENT STATES AND THE MIDDLE EAST. Added/Corp** Merkaz Le-Heker Beri. Ha-M. U-Mizrah Eropah a. Sh. Marg'ori Meirok. Vol. 17, No. 1 (1992)-. Periodical. English. mo. $40.00. Soviet and East European Resource Center, FAC-Social Sciences, Mount Scopus, Jerusalem 91905 Israel. **Tel** (011)972 2 883180, FAX (011)972 2 322545, telex 26458. **ED** Dr. Sefani Hoffman. **LC** DS63.2.S65; B84. ***Continues*** *Soviet Union and the Middle East, 0334-4142.*

US/0149-5933
**COMPARATIVE STRATEGY.** [Comp. strategy]. **Added/Corp** SRI International. Strategic Studies Center. Vol. 1 (1978)-. Periodical. English. qt. £81.00 UK; $133.00 other. Taylor & Francis Ltd., Rankine Road, Basingstoke Hampshire, RG24 8PR United Kingdom. **Tel** 011 44 256 840366, FAX 011 44 256 479438, telex 858540. **(Subscription address:** Taylor & Francis Inc., 1900 Frost Road, Suite 101, Bristol PA 19007-1598.**) ED** Richard B. Foster. **LC** JX1; .C62. **DD** 327/.05. **CODEN** COSTDY. **[CCC]. Bk Rev. Ad Acc. Pr Rev. Circ:** 800. available on microfilm and microfiche from University Microfilms International (UMI). Documents available from The Genuine Article.
**Desc:** Devoted to the elucidation of the principles and practice of grand strategy in the contemporary world. It is dedicated to a revitalization of contemporary strategic thought by way of a full integration of theoretical perspectives, empirical investigation, and historical understanding as applied to the strategic problems of the present.
**Ind/Abst** Am. Bibliogr. Slavic East Europ. Stud. (19??-19??); Arts Humanit. Citation Index [Select. Cov.]; Curr. Contents Soc. Behav. Sci.; Curr. Mil. Pol. Lit.; Int. Polit. Sci. Abstr.; PAIS Int. Print (1991-); Peace Res. Abstr. J. (1978-1983); Res. Alert [Full Cov.]; Soc. Sci. Cit. Index [Full Cov.]; U.S. Polit. Sci. Doc.

IT/0010-5066
**COMUNITA INTERNAZIONALE.** (LA COMUNITA INTERNAZIONALE : RIVISTA TRIMESTRALE DELLA SOCIETA ITALIANA PER L'ORGANIZZAZIONE INTERNAZIONALE.). [Comunita int.]. **Added/Corp** Societa Italiana per l'Organizzazione Internazionale. Vol. 1 (Jan 1946)-. Periodical. Italian. qt. L100000.00 Italy; L200000.00 other. Editoriale Scientifica SRL, Via Generale Orsini 42, 80132 Naples Italy. **Tel** 011 39 81 7646084. **LC** JX1903; .C65. **DD** 341.105.
**Ind/Abst** ABC POL SCI; Am. Hist. Life (1955-1978); Foreign Lang. Index; Index Foreign Leg. Per.

UK/0963-1674
**CONFLICT INTERNATIONAL.** [Confl. int.]. (1991)-. Periodical. English. mo. £125.00 UK; $240.00 US. Conflict International Publications, 59 Gloucester Place, London W1H 3PE England. **Tel** 011 44 71 723-5830. **ED** Ian Geldard. **DD** 303.605. Index available. cum. index. **Bk Rev. Ad Acc. Circ:** 12,000. ***Continues*** *Terror Update, 0960-0159.*
**Desc:** Provides information, news, and analysis of low intensity conflicts worldwide. It contains articles on relevant security matters, a world review of events, and a monthly chronology of international terrorist incidents written by professionals and recognized experts.

US/0738-8942
**CONFLICT MANAGEMENT AND PEACE SCIENCE.** [Confl. manage. peace sci.]. **Added/Corp** World Research Center (Cambridge, Mass.). World University Division. World University. Cornell University. Field of Peace Studies and Peace Science. Peace Science Society (International). Vol. 5, No. 1 (Fall 1980)-. Periodical. English. Twice a year. Peace Science Society International SUNY, Department of Political Science, PO Box 6000, Binghamton NY 13902. **Tel** (607) 777-2303. **LC** JX1291; .J68. **DD** 327.1/7/072. **Pr Rev.** Documents available from The Genuine Article. ***Continues*** *Journal of Peace Science, 0094-3738.*
**Ind/Abst** ABC POL SCI; J. Econ. Lit.; J. Plan. Lit.; Middle East Abstr. Index; PAIS Int. Print (1991-?); Res. Alert [Full Cov.]; Soc. Sci. Cit. Index [Full Cov.]; U.S. Polit. Sci. Doc. (199?-).

CN/0227-1311
**CONFLICT QUARTERLY.** ***Title Change.*** (CONFLICT QUARTERLY : JOURNAL OF THE CENTRE FOR CONFLICT STUDIES, UNIVERSITY OF NEW BRUNSWICK.). [Conflict quarterly]. **Added/Corp** University of New Brunswick. Centre for Conflict Studies. Vol. 1, No. 1 (Summer 1980)-(Jan. 1995). Periodical. English. qt. University of New Brunswick Centre for Conflict Studies, PO Box 4400, Fredericton NB E3B 5A3 Canada. **Tel** (506)453-4587, FAX (506)453-4599, telex 014-46202. **ED** David Charters. **LC** D839; .C8425. **DD** 327.1/6. **[CCC].** Index available. **Bk Rev. Ad Acc. Pr Rev. Circ:** 500. ***Continued by*** *Journal of Conflict Studies.*
**Desc:** Low intensity conflict: terrorism, propaganda, unconventional warfare, intelligence, special operations, counterinsurgency, revolutionary and civil wars, psychological warfare.
**Ind/Abst** Am. Bibliogr. Slavic East Europ. Stud.; Curr. Mil. Pol. Lit.; PAIS Int. Print (1991-?); Peace Res. Abstr. J. (1980-1981).

UK/0069-8792
**CONFLICT STUDIES.** [Conflict stud.]. **Added/Corp** Institute for the Study of Conflict. Current Affairs Research Services Centre (London, England) Centre for Security and Conflict Studies. Research Institute for the Study of Conflict and Terrorism. No. 1 (Dec. 1969)-. Monographic series. English. mo. $145.00 US and Canada; £75.00 UK; £80.00 Europe; £90.00 other. Research Institute for the Study of Conflict and Terrorism, 136 Baker Street, London W1M 1FH England. **Tel** 011 44 71 224 2659, FAX 011 44 71 486 3064. **(Subscription telephone:** 01-439-7381**) ED** Joan Bates. **LC** D839; .C8427. **Bk Rev. Ad Acc. Circ:** 2,000. available on microfilm and microfiche from University Microfilms International (UMI).
**Desc:** Publications on all aspects of international conflict.
**Ind/Abst** Curr. Mil. Pol. Lit.; Int. Polit. Sci. Abstr.; Middle East Abstr. Index.

US/0276-6469
**CONGRESSIONAL PRESENTATION, FISCAL YEAR.** ***Ceased.*** (CONGRESSIONAL PRESENTATION, FISCAL YEAR ... - UNITED STATES. INTERNATIONAL DEVELOPMENT COOPERATION AGENCY.). [Congr. present. fisc. year]. **Main/Corp** United States. International Development Cooperation Agency. (1982)-(19??). English. an. US International Development Cooperation Agency, Agency for International Development, Washington DC 20523. **LC** HC60; .U63a. **DD** 338.91/73/0172405.

CN/0823-8669
**CONSCIENCE CANADA NEWSLETTER.** **See** Public Administration-Public Finance and Taxation.

US/1059-8561
**CONSOLIDATED TREATIES & INTERNATIONAL AGREEMENTS. CURRENT DOCUMENT SERVICE, EUROPEAN COMMUNITY.** [Consol. treaties int. agreem., Curr. doc. serv. Eur. Community]. **Main/Corp** Council of the European Communities. **Added/Corp** Commission of the European Communities. **VFOAT** Consolidated Treaties and International Agreements. Current Document Service, European Community; Current Document Service, European Community; CTIA European Community. (1991)-. English. qt. $500.00. Oceana Publications, Inc., 75 Main Street, Dobbs Ferry NY 10522. **Tel** (914)693-1320, FAX (914)693-0402. **LC** KJE918; .C68. **DD** 341/.0264/4. available on CD-ROM.

BR
**CONSULAR LIST AND LIST OF INTERNATIONAL ORGANIZATIONS.** **Main/Corp** Burma (Union). Ministry of Foreign Affairs. English. 75.00. Ministry of Foreign Affairs / Burma, 529/531 Merchant Street, Ragoon Burma. **LC** JX1859.B8; B87A. **DD** 327/.2/025591.

CN/0832-140X
**CONTACT - CANADIAN COUNCIL FOR INTERNATIONAL COOPERATION.** (CONTACT : A PUBLICATION OF THE CANADIAN COUNCIL FOR INTERNATIONAL COOPERATION.). [Contact - Can. Counc. Int. Coop.]. **Added/Corp** Canadian Council for International Co-Operation. **VFOAT** Contact. **VAT** Contact - Conseil Canadien pour la Cooperation Internationale. Vol. 10, No. 1 (Summer 1986)-. Periodical. English (French). Ten times a year. 15.00Can$. Canadian Council for International Cooperation, 1 Nicholas Street, Suite 300, Ottawa, Ontario K1N 7B7 Canada. **Tel** (613)241-7007, FAX (613)241-5302, telex 0636700492. **DD** 327.1/7/05. ***Continues*** *The Newsletter - Canadian Council for International Cooperation, 0705-4181.*

CN/0384-9333
**CONTEMPORARY AFFAIRS (TORONTO).** ***Suspended.*** (CONTEMPORARY AFFAIRS.). No. 1 (1939)-?. Periodical. English. Canadian Institute of International Affairs, 31 Wellesley Street East, Toronto Ontario M4Y 1G9 Canada. **Tel** (416)979-1851. **Circ:** 1,500.
**Desc:** Each volume deals with some aspect of current international affairs or Canadian foreign policy.

UK
**CONTEMPORARY SECURITY POLICY.** (19??)-. English. Three times a year. $175.00. Frank Cass & Company Ltd, Newbury House, 890-900 Eastern Avenue, Newbury Park, Ilford, Essex IG2 7HH United Kingdom. **Tel** 011 44 81 599 8866, FAX 011 44 81 599 0984, telex 897719. ***Continues*** *Arms Control, 0144-0381.*

CN/0704-1926
**COOPERATION (OTTAWA).** (COOPERATION; BULLETIN OF THE STUDENTS OF I.C.I.). **Added/Corp** University of Ottawa. Institute for International Co-Operation. Vol. 1 (Jan./March 1977)-. Periodical. English (French). Free. University of Ottawa Department of Linguistics, 78 Laurier Avenue, Ottawa Ontario K1N 6N5 Canada. **Tel** (613)231-3346. **DD** 327/.17/05.

●US/1064-9093
**COUNTERTERRORISM & SECURITY REPORT.** [Counterterror. secur. rep.]. **Added/Corp** International Association of Counterterrorism & Security Professionals. **VFOAT** Counterterrorism and Security Report; Counter Terrorism and Security Report. (1992)-. Periodical. English. Six times a year (Jan., Mar., May, July, Sept., Nov.). $55.00 US; $65.00 Canada & Mexico & Panama; $67.00 other. International Association Counterterrorism & Security Professionals, PO Box 10265, Arlington VA 22210. **Tel** (703)243-0993, FAX (703)243-1197. **LC** IN PROCESS. **DD** 363. **Bk Rev. Ad Acc.** ***Continues*** *International Counterterrorism & Security.*

US/0275-309X
**COVERTACTION INFORMATION BULLETIN.** ***Title Change.*** [Covertaction inf. bull.]. **Added/Corp** Covert Action Publications, Inc. **VFOAT** Covert Action Information Bulletin; Covertaction. No. 1 (July 1978)-No. 42 (Fall 1992). Bulletin. English. bm. Covert Action Publications Inc, PO Box 34583, Washington DC 20043-4583. **Tel** (202)331-9763. **ED** Elen Ray, William Schaap, Louis Wolf and William Vornberger. **LC** JK468.I6; C68. **DD** 327.1/2/0973. Index available. **Bk Rev. Circ:** 10,000 (ctrl). available on microfilm and microfiche from University Microfilms International (UMI). ***Continued by*** *Covertaction Quarterly, 1067-7232.*
**Desc:** Reports on undercover activities of US and western intelligence agencies, revealing a usually invisible level of international policymaking.
**Ind/Abst** Altern. Press Index; Hum. Rights Intern. Rep.; PAIS Int. Print (1991-).

FR
**CROISSANCE.** No. 327 (May 1990)-. Periodical. French. mo (11 issues). 73.64Can$. Malesherbes Publications, 163 Boulevard Malesherbes, 75859 Paris France. **Tel** 011 33 1 48884600, FAX 011 33 1 48884601. **ED** Alain des Mazery. **LC** HC59.7; .C73. **DD** 909/.09724. Index available. **Bk Rev. Ad Acc. Circ:** 25,000. ***Continues*** *Croissance des Jeunes Nations, 0011-1686.*
**Desc:** Third World information, development and solidarity. Economic, political, cultural relations between developed countries and undeveloped countries.
**Ind/Abst** PAIS Int. Print; Point Repere (1990-).

US
**CSIA DISCUSSION PAPER.** **Added/Corp** John F. Kennedy School of Government. Center for Science and International Affairs. **VAT** Center for Science and International Affairs Discussion Paper. (1991)-. Monographic series. English. John F Kennedy School of Government, Harvard University, 79 John F Kennedy Street, Cambridge MA 02138. ***Formed by the union of*** *CSIA Working Papers; Discussion Paper (John F. Kennedy School of Government. Global Environmental Policy Project)* ***and*** *Discussion paper (John F. Kennedy School of Government. Science, Technology and Public Policy Program).*

US/0897-120X
**CSIA NEWS.** [CSIA news]. **Added/Corp** John F. Kennedy School of Government. Center for Science and International Affairs. **VAT** Center for Science and International Affairs News. Vol. 1, No. 1 (Summer 1987)-. Periodical. English. ir. Harvard University Center for Science & International Affairs, 79 JFK Street, School of Government, Cambridge MA 02138. **Tel** (617)495-1400. **DD** 327.

US
**CSIA STUDIES IN INTERNATIONAL SECURITY.** **Added/Corp** John E. Kennedy School of Government. Center for Science and International Affairs. **VFOAT** International Security; Center for Science and International Affairs Studies in International Security. No. 1 (Nov. 1991)-. Monographic series. English. John F Kennedy School of Government, Harvard University, 79 John F Kennedy Street, Cambridge MA 02138.

US/0195-8135
**CUBAN CHRONOLOGY.** (CUBAN CHRONOLOGY / NATIONAL FOREIGN ASSESSMENT CENTER.). English. Document Expediting Project, Exchange and Gift Division, Library of Congress, Photoduplication Service, Washington DC 20540. **Tel** (202)287-9527. **LC** F1788; .U43A. **DD** 327.7291.

RU
**CULTURE AND LIFE.** **Added/Corp** Vsesoiuznoe Obshchestvo Kulturnoi Sviazi s Zagranitsei, Moscow. Soiuz Sovetskikh Obshchestv Druzhby i Kulturnoi Svia s Zarubezhnymi Stranami. (1957)-. Periodical. English (French, German, Russian and Spanish). Four times a year. $89.95. Izdatelstvo Sovetskaia Rossiia, Proezd Sapunova 13-15, Moscow K-12, Russia. **(Subscription address:** East View Publications Inc., 3020 Harbor Lane North, Suite 110, Minneapolis MN 55447.) **LC** DK1; .C8. **DD** 327.47. ***Supersedes*** *Voks Bulletin.*
**Desc:** Deals with the participation of Russian people in public life and national economy. Scientific news and international cultural ties also receive extensive coverage.
**Ind/Abst** Middle East Abstr. Index.

FR/1157-996X
**CULTURES ET CONFLITS.** **Added/Corp** Centre d'Etude des Conflits (Paris, France). **VFOAT** Culturas y Conflictos; Cultures and Conflicts; C & C; C et C. No 1 (Winter 1991)-. Periodical. French. qt. 300.00F (France); 340.00f (other). L'Harmatten, 7 Rue de L'Ecole-Polytechnique, 75005 Paris France. **Tel** 11 33 1 43257651.
**Ind/Abst** PAIS Int. Print.

US
**CURRENT BRITISH FOREIGN POLICY.** (1970)-. English. Glendessary Press, Berkeley CA. **LC** DA592; .C852.

US/0731-8189
**CURRENT TREATY INDEX.** **See** Law-Abstracting, Bibliographies and Statistics.

US/0192-6802
**CURRENT WORLD LEADERS.** **Added/Corp** International Academy at Santa Barbara. **VFOAT** Biography & News. Vol. 21, No. 4 (Apr. 1978)-. Directory. English. bm. $248.00 (institutions), $193.00 (individuals), US; $258.00 (institutions), $203.00 (individuals). International Academy at Santa Barbara, 800 Garden Street, Suite D, Santa Barbara CA 93101. **Tel** (805)965-5010, FAX (805)965-6071. **ED** Thomas S. Garrison. **LC** D839; .C875. **DD** 327/.09045. **CODEN** CWOLED. **[CCC]. Circ:** 2,500. available on microfilm and microfiche from University Microfilms International (UMI). Documents available. ***Formed by the union of*** *Current World Leaders. Almanac, 0002-6255; Current World Leaders. Biography and News, 0002-6263* ***and*** *Current World Leaders. Speeches and Reports, 0092-1386.*
**Desc:** Current directory of world leaders, with issues focusing on special topics or geopolitical areas; includes original articles, commentary, socioeconomic-political backgrounders, speeches, and reports.
**Ind/Abst** Int. Polit. Sci. Abstr.; Linguist. Lang. Behav. Abstr.; Soc. Plann. Policy Dev. Abstr.; Sociol. Abstr.

CY
**CYPRUS REVIEW, THE.** **See** Social Sciences.

GW/0418-3894
**DARSTELLUNGEN ZUR AUSWARTIGEN POLITIK.** 1- 1960-. Periodical. German. ir. W Kohlhammer Verlag GmbH, Postfach 800430, D 70549 Stuttgart Germany. **Tel** 011 49 711 78631, FAX 011 49 711 7863263, telex 7-255820.

US/0738-2901
**DEADLINE (CHICAGO, ILL.).** **See** Journalism.

US/0364-9008
**DEFENSE & ECONOMY : WORLD REPORT AND SURVEY.** ***Title Change.*** (1984)-(19??)-. English. ir. Government Business Worldwide Reports, PO Box 5997, Washington DC 20016. **Tel** (202)244-7050, FAX (202)244-5410. **ED** J H Wagner. Index available. cum. index. **Bk Rev.** ***Continued by*** *International Observer, 1061-0324.*
**Desc:** Information on international defense and military economic affairs with special emphasis on defense plans and requirements.

US/0884-4054
**DEFENSE & FOREIGN AFFAIRS WEEKLY.** ***Ceased.*** **See** Military and Defense.

US/0193-9181
**DEFENSE & FOREIGN AFFAIRS' WEEKLY REPORT ON STRATEGIC AFRICAN AFFAIRS.** **VFOAT** Weekly Report on Strategic African Affairs; Strategic African Affairs. **VAT** Defense and Foreign Affairs' Weekly Report on Strategic African Affairs. Periodical. English. wk. $197.00. Copley & Associates S A, 2030 M Street NW, Washington DC 20036.

US
**DESSAUER'S JOURNAL.** (19??)-. Newsletter. English. mo. $195.00. Phillips Publishing Inc, 7811 Montrose Road, Potomac MD 20854. **Tel** (800)722-9120, (301)340-2100. **ED** John Dessauer (editor's address: PO Box 1718, Orleans, MA 02653; Phone: (508)255-1651). **Circ:** 4,000 (ctrl).

GW/0011-9881
**DEUTSCHE AUSSENPOLITIK.** [Dtsch. Aussenpolit.]. Vol. 1- ; Jan. 1956-. Periodical. German. mo. Deutscher Judo Verband, Redaktion Ippon Segewaldweg 40, D 12557 Berlin Germany. **Tel** 011 49 711 210770, telex 051 678. **LC** DD261.4; .D35. **DD** 327.
**Ind/Abst** Am. Hist. Life (1962-1970); Energy Res. Abstr. (Sept. 1980-).

US/8756-7466
**DEVELOPMENT AND FOREIGN POLICY REPORT.** [Dev. foreign policy rep.]. Began with V. 1, No. 1 (May/June 1984). Periodical. English. qt. $15.00. Association for Development Research, 1309 L Street NW, Washington DC 20005. **DD** 327.

SZ
**DHA UNDRO NEWS / UNITED NATIONS, DEPT. OF HUMANITARIAN AFFAIRS.** ***Title Change.*** **Added/Corp** United Nations. Dept. of Humanitarian Affairs. Office of the United Nations Disaster Relief Co-ordinator. **VFOAT** DHA-UNDRO News. (July/Aug. 1992)-(1992). Government Publication. English (French). bm. United Nations Publ, Geneva Palais des Nations, C-109, CH-1211 Geneva 10 Switzerland. **Tel** 011 41 22 7988400. **LC** HV553; .U16. **DD** 363.3/4526/05. ***Continues*** *UNDRO News, 0250-9377.* ***Continued by*** *DHA News (Geneva, Switzerland).*

IT/0394-901X
**DIABETE MILANO, IL.** [DiabeteMilano]. **VFOAT** Il Diabete. Aggiornamento Medico. (1989)-. Periodical. Italian. qt (Mar., June, Sept., Dec.). L80000. Editrice Kurtis Srl, Via Luigi Zoja 30, 20153 Milan Italy. **Tel** 011 39 2 48202740, FAX 011 39 2 48201219. **UDC** 616.379.

CN/1184-8758
**DIALOGUE - FONDATION ASIE PACIFIQUE DU CANADA.** (DIALOGUE.). [Dialogue - Fond. Asie Pac. Can.]. **Added/Corp** Fondation Asie Pacifique du Canada. Vol. 5, No 1 (Sept.

## Political Science — International Relations

1990)-. Periodical. French. qt. Limited free distribution. Asia Pacific Foundation of Canada, 666-999 Canada Pl., Vancouver, British Columbia V6C 3E1 Canada. **DD** 327.7105. *Continues* Point (Fondation Asie Pacifique du Canada)., 0835-8338.

SU
### DIBLUMASI (JIDDAH, SAUDI ARABIA).
(AL-DIBLUMASI / YUSDIRUHA MAHAD AL-DIRASAT AL-DIBLUMASIYAH, WIZARAT AL-KHARIJIYAH, AL-MAMLAKAH AL-ARABIYAH AL-SAUDIYAH.). Periodical. Arabic. Al-Diblumasi, PO Box 7954, Juddah Saudi Arabia. **LC** JX18; .D52.

UY
### DIPLOMACIA EN ACCION.
Vol. 1, No. 1 (July 1991)-. Periodical. Spanish. qt. $18.00 South America; $25.00 other. Diplomacia en Accion, 18 de Julio 2103, Apto. 1002, Montevideo Uruguay. **ED** Sergio Jellinek. **LC** K4; .I6912.

KO
### DIPLOMACY.
(19??)-. Periodical. English. Twelve times a year. $7.00. Diplomacy Company, Samduck Building 906, 131 Da Dong, Seoul South Korea. **Tel** 777-3370-4906. **LC** D839; .D515. **DD** 327/.05.

UK/0959-2296
### DIPLOMACY AND STATECRAFT. VFOAT
Diplomacy & Statecraft. Vol. 1, No. 1 (Mar. 1990)-. Periodical. English. Three times a year. $135.00. Frank Cass & Company Ltd, Newbury House, 890-900 Eastern Avenue, Newbury Park, Ilford, Essex IG2 7HH United Kingdom. **Tel** 011 44 81 599 8866, FAX 011 44 81 599 0984, telex 897719. **ED** David Armstrong and Erik Goldstein. **Ad Acc, Adv Mgr:** Anne Kidson.
**Desc:** A new international journal which should be read by all those who have a professional or general concern with international history and the contemporary conduct of international affairs.
**Ind/Abst** Am. Hist. Life (1990-); PAIS Int. Print (1991-).

UK
### DIPLOMAT (LONDON, ENGLAND), THE.
(THE DIPLOMAT.). (March/April 1986)-. Periodical. English. Six times a year. £40.00. Diplomatist Associates Ltd, 58 Theobalds Road, London WC1X 8SF England. **Tel** 071 405 4878. **ED** Wendy Holden. **LC** JX1; .D55. **DD** 351.8/92/05. **Bk Rev**. **Ad Acc. Circ:** 2,197 (ctrl). available on microfilm from University Microfilms International (UMI). *Continues* Diplomatist.
**Desc:** A monthly newsletter on international business protocol and social etiquette. Each month a different country is profiled. This includes a country briefing, doing business in that country, its customs - dining, giftgiving, etiquette, holidays/festivals - and important facts and addresses.

MW
### DIPLOMATIC AND CONSULAR DIRECTORY (LILONGWE, MALAWI).
(DIPLOMATIC AND CONSULAR DIRECTORY / MINISTRY OF EXTERNAL AFFAIRS, LILONGWE.). Directory. English. Ministry of External Affairs / Malawi, PO Box 30315, Lilongwe 3 Malawi. **LC** JX1865.M3; D56. **DD** 351.89/2/096897. *Continues* Diplomatic and Consular List (Zomba, Malawi).

PK
### DIPLOMATIC CORPS AND CONSULAR, TRADE, AND OTHER FOREIGN REPRESENTATIVES IN PAKISTAN / MINISTRY OF FOREIGN AFFAIRS.
English. NGM Communication, PO Box 2627, Karachi 75900 Pakistan. **Tel** 011 92 21 428625. **LC** JX1859.P3; D56. **DD** 351.89/2/095491. *Continues* List of the Diplomatic Corps and Consular, Trade and Other Foreign Representatives.

JM/0376-8384
### DIPLOMATIC CORPS. MINISTRY OF EXTERNAL AFFAIRS (KINGSTON).
(DIPLOMATIC CORPS - MINISTRY OF EXTERNAL AFFAIRS.). **Main/Corp** Jamaica. Ministry of External Affairs. (19??)-. English. 24 East Race Course, PO Box 624, Kingston Jamaica. **LC** JX1753; .A34a. **DD** 327/.2/0257292.

UK/0417-5131
### DIPLOMATIC PRESS DIRECTORY OF THE REPUBLIC OF CYPRUS INCLUDING TRADE INDEX AND BIOGRAPHICAL SECTION. VFOAT
Directory of the Republic of Cyprus including Trade Index and Biographical Section. Began with 1962/63 issue. Directory. English. Diplomatic Press & Publishing Company, 29 March Lane, London NW7 England.

US/0363-8200
### DIPLOMATIC WORLD BULLETIN AND DELEGATES WORLD BULLETIN, THE.
**VFOAT** Diplomatic World Bulletin; Diplomatic World. (1975)-. Periodical. English. Twenty-one times a year. $72.00. Diplomatic World Bulletin, 99 Wall Street, New York NY 10005. **Tel** (212)952-4824. **LC** JX1977.A1; D56. **DD** 341.23/05. **Ad Acc. Circ:** 13,500. *Continues* Delegates World Bulletin.

TI
### DIRASAT DAWLIYAH. VFOAT
Etudes Internationales. No. 1 (1981)-. Periodical. Arabic (French). qt. $19.00. 1 rue du Venezuala, Tunis Tunisia. **LC** D839; .D526.
**Ind/Abst** Middle East J.

SJ
### DIRECTORY OF PERSONNEL OF UNITED NATIONS ORGANIZATIONS AND THE INTERNATIONAL MONETARY FUND IN THE DEMOCRATIC REPUBLIC OF THE SUDAN.
Directory. English. Office of the Resident Representative of United Nations Development Program, PO Box 913, Khartoum Sudan. **LC** JX1977.2.S83; D57. **DD** 354.1/2/09624.

TU
### DIS POLITIKA. VFOAT
Foreign Policy. Vol. 1 (1971)-. Periodical. Turkish (English). qt. **LC** DR471; .D48. **DD** 327.56.
**Ind/Abst** Middle East J. (?-?).

US/0363-3721
### DISARMAMENT NEWS & INTERNATIONAL VIEWS. VAT
Disarmament News and International Views. Periodical. English. mo. $20.00. Council on Religion and International Affairs, 170 East 64th Street, New York NY 10021. **LC** JX1974.7; .D577. **DD** 327/.174/05. available on microfilm and microfiche from University Microfilms International (UMI). *Continues* Disarmament News & Views, 0275-794X.

US/0251-9518
### DISARMAMENT - UNITED NATIONS.
(DISARMAMENT.). [Disarmament - U. N.]. **Added/Corp** United Nations. United Nations. Dept. for Disarmament Affairs. Vol. 1 (May 1978)-. Government Publication. English. qt. $15.00. United Nations Publications, 2 United Nations Plaza, Room DC2 0853, Department 007C, New York NY 10017. **Tel** (212)963-8303, (800)253-9646. **LC** JX1974; .D48. **DD** 327/.174/05.
**Desc:** Multilingual volume in which disarmament terms used by the UN are fully compiled.
**Ind/Abst** PAIS Int. Print; Peace Res. Abstr. J. (1964-1967).

CL
### DOCUMENTO DE TRABAJO. SERIE RELACIONES INTERNACIONALES Y POLITICA EXTERIOR / FLACSO, PROGRAMA CHILE. Added/Corp
Facultad Latinoamericana de Ciencias Sociales. Programa Chile. **VFOAT** Serie Relaciones Internacionales y Politica Exterior; Documentos de Trabajo. Serie Relaciones Internacionales y Politica Exterior. No. 1 (1990)-. Monographic series. Spanish. Price varies per volume. **LC** HC1414.2; .D6. **DD** 327.8.

CN
### DOCUMENTS ON CANADIAN EXTERNAL RELATIONS. Main/Corp
Canada. Department of External Affairs. **VFOAT** Documents on Canadian External Affairs. Vol. 1 (1967)-. English (French). ir. 15.00Can$ Canada; 18.00Can$ other. Canada Communication Group Publishers, Order Processing, Ottawa Ontario K1A 0S9 Canada. **Tel** (819)956-4800, (819)956-4802.

II
### DOGAR MONTHLY GENERAL KNOWLEDGE DIGEST. VFOAT
General Knowledge Digest. Periodical. English. mo. Dogar Brothers, 17 Urdu Bazar, Lahore Pakistan. **LC** D839; .D63. **DD** 909.82/8. *Continues* Dogar's Monthly General Knowledge Digest.

US/1053-5829
### DONALD R. MORRIS NEWSLETTER.
[Donald R. Morris newsl.]. (Aug. 1989)-. Newsletter. English. Fifty times a year (Except the last 2 weeks of Dec.). $53.50 (one year) Texas; $54.13 (one year) Houston; $50.00 (one year) other. The Trident Syndicate, PO Box 19909, Houston TX 77224. **Tel** (713)871-7094. **DD** 327.

CN/0318-1316
### EAST-WEST COMMERCIAL RELATIONS SERIES.
Began publication in Aug. 1973. Monographic series. English. Price varies per volume. Institute of Soviet and East European Studies, Carleton University, Ottawa Ontario K1S 5B6 Canada. **Tel** (613)564-3798. **ED** C H McMillan. **DD** 382/.091713/01717. **Circ:** 300.
**Desc:** East-West commercial relations. Political aspects of Soviet energy resources.

UK/0142-9310
### EGYPT NEWSLETTER.
[Egypt newsl.]. **VFOAT** Newsletter Egypt. Newsletter. English. bw. $350.00. IC Publications Ltd, 7 Coldbath Square, London EC1R 4LQ England. **Tel** 011 44 71 713-7711, FAX 011 44 71 713-7898, telex 8811757.

RU/0234-1670
### EKHO PLANETY. Added/Corp
Telegrafnoe Agentstvo SSSR. Soiuz Zhurnalistov SSSR. (April 1988)-. Periodical. Russian. wk. **LC** D839; .E37.

UK
### EMBASSY.
Periodical. English. **LC** JX1; .E4. **DD** 327/.05.

US/0883-1815
### EMBASSY REPORT (AFRICA ED.).
(EMBASSY REPORT.). [Embassy rep.]. Vol. 1, No. 1 (Saturday Feb. 26-Friday Mar. 4, 1983)-. Periodical. English. wk. Embassy Report, PO Box 6802, Falls Church VA 22046. **DD** 327.

US/0883-1823
### EMBASSY REPORT (ASIA & OCEANIA ED.).
(EMBASSY REPORT.). [Embassy rep.]. Vol. 1, No. 1 (Feb. 26, 1983)-. Periodical. English. wk. Embassy Report, PO Box 6802, Falls Church VA 22046. **DD** 327.

US/0883-1807
### EMBASSY REPORT (ED. : AUSTRALIA, CANADA, JAPAN NEW ZEALAND, SCANDINAVIA & WESTERN EUROPE).
(EMBASSY REPORT.). [Embassy rep.]. Vol. 1, No. 1 (Saturday Feb. 26-Friday Mar. 4, 1983)-. Periodical. English. wk. Embassy Report, PO Box 6802, Falls Church VA 22046. **DD** 327.

US/0882-9683
### EMBASSY REPORT (LATIN AMERICA & CARIBBEAN ED.).
(EMBASSY REPORT.). [Embassy rep.]. Periodical. English. ir. Embassy Report, PO Box 6802, Falls Church VA 22046. **DD** 327.

US/0883-1793
### EMBASSY REPORT (MIDDLE EAST ED.).
(EMBASSY REPORT.). [Embassy rep.]. Vol. 1, No. 1 (Saturday Feb. 26-Friday Mar. 4, 1983)-. Periodical. English. wk. Embassy Report, PO Box 6802, Falls Church VA 22046.

UK/0140-2935
### ENVOY INTERNATIONAL (ASHFORD, KENT : 1981). (ENVOY INTERNATIONAL.).
Vol. 4, No. 1 (Mar. 1981)-. Periodical. English. mo. $42.50. Envoy International, PO Box 1305, Long Island City NY 11101. **LC** AP4; .A44. **DD** 052. *Continues* Ambassador & Envoy International.

FR/0014-1267
### EST & OUEST : BULLETIN DE L'ASSOCIATION D'ETUDES ET D'INFORMATIONS POLITIQUES INTERNATIONALES. Ceased. Added/Corp
Association d'Etudes et I'informations Politiques Internationales. **VFOAT** Horizons Nouveaux; Est et Ouest. **VAT** Est et Ouest. No. 143-145 (1956)-(1993). Bulletin. French. mo. **LC** D839; .A822. *Continues* B.E.I.P.I.
**Ind/Abst** Hum. Rights Intern. Rep. (?-?).

US/1043-1667
### ESTIMATE, THE.
English. bw. $295.00 North America; $330.00 other. The International Estimate, 1514 17th Street NW, Suite 115, Washington DC 20036. **Tel** (202)332-0849. **ED** Michael Collins Dunn. **Bk Rev. Circ:** 200.
**Desc:** Political and security intelligence analysis of North Africa, the Middle East, South Asia, East Asia and the Pacific Rim.

MX
### ESTUDIOS INTERNACIONALES.
**Added/Corp** Universidad Nacional Autonoma de Mexico. Facultad de Ciencias Politicas y Sociales. (19??)-. Spanish. ir. $18.00. Colegio de Mexico AC, Camino Al Ajusco No 20, 10740 Mexico DF Mexico. **Tel** 011 52 5 6455955 Ext. 3133, telex 1777585 COLME. **LC** JX9; .E69. **DD** 327/.05.

CN/0712-1180
### ETAT DU MONDE. (L'ETAT DU MONDE :
ANNUAIRE ECONOMIQUE ET GEOPOLITIQUE MONDIAL / SOUS LA DIRECTION DE FRANCOIS GEZE, YVES LACOSTE, ALFREDO G.A. VALLADAO.). [Etat monde]. (1981)-. French. an. 24.95Can$. Editions du Boreal, 4447 St. Denis, Montreal Quebec H2J 2L2 Canada. **Tel** (514)287-7401. **ED** Francois Geze, Yves Lacoste, Annie Lennkh, Thierry Paquot and Alfredo Valladao. **DD** 909.82/8/05.

US/0892-6794
### ETHICS & INTERNATIONAL AFFAIRS.
[Ethics int. aff.]. **Added/Corp** Carnegie Council on Ethics & International Affairs. **VFOAT** Ethics and International Affairs. Vol. 1 (1987)-. Periodical. English. an (Apr.). $10.00 US; $12.00 other. Carnegie Council on Ethics and International Affairs, 170 East 64th Street, New York NY 10021. **Tel** (212)838-4120, FAX (212)752-2432, telex CRIAPAX NEW YORK. **ED** Robert J. Myers. **LC** JX1255; .E73. **DD** 172/.4/05. **Ad Acc, Adv Mgr:** C. Wakeman. **Pr Rev. Circ:** 500 (ctrl).
**Desc:** A journal that examines the concrete application of ethics to various key international problems from a variety

of perspectives. The current issue features a section on the changing terms of sovereignty and intervention, and includes pieces by several authors.
**Ind/Abst** Hum. Rights Intern. Rep.; Int. Polit. Sci. Abstr.; PAIS Int. Print (1991-?).

CH/0256-5552
**ETUDES ET DOCUMENTS - INSTITUT DE RELATIONS INTERNATIONALES.** [Etud. doc. - Inst. relat. int.]. (1980)-. Periodical. French. Four times a year (Jan., April, July, October). $10.00. Institute of International Relations, Editorial and Publishing Section, 64 Wan Shou Road Mucha, Taipei Taiwan. **UDC** 327. **Circ:** 1,200.
**Ind/Abst** PAIS Int. Print.

CN/0014-2123
**ETUDES INTERNATIONALES (QUEBEC).** (ETUDES INTERNATIONALES.). [Etud. int.]. Vol. 1 (Feb. 1970)-. Periodical. French. qt. $41.31 (institutions), $32.71 (individuals) Canada; $41.44 (institutions), $36.84 (individuals) other. Centre Quebecois de Relations Internationales, Pavillon de Koninck/Bureau 5460, Universite Laval, Laval Quebec G1K 7P4 Canada. **Tel** (418)656-2462, FAX (418)656-3634. **LC** D849; E88. Index available. cum. index. **Bk Rev**. **Ad Acc**. **Circ:** 1,500 (ctrl).
**Desc:** A multidisciplinary journal devoted to international affairs.
**Ind/Abst** ABC POL SCI; Am. Hist. Life (1970-); Int. Labour Doc.; Int. Polit. Sci. Abstr.; PAIS Int. Print (1991-); Peace Res. Abstr. J. (1980-); Point Repere; Sage Public Adm. Abstr.; Middle East J.

SZ
**ETUDES POLITIQUES.** ***Ceased.*** Yearly Vol. 5 (Feb. 1974)-. French. ir. Institut Suisse de Recherche Sur les Pays de l'Est, Jubilaumsstrasse 41, CH-3000 6 Berne Switzerland. **LC** D839; .E84. **DD** 327/.05. ***Continues*** *Bulletin d'Etudes Politiques.*

●LU/1021-1667
**EUR-OP NEWS DEUTSCHE AUSG. See** Economics.

LU
**EUR PUBLICATION.** English. European Communities Commission, Case Postale 1003, Luxembourg Luxembourg. **Tel** (352)48 80 41, FAX (352)48 80 40, telex 2181.
**Ind/Abst** Postharvest News Inf.

LU
**EUR REPORT.** English. European Communities Commission, Case Postale 1003, Luxembourg Luxembourg. **Tel** (352)48 80 41, FAX (352)48 80 40, telex 2181.
**Ind/Abst** Postharvest News Inf.

UK
**EUROLINK AGE BULLETIN.** Bulletin. English (French and German; summaries and/or abstracts in Dutch, Italian and Spanish). Three times a year. £24.00. Eurolink Age, 1268 London Road, London SW16 4ER England. **Tel** 011 44 81 6798000, FAX 011 44 81 6796727.

GW/0014-2476
**EUROPA-ARCHIV.** [Europa Archiv]. **Added/Corp** Deutsche Gesellschaft fuer Auswaertige Politik. Forschungsinstitut. Deutsche Gesellschaft fuer Auswaertige Politik. Institut fuer Europaeische Politik und Wirtschaft. **VFOAT** Europa Archiv. (July 1946)-. Periodical. German. sm. DM224.80, DM244.80 (with covers) Germany; DM247.60, DM267.60 (with covers) other. Verlag fuer Internationale Politik GmbH, Postfach 1529, D 53005 Bonn Germany. **Tel** 011 49 228 7290010, FAX 011 49 28 695734, telex 8-86822. **ED** Wolfgang Wagner. **LC** D839; .E86. **[CCC]**. Index available. cum. index. **Bk Rev**. **Ad Acc**. **Pr Rev**. **Circ:** 4,500 (ctrl). Documents available from The Genuine Article.
**Desc:** Contains articles and documents on international relations, a current chronology of world events and a bibliography of recent publications in the field of international relations.
**Ind/Abst** ABC POL SCI; Am. Hist. Life (1955-1978); Curr. Contents Soc. Behav. Sci.; Energy Res. Abstr. (March 1979-); Int. Bibliogr. Sociol.; Int. Polit. Sci. Abstr.; PAIS Int. Print (1991-); Peace Res. Abstr. J. (1965-1967, 1969-1973); Res. Alert [Full Cov.]; Soc. Sci. Cit. Index [Full Cov.].

IT
**EUROPA E LA CEE, L'.** ***Ceased.*** (19??)-(Dec. 1993). Italian. mo. Pirola Editore, CP 10444, Via Parabiago 19, 20151 Milan Italy. **Tel** 011 39 2 3022888. **Bk Rev**. **Ad Acc, Adv Mgr:** V Systeece.

LU/1016-572X
**EUROPA FORUM LUXEMBOURG.** [Eur. forum Luxembg.]. (19??)-. Periodical. German. mo. **UDC** 328(4). **CODEN** CE. ***Continues*** *Das Europaische Parlament, 0250-5762.*
**Ind/Abst** PAIS Int. Print.

IT
**EUROPA RITROVATA : BIMESTRALE DELL'ISCOS SULL'EUROPA CENTRALE E DELL'EST, L'.** ***Ceased.*** **Added/Corp** Istituto Sindacale per la Cooperazione allo Sviluppo. Vol. 1, No. 1 (1990)-(Dec. 1993). Periodical. Italian. bm. Iscos Srl, Via Boncompagni 19, 00187 Rome Italy. **Tel** 011 39 6 4885639. **LC** DJK51; .E94.

AU/0304-2782
**EUROPAEISCHE RUNDSCHAU.** [Eur. Rundsch.]. Vol. 1 (July 1973)-. Periodical. German. qt. S370.00 Austria; S390.00 other Europe; S614.00 other. Europa Verlag Gesellschaft MBH, Altmannsdorferstr 154 156, A1232 Vienna 23 Austria. **Tel** 011 43 222 672622276. **LC** JN12; .E85a. Index available. **Bk Rev**. **Ad Acc**. **Circ:** 2,500 (ctrl).
**Desc:** Covers East-West affairs, with stress on developments in East Bloc. Contributions by authors from East and West on economics, politics and contemporary history.
**Ind/Abst** PAIS Int. Print.

UK
**EUROPE AND LATIN AMERICA.** 1980-. English. an. £1.95. **LC** F1416.G7; B7. **DD** 327.4108. ***Continues*** *Britain and Latin America.*

FR/0014-2808
**EUROPE EN FORMATION, L'.** [Eur. form.]. No. 1 (Mar. 1960)-. Periodical. French. mo. 160.00F. CIFE, Departement Presses d'Europe, 4 Boulevard Carabacel, F-06000 Nice France. **Tel** 93 858557, FAX 93 62 28 09. **Bk Rev**. **Ad Acc**. **Circ:** 2,000.
**Desc:** Problems of European unity and international relationships, federalism and regionalism.
**Ind/Abst** Am. Hist. Life (1972-1975); PAIS Int. Print.

BE
**EUROPE INFORMATION. EXTERNAL RELATIONS / COMMISSION OF THE EUROPEAN COMMUNITIES, SPOKESMAN'S GROUP, AND DIRECTORATE-GENERAL FOR INFORMATION.** **Added/Corp** Commission of the European Communities. Directorate General of Information. Commission of the European Communities. Spokesman's Group. (19??)-. Periodical. English. ir. Free on request. Office for Official Publications of the European Communities, 2 Rue Mercier, 2985 Luxembourg Luxembourg. **Tel** 011 352 499281, FAX 011 352 488573. **LC** KJE5105.A13; E97.

US/0191-4545
**EUROPE (WASHINGTON, D.C.). See** Business-Commerce.

UK/0955-534X
**EUROPEAN BUSINESS REVIEW. See** Business.

●UK
**EUROPEAN COMPANION, THE.** (1992)-. English. an. £130.00. Dods Publishing & Research Ltd, 31-A Saint James's Square, London WC1Y 4JR England. **Tel** 011 44 71 9306640, FAX 011 44 71 9309166. **ED** I. Smythe-Wood. Index available. **Bk Rev**, (Qty: 6-10). **Ad Acc**. **Pr Rev**. ***Continues*** *Dod's European Companion.*
**Desc:** Information on European communities.

NE
**EUROPEAN CONTRIBUTIONS TO AMERICAN STUDIES.** **Added/Corp** Universiteit van Amsterdam. Amerika Instituut. (1979)-. Monographic series. English.
**Ind/Abst** Am. Hist. Life (1986-).

FR
**EUROPEAN CONVENTIONS AND AGREEMENTS.** **Added/Corp** Council of Europe. **VFOAT** Conventions et Accords Europeens. (1961)-. English (French). ir. Council of Europe / Group Pact ED, Pharmacopoeia BP 907, 67029 Strasbourg Cedex 01 France. **Tel** 011 33 88 412036, FAX 011 33 88 41277181, telex 880388.

●UK/0966-2839
**EUROPEAN SECURITY.** Vol. 1, No. 1 (Spring 1992)-. Periodical. English. qt. $135.00. Frank Cass & Company Ltd, Newbury House, 890-900 Eastern Avenue, Newbury Park, Ilford, Essex IG2 7HH United Kingdom. **Tel** 011 44 81 599 8866, FAX 011 44 81 599 0984, telex 897719. **LC** IN PROCESS; UA646.3; .E9.

US/0730-0247
**EVOLUTIONARY BLUES.** **Added/Corp** Ten Directions Foundation. Vol. 1, No. 1 (Summer/Fall 1981)-. Periodical. English. qt. $12.00. Evolutionary Blues, PO Box 4448, Arcata CA 95521. **LC** JX1974.7; .E93. **DD** 327.1/74/05.

US
**FAR EASTERN AND RUSSIAN RESEARCH SERIES.** **Main/Corp** University of Southern California, Los Angeles. School of International Relations. No. 1 (1956)-. Monographic series. English. ir. Price varies per volume. School of International Relations, Far Eastern and Russian Research, Los Angeles CA 90089.

IT/0392-1042
**FEDERALISTA, IL.** [Federalista]. **Added/Corp** Movimento Federalista Europeo (Italy). Vol. 17 (March 1975)-. Periodical. Italian (English). tq (Mar., July, Nov.). L30000 Europe; L40000 other. Editrice Libera Associazione Il Federalista (EDIF), Via Porta Pertusi 6, 27100 Pavia Italy. **Tel** 011 39 382 20092, FAX 011 39 382 303784. **ED** Mario Albertini. **LC** D839; .F38. **DD** 327/.05. cum. index. **Circ:** 1,500. ***Continues*** *Federaliste (Pavia, Italy).*

US/0014-9810
**FELLOWSHIP (NEW YORK).** (FELLOWSHIP.). **Added/Corp** Fellowship of Reconciliation (U.S.) Women's International League for Peace and Freedom. Vol. 1 (March 1935)-. Periodical. English. Eight times a year. $15.00 US; $23.00 other. Fellowship of Reconciliation / Nyack, Box 271, Nyack NY 10960. **Tel** (914)358-4601, FAX (914)358-4924. **LC** JX1901; .F45. **DD** 172.405. Index available. **Bk Rev**. **Ad Acc**. available on microfilm and microfiche from University Microfilms International (UMI).
**Ind/Abst** Hum. Rights Intern. Rep.; Index Book Rev. Relig.; Peace Res. Abstr. J. (1964-1967).

LE
**FILASTIN.** **VFOAT** Falastine. Periodical. Arabic. £L20.00. Al-Hayah Al-Arabiyah Al-Ulya Li-Filastin, PO Box 113/6052, Beirut Lebanon. **LC** DS101; .F47.

RU
**FILOSOFSKIE OSNOVANIIA TEORII MEZHDUNARODNYKH OTNOSHENII.** **Added/Corp** Institut Nauchnoi Informatsii po Obshchestvennym Naukam (Akademiia Nauk SSSR). Vol. 1 (1987)-. Academic Scholarly Publication. Russian. Izdatelstvo Nauka / Akademiia Nauk, Publishing House of the Russian Academy of Sciences, Leninskii Porspekt 14, 117901 Moscow Russia. **Tel** 011 95 954-21-53, FAX 011 95 938-21-44, telex 411964. **LC** JX1246; .F48.

US/0094-3029
**FINANCIAL REPORT - CARNEGIE ENDOWMENT FOR INTERNATIONAL PEACE.** **Main/Corp** Carnegie Endowment for International Peace. English. an. Carnegie Endowment for International Peace, 345 East 46 Street, New York NY 10017. **LC** JX1906; .A462A. **DD** 327/.172/06273.

US/1046-1868
**FLETCHER FORUM OF WORLD AFFAIRS, THE.** [Fletcher forum world aff.]. **Added/Corp** Fletcher School of Law and Diplomacy. **VFOAT** Fletcher Forum. Vol. 13, No. 1 (Winter 1989)-. Periodical. English. Twice a year (Winter & Spring). $25.00 (institutions), $16.00 (individuals). Tufts University / Law, The Fletcher School of Law Diplomacy, Medford MA 02155. **Tel** (617)623-3610, FAX (617)623-3610. **ED** Professor Richard H. Shultz, Robert M. Flanagan, Joanne Giordano, Junko Shiota, and Tammy Halevy. **DD** 327. **Bk Rev**. **Ad Acc**. ***Continues*** *Fletcher Forum, 0147-0981.*
**Desc:** Analyzes outstanding problems of international law, politics, economics and diplomacy. Each issue provides penetrating and insightful articles, commentaries and reviews.
**Ind/Abst** ABC POL SCI; Am. Hist. Life (1987-); Leg. Resour. Index (1989-); LegalTrac (1989-).

IT
**FOGLI DI COLLEGAMENTO DELLA L O C.** Italian. mo (11 issues per year). L20000. Fogli Collegamento L O C, Via Scuri 1/C, 24100 Bergamo Italy. **Tel** 011 39 35 260073. **Bk Rev**, (Qty: 4-5). **Ad Acc, Adv Mgr:** Annalisa Marini. **Circ:** 2,000.
**Desc:** Articles deal with issues such as peace, defence, disarmament, and non-violence.

US/0015-7120
**FOREIGN AFFAIRS (NEW YORK, N.Y.).** (FOREIGN AFFAIRS.). [Foreign aff.]. **Added/Corp** Council on Foreign Relations. Vol. 1 (Sept. 1922)-. Periodical. English. Five times a year. $38.00 US; $47.00 Canada; $68.00 other. Foreign Affairs, 58 East 68th Street, New York NY 10021. **Tel** (212)734-0400. **(Subscription address:** Palm Coast Data, PO Box 420235, Agency Department, Palm Coast FL 32142.**)** **LC** D410; .F6. **DD** 327/.05. **CODEN** FRNAA3. cum. index. **Pr Rev**. available on microfilm and microfiche from University Microfilms International (UMI). Documents available from UMI Article Clearinghouse, Magazine Collection. ***Continues*** *Journal of International Relations (Clark University, (Worcester, Mass.)), 0148-8937.*
**Ind/Abst** ABI/INFORM Glob. Ed.; ABI Inform Ondisc (July 1976-); Abr. Read. Guide Period. Lit.; Acad. Abstr. Full Text Elite (Jan. 1984-); Acad. Abstr. (Jan. 1984-); Acad. Ind. [Computer File] (1984-); Acad. Search (Jan. 1984-); Am. Hist. Life (1954-); Am. Bibliogr. Slavic East Europ. Stud.; Econ. Lit. Index (-199?); Energy Res. Abstr. (1975-); Expand. Acad. Index (1984-); Fut. Surv.; Gen. Period. Index (1985-); Hum. Rights Intern. Rep.; Index Period. Artic. Relat. Law (19??-); INFO-SOUTH Abstr.; Infobank (Jan. 1969-); INIS Atomindex [Micro.]; LABORDOC; Mag. Artic. Summar. Elite (Jan. 1984-); Mag. Artic. Summar. Select (Jan. 1984-); Mag. Artic.

Summar. CD-ROM (Jan. 1984-); Mag. Index Plus (1989-); Mag. Index Sel. Microfiche (1986-) [Full Txt.]; Mag. Index. Sel. (1986-); Mag. Search; Manage. Market. Abstr.; Newsp. Period. Abstr. (1986-); Peace Res. Abstr. J. (1964-1975; 1977-1980; 1985-1986); Read. Guide Abstr. Select Ed.; Read. Guide Period. Lit.; Selec. Coop. Index Manage. Period; Soc. Sci. Source (Jan. 1984-); Soc. Sci. Index; Soc. Sci. Index Fulltext (Winter 1989-) [Full Txt.]; Mag. Index (1979-); Middle East J.; TOM Gen. Index (1985-) [Full Txt.]; UMI ABI/Inform--Bus. Period. Ondisc (1986-) [Full Txt.]; U.S. Polit. Sci. Doc. (199?-); Vocat. Search (Jan. 1984-).

II/0536-9258
**FOREIGN AFFAIRS RECORD. Main/Corp** India (Republic). Ministry of External Affairs. V. 1- Jan. 1955-. Periodical. English. General Manager Government of India Press, Ministry of External Affairs, Minto Road, New Delhi India. **LC** DS448; .A25. **DD** 327.54.

II/0015-7155
**FOREIGN AFFAIRS REPORTS. Added/Corp** Indian Council of World Affairs. Asian Relations Organization. (July/Aug. 1952)-. Periodical. English. Twelve times a year. $45.00. Indian Council of World Affairs, Sapru House, Barakhamba Road, New Delhi 110001 India. **Tel** 011 91 11 3319055, 3311902, 3317246, 3317249. **ED** S.C. Parasher. **LC** D839; .F65. **Circ:** 1,000.
**Ind/Abst** Int. Polit. Sci. Abstr.

US/0071-7320
**FOREIGN CONSULAR OFFICES IN THE UNITED STATES.** [Foreign consul. off. U. S.]. **Added/Corp** United States. Dept. of State. (Jan. 1932)-. Government Publication. English. sa. Superintendent of Documents, US Government Printing Office, Washington DC 20402. **Tel** (202)275-3328, FAX (202)786-2377. **LC** JX1705; .A28. **DD** 351/.892. ***Continues*** *Foreign Consular Offices in the United States Corrected to Dec. 30, ... .*

US/0749-9132
**FOREIGN INTELLIGENCE LITERARY SCENE.** ***Title Change.*** [Foreign intell. lit. scene]. **VFOAT** FILS; F.I.L.S. Vol. 1, No. 1 (Feb. 1982)-. Periodical. English. Six times a year. National Intelligence Study Center, 1800 K Street Northwest, Suite 1102, Washington DC 20006. **Tel** (202)466-6029. **ED** Marjorie W. Cline. **LC** JF1525.I6; F67. **DD** 327.1/2/05. **Bk Rev**, (Qty: up to 20/yr). ***Continued by*** *World Intelligence Review, 1076-9285.*
**Desc:** Newsletter of book reviews and bibliographic references to articles in current intelligence literature.

●US
**FOREIGN MILITARY MARKETS, ASIA & PACIFIC RIM. See** Military and Defense.

●US
**FOREIGN MILITARY MARKETS, LATIN AMERICA & CARIBBEAN BASIN. See** Military and Defense.

US
**FOREIGN MILITARY MARKETS, MIDDLE EAST & AFRICA. See** Military and Defense.

US
**FOREIGN MILITARY MARKETS, NATO & EUROPE. See** Military and Defense.

US/0015-7228
**FOREIGN POLICY.** [Foreign policy]. **Added/Corp** Carnegie Endowment for International Peace. National Affairs, Inc. No. 1 (Winter 1971)-. Periodical. English. qt. $33.00 US; $41.00 Canada and Mexico; $46.00 other. Foreign Policy, 2400 N Street NW, Suite 700, Washington DC 20037. **Tel** (202)862-7940, FAX (202)862-2610. **(Subscription address:** Foreign Policy, PO Box 56616, Boulder, CO 80322-6616) **ED** Charles William Maynes. **LC** E744; .F75. **DD** 327.73. **[CCC].** Index available. **Ad Acc. Pr Rev. Circ:** 28,000. available on microfilm and microfiche from University Microfilms International (UMI); available on CD-ROM. Documents available from The Genuine Article, UMI Article Clearinghouse, Documents on Demand, Magazine Collection.
**Desc:** Covers the complex arena of international affairs, presenting views on important world events from prominent people in the news. Features articles from across the political spectrum that attempt to explain foreign policy as well as shape the debate.
**Ind/Abst** ABC POL SCI; Acad. Abstr. Full Text Elite (Jan. 1984-) [Full Txt.]; Acad. Abstr. (Jan. 1984-); Acad. Ind. [Computer File] (1984-); Acad. Search (Jan. 1984-); Am. Hist. Life (1970-); Am. Bibliogr. Slavic East Europ. Stud.; Crim. Justice Abstr. (-199?); Crim. Penol. Police Sci. Abstr.; Curr. Contents Soc. Behav. Sci.; Curr. Mil. Pol. Lit.; Energy Inf. Abstr.; Energy Res. Abstr. (1975-); Environ. Abstr.; Expand. Acad. Index (1984-); Gen. Period. Index (1985-); Hum. Rights Intern. Rep.; Index Islam. Lit.; INFO-SOUTH Abstr.; Infobank (1971-); INIS Atomindex [Micro.]; Int. Polit. Sci. Abstr.; Leis. Recreat. Tour. Abstr.; Mag. Artic. Summar. Elite (Jan. 1984-) [Full Txt.]; Mag. Artic. Summar. Select (Jan. 1984-) [Full Txt.]; Mag. Artic. Summar. CD-ROM (Jan. 1984-); Mag. Index Plus (1989-); Mag. Index. Sel. (1986-); Mag. Search; Middle East Abstr. Index; Newsp. Period. Abstr. (1986-); PAIS Int. Print (1991-); Peace Res. Abstr. J. (1973-1986); Read. Guide Abstr. Select Ed.; Read. Guide Period. Lit.; Res. Alert [Full Cov.]; Rural Dev. Abstr.; Soc. Sci. Source (Jan. 1984-) [Full Txt.]; Soc. Sci. Cit. Index [Full Cov.]; Soc. Sci. Index; Soc. Sci. Index Fulltext (Fall 1988-) [Full Txt.]; Mag. Index (1977-); Middle East J.; TOM Gen. Index (1993-) [Full Txt.]; U.S. Polit. Sci. Doc.; Vocat. Search (Jan. 1984-) [Full Txt.]; World Agric. Econ.

US/1052-7036
**FOREIGN POLICY BULLETIN (WASHINGTON, D.C.).** (FOREIGN POLICY BULLETIN : THE DOCUMENTARY RECORD OF UNITED STATES FOREIGN POLICY.). [Foreign policy bull.]. Vol. 1, No. 1 (July/Aug. 1990)-. Periodical. English. bm (Combined Jan./Feb. and Mar./Apr.). $54.00 US; $69.60 other. Mediacom Inc., 4812 Butterworth Place NW, Washington DC 20016. **Tel** (202)686-5230, FAX (301)229-3036. **ED** Paul E Auerswald. **LC** E840; .F676. **DD** 327.73. Index available (Each issue; additional annual index in sixth issue each volume). cum. index. **Bk Rev**, (Qty: 25). available on microfilm from University Microfilms International (UMI).
**Desc:** Systematically documents all major events in U.S. foreign relations, including important materials from other governments and international organizations. Same format and subject headings as former department of state bulletin, but much more comprehensive. Privately published.
**Ind/Abst** PAIS Int. Print.

PH
**FOREIGN RELATIONS JOURNAL. Added/Corp** Philippine Council for Foreign Relations. Vol. 1, No. 1 (Jan. 1986)-. Periodical. English. qt. $40.00. Solidaridad Publishing House, PO Box 3959, 531 P Faura Ermita, Manila Philippines. **Tel** 63 2 591241, 63 2 586581. **LC** DS686.5; .F675. **DD** 327.599/005.
**Ind/Abst** Index Philip. Period.

US/0071-7355
**FOREIGN RELATIONS OF THE UNITED STATES.** (FOREIGN RELATIONS OF THE UNITED STATES / DEPARTMENT OF STATE, UNITED STATES OF AMERICA.). [Foreign relat. U. S.]. **Main/Corp** United States. Dept. of State. (1932)-. English. an. F438.00. US Department of State, 2201 C Street NW, Room 5819, Washington DC 20520. **Tel** (202)647-9859. **LC** JX233; .A3. **DD** 327.73. Each issue contains an index to its own contents (no volume index)--loose. ***Continues*** *Papers Relating to the Foreign Relations of the United States, 1048-6445.*

US/0146-3543
**FOREIGN SERVICE JOURNAL.** [Foreign serv. j.]. **Added/Corp** American Foreign Service Association. **VFOAT** FSJ. Vol. 28, No. 8 (Aug. 1951)-. Periodical. English. Twelve times a year. $40.00 US & Canada; $58.00 other. American Foreign Service Association, 2101 E Street Northwest, Washington DC 20037. **Tel** (202)338-4045, FAX (202)338-6820. **ED** Anne Stevenson-Yang. **LC** JX1; .A53. Index available. **Bk Rev. Ad Acc, Adv Mgr Tel** (202)338-4045. **Circ:** 9,700 (ctrl). available on microfilm. ***Continues*** *American Foreign Service Journal, 0360-8425.*
**Desc:** Articles and news on foreign policy and current affairs by and for the diplomats.
**Ind/Abst** Acad. Search (Jan. 1994-); Am. Hist. Life (1971-1978); Am. Bibliogr. Slavic East Europ. Stud.; INFO-SOUTH Abstr.; Mag. Search; Middle East Abstr. Index; PAIS Int. Print.

CN/1183-1359
**FORUM INTERNATIONAL (MONTREAL. 1991).** (FORUM INTERNATIONAL : BULLETIN DE LA FONDATION JEANNE-SAUVE POUR LA JEUNESSE.). [Forum int.]. **Added/Corp** Fondation Jeanne-Sauve pour la Jeunesse. **VFOAT** International Forum. **VAT** International Forum (Montreal. 1991). No 1 (Oct. 1991)-. Bulletin. French (English). sa. Limited Free Distribution. Fondation Jeanne-Suave pour la Jeunesse, Bureau 330, 680 Ouest Rue Sherbrooke, Montreal Quebec H3A 2S6 Canada. **DD** 327.1/7/05.

KO
**FREEDOM DIGEST.** Periodical. English. qt. $10.00. Freedom Center C, PO Box 72733, Seoul Korea. **LC** D839; .W554. **DD** 320.9/047. ***Continues*** *World Anti-Communist League. WACL Bulletin.*

US/0898-9265
**FREEDOM MONITOR.** ***Ceased.*** (FREEDOM MONITOR : FREEDOM HOUSE REPORT TO MEMBERS.). [Freedom monit.]. **Added/Corp** Freedom House (U.S.). (Mar. 1984)-(19??). Periodical. English. bm. Freedom House Inc, 120 Wall Street, New York NY 10005. **Tel** (212)514-8040. **DD** 324. ***Continues*** *Freedom House (U.S.) Memo to Members.*
**Ind/Abst** Hum. Rights Intern. Rep.

US/0532-6729
**FRENCH FOREIGN POLICY.** (1966)-. Periodical. English. sa. Ambassade de France, 4101 Resevoir Road NW, Washington DC 20007. **LC** WMLC L 83/2966.

SZ/0340-0255
**FRIEDENSWARTE, DIE. See** Law-International Law.

II/0016-4437
**GANDHI MARG (ENGLISH ED.).** (GANDHI MARG.). [Gandhi Marg]. **Added/Corp** Gandhi Peace Foundation (New Delhi, India). Vol. 1 (April 1979)-. Periodical. English. qt. $30.00. Gandhi Peace Foundation, 221-223 Deen Dayal Upadhyaya Marg, New Delhi 110002 India. **(Subscription address:** Prints India, 11 Darya Ganj, New Delhi, 110002 India, (Phone: 011 91 11 3268645)) **LC** DS481.G3; G2199. **DD** 909.82. available on microfilm from University Microfilms International (UMI). ***Continues*** *Gandhi Marg, 0016-4437.*
**Ind/Abst** Am. Hist. Life (1972-1979); MLA Int. Bibl. Books Artic. Mod. Lang. Lit.; Peace Res. Abstr. J. (1967-1975).

FR/0752-1693
**GEOPOLITIQUE.** (GEOPOLITIQUE : REVUE DE L'INSTITUT INTERNATIONAL DE GEOPOLITIQUE.). [Geopolitique]. No. 1 (Jan. 1983). Periodical. French (English). qt. 180.00F. International Institute of Geopolitics, 2800 Shirlington Road/Suite 405-A, Arlington VA 22206. **Tel** (703)998-7829, 011-33-14-705-6035, FAX (703)931-6432 US, 33-14-998-7829 PARIS. **ED** Christine Morel-Maroger. **LC** D839; .G46. **DD** 327/.05. **Bk Rev. Ad Acc. Circ:** 20,000 (ctrl).
**Desc:** Publicizes the research and activities of the international institute of geopolitics. Disseminates information on east-west relations, and their impact on western security.

US/0748-4305
**GEORGE WASHINGTON JOURNAL OF INTERNATIONAL LAW AND ECONOMICS, THE. See** Law-International Law.

UY
**GEOSUR / [ASOCIACION SUDAMERICANA DE ESTUDIOS GEOPOLITICOS E INTERNACIONALES]. Added/Corp** Asociacion Sudamericana de Estudios Geopoliticos e Internacionales. Year 1, No. 1 (Sept. 1979)-. Periodical. Spanish. bm (Jan., Mar., May, July, Sept., Nov.). $116.00. Geosur, Casilla de Correos 5006, Montevideo Uruguay. **Tel** 011 598 2 692953, FAX 011 598 2 961923. **ED** Bernardo Quagliotti de Bellis. **LC** HC121; .G46. **DD** 330.98/0005. Index available. cum. index. **Bk Rev. Ad Acc. Pr Rev. Circ:** 3,000 (ctrl). available on audiocassette; available on photocopies.
**Desc:** Journal of the South-American Association for Geopolitical and International Studies, featuring analyses of the international relations of South America.

GW
**GERMAN COMMENTS.** (Apr. 1983)-. Periodical. English. Four times a year (Jan., Apr., July, Oct.). DM36.00 Germany; DM60.00 other. Verlag A Fromm GmbH, Postfach 1948, 49009 Osnabrueck Germany. **Tel** 011 49 541 310334, FAX 011 49 541 310440. **ED** Dr. Bernhard Vogel (editor's address: KAS, Postfach 1260, 53730 Sankt Augustin Germany). **LC** DD259.4; .G3473. **DD** 327.43.

US/0886-6198
**GLOBAL AFFAIRS.** ***Ceased.*** [Glob. aff.]. **Added/Corp** International Security Council. Vol. 1, No. 1 (Winter 1986)-Vol. 8, No. 4. Periodical. English (Spanish, Japanese and Korean). qt (Jan., Apr., Jun/Jul, Sept.). International Security Council, 2000 L Street, NW, Suite 506, Washington DC 20036-2563. **Tel** (202)828-0802, FAX (202)429-2563, telex 229115 AUIS. **ED** Joseph Churba. **LC** D839; .G56. **DD** 327/.09/04. **Bk Rev. Ad Acc. Circ:** 4,000.
**Desc:** Provides an open forum for discussion of the issues of international security that affect free societies today.
**Ind/Abst** ABC POL SCI (Sept. 1989-); Int. Polit. Sci. Abstr.; PAIS Int. Print (1991-); Sage Public Adm. Abstr. (?-?).

●US/1057-1213
**GLOBAL AGENDA, A.** (A GLOBAL AGENDA: ISSUES BEFORE THE ... GENERAL ASSEMBLY OF THE UNITED NATIONS : AN ANNUAL PUBLICATION OF THE UNITED NATIONS ASSOCIATION OF THE UNITED STATES OF AMERICA.). [Glob. agenda]. **Added/Corp** United Nations. General Assembly. United Nations Association of the United States of America. **VFOAT** Issues Before the United Nations. 46th (1991/1992)-. English. an (September). $16.00. United Nations Association of USA, 485 Fifth Avenue, New York NY 10017. **Tel** (212)697-3232, FAX (212)682-9185. **LC** JX1977.A1; U5244a. **DD** 341.23/05. ***Continues*** *Issues Before the ... General Assembly of the United Nations, 0193-8096.*
**Desc:** Offers the reader an insightful and highly detailed study of the entire spectrum of UN activities during the last year as well as a look at the agenda of the year to come.

US
**GLOBAL ASSESSMENT.** ***Title Change.*** No. 1 (June 1986)-(19??). Periodical. English (Italian). sa. Global Assessments Inc, 15 Village Plaza/Suite 2A, South Orange NJ 07079. **Tel** (201)762-2464, FAX (201)762-6917. **ED** Jay N Woodworth and Sally Shelton-Colby. **LC** D839; .C837a. **DD** 909.82. ***Continues*** *Global Political Assessment, 0147-9512.* ***Split into*** *Global Assessment Forecast* **and** *Global Assessment*

*Special Analysis.*
**Desc:** Review by field's experts of significant political and economic trends from Global and regional perspectives; most relevant to financial, business, and academic contexts.

US/0017-1190
**GLOBAL DIALOGUE.** V. 1- Jan. 1968-. Periodical. English. mo. Global Dialogue Publishing Inc. **LC** JX1901; .G56. **DD** 327/.05. available on microfilm from University Microfilms International (UMI).

US/1060-0884
**GLOBAL JUSTICE.** (GLOBAL JUSTICE : BULLETIN FROM THE CENTER ON RIGHTS DEVELOPMENT.). [Glob. justice]. **Added/Corp** University of Denver. Center on Rights Development. (1990)-. Bulletin. English. Three times a year (Jan., Apr., Oct.). $10.00 (individuals); $15.00 (institutions). University of Denver Cnt Rights Devl., Graduate School of, International Studies, Denver CO 80208. **Tel** (303)871-2523, FAX (303)871-2456. **ED** Joy Sobrepena and Nikhil Aziz Hemmady. **DD** 323. Index available (Bound in 1st iss. (Fall)). **Bk Rev**, (Qty: 3-6). **Ad Acc**, **Adv Mgr Tel** (303)871-2523. **Pr Rev. Circ:** 300.
**Desc:** Forum for academics, activists, and professional concerned with the global human rights.

US/1060-3891
**GLOBAL VISIONS.** (GLOBAL VISIONS : THE NEWSLETTER OF BLACK PROFESSIONALS IN INTERNATIONAL AFFAIRS.). [Glob. vis.]. **Added/Corp** International Association of Black Professionals in International Affairs. (1991)-. Newsletter. English. BPIA, PO Box 11675, Washington DC 20008-0875. **DD** 327.

US/0072-727X
**GREAT DECISIONS.** **Main/Corp** Foreign Policy Association. **Added/Corp** Foreign Policy Association. Decisions. (1956)-. English. an. $15.00 (one year), $25.00 (two year), $30.00 (three year). Foreign Policy Association Inc, 729 Seventh Avenue, New York NY 10019. **Tel** (212)764-4050, FAX (212)302-6123. **ED** Nancy Hoepli. **DD** 327/.05. **Circ:** 80,000 (ctrl). available on microfilm and microfiche from University Microfilms International (UMI).
**Desc:** Provides impartial background and analyses of eight of the most important international issues facing the United States each year.
**Ind/Abst** Stat. Ref. Index.

US
**GROENE AMSTERDAMMER; ONAFHANKELIJK WEEKBLAD VOOR NEDERLAND. (MICROFICHE), DE.** (1977)-. Dutch. De Groene Amsterdammer, Westeinde 16, 1017 ZP Amsterdam Netherlands. **ED** Editor: A. C. J. Jitta; R. H. Dijkstra and others. **LC** Microfilm 01301D.

FR
**GUERRES ET CONFLITS D'AUJOURD'HUI.** **See** Military and Defense.

NZ
**GUIDE TO NEW ZEALAND'S FOREIGN RELATIONS, A.** **VFOAT** New Zealand's Foreign Relations. English. an. New Zealand Ministry of Foreign Affairs, Private Bag, Wellington 1 New Zealand. **Tel** 64 4 728877, FAX 64 4 729596, telex NZ 3441. **LC** DU421; .G84. **DD** 327.931.

GW/0936-0018
**HAMBURGER BEITRAEGE ZUR FRIEDENSFORSCHUNG UND SICHERHEITSPOLITIK.** [Hambg. Beitr. Friedensforsch. Sicherh.polit.]. (1986)-. Monographic series. German (English). ir. Price varies per volume. Institut fuer Friedenforschung und Sicherheitspolitik, An der Universitaet Hamburg, Falkenstein 1, W-2000 Hamburg 55 Germany. **Tel** (040)869054, FAX (040)866 36 15. **UDC** 327.36. Index available. cum. index. **Ad Acc. Circ:** 500 (ctrl).

KO
**HANGUK KWA KUKCHE CHONGCHI.** **VFOAT** Korea and World Politics. V. 1-Series (1985)-. Periodical. Korean. sa. W6000. Kyongnam Taehakkyo Kuktong Munje Yonguso, 28-42 Samchong-dong Chongno-ku, Seoul 110-230 Korea. **Tel** 735-3202/3, FAX 735-4359, telex KIFES K26834. **ED** Jae Kyu Park. **LC** DS917.6; .H36. Index available. cum. index. **Bk Rev. Circ:** 1,000.
**Desc:** Provides Korean scholars with the opportunity to materialize their intellectual contributions in the area of world politics; intends to play a practical role in resolving contradictions that entangle the Korean Peninsula.

US/0017-8063
**HARVARD INTERNATIONAL LAW JOURNAL.** **See** Law-International Law.

US/0739-1854
**HARVARD INTERNATIONAL REVIEW.** [Harvard int. rev.]. **Added/Corp** Harvard International Relations Council. Vol. 1, No. 1 (Feb. 1979)-. Periodical. English. Four times a year (Jan., Apr., July, Nov.). $16.00 (one year), $30.00 (two year), $42.00 (three year) individuals; $26.00 (one year), $50.00 (two year), $72.00 (three year) institutions. Harvard International Review, PO Box 401, Cambridge MA 02138. **Tel** (617)495-9607, FAX (617)496-4472. **ED** Jay Stewart. **LC** D839; .H29. **DD** 909.82. **[CCC]. Bk Rev**, (Qty: 8). **Ad Acc, Adv Mgr:** Matt Price, **Tel** (617)495-9607. **Circ:** 14,000. available on microfilm, microfiche, and CD-ROM from UMI Article Clearinghouse.
**Desc:** Journal of international affairs covering issues in international affairs.
**Ind/Abst** Am. Bibliogr. Slavic East Europ. Stud.; PAIS Int. Print.

●US
**HARVARD JOURNAL OF WORLD AFFAIRS : AN INTERNATIONAL POLICY FORUM OF THE JOHN F. KENNEDY SCHOOL OF GOVERNMENT.** **Added/Corp** John F. Kennedy School of Government. (Summer 1992)-. Periodical. English. John F Kennedy School of Government, Harvard University, 79 John F Kennedy Street, Cambridge MA 02138.

US/0017-8780
**HEADLINE SERIES.** **Added/Corp** Foreign Policy Association. No. 41 (Aug. 20, 1943)-. Monographic series. English. qt (published seasonally). $20.00 (one year), $35.00 (two year), $50.00 (three year). Foreign Policy Association, 729 Seventh Avenue, New York NY 10019. **Tel** (212)764-4050, FAX (212)302-6123. **ED** Nancy L. Hoepli. **LC** E744; .H43. **DD** 327.73. **Circ:** 11,500 (ctrl). available on microfilm and microfiche from University Microfilms International (UMI). ***Continues*** *Headline Books, 0884-4402.*
**Desc:** Current world problems and areas of critical importance, written by scholars and other experts.
**Ind/Abst** Hum. Rights Intern. Rep.; Peace Res. Abstr. J. (1965-1973).

US
**HEIN'S U.S. TREATY INDEX ON CD-ROM [COMPUTER FILE].** **Added/Corp** William S. Hein & Company. **VFOAT** U.S. Treaty Index on CD-ROM; Hein's United States Treaty Index on CD-ROM; Hein's US Treaty Index on CD-ROM; US Treaty Index on CD-ROM. (199?)-. English. sa. $800.00 non-subscribers; $200.00 subscribers. William S. Hein & Company Inc., 1285 Main Street, Buffalo NY 14209. **Tel** (716)882-2600, (800)828-7571, FAX (716)883-8100, telex 91-209 WM S HEIN BUF.

GW/0943-691X
**HISTORISCH POLITISCHE MILLEILUNGEN.** (19??)-. German. ir. DM38.00. Boehlau Verlag GmbH & Cie / Koeln, Theodor Heuss STR 76, D-51149 Cologne Germany. **Tel** 011 49 2203 307021, FAX 011 49 2203 307349. **(Subscription address:** BDK Buecherdienst GmBh, Postfach 900120, D 51111 Cologne Germany.**)**

SW
**HORN OF AFRICA BULLETIN.** **See** History(General)-History of Africa.

FR
**I & P.** **VFOAT** I and P; Israel and Palestine. (1971)-. Periodical. English. ir. 1000F. Israel & Palestine / I & P, c/o Mashrek, Boite Postale 5, 75462 Paris Cedex 10 France. **Tel** 331 4800 9660, FAX 331 4660 9645. **ED** Maxim Ghilan. **LC** DS119.7; .I825. **DD** 956.94/05/05. **Bk Rev. Ad Acc. Circ:** 5,000. available on microfilm from University Microfilms International (UMI); available in braille. ***Continues*** *Israel & Palestine.*
**Desc:** Analysis and background of Middle East Conflict, with emphasis on Israeli-Palestinian relations, and US Mideast policy. Exclusive investigative reporting.

II
**ICSSR JOURNAL OF ABSTRACTS AND REVIEWS : ECONOMICS.** **See** Economics-Abstracting, Bibliographies and Statistics.

II
**IDSA NEWS REVIEW ON AFRICA.** **VFOAT** News Review on Africa. Vol. 1, No. 1 (Jan. 1987)-. Periodical. English. mo. Rs10.00. Institute for Defence Studies and Analyses, Sapru House, Barakhamba Road, New Delhi 110001 India. **Tel** 011 91 11 3314951. **ED** C Jasjitsmah. Index available. **Circ:** 100.
**Desc:** Highly recommended for students of political science, defense studies and for all those interested in strategic developments in particular regions and security issues, national and international.

SZ
**IFDA DOSSIER / INTERNATIONAL FOUNDATION FOR DEVELOPMENT ALTERNATIVES.** ***Suspended.*** **Added/Corp** International Foundation for Development Alternatives. (Jan. 1978)-Suspended (April 1991). Periodical. English (French and Spanish). bm. 48.00F (individuals), 96.00F (libraries), 192.00F (institutions) Switzerland; $32.00 (individuals), $64.00 (libraries), $128.00 (institutions) US. International Foundation Development Alternatives, 4 Place du Marche, CH-1260 Nyon Switzerland. **Tel** 11 41 22 3618281, telex 419 953 IFDA CH. **ED** Marc Nerfin. Index available. **Bk Rev. Ad Acc. Circ:** 24,500. available on microfiche.
**Desc:** Articles and information on the development of alternative concepts, activities and actors, from local to global space (including the future of the United Nations). It is essentially a vehicle for mutually-educating dialogues.
**Ind/Abst** Geogr. Abstr. Human Geogr.; Hum. Rights Intern. Rep.; Int. Dev. Abstr.; Leis. Recreat. Tour. Abstr.; Rural Dev. Abstr.; World Agric. Econ.

UK/0046-8703
**IMPACT INTERNATIONAL.** Vol. 7(Jan. 1977)-. Periodical. English. sm. £24.00 (institutions), £16.00 (individuals), £14.00 (students) UK; £32.00 (institutions), £23.00 (individuals), £21.00 (students) Europe and Ireland; £39.00 (institutions), £25.50 (individuals), £23.50 (students) Canada, Latin America, Asia, Africa, and Middle East; $70.00 (institutions), $52.00 (individuals), $50.00 (students) US. News and Media Ltd, 33 Strouf Green Road, London N4 3EF England. **Tel** (01)263-1417. **ED** A Irfan. **LC** BP1; .I496. **DD** 909/.97671082. **Bk Rev. Ad Acc.** ***Continues*** *Impact.*
**Desc:** An independent Muslim news magazine providing worldwide coverage of news/current affairs, analysis of economic and social development and other issues affecting the Muslim world.
**Ind/Abst** Hum. Rights Intern. Rep.

US/0082-8084
**INDEX TO PROCEEDINGS OF THE ECONOMIC AND SOCIAL COUNCIL.** **Added/Corp** Dag Hammarskjold Library. United Nations Library (New York, N.Y.). (Dec. 1952)-. Government Publication. English. ir. $20.00. United Nations Publications, 2 United Nations Plaza, Room DC2 0853, Department 007C, New York NY 10017. **Tel** (212)963-8303, (800)253-9646. **LC** Z7161; .I5; HC59. **DD** 341.7/59. Index Available Published separately--free--upon request. ***Continues*** *United Nations. Economic and Social Council. Disposition of Agenda Items.*
**Desc:** Proceedings of the economic and social council of the United Nations.

US
**INDEX TO PROCEEDINGS OF THE GENERAL ASSEMBLY.** **Added/Corp** United Nations Library (New York, N.Y.) Dag Hammarskjold Library. 5th Session (Sept. 19, 1950 to Nov. 5, 1951)-. Government Publication. English. ir. $20.00. United Nations Publications, 2 United Nations Plaza, Room DC2 0853, Department 007C, New York NY 10017. **Tel** (212)963-8303, (800)253-9646. **LC** JX1977; .A44. **DD** 341.23/22. ***Continues*** *United Nations. General Assembly. Disposition of Agenda Items.*
**Desc:** Indexes the meeting records, reports, resolutions and documents of the Assembly. Indexes are by subject and by country, the latter detailing names of delegate speakers and voting records of member states.

US/0082-8408
**INDEX TO PROCEEDINGS OF THE SECURITY COUNCIL / DAG HAMMARSKJOLD LIBRARY.** **Added/Corp** Dag Hammarskjold Library. (1964)-. Government Publication. English. an. $15.00. United Nations Publications, 2 United Nations Plaza, Room DC2 0853, Department 007C, New York NY 10017. **Tel** (212)963-8303, (800)253-9646. **LC** JX1977; .A5. **DD** 341.23/23.
**Desc:** Indexes the meeting records, reports, resolutions and documents of the Council. Indexes are by subject and by country, the latter detailing names of delegate speakers and voting records of the member states.

II
**INDIA PERSPECTIVES.** **Added/Corp** India. Ministry of External Affairs. Vol. 1, No. 1 (July 1988)-. Periodical. English. mo. $60.00. Ministry of Information and Broadcasting, Government of India, Patiala House, New Delhi 110 001 India. **Tel** 387983. **(Subscription address:** Prints India, 11 Darya Ganj, New Delhi, 110002 India, (Phone: 011 91 11 3268645)**) LC** DS401; .I2754. **DD** 954/.005. ***Continues*** *Indian and Foreign Review.*

II/0251-3048
**INDIA QUARTERLY.** [India q.]. **Added/Corp** Indian Council of World Affairs. Vol. 1 (Jan. 1945)-. Periodical. English. Four times a year (Feb., May, Aug., Nov.). $40.00. Indian Council of World Affairs, Sapru House, Barakhamba Road, New Delhi 110001 India. **Tel** 011 91 11 3319055, 3311902, 3317246, 3317249. **(Subscription address:** Prints India, 11 Darya Ganj, New Delhi 110002 India.**) LC** D410; .I44. **DD** 052.
**Ind/Abst** ABC POL SCI (1956-); Acad. Search (July 1993-); Am. Hist. Life (1956-); Humanit. Source (July 1993-); Index Islam. Lit.; INFO-SOUTH Abstr.; Int. Polit. Sci. Abstr. (1956-); Middle East Abstr. Index; Middle East J.

II/0019-4735
**INDIAN EXPORT TRADE JOURNAL, THE.** [Indian export trade j.]. **Added/Corp** Indian Manufacturers' Export Association. (July 1948)-. Periodical. English. Twelve times a year. $50.00. Indian Export Trade Journal, Savajuganj, Baroda 5 India. **Tel** 329158. **ED** C. M. Pandit. **Bk Rev. Ad Acc. Circ:** 7,500 (ctrl). ***Continues*** *Indian Export Trade Bulletin.*

**Desc:** Promotes international trade and development of exports. Puts traders in contact with each other.
**Ind/Abst** AGRICOLA.

II/0251-303X
**INDIAN JOURNAL OF POLITICAL STUDIES, THE. See** Political Science.

II/0537-2704
**INDIAN YEAR BOOK OF INTERNATIONAL AFFAIRS, THE.**
**Added/Corp** University of Madras. Indian Study Group of International Affairs. University of Madras. Indian Study Group of International Law and Affairs. Vol. 1 (1952)-. English. ir. University of Madras Registrar, University Building Chepauk, Madras 600 005 India. **LC** JX21; .I6.
**Ind/Abst** Index Foreign Leg. Per.

HU
**INDIANA UNIVERSITY STUDIES ON HUNGARY.** English. Humanities Press, 165 1st Avenue, Atlantic Highlands NJ 07716. **Tel** (908)872-1441, (800)221-3845, FAX (908)872-0717, telex 752233. Index available.

SI/0217-8451
**INDOCHINA REPORT.** ***Suspended.***
**Added/Corp** Information & Resource Center (Singapore). No. 1 (Jan.-Mar. 1985)- Suspended No. 32 (Jul.-Sept. 1992). Periodical. English. qt. Information & Resource Center, 6 Nassim Road, Singapore 1025 Singapore. **Tel** 011 65 7349600. **LC** DS550; .I543.

●AT/1038-6726
**INSIGHT : AUSTRALIAN FOREIGN AFFAIRS AND TRADE ISSUES.**
**Added/Corp** Australia. Dept. of Foreign Affairs and Trade. Overseas Information Branch. Vol. 1, No. 1 (24 July 1992)-. Periodical. English. Twenty-four times a year. 80.00Aus$. Australia Department of Foreign Affairs, Publication Manager - Rod Perry, Parkes Act 2600, Australia. **Tel** 011 61 6 2613983. **(Subscription address:** Australian Government Publishing Service, GPO Box 84, Canberra ACT 2601 Australia; Phone: 011 61 6 2954411**) ED** Sam Leone. **LC** JX1162; .A33. **Circ:** 7,000 (ctrl). ***Continues*** *Australian Foreign Affairs and Trade, 1033-5722;* ***Continues in part*** *Backgrounder (Canberra, A.C.T. : 1989).*

UK/0268-4527
**INTELLIGENCE AND NATIONAL SECURITY.** [Intell. natl. secur.]. Vol. 1, No. 1 (Jan. 1986)-. Academic Scholarly Publication. English. qt. $185.00. Frank Cass & Company Ltd, Newbury House, 890-900 Eastern Avenue, Newbury Park, Ilford, Essex IG2 7HH United Kingdom. **Tel** 011 44 81 599 8866, FAX 011 44 81 599 0984, telex 897719. **ED** Christopher Andrew and Michael Handel. **Ad Acc, Adv Mgr:** Anne Kidson. available on microfilm and microfiche from University Microfilms International (UMI).
**Desc:** This journal has broken new ground in being the first scholarly journal devoted to the past history of intelligence and counter-intelligence work by the major powers... The journal began with the joint objectives of showing that intelligence was a proper field for scholarly research and that any analysis of foreign or security policy which left out intelligence was missing a dimension. Both of these objectives have already been met.
**Ind/Abst** Am. Hist. Life (1986-); Br. Humanit. Index; Int. Polit. Sci. Abstr.; Soc. Plann. Policy Dev. Abstr.

US/0094-5072
**INTER DEPENDENT, THE.** Vol. 1; April 1974-. English. bm (Feb., April, June, Aug., Oct., Dec.). $10.00 (one year), $30.00 (three year). United Nations Association of USA, 485 Fifth Avenue, New York NY 10017. **Tel** (212)697-3232, FAX (212)682-9185. **ED** John Tessitore. **LC** D839; .I4555. **DD** 327/.05. **Bk Rev**, (Qty: 12). **Ad Acc, Adv Mgr:** Susan Woolfson. **Circ:** 30,000. ***Supersedes*** *Vista of the United Nations Association.*
**Desc:** Covers United Nations and international affairs.
**Ind/Abst** Peace Res. Abstr. J. (1979-1982).

SZ/0020-5079
**INTER-PARLIAMENTARY BULLETIN.**
(INTER-PARLIAMENTARY BULLETIN : OFFICIAL PUBLICATION OF THE BUREAU OF THE INTER-PARLIAMENTARY UNION.). [Inter-parliam. bull.]. **Added/Corp** Inter-Parliamentary Union. 6th Year, No. 1 (Jan./Feb. 1926)-. English (French). Four times a year. 24.00F. Inter-Parliamentary Union, Place du Petit Saconnex, Ch 1211 Geneva 19 Switzerland. **Tel** 011 41 22 7344150, telex 789784. **ED** Michel Barton. **LC** JX1930; .I68215. Index available. **Bk Rev. Circ:** 1,950. ***Continues*** *Bulletin Interparlementaire.*
**Desc:** Contains information on the work of the union and the activities of the organization, as well as articles on topical subjects.
**Ind/Abst** Middle East Abstr. Index.

NO/0020-577X
**INTERNASJONAL POLITIKK (OSLO, NORWAY).** (INTERNASJONAL POLITIKK.). [Int. polit.]. **Added/Corp** Chr. Michelsens Institutt. Norsk Utenrikspolitisk Institutt. (1947)-. Periodical. Norwegian (Swedish and Danish). Six times a year. $40.00 one year. Norsk Utenrikspolitisk Institute, Postboks 8159, Dep 0033 Oslo 1 Norway. **Tel** 47 2 1770 50, FAX 17 70 15. **ED** Olar Fagelund Knudsen. **LC** D839; .I46. **[CCC].** Index available. **Bk Rev. Ad Acc. Pr Rev. Circ:** 2,500. available on microfilm and microfiche from University Microfilms International (UMI). Documents available from The Genuine Article. ***Continues*** *Internasjonal Politikk (Bergen, Norway).*
**Desc:** Features articles on foreign affairs. Issues include arms control, military situation in Northern Europe, development programs for the Third World, European Economic Community and international trade and economics.
**Ind/Abst** ABC POL SCI; Am. Hist. Life (1954-); Arts Humanit. Citation Index [Select. Cov.]; Curr. Contents Soc. Behav. Sci.; Energy Res. Abstr. (Sept. 1980-); Int. Polit. Sci. Abstr.; Res. Alert [Full Cov.]; Soc. Sci. Cit. Index [Full Cov.].

US/0737-3767
**INTERNATIONAL AFFAIRS AND DEFENSE.** (INTERNATIONAL AFFAIRS AND DEFENSE. MICROFORM / NEWSBANK, INC.). [Int. aff. def.]. Vol. 14, INT 1 (Jan. 1983)-. Periodical. English. mo. Newsbank Inc, 58 Pine Street, New Canaan CT 06840. **Tel** (800)243-7694, (800)762-8182, FAX (203)966-6254.

SA/0258-7270
**INTERNATIONAL AFFAIRS BULLETIN.**
***Title Change.*** **Added/Corp** South African Institute of International Affairs. Vol. 1, No. 1 (1977)-Vol. 16, No. 3 (1992). Periodical. Afrikaans (English). Three times a year. South African Institute of International Affairs, PO Box 31596, Braamfontein 2017 South Africa. **Tel** 011 27 11 3392021, telex 4-27291 SA. **ED** Alan Begg. **LC** DT30.5; .I57. **DD** 960/.05. Index available. **Bk Rev. Ad Acc. Circ:** 3,500 (ctrl). ***Continues*** *Newsletter (South African Institute of International Affairs).* ***Merged with*** *Southern Africa Record* ***to form*** *South African Journal of International Affairs, 1022-0461.*
**Desc:** All aspects of international affairs generally in relation to South Africa and Southern Africa.
**Ind/Abst** Abstr. Anthropol. (19??-).

UK/0020-5850
**INTERNATIONAL AFFAIRS (LONDON).**
(INTERNATIONAL AFFAIRS.). [Int. aff.]. **Added/Corp** Royal Institute of International Affairs. Vol. 20, No. 1 (Jan. 1944)-. Academic Scholarly Publication. English. qt (4 issues). $83.00 US, Canada & Mexico; £51.00 other. Cambridge University Press, The Edinburgh Building, Shaftesbury Road, Cambridge CB2 2RU United Kingdom. **Tel** 011 44 223 312393, FAX 011 44 223 325959. **(Subscription address:** Cambridge University Press / North America, 110 Midland Avenue, Port Chester NY 10573.**) ED** Lucy Seton-Watson. **LC** JX1; .I53. **DD** 327/.05. **[CCC].** Index available. **Bk Rev. Ad Acc. Pr Rev.** available on microfilm and microfiche from University Microfilms International (UMI). Documents available from UMI Article Clearinghouse. ***Continues*** *International Affairs Review Supplement.*
**Desc:** Journal of the Royal Institute of International Affairs. It combines broad-based coverage of global policy questions with up-to-date and penetrating analysis of the key processes shaping world developments. Articles by practicing policy-makers and academic specialists keep both general and specialist readers in touch with the leading edge of European debates, as well as with thinking elsewhere on current international issues.
**Ind/Abst** ABC POL SCI; Acad. Abstr. Full Text Elite (July 1990-); Acad. Abstr. (July 1990-); Acad. Ind. [Computer File] (1987-); Acad. Search (July 1990-); Am. Hist. Life (1954-); Arts Humanit. Citation Index [Select. Cov.]; Br. Humanit. Index; Expand. Acad. Index (1987-); Index Islam. Lit.; INFO-SOUTH Abstr.; Int. Polit. Sci. Abstr.; Leis. Recreat. Tour. Abstr.; Middle East Abstr. Index; Newsp. Period. Abstr. (1991-); PAIS Int. Print (1991-); Peace Res. Abstr. J. (1966-1967, 1971-1974, 1981-1982); Rural Dev. Abstr.; Selec. Coop. Index Manage. Period; Soc. Plann. Policy Dev. Abstr.; Soc. Sci Source (Jul. 1990-); Soc. Sci. Cit. Index [Full Cov.]; Soc. Sci. Index; Soc. Sci. Index Fulltext (Autumn 1988-) [Full Txt.]; Sociol. Abstr. (?-?); Middle East J.; World Agric. Econ.

RU/0130-9641
**INTERNATIONAL AFFAIRS (MOSCOW).**
(INTERNATIONAL AFFAIRS.). [Int. aff.]. **Added/Corp** Vsesoiuznoe Obshchestvo "Znanie." Izdatelstvo "Znanie." Vsesoiuznoe Obshchestvo po Rasprostraneniiu Politicheskikh i Nauchnykh Znanii. **VFOAT** Mezhdunarodnaia Zhizn. (January 1955)-. Periodical. English (Russian). mo. $99.00. Izdatelstvo Znanie, Novaya Pl., 3-4,, 101835 Moscow Russia. **(Subscription address:** East View Publications Inc., 3020 Harbor Lane North, Suite 110, Minneapolis MN 55447.**) LC** D839; .I465. **DD** 909.82. cum. index. available on microfilm and microfiche from University Microfilms International (UMI). Documents available from The Genuine Article.
**Desc:** Presents the fundamentals of Russian foreign policy and carries a vast amount of informative and reference material on international politics.
**Ind/Abst** ABC POL SCI; Acad. Search (Jan. 1993-); Am. Hist. Life (1972-1978); Middle East Abstr. Index; PAIS Int. Print (1991-); Res. Alert [Full Cov.]; Sage Public Adm. Abstr.

US/0534-6541
**INTERNATIONAL AFFAIRS REPORTS FROM QUAKER WORKERS.** Vol. 1; 1954-. Periodical. English. American Friends Service Committee / Pennsylvania, 1501 Cherry Street, Philadelphia PA 19102. **Tel** (215)241-7275.

PL/0867-4493
**INTERNATIONAL AFFAIRS STUDIES.**
**Added/Corp** Polski Instytut Spraw Miedzynarodowych. Vol. 1, No. 1 (1991)-. Periodical. English. qt. Z10,000 Poland; $16.50 other. Polish Institute of International Affairs, Ul Warecka 1A, POB 1000, 00-950 Warsaw Poland. Index available. **Bk Rev. Ad Acc. Pr Rev. Circ:** 1,000 (ctrl). ***Continues*** *Activity of the Polish Institute of International Affairs.*
**Desc:** International relations with special reference to Poland.

DK
**INTERNATIONAL BULLETIN.** Bulletin. Danish (Danish). 60.00. Forlaget Solidaritet, Raadhusstraede 13, 3 Copenhagen K 1466 Denmark. **LC** D839; .I467. **DD** 327/.05.

LE
**INTERNATIONAL DOCUMENTS ON PALESTINE. Added/Corp** Muassasat al-Dirasat al-Filastiniyah. Jamiat al-Kuwayt. (1967)-. Monographic series. English (French). ir. Price varies per volume. Institute for Palestine Studies, PO Box 7164, Beirut Lebanon. **Tel** 01 - 814174, 01 - 312512. **LC** DS119.7; .I494. **DD** 327.5694. **Circ:** 3,000.
**Desc:** Includes a selection of documentary material on the Palestine question and Arab-Israeli conflict, such as treaties, joint communiques, speeches and interviews.

US/1054-4933
**INTERNATIONAL DOCUMENTS REVIEW.** (INTERNATIONAL DOCUMENTS REVIEW : THE WEEKLY NEWSLETTER ON THE UNITED NATIONS.). [Int. doc. rev.]. (1990)-. Newsletter. English. Forty-six times a year. $200.00 US & Canada; $250.00 other. Impact Communication Consultants, 318 Edgewood Avenue, Teaneck NJ 07666. **Tel** (201)833-1881, , FAX (201)833-1835. **ED** Bhaskar Menon, Lauren Carner. **DD** 341. Index available. cum. index. **Bk Rev**, (Qty: 46). **Ad Acc, Adv Mgr:** Lauren Carner, **Tel** (212)355-5510. **Circ:** 200.
**Desc:** The only weekly newsletter on the United Nations, reviewing major documents, activities of the Secretary-General and senior staff, and all major inter-government meetings. Books by outside publishers on the UN are reviewed.

US/0898-4336
**INTERNATIONAL ECONOMY, THE. See** Economics-International Economics.

SA/0897-5086
**INTERNATIONAL FREEDOM FOUNDATION.** ***Title Change.*** **See** Economics-International Economics.

US
**INTERNATIONAL INFORMATION REPORT.** English. Twelve times a year. $260.00 Washington DC; $160.00 other. Washington Researchers, PO Box 19005, 20th Street Station, Washington DC 20036. **Tel** (202)333-3533, (202)333-3499, FAX (202)625-0656.

CN/0829-321X
**INTERNATIONAL INSIGHTS.**
(INTERNATIONAL INSIGHTS :A DALHOUSIE JOURNAL ON INTERNATIONAL AFFAIRS.). [Int. insights]. **Added/Corp** Dalhousie University. Faculty of Law. John E. Read International Law Society. Vol. 1, No. 1 (Spring Issue 1985)-. Periodical. English. sa. $10.00 (students), $14.02 (regular). Dalhousie Law School, Dalhousie University, Halifax Nova Scotia B3H 4H9 Canada. **Tel** (902)424-6552. **DD** 327.71/005.

UK/0305-0629
**INTERNATIONAL INTERACTIONS.** [Int. interact.]. Vol. 1 (1974)-. English. Four times a year (1 volume). $339.00 (academic institutions), $529.00 (corporate institutions). Gordon & Breach Science Publishers, PO Box 90, Reading RG1 8JL England. **Tel** 011 44 734 560080, FAX 011 44 734 568211. **(Subscription address:** International Publishers Distributor at one of the following addresses: 820 Town Center Drive, Langhorne, PA 19047; or PO Box 90, Reading Berkshire RG1 8JL UK; or Kent Ridge PO Box 1180, Singapore 9111, Republic of Singapore**) ED** Edward E. Azar. **LC** JX1; .I54. **DD** 327/.07/2. **CODEN** INIAAH. **[CCC]. Bk Rev. Ad Acc.**
**Ind/Abst** Middle East Abstr. Index; Peace Res. Abstr. J. (1974-); Soc. Sci. Cit. Index [Full Cov.].

US/0742-4698
**INTERNATIONAL JOURNAL OF WORLD STUDIES, THE.** [Int. j. world stud.]. **VFOAT** World Studies. Vol. 1, No. 1 (Winter 1984)-. Periodical. English. qt. $20.00 general, $12.00 students, $25.00 libraries (for U.S. and Canada). International Center for Democracy, 7676 New Hampshire Avenue/Suite 304, Langley Park MD 20783. **DD** 327.

US/0742-3640
**INTERNATIONAL JOURNAL ON WORLD PEACE.** [Int. j. world peace]. **Added/Corp** Professors World Peace Academy. Vol. 1, No. 1 (Autumn 1984)-. Academic Scholarly Publication. English. qt. $30.00. Professors World Peace Academy, 2700 University Avenue West, #47, St. Paul MN 55114. **Tel** (612)644-2809, FAX (612)644-0997. **ED** Panos D. Bardis (editor's address: The University of Toledo, Toledo, OH 43606). **LC** WMLC 93/304. **DD** 327. Index available. **Bk Rev**. **Pr Rev. Circ:** 1,000. Documents available from The Genuine Article, UMI Article Clearinghouse.
**Desc:** A scholarly, multi-disciplinary, and cross-cultural publication dealing with all aspects of peace from both theoretical and practical perspectives.
**Ind/Abst** Curr. Contents Soc. Behav. Sci.; Expand. Acad. Index (1992-); Int. Dev. Abstr.; Int. Polit. Sci. Abstr.; Newsp. Period. Abstr. (1989-); PAIS Int. Print (1991-); Peace Res. Abstr. J. (1985-); Psychol. Abstr.; Res. Alert [Full Cov.]; Soc. Plann. Policy Dev. Abstr.; Soc. Work Abstr. [Select. Cov.]; Sociol. Abstr.; Sociol. Educ. Abstr.

GW
**INTERNATIONAL LAW OF ARMS CONTROL.** See Law-International Law.

UK/0957-1299
**INTERNATIONAL MINDS : THE QUARTERLY JOURNAL OF PSYCHOLOGICAL INSIGHT INTO INTERNATIONAL AFFAIRS.** (July-Oct. 1989)-. Periodical. English. Four times a year. $60.00 US and Canada. International Minds, 19 Hugh Street, London SW1V 1QJ England. **Tel** 011 44 71 828 4840. **LC** K9; .N854. **DD** 327/.01/9.
**Desc:** Multi-disciplinary, psychological analysis of contemporary international issues of relevance to politics and diplomacy.
**Ind/Abst** Int. Bibliogr. Sociol.

US/0363-7123
**INTERNATIONAL ORGANISATIONS IN WORLD POLITICS YEARBOOK.** English. an. $27.50. Westview Press Inc, 5500 Central Avenue, Boulder CO 80301. **Tel** (303)444-3541, FAX (303)449-3356. **LC** JX1995; .I535. **DD** 341.2/05.

US/0020-8183
**INTERNATIONAL ORGANIZATION.** [Int. organ.]. **Added/Corp** World Peace Foundation. University of Wisconsin--Madison. Vol. 1 (Feb. 1947)-. Periodical. English. qt. $36.00 (individuals), $92.00 (institutions). Massachusetts Institute of Technology (MIT) Press, 55 Hayward Street, Cambridge MA 02142-1399. **Tel** (617)253-2889, (617)625-8481, FAX (617)258-6779. **ED** John S. Odell. **LC** JX1901; .I55. **DD** 341.105. **[CCC]. Bk Rev. Ad Acc. Pr Rev. Circ:** 2,700 (ctrl). available on microfilm and microfiche from University Microfilms International (UMI). Documents available from The Genuine Article, UMI Article Clearinghouse.
**Desc:** Presents articles on international institutions and cooperation and on economic policy issues, security policies, and other aspects of international relations and foreign policy.
**Ind/Abst** ABC POL SCI; Acad. Abstr. Full Text Elite (Jan. 1992-); Acad. Abstr. (Jan. 1992-); Acad. Search (Jan. 1992-); Am. Hist. Life (1954-); Am. Bibliogr. Slavic East Europ. Stud.; Appl. Soc. Sci. Index Abstr.; Arts Humanit. Citation Index [Select. Cov.]; Commun. Abstr. (?-?); Curr. Contents Soc. Behav. Sci.; Curr. Geogr. Publ. (199?-); Curr. Law Index (1980-); Econ. Lit. Index; Energy Res. Abstr. (Oct. 1976-); Expand. Acad. Index (1984-); Hum. Rights Intern. Rep.; Index Period. Artic. Relat. Law; INFO-SOUTH Abstr.; INIS Atomindex [Micro.]; Int. Aerosp. Abstr.; Int. Labour Doc.; Int. Polit. Sci. Abstr.; J. Econ. Lit. (1985-); J. Plan. Lit.; LABORDOC; Leg. Resour. Index (1980-); LegalTrac (1980-); Leis. Recreat. Tour. Abstr.; Middle East Abstr. Index; Newsp. Period. Abstr. (1991-); PAIS Int. Print (1991-); Peace Res. Abstr. J. (1965-); Res. Alert [Full Cov.]; Rural Dev. Abstr.; Selec. Coop. Index Manage. Period; Soc. Sci. Source (Jan. 1992-); Soc. Sci. Cit. Index [Full Cov.]; Soc. Sci. Index; Soc. Sci. Index Fulltext (Autumn 1988-) [Full Txt.]; Mag. Index (?-?); World Agric. Econ.

RU
**INTERNATIONAL PEACE AND DISARMAMENT SERIES.** **Added/Corp** Nauchnyi Sovet po Issledovaniiu Problem Mira i Razoruzheniia (Akademiia Nauk SSSR). **VFOAT** International Peace and Disarmament. (19??)-. Monographic series. English. ir. Price varies per volume.

US
**INTERNATIONAL PEACE RESEARCH NEWSLETTER.** Vol. 27, No. 2 (April 1989)-. Newsletter. English. qt (Jan., Apr., Jul., Oct.). $24.00. International Peace Research Association / Ohio, Antioch College / Paul Smoker, Yellow Springs OH 45387. **Tel** (513)767-6444, FAX (513)767-1891. available on microfilm and microfiche from University Microfilms International (UMI). ***Continues** IPRA Newsletter.*
**Ind/Abst** Hum. Rights Intern. Rep.

US
**INTERNATIONAL PEACE STUDIES NEWSLETTER.** (1971)-. Newsletter. English.
**Ind/Abst** Hum. Rights Intern. Rep.

NE/1380-748X
**INTERNATIONAL PEACEKEEPING.** (19??)-. English. bm. $175.00. Kluwer Academic Publishers, Postbus 322, 3300 AH Dordrecht, The Netherlands. **Tel** 011 (31) 78 524400, FAX 011 31 78 183273, telex 20083.

UK/1353-3312
**INTERNATIONAL PEACEKEEPING.** (19??)-. English. qt. $145.00. Frank Cass & Company Ltd, Newbury House, 890-900 Eastern Avenue, Newbury Park, Ilford, Essex IG2 7HH United Kingdom. **Tel** 011 44 81 599 8866, FAX 011 44 81 599 0984, telex 897719.

US/0738-6508
**INTERNATIONAL POLICY REPORT.** [Int. policy rep.]. **Added/Corp** Center for International Policy (Washington, D.C.) Institute for International Policy. Vol. 1, (Dec. 1975)-. Periodical. English. ir. $9.00. Center for International Policy, 1755 Massachusetts Avenue Northwest, Suite 505, Washington DC 20036. **Tel** (202)232-3317, FAX (202)232-3440. **Circ:** 1,500.
**Desc:** Reports on the US policy towards the Third World and it impact on the human rights and human needs.
**Ind/Abst** Hum. Rights Intern. Rep.

IS/0020-840X
**INTERNATIONAL PROBLEMS.** (BEAYOT BENLEUMIYOT.). [Int. probl.]. **Added/Corp** Makhon ha-Yisreeli li-Veayot Benleumiyot. **VFOAT** International Relations; International Problems. Vol. 1 (1963)-. Periodical. Hebrew (English and French). ir. $30.00. Israel Association of Graduates, 21 Hess Street, Tel Aviv 63324 Israel. **Tel** 11 972 3 296482, FAX 11 972 3 5551074. **ED** Marion Mushkat, 11 972 3 6414256. **DD** 327. Index available. **Bk Rev**, (Qty: 40). **Ad Acc. Circ:** 2,100 (ctrl). available in microform from University Microfilms International (UMI); available on microfiche.
**Desc:** Fosters the study of political thought and international relations and problems of developing countries.
**Ind/Abst** Am. Hist. Life (1976-); Foreign Lang. Index; Middle East Abstr. Index; PAIS Int. Print; Peace Res. Abstr. J. (1967-1975); Public Aff. Inf. Serv. Bull.

IT
**INTERNATIONAL RECORDS NEWS.** **VFOAT** Int'l Records News. Vol. 1, No. 1 (May 1982)-. Periodical. English. mo. $25.00 US and Canada, surface mail, $35.00 airmail. Fini Editions, 18 Via Monte Battaglia, I-40046 Imola Italy. **LC** PAR.

BU
**INTERNATIONAL RELATIONS (BULGARSKA AKADEMIIA NA NAUKITE. INSTITUT PO MEZHDUNARODNI OTNOSHENIIA I SOTSIALISTICHESKA).** (INTERNATIONAL RELATIONS : REVIEW OF THE INSTITUTE OF INTERNATIONAL RELATIONS AND SOCIALIST INTEGRATION WITH THE BULGARIAN ACADEMY OF SCIENCES / MEZHDUNARODNI OTNOSHENIIA.). **Added/Corp** Institut po Mezhdunarodni Otnosheniia i Sotsialisticheska Integratsiia (Sofia, Bulgaria). **VFOAT** Mezhdunarodni Otnosheniia. (1959)-. Periodical. English (English). ir. $10.00. **(Subscription address:** Hemus Foreign Trade Organization, 6 Tzar Osvoboditel Boulevard, 1000 Sofia Bulgaria.**) LC** D839; .I536. **DD** 327/.05.
**Desc:** Scientific theoretical magazine on the international relations, intended for scientific workers, teachers and libraries, etc.

UK/0047-1178
**INTERNATIONAL RELATIONS (LONDON).** (INTERNATIONAL RELATIONS : THE JOURNAL OF THE DAVID DAVIES MEMORIAL INSTITUTE OF INTERNATIONAL STUDIES.). [Int. relat.]. **Added/Corp** David Davies Memorial Institute of International Studies. Vol. 1, No. 1 (April 1954)-. Periodical. English. Three times a year. £20.00 UK; $40.00 (surface), $55.00 (air mail) other. David Davies Memorial Institute of International Studies, 2 Chadwick Street, London SW1P 2EP England. **Tel** 011 44 71 222 4063. **ED** Sheila Harden. **LC** JX1; .I64. **DD** 327.05. **Bk Rev**. **Ad Acc. Circ:** 1,000.
**Desc:** This journal covers a wide variety of international relations including politics, defense and strategic law, economics and environment issues.
**Ind/Abst** ABC POL SCI; Am. Hist. Life (1984-)(1983-); Int. Polit. Sci. Abstr.; Middle East Abstr. Index; PAIS Int. Print (1991-).

II/0020-8574
**INTERNATIONAL REVIEW OF HISTORY AND POLITICAL SCIENCE.** ***Suspended.*** [Int. rev. hist. polit. sci.]. Vol. 1, No. 1 (June 1964)-Suspended 1989. Periodical. English. qt. Review Publications, Rastogi Subash Bazar, Meerut UP 250002 India. **Tel** 011 91 20895 23881. **LC** D839; .I54. available on microfilm and microfiche from University Microfilms International (UMI).

**Ind/Abst** Am. Hist. Life (1972-1975, 1988-); Int. Polit. Sci. Abstr. (1972-); Middle East Abstr. Index (1972-); Soc. Plann. Policy Dev. Abstr.; Sociol. Abstr. (1972-).

US/0162-2889
**INTERNATIONAL SECURITY.** [Int. secur.]. **Added/Corp** Harvard University. Program for Science and International Affairs. John F. Kennedy School of Government. Center for Science and International Affairs. (Summer 1976)-. Periodical. English. qt. $34.00 (individuals), $92.00 (institutions). Massachusetts Institute of Technology (MIT) Press, 55 Hayward Street, Cambridge MA 02142-1399. **Tel** (617)253-2889, (617)625-8481, FAX (617)258-6779. **ED** Steven E. Miller. **LC** JX1901; .I67. **DD** 327.1. **[CCC]. Ad Acc. Pr Rev. Circ:** 3,900. available on microfilm and microfiche from University Microfilms International (UMI). Documents available from The Genuine Article, UMI Article Clearinghouse.
**Desc:** Provides analyses of world issues such as arms control, military strategy, nuclear weapons proliferation, foreign defense policies, satellite warfare, and the peace movement.
**Ind/Abst** ABC POL SCI; Acad. Search (July 1993-); Air Univ. Libr. Index Mil. Period.; Am. Hist. Life (1976-); Am. Bibliogr. Slavic East Europ. Stud.; Curr. Contents Soc. Behav. Sci.; Curr. Geogr. Publ. (199?-); Curr. Mil. Pol. Lit.; Energy Res. Abstr. (June 1977-); Expand. Acad. Index (1989-); Index Period. Artic. Relat. Law; INFO-SOUTH Abstr.; INIS Atomindex [Micro.]; Int. Polit. Sci. Abstr.; Middle East Abstr. Index; Newsp. Period. Abstr. (1990-); PAIS Int. Print (1991-); Res. Alert [Full Cov.]; Soc. Sci. Source (Jul. 1993-); Soc. Sci. Cit. Index [Full Cov.]; Soc. Sci. Index; Soc. Sci. Index Fulltext (Winter 1988-) [Full Txt.]; U.S. Polit. Sci. Doc.

IT/0393-2729
**INTERNATIONAL SPECTATOR, THE.** (THE INTERNATIONAL SPECTATOR : A QUARTERLY JOURNAL OF THE ISTITUTO AFFARI INTERNAZIONALI.). [Int. spect.]. **Added/Corp** Istituto Affari Internazionali. Vol. 18, No. 1-2 (Jan./June 1983)-. Periodical. English. qt. 75.00Can$. Organizzazione RAB SRL, Via Crocifisso 51, 00165 Rome Italy. **Tel** 011 39 6 632595, 6381177. **(Subscription address:** Canada: University of Toronto Press, 5201 Dufferin Street, North York ONT M3H 5T8 Canada**) ED** G. Bonvicini. **LC** D839; .S68. **DD** 909.82/05. ***Continues** Spettatore Internazionale, 0584-8776.*
**Desc:** Italian review of international affairs in English. Presents in-depth analyses by leading Italian and foreign experts on regional and global issues of major interest to Italy and Europe.
**Ind/Abst** PAIS Int. Print (1991-).

SW/0345-4975
**INTERNATIONAL STUDIES IN THE NORDIC COUNTRIES NEWSLETTER.** ***Ceased.*** **Added/Corp** Nordic Cooperation Committee for International Politics, including Peace and Conflict Research. (19??)-(19??). Newsletter. English. sa. Nordic Cooperation Committee for International Politics, Box 1253, S-111 82 Stockholm Sweden. **Tel** 08/23 40 60. **ED** Karin Lindgren. **LC** D839; .I547. **DD** 907/.2048. **Circ:** 1,500.
**Desc:** Brief presentations of research projects, institutions, scientific seminars and conferences; includes bibliographical section listing recent books, articles and research reports.

US/0097-8965
**INTERNATIONAL STUDIES NEWSLETTER.** **Added/Corp** International Studies Association. (Mar. 1974)-. Newsletter. English. mo (10 issues). $25.00. International Studies Association, 216 HRCB, Brigham Young University, Provo UT 84602. **Tel** (801)378-5459, FAX (801)378-7075. **LC** JX1291; .I615. **DD** 327/.07. ***Supersedes** International Studies Association. ISA Newsletter.*

US/0094-7768
**INTERNATIONAL STUDIES NOTES.** [Int. stud. notes]. **Added/Corp** International Studies Association. University of Pittsburgh. University Center for International Studies. Vol. 1 (Spring 1974)-. Periodical. English. Three times a year. $20.00 (one year), $36.00 (two year). International Studies Notes, c/o Professor Howell, 15249 North 59th Avenue, Glendale AZ 85306. **Tel** (602)978-7182, FAX (602)439-9622. **ED** Llewellyn D Howell. **LC** JX1291; .I617. **DD** 327/.05. cum. index. **Ad Acc. Pr Rev. Circ:** 3,000.
**Desc:** Challenging multi-disciplinary forum for exchange of research, curricular and program reports on international affairs.
**Ind/Abst** ABC POL SCI; Am. Hist. Life (1974-); Curr. Index J. Educ. (March 1990).

US/0020-8833
**INTERNATIONAL STUDIES QUARTERLY.** [Int. stud. q.]. **Added/Corp** International Studies Association. Vol. 11, (March 1967)-. Periodical. English. Six times a year (Jan., Mar., May, July, Sept., Nov.). $197.00 North America; $205.00 other. Blackwell Publishers, 238 Main Street, Cambridge MA 02142. **Tel** (617)547-7110, (800)835-6770, FAX (617)547-0789. **ED** Pat Lauderdale (editor's address: Center for the Study of Justice, Arizona State University, Tempe AZ 85287). **LC** D839; .B2. **[CCC]**. Index available. **Ad Acc. Pr Rev.** available on microfilm and microfiche

from University Microfilms International (UMI). Documents available from The Genuine Article, UMI Article Clearinghouse. ***Continues*** *Background, 0361-5448.*
**Desc:** This journal seeks to acquaint a broad audience of readers with work being done in the variety of intellectual traditions.
**Ind/Abst** ABC POL SCI; Acad. Abstr. Full Text Elite (Jan. 1992-); Acad. Abstr. (Jan. 1992-); Acad. Search (Jan. 1992-); Am. Hist. Life (1970-); Am. Bibliogr. Slavic East Europ. Stud.; Br. Humanit. Index; Curr. Contents Soc. Behav. Sci.; Curr. Index J. Educ. (March 1990-199?); Expand. Acad. Index (1989-); Geogr. Abstr. Human Geogr.; Hum. Resour. Abstr. (?-?); Hum. Rights Intern. Rep.; Index Islam. Lit.; Int. Bibliogr. Sociol.; Int. Dev. Abstr.; Int. Polit. Sci. Abstr.; Middle East Abstr. Index; Newsp. Period. Abstr. (1991-); PAIS Int. Print (1991-); Peace Res. Abstr. J. (1967-); Res. Alert [Full Cov.]; Sage Public Adm. Abstr.; Sage Urban Stud. Abstr (?-?); Soc. Sci. Cit. Index [Full Cov.]; Soc. Sci. Index; Soc. Sci. Index Fulltext (Dec. 1988-) [Full Txt.]; Stud. Women Abstr.; U.S. Polit. Sci. Doc.; West. Hist. Q.

US/1041-3944
**INTERNATIONAL THIRD WORLD STUDIES JOURNAL & REVIEW.** ***Ceased.*** [Int. Third World stud. j. rev.]. **VFOAT** Journal & Review; Journal and Review. (1989)-Ceased ?. English. sa. Media Productions & Marketing Inc, 2440 O Street/Suite 202, Lincoln NE 68510-1125. **Tel** (402)474-2676, (800)627-9919. **ED** Peter Suzuki. **DD** 327. **Bk Rev. Ad Acc. Pr Rev. Circ:** 200 (ctrl).
**Desc:** A professionally published and refereed journal to serve students and faculty, researchers and observers, and all others interested in Third World issues.

AU
**INTERNATIONAL (VIENNA, AUSTRIA).** (INTERNATIONAL.). **VFOAT** Zeitschrift fur Internationale Politik. (198?)-. Periodical. German (summaries and/or abstracts in English). bm. **LC** D839; .I55. **DD** 909.82/05.

US/0095-1471
**INTERNATIONAL YEARBOOK OF FOREIGN POLICY ANALYSIS, THE.** Vol. 1 (1974)-. Periodical. English. ir. John Wiley & Sons, Inc., 605 Third Avenue, New York NY 10158-0012. **Tel** (212)850-6000, (212)850-6645, FAX (212)850-6088, telex 12-7063. **(Subscription address:** John Wiley / Philadelphia, PO Box 7247, Philadelphia PA 19170.**) LC** JX21; .I63. **DD** 327/.09/04.

GW/0020-9430
**INTERNATIONALES AFRIKA-FORUM.** (INTERNATIONALES AFRIKAFORUM.). [Int. Afr.-Forum]. **Added/Corp** Europaisches Institut fuer Politische, Wirtschaftliche und Soziale Fragen. Central Asian Research Centre (London, England). Vol. 1 (Jan. 1965)-. Periodical. German. qt. DM145.50. Weltforum Verlagsgesellschaft, Marienburger Strasse 22, D 50968 Cologne Germany. **Tel** 011 49 221 376950. **LC** DT1; .I6.
**Ind/Abst** Leis. Recreat. Tour. Abstr.

GW/0020-9503
**INTERNATIONALES RECHT UND DIPLOMATIE.** ***Ceased.*** [Int. Recht Dipl.]. **VFOAT** Droit International et Diplomatie; International Law and Diplomacy. Vol. 1/2 (1956)-(19??). German (French, English and Russian). an. Verlag Wissenschaft & Politik, Salierring 14 16, D 50677 Cologne Germany. **Tel** 011 49 221 312878.
**Ind/Abst** Am. Hist. Life (1970, 1974, 1970-); Index Foreign Leg. Per.

SW/0020-952X
**INTERNATIONELLA STUDIER.** **Added/Corp** Utrikespolitiska Institutet (Sweden). **VFOAT** IS, Internationella Studier. (1968)-. Periodical. Swedish. Four times a year. $24.91. Bibliotekstjanst AB, Box 200, S-221 00 Lund Sweden. **Tel** 011 46 46 180000.

NE/0074-7289
**IPRA STUDIES IN PEACE RESEARCH.** **Main/Corp** International Peace Research Association. (1960)-. Monographic series. English. ir. Price varies per volume. International Peace Research Association / Ohio, Antioch College / Paul Smoker, Yellow Springs OH 45387. **Tel** (513)767-6444, FAX (513)767-1891.

LE
**IPS PAPERS.** **Added/Corp** Muassasat al-Dirasat al-Filastiniyah. **VFOAT** Institute for Palestine Studies Papers; I.P.S. Papers. No. 1 (1979)-. Monographic series. English (Arabic and French). ir. Price varies per volume. Institute for Palestine Studies, PO Box 7164, Beirut Lebanon. **Tel** 01 - 814174, 01 - 312512. **Circ:** 5,000.
**Desc:** A series of analytical essays dealing with selected current aspects of the Palestine problem and the Arab-Israeli conflict.

US
**IRAN VOICE.** **VFOAT** Iranvoice. V. 1- 1979-. Periodical. English. bw. $15.00. Embassy of Islamic Republic of Iran, 3005 Massachusetts Avenue NW, Washington DC 20008. **Tel** (202)797-6561. **LC** WMLC L 83/7986.

IR
**IRANIAN JOURNAL OF INTERNATIONAL AFFAIRS, THE.** **Added/Corp** Daftar-i Mutalaat-i Siyasi va Bayn al-Milali (Iran). Vol. 1, No. 1 (Spring 1989)-. Periodical. English (French). qt. $30.00. IJIA, PO Box 19395-1793, Tajrish, Tehran Iran.
**Ind/Abst** PAIS Int. Print; Middle East J.

IE/0332-1460
**IRISH STUDIES IN INTERNATIONAL AFFAIRS.** **Added/Corp** Royal Irish Academy. Vol. 1, No. 1 (1979)-. Periodical. English. an. 10p institutions; 6p individuals. Royal Irish Academy, 19 Dawson Street, Dublin 2 Ireland. **Tel** 011 353 1 762570. **ED** John Bradley. **LC** DA964.A2; I74. **DD** 327/.05. **Circ:** 500.
**Desc:** A specialist journal of studies in foreign policy and international affairs.
**Ind/Abst** Am. Hist. Life (1985-).

II
**ISAAS NEWSLETTER / INDIAN SOCIETY FOR AFRO-ASIAN STUDIES.** **Main/Corp** Indian Society for Afro-Asian Studies. **VFOAT** I.S.A.A.S. Newsletter. No. 1 (1983)-. Newsletter. English. an. Indian Society for Afro-Asian Studies, 75 Defence Enclave Vikas Marg, New Delhi 110092 India. **Tel** 382601, telex (031)4587 LAW IN. **ED** Dharampal. **LC** DS32.9.I4; I53a. **DD** 950/.0496. **Bk Rev. Ad Acc. Circ:** 5,000.
**Desc:** Covers general interest activities about African and Asian countries and cooperation between them.

TS
**ISLAH (DUBAYY, UNITED ARAB EMIRATES).** (AL-ISLAH.). **VFOAT** Al-Eslah; Eslah. Periodical. Arabic. wk. 40.00. Dubayy Shari Al-Qassis, SB 4663, United Arab Emirates. **Tel** 665962. **ED** Mohammed Saleh Rais. **LC** DS1; .I78 . **Ad Acc. Circ:** 20,000.
**Desc:** Discusses the trends of politics and economics and tries to review the development of thought in this field with the fundamental of Islam.

FR/0294-1341
**ISRAEL & PALESTINE POLITICAL REPORT : I & P.** **VFOAT** I. & P.; I & P; Israel & Palestine; Israel and Palestine Political Report. No. 85 (Sept. 1981)-. Periodical. English. Ten times a year. 875.00F. Magelan S A R L, Boite Postale 130-10, 75463 Paris Cedex 10 France. **Tel** 011 33 1 42468903, FAX 011 33 1 42465177. **ED** Maxim Ghilan. **Circ:** 10,000. available on microfilm and microfiche from University Microfilms International (UMI). ***Continues*** *Israel & Palestine Monthly Review.*
**Desc:** Concerned with contemporary conflicts in the Near East, Israeli peace-camps, PLO internal politics, US involvement in the area. A conflict-resolution oriented magazine.
**Ind/Abst** Hum. Rights Intern. Rep.; Middle East J.

US/0883-9832
**ISRAELI FOREIGN AFFAIRS.** [Isr. foreign aff.]. Vol. 1, No. 1 (Dec. 1984)-. Periodical. English. Twelve times a year. $42.00 one year (institutions); $52.00 (airmail); $58.00 (seamail). Israeli Foreign Affairs, PO Box 19580, Sacramento CA 95819. **Tel** (916)736-0274. **ED** Jane Hunter. **DD** 956. Index available. cum. index. **Bk Rev. Circ:** 1,000.
**Desc:** Independent report on Israel's political, military and economic activities outside the Middle East with emphasis on Southern Africa, Latin America and Asia.

UN
**ISSLEDOVANIIA PO ISTORII RUSSKO-GERMANSKIKH OTNOSHENII / MINISTERSTVO VYSSHEGO I SREDNEGO SPETSIALNOGO OBRAZOVANIIA SSSR, DNEPROPETROVSKII GOSUDARSTVENNYI UNIVERSITET IMENI 300-LETIIA VOSSOEDINENIIA UKRAINY S ROSSIEI.** **Added/Corp** Dnipropetrovskyi Derzhavnyi Universytet Imeni 300-Richchia Voz. (1978)-. Russian. **LC** DK67.5.G3; I84. **DD** 327.47043/05.

CH/1013-2511
**ISSUES & STUDIES.** [Issues stud. - Inst. Int. Relat.]. **VFOAT** Issues and Studies. Vol. 1, No. 1 (Oct. 1964)-. Periodical. English (Spanish and French). mo. NT$700.00 (individuals), NT$1,000 (institutions) China; $44.00 (surface mail), $66.00 (airmail) individuals, $64.00 (surface mail), $86.00 (airmail) institutions other. Institute of International Relations, Editorial and Publishing Section, 64 Wan Shou Road Mucha, Taipei Taiwan. **ED** David S Chou. Index available. **Bk Rev. Pr Rev. Circ:** 3,000 (ctrl). available on microfilm. Documents available from The Genuine Article. ***Continues*** *Analysis of Current Chinese Communist Problems, 0517-7065;* ***Absorbed*** *Chinese Communist Affairs, Facts and Features, 0577-9006; Catalog of Current Research Publications on Modern China, 0576-8845.*
**Desc:** An inter-disciplinary journal devoted to the discussion and analysis of problems relating to Chinese communism and other communist systems.
**Ind/Abst** ABC POL SCI; Am. Hist. Life (1969-); Arts Humanit. Citation Index [Select. Cov.]; Asia.-Pac. Econ. Lit.; Curr. Contents Soc. Behav. Sci.; Int. Polit. Sci. Abstr.; Leis. Recreat. Tour. Abstr.; Maize Abstr.; Res. Alert [Full Cov.]; Rural Dev. Abstr.; Soc. Sci. Cit. Index [Full Cov.]; World Agric. Econ.

IT/0303-4933
**ITALIA NELLA POLITICA INTERNAZIONALE, L'.** **Added/Corp** Istituto affari internazionali. Vol. 1 (1973)-. Italian. an. Edizioni di Comunita, Via Manzoni 12, 20121 Milan Italy. **LC** D839; .I74. **DD** 320.9/04.

GW
**JAHRBUCHER DER INTERNATIONALEN POLITIK.** (1955)-. Academic Scholarly Publication. German. be. DM98.00. R Oldenbourg Verlag, Postfach 801360, D 81613 Munich Germany. **Tel** 011 49 89 450190, FAX 011 49 89 45019305. **Acid Free. Circ:** 1,000.

GW
**JAHRESBERICHT - DEUTSCHE GESELLSCHAFT FUER AUSWAERTIGE POLITIK.** **Main/Corp** Deutsche Gesellschaft fuer Auswaertige Politik. (19??)-. German (summaries and/or abstracts in English and French). an. Free. Gesellschaft fuer Auswaertige Politik, Adenaueralle 131, Postfach 1425, W-5304 Bonn Germany. **Tel** 011 49 228 2675 0, FAX 011 49 228 2675 173. **LC** PAR. **Ad Acc. Circ:** 3,500.
**Desc:** Report on the activities of the German Society for foreign affairs.

JA/0024-127X
**JAPAN FORUM.** (19??)-. Periodical. English. sa. Shigeo Urabe, 3-3-14 Mejirodai Hachioju-shi Tokyo Japan.

JA/0913-8773
**JAPAN REVIEW OF INTERNATIONAL AFFAIRS.** **Added/Corp** Nihon Kokusai Mondai Kenkyujo. Vol. 1, No. 1 (Spring/Summer 1987)-. Periodical. English. Four times a year. $60.00. **(Subscription address:** Maruzen Company Ltd., PO Box 5050, Import & Export Department, Tokyo 100 31 Japan.**) LC** D839; .J37. **DD** 327/.09/04.
**Ind/Abst** LABORDOC.

US/0363-2865
**JERUSALEM JOURNAL OF INTERNATIONAL RELATIONS, THE.** ***Ceased.*** [Jerus. j. int. relat.]. Vol. 1 (Fall 1975)- Ceased with Vol. 14, No. 4 (Dec. 1992). Periodical. English. qt. Johns Hopkins University Press, 2715 North Charles Street, Baltimore MD 21218-4319. **Tel** (410)516-6987, FAX (410)516-6968. **ED** Gabriel Sheffer. **LC** JX18; .J47. **DD** 327/.05. **[CCC].** Index available. **Bk Rev. Ad Acc. Circ:** 800. available in microform.
**Desc:** Takes an interdisciplinary approach to the study of international politics. Examines the politics of small and medium-sized countries, reflecting primarily on the economic aspects of politics, problems of war and peace, the global significance of the Middle East conflict, and Israel's foreign policy.
**Ind/Abst** ABC POL SCI; Am. Hist. Life (1976-1992); Int. Polit. Sci. Abstr.; Middle East Abstr. Index; Peace Res. Abstr. J. (1979-1992); Middle East J.

IS
**JERUSALEM LETTER.** **See** Religion and Theology-Judaism.

FR/0021-6089
**JEUNE AFRIQUE (PARIS, FRANCE : 1980).** (JEUNE AFRIQUE.). [Jeune Afr.]. **VFOAT** Jeune Afrique Plus. Vol. 20, No. 992 (Jan. 9, 1980)-. Periodical. French. wk. 695.40F France; 710.00F Europe; 1300.00F others. Groupe Jeune Afrique, 57 Bis rue d Auteuil, 75016 Paris France. **Tel** 011 33 1 44301960. **(Subscription address:** Jeune Afrique, Serv Abon, 36 rue de Picpus, 75012 Paris France**) LC** AP27; .J4. **DD** 054/.1. ***Continues*** *J.A., Jeune Afrique.*
**Ind/Abst** LABORDOC; PAIS Int. Print (1991-); Peace Res. Abstr. J. (1969-1974); Point Repere.

SA
**JOURNAL FOR CONTEMPORARY HISTORY / JOERNAAL VIR EIETYDSE GESKIEDENIS.** **VFOAT** Joernaal vir Eietydse Geskiedenis. Vol. 4, No. 1 (Mar. 1979)-. Periodical. English (Afrikaans). sa (2 issues). R42.00. Institute for Contemporary History, PO Box 2320, Bloemfontein 9300 South Africa. **Tel** 011 27 51 4019111, FAX 011 27 51 473416. **ED** W. Coetler (Editor's Phone: (051)401-2550). Index available. **Bk Rev. Ad Acc. Circ:** 250 (ctrl). ***Continues*** *Joernaal vir Eietydse Geskiedenis en Internasionale Verhoudinge.*
**Desc:** Articles with a historical or political nature and a tendency of international relations.

US
**JOURNAL FOR PEACE & JUSTICE STUDIES.** **Added/Corp** Villanova University. Center for Peace and Justice Education. **VFOAT** Journal for Peace and Justice Studies. Vol. 1, No. 1 (1988)-. Periodical. English. Twice a year (Spring & Fall). $30.00

(institutions), $15.00 (individuals). Journal for Peace & Justice Studies, Villanova University, Center for Peace and Justice Education, Villanova PA 19085. **Tel** (215)645-4499. **ED** Joseph R. Des Jardins and Barbara Wall. **LC** WMLC 93/1509. **Bk Rev. Ad Acc. Pr Rev. Circ:** 150.
**Desc:** Interdisciplinary study of world peace and social justice issues.

●US/1058-3947
**JOURNAL OF AMERICAN-EAST ASIAN RELATIONS, THE.** (1992)-. $60.00 (institutions), $30.00 (individuals). Imprint Publications, Inc., 100 East Ohio Street, Suite 630, Chicago IL 60611. **LC** DS518.8; .J68. **DD** 327.

US/0275-3588
**JOURNAL OF ARAB AFFAIRS.** ***Ceased.*** [J. Arab aff.]. **Added/Corp** Middle East Research Group. Vol. 1, No. 1 (Oct. 1981)-(Fall 1993). Periodical. English. sa. Journal of Arab Affairs, 7872 Fairview Road, Boulder CO 80303. **Tel** (303)499-7295. **ED** Tawfic E Farah. **LC** DS36; .J68. **DD** 909/.04927082. Index available. cum. index. **Bk Rev. Ad Acc. Pr Rev. Circ:** 1,000. available on microfilm and microfiche from University Microfilms International (UMI). Documents available from The Genuine Article, UMI Article Clearinghouse.
**Desc:** Current affairs of Middle East, Arab culture and political thought.
**Ind/Abst** ABC POL SCI; Am. Hist. Life (1987-); Curr. Contents Soc. Behav. Sci.; Expand. Acad. Index (1992-); Index Islam. Lit.; Int. Polit. Sci. Abstr.; Middle East Abstr. Index; Newsp. Period. Abstr. (1992-); PAIS Int. Print (1991-); Res. Alert [Full Cov.]; Soc. Plann. Policy Dev. Abstr.; Soc. Sci. Cit. Index [Full Cov.]; Middle East J.

US/1044-2979
**JOURNAL OF ASIAN AND AFRICAN AFFAIRS.** ***Title Change.*** [J. Asian Afr. aff.]. Vol. 1, No. 1, July (1989)-(1993). Periodical. English. Twice a year (Fall & Spring). Journal Asian & African Affairs, PO Box 44843, Washington DC 20026. **Tel** (202)806-7649. **ED** Dr. Feraidoon Shams. **LC** DS1; .J6374. **DD** 950/.05. **Pr Rev.** ***Continued by*** *Journal of Third World World Spectrum, 1072-5040.*
**Desc:** This is an independent, multidisciplinary, refereed journal designed to promote critical studies on problems and prospects of the Afro-Asian world. The journal reflects contemporary and non-contemporary research and analyses on a broad range of national and international issues confronting Asia and Africa.
**Ind/Abst** Am. Hist. Life (1989-); Int. Bibliogr. Sociol.; PAIS Int. Print (1991-); Middle East J.

US/0022-0027
**JOURNAL OF CONFLICT RESOLUTION, THE.** [J. confl. resolut.]. **Added/Corp** University of Michigan. Center for Research on Conflict Resolution. University of Michigan. Dept. of Journalism. University of Michigan. Peace Science Society (International). **VFOAT** Conflict Resolution. Vol. 1, No. 4 (Dec. 1957)-. English. qt (Mar., June, Sept., Dec.). $193.00. SAGE Periodical Press, 2455 Teller Road, Thousand Oaks CA 91320. **Tel** (805)499-0721, FAX (805)499-0871, telex 100799. **ED** Bruce M. Russett (Yale University). **DD** 302. **NLM** W1 JO595M. **CODEN** JCFRAL. **[CCC].** Index available. cum. index. **Pr Rev. Acid Free.** available on microfilm and microfiche from University Microfilms International (UMI). Documents available from The Genuine Article, UMI Article Clearinghouse. ***Continues*** *Conflict Resolution, 0731-4086.*
**Desc:** Draws from interdisciplinary sources in its focus on the analysis of causes, prevention and solutions to international, domestic and interpersonal conflicts.
**Ind/Abst** ABC POL SCI; Acad. Abstr. Full Text Elite (July 1990-); Acad. Abstr. (July 1990-); Acad. Ind. [Computer File] (1987-); Acad. Search (July 1990-); Am. Hist. Life (1957-); Am. Bibliogr. Slavic East Europ. Stud.; Crim. Penol. Police Sci. Abstr.; Curr. Contents Soc. Behav. Sci.; Curr. Mil. Pol. Lit.; Econ. Lit. Index; Expand. Acad. Index (1987-); Index Period. Artic. Relat. Law; INFO-SOUTH Abstr.; Int. Bibliogr. Sociol.; Int. Polit. Sci. Abstr.; J. Econ. Lit.; J. Plan. Lit.; Mag. Search; Middle East Abstr. Index; Newsp. Period. Abstr. (1991-); PAIS Int. Print (1991-); Peace Res. Abstr. J. (1957-); Psychol. Abstr. (1959-); PsycINFO; PsycLit; PsycScan: Appl. Psych.; Res. Alert [Full Cov.]; Sage Public Adm. Abstr.; Sage Urban Stud. Abstr (?-?); Soc. Plann. Policy Dev. Abstr.; Soc. Sci. Source (Jul. 1990-); Soc. Sci. Cit. Index [Full Cov.]; Soc. Sci. Index; Soc. Sci. Index Fulltext (Sept. 1988-) [Full Txt.]; Soc. Work Abstr. (Spring, Summer 1986-) [Select. Cov.]; Sociol. Abstr. (?-?); U.S. Polit. Sci. Doc.; West. Hist. Q.

●CN/1198-8614
**JOURNAL OF CONFLICT STUDIES.** (199?)-. English. sa. 25.00Can$. University of New Brunswick Centre for Conflict Studies, PO Box 4400, Fredericton NB E3B 5A3 Canada. **Tel** (506)453-4587, FAX (506)453-4599, telex 014-46202.

US/0022-1937
**JOURNAL OF INTERAMERICAN STUDIES AND WORLD AFFAIRS.** [J. inter-Am. stud. world aff.]. **Added/Corp** University of Miami. Center for Advanced International Studies. University of Miami. Institute of Interamerican Studies. **VFOAT** Journal of Inter-American Studies and World Affairs. Vol. 12 (1970)-. Periodical. English. qt. $96.00 (institutions), $42.00 (individuals) US; $120.00 (institutions), $66.00 (individuals). University of Miami / North-South Center, PO Box 248205, Mercy Vega, Coral Gables FL 33124-3027. **Tel** (305)284-8914. **(Subscription address:** Transaction Publishers, Rutgers State University, New Brunswick NJ 08903.**) ED** Jaime Suchlicki. **LC** F1401; .J68. **DD** 980/.005. **[CCC]. Ad Acc, Adv Mgr Tel** (908)932-2280. **Pr Rev. Circ:** 1500. available on microfilm and microfiche from University Microfilms International (UMI). Documents available from The Genuine Article, UMI Article Clearinghouse. ***Continues*** *Journal of Inter-American Studies, 0885-3118.*
**Desc:** Provides in-depth insights and analyses on the latest policy issues. Offers a variety of informed viewpoints on major issues.
**Ind/Abst** ABC POL SCI; Acad. Abstr. Full Text Elite (Jan. 1992-); Acad. Abstr. (Jan. 1992-); Acad. Search (Jan. 1992-); Am. Hist. Life (1959-); Am. Bibliogr. Slavic East Europ. Stud.; Crim. Justice Abstr.; Crim. Penol. Police Sci. Abstr.; Curr. Contents Soc. Behav. Sci.; Curr. Geogr. Publ. (199?-); Expand. Acad. Index (1989-); HAPI Hisp. Am. Period. Index; Hist. Abstr.; INFO-SOUTH Abstr.; Int. Polit. Sci. Abstr.; Mag. Search; Middle East Abstr. Index; Newsp. Period. Abstr. (1991-); PAIS Int. Print; Res. Alert [Full Cov.]; Soc. Sci. Source (Jan. 1992-); Soc. Sci. Cit. Index [Full Cov.]; Soc. Sci. Index; Soc. Sci. Index Fulltext (Spring 1988-) [Full Txt.]; U.S. Polit. Sci. Doc.; West. Hist. Q.

US/0022-197X
**JOURNAL OF INTERNATIONAL AFFAIRS (NEW YORK).** (JOURNAL OF INTERNATIONAL AFFAIRS.). [J. int. aff.]. **Added/Corp** Columbia University. School of International and Public Affairs. Columbia University. School of International Affairs. Vol. 6 (Winter 1952)-. Periodical. English. sa. $28.00 (one year), $54.00 (two years), $76.00 (three years) institutions US, Canada and Mexico; $33.00 (one year), $64.00 (two years), $91.00 (three years) institutions other; $14.00 (one year), $27.00 (two years), $38.00 (three years) individuals US, Canada and Mexico; $19.00 (one year), $37.00 (two years), $53.00 (three years) individuals other. Columbia University / International Affairs, Box 4, International Affairs Building, New York NY 10027. **Tel** (212) 854-4775. **ED** Martin Malin and Christine Demkowych. **LC** JX1; .C6. **DD** 341. **[CCC]. Bk Rev. Ad Acc. Pr Rev. Circ:** 4,500. available on microfilm from University Microfilms International (UMI). ***Continues*** *Columbia Journal of International Affairs, 1045-3466.*
**Desc:** With its distinctive single topic format, provides readers with timely and insightful analysis of significant international issues. Brings together scholars and policy makers with thoughtful and provocative analysis of a current topic of international concern.
**Ind/Abst** ABC POL SCI; Acad. Abstr. Full Text Elite (Jan. 1992-); Acad. Abstr. (Jan. 1992-); Acad. Search (Jan. 1992-); Am. Bibliogr. Slavic East Europ. Stud.; Am. Hist. Life (1954-); Curr. Contents Soc. Behav. Sci.; Curr. Geogr. Publ. (199?-); Curr. Law Index; Curr. Mil. Pol. Lit.; Expand. Acad. Index (1984-); Hum. Rights Intern. Rep.; Humanit. Index; Index Islam. Lit.; INFO-SOUTH Abstr.; Int. Polit. Sci. Abstr.; J. Plan. Lit.; Leg. Resour. Index (1980-); LegalTrac (1980-); Mag. Search; Middle East Abstr. Index; Newsp. Period. Abstr. (1991-); PAIS Int. Print; Peace Res. Abstr. J.; Soc. Sci. Source (Jan. 1992-); Res. Alert [Full Cov.]; Soc. Sci. Index; Soc. Sci. Index Fulltext (Fall 1988-) [Full Txt.]; West. Hist. Q.

US
**JOURNAL OF INTERNATIONAL AFFAIRS (NEW YORK). [MICROFILM].** (JOURNAL OF INTERNATIONAL AFFAIRS.). **Added/Corp** Columbia University. School of International Affairs. Vol. 1- (Spring 1947)-. Periodical. English. sa. Washington & Jefferson College, 45 S Lincoln Dr., Washington PA 15301. **Tel** (412)222-4400. **LC** JX1; .C6. available in print.

NO/0022-3433
**JOURNAL OF PEACE RESEARCH.** [J. peace res.]. **Added/Corp** International Peace Research Institute. **VFOAT** JPR. Vol. 1 (1964)-. Periodical. English (summaries and/or abstracts in Russian). qt. £95.00. Sage Publications Ltd., 6 Bonhill Street, London EC2A 4PU, UK. **Tel** 071 374 0645, FAX 071 374 8741, telex 296207 SAGE G. **ED** Nils Petter Gleditsch. **LC** AS9; .J6. **DD** 327.1/72/05. Index available. **Bk Rev. Ad Acc. Pr Rev. Acid Free. Circ:** 1,200. available on microfilm and microfiche from University Microfilms International (UMI). Documents available from The Genuine Article, UMI Article Clearinghouse.
**Desc:** Articles directed towards ways and means of promoting peace.
**Ind/Abst** ABC POL SCI; Acad. Abstr. Full Text Elite (Jan. 1992-); Acad. Abstr. (Jan. 1992-); Acad. Search (Jan. 1992-); Am. Hist. Life (1969-); Curr. Contents Soc. Behav. Sci.; Curr. Mil. Pol. Lit.; Expand. Acad. Index (1989-); Hum. Rights Intern. Rep.; INFO-SOUTH Abstr.; Int. Bibliogr. Sociol.; Int. Polit. Sci. Abstr.; J. Plan. Lit.; Mag. Search; Middle East Abstr. Index; Newsp. Period. Abstr. (1991-); PAIS Int. Print (1991-?); Peace Res. Abstr. J. (1964-1974, 1977-); Res. Alert [Full Cov.]; Sage Public Adm. Abstr.; Soc. Plann. Policy Dev. Abstr.; Soc. Sci. Source (Jan. 1992-); Soc. Sci. Cit. Index [Full Cov.]; Soc. Sci. Index; Soc. Sci. Index Fulltext (Sept. 1988-) [Full Txt.]; Soc. Work Abstr. [Select. Cov.]; Sociol. Abstr.

US
**JOURNAL OF THE FOREIGN POLICY RESEARCH ASSOCIATION OF THE UNIVERSITY OF REDLANDS.** **Main/Corp** Redlands, Calif. University. Foreign Policy Research Association. **VFOAT** Journal of Foreign Affairs. Vol. 1 (Spring 1971)-. Periodical. English. sa. **LC** JX1; .R4.

YU/0022-5452
**JOURNAL OF THE YUGOSLAV FOREIGN TRADE.** [J. Yugosl. for. trade]. (196?)-. Periodical. English. mo. $120.00. Export Press, Ulica 27, Belgrade Yugoslavia. **Tel** FAX 011 38 11 321321. **ED** Bozidar Milosavljevic. **Bk Rev. Ad Acc. Circ:** 24,000 (ctrl). ***Continues*** *Journal of Yugoslav Foreign Trade, 0022-5452.*
**Desc:** Dedicated to economic and political relations between Yugoslavia and different countries of the world with special interest on joint ventures and export.

●US/1072-5040
**JOURNAL OF THIRD WORLD SPECTRUM.** [J. third world spect.]. Vol. 1, No. 1 (Spring 1994)-. Periodical. English (French). Twice a year. $53.00 (institutions), $28.00 (individuals) US; $63.00 (institutions), $37.00 (individuals) other. Journal Asian & African Affairs, PO Box 44843, Washington DC 20026. **Tel** (202)806-7649. **ED** Feraidoon Shams. **LC** IN PROCESS; HC59.7; .J68. **DD** 909. cum. index. **Bk Rev. Ad Acc. Circ:** 300. ***Continues*** *Journal of Asian and African Affairs.*
**Desc:** Independent, multidisciplinary, refereed journal designed to promote critical studies on problems and prospects of the Afro-Asian world. The journal reflects contemporary and non-contemporary research and analyses on a broad range of national and international issues confronting Asia and Africa.

US/8756-8691
**JOURNAL OF WORLD PEACE, THE.** ***Suspended.*** [J. world peace]. Vol. 1, No. 1 (Spring 1984)-Suspended with Vol. 7, No. 2. Periodical. English. sa. $13.00. Journal of World Peace, Social Science Division, University of Minnesota, Morris MN 56267. **Tel** (612)589-1091. **DD** 327.
**Ind/Abst** Peace Res. Abstr. J. (1984).

JA
**KABUKI.** (1???)-. Periodical. English. mo. Foreign Affairs Association of Japan, Tokyo Kaikan, 1-7 Yuraku-cho, Chiyoda-ku Tokyo Japan.

UK/0952-195X
**KEESING'S UK RECORD.** [Keesing's UK rec.]. **VFOAT** Keesing's United Kingdom Record. (1988)-. Periodical. English. bm (6 issues). $200.00. CIRCA, 13-17 Sturton Street, Cambridge CB1 2SN England. **Tel** 011 44 223 568017, FAX 011 44 223 354643. **ED** Robert Fraser. available on microfilm and microfiche from University Microfilms International (UMI).
**Desc:** Record of current events in the UK. Subject headings cover government and politics, external relations, defense and internal security, local government and regional affairs.

JA
**KOKUSAI KANKEI-GAKU KENKYU.** **Added/Corp** Tsuda-juku Daigaku. **VFOAT** Study of the International Relations. No. 1 (1974)-. Multiple languages (Japanese and English). an. Free. Tsuda-Juku Daigaku, 1491 Tsudamachi 189, Kodaira Japan. **Tel** 0423-42-5155. **LC** D410; .D58. **Bk Rev.** ctrl circ.

JA/0388-4279
**KOKUSAI KANKEI GAKUBU KENKYU NENPO.** **VFOAT** Journal of the College of International Relations. No. 1 (1980)-. Periodical. Japanese (Spanish and English). an. Nihon Daigaku Mishima Gakuen, Bunkyo-cho 2-chome, Mishima-shi, Shizuoka-ken 411, Tokyo Japan. **LC** JX18; .K59. ctrl circ.

JA/0916-3654
**KOKUSAI KANKEI KENKYU. KOKUSAI BUNKA-HEN.** **VFOAT** Studies on International Relations. Intercultural Relations. (1989)-. Periodical. Multiple languages. sa. Nihon University / College of International Relations, Mishima, Shizuoka, 411, Japan. **DD** 060. ***Continues in part*** *Kokusai Kankei Kenkyu, 0389-2603.*

JA/0916-3646
**KOKUSAI KANKEI KENKYU. KOKUSAI KANKEI-HEN.** **VFOAT** Studies on International Relations. International Relations. (1989)-. Periodical. Multiple languages. sa. Nihon University / College of

International Relations, Mishima, Shizuoka, 411, Japan. **DD** 327. ***Continues in part*** *Kokusai Kankei Kenkyu, 0389-2603.*

JA/0389-2603
**KOKUSAI KANKEI KENKYU (MISHIMA-SHI, JAPAN).** (KOKUSAI KANKEI KENKYU.). **VFOAT** Studies on International Relations. Periodical. English (Japanese and German). Three times a year. Nihon Daigaku Kokusai Kankei Gakubu Kokusai Kankei, Mishima-shi, Shizuoka-ken 411 Japan. **LC** JX18; .K594. ctrl circ.

JA
**KOKUSAI MONDAI SHIRYO. Added/Corp** Japan. Gaimusho. Joho Bunkakyoku. (19??)-. Periodical. Japanese. mo. Gaimusho Joho Bunkakyoku, 2-1 Kasumigaseki 2, Chiyoda-ku Tokyo-to 100 Japan. **LC** JX1954; .K64.

JA
**KOKUSAI SEIKEI JOHO.** 1st Ed.- 1984-. Japanese. mo. Gaimusho Joho Bunkakyoku, 2-1 Kasumigaseki 2, Chiyoda-ku Tokyo-to 100 Japan. **LC** D839; .K644.

KO/0251-3072
**KOREA & WORLD AFFAIRS.** [Korea world aff.]. **Added/Corp** Pyonghwa Tongil Yonguso (Korea). **VAT** Korea and World Affairs. Vol. 1 (Spring 1977)-. Periodical. English. qt. $35.60. Research Center of Peace and Unification of Korea, CPO Box 6545, Seoul 100 Korea. **LC** DS916.6; .K67. **DD** 951.9/005.
**Ind/Abst** Am. Hist. Life (1978-); Int. Polit. Sci. Abstr.; PAIS Int. Print.

KO/0377-0451
**KOREAN JOURNAL OF INTERNATIONAL STUDIES, THE. Added/Corp** Hanguk Kukche Kwangye Yonguso. (Summer 1970)-. Periodical. English. qt (4 issues). $55.00. Korean Institute of International Studies, KPO 426, Seoul 110-604 Korea. **Tel** 011 82 2 7527727. **ED** Chong-Ki Choi. **LC** JX1; .K66. **DD** 327/.05. **Ad Acc. Circ:** 1,500.
**Desc:** Covers the articles of many fields, which are international politics, economics, social, strategic and security affairs, by the distinguished scholars and statesmen.
**Ind/Abst** Geogr. Abstr. Human Geogr.; Int. Dev. Abstr.; Int. Polit. Sci. Abstr.; Peace Res. Abstr. J. (1974-1975).

KO
**KUKCHE MUNJE. VFOAT** Journal of International Studies. Periodical. Korean. W40.00. Kukche Munje Sa, 95 Yonji-dong Korea. **Tel** 763-7401/2. **ED** Ho-Jik Hwang. **LC** D839; .K82. **Ad Acc. Circ:** 20,000 (ctrl).
**Desc:** Publishes articles on contemporary political, military, and international relation issues representing divergent ideas and opinions.

GW
**KULTUR UND GESELLSCHAFT. Added/Corp** Demokratischer Kulturbund Deutschlands. (19??)-. Periodical. German. ir. Price varies. Friedrich Frommann Verlag, Koenig Karlstrasse 27, D 70372 Stuttgart 50 Germany. **Tel** 011 49 711 9559690. **LC** DD259.4; .K86.

RU/0023-5199
**KULTURA I ZHIZN. Added/Corp** Soiuz Sovetskikh Obshchestv Druzhby i Kulturnoi Sviazi s Zarubezhnymi Stranami. Vsesoiuznoe Obshchestvo Kulturnoi Sviazi Szagranitsei (Soviet Union). (1957)-. Periodical. Russian. Four times a year. $89.95. **(Subscription address:** East View Publications Inc., 3020 Harbor Lane North, Suite 110, Minneapolis MN 55447.**) Bk Rev.**

CH
**KUO CHI HSING SHIH NIEN CHIEN / SHANG-HAI KUO CHI WEN TI YEN SHIU SO PIEN. VFOAT** Survey of International Affairs. 1982-. Chinese. an. NT$3.75. Hsin Hua Shu Tien / Shang-Hai Fa Hsing So, Shanghai, People's Republic of China. **LC** D839; .K845. **DD** 327/.09/047.

CH
**KUO CHI KUAN HSI HSUEH PAO. VFOAT** Journal of International Relations. Vol. 1- ; 1978-. Periodical. Chinese (Chinese). an. NT$100.00 single issue. **LC** JX91.C5; K86.

CC
**KUO CHI WEN TI YEN CHIU. Added/Corp** Kuo Chi Wen ti Yen Chiu So (China). **VFOAT** Journal of International Studies; International Studies; Guoji Wenti Yanjiu. No. 1 (Jan. 1981)-. Periodical. Chinese (table of contents in English). mo. $8.36. **(Subscription address:** China International Book Trading Corporation, PO Box 399, Library Service Department, Beijing 100044 People's Republic of China.**) LC** D849; .K866. **DD** 909.82/8.

IT
**LABORATORIO POLITICA INDUSTRIALE.** Italian. L800000 Italy; L850000 other. Nomisma, Strada Maggiore 44, 40125 Bologna, Italy. **Tel** 011 39 51 239422.

AT/0817-8798
**LABOUR STUDIES BRIEFING.** [Labour stud. brief.]. (1986)-. Abstracting/Indexing Service. English. Four times a year (Mar., June, Sept., Dec.). 25.00Aus$. Centre for Labour Studies, University of Adelaide, Adelaide 5005 Australia. **Tel** 011 61 8 303 3715, FAX 011 61 8 303 4346. **DD** 322.20994. **Circ:** 400.
**Desc:** This journal contains abstracts of current articles in the field of labour studies. Subject areas include Australian political economy , Australian trade unions, work issues in Australia and international labor issues.

CN/0820-0726
**LETTRE AFRICAINE, LA.** [Lett. afr.]. Vol. 1, No. 1 (Nov. 1982)-. Periodical. French. ir. $30.00. Institut Canadien Des Affaires Africaines, 1080 Montee Du Beaver Hall, Suite 1440, Montreal Quebec H2Z 1S8. **DD** 327.6071/05.

SP/0210-6337
**LEVIATAN (MADRID, SPAIN).** (LEVIATAN.). **Added/Corp** Fundacion Pablo Iglesias. (19??)-. Spanish. Four times a year. 2000.00ptas Spain; 3200.00ptas Europe; 4800.00ptas the Americas. Fundacion Pablo Iglesias, Monte Esquinza, 30-2nd D. Madrid Spain. **Tel** 11 34 1 3104313, 5344573, FAX 11 34 1 3194585. **ED** Salvador Clotas I Cierco and Manuel Ortuno Armas. **LC** D839; .L48. **DD** 909.82. **Ad Acc, Adv Mgr:** Mercedes Garcia Lenberg. **Circ:** 5,000.
**Ind/Abst** Int. Bibliogr. Sociol.; Int. Polit. Sci. Abstr.

BE/0770-450X
**LIAISONS INTERNATIONALES / CENTRE OECUMENIQUE DE LIAISONS INTERNATIONALES. Added/Corp** Centre Oecumenique de Liaisons Internationales. **VFOAT** International Intercommunications; Comunicaciones Internacionales. (19??)-. Periodical. French (English and Spanish). qt. $12.00. COELI, rue du Boulet 31, B-1000 Brussels Belgium. **Tel** 011 32 2 5120489.

EC
**LISTA DIPLOMATICA Y DE LOS ORGANISMOS INTERNACIONALES / DIRECCION GENERAL DE PROTOCOLO.** Spanish. **LC** JX1769; .A285. **DD** 351.8/92/09866. ***Continues*** *Lista Diplomatica (Ecuador. Ministerio de Relaciones Exteriores).*

NG
**LISTE DES MEMBRES DES CORPS DIPLOMATIQUE ET CONSULAIRE ET DES ORGANISATIONS INTERNATIONALES. Main/Corp** Niger. Ministere des Affaires Etrangeres et de la Cooperation. French. **LC** JX1867.N5; N54A. **DD** 327/.2/0256626.

US/0192-1460
**MACNEIL/LEHRER REPORT. BROADCAST REVIEW AND INDEX, THE.** [MacNeil/Lehrer rep., Broadcast rev. index]. Periodical. English. qt. $20.00. Microfilming Corporation of America, 21 Harristown Road, Glen Rock NJ 07452. **LC** D839; .M323. **DD** 909.82.

II
**MAINSTREAM.** (1963)-. Periodical. English. wk. $44.00. Mainstream India, 77 Connaught Circus, Box 541, New Delhi 1 India. **(Subscription address:** Prints India, 11 Darya Ganj, New Delhi 110002 India.**)**

CN/1183-3661
**MARTELLO PAPERS. Added/Corp** Queen's University (Kingston, Ont.). Centre for International Relations. Queen's University (Kingston, Ont.). School of Policy Studies. (1991)-. Monographic series. English. Price varies per volume.

IO
**MASALAH-MASALAH INTERNASIONAL MASAKINI. Added/Corp** Lembaga Research Kebudayaan Nasional (Indonesia). (19??)-. Indonesian. Lembaga Research Kebudayaan Nasional, Jln Pejambon No 2, Jakarta Indonesia. **LC** D839; .M35.

CN/0710-457X
**MCIC NEWS.** [MCIC news]. **VAT** Manitoba Council for International Cooperation News. Periodical. English. Six times a year. Free. Manitoba Council for International Cooperation, 418 Wardlaw Avenue, Winnipeg Manitoba R3L 0L7 Canada. **Tel** (204)786-2106. **ED** Doug Smith. **DD** 327.1/7/05. **Circ:** 500 (ctrl).
**Desc:** Informs membership of activities of council related to international development.

UK/0748-8009
**MEDICINE AND WAR.** **See** Medical Science and Technology.

US/1047-4552
**MEDITERRANEAN QUARTERLY.** (MEDITERRANEAN QUARTERLY : A JOURNAL OF GLOBAL ISSUES.). [Mediterr. q.]. **Added/Corp** Mediterranean Affairs Inc. **VFOAT** MQ. Vol. 1, No. 1 (Winter 1990)-. Periodical. English. qt (4 issues). $44.00 (institutions), $24.00 (individuals) US; $56.00 (institutions), $36.00 (individuals) other. Duke University Press, PO Box 90660, Durham NC 27708-0660. **Tel** (919)687-3600, (919)688-5134 (orders), FAX (919)688-4574, telex 802829. **ED** Nikolaos A. Stavrou. **LC** D839; .M42; IN PROCESS. **DD** 327.
**Desc:** Provides an open forum for reasoned, contrasting, provocative analysis and commentary on tropics of international interest.
**Ind/Abst** Middle East J.; U.S. Polit. Sci. Doc. (199?-).

RU/0026-1874
**MEZHDUNARODNAIA ZHIZN. Added/Corp** Russian S.F.S.R. Narodnyi Komissariat po Inostrannym Delam. Soviet Union. Narodnyi Komissariat po Inostrannym Delam. Vsesoiuznoe Obshchestvo po Rasprostraneniiu Politicheskikh i Nauchnykh Znanii. (March 20, 1992)-. Periodical. Russian (French, German and Chinese; table of contents in English, French, German and Chinese). mo. $99.00. **(Subscription address:** East View Publications Inc., 3020 Harbor Lane North, Suite 110, Minneapolis MN 55447.**)** available on microfilm from University Microfilms International (UMI).
**Ind/Abst** Am. Hist. Life (1955,1966-1971); Curr. Mil. Pol. Lit.

BU
**MEZHDUNARODNI OTNOSHENIIA. Added/Corp** Institut za Vunshna Politika Ivan Bashev. **VFOAT** International Relations Journal. Vol. 1 (1972)-. Periodical. Bulgarian (summaries and/or abstracts in English, French and Russian). Six times a year. DM83.00. Institut za Mezhdunarodni Otnosheniia i Sotsialisticheska Intergratsiia, 7 Noemuri 1, Sofia Bulgaria. **(Subscription address:** Kubon & Sagner, ABT Zeitschriftenimport, D 80328 Munich Germany.**) LC** D839; .M455.
**Desc:** Publications covering world politics.

US
**MIDDLE EAST DIARY. CD-ROM.** English. $106.95. Quanta Press, Inc., 1313 Fifth Street Southeast, Suite 208C, Minneapolis MN 55414. **Tel** (612)379-3956, FAX (612)623-4570.
**Desc:** Represents a lengthy review of Middle East history, personalities, and conflicts. This "diary" gives the end-user the background needed to make competent decisions on travel, business, and relationships in the Middle East. Available in DOS and MAC formats.

CN/0705-8594
**MIDDLE EAST FOCUS. *Ceased.* Added/Corp** Canadian Academic Foundation for Peace in the Middle East. Vol. 1 (May 1978)-Vol. 14, No. 3 (July 1992). Periodical. English. qt. Canadian Academic Foundation, PO Box 81509, 1057 Steeles Avenue West, North York, Ontario M2R 3X1 Canada. **Tel** (416)963-9477. **LC** DS63.1; .M488. **DD** 327.5694/017/4927. **Bk Rev. Circ:** 4,000 (ctrl).
**Desc:** A study and analysis of the social, political and economic issues underlying the conflict areas of the Middle East.
**Ind/Abst** Fluid Abstr., Civil Eng.; Fluid Abstr. Proc. Eng.; FLUIDEX (199?-); Index Islam. Lit.; Middle East Abstr. Index.

UK/0047-7249
**MIDDLE EAST INTERNATIONAL.** No. 1 (April 1971)-. Periodical. English. Twenty-five times a year (every two weeks). £105.00 institutions, £60.00 individuals UK; £105.00 institutions, £65.00 individuals Europe; £115.00 institutions, £90.00 individuals other. Middle East International Publishers Ltd, 21 Collingham Road, London SW5 0NU England. **Tel** 011 44 71 3735228, FAX 011 44 71 3705956, telex 8953551. **(Subscription address:** PO Box 53365, Temple Heights Station, Washington DC 20009**) ED** Michael Wall. **DD** 915.6/005. Index available. cum. index. **Bk Rev. Circ:** 5,000 (ctrl). available on microfilm and microfiche from University Microfilms International (UMI).
**Desc:** Middle East current affairs.
**Ind/Abst** Middle East Abstr. Index.

●US/1061-1924
**MIDDLE EAST POLICY.** [Middle East policy]. **Added/Corp** Middle East Policy Council (U.S.). Vol. 1, No. 1 (1992)-. Periodical. English. Four times a year. $35.00 US; $55.00 other. Middle East Policy Council, 1730 M Street NW, Suite 512, Washington DC 20036. **Tel** (202)296-6767, FAX (202)296-5791, telex 440506. **ED** Anne Joyce. **LC** DS41; .M518. **DD** 956/.005. Index available. cum. index. **Bk Rev**, (Qty: various). **Ad Acc. Circ:** 8,000. available on microfiche from University Microfilms International (UMI). Documents available from UMI Article Clearinghouse. ***Continues*** *American-Arab Affairs, 0731-6763.*
**Ind/Abst** ABC POL SCI; Book Rev. Index; Newsp. Period. Abstr. (1992-); PAIS Int. Print; Middle East J.

US/0731-4655
**MIDEAST PRESS REPORT.** [Mideast press rep.]. (19??)-. Periodical. English. Fifty-two times a year. $3,400.00. Claremont Research & Publishing, 160

Claremont Avenue, New York NY 10027. **Tel** (212)662-0707. **ED** George Cavalletto.
**Desc:** A press clipping compilation of all coverage of Middle East and North Africa from over 100 US and European sources, including the major newspapers of the US, England, France, as well as English language Middle East sources.

UK/0305-8298
**MILLENNIUM.** [Millennium]. **Added/Corp** London School of Economics and Political Science. (1971)-. English. Three times a year. £10.00 (student), £16.00 (individual), £35.00 (institution) UK; $16.00 (student), $26.00 (individual), $56.00 (institution) US; 20.00Can$ (student), 30.00Can$ (individual), 67.00 (institution) Canada. London School of Economics, Houghton Street, London WC2A 2AE England. **Tel** 011 44 71 9557438, FAX 011 44 71 9557446. **ED** Malory Greene and Ian Rowlands. **LC** JX1; .M54. **DD** 327/.05. **Bk Rev. Ad Acc. Pr Rev. Circ:** 800 (ctrl). available on microfilm and microfiche from University Microfilms International (UMI). Documents available from The Genuine Article.
**Desc:** Combines extended academic articles, discussion pieces, review articles and book reviews to provide extensive coverage of international relations.
**Ind/Abst** ABC POL SCI; Am. Hist. Life (1975-); Anthropol. Index; Arts Humanit. Citation Index [Select. Cov.]; BHA : Biblio. Hist. Art; Br. Humanit. Index; Int. Bibliogr. Sociol.; Int. Polit. Sci. Abstr.; PAIS Int. Print (1991-); Res. Alert [Full Cov.]; Soc. Sci. Cit. Index [Full Cov.].

FR/0026-9395
**MONDE DIPLOMATIQUE, LE.** [Monde dipl.]. (May 1954)-. Periodical. French. mo. $135.00. Le Monde / Immeuble Sirius, 1 Place Hubert Beuve Mery, 94852 Ivry-sur-Seine CX France. **Tel** 011 33 1 49603000, 011 33 1 49603290. **LC** JX3; .M65. **DD** 327/.05.
**Ind/Abst** GeoRef; Hum. Rights Intern. Rep.; Int. Labour Doc.; LABORDOC; Point Repere (1983-).

MX
**MONDE DIPLOMATIQUE, LE.** ***Ceased.*** **VFOAT** Monde Diplomatique en Espanol. No. 1 (Jan. 1979)-Ceased (June 1990). Spanish. mo. Ediciones Diadema SA, Capitan Haya 49-9A, 28020 Madrid Spain. **LC** JX3; .M65.
**Ind/Abst** PAIS Int. Print.

US/0077-0582
**MONOGRAPH SERIES IN WORLD AFFAIRS.** (MONOGRAPH SERIES IN WORLD AFFAIRS / THE SOCIAL SCIENCE FOUNDATION AND GRADUATE SCHOOL OF INTERNATIONAL STUDIES, UNIVERSITY OF DENVER.). **Added/Corp** University of Denver. Social Science Foundation. University of Denver. Dept. of International Relations. University of Denver. Graduate School of International Studies. (1963/64)-. Monographic series. English. ir. Price varies per volume. Lynne Rienner Publishers, 1800 30th Street, Suite 314, Boulder CO 80301. **Tel** (303)444-6684, FAX (303)444-0824. **ED** Karen A. Feste. **Ad Acc.**
**Desc:** Analytical studies in historical and social science frameworks dealing with contemporary problems of international relations.
**Ind/Abst** Int. Polit. Sci. Abstr.

LE
**MONOGRAPH SERIES - INSTITUTE FOR PALESTINE STUDIES.** **Main/Corp** Mu'Assasat Al-Dirasat Al-Filastiniyah. (19??)-. Monographic series. English. ir. Price varies per volume. Institute for Palestine Studies, PO Box 7164, Beirut Lebanon. **Tel** 01 - 814174, 01 - 312512. **Circ:** 5,000.
**Desc:** Series of analytical studies dealing with various aspects of the Palestine question and the Arab-Israeli conflict.

UK
**MONTAGUE BURTON LECTURE ON INTERNATIONAL RELATIONS.** **Added/Corp** Leeds, England. University. 1 (1942)-. Monographic series. English. Price varies per volume.

SZ/0251-6624
**MONTHLY BIBLIOGRAPHY. PART II, SELECTED ARTICLES / UNITED NATIONS, LIBRARY.** **Main/Corp** United Nations Library (Geneva, Switzerland). **VFOAT** Selected Articles; Articles Selectionnes; Bibliographie Mensuelle. Partie II, Articles Selectionnes; Publications. Part II, Selected Articles; Publications. Partie II, Articles Selectionnes. No. 1-2 (Jan./Feb. 1978)-. Government Publication. English (French). mo (combined issues occasionally). $60.00. United Nations Publications, 2 United Nations Plaza, Room DC2 0853, Department 007C, New York NY 10017. **Tel** (212)963-8303, (800)253-9646. **(Subscription address:** United Nations Publications, Subscription Office, PO Box 361, Birmingham AL 35201-0361.**)** **LC** Z6472; .U55; JX1977. **DD** 016.34123. ***Continues*** *United Nations Library (Geneva, Switzerland). Liste Mensuelle d'Aticles Slectionnes.*
**Desc:** A worldwide list of selected journal articles on political, legal, economic, financial and other topics of current United Nations interest.

CN/0227-8715
**MOT A MOT (QUEBEC).** (MOT A MOT.). **Added/Corp** Association Quebec-France. (1979)-. Periodical. French. mo. Association Quebec-France, 9 Place Royale, Quebec Quebec G1X 4G2 Canada. **DD** 327.714044.

DK
**MS BIBLIOTEKSNYT.** **Main/Corp** Mellemfolkeligt Samvirke. **Added/Corp** Mellemfolkeligt Samvirke. Biblioteksnyt. **VAT** Mellemfolkeligt Samvirkes Biblioteksnyt. (19??)-. Multiple languages (Danish and Multiple languages). an. Mellemfolkeligt Samvirke, Borgergade 10-14, DK-1300 Kobenhavn K Denmark. **Tel** 33 32 62 44, telex 159 28 MS DK. **ED** Helle Leth-Moller. **LC** Z7164.U5; M43a; HC59.7. Index available. cum. index. **Bk Rev. Circ:** 500.
**Desc:** Registrate (including annotations) annually 2,000 books and 3,500 articles on Third World topics, which are accessioned in the library at Mellemfolkeligt Samvirke (Danish Association for International Co-operation).

VE/0379-6922
**MUNDO NUEVO.** **Added/Corp** Universidad Simon Bolivar. Instituto de Altos Estudios de America Latina. (July/Sept. 1978)-. Periodical. Spanish (French and English). Four times a year. Instituto de Altos Estudios America, Parque Central Nivel Oficina 220, El Conde Caracas Venezuela. **Tel** 011 58 2 5738824. **ED** Delia Colombo de Puig. **LC** F1401; .M865. **DD** 980/.005. Index available. **Bk Rev. Pr Rev. Circ:** 1,000 (ctrl).
**Desc:** Covers social sciences, economics and politics related to Latin America.
**Ind/Abst** HAPI Hisp. Am. Period. Index.

US/0894-6442
**MYTHS AND FACTS.** [Myths facts]. (1964)-. English. ir. Price varies. Near East Research Inc, 440 First Street NW, Suite 607, Washington DC 20001. **Tel** (202)639-5200, (202)639-5300. **LC** IN PROCESS. **DD** 956/.04.
**Desc:** Contains information on Jewish-Arab relations.

US/0742-8170
**N.Y. JOURNAL JAPAN.** [N.Y. j. Jap.]. **VFOAT** NY Journal Japan. (19??)-. Periodical. Japanese (English). Twelve times a year. $12.00. Japan Editorial Track, 310 East 46th Street, Suite 15H, New York NY 10017. **Tel** (212)557-5547. ***Continues*** *J.O.P.*

II
**NATION AND THE WORLD.** **VFOAT** Nation. (June 16, 1991)-. Periodical. English. Twenty-six times a year. $40.00. **(Subscription address:** Prints India, 11 Darya Ganj, New Delhi, 110002 India, (Phone: 011 91 11 3268645)**)** **LC** IN PROCESS.

US/0884-9382
**NATIONAL INTEREST, THE.** [Natl. interest]. **Added/Corp** National Affairs, inc. No. 1 (Fall 1985)-. Periodical. English. qt. $21.00 (one year), $38.00 (two year), $54.00 (three year) US; $31.00 (one year), $48.00 (two year), $64.00 (three year) other. National Affairs Inc., 1112 16th Street Northwest, Suite 540, Washington DC 20036. **Tel** (202)467-4884, FAX (202)467-0006. **(Subscription address:** Fulco, PO Box 3000, Department NI, Denville, NJ 07834-9913**)** **ED** Owen Harries. **LC** E840; .N34. **DD** 327.73/005. **Bk Rev. Ad Acc. Circ:** 5,000. available on microfilm and microfiche from University Microfilms International (UMI). Documents available from UMI Article Clearinghouse.
**Desc:** A foreign affairs journal addressing American foreign policy, defense, and national security issues.
**Ind/Abst** Am. Hist. Life (1988-); Am. Bibliogr. Slavic East Europ. Stud.; Curr. Mil. Pol. Lit.; Expand. Acad. Index (1992-); Index Period. Artic. Relat. Law; Int. Polit. Sci. Abstr.; Newsp. Period. Abstr. (1992-); PAIS Int. Print (1991-).

BE/0255-3813
**NATO REVIEW.** [NATO rev.]. **VFOAT** N.A.T.O. Review. **VAT** North Atlantic Treaty Organization Review. (May/June 1971)-. Periodical. English (French, Dutch, German, Italian and Spanish). Six times a year (Feb., Apr., June, Aug., Oct., Dec.). Free on request. OTAN/NATO Information Service, North Atlantic Treaty Organization, Distribution Unit, 1110 Brussels Belgium. **Tel** 011 32 2 2414400. **ED** Peter A. Jenner. **LC** UA646.3; .A525. **DD** 355.03/1/091821. **Circ:** 10,000. available on microfilm and microfiche from University Microfilms International (UMI). Documents available from UMI Article Clearinghouse. ***Continues*** *NATO Letter, 0027-6057.*
**Desc:** Subjects relating to the North Atlantic Treaty Organization, East-West Relations, and Disarmament Talks and Economic Affairs.
**Ind/Abst** ABC POL SCI; Acad. Abstr. Full Text Elite (Oct. 1984-June 1989); Acad. Abstr. (Oct. 1984-June 1989); Acad. Search (Oct. 1984-June 1989); Curr. Mil. Pol. Lit.; Index Free Period.; Index Period. Artic. Relat. Law; INFO-SOUTH Abstr.; Mag. Artic. Summar. Elite (Jan. 1984-June 1989); Mag. Artic. Summar. Select (Jan. 1984-June 1989); Mag. Artic. Summar. CD-ROM (Oct. 1984-June 1989); Mag. Search; Middle East Abstr. Index; Newsp. Period. Abstr. (1992-); PAIS Int. Print (1991-); Peace Res. Abstr. J. (1971-1972); Soc. Sci. Source (Oct. 1984-Jun. 1989).

GW/0027-6065
**NATO'S FIFTEEN NATIONS.** No. 1-21, Feb. 1956-Aug./Sept. 1961; V. 6- 1961-. Periodical. English. ir. $38.00. Monch Media Inc, 1701 K Street/#900, Washington DC 20006-1503. **Tel** (703)790-5252. **ED** Marvin Leibstone. **Ad Acc. Circ:** 23,800 (ctrl). available on microfilm from University Microfilms International (UMI).
**Desc:** Reporting the development and activities of the NATO alliance. Reports on the entire spectrum of strategic decision making within the alliance.

CN/0824-4456
**NDP ANTI-WAR NEWSLETTER.** [NDP anti-war newsl.]. April 1983-. Newsletter. English. qt. NDP Anti-War Committee, 184 Main Street, Toronto Ontario M4E 2W1 Canada. **DD** 327.1/74/05.

US/0028-176X
**NEAR EAST REPORT.** Vol. 1 (June 3, 1957)-. Periodical. English. wk. $50.00 US; $65.00 other. Near East Research Inc, 440 First Street NW, Suite 607, Washington DC 20001. **Tel** (202)639-5200, (202)639-5300. **ED** Eric Rozenman and Mitchell G. Bard. **LC** DS41; .N385. **DD** 320.9/56. Index available. cum. index. **Ad Acc. Circ:** 55,000 (ctrl). available in bound issues; available on microfilm and microfiche from University Microfilms International (UMI).
**Desc:** Covers American policy in the Middle East.
**Ind/Abst** Hum. Rights Intern. Rep.; Index Jew. Period.

US/0882-6331
**NETWORK NEWS (WASHINGTON, D.C. 1982).** (NETWORK NEWS / UCAM.). [Netw. news]. **VFOAT** UCAM Network News. Vol. 2, No. 7 (May 1, 1982)-. Periodical. English. mo. United Campuses To Prevent Nuclear War, 1346 Connecticut Avenue, Suite 706, Washington DC 20036. **DD** 327. available on microfilm from The State Historical Society of Wisconsin. ***Continues*** *Network News (Union of Concerned Scientists).*

GW/0548-2801
**NEUE HEIMAT.** **Added/Corp** Burgern Deutscher Herkunft im Ausland. (197?)-. Periodical. German. bm. DM13.60. Verlag Zeit Im Bild, Franklinstr 17 19, D 01069 Dresden Germany. **Tel** 011 49 351 48640.

US
**NEW AMERICAN VIEW.** Vol. 3, No. 1 (Apr. 1, 1988)-. Periodical. English. Twenty-three times a year. $60.00. New American View, PO Box 999, Herndon VA 22070. **Tel** (703)478-0592, FAX (703)478-0142. **ED** Victor Marchetti. **LC** E183.8.I75; Z56. **DD** 327.7305694/05. ***Continues*** *Zionist Watch, 1056-957X.*

UK/0305-9529
**NEW INTERNATIONALIST.** [New int.]. No. 1 (March 1973)-. Periodical. English. mo. $60.00 (institution), $36.00 (individual). New Internationalist, 120 126 Lavender Avenue, Mitcham Surrey CR4 3HP England. **Tel** 011 44 81 685 0372. **ED** Wayne Ellwood. **LC** D839; .I64. **DD** 052. Index available. cum. index. **Bk Rev. Ad Acc. Circ:** 80,000. available on microfiche. ***Continues*** *Internationalist.*
**Desc:** Exists to campaign against world poverty and for social equality and ecological sanity. For those concerned with the fate of the Third World.
**Ind/Abst** Altern. Press Index (19??-); Br. Humanit. Index (19??-); Can. Index (19??-); Can. Period. Index (19??-); Energy Res. Abstr. (Nov. 1981-); Int. Bibliogr. Sociol. (19??-); Peace Res. Abstr. J. (1973-).

US/0890-1619
**NEW OPTIONS.** ***Ceased.*** [New options]. (1984)-(19??). Periodical. English. mo. New Options Inc, PO Box 19324, Washington DC 20036. **Tel** (202)822-0929. **ED** Mark Satin. **DD** 327. Index available. cum. index. **Bk Rev.** available on microfilm; available on microfiche; available in microform.
**Ind/Abst** Hum. Rights Intern. Rep. (?-?).

IS/0028-6427
**NEW OUTLOOK (TEL AVIV).** ***Ceased.*** (NEW OUTLOOK.). [New outlook (Tel Aviv)]. Vol.1, No.1 (July 1957)-(Jan. 1993). Periodical. English. bm (except two double issues). Hillel Schenker, US Representative, Friends of New Outlook, 150 Fifth Avenue/Suite 911, New York NY 10011. **Tel** (212)929-0612 US, 972 3 236496 ISRAEL. **ED** Chaim Shur. **LC** DS41; .N5. **DD** 956/.04/005. **Bk Rev. Ad Acc. Circ:** 5,000. available on microfilm and microfiche from University Microfilms International (UMI).
**Desc:** Serves as a medium for the clarification of problems concerning peace and cooperation among all the peoples of the Middle East.
**Ind/Abst** Altern. Press Index; Hum. Rights Intern. Rep.; PAIS Int. Print (1991-?); Peace Res. Abstr. J. (1960-1961, 1977-1987).

RU/0206-1473
**NEW TIMES.** ***Title Change.*** (1943-1992). Periodical. English (French, German, Spanish, Portuguese, Italian and Russian). wk. **(Subscription address:** Victor Kamkin, 4956 Boiling Brook Parkway, Rockville MD 20852.**)** **LC** D839; .N483. **DD** 940.5505. available on microfilm from University Microfilms International (UMI). ***Continued by*** *New Times International.*
**Desc:** Covers current international events, discussing

key problems of today and printing economic reviews and world news analysis.
**Ind/Abst** PAIS Int. Print.

●RU
**NEW TIMES INTERNATIONAL.** No. 16 (Apr. 1992)-. Periodical. English. wk. $120.95. **(Subscription address:** East View Publications Inc., 3020 Harbor Lane North, Suite 110, Minneapolis MN 55447.) **LC** D839; .N483. ***Continues*** *New Times (Moscow, R.S.F.S.R.).*
**Ind/Abst** PAIS Int. Print.

US/0732-1848
**NEW TREND (BALTIMORE, MD.).** (NEW TREND.). [New trend]. **VFOAT** UMMAH. Began in May 1977. Periodical. English (Arabic). mo. $7.50 U.S. and Canada; $13.50 other. American Society for Education and Religion Inc, PO Box 356, Kingsville MD 21087. **Tel** (410)256-1349. **ED** Kaukab Siddique and Ali Siddiqui. **LC** BP1; .N5. **DD** 909/.097671082. **Bk Rev. Ad Acc. Circ:** 5,000 (ctrl).
**Desc:** Islamic viewpoint on the politics, economics, and religion of the Middle East, South Asia, and Afghanistan. Includes studies on Qur'an and Hadith.

NZ/0110-0262
**NEW ZEALAND INTERNATIONAL REVIEW.** [N.Z. int. rev.]. **Added/Corp** New Zealand Institute of International Affairs. Vol. 1 (Jan./Feb. 1976)-. Periodical. English. Six times a year. 43.00NZ$ surface mail; 51.00NZ$ (Australia and South Pacific), 69.00NZ$ (US, Canada and Asia), 74.00NZ$ (other) airmail. New Zealand Institute of International Affairs, Victoria University of Wellington, Private Bag, PO Box 600, Wellington New Zealand. **Tel** 11 64 4 4727430, FAX 11 64 4 4712070. **ED** Ian McGibbon. **LC** D839; .N485. **DD** 327/.05. **[CCC].** Index available in last issue of volume--attached. **Bk Rev. Ad Acc. Circ:** 1,500 (ctrl).
**Desc:** Review of international affairs as they affect New Zealand with an independent, non-partisan outlook.
**Ind/Abst** Int. Bibliogr. Sociol.; Int. Polit. Sci. Abstr.

NZ/0110-201X
**NEW ZEALAND REPRESENTATIVES OVERSEAS.** ***Title Change.*** English. sa. New Zealand Ministry of Foreign Affairs, Private Bag, Wellington 1 New Zealand. **Tel** 64 4 728877, FAX 64 4 729596, telex NZ 3441. **LC** JX1875; .A1545. **DD** 354/.931/00892. **Circ:** 2,400. ***Continued by*** *Overseas Posts.*
**Desc:** Lists diplomatic/consular posts of New Zealand government, including staff, addresses and other contact details.

AT
**NEWS DIGEST INTERNATIONAL.** ***Title Change.*** **See** History(General)-History of Australia and Oceania.

US/1064-1556
**NEWS NOTES - MARYKNOLL JUSTICE AND PEACE OFFICE.** (NEWS NOTES : A BI-MONTHLY NEWSLETTER OF INFORMATION ON NATIONAL AND INTERNATIONAL JUSTICE AND PEACE ISSUES / MARYKNOLL JUSTICE AND PEACE OFFICE.). [News notes - Maryknoll Justice Peace Off.]. **Added/Corp** Maryknoll Justice and Peace Office. **VFOAT** Newsnotes. (19??)-. Periodical. English. bm (Jan., Mar., May, July, Sept., Nov.). $10.00. Maryknoll Fathers and Brothers Justice and Peace Office, PO Box 29132, Washington DC 20017. **Tel** (202)832-1780, FAX (202)832-5195. **DD** 327. **Circ:** 1,500 (ctrl).
**Desc:** A bi-monthly newsletter covering information on international justice and peace issues.
**Ind/Abst** Hum. Rights Intern. Rep.

US/0545-8617
**NEWS ON INDONESIA.** **Added/Corp** Indonesia. Consulate, San Francisco. Information and Trade Bureau. (19??)-. Periodical. English. bm. Free on request. Indonesian Consulate, 1111 Columbus Avenue, San Francisco CA 94133. **Tel** (415)474-9571.

US/0896-9825
**NEWSLETTER / CONFERENCE GROUP ON ITALIAN POLITICS & SOCIETY.** ***Title Change.*** [Newsl. - Conf. Group Ital. Polit. Soc.]. **Added/Corp** Conference Group on Italian Politics and Society. McGill University. Dept. of Political Science. **VFOAT** Italian Politics and Society Newsletter; Italian Politics and Society; CONGRIPS Newsletter; Italian Politics & Society Newsletter; Italian Politics & Society. (198?)-(19??). Newsletter. English (Italian). Twice a year. University of Pittsburgh University Center for International Studies, A. Sbraggia, Pittsburgh PA 15260. **ED** K. Robert Nilsson (Editor's telephone: (717)245-1564). **LC** JN5201; .N48. **DD** 320.945/005. **Bk Rev. Ad Acc.** ctrl circ. ***Continues*** *Newsletter (Conference Group on Italian Politics).* ***Continued by*** *Biannual Newsletter of the Conference Group on Italian Politics & Society, 1077-9043.*

US/0740-6169
**NEWSLETTER - SOCIETY FOR HISTORIANS OF AMERICAN FOREIGN RELATIONS.** [Newsl. - Soc. Hist. Am. Foreign Relat.]. **Main/Corp** Society for Historians of American Foreign Relations. **VFOAT** SHAFR Newsletter. Vol. 1 (Dec. 1969)-. Newsletter. English. qt. $15.00. Tennessee Technological University / Biology Department, c/o John Harris, PO Box 5063, Cookeville TN 38505. **Tel** (615)372-3143. **ED** William J Brinker. **LC** E183.7; .S66a. **DD** 327.73. **Ad Acc. Circ:** 1,600.
**Desc:** Personals, announcements, abstracts, bibliographic or historiographical essays, essays about foreign depositories, biographies, autobiographies of "elder statesmen" in the field, jokes, etc.
**Ind/Abst** Am. Hist. Life (1977-).

NR/0331-3646
**NIGERIAN JOURNAL OF INTERNATIONAL AFFAIRS.** [Niger. j. int. aff.]. **Added/Corp** Nigerian Institute of International Affairs. Vol. 1 (1975)-. English. ir. N20.00. Nigerian Bar Association, Ozumba Mbadiwe Street, PMB 12610, Lagos Nigeria. **Tel** 01 610783 or 01 610778. **ED** R. A. Akindele and B. E. Ate. **LC** JX18; .N52. **DD** 327/.05. **Bk Rev. Circ:** 3,000.
**Desc:** Covers political science, international relations and studies.
**Ind/Abst** Int. Polit. Sci. Abstr.

GW/0933-1743
**NORD-SUD AKTUELL.** **Added/Corp** Deutsches Ubersee-Institut. Vol. 1, No. 1 (1987)-. Periodical. German. qt. Deutsches Uebersee Institut, Neuer Jungfernstieg 21, D 20354 Hamburg Germany. **Tel** 011 49 40 3562581.
**Ind/Abst** PAIS Int. Print.

NO
**NORSK UTENRIKSPOLITISK ARBOK.** **Added/Corp** Norsk Utenrikspolitisk Institutt. (1973)-. Norwegian. an. Kr210.00. Norsk Utenrikspolitisk Institute, Postboks 8159, Dep 0033 Oslo 1 Norway. **Tel** 47 2 1770 50, FAX 17 70 15. **ED** Torillegge Grung. **LC** DL458; .N73. Index available. **Circ:** 1,000.
**Desc:** Comprehensive collection of materials, articles and documentation on Norwegian foreign policy.
**Ind/Abst** Int. Polit. Sci. Abstr.

US/1060-4189
**NOTISUR (ALBUQUERQUE, N.M.).** (NOTISUR [COMPUTER FILE] : SOUTH AMERICAN & CARIBBEAN POLITICAL AFFAIRS.). [NotiSur]. **Added/Corp** University of New Mexico. Latin America Data Base. Vol. 1, No. 1 (Nov. 13, 1991)-. Periodical. English. sm. $175.00 (institutions). Latin America Data Base, University of New Mexico, LABD 801 Yale NE, Albuquerque NM 87131. **Tel** (505)277-6839, FAX (505)277-5989. **DD** 320.
**Desc:** Electronic newsletter available directly through the Latin America Data Base by subscription or as it appears on commercial databases, such as BITNET, NewsNet, or Predicasts.
**Ind/Abst** PTS Newsl. Database [Full Txt.].

RU/0137-0723
**NOVOE VIEMIA (MOSCOW, R.S.F.S.R.).** (NOVOE VREMIA.). (1945)-. Periodical. Russian. Twenty-four times a year. $120.95. **(Subscription address:** East View Publications Inc., 3020 Harbor Lane North, Suite 110, Minneapolis MN 55447.) **LC** D410; .V84. ***Continues*** *Voina I Rabochii Klass.*

RU/0137-0723
**NOVOE VREMIA.** (1943)-. Periodical. Russian. wk. $149.95. **(Subscription address:** East View Publications Inc., 3020 Harbor Lane North, Suite 110, Minneapolis MN 55447.) **LC** D410; .N653.

US/0734-5836
**NUCLEAR TIMES (NEW YORK, N.Y.).** ***Ceased.*** **See** Political Science.

SP
**NUESTRA BANDERA : REVISTA TEORICA Y POLITICA DEL PARTIDO COMUNISTA DE ESPANA.** Periodical. Spanish. Partido Comunista de Espana, Santisima Trinidad 5, Madrid 10 Spain. **LC** JN8395.C6; N83. **DD** 327.246/075.

US
**OCCASIONAL PAPER.** **Added/Corp** Cuban American National Foundation (U.S.). (1989)-. Monographic series. English. Price varies per volume. The Cuban American National Foundation, 1000 Thomas Jefferson Street NW/Suite 601, Washington DC 20007. ***Continues*** *Cuban-American National Foundation (Series).*

US
**OCCASIONAL PAPER / INDIANA CENTER ON GLOBAL CHANGE AND WORLD PEACE.** **Added/Corp** Indiana Center on Global Change and World Peace. No. 1 (Aug. 1991)-. Monographic series. English. Price varies per volume. **LC** JX1904.5; .O3.

UK
**OCCASIONAL PAPER (INSTITUTE FOR EUROPEAN DEFENCE & STRATEGIC STUDIES (LONDON, ENGLAND)).** (OCCASIONAL PAPER.). **Added/Corp** Institute for European Defence & Strategic Studies. (1982)-. Monographic series. English. Eight times a year. £40.00 Europe; $70.00 US and Canada; £45.00 other (Subscription also includes European Security Studies.). Institute for European Defence & Strategic Studies, St. George's House, 14/17 Wells Street, London W1P 3FP England. **Tel** 011 44 71 6372152, FAX 011 44 71 6372155. **ED** Andrew McHallam. **LC** UNC. **Circ:** 750.

NZ/0113-1044
**OCCASIONAL PAPER / NEW ZEALAND INSTITUTE OF INTERNATIONAL AFFAIRS.** **See** Political Science.

US/0082-8092
**OFFICIAL RECORDS - ECONOMIC AND SOCIAL COUNCIL.** (OFFICIAL RECORDS / UNITED NATIONS, ECONOMIC AND SOCIAL COUNCIL.). **Main/Corp** United Nations. Economic and Social Council. (1946)-. Government Publication. English. ir. $13.50. United Nations Publications, 2 United Nations Plaza, Room DC2 0853, Department 007C, New York NY 10017. **Tel** (212)963-8303, (800)253-9646. **LC** HC59; .A193. **DD** 330.611.
**Desc:** Records of the meetings of the Economic and Social Council. Contains 1) verbatim or summary records of the meetings, 2) annexes, important documents used in the meetings, and 3) supplements.

US
**OFFICIAL RECORDS. SUPPLEMENT FOR ... / UNITED NATIONS, SECURITY COUNCIL.** **Main/Corp** United Nations. Security Council. **VFOAT** Supplement. (1970)-. Government Publication. English. ir. Price varies per volume. United Nations Publications, 2 United Nations Plaza, Room DC2 0853, Department 007C, New York NY 10017. **Tel** (212)963-8303, (800)253-9646. ***Continues*** *United Nations. Security Council. Official Records. Supplement.*

US/0472-3724
**ONU CRONICA MENSUAL.** **Added/Corp** United Nations. Office of Public Information. Vol. 1 (May 1964)-. Periodical. Spanish. mo. United Nations Disaster Relief Company, Palais des Nations, CH 1211 Geneva 10 Switzerland. ***Continues*** *Revista de las Naciones Unidas.*

CN/0823-9703
**OPTION PAIX.** [Option paix]. **Added/Corp** Comite Quebecois pour le Desarmement. Vol. 1, No. 3 (1983)-. Periodical. French. qt. 32.71Can$ (institutions), 18.69Can$ (individuals) Canada; 40.00Can$ (institutions), 25.00Can$ (individuals) other. Mouvement Option Paix Inc., CP 1037, Succursale B, Hull Quebec J8X 3X5 Canada. **Tel** (819)777-5201, (819)776-2779. **ED** Marc Bonhomme. **DD** 327.1/74/05. **Bk Rev. Ad Acc. Circ:** 3,000. ***Continues*** *Arme A l'Oeil.*
**Desc:** Information on peace and disarmament. Investigates these issues, especially as they relate to the situation in Quebec and Canada.

AU/1015-616X
**OSTERREICHISCHES JAHRBUCH FUER INTERNATIONALE POLITIK.** [Osterr. Jahrb. Int. Polit.]. **Added/Corp** Osterreichische Gesellschaft fur Aussenpolitik und Internationale Beziehungen. Osterreichisches Institut fur Internationale Politik. (1984)-. German. an. **LC** DB47; .O43. **DD** 327.436. ***Continues*** *Osterreichische Zeitschrift fur Aussenpolitik.*
**Ind/Abst** ABC POL SCI (1984-).

CN/1184-2644
**P.A.G.E. JOURNAL.** (P.A.G.E. JOURNAL : PEACE AND GLOBAL EDUCATION PROVINCIAL SPECIALIST TEACHERS' ASSOCIATION.). [P.A.G.E. j.]. **Added/Corp** B.C. Teachers for Peace and Global Education. **VFOAT** Peace and Global Education Journal. (Fall 1990)-. Periodical. English. ir. British Columbia Teachers Federation, 100-550 West 6th Avenue, Vancouver British Columbia V5Z 4P2 Canada. **Tel** (604)871-2283, (800)663-9163, FAX (604)871-2294, (604)871-2290. **DD** 327.1/72/07. ***Continues*** *The B.C. Peace and Global Educator., 0849-9896.*

AT/1031-9379
**PACIFIC RESEARCH : A PERIODICAL OF THE PEACE RESEARCH CENTRE, AUSTRALIAN NATIONAL UNIVERSITY.** Vol. 1, No. 1 (Aug. 1988)-. Periodical. English. Four times a year (Feb., May, Aug., Nov.). 20.00Aus$. Peace Research Centre, Australian National University, GPO Box 4, Canberra Australian Capital Territory 2601 Australia. **Tel** 011 61 6 2493098, FAX 011 61 6 2571893. **ED** K. P. Clements. **Bk Rev**, (Qty: 20). **Pr Rev. Circ:** 2,000. ***Continues*** *Peace Research Centre Newsletter, 0018-2469.*
**Desc:** Covers issues of peace and security , particularly as they relate to the Asia-Pacific regions.

UK/0048-265X
**PACIFIST, THE.** ***Ceased.*** Vol. 1 (April 1961)-(1993). Periodical. English. mo. **LC** JX1901; .P23. ***Supersedes*** *Journal of the Peace Pledge Union.*

CN/0826-2764
**PAIX D'URGENCE.** (LA PAIX D'URGENCE : BULLETIN DU MRPDQ.). [Paix urgence]. No. 1

(Feb./March 84)-. Bulletin. French. bm. $6.00. MRPDQ, c/o Carrefour Tiers-Monde 454 rue Caron, Quebec Quebec G1K 8K8 Canada. **DD** 327.1/72/05.

LE/0377-2616
**PALESTINE (BEIRUT).** (PALESTINE.). **Added/Corp** Munazzamat al-Tahrir al-Filastiniyah. **VFOAT** Palestine Bulletin. (19??)-. Periodical. English. bm. $20.00. Palestine Liberation Organization United Information, PO Box 145168, Beirut Lebanon. **LC** DS119.7; .P2687. **DD** 327.5694/017/4927.

US/0191-7900
**PALESTINE (NEW YORK. 1976).** ***Ceased.*** (PALESTINE.). [Palestine]. Vol. 1 (April 1, 1976)-?. Periodical. English. ir (10 no. a year). Palestine Solidarity Committee, PO Box 372, Peck Slip Station, New York NY 10272. **Tel** (212)850-5296, (212)227-1435. **LC** WMLC L 83/976.

US/0163-3716
**PALESTINE PERSPECTIVES. Added/Corp** Palestine Research and Educational Center (Washington, D.C.) Palestine Information Office (Washington, D.C.). Vol. 1-4 (May 1978)-(July/Aug. 1983)-. Periodical. English. bm. $15.00. Palestine Research and Educational Center, 2050 Eye Street NW, Suite 415, Washington DC 20006. **ED** Muhammad Hallaj. **LC** DS119.7; .P278. **DD** 327.5694/017/4927. **Bk Rev. Ad Acc. Circ:** 7,500. ***Supersedes*** *Free Palestine.*
**Desc:** Deals with the Palestine question, the Arab-Israeli conflict, and the Israeli-occupied territories. Includes articles, news, and commentaries.
**Ind/Abst** Hum. Rights Intern. Rep.

US/0031-0336
**PALESTINE REFUGEES TODAY. See** Sociology-Social Services and Welfare.

US/0149-0508
**PEACE AND CHANGE.** [Peace change]. **Added/Corp** Conference on Peace Research in History. Consortium on Peace Research, Education, and Development (U.S.) Council on Peace Research in History. Kent State University. Center for Peaceful Change. **VFOAT** PC; P.C.; Peace & Change. Vol. 1, No. 1 (Fall 1972)-. Academic Scholarly Publication. English. qt (Jan., Apr., July, Oct.). $126.00. SAGE Periodical Press, 2455 Teller Road, Thousand Oaks CA 91320. **Tel** (805)499-0721, FAX (805)499-0871, telex 100799. **ED** Scott L. Bills and Sudarshan Kapoor. **LC** JX1901; .P248. **DD** 327.1/72/05. **CODEN** PCHAEG. Index available. cum. index. **Bk Rev. Ad Acc. Acid Free. Circ:** 1,061. available on microfilm and microfiche from University Microfilms International (UMI).
**Desc:** Publishes scholarly and interpretive articles on achieving a peaceful, just and humane society. It seeks to transcend national, disciplinary and occupational boundaries and build bridges between peace research, education and action.
**Ind/Abst** Am. Hist. Life (1975-); Hum. Rights Intern. Rep.; Int. Polit. Sci. Abstr.; J. Plan. Lit.; Middle East Abstr. Index; PAIS Int. Print (1991-); Peace Res. Abstr. J. (1972-1977, 1981); Sage Public Adm. Abstr.; Soc. Plann. Policy Dev. Abstr.

SA
**PEACE AND CONFLICT REPORT.** English. Nine times a year. R113.00. Peace and Conflict Studies, PO Box 95824, 0154 Waterkloof South Africa.

US/0749-5900
**PEACE & DEMOCRACY NEWS.** (PEACE & DEMOCRACY NEWS : THE BULLETIN OF THE CAMPAIGN FOR PEACE AND DEMOCRACY/EAST AND WEST.). [Peace democr. news]. **Added/Corp** Campaign for Peace and Democracy/East and West. Campaign for Peace and Democracy. **VFOAT** Peace and Democracy News; Journal of the Campaign for Peace and Democracy. Vol. 1, No. 1 (Spring 1984)-. Periodical. English. sa. $15.00 (institutions), $7.00 (individuals). Campaign for Peace and Democracy, PO Box 1640 Cathedral Station, New York NY 10025. **Tel** (212)666-5924. **ED** Gail Daneker. **LC** JX1901; .P43. **DD** 361. **Bk Rev. Ad Acc. Circ:** 5,000.
**Ind/Abst** Altern. Press Index; Hum. Rights Intern. Rep.; Left Index.

CN/0831-1846
**PEACE & SECURITY.** ***Ceased.*** [Peace secur.]. **Added/Corp** Canadian Institute for International Peace and Security. **VFOAT** Paix et Securite; Peace and Security. Vol. 1, No. 1 (Spring 1986)-Vol. 7, No. 1 (Spring 1992). Periodical. English (French). qt. Canadian Institute for International Peace and Security, 360 Albert Street, Suite 900, Ottawa Ontario K1R 7X7 Canada. **DD** 327.1/7/05.
**Ind/Abst** Can. Period. Index (19??-).

AU
**PEACE AND THE SCIENCES. Added/Corp** International Institute for Peace. (July/Sept. 1964)-. Periodical. English (German). qt. $54.00. International Institute for Peace, Moellwaldplatz 5, A-1040 Vienna Austria. **Tel** 11 43 222 50464370, FAX 11 43 222 505323622. **ED** Prof Dr Lev Voronkov, Peter Stania, M A (editors telephone: 504 43 76 or 77). **LC** JX1901; .P25. **Circ:** 500 (ctrl). ***Continues*** *Nuclear Energy.*
**Desc:** Appears in English and German containing contributions and discussions concerning East and West relations and shared concerns.
**Ind/Abst** Int. Polit. Sci. Abstr.; Peace Res. Abstr. J. (1972-1973, 1978-1980).

FI/0031-594X
**PEACE COURIER.** No. 1 (Sept. 1970)-. Periodical. English. ir. $30.00 (institutions), $12.00 (individuals). Information Centre of the World Peace Council, Lonnrotinkatu 25 A 5 KRS, PO Box 1811, 00180 Helsinki 18 Finland. **Bk Rev.**
**Ind/Abst** Hum. Rights Intern. Rep.

CN/0826-9521
**PEACE MAGAZINE.** [Peace mag.]. **Added/Corp** Canadian Disarmament Information Service. Vol. 1 Issue 1 (March 1985)-. Periodical. English. bm. 16.36Can$ (one year), 28.04Can$ (two year) Canada; 20.00Can$ (one year), 36.00Can$ (two year) US; 25.00Can$ (one year), 45.00Can$ (two year). Canadian Disarmament Information Service, 736 Bathurst Street, Toronto Ontario M5S 2R4 Canada. **Tel** (416)573-7581, FAX (416)531-6214. **ED** Metta Spencer. **DD** 327.1/72/05. Index available. cum. index. **Bk Rev**, (Qty: 12). **Ad Acc, Adv Mgr:** Jean Smith. **Circ:** 2,000 (ctrl). ***Continues*** *The Peace Calendar, 0824-3107.*
**Desc:** Covers issues relating to nuclear disarmament. Offers interviews, commentary and topical feature articles. Represents the diversity of views of Canadians working to reverse the nuclear arms race.
**Ind/Abst** Altern. Press Index (199?-); Can. Index; Can. Period. Index (19??-); Peace Res. Abstr. J. (1985-).

US/0735-4134
**PEACE NEWSLETTER (SYRACUSE, N.Y.).** (PEACE NEWSLETTER.). [Peace newsl.]. **Added/Corp** Syracuse Peace Council. (19??)-. Periodical. English. Twelve times a year. $25.00 profiteers; $12.50 other. Syracuse Peace Council, 924 Burnet Avenue, Syracuse NY 13203. **Tel** (315)472-5478. **ED** Bill Mazza. **Bk Rev**, (Qty: 6-8). **Ad Acc. Circ:** 4,000. available on diskette; available on microfilm from University Microfilms International (UMI).
**Desc:** Offers alternative analysis of political issues which cover local organizing events, and discuss peace movement issues. Focuses on South Africa, Central America, disarmament and environmental issues.
**Ind/Abst** Altern. Press Index.

CN/0008-4697
**PEACE RESEARCH.** (PEACE RESEARCH.). [Peace res.]. **Added/Corp** Canadian Peace Research Institute. Canadian Peace Research and Education Association. Vol. 1 (Nov. 1969)-. Academic Scholarly Publication. English. qt (Feb., May, Aug., Nov.). 30.00Can$ (individual) 45.00Can$ (institution) US; 27.00Can$ (individual), $42.00 (institution) Canada. Brandon University, c/o M.V. Naidu, Brandon Manitoba R7A 6A9 Canada. **Tel** (204)727-9720, FAX (204)726-0473, telex 07 502271. **ED** Dr. M. V. Naidu. **LC** JX1904.5; .P4. **DD** 327/.172/072. Index available (Bound in 4th issue in November). cum. index. **Bk Rev**, (Qty: 4). **Ad Acc, Adv Mgr:** Mrs. T. Sowia, **Tel** (204)729-9010. **Pr Rev. Circ:** 500. available in microform (as Peace Research Brandon, Ontario); available on microfiche (as Peace Research Brandon, Ontario).
**Desc:** Publishes scientific and scholarly work on world peace, focusing upon problems of violence, war, international organizations, development, and a better world order.
**Ind/Abst** Am. Hist. Life; Can. Index; Can. Period. Index (Nov. 1989-); Peace Res. Abstr. J. (1969-).

CN
**PEACE RESEARCH ABSTRACTS. CD-ROM.** Abstracting/Indexing Service. English. $400.00. Peace Research Institute, 25 Dundana Avenue, Dundas Ontario L9H 4E5 Canada. **Tel** (416)628-2356, FAX (416)628-1830. available in print.
**Desc:** Contains more than 180,000 abstracts to date, concerning peace and war issues.

US/0031-3599
**PEACE RESEARCH ABSTRACTS JOURNAL. See** Political Science-Abstracting, Bibliographies and Statistics.

JA
**PEACE RESEARCH IN JAPAN. Added/Corp** Nihon Heiwa Kenkyu Kondankai. (1967)-. Periodical. English. an. Japan Peace Research Group, University of Tokyo, Faculty of Law, Tokyo Japan. **LC** JX1903; .P4. **DD** 327/.172/05.
**Ind/Abst** Peace Res. Abstr. J. (1967, 1970-1971, 1973).

US/1040-2659
**PEACE REVIEW (PALO ALTO, CALIF.).** (PEACE REVIEW.). [Peace rev.]. Vol. 1, No. 1 (Winter 1989)-. Periodical. English. qt. $28.00 (individual), $60.00 (institution). Lynne Rienner Publishers, 1800 30th Street, Suite 314, Boulder CO 80301. **Tel** (303)444-6684, FAX (303)444-0824. **ED** John L Harris and Robert Elias. **DD** 327. **Bk Rev. Ad Acc. Circ:** 700.
**Desc:** Magazine of international peace research.
**Ind/Abst** PAIS Int. Print (1991-); Soc. Plann. Policy Dev. Abstr.; U.S. Polit. Sci. Doc. (199?-).

CN/1187-3485
**PEACEKEEPING & INTERNATIONAL RELATIONS.** [Peacekeep. int. relat.]. **Added/Corp** Canadian Institute of Strategic Studies. **VFOAT** Peacekeeping and International Relations. Vol. 20, No. 2 (Mar./Apr. 1991)-. Periodical. English. bm. 25.00Can$ (one year), 40.00Can$ (two year) Canada; $25.00 (one year), $40.00 (two years) other. Peacekeeping & International Relations, 76 St Clair Avenue West, Suite 502, Toronto Ontario M4V 1N2 Canada. **Tel** (416)964-6632, FAX (416)964-5833. **ED** Alex Morrison. **LC** JX1; .I635. **DD** 327.1/05. **Bk Rev**, (Qty: 6). **Ad Acc, Adv Mgr:** Fred Russell. **Pr Rev. Circ:** 1,100. available on microfilm from University Microfilms International (UMI); available on microfiche from Micromedia Limited; available on an online database from University Microfilms International (UMI). Documents available from UMI Article Clearinghouse. ***Continues*** *International Perspectives, 0381-4874.*
**Ind/Abst** Acad. Search (July 1993-); INFO-SOUTH Abstr.; Newsp. Period. Abstr. (1992-).

UK
**PEOPLE IN POWER : A COMPREHENSIVE GUIDE TO THE POLITICAL LEADERSHIP IN ALL SOVEREIGN COUNTRIES OF THE WORLD ... .** (19??)-. Directory. English. bm. £160.00 (printed or disk version); £232.00 (both versions). CIRCA, 13-17 Sturton Street, Cambridge CB1 2SN England. **Tel** 011 44 223 568017, FAX 011 44 223 354643. **Ad Acc, Adv Mgr:** M. Bellinello, **Tel** 0223 568019. **Circ:** 200. available on diskette.
**Desc:** A directory of the current political leadership in each sovereign country of the world. Includes ambassador names to the UK and the US with addresses, telephone and fax numbers to the embassy.

US/0252-0079
**PERMANENT MISSIONS TO THE UNITED NATIONS (UNITED STATES. MISSION TO THE UNITED NATIONS : 1967).** (PERMANENT MISSIONS TO THE UNITED NATIONS.). **Added/Corp** United States. Mission to the United Nations. (1963)-. Government Publication. English. sa. $25.00 (non-profit organizations), $50.00 (profit organizations). United Nations Publications, 2 United Nations Plaza, Room DC2 0853, Department 007C, New York NY 10017. **Tel** (212)963-8303, (800)253-9646. **(Subscription address:** United Nations Publications, Subscription Office, PO Box 361, Birmingham AL 35201-0361.**) LC** JX1977.2.A1; P47. ***Continues*** *Members of Permanent Missions to the United Nations Entitled to Diplomatic Privileges and Immunities.*
**Desc:** Directory containing a list of names, addresses and phone numbers of all Delegations and Permanent Missions to the United Nations.

US/1071-4154
**PERSPECTIVE (BOSTON, MASS. 1990).** (PERSPECTIVE.). [Perspective (Boston Mass. 1990)]. **Added/Corp** Boston University. Institute for the Study of Conflict, Ideology & Policy. Vol. 1, No. 1 (Oct. 1990)-. Periodical. English. qt (During the academic year). $10.00. Institute Study Conflict Ideology Policy, 141 Bay State Road, Boston University, Boston MA 02215. **Tel** (617)353-5815, FAX (617)353-7185. **ED** Dr. Keith Armes. **LC** D34; .P47. **DD** 320. **Bk Rev.**
**Desc:** Carries analyses of significant trends in the CIS by prominent Russian and western contributors, as well by members of the institute.

US/1041-9039
**PHILADELPHIA PAPERS, THE.** [Phila. pap.]. **Added/Corp** Foreign Policy Research Institute. **VFOAT** Philadelphia Paper. (1989)-. Monographic series. English. ir. Price varies per volume. Foreign Policy Research Institute, 3615 Chestnut Street, Philadelphia PA 19104. **Tel** (215)382-0685, FAX (215)382-0131. **ED** Daniel Pipes and Adam Garfinkle. **LC** UNC. **DD** 327. **Circ:** 2,500. ***Continues*** *Philadelphia Policy Papers, 0733-3218.*
**Desc:** Features authoritative studies of world politics.

LV
**PLANATAS PULSS.** (1974)-. Periodical. Latvian. ir. 0.26rub. Liesma / Flame Publishing House, Aspazijas Bulv 24, Riga Latvia 1455. **Tel** 3712 223 063. **LC** D849.5; .P55.

US
**PLANECON REVIEW & OUTLOOK.** (19??)-. English. Twice a year. $7500.00. PlanEcon Inc., 1111 14th Street Northwest, Suite 801, Washington DC 20005. **Tel** (202)898-0471.

**Desc:** Information on present and future developments in the former Soviet republics and Eastern Europe, with emphasis on related political and social developments. Includes projections of major economic indicators and a forecast risk assessment.

CN/0703-1866
**PLOUGHSHARES MONITOR.** [Ploughshares monit.]. **Added/Corp** Project Ploughshares. **VFOAT** Ploughshares Monitor Newsreport. Vol. 1 (Apr. 1977)-. Periodical. English. qt. $25.00 US; 25.00Can$ Canada; $28.00 other. Project Ploughshares, Conrad Grebel College, Waterloo Ontario N2G 9Z9 Canada. **Tel** (519)888-6541, FAX (519)885-0014. **ED** Ernie Regehr. **DD** 327/.174/05. **Bk Rev**. ctrl circ.
**Desc:** Provides information on disarmament, militarism, regional conflict, global security, Canadian military production and exports, and alternatives to Canadian security policies.
**Ind/Abst** Can. Period. Index (1989-); Hum. Rights Intern. Rep.

HU
**POLICY PAPERS. Main/Corp** Hungarian Institute of International Affairs. **VFOAT** Constitutionalism and Political Change in Hungary N.(No.1); Eastern European Party Census N.(No.2). No. 1 (January 1990)-. Monographic series. English. ir. Price varies per volume. Magyar Kulugyilntezet, 1125 Budapest, Szilagyi E. fasor Hungary. **Tel** 36 1 176 46 47, FAX 36 1 176 43 38. **Circ:** 200 (ctrl).
**Desc:** Contains studies about political science or international relations.

US/0731-6321
**POLICY PAPERS IN INTERNATIONAL AFFAIRS.** [Policy pap. int. aff.]. **Added/Corp** University of California, Berkeley. Institute of International Studies. No. 1 (1977)-. Monographic series. English. ir. Price varies per volume. IAS Publications Office / University of California, 223 Fulton Street, 3rd Floor, Berkeley CA 94720. **Tel** (415)642-7189. **ED** Paul Gilchrist.

BL/0102-2636
**POLITICA E ESTRATEGIA.** [Polit. estrateg.]. **Added/Corp** Centro de Estudos Estrategicos (Sao Paulo, Brazil) Convivio (Organization) Sociedade Brasileira de Cultura. Vol. 1, No. 1 (Oct.-Dec. 1983)-. Periodical. Portuguese (summaries and/or abstracts in English). Four times a year. $50.00. Societe Brasileira de Cultura, Al Eduardo Prado 705, 01218 Sao Paulo SP Brazil. **Tel** 011 55 11 8267577.
**Ind/Abst** Curr. Mil. Pol. Lit.; HAPI Hisp. Am. Period. Index.

SP/0213-6856
**POLITICA EXTERIOR. Added/Corp** Centro de Estudios de Politica Exterior (Spain). Vol. 1, No. 1 (Winter 1987)-. Periodical. Spanish (summaries and/or abstracts in English). Six times a year. 6000ptas Spain; 8400ptas European Economic Communities; 10200ptas other. Estudios de Politica Exterior, Calle Padilla 6 1IZ, 28006 Madrid Spain. **Tel** 011 34 1 431-2711, 431-2618, FAX 011 34 1 577-7252. **LC** DP85.8; .P58. **DD** 327.46/009/04. Index available. cum. index. **Ad Acc, Adv Mgr:** Jaime Garcia de Vinuesa. **Circ:** 10,000.
**Ind/Abst** PAIS Int. Print (1991-).

●BL
**POLITICA EXTERNA. Added/Corp** Universidade de Sao Paulo. Programa de Politica Internacional e Comparada. Vol. 1, No. 1 (June 1992)-. Periodical. Portuguese. qt. Politica Externa, Rua do Triunfo 177, Sta. Ifigenia, 01212, Sao Paulo SP Brazil. **Tel** 011 223-5522, FAX 011 233 6290. **LC** F2537; .P7. **DD** 327.81/005.
**Desc:** Covers Brazilian foreign policy and international issues.

US/1053-8771
**POLITICAL RISK YEARBOOK. VOL. 6, EUROPE. COUNTRIES OF THE EUROPEAN COMMUNITY.** [Polit. risk yearb., Vol. 6 Eur., Ctry. Eur. Community]. **Added/Corp** Political Risk Services (IBC USA (Publications) Inc.). **VFOAT** Europe, Countries of the European Community; Countries of the European Community. (1991)-. English. an. $250.00 (per volume), $1000.00 (full set). Political Risk Services, 6320 Fly Road, Suite 102, PO Box 248, East Syracuse NY 13057-0248. **Tel** (315)431-0511, FAX (315)431-0200. **LC** JN12; .P644. **DD** 940. ***Continues*** *Political Risk Yearbook. Western Europe, 0897-8522.*

US/1056-3334
**POLITICAL WARFARE.** ***Ceased.*** **Added/Corp** Institute for International Studies (Washington, D.C.). (1991)-No. 21 (Oct. 1993). Periodical. English. Three times a year. Institute for International Studies, 1718 M Street NW, Suite 244, Washington DC 20036. **Tel** (202)785-3606, FAX (202)659-5429. **ED** Tom Diaz. **LC** JF1525.I6; P64. **DD** 327.1/2/05. **Bk Rev**, (Qty: 10). **Pr Rev. Circ:** 2500 (ctrl). ***Continues*** *Soviet Intelligence & Active Measures, 1050-2866.*
**Desc:** A unique magazine about intelligence, active measures and terrorism-- topics that are growing in importance as the world is buffeted by new kinds of turmoil. It covers these topics with original articles and excerpts from the best current literature around the world.

FR/0032-342X
**POLITIQUE ETRANGERE.** [Polit. etrang.]. **Added/Corp** Institut Francais des Relations Internationales. Centre d'Etudes de Politique Etrangere (Paris, France). Vol. 1 (Feb. 1936)-. Periodical. French. qt. $109.00. Librairie Armand Colin, BP 22, 41354 Vineuil Cedex France. **Tel** 011 33 54 438994. **LC** JX3; .P6. **Bk Rev. Ad Acc. Circ:** 3,000.
**Desc:** Publishes articles on major current international issues as well as reference material (official texts, treaties, etc.). Also includes bibliographical section.
**Ind/Abst** ABC POL SCI; Am. Hist. Life (1954-1978); Int. Bibliogr. Sociol.; Int. Labour Doc.; Int. Polit. Sci. Abstr.; PAIS Int. Print (1991-); Point Repere (1983-); Middle East J.

FR/0221-2781
**POLITIQUE INTERNATIONALE.** (Autumn 1978)-. Periodical. French (summaries and/or abstracts in English). Four times a year. 315.00F (institutions), 265.00F (individuals) France; 440.74F (institutions), 411.36F (individuals) French territories; 352.60F (institutions), 308.52F (individuals) other. SARL Politique Intle, 11 rue du Bois de Boulogne, 75116 Paris France. **Tel** 011 33 1 45001526. **ED** Gurselves. **LC** D839; .P643. **DD** 327/.05. **Bk Rev. Ad Acc. Circ:** 100,000.
**Desc:** Influential French publication dealing with international affairs, read by decision makers throughout the world.
**Ind/Abst** Int. Bibliogr. Sociol.; Int. Polit. Sci. Abstr.; PAIS Int. Print (1991-).

FR/0152-0768
**POUVOIRS.** [Pouvoirs]. Vol. 1 (1977)-. Monographic series. French. qt. 318.32F France; 415.00F other. Editions du Seuil, 27 rue Jacob, 75261 Paris Cedex 06 France. **Tel** 011 33 1 69092409 or, 40465050. **ED** Philippe Ardant and Oliver Duhamel. **LC** UNC. **[CCC].**
**Desc:** Review of constitutional and political studies; looks behind the scenes of contemporary political confusion and the over-abundance of news in order to highlight the actions of the political powers of our day.
**Ind/Abst** ABC POL SCI; Int. Bibliogr. Sociol.; Int. Polit. Sci. Abstr.

XR
**PRAHA-MOSKVA.** Began in 1951. Periodical. Czech. mo. **(Subscription address:** Artia Pegas Press Ltd., Palac Metro Narodni Trida 25, 11210 Prague 1 Czech Republic.) **LC** AP52; .P7.
**Ind/Abst** Am. Hist. Life (1955-1957).

GW
**PRIF REPORTS. Added/Corp** Hessische Stiftung Friedens- und Konfliktforschung. (1987)-. Monographic series. English (German). DM100.00. Peace Research Institute Frankfurt, Leimenrode 29, D 60322 Frankfurt Germany. **Tel** 011 49 69 550191, FAX 011 49 69 558481. **ED** (phone:069-95 91 04-0). **Circ:** 200. ***Continues*** *PRIF Reports in English.*
**Desc:** Written principally for the policy-making community and are distributed mainly to government and political party officials, journalists, and public interest groups.

US/0742-4191
**PRIME SOURCE MINI REFERENCE DIRECTORY. MOST WANTED NAMES AND ADDRESSES OF--FOREIGN CONSULATE [I.E. CONSULATES] IN U.S.A. Added/Corp** North American Register. **VFOAT** Most Wanted Names and Addresses of--Foreign Consulate in U.S.A.; Foreign Consulate in U.S.A.; Foreign Consulate in USA. (1983)-. Directory. English. an. $19.95 US; $24.95 other. EGW Publishing Company, 1041 Shary Circle, Concord CA 94518. **Tel** (510)671-9852, (800)777-1164, FAX (510)671-0692. **LC** JX1705; .A158. **DD** 351.8/92/0973.

CU
**PRISMA LATINOAMERICANO. Added/Corp** Prensa Latina. Vol. 4, No. 68 (April 1978)-. Periodical. Spanish. mo. 45.29Cub$ North America; 39.96Cub$ South America; 63.94Cub$ other. Ediciones Cubanas, Obispo 527, Altos ESQ Bernaza, CP 10100 Havana Cuba. **Tel** 011 632980, 631942, FAX 011 631011, telex 512337, 6540. **Bk Rev. Ad Acc. Circ:** 30,000. ***Continues*** *Prisma del Meridiano 80.*
**Desc:** A magazine of Latin-American, world information and current events.

US
**PROBLEMY DAL'NEGO VOSTOKA.** (USSR REPORT. PROBLEMS OF THE FAR EAST. MICROFORM.). **Added/Corp** United States. Foreign Broadcast Information Service. United States. Joint Publications Research Service. **VFOAT** Problems of the Far East. **VAT** Union of Soviet Socialist Republics Report. Problems of the Far East. (1979)-. Periodical. English (translations available in Russian). ir. National Technical Information Service - NTIS, Room 2027S, 5285 Port Royal Road, Springfield VA 22161. **Tel** (703)487-4630, (703)487-4660, (703)487-4650, FAX (703)321-8547, telex 89-9405. available on microfiche (Vols. for 1987- distributed to depository libraries). ***Continues*** *Problems of the Far East.*

NE
**PROCEEDINGS OF THE INTERNATIONAL PEACE RESEARCH ASSOCIATION.** ***Ceased.*** **Main/Corp** International Peace Research Association. (1???)-(19??). Proceedings. English. International Peace Research Association / Colorado, Campus Box 327, University of Colorado, Boulder CO 80309.

CN/0576-3819
**PROCEEDINGS OF THE STANDING SENATE COMMITTEE ON FOREIGN AFFAIRS. Main/Corp** Canada. Parliament. Senate. Standing Committee on Foreign Affairs. **VFOAT** Deliberations du Comite Senatorial Permanent des Affairs Etrangeres. **VAT** Proceedings of the Senate Committee on Foreign Affairs; Deliberations du Comite Senatorial Permanent des Affairs Etrangeres (Editions Anglaise et Francaise). (Feb. 6, 1969)-. English (French). Canada Communication Group Publishers, Order Processing, Ottawa Ontario K1A 0S9 Canada. **Tel** (819)956-4800, (819)956-4802. **LC** JX354; .A46a. **DD** 327.71. ***Absorbed*** *Canada. Parliament. Senate. Standing Committee on Foreign Affairs. Deliberations du Comite Senatorial Permanent des Affaires Etrangeres, 0226-8191.*

FR
**PROGRAMME OF ACTION / WORLD PEACE COUNCIL. Main/Corp** World Peace Council. English. an. Information Centre of the World Peace Council, Lonnrotinkatu 25 A 5 KRS, PO Box 1811, 00180 Helsinki 18 Finland. **LC** JX1907; .W672. **DD** 327.1/72/0601.

US/0033-0736
**PROGRESSIVE (MADISON), THE.** (THE PROGRESSIVE.). [Progressive]. Vol. 1-4; (Dec. 7, 1929)-(May 16, 1936); New Series, Vol. 1, (May 23, 1936)-. Periodical. English. mo. $50.00 (institutions), $30.00 (individuals) US, Canada & Mexico; $56.00 (institutions), $36.00 (individuals) other. The Progressive, 409 East Main Street, Madison WI 53703. **Tel** (608)257-4626, FAX (608)257-3373. **(Subscription address:** Kable Publishers Aide, 308 East Hitt Street, Subscriptions Department, Mt. Morris, IL 61054) **ED** Erwin Knoll. **LC** AP2; .P8655. **DD** 051. Index available. cum. index. **Bk Rev. Ad Acc. Circ:** 50,000. available on microfilm and microfiche from University Microfilms International (UMI). Documents available from UMI Article Clearinghouse, Documents on Demand, Magazine Collection. ***Supersedes*** *La Follette's Magazine.*
**Desc:** Committed to the publication of articles and editorials that promote peaceful solutions to international disputes, the attainment of economic justice, and the protection of individual rights.
**Ind/Abst** Acad. Abstr. Full Text Elite (Feb. 1984-) [Full Txt.]; Acad. Abstr. (Feb. 1984-); Acad. Ind. [Computer File] (1984-); Acad. Search (Feb. 1984-); Altern. Press Index; Am. Bibliogr. Slavic East Europ. Stud.; Book Rev. Index; Energy Inf. Abstr.; Environ. Abstr.; Expand. Acad. Index (1984-); Gen. Period. Index (1985-); Humanit. Source (Jul. 1993-) [Full Txt.]; Index Period. Artic. Relat. Law; INFO-SOUTH Abstr.; Mag. Artic. Summar. Elite (Feb. 1984-) [Full Txt.]; Mag. Artic. Summar. Select (Feb. 1984-) [Full Txt.]; Mag. Artic. Summar. CD-ROM (Feb. 1984-); Mag. Express (1988-) [Full Txt.]; Mag. Index Plus (1989-); Mag. Index. Sel. (1986-); Mag. Search; Med. Rev. Dig.; Middle East Abstr. Index; Newsp. Period. Abstr. (1988-); Peace Res. Abstr. J. (1964-1967, 1970-1971, 1976-1983); Read. Guide Abstr. Select Ed.; Read. Guide Period. Lit.; Resource/One Ondisc; Soc. Sci. Source (Feb. 1984-) [Full Txt.]; Mag. Index (1977-); Urban Aff. Abstr.; Vocat. Search (Feb. 1984-) [Full Txt.].

PL
**PRZEGLAD STOSUNKOW MIEDZYNARODOWYCH. Added/Corp** Instytut Slaski w Opolu. Zakad Stosunkow Miedzynarodowych. (19??)-. Periodical. Polish. RSW Prasa-Kriazka-Ruch, Centrala Kolportazu Prasy i Wydawnictw, Towarowa 28, 00-958 Warsaw Poland. **LC** D839; .P75.

US
**PUBLICATION. Main/Corp** Hoover Institution on War, Revolution, and Peace. (1932)-. Monographic series. English. ir. Price varies per volume. Hoover Institution Press, Stanford University, HHMB Room 28, Stanford CA 94305. **Tel** (415)723-3373.

FR/0252-0524
**PUBLICATIONS / COUNCIL OF EUROPE.** ***Title Change.*** **Main/Corp** Council of Europe. (1988-1992). English. an. Publications Section, Council of Europe, 67006 Strasbourg Cedex France. **Tel** (914)271-5194. **LC** Z2000; .C6; JN24. **DD** 016.34124/2.

*Continues Council of Europe.; Catalogue of Publications.* ***Continued by*** *Council of Europe.; Catalog of Publications (1991).*

BS/0256-2316
**PULA.** [Pula]. V. 1- ; June 1978-. Periodical. English (English). bm. P4.65. Editor Pula, Department of Sociology, University College of Botswana and Swaziland, Private Bag 0022, Gaberone Botswana. **LC** DT1; .P84. **DD** 960/.05.

●CN/1188-6870
**QUARTERLY / WORLD AFFAIRS CANADA, THE.** [Q. - World Aff. Can.]. **Added/Corp** World Affairs Canada. **VFOAT** Revue; World Affairs Canada Quarterly; Revue de Canada Mondial. **VAT** Revue - Canada Mondial. Vol. 1, No. 1 (Spring 1992)-. Periodical. English (French). qt. World Affairs Canada, 6 Hoskin Avenue, Toronto Ontario M5S 1H8 Canada. **DD** 361.2/0971/05.

●CN/1188-6870
**QUARTERLY / WORLD AFFAIRS CANADA, THE.** [Q. - World Aff. Can.]. **Added/Corp** Canada Mondial. **VFOAT** Revue; World Affairs Canada Quarterly; Revue de Canada Mondial. Vol. 1, No. 1 (Spring 1992)-. Periodical. French (English). qt. Canada Mondial, 6 Avenue Hoskin, Toronto Ontario M5S 1H8 Canada. **DD** 361.2/0971/05.

CN/0225-9745
**QUEBEC INTER.** (QUEBEC INTER / PREPARE PAR LA DIRECTION DES COMMUNICATIONS DU MINISTERE DES AFFAIRES INTERGOUVERNEMENTALES DU QUEBEC.). V. 1, No. 1 (Jan. 1980)-. Periodical. French. mo. Free. Ministere des Affaires Intergouvernementales du Quebec, 1225 Place George V, Quebec Quebec G1R 4Z7 Canada. **DD** 327.714/005.

MX
**RAZONES (MEXICO CITY, MEXICO).** (RAZONES.). 1 (Jan. 1980)-. Periodical. Spanish. bw. Av Coyacan 1535, Mexico 12 DF.

US/0748-0644
**RDI MONOGRAPHS ON FOREIGN AID AND DEVELOPMENT.** [RDI monogr. for. aid dev.]. **VFOAT** R.D.I. Monographs on Foreign Aid and Development. **VAT** Rural Development Institute Monographs on Foreign Aid and Development. #1-. Monographic series. English. ir. Price varies per volume. Rural Development Institute, 4120 Brooklyn Avenue NE #508, Seattle WA 98105. **DD** 338. **Circ:** 300 (ctrl).
**Desc:** Occasional papers on foreign aid and development issues.

IO
**REKAMAN SEJARAH.** Indonesian. an. Pt Gunung Argung, Kwitang 8, Jakarta Pusat Indonesia. **LC** DS644.4; .R44.

MX/0185-0814
**RELACIONES INTERNACIONALES.** [Relac. int.]. **Added/Corp** Universidad Nacional Autonoma de Mexico. Centro de Relaciones Internacionales. New Series Vol. 1 (April/June 1973)--. Periodical. Spanish. Four times a year. $90.00. Facultad de Ciencias Politicas y Sociales, EDIF C Piso 2 UNAM, 04510 Mexico DF Mexico. **Tel** 011 52 5 6656211 Ext. 7965. **LC** JX9; .R37. **Bk Rev**. **Ad Acc**. **Circ:** 2,000.
**Desc:** Monographic studies on international relations, theoretical and practical subjects. Latin American politics and foreign policy of Mexico.
**Ind/Abst** HAPI Hisp. Am. Period. Index; Int. Polit. Sci. Abstr.; PAIS Int. Print.

GW
**RELATIONS BETWEEN THE PEOPLE'S REPUBLIC OF CHINA AND I. FEDERAL REPUBLIC OF GERMAN, II. GERMAN DEMOCRATIC REPUBLIC IN ... AS SEEN BY XINHUA NEWS AGENCY : A DOCUMENTATION, THE.** **VFOAT** Xinhua News Agency on FRG and GDR. 1980-. English. an. **ED** Wolfgang Bartke. **LC** DD258.85.C6; R44. **DD** 327.43051. ***Continues*** *Relations Between the Federal Republic of Germany and the People's Republic of China in ... as Seen by Hsinhua News Agency.*

FR/0335-2013
**RELATIONS INTERNATIONALES.** [Relat. int.]. **Added/Corp** S.E.H.R.I.C. Graduate Institute of International Studies. Universite de Paris I: Panth,eon-Sorbonne. Institut d'histoire des Relations Internationales Contemporaines. No. 1 (May 1974)-. Periodical. French. qt. 300.00F. SEHRIC Relations Internationales, 11 cite Veron, F-75018 Paris France. **LC** D410; .R37. **DD** 327/.05. **Bk Rev**, (Qty: 4).
**Ind/Abst** Am. Hist. Life (1974-1978); Int. Polit. Sci. Abstr.; PAIS Int. Print.

FR/1157-5417
**RELATIONS INTERNATIONALES ET STRATEGIQUES.** **Added/Corp** Instituts de Relations Internationales et Strategiques. No. 1 (1991)-. Periodical. French. qt. Dunod Gauthier Villars, 15 rue Gossin, 92543 Montrouge cedex France. **Tel** 011 33 1 46 56 52 66, FAX 011 33 1 46 57 40 69. **LC** JX3; .R15. **DD** 327/.05.
**Ind/Abst** PAIS Int. Print.

IT/0034-3846
**RELAZIONI INTERNAZIONALI.** [Relaz. int.]. **Added/Corp** Istituto per Gli Studi di Politica Internazionale (Milan, Italy). (Jan. 1, 1935)-. Periodical. Italian (English). Six times a year. L130000 Italy; $120.00 Europe; $150.00 other. Istituto per Gli Studi di Politica Internazionale SRL, Via Clerici 5, 20121 Milan Italy. **Tel** 011 39 2 878266, 72001705, FAX 011 39 2 8692055. **ED** Dott Gerolamo Fiori. **LC** D410; .R38. **DD** 055. Index available. cum. index. **Bk Rev**. **Ad Acc**. **Circ:** 5,000.
**Ind/Abst** Am. Hist. Life (1954-1959).

US/0712-4767
**RENAISSANCE UNIVERSAL JOURNAL.** [Renaiss. Univers. j.]. **Added/Corp** Renaissance Universal. (1976)-. Periodical. English. qt. $16.00, $30.00 (institutions). Renaissance Universal Journal, 904 Sanford Drive, Burlington Ontario L7T 3G6 Canada. **Tel** (416)632-5602. **ED** Dhanjoo N. Ghista. **LC** HN1; .R46a. **DD** 301.24. Index available. **Bk Rev**. **Ad Acc**. **Circ:** 1,000.
**Desc:** Covers political order to promote cultural expression, economic democracy, reorganization of nations into economically self-reliant zones under world government, cosmology and the science of evolution, astrophysics and geophysics and their influence on climatology and human psychology, art, literature and science for human progress.

CM
**REPERTOIRE DES ORGANISATIONS INTERNATIONALES ET DE LEUR PERSONNEL PARTICIPANT AUX PROGRAMMES DE COOPERATION TECHNIQUE DES NATIONS-UNIES AU CAMEROUN / PROGRAMMES DES NATIONS UNIES POUR LE DEVELOPPEMENT, BUREAU DU REPRESENTANT RESIDENT, CAMEROUN.** French. Programme des Nations Unies pour de Developpement Bureau du Representant Resident Cameroun, Rue Joseph Clere Face au College de la RetraiteRetraite, BP 836 Yaounde Cameroun. **LC** HC995.A1; R44.

US/0748-0571
**REPORT OF A VANTAGE CONFERENCE.** (REPORT OF A VANTAGE CONFERENCE / SONSORED BY THE STANLEY FOUNDATION.). [Rep. Vantage conf.]. **Main/Conf** Vantage Conference. **Added/Corp** Stanley Foundation. (May 1984)-. Monographic series. English. ir. Price varies per volume. The Stanley Foundation, 216 Sycamore Street, Suite 500, Muscatine IA 52761-3838. **Tel** (319)264-1500, FAX (319)264-0864. **LC** JX1932; .V36. **DD** 327. **Circ:** 10,000 (ctrl). available on microfiche. ***Continues*** *Vantage Conference Report, 0145-8833.*
**Desc:** Report from a conference discussing the evolving world situation and addressing timely, emerging issues.

US
**REPORT OF THE COMMISSION TO STUDY THE ORGANIZATION OF PEACE.** **Main/Corp** Commission to Study the Organization of Peace. **VFOAT** Transitional Period; United Nations and the Organization of Peace; Fundamentals of the International Organization: General Statement; Security and World Organization; Economic Organization of Welfare. 1st (Nov. 1940)-. Monographic series. English. ir. Price varies per volume. Commission to Study the Organization of Peace, 866 United Nations Plaza, New York NY 10017. **Tel** (212)755-7361. **LC** JX1908.U6; C62. **DD** 940.53144.

ZA
**REPORT OF THE COMMITTEE ON FOREIGN AFFAIRS FOR THE ... SESSION OF THE ... NATIONAL ASSEMBLY APPOINTED ON ... / REPUBLIC OF ZAMBIA.** **Main/Corp** Zambia. National Assembly. Committee on Foreign Affairs. 2nd Session, 4th National Assembly (1980)-. English. an. K3.50. Zambia Government Printer, POB 30136, Lusaka Zambia. **LC** JX1865.Z332; Z35A. **DD** 328.6894/07658. **Bk Rev**. **Ad Acc**.
**Desc:** The committee on foreign affairs shall enjoy all the powers of a sessional committee as provided for the national assembly standing orders, the Constitution of Zambia and the National Assembly (powers and privileges) CAP 17 of the Laws of Zambia.

US
**REPORT OF THE COMMITTEE ON INFORMATION / UNITED NATIONS.** **Main/Corp** United Nations. General Assembly. Committee on Information. (1980)-. Government Publication. English. an. United Nations Publications, 2 United Nations Plaza, Room DC2 0853, Department 007C, New York NY 10017. **Tel** (212)963-8303, (800)253-9646. ***Continues*** *Report of the Committee to Review United Nations Public Information Policies and Activities.*

US/0539-6476
**REPORT OF THE SENATE DELEGATION ON THE MEETING-MEXICO-UNITED STATES INTERPARLIAMENTARY GROUP. DELEGATION FROM THE UNITED STATES.** (REPORT OF THE SENATE DELEGATION ON THE MEETING - MEXICO-UNITED STATES INTERPARLIAMENTARY GROUP.). **Main/Corp** Mexico-United States Interparliamentary Group. Delegation from the United States. No. 1; 1961-. English. an. Committee on Foreign Relations, Dirksen Senate Office Building, 1st and Constitution Avenue NE/Room SD-423, Washington DC 20510. **Tel** (202)224-3121. **ED** M Mansfield and J Sparkman. **LC** E183.8.M6; M65. **DD** 328/.3/0601.

US/0748-9641
**REPORT OF THE ... STRATEGY FOR PEACE US FOREIGN POLICY CONFERENCE.** [Rep. Strategy Peace US Foreign Policy Conf.]. **Main/Conf** Strategy for Peace (Conference). **Added/Corp** Stanley Foundation. **VAT** Report of the Strategy for Peace United States Foreign Policy Conference. 27th (Oct. 16-18, 1986)-. English. an. Free. Stanley Foundation, 216 Sycamore Street, Suit 500, Muscatine IA 52761-3838. **Tel** (319)264-1500, FAX (319)264-0864. **LC** JX1932; .S7. **DD** 327. **Circ:** 20,000 (ctrl). available on microfiche. ***Continues*** *Strategy for Peace US Foreign Policy Conference. Strategy for Peace US Foreign Policy Conference : [Report], 0895-7029.*
**Desc:** Reports of four discussion topics on issues that are timely and important to develop policies for their effective management.

US/0743-9180
**REPORT OF THE ... UNITED NATIONS ISSUES CONFERENCE.** [Rep. U.N. Issues Conf.]. **Main/Conf** United Nations Issues Conference. 15th (April 13-15, 1984)-. English. an. Free. The Stanley Foundation, 216 Sycamore Street, Suite 500, Muscatine IA 52761-3838. **Tel** (319)264-1500, FAX (319)264-0864. **DD** 327. **Circ:** 15,000 (ctrl). available on microfiche. ***Continues*** *Report of the ... United Nations Procedures Conference, 0748-2361.*
**Desc:** Report of an informal three-day conference where 25 UN diplomats, secretariat officials, and academic specialists discussed a current UN concern or organizational procedure.

US/0748-433X
**REPORT OF THE ... UNITED NATIONS OF THE NEXT DECADE CONFERENCE.** [Rep. U. N. Next Decade Conf.]. **Main/Conf** United Nations of the Next Decade Conference. **Added/Corp** Stanley Foundation. 19th, (June 17-22, 1984)-. English. an (Aug.). Free. Stanley Foundation, 216 Sycamore Street, Suit 500, Muscatine IA 52761-3838. **Tel** (319)264-1500, FAX (319)264-0864. **DD** 354. **Circ:** 15,000 (ctrl). available on microfiche. ***Continues*** *Conference on the United Nations of the Next Decade. [Report] -Conference on the United Nations of the Next Decade, 0069-8733.*
**Desc:** Brings together 25 UN ambassadors, secretariat officials, foreign ministry officials, and international experts from the private sector to discuss a major UN issue and its future implications.

BE
**REPORT OF THE ... WORLD CONGRESS / INTERNATIONAL CONFEDERATION OF FREE TRADE UNIONS.** **Main/Corp** International Confederation of Free Trade Unions. English. bm. 650F Belgium; $15.00 US. ICFTU, Rue de la Montagen Aux Herbes Potageres 37-41, Bruxelles Belgium. **Tel** 217-80-85. **LC** HD6475.A1; I234. ctrl circ.
**Desc:** Activities in worldwide international trade union movement.

US/0084-8921
**REPORT ON PUBLICATIONS OF THE SCHOOL OF INTERNATIONAL AFFAIRS AND THE REGIONAL INSTITUTES.** **Main/Corp** Columbia University. School of International Affairs. Vol. 1 1962/63. Periodical. English. sa. $22.00. Columbia University / International Affairs, Box 4, International Affairs Building, New York NY 10027. **Tel** (212) 854-4775. **ED** James Ryan. **Bk Rev**. **Ad Acc**. **Circ:** 4,000.
**Desc:** Each issue we invite distinguished experts to analyze a different topic in world affairs.

UK/0034-4737
**REPORT ON WORLD AFFAIRS.** Began in 1919. Periodical. English. qt. £15.00. R W A, 3 Alma Square, London NW8 9QD England. **LC** D410; .R39. **DD** 327/.09/04. ***Absorbed*** *Report on Foreign Affairs.*

US/1053-1254
**RESEARCH IN INTERNATIONAL BUSINESS AND INTERNATIONAL RELATIONS.** **See** Economics-International Economics.

US
**RESEARCH NOTE (UNIVERSITY OF CALIFORNIA, LOS ANGELES. CENTER FOR INTERNATIONAL AND STRATEGIC AFFAIRS).** (RESEARCH NOTE.). No. 6-. Monographic series. English. Price varies per volume. Center for International and Strategic Affairs, UCLA, 11383 Bunche Hall, Los Angeles CA 90024-1486. **Tel** (310)825-0604. ***Continues*** *ACIS Research Notes.*

●US/1062-9300
**RESEARCH NOTES.** **VFOAT** Notes on Terrorism & Conflict. (1992)-. Periodical. English. mo. $85.00. Research Associates, PO Box 4745, East Lansing MI 48826.

IS
**RESEARCH PAPER - HEBREW UNIVERSITY OF JERUSALEM, SOVIET AND EAST EUROPEAN RESEARCH CENTRE.** **Main/Corp** Jerusalem. Hebrew University. Soviet and East European Research Centre. (1???)-. Monographic series. English. ir. Price varies per volume. Soviet and East European Resource Center, FAC-Social Sciences, Mount Scopus, Jerusalem 91905 Israel. **Tel** (011)972 2 883180, FAX (011)972 2 322545, telex 26458. **ED** Edith Rogovin Frankel. **Circ:** 600.
**Desc:** Occasional papers on wide variety of Soviet and East Europe related themes historical, contemporary, internal, international, economic and political.

UK
**RESEARCH REPORT (INSTITUTE OF JEWISH AFFAIRS).** **See** Religion and Theology-Judaism.

US/0068-6093
**RESEARCH SERIES - UNIVERSITY OF CALIFORNIA, BERKELEY. INSTITUTE OF INTERNATIONAL STUDIES.** (RESEARCH SERIES.). [Res. ser. - Univ. Calif., Berkeley, Inst. Int. Stud.]. **Added/Corp** University of California, Berkeley. Institute of International Studies. No. 3 (1963)-. Monographic series. English. ir. Price varies per volume. Regents of the University of California / Institute of International Studies, 215 Moses Hall, Berkeley CA 94720. **Tel** (510)642-4466. **ED** Paul M. Gilchrist. ***Continues*** *Research Series (University of California, Berkeley. Center for Chinese Studies).*
**Desc:** Scholarly research studies in the social sciences relating to international and comparative themes, especially political science and economics.
**Ind/Abst** GeoRef.

YU/0486-6096
**REVIEW OF INTERNATIONAL AFFAIRS.** [Rev. int. aff.]. Vol. 1; June 7, 1950-. Periodical. English (Serbo-Croatian (Roman), French, Spanish, German and Russian). sm. $18.00 (surface mail), 24.50 (airmail) US. Review of International Affairs, PO Box 413, 11001 Belgrade Yugoslavia. **LC** D839; .R4. Index available. **Bk Rev.**
**Desc:** A free tribune for exchange of opinions on various questions from the spheres of international politics, economics, law and science. It is a source of information about Yugoslavia life and development.
**Ind/Abst** Index Islam. Lit.; Middle East Abstr. Index; PAIS Int. Print; Peace Res. Abstr. J. (1964-1970).

UK/0969-2290
**REVIEW OF INTERNATIONAL POLITICAL ECONOMY.** (19??)-. English. Four times a year. $112.00 (US & Canada); £74.00 (UK); £80.00 (other). Routledge, 11 New Fetter Lane, London EC4P 4EE England. **Tel** 071 583 9855, FAX 071 842 2298. **(Subscription address:** Kinokuniya Company Ltd., 38-1 Sakuragaoka 5, chome Setagaya-ku, Tokyo 156 Japan.**)**

UK/0260-2105
**REVIEW OF INTERNATIONAL STUDIES.** (REVIEW OF INTERNATIONAL STUDIES / [PUBLISHED FOR THE BRITISH INTERNATIONAL STUDIES ASSOCIATION].). [Rev. int. stud.]. **Added/Corp** British International Studies Association. Vol. 7, No. 1 (Jan. 1981)-. Academic Scholarly Publication. English. qt. $85.00 US, Canada and Mexico; £51.00 other. Cambridge University Press, The Edinburgh Building, Shaftesbury Road, Cambridge CB2 2RU United Kingdom. **Tel** 011 44 223 312393, FAX 011 44 223 325959. **(Subscription address:** Cambridge University Press / North America, 110 Midland Avenue, Port Chester NY 10573.**) ED** Richard Little. **LC** JX1; .B74. **DD** 327/.05. **[CCC].** Index available. **Ad Acc.** available on microfilm and microfiche from University Microfilms International (UMI). ***Continues*** *British Journal of International Studies, 0305-8026.*
**Desc:** Journal of the British International Studies Association. Serves the needs of scholars in politics, law, history and all other areas of social science in the international arena. Takes a strong interdisciplinary perspective. Has an established reputation for serious scholarship, attracting contributions from academics of international standing. Each issue includes substantial articles and reviews which survey and analyze the literature of relevant fields and disciplines. Every volume carries an author and title index for the year.
**Ind/Abst** ABC POL SCI; Am. Hist. Life (1981-); Br. Humanit. Index; Econ. Lit. Index; PAIS Int. Print.

BL/0034-7329
**REVISTA BRASILEIRA DE POLITICA INTERNACIONAL.** [Rev. bras. polit. int.]. **Added/Corp** Instituto Brasileiro de Relacoes Internacionais. Vol. 1 No. 1 (1958)-No. 139/140; New series (Aug. 1993)-. Periodical. Portuguese. qt. $15.00 Brazil; $30.00 other. Inst Brasiliero Relacoes Int, Caixa Postal 4602, 70919 970 Brasilia DF Brazil. **Tel** 011 56 61 3482590. **LC** D839; .R44. **DD** 327/.05. available on microfilm from University Microfilms International (UMI).
**Ind/Abst** Am. Hist. Life (1965-1977,1980-).

UY
**REVISTA URUGUAYA DE ESTUDIOS INTERNACIONALES.** **Added/Corp** Instituto de Estudios Internacionales (Montevideo, Uruguay). Vol. 1, No. 1 (July/Aug./Sept. 1982)-. Periodical. Spanish (summaries and/or abstracts in English). Plaza Independencia, 830 P 8 Casilla de Correo 903, Montevideo Uruguay. **Tel** 980882-900351. **ED** Alphonse Max. **LC** D839; .R446. **DD** 909.82. **Bk Rev. Ad Acc. Circ:** 10,000.
**Desc:** Analysis of Uruguayan and international affairs in the fields of politics, geostrategy, science, history, sociology, law, communism, terrorism, public administration, economy, and Agrarian problems.

YU
**REVUE DE POLITIQUE INTERNATIONALE. FRENCH EDITION, LA.** ***Suspended.*** (19??)-(May 1992). French (English). sm. Revue Politique Internationale, B P 413, Belgrade Yugoslavia.

FR/1152-9172
**REVUE DES AFFAIRES EUROPEENNES.** [Rev. aff. eur.]. (1990)-. Periodical. French. 920.00F France; 940.00F Europe and French overseas territories; 1060.00F other. Editions Juridiques Associees, 26 rue Vercingetorix, 75014 Paris France. **Tel** 011 33 1 43350167. **UDC** 340(4).
**Ind/Abst** PAIS Int. Print.

BE/0303-9617
**REVUE DES PAYS DE L'EST.** ***Title Change.*** [Rev. pays est]. **Added/Corp** Universite Libre de Bruxelles. Centre d'Etude des Pays de l'Est. Centre National pour l'Etude des Etats de l'Est. Vol. 13 (1972)-(1992). Periodical. French. sa. Centre National Etude Etats, 44 Avenue Jeanne, 1050 Bruxelles Belgium. **LC** DJK1; .R47. **DD** 909/.09/71708205. ***Continues*** *Revue du Centre d'Etude des Pays de l'Est et du Centre National pour l'Etude des Etats de l'Est.* ***Continued by*** *Transitions (Brussels, Belgium).*
**Ind/Abst** Am. Hist. Life (19??-19??); Int. Labour Doc. (19??-19??); Int. Polit. Sci. Abstr. (19??-19??); PAIS Int. Print (19??-19??).

LE/0252-8290
**REVUE D'ETUDES PALESTINIENNES.** (REVUE D'ETUDES PALESTINIENNES : REVUE TRIMESTRIELLE PUBLIEE PAR L'INSTITUT DES ETUDES PALESTINIENNES.). [Rev. etud. palest.]. **Added/Corp** Muassasat al-Dirasat al-Filastiniyah. **VFOAT** Palestiniennes. No. 1 (Autumn 1981)-. Periodical. French. Four times a year. 236.97F France; 250.00F others. Les Editions de Minuit, 7 rue Bernard-Palissy, 75006 Paris France. **Tel** 011 33 1 44393920, FAX 011 33 1 45448236. **ED** Elias Sanbar. **LC** DS119.7; .R45. **DD** 909/.049245694. **Bk Rev. Ad Acc. Circ:** 6,000.
**Desc:** Deals exclusively with the Palestine question and the Arab-Israeli conflict.
**Ind/Abst** Hum. Rights Intern. Rep.; Middle East J.

FR/0035-2365
**REVUE D'HISTOIRE DIPLOMATIQUE.** [Rev. hist. dipl.]. **Added/Corp** Societe d'Histoire Generale et d'Histoire Diplomatique. Societe d'Histoire Diplomatique (Paris, France). (1887)-. French. Four times a year. 246.45F France; 320.00F others. Editions A Pedone, 13 rue Soufflot, 75005 Paris France. **Tel** 011 33 1 43540597. **ED** G. Dethan. **LC** JX3; .R3. **DD** 327.2/05. **[CCC].** Index available. cum. index. **Bk Rev. Ad Acc.** ctrl circ.
**Ind/Abst** Am. Hist. Life (1954-).

MG
**REVUE DIPLOMATIQUE DE L'OCEAN INDIEN.** Vol. 1, No. 29 (July 1982)-. Periodical. French. qt. $29.00. Communication et Media-Ocean Indien, rue H Rabesahala, BP 46, Antsakaviro 101 Antannarivo Malagasy Republic. **Tel** 22536, telex 22350 MALAKY MG. **ED** Georges Ranaivosoa. **LC** DS341; .R48. **DD** 327/.09182/4. Index available. **Bk Rev. Ad Acc. Circ:** 3,000 (ctrl).
**Desc:** Politics and diplomatic relationships in the Indian Ocean region.

RM/0048-8178
**REVUE ROUMAINE D'ETUDES INTERNATIONALES.** (REVUE ROUMAINE D'ETUDES INTERNATIONALES / ACADEMIE DES SCIENCES SOCIALES ET POLITIQUES DE LA REPUBLIQUE SOCIALISTE DE ROUMANIE, ASSOCIATION DE DROIT INTERNATIONAL ET RELATIONS INTERNATIONALES DE LA REPUBLIQUE SOCIALISTE DE ROUMANIE.). [Rev. roum. etud. int.]. **Added/Corp** Academia de Stiinte Sociale si Politice a Republicii Socialiste Romania. Asociatia de Drept International si Relatii Internationale din RSR. (1967)-. Periodical. Multiple languages (French, Russian and English). Six times a year. DM285.00. **(Subscription address:** Kubon & Sagner, ABT Zeitschriftenimport, D 80328 Munich Germany.**) LC** DR201; .R487.
**Desc:** Publishes studies on international relations.
**Ind/Abst** Am. Hist. Life (1967-).

IT/0035-6611
**RIVISTA DI STUDI POLITICI INTERNAZIONALI.** [Riv. stud. polit. int.]. **Added/Corp** R. Istituto Superiore di Scienze Sociali e Politiche "Cesare Alfieri." Facolta di Scienze Politiche "Cesare Alfieri." Studio Fiorentino di Politica Estera. Studio Fiorentino di Politica Estera del Reale Istituto Superiore di Scienze Soczli e Politiche "Cesare Alfieri" di Firenze. (1934)-. Periodical. Italian. qt (4 issues). L60000 Italy; L80000 other. Rivista di Studi Politici Internazionali, Lungarno del Tempio 40, 50121 Florence, Italy. **Tel** 011 39 55 666384. **LC** JX7; .R63. cum. index. **Bk Rev**, (Qty: 80). **Circ:** 1,000 (ctrl).
**Desc:** Covers international law and relations, diplomatic history, European and world economic financial relations, East-West relations, Third World, Latin America, European Economic Community and regional organizations.
**Ind/Abst** ABC POL SCI; Am. Hist. Life (1954-1963, 1966-); Int. Labour Doc.; World Agric. Econ.

RM
**ROMANIA VIEWPOINTS.** (19??)-. Periodical. English. Agerpres, Scinteia Square, Bucharest 1 Romania. **LC** D839; .R55. **DD** 327/.05.

UK/0035-8533
**ROUND TABLE, THE.** [Round table]. (1910)-. Periodical. English. qt (Jan., Apr., July, Oct.). £124.00. Carfax Publishing Company, PO Box 25 Abingdon, Oxfordshire OX14 3UE England. **Tel** 011 44 235 555335, FAX (0279)31067, telex 817484. **(Subscription address:** US and Canada/ PO Box 2025, Dunnellon, FL 34430-2025; telephone:(904)489-6996**) ED** Peter Lyon (editor's address: Institute of Commonwealth Studies, University of London). **LC** AP4; .R6. **DD** 917.1/241. **[CCC].** Index available. cum. index. **Bk Rev. Ad Acc.** available on microfiche.
**Desc:** Provides lucid and well written analysis and commentary principally about the contemporary commonwealth, with occasional articles on themes of historical interest.
**Ind/Abst** ABC POL SCI; Am. Hist. Life (1955-1981, 1983-); Curr. Mil. Pol. Lit.; Energy Res. Abstr. (Sept. 1980-); Geogr. Abstr. Human Geogr.; Int. Dev. Abstr.; Int. Polit. Sci. Abstr.; Middle East Abstr. Index; PAIS Int. Print; Soc. Sci. Index.

GW/0175-274X
**S + F.** **VFOAT** S und F; Sicherheit und Frieden; Vierteljahresschrift fuer Sicherheit und Frieden. Vol. 1, No. 1 (1983)-. Periodical. German. qt. Verlagsgesellschaft mbH & Co. KG, Waldseestr. 3-5, 7570 Baden-Baden Germany. **LC** JX1903; .S2. **DD** 327.1/7/05.
**Ind/Abst** PAIS Int. Print.

US/0036-0775
**SAIS REVIEW (JOHNS HOPKINS UNIVERSITY. SCHOOL OF ADVANCED INTERNATIONAL STUDIES: 1981).** (SAIS REVIEW.). [SAIS rev.]. **Added/Corp** Johns Hopkins University. School of Advanced International Studies. **VFOAT** S.A.I.S. Review. **VAT** School of Advanced International Studies Review. No. 1 (Winter 1981)-. Periodical. English. sa (2 issues). $28.00 institution, $14.00 individual. SAIS Review, Johns Hopkins Foreign Policy Institute, 1619 Massachusetts Avenue Northwest, Washington DC 20036. **Tel** (202)663-5766, (202)663-5767, FAX (202)663-5782. **ED** Thomas Conroy. **LC** D839; .S353. **DD** 327/.09/04. (each issue). cum. index. **Bk Rev**, (Qty: 20). **Ad Acc, Adv Mgr:** Sheila Ward, **Tel** same as publisher. **Circ:** 2,500. Documents available from UMI Article Clearinghouse. ***Continues*** *SAIS Review (Johns Hopkins University. School of Advanced International Studies : 1956), 0036-0775.*
**Desc:** Journal of international affairs featuring articles on international politics, trade and monetary matters, security, developing countries and U.S. foreign policy.
**Ind/Abst** ABC POL SCI; Am. Hist. Life (1981-); Am. Bibliogr. Slavic East Europ. Stud. (1981-); Expand. Acad. Index (1992-); Index Islam. Lit.; Int. Polit. Sci. Abstr.; Newsp. Period. Abstr. (1992-); PAIS Int. Print; Middle East J. (1981-).

LE
**SAMID.** ***Title Change.*** **Added/Corp** Jamiyat Maamil Abna Shuhada Filastin (Lebanon). **VFOAT** Samed.

(19??)-?. Periodical. Arabic. mo. Jamiyat Maamil Abna Shuhada Filastin, PO Box 155024, Beirut Lebanon. **LC** DS119.7; .S3375. ***Continued by*** *Samid Al-Iqtisadi.*

CN/0820-7887
**SCANDALOUS INTERNATIONAL NEWS.** (SCANDALOUS INTERNATIONAL NEWS NEWS : SIN.). **VFOAT** Nouvelles. Internationales Scandaleuses. Vol. 1, No. 2 (Jan./Feb. 1983)-. Periodical. English. mo. $25.00 per year, $13.00 for 6 months. **DD** 320/.02/07. ***Continues in part*** *Scandalous International News. English, French & Arabic, 0820-7887.*

SW/0280-2791
**SCANDINAVIAN JOURNAL OF DEVELOPMENT ALTERNATIVES.**
**Added/Corp** Institute for Alternative Development Research. Vol. 2, No. 1 (Mar. 1983)-. Periodical. English. Four times a year. $75.00 Europe; $100.00 other. Scandinavian Journal of Development Alternatives, PO Box 7444, S103 91 Stockholm Sweden. **Tel** 011 46 758 19687. **ED** Dr. Franklin Vivekananda Ph.D. **LC** HC59.69; .S28. **DD** 337/.05. Index available. cum. index. **Bk Rev. Ad Acc. Pr Rev. Circ:** 200. ***Continues*** *Scandinavian Journal of Developing Countries.*
**Desc:** A interdisciplinary social science focus devoted to studies of genuine development, especially as the latter is related to such issues as human rights, human migration, the environment, North-South relations, basic human need satisfaction, the nature and evolution of human societies, conflict and peace.
**Ind/Abst** Int. Labour Doc.; LABORDOC; PAIS Int. Print; Soc. Plann. Policy Dev. Abstr.; World Agric. Econ.

US/0892-9882
**SCIENCE & GLOBAL SECURITY.**
(SCIENCE & GLOBAL SECURITY : THE TECHNICAL BASIS FOR ARMS CONTROL AND ENVIRONMENTAL POLICY INITIATIVES.). [Sci. glob. secur.]. **VFOAT** Science and Global Security. Vol. 1, Nos. 1/2 (1989)-. Periodical. English (Russian). ir. Gordon & Breach Science Publishers, Inc., PO Box 786, Cooper Station, New York NY 10276. **Tel** (212)206-8900, FAX (212)645-2459. **ED** Harold A. Feiveson. **LC** UA12.5; .S258. **DD** 327.1/74/028. **CODEN** SGSEE8. **[CCC]. Pr Rev.**
**Desc:** An archival source for scientific analyses relating to arms control and global environmental policy. The goal is to improve the quality and the cumulative impact of communication on these subjects between the scientific communities of East and West and to help create a common understanding of the technical basis for new policy initiatives.

CN/0828-6604
**SCREAM (OTTAWA, ONT.).** (SCREAM.). [Scream]. No. 1-. Periodical. English. $1.00 per no., Free to unemployed. Youth Information Network, PO Box 4136, Station E, Ottawa Ontario K1S 5B2. **DD** 327.1/72/05.

UK/0262-4591
**SEARCHLIGHT (LONDON).** **See** Sociology.

CN/1183-2754
**SECURITE & STRATEGIES, ASIE.** [Secur. strateg. Asie]. **Added/Corp** Centre de Recherches sur l'Asie. **VFOAT** Securite et Strategies, Asie. (Jan 1991)-. Periodical. French. Centre de Recherches sur L'Asie, 24 Rue du Ravin Bleu, Hull Quebec J8Z 1X8 Canada. **DD** 950/.05.

US/0889-4876
**SECURITY AFFAIRS.** (SECURITY AFFAIRS / JINSA.). [Secur. aff.]. **Added/Corp** Jewish Institute for National Security Affairs (Washington, D.C.). **VFOAT** JINSA Security Affairs. (198?)-. Periodical. English. Ten times a year (Jan./Feb & July/Aug. issues combined). $30.00 (one year), $60.00 (two years), $75.00 (three years). Jewish Institute of National Security Affairs, 1100 Seventeenth Street Northwest, Suite 330, Washington DC 20036. **Tel** (202)833-0020, FAX (202)331-7702. **DD** 327. **Bk Rev. Ad Acc. Circ:** 15,000 (ctrl).

UK/0963-6412
**SECURITY STUDIES.** (1991)-. Periodical. English. qt. $155.00. Frank Cass & Company Ltd, Newbury House, 890-900 Eastern Avenue, Newbury Park, Ilford, Essex IG2 7HH United Kingdom. **Tel** 011 44 81 599 8866, FAX 011 44 81 599 0984, telex 897719. **ED** Amos Perlmutter and Benjamin Frankel. **Ad Acc, Adv Mgr:** Ann Kidson. **Pr Rev.**
**Desc:** Aims to play an important role in advancing and strengthening security studies. It will be dedicated to the careful and focused exploration of the enduring theme of international security: the role of force in international politics. It will do so by presenting theoretical and historical examinations of the contexts, sources, causes, dynamics, uses, ramifications an outcomes of crisis and conflict of war.
**Ind/Abst** PAIS Int. Print.

CC
**SHIH CHIEH CHIH SHIH / SHIJIE ZHISHI.**
**VFOAT** Shijie Zhishi. (19??)-. Periodical. Chinese. sm. $48.70. World Affairs Press, (Shijie Zhishi Chubanshe), 31-A Wiajiaobu Jie, Dongchend Qu, Biejing 100005, People's Republic of China. **ED** Yao Donggiao. **LC** AP95.C4; S434. **DD** 909. **Bk Rev. Ad Acc. Circ:** 250,000 (ctrl). available on microfilm from University Microfilms International (UMI).
**Desc:** Explains China's foreign policies, comments on current world events, analyses the world situation, and provides information on individual countries and helps it's readers to understand what is happening in the world.
**Ind/Abst** Am. Hist. Life (1954-).

US/0736-7163
**SIGNIFICANT ISSUES SERIES.**
(SIGNIFICANT ISSUES SERIES / [CENTER FOR STRATEGIC AND INTERNATIONAL STUDIES].). [Signif. issues ser.]. **Added/Corp** Georgetown University. Center for Strategic and International Studies. (19??)-. Monographic series. English. ir (12-15 issues per year). $125.00 North America; $135.50 Europe; $191.00 other. Center for Strategic and International Studies, 1800 K Street NW / Suite 520, Washington DC 20006. **Tel** (202)887-0200 Ext. 306. **ED** Susan Sojourner. **LC** UNC. cum. index.
**Desc:** Covers a diversity of topics of interest to both the academic and policy-making communities; often the direct product of CSIS research programs.

CH
**SINO-AMERICAN RELATIONS.**
**Added/Corp** Chung-kuo Wen Hua Hsueh Yuan. Institute of Sino-American Relations. Vol. 1, (Spring 1975)-. Periodical. English. Four times a year (Jan., Apr., July, Oct.). $33.00. Chinese Culture University Press, PO Box 12, Yang Ming Shan, Taipei Taiwan. **Tel** 011 886 2 8611861. **ED** Yu-Tang Daniel Lew. **LC** E183.8.T3; S56. **DD** 327.51/249/073. **Bk Rev. Ad Acc. Circ:** 1,500 (ctrl).
**Desc:** Includes international affairs, history, humanities, economic relations, memoirs and culture.
**Ind/Abst** Bibliogr. Mission.

US/1041-875X
**SINO-WESTERN CULTURAL RELATIONS JOURNAL.** (SINO-WESTERN CULTURAL RELATIONS (1500-1800) JOURNAL.). [Sino-West. cult. relat. j.]. **VFOAT** Chung Hsi Wen Hua Chiao Liu Shih. (1989)-. English (Chinese, German and French). an. $12.00. Sino-Western Cultural Relation, c/o D E Mungello, Coe College, History Department, Cedar Rapids IA 52402. **Tel** (319)399-8615, (319)362-9015, FAX (319)399-8748. **ED** D E Mungello. **LC** BV3410; .C44. **DD** 306. cum. index. **Bk Rev. Pr Rev. Circ:** 200 (ctrl). ***Continues*** *China Mission Studies (1550-1800) Bulletin, 0734-1946.*
**Desc:** Research in the history of cultural relations (1550-1800) between China and Europe, with emphasis on Christian missionaries as mediators.

UK/0953-0282
**SIPRI YEARBOOK 1987.** [SIPRI yearb. 1987]. **VFOAT** Stockholm International Peace Research Institute Yearbook. (1987)-. Periodical. English. an. £40.00 - £50.00 (depending on Volume number). Oxford University Press, Walton Street, Oxford OX2 6DP England. **Tel** 011 44 865 56767, FAX 011 44 865 267773, telex 837330 OXPRES G. **(Subscription address:** Oxford University Press / USA, Journals Marketing Department, Oxford University Press, 2001 Evans Road, Cary NC 27513.**) DD** 327.17405. ***Continues*** *World Armaments and Disarmament, 0347-2205.*

US/1058-1731
**SIRS GLOBAL PERSPECTIVES.**
**Added/Corp** Social Issues Resources Series, Inc. **VAT** Social Issues Resources Series Global Perspectives. (1991)-. English. $80.00. Social Issues Resources Series Inc, PO Box 2348, Boca Raton FL 33427. **Tel** (800)327-0513, (407)994-0079.

IT
**SOCIALISMO OGGI.** Vol. 1, No. 1 (1984)-. Periodical. Italian. sm. L50.000. Via di Ripetta 66, Rome Italy. **LC** HX286; .S64. **DD** 335/.00945.

●SA/1022-0461
**SOUTH AFRICAN JOURNAL OF INTERNATIONAL AFFAIRS, THE.**
**Added/Corp** South African Institute of International Affairs. **VFOAT** SAJIA. Vol. 1, No. 1 (Spring 1993)-. Periodical. English. Twice a year. $20.00 (individuals); $30.00 (institutions). South African Institute of International Affairs, PO Box 31596, Braamfontein 2017 South Africa. **Tel** 011 27 11 3392021, telex 4-27291 SA. **LC** IN PROCESS; DT1945; .S68. ***Formed by the union of*** *International Affairs Bulletin, 0258-7270* ***and*** *Southern Africa Record.*

SA
**SOUTHERN AFRICA RECORD.** ***Title Change.*** **Added/Corp** South African Institute of International Affairs. No. 1-64 (Mar. 1975)-(1992). Periodical. Afrikaans (English). qt. South African Institute of International Affairs, PO Box 31596, Braamfontein 2017 South Africa. **Tel** 011 27 11 3392021, telex 4-27291 SA. **ED** Alan Begg. **LC** DT746; .S6. **DD** 327.68. Index available. **Ad Acc. Circ:** 800 (ctrl). ***Merged with*** *International Affairs Bulletin, 0258-7270* ***to form*** *South African Journal of International Affairs, 1022-0461.*
**Desc:** Dissemination of textual information: official treaties/negotiations/private groupings, without editorial comment or distortion.

US
**SOVIET FOREIGN POLICY TODAY : REPORTS AND COMMENTARIES FROM THE SOVIET PRESS.** 4th Ed. (Aug. 1990)-. English. $20.00 (college bookstores), $16.00 (five or more copies), $28.00 (single issue). Current Digest of Soviet Press, 3857 North High Street, Columbus OH 43214. **Tel** (614)292-4234. **LC** DK285.5. **DD** 327.47.
**Desc:** Reflects the changes in US-Soviet relations and the Soviet response to the past year's dramatic events in Eastern Europe. It includes up-to-date material on developments in Soviet foreign policy.

US/1050-2866
**SOVIET INTELLIGENCE & ACTIVE MEASURES.** ***Title Change.*** [Sov. intell. act. meas.]. **VFOAT** Soviet Intelligence and Active Measures. No. 14 (Spring 1990)-?. Periodical. English. qt. Institute for International Studies, 1718 M Street NW, Suite 244, Washington DC 20036. **Tel** (202)785-3606, FAX (202)659-5429. **DD** 327. ***Continues*** *Disinformation, 0885-2529.* ***Continued by*** *Political Warfare, 1056-3334.*

UK
**SPEARHEAD.** No. 1- Aug. 1964-. Periodical. English. mo. £10.00 UK; £16.40 North America; £18.38 Australia; £15.28 Middle East; £11.66 Europe. Spearhead, PO Box 117, Welling Kent DA16 3DW United Kingdom. **Tel** 01 316 4721. **ED** John Tyndall. **Bk Rev. Ad Acc. Circ:** 2,000. ***Absorbed*** *Combat.*
**Desc:** Commentaries on British and international affairs.

US/0271-1486
**SPECIAL REPORT - UNITED STATES DEPARTMENT OF STATE, BUREAU OF PUBLIC AFFAIRS.** (SPECIAL REPORT.). [Spec. rep. - U.S. Dep. State, Bur. Public Aff.]. **Added/Corp** United States. Dept. of State. Bureau of Public Affairs. (19??)-. Monographic series. English. Price varies per volume. US Department of State / Bureau of Public Affairs, Washington DC 20520. **LC** E840; .U614b. **DD** 327.73/005. ***Continues*** *Special Report - Department of State, Bureau of Public Affairs, Office of Public Communication, 0271-1508.*

PL/0038-853X
**SPRAWY MIEDZYNARODOWE.** [Spr. miedzynar.]. **Added/Corp** Polski Instytut Spraw Miedzynarodowych. **VFOAT** Mezhdunarodnye Voprosy. Vol. 1 (Oct. 1948)-. Periodical. Polish (summaries and/or abstracts in English and Russian; table of contents in English, Russian, French and German). qt. $54.00. **(Subscription address:** ARS Polona, PO Box 1001, 00068 Warsaw Poland.**)** available on microfilm and microfiche from University Microfilms International (UMI).
**Ind/Abst** Am. Hist. Life (1954-1956, 1968-1971); Int. Polit. Sci. Abstr.; Peace Res. Abstr. J. (1963-1966).

CN/0712-0761
**STATEMENTS AND SPEECHES / EXTERNAL AFFAIRS, CANADA.**
[Statements and speeches - Extern. Aff. Can.]. **Main/Corp** Canada. Dept. of External Affairs. Began with issue No. 80/6. Periodical. English. **LC** JX351; .C36B. **DD** 327.71/005. ***Continues*** *Statements and Speeches, 0712-0761.*
**Ind/Abst** Peace Res. Abstr. J. (1962-1967).

UK
**STATISTICS ON THE OPERATION OF THE PREVENTION OF TERRORISM LEGISLATION.** **See** Law.

IT/1120-0677
**STORIA DELLE RELAZIONI INTERNATIONALI.** Yearly Vol. 1 (1985)-. Italian. L67.000 (Italy); L85.000 (other). Casa Editrice Leo S. Olschki, Viuzzo del Pozzetto, Casella Postale 66, 50126 Florence Italy. **Tel** 011 39 55 6530684, FAX 011 39 55 6530214.
**Ind/Abst** Am. Hist. Life (1986-).

UK/0459-7230
**STRATEGIC SURVEY.** **See** Military and Defense.

US/0580-4105
**STRATEGY PAPERS (NATIONAL STRATEGY INFORMATION CENTER).**
(STRATEGY PAPERS.). **Added/Corp** National Strategy Information Center. No. 1 (1969)-. Monographic series. English. Five times a year. Free on request. National Strategy Information Center, 150 East 58th Street, New York NY 10155. **Tel** (212)838-2912.

GW
**STREITKRAFTEVERGLEICH NATO-WARSCHAUER PAKT.** **VFOAT** Streitkraftevergleich Nato Warschauer Pakt; Kraftevergleich Nato-Warschauer Pakt; Kraftevergleich Nato Warschauer Pakt. German. Free. Streitkrafteamt Offentlichkeitsarbeit, Wiesenpfad 49, W-5309 Meckenheim Germany. **LC** UA646.3; .S787. **DD** 355/.031/091821.

NE
**STUDIEN ZUR REGIERUNGSLEHRE UND INTERNATIONALEN POLITIK.**
German. ir. Martinus Nijhoff Publishers, Subsidiary of Kluwer Academic Publishers, Koraalrood 50, 2718 SC Zoetermeer Netherlands. **Tel** 011 31 79 684400.

US/0081-802X
**STUDIES IN INTERNATIONAL AFFAIRS.** ***Ceased.*** **Main/Corp** Washington Center of Foreign Policy Research. No. 1 (1967)-Series complete (Vol. 26, 1993). Monographic series. English. ir. Johns Hopkins University Press, 2715 North Charles Street, Baltimore MD 21218-4319. **Tel** (410)516-6987, FAX (410)516-6968. **DD** 327.

IS
**SURVEY OF ARAB AFFAIRS. See** Religion and Theology-Judaism.

US/0895-6286
**SURVIVING TOGETHER.** (SURVIVING TOGETHER / ISSUED PERIODICALLY BY THE FRIENDS COMMITTEE ON NATIONAL LEGISLATION (FCNL) AND THE INSTITUTE FOR SOVIET AMERICAN RELATIONS (ISAR).). [Surviv. together]. **Added/Corp** Friends Committee on National Legislation (U.S.) Institute for Soviet American Relations (U.S.). No. 1 (Nov. 10, 1983)-Issue No. 25 (Sutumn 1991) ; Vol. 10, Issue 1 (Winter 1992)-. Periodical. English (Russian). qt. $25.00 (individuals), $35.00 (institutions) US; $35.00 Canada & Mexico; $45.00 other. ISAR / Institute for Soviet-American Relations, 1601 Connecticut Avenue, Suite 301, Washington DC 20009. **Tel** (202)387-3034, FAX (202)667-3291. **ED** Leanne Grossman. **LC** E183.8.R9; S95. **DD** 327. cum. index. **Ad Acc**, **Adv Mgr:** T. Speiser. **Circ:** 4,500.
**Desc:** Chronicles the multi-faceted relationship between Americans and the people of the former Soviet Union.
**Ind/Abst** Hum. Rights Intern. Rep.

SZ/0039-7490
**SWISS REVIEW OF WORLD AFFAIRS.**
[Swiss rev. world aff.]. Vol. 1, No. 1 (Apr. 1951)-. Periodical. English. Twelve times a year. 78.00F. Neue Zuercher Zeitung, Auslandvertrieb, Postfach 660, CH-8021 Zuerich Switzerland. **Tel** 011 41 1 2581111, , telex 816 570 NZZV. **LC** D839; .S9. Index Available, published separately, free-automatically sent.
**Ind/Abst** Curr. Geogr. Publ. (199?-); Index Islam. Lit.; Int. Labour Doc.; LABORDOC; Middle East Abstr. Index.

US/1063-133X
**SWORDS & PLOUGHSHARES.** (SWORDS & PLOUGHSHARES : A CHRONICLE OF INTERNATIONAL AFFAIRS.). **Added/Corp** American University. School of International Service. Graduate Student Council. **VFOAT** Swords and Ploughshares. Vol. 1, No. 1 (Autumn 1991)-. Periodical. English. sa. Free. American University / International Service, Graduate Student Council, School of International Service, 4400 Massachusetts Avenue NW, Washington DC 20016-8071. **DD** 327.

BE
**TELEX AFRICA. Added/Corp** A.S.B.L. Informations Mediterraneennes. No. 1 (Sept. 24, 1973)-. Periodical. English. bw. 13000.00F. Bureau d'Info Europeennes, Rue Venizelos 20, 1070 Brussels Belgium. **Tel** 011 32 2 5207232, FAX 011 32 5200314. **LC** HC241.25.A3; T44. **DD** 330.9/6/03.
**Desc:** Offers in-depth coverage of political and economic relations between the European community and Africa with an emphasis on national co-operative efforts concerning Africa.

IT
**TELEX COOPERAZIONE.** English. bm. L50000. COSV, Via Iglesias 33, 20128 Milan Italy. **Tel** 011 39 2 2551270.

BE
**TELEX DEVELOPMENT.** (19??)-. English. Twenty-four times a year. 13000.00F. Bureau d'Info Europeennes, Rue Venizelos 20, 1070 Brussels Belgium. **Tel** 011 32 2 5207232, FAX 011 32 5200314.
**Desc:** Concise, factual reporting on the week's main events regarding relations between the Community and the Third World - Asia and Latin America.

BE
**TELEX MEDITERRANNEE.** (19??)-. French and English. Twenty-four times a year. 13000.00F. Bureau d'Info Europeennes, Rue Venizelos 20, 1070 Brussels Belgium. **Tel** 011 32 2 5207232, FAX 011 32 5200314. **Pr Rev.**
**Desc:** Detailed coverage of economic relations between the EEC and the countries of the Mediterranean Basin.

US/1056-8018
**TERRA NOVA (WASHINGTON, D.C.).** ***Ceased.*** (TERRA NOVA : A QUARTERLY JOURNAL OF FREE-MARKET ECONOMIC AND POLITICAL THOUGHT.). [Terra nova]. **Added/Corp** International Freedom Foundation. Vol. 1, No. 1 Summer North Winter South (1991)-(1992). Periodical. English. qt. International Freedom Foundation, PO Box 15439, Washington DC 20002. **Tel** (301)699-0703. **LC** D860; .T47. **DD** 327/.09/045. ***Formed by the union of*** *International Freedom Review, 0897-506X* ***and*** *Southern African Freedom Review.*

US/1048-3276
**TERRORISM, AN INTERNATIONAL RESOURCE FILE. INDEX.** [Terror. int. resour. file, Index]. (1986)-. English. an. University Microfilms International, 300 North Zeeb Road, Ann Arbor MI 48106-1346. **Tel** (313)761-4700, (800)521-0600 Exts. 2490, 2491, FAX (313)973-1540. **LC** Z7164.T3; T47; HV6431. **DD** 016.3036/25.

UK/0954-6553
**TERRORISM AND POLITICAL VIOLENCE. VFOAT** Journal of Terrorism Research. Vol. 1, No. 1 (Jan. 1989)-. Periodical. English. qt. $175.00. Frank Cass & Company Ltd, Newbury House, 890-900 Eastern Avenue, Newbury Park, Ilford, Essex IG2 7HH United Kingdom. **Tel** 011 44 81 599 8866, FAX 011 44 81 599 0984, telex 897719. **ED** David C. Rapoport and Paul Wilkinson. **Ad Acc**, **Adv Mgr:** Anne Kidson.
**Desc:** Aims to study terrorism in all of its aspects, recognising that comprehending the motivation of terrorists helps us have a better understanding of society. The scope of the journal is interdisciplinary, including contributions from philosophy, sociology, political science, history, psychology, law, economics and criminology.
**Ind/Abst** Am. Hist. Life (1989-); Br. Humanit. Index.

US
**TERRORIST GROUP PROFILES.** English. $81.28. Quanta Press, Inc., 1313 Fifth Street Southeast, Suite 208C, Minneapolis MN 55414. **Tel** (612)379-3956, FAX (612)623-4570.
**Desc:** Takes the user inside some of today's most dangerous organizations. Included on this disc are group name, date formed, membership, headquarters, area of operation, leadership, sponsors, objectives, targets, background and a chronology of terror incidents. Available in DOS and MAC formats.

BE
**TEXTES ET DOCUMENTS - MINISTERE DES AFFAIRES ETRANGERES, DU COMMERCE EXTERIEUR ET DE LA COOPERATION AU DEVELOPPEMENT.**
**Added/Corp** Belgium. Ministere des Affaires Etrangeres, du Commerce Exterieur et de la Cooperation au Developpement. (19??)-. Government Publication. French (English, Dutch and German). Four times a year. Free. Ministere des Affaires Etrangeres du Commerce Exterieur et de la Cooperation Technique, Rue des Quatre-Bras 2, 1000 Bruxelles Belgium. **Tel** (02)516-8111. **LC** DH403; .A26. **DD** 354/.493/00892. Index available. **Circ:** 10,000 (ctrl). ***Continues*** *Belgium. Ministere des Affaires Etrangeres et du Commerce Exterieur. Textes et Documents.*
**Desc:** Government issues dealing mainly with foreign relations.
**Ind/Abst** Int. Polit. Sci. Abstr.

US
**THIRD PRESS REVIEW OF THIRD WORLD DIPLOMACY. VFOAT** Third World Diplomacy. Vol. 1, No. 1 (Winter 1982)-. Periodical. English. qt. Third World Diplomacy, 222 Forest Avenue, New Rochelle NY 10804.

UY
**THIRD WORLD GUIDE. Added/Corp** Third World Editors (Association). **VFOAT** Yearbook Third World. (1984)-. English. an. $80.00. Iberique SA, Mercedes 1125, CP 11100 Montevideo Uruguay. **LC** HC59.69; .G843. **DD** 909/.09724/005.
**Desc:** Covers politics, culture, economics and the environment covering the Third World from a Third World perspective.

II
**THIRD WORLD UNITY.** No. 1- Jan. 1978-. Periodical. English. $25.00. M C Menon, 20/3771 Regharpura Karol Bagh, New Delhi 110005 India. **LC** D839; .T55.

US/0040-9898
**TOWARD FREEDOM.** ***Title Change.*** Periodical. English. mo. Toward Freedom, 209 College Street, #202-A, Burlington VT 05401. **Tel** (802)658-2523, FAX (802)658-3738. **ED** William B Lloyd. **LC** D839; .T66. **DD** 327/.05. **Bk Rev. Circ:** 1,000. ***Continued by*** *Toward Freedom Eurofile.*
**Desc:** Economic, social and political progress of third world countries; also affairs of Soviet satellite nations.

US/1063-4134
**TOWARD FREEDOM (1990).** (TOWARD FREEDOM.). [Toward freedom]. Vol. 39, No. 6 (Aug./Sept. 1990)-. Periodical. English. Eight times a year. $25.00 (US); $35.00 (other). Toward Freedom, 209 College Street, #202-A, Burlington VT 05401. **Tel** (802)658-2523, FAX (802)658-3738. **ED** Kevin J Keller. **LC** D839; .T66. **DD** 909.82/05. **Bk Rev**, (Qty: 12 /year). **Ad Acc**, **Adv Mgr:** Pamela Polston. **Circ:** 1,000. available on microfiche from Historical Society of Wisconsin. ***Continues*** *Toward Freedom Eurofile.*
**Desc:** Progressive internationalist newsletter with news & analysis of political, cultural, and environmental events in the third world and Europe.
**Ind/Abst** Hum. Rights Intern. Rep.

US
**TOWARD FREEDOM EUROFILE.** ***Title Change.*** **VFOAT** Toward Freedom Euro File; EuroFile; Euro File; Toward Freedom/EuroFile. (19??)-(19??). Periodical. English. mo. Toward Freedom, 209 College Street, #202-A, Burlington VT 05401. **Tel** (802)658-2523, FAX (802)658-3738. **ED** Kevin J. Kelley. **LC** D839; .T66. **DD** 909.82/05. **Bk Rev. Ad Acc. Circ:** 2,000. ***Continues*** *Toward Freedom, 0040-9898.* ***Continued by*** *Toward Freedom (Burlington, Vt. : 1990), 1063-4134.*

US/0041-0063
**TOWSON STATE JOURNAL OF INTERNATIONAL AFFAIRS.** [Towson State j. intern. aff.]. **Added/Corp** Towson State College. Towson State University. (19??)-. Periodical. English. sa. $6.00. Towson State University / Political Science Department, c/o M. Kumar, Baltimore MD 21204. **Tel** (410)830-2955. **ED** Jennifer Bowers. **LC** JX1; .T68a. **DD** 327/.05. Index available. cum. index. **Bk Rev. Ad Acc. Circ:** 1,500. ***Continues*** *Journal of International Affairs (Baltimore, Md.).*
**Desc:** It is the purpose of this journal to speak on matters involving international problems with many academic voices, and possibly suggesting solutions to the problems.
**Ind/Abst** Am. Hist. Life (1969-); Am. Bibliogr. Slavic East Europ. Stud.; Middle East Abstr. Index.

BE
**TRACTION.** (19??)-. English. ir (3 issues). $10.00. International Coalition Develop Action, 115 rue Stevin, 1040 Brussels Belgium. **Tel** 011 32 2 2311659.

US/0730-8876
**TRANSAFRICA FORUM. Added/Corp** Transafrica Forum (Organization). Vol. 1, No. 1 (Summer 1982)-. Periodical. English. Four times a year. Fl130.00 (individual), Fl195.00 (institution). Transaction Publishers / Rutgers State University, New Brunswick NJ 08903. **Tel** (908)932-2280 Ext. 105, FAX (908)932-3138. **ED** Randall Robinson. **LC** DT38.7; .T73. **DD** 327.6073. **[CCC]. Bk Rev. Ad Acc. Circ:** 1,200. available on labels; available on microfilm and microfiche from University Microfilms International (UMI).
**Desc:** Presents an independent review of U.S. policy toward Africa and the Caribbean. Offers information on political, economic, and cultural matters affecting black communities globally for a better understanding of policy issues and their impact worldwide.
**Ind/Abst** Am. Hist. Life (1982-); Geogr. Abstr. Human Geogr.; Hum. Rights Intern. Rep.; Int. Dev. Abstr.; Int. Polit. Sci. Abstr.; PAIS Int. Print.

NE/0165-2230
**TRANSAKTIE : PUBLIKATIE VAN HET POLEMOLOGISCH INSTITUUT VAN DE RIJKSUNIVERSITEIT GRONINGEN.**
**Added/Corp** Rijksuniversiteit te Groningen. Polemologisch Instituut. (19??)-. Periodical. Dutch. ir. F75.00. Instituut Internationale Stud, Postbus 9555, 2300 RB Leiden Netherlands. **Tel** 011 31 71 273411. **LC** D839; .T67. **CODEN** TRNKEL.

US/0192-477X
**TRANSATLANTIC PERSPECTIVES. See** Philanthropy.

●BE
**TRANSITIONS. Added/Corp** Centre de Recherches Interdisciplinaires sur la Transition vers l'Economie de Marche des Pays de l'Est. (1993)-. Periodical. French. Twice a year. 1500F (institutions), 1000F (individuals) Belgium; 1750F (institutions), 1250F (individuals) other. Centre National d'Etude d'Etats, Institut de Sociologie, 44 avenue Jeanne, 1050 Brussels Belgium. **Tel** 011 32 2 6503360, FAX 011 32 2 6503521. **LC** DJK1; .R47. ***Continues*** *Revue des Pays de l'Est, 0303-9617.*

US
**TRANSLATIONS ON JAPAN. Added/Corp** United States. Joint Publications Research Service. No. 1, (Oct. 28, 1975)-. Periodical. English (Japanese). General Secretariat, PO Box 1738, Burg Oudlaan 50, 3016 Rotterdam Netherlands.

FR/0298-8879
**TRAVAUX ET DOCUMENTS. Added/Corp** Centre d'Etude d'Afrique Noire (Institut d'Etudes Politiques de Bordeaux). **VFOAT** Travaux et Documents du Centre d'Etude d'Afrique Noire. (1982)-. Academic Scholarly Publication. French (English). ir. Price varies. Centre d'Etudes d'Afrique Noire, Institut d'Etudes Politiques de Bordeaux, Domaine Universitaire, BP 101, 33405 Talence Cedex France. **Tel** 011 33 56 84 4282, FAX 011 33 56 84 4321. **ED** Daniel Bach. **LC** UNC. **Bk Rev**, (Qty: 4). **Pr Rev. Circ:** 300 (ctrl).
**Desc:** Short academic studies about the political field and other problems in Africa.

FR
**TRAVAUX ET RECHERCHES - CENTRE DE RECHERCHES RELATIONS INTERNATIONALES DE L'UNIVERSITE DE METZ.** **Main/Corp** Universite de Metz. Centre de Recherches Relations Internationales. Multiple languages (French and German). 40.00F. Editions Insep, 11 Avenue du Trembley, 75012 Paris France. **Tel** 011 33 1 43741121. **LC** D1; .M56A. **DD** 327/.05.

US/0083-0186
**TREATIES AND OTHER INTERNATIONAL ACTS SERIES.**
**Main/Corp** United States. **Added/Corp** United States. Dept. of State. (1946)-. Monographic series. English. ir. $220.00 US; $275.00 other. Superintendent of Documents, US Government Printing Office, Washington DC 20402. **Tel** (202)275-3328, FAX (202)786-2377. **LC** JX235.9; .A32. **DD** 341.273.
**Desc:** Contains the texts of agreements entered into by the United States with other nations.

US
**TREATIES IN FORCE. COPY A.** **Main/Corp** United States. Department of State. Office of the Legal Adviser. English.

US/1041-8474
**TVI REPORT.** [TVI rep.]. **VFOAT** Terrorism, Violence, and Insurgency. **VAT** Terrorism, Violence, and Insurgency Report. Vol. 6, No. 2 (Fall 1985)-. Periodical. English. qt. $85.00. Terrorism Violence Insurgency, PO Box 849, Klamath Falls OR 97601. **Tel** (310)276-3378. **LC** HV6431; .T87. **DD** 303.6/25/05. ***Continues*** *TVI Journal, 0195-8003.*
**Ind/Abst** PAIS Int. Print; U.S. Polit. Sci. Doc. (199?-).

US
**U.S. CHINA RELATIONS. NOTES FROM THE NATIONAL COMMITTEE.** **VFOAT** US China Relations; U.S.-China News; US-China; Notes from the National Committee; Chung-Mei Kuan Hsi Tung Hsun. **VAT** United States China Relations. Vol. 1 No. 1 (Fall 1970)-. English. qt. Free on request (libraries); $5.00 other. National Committee on US & China Relations, 777 United Nations Plaza 9B, New York NY 10017. **Tel** (212)992-1385.

US/0083-0208
**U.S. PARTICIPATION IN THE UN.** [U.S. particip. UN]. **Added/Corp** United States. Dept. of State. Bureau of International Organization Affairs. **VFOAT** Report on the United Nations. **VAT** United States Participation in the United Nations. (1948)-. English. an. US Department of State / Bureau of International Organization Affairs, 2201 C Street Northwest, Washington DC 20520. ***Continues*** *United States and the United Nations, 0272-6769.*

US
**U.S.-THIRD WORLD POLICY PERSPECTIVES.** **Added/Corp** Overseas Development Council. No. 1 (1984)-. Monographic series. English. ir (two-three editions annually). $24.95 (cloth), $15.95 (paper). Transaction Publishers / Rutgers State University, New Brunswick NJ 08903. **Tel** (908)932-2280 Ext. 105, FAX (908)932-3138. **ED** Sheldon Annis.

UN/0964-4326
**UKRAINIAN REPORTER.** ***Title Change.***
**Added/Corp** Ukrainian Press Agency. Vol. 1, No. 1 (1991)-Vol. 2, No. 9 (1992). Periodical. English. Twenty-four times a year. Ukraine Business Agency, Vigiant House 120, Wilton Road, London SW1V 1JZ England. **Tel** 011 44 71 931-0665. **ED** T. Kuzio. **Bk Rev. Ad Acc. Pr Rev. Circ:** 300. ***Absorbed by*** *Ukraine Business Review, 0969-3483.*
**Desc:** Contemporary analysis in the political economic and foreign affairs fields of developments in the Ukraine.

US/0251-7329
**UN CHRONICLE.** [UN chron.]. **VAT** United Nations Chronicle. Vol. 12, No. 4 (April 1975)-. Government Publication. English (French, Spanish and Arabic). qt. $20.00. United Nations Publications, 2 United Nations Plaza, Room DC2 0853, Department 007C, New York NY 10017. **Tel** (212)963-8303, (800)253-9646. **(Subscription address:** United Nations Publications, Subscription Office, PO Box 361, Birmingham AL 35201-0361.**)** **LC** JX1977.A1; U564. **DD** 341.23/05. available on microfilm and microfiche from University Microfilms International (UMI); available on an online database (files 647,648/Full-Text) from DIALOG. Documents available from UMI Article Clearinghouse. ***Continues*** *UN Monthly Chronicle.*
**Desc:** Gives regular reports on the activities of the UN system as it deals with problems ranging from food and health to nuclear disarmament and the world economy.
**Ind/Abst** Acad. Abstr. Full Text Elite (Jan. 1989-) [Full Txt.]; Acad. Abstr. (Jan. 1989-); Acad. Ind. [Computer File] (1984-); Acad. Search (Jan. 1989-); Expand. Acad. Index (1984-); Gen. Period. Index (1985-); Hum. Rights Intern. Rep.; INFO-SOUTH Abstr.; Mag. Artic. Summar. Elite (Jan. 1989-) [Full Txt.]; Mag. Artic. Summar. Select (Jan. 1989-); Mag. Artic. Summar. CD-ROM (Jan. 1989-); Mag. Index Plus (1989-); Mag. Search; Middle East Abstr. Index; Newsp. Period. Abstr. (1988-); Peace Res. Abstr. J. (1975-1981); Read. Guide Abstr. Select Ed.; Read. Guide Period. Lit.; Soc. Sci. Source (Jan. 1989-); Soc. Sci. Index; Soc. Sci. Index Fulltext (Sept. 1988-) [Full Txt.]; Mag. Index (1977-); TOM Gen. Index (1993-) [Full Txt.]; Trade Ind. Index; Vocat. Search (Jan. 1989-) [Full Txt.].

FR
**UNESCO PRIZE FOR PEACE EDUCATION.** **Added/Corp** Unesco. **VFOAT** Prize for Peace Education. (1981)-. English. ir. UNESCO / France, 31 rue Francois Bonvin, 75732 Paris Cedex 15 France. **Tel** 011 33 1 45684564, 011 33 1 45684565, FAX 011 33 1 42733007, telex 204461 Paris. **LC** JX1904.5; .U5. **DD** 327.1/72/07.

SZ/1012-4934
**UNIDIR NEWSLETTER / UNITED NATIONS INSTITUTE FOR DISARMAMENT RESEARCH.** **See** Military and Defense.

US
**UNITED NATIONS DISARMAMENT YEARBOOK, THE.** **Added/Corp** United Nations Centre for Disarmament. Vol. 1 (1976)-. Government Publication. English. an. price varies per volume. United Nations Publications, 2 United Nations Plaza, Room DC2 0853, Department 007C, New York NY 10017. **Tel** (212)963-8303, (800)253-9646. **LC** JX1974; .U546. **DD** 327/.174/05.
**Desc:** Reviews the main developments and negotiations during the year. Covers disarmament, nuclear arms limitations, prohibition of chemical, biological and radiological weapons and reduction of military budget.

NZ/0110-1951
**UNITED NATIONS HANDBOOK.** **Main/Corp** New Zealand. Ministry of Foreign Affairs. (19??)-. English. an. $16.00. New Zealand Ministry of Foreign Affairs, Private Bag, Wellington 1 New Zealand. **Tel** 64 4 728877, FAX 64 4 729596, telex NZ 3441. **(Subscription address:** New Zealand Mission to the United Nations, One UN Plaza, 25th Floor, New York NY 10017; phone: (212)826-1960; fax: (212)758-0827**)** **LC** DU400; .A33 subser; JX1977. **DD** 341.23. **Circ:** 5000 (ctrl). ***Continues*** *United Nations and Specialised Agencies Handbook.*
**Desc:** Historical and up-to-date information on all the organisations and committees of the United Nations is incorporated in this book, which sets out each organisation's aims, describes its activities and its relationship with other bodies.

US
**UNITED NATIONS NEWS DIGEST.**
**Added/Corp** United Nations. Dept. of Public Information. **VFOAT** News Digest. (Jan. 4, 1985)-. Government Publication. English. wk. United Nations Publications, 2 United Nations Plaza, Room DC2 0853, Department 007C, New York NY 10017. **Tel** (212)963-8303, (800)253-9646.

●US/1051-399X
**UNITED NATIONS RESOLUTIONS.SERIES 3, RESOLUTIONS AND DECISIONS OF THE ECONOMIC AND SOCIAL COUNCIL.** **VFOAT** Resolutions and Decisions of the Economic and Social Council. (1992)-. English. $65.00. Oceana Publications Inc, 75 Main Street, Dobbs Ferry NY 10522. **Tel** (914)693-1320, FAX (914)693-0402, telex (914)693-81007105640834.

AT/0817-9751
**UNITED NATIONS REVIEW.** **Added/Corp** United Nations Information Centre (Sydney, Australia). **VFOAT** UN Review. (19??)-. Periodical. English. bm (6 issues). Free on request. United Nations Information Centre, 44 Market Street, Sydney 2000 Australia. **Tel** 011 61 2 292151, 011 61 2 2831144. **LC** JX1977.A1; U63.

US/1046-7513
**UNITED STATES INSTITUTE OF PEACE JOURNAL.** [U. S. Inst. Peace j.]. **Added/Corp** United States Institute of Peace. **VFOAT** Journal. (1988)-. Periodical. English. mo. Free. United Institute of Peace, 1550 M Street NW, Suite 700, Washington DC 20005. **Tel** (202)457-1700. **ED** P. M. Jensen. **LC** WMLC 93/3886. **DD** 327.
**Desc:** A newsletter reporting on the activities of the US Institute of Peace in fulfilling its mandate to expand knowledge about international peace and the management, prevention and cessation of conflict.

BE
**UP INFORMATION.** **See** Political Science.

US/0164-3886
**US-CHINA REVIEW.** [U. S.-China rev.].
**Added/Corp** U.S.-China Peoples Friendship Association. **VFOAT** U.S.-China Review. **VAT** United States-China Review. Vol. 4, No. 3 (May-June 1980)-. Periodical. English. qt (Jan., Apr., July and Oct.). $18.00 institutions, $15.00 individuals US; $20.00 other. US China Peoples Friendship, 306 West 38th Street, Suite 603, New York NY 10018-2903. **Tel** (212)736-7355. **ED** Duncan McFarland. **LC** DS701; .U82. **DD** 951/.005. **Bk Rev. Ad Acc. Circ:** 7,000. ***Absorbed*** *New China, 0161-0643.*

US/0093-7517
**USC/FAR CONSOLIDATED PLAN FOR FOREIGN AFFAIRS RESEARCH.**
**Main/Corp** United States. National Security Council. Subcommittee on Foreign Affairs Research. English. National Security Council, Subcommittee on Foreign Affairs Research, Washington DC 20520. **LC** JX1293.U6; U48A. **DD** 327/.07/2073.

US/1059-4604
**USCSAR REPORTS / THE UNITED STATES CENTER FOR SOVIET-AMERICAN RELATIONS.**
[USCSAR rep.]. **Added/Corp** United States Center for Soviet-American Relations. **VAT** United States Center for Soviet American Relations Reports. (1991)-. Periodical. English. qt. $25.00. **DD** 327.

UK/0041-5545
**USSR AND THIRD WORLD.** ***Title Change.***
**Added/Corp** Central Asian Research Centre (London, England). Vol. 1 (Dec. 7, 1970-Jan. 10, 1971)-(19??). Periodical. English. bm. Central Asian Research Centre, 8 Wakley Street, Islington London EC1 England. **Tel** 01 278 9441. **ED** David L Morison. **LC** DK266.A2; U16. **DD** 327.47. **Ad Acc.** ***Continued by*** *Soviet Asia, 0957-9516.*
**Desc:** Comprehensive current development of relations of the USSR and of China with all Third World countries comprehensively.
**Ind/Abst** Middle East Abstr. Index.

US
**UST CUMULATIVE INDEXING SERVICE : CUMULATIVE INDEX TO UNITED STATES TREATIES AND OTHER INTERNATIONAL AGREEMENTS.** **VFOAT** Cumulative Index to United States Treaties and Other International Agreements; United States Treaties and Other International Agreements: Cumulative Index Current Supplement. (1976)-. English. ir. William S. Hein & Company Inc., 1285 Main Street, Buffalo NY 14209. **Tel** (716)882-2600, (800)828-7571, FAX (716)883-8100, telex 91-209 WM S HEIN BUF. **ED** I.I. Kavass and A. Sprudzs.

RU/0320-8001
**VEK XX I MIR.** (VEK XX I MIR / SOVETSKII KOMITET ZASHCHITY MIRA.). [Vek. XX mir]. **Added/Corp** Sovetskii Komitet Zashchity Mira. **VFOAT** Vek 20. i Mir; Vek Dvadtsatyi i Mir. (1967)-. Periodical. Russian. mo. $59.95. **(Subscription address:** East View Publications Inc., 3020 Harbor Lane North, Suite 110, Minneapolis MN 55447.**)**

GW/0042-384X
**VEREINTE NATIONEN.** [V. N.]. **Added/Corp** Deutsche Gesellschaft fuer die Vereinten Nationen. 10. Jahrg., 1 (Feb. 1962)-. Periodical. German. bm (6 issues). DM49.00 Germany; DM52.45 other. Nomos Verlagsgesellschaft, Postfach 610, D-76484 Baden Baden Germany. **Tel** 011 49 7221 21040. **ED** Volker Weyel. Index available. cum. index. **Bk Rev. Ad Acc. Circ:** 3,400. ***Continues*** *Mitteilungsblatt (Deutsche Gesellschaft fuer die Vereinten Nationen), 0505-2955.*
**Desc:** Journal dealing with United Nation's affairs.

SZ
**VERS UN DEVELOPPEMENT SOLIDAIRE.** French. bm. 40.00F (Switzerland); 45.00F (other). La Declaration de Berne, CP 81, 1000 Lausanne 9 Switzerland. **Tel** 011 41 21245419. **Bk Rev,** (Qty: 25). **Circ:** 5,500 (ctrl).
**Desc:** Topics on north-south relations, specifically between Switzerland and the Third World.

CN
**VIDEAZIMUT CLIPS.** (19??)-. Newsletter. English. Three times a year. $10.00. Videazimut, 3680 rue Jeanne-Mance, Bureau 430, Montreal Quebec H2X 2K5 Canada. **Tel** (514)982-6660, FAX (514)982-6122. **ED** Sylvia Roy.
**Desc:** Strives to promote audiovisual communication for democracy and development.

GW/0936-451X
**VIERTELJAHRESBERICHTE PROBLEMS OF INTERNATIONAL COOPERATION.** [Vierteljahresber. probl. int. coop.]. **VFOAT** Vierteljahresberichte Probleme der Internationalen Zusammenarbeit. (1983)-. Periodical. Multiple languages. qt. DM62.00. Verlag JHW Dietz Nachf GmbH, In der Raste 2, D 53129 Bonn Germany. **Tel** 011 49 228 238083, FAX 011 49 228 234104. **Ad Acc, Adv Mgr:** Margret Reichert. ***Continues*** *Vierteljahresberichte Probleme der Entwicklungslander, 0015-7910.*
**Ind/Abst** World Agric. Econ.

VM
**VIETNAM REPORT.** V. 1- 1972-. Periodical. English. available on microfilm from University Microfilms International (UMI). ***Formed by the union of*** *Vietnam Newsletter* ***and*** *Vietnam Economic Report.*

AT/1030-9985
**VIETNAM TODAY.** **Added/Corp** Australia-Vietnam Society. Vol. 1 (1977)-. Periodical. English. Four times a year (Feb., May, Aug., Nov.). 12.00Aus$ (individuals), 30.00Aus$ (institutions) Australia, 15.00Aus$ (individuals) others (surface mail); 20.00Aus$ (individuals), 40.00Aus$ (institutions) (airmail). Vietnam Today, 29 Eumeralla Road, Caulfield South Victoria 3162 Australia. **Tel** 011 61 3 5789246. **ED** David Marr. **LC** DS556; .V54. Index available. cum. index. **Bk Rev. Ad Acc. Circ:** 1,000 (ctrl).
**Desc:** Vietnam's international relations and internal politics and society given an Australian slant by writers from many fields.

KE
**VOICE OF EGYPT.** **See** History(General)-History of Asia.

CN/0706-1048
**VRAC, EN.** (EN VRAC / ASSOCIATION QUEBECOISE DES ORGANISMES DE COOPERATION INTERNATIONALE.). [En vrac]. **Added/Corp** Association Quebecoise des Organismes de Cooperation Internationale. (March 1979)-. Periodical. French. bm. Free. Association Quebecoise des Organismes de Cooperation Internationale, Bureau 200/1115 Est Boul Gouin, Montreal Quebec H2C 1B3 Canada. **DD** 327.1/7/060714. ctrl circ.

US/0749-1050
**WASHINGTON INQUIRER.** [Wash. inq.]. Periodical. English. wk. $30.00 first class, $20.00 third class. Washington Inquirer, POB 28526, Washington DC 20038. **Tel** (202)789-4294. **ED** Peter LaBarbera. **LC** NEWSPAPER. **DD** 320. Index available. **Bk Rev. Ad Acc. Circ:** 7,000 (ctrl). available on microfilm from The State Historical Society of Wisconsin.
**Desc:** Foreign affairs and economic news and columns that are rarely found anywhere else. We print the news that the big media does not.

US/0163-660X
**WASHINGTON QUARTERLY, THE.** [Wash. q.]. **Added/Corp** Georgetown University. Center for Strategic and International Studies. Vol. 1, No. 4 (Autumn 1978)-. Periodical. English. qt. $32.00 (individuals), $82.00 (institutions). Massachusetts Institute of Technology (MIT) Press, 55 Hayward Street, Cambridge MA 02142-1399. **Tel** (617)253-2889, (617)625-8481, FAX (617)258-6779. **ED** Brad Roberts. **LC** D839; .W33. **DD** 327/.09045. **[CCC]. Bk Rev. Ad Acc. Pr Rev. Circ:** 1,800 (ctrl). available on microfilm and microfiche from University Microfilms International (UMI). Documents available from The Genuine Article, UMI Article Clearinghouse, Documents on Demand. ***Continues*** *Washington Review of Strategic and International Studies, 0147-1465.*
**Desc:** Foreign policy journal focusing on strategic balance between East and West. Coverage of defense and international problems.
**Ind/Abst** ABC POL SCI; Am. Hist. Life (1983-); Am. Bibliogr. Slavic East Europ. Stud.; Curr. Contents Soc. Behav. Sci.; Curr. Mil. Pol. Lit.; Energy Inf. Abstr.; Environ. Abstr.; Expand. Acad. Index (1992-); Int. Polit. Sci. Abstr.; Middle East Abstr. Index; Newsp. Period. Abstr. (1992-); NEXIS (Jan. 1982-); PAIS Int. Print; Res. Alert [Full Cov.]; Soc. Sci. Cit. Index [Full Cov.]; U.S. Polit. Sci. Doc.

US/0893-1232
**WASHINGTON REPORT ON LATIN AMERICA & THE CARIBBEAN.** **See** Business-Commerce.

US/8755-4917
**WASHINGTON REPORT ON MIDDLE EAST AFFAIRS, THE.** **See** General Interest-General Interest-Middle East.

KE
**WEEKLY REVIEW, THE.** (Feb. 8, 1975)-. Periodical. English. wk. $200.00 Africa; $230.00 Europe and India; $270.00 other. Weekly Review Ltd, PO Box 42271, Nairobi Kenya Africa. **Tel** 11 254 2 552233, 552266. **ED** Hilary Ngweno. **LC** HF1410; .W4. **DD** 338.91. **Bk Rev. Ad Acc.** ctrl circ.

GW/0020-9465
**WELTGESCHEHEN.** (Jan./Mar. 1976)-. Periodical. German. qt. Siegler & Co. Verlag fuer Zeitarchive, PF 3120 Einsteinstr. 10, W 5205 St. Augustin 3 Germany. **Tel** 011 49 2241 31640. ***Continues*** *Weltgeschehen. Internationales Europaforum.*
**Ind/Abst** PAIS Int. Print (19??-).

GW
**WEST OESTLICHE SPIEGELUNGEN.** (19??)-. Monographic series. German. ir. Price varies per volume. Wilhelm Fink Verlag, Ohmstrasse 5, D 80802 Munich Germany. **Tel** 011 49 89 348017, 348018.

UK
**WHO'S WHO IN INTERNATIONAL AFFAIRS.** ***Suspended.*** **Added/Corp** Europa Publications Limited. **VFOAT** International Affairs. (1990)-(19??). English. $295.00. Europa Publications Ltd, 18 Bedford Square, London WC1B 3JN England. **Tel** 011 44 71 5808236, telex 21540 EUROPA G. **(Subscription address:** Gale Research Co, 835 Penobscot Bldg., Detroit, MI 48226) **LC** JX1995; .W489. **DD** 327.2/025.
**Desc:** Profiles 7,000 leading diplomats, politicians, government ministers, heads of state, professors and journalists specializing in international politics.

US/0274-5852
**WILLIAM WINTER COMMENTS (1976).** (WILLIAM WINTER COMMENTS; A TWICE-MONTHLY PERSONAL NEWSLETTER ON CURRENT WORLD AFFAIRS.). (Aug. 11, 1976)-. Newsletter. English. Twenty-four times a year. $33.50 US; $38.00 Canada; $39.75 other. William Winter Comments, 6025 El Escorpion Road, Woodland Hills CA 91367-1199. **Tel** (818)347-7417, FAX (818)347-7417. **ED** William Winter. **Circ:** 10,000. available on microfilm from University Microfilms International (UMI). ***Continues*** *William Winter Comments on Current World Affairs.*
**Desc:** Analysis of current world news by William Winter (over 40 years, commentator, CBS/ABC radio-TV networks, foreign correspondent for leading metropolitan newspapers). Includes background and interpretation.

UK/0953-8542
**WILTON PARK PAPERS.** No. 14 (1990)-. English. ir. price varies per volume. Her Majesty's Stationery Office, 51 Nine Elms Lane, London SW8 5DR England. **Tel** 011 44 71 873 8459, 011 44 71 873 8499, FAX 011 44 71 873 8499, 011 44 71 873 8456, telex 297138. **(Subscription address:** Her Majesty's Stationery Office, PO Box 276, Publications Centre, London SW8 5DT England.**)**
**Ind/Abst** World Agric. Econ.

US
**WORKING PAPER SERIES / THE CENTER FOR INTERNATIONAL AFFAIRS, HARVARD UNIVERSITY.** **Added/Corp** Harvard University. Center for International Affairs. **VFOAT** Working Paper. Spring (1991)-. Monographic series. English.

II
**WORLD AFFAIRS.** **Added/Corp** Lancer International. Vol. 1 (Dec. 1990)-. Periodical. English. sa. $35.00. Lancer International, PO Box 3802, New Delhi, 110 049 India. **Tel** 664933, FAX 6862077. **(Subscription address:** Prints India, 11 Darya Ganj, New Delhi, 110002 India, (Phone: 011 91 11 3268645)**) LC** AP8; .W64. **DD** 052.

US/1058-1766
**WORLD AFFAIRS (BOCA RATON, FLA.).** (WORLD AFFAIRS.). [World aff.]. **Added/Corp** Social Issues Resources Series, inc. **VFOAT** SirS Global Perspectives, World Affairs. (1991)-. English. $80.00. Social Issues Resources Series Inc, PO Box 2348, Boca Raton FL 33427. **Tel** (800)327-0513, (407)994-0079. **DD** 327.
**Ind/Abst** Geogr. Abstr. Human Geogr.

US/0731-4728
**WORLD AFFAIRS JOURNAL.** [World aff. j.]. **Added/Corp** Los Angeles World Affairs Council. Vol. 1, No. 1 (Spring 1982)- Vol. 6, No. 4 (Spring 1988)-. Periodical. English. mo. $50.00 (comes with Los Angeles World Affairs Council Membership). Los Angeles World Affairs Council, 900 Wilshire Boulevard/Suite 2301, Los Angeles CA 90017. **Tel** (213)628-2333. **ED** Robin G. Beeby. **LC** D839; .W5523. **DD** 327/.09/04. Index available. **Circ:** 10,000 (ctrl).
**Desc:** Compendium of addresses delivered to Los Angeles World Affairs Council by world leaders, statesmen, diplomats, scientists, journalists, and business leaders.

US/8755-0687
**WORLD AFFAIRS QUARTERLY.** [World aff. q.]. **Added/Corp** University of Southern California. School of International Relations. Vol. 26, No. 3 (Oct. 1955)-. Periodical. English. qt. **LC** AP2; .W74825. **DD** 051. ***Continues*** *World affairs interpreter.*
**Ind/Abst** Am. Hist. Life (1958-1959).

US/0043-8200
**WORLD AFFAIRS (WASHINGTON).** (WORLD AFFAIRS.). **VFOAT** Advocate of Peace Through Justice. Vol. 1 (June 1837)-. Periodical. English. qt. $38.00 (individual), $58.00 (institutional), add $12.00 (foreign postage). Heldref Publications, 1319 Eighteenth Street Northwest, Washington DC 20036-1802. **Tel** (202)296-6267, (800)365-9753, FAX (202)296-5149. **ED** Evron M Kirkpatrick. **LC** JX1901; .W7. **DD** 341.05. **Bk Rev. Ad Acc. Pr Rev. Circ:** 665. available on microfilm and microfiche from University Microfilms International (UMI). Documents available from UMI Article Clearinghouse. ***Supersedes*** *American Advocate of Peace.*
**Desc:** The oldest journal of international affairs in the US. Illuminates issues involved in international conflict, and special issues bring together divergent view and analyses of important topics.
**Ind/Abst** ABC POL SCI; Acad. Abstr. Full Text Elite (Jan. 1994-) [Full Txt.]; Acad. Abstr. (Jan. 1994-); Acad. Search (Jan. 1994-); Am. Hist. Life (1962-1968, 1970-); Am. Bibliogr. Slavic East Europ. Stud.; Appl. Soc. Sci. Index Abstr.; Expand. Acad. Index (1989-); INFO-SOUTH Abstr.; Int. Polit. Sci. Abstr.; Mag. Artic. Summar. Elite (Jan. 1994-) [Full Txt.]; Mag. Search; Middle East Abstr. Index; Newsp. Period. Abstr. (1991-); Soc. Sci. Source (Jul. 1993-); Soc. Sci. Index; Soc. Sci. Index Fulltext (Winter 1987-) [Full Txt.]; U.S. Polit. Sci. Doc.

GW
**WORLD DEFENCE ALMANAC : THE BALANCE OF MILITARY POWER.** **See** Military and Defense.

US
**WORLD GUIDE TO FOREIGN SERVICES.** **VFOAT** Internationales Verzeichnis der Auswartigen Dienste. 1st Ed. (1986/87) -. Monographic series. English. ir. price varies per volume. Gale Research Inc., 835 Penobscot Building, Detroit MI 48226. **Tel** (800)877-GALE, (313)961-2242, FAX (313)961-6083, telex TWX 810-221-7086. **LC** JX1631; .W67. **DD** 351.8/92/025.

US/0043-8561
**WORLD INDUSTRIAL REPORTER.** (19??)-. English. Nine times a year. $60.00 US; $120.00 other. Keller Publishing Corporation, 150 Great Neck Road, Great Neck NY 11021. **Tel** (516)829-9210, FAX (516)829-5414, telex 221574 KELLE. **[CCC].**

US/0193-3329
**WORLD OPINION UPDATE.** [World opin. update]. Vol. 1, (Sept. 1977)-. Periodical. English. Twelve times a year. $45.00 one year; $60.00 other. Survey Research Consultants International Inc, PO Box 25, Williamstown MA 01267. **Tel** (413)458-4414, telex 951-443. **ED** Philip K. Hastings. **LC** D839; .W568. **DD** 309.1/047. Index available. **Circ:** 500.
**Desc:** Opinion data worldwide on social, political, economic issues. Data is drawn from 100 survey organizations in 60 countries.

NR
**WORLD PEACE.** **Added/Corp** International Society of United Modern Enterprise. (19??)-. Periodical. English. qt. International Society of United Modern Enterprise, 60 A Campbell Street, PO Box 1944, Lagos Nigeria. **LC** JX1901; .W84. **DD** 327/.172/05.

US/0049-8130
**WORLD PEACE NEWS.** [World peace news]. **Added/Corp** American Movement for World Government. (Nov. 1970)-. Periodical. English. bm. $14.00 (one year), $17.00 (two year), $20.00 (three year) US; $18.50 (one year), $26.00 (two year), $33.50 (three year) other. World Peace News, 777 United Nations PL, 11th Floor, New York NY 10017. **Tel** (212)686-1069. **ED** Thomas Liggett. **DD** 327. **Bk Rev. Circ:** 2,000.
**Desc:** The development of world political unity- as seen at the U.N., with national governments, and among non-governmental "peace" organizations worldwide.
**Ind/Abst** Peace Res. Abstr. J. (1979-1980).

CN/0229-6942
**WORLD POLICY.** [World policy]. No. 1 (1983)-. English. an. $10.00. World Policy, c/o Dr P Sarbadhikari, Department of Political Studies, Lakehead University, Thunder Bay Ontario P7B 5E1 Canada. **DD** 327/.05.

US/0740-2775
**WORLD POLICY JOURNAL.** [World policy j.]. Vol. 1, No. 1 (Fall 1983)-. Periodical. English. Four times a year. $35.00 (institution), $28.00 (individual) US; $40.00 (institution), $33.00 (individual) other. World Policy Institute, 65 Fifth Avenue, Suite 413, New York NY 10017. **Tel** (212)229-5808, FAX (212)986-1482. **ED** Sherle Schwenninger. **LC** D839; .W5687. **DD** 327/.09/047. Index available. cum. index. **Ad Acc. Pr Rev. Circ:** 8,600. available on microfilm and microfiche from University Microfilms International (UMI). Documents available from The Genuine Article, UMI Article Clearinghouse.
**Desc:** The leading progressive international affairs quarterly in the U.S., World Policy Journal publishes essays, interviews and debates covering global security issues, international trade and economic policy, environmental concerns and developments in Europe, Latin America, Asia and Africa. Read widely by political leaders, policymakers, scholars, the media, and concerned citizens.
**Ind/Abst** ABC POL SCI; Acad. Abstr. Full Text Elite (July 1990-); Acad. Abstr. (July 1990-); Acad. Search (July 1990-); Altern. Press Index; Am. Hist. Life (1983-); Am. Bibliogr. Slavic East Europ. Stud.; Curr. Contents Soc. Behav. Sci.; Expand. Acad. Index (1992-); Hum. Rights Intern. Rep.; INFO-SOUTH Abstr.; Int. Polit. Sci. Abstr.; J. Plan. Lit.; Left Index; Mag. Search; Newsp. Period. Abstr. (1988-); PAIS Int. Print; Peace Res. Abstr. J. (1983-1984); Res. Alert [Full Cov.]; Sage Public Adm. Abstr.; Soc. Plann. Policy Dev. Abstr.; Soc. Sci. Source (Jul. 1990-); Soc. Sci. Cit. Index [Full Cov.]; Sociol. Abstr.; Middle East J.; U.S. Polit. Sci. Doc.

US/0043-8871
**WORLD POLITICS.** [World polit.]. **Added/Corp** Yale University. Institute of International Studies. Woodrow Wilson School of Public and International Affairs. Center of International Studies. Vol. 1 (Oct.

1948)-. Periodical. English. Four times a year (Oct., Jan., April, & July). $51.00 US; $55.00 Canada & Mexico; $61.00 other. Johns Hopkins University Press, 2715 North Charles Street, Baltimore MD 21218-4319. **Tel** (410)516-6987, FAX (410)516-6968. **(Subscription address:** John Hopkins University Press, Journals Publishing Division, PO Box 19966, Baltimore MD 21211.) **ED** Henry Bienen. **LC** D839; .W57. **DD** 909.82. **[CCC]**. Index available. **Bk Rev. Ad Acc. Pr Rev. Circ:** 3,700. available on microfilm and microfiche from University Microfilms International (UMI); available on photocopies from University Microfilms International (UMI); available on microfiche from Johnson Associates. Documents available from The Genuine Article, UMI Article Clearinghouse.
**Desc:** A multidisciplinary journal offering analytical and theoretical articles in international relations, comparative politics, political theory, foreign policy, and national development.
**Ind/Abst** ABC POL SCI; Acad. Abstr. Full Text Elite (July 1990-); Acad. Abstr. (July 1990-); Acad. Search (July 1990-); Am. Hist. Life (1954-); Am. Bibliogr. Slavic East Europ. Stud.; Book Rev. Digest; Book Rev. Index; Curr. Contents Soc. Behav. Sci.; Index Period. Artic. Relat. Law; INFO-SOUTH Abstr.; Int. Labour Doc.; Int. Polit. Sci. Abstr.; Mag. Search; Newsp. Period. Abstr. (1989-); PAIS Int. Print; Peace Res. Abstr. J. (1965-1971, 1973-1977); Res. Alert [Full Cov.]; Soc. Sci. Source (Jul. 1990-); Soc. Sci. Cit. Index [Full Cov.]; Soc. Sci. Index; Soc. Sci. Index Fulltext (Oct. 1988-) [Full Txt.]; Middle East J. (?-?); U.S. Polit. Sci. Doc.

US/0195-8895
**WORLD PRESS REVIEW.** [World press rev.]. **Added/Corp** Stanley Foundation. Vol. 27, No. 3 (March 1980)-. Periodical. English. mo. $24.97 (1 year), $44.97 (2 year). World Press Review, 200 Madison Avenue, Suite 2104, New York NY 10016. **Tel** (212)889-5155. **(Subscription address:** 205 West Center Street, Marion, OH 43302; telephone: (800)669-1002 or (614)383-5231) **ED** R. Edward Jackson. **LC** AP2; .A833. **DD** 051. **Bk Rev. Ad Acc. Circ:** 80,000. available on microfilm and microfiche from University Microfilms International (UMI). Documents available from UMI Article Clearinghouse, Magazine Collection. ***Continues*** *Atlas World Press Review, 0161-6528.*
**Desc:** A forum for expressing the ideas and opinions of the global community. Each month, articles selected from hundreds of different foreign publications are translated into English, providing a comprehensive international perspective which is quite unique.
**Ind/Abst** Acad. Abstr. Full Text Elite (Jan. 1984-) [Full Txt.]; Acad. Abstr. (Jan. 1984-); Acad. Ind. [Computer File] (1984-); Acad. Search (Jan. 1984-); Expand. Acad. Index (1984-); Gen. Period. Index (1985-); Guide Soc. Sci. Relig.; Hum. Rights Intern. Rep.; Index Period. Artic. Relat. Law; INFO-SOUTH Abstr.; Infobank (1980-); Mag. Artic. Summar. Elite (Jan. 1984-) [Full Txt.]; Mag. Artic. Summar. Select (Jan. 1984-) [Full Txt.]; Mag. Artic. Summar. CD-ROM (Jan. 1984-); Mag. Express (1986-) [Full Txt.]; Mag. Index Plus (1989-); Mag. Index Sel. Microfiche (1989-) [Full Txt.]; Mag. Index. Sel. (1986-); Mag. Search; Newsp. Period. Abstr. (1986-); PAIS Int. Print (?-?); Peace Res. Abstr. J.; Read. Guide Abstr. Select Ed.; Read. Guide Period. Lit.; Resource/One Ondisc; Soc. Sci. Source (Jan. 1984-) [Full Txt.]; Mag. Index (1980-); TOM Gen. Index (1989-) [Full Txt.]; Vocat. Search (Jan. 1984-) [Full Txt.].

UK/0043-9134
**WORLD TODAY, THE.** [World today]. **VFOAT** Chatham House Review. Vol. 1; July 1945-. Periodical. English. mo. £22.00 (individuals), £27.00 (institutions), £17.00 (students) UK and Eire; $43.00 (individuals), $65.00 (institutions), $28.00 (students) US and Canada; £28.00 (individuals), £33.00 (institutions), £25.00 (students) Europe and other. The Royal Institute of International Affairs, Chatham House, 10 St James's Square, London SWIY 4LE England. **Tel** (071)930-2233, FAX (071)839-3593. **ED** Christopher Cviic. **LC** D410; .W63. **DD** 940.55/05. **UDC** 327. **[CCC]**. Index available. cum. index. **Bk Rev. Ad Acc. Pr Rev. Circ:** 4,000 (ctrl). available on microfilm and microfiche from University Microfilms International (UMI). Documents available from The Genuine Article, UMI Article Clearinghouse. ***Supersedes in part*** *Bulletin of International News.*
**Desc:** Journal of Royal Institute of International Affairs. Read in over 70 countries by political and business leaders, academics, and media. Also libraries and research institutions.
**Ind/Abst** ABC POL SCI; Acad. Search (July 1993-); Am. Hist. Life (1967-1978); Appl. Soc. Sci. Index Abstr.; Curr. Contents, Agric. Biol. Environ. Sci.; Curr. Contents Soc. Behav. Sci.; Curr. Mil. Pol. Lit.; Expand. Acad. Index (1989-); Geogr. Abstr. Human Geogr.; INFO-SOUTH Abstr.; Int. Bibliogr. Sociol.; Int. Dev. Abstr.; Int. Labour Doc.; Int. Polit. Sci. Abstr.; Mag. Search; Middle East Abstr. Index; Newsp. Period. Abstr. (1989-); PAIS Int. Print; Peace Res. Abstr. J. (1966-1973); Res. Alert [Full Cov.]; Soc. Sci. Source (Jul. 1993-); Soc. Sci. Cit. Index [Full Cov.]; Soc. Sci. Index; Soc. Sci. Index Fulltext (Dec. 1988-) [Full Txt.]; SportSearch; World Agric. Econ.

II
**WORLD UNION. Added/Corp** World Union (Organization). Vol. 8 (1968)-. Periodical. English. mo. $10.00. World Union, Pondicherry, India. **(Subscription address:** Prints India, 11 Darya Ganj, New Delhi, 110002 India, (Phone: 011 91 11 3268645)) **LC** B1; .E67. **DD** 200/.5. ***Continues*** *=1 [i.e. Equals one];* ***Absorbed*** *World Union Focus.*

FI/0355-0079
**YEARBOOK OF FINNISH FOREIGN POLICY.** [Yearb. Finn. foreign policy]. 1973-. English. an. Fmk70.00 Finland; $15.00 US. Finnish Institute of International Affairs, Pursimiehenkatu 8, SF-00150 Helsinki Finland. **Tel** 358-0-170-434, FAX 358-0-669375. **ED** Paavo Lipponen. **LC** DK451.7; .Y4. **DD** 327.471. **Bk Rev. Circ:** 3,500 (ctrl).
**Desc:** Deals with domestic and international questions that have during the year been important from the point of view of Finland's foreign policy. Articles are written by both Finnish and foreign specialists.
**Ind/Abst** ABC POL SCI; Int. Polit. Sci. Abstr.

BE/0084-3814
**YEARBOOK OF INTERNATIONAL ORGANIZATIONS. Added/Corp** Union of International Associations. **VFOAT** Annuaire des Organisations Internationales. Vol. 1 (1948)-. Monographic series. English. ir. Price varies per volume. Union of International Associations, Rue Washington 40, 1050 Brussels Belgium. **Tel** 011 32 2 6404109, FAX 011 32 2 646 05 25, telex 65080 INAC B. **(Subscription address:** Reed Reference Publishing / Pennsylvania, PO Box 7247 8604, Philadelphia PA 19170.) **ED** Editors: 1948, M. Henchoz, R.-H. WEust. **LC** JX1904; .A42. ***Absorbed*** *Who's Who in International Organizations.*
**Desc:** Vol. 1 contains a comprehensive directory of nearly 20,000 international organizations. Vol. 2 is a country-by-country arrangement of secretariates and memberships. Vol. 3 contains organizations which are classified by subject and region.

II/8756-5307
**YEARBOOK ON INDIA'S FOREIGN POLICY.** [Yearb. India's foreign policy]. 1982-83-. English. an. Rs250.00. SAGE Periodical Press, 2455 Teller Road, Thousand Oaks CA 91320. **Tel** (805)499-0721, FAX (805)499-0871, telex 100799. **LC** DS480.832; .Y42. **DD** 327.54. **Acid Free.**
**Ind/Abst** Int. Polit. Sci. Abstr.

RU
**ZA RUBEZHOM. Added/Corp** Soiuz Zhurnalistov SSSR. No. 1 (June 18, 1960)-. Periodical. Russian. wk. $109.95. **(Subscription address:** East View Publications Inc., 3020 Harbor Lane North, Suite 110, Minneapolis MN 55447.)

---

## SOCIALISM, COMMUNISM, ANARCHISM, UTOPIANISM

---

UK
**7 DAYS (LONDON, ENGLAND).** (7 DAYS.). **Added/Corp** Communist Party of Great Britain. **VFOAT** Seven Days. (19??)-. Newspaper. English. Fifty times a year (Thursdays). £20.00 UK; £35.00 Europe; £36.00 other. 7 Days Communist Party Weekly, 16 St. John Street, London EC1M 4AY England. **Tel** 011 44 1 251 4170. **LC** HX241; .A15. **DD** 335.43/0941.

GW/0930-9977
**1999. VFOAT** Neunzehnhundertneunundneunzig; Zeitschrift fur Sozialgeschichte des 20. und 21. Jahrhunderts. Vol. 1 (1986)-. Periodical. German. qt. DM12.00 per issue. Hamburger Stiftung fur Sozialgeschichte des 20. Jahrhunderts, Mittelweg 36, W-2000 Hamburg 13 Germany. **LC** HN1; .A18. ***Continues*** *Mitteilungen (Dokumentationsstelle zur NS-Sozialpolitik), 0179-4299.*
**Ind/Abst** Am. Hist. Life (1991-).

PO
**A IDEIA.** Periodical. Portuguese. qt. 1,500$00 Portugal; $10.00 US. A Ideia, Av Guerra Junqueiro 19 5o Esq, P-1000 Lisbon Portugal. **ED** Joao Freire. **LC** HX739.A3; I35. **DD** 335/.83/09469. cum. index. **Bk Rev. Circ:** 1,000.
**Desc:** This is an ideologically oriented journal, offering reflections on contemporary themes such as ecology, education, politics and economics.

CN/0229-1347
**A.N.CH.A. AGENCIA NOTICIOSA CHILENA ANTIFASCISTA (EDICION INGLESA).** (A.N.CH.A. : AGENCIA NOTICIOSA CHILENA ANTIFASCISTA.). (1977)-. Periodical. English. mo. National Publications Centre, PO Box 727 Adelaide Station, Toronto Ontario M5C 2J8 Canada. **Tel** (416)252-3658. **DD** 335.43/0983.

FR/0398-2882
**ACTUALITES SOVIETIQUES PARIS.** [Actual. sov. Paris]. (1976)-. Periodical. French. sw. 120.00F France; 70.00F other. Editions Etudes Sovietiques, 14 Place du General Catroux, 75017 Paris France. **UDC** 32. ***Continues*** *Etudes Sovietiques. Actualites, 0395-2002.*

FR
**ACTUEL MARX.** (1987)-. Monographic series. French. sa. 280.00F France; 330.00F other. Presses Universitaires de France, Department des Revues, 14 Avenue du Bois de l'Epine, BP 90, 91003 Evry Cedex France. **Tel** (1)60 77 82 05, FAX (1) 60 79 20 45, telex PUF 600 474 F. **LC** UNC.

MG
**ADY FARANY.** Multiple languages (French and Malayalam). 1200. CCP 16 434, Tananarive Malagasy Republic. **LC** JQ3469.A515; A82.

UK/0001-9976
**AFRICAN COMMUNIST.** (THE AFRICAN COMMUNIST.). [Afr. communist]. **Added/Corp** South African Communist Party. No. 1 (1960)-. Periodical. English. qt (Feb., May, Oct., Nov.). R24.00 surface mail; R30.00 air mail. Inkululeko Publications, PO Box 1027, 3rd Floor, No. 1 Leyds Street, Braamfontein, Johannesburg 2000. **Tel** 011 339-3621, 339-3622, FAX 011 339-4244, 339-6880. **ED** Brian Bunting. **LC** HX3; .A3. **DD** 335.43/096. Index available. cum. index. **Bk Rev. Circ:** 10,000. available on microfilm and microfiche from University Microfilms International (UMI).
**Desc:** A forum for Marxist-Leninist thought in Africa.
**Ind/Abst** Int. Bibliogr. Sociol.; Recent. Publ. Artic.

UK
**AFRICAN RED FAMILY. Added/Corp** All-African Revolutionary Marxist Leninist Movement. Vol. 1 (Oct./Dec. 1972)-. Periodical. English. ir (2 to 3 issues per year). $12.00. Hamibantu Publications, 107 Pevensey Road, E7 0AH London England. **ED** Shongo Gboguntiwon. **LC** HX3; .A34. **DD** 335.43/096. **Bk Rev. Circ:** 4,000.

RU
**AFRICAN STUDIES BY SOVIET SCHOLARS.** No. 1-. Monographic series. English (Portuguese and Spanish). Price varies per volume. Social Sciences Today Editorial Board, Academy of Sciences, 33/12 Arbat, Moscow 121002 Russia. **Tel** 241-09-06. **ED** Iosiph R Grigulevich. **Bk Rev. Ad Acc. Circ:** 3,000 (ctrl).

SZ
**AGITATION.** (19??)-. Periodical. German. US Department of the Treasury, 15 Pennsylvania Avenue NW, Washington DC 20220. **LC** HX6; .A4.

SJ
**AL-BARLAMAN.** No. 1, (May 25, 1983)-. Periodical. Arabic. Sudanese Socialist Union, PO Box 1850, Khartoum Sudan. **LC** J868; .H33.

SJ
**AL-ISHTIRAKI.** V. 1.- ; Jan. 1973-. Periodical. Arabic. Al-Ittihad Al-Ishtiraki Al-Sudani, S B 185, Al-Khartum Sudan. **LC** HX9.A7; I8.

US
**AMERICAN LEGION FIRING LINE, THE. Main/Corp** American Legion. **Added/Corp** American Legion. National Americanism Commission. Vol. 1 (1952)-. Periodical. English. mo (11 issues). $7.00. National Americanism Commission, PO Box 1055, Indianapolis IN 46206. **Tel** (317)630-1200. **LC** HX81; .A54. **DD** 335.405. **Bk Rev. Circ:** 8,500. ***Continues*** *Firing Line.*

UK/0267-6141
**ANARCHIST ENCYCLOPAEDIA.** (THE ANARCHIST ENCYCLOPAEDIA : MONOGRAPH.). [Anarchist encycl.]. No. 1 (Nov. 1985)-. Monographic series. English. bm. Price varies per volume. Cambridge Free Press, 25 Gwydir Street, Cambridge CB1 2LG England.

●UK/0967-3393
**ANARCHIST STUDIES.** Vol. 1, No. 1 (Spring 1993)-. Periodical. English. sa (Spring and Autumn). £32.00. The White Horse Press, 10 High Street, Knapwell, Cambridge CB3 8NR England. **Tel** 011 44 9 547527. **(Subscription address:** White Horse Press, 1 Stronde Isle of Harris, W Isles PA83 3UD Scotland.) **ED** Thomas. V. Cahill, Lancaster University, UK.
**Desc:** Covers all aspects of contemporary anarchist research and theory.

UK/0003-2751
**ANARCHY. Added/Corp** Anarchy Collective (Great Britain). No. 1 (1971)-. Periodical. English. ir. £5.00. Anarchy Magazine, 846 White Chapel High Street, Box A, London E1 England. **LC** HX821; .A5. **Bk Rev. Circ:** 2,000 (ctrl).
**Desc:** Britain's longest running anarchist magazine, with investigative journalism on fascism, the state, counter-insurgency, terrorism, etc., and in-depth analysis of contemporary events from an anarchist perspective.

US/1044-1387
**ANARCHY (COLUMBIA, MO.).** (ANARCHY.). [Anarchy]. **Added/Corp** Columbia Anarchist League (Columbia, Mo.). Vol. 1 No. 1 (Jan. 10, 1980)-. Periodical. English. qt. $18.00. C. A. L. Press, PO Box 1446, Columbia MO 65205. **Tel** (314)442-4352. **DD** 321.
**Ind/Abst** Altern. Press Index (199?-).

IT/0393-3954
**ANNALI - FONDAZIONE GIANGIACOMO FELTRINELLI. Main/Corp** Fondazione Giangiacomo Feltrinelli. **Added/Corp** Fondazione Giangiacomo Feltrinelli. Vol. 16 (1974/75)-. Periodical. Italian (summaries and/or abstracts in English and French). an. Price varies. Feltrinelli Editore, Via Andegari 6, 20121 Milan Italy. **Tel** 011 39 2 866606. **LC** HX15; .M5. **DD** 335. **Circ:** 2,000. ***Continues*** *Annali-Istituto Giangiacomo Feltrinelli, 0544-1374.*
**Desc:** One of the most significant scientific publications on labour movement history in Italy and abroad. Also including descriptions of Feltrinelli Foundation archives and funds.
**Ind/Abst** Am. Hist. Life (1975-).

GW
**ARCHIPELAG : A. VFOAT** A. Periodical. Polish. mo. DM152.10 Europe, $67.60 other. Andrzej Wieckowski, Wilhelmsruher Damm 139, W-1000 Berlin 26 Germany. **Tel** 4151623. **ED** Andrzej Wieckowski. **LC** AP54; .A7. **Bk Rev. Ad Acc. Circ:** 10,000 (ctrl).
**Desc:** Covers socialism, communism, anarchism, utopianism.

AT
**ARENA JOURNAL.** (19??)-. English. Twice a year. 25.00Aus$; 60.00Aus$ combined subscription with Arena Magazine. Arena Publishing Association, PO Box 18, North Carlton Victoria 3054 Australia. **Tel** 011 61 3 4160232. **ED** J. H. Hinkson, G. Sharp, D. White. **Bk Rev**, (Qty: 2). **Ad Acc, Adv Mgr:** G. Rundle. **Circ:** 1,000 (ctrl).

●AT/1039-1010
**ARENA MAGAZINE.** No. 1 (Oct./Nov. 1992)-. Periodical. English. bm. 45.00Aus$ (one year); 80.00Aus$ (two years); 60.00Aus$ Australia, 76.00Aus$ others combined subscription with Arena Journal. Arena Publishing Association, PO Box 18, North Carlton Victoria 3054 Australia. **Tel** 011 61 3 4160232. **Bk Rev**, (Qty: 6). **Ad Acc, Adv Mgr:** G. Rundle. **Circ:** 2,000 (ctrl). ***Continues in part*** *Arena, 0004-0932.*

SP
**ARGUMENTOS.** Vol. 1 No. 1 (May 1977)-. Periodical. Spanish. mo. 1.2000ptas. **LC** HC381; .A8.

RU
**ARGUMENTY (MOSCOW, R.S.F.S.R.).** (ARGUMENTY.). (19??)-. Russian. 0.25rub. Politizdat, A-47 Miusskaia Pl 7, 125811 GSP Moscow Russia. **LC** HX536; .A715.

US/0361-3968
**ASIAN THOUGHT & SOCIETY.** [Asian thought soc.]. **VAT** Asian Thought and Society. V. 1- Apr. 1976-. Periodical. English (French, German and Spanish). Three times a year. $47.00 US; $50.00 other. Asian Thought and Society, University of New York, Department of Political Science, Oneonta NY 13820. **Tel** (607)431-3550, (607)431-3512. **ED** Ignatius J. H. Tsao. **LC** DS1; .A493. **DD** 950/.05. Index available. **Bk Rev. Ad Acc.** available on microfilm and microfiche from University Microfilms International (UMI).
**Desc:** Intellectual development and societal structures and changes in East, South and Southeast Asia.
**Ind/Abst** ABC POL SCI; Am. Hist. Life (1976-); Am. Bibliogr. Slavic East Europ. Stud.; Index Islam. Lit.; Int. Bibliogr. Sociol.; Int. Polit. Sci. Abstr.

SP
**AUTOGESTION Y SOCIALISMO.** No. 1-. Periodical. Spanish. M Castellote, Editor, Rios Rosas, 51 Bajo B, Madrid Spain. **LC** HX9.S7; A93. **DD** 335/.005.

GW
**AUTONOMIE.** German. 6.00 single issue. Trikont-Verlag, Josephburgstr 16, W-8 Munchen 80 Germany. **LC** HX6; .A85.

IT/0404-8172
**BANDIERA ROSSA. Added/Corp** Gruppi Comunisti Rivoluzionari. Sezione Italiana della IV Internazionale. (19??)-. Periodical. Italian. Ten times a year. L30000 Italy; L40000 other. Bandiera Rossa, Via B Varchi 3, 20158 Milan Italy. **Tel** 011 39 2 3760027.

DK
**BIDRAG.** V. 1- (No. 1- ). Danish. 19 single issue. Blabaervej 206, 5260 Jallese Denmark. **LC** HX9.D3; B5.

UK
**BIG RED DIARY.** English. **LC** HX3; .B54. **DD** 335.43/05.

GW
**BIOGRAPHIC DIRECTORY OF SOVIET REGIONAL PARTY LEADERS.** 1st Ed. (Aug. 1987)-. Directory. English. Radio Free Europe, Radio Liberty, 1775 Broadway, New York NY 10019. **Tel** (212)397-5300. **LC** JN6521; .B56. **DD** 354.47/002.

US
**BLACK ROSE. Added/Corp** Black Rose Lectures and Learning. Vol. 1, No. 1 (Spring 1979)-. Periodical. English. qt. $17.00 (institutions), $11.00 (individuals). Black Rose Lectures and Learning, PO Box 1075, Boston MA 02103.
**Ind/Abst** Altern. Press Index.

SZ
**BULLETIN - CENTRE INTERNATIONAL DE RECHERCHES SUR L'ANARCHISME. Main/Corp** Centre International de Recherches sur l'Anarchisme. 29- Spring 1975-. Bulletin. French. sa. 10.00F. Bibliotheque du C I R A, Case Postale 51, CH-1211 Geneve 13 Switzerland. **LC** HX821; .C4A. **DD** 335/.83/05. ***Continues*** *CIRA Bulletin.*

AU
**BULLETIN DER BOLSCHEWIKI-LENINISTEN. Main/Corp** Osterreichische Bolschewiki-Leninisten. (1973)-. German. ir. Bulletin der Bolshewik-Leninisten, 2320 Schwechat, Ehbrungsterg 1. **LC** HX6; .O35a.

UK
**BULLETIN OF THE MARX MEMORIAL LIBRARY - LONDON. VFOAT** MML, Bulletin of the Marx Memorial Library - London. No. 101 (Sept. 1982)-. Bulletin. English. ir (two to three issues per year). £5.00 UK; £9.00 North America; £8.00 other. Marx House, 37A Clerkenwell Green, London ECIR ODU England. **Tel** 01 253 1485. **ED** Mary Rosser. **Bk Rev. Circ:** 2,000 (ctrl). ***Continues*** *Marx Memorial Library Quarterly Bulletin.*

US/0279-0165
**BULLETIN - WORKERS LEAGUE (U.S.). CENTRAL COMMITTEE. *Title Change.*** (BULLETIN : TWICE WEEKLY ORGAN OF THE CENTRAL COMMITTEE OF THE WORKERS LEAGUE.). [Bull. - Work. Leag. (U.S.), Cent. Comm.]. **Added/Corp** Workers League (U.S.). Central Committee. Workers League (U.S.). Began in Oct. (1973)-(1993). Bulletin. English. sw. Labor Publications, PO Box 33023, Detroit MI 48216. **Tel** (313)875-4745. **ED** M McLaughlin. **DD** 324. **Bk Rev. *Continues*** *Bulletin (Workers League (U.S.)), 0894-3028.* ***Continued by*** *International Workers Bulletin, 1068-6575.*
**Desc:** Newspaper of the Workers League, the American Trotskyist movement, with is in solidarity with the International Committee of the Fourth International.

FR/0221-5047
**CAHIERS D'HISTOIRE DE L'INSTITUT DE RECHERCHES MARXISTES. See** History(General)-History of Europe.

FR/0008-0136
**CAHIERS DU COMMUNISME.** [Cah. communisme]. **Added/Corp** Parti Communiste Francais. Comite Central. Vol. 16, No. 7 (July 1939)-. Periodical. French. ir. 333.01F France; $77.93 other. Cahiers du Communisme, 2 Place du Colonel Fabien, 75940 Paris Cedex 19 France. **Tel** 011 33 1 40401304. **LC** HX5; .C26. **DD** 335.405. ***Continues*** *Cahiers du Bolchevisme.*
**Ind/Abst** Int. Dev. Abstr. (?-?).

FR/0181-0790
**CAHIERS LEON TROTSKY.** [Cah. Leon Trotsky]. **Added/Corp** Institut Leon Trotsky. No. 1 (Jan. 1979)-. Periodical. French. qt. 350.00F (institutions), 250.00F (individuals) France; 400.00F (institutions), 250.00F (individuals) other. Paule Gautier, 63 rue Thiers, 3800 Grenoble France. **Tel** 33 76 444303. **ED** Pierre Breue. **LC** HX5; .C276. cum. index. **Circ:** 800.
**Desc:** Publication of texts and documents concerning Leon Trotsky and the open movement.
**Ind/Abst** Am. Hist. Life.

BE
**CAHIERS MARXISTES. VFOAT** C.M.; CM. (19??)-. Periodical. French. Ten times a year. Fondation Joseph Jacquemotte, Avenue de Stalingrad 20, 1000 Brussels Belgium. **LC** HX5; .C28. **DD** 335.4/05.

UY
**CAMINOS.** Vol. 1, No. 1 (Sept. 1991)-. Periodical. Spanish. mo. 2500ru$ per issues. Caminos, Pando 2694, Montevideo Uruguay. **ED** Omar Rovira. **LC** F2729; .C36.

US/0045-4109
**CAMPAIGNER (NEW YORK).** (THE CAMPAIGNER.). V. 1- Sept./Oct. 1973-. Periodical. English. mo (ten no. a year). $19.00. Campaigner Publications Inc, PO Box 9063, McLean VA 22102-0063. **Tel** (703)777-9401. **LC** HX1; .C33. **DD** 320.5/31/05.

YU/0351-4285
**CASOPIS ZA KRITIKO ZNANOSTI. Added/Corp** Univerzitetna Konferenca ZSMS. (19??)-. Slovenian (summaries and/or abstracts in English, French and German). ir.

CC
**CHIEH FANG CHUN HUA PAO. VFOAT** Jiefangjun Huabao. (19??)-. Periodical. Chinese. mo. Science Press, 16 Donghuangchenggen North Street, Beijing 100707, People's Republic of China. **Tel** 011 86 1 4019821, 011 86 1 4010642, FAX 011 86 1 4012180, 011 86 1 4019810, telex 210147. **LC** UA837; .C4478. **DD** 355.1/0951.

US
**CHINAFRICA : A MONTHLY MAGAZINE OF NEWS AND VIEWS. VFOAT** China Africa. (19??)-. Periodical. English. mo. $14.00. **(Subscription address:** China International Book Trading Corporation, PO Box 399, Library Service Department, Beijing 100044 People's Republic of China.)
**Desc:** Highlights new developments in China's politics and economic construction and the new experiences of the Chinese people in building socialism.

US/0195-9387
**CHRISTIAN ANTI-COMMUNISM CRUSADE. Main/Corp** Christian Anti-Communism Crusade. 1961-. Periodical. English. sm. Free. Christian Anti-Communism, PO Box 890, 227 East 6th Street, Long Beach CA 90801. **Tel** (310)437-0941. **ED** Fred C Schwarz. **Circ:** 55,000. available on microfilm and microfiche from University Microfilms International (UMI).
**Desc:** Accurate, up-to-date, documented information concerning doctrines, organizations, methods, programs and objectives of communism, both within the United States and internationally.

UK/0009-5648
**CHRISTIAN SOCIALIST, THE. Added/Corp** Christian Socialist Movement. No. 15 (1963)-. Periodical. English. Four times a year. £6.00. Christian Socialist Movement, 36 Cross Flatts Avenue, Leeds LS11 7BG England. **LC** HX51; .C47. **DD** 335/.7/05. ***Continues*** *CSM News.*

CH/0014-9667
**CHUNG KUNG YEN CHIU = STUDIES ON CHINESE COMMUNISM. Added/Corp** Chung Kung Yen Chiu Tsa Chih She. **VFOAT** Studies on Chinese Communism. Vol. 3, No. 5 (May 1969)-. Periodical. Chinese. mo. $53.00. Institute for Study of Chinese Communist Problems, PO Box 351, Tapei Tawian. **Tel** 011 886 3 832-5726. ***Continues*** *Fei Ching Yen Chiu.*

CH
**CHUNG-KUO CHING NIEN (PEKING, CHINA : 1948).** (CHUNG-KUO CHING NIEN.). **VFOAT** Zhongguo Quignian. Began in 1948. Periodical. Chinese. mo. $6.21. Science Press, 16 Donghuangchenggen North Street, Beijing 100707, People's Republic of China. **Tel** 011 86 1 4019821, 011 86 1 4010642, FAX 011 86 1 4012180, 011 86 1 4019810, telex 210147. **LC** HX9.C5; C56. **DD** 305.2/35/0951. ***Continues*** *Chung-Kuo Ching Nien.*

IT
**CITTA FUTURA, LA.** Vol. 1 (May 11, 1977)-. Periodical. Italian. L17500. Federazione Giovanile Comunista Italian, Conto Corrente N 24124000, La Citta Futura Via Delle Vite 13, 001 Rome Italy. **LC** HX547; .C53.

NE/0030-3283
**CIVIS MUNDI. Added/Corp** Oost-West Instituut (Hague, Netherlands) Stichting Civis Mundi (Hague, Netherlands). (Jan. 1971)-. Periodical. Dutch. qt. Fl41.98 (individuals) Netherlands; Fl45.28 (individuals), Fl54.72 (institutions) other. Stichting Civis Mundi, Akkerwindestraat 23, 3051 La Rotterdam Netherlands. **Tel** 011 31 10 4182580. **LC** AP15; .O54. cum. index. **Bk Rev. Ad Acc. *Continues*** *Oost-West.*

US
**CLASS STRUGGLE.** No. 1 (Spring 1975)-. English. Four times a year. $6.00. Class Struggle, PO Box 5539, Chicago IL 60680.

UK
**COMBAT. Main/Corp** Communist League (Gt. Brit.). No. 1- March 1975-. English. qt. Communist League, 26 Cambridge Road, Ilford Essex England.

UK
**COMMUNES.** (19??)-. Periodical. English. bm. Commune Movement, 3 Russell Way, Wotton Bedford England. **DD** 335.

FR/0751-3496
**COMMUNISME (PARIS, FRANCE : 1982).** (COMMUNISME.). (1982)-. Periodical. French (English). qt. 244.86F France; $54.37 other. Editions l'Age d'Homme / France, 5 rue Ferou, 75006 Paris France. **Tel** 011 33 1 46341851, FAX 011 33 1 40517102. **ED** Monsieur Stephane Courtois. **LC** HX5; .C56. **DD** 335.43/0944. **Bk Rev. Circ:** 800.
**Desc:** A title of history, sociology and political science that studies the communist phenomenon in a scientific way.
**Ind/Abst** Int. Bibliogr. Sociol.; Int. Polit. Sci. Abstr.

●UK/0967-067X
**COMMUNIST AND POST-COMMUNIST STUDIES. VFOAT** Communist and Post Communist Studies. Vol. 26, No. 1 (Mar. 1993)-. Periodical. English. qt. $179.00 The Americas; £120.00 other. Butterworth Heinemann Publishers, Linacre House, Jordan Hill, Oxford OX2 8DP England. **Tel** 011 44 865 310366. **(Subscription address:** Elsevier Science Ltd. Oxford Fulfillment Centre, PO Box 800, Kidlington, Oxford OX5 1DX United Kingdom.) **LC** HX1; .S74. **DD** 335.43/05.

***Continues*** *Studies in Comparative Communism, 0039-3592.*
**Ind/Abst** ABC POL SCI; Acad. Search (Mar. 1993-); Int. Polit. Sci. Abstr.; Mag. Artic. Summar. Elite (Mar. 1993-); Mag. Artic. Summar. CD-ROM (March 1993-); Soc. Sci. Cit. Index.

FR
**COMMUNIST PROGRAM : ORGAN OF THE INTERNATIONAL COMMUNIST PARTY.** No. 1 (Oct. 1975)-. Periodical. English. an. $4.00. Editions Programme, 20 rue Jean-Bouton, Paris France 75012. **LC** HX3; .C77. **DD** 324/.1.

US/0148-2998
**COMMUNIST STATES AND DEVELOPING COUNTRIES, AID AND TRADE.** **Main/Corp** United States. Dept. of State. Bureau of Intelligence and Research. English. an. US Department of State / Bureau of Intelligence and Research, 2201 C Street Northwest, Room 6533, Washington DC 20520. **Tel** (202)647-9176. **LC** HC60; .U4846. **DD** 338.91/172/401717.

CN/0709-3845
**COMMUNISTE (MONTREAL).** (LE COMMUNISTE.). **Added/Corp** Parti Communiste du Quebec. Vol. 1 (Jan./Feb./March 1979)-. Periodical. French. qt. 10.00Can$ Canada; 15.00Can$ other. Communiste, 4164 rue Parthenais, Montreal Quebec H2K 3T9 Canada. **Tel** (514)524-2896. **DD** 335.43/05.

CN/0229-1185
**CORRESPONDANCE INTERNATIONALE (MONTREAL).** (CORRESPONDANCE INTERNATIONALE.). [Corresp. int.]. **Added/Corp** Union Bolchevique du Canada. No. 1 (Spring/Summer 1980)-. Periodical. French. qt. $3.50 per no. Correspondance Internationale, CP 892 Succursale Tour de la Bourse, Montreal Quebec H4Z 1K2 Canada. **DD** 335.43/05.

US/0010-955X
**COSMOPOLITAN CONTACT.** Periodical. English. ir. $5.00. Cosmopolitan Contact, PO Box 1566, Fontana CA 92335. **ED** Romulus Rexner. **Bk Rev. Ad Acc. Circ:** 1,500.
**Desc:** A polyglot magazine with worldwide circulation, established in 1961 by Planetary Legion for Peace to promote intercultural understanding and bonds of spiritual unity by means of contacts.

IT/0011-152X
**CRITICA MARXISTA.** Vol. 1 (Jan./Feb. 1963)-. Periodical. Italian. bm (6 issues). L60000 Italy; L100000 other. Ciemme Ed, Via Dei Polacchi 41, 00186 Rome Italy. **Tel** 011 39 6 6789680. **LC** HX7; .C78. cum. index. **Ad Acc. Circ:** 6,000 (ctrl).
**Desc:** Reflections on the leading idea of the present, political theory, economy and culture.
**Ind/Abst** Int. Bibliogr. Sociol.; Int. Polit. Sci. Abstr.

IT/0011-1538
**CRITICA SOCIALE.** [Crit. soc.]. (1891)-. Periodical. Italian. Ten times a year. L60000.00 Italy; L120000.00 other. Critica Sociale, Via Olmetto 5, 20123 Milan Italy. **Tel** 011 39 2 86450005. ***Supersedes*** *Cuore e Critica.*

FR
**CRITIQUE COMMUNISTE.** **Added/Corp** Ligue Communiste Revolutionnaire. Nos 8/9 (Sept./Oct. 1976)-No. 34 (July 1981); New Series, No 1 (Oct. 1981)-. Periodical. French. mo. 235.06F France; 300.00F other. Presse Edition Communication, 2 rue Richard Lenoir, 93108 Montreuil France. **Tel** 011 33 1 48590080. **LC** HX5; .C69. **DD** 335.43/05. **Bk Rev. *Continues*** *Marx ou Creve.*
**Desc:** Review of political analysis on French and foreign political life.

UK/0261-0183
**CSP. CRITICAL SOCIAL POLICY.** (CRITICAL SOCIAL POLICY : CSP.). [CSP, Crit. soc. policy]. **VFOAT** CSP. Vol. 1, No. 1 (Summer 1981)-. Periodical. English. Three times a year. £56.00 Europe; £59.00 Other (Institutions). Longman Group Ltd., Fourth Avenue, Longman House, Harlow Essex CM19 5SR England. **Tel** 011 44 279 429655, FAX 011 44 279 431059, telex 81259. **ED** Norman Ginsburg. **[CCC].** Index available. cum. index. **Bk Rev. Ad Acc. Circ:** 1,700. available on microfilm and microfiche from University Microfilms International (UMI). Documents available.
**Desc:** Presents an analysis of social policy and welfare issues from a socialist viewpoint.
**Ind/Abst** Geogr. Abstr. Human Geogr.; Linguist. Lang. Behav. Abstr.; Multicult. Educ. Abstr.; PAIS Int. Print (1991-); School Organ. Manage. Abstr.; Soc. Plann. Policy Dev. Abstr.; Sociol. Abstr.; Stud. Women Abstr.

CU
**CUBA SOCIALISTA (HAVANA, CUBA : 1981).** (CUBA SOCIALISTA.). Began in 1981. Periodical. Spanish (summaries and/or abstracts in English and French). bm. $14.00 North America; $16.00 South America; $17.00 Europe; $24.00 other. Ediciones Cubanas, Obispo 527, Altos ESQ Bernaza, CP 10100 Havana Cuba. **Tel** 011 632980, 631942, FAX 011 631011, telex 512337, 6540.
**Desc:** Realizes and exposes the analysis of the political, economic, and social reality of Cuba and that of the international life of today.

US/0196-0830
**CUBA UPDATE.** (CUBA UPDATE : A PUBLICATION OF THE CENTER FOR CUBAN STUDIES.). [Cuba update]. **Added/Corp** Center for Cuban Studies. **VFOAT** Main Report, Second Congress of the Communist Party of Cuba. Vol. 1, No. 1 (Apr. 1980)-. Periodical. English. Four times a year. $45.00 (institutions), $35.00 (individuals). Center for Cuban Studies, 124 West 23rd Street, New York NY 10011. **Tel** (212)242-0559. **LC** F1751; .C9855. **DD** 972.91/005. **Bk Rev. Ad Acc.** ctrl circ. ***Continues*** *Cuba Update, 0196-0830;* ***Absorbed*** *Cuba in Focus, 0197-5277.*
**Desc:** Provides current information on Cuba, US-Cuba relations, the economy, the arts, health care, etc.
**Ind/Abst** Hum. Rights Intern. Rep.

US/0590-3890
**CURRENT SOVIET POLICIES.** **Added/Corp** Kommunisticheskaia Partiia Sovetskogo Soiuza. S"ezd. American Association for the Advancement of Slavic Studies. (1953)-. English. ir (Published every 5 years). $12.50 each (Vols. 5-8). Current Digest of the Soviet Press, 3857 North High Street, Columbus OH 43214. **Tel** (614)292-4234, FAX (614)267-6310. **LC** IN PROCESS.
**Desc:** Covers the post-World War II Congresses of the CPSU.

US
**DANDELION, THE.** (Spring 1977)-. Periodical. English. ir. $4.50. Michael Coughlin, 1985 Selby Avenue, St Paul MN 55104. **Tel** (612)646-8917. **ED** Michael E. Coughlin. **Circ:** 400.
**Desc:** An anarchist journal with articles on history, political thought, and individuals.

AG
**DEFENSA DEL MARXISMO, EN.** Vol. 1, No. 1 (Oct. 1991)-. Periodical. Spanish.

RU/0236-0942
**DIALOG (MOSCOW, R.S.F.S.R.).** (DIALOG : ZHURNAL TSK KPSS.). **Added/Corp** TSK KPSS. Vol. 1 (1990)-. Periodical. Russian. mo. $89.95. Izdatelstvo Pressa, Myasnitskaia 24, 101877 Moscow Russia. **Tel** 011 95 923 2122, FAX 011 95 200 2259. **(Subscription address:** East View Publications Inc., 3020 Harbor Lane North, Suite 110, Minneapolis MN 55447.) **LC** DK266.A2; D49. **CODEN** DIALEQ. ***Formed by the union of*** *Politicheskoe Obrazovanie, 0235-327X and Agitator (Moscow, R.S.F.S.R.), 0320-7161.*

US/0012-3846
**DISSENT (NEW YORK).** (DISSENT.). [Dissent]. Vol. 1 (Winter 1954)-. Periodical. English. qt (Jan., Apr., July, Oct.). $30.00 (one year), $50.00 (two year) institutions, $22.00 (one year), $40.00 (two year) individuals. Foundation for the Study of Independent Social Ideas, 521 Fifth Avenue, New York NY 10017. **Tel** (212)595-3084. **ED** Irving Howe and Michael Walzer. **LC** HX1; .D58. **DD** 335.05. Index available. cum. index. **Bk Rev. Ad Acc. Pr Rev. Circ:** 10,000. available on microfilm and microfiche from University Microfilms International (UMI). Documents available from UMI Article Clearinghouse, The Genuine Article.
**Desc:** A magazine of political and social concern. It stands for unyielding opposition to all forms of authoritarianism, with an emphasis on the importance of democratic values.
**Ind/Abst** ABC POL SCI; Acad. Abstr. Full Text Elite (March 1987-June 1989); Acad. Abstr. (Mar. 1987-June 1989); Acad. Ind. [Computer File] (1987-); Acad. Search (Mar. 1987-June 1989); Altern. Press Index; Am. Hist. Life (1968-1988); Am. Bibliogr. Slavic East Europ. Stud.; Arts Humanit. Citation Index [Select. Cov.]; Book Rev. Index; Expand. Acad. Index (1985-); Film Lit. Index; Index Period. Artic. Relat. Law (19??-19??); INFO-SOUTH Abstr.; Int. Bibliogr. Sociol.; Int. Polit. Sci. Abstr.; Left Index; Linguist. Lang. Behav. Abstr.; Mag. Artic. Summar. Elite (March 1987-June 1989); Mag. Artic. Summar. Select (March 1987-June 1989); Mag. Artic. Summar. CD-ROM (March 1987-June 1989); Mag. Search; Middle East Abstr. Index; Newsp. Period. Abstr. (1990-); PAIS Int. Print (1991-); Peace Res. Abstr. J. (1963-1967); Res. Alert [Full Cov.]; Soc. Plann. Policy Dev. Abstr.; Soc. Sci. Source (Mar. 1987-Jun. 1989); Soc. Sci. Cit. Index [Full Cov.]; Soc. Sci. Index; Soc. Sci. Index Fulltext (Fall 1988-) [Full Txt.]; Soc. Work Abstr. (Spring, Summer 1987-?) [Select. Cov.]; Sociol. Abstr.; West. Hist. Q.

CH
**EAST ASIA QUARTERLY.** (19??)-. Periodical. English. qt. $8.00. Institute of International Relations, Editorial and Publishing Section, 64 Wan Shou Road Mucha, Taipei Taiwan. Index available. **Ad Acc. Circ:** 1,500.
**Desc:** Devoted to East Asian politics with emphasis on the Communist movement in the area.

FR/0424-3226
**ECONOMIE ET SOCIALISME.** **See** Economics.

US
**ELTA INFORMATION BULLETIN / OF THE SUPREME COMMITTEE FOR LIBERATION OF LITHUANIA.** **Added/Corp** ELTA. Vyriausias Lietuvos Islaisvinimo Komitetas. Lithuanian National Foundation (U.S.). (1956)-. Bulletin. English. mo. **LC** DK502.3; .E38.
**Ind/Abst** Hum. Rights Intern. Rep.

RM
**ERA SOCIALISTA.** ***Ceased.*** (19??-19??). Periodical. Romanian. Rompres-Filatelia Serviciul Import-Export-Presa, Calea Grivitei NR 64-66, POB 2001, Bucharest Romania. **LC** HX8; .L8. ***Continues*** *Lupta de Clasa.*
**Desc:** Theoretical and socio-political magazine of the Central Committee of the Romanian Communist Party.

FR/0014-1267
**EST & OUEST.** ***Ceased.*** **Added/Corp** Association d'Etudes et d'Informations Politiques Internationales. Association d'Etudes et d'Informations Politiques Internationales. B.E.I.P.I. **VAT** Est et Ouest. Vol. 1 No. 1 (Apr. 1949)-(19??). Periodical. French. sm. Est et Quest, 53 rue Sainte Anne, 75002 Paris France. **Tel** 011 33 1 46140937. **ED** M. Morvan Duhamel. **LC** D839; .A822. **DD** 327/.0904. Index available. cum. index.
**Desc:** Journal of international political studies.

UK
**EUROPE ASIA STUDIES.** (19??)-. English. Six times a year. £133.00 (EEC countries); £148.00 (other except US & Canada). Carfax Publishing Company, PO Box 25 Abingdon, Oxfordshire OX14 3UE England. **Tel** 011 44 235 555335, FAX (0279)31067, telex 817484. **(Subscription address:** US and Canada/ PO Box 2025, Dunnellon, FL 34430-2025; telephone:(904)489-6996**)** ***Continues*** *Soviet Studies, 0038-5859.*
**Ind/Abst** Curr. Contents Soc. Behav. Sci.; Curr. Geogr. Publ. (19??-); Mag. Search.

FR
**EVENEMENT EUROPEEN, L'.** Vol. 1; 1988-. Periodical. French. qt. Editions du Seuil, 27 rue Jacob, 75261 Paris Cedex 06 France. **Tel** 011 33 1 69092409 or, 40465050. **LC** HX236; .E93. **DD** 335/.0094.
**Ind/Abst** PAIS Int. Print.

RU
**EXPERIENCE OF THE SOVIET COMMUNIST PARTY.** **Added/Corp** Kommunisticheskaia Partiia Sovetskogo Soiuza. (19??)-. Monographic series. English. Price varies per volume. Novosti Press Agency Publishing House, 4 Zubovski Boulevard, Moscow Russia. **Tel** 095-201-2424, FAX 095-201-2119, telex 411321.

UK
**FABIAN REVIEW.** **Added/Corp** Fabian Society (Great Britain). Vol. 103, No. 1 (Jan 1991)-. Periodical. English. bm (Feb., Apr., June, Aug., Oct. Dec.). £17.00. Fabian Society, 11 Dartmouth Street, London SW1H 9BN England. **Tel** 011 44 071 2228877, FAX 011 44 071 9767153. **ED** Stephen Pollard. **LC** HX3; .F2. **Bk Rev**, (Qty: 6). **Ad Acc, Adv Mgr:** T. Upton. **Circ:** 6,000. ***Continues*** *Fabian News.*

US/0015-0800
**FIFTH ESTATE.** [Fifth estate]. (1966)-. Periodical. English. qt (Jan., Apr., July, Oct.). $10.00. The Fifth Estate, 4632 Second Avenue, Detroit MI 48202. **Tel** (313)831-6800. **Bk Rev**, (Qty: 10). **Circ:** 5000. available on microfilm from University Microfilms International (UMI).
**Desc:** Journal of radical anarchy which views state and capitalism along with technology and modernity as the enemy of human freedom. Seeks solutions in a decentralized, stateless society in which cooperation and freedom replace coercion and hierarchy. Models seen in primitive and other pre-technological cultures.
**Ind/Abst** Altern. Press Index.

BW/0868-6718
**FILOSOFIIA I SOVREMENNYI MIR / MINISTERSTVO NARODNOGO OBRAZOVANIIA BSSR [I] BELORUSSKII ORDENA TRUDOVOGO KRASNOGO ZNAMENI GOSUDARSTVENNYI UNIVERSITET IMENI V.I. LENINA.**
**Added/Corp** Byelorussian S.S.R. Ministerstvo Narodnogo Obrazovaniia. Belaruski Dziarzhauny Universitet Imia Ul.I. Lenina. (1990)-. Periodical. Russian. **LC** HX8; .F48. ***Continues*** *Filosofiia i Nauchnyi Kommunizm.*

KZ/0320-5452
**FILOSOFSKIE NAUKI (ALMA-ATA).** **See** Philosophy.

CN/0703-4520
**FORGE (MONTREAL).** (THE FORGE.). **VFOAT** Forge. V. 1- Dec. 1975-. Periodical. English (French). bw. $7.00. Canadian Communist League, PO Box 364, Station Place D'Armes, Montreal Quebec H2Y 3H2 Canada. **DD** 335.43/0971.

CN/0703-4539
**FORGE (MONTREAL. EDITION FRANCAISE).** (LA FORGE.). **VFOAT** Forge. V. 1- Dec. 1975-. Periodical. French (English). bw. 0.25Can$ per no. Ligue Communiste, CP 364, Montreal Quebec H2Y 3H2 Canada. **DD** 335.43/0971.

CN/0229-172X
**FORO INTERNACIONAL (IN STRUGGLE (ORGANIZATION)).** (FORO INTERNACIONAL : POR LA UNIDAD DEL MOVIMIENTO MARXISTA-LENINISTA.). V. 1, No. 1 (April 1980)-. Periodical. Spanish. ir. $9.00 Canada and US; 36.00F France. May First Distribution, 1407 D'Iberville Street, Montreal Quebec H2K 3B1 Canada. **DD** 320.5/322/05.

US/0015-9204
**FOURTH INTERNATIONAL (LONDON, ENGLAND).** **See** Political Science.

HT
**FRATERNITE (PARTI SOCIAL CHRETIENE D'HAITI).** (FRATERNITE / ORGANE DU PARTI SOCIAL CHRETIENE D'HAITI.). **Added/Corp** Parti Social Chretiene d'Haiti. (197?)-. Periodical. French. mo. Le Parti, 17 Fontamara, PO Box 609, Port-Au-Prince Haiti. **ED** G Eugene.

US/0272-4367
**FREEDOM SOCIALIST, THE.** [Freedom social.]. **Added/Corp** Freedom Socialist Party (U.S.). Vol. 1 (Aug. 1966)-. Newspaper. English (Spanish). qt. $5.00 (individual), $10.00 (institution) US; $10.00 other. The Freedom Socialist, New Freeway Hall, 5018 Rainier Avenue South, Seattle WA 98118-1927. **Tel** (206)722-2453, FAX (206)723-7691. **ED** Andrea Bauer. Index available (Published separately). **Bk Rev. Circ:** 5,000 (ctrl). available on microfiche (University of Washington, Seattle).
**Desc:** The voice of revolutionary socialist feminism.
**Ind/Abst** Altern. Press Index (-1985); Left Index.

UK/0951-7677
**FRONTIER.** **Added/Corp** Keston College. (Mar.-Apr. 1987)-. Periodical. English. bm. £17.95 UK and Europe; £17.95 (surface mail), £22.95 (air mail) other. Keston College, Heathfield Road, Keston Kent BR2 6BA England. **Tel** 011 44 0689 850116, FAX (0689)53662, telex 897684 KESCOL. **LC** HX536; .F857. **DD** 335.43/05.
**Desc:** Study of religious life in the former Soviet Union and eastern Europe.
**Ind/Abst** Am. Hist. Life (1971-1972); Hum. Rights Intern. Rep.

CN/1183-2053
**GAUCHE, LA.** [Gauche]. No 1 (Feb. 1991)-. Periodical. French. mo. 10.00Can$ per year. Nouvelles Publications Internationales, Bureau 907, 3575 Rue St-Laurent, Montreal Quebec H2X 2T7 Canada. **DD** 335.43/09714/05.

CN/0823-9177
**GAUCHE SOCIALISTE.** [Gauche social.]. Vol. 1, No. 1 (Mar. 1984)-. Periodical. French. mo. 20.00Can$. Gauche Socialiste NPI, 3575 Boulevard St-Laurent/Suite 908 Canada. **Tel** (514)845-6797. **DD** 320.5/31/05. **Circ:** 1,000.
**Desc:** On issues and topics of international and local political actuality; on worker's, youth's and women's movements; on national liberation and anti-imperialist struggles.

JA
**GEKKAN SHAKAITO.** **Added/Corp** Nihon Shakaito (1945- ). **VFOAT** Shakaito. (1957)-. Periodical. Japanese. ¥250. Nihon Shakaito Kikanshikyoku, 8-1 Nagatacho 1-chome Chiyoda-ku, Tokyo Japan. **LC** HX411; .G44.

AT/1036-126X
**GREEN LEFT WEEKLY.** **VFOAT** Green Left; GL; GLW. No. 1 (Feb. 18, 1991)-. Periodical. English. Forty-Four times a year. 80.00Aus$ (institutions), 50.00Aus$ (individuals). Green Left, PO Box 394, Broadway NSW 2007 Australia. **Tel** 02 690 1230.

US/0017-3983
**GREEN REVOLUTION (YORK, PA.).** (GREEN REVOLUTION.). [Green revolut.]. **Added/Corp** School of Living (York, Pa.). (19??)-. Periodical. English. qt (Mar., June, Sept., Dec.). $20.00 (US); $22.00 (Canada); $24.00 (other). Green Revolution / School of Living, Route 1 Box 185A, Cochranville PA 19330. **Tel** (215) 593-6988. **ED** Tom Greco and Ginny Green. **DD** 051. **Bk Rev,** (Qty: 1). **Circ:** 400 (ctrl). ***Continues*** *The Interpreter; Balanced Living, 0404-6749.*
**Desc:** Cooperative alternatives to the present economy, such as land trusts and local money systems. Decentralization of government and industry. Self reliant nutritional gardening and global peace plans.
**Ind/Abst** Altern. Press Index (-199?).

US/0894-4547
**GUIDE TO THE AMERICAN LEFT (KANSAS CITY, MO. 1984).** **See** Political Science-Abstracting, Bibliographies and Statistics.

DR
**HABLAN LOS COMUNISTAS.** Vol. 1, No. 1 (June 1978)-. Periodical. Spanish. St Andres Hirujo, c/o Partido Comunista Dom, Av Independ 258 Dominica.

SO
**HALGAN : ORGAN OF THE SOMALI REVOLUTIONARY SOCIALIST PARTY.** **VFOAT** Struggle. Vol. 1, No. 1 (Oct. 1976)-. Periodical. English. $30.00. Somali Revolutionary Socialist Party, Peoples Hall, PO Box 1204, Mogadishu SRD Somalia. **LC** DT407; .H34. **DD** 967/.73005.

GW/0138-1091
**HALLESCHE STUDIEN ZUR GESCHICHTE DER SOZIALDEMOKRATIE.** **Added/Corp** Martin-Luther-Universitat Halle-Wittenberg. Forschungsgruppe Sozialdemokratie. (197?)-. Periodical. German. Martin-Luther-Universitat Halle-Wittenberg, August-Bebel-Strasse 13, DDR-4010 Halle Germany. **Tel** 895 271, telex 04 353 UNI HAL DD. **LC** HX6; .H34. **DD** 335.5/05.

PL
**IDEOLOGIA I POLITYKA.** Polish. 72.00. Wiejska 12, Warszawa Poland. **LC** HX40; .I38.

IT
**IN FORMAZIONE.** **Added/Corp** Istituto Storico Della Resistenza in Toscana. **VFOAT** Informazione. Anno 1, N. 1 (Magg. 1982)-. Periodical. Italian. sa.

BE
**INTERNATIONAAL MARXISTISCH TIJDSCHRIFT.** Periodical. Dutch. mo. 40F single issue. Institut voor Marxistische Vorming, Stalingraadlaan 18-20, 1000 Brussels Belgium. **LC** HX9.D8; I59.

CN/0228-9962
**INTERNATIONAL CORRESPONDANCE (MONTREAL).** (INTERNATIONAL CORRESPONDANCE.). [Int. corresp.]. **Added/Corp** Bolshevik Union of Canada. No. 1 (Spring-Summer 1980)-. Periodical. English. qt. $3.50 per issue. International Correspondance, PO Box 892, Succursale Tour de la Bourse, Montreal Quebec H4Z 1K2 Canada. **DD** 335.43/05.

CN/0227-633X
**INTERNATIONAL FORUM (EN LUTTE (ORGANISATION)).** (INTERNATIONAL FORUM : POUR L'UNITE DU MOUVEMENT MARXISTE-LENINISTE.). [Int. forum unite mouvement marx.-leniniste]. V. 1, No. 1, (April 1980)-. Periodical. French. ir. $8.00 Canada. Organisation Marxiste-Leniniste Du Canada, 1407 Rue D'Iberville, Montreal Quebec H2K 3B1. **DD** 320.5/322/05.

GW
**INTERNATIONALE, DIE.** Periodical. German. DM1.00 single issue. Verlag Arbeiterkampf, Rutschbahn 35, W-2000 Hamburg 13 Germany. **LC** HX6; .I5434.

UN/0135-2202
**ISTORYCHNI DOSLIDZHENNIA. ISTORIIA ZARUBIZHNYKH KRAIN / AKADEMIIA NAUK UKRAINSKOI RSR, INSTYTUT ISTORII.** **See** History(General).

RU
**IZ ISTORII SOTSIALISTICHESKOGO I KOMMUNISTICHESKOGO STROITELSTVA V SSSR.** **Added/Corp** Institut Istorii SSSR (Akademiia Nauk SSSR). (19??)-. Academic Scholarly Publication. Russian. 0.80rub single issue. Izdatelstvo Nauka / Akademiia Nauk, Publishing House of the Russian Academy of Sciences, Leninskii Porspekt 14, 117901 Moscow Russia. **Tel** 011 95 954-21-53, FAX 011 95 938-21-44, telex 411964. **LC** DK266; .I96.

US/0449-0754
**JOHN BIRCH SOCIETY BULLETIN, THE.** [John Birch Society bull.]. **VFOAT** JBS Bulletin. No. 193 (April 1975)-. Bulletin. English. mo. $20.00 North America; $32.00 (airmail) other. John Birch Society, PO Box 8040, Appleton WI 54913. **Tel** (414)749-3780. **LC** E740.J6; A24. **DD** 324. available on microfilm from The State Historical Society of Wisconsin. ***Continues*** *Bulletin (John Birch Society).*

UK/0268-4535
**JOURNAL OF COMMUNIST STUDIES, THE.** ***Title Change.*** [J. communist stud.]. Vol. 1, No. 1 March (1985)-(19??). Periodical. English. qt. Frank Cass & Company Ltd, Newbury House, 890-900 Eastern Avenue, Newbury Park, Ilford, Essex IG2 7HH United Kingdom. **Tel** 011 44 81 599 8866, FAX 011 44 81 599 0984, telex 897719. **ED** Michael Waller and Richard Gillespie. **LC** HX3; .J65. **DD** 335.43/05. available on microfilm and microfiche from University Microfilms International (UMI). ***Continued by*** *The Journal of Communist Studies and Transitional Politics.*
**Desc:** Devotes particular attention to the ongoing process of transformation and reform and aims to provide a perspective within which current events can be understood.
**Ind/Abst** ABC POL SCI; Am. Hist. Life (1987-?); Br. Humanit. Index; Geogr. Abstr. Human Geogr.; Int. Bibliogr. Sociol.; Int. Dev. Abstr.; Int. Polit. Sci. Abstr. (1988-?).

UK
**JOURNAL OF COMMUNIST STUDIES AND TRANSITION POLITICS, THE.** English. qt. $160.00. Frank Cass & Company Ltd, Newbury House, 890-900 Eastern Avenue, Newbury Park, Ilford, Essex IG2 7HH United Kingdom. **Tel** 011 44 81 599 8866, FAX 011 44 81 599 0984, telex 897719. ***Continues*** *Journal of Communist Studies, 0268-4535.*

IS/5792-7290
**KIBBUTZ TRENDS.** **Added/Corp** Yad Tabenkin. Kibbutz Study Center (Efal, Israel) Berit Ha-Tenuah Hakibutsit. (1991)-. English. qt (Mar., June, Sept., Dec.). IL30.00 Israel; $21.00 (surface mail), $29.00 (airmail) other. Kibbutz Trends, Yad Tabenkin, Efal Seminar Center, Ramat Efal 52960 Israel. **Tel** 011 972 3 343311, FAX 011 972 3 346376. **ED** Idit Paz & Ruth Lacey. **LC** HX742.2.A3; K4932. **DD** 307.77/6/05. **Bk Rev. Ad Acc. Circ:** 1,500. ***Formed by the union of*** *Kibbutz Currents and Kibbutz Studies, 0333-6379.*
**Desc:** Information on life and culture inside a kibbutz.

IS
**KIBUTS, HA-.** **VFOAT** Kibbutz. Vol. 1 July (1973)-. Hebrew (summaries and/or abstracts in English). Ha-Rashut Le-Haskalah Ve-Heker, Shel Berit Ha-Tenuah Ha-Kibutsit, POB 303, Tel-Aviv Israel. **LC** HX765.P3; K513.
**Ind/Abst** Soc. Plann. Policy Dev. Abstr.; Sociol. Abstr. (?-?).

CN/0823-6526
**KICK IT OVER.** [Kick it over]. **Added/Corp** Kick It Over Collective. (1981)-. Periodical. English. qt. 9.00Can$ individuals; 15.00Can$ other. Kick It Over, PO Box 5811 Station A, Toronto Ontario M5W 1P2 Canada. **Tel** (416)654-0113. **ED** Bob Melcombe. **DD** 335/.83/05. **Bk Rev,** (Qty: 6-10). **Circ:** 1,300.
**Desc:** Covers native struggles, cultural politics, alternative economics, strategies for social change. Promotes new living order based on personal responsibility and mutual cooperation.
**Ind/Abst** Altern. Press Index.

AU
**KOMMUNIST.** **Added/Corp** Kommunistischer Bund Osterreichs. Vol. 1 (Aug. 1976)-. German. $5.00 single issue. **LC** HX6; .K542. ***Supersedes*** *Kommunist.*

LI/0321-2114
**KOMMUNIST.** **Added/Corp** Lietuvos Komunistu Partija. Centro Komitetas. (1946)-. Periodical. Russian. mo. $19.00. **(Subscription address:** **Victor Kamkin, 4956 Boiling Brook Parkway, Rockville MD 20852.)**

LV/0321-2092
**KOMMUNIST SOVETSKOJ LATVII.** ***Ceased.*** (KOMMUNIST SOVETSKOI LATVII : OBSHCHESTVENNO-POLITICHESKII ZHURNAL TSK KOMMUNISTICHESKOI PARTII LATVII.). [Kommunist Sov. Latvii]. **Added/Corp** Latvijas Komunistiska Partija. Centrala Komiteja. (1952)-(199?). Periodical. Russian. mo. **(Subscription address:** Victor Kamkin, 4956 Boiling Brook Parkway, Rockville MD 20852.**)** ***Continues*** *Bolshevik Sovetskoi Latvii.*

UN/0130-2434
**KOMUNIST UKRAINY.** [Komunist Ukr.]. **Added/Corp** Komunistychna Partiia Ukrainy. Tsentralnyi Komitet. (1946)-. Periodical. Ukrainian. mo. $12.00. **(Subscription address:** Victor Kamkin, 4956 Boiling Brook Parkway, Rockville MD 20852.**)** **LC** HX8; .K586. ***Continues*** *Bilshovyk Ukrainy.*

US/0094-582X
**LATIN AMERICAN PERSPECTIVES.** [Lat. Am. perspect.]. Vol. 1, Issue 1 (Spring 1974)-. Periodical. English. qt (Jan., Apr., July, Oct.). $153.00. SAGE Periodical Press, 2455 Teller Road, Thousand Oaks CA 91320. **Tel** (805)499-0721, FAX (805)499-0871, telex 100799. **ED** Ronald H. Chilcote (University of California, Riverside). **LC** F1401; .L335. **DD** 320.9/8/003. **Bk Rev. Ad Acc. Pr Rev. Acid Free. Circ:** 1,800. available on microfilm and microfiche from University Microfilms International (UMI). Documents available from The Genuine Article, UMI Article Clearinghouse.
**Desc:** Publishes discussions, debates and critical issues relating to capitalism, imperialism and socialism as they affect individuals, societies and nations throughout the Americas.
**Ind/Abst** ABC POL SCI; Acad. Abstr. Full Text Elite (Jan. 1992-); Acad. Abstr. (Jan. 1992-); Acad. Search (Jan. 1992-); Altern. Press Index; Am. Hist. Life (1974-); Arts Humanit. Citation Index [Select. Cov.]; Curr. Contents Soc. Behav. Sci.; Expand. Acad. Index (1989-); Geogr. Abstr. Human Geogr.; HAPI Hisp. Am. Period. Index; Hum. Resour. Abstr. (?-?); INFO-SOUTH Abstr.; Int. Dev. Abstr.; Int. Labour Doc.; Int. Polit. Sci. Abstr.; Left Index; Mag. Search; Newsp. Period. Abstr. (1991-); PAIS Int. Print (1991-); Res. Alert [Full Cov.]; Sage Public Adm.

Abstr.; Soc. Sci. Source (Jan. 1992-); Soc. Sci. Cit. Index [Full Cov.]; Soc. Sci. Index; Soc. Sci. Index Fulltext (Fall 1988-) [Full Txt.]; Wheat Barley Trit. Abstr.

US/0733-2998
**LEFT INDEX. See** Political Science-Abstracting, Bibliographies and Statistics.

US/0195-7333
**LEFT REVIEW (KENT).** (LEFT REVIEW.). V. 1-MAR. 1977-. Periodical. English. Three times a year. $5.00. Kent Left History Forum, Kent State University, Department of History, Kent OH 44242. **LC** HX1; .L43. **DD** 335/.005.

CN/0381-7350
**LEFTWARD.** V. 1- 1974-. Periodical. English. Leftward, PO Box 429 Station E Toronto Ontario M6H 4E3 Canada. **DD** 335/.005.

UK
**LENINIST (LONDON, ENGLAND).** ***Ceased.*** (LENINIST.). (19??)-(Oct. 1993). English. bw. November Publications Ltd, BCM Box 928, London WC1N 3XX England.
**Desc:** Monthly paper of the Leninists of the Communist Part of Great Britain.

IT
**LEVIATANO, IL.** 1- May/June 1976-. Periodical. Italian. L9000. **LC** HX7; .L48.

CC
**LI SHIH WEI WU CHU I YEN CHIU.** **Added/Corp** Chung-Kuo Li Shih Wei Wu Chu i Yen Chiu Hui. Pei-Ching Kang Tieh Hsueh Yuan. She Hui Ko Hsueh Hsi. (1987)-. Periodical. Chinese. Ching Hua Ta Hsueh Chu Pan, She Fa Hsing Ko, Beijing, People's Republic of China. **LC** D16.9; .L4385. **DD** 335.4/112/05. ***Continues*** *Li Shih Wei Wu Chu I Lun Tsung.*

UK
**LIBERAL DEMOCRATS NEWS : THE PAPER OF THE SOCIAL AND LIBERAL DEMOCRATS.** Periodical. English. wk. ***Continues*** *Social and Liberal Democrats News.*

US/1051-7871
**LIBERATION AND MARXISM.** [Lib. Marx.]. No. 5 (June/July 1990)-. Periodical. English. bm. $10.00 (other), $30.00 (institutions). Workers World, 55 West 17th Street, 5th Floor, New York NY 10011. **Tel** (212)255-0352. **LC** HX1; .L48. **DD** 320.5/32. available on microfilm and microfiche from University Microfilms International (UMI). ***Continues*** *Liberation (New York, N.Y.).*
**Ind/Abst** Altern. Press Index (199?-).

CN/0704-1969
**LIGNE DE MASSE, LA.** V. 1- July 24, 1970-. Periodical. French. National Publications Centre, PO Box 727 Adelaide Station, Toronto Ontario M5C 2J8 Canada. **Tel** (416)252-3658. **DD** 335.43/05.

GW/0024-404X
**LINKS : SOZIALISTISCHE ZEITUNG.** **Added/Corp** Sozialistisches Buro. (19??)-. Newspaper. German. mo. DM75.00. Sozialistisches Buro, Verleger: Verlag 2000 GmbH, Postfach 10 20 62, 6050 Offenbach 1 Germany. **Tel** 011 49 69 885006, FAX 011 49 69 821116. **LC** HX6; .L48. Index available. cum. index. **Bk Rev**, (Qty: 6 per year). **Ad Acc**, **Adv Mgr:** Sigrid Schoenecker. **Pr Rev.** **Acid Free.** Documents available from FAXON Xpress.
**Desc:** Newspaper for politics and economics - critical theories.

UK/0955-2448
**LIVING MARXISM.** **Added/Corp** Revolutionary Communist Party (Great Britain). (1988)-. Periodical. English. mo. £19.50 Britain and Northern Ireland; £27.00 Europe (airmail); £23.00 overseas (surface mail); (institutions add £7.00). Junius Publications Ltd., BCM JPLTD, London WC1N 3XX England. **Tel** FAX (071)278-9844. **(Subscription address:** US/Junius Publications Ltd, PO Box 769, Murray Hill Station, New York, NY 10156**)** **ED** Mick Hume. **LC** HX3; .L58. **DD** 335.43/05. Index available. **Bk Rev.** **Ad Acc.**
**Desc:** Monthly review of the Revolutionary Communist Party.

US
**LORTON PAPERS.** (1991)-. Periodical. English. ORP, Box 158, Newtonville MA 02158. **Tel** (617)868-1069. **LC** HX1; .L7.

FR/0295-5385
**LUTTE DE CLASSE 1986.** [Lutte cl. 1986]. **VFOAT** Class Struggle; Lucha de Clase. (1986)-. Periodical. Multiple languages. mo (10 issues). 100.00F Europe and French overseas departments and territories; 140.00F other. Class Struggle/Lutte Ouvriere, BP 233, 75865 Paris Cedex 18 France. **UDC** 329.13. ***Formed by the union of*** *Lutte de Classe (Paris. 1942), 0458-5143; Class Struggle (Paris. 1972), 0224-6392* ***and*** *Lucha de Clase (Paris. 1978), 0224-6384.*

CN/0701-8746
**LUTTE OUVRIERE (MONTREAL).** (LUTTE OUVRIERE.). [Lutte ouvriere]. Vol. 1 (Nov. 1964)-. Periodical. French. bw. 0.25Can$ per no. Societe d'Editions AGPP, CP 280, Succ de Lorimier, Montreal Quebec H2H 2N7 Canada. **DD** 335.43/09714. ***Absorbed*** *Liberation, 0048-0029; Combat Socialiste pour la Republique des Travailleurs du Quebec, 0821-4972.*

CC
**MA-KO-SSU CHU I YEN CHIU TSUNG KAN / MAKESIZHUYIYANJIU.** **Added/Corp** Chung-Kuo She Hui Ko Hsueh Yuan. Ma-ko-ssu Lieh-ning Mao Tse-Tung Ssu Hsiang Yen Chiu So. **VFOAT** Ma-ko-ssu Chu i Yen Chiu.; Makesizhuyiyanjiu; Studies on Marxism. (1983)-. Periodical. Chinese. Hsin Hua Shu Tien, Beijing, People's Republic of China. **Tel** 551253. **LC** HX9.C5; M34. **DD** 335.4/05.

II
**MALEMA RIBHOLUSANA PAOJELA.** **VFOAT** Malem Revolution Paojel. Periodical. Sino-Tibetan (Manipuri). mo. Rs20.00. Manipur State Council Communist Party of India, Irabat Road, Imphal 795001 India. **LC** HX9.S26; M34.

IT
**MARXISMO OGGI.** (Nov. 1987)-. Periodical. Italian. Three times a year. L50000 Italy; L80000 others. Teti Editore, Via Comelico 30, 20135 Milan Italy. **Tel** 011 39 2 55015575.

II/0542-7762
**MARXIST REVIEW, THE.** Vol. 1 July (1967)-. Periodical. English. mo. Marxist Review, BCM Box 747, London WC1N 3XX England. **Tel** 44 71 928-3218. **LC** HX3; .M36. **DD** 335.43/05.

UK/0965-9749
**MARXIST REVIEW. LONDON.** [Marx rev. Lond.]. (1986)-. Periodical. English. mo. £15.00 UK; £18.00 other. Marxist Review, BCM Box 747, London WC1N 3XX England. **Tel** 44 71 928-3218. **ED** Ray Athon. **Bk Rev**, (Qty: approx. 35). **Ad Acc.**
**Desc:** A monthly political magazine featuring history, philosophy and economics.

GW/0542-7770
**MARXISTISCHE BLATTER.** [Marx. Bl.]. **Added/Corp** Europaische Verlagsanstalt. August-Bebel-Gesellschaft. Vol. 1 (Nov./Dec. 1963)-. Periodical. German. Twelve times a year. DM45.00 Germany; DM75.00 others. Neue Impulse Verlag GmBh., Hoffnungstr 18, 45127 Essen Germany. **Tel** 011 49 201 236757. **LC** HX6; .M32. **[CCC].** **Bk Rev.** **Ad Acc.** ctrl circ.
**Desc:** Marxist review on problems of society, politics, economies and scientific discussions.
**Ind/Abst** Energy Res. Abstr. (Oct. 1981-); Int. Bibliogr. Sociol.

UN
**MATERIALY ... ZIZDU KOMUNISTYCHNOI PARTII UKRAINY.** **Main/Corp** Komunistychna Partiia Ukrainy. Zizd. Ukrainian. **LC** JN6598.K75; M3. **DD** 335.43/0947/71.

CN/0702-8415
**META (TORONTO).** (META.). Vol. 1 (Sept. 1975)-. Periodical. English. qt. $6.00 Canada and US. Meta Editorial Collective, PO Box 324 Station P, Toronto Ontario Canada. **DD** 320.9/47.
**Ind/Abst** Curr. Contents Arts Humanit.

IS
**MIBI-FNIM.** ***Title Change.*** **Added/Corp** En Harod, Israel. Kibuts ha-Meuhad. Makhon ha-Bibliyografi. Arkhiyon ha-Avodah. (1969)-?. Hebrew. qt. Hakibbutz Hameuchad Publishing House, PO Box 40016, Tel-Aviv 61400 Israel. **Tel** 972-3-7515819. **ED** Dani Hadazi. **LC** HX765.P32; E49. Index available. **Bk Rev.** **Circ:** 5,000. ***Superseded by*** *Mibi-Fenim.*
**Desc:** Journal of the United Kibbutz movement. Discusses political, economic, social, and cultural issues of Israeli society, especially from the Kibbutz point of view.

IT
**MICROMEGA.** **VFOAT** Micro Mega. No. 1 (Jan./March 1987)-. Periodical. Italian. Five times a year. L80000.00 Italy; L100000.00 other. Editrice Periodici Culturali, Via di Repetta 142, 00186 Rome Italy. **Tel** 011 39 6 68804441. **LC** HX7; .M5. **DD** 335/.005.

US/0026-4474
**MINDSZENTY REPORT, THE. See** Religion and Theology.

MV/0132-6627
**MOLDOVA SI LUMEA.** (Sept. 1991)-. Periodical. Romanian. mo. $109.95. **(Subscription address:** East View Publications Inc., 3020 Harbor Lane North, Suite 110, Minneapolis MN 55447.**)** **LC** HX8; .K567. ***Continues*** *Politika (Chisinau, Moldova : 1991). Romanian. Politica, 0868-9679.*

IT
**MONDOPERAIO.** ***Ceased.*** **Added/Corp** Partito Socialista Italiano. (19??)-(Dec. 1993). Periodical. Italian. mo. CCP N 1/32239, Intestato A Mondo Operaio, Via Dei Pontefici 3, 00188 Rome Italy. **LC** HX7; .M6. ***Continues*** *Mondo Operaio.*

US/0027-0520
**MONTHLY REVIEW (NEW YORK. 1949).** (MONTHLY REVIEW.). [Mon. rev.]. (May 1949)-. Periodical. English. Eleven times a year. $65.00 (airmail), $45.00 (surface mail) institutions; $45.00 (airmail), $25.00 (surface mail) individuals. Monthly Review Foundation Inc., 122 West 27th Street/10th Floor, New York NY 10001. **Tel** (212)691-2555. **ED** Paul M Sweezy and Harry Magdoff. **LC** HX1; .M66. **DD** 335.05. **Bk Rev.** **Ad Acc.** **Pr Rev.** **Circ:** 10,000. available on an online database from DIALOG; available on microfilm and microfiche from University Microfilms International (UMI). Documents available from The Genuine Article, UMI Article Clearinghouse.
**Desc:** Independent socialist providing analysis of world and national events from a political and economic point of view.
**Ind/Abst** Acad. Ind. [Computer File] (1984-); Acad. Search (July 1993-); Altern. Press Index; Am. Hist. Life (1973-); Arts Humanit. Citation Index [Select. Cov.]; Bus. ASAP (1990-) [Full Txt.]; Bus. Index (1985-); Commun. Abstr.; Expand. Acad. Index (1984-); Gen. BusinessFile (1985-); Gen. Period. Index (1985-); INFO-SOUTH Abstr.; Left Index (19??-); Mag. ASAP Plus; Mag. Index Plus (1989-); Mag. Search; Middle East Abstr. Index; Newsp. Period. Abstr. (1988-); PAIS Int. Print (1991-); Peace Res. Abstr. J. (1963-1964); Res. Alert [Full Cov.]; Sage Race Relat. Abstr.; Soc. Plann. Policy Dev. Abstr.; Soc. Sci. Source (Jul. 1993-); Soc. Sci. Cit. Index [Full Cov.]; Soc. Sci. Index; Soc. Sci. Index Fulltext (Oct. 1988-) [Full Txt.]; Sociol. Abstr.; Mag. Index (1977-); Trade Ind. Index (1981-?).

HU
**MULTUNK : AZ MSZMP KOZPONTI BIZOTTSAGA PARTTORTENETI INTEZETENEK FOLYOIRATA.** Vol. 34, No. 1-2 (April 1989)-. Hungarian. qt. **LC** JN2191.S92; A34. ***Continues*** *Parttorteneti Kozlemenyek, 0464-476X.*
**Ind/Abst** Am. Hist. Life (1972-).

FR
**N.R.S., LA NOUVELLE REVUE SOCIALISTE.** No.33- Sept. 1978-. Periodical. French. ir. 270.00F. La Nouvelle Revue Socialiste, 10 rue de Solferino, 75333 Cedex 07 Paris France. **Bk Rev.** **Ad Acc.** ***Continues*** *Nouvelle Revue Socialiste.*
**Desc:** General and specific political and social problems.

FR
**NASHRIYAH-I ANJUMANHA-YI DANISHJUYAN-I MUSALMAN, URUPA VA AMRIKA.** Periodical. Persian. wk. BP 18, 95430 Auvers-Sur-Oise France.

US/0740-9508
**NATIONAL SOCIALIST (ARLINGTON, VA.), THE.** (THE NATIONAL SOCIALIST.). [Nat. social.]. English. qt. World Union of National Socialists, Box 88, Arlington VA 22210. **LC** DD256.5; .N316. **DD** 320.5/33.

RU/0548-0108
**NAUCHNOE UPRAVLENIE OBSHCHESTVOM.** **Added/Corp** Akademiia Obshchestvennykh Nauk (Moscow, R.S.F.S.R.). Kafedra Nauchnogo Kommunizma. Vol. 1 (1967)-. Russian. an. **LC** HX542; .N365. **DD** 361.6/1/0947.

GW
**NEUE ARBEITERPRESSE. See** Economics-Labor.

US/0737-3724
**NEW INTERNATIONAL (NEW YORK, N.Y. : 1983).** (NEW INTERNATIONAL.). [New int.]. Vol. 1, No. 1 (Fall 1983)-. Periodical. English. ir. $12.00. 408 Printing and Publishing Inc, 410 West Street, New York NY 10014. **Tel** (212)243-6392, FAX (212)727-0150. **ED** Mary-Alice Waters and Steve Clark. **LC** HX1; .N353. **DD** 320.5/32/05. **Bk Rev.** **Circ:** 6,000. available on microfilm from University Microfilms International (UMI). ***Absorbed in part*** *Intercontinental Press (New York, N.Y. : 1985).*
**Desc:** Journal of Marxist theory and politics.

US/0028-6044
**NEW LEADER (NEW YORK, N.Y.), THE.** (THE NEW LEADER.). [New lead.]. **Added/Corp** American Labor Conference on International Affairs. Social Democratic Federation of America. Vol. 18, No. 12 (Mar. 23, 1935)-. Periodical. English. bw (25 issues). $34.00 (one year), $66.00 (two year), $97.00 (three year). American Labor Conference on International Affairs, 275 Seventh Avenue/17th Floor, New York NY 10001. **Tel** (212)807-8240, FAX (212)727-2229. **ED** Myron Kolatch. **DD** 320. Index available (bound in last issue). cum. index. **Bk Rev.** **Ad Acc.** **Circ:** 24,000 (ctrl). available on microfilm and microfiche from University Microfilms International (UMI); available on an online database (files 647,648/Full-Text) from DIALOG. Documents available from UMI Article Clearinghouse. ***Continues*** *New Leader with Which is Combined the American Appeal;* ***Absorbed***

*Russian Affairs.*
**Desc:** An independent, liberal, democratic forum covering all facets of domestic and international affairs, literature and the arts.
**Ind/Abst** Acad. Abstr. Full Text Elite (Jan. 1988-); Acad. Abstr. (Jan. 1988-); Acad. Ind. [Computer File] (1992-); Acad. Search (Jan. 1988-); Am. Bibliogr. Slavic East Europ. Stud.; Annu. Bibliogr. Engl. Lang. Lit.; Book Rev. Digest; Book Rev. Index; Expand. Acad. Index (1992-); Film Lit. Index; Gen. Period. Index (1985-); INFO-SOUTH Abstr.; Mag. Artic. Summar. Elite (Jan. 1988-); Mag. Artic. Summar. Select (Jan. 1988-); Mag. Artic. Summar. CD-ROM (Jan. 1988-); Mag. ASAP Plus [Full Txt.]; Mag. ASAP Sel. [Full Txt.]; Mag. Index Plus (1989-); Mag. Index. Sel. (1986-); Mag. Search; Med. Rev. Dig.; Middle East Abstr. Index; MLA Int. Bibl. Books Artic. Mod. Lang. Lit.; Newsp. Period. Abstr. (1988-); PAIS Int. Print (1991-?); Peace Res. Abstr. J. (1965-1968, 1971); Read. Guide Abstr. Select Ed.; Read. Guide Period. Lit.; Soc. Sci. Source (Jan. 1988-); Mag. Index (1977-); Vocat. Search (Jan. 1988-); Work Relat. Abstr.

UK/0028-6060
**NEW LEFT REVIEW.** [New Left rev.]. No. 1 (Jan./Feb. 1960)-. Periodical. English. bm. $47.00 (individuals), $93.00 (institutions). New Left Review, 6 Meard Street, London W1V 3HR England. **Tel** 011 44 71 7348830. **(Subscription address:** New Left Review Subscriptions, 120 126 Lavendar Avenue, Mitcham Surrey CR4 3HP England.**) ED** Robin Blackburn, Tarig Ali, Perry Anderson, Victoria Brittain, Patrick Camiller, Alexander Cockburn, Mike Davis, Peter Dews, Norman Geras, Quintin Hoare, Oliver MacDonald, Branka Magas, and Ellen Meiksins Wood. **LC** HX3; .N36. **DD** 335/.005. **[CCC].** cum. index. **Pr Rev.** available on microfiche. Documents available from The Genuine Article, UMI Article Clearinghouse. ***Formed by the union of*** *New Reasoner, 0548-6556* ***and*** *Universities & Left Review.*
**Desc:** International journal of socialist politics and culture.
**Ind/Abst** Acad. Search (July 1993-); Altern. Press Index; Am. Hist. Life (1971-1976, 1982-); Appl. Soc. Sci. Index Abstr.; Arts Humanit. Citation Index [Select. Cov.]; Br. Humanit. Index; Curr. Contents Soc. Behav. Sci.; Expand. Acad. Index (1992-); Index Period. Artic. Relat. Law; INFO-SOUTH Abstr.; Int. Bibliogr. Sociol.; Int. Labour Doc.; Int. Polit. Sci. Abstr.; Left Index; Mag. Search; Middle East Abstr. Index; Multicult. Educ. Abstr.; Newsp. Period. Abstr. (1992-); PAIS Int. Print (1991-?); Res. Alert [Full Cov.]; Romant. Move.; Soc. Sci. Cit. Index [Full Cov.]; Stud. Women Abstr.

CN/0702-7532
**NEW LITERATURE & IDEOLOGY. See** Literature.

US/0740-3283
**NEW ORDER (LINCOLN, NEB.), THE.** (THE NEW ORDER.). [New order]. **Added/Corp** Nationalsozialistische Deutsche Arbeiter-Partei. Auslands-Organisation. No. 13 (Apr./May 1978)-. Periodical. English. mo. $10.00 (US & Canada); $30.00 (other) 2 years. NSDAP-AO, PO Box 6414, Lincoln NE 68506. **ED** Gerhard Lauck. **Bk Rev.** ctrl circ. ***Continues*** *NS Report.*
**Desc:** Organ of the National Socialist, German foreign branch. Covers international National Socialist (NS) activism, legalization of NSDAP in Germany, creation of a NS state and world wide Aryan new order.

US/0028-6494
**NEW POLITICS.** [New polit.]. Vol. 1 No. 1 (Fall 1961)-. Periodical. English. sa. $30.00 (institutions), $20.00 (individuals) US; $34.00 (institutions), $24.00 (individuals) other. New Politics, Attention Circulation Manager, PO Box 98, Brooklyn NY 11231. **Tel** (718)237-2048. **LC** HX1; .N57. **DD** 335/.005. **CODEN** NEPOEM. available on microfilm and microfiche from University Microfilms International (UMI).
**Ind/Abst** Altern. Press Index (1987-); Int. Bibliogr. Sociol.; Left Index (19??-).

US/0731-034X
**NEW SOCIALIST (DENVER, COLO.), THE.** (THE NEW SOCIALIST : S.). [New socialist]. **VFOAT** S. Periodical. English. sa. New Socialist / Denver, Box 18026, Denver CO 80218. **Tel** (303)333-1095.

CN/0712-5275
**NEWSLETTER / COMMITTEE ON SOCIALIST STUDIES.** [Newsl. - Comm. Social. Stud.]. **Added/Corp** Committee on Socialist Studies. (1979)-. Newsletter. English (French). Three times a year. Society for Socialist Studies, 471 University College, University of Manitoba, Winnipeg Manitoba R3T 2M8 Canada. **Tel** (204)474-9119. **ED** Paul Stevenson, Elizabeth Comack and Nolan Reilly. **DD** 335/.006/071. **Bk Rev. Circ:** 500.
**Desc:** A forum for debate and exchange through the publication of short essays, reviews, debates and letters on topics of interest and concern to socialist educators and researchers.

JA
**NIHON KYOSANTO KOKUSAI MONDAI JUYO ROMBUN SHU. Added/Corp** Nihon Kyosanto. Akahata, Tokyo. Nihon Kyosanto. Shuppankyoku. (1972/75)-. Periodical. Japanese. ¥960. Nihon Kyosanto, 26-7 Sendagaya 4, Shibuya-ku, 151 Tokyo Japan. **LC** HX411; .N49c . ***Continues*** *Nihon Kyosanto Juyo Rombun Shu.*

FR/0048-0975
**NOUVELLE REVUE INTERNATIONALE; PROBLEMES DE LA PAIX ET DU SOCIALISME, LA.** Vol. 1 (Sept. 1958)-. Periodical. French. mo. 600.00F. Cope, Boite Postale 2106, L 1021 Luxembourg Belgium. **Tel** 492101.

XR/0322-905X
**NOVA MYSL.** [Nova mysl]. 1947-. Periodical. Czech (Russian). mo. **(Subscription address:** Artia Pegas Press Ltd., Palac Metro Narodni Trida 25, 11210 Prague 1 Czech Republic.**) LC** HX8; .N57. **DD** 335.43/05.
**Ind/Abst** Am. Hist. Life (1955-1958).

CN/0384-1499
**NUTCRACKER, THE. Added/Corp** Woodsworth-Irvine Socialist Fellowship. Vol. 1 (Nov. 17, 1916)-. Periodical. English. ir. Woodsworth-Irvine Socialist Fellowship, Box 1602, Edmonton Alta. T5J 2N9. **DD** 335/.0097123.

RU/0869-0499
**OBSHCHESTVENNYE NAUKI I SOVREMENNOST : ONS. See** Social Sciences.

RU
**OBSHCHESTVENNYE NAUKI ZA RUBEZHOM. SERIIA 1: PROBLEMY NAUCHNOGO KOMMUNIZMA. Added/Corp** Akademiia Nauk SSSR. Institut Nauchnoi Informatsii i Fundamentalnaia Biblioteka po Obshchestvennym Naukam. **VAT** Obshchestvennye Nauki za Rubezhom. Seriia Odin : Problemy Nauchnogo Kommunizma. (1972)-. Russian. qt. Izdatelstvo Nauka / Akademiia Nauk, Publishing House of the Russian Academy of Sciences, Leninskii Porspekt 14, 117901 Moscow Russia. **Tel** 011 95 954-21-53, FAX 011 95 938-21-44, telex 411964. **LC** HX8; .O27.

RU
**OBSHCHESTVENNYE NAUKI ZA RUBEZHOM. SERIIA 2 : EKONOMIKA.** ***Title Change.*** **See** Economics.

CN/0226-112X
**OCTOBER (MONTREAL).** (OCTOBER : THEORETICAL JOURNAL OF MARXISM-LENINISM AND MAO-TSETUNG THOUGHT / CANADIAN COMMUNIST LEAGUE (MARXIST-LENINIST).). [October]. Vol. 1, No. 1 (Summer 1977)-. Periodical. English. qt. Red Flag Publications, PO Box 40 Station N, Montreal Quebec Canada. **DD** 335.43/05.

CN/0226-1138
**OCTOBRE (MONTREAL).** (OCTOBRE : REVUE THEORIQUE DU MARXISME-LENINISME ET DE LA PENSEE MAOTSETOUNG / LIGUE COMMUNISTE (MARXISTE-LENINISTE) DU CANADA.). [Octobre]. V. 1, No. 1 Summer 1977-. Periodical. French. qt. Red Flag Publications, PO Box 40 Station N, Montreal Quebec Canada. **DD** 335.43/05.

AU
**OFFENSIV LINKS. Added/Corp** Freie Osterreichische Jugend. Bewegung fuer Sozialismus. (1974)-. Periodical. German. mo. S50.00. Bewegung fur Sozialimus, Franz Hockedlngerasse 6, 1020 Vienna, Austria. **LC** HX6; .O37.

RU
**ONI BOROLIS ZA SCHASTE NARODNOE. Added/Corp** Chuvashskaia A.S.S.R. (R.S.F.S.R.). Nauchno-Issledovatelskii Institut Iazyka, Literatury, Istorii i Ekonomiki. (1980)-. Russian. ir.

US/0097-8906
**OSAWATOMIE.** [Osawatomie]. **Added/Corp** Weather Underground Organization. (Spring 1975)-. Periodical. English. qt. **LC** HX1; .O8. **DD** 322.4/2/0973.

GW
**OSTEUROPA UND DER INTERNATIONALE KOMMUNISMUS. Added/Corp** Bundesinstitut fur Ostwissenschaftliche und Internationale Studien (Germany). (1978)-. Monographic series. German. Price varies per volume.

CN/0030-686X
**OUR GENERATION (MONTREAL).** (OUR GENERATION.). [Our gener.]. **Added/Corp** Student Union for Peace Action. Vol. 3, No. 4 (1966)-. Periodical. English. Twice a year (Mar., Sept.). $23.00 (institutions) one year; $31.00 (individuals) two years; $44.00 (individuals) one year. Our Generation, CP 1258, Montreal Quebec H2W 2R3 Canada. **Tel** (514)844-4076. **(Subscription address:** C.P 1258, Succ. Place du Parc, Montreal, Quebec, H2W 2R3 Canada**) ED** Dimitrios Rovssopoulos. **DD** 327.1/72/05. **Bk Rev. Ad Acc. Circ:** 4,800. available on microfilm and microfiche from University Microfilms International (UMI). ***Continues*** *Our Generation Against Nuclear War, 0383-8765.*
**Desc:** Offers critical, thoroughly researched articles with a radical analysis, linking practical experience to ideas, theory to day-to-day work. Includes translations of social and political analysis appearing in Quebec; reviews of key books; discussions of the urban crisis; community organizing; libertarian socialism; social ecology; feminism and its future; international politics; and more.
**Ind/Abst** Altern. Press Index; Can. Index; Can. Period. Index; Int. Bibliogr. Sociol.; Peace Res. Abstr. J. (1962-1964, 1969-1973).

US/0738-3436
**OUT SOCIALISM.** (OUR SOCIALISM / DEMOCRATIC WORKERS PARTY.). [Our social.]. Vol. 1, No. 1 (Mar. 1983)-. Periodical. English. mo. $25.00. OS Publications, PO Box 42489, San Francisco CA 94142. **LC** HX1; .O93. **DD** 335/.005. ***Continues*** *Plain Speaking, 0275-4401.*

US
**PAROLA DEL POPOLO, LA.** Periodical. Multiple languages (English and Italian). bm. $6.00. **LC** HX7; .P28.

•IT
**PAROLECHIAVE. Added/Corp** Fondazione Lelio e Lisli Basso-ISSOCO. Vol. 1 (Apr. 1993)-. Periodical. Italian. Three times a year. L70000 Italy; L110000 others. Donzelli Editore, Via Mentana 2, 00185 Rome Italy. **Tel** 011 39 6 440610. **LC** HX7; .P283. **DD** 335/.005. ***Continues*** *Problemi del Socialismo, 0552-1807.*

US/0031-2525
**PARTISAN REVIEW (1936).** (PARTISAN REVIEW.). [Partis. rev.]. **VFOAT** PR. Vol. 3, No. 6 (Oct. 1936)-. Periodical. English. qt (4 issues). $32.00 (institution), $22.00 (individual). Boston University Scholarly Publications, 881 Commonwealth Avenue, Room 230, Boston MA 02215. **Tel** (617)353-4106. **ED** William Phillips. Index available. cum. index. **Bk Rev. Ad Acc. Pr Rev. Circ:** 8,000. available on microfilm and microfiche from University Microfilms International (UMI). Documents available from The Genuine Article, UMI Article Clearinghouse. ***Continues*** *Partisan Review & Anvil.*
**Desc:** Literary and intellectual journal.
**Ind/Abst** Abstr. Engl. Stud.; Acad. Abstr. Full Text Elite (July 1990-); Acad. Abstr. (July 1990-); Acad. Ind. [Computer File] (1987-); Acad. Search (July 1990-); Am. Hist. Life (1954-1958, 1970-); Am. Bibliogr. Slavic East Europ. Stud.; Am. Humanit. Index; Annu. Bibliogr. Engl. Lang. Lit.; ARTbibliogr. Mod.; Arts Humanit. Citation Index [Full Cov.]; Book Rev. Index; Curr. Contents Arts Humanit.; Expand. Acad. Index (1987-); Film Lit. Index; Humanit. Index; Index Am. Period. Verse; Index Period. Artic. Relat. Law (19??-19??); INFO-SOUTH Abstr.; Lit. Crit. Regist.; Mag. Search; Middle East Abstr. Index; MLA Int. Bibl. Books Artic. Mod. Lang. Lit.; Newsp. Period. Abstr. (1991-); Res. Alert [Full Cov.]; Romant. Move.; Soc. Plann. Policy Dev. Abstr.; Soc. Sci. Source (Jul. 1990-); Soc. Sci. Cit. Index [Select. Cov.]; Soc. Sci. Index; Sociol. Abstr.

II/0377-2667
**PARTY LIFE.** Periodical. English. bw. People's Publishing House Pvt Ltd, 5E Rani Jhansi Road, New Delhi 110055 India. **Tel** 011 91 11 523349. **LC** HX3; .P37. **DD** 329.9/54.

IT
**PASSATO E PRESENTE.** (19??)-. Periodical. Italian. sa (June, Dec.). L3.000. Coop Il Chiese Scrl, Piazza Europa 3, 38089 Storo Trento Italy. **Tel** 011 39 465 686760. **LC** HX7; .P29. **DD** 335.43/05. cum. index. **Ad Acc.** ctrl circ.

•US
**PEOPLE FOR A NEW SYSTEM. Added/Corp** Industrial Union Party (U.S.). **VFOAT** New System. No. 36 (Fall 1992)-. Periodical. English. sa. $4.00. Socialist Republic, PO Box 711, Red Bank NJ 07701. **Tel** (201)758-0449. **LC** HX1; .P46. ***Continues*** *Socialist Republic, 0090-7405.*
**Desc:** Journal aimed at those interested in socialism and the socialist movement.

US/0199-350X
**PEOPLE (PALO ALTO. 1979), THE.** ***Suspended.*** (THE PEOPLE.). **Added/Corp** Socialist Labor Party. (Dec. 15, 1979)-Vol. 104 (May 3, 1994). English. Twenty-two times a year (semi-monthly except monthly in Jan. and July). $4.00 (one year), $7.00 (two year), $10.00 (three year). Socialist Labor Party, 11 West Evelyn Avenue, Suite 209, Sunnyvale CA 94086. **Tel** (415)494-1532. **ED** Richard Whitney, 914 Industrial Avenue, Palo Alto, CA 94303. **LC** HX1; .W38. **DD** 335/.005. **Bk Rev. Circ:** 12,610. available on microfilm from University Microfilms International (UMI). ***Continues*** *Weekly People, 0043-1885.*
**Desc:** Covers domestic and international events offering clear Marxist analyses of political and economic events.

US/1071-7250
**PEOPLE'S CULTURE (KANSAS CITY, KAN.).** (PEOPLE'S CULTURE.). [People's cult.]. New Ser., No. 1 (Jan./Feb. 1991)-. Periodical. English. bm (6 issues). $15.00. People's Culture, PO Box 5224, Kansas City KS 66119. **ED** Fred Whitehead. **DD** 306. ***Continues*** *People's Culture (Albuquerque, N.M.).*

## Political Science —Socialism, Communism, Anarchism, Utopianism

**Desc:** Collects news and information on all aspects of progressive and radical culture, including poetry, book reviews, news and notes, and scholarly or critical essays.

II
**PEOPLE'S DEMOCRACY.** Added/Corp Communist Party of India. Vol. 1 (June 27, 1965)-. Periodical. English. wk. $40.00. Communist Party of India (Marxist), Calcutta, India. (**Subscription address:** Prints India, 11 Darya Ganj, New Delhi, 110002 India, (Phone: 011 91 11 3268645)) **LC** DS480.84; .P43. **DD** 320.5/323/0954.

UK/0958-3939
**PERESTROIKA ANNUAL.** *Ceased.* See Political Science.

UK/0264-2778
**PERMANENT REVOLUTION (LONDON, ENGLAND : 1983).** *Ceased.* See Economics-Labor.

RU/0131-2278
**PERSPEKTIVY.** Added/Corp Vsesoiuznyi Leninskii Kommunisticheskii Soiuz Molodezhi. Tsentralnyi Komitet. (1990)-. Periodical. Russian. mo. $54.00. (**Subscription address:** Victor Kamkin, 4956 Boiling Brook Parkway, Rockville MD 20852.) **LC** HQ799.R9; M6. *Continues Molodoi Kommunist, 0026-9077.*

SZ
**POCH.** Periodical. German. Progressiven Organisationen, Postfach 338, 4001 Basel Switzerland. **LC** HX6; .P57.

US/1069-093X
**POLITICAL ARCHIVES OF RUSSIA.** *Title Change.* [Polit. arch. Russ.]. Vol. 2, No. 3 (1991)-(199?). Periodical. English. qt. Nova Science Publishers Inc., 6080 Jericho Turnpike, Suite 207, Commack NY 11725-2808. **Tel** (516)499-3103, (516)499-3106, FAX (516)499-3146. **LC** JN6598.K4; P62. **DD** 324.247/075/09. *Continues Political Archives of the Soviet Union, 1049-7714. Continued by Political History of Russia.*

US
**POLITICAL HISTORY OF RUSSIA.** (199?)-. English. Four times a year. $230.00. Nova Science Publishers Inc., 6080 Jericho Turnpike, Suite 207, Commack NY 11725-2808. **Tel** (516)499-3103, (516)499-3106, FAX (516)499-3146. **ED** Nadya Gotsiridze. *Continues Political Archives of Russia, 1069-093X.*
**Desc:** Presents articles which are deemed of interest to scholarship and general knowledge about the Soviet Union from 1917 to 1991.

LI
**POLITIKA.** Added/Corp Lietuvos Komunistu Partija. (1990)-. Periodical. Lithuanian. ir. (**Subscription address:** Victor Kamkin, 4956 Boiling Brook Parkway, Rockville MD 20852.) **LC** IN PROCESS. *Continues Komunistas.*

UN/0868-8273
**POLITYKA I CHAS : ZHURNAL T SK KOMPARTII UKRAINY.** Added/Corp Komunistychna Partiia Ukrainy. T Sentralnyi Komitet. (1991)-. Ukrainian. wk. $63.00. Ukrainian National Association Inc, 30 Montgomery Street, PO Box 76, Jersey City NJ 07303. **Tel** (201)451-2200. **LC** JN6639.A8; K6659. *Continues Pid Praporom Leninizmu, 0132-5949.*

MX
**POR ESTO.** See Economics-Labor.

US/0149-0893
**POTOMAC (CHICAGO).** (POTOMAC.). (May 1975)-. Periodical. English. qt. Editor Alexander E Ronnett MD, 502 Garwood Avenue, Mount Prospect IL 60056. **LC** HX1; .P64. **DD** 335.43/05.

US/0742-9940
**PRACTICE (NEW YORK, N.Y.).** (PRACTICE.). [Practice]. Added/Corp New York Institute for Social Therapy and Research. Institute for Social Therapy and Research. Vol. 1, No. 1 (Spring 1983)-. Periodical. English. Twice a year (March and Nov.). $10.00 (institutions), $8.50 (individuals). Castillo Publications, 500 Greenwich Street, Suite 202, New York NY 10013. **Tel** (212)941-8906, FAX (212)941-8340. **ED** Lois Holzman. **LC** HX1; .P73. **DD** 335.43/05. **Bk Rev**, (Qty: 2). **Ad Acc**, **Adv Mgr:** C Helm, **Tel** (212)941-8844. **Circ:** 1,000.
**Ind/Abst** Altern. Press Index; Appl. Soc. Sci. Index Abstr.; Soc. Plann. Policy Dev. Abstr.; Sociol. Abstr.

RU
**PRIMERNYE TEMATIKA I PLANY TEORETICHESKIKH SEMINAROV.** Main/Corp Dom Politicheskogo Prosveshcheniia Mk I Mgk Kpss. (19??)-. Russian. 0.22rub. Moskovskii Rabechii, Ulitsa Kuibysheva 21, Moscow Russia. **LC** HX19; .D58a.

XV
**PRISPEVKI ZA NOVEJSO ZGODOVINO.** See Economics-Labor.

IT/0552-1807
**PROBLEMI DEL SOCIALISMO.** *Title Change.* Added/Corp Fondazione Lelio e Lisli Basso-ISSOCO. Vol. 1, No. 1 (Jan. 1958)-(199?). Periodical. Italian. qt. Franco Angeli Riviste SRL, Viale Monza 106, 20127 Milan Italy. **Tel** 011 39 2 2827651, 011 39 2 289562. **LC** HX7; .P67. **DD** 335/.005. *Continued by Parolechiave.*
**Ind/Abst** Am. Hist. Life (1985-); Int. Polit. Sci. Abstr.

UK
**PROBLEMS OF COMMUNISM.** Added/Corp British and Irish Communist Organisation. (1974)-. Periodical. English. Four times a year. 17p. Problems of Communism Committee, 10 Athol Street, Belfast BT12 4GX Northern Ireland. **LC** HX3; .P7. **DD** 335.43/05. **Bk Rev**. **Ad Acc**. **Circ:** 1,000.
**Desc:** Examines particular political/historical problems for the communist movement in depth; not to be confused with its American namesake.
**Ind/Abst** Acad. Ind. [Computer File] (1987-); Am. Bibliogr. Slavic East Europ. Stud. (19??-); Curr. Contents Soc. Behav. Sci.; Expand. Acad. Index (1987-).

US/0032-941X
**PROBLEMS OF COMMUNISM (WASHINGTON, D.C.).** *Ceased.* (PROBLEMS OF COMMUNISM.). [Probl. communism]. No. 1 (1952)-(1992). Government Publication. English. bm. Superintendent of Documents, US Government Printing Office, Washington DC 20402. **Tel** (202)275-3328, FAX (202)786-2377. **LC** HX1. **DD** 335.43/05; 335.4082. Index available in last issue of volume--attached. cum. index. **Pr Rev.** available on microfilm and microfiche from University Microfilms International (UMI). Documents available from The Genuine Article, UMI Article Clearinghouse.
**Desc:** Provides analyses and significant background information on various aspects of world communism today.
**Ind/Abst** ABC POL SCI; Acad. Abstr. Full Text Elite (Nov. 1990-May 1992); Acad. Abstr. (Nov. 1990-May 1992); Acad. Search (Nov. 1990-May 1992); Am. Hist. Life (1963-); Am. Bibliogr. Slavic East Europ. Stud. (19??-1992); Curr. Contents Soc. Behav. Sci.; Curr. Mil. Pol. Lit.; Hum. Rights Intern. Rep.; INFO-SOUTH Abstr.; Int. Bibliogr. Sociol.; Int. Polit. Sci. Abstr.; Mag. Artic. Summar. Elite (Nov. 1990-May 1992); Mag. Artic. Summar. Select (July 1990-); Mag. Artic. Summar. CD-ROM (Nov. 1990-May 1992); Mag. Search; Newsp. Period. Abstr. (1990-1992); PAIS Int. Print (1991-); Peace Res. Abstr. J. (1963-1973, 1984); Res. Alert [Full Cov.]; Soc. Sci. Source (Jul. 1990-); Soc. Sci. Index; Soc. Sci. Index Fulltext (May 1988-June 1992) [Full Txt.]; U.S. Polit. Sci. Doc.

II
**PROBLEMS OF NATIONAL LIBERATION.** V. 1- Nov. 1974-. English. 3.00. R Dasgupta, 10 Bondel Road, Calcutta 700019 India. **LC** HX3; .P72. **DD** 335.43/05.

US/1075-8216
**PROBLEMS OF POST-COMMUNISM.** English. Six times a year. $120.00 US/ $150.00 other. M. E. Sharpe Inc., 80 Business Park Drive, Armonk NY 10504. **Tel** (914)273-1800, (800)541-6563, FAX (914)273-2106.

RU
**PROBLEMY MIROVOGO REVOLIUTSIONNOGO PROTSESSA / AKADEMIIA OBSHCHESTVENNYKH NAUK PRI TSK KPSS.** Added/Corp Akademiia Obshchestvennykh Nauk (Moscow, R.S.F.S.R.). Vol. 1 (1981)-. Periodical. Russian. 1.20rub. **LC** HX8; .P722. **DD** 335.43/05.

US/0735-9381
**PROCESSED WORLD.** See Literature.

SZ/0555-3482
**PROFIL : SOZIALDEMOKRATISCHE ZEITSCHRIFT FUR POLITIK, WIRTSCHAFT UND KULTUR.** Added/Corp Sozialdemokratische Partei der Schweiz. Vol. 46, (1967)-. Periodical. German. mo. 30.00F. Fr Sozialdemokratische Partei der Schweiz, Pavillonweg 3 3012 Berne Switzerland. **Tel** 031 24 11 15, FAX 031 230 065. **ED** Toya Massen, Andre Haguet, and Rolf Zimmerman. **LC** HX6; .R67. **Bk Rev**. **Ad Acc**. **Circ:** 3,000 (ctrl). *Continues Rote Revue.*

II
**PROLETARIAN PATH.** Periodical. English. bm. Rs2.00 single issue. Moni Guha, 25/1, Jyotish Roy Road, 53 Calcutta India. **LC** HX3; .P76. **DD** 335.43/05.

CN/0229-0685
**PROLETARIAN REVOLUTION (MONTREAL).** (PROLETARIAN REVOLUTION.). [Prolet. revolut.]. Added/Corp Bolshevik Union of Canada. (1978)-. Periodical. English. mo. $6.00. Lines of Demarcation, PO Box 892, Tour de la Bourse, Montreal Quebec H4Z 1K2 Canada. **DD** 335.43/05.

SW
**PUENTE (LUND, SWEDEN).** (PUENTE.). Vol. 1 (Jan. 1989)-. Periodical. Spanish. Three times a year.

KO
**PUKPANG CHONOL.** Added/Corp Han-Chung-So Hyophoe (Korea). VFOAT Northern Magazine; Wolgan Pukpang Chonol. Vol. 1 No. 1 (1991)-. Periodical. Korean. mo. **LC** D839; .P84.

US/0896-9795
**QUARTERMASTER PROFESSIONAL BULLETIN.** [Quart.master prof. bull.]. Added/Corp US Army Quartermaster School. U.S. Army Quartermaster Center and School. (Mar. 1988)-. Government Publication. English. qt. $9.50 US; $11.90 other. Superintendent of Documents, US Government Printing Office, Washington DC 20402. **Tel** (202)275-3328, FAX (202)786-2377. **DD** 355.
**Desc:** Presents material designed to keep Quartermasters knowledgeable of current and emerging developments to enhance their professional development.

FR
**QUATRIEME INTERNATIONALE.** Main/Corp Fourth International. International Executive Committee. Added/Corp Parti Ouvrier Internationaliste (Bolchevik-Leniniste). No. 1, (Oct. 1936)-. Periodical. French. Four times a year. 195.89F France; 200.00F other. Presse Edition Communication, 2 rue Richard Lenoir, 93108 Montreuil France. **Tel** 011 33 1 48590080. **LC** HX5; .Q3. **DD** 335/.005. *Supersedes Lutte de Classes.*

NE
**QUE FAZER?.** No. 1- Nov. 1974-. Portuguese. $480.00. Edicoes Maria da Fonte, rua de Fe 26 -20 2, Lisbon Portugal. **LC** HX9.P65; Q4.

YU/0033-6351
**QUESTIONS ACTUELLES DU SOCIALISME.** [Quest. actuelles social.]. Periodical. French. mo. $47.20 (airmail), $43.20 (surface mail). (**Subscription address:** Jugoslovenska Knjiga, PO Box 36, YU 11001 Belgrade Yugoslavia.) **LC** HX365.5; .Q4.
**Ind/Abst** Int. Labour Doc.

RU
**RABOCHII KLASS I SOTSIALNYI PROGRESS.** See Economics-Labor.

US/0163-6545
**RADICAL HISTORY REVIEW.** [Radic. hist. rev.]. Added/Corp MARHO (Organization). Vol. 2, No. 4 (Spring 1975)-. Academic Scholarly Publication. English. Three times a year. $53.00 US, Canada and Mexico; £37.00 other. Cambridge University Press / New York, 40 West 20th Street, New York NY 10011-4211. **Tel** (212)924-3900, (800)221-4512. (**Subscription address:** Cambridge University Press / Outside of North America, Journal Fulfillment Department, The Edinburgh Building, Cambridge CB2 2RU United Kingdom.) **ED** Barbara Smith. **LC** HX1; .R33. **DD** 909.08. Index available. **Bk Rev**. **Ad Acc**. **Circ:** 4,500. available in microform. Documents available from The Genuine Article. *Continues MARHO (Organization). MARHO Newsletter.*
**Desc:** Presents scholarship and commentary that looks critically at the past and its historians from a non-sectarian perspective drawn from the political left. Scrutinizes conventional history and seeks to broaden and advance the discussion of crucial issues such as the role of race, class and gender in history. Offers original articles; review essays that examine the uses and abuses of history in the popular media, history museums and other public forums; and interviews with leading radical historians. Each volume is illustrated with drawings, cartoons, photographs and other graphic art. Issues are often thematic and cover a wide range of geographic areas and subjects.
**Ind/Abst** Altern. Press Index; Am. Hist. Life (1978-); Arts Humanit. Citation Index [Full Cov.]; Curr. Contents Arts Humanit.; Film Lit. Index (19??-); Left Index; Middle East Abstr. Index; Res. Alert [Full Cov.]; Soc. Plann. Policy Dev. Abstr.; Soc. Sci. Cit. Index [Select. Cov.].

YU
**RADNICI U DRUSTVENOM SEKTORU, VANPRIVREDA, PREMA POPISU RADNIKA SA STANJEM ... GODINE / SOCIJALISTICKA REPUBLIKA SRBIJA, REPUBLICKI ZAVOD ZA STATISTIKU.** Added/Corp Republicki Zavod za Statistiku SR Srbije. Serbo-Croatian (Roman). University of Beograd, International University Center for Social Sciences, Belgrad Yugoslavia.

RU
**RAZVITIE LICHNOSTI V USLOVIIAKH SOTSIALIZMA.** See Psychology.

RU
**RAZVITIE SOTSIALNOI SFERY V SSSR.** Added/Corp Institut Nauchnoi Informatsii po Obshchestvennym Naukam (Akademiia Nauk SSSR). (19??)-. Russian. an. **LC** HN521; .R39.

US/1061-656X
**RCDA (NEW YORK, N.Y.).** **See** Religion and Theology.

US/0034-3978
**RCDA. RELIGION IN COMMUNIST DOMINATED AREAS.** [Relig. Communist domin. areas]. **VFOAT** Religion in Communist Dominated Areas. Vol 11 No 1 (1972)-. Periodical. English (Multiple languages). qt. $28.00. RCDA, Religion in Communist Dominated Areas, 475 Riverside Drive, New York NY 10115-0050. **Tel** (212)870-2481. **ED** Blahoslav Hrudy and Olga S Hruby. **DD** 200. Index available. **Bk Rev. Ad Acc. Pr Rev. Circ:** 3,000. available on microfilm from University Microfilms International (UMI). ***Continues*** *Religion in Communist Dominated Areas, 0034-3978.*
**Desc:** Information on the attitudes and practices of communist parties with respect to the life, work and vital concerns of believers in communist countries.
**Ind/Abst** Am. Bibliogr. Slavic East Europ. Stud.; Hum. Rights Intern. Rep.; Index Book Rev. Relig.; Middle East Abstr. Index; Relig. Index One Period.

FR
**RECHERCHES INTERNATIONALES : CAHIERS DE L'INSTITUT DE RECHERCHES MARXISTES.** **Added/Corp** Institut de Recherches Marxistes (Paris, France). (1981)-. Periodical. French. Four times a year. 244.86F France; 500.00F others. IRM / Institut de Recherches Marxistes, 64 Boulevard Auguste Blanqui, 75013 Paris France. **Tel** 011 33 1 43364534. ***Continues*** *Recherches Internationales a la Lumiere du Marxisme, 0486-1345.*

CN/0711-2270
**RED MENACE.** (THE RED MENACE / TORONTO LIBERATION SCHOOL.). [Red menace]. **Added/Corp** Toronto Liberation School. Libertarian Socialist Collective. Vol. 1 No. 1 (Feb. 1976)-. Periodical. English. ir. 2.00Can$ per number. The Red Menace, PO Box 171 Station D, Toronto Ontario M6P 3J8 Canada. **DD** 335/.00971. **Bk Rev.** ctrl circ.
**Desc:** A libertarian socialist journal devoted to critical, iconoclastic and frequently humourous examination of serious social issues.

●UK/0963-7494
**RELIGION, STATE & SOCIETY : THE KESTON JOURNAL.** **See** Religion and Theology.

US/0278-7784
**RELIGIOUS SOCIALISM.** [Relig. social.]. V. 1-Spring 1977-. Periodical. English. qt. $5.00. Religious Socialism, 45 Thorton Street, Roxbury MA 02119. **Tel** (617)427-7953. **ED** John C Cort and Ralph Pagnucco. **Bk Rev. Circ:** 800.
**Desc:** Published by Religion & Socialism Commission of the Democratic Socialists of America.

UN
**REPORT OF THE CENTRAL COMMITTEE OF THE COMMUNIST PARTY OF UKRAINE TO THE CONGRESS OF THE COMMUNIST PARTY OF UKRAINE.** **Main/Corp** Komunistychna Partiia Ukrainy. Tsentralavi Komitet. (19??)-. English. 0.20rub each copy. Ukraine Society, 6 Zoloti Vorota Street, Kiev, Ukraine. **LC** JN6598.K77; R46. **DD** 329.9/47/71.

FR
**REVEIL ANARCHISTE, LE.** Began in 1900. Periodical. French. qt. 20F. BP 121, 25014 Besancon Cedex France. **LC** HX821; .R29. **DD** 335/.83/05.

CU/0138-6425
**REVISTA CUBANA DE CIENCIAS SOCIALES.** **VFOAT** Ciencias Sociales. 1983/1-. Periodical. Spanish (summaries and/or abstracts in English). Three times a year. $13.00 North and South America; $14.00 Europe; $16.00 other. Ediciones Cubanas, Obispo 527, Altos ESQ Bernaza, CP 10100 Havana Cuba. **Tel** 011 632980, 631942. FAX 011 631011, telex 512337, 6540.
**Desc:** Offers the result of fundamental researches and studies. Orientated and applied to the field of the philosophy and other social sciences of particular interest.

FR
**REVOLUTION PROLETARIENNE, LA.** V. 1, 1925-. Periodical. French. **LC** HX821. available on microfilm.

CN/0229-0693
**REVOLUTION PROLETARIENNE (MONTREAL).** (REVOLUTION PROLETARIENNE.). **Added/Corp** Union Bolchevique du Canada. Vol. 1, No. 1 (May 1, 1978)-. Periodical. French. mo. $6.00. Lignes de Demarcation, CP 892, Succursale Tour de la Bourse, Montreal Quebec H4Z 1K2 Canada. **DD** 335/.43/05.

US/0556-7165
**REVOLUTIONARY AGE.** V. 1- 1968-. Periodical. English. qt. Freedom Socialist Publishing, 3117 E Thomas, Seattle WA 98102. **LC** HX1; .R54. **DD** 335.4.

FR/0338-0599
**REVUE D'ETUDES COMPARATIVES EST-OUEST.** [Rev. etud. comp. est-ouest]. Vol. 6 (March 1975)-. Periodical. English (French; summaries and/or abstracts in English). qt. 605.00F France; 730.00F other. Editions du CNRS, 22 rue Saint Armand, F 75015 Paris France. **Tel** 011 33 1 45075050. **(Subscription address:** Centrale des Revues, 11 rue Gossin, 92543 Montrouge Cedex France.**) ED** E. Zaleski. **LC** HC244.A1; R48. **Bk Rev. Pr Rev.** Documents available from The Genuine Article. ***Continues*** *Revue de l'Est.*
**Desc:** Fills in the gaps of information on socialist countries.
**Ind/Abst** ABC POL SCI; Am. Hist. Life (1973-); Curr. Contents Soc. Behav. Sci.; Int. Bibliogr. Sociol.; Int. Labour Doc.; Int. Polit. Sci. Abstr.; LABORDOC; PAIS Int. Print; Res. Alert; Soc. Sci. Cit. Index.

JA
**RIBERUTERU.** **VFOAT** Libertaire. Edition No. 1 (1969)-. Periodical. Japanese. mo. ¥100. Riberuteru No Kai, 2190 Oizum Gakuencho Nerima-ku, Tokyo Japan. **LC** HX947; .R52.

CN/0227-6089
**ROAD OF THE PARTY.** ***Ceased.*** (THE ROAD OF THE PARTY : THEORETICAL ORGAN OF THE CENTRAL COMMITTEE OF THE COMMUNIST PARTY OF CANADA (MARXIST-LENINIST).). [Road party]. **Added/Corp** Communist Party of Canada (Marxist-Leninist). Central Committee. Vol. 1, No. 1 (March 1980)-(199?). Periodical. English. National Executive Committee of CPC, PO Box 666 Station C, Montreal Quebec H2L 4L5 Canada. **DD** 324.271/0975.

US
**RORAIMA.** Periodical. English (English). **LC** HX1; .R67. **DD** 335/.00988/1.

FR
**ROUGE & VERT.** **Added/Corp** Parti Socialiste Unifie (France) Alternative Rouge et Verte (Group). **VFOAT** Rouge et Vert; Autogestion l'Alternative. (May 22, 1989)-. Periodical. French. wk. PSU Service des Abonnements, 9 rue Borromee, 75015 Paris France. **LC** HX5; .R58. ***Continues*** *Autogestion, l'Alternative, 0294-0698.*

AA
**RRUGA E PARTISE.** **Added/Corp** Partia e Punes se Shqiperise. Komiteti Qendror. (19??)-. Periodical. Albanian. mo. $10.91. Book Distribution Enterprise, Rruga Kavajes, Tirana, Albania. **Tel** 011 355 42 27246. **LC** HX8; .R7. **DD** 335.43/05.

NE
**S & D : MAANDBLAD VAN DE WIARDI BECKMAN STICHTING.** **Added/Corp** Wiardi Beckman Stichting. **VFOAT** S en D; Socialisme en Democratie; Socialisme & Democratie. (19??)-. Periodical. Dutch. mo. **LC** HX8; .S47. **DD** 320.5/315/05. ***Continues*** *Socialisme en Democratie.*
**Desc:** Primarily deals with socialism.

KG
**SAIASII TRIBUNA.** **Added/Corp** Kyrgyzstan KP BK. **VFOAT** Politicheskaia Tribuna. (1991)-. Periodical. Kirghiz. mo. Izdatelstvo TSK Kompartii Kyrgyzstana, Bishkek Kyrgyzstan. **LC** HX9.K57; S24. ***Continues*** *Kyrgyzstan Kommunisti.*

XR
**SBORNIK PRACI. MARXISMUS-LENINISMUS.** **Main/Corp** Universita Palackeho v Olomouci. Pedagogicka Fakulta. **VFOAT** Marxismus-Leninismus. (19??)-. Czech (summaries and/or abstracts in Russian and German). qt. $50.40. **(Subscription address:** Artia Pegas Press Ltd., Palac Metro Narodni Trida 25, 11210 Prague 1 Czech Republic.**) LC** HX15; .U55a.

UK/0954-3384
**SEARCHLIGHT SOUTH AFRICA.** ***Ceased.*** No. 1 (Sept. 1988)-(1993). Periodical. English. qt. Searchlight South Africa, BCM 7646, London WC1N 3XX England.

RU
**SEZD MONGOLSKOI NARODNO-REVOLIUTSIONNOI PARTII.** **Main/Corp** Mongolskaia. (19??)-. Russian. **LC** JQ1519.M6; A35.

IS
**SHAVUA, HA-.** **Added/Corp** Kibuts Ha-Artzi Ha-Shomer Ha-Tsair (Israel). (19??)-. Periodical. Hebrew. wk. Leonardo de Vinci 13, PO Box 40009, Tel-Aviv Israel. **LC** HX765.P3; S43. ***Continues*** *Shavua Ba-Kibuts Ha-Artsi.*

US/0196-4801
**SOCIAL ANARCHISM.** (SOCIAL ANARCHISM : A JOURNAL OF PRACTICE AND THEORY.). [Soc. anarchism]. **Added/Corp** Atlantic Center for Research and Education (Baltimore, Md.). Vol. 1, No. 1 (Winter 1980)-. Periodical. English. sa (May, and Oct.). $14.00 (institutions), $10.00 (individuals). Social Anarchism, 2743 Maryland Avenue, Baltimore MD 21218. **Tel** (410)243-6987. **ED** Chris Stadler, Mark Bevis and Howard J. Ehrlich. **LC** HX821; .S65. **DD** 335/.83/05. Index available. **Bk Rev. Ad Acc. Pr Rev. Circ:** 1,200.
**Desc:** Articles, interviews, investigative reporting, essays, historical notes, practical proposals, poetry, short fiction and book reviews relating to social anarchism and anarchist-feminism.
**Ind/Abst** Altern. Press Index.

RH
**SOCIAL CHANGE AND DEVELOPMENT.** **VFOAT** Journal on Social Change and Development. Issue 2 (Aug. 1981)-. Periodical. English. qt. $20.00 (institutions), $15.00 (individuals). Journal on Social Change and Development, PO Box 4405, Harare Zimbabwe. **Tel** 011 263 0 700047, FAX 011 263 0 725565, telex 22055. Index available. cum. index. **Bk Rev. Ad Acc. Circ:** 4,500. ***Continues*** *Journal on Social Change & Development.*
**Desc:** Aims to promote discussion and debate about change and development in Zimbabwean society.

US/0885-4300
**SOCIALISM AND DEMOCRACY.** ***Ceased.*** (SOCIALISM AND DEMOCRACY : THE JOURNAL OF THE RESEARCH GROUP ON SOCIALISM AND DEMOCRACY.). [Social. democr.]. **Added/Corp** City University of New York. Research Group on Socialism and Democracy. (Fall 1985)-(Winter 1992). Periodical. English. Three times a year. Research Group on Socialism and Democracy, 160 East 84th Street 7D, New York NY 10028. **Tel** (212)879-4735. **ED** Frank Rosengarten and Michael E. Brown. **LC** HX1; .S16. **DD** 320.5/315/05. Index available. cum. index. **Bk Rev. Ad Acc. Pr Rev. Circ:** 750. available on microfilm from University Microfilms International (UMI). Documents available from UMI Article Clearinghouse.
**Desc:** A journal concerned with the relationship between socialism and democracy, both theoretically and in practice.
**Ind/Abst** Altern. Press Index; Am. Hist. Life (1987-); Am. Bibliogr. Slavic East Europ. Stud.; Expand. Acad. Index (1992-); Int. Polit. Sci. Abstr.; Left Index; Newsp. Period. Abstr. (1992-); PAIS Int. Print; Soc. Plann. Policy Dev. Abstr.; Sociol. Abstr. (1987-) [Full Cov.].

●UK
**SOCIALISM OF THE FUTURE.** (1992)-. English. Twice a year. £25.00 (individuals), £50.00 (institutions) UK; £30.00 or $60.00 (individuals), £60.00 or $120.00 (institutions) other. Pluto Press, 345 Archway Road, London N6 5AA. **Tel** (081)348 2724, FAX (081)348-9133. **ED** Tom Bottomore.
**Desc:** Wide-ranging and not narrowly European in outlook, the journal covers many global problems, particularly those to do with the North/South divide. Crucial issues are examined such as socialism and ideology, the new industrial revolution, the changing nature of work, the upheavals in Eastern Europe, and the new social order socialists might now begin to visualize.

RU/0583-7138
**SOCIALISM, THEORY AND PRACTICE.** ***Ceased.*** **VFOAT** Soviet Monthly Digest of Theoretical and Political Press; STP; S.T.P. No. 1 (1965)-Ceased with Jan. (1991). Periodical. English (French, Spanish and German). mo. **(Subscription address:** Victor Kamkin, 4956 Boiling Brook Parkway, Rockville MD 20852.**) LC** HX1; .S18. **DD** 335.43/05.
**Desc:** Covers theoretical and political aspects of Marxism-Leninism, practice of socialist and communist construction, and the struggle for peace and socialism.

BE/0037-8127
**SOCIALISME (BRUXELLES).** (SOCIALISME.). [Socialisme]. **Added/Corp** Institut Emile Vandervelde. (Jan. 1954)-. Periodical. French. Six times a year. Van Loghum Slaterus, Santvoortbeeklaan 21 23, B 2100 Deurne Belgium. **(Subscription address:** Libresso BV, Postbus 23, 7400 GA Deventer Netherlands.**) LC** HX5; .S58. ***Supersedes*** *Cahiers Socialistes.*
**Ind/Abst** Int. Bibliogr. Sociol.; Int. Polit. Sci. Abstr.

NE
**SOCIALISME EN DEMOCRATIE.** ***Title Change.*** **Added/Corp** Sociaal-Democratische Arbeiders-Partij. Partij van de Arbeid. Wiardi Beckman Stichting. **VFOAT** S & D. Socialisme en Democratie. Vol. 1-Jan. 7, (1939)-(19??). Periodical. Dutch. mo. Kluwer Academic Publishers, Postbus 322, 3300 AH Dordrecht, The Netherlands. **Tel** 011 (31) 78 524400, FAX 011 31 78 183273, telex 20083. **LC** HX8; .S47. **DD** 320.5/315/05. ***Continues*** *Socialsitische Gids.* ***Continued by*** *S & D.*
**Ind/Abst** World Agric. Econ.

CN/0318-1685
**SOCIALISME MONDIAL.** V. 1- 1973-. French. $1.00 for 6 numbers. Socialisme Mondial, CP 244, Pointe-Aux-Trembles Quebec H1B 5K3 Canada. **DD** 335/.005.

PE
**SOCIALISMO Y PARTICIPACION.**
**Added/Corp** Ediciones Socialismo y Participacion. Centro de Estudios para el Desarrollo y la Participacion. (Oct. 1977)-. Periodical. Spanish. Four times a year. $55.00 Latin America; $60.00 other. CEDEP / Centro de Desarrollos para la Participation, Apartado 110201, Lima 17 Peru. **Tel** 011 51 14 623846, 629833. **LC** JL3401; .S62. **DD** 985/.0633. **Bk Rev. Ad Acc. Circ:** 1,100 (ctrl).
**Desc:** Covers Peruvian and other economic conditions, labor movements, trade, class struggle, religious influences, minorities and demographics.
**Ind/Abst** Int. Bibliogr. Sociol.; Int. Polit. Sci. Abstr.

UK
**SOCIALIST ACTION.** No. 1 (March 18, 1983)-. English. qt. £22.00 institutions; £10.00 individuals. Socialist Action / London, PO Box 50, London N1 2XP England. **Tel** 011 44 71 2540128. **Bk Rev. Circ:** 5,000. ***Continues*** *Socialist Challenge.*

UK
**SOCIALIST AFFAIRS AND WOMEN & POLITICS. Added/Corp** Socialist International. Socialist International Women (Organization). **VFOAT** Women & Politics; Socialist Affairs; Socialist Affairs and Women and Politics. (1990)-. Periodical. English. qt. International Secretary, Socialist International, Maritime House, Olde Town, Clapham London SW4 0JW England. **Tel** 01-586-1101. ***Continues*** *Socialist Affairs, 0049-0946.*

CN
**SOCIALIST ALTERNATIVES. Added/Corp** McGill University. Centre for Developing-Area Studies. **VFOAT** Alternatives; Alternativy. Vol. 1, No. 1 (Fall 1991)-. Periodical. English. Twice a year. 53.00Can$ institutions; 21.00Can$ individuals. McGill University / Centre for Developing Area Studies, 3715 Peel Street Room 219, Montreal H3A 1X1 Canada. **Tel** (514)398-3508. **CODEN** SALTEA.

UK
**SOCIALIST CHALLENGE.** ***Title Change.*** No. 1 (1977)-?. Periodical. English. wk. Socialist Action / London, PO Box 50, London N1 2XP England. **Tel** 011 44 71 2540128. ***Supersedes*** *Red Weekly.* ***Continued by*** *Socialist Action.*

CN/0821-4980
**SOCIALIST CHALLENGE (MONTREAL).** (SOCIALIST CHALLENGE.). [Social. chall.]. No. 1 (Nov. 20, 1980)-. Periodical. English. ir. $10.00 Canada; $15.00 other. Socialist Challenge / Canada, PO Box 152 Terminal N, Montreal Quebec H2X 3M6 Canada. **DD** 335.43/0971.

CN/0707-5472
**SOCIALIST FULCRUM. Added/Corp** Socialist Party of Canada. Vol. 10, No. 3 (1977)-. Periodical. English. Four times a year. 3.00Can$. Socialist Party of Canada, Box 4280 Station A, Victoria British Columbia V8X 3X8 Canada. **Tel** (604)652-3863. **DD** 335/.005. ***Continues*** *Fulcrum., 0707-5464.*

UK/0954-3635
**SOCIALIST LAWYER.** [Social. lawyer]. (1986)-. Periodical. English. Three times a year. £8.00. Haldane Society of Lawyers, Panther House 38 Mount Pleasant, London WC1X 0AP England. **Tel** 011 44 71 3539328. **DD** 344.1.

US/0884-6154
**SOCIALIST (LOS ANGELES, CALIF.).** (THE SOCIALIST.). **Added/Corp** Socialist Party of California. State Committee. Vol. 9, No. 6 (July/Aug. 1985)-. Newspaper. English. Ten times a year (July/Aug. issues combined). $5.00. Socialist, 5502 West Adams, Los Angeles CA 90016. **Tel** (310)939-8281. **Bk Rev.** ***Continues*** *California Socialist and Socialist Tribune.*

II
**SOCIALIST PERSPECTIVE. Added/Corp** Council for Political Studies. Vol. 1 (June 1973)-. Academic Scholarly Publication. English. qt. $40.00 (institution), $20.00 (individual) US; £20.00 (institution), £10.00 (individual) other. Socialist Perspective, 140/20E South Sinthee Road, 1st Floor, Calcutta 700050 India. **Tel** 525351. **ED** A. K. Mukhopadhyay. **LC** HX3; .S75. **DD** 335/.00954. Index available. cum. index. **Bk Rev**, (Qty: 2-4). **Ad Acc, Adv Mgr Tel** 525196. **Circ:** 1,000 (ctrl). Documents available from FAXON Xpress. ***Supersedes*** *Transition; A Quarterly Journal of Social Sciences.*
**Desc:** Covers articles on theoretical and empirical issues of contemporary social science. Marxism is a special interest.

NZ
**SOCIALIST POLITICS.** ***Suspended.*** (1970)-. Periodical. English. qt. $2.26. Zew Zealand Socialist Publishing Distribution, PO Box 1987, Auckland 1 New Zealand. **Tel** 734 046.

UK/0081-0606
**SOCIALIST REGISTER.** (THE SOCIALIST REGISTER.). [Social. regist.]. **VFOAT** Socialist Register. (1964)-. English. an. $60.00. Sheed & Ward Ltd., 14 Coopers Row, London EC3N 2BH England. **Tel** 011 44 71 702 9799. **ED** Ralph Miliband, Leo Panitch and John Saville. **LC** HX15; .S59. **DD** 320. **[CCC].**
**Desc:** A collection of essays covering issues of major significance for socialist theory and practice.
**Ind/Abst** Altern. Press Index (-199?); Int. Polit. Sci. Abstr.

UK
**SOCIALIST REVIEW.** Issue 145 (Sept. 1991)-. Periodical. English. Eleven times a year. £40.00 UK; £45.00 other. Socialist Workers Party, PO Box 82, London E3 3LH England. **Tel** 011 44 71 538-1626, FAX 011 44 71 538-0018. **LC** HX3; .S758. ***Continues*** *Socialist Worker Review.*

US/0161-1801
**SOCIALIST REVIEW (SAN FRANCISCO).** (SOCIALIST REVIEW.). [Social. rev.]. Vol. 8, No. 37 (Jan./Feb. 1978)-. Periodical. English. qt (4 issues). $65.00 (institutions), $28.00 (individuals) US; $77.00 (institutions), $40.00 (individuals) other. Duke University Press, PO Box 90660, Durham NC 27708-0660. **Tel** (919)687-3600, (919)688-5134 (orders), FAX (919)688-4574, telex 802829. **ED** David Trend. **LC** HX1; .S35. **DD** 335/.005. Index available. **Bk Rev. Ad Acc. Pr Rev. Circ:** 5,000. available on microfilm and microfiche from University Microfilms International (UMI). Documents available from The Genuine Article, UMI Article Clearinghouse. ***Continues*** *Socialist Revolution, 0037-8240;* ***Absorbed*** *Marxist Perspectives, 0149-8681.*
**Desc:** Covers American politics, feminism, democratic movements, labor struggles, organizing strategies and leftists, with perspectives on culture.
**Ind/Abst** Acad. Abstr. Full Text Elite (Dec. 1990-); Acad. Abstr. (Dec. 1990-); Acad. Ind. [Computer File] (1987-); Acad. Search (Dec. 1990-); Altern. Press Index; Chicano Index; Curr. Contents Soc. Behav. Sci.; Expand. Acad. Index (1987-); INFO-SOUTH Abstr.; Int. Polit. Sci. Abstr.; Left Index; Mag. Search; Middle East Abstr. Index; Newsp. Period. Abstr. (1989-); Res. Alert [Full Cov.]; Soc. Plann. Policy Dev. Abstr.; Soc. Sci. Source (Jul. 1990-); Soc. Sci. Cit. Index [Full Cov.]; Sociol. Abstr.

UK/0037-8259
**SOCIALIST STANDARD. Added/Corp** Socialist Party of Great Britain. World Socialist Party of Ireland. Vol. 1 (1904)-. Periodical. English. Twelve times a year. £8.00 UK; £11.00 (airmail) Europe; £15.00 (airmail) other. Socialist Party Great Britain, 52 Clapham High Street, London SW4 England. **Tel** 011 44 1 622 3811. **LC** HX3; .S76. **DD** 335.05. **Bk Rev. Circ:** 4,000.
**Desc:** Maintains a critical analysis of and a revolutionary approach to Capitalist Society, private or state, with opposition to reformism.

CN
**SOCIALIST STUDIES BULLETIN. VFOAT** Bulletin d'Etudes Socialistes. No. 1 (Winter 1985)-. Bulletin. English (French). Four times a year. $12.00 US and Canada; $20.00 other. Society for Socialist Studies, 471 University College, University of Manitoba, Winnipeg Manitoba R3T 2M8 Canada. **Tel** (204)474-9119. **ED** Barbara Levy, Jim Sacoumah, Anthony Thomson. **DD** 320.5/31/06071. **Pr Rev.**
**Desc:** A forum for debate and exchange through the publication of short essays, reviews, debates and letters on topics of interest and concern to socialist educators and researchers.

US/0885-1468
**SOCIALIST WORKER (CHICAGO, ILL.), THE.** (SOCIALIST WORKER.). [Social. work.]. **Added/Corp** International Socialist Organization. No. 1 (April 1977)-. Periodical. English. mo. $18.00 institutions, $12.50 individual, US; $25.00 Canada and Mexico; $37.50 other. Socialist Worker / Chicago, P.O.Box 16085, Chicago IL 60616. **Tel** (312)666-7337. **DD** 320.
**Ind/Abst** Altern. Press Index.

CN/0836-7094
**SOCIALIST WORKER (TORONTO).** (SOCIALIST WORKER : PAPER OF THE INTERNATIONAL SOCIALISTS.). [Social. work.]. **Added/Corp** International Socialists (Toronto, Ont.). (1985)-. Newspaper. English. Eleven times a year. 10.00Can$ Canada; 20.00Can$ other. International Socialists, PO Box 339 Station E, Toronto Ontario M6H 4E3 Canada. **Tel** (416)972-6391. **ED** Paul Kellogg and David McNally. **DD** 331/.05. **Bk Rev**, (Qty: 12/yr). **Circ:** 2,000. ***Continues*** *Workers' Action, 0823-6038.*
**Desc:** Current events, working class and socialist history from the perspective of three "classical" narrators.

II
**SOCIALIST WORLD PERSPECTIVES.** Vol. 1 (Aug. 1977)-. Periodical. English. qt. $16.00. S. S. Chauhan, C-19 Amar Colony, Lajpat Nagar-4, New Delhi 110024 India. **LC** HX3; .S78. **DD** 335/.005.

SP
**SOCIALISTA (P.S.O.E. (POLITICAL PARTY) : WEEKLY).** (EL SOCIALISTA.). **Added/Corp** P.S.O.E. (Political Party). (19??)-. Periodical. Spanish. Twenty-four times a year. 1300ptas Spain; 2600ptas Europe; 2000ptas others. El Socialista, Santa Engracia 165, 28003 Madrid Spain. **Tel** 011 34 1 2348740. **ED** Ana Checa. **LC** JN8101; .S65. **Ad Acc. Circ:** 250,000 (per edition) (ctrl).

BE
**SOCIALISTISCHE STANDPUNTEN.**
**Added/Corp** Institut Emile Vandervelde. (1954)-. Periodical. Dutch. bm. Emile Vandervelde-Institut, Grasmarkt 105 Bus 55, B-1000 Brussels Belgium. **Tel** 011 32 2 5131827. **LC** WMLC 93/2903. cum. index.

CI/0560-6675
**SOCIJALIZAM. Added/Corp** Savez Komunista Jugoslavije. Savez Komunista Jugoslavije. Centralni Komitet. Vol. 1 (1958)-. Periodical. Serbo-Croatian (Cyrillic). mo. **(Subscription address:** Mladost Export Import, PO Box 1028, Ilica 30, 41000 Zagreb Croatia.**) LC** HX365.5; .S63. ***Absorbed*** *Nasa Stvarnost.*

II
**SOSALISTA PANORAMA. VFOAT** Socialist Panorama. Periodical. Hindi. mo. Rs10.00. Omaprakasa Mantri, B-71 Gulmohar Park, Journalists' Colony 49, Nai Dilli India. **LC** H8; .S643.

NO
**SOSIALT FORUM/SOSIALT ARBEID.** 46.-Yearly volume; 1972-. Periodical. Norwegian. ir. Olaf Norlis Forlag, KR Augusts GY 7A, Oslo Norway. ***Formed by the union of*** *Sosialt Forum* ***and*** *Sosialt Arbeid.*

RU/0868-5797
**SOTSIALNO-POLITICHESKIE NAUKI.**
***Title Change.*** **Added/Corp** Soviet Union. Gosudarstvennyi Komitet po Narodnomu Obrazovaniiu. (1990)-(1992). Periodical. Russian. mo. **(Subscription address:** Victor Kamkin, 4956 Boiling Brook Parkway, Rockville MD 20852.**) LC** HX8; .R87a. ***Continues*** *Nauchnyi Kommunizm (Soviet Union. Gosudarstvennyi Komitet po Narodnomu Obrazovaniiu), 0235-1196.* ***Continued by*** *Sotsialno-Politicheskii Zhurnal.*

●RU
**SOTSIALNO-POLITICHESKII ZHURNAL.**
**Added/Corp** Russia (Federation). Komitet po Vysshei Shkole. Moskovskii Nezavisimyi Institut Ekologii, Konfliktologii i Otkrytogo Obrazovaniia. (1992)-. Periodical. Russian. mo. **(Subscription address:** Victor Kamkin, 4956 Boiling Brook Parkway, Rockville MD 20852.**)** ***Continues*** *Sotsialno-Politicheskie Nauki, 0868-5797.*

UK/0038-5859
**SOVIET STUDIES.** ***Title Change.*** [Sov. stud.]. Vol. 1 (June 1949)-(19??). Periodical. English. qt. Carfax Publishing Company, PO Box 25 Abingdon, Oxfordshire OX14 3UE England. **Tel** 011 44 235 555335, FAX (0279)31067, telex 817484. **(Subscription address:** US and Canada/ PO Box 2025, Dunnellon, FL 34430-2025; telephone:(904)489-6996**) ED** R A Clarke. **LC** DK266.A2; S74. **DD** 947/.005. **[CCC].** Index available. **Bk Rev. Ad Acc. Pr Rev. Circ:** 2,000. available on microfilm; available on microfiche. Documents available from The Genuine Article, UMI Article Clearinghouse. ***Continued by*** *Europe Asia Studies.*
**Desc:** An academic publication devoted to the political, economic and social affairs of the Soviet Union and the communist countries of Eastern Europe.
**Ind/Abst** ABC POL SCI; Am. Hist. Life (1955-); Br. Humanit. Index; Curr. Contents Soc. Behav. Sci.; Curr. Geogr. Publ. (199?-19??); Expand. Acad. Index (1989-); Geogr. Abstr. Human Geogr.; Humanit. Index; Index Period. Artic. Relat. Law; Int. Bibliogr. Sociol.; Int. Dev. Abstr.; Int. Polit. Sci. Abstr.; Middle East Abstr. Index; Newsp. Period. Abstr. (1991-); PAIS Int. Print; Res. Alert [Full Cov.]; Soc. Sci. Index; Soc. Sci. Index Fulltext (July 1988-) [Full Txt.].

US/0038-6596
**SPARTACIST.** [Spartacist]. No. 1 (Feb.-March 1964)-. Periodical. English (French, Spanish and German). ir. Free with $7.00 subscription to Workers Vanguard. Spartacist Publishing Company, Box 1377 General Post Office, New York NY 10016. **Tel** (212)732-7862. **ED** James Robertson, Helene Brosius, and Emily Tanner. **LC** WMLC L 83/3400. Index available. **Bk Rev.** available on microfilm.
**Desc:** An organ of revolutionary Marxism. Organ of the International Executive Committee of the international Spartacist tendency.

CN/0229-5415
**SPARTACIST CANADA.** [Sparticist Can.]. **VFOAT** Spartacist. **VAT** Sparticist (Toronto). No. 1 (Oct. 1975)-. Periodical. English. qt. $2.00 Canada; $2.00 (surface mail), $5.00 (air mail) other. Spartacist Canada Publishing Association, PO Box 6867 Station A, Toronto Ontario M5W 1X6 Canada. **Tel** (416)593-1529. **DD** 335.43/0971.

## Political Science — Socialism, Communism, Anarchism, Utopianism

GW/0170-4613
**SPW.** VFOAT S.P.W.; Sozialistische Politik und Wirtschaft. Periodical. German. ir. 7.70 each issue. SPW-Verlag/Redaktion GmbH, Moltkestr 21, O-1000 Berlin 45 Germany. **LC** HX6; .S68. **DD** 335/.005.

CE
**STATE.** Periodical. English. qt. Rs16.00. 457 Union Place 2, Colombo Sri Lanka Ceylon. **LC** HX385.8.A75; S7. **DD** 335.43/09549/3.

UK/0039-3592
**STUDIES IN COMPARATIVE COMMUNISM.** *Title Change.* [Stud. comp. communism]. Vol. 1 (July/Oct. 1968)-(19??). Periodical. English. qt. Butterworth Heinemann Publishers, Linacre House, Jordan Hill, Oxford OX2 8DP England. **Tel** 011 44 865 310366. **ED** David T Cattell. **LC** HX1; .S74. **DD** 335.43/05. **[CCC].** Index available. cum. index. **Bk Rev**. **Ad Acc**. **Pr Rev**. available on microfilm and microfiche from University Microfilms International (UMI). Documents available from The Genuine Article, UMI Article Clearinghouse. **Supersedes** Communist Affairs, 0588-8174. **Continued by** Communist and Post-Communist Studies, 0976-067X.
**Desc:** A international journal covering all communist states and communist movements including both their internal developments and their international relations. The aim of the editors is to provide comparative foci on a given subject by inviting or soliciting comments of a comparative character from scholars specializing in the same subject matter but in different communist countries.
**Ind/Abst** ABC POL SCI; Acad. Abstr. Full Text Elite (Jan. 1992-Dec. 1992); Acad. Abstr. (Jan. 1992-Dec. 1992); Acad. Search (Jan. 1992-Dec. 1992); Am. Hist. Life (1971-); Am. Bibliogr. Slavic East Europ. Stud.; Curr. Contents Soc. Behav. Sci.; Curr. Geogr. Publ. (-19??); Expand. Acad. Index (1989-); Hist. Source (Jan. 1992-); INFO-SOUTH Abstr.; Int. Bibliogr. Sociol.; Int. Polit. Sci. Abstr.; Mag. Search; Middle East Abstr. Index; Newsp. Period. Abstr. (1991-); PAIS Int. Print; Res. Alert [Full Cov.]; Soc. Sci. Source (Jan. 1992-); Soc. Sci. Cit. Index (19??-19??) [Full Cov.]; Soc. Sci. Index; Soc. Sci. Index Fulltext (Summer 1988-) [Full Txt.]; U.S. Polit. Sci. Doc.

KO
**SUNGGONG NONMUNJIP.** V. 1-. Periodical. Korean. W7,000. Tongil Sasang Yonguwon, 8-3 Chongpa-dong 2-ka Yongsan-ku, Seoul Korea. **LC** HX9.K65; S85.

HU
**SZAKSZERVEZETI SZEMLE.** Vol. 1- ; 1972-. Periodical. Hungarian. 40.00ft. Tancsics Konyvkiado, Dozsa Gyorgy UT 84/B, Budapest Hungary. **LC** HX9.H8; S9.

HU/0039-971X
**TARSADALMI SZEMLE.** [Tars. szle.]. Vol. 1- ; Jan. 1946-. Periodical. Hungarian. mo. **LC** HX8; .T3.
**Ind/Abst** Am. Hist. Life (1964-1983).

XR
**TEORIE SOCIALISMU / USTAV MARKXISMU-LENINISMU UV KSC A USTAV MARXIZMU-LENINIZMU UV KSS.** **Added/Corp** Ustav Marxismu-Leninismu UV KSC. Ustav Marxizmu-Leninismu UV KSS. (1986-). Periodical. Czech (Slovak; table of contents in German and Russian). bm. **(Subscription address:** Artia Pegas Press Ltd., Palac Metro Narodni Trida 25, 11210 Prague 1 Czech Republic.**)**

BU
**TEORIIA I PRAKTIKA NA PROPAGANDATA I AGITASIIA.** **Added/Corp** Institut za Propaganda na Marksizma-Leniniza. (1946)-. Bulgarian. UL Gurko 1, Sofia Bulgaria. **LC** Z7164.S67; T46; HX44.

GW
**TEUTONIC UNITY.** **Added/Corp** German Citizen's Initiative. No. 1 (1979)-. Periodical. English.

US/0725-5136
**THESIS ELEVEN.** See Sociology.

NE/0303-9935
**TIJDSCHRIFT VOOR SOCIALE GESCHIEDENIS.** [Tijdschr. soc. geschied.]. Vol. 1- ; May 1975-. Periodical. Dutch. Three times a year. Fl20.00. Nederlandse Vereniging Tot Beoefening Vau de Sociale Gerschiedenis, Herengracht 262-266, Amsterdam Netherlands. **LC** HX9.D8; T54.
**Ind/Abst** Int. Bibliogr. Sociol.

FR
**TRAVAUX DE L'ATELIER PROUDHON / ECOLE DES HAUTES ETUDES EN SCIENCES SOCIALES, LES.** 1- 1986-. Monographic series. French. Price varies per volume. Mme M Aymard, Centre d'Etudes sur l'URSS et l'Europe Orientale, Ecole des Hautes Etudes en Sciences Sociales, 54 Boulevard Raspail, 75270 Paris Cedex 06 France. **LC** HX261; .T77. **DD** 335.2.

FR
**TRIBUNE SOCIALISTE.** Periodical. French. 130F. **LC** HX5; .T73. **DD** 335/.005. **Continues** TS, Tribune Socialiste.

UK/0953-7554
**TROTSKYIST INTERNATIONAL.** [Trotsky. int.]. (1988)_. Periodical. English. Three times a year (Spring & Autumn & Winter). $25.49. Trotskyist International, c/o MCRI, BCM 7750, London WC1N 3XX England.

UK
**TURKEY NEWSLETTER : MONTHLY PUBLICATION OF THE COMMITTEE FOR DEFENCE OF DEMOCRATIC RIGHTS IN TURKEY.** **Added/Corp** Committee for the Defence of Democratic Rights in Turkey. No. 26 (Sept. 1982)-. Newsletter. English. bm. **Continues** Newsletter (Committee for the Defence of Democratic Rights in Turkey).
**Ind/Abst** Hum. Rights Intern. Rep.

RU/0502-9988
**UCHENYE ZAPISKI KAFEDR MARKSISTSKO-LENINSKOI FILOSOFII VYSSHEI PARTIINOI SHKOLY PRI TSK KPSS I MESTNYKH VYSSHIKH PARTIINYKH SHKOL.** See Philosophy.

RU
**UCHENYE ZAPISKI / ORDENA LENINA VYSSHAIA PARTIINAIA SHKOLA PRI TSK KPSS.** **Main/Corp** TSK. KPSS. Vysshaia Partiinaia Shkola. **Added/Corp** TSK KPSS. Vysshaia Partiinaia Shkola. Vol. 2 (1974)-. Russian. sa. MYSL, 117071 B-71 Leninskii Prospekt 15, Moscow Russia. **LC** HX15; .K65a. **Continues** Uchenye Zapiski Kafedr Istorii Kommunisticheskoi Partii Sovetskogo Soiuza Vysshei Partiinoi Shkoly Pri TSK KPSS i Mestnykh Vysshikh Partiinykh Shkol.

CN/0707-7696
**UNITE PROLETARIENNE.** 1st Edition in 1976. Periodical. French. bm. $1.50 each number. En Lutte, 4933 De Grand Pre, Montreal Quebec H2T 2H9 Canada. **DD** 335.43/0971.

GW
**UNTER DEM PFLASTER LIEGT DER STRAND.** V. 1- ; 1974-. German. Karin Kramer Verlag, Postfach 106, 1000 Berlin 44 Germany. **LC** HX821; .U53. **DD** 335/.83/05.

FR
**UNZER SHTIME / NOTRE VOIX.** See Religion and Theology-Judaism.

US/1045-991X
**UTOPIAN STUDIES.** (UTOPIAN STUDIES : JOURNAL OF THE SOCIETY FOR UTOPIAN STUDIES.). [Utop. stud.]. Vol. 1, No. 1 (1990)-. Periodical. English. Twice a year. $45.00 Comes with Society for Utopian Studies membership. Society of Utopian Studies / Department of Political Science, University of Missouri, St Louis MO 63121. **Tel** (314)553-5521. **ED** Lyman Tower Sargent (editor's address: 8001 Natural Bridge, St. Louis, MO 63121, phone: (314)553-5835). **DD** 335. **Bk Rev** (Qty: 40). **Circ**: 450. **Continues** Utopian Studies, 1045-991X.
**Ind/Abst** Am. Hist. Life (1990-).

FR/0995-0583
**VENDREDI.** (1989)-. French. wk. **Continues** L'Unite.

IT/1121-0680
**VENTESIMO SECOLO.** **Added/Corp** Centro Ligure di Storia Sociale. VFOAT 20. Secolo; XX. Secolo. (1991)-. Periodical. Italian (summaries and/or abstracts in English). tq. L60000 Italy; L100000 Europe; L120000 (other). Centro Ligure Storia Sociale, Piazza Campetto 8 A, 16100 Genoa Italy. **Tel** 011 39 10 297408. **LC** HX7; .V46. **DD** 335/.005. **Continues** Movimento Operaio e Socialista.
**Ind/Abst** Am. Hist. Life (1991-).

RU
**VESTNIK MOSKOVSKOGO UNIVERSITETA. SERIIA 12, SOTSIALNO-POLITICHESKIE ISSLEDOVANIIA.** **Added/Corp** Moskovskii Gosudarstvennyi Universitet im. M.V. Lomonosova. VFOAT Sotsialno-Politicheskie Issledovaniia. (1990)-. Periodical. Russian. Six times a year. $119.95. Izdatelstvo Moskovskogo Universiteta, K-9 Ulitsa Gertsena 5/7, Moscow Russia. **Tel** (301)881-5973. **(Subscription address:** East View Publications Inc., 3020 Harbor Lane North, Suite 110, Minneapolis MN 55447.**) LC** HX8; .V48. **Continues** Moskovskii Gosudarstvennyi Universitet Im. M.V. Lomonosova Vestnik Moskovskogo Universiteta. Seriia XII: Teoriia Nauchnogo Kommunizma.

GW
**VOGTLAND-JAHRBUCH ... FUER SOZIALISTISCHE HEIMATGESCHICHTE UND HEIMATKUNDE.** **Added/Corp** Kulturbund der DDR. Bezirksleitung Karl-Marx-Stadt. 1988-. German. **Continues** Unser Vogtland Jahrbuch.

CN/0229-4834
**VOICE OF THE YOUTH.** (THE VOICE OF THE YOUTH : ORGAN OF THE COMMUNIST YOUTH UNION OF CANADA (MARXIST-LENINIST).). [Voice youth]. Vol. 1, No. 1 (June 1979)-. Periodical. English. $0.25 each issue. National Publications Centre, PO Box 727 Adelaide Station, Toronto Ontario M5C 2J8 Canada. **Tel** (416)252-3658. **DD** 320.5/322/05.

CN/0229-4842
**VOIX DES JEUNES (TORONTO. 1979).** (LA VOIX DES JEUNES : ORGANE DE L'UNION DE LA JEUNESSE COMMUNISTE DU CANADA (MARXISTE-LENINISTE).). [Voix jeunes]. **Added/Corp** Union de la Jeunesse Communiste du Canada (Marxiste-Leniniste). Vol. 1, No 1 (June 15, 1979)-. Periodical. French. Centre National de Publications, CP 727 Succursale Adelaide, Toronto Ontario M5C 2J8 Canada. **DD** 320.5/322/05.

CN/0824-247X
**VOIX DU PEUPLE (TORONTO).** (LA VOIX DU PEUPLE : JOURNAL NATIONAL DU FRONT DU PEUPLE CONTRE LA VIOLENCE RACISTE ET FASCISTE.). [Voix peuuple]. Vol. 1, No 1 (Sept. 1982)-. Periodical. French. Front du Peuple, CP 37 Succursale P, Toronto Ontario M5S 2S6 Canada. **DD** 335.4/0971.

RU/0042-8744
**VOPROSY FILOSOFII.** See Philosophy.

US/0043-4191
**WESTERN SOCIALIST, THE.** [West. social.]. V. 1- (No. 1- ). Periodical. English. bm. $2.00. Workers World Party, 186 Lincoln Street/#602, Boston MA 02111-2485. **LC** HX1; .W46. **DD** 335.05. available on microfilm and microfiche from University Microfilms International (UMI).

SZ
**WIDERSPRUCH.** No. 1 (March 1981)-. Periodical. German. sa. 7.00F each issue. Redaktionskollektiv Widerspruch, Postfach 8026, Zurich Switzerland. **LC** HX6; .W5. **DD** 335/.005.

SZ
**WIDERSPRUCH. SONDERBAND.** VFOAT Widerspruch-Sonderband. German. Redaktionskollektiv Widerspruch, Postfach 8026, Zurich Switzerland.

US/0276-363X
**WORKER'S ADVOCATE, THE.** (THE WORKERS' ADVOCATE : VOICE OF THE MARXIST-LENINIST PARTY OF THE U.S.A.). [Work. advocate]. **Added/Corp** Marxist-Leninist Party, USA. (19??)-. Periodical. English (summaries and/or abstracts in Spanish). Eight times a year. $9.00. Marxist-Leninist Publications, Ontario Street Station, PO Box 11972, Chicago IL 60611. **ED** S T Simpson. **LC** Discard. **DD** 322. cum. index. **Bk Rev**, (Qty: 3-4).
**Desc:** A newspaper of the Marxist- Leninist party, USA which guides the American workers in developing their revolutionary struggle to overthrow the bourgeoisie and establish socialism.

US/0084-2257
**WORLD STRENGTH OF THE COMMUNIST PARTY ORGANIZATIONS.** English. an. US Department of State, 2201 C Street NW, Room 5819, Washington DC 20520. **Tel** (202)647-9859.

UK
**YEAR LEFT, THE.** *Ceased.* Vol. 1 (1985)-?. English. Routledge Chapman & Hall Inc, 29 West 35th Street, New York NY 10001. **Tel** (212)244-3336, (212)244-6412. **LC** HX1; .Y38. **DD** 335/.00973.
**Ind/Abst** Left Index.

US/0360-0157
**YOUNG SOCIALIST (NEW YORK. 1972).** *Suspended.* See Literary and Political Reviews.

YU
**YUGOSLAV INFORMATION BULLETIN OF THE LEAGUE OF COMMUNISTS OF YUGOSLAVIA & THE SOCIALIST ALLIANCE OF WORKING PEOPLE OF YUGOSLAVIA.** Bulletin. English. ir. League of Communists of Yugoslavia and the Socialist Alliance of Working People of Yugoslavia, POB 23, Belgrad 11000 Yugoslavia. **LC** DR370; .S37A. **DD** 949.7/02.

●US/1060-2070
**Z PAPERS.** [Z pap.]. **Added/Corp** Institute for Social and Cultural Communications. Vol. 1 No. 1 Jan./Mar. (1992)-. Periodical. English. qt. $30.00 (institutions). Institute for Social and Cultural Communications, 150 West Canton, Boston MA 02118. **DD** 322.

PL/0044-149X
**Z POLA WALKI.** [Z pola walki]. Vol. 1- (No. 1- ); 1958-. Periodical. Multiple languages (table of contents in French, German and Russian). qt. $20.00. **(Subscription address:** ARS Polona, PO Box 1001, 00068 Warsaw Poland.**)** **LC** HX315.7; .Z2. cum. index.
**Ind/Abst** Am. Hist. Life (1959-).

XR
**ZBIERKA ZAKONOV, CESKOSLOVENSKA SOCIALISTICKA REPUBLIKA.** **Main/Corp** Czechoslovakia. Slovak. kcs68.00. Federalni Statisticky Urad, Trziste 8, Prague 1 Mala Strana, Prague Czecholsovakia. **LC** LAW. ***Continues*** *Zbierka Zakonov Republiky Ceskoslovenskej.*

UK
**ZERO.** ***Ceased.*** **See** Women's Interests.

## POPULATION STUDIES

●CN/1193-2732
**1991 CENSUS OF CANADA, INFORMATION RELEASE.** [1991 Census Can. inf. release]. **Added/Corp** Nova Scotia. Dept. of Economic Development. Statistics Branch. **VAT** Nineteen Ninety-one Census of Canada, Information Release. (Apr. 1992)-. Periodical. English. **DD** 304.6/09716/021.

ET
**AFRICAN POPULATION NEWSLETTER.** **Added/Corp** United Nations. Economic Commission for Africa. Population Programme Centre. United Nations. Economic Commission for Africa. Population Division. **VFOAT** Information sur la Population en Afrique. Vol. 1, No. 1 (May 1970)- Vol. 1, No. 3 (Jan. 1971)- No. 4 (July 1971)-. Newsletter. English. Twice a year. Free. Economic Commissions for Africa, Popul Div, PO Box 3001, Addis Ababa Ethiopa.

CN/0848-2845
**ALBERTA POPULATION GROWTH.** ***Title Change.*** [Alta. popul. growth]. **Added/Corp** Alberta. Bureau of Statistics. 1st quarter (1986)-(199?). English. qt. Alberta Bureau of Statistics / Canada, Alberta Treasury, 7th Floor/9811-109 Street, Edmonton Alberta T5K OC8 Canada. **Tel** (403)427-3058, FAX (403)427-0409. **LC** HB1990.A4; A43. **DD** 304.6/2/097123. ***Continues*** *Alberta Quarterly Population Growth.* ***Continued by*** *ABS Probe, 1191-6893.*
**Desc:** Provides up-to-date information on population estimates and population growth components (births, deaths and migration) for the province of Alberta.

US
**ALUMNI DIRECTORY - POPULATION COUNCIL.** **See** College and School Publications-Alumni.

US/0163-4089
**AMERICAN DEMOGRAPHICS.** [Am. demogr.]. **Added/Corp** Dow Jones & Co. Vol. 1, (Jan. 1979)-. Periodical. English. Twelve times a year. $69.00 US and Canada; $89.00 other. American Demographics / New York, PO Box 68, Ithaca NY 14851. **Tel** (607)273-6343, (800)828-1133. **(Subscription address:** P.O. Box 2888, Boulder, CO 80322-2606**)** **ED** Cheryl Russell. **LC** HB3505; .A66. **DD** 301.32/9/73. **CODEN** AMDEEF. **[CCC].** Index available. cum. index. **Bk Rev. Ad Acc. Circ:** 34,000 (ctrl). available on microfilm and microfiche from University Microfilms International (UMI); available on an online database from DIALOG. Documents available from UMI Article Clearinghouse, Documents on Demand.
**Desc:** Examines, in non-technical language, population trends, techniques of demographic analysis, and sources of data. Monthly columns discuss demographic surveys, how-to approaches to using demographics, and new developments in the field.
**Ind/Abst** ABI/INFORM Glob. Ed.; ABI Inform Ondisc (March 1980-); ABI/INFORM Ondisc: Expr. Ed. (Jan. 1987-); Abstr. Soc. Gerontol.; Acad. Abstr. Full Text Elite (Jan. 1992-); Acad. Abstr. (Jan. 1992-); Acad. Ind. [Computer File] (1992-); Acad. Search (Jan. 1992-); Bus. Index (1985-); Bus. Period. Index; Bus. Source (Jan. 1992-); Chicano Index; Cumul. Index Nurs. Allied Health Lit.; Curr. Lit. Fam. Plan.; Curr. Thoughts Trends; Energy Inf. Abstr.; Environ. Abstr.; Expand. Acad. Index (1984-); F&S Index Plus Text, Int. [Select. Cov.]; Foods Adlibra; Gen. BusinessFile (1985-); Gen. Period. Index (1985-); Hospit. Manage. Rev.; INFO-SOUTH Abstr.; Infobank (Jan. 1979-); Mag. Search; Manage. Contents; Mark. Advert. Ref. Serv.; Newsp. Period. Abstr. (1986-); PAIS Int. Print (1991-); Person. Manage. Abstr.; Popul. Index; PROMT; Sage Race Relat. Abstr.; Soc. Sci. Source (Jan. 1992-); Soc. Sci. Index; Soc. Sci. Index Fulltext (Oct. 1988-) [Full Txt.]; Trade Ind. Index [Full Txt.]; UMI ABI/Inform--Bus. Period. Ondisc (Jan. 1987-) [Full Txt.]; Wilson Bus. Abstr.

FI
**AMMATILLISIIN OPPILAITOKSIIN SEKA KANSANOPISTOIHIN JA KANSANKORKEAKOULUTHIN PYUKINEET JAOTETUT.** **See** Education-Vocational Education.

FR/0066-2062
**ANNALES DE DEMOGRAPHIE HISTORIQUE.** [Ann. demogr. hist.]. **Added/Corp** Societe de Demographie Historique (France). (1965)-. Periodical. French. an. 230.00F. Editions EHESS, 131 Boulevard Saint Michel, 75005 Paris France. **Tel** 011 33 43 544715. **(Subscription address:** CID, 131 Boulevard Saint Michel, 75005 Paris France.**)** **LC** HB848; .A5. **NLM** W1 AN333F. Index available. **Bk Rev. Circ:** 1,100. Documents available from BIOSIS Document Express.
**Ind/Abst** Am. Hist. Life (1979-); Anim. Breed. Abstr.; Biol. Abstr.; Dairy Sci. Abstr.; Field Crop Abstr.; For. Prod. Abstr.; For. Abstr.; Grasslands For. Abstr.; Index Vet.; Nutr. Abstr. Rev., Ser. B, Live Feeds and Feed.; Nutr. Abstr. Rev., Ser. A, Hum. Exp.; Popul. Index; Protozoolog. Abstr.; Vet. Bull.

CN/0225-2716
**ANNUAIRE ET RAPPORT D'ACTIVITES - DEPARTEMENT DE DEMOGRAPHIE, UNIVERSITE DE MONTREAL.** [Annu. rapp. act. - Dep. demogr., Univ. Montreal]. **Main/Corp** Universite de Montreal. Departement de Demographie. First issue in 1971?. French. an. Dep de Demographie, Universite de Montreal, CP 6128 Montreal Succursale A, Montreal Quebec H3C 3J7 Canada. **DD** 304/.6/07/11714281. ***Absorbed*** *Universite de Montreal. Departement de Demographie. Bulletin d'Information, 0700-3064.*

US
**ANNUAL DEMOGRAPHIC DATA FOR MIGRANT FAMILY HOUSING CENTERS.** English. an. California Department of Housing & Community Development, PO Box 951050, Sacramento CA 94252. **Tel** (916)445-4775, FAX (916)323-2815. **LC** HD7289.U7; C32. **DD** 305.5/63.
**Desc:** Migrant farmworkers and family composition.

US/0361-6053
**ANNUAL ESTIMATE OF POPULATION FOR THE STATE OF GEORGIA.** **Main/Corp** Georgia. State Data Center. English. an. Georgia State Data Center, 270 Washington Street SW, Atlanta GA 30334. **LC** HA321; .S7A. **DD** 312/.09758.

US/0097-6032
**ANNUAL REPORT - EAST-WEST POPULATION INSTITUTE.** **Main/Corp** East-West Population Institute. English. an. East-West Population Institute, 1777 East-West Road, Honolulu HI 96848. **Tel** (808)944-7401, (808)944-7444, FAX (808)944-7970, telex 989171. **LC** HB850; .E27A. **DD** 301.32.

UK
**ANNUAL REPORT / INTERNATIONAL PLANNED PARENTHOOD FEDERATION.** **Main/Corp** International Planned Parenthood Federation. (198?)-. Periodical. English. International Planned Parenthood Federation / New York, Western Hemisphere Region Inc, 902 Broadway/10th Floor, New York NY 10010. **Tel** (212)995-8800, telex 620661. ***Continues*** *IPPF in Action.*

US/0361-7858
**ANNUAL REPORT / THE POPULATION COUNCIL.** ***Title Change.*** [Annu. Rep. - Popul. Counc. (N. Y. N. Y.)]. **Main/Corp** Population Council. **Added/Corp** University of California (System). Water Resources Center. **VFOAT** Population Council Annual Report. (1968)-(?). English. an. Population Council, One Dag Hammarskjold Plaza, New York NY 10017. **Tel** (212)644-1300, FAX (212)755-6052, telex 9102900660 POPCO. **ED** Robert Heidel. **NLM** W1 PO645. **CODEN** POPCA6. Documents available from BIOSIS Document Express. ***Continues*** *Population Council (New York, N.Y.). Annual Report for the Year Ended December 31 ... .* ***Continued by*** *Report (California Water Resources Center), 0575-4968.*
**Desc:** Reports on activities of the Population Council during the relevant year.
**Ind/Abst** Biol. Abstr.

US/0891-0847
**APLICOMMUNICATOR.** [APLICommunicator]. **VFOAT** APLI Communicator. **VAT** Association for Population/Family Planning Libraries and Information Centers-International Communicator. (1975)-. Periodical. English. qt. $15.00. University of Wisconsin-Madison Center for Demography, 4457 Social Science Building, 1180 Observatory Drive, Madison WI 53706. **DD** 026.
**Ind/Abst** Curr. Lit. Fam. Plan.

US
**APPLIED DEMOGRAPHY.** English. Three times a year. $5.00 (members), $10.00 (nonmembers). Population Association of America, 1722 N Street Northwest, Washington DC 20036. **Tel** (202)429-0891.

US/0731-3721
**ARBITRON TELEVISION POPULATION BOOK.** [Arbitron telev. popul. book]. **Main/Corp** Arbitron Company. **VFOAT** Population Book. English. an. Arbitron Ratings, 142 West 57th Street/14th Floor, New York NY 10019-3301.

US/0891-6683
**ASIA-PACIFIC POPULATION & POLICY.** [Asia Pac. pop. policy]. **VFOAT** Asia Pacific Population and Policy. No. 1 (Jan. 1987)-. Periodical. English. qt. Free. Center for Cultural and Technical Interchange between East and West Inc, 1777 East-West Road, Honolulu HI 96848. **Tel** (808)944-7401, FAX (808)944-7490, telex 230-980-171. **ED** Bryant Robey. **DD** 303. **Circ:** 3,500 (ctrl).
**Desc:** Reports research of interest to policymakers and other professionals concerned with population trends, family planning, and development.
**Ind/Abst** Geogr. Abstr. Human Geogr.; Int. Dev. Abstr.; Trop. Dis. Bull.

TH/0259-238X
**ASIA-PACIFIC POPULATION JOURNAL.** (ASIA-PACIFIC POPULATION JOURNAL / UNITED NATIONS.). [Asia-Pac. popul. j.]. **Added/Corp** United Nations. Economic and Social Commission for Asia and the Pacific. Population Division. United Nations Fund for Population Activities. Vol. 1, No. 1 (March 1986)-. Periodical. English. Four times a year. Free on request. ESCAP / United Nations Economic and Social Commission for Asia and the Pacific, United Nations Building, Rajdamnern Nok Avenue, Bangkok 10200 Thailand. **Tel** 011 66 2 2829161. **ED** Nibhon Debavalya. **LC** HA4551; .A83. **DD** 304.6/095. **NLM** W1; AS1394. Index available. cum. index. **Bk Rev. Circ:** 2,500.
**Desc:** Provides a medium for the international exchange of knowledge, experience, ideas, technical information and data on all aspects of the field of population in order to assist developing countries in the region to improve the utilization of data and information at the national level.
**Ind/Abst** Int. Dev. Abstr. (?-?); Popul. Index.

US/0891-2823
**ASIAN AND PACIFIC POPULATION FORUM.** ***Ceased.*** (ASIAN AND PACIFIC POPULATION FORUM / EAST-WEST POPULATION INSTITUTE, EAST-WEST CENTER.). [Asian Pac. popul. forum]. **Added/Corp** East-West Population Institute. **VFOAT** Population Forum. Vol. 1, No. 1 (Nov. 1986)-Vol. 6, No. 4 (Winter 1993). Periodical. English. qt. East-West Population Institute, 1777 East-West Road, Honolulu HI 96848. **Tel** (808)944-7401, (808)944-7444, FAX (808)944-7970, telex 989171. **ED** Sandra E. Ward. **LC** HB3633.A3; A774. **DD** 304.6/095. **Circ:** 2,000 (ctrl). ***Continues*** *Asian and Pacific Census Forum, 0732-0515.*
**Desc:** This journal brings articles of potential value in policy formulation, program administration, and research to the notice of professionals concerned with population matters, particularly in Asia, the Pacific, and the United States.
**Ind/Abst** Geogr. Abstr. Human Geogr.; Int. Dev. Abstr.; Popul. Index.

TH/0125-6718
**ASIAN-PACIFIC POPULATION PROGRAMME NEWS.** ***Ceased.*** [Asian-Pac. popul. programme news]. **VFOAT** Asian & Pacific Population Programme News; Asian and Pacific Population Programme News. **VAT** Asian Pacific Population Programme News. Vol. 7, No. 1 (1978)- Vol. 14, No. 4 (Dec. 1992). Periodical. English. qt. ESCAP / United Nations Economic and Social Commission for Asia and the Pacific, United Nations Building, Rajdamnern Nok Avenue, Bangkok 10200 Thailand. **Tel** 011 66 2 2829161. **LC** HB850.5.A75; A74. **DD** 304.6/095. **NLM** W1 AS139C. ***Continues*** *Asian Population Programme News.*
**Ind/Abst** Trop. Dis. Bull. (-19??).

US/0066-8451
**ASIAN POPULATION STUDIES SERIES.** [Asian popul. stud. ser.]. **Added/Corp** United Nations. Economic Commission for Asia and the Far East. United Nations. Economic and Social Commission for Asia and the Pacific. **VFOAT** Asian Population Study Series. No. 1 (1966)-. Government Publication. English. mo. United Nations Publications, 2 United Nations Plaza, Room DC2 0853, Department 007C, New York NY 10017. **Tel** (212)963-8303, (800)253-9646. **LC** JX1977; .A2. **DD** 301.3/29/5. **NLM** W1; AS14S.
**Ind/Abst** Popul. Index (?-?); Rural Dev. Abstr.

AT/0814-4370
**AUSTRALIA'S POPULATION TRENDS AND PROSPECTS.** [Aust. popul. trends prospects]. **Added/Corp** Australia. Dept. of Immigration and Ethnic Affairs. (1984)-. English. an. 8.95Aus$. Australian Government Publishing Service, GPO Box 84, Canberra ACT 2601 Australia. **Tel** 011 61 6 2954411, FAX 011 61 6 2954455. **LC** HB3675; .A98. **DD** 304.6/0994. ***Formed by the union of*** *Review of Australia's Demographic Trends, 0727-7982* ***and*** *Population Forecasts ... with Projections for Selected Years to 2021, 0810-9559.*

US
**BALANCE REPORT, THE.** **VFOAT** Population Environment Balance Report. No. 48 (May/June 1986)-. Periodical. English. qt. $25.00 (membership). Population-Environment Balance Inc, 1325 G Street NW, Suite 1003, Washington DC 20005. **Tel** (202)879-3000, FAX (202)879-3019. **ED** Dayha Petete and Kent Karstadt. **Circ:** 10,000. ***Continues*** *Other Side.*
**Desc:** Newsletter covering a variety of population issues, including birth control, and immigration.

GW/0005-7215
**BAYERN IN ZAHLEN.** [Bayern Zahlen]. V. 1- Jan. 1947-. Periodical. German. mo. Munchen Bayerisches Statistisches Landesamt, Neuhauser Str 51, 8 Munchen 2 Germany.

DK/0108-8076
**BEFOLKNINGEN I KOMMUNERNE.** Vol. 1 (1983)-. Danish. an. kr77.87. Danmarks Statistik, Sejrgade 11, DK-2100 Copenhagen Denmark. **Tel** 011 45 3 9173917, FAX 011 45 31 18 48 01, telex 1 62 36. **LC** HA1471; .B43. **Circ:** 1,550. ***Continues*** *Befolkningen I de Enkelte Kommuner Pr. ... Fordelt Efter Kn, Alder Og Gteskabelig Stilling, 0107-1041.*
**Desc:** Populations of municipalities.

GW
**BEITRAEGE ZUR DEMOGRAPHIE.** 1977-. Monographic series. German. Price varies per volume. Akademie-Verlag GmbH, Muehlenstrasse 33 34, D 13162 Berlin Germany. **Tel** 011 49 30 47889300, FAX 011 49 30 47889357. **(Subscription address:** VCH Publishers Inc., 303 Northwest 12th Avenue, Journals Department, Deerfield FL 33442.**)**

GW
**BEVOELKERUNG & ERWERBSTATIGKEIT : POPULATION AND EMPLOYMENT. FACHSERIE 1. EINZELVEROEFFENTLICHUNGEN.** (19??)-. German. ir. DM18.50 (latest issue). Metzler Poeschel Verlag Veroeffen, Statist Bundesamt Kernerstr 43, D 70182 Stuttgart Germany. **Tel** 011 49 7071 935350.

GW/0072-1867
**BEVOELKERUNGSSTRUKTUR UND WIRTSCHAFTSKRAFT DER BUNDESLAENDER.** (BEVOELKERUNGSSTRUKTUR UND WIRTSCHAFTSKRAFT DER BUNDESLAENDER / STATISTICHES BUNDESAMT WIESBADEN.). **Added/Corp** Germany (West). Statistisches Bundesamt. (1961)-. Periodical. German. an. DM22.80. Metzler Poeschel Verlag Veroeffen, Statist Bundesamt Kernerstr 43, D 70182 Stuttgart Germany. **Tel** 011 49 7071 935350. **LC** HA1235; .A3. ***Continues*** *Statistische Unterlagen zur Beurteilung der Bevolkerungsstruktur und Wirtschaftskraft der Bundeslander.*
**Desc:** Contains selected numerical data from all spheres of official statistics, with an emphasis on demographic and economic data.

GW
**BEVOLKERUNG UND ERWERBSTATIGKEIT. REIHE 1, GEBIET UND BEVOLKERUNG / HERAUSGEBER STATISTISCHES BUNDESAMT.** **VFOAT** Gebiet und Bevolkerung; Fachserie 1. Periodical. German. qt. DM19.50. Messrs W Kohlhammer GmbH, Publications of the Federal Statistical Office, Philipp-Reis-Strabe 3, Postfach 42 11 20, W-6500 Mainz 42 Germany. **Tel** 06131/59094-95, telex 4187768 DGV. **LC** HA1231; .B48.

BE/0772-764X
**BEVOLKING EN GEZIN.** [Bevolking gezin]. **Added/Corp** Centre d'Etude de la Population et de la Famille (Belgium). Nederlands Interuniversitair Demografisch Instituut. (1972)-. Dutch. Three times a year. 640.00F. Uitgeverij Pelckmans NV, Kapelsestraat 222, C 2950 Kapellen Belgium. **Tel** 011 32 3 6645320, FAX 011 32 3 6650263. **LC** HB3603; .B43. ***Supersedes in part*** *Bevolking en Gezin, 0523-1159.*
**Ind/Abst** Int. Bibliogr. Sociol.; Popul. Index.

BE/0304-8888
**BEVOLKINGSSTATISTIEKEN - NATIONAAL INSTITUUT VOOR DE STATISTIEK.** **See** Population Studies-Abstracting, Bibliographies and Statistics.

SZ
**BIENNIAL REPORT / SPECIAL PROGRAMME OF RESEARCH, DEVELOPMENT AND RESEARCH TRAINING IN HUMAN REPRODUCTION.** **See** Birth Control.

US/0149-0915
**BIORESEARCH TODAY. POPULATION, FERTILITY & BIRTH CONTROL.** ***Ceased.*** **VFOAT** Population, Fertility & Birth Control. **VAT** BioResearch Today. Population, Fertility and Birth Control. Ceased (Dec. 1991). English. mo. BioSciences Information Service, Biological Abstracts / BIOSIS, 2100 Arch Street, Philadelphia PA 19103-1399. **Tel** (800)523-4806 US, (215)587-4800 Pennsylvania and worldwide, FAX (215)587-2016, telex 831739.
**Desc:** Current awareness journal including abstracts and content summaries of studies involving population, fertility and birth control.

US/0891-3641
**BIRTH-ORIGIN STUDY OF TEXAS NEWBORNS, A.** (A BIRTH-ORIGIN STUDY OF TEXAS NEWBORNS DURING ... / TEXAS DEPARTMENT OF HEALTH.). [Birth-orig. study Tex. newborns]. **Added/Corp** Texas. Bureau of State Health Planning & Resource Development. **VFOAT** Migration for Birth; Birth Origin Study of Texas Newborns During ... . (19??)-. English. an. Free. Bureau of State Health Data and Policy Analysis, Texas Department of Health, 1100 Westes 49th Street, Austin TX 78756-3180. **Tel** (512)458-7261. **LC** RG530.3.U52; T47. **DD** 312. **NLM** W2; AT4 B8b. **Circ:** 250 (ctrl). ***Continues*** *Birth-Origin Survey of Texas Newborns.*
**Desc:** Shows county of residence for mothers and county of birth for all Texas births. Also gives number and percent of births occurring in hospitals and outside hospitals.

AT
**BIRTHS, AUSTRALIA.** **See** Population Studies-Abstracting, Bibliographies and Statistics.

SP/0213-1145
**BOLETIN DE LA ASOCIACION DE DEMOGRAFIA HISTORICA.** [Bol. Asoc. Demogr. Hist.]. **Added/Corp** Asociacion de Demografia Historica. Societa Italiana di Demografia Storica. (1984)-. Periodical. Spanish (English). tq. $30.00 (individual membership), $35.00 (institutional membership). Asociacion de Demografia Historica, Facultad de Ciencias Politicas y Sociologia, Universidad Complutense, Campus de Somosaguas, 28023 Madrid Spain.
**Ind/Abst** Popul. Index.

CL
**BOLETIN DEL BANCO DE DATOS.** **Main/Corp** Celade (Organization). Banco de Datos. Spanish (English). ir. $6.00 (per issue). Centro Latinoamericano Demografia, Casilla 91, Santiago Chile. **Tel** 011 56 2 2085051, FAX 011 56 2 480252, telex 340295 UNSTGO CK. **LC** HB3530.5; .C42A. **Circ:** 900.
**Desc:** Information on censuses and population surveys of Latin America and the Caribbean stored in the Celade population data bank.

AG
**BOLETIN DEL PROLAP.** **Added/Corp** Programa Latinoamericano de Actividades en Poblacion. (1986)-. Periodical. Spanish. Three times a year. $15.00. Centro de Estudios Poblacion, Casilla 4397 Correo Central, 1000 Buenos Aires Argentina. **Tel** FAX 54 1 961 8195. **LC** HB850.5.L37; B6. **Circ:** 500.

CL/0378-5386
**BOLETIN DEMOGRAFICO - CENTRO LATINOAMERICANO DE DEMOGRAFIA.** (BOLETIN DEMOGRAFICO.). [Bol. demogr. - Cent. Latinoam. Demogr.]. **Main/Corp** Celade (Organization). **Added/Corp** CELADE (Organization). Year 1 (Jan. 1968)-. Periodical. Spanish (English). sa. $10.00. Centro Latinoamericano Demografia, Casilla 91, Santiago Chile. **Tel** 011 56 2 2085051, FAX 011 56 2 480252, telex 340295 UNSTGO CK. **LC** HB3530.5.A3; B65. **Circ:** 1,000. available on microfiche.
**Desc:** Contains population projections and estimates, birth and death rates, for the Latin American and Caribbean countries.
**Ind/Abst** PAIS Int. Print; Popul. Index.

DK/0107-8909
**BOLIGTLLINGEN.** Vol. 1 (Jan. 1980)-. Danish. kr33.61. Danmarks Statistik, Sejrgade 11, DK-2100 Copenhagen Denmark. **Tel** 011 45 3 9173917, FAX 011 45 31 18 48 01, telex 1 62 36. **LC** HD7347.A3; B685. **Circ:** 1,800.
**Desc:** Population and housing census, national tables.

CN/1186-7965
**BRITISH COLUMBIA MIGRATION HIGHLIGHTS.** [B.C. migr. highlights]. **Added/Corp** British Columbia. Population Section. Issue 91/1 (May 1991)-. Periodical. English. qt. **DD** 304.8/711/0021.

CX
**BULLETIN DE LIAISON / CENTRE REGIONAL D'ETUDES DE POPULATION.** ***Title Change.*** **Added/Corp** Centre Regional d'Etudes de Population. (19??)-(19??). Bulletin. French. qt. Centre Regional d'Etudes de Population, BP 1418, Bangui Central African Republic. **LC** HB3664.8.A3; B84. **DD** 304.6/0966/0097541. ***Continued by*** *Bulletin de Liaison (Union Douaniere et Economique de l'Afrique Centrale. Departement des Etudes de Population).*

CM/1013-1396
**BULLETIN DE LIAISON DE DEMOGRAPHIE AFRICAINE.** [Bull. liaison demogr. afr.]. **Added/Corp** Institut de Formation et de Recherche Demographiques (Yaounde, Cameroon). **VFOAT** Demographie Africaine. No. 29 (March/April 1979)-. Bulletin. French (French). Three times a year. Free. Institut de Formation et de Recherche Demographiques, Service des Publications, B P 1556, Yaounde Cameroun. **Tel** 22.24.71. **ED** M Sala-Diakanda. **LC** HB3661.A3; D44. **DD** 304.6/096. **Bk Rev. Circ:** 1,000. ***Continues*** *Demographie Africaine, 0151-1394.*
**Desc:** List of searchers interested African population problems. Population projects in Africa. Recent publications on population studies. Reports on seminars, workshops, and the congress on population issues.
**Ind/Abst** Popul. Index.

CX
**BULLETIN DE LIAISON / DEPARTEMENT DES ETUDES DE POPULATION.** **Added/Corp** Union Douaniere et Economique de l'Afrique Centrale. Departement des Etudes de Population. (19??)-. Bulletin. French. qt. Centre Regional d'Etudes de Population, BP 1418, Bangui Central African Republic. **LC** HB3664.8.A3; B84. **DD** 304.6/0966/0097541. ***Continues*** *Bulletin de Liaison (Centre Regional d'Etudes de Population).*

CN/0380-1721
**CAHIERS QUEBECOIS DE DEMOGRAPHIE.** [Cah. que. demogr.]. **Added/Corp** Association des demographes du Quebec. Vol. 4 (March 1975)-. Periodical. French. sa. 18.00Can$ Canada; 30.00Can$ other. Bureau of Statistics / Quebec, Publications, 117 rue Saint Andre, Quebec Quebec G1K 3Y3 Canada. **Tel** (418)691-2401, (800)463-4090. **ED** Claude Dionne (editor's phone: (418)691-2406). **DD** 301.32/05. **Circ:** 800 (ctrl). ***Continues*** *Bulletin de l'Association des Demographes du Quebec, 0380-1713.*
**Desc:** Topics covered: fertility, migration, mortality, historical demography, demolinguistics, health, social demography, methods and models of population analysis.
**Ind/Abst** Foreign Lang. Index; PAIS Int. Print (1991-); Point Repere (1983-); Popul. Index.

UK/0954-0547
**CAMBRIDGE STUDIES IN POPULATION, ECONOMY AND SOCIETY IN PAST TIME.** [Camb. stud. popul. econ. soc. past time]. (1984)-. Monographic series. English. ir. Price varies per volume. Cambridge University Press, The Edinburgh Building, Shaftesbury Road, Cambridge CB2 2RU United Kingdom. **Tel** 011 44 223 312393, FAX 011 44 223 325959. **(Subscription address:** North America: Cambridge University Press, 110 Midland Avenue, Port Chester, NY 10573**)**

CN/0380-1489
**CANADIAN STUDIES IN POPULATION.** [Can. stud. popul.]. **Added/Corp** University of Alberta. Population Research Laboratory. Canadian Population Society. Vol. 1 (1974)-. English (French). sa (June and November). $35.00 (institution), $22.00 (individual), $10.00 (student) US and Canada; $36.00 (institution), $23.00 (individual), $11.00 (student) other. Canadian Studies in Population, Department of Sociology, Population Research Laboratory, Edmonton Alberta T6G 2H4 Canada. **Tel** (403)492-4659, FAX (403)492-2589. **ED** H. Northcott, University of Alberta. **LC** HB848; .C36. **DD** 304.6/0971. cum. index. **Bk Rev.** ctrl circ.
**Desc:** International in scope, this journal publishes articles of quality in any area of population - methodological or substantive - that contributes to the growth of the discipline. In addition to major articles, it presents research notes, a forum section, and news and notes on population activities, as well as a book review section.
**Ind/Abst** Popul. Index.

US
**CAROLINA POPULATION CENTER PAPERS.** No. 1 (March 1978)-. Periodical. English.
**Ind/Abst** Popul. Index (?-?).

US
**CASE STUDIES OF ARRANGEMENTS FOR EVALUATION AND UTILIZATION OF POPULATION CENSUS RESULTS; REPORT.** **Main/Corp** United Nations. Department of Economic and Social Affairs. (1959)-. Government Publication. English. ir. United Nations Publications, 2 United Nations Plaza, Room DC2 0853, Department 007C, New York NY 10017. **Tel** (212)963-8303, (800)253-9646. **LC** JX1977; .A2; HA46; .U5. **DD** 312.09624.
**Desc:** Census results from the Republic of Sudan, Guatemala, and Edcuador.

AT
**CAUSES OF DEATH, AUSTRALIA.** **See** Population Studies-Abstracting, Bibliographies and Statistics.

US/0565-0828
**CENSUS BUREAU METHODOLOGICAL RESEARCH.** **Main/Corp** United States. Bureau of the Census. Began with 1963-1966. Government Publication. English. an. US Department of Commerce / Bureau of the Census, Data User Services Division, Customer Services, Washington DC 20233-0800. **Tel** (301)763-4100. **(Subscription address:** Superintendent of Documents, US Government Printing Office, Washington DC 20402.**)** **LC** Z7554.U5; U58a; HA37. **DD** 016.0014/33. **NLM** Z 7554.U5 C396.

US
**CENSUS OF POPULATION AND HOUSING (1980).** (1980 CENSUS OF POPULATION AND HOUSING. CENSUS TRACTS.). **Added/Corp** United States. Bureau of the Census. (198?)-. Government Publication. English. ir. Free. US Department of Commerce / Bureau of the Census, Data User Services Division, Customer Services, Washington DC 20233-0800. **Tel** (301)763-4100. **(Subscription address:** Superintendent of Documents, US Government Printing Office, Washington DC 20402.**)** available on microfiche.
**Desc:** These reports present demographic, social, economic, and housing statistics for census tracts from the 1980 Census of Population and Housing; maps included.

US/0513-1529
**CENTER PAPER (PRINCETON, N.J.).** (CENTER PAPER.). [Cent. pap.]. **Main/Corp** Yale University. Economic Growth Center. No. 1-. Monographic series. English. ir. Price varies per volume. Yale University Economic Growth Center, 27 Hillhouse Avenue, Box 1987 Yale Station, New Haven CT 06520-1987. **Tel** (203)432-3610, FAX (203)432-3898, telex 9102508365. **DD** 330. cum. index. **Bk Rev. Ad Acc. Circ:** 400.
**Ind/Abst** Popul. Index (?-?).

US
**CERTIFIED POPULATION OF TENNESSEE INCORPORATED MUNICIPALITIES.** English. an. Local Planning Assistance Office, 1800 James K. Polk Street, Office Building, Nashville TN 37219. **LC** HA641; .C47. **DD** 304.6/2/09768021.

US/1044-8403
**CHINESE JOURNAL OF POPULATION SCIENCE.** [Chin. j. popul. sci.]. **Added/Corp** Population Research Institute. Vol. 1, No. 1 (1989)-. Periodical. English (translations available in Chinese). Four times a year. $270.00. Allerton Press, Inc., 150 Fifth Avenue, New York NY 10011. **Tel** (212)924-3950, FAX (212)463-9684, telex 427441 ALPRES. **LC** HB3654.A3; C486. **DD** 304.6/0951/05. **[CCC].**
**Ind/Abst** Popul. Index.

CC
**CHUNG-KUO JEN KUO TUNG CHI NIEN CHIEN.** **Added/Corp** China. Kuo Chia Tung Chi Chu. Jen Kou Tung Chi Ssu. **VFOAT** China Population Statistics Yearbook. (1988)-. Chinese. an. China National Publishing Import & Export Corporation, 16 Gongti E Rd., Chaoyang Dist., Beijing 100704, People's Republic of China. **Tel** 011 8601 50630169, 5066688, FAX 011 8601 5063101, 5063010, telex 22313. **LC** HA4635; .C48.

US/0362-3904
**CITY POPULATION ESTIMATES - GEORGIA. STATE DATA CENTER.** **Main/Corp** Georgia. State Data Center. English. Georgia Office of Planning and Budget, 270 Washington Street Southwest, Room 611, Atlanta GA 30334. **Tel** (404)656-3820. **LC** HA321; .S7B. **DD** 312/.09758.

TR/0564-2612
**CONTINUOUS SAMPLE SURVEY OF POPULATION.** Began with: No. 1, published in 1964?. English. an. $3.00. Central Statistical Office / Trinidad and Tobago, PO Box 98, 23 Park Street, Port of Spain Trinidad. **Tel** 62-54970, FAX 62-53802. **LC** HA867; .A385. **DD** 304.6/097298/3021. **Circ:** 400 (ctrl).
**Desc:** Provides a description of the labor force in Trinidad and Tobago. Published in the series of labor force size and structure; and housing and income.

US/0360-8514
**COUNTRY DEMOGRAPHIC PROFILES.** [Ctry. demogr. profiles]. **Added/Corp** International Statistical Programs Center (U.S.). Vol. 1 (1973)-. Government Publication. English. Price varies per volume. US Department of Commerce / Bureau of the Census, Data User Services Division, Customer Services, Washington DC 20233-0800. **Tel** (301)763-4100. **(Subscription address:** Superintendent of Documents, US Government Printing Office, Washington DC 20402.**)** **LC** HB848; .C68. **DD** 312.
**Ind/Abst** Popul. Index (?-?).

US/0097-305X
**COUNTRY PROFILES.** [Ctry. profiles]. **Added/Corp** Population Council. International Institute for the Study of Human Reproduction. (19??)-. Monographic series. English. Population Council, One Dag Hammarskjold Plaza, New York NY 10017. **Tel** (212)644-1300, FAX (212)755-6052, telex 9102900660 POPCO. **NLM** W1 CO968K.

US
**COUNTY AND CITY COMPENDIUM. CD-ROM.** English. an. $670.00 (nonprofit institutions), $745.00 other. Slater Hall Information Products, 1301 Pennsylvania Avenue Northwest, Washington DC 20004. **Tel** (202)393-2666.
**Desc:** Economic and social statistics for counties, cities, metroareas; census bureau and other federal agencies. Retrieval software included.

US
**COUNTY-CITY PLUS. CD-ROM.** English. an. $199.00. Slater Hall Information Products, 1301 Pennsylvania Avenue Northwest, Washington DC 20004. **Tel** (202)393-2666.
**Desc:** Latest 1990 census data plus other key economic and demographic data for U.S. counties and cities. Retrieval software included.

US/0190-7190
**CPR POPULATION RESEARCH.** **Main/Corp** United States. National Institute of Child Health and Human Development. Center for Population Research. **VFOAT** Population Research. **VAT** Center for Population Research. Monographic series. English. Price varies per volume. National Institute of Child Health and Human Development / Population Research, Center for Population Research, 9000 Rockville Pike, Bethesda MD 20014. **NLM** W1 C548.

US/0748-7819
**CURRENT DEVELOPMENTS IN ANTHROPOLOGICAL GENETICS.** **See** Biology-Genetics.

US
**CURRENT POPULATION REPORTS : FARM POPULATION. SERIES P-27.** **Main/Corp** United States. Bureau of the Census. **Added/Corp** United States. Bureau of Agricultural Economics. United States. Agricultural Marketing Service. United States. Dept. of Agriculture. Economic Research Service. United States. Dept. of Agriculture. Economics, Statistics, and Cooperatives Service. **VFOAT** Farm Population. No. 1 (Jan. 14, 1945)-. English. Comes with Population Characteristics Special Studies and Consumer Income. Superintendent of Documents, US Government Printing Office, Washington DC 20402. **Tel** (202)275-3328, FAX (202)786-2377.
**Ind/Abst** Curr. Lit. Fam. Plan.; Popul. Index.

US/0738-453X
**CURRENT POPULATION REPORTS. SER. P-25, POPULATION ESTIMATES AND PROJECTIONS.** (CURRENT POPULATION REPORTS. SERIES P-25, POPULATION ESTIMATES AND PROJECTIONS.). [Curr. popul. rep., P-25 Popul. estim. proj.]. **Added/Corp** United States. Bureau of the Census. **VFOAT** Population Estimates and Projections. (19??)-. Monographic series. English. mo. $27.00 domestic; $33.75 other. Superintendent of Documents, US Government Printing Office, Washington DC 20402. **Tel** (202)275-3328, FAX (202)786-2377. **LC** HA195; .A533. **DD** 312/.0973. **NLM** W2 A B9CUB. Documents available from Documents on Demand. ***Continues*** *Current Population Reports. Series P-25, Population Estimates.*
**Desc:** Estimates of the total population of the United States; annual mid-year estimates of the United States by age, color, and sex; states by broad age groups; annual estimates of the components of population change; projections of the future population of the United States.
**Ind/Abst** Am. Stat. Index; Curr. Lit. Fam. Plan.; Popul. Index.

US/0363-6836
**CURRENT POPULATION REPORTS. SERIES P-20, POPULATION CHARACTERISTICS.** [Curr. popul. rep., Ser. P-20, Popul. char.]. **Added/Corp** United States. Bureau of the Census. **VFOAT** Population Characteristics. (1947)-. Monographic series. English. ir. $101.00 domestic; $126.25 other. Superintendent of Documents, US Government Printing Office, Washington DC 20402. **Tel** (202)275-3328, FAX (202)786-2377. **LC** HA195; .A53. **DD** 312.9. **NLM** W2 A B9CU. Documents available from Documents on Demand. ***Absorbed*** *Current Population Reports. Series P-27, Farm Population, 1048-6283.*
**Desc:** Current national and regional data on geographic residence and mobility, fertility, education, school enrollment, marital status, numbers and characteristics of household and families.
**Ind/Abst** Am. Stat. Index; Curr. Lit. Fam. Plan.; Popul. Index.

US/0498-8485
**CURRENT POPULATION REPORTS. SERIES P-23, SPECIAL STUDIES.** [Curr. popul. rep., Ser. P-23, Spec. stud.]. **Added/Corp** United States. Bureau of the Census. **VFOAT** Special Studies. (1969)-. Government Publication. English. ir. $101.00 domestic; $126.25 other. Superintendent of Documents, US Government Printing Office, Washington DC 20402. **Tel** (202)275-3328, FAX (202)786-2377. **LC** HA203; .A218. **NLM** W2 A B9CUE. Documents available from Documents on Demand. ***Continues*** *Current Population Reports. Series P-23, Technical Studies.*
**Desc:** Infrequent reports on methods, concepts, or specialized data.
**Ind/Abst** Am. Stat. Index; Curr. Lit. Fam. Plan.; Popul. Index.

US/0270-6660
**CURRENT POPULATION REPORTS. SERIES P-28, SPECIAL CENSUSES.** [Curr. popul. rep., Ser. P-28, Spec. censuses]. **VFOAT** Special Censuses. Began with No. 232. Government Publication. English. ir. Price varies per volume. US Department of Commerce / Bureau of the Census, Data User Services Division, Customer Services, Washington DC 20233-0800. **Tel** (301)763-4100. **(Subscription address:** Superintendent of Documents, US Government Printing Office, Washington DC 20402.**)** **NLM** W2 A B9CUC. available on microfiche. Documents available from Documents on Demand. ***Continues*** *Current Population Reports. Series P-SC, Special Censuses.*
**Ind/Abst** Am. Stat. Index; Popul. Index (?-?).

US/0730-4803
**CURRENT POPULATION REPORTS. SERIES P-60, CONSUMER INCOME.** **See** Economics.

US/0886-5698
**CURRENT POPULATION REPORTS. SERIES P-70, HOUSEHOLD ECONOMIC STUDIES.** [Curr. popul. rep., Ser. P-70, Househ. econ. stud.]. **Added/Corp** United States. Bureau of the Census. **VFOAT** Household Economic Studies. No. 1 (1983)-. Government Publication. English. bm. $21.00 domestic; $26.25 other. Superintendent of Documents, US Government Printing Office, Washington DC 20402. **Tel** (202)275-3328, FAX (202)786-2377. **LC** HA203; .C87. **DD** 339.2/2.

AT
**DEATHS, AUSTRALIA.** **See** Population Studies-Abstracting, Bibliographies and Statistics.

AT/0816-0465
**DEATHS, QUEENSLAND.** **See** Population Studies-Abstracting, Bibliographies and Statistics.

TR
**DEATHS REPORT / REPUBLIC OF TRINIDAD & TOBAGO, CENTRAL STATISTICAL OFFICE.** **Added/Corp** Trinidad and Tobago. Central Statistical Office. (1985)-. Statistical Publication. English. an. Central Statistical Office / Trinidad and Tobago, PO Box 98, 23 Park Street, Port of Spain Trinidad. **Tel** 62-54970, FAX 62-53802. **LC** RA407.5.T7; D43. **DD** 614.4/272983/021. ***Continues in part*** *Population and Vital Statistics Report.*
**Desc:** This report contains the births registered in the country. Also contained is the cause of death.

HU/0011-8249
**DEMOGRAFIA.** [Demografia]. **Added/Corp** Magyar Tudomanyos Akademia. Demografiai Elnoksegi Bizottsag. Hungary. Kozponti Statisztikai Hivatal. (1958)-. Periodical. Hungarian (summaries and/or abstracts in English and Russian). Four times a year. $19.50. **(Subscription address:** Kultura, PO Box 149, H 1389 Budapest 62 Hungary**)** **LC** HB3592.H8; D4. **DD** 312. **NLM** W1 DE134R.
**Ind/Abst** Am. Hist. Life (1958-); Int. Bibliogr. Sociol.; Popul. Index; Rural Dev. Abstr.; Soc. Plann. Policy Dev. Abstr.; Sociol. Abstr. (?-?); World Agric. Econ.

UN
**DEMOGRAFICHESKIE ISSLEDOVANIIA / ACADEMIIA NAUK UKRAINSKOI SSR, INSTITUT EKONOMIKI.** Vol. 11 (1987)-. Russian (Russian). an. **LC** HB3608.U5; D42. ***Continues*** *Demohrafichni Doslidzhennia.*
**Ind/Abst** Popul. Index.

XR/0011-8265
**DEMOGRAFIE.** (DEMOGRAFIE; REVUE PRO VYZKUM POPULACNIHO VYVOJE.). [Demografie]. Vol. 1- 1959-. Periodical. Czech (English; table of contents in English and Russian). qt. kcs40.00. **(Subscription address:** Artia Pegas Press Ltd., Palac Metro Narodni Trida 25, 11210 Prague 1 Czech Republic.**)** **LC** HB3592.C9. **NLM** W1 DE134U. cum. index. **Bk Rev. Circ:** 1,800 (ctrl).
**Desc:** A review dealing with contemporary and past population development; provides the latest demographic data concerning Czechoslovakia.
**Ind/Abst** Popul. Index.

CN/0702-0031
**DEMOGRAPHIC BULLETIN (TORONTO).** (DEMOGRAPHIC BULLETIN.). [Demogr. bull.]. **Added/Corp** Ontario. Ministry of Treasury, Economics and Intergovernmental Affairs. Social and Economic Unit. Ontario. Ministry of Treasury, Economics and Intergovernmental Affairs. Social and Economic Data. Ontario. Ministry of Treasury and

Economics. Social and Economic Data. Vol. 1 (Aug. 1977)-. Monographic series. English. mo. Price varies per volume. Ontario Government Bookstore, 880 Bay Street, Toronto Ontario M7A 1N8 Canada. **LC** HA747.O6; D45. **DD** 304.6/09713.

US/0275-9594
**DEMOGRAPHIC MONOGRAPHS.** [Demogr. monogr.]. V. 1-. Monographic series. English. ir. Price varies per volume. Gordon & Breach Science Publishers, Inc., PO Box 786, Cooper Station, New York NY 10276. **Tel** (212)206-8900, FAX (212)645-2459. **(Subscription address:** International Publishers Distributor at one of the following addresses: 820 Town Center Drive, Langhorne, PA 19047; or PO Box 90, Reading Berkshire RG1 8JL UK; or Kent Ridge PO Box 1180, Singapore 9111, Republic of Singapore**)**

US
**DEMOGRAPHIC PROFILES, SOCIOECONOMIC PROFILES, AND PER CAPITA INCOMES OF THE RESIDENT POPULATIONS OF WASHINGTON STATE SCHOOL DISTRICTS. Main/Corp** Washington (State). Superintendent of Public Instruction. **VFOAT** Demographic Profiles, Washington State School Districts. English. State Superintendent of Public Instruction, 650 West State, Boise ID 83702. **LC** LC132.W3; W37A. **DD** 371.2/19/797.
**Desc:** Vols. for 1976-77 include comparative data for earlier years., e.g. 1970.

US/0148-6284
**DEMOGRAPHIC REPORT, HEW. Main/Corp** United States. Dept. of Health, Education, and Welfare. Region III. **VAT** Demographic Report, Health, Education, and Welfare. English. PO Box 13716, Philadelphia PA 19101. **LC** HB3509; .U55A. **DD** 301.32/9/74.

NZ/0113-3667
**DEMOGRAPHIC TRENDS. Added/Corp** New Zealand. Dept. of Statistics. (1987)-. English. an. 44.40NZ$ New Zealand; 63.40NZ$ other. Department of Statistics / New Zealand, PO Box 2922, Wellington New Zealand. **Tel** 011 64 4 4954600. **LC** HA3171; .D46. **DD** 304.6/09931/021. ***Continues*** *Demographic Trends Bulletin, 0112-9155.*

US/0082-8041
**DEMOGRAPHIC YEARBOOK. See** Population Studies-Abstracting, Bibliographies and Statistics.

AU
**DEMOGRAPHISCHE INFORMATIONEN / HRSG. VOM INSTITUT FUER DEMOGRAPHIE, OSTERREICHISCHE AKADEMIE DER WISSENSCHAFTEN.** **Added/Corp** Osterreichische Akademie der Wissenschaften. Institut fuer Demographie. (1981)-. German. Akademie der Wissenschaften Zentinst, Permoserstrasse 15, O-7010 Leipzig Germany. **LC** HB3591; .D44.
**Ind/Abst** Popul. Index.

US/0070-3370
**DEMOGRAPHY.** [Demography]. **Added/Corp** Population Association of America. Vol. 1 (1964)-. Periodical. English (summaries and/or abstracts in Spanish). Four times a year (Feb., May, Aug., & Nov.). $85.00. Population Association of America, 1722 N Street Northwest, Washington DC 20036. **Tel** (202)429-0891. **LC** HB881.A1; D53. **DD** 304.6/05. **NLM** W1 DE136K. cum. index. available on microfilm and microfiche from University Microfilms International (UMI). Documents available from The Genuine Article, UMI Article Clearinghouse, Documents on Demand.
**Ind/Abst** ABI/INFORM Glob. Ed.; ABI Inform Ondisc (Nov. 1971-Dec. 1976); Abstr. Anthropol.; Acad. Search (July 1993-); Appl. Soc. Sci. Index Abstr.; Biostatistica (19??-19??); Chicano Index; Curr. Contents Soc. Behav. Sci.; Curr. Lit. Fam. Plan.; Econ. Lit. Index; Energy Inf. Abstr.; Energy Res. Abstr. (Aug. 1982-); Environ. Abstr.; Expand. Acad. Index (1989-); Geogr. Abstr. Human Geogr.; Health Plan. Adminis.; Index Med.; Int. Bibliogr. Sociol.; Int. Dev. Abstr.; Int. Labour Doc.; J. Econ. Lit.; J. Plan. Lit.; LABORDOC; Mag. Search; Middle East Abstr. Index; Newsp. Period. Abstr. (1991-); PAIS Int. Print (1991-); Popul. Index; Res. Alert [Full Cov.]; Soc. Sci. Cit. Index [Full Cov.]; Soc. Sci. Index; Soc. Sci. Index Fulltext (1989-) [Full Txt.]; Stat. Theory Method Abstr. (1987); Trop. Dis. Bull.; West. Hist. Q.; Women Stud. Abstr.

II/0970-454X
**DEMOGRAPHY INDIA.** [Demogr. India]. **Added/Corp** Indian Association for the Study of Population. Vol. 1 (Oct. 1972)-. Periodical. English. sa. $40.00. Hindustan Publishing Corporation, 6 UB Jawahar Nagar, Delhi 110 007 India. **Tel** (11)2915059, FAX (11)6863511. **(Subscription address:** Prints India, 11 Darya Ganj, New Delhi, 110002 India, (Phone: 011 91 11 3268645)**) ED** P B Desai. **LC** HB848; .D46. **DD** 301.32/0954.
**Ind/Abst** Popul. Index; Trop. Dis. Bull.

AT/1036-2649
**DEMOGRAPHY, QUEENSLAND. See** Population Studies-Abstracting, Bibliographies and Statistics.

AT/1036-2657
**DEMOGRAPHY, SOUTH AUSTRALIA. See** Population Studies-Abstracting, Bibliographies and Statistics.

US/0732-9830
**DETAILED MORTALITY STATISTICS, ALABAMA.** [Detail. mortal. stat., Ala.]. **Added/Corp** Alabama. Bureau of Vital Statistics. Alabama. Division of Vital Statistics. **VFOAT** Alabama, Detailed Mortality Statistics. (19??)-. English. an. $5.00. Center for Health Statistics, State Office Building, 434 Monroe Street, Montgomery AL 36130. **Tel** (205)242-5253. **LC** HB1355.A2; D47. **DD** 312/.2/09761. **NLM** W2 AA4 D6D.

UA
**DIRASAT SUKKANIYAH. Added/Corp** Egypt. Jihaz Tanzim al-Usrah wa-al-Sukkan. Maktab al-Buhuth. Majlis al-Qawmi lil-Sukkan (Egypt). **VFOAT** Population Studies. (1974)-. Periodical. Arabic (English). qt. National Population Council of Egypt, PO Box 1036, Cairo, Egypt. **LC** HB3661.7.A3; D57. ***Continues*** *Egypt. Jihaz Tanzim al-Usrah wa-al-Sukkan. Maktab al-Buhuth. Dirasat -- Jihaz Tanzim al-Usrah wa-al-Sukkan, Maktab al-Buhuth.*
**Ind/Abst** Popul. Index.

CL/0378-5378
**DOCPAL RESUMENES SOBRE POBLACION EN AMERICA LATINA.** (RESUMENES SOBRE POBLACION EN AMERICA LATINA.). [DOCPAL Resum. pobl. Am. Lat.]. **VFOAT** Latin American Population Abstracts; Docpal. V. 1-June 1977-. Spanish (English). sa. $20.00. Centro Latinoamericano Demografia, Casilla 91, Santiago Chile. **Tel** 011 56 2 2085051, FAX 011 56 2 480252, telex 340295 UNSTGO CK. **LC** HB3530.5; .R48. **DD** 301.32/9/8. **NLM** Z 7164.D3 D11. **Circ:** 1,000. available on CD-ROM.
**Desc:** Detailed abstracts of published and unpublished literature on population written in or about Latin America and the Caribbean.
**Ind/Abst** Popul. Index.

FR/0993-6165
**DOSSIERS DU CEPED, LES. Added/Corp** Centre Francais sur la Population et le Developpement. **VAT** Dossiers du Centre Francais sur la Population et le Developpement. No 1 (Sept. 1988)-. Monographic series. French. Four times a year. Price varies per volume. Centre Francais sur la Population et la Developpement, 15 rue de l'Ecole de Medecine, 75270 Paris Cedex 06 France. **Tel** 011 33 1 46 33 9941, FAX 011 33 1 43 25 4578. **LC** IN PROCESS. Index available. cum. index. **Pr Rev. Acid Free. Circ:** 600 (ctrl). available on diskette.
**Desc:** Monographs in the fields of population and development, demographic transition, health policy and data collection in developing countries.
**Ind/Abst** Popul. Index.

US/1050-8627
**ECONOMIC AND DEMOGRAPHIC ALMANAC OF WASHINGTON COUNTIES AND CITIES.** [Econ. demogr. alm. Wash. cties. cities]. **VFOAT** Economic & Demographic Almanac of Washington Counties & Cities. (1989)-. English. Information Press, PO Box 1422, Eugene OR 97440. **Tel** (503)689-0188. **LC** HC107.W2; E25. **DD** 330. ***Continues*** *Economic and Demographic Almanac of Washington Counties.*

CN/0703-8763
**EDMONTON AREA SERIES REPORT.** No. 1-. Monographic series. English. Price varies per volume. Population Research Laboratory / Department of Social Science, University of Alberta 1 62, Edmonton Alberta T6G 2H4 Canada. **Tel** (403)492-4659. **DD** 309.1/7123/3. **Circ:** 100.
**Desc:** Reports on the findings of our annual Edmonton area study. This is a survey of Edmonton residents gathering basic demographic data plus information on a special topic each year.

UA
**EGYPTIAN POPULATION AND FAMILY PLANNING REVIEW, THE. Added/Corp** Jamiyah al-Misriyah lil-Buhuth al-Sukkaniyan. Jamiat al-Qahirah. Mahad al-Dirasat wa-al-Buhuth al-Ihsaiyah. (19??)-. English. Twice a year. Institute of Statistical Studies & Research, PO Box 1017, 5 Tharwat St/Giza, Cairo Egypt. **Tel** 011 20 2 718355, 718496. **ED** A.A. Sorhan, A.M. Khalifa, and H.H. Makhlouf. **LC** HQ766.5.E3; E38. **DD** 362.8/2. **Ad Acc.**
**Ind/Abst** PAIS Int. Print; Popul. Index.

US/0190-3896
**ELDERLY POPULATION: ESTIMATES BY COUNTY, THE.** (THE ELDERLY POPULATION, ESTIMATES BY COUNTY / U.S. DEVELOPMENT [I.E. DEPARTMENT] OF HEALTH AND HUMAN SERVICES, OFFICE OF HUMAN DEVELOPMENT SERVICES, ADMINISTRATION ON AGING, NATIONAL CLEARINGHOUSE ON AGING.). **Added/Corp** National Clearinghouse on Aging (U.S.). (1976)-. English. an. National Clearinghouse on Aging, 330 Independence Avenue Southwest, Washington DC 20201. **LC** HQ1064.U5; N24a. **DD** 312/.92/0973.

SP
**ENCUESTA DE POBLACION ACTIVA.** **Added/Corp** Spain. Instituto Nacional de Estadistica. **VFOAT** Poblacion Activa, Encuesta. (19??)-. Spanish. Instituto Nacional de Estadistica Spain, Paseo de la Castellana 183, 28071 Madrid Spain. **LC** HD5807; .E5. ***Continues*** *Encuesta Sobre Poblacion Activa.*

US/0090-7871
**EQUILIBRIUM (WASHINGTON, D.C.).** (EQUILIBRIUM.). [Equilibrium]. V. 1- Jan. 1973-. Periodical. English. qt. $3.00. Zero Population Growth / Washington DC, 1400 Sixteenth Street Northwest, Suite 320, Washington DC 20036. **Tel** (202)332-2200, FAX (202)332-2302. **LC** HB848; .E67. **DD** 301.32/9/73.

FR/0755-7809
**ESPACE POPULATIONS SOCIETES.** [Espace popul. soc.]. **Added/Corp** Universite des Sciences et Techniques de Lille. U.E.R. de Geographie. Universite des Sciences et Techniques de Lille-Flandres-Artois. U.F.R. de Geographie. (19??)-. Periodical. French. Three times a year. 340.00F France; 360.00 other. Univ Sci Tech, Lille-Flanders-Artois, Ufr Geog Amenagmnt, Batiment 2, 59655 Villenv d'Ascq Cedex France. **Tel** 011 33 1 20 436552, FAX 011 33 1 20 434995. **LC** HB848; .E83. Index available. **Circ:** 800.
**Ind/Abst** Am. Hist. Life (1983-); Geogr. Abstr. Phys. Geogr.; Geogr. Abstr. Human Geogr.; Int. Bibliogr. Sociol.; Int. Dev. Abstr.; Popul. Index.

BL
**ESTATISTICAS DE MORTALIDADE, BRASIL / MINISTERIO DA SAUDE, SECRETARIA NACIONAL DE ACOES BASICAS DE SAUDE, DIVISAO NACIONAL DE EPIDEMIOLOGIA.** 1979-. Portuguese. an. Free. Centro de Documenta Cao do Ministerio da Saude, Esplanada dos Ministerios Bloco G Terreo rreo, 70058 Brasilia DF Brazil. **LC** HB1393; .E87. **DD** 312/.2/0981. **NLM** W2; DB8 D62e. **Circ:** 2,000 (ctrl).

TR/0303-4410
**ESTIMATED INTERNAL MIGRATION BULLETIN (PORT OF SPAIN).** (ESTIMATED INTERNAL MIGRATION BULLETIN (TRINIDAD AND TOBAGO).). **Main/Corp** Trinidad and Tobago. Central Statistical Office. 1- 1973-. Bulletin. English. Central Statistical Office / Trinidad and Tobago, PO Box 98, 23 Park Street, Port of Spain Trinidad. **Tel** 62-54970, FAX 62-53802. **(Subscription address:** Government Printing Office, 48 St Vincent Street, Port of Spain Trinidad**) LC** HA867; .A385 subser; HB2017. **DD** 317.29/83 S; 312/.8. **Circ:** 400.
**Desc:** Shows data on net international migration by age group, sex and area, also shows migrant gain to administrative areas.

AT
**ESTIMATED RESIDENT POPULATION BY AGE AND SEX IN STATISTICAL LOCAL AREAS, WESTERN AUSTRALIA / AUSTRALIAN BUREAU OF STATISTICS. See** Population Studies-Abstracting, Bibliographies and Statistics.

AT/1030-9179
**ESTIMATED RESIDENT POPULATION BY COUNTRY OF BIRTH, AGE AND SEX, AUSTRALIA / AUSTRALIAN BUREAU OF STATISTICS. Added/Corp** Australian Bureau of Statistics. (1976)-. English. an. 15.30Aus$. Australian Bureau of Statistics, PO Box 10, Belconnen Australian Capital Territory, 2616 Australia. **Tel** 011 61 6 2527911, FAX 011 61 6 2516009. **LC** HA3001; .E875.
**Desc:** Estimated resident population of Australia by country of birth, 5-year age groups and sex.

AT/1030-8989
**ESTIMATED RESIDENT POPULATION BY MARITAL STATUS, AGE AND SEX, AUSTRALIA. Added/Corp** Australian Bureau of Statistics. (19??)-. English. an. 11.70Aus$. Australian Bureau of Statistics, PO Box 10, Belconnen Australian Capital Territory, 2616 Australia. **Tel** 011 61 6 2527911, FAX 011 61 6 2516009. **LC** HA3001; .E876.
**Desc:** Estimated resident population by marital status, single years of age and sex.

AT/0810-0039
**ESTIMATED RESIDENT POPULATION BY SEX AND AGE, STATES AND TERRITORIES OF AUSTRALIA.** **Added/Corp** Australian Bureau of Statistics. (1968)-. English. an. 12.20Aus$. Australian Bureau of Statistics, PO Box 10, Belconnen Australian Capital Territory, 2616 Australia. **Tel** 011 61 6 2527911, FAX 011 61 6 2516009. **LC** HA3001; .E877.

**Desc:** Estimates of population for each State and Territory classified by sex and single years of age (0 to 84).

AT
**ESTIMATED RESIDENT POPULATION IN LOCAL GOVERNMENT AREAS / AUSTRALIAN BUREAU OF STATISTICS, SOUTH AUSTRALIAN OFFICE.** **See** Population Studies-Abstracting, Bibliographies and Statistics.

MX/0186-7210
**ESTUDIOS DEMOGRAFICOS Y URBANOS.** **Added/Corp** Colegio de Mexico. Centro de Estudios Demograficos y de Desarrollo Urbano. (Jan./Apr., 1986)-. Periodical. Spanish (summaries and/or abstracts in English). Three times a year. $55.00 (institutions), $35.00 (individuals) US and Canada; $35.00 (institutions), $28.00 (individuals) Latin America; $62.00 (institutions), $45.00 (individuals) other. Colegio de Mexico AC, Camino Al Ajusco No 20, 10740 Mexico DF Mexico. **Tel** 011 52 5 6455955 Ext. 3133, telex 1777585 COLME. **LC** HB3531; .E84. ***Continues in part*** *Demografia y Economia.*
**Ind/Abst** Popul. Index.

FR/0014-2247
**ETUDES TSIGANES.** **Added/Corp** Association des Etudes Tsiganes. Vol. 1 (Apr. 1955)-. Periodical. French (English). sa. 208.00F. Etudes Tsiganes, 2 rue d'Hautpoul, 75019 Paris France. **Tel** 1 40 40 09 05. **LC** DX101; .E79. **DD** 909/.0491497. **Bk Rev. Circ:** 1,500.
**Desc:** Presents studies of the "Tsiganes" population of France and other countries. Covers history, linguistics, sociology, ethnology, art, literature, music and social actions. Includes chronicles and bibliographies.

NE/0168-6577
**EUROPEAN JOURNAL OF POPULATION.** **Added/Corp** European Association for Population Studies. **VFOAT** Revue Europeenne de Demographie. Vol. 1, No. 1 (Jan. 1985)-. Periodical. English (French). qt. $380.00. Kluwer Academic Publishers, Postbus 322, 3300 AH Dordrecht, The Netherlands. **Tel** 011 (31) 78 524400, FAX 011 31 78 183273, telex 20083. **ED** Daniel Courgeau, David Coleman, Paolo de Sandre, Hella Courgeau. **LC** Z7164.D3; E85. **DD** 304.6/094/05. **NLM** W1; EU72EC. **[CCC]. Pr Rev. Acid Free.** available on microfilm and microfiche from University Microfilms International (UMI). Documents available from The Genuine Article. ***Continues*** *European Demographic Information Bulletin, 0046-2756.*
**Desc:** Aims to improve understanding of population processes and their correlates, more particularly with respect to issues of scientific and policy concern in Europe.
**Ind/Abst** Appl. Soc. Sci. Index Abstr.; Curr. Contents Soc. Behav. Sci.; Geogr. Abstr. Human Geogr.; Int. Bibliogr. Sociol.; Int. Dev. Abstr.; J. Plan. Lit.; PAIS Int. Print (1991-); Popul. Index; Res. Alert [Full Cov.]; Sage Fam. Stud. Abstr.; Soc. Plann. Policy Dev. Abstr.; Soc. Sci. Cit. Index [Full Cov.]; Trop. Dis. Bull.

US/0193-8762
**FACTFINDER FOR THE NATION.**
**Main/Corp** United States. Bureau of the Census. Government Publication. English. US Department of Commerce / Bureau of the Census, Data User Services Division, Customer Services, Washington DC 20233-0800. **Tel** (301)763-4100. **(Subscription address:** Superintendent of Documents, US Government Printing Office, Washington DC 20402.**)**
**Desc:** Describes, in a series of reports, the range of Census Bureau materials available on a given subject and suggests some of their uses.

US/1063-0961
**FEDSTAT (ALEXANDRIA, VA.).** (FEDSTAT [COMPUTER FILE].). [FEDSTAT]. **Added/Corp** U.S. Statistics, Inc. University of Alabama. JVC Disc America Co. (198?)-. English. US Statistics Inc, PO Box 816, Alexandria VA 22313. **Tel** (703)979-9699, FAX (703)548-4585. **LC** HB848. **DD** 304.
**Desc:** Contains county and city data files, current population survey files, county business pattern files, regional economic information system files, TIGER and decennial census files, intercensal population estimates files, and ZIP-city-county reference files. System requirements: IBM PC, XT, AT or compatible; 512K of memory; 1.2MB of hard disk space; MS-DOS 3.1 or higher; any ISO 9660 CD-ROM drive.

US/0145-4668
**FLORIDA ESTIMATES OF POPULATION / PREPARED BY THE POPULATION PROGRAM, BUREAU OF ECONOMIC AND BUSINESS RESEARCH, COLLEGE OF BUSINESS ADMINISTRATION, UNIVERSITY OF FLORIDA.** **Added/Corp** University of Florida. Population Division. (Apr. 1, 1987)-. English. an (Feb.). $21.20 (taxable) Florida; $20.00 (non-taxable) others. Bureau of Economic & Business Research / Florida, University of Florida, 221 Matherly Hall, Gainesville FL 32611. **Tel** (904)392-0171, FAX (904)392-4739. **LC** HB3525.F6; F57. **DD** 312/.09759. ***Continues*** *Florida Estimates of Population, State, Counties, and Municipalities, 0145-4668.*

●US
**FLORIDA POPULATION STUDIES.**
**Added/Corp** University of Florida. Population Program. Bulletin No. 104 (Mar. 1993)-. Periodical. English. Three times a year. $31.80 Florida; $30.00 others. Bureau of Economic & Business Research / Florida, University of Florida, 221 Matherly Hall, Gainesville FL 32611. **Tel** (904)392-0171, FAX (904)392-4739. **LC** HB3525.F6; F55a. ***Continues*** *Population Studies (University of Florida. Population Program).*

CN/0843-7548
**FOCUS ON CULTURE.** [Focus cult.]. **Added/Corp** Statistics Canada. **VFOAT** Culture en Perspective. Vol. 1, No. 1 (Autumn 1989)-. Periodical. English (French). qt. 26.00Can$ Canada; $32.00 US; $37.00 other. Statistics Canada, Publications Sales & Services, Main Building Room 1710, Ottawa Ontario K1A 0T6 Canada. **Tel** (613)951-5078, (800)267-6677, FAX (613)951-1584, telex 053-3585. **DD** 306/.0971.
**Desc:** Provides readers with articles based on the surveys of cultural industries, institutions and activities available through the Culture Statistics Program.

AU
**GEMEINDEUBERSICHT.** **Main/Corp** Osterreichisches Statistisches Zentralamt. (19??)-. German. an. S140.00. Osterreichisches Statistisches Zentralamt, Hintere Zollamtsstrasse 2B, Postfach 9000, Vienna 1033 Austria. **Tel** (0222)71128-7628, FAX (0222)71128-7728, telex 0132600. **LC** G108.7; .A95a. **DD** 910/.5. Index available. **Circ:** 230 (ctrl).
**Desc:** Lists 2,350 communities of Austria with their post codes and population figures divided in political districts and federal countries.

GW/0177-2082
**GEMEINDEWACHSTUM.**
[Gemeindewachstum]. **VFOAT** Dynamische Gemeinde. (1979)-. Periodical. German. ir (4 issues). DM18.00 (latest issue). Jorg Knoblauch, Postfach 1108, W 7928 Gingen FR Germany. **Tel** 011 49 7322 13650. **UDC** 284.

IT/0016-6987
**GENUS.** [Genus]. V. 1- June 1934-. Periodical. English (Italian, French and German). sa. L80000 Italy; 100.00F other. ESIA Books and Journals, Via Palestro 30, 00185 Rome Italy. **Tel** 011 39 6 4441220, 011 39 6 4441221, FAX 011 39 6 4747743. **ED** Nora Federici. **LC** HB881; .G4. **DD** 304.6/05. **NLM** W1 GE357. **CODEN** GNUSA7. **Bk Rev. Circ:** 3,000. Documents available from BIOSIS Document Express.
**Desc:** Demographical analysis, as well as historical demography, bio-demography, economical demography, social demography, theory of population and demographical models.
**Ind/Abst** Am. Hist. Life (1975-); Anthropol. Index; Anthropol. Lit.; Biol. Abstr.; Int. Bibliogr. Sociol.; PAIS Int. Print (1991-); Popul. Index; Stat. Theory Method Abstr. (1959-1963); Trop. Dis. Bull.

NO/0435-3684
**GEOGRAFISKA ANNALER. SERIES B, HUMAN GEOGRAPHY.** **See** Housing and Urban Development.

US
**GEOGRAPHICAL MOBILITY.** Began with Mar. 1975 - Mar. 1976. Government Publication. English. an. US Department of Commerce, 14th Street & Constitution Avenue NW, Washington DC 20230. **Tel** (202)482-2000, FAX (202)482-3772. ***Continues*** *Mobility of the Population of the United States.*

DK/0017-4556
**GRNLAND (1953).** (GRNLAND.). [Grnland]. (1953)-. Periodical. Danish. mo (ten issues per year). Kr255.00 Denmark; Kr365.00 other. Det Gronlakdske Seldkab, Le Bruunsvej 10, 2920 Charlottenlund Denmark. **Tel** 009451635733. **ED** Keld Hansen. **LC** G725; .G8233. **CODEN** GRGSAX. Index available. cum. index (ten year). **Bk Rev. Ad Acc. Circ:** 2,000.
**Desc:** Greenland and the Arctic environments and populations.
**Ind/Abst** ASTIS Curr. Aware. Bull. (1978-); Am. Hist. Life (1989-1990); ASTIS Bibliogr. (1978-); Energy Res. Abstr. (Jan. 1982-); GeoRef.

US
**GUIDE TO SOURCES OF INTERNATIONAL POPULATION ASSISTANCE.** 1976-. English (French and English). te. Free to libraries in both developed and developing countries; $20.00 other. United Nations Population Fund, 220 East 42nd Street/17th Floor, New York NY 10017. **Tel** (212)297-5026, FAX (212)557-6416, telex 422031. **LC** HB848; .G83. **DD** 309.2/23. **NLM** HQ 766.7; P831. Index available. **Circ:** 3,000 (ctrl). available on microfilm.
**Desc:** Shows the types of population activities which various organizations and agencies (multilateral, regional, bilateral, non-governmental) and research and training institutions can provide.

US
**HAVE YOU HEARD?.** (19??)-. English. qt. Free to members. Population Environment Balance Inc, 1325 G Street Northwest, Suite 1003, Washington DC 20005. **Tel** (202)879-3000, FAX (202)879-3019. **ED** M. Nowak. **Circ:** 10,000.
**Desc:** A humorous, short takes newsletter, focusing on US population and emvironmental issues.

CN/1180-2421
**HEALTH REPORTS. SUPPLEMENT. CAUSES OF DEATH.** (HEALTH REPORTS. SUPPLEMENT. CAUSES OF DEATH / STATISTICS CANADA, CANADIAN CENTRE FOR HEALTH INFORMATION.). [Health rep., Suppl., Causes death]. **Added/Corp** Canadian Centre for Health Information. **VFOAT** Causes of Death; Causes de Deces; Rapports sur la Sante. Causes de Deces. (1987)-. English (French). an. 30.00Can$ Canada; $36.00 US; $42.00 other. Statistics Canada, Publications Sales & Services, Main Building Room 1710, Ottawa Ontario K1A 0T6 Canada. **Tel** (613)951-5078, (800)267-6677, FAX (613)951-1584, telex 053-3585. **LC** RA407.5.C2; H42. **DD** 614.4/271/021. **NLM** W2; DC2 V8C. ***Continues*** *Causes of Death, Vital Statistics, Volume IV, 0380-7533.*
**Desc:** Presents the number of deaths by three-digit categories and four-digit sub-categories of the International Classification of Diseases (ICD).

CN/1180-307X
**HEALTH REPORTS. SUPPLEMENT. LIFE TABLES, CANADA AND PROVINCES.** **See** Population Studies-Abstracting, Bibliographies and Statistics.

SA
**HUWELIKE EN EGSKEIDINGS / REPUBLIEK VAN SUID-AFRIKA, SENTRALE STATISTIEKDIENS / MARRIAGES AND DIVORCES / REPUBLIC OF SOUTH AFRICA, CENTRAL STATISTICAL SERVICE.**
**Added/Corp** South Africa. Central Statistical Services. **VFOAT** Marriages and Divorces. (1990)-. Statistical Publication. Afrikaans (English). Central Statistical Service, The Government Printer, Private Bag X85, Pretoria 0001 South Africa. **Tel** 012-3228622, FAX 012-3226325, telex 320450. **LC** HB1283.4.A3; H88. ***Continues*** *Huwelike en Egskeidings, Blankes, Kleurlinge en Asieers ... Suid-Afrika.*

CN/0251-0464
**IGU NEWSLETTER.** **See** Geography.

II
**IIPS NEWSLETTER.** **Main/Corp** International Institute for Population Studies. **Added/Corp** International Institute for Population Studies. Newsletter. Vol. 19 (Jan. 1978)-. Newsletter. English. qt. Free. International Institute for Population Studies, Govandi Station Road, Deonar Bombay 400 088 India. **Tel** 22 5563254. **ED** Parveen Nangia and B.M. Ramesh. **LC** HB850.5.I4; I54a. **DD** 304.6/072054. **Bk Rev. Circ:** 1,300 (ctrl). available with charts; available with illustrations. ***Continues*** *Newsletter - International Institute for Population Studies, 0047-0716.*
**Desc:** Details about the teaching and research activities of the International Institute for Population Sciences.

US
**ILLINOIS POPULATION TRENDS FROM ... TO ... .** **Added/Corp** Illinois. Bureau of the Budget. (1982)-. English. an. Illinois Bureau of the Budget, Division of Planning and Financial Analysis, 605 Stratton Building, Springfield IL 62706. **LC** HA341; .I44. **DD** 312/.8/09773. ***Continues*** *Illinois Population Projections.*

KO/0537-6998
**INGU MUNJE NONJIP.** **Added/Corp** Ingu Munje Yonguso. **VFOAT** Journal of Population Studies. (1965)-. Periodical. Korean (English and Korean). **LC** HB848; .I516.
**Ind/Abst** Trop. Dis. Bull.

PH/0115-2181
**INITIATIVES IN POPULATION.** (INITIATIVES IN POPULATION : QUARTERLY MAGAZINE OF THE POPULATION CENTER FOUNDATION OF THE PHILIPPINES.). **Added/Corp** Population Center Foundation. Vol. 1, No. 1 (Sept. 1975)-. Periodical. English. qt. P20.00. Population Center Foundation, PO Box 2065, Makati Central Puyat Avenue, Makati Philippines. **Tel** 855-111. **ED** Virgilio F Lacaba. **LC** HQ763; .I58. **DD** 363.9/6/09599. **NLM** W1 IN4511. **Bk Rev. Ad Acc. Circ:** 10,000 (ctrl).
**Desc:** Seeks to bring scientific, technical and population program information to professionals, workers and managers.

FR/0998-4860
**INSEE CADRAGE. DEMOGRAPHIE-SOCIETE.** ***Title Change.***
**VFOAT** Institut National de la Statistique et des Etudes Economiques Cadrage, Demographie-Societe. (1989)-(19??). French. Institut National de la Statistique

# Population Studies

et des Etudes Economiques, 18 Bc Adolphe Pinard, 75675 Paris 14 France. **UDC** 31(44). *Merged into INSEE Resultats.*

JA
**INTEGRATION / JOICFP.** See Birth Control.

US/0163-7223
**INTERCOM (WASHINGTON. EDICION ESPANOL).** (INTERCOM.). V. 1- Jan. 1979-. Periodical. Spanish. mo. Population Reference Bureau, 1875 Connecticut Avenue Northwest, Suite 520, Washington DC 20009. **Tel** (202)483-1100, (800)877-9881, FAX (202)328-3937.

US/0363-5155
**INVENTORY OF POPULATION PROJECTS IN DEVELOPING COUNTRIES AROUND THE WORLD.** 1973/74-. English. an. Free to all libraries; $20.00 other. United Nations Population Fund, 220 East 42nd Street/17th Floor, New York NY 10017. **Tel** (212)297-5026, FAX (212)557-6416 telex 422031. **LC** HQ763. **DD** 363.9/6/091724. **NLM** HQ 763.5; P831. Index available. **Circ:** 3,000 (ctrl). available on microfilm.
**Desc:** Gives description of population activities supported by a number of organizations and agencies (multilateral, bilateral, regional, and non-governmental) to over 137 developing countries and/or territories.

US
**IREDELL COUNTY TRACKS / GENEALOGICAL SOCIETY OF IREDELL COUNTY, N.C.** Added/Corp Genealogical Society of Iredell County, N.C. (19??)-. Periodical. English. qt. **LC** F262.I7; G46a. **DD** 929/.1/0720756793. *Continues Genealogical Society of Iredell County, N.C.; Genealogical Society of Iredell County, N.C., 0740-5006.*

BE/0253-4010
**IUSSP PAPERS.** (IUSSP PAPERS / INTERNATIONAL UNION FOR THE SCIENTIFIC STUDY OF POPULATION.). [IUSSP pap.]. **Added/Corp** International Union for the Scientific Study of Population. (19??)-. Monographic series. English (French). ir. Price varies per volume. International Union for the Scientific Study of Population, 34 rue Augustins, B-4000 Liege Belgium. **Tel** (41)224080, FAX (41)223847, telex 42648 POPUN B. **NLM** W1 I41. **Circ:** 2,300.
**Ind/Abst** Popul. Index (?-?).

II
**JANASAMKHYA.** Added/Corp University of Kerala. Dept. of Demography. Vol. 1, No. 1 (June 1983)-. Periodical. English. Twice a year. $15.00. Professor & Head of Department of Demography and Population Studies, University of Kerala, Kariavattom 695581 India. **Tel** (0471)8057. **ED** R. Ramakumar. Index available. **Ad Acc. Pr Rev. Circ:** 200 (ctrl).
**Desc:** Research articles in demography toward methodology, technical demography and statistical models. Results of population studies from any part of the world.
**Ind/Abst** Popul. Index.

CH
**JEN KOU HSUEH KAN / KUO LI TAI-WAN TA HSUEH.** Added/Corp Kuo li Tai-wan ta Hsueh. Jen ko Yen Chiu Chung Hsin. VFOAT Journal of Population Studies. (19??)-. Chinese (English). an. $15.00. Population Study Center, National Taiwan University, Taipei Taiwan. **Tel** (02)3630197, FAX (02)3639565. **ED** Lan-hung Nora Chiang. **LC** HB3656.A3; J46. **DD** 304.6/0951/249. Index available. cum. index. **Bk Rev. Pr Rev. Circ:** 1,000.
**Desc:** Articles of population studies from all over the world.
**Ind/Abst** Popul. Index.

JA/0387-2793
**JINKO MONDAI KENKYU.** [Jinko mondai kenkyu]. Added/Corp Jinko Mondai Kenkyujo (Japan). VFOAT Journal of Population Problems. Vol. 1 No. 1 (1940)-. Periodical. Japanese (table of contents in English). qt. Ministry of Health and Welfare, Institute of Population Problems, 2-2, 1-chome, Kasumigaseki, Chiyoda-ku, Tokyo, Japan. **NLM** W1 JI645P.
**Ind/Abst** Popul. Index.

JA/0449-0339
**JINKO MONDAI KENKYUJO NENPO.** Main/Corp Jinko Mondai Kenkyuho (Japan). VFOAT Annual Report of the Institute of Population Problems. Japanese (summaries and/or abstracts in English). an. 2-2 Kasumigaseki 1-chome, Chiyoda-ku Tokyo 100 Japan. **LC** HB850.5.J3; J55D.

JA
**JINKO MONDAI KENKYUJO YORAN.** Main/Corp Jinko Mondai Kenkyujo (Japan). VFOAT Brochure of the Institute of Population Problems, Ministry of Health and Welfare. Multiple languages (Japanese and English). 2-2 Kasumigaseki 1-chome, Chiyoda-ku, Tokyo 100 Japan. **LC** HB850.5.J3; J55A.
**Ind/Abst** Popul. Index (?-?).

JA/0386-8311
**JINKOGAKU KENKYU.** (JINKOGAKU KENKYU / NIHON JINKO GAKKAI HENSHU.). [Jinkogaku kenkyu]. VFOAT Journal of Population Studies. No. 1- (March, 1978)-. Japanese (summaries and/or abstracts in English). an. Kokon Shoin, 2-10 Kanda Surugadai, Chiyoda-ku 100, Tokyo Japan. **LC** HB3651; .J535.
**Ind/Abst** Popul. Index.

TH
**JOURNAL OF POPULATION AND SOCIAL STUDIES.** English. sa. $36.00. Inst Population Social Research, Mahidol University, Salaya Nakhonch, Nakhonpathom 73170 Thailand. **Tel** 011 66 2 4419521.
**Ind/Abst** Popul. Index; Trop. Dis. Bull.

GW/0933-1433
**JOURNAL OF POPULATION ECONOMICS.** [J. popul. econ.]. VFOAT Population Economics. Vol. 1, No. 1 (June 1988)-. Periodical. English. qt. DM360.00. Springer-Verlag GmbH & Company KG, Heidelberger Platz 3, D 14197 Berlin Germany. **Tel** 011 49 30 8207223, FAX 011 49 30 8214091, telex 183 319 SPBLN D. **(Subscription address:** Springer Verlag New York Inc. for North America, 44 Hartz Way, Secaucus NJ 07096.) **ED** A Cigno, P Pestieau, B M S van Praag, R Willis, and K F Zimmermann. **LC** HB849.41; .J68. **DD** 304.6/05. **CODEN** JPECEW. **[CCC].** cum. index. **Ad Acc. Pr Rev. Circ:** 500. available on magnetic tape, an online database, and CD-ROM; available on microfilm and microfiche from University Microfilms International (UMI). Documents available from The Genuine Article.
**Desc:** Focuses on the relation between economics and demographics and addresses diverse topics in this area.
**Ind/Abst** Curr. Contents Soc. Behav. Sci.; Econ. Lit. Index (199?-); Geogr. Abstr. Human Geogr.; Int. Bibliogr. Sociol.; Int. Dev. Abstr. (?-?); J. Econ. Lit. (1991-); Popul. Index; Res. Alert [Full Cov.]; Soc. Sci. Cit. Index [Full Cov.].

AT/0814-5725
**JOURNAL OF THE AUSTRALIAN POPULATION ASSOCIATION.** [J. Aust. Popul. Assoc.]. Added/Corp Australian Population Association. (1984)-. Periodical. English. Twice a year (June & Nov.). 50.00Aus$ Australia, 60.00Aus$ others (members); 100.00aus$ Australia, 110.00Aus$ (corporate) others Comes with Australian Population Association membership. Australian Population Association, PO Box 583, Indooroopilly Queensland 4068 Australia. **Tel** 011 61 7 2370888, FAX 011 61 7 2354071. **DD** 304.60994.

UK
**KEY POPULATION AND VITAL STATISTICS. LOCAL AND HEALTH AUTHORITY AREAS / OFFICE OF POPULATION CENSUSES AND SURVEYS.** Added/Corp Great Britain. Office of Population Censuses and Surveys. VFOAT Local and Health Authority Areas. (1986)-. English. an. £8.60. Her Majesty's Stationery Office, 51 Nine Elms Lane, London SW8 5DR England. **Tel** 011 44 71 873 8459, 011 44 71 873 8499, FAX 011 44 71 873 8499, 011 44 71 873 8456, telex 297138. **LC** HA1123; .P64. **DD** 304.6/0942/021. *Continues Population and Vital Statistics. Local and Health Authority Area Summary.*

JA/0386-4561
**KOTAIGUN SEITAI GAKKAI KAIHO.** Added/Corp Kotaigun Seitai Gakkai (Japan). (19??)-. Periodical. Japanese. ir. Kotaigun Seitai Gakkai / Society of Population Ecology, Ogawa Higashi Iru, Shimordachuri Dori, Kamigayo-ku, Kyoto 602 Japan. **LC** QH352; .K67.

US/1050-2351
**LATIN AMERICAN POPULATION HISTORY BULLETIN.** See History(General)-History of North, South, and Central America.

US/0148-6136
**LAW AND POPULATION PROGRAMME NEWSLETTER.** See Law.

RU
**LITERATURA O NARODONASELENII.** (1983)-. Russian. MYSL, 117071 B-71 Leninskii Prospekt 15, Moscow Russia. *Continues Literatura o Naselenii.*

UK/0143-2974
**LOCAL POPULATION STUDIES.** [Local popul. stud.]. Added/Corp University of Nottingham. Dept. of Adult Education. No. 5 (Autumn 1970)-. Periodical. English. Twice a year (May & Nov.). £7.00. Local Population Studies - M. Charlton, 27 St. Margarets Road, St. Mary Church, Torquay Devon England. **Tel** 011 44 803 38112. **ED** Tom Arkell, Christopher Charlton, Terry Gwynne, May Pickles, Roger Schofield, Kevin Schurer, Malcolm Smith and Geoffrey Stevenson. **LC** HB3583; .L63. **DD** 304.6/0941/021. **NLM** W1 LO1016H. Index available. **Bk Rev. Ad Acc. Circ:** 1,500. *Continues Local Population Studies Magazine and Newsletter.*

**Ind/Abst** Am. Hist. Life (1976-); Br. Humanit. Index; Geogr. Abstr. Human Geogr. (?-?); Humanit. Index; Int. Bibliogr. Sociol.; Popul. Index.

FI
**MAASAAMUUTTO MUUTON SUUNNAN MUKAAN KUNNITTAIN ... .** Added/Corp Finland. Tilastotiedotus. VFOAT Inrikes Omflyttning Efter Flyttningens Riktning Kommunvis ... . (19??)-. Finnish (Swedish). an. Government Printing Centre, PO Box 516, SF-00101 Helsinki 10 Finland. **LC** HB3608.3.A3; T55 subser.; HB2068.3.A3. *Continues Finland. Tilastotiedotus. Maassamuutto Kunnittain.*

IO/0126-0251
**MAJALAH DEMOGRAFI INDONESIA.** [Maj. demogr. Indones.]. Added/Corp Universitas Indonesia. Lembaga Demografi. Ikatan Peminat dan Ahli Demografi Indonesia. VFOAT Journal of Indonesian Demography. Vol. 1 (June 1974)-. English (Indonesian). Twice a year (June & Dec.). $35.00. Demographic Institute, PO Box 427, Jakarta 10002 Indonesia. **Tel** 011 62 21 336434, 011 62 21 336539, 33102457. **ED** M. Djuhari Wirakartakusumah. **LC** HA1815; .M33; HA4601; .M35. Index available. **Bk Rev. Ad Acc. Circ:** 1,000 (ctrl).
**Ind/Abst** Asia.-Pac. Econ. Lit.; Int. Bibliogr. Sociol.; Int. Labour Doc.; Popul. Index.

US/0580-9029
**MARYLAND STATISTICAL ABSTRACT.** See Economics.

US/0889-8480
**MATHEMATICAL POPULATION STUDIES.** [Math. popul. stud.]. Vol. 1/No. 1 (1988)-. Periodical. English. qt (1 volume). $373.00 (academic institutions), $582.00 (corporate institutions). Gordon & Breach Science Publishers, Inc., PO Box 786, Cooper Station, New York NY 10276. **Tel** (212)206-8900, FAX (212)645-2459. **ED** William Brass, Nathan Keyfitz, Herve Le Bras, Ronald D. Lee and John H. Pollard. **LC** HB849.51; .M38. **DD** 304.6/01/51. **CODEN** MPSTEG. **[CCC].**
**Ind/Abst** Popul. Index; Soc. Res. Methodol. Abstr. (1990-).

US/0749-9868
**MEDIA AUDIT. CORPUS CHRISTI, TEXAS. QUARTERLY REPORT, THE.** Periodical. English. qt. International Demographics Inc, 3000 Richmond Avenue, Suite 170, Houston TX 77098.

US/0734-032X
**MISSOURI POPULATION ESTIMATES, BY COUNTY, BY AGE, BY SEX.** VFOAT Missouri Population Estimates. Began with: 1971-1975. English. an. $10.00. Missouri Center for Health Statistics, PO Box 570, Jefferson City MO 65102. **ED** Garland Land and Wayne Schramm. **NLM** W2 AM8 C4MC. Index available. cum. index. **Circ:** 750.

NE
**MOBILITEIT VAN DE NEDERLANDSE BEVOLKING IN ... / CENTRAAL BUREAU VOOR DE STATISTIEK, HOOFDAFDELING STATISTIEKEN VAN VERKEER EN VERVOER, DE.** VFOAT Mobility of Dutch Population in ... . Dutch. Fl15.90. Centraal Bureau voor de Statistiek, AFD ALG Zaken, Postbus 959, 2270 AZ Voorburg Netherlands. **Tel** 011 31 70 3373800, FAX 011 31 038 7429, telex 32692 CBS NL. **LC** HB2065; .M6.

US
**MONEY INCOME AND POVERTY STATUS OF FAMILIES AND PERSONS IN THE UNITED STATES.** Government Publication. English. an. US Department of Commerce, 14th Street & Constitution Avenue NW, Washington DC 20230. **Tel** (202)482-2000, FAX (202)482-3772. **LC** HC110.I5; M62. **DD** 339.2/2/0973.

US
**MONEY INCOME OF HOUSEHOLDS, FAMILIES, AND PERSONS IN THE UNITED STATES.** Added/Corp United States. Bureau of the Census. (1980)-. Government Publication. English. ir. $16.00 (latest per copy). Superintendent of Documents, US Government Printing Office, Washington DC 20402. **Tel** (202)275-3328, FAX (202)786-2377. *Continues Money Income of Families and Persons in the United States.*

US/0745-5429
**MONTANA MORBIDITY REPORT.** [Mont. morb. rep.]. English. mo. Free to Qualified Personnel. Montana Department of Health & Environmental Sciences, 1400 Broadway, Cogswell Building, Room C108, Helena MT 59620. **Tel** (406)444-2544, FAX (406)444-2606. **DD** 353.

# Population Studies

US
## MONTHLY PRODUCT ANNOUNCEMENT / U.S. DEPARTMENT OF COMMERCE, BUREAU OF THE CENSUS.
**Added/Corp** United States. Bureau of the Census. No. 1 (Jan. 1981)-. Government Publication. English. Twelve times a year. Free. US Department of Commerce / Bureau of the Census, Data User Services Division, Customer Services, Washington DC 20233-0800. **Tel** (301)763-4100. **(Subscription address:** Superintendent of Documents, US Government Printing Office, Washington DC 20402.) **ED** Bernice L. Baker.
**Desc:** Lists all the Census Bureau's publications, microfiche, maps, data files and documentation that became available during the previous month.

UK
## MORTALITY STATISTICS.
(MORTALITY STATISTICS. CHILDHOOD / OFFICE OF POPULATION CENSUSES AND SURVEYS.). **Added/Corp** Great Britain. Office of Population Censuses and Surveys. (1980)-. Periodical. English. ir. £10.30. Her Majesty's Stationery Office, 51 Nine Elms Lane, London SW8 5DR England. **Tel** 011 44 71 873 8459, 011 44 71 873 8499, **FAX** 011 44 71 873 8499, 011 44 71 873 8456, telex 297138. **(Subscription address:** Her Majesty's Stationery Office, PO Box 276, Publications Centre, London SW8 5DT England.) **LC** HB1323.I4; M628. **DD** 312/.2/088054. **Continues in part** Mortality Statistics. Childhood and Maternity.

UK
## MORTALITY STATISTICS. PERINATAL AND INFANT : SOCIAL AND BIOLOGICAL FACTORS.
See Population Studies-Abstracting, Bibliographies and Statistics.

CN/1195-4108
## MORTALITY, SUMMARY LIST OF CAUSES / STATISTICS CANADA, CANADIAN CENTRE FOR HEALTH INFORMATION.
**Added/Corp** Canadian Centre for Health Information. **VFOAT** Mortalite, List Sommaire des Causes. (1991)-. English (French). 31.00Can$ Canada; $32.00 other. Statistics Canada, Publications Sales & Services, Main Building Room 1710, Ottawa Ontario K1A 0T6 Canada. **Tel** (613)951-5078, (800)267-6677, **FAX** (613)951-1584, telex 053-3585. **LC** RA407.5.C2; H424. **DD** 614.4/271/021. **Continues** Health Reports. Supplement. Mortality, Summary List of Causes, 1180-2448.

BU/0205-0617
## NASELENIE.
**Added/Corp** Koordinatsionen Suvet po Demografiia (Bulgarska Akademiia na Naukite). (1983)-. Periodical. Bulgarian (summaries and/or abstracts in English and Russian). Six times a year. DM132.00. Bulgarian Academy of Sciences, 1 rue 15 Noemvri, 1040 Sofia Bulgaria. **Tel** 011 359 2 803127. **(Subscription address:** Kubon & Sagner, ABT Zeitschriftenimport, D 80328 Munich Germany.) **LC** HB3627; .N37.
**Ind/Abst** Popul. Index.

UK/0263-5429
## NEW GENERATION.
[New gener.]. (1982)-. Periodical. English. qt. £3.00. National Child Birth Trust, Alexandra House Oldham Terrace, Acton London W3 6HN England. **Tel** 011 44 81 9928637. **DD** 618.2005.

US
## NEW JERSEY DIVISION OF LABOR MARKET AND DEMOGRAPHIC RESEARCH POPULATION ESTIMATES FOR NEW JERSEY.
English. an. Division of Labor Market and Demographic Research, New Jersey Department of Labor, CN 388, Trenton NJ 08625-0388. **Tel** (609)292-0076, **FAX** (609)984-6833. **ED** Sen-Yuan Wu. **Circ:** 3,800 (ctrl). available on diskette.
**Desc:** Presents the official estimates of total population for the state of New Jersey, it's 21 counties and 567 municipalities based on the lastest information.

NZ/0111-199X
## NEW ZEALAND POPULATION REVIEW.
(NEW ZEALAND POPULATION REVIEW / NEW ZEALAND DEMOGRAPHIC SOCIETY (INC.).). [N.Z. popul. rev.]. **Added/Corp** New Zealand Demographic Society. **VFOAT** Population Review. Vol. 6, No. 1 (March 1980)-. Periodical. English. sa. 50.00NZ$ New Zealand; 75.00NZ$ other. New Zealand Demographic Society, PO Box 225, Wellington New Zealand. **Tel** 04-729119, **FAX** 04-729135, telex 31313. **ED** Janet Cameron. **LC** HB3692.5.A3; N58. cum. index. **Bk Rev. Circ:** 250 (ctrl). **Continues** New Zealand Population Newsletter.
**Desc:** Research articles and methodological and topical comments, and summaries of key statistics on the demography of New Zealand and the South Pacific.
**Ind/Abst** Geogr. Abstr. Human Geogr.; Int. Dev. Abstr. (?-?); Popul. Index.

II
## NEWS LETTER / POPULATION CENTRE BANGALORE.
See Birth Control.

BE/0771-2022
## NEWSLETTER / INTERNATIONAL UNION FOR THE SCIENTIFIC STUDY OF POPULATION.
**Main/Corp** International Union for the Scientific Study of Population. **VFOAT** Bulletin de Liaison. No. 1 (1972)-. Newsletter. English (French). Three times a year. International Union for the Scientific Study of Population, 34 rue Augustins, B4000 Liege Belgium. **Tel** 011 32 41 224080. **LC** HB848; .I55a. **DD** 304.6/05.

US/1069-9317
## NEWSLETTER - SOUTH BEND AREA GENEALOGICAL SOCIETY.
(NEWSLETTER.). [Newsl. - South Bend Area Geneal. Soc.]. **Added/Corp** South Bend Area Genealogical Society. (19??)-. Newsletter. English. mo. **LC** F534.S7; S685. **DD** 929/.377289. **Continues** South Bend Area Genealogical Society : [Newsletter], 0737-2973.
**Desc:** Newsletter for the South Bend Area Genealogical Society providing information on registers of birth, etc.

NE/0922-7210
## NIDI RAPPORT.
[NiDi rapp.]. **VFOAT** Nederlands Interdisciplinair Demografisch Instituut Rapport; NiDi Report. (1988)-. Monographic series. Miscellaneous. ir. Free on request. Netherlands Interuniversity Demographic Institute, POB 11650, 2502 AR Gravenhage Netherlands. **Tel** 011 31 70 3565200. **UDC** 314. **Formed by the union of** Working Papers of the NIDI, 0920-9719 **and** Intern Rapport - Nederlands Interuniversitair Demografisch Instituut, 0925-6954.

US
## NORTH CAROLINA POPULATION PROJECTIONS.
**Main/Corp** North Carolina. Division of State Budget and Management. Research and Planning Services. English. be. $3.50. Division of State Budget and Management, Librarian, 116 West Jones Street, Raleigh NC 27603. **LC** HA554; .D57A. **DD** 312/.8/09756.

CL/0303-1829
## NOTAS DE POBLACION.
[Notas pobl.]. Vol. 1- Apr. 1973-. Periodical. Spanish (summaries and/or abstracts in English). Three times a year. $20.00 US. Centro Latinoamericano Demografia, Casilla 91, Santiago Chile. **Tel** 011 56 2 2085051, **FAX** 011 56 2 480252, telex 340295 UNSTGO CK. **ED** Jorge Arevalo. **LC** HB3530.5.A3. **Circ:** 1,000. available on microfiche. **Supersedes** Centro Latinoamericano de Demografia. Boletin Informativo.
**Desc:** Recent studies on population dynamics in Latin America and the Caribbean; information on work being carried out in the field of population.
**Ind/Abst** PAIS Int. Print (1991-); Popul. Index.

TU/0259-6334
## NUFUSBILIM DERGISI. THE TURKISH JOURNAL OF POPULATION STUDIES.
**Added/Corp** Hacettepe Universitesi. Nufus Etutleri Enstitusu. **VFOAT** Turkish Journal of Population Studies. (1979)-. Periodical. English (Turkish). an. $11.00. Hacettepe Universitesi, Nufus Etutleri Enstitusu, Ankara Turkey. **Tel** 011 90 312 3197906, **FAX** 011 90 312 311 81 41, telex 42237. **LC** HB3633.4.A3; N83.
**Ind/Abst** Popul. Index; Trop. Dis. Bull.

US/0732-1597
## NUMBERS NEWS, THE.
[Numbers news]. Vol. 1, No. 1 (Dec. 15, 1980)-. Periodical. English. mo. $149.00 US, Canada and Mexico; $169.00 other. American Demographics / New York, PO Box 68, Ithaca NY 14851. **Tel** (607)273-6343, (800)828-1133. **ED** Martha Farnsworth Riche and Diane Crispell. **[CCC]**. Index available (bound in Dec. issue). cum. index. **Circ:** 1,500.
**Desc:** Covers consumer trends, demographic-oriented publications, and the marketing information industry.

US/0149-1520
## OHIO POPULATION ESTIMATES.
**Main/Corp** Ohio. Dept. of Economic and Community Development. (19??)-. English. an. Ohio Department of Economic and Community Development, PO Box 1001, Columbus OH 43266. **Tel** (614)466-2285. **LC** HB3525.O3; O34a. **DD** 312/.8/09771.

UK
## OPCS MONITOR. ADOPTIONS.
**Main/Corp** Great Britain. Office of Population Censuses & Surveys. **VFOAT** Adoptions. English. Information Branch / London, Office of Population Censuses & Surveys, St Catherines House, 10 Kingsway, London WC2B 6JP England. **Tel** 011 44 71 242 0262.

UK
## OPCS MONITOR. BIRTHS AND DEATHS.
**Main/Corp** Great Britain. Office of Population Censuses & Surveys. **VFOAT** Births and Deaths. English. Information Branch / London, Office of Population Censuses & Surveys, St Catherines House, 10 Kingsway, London WC2B 6JP England. **Tel** 011 44 71 242 0262.

UK
## OPCS MONITOR. BIRTHS BY BIRTH PLACE OF PARENT.
**Main/Corp** Great Britain. Office of Population Censuses & Surveys. **VFOAT** Births by Birth Place of Parent. English. Information Branch / London, Office of Population Censuses & Surveys, St Catherines House, 10 Kingsway, London WC2B 6JP England. **Tel** 011 44 71 242 0262.

UK/0144-5537
## OPCS MONITOR. CENSUS MONITORS.
[OPCS monit. 1981 census]. **VFOAT** Census Monitors. (1978)-. English. Information Branch / London, Office of Population Censuses & Surveys, St Catherines House, 10 Kingsway, London WC2B 6JP England. **Tel** 011 44 71 242 0262.
**Ind/Abst** Popul. Index (?-?).

UK
## OPCS MONITOR. CONGENITAL MALFORMATIONS.
**Main/Corp** Great Britain. Office of Population Censuses & Surveys. **VFOAT** Congenital Malformations. English. Information Branch / London, Office of Population Censuses & Surveys, St Catherines House, 10 Kingsway, London WC2B 6JP England. **Tel** 011 44 71 242 0262.

UK
## OPCS MONITOR. DEATHS BY CAUSE.
**Main/Corp** Great Britain. Office of Population Censuses & Surveys. **VFOAT** Deaths by Cause. English. Information Branch / London, Office of Population Censuses & Surveys, St Catherines House, 10 Kingsway, London WC2B 6JP England. **Tel** 011 44 71 242 0262.

UK
## OPCS MONITOR. DEATHS FROM ACCIDENTS.
**Ceased. Main/Corp** Great Britain. Office of Population Censuses & Surveys. **VFOAT** Deaths from Accidents. (197?)-(19??). English. Information Branch / London, Office of Population Censuses & Surveys, St Catherines House, 10 Kingsway, London WC2B 6JP England. **Tel** 011 44 71 242 0262.

UK
## OPCS MONITOR. INFANT AND PERINATAL MORTALITY.
**Main/Corp** Great Britain. Office of Population Censuses & Surveys. **VFOAT** Infant and Perinatal Mortality. English. Information Branch / London, Office of Population Censuses & Surveys, St Catherines House, 10 Kingsway, London WC2B 6JP England. **Tel** 011 44 71 242 0262.

UK
## OPCS MONITOR. INFECTIOUS DISEASES.
**Main/Corp** Great Britain. Office of Population Censuses & Surveys. **VFOAT** Infectious Diseases. English. Information Branch / London, Office of Population Censuses & Surveys, St Catherines House, 10 Kingsway, London WC2B 6JP England. **Tel** 011 44 71 242 0262. **NLM** W2; FA1 O3ob.

UK/0953-3362
## OPCS MONITOR. LEGAL ABORTIONS / OFFICE OF POPULATION CENSUS & SURVEYS.
**Main/Corp** Great Britain. Office of Population Censuses & Surveys. **Added/Corp** Great Britain. Government Statistical Service. Great Britain. Office of Population Censuses & Surveys. **VFOAT** Legal Abortions. (19??)-. Periodical. English. ir. Price varies. Information Branch / London, Office of Population Censuses & Surveys, St Catherines House, 10 Kingsway, London WC2B 6JP England. **Tel** 011 44 71 242 0262. **NLM** W2; FA1 O3o.

UK
## OPCS MONITOR. MID-YEAR ESTIMATES OF THE POPULATION OF NEW COMMONWEALTH AND PAKISTANI ETHNIC ORIGIN.
**Main/Corp** Great Britain. Office of Population Censuses & Surveys. **VFOAT** Mid-Year Estimates of the Population of New Commonwealth and Pakistani Ethnic Origin. English. Information Branch / London, Office of Population Censuses & Surveys, St Catherines House, 10 Kingsway, London WC2B 6JP England. **Tel** 011 44 71 242 0262.

UK
## OPCS MONITOR. POPULATION PROJECTIONS.
**Main/Corp** Great Britain. Office of Population Censuses & Surveys. **VFOAT** Population Projections. English. Information Branch / London, Office of Population Censuses & Surveys, St Catherines House, 10 Kingsway, London WC2B 6JP England. **Tel** 011 44 71 242 0262.

UK
## OPCS MONITOR. REGISTRAR GENERAL'S WEEKLY RETURN FOR ENGLAND AND WALES.
**Main/Corp** Great Britain. Office of Population Censuses & Surveys. **VFOAT** Registrar General's Weekly Return for England and Wales. English. Information Branch / London, Office of Population Censuses & Surveys, St Catherines House, 10 Kingsway, London WC2B 6JP England. **Tel** 011 44 71 242 0262.

US/0300-6816
**P.A.A. AFFAIRS.** (P.A.A. AFFAIRS / POPULATION ASSOCIATION OF AMERICA.). **Main/Corp** Population Association of America. **VFOAT** PAA Affairs; Population Association of America Affairs. **VAT** Population Association of America Affairs. (1968)-. Periodical. English. Four times a year (published seasonally). $5.00. Population Association of America, 1722 N Street Northwest, Washington DC 20036. **Tel** (202)429-0891. **ED** David and Marilyn McMillen. **LC** HB848; .P66. **Circ:** 3,000 (ctrl).
**Desc:** Newsletter containing association and member news, etc.

PK
**PAKISTAN POPULATION REVIEW.** **Added/Corp** National Institute of Population Studies (Pakistan). Vol. 1, No. 1 (Autumn 1990)-. Periodical. English. National Institute of Population Studies, House No. 8, St. 70, F-8/3, PO Box 2197, Islamabad, Pakistan. **LC** HB1050.5.A3; P35. **DD** 304.6/095491/05. **NLM** W1; PA361G.
**Ind/Abst** Popul. Index.

US/0732-0531
**PAPERS OF THE EAST-WEST POPULATION INSTITUTE.** [Pap. East-West Popul. Inst.]. **Main/Corp** East-West Population Institute. No. 28 (1973)-. Monographic series. English. ir (four to eight issues per year). Price varies per volume. East-West Population Institute, 1777 East-West Road, Honolulu HI 96848. **Tel** (808)944-7401, (808)944-7444, FAX (808)944-7970, telex 989171. **ED** Sandra E Ward. **Circ:** 600 (ctrl). ***Continues*** *Working Papers - East-West Population Institute.*
**Desc:** Disseminates research findings and policy recommendations on the populations of Asia, the Pacific, and the United States. Topics include demographic trends and estimation, fertility, family structure, economic development, human resources, urbanization, migration, and population policies and programs.
**Ind/Abst** Geogr. Abstr. Human Geogr.; Int. Dev. Abstr.; Popul. Index (?-?).

IO
**PENDUDUK CINA JAWA-MADURA : HASIL REGISTRASI PENDUDUK.** **Main/Corp** Indonesia. Biro Pusat Statistik. **VFOAT** Chinese Population of Java-Madura : Results of Population Registration. 1973/75-. Indonesian (English and Indonesian). an. Rp1500 Indonesia; $1.00 US. Central Bureau of Statistics / Indonesia, c/o Dr. Sutomo, 8 Jalan, PO Box 3, Jakarta Indonesia. **Tel** 372808 374908 Ext.342. **LC** HA1817.J3; I53C. ctrl circ.

●UK/0968-1655
**PEOPLE & THE PLANET / IPPF, UNFPA, IUCN.** **Added/Corp** International Planned Parenthood Federation. United Nations Population Fund. International Union for Conservation of Nature and Natural Resources. **VFOAT** People and the Planet. Vol. 1, No. 1/2 (1992)-. Periodical. English. Four times a year (Jan., Apr., July, Oct.). $20.00 US; £10.00 UK. International Planned Parenthood Federation, Regent's College, Inner Circle, Regent's Park, London NW1 4NS England. **Tel** 011 44 71 486 0741, FAX 011 44 71 487 7950, telex 919573 IPEPEE G. **ED** John Rowley, (phone: (447 485 3136). **LC** GF1; .P46. **Bk Rev**, (Qty: varies). **Ad Acc. Circ:** 20,000 (ctrl). ***Continues*** *Earthwatch.*
**Desc:** Studies on the population, environment and development.

AT
**PERINATAL DEATHS, AUSTRALIA.** **See** Population Studies-Abstracting, Bibliographies and Statistics.

KO
**POGON SAHOE NONJIP.** **Added/Corp** Hanguk Pogon Sahoe Yonguwon. **VFOAT** Journal of Population, Health, and Social Welfare. (1990)-. Periodical. Korean (English). sa. Korea Institute for Health and Social Affairs, San 42-14 Bulgwang-Dong Eunpyung-Ku, Seoul 122-040 Korea. **Tel** 355-8003-7, FAX 352-9129. ***Continues*** *Ingu Pogon Nonjip.*
**Ind/Abst** Popul. Index.

PL/0867-7905
**POLISH POPULATION REVIEW / POLISH DEMOGRAPHIC SOCIETY [AND] CENTRAL STATISTICAL OFFICE.** **Added/Corp** Polskie Towarzystwo Demograficzne. Poland. Gowny Urzad Statystyczny. No. 1 (1991)-. Statistical Publication. English. Polish Demographic Society, Ulitsa Wisniowa 41, Room 76, 02-520 Warsaw Poland.
**Ind/Abst** Popul. Index.

BE
**POLITIQUES DE POPULATION.** **Added/Corp** Universite Catholique de Louvain (1970- ). Departement de Demographie. Universite de Montreal. Departement de Demographie. Institut National d'Etudes Demographiques (France). **VFOAT** Etudes et Documents. No. 1 (Nov. 1983)-. Academic Scholarly Publication. French (English). Four times a year. 350F Belgium; 700F others. Academia Erasme s.a. Edition et Diffusion, Grand rue, 25/115, B-1348 Louvain-La-Neuve Belgium. **Tel** 010 45239596, FAX 010 454480. **LC** HB883.5; .P64. **Pr Rev. Circ:** 500.
**Ind/Abst** Popul. Index.

US
**POPLINE.** **Added/Corp** Population Action Council. Vol. 1 (1979)-. Periodical. English (Spanish and French). Six times a year. $25.00. Population Action Council, 110 Maryland Avenue NE, Washington DC 20002. **Tel** (202)544-3300. **ED** Hal Burdett. **LC** WMLC 93/218. **Bk Rev. Circ:** 56,500 (ctrl).
**Desc:** Researches and evaluates policies and facts related to international population studies.

XR/0231-5513
**POPULACNI ZPRAVY.** [Popul. zpr.]. Periodical. Czech (English and Russian). ir (issued once or twice a year). Free. Prace / Labour, Vaclavske Nam 17, 112 58 Prague 1 Czech Republic. **Tel** telex 121134. **ED** Vladimir Marik. **LC** HB848; .P6.
**Ind/Abst** Popul. Index (?-?).

IO/0853-0262
**POPULASI.** **Added/Corp** Universitas Gadjah Mada. Pusat Penelitian dan Studi Kependudukan. (1990)-. Periodical. Indonesian. sa. Populasi, Bulaksumur Blok G-7, Yogyakarta 55281 Indonesia. **LC** HB3647; .P64.
**Ind/Abst** Popul. Index.

FR/0032-4663
**POPULATION.** [Population]. **Added/Corp** Institut National d'Eetudes Demographiques (France). (Jan./Mar. 1946)-. Periodical. French. bm. 342.81F (without English issue), 489.72F (including English issue) France; 405.00F (without English issue), 570.00F (including English issue) other. Institut National d'Etudes Demographiques, 27 rue du Commandeur, 75675 Paris Cedex 14 France. **Tel** 011 33 1 42182000. **LC** HB881; .P67. **DD** 312.05. **NLM** W1 PO592. **CODEN** POPUAQ. Index available. cum. index. **Bk Rev. Circ:** 4,000 (ctrl). Documents available from BIOSIS Document Express.
**Desc:** Populations studies and demographics.
**Ind/Abst** Am. Hist. Life (1979-); Arts Humanit. Citation Index [Select. Cov.]; Biol. Abstr.; Curr. Contents Soc. Behav. Sci.; Curr. Lit. Fam. Plan.; Geogr. Abstr. Human Geogr.; Int. Bibliogr. Sociol.; Int. Dev. Abstr.; Int. Labour Doc.; PAIS Int. Print (1991-); Popul. Index; Soc. Sci. Cit. Index [Full Cov.]; Trop. Dis. Bull.

US/0897-3849
**POPULATION & DEVELOPMENT.** (POPULATION & DEVELOPMENT / COLLEGE OF AGRICULTURE AND LIFE SCIENCES AT CORNELL UNIVERSITY, DEPT. OF RURAL SOCIOLOGY.). [Popul. dev.]. **Added/Corp** New York State College of Agriculture and Life Sciences. Dept. of Rural Sociology. **VFOAT** Population and Development. No. 1 (Oct. 1987)-. Periodical. English. Five times a year. $20.00 (one year), $30.00 (two years). Cornell University / Warren Hall, 333 Warren Hall, c/o T. Hirschl, Ithaca NY 14853. **Tel** (607)255-3163, FAX (607)255-9984. **ED** Tom Hirschl. **DD** 304.

US/0098-7921
**POPULATION AND DEVELOPMENT REVIEW.** [Popul. dev. rev.]. **Added/Corp** Population Council. Vol. 1 (Sept. 1975)-. Periodical. English (summaries and/or abstracts in Spanish and French). Four times a year. $32.00 (one year); $60.00 (two years). The Population Council, One Dag Hammarskjold Plaza, New York NY 10017. **Tel** (212)644-1614, (212)339-0500, FAX (212)755-6052, telex 9102900660 POPCO. **ED** Ethel P. Churchill. **LC** HB848; .P62. **DD** 301.32/07/2. **NLM** W1 PO597. Index available. cum. index. **Bk Rev. Pr Rev. Circ:** 5,000 (ctrl). available on microfilm and microfiche from University Microfilms International (UMI). Documents available from The Genuine Article, UMI Article Clearinghouse, Documents on Demand.
**Desc:** Advances knowledge on the relationship between population growth and socioeconomic change. Discusses related issues of public policy.
**Ind/Abst** ABC POL SCI; AGRICOLA; Am. Hist. Life (1981-); Am. Bibliogr. Slavic East Europ. Stud.; Anthropol. Lit.; Appl. Soc. Sci. Index Abstr.; Chicano Index; Curr. Contents Soc. Behav. Sci.; Curr. Lit. Fam. Plan.; Econ. Lit. Index; Environ. Abstr.; Expand. Acad. Index (1992-); Geogr. Abstr. Human Geogr.; Int. Bibliogr. Sociol.; Int. Dev. Abstr.; Int. Labour Doc.; J. Econ. Lit.; J. Plan. Lit.; LABORDOC; Middle East Abstr. Index; Newsp. Period. Abstr. (1992-); PAIS Int. Print (1991-); Popul. Index; Res. Alert [Full Cov.]; Sage Fam. Stud. Abstr.; Soc. Plann. Policy Dev. Abstr.; Soc. Sci. Cit. Index [Full Cov.]; Sociol. Abstr.; Trop. Dis. Bull.; Urban Aff. Abstr.; World Agric. Econ.

SZ
**POPULATION AND EMPLOYMENT WORKING PAPER.** **VFOAT** World Employment Programme: Population and Employment Project. (1974)-. Monographic series. English. ir. Price varies per volume. ILO Publications, 1828 L Street Northwest, Suite 801, Washington DC 20036. **Tel** (202)653-7652, FAX (202)653-7687. **(Subscription address:** ILO Publications, International Labour Office, CII-1211 Geneva 22 Switzerland**)**

US/0199-0039
**POPULATION AND ENVIRONMENT.** [Popul. environ.]. **Added/Corp** American Psychological Association. Division of Population and Environmental Psychology. Vol. 3 (Spring 1980)-. Academic Scholarly Publication. English. bm. £40.00 (individuals), £199.00 (institutions) UK; $255.00 US; $300.00 other. Human Sciences Press, PO Box 735, 233 Spring Street, New York NY 10013. **Tel** (212)620-8000, FAX (212)807-1047, telex 23421139. **(Subscription address:** Eurospan Ltd., Journals and Serials Division, 3 Henrietta Street, Covent Garden, London WC2E 8LU England.**) LC** HB848; .J68. **DD** 304.6/05. **NLM** W1 PO597E. **CODEN** PENVDK. **[CCC]. Pr Rev.** available on microfilm and microfiche from University Microfilms International (UMI). Documents available from The Genuine Article, BIOSIS Document Express, UMI Article Clearinghouse, Documents on Demand. ***Continues*** *Journal of Population, 0146-1052.*
**Desc:** Devoted to scholarly, empirical and theoretical articles on population and environmental phenomena and issues, from architectural impacts to wilderness perception, from reproductive behavior to migration. While primary emphasis is on psychological treatment of population and environment behavior phenomena, articles from related disciplines.
**Ind/Abst** Acad. Search (July 1993-); Biol. Abstr.; Crim. Penol. Police Sci. Abstr.; Curr. Contents Soc. Behav. Sci.; Curr. Index J. Educ.; Curr. Lit. Fam. Plan.; EMBASE; Environ. Abstr.; Environ. Period. Bibliogr.; Expand. Acad. Index (1992-); Gen. Sci. Source (Jul. 1993-); Guide Soc. Sci. Relig.; Health Saf. Sci. Abstr.; High. Educ. Abstr.; INFO-SOUTH Abstr.; Int. Bibliogr. Sociol.; J. Plan. Lit.; Mag. Search; Newsp. Period. Abstr. (1992-); PAIS Int. Print (1991-); Pollut. Abstr. Indexes; Popul. Index; Psychol. Abstr. (1980-); PsycINFO (1990-); PsycLit; PsycScan: Appl. Psych.; Res. Alert [Full Cov.]; Soc. Plann. Policy Dev. Abstr.; Soc. Sci. Cit. Index [Full Cov.]; Soc. Work Abstr. [Select. Cov.]; Sociol. Abstr.; Trop. Dis. Bull.

IE/0790-9969
**POPULATION AND LABOUR FORCE PROJECTIONS / CENTRAL STATISTICS OFFICE.** **Added/Corp** Ireland. Central Statistics Office. (1991)-. English. te. Government Publications, 4 5 Harcourt Road, Dublin 2 Ireland. **Tel** 011 353 1 6613111 Ext.4005. **LC** HA1170.3; .P67. **DD** 304.6/2/0941705.

US
**POPULATION AND LABOUR RESEARCH NEWS : A REPORT ON RESEARCH AND RELATED POLICY ACTIVITIES IN THE ILO'S POPULATION LABOUR POLICIES PROGRAMME.** English. ILO Publications, 1828 L Street Northwest, Suite 801, Washington DC 20036. **Tel** (202)653-7652, FAX (202)653-7687. **(Subscription address:** ILO Publications, International Labour Office, CII-1211 Geneva 22 Switzerland**)**

US/0273-2548
**POPULATION (BOCA RATON).** (POPULATION.). [Population]. Vol. 1, Article 1-. English. an. Social Issues Resources Series Inc, PO Box 2348, Boca Raton FL 33427. **Tel** (800)327-0513, (407)994-0079. **ED** E C Goldstein. **LC** HB848; .P618. **DD** 304.6/05. Documents available from The Genuine Article.
**Desc:** Interdisciplinary resource material consisting of reprinted articles from popular and professional journals, newspapers, magazines and government documents.
**Ind/Abst** Curr. Contents Soc. Behav. Sci.; J. Plan. Lit.; Res. Alert [Full Cov.].

US/0032-468X
**POPULATION BULLETIN.** [Popul. bull.]. **Added/Corp** Population Reference Bureau. Vol. 1, (Sept. 1945)-. Periodical. English. qt. Free to members of the Population Reference Bureau. Population Reference Bureau, 1875 Connecticut Avenue Northwest, Suite 520, Washington DC 20009. **Tel** (202)483-1100, (800)877-9881, FAX (202)328-3937. **LC** HB881.A1; P65. **DD** 312.05. **NLM** W1 PO643. **CODEN** POPBA3. **Pr Rev.** available on microfilm and microfiche from University Microfilms International (UMI). Documents available from The Genuine Article, BIOSIS Document Express, UMI Article Clearinghouse, Documents on Demand. ***Supersedes*** *Population Bulletin, 0032-468X.*
**Ind/Abst** Acad. Abstr. Full Text Elite (July 1990-); Acad. Abstr. (July 1990-); Acad. Ind. [Computer File] (1987-); Acad. Search (July 1991-); Am. Bibliogr. Slavic East Europ. Stud.; Appl. Soc. Sci. Index Abstr.; Biol. Abstr.; Curr. Contents Soc. Behav. Sci.; Curr. Lit. Fam. Plan.; Environ. Abstr.; Expand. Acad. Index (1987-); Geogr. Abstr. Human Geogr.; Index Period. Artic. Relat. Law; INFO-SOUTH Abstr.; Int. Dev. Abstr.; Int. Labour Doc.; Mag. Artic. Summar. Elite (July 1991-); Mag. Artic. Summar. Select (July 1990-); Mag. Artic. Summar. CD-ROM (July 1990-); Mag. Search; Middle East Abstr. Index; Newsp. Period. Abstr. (1986-); Popul. Index; Res. Alert [Full Cov.]; Soc. Sci. Source (Jul. 1990-); Soc. Sci. Cit. Index [Full Cov.]; Soc. Sci. Index; Soc. Sci. Index Fulltext (Dec. 1988-) [Full Txt.]; Stat. Ref. Index.

US/0251-7604
**POPULATION BULLETIN OF THE UNITED NATIONS.** [Popul. bull. U. N.]. **Added/Corp** United Nations. Dept. of International Economic and Social Affairs. United Nations. Dept. of Economic and Social Affairs. United Nations. Dept. of

Social Affairs. Population Division. No. 3 (Oct. 1953)-. Government Publication. English. sa. price varies per volume. United Nations Publications, 2 United Nations Plaza, Room DC2 0853, Department 007C, New York NY 10017. **Tel** (212)963-8303, (800)253-9646. **LC** HB848; .P619. **DD** 304.6/05. ***Continues*** *Population Bulletin.*
**Desc:** Presents brief articles on population which are aimed at research institutions and individuals engaged in social and economic research.
**Ind/Abst** PAIS Int. Print; Popul. Index.

TH
**POPULATION EDUCATION IN ASIA AND THE PACIFIC NEWSLETTER. Added/Corp** Unesco. Regional Office for Education in Asia and the Pacific. Unesco. Principal Regional Office for Asia and the Pacific. No. 13 (Dec. 1980)-. Periodical. English. Twice a year. Free on request. UNESCO Population Education Clearing House, GPO Box 1425, Bangkok 10500 Thailand. **Tel** 3910577, telex 20591. **ED** Carmelita L. Villanueva. **LC** HQ763.6.A78; P66. **NLM** W1; PO646. **Bk Rev**. ctrl circ. ***Continues*** *Population Education in Asia and Oceania Newsletter.*

TH
**POPULATION EDUCATION IN ASIA AND THE PACIFIC NEWSLETTER AND FORUM. Added/Corp** Unesco. Regional Office for Education in Asia and the Pacific. No. 24 (198?)-. Newsletter. English. sa. (free upon request). UNESCO Population Education Clearing House, GPO Box 1425, Bangkok 10500 Thailand. **Tel** 3910577, telex 20591. ***Continues*** *Population Education in Asia and the Pacific Newsletter.*
**Ind/Abst** Curr. Index J. Educ.

US
**POPULATION EDUCATION INTERCHANGE. Added/Corp** Population Reference Bureau. **VFOAT** Interchange. Vol. 15, No. 1 (April 1986)-. Periodical. English. qt. Population Reference Bureau, 1875 Connecticut Avenue Northwest, Suite 520, Washington DC 20009. **Tel** (202)483-1100, (800)877-9881, FAX (202)328-3937. **LC** HB850; .I57. ***Continues*** *Interchange, 0047-0465.*
**Ind/Abst** Curr. Lit. Fam. Plan. (19??-199?).

TH
**POPULATION EDUCATION PROGRAMME SERVICE. VFOAT** Abstract-Bibliography. (1981)-. Monographic series. English. Price varies per volume. UNESCO / Thailand, Principal Regional Office for Asia and the Pacific, PO Box 967, Library and Document Service, Bangkok 10110 Thailand. **Circ:** 2,000 (ctrl). ***Continues*** *Abstract Bibliography / Population Education Clearing House.*

US
**POPULATION ESTIMATE AND HOUSING INVENTORY FOR THE CITY OF LOS ANGELES AS OF OCTOBER 1 ... (LOS ANGELES (CALIF.)). See** Housing and Urban Development.

US
**POPULATION ESTIMATES AND ... PER CAPITA INCOME ESTIMATES FOR COUNTIES, INCORPORATED PLACES, AND MINOR CIVIL DIVISIONS. OHIO / U.S. DEPARTMENT OF COMMERCE, BUREAU OF THE CENSUS.** 1982-. Government Publication. English. be. US Department of Commerce, 14th Street & Constitution Avenue NW, Washington DC 20230. **Tel** (202)482-2000, FAX (202)482-3772.

US
**POPULATION ESTIMATES AND ... PER CAPITA INCOME ESTIMATES FOR COUNTIES, INCORPORATED PLACES, AND SELECTED MINOR CIVIL DIVISIONS. INDIANA / U.S. DEPARTMENT OF COMMERCE, BUREAU OF THE CENSUS.** 1982-. Government Publication. English. be. US Department of Commerce, 14th Street & Constitution Avenue NW, Washington DC 20230. **Tel** (202)482-2000, FAX (202)482-3772.

US
**POPULATION ESTIMATES FOR NEW JERSEY (TRENTON, N.J. : 1981).** (POPULATION ESTIMATES FOR NEW JERSEY.). English. an. Division of Labor Market and Demographic Research, New Jersey Department of Labor, CN 388, Trenton NJ 08625-0388. **Tel** (609)292-0076, FAX (609)984-6833. **LC** HA521; .N55A. **DD** 312/.8/09749. **Circ:** 2,500. available on diskette. ***Continues*** *Provisional Population Estimates for New Jersey.*
**Desc:** Population estimates for New Jersey, its counties, and its municipalities.

US
**POPULATION ESTIMATES FOR OREGON. Added/Corp** Portland State University. Center for Population Research and Census. (1980/1989)-. English. an (Mar.). $6.00. Center for Population Research and Census, Portland State University, PO Box 751, Portland OR 97207. **Tel** (503)725-3922, FAX (503)725-5199. **ED** Howard Wineberg (phone: (503)725-5157). **LC** HA597; .P67. **Pr Rev. Circ:** 1,000 (ctrl). available on diskette. ***Continues*** *Official Population Estimates for Oregon Counties and Cities.*

BE/0523-1159
**POPULATION ET FAMILLE. *Suspended.*** [Popul. fam.]. 26/27-Suspended with (1984). Periodical. French (summaries and/or abstracts in English). Three times a year. 500F. Centre d'Etude de la Population et de la Famille, Office International de Librairie, Avenue Marnix 30-1050, Bruxelles Belgium. **LC** HB848. **DD** 301.32/05. **NLM** W1 PO648. ***Supersedes in part*** *Bevolking en Gezin, 0523-1159.*
**Ind/Abst** Popul. Index (?-?); Soc. Plann. Policy Dev. Abstr.; Sociol. Abstr. (?-?).

FR/0184-7783
**POPULATION ET SOCIETES.** [Popul. soc.]. **Added/Corp** Institut National d'Etudes Demographiques (France). No. 1, (March 1968)-. Periodical. French. Eleven times a year. 58.77F France; 90.00F other. Institut National d'Etudes Demographiques, 27 rue du Commandeur, 75675 Paris Cedex 14 France. **Tel** 011 33 1 42182000. **LC** HB848; .P637. **NLM** W1 PO649. Index available. **Bk Rev. Ad Acc. Circ:** 41,500 (ctrl).
**Desc:** Contains science, French society, demography, world population, and development.
**Ind/Abst** Popul. Index.

II
**POPULATION GEOGRAPHY : A JOURNAL OF THE ASSOCIATION OF POPULATION GEOGRAPHERS OF INDIA. Added/Corp** Association of Population Geographers of India. Vol. 1, No. 1 and 2 (June/Dec. 1979)-. Periodical. English. sa. $50.00. Association of Population Geographers of India, Department of Geography, Punjab University, Chandigarh, 160 014 India. **(Subscription address:** Prints India, 11 Darya Ganj, New Delhi, 110002 India, (Phone: 011 91 11 3268645)) **LC** HB1951; .P65. **DD** 304.6/05.
**Ind/Abst** Popul. Index.

US/0032-4701
**POPULATION INDEX. See** Population Studies-Abstracting, Bibliographies and Statistics.

US/0094-0348
**POPULATION MOBILITY IN HAWAII. Main/Corp** Hawaii. Dept. of Health. **Added/Corp** Hawaii. Dept. of Planning and Economic Development. (1971)-. English. Hawaii Department of Health, PO Box 3378, Honolulu HI 96801. **LC** HB1985.H3; H33a. **DD** 301.32/6/09969.

US/0048-4849
**POPULATION NEWSLETTER. Added/Corp** United Nations. Dept. of International Economic and Social Affairs. Population Division. United Nations. Dept. of Economic and Social Affairs. Population Division. No. 1 (Apr. 1968)-. Newsletter. English. sa. Free on request. United Nations Population Division, DC2 1960, New York NY 10017. **Tel** (212)963-3186. **LC** HB848; .P64. **DD** 312. **NLM** W1 PO654.
**Ind/Abst** Trop. Dis. Bull.

US/0091-5610
**POPULATION : PERSPECTIVE. Main/Corp** American Universities Field Staff. 1971-. English. Freeman Cooper and Company, 1736 Stockton Street, San Francisco CA 94133. **LC** HB871; .A45A. **DD** 301.32.

US
**POPULATION PROFILE OF THE UNITED STATES. Added/Corp** United States. Bureau of the Census. United States. Bureau of the Census. Population Division. (1974)-. Government Publication. English. an. Superintendent of Documents, US Government Printing Office, Washington DC 20402. **Tel** (202)275-3328, FAX (202)786-2377. **LC** HA195; .A53 subser.; HA203; .A218 subser. **DD** 304.6/0973/05. **NLM** W2; A B9cu no.374 etc.

UK/0950-7582
**POPULATION PROJECTIONS AREA.** [Popul. proj., Area]. **Added/Corp** Great Britain. Office of Population Censuses and Surveys. **VFOAT** Population Projections. (1991)-. Periodical. English. an. £11.30. Her Majesty's Stationery Office, 51 Nine Elms Lane, London SW8 5DR England. **Tel** 011 44 71 873 8459, 011 44 71 873 8499, FAX 011 44 71 873 8499, 011 44 71 873 8456, telex 297138. **(Subscription address:** Her Majesty's Stationery Office, PO Box 276, Publications Centre, London SW8 5DT England.**) LC** HA1123; .P66. **DD** 304.6/2/0942021.

US
**POPULATION PROJECTIONS BY MINOR CIVIL DIVISIONS, SEX, AGE GROUP, AND COUNTY. Added/Corp** Maine. Bureau of Health Planning and Development. Division of Data and Research. (19??)-. English. an. Office of Data and Research and Vital Statistics, Department of Human Services, Station 11/State House, Augusta ME 04333. **Tel** (207)289-3001. **ED** Dale Welch. **LC** HA415; .P66. **DD** 312/.8/09741. **Circ:** 400 (ctrl).
**Desc:** Population projections for 1988-1997, by minor civil division, sex, age group and county. Estimated population for 1987 is also included.

US/0097-9090
**POPULATION REPORT. SERIES I, PERIODIC ABSTINENCE (ENGLISH ED.). *Ceased.*** (POPULATION REPORTS. PERIODIC ABSTINENCE - SERIES I.). [Popul. rep., I, Period. abstin.]. **Added/Corp** George Washington University. Population Information Program. George Washington University. Dept. of Medical and Public Affairs. Johns Hopkins University. Population Information Program. **VFOAT** Periodic Abstinence. No. 1 (June 1974)-(19??). Periodical. English. ir. Johns Hopkins University / Population Information Program, 111 Market Place, Suite 310, Baltimore MD 21202. **Tel** (410)659-6300, FAX (410)659-6311. **ED** Ward Rinehart. **LC** RG136.5; .P66. **DD** 613. **NLM** W1 PO671R.
**Ind/Abst** Index Med. (?-?); Popul. Index (?-?).

US/0887-0241
**POPULATION REPORTS (BALTIMORE, MD.).** (POPULATION REPORTS.). [Popul. rep.]. **Added/Corp** George Washington University. Population Information Program. George Washington University. Dept. of Medical and Public Affairs. Johns Hopkins University. Population Information Program. (1972)-. Monographic series. English (French, Spanish, Portuguese and Arabic). qt. Price varies per volume. Johns Hopkins University / Population Information Program, 111 Market Place, Suite 310, Baltimore MD 21202. **Tel** (410)659-6300, FAX (410)659-6311. **ED** Ward Rinehart. **DD** 304. **Circ:** 110,000 (ctrl). Documents available from UMI Article Clearinghouse, Documents on Demand.
**Desc:** International reviews of important issues in population and family planning.
**Ind/Abst** Acad. Ind. [Computer File] (1992-); Curr. Lit. Fam. Plan.; Environ. Abstr.; Expand. Acad. Index (1992-); Gen. Period. Index (1992-); Health Index (1989-); Health Period. Database [Full Txt.]; Health Ref. Cent. (Jan. 1989-) [Full Txt.] [Full Cov.]; Index Period. Artic. Relat. Law; Mag. ASAP Plus [Full Txt.]; Mag. Index Plus (1992-); Newsp. Period. Abstr. (1992-); Popul. Index.

US/0097-9074
**POPULATION REPORTS. SERIES A, ORAL CONTRACEPTIVES (ENGLISH ED.).** (POPULATION REPORTS. SERIES A, ORAL CONTRACEPTIVES.). [Popul. rep., A, Oral contracept.]. **Added/Corp** George Washington University. Population Information Program. George Washington University. Dept. of Medical and Public Affairs. Johns Hopkins University. Population Information Program. **VFOAT** Oral Contraceptives. No. 1 (April 1974)-. Periodical. English (French, Spanish and Portuguese). ir. Free on request. Johns Hopkins University / Population Information Program, 111 Market Place, Suite 310, Baltimore MD 21202. **Tel** (410)659-6300, FAX (410)659-6311. **ED** Ward Rinehart. **LC** RG137.5; .P65. **DD** 613.9/432. **NLM** W1 PO671H.
**Ind/Abst** EMBASE; Energy Res. Abstr. (Aug. 1982-); Index Med.; Popul. Index.

US/0092-9344
**POPULATION REPORTS. SERIES B, INTRAUTERINE DEVICES (ENGLISH ED.).** (POPULATION REPORTS. SERIES B, INTRAUTERINE DEVICES.). [Popul. rep., B Intrauter. devices]. **Added/Corp** George Washington University. Population Information Program. George Washington University. Dept. of Medical and Public Affairs. Johns Hopkins University. Population Information Program. **VFOAT** Intrauterine Devices. No. 1 (Dec. 1973)-. Periodical. English. ir. Free on request; comes with Population Reports (entire series). Johns Hopkins University / Population Information Program, 111 Market Place, Suite 310, Baltimore MD 21202. **Tel** (410)659-6300, FAX (410)659-6311. **LC** RG137.3; .P63. **DD** 613.9/435. **NLM** W1 PO671I.
**Ind/Abst** EMBASE; Energy Res. Abstr. (Aug. 1982-); Index Med.; Popul. Index.

US/0891-0030
**POPULATION REPORTS. SERIES C, FEMALE STERILIZATION (ENGLISH ED.).** (POPULATION REPORTS. SERIES C, FEMALE STERILIZATION.). [Popul. rep., C, Female steriliz.]. **Added/Corp** Johns Hopkins University. Population Information Program. **VFOAT** Female Sterilization. No. 8 (Sept. 1980)-. Periodical. English. ir. Free on request, (comes with Population Reports entire series). Johns Hopkins University / Population Information Program, 111 Market Place, Suite 310, Baltimore MD 21202. **Tel** (410)659-6300, FAX (410)659-6311. **ED** Ward Rinehart.

**DD** 614. **NLM** W1; PO671KB. ***Continues** Population Reports (Washington, D.C.). Series C, Sterilization (Female), 0091-9268.*
**Ind/Abst** Energy Res. Abstr. (Aug. 1982-); Index Med.; Popul. Index.

US/0891-0049
**POPULATION REPORTS. SERIES D, MALE STERILIZATION (ENGLISH ED.).** (POPULATION REPORTS. SERIES D, MALE STERILIZATION.). [Popul. rep., D, Male steriliz.]. **Added/Corp** Johns Hopkins University. Population Information Program. **VFOAT** Male Sterilization. No. 4 (Nov./Dec. 1983)-. Periodical. English. ir. Free on request, (comes with Population Reports entire series). Johns Hopkins University / Population Information Program, 111 Market Place, Suite 310, Baltimore MD 21202. **Tel** (410)659-6300, FAX (410)659-6311. **ED** Ward Rinehart. **LC** RG136; .P66 ser.D. **DD** 613. **NLM** W1; PO671MB. ***Continues** Population Reports (Washington, D.C). Series D, Sterilization, 0093-4488.*
**Ind/Abst** Energy Res. Abstr. (Aug. 1982-); Index Med.; Popul. Index.

US/0097-9082
**POPULATION REPORTS. SERIES E, LAW AND POLICY (ENGLISH ED.).** (POPULATION REPORTS. SERIES E, LAW AND POLICY.). [Popul. rep., E Law policy]. **Added/Corp** George Washington University. Population Information Program. George Washington University. Dept. of Medical and Public Affairs. Johns Hopkins University. Population Information Program. **VFOAT** Law and Policy. No. 1 (July 1974)-. Periodical. English. ir. Free on request (comes with Population Reports entire series). Johns Hopkins University / Population Information Program, 111 Market Place, Suite 310, Baltimore MD 21202. **Tel** (410)659-6300, FAX (410)659-6311. **ED** Ward Rinehart. **LC** K2000.A13; P65. **DD** 344/.048; 342.448. **NLM** W1 PO671ME.
**Ind/Abst** Crim. Justice Abstr. (-199?); Curr. Law Index (1984-); EMBASE; Energy Res. Abstr. (Aug. 1982-); Index Med.; Leg. Resour. Index (1984-?); Popul. Index; Sage Urban Stud. Abstr (?-?).

US/0093-4496
**POPULATION REPORTS. SERIES H, BARRIER METHODS (ENGLISH ED.).** (POPULATION REPORTS. BARRIER METHODS - SERIES H.). [Popul. rep., H Barrier methods]. **Added/Corp** George Washington University. Population Information Program. George Washington University. Dept. of Medical and Public Affairs. Johns Hopkins University. Population Information Program. **VFOAT** Barrier Methods. No. 1 (Dec. 1973)-. Periodical. English (Spanish, French, Arabic and Portuguese). ir. Free on request, (comes with Population Reports entire series). Johns Hopkins University / Population Information Program, 111 Market Place, Suite 310, Baltimore MD 21202. **Tel** (410)659-6300, FAX (410)659-6311. **ED** Ward Rinehart. **LC** RC888; .P67. **DD** 613. **NLM** W1 PO671Q. **CODEN** PRSHDQ.
**Ind/Abst** EMBASE; Index Med.; Popul. Index.

US/0091-925X
**POPULATION REPORTS. SERIES J, FAMILY PLANNING PROGRAMS (ENGLISH ED.).** (POPULATION REPORTS. SERIES J, FAMILY PLANNING PROGRAMS.). [Popul. rep., J, Fam. plan. programs]. **Added/Corp** George Washington University. Population Information Program. George Washington University. Dept. of Medical and Public Affairs. Johns Hopkins University. Population Information Program. **VFOAT** Family Planning Programs. No. 1 (Aug. 1973)-. Periodical. English (French, Spanish and Portuguese). ir. Free on request, (comes with Population Reports entire series). Johns Hopkins University / Population Information Program, 111 Market Place, Suite 310, Baltimore MD 21202. **Tel** (410)659-6300, FAX (410)659-6311. **ED** Ward Rinehart. **LC** HQ763; .P616. **DD** 304. **NLM** W1 PO671S. **CODEN** PLNRAK.
**Ind/Abst** Index Med.; Popul. Index.

US/0097-9104
**POPULATION REPORTS. SERIES K, INJECTABLES AND IMPLANTS (ENGLISH ED.).** (POPULATION REPORTS. SERIES K, INJECTABLES AND IMPLANTS.). [Popul. rep., K, Inject. implants]. **Added/Corp** George Washington University. Population Information Program. George Washington University. Dept. of Medical and Public Affairs. Johns Hopkins University. Population Information Program. **VFOAT** Injectables and Implants. No. 1 (March 1975)-. Periodical. English. ir. Free on request (comes with Population Reports entire series). Johns Hopkins University / Population Information Program, 111 Market Place, Suite 310, Baltimore MD 21202. **Tel** (410)659-6300, FAX (410)659-6311. **ED** Ward Rinehart. **LC** RG137.55; .P66. **DD** 613. **NLM** W1 PO671SC. **CODEN** PRSIDT.
**Ind/Abst** Index Med.; Popul. Index.

US/0197-5838
**POPULATION REPORTS. SERIES L, ISSUES IN WORLD HEALTH (ENGLISH ED.).** (POPULATION REPORTS. SERIES L, ISSUES IN WORLD HEALTH.). [Popul. rep., L Issues world health]. **Added/Corp** Johns Hopkins University. Population Information Program. **VFOAT** Issues in World Health. No. 1 (March 1979)-. Academic Scholarly Publication. English. ir. Free on request, (comes with Population Reports entire series). Johns Hopkins University / Population Information Program, 111 Market Place, Suite 310, Baltimore MD 21202. **Tel** (410)659-6300, FAX (410)659-6311. **ED** Ward Rinehart. **LC** RC889; .P59. **DD** 616.6/92. **NLM** W1 PO671SD.
**Ind/Abst** EMBASE; Index Med.; Popul. Index.

US/0733-9135
**POPULATION REPORTS. SERIES M, SPECIAL TOPICS (ENGLISH ED.).** (POPULATION REPORTS. SPECIAL TOPICS - SERIES M.). [Popul. rep., M, Spec. top.]. **Added/Corp** Johns Hopkins University. Population Information Program. **VFOAT** Special Topics. No. 5 (May/June 1981)-. Academic Scholarly Publication. English (Spanish, French, Arabic and Portuguese). ir. Free on request, (comes with Population Reports entire series). Johns Hopkins University / Population Information Program, 111 Market Place, Suite 310, Baltimore MD 21202. **Tel** (410)659-6300, FAX (410)659-6311. **ED** Ward Rinehart. **LC** RG136; .P6 Ser. M. **DD** 304. **NLM** W1 PO671SE. **Pr Rev.** ***Continues** Population Reports (Washington, D.C.). Series M, Special Topic Monographs, 0275-8792.*
**Ind/Abst** EMBASE; Index Med.; Popul. Index.

CN/0317-3100
**POPULATION REPRINTS.** No. 1- 1972-. Monographic series. English. ir. Price varies per volume. Population Research Laboratory / Department of Social Science, University of Alberta 1 62, Edmonton Alberta T6G 2H4 Canada. **Tel** (403)492-4659. **DD** 301.3/2. **Circ:** 125.

CC
**POPULATION RESEARCH.** ***Ceased.*** **Added/Corp** China Scientific and Technical Document Translation Co. Vol., No. 1 (1983)-?. Periodical. English (translations available in Chinese). bm. China National Publishing Import & Export Corporation, 16 Gongti E Rd., Chaoyang Dist., Beijing 100704, People's Republic of China. **Tel** 011 8601 50630169, 5066688, FAX 011 8601 5063101, 5063010, telex 22313.

II/0971-1996
**POPULATION RESEARCH ABSTRACT.** [Popul. Res. Abstr.]. (1990)-. Periodical. English. sa. Applied Population Research Trust, 79/3 Benson Cross Road, Bangalore 560 046 India. **UDC** 312.
**Ind/Abst** Popul. Index.

NE/0167-5923
**POPULATION RESEARCH AND POLICY REVIEW.** [Popul. res. policy rev.]. Vol. 1, No. 1 (Jan. 1982)-. Periodical. English. qt. $436.00. Kluwer Academic Publishers, Postbus 322, 3300 AH Dordrecht, The Netherlands. **Tel** 011 (31) 78 524400, FAX 011 31 78 183273, telex 20083. **ED** Larry D Barnett and Eric Moore. **LC** HB848; .P65. **DD** 304.6/05. **[CCC]. Pr Rev. Acid Free.** available on microfilm and microfiche from University Microfilms International (UMI). Documents available from The Genuine Article.
**Desc:** Provides a convenient source for government officials and scholars to learn about the policy implications of recent research relevant to the causes and consequences of changing population size and composition.
**Ind/Abst** Chicano Index; Curr. Contents Soc. Behav. Sci.; Econ. Lit. Index (19??-); Geogr. Abstr. Human Geogr. (1988-); Index Period. Artic. Relat. Law (19??-19??); Int. Bibliogr. Sociol.; Int. Dev. Abstr.; Int. Polit. Sci. Abstr. (1988-); J. Econ. Lit. (1988-); Middle East Abstr. Index; PAIS Int. Print (1991-); Popul. Index; Res. Alert [Full Cov.]; Soc. Plann. Policy Dev. Abstr.; Soc. Sci. Cit. Index [Full Cov.]; Soc. Work Abstr. (1988-?); Sociol. Abstr.

US/0032-471X
**POPULATION REVIEW.** [Popul. rev.]. **Added/Corp** Indian Institute for Population Studies. Vol. 1 Jan. (1957)-. Periodical. English. sa (each September in a double issue). $25.00. Indian Institute for Population Studies, 8976 Cliffridge Avenue, La Jolla CA 92037. **Tel** (619)455-6283. **(Subscription address:** PO Box 8093, La Jolla, CA 92083-8093) **ED** S Chandrasekhar. **LC** HB881; .P7. **DD** 301.32/05. **NLM** W1 PO672. cum. index. **Bk Rev. Ad Acc. Circ:** 2,500.
**Desc:** Deals with Asia and other developing countries. Subjects include: population, family planning, economics, environment, sociology and public health.
**Ind/Abst** Int. Bibliogr. Sociol.; PAIS Int. Print; Popul. Index; Soc. Plann. Policy Dev. Abstr.; Sociol. Abstr.

UA
**POPULATION SCIENCES : JOURNAL OF INTERNATIONAL ISLAMIC CENTER FOR POPULATION STUDIES AND RESEARCH, AL-AZHAR UNIVERSITY, CAIRO.** **Added/Corp** Markaz al-Dawli al-Islami lil-Dirasat wa-al-Buhuth al-Sukkaniyah. **VFOAT** Ulum al-Sakkaniyah. No. 1 (1979)-. Periodical. English (Arabic). sa. International Islamic Centre for Population Studies and Research, Al-Azhar University, PO Box 1894, Cairo, Egypt. **LC** RG136.A1; P66. **DD** 363.9/05.
**Ind/Abst** Popul. Index.

US
**POPULATION STATISTICS. CD-ROM.** English. $990.00 (nonprofit institutions), $1200.00 other. Slater Hall Information Products, 1301 Pennsylvania Avenue Northwest, Washington DC 20004. **Tel** (202)393-2666.

UK/0032-4728
**POPULATION STUDIES.** [Popul. stud.]. **Added/Corp** London School of Economics and Political Science. Population Investigation Committee. (June 1947)-. Academic Scholarly Publication. English. Three times a year (Mar., July, Nov.). $110.00 US; £48 other. Population Investigation Committee, London School of Economics, Houghton Street, London WC2A 2AE England. **Tel** 11 44 71 9557666, FAX 11 44 71 9556833, telex 24655 BLPES C. **ED** E. Grebenik, T. Dyson, J. Hobcraft, M. Murphy and R. Schofield. **LC** HB848; .P66. **DD** 304.6/05. **NLM** W1 PO675. **CODEN** POSTA4. **[CCC].** Index available. **Bk Rev. Ad Acc. Pr Rev. Circ:** 3,000. available on microfilm and microfiche from University Microfilms International (UMI). Documents available from The Genuine Article, BIOSIS Document Express, UMI Article Clearinghouse, Documents on Demand.
**Desc:** Covers socio-economic and biomedical causes and consequences of fertility, family, marriage, mortality, migration theory, methods and models; worldwide trends.
**Ind/Abst** Am. Hist. Life (1955-); Anthropol. Index; Appl. Soc. Sci. Index Abstr.; Biol. Abstr.; Biostatistica; Curr. Lit. Fam. Plan.; Econ. Lit. Index; EMBASE; Environ. Abstr.; Environ. Period. Bibliogr.; Expand. Acad. Index (1992-); Geogr. Abstr. Human Geogr.; Int. Bibliogr. Sociol.; Int. Dev. Abstr.; Int. Labour Doc.; J. Econ. Lit.; J. Plan. Lit.; LABORDOC; Newsp. Period. Abstr. (1992-); PAIS Int. Print (1991-); Popul. Index; Res. Alert [Full Cov.]; Soc. Plann. Policy Dev. Abstr.; Soc. Sci. Cit. Index [Full Cov.]; Soc. Work Abstr. (?-?); Sociol. Abstr. [Full Cov.]; Stat. Theory Method Abstr. (1959-1963, 1970); Trop. Dis. Bull.; Women Stud. Abstr.

II
**POPULATION STUDIES.** English. Professor & Head of Department of Demography and Population Studies, University of Kerala, Kariavattom 695581 India. **Tel** (0471)8057. **ED** R Ramakumar. **LC** HB3640.K4; P66. **DD** 301.32/9/5483. **Ad Acc. Circ:** 200 (ctrl).
**Desc:** Research articles in demography slant towards methodology, technical demography, statistical models. Results of population studies from any part of the world.

US
**POPULATION STUDIES.** ***Title Change.*** **Added/Corp** University of Florida. Population Program. Bulletin No. 69 (July 1984)-Bulletin No. 101-102 (May 1992). Periodical. English. qt. Bureau of Economic & Business Research / Florida, University of Florida, 221 Matherly Hall, Gainesville FL 32611. **Tel** (904)392-0171, FAX (904)392-4739. **LC** HB3225.F6; F55a. ***Continues** Population Studies (University of Florida. Population Division).* ***Continued by*** *Florida Population Studies.*

FR
**POPULATION STUDIES (STRASBOURG, FRANCE).** (POPULATION STUDIES.). **VFOAT** Council of Europe Population Studies. (1976)-. Monographic series. English. Price varies per volume. Manhattan Publishing Company, PO Box 650, Croton-on-Hudson NY 10520. **Tel** (914)271-5194.
**Desc:** Demographic aspects of labor force and employment in Europe.

US/0082-805X
**POPULATION STUDIES - UNITED NATIONS.** (POPULATION STUDIES.). [Popul. stud. - U. N.]. **Main/Corp** United Nations. Dept. of Economic and Social Affairs. **Added/Corp** United Nations. Dept. of Social Affairs. United Nations. Dept. of Social Affairs. Population Division. United Nations. Dept. of Economic and Social Affairs. Population Branch. United Nations. Dept. of International Economic and Social Affairs. **VFOAT** Demographic Studies; Reports on the Population of the Trust Territories. No. 1, (1948)-. Government Publication. English. ir. Price varies per volume. United Nations Publications, 2 United Nations Plaza, Room DC2 0853, Department 007C, New York NY 10017. **Tel** (212)963-8303, (800)253-9646. **LC** JX1977; .A2.
**Desc:** Covers all aspects of population trends, problems and policies.
**Ind/Abst** Index Med.; Women Stud. Abstr.

US/0749-2448
**POPULATION TODAY.** [Popul. today]. **Added/Corp** Population Reference Bureau. Vol. 12, No. 1 (Jan. 1984)-. Periodical. English. Eleven times a year (July/Aug. issues combined). $55.00 (non-profit organization & libraries); $45.00 (individuals); $200.00 (corporations) Comes with Population Reference Bureau membership. Population Reference Bureau, 1875 Connecticut Avenue Northwest, Suite 520, Washington DC 20009. **Tel** (202)483-1100, (800)877-9881, FAX (202)328-3937. **ED** Arthur Hauph. **DD** 304. **NLM** W1; PO675P. Index available. **Bk Rev. Circ:** 5,000. available on microfilm. Documents available from UMI Article Clearinghouse, Documents on Demand. ***Continues** Intercom, 0092-444X.*
**Desc:** Covers US and international population news and issues, including demography, party planning, economic development and the environment.

# Population Studies

**Ind/Abst** Acad. Search (July 1993-); Curr. Lit. Fam. Plan.; Environ. Abstr.; INFO-SOUTH Abstr.; Mag. Search; Middle East Abstr. Index; Newsp. Period. Abstr. (1990-); Popul. Index; Stat. Ref. Index.

US/0736-7716
## POPULATION TRENDS AND PUBLIC POLICY.
[Popul. trends public policy]. **Added/Corp** Population Reference Bureau. No. 1 (Jan. 1981)-. Monographic series. English. Price varies per volume. Population Reference Bureau, 1875 Connecticut Avenue Northwest, Suite 520, Washington DC 20009. **Tel** (202)483-1100, (800)877-9881, FAX (202)328-3937. **NLM** W1; PO677.
**Ind/Abst** Popul. Index; Stat. Ref. Index.

US/0251-8996
## POPULATION - UNITED NATIONS FUND FOR POPULATION ACTIVITIES.
Ceased. (POPULATION : UNFPA NEWSLETTER.). **Added/Corp** United Nations Fund for Population Activities. **VFOAT** UNFPA Newsletter. (197?)-(1992). Newsletter. English. mo. UN Fund for Population Activities, 220 East 42nd Street/17th Floor, New York NY 10017. **LC** HB848; .P6185. **DD** 304/.05. Documents available from Documents on Demand. **Continues** United Nations Fund for Population Activities. UNFPA Newsletter.
**Ind/Abst** Environ. Abstr.

US/0251-6861
## POPULI (ENGLISH ED.).
(POPULI.). [Populi]. **Added/Corp** United Nations Fund for Population Activities. **VFOAT** United Nations Population Fund. (19??)-. English. qt. free on request. United Nations Population Fund, 220 East 42nd Street/17th Floor, New York NY 10017. **Tel** (212)297-5026, FAX (212)557-6416, telex 422031. **ED** Abid Aslam. **LC** HB848; .P68. **DD** 301.32/05. **NLM** W1 PO678. available on microfilm and microfiche from University Microfilms International (UMI). Documents available from Documents on Demand.
**Desc:** Provides up-to-date coverage of demographic trends and population problems throughout the world.
**Ind/Abst** Curr. Lit. Fam. Plan.; Environ. Abstr.; PAIS Int. Print (1991-); Popul. Index; Trop. Dis. Bull.

●US
## POPULI / UNITED NATIONS POPULATION FUND.
See Public Administration-Public Finance and Taxation.

CN/0827-9624
## POSTCENSAL ANNUAL ESTIMATES OF POPULATION BY MARITAL STATUS, AGE, SEX AND COMPONENTS OF GROWTH FOR CANADA, PROVINCES AND TERRITORIES.
See Population Studies-Abstracting, Bibliographies and Statistics.

US/0146-7646
## PRB REPORT.
**Main/Corp** Population Reference Bureau. **VAT** Population Reference Bureau Report. Vol. 1, No. 1 (1975)-. Periodical. English. ir. $20.00 (Individuals) $25.00 (Libraries) $50.00 (Institutions). Population Reference Bureau, 1875 Connecticut Avenue Northwest, Suite 520, Washington DC 20009. **Tel** (202)483-1100, (800)877-9881, FAX (202)328-3937. **Formed by the union of** Population Profile **and** PRB Selection.

RU
## PROBLEMY REGIONALNOGO DEMOGRAFICHESKOGO PROGNOZIROVANIIA V SISTEME NARODNOKHOZIAISTVENNOGO PLANIROVANIIA / GOSPLAN TADZHIKSKOI SSR, NAUCNHO-ISSLEDOVATELSKII INSTITUT EKONOMIKI I EKONOMIKO-MATEMATICHESKIKH METODOV PLANIROVANIIA S VYCHISLITELNYM TSENTROM.
**Added/Corp** Nauchno-Issledovatelskii Institut Ekonomiki i Ekonomiko-Matematicheskikh Metodov Planirovaniia (Dushanbe, Tajik S.S.R.). (19??)-. Russian. **LC** HB3607; .P8.

US
## PROJECTIONS OF THE POPULATION OF THE UNITED STATES ... (ADVANCE REPORT).
1982 to 2050-. Government Publication. English. US Department of Commerce, 14th Street & Constitution Avenue NW, Washington DC 20230. **Tel** (202)482-2000, FAX (202)482-3772.

US
## PROJECTIONS OF THE POPULATION OF VOTING AGE FOR STATES / U.S. DEPARTMENT OF COMMERCE, BUREAU OF THE CENSUS.
Began with Nov. 1966-1968. Government Publication. English. be. US Department of Commerce, 14th Street & Constitution Avenue NW, Washington DC 20230. **Tel** (202)482-2000, FAX (202)482-3772. **Continues** Estimates of the Civilian Population of Voting Age, for States.

AT/0816-3391
## PROJECTIONS OF THE POPULATIONS OF AUSTRALIA, STATES AND TERRITORIES.
**Added/Corp** Australian Bureau of Statistics. (1984)-. Periodical. English. ir. 26.00Aus$. Australian Bureau of Statistics, PO Box 10, Belconnen Australian Capital Territory, 2616 Australia. **Tel** 011 61 6 2527911, FAX 011 61 6 2516009. **LC** HB3675; .P76.
**Desc:** Four alternative projections of the resident population of Australia, States and Territories for each year to 1993 and from 1996 at five-yearly intervals to 2031. Number and percentage of population at selected ages, sex, sex ratios, mean and median ages. Detailed notes on methodology and background to the assumptions.

CN/0835-4057
## QUARTERLY DEMOGRAPHIC STATISTICS.
See Population Studies-Abstracting, Bibliographies and Statistics.

LU
## RAPID REPORTS. POPULATION AND SOCIAL CONDITIONS / EUROSTAT.
**Added/Corp** Statistical Office of the European Communities. **VFOAT** Population and Social Conditions. (1989)-. Periodical. English. ir. ECU 206.00 (complete set). Office for Official Publications of the European Communities, 2 Rue Mercier, 2985 Luxembourg Luxembourg. **Tel** 011 352 499281, FAX 011 352 488573. **LC** HB2672.5.A3; R37.

LU
## RAPID REPORTS. REGIONS / EUROSTAT.
**Added/Corp** Statistical Office of the European Communities. **VFOAT** Regions. (19??)-. Periodical. English. ir. ECU 206.00 (complete set). Office for Official Publications of the European Communities, 2 Rue Mercier, 2985 Luxembourg Luxembourg. **Tel** 011 352 499281, FAX 011 352 488573.

II/0376-5288
## REGISTRATION OF BIRTHS & DEATHS ACT. ANNUAL REPORT.
(REGISTRATION OF BIRTHS & DEATHS ACT, ANNUAL REPORT / UNION TERRITORY OF DELHI.). **Added/Corp** Delhi (India : Union Territory). Office of the Chief Registrar, Births & Deaths. Delhi (India : Union Territory). Bureau of Economics & Statistics. **VFOAT** Registration of Births and Deaths Act, Annual Report. (1969)-. English. an. Delhi Administration, Room No 148/Old Secretariat, New Delhi 110054 India. **LC** HB3640.D4; R43. **DD** 312/.0954/56.

CC/1000-6087
## RENKOU YANJIU.
(JEN KOU YEN CHIU.). [Renkou yanjiu]. **VFOAT** Renkou Yanjiu; Population Research. (1977)-. Periodical. Chinese. bm. $12.55. Science Press, 16 Donghuangchenggen North Street, Beijing 100707, People's Republic of China. **Tel** 011 86 1 4019821, 011 86 1 4010642, FAX 011 86 1 4012180, 011 86 1 4019810, telex 210147. **(Subscription address:** China International Book Trading Corporation, PO Box 399, Library Service Department, Beijing 100044 People's Republic of China.) **LC** HB3654.A3; J467. **DD** 304.6/0951.
**Ind/Abst** Popul. Index.

CC/1000-4149
## RENKOU YU JINGJI.
(JEN KOU YU CHING CHI.). [Renkou yu jingji]. **VFOAT** Renkou yu Jingji; Population and Economics. (1980)-. Periodical. Chinese. bm. $24.30. Beijing Jingji Xueyuan, Renkou Jingji Yanjiusuo, Beijing Institute of Economics, Hongmiao, Chaoyangmen, Beijing 100026, People's Republic of China. **Tel** 5005511. **(Subscription address:** China International Book Trading Corporation, PO Box 399, Library Service Department, Beijing 100044 People's Republic of China.) **ED** F. Litian. **LC** HB3654.A3; J468. **DD** 304.6/0951. Documents available from The UnCover Company.
**Desc:** Contains information compiled from economic and population studies.

BE
## REPERTOIRE DES ACTIVITES SCIENTIFIQUES DES MEMBRES / UNION INTERNATIONALE POUR L'ETUDE SCIENTIFIQUE DE LA POPULATION.
**Main/Corp** International Union for the Scientific Study of Population. **VFOAT** Directory of Members' Scientific Activities. French. International Union for the Scientific Study of Population, 34 rue Augustins, B4000 Liege Belgium. **Tel** 011 32 41 224080. **LC** HB849.3; .I58A. **DD** 304.6/025.

US
## REPORT OF PENNSYLVANIA COUNCIL FOR SEXUAL MINORITIES.
**Main/Corp** Pennsylvania. Council for Sexual Minorities. (1977)-. English. an. Pennsylvania Council for Sexual Minorities, PO Box 7319, Pittsburgh PA 15213. **LC** HQ75; .P46a. **DD** 353.9/748/00996.

US
## REPORT OF THE POPULATION COMMISSION / ECONOMIC AND SOCIAL COUNCIL, UNITED NATIONS.
**Main/Corp** United Nations. Economic and Social Council. Population Commission. **VFOAT** Report to the Economic and Social Council on the ... Session of the Commission. 1st Session (Feb. 6/19, 1947)-. Government Publication. English (French; table of contents in French). ir. United Nations Publications, 2 United Nations Plaza, Room DC2 0853, Department 007C, New York NY 10017. **Tel** (212)963-8303, (800)253-9646. **LC** JX1977; .A2 E/267, etc. **DD** 312.0611.

US/0275-2050
## REPORT ON FAMILY PLANNING SERVICES AND POPULATION RESEARCH, A.
See Birth Control.

FR
## REPORT ON THE ACTIVITIES OF THE IGU COMMISSION ON POPULATION GEOGRAPHY.
**Main/Corp** International Geographical Union. Commission of Population Geography. (1980)-. Newsletter. English (French). Twice a year. Free on request. University of Paris, Professor Daniel Noin, 191 rue Saint-Jacques, 75005 Paris France. **Tel** 011 33 1 44211416, FAX 011 33 1 44321454. **ED** Prof. Daniel Noin. **LC** HB848; .I525a. **DD** 301.32/06/01. **Circ:** 380.
**Desc:** Newsletter of the International Geographical Union's Commission on Population Geography; contains information on activities, events and other population information.

CN/0715-9293
## REPORT ON THE DEMOGRAPHIC SITUATION IN CANADA.
See Population Studies-Abstracting, Bibliographies and Statistics.

SQ
## REPORT ON THE SWAZILAND POPULATION CENSUS.
See Population Studies-Abstracting, Bibliographies and Statistics.

II
## RES. PUB. (NATIONAL GEOGRAPHICAL SOCIETY OF INDIA).
See Geography.

US/0163-7878
## RESEARCH IN POPULATION ECONOMICS.
[Res. popul. econ.]. Vol. 1 (1978)-. Monographic series. English. ir. price varies per volume. JAI Press Inc., 55 Old Post Road, Suite 2, PO Box 1678, Greenwich CT 06836-1678. **Tel** (203)661-7602, FAX (203)661-0792. **ED** Paul Shultz. **LC** HB848; .R47. **DD** 301.32/05. **[CCC]**.
**Ind/Abst** Popul. Index.

US/0886-9014
## RESEARCH REPORT - UNIVERSITY OF MICHIGAN. POPULATION STUDIES CENTER.
(RESEARCH REPORT.). [Res. rep. - Univ. Mich., Popul. Stud. Cent.]. **Added/Corp** University of Michigan. Population Studies Center. (19??)-. Monographic series. English. Price varies per volume. Population Studies Center, University of Michigan, Ann Arbor MI 48104. **DD** 304.
**Ind/Abst** Geogr. Abstr. Human Geogr.

AG
## RESENA DE ACTIVIDADES - CENEP.
**Main/Corp** Centro de Estudios de Poblacion, (Buenos Aires, Argentina). Spanish. be. Casilla 4397, Correo Central, 1000 Buenos Aires Argentina. **Tel** (54)1 961-0309, FAX (54)1-961-8195, telex 23854 GECOPAR CEP. **LC** HB850.5.A7; C46A. **DD** 304.6/072082. Index available. cum. index. **Bk Rev. Circ:** 400 (ctrl).

UK
## RESIDENT ABROAD.
English. Financial Times Business Information Ltd, Central House, 27 Park Street, Croydon CR0 1YD England. **Tel** 011 44 81 680 3786.

DR
## RESUMENES SOBRE POBLACION DOMINICANA.
V. 1, No. 1 (June 1984)-. Spanish. sa. Profamilia, Apartado Postal 1053, Saint Domingo Dominican Republic. **Tel** (809)682-9611, (809)689-2723. **LC** HB3552.A3; R47. **DD** 304.6/097293.

FR/0377-8967
## REVIEW OF POPULATION REVIEWS.
[Rev. popul. rev.]. **Added/Corp** CICRED. United Nations Fund for Population Activities. No. 7 (Jan./March 1978)-. Periodical. English (French). qt. Free. Committee for International Cooperation in National Research in

Demography, 27 rue du Commandeur, 75675 Paris Cedex 44 France. **Tel** (33) (1) 43.20.13.45. **LC** HB848; .R48. **DD** 304.6/05. **Circ:** 600 French, 900 English.
**Desc:** Presents summaries of articles published in periodical population reviews. Each summary consists of 100 to 150 words of brief description of the article. Between 275 and 300 summaries are given in each issue.
**Ind/Abst** Popul. Index.

BL/0102-3098
**REVISTA BRASILEIRA DE ESTUDOS DE POPULACAO.** **Added/Corp** Associacao Brasileira de Estudos Populacionais. Vol. 1, No. 1/2 (Jan./Dec. 1984)-. Periodical. Portuguese. Three times a year. $22.00. Assoc Brasileira Estudos Popul Belo Horizonte, Rua General Jandim 770 Conj 3D, 01223 Sao Paulo SP Brazil. **Tel** 011 55 31 2551820. **LC** HB3563; .R48. **NLM** W1; RE317G.
**Ind/Abst** Int. Bibliogr. Sociol.; Popul. Index.

PO/0079-4082
**REVISTA DO CENTRO DE ESTUDOS DEMOGRAFICOS.** (REVISTA.). [Rev. Cent. Estud. Demogr.]. **Main/Corp** Centro de Estudos Demograficos (Portugal). (1944)-. Portuguese. Instituto Nacional de Estatistica, Servicos Centrais, Avenida Antonio Jose de Almeida 1, 1078 Lisbon Portugal. **Tel** 80 20 80, FAX 8489480, telex 63738 PCDINE. **LC** HB3621; .A33.
**Ind/Abst** Popul. Index.

BL/0101-7217
**REVISTA DOCPOP.** (REVISTA DOCPOP / SEADE.). [Rev. DOCPOP]. **Added/Corp** Sao Paulo (Brazil : State). Fundacao Sistema Estadual de Analise de Dados. **VFOAT** DOCPOP. Vol. 1, No. 1 (Dec. 1982)-. Periodical. Portuguese (English). sa. $18.00. SEADE, Av Casper Libero 464, 01033 Sao Paulo SP Brazil. **Tel** 011 55 11 2279788.

●PE
**REVISTA PERUANA DE POBLACION.** (1992)-. Spanish. sa. Asociation Multidisciplinaria de Investigacion y Docencia en Poblacion, Ave. Salaverry 2461, Lima 27 Peru. **Tel** 705145, FAX 222950. **Bk Rev.**

YU
**REZULTATI SAMOPOPISIVANJA I POSTANSKIH METODA U BEOGRADU ... GODINE.** **VFOAT** Results of Self-Enumeration and Mail Methods in Beograd. Serbo-Croatian (Roman). 50.00 Din. Savezni Zavod za Statistiku, Kneza Milosa 20, Belgrad Yugoslavia. **LC** HA37.Y8; A37 subser; HA1635.B4.

PL
**ROCZNIKI STATYSTYCZNE. DEMOGRAFIA / GOWNY URZAD STATYSTYCZNY.** **Added/Corp** Poland. Gowny Urzad Statystyczny. **VFOAT** Demografia. (1990)-. Polish. Zaklad Wydawnictw Statystycznych, Al Niepodleglosci 208, 00-925 Warszawa Poland. **Tel** 253241, telex 814581A GUS. **LC** HB3608.7; .A33. ***Continues*** *Poland. Gowny Urzad Statystyczny.; Rocznik Demograficzny, 0079-2616.*

BG/1010-3783
**RURAL DEMOGRAPHY.** [Rural demogr.]. V. 1-Summer 1974-. Periodical. English. sa. $6.00. Institute of Statistical Research & Training, Secretary, Dacca 2 Bangladesh. **LC** HB850.5.B3; R85. **DD** 301.32/9/5492.
**Ind/Abst** Popul. Index.

IT
**SERVIZI DEMOGRAFICI.** Maggioli Editore, Casella Postale 290, 47037 Rimini, Italy. **Tel** 011 39 541 628666, FAX 011 39 541 742217.

YU/0038-982X
**STANOVNISTVO.** [Stanovnistvo]. **Added/Corp** Centar za Demografska Istrazivanja (Institut Drustvenih Nauka). **VFOAT** Population; Naselenie. (Jan./Mar. 1963)-. Periodical. Serbo-Croatian (Roman) (summaries and/or abstracts in English, French and Russian; table of contents in English, French and Russian). qt. Institut Drustvenih Nauka, Centar za Demografska Istrazivanja, Narodnog Fronta 45, p.f. 927, 11000 Belgrade Yugoslavia. **LC** HB848; .S7.
**Ind/Abst** Popul. Index.

US
**STATE OF WORLD POPULATION / RAFAEL M. SALAS, EXECUTIVE DIRECTOR OF THE UNITED NATIONS FUND FOR POPULATION ACTIVITIES, THE.** **Added/Corp** United Nations Fund for Population Activities. (19??)-. English (French, Spanish, Arabic and Portuguese). an. Free. United Nations Population Fund, 220 East 42nd Street/17th Floor, New York NY 10017. **Tel** (212)297-5026, FAX (212)557-6416, telex 422031. **ED** Alex Marshall. ctrl circ.

IT
**STATISTICHE DEMOGRAFICHE.** **See** Population Studies-Abstracting, Bibliographies and Statistics.

BE/0067-5490
**STATISTIQUES DEMOGRAPHIQUES.** **See** Population Studies-Abstracting, Bibliographies and Statistics.

PL/0039-3134
**STUDIA DEMOGRAFICZNE.** [Stud. demogr.]. **Added/Corp** Polska Akademia Nauk. Komitet Nauk Demograficznych. (1963)-. Periodical. Polish (summaries and/or abstracts in English and Russian; table of contents in English and Russian). qt. $39.00. **(Subscription address:** ARS Polona, PO Box 1001, 00068 Warsaw Poland.) **LC** HB881.A1; S8.
**Ind/Abst** Int. Bibliogr. Sociol.; Popul. Index.

AT
**STUDIES IN DEMOGRAPHY AT THE AUSTRALIAN NATIONAL UNIVERSITY.** English. ir. Anutech Pty Limited, GPO Box 4, Canberra Act, 2601 Australia. **Tel** 011 61 6 2492479, FAX 011 61 6 2575088.

US/0039-3665
**STUDIES IN FAMILY PLANNING.** **See** Birth Control.

CN/1194-6164
**SUSPOP NEWS.** (SUSPOP NEWS : THE SUSTAINABLE POPULATION SOCIETY NEWSLETTER.). [SusPop news]. **Added/Corp** Sustainable Population Society. **VFOAT** Sustainable Population Society Newsletter. Issue No. 1 (Aug. 1991)-. Periodical. English. ir. $24.00 Comes with Sustainable Population Society membership. Sustainable Population Society, PO Box 11964, Main PO, Edmonton Alberta T5J 3L1 Canada. **Tel** (403)466-2196, FAX (403)466-2196. **DD** 363.9/1/06. **Circ:** 100.

US/0363-3144
**TEACHING NOTES ON POPULATION.** V. 1- Spring/Summer 1972-. English. St Lawrence University, Department of Sociology, c/o Parker Marden, Canton NY 13617.

NE/1012-8727
**TECHNICAL BULLETINS / WORLD FERTILITY SURVEY.** [Tech. bull. - World Fertil. Surv.]. No. 1; Oct. 1976-. Monographic series. English. Price varies per volume. International Statistical Institute, 428 Prinses Beatrixlaan, 2270 AZ Voorburg Netherlands. **Tel** 011 31 70 3375737, FAX 011 31 70 3860025, telex 32260 ISI NL. **NLM** W1; TE134. **CODEN** TBWSDB. Documents available from BIOSIS Document Express.
**Ind/Abst** Biol. Abstr. (-1983); Popul. Index (?-?).

CN/1181-6643
**TELEVISION VIEWING.** (TELEVISION VIEWING / STATISTICS CANADA, EDUCATION, CULTURE AND TOURISM DIVISION.). [Telev. viewing]. **Added/Corp** Statistics Canada. Education, Culture and Tourism Division. **VFOAT** Ecoute de la Television. (1989)-. English (French). an. 28.00Can$ Canada; $34.00 US; $40.00 other. Statistics Canada, Publications Sales & Services, Main Building Room 1710, Ottawa Ontario K1A 0T6 Canada. **Tel** (613)951-5078, (800)267-6677, FAX (613)951-1584, telex 053-3585. **DD** 384.55/0971/021. ***Continues*** *Television Viewing in Canada., 1180-3304.*
**Desc:** An annual analysis of the television viewing patterns of Canadians, including charts and tables, beginning with survey data from the fall of 1985.

US/0040-5809
**THEORETICAL POPULATION BIOLOGY.** [Theor. popul. biol.]. Vol. 1 (May 1970)-. Academic Scholarly Publication. English. bm (6 issues). $380.00 US and Canada; $470.00 other. Academic Press, Inc., 6277 Sea Harbor Drive, Orlando FL 32887. **Tel** (800)543-9534, (407)345-4100, FAX (407)363-9661. **ED** P. Chesson, K. Dietz, J. Gillespie, S. Karlin and M. Feldman. **LC** QH301; .T5. **DD** 575.1. **NLM** W1 TH12K. **CODEN** TLPBAQ. **[CCC]. Pr Rev.** Documents available from The Genuine Article, BIOSIS Document Express.
**Desc:** Presents articles on the theoretical aspects of the biology of populations, particularly in the areas of ecology, genetics, demography, and epidemiology. Primary emphasis is on developments of the theory, but also presented are experimental results directly impinging on the theory.
**Ind/Abst** AGRICOLA; Anim. Breed. Abstr.; Biocont. News Inf.; Biol. Abstr.; Curr. Aware. Biol. Sci., CABS; Curr. Contents, Agric. Biol. Environ. Sci.; Curr. Contents Life Sci.; Ecology Abstr.; For. Abstr.; Genet. Abstr.; Geogr. Abstr. Human Geogr.; Index Med.; Key Word Index Wildl. Res.; Math. Rev.; Life Sci. Collect.; Plant Breed. Abstr.; Plant Genet. Resour. Abstr.; Popul. Index; Res. Alert [Full Cov.]; Rev. Agric. Entomol.; Rev. Med. Vet. Entomol.; Sci. Cit. Index; SCISEARCH; Soc. Sci. Cit. Index [Select. Cov.]; Wildl. Rev.; Zentralbl. Math. Ihre Grenzgeb.

FR/0071-8823
**TRAVAUX ET DOCUMENTS / INSTITUT NATIONAL D'ETUDES DEMOGRAPHIQUES.** [Trav. doc. - Inst. natl. ,etud. d,emogr.]. **Added/Corp** Institut National d'Etudes Demographiques (France). (1946)-. Monographic series. French. ir. Presses Universitaires de France, Department des Revues, 14 Avenue du Bois de l'Epine, BP 90, 91003 Evry Cedex France. **Tel** (1)60 77 82 05, FAX (1) 60 79 20 45, telex PUF 600 474 F. **LC** UNC.

US/1058-0018
**U.S. DEPARTMENT OF STATE INDEXES OF LIVING COSTS ABROAD, QUARTERS ALLOWANCES, AND HARDSHIP DIFFERENTIALS.** (U.S. DEPARTMENT OF STATE INDEXES OF LIVING COSTS ABROAD, QUARTERS ALLOWANCES, AND HARDSHIP DIFFERENTIALS / U.S. DEPARTMENT OF LABOR, BUREAU OF LABOR STATISTICS.). [U. S. Dept. State indexes living costs abroad, quart. allow. hardship differ.]. **Added/Corp** United States. Bureau of Labor Statistics. United States. Dept. of State. Allowances Staff. United States. Dept. of State. Office of Allowances. **VFOAT** US Department of State Indexes of Living Costs Abroad, Quarters Allowances, and Hardship Differentials. (July 1982)-. Government Publication. English. qt. $5.50. Superintendent of Documents, US Government Printing Office, Washington DC 20402. **Tel** (202)275-3328, FAX (202)786-2377. **LC** HD8051; .A7876 subser.; JK774. **DD** 353. Documents available from Documents on Demand. ***Continues*** *U.S. Department of State Indexes of Living Costs Abroad and Living Quarters Allowances.*
**Ind/Abst** Am. Stat. Index.

US
**UNITED STATES LIFE TABLES.** **Main/Corp** National Center for Health Statistics (U.S.). **Added/Corp** National Center for Health Statistics (U.S.) U.S. Decennial Life Tables. **VFOAT** U.S. Decennial Life Tables. Vol. 1 (1969/1971)-. English. an. $1.75. Superintendent of Documents, US Government Printing Office, Washington DC 20402. **Tel** (202)275-3328, FAX (202)786-2377. **LC** HB1355; .U53a. **DD** 312/.2/0973. **NLM** HG 8781 U58L.

US
**VERMONT POPULATION ESTIMATES, STATE, COUNTY, CITIES, TOWNS, VILLAGES.** **Main/Corp** Vermont. Dept. of Health. English. 115 Colchester Avenue, Burlington VT 05401. **LC** HA674; .V47A. **DD** 312/.8/09743.

US/0278-5234
**VITAL AND HEALTH STATISTICS. SERIES 23. DATA FROM THE NATIONAL SURVEY OF FAMILY GROWTH.** (VITAL AND HEALTH STATISTICS. SERIES 23, DATA FROM THE NATIONAL SURVEY OF FAMILY GROWTH.). [Vital health stat. Ser. 23. Data natl. surv. fam. growth]. **Added/Corp** National Center for Health Statistics (U.S.). **VFOAT** Data from the National Survey of Family Growth; National Survey of Family Growth. **VAT** Vital and Health Statistics. Series Twenty Three. Data from the National Survey of Family Growth. No. 1 (Nov. 1977). Monographic series. English. ir. Free on request for libraries. National Center for Health Statistics, 6525 Belcrest Road, Hyattsville MD 20782. **Tel** (301)436-8500. **DD** 363.9/90973. **NLM** W2 A N148VW.
**Ind/Abst** Index Med. (19??-); Popul. Index (19??-).

CN/0317-3143
**VITAL STATISTICS. PRELIMINARY ANNUAL REPORT (OTTAWA).** **See** Population Studies-Abstracting, Bibliographies and Statistics.

IO
**WARTA DEMOGRAFI.** Periodical. Indonesian. mo. $10.00 Indonesia; $20.00 other. Lembaga Demografi, Fakultas Ekonomi Universitas Indonesia, Jl Salemba Raya 4, Jakarta 10430 Indonesia. **Tel** 336434. **ED** M Djuhari Wirakartakusumah. **LC** HB848; .W37. Index available. **Bk Rev. Circ:** 800 (ctrl).

US/0099-2046
**WASHINGTON REGION.** **Main/Corp** Washington Center for Metropolitan Studies. 1974-. English. Washington Center for Metropolitan Studies, 1717 Massachusetts Avenue NW, Washington DC 20036. **LC** HB3527.W3; W33A. **DD** 312/.09753.

US/1041-4037
**WEST COAST STUDIES.** [West Coast stud.]. (1989)-. Monographic series. English. Price varies per volume. Borgo Press, PO Box 2845, San Bernardino CA 92406. **Tel** (714)884-5813, (714)885-1161. **DD** 979. Index available. ***Continues*** *San Bernardino County Studies, 0748-0784.*
**Desc:** Monographs, directories, histories, and indexes dealing with the West Coast of the United States.

UA
**WORKING PAPER / CAIRO DEMOGRAPHIC CENTRE.** **VFOAT** CDC Working Papers. No. 1 (1981)-. Monographic series. English. ir. Price varies per volume. Cairo Demographic

Center, PO Box 73, 2 Lebanon Street, Mohandiseen Cairo 12655 Egypt. **Tel** 3462002, telex 92034 DP UN. **LC** HB848; .W65.

US/0740-9095
**WORKING PAPER - FLORIDA STATE UNIVERSITY. CENTER FOR THE STUDY OF POPULATION.** (WORKING PAPER / INSTITUTE FOR SOCIAL RESEARCH, CENTER FOR THE STUDY OF POPULATION.). [Work. pap. - Fl. State Univ., Cent. Stud. Popul.]. Monographic series. English. ir. Price varies per volume. Director Center for the Study of Population, Institute for Social Research, Florida State University, 659 Bellamy, Tallahassee FL 32306. **Tel** (904)644-1762. **ED** Robert H Weller. Index available. cum. index. ctrl circ.
**Ind/Abst** Popul. Index (?-?).

AT
**WORKING PAPERS IN DEMOGRAPHY.** 1-. Monographic series. English. Price varies per volume. Anutech Pty Limited, GPO Box 4, Canberra Act, 2601 Australia. **Tel** 011 61 6 2492479, FAX 011 61 6 2575088. **DD** 304.6.

US
**WORLD POPULATION. ADVANCE REPORT / U.S. DEPARTMENT OF COMMERCE, BUREAU OF THE CENSUS.** Government Publication. English. be. US Department of Commerce / Bureau of the Census, Data User Services Division, Customer Services, Washington DC 20233-0800. **Tel** (301)763-4100. **(Subscription address:** Superintendent of Documents, US Government Printing Office, Washington DC 20402.**)**

US/0085-8315
**WORLD POPULATION DATA SHEET OF THE POPULATION REFERENCE BUREAU, INC.** [World popul. data sheet Popul. Ref. Bur. Inc.]. **Main/Corp** Population Reference Bureau. (19??)-. English (French). an. $45.00 (corporations); $55.00 (individuals); $200.00 (others). Population Reference Bureau, 1875 Connecticut Avenue Northwest, Suite 520, Washington DC 20009. **Tel** (202)483-1100, (800)877-9881, FAX (202)328-3937. **DD** 312.
**Ind/Abst** F&S Index Plus Text, Int. [Select. Cov.]; Predicasts Forecasts; Stat. Ref. Index.

US/0163-2361
**WORLD POPULATION ESTIMATES.** **Added/Corp** Environmental Fund (U.S.). (19??)-. Periodical. English. an. Environmental Fund, 1325 G Street NW/1003, Washington DC 20005-3157. **LC** HA155; .W67. **DD** 312/.8/05.

US
**WYOMING POPULATION AND EMPLOYMENT FORECAST REPORT.** **Main/Corp** Wyoming. Dept. of Administration and Fiscal Control. Statistics and Research Division. (1978)-. Periodical. English. an (Sept.). Free on request. Wyoming Research DAFC, 302 Emerson Building, Cheyenne WY 82002. **Tel** (307)777-7201. **LC** HA721; .D46b. **DD** 304.6/2/09787.

FI/0506-3590
**YEARBOOK OF POPULATION RESEARCH IN FINLAND.** (VAESTONTUTKIMUKSEN VUOSIKIRJA.). [Yearb. popul. res. Finl.]. **Added/Corp** Vaestontutkimuslaitos (Finland). **VFOAT** Yearbook of Population Research in Finland. (1946)-. English. an. Fmk110. Vaestontutkimuslaitos, Kalevankatu 16, SF-00100 Helsinki 10 Finland. **Tel** 358 0 640 235, FAX 358 0 612 1211. **ED** Jarl Lindgren. **LC** HB848; .V34. **DD** 304.6/05. **Bk Rev**, (Qty: 1-3 per year). **Circ:** 700 (ctrl). ***Continues*** *Vaestoliiton Vuosikirja.*
**Ind/Abst** Popul. Index.

GW/0340-2398
**ZEITSCHRIFT FUER BEVOELKERUNGSWISSENSCHAFT.** [Z. Bevoelkerungswiss.]. **Added/Corp** Bundesinstitut fuer Bevoelkerungsforschung. (1975)-. Periodical. German. Four times a year. DM96.00. Harald Boldt Verlag, Postfach 1110, D 56135 Boppard Germany. **Tel** 011 49 67422511. **LC** HB848; .Z44. **[CCC].**
**Ind/Abst** PAIS Int. Print; Popul. Index.

US
**ZERO POPULATION GROWTH NEWSLETTER.** (1971)-. Periodical. English. ir. $10.00. Zero Population Growth, 2008 1 2 Preuss, Los Angeles CA 90034. **Tel** (213)839-1976.
**Ind/Abst** Curr. Lit. Fam. Plan.

US/0199-0071
**ZPG REPORTER.** **See** Family and Marriage.

## ABSTRACTING, BIBLIOGRAPHIES AND STATISTICS

US
**ARIZONA SUICIDE STATISTICS.** **Main/Corp** Arizona. Dept. of Health Services. Planning and Analysis Management Information Systems. English. Planning & Analysis Management Information Systems Services, 1740 West Adams Street, Phoenix AZ 85007. **LC** HB1323.S8; A74A. **DD** 312/.276.

GW
**BEVOLKERUNG IN NORDRHEIN-WESTFALEN, DIE.** **Main/Corp** North Rhine-Westphalia (Germany). Landesamt fur Datenverarbeitung und Statistik. German. $6.00 US. Landesamt fuer Datenverarbeitung und Statistik Nordrhein-Westfalen, Postfach 101105, 40002 Duesseldorf Germany. **Tel** (0211)944901, FAX (0211)442006, telex 8586654 LDST D. **LC** HB2056.N6; N67A. **Ad Acc. Circ:** 1,100.
**Desc:** Statistical returns on the population.

BE/0304-8888
**BEVOLKINGSSTATISTIEKEN - NATIONAAL INSTITUUT VOOR DE STATISTIEK.** **Main/Corp** Institut National de Statistique (Belgium). (1973)-. Dutch (French). ir. 250F Belgium; 400F other. Nationaal Instituut voor de Statistiek, Leuvenseweg 44, 1000 Brussels Belgium. **Tel** 011 32 2 5139650. **LC** HA1391; .I57a. **Circ:** 525 (ctrl).

BE/0255-0849
**BIBLIOGRAPHIE INTERNATIONALE DE LA DEMOGRAPHIE HISTORIQUE.** [Bibliogr. int. demogr. hist.]. **VFOAT** International Bibliography of Historical Demography; Historical Demography. French (Multiple languages and English). an. $10.00. International Union Scientific Study Pop, 34 rue des Augustins, B-4000 Liege Belgium. **Tel** (041)224080, FAX (041)223847. **ED** E Helin. **LC** Z7164.D3; B525; HB871. **DD** 016.3046/09. Index available. **Bk Rev. Circ:** 4,000 (ctrl).
**Desc:** International bibliography covering historical demography and methodology; includes a subject index, author index, geographical index and abstracts.
**Ind/Abst** Popul. Index.

SZ
**BILANZ DER WOHNBEVOELKERUNG IN DEN GEMEINDEN DER SCHWEIZ.** **VFOAT** Bilan Demographique des Communes Suisses. 1981-. French (German). an. 26.00F. Bundesamt fuer Statistik, Schwarztorstrasse 96, CH 3003 Bern Switzerland. **Tel** 031 3236011, FAX 031 3236061. **LC** HA1593; .S72B. **DD** 312/.09494. **Ad Acc. Circ:** 900. ***Continues*** *Switzerland. Eidgenossisches Statistisches Amt. Heiraten, Lebendgeborene und Gestorbene in den Gemeinden.*
**Desc:** Resident population, live births, deaths, marriages, internal migration, emigration, immigration, population change, regionalized data on population change.

AT
**BIRTHS, AUSTRALIA.** **Added/Corp** Australian Bureau of Statistics. (1978)-. English. an. 12.20Aus$. Australian Bureau of Statistics, PO Box 10, Belconnen Australian Capital Territory, 2616 Australia. **Tel** 011 61 6 2527911, FAX 011 61 6 2516009. **LC** HB1085; .A9b. ***Continues*** *Australian Bureau of Statistics. Births.*
**Desc:** Detailed statistics on confinements and live births presented in 26 tables -- male and female births, age and birthplace of parents, duration of marriage, previous issue of mother, nuptial and ex-nuptial births, single and multiple births, usual residence of mother, and more.

US/0195-4520
**CALIFORNIA POLL, THE.** ***Title Change.*** **Added/Corp** Field Research Corporation. Field Institute. (19??)-(1992). English. ir. The Field Institute, 550 Kearny Street, San Francisco CA 94108-2527. **Tel** (415)392-5763, FAX (415)434-2541. **ED** Mark DiCamillo. **LC** HN90.P8; C34. **Circ:** 300 (ctrl). ***Continued by*** *Field Poll.*
**Desc:** Regular statewide public opinion reports in California on political, social, economic and other topics.

AT
**CAUSES OF DEATH, AUSTRALIA.** **Added/Corp** Australian Bureau of Statistics. (1978)-. Periodical. English. an. 17.30Aus$. Australian Bureau of Statistics, PO Box 10, Belconnen Australian Capital Territory, 2616 Australia. **Tel** 011 61 6 2527911, FAX 011 61 6 2516009. ***Continues*** *Australian Bureau of Statistics. Causes of Death.*
**Desc:** Number of deaths by sex, selected age groups, and cause of death classified to the World Health Organization's International Classification of Diseases.

US/1057-9656
**CENSUS AND YOU.** (CENSUS AND YOU : MONTHLY NEWS FROM THE U.S. BUREAU OF THE CENSUS.). [Census you]. **Added/Corp** United States. Bureau of the Census. **VFOAT** Census. Vol. 23, No. 4/5 (April/May 1988)-. Government Publication. English. mo. $21.00 US; $26.25 other. Superintendent of Documents, US Government Printing Office, Washington DC 20402. **Tel** (202)275-3328, FAX (202)786-2377. **LC** HA203; .B8b. **DD** 001.4/22/0973. Documents available from Documents on Demand. ***Continues*** *Data User News, 0096-9877.*
**Desc:** For users of Census Bureau statistics; gives up-to-date information on Bureau programs, products, and services and the latest news about demographic and economic data. Especially helpful for users interested in computer tape files, online data systems, and micro-computer data diskettes, it also identifies local data contacts. Statistical products from other Federal agencies are described periodically.
**Ind/Abst** Am. Stat. Index.

AT
**DEATHS, AUSTRALIA.** **Added/Corp** Australian Bureau of Statistics. (197?)-. English. an. 18.40Aus$. Australian Bureau of Statistics, PO Box 10, Belconnen Australian Capital Territory, 2616 Australia. **Tel** 011 61 6 2527911, FAX 011 61 6 2516009. ***Continues*** *Australian Bureau of Statistics. Deaths.*
**Desc:** Number of deaths classified by age, sex, birthplace, marital status, occupation, cause of death and usual residence of deceased by State or Territory.

AT/0816-0465
**DEATHS, QUEENSLAND.** [Deaths Qld.]. **Added/Corp** Australian Bureau of Statistics. Queensland Office. (1983)-. English. an. 14.80Aus$. Australian Bureau of Statistics, PO Box 10, Belconnen Australian Capital Territory, 2616 Australia. **Tel** 011 61 6 2527911, FAX 011 61 6 2516009. **DD** 312.209943. ***Absorbed*** *Causes of Death, Queensland, 0811-8655.*
**Desc:** All deaths classified by age and sex.

AT/0814-8155
**DEATHS, TASMANIA.** 1983-. English. an. 5.00Aus$ Australia; 6.50Aus$ other. Australian Bureau Statistics / Tasmanian Office, Commonwealth Government Centre, 188 Collins Street, Hobart GPO Box 66A, Hobart Tasmania 7001 Australia. **Tel** (002)205889. ctrl circ. ***Continues*** *Causes of Deaths, Tasmania.*

MM
**DEMOGRAPHIC REVIEW OF THE MALTESE ISLANDS / CENTRAL OFFICE OF STATISTICS, MALTA.** (1959)-. Statistical Publication. English. an. Central Office of Statistics / Malta, Auberge de Castille, Merchants Street, Valletta Malta. **LC** WMLC L 82/28.

JM
**DEMOGRAPHIC STATISTICS.** **Main/Corp** Jamaica. Dept. of Statistics. **Added/Corp** Jamaica. Dept. of Statistics. Statistical Institute of Jamaica. (19??)-. Statistical Publication. English. an. $30.00. Statistical Institute of Jamaica, 9 Swallowfield Road, PO Box 643, Kingston 5 Jamaica. **Tel** (809)92-62175-6, FAX (809)92-64859. **LC** HA891; .D46a. **DD** 312/.097292.

US/0082-8041
**DEMOGRAPHIC YEARBOOK.** **Added/Corp** United Nations. Statistical Office. United Nations. Statistical Division. United Nations. Dept. of Social Affairs. United Nations. Dept. of Economic Affairs. United Nations. Dept. of Economic and Social Affairs. United Nations. Dept. of International Economic and Social Affairs. **VFOAT** Annuaire Demographique. 1st Ed. (1948)-. Government Publication. English (French). an. Price varies per volume. United Nations Publications, 2 United Nations Plaza, Room DC2 0853, Department 007C, New York NY 10017. **Tel** (212)963-8303, (800)253-9646. **LC** HA17; .D45. **DD** 312.058. **NLM** W2 MU5 S7d.
**Desc:** International demographic statistics covering 250 countries or areas. Tables give world summaries and country data on population, natality, infant mortality, nuptiality and divorce.

AT/1036-2649
**DEMOGRAPHY, QUEENSLAND.** [Demogr. Qld.]. **Added/Corp** Australian Bureau of Statistics. Queensland Office. (1990)-. English. an. 27.50Aus$. Australian Bureau of Statistics, PO Box 10, Belconnen Australian Capital Territory, 2616 Australia. **Tel** 011 61 6 2527911, FAX 011 61 6 2516009. **DD** 304.609943. ***Formed by the union of*** *Births, Queensland, 0815-8681; Divorces Queensland, 0816-0783; Demographic Summary, Queensland, 0816-3537* ***and*** *Demography. Small Area Summary, Queensland, 1031-217X.*
**Desc:** Detailed statistics on births, deaths, infant deaths, marriages and divorces.

AT/1036-2657
**DEMOGRAPHY, SOUTH AUSTRALIA.** [Demogr. S. Aust.]. **Added/Corp** Australian Bureau of Statistics. South Australian Office. (1990)-. English. an. 27.50Aus$. Australian Bureau of Statistics, PO Box 10, Belconnen Australian Capital Territory, 2616 Australia. **Tel** 011 61 6 2527911, FAX 011 61 6 2516009. **DD** 304.6099423. ***Formed by the union of*** *Births. South Australia, 0067-088X; Marriages, South Australia, 1031-2706* ***and*** *Divorces, South Australia, 1031-2218.*
**Desc:** Detailed statistics on births, deaths, infant deaths, marriages and divorces. Contains detailed population statistics and population projections.

NO/0550-032X
**DOEDSARSAKER. HOVEDTABELLER.**
**Main/Corp** Norway. Statistisk Sentralbyra. **VFOAT** Causes of Death. Main Tables. 1964-. Norwegian (English). an. Kr40.00. Central Bureau of Statistics / Norway, PO Box 8131 DEP, N-0033 Oslo 1 Norway. **Tel** 011 47 2 2864964, FAX 011 47 2 864973. **LC** HA1501; RA407.5.N. **DD** 314.81 S; 312/.2/09481. **NLM** W2 GN6 S6D. ***Continues in part*** *Helsestatistikk;* ***Continues*** *Health Statistics.*

BE
**ENQUETE SOCIO-ECONOMIQUE.**
**Main/Corp** Institut National de Statistique (Belgium). (19??)-. Periodical. French. 550F Belgium; 660F other. Institut National de Statistique / Belgium, rue de Louvain, 44, Centre Albert, 8e Etage, 1000 Brussels Belgium. **Tel** 011 32 2 5486211. **LC** HA1393 .I57b. **DD** 314.93. **Bk Rev. Ad Acc. Circ:** 700 (ctrl).
**Desc:** Statistics about population, employment, families, housing, strangers, and instruction.

AT
**ESTIMATED RESIDENT POPULATION BY AGE AND SEX IN STATISTICAL LOCAL AREAS, WESTERN AUSTRALIA / AUSTRALIAN BUREAU OF STATISTICS.** **Added/Corp** Australian Bureau of Statistics. (June 1986)-. Statistical Publication. English. an. 13.80Aus$. Australian Bureau of Statistics, PO Box 10, Belconnen Australian Capital Territory, 2616 Australia. **Tel** 011 61 6 2527911, FAX 011 61 6 2516009. ***Continues*** *Estimated Resident Population in Local Government Areas, Western Australia.*
**Desc:** Estimated resident population, by age and sex, of statistical local areas in Western Australia and percentage increases in total population from the previous year.

AT
**ESTIMATED RESIDENT POPULATION IN LOCAL GOVERNMENT AREAS / AUSTRALIAN BUREAU OF STATISTICS, SOUTH AUSTRALIAN OFFICE.** **Added/Corp** Australian Bureau of Statistics. South Australian Office. (19??)-. English. ir. 10.00Aus$. Australian Bureau of Statistics, PO Box 10, Belconnen Australian Capital Territory, 2616 Australia. **Tel** 011 61 6 2527911, FAX 011 61 6 2516009. **LC** HA3091; .A2. **DD** 312/.099423. ***Continues*** *Population in Local Government Areas.*
**Desc:** Post censal revisions of annual statistical local area population estimates.

SW
**FOLKMANGD.** **Main/Corp** Sweden. Statistiska Centralbyran. **VFOAT** Population. Swedish (summaries and/or abstracts in English). PO Box 23116, 10435 Stockholm 23 Sweden. **LC** HA1523; .S94A. **DD** 312/.09485. ***Continues*** *Folkmangden Inom Administrativa Omraden.*

CN/1180-307X
**HEALTH REPORTS. SUPPLEMENT. LIFE TABLES, CANADA AND PROVINCES.** (HEALTH REPORTS. SUPPLEMENT. LIFE TABLES, CANADA AND PROVINCES / STATISTICS CANADA, CANADIAN CENTRE FOR HEALTH INFORMATION.). [Health rep., Suppl., Life tables Can. prov.]. **Added/Corp** Canadian Centre for Health Information. **VFOAT** Life Tables, Canada and Provinces; Tables de Mortalite, Canada et Provinces; Rapports sur la Sante. Tables de Mortalite, Canada et Provinces. (1987)-. English (French). an. 6.65Can$ Canada; $8.00 other. Statistics Canada, Publications Sales & Services, Main Building Room 1710, Ottawa Ontario K1A 0T6 Canada. **Tel** (613)951-5078, (800)267-6677, FAX (613)951-1584, telex 053-3585. **DD** 304.6/4571/021. ***Continues*** *Life Tables, Canada and Provinces., 0827-990X.*
**Desc:** Contains tables generated on the basis of age-sex-specific mortality rates for Canada and the provinces prevailing in the period studied.

AT
**JOURNAL OF THE AUSTRALIAN POPULATION ASSOCIATION.** **Added/Corp** Australian Population Association. (Autumn 1984)-. Periodical. English. sa (June & Nov.). 50.00Aus$ Australia; 60.00Aus$ other. Australian Population Association, PO Box 583, Indooroopilly Queensland 4068 Australia. **Tel** 011 61 7 2370888, FAX 011 61 7 2354071. **ED** Don Rowland.
**Ind/Abst** APAIS, Aust. Public Aff. Inf. Ser. (1984-); Int. Bibliogr. Sociol.; Popul. Index.

US/0077-1198
**MONTANA VITAL STATISTICS.** **Main/Corp** Montana. Dept. of Health and Environmental Sciences. Bureau of Records & Statistics. 1970-. English. an. Montana Department of Health & Environmental Sciences, 1400 Broadway, Cogswell Building, Room C108, Helena MT 59620. **Tel** (406)444-2544, FAX (406)444-2606. **ED** Sam H Sperry. **LC** HA481; .A3. **DD** 312/.09786. **NLM** W2 AM9 S7A. **Circ:** 800 (ctrl). ***Continues*** *Montana. State Dept. of Health. Annual Statistical Supplement.*

US/0364-0396
**MONTHLY VITAL STATISTICS REPORT.** (MONTHLY VITAL STATISTICS REPORT : PROVISIONAL STATISTICS FROM THE NATIONAL CENTER FOR HEALTH STATISTICS.). [Mon. vital sta. rep.]. **Added/Corp** National Center for Health Statistics (U.S.) United States. National Office of Vital Statistics. United States. National Vital Statistics Division. United States. Public Health Service. **VFOAT** Annual Summary of Births, Marriages, Divorces, and Deaths. Vol. 1, No. 1, Jan. (1952)-. Periodical. English. Twelve times a year. Free. National Center for Health Statistics, 6525 Belcrest Road, Hyattsville MD 20782. **Tel** (301)436-8500. **LC** HA203; .A43. **DD** 312/.0973. **NLM** W2 A N148M. Documents available from Documents on Demand. ***Formed by the union of*** *Current Mortality Analysis; Monthly Marriage Report* ***and*** *Monthly Vital Statistics Bulletin.*
**Ind/Abst** Am. Stat. Index; Curr. Lit. Fam. Plan.; Popul. Index; Trop. Dis. Bull.

UK
**MORTALITY STATISTICS. PERINATAL AND INFANT : SOCIAL AND BIOLOGICAL FACTORS.** **Added/Corp** Great Britain. Office of Population Censuses and Surveys. **VFOAT** Perinatal and Infant. (197?)-. Statistical Publication. English. an. £9.50. Her Majesty's Stationery Office, 51 Nine Elms Lane, London SW8 5DR England. **Tel** 011 44 71 873 8459, 011 44 71 873 8499, FAX 011 44 71 873 8499, 011 44 71 873 8456, telex 297138. **(Subscription address:** Her Majesty's Stationery Office, PO Box 276, Publications Centre, London SW8 5DT England.**) LC** PAR.

CN
**ONTARIO POPULATION STATISTICS.**
**Main/Corp** Ontario. Ministry of Treasury, Economics and Intergovernmental Affairs. Municipal Planning & Development Branch. English. an. $2.00. Ministry of Treasury Municipal Planning & Development Branch, Parliament Buildings, Toronto Ontario Canada. **LC** HB3530.O5; O55A. **DD** 312/.09713.

AT
**PERINATAL DEATHS, AUSTRALIA.**
**Added/Corp** Australian Bureau of Statistics. (1978)-. English. an. 14.80Aus$. Australian Bureau of Statistics, PO Box 10, Belconnen Australian Capital Territory, 2616 Australia. **Tel** 011 61 6 2527911, FAX 011 61 6 2516009. ***Continues*** *Australian Bureau of Statistics Perinatal Deaths.*
**Desc:** Number of stillbirths and deaths at ages under four weeks classified by sex, age, weight at birth, and usual residence of mother, period of gestation, time of cessation of heartbeat, and more.

US
**POPULATION AND VITAL STATISTICS REPORT (NEW YORK, N.Y.).** (POPULATION AND VITAL STATISTICS REPORT.). **Main/Corp** United Nations. Statistical Office. **Added/Corp** United Nations. Statistical Office. **VFOAT** A.Population and vital statistics reports. (Jan. 1949)-. Government Publication. English. qt. $30.00. United Nations Publications, 2 United Nations Plaza, Room DC2 0853, Department 007C, New York NY 10017. **Tel** (212)963-8303, (800)253-9646. **(Subscription address:** United Nations Publications, Subscription Office, PO Box 361, Birmingham AL 35201-0361.**) LC** HA13; .U5 subser.; HA154. **DD** 310 S; 304.6/021. available on microfilm and microfiche from University Microfilms International (UMI).
**Desc:** Provides latest worldwide demographic statistics on birth and mortality.

US/0032-4701
**POPULATION INDEX.** [Popul. index]. **Added/Corp** Princeton University. Office of Population Research. Princeton University. School of Public Affairs. Population Association of America. Vol. 3 (Jan. 1937)-. Abstracting/Indexing Service. English. qt (published within seasons of the year). $90.00. Princeton University Office of Population Research, Woodrow Wilson School of Public and International Affairs, 21 Prospect Avenue, Princeton NJ 08544-2091. **Tel** (609)258-4873, FAX (609)258-1039. **ED** Richard Hankinson (association's address: Population Association of America, Inc., 1722 N Street NW, Washington, DC 20036). **LC** Z7164.D3; P83. **DD** 016.3046. **NLM** Z 7164.D3 P831. Index available. cum. index. **Ad Acc, Adv Mgr:** G Hancock. **Pr Rev. Circ:** 4,400. available on microfilm and microfiche from University Microfilms International (UMI). Documents available from The Genuine Article, Documents on Demand. ***Continues*** *Population Literature.*
**Desc:** A comprehensive annotated bibliographic journal of world literature on population and demography. Includes articles on items of current interest. Primary reference tool to world's population literature. Annotated bibliography of about 4,000 recently published books, journal articles, etc., per year. Entries by subject, with author and geographical indexes.
**Ind/Abst** Curr. Contents Soc. Behav. Sci.; Curr. Lit. Fam. Plan.; Energy Inf. Abstr.; Environ. Abstr.; PAIS Int. Print; Res. Alert [Full Cov.]; Soc. Sci. Cit. Index [Full Cov.].

UK/0307-4463
**POPULATION TRENDS.** [Popul. trends]. **Main/Corp** Great Britain. Office of Population Censuses and Surveys. (Autumn 1975)-. Periodical. English. qt. £31.60. Her Majesty's Stationery Office, 51 Nine Elms Lane, London SW8 5DR England. **Tel** 011 44 71 873 8459, 011 44 71 873 8499, FAX 011 44 71 873 8499, 011 44 71 873 8456, telex 297138. **(Subscription address:** Her Majestys Stationery Offic, PO Box 276 Public Centre, London SW8 5DT England**) LC** HB3583; .G66b. **DD** 301.32/9/41. **NLM** W1 PO676.
**Desc:** Contains regular series of statistical tables on population change, vital statistics summaries, births, marriages, divorces, migration, deaths and abortions.
**Ind/Abst** Appl. Soc. Sci. Index Abstr.; Popul. Index; Public Aff. Inf. Serv. Bull.; Sage Race Relat. Abstr.; Soc. Plann. Policy Dev. Abstr.; Soc. Welf. Soc. Plan./Policy Soc. Dev.; Sociol. Abstr. (?-?); Trop. Dis. Bull.

CN/0827-9624
**POSTCENSAL ANNUAL ESTIMATES OF POPULATION BY MARITAL STATUS, AGE, SEX AND COMPONENTS OF GROWTH FOR CANADA, PROVINCES AND TERRITORIES.** (POSTCENSAL ANNUAL ESTIMATES OF POPULATION BY MARITAL STATUS, AGE, SEX, AND COMPONENTS OF GROWTH FOR CANADA, PROVINCES, AND TERRITORIES, JUNE 1, ... / STATISTICS CANADA, DEMOGRAPHY DIVISION, POPULATION ESTIMATES SECTION.). [Postcensal annu. estim. popul. marital status age sex compon. growth Can. prov. territ.]. **Added/Corp** Statistics Canada. Population Estimates Section. **VFOAT** Estimations Annuelles Postcensitaires de la Population Suivant l'Etat Matrimonial, l'Age, le Sexe et Composantes de l'Accroissement, Canada, Provinces et Territoires au 1er Juin ... . Vol. 2 (1984)-. English (French). 29.00Can$ Canada; $35.00 US; $41.00 other. Statistics Canada, Publications Sales & Services, Main Building Room 1710, Ottawa Ontario K1A 0T6 Canada. **Tel** (613)951-5078, (800)267-6677, FAX (613)951-1584, telex 053-3585. **LC** HA741; .P67. **DD** 312/.0971. ***Continues*** *Postcensal Annual Estimates of Population by Marital Status, Age, Sex, and Components of Growth for Canada and the Provinces, 0824-9563.*

CN/0835-4057
**QUARTERLY DEMOGRAPHIC STATISTICS.** [Q. demogr. stat.]. **Added/Corp** Statistics Canada. Population Estimates Section. Statistics Canada. Vital Statistics and Health Status Section. Statistics Canada. Health Status, Vital Statistics Section. Statistics Canada. Vital Statistics and Disease Registries Section. Canadian Centre for Health Information. **VFOAT** Statistiques Demographiques Trimestrielles. Vol. 1, No. 1 (Jan./Mar. 1987)-. English (French). qt. 32.00Can$ Canada; $39.00 US; $45.00 other. Statistics Canada, Publications Sales & Services, Main Building Room 1710, Ottawa Ontario K1A 0T6 Canada. **Tel** (613)951-5078, (800)267-6677, FAX (613)951-1584, telex 053-3585. **LC** HA741; .Q36. **DD** 304.6/0971/021. ***Formed by the union of*** *Vital Statistics Quarterly, 0829-657X* ***and*** *Quarterly Estimates of Population for Canada, the Provinces and the Territories, 0830-0038.*
**Desc:** Presents quarterly estimates of population for Canada, the provinces and territories as well as statistics on the following components of population change: births, deaths, deaths, emigration and interprovincial migration, the latter by origin and destination.

CN/0715-9293
**REPORT ON THE DEMOGRAPHIC SITUATION IN CANADA.** [Rep. demogr. situat. Can.]. **Added/Corp** Statistics Canada. (1983)-. English. an. 30.00Can$ Canada; $36.00 US; $42.00 other. Statistics Canada, Publications Sales & Services, Main Building Room 1710, Ottawa Ontario K1A 0T6 Canada. **Tel** (613)951-5078, (800)267-6677, FAX (613)951-1584, telex 053-3585. **LC** HB3529; .R46. **DD** 304.6/0971.

SQ
**REPORT ON THE SWAZILAND POPULATION CENSUS.** **Main/Corp** Swaziland Population Census. English. ir (every ten years). E15.00. Economics Statistics Library, PO Box 456, Mbabane Swaziland. **Tel** 011 43765. **DD** 912.68/3. **Ad Acc.**

JA
**SEAMIC HEALTH STATISTICS.** **Main/Corp** Nihon Kokusai Iryodan. Tonan Ajia Iryo Joho Senta. Committee on Health Statistics. **VAT** Southeast Asian Medical Information Center Health Statistics. 1979-. English. Southeast Asian Medical Information Center, International Medical Foundation of Japan, No 6 Toyo-Kaiji Building, 7-2 Shinbashi 4-chome, Minato-ku 105, Tokyo Japan. **Tel** (03)432-2888, telex IMFJ J34484. **LC** RA407.5.A7842; N48A. **DD** 362.1/0959. **NLM** W1; S48H no. 17 etc.

NE/0167-4757
**SELECTED ANNOTATED BIBLIOGRAPHY OF POPULATION STUDIES IN THE NETHERLANDS.** [Sel. annot. bibl. popul. stud. Neth.]. 1974-. Bibliography.

Dutch (English). an. Netherlands Interuniversity Demographic Institute, POB 11650, 2502 AR Gravenhage Netherlands. **Tel** 011 31 70 3565200. **LC** Z7164.D3; B48; HD881. ***Continues*** *Bibliografie van in Nederland Verschenen Demografische Studies.*
**Ind/Abst** Popul. Index.

US/1047-3394
**STATE AND LOCAL STATISTICS SOURCES.** ***Ceased.*** **Added/Corp** Gale Research Inc. 1st Ed. (1990/1991)-2nd Ed. English. be. Gale Research Inc., 835 Penobscot Building, Detroit MI 48226. **Tel** (800)877-GALE, (313)961-2242, FAX (313)961-6083, telex TWX 810-221-7086. **ED** M. Balchandran and S. Balachandran. **LC** HA203; .S7. **DD** 016.3173.
**Desc:** Contains 40,000 citations to state and local statistics sources arranged in 54 state and territorial chapters. Provides an annotated bibliography of source material.

AT/1032-8793
**STATE AND REGIONAL PROJECTIONS. BULLETIN.** [State reg. proj. bull.]. (1989)-. Periodical. English. ir. free. Department of Environment and Planning, GPO Box 667, Adelaide SA 5001 Australia. **Tel** (08)216-7559, FAX (08)212-3962. **DD** 304.6099423. **Circ:** 200.
**Desc:** Population projections for the adelaide statistical division by age group in 5 year intervals, low, medium and high series to the year 2021.

IT
**STATISTICHE DEMOGRAFICHE.**
**Added/Corp** Istituto Centrale di Statistica (Italy). **VFOAT** Annuario di Statistiche Demografiche. (1989). Periodical. Italian. ir. Istituto Nazionale Statistica, GBP SEZ4 Via Cesare Balbo 16, 00184 Rome Italy. **Tel** 011 39 6 46735118. **LC** HA1363; .A36. ***Continues*** *Annuario di Statistiche Demografiche, 0075-1685.* ***Continued in part by*** *Nascite e Decessi* ***and*** *Matrimoni, Separazioni e Divorzi.*

BE/0067-5490
**STATISTIQUES DEMOGRAPHIQUES.**
[Stat. demogr.]. **Main/Corp** Institut National de Statistique (Belgium). **Added/Corp** Institut National de Statistique (Belgium) Bevolkings-Statistieken. **VFOAT** Bevolkings-Statistieken. (1969)-. Periodical. French. Four times a year. 1000F Belgium; 1250F other. Institut National de Statistique / Belgium, rue de Louvain, 44, Centre Albert, 8e Etage, 1000 Brussels Belgium. **Tel** 011 32 2 5486211. **NLM** W2 GB4 I5SF. **Bk Rev. Ad Acc. Circ:** 650 (ctrl).
**Ind/Abst** Foreign Lang. Index.

TU
**TURKIYE OZETLI NUFUS BIBLIOGRAFYAS.** Vol. 1- 1970-. Multiple languages (Turkish and English). $4.00. Hacettepe Universitesi, Nufus Etutleri Enstitusu, Ankara Turkey. **Tel** 011 90 312 3197906, FAX 011 90 312 311 81 41, telex 42237. **ED** Ergul Tuncbilek. **LC** Z7165.T9; B342. **Bk Rev. Circ:** 1,000 (ctrl).
**Desc:** Population studies, contraceptive usage, family planning, fertility, infant mortality, public health, and statistics.

FI
**VAESTO.** **Added/Corp** Finland. Tilastokeskus. **VFOAT** Befolkning; Population. (19??)-?. English (Finnish and Swedish). an. Tilastokeskus, PL 504, Annankatu 44, 00101 Helsinki Finland. **Tel** 358-0-17341, FAX 358-0-17342474, telex 1002111 TILASTO SF. **LC** HA1448; .F4 subser; HB3608.3.A3. **DD** 314.897 S; 312/.094897. **NLM** W2; GF5 T5v. ***Continues*** *V2aest2onmuutokset.* ***Continued in part by*** *V2aest2orakenne ja V2aest2onmuutokset; V2aest2oradenne Kunnittain.*

VI
**VIRGIN ISLANDS VITAL STATISTICS ... DEATHS.** English.

US/1057-7629
**VITAL AND HEALTH STATISTICS. SERIES 21. DATA ON NATALITY, MARRIAGE, AND DIVORCE.** (VITAL AND HEALTH STATISTICS. SERIES 21). **Added/Corp** National Center for Health Statistics (U.S.). **VFOAT** Data on Natality, Marriage, and Divorce. (1989)-. Monographic series. English. ir. Free on request to libraries. National Center for Health Statistics, 6525 Belcrest Road, Hyattsville MD 20782. **Tel** (301)436-8500. **DD** 300. **NLM** W2; A N148vu. ***Continues*** *Vital and Health Statistics. Series 21, Data from the National Vital Statistics System, 0083-2030.*
**Ind/Abst** Index Med. (1989-).

CN/0317-3143
**VITAL STATISTICS. PRELIMINARY ANNUAL REPORT (OTTAWA).** (VITAL STATISTICS : PRELIMINARY ANNUAL REPORT.). **Added/Corp** Statistics Canada. Vital Statistics Section. Canada. Vital Statistics Section. **VFOAT** Statistique de l'Etat Civil; Rapport Annuel Preliminaire. (1950)-. English (French). ir. 5.00Can$ Canada; $6.00 other. Statistics Canada, Publications Sales & Services, Main Building Room 1710, Ottawa Ontario K1A 0T6 Canada. **Tel** (613)951-5078, (800)267-6677, FAX (613)951-1584, telex 053-3585. **NLM** W2 DC2 S83V. ***Formed by the union of*** *Quarterly Report of Births, Marriages and Deaths* ***and*** *Preliminary Annual Report of Vital Statistics of Canada.*

---

## PRINTING INDUSTRY

---

US/0161-0988
**AAUP BOOK SHOW CATALOGUE.** [AAUP book show cat.]. **Added/Corp** Association of American University Presses. Book Show Committee. **VAT** Association of American University Presses Book Show Catalogue. (19??)-. English. **LC** Z231.5.U6; A17. **DD** 011.

US
**ABSTRACTS (GRAPHIC ARTS TECHNICAL FOUNDATION).** **See** Printing Industry-Abstracting, Bibliographies and Statistics.

UK
**ADVANCES IN PRINTING SCIENCE AND TECHNOLOGY : PROCEEDINGS OF THE ... INTERNATIONAL CONFERENCE OF PRINTING RESEARCH INSTITUTES.** **Main/Conf** International Conference of Printing Research Institutes. 13th (May 1975)-. Proceedings. English. be. Pentech Press, 4 Graham House, Graham Road, London NW43DG England. **Tel** (01)202-5373. **ED** W H Banks. **LC** Z120.5; .I57A. **DD** 338.8/2616862. **Circ:** 600. ***Continues*** *Proceedings of the ... International Conference of Printing Research Institutes.*
**Desc:** A source of new information for scientists, technologists, and managers in the manufacturing and printing industries. Covers a wide spectrum of graphic arts research and development.

UK
**ALBION.** (19??)-. Periodical. English. Three times a year. £5.00 (individuals), £10.00 (institutions) UK; $10.00 (individuals), $20.00 (institutions) US. Dodman Press, 26 West Hill, Hitchin Hertfordshire England. **Tel** 0462-53627. **ED** David Goss. **Bk Rev. Ad Acc. Circ:** 450 (ctrl).
**Desc:** A journal about printing history and practice, publishing and literary reviews.

US/0002-8916
**AMERICAN INKMAKER.** (AMERICAN INK MAKER.). [Am. inkmak.]. **Added/Corp** National Association of Printing Ink Manufacturers. Vol. 59, No. 6 (June 1981)-. Periodical. English. Twelve times a year. $60.00 US; $75.00 Canada; $95.00 other. PTN Publishing Company, 445 Broad Hollow Road, Melville NY 11747. **Tel** (516)845-2700, FAX (516)845-7109. **LC** TP949; .A1A5. **DD** 667. available on microfilm from University Microfilms International (UMI). Documents available from CASDDS. ***Continues*** *American Inkmaker, 0002-8916.*
**Ind/Abst** Abstr. Bull. Inst. Pap. Sci. Tech.; Abstr. Graphic Arts Tech. Found. (1984); Chem. Abstr.; F&S Index Plus Text, Int. [Select. Cov.]; Graph. Arts Bull. Inst. Pap. Sci. Technol. (Jan. 1989-Mar. 1989, May 1989-June 1989, Aug. 1989-Sept. 1989, Nov. 1989); Print. Abstr.; PROMT; World Surf. Coat. Abstr.

US/0744-6616
**AMERICAN PRINTER (1982).** (AMERICAN PRINTER.). [Am. print.]. Vol. 188, No. 4 (Jan. 1982)-. Periodical. English. mo. $50.00 (one year), $75.00 (two year), $100.00 (three year) US; $60.00 (one year), $85.00 (two year), $110.00 (three year) Canada; $100.00 (one year), $150.00 (two year), $200.00 (three year) other. MacLean Hunter Publishing Corporation / Chicago, IL, 29 North Wacker Drive, Chicago IL 60606-3298. **Tel** (312)726-2802, FAX (312)726-3091. **ED** Jill Roth. **LC** Z119; .I56. **DD** 686.2/05. **[CCC]. Bk Rev. Ad Acc. Circ:** 93,664 (ctrl). available on microfilm and microfiche from University Microfilms International (UMI). Documents available from UMI Article Clearinghouse. ***Continues*** *American Printer and Lithographer (Chicago, Ill.), 0192-9933.*
**Desc:** Information on trends and insight into management and production techniques of the printing, publishing and graphic arts industries.
**Ind/Abst** ABI/INFORM Glob. Ed.; ABI Inform Ondisc (Nov. 1987-); Abstr. Bull. Inst. Pap. Sci. Tech.; Abstr. Graphic Arts Tech. Found. (1984-); Bus. ASAP (1990-) [Full Txt.]; Bus. Index (1985-); Bus. Period. Index; Gen. BusinessFile (1985-); Gen. Period. Index (1985-); Graph. Arts Bull. Inst. Pap. Sci. Technol. (Jan. 1989-April 1989, July 1989-Aug. 1989, Nov. 1989-Dec. 1989); Imaging Abstr.; Mag. Search; Print. Abstr.; Trade Ind. ASAP [Full Txt.]; Trade Ind. Index (1982-) [Full Txt.]; UMI ABI/Inform--Bus. Period. Ondisc (Nov. 1987-) [Full Txt.]; Vocat. Search (July 1993-); Wilson Bus. Abstr.

US/0094-7490
**AMERICAN PRINTMAKERS.** 1st- Ed.; 1974-. English. an. KDM Graphics, 149 E St Joseph Street/#C, Arcadia CA 91006. **LC** NE508; .A585. **DD** 769/.973.

US/0276-5519
**AMERICAN REGISTER OF PRINTING AND GRAPHIC ARTS SERVICES, THE.** ***Ceased.*** [Am. regist. print. graph. arts serv.]. **VFOAT** American Register. (1981)-(1987). English. an. Interface References Inc, 305 Madison Avenue/Suite 1166, New York NY 10165. **Tel** (212)316-7001. **ED** Howard Samelsan. **LC** Z244.6.U5; A43. **DD** 686.2/025/73. **Ad Acc. Circ:** 55,000 (ctrl).
**Desc:** A sourcebook for locating suppliers of printing, color separations, paper, book manufacturers, letter shops, mailing lists, fulfillment companies, etc.

US/0740-5804
**AMPERSAND (SAN FRANCISCO, CALIF.), THE.** (THE AMPERSAND / PACIFIC CENTER FOR THE BOOK ARTS.). [Ampersand]. **Added/Corp** Pacific Center for the Book Arts. Vol. 1, No. 1 (Jan. 1980)-. Periodical. English. Four times a year (Feb., May, Sept., Dec.). $30.00 (associate); $40.00 (institution). Pacific Center for Book Arts, PO Box 424431, San Francisco CA 94142. **Tel** (415)386-3044. **ED** A. M. Johnston, (editor's address: P. O. Box 8701, Oakland, CA 94662-8701). **LC** Z116.A3; A53. **DD** 686. **Bk Rev. Circ:** 390.

US/0892-4201
**AMS STUDIES IN THE EMBLEM.** No. 1 (1988)-. Monographic series. English. ir. Price varies per volume. AMS Press Inc., 56 East 13th Street, New York NY 10003. **Tel** (212)777-4700, FAX (212)995-5413, telex 710 581 2302. **ED** Peter M. Daly, Daniel Russell. **DD** 686.
**Desc:** Covers the spectrum of emblem books and the related iconography.
**Ind/Abst** MLA Int. Bibl. Books Artic. Mod. Lang. Lit.

PO
**ANAIS DO ... CONGRESSO LATINO-AMERICANO DE MICROGRAFICA.** **Main/Conf** Congresso Latino-Americano de Industria Micrografica. Began with Vol. for 1978. Portuguese (Spanish). **LC** Z265; .C63A. **DD** 686.4/3.

IT
**ANNUNCIATORE POLIGRAFICO.** ***Ceased.*** (19??)-(Dec. 1992). Etas Periodici Spa, Via Mecenate 91, 20138 Milan Italy.

SP
**ANUARIO ESPANOL DE LAS ARTES GRAFICAS.** Spanish. an. 4.500ptas Spain; 9.00ptas North America; 6.500ptas other. Puntex SA, c/ Mare de Deu del Coll 14, 08023 Barcelona Spain. **Tel** (93)237 71 24, FAX (93)217 55 73, telex 97131 GPMM E. **Bk Rev. Ad Acc. Circ:** 10,000.
**Desc:** Printing companies, distributors, trademarks and products.

US
**APHA NEWSLETTER : A PUBLICATION OF THE AMERICAN PRINTING HISTORY ASSOCIATION, THE.** **Added/Corp** American Printing History Association. **VAT** American Printing History Association Newsletter. Vol. 69 (Jan. 1986)-. Newsletter. English. ir. $30.00 (individuals), $35.00 (institutions) Comes with American Printing History Association membership. American Printing History Association, PO Box 4922, Grand Central Station, New York NY 10163. **Tel** (212)930-0802, FAX (212)302-4815. **ED** David Pankow (editor's address: Rochester Institute of Technology, Rochester, New York 14623, phone: (716)475-2408). **Bk Rev. Ad Acc. Circ:** 900 (ctrl). ***Continues*** *APHA Letter, 0898-1078.*

AG
**ARTES GRAFICAS.** **See** The Arts-Graphic Arts.

AT
**AUSTRALIAN LITHOGRAPHER, PRINTER AND PACKAGER, THE.** ***Suspended.*** 1964-Suspended. Periodical. English. bm. 26.00Aus$ Australia; 35.00Aus$ other. Prestige Publishing Pty Ltd, GPO 5158, Sydney New South Wales 2001 Australia. **Tel** (2)211-4052, FAX (2)2811183. **ED** F Stern. Index available. cum. index. **Bk Rev. Ad Acc. Circ:** 8,960 (ctrl). ***Continues*** *Australian Lithographer.*
**Desc:** Covers printing, publishing, packaging, and converting.
**Ind/Abst** Abstr. Graphic Arts Tech. Found. (1984); Graph. Arts Bull. Inst. Pap. Sci. Technol. (March 1989, July 1989, Dec. 1989); Int. Packag. Abstr.; Print. Abstr.

AT
**AUSTRALIAN PRINTER MAGAZINE.** Vol. 39, No. 11 (Dec. 1988/Jan. 1989)-. Periodical. English. mo (11 issues). 50.00Aus$ Australia; 80.00Aus$ other. Calmor & Associates Pty Ltd, PO Box 1316, North Sydney NSW 2059 Australia. **Tel** 011 61 2 9226133, FAX 011 61 2 9224734. **ED** Patrick Howard. **Ad Acc. Circ:** 9,814 (ctrl). ***Continues*** *Australian Printer.*
**Desc:** Directed to senior management and production managers in the printing industry and allied areas such as typesetters, publishers, art studios, advertisement agencies, repro houses, etc.
**Ind/Abst** Graph. Arts Bull. Inst. Pap. Sci. Technol. (July 1989-); Print. Abstr.

FR/0180-4979
**B.A.T. BON A TIRER.** **VFOAT** Bon a Tirer. (1978)-. Periodical. French. mo. 597.45F France; 760.00F other Europe; 1038.00F other. BAT, 5 rue la Boetie, 75008 Paris France. **Tel** 011 33 1 44563186. **UDC** 65.

UK/0954-9226
**BASELINE LONDON.** (BASELINE). [Baseline Land]. (19??)-. English. Twice a year (Spring and Autumn). £34.50 Europe; £27.00 UK; £38.00 other. Esselte Letraset LTD, Wotton Road, Ashford, Kent England TN23 2FL. **Tel** 011 44 233 624421, FAX 011 44 233 633364. **ED** Mr. M. D. Daines, (Telephone # 011 44 71 922 8805). **Bk Rev**, (Qty: 12-15). **Ad Acc, Adv Mgr:** M. D. Daines. **Circ:** 9,500.
**Desc:** The desktop typographer is being invited with increasing frequency and volume, to remember his type heritage. Nostalgia reveal the contributions of inspired individuals to typographic art and scholarship. The dedication of one scholar, James Mosley, has created a collection at St. Bride's which will enable future typographers to complement an awareness of contemporary influences with a productive study of the past.

GW/0067-5091
**BEITRAEGE ZUR INKUNABELKUNDE : IM AUFTRAGE DER DEUTSCHEN STAATSBIBLIOTHEK ZU BERLIN.**
**Added/Corp** Deutsche Staatsbibliothek. Gesellschaft fuer Typenkunde des XV. Jahrhunderts. Gesellschaft fuer Typenkunde des XV. Jahrhunderts-Wiegendruckgesellschaft. Prussia (Germany). Kommission fuer den Gesamtkatalog der Wiegendrucke. Gesellschaft fuer Typenkunde des XV. Jahrhunderts. Veroeffentlichungen der Gesellschaft fuer Typenkunde des XV. Jahrhunderts. (1907)-. Monographic series. German (English). ir. Price varies per volume. Akademie-Verlag GmbH, Muehlenstrasse 33 34, D 13162 Berlin Germany. **Tel** 011 49 30 47889300, FAX 011 49 30 47889357. **(Subscription address:** VCH Publishers Inc., 303 Northwest 12th Avenue, Journals Department, Deerfield FL 33442.**)** **LC** Z240; .B42.
**Desc:** Monograph series covering type and type-founding.

UK
**BOOK PRODUCTION (BENN PUBLICATIONS LTD.).** **See** Publishing-Books and Bookmaking.

UK/0007-1684
**BRITISH PRINTER, THE.** [Br. print.]. (1888)-. Periodical. English. mo. £60.00. Maclean Hunter Ltd. / UK, Chalk Lane Cockfosters Road, Barnet Herts EN4 0BU England. **Tel** 011 44 81 2423000, FAX 011 44 81 9759753, telex 299072. **ED** Andrew Parker. **LC** Z119; .B86. **Bk Rev**. **Ad Acc. Circ:** 13,926 (ctrl). ***Absorbed*** *British Bookmaker; British Lithographer; Printers' International Specimen Exchange.*
**Desc:** Serves executive and technical management in commercial printing companies and major in-plant departments, keeping them informed of all technological development across all printing processes.
**Ind/Abst** Abstr. Bull. Inst. Pap. Sci. Tech.; Abstr. Graphic Arts Tech. Found. (1979, 1984); Curr. Technol. Index; Graph. Arts Bull. Inst. Pap. Sci. Technol. (Jan. 1989-March 1989, Oct. 1989, Dec. 1989); Print. Abstr.

FR
**BULLETIN BIMENSUEL DES TIRAGES.** Bulletin. French. sm. DAFSA Documentation, 25 Rue Leblanc, 75510 Paris Cedex 15 France. **Tel** 011 33 1 40605129.

US/0020-904X
**BULLETIN - INTERNATIONAL TYPOGRAPHICAL UNION, THE.** **Main/Corp** International Typographical Union of North America. V. 1-Aug. 1, 1912-. Bulletin. English. mo. International Typographical Union / Colorado, 301 South Union Boulevard, Colorado Springs CO 80910-3123.

UK/0144-7505
**BULLETIN / PRINTING HISTORICAL SOCIETY.** **Added/Corp** Printing Historical Society. No. 1 (Sept. 1980)-. Periodical. English. Twice a year (May & Dec.). £20.00 Comes with Printing Historical Society membership. Printing Historical Society, 3 Greenstead Sawbridgeworth, Herts CM21 9NY England. **Tel** 011 44 865 510628. **Bk Rev**. **Ad Acc. Circ:** 1,000. ***Continues*** *Newsletter (Printing Historical Society).*

CN/0849-0767
**CANADIAN PRINTER.** [Can. print.]. Vol. 97, No. 9 (Sept. 1989)-. Periodical. English. mo. 45.00Can$ Canada; 90.00Can$ other. MacLean Hunter Ltd. Business Publishers / Canada, Box 9100, Station A, Toronto ONT M5W 1A5 Canada. **Tel** (416)946-8420, (800)567-0444. **(Subscription address:** Indas, 35 Riviera Drive, Building 17, Markham Ontario L3R 8N4 Canada.**)** **DD** 338.4/76862/0971. **[CCC].** available on microfilm and microfiche from University Microfilms International (UMI). ***Continues*** *Canadian Printer & Publisher., 0008-4816.*
**Ind/Abst** Abstr. Bull. Inst. Pap. Sci. Tech.

CN/0068-9491
**CANADIAN PULP AND PAPER ASSOCIATION. NEWSPRINT DATA.** **See** Paper and Pulp Industry.

FR/0008-6126
**CARACTERE.** (CARACTERE; REVUE ... DES INDUSTRIES GRAPHIQUES ET PAPETIERES.). [Caractere]. Vol. 1 (April/May 1949)-. Periodical. French. mo. 510.00F France; 715.00F other. CEP Information Professions, 1 Cite Bergere, 75311 Paris Cedex 09 France. **Tel** 011 33 1 44695550. **ED** Edited 1949-50 by M. Vox. **LC** Z119; .C35. ***Supersedes*** *Industries et Techniques Graphiques.*
**Ind/Abst** Abstr. Bull. Inst. Pap. Sci. Tech.; Print. Abstr.

FR/0247-039X
**CARACTERE 1980.** [Caractere 1980]. (1980)-. Periodical. French. Twenty-four times a year. 548.48F France, 763.00F other (surface mail); 1023.00F US & Canada, 853.00F Europe, 1193.00F Asia & France, 1373.00F others (airmail). CEP Information Professions, 1 Cite Bergere, 75311 Paris Cedex 09 France. **Tel** 011 33 1 44695550. **UDC** 655. **[CCC].** ***Continues*** *Caractere, T.P.G, 0151-1041; L'Imprimerie Nouvelle, 0019-302X.*
**Ind/Abst** Infomat Int. Bus.

CC
**CHING TSAO MU KO.** **See** The Arts-Graphic Arts.

DK
**DANSK GRAFIA.** Danish. kr160.00. Grafisk Kartel, Lytgten 16, 2400 Kbenhavn NV Denmark. **LC** Z119; .D35. ***Supersedes*** *Typograf-Tidende.*

US/1050-6993
**DATEK IMAGING SUPPLIES MONTHLY, THE.** ***Title Change.*** [Datek imaging supplies mon.]. **Added/Corp** Datek Information Services, Inc. **VFOAT** Imaging Supplies Monthly. (1987)-Sept. (1992). Periodical. English. mo. BIS CAP International, PO Box 68, Newtonville MA 02160. **Tel** (617)893-9130, FAX (617)894-5093, telex 9102401640 DATEK UQ. **ED** Robert Leahey. **DD** 338. **[CCC].** **Bk Rev**. ***Continued by*** *Imaging Supplies Monthly.*
**Desc:** Covers consumables for electronic printers, copiers, and other imaging equipment for the office, industry, and home.

CN/0225-7874
**DEVIL'S ARTISAN, THE.** [Devil's artis.]. No. 1 (Feb. 1980)-. Periodical. English. ir. The Devil's Artisan, 354 Markham Street, Toronto Ontario M6G 2K9 Canada. **DD** 686.2/05.

US/1063-9276
**DICK VINOCUR'S FOOTPRINTS.** (DICK VINOCUR'S FOOTPRINTS : A TWICE MONTHLY INTELLIGENCE SERVICE FOR THE PRINTING INDUSTRIES.). [Dick Vinocur's footpr.]. **VFOAT** Footprints. (19??)-. Periodical. English. Twenty-four times a year (twice a month). $247.00 one year; $452.00 two year. Footprints Communications Inc., 2400 Lemoine Avenue, Fort Lee NJ 07024. **Tel** (201)461-5252, FAX (201)947-5812. **ED** M. Richard Vinocur. **DD** 686. **Bk Rev**, (Qty: 6). **Circ:** 1,200.
**Desc:** Marketing and planning by graphic arts firms. A ranking of the largest printing companies in North America. His monthly column was a regular feature in the magazine.

US
**DIPPY. DIRECT INPUT PHOTOTYPESETTING NEWSLETTER.** ***Title Change.*** **VFOAT** Direct Input Phototypesetting Newsletter; DIPPY; DIPPY. Direct Input Phototypesetting Publication. 1975-?. Newsletter. English. Ten times a year. Graphic Dimensions, 134 Caversham Woods, Pittsford NY 14534-2834. **Tel** (716)381-3428. **ED** Michael Kleper. **Bk Rev**. ***Continued by*** *Personal Composition Report.*
**Desc:** Covers the desktop publishing and personal typesetting field for word processing, micro, and typesetting users worldwide.

US/0895-139X
**DIRECTORY OF BOOK, CATALOG, AND MAGAZINE PRINTERS.** ***Title Change.*** [Dir. book cat. mag. print.]. (1988)-?. Catalog. English. an. Ad-Lib Publications, 51 North Fifth Street, PO Box 1102, Fairfield IA 52556-1102. **Tel** (515)472-6617, FAX (515)472-3186. **ED** John Kremer. **LC** Z475; .D644. **DD** 686. Index available. **Bk Rev**. **Ad Acc. Circ:** 5,000. available on diskette. ***Continues*** *Directory of Short-Run Book Printers, 0892-0958.* ***Continued by*** *Directory of Book Printers.*
**Desc:** Lists the names, addresses, and capabilities of over 990 US and Canadian printers of books, catalogs, magazines, and other publications. With this directory, you can locate a quality printer who specializes in the quantities, sizes, and bindings you want to use-at a price you can afford.

US
**DIRECTORY OF BOOK PRINTERS.** Directory. The Juniper Tree Press, 4830 Carol Drive, Troy MI 48098.

US/1053-3699
**DISCOUNT AND WHOLESALE PRINTING NEWSLETTER.** [Discount wholes. print. newsl.]. Vol. 1 (1990)-. Newsletter. English. be. $4.50 US; $8.50 other. Wellthe Publishing, PO Box 570213, Houston TX 77257-0213. **Tel** (713)867-3438. **(Subscription address:** Prosperity and Profits Unlimited, Box 570213, Houston TX 77257**)** **ED** A Doyle. **DD** 686. **Circ:** 1,500.
**Desc:** A source for finding or locating discount and wholesale printers.

GW/0012-6462
**DRUCK PRINT.** [Druck Print]. **VFOAT** Druck-Print; Druck. Vol. 105- ; Jan. 1968-. Trade Publication. German (summaries and/or abstracts in French and English). mo. DM170.40. P Keppler KG, Industriestrasse 2, D 63150 Heusenstamm Germany. **Tel** 011 49 6104 6060, telex 410 131. **ED** Heinz Schloesser and Herta Koehler. **LC** Z119; .A674. **[CCC].** Index available. **Ad Acc. Circ:** 9,420 (ctrl). ***Continues*** *Archiv fur Drucktechnik.*
**Desc:** Trade journal for the printing industry, with technical articles on recent equipment, new processes, and paper technology. Biographies, meetings, columns on recycling, cleaning techniques and ticket printing.
**Ind/Abst** Abstr. Bull. Inst. Pap. Sci. Tech.; Graph. Arts Bull. Inst. Pap. Sci. Technol. (June 1989-July 1989, Sept. 1989, Dec. 1989); Print. Abstr.

SZ/0046-0737
**DRUCKINDUSTRIE (ST. GALLEN).** (DRUCKINDUSTRIE.). [Druckindustrie]. **Added/Corp** Verbandes der Schweizer Druckindustrie. Grafischen Forums Zurich. **VFOAT** Druck Industrie. (Jan. 7, 1971)-. Periodical. German (French). Twenty-two times a year. 75.00F Switzerland; 95.00F other. Zollikofer AG, Fuerstenlandstr 122, CH-9001 St. Gallen Switzerland. **Tel** 011 41 71 297777, FAX 011 41 71 257487, telex 77537. **Bk Rev. Ad Acc. Circ:** 13,000.
**Ind/Abst** Print. Abstr.

GW/0012-6500
**DRUCKSPIEGEL, DER.** (DER DRUCKSPIEGEL : DIE ZEITSCHRIFT FUER DEUTSCHE UND INTERNATIONALE DRUCKTECHNIK.). [Druckspiegel]. Began with 1. Year. (May 30, 1946). Periodical. German. mo. **LC** Z119; .D79.
**Ind/Abst** Graph. Arts Bull. Inst. Pap. Sci. Technol. (May 1989-June 1989, Aug. 1989, Oct. 1989, Dec. 1989); Print. Abstr.

GW/0012-6519
**DRUCKWELT.** [Druckwelt]. (1969)-. Periodical. German. mo. DM120.00 Germany; DM152.00 other. Schluetersche Verlag Druckerei, Postfach 5440, D-30054 Hannover Germany. **Tel** 011 49 511 85500, FAX 011 49 511 1236400, telex 923978. **LC** Z119; .G94. **[CCC].** Index available (free). **Bk Rev**. **Ad Acc.** ctrl circ. ***Continues*** *Graphische Woche.*
**Desc:** Journal for contractors and managers of the printing industry.
**Ind/Abst** F&S Index Plus Text, Int. [Select. Cov.]; Infomat Int. Bus.; Print. Abstr.; PROMT.

US/0197-470X
**DURBIN DATA SHEETS.** **See** The Arts-Graphic Arts.

US/0195-5896
**EDUCATIONAL MARKETER YELLOW PAGES.** 1974/75-. English. an. $17.95. Knowledge Industry Publications Inc, 701 Westchester Avenue, White Plains NY 10604. **Tel** (914)328-9157, (800)800-5474, FAX (914)328-9093. **LC** HD9999.I573; U544. **DD** 381/.45/68.

NE/0921-383X
**EFM. EURO FLEXO MAGAZINE.** (EFM). [EFM, Euro flexo mag.]. **VFOAT** Euro Flexo Magazine. (1985)-. Periodical. Multiple languages (English, French, German and Italian). mo (10 issues per year). Fl120.00. Uitgeverij Compres, PO Box 55, 2300 AB Leiden, Netherlands. **Tel** 011 31 71 161515, FAX 011 31 71 121550. **UDC** 655.3. Index available. cum. index. **Pr Rev. Circ:** 9,500.
**Desc:** Technical and other information on the flexographic printing industry.
**Ind/Abst** Abstr. Bull. Inst. Pap. Sci. Tech.

US
**ELECTRONIC PUBLISHING.** **See** Computers-Desktop Publishing.

US/0099-0043
**ENGRAVERS JOURNAL, THE.** Vol. 1 (July/Aug. 1975)-. Periodical. English. Ten times a year. $49.00 (US); $60.75 (Canada); $78.00 (other). Engravers Journal, PO Box 318, 26 Summit Street, Brighton MI 48116. **Tel** (313)229-5725, FAX (313( 229-8320. **ED** James J Farrell. **LC** NE2720; .E5. **DD** 338.4/7/739. **Ad Acc.**
**Desc:** Education and advancement of the engraving industry.

GW/0938-1236
**EURO PRINTER.** English. Four times a year. $36.00 US, DM58.00 Germany (surface mail); $66.00 US, DM96.00 (airmail). Deutscher Drucker Verlag International, Postfach 4124/Senefelderstr 12, D 73744

Ostfildern 1 Germany. **Tel** 011 49 711 448170, FAX 011 49 711 415299, telex 841 177111490. **ED** Andrew Bluhm. **Bk Rev. Ad Acc.**
**Desc:** Aimed primarily at top European printing management. It shows how markets are changing and what this implies in technology, environmental matters and the legal background it faces.

US/0741-7160
**EXPORT GRAFICAS USA.** **See** The Arts-Graphic Arts.

GW/0937-9924
**EXPORT-POLYGRAPH INTERNATIONAL 1990.** [Export-Polygr. int. 1990]. **VFOAT** Polygraph International. (1990)-. Periodical. Multiple languages. bm (6 issues). DM102.00. Polygraph Verlag GmbH, Schaumainkai 85, D 60596 Frankfurt Germany. **Tel** 011 49 69 6300860, FAX 011 49 69 6313502. **UDC** 655. ***Continues*** *EPI. Export-Polygraph International, 0343-5199.*
**Ind/Abst** Abstr. Bull. Inst. Pap. Sci. Tech.

SZ/0367-1933
**FACHHEFTE. CHEMIGRAPHIE, LITHOGRAPHIE UND TIEFDRUCK.** ***Title Change.*** (FACHHEFTE, BULLETIN TECHNIQUE / HERAUSGEGEBEN VOM SCHWEIZERISCHEN LITHOGRAPHENBUND UND VOM VEREIN SCHWEIZERISCHER LITHOGRAPHIEBEZITZER.). [Fachh., Chemigr. Lithogr. Tiefdruck]. **Added/Corp** Schweizerischer Lithographenbund. Verein Schweizerischer Lithographiebesitzer. Verband der Schweizer Druckindustrie. **VFOAT** Fachhefte; Bulletin Technique. (1973)-(199?). Bulletin. German (French). qt. Conzett + Huber AG, Baslerstrasse 30, Postfach 8048, Zurich Switzerland. ***Formed by the union of*** *Fachhefte (Schweizerischer Lithographenbund)* ***and*** *Bulletin Technique (Schweizerischer Lithographenbund).* ***Continued by*** *Fachhefte Grafische Industrie Bulletin Technique.*
**Ind/Abst** Abstr. Bull. Inst. Pap. Sci. Tech.; Art Archaeol. Tech. Abstr.; Print. Abstr.

US/0361-3801
**FINE PRINT (SAN FRANCISCO).** (FINE PRINT.). [Fine print]. Began with Jan. 1975 issue. Periodical. English. qt. $58.00 US, Canada and Mexico; $62.00 other. Fine Print, PO Box 3394, San Francisco CA 94119. **Tel** (415)543-4455. **ED** Sandra Kirshenbaum. **LC** Z119; .F55. **DD** 686.2/0973. **Bk Rev. Ad Acc. Circ:** 3,500.
**Desc:** Provocative articles about contemporary fine printing, typography, graphic design, illustration, papermaking, calligraphy, bookbinding, and the history of books and printing, as well as critical reviews of fine books.
**Ind/Abst** Abstr. Graphic Arts Tech. Found. (1984); Annu. Bibliogr. Engl. Lang. Lit.; Art Archaeol. Tech. Abstr.; Art Index; ARTbibliogr. Mod. (1977-); ARTbibliogr. Curr. Titles; Book Rev. Index.

US/1051-7324
**FLEXO (RONKONKOMA, N.Y.).** (FLEXO.). **Added/Corp** Flexographic Technical Association. Vol. 9, No. 1 (Jan. 1984)-. Periodical. English. mo. $33.00. Flexographic Technical Association, 900 Marconi Avenue, Ronkonkoma NY 11779. **Tel** (516)737-6023, FAX (516)737-6813. **DD** 686. ***Continues*** *Flexographic Technical Journal, 0734-6980.*
**Ind/Abst** Abstr. Bull. Inst. Pap. Sci. Tech.

US/1054-1756
**FORGING (CLEVELAND, OHIO).** (FORGING.). [Forging]. Vol. 1, No. 1 (Fall 1990)-. Periodical. English. Four times a year. $20.00 US; $30.00 Canada; $40.00 Mexico; $50.00 other. Penton Publishing, 1100 Superior Avenue, Cleveland OH 44114-2543. **Tel** (216)696-7000, FAX (216)696-0836. **(Subscription address:** Penton Publishing, PO Box 96732, Chicago IL 60693.**)** **LC** WMLC 93/1883. **DD** 682. available on microfiche from University Microfilms International (UMI).

US/0532-1700
**FORM (ALEXANDRIA).** (FORM.). **Added/Corp** National Business Forms Asociation. (19??)-. Periodical. English. mo. $24.00 (one year), $39.00 (two year) National Business Form Association members; $44.00 (one year), $64.00 (two year), $76.00 (three year) US; $64.00 (one year), $104.00 (two year), $136.00 (three year) Canada; $74.00 (one year), $124.00 (two year), $166.00 (three year) other, non-members. National Business Forms Association, 433 East Monroe Avenue, Alexandria VA 22301. **Tel** (703)836-6232, FAX (703)836-2241. **ED** Brad Holt. cum. index. **Ad Acc, Adv Mgr:** Katie Davis. **Circ:** 11,500.
**Desc:** Published for management and marketing pros in the printing industry, particularly business forms and related business printing.
**Ind/Abst** Abstr. Bull. Inst. Pap. Sci. Tech.; Abstr. Graphic Arts Tech. Found. (1984).

FR/0015-9565
**FRANCE GRAPHIQUE, LA.** [Fr. graph.]. (1946)-. Periodical. French. ir. 400.00F France; 780.00F other. Edipresse, 16 rue Guillaume Tell, 75017 Paris France. **Tel** 011 33 1 47660005 ext. 246.
**Ind/Abst** Print. Abstr.

US/0738-6427
**FRANKLIN OFFSET CATALOG.** (19??)-. Catalog. English. ir. $145.00. Franklin Estimating Systems, 952 East 21st Street South, PO Box 16690, Salt Lake City UT 84106-0199. **Tel** (801)355-5954. **Circ:** 15,000.
**Desc:** Estimating and pricing guide for the offset worker of different types of printing, binding and also a section for commercial printing plants, with 16 different sections.

US/0161-5181
**GOVERNMENT PRINTING & BINDING REGULATIONS.** **Main/Corp** United States. Congress. Joint Committee on Printing. **VAT** Government Printing and Binding Regulations. No. 1 (July 1, 1948)-. Government Publication. English. Superintendent of Documents, US Government Printing Office, Washington DC 20402. **Tel** (202)275-3328, FAX (202)786-2377. **LC** Z232.U6; U7082. **DD** 655.173. ***Supersedes*** *Regulations of the Joint Committee on Printing Relative to Periodicals and Field Printing.*

FI/0785-0522
**GRAAFINEN TEOLLISUUS.** **Added/Corp** Finland. Tilastokeskus. **VFOAT** Grafisk Industri. Finnish (Swedish). Tilastokeskus, PL 504, Annankatu 44, 00101 Helsinki Finland. **Tel** 358-0-17341, FAX 358-0-17342474, telex 1002111 TILASTO SF. **LC** Z244.6.F5; G52.

SP/0017-2901
**GRAFICAS.** (GRAFICA; REVISTA DE LAS TECNICAS DELL LIBRO.). [Graficas]. (July 1944)-. Periodical. Spanish. mo. $16.35. Felipe de Pablo Cereceda, C/Blasco Degaray 76 F, Madrid 15 Spain. **LC** Z119; .G7.
**Ind/Abst** Abstr. Bull. Inst. Pap. Sci. Tech.

NE/0017-2936
**GRAFICUS.** [Graficus]. (1917)-. Periodical. Dutch. ir (46 issues). Fl250.00. Wegener Tijl Tijdschriften Group, Postbus 9943, 1006 AP Amsterdam Netherlands. **Tel** 011 31 20 5182828. **UDC** 655.

NE
**GRAFICUS MAGAZINE.** (19??)-. Dutch. qt (4 issues). Fl135.95. Wegener Tijl Tijdschriften Group, Postbus 9943, 1006 AP Amsterdam Netherlands. **Tel** 011 31 20 5182828.

BE
**GRAFIEK.** Periodical. Dutch. Three times a year. Grafiek, Industrieweg 226, 9910 Gent Mariakerke Belgium. **LC** WMLC L 83/4755.
**Ind/Abst** Print. Abstr.

DK
**GRAFISKE FAG, DE.** (19??)-. Periodical. Danish. Ten times a year. kr400.00. Grafisk Arbejdsgiverforening, Helgavej 26,, DK 5230 Odense M, Denmark. **Tel** 011 45 66 130601, FAX 011 45 66 136115. ***Continues*** *Bogtrykkerbladet.*
**Ind/Abst** Print. Abstr.

US/1044-7970
**GRAPHIC ARTS BLUE BOOK.** [Graph. arts blue book]. **VFOAT** GABB. (1990)-. English. be. $75.00. A F Lewis, 79 Madison Avenue, New York NY 10016. **Tel** (212)679-0770. **LC** Z244.6.U5; P74. **DD** 338.8/2616862/02574. ***Continues*** *Printing Trades Blue Book., 0193-3949.*

US/1044-8527
**GRAPHIC ARTS BLUE BOOK (METROPOLITAN NEW YORK-NEW JERSEY ED.).** (GRAPHIC ARTS BLUE BOOK : GABB.). [Graph. arts blue book]. **VFOAT** GABB. (1989)-. English. an. $80.00. A. F. Lewis & Company, 79 Madison Avenue, New York NY 10016. **Tel** (212)697-0770, FAX (212)545-7963. **ED** Doris Keyes. **LC** Z475; .P8N. **DD** 338.8/2616862/025747. **Ad Acc. Circ:** 6,000 (ctrl). ***Continues*** *Printing Trades Blue Book; Metropolitan New York Edition, 0079-5348.*
**Desc:** Buying and reference listings of products, services, equipments, supplies for printers.

US/1044-7989
**GRAPHIC ARTS BLUE BOOK (SOUTHEASTERN ED.).** **See** The Arts-Graphic Arts.

US/1046-8005
**GRAPHIC ARTS BLUE BOOK (WEST COAST ED.).** **See** The Arts-Graphic Arts.

US/1047-9325
**GRAPHIC ARTS MONTHLY (1987).** **See** The Arts-Graphic Arts.

US/0072-5498
**GRAPHIC ARTS TRADE DIRECTORY & REGISTER.** **See** The Arts-Graphic Arts.

US/0884-6901
**GRAPHIC COMMUNICATIONS WORLD.** [Graph. commun. world]. Vol. 9, No. 1 (Jan. 6, 1976)-. Periodical. English. Twenty-four times a year. $172.00 schools, $247.00 other. Green Sheet Communications Inc., PO Box 727, Hartsdale NY 10530. **Tel** (914)472-3051, FAX (914)472-3880. **ED** John R. Werner. **DD** 686. **Bk Rev.** ***Continues*** *Graphic Communications Weekly.*
**Ind/Abst** Abstr. Bull. Inst. Pap. Sci. Tech.; Graph. Arts Bull. Inst. Pap. Sci. Technol. (April 1989).

CN/0227-2806
**GRAPHIC MONTHLY, THE.** [Graph. mon.]. Vol. 1, No. 1 (Jan. 1980)-. Periodical. English. bm. $19.35. The Graphic Monthly, 2065 Dundas Street East/Suite 205, Mississauga Ontario L4X 2W1 Canada. **Tel** (416)625-7070. **ED** Sandy Donald. **DD** 686.2/05. **Bk Rev. Ad Acc. Circ:** 7,000 (ctrl).
**Desc:** Graphic arts publication to the Canadian industry. 'How to' approach editorial.

SZ
**GRAPHIS LOGO.** **See** The Arts-Graphic Arts.

US/0894-4946
**GRAVURE (NEW YORK, N.Y. 1987).** (GRAVURE.). [Gravure]. **Added/Corp** Gravure Association of America. (Spring 1987)-. Periodical. English. Four times a year. $42.00 one year; $76.00 two year;. Gravure Association of America, 1200 A Scottsville Road, Rochester NY 14624. **Tel** (716)436-2150, FAX (716)436-7689. **ED** John Sippel. **LC** Z258; .G7. **DD** 686.2/3042/05. **Ad Acc. Circ:** 7,000 (ctrl). ***Continues*** *Gravure Bulletin, 0160-8789.*
**Desc:** Report on latest technology and general news of interest to the Gravure Printing Industry.
**Ind/Abst** Abstr. Bull. Inst. Pap. Sci. Tech.; Graph. Arts Bull. Inst. Pap. Sci. Technol. (March 1989, June 1989, Nov. 1989).

US/0534-0489
**GRI NEWSLETTER.** [GRI newsl.]. **Main/Corp** Gravure Research Institute. No. 1- 196-. Newsletter. English. Gravure Research Institute, 22 Manhasset Avenue, Port Washington NY 11050. **LC** TR980; .G72. **DD** 686.
**Ind/Abst** Print. Abstr.

GW/0072-9094
**GUTENBERG-JAHRBUCH.** (GUTENBERG JAHRBUCH.). [Gutenberg-Jahrb.]. **Added/Corp** Gutenberg-Gesellschaft. (1926)-. German (English, French, Italian and Spanish). an (Published in June). free (members), DM136.00 (non-members) Germany; DM139 (non-members) other. Gutenberg Gesellschaft, Internationale Vereinigung fuer Geschichte und Gegenwart der Druckkunst eV, Liebfrauenplatz 5, D-55116 Mainz Germany. **Tel** 011 49 6131 226420. **ED** Hans-Joachim Koppitz. **LC** Z1008; .G98. Index available. cum. index. **Ad Acc.** ctrl circ.
**Desc:** Disseminates the results of the research on the past and present history of printing and the book in all countries of the world.
**Ind/Abst** Am. Hist. Life (1986-); BHA : Biblio. Hist. Art; MLA Int. Bibl. Books Artic. Mod. Lang. Lit.

GW
**HIGH QUALITY : HQ.** (1985)-. German (English). Three times a year. DM69.00 Germany; DM79.00 other Europe; DM117.00 other. Verlag und Vertrieb GGMBH, Zahringerstrasse 2, W-6900 Heidelberg 1 Germany. **Tel** 011 49 6221 184020. ctrl circ.
**Desc:** Magazine on design and printing.

US/0737-1020
**HIGH VOLUME PRINTING.** (HIGH VOLUME PRINTING : HVP.). [High vol. print.]. **VFOAT** HVP; H.P.V. Vol. 1, No. 1 (July/Aug. 1982)-. Periodical. English. bm (6 issues). $45.00 US; $50.00 Canada; $65.00 other. Innes Publishing Company, PO Box 1387, Northbrook IL 60065. **Tel** (708)564-5940, (800)247-3306, FAX (708)564-8361. **ED** Catherine Stanulis. **LC** Z119; .H54. **DD** 070.5/05. **Bk Rev. Ad Acc. Circ:** 38,000 (ctrl). available on microfilm. ***Continues*** *Book and Magazine Production, 0273-8724.*
**Desc:** Covers the printing industry and software related to the field.
**Ind/Abst** Abstr. Bull. Inst. Pap. Sci. Tech.; Abstr. Graphic Arts Tech. Found. (1984); Graph. Arts Bull. Inst. Pap. Sci. Technol. (Jan. 1989, March 1989, May 1989, Sept. 1989, Dec. 1989); Print. Abstr.

US/0889-9142
**IMAGING UPDATE.** ***Ceased.*** [Imaging update]. June (1986)-?. Periodical. English. mo. Imaging Update, PO Box 2287, Fair Oaks CA 95628. **Tel** (916)966-6024. **ED** Kristin E Hill. **DD** 338. **Bk Rev. Ad Acc.** available on an online database (file 636/Full-Text) from DIALOG.
**Desc:** Abstracts of US patents, bibliographies and abstracts of relevant papers.
**Ind/Abst** Print. Abstr.; PTS Newsl. Database [Full Txt.].

●US/1071-832X
**IN-PLANT PRINTER (1993).** (IN-PLANT PRINTER.). [In-plant print.]. **VFOAT** In Plant Printer; In-Plant Printer & Electronic Publisher. Vol. 33, No. 3 (June 1993)-. Periodical. English. bm. Innes Publishing Company, PO Box 1387, Northbrook IL 60065. **Tel** (708)564-5940, (800)247-3306, FAX (708)564-8361. **DD** 070. ***Continues*** *In-Plant Printer & Electronic Publisher, 0891-8996.*

US/0891-8996
**IN-PLANT PRINTER & ELECTRONIC PUBLISHER.** ***Title Change.*** [In-plant print. elec. pub.]. **VFOAT** In Plant Printer and Electronic Publisher. Vol. 26, No. 5 (Oct. 1986)-(1993). Periodical. English. Six times a year. Innes Publishing Company, PO Box 1387, Northbrook IL 60065. **Tel** (708)564-5940, (800)247-3306, FAX (708)564-8361. **ED** Michael Angelo. **LC** Z119; .I58. **DD** 070.5/0285. **Ad Acc. Circ:** 38,692 (ctrl). available on microfilm and microfiche from University Microfilms International (UMI). ***Continues*** *In-Plant Printer, 0019-3232.* ***Continued by*** *In-Plant Printer (Northbrook, Ill. : 1993), 1071-832X.*
**Desc:** Serves printing, graphics, and typesetting in-plant facilities.
**Ind/Abst** Abstr. Bull. Inst. Pap. Sci. Tech.; Graph. Arts Bull. Inst. Pap. Sci. Technol. (Mar. 1989-Apr.1989, Sept. 1989, Dec. 1989); Print. Abstr.

US/1043-1942
**IN-PLANT REPRODUCTIONS (1988).** (IN-PLANT REPRODUCTIONS.). [In-plant reprod.]. **VFOAT** In-Plant Reproductions and Electronic Publishing; In-Plant Reproductions & Electronic Publishing. **VAT** In Plant Reproductions; In Plant Reproductions & Electronic Publishing. Vol. 38 No. 12 (Dec. 1988)-. Periodical. English. Twelve times a year. $65.00. North American Publishing Company, 401 North Broad Street, Philadelphia PA 19108. **Tel** (215)238-5300, (800)777-8074, FAX (215)238-5283. **LC** Z252.5.O5; R39. **DD** 686.2/315/05. ***Continues*** *In-Plant Reproductions & Electronic Publishing, 0886-3121.*
**Desc:** Written for management and technical personnel concerned with basic printing and production processes and techniques. Examines in-plant and electronic publishing concerns for business, industry and government.
**Ind/Abst** Abstr. Bull. Inst. Pap. Sci. Tech.; Graph. Arts Bull. Inst. Pap. Sci. Technol. (May 1989); Print. Abstr.

GW
**INDEX AURELIENSIS.** (1965)-. Catalog. Multiple languages. ir. DM280.00. Verlag Valentin Koerner GmbH, Postfach 304, D-76482 Baden Baden Germany. **Tel** 011 49 7221 22423. **ED** Valentin Koerner.
**Desc:** Catalog of books printed all over the world during the 16th century, listed alphabetically (not included books printed entirely in Hebrew, Greek, and Cyrillic).

FR/1164-0863
**INDUSTRIES GRAPHIQUES PARIS.** (INDUSTRIES GRAPHIQUES.). (1991)-. Periodical. French. Ten times a year. 400.00F (France); 391.77 (other). Fed Imprimerie Comm Graphique, 115 BD Saint Germain, 75006 Paris France. **Tel** 33 1 46342115. **UDC** 655(44). ***Continues*** *IG Revue (Paris), 0991-9325.*

UK/0263-497X
**INK & PRINT.** ***Title Change.*** [Ink print]. **Added/Corp** Society of British Printing Ink Manufacturers. **VFOAT** Ink and Print. Vol. 1 No. 1 (Summer 1982)-(19??). Periodical. English. qt. Batiste Publications Ltd, Pembroke House, Campsbourne Road, Hornsey London N8 7PE England. **Tel** 011 44 81 3403291, FAX 011 44 81 3414840, telex 267727. **LC** TP949; .I53. **DD** 667/.4/05. ***Continues*** *British Ink Maker, 0007-0831.* ***Continued by*** *Ink & Print International.*
**Ind/Abst** Abstr. Bull. Inst. Pap. Sci. Tech.; Abstr. Graphic Arts Tech. Found. (1984); F&S Index Plus Text, Int. [Select. Cov.]; Graph. Arts Bull. Inst. Pap. Sci. Technol. (Sept. 1989); Print. Abstr.; PROMT; World Surf. Coat. Abstr.

UK/0263-497X
**INK & PRINT INTERNATIONAL.** **VFOAT** Ink and Print International. (19??)-. Periodical. English. qt. £18.00 UK; £22.00 other. Batiste Publishing Ltd, Pembroke House, Campsbourne Road, Hornsey, London N8 7PE England. **Tel** 011 44 81 340 3291. **LC** TP949; .I53. **DD** 667/.4/05. ***Continues*** *Ink & Print, 0263-497X.*
**Ind/Abst** Abstr. Bull. Inst. Pap. Sci. Tech.; Trade Ind. ASAP [Full Txt.]; Trade Ind. Index [Full Txt.].

JA/0367-8547
**INSATSU-KYOKU KENKYUJO HOKOKU.** [Insatsu-kyoku Kenkyujo hokoku]. **VFOAT** Research Bulletin of the Government Printing Bureau.; Research Bulletin of the Printing Bureau, Ministry of Finance. (1948)-. Academic Scholarly Publication. Japanese. sa. The Research Institute, Printing Bureau, Ministry of Finance, 1-6-1 Oji, Kita-ku, Tokyo Japan. **CODEN** IKKHAR. Documents available from CASDDS.
**Ind/Abst** Abstr. Bull. Inst. Pap. Sci. Tech.; Chem. Abstr. (1948-1977).

JA
**INSATSU ZASSHI.** **Added/Corp** Nihon Insatsu Gakkai. **VFOAT** Japan Printer. (1917)-. Periodical. Japanese (Japanese). mo. $273.50. Insatsu Gakkai Shuppanbu, c/o Shippo Building, 6-2 Ginza 5, Chuo-ku Tokyo-to 104 Japan. **Tel** (03)571-6025. **(Subscription address:** Japan Publications Trading Company, Ltd., PO Box 5030, Tokyo International, Tokyo 100-31 Japan.**)** **ED** Akio Sato. **LC** Z119; .I585. **Ad Acc.**

US/1044-3746
**INSTANT AND SMALL COMMERCIAL PRINTER.** [Instant small commer. printer]. **VFOAT** Instant Printer. (1983)-. Periodical. English. mo. $45.00 US; $50.00 Canada; $65.00 other. Innes Publishing Company, PO Box 1387, Northbrook IL 60065. **Tel** (708)564-5940, (800)247-3306, FAX (708)564-8361. **LC** Z252.5.I49; I57. **DD** 686.4/4. ***Continues*** *Instant Printer, 0744-3854.*
**Ind/Abst** Abstr. Bull. Inst. Pap. Sci. Tech.; Graph. Arts Bull. Inst. Pap. Sci. Technol. (March 1989, April 1989).

KO
**INSWAEGYE.** (19??)-. Periodical. Korean. bm. **LC** Z119; .I595.

FR/0397-1392
**INTEGREE, L'.** (1976)-. Periodical. French. bm. 290.89F France; 343.00F other. IRED, 13 rue Rougemont, 75009 Paris France. **Tel** 011 33 1 47704038. **UDC** 65.

UK
**INTERNATIONAL PRINT BUYER'S DIRECTORY.** (1983)-. Directory. English (French and German). £30.00 UK; $78.60 (surface mail), $88.20 (airmail) US. Metal Bulletin PLC, PO Box 28E, Worcester Park, Surrey KT4 7HX England. **Tel** 011 44 71 827 9977, FAX 011 44 81 337 8943. **ED** Andrew Ivett. **LC** Z282; .I6. **DD** 686.2/025. Index available. **Circ:** 500.
**Desc:** The unique worldwide directory of printers and print-binders.

US
**INTERNATIONAL STEREOTYPERS AND ELECTROTYPERS UNION JOURNAL, THE.** Began publication with Vol. 1 in 1906?. Periodical. English. mo. J J Kelley, 90 East 214th Street, Cleveland OH 44123.

IT/0021-2784
**ITALIA GRAFICA, L'.** [Ital. graf.]. **Added/Corp** Associazione Nazionale Industrie Grafische Cartoteiche Ed Affini. Associazione Nazionale Industrie Grafiche Cartotecniche e Transformatrici. (1946)-. Italian. bm. L42000 Italy; L84000 other. Editing Spa, Via Cassia 1328, 00123 Rome Italy. **Tel** 011 39 6 30311464, FAX 011 39 6 30311473. **LC** Z119; .A86a. **DD** 686.2/0945. **Bk Rev. Ad Acc. Circ:** 12,000.
**Desc:** Information concerning labor, economic and technical aspects, as well as taxes and law for the printing, paper and cardboard converting industries.
**Ind/Abst** Print. Abstr.

NE
**JAARVERSLAG - KONINKLIJK NEDERLANDS VERBOND VAN DRUKKERIJEN.** **Main/Corp** Nederlands Verbond Van Drukkerijen. Dutch. Koninklijk Nederlands Verbond van Graf Ond, Postbus 220, 1180 AE Amstelveen, Startbaan 10 Amstelveen. **Tel** (020)5475678. **LC** Z244.6.N4; N44A.

AU/0075-2266
**JAHRBUCH DER GRAPHISCHEN UNTERNEHMUNGEN OSTERREICHS.** **Added/Corp** Hauptverband der Graphischen Unternehmungen Osterreichs. (19??)-. German. an. Hamptverband der Graphischen Undernehmnnpl, Grinangergasse 4, A-1010 Vienna Austria. **Tel** 0222/526609. **LC** Z119; .J3. **Ad Acc.**
**Desc:** Address index of Austrian printing houses, presses and word processing facilities.

JA
**JAPAN GRAPHIC ARTS.** **Added/Corp** Japan Federation of Printing Industries. (1989)-. English. an (Nov.). $45.00. Japan Printings News Company Ltd., 16 8 1 Chome Shintomi, Chuo KU Tokyo Japan. **Tel** 011 81 3 35535681, FAX (03)553 5684. **ED** Hiroshi Kurihara. **Ad Acc. Circ:** 5,000 (ctrl). ***Continues*** *Graphic Arts Japan.*
**Desc:** Design for the printers, traders and managers of dealing with machinery related printing all over the world.
**Ind/Abst** Abstr. Bull. Inst. Pap. Sci. Tech.

US/0737-7436
**JOURNAL OF THE PRINT WORLD.** [J. print world]. (1978)-. Periodical. English. qt. Regular Mail: $10.00 (non profit institutes), $12.00 US; $20.00 other. Journal of the Print World, 1008 Winona Road, Meredith NH 03253. **Tel** (603)279-6479, FAX (603)279-1337. **Bk Rev**, (Qty: 4-6). **Ad Acc, Adv Mgr:** Sophia Lane, **Tel** (603)279-6479. ctrl circ.

US/0453-4867
**KEMBLE OCCASIONAL, THE.** ***Ceased.*** (1964)-(19??). English. ir. The Kemble Collections, California Historical Society Library, 2099 Pacific, San Francisco CA 94109. **Tel** (415)567-1848. **ED** Charles N Johnson. **Bk Rev. Circ:** 200 (ctrl).
**Desc:** Devoted to printing, publishing, and ancillary trades in the Western United States
**Ind/Abst** Am. Hist. Life.

US/1054-3724
**LASERJET JOURNAL.** ***Ceased.*** [Laserjet j.]. **Added/Corp** Hewlett-Packard Company. (19??)-(Dec. 1993). Periodical. English. Twelve times a year. Laserjet Journal, 1945 Techny Road, Number 4, Northbrook IL 60062. **Tel** (312)498-0920, (800)323-2686. **DD** 004.

US
**LASERTONE NEWS.** Periodical. English. Spectrum Inc, Spectrum Color Center, 6275 Joyce Drive, Golden CO 80403. **Tel** (800)426-5677, FAX (303)425-0655. **Circ:** 15,000 (ctrl).
**Desc:** Contains practical tips for color buyers and trends in electronic pre-press.

SP
**LATINGRAFICA.** (1975)-. Spanish. Parana 140 2 Piso, Buenos Aires Argentina. **LC** Z244.6.L35; L37.

CK/0121-1242
**LIBRO EN AMERICA LATINA Y EL CARIBE, EL.** **See** Publishing-Books and Bookmaking.

UK/0264-732X
**LITHOWEEK.** ***Title Change.*** [Lithoweek]. Vol. 4, No. 40 (Oct. 1982)-(19??). Trade Publication. English. wk. Haymarket Publishing Ltd., 12 14 Ansdell Street, London W8 5TR England. **Tel** 011 44 483 733800, FAX 011 44 483 776573. **ED** Simon Kanter and Paul Simpson. **Circ:** 13,000. ***Continues*** *Lithoprinter Week.* ***Continued by*** *Printweek.*
**Desc:** News magazine for the printing trade.
**Ind/Abst** Curr. Technol. Index; Fluid Abstr., Civil Eng.; Fluid Abstr. Proc. Eng.; FLUIDEX (1982-); Graph. Arts Bull. Inst. Pap. Sci. Technol. (Jan. 1989, April 1989-Nov. 1989); Infomat Int. Bus.; Print. Abstr.

GW
**M.A.N-ROLAND REVUE.** **VFOAT** Revue. (19??)-. Consumer Publication. English (French, German, Italian and Spanish). ir. MAN Roland Druckmaschinen AG, Christian-Pless-Str, Postfach 10 1264, D-63012 Offenbach/Main Germany. ***Continues*** *Roland Offset Revue.*
**Desc:** Information and news about printing presses and other products for our customers.
**Ind/Abst** Abstr. Bull. Inst. Pap. Sci. Tech.

CN/0025-0996
**MAITRE IMPRIMEUR, LE.** [Maitre impr.]. **Added/Corp** Association des Maitre-Imprimeurs de Montreal. (1937)-. Periodical. French. Twelve times a year. 25.00Can$ Canada; 30.00Can$ US; 45.00Can$ others. Association des Arts Graphiques du Quebec Inc, 65 rue de Castelnau Ouest #101, Montreal QUE H2R 2W3 Canada. **Tel** (514)274-7446, FAX (514)274-7482. **ED** Charles Henri Dube (editor's address: 3342 Montpetit, Ste Foy, P-Q G1W 2T2 Canada, phone: (418)654-0010). **Ad Acc, Adv Mgr:** J. Cote, **Tel** (514)227-7300. **Circ:** 4,800 (ctrl).
**Desc:** All matters related to printing and allied trades, new technological developments, trends in the industry, and who's who in the printing world.
**Ind/Abst** Point Repere (1983-);(1984-v. 54, no 12 (d,ec. 1990)).

US/1050-2114
**MANAGEMENT PORTFOLIO.** **See** Business-General Management.

UK
**MICROINFO, MICROFILM NEWS.** ***Title Change.*** **VFOAT** MMN. Vol. 18, No. 1 (Jan. 1987)-?. Periodical. English. mo. MicroInfo Ltd., PO Box 3, Omega Park, Alton Hants GU34 2PG England. **Tel** 011 44 420 86848, FAX 011 44 420 89889, telex 858431 MINFO G. **LC** TR835; .M54. **DD** 686.4/3/05. ***Continues*** *MicroInfo.* ***Continued by*** *Document Image Processing (DIP).*

GW/0175-6869
**MITTEILUNGEN - DEUTSCHE FORSCHUNGSGESELLSCHAFT FUER DRUCK- UND REPRODUKTIONSTECHNIK E.V.** **VFOAT** Mitteilungen - Fogra. (1983)-. Periodical. German. qt. Fogra, Streitfeldstrasse 19, D 81673 Munich Germany. **Tel** 011 49 89 431623. **UDC** 655.1.

US/0889-7565
**MONTHLY NEWSPRINT STATISTICAL REPORT.** [Mon. newspr. stat. rep.]. **VFOAT** ANPA Monthly Newsprint Statistical Report. (Aug. 1980)-. Statistical Publication. English. mo. Free. American Newspapers Publishing Association, PO Box 17407, Dulles International, Washington DC 20041. **Tel** (703)648-1104. **DD** 338.
**Ind/Abst** Predicasts Forecasts.

US/0148-5539
**MOSSTYPER, THE.** **Main/Corp** Mosstype Corporation. Periodical. English. sa. Mosstype Corporation, Waldwick NJ 07463. **LC** Z119; .M76A. **DD** 686.2/05.
**Ind/Abst** Print. Abstr.

US/0893-4975
**NAPL SPECIAL REPORT.** [NAPL spec. rep.]. **Added/Corp** National Association of Printers and Lithographers. **VAT** National Association of Printers and Lithographers Special Report. (197?)-. Monographic

# Printing Industry

series. English. National Association of Printers and Lithographers, 780 Palisade Avenue, Teaneck NJ 07666. **Tel** (201)342-0707, (800)642-6275.
**Ind/Abst** Abstr. Bull. Inst. Pap. Sci. Tech.

US/0162-8771
**NEW ENGLAND PRINTER & PUBLISHER. VFOAT** New England Printer and Publisher. (19??)-. Periodical. English. Twelve times a year. $11.00 one year; $19.00 two years; $25.00 three years. New England Printer & Publisher, 12 Carlton Drive, PO Box 810, Newburyport MA 01950. **Tel** (508)462-9461, FAX (508)462-9160. **ED** Jean Hansen. **LC** Z119; .N4. **DD** 681.6. **Bk Rev**. **Ad Acc**. **Circ:** 4,200. *Continues New England Printer and Lithographer.*
**Desc:** News of people, clubs, events and products pertinent to the graphic arts community for New England printers, marketing, and business management.
**Ind/Abst** Abstr. Bull. Inst. Pap. Sci. Tech.; Abstr. Graphic Arts Tech. Found. (1984); Graph. Arts Bull. Inst. Pap. Sci. Technol. (Jan. 1989-March 1989, May 1989-July 1989, Sept. 1989, Nov.1989).

UK
**NEW IN PRINTING.** Vol. 1, No. 1 (June 1985)-. Periodical. English. mo (12 issues). Haymarket Publishing Ltd., 12 14 Ansdell Street, London W8 5TR England. **Tel** 011 44 483 733800, FAX 011 44 483 776573. **(Subscription address:** Haymarket Publishing Ltd, PO Box 219, Subscriptions Department, Woking Surrey GU21 1ZW, United Kingdom.**)**
**Desc:** Information on printing machinery and supplies.
**Ind/Abst** Graph. Arts Bull. Inst. Pap. Sci. Technol. (July 1989); Print. Abstr.

NZ/1171-0829
**NEW ZEALAND PRINTER MAGAZINE.** [N.Z. print. mag.]. **VFOAT** New Zealand Printer; Printer. (1991)-. Periodical. English. bm (6 issues). 40.00Aus$ New Zealand; 80.00Aus$ (zone 1), 100.00Aus$ (zones 2 & 3), 105.00Aus$ (zone 4), 115.00Aus$ (zone 5) airmail; 50.00Aus$ surface mail other. Calmor & Associates Pty Ltd, PO Box 1316, North Sydney NSW 2059 Australia. **Tel** 011 61 2 9226133, FAX 011 61 2 9224734. **ED** Patrick Howard. **DD** _a686.205 _a338.47686205. **Ad Acc, Adv Mgr:** P. Callahan, **Tel** 922-6133. **Circ:** 3,600 (ctrl).

US/0271-1699
**NEWSLETTER, GRAVURE ENVIRONMENTAL.** [Newsl. grav. environ.]. **VFOAT** Environmental Newsletter of the Gravure Industry; Gravure Environmental Letter; GRI-GTA Environmental Letter. No. 9- Aug. 1979-. Newsletter. English. mo. Gravure Association of America, 1200 A Scottsville Road, Rochester NY 14624. **Tel** (716)436-2150, FAX (716)436-7689. **ED** David A Smith. **LC** TD195.P7; G7. **DD** 686.2. **Circ:** 2,000 (ctrl). *Continues Gravure Environmental and O.S.H.A. Newsletter, 0091-5203.*
**Desc:** Flash reports covering environmental regulations, updates, alerts, status, health and safety.
**Ind/Abst** Print. Abstr.

JA/0914-3319
**NIPPON INSATSU GAKKAISHI.** [Nippon Insatsu Gakkaishi]. **VFOAT** Bulletin of the Japanese Society of Printing Science and Technology (1987). (1987)-. Academic Scholarly Publication. Multiple languages. qt. $130.00. **(Subscription address:** Kyowa Book Company Inc., 1-38 Kanda Jinbocho Chiyoda-ku, Tokyo 101 Japan**) DD** 686. Documents available from CASDDS. *Continues Nippon Insatsu Gakkai Ronbunshu, 0040-0874.*
**Ind/Abst** Chem. Abstr.

US/0889-9819
**NORTH AMERICAN COPIER & COPYBOARD GUIDE. VFOAT** North American Copier and Copyboard Guide. (198?)-. Periodical. English. sa. $65.00 US; $87.00 Canada; $80.00 other. Info-Market, 13935 Rancheros, Reno NV 89511. **Tel** (702)851-0356. **DD** 686. *Continues North American Copier Catalog, 8755-1071.*

FR/0029-4888
**NOUVELLES DE L'ESTAMPE.** [Nouv. estampe]. (Jan. 1963). Periodical. French. Five times a year. 329.32F France; 450.00F other. Comite Natl Gravure Francaise, 58 rue de Richelieu, 75084 Paris Cedex 02 France. **Tel** 33 1 47 03 83 88. **ED** Gerard Sourd. **LC** NE1; .N67. **Bk Rev**, (Qty: 5/yr). **Ad Acc**. **Circ:** 1000-2000.
**Ind/Abst** Art Archaeol. Tech. Abstr.; ARTbibliogr. Mod.; ARTbibliogr. Curr. Titles; BHA : Biblio. Hist. Art.

UK
**OCTAVO (LONDON, ENGLAND).** (OCTAVO.). (1986)-. Periodical. English. sa. $32.00. Octavo, 3 Morocco Street, London SE1 3HP England. **ED** Mr. Johnston, Mr. Holt, Mr. Muir and Mr. Burke. **Circ:** 3,000.
**Desc:** International journal of typography.

UK/0964-0746
**OFFSET PRINTING & REPRODUCTION.** [Offset print. reprod.]. **VFOAT** Offset Printing and Reproduction. (1990)-. Periodical. English. mo. £50.00 (surface mail); £85.00 (airmail). Maclean Hunter Ltd. / UK, Chalk Lane Cockfosters Road, Barnet Herts EN4 0BU England. **Tel** 011 44 81 2423000, FAX 011 44 81 9759753, telex 299072. *Continues Offset Printing and Reprographics, 0263-4384.*
**Ind/Abst** Abstr. Bull. Inst. Pap. Sci. Tech.

GW/0178-1197
**OFFSET-TECHNIK.** (1968)-. Periodical. German. Eleven times a year. DM80.20. Support GMBH, Grethenweg 32, W 6000 Frankfurt 70 Germany. **Tel** 011 49 69 615469. **UDC** 655.

GW/0030-0594
**OFFSETPRAXIS. See** Photography and Video.

US/0891-7604
**OLD PRINT SHOP PORTFOLIO, THE.** [Old Print Shop portf.]. **Main/Corp** Old Print Shop (New York, N.Y.). **VFOAT** Old Print Shop Portfolio. V. 1- Sept. 1941-. Periodical. English. mo. Old Print Shop, 150 Lexington Avenue at 30th Street, New York NY 10016. **LC** NE1; .O63. **DD** 760.5.

NE
**P-IM : PROFESSIONAL IMAGING.** Dutch. Four times a year. FL55.00. P/F Publishing BV, Postbus 773, 2700 At Zoetermeer, Netherlands. **Tel** 79 612930, FAX 79.611737. **ED** Jan J. Van der Schans. **Circ:** 9,000 (ctrl).

US/0552-7511
**PACIFIC PRINTERS PILOT.** Periodical. English. mo. Pacific Printers Pilot, 583 Monterey Pass Road, Monterey Park CA 91754. **Tel** (310)576-1538. **ED** Elaine Past.

SA
**PACK & PRINT. See** Packaging.

US/0895-1608
**PACKAGE PRINTING AND CONVERTING. See** Packaging.

II/0556-4409
**PAINTINDIA. See** Paints and Painting.

II/0030-9540
**PAINTINDIA. ANNUAL. See** Paints and Painting.

AU
**PAPIER & DRUCK. See** Paper and Pulp Industry.

GW/0031-1375
**PAPIER UND DRUCK.** *Ceased.* **See** Paper and Pulp Industry.

HU/0231-0740
**PAPRIPARI ES NYOMDAIPARI SZAKIRODALMI TAJEKOZTATO. See** Paper and Pulp Industry.

US/0194-2530
**PDQ.** *Ceased.* (1979)-?. Periodical. English. mo. Printing Industries of America, 100 Daingerfield Road, Alexandria VA 22314. **Tel** (703)519-8146.

NE
**PERS.** Dutch. bw. Utigeverij Compres, Postbus 55, Leiden Netherlands. **Tel** 011 31 71 161515.

US
**PERSONAL COMPOSITION REPORT, THE. VFOAT** PCR. Vol. 7, No. 6 (Sept. 1985)-. Periodical. English. Ten times a year. $75.00 US; $600.00 OPEC countries; $90.00 other. Graphic Dimensions, 134 Caversham Woods, Pittsford NY 14534-2834. **Tel** (716)381-3428. **ED** Michael L Kleper. **Bk Rev**.
*Continues Digest of Information on Phototypesetting.*
**Desc:** Covers the desktop publishing and personal typesetting field for word processing, personal computer and typesetting users worldwide.
**Ind/Abst** Graph. Arts Bull. Inst. Pap. Sci. Technol. (March 1989, July 1989, Sept. 1989, Dec. 1989).

US/0032-0595
**PLAN AND PRINT.** *Title Change.* **See** Computers-Computer Graphics and Design.

RM/0032-2695
**POLIGRAFIA.** [Poligrafia]. **Added/Corp** Romania. Comitetul de Stat pentru Cultura si Arta. (19??)-. Periodical. Romanian. Six times a year. $89.95. **(Subscription address:** East View Publications Inc., 3020 Harbor Lane North, Suite 110, Minneapolis MN 55447.**) LC** Z1191; .P74.
**Ind/Abst** Abstr. Bull. Inst. Pap. Sci. Tech.; Print. Abstr.

RU/0134-9147
**POLIGRAFICESKAJA PROMYSLENNOST. OBZORNAJA INFORMACIJA.** (POLIGRAFICHESKAIA PROMYSHLENNOST. OBZORNAIA INFORMATSIIA.). [Poligr. prom., Obz. inf.]. **Added/Corp** Gosudarstvennyi Komitet SSSR po Delam Izdatelstvu, Poligrafii i Knizhnoi Torgovli. Vsesoiuznaia Knizhnaia Palata. Nauchno-Informatsionnyi Tsentr po Izdatelskomu Delu, Poligraficheskoi Promyshlennosti i Knizhnoi Torgovle. **VFOAT** Poligraficheskaia Promyshlennost. (1970)-. Academic Scholarly Publication. Russian. mo. Izdatelstvo Kniga, 50 Gorky Ulitsa, 125047 Moscow Russia. **CODEN** OIPPDT. Documents available from CASDDS.
**Ind/Abst** Chem. Abstr. (1970-1984).

RU
**POLIGRAFICHESKAIA PROMYSHLENNOST. BIBLIOGRAFICHESKAIA INFORMATSIIA: NOVOSTI TEKHNICHESKOI LITERATURY. Added/Corp** Gosudarstvennyi Komitet Soveta Ministrov SSSR po Delam Izdatelstv, Poligrafii i Knizhnoi Torgovli. Vsesoiuznaia Knizhnaia Palata. Tsentralnoe Biuro Nauchno-Tekhnicheskoi Informatsii i Tekhniko-Ekonomicheskikh Issledovanii po Poligraficheskoi Promyshlennosti, Izdatelskomu Delu, Knigovedeniiu i Knizhnoi Torgovle. **VFOAT** Novosti Tekhnicheskoi Literatury. (1969)-. Multiple languages (Russian and Multiple languages). mo. 0.10rub (single issue). Izdatelstvo Kniga, 50 Gorky Ulitsa, 125047 Moscow Russia. **LC** Z117; .P63.

IT
**POLIGRAFICO ITALIANO, IL.** (1960)-. Periodical. Italian. mo (11 issues). L81730 Italy; L170000 other. Zetas, Via Kolbe 8, 20137 Milan Italy. **Tel** 011 39 2 76110075. **LC** Z119; .P753.
**Ind/Abst** Print. Abstr.

PL/0373-9864
**POLIGRAFIKA.** [Poligrafika]. (1947)-. Periodical. Polish (summaries and/or abstracts in Russian and German). mo. Price on Request. **(Subscription address:** ARS Polona, PO Box 1001, 00068 Warsaw Poland.**) CODEN** POLGDZ. Documents available from CASDDS.
**Ind/Abst** Chem. Abstr. (1947-1981).

GW/0032-3845
**POLYGRAPH, DER.** [Polygraph]. Vol. 1 (March 1948)-. Academic Scholarly Publication. German. sm. DM186.00. Polygraph Verlag GmbH, Schaumainkai 85, D 60596 Frankfurt Germany. **Tel** 011 49 69 6300860, FAX 011 49 69 6313502. **ED** Ulrike Schulz. **LC** Z119; .P767. **[CCC]**. Index available. **Bk Rev**. **Ad Acc**. **Circ:** 13,000 (ctrl). *Supersedes Klimschs Druckerei-Anzeiger.*
**Desc:** Trade magazine for the printing industry and communication technology; deals with topics and professional sectors, from typesetting, reproduction and printing techniques to bookbinding and paper industries, typography, business management, environment protection and communication technology.
**Ind/Abst** Bibliogr. Carto.; EMBASE; Infomat Int. Bus.; Saf. Health Work.

US/8750-2224
**PREPRESS BULLETIN, THE. Added/Corp** International Prepress Association. Vol. 74, No. 2 (July/Aug. 1984)-. Bulletin. English. bm (6 issues). $15.00 US; $17.00 other. International Prepress Association, 552 West 167th Street, South Holland IL 60473. **Tel** (708)596-5110, FAX (708)596-5112. **ED** Bessie Halfacre. **DD** 686. **Bk Rev**, (Qty: 3-4). **Ad Acc, Adv Mgr:** H. Yocherer, **Tel** (708)369-7442. **Circ:** 1,450 (ctrl). *Continues Photoplatemakers Bulletin, 0031-8841.*
**Desc:** Management and technical information for companies producing color separations and other prepress preparatory materials for the graphic arts.
**Ind/Abst** Abstr. Bull. Inst. Pap. Sci. Tech.; Graph. Arts Bull. Inst. Pap. Sci. Technol. (Jan. 1989, March 1989, May 1989, Aug. 1989, Oct. 1989, Dec. 1989); Imaging Abstr.; Print. Abstr.

AU
**PRESSE HANDBUCH / VERBAND OSTERREICHISCHER ZEITUNGSHERAUSGEBER UND ZEITUNGSVERLEGER. Added/Corp** Verband Osterreichischer Zeitungsherausgeber und Zeitungsverleger. (1985)-. German. an. S1,089.00. Verband Osterreichischer Zeitungsherausgeber und Zeitungsverleger, Schreyvogelgasse 3, 1010 Vienna 1 Austria. **Tel** 0222/533 61 78, FAX 0222/533 61 78-22. **LC** Z6956.A9; H3; PN5164. **DD** 073/.6/025. **Ad Acc**. **Acid Free**. **Circ:** 2,800 (ctrl). available on diskette. *Continues Osterreichs Presse, Werbung, Graphik Handbuch, 0030-0004.*
**Desc:** General information about the Austrian press, newspapers and advertisers.

CN/0380-2752
**PRINT ACTION.** Vol. 1 (Oct. 1971)-. Periodical. English (French). Twelve times a year. 42.00Can$ Canada; 52.00Can$ others. Youngblood Publishing Company, 2240 Midland Avenue, Suite 201,

Scarborough, Ontario M1P 4R8 Canada. **Tel** (905)299-6007. **ED** Pat Trusty. **Ad Acc. Circ:** 16,000 (ctrl).
**Desc:** Fast-breaking news coverage aimed at all segments of the Canadian graphic arts industry. Includes case histories and studies of companies, the latest technological developments, in-depth feature issues directed to segments of the industry.

US/0273-9550
**PRINT & GRAPHICS.** [Print graph.]. **VAT** Print and Graphics. (Nov. 1980)-. Periodical. English. mo. Free to print and graphics business subscribers; $39.00 other. East West Communications, 1432 Duke Street, Alexandria VA 22314. **Tel** (703)683-8800.
**Ind/Abst** Abstr. Bull. Inst. Pap. Sci. Tech.; Graph. Arts Bull. Inst. Pap. Sci. Technol. (Jan. 1989-Mar.1989, June 1989-Sept. 1989, Nov. 1989).

US
**PRINT BUSINESS REGISTER.** (19??)-. Periodical. English. Twenty-four times a year. $397.00 US, Canada and Mexico; $637.00 other. Quoin Research, 800 West Huron Street, Suite 3N, Chicago IL 60622. **Tel** (312)226-5600, FAX (312)226-4640. **ED** Rod Piechowski. Index available (published separately). cum. index.
**Desc:** Designed for top decision makers in the printing industry. News stories cover mergers, acquisitions, financial analysis, government contracts awarded, personal moves, bankruptcies and failures.

UK/0264-5424
**PRINT BUYER (1982).** (PRINT BUYER.). [Print buy.]. Vol. 17, No. 1 (Oct. 1982)-. Periodical. English. qt. £45.00 UK; £75.00 others. Macro Publishing Ltd., Conbar House, Mead Lane, Hertford SG13 7AS England. **Tel** 011 44 992 584233. ***Continues*** *Print & Promotion.*
**Ind/Abst** Infomat Int. Bus.; Print. Abstr.

UK
**PRINT BUYING.** English. £75.00. Marco Publishing Ltd, Conbar House Mead Lane, Hertford Herts SG13 7AS England. **Tel** 0992 584233, FAX 0992 500717. **ED** H Attrill. **LC** Z249 .B66. **DD** 681/.6. **Bk Rev. Ad Acc. Circ:** 7,000.
**Desc:** The United Kingdom's only magazine for buyers of print paper and promotional material.
**Ind/Abst** Print. Abstr.

US
**PRINT EDUCATION MAGAZINE.** V. 1- Oct. 1976-. Periodical. English. mo. $13.00. Westana Publications, 298 Harbor Drive, PO Box Drawer G, Sausalito CA 94965. **LC** Z119; .P8987. **DD** 686.2/05.

AT/1033-6885
**PRINT PRODUCTION DIRECTORY.** [Print prod. dir.]. (1989)-. Periodical. English. Four times a year. 345.00Aus$ (Australia); 400.00Aus$ (other). Thomson Publications / Australia, 47 Chippen Street, Chippendale New South Wales, 2008 Australia. **Tel** 011 61 2 6992411, FAX 011 61 2 698 3920, telex 122226. **(Subscription address:** Thomson Publications Australia, PO Box 815, Strawberry Hills, New South Wales, 2012 Australia.**) ED** Caroline Mackie. **DD** 686.02594. **Ad Acc. Circ:** 500.
**Desc:** Gives full details on more than 2,500 magazines and 1,200 newspapers, all mechanical specifications and production data, after hours contact numbers, names of key personnel, booking and cancellation deadlines, circulation and distribution figures, artwork delivery point, state-of-the-art glossary and specialist printers covering everything from non-paper printing to holography.

UK/0265-8305
**PRINT QUARTERLY.** [Print q.]. **VFOAT** PQ. Vol. 1, No. 1 (March 1984)-. Periodical. English. qt (4 issues). $66.00. Print Quarterly, 80 Carlton Hill, London MN8 0ER England. **Tel** 011 44 71 625 6332. **ED** David Landau. **LC** NE1; .P757. **DD** 760/.5. Index available. **Bk Rev. Ad Acc. Circ:** 1,000. Documents available from The Genuine Article.
**Desc:** The history of printmaking from the 1400s to the present.
**Ind/Abst** Am. Hist. Life (1984-); Art Archaeol. Tech. Abstr.; ARTbibliogr. Mod. (1984-); Arts Humanit. Citation Index [Full Cov.]; BHA : Biblio. Hist. Art; Curr. Contents Soc. Behav. Sci.; Res. Alert [Full Cov.]; Romant. Move.

US/0192-6314
**PRINTERS HOT LINE.** [Print. hot line]. (1978)-. English. wk. $69.00 US; $119.00 Canada; $349.00 other. United Advertising Periodicals, 15400 Knoll Trail Suite 400, Dallas TX 75248. **Tel** (214)233-5131. **DD** 338. Index available. **Ad Acc.** ctrl circ.

NZ/0048-5330
**PRINTER'S NEWS (WELLINGTON).** (PRINTER'S NEWS.). [Print. news]. **Added/Corp** Auckland Master Printer's Association. Federation of Master Printers of New Zealand. Vol. 1 (Aug. 1943)-. Periodical. English. Six times a year (Feb., Apr., June, Aug., Oct., Dec.). 25.00NZ$ (members or non-printers); 100.00NZ$ (printers or non-members). Printing Industries Federation of New Zealand Inc., PO Box 1422, Wellington New Zealand. **Tel** 011 64 4 723497, FAX 011 64 4 723534. **ED** W. R. Johnson. **LC** Z119; .P9516. **DD** 655.305. **Bk Rev. Ad Acc. Circ:** 1,100 (ctrl). ***Absorbed*** *Typonews.*
**Desc:** Information for members of the printing industry, and suppliers of machinery and supplies.
**Ind/Abst** Abstr. Graphic Arts Tech. Found. (1979, 1984); Print. Abstr.

UK
**PRINTERS YEARBOOK : THE COMPREHENSIVE GUIDE TO THE PRINTING INDUSTRY.** **Added/Corp** British Printing Industries Federation. (1983)-. English. an (July). £40.00 UK; $75.00 US. British Printing Industries Federation, 11 Bedford Row, London WC1 R4DX England. **Tel** 011 44 71 242 6904, FAX 011 44 71 405 7784. **ED** Alison Harmer. **LC** Z119.5; .M42. **DD** 686.2/0941. Index available. **Ad Acc. Circ:** 3,700 (ctrl). ***Continues*** *Printing Industries Annual.*
**Desc:** A guide to suppliers, education and training, printer's law, technical information, printer's costs and prices, who's who and BPIF services to printers and customers.

UK/0031-109X
**PRINTING ABSTRACTS.** **See** Printing Industry-Abstracting, Bibliographies and Statistics.

UK
**PRINTING & CONVERTING MATTERS.** (19??)-. English. Nine times a year. £9.00. A E Morgan Publications Ltd, Stanley House, 9 West Street, Epsom Surrey KT18 7RL England. **Tel** 011 44 3727 41411, FAX 0372 744493, telex 291561 VIA SOS G.

US/0741-1979
**PRINTING AND GRAPHIC ARTS BUYERS : PGAB.** [Print. graph. arts buy.]. **VFOAT** PGAB; P.G.A.B. 1984 ed.-. English. an. $79.00. Hilary House Publishers Inc, 980 North Federal Highway/Suite 206, Boca Raton FL 33432-2704. **Tel** (407)338-2120. **ED** Edward L Stern. **LC** Z475; .P677. **DD** 070.5/025/73. **Ad Acc. Circ:** 2,500.
**Desc:** Names, addresses, and phone numbers of over 5,800 national key buyers and purchasing agents, of printing, advertising, direct mail, catalogs, sales promotion, displays, papers, ink, envelopes, composition, separations, etc.

US
**PRINTING BUSINESS REPORT.** (19??)-. English. qt. $150.00. National Association of Printers and Lithographers, 780 Palisade Avenue, Teaneck NJ 07666. **Tel** (201)342-0707, (800)642-6275. ***Continues*** *Quarterly Printing Industry Business Indicator Report;* ***Absorbed*** *Printing Sales Index.*
**Ind/Abst** Abstr. Bull. Inst. Pap. Sci. Tech.

US/0192-9275
**PRINTING HISTORY.** [Print. hist.]. **Added/Corp** American Printing History Association. Vol. 1 (1979)-. Periodical. English. Twice a year. $30.00 (individuals), $35.00 (institutions) Comes with American Printing History Association membership. American Printing History Association, PO Box 4922, Grand Central Station, New York NY 10163. **Tel** (212)930-0802, FAX (212)302-4815. **ED** David Pankow (editor's address: Rochester Institute of Technology, Rochester, New York 14623, phone: (716)475-2408). **LC** Z124.A2; P74. **DD** 686.2/09. **Bk Rev. Ad Acc. Circ:** 900 (ctrl).
**Ind/Abst** Libr. Inf. Sci. Abstr.; Libr. Lit.; MLA Int. Bibl. Books Artic. Mod. Lang. Lit.

US/0032-860X
**PRINTING IMPRESSIONS.** [Print. impress.]. Vol. 1, No. 1 (June 1958)-. Periodical. English. Twelve times a year. $75.00 US; $100.00 Canada; $115.00 other. North American Publishing Company, 401 North Broad Street, Philadelphia PA 19108. **Tel** (215)238-5300, (800)777-8074, FAX (215)238-5283. **ED** Mark Michelson. **DD** 338. **Ad Acc. Circ:** 95,000 (ctrl). available on microfilm and microfiche from University Microfilms International (UMI). Documents available from UMI Article Clearinghouse. ***Absorbed*** *Web; Newspaper and Magazine Production, 0191-4634.*
**Desc:** News and feature material on management, marketing, and technical aspects of printing and publishing operations. Departments include: new products, equipment and supply review, people in the news, supplier news, industry news, calendar.
**Ind/Abst** ABI/INFORM Glob. Ed.; ABI Inform Ondisc (March 1975-Dec. 1977); Abstr. Bull. Inst. Pap. Sci. Tech.; Abstr. Graphic Arts Tech. Found. (1984); Graph. Arts Bull. Inst. Pap. Sci. Technol. (Jan. 1989-June 1989, Sept. 1989, Dec. 1989); Print. Abstr.

UK/0307-7195
**PRINTING INDUSTRIES.** [Print. ind.]. **Added/Corp** British Printing Industries Federation. Vol. 73, No. 2 (Feb. 1974)-. Periodical. English. Ten times a year. £40.00 members, £50.00 (nonmembers) UK; £70.00 other. British Printing Industries Federation, 11 Bedford Row, London WC1 R4DX England. **Tel** 011 44 71 242 6904, FAX 011 44 71 405 7784. **ED** Louise Taylor. **LC** Z120; .B78. **DD** 331.88/11/68620941. Index available. **Bk Rev. Ad Acc. Circ:** 4,800 (ctrl). ***Continues*** *British Federation of Master Printers. Members Circular.*
**Desc:** Unique source of management information directly related to the printing industry.
**Ind/Abst** Abstr. Bull. Inst. Pap. Sci. Tech.; Abstr. Graphic Arts Tech. Found. (1984); Graph. Arts Bull. Inst. Pap. Sci. Technol. (Jan. 1989-Feb. 1989, June 1989, Aug. 1989, Oct. 1989); Print. Abstr.

US/0191-8273
**PRINTING JOURNAL.** [Print. j.]. (1974)-. Periodical. English. Twelve times a year. Wells Publishing, PO Box 91447, Pasadena CA 91109-1447. **Tel** (818)793-7717, FAX (818)793-1462. **ED** Noel Jeffrey. **Bk Rev. Ad Acc. Circ:** 25,000 (ctrl).
**Desc:** Printing industry news and advertising journal for western states.
**Ind/Abst** Abstr. Bull. Inst. Pap. Sci. Tech.; Abstr. Graphic Arts Tech. Found. (1984); Graph. Arts Bull. Inst. Pap. Sci. Technol. (Jan. 1989, March 1989-July 1989, Sept. 1989, Nov. 1989).

US
**PRINTING MANAGER.** English. bm. Free to members; $30.00 (nonmembers). National Association of Printers and Lithographers, 780 Palisade Avenue, Teaneck NJ 07666. **Tel** (201)342-0707, (800)642-6275.
**Ind/Abst** Abstr. Bull. Inst. Pap. Sci. Tech.

CN/0575-9412
**PRINTING, PUBLISHING AND ALLIED INDUSTRIES.** [Print. publ. allied ind.]. **Main/Corp** Canada. Statistique Canada. Division des Industries Manufacturieres et Primaires. **Added/Corp** Canada. Bureau Federal de la Statistique. Division de l'Industrie. Canada. Bureau Federal de la Statistique. Division des industries Manufacturieres et Primaires. Statistique Canada. Division des Industries Manufacturieres et Primaires. Statistique Canada. Section du Recensement des Manufactures. Statistique Canada. Division de l'Industrie. Statistique Canada. Section de l'Enquete Annuelle des Manufactures. **VFOAT** Imprimerie, Edition et Industries Connexes; Imprimerie, Edition et Activites Annexes. (1963)-. French (English). an. 38.00Can$ Canada; $46.00 US; $54.00 other. Statistics Canada, Publications Sales & Services, Main Building Room 1710, Ottawa Ontario K1A 0T6 Canada. **Tel** (613)951-5078, (800)267-6677, FAX (613)951-1584, telex 053-3585. **DD** 338.4/70705/0971. ***Formed by the union of*** *Commercial Printing Industries, 0527-4923; Engraving, Stereotyping and Allied Industries, 0527-5075; Printing and Publishing Industry, 0575-9404; Publishing Industry, 0383-4409* ***and*** *General Review of the Printing, Publishing and Allied Industries, 0383-4395.*

CN/1188-3030
**PRINTING SOURCE.** [Print. source]. **VFOAT** Canadian Printing Source. (1991)-. English. Wilcord Publications Limited, #110, 511 King Street West, Toronto Ontario M5V 2Z4 Canada. **DD** 741.6/02571.

UK
**PRINTING TRADES DIRECTORY.** (19??)-. English. an. £88.00. Benn Business Information Service Ltd, Riverbank House, Angel Lane, Tonbridge Kent TN9 1SE England. **Tel** 011 44 732 362666, FAX 011 44 732 770483, telex 95454 BBIS. **ED** Caroline Miles. **LC** Z327; .P73. **DD** 686.2/025/41. **Ad Acc. Circ:** 2,950.
**Desc:** Covers every aspect of the British printing industry. Suppliers of equipment, materials and services together with a buyers guide to their products and services.

UK/0032-8715
**PRINTING WORLD.** [Print. world]. Vol. 154, No. 1 (Jan. 1, 1954)-. Periodical. English. wk. £73.00 UK; £108.00 other. Benn Publications Ltd., Sovereign Way, Tonbridge TNQ 1RW England. **Tel** 011 44 732 364422, FAX 011 44 732 361534, telex 0732 95132 BENTON G. **ED** Roy Coxhead. **LC** Z119; .B83. **Bk Rev. Ad Acc. Circ:** 12,200 (ctrl). available on microfilm and microfiche from University Microfilms International (UMI). ***Continues*** *British & Colonial Printer;* ***Absorbed*** *Printing Today; Printing Trades Journal (London, England), 0032-8707.*
**Desc:** News weekly for the printing industry.
**Ind/Abst** Abstr. Bull. Inst. Pap. Sci. Tech.; Abstr. Graphic Arts Tech. Found. (1979, 1984); Curr. Technol. Index; Graph. Arts Bull. Inst. Pap. Sci. Technol. (Jan. 1989-Oct. 1989); Infomat Int. Bus.; Print. Abstr.; PROMT.

US/1046-8595
**PRINTINGNEWS. EAST.** [PrintingNews, East]. **VFOAT** East; Printing News; PrintingNews. Vol. 123, No. 15 (Oct. 7, 1989)-. Periodical. English. wk. $24.95 US; $30.95 Canada; $39.95 other. PTN Publishing Company, 445 Broad Hollow Road, Melville NY 11747. **Tel** (516)845-2700, FAX (516)845-7109. **LC** Z119; .P9562. **DD** 686.2. **[CCC].** ***Continues*** *Printing News, 0032-8626.*
**Ind/Abst** Abstr. Bull. Inst. Pap. Sci. Tech.

US/1048-6860
**PRINTINGNEWS. MIDWEST.** (PRINTINGNEWS. MIDWEST : THE MONTHLY NEWSPAPER OF GRAPHIC COMMUNICATIONS.). [Print.News, Midwest]. **VFOAT** Printing News Midwest; Printingnews. Vol. 56, No. 1 (Jan. 1990)-. Trade Publication. English. mo. $36.00 (one year), $56.00 (two year), $76.00 (three year) US; $56.00 (one year), $76.00 (two year), $96.00 (three year) Canada & Mexico; $80.00

other. Quoin Research, 800 West Huron Street, Suite 3N, Chicago IL 60622. **Tel** (312)226-5600, FAX (312)226-4640. **ED** Vicki Bolton Cessna. **DD** 686. **Ad Acc, Adv Mgr:** Steve Lovie. **Circ:** 20,000 (ctrl). Documents available from UMI Article Clearinghouse. ***Continues*** *P.V. Printing Views, 0030-8439.*
**Desc:** News magazine of the printing and graphic communications industries in Illinois, Indiana, Ohio, Michigan, Wisconsin and Iowa. Each issue contains regional news, economic forecasts, upcoming trade shows, services to the trade, awards and local organization events, and the largest classified section for the industry.
**Ind/Abst** ABI/INFORM Glob. Ed.; ABI Inform Ondisc; Abstr. Bull. Inst. Pap. Sci. Tech.

US
**PRINTING'S PC QUARTERLY.** **Added/Corp** National Association of Printers and Lithographers. Vol. 1, No. 1 (1984)-. Periodical. English. qt. National Association of Printers and Lithographers, 780 Palisade Avenue, Teaneck NJ 07666. **Tel** (201)342-0707, (800)642-6275.
**Ind/Abst** Abstr. Bull. Inst. Pap. Sci. Tech.

US/0738-6613
**PRINTOUT (NEWTONVILLE, MASS.).** (PRINTOUT.). (19??)-. Periodical. English. mo. $367.00 US and Canada; $417.00 other. BIS Strategic Decisions, 1 Longwater Circle, Norwell MA 02061. **Tel** (617)982-9500. **(Subscription address:** PO Box 5 0075, Woburn, MA 01815**)** **[CCC]**. Index available.
**Desc:** Survey of developments in the computer printer industry.
**Ind/Abst** Abstr. Bull. Inst. Pap. Sci. Tech.

US/0274-5097
**PRINTS (ALTON).** ***Suspended.*** (PRINTS.). [Prints]. Vol. 1 (Winter 1978/79)-Suspended. Periodical. English. bm. $20.00 US; $24.00 Canada and Mexico; $40.00 other. Art on Paper Inc, PO Box 1468, Alton IL 62002. **LC** NE1; .P768. **DD** 760/.5.

●UK/0967-2486
**PRINTWEAR & PROMOTION.** [Printwear promot.]. **VFOAT** Printwear and Promotion. (1992)-. Periodical. English. mo. Batiste Publishing Ltd, Pembroke House, Campsbourne Road, Hornsey, London N8 7PE England. **Tel** 011 44 81 340 3291. **DD** 338.476862316. ***Continues*** *Screenprint Wear, 0967-2494.*

UK
**PRINTWEEK.** (19??)-. English. wk (52 issues). £64.00 UK; £75.00 Eire & Europe; £136.00 America, Middle East, Africa & India; £165.00 Australia, New Zealand & Japan. Haymarket Publishing Ltd., 12 14 Ansdell Street, London W8 5TR England. **Tel** 011 44 483 733800, FAX 011 44 483 776573. **(Subscription address:** Haymarket Publishing Ltd, PO Box 219, Subscriptions Department, Woking Surrey GU21 1ZW, United Kingdom.**)** ***Continues*** *Lithoweek, 0264-732X.*

US/0734-2721
**PRINTWORLD DIRECTORY OF CONTEMPORARY PRINTS AND PRICES.** **See** The Arts-Graphic Arts.

UK
**PRIVATE PRESS BOOKS.** **See** Publishing-Books and Bookmaking.

US/0277-4119
**PRODUCTION EMPLOYEES COST SURVEY.** **See** Economics-Labor.

UK/0308-4205
**PROFESSIONAL PRINTER.** [Prof. print.]. **Added/Corp** Institute of Printing. Vol. 17, (Jan. 1973)-. Periodical. English. bm. £14.00 UK; £20.00 other. Institute of Printing, 8 Lonsdale Gardens, Tunbridge Wells Kent TN1 1NU England. **Tel** 011 44 892 538118. **ED** Dennis Griffiths. **LC** Z120; .A8. **DD** 686.2/05. Index available. **Bk Rev. Ad Acc. Circ:** 3,000 (ctrl). available on microfilm and microfiche from University Microfilms International (UMI). ***Continues*** *Printing Technology.*
**Desc:** Journal of the Institute of Printing for members and subscribers. Published six times per year, alternate months from January.
**Ind/Abst** Abstr. Bull. Inst. Pap. Sci. Tech.; Abstr. Graphic Arts Tech. Found. (1979, 1984); Curr. Technol. Index; Graph. Arts Bull. Inst. Pap. Sci. Technol. (Jan. 1989, April 1989-May 1989, Sept. 1989-Oct. 1989, Dec. 1989); Libr. Inf. Sci. Abstr.; Print. Abstr.

US/0739-6732
**QUALITY CONTROL SCANNER, THE.** [Qual. control scanner]. **VFOAT** QCS. Vol. 1 (Oct. 1981)-. Periodical. English. mo. $100.00 (one year) $175.00 (two year), $250.00 (three year) US, Canada, and Mexico except individuals, schools, colleges and research oragnizations; $65.00 (one year) individuals, schools, colleges, and research organizations; $115.00 (one year), $205.00 (two year) $295.00 (three year) other. Graphic Arts Publishing Company, 3100 Bronson Hill Road, Livonia NY 14487. **Tel** (716)346-2276, FAX (716)346-2276. **ED** Miles and Donna Southworth. **LC** Z119; .Q34. **DD** 686.2/05. Index Available in first issue of next volume--attached. **Circ:** 600.
**Desc:** Practical ideas for improving quality and productivity.
**Ind/Abst** Graph. Arts Bull. Inst. Pap. Sci. Technol. (Feb.-April 1990); Print. Abstr.

US
**QUARTERLY PRINTING INDUSTRY BUSINESS INDICATOR REPORT.** ***Title Change.*** **Added/Corp** National Association of Printers and Lithographers. (19??)-(1992). Periodical. English. qt. National Association of Printers and Lithographers, 780 Palisade Avenue, Teaneck NJ 07666. **Tel** (201)342-0707, (800)642-6275. ***Continued by*** *Printing Business Report.*
**Ind/Abst** Abstr. Bull. Inst. Pap. Sci. Tech.; Graph. Arts Bull. Inst. Pap. Sci. Technol. (Jan. 1989).

US/0191-4588
**QUICK PRINTING.** (1977)-. Periodical. English. Fourteen times a year (except semimonthly in Jan.). $30.00 US; $110.00 others. Coast Publishing Inc, 1680 Southwest Bayshore Boulevard, Port St Lucie FL 34984. **Tel** (407)879-6666, FAX (407)879-7388. **ED** Bob Hall. **[CCC]. Bk Rev. Ad Acc. Circ:** 53,000 (ctrl).
**Desc:** The information source for commercial copyshops and printshops.
**Ind/Abst** Abstr. Bull. Inst. Pap. Sci. Tech.; Abstr. Graphic Arts Tech. Found. (1984); Graph. Arts Bull. Inst. Pap. Sci. Technol. (Jan. 1989-April 1989, July 1989-Nov. 1989).

IT
**RASSEGNA GRAFICA.** Arti Poligrafiche Europee SAS, Via Casella 16, 20156 Milan Italy. **Tel** 011 39 02 330221, FAX 011 39 02 394341, telex 326544 ANTO I. **ED** Antonio Ghiorzo. **Ad Acc. Circ:** 13,000 (ctrl).
**Desc:** Printing industry and graphic arts field.

●US/1064-7120
**READY, SET, GO! IN-DEPTH (1992).** (READY, SET, GO! IN-DEPTH : THE JOURNAL FOR INVOLVED USERS OF READY, SET, GO! AND DESIGNSTUDIO.). [Ready Set Go! in-depth]. **VFOAT** Ready, Set, Go! In Depth; In-Depth; In Depth. Vol. 3, No. 6 (1992)-. Periodical. English. mo. MindCraft Publishing Corporation, PO Box 256, Lincoln MA 01773-0256. **DD** 686. ***Continues*** *Ready, Set, Go! DesignStudio In-Depth, 1055-7741.*

US/0428-5670
**REPORT OF THE PROCEEDINGS : ANNUAL MEETING AND TECHNICAL FORUM.** **Main/Corp** Flexographic Technical Association. 1st- 1959-. Proceedings. English. an. Flexographic Technical Association, 900 Marconi Avenue, Ronkonkoma NY 11779. **Tel** (516)737-6023, FAX (516)737-6813. **LC** Z252.5.F6; F55A. **DD** 686.2/31.

UK/0034-4958
**REPRODUCTION.** Vol. 1, No. 1 (Jan. 1964)-. Periodical. English. Twelve times a year. £50.00 Europe; £85.00 others. Maclean Hunter Ltd. / UK, Chalk Lane Cockfosters Road, Barnet Herts EN4 0BU England. **Tel** 011 44 81 2423000, FAX 011 44 81 9759753, telex 299072. **ED** Charles Walker. **Bk Rev. Ad Acc. Circ:** 16,000 (ctrl). ***Absorbed*** *Small Offset User; Repro: The Journal of the Institute of Reprographic Technology.*
**Desc:** The only magazine in UK which deals expertly with inplant reprographics and the whole spectrum of the reproduction market.
**Ind/Abst** Curr. Technol. Index; Print. Abstr.; World Surf. Coat. Abstr.

US/1069-1510
**REPROGRAPHICS & DESIGN IMAGING.** ***Ceased.*** [Reprogr. des. imaging]. **Added/Corp** International Reprographic Association. **VFOAT** Reprographics and Design Imaging. Vol. 66, No. 1 (Jan. 1993)-(April 1993). Periodical. English. mo. International Reprographic Association, 434 W Downer, Aurora IL 60506. **Tel** (708)571-4685. **LC** TR921.A1; I6. **DD** 621. ***Continues*** *Plan and Print, 0032-0595.*
**Ind/Abst** Abstr. Bull. Inst. Pap. Sci. Tech.

UK/0306-2880
**REPROGRAPHICS QUARTERLY.** ***Title Change.*** [Reprogr. q.]. V. 7- Winter 1973/74-. Periodical. English (summaries and/or abstracts in French and German). qt. National Reprographic Centre for Documentation, The Hatfield Polytechnic, Endymion Road Annex, Herts AL10 8 England. **LC** Z48; .N3. **DD** 686.4/3/05. **CODEN** RPGQAW. Documents available from Ask*IEEE. ***Continues*** *NRCD Bulletin.* ***Continued by*** *Information Media & Technology.*
**Ind/Abst** Consum. Index Prod. Eval. Inf. Source; INSPEC (Spring 1974-); Libr. Inf. Sci. Abstr.; Print. Abstr.

US
**SCREEN PRINTING.** [Screen print.]. (1984)-. Trade Publication. English. mo (except two issues in July). $39.00 US; $58.00 Canada; $60.00 other. Signs of the Times Publishing Company, 407 Gilbert Avenue, Cincinnati OH 45202. **Tel** (513)421-2050, (800)925-1110, FAX (513)421-5144. **ED** Susan Venell. **LC** TT273; .S33. **DD** 686.2/316/05. Index available. **Bk Rev. Ad Acc. Circ:** 15,000. available on microfiche. ***Continues*** *Screen Printing Technology and Management.*
**Desc:** Technical trade journal dealing with the products and process and screen printing.
**Ind/Abst** Abstr. Bull. Inst. Pap. Sci. Tech.; Abstr. Graphic Arts Tech. Found. (1984); Graph. Arts Bull. Inst. Pap. Sci. Technol. (Jan. 1989-Feb. 1989, May 1989, July 1989-Sept. 1989, Nov. 1989-Dec. 1989); Imaging Abstr.; Print. Abstr.

US/0362-160X
**SCREEN PRINTING TECHNIQUES.** (19??)-. English. ir. $21.00. Signs of the Times Publishing Company, 407 Gilbert Avenue, Cincinnati OH 45202. **Tel** (513)421-2050, (800)925-1110, FAX (513)421-5144. **ED** Tamas S. Frecska. **LC** TT273; .K659. **DD** 686.2/316. **Bk Rev. Ad Acc. Circ:** 12,000. ***Supersedes*** *Screen Process Printing.*
**Desc:** Technical magazine for the screen printing industry, dealing with the process and products used in its application.

UK/0487-9775
**SCREEN PROCESS PRINTING.** (1951)-. English. an. **ED** F. W. Mackenzie and P. Mytton-Davies. **LC** TT273; .S35. **DD** 745.7; 655.3.

UK
**SCREENPRINTING.** English. Batiste Publications Ltd, Pembroke House, Campsbourne Road, Hornsey London N8 7PE England. **Tel** 011 44 81 3403291, FAX 011 44 81 3414840, telex 267727.

IT
**SERIGRAFIA (MILANO, ITALY).** (SERIGRAFIA.). Began in 1956. Periodical. Italian. bm. L25000 Italy; L60000 other. Via Kolbe 8, 20137 Milan Italy. **Tel** 02/76110075, FAX 02/7387371. **ED** Ruggero Zuliani. **LC** TT273; .S47. **DD** 686.2/316. **Bk Rev. Ad Acc. Circ:** 2,500.
**Desc:** A magazine for the screen printing field.

GW/0178-2835
**SIEBDRUCK, DER.** [Siebdruck]. (19??)-. Periodical. German. Twelve times a year. DM69.00 Germany; DM96.00 other. Graphische Werkstaetten, Schwertfegerstr 7, W 2400 Luebeck 7 F R Germany. **Tel** 49 451 87999. **UDC** 655.332. ***Absorbed*** *Sieb + Rakel, 0342-7013.*
**Ind/Abst** Biodeter. Abstr.

US/1068-1957
**SIGNATURE (PRAIRIE VILLAGE, KAN.).** ***Ceased.*** (SIGNATURE : FOR MAGAZINE AND CATALOG PRODUCTION MANAGEMENT.). [Signature]. Vol. 9, No. 1 (Jan./Feb. 1993)-(May 1994). Catalog. English. Nine times a year. Signature, 8340 Mission Road, Suite 106, Prairie Village KE 66206. **Tel** (913)642-6611. **ED** Maureen Waters. **DD** 686. **Ad Acc.** ctrl circ. ***Continues*** *Magazine Design & Production, 0882-049X.*
**Ind/Abst** Abstr. Bull. Inst. Pap. Sci. Tech.

US/0000-0485
**SMALL PRESS.** [Small press]. Vol. 1, No. 1 (Sept./Oct. 1983)-. Periodical. English. Four times a year. $29.00 US; $39.00 Canada, Mexico and South America; $44.00 other. Moyer Bell Limited, Kymbolde Way, Wakefield RI 02879. **Tel** (401)789-0074, FAX (401)789-3793. **ED** Evie Righter. **LC** Z231.5.L5; S58. **DD** 070.5. **Bk Rev**, (Qty: 640). **Ad Acc, Adv Mgr:** Lisa Phelps. **Circ:** 15,000. available on microfilm and microfiche from University Microfilms International (UMI).
**Desc:** Reviews of independently published works, plus important articles and interviews dealing with all facets of the independent publishing process.
**Ind/Abst** Book Rev. Digest; Book Rev. Index (1988-); Graph. Arts Bull. Inst. Pap. Sci. Technol. (Oct. 1989, Dec. 1989); Libr. Lit.

SI/0129-1262
**SOUTH EAST ASIAN PRINTER MAGAZINE.** [South east asian print. mag.]. (1988)-. Periodical. English. bm (6 issues). 30.00Sing$ Singapore; 50.00Mal$ Malaysia; 200.00HK$ Hong Kong; $20.00 Philippines, Indonesia & Thailand; $30.00 Asia; £30.00 Europe; $50.00 US; 60.00Aus$ Australasia. Calmor & Associates Pty Ltd, PO Box 1316, North Sydney NSW 2059 Australia. **Tel** 011 61 2 9226133, FAX 011 61 2 9224734. **ED** Peter Loh. **DD** 338.4768620959. **Ad Acc, Adv Mgr:** C. Chong, **Tel** 299-8577. **Circ:** 15,249 (ctrl).

CN/1185-8834
**SPANZINE (VANCOUVER).** (SPANZINE : THE NEWSLETTER OF THE SMALL PRESS ACTION NETWORK.). [SPANzine]. **Added/Corp** Small Press Action Network. No. 1 (Sept. 1991)-. Newsletter. English. qt. Free to members. Small Press Action Network, PO Box 24953, Station C, Vancouver British Columbia V5T 4G3 Canada. **DD** 070.5.

US
**SWOP HI LO INK REFERENCE.** (19??)-. English. $52.00. International Prepress Association, 552 West 167th Street, South Holland IL 60473. **Tel** (708)596-5110, FAX (708)596-5112.

US/0279-053X
**TABLOID (FAIRFAX, VA.), THE.** (THE TABLOID / SCREEN PRINTING ASSOCIATION INTERNATIONAL.). [Tabloid]. **Added/Corp** Screen Printing Association International. (19??)-. Periodical. English. mo. $10.00. Screen Printing Association International, 10015 Main Street, Fairfax VA 22031. **Tel** (703)285-1335, FAX (703)273-0456. **ED** Bruce H Joffe.

**Bk Rev. Circ:** 3,500 (ctrl).
**Desc:** Membership newsletter about the screen printing industry for members of the Screen Printing Association Int.
**Ind/Abst** Abstr. Bull. Inst. Pap. Sci. Tech.

US/1043-2302
**TEXAS PRINTER.** [Tex. print.]. 1989-. Periodical. English. qt. Free. Printing Industry, 120 St Louis, PO Box 1868, Ft Worth TX 76101. **Tel** (214)630-8871. **(Subscription address:** 910 W Mockingbird, Dallas, TX 75247**) ED** Nolan Moore. **DD** 681. **Bk Rev. Ad Acc. Circ:** 4,000.
**Desc:** Serves 4,000 Texas printers.

US
**TGC TYPEFACE DIRECTORY. Main/Corp** Typographics Communications, Inc. **VFOAT** Typeface Directory. (19??)-. Directory. English. Typographers Association of New York Inc, 461 Eighth Avenue, New York NY 10001.

IT/0391-2159
**TRIBUNA STAMPA.** [Trib. stamp.]. (1966)-. Periodical. Italian. mo. L30000 Italy; L60000 other. Tribuna Stampa Soc Coop Arl, Via Egadi 3-5, 20144 Milan Italy. **Tel** 011 39 2 48000648. **UDC** 655.

US/0194-4851
**TYPE WORLD.** ***Title Change.*** [TypeWorld]. Vol. 1 (1977)-(19??). Periodical. English. Two issues per month. PennWell Publishing Company, 1421 South Sheridan, PO Box 1260, Tulsa OK 74101. **Tel** (918)835-3161, (800)331-4463, FAX (918)831-9497. **DD** 070. available on microfilm and microfiche from University Microfilms International (UMI). ***Continued by*** *Electronic Publishing.*
**Desc:** Focuses on typesetting and electronic publishing systems for both commercial and corporate markets.
**Ind/Abst** Graph. Arts Bull. Inst. Pap. Sci. Technol. (April-May 1989); Pollut. Abstr. Indexes; Print. Abstr.

SZ
**TYPOGRAFISCHE MONATSBLATTER. Added/Corp** Schweizerischer Typografenbund zur Forderung der Berufsbildung. Gewerkschaft Druck und Papier zur Forderung der Berufsbildung (Switzerland). **VFOAT** Schweizer Grafische Mitteilungen; Revue Suisse de l'Imprimerie; TM; TM/SGM; RSI. (19??)-. Periodical. English (French and German). bm. 105.00F (SZ); 135.00F (other). Zollikofer AG, Fuerstenlandstr 122, CH-9001 St. Gallen Switzerland. **Tel** 011 41 71 297777, FAX 011 41 71 257487, telex 77537. **Bk Rev. Ad Acc. Circ:** 4,000. ***Continues*** *Typographische Monatsblatter.*
**Ind/Abst** Print. Abstr.

UK/0143-7623
**TYPOGRAPHIC SOCIETY OF TYPOGRAPHIC DESIGNERS.** [Typographic Soc. Typogr. Des.]. (1972)-. Periodical. English. Three times a year. £40.00. Society of Typographic Designers, Chapelfield Cottage / Randwick, Stroud, Gloucestershire GL6 6HS England. **Tel** 011 44 453 759311, FAX 011 44 453 759311. **DD** _a686.22. Index available. cum. index. **Circ:** 1,000 (ctrl).
**Desc:** Contains articles on typography, printing and other related topics.

UK
**TYPOGRAPHIC : THE JOURNAL OF THE SOCIETY OF TYPOGRAPHIC DESIGNERS.** English. Three times a year. £40.00. Society of Typographic Designers, Chapelfield Cottage / Randwick, Stroud, Gloucestershire GL6 6HS England. **Tel** 011 44 453 759311, FAX 011 44 453 759311. **Bk Rev. Ad Acc. Circ:** 800 (ctrl).

US/0275-6870
**TYPOGRAPHY (NEW YORK, N.Y.).** (TYPOGRAPHY : THE ANNUAL OF THE TYPE DIRECTORS CLUB.). [Typography]. **Added/Corp** Type Directors Club (U.S.). (1980)-. English. an. $57.50. Watson Guptill Publications, PO Box 2014, Lakewood NJ 08701. **Tel** (800)451-1741, (908)363-5679. **(Subscription address:** RC Publications, 3200 Tower Oaks Boulevard, Rockville MD 20852-9789.**) LC** Z243.A2; T9a. **DD** 686.2/24.

US/0362-6245
**U & LC.** [U lc]. **Added/Corp** International Typeface Corporation. **VAT** Upper and Lower Case. (1974)-. Periodical. English. qt. $6.00. International Typeface Corporation, 2 Hammarskjold Plaza, New York NY 10017. **Tel** (212)371-0699. **LC** Z119; .U14. **DD** 686.2/05. **CODEN** ULCCDC. available on microfilm and microfiche from University Microfilms International (UMI).
**Ind/Abst** Abstr. Bull. Inst. Pap. Sci. Tech.; Abstr. Graphic Arts Tech. Found. (1984); ARTbibliogr. Mod.; Print. Abstr.

SZ/1019-4754
**UGRA MITTEILUNGEN.** [UGRA Mitt.]. **VFOAT** Verein zur Forderung Wissenschaftlicher Untersuchungen in der Graphischen Industrie Mitteilungen. (1963)-. Periodical. Multiple languages. tq. Forschungsstelle der UGRA EMPA, Postfach 977, Unterstrasse 11, CH 9001 St Gallen Switzerland. **Tel** 41 71 300434. **UDC** 686.
**Ind/Abst** Abstr. Bull. Inst. Pap. Sci. Tech.

•US/1064-6868
**V.P.I.'S IMPRINTABLES TODAY.** [V.P.I.'s impr. today]. **Added/Corp** Virgo Publishing, Inc. **VFOAT** Imprintables Today; V.P.I.'s Imprintable Today. (July 20, 1992)-. Periodical. English. Twenty-six times a year. $65.00 US; $100.00 Canada; $192.00 other. Virgo Publishing Inc., 4141 North Scottsdale Road, Suite 316, Scottsdale AZ 85251. **Tel** (602)483-0014, (602)990-1101, FAX (602)990-0819. **DD** 384. ***Continues*** *Screen Printing Today, 1063-5521.*

NE/0042-3904
**VERFKRONIEK.** [Verfkroniek]. **Added/Corp** Vereniging van Verf en Drukinktfabrikanten (Netherlands). **VFOAT** Verf Kroniek. Academic Scholarly Publication. Dutch. mo. Verfkroniek, Groot Haesebroekseweg 1 POB 71, 2240 AB Wassenaar Netherlands. **CODEN** VERFAL. Documents available from CASDDS.
**Ind/Abst** Chem. Abstr.; EMBASE; Print. Abstr.; Saf. Health Work.

US/0022-2224
**VISIBLE LANGUAGE.** [Visible lang.]. Vol. 5, (Winter 1971)-. Periodical. English. Four times a year (Jan., Apr., July, Oct.). $30.00 (individuals); $55.00 (institutions). Visible Language Rhode Island School, Des Grph Design, Department 2 Coll Street, Providence RI 02903. **Tel** (401)454-6171. **(Subscription address:** Rhode Island School of Design, Graphic Design Department, 2 College Street, Providence, RI 02903**) ED** Sharon Poggenpohl (phone: (312)285-1205). **LC** Z119; .J88. **DD** 001.5/52/05. **CODEN** VSLGAO. **[CCC].** Index available (Bound in 4th iss. (Free)). cum. index. **Bk Rev**, (Qty: 4-6). **Ad Acc, Adv Mgr:** Carrie Harris, **Tel** (401)454-6171. **Pr Rev. Circ:** 1,200. available on microfilm and microfiche from University Microfilms International (UMI). Documents available from The Genuine Article, Ask*IEEE. ***Continues*** *Journal of Typographic Research.*
**Desc:** Research and ideas that help to define the unique role and properties of written language. Articles published that deal with typography and type design, linguistics, information design, diagrams, bi-lingualism, anthropological investigation of scripts, the inter-relationships between reading and writing.
**Ind/Abst** Abstr. Graphic Arts Tech. Found.; Abstr. Engl. Stud.; Art Index; ARTbibliogr. Mod.; ARTbibliogr. Curr. Titles; Arts Humanit. Citation Index [Full Cov.]; BHA : Biblio. Hist. Art; Curr. Contents Arts Humanit.; Curr. Index J. Educ.; Electron. Pub. Abstr.; Ergon. Abstr.; INSPEC (Autumn 1971-); Lang. Lang. Behav. Abstr.; Math. Rev.; MLA Int. Bibl. Books Artic. Mod. Lang. Lit.; Print. Abstr.; Res. Alert [Full Cov.]; Romant. Move.; Soc. Plann. Policy Dev. Abstr.; World Publ. Monit.

US/0507-1658
**VISUAL COMMUNICATIONS JOURNAL. Added/Corp** International Graphic Arts Education Association. Vol. 1 (1965)-. Periodical. English. an. $7.50. International Graphic Arts Education Association Inc, 4615 Forbes Avenue, Pittsburgh PA 15213. **Tel** (412)682-5170. **LC** Z122; .V57. **DD** 686.2/2. ctrl circ.
**Desc:** Professional journal articles of interest to graphic arts/printing teachers and others interested in graphic arts education.

CN/0715-4720
**WAYZGOOSE.** (WAYZGOOSE ANTHOLOGY.). '81-. English. an. 60.00Can$. Wayzgoose, c/o Grimsby Public Art Gallery, 25 Adelaide Street, Grimsby Ontario L3M 1X2 Canada. **Tel** (416)945-3246. **DD** 686.2. **Circ:** 135 (ctrl).
**Desc:** A collection of signatures representing the scope of private press printers talents and includes a portfolio of limited edition prints.

US/1057-803X
**WHO'S PRINTING WHAT (DIRECTORY).** (WHO'S PRINTING WHAT : THE GUIDE TO NORTH AMERICAN PUBLICATION PRINTERS AND THEIR CLIENTS.). [Who's print. what]. (1991)-. English. $195.00. Oxbridge Communications Inc., 150 5th Avenue, Room 302, New York NY 10011. **Tel** (212)741-0231, FAX (212)633-2938. **DD** 686.

US/1056-6376
**WHO'S PRINTING WHAT? (NEWSLETTER).** (WHO'S PRINTING WHAT?.). [Who's print. what?]. Vol. 1, No. 1 (May 1991)-. Periodical. English. mo. $195.00. Oxbridge Communications Inc., 150 5th Avenue, Room 302, New York NY 10011. **Tel** (212)741-0231, FAX (212)633-2938. **DD** 686.

GW/0147-4804
**WORLD-WIDE PRINTER.** [World-wide print.]. **VAT** Worldwide Printer. (197?)-. Trade Publication. English (Spanish; table of contents in Spanish, Arabic, French, Japanese, Italian, Russian and German). bm. DM72.00 (one year), DM130.00 (two year), DM180.00 (three year). Deutscher Drucker Verlag International, Postfach 4124/Senefelderstr 12, D 73744 Ostfildern 1 Germany. **Tel** 011 49 711 448170, FAX 011 49 711 415299, telex 841 177111490. **LC** Z119; .W67. **DD** 686.2/05. **Ad Acc. Circ:** 22,000. ***Absorbed*** *Arte Tipografico.*
**Desc:** For the printing and graphic communications industries. Published in association with the Spanish language edition El Arte Tipografico.
**Ind/Abst** Abstr. Graphic Arts Tech. Found. (1984); Graph. Arts Bull. Inst. Pap. Sci. Technol. (July 1989); Print. Abstr.

US/0897-5256
**WRIGHT/CHAMBERS REPORT, THE.** [Wright/Chambers rep.]. Vol. 1, No. 1 (Jan. 1988)-. Periodical. English. Ten times a year. $150.00. The Wright/Chambers Group, PO Box 861, West Branch IA 52358. **Tel** (319)643-5737. **DD** 686.

## ABSTRACTING, BIBLIOGRAPHIES AND STATISTICS

US
**ABSTRACTS (GRAPHIC ARTS TECHNICAL FOUNDATION). VFOAT** Graphic Arts Abstracts. (198?)-. Abstracting/Indexing Service. English. mo. $90.00 (one year), $160.00 (two year) US; $95.00 (one year), $170.00 (two year) Canada; $105.00 (one year), $190.00 (two year) other. Graphic Arts Technical Foundation Inc, 4615 Forbes Avenue, Pittsburgh PA 15213. **Tel** (412)621-6941, FAX (412)621-3049, telex 9103509221. **LC** Z119; .G84. **DD** 686.2/05. ***Continues*** *Graphic Arts Abstracts (Pittsburgh, PA. : 1968).*

BE
**GULDEN PASSER, DE. Added/Corp** Vereeniging der Antwerpsche Bibliophielen, Antwerp. Vol. 1 (1923)-. Academic Scholarly Publication. Multiple languages (Dutch and French). an. 800F. Vereeniging der Antwerpsche Bibliophielen, Vrijdagmarkt 22, Museum Plantin-Moretus, Antwerpen B 2000 Belgium. **Tel** 03 233 02 94, FAX 03 226 25 16. **LC** Z1007; .G93. **DD** 010.5. cum. index. **Bk Rev**, (Qty: 1). ctrl circ.
**Desc:** Publication for the study of Western printing history.
**Ind/Abst** BHA : Biblio. Hist. Art.

SP
**LIBROS MEJOR EDITADOS, ESPANA.** 1983-. Spanish. **LC** Z173; .L5. **DD** 686.2/0946.

UK/0031-109X
**PRINTING ABSTRACTS.** [Print. abstr.]. **Added/Corp** Printing, Packaging & Allied Trades Research Association (Great Britain) PATRA Library. Printing, Packaging & Allied Trades Research Association (Great Britain). Printing Division. Pira (Association). (1946)-. Abstracting/Indexing Service. English. mo. £671.00, $1,105.20. Pira International, Randalls Road, Leatherhead, Surrey KT22 7RU England. **Tel** 011 44 372 376161, FAX 011 44 372 377526. **ED** Kathy Young (editor's address: PIRA, The Research Association for the Paper and Board, Printing, and Packaging Industries, Randalls Road, Leatherhead Surrey KT22 7RU UK). **LC** Z118.A3; P7. **DD** 686.2/05. **[CCC]. Bk Rev. Pr Rev.** available on CD-ROM; available on microfilm and microfiche from University Microfilms International (UMI); available on an online database. Documents available.
**Desc:** Contains summaries of publications and documents issued throughout the world relating to all aspects of printing including commercial information.
**Ind/Abst** Abstr. Bull. Inst. Pap. Sci. Tech. (19??-); World Surf. Coat. Abstr. (19??-); World Text. Abstr. (19??-).

# PSYCHOLOGY

FR/0296-9955
**ABSTRACT NEURO ET PSY PARIS. See** Medical Science and Technology-Neurology.

US/0733-2599
**ABSTRACTS OF RESEARCH IN PASTORAL CARE AND COUNSELING. See** Religion and Theology-Abstracting, Bibliographies and Statistics.

US/0737-5166
**ACTA PAEDOLOGICA.** [Acta paedolog.]. **Added/Corp** Eterna International (Organization). Vol. 1, No. 1 (Jan. 1984)-. Periodical. English. qt. $35.00 individuals, $50.00 institutions. Eterna Press, PO Box 157941, Chicago IL 60615. **Tel** (312)969-0318. **DD** 155. **NLM** W1; AC905P.
**Ind/Abst** PsycINFO.

AG/0001-6896
**ACTA PSIQUIATRICA Y PSICOLOGICA DE AMERICA LATINA. See** Medical Science and Technology-Psychiatry.

NE/0001-6918
**ACTA PSYCHOLOGICA.** [Acta psychol.]. Vol. 1, No. 1 (1935)-. Academic Scholarly Publication. English (French and German). Nine times a year (3 volumes). Fl831.00. Elsevier Science Publishers BV, PO Box 211,

1000 AE Amsterdam Netherlands. **Tel** 011 31 20 5803642, FAX 011 31 20 5862696, telex 15682. **ED** G A M Kempen, P J G Keuss, J G W Raaymakers, A F Sanders, C A J Vlek, and Ch M M de Weert. **LC** BF1; .A12. **DD** 150.5; 159.905. **NLM** W1 AC933. **CODEN** APSOAZ. **[CCC]. Pr Rev.** available on microfilm and microfiche from University Microfilms International (UMI). Documents available from The Genuine Article.
**Desc:** Represents a long and outstanding history of written communication in psychology. An important feature of the journal has always been its international character, guaranteed by an international editorial board.
**Ind/Abst** Appl. Soc. Sci. Index Abstr.; Curr. Contents Soc. Behav. Sci.; Ergon. Abstr.; Health Plan. Adminis.; HILITES; Index Med.; Int. Aerosp. Abstr.; Linguist. Lang. Behav. Abstr.; Middle East Abstr. Index; Life Sci. Collect.; Psychol. Abstr. (1950-); PsycINFO; PsycLit; Res. Alert [Full Cov.]; Res. High. Educ. Abstr.; Risk Abstr. (19??-19??); Soc. Plann. Policy Dev. Abstr.; Soc. Sci. Cit. Index [Full Cov.]; Sociol. Abstr.

●US/1059-7123
**ADAPTIVE BEHAVIOR.** [Adapt. behav.]. Vol. 1, No. 1 (Summer 1992)-. Periodical. English. qt (4 issues). $50.00 (individuals), $135.00 (institutions). Massachusetts Institute of Technology (MIT) Press, 55 Hayward Street, Cambridge MA 02142-1399. **Tel** (617)253-2889, (617)625-8481, FAX (617)258-6779. **ED** Jean-Arcady Meyer. **LC** QL750; .A36. **DD** 591.51/05. **CODEN** ADBEEA. **[CCC]. Ad Acc. Pr Rev.**
**Desc:** Provides the first international forum for research on adaptive behavior in animals and autonomous, artificial systems. Offering ethologists, psychologists, computer scientists, and robotic scientists the chance to compare insights.
**Ind/Abst** ACM Guide Comput. Lit.; Comput. Rev.; Ergon. Abstr.

US
**ADHD NEWSLETTER.** English. qt. $18.00. Gordon Systems, Inc., PO Box 746, De Witt NY 13214. **Tel** (315)446-4849, FAX (315)446-2012. **ED** Michael Gordon, Ph.D. **Bk Rev. Circ:** 1,000. ***Continues*** *Hyperactivity Newsletter.*
**Desc:** For professionals involved in ADHD/hyperactivity research - includes current issues, etc.

●US
**ADOLESCENCE MAGAZINE. See** Drug Abuse and Alcoholism.

FR/0751-7696
**ADOLESCENCE (PARIS, FRANCE).** (ADOLESCENCE.). Vol. 1, No. 1 (Spring 1983)-. Periodical. French. sa (Spring & Fall). 220.00F France; 280.00F other. GREUPP, Centre Censier, 13 rue de Santeuil, 75231 Paris Cedex 05 France. **Tel** 011 33 1 45874114. **ED** Philippe Gutton. **NLM** W1; AD37C.
**Desc:** Information on adolescent psychology.

US/1042-7589
**ADOLESCENT COUNSELOR.** ***Title Change.*** [Adolesc. couns.]. **VFOAT** Adolescent Counselor Magazine. Began in 1988-Vol. 5, No. 2 (July 1992). Periodical. English. bm. Adolescent Counselor, PO Box 2079, Redmond VA 98073. **Tel** (206)867-5024. **DD** 155. **NLM** W1; AD37EG. ***Continued by*** *Adolescence Magazine.*
**Desc:** Educates those who work with kids about alcohol, drugs and other addictions.

IT/1120-3714
**ADOLESCENZA. See** Children and Youth Interests.

US/0891-9879
**ADVANCES IN ADOLESCENT MENTAL HEALTH.** [Adv. adolesc. mental health]. Vol. 1 (1986)-. English. ir. price varies per volume. Jessica Kingsley Publishers, 118 Pentonville Road, London N1 9JN England. **Tel** 011 44 71 833 2307, FAX 011 44 71 837 2917. **LC** RJ499.A1; A3. **DD** 616/89/022. **NLM** W1; AD43E.

UK/0271-9738
**ADVANCES IN ANALYSIS OF BEHAVIOUR.** [Adv. anal. behav.]. **VFOAT** Wiley Series on Advances in Analysis of Behaviour. Vol. 1-. Monographic series. English. ir. Price varies per volume. John Wiley & Sons Ltd., Baffins Lane, Chichester West Sussex PO19 1UD England. **Tel** 0243 779777, FAX 0243 776128 BTG:JWP001, telex 86290 WIBOOKG. **(Subscription address:** North, South and Central America/ John Wiley & Sons, Inc., Subscription Department, 605 Third Avenue, New York, NY 10158-0012, USA; telephone: (212)850-6645; FAX: (212)850-6021**) ED** P Harzem and Michael D Zeiler. **DD** 150. **NLM** W1 AD432M.

US/0883-3656
**ADVANCES IN APPLIED SOCIAL PSYCHOLOGY.** [Adv. appl. soc. psychol.]. Vol. 1 (1980)-. English. ir. $36.00. Lawrence Erlbaum Associates, 365 Broadway, Suite 102, Hillsdale NJ 07642. **Tel** (201)666-4110, (800)926-6579, FAX (201)666-2394. **LC** HM251; .A33. **DD** 302.

US/0893-6110
**ADVANCES IN BEHAVIORAL ASSESSMENT OF CHILDREN AND FAMILIES.** [Adv. behav. assess. child. fam.]. Vol. 2 (1986)-. Monographic series. English. an. Jessica Kingsley Publishers, 118 Pentonville Road, London N1 9JN England. **Tel** 011 44 71 833 2307, FAX 011 44 71 837 2917. **(Subscription address:** Taylor & Francis Inc., 1900 Frost Road, Suite 101, Bristol PA 19007-1598.**) LC** BF721; .A47. **DD** 155.4. **NLM** W1; AD879TH. **CODEN** ABAFES. **[CCC].** Documents available from BIOSIS Document Express. ***Continues*** *Advances in Behavioral Measurement of Children.*
**Ind/Abst** Biol. Abstr. (1986-).

US/0099-6246
**ADVANCES IN BEHAVIORAL BIOLOGY. See** Biology.

US/0885-0836
**ADVANCES IN BEHAVIORAL MEDICINE.** [Adv. behav. med.]. Vol. 1 (1985)-. Periodical. English. an. $38.00 (latest volume). Jessica Kingsley Publishers, 118 Pentonville Road, London N1 9JN England. **Tel** 011 44 71 833 2307, FAX 011 44 71 837 2917. **LC** R726.5; .A38. **DD** 616/.001/9. **NLM** W1; AD436EH. **[CCC].**

US/0147-071X
**ADVANCES IN BEHAVIORAL PHARMACOLOGY.** ***Ceased.*** [Adv. behav. pharmacol.]. **VFOAT** Developmental Behavioral Pharmacology. Vol. 1 (1977)-(1994). Monographic series. English. ir. Lawrence Erlbaum Associates, 365 Broadway, Suite 102, Hillsdale NJ 07642. **Tel** (201)666-4110, (800)926-6579, FAX (201)666-2394. **ED** Krasnegor. **LC** RC483; .A28. **DD** 615/.78/05. **NLM** W1 AD436G. **CODEN** ABPHD6. Documents available from CASDDS.
**Ind/Abst** Chem. Abstr. (?-?); Life Sci. Collect. (?-?).

UK/0146-6402
**ADVANCES IN BEHAVIOUR RESEARCH AND THERAPY.** [Adv. behav. res. therapy]. Vol. 1 (1977)-. Periodical. English. qt. $336.00 The Americas; £225.00 other. Pergamon Press, An Imprint of Elsevier Science Ltd., The Boulevard, Langford Lane, Kidlington, Oxford OX5 1GB United Kingdom. **Tel** 011 44 865 843000, 011 44 865 843699, FAX 011 44 865 843010. **(Subscription address:** Elsevier Science Ltd. Oxford Fulfillment Centre, PO Box 800, Kidlington, Oxford OX5 1DX United Kingdom.**) ED** S. Rachman and T. Wilson. **LC** RC489.B4; A33. **DD** 616.8/914. **NLM** W1 AD436I. **CODEN** ABRTDI. **[CCC]. Pr Rev.** available on microfilm and microfiche from University Microfilms International (UMI). Documents available from The Genuine Article.
**Desc:** Publishes extended reports and reviews of research in the theory and practice of behaviour therapy. The aim is to encourage and facilitate the dissemination of new ideas, findings and formulations in the field.
**Ind/Abst** Appl. Soc. Sci. Index Abstr.; Crim. Penol. Police Sci. Abstr.; Curr. Aware. Biol. Sci., CABS; Curr. Contents Soc. Behav. Sci.; EMBASE; Psychol. Abstr. (1977-); PsycINFO; PsycLit; Res. Alert [Full Cov.]; Soc. Sci. Cit. Index [Full Cov.].

US/0739-7313
**ADVANCES IN CHILD BEHAVIORAL ANALYSIS AND THERAPY.** [Adv. child behav. anal. ther.]. Vol. 1 (1982)-. Monographic series. English. ir. Price varies per volume. Lexington Books, 125 Spring Street, Lexington MA 02173. **Tel** (800)235-3565, (617)862-6650. **ED** Paul Karoly and John J. Steffen. **NLM** W1 AD53NM.
**Ind/Abst** Psychol. Abstr. (1982-); PsycINFO.

US/0065-2407
**ADVANCES IN CHILD DEVELOPMENT AND BEHAVIOR.** [Adv. child dev. behav.]. Vol. 1 (1963)-. Monographic series. English. ir. Price varies per volume. Academic Press, Inc., 6277 Sea Harbor Drive, Orlando FL 32887. **Tel** (800)543-9534, (407)345-4100, FAX (407)363-9661. **ED** Lewis P. Lipsitt and Charles C. Spiker. **LC** BF721; .A45. **DD** 136.7082. **NLM** W1 AD53P. **CODEN** ADCDA8. **[CCC]. Pr Rev.** Documents available from The Genuine Article, BIOSIS Document Express.
**Ind/Abst** Biol. Abstr.; Health Plan. Adminis.; Index Med.; Res. Alert [Full Cov.]; Soc. Sci. Cit. Index [Full Cov.].

●US/0940-8606
**ADVANCES IN CHILD NEUROPSYCHOLOGY.** Vol. 1 (1992)-. Monographic series. English. ir. Price varies per volume. Springer-Verlag New York Inc., 175 5th Avenue, New York NY 10010. **Tel** (212)460-1500, telex 232 235 SPB UR. **(Subscription address:** Springer Verlag New York Inc. / for North America, 44 Hartz Way, Secaucus NJ 07096.**) LC** RJ486.5; .A38. **DD** 618.92//8/05. **NLM** W1; AD53S.
**Desc:** Series covering pediatric neuropsychology.

US/0149-4732
**ADVANCES IN CLINICAL CHILD PSYCHOLOGY.** [Adv. clin. child psychol.]. (1977)-. Monographic series. English. ir. Price varies per volume. Plenum Press, 233 Spring Street, New York NY 10013-1578. **Tel** (212)620-8000, (800)221-9369, FAX (212)463-0742, (212)807-1047, telex 23/421139. **LC** RJ503.3; .A37. **DD** 618.9/28/9. **NLM** W1 AD54H. Documents available from The Genuine Article.
**Ind/Abst** Res. Alert [Full Cov.]; Soc. Sci. Cit. Index [Full Cov.].

US/0748-4410
**ADVANCES IN CLINICAL NEUROPSYCHOLOGY. See** Medical Science and Technology-Neurology.

●US
**ADVANCES IN COGNITION AND EDUCATIONAL PRACTICE. VFOAT** Cognition and Educational Practice. Vol. 1 (1992)-. English. ir. $73.25. JAI Press Inc., 55 Old Post Road, Suite 2, PO Box 1678, Greenwich CT 06836-1678. **Tel** (203)661-7602, FAX (203)661-0792. **ED** Jerry Carlson. **LC** LB1051; .A316; BF311; .A38. **DD** 370.15/2/05.

●NE
**ADVANCES IN CONSCIOUSNESS RESEARCH. See** Linguistics.

US/0276-9913
**ADVANCES IN DESCRIPTIVE PSYCHOLOGY.** (ADVANCES IN DESCRIPTIVE PSYCHOLOGY : OFFICIAL ANNUAL PUBLICATION OF THE SOCIETY FOR DESCRIPTIVE PSYCHOLOGY.). [Adv. descr. psychol.]. **Added/Corp** Society for Descriptive Psychology (U.S.). Vol. 1 (1981)-. English. ir. Price varies. University of South Carolina / College of Education, c/o D. G. Turner, Columbia SC 29208. **Tel** (803)777-3828. **(Subscription address:** Descriptive Psychology Press, 1019 Baldwin Avenue, c/o Dr. Putman, Ann Arbor MI 48014.**) ED** Keith E. Davis and Anthony O. Patman. **LC** BF1; .A45. **DD** 150.19. **NLM** W1 AD546M. **[CCC].** Index available. **Bk Rev. Pr Rev. Circ:** 300.
**Ind/Abst** Psychol. Abstr. (1982-); PsycINFO.

US/0737-7452
**ADVANCES IN DEVELOPMENTAL AND BEHAVIORAL PEDIATRICS. See** Medical Science and Technology-Pediatrics.

US/0275-3049
**ADVANCES IN DEVELOPMENTAL PSYCHOLOGY.** ***Ceased.*** [Adv. dev. psychol.]. Vol. 1 (1981)-Completed Series Vol. 4 (19??). English. ir. Lawrence Erlbaum Associates, 365 Broadway, Suite 102, Hillsdale NJ 07642. **Tel** (201)666-4110, (800)926-6579, FAX (201)666-2394. **ED** M. E. Lamb and A. L. Brown. **LC** BF712; .A38. **DD** 155. **NLM** W1 AD548.
**Desc:** Information on human development and developmental psychology.
**Ind/Abst** AGRICOLA (?-?) [Select. Cov.].

GW/0931-4202
**ADVANCES IN ETHOLOGY (1987).** (ADVANCES IN ETHOLOGY.). [Adv. ethol.]. **VFOAT** Supplement ... to Ethology. (1987)-. Monographic series. English (summaries and/or abstracts in German). ir. Price varies per volume. Blackwell Wissenschafts-Verlag, Kurfuerstendamm 57, D 10707 Berlin Germany. **Tel** 011 49 30 32790623, 011 49 30 32790624, FAX 011 49 30 327 90610. **LC** BF1; .F61. **CODEN** AEHYAZ. Documents available from BIOSIS Document Express. ***Continues*** *Fortschritte der Verhaltensforschung, 0301-2808.*
**Ind/Abst** Biol. Abstr. (1991-).

US/0065-2601
**ADVANCES IN EXPERIMENTAL SOCIAL PSYCHOLOGY.** [Adv. exp. soc. psychol.]. **VFOAT** Experimental Social Psychology. Vol. 1 (1964)-. Monographic series. English. ir. Price varies per volume. Academic Press, Inc., 6277 Sea Harbor Drive, Orlando FL 32887. **Tel** (800)543-9534, (407)345-4100, FAX (407)363-9661. **LC** HM251; .A35. **DD** 301.1/05. **NLM** W1 AD561. **CODEN** AXSPAQ. **[CCC].** Documents available from The Genuine Article, BIOSIS Document Express.
**Ind/Abst** Biol. Abstr.; Res. Alert [Full Cov.]; Soc. Sci. Cit. Index [Full Cov.].

US/0747-6353
**ADVANCES IN FORENSIC PSYCHOLOGY AND PSYCHIATRY.** [Adv. forensic psychol. psychiatr.]. Vol. 1 (1984)-. English. ir. $35.00. Ablex Publishing Corporation, 355 Chestnut Street, Norwood NJ 07648. **Tel** (201)767-8450, (201)767-8455 (Customer Service), FAX (201)767-6717. **ED** Robert W. Rieber. **LC** HV6001; .A38. **DD** 347.
**Desc:** Focuses on current research in forensic psychology and psychiatry.
**Ind/Abst** PsycINFO.

US/0272-068X
**ADVANCES IN HUMAN PSYCHOPHARMACOLOGY. See** Pharmacy and Pharmacology.

US/0732-9598
**ADVANCES IN INFANCY RESEARCH.** [Adv. infancy res.]. Vol. 1 (1981)-. English. an. $45.00. Ablex Publishing Corporation, 355 Chestnut Street, Norwood NJ 07648. **Tel** (201)767-8450, (201)767-8455 (Customer Service), FAX (201)767-6717. **ED** Lewis P. Lipsitt and Carolyn Rovee-Collier. **LC** BF719; A33. **DD**

155.4/22. **NLM** W1 AD647M.
**Desc:** Book series devoted exclusively to infancy research.
**Ind/Abst** Psychol. Abstr. (1981-); PsycINFO.

US/0163-5379
**ADVANCES IN INSTRUCTIONAL PSYCHOLOGY.** [Adv. instr. psychol.]. Vol. 1 (1978)-. Monographic series. English. ir. Price varies per volume. Lawrence Erlbaum Associates, 365 Broadway, Suite 102, Hillsdale NJ 07642. **Tel** (201)666-4110, (800)926-6579, FAX (201)666-2394. **ED** Glaser Resnick. **LC** LB1051; .A3176. **DD** 370.15. **NLM** W1 AD652.

US/0732-3565
**ADVANCES IN LAW AND CHILD DEVELOPMENT.** ***Ceased.*** **See** Law-Family Law.

US/0888-9287
**ADVANCES IN MOTOR DEVELOPMENT RESEARCH.** [Adv. motor dev. res.]. Vol. 1 (1987)-. English. an. $37.50. AMS Press Inc., 56 East 13th Street, New York NY 10003. **Tel** (212)777-4700, FAX (212)995-5413, telex 710 581 2302. **ED** Jane E Clark. **LC** RJ133; .A35. **DD** 155.4/12. **NLM** W1; AD683H.
**Desc:** Strives to supplement and support journals and annual reviews which report on similar topics in motor development research.

US/8755-0032
**ADVANCES IN NEURAL AND BEHAVIORAL DEVELOPMENT.** ***Ceased.*** **See** Medical Science and Technology-Neurology.

US/0741-8957
**ADVANCES IN NEUROPSYCHOLOGY AND BEHAVIORAL NEUROLOGY.** **See** Medical Science and Technology-Neurology.

US/0278-2367
**ADVANCES IN PERSONALITY ASSESSMENT.** [Adv. pers. assess.]. Vol. 1 (1982)-. Periodical. English. an. Price varies per volume. Lawrence Erlbaum Associates, 365 Broadway, Suite 102, Hillsdale NJ 07642. **Tel** (201)666-4110, (800)926-6579, FAX (201)666-2394. **ED** Charles D. Spielberger and James N. Butcher. **LC** BF698.4; .A328. **DD** 155.2/8. Index available. **Pr Rev. Circ:** 1,000.
**Desc:** Covers personality assessment.

US/0065-325X
**ADVANCES IN PSYCHOLOGICAL ASSESSMENT.** ***Ceased.*** [Adv. psychol. assess.]. (1968)-(1984). English. Jossey Bass Inc., 350 Sansome Street, San Francisco CA 94104. **Tel** (415)433-1767, FAX (415)433-0499. **LC** BF698.4; .A33. **DD** 150/.28. **NLM** W1 AD798.

NE/0166-4115
**ADVANCES IN PSYCHOLOGY.** [Adv. psychol.]. (1979)-. Monographic series. English. ir. Price varies per volume. Elsevier Science Publishers BV, PO Box 211, 1000 AE Amsterdam Netherlands. **Tel** 011 31 20 5803642, FAX 011 31 20 5862696, telex 15682. **LC** UNC. **DD** 150. **NLM** W1 AD798L. **CODEN** ADPSEK.

UK/0892-7901
**ADVANCES IN PSYCHOPHYSIOLOGY.** **See** Biology-Physiology.

SZ/0065-3268
**ADVANCES IN PSYCHOSOMATIC MEDICINE.** [Adv. psychosom. med.]. Vol. 5 (1967)-. Monographic series. English. an. 120.00F (approx. per volume). S. Karger AG, Allschwilerstrasse 10, PO Box - Postfach - Case Postale, CH-4009 Basel Switzerland. **Tel** 011 41 61 306-1111, FAX 011 41 61 306-1234, telex CH 962 652. **ED** T. N. Wise. **LC** UNC. **NLM** W1 AD81. **[CCC].** Documents available from BIOSIS Document Express. ***Continues*** *Fortschritte der Psychosomatischen Medizin.*
**Desc:** Recognizing the complexity of interactions between personality and physical illness, this series employs an interdisciplinary strategy to explore areas where knowledge from psychosomatic medicine may aid the prevention of specific diseases or help meet the emotional demands of hospitalized patients. In each work, the editor strives to bring together distinguished contributors, creating a series of coherent and comprehensive reviews on a variety of novel topics.
**Ind/Abst** Biol. Abstr.; Health Plan. Adminis.; Index Med.; Ref. Upd. Deluxe Ed.

US/0270-3920
**ADVANCES IN SCHOOL PSYCHOLOGY.** ***Ceased.*** [Adv. sch. psychol.]. Vol. 1 (1981)-Vol. 9 (1992). English. an. Lawrence Erlbaum Associates, 365 Broadway, Suite 102, Hillsdale NJ 07642. **Tel** (201)666-4110, (800)926-6579, FAX (201)666-2394. **LC** LB1027.55; A42. **NLM** W1; AD842.

US/0272-1740
**ADVANCES IN SUBSTANCE ABUSE, BEHAVIORAL AND BIOLOGICAL RESEARCH.** **See** Drug Abuse and Alcoholism.

NE/0923-019X
**ADVANCES IN TEST ANXIETY RESEARCH.** [Adv. test anxiety res.]. **Added/Corp** International Society for Test Anxiety Research. **VFOAT** Test Anxiety Research. Vol. 1 (1982)-. English. an. Price varies. Swets & Zeitlinger BV, Heereweg 347B PO Box 825, 2160 SZ Lisse Holland. **Tel** 011 31 2521 35111, FAX 02521-15888, telex 41325. **(Subscription address:** Taylor & Francis Inc., 1900 Frost Road, Suite 101, Bristol PA 19007-1598.**) LC** BF575.A6; A37. **DD** 152/.28/7. **NLM** W1; AD879N. **CODEN** ATRSE6. Documents available from BIOSIS Document Express.
**Ind/Abst** Biol. Abstr. (1987-).

US/0196-1934
**ADVANCES IN THANATOLOGY.**
**Added/Corp** Foundation of Thanatology. Center for Thanatology. Foundation Book and Periodical Division. Vol. 4, No. 1 (1977)-. Periodical. English. Four times a year. $73.00. Foundation Book & Periodical, 391 Atlantic Avenue, Brooklyn NY 11217. **Tel** (718)270-3725. **ED** Austin H. Kutscher. **LC** BD444; .J63. **DD** 128/.5. **NLM** W1 AD879T. Index available. **Ad Acc. Circ:** 590. available on microfilm and microfiche from University Microfilms International (UMI). ***Continues*** *Journal of Thanatology, 0047-2832.*
**Desc:** Subject centered essays on various aspects of life-threatening disease, dying and bereavement.

US/0278-2359
**ADVANCES IN THE PSYCHOLOGY OF HUMAN INTELLIGENCE.** ***Ceased.*** [Adv. psychol. hum. intell.]. Vol. 1 (1982)-(1994). English. an. Lawrence Erlbaum Associates, 365 Broadway, Suite 102, Hillsdale NJ 07642. **Tel** (201)666-4110, (800)926-6579, FAX (201)666-2394. **LC** BF431; .A46. **DD** 153.9/05. **NLM** W1; AD8793D. **Pr Rev. Circ:** 1,200.

US/0065-3454
**ADVANCES IN THE STUDY OF BEHAVIOR.** [Adv. study behav.]. Vol. 1 (1965)-. Academic Scholarly Publication. English. ir. $69.95 (Vol. 23). Academic Press, Inc., 6277 Sea Harbor Drive, Orlando FL 32887. **Tel** (800)543-9534, (407)345-4100, FAX (407)363-9661. **ED** Daniel S. Lehman, Robert A. Hinde and Evelyn Shaw. **LC** QL750; .A38. **DD** 591.51. **NLM** W1 AD88. **CODEN** ADSBBF. **[CCC].** Documents available from The Genuine Article, BIOSIS Document Express, CASDDS.
**Ind/Abst** AGRICOLA [Select. Cov.]; Biol. Abstr.; Chem. Abstr. (1965-1983); Curr. Aware. Biol. Sci., CABS; Dairy Sci. Abstr.; Index Sci. Rev. [Full Cov.]; Key Word Index Wildl. Res.; Life Sci. Collect.; Res. Alert [Full Cov.]; Sci. Cit. Index; SCISEARCH; Soc. Sci. Cit. Index [Select. Cov.].

US/0190-9703
**ADVANCES IN THE STUDY OF COMMUNICATION AND AFFECT.** [Adv. study commun. affect]. Vol. 1 (1974)-. Monographic series. English. ir. Price varies per volume. Plenum Press, 233 Spring Street, New York NY 10013-1578. **Tel** (212)620-8000, (800)221-9369, FAX (212)463-0742, (212)807-1047, telex 23/421139. **LC** UNC. **DD** 152. **NLM** W1 AD8801.

US/0883-5659
**ADVENTURES IN TOTAL DEVELOPMENT.** (ADVENTURES IN TOTAL DEVELOPMENT: ATD.). [Adventures total dev.]. **Added/Corp** Asbury Associates. **VFOAT** ATD. (198?)-. Periodical. English. Six times a year. $30.00. The Asbury Theological Journal, Asbury Theological Seminary, 204 North Lexington Avenue, Wilmore KY 40390. **Tel** (606)858-3581, FAX (606)858-3581. **DD** 158.

US/1044-0534
**AFTERLOSS (RANCHO MIRAGE, CALIF.).** (AFTERLOSS.). **VFOAT** After Loss. Vol. 1, No. 1 (1989)-. Periodical. English. Twelve times a year. $78.00. Harbor House Publishers West, 40 781 Smoke Tree Lane, Rancho Mirage CA 92270. **Tel** (619)321-0270, FAX (619)321-0019. **ED** Margie Kennedy Reeves. **DD** 158. Index available. cum. index. **Bk Rev.**

UK
**AGGRESSION AND ANTI-SOCIAL BEHAVIOR IN CHILDHOOD AND ADOLESCENCE.** 1st Ed. (1978)-. English. Pergamon Press, An Imprint of Elsevier Science Ltd., The Boulevard, Langford Lane, Kidlington, Oxford OX5 1GB United Kingdom. **Tel** 011 44 865 843000, 011 44 865 843699, FAX 011 44 865 843010. **(Subscription address:** US/ 395 Saw Mill River Road, Elmsford, NY 10523; Can/ 150 Consumers Road/Suite 104, Willowdale Ontario M2J 1P9; Aus-NZ/ POB 544, Potts Point NSW 2011**) LC** RJ506.A35; A35. **DD** 305.2/3.

US/0096-140X
**AGGRESSIVE BEHAVIOR.** [Aggress. behav.]. **Added/Corp** International Society for Research on Aggression. Vol. 1 (1974)-. Academic Scholarly Publication. English. bm. $576.00 US; $636.00 Canada and Mexico; $658.50 other. John Wiley & Sons, Inc., 605 Third Avenue, New York NY 10158-0012. **Tel** (212)850-6000, (212)850-6645, FAX (212)850-6088, telex 12-7063. **(Subscription address:** John Wiley & Sons / England, Baffins Lane, Chichester, West Sussex PO19 1UD England.**) ED** Ronald Baenninger. **LC** BF575.A3; A57. **DD** 152.5/2. **NLM** W1 AG341. **CODEN** AGBEDUAGBED. **[CCC]. Bk Rev. Ad Acc. Pr Rev.** Documents available from The Genuine Article, BIOSIS Document Express, UMI Article Clearinghouse, CASDDS.
**Desc:** A multidisciplinary journal with an editorial board drawn from a broad range of academic fields. Devoted to the empirical and theoretical analysis of conflict and the scientific understanding of aggression in humans and animals.
**Ind/Abst** Anim. Behav. Abstr.; Biol. Abstr.; Chem. Abstr.; Commun. Abstr. (?-?); Crim. Justice Abstr.; CSA Neuro. Abstr.; Curr. Contents Life Sci.; Curr. Contents Soc. Behav. Sci.; EMBASE [Select. Cov.]; Expand. Acad. Index (1992-); Fish Rev.; Index Vet.; Middle East Abstr. Index; Newsp. Period. Abstr. (1992-); Nutr. Abstr. Rev., Ser. B, Live Feeds and Feed.; Peace Res. Abstr. J. (1977-); Life Sci. Collect.; Pig News Inf.; Psychol. Abstr. (1974-); PsycINFO; PsycLit; Ref. Upd. Deluxe Ed.; Res. Alert [Full Cov.]; Sci. Cit. Index; SCISEARCH; Soc. Sci. Cit. Index [Full Cov.]; SportSearch; Vet. Bull.; Wildl. Rev.

NE/0928-9917
**AGING AND COGNITION.** (19??)-. English. Four times a year. Fl330.00 (institution). Swets & Zeitlinger BV, Heereweg 347B PO Box 825, 2160 SZ Lisse Holland. **Tel** 011 31 2521 35111, FAX 02521-15888, telex 41325. **(Subscription address:** Swets Publishing Service, PO Box 825, 2160 SZ Lisse The Netherlands**)**

FR/0002-1148
**AGRESSOLOGIE.** [Agressologie]. Vol. 1 (April 1960)-. Periodical. French (English, French, German and Spanish). mo. 587.66F France; 800.00F others. Societe de Presse Medicale, 14 rue Drouot, 75009 Paris France. **Tel** 011 33 1 48249693, 011 33 1 47703994. **LC** BF575.A3; A6. **NLM** W1 AG38. **CODEN** AGSOA6. **[CCC].** available on microfilm and microfiche from University Microfilms International (UMI). Documents available from BIOSIS Document Express, CASDDS.
**Ind/Abst** Biol. Abstr.; Chem. Abstr.; EMBASE; Health Plan. Adminis.; Index Med.; Nutr. Abstr. Rev., Ser. B, Live Feeds and Feed.; Nutr. Abstr. Rev., Ser. A, Hum. Exp.; Life Sci. Collect.; PESTDOC.

UA
**AL-INSAN WA-AL-TATAWWUR / TUSDIRUHA JAMIYAT AL-TIBB AL-NAFSI AL-TATAWWURI.** **VFOAT** Man and Evolution; Man & Evolution. Periodical. Arabic. qt. 1.20. Al-Jamiyah, 17 Shari 19 Madinat Al-Muqattam, Al-Qahirah Egypt. **LC** BF8.A73; I57.

US/1066-4076
**AMERICAN ART THERAPY ASSOCIATION NEWSLETTER.** [Am. Art Ther. Assoc. newsl.]. **Added/Corp** American Art Therapy Association. (1967)-. Newsletter. English. qt. $16.00 US; $28.00 other. American Art Therapy Assn Inc, 1202 Allanson Road, Mundelein IL 60060. **Tel** (708)949-6064, FAX (708)566-4580. **ED** Debra Paskind. **DD** 618. **Ad Acc. Circ:** 4,100 (ctrl).
**Desc:** Matters of interest to AATA members as well as those considering a career in art therapy.

●US/1059-3497
**AMERICAN COUNSELOR.** ***Suspended.*** (AMERICAN COUNSELOR / AMERICAN ASSOCIATION FOR COUNSELING AND DEVELOPMENT.). [Am. couns.]. **Added/Corp** American Association for Counseling and Development. Vol. 1, No. 1 (Winter 1992)-Suspended with Vol. 2, No. 4 (1993). Periodical. English. qt. American Counseling Association, 5999 Stevenson Avenue, Alexandria VA 22304. **Tel** (703)823-9800, (800)347-6647, FAX (703)823-0252. **ED** Gerry Romano. **DD** 361.

US/0065-860X
**AMERICAN IMAGO.** [Am. imago]. **Added/Corp** Association for Applied Psychoanalysis. Vol. 1 (Nov. 1939)-. Periodical. English. Four times a year. $65.00 US; $68.35 Canada and Mexico; $71.40 other. Johns Hopkins University Press, 2715 North Charles Street, Baltimore MD 21218-4319. **Tel** (410)516-6987, FAX (410)516-6968. **(Subscription address:** John Hopkins University Press, Journals Publishing Division, PO Box 19966, Baltimore MD 21211.**) ED** Martin Gliserman, Louise Kaplan and Donald Moss. **LC** BF173.A2; A55. **DD** 150. **NLM** W1 AM435I. **CODEN** AMIAAO. **[CCC].** cum. index. **Bk Rev. Circ:** 1,000 (ctrl). available on microfilm and microfiche from University Microfilms International (UMI). Documents available from The Genuine Article, UMI Article Clearinghouse, Magazine Collection.
**Desc:** Journal of psychoanalysis and culture.
**Ind/Abst** Abstr. Engl. Stud.; Acad. Abstr. Full Text Elite (Jan. 1992-); Acad. Abstr. (Jan. 1992-); Acad. Search (Jan. 1992-); Annu. Bibliogr. Engl. Lang. Lit.; Arts Humanit. Citation Index [Full Cov.]; BHA : Biblio. Hist. Art; Child. Lit. Abstr. (19??-); Curr. Contents Arts Humanit.; Film Lit. Index; Gen. Period. Index (1985-); Hist. Source (Jan. 1992-); Humanit. Source (Jan. 1992-); Index Med.; INFO-SOUTH Abstr.; Lit. Crit. Regist.; Mag. Index Plus (1989-); Mag. Search; Middle East Abstr. Index; MLA Int. Bibl. Books Artic. Mod. Lang. Lit.; Newsp. Period. Abstr. (1988-); Psychol. Abstr. (1939-); PsycINFO; PsycLit;

Read. Guide Period. Lit.; Res. Alert [Full Cov.]; Romant. Move.; Soc. Sci. Cit. Index [Full Cov.]; Mag. Index (1977-); TOM Gen. Index (1992-) [Full Txt.].

US/0091-0562
**AMERICAN JOURNAL OF COMMUNITY PSYCHOLOGY.** [Am. j. community psychol.]. **Added/Corp** American Psychological Association. Division of Community Psychology. Vol. 1 (Jan./Mar. 1973)-. Periodical. English. Six times a year. $370.00 institutions, $92.00 individuals US; $435.00 institutions, $108.00 individuals other. Plenum Press, 233 Spring Street, New York NY 10013-1578. **Tel** (212)620-8000, (800)221-9369, FAX (212)463-0742, (212)807-1047, telex 23/421139. **ED** Julian Rappaport. **LC** RA790.A1; A47. **DD** 361/.001/9. **NLM** W1 AM45LE. **CODEN** AJCPCK. **[CCC].** Index available. **Pr Rev.** available on microfilm and microfiche from University Microfilms International (UMI). Documents available from The Genuine Article, UMI Article Clearinghouse.
**Desc:** Devoted to research and theory concerned with interaction between individuals and communities, organizations, institutions and human groups.
**Ind/Abst** Acad. Search (July 1993-); Appl. Soc. Sci. Index Abstr.; Coal Abstr.; Crim. Justice Abstr.; Crim. Penol. Police Sci. Abstr.; Cumul. Index Nurs. Allied Health Lit.; Curr. Contents Soc. Behav. Sci.; Educ. Adm. Abstr.; EMBASE; Expand. Acad. Index (1989-); Health Source (Jul. 1993-); Hum. Resour. Abstr. (?-?); Index Med.; INFO-SOUTH Abstr.; INIS Atomindex [Micro.]; Linguist. Lang. Behav. Abstr.; Mag. Search; Middle East Abstr. Index; Multicult. Educ. Abstr.; Newsp. Period. Abstr. (1989-); Pollut. Abstr. Indexes; Psychol. Abstr. (1974-); PsycINFO; PsycLit; Res. Alert [Full Cov.]; Risk Abstr.; Sage Fam. Stud. Abstr.; Sage Urban Stud. Abstr; Soc. Plann. Policy Dev. Abstr.; Soc. Sci. Source (Jul. 1993-); Soc. Sci. Cit. Index [Full Cov.]; Soc. Sci. Index Fulltext (Aug. 1988-) [Full Txt.]; Soc. Work Abstr. (Spring, Summer 1987-) [Select. Cov.]; Sociol. Abstr.; Spec. Educ. Needs Abstr.

US/0146-3721
**AMERICAN JOURNAL OF DANCE THERAPY.** [Am. j. dance ther.]. **Added/Corp** American Dance Therapy Association. Vol. 1 (Spring/Summer 1977)-. Periodical. English. sa. £25.00 (individual), £75.00 (institutions) UK & Europe; $95.00 US; $110.00 other. Human Sciences Press, PO Box 735, 233 Spring Street, New York NY 10013. **Tel** (212)620-8000, FAX (212)807-1047, telex 23421139. **(Subscription address:** UK & European Subscriptions: Eurospan Group, Journals and Serials Division, 3 Henrietta Street, Covent Garden, London WC2E 8LU England: Telephone: 011 44 71 240-0856 FAX: 011 44 71 379-0609**) ED** Miriam Roskin Berger and Marcia Leventhal. **LC** RC489.D3; A42. **DD** 615/.8515. **NLM** W1 AM45LT. **[CCC].** available on microfilm and microfiche from University Microfilms International (UMI). Documents available from The Genuine Article.
**Desc:** Devoted to the psychotherapeutic use of movement as a process that furthers the emotional and physical integration of the individual. Publishes original contributions related to the clinical use of dance therapy with a wide variety of populations; theoretical considerations that provide a framework for dance therapy intervention; and research in dance therapy.
**Ind/Abst** Arts Humanit. Citation Index [Select. Cov.]; Curr. Contents Soc. Behav. Sci.; Psychol. Abstr. (1977-); PsycINFO; PsycLit; Res. Alert [Full Cov.]; Soc. Sci. Cit. Index [Full Cov.].

US/0192-6187
**AMERICAN JOURNAL OF FAMILY THERAPY, THE.** [Am. j. fam. ther.]. Vol. 7, No. 1 (Spring 1979)-. Periodical. English. qt. $80.00 (institution), $38.00 (individual). Brunner Mazel, 19 Union Square West, New York NY 10003. **Tel** (212)924-3344, (800)825-3089. **ED** S. Richard Sauber. **LC** RC488.5; .I54. **DD** 616.89/156. **NLM** W1 AM451I. **CODEN** IJFPDM. **Bk Rev. Ad Acc. Pr Rev. Circ:** 2,800 (ctrl). available on microfilm and microfiche from University Microfilms International (UMI). Documents available from The Genuine Article, BIOSIS Document Express, UMI Article Clearinghouse. ***Continues** International Journal of Family Counseling, 0147-1775.*
**Desc:** Theory, research and clinical practice of family therapy.
**Ind/Abst** Acad. Abstr. Full Text Elite (Jan. 1992-); Acad. Abstr. (Jan. 1992-); Acad. Search (Jan. 1992-); Biol. Abstr. (1986-1990); Commun. Abstr. (?-?); Curr. Contents Soc. Behav. Sci.; Curr. Index J. Educ.; Expand. Acad. Index (1989-); Health Source (Jan. 1992-); INFO-SOUTH Abstr.; Linguist. Lang. Behav. Abstr.; Mag. Search; Middle East Abstr. Index; Multicult. Educ. Abstr.; Newsp. Period. Abstr. (1991-); Psychol. Abstr. (1979-); PsycINFO; PsycLit; Res. Alert [Full Cov.]; Sage Fam. Stud. Abstr.; Soc. Plann. Policy Dev. Abstr.; Soc. Sci. Source (Jan. 1992-); Soc. Sci. Cit. Index [Full Cov.]; Soc. Sci. Index; Soc. Sci. Index Fulltext (Winter 1988-) [Full Txt.]; Soc. Work Abstr. (Spring, Summer 1987-) [Select. Cov.]; Sociol. Abstr.; Spec. Educ. Needs Abstr.

US/0733-1290
**AMERICAN JOURNAL OF FORENSIC PSYCHOLOGY, THE. See** Medical Science and Technology-Forensic Medicine, Medical Jurisprudence.

US/0002-9556
**AMERICAN JOURNAL OF PSYCHOLOGY, THE.** [Am. j. psychol.]. Vol. 1 (Nov. 1887)-. Periodical. English. qt. $80.00 (one year), $144.00 (two year) institutions; $35.00 (one year), $63.00 (two year) individuals. University of Illinois Press, 1325 South Oak Street, Champaign IL 61820. **Tel** (217)333-0950, FAX (217)244-8082. **ED** D. Dulany. **LC** BF1; .A5. **DD** 150.5. **NLM** W1 AM517. **CODEN** AJPCAA. **[CCC].** Index available. cum. index. **Bk Rev. Ad Acc. Pr Rev. Circ:** 2,900. available on microfilm and microfiche from University Microfilms International (UMI). Documents available from The Genuine Article, BIOSIS Document Express, UMI Article Clearinghouse.
**Desc:** Articles on general experimental psychology, original research and theoretical issues.
**Ind/Abst** Acad. Abstr. Full Text Elite (July 1990-); Acad. Abstr. (July 1990-); Acad. Ind. [Computer File] (1987-); Acad. Search (July 1990-); Appl. Soc. Sci. Index Abstr.; Biol. Abstr.; Book Rev. Index; Commun. Abstr. (?-?); Curr. Contents Soc. Behav. Sci.; Ergon. Abstr.; Expand. Acad. Index (1987-); Gen. Sci. Index (1992-); Gen. Sci. Source (Jul. 1990-); Health Index (1989-); Health Plan. Adminis.; Health Ref. Cent. (Jan. 1989-) [Full Cov.]; Index Med.; Index Period. Artic. Relat. Law (199?-); INFO-SOUTH Abstr.; Int. Aerosp. Abstr.; Mag. Search; Middle East Abstr. Index; Multicult. Educ. Abstr.; Newsp. Period. Abstr. (1986-); Psychol. Abstr. (1925-); PsycINFO; PsycLit; Res. Alert [Full Cov.]; Saf. Health Work; Soc. Plann. Policy Dev. Abstr.; Soc. Sci. Source (Jul. 1990-); Soc. Sci. Cit. Index [Full Cov.]; Soc. Sci. Index; Soc. Sci. Index Fulltext (Fall 1987-) [Full Txt.]; Sociol. Abstr. (?-?).

US/1052-7958
**AMERICAN PSYCHOANALYST, THE.** (THE AMERICAN PSYCHOANALYST : QUARTERLY NEWSLETTER OF THE AMERICAN PSYCHOANALYTIC ASSOCIATION.). [Am. psychoanal.]. **Added/Corp** American Psychoanalytic Association. Vol. 24, No. 1 (Winter 1990)-. Newsletter. English. qt. $50.00 US & Canada; $70.00 other. Lawrence Erlbaum Associates, 365 Broadway, Suite 102, Hillsdale NJ 07642. **Tel** (201)666-4110, (800)926-6579, FAX (201)666-2394. **LC** RC500; .A4915. **DD** 616.89/17/05. ***Continues** American Psychoanalytic Association. Newsletter.*

US/0003-066X
**AMERICAN PSYCHOLOGIST, THE.** [Am. psychol.]. **Added/Corp** American Psychological Association. American Psychological Association. Proceedings. Vol. 1 (Jan. 1946)-. Periodical. English. mo. $286.00 (institution, nonmember) US. American Psychological Association, 750 First Street Northeast, Washington DC 20002. **Tel** (800)374-2721, (202)336-5600, (subscriptions - (202)336-5600. **ED** Raymond D. Fowler. **LC** BF1; .A55. **DD** 150.5. **NLM** W1 AM7297. **CODEN** AMPSAB. **[CCC].** Index available (free). **Ad Acc. Circ:** 70,000. available on microfilm and microfiche from University Microfilms International (UMI). Documents available from The Genuine Article, UMI Article Clearinghouse. ***Continued in part by** Proceedings of the Annual Convention of the American Psychological Association, 0065-9878.*
**Desc:** The American Psychologist is the authoritative source for substantive, feature, and non-integrative articles that advance psychology. Readers will find articles on: new concepts relevant to all scientific specialities; theories linking subfield; psychology, public interests, and practice; studies of professionals training and demography; and awards and other distinguished presentations.
**Ind/Abst** Abstr. Res. Pastor. Care Couns. (19??-); Acad. Abstr. Full Text Elite (July 1990-); Acad. Abstr. (July 1990-); Acad. Ind. [Computer File] (1987-); Acad. Search (July 1990-); Appl. Soc. Sci. Index Abstr.; Commun. Abstr. (?-?); Crim. Justice Abstr.; Curr. Contents Soc. Behav. Sci.; Curr. Index J. Educ.; Educ. Technol. Abstr.; Expand. Acad. Index (1987-); Gen. Sci. Index; Gen. Sci. Source (Jul. 1990-); Health Saf. Sci. Abstr.; Health Plan. Adminis.; High. Educ. Abstr. (19??-); Hum. Resour. Abstr. (?-?); Index Med.; Index Period. Artic. Relat. Law; INFO-SOUTH Abstr.; Int. Aerosp. Abstr.; Int. Bibliogr. Sociol.; J. Plan. Lit.; Mag. Search; Med. Abstr. Newsl.; Middle East Abstr. Index; MLA Int. Bibl. Books Artic. Mod. Lang. Lit.; Multicult. Educ. Abstr.; Newsp. Period. Abstr. (1988-); Peace Res. Abstr. J. (1973-); Life Sci. Collect.; Psychol. Abstr. (1946-); PsycINFO; PsycLit; Res. Alert [Full Cov.]; Res. High. Educ. Abstr.; Risk Abstr.; Sage Fam. Stud. Abstr. (?-?); Sage Public Adm. Abstr. (?-?); Sage Race Relat. Abstr.; Soc. Plann. Policy Dev. Abstr.; Soc. Sci. Source (Jul. 1990-); Soc. Sci. Cit. Index [Full Cov.]; Soc. Sci. Index; Soc. Sci. Index Fulltext (Sept. 1988-) [Full Txt.]; Soc. Work Abstr. [Select. Cov.]; Sociol. Abstr. (?-?); Sociol. Educ. Abstr.; SportSearch; Tech. Educ. Train. Abstr.; Virol. AIDS Abstr.; Women Stud. Abstr.; Work Relat. Abstr.

RM
**ANALELE UNIVERSITATII BUCURESTI: PSIHOLOGIE. Main/Corp** Universitatea Din Bucuresti. (19??)-. Romanian (summaries and/or abstracts in French and Russian). an. University of Bucharest / Universitatea din Bucuresti, B-Dul Gh Gheorghiu-Dej Nr 64, Bucharest Romania. **LC** BF8.R7; B8a.

PO/0870-8231
**ANALISE PSICOLOGICA.** V. 1- Oct. 1977-. Periodical. Portuguese. 2500$00 Portugal; $30.00 rest of Europe. Analise Psicologica, R Jardim do Tabaco, 44-1100 Lisbon Portugal. **Tel** 863184. **ED** Frederico Pereira. **LC** RC500; .A55. **Bk Rev. Ad Acc. Circ:** 1,000.
**Desc:** Educational, clinical, social psychology, organizational psychology, general psychology, epistemology/history of psychology, developmental psychoanalysis, comparative psychology.

SP/0211-7339
**ANALISIS Y MODIFICACION DE CONDUCTA.** [Anal. modif. conducta]. (1975)-. Periodical. Multiple languages. sa. Analisis y Modificacion de Conducta, 46010 Valencia Spain. **UDC** 159.9.
**Ind/Abst** Psychol. Abstr.; PsycINFO.

US/0889-9401
**ANALYSIS OF VERBAL BEHAVIOR, THE.** [Anal. verbal behav.]. **Added/Corp** Association for Behavior Analysis. Verbal Behavior Special Interest Group. Vol. 3, No. 1 (Spring 1985)-. Periodical. English. an (Dec.). $50.00. Verbal Behavior Special Interest Group, 1236 Stafford Avenue, Concord CA 94521. **Tel** (510)682-5256, FAX (510)825-1933. **ED** Mark L. Sundbery. **DD** 150. **Pr Rev. Circ:** 500. ***Continues** VB News.*
**Desc:** Contains empirical and conceptual papers relevant to a behavioral analysis of language. Applications to human communication are stressed.

FR/0246-2826
**ANALYTICA. *Suspended.*** [Analytica]. Suspended Nov. (1990). Periodical. French. Parva, 31 rue de Navarin, 75009 Paris France. **Tel** 011 33 1 48780565. **NLM** W1; AN191H.

SZ/0301-3006
**ANALYTISCHE PSYCHOLOGIE.** (ANALYTISCHE PSYCHOLOGIE : OFFIZIELLES ORGAN DER DEUTSCHEN GESELLSCHAFT FUER ANALYTISCHE PSYCHOLOGIE, DER SCHWEIZERISCHEN GESELLSCHAFT FUER ANALYTISCHE PSYCHOLOGIE UND DER INTERNATIONALEN GESELLSCHAFT ARZT UND SEELSORGER.). [Anal. Psychol.]. **Added/Corp** Deutsche Gesellschaft fuer Analytische Psychologie. Schweizerische Gesellschaft fuer Analytische Psychologie. Internationale Gesellschaft Arzt und Seelsorger Stuttgart. Internationale Gesellschaft fuer Tiefenpsychologie. Vol. 5 , No. 1 (1974)-. Periodical. German (summaries and/or abstracts in English). qt. $75.00. S. Karger AG, Allschwilerstrasse 10, PO Box - Postfach - Case Postale, CH-4009 Basel Switzerland. **Tel** 011 41 61 306-1111, FAX 011 41 61 306-1234, telex CH 962 652. **ED** H. Dieckmann and C. A. Meier. **LC** RC500; .Z42. **DD** 616.89/17/05. **NLM** W1 AN1919J. **CODEN** ANAPC4. **[CCC]. Ad Acc. Pr Rev. Circ:** 5,500 (ctrl). Documents available from The Genuine Article, BIOSIS Document Express. ***Continues** Zeitschrift fur Analytische Psychologie und Ihre Grenzgebiete, 0049-8580.*
**Desc:** Publishes important contributions in the tradition of C G Jung's analytical psychology.
**Ind/Abst** Biol. Abstr.; Curr. Contents Soc. Behav. Sci.; Life Sci. Collect.; Psychol. Abstr. (1974-); PsycINFO (1990-); Ref. Upd. Deluxe Ed.; Res. Alert [Full Cov.]; Soc. Sci. Cit. Index [Full Cov.].

IO
**ANDA. Added/Corp** Yayasan Bina Psikologi. (19??)-. Indonesian. ir. Mulyono & Associates, Gedung Pant Trisula, Jl Menteng Raya 35, PO Box 3216, Jakarta Pusat Indonesia. **LC** BF8.I5; A5.

US/0090-4996
**ANIMAL LEARNING & BEHAVIOR. See** Zoology.

FR/0338-9375
**ANNALES DE PSYCHOTHERAPIE. See** Medical Science and Technology-Psychiatry.

FR/0003-4487
**ANNALES MEDICO PSYCHOLOGIQUES.** [Ann. med. psychol.]. **Added/Corp** Societe Medico-Psychologique. (1843)-. Academic Scholarly Publication. French. Ten times a year. $282.00. Masson Editeur, Box Postale 22, 41353 Vineuil 16 France. **Tel** 011 33 54 438994. **(Subscription address:** 7A Boulevard de Perolles, CH-1701 Fribourg Switzerland**) NLM** W1 AN457P. **CODEN** AMPYAT. **[CCC]. Pr Rev.** available on microfilm and microfiche from University Microfilms International (UMI). Documents available from The Genuine Article.
**Ind/Abst** Curr. Contents Clin. Med.; EMBASE; Health Plan. Adminis.; Index Med.; Life Sci. Collect.; PESTDOC; Psychol. Abstr. (1927-); PsycINFO; PsycLit; Res. Alert [Full Cov.]; Saf. Health Work; SCISEARCH; Soc. Sci. Cit. Index [Select. Cov.]; Virol. AIDS Abstr.

US/0883-6612
**ANNALS OF BEHAVIORAL MEDICINE. See** Medical Science and Technology-Abstracting, Bibliographies and Statistics.

UK/0747-7902
**ANNALS OF CHILD DEVELOPMENT.** [Annals child dev.]. Vol. 1 (1984)-. Periodical. English. an.

$75.00. Jessica Kingsley Publishers, 118 Pentonville Road, London N1 9JN England. **Tel** 011 44 71 833 2307, FAX 011 44 71 837 2917. **(Subscription address:** Taylor & Francis Inc., 1900 Frost Road, Suite 101, Bristol PA 19007-1598.**) ED** Grover Whitehurst. **LC** BF712; .A56. **DD** 155.4/05. **NLM** W1; AD57F. **CODEN** ACDEED. **[CCC].** Documents available from BIOSIS Document Express.
**Ind/Abst** Biol. Abstr. (1986-).

CN/0843-4611
**ANNALS OF SEX RESEARCH.** ***Title Change.*** **See** Sexual Life.

US/0747-5241
**ANNALS OF THEORETICAL PSYCHOLOGY.** [Ann. theor. psychol.]. Vol. 1 (1984)-. Monographic series. English. ir. Price varies per volume. Plenum Press, 233 Spring Street, New York NY 10013-1578. **Tel** (212)620-8000, (800)221-9369, FAX (212)463-0742, (212)807-1047, telex 23/421139. **LC** BF38; .A53. **DD** 150/.5. **NLM** W1; AN627G.

FR/0003-5033
**ANNEE PSYCHOLOGIQUE, L'.** [Annee psychol.]. **Added/Corp** Ecole Pratique des Hautes Etudes (France). Laboratoire de Psychologie Physiologique. Centre National de la Recherche Scientifique (France). Vol. 1 (1894)-. French. Four times a year. 520.00F France; 630.00F other. Presses Universitaires de France, Department des Revues, 14 Avenue du Bois de l'Epine, BP 90, 91003 Evry Cedex France. **Tel** (1)60 77 82 05, FAX (1) 60 79 20 45, telex PUF 600 474 F. **ED** Paul Fraisse and George Noizet. **LC** BF2; .A6. **DD** 150/.5. **NLM** W1 AN673. **CODEN** ANPQAX. **[CCC].** cum. index. **Pr Rev.** Documents available from The Genuine Article.
**Desc:** Contains research reports and findings, critical reviews and biographical analyses.
**Ind/Abst** Curr. Contents Soc. Behav. Sci.; Index Med.; Linguist. Lang. Behav. Abstr.; Psychol. Abstr. (1925-); PsycINFO; PsycLit; Res. Alert [Full Cov.]; Soc. Plann. Policy Dev. Abstr.; Soc. Sci. Cit. Index [Full Cov.]; Sociol. Abstr.

US/0733-3609
**ANNUAL REPORT - OKLAHOMA. STATE BOARD OF EXAMINERS OF PSYCHOLOGISTS.** (ANNUAL REPORT FOR FY ... / STATE BOARD OF EXAMINERS OF PSYCHOLOGISTS.). **Main/Corp** Oklahoma. State Board of Examiners of Psychologists. English. an. State Board of Examiners of Psychologists, Room 503/NE Tenth and Stonewall, PO Box 53551, Oklahoma City OK 73152. **LC** BF80.8; .O37A. **DD** 353.9766008243046.

US
**ANNUAL REPORT TO THE GOVERNOR / NEW MEXICO STATE BOARD OF PSYCHOLOGIST EXAMINERS.** **Main/Corp** New Mexico State Board of Psychologist Examiners. (19??)-. English. an. **LC** BF80.8; .N48a. **DD** 353.97890082/43.

US/0066-4308
**ANNUAL REVIEW OF PSYCHOLOGY.** [Annu. rev. psychol.]. Vol. 1 (1950)-. English. an (Feburary). $46.00 US; $51.00 other. Annual Reviews Inc., 4139 El Camino Way, PO Box 10139, Palo Alto CA 94303-0139. **Tel** (415)493-4400, (800)523-8635, FAX (415)855-9815. **ED** Mark R. Rosenzweig and Lyman W. Porter. **LC** BF30; .A56. **DD** 150.58. **NLM** W1 AN7796. **CODEN** ARPSAC. **[CCC].** Index available. cum. index. **Pr Rev.** ctrl circ. available on microfilm and microfiche from University Microfilms International (UMI). Documents available from The Genuine Article, BIOSIS Document Express, UMI Article Clearinghouse, CASDDS, Documents on Demand.
**Desc:** Comprehensive, thorough coverage of latest advances in psychology, written by acknowledged experts in the field. Extensive literature citations included.
**Ind/Abst** Acad. Abstr. Full Text Elite (July 1990-); Acad. Abstr. (July 1990-); Acad. Search (July 1990-); Biol. Abstr.; Chem. Abstr.; Curr. Aware. Biol. Sci., CABS; Curr. Contents Life Sci.; Curr. Contents Soc. Behav. Sci.; Environ. Abstr.; Expand. Acad. Index (1989-); Gen. Sci. Source (Jul. 1990-); Health Period. Database; Health Plan. Adminis.; Index Med.; Index Sci. Rev. [Full Cov.]; INFO-SOUTH Abstr.; Int. Bibliogr. Sociol.; Linguist. Lang. Behav. Abstr.; Mag. Search; Newsp. Period. Abstr. (1990-); Life Sci. Collect.; Psychol. Abstr. (1950-); PsycINFO; PsycLit; PsycScan: Develop. Psych.; Ref. Upd. Basic Ed.; Ref. Upd. Deluxe Ed.; Res. Alert [Full Cov.]; Saf. Health Work; Sci. Cit. Index; SCISEARCH; Soc. Plann. Policy Dev. Abstr.; Soc. Sci. Source (Jul. 1990-); Soc. Sci. Cit. Index [Full Cov.]; Soc. Sci. Index; Soc. Sci. Index Fulltext (1988-) [Full Txt.]; Sociol. Abstr.; SportSearch.

US
**ANNUAL REVIEW OF PSYCHOPATHOLOGY.** Vol. 1 (1991)-. Monographic series. English. Price varies per volume. SAGE Periodical Press, 2455 Teller Road, Thousand Oaks CA 91320. **Tel** (805)499-0721, FAX (805)499-0871, telex 100799. **LC** RC435; .A55. **NLM** W1; AN7796H. **Acid Free.**

XV/0587-5161
**ANTHROPOS (LJUBLJANA).** (ANTHROPOS.). [Anthropos]. **Added/Corp** Drustvo Psihologov Slovenije. Slovensko Filozofsko Drustvo. (1969)-. Periodical. Slovenian (summaries and/or abstracts in English, French and German). bm. **LC** B6; .A5. **CODEN** ATHRAH.
**Ind/Abst** Psychol. Abstr. (1972-); Soc. Plann. Policy Dev. Abstr.; Sociol. Abstr.

SP
**ANUARIO DE PSICOLOGIA.** **Main/Corp** Universidad de San Carlos de Guatemala. Facultad de Humanidades. Vol. 1 (1962)-. Spanish. Four times a year. 4500.00ptas. Editorial Fontalba SA, Valencia 359 6TO 1, 08009 Barcelona Spain. **Tel** 011 34 3 4585508. **ED** Miguel Siguan. Index available. cum. index. **Bk Rev. Ad Acc. Pr Rev. Circ:** 1,500 (ctrl).
**Desc:** Publishes theoretical and empirical studies relating to general psychology.
**Ind/Abst** Indice Med. Esp.; Psychol. Abstr. (1962-); PsycINFO (1990-); PsycLit.

●US/1070-9797
**ANXIETY (NEW YORK, N.Y.).** (ANXIETY.). (1994)-. Periodical. English. bm. $180.00 US; $240.00 Canada and Mexico; $262.50 other. John Wiley & Sons, Inc., 605 Third Avenue, New York NY 10158-0012. **Tel** (212)850-6000, (212)850-6645, FAX (212)850-6088, telex 12-7063. **(Subscription address:** John Wiley & Sons / England, Baffins Lane, Chichester, West Sussex PO19 1UD England.**) ED** Thomas Uhde (editor-in-chief), Sandra E. File (associate editor for basic science), John J. Bartko (consulting editor for statisitcs), Manuel Tancer (book review editor). **NLM** W1; AN958E. **Bk Rev. Pr Rev.**
**Desc:** Publishes reports of novel research on the etiology, pathophysiology, epidemiology, nosology, symptomatology and treatment of anxiety disorders.

●SZ/1061-5806
**ANXIETY, STRESS AND COPING.** [Anxiety stress coping]. Vol. 5, No. 1 (May 1992)-. Periodical. English. qt. $255.00 (academic institutions), $397.00 (corporate institutions). Harwood Academic Publishers, PO Box 90, Reading RG1 8JL England. **Tel** 011 44 734 560080. **(Subscription address:** International Publishers Distributor at one of the following addresses: 820 Town Center Drive, Langhorne, PA 19047; or PO Box 90, Reading Berkshire RG1 8JL UK; or Kent Ridge PO Box 1180, Singapore 9111, Republic of Singapore**) LC** BF575.A6; A59. **DD** 152.4. **NLM** W1; AN958L. **CODEN** AXSCEP. **[CCC].** Documents available from The Genuine Article. ***Continues*** *Anxiety Research, 0891-7779.*
**Ind/Abst** Curr. Contents Soc. Behav. Sci.; Res. Alert [Full Cov.]; Soc. Sci. Cit. Index [Full Cov.].

US/0737-1446
**APA MEMBERSHIP REGISTER.** [APA membsh. reg.]. **Main/Corp** American Psychological Association. **VFOAT** A.P.A. Membership Register. **VAT** American Psychological Association Membership Register. (1982)-. English. ir. $35.00. American Psychological Association, 750 First Street Northeast, Washington DC 20002. **Tel** (800)374-2721, (202)336-5600, (subscriptions - (202)336-5600. **(Subscription address:** American Psychological Association, Order Department, PO Box 2710, Hyattsville MD 20784.**) ED** John A. Lazo. **LC** BF30; .A49. **DD** 150/.25/73. **NLM** BF 11 A51M. **Ad Acc. Circ:** 5,000. ***Continues*** *American Psychological Association. Membership Register, 0569-714X.*
**Desc:** Published to provide a current record of the association membership including mailing addresses, telephone numbers and membership status.

US/0001-2114
**APA MONITOR.** [APA monit.]. **Main/Corp** American Psychological Association. **VAT** American Psychological Association Monitor. Vol. 1 (Oct. 1970)-. English. mo. $32.50 (nonmember, institution) US. American Psychological Association, 750 First Street Northeast, Washington DC 20002. **Tel** (800)374-2721, (202)336-5600, (subscriptions - (202)336-5600. **ED** Jeffrey Mervis. **LC** BF1; .A54. **DD** 150/.5. **NLM** W1 A142V. **Ad Acc. Circ:** 76,400. available on microfilm from University Microfilms International (UMI).
**Desc:** The official newspaper of the American Psychological Association. Reports on the science, profession, and social impact of psychology, plus legislative developments affecting health services, education, and research are all covered regularly. Prominent psychologists discuss issues facing the field and other features bring in-depth articles on psychology in the United States and abroad.

●US/1078-7178
**APPIC DIRECTORY.** (APPIC DIRECTORY : INTERNSHIP AND POSTDOCTORAL PROGRAMS IN PROFESSIONAL PSYCHOLOGY.). [APPIC dir.]. **Added/Corp** Association of Psychology Postdoctoral and Internship Centers (U.S.). **VFOAT** Association of Psychology Postdoctoral and Internship Centers Directory; Internship and Postdoctoral Programs in Professional Psychology. 22nd Ed. (1993/1994)-. Directory. English. Association of Psychology Internship Centers, 733 15th Street NW, Suite 717, Washington DC 20005. **Tel** (202)347-0022. **DD** 150. ***Continues*** *Directory, Internship and Postdoctoral Programs in Professional Psychology.*

●US/0962-1849
**APPLIED & PREVENTIVE PSYCHOLOGY : JOURNAL OF THE AMERICAN ASSOCIATION OF APPLIED AND PREVENTIVE PSYCHOLOGY.** **Added/Corp** American Association of Applied and Preventive Psychology. **VFOAT** Applied and Preventive Psychology. Vol. 1, No. 1 (Winter 1992)-. Academic Scholarly Publication. English. qt. $96.00 US, Canada & Mexico; £56.00 other. Cambridge University Press / New York, 40 West 20th Street, New York NY 10011-4211. **Tel** (212)924-3900, (800)221-4512. **(Subscription address:** Cambridge University Press / Outside of North America, Journal Fulfillment Department, The Edinburgh Building, Cambridge CB2 2RU United Kingdom.**) ED** Samuel Osipow. **LC** IN PROCESS. **NLM** W1; AP51BP.
**Desc:** Intended for the scientist-practitioner engaged in the scientific, epidemiological or public health approach to psychological problems.

●US/1068-8595
**APPLIED BEHAVIORAL SCIENCE REVIEW.** (1993)-. Periodical. English. Twice a year. $125.00 (institutions), $60.00 (individuals) US; $135.00 (institutions), $70.00 (individuals) (surface mail), $145.00 (institutions), $80.00 (individuals) (air mail) other. JAI Press Inc., 55 Old Post Road, Suite 2, PO Box 1678, Greenwich CT 06836-1678. **Tel** (203)661-7602, FAX (203)661-0792. **ED** David Britt. **LC** IN PROCESS. **CODEN** ABSREI.
**Desc:** A multidisciplinary journal with a focus on policy studies, intervention strategies, and the assumptions and ideologies which undergird policy formation and options. A forum for dialogue between basic and applied approaches; seeks manuscripts devoted to theoretical explorations, reviews and meta-analyses, interpretive studies, and empirical investigations using historical, quantitative, and qualitative methods.

UK/0888-4080
**APPLIED COGNITIVE PSYCHOLOGY.** [Appl. cogn. psychol.]. **VFOAT** ACP. Vol. 1, No. 1 (Jan./March 1987)-. Periodical. English. Seven times a year. $365.00. John Wiley & Sons Ltd., Baffins Lane, Chichester West Sussex PO19 1UD England. **Tel** 0243 779777, FAX 0243 776128 BTG:JWP001, telex 86290 WIBOOKG. **(Subscription address:** John Wiley / Philadelphia, PO Box 7247, Philadelphia PA 19170.**) ED** Graham Davies and Michael Pressley. **LC** BF311; .A637. **DD** 153/.05. **NLM** W1; AP522C. **CODEN** ACPSED. **[CCC].** Index available. **Bk Rev. Ad Acc. Pr Rev.** available on microfilm and microfiche from University Microfilms International (UMI). Documents available from The Genuine Article, BIOSIS Document Express. ***Continues*** *Human Learning, 0277-6707.*
**Desc:** Seeks to publish the papers dealing with psychological analyses of problems of memory, learning, thinking, language and consciousness as they are reflected in the real world.
**Ind/Abst** Abstr. Hum. Comput. Interact.; Appl. Soc. Sci. Index Abstr.; Biol. Abstr.; Curr. Contents Soc. Behav. Sci.; Educ. Technol. Abstr.; Ergon. Abstr.; HILITES; Linguist. Lang. Behav. Abstr.; Psychol. Abstr. (1983-); PsycINFO; PsycLit; Res. Alert [Full Cov.]; Soc. Plann. Policy Dev. Abstr.; Soc. Sci. Cit. Index [Full Cov.]; Sociol. Abstr.

DK
**APPLIED NEUROPSYCHOLOGY.** Vol. 1 (1994)-. English. qt. kr730.00 US, Canada and Japan; kr720.00 other. Munksgaard International Publishers Ltd, PO Box 2148, DK-1016 Copenhagen K Denmark. **Tel** 011 45 33 12 70 30, FAX 011 45 33 12 93 87, telex 19431 MUNKS DK.

US/0146-6216
**APPLIED PSYCHOLOGICAL MEASUREMENT.** [Appl. psychol. meas.]. **Added/Corp** West Publishing Company. Vol. 1 (Winter 1977)-. Periodical. English. qt. $55.00. Applied Psychological Measurement, N657 Elliot Hall, University of Minnesota, Minneapolis MN 55455. **Tel** (612)625-0862. **ED** David J. Weiss. **LC** BF39; .A66. **DD** 150.1/82. **NLM** W1 AP528N. **[CCC].** Index available. cum. index. **Bk Rev. Ad Acc. Pr Rev. Circ:** 975 (ctrl). available on microfilm and microfiche from University Microfilms International (UMI). Documents available from The Genuine Article.
**Desc:** Research and reviews on methodologies for the measurement of psychological variables in all settings. Applications of psychological measurement to all areas of psychology and education.
**Ind/Abst** Curr. Contents Soc. Behav. Sci.; Curr. Index J. Educ. (March 1990); Psychol. Abstr. (1977-); PsycINFO; PsycLit; PsycScan: Appl. Psych.; Res. Alert [Full Cov.]; Soc. Sci. Cit. Index [Full Cov.]; Soc. Res. Methodol. Abstr. (1983-).

UK/0269-994X
**APPLIED PSYCHOLOGY.** **Added/Corp** International Association of Applied Psychology. **VFOAT** Psychologie Appliquee. Vol. 36, Issue 1 (Jan. 1987)-. Periodical. English (French). qt. $200.00 US; £108.00 Europe; £113.00 other. Lawrence Erlbaum Associates

Ltd., 27 Palmeira Mansions, Church Road, Hove East Sussex BN3 2FA England. **Tel** 011 44 273 207411. **(Subscription address:** Turpin Distribution Services Limited, Blackhorse Road, Letchworth, Hertfordshire SG6 1HN, United Kingdom.**) ED** Michael Frese. **LC** BF636.A1; I53. **DD** 158/.05. **NLM** W1; AP516H. **CODEN** ADPYE4. **Ad Acc. Pr Rev.** Documents available from The Genuine Article. ***Continues*** *International Review of Applied Psychology.*
**Desc:** Contains research findings in the field of applied psychology. Includes advances in psychological research, work and organizational psychology, environmental issues, health, gerontology, education, community problems, and intergroup relations.
**Ind/Abst** Contents Pages Manage.; Curr. Contents Soc. Behav. Sci.; Linguist. Lang. Behav. Abstr. (1992-); Psychol. Abstr. (1968-); PsycINFO (1968-); PsycLit; Res. Alert [Full Cov.]; Soc. Plann. Policy Dev. Abstr. (1992-); Soc. Sci. Cit. Index [Full Cov.]; Sociol. Abstr. (1992-).

●US/1070-6585
**APPLIED SOCIAL PROBLEMS AND INTERVENTION STRATEGIES.** (1994)-. Periodical. English. Harwood Academic Publishers / New York, PO Box 786, Cooper Station, New York NY 10276. **Tel** (212)206-8900, (201)643-7500. **(Subscription address:** International Publishers Distributor at one of the following addresses: 820 Town Center Drive, Langhorne, PA 19047; or PO Box 90, Reading Berkshire RG1 8JL UK; or Kent Ridge PO Box 1180, Singapore 9111, Republic of Singapore**)**

US
**APPLIED SOCIAL PSYCHOLOGY.** (19??)-. English. ir. $36.00. Lawrence Erlbaum Associates, 365 Broadway, Suite 102, Hillsdale NJ 07642. **Tel** (201)666-4110, (800)926-6579, FAX (201)666-2394. ***Continues*** *Advances in Applied Social Psychology, 0883-3656.*

US/1050-4672
**APS OBSERVER.** [APS obs.]. **Added/Corp** American Psychological Society. **VAT** American Psychological Society Observer. (19??)-. English. Ten times a year (Except June, & Aug.). $35.00. American Psychological Society, 1010 Vermont Avenue Northwest, Suite 1100, Washington DC 20005. **Tel** (202)783-2077, FAX (202)783-2083. **ED** K. Lee Herring. **DD** 150. **Ad Acc. Circ:** 15,000 (ctrl).
**Desc:** This newsletter features the current activities of the society national and international events and policy affecting the society or psychology, noteworthy psychological research, announcements, and the position opening for employment.

US/0895-1268
**ARCHAEUS.** [Archaeus]. **Added/Corp** Archaeus Project. (1983)-. English. $20.00 (includes Artifex). Archaeus Project, 629 Twelfth Avenue SE, Minneapolis MN 55414. **LC** R726.5; .A73. **DD** 610.
**Ind/Abst** Except. Hum. Exp.

UK
**ARCHITECTURAL PSYCHOLOGY NEWSLETTER.** ***Suspended.*** **Added/Corp** Kingston Polytechnic. School of Architecture. Psychology Reseach Unit. Vol. 1 (July 1969)-(19??). Newsletter. English. qt. $12.26. Kingston Polytechnic, Kingston Upon Thames, Surrey KT1 2QJ England. **Tel** 01 549 6151. **ED** Sue-Ann Lee. **Bk Rev. Circ:** 300.
**Desc:** Research summaries, articles, reviews, and information on courses, meetings and publications concerning the inter-relationship between people and their physical environment.

GW
**ARCHIV FUER RELIGIONSPSYCHOLOGIE.** **See** Religion and Theology.

SZ/0003-9640
**ARCHIVES DE PSYCHOLOGIE.** [Arch. psychol.]. Vol. 1 (1902)-. Periodical. English (French). Four times a year. 146.00F (institutions); 86.00F (individual). Medecine et Hygiene, Case Postale 456, CH-1211 Geneve 4 Switzerland. **Tel** 011 41 22 3469355, 011 41 22 3469356. **LC** BF2; .A75. **NLM** W1 AR343. **[CCC]**. cum. index.
**Ind/Abst** Psychol. Abstr. (1959-); PsycINFO; PsycLit; Soc. Plann. Policy Dev. Abstr.; Sociol. Abstr. (?-?).

IT/0004-0150
**ARCHIVIO DI PSICOLOGIA, NEUROLOGIA E PSICHIATRIA.** [Arch. psicol. neurol. psichiatr.]. **Added/Corp** Universita Cattolica del Sacro Cuore. (1957)-. Periodical. Italian. Four times a year. L120000 Italy; $110.00 others. Vita e Pensiero, Pubblic University, Largo Gemelli 1, 20123 Milan Italy. **Tel** 011 39 2 72342310, 011 39 2 72342370. **NLM** W1 AR553. **CODEN** APNPAD. Documents available from BIOSIS Document Express. ***Continues*** *Archivio de Psicologia, Neurologia, Psichiatria e Psicoterapia.*
**Ind/Abst** Biol. Abstr.; Linguist. Lang. Behav. Abstr.; Psychol. Abstr. (1957-); PsycINFO (1990-); PsycLit; Soc. Plann. Policy Dev. Abstr.; Sociol. Abstr.

CL/0577-8557
**ARCHIVOS.** **Main/Corp** Chile. Universidad, Santiago. Instituto de Psicologia. V. 3, No. 1- 1965-). Periodical. Spanish. Editorial Universitaria SA de Chile, Casilla 10220, Santiago Chile. **Tel** 011 56 2 223-4555.

IT
**ARGONAUTI, GLI.** Yearly Vol. 1, No. (June 1979)-. Periodical. Italian. qt. L62000.00. Centro Informazione Sanitaria, Via San Siro 1, 20149 Milan Italy. **Tel** 011 39 2 4694542.

US/0742-1656
**ART THERAPY : JOURNAL OF THE AMERICAN ART THERAPY ASSOCIATION.** [Art ther.]. **Added/Corp** American Art Therapy Association. Vol. 1, No. 1 (Oct. 1983)-. Academic Scholarly Publication. English. qt. $57.00 (institutions), $40.00 (individuals) US; $80.00 (institutions), $64.00 (individuals) other. American Art Therapy Assn Inc, 1202 Allanson Road, Mundelein IL 60060. **Tel** (708)949-6064, FAX (708)566-4580. **ED** Cathy Malchiodi. **NLM** W1; AR9482. cum. index. **Bk Rev**, (Qty: 8-12). **Ad Acc, Adv Mgr:** C. Fryer. **Pr Rev. Circ:** 4,200 (ctrl).
**Desc:** Scholarly papers, viewpoints, books, and media reviews and Association news regarding the adjunct of art therapy to psychological well-being.
**Ind/Abst** ARTbibliogr. Mod.; ARTbibliogr. Curr. Titles; Except. Child Educ. Resour.; PsycINFO.

US/0895-125X
**ARTIFEX (MINNEAPOLIS, MINN.).** (ARTIFEX / ARCHAEUS PROJECT.). [Artifex]. **Added/Corp** Archaeus Project. (1985)-. Periodical. English. bm. $20.00 (includes Archaeus). Archaeus Project, 629 Twelfth Avenue SE, Minneapolis MN 55414. **DD** 130. ***Continues*** *Archaeus Project Newsletter.*
**Ind/Abst** Except. Hum. Exp.

II
**ASIAN JOURNAL OF PSYCHOLOGY & EDUCATION, THE.** **Added/Corp** Agra Psychological Research Cell. **VFOAT** Asian Journal of Psychology and Education. Vol. 1, No. 1 (Mar. 1976)-. Periodical. English. Eight times a year. $179.95. Agra Psychological Research Cell, Agra, India. **(Subscription address:** Prints India, 11 Darya Ganj, New Delhi, 110002 India, (Phone: 011 91 11 3268645)**)**

US/0890-7854
**ASSERT.** ***Ceased.*** [Assert]. Issue 1 (Jan. 1975)-Issue 66 (Fall 1987). Periodical. English. qt. Assert, PO Box 1094, San Lius Obispo CA 93406. **Tel** (805)543-5911. **ED** Robert Alberti. **DD** 155. **Circ:** 600.

US/1047-0387
**ATTENTION AND PERFORMANCE.** [Atten. perform.]. **Added/Corp** Instituut voor Zintuigfysiologie RVO-TNO. International Association for the Study of Attention and Performance. (1967)-. English. ir. Lawrence Erlbaum Associates, 365 Broadway, Suite 102, Hillsdale NJ 07642. **Tel** (201)666-4110, (800)926-6579, FAX (201)666-2394. **LC** BF321; .A79. **DD** 153.7/33. Documents available from The Genuine Article.
**Ind/Abst** Res. Alert [Full Cov.]; Soc. Sci. Cit. Index [Full Cov.].

IT
**ATTUALITA IN PSICOLOGICA.** (19??)-. Italian. Edizioni Universitarie Romane, Via M Poggioli 3, 00161 Rome Italy.

US/0148-3420
**AUDIT REPORT. BOARD OF PSYCHOLOGY.** (AUDIT REPORT, BOARD OF PSYCHOLOGY (TENNESSEE).). **Main/Corp** Tennessee. Division of State Audit. English. Tennessee Comptroller of the Treasury, Nashville TN 37219. **LC** RA790.65.T35; T43A. **DD** 353.97/68/00842.

AT/0726-3864
**AUSTRALIA AND NEW ZEALAND JOURNAL OF DEVELOPMENTAL DISABILITIES.** **See** Physically Impaired.

AT/0312-8857
**AUSTRALIAN AUTISM REVIEW.** ***Ceased.*** [Aust. autism rev.]. Vol. 1 (Sept. 1975)-?. Periodical. English. an. National Association for Autism, PO Box 607, Chatswood New South Wales 2067 Australia. **Tel** (61) (2) 412 4766. **ED** R Q Allen & K F Kennett. **NLM** W1 AU516. **Bk Rev. Ad Acc. Circ:** 1,000.
**Desc:** Medical and educational research into problems of autism including services to autistic persons and their families.
**Ind/Abst** Aust. Educ. Index (1977-19??).

AT/0816-5122
**AUSTRALIAN EDUCATIONAL AND DEVELOPMENTAL PSYCHOLOGIST.** [Aust. educ. dev. psychol.]. **Added/Corp** Australian Psychological Society. Board of Educational and Development Psychologists. (1984)-. Periodical. English. Twice a year (May & Nov.). 25.00Aus$ (institutions), 15.00Aus$ (individuals) Australia; 30.00Aus$ (institutions) other. Australian Psychological Society Division of Education, Griffith University, Nathan QLD 4111 Aystrakua Australia. **Tel** 011 61 7 8755834, FAX 011 61 7 8755910. **(Subscription address:** Australian Psychological Society, PO Box 126, Carlton South Victoria, 3053 Australia.**) ED** Fiona Bryer PhD. **DD** 370.1505.
**Ind/Abst** Aust. Educ. Index (199?-).

AT/0004-9530
**AUSTRALIAN JOURNAL OF PSYCHOLOGY.** [Aust. j. psychol.]. **Added/Corp** British Psychological Society. Australian Branch. Australian Psychological Society. Vol. 1 (June 1949)-. Periodical. English. Three times a year (Apr., Aug., & Dec.). 55.00Aus$ (individuals), 65.00Aus$ (institutions) Australia; 70.00Aus$ others. Australian Psychological Society, 1 Grattan Street, Carlton Victoria 3053 Australia. **Tel** 011 61 3 6636166, FAX 011 61 3 3474841. **ED** P. Sheehan. **LC** BF1; .B74. **DD** 150/.5. **NLM** W1 AU618. **CODEN** ASJPAE. Index available. cum. index. **Bk Rev. Ad Acc. Pr Rev. Circ:** 5,600 (ctrl). Documents available from The Genuine Article, BIOSIS Document Express.
**Desc:** Presents articles and book reviews on any topic with a central reference to psychology and an emphasis on academic or archival functions.
**Ind/Abst** Abstr. Anthropol.; APAIS, Aust. Public Aff. Inf. Ser. (1963-); Appl. Soc. Sci. Index Abstr.; Aust. Educ. Index (1978-); Biol. Abstr.; Curr. Contents Soc. Behav. Sci.; Ergon. Abstr.; Linguist. Lang. Behav. Abstr.; Middle East Abstr. Index; Life Sci. Collect.; Psychol. Abstr. (1949-); PsycINFO; PsycLit; Res. Alert [Full Cov.]; Res. High. Educ. Abstr.; Soc. Plann. Policy Dev. Abstr.; Soc. Sci. Cit. Index [Full Cov.]; Sociol. Abstr.; Sociol. Educ. Abstr.; SportSearch; Stud. Women Abstr.; Women Stud. Abstr.

AT/0728-6155
**AUSTRALIAN JOURNAL OF PSYCHOTHERAPY.** [Aust. j. psycho.-ther.]. **Added/Corp** Psychotherapy Association of Australia. Vol. 1, No. 1, (1982)-. Periodical. English. sa. 70.00Aus$ (institutions), 45.00Aus$ (individuals). Australian Journal of Psychotherapy, 24 140 Church Street, Richmond VIC 3121 Australia. **Tel** 011 61 3 6623165. **ED** E. Sebel. **NLM** W1; AU624H. **Bk Rev. Ad Acc. Circ:** 1,000 (ctrl).
**Desc:** Publishes original articles devoted to individual and group psycotherapy and related topics.

AT/0005-0067
**AUSTRALIAN PSYCHOLOGIST.** [Aust. psychol.]. **Added/Corp** Australian Psychological Society. Vol. 1 (July 1966)-. Periodical. English. Three times a year (Mar., July, Nov.). 55.00Aus$ (individuals), 65.00Aus$ (institutions) Australia; 70.00Aus$ (institutions) other. Australian Psychological Society, 1 Grattan Street, Carlton Victoria 3053 Australia. **Tel** 011 61 3 6636166, FAX 011 61 3 3474841. **ED** Graham Davidson. **NLM** W1 AU644G. **CODEN** AUPCBK. Index available. cum. index. **Bk Rev. Ad Acc. Pr Rev. Circ:** 5,800 (ctrl). Documents available from The Genuine Article.
**Desc:** Publishes articles and reviews of applied and professional interest to psychologists.
**Ind/Abst** APAIS, Aust. Public Aff. Inf. Ser. (1974-); Appl. Soc. Sci. Index Abstr.; Aust. Educ. Index (1978-); Curr. Contents Soc. Behav. Sci.; Hum. Resour. Abstr. (?-?); Psychol. Abstr. (1966-); PsycINFO; PsycLit; Res. Alert [Full Cov.]; Res. High. Educ. Abstr.; Soc. Sci. Cit. Index [Full Cov.]; SportSearch.

US/0893-8474
**AUTISM RESEARCH REVIEW INTERNATIONAL, THE.** (THE AUTISM RESEARCH REVIEW INTERNATIONAL : A QUARTERLY PUBLICATION OF THE INSTITUTE FOR CHILD BEHAVIOR RESEARCH.). [Autism res. rev. int.]. **Added/Corp** Institute for Child Behavior Research (San Diego, Calif.). Vol. 1, No. 1 (1987)-. Periodical. English. Four times a year (Mar., June, Sept., Dec.). $16.00 US; $18.00 other. Autism Research Institute, 4182 Adams Avenue, San Diego CA 92116. **Tel** (619)281-7165, FAX (619)563-6840. **ED** Bernard Rimland & Alison Blake. **DD** 155. **Bk Rev**, (Qty: 4-5). **Circ:** 6,200.
**Desc:** Succinct reviews of current biomedical and educational research on autistic children, based on computer search of world literature.

CK/0120-3797
**AVANCES EN PSICOLOGIA CLINICA LATINOAMERICANA.** **VFOAT** APCL. Vol. 1 (1982)-. Spanish (summaries and/or abstracts in English). an. 1.800Col$ Colombia; $25.00 other. Apartado 92621, Bogota Colombia. **ED** Ruben Ardila. **NLM** W1; AV219. Index available. cum. index. **Bk Rev. Ad Acc.**
**Ind/Abst** PsycINFO (1990-).

FR
**AVE: LE MAGAZINE FREUDIEN, L'.** No. 1 (April/May 1981)-. Periodical. French. qt. 240.00F (individuals) France; 280.00F (individuals) other. L Ane, 74 rue d Assas, 75006 Paris France. **Tel** 011 33 1 45485672, FAX 011 33 1 45487938. **ED** J. Miller. Index available. **Bk Rev**, (Qty: 4). **Ad Acc.**

GW
**BALINT-GRUPPE IN KLINIK UND PRAXIS, DIE.** **See** Medical Science and Technology.

US/0197-3533
**BASIC AND APPLIED SOCIAL PSYCHOLOGY.** [Basic appl. soc. psychol.]. Vol. 1, No. 1 (March 1980)-. Periodical. English. qt. $395.00 US & Canada; $440.00 other. Lawrence Erlbaum Associates, 365 Broadway, Suite 102, Hillsdale NJ 07642. **Tel** (201)666-4110, (800)926-6579, FAX (201)666-2394. **ED** Paul B Paulus. **LC** HM251; .B4413. **DD** 302/.05. **CODEN** BASPEG. **Ad Acc. Pr Rev.** available on CD-ROM; available on microfilm and microfiche from University Microfilms International (UMI). Documents available from The Genuine Article, BIOSIS Document Express.
**Ind/Abst** Biol. Abstr. (1986-); Cumul. Index Nurs. Allied Health Lit.; Curr. Contents Soc. Behav. Sci.; High. Educ. Abstr. (1986-); Index Period. Artic. Relat. Law (19??-19??); Psychol. Abstr. (1980-); PsycINFO; PsycLit; PsycScan: Appl. Psych.; Res. Alert [Full Cov.]; Soc. Sci. Cit. Index [Full Cov.]; SportSearch.

US/1052-0082
**BEHAVIOR ANALYSIS DIGEST.** [Behav. anal. dig.]. Vol. 1, No. 1 (Dec. 1989)-. Periodical. English. qt. $12.00 (institutions), $8.00 (individuals). Behavior Analysis Digest, 509 Hurricane Court, Hurricane WV 25526. **Tel** (304)766-8787. **ED** W Joseph Wyatt. **LC** BF1; .B38. **DD** 150/.5. **Bk Rev**, (Qty: 3). **Circ:** 200 (ctrl).
**Desc:** Serves as an exchange and clearing house for information about the experimental, theoretical and applied analysis of behavior.

US/0738-6729
**BEHAVIOR ANALYST, THE.** (BEHAVIOR ANALYST / MABA.). [Behav. anal.]. **Added/Corp** Society for the Advancement of Behavior Analysis. Association for Behavior Analysis. Midwestern Association of Behavior Analysis. Vol. 1, No. 1 (Spring 1978)-. Periodical. English. sa (May and December). $42.50 (institution), $25.00 (individual), $15.00 (student) US; $57.50 (institution), $40.00 (individual), $30.00 (student) other. Society for the Advancement of Behavior Analysis, Western Michigan University, 258 Wood Hall, Kalamazoo MI 49008. **Tel** (616)387-4584. **ED** Samuel M Deitz. **LC** BF199; .B35. **DD** 150/.5. **NLM** W1 BE122D. Index available. cum. index. **Bk Rev. Ad Acc. Pr Rev. Acid Free. Circ:** 2,500 (ctrl). available on audiocassette. Documents available from The Genuine Article.
**Desc:** Contains articles on trends, issues, policies, and developments in the field of behavior analysis.
**Ind/Abst** Abstr. Res. Pastor. Care Couns. (19??-); Crim. Justice Abstr.; Curr. Contents Soc. Behav. Sci.; Psychol. Abstr. (1982-); PsycINFO (1990-); PsycLit; Res. Alert [Full Cov.].

US/1053-8348
**BEHAVIOR AND PHILOSOPHY.** [Behav. philos.]. **Added/Corp** Cambridge Center for Behavioral Studies. Vol. 18, No. 1 (Spring/Summer 1990)-. Periodical. English. sa (2 issues). $28.00 (individuals), $48.00 (institutions) US; $30.50 (individuals), $50.50 (institutions) Canada and Mexico; $33.00 (individuals), $53.00 (institutions) other. Cambridge Center for Behavioral Studies, 11 Waterhouse Street, Cambridge MA 02138. **Tel** (617)491-9020, FAX (617)491-1072. **DD** 150. **CODEN** BEPHE5. available on microfilm and microfiche from University Microfilms International (UMI); available on CD-ROM. Documents available from The Genuine Article, BIOSIS Document Express. ***Continues*** *Behaviorism, 0090-4155.*
**Ind/Abst** Biol. Abstr. (1991-); Curr. Contents Soc. Behav. Sci.; PsycLit; Res. Alert [Full Cov.]; Soc. Sci. Cit. Index [Full Cov.].

US/1064-9506
**BEHAVIOR AND SOCIAL ISSUES.** [Behav. soc. issues]. **Added/Corp** Cambridge Center for Behavioral Studies. (1991)-. Periodical. English. sa (Mar. and Sept.). $28.00 (individual), $48.00 (institutions) US; $30.50 (individual), $50.50 (institutions) Canada and Mexico; $33.00 (individual), $53.00 (institutions) other. Cambridge Center for Behavioral Studies, 11 Waterhouse Street, Cambridge MA 02138. **Tel** (617)491-9020, FAX (617)491-1072. **(Subscription address:** Johnson Press, 49 Sheridan Avenue, Albany NY 12210.) **LC** BF199; .B376. **DD** 150.19/43. **Bk Rev. Circ:** 250. available on CD-ROM. ***Continues*** *Behavior Analysis & Social Action, 1065-1047.*
**Desc:** Publishes scholarly articles that advance the analysis of human social behavior, particularly with application to understanding existing social problems.
**Ind/Abst** PsycLit.

US/0193-6271
**BEHAVIOR IMPROVEMENT NEWS.** (BEHAVIOR IMPROVEMENT NEWS : THE BEHAVIOR MODIFICATION NEWSLETTER.). V. 1, No. 1- Sept. 1977-. Newsletter. English. mo. $36.00. Subscription Desk, Research Press Company, 2612 North Mattis Avenue, Champaign IL 61820.

US/0145-4455
**BEHAVIOR MODIFICATION.** [Behav. modif.]. Vol. 1 (Jan. 1977)-. Periodical. English. qt (Jan., Apr., July, Oct.). $174.00. SAGE Periodical Press, 2455 Teller Road, Thousand Oaks CA 91320. **Tel** (805)499-0721, FAX (805)499-0871, telex 100799. **ED** Michel Hersen and Alan S. Bellack (associate editor). **LC** BF637.B4; B43. **DD** 158. **NLM** W1 BE124T. **[CCC].** Index available in last issue of volume--attached. **Pr Rev. Acid Free.** available on microfilm and microfiche from University Microfilms International (UMI). Documents available from The Genuine Article.
**Desc:** Describes assessment and modification techniques for problems in psychiatric, clinical, educational and rehabilitational settings.
**Ind/Abst** Abstr. Anthropol. (19??-); Cumul. Index Nurs. Allied Health Lit.; Curr. Contents Soc. Behav. Sci.; Educ. Index; Educ. Adm. Abstr. (?-?); EMBASE; Except. Child Educ. Resour.; Health Plan. Adminis.; Hum. Resour. Abstr.; Index Med. (1983-); Middle East Abstr. Index; Multicult. Educ. Abstr.; Psychol. Abstr. (1977-); PsycINFO; PsycLit; Res. Alert [Full Cov.]; Sage Fam. Stud. Abstr.; Soc. Sci. Cit. Index [Full Cov.]; SportSearch; Work Relat. Abstr.

US/0743-3808
**BEHAVIOR RESEARCH METHODS, INSTRUMENTS, & COMPUTERS : A JOURNAL OF THE PSYCHONOMIC SOCIETY, INC.** [Behav. res. meth. instrum. comput.]. **Added/Corp** Psychonomic Society. **VFOAT** Behavior Research Methods, Instruments, and Computers. Vol. 16, No. 1 (Feb. 1984)-. Periodical. English. Four times a year (Feb., May, Aug., Nov.). $112.00 US; $119.00 other. Psychonomic Society Publications, 1710 Fortview Road, Austin TX 78704. **Tel** (512)462-2442, FAX (512)462-1101. **ED** Joseph B. Sidowski. **LC** BF180; .B4. **DD** 150/.72. **NLM** W1 BE126H. **CODEN** BRMCEW. **[CCC].** Index available. **Ad Acc. Circ:** 1,300. available on microfilm and microfiche from University Microfilms International (UMI). Documents available from The Genuine Article, Ask*IEEE. ***Continues*** *Behavior Research Methods and Instrumentation, 0005-7878.*
**Desc:** Deals with methods, techniques, and instrumentation of research in experimental psychology with special focus on the use of computer technology in experimental psychology.
**Ind/Abst** Acad. Search (July 1993-); Curr. Contents Soc. Behav. Sci.; Ei Page One; Ergon. Abstr.; Fish Rev. (Jan. 1989-July 1992); Index Vet.; INFO-SOUTH Abstr.; INSPEC (1985-); Linguist. Lang. Behav. Abstr.; Life Sci. Collect. (1984-); Psychol. Abstr. (1968-); PsycINFO; PsycLit; Res. Alert [Full Cov.]; Soc. Plann. Policy Dev. Abstr.; Soc. Sci. Source (Jul. 1993-); Soc. Sci. Cit. Index [Full Cov.]; Sociol. Abstr.; Soc. Res. Methodol. Abstr. (1981-); Wildl. Rev. (Jan. 1989-July 1992).

US/0278-8403
**BEHAVIOR THERAPIST, THE.** [Behav. ther.]. **Added/Corp** Association for Advancement of Behavior Therapy. (197?)-. Periodical. English. Ten times a year. $38.00 institution. Association for the Advancement of Behavior Therapy, 305 7th Avenue, New York NY 10001. **Tel** (212)647-1890, FAX (212)647-1865. **ED** Alan M. Gross. **DD** 155. **NLM** W1 BE128C. Index available. cum. index. **Bk Rev. Ad Acc. Circ:** 3,800 (ctrl).
**Desc:** News magazine specializing in developments in behavior therapy/modification, special education, & mental health.
**Ind/Abst** Psychol. Abstr. (1979-); PsycINFO (1979-?).

US/0005-7894
**BEHAVIOR THERAPY.** [Behav. ther.]. **Added/Corp** Association for Advancement of Behavior Therapy. Vol. 1, No. 1 (March 1970)-. Academic Scholarly Publication. English. Four times a year (Feb., May, Aug., Nov.). $130.00 institution. Association for the Advancement of Behavior Therapy, 305 7th Avenue, New York NY 10001. **Tel** (212)647-1890, FAX (212)647-1865. **ED** Edward Blanchard. **LC** RC489.B4; B435. **DD** 616.89. **NLM** W1 BE128D. **CODEN** BHVTAK. **[CCC].** Index available. cum. index. **Bk Rev. Ad Acc. Pr Rev. Acid Free. Circ:** 3,200. Documents available from The Genuine Article, BIOSIS Document Express, UMI Article Clearinghouse.
**Desc:** An interdisciplinary journal which presents original research, both clinical and experimental, treatment procedures and methodological evaluation employed in the field of behavior therapy. Topics include alcohol and drug abuse, anxiety, depression, marital therapy, phobia and panic disorders, relaxation, smoking cessation, and weight control.
**Ind/Abst** Annals Behav. Med.; Biol. Abstr.; Curr. Contents Soc. Behav. Sci.; EMBASE; Expand. Acad. Index (1992-); Newsp. Period. Abstr. (1992-); Psychol. Abstr. (1970-); PsycLit; PsycScan: Clin. Psych.; Res. Alert [Full Cov.]; Soc. Sci. Cit. Index [Full Cov.]; Spec. Educ. Needs Abstr.; Women Stud. Abstr.

US/0360-6341
**BEHAVIOR THERAPY WITH CHILDREN.** Vol. 1 (1971)-. English. Aldine Publishing Company, 200 Saw Mill River Road, Hawthorne NY 10532. **LC** RJ505.B4; B43. **DD** 618.9/28/91.

US/0140-525X
**BEHAVIORAL AND BRAIN SCIENCES, THE.** [Behav. brain sci.]. Vol. 1 (March 1978)-. Academic Scholarly Publication. English. qt (March, June, September and December). $222.00 US, Canada & Mexico; £150.00 other. Cambridge University Press / New York, 40 West 20th Street, New York NY 10011-4211. **Tel** (212)924-3900, (800)221-4512. **(Subscription address:** Cambridge University Press / Outside of North America, Journal Fulfillment Department, The Edinburgh Building, Cambridge CB2 2RU United Kingdom.) **ED** Stevan Harnad. **LC** QP360; .B425. **DD** 152/.05. **NLM** W1 BE129K. **CODEN** BBSCDH. **Pr Rev.** available on microfilm and microfiche from University Microfilms International (UMI). Documents available from The Genuine Article, BIOSIS Document Express, Ask*IEEE, UMI Article Clearinghouse.
**Desc:** Open peer commentary format; work published from researchers in any area of psychology, neuroscience, behavioral biology or cognitive science. Commentaries from specialists within and across these disciplines, plus the author's response are provided on each article. Contributes to the communication, criticism, stimulation, and unification of research in behavioral and brain sciences, from molecular neurobiology to artificial intelligence and the philosophy of the mind.
**Ind/Abst** Anim. Behav. Abstr.; Anim. Breed. Abstr.; Biol. Abstr.; CSA Neuro. Abstr.; Curr. Aware. Biol. Sci., CABS; Curr. Contents Life Sci.; Curr. Contents Soc. Behav. Sci.; EMBASE; Expand. Acad. Index (1992-); Index Vet.; INSPEC (1987-); Int. Bibliogr. Sociol.; Linguist. Lang. Behav. Abstr.; Newsp. Period. Abstr. (1992-); Life Sci. Collect.; Psychol. Abstr. (1978-); PsycINFO; PsycLit; Ref. Upd. Deluxe Ed.; Res. Alert [Full Cov.]; Sci. Cit. Index; SCISEARCH; Soc. Plann. Policy Dev. Abstr.; Soc. Sci. Cit. Index [Full Cov.]; Sociol. Abstr.

US/0163-9269
**BEHAVIORAL & SOCIAL SCIENCES LIBRARIAN.** See Library and Information Sciences.

US/0191-5401
**BEHAVIORAL ASSESSMENT.** ***Title Change.*** [Behav. assess.]. Vol. 1- (1979)-(19??). Periodical. English. qt. Pergamon Press Inc., 660 White Plains Road, Tarrytown NY 10591-5153. **Tel** (914)524-9200, FAX (914)333-2444, telex 13-7328. **(Subscription address:** UK/ Headington Hill Hall, Oxford OX3 0BW; Can/ 150 Consumers Road/Suite 104, Willowdale Ontario M2J 1P9; Aus-NZ/ POB 544, Potts Point NSW 2011) **ED** John D Cone. **LC** RC489.B4; B4353. **DD** 616.89/142/05. **NLM** W1 BE129T. **CODEN** BEHSDV. **[CCC]. Pr Rev.** available on microfilm and microfiche from University Microfilms International (UMI). Documents available from The Genuine Article, BIOSIS Document Express. ***Merged into*** *Behavior Research and Therapy., 0005-7967.*
**Ind/Abst** Annals Behav. Med.; Biol. Abstr.; Crim. Justice Abstr.; Curr. Aware. Biol. Sci., CABS; Curr. Contents Soc. Behav. Sci.; EMBASE; Psychol. Abstr. (1980-); PsycINFO; PsycLit; Res. Alert [Full Cov.]; Soc. Sci. Cit. Index (19??-19??) [Full Cov.].

US/0197-7717
**BEHAVIORAL MEDICINE ABSTRACTS.** ***Title Change.*** See Medical Science and Technology-Abstracting, Bibliographies and Statistics.

US/0735-7044
**BEHAVIORAL NEUROSCIENCE.** [Behav. neurosci.]. **Added/Corp** American Psychological Association. Vol. 97, No. 1 (Feb. 1983)-. Academic Scholarly Publication. English. bm. $292.00 (nonmember, institution) US. American Psychological Association, 750 First Street Northeast, Washington DC 20002. **Tel** (800)374-2721, (202)336-5600, (subscriptions - (202)336-5600. **ED** Larry R. Squire, PhD. **LC** BF1; .B39. **DD** 152. **NLM** W1 BE13M. **CODEN** BENEDJ. **[CCC]. Ad Acc. Pr Rev. Circ:** 2,600. available on microfilm and microfiche from University Microfilms International (UMI). Documents available from The Genuine Article, UMI Article Clearinghouse, CASDDS. ***Continues in part*** *Journal of Comparative and Physiological Psychology, 0021-9940.*
**Desc:** Features include reproduction of photomicrographs, technical exchanges between authors and readers, and original studies of behavioral neuroscience. Also research in anatomy, chemistry, endocrinology, genetics, pharmacology, physiology, vertebrates and invertebrates, patient populations, and normal human subjects.
**Ind/Abst** Acad. Search (July 1993-); AGRICOLA [Select. Cov.]; Anim. Breed. Abstr.; Biol. Agric. Index; Chem. Abstr. (1983-); Chemorecept. Abstr.; CSA Neuro. Abstr. (?-?); Curr. Aware. Biol. Sci., CABS; Curr. Contents Life Sci.; Curr. Ref. Fish Res.; EMBASE; Expand. Acad. Index (1989-); Fish Rev. (Jan. 1989-July 1992); Gen. Sci. Source (Jul. 1993-); Health Plan. Adminis.; Index Med.; INFO-SOUTH Abstr.; INIS Atomindex [Micro.]; Newsp. Period. Abstr. (1990-); Nutr. Abstr. Rev., Ser. A, Hum. Exp.; Life Sci. Collect.; Psychol. Abstr. (1983-); PsycINFO; PsycLit; Ref. Upd. Deluxe Ed.; Res. Alert [Full Cov.]; Sci. Cit. Index; SCISEARCH; Soc. Sci. Source (Jul. 1993-); Soc. Sci. Cit. Index [Select. Cov.]; Soc. Sci. Index; Soc. Sci. Index Fulltext (Aug. 1988-) [Full Txt.]; Wildl. Rev. (Jan. 1989-July 1992).

US/0005-7940
**BEHAVIORAL SCIENCE.** [Behav. sci.]. **Added/Corp** University of Michigan. Mental Health Research Institute. Fund for the Behavioral Sciences (U.S.) Institute of Management Sciences. Society for General Systems Research. Vol. 1, No. 1 (Jan. 1956)-. Periodical. English. Four times a year (Jan., Apr., July, Oct.). $41.00 (individuals), $76.00 (institutions) US; $81.50 others. Behavioral Science, PO Box 26519, San Diego CA 92126. **Tel** (619)549-2901, FAX (619)549-3094. **LC** BF1; .B4. **DD** 150/.5. **NLM** W1 BE132. **CODEN** BEHSAS. **[CCC]. Pr Rev.** available on microfilm and microfiche from University Microfilms International (UMI). Documents available from The Genuine Article, Ask*IEEE, UMI Article Clearinghouse.

**Desc:** Articles dealing with animal or human behavior with emphasis on biological and social systems and cross-level formal identities among them.
**Ind/Abst** ABC POL SCI; ABI/INFORM Glob. Ed.; ABI Inform Ondisc (Sept. 1971-Sept. 1973); Acad. Search (July 1993-); ACM Guide Comput. Lit.; Am. Hist. Life (1972-1974); Anthropol. Index; Appl. Soc. Sci. Index Abstr.; Comput. Rev.; Contents Pages Manage.; Curr. Contents Soc. Behav. Sci.; EMBASE; Energy Res. Abstr.; Ergon. Abstr. (?-?); Expand. Acad. Index (1989-); Gen. Sci. Source (Jul. 1993-); Geogr. Abstr. Human Geogr.; Health Plan. Adminis.; Hum. Resour. Abstr. (?-?); Index Med.; INFO-SOUTH Abstr.; INIS Atomindex [Micro.]; INSPEC (Jan. 1972-); Int. Aerosp. Abstr.; Int. Bibliogr. Sociol.; Int. Dev. Abstr.; Int. Polit. Sci. Abstr.; J. Plan. Lit.; Key Word Index Wildl. Res.; Linguist. Lang. Behav. Abstr.; Mag. Search; Middle East Abstr. Index; MLA Int. Bibl. Books Artic. Mod. Lang. Lit.; Newsp. Period. Abstr. (1991-); Psychol. Abstr. (1956-); PsycINFO; PsycLit; Res. Alert [Full Cov.]; Selec. Coop. Index Manage. Period; Soc. Plann. Policy Dev. Abstr.; Soc. Sci. Source (Jul. 1993-); Soc. Sci. Cit. Index [Full Cov.]; Soc. Sci. Index; Soc. Sci. Index Fulltext (Oct. 1988-) [Full Txt.]; Sociol. Abstr.; Sociol. Educ. Abstr.; U.S. Polit. Sci. Doc.

UK/0735-3936
**BEHAVIORAL SCIENCES & THE LAW.** See Law.

US/0361-4646
**BEHAVIORAL SCIENCES NEWSLETTER.** ***Ceased.*** (1972)-(19??). Newsletter. English (Spanish). sm. Roy W Walter & Associates, Whitney Road, Mahwah NJ 07430. **Tel** (201)891-5757. **ED** John V Hickey. **[CCC].** Index available. cum. index. **Bk Rev. Circ:** 10,000.
**Desc:** Reports ways to increase productivity, motivate employees, and reduce absenteeism. Special areas of interest include organizational development, work effectiveness and change implementation.

JA/0385-7417
**BEHAVIORMETRIKA. Added/Corp** Behaviormetric Society of Japan. (July 1974)-. Periodical. English. sa. $40.00. Nihon Kodo Keiryo Gakkai, (Behaviormetric Society of Japan), 6-7, Minamiazabu, 4 Chome, Minatoku, Tokyoto 106 Japan. **(Subscription address:** Japan Publications Trading Company, Ltd., PO Box 5030, Tokyo International, Tokyo 100-31 Japan.) **LC** BF76.5; .B438. **DD** 150/.72.
**Ind/Abst** Linguist. Lang. Behav. Abstr.; Psychol. Abstr. (1983-); PsycINFO; PsycLit; Soc. Plann. Policy Dev. Abstr.; Sociol. Abstr.; Stat. Theory Method Abstr. (1983-1984, 1987).

●US/1047-8663
**BEHAVIOROLOGY (MORGANTOWN, W. VA.).** (BEHAVIOROLOGY: A JOURNAL OF THE INTERNATIONAL BEHAVIOROLOGY ASSOCIATION). **Added/Corp** International Behaviorology Association. (1992)-. Periodical. English. ir. University of West Virginia, 609-C Allen Hall, Morgantown WV 26506-6122. **NLM** W1; BE1333.

AT/0813-4839
**BEHAVIOUR CHANGE.** (BEHAVIOUR CHANGE : JOURNAL OF THE AUSTRALIAN BEHAVIOUR MODIFICATION ASSOCIATION.). [Behav. change]. **Added/Corp** Australian Behaviour Modification Association. **VFOAT** BC. (1984)-. Periodical. English. Four times a year (Feb., May, Aug., Nov.). 33.00Aus$ (individuals), 63.00Aus$ (institutions) Australia; 43.00Aus$ (individuals), 74.00Aus$ (institutions) New Zealand; 60.00Aus$ (individuals) 83.00Aus$ (institutions) other. Australian Academic Press Pty. Ltd., 32 Jeays Street, Bowen Hills Queensland 4006 Australia. **Tel** 011 61 7 2571176, FAX 011 61 7 2525908. **ED** Matthew R. Sanders. **LC** RC489.B4; B4378. **DD** 616.89/142/05. **NLM** W1; BE1342AE. **CODEN** BHCAE8. **[CCC]. Bk Rev. Ad Acc. Pr Rev. Circ:** 900. available on microfilm and microfiche from University Microfilms International (UMI).
**Desc:** Publishes original contributions on behavioural assessment and intervention in a diverse range of settings which are of interest and use to psychologists, psychiatrists, nurses, occupational therapists, social workers and teachers.
**Ind/Abst** Aust. Educ. Index; EMBASE; Psychol. Abstr. (1984-); PsycINFO (1990-); PsycLit; Spec. Educ. Needs Abstr.

UK
**BEHAVIOURAL AND COGNITIVE PSYCHOTHERAPY. Added/Corp** British Association for Behavioural and Cognitive Psychotherapies. Vol. 21, No. 3 (1993)-. Periodical. English. qt. $125.00. Wisepress Ltd., Old Church Hall, 89A Quicks Road, Wimbledon SW19 1EX United Kingdom. **Tel** 011 44 81 715 1812. **LC** RC489.B4; B45. **DD** 616.89/142/05. **NLM** W1; BE135CR. ***Continues*** *Behavioural Psychotherapy, 0141-3473.*

UK/0141-3473
**BEHAVIOURAL PSYCHOTHERAPY.** ***Title Change.*** [Behav. psychother.]. **Added/Corp** British Association for Behavioural Psychotherapy. Vol. 6, No. 1 (Jan. 1978)-Vol. 21, No. 2 (1993). Periodical. English. qt. Wisepress Ltd., Old Church Hall, 89A Quicks Road, Wimbledon SW19 1EX United Kingdom. **Tel** 011 44 81 715 1812. **LC** RC489.B4; B45. **DD** 616.89/142/05. **NLM** W1 BE135H. **CODEN** BEPSD3. **[CCC]. Pr Rev.** Documents available from The Genuine Article, BIOSIS Document Express. ***Continues*** *BABP Bulletin.* ***Continued by*** *Behavioural and Cognitive Psychotherapy.*
**Desc:** A journal for the publication of original experimental or clinical research that contributes to the theory, practice, and evaluation of behavior therapy.
**Ind/Abst** Appl. Soc. Sci. Index Abstr.; Biol. Abstr. (1986-); Cumul. Index Nurs. Allied Health Lit.; Curr. Contents Soc. Behav. Sci.; EMBASE; Psychol. Abstr. (1981-); PsycINFO; PsycLit; Res. Alert [Full Cov.]; Soc. Sci. Cit. Index [Full Cov.]; Spec. Educ. Needs Abstr.

GW/0085-1302
**BEIHEFT ZUR ZEITSCHRIFT GRUPPENPSYCHOTHERAPIE UND GRUPPENDYNAMIK.** [Beihef.t Z. Gruppenpsychother. Gruppendyn.]. (1972)-. Monographic series. German. Price varies per volume. Vandenhoeck & Ruprecht, Robert Bosch Breite 6, D-37079 Goettingen Germany. **Tel** 011 49 551 695911, FAX 011 49 551 695917, telex 965226 VAN d. Documents available from The Genuine Article.
**Ind/Abst** Res. Alert [Full Cov.]; Soc. Sci. Cit. Index [Full Cov.].

GW/0522- 7194
**BEITRAGE ZUR VERHALTUNGSFORSCHUNG.** No. 1-. Monographic series. German. ir. Price varies per volume. Duncker und Humblot Verlag, Postfach 410329, D-12113 Berlin Germany. **Tel** 011 49 30 79000612, 011 49 30 79000613.

US/0277-0032
**BENCHMARK PAPERS IN BEHAVIOR.** [Benchmark pap. behav.]. (1980)-. Monographic series. English. ir. Price varies per volume. Academic Press, Inc., 6277 Sea Harbor Drive, Orlando FL 32887. **Tel** (800)543-9534, (407)345-4100, FAX (407)363-9661. **ED** M. W. Schein and S. W. Porges. **LC** UNC. **DD** 591.51. **NLM** W1 BE514B. ***Continues*** *Benchmark Papers in Animal Behavior, 0093-4720.*

US/1071-7366
**BEREAVEMENT & LOSS RESOURCES.** [Bereave. loss resour.]. **Added/Corp** Rivendell Resources. **VFOAT** Bereavement and Loss Resources. (19??)-. Periodical. English. Four times a year. $25.00 (one year), $45.00 (two years). Rivendell Resources, PO Box 3272, Ann Arbor MI 48106-3272. **Tel** (313)761-1960. **ED** Cendra Lynn. **DD** 155. **Bk Rev**, (Qty: 20). **Ad Acc. Circ:** 1,000. available on an online database.

US/0897-9588
**BEREAVEMENT (CARMEL, IND.).** (BEREAVEMENT : A MAGAZINE OF HOPE AND HEALING.). [Bereavement]. Vol. 1, No. 1 (Nov./Dec. 1987)-. Periodical. English. Six times a year (Jan., Mar., May, July, Sept., Nov.). $29.00 (one year); $53.00 (two years). Bereavement Publishing, 8133 Telegraph Drive, Colorado Springs CO 80920. **Tel** (719)282-1948. **ED** Andrea Gambill. **DD** 155. **Bk Rev**, (Qty: 6). **Ad Acc, Adv Mgr Tel** (719)282-1948. **Circ:** 5,000.
**Desc:** A magazine of hope and healing, dedicated to the concerns of people who are grieving the loss by death of any significant relationship.

US/1061-396X
**BETTER WORLD.** ***Ceased.*** [Better world]. **Added/Corp** Intergroup for Planetary Oneness. Vol. 1, No. 1 (1991)-(199?). Periodical. English. bm. Better World, 17211 Orozco Street, Granada Hills CA 91344-1132. **DD** 158. ***Continues*** *Meditation, 0886-3830.*

GW/0303-5999
**BIBLIOGRAPHIE DER DEUTSCHSPRACHIGEN PSYCHOLOGISCHEN LITERATUR.** See Psychology-Abstracting, Bibliographies and Statistics.

US/0742-681X
**BIBLIOGRAPHIES AND INDEXES IN PSYCHOLOGY.** [Bibliogr. indexes psychol.]. No. 1 (1985)-. Monographic series. English. ir. Price varies per volume. Greenwood Press Inc., PO Box 5007, Westport CT 06881-5007. **Tel** (203)226-3571, FAX (203)222-1502. **DD** 016.

US
**BIENNIAL REPORT OF EXAMINING AND LICENSING BOARDS / MINNESOTA BOARD OF PSYCHOLOGY. Main/Corp** Minnesota. Board of Psychology. English. be. Minnesota Board of Psychology, 2700 University Avenue West #101, St Paul MN 55114-1095. **Tel** (612)642-0587. **LC** BF80.8; .M562A. **DD** 353.97760082/43. **Bk Rev. Ad Acc. Circ:** 20 (ctrl).
**Desc:** A report to Governor re-licensure. Data, activities, time spent of board members and disciplinary actions taken by the board of psychology.

US/0743-4804
**BIOENERGETIC ANALYSIS.** See Medical Science and Technology-Psychiatry.

US/0363-3586
**BIOFEEDBACK AND SELF-REGULATION.** [Biofeedback self-regul.]. **Added/Corp** Biofeedback Research Society. Biofeedback Society of America. **VFOAT** Biofeedback and Self Regulation. Vol. 1, (Mar. 1976)-. Periodical. English. Four times a year. $245.00 institutions, $55.00 individuals US; $285.00 institutions, $64.00 individuals other. Plenum Press, 233 Spring Street, New York NY 10013-1578. **Tel** (212)620-8000, (800)221-9369, FAX (212)463-0742, (212)807-1047, telex 23/421139. **ED** Robert Freedman. **LC** BF319.5.B5; B55. **DD** 615/.851. **NLM** W1 BI664R. **CODEN** BSELDP. **[CCC].** available on microfilm and microfiche from University Microfilms International (UMI). Documents available from The Genuine Article, BIOSIS Document Express, Ask*IEEE.
**Desc:** Provides rapid dissemination of information in the field of biofeedback. Original papers, clinical case studies, and review articles address all relevant aspects of psychology, psychiatry, psychosomatic and physical medicine, and cybernetics.
**Ind/Abst** Biol. Abstr. (March 1979-); Curr. Contents Eng. Tech. Appl. Sci.; EMBASE (1976-); Health Plan. Adminis.; Index Med.; INSPEC (March 1979-); Life Sci. Collect. (March 1979-); Psychol. Abstr.; PsycLit; Res. Alert [Full Cov.]; Soc. Sci. Cit. Index [Full Cov.]; Spec. Educ. Needs Abstr.

NE/0301-0511
**BIOLOGICAL PSYCHOLOGY.** [Biol. psychol.]. Vol. 1 (1973)-. Academic Scholarly Publication. English. Six times a year (2 volumes). Fl844.00. Elsevier Science Publishers BV, PO Box 211, 1000 AE Amsterdam Netherlands. **Tel** 011 31 20 5803642, FAX 011 31 20 5862696, telex 15682. **ED** D Siddle and P H Venables. **NLM** W1 BI754P. **CODEN** BLPYAX. **[CCC]. Pr Rev.** available on microfilm and microfiche from University Microfilms International (UMI). Documents available from The Genuine Article, BIOSIS Document Express, CASDDS.
**Desc:** Publishes original scientific papers dealing with the biological correlates of psychological states.
**Ind/Abst** Annals Behav. Med.; Biol. Abstr.; Chem. Abstr. (1973-1982); Commun. Abstr. (?-?); CSA Neuro. Abstr. (?-?); Curr. Aware. Biol. Sci., CABS; Curr. Contents Soc. Behav. Sci.; Dev. Med. Child Neurol. (-1990); EMBASE; Health Plan. Adminis.; Index Med.; Life Sci. Collect.; Psychol. Abstr. (1973-); PsycINFO; PsycLit; Ref. Upd. Deluxe Ed.; Res. Alert [Full Cov.]; Soc. Sci. Cit. Index [Full Cov.].

US/0734-3124
**BIRTH PSYCHOLOGY BULLETIN.** See Medical Science and Technology-Gynecology and Obstetrics.

CU/0253-5742
**BOLETIN DE PSICOLOGIA.** (BOLETIN DE PSICOLOGIA / REPUBLICA DE CUBA, MINISTERIO DE SALUD PUBLICA, HOSPITAL PSIQUIATRICO DE LA HABANA.). [Bol. psicol.]. **Added/Corp** Hospital Psiquiatrico de la Habana. (1978)-. Spanish (summaries and/or abstracts in English). Three times a year (Jan., May, Sept.). Free. Hspt Psiquiatrico de la Habana, Ministerio de Salud Publica, Habana Cuba. **Tel** 45-16-88. **ED** Dr. Noemi Perez Valdes. **NLM** W1 BO266. Index available. **Bk Rev. Circ:** 2,000.
**Ind/Abst** Psychol. Abstr. (1978-); PsycINFO; PsycLit.

IT/0006-6761
**BOLLETTINO DI PSICOLOGIA APPLICATA.** [Boll. psicol. appl.]. No. 37/39 (Feb./June 1960)-. Periodical. Italian. Four times a year. L60000 (individuals), L90000 (institutions) Italy; 120000 (individuals), L150000 (institutions) others. Orginizzazioni Speciali, Via Scipione Ammirato 37, Florence Italy. **Tel** 011 39 55 660997, FAX 011 39 55 268312, telex 571438. **NLM** W1 BO563. Index available. **Bk Rev. Ad Acc. Circ:** 1,000 (ctrl). Documents available. ***Continues*** *Bollettino di Psicologia e Sociologia Applicata.* ***Continued in part by*** *Rassegna Italiana di Sociologia.*
**Desc:** Publishes articles on general psychology, psychometrics, developmental psychology, social processes, personality, educational psychology, industrial psychology, and clinical psychology.
**Ind/Abst** Linguist. Lang. Behav. Abstr.; Psychol. Abstr. (1960-); PsycINFO; PsycLit; Soc. Plann. Policy Dev. Abstr.; Sociol. Abstr.

US/0278-2626
**BRAIN AND COGNITION.** [Brain cogn.]. Vol. 1, No. 1 (Jan. 1982)-. Academic Scholarly Publication. English. Nine times a year. $255.00 US and Canada; $305.50 other. Academic Press, Inc., 6277 Sea Harbor Drive, Orlando FL 32887. **Tel** (800)543-9534, (407)345-4100, FAX (407)363-9661. **ED** Harry A. Whitaker and Jeffery L. Cummings. **LC** QP376; .B69595. **DD** 612/.82/05. **NLM** W1; BR112F. **[CCC]. Bk Rev. Pr Rev.** Documents available from The Genuine Article.
**Desc:** This journal deals with the nonlinguistic aspects of neuropsychology during the past decade. Presenting clinical case histories, original experimental research papers, reviews, notes, and commentaries, it provides a forum for the discussion of timely and important advances in the field.
**Ind/Abst** Arts Humanit. Citation Index [Select. Cov.]; Curr. Aware. Biol. Sci., CABS; Curr. Contents Life Sci.; Curr. Contents Soc. Behav. Sci.; Dev. Med. Child Neurol.;

Health Plan. Adminis.; Index Med. (1984-); Psychol. Abstr. (1982-); PsycINFO; PsycLit; Res. Alert [Full Cov.]; Sci. Cit. Index; SCISEARCH; Soc. Sci. Cit. Index [Full Cov.].

●US/1064-671X
**BRAIN, MIND & COMMON SENSE.** [Brain mind common sense]. **VFOAT** Brain, Mind and Common Sense; Brain Mind; Brain/Mind & Common Sense. Vol. 17, No. 8 (May 1992)-. Periodical. English. mo. Brain, Mind & Common Sense, PO Box 42211, Los Angeles CA 90042. **LC** BP605.N48; B7. **DD** 133. ***Continues*** *New Sense Bulletin, 1057-0705.*

NE/0924-0314
**BRILL'S STUDIES IN EPISTEMOLOGY, PSYCHOLOGY AND PSYCHIATRY.** [Brill's stud. epistemol. psychol. psychiatry]. (1989)-. Monographic series. English. ir. Price varies per volume. E. J. Brill, Postbus 9000, 2300 PA Leiden Netherlands. **Tel** 011 31 71 312624, FAX 011 31 71 317532, telex 39296 BRILL NL. **UDC** 159.0 :165.

UK/0144-6657
**BRITISH JOURNAL, THE. OF CLINICAL PSYCHOLOGY, THE.** [Br. j. clin. psychol.]. **Added/Corp** British Psychological Society. Vol. 20, Pt. 1 (Feb. 1981)-. Periodical. English. qt (Feb., May, Sep., Nov.). £110.00 Canada & EEC Countries; £204.00 others. British Psychological Society, St. Andrews House, 48 Princess Road, Leicester LE1 7DR England. **Tel** 011 44 533 549568. **(Subscription address:** Turpin Distribution Services Limited, Blackhorse Road, Letchworth, Hertfordshire SG6 1HN, United Kingdom.**)** **ED** Chris R. Brewin. **LC** BF1; .B723. **DD** 616.89/005. **NLM** W1 BR519V. **CODEN** BJCPDW. **[CCC].** Index available (Bound in last issue). cum. index. **Bk Rev. Ad Acc. Pr Rev. Circ:** 3,100. available on microfiche. Documents available from The Genuine Article, BIOSIS Document Express. ***Continues in part*** *British Journal of Social and Clinical Psychology, 0007-1293.*
**Desc:** A special section devoted to health psychology, regular "practice reviews" to acquaint practitioners with clinically relevant research findings and the publication of brief lists of references on the treatment of different disorders selected by experts in the field.
**Ind/Abst** Annals Behav. Med. (19??-); Appl. Soc. Sci. Index Abstr. (19??-); Biol. Abstr. (19??-); Crim. Penol. Police Sci. Abstr. (19??-); Cumul. Index Nurs. Allied Health Lit. (19??-); Curr. Contents Soc. Behav. Sci. (19??-); Dev. Med. Child Neurol. (19??-); EMBASE (19??-); Health Plan. Adminis. (19??-); Index Med. (19??-); Int. Bibliogr. Sociol. (19??-); Linguist. Lang. Behav. Abstr. (19??-); Middle East Abstr. Index (19??-); Life Sci. Collect. (19??-); Psychol. Abstr. (1981-); PsycINFO (19??-); PsycLit (19??-); PsycScan: Clin. Psych. (19??-); Res. Alert (19??-) [Full Cov.]; Soc. Plann. Policy Dev. Abstr. (19??-); Soc. Sci. Cit. Index (19??-) [Full Cov.]; Sociol. Abstr. (19??-).

UK/0261-510X
**BRITISH JOURNAL OF DEVELOPMENTAL PSYCHOLOGY, THE.** [Br. j. dev. psychol.]. **Added/Corp** British Psychological Society. Vol. 1, Pt. 1 (March 1983)-. Periodical. English. Four times a year. £97.00 Canada & EEC Countries, £180.00 other. British Psychological Society, St. Andrews House, 48 Princess Road, Leicester LE1 7DR England. **Tel** 011 44 533 549568. **(Subscription address:** Turpin Transactions Ltd., Blackhorse Road, Letchworth, Hertfordshire SG6 1HN United Kingdom; Telephone: (0462) 672555, FAX: (0462) 480947**)** **ED** George Butterworth. **LC** BF712; .B75. **DD** 155/.05. **[CCC].** Index available. **Bk Rev. Ad Acc. Pr Rev. Circ:** 1,200. available on microfilm. Documents available from The Genuine Article.
**Desc:** This journal aims to publish full length, empirical, conceptual, review and discussion papers, as well as brief reports on work in progress.
**Ind/Abst** Appl. Soc. Sci. Index Abstr.; Br. Educ. Index; Curr. Contents Soc. Behav. Sci.; Dev. Med. Child Neurol.; Linguist. Lang. Behav. Abstr.; Psychol. Abstr. (1983-); PsycINFO; PsycLit; PsycScan: Develop. Psych.; Res. Alert [Full Cov.]; Soc. Plann. Policy Dev. Abstr.; Soc. Sci. Cit. Index [Full Cov.]; Sociol. Abstr.

UK/0007-0998
**BRITISH JOURNAL OF EDUCATIONAL PSYCHOLOGY, THE.** [Br. j. educ. psychol.]. **Added/Corp** British Psychological Society. Training College Association (Great Britain). Vol. 1 (Feb. 1931)-. Periodical. English. qt. £97.00, $109.00. British Psychological Society, St. Andrews House, 48 Princess Road, Leicester LE1 7DR England. **Tel** 011 44 533 549568. **(Subscription address:** Turpin Distribution Services Limited, Blackhorse Road, Letchworth, Hertfordshire SG6 1HN, United Kingdom.**)** **ED** Dr. Michael Youngman. **LC** LB1051.A2; B7. **NLM** W1 BR527. **CODEN** BJESAE. **[CCC].** Index available (Bound in last issue). cum. index. **Bk Rev. Ad Acc. Pr Rev.** ctrl circ. Documents available from The Genuine Article. ***Continues*** *Forum of Education.*
**Desc:** Publishes a wide spectrum of educational research.
**Ind/Abst** Appl. Soc. Sci. Index Abstr. (19??-); Arts Humanit. Citation Index [Select. Cov.]; Br. Educ. Index (19??-); Curr. Contents Soc. Behav. Sci. (19??-); Curr. Index J. Educ. (19??-); Educ. Index (19??-); Educ. Technol. Abstr. (19??-); Health Plan. Adminis. (19??-); High. Educ. Abstr. (1965-); Index Med. (19??-); Lang. Teach. (19??-); Linguist. Lang. Behav. Abstr. (19??-); Multicult. Educ. Abstr. (19??-); Psychol. Abstr. (1931-); PsycINFO (19??-); PsycLit (19??-); Res. Alert (19??-) [Full Cov.]; Res. High. Educ. Abstr. (19??-); School Organ. Manage. Abstr. (19??-); Soc. Plann. Policy Dev. Abstr. (19??-); Soc. Sci. Cit. Index (19??-) [Full Cov.]; Sociol. Abstr. (?-?); Sociol. Educ. Abstr. (19??-); Stat. Theory Method Abstr. (1983); Stud. Women Abstr. (19??-); Tech. Educ. Train. Abstr. (19??-); Women Stud. Abstr. (19??-).

UK/0007-1102
**BRITISH JOURNAL OF MATHEMATICAL & STATISTICAL PSYCHOLOGY, THE.** **See** Psychology-Abstracting, Bibliographies and Statistics.

UK/0007-1129
**BRITISH JOURNAL OF MEDICAL PSYCHOLOGY.** [Br. j. med. psychol.]. **Added/Corp** British Psychological Society. British Psychological Society. Medical Section. **VFOAT** Medical Section. Vol. 3 (Jan. 1923)-. Academic Scholarly Publication. English. Four times a year (Mar., June, Sept., Dec.). £106.00 UK, Canada, & EEC Countries, £197.00 others. British Psychological Society, St. Andrews House, 48 Princess Road, Leicester LE1 7DR England. **Tel** 011 44 533 549568. **(Subscription address:** Turpin Transactions Ltd., Blackhorse Road, Letchworth, Hertfordshire SG6 1HN United Kingdom; Telephone (0462) 672555, FAX: (0462) 480947**)** **ED** John Birtchnell. **LC** RC321; .B83. **NLM** W1 BR581. **CODEN** BJMPAB. **[CCC].** Index available (Bound in last issue). cum. index. **Bk Rev. Ad Acc. Pr Rev. Circ:** 2,300. available on microfiche. Documents available from The Genuine Article, BIOSIS Document Express, CASDDS. ***Continues*** *British Journal of Psychology. Medical Section.*
**Desc:** An international journal with a traditional orientation towards psychodynamic issues. The journal aims to bring together other medical and psychological disciplines and this is reflected in the composition to the editorial team.
**Ind/Abst** Annals Behav. Med.; Arts Humanit. Citation Index [Select. Cov.]; Biol. Abstr.; Chem. Abstr.; Cumul. Index Nurs. Allied Health Lit.; Curr. Contents Clin. Med.; Curr. Contents Soc. Behav. Sci.; Dev. Med. Child Neurol.; EMBASE; Health Plan. Adminis.; Index Med.; Linguist. Lang. Behav. Abstr.; Med. Abstr. Newsl.; Middle East Abstr. Index; Nutr. Abstr. Rev., Ser. B, Live Feeds and Feed.; Nutr. Abstr. Rev., Ser. A, Hum. Exp.; Psychol. Abstr. (1926-); PsycINFO; PsycLit; Res. Alert [Full Cov.]; Sci. Cit. Index; SCISEARCH; Soc. Plann. Policy Dev. Abstr.; Soc. Sci. Cit. Index [Full Cov.]; Sociol. Abstr.

UK
**BRITISH JOURNAL OF PROJECTIVE PSYCHOLOGY.** **Added/Corp** British Society for Projective Psychology. Vol. 31, No. 2 (Dec 1986)-. Periodical. English. sa. $40.00 (institutions), $30.00 (individuals) US and Canada; $36.24 other. British Rorschach Forum Trust, 81 Salamanca Street, Parkhead Hospital, Glasgow G31 5ES Scotland. **Tel** 011 41 5547951. **ED** Zahid Mahmood (editor's address: Department of Psychology, 155 Crail Street, Glasgow G31 5RB Scotland). **NLM** W1; BR613M. **Bk Rev. Ad Acc.** ***Continues*** *British Journal of Projective Psychology and Personality Study, 0309-7757.*
**Desc:** Articles on clinical and research work related to projective psychology.
**Ind/Abst** PsycLit.

UK/0007-1269
**BRITISH JOURNAL OF PSYCHOLOGY (1955).** (THE BRITISH JOURNAL OF PSYCHOLOGY.). [Br. j. psychol.]. **Added/Corp** British Psychological Society. (1953)-. Periodical. English. qt. $141.00 Canada and EEC; $262.00 other. British Psychological Society, St. Andrews House, 48 Princess Road, Leicester LE1 7DR England. **Tel** 011 44 533 549568. **(Subscription address:** British Psychological Society Distribution Center; Blackhorse Road, Letchworth, Hertfordshire SG6 1HN United Kingdom; Telephone: (0462) 672555, FAX: (0462) 480947**)** **ED** Antony J. Chapman. **CODEN** BJSGAE. **[CCC].** Index available. cum. index. **Bk Rev. Ad Acc. Pr Rev. Circ:** 3,400. available on microfilm. Documents available from The Genuine Article, BIOSIS Document Express, UMI Article Clearinghouse. ***Continues*** *British Journal of Psychology. General Section, 0373-2460.*
**Desc:** Publishes reports of empirical studies, critical reviews of the literature and theoretical distributions.
**Ind/Abst** Acad. Search (July 1993-); Appl. Soc. Sci. Index Abstr.; Biol. Abstr.; Br. Educ. Index; Dev. Med. Child Neurol.; Ergon. Abstr.; Expand. Acad. Index (1989-); Health Period. Database; Health Plan. Adminis.; High. Educ. Abstr. (1965-); Index Med.; INFO-SOUTH Abstr.; Int. Bibliogr. Sociol.; Linguist. Lang. Behav. Abstr.; Middle East Abstr. Index; MLA Int. Bibl. Books Artic. Mod. Lang. Lit.; Newsp. Period. Abstr. (1991-); Psychol. Abstr. (1926-); PsycINFO; PsycLit; Res. Alert [Full Cov.]; Res. High. Educ. Abstr.; Soc. Plann. Policy Dev. Abstr.; Soc. Sci. Source (Jul. 1993-); Soc. Sci. Cit. Index [Full Cov.]; Soc. Sci. Index; Soc. Sci. Index Fulltext (Nov. 1988-) [Full Txt.]; Sociol. Abstr.; Sociol. Educ. Abstr.; SportSearch.

UK/0144-6665
**BRITISH JOURNAL OF SOCIAL PSYCHOLOGY, THE.** [Br.j. soc. psychol.]. **Added/Corp** British Psychological Society. Vol. 20, Pt. 1 (Feb. 1981)-. Academic Scholarly Publication. English. Four times a year (Feb., June, Sept., Nov.). £95.00 Canada & EEC Countries; £176.00 others. British Psychological Society, St. Andrews House, 48 Princess Road, Leicester LE1 7DR England. **Tel** 011 44 533 549568. **(Subscription address:** Turpin Transactions Ltd., Blackhorse Road, Letchworth, Hertfordshire SG6 1HN United Kingdom; Telephone: (0462) 672555, FAX: (0462) 480947**)** **ED** Miles Hewstone. **LC** BF1; .B727. **DD** 302/.05. **NLM** W1 BR635F. **CODEN** BJSPDA. **[CCC].** Index available. **Bk Rev. Ad Acc. Pr Rev. Circ:** 2,300. available on microfiche. Documents available from The Genuine Article, BIOSIS Document Express. ***Continues*** *British Journal of Social and Clinical Psychology, 0007-1293.*
**Desc:** Publishes articles which contribute to the basic methodological and theoretical issues confronting the discipline. In addition, it encourages: theoretical and review papers, papers describing applied social psychology in a variety of settings, on controversial issues, and guest-edited issues on research in growth areas of social psychology.
**Ind/Abst** Appl. Soc. Sci. Index Abstr.; Biol. Abstr.; Crim. Justice Abstr.; Crim. Penol. Police Sci. Abstr.; Curr. Contents Soc. Behav. Sci.; Dev. Med. Child Neurol.; EMBASE; Health Plan. Adminis.; High. Educ. Abstr. (1981-); Index Med.; Int. Bibliogr. Sociol.; Linguist. Lang. Behav. Abstr.; Middle East Abstr. Index; Multicult. Educ. Abstr.; Life Sci. Collect.; Psychol. Abstr. (1981-); PsycINFO; PsycLit; Res. Alert [Full Cov.]; Res. High. Educ. Abstr.; Soc. Plann. Policy Dev. Abstr.; Soc. Sci. Cit. Index [Full Cov.]; Sociol. Abstr.; Sociol. Educ. Abstr.; Stud. Women Abstr.

US/1058-1073
**BROWN UNIVERSITY CHILD AND ADOLESCENT BEHAVIOR LETTER, THE.** (THE BROWN UNIVERSITY CHILD AND ADOLESCENT BEHAVIOR LETTER : MONTHLY REPORTS ON THE PROBLEMS OF CHILDREN AND ADOLESCENTS GROWING UP.). [Brown Univ. child adolesc. behav. lett.]. **Added/Corp** Brown University. Manisses Communications Group. **VFOAT** Child and Adolescent Behavior Letter. Vol. 7, No. 7 (July 1991)-. Periodical. English. mo. $129.00 (institutions), $99.00 (individuals) US; $139.00 (institutions), $119.00 (individuals) Canada; $149.00 (institutions), $139.00 (individuals) other. Manisses Communications Group Inc., PO Box 3357, Providence RI 02906-0757. **Tel** (401)831-6020, (800)333-7771, FAX (401)861-6370. **ED** Lewis P. Lipsitt. **LC** HQ767.8; .B76. **DD** 362. Index available. available on an online database (file 149/Full-Text) from DIALOG. ***Continues*** *Brown University Child Behavior and Development Letter, 0898-2562.*
**Desc:** Updates on research and theories on the problems of children and adolescents.
**Ind/Abst** Health Index (1991-); Health Period. Database [Full Txt.].

US/1068-4409
**BULLETIN - ALBERT HOFMANN FOUNDATION.** (BULLETIN / THE ALBERT HOFMANN FOUNDATION.). [Bull. - Albert Hofmann Found.]. **Added/Corp** Albert Hofmann Foundation. **VFOAT** Bulletin of the Albert Hofmann Foundation. Vol. 2 No. 2/3 (Spring/Summer 1991)-. Bulletin. English. qt. $30.00 (membership). The Albert Hofmann Foundation, 291 South La Cienega Boulevard, #615, Beverly Hills CA 90211-3325. **Tel** FAX (310) 854-1840. **LC** IN PROCESS. **DD** 026. **Bk Rev**, (Qty: 8). **Circ:** 1,000. ***Continues*** *Newsletter (Albert Hofmann Foundation), 1047-6245.*
**Desc:** Scientific study of human consciousness, synthetic and naturally occuring hallucinogen and their effects on human consciousness.

FR/0373-6261
**BULLETIN DE LA SOCIETE FRANCAISE DU RORSCHACH ET DES METHODES PROJECTIVES.** [Bull. soc. fr. Rorschach methodes proj.]. (1962)-. Periodical. French. ir. Societe Francaise du Rorschach et des Methodes Projectives, 28 Rue Serpente, F-75006 Paris France. **UDC** 159.9. ***Continues*** *Bulletin du Groupement Francais du Rorschach, 1148-828X.*
**Ind/Abst** PsycINFO (1963-); PsycLit.

FR/0007-4403
**BULLETIN DE PSYCHOLOGIE.** [Bull. psychol.]. **Added/Corp** Universite de Paris. Groupe d'Etudes de Psychologie. (195?)-. Bulletin. French. bm. 530.00F individuals, 805.00F societies, 705.00F institutions. Groupe Etudes Psychologie Universite, 17 rue de la Sorbonne, 75005 Paris France. **NLM** W1 BU564. **Bk Rev.** ctrl circ. ***Continues*** *Bulletin (Universite de Paris. Groupe d'Etudes de Psychologie).*
**Ind/Abst** Psychol. Abstr. (1962-); PsycINFO; PsycLit.

BE/0007-4411
**BULLETIN DE PSYCHOLOGIE SCOLAIRE ET D'ORIENTATION.** [Bull. psychol. sc. orientat.]. Vol. 1 (1952)-. Periodical. French (English). Four times a year. 700F Belgium; 900F other.

Federation de Centres Psycho-Medico-Sociaux et d'Orientation Libres, Avenue de Tervueren 222, Bte 8, 1150 Bruxelles Belgium. **ED** R. Andre. **DD** 150. Index available. cum. index. **Bk Rev. Ad Acc. Circ:** 350 (ctrl).
**Ind/Abst** Psychol. Abstr. (1955-); PsycINFO; PsycLit.

US/0077-5339
**BULLETIN - NATIONAL PSYCHOLOGICAL ASSOCIATION FOR PSYCHOANALYSIS.** [Bull. - Natl. Psychol. Assoc. Psychoanal.]. **Main/Corp** National Psychological Association for Psychoanalysis. Bulletin. English. an. National Psychological Association for Psychoanalysis, 140 West 13th Street, New York NY 10011. **Tel** (212)924-7440. **ED** Annabella B Nelken. **Circ:** 5,000 (ctrl).
**Desc:** Catalogue and course description for training program in psycho analysis.

AT
**BULLETIN OF THE AUSTRALIAN PSYCHOLOGICAL SOCIETY. Added/Corp** Australian Psychological Society. Vol. 1, Issue 1 (May 1979)-. Periodical. English. Six times a year (Feb., Apr., June, Aug., Oct., Dec.). 65.00Aus$ (institutions) Australia; 70.00Aus$ (institutions) other; 55.00Aus$ (individuals). Australian Psychological Society, 1 Grattan Street, Carlton Victoria 3053 Australia. **Tel** 011 61 3 6636166, FAX 011 61 3 3474841. **ED** Allan Anderson. **Ad Acc. Circ:** 5,400 (ctrl).
**Desc:** Articles regarding professional matters and informs its members of matters which related to their society and what it is doing for them.
**Ind/Abst** Aust. Educ. Index (199?-).

II/0376-6675
**BULLETIN OF THE BUREAU OF EDUCATIONAL AND PSYCHOLOGICAL RESEARCH, CALCUTTA. Main/Corp** Bureau of Educational and Psychological Research, Calcutta. No. 1- Jan. 1971-. Bulletin. English. Bureau of Educational and Psychological Research, 25/3 Ballygunge Circular Road, Calcutta 19 India. **LC** LB7; .B83A. **DD** 370/.5.

FR/1013-9974
**BULLETIN OF THE INTERNATIONAL TEST COMMISSION AND OF THE DIVISION OF PSYCHOLOGICAL ASSESSMENT OF THE IAAP.** [Bull. Int. Test Comm. Div. Psychol. Assess IAAP]. **VFOAT** Bulletin de la Commission Internationale des Tests et de la Division Evaluation en Psychologie de l'AIPA. No. 20 (Sept. 1984)-. Academic Scholarly Publication. English (French). sa. Editions du Centre de Psychologie Apliquee, 48 Avenue Victor-Hugo, 75783 Paris France. ***Continues*** *Newsletter of the International Test Commission and of the Division Psychological Assessment of the IAAP.*
**Ind/Abst** EMBASE.

US/0090-5054
**BULLETIN OF THE PSYCHONOMIC SOCIETY.** ***Title Change.*** [Bull. Psychon. Soc.]. **Main/Corp** Psychonomic Society. Vol. 1-31 (Jan. 1973)-(Nov. 1993). Academic Scholarly Publication. English. bm. Psychonomic Society Publications, 1710 Fortview Road, Austin TX 78704. **Tel** (512)462-2442, FAX (512)462-1101. **ED** Anne Dossett. **LC** BF1; .P883a. **DD** 150/.5. **NLM** W1 BU886V. **CODEN** BPNSBY. **[CCC].** Index available. **Pr Rev. Circ:** 1,400. available on microfilm and microfiche from University Microfilms International (UMI). Documents available from The Genuine Article, BIOSIS Document Express, CASDDS. ***Supersedes in part*** *Psychonomic Science, 0033-3131.* ***Continued by*** *Psychonomic Bulletin & Review, 1069-9384.*
**Desc:** A short-report journal providing prompt publication of articles covering all areas of experimental psychology. All articles authored or sponsored by members of the Psychonomic Society.
**Ind/Abst** Biol. Abstr.; Chem. Abstr.; Curr. Contents Soc. Behav. Sci.; EMBASE; Ergon. Abstr.; High. Educ. Abstr. (1977-?); Int. Aerosp. Abstr.; Linguist. Lang. Behav. Abstr.; Middle East Abstr. Index; MLA Int. Bibl. Books Artic. Mod. Lang. Lit.; Life Sci. Collect.; Psychol. Abstr. (1973-?); PsycINFO; PsycLit; Res. Alert [Full Cov.]; Soc. Plann. Policy Dev. Abstr.; Soc. Sci. Cit. Index [Full Cov.]; Sociol. Abstr.; Stat. Theory Method Abstr. (1980-1981).

CN
**BULLETIN - YORK UNIVERSITY, TORONTO. INSTITUTE FOR BEHAVIOURAL RESEARCH. Main/Corp** York University (Toronto, Ont.) Institute for Behavioural Research. No. 1- 196 -. Bulletin. English. ir. Institute for Social Research / Ontario, York University, 4700 Keele Street, North York Ontario M3J 1P3 Canada. **Tel** (416)736-5061, FAX (416)736-5687.

PO/0871-7516
**CADERNOS DE CONSULTA PSICOLOGICA. Added/Corp** Universidade do Porto. Servico de Consulta Psicologica e Orientacao Vocacional. Universidade do Porto. Instituto de Consulta Psicologica, Formacao e Desenvolvimento. (1985)-. Periodical. Portuguese (English and French). Faculdade de Psicologia e Ciencias da Educacao, Universidade do Porto, Rua de Ceuta, 118-6, 4000 Porto Portugal. **LC** RC467; .C3. **DD** 616.89.
**Ind/Abst** PsycINFO (1985-); PsycLit.

BL
**CADERNOS DE PSICOLOGIA APLICADA.** V. 1- Jan./July 1973-. Periodical. Multiple languages (English, Portuguese and Spanish). Centro de Orientacao e Selecao Psicotecnica, rua Jacinto Gomes 540 5 Andar, Porto Alegre Brazil. **LC** BF636.A1; C33.

FR
**CAHIERS BINET SIMON. Added/Corp** Societe Alfred Binet & Theodore Simon. No 626/627 (1991)-. Periodical. French. qt. Editions Eres, 11 rue des Alouettes, Ramonville St. Agne France. **Tel** 011 33 61 751576. **NLM** W1; CA1333C. ***Continues*** *Binet Simon.*

FR
**CAHIERS CONFRONTATION.** ***Ceased.*** **VFOAT** Confrontation. No. 1, Spring 1979-Ceased with No. 20. Periodical. French. sa. Aubier Montaigne, 13 Quai de Conti, Paris 6 France. **LC** BF173.A2; C33. **DD** 150.19/5/05.
**Ind/Abst** MLA Int. Bibl. Books Artic. Mod. Lang. Lit. (?-?).

BE/0241-5453
**CAHIERS CRITIQUES DE THERAPIE FAMILIALE ET DE PRATIQUES.** [Cah. crit. ther. fam. prat. reseaux]. No. 1 (1979)-. Periodical. French. sa. 290.00F. Dunod Gauthier Villars, 15 rue Gossin, 92543 Montrouge cedex France. **Tel** 011 33 1 46 56 52 66, FAX 011 33 1 46 57 40 69. **(Subscription address:** Centrale des Revues, 11 rue Gossin, Gauthier Villars, 92543, Montrouge Cedex France**) NLM** W1; CA1333E.

FR/0249-9185
**CAHIERS DE PSYCHOLOGIE COGNITIVE.** [Cah. psychol. cogn.]. **VFOAT** European Bulletin of Cognitive Psychology; CPC. Vol. 1, No. 1 (Apr. 1981)-. Periodical. French (English). Six times a year (Feb., Apr., June, Aug., Oct., Dec.). 685.60F France; 700.00F others. ADRSC, IBHOP Traverse Charles Susini, 13388 Marseille CDX 13 France. **Tel** 011 33 91 660069, FAX 011 33 91 611420. **ED** Jean Pailhous. **NLM** W1; CA1395C. Index available. cum. index. **Ad Acc. Pr Rev. Circ:** 400. Documents available from The Genuine Article. ***Continues*** *Cahiers de Psychologie.*
**Desc:** Cognition, psychophysiology, neuropsychology, neurophysiology, psycholinguistics, ethology, and social psychology. All cognitive approaches of behaviors.
**Ind/Abst** Curr. Contents Soc. Behav. Sci.; Linguist. Lang. Behav. Abstr.; Psychol. Abstr. (1981-); PsycINFO; PsycLit; Res. Alert [Full Cov.]; Soc. Plann. Policy Dev. Abstr.; Soc. Sci. Cit. Index (19??-19??) [Full Cov.]; Sociol. Abstr.

FR/0761-9871
**CAHIERS DE SOCIOLOGIE ECONOMIQUE ET CULTURELLE, ETHNOPSYCHOLOGIE.** **See** Sociology.

BE/0777-0707
**CAHIERS INTERNATIONAUX DE PSYCHOLOGIE SOCIALE, LES.** [Cah. int. psychol. soc.]. (1989)-. Periodical. French. qt. 2830.00F Belgium; 3080.00F Europe; 3130.00F other. Universite de Liege Institut Psy Science, Education Svc Psychologie Soc, 4000 Liege Belgium. **(Subscription address:** Editions de Boeck Wesmael, 4 Rue Fonds, Jean Paques, 1348 Louvain la Neuve Belgium**) UDC** 301.151. ***Continues*** *Les Cahiers de Psychologie Sociale, 0774-6288.*
**Ind/Abst** Psychoanal. Abstr.; PsycINFO (1991-); PsycScan: Appl. Exp. Eng. Psych.; PsycScan: LD/MR; PsycScan: Neuropsych.

BE/0008-0284
**CAHIERS INTERNATIONAUX DE SYMBOLISME.** [Cah. int. symb.]. **Added/Corp** Universite de Mons. Centre Interdisciplinaire d'Etudes Philosophiques. Societe de Symbolisme. No. 1 (1963)-. Periodical. French. Three times a year. 600F (individuals), 1200F (institutions) Belgium; 900F (individuals), 1500F (institutions) other. Ciephum, 20 Place du Parc, B 7000 Mons Belgium. **Tel** 011 32 65 373736. **LC** BF458; .C3. **DD** 001.51.
**Desc:** Interdisciplinary research on the symbol in its relationship with exact sciences, human sciences, tradition, art, and religions.
**Ind/Abst** Annu. Bibliogr. Engl. Lang. Lit.; BHA : Biblio. Hist. Art; MLA Int. Bibl. Books Artic. Mod. Lang. Lit.; Romant. Move.; Soc. Plann. Policy Dev. Abstr.; Sociol. Abstr. (?-?).

US/0890-0302
**CALIFORNIA PSYCHOLOGIST, THE.** (THE CALIFORNIA PSYCHOLOGIST : NEWSLETTER OF THE CALIFORNIA STATE PSYCHOLOGICAL ASSOCIATION.). [Calif. psychol.]. **Added/Corp** California State Psychological Association. (19??)-. Newsletter. English. Eleven times a year. $80.00 (out of state & affiliate membership); $120.00 (regular, doctorate, & associate) Comes with California Pyschological Association membership. California State Psychological Association, 1010 11th Street, Suite 202, Los Angeles CA 95814. **Tel** (916)325-9786. **ED** Win Schachter. **DD** 150. **Bk Rev. Ad Acc. Circ:** 3,200 (ctrl). ***Continues*** *California State Psychologist.*
**Desc:** A compendium of current events in psychology and related fields. Offers in-depth coverage of the state association's legislative and political programs conducted on behalf of psychologists, the development of professional standards, and the development of professional practices and knowledge.

CN/0008-400X
**CANADIAN JOURNAL OF BEHAVIOURAL SCIENCE.** [Can. j. behav. sci.]. **Added/Corp** Canadian Psychological Association. **VFOAT** Revue Canadienne des Sciences du Comportement. Vol. 1 (Jan. 1969)-. Periodical. English (French). Four times a year (Jan., Apr., July, Oct.). 73.84Can$ Canada; 77.00Can$ US; 80.00Can$ other. Canadian Psychological Association, Chemin Vincent Road, Old Chelsea Quebec J0X 2N0 Canada. **Tel** (819)827-3927. **ED** Kenneth Craig. **NLM** W1 CA569P. **CODEN** CJBSAA. **[CCC].** Index available. cum. index. **Bk Rev. Ad Acc. Pr Rev. Circ:** 2,500 (ctrl). available on microfiche from Micromedia Limited; available on microfilm and microfiche from University Microfilms International (UMI). Documents available from The Genuine Article, BIOSIS Document Express.
**Desc:** Publishes original contributions in the applied areas of psychology.
**Ind/Abst** Biol. Abstr.; Biostatistica (19??-19??); Can. Index; Can. Period. Index (19??-); Crim. Justice Abstr.; Curr. Contents Soc. Behav. Sci.; Linguist. Lang. Behav. Abstr.; Middle East Abstr. Index; Multicult. Educ. Abstr.; Peace Res. Abstr. J. (1973-1974, 1982-1985); Psychol. Abstr. (1969-); PsycINFO; PsycLit; Res. Alert [Full Cov.]; Sage Race Relat. Abstr.; Soc. Plann. Policy Dev. Abstr.; Soc. Sci. Cit. Index [Full Cov.]; Sociol. Abstr.; Spec. Educ. Needs Abstr.; Stud. Women Abstr.; Women Stud. Abstr.

●CN/1196-1961
**CANADIAN JOURNAL OF EXPERIMENTAL PSYCHOLOGY.** [Can. j. exp. psychol.]. **Added/Corp** Canadian Psychological Association. **VFOAT** Revue Canadienne de Psychologie Experimentale. Vol. 47, No. 1 (Mar. 1993)-. Periodical. English (summaries and/or abstracts in French). Four times a year (Mar., June, Sept., Dec.). 73.84Can$ Canada; 77.00Can$ US; 80.00Can$ other. Canadian Psychological Association, Chemin Vincent Road, Old Chelsea Quebec J0X 2N0 Canada. **Tel** (819)827-3927. **DD** 150/.5. **CODEN** CJEPEK. Index available (Bound in issue). cum. index. **Ad Acc. Pr Rev.** ctrl circ. available on microfilm and microfiche from Micromedia Limited. ***Continues*** *Canadian Journal of Psychology, 0008-4255.*
**Ind/Abst** Can. Index; Soc. Sci. Cit. Index [Full Cov.].

CN/0008-4255
**CANADIAN JOURNAL OF PSYCHOLOGY.** ***Title Change.*** (CANADIAN JOURNAL OF PSYCHOLOGY. REVUE CANADIENNE DE PSYCHOLOGIE.). [Can. j. psychol.]. **Added/Corp** Canadian Psychological Association. **VFOAT** Revue Canadienne de Psychologie. Vol. 1-46 (Mar. 1947)-(Dec. 1992). Periodical. English (French; summaries and/or abstracts in French). Four times a year. Canadian Psychological Association, Chemin Vincent Road, Old Chelsea Quebec J0X 2N0 Canada. **Tel** (819)827-3927. **ED** Vince DiLollo. **LC** BF1; .C3. **NLM** W1 CA603. **CODEN** CJPSAC. **[CCC].** Index available. **Bk Rev. Ad Acc. Pr Rev. Circ:** 2,200 (ctrl). available on microfilm and microfiche from University Microfilms International (UMI). Documents available from The Genuine Article, BIOSIS Document Express, UMI Article Clearinghouse. ***Supersedes*** *Canadian Psychological Association. Bulletin of the Canadian Psychological Association, 0382-8654.* ***Continued by*** *Canadian Journal of Experimental Psychology, 1196-1961.*
**Desc:** Publishes reports of empirical research in general experimental psychology, focussing on studies of learning, perception, motivation, and cognition in animals and humans.
**Ind/Abst** Acad. Abstr. (Jan. 1992-); Acad. Search (Jan. 1992-Dec. 1993); Appl. Soc. Sci. Index Abstr.; Biol. Abstr.; Can. Index (?-?); Can. Period. Index (19??-); CSA Neuro. Abstr. (?-?); Curr. Contents Soc. Behav. Sci.; Ergon. Abstr. (?-?); Expand. Acad. Index (1989-); Health Plan. Adminis.; Index Med.; INFO-SOUTH Abstr.; Int. Aerosp. Abstr.; Linguist. Lang. Behav. Abstr.; Mag. Search; Middle East Abstr. Index; Multicult. Educ. Abstr.; Newsp. Period. Abstr. (1991-); Peace Res. Abstr. J. (1968-1973, 1983-1985); Life Sci. Collect.; Psychol. Abstr. (1947-); PsycINFO; PsycLit; Res. Alert [Full Cov.]; Soc. Plann. Policy Dev. Abstr.; Soc. Sci. Source (Jan. 1992-); Soc. Sci. Cit. Index (19??-19??) [Full Cov.]; Soc. Sci. Index; Soc. Sci. Index Fulltext (Sept. 1988-) [Full Txt.]; Sociol. Abstr.; Spec. Educ. Needs Abstr.; Stud. Women Abstr.

CN/0829-5735
**CANADIAN JOURNAL OF SCHOOL PSYCHOLOGY.** **See** Education.

CN/0708-5591
**CANADIAN PSYCHOLOGY.** (CANADIAN PSYCHOLOGY. PSYCHOLOGIE CANADIENNE.). [Can. psychol.]. **Added/Corp** Canadian Psychological Association. **VFOAT** Psychologie Canadienne. Vol. 21

(Jan. 1980)-. Periodical. English (French; summaries and/or abstracts in French). Four times a year (Jan., Apr., July, Oct.). 73.84Can$ Canada; 77.00Can$ US; 80.00Can$ other. Canadian Psychological Association, Chemin Vincent Road, Old Chelsea Quebec J0X 2N0 Canada. **Tel** (819)827-3927. **ED** John Conway. **LC** BF1; .A15. **DD** 150/.5. **NLM** W1 CA647H. **CODEN** CPSGD2. **[CCC].** Index available (Bound in all issues). cum. index. **Bk Rev. Ad Acc. Circ:** 3,500 (ctrl). available on microfilm and microfiche from University Microfilms International (UMI). Documents available from The Genuine Article, BIOSIS Document Express. ***Continues** Canadian Psychological Review, 0318-2096.*
**Desc:** A generalist professional affairs and applied journal published by the Canadian Psychological Association.
**Ind/Abst** Abstr. Res. Pastor. Care Couns. (19??-); Appl. Soc. Sci. Index Abstr.; Biol. Abstr.; Can. Index; Can. Period. Index; Curr. Contents Soc. Behav. Sci.; Linguist. Lang. Behav. Abstr.; Middle East Abstr. Index; Peace Res. Abstr. J. (1983-1984); Psychol. Abstr. (1980-); PsycINFO; PsycLit; Res. Alert [Full Cov.]; Sage Race Relat. Abstr.; Soc. Plann. Policy Dev. Abstr.; Soc. Sci. Cit. Index [Full Cov.]; Sociol. Abstr.

US/0149-6948
**CASE ANALYSIS IN SOCIAL SCIENCE N SOCIAL THERAPY.** ***Ceased.*** **See** Sociology.

US/0271-9223
**CENTURY PSYCHOLOGY SERIES.**
[Century psychol. ser.]. Monographic series. English. Price varies per volume. Irvington Publishers Inc, Lower Mill Road, North Stratford NH 03590.

XR/0009-062X
**CESKOSLOVENSKA PSYCHOLOGIE.**
[Cesk. psychol.]. **Added/Corp** Ceskoslovenska Akademie Ved. Psychologicky Ustav. Vol. 1 (1957)-. Periodical. Czech (summaries and/or abstracts in English and Russian; table of contents in Russian). bm. DM141.00. Academia, Publishing House of the Czechoslovak Academy of Sciences, Czech AC SCI, Vodickova 40, PO Box 896, 112 29 Prague 1, Czech Republic. **Tel** 011 42 2 245117. **(Subscription address:** Kubon & Sagner, ABT Zeitschriftenimport, D 80328 Munich Germany.) **ED** J. Linhart. **LC** BF8.C9; C4. **DD** 150. **NLM** W1 CE902S. **CODEN** CEPSBC. Index available. **Bk Rev. Ad Acc. Circ:** 2,800 (ctrl). Documents available from The Genuine Article, BLDSC.
**Desc:** Articles cover a wide range of subjects in theoretical and applied psychology. General preference is given to basic research studies and surveys.
**Ind/Abst** Arts Humanit. Citation Index [Select. Cov.]; Curr. Contents Soc. Behav. Sci.; Ergon. Abstr.; Psychol. Abstr. (1957-); PsycINFO; PsycLit; Res. Alert [Full Cov.]; Saf. Health Work; Soc. Sci. Cit. Index [Full Cov.].

CH
**CHANG LAO SHIH YUEH KAN. VFOAT**
Living Psychology. (1987)-. Periodical. Chinese. mo. Chang Lao Shih Yueh Kan, #131 Tunhua N Road, Taipei Taiwan. **Tel** 011 886 2 7174355.

UK/0263-8371
**CHANGES : AN INTERNATIONAL JOURNAL OF PSYCHOLOGY AND PSYCHOTHERAPY.** **Added/Corp** Psychology and Psychotherapy Association. (1982)-. Periodical. English. qt (4 issues). $95.00 (institution) US. John Wiley & Sons Ltd., Baffins Lane, Chichester West Sussex PO19 1UD England. **Tel** 0243 779777, FAX 0243 776128 BTG:JWP001, telex 86290 WIBOOKG. **(Subscription address:** John Wiley / Philadelphia, PO Box 7247, Philadelphia PA 19170.) **NLM** W1; CH1234G. ***Continues** New Forum.*

●US/1062-9548
**CHEAP RELIEF.** [Cheap relief]. (1992)-. Periodical. English. mo. $48.00. Cheap Relief, PO Box 11501, Washington DC 20008. **DD** 155.

UK/0952-9136
**CHILD ABUSE REVIEW.** ***Title Change.*** **See** Sociology-Social Services and Welfare.

US
**CHILD ANALYSIS.** English. an (Jan.). $25.00. Cleveland Center for Research in Child Development, 2084 Cornell Road, Cleveland OH 44106. **Tel** (216)421-7880, FAX (216)421-8880. **ED** Deborah Paris. Index available. cum. index. ctrl circ.
**Desc:** Dedicated to furthering understanding of personality development and ongoing exploration of effective, psychoanalytically oriented work with children and parents in both clinical and community settings.

●US/1071-2828
**CHILD AND ADOLESCENT MENTAL HEALTH CARE.** [Child adolesc. ment. health care]. **Added/Corp** Devereux Foundation. Vol. 3, No. 1 (Spring 1993)-. Periodical. English. Three times a year. $39.00 (individuals, 1 year), $69.00 (individuals, 2 year), $74.00 (institutions, 1 year), $129.00 (institutions, 2 year) US; $44.00 (individuals, 1 year), $79.00 (individuals, 2 year), $85.00 (institutions, 1 year), $149.00 (institutions, 2 year) other. Springer Publishing Company, 536 Broadway, New York NY 10012-3955. **Tel** (212)431-4370, FAX (212)941-7842. **ED** Steven L. Pfeiffer, PhD. **DD** 616. **NLM** W1; CH642RQ. **CODEN** CAMCEQ. ***Continues** Comprehensive Mental Health Care, 1051-7782.*
**Desc:** Among the specific areas addressed by the contributors to this Journal are diagnosis and assessment, intervention techniques, education, habilitation and rehabilitation social and recreational services, supervision, consultation/liaison, funding and policy analysis, administration, ethical, legal, and other professional concerns.

US/0731-7107
**CHILD & FAMILY BEHAVIOR THERAPY.**
[Child fam. behav. ther.]. **VFOAT** Child and Family Behavior Therapy. Vol. 4, No. 1 (Spring 1982)-. Academic Scholarly Publication. English. qt. $260.00 US; $364.00. The Haworth Press Inc, 10 Alice Street, Binghamton NY 13904-1580. **Tel** (607)722-5857, (800)3-HAWORTH, FAX (607)722-1424. **ED** Cyril M. Franks (editor's address: Graduate School of Applied and Professional Psychology, Rutgers University, Busch Campus, PO Box 819, Piscataway, NJ 08855-0819). **LC** RJ504; .C467. **DD** 618.92/89142/05. **Bk Rev. Ad Acc. Pr Rev. Acid Free. Circ:** 532. available on microfilm and microfiche from University Microfilms International (UMI). Documents available from The Genuine Article, Haworth Document Delivery Service. ***Continues** Child Behavior Therapy, 0162-1416.*
**Desc:** Scholarly and interdisciplinary journal devoted to research and clinical applications in behavior therapy with children and adolescents, as well as the enhancement of parenting.
**Ind/Abst** Abstr. Res. Pastor. Care Couns.; Acad. Search (July 1993-); Annals Behav. Med.; Child Dev. Abstr. Bibliogr.; Crim. Justice Abstr.; Crim. Penol. Police Sci. Abstr.; Curr. Contents Soc. Behav. Sci.; Curr. Index J. Educ.; Educ. Index; Except. Child Educ. Resour.; INFO-SOUTH Abstr.; Linguist. Lang. Behav. Abstr.; Psychol. Abstr. (1982-); PsycINFO; PsycLit; Res. Alert [Full Cov.]; Sage Fam. Stud. Abstr.; Soc. Plann. Policy Dev. Abstr.; Soc. Sci. Cit. Index [Full Cov.]; Soc. Work Abstr. (Summer 1987-) [Select. Cov.]; Sociol. Abstr.; Sociol. Educ. Abstr.; Spec. Educ. Needs Abstr.; Stud. Women Abstr.

CN
**CHILD AND YOUTH PSYCHIATRY, EUROPEAN PERSPECTIVES.** **See** Medical Science and Technology-Psychiatry.

US/1055-0518
**CHILD ASSESSMENT NEWS.** [Child assess. news]. Vol. 1, No. 1 (1991)-. Periodical. English. Six times a year. $80.00 (institutions); $85.00 others. Guilford Publications Inc., 72 Spring Street, New York NY 10012. **Tel** (212)431-9800, (800)365-7006, FAX (212)966-6708. **ED** Randy Kamphaus. **DD** 153. **NLM** W1; CH6444. **[CCC].**
**Desc:** Offers the latest and most relevant information on child assessment by providing critiques of existing and new instruments as well as clinical advice, legislation news, and timely reference lists.

US/0009-3920
**CHILD DEVELOPMENT.** [Child dev.]. **Added/Corp** Society for Research in Child Development. Vol. 1 (March 1930)-. Periodical. English. bm (6 issues). $142.00 US; $163.94 Canada, including GST and postage; $154.00 other, including postage. University of Chicago Press / Journals Division, PO Box 37005, 5720 South Woodlawn, Chicago IL 60637. **Tel** (312)753-3347, FAX (312)753-0811. **(Subscription telephone:** (312)753-8083) **ED** Susan Clare Somerville. **LC** HQ750.A1; C45. **DD** 136.705. **NLM** W1 CH647. **CODEN** CHDEAW. **[CCC].** cum. index. **Ad Acc. Pr Rev. Acid Free. Circ:** 8,500. available on microfilm (Reprinted Vols. 1-40 Kraus Reprints) from Kraus Reprint Co.; available on microfilm and microfiche from University Microfilms International (UMI). Documents available from The Genuine Article, BIOSIS Document Express, UMI Article Clearinghouse.
**Desc:** Devoted to original contributions on topics in child development from the fetal period through adolescence. It is a vital source of information not only for researchers and theoreticians, but for child psychiatrists, clinical psychologists, and other researchers in the field.
**Ind/Abst** Abstr. Anthropol.; Acad. Abstr. Full Text Elite (Jan. 1990-); Acad. Abstr. (Jan. 1990-); Acad. Ind. [Computer File] (1987-); Acad. Search (Jan. 1990-); AGRICOLA [Select. Cov.]; Annals Behav. Med.; Appl. Soc. Sci. Index Abstr.; Arts Humanit. Citation Index [Select. Cov.]; Biol. Abstr.; Commun. Abstr.; Crim. Justice Abstr.; Curr. Contents Soc. Behav. Sci.; Curr. Index J. Educ.; Dev. Med. Child Neurol.; Educ. Index; Educ. Adm. Abstr. (?-?); Except. Child Educ. Resour. (19??-19??); Expand. Acad. Index (1987-); Health Plan. Adminis.; Health Ref. Cent. (1987-) [Select. Cov.]; Health Source (Jul. 1990-); Hum. Resour. Abstr. (?-?); Index Med.; INFO-SOUTH Abstr.; Int. Bibliogr. Sociol.; Linguist. Lang. Behav. Abstr.; Mag. Search; Middle East Abstr. Index; MLA Int. Bibl. Books Artic. Mod. Lang. Lit.; Multicult. Educ. Abstr.; Newsp. Period. Abstr. (1988-); Nutr. Abstr. Rev., Ser. B, Live Feeds and Feed.; Nutr. Abstr. Rev., Ser. A, Hum. Exp.; Life Sci. Collect.; Psychol. Abstr. (1930-); PsycINFO; PsycLit; PsycScan: Develop. Psych.; Res. Alert [Full Cov.]; Risk Abstr.; Sage Fam. Stud. Abstr.; School Organ. Manage. Abstr.; Soc. Plann. Policy Dev. Abstr.; Soc. Sci. Source (Jul. 1990-); Soc. Sci. Cit. Index [Full Cov.]; Soc. Sci. Index; Soc. Sci. Index Fulltext (Oct. 1988-) [Full Txt.]; Soc. Work Abstr. (?-?); Sociol. Abstr.; Sociol. Educ. Abstr.; Spec. Educ. Needs Abstr.; Stud. Women Abstr.; Women Stud. Abstr.

US/0093-2175
**CHILD PERSONALITY AND PSYCHOPATHOLOGY.** **See** Medical Science and Technology-Pediatrics.

US/0009-398X
**CHILD PSYCHIATRY AND HUMAN DEVELOPMENT.** **See** Medical Science and Technology-Psychiatry.

US/0009-4005
**CHILD STUDY JOURNAL.** [Child study j.]. **Added/Corp** State University College at Buffalo. Faculty of Applied and Professional Studies. State University College at Buffalo. Faculty of Professional Studies. State University College at Buffalo. Child Study Center. State University College at Buffalo. Dept. of Behavioral and Humanistic Studies. Vol. 1 (Fall 1970)-. Periodical. English. qt (Mar., June, Sept., Dec.). $6.00 (student), $16.00 (individuals), $33.00 (institutions) US and Canada; $10.00 (students or APA Member subscription), $38.00 (institutions) other. State University College at Buffalo / Educational Foundation Department, Bacon Hall 306, Buffalo NY 14222. **Tel** (716)878-4000. **ED** Donald E Carter. **LC** LB1101; .C43. **DD** 115.4/05. **NLM** W1 CH6911. **CODEN** CSJOD2. **Bk Rev. Circ:** 600. available on microfilm and microfiche from University Microfilms International (UMI). Documents available. ***Supersedes** Child Study Center Bulletin, 0193-8924.*
**Desc:** Covers educational and psychological aspects of human development (child and adolescent).
**Ind/Abst** Acad. Search (July 1993-); Contents Pages Educ.; Curr. Index J. Educ.; Educ. Index; INFO-SOUTH Abstr.; Linguist. Lang. Behav. Abstr.; Mag. Search; Middle East Abstr. Index; Multicult. Educ. Abstr.; Psychol. Abstr. (1970-); PsycINFO; PsycLit; PsycScan: Develop. Psych.; Soc. Plann. Policy Dev. Abstr.; Sociol. Abstr.; Sociol. Educ. Abstr.; Spec. Educ. Needs Abstr.; Stud. Women Abstr.

US/1072-6241
**CHILD THERAPY NEWS, THE.** (1993)-. Periodical. English. bm (6 issues). $65.00. Center for Applied Psychology, PO Box 61586, King of Prussia PA 19406. **Tel** (800)962-1141.

US/0882-942X
**CHILDREN & TEENS TODAY.** ***Ceased.*** **See** Sociology-Social Services and Welfare.

AT/0814-9127
**CHILDREN IN HOSPITAL.** [Child. hosp.]. **Added/Corp** Association for the Welfare of Children in Hospital, New South Wales. (1984)-. Periodical. English. Four times a year (Mar., June, Sept., Dec.). 25.00Aus$ Australia; 30.00Aus$ others. Association of Welfare Children Hospital, 191/207 Forest Way, Belrose New South Wales 2085 Australia. **Tel** 011 61 2 4500141, FAX 011 61 2 4500141. **ED** Eva M. Langley. **DD** 362.1109944. **Bk Rev**, (Qty: varies). **Circ:** 800. ***Continues** A.W.C.H.N.S.W. Newsletter, 0814-9119.*
**Desc:** News and information about children health and psychology.

CC
**CHINESE JOURNAL OF PSYCHOLOGY.**
**VFOAT** Chinese Journal of Psychology. Vol. 1, (1922)-. Periodical. Chinese. sa. Chinese Psychological Association, National Taiwan University, Department of Psychology, Taipei 107 Taiwan. **Tel** (02)3510231. **(Subscription address:** No 175 Chung-Cheng Road, Chung-Li 320 Taiwan) **ED** Chia-Hung Hsu. **Circ:** 500 (ctrl).

KO
**CHONGSIN PAKYAK YONGU.** **See** Medical Science and Technology-Psychiatry.

US/0892-4686
**CHRISTIAN PSYCHOLOGY FOR TODAY.** ***Title Change.*** [Christ. psychol. today]. **Added/Corp** Dallas Graduate School of Psychology. Minirth-Meier Clinic. **VFOAT** Christian Psychology. (198?)-. Periodical. English. qt. Minirth-Meier Clinic, 2100 North Collins Boulevard, Richardson TX 75080. **Tel** (214)669-1733. **ED** Frank Minirth, Paul Meier, Don Hawkins, Jane Mack and Marty Anderson. **DD** 150. **Ad Acc. Circ:** 5,600 (ctrl). ***Continued by** Today's Better Life.*
**Desc:** Designed to provide practical help and insight into applying Christian psychology to the stresses of everyday life.
**Ind/Abst** Christ. Period. Index.

FR/0529-7788
**CIRCE: CAHIERS DU CENTRE DE RECHERCHE SUR L'IMAGINAIRE.**
**Added/Corp** Centre de Recherche sur l'Imaginaire (Chambery, France). Vol. 1 (1969)-. Monographic series. French. ir. Price varies per volume. Lettres Modernes Minard, 45 rue de Saint Andre, 14123 Fleury Surrey Orne France. **Tel** 011 33 31 844706. **LC** BF408; .C55. **DD** 100; 700.

SW
**CIVIL.** **Added/Corp** Sveriges Civilforsvarsforbund. No. 1 (1991)-. Periodical. Swedish. mo. **LC** UA929.S5; C58. ***Continues*** *Civila Forsvarstidningen.*

US/0735-0341
**CLASSICS IN PSYCHOANALYSIS.** ***Ceased.*** **Added/Corp** Institute for Psychoanalysis. Monograph No. 1 (1983)-(19??). Monographic series. English. ir. International Universities Press Inc., 59 Boston Post Road, PO Box 1524, Madison CT 06443-1524. **Tel** (203)245-4000, FAX (203)245-0775, telex 282986 IUP BK. **NLM** W1; CL122D.

SP/0210-0657
**CLINICA Y ANALISIS GRUPAL.** (19??)-. Periodical. Spanish (summaries and/or abstracts in English). Three times a year. 5300ptas. Grupo Quipu de Psicoterapia Soc Coop Ltda, C Principe de Vergara 35BJO DCHA, 28001 Madrid Spain. **Tel** 011 34 1 5776039. **ED** Isabel Sanfeliu. **LC** RC475; .C53. **DD** 616.89/14/05. **NLM** W1 CL613W. Index available. cum. index. **Bk Rev. Pr Rev. Circ:** 1,000 (ctrl).
**Desc:** Follows group psychotherapy, psychoanalysis and social psychology.
**Ind/Abst** Psychol. Abstr.; PsycINFO; PsycLit.

CN/0827-1038
**CLINICAL BIOFEEDBACK AND HEALTH.** ***Ceased.*** [Clin. biofeedback health]. Vol. 8, No. 1 (1985)-Vol. 10, No. 2 (1987). Academic Scholarly Publication. English. sa. Hogrefe and Huber Publishers, PO Box 2487, Kirkland WA 98083. **Tel** (800)228-3749, (206)820-1500, FAX (206)823-8324. **(Subscription address:** US/ PO Box 51, Lewiston, NY 14092; Germany/ Daimlerstrasse 40, W-7000 Stuttgart 50; Switzerland/ Laenggass Strasse 76, CH-3000 Bern 9**)** **ED** K N Anchor. **LC** RC489.B53; A44. **DD** 615.8/51. **CODEN** CBHEEE. **Bk Rev. Ad Acc. Circ:** 2,000. available on microfilm from University Microfilms International (UMI). Documents available from BIOSIS Document Express. ***Continues*** *American Journal of Clinical Biofeedback, 0190-4019.*
**Desc:** The journal publishes original articles dealing with the practice, research and theory of behavioral medicine and health enhancement.
**Ind/Abst** Biol. Abstr. (1986-); EMBASE; PsycINFO.

US/0735-2530
**CLINICAL INFANT REPORTS.** (CLINICAL INFANT REPORTS : SERIES OF THE NATIONAL CENTER FOR CLINICAL INFANT PROGRAMS.). [Clin. infant rep.]. **Added/Corp** National Center for Clinical Infant Programs (U.S.). **VFOAT** Series of the National Center for Clinical Infant Programs. No. 1 (1981)-. Monographic series. English. ir. Price varies per volume. International Universities Press Inc., 59 Boston Post Road, PO Box 1524, Madison CT 06443-1524. **Tel** (203)245-4000, FAX (203)245-0775, telex 282986 IUP BK.
**Ind/Abst** Psychol. Abstr. (1981-); PsycLit.

NE/0920-1637
**CLINICAL NEUROPSYCHOLOGIST, THE.** **See** Medical Science and Technology-Neurology.

●UK/1063-3995
**CLINICAL PSYCHOLOGY AND PSYCHOTHERAPY.** (CLINICAL PSYCHOLOGY AND PSYCHOTHERAPY : AN INTERNATIONAL JOURNAL OF THEORY AND PRACTICE.). Vol. 1 (1993)-. Periodical. English. Four times a year. $145.00 institution. John Wiley & Sons Ltd., Baffins Lane, Chichester West Sussex PO19 1UD England. **Tel** 0243 779777, FAX 0243 776128 BTG:JWP001, telex 86290 WIBOOKG. **(Subscription address:** John Wiley / Philadelphia, PO Box 7247, Philadelphia PA 19170.**)** **ED** Paul Emmelkamp and Mick Power.
**Desc:** Provides an integrative impetus both between theory and practice and between different orientations within clinical psychology and psychotherapy.

US/0272-7358
**CLINICAL PSYCHOLOGY REVIEW.** [Clin. psychol. rev.]. **Added/Corp** American Psychological Association. Division of Clinical Psychology. Vol. 1, No. 1 (1981)-. Periodical. English. Eight times a year. $453.00 The Americas; £305.00 other. Pergamon Press, An Imprint of Elsevier Science Ltd., The Boulevard, Langford Lane, Kidlington, Oxford OX5 1GB United Kingdom. **Tel** 011 44 865 843000, 011 44 865 843699, FAX 011 44 865 843010. **(Subscription address:** Elsevier Science Ltd. Oxford Fulfillment Centre, PO Box 800, Kidlington, Oxford OX5 1DX United Kingdom.**)** **ED** Alan S. Bellack and Michel Hersen. **LC** RC467; .C587. **DD** 616.89/005. **NLM** W1 CL768E. **CODEN** CPSRDZ. **[CCC]. Bk Rev. Ad Acc. Pr Rev.** available on microfilm and microfiche from University Microfilms International (UMI). Documents available from The Genuine Article, BIOSIS Document Express.
**Desc:** Covers diverse issues, including: psychotherapy, psychopathology, behavior therapy, behavioral medicine, community mental health, assessment and child development.
**Ind/Abst** Annals Behav. Med.; Biol. Abstr. (1986-); Crim. Justice Abstr.; Curr. Contents Soc. Behav. Sci.; EMBASE; Psychol. Abstr. (1981-); PsycINFO; PsycLit; PsycScan: Clin. Psych.; Res. Alert [Full Cov.]; Soc. Sci. Cit. Index [Full Cov.].

US/0969-5893
**CLINICAL PSYCHOLOGY : SCIENCE AND PRACTICE.** (19??)-. English. Four times a year. $135.00 institutions, $45.00 individuals US; $147.00 institutions, $57.00 individuals other. Oxford University Press / New York, 200 Madison Avenue, New York NY 10016. **Tel** (212)679-7300, (919)677-0977, (800)451-7556, (800)445-9714, FAX (919)677-1303. **(Subscription address:** Oxford University Press / USA, Journals Marketing Department, Oxford University Press, 2001 Evans Road, Cary NC 27513.**)**

US/0732-5223
**CLINICAL SUPERVISOR, THE.** [Clin. superv.]. Vol. 1, No. 1 (Spring 1983)-. Periodical. English. sa. $200.00 US; $280.00 other. The Haworth Press Inc, 10 Alice Street, Binghamton NY 13904-1580. **Tel** (607)722-5857, (800)3-HAWORTH, FAX (607)722-1424. **ED** Carlton Munson (editor's address: Graduate School of Social Service, Fordham University, University of Lincoln Center, 113 W 60th Street, New York, NY 10023). **LC** RC336; .C55. **DD** 616.89/0068/3. **NLM** W1 CL795R. **CODEN** CLSUEH. **Bk Rev. Ad Acc. Pr Rev. Acid Free. Circ:** 200. available on microfilm and microfiche from University Microfilms International (UMI). Documents available from Haworth Document Delivery Service.
**Desc:** Designed to reflect the concerns, needs, and interests of supervisors in a variety of professional settings. Provides the latest supervisory techniques and methods.
**Ind/Abst** Abstr. Res. Pastor. Care Couns. (19??-); Cumul. Index Nurs. Allied Health Lit.; Linguist. Lang. Behav. Abstr.; Pollut. Abstr. Indexes; Psychol. Abstr. (1983-); PsycINFO; PsycLit; Soc. Plann. Policy Dev. Abstr.; Soc. Work Abstr. [Select. Cov.]; Sociol. Abstr.

US/8756-3207
**CLINICIAN'S RESEARCH DIGEST.** [Clin. res. dig.]. **Added/Corp** American Psychological Association. (1983)-. Periodical. English. mo. $97.00 (nonmember, institution) US. American Psychological Association, 750 First Street Northeast, Washington DC 20002. **Tel** (800)374-2721, (202)336-5600, (subscriptions - (202)336-5600. **ED** George Stricker, PhD. **DD** 157. Index available. cum. index (annual). **Bk Rev. Pr Rev.**
**Desc:** Selections from over 50 journals each month are high-lighted. Subscribers recieve the most up-to-date information in a format that is inviting to read. Complete citations and the author's address accompany each summary. This newsletter is APA-approved for continuing education credits.

UK/0957-9664
**CMBH CRIMINAL BEHAVIOUR AND MENTAL HEALTH.** **See** Law-Law Enforcement and Criminology.

SZ/0010-0277
**COGNITION.** [Cognition]. Vol. 1 (1972)-. Academic Scholarly Publication. English (summaries and/or abstracts in French). Twelve times a year (4 volumes). Fl1260.00. Elsevier Science Publishers BV, PO Box 211, 1000 AE Amsterdam Netherlands. **Tel** 011 31 20 5803642, FAX 011 31 20 5862696, telex 15682. **ED** J Mehler. **LC** BF311; .C545. **DD** 153/.05. **NLM** W1 CO107N. **CODEN** CGTNAU. **[CCC]. Pr Rev.** available on microfilm and microfiche from University Microfilms International (UMI). Documents available from The Genuine Article, BIOSIS Document Express.
**Desc:** Publishes theoretical and experimental papers covering all aspects of the study of the mind.
**Ind/Abst** Biol. Abstr.; Curr. Contents Soc. Behav. Sci.; Health Plan. Adminis.; Int. Bibliogr. Sociol.; Lang. Teach.; Linguist. Lang. Behav. Abstr.; MLA Int. Bibl. Books Artic. Mod. Lang. Lit.; Life Sci. Collect.; Philos. Index; Psychol. Abstr. (1972-); PsycINFO (1990-); PsycLit; Res. Alert [Full Cov.]; Soc. Plann. Policy Dev. Abstr.; Soc. Sci. Cit. Index [Full Cov.]; Sociol. Abstr.

UK/0269-9931
**COGNITION & EMOTION.** [Cogn. emot.]. **VFOAT** Cognition and Emotion. Vol. 1, Issue 1 (March 1987)-. Periodical. English. bm (6 issues). $236.00 US; £134.00 Europe; £139.00 other. Lawrence Erlbaum Associates Ltd., 27 Palmeira Mansions, Church Road, Hove East Sussex BN3 2FA England. **Tel** 011 44 273 207411. **(Subscription address:** Turpin Distribution Services Limited, Blackhorse Road, Letchworth, Hertfordshire SG6 1HN, United Kingdom.**)** **ED** Fraser N. Watts. **LC** BF309; .C6172. **NLM** W1; CO107PD. **CODEN** COEMEC. **Bk Rev. Ad Acc. Circ:** 600. Documents available from The Genuine Article.
**Ind/Abst** Curr. Contents Soc. Behav. Sci.; Linguist. Lang. Behav. Abstr.; Psychol. Abstr. (1987-); PsycINFO (1990-); PsycLit; Res. Alert [Full Cov.]; Soc. Plann. Policy Dev. Abstr.; Soc. Sci. Cit. Index [Full Cov.]; Sociol. Abstr.

SP/0214-3550
**COGNITIVA MADRID.** [Cognitiva Madr.]. (1988)-. Periodical. Multiple languages. sa. Comes with Estudios Psicologia and Revista de Psicologia Social. Aprendizaje SA, Carretera de Canillas 138 16 C, 28033 Madrid Spain. **Tel** 011 34 1 3883874, 011 34 1 2009338, FAX 011 34 1 3003527. **UDC** 159.9.
**Ind/Abst** PsycINFO (1988-); PsycLit.

●US
**COGNITIVE AND BEHAVIORAL PRACTICE.** Vol. 1 (1994)-. English. sa (March and Sept.). $75.00 institution. Association for the Advancement of Behavior Therapy, 305 7th Avenue, New York NY 10001. **Tel** (212)647-1890, FAX (212)647-1865.

●NE/0926-6410
**COGNITIVE BRAIN RESEARCH.** **See** Medical Science and Technology-Neurology.

US/0885-2014
**COGNITIVE DEVELOPMENT.** [Cogn. dev.]. Vol. 1, No. 1 (Jan. 1986)-. Periodical. English. qt. $115.00 institution. Ablex Publishing Corporation, 355 Chestnut Street, Norwood NJ 07648. **Tel** (201)767-8450, (201)767-8455 (Customer Service), FAX (201)767-6717. **ED** Wendell E. Jeffrey. **LC** BF1; .C48. **DD** 155.4/13/06. **NLM** W1; CO107PN. **[CCC].** Index available. cum. index. **Bk Rev. Ad Acc. Pr Rev. Circ:** 500. Documents available from The Genuine Article.
**Desc:** Articles on the most timely and significant issues in the broad field of cognitive studies.
**Ind/Abst** Curr. Contents Soc. Behav. Sci.; Psychol. Abstr. (1983-); PsycINFO; PsycLit; Res. Alert [Full Cov.]; Soc. Sci. Cit. Index [Full Cov.].

UK/0264-3294
**COGNITIVE NEUROPSYCHOLOGY.** [Cogn. neuropsychol.]. Vol. 1, No. 1 (Feb. 1984)-. Periodical. English. bm (6 issues). $399.00 US; £230.00 Europe; £235.00 other. Lawrence Erlbaum Associates Ltd., 27 Palmeira Mansions, Church Road, Hove East Sussex BN3 2FA England. **Tel** 011 44 273 207411. **(Subscription address:** Turpin Distribution Services Limited, Blackhorse Road, Letchworth, Hertfordshire SG6 1HN, United Kingdom.**)** **ED** Max Coltheart. **NLM** W1; CO107Q. **CODEN** COGNEP. **Pr Rev.** Documents available from The Genuine Article, BIOSIS Document Express.
**Ind/Abst** Biol. Abstr.; Curr. Contents Soc. Behav. Sci.; Dev. Med. Child Neurol.; Linguist. Lang. Behav. Abstr.; MLA Int. Bibl. Books Artic. Mod. Lang. Lit.; Psychol. Abstr. (1984-); PsycINFO; PsycLit; Res. Alert [Full Cov.]; Soc. Plann. Policy Dev. Abstr.; Soc. Sci. Cit. Index [Full Cov.]; Sociol. Abstr.

US/0010-0285
**COGNITIVE PSYCHOLOGY.** [Cogn. psychol.]. Vol. 1 (Jan. 1970)-. Academic Scholarly Publication. English. bm (6 issues). $222.00 US and Canada; $267.00 other. Academic Press, Inc., 6277 Sea Harbor Drive, Orlando FL 32887. **Tel** (800)543-9534, (407)345-4100, FAX (407)363-9661. **ED** Douglas L. Medin. **LC** BF309; .C62. **DD** 150; 153.4/05. **NLM** W1 CO107R. **CODEN** CGPSBQ. **[CCC]. Pr Rev.** Documents available from The Genuine Article, Ask*IEEE, UMI Article Clearinghouse.
**Desc:** Concerned with advances in the study of memory, language processing, perception, problem solving, and thinking. Presents original empirical, theoretical and tutorial papers, methodological articles, and critical reviews.
**Ind/Abst** Acad. Abstr. Full Text Elite (Jan. 1992-); Acad. Abstr. (Jan. 1992-); Acad. Search (Jan. 1992-); Curr. Contents Soc. Behav. Sci.; Curr. Index J. Educ.; Educ. Index (1992-); Ergon. Abstr.; Expand. Acad. Index (1989-); Health Plan. Adminis.; INFO-SOUTH Abstr.; INSPEC (July 1974-); Linguist. Lang. Behav. Abstr.; Mag. Search; Middle East Abstr. Index; MLA Int. Bibl. Books Artic. Mod. Lang. Lit.; Newsp. Period. Abstr. (1992-); Psychol. Abstr. (1970-); PsycINFO; PsycLit; PsycScan: Develop. Psych.; Res. Alert [Full Cov.]; Soc. Plann. Policy Dev. Abstr.; Soc. Sci. Source (Jan. 1992-); Soc. Sci. Cit. Index [Full Cov.]; Soc. Sci. Index; Soc. Sci. Index Fulltext (Jan. 1989-) [Full Txt.]; Sociol. Abstr.

NE/0256-663X
**COGNITIVE SYSTEMS.** [Cogn. syst.]. (1985)-. Periodical. English. ir. Fl120.00. European Society for the Study of Cognitive Systems, Groningen University, PO Box 41096, 9701 CB Groningen Netherlands. **Tel** 011 31 50 636472. **UDC** 159.9.
**Ind/Abst** Psychol. Abstr. (1988-); PsycLit.

US/0163-2035
**COGNITIVE THEORY.** ***Ceased.*** [Cogn. theory]. Vol. 1 (1975)-(1994). English. ir. Lawrence Erlbaum Associates, 365 Broadway, Suite 102, Hillsdale NJ 07642. **Tel** (201)666-4110, (800)926-6579, FAX (201)666-2394. **ED** A. Norman Ortony. **LC** BF309; .C65. **DD** 153.4/05.

US/0147-5916
**COGNITIVE THERAPY AND RESEARCH.** [Cogn. ther. res.]. Vol 1 (March 1977)-. Periodical. English. Six times a year. $265.00 institutions, $49.00 individuals US; $310.00 institutions, $57.00 individuals other. Plenum Press, 233 Spring Street, New York NY 10013-1578. **Tel** (212)620-8000, (800)221-9369, FAX (212)463-0742, (212)807-1047, telex 23/421139. **ED** Philip C. Kendall. **LC** BF311; .C5535. **DD** 616.8/117/05. **NLM** W1 CO107W. **CODEN** CTHRD8. **[CCC].** Index available. **Pr Rev.** available on microfilm and microfiche from University Microfilms International (UMI). Documents available from The Genuine Article, BIOSIS Document Express.
**Desc:** Broadly conceived interdisciplinary journal whose

main function is to stimulate and communicate research and theory on the role of cognitive processes in human adaptation and adjustment.
**Ind/Abst** Acad. Search (July 1993-); Biol. Abstr.; Curr. Contents Soc. Behav. Sci.; EMBASE [Select. Cov.]; INFO-SOUTH Abstr.; Mag. Search; Psychol. Abstr. (1977-); PsycINFO; PsycLit; PsycScan: Clin. Psych.; Ref. Z.; Res. Alert [Full Cov.]; Soc. Sci. Cit. Index [Full Cov.]; Spec. Educ. Needs Abstr.; SportSearch.

US
**COLLEAGUE.** No. 1 1976-. Periodical. English. Rational Island Publishers, 719 2nd Avenue North, Seattle WA 98109. **ED** P Roby.

US/0885-8500
**COMMON BOUNDARY, THE.** [Common bound.]. (19?)-. Periodical. English. bm. $22.00 (one year), $40.00 (two year), $50.00 (three year). Common Boundary Inc, 4304 East-West Highway, Bethesda MD 20814. **Tel** (301)652-9495. **ED** Anne A Sompkinson. **DD** 158. **Bk Rev**. **Ad Acc. Circ:** 11,000. ***Continues** Kindred Spirit Network Newsletter.*
**Desc:** Explores the relationship of psychology and spirituality. Each issue contains feature articles; reviews of books and tapes; and sections such as innovations, trends, opinion, in your own words (1st person narratives), etc. as well as letters to the editor and a calendar of events.

US
**COMMON FOCUS.** **Added/Corp** University of North Carolina at Chapel Hill. Center for Early Adolescence. (19??)-. Periodical. English. qt (five issues yearly Jan., March, May, Sept., and Nov.). Free. Center for Early Adolescence, Department of Maternal and Child Health, School of Public Health, University of North Carolina at Chapel Hill, Chapel Hill NC 27514. **Tel** (919)966-1148. **ED** K Marley. **LC** HQ796; .C695. **DD** 305.2/35. **Bk Rev. Circ:** 8,000 (ctrl).
**Desc:** Provides in-depth reports on Center for Early Adolescence projects concerning education, literacy, dropout prevention, after school issues with a focus on ten to fifteen year olds. It also contains information in resources and reviews.
**Ind/Abst** Curr. Lit. Fam. Plan. (19??-19??).

US/0164-775X
**COMMUNIQUE (KENT).** (COMMUNIQUE.). [Communique]. **Main/Corp** National Association of School Psychologists. (1973)-. Periodical. English. Eight times a year. $30.00. National Association of School Psychologists, 8455 Colesville Road 1000, Silver Spring MD 20910. **Tel** (301)608-0500. **ED** Alex Thomas. **DD** 370. **Bk Rev**. **Ad Acc. Circ:** 15,000 (ctrl).
**Desc:** Describes practices of school psychologists who consult about behavior or learning problems, help develop remedial and prevention programs for pupils, parents, teachers and other staff.

US/0190-1079
**COMPARATIVE STUDIES IN BEHAVIORAL SCIENCE.** (19??)-. Monographic series. English. ir. Price varies per volume. John Wiley & Sons, Inc., 605 Third Avenue, New York NY 10158-0012. **Tel** (212)850-6000, (212)850-6645, FAX (212)850-6088, telex 12-7063. **(Subscription address:** John Wiley & Sons / England, Baffins Lane, Chichester, West Sussex PO19 1UD England.**)**

US/0271-9193
**COMPLEX HUMAN BEHAVIOR.** [Complex hum. behav.]. Monographic series. English. ir. Price varies per volume. John Wiley & Sons, Inc., 605 Third Avenue, New York NY 10158-0012. **Tel** (212)850-6000, (212)850-6645, FAX (212)850-6088, telex 12-7063. **(Subscription address:** John Wiley & Sons / England, Baffins Lane, Chichester, West Sussex PO19 1UD England.**)**

CN/0832-929X
**COMPORTEMENT HUMAIN.** [Comport. hum.]. (1987)-. Periodical. French. Twice a year. 60.00Can$. Editions Behaviora, 6955 boulevard Taschereau, Suite 100-C, Brossard QUE J4Z 1A7 Canada. **Tel** (514)678-8100, FAX (514)678-8106. **DD** 616.89.42. ***Continues** Technologie et Therapie du Comportement, 0831-6570.*

US/1051-7782
**COMPREHENSIVE MENTAL HEALTH CARE.** ***Title Change.*** [Compr. ment. health care]. **Added/Corp** Devereux Foundation. Vol. 1, No. 1 (Spring 1991)-Vol. 2, No. 3 (Winter 1992). Periodical. English. Three times a year. Springer Publishing Company, 536 Broadway, New York NY 10012-3955. **Tel** (212)431-4370, FAX (212)941-7842. **DD** 616. **NLM** W1; CO4527. **CODEN** CHCAEJ. ***Continued by** Child and Adolescent Mental Health Care, 1071-2828.*
**Ind/Abst** Psychoanal. Abstr.; PsycScan: Appl. Exp. Eng. Psych.; PsycScan: LD/MR; PsycScan: Neuropsych.

US/0747-5632
**COMPUTERS IN HUMAN BEHAVIOR.** [Comput. hum. behav.]. Vol. 1, No. 1 (1985)-. Academic Scholarly Publication. English. qt. $388.00 The Americas; £260.00 other. Pergamon Press, An Imprint of Elsevier Science Ltd., The Boulevard, Langford Lane, Kidlington, Oxford OX5 1GB United Kingdom. **Tel** 011 44 865 843000, 011 44 865 843699, FAX 011 44 865 843010. **(Subscription address:** Elsevier Science Ltd. Oxford Fulfillment Centre, PO Box 800, Kidlington, Oxford OX5 1DX United Kingdom.**) ED** Robert D. Tennyson. **LC** BF39.5; .C663. **DD** 150/.28/5. **NLM** W1; CO457YB. **CODEN** CHBEEQ. **[CCC].** available on microfilm and microfiche from University Microfilms International (UMI). Documents available from Article Express International, The Genuine Article, Ask*IEEE.
**Desc:** Dedicated to examining the use of computers from a psychological perspective.
**Ind/Abst** Abstr. Hum. Comput. Interact.; Curr. Contents Soc. Behav. Sci.; Curr. Index J. Educ. (March 1990); Ei Page One; EMBASE; Eng. Index Annu. [Select. Cov.]; Ergon. Abstr.; HILITES; Inf. Sci. Abstr.; INSPEC (1985-); Linguist. Lang. Behav. Abstr.; Psychol. Abstr. (1985-); PsycINFO; PsycLit; Res. Alert [Full Cov.]; Soc. Plann. Policy Dev. Abstr.; Soc. Sci. Cit. Index [Full Cov.]; Sociol. Abstr.

US/0738-3614
**COMPUTERS IN PSYCHIATRY/PSYCHOLOGY.** **See** Medical Science and Technology-Psychiatry.

FR/0337-3126
**CONNEXIONS (PARIS).** (CONNEXIONS; PSYCHOSOCIOLOGIE, SCIENCES HUMAINES.). [Connexions]. **Added/Corp** Association pour la Recherche et l'Intervention Psychosociologiques. (1972)-. Periodical. French. sa. 280.00F France; 320.00F France. Editions Eres, 11 rue des Alouettes, Ramonville St. Agne France. **Tel** 011 33 61 751576. **ED** Dodei se Brouvne. **NLM** W1 CO728.
**Ind/Abst** Int. Labour Doc.; Psychol. Abstr. (1974-).

●US/1053-8100
**CONSCIOUSNESS AND COGNITION.** [Conscious. cogn.]. Vol. 1, No. 1 (Mar. 1992)-. Academic Scholarly Publication. English. qt (4 issues). $176.00 US and Canada; $205.00 other. Academic Press, Inc., 6277 Sea Harbor Drive, Orlando FL 32887. **Tel** (800)543-9534, (407)345-4100, FAX (407)363-9661. **ED** Bernard J. Baars and William P. Banks. **LC** BF309; .C66. **DD** 153.4/05. **NLM** W1; CO736L. **[CCC].** Documents available from The Genuine Article.
**Desc:** Provides a forum for a natural-science approach to the issues of consciousness, volumtary control, and self. Features both empirical research and theoretical articles. Integrative theoretical and critical literature reviews, and tutorial reviews are also published. Both scientifically rigorous and open to novel contributions.
**Ind/Abst** Arts Humanit. Citation Index [Select. Cov.]; Curr. Contents Soc. Behav. Sci.; Res. Alert [Full Cov.]; Soc. Sci. Cit. Index [Full Cov.].

US/0146-5457
**CONSCIOUSNESS AND SELF-REGULATION.** [Conscious. self-regul.]. Vol. 1 (1976)-. Monographic series. English. ir. Price varies per volume. Plenum Press, 233 Spring Street, New York NY 10013-1578. **Tel** (212)620-8000, (800)221-9369, FAX (212)463-0742, (212)807-1047, telex 23/421139. **ED** G.E. Schwartz and D. Shapiro. **LC** QP411; .C58. **DD** 153. **NLM** W1 CO737.

US/1052-8164
**CONSTRUCTIVE CRITICISM.** (CONSTRUCTIVE CRITICISM : A JOURNAL OF CONSTRUCT PSYCHOLOGY AND THE ARTS.). [Constr. crit.]. **Added/Corp** Center for the Study of Construct Psychology and the Arts. Vol. 1, No. 1 (Mar. 1991)-. Periodical. English. qt. $30.00. Center for the Study of Construct Psychology and the Arts, PO Box 162, Gambier OH 43022. **LC** NX165; .C65. **DD** 700/.1/9.

●US/1065-9293
**CONSULTING PSYCHOLOGY JOURNAL.** [Consult. psychol. j.]. **Added/Corp** Educational Publishing Foundation. American Psychological Association. Division of Consulting Psychology. Vol. 44, No. 2 (1992)-. Periodical. English. qt. $76.00 (institutions), $54.00 (individuals). American Psychological Association, 750 First Street Northeast, Washington DC 20002. **Tel** (800)374-2721, (202)336-5600, (subscriptions - (202)336-5600. **LC** IN PROCESS. **DD** 158. **NLM** W1; CO754R. ***Continues** Journal (American Psychological Association. Division of Consulting Psychology), 1061-4087.*
**Desc:** Provides a current exchange of knowledge and ideas regarding the field of consultation and the community of psychologists and others interested in consultation. Contains in-depth reviews of the research and literature in specific areas of consultation practice.

US
**CONTACT : A NEWSLETTER AND NETWORKING TOOL FOR THE GESTALT COMMUNITY.** Vol. 1, No. 1 (1990)-. Newsletter. English. **NLM** W1; CO769G.

US/0361-476X
**CONTEMPORARY EDUCATIONAL PSYCHOLOGY.** [Contemp. educ. psychol.]. Vol. 1 (Jan. 1976)-. Academic Scholarly Publication. English. qt (4 issues). $190.00 US and Canada; $236.00 other. Academic Press, Inc., 6277 Sea Harbor Drive, Orlando FL 32887. **Tel** (800)543-9534, (407)345-4100, FAX (407)363-9661. **ED** Raymond W. Kulhavy. **LC** LB1051; .C678. **DD** 370.15/05. **NLM** W1 CO769MP. **[CCC]. Pr Rev.** Documents available from The Genuine Article.
**Desc:** Empirical research and theory that demonstrates the application of psychological methods and research to problems in education. Articles and reviews cover the process of education through the lifespan, presenting a clear relationship of topic to data and theory.
**Ind/Abst** Acad. Search (Jan. 1994-); Arts Humanit. Citation Index [Select. Cov.]; Contents Pages Educ.; Curr. Contents Soc. Behav. Sci.; Curr. Index J. Educ.; Educ. Index; Educ. Technol. Abstr.; INFO-SOUTH Abstr.; Mag. Search; Multicult. Educ. Abstr.; Psychol. Abstr. (1976-); PsycINFO; PsycLit; Res. Alert [Full Cov.]; Res. High. Educ. Abstr.; School Organ. Manage. Abstr.; Soc. Sci. Cit. Index [Full Cov.]; Sociol. Educ. Abstr.; Stud. Women Abstr.; Tech. Educ. Train. Abstr.

US/0892-2764
**CONTEMPORARY FAMILY THERAPY.** **See** Family and Marriage.

US/0147-1082
**CONTEMPORARY PROBLEMS OF CHILDHOOD.** No. 1 (1977)-. Monographic series. English. ir. Price varies per volume. Greenwood Press Inc., PO Box 5007, Westport CT 06881-5007. **Tel** (203)226-3571, FAX (203)222-1502. **ED** Carol Ann Winchell. **LC** UNC. **NLM** ZWA 320 C761.

US/0010-7549
**CONTEMPORARY PSYCHOLOGY.** [Contemp. psychol.]. **Added/Corp** American Psychological Association. Vol. 1 (Jan. 1956)-. Academic Scholarly Publication. English. mo. $255.00 (nonmember, institution) US. American Psychological Association, 750 First Street Northeast, Washington DC 20002. **Tel** (800)374-2721, (202)336-5600, (subscriptions - (202)336-5600. **ED** John G. Gallup. **LC** BF1; .C53. **DD** 150.5. **NLM** Z 7203 C761. **[CCC].** Index available (free). **Bk Rev**. **Ad Acc**. **Pr Rev. Circ:** 6,000. available in microform from Johnson Associates; available on microfilm and microfiche from University Microfilms International (UMI). Documents available from The Genuine Article.
**Desc:** A journal of reviews. Readers will find recent books on scholarly, professional, and self-help materials; new insights from other disciplines; and 50-60 in depth reviews in every area of psychological application -- counseling, sociology, psychobiology, education, criminology, psychiatry, human development, media, substance abuse, aging, linguistics, computers, neuroscience, and more.
**Ind/Abst** Arts Humanit. Citation Index [Select. Cov.]; Book Rev. Index; Curr. Contents Soc. Behav. Sci.; Health Period. Database; Middle East Abstr. Index; Multicult. Educ. Abstr.; Res. Alert [Full Cov.]; Soc. Sci. Cit. Index [Full Cov.]; Soc. Res. Methodol. Abstr. (1975-); Women Stud. Abstr.

UK
**CONTEMPORARY PSYCHOLOGY SERIES.** (1991)-. Monographic series. English. **NLM** W1; CO769WH.

US/1041-3030
**CONTEMPORARY SSOCIAL PSYCHOLOGY.** (CONTEMPORARY SOCIAL PSYCHOLOGY : A PUBLICATION OF THE SOCIETY FOR THE ADVANCEMENT OF SOCIAL PSYCHOLOGY.). [Contemp. soc. psychol.]. **Added/Corp** Society for the Advancement of Social Psychology. (19??)-. Periodical. English. qt. $22.00. Society for the Advancement of Social Psychology, Department of Psychology, Mercer University, Macon GA 31207. **Tel** (912)752-2972, FAX (912)752-2108. **ED** Francis C. Dane. **DD** 302. Index available. **Bk Rev**, (Qty: 5 per year). **Ad Acc, Adv Mgr:** Editor. **Pr Rev. Circ:** 400. ***Continues** SASP Newsletter.*
**Desc:** Reports of research, theory, and announcements of interest to social psychologists and those who teach social psychology.
**Ind/Abst** Psychol. Abstr. (1986-); PsycINFO (1990-); PsycLit.

US
**CONTEMPORARY STUDIES IN APPLIED BEHAVIORAL SCIENCE.** (1983)-. Monographic series. English. ir. Price varies per volume. JAI Press Inc., 55 Old Post Road, Suite 2, PO Box 1678, Greenwich CT 06836-1678. **Tel** (203)661-7602, FAX (203)661-0792. **ED** Judith Levy.
**Desc:** Analysis of securities and commodities markets from a sociological perspective, with consideration given to economic and psychological theories of human behavior and market functioning.

US/0889-468X
**CONTINUING THE CONVERSATION.** ***Ceased.*** **See** Philosophy.

US/0736-2714
**CONTRIBUTIONS IN PSYCHOLOGY.** [Contrib. psychol.]. No. 1 (1983)-. Monographic series. English. ir. Price varies per volume. Greenwood Press

Inc., PO Box 5007, Westport CT 06881-5007. **Tel** (203)226-3571, FAX (203)222-1502. **NLM** W1; CO778NHH.

SZ/0301-4193
**CONTRIBUTIONS TO HUMAN DEVELOPMENT.** [Contrib. hum. dev.]. Vol. 1 (1974)-. Monographic series. English. an. 70.00F (approx. per volume). S. Karger AG, Allschwilerstrasse 10, PO Box - Postfach - Case Postale, CH-4009 Basel Switzerland. **Tel** 011 41 61 306-1111, FAX 011 41 61 306-1234, telex CH 962 652. **ED** D. Kuhn. **NLM** W1 CO778S. **CODEN** CHDEDZ. **[CCC].** Documents available from BIOSIS Document Express. ***Continues** Bibliotheca Vita Humana, 0523-4867.*
**Desc:** In all respects but size, theoretical contributions and research reports resemble articles commonly found in scientific journals. The editors have selected topics from all areas of developmental psychology as well as border areas of biology, sociology, anthropology, and education. Preference is given to interdisciplinary and cross-cultural studies.
**Ind/Abst** Biol. Abstr.; Psychol. Abstr. (1983-); PsycINFO; PsycLit; Ref. Upd. Deluxe Ed.

UK/0191-2488
**CONTRIBUTIONS TO MEDICAL PSYCHOLOGY.** Vol. 1 (1977)-. English. Pergamon Press, An Imprint of Elsevier Science Ltd., The Boulevard, Langford Lane, Kidlington, Oxford OX5 1GB United Kingdom. **Tel** 011 44 865 843000, 011 44 865 843699, FAX 011 44 865 843010. **DD** 610/.1/9. **NLM** W1 CO778TM. **CODEN** CMEPD6. Documents available from BIOSIS Document Express.
**Ind/Abst** Biol. Abstr. (-1977).

US/0273-124X
**CONTRIBUTIONS TO THE STUDY OF CHILDHOOD AND YOUTH.** [Contrib. study child. youth]. No. 1 (1982)-. Monographic series. English. ir. Price varies per volume. Greenwood Press Inc., PO Box 5007, Westport CT 06881-5007. **Tel** (203)226-3571, FAX (203)222-1502. **Bk Rev. Ad Acc.**
**Desc:** This series examines childhood and adolescence throughout the world within a historical as well as contemporary perspective.

US/1055-7873
**CORPORATE PSYCHOLOGY.** (1991)-. Periodical. English. mo. Corporate Psychology, 11735 Bowman Green Drive, Reston VA 22090. ***Continues** Management Productivity Review.*

US/0093-1551
**CORRECTIVE AND SOCIAL PSYCHIATRY AND JOURNAL OF BEHAVIOR TECHNOLOGY METHODS AND THERAPY.** **See** Medical Science and Technology-Psychiatry.

US/0160-7960
**COUNSELING AND VALUES.** [Couns. values]. **Added/Corp** American Association for Counseling and Development. Association for Religious and Value Issues in Counseling (U.S.). Vol. 16 (Fall 1971)-. Academic Scholarly Publication. English. Three times a year. $24.00 (institution), $18.00 (individual) US. American Counseling Association, 5999 Stevenson Avenue, Alexandria VA 22304. **Tel** (703)823-9800, (800)347-6647, FAX (703)823-0252. **(Subscription address:** American Counseling Association, Subscription Office, PO Box 2513, Birmingham AL 35201-2513.**) ED** Harry Daniels. **LC** LC461; .N438. **DD** 371.4/05. **CODEN** COVADQ. **[CCC].** Index available (free). **Ad Acc. Circ:** 3,998. available on microfilm and microfiche from University Microfilms International (UMI). ***Continues** National Catholic Guidance Conference Journal.*
**Desc:** Focuses exclusively on the role of values and religion in counseling and psychology. It provides scholarly, thoughtful discussion with invited papers by leading scholars. Features articles on topics such as the moral nature of psychotherapy, equality for women seminars, Marxism and liberation theology, pastoral counseling, and confidentiality keep you well informed.
**Ind/Abst** Abstr. Res. Pastor. Care Couns. (19??-); Curr. Index J. Educ.; High. Educ. Abstr. (1972-); Psychol. Abstr. (1971-); PsycINFO; PsycLit; Sage Fam. Stud. Abstr. (?-?); Soc. Work Abstr. [Select. Cov.]; Abr. Cathol. Period. Lit. Index; Cathol. Period. Lit. Index.

US/0160-6794
**COUNSELING INTERVIEWER, THE.** **Added/Corp** Missouri Guidance Association. (19??)-. Periodical. English. Four times a year. $20.00. Missouri School Counselor Association, PO Box 402, Jackson MO 63755. **Tel** (314)243-3611. **ED** Pat Ferris. **Bk Rev. Ad Acc. Pr Rev. Circ:** 1,000.
**Desc:** Provides up-to-date counseling information and materials for the school counselor. Current trends, theories and applications are discussed.

US/0011-0000
**COUNSELING PSYCHOLOGIST, THE.** [Couns. psychol.]. **Added/Corp** American Psychological Association. Division of Counseling Psychology. Vol. 1 (1969)-. English. qt (Jan., Apr., July, Oct.). $163.00. SAGE Periodical Press, 2455 Teller Road, Thousand Oaks CA 91320. **Tel** (805)499-0721, FAX (805)499-0871, telex 100799. **ED** Gerald L. Stone (University of Iowa). **LC** BF637.C6; C64. **DD** 158. **NLM** W1 CO964. **CODEN** CPSYB. **Pr Rev. Acid Free.** available on microfilm and microfiche from University Microfilms International (UMI). Documents available from The Genuine Article, UMI Article Clearinghouse.
**Desc:** Presents timely coverage in new or developing areas of practice and research of topics of immediate interest to counseling psychologists. Defines the field and communicates that identity to the profession, as well as to those in other disciplines.
**Ind/Abst** Acad. Abstr. Full Text Elite (Jan. 1992-); Acad. Abstr. (Jan. 1992-); Acad. Search (Jan. 1992-); Curr. Contents Soc. Behav. Sci.; Curr. Index J. Educ.; Educ. Adm. Abstr.; Expand. Acad. Index (1989-); High. Educ. Abstr. (1973-); Hum. Resour. Abstr.; INFO-SOUTH Abstr.; Mag. Search; Middle East Abstr. Index; Newsp. Period. Abstr. (1991-); Psychol. Abstr. (1969-); PsycINFO; PsycLit; Res. Alert [Full Cov.]; Soc. Sci. Source (Jan. 1992-); Soc. Sci. Cit. Index [Full Cov.]; Soc. Sci. Index; Soc. Sci. Index Fulltext (Oct. 1988-) [Full Txt.]; Women Stud. Abstr.

●US
**COUNSELING TODAY.** (1993)-. English. mo. $49.00 (institution), $37.00 (individual) US. American Counseling Association, 5999 Stevenson Avenue, Alexandria VA 22304. **Tel** (703)823-9800, (800)347-6647, FAX (703)823-0252. **(Subscription address:** American Counseling Association, Subscription Office, PO Box 2513, Birmingham AL 35201-2513.**) *Continues*** *Guideposts, 0017-5323.*

UK/0264-9977
**COUNSELLING.** [Counselling]. (1981)-. Periodical. English. qt. £26.00. British Association for Counselling, 1 Regent Place, Rugby CV21 2PJ England. **Tel** 011 44 788 578328, FAX 011 44 788 562189. **DD** 361.32305. ***Continues** Counselling News.*

UK/0951-5070
**COUNSELLING PSYCHOLOGY QUARTERLY.** **VFOAT** Counseling Psychology Quarterly; CPQ. Vol. 1, No. 1 (1988)-. Periodical. English. qt. £164.00. Carfax Publishing Company, PO Box 25 Abingdon, Oxfordshire OX14 3UE England. **Tel** 011 44 235 555335, FAX (0279)31067, telex 817484. **(Subscription address:** US and Canada/ PO Box 2025, Dunnellon, FL 34430-2025; telephone:(904)489-6996**) ED** W. J. Alladin. **NLM** W1; CO964H. **CODEN** CPQUEZ. **[CCC].** available on microfiche.
**Desc:** Covers practice, theory and research in counselling psychology.
**Ind/Abst** EMBASE; Psychol. Abstr. (1988-); PsycINFO; PsycLit; Spec. Educ. Needs Abstr.

UK
**COUNSELLING : THE JOURNAL OF THE BRITISH ASSOCIATION FOR COUNSELLING.** **See** Sociology-Social Services and Welfare.

CN/0821-0101
**COURRIER P.R.H. MONTREAL.** [Courr. P.R.H.-Montr.]. **VAT** Courrier Personnalite et Relations Humaines-Montreal. No. 1 (Oct. 1977)-. Periodical. French. sm. 12.00Can$. Sessions P R H, Bureau 1, 2130 Boul, Rosemont Quebec H2G 1T4 Canada. **Tel** (514)273-8361. **DD** 158/.1/060714281. **Circ:** 500 (ctrl).

US/0740-7947
**CPI NATIONAL REPORT.** ***Title Change.*** [CPI natl. rep.]. **Added/Corp** Crisis Prevention Institute (U.S.). **VFOAT** C.P.I. National Report. **VAT** Crisis Prevention Institute National Report. (19??)-(199?). Periodical. English. Four times a year (Jan., Apr., July, Oct.). Crisis Prevention Institute, 3315 K North 124th Street, Brookfield WI 53005. **Tel** (414)783-5787, (800)558-8976, FAX (414)783-5906. **ED** Diana Kahn and Sandra Christensen. **LC** WMLC 93/1916. **Circ:** 5,000 (ctrl). ***Continues** Journal of Safe Management of Disruptive and Assaultive Behavior, 1065-3341. **Continued by** Journal of Safe Management of Disruptive and Assaultive Behavior, 1065-3341.*
**Desc:** The safe management of disruptive and assaultive behavior.

CN/1186-0391
**CREATE: JOURNAL OF THE CREATIVE AND EXPRESSIVE ARTS THERAPIES EXCHANGE.** [Create]. **Added/Corp** Creative and Expressive Arts Therapies Exchange. Vol. 1 (1991)-. English. $10.00 per volume. Creative and Expressive Arts Therapies Exchange, 118 Wells Street, Toronto Ontario M5R 1P3 Canada. **DD** 616.89/165/05.

US/8755-884X
**CREATIVE LIVING TODAY.** [Creat. living today]. (19??)-. Periodical. English. bm (6 issues). $9.00. Creative Living Today, PO Box 808, Gatlinburg TN 37738. **Tel** (615)436-4762, (615)436-7478. **DD** 158.

US/0093-5263
**CREATIVITY IN ACTION.** [Creat. act.]. (1972)-. Newsletter. English. mo. $50.00 US; $55.00 Canada and Mexico; $60.00 other. Creative Education Foundation, 1050 Union Road, Buffalo NY 14224. **Tel** (716)675-3181, FAX (716)675-3209. **ED** Grace Guzzetta. **DD** 153. **Circ:** 1,000.
**Desc:** Ideas, assistance for enhancement of creative thinking and action for individuals and groups. Tools for creativity, participation programs, creative puzzles, "Creativity Fitness Program" (copyrighted).

US/0093-8548
**CRIMINAL JUSTICE AND BEHAVIOR.** [Crim. justice behav.]. **Added/Corp** American Association of Correctional Psychologists. Vol. 1 (Mar. 1974)-. Periodical. English. qt (Mar., June, Sept., Dec.). $158.00. SAGE Periodical Press, 2455 Teller Road, Thousand Oaks CA 91320. **Tel** (805)499-0721, FAX (805)499-0871, telex 100799. **ED** David S. Glenwick (Fordham University). **LC** HV9261; .C74. **DD** 364.6/01/9. **NLM** W1 CR194J. **CODEN** CJBHAB. **[CCC]. Pr Rev. Acid Free.** available on microfilm and microfiche from University Microfilms International (UMI). Documents available from The Genuine Article, UMI Article Clearinghouse. ***Supersedes** Correctional Psychologist, 0589-8218.*
**Desc:** Provides a means of communication among mental health professionals, behavioral scientists, researchers and practitioners in the area of criminal justice.
**Ind/Abst** Acad. Abstr. Full Text Elite (July 1990-); Acad. Abstr. (July 1990-); Acad. Search (July 1990-); Appl. Soc. Sci. Index Abstr.; Crim. Justice Abstr.; Crim. Justice Period. Index; Crim. Penol. Police Sci. Abstr.; Curr. Contents Soc. Behav. Sci.; Curr. Index J. Educ.; Curr. Law Index (1980-); EMBASE; Expand. Acad. Index (1984-); Index Period. Artic. Relat. Law; INFO-SOUTH Abstr.; Leg. Resour. Index (1980-); LegalTrac (1980-); Mag. Search; Middle East Abstr. Index; Multicult. Educ. Abstr.; Newsp. Period. Abstr. (1988-); Psychol. Abstr. (1974-); PsycINFO; PsycLit; Res. Alert [Full Cov.]; Sage Urban Stud. Abstr; Soc. Sci. Source (Jul. 1990-); Soc. Sci. Cit. Index [Full Cov.]; Soc. Sci. Index Fulltext (Sept. 1988-) [Full Txt.]; Spec. Educ. Needs Abstr.

CN/0227-5910
**CRISIS (TORONTO).** (CRISIS : INTERNATIONAL JOURNAL OF SUICIDE- AND CRISIS- STUDIES.). [Crisis]. **Added/Corp** International Association for Suicide Prevention. **VFOAT** International Zeitschrift fur Selbstmord- und Krisen-StudienRevue International Sic pour l'Etude du Suicide et des Etats de Crise. Vol. 1, No. 1 (Apr. 1980)-. Periodical. English (French and German; summaries and/or abstracts in French and German). Four times a year. DM79.00. Hogrefe Verlag fuer Psychologie, Rohnsweg 25, D 37085 Goettingen Germany. **Tel** 011 49 551 496090, FAX 011 49 551 4960988. **(Subscription address:** Hogrefe & Huber Publishers, Seattle Office, Box 2487, Kirkland WA 98083.**) ED** David Clark, Chefredaktoren Ad Kerkhof. **LC** PAR. **DD** 364.1/522/05. **NLM** W1 CR202M. **Bk Rev. Ad Acc. Circ:** 3,000. ***Continues** Vita.*
**Desc:** Serves as a forum for suicide studies; for the exchange and discussion of information, investigations and results of suicide researchers from around the world.
**Ind/Abst** Health Plan. Adminis.; Index Med. Vol. 6, No. 1, 1985-; Psychol. Abstr. (1980-).

US/0276-5330
**CRITICAL PERSPECTIVES ON CONTEMPORARY PSYCHOLOGY.** [Crit. perspect. contemp. psychol.]. **Added/Corp** New School for Social Research (New York, N.Y.). Graduate Faculty. Vol. 1, No. 1 (Spring 1980)-. Periodical. English. sa. $3.50 US; $4.00 other. Graduate Faculty of the New School for Social Research, 65-5th Avenue, New York NY 10003. **LC** BF1; .C75. **DD** 150/.5.

CN/0710-068X
**CROSS-CULTURAL PSYCHOLOGY BULLETIN.** (CROSS-CULTURAL PSYCHOLOGY BULLETIN : OFFICIAL PUBLICATION / INTERNATIONAL ASSOCIATION FOR CROSS-CULTURAL PSYCHOLOGY.). [Cross-cult. psychol. bull.]. **Added/Corp** International Association for Cross-Cultural Psychology. Vol. 15, No. 1/2 (Feb./May 1981)-. Periodical. English. Four times a year (Mar., June, Sept., Dec.). $15.00. C O R Annis, Brandon University Native Studies, Brandon Manitoba R7A 6A9 Canada. **Tel** (204)727-3076. **ED** R. C. Annis and B. Corenblum. **DD** 155.8/06/01. **Bk Rev. Circ:** 500. ***Continues** Cross-Cultural Psychology Newsletter, 0702-6056.*

SP/0211-3481
**CUADERNOS DE PSICOLOGIA (BARCELONA, SPAIN).** (CUADERNOS DE PSICOLOGIA.). [Cuad. psicol.]. **VFOAT** Quaderns de Psicologia. Spanish (Catalan). **NLM** W1; CU137M.
**Ind/Abst** Psychol. Abstr. (1982-); PsycINFO.

AG
**CUADERNOS SIGMUND FREUD.** (May 1971)-. Monographic series. Spanish. ir. Price varies per volume. Ediciones Nueva Vision, Tucuman 3748, Buenos Aires Argentina.

US/0092-6361
**CURRENT CONTENTS. SOCIAL & BEHAVIORAL SCIENCES.** **See** Social Sciences-Abstracting, Bibliographies and Statistics.

●US/0963-7214
**CURRENT DIRECTIONS IN PSYCHOLOGICAL SCIENCE : A JOURNAL OF THE AMERICAN PSYCHOLOGICAL SOCIETY.** **Added/Corp** American Psychological Society. Vol. 1, No. 1 (Feb. 1992)-. Academic Scholarly Publication. English. bm (6 issues). $125.00 US, Canada & Mexico; £74.00 other. Cambridge University Press / New York, 40 West 20th Street, New York NY 10011-4211. **Tel** (212)924-3900, (800)221-4512. **(Subscription address:** Cambridge University Press / Outside of North America, Journal Fulfillment Department, The Edinburgh Building, Cambridge CB2 2RU United Kingdom.**)** **ED** Sandra W. Scarr and Charles R. Gallistel. **LC** BF1; .C86. **DD** 150/.5. **NLM** W1; CU788DU. **CODEN** CDPSE8.
**Desc:** Serves as a timely source of information about the broad field of psychology, covering emerging trends, controversies, and topics of enduring importance to psychologists.

US/0741-9724
**CURRENT ISSUES IN CLINICAL PSYCHOLOGY.** [Curr. issues clin. psychol.]. **Main/Conf** Merseyside Course in Clinical Psychology. (1983)-. Monographic series. English. ir. Price varies per volume. Plenum Press, 233 Spring Street, New York NY 10013-1578. **Tel** (212)620-8000, (800)221-9369, FAX (212)463-0742, (212)807-1047, telex 23/421139. **ED** Eric Karas. **LC** RC469; .M45a. **DD** 616.89/005. **NLM** W3 ME56.

UK/0264-4517
**CURRENT ISSUES IN EUROPEAN SOCIAL PSYCHOLOGY.** [Curr. issues Eur. soc. psychol.]. Vol. 1-. Academic Scholarly Publication. English. ir. Cambridge University Press, The Edinburgh Building, Shaftesbury Road, Cambridge CB2 2RU United Kingdom. **Tel** 011 44 223 312393, FAX 011 44 223 325959. **(Subscription address:** US/ 110 Midland Avenue, Port Chester, NY 10573**)** **LC** HM251; .C947. **DD** 302/.05.

US
**CURRENT ISSUES IN PSYCHOANALYTIC PRACTICE.** (CURRENT ISSUES IN PSYCHOANALYTIC PRACTICE : MONOGRAPHS OF THE SOCIETY FOR PSYCHOANALYTIC TRAINING.). **VFOAT** Monographs of the Society for Psychoanalytic Training. (1989)-. Monographic series. English. Price varies per volume. Brunner Mazel, 19 Union Square West, New York NY 10003. **Tel** (212)924-3344, (800)825-3089. **NLM** W1; CU788LD. ***Continues** Current Issues in Psychoanalytic Practice, 0737-7851.*

US/1046-1310
**CURRENT PSYCHOLOGY (NEW BRUNSWICK, N.J.).** (CURRENT PSYCHOLOGY : RESEARCH & REVIEWS.). [Curr. psychol.]. **VFOAT** Current Psychology Research & Reviews; Current Psychology Research and Reviews. Vol. 7, No. 1 (Spring 1988)-. Periodical. English. Four times a year. Fl195.00 (individual), Fl372.00 (institution). Transaction Publishers / Rutgers State University, New Brunswick NJ 08903. **Tel** (908)932-2280 Ext. 105, FAX (908)932-3138. **ED** Noel P. Sheehy, Nathaniel J. Pallone. **LC** BF1; .C87. **DD** 150/.5. **NLM** W1; CU807J. **[CCC]. Pr Rev. Circ:** 550. available on labels; available on microfilm and microfiche from University Microfilms International (UMI). Documents available from The Genuine Article. ***Continues** Current Psychological Research & Reviews, 0737-8262.*
**Desc:** An international forum for rapid dissemination of information in psychology. Significant empirical contributions from all areas of psychology including social psychology; small groups and personality; human development; sensation, perception, and cognition; clinical and abnormal psychology; and methodology and field research.
**Ind/Abst** ABC POL SCI (19??-19??); Curr. Contents Soc. Behav. Sci.; Highw. Res. Abstr.; Psychol. Abstr. (1988-); PsycINFO (1990-); PsycLit; Res. Alert [Full Cov.]; Sage Fam. Stud. Abstr.; Soc. Sci. Cit. Index [Full Cov.]; Soc. Sci. Index.

US/8755-0040
**CURRENT TOPICS IN HUMAN INTELLIGENCE.** [Curr. top. hum. intell.]. Vol. 1 (1985)-. English. ir. Price varies per volume. Ablex Publishing Corporation, 355 Chestnut Street, Norwood NJ 07648. **Tel** (201)767-8450, (201)767-8455 (Customer Service), FAX (201)767-6717. **ED** Douglas Detterman. **LC** BF431; .C86. **DD** 153.9/05. **Bk Rev. Ad Acc.**
**Desc:** A book series focusing on selected topics on human intelligence of current interest to researchers.
**Ind/Abst** Psychol. Abstr. (1985-); PsycINFO; PsycLit.

US/8750-8699
**CURRENTS IN AFFECTIVE ILLNESS.** [Curr. affective illn.]. **VFOAT** Currents. Vol. 1, No. 1 (July 1982)-. Periodical. English. mo. $115.00 US; $125.00 Canada and Mexico; $180.00 other. Currents Publications Inc, 7000 Carmichael Avenue, Bethesda MD 20817. **Tel** (301)320-6915, FAX (301)320-6915. **ED** J.E. Rosenblatt. **DD** 626. **NLM** ZWM 207; C976. Index available.
**Desc:** Review of the latest literature in biological psychiatry and monthly authoritative interviews.

US/0748-1187
**DEATH STUDIES.** [Death stud.]. **Added/Corp** University of Florida. Center for Gerontological Studies. Vol. 9, No. 1 (1985)-. Periodical. English. bm. £97.00 UK; $160.00 other. Taylor & Francis Ltd., Rankine Road, Basingstoke Hampshire, RG24 8PR United Kingdom. **Tel** 011 44 256 840366, FAX 011 44 256 479438, telex 858540. **(Subscription address:** Taylor & Francis Inc., 1900 Frost Road, Suite 101, Bristol PA 19007-1598.**)** **ED** Robert A. Neimeyer (editor's address: Memphis State University, Department of Psychology, Memphis, TN 38152). **LC** BF789.D4; D45. **DD** 306. **NLM** W1; DE107H. **CODEN** DESTEA. **[CCC]. Bk Rev. Ad Acc. Pr Rev. Circ:** 1,100. available on microfilm and microfiche from University Microfilms International (UMI). Documents available from The Genuine Article, UMI Article Clearinghouse. ***Continues** Death Education, 0145-7624.*
**Desc:** Publishes refereed papers on significant concerns and practical approaches in the ever-growing field of death education and counseling. It provides an international, interdisciplinary forum in which a variety of professionals share experiences, techniques, successes, failures, and ideas with the aim of significantly helping those who work with the dying and their families.
**Ind/Abst** Abstr. Res. Pastor. Care Couns. (19??-); Acad. Search (July 1993-); Contents Pages Educ.; Cumul. Index Nurs. Allied Health Lit.; Curr. Contents Soc. Behav. Sci.; Curr. Index J. Educ.; EMBASE; Expand. Acad. Index (1989-); Health Plan. Adminis.; Hospit. Health Admin. Index (1985-); Hum. Resour. Abstr. (?-?); Humanit. Source (Jul. 1993-); INFO-SOUTH Abstr.; Linguist. Lang. Behav. Abstr.; Mag. Search; Multicult. Educ. Abstr.; Newsp. Period. Abstr. (1991-); Psychol. Abstr. (1977-); PsycINFO; PsycLit; Res. Alert [Full Cov.]; Res. High. Educ. Abstr.; Sage Fam. Stud. Abstr.; Soc. Plann. Policy Dev. Abstr.; Soc. Sci. Source (Jul. 1993-); Soc. Sci. Cit. Index [Full Cov.]; Soc. Sci. Index; Soc. Sci. Index Fulltext (Nov. 1988-) [Full Txt.]; Soc. Work Abstr. [Select. Cov.]; Sociol. Abstr.

●US/1066-5056
**DEMENTIA REVIEWS.** **See** Medical Science and Technology-Psychiatry.

NE
**DENKBEELD.** **See** Medical Science and Technology-Geriatrics.

●US/1062-6417
**DEPRESSION (NEW YORK, N.Y.).** (DEPRESSION.). [Depression]. (1993)-. Periodical. English. Six times a year (Jan., Mar., May., July, Sept., Nov.). $168.00 (US); $228.00 (Canada and Mexico); $250.50 (other). John Wiley & Sons, Inc., 605 Third Avenue, New York NY 10158-0012. **Tel** (212)850-6000, (212)850-6645, FAX (212)850-6088, telex 12-7063. **(Subscription address:** John Wiley & Sons / England, Baffins Lane, Chichester, West Sussex PO19 1UD England.**)** **ED** Charles B. Nemeroff. **DD** 362. **NLM** W1; DE467D. **CODEN** DRESES. **Pr Rev.**
**Desc:** Publishes peer-reviewed reports of novel research on the etiology, symptomatology, and treatment of mood disorders, including bipolar disorders, major depression, and dysthymia. Welcomes original research and synthetic review articles on the neuropsychobiological precipitants of depression and its comorbid disorders; somatic, psychodynamic, behavioral, and cognitive aspects of the disorder; and pharmacotherapeutic and psychotherapeutic treatment techniques.

US/0954-5794
**DEVELOPMENT AND PSYCHOPATHOLOGY.** [Dev. psychopathol.]. Vol. 1, No. 1 (1989)-. Academic Scholarly Publication. English. qt (March, June, September and December). $121.00 US, Canada & Mexico; £69.00 other. Cambridge University Press / New York, 40 West 20th Street, New York NY 10011-4211. **Tel** (212)924-3900, (800)221-4512. **(Subscription address:** Cambridge University Press / Outside of North America, Journal Fulfillment Department, The Edinburgh Building, Cambridge CB2 2RU United Kingdom.**)** **ED** Dante Cicchetti and Barry Nurcombe. **LC** RC454.4; .D479. **DD** 616.89/005. **NLM** W1; DE997NAF. **Ad Acc.** available on microfilm and microfiche from University Microfilms International (UMI). Documents available from The Genuine Article.
**Desc:** Multidisciplinary journal devoted to the publication of original, empirical, theoretical and review papers which address the interrelationship of normal and pathological development in adults and children. Intended to serve and integrate the emerging field of developmental psychopathology which strives to understand patterns of adaptation and maladaptation throughout the life span.
**Ind/Abst** Curr. Contents Soc. Behav. Sci.; Psychol. Abstr. (1989-); PsycINFO; PsycLit; Res. Alert [Full Cov.]; Soc. Sci. Cit. Index [Full Cov.].

US/0892-8150
**DEVELOPMENTAL CLINICAL PSYCHOLOGY AND PSYCHIATRY.** [Dev. clin. psychol. psychiatry]. **VFOAT** Developmental Clinical Psychology and Psychiatry Series. Vol. 1 (1985)-. Monographic series. English. ir. Price varies per volume. SAGE Periodical Press, 2455 Teller Road, Thousand Oaks CA 91320. **Tel** (805)499-0721, FAX (805)499-0871, telex 100799. **DD** 618. **NLM** W1; DE997NC. **CODEN** DCPPE3.
**Ind/Abst** Biol. Abstr. (1988-).

US/0012-1630
**DEVELOPMENTAL PSYCHOBIOLOGY.** **See** Biology.

US/0012-1649
**DEVELOPMENTAL PSYCHOLOGY.** [Dev. psychol.]. **Added/Corp** American Psychological Association. Vol. 1 (Jan. 1969)-. Periodical. English. bm. $243.00 (nonmember, institution) US. American Psychological Association, 750 First Street Northeast, Washington DC 20002. **Tel** (800)374-2721, (202)336-5600, (subscriptions - (202)336-5600. **ED** Carolyn Zahn-Waxler, PhD. **LC** BF699; .D46. **DD** 155/.05. **NLM** W1 DE997US. **CODEN** DEVPA9. **[CCC].** Index available (free). **Ad Acc. Pr Rev. Circ:** 5,100. available on microfilm and microfiche from University Microfilms International (UMI). Documents available from The Genuine Article, BIOSIS Document Express, UMI Article Clearinghouse.
**Desc:** Covers new research on developmental processes in such areas as gender, age, and cultural differences. Provides board coverage of developmental psychology for advances in language processes, cognitive development, emotional development, moral development, understanding relationships, and social development.
**Ind/Abst** Acad. Abstr. Full Text Elite (July 1990-); Acad. Abstr. (July 1990-); Acad. Ind. [Computer File] (1992-); Acad. Search (July 1990-); AGRICOLA; Appl. Soc. Sci. Index Abstr.; Arts Humanit. Citation Index [Select. Cov.]; Biol. Abstr.; Crim. Justice Abstr.; Crim. Penol. Police Sci. Abstr.; Curr. Contents Soc. Behav. Sci.; Curr. Index J. Educ.; Dev. Med. Child Neurol.; Educ. Index; Expand. Acad. Index (1989-); Gen. Sci. Source (Jul. 1990-); Health Period. Database; High. Educ. Abstr. (1973-19??); Index Period. Artic. Relat. Law (19??-19??); INFO-SOUTH Abstr.; Mag. Search; Middle East Abstr. Index; MLA Int. Bibl. Books Artic. Mod. Lang. Lit.; Multicult. Educ. Abstr.; Newsp. Period. Abstr. (1990-); Life Sci. Collect.; Psychol. Abstr. (1969-); PsycINFO; PsycLit; PsycScan: Develop. Psych.; Res. Alert [Full Cov.]; Soc. Sci. Source (Jul. 1990-); Soc. Sci. Cit. Index [Full Cov.]; Soc. Sci. Index; Soc. Sci. Index Fulltext (July 1988-) [Full Txt.]; Soc. Work Abstr. [Select. Cov.]; Sociol. Educ. Abstr.; Spec. Educ. Needs Abstr.; Stud. Women Abstr.; Women Stud. Abstr.

US/0273-2297
**DEVELOPMENTAL REVIEW.** (DEVELOPMENTAL REVIEW : DR.). [Dev. rev.]. **VFOAT** DR. Vol. 1, No. 1 (March 1981)-. Academic Scholarly Publication. English. qt (4 issues). $127.50 US and Canada; $156.50 other. Academic Press, Inc., 6277 Sea Harbor Drive, Orlando FL 32887. **Tel** (800)543-9534, (407)345-4100, FAX (407)363-9661. **ED** Grover J. Whitehurst. **LC** BF721; .D45. **DD** 155. **NLM** W1 DE997UU. **[CCC]. Pr Rev.** Documents available from The Genuine Article.
**Desc:** Presents research that bears on important conceptual issues in developmental psychology; provides child and developmental psychologists, child clinical psychologists, and educational psychologists with authoritative articles that reflect current thinking and cover significant scientific developments.
**Ind/Abst** AGRICOLA; Curr. Contents Soc. Behav. Sci.; Psychol. Abstr. (1981-); PsycINFO; PsycLit; PsycScan: Develop. Psych.; Res. Alert [Full Cov.]; Soc. Sci. Cit. Index [Full Cov.].

SZ/0378-7931
**DEVIANCE ET SOCIETE.** V. 1- May 1977-. Periodical. French. qt. 73.00F (individuals), 128.00F (institutions). Medecine et Hygiene, Case Postale 456, CH-1211 Geneve 4 Switzerland. **Tel** 011 41 22 3469355, 011 41 22 3469355. **LC** HM291; .D4833. **DD** 301.6/2/05. **[CCC]. Bk Rev. Ad Acc. Circ:** 750 (ctrl).
**Desc:** Articles resulting from recent research studies. Debates between supporters of different points of view on deviance and social control problems. Bibliographical syntheses in different fields of research.
**Ind/Abst** Crim. Justice Abstr.

US/0163-9625
**DEVIANT BEHAVIOR.** [Deviant behav.]. Vol. 1 (1979)-. Periodical. English. qt. £80.00 UK; $132.00 other. Taylor & Francis Ltd., Rankine Road, Basingstoke Hampshire, RG24 8PR United Kingdom. **Tel** 011 44 256 840366, FAX 011 44 256 479438, telex 858540. **(Subscription address:** Taylor & Francis Inc., 1900 Frost Road, Suite 101, Bristol PA 19007-1598.**)** **ED** C. Eddie Palmer. **LC** HM1; .D48. **DD** 302.5. **NLM** W1 DE999H. **CODEN** DEBEDF. **[CCC]. Bk Rev. Ad Acc. Pr Rev. Circ:** 450. available on microfilm and microfiche from University Microfilms International (UMI). Documents available from The Genuine Article.
**Desc:** The only journal which specifically and exclusively addresses social deviance. It is international and interdisciplinary in scope and publishes refereed theoretical, descriptive, methodological, conceptual, and applied papers on all aspects of deviant behavior including crime, juvenile delinquency, alcohol abuse and narcotic addiction, sexual deviance, societal reaction to handicap and disfigurement, mental illness, and socially inappropriate behavior.

**Ind/Abst** Abstr. Res. Pastor. Care Couns. (19??-); Crim. Justice Abstr.; Curr. Contents Soc. Behav. Sci.; Index Period. Artic. Relat. Law (19??-19??); Linguist. Lang. Behav. Abstr.; Psychol. Abstr. (1981-); PsycINFO; PsycLit; Res. Alert [Full Cov.]; Sage Urban Stud. Abstr; Soc. Plann. Policy Dev. Abstr.; Soc. Sci. Cit. Index [Full Cov.]; Sociol. Abstr.

GW/0012-1924
**DIAGNOSTICA (GOTTINGEN).**
(DIAGNOSTICA.). [Diagnostica]. (April 1955)-. Periodical. German. Four times a year. DM94.00. Hogrefe Verlag fuer Psychologie, Rohnsweg 25, D 37085 Goettingen Germany. **Tel** 011 49 551 496090, FAX 011 49 551 4960988. **(Subscription address:** Hogrefe & Huber Publishers, Seattle Office, Box 2487, Kirkland WA 98083.) **ED** Hans Westmeyer. **DD** 150. **NLM** ZBF 431 D536. **CODEN** DGNSAQ. **Circ:** 1,000.
**Desc:** Pertains to the practical side of psychology: diagnostics and differential psychology. Special attention is paid to the development of tests and their application.
**Ind/Abst** Int. Aerosp. Abstr.; Psychol. Abstr. (1964-); PsycINFO; PsycLit.

US/1062-0788
**DIRECTIONS IN MENTAL HEALTH COUNSELING.** [Dir. ment. health couns.]. (1991)-. Periodical. English. mo. $195.00. Hatherleigh Co., 420 51st Street, New York NY 10022. **DD** 362.

US/0149-4368
**DIRECTORIO DE MIEMBROS - SOCIEDAD INTERAMERICANA DE PSICOLOGIA.** **Main/Corp** Interamerican Society of Psychology. **VFOAT** Directory of Members - Interamerican Society of Psychology; Catalogo de Membros - Sociedade Interamericana de Psicologia. Multiple languages (English, Portuguese and Spanish). Interamerican Society of Psychology, Department of Psychology, De Paul University Chicago IL 60614. **LC** BF15; .I5814. **DD** 150/.6/21.

US/0193-7561
**DIRECTORY, HANDBOOK - CALIFORNIA STATE PSYCHOLOGICAL ASSOCIATION.** **Main/Corp** California State Psychological Association. **VFOAT** CSPA Directory, Handbook. Directory. English. $10.00. California State Psychological Association, 1010 11th Street, Suite 202, Los Angeles CA 95814. **Tel** (916)325-9786. **LC** BF30; .C34A. **DD** 150/.6/2794.

US
**DIRECTORY, INTERNSHIP PROGRAMS IN PROFESSIONAL PSYCHOLOGY (INCLUDING POST-DOCTORAL TRAINING PROGRAMS).** ***Title Change.***
**Main/Corp** Association of Psychology Internship Centers (U.S.). **VFOAT** Internship Programs in Professional Psychology (Including Post-Doctoral Training Programs); APIC Directory. (19??)-(199?). Directory. English. an. Association of Psychology Internship Centers, 733 15th Street NW, Suite 717, Washington DC 20005. **Tel** (202)347-0022. **Circ:** 1,500. ***Continued by*** *APPIC Directory, 1078-7178.*

US/0732-1333
**DIRECTORY OF PSYCHOLOGISTS AND PSYCHOLOGICAL EXAMINERS LICENSED AND REGISTERED IN TENNESSEE.** (DIRECTORY OF PSYCHOLOGISTS AND PSYCHOLOGICAL EXAMINERS LICENSED AND REGISTERED IN TENNESSEE / STATE LICENSING BOARD FOR THE HEALING ARTS.). **Added/Corp** Tennessee. State Licensing Board for the Healing Arts. Tennessee. State Licensing Board for the Healing Arts Act. Tennessee. State Board of Examiners in Psychology Act. (1976)-. Directory. English. an. State Licensing Board for the Healing Arts, TDPH State Office Building, Ben Allen Road, Nashville TN 37216. **NLM** BF 109 D615. ***Continues*** *Directory of Psychologists and Psychological Examiners Licensed in Tennessee, 0163-8556.*

US/0361-3771
**DIRECTORY OF PSYCHOSOCIAL INVESTIGATORS.** **Added/Corp** Center for Psychosocial Studies. (July 1975)-. English. Center for Psychosocial Studies, 233 North Michigan Avenue, Chicago IL 60601. **LC** BF30; .D533. **DD** 301.1/025.

US/0196-6545
**DIRECTORY OF THE AMERICAN PSYCHOLOGICAL ASSOCIATION (1978).** **See** Encyclopedias and General Reference Books.

CN/0068-9475
**DIRECTORY OF THE CANADIAN PSYCHOLOGICAL ASSOCIATION.**
**Main/Corp** Canadian Psychological Association. **VFOAT** Repertoire de la Societe Canadienne de Psychologie; Directory; Annuaire. 1981 Ed.-. Directory. English (French). te. Free to members. Canadian Psychological Association, Chemin Vincent Road, Old Chelsea Quebec J0X 2N0 Canada. **Tel** (819)827-3927. **DD** 150/.6/071. ***Continues*** *Canadian Psychological Society. Directory, 0068-9475.*

CN/0316-7569
**DIRECTORY - ONTARIO PSYCHOLOGICAL ASSOCIATION.**
**Main/Corp** Ontario Psychological Association. (1???)-. Directory. English. be. $25.00 (two year). Ontario Psychological Association, 730 Yonge Street/Suite 221, Toronto Ontario M4Y 2B7 Canada. **Tel** (416)961-5552, FAX (416)961-5516. **DD** 150/.6/2713.

US/0545-6371
**DIRECTORY - THE NEW YORK SOCIETY OF CLINICAL PSYCHOLOGISTS, INC.**
[Dir. - New York Soc. Clin. Psychol., inc.]. **Main/Corp** New York Society of Clinical Psychologists. Feb. 1950-. Directory. English. an. New York Society of Clinical Psychologists, 30 West 60th Street, New York NY 10023. **NLM** WM 22 AA1 N5D.

CN/1182-946X
**DISENPLUS (MONTREAL).** **See** Medical Science and Technology-Psychiatry.

US/0896-2863
**DISSOCIATION (SMYRNA, GA.).**
(DISSOCIATION: THE OFFICIAL JOURNAL OF THE INTERNATIONAL SOCIETY FOR THE STUDY OF MULTIPLE PERSONALITY & DISSOCIATION.). **Added/Corp** International Society for the Study of Multiple Personality and Dissociation. Ridgeview Institute. Vol. 1, No. 1 (March 1988)-. Periodical. English. qt. $60.00 individuals, $65.00 institutions, US; $65.00 other. Ridgeview Institute, 3995 South Cobb Dr., Smyrna GA 30080. **Tel** (404)434-4567. **ED** Richard Kluft. **DD** 616. **NLM** W1; DI182I.
**Desc:** Current information regarding the study of multiple personality disorder and dissociative disorders.
**Ind/Abst** Except. Hum. Exp.; Psychoanal. Abstr.; Psychol. Abstr. (1988-); PsycINFO; PsycLit; PsycScan: Appl. Exp. Eng. Psych.; PsycScan: LD/MR; PsycScan: Neuropsych.

JA/0003-5130
**DOBUTSU SHINRIGAKU NENPO.** [Dobutsu shinrigaku nenpo]. **Added/Corp** Nihon Dobutsu Shinri Gakkai. **VFOAT** Annual of Animal Psychology. Vol. 1 (1951)-. Periodical. Japanese (English). sa. $30.00. Nihon Dobutsu Shinri Gakkai, (Japanese Society for Animal Psychology), Tokyo Daigaku Bungakubu, 3-1, Hongo 7 Chome, Bunkyoku, Tokyoto 113 Japan. **(Subscription address:** Japan Publications Trading Company, Ltd., PO Box 5030, Tokyo International, Tokyo 100-31 Japan.) **NLM** W1 DO157.
**Ind/Abst** Life Sci. Collect.; Psychol. Abstr. (1956-); PsycINFO (1956-); PsycLit.

US/0162-2315
**DOWNSTATE SERIES OF RESEARCH IN PSYCHIATRY AND PSYCHOLOGY, THE.** **See** Medical Science and Technology-Psychiatry.

US/0190-7093
**DRAGONFLIES.** V. 1- Fall 1978-. Periodical. English. $5.00. Editor Dragonflies, Department of Psychology, University of Dallas, Irving TX 75061. **LC** BF455.A1; D7. **DD** 150/.19/2.

US/1053-0797
**DREAMING (NEW YORK, N.Y.).** **See** Biology-Physiology.

CN/0823-2180
**DREAMWEAVER MAGAZINE.** [Dreamweaver mag.]. Vol. 1, No. 1 (Spring 1983)-. Periodical. English. qt. Dreamweaver Magazine, 6 Charles Street East, Toronto Ontario M4Y 1T2 Canada. **DD** 154.6/05/. ***Continues*** *Dreamweaver (Toronto, Ont.), 0228-9342.*

AT/1030-2883
**DULWICH CENTRE NEWSLETTER.**
[Dulwich Cent. newsl.]. (1987)-. Newsletter. English. qt. 40.00Aus$. Dulwich Centre, Hutt Street, Box 7192, Adelaide South Australia 5000. **Tel** 08 223 3966, FAX 08 223 4441. **(Subscription address:** Dulwich Centre, PO Box 7192, Adelaide SA 5000 Australia.) **DD** 362.8205.
**Desc:** Covers a range of themes and issues of interest to family therapists.

US/0070-7716
**DUQUESNE STUDIES. PSYCHOLOGICAL SERIES.** Vol. 1 (1963)-. Monographic series. English. ir. Price varies per volume. Humanities Press, 165 1st Avenue, Atlantic Highlands NJ 07716. **Tel** (908)872-1441, (800)221-3845, FAX (908)872-0717, telex 752233. **ED** Albert C. Labriola. **DD** 150.
**Desc:** Publishes monographs on Spenser and Milton which clarify or influence their works, i.e. Green and Roman classics, commentary by church fathers, medieval secular and religious literature and drama.

●UK/1057-3593
**EARLY DEVELOPMENT AND PARENTING.** **See** Education-Early Childhood and Primary Education.

●US/1064-0266
**EATING DISORDERS.** [Eat. disord.]. Vol. 1, No. 1 (Spring 1993)-. Periodical. English. qt. $80.00 (institution), $38.00 (individual). Brunner Mazel, 19 Union Square West, New York NY 10003. **Tel** (212)924-3344, (800)825-3089. **DD** 641.

UK/1067-1633
**EATING DISORDERS REVIEW (CHICHESTER, ENGLAND).** ***Title Change.***
(EATING DISORDERS REVIEW.). [Eat. disord. rev.]. **Added/Corp** Eating Disorders Association (Great Britain). Vol. 1, No. 1 (May 1993)-(1993). Periodical. English. Four times a year. $100.00 institution. John Wiley & Sons Ltd., Baffins Lane, Chichester West Sussex PO19 1UD England. **Tel** 0243 779777, FAX 0243 776128 BTG:JWP001, telex 86290 WIBOOKG. **(Subscription address:** John Wiley / Philadelphia, PO Box 7247, Philadelphia PA 19170.) **ED** Carol Bowyer, Alan Cockett, Pat Hartley and Jill Welbourne. **LC** RC552.E18; B75. **DD** 613. **NLM** W1; EA874. **CODEN** EDIREQEDEVEI. ***Continues*** *British Review of Bulimia + Anorexia Nervosa, 0950-3005.* ***Continued by*** *European Eating Disorders Review, 1072-4133.*
**Desc:** Provides practical help and new ideas for professionals who treat or care for anyone who suffers from bulimia or anorexia nervosa or related eating disorders.

US/1040-7413
**ECOLOGICAL PSYCHOLOGY.**
(ECOLOGICAL PSYCHOLOGY : A PUBLICATION OF THE INTERNATIONAL SOCIETY FOR ECOLOGICAL PSYCHOLOGY.). [Ecol. psychol.]. **Added/Corp** International Society for Ecological Psychology. Vol. 1, No. 1 (1989)-. Periodical. English. qt. $180.00 US & Canada; $205.00 other. Lawrence Erlbaum Associates, 365 Broadway, Suite 102, Hillsdale NJ 07642. **Tel** (201)666-4110, (800)926-6579, FAX (201)666-2394. **LC** BF353; .E26. **DD** 155. **NLM** W1; EC912G. **CODEN** ECPSEN. Documents available from BIOSIS Document Express.
**Ind/Abst** Biol. Abstr. (1991-); Ergon. Abstr.; Psychol. Abstr. (1989-); PsycINFO; PsycLit; Soc. Sci. Cit. Index [Full Cov.].

UK/0262-4087
**EDUCATION SECTION REVIEW - BRITISH PSYCHOLOGICAL SOCIETY.**
[Educ. Sect. rev. - Br. Psychol. Soc.]. **VFOAT** Educational Section Review - British Psychological Society; Review - Education Section, British Psychological Society. (1981)-. English. sa. British Psychological Society, St. Andrews House, 48 Princess Road, Leicester LE1 7DR England. **Tel** 011 44 533 549568. **DD** 150.5. ***Continues*** *Newsletter - Educatio Section, British Psychological Society.*
**Ind/Abst** Br. Educ. Index.

UK/0267-1611
**EDUCATIONAL AND CHILD PSYCHOLOGY.** (EDUCATIONAL AND CHILD PSYCHOLOGY / DIVISION OF EDUCATIONAL AND CHILD PSYCHOLOGY.). [Educ. child psychol.]. **Added/Corp** British Psycological Society. Division of Educational and Child Psychology. Vol. 1, No. 1 (1984)-. Periodical. English. Four times a year. £18.50. British Psychological Society, St. Andrews House, 48 Princess Road, Leicester LE1 7DR England. **Tel** 011 44 533 549568. ***Continues*** *Occasional Papers (British Psychological Society. Division of Educational and Child Psychology), 0144-5219.*
**Ind/Abst** Br. Educ. Index; Psychol. Abstr. (1985-); PsycINFO (1990-); PsycLit; Spec. Educ. Needs Abstr.

SW/0070-9263
**EDUCATIONAL AND PSYCHOLOGICAL INTERACTIONS.** **See** Education.

US/1013-1644
**EDUCATIONAL AND PSYCHOLOGICAL MEASUREMENT.** [Educ. psychol. meas.]. **Added/Corp** American College Personnel Association. Proceedings. Science Research Associates. **VFOAT** EPM. Vol. 1 (Jan. 1941)-. English. bm (Feb., Apr., June, Aug., Oct., Dec.). $128.00. SAGE Periodical Press, 2455 Teller Road, Thousand Oaks CA 91320. **Tel** (805)499-0721, FAX (805)499-0871, telex 100799. **ED** William Michael (University of Southern California). **LC** BF1; .E3. **DD** 151.205. **NLM** W1 ED855. **CODEN** EPMEAJ. **Bk Rev**. **Pr Rev**. **Acid Free**. **Circ:** 2,400. available on microfilm and microfiche from University Microfilms International (UMI). Documents available from The Genuine Article, UMI Article Clearinghouse.
**Desc:** Discussion of problems in the field of the measurement of individual differences. Reports of research on the development and use of tests and measurements in education, industry, and government. Descriptions of testing programs being used for various purposes, and reports which are pertinent to the measurement field.
**Ind/Abst** Acad. Abstr. Full Text Elite (July 1990-); Acad. Abstr. (July 1990-); Acad. Ind. [Computer File] (1989-); Acad. Search (July 1990-); Chicano Index; Compumath Citation Index [Full Cov.]; Contents Pages Educ.; Cumul. Index Nurs. Allied Health Lit.; Curr. Contents Soc. Behav. Sci.; Curr. Index J. Educ.; Educ. Index; Except. Child Educ. Resour. (19??-19??); Expand. Acad. Index (1987-);

High. Educ. Abstr. (1965-); INFO-SOUTH Abstr.; Mag. Search; Middle East Abstr. Index; Newsp. Period. Abstr. (1989-); Psychol. Abstr. (1941-); PsycINFO; PsycLit; PsycScan: Appl. Psych.; Res. Alert [Full Cov.]; Res. High. Educ. Abstr.; Soc. Sci. Source (Jul. 1990-); Soc. Sci. Cit. Index [Full Cov.]; Soc. Work Abstr. (?-?); Spec. Educ. Needs Abstr.; Soc. Res. Methodol. Abstr. (1975-); Women Stud. Abstr.

US/0046-1520
**EDUCATIONAL PSYCHOLOGIST.** [Educ. psychol.]. **Added/Corp** American Psychological Association. Division of Educational Psychology. (1963)-. Periodical. English. qt. $190.00 US & Canada; $215.00 other. Lawrence Erlbaum Associates, 365 Broadway, Suite 102, Hillsdale NJ 07642. **Tel** (201)666-4110, (800)926-6579, FAX (201)666-2394. **ED** Gavriel Salomon. **LC** LB1051; .E35. **DD** 370.15/05. **NLM** W1 ED875K. **CODEN** EDPSDT. **Ad Acc. Pr Rev. Circ:** 1,200. available on microfilm and microfiche from University Microfilms International (UMI). Documents available from The Genuine Article.
**Desc:** Essays, critiques and articles of a theoretical, conceptual nature contributing to understanding of issues and research in educational psychology.
**Ind/Abst** Acad. Search (July 1993-); Curr. Contents Soc. Behav. Sci.; Educ. Index; High. Educ. Abstr. (1985-19??); INFO-SOUTH Abstr.; Mag. Search; Psychol. Abstr. (1973-); PsycINFO; PsycLit; Res. Alert [Full Cov.]; Soc. Sci. Cit. Index [Full Cov.]; Tech. Educ. Train. Abstr.

UK/0144-3410
**EDUCATIONAL PSYCHOLOGY (DORCHESTER-ON-THAMES).** (EDUCATIONAL PSYCHOLOGY.). [Educ. psychol.]. Vol. 1, No. 1 (1981)-. English. qt (Mar., June, Sept., Dec.). £164.00. Carfax Publishing Company, PO Box 25 Abingdon, Oxfordshire OX14 3UE England. **Tel** 011 44 235 555335, FAX (0279)31067, telex 817484. **(Subscription address:** US and Canada/ PO Box 2025, Dunnellon, FL 34430-2025; telephone:(904)489-6996) **ED** Richard Riding & Kevin Wheldall. **LC** LB1051; .E358. **DD** 370.15. **NLM** W1 ED875N. **[CCC].** available on microfiche.
**Desc:** The aim of the journal is to be a primary source for articles dealing with the psychological aspects of education ranging from preschool to tertiary provision and the education of children with special needs.
**Ind/Abst** Br. Educ. Index; Curr. Index J. Educ.; Educ. Technol. Abstr.; Multicult. Educ. Abstr.; Psychol. Abstr. (1981-); School Organ. Manage. Abstr.; Sociol. Educ. Abstr.; Spec. Educ. Needs Abstr.; Stud. Women Abstr.; Tech. Educ. Train. Abstr.

US/0731-1141
**EDUCATIONAL PSYCHOLOGY GUILFORD, CONN.** (EDUCATIONAL PSYCHOLOGY.). [Educ. psychol.]. **VFOAT** Annual Editions. Educational Psychology. 82/83-. Periodical. English. an. $10.95. Dushkin Publishing Group Inc., Sluice Dock, Guilford CT 06437. **Tel** (203)453-4351, (800)243-6532, FAX (203)453-6000. **ED** Kathleen M Cauley, Fredric Linder and James McMillan. **LC** LB1051; .E362. **DD** 370.15/05. Index available.
**Desc:** An updated collection of public press articles covering current issues in the wide range of topics comprising the interdisciplinary field of educational psychology.
**Ind/Abst** PsycLit.

UK/0266-7363
**EDUCATIONAL PSYCHOLOGY IN PRACTICE. Added/Corp** Association of Educational Psychologists. (198?)-. Periodical. English. qt. £39.00 Europe; £43.00 Other (Institutions). Longman Group Ltd., Fourth Avenue, Longman House, Harlow Essex CM19 5SR England. **Tel** 011 44 279 429655, FAX 011 44 279 431059, telex 81259. **ED** Peter Love. Index available. **Bk Rev. Ad Acc. Circ:** 2,350. available on microfilm from University Microfilms International (UMI).
**Desc:** A lively, relevant and readable journal specifically geared to reflect your professional interests and supply your need for information at a time of considerable change in the education world.
**Ind/Abst** Br. Educ. Index; Educ. Adm. Abstr.; Psychol. Abstr. (1974-); PsycINFO (1990-); PsycLit.

US/1040-726X
**EDUCATIONAL PSYCHOLOGY REVIEW.** [Educ. psychol. rev.]. Vol. 1, No. 1 (Mar. 1989)-. Periodical. English. Four times a year. $155.00 institutions, $39.00 individuals US; $180.00 institutions, $36.00 individuals other. Plenum Press, 233 Spring Street, New York NY 10013-1578. **Tel** (212)620-8000, (800)221-9369, FAX (212)463-0742, (212)807-1047, telex 23/421139. **ED** Stephen L. Benton. **LC** LB1051; .E374. **DD** 370.15/05. **CODEN** EPSREO. **[CCC].** available on microfilm and microfiche from University Microfilms International (UMI).
**Desc:** Journal containing state-of-the-art review articles in general education psychology - learning, cognition, measurement, school-related counseling, and development.
**Ind/Abst** Acad. Search (July 1993-); Educ. Index (1992-); INFO-SOUTH Abstr.; Mag. Search; Psychol. Abstr. (1989-); PsycINFO; PsycLit; Soc. Plann. Policy Dev. Abstr.; Spec. Educ. Needs Abstr.

RU
**EKSPERIMENTALNOE ISSLEDOVANIE LICHNOSTI I TEMPERAMENTA. Added/Corp** Permskii Gosudarstvennyi Pedagogicheskii Institut. Obshchestvo Psikhologov. Uralskoe Otdelenie. **VFOAT** Eksperimentalnye Issledovaniia Lichnosti I Temperamenta. (19??)-. Russian. **LC** AS262.P37; A37 subser; BF798.

US
**EMOTION.** Vol. 1 (1980)-. Monographic series. English. ir. Price varies per volume. Academic Press, Inc., 6277 Sea Harbor Drive, Orlando FL 32887. **Tel** (800)543-9534, (407)345-4100, FAX (407)363-9661. **ED** Robert Plutchik and Henry Kellerman. **NLM** W1 EM668.

US/0739-828X
**EMOTIONAL FIRST AID.** ***Suspended.*** (EMOTIONAL FIRST AID / AMERICAN ACADEMY OF CRISIS INTERVENERS, SOUTHWESTERN ACADEMY OF CRISIS INTERVENERS.). [Emot. first aid]. Vol. 1, No. 1 (Spring 1984)-?. Periodical. English. qt. $50.00. AACI SWACI, c/o J Greenstone, PO Box 670292, Dallas TX 75367. **ED** James L Greenstone. **DD** 616. **NLM** W1; EM668R. **Bk Rev. Ad Acc.** ***Continues*** *Emotional First Aid, 0739-828X.*
**Desc:** Offers a wide range of topics, both theoretical and practical, related to crisis intervention.
**Ind/Abst** PsycINFO; PsycLit.

US/0734-9890
**EMOTIONS AND BEHAVIOR MONOGRAPHS.** [Emot. behav. monogr.]. **VFOAT** Emotions & Behavior. Monograph No. 1 (1983)-. Monographic series. English. ir. Price varies per volume. International Universities Press Inc., 59 Boston Post Road, PO Box 1524, Madison CT 06443-1524. **Tel** (203)245-4000, FAX (203)245-0775, telex 282986 IUP BK. **LC** UNC. **NLM** W1; EM673. **CODEN** EBMOEN. Documents available from BIOSIS Document Express.
**Ind/Abst** Biol. Abstr. (1987-); PsycINFO.

UK/0933-8217
**EMPLOYEE COUNSELLING TODAY. Added/Corp** Employee Assistance Resource (Great Britain). (1989)-. Periodical. English. bm. $1159.00. MCB University Press, 60 62 Toller Lane, Bradford West Yorkshire BD8 9BX England. **Tel** 011 44 274 499821, FAX 011 44 274 547143, telex 51317 MCBUNI G. **(Subscription address:** MCB University Press / US and Canada Subscriptions, PO Box 10812, Birmingham AL 35201-0812.) **ED** Mike Megranahan. Index available. cum. index. **Pr Rev. Circ:** 400 (ctrl). available on microfilm from University Microfilms International (UMI).
**Desc:** By drawing on the practical experiences of people in the field, it keeps readers up-to-date with developments, as well as examining the results of workplace counselling. In addition to a selection of in depth articles the journal regularly carries news items, book and video reviews, and abstracts of articles published in other leading journals.

UK/0013-7472
**ENERGY AND CHARACTER.** Vol. 1, (Jan. 1970)-. Periodical. English. Twice a year (Apr., Oct.). £16.00. Abbotsbury Publications, 6 Surrey Close Granby Industrial Estate, Weymouth Dorset DT4 9TY England. **Tel** 011 44 305 771718. **ED** David Boadella. **NLM** W1 EN45. Index available in last issue of volume--attached. cum. index. **Circ:** 1,000 (ctrl).
**Desc:** Covers somatic psychology, bioenergetics, remedial work and prevention of neurosis.

FR/0013-7545
**ENFANCE.** [Enfance]. **Added/Corp** Ecole Ppratique des Hautes Etudes (France). Laboratoire de Psychobiologie de l'Enfant. (1948)-. Periodical. French. qt. 340.00F France; 395.00F other. Presses Universitaires de France, Department des Revues, 14 Avenue du Bois de l'Epine, BP 90, 91003 Evry Cedex France. **Tel** (1)60 77 82 05, FAX (1) 60 79 20 45, telex PUF 600 474 F. **LC** HQ768; .E5. **NLM** W1 EN531.
**Ind/Abst** Psychol. Abstr. (1948-); PsycINFO; PsycLit.

●US
**ENNEIGRAM EDUCATOR.** (1994)-. Periodical. English. Four times a year. $15.00. National Catholic Reporter Publishing Company, PO Box 419281, 115 East Armour Boulevard, Kansas City MO 64141-6281. **Tel** (816)531-0538, (800)444-8910, (800)333-7373, FAX (816)531-7466. **ED** Clarence Thomson.
**Desc:** Studies in personality types.

MX/0185-1594
**ENSENANZA E INVESTIGACION EN PSICOLOGIA.** [Ensen. invest. psicol.]. Vol. 1, No. 1-June 1975-. Periodical. Spanish. sa. $12.00. Ensenanza Investigacion, Apdo Postal 19 174, 03910 Mexico DF Mexico. available on microfilm from University Microfilms International (UMI).
**Ind/Abst** Psychol. Abstr. (1975-); PsycINFO; PsycLit.

US/0743-586X
**ERANOS LECTURES.** [Eranos lect.]. Monographic series. English. ir. Price varies per volume. Spring Journal, PO Box 583, Putnam CT 06260. **Tel** (203)974-3229, FAX (203)974-3195. **ED** James Hillman. **Circ:** 1,800.
**Desc:** Large-format reproductions of lectures originally included in editions of the Eranos Jahrbuch.

SP/0210-9395
**ESTUDIOS DE PSICOLOGIA.** [Estud. psicol.]. (1980)-. Periodical. Spanish (summaries and/or abstracts in English and French). bm. 8500.00ptas (institutions), 12500.00 (individuals) Latin America; 18500.00ptas (institutions), 9900.00ptas (individuals) Spain; 20000.00ptas (institutions), 11400.00ptas (individuals) other. Aprendizaje SA, Carretera de Canillas 138 16 C, 28033 Madrid Spain. **Tel** 011 34 1 3883874, 011 34 1 2009338, FAX 011 34 1 3003527. **LC** BF5; .E84. **DD** 150/.5. **NLM** W1 ES96SG.
**Ind/Abst** PsycINFO; PsycLit.

GW/0179-1613
**ETHOLOGY.** **See** Zoology.

US/0162-3095
**ETHOLOGY AND SOCIOBIOLOGY.** [Ethol. sociobiol.]. Vol. 1 (Oct. 1979)-. Academic Scholarly Publication. English. Six times a year (1 volume). $354.00 US; $394.00 other. Elsevier Science Publishing Company Inc, Madison Square Station, PO Box 882, New York NY 10159-0882. **Tel** (212)633-3950, FAX (212)633-3990. **ED** Michael T. McGuire, N.G. Blurton Jones, and W.C. McGrew. **LC** BF1; .E73. **DD** 150/.5. **NLM** W1 ET448. **CODEN** ETSOD8. **[CCC]. Pr Rev.** available on microfilm and microfiche from University Microfilms International (UMI). Documents available from The Genuine Article.
**Desc:** Publishes new studies on ethological and sociobiological theories using comparative data, experimental results and literature reviews.
**Ind/Abst** Anthropol. Lit.; Appl. Soc. Sci. Index Abstr.; Curr. Contents, Agric. Biol. Environ. Sci.; Fish Rev. (Jan. 1989-July 1992); Geogr. Abstr. Human Geogr.; Index Period. Artic. Relat. Law (19??-19??); Int. Bibliogr. Sociol.; Life Sci. Collect.; Psychol. Abstr. (1980-); PsycINFO; PsycLit; Ref. Upd. Deluxe Ed.; Res. Alert [Full Cov.]; SCISEARCH; Soc. Plann. Policy Dev. Abstr.; Soc. Sci. Cit. Index [Full Cov.]; Sociol. Abstr.; SportSearch; Wildl. Rev. (Jan. 1989-July 1992).

US/0091-2131
**ETHOS.** [Ethos]. **Added/Corp** Society for Psychological Anthropology. Vol. 1, Spring (1973)-. Periodical. English. qt. $60.00 (institutions), $44.00 (individuals). American Anthropological Association, 4350 North Fairfax Dr, Suite 640, Arlington VA 22203. **Tel** (703)528-1902 ext. 3031, FAX (703)528-3546. **ED** Robert A. Paul and Susan Valenza. **LC** GN270; .E85. **DD** 155.8/05. **CODEN** ETHSAU. **[CCC]. Bk Rev. Ad Acc. Pr Rev. Circ:** 1,200 (ctrl). available on microfilm and microfiche from University Microfilms International (UMI). Documents available from The Genuine Article.
**Desc:** Thought and research in psychological anthropology and cross-cultural psychology. Encompassing culture and cognition, transcultural psychiatry, ethnopsychiatry, socialization, psychoanalytic, anthropology and other psychocultural topics.
**Ind/Abst** Curr. Contents Soc. Behav. Sci.; Int. Bibliogr. Sociol.; Middle East Abstr. Index; Psychol. Abstr. (1973-); PsycLit; Res. Alert [Full Cov.]; Soc. Plann. Policy Dev. Abstr.; Soc. Sci. Cit. Index [Full Cov.]; Sociol. Abstr.

FR
**ETUDES DE PSYCHOLOGIE ET DE PHILOSOPHIE.** **See** Philosophy.

GW/0531-7347
**EUROPAISCHE HOCHSCHULSCHRIFTEN. REIHE 6, PSYCHOLOGIE.** [Eur. Hochsch.schr.. Reihe 6 Psychol.]. **VFOAT** Psychologie; Psychology; Publications Universitaires Europeennes. Serie 6, Psychologie; European University Papers. Series 6, Psychology. Began with: V. 1, in 1968. Monographic series. German. ir. Price varies per volume. **NLM** W1 EU586D.
**Ind/Abst** Math. Rev.

●CN
**EUROPEAN CHILD & ADOLESCENT PSYCHIATRY. SUPPLEMENT.** **See** Medical Science and Technology-Psychiatry.

●UK/1072-4133
**EUROPEAN EATING DISORDERS REVIEW.** (EUROPEAN EATING DISORDERS REVIEW : THE JOURNAL OF THE EATING DISORDERS ASSOCIATION.). [Eur. eat. disord. rev.]. **Added/Corp** Eating Disorders Association (Great Britain). **VFOAT** Eating Disorders Review. Vol. 1, No. 3 (Dec. 1993)-. Periodical. English. qt. $90.00. John Wiley & Sons Ltd., Baffins Lane, Chichester West Sussex PO19 1UD England. **Tel** 0243 779777, FAX 0243 776128 BTG:JWP001, telex 86290 WIBOOKG. **(Subscription address:** John Wiley / Philadelphia, PO Box 7247, Philadelphia PA 19170.) **LC** RC552.E18; B75. **DD** 613. **CODEN** EEDRE8. ***Continues*** *Eating Disorders Review (Chichester, England), 1067-1633.*

UK/0954-1446
**EUROPEAN JOURNAL OF COGNITIVE PSYCHOLOGY, THE. Added/Corp** European Society for Cognitive Psychology. Vol. 1, Issue 1 (March

1989)-. Periodical. English. qt (4 issues). $178.50 US; £100.00 Europe; £105.00 other. Lawrence Erlbaum Associates Ltd., 27 Palmeira Mansions, Church Road, Hove East Sussex BN3 2FA England. **Tel** 011 44 273 207411. **(Subscription address:** Turpin Distribution Services Limited, Blackhorse Road, Letchworth, Hertfordshire SG6 1HN, United Kingdom.**) ED** Lars-Goran Nilsson. **LC** BF309; .E97. **NLM** W1; EU72DC. **CODEN** EJCPEW. **Bk Rev. Ad Acc. Circ:** 1,000. Documents available from The Genuine Article, BIOSIS Document Express.
**Desc:** Encourages the exchange and integration of ideas, research and training in cognitive psychology throughout Europe.
**Ind/Abst** Abstr. Soc. Gerontol.; Arts Humanit. Citation Index [Select. Cov.]; Biol. Abstr.; Ergon. Abstr.; Psychoanal. Abstr.; Psychol. Abstr. (1989-); PsycINFO; PsycScan: Appl. Exp. Eng. Psych.; PsycScan: LD/MR; PsycScan: Neuropsych.; Res. Alert [Full Cov.]; Soc. Plann. Policy Dev. Abstr.; Soc. Sci. Cit. Index [Full Cov.].

UK/0890-2070
**EUROPEAN JOURNAL OF PERSONALITY.** [Eur. j. pers.]. **Added/Corp** European Association of Personality Psychology. (1987)-. Periodical. English (summaries and/or abstracts in French and German). Five times a year. $375.00. John Wiley & Sons Ltd., Baffins Lane, Chichester West Sussex PO19 1UD England. **Tel** 0243 779777, FAX 0243 776128 BTG:JWP001, telex 86290 WIBOOKG. **(Subscription address:** John Wiley / Philadelphia, PO Box 7247, Philadelphia PA 19170.**) ED** Guus L. Van Heck. **LC** WMLC 93/1303; BF698.A1; E87. **DD** 155. **NLM** W1; EU72DPF. **[CCC].** Index available. cum. index. **Bk Rev. Ad Acc. Pr Rev. Circ:** 500. available on microfilm and microfiche from University Microfilms International (UMI). Documents available from The Genuine Article.
**Desc:** Reflects all areas of current personality psychology with emphasis on human individuality as manifested in cognitive processes, emotional and motivational functioning and personal ways of interacting with the environment. Covers individual differences in personality structure and dynamics. Studies of intelligence and interindividual differences in cognitive functioning are also included.
**Ind/Abst** Curr. Contents Soc. Behav. Sci.; Psychol. Abstr. (1987-); PsycINFO (1990-); PsycLit; Res. Alert [Full Cov.]; Soc. Plann. Policy Dev. Abstr.; Soc. Sci. Cit. Index [Full Cov.].

GW/1015-5759
**EUROPEAN JOURNAL OF PSYCHOLOGICAL ASSESSMENT.** (19??)-. English. Three times a year. DM123.00 (institutions), DM87.00 (individuals). Hogrefe Verlag fuer Psychologie, Rohnsweg 25, D 37085 Goettingen Germany. **Tel** 011 49 551 496090, FAX 011 49 551 4960988. **(Subscription address:** Hogrefe & Huber Publishers, Seattle Office, Box 2487, Kirkland WA 98083.**) ED** R. Fernandez-Ballesteros, F. Silva. **Circ:** 800.
**Desc:** Provides an active forum for the important issues in the field of psychological assessment. Presents articles on theoretical as well as practical subjects and is therefore clearly directed at both researchers and practitioners.

PO/0256-2928
**EUROPEAN JOURNAL OF PSYCHOLOGY OF EDUCATION. See** Education-Special Education and Rehabilitation.

UK/0046-2772
**EUROPEAN JOURNAL OF SOCIAL PSYCHOLOGY. See** Sociology.

UK/0892-7286
**EUROPEAN MONOGRAPHS IN SOCIAL PSYCHOLOGY.** [Eur. monogr. soc. psychol.]. 1-1971-. Monographic series. English. ir. Price varies per volume. Academic Press Ltd., A Division of Harcourt Brace & Company Ltd., 24-28 Oval Road, London NW1 7DX England. **Tel** 071 267 4466, FAX 071 482 2293, 071 485 4752, telex 25775 ACPRES G. **(Subscription address:** Harcourt Brace Jovanovich Limited, Footscray High Street, Sidcup, Kent DA14 5HP UK, (Phone: 081-300-3322)) **DD** 302. **NLM** W1 EU721F. ***Absorbed*** *European Studies in Social Psychology.*
**Ind/Abst** Psychol. Abstr. (1981-).

FR
**EUROPEAN REVIEW OF APPLIED PYCHOLOGY / REVUE EUROPEENNE DE PSYCHOLOGIE APPLIQUEE. VFOAT** Revue Europeenne de Psychologie Appliquee. Vol. 41, No 1 (1991)-. Periodical. French (English). Four times a year. 401.57F. Centre de Psychology Appliquee, 25 rue de la Plaine, 75680 Paris Cedex 20 France. **Tel** 011 33 1 40096262. **LC** BF636.A1; R4. Documents available from The Genuine Article. ***Continues*** *Revue de Psychologie Appliquee, 0035-1709.*
**Ind/Abst** Curr. Contents Soc. Behav. Sci.; Ergon. Abstr.; Res. Alert [Full Cov.]; Soc. Sci. Cit. Index [Full Cov.].

UK/0960-2003
**EUROPEAN WORK AND ORGANISATIONAL PSYCHOLOGIST, THE. Added/Corp** International Association of Applied Psychology. European Association of Work and Organizational Psychology. Vol. 1, Issue 1 (1991)-. Periodical. English. qt. $110.00 US; £60.00 Europe; £65.00 other. Lawrence Erlbaum Associates Ltd., 27 Palmeira Mansions, Church Road, Hove East Sussex BN3 2FA England. **Tel** 011 44 273 207411. **(Subscription address:** Turpin Distribution Services Limited, Blackhorse Road, Letchworth, Hertfordshire SG6 1HN, United Kingdom.**) ED** Charles de Wolff. **NLM** W1; EU736. **CODEN** EWOPED.
**Desc:** Published in association with the International Association of Applied Psychology. This journal publishes articles with a European focus that provide a bridge between academics, who enlarge the knowledge to clients and organizations. Should be of interest to all researchers in the field of work and organizational psychology, work psychologists in the public and private sector, personnel managers and organizational consultants.
**Ind/Abst** Ergon. Abstr.; Soc. Plann. Policy Dev. Abstr.

SP
**EVALUACION PSICOLOGICA. VFOAT** Psychological Assessment. Vol. 1, No. 1/2 (1985)-. Periodical. English (Spanish). tq. $25.00. Edisa, Calle Lopez de Hoyos 141, 28002 Madrid Spain. **Tel** 011 34 1 4159712, 011 34 1 5196776. **LC** BF176; .E93.
**Ind/Abst** Psychol. Abstr. (1985-); PsycINFO (1985-); PsycLit.

●US/1064-1297
**EXPERIMENTAL AND CLINICAL PSYCHOPHARMACOLOGY.** [Exp. clin. psychopharmacol.]. **Added/Corp** American Psychological Association. Vol. 1, Nos. 1-4 (Oct. 1993)-. Periodical. English. qt. $120.00 (nonmember, institution) US. American Psychological Association, 750 First Street Northeast, Washington DC 20002. **Tel** (800)374-2721, (202)336-5600, (subscriptions - (202)336-5600. **DD** 615. **NLM** W1; EX467.

●US/1066-4807
**FAMILY JOURNAL (ALEXANDRIA, VA.), THE. See** Family and Marriage.

US/0277-6464
**FAMILY THERAPY NEWS.** (FAMILY THERAPY NEWS : NEWSPAPER OF THE AMERICAN ASSOCIATION FOR MARRIAGE AND FAMILY THERAPY.). [Fam. ther. news]. **Added/Corp** American Association for Marriage and Family Therapy. (198?)-. Periodical. English. Six times a year. $40.00 (institution), $25.00 (individual) US, Canada and Mexico. American Association for Marriage and Family Therapy, 1100 17th Street Northwest, 10th Floor, Washington DC 20036-4601. **Tel** (202)452-0109, FAX (202)223-2329. ***Continues*** *American Association for Marriage and Family Therapy Newsletter, 0273-575X.*
**Desc:** Offers broad coverage of recent news developments in the field of marriage and family therapy. Features interviews with leading therapists and reports from international correspondents, with reports on legislative developments affecting the field of marital and family therapy, and current data on trends in marriage, divorce and other family-related factors.

UK/0959-3535
**FEMINISM & PSYCHOLOGY. See** Women's Interests.

CN/0227-7751
**FITNESS AND LIFESTYLE RESEARCH REVIEWS. See** Health and Personal Fitness.

US/0046-4171
**FLORIDA PSYCHOLOGIST, THE. VFOAT** FP; F.P. Vol. 10, No. 3 (1960)-. English. qt. Florida Psychological Association, 1731 Mockingbird Lane Gessner, Lakeland FL 33801. ***Continues*** *F.P.A. Newsletter.*

US
**FOCUS. Added/Corp** Illinois. Dept. of Mental Health and Developmental Disabilities. **VFOAT** Illinois Department of Mental Health and Developmental Disabilities Focus. (19??)-. Periodical. English. qt.
**Ind/Abst** Spec. Educ. Needs Abstr.

US
**FOCUS ON BEHAVIORAL HEALTH. Main/Corp** New Mexico. Behavioral Health Services Division. 1-. English. PO Box 968, 724 Saint Michaels Drive, Crown Building, Santa Fe NM 87503. ***Supersedes*** *MH-MR Digest.*

GW
**FORTSCHRITTE DER VERHALTENSFORSCHUNG. See** Veterinary Sciences.

GW/0178-7667
**FORUM DER PSYCHOANALYSE.** Vol. 1, No. 1 (July 1985)-. Periodical. German (summaries and/or abstracts in English). Four times a year. DM158.00. Springer-Verlag GmbH & Company KG, Heidelberger Platz 3, D 14197 Berlin Germany. **Tel** 011 49 30 8207223, FAX 011 49 30 8214091, telex 183 319 SPBLN D. **(Subscription address:** Springer Verlag New York Inc. / for North America, 44 Hartz Way, Secaucus NJ 07096.**) ED** M Ermann, S O Hoffmann, and J Koerner. **NLM** W1; FO946H. **[CCC].** available on microfilm and microfiche from University Microfilms International (UMI). Documents available from The Genuine Article.
**Desc:** Covers various schools of thought. Presents articles on the theory and practice of psychoanalysis and on current research in the field.
**Ind/Abst** Curr. Contents Soc. Behav. Sci.; EMBASE; Res. Alert [Full Cov.]; Soc. Sci. Cit. Index [Full Cov.].

GW/0720-0447
**FORUM KRITISCHE PSYCHOLOGIE.** (1977)-. Monographic series. German. ir. Price varies per volume. Argument Verlag GmbH, Rentzelstr 1, D 21046 Hamburg Germany. **Tel** 011 49 40 453680, 011 49 40 456018. **(Subscription address:** IA Inter ABO Betreuungs GmBh, Postfach 103245, D 20022 Hamburg Germany.**) LC** UNC. ***Continues*** *Kritische Psychologie.*

UK
**FURTHER ASPECTS OF PIAGET'S WORK.** ***Ceased.*** **Added/Corp** National Froebel Foundation. (19??)-(19??). English. Routledge, 11 New Fetter Lane, London EC4P 4EE England. **Tel** 071 583 9855, FAX 071 842 2298. **(Subscription address:** Kinokuniya Company Ltd., 38-1 Sakuragaoka 5, chome Setagaya-ku, Tokyo 156 Japan.**) LC** BF721; .F83. **DD** 155.4.

NE/0921-5360
**GEDRAG & GEZONDHEID.** [Gedrag gezond.]. **Added/Corp** Stichting Gawein (Nijmegen, Netherlands). **VFOAT** Gedrag en Gezondheid. Vol. 14, No. 1 (April 1986)-. Periodical. Dutch (summaries and/or abstracts in English). Six times a year. Fl130.66 institutions; Fl84.43 individuals. Uitgeverij Tidjdstroom BV, Postbus 19135, 3501 DC Utrecht Netherlands. **Tel** 011 33 70 3819900. **(Subscription address:** Infolio BV, Postbus 16500, 2500 DM Den Haag Netherlands.**) LC** BF8.D8; G42. **CODEN** GEGEE6. Documents available from The Genuine Article, BIOSIS Document Express. ***Continues*** *Gedrag, 0377-7308.*
**Ind/Abst** Biol. Abstr.; Curr. Contents Soc. Behav. Sci.; Psychol. Abstr. (1973-); PsycINFO (1990-); PsycLit; Res. Alert [Full Cov.].

NE/0921-5077
**GEDRAG EN ORGANISATIE.** [Gedrag organ.]. (1988)-. Periodical. Dutch. bm (6 issues). Fl97.00 (latest issue). Infolio BV, Postbus 16500, 2500 BM Den Haag Netherlands. **Tel** 011 31 70 3819900, FAX 011 31 70 3632338. **UDC** 316.6.

US/0195-5594
**GENESIS OF BEHAVIOR.** (1978)-. Monographic series. English. ir. Price varies per volume. Plenum Press, 233 Spring Street, New York NY 10013-1578. **Tel** (212)620-8000, (800)221-9369, FAX (212)463-0742, (212)807-1047, telex 23/421139. **LC** UNC. **NLM** W1 GE275.

GW/0740-9583
**GENETIC EPISTEMOLOGIST, THE. See** Biology-Genetics.

US/8756-7547
**GENETIC, SOCIAL, AND GENERAL PSYCHOLOGY MONOGRAPHS.** (GENETIC, SOCIAL, AND GENERAL PSYCHOLOGY MONOGRAPHS.). [Genet. soc. gen. psychol. monogr.]. Vol. 111, No. 1 (Feb. 1985)-. Academic Scholarly Publication. English. qt. $98.00. Heldref Publications, 1319 Eighteenth Street Northwest, Washington DC 20036-1802. **Tel** (202)296-6267, (800)365-9753, FAX (202)296-5149. **ED** John E Horrocks. **LC** LB1101; .G4. **DD** 150/.5. **NLM** W1; GE283. **CODEN** GSGMEQ. **Ad Acc. Circ:** 875. available on microfilm and microfiche from University Microfilms International (UMI). Documents available from The Genuine Article, BIOSIS Document Express. ***Continues*** *Genetic Psychology Monographs, 0016-6677.*
**Desc:** Publishes articles of monograph length that make an outstanding contribution to the field of psychology. Articles may deal with the biological as well as the behavioral and social aspects of psychology and may present a series of research studies, a new theory, or an in-depth criticism of an existing theory.
**Ind/Abst** Arts Humanit. Citation Index [Select. Cov.]; Biol. Abstr. (1985-); Child Dev. Abstr. Bibliogr.; Curr. Aware. Biol. Sci., CABS; Curr. Contents Soc. Behav. Sci.; Dev. Med. Child Neurol. (-1990); EMBASE; Except. Child Educ. Resour. (19??-19??); Health Plan. Adminis.; Index Med. (1985-); Multicult. Educ. Abstr.; Psychol. Abstr. (1926-); PsycINFO; PsycLit; PsycScan: Develop. Psych.; Res. Alert [Full Cov.]; Soc. Plann. Policy Dev. Abstr.; Soc. Sci. Cit. Index [Full Cov.]; Soc. Work Abstr. [Select. Cov.]; Sociol. Educ. Abstr.

US
**GENETIC STUDIES OF GENIUS.** (1925)-. English. Stanford University Press, Courtyard Santa Teresa Street, Stanford CA 94305. **Tel** (415)723-9434.

GW/0705-5870
**GERMAN JOURNAL OF PSYCHOLOGY, THE.** [Ger. j. psychol.]. Vol. 1 (Jan. 1977)-. English. Four times a year. DM122.00. Hogrefe Verlag fuer Psychologie, Rohnsweg 25, D 37085 Goettingen Germany. **Tel** 011 49 551 496090, FAX 011 49 551 4960988. **(Subscription address:** Hogrefe & Huber Publishers, Seattle Office, Box 2487, Kirkland WA 98083.**) ED** B. Dahme, D. Frey, W. Krause, G. Luer, E. Mittenecker, K. Pawlik, M. Perrez, H. Reinecker, F. Rosler, H. Sydow, W. Tack. **LC** BF1; .G47. **DD** 150/.5; 150/.8. **NLM** Z 7203 G373. Index available. **Bk Rev. Ad Acc. Circ:** 2,000.
**Desc:** Each issue contains a comprehensive look at a particular field of modern German psychology in the form of a review article or report.
**Ind/Abst** Psychol. Abstr. (1981-); PsycINFO; PsycLit.

US/0190-0412
**GESTALT JOURNAL, THE.** [Gestalt j.]. **Added/Corp** Center for Gestalt Development. Vol. 1 (Winter 1978)-. Periodical. English. sa. $30.00 (individual), $45.00 (institution) US; $35.00 (individual), $50.00 (institution) includes GST and provincial taxes, Canada; $40.00 (individual), $55.00 (institution) other. Center for Gestalt Development, PO Box 990, Highland NY 12528. **Tel** (914)691-7192, FAX (914)691-6530. **ED** Joe Wysung. **NLM** W1 GE826. **Bk Rev. Circ:** 2,600.
**Desc:** The only professional publication devoted to the exploration of the theory and practice of Gestalt therapy.
**Ind/Abst** Psychol. Abstr. (1978-); PsycINFO (1978-); PsycLit.

GW/0170-057X
**GESTALT THEORY.** (GESTALT THEORY : OFFICIAL JOURNAL OF THE SOCIETY FOR GESTALT THEORY AND ITS APPLICATIONS (GTA).). [Gestalt theory]. **Added/Corp** Society for Gestalt Theory and Its Applications. Vol. 1, No. 1 (Oct. 1979)-. Periodical. English (German). Four times a year. DM159.60 Germany; DM173.40 other. Westdeutscher Verlag GmbH, Postfach 5829, D 65048 Wiesbaden Germany. **Tel** 011 49 611 160220. **(Subscription address:** VVA Bertelsmann Dist GmbH, Postfach 7600, D 33310 Guetersloh Germany**) LC** BF203; .G46. **DD** 150.19/82/05. **NLM** W1 GE831. **[CCC].**
**Ind/Abst** Psychol. Abstr. (1979-); PsycINFO; PsycLit.

IT/0392-4483
**GIORNALE DI NEUROPSICHIATRIA DELL'ETA EVOLUTIVA : ORGANO UFFICIALE DELLA SOCIETA ITALIANA DI NEUROPSICHIATRIA INFANTILE. See** Medical Science and Technology-Neurology.

IT/0390-5349
**GIORNALE ITALIANO DI PSICOLOGIA.** [G. ital. psicol.]. **VFOAT** Italian Journal of Psychology. Vol. 1, No. 1 (April 1974)-. Periodical. Italian (English). Five times a year. L100000.00 Italy; L140000.00 (surface mail), L160000.00 (airmail) other. Societa Editrice il Mulino, Strada Maggiore 37, 40125 Bologna Italy. **Tel** 011 39 51 256011, FAX 011 39 51 256034. **LC** BF1; .A155. **DD** 150/.5. **NLM** W1 GI814G. ***Continued in part by*** *Italian Journal of Psychology.*
**Ind/Abst** Psychol. Abstr. (1974-); PsycINFO; PsycLit; Soc. Plann. Policy Dev. Abstr.

IT/0391-2515
**GIORNALE STORICO DI PSICOLOGIA DINAMICA.** [G. stor. psicol. din.]. V. 1- (Issue 1- ); Jan. 1977-. Periodical. Italian (summaries and/or abstracts in English). sa. L50000 Italy; $100.00 US. C C Postale No 19932003, Intestato a Rivista di Psicologia Analitica, Via Gallonio 8, 00161 Rome Italy. **Tel** 4270177. **ED** Aldo Carotenuto. **LC** BF84; .G56. Index available. cum. index. **Bk Rev. Ad Acc. Circ:** 1,000 (ctrl).
**Desc:** Publishes articles about the most important problems of dynamic psychology from an historical point of view.
**Ind/Abst** Psychol. Abstr. (1981-); PsycINFO (1990-); PsycLit.

●US
**GRADUATE STUDY IN PSYCHOLOGY.** **Added/Corp** American Psychological Association. (1992)-. English. **LC** BF77; .G73. ***Continues*** *Graduate Study in Psychology and Associated Fields.*

US/0362-4021
**GROUP (NEW YORK. 1977).** (GROUP.). [Group]. **Added/Corp** Eastern Group Psychotherapy Society. Vol. 1 Spring (1977)-. Periodical. English. qt. $70.00 (institution), $34.00 (individuals). Brunner Mazel, 19 Union Square West, New York NY 10003. **Tel** (212)924-3344, (800)825-3089. **ED** Dorothy Flapan and Peter Schlachet. **LC** RC488.A1; G7. **DD** 616.8/915. **NLM** W1 GR799. **CODEN** GROUDE. **Bk Rev. Ad Acc. Pr Rev. Circ:** 1,000 (ctrl). available on microfilm and microfiche from University Microfilms International (UMI). Documents available from The Genuine Article.
**Desc:** Group psychotherapy-its conceptualizations and clinical applications to diverse populations.
**Ind/Abst** EMBASE; Psychol. Abstr. (1982-); PsycINFO (1990-); PsycLit; Res. Alert [Full Cov.]; Soc. Sci. Cit. Index [Full Cov.].

UK/0046-6468
**GROUP PROCESS.** [Group process]. Periodical. English. sa. $18.00. Gordon & Breach Science Publishers, PO Box 90, Reading RG1 8JL England. **Tel** 011 44 734 560080, FAX 011 44 734 568211. **(Subscription address:** International Publishers Distributor at one of the following addresses: 820 Town Center Drive, Langhorne, PA 19047; or PO Box 90, Reading Berkshire RG1 8JL UK; or Kent Ridge PO Box 1180, Singapore 9111, Republic of Singapore**) LC** RC488.A1; G72. **DD** 616.8/915. **NLM** W1 GR6588. **CODEN** GPCSA. ***Continues*** *Journal of Group Psychoanalysis and Process.*

UK/0951-824X
**GROUPWORK LONDON. See** Sociology-Social Services and Welfare.

GW/0046-6514
**GRUPPENDYNAMIK.** [Gruppendynamik]. (1970)-. Periodical. German. qt (4 issues). DM67.00 Germany; DM72.60 other. Leske Verlag & Budrich GmbH, Postfach 300551, Gerhart Hauptmann Strasse 27, W-5090 Leverkusen 3 Opladen Germany. **Tel** 011 49 21712079. **CODEN** GRUPDT. **[CCC].** Documents available from The Genuine Article.
**Ind/Abst** Psychol. Abstr. (1970-); PsycINFO; PsycLit; Res. Alert [Full Cov.]; Soc. Sci. Cit. Index [Full Cov.].

CN/0831-5493
**GUIDANCE & COUNSELLING. See** Education.

CN/1187-502X
**GUIDE RESSOURCES (1991).** (GUIDE RESSOURCES.). [Guide ressour.]. Vol. 7, No 1 (Sept. 1991)-. Periodical. French. Ten times a year (published monthly except Feb. and Aug.). 27.60Can$ Canada; 39.95Can$ other. Guide Ressources, 7388 rue St Denis Bereau 305, Montreal Quebec H2J 2L1 Canada. **Tel** (514)847-0060, FAX (514)847-0062. **ED** Christian Lamontagne. **DD** 613. ***Continues*** *Guide Ressources Pour une Conscience Globale., 1184-1818.*

US/0017-5323
**GUIDEPOST (WASHINGTON, D.C.).** ***Title Change.*** (GUIDEPOST.). [Guidepost]. **Added/Corp** American Counseling Association. American Association for Counseling and Development. American Personnel and Guidance Association. Vol. 1 (1958)-(1993). Periodical. English. Fourteen times a year. American Counseling Association, 5999 Stevenson Avenue, Alexandria VA 22304. **Tel** (703)823-9800, (800)347-6647, FAX (703)823-0252. **ED** Jennifer L. Sacks. **[CCC]. Bk Rev. Ad Acc. Circ:** 57,000 (ctrl). ***Continued by*** *Counseling Today.*
**Desc:** Timely articles on national counseling and development issues, and legislative and governmental activities affecting counselors, as well as information on association activities.

US
**HANDBOOK OF CERTIFICATION/LICENSURE REQUIREMENTS FOR SCHOOL PSYCHOLOGISTS, THE. Added/Corp** National Association of School Psychologists. Madison College, Harrisonburg, Va. 1st Ed. (1976)-. English. ir. $30.00. National Association of School Psychologists / Connecticut, 10 Overland Drive, Stratford CT 06497. **Tel** (203)377-4249. **ED** Timothy J. Sewall and Douglas T. Brown. **Bk Rev. Ad Acc. Circ:** 9,000.

JA/0017-7547
**HANZAI SHINRIGAKU KENKYU. VFOAT** Japanese Journal of Criminal Psychology. (1963)-. Periodical. Multiple languages. ir. Japanese Association of Criminal Psychology, 11-7, 2-Chome Hikawadai, Nerima-ku Tokyo 179 Japan. **DD** 157.
**Ind/Abst** PsycINFO (1969-); PsycLit.

US/1057-5022
**HARVARD MENTAL HEALTH LETTER, THE. See** Medical Science and Technology-Psychiatry.

IT
**HD : GIORNALE DI PSICOLOGIA E PEDAGOGIA DELL HANDICAPPATO E DELLE DISABILITA DI APPRENDIMENTO.** (19??)-. Italian. bm (6 issues). L65000 (institutions), L50000 (individuals) Italy; L75000 other. Editrice Tecnoscuola Sas, Via Buonarroti 10, 34170 Gorizia Italy. **Tel** 011 39 481 536915.

US/0278-6133
**HEALTH PSYCHOLOGY.** (HEALTH PSYCHOLOGY : THE OFFICIAL JOURNAL OF THE DIVISION OF HEALTH PSYCHOLOGY, AMERICAN PSYCHOLOGICAL ASSOCIATION.). [Health psychol.]. **Added/Corp** American Psychological Association. Division of Health Psychology. Vol. 1, No. 1 (Winter 1982)-. Periodical. English. bm. $180.00 (nonmember, institution) US. American Psychological Association, 750 First Street Northeast, Washington DC 20002. **Tel** (800)374-2721, (202)336-5600, (subscriptions - (202)336-5600. **ED** Karen A. Matthews, PhD. **LC** R726.5; .H434. **DD** 610/.19. **NLM** W1 HE488. **[CCC].** Index available (free). **Ad Acc. Pr Rev.** available on microfilm and microfiche from University Microfilms International (UMI). Documents available from The Genuine Article.
**Desc:** Promotes the understanding of scientific relationships between behavioral principles on the one hand and physical health and illness on the other. Readership has a broad range of backgrounds, interests, and specializations, often interdisciplinary in nature.
**Ind/Abst** Annals Behav. Med.; Cumul. Index Nurs. Allied Health Lit.; Curr. Contents Soc. Behav. Sci.; Health Plan. Adminis.; Index Med. (Vol. 3, No. 1, 1984-); Nutr. Res. Newsl.; Psychol. Abstr. (1982-); PsycINFO; PsycLit; Res. Alert [Full Cov.]; Soc. Sci. Cit. Index [Full Cov.].

CN/1180-3037
**HEALTH REPORTS. SUPPLEMENT. MENTAL HEALTH STATISTICS.** (HEALTH REPORTS. NO. 3, SUPPLEMENT. MENTAL HEALTH STATISTICS / STATISTICS CANADA, CANADIAN CENTRE FOR HEALTH INFORMATION). [Health rep., Suppl., Ment. health stat.]. **Added/Corp** Canadian Centre for Health Information. **VFOAT** Mental Health Statistics; Statistique de l'Hygiene Mentale; Rapports sur la Sante. No 3, La Statistique de l'Hygiene Mentale. (1985/1986)-. English (French). an. 15.00Can$ Canada; $18.00 US; $21.00. Statistics Canada, Publications Sales & Services, Main Building Room 1710, Ottawa Ontario K1A 0T6 Canada. **Tel** (613)951-5078, (800)267-6677, FAX (613)951-1584, telex 053-3585. **LC** RA790.7.C2; H43. **DD** 362.2/0971/021. ***Continues*** *Mental Health Statistics (Statistics Canada), 0835-6092.*

CN/0825-5318
**HEARTWOOD.** ***Ceased.*** [Heartwood]. Vol. 1, No. 1 (Autumn 1982)-Ceased ?. Periodical. English. Box 90, Mason's Landing, Cortes Island British Columbia N0P 1K0 Canada. **DD** 155.2/5/05.

US/0891-6144
**HIMALAYAN INSTITUTE QUARTERLY GUIDE TO PROGRAMS AND OTHER OFFERINGS. See** Philosophy.

JA/0386-3158
**HIROSHIMA FORUM FOR PSYCHOLOGY.** [Hiroshima forum psychol.]. **Added/Corp** Hiroshima Daigaku. Shinrigaku Kenkyushitsu. Vol. 1 (1974)-. Periodical. English. Hiroshima University / Psychology, Department of Psychology, Faculty of Education, Kagamiyama, Higashi Hiroshima 724 Japan. **LC** BF1; .H57. **DD** 150/.5.
**Ind/Abst** Psychol. Abstr. (1975-); PsycLit.

US/0734-9831
**HISTORY OF PSYCHOANALYSIS MONOGRAPH.** ***Ceased.*** **See** Medical Science and Technology-Psychiatry.

US/0097-6091
**HISTORY OF PSYCHOLOGY IN AUTOBIOGRAPHY.** (A HISTORY OF PSYCHOLOGY IN AUTOBIOGRAPHY.). (1930)-. English. Prentice-Hall Law and Business, 270 Sylvan Avenue, Englewood Cliffs NJ 07632. **Tel** (800)223-0231, (201)894-8538, FAX (201)894-8666. **LC** BF105; .H5. **DD** 150/.92/2; B. **NLM** W1 HI86.

US/0146-0331
**HISTORY OF PSYCHOLOGY SERIES.** Monographic series. English. ir. Price varies per volume. Scholars Facsimiles and Reprints Inc, PO Box 344, Delmar NY 12054-0344. **Tel** (513)439-5978.

HK/0379-4490
**HONG KONG PSYCHOLOGICAL SOCIETY BULLETIN.** [Hong Kong Psychol. Soc. bull.]. (1978)-. Periodical. English. sa. Hong Kong Psychological Society, University of Hong Kong, Department of Psychology, Hong Kong, Hong Kong. **UDC** 159.9.
**Ind/Abst** Psychol. Abstr.; PsycLit.

CC/1000-6648
**HSIN LI KO HSUEH. Added/Corp** Chung-Kuo Hsin li Hsueh Hui. **VFOAT** Psychological Science. (1991)-. Periodical. Chinese (summaries and/or abstracts in English). bm. Hsin Li Ko Hsueh Pien Wei Hui, Chung-Kuo Kuo Chi Tu Shu Mao I Tsung Kung Ssu, PO Box 2820, Pei-Ching, People's Republic of China. **LC** BF8.C5; H76. **DD** 150/.5. ***Continues*** *Hsin li Ko Hsueh Tung Hsun.*
**Ind/Abst** Psychol. Abstr. (1984-); PsycINFO.

US/0148-8686
**HUMAN BEHAVIOR AND ENVIRONMENT. See** Sociology.

US/0737-0024
**HUMAN-COMPUTER INTERACTION. See** Computers.

SZ/0018-716X
**HUMAN DEVELOPMENT.** [Hum. dev.]. Vol. 8, No. 1 (1965)-. Academic Scholarly Publication. English (French and German; summaries and/or abstracts in French, German and English). bm. $200.00. S. Karger AG, Allschwilerstrasse 10, PO Box - Postfach - Case

Postale, CH-4009 Basel Switzerland. **Tel** 011 41 61 306-1111, FAX 011 41 61 306-1234, telex CH 962 652. **ED** D. Kuhn, J. Brandtstadter, G. Hatano. **NLM** W1 HU446C. **CODEN** HUDEA8. **[CCC]**. Index available. **Ad Acc. Pr Rev.** available on microfilm from University Microfilms International (UMI). Documents available from The Genuine Article, BIOSIS Document Express, UMI Article Clearinghouse. ***Continues*** *Vita Humana, 0375-4774.*
**Desc:** Publishes original articles on all aspects of development throughout the human life span, from infancy to aging. Both social and cognitive development are covered. Included are theoretical contributions, commentaries and integrative reviews of literature in the behavioral and social sciences. Book reviews and special issues covering particular topics of interest are published regularly. Contributions from the fields of history, philosophy, biology, anthropology, sociology, and education are included to provide a truly encompassing picture of human development.
**Ind/Abst** Biol. Abstr.; Br. Educ. Index; Curr. Contents Soc. Behav. Sci.; Curr. Index J. Educ.; Dev. Med. Child Neurol.; Educ. Index; EMBASE; Expand. Acad. Index (1992-); Health Plan. Adminis.; Index Med.; Middle East Abstr. Index; MLA Int. Bibl. Books Artic. Mod. Lang. Lit.; Newsp. Period. Abstr. (1992-); Life Sci. Collect.; Psychol. Abstr. (1965-); PsycScan: Develop. Psych.; Ref. Upd. Deluxe Ed.; Res. Alert [Full Cov.]; Soc. Plann. Policy Dev. Abstr.; Soc. Sci. Cit. Index [Full Cov.]; Sociol. Abstr. (?-?); Women Stud. Abstr.

US/0278-4661
**HUMAN DEVELOPMENT (GUILFORD, CT.).** (HUMAN DEVELOPMENT ...). [Hum. dev.]. **VFOAT** Annual Editions Human Development. 80/81-. English. an. $8.95. Dushkin Publishing Group Inc., Sluice Dock, Guilford CT 06437. **Tel** (203)453-4351, (800)243-6532, FAX (203)453-6000. **ED** Hiram Fitzgerald and Michael Walraven. **LC** HQ768; .A55. **DD** 305.2. ***Continues*** *Annual Editions. Readings in Human Development, 0090-5348.*
**Desc:** Updated collection of public press articles covering current issues in human development. Includes topic guide and complete index.

US/0197-3096
**HUMAN DEVELOPMENT (NEW YORK).** (HUMAN DEVELOPMENT / THE JESUIT EDUCATIONAL CENTER FOR HUMAN DEVELOPMENT.). [Hum. dev.]. **Added/Corp** Jesuit Educational Center for Human Development (New York, N.Y.). Vol. 1, No. 1 (Spring 1980)-. Periodical. English. qt. $20.00 US; $27.00 other. Human Development / Connecticut, 400 Washington Street, Hartford CT 06106. **Tel** (203)241-8041, FAX (203)241-8042. **ED** James J Gill. **LC** BV4012; .H82. **DD** 253.5. **Bk Rev. Circ:** 10,000 (ctrl).
**Ind/Abst** Acad. Search (July 1993-); INFO-SOUTH Abstr.; Mag. Search; PsycINFO; PsycLit; Abr. Cathol. Period. Lit. Index; Cathol. Period. Lit. Index.

US/0739-2036
**HUMAN ETHOLOGY NEWSLETTER.** **See** Anthropology.

US/0895-9285
**HUMAN PERFORMANCE.** [Hum. perform.]. Vol. 1, No. 1 (1988)-. Periodical. English. qt. $210.00 US & Canada; $235.00 other. Lawrence Erlbaum Associates, 365 Broadway, Suite 102, Hillsdale NJ 07642. **Tel** (201)666-4110, (800)926-6579, FAX (201)666-2394. **DD** 152. **NLM** W1; HU46M.
**Ind/Abst** Ergon. Abstr.; Psychol. Abstr. (1988-); PsycINFO (1990-); PsycLit.

UK/0461-5905
**HUMAN PERFORMANCE REPORTS (1960).** (HUMAN PERFORMANCE REPORTS / MEDICAL RESEARCH COUNCIL, APPLIED PSYCHOLOGY UNIT.). [Human perform. rep.]. **Added/Corp** Medical Research Council (Great Britain). Applied Psychology Unit. Medical Research Council (Great Britain). Perceptual and Cognitive Performance Unit. (1960)-. Periodical. English. Medical Research Council, 20 Park Cresent, London W1N 4AL England. **Tel** 011 44 71 636 5422. ***Continues*** *Human Performance Progress Reports.*
**Ind/Abst** HILITES.

UK/0885-6222
**HUMAN PSYCHOPHARMACOLOGY.** **See** Pharmacy and Pharmacology.

US/0885-1174
**HUMAN STRESS.** [Hum. stress]. Vol. 1 (1986)-. English. an. $37.50. AMS Press Inc., 56 East 13th Street, New York NY 10003. **Tel** (212)777-4700, FAX (212)995-5413, telex 710 581 2302. **ED** James H Humphrey. **LC** BF575.S75; H84. **DD** 155.9/05. **NLM** W1; HU464. Index available. **Bk Rev.**
**Desc:** Behavioral, environmental and physiological original studies examining causes of human stress and techniques of stress reduction.

US/0887-3267
**HUMANISTIC PSYCHOLOGIST, THE.** [Humanist. psychol.]. **Added/Corp** American Psychological Association. Division of Humanistic Psychology. (19??)-. Periodical. English. tq (Mar., July, Nov.). $20.00 (individuals); $40.00 (institutions). The Humanistic Psychologist, West Georgia College, Psychology Department, Carrollton GA 30118. **Tel** (404)836-6510, FAX (404)836-6791. **ED** Christopher M. Aanstoos. **LC** WMLC 93/1089. **DD** 150. Index available. cum. index. **Bk Rev**, (Qty: 12-18). **Ad Acc. Pr Rev. Circ:** 1,200 (ctrl). ***Continues*** *Newsletter (American Psychological Association. Division of Humanistic Psychology).*
**Desc:** Articles, interviews, comments, reports and other reviews that contribute to advancing the field of humanistic psychology, broadly defined, especially with respect to methods and other findings.
**Ind/Abst** Psychol. Abstr. (1986-); PsycINFO; PsycLit.

GW/0933-1719
**HUMOR (BERLIN, GERMANY).** (HUMOR.). Vol. 1, No. 1 (1988)-. Periodical. English. qt. $157.60. Walter de Gruyter Inc., PO Box 303421, D 10728 Berlin Germany. **Tel** 011 49 30 260050, FAX 011 49 30 26005251. **ED** Victor Raskin. **LC** PN6149.P5; H847. **DD** 152.4. **CODEN** HUMRES. **[CCC]**. Index available. **Pr Rev. Circ:** 1,000.
**Desc:** An international interdisciplinary forum for the publication of research papers on humor as an important and universal human faculty.
**Ind/Abst** Arts Humanit. Citation Index [Full Cov.]; Int. Bibliogr. Sociol.; Soc. Plann. Policy Dev. Abstr.; Soc. Sci. Cit. Index [Select. Cov.].

US/8756-2189
**IACD QUARTERLY.** [IACD q.]. **VAT** Illinois Association for Counseling and Development Quarterly. Periodical. English. qt. $15.00 libraries, $30.00 private (includes membership). IACD, Box 220, Charleston IL 61920. **ED** John DeVolder. **DD** 158. **Bk Rev. Ad Acc.** ***Continues*** *Illinois Guidance and Personnel Association Quarterly.*
**Desc:** Official publication of the Illinois Association for Counseling and Development. Serves common interests of counselors and personnel workers in the state.

US/0019-2198
**ILLINOIS PSYCHOLOGIST : NEWSLETTER OF THE ILLINOIS PSYCHOLOGICAL ASSOCIATION.** [Ill. psychol.]. **Added/Corp** Illinois Psychological Association. (19??)-. Newsletter. English. Four times a year (Jan., Apr., July, Oct.). $20.00. Illinois Psychological Association, 203 North Wabash Avenue, Suite 1200, Chicago IL 60601. **Tel** (312)372-7610, FAX (312)372-6787. **ED** Bruce E. Bennett, Ph.D. **Bk Rev. Ad Acc. Circ:** 1,500. ***Continues*** *Illinois Psychological Association Newsletter.*
**Desc:** To design and coordinate the strategy for assuring psychology's has the appropriate role in national health care reform. activities to promote the professional practice of psychology.

US/0276-2366
**IMAGINATION, COGNITION AND PERSONALITY.** [Imagin. cogn. pers.]. **VFOAT** Journal of Imagination, Cognition, and Personality. Vol. 1, No. 1 (1981-82)-. Academic Scholarly Publication. English. qt. $118.00. Baywood Publishing Company Inc., 26 Austin Avenue, PO Box 337, Amityville NY 11701. **Tel** (516)691-1270, (800)638-7819, FAX (516)691-1770. **ED** Jerome L Singer and Kenneth S Pope. **LC** BF311; .I44. **DD** 153/.05. **NLM** W1 IM457T. cum. index. **Bk Rev.** ***Continues*** *Journal of Altered States of Consciousness.*
**Desc:** Presents the current understanding of the nature, functions and resources of the stream of consciousness, along with practice, scientifically based applications and interventions.
**Ind/Abst** EMBASE; Except. Hum. Exp.; Psychol. Abstr. (1981-); PsycINFO; PsycLit.

US/0279-0408
**IMPRINT (HILLSDALE, N.J.).** (IMPRINT.). Periodical. English. mo. Northern New Jersey Mensa, c/o Janet Cuccineli, 17 Wierimus Lane, Hillsdale NJ 07642.

US
**INDEX OF PSYCHOANALYTIC WRITINGS (WITH PREFACE BY ERNEST JONES), THE.** (1956)-. Periodical. English. ir. International Universities Press Inc., 59 Boston Post Road, PO Box 1524, Madison CT 06443-1524. **Tel** (203)245-4000, FAX (203)245-0775, telex 282986 IUP BK.

II/0019-5073
**INDIAN JOURNAL OF APPLIED PSYCHOLOGY.** [Indian j. appl. psychol.]. **Added/Corp** Madras Psychology Society. Vol. 1, No. 1 (Jan. 1964)-. Periodical. English. sa. $50.00. The Madras Psychology Society, University of Madras, Department of Psychology, Madras 600 005 India. **Tel** 011 91 44 568778 Ext. 306. **(Subscription address:** Prints India, 11 Darya Ganj, New Delhi, 110002 India, (Phone: 011 91 11 3268645)) **ED** P Ananthakrishnan. **LC** BF636.A1; I47. **DD** 158/.05. **NLM** W1 IN206PH. **CODEN** IJAPBI. **Pr Rev. Circ:** 100. available on microfilm from University Microfilms International (UMI). Documents available from BIOSIS Document Express.
**Desc:** Papers refereed and published or sent back to the author for revision as suggested by the referees and the revised articles published.
**Ind/Abst** Biol. Abstr.; Psychol. Abstr. (1964-); PsycINFO; PsycLit; Spec. Educ. Needs Abstr.

II/0970-0897
**INDIAN JOURNAL OF BEHAVIOUR.** [Indian j. behav.]. (1976)-. Periodical. English. qt. $200.00. Indian Journal of Behaviour, Dr T R Rao, 780 First Cross Road, Mahalakphmi Layout, Bangalore 560086 India. **(Subscription address:** Prints India, 11 Darya Ganj, New Delhi, 110002 India, (Phone: 011 91 11 3268645)) **ED** T R Rao. **LC** BF1; .I37. **DD** 150/.5. **NLM** W1; IN206PK. cum. index. **Bk Rev. Ad Acc. Circ:** 500 (ctrl). available on microfilm.
**Desc:** A journal of interdisciplinary character.
**Ind/Abst** Psychol. Abstr. (1976-); PsycINFO; PsycLit.

II/0303-2582
**INDIAN JOURNAL OF CLINICAL PSYCHOLOGY.** [Indian j. clin. psychol.]. **Added/Corp** Indian Association of Clinical Psychologists. Vol. 1 (Mar. 1974)-. Periodical. English. sa. $50.00. Impex India, 2118 Ansari Road, New Delhi 110002 India. **Tel** 278034. **(Subscription address:** Prints India, 11 Darya Ganj, New Delhi, 110002 India, (Phone: 011 91 11 3268645)) **ED** A C Moudgil. **LC** RC467; .I53. **DD** 616.8/9/005. **NLM** W1 IN207B. **Bk Rev. Ad Acc. Circ:** 700.
**Desc:** Devoted to research in areas of clinical psychology, mental health, psychiatry, and other allied and behavioural sciences.
**Ind/Abst** Psychol. Abstr. (1974-); PsycINFO; PsycLit; Soc. Plann. Policy Dev. Abstr.; Sociol. Abstr. (?-?).

II
**INDIAN JOURNAL OF CURRENT PSYCHOLOGICAL RESEARCH.** Vol. 1, No. 1 (1986)-. Periodical. English. sa. $40.00. S. N. Rai, Meerut Univeristy, Meerut, U.P. 250005 India. **(Subscription address:** Prints India, 11 Darya Ganj, New Delhi, 110002 India, (Phone: 011 91 11 3268645))
**Ind/Abst** Psychol. Abstr. (1986-); PsycLit.

II/0019-5553
**INDIAN JOURNAL OF PSYCHOLOGY.** **Added/Corp** Indian Psychological Association. Vol. 1 (Jan. 1926)-. Periodical. English. qt. $35.00. Indian Psychological Association, 27 A Masjid Moth Vill, New Delhi 110049 India. **(Subscription address:** Prints India, 11 Darya Ganj, New Delhi, 110002 India, (Phone: 011 91 11 3268645)) **LC** BF1; .I39. **NLM** W1 IN227M. available on microfilm and microfiche from University Microfilms International (UMI).

II
**INDIAN JOURNAL OF PSYCHOPHYSIOLOGY.** Calcutta Psychophysiological Research Society, 83/B Deb Lane, Calcutta I-700014 India.
**Ind/Abst** Psychol. Abstr. (1983-); PsycLit.

II
**INDIAN PSYCHOLOGICAL ABSTRACTS.** **Added/Corp** Indian Council of Social Science Research. Indian Psychological Association. Vol. 1 (Jan./Feb. 1972)-. English. qt. $10.00. Indian Council of Social Science Research, 35 Ferozshah Road, New Delhi 110 001 India. **Tel** 011 91 11 38959, 011 91 11 381571. **(Subscription address:** Prints India, 11 Darya Ganj, New Delhi, 110002 India, (Phone: 011 91 11 3268645)) **ED** Udai Pareek. **LC** BF1; .I392. **DD** 150/.954. **Bk Rev. Ad Acc. Circ:** 500.
**Desc:** Publishes brief abstracts of research done on Indian themes.

US/0971-524X
**INDIAN PSYCHOLOGICAL ABSTRACTS AND REVIEWS.** English. sa (Apr. and Oct.). $95.00. SAGE Periodical Press, 2455 Teller Road, Thousand Oaks CA 91320. **Tel** (805)499-0721, FAX (805)499-0871, telex 100799.

II/0019-6215
**INDIAN PSYCHOLOGICAL REVIEW.** [Indian psychol. rev.]. **Added/Corp** Indian Psychological Society. Vol. 1 (July 1964)-. Periodical. English. mo. $431.00. Indian Psychological Review, Tiwari Kothi Belanganj, Agra 282004 India. **(Subscription address:** Prints India, 11 Darya Ganj, New Delhi 110002 India.) **ED** S. Jalota and M. C. Joshi. **LC** BF1; .I395. **NLM** W1 IN27R. **Bk Rev. Ad Acc. Circ:** 2,000. available on microfilm.
**Desc:** The first regular journal of India covering all the fields of psychology.
**Ind/Abst** Psychol. Abstr. (1978-); PsycINFO (1978-); PsycLit.

II/0970-2520
**INDIAN PSYCHOLOGIST.** [Indian psychol.]. **Added/Corp** Utkal University. Centre of Advanced Study in Psychology. Vol. 1, No. 1 (Apr. 1982)-. Periodical. English. sa. $40.00. Centre of Advanced Study in Psychology, Utkal University, Van Vihar, Bhubaneswar 751004 Orissa India. **Tel** 53639. **(Subscription address:** Prints India, 11 Darya Ganj, New Delhi 110002 India.) **ED** S Sahu. **LC** BF1; .I396. **DD** 150/.5. Index available. **Bk Rev. Circ:** 700.
**Desc:** The journal publishes empirical and theoretical

research articles of high standard. American Psychological Association's style is followed strictly.
**Ind/Abst** Psychol. Abstr. (1982-); PsycINFO; PsycLit.

SP/0213-019X
**INDICE ESPANOL DE CIENCIAS SOCIALES. SERIE A, PSICOLOGIA Y CIENCIAS DE LA EDUCACION.** **See** Social Sciences.

US/0277-7010
**INDIVIDUAL PSYCHOLOGY.** [Individ. psychol.]. **Added/Corp** North American Society of Adlerian Psychology. Vol. 38, No. 1 (March 1982)-. Periodical. English. qt. $59.00 (institutions), $30.00 (individuals) US; add $6.00 postage other. University of Texas Press, PO Box 7819, Austin TX 78713. **Tel** (512)471-4531, FAX (512)320-0668, telex 776453 UTEXPRES AUS. **ED** Guy J. Manaster. **LC** BF1; .I415. **DD** 150/19/54/05. **NLM** W1 IN352W. **[CCC].** Index available. **Bk Rev. Ad Acc. Circ:** 700 (ctrl). available on microfilm and microfiche from University Microfilms International (UMI). Documents available from The Genuine Article. ***Formed by the union of*** *Journal of Individual Psychology, 0022-1805* ***and*** *The Individual Psychologist, 0019-7149.*
**Desc:** The only journal exclusively devoted to all aspects of the social, psychological and personality theory founded by Alfred Adler. The journal of the North American Society of Adlerian Psychology, Inc.
**Ind/Abst** Abstr. Anthropol.; Abstr. Res. Pastor. Care Couns. (19??-); Acad. Search (July 1993-); Cumul. Index Nurs. Allied Health Lit.; Curr. Contents Soc. Behav. Sci.; INFO-SOUTH Abstr.; Mag. Search; Middle East Abstr. Index; Psychol. Abstr. (1982-); PsycINFO; PsycLit; Res. Alert [Full Cov.]; Soc. Plann. Policy Dev. Abstr.; Soc. Sci. Cit. Index [Full Cov.]; Soc. Work Abstr. [Select. Cov.]; Sociol. Abstr.

US/0888-4595
**INDIVIDUAL PSYCHOLOGY REPORTER.** (INDIVIDUAL PSYCHOLOGY REPORTER : A PUBLICATION OF THE AMERICAS INSTITUTE OF ADLERIAN STUDIES, LTD.). [Individ. psychol. report.]. **Added/Corp** Americas Institute of Adlerian Studies (Chicago, Ill.). **VFOAT** IP Reporter. (198?)-. Periodical. English. Four times a year. $15.00 US; $17.00 others. Adlerian Psycology Association Ltd., 600 North McClurg, Suite 2502 A, Chicago IL 60611-3027. **Tel** (321)337-5066. **ED** Jane Griffith. **DD** 150. Index available. cum. index. **Bk Rev. Pr Rev. Circ:** 1,000.
**Desc:** Publishes essays, case reports, book reviews, letters and interviews relating to the theory and applications of Alfred Adler's individual psychology for an audience of clinicians, educators and organizational managers.

US/0739-1110
**INDUSTRIAL ORGANIZATIONAL PSYCHOLOGIST, THE.** [Ind. organ. psychol.]. **Added/Corp** American Psychological Association. Division of Industrial-Organizational Psychology. Society for Industrial and Organizational Psychology (U.S.). **VFOAT** T.I.P.; Division Fourteen A.P.A. Newsletter; TIP; Division 14 APA Newsletter. (Dec. 1972)-. Periodical. English. qt. $30.00 (institutions), $20.00 (individuals). Industrial Organizational Psychologist, 129 Psych Research Building/ MSU, East Lansing MI 48824. **Tel** (517)353-8855. **ED** Kurt Kraiger PhD (editor's address: Department of Psychology, Box 173, University of Colorado at Denver, PO Box 173364, Denver CO 80217-3364; editor's phone; (303)556-2965). **LC** HF5548.7; .I53. **DD** 158.7/05. **Ad Acc, Adv Mgr:** Jennifer Rinas, **Tel** (708)640-0068. **Circ:** 5,000 (ctrl). ***Continues*** *Industrial Psychologist.*
**Desc:** Provides up-to-date information on human resources issues in industrial-organizational psychology-selection, productivity, careers, graduate programs, international issues.

SA/0258-5200
**INDUSTRIAL PSYCHOLOGY. Added/Corp** Randse Afrikaanse Universiteit. Departement Bedryfsielkunde. **VFOAT** Bedryfsielkunde; Tydskrif Vir Bedryfsielkunde; Journal of Industrial Psychology. (198?)-. Periodical. Afrikaans (English). tq (3 issues). R30.00 South Africa; $60.00 other. Department of Industrial Psychology, Rand Afrikaanse University, PO Box 524, Auckland Park 2006 South Africa. **Tel** 011 27 11 489-2033, 011 27 11 489-2858, FAX 011 27 11 489-2710. **ED** Prof. I. van W. Raubenheimer. **LC** HF5548.8; .P417. **DD** 158.7/05. **Bk Rev**, (Qty: 3). **Ad Acc, Adv Mgr:** F. Crous. ctrl circ. ***Continues*** *Perspektiewe in die Bedryfsielkunde.*
**Desc:** Serves as independent publication for scientific contributions to the field of industrial psychology.

SP/0210-3702
**INFANCIA Y APRENDIZAJE.** [Infanc. aprendiz.]. **Added/Corp** Equipo Aprendizaje, Madrid. (1977)-. Periodical. Spanish. qt. 6000.00ptas (institutions), 9000.00ptas (individuals) Latin America; 13200.00ptas (institutions), 7200.00ptas (individuals) Spain; 14700.00ptas (institutions), 8700.00ptas (individuals) other. Aprendizaje SA, Carretera de Canillas 138 16 C, 28033 Madrid Spain. **Tel** 011 34 1 3883874, 011 34 1 2009338, FAX 011 34 1 3003527. **LC** LB1051; .I466. Index available. cum. index. **Bk Rev. Ad Acc. Pr Rev. Circ:** 3,000.
**Ind/Abst** Psychol. Abstr. (1982-); PsycINFO (1982-); PsycLit.

US/0163-6383
**INFANT BEHAVIOR & DEVELOPMENT.** [Infant behav. dev.]. **VAT** Infant Behavior and Development. Vol. 1 (Jan. 1978)-. Academic Scholarly Publication. English. qt. $135.00 institution. Ablex Publishing Corporation, 355 Chestnut Street, Norwood NJ 07648. **Tel** (201)767-8450, (201)767-8455 (Customer Service), FAX (201)767-6717. **ED** Carolyn Rovee-Collier. **LC** BF719; .I53. **DD** 155.4/22/05. **NLM** W1 IN3994. **CODEN** IBDEDP. **[CCC].** Index available. **Bk Rev. Ad Acc. Pr Rev. Circ:** 800. Documents available from The Genuine Article, BIOSIS Document Express.
**Desc:** First journal devoted exclusively to infancy, providing original empirical and theoretical studies.
**Ind/Abst** AGRICOLA; Arts Humanit. Citation Index [Select. Cov.]; Biol. Abstr.; Curr. Contents Soc. Behav. Sci.; Dev. Med. Child Neurol.; EMBASE; MLA Int. Bibl. Books Artic. Mod. Lang. Lit.; Psychol. Abstr. (1979-); PsycINFO; PsycLit; PsycScan: Develop. Psych.; Res. Alert [Full Cov.]; Soc. Plann. Policy Dev. Abstr.; Soc. Sci. Cit. Index [Full Cov.]; Sociol. Abstr.; Spec. Educ. Needs Abstr.

US/0163-9641
**INFANT MENTAL HEALTH JOURNAL.** [Infant ment. health j.]. **Added/Corp** International Association for Infant Mental Health. Michigan Association for Infant Mental Health. World Association for Infant Psychiatry and Allied Disciplines. Vol. 1 (Spring 1980)-. Periodical. English. Four times a year. $109.00 US; $122.50 other. Clinical Psychology Publishing Company, 4 Conant Square, Brandon VT 05733. **Tel** (802)247-6871, (800)433-8234. **ED** Hiram Fitzgerald. **LC** RJ502.5; .I5. **DD** 618.92/89/005. **NLM** W1 IN3996. **CODEN** IMHJDZ. Index available (bound in last volume of each issue). **Bk Rev. Ad Acc. Pr Rev. Circ:** 650. available on microfilm and microfiche from University Microfilms International (UMI). Documents available from The Genuine Article, BIOSIS Document Express.
**Desc:** Research on infant mental health.
**Ind/Abst** Biol. Abstr. (1987-); Curr. Contents Soc. Behav. Sci.; Psychol. Abstr. (1980-); PsycINFO; PsycLit; Res. Alert [Full Cov.]; Soc. Sci. Cit. Index [Full Cov.].

IT/0390-2420
**INFANZIA.** [Infanzia]. (1973)-. Periodical. Italian. Twelve times a year. L50000 Italy; L60000 other. La Nuova Italia Editrice Spa, Via Ernesto Codignola, 50018 Scandicci Florence Italy. **Tel** 011 39 55 75901, FAX 011 39 55 7590208. **UDC** 372.

US/0737-125X
**INNOVATIONS IN CLINICAL PRACTICE : A SOURCE BOOK.** [Innov. clin. pract.]. (1982)-. English. an (October). $54.20 hardbound; $59.20 looseleaf. Professional Resource Exchange Inc, PO Box 15560, Sarasota FL 34277-1560. **Tel** (813)366-7913, FAX (813)366-7971. **ED** Leon VandeCreek. **LC** RC467; .I55. **NLM** W1 IN455C. Index available (Bound in next issue). cum. index. **Circ:** 2,000.
**Desc:** List of books and articles that are specialize in the publication and distribution of highly applied books and other resources for practicing mental health professionals.

US/1061-7132
**INSIDER'S GUIDE TO GRADUATE PROGRAMS IN CLINICAL PSYCHOLOGY.** [Insid. guide grad. prog. clin. psychol.]. (1991)-. English. $17.95 (single issue). Guilford Press, A Division of Guildord Publications, Inc., 72 Spring Street, New York NY 10012. **DD** 616.

US/0737-7215
**INSIGHT & HINDSIGHT. Added/Corp** Governors State University. Division of Psychology and Counseling. **VFOAT** Insight and Hindsight. Vol. 1, No. 1 (Spring 1982)-. Periodical. English. $6.00. Governors State University, Division of Psychology and Counseling, Park Forest South IL. **LC** BF1; .I43. **DD** 150/.5.

US/0093-2213
**INTEGRATIVE PHYSIOLOGICAL AND BEHAVIORAL SCIENCE.** [Integr. physiol. behav. sci.]. **Added/Corp** Pavlovian Society of America. Vol. 26, No. 1 (Jan./March 1991)-. Academic Scholarly Publication. English. Twice a year. Fl116.00 (individual), Fl199.00 (institution). Transaction Publishers / Rutgers State University, New Brunswick NJ 08903. **Tel** (908)932-2280 Ext. 105, FAX (908)932-3138. **ED** Stewart G Wolf, Jr. **DD** 150. **NLM** W1; IN645T. **[CCC]. Circ:** 550. Documents available from The Genuine Article, BIOSIS Document Express, CASDDS. ***Continues*** *Pavlovian Journal of Biological Science, 0093-2213.*
**Desc:** Contains articles pertaining to empirical, theoretical, review, apparatus, and historical topics. The journal is dedicated to the advancement of biological science, including the behavioral and physiological sciences of physiology, physiological psychology, psychophysiology, psychopharmacology, ethology, behavioral medicine, biological psychiatry and medicine. The official journal of The Pavlovian Society.
**Ind/Abst** Biol. Abstr.; Chem. Abstr.; EMBASE (1991-); Energy Res. Abstr.; Health Plan. Adminis.; Index Med.; Life Sci. Collect.; Psychol. Abstr. (1966-); PsycINFO; PsycLit; Res. Alert [Full Cov.]; Soc. Sci. Cit. Index [Select. Cov.].

US/0160-2896
**INTELLIGENCE (NORWOOD).** (INTELLIGENCE.). [Intelligence]. Vol. 1 (Jan. 1977)-. Periodical. English. qt. $140.00 institution. Ablex Publishing Corporation, 355 Chestnut Street, Norwood NJ 07648. **Tel** (201)767-8450, (201)767-8455 (Customer Service), FAX (201)767-6717. **ED** Douglas Detterman. **LC** BF431; .I524. **DD** 153.9/05. **NLM** W1 IN651K. **CODEN** NTLLDT. **[CCC].** Index available. **Bk Rev. Ad Acc. Pr Rev. Circ:** 700. Documents available from The Genuine Article, BIOSIS Document Express, UMI Article Clearinghouse.
**Desc:** Journal devoted to original research in all facets of intelligence studies.
**Ind/Abst** Biol. Abstr.; Curr. Index J. Educ.; Newsp. Period. Abstr. (1992-); Psychol. Abstr. (1977-); PsycINFO (1990-); PsycLit; Res. Alert [Full Cov.]; Soc. Plann. Policy Dev. Abstr.; Soc. Sci. Cit. Index [Full Cov.].

US/0146-034X
**INTERAMERICAN PSYCHOLOGIST.** Periodical. Multiple languages (English and Spanish). Interamerican Society of Psychology, Department of Psychology, De Paul University Chicago IL 60614.

US/8755-612X
**INTERBEHAVIORIST, THE.** [Interbehaviorist]. **Added/Corp** University of Kansas. Dept. of Human Development. (19??)-. Periodical. English. Four times a year (Jan., Apr., July, Oct.). $7.50 (individuals), $12.00 (institutions). Interbehaviorist, Department of Human Development, University of Kansas, Lawrence KS 66045. **Tel** (913)864-4840, , FAX (607)722-1424. **ED** Edward K. Morris. **DD** 150. **Bk Rev. Ad Acc. Pr Rev. Circ:** 150.
**Desc:** A publication of news, discussion, reviews, and articles on interbehavioral psychology. A contextualistic, field-theory approach to a natural science of psychology.

AG/0325-8203
**INTERDISCIPLINARIA.** (19??)-. Periodical. Spanish (summaries and/or abstracts in English). sa. $20.00. Fernando Garcia Cambeiro, Cochabamba 244, 1150 Buenos Aires Argentina. **Tel** 011 54 1 3610473. **(Subscription address:** Fernando Garcia Cambeiro, 7331 Northwest 35th Street, PO Box 014, Miami FL 33122.**) LC** BF5; .I57. **DD** 150/.5.
**Ind/Abst** Psychol. Abstr. (1983-); PsycINFO (1990-).

US/0743-2135
**INTERFACES IN PSYCHOLOGY.** (INTERFACES IN PSYCHOLOGY / TEXAS TECH UNIVERSITY.). [Interfaces psychol.]. No. 1 (Sept. 1984)-. Periodical. English. an. $24.95 cloth, $14.95 paper. Texas Tech University Press, Administrative Education Room 43, West Basement, Lubbock TX 79409-1037. **Tel** (800)832-4042, (806)742-2982. **ED** John Harvey. **LC** BF1; .I437. **DD** 150/.5. **Circ:** 500.
**Desc:** The series results from annual symposia organized by the Texas Tech University Department of Psychology. They are numbered serially, paged separately and priced individually.

US/1046-5448
**INTERNATIONAL BRAIN DOMINANCE REVIEW.** ***Ceased.*** [Int. brain domin. rev.]. **Added/Corp** Brain Dominance Institute. **VFOAT** IBDR. (Jan. 1984)-(19??). Periodical. English. Twice a year (June & Dec.). The Ned Herrmann Group, 2075 Buffalo Creek Road, Lake Lure NC 28746. **Tel** (704)625-9153, FAX (704)625-2198. **ED** Laura Herrman. **DD** 152. Index available ($6.00). cum. index. **Bk Rev**, (Qty: 2). **Circ:** 500.
**Desc:** News and information on the cerebral dominance and creative thinking.

CN/0847-415X
**INTERNATIONAL BULLETIN OF MORITA THERAPY.** [Int. bull. Morita ther.]. **Added/Corp** International Network of Morita Therapists. University of British Columbia. Dept. of Counselling Psychology. Vol. 1, No. 1 (May 1988)-. Periodical. English. Twice a year (June & Dec.). 18.00Can$ (individuals), 39.00Can$ (instititutions) US & Canada; 20.00Can$ (individuals), 41.00Can$ (institutions) others. University of British Columbia / Department of Counseling, 5780 Toronto Road, Vancouver BC V6T 1L2 Canada. **Tel** (604)822-5329. **DD** 616.89/14.

UK/0268-1315
**INTERNATIONAL CLINICAL PSYCHOPHARMACOLOGY.** **See** Pharmacy and Pharmacology.

US/0738-8217
**INTERNATIONAL FORUM FOR PSYCHOANALYSIS.** [Int. forum psychoanal.]. Vol. 1, No. 1 (1984)-. Periodical. English. qt. Kr710.00, $109.00. Scandinavian University Press, PO Box 2959 Toeyen, N 0608 Oslo 6 Norway. **Tel** 011 47 2 2575400, FAX 011 47 2 2575353, telex 71896 UROR N. **(Subscription address:** Scandinavian University Press, 200 Meacham Ave., Elmont NY 11003.**) NLM** W1; IN7268H.

●NO/0803-706X
**INTERNATIONAL FORUM OF PSYCHOANALYSIS.** **Added/Corp** International Federation of Psychoanalytic Societies. **VFOAT** IFP. Vol 1, No. 1 (June 1992)-. Periodical. English. qt. Kr710.00, $109.00. Scandinavian University Press, PO Box 2959 Toeyen, N 0608 Oslo 6 Norway. **Tel** 011 47 2 2575400, FAX 011 47 2 2575353, telex 71896 UROR N. **(Subscription address:** Scandinavian University Press, 200 Meacham Ave., Elmont NY 11003.**)** **NLM** W1; IN7268M.

NE/0165-0653
**INTERNATIONAL JOURNAL FOR THE ADVANCEMENT OF COUNSELLING.** [Int. j. adv. couns.]. **Added/Corp** International Round Table for the Advancement of Counselling. International Association for Educational and Vocational Guidance. Vol. 1 (1978)-. Periodical. English. qt. $306.00. Kluwer Academic Publishers, Postbus 322, 3300 AH Dordrecht, The Netherlands. **Tel** 011 (31) 78 524400, FAX 011 31 78 183273, telex 20083. **ED** Len Stewin, Lothar Martin, Peter Weerdt, Beatrice Wehrly. **LC** BF637.C6; I53. **DD** 158/.3. **NLM** W1 IN7652L. **CODEN** IJACER. **[CCC]. Pr Rev. Acid Free.** available on microfilm and microfiche from University Microfilms International (UMI). Documents available from The Genuine Article.
**Desc:** Published under the auspices of the International Round Table for the Advancement of Counseling and the International Association for Educational and Vocational Guidance. The journal promotes the exchange of information about counseling activities throughout the world. Papers published in the journal provide conceptual, practical or research contributions, providing an international perspective.
**Ind/Abst** Br. Educ. Index; Commun. Abstr.; Curr. Contents Soc. Behav. Sci.; Educ. Adm. Abstr.; Hum. Resour. Abstr.; Psychol. Abstr. (1981-); PsycINFO (1990-); PsycLit; Res. Alert [Full Cov.]; Soc. Sci. Cit. Index [Full Cov.]; Soc. Work Abstr. (Summer 1987-?) [Select. Cov.].

US/1050-8414
**INTERNATIONAL JOURNAL OF AVIATION PSYCHOLOGY, THE.** [Int. j. aviat. psychol.]. **Added/Corp** Lawrence Erlbaum Associates. Vol. 1, No. 1 (1991)-. Periodical. English. qt. $165.00 US & Canada; $190.00 other. Lawrence Erlbaum Associates, 365 Broadway, Suite 102, Hillsdale NJ 07642. **Tel** (201)666-4110, (800)926-6579, FAX (201)666-2394. **ED** Richard S Jensen. **LC** TL553.6; .I57. **DD** 155.9/65/05. **NLM** W1; IN7652CG.
**Desc:** Publishes scholarly papers concerned with the development and management of safe, effective aviation systems from the standpoint of the human operators.
**Ind/Abst** Aviat. Tradescan [Full Cov.]; Ergon. Abstr.; Int. Aerosp. Abstr.

NE/0165-0254
**INTERNATIONAL JOURNAL OF BEHAVIORAL DEVELOPMENT.** (INTERNATIONAL JOURNAL OF BEHAVIORAL DEVELOPMENT : IJBD.). [Int. j. behav. dev.]. **Added/Corp** International Society for the Study of Behavioral Development. **VFOAT** IJBD. Vol. 1, No. 1 (Jan. 1978)-. Periodical. English. qt. $270.00 US; £154.00 Europe; £159.00 other. Lawrence Erlbaum Associates Ltd., 27 Palmeira Mansions, Church Road, Hove East Sussex BN3 2FA England. **Tel** 011 44 273 207411. **(Subscription address:** Turpin Distribution Services Limited, Blackhorse Road, Letchworth, Hertfordshire SG6 1HN, United Kingdom.**)** **ED** Linda Siegel. **LC** BF712; .I55. **DD** 155/.05. **NLM** W1 IN7655L. **CODEN** IJBDDY. **[CCC]. Pr Rev.** available on microfilm and microfiche from University Microfilms International (UMI). Documents available from The Genuine Article, BIOSIS Document Express.
**Ind/Abst** Appl. Soc. Sci. Index Abstr.; Biol. Abstr.; Cumul. Index Nurs. Allied Health Lit.; Curr. Contents Soc. Behav. Sci.; Curr. Index J. Educ.; Multicult. Educ. Abstr.; Psychol. Abstr. (1978-); PsycINFO; PsycLit; PsycScan: Develop. Psych.; Res. Alert [Full Cov.]; Soc. Plann. Policy Dev. Abstr.; Soc. Sci. Cit. Index [Full Cov.]; Sociol. Educ. Abstr.; Stud. Women Abstr.

●US/1070-5503
**INTERNATIONAL JOURNAL OF BEHAVIORAL MEDICINE.** (INTERNATIONAL JOURNAL OF BEHAVIORAL MEDICINE : OFFICIAL JOURNAL OF THE INTERNATIONAL SOCIETY OF BEHAVIORAL MEDICINE.). [Int. j. behav. med.]. **Added/Corp** International Society of Behavioral Medicine. **VFOAT** IJBM. Vol. 1, No. 1 (1994)-. Periodical. English. qt. $115.00 US & Canada; $140.00 other. Lawrence Erlbaum Associates, 365 Broadway, Suite 102, Hillsdale NJ 07642. **Tel** (201)666-4110, (800)926-6579, FAX (201)666-2394. **LC** IN PROCESS. **DD** 616.

US/0749-8470
**INTERNATIONAL JOURNAL OF CLINICAL NEUROPSYCHOLOGY, THE.** ***Ceased.*** [Int. j. clin. neuropsychol.]. Vol. 6, No. 1 (1984)-(19??). Periodical. English. qt. Melnic Press Inc, PO Box 6216, Madison WI 53716. **Tel** (608)222-6611. **ED** Charles J Golden. **DD** 616. **NLM** W1; IN766DJE. **[CCC]. Bk Rev. Ad Acc. Pr Rev. Circ:** 1,500 (ctrl). available on microfilm and microfiche from University Microfilms International (UMI). Documents available from The Genuine Article. ***Continues** Clinical Neuropsychology, 0197-3681.*
**Desc:** Devoted to the understanding, measurement and treatment of maladaptive human behavior dependent upon brain functioning.
**Ind/Abst** Curr. Contents Clin. Med.; Curr. Contents Soc. Behav. Sci.; EMBASE; Life Sci. Collect.; Psychol. Abstr. (1979-); PsycINFO; PsycLit; Res. Alert [Full Cov.]; SCISEARCH.

US/0889-3667
**INTERNATIONAL JOURNAL OF COMPARATIVE PSYCHOLOGY.** (INTERNATIONAL JOURNAL OF COMPARATIVE PSYCHOLOGY / ISCP; SPONSORED BY THE INTERNATIONAL SOCIETY FOR COMPARATIVE PSYCHOLOGY AND THE UNIVERSITY OF CALABRIA.). [Int. j. comp. psychol.]. **Added/Corp** International Society for Comparative Psychology. Universita Degli Studi Della Calabria. **VFOAT** ISCP International Journal of Comparative Psychology. Vol. 1, No. 1 (Fall 1987)-. Periodical. English. qt. $95.00 US; $110.00 other. International Society for Comparative Psychology. **(Subscription address:** International Journal of Comparative Psychology, PO Box 1897, Lawrence KS 66044-8897.**)** **LC** BF671; .I56. **DD** 156. **NLM** W1; IN766DS. **CODEN** IJCPE8IJCP8. **[CCC].** available on microfilm and microfiche from University Microfilms International (UMI).
**Desc:** Contains authors and editors from more than 20 countries, this journal studies the evolution and development in all species, including human.
**Ind/Abst** Acad. Abstr. Full Text Elite (July 1991-); Acad. Abstr. (July 1991-); Acad. Search (July 1991-); INFO-SOUTH Abstr.; Psychol. Abstr. (1987-); PsycINFO (1990-); PsycLit; Soc. Sci. Source (Jul. 1991-); Soc. Work Abstr. [Select. Cov.].

US/0047-0732
**INTERNATIONAL JOURNAL OF GROUP TENSIONS.** **See** Sociology.

UK/0893-603X
**INTERNATIONAL JOURNAL OF PERSONAL CONSTRUCT PSYCHOLOGY.** ***Title Change.*** [Int. j. pers. constr. psychol.]. Vol. 1, No. 1 (July 1988)-(1994). Periodical. English. qt (4 issues). Taylor & Francis Ltd., Rankine Road, Basingstoke Hampshire, RG24 8PR United Kingdom. **Tel** 011 44 256 840366, FAX 011 44 256 479438, telex 858540. **(Subscription address:** Taylor & Francis Inc., 1900 Frost Road, Suite 101, Bristol PA 19007-1598.**)** **ED** Robert A. Neimeyer (editor's address: Department of Psychology, Memphis State University, Memphis, TN 38152); Greg J. Neimeyer (editor's address: Department of Psychology, University of Florida) Florida, Gainesville, FL 32611). **LC** BF698.9.P47; I58. **DD** 150.19/8. **NLM** W1; IN771RT. **CODEN** IPCPEG. **[CCC].** available on microfilm and microfiche from University Microfilms International (UMI). ***Continued by** Journal of Constructivist Psychology.*
**Desc:** Provides readers with the latest research and scholarship in this fast growing specialty. Serves the key, dual purpose of making the latest research findings accessible to professionals, and promoting a critical and informed exchange between construct theory and related specialties in the social sciences. The journal features such topics as the relation of cognitive structure to behavior, the role of construing in the development and breakdown of close relationships, then use of construct theory in business and educational settings, methodological studies of repertory grid technique, and constructivist models of psychotherapy and psychopathology.
**Ind/Abst** Psychol. Abstr. (1988-?); PsycINFO (19?-19?); PsycLit (19?-19?).

●US/1061-530X
**INTERNATIONAL JOURNAL OF PHILOSOPHY, PSYCHOLOGY, AND SPIRITUALITY.** **See** Philosophy.

UK/0020-7578
**INTERNATIONAL JOURNAL OF PSYCHO-ANALYSIS, THE.** [Int. j. psycho-anal.]. **Added/Corp** International Psycho-Analytical Association. Institute of Psycho-analysis (London, England) International Psycho-Analytical Association. Bulletin. Vol. 1 (1920)-. Academic Scholarly Publication. English. Six times a year. £135.00 EEC; $269.00 US; £170.00 other. Institute of Psycho-Analysis, 63 New Cavendish Street, London W1M 7RD England. **Tel** 11 44 71 580 4952, FAX 11 44 71 323 5312. **ED** David Tuckett. **LC** BF173.A2; I6. **NLM** W1 IN777. **CODEN** IJPSAA. **[CCC].** cum. index. **Bk Rev. Ad Acc. Pr Rev. Circ:** 7,000. available on microfilm and microfiche from University Microfilms International (UMI). Documents available from The Genuine Article, BIOSIS Document Express. ***Absorbed** International Review of Psycho-Analysis, 0306-2643.*
**Desc:** Contributions to the theory and practice of psychoanalysis.
**Ind/Abst** Arts Humanit. Citation Index [Select. Cov.]; Biol. Abstr.; Curr. Contents Soc. Behav. Sci.; EMBASE; Index Med.; Int. Bibliogr. Sociol.; Middle East Abstr. Index; Multicult. Educ. Abstr. (1929-); Psychol. Abstr. (1929-); PsycINFO; PsycLit; Res. Alert [Full Cov.]; Soc. Plann. Policy Dev. Abstr.; Soc. Sci. Cit. Index [Full Cov.].

JA/0165-4055
**INTERNATIONAL JOURNAL OF PSYCHOLINGUISTICS.** **See** Linguistics.

NE/0020-7594
**INTERNATIONAL JOURNAL OF PSYCHOLOGY.** (INTERNATIONAL JOURNAL OF PSYCHOLOGY / INTERNATIONAL UNION OF PSYCHOLOGICAL SCIENCE.). [Int. J. Psychol.]. **Added/Corp** International Union of Psychological Science. **VFOAT** Journal International de Psychologie. Vol. 1, No. 1 (1966)-. Periodical. English (French). bm. $220.00 US; £116.00 Europe; £121.00 other. Lawrence Erlbaum Associates Ltd., 27 Palmeira Mansions, Church Road, Hove East Sussex BN3 2FA England. **Tel** 011 44 273 207411. **(Subscription address:** Turpin Distribution Services Limited, Blackhorse Road, Letchworth, Hertfordshire SG6 1HN, United Kingdom.**)** **ED** Michel E. Sabourin. **LC** BF1; .A158. **DD** 150.5. **NLM** W1; IN777K. **CODEN** IJPSBB. **[CCC]. Pr Rev.** available on microfilm and microfiche from University Microfilms International (UMI). Documents available from The Genuine Article, BIOSIS Document Express.
**Desc:** Publishes scientific and theoretical papers in all fields of psychology, with emphasis on topics where the social or cultural context is important. Fields covered include general psychology, developmental psychology and social psychology.
**Ind/Abst** Appl. Soc. Sci. Index Abstr.; Biol. Abstr.; Curr. Contents Soc. Behav. Sci.; Ergon. Abstr.; Middle East Abstr. Index; Peace Res. Abstr. J. (1966-1977); Psychol. Abstr. (1966-); PsycINFO; PsycLit; Res. Alert [Full Cov.]; Sage Race Relat. Abstr.; Soc. Sci. Cit. Index [Full Cov.]; Sociol. Educ. Abstr.; Stud. Women Abstr.

●US
**INTERNATIONAL JOURNAL OF PSYCHOLOGY RESEARCH.** (1994)-. Periodical. English. Four times a year. $65.00. Nova Science Publishers Inc., 6080 Jericho Turnpike, Suite 207, Commack NY 11725-2808. **Tel** (516)499-3103, (516)499-3106, FAX (516)499-3146.

UK/0884-724X
**INTERNATIONAL JOURNAL OF SHORT-TERM PSYCHOTHERAPY.** [Int. j. short-term psychother.]. Vol. 1, No. 1 (Jan. 1986)-. Periodical. English. Four times a year. $245.00. John Wiley & Sons Ltd., Baffins Lane, Chichester West Sussex PO19 1UD England. **Tel** 0243 779777, FAX 0243 776128 BTG:JWP001, telex 86290 WIBOOKG. **(Subscription address:** John Wiley / Philadelphia, PO Box 7247, Philadelphia PA 19170.**)** **ED** Paul Jay Fink. **LC** RC480.55; .I57. **DD** 616.89/14. **NLM** W1; IN7884E. **CODEN** IJTPEP. available on microfilm and microfiche from University Microfilms International (UMI). ***Continues** International Journal of Short-Term Dynamic Psychotherapy.*
**Desc:** Offers the researcher and the practitioner access to ongoing systematic research and developments in the spectrum of short-term psychotherapies. The journal covers the use of psychotherapy in a variety of settings: individual, family, and group. It also presents assessments of specific patient selection criteria, vital patient-history, ground outlines and interviews with prominent figures in the field.
**Ind/Abst** Psychoanal. Abstr.; Psychol. Abstr. (1990-); PsycINFO; PsycScan: Appl. Exp. Eng. Psych.; PsycScan: LD/MR; PsycScan: Neuropsych.

●US/1072-5245
**INTERNATIONAL JOURNAL OF STRESS MANAGEMENT.** [Int. j. stress manag.]. **Added/Corp** International Stress Management Association. Vol. 1, No. 1 (Jan. 1994)-. Periodical. English. qt. $75.00 US; $90.00 other. Human Sciences Press, PO Box 735, 233 Spring Street, New York NY 10013. **Tel** (212)620-8000, FAX (212)807-1047, telex 23421139. **(Subscription address:** Eurospan Ltd., Journals and Serials Division, 3 Henrietta Street, Covent Garden, London WC2E 8LU England.**)** **LC** IN PROCESS. **DD** 616. **NLM** W1; IN791FM.

US/0047-116X
**INTERNATIONAL PSYCHOLOGIST.** **Added/Corp** International Council of Psychologists. (19??)-. Periodical. English. qt. $24.00. International Council of Psychologists Inc., Department of Psychology, Southwest Texas State University, San Marcos TX 78666. **Tel** (512)245-3162, (512)245-2526, FAX (512)245-3153. **LC** BF1; .I53. **NLM** W1 IN827Y. **Bk Rev. Ad Acc. Circ:** 1,700 (ctrl).
**Desc:** News of the organization and of the practice of psychology in different countries.

UK/0886-1528
**INTERNATIONAL REVIEW OF INDUSTRIAL AND ORGANIZATIONAL PSYCHOLOGY.** [Int. rev. ind. organ. psychol.]. (1986)-. English. an. $90.00. John Wiley & Sons Ltd., Baffins Lane, Chichester West Sussex PO19 1UD England. **Tel** 0243 779777, FAX 0243 776128 BTG:JWP001, telex 86290 WIBOOKG. **(Subscription address:** John Wiley / Philadelphia, PO Box 7247,

Philadelphia PA 19170.) **ED** Cary L. Cooper and Ivan T. Robertson. **LC** HF5548.7; .I57. **DD** 158.7/05. **NLM** W1; IN832U. **[CCC]**. available on microfilm and microfiche from University Microfilms International (UMI).
**Desc:** Provides reviews in the field of industrial and organizational psychology. The chapters are written by established experts and the topics are carefully chosen to reflect the major concerns in the research literature and in current practice.

UK/0306-2643
**INTERNATIONAL REVIEW OF PSYCHO-ANALYSIS, THE.** ***Title Change.*** [Int. rev. psycho-anal.]. **Added/Corp** Institute of Psycho-Analysis (London, England). Vol. 1 (1974)-Vol. 19 (1992). Periodical. English. qt. Institute of Psycho-Analysis, 63 New Cavendish Street, London W1M 7RD England. **Tel** 11 44 71 580 4952, FAX 11 44 71 323 5312. **LC** BF173.A2; I65. **DD** 616.8/917/05. **NLM** W1 IN834H. **CODEN** IRPADF. **Pr Rev.** available on microfilm and microfiche from University Microfilms International (UMI). Documents available from The Genuine Article. ***Absorbed by*** *International Journal of Psycho-Analysis, 0020-7578.*
**Ind/Abst** Abstr. Res. Pastor. Care Couns. (19??-); Curr. Contents Soc. Behav. Sci.; Int. Bibliogr. Sociol.; Middle East Abstr. Index; Psychol. Abstr. (1974-); PsycINFO (1974-); PsycLit; Res. Alert [Full Cov.]; Soc. Plann. Policy Dev. Abstr.; Soc. Sci. Cit. Index (19??-19??) [Full Cov.].

UK/1058-4994
**INTERNATIONAL REVIEW OF STUDIES ON EMOTION.** [Int. rev. stud. emot.]. **VFOAT** Review of Studies on Emotion. Vol. 1 (1991)-. English. be. John Wiley & Sons Ltd., Baffins Lane, Chichester West Sussex PO19 1UD England. **Tel** 0243 779777, FAX 0243 776128 BTG:JWP001, telex 86290 WIBOOKG. **(Subscription address:** North, South and Central America/ John Wiley & Sons, Inc., Subscription Department, 605 Third Avenue, New York, NY 10158-0012, USA; telephone: (212)850-6645; FAX: (212)850-6021**)** **LC** BF531; .I58. **DD** 152.4/05.

UK/0364-0841
**INTERNATIONAL SERIES IN EXPERIMENTAL PSYCHOLOGY.** **VFOAT** International Series of Monographs in Experimental Psychology. Vol. 20 (1975)-. Monographic series. English. Price varies per volume. Pergamon Press, An Imprint of Elsevier Science Ltd., The Boulevard, Langford Lane, Kidlington, Oxford OX5 1GB United Kingdom. **Tel** 011 44 865 843000, 011 44 865 843699, FAX 011 44 865 843010. **DD** 150/.724. **NLM** W1 IN835JE. ***Continues*** *International Series of Monographs on Experimental Psychology, 0074-8137.*

UK/0892-3175
**INTERNATIONAL SERIES IN EXPERIMENTAL SOCIAL PSYCHOLOGY.** [Int. ser. exp. soc. psychol.]. Vol. 1 (1982)-. Monographic series. English. Price varies per volume. Pergamon Press, An Imprint of Elsevier Science Ltd., The Boulevard, Langford Lane, Kidlington, Oxford OX5 1GB United Kingdom. **Tel** 011 44 865 843000, 011 44 865 843699, FAX 011 44 865 843010. **(Subscription address:** US/ 395 Saw Mill River Road, Elmsford, NY 10523; Can/ 150 Consumers Road/Suite 104, Willowdale Ontario M2J 1P9; Aus-NZ/ POB 544, Potts Point NSW 2011**)** **DD** 302.
**Ind/Abst** Math. Rev.

●US/1060-7978
**INTERPRET YOUR DREAMS.** **VFOAT** IYDI. (1992)-. Periodical. English. wk. Free. Unlimited Concepts, 6050 Peachtree Parkway, Suite 340, Norcross GA 30092.

SP
**INVESTIGACIONES PSICOLOGICAS (MADRID, SPAIN).** (INVESTIGACIONES PSICOLOGICAS / FACULTAD DE PSICOLOGIA.). **Added/Corp** Universidad Complutense de Madrid. Facultad de Psicologia. (198?)-. Periodical. Spanish (summaries and/or abstracts in English). Editorial Complutense, Donoso Cortes 65 1RA Planta, 28003 Madrid Spain. **Tel** 011 34 1 3946372. **NLM** W1; IN994K.
**Ind/Abst** PsycINFO (1990-).

UK/0309-152X
**IRCS MEDICAL SCIENCE. PSYCHOLOGY AND PSYCHIATRY.** **See** Medical Science and Technology-Psychiatry.

IE/0303-3910
**IRISH JOURNAL OF PSYCHOLOGY, THE.** [Ir. j. psychol.]. **Added/Corp** Psychological Society of Ireland. Vol. 1, (May 1971)-. Periodical. English. Four times a year (Feb., May, Aug., Nov.). $70.00. The Irish Journal of Psychology, Department of Psychology, Trinity College, 25 Westland Row, Dublin 2 Ireland. **Tel** 353 1 772941. **ED** Howard Smith. **NLM** W1 IR434. **CODEN** IRJPAR. Index available. **Bk Rev. Ad Acc. Pr Rev. Circ:** 900. available on diskette. Documents available from The Genuine Article, BIOSIS Document Express.
**Desc:** Publishes original articles dealing with theory, methodology or empirical findings in any pure or applied field of psychology, as well as review articles, abstracts of theses for which higher degrees in psychology are awarded by Irish Universities and book reviews.
**Ind/Abst** Biol. Abstr.; Br. Educ. Index; Curr. Contents Soc. Behav. Sci.; Psychol. Abstr. (1971-); PsycINFO; PsycLit; Ref. Z.; Res. Alert [Full Cov.]; Soc. Sci. Cit. Index [Full Cov.].

II
**ISPT JOURNAL OF RESEARCH.** **Main/Corp** Institute for Studies in Psychological Testing. V. 1- Jan. 1977-. Periodical. English. sa. Rs50.00. Institute for Studies in Psychological Testing, 17 Karanpur, Dehradun 248001 India. **Tel** 27404. **ED** SP Kulshestha. **LC** BF176; .I58A. **DD** 150/.28/7. **Bk Rev. Ad Acc. Circ:** 1,000.
**Desc:** Journal of research in educational and psychological testing and measurement assessment.

UK/0266-6863
**ISSUES IN CRIMINOLOGICAL AND LEGAL PSYCHOLOGY.** [Issues criminol. legal psychol.]. (1981)-. Monographic series. English. sa. Price varies per volume. British Psychological Society, St. Andrews House, 48 Princess Road, Leicester LE1 7DR England. **Tel** 011 44 533 549568.
**Ind/Abst** Psychol. Abstr. (1981-); PsycLit.

US/0097-6555
**ISSUES IN EGO PSYCHOLOGY.** ***Title Change.*** [Issues ego psychol.]. **Added/Corp** Washington Square Institute for Psychotherapy and Mental Health. (19??)-(199?). English. sa. Washington Institute, 1015 18th Street Northwest, Suite 300, Washington DC 20036-5204. **Tel** (202)293-7440, FAX (202)293-9393. **LC** RC475; .I88. **DD** 616.8/914/08. **NLM** W1 IS668E. ***Continued by*** *Issues in Psychoanalytic Psychology, 1075-0754.*
**Ind/Abst** Psychol. Abstr. (1975-?); PsycLit.

US/0161-2840
**ISSUES IN MENTAL HEALTH NURSING.** **See** Medical Science and Technology-Nursing.

●US/1075-0754
**ISSUES IN PSYCHOANALYTIC PSYCHOLOGY.** [Issues psychoanal. psychol.]. **Added/Corp** Washington Square Institute for Psychotherapy and Mental Health (New York, N.Y.). Vol. 15, No. 2 (1993)-. Periodical. English. sa. $16.00. Washington Square Institute, 41 East 11th Street, New York NY 10003. **Tel** (212)477-2600. **LC** RC475; .I88. **DD** 616.8/914/08. ***Continues*** *Issues in Ego Psychology, 0097-6555.*

IT
**ITALIAN JOURNAL OF PSYCHOLOGY, THE.** Vol. 5, No. 1 (April 1978)-. Periodical. English. Three times a year. Societa Editrice il Mulino, Strada Maggiore 37, 40125 Bologna Italy. **Tel** 011 39 51 256011, FAX 011 39 51 256034. **NLM** W1 GI814G. ***Separated from*** *Giornale Italiano di Psicologia, 0390-5349.*
**Ind/Abst** Psychol. Abstr. (1978-).

GW/0075-2924
**JAHRESKATALOG PSYCHOLOGIE UND VERWANDTE WISSENSCHAFTEN.** **VFOAT** Psychologie Jahreskatalog. (1964)-. Periodical. German. an. Buchwerbung In Berlin GmbH, Luetzowstrasse 105 106, D 10785 Berlin Germany. **Tel** 011 49 30 2619257, 011 49 30 2614933.

JA
**JAPANESE JOURNAL OF BEHAVIOR THERAPY.** ir. Japanese Association of Behavior Therapy, University of Hiroshima, Higashi Senda-cho, Naka-ku, Hiroshima 730 Japan.
**Ind/Abst** PsycINFO (1984-); PsycLit.

JA
**JAPANESE JOURNAL OF BEHAVIORMETRICS.** Twice a year. Behaviormetric Society of Japan, 6-7 Minami-Azabu 4-Chome Minato-ku, Tokyo 106 Japan.
**Ind/Abst** PsycINFO (1983-); PsycLit.

JA/0021-5368
**JAPANESE PSYCHOLOGICAL RESEARCH.** [Jpn. psychol. res.]. **Added/Corp** Nihon Shinri Gakkai. Vol. 1 (March 1954)-. Periodical. English. qt. $90.00. Nihon Shinri Gakkai, (Japanese Psychological Assoc.), 40-14-901, Hongo 2 Chome, Bunkyoku, Tokyoto 113 Japan. **(Subscription address:** Kyowa Book Company Inc., 1 38 Kanda Jinbocho Chiyoda-ku, Tokyo 101 Japan.**)** **LC** BF76.5; .J3. **NLM** W1 JA979. **CODEN** JPREAV. **Pr Rev.** Documents available from The Genuine Article, BIOSIS Document Express.
**Ind/Abst** Biol. Abstr.; Curr. Contents Soc. Behav. Sci.; Life Sci. Collect.; Psychol. Abstr. (1954-); PsycINFO; PsycLit; Res. Alert [Full Cov.]; Soc. Plann. Policy Dev. Abstr.; Soc. Sci. Cit. Index [Full Cov.].

JA
**JAPANESE PSYCHOLOGICAL REVIEW.** Twice a year. Kyoto University / Department of Psychology, Daigaku Bungakubu Shinrigaku Kyushitsu, 54 Shogoin Kawara-cho, Sakyo-ku Kyoto 606 Japan.
**Ind/Abst** PsycINFO (1969-); PsycLit.

CH/1011-5714
**JIAOYU XINLIXUEBAO.** (CHIAO YU HSIN LI HSUEH PAO. BULLETIN OF EDUCATIONAL PSYCHOLOGY.). [Jiaoyu xinlixuebao]. **Added/Corp** Kuo li T'ai-Wan Shih fan ta Hsueh. Chiao yu Hsin li Hsueh Hsi. **VFOAT** Bulletin of Educational Psychology. Vol. 6 (1973)-. Academic Scholarly Publication. Chinese (English). an. National Taiwan Normal University, 162 Ho-ping East Road. Sec.1, Department of Educational Pshchology & Counseling, Taipie, Taiwan 106. **Tel** 02 351 1263, 02 395 2445, FAX 02 341-3865. **ED** Lan Ming-Chih. **LC** LB1051; .C332886. ***Continues*** *Hsin li yu Chiao yu.*
**Desc:** A major portion of their researches relates to educational testing measurements and practice issues on guidance problems of adolescence.
**Ind/Abst** Psychol. Abstr. (1973-); PsycINFO (1973-); PsycLit.

JA/0387-7973
**JIKKEN SHAKAI SHINRIGAKU KENKYU.** [Jikken shakai shinrigaku kenkyu]. **VFOAT** Japanese Journal of Experimental Social Psychology. Periodical. Japanese (summaries and/or abstracts in English). Three times a year. $40.00 US. The Japanese Group Dynamics Association, Nishinippon Shimbun Kaikan Building/14-F, Institute for Group Dynamics, 4-ban 1-go Tenjin 1-chome Chuo-ku, Fukuoka-shi 810 Japan. **Tel** 092-713-1308. **ED** Jyuji Misumi. **LC** HM251; .J43. **Bk Rev. Ad Acc.** ctrl circ.
**Ind/Abst** Psychol. Abstr. (1972-); PsycINFO (1972-).

BL/0047-2085
**JORNAL BRASILEIRO DE PSIQUIATRIA.** **See** Medical Science and Technology-Psychiatry.

PO/0870-4783
**JORNAL DE PSICOLOGIA.** **Added/Corp** Universidade do Porto. Grupo de Estudos e Reflexao em Psicologia. Vol. 1, No. 1 (Mar./April 1982)-. Periodical. Portuguese (summaries and/or abstracts in English and French). bm. $25.00. Jornal de Psicologia, Rua das Taipas 76, 4000 Porto, Portugal. **NLM** W1; JO199HH.
**Ind/Abst** PsycINFO (1984-); PsycLit.

US/1061-4087
**JOURNAL - AMERICAN PSYCHOLOGICAL ASSOCIATION. DIVISION OF CONSULTING PSYCHOLOGY.** ***Title Change.*** (CONSULTING PSYCHOLOGY JOURNAL.). [J. - Am. Psychol. Assoc., Div. Consult. Psychol.]. **Added/Corp** American Psychological Association. Division of Consulting Psychology. Educational Publishing Foundation. **VFOAT** Consulting Psychology Journal. (1992)-. Periodical. English. qt. Educational Publishing Foundation, 750 First Street NE, Washington DC 20002-4242. **DD** 158. **NLM** W1; JO222VM. ***Continues*** *Bulletin (American Psychological Association. Division of Consulting Psychology), 1049-9067.* ***Continued by*** *Consulting Psychology Journal, 1065-9293.*

FR
**JOURNAL DE LA PSYCHANALYSE DE L'ENFANT.** (1986)-. Periodical. French. ir. 300.00F France; 350.00F other. Bayard Presse, Svc Client, 3 rue Bayard/Dept 2, 75393 Paris Cedex 08 France. **Tel** 011 33 1 44356060, 011 33 1 44356262.

FR
**JOURNAL DE THERAPIE COMPORTEMENTALE ET COGNITIVE.** French. qt. 500.00F France; $114.00 US; £97.00 other. Masson SA, Avenue Beauregard 12, CH-1701 Fribourg Switzerland. **Tel** 011 41 37 249585, FAX 011 41 37 247559, telex 942658 SEMI CH.

FR/0752-501X
**JOURNAL DES PSYCHOLOGUES, LE.** [J. psychol.]. (1982)-. Periodical. French. mo. 300.00F France; 350.00F (surface mail), 400.00F (air mail) other. Psychologie et Avenir, 18 Boulevard Camille Flammarion, 13001 Marseille France. **Tel** 011 33 1 91622277, FAX 011 33 1 91622282. **UDC** 159.9.

US/0193-3922
**JOURNAL FOR SPECIALISTS IN GROUP WORK, THE.** [J. spec. group work]. **Added/Corp** Association for Specialists in Group Work (U.S.). Vol. 3, No. 2 (Summer 1978)-. Periodical. English. qt (4 issues). $24.00 (institution), $18.00 (individual) US. American Counseling Association, 5999 Stevenson Avenue, Alexandria VA 22304. **Tel** (703)823-9800, (800)347-6647, FAX (703)823-0252. **(Subscription address:** American Counseling Association, Subscription Office, PO Box 2513, Birmingham AL 35201-2513.**)** **ED** Arthur M. Horne. **LC** BF637.C6; T63. **DD** 158. **[CCC]. Ad Acc. Circ:** 264 (ctrl). available on microfilm and microfiche from University Microfilms International (UMI). ***Continues*** *Together (Washington. 1975), 0161-0333.*
**Desc:** Reports on a regular basis group processes that have been demonstrated to be effective. Read by counselors who specialize in group work and those who use group therapy specific situations.
**Ind/Abst** Curr. Index J. Educ.; High. Educ. Abstr.

(1984-); Psychol. Abstr. (1979-); PsycINFO; PsycLit; Soc. Plann. Policy Dev. Abstr.; Soc. Work Abstr. [Select. Cov.]; Sociol. Abstr.; Spec. Educ. Needs Abstr.

UK/0021-8308
**JOURNAL FOR THE THEORY OF SOCIAL BEHAVIOUR.** [J. theory soc. behav.]. Vol. 1 (April 1971)-. Academic Scholarly Publication. English. Four times a year. £97.00 UK and Europe; $164.00 North America; £121.00 other. Basil Blackwell Publishers Ltd, 108 Cowley Road, Oxford 0X4 1JF England. **Tel** 011 44 865 791100, FAX 011 44 865 791347, telex 837022 OXBOOK G. **(Subscription address:** Blackwell Publishers / UK, Marston Book Services, PO Box 87, Oxford OX2 0DT England.**) ED** Charles W Smith. **NLM** W1 JO404. **[CCC]. Bk Rev. Ad Acc. Pr Rev.** available on microfilm and microfiche from University Microfilms International (UMI). Documents available from The Genuine Article.
**Desc:** Interdisciplinary journal publishing original theoretical and methodological articles relating to social behaviour.
**Ind/Abst** Appl. Soc. Sci. Index Abstr.; Curr. Contents Soc. Behav. Sci.; Int. Bibliogr. Sociol.; Int. Polit. Sci. Abstr.; Middle East Abstr. Index; Philos. Index; Psychol. Abstr. (1971-); PsycINFO; PsycLit; Res. Alert [Full Cov.]; Res. High. Educ. Abstr.; Soc. Plann. Policy Dev. Abstr.; Soc. Sci. Cit. Index [Full Cov.]; Sociol. Abstr.; Sociol. Educ. Abstr.

CN/0849-3588
**JOURNAL L'ARISTOCRATE.** [J. aristocr.]. Vol. 1, No 1 (June 1990)-. Periodical. French. bm. 1.25Can$ per issue. Editions E=MC2, 7483 St.-Denis, Montreal, Quebec H2R 2E5 Canada. **DD** 155/.05.

US/0091-0627
**JOURNAL OF ABNORMAL CHILD PSYCHOLOGY.** [J. abnorm. child psychol.]. **Added/Corp** American Psychological Association. (Jan./Mar. 1973)-. Academic Scholarly Publication. English. Six times a year. $345.00 institutions, $62.00 individuals US; $405.00 institutions, $73.00 individuals other. Plenum Press, 233 Spring Street, New York NY 10013-1578. **Tel** (212)620-8000, (800)221-9369, FAX (212)463-0742, (212)807-1047, telex 23/421139. **ED** Herbert C. Quay. **LC** RJ499.A1; J57. **DD** 618.9/28/9005. **NLM** W1 JO533L. **CODEN** JABCAA. **[CCC].** Index available. **Pr Rev.** available on microfilm and microfiche from University Microfilms International (UMI). Documents available from The Genuine Article, BIOSIS Document Express, UMI Article Clearinghouse.
**Ind/Abst** Acad. Search (July 1993-); Annals Behav. Med.; Appl. Soc. Sci. Index Abstr.; Biol. Abstr.; Crim. Justice Abstr.; Crim. Penol. Police Sci. Abstr.; Curr. Contents Soc. Behav. Sci.; Dev. Med. Child Neurol.; EMBASE; Except. Child Educ. Resour.; Expand. Acad. Index (1989-); Health Period. Database; Index Med.; Mag. Search; Middle East Abstr. Index; Multicult. Educ. Abstr.; Newsp. Period. Abstr. (1989-); Psychol. Abstr. (1977-); PsycINFO; PsycLit; PsycScan: Develop. Psych.; Res. Alert [Full Cov.]; Soc. Sci. Cit. Index [Full Cov.]; Soc. Sci. Index Fulltext (Oct. 1988-) [Full Txt.]; Spec. Educ. Needs Abstr.

US/0021-843X
**JOURNAL OF ABNORMAL PSYCHOLOGY (1965).** (JOURNAL OF ABNORMAL PSYCHOLOGY.). [J. abnorm. psychology]. **Added/Corp** American Psychological Association. Vol. 70 (Feb. 1965)-. Academic Scholarly Publication. English. Four times a year (Feb., May, Aug., Nov.). $158.00 (nonmember, institution) US. American Psychological Association, 750 First Street Northeast, Washington DC 20002. **Tel** (800)374-2721, (202)336-5600, (subscriptions - (202)336-5600. **ED** Susan Mineka, Ph.D. **LC** RC321; .J7. **DD** 157. **NLM** W1 JO533P. **CODEN** JAPCAC. **[CCC].** Index available (bound in last issue). **Ad Acc. Pr Rev. Circ:** 5,800. available on microfilm from Johnson Associates; available on microfilm and microfiche from University Microfilms International (UMI). Documents available from The Genuine Article, BIOSIS Document Express, UMI Article Clearinghouse. ***Continues in part*** *Journal of Abnormal and Social Psychology, 0096-851X.*
**Desc:** Keeps readers up-to-date on research in psychopathology. Normal processes in abnormal individuals, and pathological or atypical features of the behavior of normal persons. Coverage includes cognitive, behavioral and psychodynamic perspectives.
**Ind/Abst** Acad. Abstr. Full Text Elite (July 1990-); Acad. Abstr. (July 1990-); Acad. Ind. [Computer File] (1987-); Acad. Search (July 1990-); Annals Behav. Med.; Appl. Soc. Sci. Index Abstr.; Biol. Abstr.; Biol. Dig.; Crim. Justice Abstr.; Curr. Contents Soc. Behav. Sci.; EMBASE; Except. Child Educ. Resour. (1965-); Expand. Acad. Index (1987-); Health Index (1989-1991); Health Period. Database; High. Educ. Abstr. (1965-); Index Med.; INFO-SOUTH Abstr.; Int. Aerosp. Abstr.; Mag. Search; Middle East Abstr. Index; MLA Int. Bibl. Books Artic. Mod. Lang. Lit.; Multicult. Educ. Abstr.; Newsp. Period. Abstr. (1986-); Psychol. Abstr. (1965-); PsycINFO; PsycLit; PsycScan: Clin. Psych.; Res. Alert [Full Cov.]; Soc. Sci. Source (Jul. 1990-); Soc. Sci. Cit. Index [Full Cov.]; Soc. Sci. Index; Soc. Sci. Index Fulltext (Nov. 1988-) [Full Txt.]; Soc. Work Abstr. (Summer 1987-) [Select. Cov.]; Sociol. Educ. Abstr.; Spec. Educ. Needs Abstr.; Stud. Women Abstr.; Women Stud. Abstr.

US/1055-3835
**JOURNAL OF ADDICTIONS & OFFENDER COUNSELING.** [J. addict. offender couns.]. **Added/Corp** International Association of Addictions and Offender Counselors. **VFOAT** Journal of Addictions and Offender Counseling; Addictions & Offender Counseling; Addictions and Offender Counseling. Vol. 11, No. 1 (Oct. 1990)-. Periodical. English. sa (Apr. and Oct.). $15.00 (institution), $9.00 (individual) US. American Counseling Association, 5999 Stevenson Avenue, Alexandria VA 22304. **Tel** (703)823-9800, (800)347-6647, FAX (703)823-0252. **(Subscription address:** American Counseling Association, Subscription Office, PO Box 2513, Birmingham AL 35201-2513.**) ED** Bob Shearer. **LC** HV9275; .J68. **DD** 365/.66. **NLM** W1; JO533PT. **[CCC].** available on microfilm and microfiche from University Microfilms International (UMI). ***Continues*** *Journal of Offender Counseling, 0275-8598.*
**Ind/Abst** Crim. Justice Abstr. (199?-); Curr. Index J. Educ.; Psychoanal. Abstr.; PsycScan: Appl. Exp. Eng. Psych.; PsycScan: LD/MR; PsycScan: Neuropsych.; Soc. Work Abstr. [Select. Cov.].

UK/0140-1971
**JOURNAL OF ADOLESCENCE (LONDON, ENGLAND).** **See** Medical Science and Technology-Pediatrics.

US/0743-5584
**JOURNAL OF ADOLESCENT RESEARCH.** [J. adolesc. res.]. Vol. 1, No. 1 (Spring 1986)-. Periodical. English. qt (Jan., Apr., July, Oct.). $118.00. SAGE Periodical Press, 2455 Teller Road, Thousand Oaks CA 91320. **Tel** (805)499-0721, FAX (805)499-0871, telex 100799. **ED** E. Ellen Thornburg. **LC** HQ796; .J6237. **DD** 305.23/5/05. **NLM** W1; JO533SE. Index available. cum. index. **Ad Acc. Acid Free. Circ:** 1,000 (ctrl). available on microfilm and microfiche from University Microfilms International (UMI); available on photocopies from University Microfilms International (UMI).
**Desc:** Provides scholars with the most current and relevant information on ways in which individuals age 10-20 develop, behave and are influenced by societal and cultural perspectives.
**Ind/Abst** AGRICOLA [Full Cov.]; Educ. Adm. Abstr.; Psychol. Abstr. (1986-); PsycINFO; PsycLit; Sage Fam. Stud. Abstr.; Soc. Plann. Policy Dev. Abstr.; Soc. Work Abstr. [Select. Cov.]; Sociol. Abstr.

●US/1068-0667
**JOURNAL OF ADULT DEVELOPMENT.** (1993)-. Periodical. English. Four times a year. $100.00 institutions, $35.00 individuals US; $115.00 institutions, $41.00 individuals other. Plenum Press, 233 Spring Street, New York NY 10013-1578. **Tel** (212)620-8000, (800)221-9369, FAX (212)463-0742, (212)807-1047, telex 23/421139. **NLM** W1; JO533T.
**Desc:** Explores positive aspects of development in adults across the lifespan using a broad range of developmental perspectives. Reporting both theoretical and empirical reserach, the journal focuses on adult social and interpersonal development, including the acquisition of moral ideas and principles, the development and character of the ego, and the depth and changing nature of human relationships across the lifespan. Combines the work of investigators in numerous core developmental fields, as well as applied disciplines such as education, counseling, psychology and psychiatry, gerontology, and industrial psychology.

NR/0795-3097
**JOURNAL OF AFRICAN PSYCHOLOGY (SOUTH OF THE SAHARA, THE CARIBBEAN, AND AFRO-LATIN AMERICA).** **Added/Corp** Working Group for African Psychology (Enugu, Nigeria). **VFOAT** Journal of African Psychology. Vol. 1, No. 1 (1988)-. Periodical. English (French and Portuguese). sa. **LC** IN PROCESS; BF108.A3; J6.
**Ind/Abst** Soc. Plann. Policy Dev. Abstr.

●US/1052-9950
**JOURNAL OF ANALYTIC SOCIAL WORK.** **See** Sociology-Social Services and Welfare.

UK/0021-8774
**JOURNAL OF ANALYTICAL PSYCHOLOGY.** [J. anal. psychol.]. **Added/Corp** Society of Analytical Psychology. Vol. 1 (1955)-. Academic Scholarly Publication. English. Four times a year (Jan., Apr., Jul., Oct.). $110.00 (US & Canada); £75.00 (UK); £80.00 (other). Routledge, 11 New Fetter Lane, London EC4P 4EE England. **Tel** 071 583 9855, FAX 071 842 2298. **(Subscription address:** Kinokuniya Company Ltd., 38-1 Sakuragaoka 5, chome Setagaya-ku, Tokyo 156 Japan.**) ED** Rosemary Gordon. **LC** BF173.A2; S6. **DD** 131.3405. **NLM** W1 JO536. **CODEN** JANPA7. **[CCC]. Bk Rev. Pr Rev.** Documents available from The Genuine Article, BIOSIS Document Express.
**Desc:** The principal aim of this journal is to disseminate the thoughts, theories, and clinical work of C.G. Jung as well as the development of his ideas as they occur and are being worked out in England and in all other countries by analytical psychologists and by those interested in analytical psychology.
**Ind/Abst** Abstr. Res. Pastor. Care Couns. (19??-); Appl. Soc. Sci. Index Abstr.; Arts Humanit. Citation Index [Select. Cov.]; Biol. Abstr. (-1989); Curr. Contents Soc. Behav. Sci.; EMBASE; Except. Hum. Exp.; Index Med.; Int. Bibliogr. Sociol.; Middle East Abstr. Index; Psychol. Abstr. (1955-); PsycINFO; PsycLit; Res. Alert [Full Cov.]; Soc. Sci. Cit. Index [Full Cov.].

US/0887-6185
**JOURNAL OF ANXIETY DISORDERS.** [J. anxiety disorders]. **VFOAT** Anxiety Disorders. Vol. 1, No. 1 (1987)-. Periodical. English. Six times a year. $249.00 The Americas; £167.00 other. Pergamon Press, An Imprint of Elsevier Science Ltd., The Boulevard, Langford Lane, Kidlington, Oxford OX5 1GB United Kingdom. **Tel** 011 44 865 843000, 011 44 865 843699, FAX 011 44 865 843010. **(Subscription address:** Elsevier Science Ltd. Oxford Fulfillment Centre, PO Box 800, Kidlington, Oxford OX5 1DX United Kingdom.**) ED** Cynthia G. Last and Michel Hersen. **LC** RC531; .J68. **DD** 616.85/223. **NLM** W1; JO538S. **CODEN** JADIE8. **[CCC]. Ad Acc. Pr Rev. Circ:** 1,000. available on microfilm and microfiche from University Microfilms International (UMI). Documents available from The Genuine Article, BIOSIS Document Express.
**Desc:** Publishes research papers dealing with all aspects of anxiety disorders for all age groups. Areas of focus include: traditional, behavioural, cognitive, and biological assessment; diagnosis and classification; psychosocial and psychopharmacological treatment; genetics; epidemiology; and prevention.
**Ind/Abst** Abstr. Res. Pastor. Care Couns. (19??-); Biol. Abstr. (1990-); Curr. Aware. Biol. Sci., CABS; Curr. Contents Soc. Behav. Sci.; EMBASE; Psychol. Abstr. (1987-); PsycINFO (1990-); PsycLit; Res. Alert [Full Cov.]; Soc. Sci. Cit. Index [Full Cov.].

US/0021-8855
**JOURNAL OF APPLIED BEHAVIOR ANALYSIS.** [J. appl. behav. anal.]. **Added/Corp** Society for the Experimental Analysis of Behavior. Vol. 1 (Spring 1968)-. Periodical. English. qt. $64.00 US; $70.00 Canada; $74.00 other. Journal of Applied Behavior Analysis, Department of Human Development, University of Kansas, Lawrence KS 66045. **Tel** (913)843-0008. **ED** E. Scott Geller. **LC** BF636.A1; J6. **DD** 159/.05. **NLM** W1 JO539N. **CODEN** JOABAW. Index available. cum. index. **Bk Rev. Ad Acc. Pr Rev. Circ:** 6,000. available on microfiche. Documents available from The Genuine Article, BIOSIS Document Express, UMI Article Clearinghouse.
**Desc:** Publishes primarily original reports of experimental research involving applications of the experimental analysis of behavior to problems of social importance.
**Ind/Abst** ABI/INFORM Glob. Ed.; ABI Inform Ondisc (Winter 1973-Fall 1974); ABI/INFORM Ondisc: Expr. Ed.; Acad. Abstr. Full Text Elite (Jan. 1992-); Acad. Abstr. (Jan. 1992-); Acad. Search (Jan. 1992-); Appl. Soc. Sci. Index Abstr.; Biol. Abstr.; Curr. Contents Soc. Behav. Sci.; Curr. Index J. Educ.; Energy Res. Abstr. (Aug. 1982-); Except. Child Educ. Resour.; Expand. Acad. Index (1989-); Index Med.; INFO-SOUTH Abstr.; INIS Atomindex [Micro.]; Int. Nurs. Index; Middle East Abstr. Index; Newsp. Period. Abstr. (1991-); Psychol. Abstr. (1968-); PsycINFO; PsycLit; PsycScan: Appl. Psych.; Res. Alert [Full Cov.]; Soc. Sci. Source (Jan. 1992-); Soc. Sci. Cit. Index [Full Cov.]; Soc. Sci. Index; Soc. Sci. Index Fulltext (Summer 1988-) [Full Txt.]; SportSearch; Work Relat. Abstr.

US/0193-3973
**JOURNAL OF APPLIED DEVELOPMENTAL PSYCHOLOGY.** [J. appl. dev. psychol.]. Vol. 1 (Winter 1980)-. Periodical. English. qt. $165.00 institution. Ablex Publishing Corporation, 355 Chestnut Street, Norwood NJ 07648. **Tel** (201)767-8450, (201)767-8455 (Customer Service), FAX (201)767-6717. **ED** Irving Sigel. **LC** BF636.A1; J63. **DD** 155/.05. **NLM** W1 JO541E. **[CCC].** Index available. **Bk Rev. Ad Acc. Circ:** 600.
**Desc:** Devoted to study of humans over time to bridge gap between research in developmental psychology and application of such research.
**Ind/Abst** Psychol. Abstr. (1980-); PsycINFO; PsycLit; PsycScan: Develop. Psych.; Soc. Plann. Policy Dev. Abstr.

US/0021-9010
**JOURNAL OF APPLIED PSYCHOLOGY.** [J. appl. psychol.]. **Added/Corp** American Psychological Association. American Association for Applied Psychology. Vol. 1 (March 1917)-. Periodical. English. bm. $243.00 (nonmember, institution) US. American Psychological Association, 750 First Street Northeast, Washington DC 20002. **Tel** (800)374-2721, (202)336-5600, (subscriptions - (202)336-5600. **ED** Neal Schmitt, PhD. **LC** BF1; .J55. **DD** 158/.05. **NLM** W1 JO543. **CODEN** JAPGBP. **[CCC].** (free). cum. index. **Ad Acc. Pr Rev. Circ:** 6,300. available in microform from Johnson Associates; available on microfilm and microfiche from University Microfilms International (UMI). Documents available from The Genuine Article, UMI Article Clearinghouse.
**Desc:** Covers issues related to stress; decision-making; group effectiveness; group evaluation; leadership effectiveness; team dynamics; human factors; effects of gender/ethnicity/age; student ratings of faculty; lie detection; and eyewitness testimony.

**Ind/Abst** ABI/INFORM Glob. Ed.; ABI Inform Ondisc (Oct. 1971-); Acad. Abstr. Full Text Elite (Jan. 1990-); Acad. Abstr. (Jan. 1990-); Acad. Ind. [Computer File] (1984-); Acad. Search (Jan. 1990-); Appl. Soc. Sci. Index Abstr.; Bus. Index (1985-); Coal Abstr.; Commun. Abstr.; Crim. Justice Abstr.; Crim. Penol. Police Sci. Abstr.; Cumul. Index Nurs. Allied Health Lit.; Curr. Contents Soc. Behav. Sci.; Educ. Index; Educ. Adm. Abstr. (?-?); Ergon. Abstr.; Expand. Acad. Index (1984-); Gen. BusinessFile (1985-); Gen. Period. Index (1985-); Gen. Sci. Source (Jul. 1990-); Health Ref. Cent. (1987-) [Select. Cov.]; High. Educ. Abstr. (1965-); Hum. Resour. Abstr. (?-?); Index Med.; INFO-SOUTH Abstr.; Int. Bibliogr. Sociol.; Int. Labour Doc.; Mag. Search; Middle East Abstr. Index; Multicult. Educ. Abstr. (1983-); Newsp. Period. Abstr. (1986-); Psychol. Abstr. (1926-); PsycINFO; PsycLit; PsycScan: Appl. Psych.; Res. Alert [Full Cov.]; Res. High. Educ. Abstr.; Sage Urban Stud. Abstr (1926-?); School Organ. Manage. Abstr. (Oct. 1971-); Selec. Coop. Index Manage. Period; Soc. Sci. Source (Jul. 1990-); Soc. Sci. Cit. Index [Full Cov.]; Soc. Sci. Index; Soc. Sci. Index Fulltext (May 1988-) [Full Txt.]; Soc. Work Abstr. (?-?); Sociol. Educ. Abstr.; Spec. Educ. Needs Abstr.; SportSearch; Soc. Res. Methodol. Abstr. (1988-); Stud. Women Abstr.; UMI ABI/Inform--Bus. Period. Ondisc (Aug. 1987-) [Full Txt.]; Women Stud. Abstr.; Work Relat. Abstr. (1974-).

US/0021-9029
**JOURNAL OF APPLIED SOCIAL PSYCHOLOGY.** [J. appl. soc. psychol.]. Vol. 1 (Jan./March 1971)-. Periodical. English. sm (24 issues). $517.00 US; $582.00 other. V. H. Winston & Sons Inc., 7961 Eastern Avenue, Suite 202A, Silver Spring MD 20910. **Tel** (301)587-3356. **(Subscription address:** Bellwether Publishing, Ltd, 8640 Guilford Road, Suite 200, Columbia MD 21046.**) ED** Andrew Baum. **LC** HM251; .J52. **DD** 301.1/05. **NLM** W1 JO544G. **CODEN** JASPBX. **[CCC]. Pr Rev. Circ:** 1,000 (ctrl). Documents available from The Genuine Article, UMI Article Clearinghouse.
**Desc:** Devoted to application of experimental behavioral science research to problems of society.
**Ind/Abst** Acad. Search (July 1993-); Appl. Soc. Sci. Index Abstr.; Commun. Abstr. (?-?); Crim. Justice Abstr.; Crim. Penol. Police Sci. Abstr.; Curr. Contents Soc. Behav. Sci.; Educ. Technol. Abstr.; Expand. Acad. Index (1989-); High. Educ. Abstr. (1972-); Index Period. Artic. Relat. Law (19??-19??); INFO-SOUTH Abstr.; Int. Bibliogr. Sociol.; Mag. Search; Manage. Contents; Middle East Abstr. Index; Multicult. Educ. Abstr.; Newsp. Period. Abstr. (1989-); Peace Res. Abstr. J. (1971-1973); Psychol. Abstr. (1971-); PsycINFO; PsycLit; PsycScan: Appl. Psych.; Res. Alert [Full Cov.]; Risk Abstr. (19??-19??); Soc. Sci. Source (Jul. 1993-); Soc. Sci. Cit. Index [Full Cov.]; Soc. Sci. Index; Soc. Sci. Index Fulltext (Sept. 1988-) [Full Txt.]; Sociol. Educ. Abstr.; SPORT Discus; Stud. Women Abstr.; Women Stud. Abstr.

US/1041-3200
**JOURNAL OF APPLIED SPORT PSYCHOLOGY.** [J. appl. sport psychol.]. **Added/Corp** Association for the Advancement of Applied Sport Psychology. Vol. 1, No. 1 (Mar. 1989)-. Periodical. English. Twice a year. $50.00 US; $60.00 other. Allen Press Inc., 810 East 10th Street, PO Box 1897, Lawrence KS 66044-8897. **Tel** (913)843-1221, (800)627-0629, FAX (913)843-1274. **LC** GV706.4; .J66. **DD** 796/.01. **NLM** W1; JO544KAC.
**Ind/Abst** Phys. Educ. Index (1991-); SPORT Discus.

UK/0894-3257
**JOURNAL OF BEHAVIORAL DECISION MAKING.** (BEHAVIORAL DECISION MAKING.). [J. behav. decis. mak.]. **VFOAT** Behavioral Decision Making. Vol. 1 (1988)-. Periodical. English. Four times a year (Mar., June, Sept., Dec.,). $215.00. John Wiley & Sons Ltd., Baffins Lane, Chichester West Sussex PO19 1UD England. **Tel** 0243 779777, FAX 0243 776128 BTG:JWP001, telex 86290 WIBOOKG. **(Subscription address:** John Wiley / Philadelphia, PO Box 7247, Philadelphia PA 19170.**) ED** George Wright and J. Frank Yates. **DD** 001. **NLM** W1; JO555J. **CODEN** BDMAEU. **[CCC].** available on microfilm and microfiche from University Microfilms International (UMI). Documents available from UMI Article Clearinghouse, Ask*IEEE.
**Desc:** Publishes original empirical reports, theoretical analyses, methodological contributions and critical review papers. Also features book and software reviews, abstracts of important articles published elsewhere.
**Ind/Abst** ABI/INFORM Glob. Ed.; ABI Inform Ondisc; INSPEC; Psychol. Abstr.; PsycINFO; PsycLit; Soc. Plann. Policy Dev. Abstr.; Soc. Sci. Cit. Index [Full Cov.]; Sociol. Abstr.

US/1053-0819
**JOURNAL OF BEHAVIORAL EDUCATION.** **See** Education-Special Education and Rehabilitation.

US/0160-7715
**JOURNAL OF BEHAVIORAL MEDICINE.** [J. behav. med.]. **VFOAT** Behavioral Medicine. Vol. 1 (March 1978)-. Periodical. English. Six times a year. $295.00 institutions US, $47.00 individuals US; $345.00 institutions, $55.00 individuals other. Plenum Press, 233 Spring Street, New York NY 10013-1578. **Tel** (212)620-8000, (800)221-9369, FAX (212)463-0742, (212)807-1047, telex 23/421139. **ED** W. Doyle Gentry. **LC** R726.5; .J68. **DD** 616/.001/9. **NLM** W1 JO555P. **CODEN** JBMEDD. **[CCC].** Index available. **Pr Rev.** available on microfilm and microfiche from University Microfilms International (UMI). Documents available from The Genuine Article, BIOSIS Document Express.
**Desc:** An interdisciplinary publication devoted to furthering the understanding of physical health and illness through the knowledge and techniques of the behavioral sciences.
**Ind/Abst** Acad. Search (July 1993-); Annals Behav. Med.; Biol. Abstr.; Cumul. Index Nurs. Allied Health Lit.; Curr. Contents Soc. Behav. Sci.; EMBASE; Index Med.; INFO-SOUTH Abstr.; Mag. Search; Nutr. Res. Newsl.; Psychol. Abstr. (1979-); PsycINFO; PsycLit; PsycScan: Clin. Psych.; Res. Alert [Full Cov.]; Soc. Plann. Policy Dev. Abstr.; Soc. Sci. Cit. Index [Full Cov.]; Soc. Work Abstr. [Select. Cov.]; Sociol. Abstr.; SportSearch.

US/0093-3597
**JOURNAL OF BIO-FEEDBACK, THE.** English. $10.00. Bio-Feedback Technology Inc, 1804 East Ocean Boulevard, Long Beach CA 90802. **LC** BF319.5.B5; J68. **DD** 615/.8. **NLM** W1 JO564BJ.

US/0095-7984
**JOURNAL OF BLACK PSYCHOLOGY, THE.** [J. black psychol.]. **Added/Corp** Association of Black Psychologists (U.S.). Vol. 1 (Aug. 1974)-. Academic Scholarly Publication. English. qt (Feb., May, Aug., Nov.). $129.00. SAGE Periodical Press, 2455 Teller Road, Thousand Oaks CA 91320. **Tel** (805)499-0721, FAX (805)499-0871, telex 100799. **ED** Ann Kathleen Burlew (University of Cincinnati). **LC** E185.625; .J68. **DD** 155.8/4/96. **NLM** W1 JO568T. **Bk Rev. Ad Acc. Acid Free. Circ:** 1,000. available on microfilm and microfiche from University Microfilms International (UMI). Documents available from UMI Article Clearinghouse.
**Desc:** Publishes scholarly contributions within the field of psychology on the experience and behavior of black and other populations from an afrocentric or black perspective, in such areas as cognition, personality, social behavior, child development, education and clinical application.
**Ind/Abst** High. Educ. Abstr. (1981-); Newsp. Period. Abstr. (1992-); Psychol. Abstr. (1974-); PsycINFO; PsycLit.

US/0889-3268
**JOURNAL OF BUSINESS AND PSYCHOLOGY.** (JOURNAL OF BUSINESS AND PSYCHOLOGY / SPONSORED BY THE BUSINESS PSYCHOLOGY RESEARCH INSTITUTE.). [J. bus. psychol.]. **Added/Corp** Business Psychology Research Institute (Mendota, Minn.). **VFOAT** JBP. Vol. 1, No. 1 (Fall 1986)-. Periodical. English. qt. £38.00 (individuals), £170.00 (institutions) UK; $215.00 US; $250.00 other. Human Sciences Press, PO Box 735, 233 Spring Street, New York NY 10013. **Tel** (212)620-8000, FAX (212)807-1047, telex 23421139. **(Subscription address:** Eurospan Ltd., Journals and Serials Division, 3 Henrietta Street, Covent Garden, London WC2E 8LU England.**) ED** John Jones. **LC** WMLC 93/1687. **DD** 158. **NLM** W1; JO57RS. **[CCC].** available on microfilm and microfiche from University Microfilms International (UMI).
**Desc:** Publishes empirical research, case studies and literature reviews dealing with psychological programs implemented in business settings, written by psychologists, behavioral scientists, and organizational specialists employed in business, industry and academia. Articles deal with all aspects of psychology that apply to business settings, including personnel selection and training; organizational assessment and development; risk management and loss control; marketing and consumer behavior research.
**Ind/Abst** Acad. Search (July 1993-); Anbar Account. Finan. Abstr. [Full Txt.]; Anbar Mark. Distr. Abstr. [Full Txt.]; Anbar Top Manage. Abstr. [Full Txt.]; Bus. Period. Index; Bus. Source (Jul. 1993-); Commun. Abstr.; Hum. Resour. Abstr.; INFO-SOUTH Abstr.; Mag. Search; Manage. Bibliogr. Rev.; Oper. Prod. Manage. Abstr. [Full Txt.]; Person. Train. Abstr. [Full Txt.]; Psychol. Abstr. (1986-); PsycINFO; PsycLit; Wilson Bus. Abstr.; Women Manage. Rev. [Full Txt.]; Work Relat. Abstr.

US/1069-0727
**JOURNAL OF CAREER ASSESSMENT.** **See** Occupations and Careers.

US/1053-0800
**JOURNAL OF CHILD AND ADOLESCENT GROUP THERAPY.** [J. child adolesc. group ther.]. Vol. 1, No. 1 (Mar. 1991)-. Periodical. English. qt. $115.00 US; $135.00 other. Human Sciences Press, PO Box 735, 233 Spring Street, New York NY 10013. **Tel** (212)620-8000, FAX (212)807-1047, telex 23421139. **(Subscription address:** Eurospan Ltd., Journals and Serials Division, 3 Henrietta Street, Covent Garden, London WC2E 8LU England.**) ED** Edward Soo. **LC** RJ505.G7; J68. **DD** 618. **NLM** W1; JO583JE. **CODEN** JAGTEM. **[CCC].**
**Desc:** Devoted to the publication of original papers on critical issues in child, adolescent, and parent group therapy from a diverse range of approaches. The journal publishes not only clinical reports, illustrations of new developments, and research that contributes to the advancements of therapeutic results, but also articles on theoretical issues, applications of group therapy and different group methods, and the group process. In addition, it integrates new ideas, concepts, and innovations from other disciplines that enhance the treatment of the child and adolescent in a group.
**Ind/Abst** Soc. Work Abstr. [Select. Cov.].

US/1044-5463
**JOURNAL OF CHILD AND ADOLESCENT PSYCHOPHARMACOLOGY.** **See** Medical Science and Technology-Psychiatry.

US/0748-8793
**JOURNAL OF CHILD AND ADOLESCENT PSYCHOTHERAPY.** ***Ceased.*** [J. child adolesc. psychother.]. **VFOAT** Child and Adolescent Psychotherapy; JCAP. Vol. 1, No. 1 (1984)-(1988). Periodical. English. qt. Rivendell Foundation, 5180 Park/Suite 300, Memphis TN 38119. **Tel** (901)685-8142. **ED** Robert W Wood and John Bassett. **DD** 616. **NLM** W1; JO583K. Index available. **Bk Rev. Circ:** 10,000 (ctrl).
**Desc:** A forum for all disciplines in child and adolescent mental health care in which various professionals may publish to promote child and adolescent mental health care.
**Ind/Abst** Child Dev. Abstr. Bibliogr.; Psychol. Abstr.; PsycINFO; PsycLit; Sage Fam. Stud. Abstr. (?-?).

UK/0373-8086
**JOURNAL OF CHILD PSYCHOLOGY AND PSYCHIATRY.** [J. Child Psychol. Psychiatry]. (1???)-. English. Pergamon Press, An Imprint of Elsevier Science Ltd., The Boulevard, Langford Lane, Kidlington, Oxford OX5 1GB United Kingdom. **Tel** 011 44 865 843000, 011 44 865 843699, FAX 011 44 865 843010.
**Ind/Abst** Br. Educ. Index.

UK/0021-9630
**JOURNAL OF CHILD PSYCHOLOGY AND PSYCHIATRY AND ALLIED DISCIPLINES.** [J. child psychol. psychiatry allied discipl.]. **Added/Corp** Association of Child Psychology and Psychiatry. **VFOAT** Journal of Child Psychology and Psychiatry. Vol. 1 (Jan. 1960)-. Academic Scholarly Publication. English. Eight times a year. $346.00 The Americas; £232.00 other. Pergamon Press, An Imprint of Elsevier Science Ltd., The Boulevard, Langford Lane, Kidlington, Oxford OX5 1GB United Kingdom. **Tel** 011 44 865 843000, 011 44 865 843699, FAX 011 44 865 843010. **(Subscription address:** Elsevier Science Ltd. Oxford Fulfillment Centre, PO Box 800, Kidlington, Oxford OX5 1DX United Kingdom.**) ED** Eric Taylor and Dorothy Bishop. **LC** RJ499.A1; J6. **NLM** W1 JO584F. **CODEN** JPPDAI. **[CCC]. Pr Rev.** available on microfilm from Microfilms International Marketing Corp.; available on microfilm and microfiche from University Microfilms International (UMI); available on microfiche from the publisher. Documents available from The Genuine Article, BIOSIS Document Express.
**Desc:** Primarily concerned with child and adolescent psychology and psychiatry, including experimental and developmental studies and especially developmental psychopathology. Brings together interdisciplinary contributions so that more is known about the mental life and behaviour of children.
**Ind/Abst** Appl. Soc. Sci. Index Abstr.; Biol. Abstr.; Crim. Penol. Police Sci. Abstr.; Cumul. Index Nurs. Allied Health Lit.; Curr. Contents Soc. Behav. Sci.; Curr. Index J. Educ.; Dev. Med. Child Neurol. (1960-); Educ. Index; EMBASE; Index Med.; Int. Nurs. Index; Mag. Search; Middle East Abstr. Index; Life Sci. Collect.; Psychol. Abstr. (1960-); PsycINFO; PsycLit; PsycScan: Develop. Psych.; Res. Alert [Full Cov.]; Soc. Plann. Policy Dev. Abstr.; Soc. Sci. Cit. Index [Full Cov.]; Sociol. Abstr.; Spec. Educ. Needs Abstr.

US/0749-4025
**JOURNAL OF CLASSROOM INTERACTION, THE.** **See** Education.

NE/0168-8634
**JOURNAL OF CLINICAL AND EXPERIMENTAL NEUROPSYCHOLOGY.** **See** Medical Science and Technology-Neurology.

US/0047-228X
**JOURNAL OF CLINICAL CHILD PSYCHOLOGY.** [J. clin. child psychol.]. **Added/Corp** American Psychological Association. Section on Clinical Child Psychology. Vol. 1 (Winter 1972)-. Periodical. English. qt. $215.00 US & Canada; $240.00 other. Lawrence Erlbaum Associates, 365 Broadway, Suite 102, Hillsdale NJ 07642. **Tel** (201)666-4110, (800)926-6579, FAX (201)666-2394. **ED** Donald K Roth and Jan Loney. **LC** BF721; .J635. **DD** 362.7. **NLM** W1 JO587B. **CODEN** JCCPD3. **Ad Acc. Pr Rev.** available on microfilm and microfiche from University Microfilms International (UMI). Documents available from The Genuine Article, UMI Article Clearinghouse. ***Supersedes*** *Clinical Child Psychology Newsletter.*
**Ind/Abst** Acad. Search (Jan. 1994-); Appl. Soc. Sci. Index Abstr.; Commun. Abstr.; Curr. Contents Soc. Behav. Sci.; Dev. Med. Child Neurol.; Except. Child Educ. Resour.; Expand. Acad. Index (1989-); INFO-SOUTH Abstr.; Mag. Search; Middle East Abstr. Index; Newsp.

Period. Abstr. (1989-); Psychol. Abstr. (1972-); PsycINFO; PsycLit; PsycScan: Clin. Psych.; PsycScan: Develop. Psych.; Res. Alert [Full Cov.]; Sage Fam. Stud. Abstr.; Soc. Sci. Source (Jul. 1993-); Soc. Sci. Cit. Index [Full Cov.]; Soc. Sci. Index; Soc. Sci. Index Fulltext (Sept. 1988-) [Full Txt.]; Women Stud. Abstr.

●US
**JOURNAL OF CLINICAL GEROPSYCHOLOGY.** (1994)-. Periodical. English. Four times a year. $125.00 institutions, $40.00 individuals US; $145.00 institutions, $47.00 individuals other. Plenum Press, 233 Spring Street, New York NY 10013-1578. **Tel** (212)620-8000, (800)221-9369, FAX (212)463-0742, (212)807-1047, telex 23/421139.

US/0021-9762
**JOURNAL OF CLINICAL PSYCHOLOGY.** [J. clin. psychol.]. Vol. 1 (Jan. 1945)-. Academic Scholarly Publication. English. bm (6 issues). $140.00 US; $153.50 other. Clinical Psychology Publishing Company, 4 Conant Square, Brandon VT 05733. **Tel** (802)247-6871, (800)433-8234. **ED** Vladimir Pishkin. **LC** RC321; .J74. **DD** 616.805. **NLM** W1 JO591. **CODEN** JCPYAO. Index available (bound in last volume of each issue). **Bk Rev. Ad Acc. Circ:** 2,400. available on microfilm and microfiche from University Microfilms International (UMI). Documents available from The Genuine Article, BIOSIS Document Express, UMI Article Clearinghouse. ***Superseded in part by*** *Journal of Community Psychology, 0090-4392.*
**Desc:** Current research in clinical psychology.
**Ind/Abst** Acad. Abstr. Full Text Elite (Jan. 1992-); Acad. Abstr. (Jan. 1992-); Acad. Search (Jan. 1992-); Appl. Soc. Sci. Index Abstr.; Biol. Abstr.; Chicano Index; Commun. Abstr. (?-?); Crim. Justice Abstr.; Crim. Penol. Police Sci. Abstr.; Cumul. Index Nurs. Allied Health Lit.; Curr. Contents Soc. Behav. Sci.; Curr. Index J. Educ.; Educ. Adm. Abstr. (?-?); EMBASE; Expand. Acad. Index (1989-); High. Educ. Abstr. (1965-); Hum. Resour. Abstr. (?-?); Index Med.; Index Period. Artic. Relat. Law (19??-19??); Mag. Search; Middle East Abstr. Index; Newsp. Period. Abstr. (1989-); Nutr. Abstr. Rev., Ser. B, Live Feeds and Feed.; Nutr. Abstr. Rev., Ser. A, Hum. Exp.; Life Sci. Collect.; Psychol. Abstr. (1945-); PsycINFO; PsycLit; PsycScan: Clin. Psych.; Res. Alert [Full Cov.]; Sage Fam. Stud. Abstr.; Sage Urban Stud. Abstr (?-?); Soc. Plann. Policy Dev. Abstr.; Soc. Sci. Source (Jan. 1992-); Soc. Sci. Cit. Index [Full Cov.]; Soc. Sci. Index; Soc. Sci. Index Fulltext (Sept. 1988-) [Full Txt.]; Soc. Work Abstr. [Select. Cov.]; SportSearch; Women Stud. Abstr.

●US/1068-9583
**JOURNAL OF CLINICAL PSYCHOLOGY IN MEDICAL SETTINGS.** (1994)-. Periodical. English. Four times a year. $100.00 institutions, $40.00 individuals US; $115.00 institutions, $47.00 individuals other. Plenum Press, 233 Spring Street, New York NY 10013-1578. **Tel** (212)620-8000, (800)221-9369, FAX (212)463-0742, (212)807-1047, telex 23/421139.

US/0271-0749
**JOURNAL OF CLINICAL PSYCHOPHARMACOLOGY.** **See** Pharmacy and Pharmacology.

US/0889-8391
**JOURNAL OF COGNITIVE PSYCHOTHERAPY, THE.** [J. cogn. psychother.]. Vol. 1 No. 1 (Spring 1987)-. Periodical. English. qt. $39.00 (individuals, 1 year), $69.00 (individuals, 2 year), $74.00 (institutions, 1 year), $129.00 (institutions, 2 year) US; $44.00 (individuals, 1 year), $79.00 (individuals, 2 year), $85.00 (institutions, 1 year), $149.00 (institutions, 2 year) other. Springer Publishing Company, 536 Broadway, New York NY 10012-3955. **Tel** (212)431-4370, FAX (212)941-7842. **ED** E. Thomas Dowd and Windy Dryden. **DD** 616. **NLM** W1; JO5926G. **[CCC]. Bk Rev. Ad Acc, Adv Mgr:** Beth Albert. **Pr Rev. Circ:** 600. ***Formed by the union of*** *Cognitive Behaviorist* ***and*** *British Journal of Cognitive Psychotherapy, 0264-5432.*
**Desc:** Contains case studies emphasizing therapeutic procedures, measures of outcome, and follow-up; theoretical articles with clinical implications; specific techniques; practice with specific populations; and clinical relevance of topical research.
**Ind/Abst** EMBASE; Psychol. Abstr. (1987-); PsycINFO (1990-); PsycLit.

US/8756-8225
**JOURNAL OF COLLEGE STUDENT PSYCHOTHERAPY.** [J. college stud. psychother.]. Vol. 1, No. 1 (Fall 1986)-. Periodical. English. qt (Published during the academic year). $160.00 US; $224.00 other. The Haworth Press Inc, 10 Alice Street, Binghamton NY 13904-1580. **Tel** (607)722-5857, (800)3-HAWORTH, FAX (607)722-1424. **ED** Leighton Whitaker (editor's address: Psychological Services, Swarthmore College, Swarthmore, PA 19081). **DD** 616. **NLM** W1; JO5927. **Bk Rev. Ad Acc. Pr Rev. Acid Free. Circ:** 346. available on microfilm and microfiche from University Microfilms International (UMI). Documents available from Haworth Document Delivery Service.
**Desc:** Dedicated to enhancing the lives of college and university students by stimulation high quality practice, theory, and research in mental and personal development. Serves to promote greater care for and knowledge of students.
**Ind/Abst** Appl. Soc. Sci. Index Abstr.; Educ. Adm. Abstr.; High. Educ. Abstr. (1986-); Hum. Resour. Abstr. (?-?); Psychol. Abstr. (1986-); PsycINFO; PsycLit; Soc. Plann. Policy Dev. Abstr.; Soc. Work Abstr. [Select. Cov.]; Spec. Educ. Needs Abstr.; Stud. Women Abstr.

US/0734-4368
**JOURNAL OF COMMUNICATION THERAPY.** [J. commun. ther.]. Vol. 1, No. 1 (1982)-. Periodical. English. sa. $40.00 (institutions), $20.00 (individuals), $15.00 (students). Journal of Communication Therapy, University of Houston, Clear Lake, Houston TX 77058. **Tel** (713)283-3311. **ED** Tulsi B. Saral. **LC** RC475; .J58. **DD** 616.89/14. cum. index. **Bk Rev. Ad Acc. Circ:** 300 (ctrl).
**Desc:** Interdisciplinary journal presenting theoretical articles, case studies, research reports and book reviews on the role and scope of intrapersonal, interpersonal, intercultural and transpersonal communication in the therapeutic process.

UK/1052-9284
**JOURNAL OF COMMUNITY AND APPLIED SOCIAL PSYCHOLOGY.** **See** Sociology.

●II/0970-1346
**JOURNAL OF COMMUNITY GUIDANCE AND RESEARCH.** Vol. 9 No. 1 (Jan. 1992)-. Periodical. English. tq. $75.00. Journal of Community Guidance and Research, 14 Ranganathan Gardens, Annanagar Madras 600040 India. **LC** RA790.7.I5; I53. ***Continues*** *Indian Journal of Community Guidance Service.*

US/0090-4392
**JOURNAL OF COMMUNITY PSYCHOLOGY.** [J. commun. psychol.]. Vol. 1 (Jan. 1973)-. Periodical. English. Four times a year. $140.00 US; $153.50 other. Clinical Psychology Publishing Company, 4 Conant Square, Brandon VT 05733. **Tel** (802)247-6871, (800)433-8234. **ED** J. R. Newbrough. **LC** RC467; .J65. **DD** 362.2/2/05. **NLM** W1 JO593S. **CODEN** JCPSD9. Index available (bound in last volume of each issue). **Bk Rev. Ad Acc. Pr Rev. Circ:** 700. available on microfilm and microfiche from University Microfilms International (UMI). Documents available from The Genuine Article. ***Supersedes in part*** *Journal of Clinical Psychology, 0021-9762.*
**Desc:** Research and opinions in community psychology.
**Ind/Abst** Commun. Abstr. (?-?); Crim. Justice Abstr.; Curr. Contents Soc. Behav. Sci.; High. Educ. Abstr. (1978-19??); Hospit. Health Admin. Index (1975-1987); Hum. Resour. Abstr.; Index Med.; J. Plan. Lit.; Middle East Abstr. Index; Psychol. Abstr. (1973-); PsycINFO; PsycLit; Res. Alert [Full Cov.]; Risk Abstr. (19??-19??); Sage Urban Stud. Abstr (?-?); Soc. Plann. Policy Dev. Abstr.; Soc. Sci. Cit. Index [Full Cov.]; Soc. Work Abstr. (?-?); Sociol. Abstr. (?-?); Women Stud. Abstr.

US/0735-7036
**JOURNAL OF COMPARATIVE PSYCHOLOGY (1983).** (JOURNAL OF COMPARATIVE PSYCHOLOGY.). [J. comp. psychol.]. **Added/Corp** American Psychological Association. Vol. 97, No. 1 (Mar. 1983)-. Academic Scholarly Publication. English. qt. $100.00 (nonmember, institution) US. American Psychological Association, 750 First Street Northeast, Washington DC 20002. **Tel** (800)374-2721, (202)336-5600, (subscriptions - (202)336-5600. **ED** Gordon G. Gallup, PhD. **LC** BF1; .J572. **DD** 156/.05. **CODEN** JCOPDT. **[CCC]. Ad Acc. Pr Rev. Circ:** 2,100. available on microfilm and microfiche from University Microfilms International (UMI). Documents available from The Genuine Article, UMI Article Clearinghouse, CASDDS. ***Continues in part*** *Journal of Comparative and Physiological Psychology, 0021-9940.*
**Desc:** Journal for research into the behavior and cognition of organisms as they relate to evolution, ecology, adaptation and development.
**Ind/Abst** Acad. Abstr. Full Text Elite (Jan. 1992-); Acad. Abstr. (Jan. 1992-); Acad. Search (Jan. 1992-); Anim. Breed. Abstr.; Biol. Agric. Index; Chem. Abstr. (1983-); Curr. Aware. Biol. Sci., CABS; Curr. Contents Life Sci.; Ecol. Abstr.; EMBASE; Expand. Acad. Index (1989-); Index Med.; INFO-SOUTH Abstr.; INIS Atomindex [Micro.]; Mag. Search; Newsp. Period. Abstr. (1991-); Nutr. Abstr. Rev., Ser. B, Live Feeds and Feed.; Poult. Abstr.; Psychol. Abstr. (1983-); PsycINFO; PsycLit; Ref. Upd. Deluxe Ed.; Res. Alert [Full Cov.]; Sci. Cit. Index; SCISEARCH; Soc. Sci. Source (Jan. 1992-); Soc. Sci. Cit. Index [Select. Cov.]; Soc. Sci. Index; Soc. Sci. Index Fulltext (Dec. 1988-) [Full Txt.].

●US/1072-0537
**JOURNAL OF CONSTRUCTIVIST PSYCHOLOGY.** [J. constr. psych.]. Vol. 7, No. 1 (Jan.-Mar. 1994)-. Periodical. English. qt. £94.00 UK; $155.00 other. Taylor & Francis Ltd., Rankine Road, Basingstoke Hampshire, RG24 8PR United Kingdom. **Tel** 011 44 256 840366, FAX 011 44 256 479438, telex 858540. **(Subscription address:** Taylor & Francis Inc., 1900 Frost Road, Suite 101, Bristol PA 19007-1598.) **ED** Robert A. Neimeyer and Greg J. Neimeyer. **LC** BF698.9.P47; I58. **DD** 150.19/8. **CODEN** JCPYES. ***Continues*** *International Journal of Personal Construct Psychology, 0893-603X.*
**Desc:** Provides a professional forum for the "postmodern" emphasis on the role of language, human systems and personal knowledge in the construction of social realities. Embraces diverse expressions of constructivism such as personal construct theory, structural-developmental and language-based approaches to psychotherapy and narrative psychology.

US/0022-006X
**JOURNAL OF CONSULTING AND CLINICAL PSYCHOLOGY.** [J. consult. clin. psychol.]. **Added/Corp** American Psychological Association. Vol. 32, (Feb. 1968)-. Academic Scholarly Publication. English. Six times a year. $273.00 (nonmember, institution) US. American Psychological Association, 750 First Street Northeast, Washington DC 20002. **Tel** (800)374-2721, (202)336-5600, (subscriptions - (202)336-5600. **ED** Larry E. Beutler, Ph.D. **LC** BF1; .J575. **DD** 616.89/005. **NLM** W1 JO595R. **CODEN** JCLPBC. **[CCC]. Ad Acc. Pr Rev. Circ:** 11,000. available on microfilm and microfiche from University Microfilms International (UMI). Documents available from The Genuine Article, BIOSIS Document Express, UMI Article Clearinghouse. ***Continues*** *Journal of Consulting Psychology, 0095-8891.* ***Continued in part by*** *Psychological Assessment, 1040-3590.*
**Desc:** Readers will find articles on development, validity and use of techniques of diagnosis and treatment; studies of geriatric, hospital, prison and rehabilitation populations; cross-cultural and demographic studies of behavior disorders; behavior studies of gender, ethnicity, of sexual orientation of clinical that bear on the diagnosis, treatment and prevention of clinical disorders.
**Ind/Abst** Acad. Abstr. Full Text Elite (Jan. 1990-); Acad. Abstr. (Jan. 1990-); Acad. Ind. [Computer File] (1987-); Acad. Search (Jan. 1990-); Annals Behav. Med.; Appl. Soc. Sci. Index Abstr.; Biol. Abstr.; Chicano Index; Crim. Justice Abstr.; Crim. Penol. Police Sci. Abstr.; Cumul. Index Nurs. Allied Health Lit.; Curr. Contents Soc. Behav. Sci.; Curr. Index J. Educ.; EMBASE; Expand. Acad. Index (1987-); High. Educ. Abstr. (1968-); Index Med.; INFO-SOUTH Abstr.; Mag. Search; Middle East Abstr. Index; Multicult. Educ. Abstr.; Newsp. Period. Abstr. (1986-); Life Sci. Collect.; Psychol. Abstr. (1968-); PsycINFO; PsycLit; PsycScan: Clin. Psych.; Res. Alert [Full Cov.]; Risk Abstr. (19??-19??); Sage Fam. Stud. Abstr. (?-?); Soc. Sci. Source (Jul. 1990-); Soc. Sci. Cit. Index [Full Cov.]; Soc. Sci. Index; Soc. Sci. Index Fulltext (Aug. 1988-) [Full Txt.]; Soc. Work Abstr. [Select. Cov.]; Spec. Educ. Needs Abstr.; SportSearch; Women Stud. Abstr.

US/0022-0116
**JOURNAL OF CONTEMPORARY PSYCHOTHERAPY.** [J. contemp. psychother.]. **Added/Corp** Long Island Consultation Center. Long Island Institute for Mental Health. Vol. 1 (Fall 1968)-. Periodical. English. qt. $215.00 US; $250.00 other. Human Sciences Press, PO Box 735, 233 Spring Street, New York NY 10013. **Tel** (212)620-8000, FAX (212)807-1047, telex 23421139. **(Subscription address:** Eurospan Ltd., Journals and Serials Division, 3 Henrietta Street, Covent Garden, London WC2E 8LU England.) **ED** Erwin Randolph Parson. **LC** RC475; .J6. **DD** 616.89/1/05. **NLM** W1 JO595V. **CODEN** JCPTBA. **[CCC].** available on microfilm and microfiche from University Microfilms International (UMI). ***Continues*** *Journal of the Long Island Consultation Center, 0458-2365.*
**Desc:** Examines current and significant advances in therapeutic concepts and methodology. It has established an interdisciplinary forum with an eclectic approach to the promotion of emotional health and maturity.
**Ind/Abst** Psychol. Abstr. (1968-); PsycINFO; PsycLit; Soc. Work Abstr. [Select. Cov.].

US/0887-5502
**JOURNAL OF COUNSELING AND HUMAN SERVICE PROFESSIONS.** [J. couns. hum. serv. prof.]. **Added/Corp** Minnesota Association for Counseling and Leadership. Vol. 1, No. 1 (May 1986)-. Periodical. English. Twice a year. $20.00 institutions; $9.00 individuals. St. Cloud State University / Department of Applied Psychology, c/o T. Peterson, St. Cloud MN 56301. **DD** 158.

US/0022-0167
**JOURNAL OF COUNSELING PSYCHOLOGY.** [J. couns. psychol.]. **Added/Corp** American Psychological Association. Vol. 1 (Feb. 1954)-. Periodical. English. qt. $130.00 (nonmember, institution) US. American Psychological Association, 750 First Street Northeast, Washington DC 20002. **Tel** (800)374-2721, (202)336-5600, (subscriptions - (202)336-5600. **ED** Lenore W. Harmon, PhD. **LC** BF637.C6; J6. **DD** 150.13. **NLM** W1 JO602. **[CCC].** Index available (free). **Ad Acc. Pr Rev. Circ:** 6,300. available on microfilm and microfiche from University Microfilms International (UMI). Documents available from The Genuine Article, UMI Article Clearinghouse.
**Desc:** Publishes articles on counseling in colleges and universities private and public counseling agencies; and in business, school, religious and military settings. Particular attention is given to empirical studies about processes and interventions, studies on the evaluation and application of counseling programs and theoretical

articles.
**Ind/Abst** ABI/INFORM Glob. Ed.; ABI Inform Ondisc (May 1971-July 1975); Abstr. Res. Pastor. Care Couns. (19??-); Acad. Abstr. Full Text Elite (July 1990-); Acad. Abstr. (July 1990-); Acad. Search (July 1990-); Appl. Soc. Sci. Index Abstr.; Chicano Index; Crim. Justice Abstr.; Curr. Contents Soc. Behav. Sci.; Curr. Index J. Educ.; Educ. Index; Educ. Adm. Abstr. (?-?); Expand. Acad. Index (1989-); High. Educ. Abstr. (1965-); Hum. Resour. Abstr. (?-?); INFO-SOUTH Abstr.; Mag. Search; Middle East Abstr. Index; Multicult. Educ. Abstr.; Newsp. Period. Abstr. (1986-); Psychol. Abstr. (1954-); PsycINFO; PsycLit; PsycScan: Clin. Psych.; Res. Alert [Full Cov.]; Res. High. Educ. Abstr.; Soc. Sci. Source (Jul. 1990-); Soc. Sci. Cit. Index [Full Cov.]; Soc. Sci. Index; Soc. Sci. Index Fulltext (Oct. 1988-) [Full Txt.]; Soc. Work Abstr. [Select. Cov.]; Spec. Educ. Needs Abstr.; Stud. Women Abstr.; Tech. Educ. Train. Abstr.; Women Stud. Abstr.; Work Relat. Abstr.

US/0897-4446
**JOURNAL OF COUPLES THERAPY.** **See** Family and Marriage.

US/0022-0175
**JOURNAL OF CREATIVE BEHAVIOR, THE.** (THE JOURNAL OF CREATIVE BEHAVIOR.). [J. creat. behav.]. **Added/Corp** Creative Education Foundation. Vol. 1 (Winter 1967)-. Periodical. English. qt. $38.00 US; $41.00 Canada and Mexico; $48.00 other. Creative Education Foundation, 1050 Union Road, Buffalo NY 14224. **Tel** (716)675-3181, FAX (716)675-3209. **ED** Grace A. Guzzetta. **LC** BF408; .J65. **DD** 153.3/5/55. **NLM** W1 JO604. Index available. **Pr Rev. Circ:** 2,500 (ctrl). available on microfilm and microfiche from University Microfilms International (UMI). Documents available from The Genuine Article.
**Desc:** Devoted to the serious general reader with vocational/avocational interests in the fields of creativity and problem solving. Its articles deal with methods to foster creative productivity giftedness, testing, creativity in business and industry, development of creative curricula, creativity in the arts and the sciences and reviews of the literature on creativity and problem solving.
**Ind/Abst** Appl. Soc. Sci. Index Abstr.; Contents Pages Educ.; Curr. Contents Soc. Behav. Sci.; Curr. Index J. Educ.; Educ. Index; Except. Child Educ. Resour.; Except. Hum. Exp.; High. Educ. Abstr. (1969-19??); Psychol. Abstr. (1967-); PsycINFO; PsycLit; Res. Alert [Full Cov.]; Soc. Plann. Policy Dev. Abstr.; Soc. Sci. Cit. Index [Full Cov.]; Soc. Work Abstr. (Summer 1987-) [Select. Cov.]; Sociol. Abstr.

US/0022-0221
**JOURNAL OF CROSS-CULTURAL PSYCHOLOGY.** [J. cross-cult. psychol.]. **Added/Corp** Western Washington State College. Center for Cross-Cultural Research. International Association for Cross-Cultural Psychology. Vol. 1 (March 1970)-. Periodical. English. bm. $198.00. SAGE Periodical Press, 2455 Teller Road, Thousand Oaks CA 91320. **Tel** (805)499-0721, FAX (805)499-0871, telex 100799. **ED** John E. Williams and Walter J. Lonner. **LC** BF728; .J65. **DD** 155.8/05. **NLM** W1 JO612A. **CODEN** JCPGB5. **Pr Rev. Acid Free.** available on microfilm and microfiche from University Microfilms International (UMI). Documents available from The Genuine Article, UMI Article Clearinghouse.
**Desc:** Presents behavioral and social research concentrating on psychological phenomena as differentially conditioned by culture, focusing on individual members of cultural groups.
**Ind/Abst** Abstr. Anthropol.; Appl. Soc. Sci. Index Abstr.; Chicano Index; Commun. Abstr. (?-?); Crim. Penol. Police Sci. Abstr.; Curr. Index J. Educ.; Expand. Acad. Index (1992-); High. Educ. Abstr. (19??-19??); Hum. Resour. Abstr. (?-?); Middle East Abstr. Index; Multicult. Educ. Abstr.; Newsp. Period. Abstr. (1992-); Peace Res. Abstr. J. (1970-1985); Psychol. Abstr. (1970-); PsycINFO; PsycLit; Res. Alert [Full Cov.]; Sage Fam. Stud. Abstr.; Soc. Plann. Policy Dev. Abstr.; Soc. Sci. Cit. Index [Full Cov.]; Sociol. Abstr.; Stud. Women Abstr.; Women Stud. Abstr.

US
**JOURNAL OF DEPRESSION & STRESS.** **See** Medical Science and Technology-Psychiatry.

US/0272-4316
**JOURNAL OF EARLY ADOLESCENCE, THE.** [J. early adolesc.]. Vol. 1, No. 1 (Spring 1981)-. Periodical. English. qt (Feb., May, Aug., Nov.). $123.00. SAGE Periodical Press, 2455 Teller Road, Thousand Oaks CA 91320. **Tel** (805)499-0721, FAX (805)499-0871, telex 100799. **ED** E. Ellen Thornburg. **LC** HQ796; .J624. **DD** 305.2/35/0973. **NLM** W1 JO626N. Index available. cum. index. **Bk Rev. Ad Acc. Acid Free. Circ:** 1,000 (ctrl). available on microfilm and microfiche from University Microfilms International (UMI).
**Desc:** Provides a well-balanced, interdisciplinary, international perspective in early adolescent development (ages 10-14) and the factors affecting it.
**Ind/Abst** AGRICOLA [Select. Cov.]; Chicano Index; Child Dev. Abstr. Bibliogr.; Curr. Lit. Fam. Plan.; Educ. Adm. Abstr.; Psychol. Abstr. (1981-); PsycINFO; PsycLit; Sage Fam. Stud. Abstr.; Soc. Plann. Policy Dev. Abstr.; Soc. Work Abstr. [Select. Cov.]; Sociol. Abstr.

II/0022-0590
**JOURNAL OF EDUCATION & PSYCHOLOGY.** (1942)-. Periodical. English. qt. $20.00. Registrar Sardar Patel University, Vallabh Vidyanagar 38 120, Gujarat 388001 India. **Tel** 011 91 2692 388120. **(Subscription address:** Prints India, 11 Darya Ganj, New Delhi 110002 India.**) ED** T K N Menon. **LC** L61; .J5. **DD** 370.1505. **NLM** W1 JO627M. **Ad Acc. Circ:** 3,000 (ctrl).
**Ind/Abst** Appl. Soc. Sci. Index Abstr.; Commun. Abstr. (?-?).

US/0022-0663
**JOURNAL OF EDUCATIONAL PSYCHOLOGY.** [J. educ. psychol.]. **Added/Corp** American Psychological Association. Vol. 1 (Jan. 1910)-. Periodical. English. Four times a year (Mar., June, Sept., Dec.). $170.00 (nonmember, institution) US. American Psychological Association, 750 First Street Northeast, Washington DC 20002. **Tel** (800)374-2721, (202)336-5600, (subscriptions - (202)336-5600. **ED** Joel R. Levin, PhD. **LC** LB1051.A2; J6. **DD** 370.15/05. **NLM** W1 JO628. **CODEN** JLEPAX. **[CCC].** Index available. **Pr Rev. Circ:** 5,000. available in microform from University Microfilms International (UMI); and Johnson Associates. Documents available from UMI Article Clearinghouse.
**Desc:** Contains original research relevant to all levels of instruction including learning, cognition and development; testing and individual differences; classroom and social processes; instructional use of computers and other technology; empirical data, technology, and practical implications. Readers learn of innovative primary research, integrative and empirical studies.
**Ind/Abst** Acad. Abstr. Full Text Elite (July 1990-); Acad. Abstr. (July 1990-); Acad. Ind. [Computer File] (1987-); Acad. Search (July 1990-); AGRICOLA [Select. Cov.]; Contents Pages Educ.; Curr. Contents Soc. Behav. Sci.; Curr. Index J. Educ.; Educ. Index; Educ. Adm. Abstr. (?-?); Educ. Technol. Abstr.; Expand. Acad. Index (1987-); High. Educ. Abstr. (1965-); Hum. Resour. Abstr. (?-?); INFO-SOUTH Abstr.; Lang. Teach.; Middle East Abstr. Index; Multicult. Educ. Abstr.; Newsp. Period. Abstr. (1986-); Psychol. Abstr. (1926-); PsycINFO; PsycLit; PsycScan: Develop. Psych.; Res. Alert [Full Cov.]; Res. High. Educ. Abstr.; Romant. Move.; School Organ. Manage. Abstr.; Soc. Sci. Cit. Index [Full Cov.]; Sociol. Educ. Abstr.; Spec. Educ. Needs Abstr.; Stud. Women Abstr.; Women Stud. Abstr.

●US/1063-4266
**JOURNAL OF EMOTIONAL AND BEHAVIORAL DISORDERS.** [J. emot. behav. disord.]. Vol. 1, No. 1 (Jan. 1993)-. Periodical. English. qt. $85.00 (institutions), $39.00 (individuals) US & Canada; $95.00 other. Pro-Ed Inc., 8700 Shoal Creek Boulevard, Austin TX 78757-6897. **Tel** (512)451-3246, FAX (512)451-8542. **LC** RJ499.A1; J63. **DD** 618.92/89/005. **NLM** W1; JO638N. **[CCC].**

●US/1064-7023
**JOURNAL OF EMOTIONAL AND BEHAVIORAL PROBLEMS.** [J. emot. behav. probl.]. **Added/Corp** National Educational Service (U.S.). **VFOAT** JEB-P. Vol. 1, Issue 1 (Spring 1992)-. Periodical. English. Four times a year (Feb., May, Aug., Nov.). $35.00 (individual), $70.00 (institution), US; $40.00 (individual), $75.00 (institution), Canada & Mexico; $50.00 (individual), $85.00 (institution), other. National Educational Services, 1610 West 3rd Street, Box 8, Bloomington IN 47404. **Tel** (800)733-6786, (812)336-7700, FAX (812)336-7790. **ED** Dr. Larry Brendt and Dr. Nick Long. **LC** HV741; .A16. **DD** 362.7/4/097305. **Bk Rev. Ad Acc, Adv Mgr:** Nancy Shin, **Tel** (812)336-7700. **Pr Rev. Circ:** 2,000.
**Desc:** An interdisciplinary journal combining theory and practice by networking practitioners and policy leaders from diverse backgrounds who serve children and youth in conflict with self, family, school, and community.

UK/0272-4944
**JOURNAL OF ENVIRONMENTAL PSYCHOLOGY.** [J. environ. psychol.]. Vol. 1, No. 1 (Mar. 1981)-. Academic Scholarly Publication. English. qt (4 issues). $165.00. Academic Press Ltd., A Division of Harcourt Brace & Company Ltd., 24-28 Oval Road, London NW1 7DX England. **Tel** 071 267 4466, FAX 071 482 2293, 071 485 4752, telex 25775 ACPRES G. **(Subscription address:** Harcourt Brace & Company, Ltd., Foots Cray, High Street, Sidcup Kent DA14 5HP England.**) ED** D. V. Canter, K. H. Craik and C. Spencer. **LC** BF353. **DD** 155.9/05. **NLM** W1 JO644BFN. **CODEN** JEPSEO. **[CCC]. Pr Rev.** Documents available from The Genuine Article, BIOSIS Document Express.
**Desc:** Directed toward individuals with an interest in the study of the transactions and interrelationships between people and their sociophysical surroundings (including man-made and natural environments) and the relation of this field to other social and biological sciences and to the environmental professions.
**Ind/Abst** Appl. Soc. Sci. Index Abstr.; Archit. Period. Index (1981-); Biol. Abstr. (1986-); Curr. Contents Soc. Behav. Sci.; J. Plan. Lit.; Leis. Recreat. Tour. Abstr.; Psychol. Abstr. (1981-); PsycINFO; PsycLit; PsycScan: Appl. Psych.; Res. Alert [Full Cov.]; Sage Urban Stud. Abstr; Soc. Sci. Cit. Index [Full Cov.].

US/0737-4828
**JOURNAL OF EVOLUTIONARY PSYCHOLOGY.** **See** Literature.

US/0022-0965
**JOURNAL OF EXPERIMENTAL CHILD PSYCHOLOGY.** [J. exp. child psychol.]. Vol. 1 (Apr. 1964)-. Academic Scholarly Publication. English. bm. $390.00 US and Canada; $468.00 other. Academic Press, Inc., 6277 Sea Harbor Drive, Orlando FL 32887. **Tel** (800)543-9534, (407)345-4100, FAX (407)363-9661. **ED** Hayne W. Reese. **LC** BF721; .J64. **DD** 155.4. **NLM** W1 JO644IF. **CODEN** JECPAE. **[CCC]. Pr Rev.** Documents available from The Genuine Article, BIOSIS Document Express, UMI Article Clearinghouse.
**Desc:** An excellent source of information concerning all aspects of behavior in children. Dedicated to expanding psychological knowledge about children, it presents material in the form of empirical research studies and short notes on methodological issues and innovative apparatus. Particular attention is paid to definitive new information and to the value of ideas as stimulants to further research. Presents single and multiple experiments that focus on a problem of empirical and theoretical interest.
**Ind/Abst** Acad. Search (Jan. 1994-); AGRICOLA; Appl. Soc. Sci. Index Abstr.; Biol. Abstr.; Curr. Contents Soc. Behav. Sci.; Curr. Index J. Educ.; Dev. Med. Child Neurol.; Expand. Acad. Index (1989-); Index Med.; INFO-SOUTH Abstr.; Int. Bibliogr. Sociol.; Middle East Abstr. Index; Newsp. Period. Abstr. (1992-); Psychol. Abstr. (1964-); PsycINFO; PsycLit; PsycScan: Develop. Psych.; Res. Alert [Full Cov.]; Soc. Sci. Source (Jul. 1993-); Soc. Sci. Cit. Index [Full Cov.]; Soc. Sci. Index; Soc. Sci. Index Fulltext (Dec. 1988-) [Full Txt.]; Soc. Work Abstr. (?-?); Women Stud. Abstr.

US/0097-7403
**JOURNAL OF EXPERIMENTAL PSYCHOLOGY : ANIMAL BEHAVIOR PROCESSES.** [J. exp. psychol., Anim. behav. processes]. **Added/Corp** American Psychological Association. **VFOAT** Animal Behavior Processes. Vol. 1 (Jan. 1975)-. Academic Scholarly Publication. English. qt. $112.00 (nonmember, institution) US. American Psychological Association, 750 First Street Northeast, Washington DC 20002. **Tel** (800)374-2721, (202)336-5600, (subscriptions - (202)336-5600. **ED** Stewart H. Hulse, PhD. **LC** QL750; .J653. **DD** 599/.05. **NLM** W1 JO644VB. **CODEN** JPAPDG. **[CCC]. Ad Acc. Pr Rev. Circ:** 2,600. available on microfilm from Johnson Associates; available on microfilm and microfiche from University Microfilms International (UMI). Documents available from The Genuine Article, BIOSIS Document Express, UMI Article Clearinghouse, CASDDS.
***Supersedes in part** Journal of Experimental Psychology, 0022-1015.*
**Desc:** Experimental studies on the basic mechanisms of perception, learning, motivation and performance, especially in nonhuman animals.
**Ind/Abst** Acad. Search (July 1993-); Anim. Behav. Abstr.; Biol. Abstr.; Chem. Abstr.; CSA Neuro. Abstr. (?-?); Curr. Contents Life Sci.; Curr. Contents Soc. Behav. Sci.; EMBASE; Energy Res. Abstr. (Aug. 1982-); Expand. Acad. Index (1989-); Fish Rev. (Jan. 1989-July 1992); Index Med.; INFO-SOUTH Abstr.; Int. Aerosp. Abstr.; Newsp. Period. Abstr. (1991-); Life Sci. Collect.; Psychol. Abstr. (1975-); PsycINFO; PsycLit; Ref. Upd. Deluxe Ed.; Res. Alert [Full Cov.]; Sci. Cit. Index; SCISEARCH; Soc. Sci. Source (Jul. 1993-); Soc. Sci. Cit. Index [Full Cov.]; Soc. Sci. Index Fulltext (Dec. 1988-) [Full Txt.]; Wildl. Rev. (Jan. 1989-July 1992).

●US/1076-898X
**JOURNAL OF EXPERIMENTAL PSYCHOLOGY. APPLIED.** **Added/Corp** American Psychological Association. **VFOAT** Applied. (1995)-. Periodical. English. qt. $100.00 (nonmember, institution) US. American Psychological Association, 750 First Street Northeast, Washington DC 20002. **Tel** (800)374-2721, (202)336-5600, (subscriptions - (202)336-5600.
**Desc:** Publishes original empirical investigations in experimental psychology that bridge practically oriented problems and psychological theory.

US/0096-3445
**JOURNAL OF EXPERIMENTAL PSYCHOLOGY : GENERAL.** [J. exp. psychol. Gen.]. **Added/Corp** American Psychological Association. Vol. 104 (Mar. 1975)-. Academic Scholarly Publication. English. Four times a year (Mar., June, Sept., Dec.). $100.00 (nonmember, institution) US. American Psychological Association, 750 First Street Northeast, Washington DC 20002. **Tel** (800)374-2721, (202)336-5600, (subscriptions - (202)336-5600. **ED** Earl Hunt, Ph.D. **LC** BF180; .J67. **DD** 150/.5. **NLM** W1 JO644VC. **CODEN** JPGEDD. **[CCC]. Ad Acc. Pr Rev. Circ:** 3,400. available on microfilm and microfiche from University Microfilms International (UMI). Documents available from The Genuine Article, BIOSIS Document Express, UMI Article Clearinghouse, CASDDS.
***Supersedes in part** Journal of Experimental Psychology, 0022-1015.*
**Desc:** Major articles that integrate recent research and make significant contributions to the science of psychology. Features advances of interest to all

experimental psychologists; reports of major series of studies; and critiques, new insights, and rebuttals.
**Ind/Abst** Acad. Search (July 1993-); Biol. Abstr.; Chem. Abstr.; Commun. Abstr. (?-?); Curr. Contents Soc. Behav. Sci.; EMBASE; Energy Res. Abstr. (Aug. 1982-); Ergon. Abstr.; Expand. Acad. Index (1989-); Health Period. Database; Index Med.; INFO-SOUTH Abstr.; Int. Aerosp. Abstr.; Med. Abstr. Newsl.; Multicult. Educ. Abstr.; Newsp. Period. Abstr. (1991-); Peace Res. Abstr. J. (1970-1973); Life Sci. Collect.; Psychol. Abstr. (1975-); PsycINFO; PsycLit; Res. Alert [Full Cov.]; Soc. Sci. Source (Jul. 1993-); Soc. Sci. Cit. Index [Full Cov.]; Soc. Sci. Index Fulltext (Sept. 1988-) [Full Txt.].

US/0096-1523
**JOURNAL OF EXPERIMENTAL PSYCHOLOGY : HUMAN PERCEPTION AND PERFORMANCE.** [J. exp. psychol. Hum. percept. perform.]. **Added/Corp** American Psychological Association. **VFOAT** Human Perception and Performance. Vol. 1 (Feb. 1975)-. Academic Scholarly Publication. English. Six times a year (Feb., Apr., June, Aug., Oct., Dec.). $280.00 (nonmember, institution) US. American Psychological Association, 750 First Street Northeast, Washington DC 20002. **Tel** (800)374-2721, (202)336-5600, (subscriptions - (202)336-5600. **ED** James E. Cutting, Ph.D. **LC** BF311; .J64. **DD** 152/.05. **NLM** W1 JO644VF. **CODEN** JPHPDH. **[CCC]**. **Pr Rev. Circ:** 3,300. available on microfilm from Johnson Associates; and Princeton Microfilms; available on microfilm and microfiche from University Microfilms International (UMI). Documents available from The Genuine Article, BIOSIS Document Express, UMI Article Clearinghouse, CASDDS. ***Supersedes in part*** *Journal of Experimental Psychology, 0022-1015.*
**Desc:** Spotlighting current research in perception, motor performance, and related cognitive processes including all sensory modalities; all types of motor behavior; empirical studies of human action; machine and animal research; and theoretical notes and commentary.
**Ind/Abst** Acad. Search (July 1993-); Appl. Soc. Sci. Index Abstr.; Biol. Abstr.; Chem. Abstr.; Commun. Abstr. (?-?); Curr. Contents Soc. Behav. Sci.; Curr. Index J. Educ.; EMBASE; Energy Res. Abstr. (Aug. 1982-); Ergon. Abstr.; Expand. Acad. Index (1989-); Health Period. Database; Index Med.; INFO-SOUTH Abstr.; Int. Aerosp. Abstr.; MLA Int. Bibl. Books Artic. Mod. Lang. Lit.; Multicult. Educ. Abstr.; Newsp. Period. Abstr. (1991-); Psychol. Abstr. (1975-); PsycINFO; PsycLit; Res. Alert [Full Cov.]; Soc. Sci. Source (Jul. 1993-); Soc. Sci. Cit. Index [Full Cov.]; Soc. Sci. Index Fulltext (Aug. 1988-) [Full Txt.].

US/0278-7393
**JOURNAL OF EXPERIMENTAL PSYCHOLOGY. LEARNING, MEMORY, AND COGNITION.** [J. exper. psychol., Learn., mem., cogn.]. **Added/Corp** American Psychological Association. **VFOAT** Learning, Memory and Cognition. Vol. 8, No. 1 (Jan. 1982)-. Academic Scholarly Publication. English. bm. $300.00 (nonmember, institution) US. American Psychological Association, 750 First Street Northeast, Washington DC 20002. **Tel** (800)374-2721, (202)336-5600, (subscriptions - (202)336-5600. **ED** Keith Rayner, PhD. **LC** LB1051; .J647. **DD** 370.15. **NLM** W1 JO644VJ. **CODEN** JEPCEA. **[CCC]**. **Ad Acc. Pr Rev. Circ:** 3,800. available on microfilm and microfiche from University Microfilms International (UMI). Documents available from The Genuine Article, UMI Article Clearinghouse. ***Continues*** *Journal of Experimental Psychology. Human Learning and Memory, 0096-1515.*
**Desc:** This journal makes it easy for readers to stay up-to-date on cutting edge research in all cognitive processes including learning, memory, imagery, concept formation, problem-solving, decision-making, thinking, reading and language processing.
**Ind/Abst** Acad. Search (July 1993-); Curr. Contents Soc. Behav. Sci.; Curr. Index J. Educ.; EMBASE; Energy Res. Abstr. (Aug. 1982-); Ergon. Abstr.; Expand. Acad. Index (1989-); Health Period. Database; Index Med.; INFO-SOUTH Abstr.; MLA Int. Bibl. Books Artic. Mod. Lang. Lit.; Newsp. Period. Abstr. (1991-); Psychol. Abstr. (1982-); PsycINFO; PsycLit; Res. Alert [Full Cov.]; Soc. Sci. Source (Jul. 1993-); Soc. Sci. Cit. Index [Full Cov.]; Soc. Sci. Index; Soc. Sci. Index Fulltext (July 1988-) [Full Txt.].

US/0278-7393
**JOURNAL OF EXPERIMENTAL PSYCHOLOGY. LEARNING, MEMORY, AND COGNITION [MICROFORM].** **Added/Corp** American Psychological Association. **VFOAT** Learning, Memory and Cognition. Vol. 8, No. 1 (Jan. 1982)-. Periodical. English. ir. American Psychological Association, 750 First Street Northeast, Washington DC 20002. **Tel** (800)374-2721, (202)336-5600, (subscriptions - (202)336-5600. **[CCC]**. ***Continues*** *Journal of Experimental Psychology. Human Learning and Memory, 0096-1515.*

US/0022-1031
**JOURNAL OF EXPERIMENTAL SOCIAL PSYCHOLOGY.** [J. exp. soc. psychol.]. Vol. 1 (Jan. 1965)-. Academic Scholarly Publication. English. bm (6 issues). $223.00 US and Canada; $276.00 other. Academic Press, Inc., 6277 Sea Harbor Drive, Orlando FL 32887. **Tel** (800)543-9534, (407)345-4100, FAX (407)363-9661. **ED** Charles M. Judd, John M. Levine and Bernadette Park. **LC** HM251; .J53. **DD** 301. **NLM** W1 JO644X. **CODEN** JESPAQ. **[CCC]**. Index available in last issue of volume--attached. **Pr Rev.** Documents available from The Genuine Article, BIOSIS Document Express, UMI Article Clearinghouse.
**Desc:** Publishes original research and theory on human social behavior and related phenomena. The journal emphasizes empirical, conceptually based research that advances our understanding of important social psychological processes. The journal also publishes literature reviews, theoretical analyses, and methodological comments.
**Ind/Abst** Acad. Search (Jan. 1994-); Appl. Soc. Sci. Index Abstr.; Biol. Abstr.; Commun. Abstr. (?-?); Crim. Penol. Police Sci. Abstr.; Curr. Contents Soc. Behav. Sci.; Expand. Acad. Index (1989-); INFO-SOUTH Abstr.; Int. Bibliogr. Sociol.; Middle East Abstr. Index; Newsp. Period. Abstr. (1992-); Peace Res. Abstr. J. (1966-1973); Psychol. Abstr. (1965-); PsycINFO; PsycLit; Res. Alert [Full Cov.]; Soc. Plann. Policy Dev. Abstr.; Soc. Sci. Source (Jul. 1993-); Soc. Sci. Cit. Index [Full Cov.]; Soc. Sci. Index; Soc. Sci. Index Fulltext (Nov. 1988-) [Full Txt.]; Sociol. Abstr. (?-?); Women Stud. Abstr.

●US/1057-7432
**JOURNAL OF EXPRESSIVE THERAPY.** (JOURNAL OF EXPRESSIVE THERAPY: JET.). **Added/Corp** National Expressive Therapy Association. **VFOAT** JET. (1994)-. Periodical. English. qt. National Expressive Therapy Association, 1164 Bishop Street, Suite 124, Honolulu HI 96813.

US/0893-3200
**JOURNAL OF FAMILY PSYCHOLOGY.** (JOURNAL OF FAMILY PSYCHOLOGY : JFP : JOURNAL OF THE DIVISION OF FAMILY PSYCHOLOGY OF THE AMERICAN PSYCHOLOGICAL ASSOCIATION (DIVISION 43).). [J. fam. psychol.]. **Added/Corp** American Psychological Association. Division of Family Psychology. **VFOAT** JFP. Vol. 1, No. 1 (Sept. 1987)-. Periodical. English. qt. $87.00 (nonmember, institution) US. American Psychological Association, 750 First Street Northeast, Washington DC 20002. **Tel** (800)374-2721, (202)336-5600, (subscriptions - (202)336-5600. **ED** Ronald F. Levant. **DD** 362. **NLM** W1; JO6444N. **[CCC]**. Index available. cum. index. **Ad Acc. Pr Rev.** available on microfilm and microfiche from University Microfilms International (UMI).
**Desc:** Enhances theory, research and clinical practice in family psychology and deals with: family and marital theory and concepts; research and evaluation; therapeutic frameworks and methods; training and supervision; policies and legal matters concerning the family and marriage.
**Ind/Abst** Psychol. Abstr. (1987-); PsycINFO (1990-); PsycLit; Sage Fam. Stud. Abstr.; Soc. Plann. Policy Dev. Abstr.

US/0897-5353
**JOURNAL OF FAMILY PSYCHOTHERAPY.** See Family and Marriage.

US/0895-2833
**JOURNAL OF FEMINIST FAMILY THERAPY.** See Family and Marriage.

US/0891-7140
**JOURNAL OF GAY & LESBIAN PSYCHOTHERAPY.** See Homosexuality.

US/0022-1309
**JOURNAL OF GENERAL PSYCHOLOGY, THE.** [J. gen. psych.]. Vol. 1 (Jan. 1928)-. Periodical. English (German; summaries and/or abstracts in French, German and Russian). qt. $93.00. Heldref Publications, 1319 Eighteenth Street Northwest, Washington DC 20036-1802. **Tel** (202)296-6267, (800)365-9753, FAX (202)296-5149. **ED** Arthur J Riopelle. **LC** BF1; .J64. **DD** 150.5; 159.905. **NLM** W1 JO668G. **CODEN** JGPSAY. **[CCC]**. **Bk Rev. Ad Acc. Pr Rev. Circ:** 1,475. available on microfilm and microfiche from University Microfilms International (UMI). Documents available from The Genuine Article, BIOSIS Document Express, UMI Article Clearinghouse.
**Desc:** Devoted to experimental, physiological, and comparative psychology. Publishes articles that establish functional relationships, involve a series of integrated studies, or contribute to the development of new theoretical insights.
**Ind/Abst** Acad. Abstr. Full Text Elite (Jan. 1992-) [Full Txt.]; Acad. Abstr. (Jan. 1992-); Acad. Search (Jan. 1992-); Appl. Soc. Sci. Index Abstr.; Biol. Abstr.; Commun. Abstr. (?-?); Crim. Penol. Police Sci. Abstr.; Curr. Contents Soc. Behav. Sci.; Ergon. Abstr.; Except. Child Educ. Resour.; Expand. Acad. Index (1992-); Gen. Sci. Index; Gen. Sci. Source (Jan. 1992-); Index Med.; Index Period. Artic. Relat. Law (19??-19??); INFO-SOUTH Abstr.; Int. Aerosp. Abstr.; Mag. Artic. Summar. Elite (Jan. 1992-) [Full Txt.]; Mag. Artic. Summar. Select (Jan. 1992-); Mag. Artic. Summar. CD-ROM (Jan. 1992-); Middle East Abstr. Index; Newsp. Period. Abstr. (1991-); Psychol. Abstr. (1928-); PsycINFO; PsycLit; Res. Alert [Full Cov.]; Soc. Plann. Policy Dev. Abstr.; Soc. Sci. Source (Jan. 1992-) [Full Txt.]; Soc. Sci. Cit. Index [Full Cov.]; Soc. Sci. Index; Soc. Sci. Index Fulltext (Jan. 1989-) [Full Txt.]; Soc. Work Abstr. [Select. Cov.]; Sociol. Abstr.; Vocat. Search (Jan. 1992-) [Full Txt.]; Women Stud. Abstr.

US/0022-1325
**JOURNAL OF GENETIC PSYCHOLOGY, THE.** [J. genet. psychol.]. Vol. 84 (March 1954)-. Periodical. English. qt. $95.00. Heldref Publications, 1319 Eighteenth Street Northwest, Washington DC 20036-1802. **Tel** (202)296-6267, (800)365-9753, FAX (202)296-5149. **ED** John E Horrocks. **LC** L11; .P4. **DD** 370.5. **NLM** W1 JO669. **CODEN** JGPYAI. **[CCC]**. Index available. cum. index. **Ad Acc. Pr Rev. Circ:** 1,400. available on microfilm and microfiche from University Microfilms International (UMI). Documents available from The Genuine Article, BIOSIS Document Express, UMI Article Clearinghouse. ***Continues*** *Pedagogical Seminary and Journal of Genetic Psychology, 0885-6559.*
**Desc:** Devoted to research and theory in developmental and clinical psychology. Articles deal with the biological as well as the behavioral and social aspects of these fields. Emphasizes empirical research and the exposition and criticism of theory; it occasionally publishes applied and descriptive articles or briefly reported replications.
**Ind/Abst** Acad. Search (Jan. 1994-); AGRICOLA [Select. Cov.]; Biol. Abstr.; Curr. Contents Soc. Behav. Sci.; Curr. Index J. Educ.; Dev. Med. Child Neurol.; Except. Child Educ. Resour.; Expand. Acad. Index (1992-); High. Educ. Abstr. (1965-); Index Med.; Index Period. Artic. Relat. Law (19??-19??); INFO-SOUTH Abstr.; Middle East Abstr. Index; Newsp. Period. Abstr. (1991-); Psychol. Abstr. (1954-); PsycINFO; PsycLit; PsycScan: Develop. Psych.; Res. Alert [Full Cov.]; Risk Abstr.; Soc. Plann. Policy Dev. Abstr.; Soc. Sci. Source (Jul. 1993-); Soc. Sci. Cit. Index [Full Cov.]; Soc. Sci. Index; Soc. Sci. Index Fulltext (Dec. 1988-) [Full Txt.]; Soc. Work Abstr. [Select. Cov.]; Sociol. Abstr.; Sociol. Educ. Abstr.; Spec. Educ. Needs Abstr.; Stud. Women Abstr.; Women Stud. Abstr.

US/0022-1422
**JOURNAL OF GERONTOLOGY (KIRKWOOD).** See Medical Science and Technology-Geriatrics.

US/0022-1465
**JOURNAL OF HEALTH AND SOCIAL BEHAVIOR.** See Public Health and Safety.

US/0022-1678
**JOURNAL OF HUMANISTIC PSYCHOLOGY, THE.** [J. humanist. psychol.]. **Added/Corp** Association for Humanistic Psychology. Vol. 1 (Spring 1961)-. Periodical. English. qt. $153.00. SAGE Periodical Press, 2455 Teller Road, Thousand Oaks CA 91320. **Tel** (805)499-0721, FAX (805)499-0871, telex 100799. **ED** Thomas Greening (Psychological Service Associates). **LC** BF1; .J645. **DD** 150/.19/2. **NLM** W1 JO673Y. **[CCC]**. Index available. cum. index. **Pr Rev. Acid Free.** available on microfilm and microfiche from University Microfilms International (UMI). Documents available from The Genuine Article.
**Desc:** Provides an interdisciplinary forum for contributions and controversies in humanistic psychology as applied to personal growth, interpersonal encounter, social problems and philosophical issues.
**Ind/Abst** Abstr. Res. Pastor. Care Couns. (19??-); AGRICOLA; Appl. Soc. Sci. Index Abstr.; Arts Humanit. Citation Index [Select. Cov.]; Commun. Abstr. (?-?); Curr. Contents Soc. Behav. Sci.; Curr. Index J. Educ.; Educ. Adm. Abstr. (?-?); Except. Hum. Exp.; Hum. Resour. Abstr. (?-?); Multicult. Educ. Abstr.; Peace Res. Abstr. J. (1965-1967); Psychol. Abstr. (1961-); PsycINFO; PsycLit; Res. Alert [Full Cov.]; Sage Public Adm. Abstr. (?-?); Soc. Plann. Policy Dev. Abstr.; Soc. Sci. Cit. Index [Full Cov.]; Sociol. Abstr. (?-?); Sociol. Educ. Abstr.; Women Stud. Abstr.

II/0379-3885
**JOURNAL OF INDIAN PSYCHOLOGY.** [J. Indian psychol.]. **Added/Corp** Andhra University. Vol. 1 (Jan. 1978)-. Periodical. English. sa. $20.00. Andhra University Press, Waltair, Visakhapathnam 530 003, Waltair India. **(Subscription address:** Prints India, 11 Darya Ganj, New Delhi 110002 India.) **LC** BF1; .J647. **DD** 150/.954. **NLM** W1 JO703D.
**Ind/Abst** Except. Hum. Exp.; Psychol. Abstr. (1978-); PsycINFO; PsycLit.

US/0022-1805
**JOURNAL OF INDIVIDUAL PSYCHOLOGY.** **Added/Corp** North American Society of Adlerian Psychology. American Society of Adlerian Psychology. Individual Psychology Association of Chicago. Individual Psychology Bulletin. Vol. 1 (1940)-. Periodical. English. sa. **[CCC]**. cum. index. available on microfilm and microfiche from University Microfilms International (UMI).

US/0094-1956
**JOURNAL OF INSTRUCTIONAL PSYCHOLOGY.** [J. instr. psychol.]. Vol. 1 (Winter 1974)-. Periodical. English. qt. $25.00 (one year), $45.00 (two year), $65.00 (three year) institutions, $16.00 (1 year), $30.00 (2 year), $45.00 (3 year) individuals, US; $33.00 (1 year), $61.00 (2 year), $89.00 (3 year) institutions, $24.00 (1 year), $46.00 (2 year), $69.00 (3

year) individuals, other. Journal of Instructional Psychology, Box 8826 Spring Hill Station, Mobile AL 36608. **Tel** (205)343-1878. **ED** G E Uhlig. **LC** LB1051; .J65. **DD** 370.15/05. **Bk Rev. Circ:** 250. available on microfilm and microfiche from University Microfilms International (UMI).
**Desc:** Contains general and professional education research.
**Ind/Abst** Acad. Search (July 1993-); Chicano Index; Educ. Index; High. Educ. Abstr. (1976); INFO-SOUTH Abstr.; Mag. Search; Psychol. Abstr. (1974-); PsycINFO; PsycLit; Soc. Plann. Policy Dev. Abstr.; Soc. Sci. Source (Jul. 1993-); Spec. Educ. Needs Abstr.

●UK/0964-2633
**JOURNAL OF INTELLECTUAL DISABILITY RESEARCH.** (JOURNAL OF INTELLECTUAL DISABILITY RESEARCH : JIDR.). [J. intellect. disabil. res.]. **Added/Corp** Royal Society for Mentally Handicapped Children and Adults. **VFOAT** JIDR. Vol. 36, Pt. 1 (Feb. 1992)-. Academic Scholarly Publication. English. bm (6 issues). $225.00 (institutions), $72.00 (individuals) US & Canada; £132.00 (institutions), £42.00 (individuals) Europe; £145.50 (institutions), £46.50 (individuals) other. Blackwell Scientific Publications Ltd, Marston Book Services, PO Box 87, Oxford OX2 ODT UK. **Tel** 011 44 865 791155, FAX 011 44 865 791927, telex 837 515 MARDIS G. **LC** RC321; .J78. **NLM** W1; JO716CE. **CODEN** JIDREN. Index available (bound in last issue). Documents available from The Genuine Article. ***Continues** Journal of Mental Deficiency Research, 0022-264X.*
**Ind/Abst** Curr. Aware. Biol. Sci., CABS; Curr. Contents Life Sci.; Curr. Contents Soc. Behav. Sci.; EMBASE; Index Med. (1992-); Res. Alert [Full Cov.]; Sci. Cit. Index; SCISEARCH; Soc. Plann. Policy Dev. Abstr.; Soc. Sci. Cit. Index [Full Cov.].

●US/1060-6041
**JOURNAL OF INVITATIONAL THEORY AND PRACTICE.** See Education-Teaching and Curriculum.

US/0261-927X
**JOURNAL OF LANGUAGE AND SOCIAL PSYCHOLOGY.** See Linguistics.

UK/0268-3946
**JOURNAL OF MANAGERIAL PSYCHOLOGY.** Vol. 1, No. 1 (1986)-. Periodical. English. Seven times a year. $1249.00. MCB University Press, 60 62 Toller Lane, Bradford West Yorkshire BD8 9BX England. **Tel** 011 44 274 499821, FAX 011 44 274 547143, telex 51317 MCBUNI G. **(Subscription address:** MCB University Press / US and Canada Subscriptions, PO Box 10812, Birmingham AL 35201-0812.**) ED** Andrew Kakabadse. **[CCC]. Ad Acc.** available on an online database (file 15/Full-Text) from DIALOG. Documents available from UMI Article Clearinghouse.
**Desc:** Brings the latest research of importance to managers out of academia and into the workplace - providing practical guidance on managerial psychology. Articles cover subjects such as communications, interpersonal skills and motivation. They include case studies that can be applied to the reader's organisation. They are supported by research reviews, etc.
**Ind/Abst** ABI/INFORM Glob. Ed.; ABI Inform Ondisc (1986-); Ergon. Abstr.; Gen. BusinessFile (1992-); Manage. Market. Abstr.; Women Manage. Rev. [Full Txt.].

US/0194-472X
**JOURNAL OF MARITAL AND FAMILY THERAPY.** [J. marital fam. ther.]. **Added/Corp** American Association for Marriage and Family Therapy. Vol. 5 (Jan. 1979)-. Academic Scholarly Publication. English. qt (Jan., Apr., July, Oct.). $75.00 (institution); $45.00 (individual) US, Canada & Mexico; $90.00 (institution) $60.00 (individual) other. American Association for Marriage and Family Therapy, 1100 17th Street Northwest, 10th Floor, Washington DC 20036-4601. **Tel** (202)452-0109, FAX (202)223-2329. **ED** Alan Gurman. **LC** HQ1; .J47. **DD** 362.8/2. **NLM** W1 JO748NH. **CODEN** JMFTA. **Bk Rev. Ad Acc. Pr Rev. Circ:** 16,000. available on microfilm and microfiche from University Microfilms International (UMI). Documents available from The Genuine Article, UMI Article Clearinghouse. ***Continues** Journal of Marriage and Family Counseling, 0094-5102.*
**Desc:** Published to advance the professional understanding of marital and family behavior, and to improve the psychotherapeutic treatment of marital and family dysfunction. Publishes articles on clinical practice, research and theory in marital and family therapy.
**Ind/Abst** Abstr. Res. Pastor. Care Couns. (19??-); Acad. Abstr. Full Text Elite (Jan. 1992-); Acad. Abstr. (Jan. 1992-); Acad. Search (Jan. 1992-); Curr. Contents Soc. Behav. Sci.; Curr. Index J. Educ.; EMBASE; Expand. Acad. Index (1989-); INFO-SOUTH Abstr.; Mag. Search; Newsp. Period. Abstr. (1991-); Psychol. Abstr. (1979-); PsycINFO; PsycLit; Res. Alert [Full Cov.]; Sage Fam. Stud. Abstr.; Soc. Plann. Policy Dev. Abstr.; Soc. Sci. Source (Jan. 1992-); Soc. Sci. Cit. Index [Full Cov.]; Soc. Sci. Index; Soc. Sci. Index Fulltext (Oct. 1988-) [Full Txt.]; Soc. Work Abstr. [Full Cov.]; Sociol. Abstr.; Stud. Women Abstr.

US/0022-2496
**JOURNAL OF MATHEMATICAL PSYCHOLOGY.** [J. math. psychol.]. Vol. 1 (Feb. 1964)-. Academic Scholarly Publication. English. qt (4 issues). $276.00 US and Canada; $335.50 other. Academic Press, Inc., 6277 Sea Harbor Drive, Orlando FL 32887. **Tel** (800)543-9534, (407)345-4100, FAX (407)363-9661. **ED** Thomas S. Wallsten. **LC** BF1; .J657. **NLM** W1 JO748T. **CODEN** JMTPAJ. **[CCC]. Bk Rev. Pr Rev.** Documents available from The Genuine Article, BIOSIS Document Express, Ask*IEEE.
**Desc:** Concerned with empirical research directly relevant to theoretical questions within psychology. Presents research articles, monographs and reviews, and notes and comments in all areas of mathematical and theoretical psychology. The journal emphasizes the development or experimental testing of psychological process models.
**Ind/Abst** ACM Guide Comput. Lit.; Biol. Abstr.; Compumath Citation Index [Full Cov.]; Comput. Rev.; Curr. Contents Soc. Behav. Sci.; INSPEC (March 1992-); Int. Aerosp. Abstr.; Math. Rev.; Life Sci. Collect.; Psychol. Abstr. (1964-); PsycINFO; PsycLit; Res. Alert [Full Cov.]; Soc. Sci. Cit. Index [Full Cov.]; Soc. Res. Methodol. Abstr. (1990-); Stat. Theory Method Abstr. (1967, 1970); Zentralbl. Math. Ihre Grenzgeb.

US/0749-596X
**JOURNAL OF MEMORY AND LANGUAGE.** [J. mem. lang.]. Vol. 24, No. 1 (Feb. 1985)-. Academic Scholarly Publication. English. bm (6 issues). $236.00 US and Canada; $283.00 other. Academic Press, Inc., 6277 Sea Harbor Drive, Orlando FL 32887. **Tel** (800)543-9534, (407)345-4100, FAX (407)363-9661. **ED** Edward J. Shoben. **LC** BF455.A1; J6. **DD** 153. **NLM** W1; JO76IC. **[CCC]. Pr Rev.** Documents available from The Genuine Article, UMI Article Clearinghouse. ***Continues** Journal of Verbal Learning and Verbal Behavior, 0022-5371.*
**Desc:** Contribute to the formulation of scientific issues and theories in the areas of memory, language comprehension and production, and cognitive processes. Special emphasis is given to research articles that provide new theoretical insights based on a carefully laid empirical foundation. In addition, significant theoretical papers without new experimental findings may be published. A valuable tool for cognitive scientists including psychologists, linguists, and others interested in memory and learning, language, reading, and speech.
**Ind/Abst** Abstr. Anthropol.; Acad. Search (Jan. 1994-); Appl. Soc. Sci. Index Abstr.; Contents Pages Educ.; Curr. Index J. Educ.; Expand. Acad. Index (1989-1991); Health Period. Database; INFO-SOUTH Abstr.; Linguist. Lang. Behav. Abstr. (1972-) [Full Cov.]; MLA Int. Bibl. Books Artic. Mod. Lang. Lit.; Newsp. Period. Abstr. (1992-); Psychol. Abstr. (1962-); PsycINFO; PsycLit; Res. Alert [Full Cov.]; Soc. Plann. Policy Dev. Abstr.; Soc. Sci. Source (Jul. 1993-); Soc. Sci. Cit. Index [Full Cov.]; Soc. Sci. Index; Soc. Sci. Index Fulltext (Dec. 1988-) [Full Txt.].

US/0364-5541
**JOURNAL OF MENTAL IMAGERY.** [J. ment. imag.]. Vol. 1 (Spring 1977)-. Periodical. English. qt. $80.00 (1 year), $160.00 (2 year), $240.00 (3 year). Brandon House, PO Box 240, Bronx NY 10471. **Tel** (914)423-9200. **ED** Akhter Ahsen. **LC** BF367; .J68. **DD** 153.3. **NLM** W1 JO76LM. **Bk Rev. Ad Acc. Circ:** 11,000.
**Desc:** Definitive source for imagery articles by leading experts.
**Ind/Abst** Except. Hum. Exp.; Psychol. Abstr. (1977-); PsycINFO; PsycLit; Soc. Plann. Policy Dev. Abstr.

US/0271-0137
**JOURNAL OF MIND AND BEHAVIOR, THE.** [J. mind behav.]. **Added/Corp** Institute of Mind and Behavior. **VFOAT** JMB. Vol. 1, No. 1 (Spring 1980)-. Periodical. English. Four times a year (Mar., June, Sept., Dec.). $73.00 (institutions); $42.00 (individuals). Journal of Mind and Behavior, PO Box 522, Village Station, New York NY 10014. **Tel** (212)595-4853. **ED** Raymond Russ Ph.D. (editor's address: Department of Psycology Room 301, University of Maine, 5742 Little Hall, Orona, MA 04469-5772, phone: (207)581-2057). **LC** BF1; .J6575. **DD** 150/.5. **NLM** W1; JO77M. Index available (4th iss. (Aut).). cum. index. **Bk Rev. Ad Acc. Pr Rev. Circ:** 1,019 (ctrl). Documents available from The Genuine Article, Ask*IEEE.
**Desc:** An interdisciplinary journal that is in the areas of mind/body epistemology, the scientific method, psychiatry and social philosophy, and sociology of knowledge.
**Ind/Abst** Abstr. Anthropol. (19??-); INSPEC (Summer 1991-); Linguist. Lang. Behav. Abstr.; Philos. Index; Psychol. Abstr. (1981-); PsycINFO; PsycLit; Res. Alert [Full Cov.]; Soc. Plann. Policy Dev. Abstr.; Soc. Sci. Cit. Index [Full Cov.]; Soc. Work Abstr. [Select. Cov.]; Sociol. Abstr.

●UK/1057-9214
**JOURNAL OF MULTICRITERIA ANALYSIS.** (JOURNAL OF MULTICRITERIA DECISION ANALYSIS.). [multi-criteria decis. anal.]. **VFOAT** Journal of Multi Criteria Decision Analysis. (1992)-. Periodical. English. qt. $135.00. John Wiley & Sons Ltd., Baffins Lane, Chichester West Sussex PO19 1UD England. **Tel** 0243 779777, FAX 0243 776128 BTG:JWP001, telex 86290 WIBOOKG. **(Subscription address:** John Wiley / Philadelphia, PO Box 7247, Philadelphia PA 19170.**) ED** Simon French. **LC** T57.95; .J68. **DD** 658.4/0354. **CODEN** JMDAEY.
**Desc:** Provides an international forum for the presentation and discussion of all aspects of research, application and evaluation of multi-criteria decision analysis.

US/0883-8534
**JOURNAL OF MULTICULTURAL COUNSELING AND DEVELOPMENT.** [J. multicult. couns. devel.]. **Added/Corp** Association for Multicultural Counseling and Development (U.S.). Vol. 13, No. 3 (July 1985)-. Periodical. English. qt (4 issues). $19.00 (institution), $15.00 (individual) US. American Counseling Association, 5999 Stevenson Avenue, Alexandria VA 22304. **Tel** (703)823-9800, (800)347-6647, FAX (703)823-0252. **(Subscription address:** American Counseling Association, Subscription Office, PO Box 2513, Birmingham AL 35201-2513.**) ED** Frederick D. Harper. **LC** LC3701; .J68. **DD** 371. **[CCC].** available on microfilm and microfiche from University Microfilms International (UMI). ***Continues** Journal of Non-White Concerns in Personnel and Guidance, 0090-5461.*
**Desc:** Includes state-of-the-art multicultural counseling research and reports on applications of latest theoretical ideas and concepts.
**Ind/Abst** Acad. Search (July 1993-); Curr. Index J. Educ.; Educ. Index; High. Educ. Abstr. (1985-); INFO-SOUTH Abstr.; Mag. Search; Psychol. Abstr. (1973-); PsycINFO (1990-); PsycLit; Soc. Work Abstr. [Select. Cov.].

US/0191-5886
**JOURNAL OF NONVERBAL BEHAVIOR.** [J. nonverbal behav.]. Vol. 4 (Fall 1979)-. Periodical. English. qt. $225.00 US; $265.00 other. Human Sciences Press, PO Box 735, 233 Spring Street, New York NY 10013. **Tel** (212)620-8000, FAX (212)807-1047, telex 23421139. **(Subscription address:** Eurospan Ltd., Journals and Serials Division, 3 Henrietta Street, Covent Garden, London WC2E 8LU England.**) ED** Judith Hall. **LC** BF353; .E55. **DD** 153.6. **NLM** W1 JO795J. **CODEN** JNVBDV. **[CCC]. Pr Rev.** available on microfilm and microfiche from University Microfilms International (UMI). Documents available from The Genuine Article, UMI Article Clearinghouse. ***Continues** Environmental Psychology and Nonverbal Behavior, 0361-3496.*
**Desc:** Presents original theoretical and empirical research on nonverbal behavior. Specific areas include paralanguage, proxemics, facial expressions, eye contact, face-to-face interaction and emotional expression.
**Ind/Abst** Abstr. Anthropol.; Acad. Abstr. Full Text Elite (Jan. 1992-); Acad. Abstr. (Jan. 1992-); Acad. Search (Jan. 1992-); Commun. Abstr.; Curr. Contents Soc. Behav. Sci.; Expand. Acad. Index (1989-); INFO-SOUTH Abstr.; Mag. Search; MLA Int. Bibl. Books Artic. Mod. Lang. Lit.; Newsp. Period. Abstr. (1991-); Psychol. Abstr. (1979-); PsycINFO; PsycLit; Res. Alert [Full Cov.]; Sage Fam. Stud. Abstr.; Soc. Plann. Policy Dev. Abstr.; Soc. Sci. Source (Jan. 1992-); Soc. Sci. Cit. Index [Full Cov.]; Soc. Sci. Index; Soc. Sci. Index Fulltext (Spring 1988-) [Full Txt.]; Soc. Work Abstr. [Select. Cov.]; Spec. Educ. Needs Abstr.

●UK/0963-1798
**JOURNAL OF OCCUPATIONAL AND ORGANIZATIONAL PSYCHOLOGY.** **Added/Corp** British Psychological Society. Vol. 65, Pt. 1 (Mar. 1992)-. Periodical. English. qt. £95.00 UK; $176.00 US. British Psychological Society, St. Andrews House, 48 Princess Road, Leicester LE1 7DR England. **Tel** 011 44 533 549568. **ED** Dr Michael West. **LC** HF5548.8; .O26. **DD** 158.7/05. **NLM** W1; JO801NJ. **CODEN** JOCCEF. **[CCC].** Index available. **Bk Rev**, (Qty: (8-12)). **Ad Acc, Adv Mgr:** H Dauker, **Tel** 44 81 444 1040. **Pr Rev. Circ:** 2500. available on an online database, CD-ROM, magnetic tape, and microfilm from Swets & Zeitlinger; available on an online database (file 648/Full-Text) from DIALOG. Documents available from The Genuine Article, Ask*IEEE, UMI Article Clearinghouse. ***Continues** Journal of Occupational Psychology, 0305-8107.*
**Desc:** Empirical and conceptual paper which aims to increase understanding of people and organizations at work.
**Ind/Abst** Acad. Search (July 1993-); Bus. ASAP (1992-) [Full Txt.]; Bus. Index (1992-); Bus. Source (Jul. 1993-); Ergon. Abstr.; Gen. BusinessFile (1992-); Gen. Period. Index (1992-); INFO-SOUTH Abstr.; INSPEC (March 1992-); Mag. Search; Newsp. Period. Abstr. (1992-); Res. Alert [Full Cov.]; Soc. Plann. Policy Dev. Abstr.; Soc. Sci. Cit. Index [Full Cov.]; Trade Ind. Index [Full Txt.]; Work Relat. Abstr.

US/1050-9674
**JOURNAL OF OFFENDER REHABILITATION.** See Law-Law Enforcement and Criminology.

UK/0894-3796
**JOURNAL OF ORGANIZATIONAL BEHAVIOR.** [J. organ. behav.]. Vol. 1 (1988)-. Periodical. English. Seven times a year. $465.00. John Wiley & Sons Ltd., Baffins Lane, Chichester West Sussex PO19 1UD England. **Tel** 0243 779777, FAX 0243 776128 BTG:JWP001, telex 86290 WIBOOKG. **(Subscription address:** John Wiley / Philadelphia, PO Box 7247,

Philadelphia PA 19170.) **ED** Cary L. Cooper. **LC** HD6951; .J68. **DD** 158.7/05. **NLM** W1; JO804LK. **CODEN** JORBEJ. **[CCC]. Pr Rev.** available on microfilm and microfiche from University Microfilms International (UMI). Documents available from The Genuine Article, UMI Article Clearinghouse. ***Continues*** *Journal of Occupational Behaviour, 0142-2774.*
**Desc:** An international research journal dealing with problems associated with psycho-social aspects of work and occupational life. Also reflects concerns such as legal, industrial, managerial and other changes in relation to behavior and the quality of working life.
**Ind/Abst** ABI/INFORM Glob. Ed.; ABI Inform Ondisc (1988-); Acad. Search (July 1993-); Appl. Soc. Sci. Index Abstr.; Bus. Index (1988-); Contents Pages Manage.; Curr. Contents Soc. Behav. Sci.; Ergon. Abstr.; Gen. BusinessFile (1988-); Gen. Period. Index (1988-); High. Educ. Abstr. (1986-); Hum. Resour. Abstr.; Int. Labour Doc.; LABORDOC; Oper. Res./Manag. Sci.; Life Sci. Collect. (1988-); Person. Manage. Abstr.; Pollut. Abstr. Indexes (1988-); Psychol. Abstr. (1988-); PsycLit; Res. Alert [Full Cov.]; Selec. Coop. Index Manage. Period; Soc. Plann. Policy Dev. Abstr.; Soc. Sci. Cit. Index [Full Cov.]; Sociol. Abstr. (1988-); Stud. Women Abstr.; Work Relat. Abstr.

US/0160-8061
**JOURNAL OF ORGANIZATIONAL BEHAVIOR MANAGEMENT.** [J. organ. behav. manage.]. Vol. 1 (Summer 1977)-. Periodical. English. sa. $180.00 US; $252.00 other. The Haworth Press Inc, 10 Alice Street, Binghamton NY 13904-1580. **Tel** (607)722-5857, (800)3-HAWORTH, FAX (607)722-1424. **ED** Thomas Mawhinney (editor's address: College of Business Administration, University of Detroit, 4001 W McNichols, Detroit, MI 48221-9987). **LC** HD58.7; .J68. **DD** 658.3/005. **NLM** W1 JO804LM. **Bk Rev. Ad Acc. Pr Rev. Acid Free. Circ:** 574. available on microfilm and microfiche from University Microfilms International (UMI). Documents available from UMI Article Clearinghouse, Haworth Document Delivery Service.
**Desc:** Devoted entirely to behavior management in organizations. Top researchers provide proven methods backed by facts to show practical ways to apply behavior management in the workplace.
**Ind/Abst** ABI/INFORM Glob. Ed.; ABI Inform Ondisc (Spring 1981-); Acad. Search (Jan. 1993-); AGRICOLA; Bus. Index (1985-); Bus. Source (Jul. 1993-); Gen. BusinessFile (1985-); Gen. Period. Index (1985-); Hum. Resour. Abstr. (?-?); INFO-SOUTH Abstr.; Mag. Search; Person. Manage. Abstr.; Psychol. Abstr. (1978-); PsycINFO; PsycLit; PsycScan: Appl. Psych.; Sage Public Adm. Abstr. (?-?); Women Manage. Rev. [Full Txt.]; Work Relat. Abstr. (1977-).

US/0885-3924
**JOURNAL OF PAIN AND SYMPTOM MANAGEMENT.** **See** Medical Science and Technology.

US/0022-3409
**JOURNAL OF PASTORAL CARE, THE.** **See** Religion and Theology.

US/0886-5477
**JOURNAL OF PASTORAL PSYCHOTHERAPY.** ***Title Change.*** [J. pastor. psychother.]. (1987)-Vol. 2, No. 2 (19??). Periodical. English. qt. The Haworth Press Inc, 10 Alice Street, Binghamton NY 13904-1580. **Tel** (607)722-5857, (800)3-HAWORTH, FAX (607)722-1424. **ED** Robert Kriesel. **LC** BV4012; .J677. **NLM** W1; JO8288. **Bk Rev. Ad Acc. Circ:** 109. available on microfilm and microfiche from University Microfilms International (UMI). Documents available from Haworth Document Delivery Service. ***Continued by*** *Journal of Religion in Psychotherapy, 0886-5477.*
**Desc:** Presents pertinent material in the burgeoning discipline of pastoral counseling and psychotherapy.
**Ind/Abst** Abstr. Res. Pastor. Care Couns. (1987-); PsycINFO (1990-); PsycLit; Soc. Work Abstr. [Select. Cov.].

US/0146-8693
**JOURNAL OF PEDIATRIC PSYCHOLOGY.** [J. pediatr. psychol.]. **Added/Corp** Society of Pediatric Psychology. (Jan. 1976)-. Periodical. English. Six times a year. $335.00 institutions, $55.00 individuals US; $390.00 institutions, $64.00 individuals other. Plenum Press, 233 Spring Street, New York NY 10013-1578. **Tel** (212)620-8000, (800)221-9369, FAX (212)463-0742, (212)807-1047, telex 23/421139. **ED** Michael C. Roberts. **LC** RJ503.3; .J68. **DD** 618.92/89/005. **NLM** W1 JO828FG. **CODEN** JPPSDW. **[CCC].** Index available. **Pr Rev.** available on microfilm and microfiche from University Microfilms International (UMI). Documents available from The Genuine Article, BIOSIS Document Express. ***Continues*** *Pediatric Psychology.*
**Desc:** Psychological issues related to the care of children in pediatric settings and psychological aspects of childhood illness.
**Ind/Abst** Annals Behav. Med.; Biol. Abstr.; Child Dev. Abstr. Bibliogr.; Crim. Penol. Police Sci. Abstr.; Cumul. Index Nurs. Allied Health Lit.; Curr. Contents Soc. Behav. Sci.; Dev. Med. Child Neurol.; EMBASE; Except. Child Educ. Resour.; Index Med.; Psychol. Abstr. (1975-); PsycINFO; PsycLit; PsycScan: Develop. Psych.; Ref. Z.; Res. Alert [Full Cov.]; Risk Abstr.; Sage Fam. Stud. Abstr.; Soc. Plann. Policy Dev. Abstr.; Soc. Sci. Cit. Index [Full Cov.]; Soc. Work Abstr. (Summer 1987-) [Select. Cov.]; Sociol. Abstr.; Spec. Educ. Needs Abstr.

US/0022-3506
**JOURNAL OF PERSONALITY.** [J. person.]. Vol. 14 (Sept. 1945)-. Periodical. English. qt (4 issues). $96.00 (institutions), $48.00 (individuals) US; $108.00 (institutions), $60.00 (individuals) other. Duke University Press, PO Box 90660, Durham NC 27708-0660. **Tel** (919)687-3600, (919)688-5134 (orders), FAX (919)688-4574, telex 802829. **ED** Howard Tennen. **DD** 137. **NLM** W1 JO828P. **CODEN** JOPEAE. **[CCC]. Bk Rev. Ad Acc. Pr Rev. Circ:** 2,000 (ctrl). available on microfilm and microfiche from University Microfilms International (UMI). Documents available from The Genuine Article, UMI Article Clearinghouse. ***Continues*** *Character and Personality, 0730-6407.*
**Desc:** Devoted to scientific investigations in the field of personality, especially experimental studies of personality and behavior dynamics, personality development, and individual differences in the cognitive, affective, and interpersonal domains.
**Ind/Abst** Abstr. Res. Pastor. Care Couns. (19??-); Acad. Abstr. Full Text Elite (July 1990-); Acad. Abstr. (July 1990-); Acad. Ind. [Computer File] (1987-); Acad. Search (July 1990-); AGRICOLA; Appl. Soc. Sci. Index Abstr.; Curr. Contents Soc. Behav. Sci.; Expand. Acad. Index (1987-); High. Educ. Abstr. (1965-); Hum. Resour. Abstr. (?-?); Index Med.; INFO-SOUTH Abstr.; Int. Bibliogr. Sociol.; Mag. Search; Middle East Abstr. Index; Newsp. Period. Abstr. (1991-); Peace Res. Abstr. J. (1946, 1971-), (1974-); Psychol. Abstr. (1945-); PsycINFO; PsycLit; Res. Alert [Full Cov.]; Risk Abstr.; Sage Fam. Stud. Abstr. (?-?); Soc. Plann. Policy Dev. Abstr.; Soc. Sci. Source (Jul. 1990-); Soc. Sci. Cit. Index [Full Cov.]; Soc. Sci. Index; Soc. Sci. Index Fulltext (Sept. 1988-) [Full Txt.]; Sociol. Abstr.; Women Stud. Abstr.

II
**JOURNAL OF PERSONALITY AND CLINICAL STUDIES.** **Added/Corp** Association of Clinical Psychologists, Delhi. **VFOAT** Journal of Personality & Clinical Studies. (198?)-. Periodical. English. sa. $30.00. Central News Agency Private Limited, 23 90 Connaught Circus, New Delhi India. **Tel** 011 91 11 344448. **(Subscription address:** Prints India, 11 Darya Ganj, New Delhi 110002 India.)
**Ind/Abst** Psychol. Abstr. (1985-); PsycLit.

US/0022-3514
**JOURNAL OF PERSONALITY AND SOCIAL PSYCHOLOGY.** [J. pers. soc. psychol.]. **Added/Corp** American Psychological Association. Vol. 1 (Jan. 1965)-. Periodical. English. mo. $525.00 (nonmember, institution) US. American Psychological Association, 750 First Street Northeast, Washington DC 20002. **Tel** (800)374-2721, (202)336-5600, (subscriptions - (202)336-5600. **ED** Abraham Tesser, PhD, Norman Miller, PhD, and Russell Geen, PhD. **LC** HM251; .J56. **DD** 301.1. **NLM** W1 JO828PC. **CODEN** JPSPB2. **[CCC]. Ad Acc. Pr Rev. Circ:** 6,000. available on microfilm and microfiche from University Microfilms International (UMI). Documents available from The Genuine Article, UMI Article Clearinghouse. ***Supersedes in part*** *Journal of Abnormal and Social Psychology, 0096-851X.*
**Desc:** Topics include measurements of attitudes, and the relation between attitudes and behavior; interpersonal relations and group processes; psychological and structural features of a group processes; personality processes and individual differences; interaction between the individual and the social environment.
**Ind/Abst** Acad. Abstr. Full Text Elite (July 1990-); Acad. Abstr. (July 1990-); Acad. Ind. [Computer File] (1987-); Acad. Search (July 1990-); Appl. Soc. Sci. Index Abstr.; Commun. Abstr.; Crim. Justice Abstr.; Curr. Contents Soc. Behav. Sci.; Curr. Index J. Educ.; Educ. Adm. Abstr. (?-?); Expand. Acad. Index (1987-); High. Educ. Abstr. (1965-); Hum. Resour. Abstr.; Index Med.; Index Period. Artic. Relat. Law (19??-19??); INFO-SOUTH Abstr.; Int. Bibliogr. Sociol.; Int. Polit. Sci. Abstr.; Mag. Search; Middle East Abstr. Index; MLA Int. Bibl. Books Artic. Mod. Lang. Lit.; Newsp. Period. Abstr. (1986-); Psychol. Abstr. (1965-); PsycINFO; PsycLit; PsycScan: Develop. Psych.; Res. Alert [Full Cov.]; Risk Abstr.; Sage Fam. Stud. Abstr.; Soc. Sci. Source (Jul. 1990-); Soc. Sci. Cit. Index [Full Cov.]; Soc. Sci. Index; Soc. Sci. Index Fulltext (Sept. 1988-) [Full Txt.]; Soc. Work Abstr. (Spring, Summer 1987-) [Select. Cov.]; Sociol. Educ. Abstr.; Spec. Educ. Needs Abstr.; SportSearch; Stud. Women Abstr.; Women Stud. Abstr.

US/0022-3891
**JOURNAL OF PERSONALITY ASSESSMENT.** [J. pers. assess.]. **Added/Corp** Society for Personality Assessment. Vol. 35 (Feb. 1971)-. Periodical. English. bm. $230.00 US & Canada; $275.00 other. Lawrence Erlbaum Associates, 365 Broadway, Suite 102, Hillsdale NJ 07642. **Tel** (201)666-4110, (800)926-6579, FAX (201)666-2394. **ED** Irving B Weiner. **LC** BF698.4; .J67. **DD** 155.28/05. **NLM** W1 JO828R. **CODEN** JNPABX. **Bk Rev. Ad Acc. Circ:** 2,500 (ctrl). available on microfilm and microfiche from University Microfilms International (UMI). Documents available from The Genuine Article. ***Continues*** *Journal of Projective Techniques & Personality Assessment, 0091-651X.*
**Desc:** Conforms with guidelines in the Publication Manual of the American Psychological Association.
**Ind/Abst** Appl. Soc. Sci. Index Abstr.; Curr. Contents Soc. Behav. Sci.; EMBASE; High. Educ. Abstr. (1972-); Index Med.; Middle East Abstr. Index; Psychol. Abstr. (1971-); PsycINFO; PsycLit; PsycScan: Clin. Psych.; Res. Alert [Full Cov.]; Saf. Health Work; Soc. Plann. Policy Dev. Abstr.; Soc. Sci. Cit. Index [Full Cov.]; Sociol. Abstr.; SportSearch; Women Stud. Abstr.

US/0885-579X
**JOURNAL OF PERSONALITY DISORDERS.** [J. pers. disord.]. Vol. 1, No. 1 (Spring 1987)-. Periodical. English. Four times a year. $115.00 (institutions); $135.00 others. Guilford Publications Inc., 72 Spring Street, New York NY 10012. **Tel** (212)431-9800, (800)365-7006, FAX (212)966-6708. **(Subscription address:** Turpin Distribution Services Limited, Blackhorse Road, Letchworth, Hertfordshire SG6 1HN, United Kingdom.) **ED** Theodore Millon and Allen Frances. **LC** RC554; .J68. **DD** 616.89. **NLM** W1; JO828RD. **[CCC].** Index available. **Bk Rev. Ad Acc. Circ:** 1,000. available on microfilm and microfiche from University Microfilms International (UMI). Documents available from The Genuine Article.
**Desc:** Devoted exclusively to the diagnosis and treatment of clinically significant personality disorders, this new multidisciplinary journal presents research on normal and pathological personality and development, new methodologies for assisting personality, clinical nosologies for personality disorders, epidemiological research, treatment innovations, and outcome research.
**Ind/Abst** Curr. Contents Soc. Behav. Sci.; EMBASE; Psychol. Abstr. (1987-); PsycINFO (1990-); PsycLit; Res. Alert [Full Cov.]; Soc. Sci. Cit. Index [Full Cov.]; Soc. Work Abstr. [Select. Cov.].

US/0047-2662
**JOURNAL OF PHENOMENOLOGICAL PSYCHOLOGY.** [J. phenomenol. psychol.]. Vol. 1 (Fall 1970)-. Periodical. English. Twice a year (Apr., & Nov.). $50.00 (institutions); $40.00 (individual); $29.95 (Back Issues). Humanities Press, 165 1st Avenue, Atlantic Highlands NJ 07716. **Tel** (908)872-1441, (800)221-3845, FAX (908)872-0717, telex 752233. **ED** Amedeo Giorgi, University of Quebec at Montreal. **LC** BF204.5; .J68. **DD** 150/.19/2. **NLM** W1 JO831F. **CODEN** JPHPAE. **Bk Rev. Ad Acc, Adv Mgr:** J. Camlin, **Tel** (308)872-1441. **Circ:** 300. available on microfilm and microfiche from University Microfilms International (UMI). Documents available from The Genuine Article.
**Desc:** Presents papers dealing with the application of phenomenological thought to the problems of psychology.
**Ind/Abst** Psychol. Abstr. (1970-); PsycINFO; PsycLit; Res. Alert [Full Cov.]; Soc. Sci. Cit. Index [Full Cov.].

US/0889-3675
**JOURNAL OF POETRY THERAPY.** [J. poet. ther.]. **Added/Corp** National Association for Poetry Therapy (U.S.). (Fall 1987)-. Periodical. English. qt. £35.00 (individuals), £130.00 (institutions) UK; $175.00 US; $205.00 other. Human Sciences Press, PO Box 735, 233 Spring Street, New York NY 10013. **Tel** (212)620-8000, FAX (212)807-1047, telex 23421139. **(Subscription address:** Eurospan Ltd., Journals and Serials Division, 3 Henrietta Street, Covent Garden, London WC2E 8LU England.) **ED** Nicholas Mazza. **DD** 615. **NLM** W1; JO837G. **CODEN** JPTHEK. **[CCC].** available on microfilm and microfiche from University Microfilms International (UMI).
**Desc:** Emerging from the tradition of the arts and psychotherapy, this interdisciplinary journal is devoted to the use of poetics in health, mental health, education and other human service settings.
**Ind/Abst** Sage Fam. Stud. Abstr. (?-?); Soc. Plann. Policy Dev. Abstr.; Soc. Work Abstr. [Select. Cov.].

US/0737-1195
**JOURNAL OF POLYMORPHOUS PERVERSITY.** **VFOAT** JPP. Vol. 1, No. 1, (Spring 1984)-. Periodical. English. Twice a year. $14.00 US; $15.75 Canada; $21.75 other. Wry-Bred Press Inc, 10 Waterside Plaza, Suite 20-B, New York NY 10010. **Tel** (212)689-5473. **ED** Glenn C. Ellenbogen. **Ad Acc. Circ:** 3,500.
**Desc:** A humorous and satirical journal of psychology, psychiatry and medicine.

US/0278-095X
**JOURNAL OF PRIMARY PREVENTION, THE.** **See** Public Health and Safety.

US/0734-2829
**JOURNAL OF PSYCHOEDUCATIONAL ASSESSMENT.** **VFOAT** JPA. Vol. 1, No. 1 (March 1983)-. Periodical. English. Four times a year. $120.00 US; $133.50 other. Clinical Psychology Publishing Company, 4 Conant Square, Brandon VT 05733. **Tel** (802)247-6871, (800)433-8234. **LC** LB1131; .J8. **DD** 371.2/6/05. **NLM** W1; JO857E. **CODEN** JPSAES. Index available (bound in last volume of each issue). Documents available from The Genuine Article.
**Ind/Abst** Curr. Contents Soc. Behav. Sci.; Psychol. Abstr. (1983-); PsycINFO; PsycLit; Res. Alert [Full Cov.]; Soc. Plann. Policy Dev. Abstr.; Soc. Sci. Cit. Index [Full Cov.].

US/0145-3378
**JOURNAL OF PSYCHOHISTORY, THE.** [J. psychohist.]. Vol. 4 (Summer 1976)-. Periodical. English. Four times a year (Seasonally). $48.00 (individuals), $119.00 (institutions). Association Psychohistory Inc, 140 Riverside Drive, New York NY 10024-2605. **Tel** (212)799-2294, FAX (212)799-2294. **ED** Lloyd deMause. **LC** HQ768; .H56. **DD** 155. **NLM** W1 JO857H. **CODEN** JOPSDP. **[CCC]. Bk Rev. Ad Acc. Pr Rev. Circ:** 6,000. available on microfilm from Xerox. Documents available from BIOSIS Document Express. ***Continues*** *History of Childhood Quarterly, 0091-4266;* ***Absorbed*** *Journal of Psycoanalytic Anthropology, 0278-2944.*
**Desc:** A journal exploring all aspects of the rapidly developing discipline of psychohistory.
**Ind/Abst** Am. Hist. Life (1973-); Anthropol. Lit. (Vol. 11, 1989); BHA : Biblio. Hist. Art; Biol. Abstr.; Child Dev. Abstr. Bibliogr.; Child. Lit. Abstr. (19??-); Middle East Abstr. Index; Psychol. Abstr. (1976-); PsycINFO; PsycLit; Soc. Plann. Policy Dev. Abstr.; Sociol. Abstr.

US/0090-6905
**JOURNAL OF PSYCHOLINGUISTIC RESEARCH. See** Linguistics.

II/0022-3972
**JOURNAL OF PSYCHOLOGICAL RESEARCHES.** [J. psychol. res.]. **Added/Corp** Madras. University. Dept. of Psychology. Madras Psychological Society. (Jan. 1957)-. Periodical. English. Three times a year (Jan., May, Sept.,). $75.00 India; $85.00 others. The Madras Psychology Society, University of Madras, Department of Psychology, Madras 600 005 India. **Tel** 011 91 44 568778 Ext. 306. **LC** BF1; .J668. **NLM** W1 JO857T. **CODEN** JPSRB8. Index available. **Bk Rev. Ad Acc.** available on microfilm and microfiche from University Microfilms International (UMI).
**Ind/Abst** Psychol. Abstr. (1957-); PsycINFO; PsycLit.

US/0895-8750
**JOURNAL OF PSYCHOLOGICAL TYPE.** (JOURNAL OF PSYCHOLOGICAL TYPE : THE OFFICIAL RESEARCH JOURNAL OF THE ASSOCIATION FOR PSYCHOLOGICAL TYPE.). [J. psychol. type]. **Added/Corp** Association for Psychological Type (U.S.). **VFOAT** JPT. Vol. 7 (1984)-. Periodical. English. Four times a year (Mar., June, Sept., Dec.). $88.00 US; $99.00 others. American Association of Psychological Type, PO Box 6161, Mississippi State University, Psychology Department, Mississippi State MS 39762. **Tel** (601)325-7655, FAX (601)325-3299. **ED** Dr. Thomas Carskadon. **DD** 155. **Ad Acc. Circ:** 7,000 (ctrl). ***Continues*** *Research in Psychological Type.*

US/0022-3980
**JOURNAL OF PSYCHOLOGY, THE.** [J. psychol.]. Vol. 1 (1935/1936)-. Periodical. English. bm (6 issues). $110.00. Heldref Publications, 1319 Eighteenth Street Northwest, Washington DC 20036-1802. **Tel** (202)296-6267, (800)365-9753, FAX (202)296-5149. **ED** Leonard Doob, John Horrocks, and Arthur Riopelle. **LC** BF1; .J67. **DD** 150.5; 159.905. **NLM** W1 JO858. **CODEN** JOPSAM. **[CCC]. Ad Acc. Pr Rev. Circ:** 1,633. available on microfilm and microfiche from University Microfilms International (UMI). Documents available from The Genuine Article, BIOSIS Document Express, UMI Article Clearinghouse, CASDDS.
**Desc:** Publishes a variety of research and theoretical articles in the field of psychology, with an emphasis on articles that integrate divergent data and theories, explore new avenues for thinking and research present outrageous criticisms of the present status of the behavioral disciplines.
**Ind/Abst** Abstr. Res. Pastor. Care Couns.; Acad. Abstr. Full Text Elite (July 1990-) [Full Txt.]; Acad. Abstr. (July 1990-); Acad. Ind. [Computer File] (1987-); Acad. Search (July 1990-); Biol. Abstr.; Chem. Abstr.; Commun. Abstr. (?-?); Cumul. Index Nurs. Allied Health Lit.; Curr. Index J. Educ.; Ergon. Abstr.; Except. Child Educ. Resour.; Expand. Acad. Index (1987-); High. Educ. Abstr. (1965-); Index Med.; INFO-SOUTH Abstr.; Int. Aerosp. Abstr.; Int. Bibliogr. Sociol.; Int. Polit. Sci. Abstr.; Mag. Artic. Summar. Elite (July 1990-) [Full Txt.]; Mag. Search; Middle East Abstr. Index; Newsp. Period. Abstr. (1989-); Life Sci. Collect.; Psychol. Abstr. (1935-); PsycINFO; PsycLit; Res. Alert [Full Cov.]; Soc. Plann. Policy Dev. Abstr.; Soc. Sci. Source (Jul. 1990-); Soc. Sci. Cit. Index [Full Cov.]; Soc. Sci. Index; Soc. Sci. Index Fulltext (Nov. 1988-) [Full Txt.]; Soc. Work Abstr. (?-?); Sociol. Abstr.; SportSearch; Stud. Women Abstr.; Women Stud. Abstr.

US/0733-4273
**JOURNAL OF PSYCHOLOGY AND CHRISTIANITY. See** Religion and Theology.

US/0890-7064
**JOURNAL OF PSYCHOLOGY & HUMAN SEXUALITY.** [J. psychol. human sex.]. **VFOAT** Journal of Psychology and Human Sexuality. Vol. 1, No. 1 (1988)-. Periodical. English. qt. $150.00 US; $210.00 other. The Haworth Press Inc, 10 Alice Street, Binghamton NY 13904-1580. **Tel** (607)722-5857, (800)3-HAWORTH, FAX (607)722-1424. **ED** Eli Coleman (editor's address: Program in Human Sexuality, 1300 South 2nd Street, Minneapolis, MN 55414-1092). **LC** BF692; .J64. **DD** 155.3/05. **NLM** W1; JO858B. **CODEN** JPSXET. **Bk Rev. Ad Acc. Pr Rev. Acid Free. Circ:** 226. available on microfilm and microfiche from University Microfilms International (UMI). Documents available from Haworth Document Delivery Service.
**Desc:** Provides new and pertinent psychological perspectives on human sexuality issues. Articles report new theory and research, and clinical or educational methodology which cover the entire scope of the discipline of psychology.
**Ind/Abst** Biol. Dig.; Psychol. Abstr. (1988-); PsycINFO; PsycLit; Soc. Plann. Policy Dev. Abstr.; Soc. Work Abstr. [Select. Cov.].

US/0700-9801
**JOURNAL OF PSYCHOLOGY AND JUDAISM.** [J. psychol. Jud.]. **Added/Corp** Center for the Study of Psychology and Judaism. Vol. 1 (Fall 1976)-. Periodical. English. qt. $185.00 US; $215.00 other. Human Sciences Press, PO Box 735, 233 Spring Street, New York NY 10013. **Tel** (212)620-8000, FAX (212)807-1047, telex 23421139. **(Subscription address:** Eurospan Ltd., Journals and Serials Division, 3 Henrietta Street, Covent Garden, London WC2E 8LU England.**) ED** Reuven P. Bulka. **LC** BF51; .J68. **DD** 150/.5. **NLM** W1 JO858C. **CODEN** JPJUD8. **[CCC].** Index available. cum. index. **Bk Rev. Ad Acc. Circ:** 1,000 (ctrl). available on microfilm and microfiche from University Microfilms International (UMI). ***Continues*** *Journal of Aging & Judaism, 0884-8688.*
**Desc:** A provocative journal which explores the relationship between modern psychology and Judaism on a clinical as well as philosophical level. By including case histories of the distinctly Jewish problems of identity, and the unique dynamics involved in the treatment of Jewish patients, it is hoped that the capacity of all therapists, Jewish and non-Jewish, will be enhanced.
**Ind/Abst** Abstr. Res. Pastor. Care Couns. (19??-); Curr. Contents Soc. Behav. Sci.; Except. Hum. Exp.; Guide Soc. Sci. Relig.; Index Book Rev. Relig.; Index Jew. Period. (199?-); Middle East Abstr. Index; MLA Int. Bibl. Books Artic. Mod. Lang. Lit.; Psychol. Abstr. (1976-); PsycINFO (1976-); PsycLit; Relig. Index One Period.; Relig. Theol. Abstr.; Sage Fam. Stud. Abstr. (?-?); Soc. Plann. Policy Dev. Abstr.

US/0091-6471
**JOURNAL OF PSYCHOLOGY AND THEOLOGY.** [J. psychol. theol.]. **Added/Corp** Rosemead Graduate School of Psychology. Rosemead Graduate School of Professional Psychology. Vol. 1 (Jan. 1973)-. Academic Scholarly Publication. English. Four times a year (Mar., June, Sept., Dec.). $38.00 US, $40.00 others (surface mail); $50.00 (airmail). Rosemead Graduate School of Psychology, Biola University, 13800 Biola Avenue, La Mirada CA 90639. **Tel** (310)903-4727, FAX (310)903-4748. **ED** William F. Hunter. **LC** BF1; .J6695. **DD** 253.5/01/9. **NLM** W1 JO858E. **CODEN** JPSTDG. Index available ($16.00). **Bk Rev. Pr Rev. Circ:** 2,000 (ctrl). available on an online database from BRS; and DIALOG; available on microfilm and microfiche from University Microfilms International (UMI). Documents available from The Genuine Article.
**Desc:** Recent scholarly thinking and research on the interrelationships of psychological and theological concepts and their application to a variety of professional and pastoral settings.
**Ind/Abst** Abstr. Res. Pastor. Care Couns. (19??-); Arts Humanit. Citation Index [Full Cov.]; Christ. Period. Index; Curr. Contents Arts Humanit.; Curr. Contents Soc. Behav. Sci.; Except. Hum. Exp.; Guide Soc. Sci. Relig.; High. Educ. Abstr. (1981-); Index Book Rev. Relig.; Old Testam. Abstr.; Psychol. Abstr. (1973-); PsycINFO; PsycLit; Relig. Index One Period. (1973-); Relig. Theol. Abstr.; Res. Alert [Full Cov.]; Soc. Sci. Cit. Index [Full Cov.].

US/0882-2689
**JOURNAL OF PSYCHOPATHOLOGY AND BEHAVIORAL ASSESSMENT.** [J. psychopathol. behav. assess.]. Vol. 7, No. 1 (March 1985)-. Periodical. English. Four times a year. $250.00 institutions, $44.00 individuals US; $295.00 institutions, $51.00 individuals other. Plenum Press, 233 Spring Street, New York NY 10013-1578. **Tel** (212)620-8000, (800)221-9369, FAX (212)463-0742, (212)807-1047, telex 23/421139. **LC** BF698.4; .J65. **DD** 616.89/005. **NLM** W1; JO858F. **CODEN** JPBAEB. **[CCC]. Pr Rev.** available on microfilm and microfiche from University Microfilms International (UMI). Documents available from The Genuine Article, BIOSIS Document Express. ***Continues*** *Journal of Behavioral Assessment, 0164-0305.*
**Ind/Abst** Biol. Abstr. (1985-); Curr. Contents Soc. Behav. Sci.; EMBASE; Psychol. Abstr. (1985-); PsycINFO (1990-); PsycLit; Res. Alert [Full Cov.]; Soc. Sci. Cit. Index [Full Cov.]; Soc. Work Abstr. [Select. Cov.]; Spec. Educ. Needs Abstr.; Stud. Women Abstr.

US/0449-3044
**JOURNAL OF PSYCHOPHARMACOLOGY.** ***Ceased.*** **See** Pharmacy and Pharmacology.

UK/0269-8811
**JOURNAL OF PSYCHOPHARMACOLOGY (OXFORD, ENGLAND). See** Pharmacy and Pharmacology.

UK/0269-8803
**JOURNAL OF PSYCHOPHYSIOLOGY.** **Added/Corp** Psychophysiology Society (Great Britain) Deutsche Gesellschaft Fur Psychophysiologie und Ihre Anwendung. Scandinavian Psychophysiology Society. Dutch Psychophysiology Society. Vol. 1, No. 1 March (1987)-. Periodical. English. Four times a year. DM224.00. Hogrefe Verlag fuer Psychologie, Rohnsweg 25, D 37085 Goettingen Germany. **Tel** 011 49 551 496090, FAX 011 49 551 4960988. **(Subscription address:** Hogrefe & Huber Publishers, Seattle Office, Box 2487, Kirkland WA 98083.**) ED** G. Barrett. **NLM** W1; JO858T. **[CCC]. Bk Rev. Ad Acc. Circ:** 1,000. available on microfilm and microfiche from University Microfilms International (UMI). Documents available from The Genuine Article.
**Desc:** An outlet for original research in all areas employing, psychophysiological techniques, or of relevance to their interpretation, including physiology, clinical psychology, psychiatry, neurosciences, pharmacology and genetics. The journal also acknowledges the important contribution animal research makes to these areas.
**Ind/Abst** Curr. Aware. Biol. Sci., CABS; EMBASE; Psychol. Abstr. (1987-); PsycINFO (1990-); PsycLit; Ref. Upd. Deluxe Ed.; Res. Alert [Full Cov.]; Soc. Sci. Cit. Index [Select. Cov.].

UK/0022-3999
**JOURNAL OF PSYCHOSOMATIC RESEARCH. See** Medical Science and Technology.

US/1053-0479
**JOURNAL OF PSYCHOTHERAPY INTEGRATION.** [J. psychother. integr.]. **Added/Corp** Society for the Exploration of Psychotherapy Integration. Vol. 1, No. 1 (Mar. 1991)-. Periodical. English. Four times a year. $125.00 institutions, $37.00 individuals US; $145.00 institutions, $43.00 individuals other. Plenum Press, 233 Spring Street, New York NY 10013-1578. **Tel** (212)620-8000, (800)221-9369, FAX (212)463-0742, (212)807-1047, telex 23/421139. **ED** Hal Arkovitz. **LC** RC475; .J63. **DD** 616.89/14/05. **NLM** W1; JO859F. **CODEN** JPINEH. **[CCC].**
**Desc:** Seeking to look beyond the limitations of the multitude of single school approaches to psychotherapy, publishes articles that focus on enhancing understanding of the processes of change and improving the effectiveness of psychotherapy based on integrative approaches.

US/0894-9085
**JOURNAL OF RATIONAL-EMOTIVE AND COGNITIVE-BEHAVIOR THERAPY.** (JOURNAL OF RATIONAL-EMOTIVE AND COGNITIVE-BEHAVIOR THERAPY : RET.). [J. ration.-emot. cogn.-behav. ther.]. **Added/Corp** Institute for Rational-Emotive Therapy (New York, N.Y.). **VFOAT** Journal of Rational Emotive and Cognitive Behavior Therapy; RET. Vol. 6, No. 1 & 2 (Spring/Summer 1988)-. Periodical. English. qt. $210.00 US; $245.00 other. Human Sciences Press, PO Box 735, 233 Spring Street, New York NY 10013. **Tel** (212)620-8000, FAX (212)807-1047, telex 23421139. **(Subscription address:** Eurospan Ltd., Journals and Serials Division, 3 Henrietta Street, Covent Garden, London WC2E 8LU England.**) ED** Russell Grieger and Paul Woods. **LC** RC489.R3; J68. **DD** 616. **NLM** W1; JO777MT. **[CCC].** available on microfilm and microfiche from University Microfilms International (UMI). ***Continues*** *Journal of Rational Emotive Therapy, 0748-1985.*
**Desc:** A forum for stimulation and maintenance of rational-emotive therapy and other forms of cognitive-behavioral therapy.
**Ind/Abst** Psychol. Abstr. (1988-); PsycINFO (1990-); PsycLit.

US/0743-0493
**JOURNAL OF REALITY THERAPY.** (JOURNAL OF REALITY THERAPY / SPONSORED BY INSTITUTE FOR REALITY THERAPY.). [J. real. ther.]. **Added/Corp** Institute for Reality Therapy. Vol. 1, No. 1 (Sept. 1981)-. Periodical. English. Twice a year (Spring & Fall). $8.00 US; $15.00 other. Journal of Reality Therapy, 203 Lake Hall, Northeastern University, Boston MA 02115. **Tel** (617)373-3276. **ED** Larry Litwack. **LC** RC489.R37; J68. **DD** 616.89/14. **NLM** W1; JO865P. **Pr Rev. Circ:** 2,000.
**Ind/Abst** Psychol. Abstr. (1981-); PsycINFO (1990-); PsycLit.

US/1054-0830
**JOURNAL OF REGRESSION THERAPY, THE.** [J. regres. ther.]. **Added/Corp** Association for Past-Life Research and Therapy. Vol. 1, No. 1 (Spring 1986)-. Periodical. English. an (Dec.). $14.00. Association of Past-Life Research and Therapy, PO Box 20151, Riverside CA 92516. **Tel** (909)784-1570. **ED** Garrett Oppenheim. **LC** IN PROCESS. **DD** 616. **Bk Rev. Circ:** 500 (ctrl).

US/0275-1402
**JOURNAL OF RELIGION AND THE APPLIED BEHAVIORAL SCIENCES. See** Religion and Theology.

UK/0264-6838
**JOURNAL OF REPRODUCTIVE AND INFANT PSYCHOLOGY.** See Medical Science and Technology-Gynecology and Obstetrics.

US/0092-6566
**JOURNAL OF RESEARCH IN PERSONALITY.** [J. res. pers.]. Vol. 7 (June 1973)-. Academic Scholarly Publication. English. qt (4 issues). $214.00 US and Canada; $260.00 other. Academic Press, Inc., 6277 Sea Harbor Drive, Orlando FL 32887. **Tel** (800)543-9534, (407)345-4100, FAX (407)363-9661. **ED** William Griffitt. **LC** BF1; .J62. **DD** 150/.5. **NLM** W1 JO869T. **CODEN** JRPRA6. **[CCC]. Pr Rev.** Documents available from The Genuine Article, BIOSIS Document Express. ***Continues*** *Journal of Experimental Research in Personality, 0022-1023.*
**Desc:** Presents articles that examine important issues in the field of personality and in related fields basic to the understanding of personality.
**Ind/Abst** Appl. Soc. Sci. Index Abstr.; Biol. Abstr.; Commun. Abstr. (?-?); Crim. Justice Abstr.; Curr. Contents Soc. Behav. Sci.; Curr. Index J. Educ.; EMBASE; High. Educ. Abstr. (1975-); Middle East Abstr. Index; Psychol. Abstr. (1973-); PsycINFO; PsycLit; Res. Alert [Full Cov.]; Soc. Sci. Cit. Index [Full Cov.]; Soc. Work Abstr. [Select. Cov.]; SportSearch; Women Stud. Abstr.

US/1050-8392
**JOURNAL OF RESEARCH ON ADOLESCENCE.** (JOURNAL OF RESEARCH ON ADOLESCENCE : THE OFFICIAL JOURNAL OF THE SOCIETY FOR RESEARCH ON ADOLESCENCE.). [J. res. adolesc.]. **Added/Corp** Society for Research on Adolescence. Vol. 1, No. 1 (1991)-. Periodical. English. qt. $165.00 US & Canada; $190.00 other. Lawrence Erlbaum Associates, 365 Broadway, Suite 102, Hillsdale NJ 07642. **Tel** (201)666-4110, (800)926-6579, FAX (201)666-2394. **ED** Richard M Lerner. **LC** HQ796; .J6245. **DD** 305.23/5/05. **NLM** W1 JO87C. **CODEN** JRADET.
**Desc:** Presents research that employs a diverse array of methodologies published in articles that significantly advance knowledge about the second decade of life.
**Ind/Abst** Soc. Plann. Policy Dev. Abstr.

US/0895-5646
**JOURNAL OF RISK AND UNCERTAINTY.** See Economics.

US/0276-2285
**JOURNAL OF RURAL COMMUNITY PSYCHOLOGY.** ***Ceased.*** [J. rural community psychol.]. **Added/Corp** California School of Professional Psychology, Fresno. **VFOAT** Rural Community Psychology. Vol. 1, No. 1 (Spring 1980)-Vol. 12. Periodical. English. an. California School Professional Psychology, 1350 M Street, Fresno CA 93721. **Tel** (209)486-8420, FAX (209)486-0734. **ED** Mary Beth Kenkel and I M Abou-Ghorra. **LC** RA790.A1; J7. **DD** 362.2/0425. **NLM** W1 JO871J. **Bk Rev**, (Qty: 1). **Ad Acc, Adv Mgr:** Smith. **Circ:** 100.
**Desc:** Human behavior in rural environments, rural mental health interventions and psychological impact of rural environment.
**Ind/Abst** AGRICOLA [Full Cov.]; Curr. Index J. Educ.; Psychol. Abstr. (1980-); PsycINFO; PsycLit.

●US/1061-0405
**JOURNAL OF RUSSIAN AND EAST EUROPEAN PSYCHOLOGY.** [J. Russ. East Eur. psychol.]. Vol. 30, No. 1 (Jan.-Feb. 1992)-. Periodical. English (translations available in Russian). bm. $506.00 US; $557.00 other. M. E. Sharpe Inc., 80 Business Park Drive, Armonk NY 10504. **Tel** (914)273-1800, (800)541-6563, FAX (914)273-2106. **LC** BF1; .S6. **DD** 150. **NLM** W1; JO871T. Documents available from BIOSIS Document Express. ***Continues*** *Soviet Psychology, 0038-5751.*
**Ind/Abst** Biol. Abstr. (1979-); Psychol. Abstr.

●US
**JOURNAL OF SCHOOL PSYCHOLOGY.** (1994)-. English. sa. $50.00 US; $60.00 other. Human Sciences Press, PO Box 735, 233 Spring Street, New York NY 10013. **Tel** (212)620-8000, FAX (212)807-1047, telex 23421139. **(Subscription address:** UK & European Subscriptions: Eurospan Group, Journals & Serials Division, 3 Henrietta Street, Covent Garden, London WC2E 8LU England; Telephone: 011 44 77 240-0856 FAX: 011 44 71 379-0609**)**

US/0022-4405
**JOURNAL OF SCHOOL PSYCHOLOGY.** [J. sch. psychol.]. **Added/Corp** Ohio. Dept. of Education. Vol. 1 (Jan. 1963)-. Periodical. English. qt. $154.00 The Americas; £104.00 other. Pergamon Press, An Imprint of Elsevier Science Ltd., The Boulevard, Langford Lane, Kidlington, Oxford OX5 1GB United Kingdom. **Tel** 011 44 865 843000, 011 44 865 843699, FAX 011 44 865 843010. **(Subscription address:** Elsevier Science Ltd. Oxford Fulfillment Centre, PO Box 800, Kidlington, Oxford OX5 1DX United Kingdom.**) ED** Joel Meyers. **LC** LB3013.6; .J6. **DD** 370.15/05. **NLM** W1 JO874. **CODEN** JSCPAA. **[CCC]. Bk Rev. Ad Acc. Pr Rev.** available on microfilm and microfiche from University Microfilms International (UMI). Documents available from The Genuine Article.
**Ind/Abst** Acad. Search (July 1993-); Aust. Educ. Index (?-199?); Contents Pages Educ.; Curr. Contents Soc. Behav. Sci.; Curr. Index J. Educ.; Educ. Index; Except. Child Educ. Resour. (19??-19??); INFO-SOUTH Abstr.; Mag. Search; Psychol. Abstr. (1963-19??); PsycINFO; PsycLit; Res. Alert [Full Cov.]; Soc. Plann. Policy Dev. Abstr.; Soc. Sci. Cit. Index [Full Cov.]; Soc. Work Abstr. [Select. Cov.]; Sociol. Abstr.; Spec. Educ. Needs Abstr.; Women Stud. Abstr.

US/0736-7236
**JOURNAL OF SOCIAL AND CLINICAL PSYCHOLOGY.** [J. soc. clin. psychol.]. Vol. 1 No. 1 (1983)-. Periodical. English. Four times a year. $115.00 (institutions); $132.50 others. Guilford Publications Inc., 72 Spring Street, New York NY 10012. **Tel** (212)431-9800, (800)365-7006, FAX (212)966-6708. **(Subscription address:** Turpin Distribution Services Limited, Blackhorse Road, Letchworth, Hertfordshire SG6 1HN, United Kingdom.**) ED** C. R. Snyder. **LC** RC467; .J66. **DD** 616.89/005. **[CCC].** Index available. **Bk Rev. Ad Acc. Pr Rev. Circ:** 500. available on microfilm and microfiche from University Microfilms International (UMI). Documents available from The Genuine Article.
**Desc:** Designed to promote communication and scholarship at the interface of social and clinical psychology. The journal features reports of clinical and empirical research on various topics.
**Ind/Abst** Curr. Contents Soc. Behav. Sci.; High. Educ. Abstr.; Int. Bibliogr. Sociol.; Multicult. Educ. Abstr.; Psychol. Abstr. (1983-); PsycINFO; PsycLit; Res. Alert [Full Cov.]; Sage Fam. Stud. Abstr. (?-?); Soc. Sci. Cit. Index [Full Cov.]; Sociol. Educ. Abstr.; Spec. Educ. Needs Abstr.; Stud. Women Abstr.

UK/0265-4075
**JOURNAL OF SOCIAL AND PERSONAL RELATIONSHIPS.** [J. soc. pers. relatsh.]. Vol. 1, No. 1 (March 1984)-. Periodical. English. qt. £110.00. Sage Publications Ltd., 6 Bonhill Street, London EC2A 4PU, UK. **Tel** 071 374 0645, FAX 071 374 8741, telex 296207 SAGE G. **ED** Steve Duck. **NLM** W1; JO877KH. **CODEN** JSRLE9. **Bk Rev. Ad Acc. Pr Rev. Acid Free.** Documents available from The Genuine Article.
**Desc:** Meets the need for a cohesive journal in the growing field of personal relationships. This journal is multi-disciplinary, drawing material from the fields of social psychology, communications, developmental psychology and sociology.
**Ind/Abst** Appl. Soc. Sci. Index Abstr.; Curr. Contents Soc. Behav. Sci.; Psychol. Abstr. (1988-); PsycINFO; PsycLit; Res. Alert [Full Cov.]; Soc. Plann. Policy Dev. Abstr.; Soc. Sci. Cit. Index [Full Cov.]; Sociol. Educ. Abstr.; Stud. Women Abstr.

US/0886-1641
**JOURNAL OF SOCIAL BEHAVIOR AND PERSONALITY.** [J. soc. behav. pers.]. Vol. 1, No. 1 (Jan. 1986)-. Periodical. English. qt. $65.00 (US), $73.00 (other). Select Press, PO Box 37, Corte Madera CA 94976. **Tel** (415)924-1612. **ED** Rick Crandall. **LC** BF698.A1; J7. **DD** 155.2/05. **CODEN** JSBPE9. **Ad Acc. Pr Rev. Circ:** 700. Documents available from The Genuine Article.
**Desc:** Most papers will be research-based on topics of general interest within basic disciplines such as psychology, sociology, and anthropology or applied areas such as business, clinical practice and public policy.
**Ind/Abst** Abstr. Res. Pastor. Care Couns. (19??-); Arts Humanit. Citation Index [Select. Cov.]; Commun. Abstr.; Curr. Contents Soc. Behav. Sci.; High. Educ. Abstr.; Psychol. Abstr. (1986-); PsycINFO; PsycLit; Res. Alert [Full Cov.]; Soc. Plann. Policy Dev. Abstr.; Soc. Sci. Cit. Index [Full Cov.].

US/0022-4537
**JOURNAL OF SOCIAL ISSUES, THE.** See Social Sciences.

US/0022-4545
**JOURNAL OF SOCIAL PSYCHOLOGY, THE.** [J. soc. psychol.]. **Added/Corp** Helen Dwight Reid Educational Foundation. Vol. 1; (Feb. 1930)-. Academic Scholarly Publication. English (German; summaries and/or abstracts in French and German). bm. $110.00. Heldref Publications, 1319 Eighteenth Street Northwest, Washington DC 20036-1802. **Tel** (202)296-6267, (800)365-9753, FAX (202)296-5149. **ED** Leonard W Doob. **LC** HM251.A1; J6. **DD** 150.5; 159.905. **NLM** W1 JO888P. **CODEN** JSPSAG. **[CCC]. Bk Rev. Ad Acc. Pr Rev. Circ:** 2,300. available on microfilm and microfiche from University Microfilms International (UMI). Documents available from The Genuine Article, BIOSIS Document Express, UMI Article Clearinghouse.
**Desc:** Publishes experimental, empirical, and field studies of groups, cultural effects, cross-national problems, language, and ethnicity. It also publishes cross-cultural notes and briefly reported replications and refinements. Notable articles include "Power Strategies in Dual-Career and Traditional Couples" and "Arab Communal Identity in Israel and the Lebanon."
**Ind/Abst** Acad. Abstr. Full Text Elite (Jan. 1992-) [Full Txt.]; Acad. Abstr. (Jan. 1992-); Acad. Search (Jan. 1992-); Appl. Soc. Sci. Index Abstr.; Biol. Abstr.; Chicano Index; Commun. Abstr. (?-?); Crim. Justice Abstr.; Crim. Penol. Police Sci. Abstr.; Cumul. Index Nurs. Allied Health Lit.; Curr. Contents Soc. Behav. Sci.; Curr. Index J. Educ. (March 1990); Educ. Adm. Abstr. (?-?); EMBASE; Except. Child Educ. Resour. (19??-19??); Expand. Acad. Index (1989-); High. Educ. Abstr. (1965-); Hum. Resour. Abstr.; Index Med.; INFO-SOUTH Abstr.; Int. Bibliogr. Sociol.; Int. Labour Doc.; Int. Polit. Sci. Abstr.; Mag. Artic. Summar. Elite (Jan. 1992-) [Full Txt.]; Mag. Artic. Summar. Select (Jan. 1992-); Mag. Artic. Summar. CD-ROM (Jan. 1992-); Mag. Search; Middle East Abstr. Index; Multicult. Educ. Abstr.; Newsp. Period. Abstr. (1989-); Peace Res. Abstr. J. (1958-1977); Psychol. Abstr. (1930-); PsycINFO; PsycLit; Res. Alert [Full Cov.]; Res. High. Educ. Abstr.; Sage Fam. Stud. Abstr. (?-?); School Organ. Manage. Abstr.; Soc. Plann. Policy Dev. Abstr.; Soc. Sci. Source (Jan. 1992-) [Full Txt.]; Soc. Sci. Cit. Index [Full Cov.]; Soc. Sci. Index; Soc. Sci. Index Fulltext (Aug. 1988-) [Full Txt.]; Soc. Work Abstr. [Select. Cov.]; Sociol. Abstr.; Sociol. Educ. Abstr.; Stud. Women Abstr.; Tech. Educ. Train. Abstr.; Vocat. Search (Jan. 1992-) [Full Txt.]; Women Stud. Abstr.

US/0003-0651
**JOURNAL OF THE AMERICAN PSYCHOANALYTIC ASSOCIATION.** [J. Am. Psychoanal. Assoc.]. **Main/Corp** American Psychoanalytic Association. **Added/Corp** American Psychoanalytic Association. Bulletin of the American Psychoanalytic Association. Vol. 1 (Jan. 1953)-. Academic Scholarly Publication. English. qt. $112.50 (institutions), $92.50 (individuals) US; $149.00 (institutions), $126.50 (individuals) other. International Universities Press Inc., 59 Boston Post Road, PO Box 1524, Madison CT 06443-1524. **Tel** (203)245-4000, FAX (203)245-0775, telex 282986 IUP BK. **ED** Theodore Shapiro. **LC** BF173.A2; A63. **DD** 616.89/17/05. **NLM** W1 JO91K. **CODEN** JAPOAE. Index available. cum. index. **Bk Rev. Ad Acc. Pr Rev. Circ:** 2,000 (ctrl). Documents available from The Genuine Article, BIOSIS Document Express.
**Desc:** Articles on all aspects of psychoanalysis.
**Ind/Abst** Abstr. Res. Pastor. Care Couns. (19??-); Appl. Soc. Sci. Index Abstr.; Arts Humanit. Citation Index [Select. Cov.]; Biol. Abstr.; Curr. Contents Soc. Behav. Sci.; EMBASE; Index Med.; Middle East Abstr. Index; Life Sci. Collect.; Psychol. Abstr. (1953-); PsycINFO; PsycLit; Res. Alert [Full Cov.]; Soc. Plann. Policy Dev. Abstr.; Soc. Sci. Cit. Index [Full Cov.].

US
**JOURNAL OF THE AMERICAN PSYCHOANALYTIC ASSOCIATION. MONOGRAPH SERIES. Main/Corp** American Psychoanalytic Association. **VFOAT** Monograph Series. No. 1 (1958)-. Monographic series. English. ir. Price varies per volume. International Universities Press Inc., 59 Boston Post Road, PO Box 1524, Madison CT 06443-1524. **Tel** (203)245-4000, FAX (203)245-0775, telex 282986 IUP BK. **NLM** W1 JO91KB.

US/0022-5002
**JOURNAL OF THE EXPERIMENTAL ANALYSIS OF BEHAVIOR.** [J. exp. anal. behav.]. **Added/Corp** Society for the Experimental Analysis of Behavior. Vol. 1 (Jan. 1958)-. Academic Scholarly Publication. English. bm. $106.00 US; $112.00 other. Journal of the Experimental Analysis of Behavior, Psychology Department, Indiana University, Bloomington IN 47405-1301. **Tel** (812)339-4718, (812)876-9081. **ED** Edmund Fantino. **LC** BF1; .J69. **DD** 150.5. **NLM** W1 JO921. **CODEN** JEABAU. Index available. cum. index. **Bk Rev. Ad Acc. Pr Rev. Circ:** 2,750. Documents available from The Genuine Article, BIOSIS Document Express, UMI Article Clearinghouse, CASDDS.
**Desc:** A publication for the original publication of experiments relevant to the behavior of individual organisms.
**Ind/Abst** Acad. Search (July 1993-); Appl. Soc. Sci. Index Abstr.; Biol. Abstr.; Chem. Abstr.; EMBASE; Energy Res. Abstr.; Expand. Acad. Index (1989-); Index Med.; Int. Aerosp. Abstr.; Middle East Abstr. Index; Newsp. Period. Abstr. (1992-); Nucl. Sci. Abstr.; Peace Res. Abstr. J. (1969-1974); Life Sci. Collect.; Psychol. Abstr. (1958-); PsycINFO; PsycLit; Ref. Upd. Deluxe Ed.; Res. Alert [Full Cov.]; Sci. Cit. Index; SCISEARCH; Soc. Sci. Cit. Index [Full Cov.]; Soc. Sci. Index; Soc. Sci. Index Fulltext (July 1988-) [Full Txt.].

US/0022-5061
**JOURNAL OF THE HISTORY OF THE BEHAVIORAL SCIENCES.** [J. hist. behav. sci.]. Vol. 1 (Jan. 1965)-. Periodical. English. qt (4 issues). $115.00 US; $128.50 other. Clinical Psychology Publishing Company, 4 Conant Square, Brandon VT 05733. **Tel** (802)247-6871, (800)433-8234. **ED** B. Ross. **LC** BF1; .J7. **NLM** W1 JO928V. **CODEN** JHBSA5. Index available (bound in last volume of each issue). **Bk Rev. Ad Acc. Pr Rev. Circ:** 1,000. available on microfilm and microfiche from University Microfilms International (UMI). Documents available from The Genuine Article.
**Desc:** Interdisciplinary international journal on the history of the behavioral sciences.
**Ind/Abst** Abstr. Anthropol.; Acad. Search (July 1993-); Am. Hist. Life (1970-); Am. Bibliogr. Slavic East Europ. Stud.; Appl. Soc. Sci. Index Abstr.; Arts Humanit. Citation Index [Select. Cov.]; Curr. Contents Soc. Behav. Sci.; Energy Res. Abstr. (Aug. 1982-); Hist. Source (July 1993-); Index Med.; Index Period. Artic. Relat. Law (19??-19??); INFO-SOUTH Abstr.; Int. Bibliogr. Sociol.; Mag. Search; Middle East Abstr. Index; Life Sci. Collect.;

Psychol. Abstr. (1965-); PsycINFO (1970-); PsycLit; Res. Alert [Full Cov.]; Soc. Plann. Policy Dev. Abstr.; Soc. Sci. Cit. Index [Full Cov.]; Sociol. Abstr.; West. Hist. Q.

II/0019-4247
**JOURNAL OF THE INDIAN ACADEMY OF APPLIED PSYCHOLOGY.** **Main/Corp** Indian Academy of Applied Psychology. **Added/Corp** Indian Academy of Applied Psychology. **VFOAT** JIAAP. (1964)-. Periodical. English. sa. $20.00. Indian Academy of Applied Psychology, New Delhi, India. **(Subscription address:** Prints India, 11 Darya Ganj, New Delhi 110002 India.**) DD** 158/.05. **NLM** W1; JO93G.
**Ind/Abst** Psychol. Abstr. (1964-); PsycINFO; PsycLit.

UK/1355-6177
**JOURNAL OF THE INTERNATIONAL NEUROPSYCHOLOGICAL SOCIETY.** Vol. 1 (1995)-. Academic Scholarly Publication. English. Six times a year. $160.00 US, Canada & Mexico; £112.00 other. Cambridge University Press, The Edinburgh Building, Shaftesbury Road, Cambridge CB2 2RU United Kingdom. **Tel** 011 44 223 312393, FAX 011 44 223 325959. **(Subscription address:** Cambridge University Press / North America, 110 Midland Avenue, Port Chester NY 10573.**)**

US/0030-6711
**JOURNAL OF THE OTTO RANK ASSOCIATION.** [J. Otto Rank Assoc.]. **Main/Corp** Otto Rank Association. V. 1- Fall 1966-. Periodical. English. sa. $10.00. Otto Rank Association, 35 West State Street, Doylestown, Bucks County PA 18901. **LC** BF173; .O8. **CODEN** ORAJAU. available on microfilm and microfiche from University Microfilms International (UMI).
**Ind/Abst** Psychol. Abstr. (1966-).

US/0895-7673
**JOURNAL OF TRAINING & PRACTICE IN PROFESSIONAL PSYCHOLOGY, THE.** ***Ceased.*** [J. train. pract. prof. psychol.]. **Added/Corp** Forest Institute of Professional Psychology. **VFOAT** Journal of Training and Practice in Professional Psychology. Vol. 1, No. 1 (Fall 1987)-Ceased in (1993). Periodical. English. sa. Forest Institute, 2611 Leeman Ferry Road, Huntsville AL 35801. **Tel** (205)536-9088. **DD** 158.
**Ind/Abst** Abstr. Res. Pastor. Care Couns. (19??-); Psychol. Abstr. (1987-); PsycINFO; PsycLit.

US/0022-524X
**JOURNAL OF TRANSPERSONAL PSYCHOLOGY, THE.** [J. transpers. psychol.]. **Added/Corp** Transpersonal Institute. American Transpersonal Association. **VFOAT** Transpersonal Psychology. (Spring 1969)-. Periodical. English. sa. $32.00 (institutions), $24.00 (individuals). Journal of Transpersonal Psychology, PO Box 4437, Stanford CA 94305. **Tel** (415)327-2066, FAX (415)327-0535. **ED** Miles Vich. **LC** BF1; .J75. **DD** 150/.5. **NLM** W1 JO966L. **CODEN** JTPSAN. Index available. cum. index. **Bk Rev. Pr Rev. Acid Free. Circ:** 4,000. available on microfilm and microfiche from University Microfilms International (UMI). Documents available from The Genuine Article.
**Desc:** Presents theory, research, applications in full human development and awareness, especially those aspects that integrate psychological and spiritual experience, and self-transcendence.
**Ind/Abst** Curr. Contents Soc. Behav. Sci.; Except. Hum. Exp.; Psychol. Abstr. (1969-); PsycINFO; PsycLit; Res. Alert [Full Cov.]; Soc. Sci. Cit. Index (1982-) [Full Cov.].

US/0894-9867
**JOURNAL OF TRAUMATIC STRESS.** [J. trauma. stress]. **Added/Corp** Society for Traumatic Stress Studies. Vol. 1, No. 1 (Jan. 1988)-. Periodical. English. Four times a year. $185.00 institutions, $43.00 individuals US; $215.00 institutions, $50.00 individuals other. Plenum Press, 233 Spring Street, New York NY 10013-1578. **Tel** (212)620-8000, (800)221-9369, FAX (212)463-0742, (212)807-1047, telex 23/421139. **ED** Charles R. Figley. **LC** RC552.P67; J68. **DD** 616.85/21/005. **NLM** W1; JO966PT. **CODEN** JTSTEB. **[CCC].** available on microfilm and microfiche from University Microfilms International (UMI). Documents available from The Genuine Article.
**Desc:** Articles in this journal are concerned with the immediate and long-term psychosocial consequences of highly stressful events or situations. Features include special issues, brief reports, book reviews, comments, and a section of international developments.
**Ind/Abst** Curr. Contents Soc. Behav. Sci.; PsycINFO (1990-); PsycLit; Res. Alert [Full Cov.]; Soc. Sci. Cit. Index [Full Cov.].

US/0096-1337
**JOURNAL OF UNDERGRADUATE PSYCHOLOGICAL RESEARCH.** V. 1- Sept. 1974-. English. West Valley College, 14000 Fruitvale Avenue, Saratoga CA 95070. **LC** BF1; .J77. **DD** 150/.5.

US/0001-8791
**JOURNAL OF VOCATIONAL BEHAVIOR.** [J. vocat. behav.]. **VFOAT** Vocational Behavior. Vol. 1 (Jan. 1971)-. Academic Scholarly Publication. English. bm (6 issues). $308.00 US and Canada; $373.50 other. Academic Press, Inc., 6277 Sea Harbor Drive, Orlando FL 32887. **Tel** (800)543-9534, (407)345-4100, FAX (407)363-9661. **ED** Howard E. A. Tinsley. **LC** HF5381.A1; J68. **DD** 331.7/005. **NLM** W1 JO971G. **CODEN** JVBHA2. **[CCC]. Pr Rev.** Documents available from The Genuine Article.
**Desc:** Empirical and theoretical articles that expand knowledge of vocational behavior and career development across the lifespan. Research presented in the journal spans the general categories adjustment and adaptation.
**Ind/Abst** AGRICOLA; Appl. Soc. Sci. Index Abstr.; Cumul. Index Nurs. Allied Health Lit.; Curr. Contents Soc. Behav. Sci.; Curr. Index J. Educ.; High. Educ. Abstr. (1971-); Middle East Abstr. Index; Psychol. Abstr. (1971-); PsycINFO; PsycLit; PsycScan: Appl. Psych.; Res. Alert [Full Cov.]; Soc. Plann. Policy Dev. Abstr.; Soc. Sci. Cit. Index [Full Cov.]; Sociol. Abstr. (?-?); Stud. Women Abstr.; Tech. Educ. Train. Abstr.; Women Stud. Abstr.; Work Relat. Abstr.

US/0739-3563
**KENNETH COLEMAN'S REALITY THEORY NEWSLETTER.** **VFOAT** Reality Theory Newsletter. Newsletter. English. qt. Seraphim Press, 7439 La Palma Avenue/Suite 263, Buena Park CA 90620.

JA
**KIKAN GENDAI KYOIKU SHINRI.** **Added/Corp** Tanaka Kyoiku Kenkyujo. **VFOAT** Gendai Kyoiku Shinri. (1974)-. Periodical. Japanese. ¥690. Meiji Tosho Shuppan, 3-11 Irifune 3 Chuo-ku (104), Tokyo Japan. **LC** LB1051; .K53.

NE
**KIND EN ADOLESCENT.** **See** Children and Youth Interests.

●GW
**KINDHEIT UND ENTWICKLUNG.** (1993)-. Monographic series. German. Four times a year. DM98.00 Germany; DM108.00 other. Quintessenz Verlag GmbH, Ifenpfad 2 4, D 12107 Berlin Germany. **Tel** 011 49 30 740060. **NLM** W1; KI633.

US/0193-1911
**KINESIS REPORT, THE.** **Added/Corp** Institute for Nonverbal Communication Research. Vol. 2 (Fall 1979)-. Periodical. English. qt. $24.00 US; $28.00 other. Human Sciences Press, PO Box 735, 233 Spring Street, New York NY 10013. **Tel** (212)620-8000, FAX (212)807-1047, telex 23421139. **LC** BF637.C45; K52. **DD** 153.6. ***Continues*** *Kinesis.*
**Desc:** Covers the psychology of nonverbal communication.

JA/0287-7651
**KISO SHINRIGAKU KENKYU.** [Kiso shinrigaku kenkyu]. **VFOAT** Japanese Journal of Psychonomic Science. (1982)-. Periodical. Multiple languages. sa. Japanese Psychonomic Society, Department of Psychology, Teikyo University, 359 Otsuka, Hachiojishi, Tokyo, Minato-ku 192-03 Japan. **DD** 150.
**Ind/Abst** Psychol. Abstr. (1982-); PsycINFO (1982-); PsycLit.

GW/0343-9429
**KLINISCHE PSYCHOLOGIE UND PSYCHOPATHOLOGIE.** (1978)-. Monographic series. German. Price varies per volume. Ferdinand Enke Verlag, Ruedigerstrasse 14, D-70469 Stuttgart Germany. **Tel** 011 49 711 8931124, 011 49 711 893123. **ED** H Remschmidt. **LC** UNC. **NLM** W1 KL55P.

GW/0938-7986
**KOGNITIONSWISSENSCHAFT.** Vol. 1, No. 1 (Sept. 1990)-. Periodical. German. qt. DM224.00. Springer-Verlag GmbH & Company KG, Heidelberger Platz 3, D 14197 Berlin Germany. **Tel** 011 49 30 8207223, FAX 011 49 30 8214091, telex 183 319 SPBLN D. **(Subscription address:** Springer Verlag New York Inc. / for North America, 44 Hartz Way, Secaucus NJ 07096.**) ED** C Habel, S Kanngiesser, and G Strube. **LC** BF309; .K64. **CODEN** KOGNEB. **[CCC]. Bk Rev. Ad Acc. Pr Rev.**
**Desc:** Publishes articles that contribute to the development of cognitive sciences based on their perspective, quality, and relevance. Provides a forum for the discussion of cognitive sciences for psychologists, computer scientists, and philologists.

IT
**KOINOS - GRUPPO E FUNZIONE ANALITICA.** (19??)-. Periodical. Italian. sa (June and Dec.). L70000 (institution), L50000 (individual) Italy. Edizioni Borla, Via delle Fornaci 50, 00165 Rome, Italy. **Tel** 011 39 6 39376728. ***Continues*** *Gruppo e Funzione Analitica.*

KO
**KOREAN JOURNAL OF PSYCHOLOGY.** Korean Psychological Association, Department of Psychology, Seoul National University, Seoul, 151-742 South Koreo.
**Ind/Abst** Psychol. Abstr. (1979-); PsycINFO (1979-); PsycLit.

JA/0021-5015
**KYOIKU SHINRIGAKU KENKYU.** (THE JAPANESE JOURNAL OF EDUCATIONAL PSYCHOLOGY.). [Kyoiku Shinrigaku Kenkyu]. Vol. 1 (May 1953)-. Periodical. Japanese. Four times a year. $185.00. **(Subscription address:** Kyowa Book Company Inc., 1 38 Kanda Jinbocho Chiyoda-ku, Tokyo 101 Japan.**) CODEN** JJEPAP.
**Ind/Abst** Arts Humanit. Citation Index [Select. Cov.]; Psychol. Abstr. (1956-); PsycINFO (1990-?); PsycLit; Soc. Sci. Cit. Index [Full Cov.].

BE/0458-7251
**LANGAGE ET L'HOMME, LE.** **See** Linguistics.

US/0098-5961
**LAW & PSYCHOLOGY REVIEW.** **See** Law.

●US/1072-0502
**LEARNING & MEMORY (COLD SPRING HARBOR, N.Y.).** (LEARNING & MEMORY.). **VFOAT** Learning and Memory. (1994)-. Periodical. English. bm. $190.00 US; $205.00 (surface delivery), $235.00 (airlift delivery) other. Cold Spring Harbor Laboratory, 10 Skyline Drive, Plainview NY 11803. **Tel** (516)349-1930, (800)843-4388, FAX (516)349-1946.
**Desc:** Publishes research papers on all types of learning, memory, and their models, conducted in humans and vertebrate and invertebrate species.

US/0023-9690
**LEARNING AND MOTIVATION.** [Learn. motiv.]. Vol. 1 (Feb. 1970)-. Academic Scholarly Publication. English. qt (4 issues). $202.50 US and Canada; $257.00 other. Academic Press, Inc., 6277 Sea Harbor Drive, Orlando FL 32887. **Tel** (800)543-9534, (407)345-4100, FAX (407)363-9661. **ED** Steven F. Maier. **LC** BF1; .L4. **DD** 156/.3/1505. **NLM** W1 LE289G. **CODEN** LNMVAV. **[CCC]. Pr Rev.** Documents available from The Genuine Article, BIOSIS Document Express, UMI Article Clearinghouse.
**Desc:** Features original experimental research devoted to the analysis of basic phenomena and mechanisms of learning, memory, and motivation.
**Ind/Abst** Acad. Abstr. Full Text Elite (Jan. 1992-); Acad. Abstr. (Jan. 1992-); Acad. Search (Jan. 1992-); Anim. Behav. Abstr.; Biol. Abstr.; Chemorecept. Abstr.; Commun. Abstr. (?-?); Contents Pages Educ.; Curr. Contents Soc. Behav. Sci.; Expand. Acad. Index (1989-); Humanit. Source (Jan. 1992-); INFO-SOUTH Abstr.; Mag. Search; Middle East Abstr. Index; Newsp. Period. Abstr. (1992-); Life Sci. Collect.; Psychol. Abstr. (1970-); PsycINFO; PsycLit; Res. Alert [Full Cov.]; Soc. Sci. Source (Jan. 1992-); Soc. Sci. Cit. Index [Full Cov.]; Soc. Sci. Index; Soc. Sci. Index Fulltext (Nov. 1988-) [Full Txt.].

●UK/1355-3259
**LEGAL AND CRIMINOLOGICAL PSYCHOLOGY.** (1995)-. English. Twice a year (May and November). £50.00 UK; $93.00 Other. British Psychological Society, St. Andrews House, 48 Princess Road, Leicester LE1 7DR England. **Tel** 011 44 533 549568. **(Subscription address:** Turpin Distribution Services Limited, Blackhorse Road, Letchworth, Hertfordshire SG6 1HN, United Kingdom.**) ED** Dr. Mary McMurran and Dr. Sally Lloyd-Bostock.
**Desc:** Publishes theoretical, empirical and review studies which advance scientific and professional knowledge in the field broadly defined to include new legislation, legal decision- making, court processes, victimology, theories of delinquency and public attitudes.

GW
**LEHRBUCH DER DIFFERENTIELLEN PSYCHOLOGIE.** V. 1- 1978-. Monographic series. German. Price varies per volume. **ED** F Merz. **NLM** W1 LE488.

RU
**LENINSKAIA TEORIIA OTRAZHENIIA I PROBLEMY PSIKHOLOGII.** **See** Biology-Physiology.

US
**LICENSED PSYCHOLOGISTS.** **Added/Corp** Kansas. Behavioral Sciences Regulatory Board. (1987)-. English. **LC** BF30; .K36. **DD** 150/.25/781. ***Continues*** *Certified Psychologists.*

LI/0202-3326
**LIETUVOS TSR AUKSTUJU MOKYKLU MOKSLO DARBAI: PEDAGOGIKA.** **See** Education.

LI/0202-3318
**LIETUVOS TSR AUKSTUJU MOKYKLU MOKSLO DARBAI: PSICHOLOGIJA.** **VFOAT** Psichologija; Nauchnye Trudy Vysshikh Uchebnykh Zavedenii Litovskoi SSR; Sikhologiia; Psikhologiia; Transactions of the Higher Schools of the Lithuanian SSR; Psychology. Vol. 1 (1980)-. Lithuanian (Russian; summaries and/or abstracts in English and German). an. Mintis / Idea, Z Sierakausko 15, Vilnius 2600 Lithuania. **Tel** 3702 632 943. **(Subscription address:** Victor Kamkin, 4956 Boiling Brook Parkway, Rockville MD 20852.**)** ***Continues in part*** *Pedagogika Ir Psichologija.*

●US/1064-217X
**LIFE DESIGNS.** See Health and Personal Fitness.

US/0731-3772
**LIMERENCE FORUM.** Vol. 1, No. 1 (Feb. 1982)-. Periodical. English. ir. $5.00 first 3 Issues. Limerence Forum, POB 2365, Huntington CT 06484.

US/0024-4759
**LITERATURE AND PSYCHOLOGY.** See Literature.

CN/0705-4718
**LITHIUM AND ANIMAL BEHAVIOR.** *Ceased.* See Veterinary Sciences.

US/0743-0264
**LIVING ANEW.** [Living anew]. Vol. 1, No. 1-. Periodical. English. mo. $21.00 US; $26.00 other. Lafayette Publishing Company, 90 Park Avenue, New York NY 10016. **DD** 158.

US/8756-4610
**LOSS, GRIEF & CARE.** [Loss grief care]. **VFOAT** Loss, Grief and Care. Vol. 1, No. 1 (Fall 1986)-. Periodical. English. qt. $150.00 US; $210.00 other. The Haworth Press Inc, 10 Alice Street, Binghamton NY 13904-1580. **Tel** (607)722-5857, (800)3-HAWORTH, FAX (607)722-1424. **ED** Austin Kutscher (editor's address: Foundationh of Thanatology, 630 West 168 Street, New York, NY 10032). **LC** R726.5; .L685. **DD** 616. **NLM** W1; LO853F. **Bk Rev. Ad Acc. Pr Rev. Acid Free. Circ:** 253. available on microfilm and microfiche from University Microfilms International (UMI). Documents available from Haworth Document Delivery Service.
**Desc:** Explores the crucial issues of psychosocial care for chronically, critically, and terminally ill patients and their family members. Features articles on a variety of topics including research in thanatology, the state of the art in educational programs for practitioners and students in the allied health sciences who serve as caregivers for the dying and the bereaved.
**Ind/Abst** Abstr. Res. Pastor. Care Couns. (19??-); Appl. Soc. Sci. Index Abstr.; Cumul. Index Nurs. Allied Health Lit.; Psychol. Abstr. (1986-); PsycINFO; PsycLit; Soc. Plann. Policy Dev. Abstr.

US/1056-3954
**LOTUS (MUSKOGEE, ILL.).** (LOTUS.). (1991)-. Periodical. English. qt. $24.00 US; $27.00 Canada and Mexico; $32.00 other. Lotus / Texas, 4032 South Lamar Boulevard, Austin TX 78704. **Tel** (918)683-4560, FAX (918)683-2466. **ED** Mary N Stearns. **Bk Rev. Ad Acc, Adv Mgr:** J Tramel, **Tel** (918)683-4560. **Circ:** 16,500.
**Desc:** Devoted to inner peace, mindfulness and compassionate living as pathways to personal and spiritual growth. It offers fresh, thoughtful perspectives on experiencing deeper levels of self-acceptance, inner transformation and love.

US
**LOYOLA EDUCATIONAL INDEX; A READERS' GUIDE TO EDUCATION AND PSYCHOLOGY.** See Education.

GW/0933-3347
**LUZIFER-AMOR.** **VAT** Luzifer Amor. (1988)-. Periodical. German. sa (Mar. and Oct.). DM48.00. Edition Diskord, Schwarzoischerstrasse 104B, 7400 Tubingen Germany. **Tel** 011 49 7071 40102. **LC** BF173.A2; L89. **DD** 150.19/5/09. **NLM** W1; LU897.

●CN/1193-6924
**MAGAZINE LUMIERE.** [Mag. lumi-ere]. Vol. 1, No 4 (Sept./Oct. 1992)-. Periodical. French. bm. 3.50Can$ per issue. Editions le Reseau-Lu, CP 86, Cap-Rouge Quebec G1Y 3C6 Canada. **DD** 158. ***Continues*** *Porteurs de Lumiere., 1188-5300.*

HU/0025-0279
**MAGYAR PSZICHOLOGIAI SZEMLE.** [M. pszichol. szle.]. **Added/Corp** Magyar Tudomanyos Akademia, Budapest. Pszichologiai Bizottsag. Magyar Pszichologiai Tudomanyos Tarsasag. **VFOAT** Hungarian Psychological Review. (1928)-. Academic Scholarly Publication. Hungarian (summaries and/or abstracts in Russian and English). Six times a year. $39.00. Akademiai Kiado, Publishing House of the Hungarian Academy of Sciences, Prielle Kornelia u. 19-35, H-1117 Budapest Hungary. **Tel** 011 36 1 1811991, FAX 011 36 1 1811991, telex 22-6228 AKNYO H. **ED** P. Popper. **LC** BF8.H8; M3. **NLM** W1 MA408. **Bk Rev. Circ:** 3,000 (ctrl).
**Desc:** Contains information about general, developmental, pedagogical, social, labour, art, criminal, and sports psychology. Also covers the history of psychology by Hungarian and international authors.
**Ind/Abst** Psychol. Abstr. (1934-); PsycINFO; PsycLit; Soc. Plann. Policy Dev. Abstr.

II/0025-1615
**MANAB MON.** **Added/Corp** Pavlov Institute. No. 1 (1972)-. Periodical. English. qt. Rs8.00. Pavlov Institute, 132/1-A Bidhan Sarani, Calcutta-4 India. **ED** Dr. D.N. Ganguly. **LC** BF1; .M28. **DD** 150/.5. **Bk Rev. Ad Acc. Circ:** 1,000.
**Desc:** Discusses modern issues in psychology, sociology and biology.

II
**MANABAMANA.** Periodical. Bengali (Bengali). 5.00. **LC** BF8.B43; M35.

II
**MANAGERIAL PSYCHOLOGY.** **Added/Corp** Osmania University. Dept. of Psychology. (19??)-. Periodical. English. sa. $40.00. Osmania University Department of Psychology, Hyderabad -500007 India. **(Subscription address:** Prints India, 11 Darya Ganj, New Delhi 110002 India.**)**
**Ind/Abst** Psychol. Abstr. (1980-); PsycLit.

II/0025-1984
**MANAS.** (Mar. 1954)-. Periodical. English. sa. $25.00. **(Subscription address:** Prints India, 11 Darya Ganj, New Delhi 110002 India.**) LC** BF1; .M3.

CN/0711-1533
**MANITOBA PSYCHOLOGIST.** [Manit. psychol.]. **Added/Corp** Psychological Association of Manitoba. Vol. 1, No. 1 (Nov. 1981)-. Periodical. English. qt. 16.00Can$. Manitoba Psychologist, M4 409 Tache Avenue, Winnipeg Manitoba R2H 2A6 Canada. **Tel** (204)237-2901. **ED** Michael J. Kral. **DD** 150/.97127. cum. index. **Bk Rev. Ad Acc. Pr Rev. Circ:** 250 (ctrl).
**Desc:** Assists the Psychological Association of Manitoba in fulfilling its legal responsibilities concerning the protection of the public, and the regulation and advancement of professional psychology in the province.

IE/0025-2409
**MANPOWER AND APPLIED PSYCHOLOGY.** *Ceased.* Vol. 1 (1967)-Ceased ?. Periodical. English. Ergon Press, 45 South Mall, Cork Ireland. **DD** 158.7/05.

US/1042-2277
**MANY VOICES.** [Many voices]. (1989)-. Periodical. English. bm. $30.00 US; $36.00 other. Many Voices, PO Box 2639, Cincinnati OH 45201. **Tel** (513)531-5415. **DD** 616. Index available. **Bk Rev,** (Qty: 12-15). **Circ:** 3,000.
**Desc:** Self-help information for people with Multiple Personality Disorder or a Dissociative Disorder, their families and therapists. Positive healing oriented.

US/0892-0060
**MASTER LECTURE SERIES, THE.** [Master lect. ser.]. **Added/Corp** American Psychological Association. Vol. 1 (1981)-. Monographic series. English. ir. Price varies per volume. American Psychological Association, 750 First Street Northeast, Washington DC 20002. **Tel** (800)374-2721, (202)336-5600, (subscriptions - (202)336-5600. **(Subscription address:** American Psychological Association, Order Department, PO Box 2710, Hyattsville MD 20784.**) DD** 150. **NLM** W1; MA9309V.

US/0748-1756
**MEASUREMENT AND EVALUATION IN COUNSELING AND DEVELOPMENT.** See Education.

US/0894-5098
**MEDICAL HYPNOANALYSIS JOURNAL.** [Med. hypnoanal. j.]. **Added/Corp** American Academy of Medical Hypnoanalysts. Vol. 2, No. 1 (March 1987)-. Periodical. English. Four times a year (Mar., June, Sept., Dec.). $26.00 US; $32.00 other. Medical Hypnoanalysis, c/o Dr D Zelling, 80 North Miller Road, Akron OH 44313. **Tel** (800)34-HYPNO (216)867-6677. **ED** Daniel A Zelling. **LC** RC490; .J68. **DD** 615. **NLM** W1; ME341B. Index available. **Bk Rev,** (Qty: 8). **Ad Acc, Adv Mgr:** Rhonda Shipley, **Tel** (216)867-6677. **Circ:** 1,000. Documents available from BIOSIS Document Express. ***Continues*** *Journal of the American Academy of Medical Hypnoanalysts, 0894-5101.*
**Desc:** Filled with practical articles directed to and written by psychotherapists in a manner that makes the method easily understood. It is body, mind and spirit oriented. Contains at least one therapeutic script on a variety of medical, psychological, self-improvement or sports applications.
**Ind/Abst** Biol. Abstr. (1987-); Psychol. Abstr. (1987-); PsycLit.

CN/0835-3069
**MEDICAL PSYCHOTHERAPY.** *Ceased.* See Medical Science and Technology.

YU/0351-4501
**MEDITERRANEAN JOURNAL OF SOCIAL PSYCHIATRY / MEDITERRANEAN SOCIOPSYCHIATRIC ASSOCIATION.** See Medical Science and Technology-Psychiatry.

CN/0848-8479
**MELANIE KLEIN AND OBJECT RELATIONS.** [Melanie Klein object relat.]. Vol. 7, No. 1 (June 1989)-. Periodical. English. sa. 20.00Can$. Ontario Institute for Studies in Education, 252 Bloor Street West, Toronto Ontario M5S 1V6 Canada. **Tel** (416)923-6641 ext. 2334, FAX (416)926-4725, telex 06217720. **DD** 150.19/5/05. ***Continues*** *Journal of the Melanie Klein Society, 0834-9185.*
**Ind/Abst** Psychol. Abstr. (1987-); PsycLit.

AT/0814-3757
**MELBOURNE PSYCHOLOGY MONOGRAPHS.** [Melbourne psychol. monogr.]. (1983)-. Periodical. English. ir. University of Melbourne / Parkville, Parkville Victoria 3052 Australia. **Tel** 344-6000. **DD** 150.'5.
**Ind/Abst** Aust. Educ. Index (?-?).

US
**MEMBERSHIP DIRECTORY.** **Main/Corp** Association for Applied Psychophysiology and Biofeedback. **VFOAT** AAPB Directory. (1988-1989)-. Directory. English. $15.00. Association for Applied Psychophysiology and Biofeedback, 10200 West 44th Avenue, Suite 304, Wheat Ridge CO 80033. **Tel** (303)442-8436. **NLM** WL 22; AA1 B6m. ***Continues*** *Membership Directory of the Biofeedback Society of America, 0739-5280.*

US/1051-1830
**MEMBERSHIP DIRECTORY OF THE AMERICAN PSYCHOLOGICAL SOCIETY.** [Membsh. dir. Am. Psychol. Soc.]. **Main/Corp** American Psychological Society. **VFOAT** Membership Directory; Membership Directory of the APS. (1990)-. English. ir. $10.00 (members), $25.00 (nonmembers). American Psychological Society, 1010 Vermont Avenue Northwest, Suite 1100, Washington DC 20005. **Tel** (202)783-2077, FAX (202)783-2083. **(Subscription address:** American Psychological Society, PO Box 90457, Washington DC 20090.**) LC** BF30; .A493a. **DD** 150/.25/73.

US/1052-9764
**MEMBERSHIP DIRECTORY - SOCIETY FOR NEUROSCIENCE.** (MEMBERSHIP DIRECTORY.). [Membersh. dir. - Soc. Neurosci.]. (197?)-. Directory. English. ir. $27.00 (non-members), $25.00 (members). Society for Neuroscience, 11 Dupont Circle, Suite 500, Washington DC 20036. **Tel** (202)462-6688. **DD** 612. ***Continues*** *Society for Neuroscience. Directory of Members, 0098-9460.*

US/0736-4385
**MEMBERSHIP ROSTER - AMERICAN ACADEMY OF PSYCHOANALYSIS.** (MEMBERSHIP ROSTER / THE AMERICAN ACADEMY OF PSYCHOANALYSIS.). [Membsh. roster - Am Acad. Psychoanal.]. **Main/Corp** American Academy of Psychoanalysis. (1967)-. English. be. $15.00. American Academy of Psychoanalysis, 47 East 19th Street, 6th Floor, New York NY 10063. **Tel** (212)475-7980. **ED** Vivian Mendelsohn. **NLM** WM 22.1 A512M. **Circ:** 1,000.
**Desc:** Directory of members listed alphabetically and geographically.

●UK/0965-8211
**MEMORY.** (1993)-. Periodical. English. qt. $119.00 US; £65.00 Europe; £70.00 other. Lawrence Erlbaum Associates Ltd., 27 Palmeira Mansions, Church Road, Hove East Sussex BN3 2FA England. **Tel** 011 44 273 207411. **(Subscription address:** Turpin Distribution Services Limited, Blackhorse Road, Letchworth, Hertfordshire SG6 1HN, United Kingdom.**) ED** Susan E. Gathercole and Martin A. Conway (Lancaster University). **NLM** W1; ME9036.
**Desc:** International journal dedicated to the study of human memory. The aim is to provide an outlet for original and high quality research in human memory representing the full range of current influential approaches.
**Ind/Abst** Ergon. Abstr.

US/0090-502X
**MEMORY & COGNITION.** [Mem. cogn.]. **Added/Corp** Psychonomic Society. **VAT** Memory and Cognition. Vol. 1 (Jan. 1973)-. Academic Scholarly Publication. English. bm (Jan., Mar., May, July, Sept., Nov.). $121.00 US; $131.00 other. Psychonomic Society Publications, 1710 Fortview Road, Austin TX 78704. **Tel** (512)462-2442, FAX (512)462-1101. **ED** Alice Healy. **LC** BF371; .M45. **DD** 153.1/05. **NLM** W1 ME904. **CODEN** MYCGAO. **[CCC].** Index available. **Pr Rev. Circ:** 2,250. available on microfilm and microfiche from University Microfilms International (UMI). Documents available from The Genuine Article, BIOSIS Document Express, UMI Article Clearinghouse. ***Supersedes in part*** *Psychonomic Science, 0033-3131.*
**Desc:** Articles covering human memory and learning, conceptual processes, psycholinguistics, problem solving, thinking, decision making, and skilled performance.
**Ind/Abst** Acad. Search (July 1993-); Arts Humanit. Citation Index [Select. Cov.]; Biol. Abstr.; Commun. Abstr. (?-?); Curr. Contents Soc. Behav. Sci.; EMBASE; Energy Res. Abstr. (Aug. 1982-); Expand. Acad. Index (1989-); INFO-SOUTH Abstr.; Mag. Search; Middle East Abstr. Index; MLA Int. Bibl. Books Artic. Mod. Lang. Lit.; Newsp. Period. Abstr. (1991-); Life Sci. Collect.; Psychol. Abstr. (1973-); PsycINFO; PsycLit; Res. Alert [Full Cov.]; Soc. Plann. Policy Dev. Abstr.; Soc. Sci. Source (Jul. 1993-); Soc. Sci. Cit. Index [Full Cov.]; Soc. Sci. Index; Soc. Sci. Index Fulltext (Sept. 1988-) [Full Txt.]; Sociol. Abstr.

US/8750-4529
**MENSALOHA.** (MENSALOHA : MENSA HAWAII PUBLICATION.). Periodical. English. mo. $3.00 members, $8.50 nonmembers. MENSALOHA, 45-436

Makalani Street, Kaneohe HI 96744. **Tel** (808)247-1853. **ED** Jean Buckley. **Bk Rev**. **Ad Acc**. **Pr Rev. Circ:** 500 (ctrl).

US/0883-7902
**MENTAL AND PHYSICAL DISABILITY LAW REPORTER.** See Law.

UK/0261-9997
**MENTAL HANDICAP : JOURNAL OF THE BRITISH INSTITUTE OF MENTAL HANDICAP.** See Sociology-Social Services and Welfare.

US/0272-9962
**MENTAL HEALTH (BOCA RATON).** See Public Health and Safety.

US/0730-1588
**MENTAL HEALTH SERVICE SYSTEM REPORTS. SERIES DN. HEALTH / MENTAL HEALTH RESEARCH.** (MENTAL HEALTH SERVICE SYSTEM REPORTS. SERIES DN, HEALTH/MENTAL HEALTH RESEARCH / U.S. DEPARTMENT OF HEALTH AND HUMAN SERVICES, PUBLIC HEALTH SERVICE, ALCOHOL, DRUG ABUSE, AND MENTAL HEALTH ADMINISTRATION, NATIONAL INSTITUTE OF MENTAL HEALTH.). [Ment. health serv. syst. rep., Ser. DN., Health/ment. health res.]. **VFOAT** Health/Mental Health Research. No. 1-. Monographic series. English. Price varies per volume. National Institute of Mental Health, 9000 Rockville Pike, Rockville MD 20892. **Tel** (301)496-9291. **DD** 362.2/0973. **NLM** W1 ME928EP.

US/0892-0664
**MENTAL HEALTH, UNITED STATES.** (MENTAL HEALTH, UNITED STATES / NATIONAL INSTITUTE OF MENTAL HEALTH.). [Ment. health, U.S.]. **Added/Corp** National Institute of Mental Health (U.S.). Division of Biometry and Epidemiology. National Institute of Mental Health (U.S.). Division of Biometry and Applied Sciences. Center for Mental Health Services (U.S.) National Institute of Mental Health (U.S.). (1983)-. English. an. Superintendent of Documents, US Government Printing Office, Washington DC 20402. **Tel** (202)275-3328, FAX (202)786-2377. **LC** RA790.6; .M463. **DD** 362.2/0973. **NLM** W2; A N2225m

US/1058-1103
**MENTAL HEALTH WEEKLY.** [Ment. health wkly.]. **Added/Corp** Manisses Communications Group. (1991)-. Newsletter. English. wk (except four weeks of the year). $449.00 (institutions), $399.00 (individuals) US; $469.00 (institutions), $419.00 (individuals) Canada; $489.00 (institutions), $439.00 (individuals) other. Manisses Communications Group Inc., PO Box 3357, Providence RI 02906-0757. **Tel** (401)831-6020, (800)333-7771, FAX (401)861-6370. **ED** Gary Enos. **DD** 362. **[CCC].** Index available.
**Desc:** Public policy and economic issues for mental health professionals and policy makers in the public, private, and nonprofit sectors.

NZ/0111-8854
**MENTALITIES. VFOAT** Mentalites. Vol. 1, No. 1 (1982)-. Periodical. English (French and German). sa. $60.00 (one year), $115.00 (two year) institutions; $40.00 (one year), $75.00 (two year) individuals. Outrigger Publishers, PO Box 1198, Hamilton New Zealand. **Tel** 011 64 71 8567820, FAX 011 64 71 562158. **(Subscription address:** Mentalities, Robert Liris, 3 Rue Saint Saens, 03700 Bellrive Allier France**) ED** Norman Simms. **LC** AP7.5; .M45. **DD** 052. **[CCC]. Bk Rev**, (Qty: 25). **Ad Acc. Pr Rev. Circ:** 200.
**Desc:** Provides a comprehensive and multidisciplinary approach to human culture, psychology and institutions especially the long hidden aspects of personal and group experience.
**Ind/Abst** Am. Hist. Life (1982-); Annu. Bibliogr. Engl. Lang. Lit.

CN/0843-5405
**MENTORING INTERNATIONAL.** ***Ceased.*** (MENTORING INTERNATIONAL : JOURNAL OF THE INTERNATIONAL CENTRE FOR MENTORING.). [Mentor. int.]. **Added/Corp** International Centre for Mentoring. **VFOAT** MI. Vol. 3, No. 1 (Winter 1989)-(1992). Periodical. English. qt. Mentoring Institute, 675 Inglewood Avenue, West Vancouver British Columbia V7T 1X4 Canada. **Tel** (604)925-2295, FAX (604)925-1162. **DD** 158/.3. **Bk Rev. Ad Acc. *Continues*** *International Journal of Mentoring, 0835-3034.*

US/0272-930X
**MERRILL-PALMER QUARTERLY (1960).** (MERRILL-PALMER QUARTERLY.). [Merrill-Palmer q.]. **VFOAT** Merrill Palmer Quarterly. Vol. 28, No. 1 (Jan. 1982)-. Periodical. English. qt (Jan., Apr., Jul., Oct.). $75.00 (one year) $145.00 (two year) $205.00 (three year) institution; $40.00 (one year) $74.00 (two year), $115.00 (three year) individual. Wayne State University Press, 4809 Woodward Avenue, The Leonard N. Simons Building, Detroit MI 48201-1309. **Tel** (313)577-6119, (313)577-6120, FAX (313)577-6131. **ED** Carol Shantz and Keith E. Stanovich. **LC** HQ1; .M4. **DD** 155. Index available (bound in Oct. issue). **Bk Rev. Ad Acc. Pr Rev. Circ:** 1,300. available on microfilm and microfiche from University Microfilms International (UMI). Documents available from The Genuine Article. ***Continues*** *Merrill-Palmer Quarterly, Behavior and Development, 0272-930X.*
**Desc:** A journal devoted to research in the area of child development. Articles include original research, theoretical papers, and reviews of the literature in the area of child development and family-child relationships.
**Ind/Abst** Acad. Search (July 1993-); Child Dev. Abstr. Bibliogr.; Commun. Abstr. (?-?); Curr. Contents Soc. Behav. Sci.; Curr. Index J. Educ.; Dev. Med. Child Neurol.; Educ. Index; INFO-SOUTH Abstr.; Mag. Search; Middle East Abstr. Index; Psychol. Abstr. (1982-); PsycINFO; PsycLit; PsycScan: Develop. Psych.; Res. Alert [Full Cov.]; Sage Fam. Stud. Abstr. (?-?); Soc. Plann. Policy Dev. Abstr.; Soc. Sci. Cit. Index [Full Cov.]; Soc. Work Abstr. [Select. Cov.]; Sociol. Abstr.; Sociol. Educ. Abstr.; Spec. Educ. Needs Abstr.; Women Stud. Abstr.

US/1044-2634
**MICHIGAN JOURNAL OF COUNSELING AND DEVELOPMENT.** [Mich. j. couns. dev.]. **Added/Corp** Michigan Association for Counseling and Development. Vol. 17, No. 2 (Summer 1986)-. Periodical. English. sa. MACD, Box 190, St. Johns MI 48879. **DD** 371. ***Continues*** *Michigan Personnel and Guidance Journal, 0160-5577.*

US/0748-2051
**MICROPSYCH NETWORK.** ***Ceased.*** [Micropsych netw.]. Vol. 1, No. 1 (1984)-(19??). Periodical. English. tq. Human Technology Interface, c/o L Sadler, 163 Wood Wedge Way, Sanford NC 27330. **Tel** (919)499-9216, FAX (919)499-9216. **DD** 150. **Ad Acc. Circ:** 1,500 (ctrl).

US/0276-8887
**MILIEU THERAPY.** [Milieu ther.]. Vol. 1, No. 1 (Summer 1981)-. Periodical. English. sa. $12.00. Avalon Press, Old Stockbridge Road, Lennox MA 01240. **LC** RC489.M5; M545. **DD** 616.89/144.
**Ind/Abst** Except. Child Educ. Resour.; Psychol. Abstr. (1981-); PsycINFO; Soc. Work Abstr. (Summer 1987-?) [Select. Cov.].

●US/1062-1806
**MIND MATTERS.** [Mind matters]. **Added/Corp** ASCD Network on Teaching Thinking. Vol. 6, No. 2 (Winter 1992)-. Periodical. English. qt. $10.00. Skylight Publishing, 200 East Wood Street, Suite 274, Palatine IL 60067. **DD** 371. ***Continues*** *Cogitare, 0896-0380.*

●US/1065-3848
**MINDFIELD (NEW YORK, N.Y.).** (MINDFIELD : A QUARTERLY SOURCE JOURNAL FOR CONSCIOUSNESS.). [MindField]. **VFOAT** Mind Field. Vol. 1, No. 1 (Spring 1992)-. Periodical. English. qt. $24.00 US; $30.00 Canada and Mexico; $31.50 other. MindField Publishing, 270 Madison Avenue, New York NY 10016. **Tel** (212)683-5320, FAX (212)686-2182. **DD** 153.
**Desc:** Collects complete, unabridged chapters selected from current books in the areas of philosophy, physics, psychology, spirituality, mind/brain studies and the search for new paradigms.

IT/0391-1772
**MINERVA PSICHIATRICA.** See Medical Science and Technology-Psychiatry.

US/0076-9266
**MINNESOTA SYMPOSIA ON CHILD PSYCHOLOGY.** (MINNESOTA SYMPOSIA ON CHILD PSYCHOLOGY. PAPERS.). [Minn. Symp. Child Psychol.]. **Added/Corp** University of Minnesota. Institute of Child Development. **VFOAT** Child Psychology. Vol. 1 (1967)-. Monographic series. English. an. $59.95. Lawrence Erlbaum Associates, 365 Broadway, Suite 102, Hillsdale NJ 07642. **Tel** (201)666-4110, (800)926-6579, FAX (201)666-2394. **ED** Charles A. Nelson. **LC** BF721; .M545. **DD** 155.4. **NLM** W3 MI607. **CODEN** MSCRBG. Documents available from The Genuine Article, BIOSIS Document Express.
**Ind/Abst** Biol. Abstr. (?-1975); Res. Alert [Full Cov.]; Soc. Sci. Cit. Index [Full Cov.].

US/0361-5227
**MODERN PSYCHOANALYSIS.** [Mod. psychoanal.]. **Added/Corp** Manhattan Center for Advanced Psychoanalytic Studies. Vol. 1 (Spring 1976)-. Periodical. English. sa. $30.00 (institutional), $15.00 (individual) US; $35.00 (institutional), $20.00 (individual) Canada; $40.00 (institutional), $30.00 (individual) other. Center for Modern Psychoanalytie Studies, 16 West 10th Street, New York NY 10011. **Tel** (212)260-7050, FAX (212)260-7052. **ED** Phyllis W. Meadow (editor's phone: (212)242-4846). **LC** RC500; .M6. **DD** 616.8/917/05. **NLM** W1 MO1684. Index available. cum. index. **Bk Rev**, (Qty: 10-15). **Circ:** 1,200 (ctrl).
**Desc:** Dedicated to publishing articles extending the theory and practice of psychoanalysis to the full range of emotional disorders.
**Ind/Abst** Cumul. Index Nurs. Allied Health Lit.; Middle East Abstr. Index; Psychol. Abstr. (1976-); PsycINFO; PsycLit.

US/0163-2841
**MODERN PSYCHOTHERAPY.** V. 1- May 1978-. Periodical. English. Dr John B Snook, Westchester Institute for Training in Counseling and Psychotherapy, 260 Styvesant Avenue, Rye NY 10580. **LC** RC475; .M62. **DD** 616.8.914.

US/0899-6059
**MONK (SAN FRANCISCO, CALIF.).** (MONK.). [Monk]. **VFOAT** Traveling Monk; Monk Magazine. (Sept. 1986)-. Periodical. English. qt. $10.00 (one year), $18.00 (two year). Monk, 175 5th Avenue, Suite 2322, New York NY 10010. **Tel** (212)465-3231. **ED** James Crotty and Michael Lane. **DD** 158. **Bk Rev. Ad Acc, Adv Mgr:** Jim Crotty.
**Desc:** Travel magazine that seeks out the odd and notorious in an area and make fun at ideologies and then chronicle their findings.

US/0077-9008
**MONOGRAPH - NEW YORK PSYCHOANALYTIC INSTITUTE. ERNST KRIS STUDY GROUP.** (MONOGRAPH / THE KRIS STUDY GROUP OF THE NEW YORK PSYCHOANALYTIC INSTITUTE.). [Monogr. - N.Y. Psychoanal. Inst., Ernst Kris Stud. Group]. **Added/Corp** New York Psychoanalytic Institute. Kris Study Group. (1965)-. Monographic series. English. ir. Price varies per volume. International Universities Press Inc., 59 Boston Post Road, PO Box 1524, Madison CT 06443-1524. **Tel** (203)245-4000, FAX (203)245-0775, telex 282986 IUP BK. **LC** BF173.A2; N4313. **DD** 150.19/5/05. **NLM** W1 MO558N.

FR/0077-071X
**MONOGRAPHIES FRANCAISES DE PSYCHOLOGIE.** [Monogr. fr. psychol.]. 1 (1958)-. Monographic series. French. ir. Price varies per volume. Editions du CNRS, 22 rue Saint Armand, F 75015 Paris France. **Tel** 011 33 1 45075050. **NLM** W1 MO562N.
**Desc:** French monograph series on psychology and child psychology.
**Ind/Abst** Psychol. Abstr. (1960-).

US/0270-0131
**MONOGRAPHS IN PSYCHOBIOLOGY AND DISEASE.** See Biology.

US/0037-976X
**MONOGRAPHS OF THE SOCIETY FOR RESEARCH IN CHILD DEVELOPMENT.** [Monogr. Soc. Res. Child Dev.]. **Added/Corp** Society for Research in Child Development. Vol. 1 (1936)-. Monographic series. English. ir. $68.00. University of Chicago Press / Journals Division, PO Box 37005, 5720 South Woodlawn, Chicago IL 60637. **Tel** (312)753-3347, FAX (312)753-0811. **ED** Wanda C. Bronson. **LC** LB1103; .S6. **DD** 370.15. **NLM** W1 MO569RK. **CODEN** MSCDA7. **Acid Free.** available on microfilm and microfiche from University Microfilms International (UMI). Documents available from The Genuine Article, BIOSIS Document Express.
**Desc:** Presents research studies and findings in child development and its related disciplines. Each issue consists of a single study or a group of papers on a single theme, accompanied usually by commentary and discussion.
**Ind/Abst** Abstr. Res. Pastor. Care Couns. (19??-); Acad. Search (Jan. 1994-); Biol. Abstr.; Curr. Index J. Educ.; Educ. Index; Energy Res. Abstr. (Aug. 1982-); Index Med.; INFO-SOUTH Abstr.; Mag. Search; Middle East Abstr. Index; Psychol. Abstr. (1935-); PsycINFO; PsycLit; PsycScan: Develop. Psych.; Res. Alert [Full Cov.]; Soc. Plann. Policy Dev. Abstr.; Soc. Sci. Cit. Index [Full Cov.]; Sociol. Abstr.

US/0146-7239
**MOTIVATION AND EMOTION.** [Motiv. emot.]. Vol. 1 (Mar. 1977)-. Periodical. English. Four times a year. $230.00 institutions, $41.00 individuals US; $270.00 institutions, $48.00 individuals other. Plenum Press, 233 Spring Street, New York NY 10013-1578. **Tel** (212)620-8000, (800)221-9369, FAX (212)463-0742, (212)807-1047, telex 23/421139. **ED** Alice M. Isen. **LC** BF683; .M64. **DD** 153.8/05. **NLM** W1 MO944. **CODEN** MOEMDJ. **[CCC].** Index available. **Pr Rev.** available on microfilm and microfiche from University Microfilms International (UMI). Documents available from The Genuine Article, BIOSIS Document Express.
**Desc:** Primary focus is human motivation. Publishes theoretical papers, reviews position papers and original research, basic or applied, focusing on human motivation.
**Ind/Abst** Biol. Abstr.; Curr. Contents Soc. Behav. Sci.; EMBASE; Life Sci. Collect.; Psychol. Abstr. (1977-); PsycINFO; PsycLit; Ref. Z.; Res. Alert [Full Cov.]; Soc. Sci. Cit. Index [Full Cov.].

GW/0173-3532
**MOTIVATIONSFORSCHUNG.** [Motivationsforschung]. Vol. 1 (1973)-. Monographic series. German. Price varies per volume. Hans Huber Verlag, Daimlerstrasse 40, W-7000 Stuttgart 50 Germany. **Tel** (416)482-6339. **(Subscription address:** US/ PO Box 51, Lewiston, NY 14092; Canada/ 12 Bruce Park Avenue, Toronto, Ontario M4P 2S3; Switzerland/ Laenggass Strasse 76, CH-3000 Bern 9**) ED** H Heckhausen. **LC** UNC. **NLM** W1 MO79.

IT
**MOVIMENTO.** (19??)-. Italian. qt. $60.00. Edizioni Luigi Pozzi Srl, Via Panama 68, 00198 Rome Italy. **Tel** (06)8553548, FAX (06)8554105. **ED** Ferrucis Antonelli. Index available. **Bk Rev. Ad Acc. Circ:** 1,500.
**Desc:** Psychology applied to sports.

US/0098-8553
**MULTIDISCIPLINARY RESEARCH.** [Multidiscip. res.]. Periodical. English. sa. Multidisciplinary Research, 848 West Holt Avenue, Pomona CA 91768. **LC** BF11; .I615. **DD** 051. **CODEN** MRINCS. Documents available from Ask*IEEE.
**Ind/Abst** INSPEC (Sept. 1974-).

US/0027-3171
**MULTIVARIATE BEHAVIORAL RESEARCH.** [Multivariate behav. res.]. **Added/Corp** Society of Multivariate Experimental Psychology. **VFOAT** MBR. Vol. 1 (Jan. 1966)-. Periodical. English. qt. $195.00 US & Canada; $220.00 other. Lawrence Erlbaum Associates, 365 Broadway, Suite 102, Hillsdale NJ 07642. **Tel** (201)666-4110, (800)926-6579, FAX (201)666-2394. **ED** Stanley A Mulaik. **LC** BF39; .M85. **NLM** W1 MU398N. **CODEN** MVBRAV. Index available. cum. index. **Ad Acc. Pr Rev. Circ:** 1,000. available on microfilm and microfiche from University Microfilms International (UMI). Documents available from The Genuine Article, BIOSIS Document Express.
**Desc:** Substantive, theoretical and methodological articles of multivariate experimental psychology.
**Ind/Abst** Biol. Abstr.; Biostatistica; Commun. Abstr. (?-?); Compumath Citation Index [Full Cov.]; Curr. Contents Soc. Behav. Sci.; Curr. Index J. Educ.; Int. Aerosp. Abstr.; J. Plan. Lit.; Middle East Abstr. Index; Multicult. Educ. Abstr.; Psychol. Abstr. (1966-); PsycINFO; PsycLit; PsycScan: Appl. Psych.; Res. Alert [Full Cov.]; Soc. Plann. Policy Dev. Abstr.; Soc. Sci. Cit. Index [Full Cov.]; Sociol. Abstr. (?-?); Soc. Res. Methodol. Abstr. (1975-).

US/0147-3964
**MULTIVARIATE EXPERIMENTAL CLINICAL RESEARCH.** [Multivar. exp. clin. res.]. **Added/Corp** Wichita State University. Dept. of Psychology. (19??)-. Periodical. English. Three times a year. $50.00 (institutions), $29.00 (individuals) US; $56.00 (institutions), $35.00 (individuals) other. Wichita State University Department of Psychology, PO Box 34, Wichita KS 67208. **Tel** (316)689-3884. **ED** Dr. Charles A. Burdsal Jr. **LC** BF698.A1; M84. **DD** 155.2/8/0182. **NLM** W1 MU398W. **CODEN** MCREDA. **Bk Rev. Circ:** 250 (ctrl). Documents available from The Genuine Article, BIOSIS Document Express. ***Continues** Journal of Multivariate Experimental Personality and Clinical Psychology, 0149-9688.*
**Desc:** Outlet for research in areas covered by the terms personality study, clinical diagnosis and therapy, extending into their learning, social, physiological, applied and developmental aspects.
**Ind/Abst** Biol. Abstr.; Curr. Contents Soc. Behav. Sci.; EMBASE; Psychol. Abstr. (1976-); PsycINFO; PsycLit; Res. Alert [Full Cov.].

US/0734-7367
**MUSIC THERAPY (NEW YORK, N.Y.). See** Music.

GW/0177-350X
**MUSIK PSYCHOLOGIE : JAHRBUCH DER DEUTSCHEN GESELLSCHAFT FUER MUSIKPSYCHOLOGIE. See** Music.

•US/0898-1493
**NATIONAL DIRECTORY OF CERTIFIED COUNSELORS.** ***Suspended.* See** Education-Special Education and Rehabilitation.

US/1058-6776
**NATIONAL PSYCHOLOGIST, THE.** [Natl. psychol.]. Vol. 1, No. 1 (Aug. 1991)-. Periodical. English. bm. $30.00. Ohio Psychology Publications, 6100 Channingway Boulevard, Suite 201, Columbus OH 43232. **DD** 150.

US/0099-2151
**NATIONAL REGISTER OF HEALTH SERVICE PROVIDERS IN PSYCHOLOGY.** [Natl. reg. health serv. provid. psychol.]. **Added/Corp** Council for the National Register of Health Service Providers in Psychology. **VFOAT** National Register, Health Service Providers, Psychology. (1975)-. Directory. English. an. $195.00. National Register Health Service Providers, 1120 G Street Northwest, Suite 330, Washington DC 20003. **Tel** (202)783-7663. **LC** BF30; .N3. **DD** 616.89/0025/73. **NLM** BF 30 N27.

US/0730-5540
**NATIONAL REGISTER OF HEALTH SERVICE PROVIDERS IN PSYCHOLOGY. SUPPLEMENT.** Winter 1975/76-. English. sa. Council for the National Register of Health Service, Providers in Psychology, 1200 17th Street NW, Washington DC 20036. **Tel** (202)833-2377, FAX (202)296-0831. **LC** BF30. **DD** 150/.2573.

US/0146-7875
**NEBRASKA SYMPOSIUM ON MOTIVATION.** [Neb. Symp. Motiv.]. **Main/Conf** Nebraska Symposium on Motivation. **Added/Corp** University of Nebraska (Lincoln Campus). Dept. of Psychology. **VFOAT** Current Theory and Research in Motivation. Vol. 2 (1954)-. English. an. $35.00 (cloth edition); $19.95 (paper edition). University of Nebraska Press, PO Box 880484, Lincoln NE 68588-0520. **Tel** (402)472-3584, (800)755-1105, FAX (402)472-6214, (800)526-2617. **LC** BF683; .N4. **DD** 159.4082. **NLM** W3 NE16. **CODEN** NSMPB3. **Pr Rev.** Documents available from The Genuine Article, BIOSIS Document Express. ***Continues** Current Theory and Research in Motivation (Symposium). Current Theory and Research in Motivation, a Symposium, 0070-2099.*
**Ind/Abst** Biol. Abstr.; Index Med.; Psychol. Abstr. (1964-); PsycINFO; PsycLit; Res. Alert [Full Cov.]; Soc. Sci. Cit. Index [Select. Cov.].

NE/0028-2235
**NEDERLANDS TIJDSCHRIFT VOOR DE PSYCHOLOGIE EN HAAR GRENSGEBIEDEN.** [Ned. tijdschr. psychol. haar grensgeb.]. (1946)-. Periodical. Dutch (summaries and/or abstracts in English). Eight times a year. Fl240.00. Intermedia BV, Postbus 4, 2400 M Alphen Rijn Netherlands. **Tel** 011 31 1720 66855. **(Subscription address:** Intermedia BV, Postbus 4, 2400 MA Alphen Rijn Netherlands.**) LC** BF8.N2; N5. **NLM** W1 NE138N. ***Continues** Nederlands Tijdschrift voor de Psychologie en Haar Grensgebieden.*
**Ind/Abst** Psychol. Abstr. (1946-); PsycINFO (1928-); PsycLit.

FR/0296-3981
**NEURO-PSY. See** Medical Science and Technology-Neurology.

UK/0028-3932
**NEUROPSYCHOLOGIA. See** Medical Science and Technology-Neurology.

UK/0960-2011
**NEUROPSYCHOLOGICAL REHABILITATION.** Vol. 1, Issue 1 (1991)-. Periodical. English. qt. $110.00 US; £60.00 Europe; £65.00 other. Lawrence Erlbaum Associates Ltd., 27 Palmeira Mansions, Church Road, Hove East Sussex BN3 2FA England. **Tel** 011 44 273 207411. **(Subscription address:** Turpin Distribution Services Limited, Blackhorse Road, Letchworth, Hertfordshire SG6 1HN, United Kingdom.**) ED** Barbara A. Wilson. **NLM** W1; NE342B. **CODEN** NREHE3.
**Desc:** Provides an international forum for the publication of well-designed and properly evaluated intervention strategies, surveys, and arguments or models. The digest is a regular feature in Neuropsychological Rehabilitation.
**Ind/Abst** Soc. Plann. Policy Dev. Abstr.; Soc. Sci. Cit. Index [Select. Cov.].

US/0894-4105
**NEUROPSYCHOLOGY.** [Neuropsychology]. **Added/Corp** Philadelphia Clinical Neuropsychology Group. Vol. 1, No. 1 (May 1987)-. Academic Scholarly Publication. English. qt. $87.00 (nonmember, institution) US. American Psychological Association, 750 First Street Northeast, Washington DC 20002. **Tel** (800)374-2721, (202)336-5600, (subscriptions - (202)336-5600. **ED** Nelson Butters. **DD** 616. **NLM** W1; NE342D. **CODEN** NEUPEG. **[CCC]. Pr Rev.** available on microfilm from University Microfilms International (UMI). Documents available from The Genuine Article.
**Desc:** Focuses on basic and clinical research, the integration of basic and applied findings, and improving practice in the field of neuropsychology. Brings readers original, empirical papers in the field, as well as scholarly reviews and theoretical papers promoting research on the relation between brain and human cognitive, emotional and behavioral function.
**Ind/Abst** Psychol. Abstr. (1987-); PsycINFO; PsycLit; Res. Alert [Full Cov.]; Soc. Plann. Policy Dev. Abstr.

NE
**NEUROPSYCHOLOGY DEVELOPMENT AND COGNITION.** (19??)-. English. Ten times a year. Fl1675.00 (all four groups) (institution). Swets & Zeitlinger BV, Heereweg 347B PO Box 825, 2160 SZ Lisse Holland. **Tel** 011 31 2521 35111, FAX 02521-15888, telex 41325. **(Subscription address:** Swets Publishing Service, PO Box 825, 2160 SZ Lisse The Netherlands**)**

US/1040-7308
**NEUROPSYCHOLOGY REVIEW. See** Medical Science and Technology-Neurology.

US/0149-7634
**NEUROSCIENCE AND BIOBEHAVIORAL REVIEWS. See** Medical Science and Technology-Neurology.

US/0278-3738
**NEUROSCIENCE NEWSLETTER.** [Neurosci. newsl.]. (19??)-. Newsletter. English. Six times a year. $50.00. Society for Neuroscience, 11 Dupont Circle, Suite 500, Washington DC 20036. **Tel** (202)462-6688.

US/0195-2269
**NEW DIRECTIONS FOR CHILD DEVELOPMENT.** [New dir. child dev.]. No. 1 (1978)-. Periodical. English. qt. $78.00 institutions; $56.00 individuals. Jossey Bass Inc., 350 Sansome Street, San Francisco CA 94104. **Tel** (415)433-1767, FAX (415)433-0499. **ED** William Damon. **LC** BF721; .N49. **DD** 155.4. **NLM** W1 NE374DR. **CODEN** NDCDDI. **Circ:** 450 (ctrl). available on microfilm and microfiche from University Microfilms International (UMI). Documents available from BIOSIS Document Express.
**Desc:** Explores the cognitive, social, emotional, moral, and linguistic development of children from infancy through adolescence.
**Ind/Abst** Abstr. Res. Pastor. Care Couns. (19??-); AGRICOLA [Select. Cov.]; Biol. Abstr.; Curr. Index J. Educ. (1980-); Index Med. (1985-);; Psychol. Abstr. (1980-); PsycINFO (1985-); PsycLit; Soc. Plann. Policy Dev. Abstr.

US
**NEW DIRECTIONS FOR EDUCATION REFORM.** English. West Kentucky University, College of Education and Behavioral Sciences, Bowling Green KY 42101. **Tel** (502)745-4998, (502)745-4950. ***Continues** Journal of Human Behavior and Learning.*
**Ind/Abst** High. Educ. Abstr. (1990-); Psychol. Abstr. (1984-); PsycINFO.

UK/0732-118X
**NEW IDEAS IN PSYCHOLOGY.** [New ideas psychol.]. Vol. 1, No. 1 (1983)-. Periodical. English. Three times a year. $239.00 The Americas; £160.00 other. Pergamon Press, An Imprint of Elsevier Science Ltd., The Boulevard, Langford Lane, Kidlington, Oxford OX5 1GB United Kingdom. **Tel** 011 44 865 843000, 011 44 865 843699, FAX 011 44 865 843010. **(Subscription address:** Elsevier Science Ltd. Oxford Fulfillment Centre, PO Box 800, Kidlington, Oxford OX5 1DX United Kingdom.**) ED** Pierre Moessinger and Richard F. Kitchener. **LC** BF1; .N48. **DD** 150/.5. **[CCC]. Pr Rev.** available on microfiche (simultaneously with the paper edition); available on microfilm (at the end of the subscription year). Documents available from The Genuine Article.
**Desc:** Represents an authoritative source of expert information for psychologists and professionals responsible for training programs or psychological services in schools, clinics, and private practice.
**Ind/Abst** Abstr. Res. Pastor. Care Couns. (19??-); Curr. Aware. Biol. Sci., CABS; Curr. Contents Soc. Behav. Sci.; Life Sci. Collect.; Psychol. Abstr.; PsycINFO; PsycLit; Res. Alert [Full Cov.]; Soc. Sci. Cit. Index [Full Cov.].

US/0275-9578
**NEW PATTERNS OF LEARNING.** [New patterns learn.]. Monographic series. English. ir. Price varies per volume. John Wiley & Sons, Inc., 605 Third Avenue, New York NY 10158-0012. **Tel** (212)850-6000, (212)850-6645, FAX (212)850-6088, telex 12-7063. **(Subscription address:** John Wiley & Sons / England, Baffins Lane, Chichester, West Sussex PO19 1UD England.**)**

UK
**NEW PSYCHOLOGIST.** V. 1- Apr. 1978-. Periodical. English. mo. Psychologist Magazine, 167 Ferme Park Road, London N8 9BP England. **LC** BF636.A1; N48. **DD** 158/.05. ***Supersedes** Psychologist, Practical and Personal Psychology.*

US/1057-0705
**NEW SENSE BULLETIN.** ***Title Change.*** [New sense bull.]. Vol. 16, No. 8 (May 1991)-Vol. 17, No. 7 (Apr. 1992). Bulletin. English. mo. Interface Press, PO Box 42211, Los Angeles CA 90042. **Tel** (213)223-2500, (800)553-6463, FAX (213)223-2519. **LC** BP605.N48; B7. **DD** 133. available on microfilm and microfiche from University Microfilms International (UMI). ***Continues** Brain Mind Bulletin, 0273-8546.* ***Continued by** Brain, Mind & Common Sense, 1064-671X.*
**Ind/Abst** AGRICOLA.

US/0160-7162
**NEW VISTAS IN COUNSELING SERIES. See** Medical Science and Technology.

NZ/0112-109X
**NEW ZEALAND JOURNAL OF PSYCHOLOGY (CHRISTCHURCH. 1983).** (NEW ZEALAND JOURNAL OF PSYCHOLOGY.). [N.Z. j. psychol.]. **Added/Corp** New Zealand Psychological Society. Vol. 12, No. 1 (May 1983)-. Periodical. English. sa (2 issues). 25.00NZ$ New Zealand; 31.00NZ$ (airmail) Australia, South Pacific; 35.00NZ$ (airmail) Asia, US & Canada; 39.00NZ$ (airmail) Europe, Africa, South America & Middle East; 30.00NZ$ surface mail other. New Zealand Journal of Psychology, PO Box 4092, Wellington New Zealand. **Tel** FAX 011 64 4 3828763. **ED** Michael Corballis (Editor's Address: University of Auckland, Department of Psychology, Private Bag 92019, Auckland, New Zealand; Phone: 09 3737999). **NLM** W1; NE9732H. **[CCC]. Bk Rev. Pr Rev.** Documents available from The Genuine Article. ***Continues** New Zealand Psychologist, 0303-6863.*
**Ind/Abst** Curr. Contents Soc. Behav. Sci.; Psychol. Abstr. (1983-); PsycINFO; PsycLit; Res. Alert [Full Cov.]; Soc. Sci. Cit. Index [Full Cov.].

CN/0831-9510
**NEWSLETTER OF THE CPA/SCP SECTION ON WOMEN & PSYCHOLOGY.** [Newsl. CPA/SCP Sect. Women Psychol.]. **VFOAT** Section Femmes et Psychologie. **VAT** Newsletter of the Canadian Psychological Association/Societe Canadienne de Psychologie Section on Women and Psychology. Vol. 8, No. 3 (April 1984)-. Newsletter. English (French). Three times a year. Newsletter of the CPA Section on Women and Psychology, c/o Dr Lorna Larsen, Student Counseling Services, University of Calgary, 2500 University Drive NW, Calgary Alberta T2N 1N4 Canada. **Tel** (604)228-5259, telex 04 512 33. **ED** Lorette Woolsey and Carol Wilson. **DD** 155.6/33/05. **Bk Rev. Circ:** 250. ***Continues*** *Newsletter of the CPA Section on Women & Psychology, 0826-1989.*
**Desc:** Publishes information on women and psychology, CPA policies and activities, and conferences and jobs.

US
**NEWSLINK.** **Added/Corp** American Association of Suicidology. **VFOAT** News Link. (19??)-. English. qt. $80.00 (includes membership). American Association of Suicidology, 2459 South Ash, Denver CO 80222. **Tel** 303 692-0985, FAX 303 756-3299. **LC** HV6548.U5; N48. **DD** 362.28/0973/05. **Ad Acc. Pr Rev. Circ:** 1,300 (ctrl).
**Desc:** Information about suicide and association activities.

NR/0794-0831
**NIGERIAN JOURNAL OF GUIDANCE AND COUNSELLING, THE.** **Added/Corp** University of Ilorin. Dept. of Guidance and Counselling. Vol. 1 (Aug. 1985)-. English. University of Ilorin, Department of Guidance & Counselling, PMB 1515, Ilorin, Kwara State, Nigeria.
**Ind/Abst** Psychol. Abstr. (1986-); PsycINFO (1986-); PsycLit.

US/0888-9368
**NIGHT LIGHT, THE.** [Night light]. **Added/Corp** Alabama Society for Sleep Disorders. Vol. 1, Issue 1 (Apr. 1986)-. Periodical. English. qt. Alabama Society for Sleep Disorders, 800 Montclair Road, Birmingham AL 35213. **DD** 613.
**Ind/Abst** Except. Hum. Exp.

US/0897-1013
**NOETIC SCIENCES BULLETIN.** **Added/Corp** Institute of Noetic Sciences. Vol. 2, No. 2 (June/July 1987)-. Bulletin. English. qt. comes with Noetic Science Review. Institute of Noetic Sciences, 475 Gate Five Road, Suite 300, San Francisco CA 94965. **Tel** (800)383-1586, FAX (415)331-5673. **ED** Barbara McNeill. **DD** 153. **Bk Rev. Circ:** 25,000. ***Continues*** *Bulletin - Institute of Noetic Sciences.*
**Desc:** Features updates of ongoing institute research projects, awards and prizes, upcoming institute lectures, symposia, travel/study programs, and member study groups, and notices of lectures and conference presentations of institute colleagues.

US/0897-1005
**NOETIC SCIENCES REVIEW.** **Added/Corp** Institute of Noetic Sciences. No. 1 (Winter 1986)-. Periodical. English. qt. $35.00 (comes with membership and Noetic Sciences Bulletin). Institute of Noetic Sciences, 475 Gate Five Road, Suite 300, San Francisco CA 94965. **Tel** (800)383-1586, FAX (415)331-5673. **ED** Barbara McNeill. **DD** 153. **Bk Rev. Circ:** 25,000. ***Continues*** *Newsletter (Institute of Noetic Sciences), 0888-3432.*
**Desc:** Penetrating articles, interviews, research updates and reviews. Essays on the people and ideas in the forefront of consciousness research and its application to the enhancement of life on the planet.
**Ind/Abst** Except. Hum. Exp.

DK/0029-1463
**NORDISK PSYKOLOGI.** [Nord. psykol.]. **Added/Corp** Dansk Psykologforening. Suomen Psykologinen Seura. Norsk Psykologforening. Sveriges Psykologforbund. Vol. 1 (1949)-. Periodical. Danish (English). qt. kr440.00. CA Reitzels Forlag AS, Norregade 20, DK 1165 Coppenhagen K Denmark. **Tel** 011 45 3 3122400. **(Subscription address:** Munksgaard International Publishers, Inc., Norre Sogade 35, PO Box 2148, DK-1016 Copenhagen K Denmark.**)** **ED** Schultz Jorgensen. **LC** BF8.D3; N6. **NLM** W1 NO217D. **CODEN** NOPSAW. **Bk Rev. Ad Acc. Pr Rev. Circ:** 3,600 (ctrl). Documents available from The Genuine Article.
**Ind/Abst** Arts Humanit. Citation Index [Select. Cov.]; Psychol. Abstr. (1949-); PsycINFO (19??-); PsycLit (19??-); Res. Alert (19??-) [Full Cov.]; Soc. Plann. Policy Dev. Abstr. (19??-); Soc. Sci. Cit. Index (19??-) [Full Cov.].

DK/0108-271X
**NORDISK SEXOLOGI.** (19??)-. Periodical. Danish (Norwegian, Swedish and English). qt. kr296.00. Dansk Psykologisk Forlag, Hans Knudsens Plads 1A, DK 2100 Copenhagen Denmark. **Tel** 011 45 31 182757. **NLM** W1; NO218.
**Ind/Abst** Psychol. Abstr. (1987-); PsycINFO (1987-); PsycLit.

SW/0345-1402
**NORDISK TIDSKRIFT FOR BETEENDETERAPI.** [Nord. tidskr. beteendeter.]. **VFOAT** Scandinavian Journal of Behaviour Therapy. Vol. 4 (1975)-. Periodical. Swedish (English). qt. DM65.00. Nordisk Tidskrift Beteendetera. **NLM** W1 NO2197. **CODEN** NTBEDQ. Documents available from BIOSIS Document Express. ***Continues*** *Beteendeterapi.*
**Ind/Abst** Biol. Abstr. (1986-); Psychol. Abstr. (1975-); PsycINFO (1975-); PsycLit.

FR/0223-565X
**NOUVELLE REVUE DE PSYCHANALYSE.** ***Ceased.*** [Nouv. rev. psychanal.]. **Added/Corp** Association Psychanalytique de France. No. 1 (Spring 1970)-No. 50. Monographic series. French. Twice a year. Editions Gallimard, 5 rue Sebastien Bottin, 75328 Paris Cedex 7 France. **Tel** 011 33 1 49544200. **ED** J. B. Pontalis. **NLM** W1 NO834G. **Circ:** 7,000.
**Desc:** Goal is to explicate and clarify the work of the subconscious mind. There is no connection with any psychoanalytic institution or school and is not derived from any one teacher.
**Ind/Abst** Psychol. Abstr. (1973-).

US/0048-1335
**OBSERVATIONS FROM THE TREADMILL.** English. 357 Hidden River Road, Narberth PA 19072. **LC** BF1; .O27. **DD** 081.

US/0030-2228
**OMEGA (FARMINGDALE).** (OMEGA. JOURNAL OF DEATH & DYING.). [Omega]. **Added/Corp** Ars Moriendi Inc. Health and Human Values Task Force. Vol. 1 (1970)-. Academic Scholarly Publication. English. bm. $165.00. Baywood Publishing Company Inc., 26 Austin Avenue, PO Box 337, Amityville NY 11701. **Tel** (516)691-1270, (800)638-7819, FAX (516)691-1770. **ED** Robert J Kastenbaum. **LC** BF789.D4; O4. **DD** 155.9/37. **NLM** W1 OM423. **CODEN** OMGABX. cum. index. **Bk Rev. Ad Acc. Pr Rev.** Documents available from The Genuine Article, UMI Article Clearinghouse.
**Desc:** The international forum on the subject of thanatology. Terminal illness, suicide, violence and disaster, bereavement and grief, concepts and attitudes are explored. A guide for clinicians, social workers and health professionals dealing with problems in crisis management.
**Ind/Abst** Abstr. Anthropol. (19??-); Abstr. Res. Pastor. Care Couns. (19??-); Acad. Abstr. Full Text Elite (July 1990-); Acad. Abstr. (July 1990-); Acad. Ind. [Computer File] (1988-); Acad. Search (July 1990-); Anbar Account. Finan. Abstr. [Full Txt.]; Anbar Mark. Distr. Abstr. [Full Txt.]; Anbar Top Manage. Abstr. [Full Txt.]; Appl. Soc. Sci. Index Abstr.; Arts Humanit. Citation Index [Select. Cov.]; Cumul. Index Nurs. Allied Health Lit.; Curr. Contents Soc. Behav. Sci.; Curr. Index J. Educ.; EMBASE; Expand. Acad. Index (1988-); Health Index (1989-); Health Period. Database; Health Ref. Cent. (Jan. 1989-) [Full Cov.]; High. Educ. Abstr. (1975-); Index Period. Lit. Aging; INFO-SOUTH Abstr.; Mag. Search; Manage. Market. Abstr.; Manage. Bibliogr. Rev.; Middle East Abstr. Index; Newsp. Period. Abstr. (1992-); Oper. Prod. Manage. Abstr. [Full Txt.]; Person. Train. Abstr. [Full Txt.]; Psychol. Abstr. (1970-); PsycLit; Res. Alert [Full Cov.]; Soc. Plann. Policy Dev. Abstr.; Soc. Sci. Source (Jul. 1990-); Soc. Sci. Cit. Index [Full Cov.]; Soc. Sci. Index; Soc. Sci. Index Fulltext (1988-) [Full Txt.]; Sociol. Abstr.; Women Manage. Rev. [Full Txt.].

●US/1062-7049
**ON BALANCE (DENVER, COLO.).** (ON BALANCE.). (1992)-. Periodical. English. bm. $25.00 (library), $45.00 (institution, 8 copies), $25.00 (individual). On Balance, Inc., 2640 East 12th Avenue #708, Denver CO 80206. **Tel** (303)393-1049. **ED** Catherine Hart. **Bk Rev**, (Qty: (varies)). **Pr Rev. Circ:** 500 (ctrl).
**Desc:** Provides information and encouragement to readers as they travel the path toward self-discovery and well-being.
**Ind/Abst** Leis. Recreat. Tour. Abstr.

CN/0030-3054
**ONTARIO PSYCHOLOGIST, THE.** [Ont. psychol.]. **Added/Corp** Ontario Psychological Association. Vol. 1 (1969)-. Periodical. English. Six times a year (Feb., Apr., June, Aug., Oct., Dec.). 60.00Can$. Ontario Psychological Association, 730 Yonge Street/Suite 221, Toronto Ontario M4Y 2B7 Canada. **Tel** (416)961-5552, FAX (416)961-5516. **ED** Dr. Donald Rudzinski. **LC** RC467; .O6. **DD** 150/.5. **NLM** W1 ON856. **CODEN** ONPSDS. **Bk Rev. Ad Acc, Adv Mgr:** S. Traub. **Circ:** 1,600 (ctrl). available on microfilm and microfiche from University Microfilms International (UMI). ***Supersedes*** *Ontario Psychological Association O.P.A. Quarterly, 0318-2657;* ***Absorbed*** *Ontario Psychological Association. O P A Update., 0703-8895.*
**Desc:** Articles and news items about professional psychology in Ontario directed at members of the profession.
**Ind/Abst** Psychol. Abstr. (1971-); PsycINFO (?-?); PsycLit.

US/1043-3880
**OPEN MINDS.** [Open minds]. (1988)-. Periodical. English. Twelve times a year. $154.00 US; $254.00 other. Open Minds, 4465 Old Harrisburg Road, Gettysburg PA 17325. **Tel** (717)334-1329, FAX (717)334-1329. **DD** 362. cum. index. **Bk Rev**, (Qty: 12/yr).

US/0746-8822
**ORACLE (SANTA ANA, CALIF.), THE.** (THE ORACLE : NEWSLETTER OF ORANGE COUNTY MENSA.). Newsletter. English. mo. Free to Orange County MENSA Members, $7.00 other MENSA members (directory not included), $10.00 nonmembers (directory not included). The Oracle, 1371 Haight Street South, San Francisco CA 94117.

FR/0395-000X
**ORDINAIRE DU PSYCHANALYSTE, L'.** 1- May 1973-. Periodical. French. 80.00F. Librairie les Mains Libres 2, rue de Pere Corentin, 75014 Paris France. **LC** RC500; .O73. **DD** 616.8/917/05. **NLM** W1 OR271.

US/0749-5978
**ORGANIZATIONAL BEHAVIOR AND HUMAN DECISION PROCESSES.** [Org. behav. hum. decis. process.]. Vol. 35, No. 1 (Feb. 1985)-. Academic Scholarly Publication. English. mo. $599.50 US and Canada; $695.50 other. Academic Press, Inc., 6277 Sea Harbor Drive, Orlando FL 32887. **Tel** (800)543-9534, (407)345-4100, FAX (407)363-9661. **ED** James C. Naylor. **LC** BF636.A1; O7. **DD** 302.3/05. **NLM** W1; OR663FE. **[CCC].** Documents available from The Genuine Article, UMI Article Clearinghouse. ***Continues*** *Organizational Behavior and Human Performance, 0030-5073.*
**Desc:** Features articles that describe original empirical research and theoretical developments in all areas of human decision processes and organizational psychology. Emphasizes research that contributes to the development of principles or theories relevant to psychological processes.
**Ind/Abst** ABI/INFORM Glob. Ed.; ABI Inform Ondisc (Sept. 1971-); ABI/INFORM Ondisc: Expr. Ed.; Acad. Search (Jan. 1994-); Appl. Soc. Sci. Index Abstr.; Bus. Index (1985-); Bus. Period. Index; Bus. Source (Jul. 1993-); Commun. Abstr. (?-?); Contents Pages Manage.; Curr. Contents Soc. Behav. Sci.; Gen. BusinessFile (1985-); Gen. Period. Index (1985-); Hospit. Health Admin. Index (Feb. 1985-Dec. 1987); INFO-SOUTH Abstr.; Int. Bibliogr. Sociol.; J. Plan. Lit.; Mag. Search; Psychol. Abstr. (1966-); PsycINFO; PsycLit; PsycScan: Appl. Psych.; Res. Alert [Full Cov.]; Risk Abstr.; Selec. Coop. Index Manage. Period; Soc. Sci. Cit. Index [Full Cov.]; Wilson Bus. Abstr.

US/0094-6206
**ORIGINS OF BEHAVIOR, THE.** Vol. 1 (1974)-. Periodical. English. ir. Price varies. John Wiley & Sons Inc / New Jersey, 1 Wiley Drive, Somerset NJ 08875. **Tel** (800)225-5945, (908)469-4400. **(Subscription address:** John Wiley & Sons / England, Baffins Lane, Chichester, West Sussex PO19 1UD England.**)** **NLM** W1 OR687.

●PK/1019-438X
**PAKISTAN JOURNAL OF CLINICAL PSYCHOLOGY.** (1992)-. English. Twice a year. $24.00. Institute of Clinical Psychology, University of Karachi, 118 Block 20 Abul-Asar Hafeez Jalindhri Road, Gulistan-e-Jauhar, Karachi 75290 Pakistan. **Tel** 11 92 21 8113584. **ED** Farrukh Z. Ahmad.
**Desc:** Covers the clinical, theoretical and experimental aspects of psychology.

PK
**PAKISTAN JOURNAL OF PSYCHOLOGICAL RESEARCH : PJPR.** **Added/Corp** National Institute of Psychology (Pakistan). **VFOAT** PJPR. Vol. 1, No. 1-2 (Summer 1986)-. Periodical. English. sa. $15.00. Incharge Publications, National Institute of Psychology, PO Box 1511, Islamabad, Pakistan. **LC** BF1; .P28. **DD** 150/.5.
**Ind/Abst** Psychol. Abstr. (1986-); PsycLit.

PK/0030-9869
**PAKISTAN JOURNAL OF PSYCHOLOGY.** **Added/Corp** Karachi. University. Dept. of Psychology. Vol. 1 (July 1967)-. Periodical. English. Twice a year. $32.00. Institute of Clinical Psychology, University of Karachi, 118 Block 20 Abul-Asar Hafeez Jalindhri Road, Gulistan-e-Jauhar, Karachi 75290 Pakistan. **Tel** 11 92 21 8113584. **ED** Dr. Farrukh Z. Ahmad. **LC** BF1; .P3. **DD** 150/.5. **NLM** W1 PA356V. Index available. cum. index. **Bk Rev**, (Qty: 1,000). **Ad Acc.** ctrl circ.

FR
**PASCAL. 65, PSYCHOLOGIE, PSYCHOPATHOLOGIE, PSYCHIATRIE.** **Added/Corp** Institut de l'Information Scientifique et Technique (France). **VFOAT** Psychologie, Psychopathologie, Psychiatrie; Psychology, Psychopathology, Psychiatry; PASCAL International Bibliography. 65, Psychology, Psychopathology, Psychiatry. (1991)-. Periodical. French (English). Ten times a year. 1755.00F France; 1860.00F other. CNRS / Institut d'Information Scientifique et Technique, (Centre National de la Recherche Scientifique), 15 Quai Anatole France, Paris 75700 France. **Tel** 011 33 1 47531515, telex 299 356 F. **(Subscription address:** Institut d'Information Scientifique et Technique, 2 Allee du Parc

de Brabois, 54514 Vandoeuvre Nancy France) **LC** Z7203; .P233. ***Continues*** *PASCAL. E65, Psychologie, Psychopathologie, Psychiatrie, 1146-5330.*

US/0031-2789
**PASTORAL PSYCHOLOGY.** [Pastor. psychol.]. **Added/Corp** Princeton Theological Seminary. Vol. 1, No. 1 (Feb. 1950)-. Periodical. English. bm. £40.00 (individuals), £199.00 (institutions) UK; $255.00 US; $300.00 other. Human Sciences Press, PO Box 735, 233 Spring Street, New York NY 10013. **Tel** (212)620-8000, FAX (212)807-1047, telex 23421139. **(Subscription address:** Eurospan Ltd., Journals and Serials Division, 3 Henrietta Street, Covent Garden, London WC2E 8LU England.**) ED** Lewis Rambo. **LC** BV4012; .P33. **DD** 253.5. **NLM** W1 PA874H. **[CCC].** available on microfilm and microfiche from University Microfilms International (UMI).
**Desc:** Addresses itself to bringing psychological and behavioral science into relation and dialogue with the work of the ministry. Pastoral counseling along with other dimensions of the profession and the changing contours of the field are thoughtfully examined and discussed by distinguished contributors.
**Ind/Abst** Abstr. Res. Pastor. Care Couns. (19??-); Curr. Thoughts Trends; Guide Soc. Sci. Relig.; Index Book Rev. Relig.; Psychol. Abstr. (1982-); PsycINFO (1990-); PsycLit; Relig. Index One Period. (1950-); Relig. Theol. Abstr.

FR
**PATIO.** Periodical. French. Three times a year. 300.00F, 360.00F (airmail). Editions de L'Eclat / Montpellier, 4 rue du Chapeau Rouge, 34000 Montpellier France. **Tel** 011 33 66 778763. **LC** PAR. Index available. **Bk Rev. Ad Acc.**
**Desc:** Studies the implications of psychoanalysis in different research camps (pedagogy, therapy, literature, etc.).
**Ind/Abst** PsycINFO (1990-).

RU
**PEDAGOGICHESKIE PROBLEMY FORMIROVANIIA POZNAVATELNYKH INTERESOV UCHASHCHIKHSIA.**
**Added/Corp** Leningradskii Gosudartsvennyi Pedagogicheskii Institut Imeni A.I. Gertsena. Vol. 1 (1975)-. Periodical. Russian. an. 1.28rub. Leningradskii Gosudarstvennyi Pedagogicheskii Institut Imeni, 191186 Moika 48, St. Petersburg Russia. **LC** AZ711; .P44.

●US/1070-6674
**PELIZZA'S POSITIVE PRINCIPLES FOR BETTER LIVING.** [Pelizza's posit. princ. better living]. **VFOAT** Pelizza's Positive Principles. Vol. 1, No. 1 (July 1993)-. Periodical. English. bm. $12.00. Pelizza & Associates, 1903 Huntridge Drive, Clifton Park NY 12065. **Tel** (518)383-2302. **(Subscription address:** Box 225 North Chatham, NY 12132 (telephone 518-766-4849)**) ED** Phillip Niles. **DD** 155. **Bk Rev. Ad Acc, Adv Mgr:** John Pelizza. **Circ:** 1,000. available in Loose-leaf.

US
**PENSAMIENTOS.** No. 1 (1975)-. Periodical. English. an. Rational Island Publishers, 719 2nd Avenue North, Seattle WA 98109. **LC** Discard.

US/0031-5117
**PERCEPTION & PSYCHOPHYSICS.** [Percept. psychophys.]. **Added/Corp** Psychonomic Society. **VAT** Perception and Psychophysics. Vol. 1 (Jan. 1966)-. Academic Scholarly Publication. English. Eight times a year. $164.00 US; $176.00 other. Psychonomic Society Publications, 1710 Fortview Road, Austin TX 78704. **Tel** (512)462-2442, FAX (512)462-1101. **ED** Charles W. Eriksen. **LC** BF233; .P4. **DD** 153.7/05. **NLM** W1 PE78H. **CODEN** PEPSBJ. **[CCC].** Index available. **Ad Acc. Pr Rev. Circ:** 1,825. available on microfilm and microfiche from University Microfilms International (UMI). Documents available from The Genuine Article, BIOSIS Document Express.
**Desc:** Deals with sensory processes, perception and psychophysics. Although the majority of articles report experimental investigations, also included are articles that are theoretical.
**Ind/Abst** Arts Humanit. Citation Index [Select. Cov.]; Biol. Abstr.; CSA Neuro. Abstr. (?-?); Curr. Contents Soc. Behav. Sci.; EMBASE; Ergon. Abstr.; Int. Aerosp. Abstr.; Int. Bibliogr. Sociol.; MLA Int. Bibl. Books Artic. Mod. Lang. Lit.; Life Sci. Collect.; Psychol. Abstr. (1966-); PsycINFO; PsycLit; Res. Alert [Full Cov.]; Sci. Cit. Index; SCISEARCH; Soc. Plann. Policy Dev. Abstr.; Soc. Sci. Cit. Index [Full Cov.]; Spec. Educ. Needs Abstr.

UK/0301-0066
**PERCEPTION (LONDON).** (PERCEPTION.). [Perception]. Vol. 1 (1972)-. Periodical. English (French and German). mo. £290.00 UK; $480.00 US. Pion Ltd., 207 Brondesbury Park, London NW2 5JN England. **Tel** 011 44 81 459 0066, FAX 011 44 81 451 6454, telex 94016265 PION G. **ED** Richard L. Gregory. **LC** BF311; .P348. **DD** 153.7/05. **NLM** W1 PE78G. **CODEN** PCTNBA. Index available. **Bk Rev. Ad Acc. Circ:** 700. Documents available from The Genuine Article.
**Desc:** Experimental results and theoretical ideas in fields of animal, human and machine perception. Includes physiological mechanisms, psychological data, cognitive experiments and theories, and philosophical implications.
**Ind/Abst** Abstr. Hum. Comput. Interact.; Can. Index; CSA Neuro. Abstr. (?-?); Curr. Contents Soc. Behav. Sci.; EMBASE; Ergon. Abstr.; Health Period. Database; Index Med.; Middle East Abstr. Index; Life Sci. Collect.; Psychol. Abstr. (1972-); PsycLit; Res. Alert [Full Cov.]; Soc. Sci. Cit. Index [Full Cov.].

US/0031-5125
**PERCEPTUAL AND MOTOR SKILLS.** [Percept. mot. skills]. Vol. 5 (March 1955)-. Academic Scholarly Publication. English. bm (6 issues). $240.00. Southern Universities Press, Box 9229, Missoula MT 59807. **Tel** (406)728-1710. **ED** R. B. Ammons and Carol H. Ammons. **LC** BF311; .P36. **DD** 152. **NLM** W1 PE78K. **CODEN** PMOSAZ. **Bk Rev. Pr Rev.** available on microfilm. Documents available from The Genuine Article, BIOSIS Document Express, UMI Article Clearinghouse. ***Continues*** *Perceptual and Motor Skills Research Exchange, 0885-6524.*
**Desc:** Experimental or theoretical articles dealing with perception or motor skills, especially as affected by experience. Also articles on general methodology and new material listings and reviews.
**Ind/Abst** Abstr. Anthropol.; Acad. Search (July 1993-); Biol. Abstr.; Commun. Abstr.; CSA Neuro. Abstr. (?-?); Curr. Contents Soc. Behav. Sci.; Curr. Index J. Educ.; Dev. Med. Child Neurol.; Educ. Technol. Abstr.; EMBASE; Energy Res. Abstr.; Ergon. Abstr.; Expand. Acad. Index (1989-); High. Educ. Abstr. (1968-); Highw. Res. Abstr.; Index Med.; INFO-SOUTH Abstr.; Int. Aerosp. Abstr.; Lang. Lang. Behav. Abstr.; Middle East Abstr. Index; MLA Int. Bibl. Books Artic. Mod. Lang. Lit.; Multicult. Educ. Abstr.; Newsp. Period. Abstr. (1989-); Nucl. Sci. Abstr.; Life Sci. Collect.; Phys. Educ. Index; Psychol. Abstr. (1955-); PsycINFO; PsycLit; Res. Alert [Full Cov.]; Risk Abstr.; Soc. Plann. Policy Dev. Abstr.; Soc. Sci. Source (Jul. 1993-); Soc. Sci. Cit. Index [Full Cov.]; Soc. Sci. Index; Soc. Sci. Index Fulltext (Dec. 1987-) [Full Txt.]; Sociol. Abstr.; Sociol. Educ. Abstr.; Spec. Educ. Needs Abstr.; SPORT Discus; SportSearch; Stud. Women Abstr.; Women Stud. Abstr.

US/0883-2293
**PERSON-CENTERED REVIEW.** ***Ceased.*** [Person-cent. rev.]. **VFOAT** Person Centered Review. Vol. 1, No. 1 (Feb. 1986)-Vol. 5, No. 4 (1990). Periodical. English. qt. SAGE Periodical Press, 2455 Teller Road, Thousand Oaks CA 91320. **Tel** (805)499-0721, FAX (805)499-0871, telex 100799. **ED** David J Cain. **NLM** W1; PE843P. **[CCC].** Index available. cum. index. **Bk Rev. Ad Acc. Circ:** 241. available on microfilm.
**Desc:** Devoted to the continued development of person-centered theory, research, and application in the fields of psychotherapy, education, supervision and training, and human development in various group and organizational settings.
**Ind/Abst** PsycINFO (1990-).

US/0732-0779
**PERSONAL GROWTH AND BEHAVIOR.** [Pers. growth behav.]. **VFOAT** Annual Editions: Personal Growth and Behavior. (19??)-. English. an. $12.95. Dushkin Publishing Group Inc., Sluice Dock, Guilford CT 06437. **Tel** (203)453-4351, (800)243-6532, FAX (203)453-6000. **ED** Karen G. Duffy. **LC** BF698.A1; P45. **DD** 155.
**Desc:** Annually updated collection of public press articles covering current issues in personal growth and behavior. Includes topic guide and complete index.

UK/0191-8869
**PERSONALITY AND INDIVIDUAL DIFFERENCES.** [Pers. individ. differ.]. **Added/Corp** International Society for the Study of Individual Differences. Vol. 1, No. 1 (1980)-. Periodical. English. mo. $790.00 The Americas; £530.00 other. Pergamon Press, An Imprint of Elsevier Science Ltd., The Boulevard, Langford Lane, Kidlington, Oxford OX5 1GB United Kingdom. **Tel** 011 44 865 843000, 011 44 865 843699, FAX 011 44 865 843010. **(Subscription address:** Elsevier Science Ltd. Oxford Fulfillment Centre, PO Box 800, Kidlington, Oxford OX5 1DX United Kingdom.**) ED** H. J. Eysenck. **LC** BF698.A1; P49. **DD** 155.2/05. **NLM** W1 PE86T. **CODEN** PEIDD9. **[CCC]. Pr Rev.** available on microfilm and microfiche from University Microfilms International (UMI). Documents available from The Genuine Article, BIOSIS Document Express.
**Ind/Abst** Appl. Soc. Sci. Index Abstr.; Arts Humanit. Citation Index [Select. Cov.]; Biol. Abstr.; Br. Educ. Index; Crim. Justice Abstr.; Curr. Contents Soc. Behav. Sci.; Psychol. Abstr. (1980-); PsycINFO; PsycLit; Res. Alert [Full Cov.]; Soc. Sci. Cit. Index [Full Cov.]; SportSearch.

US/0146-1672
**PERSONALITY & SOCIAL PSYCHOLOGY BULLETIN.** [Pers. soc. psychol. bull.]. **Added/Corp** Society for Personality and Social Psychology. **VAT** Personality and Social Psychology Bulletin. Vol. 1, No. 2 (Feb. 1975)-. Periodical. English. mo. $440.00. SAGE Periodical Press, 2455 Teller Road, Thousand Oaks CA 91320. **Tel** (805)499-0721, FAX (805)499-0871, telex 100799. **ED** Arie Kruglanski (University of Maryland). **LC** BF698.A1; P48. **DD** 301.1/05. **NLM** W1 PE861S. **[CCC]. Pr Rev. Acid Free.** available on microfilm and microfiche from University Microfilms International (UMI). Documents available from The Genuine Article, UMI Article Clearinghouse. ***Continues*** *Proceedings of the Division of Personality and Social Psychology.*
**Desc:** Publishes theoretical articles and empirical reports of research in all areas of personality and social psychology.
**Ind/Abst** Acad. Search (Jan. 1994-); Appl. Soc. Sci. Index Abstr.; Commun. Abstr.; Curr. Contents Soc. Behav. Sci.; Expand. Acad. Index (1989-); High. Educ. Abstr. (1977-); INFO-SOUTH Abstr.; Mag. Search; Newsp. Period. Abstr. (1991-); Psychol. Abstr. (1975-); PsycINFO; PsycLit; Res. Alert [Full Cov.]; Risk Abstr.; Sage Fam. Stud. Abstr. (?-?); Sage Public Adm. Abstr. (?-?); Soc. Sci. Source (Jul. 1993-); Soc. Sci. Cit. Index [Full Cov.]; Soc. Sci. Index; Soc. Sci. Index Fulltext (Dec. 1988-) [Full Txt.]; SportSearch; Stud. Women Abstr.; Work Relat. Abstr.

US/0740-4379
**PERSONALITY ASSESSMENT SYSTEM FOUNDATION JOURNAL.** [Pers. Assess. Syst. Found. j.]. **VFOAT** Journal. Vol. 1, No. 1 (Spring 1982)-. Periodical. English. qt. $3.00 single issue. Alfred Couchon, c/o Personality Assessment, System Institute, PO Box 4164, Martinsville VA 24115. **LC** BF698.4; .P48. **DD** 155.2/8.

US/0888-9740
**PERSONALITY, PSYCHOPATHOLOGY, AND PSYCHOTHERAPY.** [Pers. psychopathol. psychother.]. Vol. 34 (1985)-. Monographic series. English. ir. Price varies per volume. Academic Press, Inc., 6277 Sea Harbor Drive, Orlando FL 32887. **Tel** (800)543-9534, (407)345-4100, FAX (407)363-9661. **DD** 150. ***Continues*** *Personality and Psychopathology, 0079-0931.*

II
**PERSONALITY STUDY AND GROUP BEHAVIOUR.** **Added/Corp** Guru Nanak Dev University. Dept. of Psychology. Vol. 1, No. 1 (Jan. 1981)-. Periodical. English. sa. $20.00. Guru Nanak Development University Department of Psychology, Amritsar 143005 India. **Tel** 62801. **(Subscription address:** Prints India, 11 Darya Ganj, New Delhi 110002 India.**) ED** Satvir Singh. **LC** BF698.9.S63; P47. **DD** 155.2/05. **Bk Rev. Circ:** 500 (ctrl).
**Ind/Abst** Psychol. Abstr. (1981-); PsycINFO; PsycLit.

US/0031-5826
**PERSONNEL PSYCHOLOGY.** [Pers. psychol.]. Vol. 1 (Spring 1948)-. Periodical. English. qt. $55.00 US; $61.00 other (surface mail); $83.00 (airmail). Personnel Psychology Inc., 745 Haskins Road, Suite A, Bowling Green OH 43402. **Tel** (419)352-1562, FAX (419)352-2645. **LC** HF5549.A2; P53. **DD** 658.305. **NLM** W1 PE8702. **CODEN** PPSYAQ. **[CCC].** Index available. **Bk Rev. Ad Acc. Pr Rev. Circ:** 3,300. available on microfilm and microfiche from University Microfilms International (UMI). Documents available from The Genuine Article, UMI Article Clearinghouse.
**Desc:** Publishes articles abount applied research in personnel plus approximately 100 book reviews each year; read by personnel managers, teachers and students in business schools and psychology departments. Refereed journal.
**Ind/Abst** ABI/INFORM Glob. Ed.; ABI Inform Ondisc (Fall 1971-); Acad. Search (July 1993-); Book Rev. Index; Bus. Index (1985-); Bus. Period. Index; Bus. Source (Jul. 1993-); Contents Pages Manage.; Curr. Contents Soc. Behav. Sci.; Curr. Index J. Educ.; Gen. BusinessFile (1985-); Gen. Period. Index (1985-); Hum. Resour. Abstr. (?-?); INFO-SOUTH Abstr.; J. Plan. Lit.; Mag. Search; Manage. Market. Abstr.; Manage. Contents; Person. Manage. Abstr.; Psychol. Abstr. (1949-); PsycINFO; PsycLit; PsycScan: Appl. Psych.; Res. Alert [Full Cov.]; Risk Abstr.; Selec. Coop. Index Manage. Period; Soc. Sci. Cit. Index [Full Cov.]; UMI ABI/Inform--Bus. Period. Ondisc (Winter 1987-) [Full Txt.]; Wilson Bus. Abstr.; Women Stud. Abstr.; Work Relat. Abstr.

CK/0120-3878
**PERSPECTIVAS EN PSICOLOGIA.** **Added/Corp** Universidad Cooperativa de Manizales. Facultad de Psicologia. Fundacion Universitaria de Manizales. Facultad de Psicologia. Vol. 1, No. 1 (May 1982)-. Periodical. Spanish (summaries and/or abstracts in English). Three times a year. $4.00. Apartado Aereo, 868 Manizales Colombia. **Tel** FAX 841443. **LC** BF5; .P46. **DD** 150/.5.
**Ind/Abst** PsycINFO.

US/0160-4422
**PERSPECTIVES IN LAW & PSYCHOLOGY.** **See** Law.

UK/1057-8994
**PERSPECTIVES IN PERSONALITY.** [Perspect. pers.]. Vol. 1 (1985)-. English. an. Jessica Kingsley Publishers, 118 Pentonville Road, London N1 9JN England. **Tel** 011 44 71 833 2307, FAX 011 44 71 837 2917. **LC** BF698.A1; P52. **DD** 155.2/05.

II/0971-1562
**PERSPECTIVES IN PSYCHOLOGICAL RESEARCHES.** [Perspect. Psychol. Res.]. (1978)-. Periodical. English. sa. $25.00. **(Subscription address:** Prints India, 11 Darya Ganj, New Delhi 110002 India.**) UDC** 159.9.

US/0735-4037
**PERSPECTIVES IN PSYCHOTHERAPY.** [Perspect. psychother.]. Vol. 1-. Monographic series. English. ir. Price varies per volume. Gordon & Breach Science Publishers, Inc., PO Box 786, Cooper Station, New York NY 10276. **Tel** (212)206-8900, FAX (212)645-2459. **(Subscription address:** International Publishers Distributor at one of the following addresses: 820 Town Center Drive, Langhorne, PA 19047; or PO Box 90, Reading Berkshire RG1 8JL UK; or Kent Ridge PO Box 1180, Singapore 9111, Republic of Singapore) **ED** P Olsen. **DD** 616.

US/0091-3057
**PHARMACOLOGY, BIOCHEMISTRY AND BEHAVIOR.** **See** Pharmacy and Pharmacology.

US
**PHARMACOLOGY BIOCHEMISTRY & BEHAVIOR. SUPPLEMENT.** **See** Pharmacy and Pharmacology.

II/0970-3926
**PHARMACOPSYCHOECOLOGIA VARANASI.** (PHARMACOPSYCHOECOLOGIA.). [Pharmacopsychoecologia Varanasi]. (1988)-. Periodical. English. Twice a year. Pharmacopsychoecological Association, B-29/12A, Lanka, Varanasi 221005 India. **UDC** 159.9 :615.
**Ind/Abst** Psychol. Abstr. (1988-); PsycLit.

PH
**PHILIPPINE JOURNAL OF COUNSELING PSYCHOLOGY.** English (Tagalog). P100.00 Philippines. Salle University, Department of Psychology, Guidance and Counselling, 2401 Taft Avenue, Manila Philippines. **ED** Rose Marie C Salazar. **Circ:** 500.
**Desc:** Publishes original contributions on counseling in different settings and for different populations. It gives special attention to empirical studies on: counseling techniques and intervention strategies; assessment instruments for use in counseling; group treatment programs; and counselor education and supervision.

PH/0115-3153
**PHILIPPINE JOURNAL OF PSYCHOLOGY.** [Philipp. j. psychol.]. **Added/Corp** Psychological Association of the Philippines. (1968)-. Periodical. English. Four times a year. $20.00. PSSC Central Subscription Service, PO Box 205 UP Diliman, Quezon City 1101 Philippines. **Tel** 011 63 2 9229621. **LC** BF1; .P36. **DD** 150/.9599. **CODEN** PJPSDM.
**Ind/Abst** Psychol. Abstr. (1969-); PsycLit.

UK/0951-5089
**PHILOSOPHICAL PSYCHOLOGY.** Vol. 1, No. 1 (1988)-. Periodical. English. qt. £138.00. Carfax Publishing Company, PO Box 25 Abingdon, Oxfordshire OX14 3UE England. **Tel** 011 44 235 555335, FAX (0279)31067, telex 817484. **(Subscription address:** US and Canada/ PO Box 2025, Dunnellon, FL 34430-2025; telephone:(904)489-6996) **NLM** W1; PH602P. **[CCC].** Index available in last issue of volume--attached. available on microfiche. Documents available from The Genuine Article.
**Desc:** Dedicated to promoting the interaction of psychologists, philosophers, and other investigators of behavioural and mental phenomena.
**Ind/Abst** Arts Humanit. Citation Index [Select. Cov.]; Curr. Contents Soc. Behav. Sci.; Philos. Index; Psychol. Abstr. (1988-); PsycLit; Res. Alert [Full Cov.]; Soc. Plann. Policy Dev. Abstr.; Soc. Sci. Cit. Index [Full Cov.]; Spec. Educ. Needs Abstr.

US
**PHILOSOPHY, PSYCHIATRY, & PSYCHOLOGY.** **See** Philosophy.

US/0893-4509
**PHOENIX (MINNEAPOLIS, MINN.), THE.** (THE PHOENIX.). [Phoenix]. **Added/Corp** Phoenix, Inc. (Minneapolis, Minn.). Phoenix Health and Recovery News (Firm : Minneapolis, Minn.). Vol. 1, No. 1 (Jan. 1, 1981)-. Periodical. English. mo. $15.00 (one year), $26.00 (two year). The Phoenix, 447 Marshall Avenue #4, St. Paul MN 55102-1766. **Tel** (612)291-2691, FAX (612)291-0533. **ED** Rosanne Bane. **DD** 158. **Bk Rev.** **Ad Acc.** **Pr Rev.** **Circ:** 120,000.
**Desc:** Aimed at people actively working on their physical, mental, emotional and spiritual well-being. Committed to providing a broad spectrum of recovery, renewal and growth information.

SP
**PHRONESIS. REVISTA DE NEUROLOGIA, NEUROCIRUGIA Y PSIQUIATRIA.** **See** Medical Science and Technology-Neurology.

US/0361-0802
**PILGRIMAGE.** **Added/Corp** Pastoral Counseling and Consultation Centers of Greater Washington. Vol. 1 (1972)-. Periodical. English. Five times a year. $39.00 (institutions); $24.00 (individuals). Pilgrimage Press, 427 Lakeshore Drive, Atlanta GA 30307. **Tel** (404)377-1088. **ED** David Barstow. **LC** BF204.5; .P54. **DD** 616.89/14/05. **CODEN** PILGDR. Index available (Nov/Dec). cum. index. **Bk Rev.** **Circ:** 1500. available on an online database, CD-ROM, magnetic tape, and microfilm from Microfilms International Marketing Corp.; available on microfilm from University Microfilms International (UMI).
**Desc:** Focuses on the image of life as a journey, as an adventure of discovery. We invite authors to dig deeply in the mines of their own personal experience for those nuggets of truth and insight that cannot be found elsewhere. We delight in casting a wide net; our broad range of articles are united by a fascination with the wonder of the journey, and a strong desire to more fully understand and celebrate that journey in all its psychological and spiritual dimensions.
**Ind/Abst** Except. Hum. Exp.

PL/0079-2993
**POLISH PSYCHOLOGICAL BULLETIN.** (POLISH PSYCHOLOGICAL BULLETIN / POLISH ACADEMY OF SCIENCES, COMMITTEE FOR PSYCHOLOGICAL SCIENCES.). [Pol. psychol. bull.]. **Added/Corp** Polska Akademia Nauk. Komitet Nauk Psychologicznych. Polskie Towarzystwo Psychologiczne. Vol. 1 (1970)-. Bulletin. English. qt. $53.00. **(Subscription address:** ARS Polona, PO Box 1001, 00068 Warsaw Poland.) **LC** BF1; .P37. **NLM** W1; PO239M. **CODEN** PPBUDY. available on microfilm.
**Ind/Abst** Psychol. Abstr. (1970-); PsycINFO; PsycLit; Sociol. Educ. Abstr.; Spec. Educ. Needs Abstr.

US/0162-895X
**POLITICAL PSYCHOLOGY.** [Polit. psychol.]. **Added/Corp** International Society of Political Psychology. Vol. 1 (Spring 1979)-. Periodical. English. qt. $288.00 (North America); $330.00 (other). Blackwell Publishers, 238 Main Street, Cambridge MA 02142. **Tel** (617)547-7110, (800)835-6770, FAX (617)547-0789. **ED** Stanley A Renshon and Alfred M Freeman. **LC** JA74.5; .P63. **DD** 320/.01/9. **CODEN** POPSEO. **[CCC].** Index available. **Pr Rev.** available on microfilm and microfiche from University Microfilms International (UMI). Documents available from The Genuine Article.
**Desc:** This is an interdisciplinary journal dedicated to examining the relationships between psychological and political phenomena.
**Ind/Abst** Am. Bibliogr. Slavic East Europ. Stud.; Arts Humanit. Citation Index [Select. Cov.]; Crim. Justice Abstr.; Curr. Contents Soc. Behav. Sci.; Int. Bibliogr. Sociol.; Int. Polit. Sci. Abstr.; Peace Res. Abstr. J. (1979-); Psychol. Abstr. (1980-); PsycINFO; PsycLit; Res. Alert [Full Cov.]; Soc. Sci. Cit. Index [Full Cov.]; U.S. Polit. Sci. Doc.

US/0091-5157
**POPULAR PSYCHOLOGY (SHERMAN OAKS).** (POPULAR PSYCHOLOGY.). Periodical. English. bm. Popular Psychology, 14018 Ventura Boulevard, Sherman Oaks CA 91403. **LC** BF1; .P377. **DD** 150/.5. available on microfilm from University Microfilms International (UMI).

US/0199-0039
**POPULATION AND ENVIRONMENT.** **See** Population Studies.

PL
**PORADNICTWO WE WSPOCZESNYM SPOECZENSTWIE.** (1979)-. Polish (Polish). be.

AG
**PORTAVOZ PICHONIANO.** (April 1990)-. Periodical. Spanish. **LC** IN PROCESS. ***Formed by the union of*** *Espacio (Primera Escuela Privada de Psicologia Social (Buenos Aires, Argentina))* ***and*** *Pichoneando.*

CN/1188-5300
**PORTEURS DE LUMIERE.** ***Title Change.*** [Porteurs lumiere]. Vol. 1, No 1 (Mar./April 1992)-Vol. 1, No 3 (July/Aug. 1992). Periodical. French. bm. Editions le Reseau-Lu, CP 86, Cap-Rouge Quebec G1Y 3C6 Canada. **DD** 158. ***Continued by*** *Magazine Lumiere, 1193-6924.*

GW/0937-2032
**PPMP. PSYCHOTHERAPIE, PSYCHOSOMATIK, MEDIZINISCHE PSYCHOLOGIE.** **VFOAT** Psychotherapie, Psychosomatik, Medizinische Psychologie (1988). Periodical. German. mo. $168.00. Georg Thieme Verlag Stuttgart, Postfach 301120, D 70451 Stuttgart Germany. **Tel** 011 49 711 89310, FAX 011 49 711 8931298, telex 7 252 275 GTVD. **(Subscription address:** Thieme Medical Publishers Inc., 381 Park Avenue South, New York NY 10016.) **UDC** 615.851. **[CCC].** ***Continues*** *Psychotherapie Psychosomatik Medizinische Psychologie, 0173-7937.*

IT
**PRATICA SOCIALE.** ***Suspended.*** (19??)-(Dec. 1991). Italian. qt. L15.000 Italy; $30.00 other. ASSCOM, Via Tonale 17, 24060 Endine BG Italy. **Tel** 035/827043. **Bk Rev.** **Ad Acc.**
**Desc:** Rsearch, projects and training on community psychology.

FR/0292-9651
**PRATIQUES CORPORELLES.** **See** Medical Science and Technology-Neurology.

GW/0032-7034
**PRAXIS DER KINDERPSYCHOLOGIE UND KINDERPSYCHIATRIE.** [Prax. Kinderpsychol. Kinderpsychiatr.]. Vol 1. (Jan. 1952)-. Periodical. German. Ten times a year. DM115.00. Vandenhoeck & Ruprecht, Robert Bosch Breite 6, D-37079 Goettingen Germany. **Tel** 011 49 551 695911, FAX 011 49 551 695917, telex 965226 VAN d. **NLM** W1 PR319. **CODEN** PKIKAZ. **[CCC].** **Pr Rev.** Documents available from The Genuine Article, BIOSIS Document Express.
**Ind/Abst** Biol. Abstr.; Curr. Contents Soc. Behav. Sci.; EMBASE; Index Med.; Psychol. Abstr. (1952-); PsycINFO (1952-); PsycLit; Res. Alert [Full Cov.]; Soc. Sci. Cit. Index [Full Cov.].

GW
**PRAXIS DER KINDERPSYCHOLOGIE UND KINDERPSYCHIATRIE BEIHEFT.** (1958)-. Periodical. German. ir. Price varies. Vandenhoeck & Ruprecht, Robert Bosch Breite 6, D-37079 Goettingen Germany. **Tel** 011 49 551 695911, FAX 011 49 551 695917, telex 965226 VAN d. **NLM** W1 PR319E.
**Ind/Abst** Index Med.

GW/0171-791X
**PRAXIS DER PSYCHOTHERAPIE UND PSYCHOSOMATIK.** ***Title Change.*** [Prax. Psycother. Psychosom.]. Vol. 24 (1979)-(19??). Periodical. German. Six times a year. Springer-Verlag GmbH & Company KG, Heidelberger Platz 3, D 14197 Berlin Germany. **Tel** 011 49 30 8207223, FAX 011 49 30 8214091, telex 183 319 SPBLN D. **(Subscription address:** Springer Verlag New York Inc. / for North America, 44 Hartz Way, Secaucus NJ 07096.) **ED** J Bastiaans, G Benedetti, P Buchheim, M Cierpka, J Cremerius, P Dettmering, M Ermann, P Hahn, S O Hoffmann, Th Seifert, H Stolze, and E Wiesenhuetter. **NLM** W1 PR321K. **CODEN** PRPPDZ. **[CCC].** **Bk Rev.** available on microfilm from University Microfilms International (UMI). Documents available from The Genuine Article, BIOSIS Document Express. ***Continues*** *Praxis der Psychotherapie, 0032-7077.* ***Continued by*** *Der Psychotherapeut.*
**Desc:** An interdisciplinary orientation to psychologists, social scientists, psychotherapists, and doctors in general. Original articles and reports, complete conference and symposium calendar.
**Ind/Abst** Biol. Abstr.; EMBASE; Psychol. Abstr. (1979-); PsycINFO (1959-); PsycLit; Res. Alert [Full Cov.]; Soc. Sci. Cit. Index [Full Cov.].

US/0164-5056
**PRIMAL INSTITUTE NEWSLETTER, THE.** **Main/Corp** Primal Institute. (1978)-. English. bm (Jan., Mar., May, July, Sept., Nov.). $11.00 US and Canada; $15.00 other. Primal Institute Newsletter, 1950 Cotner, Los Angeles CA 90025. **Tel** (213)478-0167. **ED** Cindy Naughton and Nick Barton. **Bk Rev.** **Circ:** 1,700 (ctrl).
**Desc:** Contains all information pertinent to primal therapy of the latest developments in psychology, with letters from patients, non-patients and staff. Includes comments, book reviews, events, science watch, etc.

US/0731-2326
**PROBLEM BEHAVIOR MANAGEMENT.** [Probl. behav. manage.]. (1982)-. English. $125.00. Aspen Publishers Inc., 7201 McKinney Circle, Frederick MD 21701. **Tel** (800)234-1660, (301)698-7100, FAX (301)251-5784, telex 5106014543. **(Subscription address:** Aspen Publishers Inc., PO Box 990, Frederick MD 21701.)

UK
**PROBLEMS IN THE BEHAVIOURAL SCIENCES.** (1980)-. Monographic series. English. Price varies per volume. Cambridge University Press, The Edinburgh Building, Shaftesbury Road, Cambridge CB2 2RU United Kingdom. **Tel** 011 44 223 312393, FAX 011 44 223 325959.

RU
**PROBLEMY INDUSTRIALNOI PSIKHOLOGII.** **See** Business.

US
**PROCEEDINGS AND ABSTRACTS, AMERICAN INSTITUTE FOR DECISION SCIENCES, ANNUAL MEETING, WESTERN REGIONAL CONFERENCE.** **Main/Corp** American Institute for Decision Sciences. Western Regional Conference. 1st- (1972)-. Proceedings. English. an.

US
**PROCEEDINGS / ANNUAL MEETING. ASSOCIATION FOR APPLIED PSYCHOPHYSIOLOGY.** **Main/Corp** Association for Applied Psychophysiology and Biofeedback. Meeting. 20th (Mar. 17-22, 1989)-. Proceedings. English.

Association for Applied Psychophysiology and Biofeedback, 10200 West 44th Avenue, Suite 304, Wheat Ridge CO 80033. **Tel** (303)442-8436. ***Continues*** *Proceedings / Biofeedback Society of America. Meeting, 0739-6252.*

US/0092-072X
**PROCEEDINGS OF THE ANNUAL CONVENTION - CHRISTIAN ASSOCIATION FOR PSYCHOLOGICAL STUDIES.** **See** Religion and Theology.

UK/0081-1475
**PROCEEDINGS OF THE SOCIETY FOR PSYCHICAL RESEARCH.** [Proc. Soc. Psych. Res.]. **Main/Corp** Society for Psychical Research (London, England). V. 1- (Pt. 1- ); 1882-. Proceedings. English. ir. $5.00. The Society for Psychical Research, 1 Adam and Eve Mews, London W8 6UG England. **Tel** (01)937-8984. **ED** John BeLoff. **LC** BF1011; .I4. **DD** 133.8/01/5. **CODEN** PPSRA5. Index available. **Circ:** 1,000 (ctrl).
**Desc:** The proceedings, published in parts as and when suitable material becomes available. Devoted to major pieces of research, presidential addresses and papers of a theoretical or analytical nature.
**Ind/Abst** Br. Humanit. Index; Except. Hum. Exp.; Psychol. Abstr. (1963-).

US
**PROFESSIONAL COUNSELOR.** (19??)-. Periodical. English. Six times a year. $22.00. US Journal Inc., 3201 Southwest 15th Street, Deerfield Beach FL 33442. **Tel** (305)360-0909 ext. 232, (800)851-9100, FAX (305)360-0034. **(Subscription address:** Kable Publishers Aide, 308 East Hitt Street, Subscription Department, Mt. Morris IL 61054-1473.**)** ***Continues*** *Professional Counselor Magazine.*

US/0735-7028
**PROFESSIONAL PSYCHOLOGY, RESEARCH AND PRACTICE.** [Prof. psychol. res. pract.]. **Added/Corp** American Psychological Association. Vol. 14, No. 1 (Feb. 1983)-. Periodical. English. bm. $146.00 (nonmember, institution) US. American Psychological Association, 750 First Street Northeast, Washington DC 20002. **Tel** (800)374-2721, (202)336-5600, (subscriptions - (202)336-5600. **ED** Ursula Delworth, PhD. **LC** RC467; .P69. **DD** 616.89/005. **NLM** W1 PR601B. **[CCC].** Index available (bound in last issue). **Ad Acc. Pr Rev. Circ:** 4,100. available on microfilm and microfiche from University Microfilms International (UMI). Documents available from The Genuine Article. ***Continues*** *Professional Psychology, 0033-0175.*
**Desc:** Publishes articles that address a variety of topics including current advances in application from health psychology, community psychology, clinical neuropsychology, family psychology, and forensic psychology; standards of professional practice and delivery of service; public policy; and education and training of professional psychologists training the graduate level and CE.
**Ind/Abst** Abstr. Res. Pastor. Care Couns. (19??-); Curr. Contents Soc. Behav. Sci.; Educ. Adm. Abstr. (?-?); High. Educ. Abstr. (1974-); Hum. Resour. Abstr. (?-?); Psychol. Abstr. (1983-); PsycINFO; PsycLit; PsycScan: Clin. Psych.; Res. Alert [Full Cov.]; Sage Fam. Stud. Abstr. (?-?); Soc. Sci. Cit. Index [Full Cov.].

US/0099-037X
**PROGRESS IN BEHAVIOR MODIFICATION.** [Prog. behav. modif.]. Vol. 1 (1975)-. English. ir. Price varies. Sycamore Publishing Company, PO Box 133, Sycamore IL 60178. **Tel** (815)756-5388. **ED** Michael Hersen, Richard Eisler and Peter M. Miller. **LC** BF637.B4; P66. **DD** 616.8/914. **NLM** W1 PR666GM. **CODEN** PBMOE8. **[CCC].** Documents available from The Genuine Article, BIOSIS Document Express.
**Ind/Abst** Biol. Abstr. (1985-); Index Med.; Res. Alert [Full Cov.].

US/0891-0111
**PROGRESS IN BEHAVIORAL STUDIES.** ***Ceased.*** (PROGRESS IN BEHAVIORAL STUDIES : A PUBLICATION OF THE CAMBRIDGE CENTER FOR BEHAVIORAL STUDIES.). [Prog. behav. stud.]. **Added/Corp** Cambridge Center for Behavioral Studies. Vol. 1 (1989)-(1994). Periodical. English. ir. Lawrence Erlbaum Associates, 365 Broadway, Suite 102, Hillsdale NJ 07642. **Tel** (201)666-4110, (800)926-6579, FAX (201)666-2394. **DD** 300.
**Desc:** Covers behavioral assessment and modification.

US/0363-0951
**PROGRESS IN PSYCHOBIOLOGY AND PHYSIOLOGICAL PSYCHOLOGY.** **See** Biology-Physiology.

US/0893-5483
**PROGRESS IN SELF PSYCHOLOGY.** [Prog. self psychol.]. Vol. 1 (1985)-. English. an. $29.95. Lawrence Erlbaum Associates, 365 Broadway, Suite 102, Hillsdale NJ 07642. **Tel** (201)666-4110, (800)926-6579, FAX (201)666-2394. **ED** Arnold Goldberg. **LC** BF697; .P74. **DD** 155.2. **NLM** W1; PR681CE.

IT
**PROSPETTIVE PSICOANALITICHE NEL LAVORO ISTITUZIONALE.** No. 1 (1983)-. Periodical. Italian. Three times a year. L65000 individuals; L100000 institutions. Il Pensiero Scientifico Editore s.r.l., Via Bradano 3C, 00199 Rome Italy. **Tel** 011 39 6 86207158, 86207159, 86207168, 86207169, FAX 011 39 6 86207160. **ED** M. Ammaniti, M. Bacigalupi and L. Carbone Tirelli. **NLM** W1; PR768V. Index available. cum. index. **Bk Rev. Ad Acc, Adv Mgr:** Dott Dalla. Full Page (B&W) L1300.000. **Circ:** 1,500.
**Desc:** A series devoted to social and institutional approaches to psychoanalytic problems. Major topics are adolescence and child psychoanalysis, with articles written by experts internationally known in the field.

US/1044-6893
**PROVOKING THOUGHTS.** ***Ceased.*** [Provok. thoughts]. No. 1 (Jan. 1989)-(19??). Periodical. English. bm. Sunrise Valley Press, PO Box 1004, Austin TX 55912. **Tel** (800)828-1231, (507)433-6562. **DD** 371.
**Desc:** Appeals to all ages and abilities. It helps and encourages creative thinking. Using seven different mental abilities, each issue features several dozen interesting exercises.

PL/0048-5675
**PRZEGLAD PSYCHOLOGICZNY.** [Prz. psychol.]. **Added/Corp** Polskie Towarzystwo Psychologiczne. (1952)-. Periodical. Polish (summaries and/or abstracts in English, French and Russian; table of contents in English, Russian and French). qt. Price on Request. **(Subscription address:** ARS Polona, PO Box 1001, 00068 Warsaw Poland.**) LC** BF26; .P7. **NLM** W1 PR936K. **CODEN** PRZPBF.
**Ind/Abst** Psychol. Abstr. (1952-); PsycINFO (1952-); PsycLit; Soc. Plann. Policy Dev. Abstr.; Sociol. Abstr. (?-?).

US/0033-2569
**PSI CHI NEWSLETTER.** **Main/Corp** Psi Chi. **Added/Corp** Psi Chi. Newsletter. (197?)-. Newsletter. English. ir. $6.25. Psi Chi National Office, APA Building, 1200 17th Street Northwest, Washington DC 20036. **ED** Ruth Hubbard Cousins. **LC** LJ121; .P7. **DD** 378.1/98/5415. **Bk Rev. Circ:** 13,000 (ctrl).

IT/0393-361X
**PSICHIATRIA DELL'INFANZIA E DELL-ADOLESCENZA.** **Added/Corp** Universita di Roma. Istituto di Neuropsichiatria Infantile. Vol. 51, No. 1 (Feb. 1984)-. Periodical. Italian (summaries and/or abstracts in English). bm. $130.00 (institutions), $110.00 (individuals). Edizioni Borla, Via delle Fornaci 50, 00165 Rome, Italy. **Tel** 011 39 6 39376728. **NLM** W1; PS127H. ***Continues*** *Neuropsichiatria Infantile.*

BL
**PSICO : REVISTA SEMESTRAL DO INSTITUTO DE PSICOLOGIA DA PUC RIO GRANDE DO SUL, BRASIL.** **Added/Corp** Instituto de Psicologia da PUC Rio Grande do Sul. (197?)-. Periodical. Portuguese. sa. Instituto de Psicologia de PUC-RS, 6681 Caixa Postal 1429, CEP 90001 Porto Alerge, RS Brazil. **NLM** W1; PS134.
**Ind/Abst** Psychol. Abstr. (1979-); PsycLit.

IT/0393-6902
**PSICOANALISI CONTRO.** **See** Medical Science and Technology-Psychiatry.

IT/0392-2952
**PSICOBIETTIVO ROMA.** (PSICOBIETTIVO.). (1981)-. Periodical. Italian. Three times a year. L50000 (individuals), L70000 (institutions). Cedis SRL, Via F Denza 52, 00197 Rome Italy. **Tel** 011 39 6 36307954. **UDC** 159.9.

SP/0377-8320
**PSICODEIA.** (1975)-. Periodical. Spanish. Twelve times a year. $21.43. Ediciones Inapp, Habana 66, Madrid 16 Spain. **LC** BF5; .P73. **NLM** W1 PS148.

BL/0101-6016
**PSICOLOGIA.** [Psicologia]. **Main/Corp** Universidade de Sao Paulo. Faculdade de Filosofia, Ciencias e Letras. (1975)-. Portuguese. Conselho Editorial da Sociedade de Estudos Psicologicos, Caixa Postal 20.532, CEP 01498 Sao Paulo, Brazil. **LC** BF15; .S3.
**Ind/Abst** Psychol. Abstr. (1975-?); PsycINFO (1980-); PsycLit.

IT/0390-346X
**PSICOLOGIA CONTEMPORANEA.** [Psicol. contemp.]. (1974)-. Periodical. Italian. bm. L28000.00 Italy; L39000.00 other. Giunti Editore, Via Bolognese 165, 50139 Florence Italy. **Tel** 011 39 55 6679267, FAX 011 39 55 268312, telex 571438. **UDC** 159.

FI
**PSICOLOGIA ITALIANA.** ***Ceased.*** Vol. 1, No. 1 (1979)-(1993). Periodical. Italian. Three times a year. Gio Editing SRL, via Vestri 1, 40128 Bologna Italy. **Tel** 011 39 51 355832. **LC** BF4; .P78. **DD** 150/.5.

●US
**PSICOLOGIA, PSICOPATOLOGIA & PSICOSOMATICA DELLA DONNA.** (Spring 1993)-. Periodical. English. Three times a year. L70000 institutions; L60000 individuals. Il Pensiero Scientifico Editore s.r.l., Via Bradano 3C, 00199 Rome Italy. **Tel** 011 39 6 86207158, 86207159, 86207168, 86207169, FAX 011 39 6 86207160. **Ad Acc.** Full Page (B&W) L1.650.000. **Circ:** 900.
**Desc:** Covers psychological development and disturbances of women originating from early in life, adolescence, motherhood, or later in life.

IT/0394-7904
**PSICOLOGIA SOCIALE.** [Psicol. soc.]. (1987)-. Periodical. Italian. qt. L38462.00. Centro Studi Psico Sociali, Via Rimini 25, 00182 Rome Italy. **Tel** 011 39 6 700871. **UDC** 159.9.

BL/0102-3772
**PSICOLOGIA. TEORIA E PESQUISA.** (PSICOLOGIA.). [Psicol., Teor. pesqui.]. **VFOAT** Psychology. Theory and Research. (1985)-. Periodical. Portuguese. tq. Universidade de Brasilia, 70910- Brasilia DF, Brasilia DF Brazil. **UDC** 15.
**Ind/Abst** PsycINFO (1985-); PsycLit.

SP/0211-2159
**PSICOLOGICA.** [Psicologica]. (1980)-. Periodical. Spanish. ir. Departamento de Psicologia Experimental, Fac. de Filosofia y Ciencias de la Educ., Avda. Vicente Blasco Ibanez, Valencia 10 Spain. **UDC** 159.9.
**Ind/Abst** PsycINFO (1980-); PsycLit.

US
**PSICOSI.** (19??)-. Periodical. English. Three times a year. Included with Rivista di Psichiatria: L140000 institutions; L85000 individuals. Il Pensiero Scientifico Editore s.r.l., Via Bradano 3C, 00199 Rome Italy. **Tel** 011 39 6 86207158, 86207159, 86207168, 86207169, FAX 011 39 6 86207160. **ED** M. Biondi. **Circ:** 1,200.
**Desc:** Official publication of the Italian Foundation for the Study of Schizophrenia.

SP/0214-9915
**PSICOTHEMA OVIEDO.** [Psicothema Oviedo]. (1989)-. Periodical. Multiple languages. Three times a year. 12000ptas (institutions), 6000ptas (individuals). Universidad Oviedo Dept Psilologia, C Aniceto Sela, 33005 Oviedo Spain. **(Subscription address:** Colegio Oficial de Psicologos, Ildefonso Sanchez del Rio 4, 33001 Oviedo Spain.**) UDC** 159.9.
**Ind/Abst** Soc. Sci. Cit. Index [Full Cov.].

RU/0205-9592
**PSIHOLOGICESKIJ ZURNAL.** (PSIKHOLOGICHESKII ZHURNAL.). [Psihol. z.]. **Added/Corp** Akademiia Nauk SSSR. Vol. 1, (Jan./Feb. 1980)-. Academic Scholarly Publication. Russian (summaries and/or abstracts in English). Six times a year. $132.00. Izdatelstvo Nauka / Akademiia Nauk, Publishing House of the Russian Academy of Sciences, Leninskii Porspekt 14, 117901 Moscow Russia. **Tel** 011 95 954-21-53, FAX 011 95 938-21-44, telex 411964. **(Subscription address:** East View Publications Inc., 3020 Harbor Lane North, Suite 110, Minneapolis MN 55447.**) LC** BF8.R8; P68. **NLM** W1; PS18QD. **[CCC]. Pr Rev.** Documents available from The Genuine Article.
**Ind/Abst** Curr. Contents Soc. Behav. Sci.; Psychol. Abstr. (1982-); Res. Alert [Full Cov.]; Soc. Sci. Cit. Index [Full Cov.].

BU
**PSIKHOLOGIIA.** **Added/Corp** Druzhestvo na Bulgarskite Psikholozi. **VFOAT** Psychology. (19??)-. Bulgarian (summaries and/or abstracts in English). qt. 1.60lv (single issue). Bulgarian Psychological Society, V. Levski Stadium, Sofia, Bulgaria. **(Subscription address:** Hemus Foreign Trade Organization, 6 Tzar Osvoboditel Boulevard, 1000 Sofia Bulgaria.**) LC** BF8.B9; P77. **Circ:** 500.
**Ind/Abst** PsycINFO (1985-); PsycLit.

FR/0338-2397
**PSYCHANALYSE A L'UNIVERSITE.** ***Ceased.*** [Psychoanal. univ.]. **Added/Corp** Universite de Paris VII. Laboratoire de Psychanalyse et de Psychopathologie. Universite de Paris VII. Centre de Recherches en Psychanalyse et Psychopathologie. Vol. 1, No. 1 (Dec. 1975)-(Jan. 1995). Periodical. French (summaries and/or abstracts in English and Spanish). qt. Presses Universitaires de France, Department des Revues, 14 Avenue du Bois de l'Epine, BP 90, 91003 Evry Cedex France. **Tel** (1)60 77 82 05, FAX (1) 60 79 20 45, telex PUF 600 474 F. cum. index.
**Ind/Abst** PsycINFO (1985-); PsycLit.

GW/0033-2623
**PSYCHE.** [Psyche]. **VFOAT** Psychoanalyse. Vol. 1 (July 1947)-. Periodical. German. mo. DM180.00. Klett-Cotta Verlagsgemeinschft, PO Box 106016, D 70049 Stuttgart Germany. **Tel** 011 49 711 66720. **(Subscription address:** Stuttgerter Verlagskontor, Postfatch 106016, D-70049 Stuttgart, Germany.**) LC** BF173.A2; P67. **DD** 150.19/5/05. **NLM** W1; PS225. **CODEN** PSYEDK. **[CCC].** cum. index. **Pr Rev.** Documents available from The Genuine Article.

**Ind/Abst** Index Med.; Psychol. Abstr. (1947-); PsycINFO; PsycLit; Res. Alert [Full Cov.]; Rev. Med. Vet. Entomol.; Soc. Sci. Cit. Index [Full Cov.].

UK/0033-2801
**PSYCHIC NEWS.** English. wk. $41.00 US. Psychic Press Ltd, 2 Tavistock Chamb, Bloomsbury, London WC1A 2SE England. **Tel** 011 44 71 4053340.

GW/0944-6877
**PSYCHO PHARMAKO THERAPIE. See** Pharmacy and Pharmacology.

BE/0772-9219
**PSYCHOANALYSE. Added/Corp** Ecole Belge de Psychanalyse. (Mar. 1984)-. Periodical. Dutch (Multiple languages). an. 800F. Editions Peeters SA, Bondgenotenlaan 153, BP 41, B-3000 Leuven Belgium. **Tel** 32 16 235170, FAX 32 16 228500, telex 65987 PUL B. **ED** Fr. Martens.

●GW/0941-4428
**PSYCHOANALYSE: KLINIK UND KULTURKRITIK.** (1992)-. Periodical. German (summaries and/or abstracts in English). mo. Klett-Cotta Verlagsgemeinschft, PO Box 106016, D 70049 Stuttgart Germany. **Tel** 011 49 711 66720. ***Continues*** *Psyche.*
**Ind/Abst** Index Med. (1992-).

US/0161-5289
**PSYCHOANALYSIS AND CONTEMPORARY THOUGHT.** [Psychoanal. contemp. thought]. Vol. 1 (1978)-. Academic Scholarly Publication. English. qt. $113.00 (institutions), $67.00 (individuals) US; $148.00 (institutions), $109.00 (individuals) other. International Universities Press Inc., 59 Boston Post Road, PO Box 1524, Madison CT 06443-1524. **Tel** (203)245-4000, FAX (203)245-0775, telex 282986 IUP BK. **ED** Leo Goldberger. **LC** RC500; .P79. **DD** 616.8/917/05. **NLM** W1 PS395M. **CODEN** PCTHDS. **Ad Acc. Circ:** 900 (ctrl). Documents available from BIOSIS Document Express. ***Continues*** *Psychoanalysis and Contemporary Science, 0092-864X.*
**Desc:** Aimed at broadening the scientific and intellectual horizons of psychoanalysis. Publishes original clinical, theoretical, experimental, and quantitative contributions.
**Ind/Abst** Biol. Abstr. (-1991); EMBASE; Psychol. Abstr. (1978-); PsycINFO; PsycLit; Soc. Plann. Policy Dev. Abstr.; Sociol. Abstr.

US/1062-6069
**PSYCHOANALYST : A MONOGRAPH OF THE WESTCHESTER CENTER FOR THE STUDY OF PSYCHOANALYSIS AND PSYCHOTHERAPY AND THE PSYCHOANALYTIC ASSOCIATION OF THE WESTCHESTER CENTER, THE.** [Psychoanalyst]. **Added/Corp** Westchester Center for the Study of Psychoanalysis and Psychotherapy. Psychoanalytic Association of the Westchester Center. Vol. 1, No. 1 (Apr. 1991)-. Periodical. English. The Westchester Center for the Study of Psychoanalysis and Psychotherapy and the Psychoanalytic Association of the Westchester Center, 29 Sterling Avenue, White Plains NY 10606. **LC** RC500.5; P7925. **DD** 616.89/17. **NLM** W1; PS396G.

●US/1066-9884
**PSYCHOANALYTIC ABSTRACTS. See** Psychology-Abstracting, Bibliographies and Statistics.

US/1044-2103
**PSYCHOANALYTIC BOOKS.** [Psychoanal. books]. Vol. 1, No. 1 (1990)-. Periodical. English. qt. $90.00 (institutions), $50.00 (individuals) US; $f100.00 (institutions), $60.00 (individuals) other. Psychoanalytic Books Inc, 211 East 70th Street, New York NY 10021. **Tel** (212)628-8792, FAX (212)628-8453. **ED** Joseph Reppen. **LC** BF173.A2; P676. **DD** 150.19/5. **NLM** W1; PS396L.
**Desc:** Prints timely, critical reviews of books in the broad field of psychoanalysis, including clinical and theoretical psychoanalysis, Freud studies, history of psychoanalysis, psychobiography, psychohistory, and the psychoanalytic study of literature and the arts.

US/1048-1885
**PSYCHOANALYTIC DIALOGUES.** [Psychoanal. dialogues]. Vol. 1, No. 1 (1991)-. Periodical. English. qt. $95.00 US & Canada; $120.00 other. Lawrence Erlbaum Associates, 365 Broadway, Suite 102, Hillsdale NJ 07642. **Tel** (201)666-4110, (800)926-6579, FAX (201)666-2394. **ED** Stephen A. Mitchell. **LC** RC500; .P793. **DD** 616.89/17/05. **NLM** W1; PS397.
**Desc:** Dedicated to facilitating debate among theoreticians and clinicians working within the array of relational perspectives that characterize the communities that make up the world of psychoanalysis.
**Ind/Abst** Psychol. Abstr.; PsycINFO.

US/0736-9735
**PSYCHOANALYTIC PSYCHOLOGY.** (PSYCHOANALYTIC PSYCHOLOGY : THE OFFICIAL JOURNAL OF THE DIVISION OF PSYCHOANALYSIS, AMERICAN PSYCHOLOGICAL ASSOCIATION, DIVISION 39.). [Psychoanal. psychol.]. **Added/Corp** American Psychological Association. Division of Psychoanalysis. Vol. 1, No. 1 (Winter 1984)-. Periodical. English. qt. $195.00 US & Canada; $220.00 other. Lawrence Erlbaum Associates, 365 Broadway, Suite 102, Hillsdale NJ 07642. **Tel** (201)666-4110, (800)926-6579, FAX (201)666-2394. **ED** Gerald Stechler. **NLM** W1; PS428. **Ad Acc.** available on microfilm and microfiche from University Microfilms International (UMI).
**Ind/Abst** EMBASE; Psychol. Abstr. (1984-); PsycINFO; PsycLit.

UK/0266-8734
**PSYCHOANALYTIC PSYCHOTHERAPY. See** Medical Science and Technology-Psychiatry.

US/0033-2828
**PSYCHOANALYTIC QUARTERLY, THE.** [Psychoanal. q.]. Vol. 1 (April 1932)-. Academic Scholarly Publication. English. qt. $75.00 US; $90.00 other. Psychoanalytic Quarterly, 175 Fifth Avenue Room 210, New York NY 10010. **Tel** (212)982-9358. **ED** Owen Renik. **LC** BF173.A2; P7. **DD** 131.3405. **NLM** W1 PS437. **CODEN** PSQAAX. Index available. cum. index. **Bk Rev. Pr Rev. Circ:** 4,000. Documents available from The Genuine Article.
**Desc:** Forum for developments in psychoanalysis; contains original articles, abstracts of contributions from other journals (foreign and domestic), and a notes section with summaries of papers presented at scientific meetings and announcements of important conferences.
**Ind/Abst** Arts Humanit. Citation Index [Select. Cov.]; Curr. Contents Soc. Behav. Sci.; EMBASE; Hospit. Health Admin. Index; Index Med.; Middle East Abstr. Index; Psychol. Abstr. (1932-); PsycINFO; PsycLit; Res. Alert [Full Cov.]; Soc. Plann. Policy Dev. Abstr.; Soc. Sci. Cit. Index [Full Cov.]; Soc. Work Abstr. [Select. Cov.]; Sociol. Abstr.

US/0033-2836
**PSYCHOANALYTIC REVIEW (1963).** (THE PSYCHOANALYTIC REVIEW.). [Psychoanal. rev.]. **Added/Corp** National Psychological Association for Psychoanalysis (U.S.). Vol. 50 (Spring 1963)-. Periodical. English. Six times a year. $175.00 (institutions); $200.00 others. Guilford Publications Inc., 72 Spring Street, New York NY 10012. **Tel** (212)431-9800, (800)365-7006, FAX (212)966-6708. **ED** Martin Schulman. **LC** BF1; .P5. **DD** 61689. **NLM** W1 PS411. **CODEN** PSREAG. **[CCC].** Documents available from The Genuine Article, BIOSIS Document Express. ***Continues*** *Psychoanalysis and the Psychoanalytic Review, 0885-7830.*
**Desc:** Leading forum for critical discourse in psychoanalytic theory and clinical practice and their application to art, literature, history and the creative process.
**Ind/Abst** Abstr. Anthropol.; Abstr. Engl. Stud.; Arts Humanit. Citation Index [Select. Cov.]; Biol. Abstr.; Crim. Penol. Police Sci. Abstr.; Curr. Contents Soc. Behav. Sci.; Film Lit. Index; Index Med.; Int. Bibliogr. Sociol.; Middle East Abstr. Index; Psychol. Abstr.; PsycINFO; PsycLit; Res. Alert [Full Cov.]; Soc. Sci. Cit. Index [Full Cov.]; Soc. Work Abstr. [Select. Cov.]; Sociol. Abstr.; Women Stud. Abstr.

US/0079-7308
**PSYCHOANALYTIC STUDY OF THE CHILD, THE.** [Psychoanal. study child]. Vol. 1, (1945)-. English. an (Fall). $58.00. Yale University Press, PO Box 209040, New Haven CT 06520. **Tel** (203)432-0940, (800)987-7323, FAX (203)432-0948. **LC** BF721; .P8. **DD** 131.34058. **NLM** W1 PS45. **CODEN** PYACAZ. cum. index. Documents available from The Genuine Article, BIOSIS Document Express.
**Ind/Abst** Acad. Search (July 1993-); Biol. Abstr.; Educ. Index (-1992); EMBASE; Index Med.; INFO-SOUTH Abstr.; Mag. Search; Psychol. Abstr. (1945-); PsycINFO; PsycLit; Res. Alert [Full Cov.]; Soc. Sci. Cit. Index [Full Cov.].

US/0278-1719
**PSYCHOBIOLOGY AND PSYCHOPATHOLOGY.** [Psychobiol. psychopathol.]. Vol. 1 -. Academic Scholarly Publication. English. Price varies per volume. **NLM** W1 PS498H. **CODEN** PPSYDT. Documents available from CASDDS.
**Ind/Abst** Chem. Abstr.

US/0889-6313
**PSYCHOBIOLOGY (AUSTIN, TEX.).** (PSYCHOBIOLOGY : A JOURNAL OF THE PSYCHONOMIC SOCIETY, INC.). [Psychobiology]. **Added/Corp** Psychonomic Society. Vol. 15, No. 1 (March 1987)-. Academic Scholarly Publication. English. qt (Mar., June, Sept., Dec.). $82.00 US; $88.00 other. Psychonomic Society Publications, 1710 Fortview Road, Austin TX 78704. **Tel** (512)462-2442, FAX (512)462-1101. **ED** Lynn Nadel. **LC** QP360; .P47. **DD** 152/.05. **NLM** W1; PS498G. **CODEN** PSYBEC. **[CCC].** Index available. **Bk Rev. Ad Acc. Circ:** 1,350. available on microfilm and microfiche from University Microfilms International (UMI). Documents available from The Genuine Article, BIOSIS Document Express, CASDDS. ***Continues*** *Physiological Psychology, 0090-5046.*
**Desc:** Covers neurosciences fields relating to behavior: psychology, biology, pharmacology, anatomy, physiology, neuroendocrinology, autonomic functions, etc.
**Ind/Abst** Biol. Abstr. (1987-); Chem. Abstr. (1987-); CSA Neuro. Abstr. (?-?); Curr. Aware. Biol. Sci., CABS; Curr. Contents Life Sci.; EMBASE; Life Sci. Collect. (1987-); Psychol. Abstr. (1987-); PsycINFO; PsycLit; Ref. Upd. Deluxe Ed.; Res. Alert [Full Cov.]; Sci. Cit. Index; SCISEARCH; Soc. Plann. Policy Dev. Abstr.; Soc. Sci. Cit. Index [Select. Cov.]; Sociol. Abstr.

●UK/1353-3339
**PSYCHODYNAMIC COUNSELLING.** (October 1994)-. English. Four times a year. $85.00 US and Canada; £60.00 UK; £65.00 Other. Routledge, 11 New Fetter Lane, London EC4P 4EE England. **Tel** 071 583 9855, FAX 071 842 2298. **(Subscription address:** Kinokuniya Company Ltd., 38-1 Sakuragaoka 5, chome Setagaya-ku, Tokyo 156 Japan.**)**

US/0363-891X
**PSYCHOHISTORY REVIEW, THE. See** History(General).

JA/0033-2852
**PSYCHOLOGIA.** [Psychologia]. **Added/Corp** Pushikorogia-Kai. (June 1957)-. Periodical. English (German and French). qt. $145.00. Psychologia Society, Kyoto University, Department of Psychology, Kyoto 606 Japan. **Tel** (075)753-3051. **(Subscription address:** Maruzen Company Ltd., PO Box 5050, Import & Export Department, Tokyo 100 31 Japan.**) ED** Noboru Sakano. **LC** BF1; .P63. **DD** 150/.5. **NLM** W1 PS528T. **CODEN** PYLGAY. Index available. cum. index. **Bk Rev. Ad Acc. Pr Rev. Circ:** 1,000. Documents available from The Genuine Article, BIOSIS Document Express.
**Desc:** Original works in the fields of psychology.
**Ind/Abst** Biol. Abstr.; Curr. Contents Soc. Behav. Sci.; Middle East Abstr. Index; Psychol. Abstr. (1957-); PsycINFO (1990-); PsycLit; Res. Alert [Full Cov.]; Soc. Plann. Policy Dev. Abstr.; Soc. Sci. Cit. Index [Full Cov.]; Sociol. Abstr.

XO
**PSYCHOLOGIA A PATOPSYCHOLOGIA DIETATA. See** Medical Science and Technology-Psychiatry.

GW/0555-5582
**PSYCHOLOGIA UNIVERSALIS.** [Psychol. univ.]. Monographic series. German. ir. Price varies per volume. Verlag Anton Hain Athenaeum, Wormer Strasse 99, D 55294 Bodenheim Germany. **Tel** 011 49 6135 3057. **ED** Gustav Adolf Lienert, Thomae, Wilhelm Witte Steingruber, Hans Thomae and Wilhelm Witte. **NLM** W1 PS534. **CODEN** PSUNDR. **Bk Rev. Ad Acc. Circ:** 400.
**Desc:** Covers experimental psychology.
**Ind/Abst** Psychol. Abstr. (1974-).

BE/0033-2879
**PSYCHOLOGICA BELGICA.** [Psychol. Belg.]. **Added/Corp** Societe Belge de Psychologie. Vol. 1 (1953)-. Periodical. Dutch (English, Flemish and French). sa. 850F Belgium; 900F other. Editions Peeters SA, Bondgenotenlaan 153, BP 41, B-3000 Leuven Belgium. **Tel** 32 16 235170, FAX 32 16 228500, telex 65987 PUL B. **ED** P. Coetsier, J. Costermans, T. DeBacker, W. De Coster and L. Delbeke. **LC** BF30; .P85. **DD** 150/.5. **NLM** W1 PS541. **CODEN** PBELAN. Index available. **Bk Rev. Pr Rev. Circ:** 500 (ctrl). Documents available from The Genuine Article, BIOSIS Document Express.
**Desc:** Publishes scientific contributions to various fields in psychology.
**Ind/Abst** Biol. Abstr.; CIS Abstr.; Curr. Contents Soc. Behav. Sci.; Life Sci. Collect.; Psychol. Abstr. (1961-); PsycINFO (1961-); PsycLit; Res. Alert [Full Cov.]; Saf. Health Work; Soc. Sci. Cit. Index [Full Cov.].

US/0033-2887
**PSYCHOLOGICAL ABSTRACTS. See** Psychology-Abstracting, Bibliographies and Statistics.

US/1040-3590
**PSYCHOLOGICAL ASSESSMENT.** (PSYCHOLOGICAL ASSESSMENT / AMERICAN PSYCHOLOGICAL ASSOCIATION.). [Psychol. assess.]. **Added/Corp** American Psychological Association. Vol. 1, No. 1 (March 1989)-. Periodical. English. qt. $146.00 (nonmember, institution) US. American Psychological Association, 750 First Street Northeast, Washington DC 20002. **Tel** (800)374-2721, (202)336-5600, (subscriptions - (202)336-5600. **ED** James N. Butcher, PhD. **DD** 150. **NLM** W1; PS746M. **[CCC]. Ad Acc. Pr Rev. Circ:** 4,100,000. available on microfilm and microfiche from University Microfilms International (UMI). ***Continues in part*** *Journal of Consulting and Clinical Psychology, 0022-006X.*
**Desc:** Focuses on development, validation, and evaluation of assessment techniques. The journal also presents assessment topics in the context of cross cultural studies, ethnicity, minority status, gender, and sexual orientation. Case studies identify assessment techniques that permit evaluation of the nature, course, or treatment of clinical dysfunction.
**Ind/Abst** Psychol. Abstr. (1989-); PsycINFO (1990-); PsycLit; PsycScan: Clin. Psych.

US/0033-2909
**PSYCHOLOGICAL BULLETIN.** [Psychol. bull.]. **Added/Corp** American Psychological Association. Publication Manual. Vol. 1 (Jan. 1904)-. Periodical. English. bm. $251.00 (nonmember, institution) US. American Psychological Association, 750 First Street Northeast, Washington DC 20002. **Tel** (800)374-2721, (202)336-5600, (subscriptions - (202)336-5600. **ED** Robert J. Sternberg, PhD. **LC** BF1; .P75. **DD** 150/.5. **NLM**

W1 PS557. **CODEN** PSBUAI. **[CCC].** Index available (free). **Ad Acc. Pr Rev. Circ:** 8,700. available on microfilm and microfiche from University Microfilms International (UMI). Documents available from The Genuine Article, BIOSIS Document Express, UMI Article Clearinghouse.
**Desc:** Introduces exciting developments to readers by publishing evaluative and integrative reviews and interpretations of issues in scientific psychology. This journal features thorough, cross-disciplinary articles that serve to increase the reader's understanding of substantive methodological issues. Portrays a wide variety of insights in behavioral and social issues.
**Ind/Abst** ABI/INFORM Glob. Ed.; ABI Inform Ondisc (Feb. 1973-Dec. 1974); Acad. Abstr. Full Text Elite (July 1990-); Acad. Abstr. (July 1990-); Acad. Ind. [Computer File] (1987-); Acad. Search (July 1990-); Appl. Soc. Sci. Index Abstr.; Biol. Abstr.; Crim. Justice Abstr.; Curr. Contents Life Sci.; Curr. Contents Soc. Behav. Sci.; Curr. Index J. Educ.; Ergon. Abstr.; Expand. Acad. Index (1987-); High. Educ. Abstr. (1972-19??); Index Med.; INFO-SOUTH Abstr.; Int. Aerosp. Abstr.; Int. Bibliogr. Sociol.; Int. Labour Doc.; Mag. Search; Middle East Abstr. Index; MLA Int. Bibl. Books Artic. Mod. Lang. Lit.; Multicult. Educ. Abstr.; Newsp. Period. Abstr. (1986-); Peace Res. Abstr. J. (1967-1974); Life Sci. Collect.; Psychol. Abstr. (1926-); PsycINFO; PsycLit; PsycScan: Appl. Psych.; PsycScan: Clin. Psych.; PsycScan: Develop. Psych.; Res. Alert [Full Cov.]; School Organ. Manage. Abstr.; Sci. Cit. Index; SCISEARCH; Soc. Sci. Source (Jul. 1990-); Soc. Sci. Cit. Index [Full Cov.]; Soc. Sci. Index; Soc. Sci. Index Fulltext (Sept. 1988-) [Full Txt.]; Soc. Work Abstr. (Summer 1987-) [Select. Cov.]; Spec. Educ. Needs Abstr.; Soc. Res. Methodol. Abstr. (1975-); Stud. Women Abstr.; Women Stud. Abstr.

US/1047-840X
**PSYCHOLOGICAL INQUIRY.** [Psychol. inq.]. Vol. 1, No. 1 (1990)-. Periodical. English. qt. $220.00US & Canada; $245.00 other. Lawrence Erlbaum Associates, 365 Broadway, Suite 102, Hillsdale NJ 07642. **Tel** (201)666-4110, (800)926-6579, FAX (201)666-2394. **ED** Lawrence A Pervin. **LC** BF1; .P675. **DD** 150/.5. **NLM** W1; PY559L. **CODEN** PINQEY. **Pr Rev.**
**Desc:** New international forum for scholarly inquiry, criticism, and review will publish theoretical and issue-oriented articles in the areas of personality, social, developmental, health, and clinical psychology.
**Ind/Abst** Psychoanal. Abstr.; Psychol. Abstr. (1990-); PsycINFO; PsycScan: Appl. Exp. Eng. Psych.; PsycScan: LD/MR; PsycScan: Neuropsych.

US/0048-5748
**PSYCHOLOGICAL ISSUES.** [Psychol. issues]. Monograph 1 (1959)-. Monographic series. English. ir. Price varies per volume. International Universities Press Inc., 59 Boston Post Road, PO Box 1524, Madison CT 06443-1524. **Tel** (203)245-4000, FAX (203)245-0775, telex 282986 IUP BK. **ED** Herbert J. Schlesinger. **LC** UNC. **NLM** W1 PS572. **CODEN** PSYIA.
**Ind/Abst** Index Med.; Middle East Abstr. Index; Psychol. Abstr. (1964-); PsycINFO; PsycLit.

UK/0033-2917
**PSYCHOLOGICAL MEDICINE.** [Psychol. med.]. **Added/Corp** British Medical Association. Vol. 1 (1970)-. Academic Scholarly Publication. English. Six times a year. $320.00 US, Canada and Mexico; £169.00 other. Cambridge University Press, The Edinburgh Building, Shaftesbury Road, Cambridge CB2 2RU United Kingdom. **Tel** 011 44 223 312393, FAX 011 44 223 325959. **(Subscription address:** Cambridge University Press / North America, 110 Midland Avenue, Port Chester NY 10573.**) ED** Michael Shepherd. **LC** RC321; .P92. **NLM** W1 PS591. **CODEN** PSMDCO. **[CCC]. Bk Rev. Pr Rev.** available on microfilm and microfiche from University Microfilms International (UMI). Documents available from The Genuine Article, CASDDS.
**Desc:** Publishes original research in clinical psychiatry and the basic sciences related to it. Each issue contains several guest editorials by respected scholars and researchers from a wide range of fields. Authoritative articles not only provide up-to-date surveys of recent findings and issues, but may offer a historical and interdisciplinary perspective not often found in more traditional journals.
**Ind/Abst** Annals Behav. Med.; Appl. Soc. Sci. Index Abstr.; Arts Humanit. Citation Index [Select. Cov.]; Chem. Abstr.; Cumul. Index Nurs. Allied Health Lit.; Curr. Contents Clin. Med.; Curr. Contents Life Sci.; Curr. Contents Soc. Behav. Sci.; Dev. Med. Child Neurol. (-1990); EMBASE; Index Med.; Index Period. Artic. Relat. Law; Middle East Abstr. Index; Nutr. Abstr. Rev., Ser. A, Hum. Exp.; Life Sci. Collect.; Psychol. Abstr. (1970-); PsycINFO (?-1988); PsycLit; Ref. Upd. Deluxe Ed.; Res. Alert [Full Cov.]; Res. High. Educ. Abstr.; Risk Abstr.; Sci. Cit. Index; SCISEARCH; Soc. Sci. Cit. Index [Full Cov.]; Trop. Dis. Bull.

UK/0264-1801
**PSYCHOLOGICAL MEDICINE. MONOGRAPH SUPPLEMENT.** [Psychol. med., monogr. suppl.]. **VFOAT** Monograph Supplement. (1982)-. Monographic series. English. ir. Comes with Psychological Medicine. Cambridge University Press, The Edinburgh Building, Shaftesbury Road, Cambridge CB2 2RU United Kingdom. **Tel** 011 44 223 312393, FAX 011 44 223 325959. **ED** Michael Shepherd. **NLM** W1 PS591B. **Bk Rev. Ad Acc. Circ:** 3,000.
**Desc:** Concerned with original research in clinical psychiatry and the basic sciences related to it.
**Ind/Abst** Index Med.

US/0033-2925
**PSYCHOLOGICAL PERSPECTIVES.** [Psychol. perspect.]. **Added/Corp** C.G. Jung Institute of Los Angeles (Calif.). Vol. 1 (Spring 1970)-. Periodical. English. sa (2 issues). $22.00 US; $26.00 other. C. G. Jung Institute of LA, 10349 West Pico Boulevard, Los Angeles CA 90064. **Tel** (213)556-1193, FAX (213)556-2290. **ED** Charlene Sieg (Editor's Phone: (310)556-1193). **LC** BF173.A2; P76. **DD** 150/.5. **NLM** W1; PS63H. **[CCC].** Index available. **Bk Rev. Ad Acc. Pr Rev. Circ:** 18000. available on microfilm and microfiche from University Microfilms International (UMI).
**Desc:** A journal of Jungian thought featuring articles, interviews, poetry, fiction, and book and film reviews. Themes and issues of personal, cultural, and global interest are explored from a unique perspective that integrates archetypal and leading edge thinking in the arts and sciences.
**Ind/Abst** Except. Hum. Exp.; Psychol. Abstr. (1973-); PsycINFO (?-?); PsycLit.

US/0033-2933
**PSYCHOLOGICAL RECORD, THE.** [Psychol. rec.]. **Added/Corp** Denison University. Vol. 1 (March 1937)-. Periodical. English. qt. $65.00 (institutions), $30.00 (individuals). Kenyon College, c/o Charles E. Rice, Gambier OH 43022. **Tel** (614)427-5377, FAX (614)427-4950. **ED** Charles E. Rice. **LC** BF1; .P68. **DD** 150.5; 159.905. **NLM** W1 PS632. **CODEN** PYRCAI. **[CCC].** Index available. **Bk Rev**, (Qty: 5-10). **Ad Acc. Pr Rev. Circ:** 1,475. available on magnetic tape, an online database, and CD-ROM; available on microfilm and microfiche from University Microfilms International (UMI). Documents available from The Genuine Article, BIOSIS Document Express, UMI Article Clearinghouse.
**Desc:** Theoretical and experimental articles on current development in psychology.
**Ind/Abst** Acad. Search (July 1993-); Appl. Soc. Sci. Index Abstr.; Biol. Abstr.; Curr. Contents Soc. Behav. Sci.; Expand. Acad. Index (1989-); High. Educ. Abstr. (1973-); INFO-SOUTH Abstr.; Mag. Search; Middle East Abstr. Index; Newsp. Period. Abstr. (1991-); Life Sci. Collect.; Psychol. Abstr. (1937-); PsycINFO; PsycLit; Res. Alert [Full Cov.]; Soc. Plann. Policy Dev. Abstr.; Soc. Sci. Source (Jul. 1993-); Soc. Sci. Cit. Index [Full Cov.]; Soc. Sci. Index; Soc. Sci. Index Fulltext (Fall 1988-) [Full Txt.]; Sociol. Abstr.

US/0033-2941
**PSYCHOLOGICAL REPORTS.** [Psychol. rep.]. Vol. 1 (March 1955)-. Periodical. English. bm (Feb., Apr., June, Aug., Oct., Dec.). $240.00. Southern Universities Press, Box 9229, Missoula MT 59807. **Tel** (406)728-1710. **ED** Robert B. Ammons and Carol H. Ammons. **LC** BF21; .P843. **DD** 150.82. **NLM** W1 PS635. **CODEN** PYRTAZ. Index available (bound in June issue). **Bk Rev. Pr Rev.** available on microfilm. Documents available from The Genuine Article, BIOSIS Document Express, UMI Article Clearinghouse.
**Desc:** Contains experimental, theoretical, and speculative articles. Encourages scientific originality and creativity in the field of general psychology. Also contains special reviews and listings of new books and materials received.
**Ind/Abst** Abstr. Res. Pastor. Care Couns. (19??-); Acad. Abstr. Full Text Elite (Jan. 1992-); Acad. Abstr. (Jan. 1992-); Acad. Search (Jan. 1992-); Arts Humanit. Citation Index [Select. Cov.]; Biol. Abstr.; Chicano Index; Commun. Abstr. (?-?); Crim. Penol. Police Sci. Abstr.; Cumul. Index Nurs. Allied Health Lit.; Curr. Contents Soc. Behav. Sci.; EMBASE; Ergon. Abstr.; Expand. Acad. Index (1989-); High. Educ. Abstr. (1966-); Index Med.; Index Period. Artic. Relat. Law (19??-19??); INFO-SOUTH Abstr.; Int. Aerosp. Abstr.; Lang. Lang. Behav. Abstr.; Mag. Search; Middle East Abstr. Index; Multicult. Educ. Abstr.; Newsp. Period. Abstr. (1989-); Peace Res. Abstr. J. (1969-1974); Life Sci. Collect.; Psychol. Abstr. (1955-); PsycINFO; PsycLit; Res. Alert [Full Cov.]; Res. High. Educ. Abstr.; Soc. Plann. Policy Dev. Abstr.; Soc. Sci. Source (Jan. 1992-); Soc. Sci. Cit. Index [Full Cov.]; Soc. Sci. Index; Soc. Sci. Index Fulltext (Dec. 1987-) [Full Txt.]; Soc. Welf. Soc. Plan./Policy Soc. Dev.; Sociol. Abstr. (?-?); Sociol. Educ. Abstr.; SPORT Discus; SportSearch; Stud. Women Abstr.; Women Stud. Abstr.

GW/0340-0727
**PSYCHOLOGICAL RESEARCH.** [Psychol. res.]. Vol. 37 (1974)-. Periodical. English. Four times a year. DM558.00. Springer-Verlag GmbH & Company KG, Heidelberger Platz 3, D 14197 Berlin Germany. **Tel** 011 49 30 8207223, FAX 011 49 30 8214091, telex 183 319 SPBLN D. **(Subscription address:** Springer Verlag New York Inc. / for North America, 44 Hartz Way, Secaucus NJ 07096.**) ED** E. Scheerer, B. Bridgeman, D.E. Broadbent, J. Engelkamp, A.H.C. van der Heijden, H. Heuer, and D.J.K. Mewhort. **LC** BF3; .P65. **DD** 150/.5. **NLM** W1 PS635J. **CODEN** PSREDJ. **[CCC].** available on microfilm and microfiche from University Microfilms International (UMI). Documents available from The Genuine Article, BIOSIS Document Express. ***Continues** Psychologische Forschung, 0033-3026.*
**Desc:** Publishes original contributions which emphasize the theoretical implications of the research reported.
**Ind/Abst** Biol. Abstr.; Curr. Contents Soc. Behav. Sci.; Index Med.; Lang. Lang. Behav. Abstr.; Middle East Abstr. Index; Psychol. Abstr. (1974-); PsycINFO; PsycLit; Res. Alert [Full Cov.]; Soc. Sci. Cit. Index [Full Cov.].

SW/0555-5620
**PSYCHOLOGICAL RESEARCH BULLETIN.** ***Ceased.*** [Psychol. res. bull.]. **Added/Corp** Lunds Universitet. Vol. 1 (1961)-(1993). Bulletin. English. ir. Price varies per volume. Department of Psychology, Paradisgatan 5 P, 223 50 Lund Sweden. **Tel** 046/107000. **ED** Gudmund Smith. **LC** BF21.A1; .P75. **DD** 150/.5. **CODEN** PRBUDE. Index available. cum. index. **Circ:** 550 (ctrl).
**Desc:** Empirical psychological studies, often concerned with the analysis of personality.
**Ind/Abst** Psychol. Abstr. (1963-); PsycINFO (1963-?); PsycLit.

US/0033-295X
**PSYCHOLOGICAL REVIEW.** [Psychol. rev.]. **Added/Corp** American Psychological Association. Vol. 1 (Jan. 1894)-. Periodical. English. qt (4 issues). $146.00 (nonmember, institution) US. American Psychological Association, 750 First Street Northeast, Washington DC 20002. **Tel** (800)374-2721, (202)336-5600, (subscriptions - (202)336-5600. **ED** Walter Kintsch, PhD. **LC** BF1; .P7. **DD** 150/.5. **NLM** W1 PS636. **CODEN** PSRVAX. **[CCC]. Pr Rev. Circ:** 6,500. available on microfilm and microfiche from University Microfilms International (UMI). Documents available from The Genuine Article, BIOSIS Document Express, UMI Article Clearinghouse.
**Desc:** Presents the most significant advances in theory. The journal of choice for new ideas, explanations, critical insights, and inspiration.
**Ind/Abst** Acad. Abstr. Full Text Elite (July 1990-); Acad. Abstr. (July 1990-); Acad. Ind. [Computer File] (1987-); Acad. Search (July 1990-); Appl. Soc. Sci. Index Abstr.; Biol. Abstr.; Curr. Contents Life Sci.; Curr. Contents Soc. Behav. Sci.; Curr. Index J. Educ.; Ergon. Abstr.; Expand. Acad. Index (1987-); Index Med.; INFO-SOUTH Abstr.; Int. Aerosp. Abstr.; Int. Bibliogr. Sociol.; Mag. Search; Med. Abstr. Newsl.; Middle East Abstr. Index; MLA Int. Bibl. Books Artic. Mod. Lang. Lit.; Multicult. Educ. Abstr.; Newsp. Period. Abstr. (1986-); Peace Res. Abstr. J. (1973-1974); Life Sci. Collect.; Psychol. Abstr. (1924-); PsycINFO; PsycLit; PsycScan: Develop. Psych.; Ref. Upd. Deluxe Ed.; Res. Alert [Full Cov.]; Sci. Cit. Index; SCISEARCH; Soc. Sci. Source (Jul. 1990-); Soc. Sci. Cit. Index [Full Cov.]; Soc. Sci. Index; Soc. Sci. Index Fulltext (Oct. 1988-) [Full Txt.]; Soc. Work Abstr. [Select. Cov.]; Spec. Educ. Needs Abstr.; Stud. Women Abstr.

US/0956-7976
**PSYCHOLOGICAL SCIENCE.** (PSYCHOLOGICAL SCIENCE : A JOURNAL OF THE AMERICAN PSYCHOLOGICAL SOCIETY / APS.). [Psychol. sci.]. **Added/Corp** American Psychological Society. Vol. 1, No. 1 (Jan. 1990)-. Academic Scholarly Publication. English. bm (6 issues). $128.00 US, Canada and Mexico; £84.00 other. Cambridge University Press / New York, 40 West 20th Street, New York NY 10011-4211. **Tel** (212)924-3900, (800)221-4512. **(Subscription address:** Cambridge University Press / Outside of North America, Journal Fulfillment Department, The Edinburgh Building, Cambridge CB2 2RU United Kingdom.**) ED** William K. Estes. **LC** BF1; .P816. **DD** 150/.5. **NLM** W1; PS643G. **CODEN** PSYSET. **Bk Rev. Ad Acc.** available on microfilm and microfiche from University Microfilms International (UMI). Documents available from The Genuine Article, UMI Article Clearinghouse.
**Desc:** Journal of the American Psychological Society. Founded to advance the scientific focus of psychological research. Designed to be a forum for research, theory and application in psychology and the closely related behavioral, cognitive, neural and social sciences. Also covers psychology in government and public affairs. Unlike most journals, articles of general theoretical significance are of broad interest across specialties.
**Ind/Abst** Curr. Contents Soc. Behav. Sci.; Ergon. Abstr.; Expand. Acad. Index (1992-); Newsp. Period. Abstr. (1992-); Psychol. Abstr. (1990-); PsycINFO (1990-); Res. Alert [Full Cov.]; Soc. Plann. Policy Dev. Abstr.; Soc. Sci. Cit. Index [Full Cov.].

II/0033-2968
**PSYCHOLOGICAL STUDIES.** [Psychol. stud.]. **VFOAT** A.PS. Vol. 1 (1956)-. Periodical. English. Three times a year. $30.00. Indian Books and Periodicals, 2429 Tilak Street, Pahar Ganj, New Delhi 110005 India. **(Subscription address:** Prints India, 11 Darya Ganj, New Delhi 110002 India.**) ED** M A Faroqi. **LC** BF1; .P817. **NLM** W1 PS645. **Bk Rev. Ad Acc. Circ:** 1,000.
**Desc:** Covers psychological research and empirical studies.
**Ind/Abst** Psychol. Abstr. (1956-); PsycINFO; PsycLit.

AT/1031-7511
**PSYCHOLOGICAL TEST BULLETIN.** ***Ceased.*** (1988)-(19??). Periodical. English. sa. Australian Council for Educational Research, 19 Prospect Hill Road, Camberwell VIC 3124 Australia. **Tel** 011 61 3 2775555.
**Ind/Abst** Aust. Educ. Index.

FR
**PSYCHOLOGIE & EDUCATION.** **Added/Corp** Association Francaise des Psychologues Scolaires. **VFOAT** Psychologie et Education. (1990)-. Periodical. French (summaries and/or abstracts in

English). qt (Mar., June, Sept., Dec.). 300.00F. Psychologie Scolaire, 24 rue de Bougainville, 50130 Octeville France. **Tel** 011 33 33 932502. **ED** Georges Masclet. **LC** LB1051; .P729162. **DD** 370.15/05. Index available. **Bk Rev. Ad Acc, Adv Mgr:** Herve Jo. **Circ:** 3,000 (ctrl).
**Desc:** The goal of this scientific and professional journal is to spread over current tendancies in educational psychology as they appear in France and abroad. Presents papers covering various fields related to educational psychology and school psychology, namely: child and adolescent psychology; cognitive psychology; clinical psychology; psychoanalysis; school ergonomy; ethnopsychology; therapy practices; epistemology.

NE
**PSYCHOLOGIE & MAATSCHAPPIJ.**
**VFOAT** Psychologie en Maatschappij. No. 6 (Jan. 1979)-. Periodical. Dutch. qt. Uitgeverij Sun, PO Box 1609, 6501 BP Nijmegen Netherlands. **Tel** 011 31 80 221700. ***Continues*** *Nieuwsbrief Psychologie & Maatschappij.*

●FR
**PSYCHOLOGIE CLINIQUE EG PROJECTIVE.** (1994)-. Periodical. French. Twice a year. 200.00F (institutions), 170.00F (students) France; 260.00F (institutions), 220.00F (students) other. Dunod Gauthier Villars, 15 rue Gossin, 92543 Montrouge cedex France. **Tel** 011 33 1 46 56 52 66, FAX 011 33 1 46 57 40 69. **(Subscription address:** Centrale des Revues, 11 rue Gossin, 92543 Montrouge Cedex France.**)**

FR/0033-2984
**PSYCHOLOGIE FRANCAISE.** [Psychol. fr.]. **Added/Corp** Societe Francaise de Psychologie. Vol. 1 (1956)-. Periodical. French. Four times a year. 390.00F (institutions), 195.00F (students) France; 520.00F (institutions), 260.00F (students) other. Dunod Gauthier Villars, 15 rue Gossin, 92543 Montrouge cedex France. **Tel** 011 33 1 46 56 52 66, FAX 011 33 1 46 57 40 69. **(Subscription address:** Centrale des Revues, 11 rue Gossin, 92543 Montrouge Cedex France.**) LC** BF2; .P63. **NLM** W1 PS65. **CODEN** PSFRAT. **[CCC].** Documents available from BIOSIS Document Express.
**Ind/Abst** Biol. Abstr.; Index Book Rev. Relig.; Psychol. Abstr. (1956-); PsycINFO (1956-); PsycLit; Soc. Plann. Policy Dev. Abstr.; Sociol. Abstr. (?-?).

GW/0233-0202
**PSYCHOLOGIE FUER DIE PRAXIS : ORGAN DER GESELLSCHAFT FUER PSYCHOLOGIE DER DEUTSCHEN DEMOKRATISCHEN REPUBLIK.** [Psychol. Prax. - Berl. DDR]. Vol. 1 (1983)-. Periodical. German (summaries and/or abstracts in English and Russian). **LC** BF23. **DD** 150/.5. **NLM** W1; PS65F. ***Continues*** *Probleme und Ergebnisse der Psychologie, 0048-5403.*
**Ind/Abst** PsycINFO (1984-); PsycLit.

AU
**PSYCHOLOGIE-INFORMATION / GESELLSCHAFT FUER PSYCHOLOGIE DER DEUTSCHEN DEMOKRAITISCHEN REPUBLIK.** (19??)-. Periodical. German. Gesellschaft fur Psychologie der DDR, AM Kupfergraben, Berlin Germany. **LC** BF3; .P633. **DD** 150/.5.

NE/0167-6598
**PSYCHOLOGIE LISSE.** (PSYCHOLOGIE.). [Psychologie Lisse]. (1982)-. Periodical. Dutch. Eleven times a year. Fl70.05. Swets & Zeitlinger BV, Heereweg 347B PO Box 825, 2160 SZ Lisse Holland. **Tel** 011 31 2521 35111, FAX 02521-15888, telex 41325. **(Subscription address:** Swets Publishing Service, PO Box 825, 2160 SZ Lisse The Netherlands**) UDC** 159.9.

FR/0048-5756
**PSYCHOLOGIE MEDICALE.** [Psychol. med.]. Vol. 1 (1968)-. Academic Scholarly Publication. French. Fourteen times a year. 700.00F France; 1100.00F other. Societe de Presse Medicale, 14 rue Drouot, 75009 Paris France. **Tel** 011 33 1 48249693, 011 33 1 47703994. **NLM** W1 PS651E.
**Desc:** Includes the annual report of the conference and the transactions of the Society of psychology, medical, & French language.
**Ind/Abst** EMBASE; Psychol. Abstr.; PsycINFO (1970-); PsycLit.

CN/0714-3494
**PSYCHOLOGIE PREVENTIVE.** [Psychol. prev.]. **Added/Corp** Societe de Recherche en Orientation Humaine. Vol. 1, No. 1 (1982)-. Periodical. French. Twice a year (Mar. & Nov.). 7.50Can$ (individuals), 10.00Can$ (institutions) Canada; 15.00Can$ (individuals), 20.00Can$ (institutions) others. Societe Recherche en Orientation Humaine, 2120 Est Sherbrooke, Suite 212, Montreal Quebec H2K 1C3 Canada. **Tel** (514)523-5677, FAX (514)523-9999. **DD** 150/.5. Index available. cum. index. **Ad Acc. Circ:** 1,200 (ctrl).
**Ind/Abst** Point Repere.

CN/0824-1724
**PSYCHOLOGIE QUEBEC.** [Psychol. Que.]. V. 5, No. 3, (April 1984)-. Periodical. French. bm. Free to members. Corporation Professionnelle des Psychologues du Quebec, Bureau 510/1575 Ouest Boulevard Henri-Bourassa, Montreal Quebec H3M 3A9 Canada. **DD** 150/.9714. ***Continues*** *Cahiers du Psychologue Quebecois, 0701-8932.*

FR
**PSYCHOLOGIES.** No. 1 (May 1983)-. Periodical. French. Eleven times a year. 279.14F France; 355.00F other. Loft International, 1 Rue Lord Byron, 75008 Paris France. **Tel** 011 33 1 42256520. **(Subscription address:** Psychologies Service Abonnements, B704, 60732 Ste Genevieve Cedex France.**) Bk Rev. Ad Acc. *Continues*** *Psychologie.*
**Desc:** A magazine for everyone who wants to understand himself and others.
**Ind/Abst** Point Repere (1979-1983).

GW
**PSYCHOLOGISCH GESEHEN.** No. 1 (1965)-. Periodical. German. ir. Adolph Bonz Verlag, Krahenstrasse 9, W-7013 Oeffingen Germany.

GW/0033-3018
**PSYCHOLOGISCHE BEITRAEGE.** [Psychol. Beitr.]. **Added/Corp** Deutsche Gesellschaft fuer Psychologie. Vol. 1 (1953)-. Periodical. German (English, French and Japanese). Twice a year. Price varies. Wolfgang Pabst Verlag, Am Eichengrund 28, D 49525 Lengerich Germany. **Tel** 011 49 5484 308, FAX 011 49 5484 550. **ED** Gunther Baumler, Ferdinand Merz, Manfred Ritter and Heinz Schmidtke. **LC** BF3; .P64. **NLM** W1 PS723. **Bk Rev. Ad Acc. Circ:** 50 (ctrl).
**Desc:** A journal for all fields of psychology.
**Ind/Abst** Ergon. Abstr. (?-?); Psychol. Abstr. (1953-); PsycINFO (1953-); PsycLit; Soc. Plann. Policy Dev. Abstr.; Stat. Theory Method Abstr. (1969).

SZ/0079-7413
**PSYCHOLOGISCHE PRAXIS.** [Psychol. Prax.]. No. 1 (1943)-. Monographic series. German. ir. Price varies per volume. S. Karger AG, Allschwilerstrasse 10, PO Box - Postfach - Case Postale, CH-4009 Basel Switzerland. **Tel** 011 41 61 306-1111, FAX 011 41 61 306-1234, telex CH 962 652. **ED** R. Schmitz-Scherzer. **NLM** W1 PS739. **CODEN** PSPAAS.
**Ind/Abst** Psychol. Abstr. (1976-).

GW/0033-3042
**PSYCHOLOGISCHE RUNDSCHAU.** [Psychol. Rundsch.]. **Added/Corp** Berufsverband Deutscher Psychologen. Vol. 1 (Oct. 1949)-. Periodical. German. qt. DM64.00. Hogrefe Verlag fuer Psychologie, Rohnsweg 25, D 37085 Goettingen Germany. **Tel** 011 49 551 496090, FAX 011 49 551 4960988. **ED** W.H. Tack. **LC** BF3; .P68. **DD** 150.5. **NLM** W1 PS742. **Bk Rev. Ad Acc. Pr Rev. Circ:** 5,500. Documents available from The Genuine Article.
**Desc:** Europe's largest scientific journal in the field of psychology.
**Ind/Abst** Psychol. Abstr. (1949-); PsycINFO (1929-); PsycLit; Res. Alert [Full Cov.]; Soc. Sci. Cit. Index [Full Cov.].

GW
**PSYCHOLOGISCHER INDEX / HERAUSGEBER ZENTRALSTELLE FUER PSYCHOLOGISCHE INFORMATION UND DOKUMENTATION AN DER UNIVERSITAET TRIER.**
**Added/Corp** Universitaet Trier. Zentralstelle fuer Psychologische Information und Dokumentation. (1981)-. Periodical. German. Four times a year. DM192.00. Verlag F Psychologie Testzentr, Robert Bosch Breite 25, D 37079 Goettingen FR Germany. **Tel** 011 49 5515068814.

GW/0555-5701
**PSYCHOLOGISCHES KOLLOQUIUM.**
Monographic series. German. Price varies per volume. Huber, Max-Hueber-Strasse 4, W-8045 Ismaning Bei Munich Germany. **Tel** (054)27 11 11. **NLM** W1 PS744L.

UK/0952-8229
**PSYCHOLOGIST, THE. Added/Corp** British Psychological Society. Vol. 1, No. 1 (Jan. 1988)-. Newsletter. English. Twelve times a year. £45.00 UK; £55.00 other. British Psychological Society, St. Andrews House, 48 Princess Road, Leicester LE1 7DR England. **Tel** 011 44 533 549568. **NLM** W1; PS744Y. **[CCC]. *Continues*** *Bulletin of the British Psychological Society, 0007-1692.*

CN/0713-5750
**PSYCHOLOGISTS REGISTERED IN ONTARIO.** (PSYCHOLOGISTS REGISTERED IN ONTARIO, DIRECTORY / ONTARIO BOARD OF EXAMINERS IN PSYCHOLOGY.). [Psychol. regist. Ont.]. 1982-. Directory. English. an. Free to Registered Psychologists in Ontario. Ontario Board of Examiners in Psychology, 37 Prince Arthur Avenue, Toronto Ontario M5R 1B2. **DD** 150/.25/713. ***Continues*** *Directory of Psychologists Registered in the Province of Ontario, 0316-0793.*

CN/0318-1707
**PSYCHOLOGUE QUEBECOIS, LE.** V. 6- Jan./Feb. 1974-. French. ir. Corporation des Psychologues de la Province de Quebec, 8180 Chemin Devonshire, Montreal Quebec H4P 2K3 Canada. **DD** 150/5. ***Continues*** *Corporation des Psychologues de la Province de Quebec. Bulletin de Nouvelles, 0318-1715.*

US/0882-7974
**PSYCHOLOGY AND AGING.** [Psychol. aging]. **Added/Corp** American Psychological Association. Vol. 1, No. 1 (March 1986)-. Periodical. English. qt. $155.00 (nonmember, institution) US. American Psychological Association, 750 First Street Northeast, Washington DC 20002. **Tel** (800)374-2721, (202)336-5600, (subscriptions - (202)336-5600. **ED** Timothy A. Salthouse, PhD. **LC** BF724.55.A35; P79. **DD** 155.67/05. **NLM** W1; PS746JL. **[CCC]. Ad Acc. Pr Rev. Circ:** 3,500. available on microfilm and microfiche from University Microfilms International (UMI). Documents available from The Genuine Article.
**Desc:** This journal is devoted exclusively to publishing research on the physiological and behavioral aspects of aging. Original articles in adult development and aging include reports of research including applied, biobehavioral, clinical, educational, experimental, methodological, and psychosocial issues. Addresses both practice and research issues.
**Ind/Abst** Annals Behav. Med.; Curr. Contents Soc. Behav. Sci.; Health Plan. Adminis.; Hum. Resour. Abstr.; Psychol. Abstr. (1986-); PsycINFO (1990-); PsycLit; Res. Alert [Full Cov.]; Soc. Sci. Cit. Index [Full Cov.]; SPORT Discus.

II/0971-3336
**PSYCHOLOGY AND DEVELOPING SOCIETIES. Added/Corp** University of Allahabad. Dept. of Psychology. Vol. 1, No. 1 (Jan.-June 1989)-. Periodical. English. sa (Mar. and Sept.). $70.00. SAGE Periodical Press, 2455 Teller Road, Thousand Oaks CA 91320. **Tel** (805)499-0721, FAX (805)499-0871, telex 100799. **ED** Durganand Sinha. **LC** BF1; .P847. **DD** 150/.9172/405. **NLM** W1; PS746JP. **CODEN** PDSOEI. Index available. **Ad Acc.** available on microfilm and microfiche from University Microfilms International (UMI).
**Desc:** Provides a forum for psychologists from different parts of the world who are concerned with problems of developing societies.
**Ind/Abst** Int. Bibliogr. Sociol.; Psychol. Abstr. (1989-); PsycINFO; PsycLit; Soc. Plann. Policy Dev. Abstr.

SZ/0887-0446
**PSYCHOLOGY & HEALTH. See** Public Health and Safety.

US/0277-2469
**PSYCHOLOGY & SOCIAL THEORY.**
[Psychol. soc. theory]. **VFOAT** Psychology and Social Theory. **VAT** Psychology and Social Theory. No. 1 (Spring/Summer 1981)-. Periodical. English. sa. $45.00. Psychology and Social Theory, PO Box 4387, Triphammer Mall, Ithaca NY 14852. **Tel** (415)585-8788.
**Ind/Abst** Altern. Press Index (-199?); Left Index; Psychol. Abstr. (1981-); Soc. Plann. Policy Dev. Abstr.; Sociol. Abstr. (?-?).

US/0885-7423
**PSYCHOLOGY AND SOCIOLOGY OF SPORT.** [Psychol. sociol. sport]. Vol. 1 (1986)-. English. an. $37.50. AMS Press Inc., 56 East 13th Street, New York NY 10003. **Tel** (212)777-4700, FAX (212)995-5413, telex 710 581 2302. **ED** Lee Vander Velden and James H Humphrey. **LC** GV706; .P77. **DD** 796/.01. **Bk Rev. Pr Rev.**
**Desc:** Presents original research on contemporary problems of interest to behavioral scientists in the areas of sport psychology and sport sociology.

●UK/1068-316X
**PSYCHOLOGY, CRIME & LAW.** [Psychol., crime, law]. **VFOAT** Psychology, Crime, and Law. Vol. 1, No. 1 (1994)-. Periodical. English. ir (every three months). $212.00 (institution), $150.00 (library). Harwood Academic Publishers, PO Box 90, Reading RG1 8JL England. **Tel** 011 44 734 560080. **DD** 345.
**Desc:** Promotes the study and application of psychological approaches to crime, criminal and civil law, and the influence of law on behavior.

US/0272-3794
**PSYCHOLOGY (GUILFORD).**
(PSYCHOLOGY.). [Psychology]. **VFOAT** Annual Editions: Psychology. 10th- Ed.; 1980/81-. English. an. $10.95. Dushkin Publishing Group Inc., Sluice Dock, Guilford CT 06437. **Tel** (203)453-4351, (800)243-6532, FAX (203)453-6000. **ED** Hiram Fitzgerald and Michael Walraven. **LC** BF149; .A58. **DD** 150/.5. ***Continues*** *Annual Editions. Readings in Psychology, 0197-0542.*
**Desc:** Contains high-interest articles which are easily integrated into any basic psychology course. Articles cover a broad range of current topics and are selected from a wide assortment of sources.

US/0033-3085
**PSYCHOLOGY IN THE SCHOOLS.**
[Psychol. sch.]. Vol. 1 (1964)-. Periodical. English. qt (4 issues). $100.00 US; $113.50 other. Clinical Psychology Publishing Company, 4 Conant Square, Brandon VT 05733. **Tel** (802)247-6871, (800)433-8234. **ED** G. B. Fuller. **LC** LB1101; .P75. **DD** 370.15/05. **NLM** W1 PS746S. Index available (bound in last volume of each issue). **Bk Rev. Ad Acc. Pr Rev. Circ:** 1,800. available on microfilm and microfiche from University Microfilms

International (UMI). Documents available from The Genuine Article.
**Desc:** Educational psychology research for the school psychologist, administrator, counselor, researcher and educator.
**Ind/Abst** Acad. Search (July 1993-); Contents Pages Educ.; Curr. Contents Soc. Behav. Sci.; Curr. Index J. Educ.; Educ. Index; Educ. Adm. Abstr.; Except. Child Educ. Resour. (19??-19??); INFO-SOUTH Abstr.; Mag. Search; Multicult. Educ. Abstr.; Psychol. Abstr. (1965-); PsycINFO; PsycLit; Res. Alert [Full Cov.]; Sage Fam. Stud. Abstr.; School Organ. Manage. Abstr.; Soc. Plann. Policy Dev. Abstr.; Soc. Sci. Cit. Index [Full Cov.]; Sociol. Educ. Abstr.; Spec. Educ. Needs Abstr.

US/0095-1145
**PSYCHOLOGY (MENTOR).**
(PSYCHOLOGY.). [Psychology]. **VFOAT** Core Information Series. V. 1- Jan. 1975-. Periodical. English. mo. $75.00. 7139 Hopkins Road, PO Box 138, Mentor OH 44060. **LC** Z7203; .P98; BF1. **DD** 016.15.

US/0893-164X
**PSYCHOLOGY OF ADDICTIVE BEHAVIORS.** (PSYCHOLOGY OF ADDICTIVE BEHAVIORS : JOURNAL OF THE SOCIETY OF PSYCHOLOGISTS IN ADDICTIVE BEHAVIORS.). [Psychol. addict. behav.]. **Added/Corp** Society of Psychologists in Addictive Behaviors. Vol. 1, No. 1 (1987)-. Periodical. English. qt. $60.00 (institutions), $45.00 (individuals). American Psychological Association, 750 First Street Northeast, Washington DC 20002. **Tel** (800)374-2721, (202)336-5600, (subscriptions - (202)336-5600. **LC** RC563; .P79. **DD** 616.86/005. **NLM** W1; PS746SS. **[CCC].** ***Continues** Bulletin of the Society of Psychologists in Addictive Behaviors, 0883-9646.*
**Desc:** Covers compulsive behavior, behavior therapy and substance dependence and abuse.
**Ind/Abst** Psychol. Abstr. (1981-); PsycINFO; PsycLit.

US/0079-7421
**PSYCHOLOGY OF LEARNING AND MOTIVATION, THE.** [Psychol. learn. motiv.]. (1967)-. Monographic series. English. ir. Price varies per volume. Academic Press, Inc., 6277 Sea Harbor Drive, Orlando FL 32887. **Tel** (800)543-9534, (407)345-4100, FAX (407)363-9661. **ED** K. W. Spence and J. T. Spence. **LC** BF683; .P78. **DD** 153.1/534. **NLM** W1 PS746U. **CODEN** PYLMAIPYLMA. **[CCC].** Documents available from The Genuine Article, BIOSIS Document Express.
**Ind/Abst** Biol. Abstr. (1991-); Educ. Index; Life Sci. Collect.; Res. Alert [Full Cov.]; Soc. Sci. Cit. Index [Full Cov.].

UK/0305-7356
**PSYCHOLOGY OF MUSIC.** See Music.

●US/1076-8971
**PSYCHOLOGY, PUBLIC POLICY, AND LAW.** **Added/Corp** American Psychological Association. (1995)-. Periodical. English. qt. $100.00 (nonmember, institution) US. American Psychological Association, 750 First Street Northeast, Washington DC 20002. **Tel** (800)374-2721, (202)336-5600, (subscriptions - (202)336-5600. **Pr Rev.**
**Desc:** Covers the link between psychology as a science and public policy and law.

US/0033-3077
**PSYCHOLOGY (SAVANNAH).**
(PSYCHOLOGY.). [Psychology]. (May 1964)-. Periodical. English. qt. $18.00 US; $21.00 Canada; $21.50 other. Psychology, Ohio State University, 1775 College Rd., Columbus OH 43210. **Tel** (412)675-9080. **ED** Joseph Cangemi (editor's address: PO Box U-121, College Heights Post Office, Bowling Green, KY 42101). **LC** BF1; .P845. **DD** 150/.5. **NLM** W1 PS746H. **CODEN** PYCHBR. **Bk Rev. Ad Acc. Circ:** 1,500 (ctrl). available on microfilm and microfiche from University Microfilms International (UMI). Documents available from The Genuine Article, BIOSIS Document Express.
**Desc:** Research, theory, techniques, and arts of practice in the general field of psychology. Study of human behavior.
**Ind/Abst** Arts Humanit. Citation Index [Select. Cov.]; Biol. Abstr.; Commun. Abstr.; Crim. Justice Abstr.; Curr. Index J. Educ.; Psychol. Abstr. (1965-); PsycLit; Res. Alert [Full Cov.]; Sage Fam. Stud. Abstr.; Soc. Plann. Policy Dev. Abstr.; Soc. Sci. Cit. Index [Full Cov.]; Sociol. Abstr. (?-?); SportSearch.

UK
**PSYCHOLOGY SURVEY.** ***Ceased.***
**Added/Corp** British Psychological Society. No. 1 (1978)-?. English. an. Unwin Hyman Ltd., 15 17 Broadwick Street, London W1V 1FP England. **Tel** 011 44 71 439 3126. **LC** BF1; .P853. **DD** 150/.5.

●US/0033-3107
**PSYCHOLOGY TODAY.** Vol. 25, No. 1 (Jan./Feb. 1992)-. Periodical. English. bm (6 issues). $18.00. Sussex Publishers Inc., 49 East 21st Street, 11th Floor, New York NY 10010. **Tel** (212) 260-7210. **(Subscription address:** Neodata / Colorado, PO Box 2606, Boulder Boulder CO 80322.) **ED** Owen Lipstein. ***Continues** Psychology Today, 0033-3107.*
**Desc:** The bimonthly magazine for health of mind, body, and spirit. It explores all aspects of human behavior. It is written for people who are interested in learning more about themselves as well as the people around them.
**Ind/Abst** Acad. Ind. [Computer File]; Curr. Thoughts Trends; Expand. Acad. Index (1984-); Gen. Period. Index (19??-); Health Index (1989-); Health Period. Database [Full Txt.]; Health Ref. Cent. [Full Txt.] [Full Cov.]; INFO-SOUTH Abstr.; Mag. ASAP Plus [Full Txt.]; Mag. ASAP Sel. [Full Txt.]; Mag. Index Plus (1989-); Mag. Index Sel. Microfiche (1986-) [Full Txt.]; Mag. Index. Sel. (1986-); TOM Gen. Index [Full Txt.].

US/0033-3107
**PSYCHOLOGY TODAY.** ***Title Change.***
[Psychol. today]. Vol. 1 (May 1967)-(19??). Periodical. English. bm. Sussex Publishers Inc., 49 East 21st Street, 11th Floor, New York NY 10010. **Tel** (212) 260-7210. **(Subscription address:** Neodata, PO Box 2606, Boulder CO 80322) **ED** Patrice Horn. **LC** BF1; .P855. **DD** 150. **NLM** W1 PS746W. **CODEN** PSTOAM. cum. index. **Bk Rev. Ad Acc.** ctrl circ. available on microfilm from University Microfilms International (UMI); available on an online database (files 149,647,648/Full-Text) from DIALOG. Documents available from UMI Article Clearinghouse. ***Absorbed** Careers Today. **Continued by** Psychology Today.*
**Desc:** Investigates the secrets of the human mind.
**Ind/Abst** ABI/INFORM Glob. Ed.; ABI Inform Ondisc (Aug. 1973-Jan. 1980); Abr. Read. Guide Period. Lit.; Acad. Abstr. Full Text Elite (Jan. 1984-) [Full Txt.]; Acad. Abstr. (Jan. 1984-); Acad. Search (Jan. 1984-); AGRICOLA [Select. Cov.]; Appl. Soc. Sci. Index Abstr.; Biol. Dig.; Book Rev. Digest; Book Rev. Index; Can. Index (?-?); Consum. Health Nutr. Index (?-?); Crim. Penol. Police Sci. Abstr.; Cumul. Index Nurs. Allied Health Lit.; Curr. Lit. Fam. Plan.; Dent. Abstr. (1992-); EMBASE; Film Lit. Index; Gen. Sci. Index; Guide Soc. Sci. Relig.; Health Source (Jan. 1984-); High. Educ. Abstr. (1971-19??); Index Period. Artic. Relat. Law; INFO-SOUTH Abstr.; Infobank (Jan. 1969-); Mag. Artic. Summar. Elite (Jan. 1984-) [Full Txt.]; Mag. Artic. Summar. Select (Jan. 1984-) [Full Txt.]; Mag. Artic. Summar. CD-ROM (Jan. 1984-); Mag. Express (1986-) [Full Txt.]; Mag. Search; Middle East Abstr. Index; Mid. Search (Jan. 1984-); Newsp. Period. Abstr. (1986-); Peace Res. Abstr. J. (1969-); PsycINFO (?-?); PsycLit; Read. Guide Period. Lit.; Resource/One Ondisc; Soc. Sci. Source (Jan. 1984-); Soc. Sci. Index; Soc. Sci. Index Fulltext (Oct. 1988-) [Full Txt.]; SportSearch; Mag. Index (1977-); Vocat. Search (Jan. 1984-) [Full Txt.]; Women Stud. Abstr.

NE/0033-3115
**PSYCHOLOOG.** [Psycholoog]. (1966)-. Periodical. Dutch (English). mo (except July). Fl175.00 (institutions and libraries), Fl95.00 (regular) Netherlands; Fl210.00 (institutions and libraries), Fl135.00 (regular) other. Van Gorcum & Company BV, PO Box 43, NL 9400 AA Assen Netherlands. **Tel** 011 31 5920 46846, FAX 011 31 5920 72064. **ED** E Petersma. Index available. **Ad Acc. Circ:** 6,750 (ctrl).
**Desc:** Presents scientific articles on psychology.
**Ind/Abst** PsycINFO (1972-); PsycLit.

●UK/1354-1129
**PSYCHOLOY REVIEW.** Vol. 1 (Sept. 1994)-. English. Four times a year (Sept., Nov., Feb., Apr.). £14.95 UK; £23.00 Europe; £28.50 other. Philip Allan Publishers Ltd, Market Place, Deddington Oxford, OX15 0SE England. **Tel** 011 44 869 38652, FAX 011 44 869 38803.

GW/0935-2937
**PSYCHOMED.** (198?)-. Periodical. German. qt. DM98.00 Germany; DM108.00 other. Quintessenz Verlag GmbH, Ifenpfad 2 4, D 12107 Berlin Germany. **Tel** 011 49 30 740060. **NLM** W1; PS747C.

US/0033-3123
**PSYCHOMETRIKA.** Vol. 1 (March 1936)-. Periodical. English. qt. $90.00. Psychometric Society, PO Box 168 ACT, Iowa City IA 52243. **Tel** (319)339-1095, FAX (319)339-3021. **ED** Lawrence Hubert. **LC** BF1; .P86. **DD** 150.5; 159.905. **NLM** W1 PS747D. **CODEN** PSMIAX. **[CCC].** cum. index. **Bk Rev. Pr Rev. Circ:** 3,000. available on microfilm and microfiche from University Microfilms International (UMI). Documents available from The Genuine Article.
**Desc:** Presents articles on the development of quantitative models for methodology.
**Ind/Abst** Compumath Citation Index [Full Cov.]; Curr. Contents Soc. Behav. Sci.; Curr. Index J. Educ.; Curr. Index Stat.; Math. Rev.; Middle East Abstr. Index; Psychol. Abstr. (1936-); PsycINFO; PsycLit; PsycScan: Appl. Psych.; Res. Alert [Full Cov.]; Soc. Sci. Cit. Index [Full Cov.]; Soc. Res. Methodol. Abstr. (1975-); Stat. Theory Method Abstr. (1959-1963, 1969, 1971, 1977, 1979-1981, 1983, 1986-1987); Zentralbl. Math. Ihre Grenzgeb.

FR/0151-5845
**PSYCHOMOTRICITE, LA.** ***Ceased.***
**Added/Corp** Federation francaise des psychoreeducateurs. Vol. 1 (1977)-Vol. 10 (1986/87). Periodical. French. qt. Masson SA, Avenue Beauregard 12, CH-1701 Fribourg Switzerland. **Tel** 011 41 37 249585, FAX 011 41 37 247559, telex 942658 SEMI CH. **(Subscription address:** 7A Boulevard de Perolles, CH-1701 Fribourg Switzerland) **NLM** W1 PS748E. **[CCC].**

US/0275-3987
**PSYCHOMUSICOLOGY.** See Music.

●US/1069-9384
**PSYCHONOMIC BULLETIN & REVIEW.**
[Psychon. bull. rev.]. **Main/Corp** Psychonomic Society. **Added/Corp** Psychonomic Society. **VFOAT** Psychonomic Bulletin and Review. Vol. 1, No. 1 (Mar. 1994)-. Bulletin. English. qt (Mar., June, Sept., Dec.). $95.00 US; $101.00 other. Psychonomic Society Publications, 1710 Fortview Road, Austin TX 78704. **Tel** (512)462-2442, FAX (512)462-1101. **LC** BF1; .P78. **DD** 150. **[CCC].** ***Supersedes in part** Bulletin of the Psychonomic Society, 0090-5054.*
**Desc:** A short-report journal providing prompt publication of articles covering all areas of experimental psychology. All articles authored or sponsored by members of the Psychonomic Society.

IT/0394-7912
**PSYCHOPATHOLOGIA.** [Psychopathologia]. (1983)-. Periodical. Italian. bm (6 issues). L70000.00 (institutions), L50000.00 (individuals). Associazione la Ginestra, 3 CPS, V Manara 7, 25126 Brescia Italy. **Tel** 011 39 30 2410774. **UDC** 616.89.

GW/0033-3158
**PSYCHOPHARMACOLOGIA.** See Pharmacy and Pharmacology.

NE/0167-9198
**PSYCHOPHARMACOLOGY (AMSTERDAM).** ***Ceased.*** See Pharmacy and Pharmacology.

US/0048-5764
**PSYCHOPHARMACOLOGY BULLETIN.**
[Psychopharmacol. bull.]. **Added/Corp** National Clearinghouse for Mental Health Information (U.S.) National Institute of Mental Health (U.S.). Pharmacology Research Branch. International Reference Center on Psychotropic Drugs (U.S.) National Institute of Mental Health (U.S.). Pharmacologic and Somatic Treatments Research Branch. National Institute of Mental Health (U.S.). Division of Clinical Research. United States. Alcohol, Drug Abuse, and Mental Health Administration. Vol. 3, No. 3 (July 1966)-. Academic Scholarly Publication. English. qt. $21.00 domestic; $26.25 other. Superintendent of Documents, US Government Printing Office, Washington DC 20402. **Tel** (202)275-3328, FAX (202)786-2377. **NLM** W1 PS773. **CODEN** PSYBB9. **Pr Rev.** available on microfilm and microfiche from University Microfilms International (UMI). Documents available from The Genuine Article, BIOSIS Document Express, CASDDS. ***Continues** Psychopharmacology Service Center Bulletin.*
**Desc:** Provides up-to-date and otherwise inaccessible information on ongoing research and its results in this country and abroad, to facilitate greater integration of research efforts and to make the latest findings as well as dates, places and proceedings of national and international meetings rapidly available to the scientific community in the field of psychopharmacology.
**Ind/Abst** Biol. Abstr.; Chem. Abstr.; Curr. Contents Life Sci.; EMBASE; Energy Res. Abstr. (Aug. 1982-); Index Med.; PESTDOC; Res. Alert [Full Cov.]; Sci. Cit. Index; SCISEARCH; Soc. Sci. Cit. Index [Select. Cov.].

US/0161-0139
**PSYCHOPHARMACOLOGY (NEW YORK).** See Pharmacy and Pharmacology.

GW/0931-6795
**PSYCHOPHARMACOLOGY SERIES.** See Pharmacy and Pharmacology.

US/0048-5772
**PSYCHOPHYSIOLOGY.** See Biology-Physiology.

US
**PSYCHOSCOPE.** English. Ten times a year. $44.00 (individuals, add $10.00 postage and handling), $26.00 (students, add $10.00 postage and handling). Hogrefe and Huber Publishers, PO Box 2487, Kirkland WA 98083. **Tel** (800)228-3749, (206)820-1500, FAX (206)823-8324.

NE
**PSYCHOSOMATIC MEDICINE : PROCEEDINGS OF THE ... INTERNATIONAL CONGRESS OF THE ACADEMY OF PSYCHOSOMATIC MEDICINE.** See Medical Science and Technology.

GW/0171-3434
**PSYCHOSOZIAL.** Vol. 1, No. 1 (May 1978)-. Periodical. German. Four times a year. DM98.00. Julius Beltz GmbH & Co. KG, Postfach 100161, D 69441 Weinheim Germany. **Tel** 011 49 6201 703220.

GW
**PSYCHOTHERAPEUT, DER.** (199?)-. Six times a year. DM188.00. Springer-Verlag GmbH & Company KG, Heidelberger Platz 3, D 14197 Berlin Germany. **Tel** 011 49 30 8207223, FAX 011 49 30 8214091, telex 183 319 SPBLN D. **(Subscription**

address: Springer Verlag New York Inc. / for North America, 44 Hartz Way, Secaucus NJ 07096.) ***Continues*** *Praxis der Psychotherapie und Psychosomatik.*

AU
**PSYCHOTHERAPIE FORUM.** (19??)-. German. Four times a year. $66.00 North America. Springer-Verlag Wien, Sachsenplatz 4 6, PO Box 89, A-1201 Vienna Austria. **Tel** 011 43 1 3302415. **(Subscription address:** Springer Verlag New York Inc. / for North America, 44 Hartz Way, Secaucus NJ 07096.**)**

GW/0173-7937
**PSYCHOTHERAPIE, PSYCHOSOMATIK, MEDIZINISCHE PSYCHOLOGIE.** ***Title Change.*** [Psychother., Psychosom., med. Psychol.]. **Added/Corp** Allgemeine Arztliche Gesellschaft fuer Psychotherapie. **VFOAT** PPMP. Vol. 1, No. 1 (Jan. 1980)-(1993). Periodical. German (summaries and/or abstracts in English). mo. Georg Thieme Verlag Stuttgart, Postfach 301120, D 70451 Stuttgart Germany. **Tel** 011 49 711 89310, FAX 011 49 711 8931298, telex 7 252 275 GTVD. **(Subscription address:** Thieme Medical Publishers Inc., 381 Park Avenue South, New York, NY 10016**) NLM** W1; PS83E. **[CCC].** Documents available from The Genuine Article. ***Continues*** *Psychotherapie und Medizinische Psychologie, 0302-8984.* ***Continued by*** *PPMP Psychotherapie Psychosomatik Medizinische Psychologie, 0937-2032.*
**Ind/Abst** Curr. Contents Soc. Behav. Sci.; EMBASE; Index Med.; Int. Nurs. Index; Psychol. Abstr. (1980-); PsycINFO (1951-); PsycLit; Res. Alert [Full Cov.]; Soc. Sci. Cit. Index [Full Cov.].

SZ/0033-3190
**PSYCHOTHERAPY AND PSYCHOSOMATICS. See** Medical Science and Technology-Psychiatry.

US/0163-1543
**PSYCHOTHERAPY FINANCES.** [Psychother. finances]. **Added/Corp** Ridgewood Financial Institute. Vol. 5 (Jan. 1978)-. Periodical. English. Twelve times a year. $48.00. Ridgewood Financial Institute, 1016 Clemons Street Suite 407, Jupiter FL 33477. **Tel** (201)427-3366. **DD** 362. ***Continues*** *Psychotherapy Economics, 0092-184X.*

US/0731-7158
**PSYCHOTHERAPY IN PRIVATE PRACTICE.** [Psychother. priv. pract.]. Vol. 1, No. 1 (Spring 1983)-. Periodical. English. qt. $150.00 US; $210.00 other. The Haworth Press Inc, 10 Alice Street, Binghamton NY 13904-1580. **Tel** (607)722-5857, (800)3-HAWORTH, FAX (607)722-1424. **ED** Robert Weitz (editor's address: 7566 Martinique Boulevard, Boca Raton, FL 33433). **LC** RC455.2.P73; P89. **DD** 616.89/14/068. **NLM** W1; PS86M. **Bk Rev. Ad Acc. Pr Rev. Acid Free. Circ:** 399. available on microfilm and microfiche from University Microfilms International (UMI). Documents available from Haworth Document Delivery Service.
**Desc:** Devoted entirely to issues and methods in the development of private practice for psychotherapists.
**Ind/Abst** Abstr. Res. Pastor. Care Couns. (19??-); EMBASE; Hum. Resour. Abstr. (?-?); Index Period. Artic. Relat. Law; Multicult. Educ. Abstr.; Psychol. Abstr. (1983-); PsycINFO; PsycLit; Sage Fam. Stud. Abstr.; Soc. Work Abstr. [Select. Cov.].

US/1062-9475
**PSYCHOTHERAPY LETTER, THE.** [Psychother. lett.]. (199?)-. Newsletter. English. mo. $129.00 (institutions), $99.00 (individuals) US; $139.00 (institutions), $109.00 (individuals) Canada; $149.00 (institutions), $119.00 (individuals) other. Manisses Communications Group Inc., PO Box 3357, Providence RI 02906-0757. **Tel** (401)831-6020, (800)333-7771, FAX (401)861-6370. **DD** 616. Index available. ***Continues*** *Psychotherapy Today, 1047-9848;* ***Absorbed*** *Brown University Family Therapy Letter, 1045-5051.*

US/0738-6176
**PSYCHOTHERAPY PATIENT, THE. See** Medical Science and Technology-Psychiatry.

US/1050-3307
**PSYCHOTHERAPY RESEARCH.** (PSYCHOTHERAPY RESEARCH : JOURNAL OF THE SOCIETY FOR PSYCHOTHERAPY RESEARCH.). [Psychother. res.]. **Added/Corp** Society for Psychotherapy Research. **VFOAT** Journal of the Society for Psychotherapy Research. Vol. 1, No. 1 (Spring/Summer 1991)-. Periodical. English. Four times a year. $70.00 (institutions); $85.00 others. Guilford Publications Inc., 72 Spring Street, New York NY 10012. **Tel** (212)431-9800, (800)365-7006, FAX (212)966-6708. **(Subscription address:** Turpin Distribution Services Limited, Blackhorse Road, Letchworth, Hertfordshire SG6 1HN, United Kingdom.**) ED** Hans Strupp. **LC** RC475; .P75. **DD** 616.89/14/05. **NLM** W1; PS877. **[CCC]. Bk Rev. Ad Acc. Pr Rev.** available on microfilm and microfiche from University Microfilms International (UMI).
**Desc:** Publishes original research on psychotherapy process and outcome, reviews on key topics, and theoretical papers that are closely tied to empirical data.
**Ind/Abst** Int. Bibliogr. Sociol.; Psychoanal. Abstr.; PsycScan: Appl. Exp. Eng. Psych.; PsycScan: LD/MR; PsycScan: Neuropsych.

US/1047-9848
**PSYCHOTHERAPY TODAY.** ***Title Change.*** [Psychother. today]. **Added/Corp** Association for Psychohistory. **VFOAT** Psychotherapy Today Newsletter. Vol. 1 No. 1 (Dec. 1989)-(199?). Periodical. English. mo. Manisses Communications Group Inc., PO Box 3357, Providence RI 02906-0757. **Tel** (401)831-6020, (800)333-7771, FAX (401)861-6370. **DD** 616. **[CCC].** ***Continued by*** *Psychotherapy Letter, 1062-9475.*

US/1042-4717
**PSYCHWARE SOURCEBOOK. See** Education.

US
**PSYCINFO. See** Psychology-Abstracting, Bibliographies and Statistics.

US
**PSYCLIT DATABASE. See** Psychology-Abstracting, Bibliographies and Statistics.

US/0891-0685
**PSYCSCAN: APPLIED EXPERIMENTAL AND ENGINEERING PSYCHOLOGY. See** Psychology-Abstracting, Bibliographies and Statistics.

US/0271-7506
**PSYCSCAN. APPLIED PSYCHOLOGY. See** Psychology-Abstracting, Bibliographies and Statistics.

●US
**PSYCSCAN: BEHAVIOR ANALYSIS.** (1995)-. English. qt. $66.00 (nonmember, institution) US. American Psychological Association, 750 First Street Northeast, Washington DC 20002. **Tel** (800)374-2721, (202)336-5600, (subscriptions - (202)336-5600.
**Desc:** Provides citations and abstracts for articles from journals published throughout the world on both basic and applied behavior analysis.

US/0197-1484
**PSYCSCAN. CLINICAL PSYCHOLOGY. See** Psychology-Abstracting, Bibliographies and Statistics.

US/0197-1492
**PSYCSCAN. DEVELOPMENTAL PSYCHOLOGY. See** Psychology-Abstracting, Bibliographies and Statistics.

US/0730-1928
**PSYCSCAN. LD/MR. See** Psychology-Abstracting, Bibliographies and Statistics.

●US/1058-6660
**PSYCSCAN. NEUROPSYCHOLOGY. See** Psychology-Abstracting, Bibliographies and Statistics.

US/0889-5236
**PSYCSCAN: PSYCHOANALYSIS.** ***Title Change.*** **See** Psychology-Abstracting, Bibliographies and Statistics.

DK/0107-1211
**PSYKE & LOGOS.** [Psyke & logos]. **VFOAT** Psyke og Logos. (1980)-. Periodical. Danish. sa. Dansk Psykologisk Forlag, Hans Knudsens Plads 1A, DK 2100 Copenhagen Denmark. **Tel** 011 45 31 182757. **DD** 150. **CODEN** 13.
**Ind/Abst** Psychol. Abstr. (1981-); PsycINFO (1981-); PsycLit.

FI/0355-1067
**PSYKOLOGIA.** [Psykologia]. **Added/Corp** Suomen Psykologiliitto. Suomen Psykologinen Seura. (1966)-. Periodical. Finnish. bm. Fmk35.00. Psykologia, Mariankatu 7 C, 00170 Helsinki Finland. **NLM** W1 PS96.
**Ind/Abst** Psychol. Abstr. (1981-?); PsycINFO (1981-); PsycLit.

DK/0906-219X
**PSYKOLOGISK PDAGOGISK RADGIVNING.** [Psyk. pdagog. radgiv.]. **VFOAT** PPR (Holte). (1991)-. Periodical. Danish. Dansk Psykologisk Forlag, Hans Knudsens Plads 1A, DK 2100 Copenhagen Denmark. **Tel** 011 45 31 182757. **DD** 370.15. ***Continues*** *Skolepsykologi (Kbenhavn), 0037-6493.*
**Ind/Abst** PsycINFO (1968-).

DK/0900-8527
**PSYKOLOGISK SKRIFTSERIE AARHUS.** [Psykol. skr.ser. Aarhus]. **Added/Corp** Aarhus Universitet. Psykologisk Institut. **VFOAT** Psychological Reports AARHUS. (19??)-. Periodical. Danish. ir. Price varies. Aarhus Universitet, Psykologisk Institut, DK-8000 Aarhus Denmark. **Tel** 86-175511, FAX 86-175973. Index available. **Circ:** 300 (ctrl).
**Ind/Abst** Psychol. Abstr. (1978-); PsycINFO (1990-?).

HU/0230-0508
**PSZICHOLOGIA: AZ MTA PSZICHOLOGIAI INTEZETENEK FOLYOIRATA.** **Added/Corp** Magyar Tudomanyos Akademia. Pszichologiai Intezet. (1981)-. Academic Scholarly Publication. Hungarian. qt. $17.50 Austria, Croatia, Czech Republic, Slovakia, Romania, Yugoslavia, Slovenia, & Ukraine; $23.00 other. Akademiai Kiado, Publishing House of the Hungarian Academy of Sciences, Prielle Kornelia u. 19-35, H-1117 Budapest Hungary. **Tel** 011 36 1 1811991, FAX 011 36 1 1811991, telex 22-6228 AKNYO H. **(Subscription address:** Kultura, Hungarian Foreign Trading Company, PO Box 149, H-1389 Budapest 62 Hungary (011 36 1 359370)**) ED** L Halasz. **LC** BF8.H8; P74. **Bk Rev. Circ:** 1,450.

HU
**PSZICHOLOGIAI TANULMANYOK.** **Added/Corp** Magyar Tudomanyos Akademia, Budapest. Pszichologiai Bizottsag. (1958)-. Academic Scholarly Publication. Hungarian (summaries and/or abstracts in Russian and English). ir. Price varies per volume. Akademiai Kiado, Publishing House of the Hungarian Academy of Sciences, Prielle Kornelia u. 19-35, H-1117 Budapest Hungary. **Tel** 011 36 1 1811991, FAX 011 36 1 1811991, telex 22-6228 AKNYO H.

US/0033-5010
**QUADRANT (NEW YORK).** ***Suspended.*** (QUADRANT.). [Quadrant]. **Added/Corp** C.G. Jung Foundation for Analytical Psychology. No. 1 (Spring 1968)-Suspended with Vol. 25 (1992). Periodical. English. sa (Summer & Winter). $25.00. CG Jung Foundation, 28 East 39th Street, New York NY 10016. **Tel** (212)697-6430. **ED** Dr. Stephen Martin. **LC** BF173.A2; Q3. **NLM** W1 QU158D. cum. index. **Bk Rev. Ad Acc. Circ:** 2,000 (ctrl).
**Desc:** Addresses wide spectrum of Jungian thought through articles and book reviews on mythology, literature and symbolism, religion and philosophy, social and natural sciences, and clinical practice.
**Ind/Abst** Abstr. Res. Pastor. Care Couns. (19??-); Except. Hum. Exp.; Psychol. Abstr. (1985-); PsycINFO; PsycLit.

US/8756-4599
**QUARTERLY BENCHMARKS.** [Q. benchmarks]. Began with Winter 1985. Periodical. English. qt. $25.00, $7.50 back issue. Center for Constructive Change, 16 Strafford Avenue, Durham NH 03824. **Tel** (603)868-5433. **ED** Janis P Williams. **DD** 158. Index available. cum. index. **Circ:** 1,000 (ctrl).
**Desc:** Demonstrates the difference it makes to start-at-the-end in business, family life, and civic activity. Articles illustrate the principles of The Center for Constructive Change.

UK/0272-4987
**QUARTERLY JOURNAL OF EXPERIMENTAL PSYCHOLOGY. A, HUMAN EXPERIMENTAL PSYCHOLOGY, THE.** [Q. j. exp. psychol., A, Human exp. psychol.]. **Added/Corp** Experimental Psychology Society. **VFOAT** Human Experimental Psychology; Quarterly Journal of Experimental Psychology. Section A, Human Experimental Psychology. Vol. 33A, Pt. 1 (Feb. 1981)-. Periodical. English. qt. $256.00 US; £134.00 Europe; £140.00 other. Lawrence Erlbaum Associates Ltd., 27 Palmeira Mansions, Church Road, Hove East Sussex BN3 2FA England. **Tel** 011 44 273 207411. **(Subscription address:** Turpin Distribution Services Limited, Blackhorse Road, Letchworth, Hertfordshire SG6 1HN, United Kingdom.**) ED** Glyn Humphreys. **LC** QP351; .Q37. **DD** 153/.05. **NLM** W1 QU265D. **CODEN** QJEADQ. **Pr Rev.** Documents available from The Genuine Article, BIOSIS Document Express. ***Continues in part*** *Quarterly Journal of Experimental Psychology, 0033-555X.*
**Ind/Abst** Anim. Behav. Abstr.; Biol. Abstr.; CSA Neuro. Abstr. (?-?); Ergon. Abstr.; Index Med.; Life Sci. Collect.; Psychol. Abstr. (1981-); PsycINFO; PsycLit; Res. Alert [Full Cov.]; Soc. Sci. Cit. Index [Full Cov.]; SportSearch.

UK/0272-4995
**QUARTERLY JOURNAL OF EXPERIMENTAL PSYCHOLOGY. B, COMPARATIVE AND PHYSIOLOGICAL PSYCHOLOGY, THE.** [Q. j. exp. psychol., B, Comp. physiol. psychol.]. **Added/Corp** Experimental Psychology Society. **VFOAT** Comparative and Physiological Psychology; Quarterly Journal of Experimental Psychology. Section B, Comparative and Physiological Psychology. Vol. 33B, Pt. 1 (Feb. 1981)-. Periodical. English. qt. $141.00 US; £72.00 Europe; £76.00 other. Lawrence Erlbaum Associates Ltd., 27 Palmeira Mansions, Church Road, Hove East Sussex BN3 2FA England. **Tel** 011 44 273 207411. **(Subscription address:** Turpin Distribution Services Limited, Blackhorse Road, Letchworth, Hertfordshire SG6 1HN, United Kingdom.**) ED** A. Dickinson. **LC** QP351; .Q372. **DD** 152/.05. **NLM** W1 QU265E. **CODEN** QJEBDT. **Pr Rev.** Documents available from The Genuine Article, BIOSIS Document Express. ***Continues in part*** *Quarterly Journal of Experimental Psychology, 0033-555X.*
**Ind/Abst** Anim. Behav. Abstr.; Biol. Abstr.; CSA Neuro.

Abstr. (?-?); Index Med.; Life Sci. Collect.; Psychol. Abstr. (1981-); PsycINFO; PsycLit; Res. Alert [Full Cov.]; Sci. Cit. Index; SCISEARCH; Soc. Sci. Cit. Index [Full Cov.].

US/0278-4351
**QUARTERLY NEWSLETTER OF THE LABORATORY OF COMPARATIVE HUMAN COGNITION, THE.** ***Title Change.*** [Q. newsl. Lab. Comp. Hum. Cogn.]. **Main/Corp** University of California, San Diego. Laboratory of Comparative Human Cognition. Vol. 1 (Sept. 1978)-(19??). Periodical. English. qt. Laboratory of Comparative Human Cognition, 0092 Univ of California Regents, University of California San Diego, La Jolla CA 92093. **Tel** (619)534-4006, FAX (619)534-7749. **ED** Luis Moll, Esteban Diaz, Yrjo Engestrom, Terezinha Carraher, William Hall, Giyoo Hatano, David Middleton, James Wertsch, Vladimir Zinchenko. **[CCC].** cum. index. **Bk Rev. Circ:** 550. ***Continues*** *Rockefeller University. Institute for Comparative Human Development. Quarterly Newsletter of the Institute for Comparative Human Development, 0160-3361.* ***Continued by*** *Mind, Culture and Activity : An International Journal.*
**Ind/Abst** Soc. Plann. Policy Dev. Abstr.

YU/0352-6798
**RADOVI. RAZDIO FILOZOFIJE, PSIHOLOGIJE, SOCIOLOGIJE I PEDAGOGIJE / SVEUCILISTE U SPLITU, FILOZOFSKI FAKULTET--ZADAR. See** Philosophy.

IT
**RASSEGNA DI PSICOLOGIA : QUADRIMESTRALE DEI DIPARTIMENTI DI PSICOLOGIA E DI PSICOLOGIA DI SVILUPPO E SOCIALIZZAZIONE DELL'UNIVERSITA "LA SAPIENZA" DI ROMA.** **Added/Corp** Universita Degli Studi di Roma "La Sapienza." Dipartimento di Psicologia. Universita Degli Studi di Roma "La Sapienza." Dipartimento di Psicologia di Sviluppo e Socializzazione. (1984)-. Periodical. Italian. qt. L40000 Italy; L65000 other. Franco Angeli Riviste SRL, Viale Monza 106, 20127 Milan Italy. **Tel** 011 39 2 2827651, 011 39 2 289562. **LC** BF4; .R3.

RU
**RAZVITIE LICHNOSTI V USLOVIIAKH SOTSIALIZMA.** **Added/Corp** Vladimirskii Gosudarstvennyi Pedagogicheskii Institut Imeni P.I. Lebedeva-Polianskogo. (19??)-. Periodical. Russian. 0.70rub single issue. **LC** BF698.A1; R39.

UK/0270-2711
**READING PSYCHOLOGY.** [Read. psychol.]. **Added/Corp** North Texas State University. College of Education. Pupil Appraisal Center. University of North Carolina at Asheville. Dept. of Education. Vol. 1 (Fall 1979)-. Periodical. English. qt (4 issues). £77.00 UK; $127.00 other. Taylor & Francis Ltd., Rankine Road, Basingstoke Hampshire, RG24 8PR United Kingdom. **Tel** 011 44 256 840366, FAX 011 44 256 479438, telex 858540. **(Subscription address:** Taylor & Francis Inc., 1900 Frost Road, Suite 101, Bristol PA 19007-1598.**) ED** Lance M. Gentile. **LC** BF456.R2; R34. **DD** 153.6. **CODEN** RRPSDW. **[CCC].** Index available. **Bk Rev. Ad Acc. Circ:** 600. available on microfilm and microfiche from University Microfilms International (UMI).
**Desc:** Offers an exceptional selection of material covering all levels of readers- elementary, secondary, and adult. Prepared exclusively by professionals who teach reading in schools, the journal presents empirical research, ideas for teachers and practitioners, and items of general interest.
**Ind/Abst** Contents Pages Educ.; Curr. Index J. Educ.; Educ. Adm. Abstr.; Lang. Lang. Behav. Abstr.; MLA Int. Bibl. Books Artic. Mod. Lang. Lit.; Psychol. Abstr. (1979-); PsycINFO; PsycLit; Soc. Plann. Policy Dev. Abstr.; Spec. Educ. Needs Abstr.

US
**READINGS IN BEHAVIOR MODIFICATION.** **Added/Corp** Special Learning Corporation. (1978/79)-. English. an. Special Learning Corporation, 42 Boston Post Road, Guilford CT 06437. **LC** BF637.B4; R38. **DD** 153.8/5.

US/0198-912X
**READINGS IN PERSONAL GROWTH AND ADJUSTMENT.** (READINGS IN PERSONAL GROWTH AND ADJUSTMENT : ANNUAL EDITIONS.). [Read. pers. growth adjust.]. **VFOAT** Annual Editions, Personal Growth and Adjustment. 1980/81-. English. an. Dushkin Publishing Group Inc., Sluice Dock, Guilford CT 06437. **Tel** (203)453-4351, (800)243-6532, FAX (203)453-6000. **LC** BF698.A1; A55. **DD** 158/.1/05. **NLM** W1 RE105CM. ***Continues*** *Annual Editions. Readings in Personality and Adjustment, 0361-3836.*

US
**REFERENCE GUIDE TO ADDICTION COUNSELING.** (19??)-. Periodical. English. an. $209.00. Manisses Communications Group Inc., PO Box 3357, Providence RI 02906-0757. **Tel** (401)831-6020, (800)333-7771, FAX (401)861-6370.

US
**REFERENCE GUIDE TO COUNSELING CHILDREN AND ADOLESCENTS.** (19??)-. Periodical. English. an. $209.00. Manisses Communications Group Inc., PO Box 3357, Providence RI 02906-0757. **Tel** (401)831-6020, (800)333-7771, FAX (401)861-6370.

US
**REFERENCE GUIDE TO MANAGING ADDICTION PROGRAMS.** (19??)-. Periodical. English. sa. $48.00. Manisses Communications Group Inc., PO Box 3357, Providence RI 02906-0757. **Tel** (401)831-6020, (800)333-7771, FAX (401)861-6370.

SA
**REGISTER VAN SIELKUNDLIGES EN PSIGOTEGNICI VIR DIE REPUBLIEK VAN SUID-AFRIKA.** **VFOAT** Register of Psychologists and Psycho-Technicians for the Republic of South Africa. Afrikaans (English). an. Oranje-Nassau Building, 188 Schoeman Street, Posbus 205, Pretoria 0001 South Africa. **LC** BF30; .R43. **DD** 150/.25/68.

US/0090-5550
**REHABILITATION PSYCHOLOGY.** [Rehabil. psychol.]. **Added/Corp** American Psychological Association. Division of Rehabilition Psychology. Vol. 19 (Spring 1972)-. Academic Scholarly Publication. English. qt. $74.00 (institution), $39.00 (individual) US; $85.00 (institution), $44.00 (individual). Springer Publishing Company, 536 Broadway, New York NY 10012-3955. **Tel** (212)431-4370, FAX (212)941-7842. **ED** Mary A. Jansen. **LC** RM930.A1; R415. **DD** 617. **NLM** W1 RE1749M. **Bk Rev. Ad Acc. Pr Rev. Circ:** 1,500 (ctrl). Documents available from The Genuine Article. ***Continues*** *Psychological Aspects of Disability, 0091-178X.*
**Desc:** Journal addresses psychosocial and behavioral aspects of rehabilitation in a wide range of settings.
**Ind/Abst** Annals Behav. Med.; Curr. Contents Soc. Behav. Sci.; EMBASE; Hum. Resour. Abstr.; Psychol. Abstr. (1972-); PsycINFO; PsycLit; Res. Alert [Full Cov.]; Soc. Sci. Cit. Index [Full Cov.].

SA
**REPORTS FROM THE PSYCHOLOGY DEPARTMENT, UNIVERSITY OF SOUTH AFRICA.** English. ir. University of South Africa, PO Box 392, Pretoria 0001 South Africa. **Tel** 011 27 12 4298468, FAX 011 (27)12 429 3321, telex (59)350068+.
**Ind/Abst** Psychol. Abstr. (1981-); PsycINFO (1981-).

US/0034-4907
**REPRESENTATIVE RESEARCH IN SOCIAL PSYCHOLOGY.** [Represent. res. soc. psychol.]. **Added/Corp** University of North Carolina at Chapel Hill. Dept. of Psychology. (1970)-. Periodical. English. Six times a year. $14.00 institutions; $7.00 individuals. University of North Carolina at Chapel Hill, Department of Psychology, CB 3270, Chapel Hill NC 27599-3270. **Tel** (919)962-7636. **ED** Paul Bernthal. **LC** HM251; .R46. **DD** 302/.05. **CODEN** RRSPD4. cum. index. **Bk Rev. Ad Acc. Circ:** 600.
**Desc:** Promotes methodological and theoretical improvement in the field. The journal hopes to establish a priority for ascertaining the reliability of psychological phenomena, and for disseminating a less-biased sample of methodologically-sound findings than is presently available.
**Ind/Abst** Psychol. Abstr. (1970-); PsycINFO; PsycLit.

US/0362-2428
**RESEARCH COMMUNICATIONS IN PSYCHOLOGY, PSYCHIATRY AND BEHAVIOR.** [Res. commun. psychol. psych. behav.]. Vol. 1 (1976)-. Academic Scholarly Publication. English. Four times a year. $90.00 US; $102.00 other. PJD Publications Ltd., PO Box 966, Westbury NY 11590. **Tel** (516)626-0650, FAX (516)626-5546. **LC** BF1; .R48. **DD** 150/.5. **NLM** W1 RE216HP. **CODEN** RCPBDC. **[CCC].** Documents available from BIOSIS Document Express, CASDDS. ***Continues*** *Pedagogiska Sektionens Medlemsblad - Svensk Sjukskoterskeforening.*
**Ind/Abst** Biol. Abstr.; Chem. Abstr.; CSA Neuro. Abstr. (?-?); EMBASE; Life Sci. Collect.; Psychol. Abstr. (1976-); PsycINFO; PsycLit; Sci. Cit. Index (19??-19??); SCISEARCH.

US/0192-0812
**RESEARCH IN COMMUNITY AND MENTAL HEALTH.** [Res. community ment. health]. Vol. 1 (1979)-. English. ir. $73.25. JAI Press Inc., 55 Old Post Road, Suite 2, PO Box 1678, Greenwich CT 06836-1678. **Tel** (203)661-7602, FAX (203)661-0792. **ED** James R. Greenley. **LC** RA790.A1; R48. **DD** 616.8/9. **NLM** W1 RE227FI. **[CCC].**
**Ind/Abst** Psychol. Abstr. (1981-); PsycINFO (?-?); PsycLit; Soc. Plann. Policy Dev. Abstr.; Sociol. Abstr.

US/0891-4222
**RESEARCH IN DEVELOPMENTAL DISABILITIES.** [Res. dev. disabil.]. Vol. 8, No. 1 (1987)-. Periodical. English. Six times a year. $254.00 The Americas; £170.00 other. Pergamon Press, An Imprint of Elsevier Science Ltd., The Boulevard, Langford Lane, Kidlington, Oxford OX5 1GB United Kingdom. **Tel** 011 44 865 843000, 011 44 865 843699, FAX 011 44 865 843010. **(Subscription address:** Elsevier Science Ltd. Oxford Fulfillment Centre, PO Box 800, Kidlington, Oxford OX5 1DX United Kingdom.**) ED** Johnny L. Matson. **LC** HV1570.5.U65; R45. **DD** 362.1/968. **NLM** W1; RE227FIH. **CODEN** RDDIEF. **[CCC]. Pr Rev.** available on microfilm and microfiche from University Microfilms International (UMI). Documents available from The Genuine Article, BIOSIS Document Express. ***Formed by the union of*** *Analysis and Intervention in Developmental Disabilities, 0270-4684* ***and*** *Applied Research in Mental Retardation, 0270-3092.*
**Desc:** Publishes articles on all aspects of research with the developmentally disabled, with any methodologically sound approach being acceptable. Aims to publish the most current research possible.
**Ind/Abst** Annals Behav. Med.; Biol. Abstr. (1987-); Cumul. Index Nurs. Allied Health Lit.; Curr. Aware. Biol. Sci., CABS; Curr. Contents Soc. Behav. Sci.; Curr. Index J. Educ. (March 1990); Educ. Index (1992-); EMBASE; Except. Child Educ. Resour.; Index Med. (1987-); Int. Nurs. Index; Psychol. Abstr. (1987-); PsycINFO; PsycLit; Res. Alert [Full Cov.]; Soc. Sci. Cit. Index [Full Cov.].

NZ/0069-3774
**RESEARCH PROJECT.** **Main/Corp** Christchurch, N.A. University of Canterbury. Dept. of Psychology and Sociology. Monographic series. English. ir. Price varies per volume. University of Canterbury / Psychology, Department of Psychology, Christchurch New Zealand. ctrl circ.
**Desc:** Contains variable length research reports.

AT/0155-3453
**RESEARCH REPORT - AUSTRALIAN ARMY PSYCHOLOGICAL RESEARCH UNIT.** (197?)-. Monographic series. English. ir. Price varies per volume. 1st Psychological Research Unit, Northbourne House 3-39, PO Box E33, Queen Victoria Terrace, Canberra, ACT 2600 Australia.
**Ind/Abst** Psychol. Abstr. (1966-).

US/0361-1531
**REVIEW OF EXISTENTIAL PSYCHOLOGY AND PSYCHIATRY (1972).** (REVIEW OF EXISTENTIAL PSYCHOLOGY AND PSYCHIATRY.). [Rev. existent. psychol. psychiatr.]. **Added/Corp** Association of Existential Psychology and Psychiatry. **VFOAT** Review of Existential Psychology & Psychiatry. Vol. 11, No. 3 (Oct. 1972)-. Periodical. English. Three times a year. $60.00 (institutions); $35.00 (individuals); $29.95 (Back Issue). Humanities Press, 165 1st Avenue, Atlantic Highlands NJ 07716. **Tel** (908)872-1441, (800)221-3845, FAX (908)872-0717, telex 752233. **ED** Keith Hoeller, P. O. Box 23220, Seattle, WA 98102. **NLM** W1 RE253BG. **CODEN** REXPB4. Index available. **Bk Rev. Ad Acc, Adv Mgr:** J. Camlin, **Tel** (908)872-1441. **Pr Rev. Circ:** 1,000. ***Continues*** *Human Inquiries, 0363-2326.*
**Desc:** It contains essays taken broadly from literature and philosophy, as well as psychology and psychiatry.
**Ind/Abst** Philos. Index; Psychol. Abstr. (1972-); PsycINFO; PsycLit.

US/0270-1987
**REVIEW OF PERSONALITY AND SOCIAL PSYCHOLOGY.** ***Ceased.*** [Rev. person. soc. psychol.]. **Added/Corp** Society for Personality and Social Psychology. (1980)-(19??). Periodical. English. an. SAGE Periodical Press, 2455 Teller Road, Thousand Oaks CA 91320. **Tel** (805)499-0721, FAX (805)499-0871, telex 100799. **LC** BF698; .R395. **DD** 302/.05. **NLM** W1 RE253K.

US
**REVIEWS OF RESEARCH FOR PRACTITIONERS AND PARENTS.** No. 1-. English. ir. $5.00 (per issue). Center for Early Education and Development, 226 Child Development Building, University of Minnesota, Minneapolis MN 55455. **Tel** (612)376-3229. **ED** Shirley G Moore and Kathy Kolb. ctrl circ.
**Desc:** This useful volume is a must for people who have an interest in both the practical and theoretical aspects of research in child development and early education. Parents, as well as professionals and students in elementary and preschool education, social work, psychology and other related fields will find valuable information on such topics as playfulness and thinking skills, achievement, stress, etc.

CI/0352-1605
**REVIJA ZA PSIHOLOGIJU.** (REVIJA ZA PSIHOLOGIJU / CASOPIS UDRUZENJA PSIHOLOGA JUGOSLAVIJE.). [Rev. psihol.]. **Added/Corp** Udruzenje Psihologa Jugoslavije. Drustvo Psihologa Hrvatske. Vol. 1, No. 1 (1970)-. Periodical. Serbo-Croatian (Roman) (summaries and/or abstracts in English). Association of Yugoslav Psychologists, Revija za Psihologiju, Odsjek za Psihologiju, Filosof. fak., YU-41100 Zagreb Croatia. **LC** BF8.S4; R47. **NLM** W1 RE257Q. **CODEN** RPSHDY.
**Ind/Abst** Psychol. Abstr. (1970-); PsycINFO (1970-); PsycLit.

BL/0486-641X
**REVISTA BRASILEIRA DE PSICANALISE.** [Rev. bras. psicanal.]. V. 1-. Periodical. Portuguese (Portuguese). qt. **LC** RC500. **NLM** W1 RE345I.
**Ind/Abst** Psychoanal. Abstr.; Psychol. Abstr. (1976-); PsycINFO (1976-); PsycLit; PsycScan: Appl. Exp. Eng. Psych.; PsycScan: LD/MR; PsycScan: Neuropsych.

SP/0212-9205
**REVISTA CATALANA DE PSICOANALISI.** [Rev. catalana psicoanal.]. (1984)-. Periodical. Catalan. sa. Institut de Psicoanalisi de Barcelona, Alacant 27-Entresol B, 08022 Barcelona Spain. **UDC** 159.9.
**Ind/Abst** PsycINFO (1984-); PsycLit.

CL/0716-3630
**REVISTA CHILENA DE PSICOLOGIA.** [Rev. chil. psicol.]. (1978)-. Periodical. Spanish. an. Colegio de Psicologia, Loreto No. 25, Dpto. 22, Santiago, Chile. **UDC** 159.9.
**Ind/Abst** Psychol. Abstr. (1978-); PsycLit.

CU/0257-4322
**REVISTA CUBANA DE PSICOLOGIA / UNIVERSIDAD DE LA HABANA.** **Added/Corp** Universidad de La Habana. (19??)-. Periodical. Spanish (summaries and/or abstracts in English; table of contents in English). Three times a year. Ediciones Cubanas, Obispo 527, Altos ESQ Bernaza, CP 10100 Havana Cuba. **Tel** 011 632980, 631942, FAX 011 631011, telex 512337, 6540. **NLM** W1; RE3643H.

BL
**REVISTA DA UNIVERSIDADE CATOLICA DE PETROPOLIS.** **Main/Corp** Universidade Catolica de Petropolis. Portuguese (summaries and/or abstracts in English and French). $5.00 single issue. Universidade Catolica de Petropolis, Caixa Postal 944, 25.600 Petropolis Brazil. **LC** BF5; .U54A.

SP/0211-0040
**REVISTA DE HISTORIA DE LA PSICOLOGIA.** [Rev. hist. psicol.]. **Added/Corp** Universidad de Valencia. Departamento de Psicologia General. Vol. 1, No 1. (Jan. 1980)-. Periodical. Spanish (summaries and/or abstracts in English). qt. 2500ptas. U Valencia Fac Psicologia, Basica Avenida Blasco Ibanez 21, Valencia 10 Spain. **Tel** 011 34 6 3864823. **LC** BF85; .R48. **DD** 150/.9.
**Ind/Abst** Am. Hist. Life (1981-); Psychol. Abstr. (1980-); PsycINFO (1980-); PsycLit.

AG/0034-8740
**REVISTA DE PSICOANALYSIS.** [Rev. psicoanal.]. **Added/Corp** Asociacion Psicoanalitica Argentina. (July 1943)-. Periodical. Spanish (French and English). bm. $80.00. Asociacion Psicoanal-Argentina, Rodriguez Pena 1674, 1021 Buenos Aires Argentina. **Tel** 011 54 1 443518, 011 54 1 421209. **LC** RC321; .R415. **DD** 131.3405. **NLM** W1 RE463Y. **CODEN** REPSA6. Index available. cum. index. **Bk Rev. Circ:** 1,500.
**Desc:** Covers psychoanalysis.
**Ind/Abst** EMBASE; Psychol. Abstr. (1934-); PsycINFO (1934-); PsycLit.

BL
**REVISTA DE PSICOLOGIA (FORTALEZA, BRAZIL).** (REVISTA DE PSICOLOGIA.). Vol. 1, No. 1 (Jan./Dec. 1983)-. Periodical. Portuguese. ir. **LC** BF5; .R395. **DD** 150/.5.
**Ind/Abst** PsycINFO (1987-); PsycLit.

SP/0373-2002
**REVISTA DE PSICOLOGIA GENERAL Y APLICADA.** [Rev. psicol. gen. apl.]. **Added/Corp** Instituto Nacional de Psicologia Aplicada y Orientacion Profesional (Spain) Instituto Nacional de Psicotecnia (Spain) Instituto Nacional de Psicologia Aplicada y Psicotecnia (Spain). Vol. 1 No. 1 (Jan./June 1946)-. Periodical. Spanish. qt. 6900.00ptas Spain; 9200.00ptas Europe; 11500.00ptas other. Ediciones Piramide SA, Telemaco 43, 28027 Madrid Spain. **Tel** 34 1 3200119, FAX 34 1 7426631. **LC** BF5; .R4. **DD** 150.5. **NLM** W1 RE468. **CODEN** RPGAAI. cum. index. **Bk Rev**, (Qty: 20). **Ad Acc, Adv Mgr:** Palonea Rivero. **Circ:** 2,000 (ctrl).
**Ind/Abst** Indice Med. Esp.; Psychol. Abstr. (1948-); PsycINFO (1948-); PsycLit; Soc. Plann. Policy Dev. Abstr.; Sociol. Abstr.

SP/0213-4748
**REVISTA DE PSICOLOGIA SOCIAL.** (1985)-. Periodical. Multiple languages. sa. Aprendizaje SA, Carretera de Canillas 138 16 C, 28033 Madrid Spain. **Tel** 011 34 1 3883874, 011 34 1 2009338, FAX 011 34 1 3003527. **UDC** 159.9.
**Ind/Abst** PsycINFO (1988-); PsycLit.

MX
**REVISTA DE PSICOLOGIA SOCIAL Y PERSONALIDAD.** **Added/Corp** Asociacion Mexicana de Psicologia Social. (198?)-. Periodical. Spanish. Aprendizaje SA, Carretera de Canillas 138 16 C, 28033 Madrid Spain. **Tel** 011 34 1 3883874, 011 34 1 2009338, FAX 011 34 1 3003527.
**Ind/Abst** PsycINFO (1986-); PsycLit.

UY/0255-8327
**REVISTA DE PSICOTERAPIA PSICOANALITICA.** [Rev. psicoter. psicoanal.]. (1983)-. Periodical. Spanish. Asociacion Uruguaya de Psicoterapia Psicoanalitica, Canelones 2208, Montevideo Uruguay. **UDC** 615.851.1.
**Ind/Abst** PsycINFO (1986-); PsycLit.

RM/0034-8759
**REVISTA DE PSIHOLOGIE.** [Rev. psihol.]. **Added/Corp** Academia Republicii Populare Romine. (1955)-. Periodical. Romanian (summaries and/or abstracts in French and Russian). qt. DM210.00. **(Subscription address:** Kubon & Sagner, ABT Zeitschriftenimport, D 80328 Munich Germany.**) LC** BF8.R7; R46.
**Desc:** Studies and research on psychology.
**Ind/Abst** PsycINFO (1961-); PsycLit; Saf. Health Work.

SP
**REVISTA DE PSIQUIATRIA Y PSICOLOGIA MEDICA DE EUROPA Y AMERICA LATINAS.** ***Ceased.*** **See** Medical Science and Technology-Psychiatry.

US/0034-9690
**REVISTA INTERAMERICANA DE PSICOLOGIA.** [Interam. j. psychol.]. **VFOAT** Interamerican Journal of Psychology. Vol. 1, No. 1 (March 1967)-. Periodical. Spanish (English and Portuguese). sa (July and Nov). $25.00 Latin America; $30.00 US, Europe and Canada (individuals); $50.00 Latin America; $60.00 US, Canada and Europe (instituions). Universtiy Central Venezuela / Pedro Rodriguez, Apartado 47018, Caracas 1041 A Venezuela. **Tel** FAX 011 58 2 6623961. **ED** Jose Miguel Salazar (508)662-3949. **LC** BF1. **NLM** W1 RE594G. **CODEN** RIPSBZ. cum. index. **Bk Rev**, (Qty: varies). **Ad Acc. Circ:** 1,500. Documents available from The Genuine Article.
**Ind/Abst** Psychol. Abstr. (1967-); PsycINFO (1967-); PsycLit; Res. Alert [Full Cov.]; Soc. Sci. Cit. Index [Full Cov.].

MX/0187-7690
**REVISTA INTERCONTINENTAL DE PSICOLOGIA Y EDUCACION.** [Rev. intercont. psicol. educ.]. (1988)-. Periodical. Spanish. sa. Universidad Intercontinental, Insurgentes Sur No. 4135, Tlalpan, D.F. Mexico. **DD** _a370.15.
**Ind/Abst** PsycINFO (1988-); PsycLit.

CK/0120-0534
**REVISTA LATINOAMERICANA DE PSICOLOGIA.** [Rev. latinoam. psicol.]. (1969)-. Periodical. Spanish (summaries and/or abstracts in English). Three times a year. $25.00 institutions; $15.00 individuals. Revista Latinoamericana, Apartado 92621, Bogota Colombia. **Tel** 11 57 1 256 7527. **ED** Ruben Ardila Ph D. **LC** BF5; .R43. **DD** 150/.5. **NLM** W1 RE597N. **CODEN** RLPSBM. Each issue contains an index to its own contents (no volume index)--loose. cum. index. **Bk Rev**, (Qty: 10). **Ad Acc. Pr Rev. Circ:** 2,500. Documents available from The Genuine Article, BIOSIS Document Express.
**Desc:** Publishes studies with an experimental and theoretic character in all the areas of psychology.
**Ind/Abst** Biol. Abstr.; Curr. Contents Soc. Behav. Sci.; Psychol. Abstr. (1969-); PsycINFO (1969-); PsycLit; Res. Alert [Full Cov.]; Soc. Sci. Cit. Index [Full Cov.]; Women Stud. Abstr.

CK/0120-7458
**REVISTA LATINOAMERICANA DE SEXOLOGIA.** [Rev. latinoam. sexol.]. (1986)-. Periodical. Spanish. tq. Sociedad Colombiana de Sexologia, Apartado Aereo 3441, Cali, Colombia. **DD** _a155.32.
**Ind/Abst** PsycINFO (1986-); PsycLit; Soc. Plann. Policy Dev. Abstr.

MX
**REVISTA MEXICANA DE ANALISIS DE LA CONDUCTA.** **VFOAT** Mexican Journal of Behavior Analysis. Vol. 1, No. 1 (Jan. 1975)-. Periodical. English (Spanish). Three times a year (Jan., July, & Dec.). $35.00 North & Central America, $38.00 South America, $40.00 others (institutions); $20.00 North & Central America, $23.00 South America, $25.00 others (individuals). Mexican Journal of Behavior Analysis, Universidad 3004 UNAM Dr. Ayala, 04510 Mexico DF Mexico. **Tel** 011 52 5 6222304. **ED** Javier Nieto and Florente Lopez Rodriguez. Index available. cum. index. **Bk Rev. Ad Acc. Circ:** 1,000.
**Desc:** Publishes original, systematic, basic and applied studies on behavior analysis. It includes theoretical works and methodological and technical articles in the areas of pharmacology, toxicology and psychophysiology.
**Ind/Abst** Psychol. Abstr. (1975-); PsycINFO (?-?); PsycLit.

MX/0035-0079
**REVISTA MEXICANA DE PSICOLOGIA.** V. 1- (No. 1- July 1963-. Periodical. Spanish. Ensenanza Investigacion, Apdo Postal 19 174, 03910 Mexico DF Mexico. **LC** BF5. **NLM** W1 RE685K.
**Ind/Abst** PsycINFO (1984-); PsycLit.

PR
**REVISTA PUERTORRIQUENA DE PSICOLOGIA.** **Added/Corp** Asociacion de Psicologos de Puerto Rico. **VFOAT** Psicologia. (19??)-. Periodical. Spanish. mo. Asociacion Psicologia de Puerto Rico, Apdo 363435 / Ofc. Gen de Correos, San Juan Puerto Rico 00926. **Tel** (809)751-7100.

UY/0484-8268
**REVISTA URUGUAYA DE PSICOANALISIS.** [Rev. urug. psicoanal.]. **Added/Corp** Asociacion Psicoanalitica del Uruguay. Vol. 1, No. 1 (May 1956)-. Periodical. Spanish (summaries and/or abstracts in English). sa. $25.00 (two year). AS Psicoanalitica del Uruguay, Casilla de Correo 813, Montevideo Uruguay. **Tel** 011 598 2 407418. **ED** Tomas Bedo. **NLM** W1; RE735. cum. index. **Bk Rev. Circ:** 800.
**Desc:** Publishes articles of Uruguayan and other psychoanalysts and studies presented at congresses.
**Ind/Abst** Psychol. Abstr. (1977-); PsycINFO (1977-); PsycLit.

UY
**REVISTA URUGUAYA DE PSICOLOGIA.** **Added/Corp** Asociacion de Psicologos Universitarios del Uruguay. Vol. 1 No. 1 (Dec. 1978)-. Periodical. Spanish (summaries and/or abstracts in English). qt. AS Psicoanalitica del Uruguay, Casilla de Correo 813, Montevideo Uruguay. **Tel** 011 598 2 407418. cum. index. **Bk Rev. Circ:** 800.

US
**REVITALIZED SIGNS.** **VFOAT** Newsletter for the International Association for Near Death Studies; Newsletter (International Association for Near Death Studies). English. qt. $30.00 US; $35.00 other. International Association for Near-Death Studies, PO Box 7767, Philadelphia PA 19101-7767. **ED** Leon Rhodes. **Bk Rev. Circ:** 1,000 (ctrl).
**Desc:** Personal accounts and general discussion of near-death and related experiences, including book reviews, news and notes, etc.

SG
**REVUE AFRICAINE ET MALGACHE DE PSYCHOLOGIE.** Periodical. French. ir. 5,000. Union Senegalaise de Banque, Compte Banchire, 500592 Dakar Senegal. **LC** BF2; .R48.

BE
**REVUE BELGE DE PSYCHANALYSE.** **Added/Corp** Societe Belge de Psychanalyse. (198?)-. Periodical. French. Twice a year (Spring & Fall). 708F Belgium; 1000F others. Societe Belge de Psychanalyse, rue Joseph Stallaert 6, 1160 Brussels Belgium. **Tel** 011 32 2 7347748. **(Subscription address:** Revue Belge de Psychanalyse, 29 rue du Chateau Maasart, 4000 Liege Belgium.**)**

FR/0298-3850
**REVUE DE MEDECINE PSYCHOSOMATIQUE (1985).** (REVUE DE MEDECINE PSYCHOSOMATIQUE.). [Rev. med. psychosom.]. **VFOAT** Psychosomatique. New series 26E, No. 1 (1985)-. Periodical. French (summaries and/or abstracts in English and French). qt. 350.00F (individuals), 440.00F (institutions) France; 440.00F (individuals), 530.00F (institutions) other. Editions la Pensee Sauvage, BP 141, 38002 Grenoble Cedex France. **Tel** 011 33 76 871303. **NLM** W1; RE796EH. ***Continues*** *Revue de Medecine Psychosomatique et de Psychologie Medicale, 0397-930X.*
**Ind/Abst** EMBASE.

FR/1155-4452
**REVUE DE NEUROPSYCHOLOGIE / SOCIETE DE NEUROPSYCHOLOGIE DE LANGUE FRANCAISE.** **See** Medical Science and Technology-Neurology.

FR/1152-8400
**REVUE DU LITTORAL.** No. 30 (Oct. 1990)-. Periodical. French. qt. ***Continues*** *Littoral, 0751-2090.*

FR/0035-2942
**REVUE FRANCAISE DE PSYCHANALYSE : ORGANE OFFICIEL DE LA SOCIETE PSYCHANALYTIQUE DE PARIS.** **Added/Corp** Societe Psychanalytique de Paris. (July 1927)-. Periodical. French. Five times a year. 680.00F France; 820.00F other. Presses Universitaires de France, Department des Revues, 14 Avenue du Bois de l'Epine, BP 90, 91003 Evry Cedex France. **Tel** (1)60 77 82 05, FAX (1) 60 79 20 45, telex PUF 600 474 F. **ED** Ilse Barande. **[CCC]. Pr Rev.** Documents available from The Genuine Article.
**Desc:** Publishes individual research by members of the Psychoanalytical Society of Paris and by non-members, considered as a continuation of Freudian theory and practice.
**Ind/Abst** Arts Humanit. Citation Index [Select. Cov.]; PsycINFO (1928-); PsycLit; Res. Alert [Full Cov.]; Soc. Sci. Cit. Index [Full Cov.].

FR
**REVUE FRANCAISE DE PSYCHOSOMATIQUE.** (1991)-. Monographic series. French (summaries and/or abstracts in English, German and Spanish). sa (2 issues per year). 355.00F France; 410.00F other. Presses Universitaires de France, Department des Revues, 14 Avenue du Bois de l'Epine, BP 90, 91003 Evry Cedex France. **Tel** (1)60 77 82 05, FAX (1) 60 79 20 45, telex PUF 600 474 F. **NLM** W1; RE846S.

FR/0992-986X
**REVUE INTERNATIONALE DE PSYCHOLOGIE SOCIALE.** (1988)-. Periodical. English (French). qt. 380.00F France; 425.00F other. Teknea, 204 Avenue de Fronton, 31200 Toulouse France. **NLM** W1; RE886K. ***Continues*** *Psychologie et Education.*
**Ind/Abst** Psychoanal. Abstr.; PsycINFO (1988-); PsycScan: Appl. Exp. Eng. Psych.; PsycScan: LD/MR; PsycScan: Neuropsych.

FR
**REVUE INTERNATIONALE D'HISTOIRE PSYCHANALYSE.** ***Ceased.*** (19??)-(Jan. 1994). French. an. Presses Universitaires de France, Department des Revues, 14 Avenue du Bois de l'Epine, BP 90, 91003 Evry Cedex France. **Tel** (1)60 77 82 05, FAX (1) 60 79 20 45, telex PUF 600 474 F.

FR
**REVUE PRATIQUE DE PSYCHOLOGIE DE LA VIE SOCIALE ET DE L'HYGIENE MENTALE.** French. qt. 200.00F France; 270.00F other (one year), 360.00F France; 490.00F other (two year). Fedn Natl Assn Croix Mar Aide Sante Ment, 31 rue de Liege, F-75008 Paris France. **Tel** 011 33 1 43877344.

CN/0225-9885
**REVUE QUEBECOISE DE PSYCHOLOGIE.** [Rev. quebecoise psychol.]. Vol. 1 (Feb. 1980)-. Periodical. French. Three times a year (Spring, Summer and Fall). 35.00Can$ (individuals), 50.00Can$ (institutions) Canada; 40.00Can$ (individuals). Universite du Quebec a Trois-Rivieres, CP 500, Des Forges Trois-Rivieres, Quebec G9A 5H7 Canada. **Tel** (819)376-5085, FAX (819)376-5092. **ED** P. Michaud. **DD** 158/.05. **Bk Rev. Circ:** 900.
**Desc:** General review of applied psychology for psychologists and allied professions.
**Ind/Abst** Point Repere (1983-); Psychol. Abstr. (1988-); PsycINFO (1986-); PsycLit.

●RM/1220-5419
**REVUE ROUMAINE DE PSYCHOLOGIE / ACADEMIE ROUMAINE. Added/Corp** Academia Romana. Vol. 36, No. 1 (Jan./July 1992)-. Periodical. French (English and French). Twice a year. $95.00. **(Subscription address:** Orion Press SRL, SPL Independentei 202-A, Bucharest 6 Romania.**)** **LC** BF1; .A187. **NLM** W1; RE965E. ***Continues*** *Revue de Psychologie (Bucharest, Romania).*

CN/0843-5952
**REVUE TIRES A PART.** [Rev. Tires part]. **Added/Corp** Association des Professeurs de Psychologie du Reseau Collegial du Quebec. College de Bois-de-Boulogne. **VFOAT** Tires a Part. Vol. 10, Sept. (1989)-. French (summaries and/or abstracts in English). Gratuit pour les membres de l'Association des professeurs de psychologie du Reseau Collegial du Quebec. Tires a Part, Cegep Bois-de-Boulogne, 10555 Avenue Bois-de-Boulogne, Montreal Quebec H4N 1L4 Canada. **Tel** (514)332-3000. **DD** 150/.5. ***Continues*** *Tires a Part., 0823-6291.*

CG
**REVUE ZAIROISE DE PSYCHOLOGIE ET DE PEDAGOGIE. Added/Corp** Universite Nationale du Zaire, Campus de Kisangani. Faculte des Sciences Psychologiques et Pedagogiques. Niversite Nationale du Zaire, Campus de Kisangani. Faculte des Sciences Psychologiques et Pedagogiques. Centre de Recherches. Universite Nationale du Zaire, Campus de Kisangani. Centre de Recherches Interdisciplinaires pour le Developpement de l'Education. Universite Nationale du Zaire, Campus de Kisangani. Faculte de Psychologie et des Sciences de l'Education. Vol. 1 (July 1972)-. French (summaries and/or abstracts in English). $8.00. Universite Nationale du Zaire / Congo, Boite Postale 2012, Kisangani Congo Zaire. **LC** BF2; .R485. **DD** 370.15/05.

IT/0391-6081
**RICERCHE DI PSICOLOGIA.** [Ric. psicol.]. Vol. 1, No. 1 (Jan. 1977)-. Periodical. Italian (summaries and/or abstracts in English). Four times a year. L110000 Italy; L150000 other. Franco Angeli Riviste SRL, Viale Monza 106, 20127 Milan Italy. **Tel** 011 39 2 2827651, 011 39 2 289562. **ED** Marcello Cesa-Bianchi. **LC** BF76.5; .R5. **NLM** W1 RI106. ***Continues*** *Annali dell'Istituto di Psicologia, 0391-996X.*
**Ind/Abst** Life Sci. Collect.; Psychol. Abstr. (1979-); PsycINFO (1979-); PsycLit.

●US
**RICHARD E PIGGLE. STUDI PSICOANALITICI DEL BAMBINO E DELL'ADOLESCENTE.** (Spring 1993)-. Periodical. English. Twice a year. L70000 institutions; L55000 individuals. Il Pensiero Scientifico Editore s.r.l., Via Bradano 3C, 00199 Rome Italy. **Tel** 011 39 6 86207158, 86207159, 86207168, 86207169, FAX 011 39 6 86207160.
**Desc:** Covers psychoanalysis of children and adolescents.

IT/0035-6492
**RIVISTA DI PSICOANALISI.** [Riv. psicoanal.]. (1955)-. Periodical. Italian. qt. L90.000 (individuals), L120.000 (institutions) Italy; $110.00 (individuals), $130.00 (institutions) other. Edizioni Borla, Via delle Fornaci 50, 00165 Rome, Italy. **Tel** 011 39 6 39376728. **UDC** 616.89. **CODEN** RPSAB.
**Ind/Abst** Psychoanal. Abstr.; PsycINFO (1990-); PsycScan: Appl. Exp. Eng. Psych.; PsycScan: LD/MR; PsycScan: Neuropsych.

IT/0392-9787
**RIVISTA DI PSICOLOGIA ANALITICA.** [Riv. psicol. anal.]. (1970)-. Monographic series. Italian. Twice a year (July & Oct.). L50000 Italy; L100000 others. Carotenuto Aldo, Via Gallonio 8, 00161 Rome Italy. **Tel** 11 39 6 44291151, 44290756. **LC** UNC.
**Ind/Abst** Psychol. Abstr. (1981-).

IT
**RIVISTA DI PSICOLOGIA CLINICA.** Vol. 1, No. 1 (Jan./April 1987)-. Periodical. Italian (summaries and/or abstracts in English). Three times a year. Nuova Italia Scientifica, Via Sardegna 50, 00187 Rome Italy. **NLM** W1; RE519FJ.

IT
**RIVISTA DI PSICOLOGIA DELL'ARTE.** **See** The Arts.

IT
**RIVISTA ITALIANA DI GRUPPOANALISI.** (19??)-. Italian. Three times a year. L60000 Italy; L120000 other. Societa Editrice Sgai, V Procaccini 11, 20154 Milan Italy. **Tel** 011 39 2 3495601.

IT
**RUOLO TERAPEUTICO.** Italian. Three times a year. L100000.00 institutions; L50000.00 individuals. Il Ruolo Terapeutico, Via G Milani 12, 20133 Milan Italy. **Tel** 011 39 2 70636457, FAX 011 39 2 70636457.

US/0277-4240
**RUTGERS PROFESSIONAL PSYCHOLOGY REVIEW.** (RUTGERS PROFESSIONAL PSYCHOLOGY REVIEW / THE GRADUATE SCHOOL OF APPLIED AND PROFESSIONAL PSYCHOLOGY, RUTGERS--THE STATE UNIVERSITY OF NEW JERSEY.). [Rutgers prof. psychol. rev.]. Vol. 1-. Monographic series. English. an. Price varies per volume. Transaction Publishers / Rutgers State University, New Brunswick NJ 08903. **Tel** (908)932-2280 Ext. 105, FAX (908)932-3138. **ED** Donald R Peterson. **DD** 150/.5. **NLM** W1 RU933G.

IT/0390-5179
**SAGGI NEUROPSICOLOGIA INFANTILE PSICOPEDAGOGIA RIABILITAZIONE.** [Saggi neuropsicol. infant. psicopedagog. riabil.]. (1975)-. Periodical. Multiple languages. sa. L45000.00 Italy; L55000.00 other. Instituto Scientifico e Medea, La Nostra Famiglia, 22040 Bosisio Parino Co Italy. **Tel** 011 39 31 877507, FAX 011 39 31 877559. **UDC** 159. Index available. cum. index. **Bk Rev. Ad Acc. Circ:** 1,000 (ctrl).
**Ind/Abst** Soc. Sci. Cit. Index [Select. Cov.].

II/0304-5110
**SAMIKSA.** [Samiksa]. **Added/Corp** Indian Psychoanalytical Society. (1947)-. Academic Scholarly Publication. English. qt. $15.00. Indian Psychoanalytic Society, 14 Parsabagan Lane, Calcutta India. **Tel** 91 33 508788. **ED** Dr. T K Chatterjee. **LC** BF173.A2; S3. **NLM** W1 SA449. **Bk Rev**, (Qty: 4).
**Ind/Abst** EMBASE; Psychol. Abstr. (1951-).

US/0270-6210
**SAN FRANCISCO JUNG INSTITUTE LIBRARY JOURNAL, THE. Added/Corp** Virginia Allan Detloff Library. Vol. 1, No. 1 (Autumn 1979)-. Periodical. English. qt. $50.00 (institutions), $36.00 (individuals) US; $42.00 other. CG Jung Institute of San Francisco, 2040 Gough Street, Detloff Library, San Francisco CA 94109. **Tel** (415)771-8055. **ED** John Beebe. Index available. **Bk Rev. Ad Acc, Adv Mgr Tel** (415)221-2266. **Circ:** 1,500.
**Desc:** Presents reviews of films and culture. Based on the psychology of C.G. Jung, appeals to professional and lay readers interested in myth, spirituality, gender, psychology and media.
**Ind/Abst** Film Lit. Index (19??-).

CN
**SANS FRONTIERES :LES FORCES PSYCHOLOGIQUES. Added/Corp** Institut de Formation et de Reeducation de Montreal. Vol. 1, No. 1 (Autumn 1986)-. French. sa (Spring and Fall). 7.50Can$. Sans Frontieres, 55 Ouest Boulevard Gouin, Montreal Quebec H3L 1H9 Canada. **Tel** (514)331-6861. **DD** 155.2/05.

FR
**SANTE DE L'ECOLIER.** French. Four times a year (Jan., Apr., July, and Oct.). 177.00F. La Sante de l'Ecolier, 23 rue de Lorraine, 16800 Soyaux, France. **Tel** 011 33 45 953927. ctrl circ.
**Desc:** Medical and psychological news for the health of children and family.

US/0740-0853
**SAYBROOK REVIEW.** ***Ceased.*** [Saybrook rev.]. Vol. 4, No. 1 (1982)-?. Periodical. English. an. Saybrook Institute, 1550 Sutter Street, San Francisco CA 94109. **Tel** (415)441-5034, FAX (415)441-7556. **ED** Rudolph J Melone. **LC** BF204; .H869. **NLM** W1 SA999M. **Bk Rev. Circ:** 800. ***Continues*** *Humanistic Psychology Institute Review, 0272-1627.*
**Desc:** Features the work of members of Saybrook's executive faculty. Consists of papers invited from specific scholars. Each issue revolves around a particular topic in the fields of psychology or human science.
**Ind/Abst** Psychol. Abstr. (1982-); PsycINFO; PsycLit.

XO/0083-419X
**SBORNIK FILOZOFICKEJ FAKULTY UNIVERZITY KOMENSKEHO. PSYCHOLOGICA.** [Zb. Filoz. fak. Univ. Komenskeho, Psychol.]. **Added/Corp** Univerzita Komenskeho v Bratislave. Filozoficka Fakulta. **VFOAT** Zbornik Filozofickej Fakulty Univerzity Komenskeho. Psychologica; Psychologica. (1961)-. Periodical. Slovak (summaries and/or abstracts in English, French, German and Russian; table of contents in English, French, German and Russian). **LC** BF26; .B72. **CODEN** PSYAD8. ***Continues in part*** *Sbornik Filosoficke Fakulty Univerzity Komenskeho v Bratislave.*
**Ind/Abst** Psychol. Abstr. (1963-1967); PsycLit.

SW/0284-5717
**SCANDINAVIAN JOURNAL OF BEHAVIOUR THERAPY.** [Scand. j. behav. ther.]. **VFOAT** Nordisk Tidskrift for Beteendeterapi. (1984)-. Periodical. Multiple languages. qt. Kr100.00. Swedish Association of Behaviour Therapy, Department of Psychiatry, University of Uppsala, S 75017 Uppsala Sweden. **Tel** 011 46 18 178322. **UDC** 159. ***Continues*** *Nordisk Tidskrift for Beteendeterapi, 0345-1402.*

SW/0036-5564
**SCANDINAVIAN JOURNAL OF PSYCHOLOGY.** [Scand. j. psychol.]. Vol. 1 (1960)-. Periodical. English. qt. Kr825.00, $139.00. Scandinavian University Press, PO Box 2959 Toeyen, N 0608 Oslo 6 Norway. **Tel** 011 47 2 2575400, FAX 011 47 2 2575353, telex 71896 UROR N. **(Subscription address:** Scandinavian University Press, 200 Meacham Ave., Elmont NY 11003.**)** **ED** Kenneth Hugdahl. **LC** BF1. **DD** 150/.5. **NLM** W1 SC153. **CODEN** SJPYA2. **[CCC].** Index available in last issue of volume--attached. cum. index. **Bk Rev. Ad Acc. Pr Rev. Circ:** 550 (ctrl). Documents available from The Genuine Article, BIOSIS Document Express.
**Desc:** Devoted to original scientific contributions from all fields of psychology. Publishes regular articles with theoretical and/or empirical orientation, short notes, and reviews of Scandinavian books and dissertations on psychology written in English.
**Ind/Abst** Appl. Soc. Sci. Index Abstr.; Biol. Abstr.; Curr. Contents Soc. Behav. Sci.; Ergon. Abstr.; Index Med.; Middle East Abstr. Index; Life Sci. Collect.; Psychol. Abstr. (1960-); PsycINFO; PsycLit; Res. Alert [Full Cov.]; Risk Abstr.; Soc. Plann. Policy Dev. Abstr.; Soc. Sci. Cit. Index [Full Cov.]; Sociol. Abstr.

NO/0106-2301
**SCANDINAVIAN PSYCHOANALYTIC REVIEW, THE.** [Scand. psychoanal. rev.]. Vol. 1 (1978)-. Periodical. English. sa. kr380.00. Munksgaard International Publishers Ltd, PO Box 2148, DK-1016 Copenhagen K Denmark. **Tel** 011 45 33 12 70 30, FAX 011 45 33 12 93 87, telex 19431 MUNKS DK. **ED** Lis Lind, Finn Askevold, Martin Lotz, Henning Paikin, and Jukka Valimaki. **LC** RC500; .S35. **DD** 150/.19/505. **NLM** W1 SC154N. **[CCC].** Index available. **Bk Rev. Ad Acc. Circ:** 550 (ctrl).
**Desc:** Concerns psychoanalysis and psychology.
**Ind/Abst** Psychol. Abstr. (1978-); PsycINFO; PsycLit; Romant. Move.

CN/0704-500X
**SCHEDULE-INDUCED BEHAVIOR. RESEARCH & THEORY.** (SCHEDULE-INDUCED BEHAVIOR.). [Sched.-induc. behav., Res. theory]. (1977)-. Periodical. English. ir. Human Sciences Press, PO Box 735, 233 Spring Street, New York NY 10013. **Tel** (212)620-8000, FAX (212)807-1047, telex 23421139. **ED** W. P. Christian, R. W. Schaeffer, G. D. King. **NLM** W1 SC166.

**Desc:** Information on behavior and reinforcement schedules.
**Ind/Abst** Psychol. Abstr. (1977-).

US/0160-5585
**SCHOOL PSYCHOLOGIST, THE.** [Sch. psychol.]. **Added/Corp** American Psychological Association. Division of School Psychology. American Psychological Association. Division of School Psychology. Newsletter. (19??)-. Periodical. English. qt. $25.00. American Psychological Association, 750 First Street Northeast, Washington DC 20002. **Tel** (800)374-2721, (202)336-5600, (subscriptions - (202)336-5600. **(Subscription address:** APA Division 16, 750 First Street Northeast, Washington DC 20002.**)** **CODEN** SPSYDS.

UK/0143-0343
**SCHOOL PSYCHOLOGY INTERNATIONAL.** [Sch. psychol. int.]. **VFOAT** SPI. Vol. 1 (July/Aug. 1979)-. Periodical. English. qt. £130.00. Sage Publications Ltd., 6 Bonhill Street, London EC2A 4PU, UK. **Tel** 071 374 0645, FAX 071 374 8741, telex 296207 SAGE G. **ED** Robert L. Burden and Caven S. McLoughlin. **LC** LB1051; .S3733. **DD** 370.15/05. **[CCC]. Acid Free.**
**Desc:** Highlights the concerns of those who provide quality mental health, educational, therapeutic and support services to schools and their communities throughout the world.
**Ind/Abst** Br. Educ. Index; Psychol. Abstr. (1979-); PsycINFO; PsycLit; Spec. Educ. Needs Abstr.

US/1045-3830
**SCHOOL PSYCHOLOGY QUARTERLY.** (SCHOOL PSYCHOLOGY QUARTERLY : THE OFFICIAL JOURNAL OF THE DIVISION OF SCHOOL PSYCHOLOGY, AMERICAN PSYCHOLOGICAL ASSOCIATION.). [Sch. psychol. q.]. **Added/Corp** American Psychological Association. Division of School Psychology. Vol. 5, No. 1 (Spring 1990)-. Periodical. English. Four times a year. $85.00 (institutions); $100.00 others. Guilford Publications Inc., 72 Spring Street, New York NY 10012. **Tel** (212)431-9800, (800)365-7006, FAX (212)966-6708. **ED** Joseph Witt. **LC** LB1027.55; .P76. **DD** 370.15/0973/05. **NLM** W1; SC252. **CODEN** SPSQE5. **[CCC].** available on microfilm and microfiche from University Microfilms International (UMI). ***Continues*** *Professional School Psychology, 0886-3016.*
**Ind/Abst** Psychol. Abstr. (1986-); PsycINFO; PsycLit; Soc. Plann. Policy Dev. Abstr.

US/0279-6015
**SCHOOL PSYCHOLOGY REVIEW.** [School psych. rev.]. **Added/Corp** National Association of School Psychologists. Vol. 9 (Winter 1980)-. Periodical. English. Four times a year (Feb., May, Aug., Nov.). $80.00 (institutions); $50.00 (individuals). National Association of School Psychologists, 8455 Colesville Road 1000, Silver Spring MD 20910. **Tel** (301)608-0500. **ED** Stephen Elliott. **LC** LB1051; .S373. **DD** 370.15. **Bk Rev. Ad Acc. Pr Rev. Circ:** 15,000 (ctrl). available on microfilm and microfiche from University Microfilms International (UMI). Documents available from The Genuine Article. ***Continues*** *School Psychology Digest, 0160-5569.*
**Desc:** Describes practices of school psychologists who consult behavior/learning problems, help develop remedial and prevention programs for pupils, parents, teachers and other staff.
**Ind/Abst** Acad. Search (July 1993-); Contents Pages Educ.; Curr. Contents Soc. Behav. Sci.; Curr. Index J. Educ.; Educ. Index; Except. Child Educ. Resour. (19??-19??); INFO-SOUTH Abstr.; Mag. Search; Multicult. Educ. Abstr.; Psychol. Abstr. (1980-); PsycINFO; PsycLit; Res. Alert [Full Cov.]; Soc. Sci. Cit. Index [Full Cov.].

SZ
**SCHWEIZERISCHE ZEITSCHRIFT FUER PSYCHOLOGIE. Added/Corp** Schweizerische Gesellschaft fuer Psychologie und Ihre Anwendungen. **VFOAT** Revue Suisse de Psychologie. Vol. 46, No. 1/2 (1987)-. Periodical. German (French; summaries and/or abstracts in English, French and German). Four times a year. 81.00F Germany; 85.00F other. Verlag Hans Huber Ag Bern, Laenggass Strasse 76, CH 3000 Bern 9 Switzerland. **Tel** 011 41 31 3004500. Documents available from The Genuine Article. ***Continues*** *Psychologie (Bern, Switzerland), 0033-2976; Schweizereische Zeitschrift fuer Psychologie und Ihre Anwendungen.*
**Ind/Abst** Curr. Contents Soc. Behav. Sci.; PsycINFO (1990-); PsycLit; Res. Alert [Full Cov.]; Soc. Sci. Cit. Index [Full Cov.].

SZ
**SCHWEIZERISCHE ZEITSCHRIFT FUER PSYCHOLOGIE UND IHRE ANWENDUNGEN. BEIHEFT.** ***Title Change.*** **VFOAT** Revue Suisse de Psychologie et de Psychologie Appliquee. (1943)-(19??). Monographic series. Multiple languages (French and German). qt. Verlag Hans Huber Ag Bern, Laenggass Strasse 76, CH 3000 Bern 9 Switzerland. **Tel** 011 41 31 3004500. ***Continued by*** *Schweizerische Zeitschrift fuer Psychologie, 0036-7869.*

CN/0841-7741
**SCIENCE ET COMPORTEMENT.** [Sci. comport.]. **Added/Corp** Association Scientifique pour la Modification du Comportement. Vol. 18, No 1/2 (1988)-. Periodical. French. Three times a year. 80.00Can$ Canada; 90.00Can$ other. ASMC / Association Scientifique pour la Modification du Comportement, 309 rue Godin, Repentigny Quebec J6A 5Z8 Canada. **Tel** (514)585-2247 ext. 2950. **ED** Andre Marchand. **DD** 616.89/142/05. **NLM** W1; SC693S. Index available. cum. index. **Bk Rev. Ad Acc. Circ:** 400 (ctrl). ***Continues*** *Revue de Modification du Comportement, 0383-056X.*
**Desc:** Scientific reports, case studies, and essays related to behavior modification.
**Ind/Abst** Point Repere; PsycINFO (1979-); PsycLit.

US/0586-5719
**SCIENTIFIC AMERICAN RESOURCE LIBRARY. READINGS IN PSYCHOLOGY.** (SCIENTIFIC AMERICAN RESOURCE LIBRARY: READINGS IN PSYCHOLOGY.). **VFOAT** Readings in Psychology. Vol. 1 (1969)-. English. W H Freeman & Company Publishers, 41 Madison Avenue, New York NY 10010. **LC** BF21; .S2. **DD** 150/.8.

US/0883-8941
**SECRETS OF WINNERS.** ***Suspended.*** [Secrets winners]. Premier Issue (1985)-Suspended ?. Periodical. English. mo. $36.00. Successful Publishing Company, 157 Whooping Loop, Altamonte Springs FL 32701. **DD** 158.

JA
**SEINEN SHINRI. VFOAT** Youth Problem. Feb. 1977-. Periodical. Japanese (Japanese). Kaneko Shobo, 3-7 Otsuka 3, Bunkyo-ku Tokyo 112 Japan. **LC** HQ799.J3; S324.

JA/0289-2405
**SEIRI SHINRIGAKU TO SEISHIN SEIRIGAKU.** [Seiri shinrigaku to seishin seirigaku]. **VFOAT** Japanese Journal of Physiological Psychology and Psychophysiology. (1983)-. Periodical. Multiple languages. sa. Japanese Society for Physiological Psychology and Psychophysiology, Hiroshima University, Faculty of Integrated Arts and Sciences, 1-1-89 Higashisenda-machi, Naka-ku Naka-ku, Hiroshima 730 Japan. **DD** 152.
**Ind/Abst** PsycINFO (1986-); PsycLit.

US/8756-1425
**SELF-HELP SOURCEBOOK, THE.** [Self-help sourceb.]. **Added/Corp** New Jersey Self-Help Clearinghouse. American Self-Help Clearinghouse. **VFOAT** Self Help Sourcebook. (1986)-. English. an. $9.00. Self-Help Clearinghouse, St Clares-Riverside Medical Center, Denville NJ 07834. **Tel** (201)625-9565. **ED** E. Madara and A. Meese. **LC** HV547; .S435. **DD** 361.6/025/73. **NLM** W 22; AA1 S4.
**Desc:** Directory of over 500 national and model self-help groups. Includes sections on national helplines, self-help clearinghouses, rare disorders and ideas for developing groups.

US/0160-4430
**SELF-IN-PROCESS SERIES.** Vol. 1 (1977)-. Monographic series. English. ir. Price varies per volume. Human Sciences Press, PO Box 735, 233 Spring Street, New York NY 10013. **Tel** (212)620-8000, FAX (212)807-1047, telex 23421139. **LC** UNC. **NLM** W1 SE354.

UK/0143-7526
**SENSORY PERCEPTION AND INFORMATION PROCESSING.** [Sens. percept. inf. process.]. (1979)-. English. mo. £75.00. SUBIS, Mansion House, 19 Kingfield Road, Sheffield S11 9AS England. **Tel** 011 44 114 255 4433, FAX 011 44 114 255 4626. **DD** _a016.574. **Ad Acc.**
**Desc:** Current awareness service for researchers and clinicians.

US/0146-0846
**SERIES IN CLINICAL AND COMMUNITY PSYCHOLOGY, THE.** [Ser. clin. community psychol.]. (197?)-. Monographic series. English. ir. Price varies per volume. Taylor & Francis Ltd., Rankine Road, Basingstoke Hampshire, RG24 8PR United Kingdom. **Tel** 011 44 256 840366, FAX 011 44 256 479438, telex 858540. **(Subscription address:** Taylor & Francis Inc., 1900 Frost Road, Suite 101, Bristol PA 19007-1598.**) ED** Charles D. Speilberger & Irwin G. Sarason. **LC** UNC. ***Continues*** *Series in Clinical Psychology.*
**Desc:** Series specializing in clinical and community psychology. Volumes have covered topics such as treatment test anxiety and anger disorders.

US/8756-467X
**SERIES IN HEALTH PSYCHOLOGY AND BEHAVIORAL MEDICINE, THE.** [Ser. health psychol. behav. med.]. (1985)-. Monographic series. English. ir. Price varies per volume. Taylor & Francis Ltd., Rankine Road, Basingstoke Hampshire, RG24 8PR United Kingdom. **Tel** 011 44 256 840366, FAX 011 44 256 479438, telex 858540. **(Subscription address:** Taylor & Francis Inc., 1900 Frost Road, Suite 101, Bristol PA 19007-1598.**) ED** Charles D. Spielberger. **DD** 616.
**Desc:** Series specializing in health psychology and behavioral medicine. Volumes have covered topics such as occupational stress, the ecology of stress, death anxiety, and behavioral analysis of societies and cultural practices.

●US
**SEXUAL ABUSE : A JOURNAL OF RESEARCH AND TREATMENT.** (1994)-. Periodical. English. Four times a year. $100.00 institutions, $40.00 individuals US; $115.00 institutions, $47.00 individuals other. Plenum Press, 233 Spring Street, New York NY 10013-1578. **Tel** (212)620-8000, (800)221-9369, FAX (212)463-0742, (212)807-1047, telex 23/421139. ***Continues*** *Annals of Sex Research, 0843-4611.*

JA/0388-7588
**SHINKEI SEISHIN YAKURI. See** Medical Science and Technology-Neurology.

JA
**SHINRIGAKU. Main/Corp** Tokyo Daigaku. Kyoyo Gakubu. Shinrigaku Kenkyushitsu. **VFOAT** Series of Psychology. Japanese (Japanese). Kyoyo Gakubu Shinrigaku, 865 Kombamachi Meguro-ku, Tokyo Japan. **LC** BF8.J3; T64A.

JA/0386-1058
**SHINRIGAKU HYORON.** [Shinrigaku hyoron]. **VFOAT** Japanese Psychological Review. Japanese (summaries and/or abstracts in German and English). $120.00. Kyoto University / Department of Psychology, Daigaku Bungakubu Shinrigaku Kyushitsu, 54 Shogoin Kawara-cho, Sakyo-ku Kyoto 606 Japan. **LC** BF8.J3; S45. **CODEN** SHHYDJ.
**Ind/Abst** Psychol. Abstr. (1969-).

JA/0021-5236
**SHINRIGAKU KENKYU.** [Shinrigaku kenkyu]. **Added/Corp** Nihon Shinri Gakkai. **VFOAT** Japanese Journal of Psychology. Vol. 1 (1923)-. Periodical. Japanese (English and German; summaries and/or abstracts in English and German). bm. $130.00. Japanese Psychological Association, 37 13 4 Chome 802 Hongo, Bunkyo Ku Tokyo 113 Japan. **(Subscription address:** Kyowa Book Company Inc., 1 38 Kanda Jinbocho Chiyoda-ku, Tokyo 101 Japan.**) CODEN** SHKEA5. **Pr Rev.** Documents available from The Genuine Article.
**Ind/Abst** Curr. Contents Soc. Behav. Sci.; Index Med.; Life Sci. Collect.; Psychol. Abstr. (1929-); PsycINFO (1929-); PsycLit; Res. Alert [Full Cov.]; Soc. Plann. Policy Dev. Abstr.

JA/0385-0307
**SHINSHIN IGAKU. See** Medical Science and Technology.

SP/1130-149X
**SI..., ENTONCES... .** [Si entonces]. (1985)-. Periodical. Spanish (English). Twice a year. $17.00. Si Entonces, Apartado de Correos 761, 43080 Tarragona, Spain. **Tel** 011 34 77 231165. **UDC** 159.9. Index available (bound in all issues). cum. index. **Pr Rev.**
**Desc:** Interdisciplinary journal of psychology, neuroscience, psychiatry, sociology, and philosophy.

AU
**SIGMUND FREUD HOUSE BULLETIN. Main/Corp** Sigmund Freud Society. **Added/Corp** Sigmund Freud-Gesellschaft. Vol. 1 No. 1 (1975)-. Bulletin. English (summaries and/or abstracts in German). Bergrasse 19, A-1090 Vienna Austria. **ED** Editorial committee: 1975- H. Leupold-Lowenthal.
**Ind/Abst** Psychol. Abstr. (1986-); PsycINFO (1986-); PsycLit.

US/0093-0407
**SLEEP RESEARCH.** [Sleep res.]. **Added/Corp** University of California, Los Angeles. Brain Information Service. University of California, Los Angeles. Brain Research Institute. (1972)-. English. an. $85.00. Brain Information Service, 43 367 CHS, UCLA School of Medicine, Los Angeles CA 90024. **Tel** (310)825-3417, FAX (310)206-3499. **DD** 612. **NLM** ZWL 108 S6326. ***Supersedes*** *Sleep Bibliography, 0362-0514.*

IE
**SOCIAL ATTITUDES IN NORTHERN IRELAND. See** Sociology.

NZ/0301-2212
**SOCIAL BEHAVIOR AND PERSONALITY. See** Sociology.

US/0730-6962
**SOCIAL PSYCHOLOGY (GUILFORD, CONN.).** (SOCIAL PSYCHOLOGY.). [Soc. psychol.]. **VFOAT** Annual Editions. Social Psychology. (19??)-. English. an. Dushkin Publishing Group Inc., Sluice Dock, Guilford CT 06437. **Tel** (203)453-4351, (800)243-6532, FAX (203)453-6000. **LC** HM251; .A752. **DD** 302. ***Continues*** *Annual Editions. Readings in Social Psychology.*

US/0190-2725
**SOCIAL PSYCHOLOGY QUARTERLY.** **See** Sociology.

SA/0081-2463
**SOUTH AFRICAN JOURNAL OF PSYCHOLOGY.** [S. Afr. j. psychol.]. **Added/Corp** Psychological Institute of the Republic of South Africa. South African Psychological Association. Foundation for Education, Science, and Technology (South Africa). Bureau for Scientific Publications. **VFOAT** Suid-Afrikaanse Tydskrif vir Sielkunde; Suid-Afrikaanse Joernaal vir Psigologie; Suid-Afrikaanse Joernaal vir Sielkunde; Psychology. Sielkunde. Vol. 1 (1970)-. Periodical. Afrikaans (English). qt. R108.00 South Africa; R110.00 other. Foundation for Education Science & Technology, PO Box 1758, Pretoria 0001 South Africa. **Tel** 011 27 12 3226404, FAX 011 27 12 3207803. **LC** BF1; .S58. **DD** 150/.5. **NLM** W1 SO905NP. **CODEN** SAJPDL. **[CCC].** Documents available from BIOSIS Document Express. ***Absorbed*** *Journal of Behavioral Science; South African Psychologist.*
**Ind/Abst** Biol. Abstr.; Cumul. Index Nurs. Allied Health Lit.; Ergon. Abstr.; Life Sci. Collect.; Psychol. Abstr. (1970-); PsycINFO (1970-); PsycLit; Stud. Women Abstr.

US/0891-2726
**SOVIET JOURNAL OF PSYCHOLOGY.** [Sov. j. psychol.]. **Added/Corp** Akademiia nauk SSSR. **VFOAT** Psychologicheskii Zhurnal; Psikhologicheskii Zhurnal. (1987)-. Periodical. English (Russian; translations available in Russian). bm. $622.00 (institutions), $397.00 (individuals) US; $735.00 (institutions), $485.00 (individuals) other. International Universities Press Inc., 59 Boston Post Road, PO Box 1524, Madison CT 06443-1524. **Tel** (203)245-4000, FAX (203)245-0775, telex 282986 IUP BK. **ED** B.F. Lomov, V.S. Shustikov and L.I. Antsyferova. **LC** BF1; .P44. **DD** 150/.5. **NLM** W1; PS18QV. **Bk Rev. Pr Rev.**
**Desc:** Features Soviet studies in the field of psychology. Subjects include general and educational psychology, social and medical psychology, occupational and management psychology, psychophysiology, psycholinguistics, human engineering, experimental psychology, and more.
**Ind/Abst** Psychol. Abstr. (1990-); PsycINFO (1990-).

US
**SPAB NEWSLETTER / SOCIETY OF PSYCHOLOGISTS IN ADDICTIVE BEHAVIORS.** **Added/Corp** Society of Psychologists in Addictive Behaviors. Vol. 1, No. 1 (Winter/Spring 1990)-. Newsletter. English. **NLM** W1; SP11.

NE/0167-5311
**SPANISH-LANGUAGE PSYCHOLOGY.** **VFOAT** Spanish Language Psychology. Vol. 1, No. 1 (Mar. 1981)-. Periodical. English. qt. $60.00. North-Holland Publishing Company, PO Box 211, Amsterdam The Netherlands. **LC** BF1; .A189. **DD** 150/.5. **NLM** Z 7203 S735. **CODEN** SLPSDZ.

US/1047-286X
**SPECIAL REPORT ON PERSONALITIES.** ***Title Change.*** [Spec. rep. pers.]. **VFOAT** Personalities; Special Report, Personalities; Special Report. (Nov. 1988/Jan. 1989)-(199?). Periodical. English. qt. Whittle Communications, 333 Main Avenue, Knoxville TN 37902. **Tel** (615)595-5000, FAX (615)595-5877. **LC** PAR. **DD** 051. ***Merged with*** *Special Report, Fiction, 1047-2886; Special Report on Family, 1047-2878; Special Report on Health, 1047-272X; Special Report on Living, 1047-0123* ***and*** *Special Report on Sports, 1047-2851* ***to form*** *Special Report (Whittle Communications).*

CN/0822-9252
**SPIRALE (SHERBROOKE).** (LA SPIRALE.). [Spirale]. Vol. 1, No 4 (Sept./Oct. 1983)-. Periodical. French. bm. Free. Fraternite Rosicrucienne Centre de Sherbrooke, C P 1383 Canada. **DD** 135/.43/06071466. ***Continues*** *Spirale (Fraternite Rosicrucienne. Groupe de Sherbrooke), 0822-9252.*

US/0888-4781
**SPORT PSYCHOLOGIST, THE.** [Sport psychol.]. **Added/Corp** International Society of Sport Psychology. Vol. 1, No. 1 (March 1987)-. Periodical. English. qt (Mar., June, Sept., Dec.). $36.00 (individuals), $80.00 (institutions) US; $40.00 (individuals), $84.00 (institutions) other. Human Kinetics Publishers Inc, 1607 North Market Street, PO Box 5076, Champaign IL 61825-5076. **Tel** (217)351-5076, FAX (217)351-2674. **ED** Robin S. Vealey. **LC** GV706.4; .S6. **DD** 796. **CODEN** SPPSEU. **[CCC].** Index available (Included in Dec. issue). **Bk Rev. Ad Acc. Circ:** 575.
**Desc:** Designed to meet the needs of educational and clinical sport psychologists. Focuses on applied research and the application of research in the delivery of psychological services to coaches and athletes. International in scope.
**Ind/Abst** Phys. Educ. Index; Psychol. Abstr. (1987-); PsycINFO; PsycLit; Soc. Plann. Policy Dev. Abstr.; Soc. Sci. Cit. Index [Full Cov.]; SPORT Discus.

US/1044-3118
**SPORT PSYCHOLOGY TRAINING BULLETIN.** **See** Recreation, Leisure-Sports.

SZ/0253-4533
**SPRACHE & KOGNITION.** **See** Linguistics.

US/0362-0522
**SPRING.** [Spring]. **Added/Corp** Analytical Psychology Club of New York. (1941)-. English. Twice a year (Mar. & Sept.). $30.00. Spring Journal, PO Box 583, Putnam CT 06260. **Tel** (203)974-3229, FAX (203)974-3195. **ED** James Hillman. **LC** BF173.A2; S67. **DD** 150.19/54/05. **NLM** W1 SP685. **CODEN** SAATDM. Index available. cum. index. **Bk Rev**, (Qty: 30). **Ad Acc, Adv Mgr:** Jay Livernois, **Tel** (203)974-3229. **Pr Rev. Circ:** 7,000.
**Desc:** A journal of archetypal psychology and Jungian thought covering mythology, psychotherapy, dreams, cultural psychology, and imagination in life and literature.
**Ind/Abst** Except. Hum. Exp. (1987-1990); Psychol. Abstr. (1970-); PsycINFO (?-?); PsycLit.

GW/0720-678X
**SPRINGER SERIES IN INFORMATION SCIENCES.** [Springer ser. inf. sci.]. Vol. 1 (1980)-. Monographic series. English. ir. Price varies per volume. Springer Verlag New York Inc., PO Box 19386 Books, Newark NJ 07195. **Tel** (201)348-4033. **[CCC].** Documents available from Ask*IEEE.
**Desc:** Studies on associative memory, image processing and analysis, pattern recognition, and mechanical foundations.
**Ind/Abst** Ei Page One; INSPEC; Zentralbl. Math. Ihre Grenzgeb.

US/0278-6729
**SPRINGER SERIES ON BEHAVIOR THERAPY AND BEHAVIORAL MEDICINE.** [Springer ser. behav. ther. behav. med.]. Vol. 6 (1980)-. Monographic series. English. ir. Price varies per volume. Springer Publishing Company, 536 Broadway, New York NY 10012-3955. **Tel** (212)431-4370, FAX (212)941-7842. **ED** Cyril Franks and Frederick J. Evans. **NLM** W1 SP685NB. ***Continues*** *Springer Series in Behavior Modification, 0272-9636.*
**Desc:** Provides the professional and academic community with carefully selected volumes in the broadly defined areas of behavior therapy and behavioral medicine.

AT/1035-7602
**STATISTICAL REPORT - AUSTRALIA. ARMY OFFICE. 1 PSYCHOLOGICAL RESEARCH UNIT.** (STATISTICAL REPORT.). [Stat. rep. - Aust., Army Off., 1 Psychol. Res. Unit]. **Added/Corp** Australia. Army Office. 1 Psychological Research Unit. (1991)-. Statistical Publication. English. ir. Price varies per volume. 1st Psychological Research Unit, Northbourne House 3-39, PO Box E33, Queen Victoria Terrace, Canberra, ACT 2600 Australia. **DD** 355.0099405.
**Ind/Abst** Psychol. Abstr.

NE/0924-7025
**STEM-, SPRAAK- EN TAALPATHOLOGIE.** (1993)-. Dutch. qt. Fl121.00 (institution). Swets & Zeitlinger BV, Heereweg 347B PO Box 825, 2160 SZ Lisse Holland. **Tel** 011 31 2521 35111, FAX 02521-15888, telex 41325. **ED** Drs H.F.M Peters, B. Maassen, P.P ,Devriese, S.M. Goorhuis-Brouwer.

●US/1067-9537
**STRATEGIES & SOLUTIONS.** **See** Public Health and Safety.

US/0883-0908
**STRESS AND COPING.** [Stress coping]. Vol. 1 (1985)-. English. ir. $36.00. Lawrence Erlbaum Associates, 365 Broadway, Suite 102, Hillsdale NJ 07642. **Tel** (201)666-4110, (800)926-6579, FAX (201)666-2394. **DD** 157.
**Desc:** Covers the psychology and physiology related to stress and adjustment.

US/1053-2161
**STRESS AND EMOTION.** (STRESS AND EMOTION : ANXIETY, ANGER, AND CURIOSITY.). [Stress emot.]. Vol. 14 (1991)-. Monographic series. English. Price varies per volume. Taylor & Francis Ltd., Rankine Road, Basingstoke Hampshire, RG24 8PR United Kingdom. **Tel** 011 44 256 840366, FAX 011 44 256 479438, telex 858540. **(Subscription address:** Taylor & Francis Inc., 1900 Frost Road, Suite 101, Bristol PA 19007-1598.**) LC** BF575.S75; S76. **DD** 616.8/522. **NLM** W1; ST799JP. ***Continues*** *Stress and Anxiety, 0364-1112.*
**Desc:** Ongoing research developments in the area of environmental stressors and the emotional reactions they evoke are explored.

US/0884-870X
**STRESS IN MODERN SOCIETY.** [Stress mod. soc.]. (1984)-. Monographic series. English. ir. Price varies per volume. AMS Press Inc., 56 East 13th Street, New York NY 10003. **Tel** (212)777-4700, FAX (212)995-5413, telex 710 581 2302. **ED** James H Humphrey. **DD** 155.
**Desc:** Provides information on stress and how stress affects individuals and society.

US/1056-5868
**STRESS MANAGEMENT ADVISOR.** ***Ceased.*** [Stress manage. advis.]. Vol. 1, No. 1 (Mar. 1991)-(19??). Periodical. English. mo. Genesis Communications, 11772 Sorrento Valley Road, Suite 134, San Diego CA 92121. **DD** 155.

IT/0393-6457
**STUDI DI PSICOLOGIA DELL EDUCAZIONE.** Armando Armando Srl, Viale Trastevere SRL, 00153 Rome Italy. **Tel** 011 39 6 5806420.

IT/0393-6163
**STUDI DI PSICOLOGIA DELL'EDUCAZIONE.** [Studi psicol. educ.]. (1982)-. Periodical. Italian. tq. Armando Armando Srl, Viale Trastevere SRL, 00153 Rome Italy. **Tel** 011 39 6 5806420. **UDC** 37.015.
**Ind/Abst** PsycINFO (1986-); PsycLit.

XO
**STUDIA PSYCHOLOGICA.** **Added/Corp** Universita Karlova. (1970)-. Academic Scholarly Publication. Czech (Slovak, English, Russian and Russian; summaries and/or abstracts in English and Russian). ir (five issues per year). $20.00. Veda, Publishing House of the Slovak Academy of Sciences, Klemensova 19, 814 30 Bratislava Slovakia. **Tel** (7)583-15. **(Subscription address:** Kubon & Sagner, ABT Zeitschriftenimport, D 80328 Munich Germany.**) ED** Dr. Damian Kovac. **LC** AS141; .A52 subser; BF8.C9. **DD** 909 S; [150/.5]. Index available. **Bk Rev. Ad Acc. Circ:** 1,300 (ctrl). Documents available from The Genuine Article.
**Desc:** Journal for basic research in all psychological fields. Publication of experimental and theoretical original studies of Czechoslovak as well as foreign scientists.
**Ind/Abst** Curr. Contents Soc. Behav. Sci.; Ergon. Abstr.; PsycINFO (1960-); PsycLit; Res. Alert [Full Cov.]; Soc. Sci. Cit. Index [Full Cov.].

CZ/0039-3320
**STUDIA PSYCHOLOGICA.** [Stud. psychol.]. **Added/Corp** Slovenska Akademia Vied. (1965)-. Periodical. English (German and Russian; summaries and/or abstracts in Czech). qt. **NLM** W1 ST886. **CODEN** STPSAK. Documents available from BIOSIS Document Express. ***Continues*** *Psychologicke Studie.*
**Ind/Abst** Biol. Abstr.; Psychol. Abstr. (1960-); Soc. Plann. Policy Dev. Abstr.

PL/0081-685X
**STUDIA PSYCHOLOGICZNE.** [Stud. psychol.]. **Added/Corp** Polska Akademia Nauk. Komitet Nauk Pedagogicznych i Psychologicznych. Vol. 1, (1956)-. Polish (summaries and/or abstracts in English and Russian). sa. Price on Request. **(Subscription address:** ARS Polona, PO Box 1001, 00068 Warsaw Poland.**) NLM** W1 ST886F. **CODEN** SPSLBL.
**Ind/Abst** Psychol. Abstr. (1970-); PsycINFO (1970-); PsycLit; Soc. Plann. Policy Dev. Abstr.; Sociol. Abstr. (?-?).

GW/0721-4502
**STUDIEN ZUR KRITISCHEN PSYCHOLOGIE.** Began with Vol. 1-2, 1977?. Monographic series. German. ir. Price varies per volume. Pahl Rugenstein Verlag, Gottesweg 54, W-5000 Koln 51 Germany. **Tel** 0221-360020, FAX 0221-3600248. **ED** K H Braun and K Holzkamp. **DD** 150/.5. **NLM** W1 ST913J.

US/0363-0234
**SUICIDE & LIFE-THREATENING BEHAVIOR.** [Suicide life-threat. behav.]. **Added/Corp** American Association of Suicidology. **VFOAT** Suicide and Life-Threatening Behavior; Suicide and Life Threatening Behavior. Vol. 6 (Spring 1976)-. Periodical. English. Four times a year. $140.00 (institutions); $157.50 others. Guilford Publications Inc., 72 Spring Street, New York NY 10012. **Tel** (212)431-9800, (800)365-7006, FAX (212)966-6708. **(Subscription address:** Turpin Distribution Services Limited, Blackhorse Road, Letchworth, Hertfordshire SG6 1HN, United Kingdom.**) ED** Ronald W. Maris. **LC** RC569; .S93. **DD** 616.8/5844. **NLM** W1 SU283L. **CODEN** SLBEDP. **[CCC]. Bk Rev. Ad Acc. Circ:** 1,000. available on microfilm and microfiche from University Microfilms International (UMI). Documents available from The Genuine Article, UMI Article Clearinghouse. ***Continues*** *Suicide, 0360-1390.*
**Desc:** Devoted to emergent approaches in theory and practice to life-threatening behaviors. Multi-disciplinary topics: suicide, suicide prevention, accidents, sub-intentional destruction, etc.
**Ind/Abst** Acad. Search (July 1993-); Chicano Index; Curr. Contents Soc. Behav. Sci.; Curr. Index J. Educ.; EMBASE; Expand. Acad. Index (1989-); Index Med.; INFO-SOUTH Abstr.; Newsp. Period. Abstr. (1991-); Pollut. Abstr. Indexes; Psychol. Abstr. (1971-); PsycINFO; PsycLit; Res. Alert [Full Cov.]; Sage Fam. Stud. Abstr.; Soc. Plann. Policy Dev. Abstr.; Soc. Sci. Source (Jul. 1993-); Soc. Sci. Cit. Index [Full Cov.]; Soc. Sci. Index Fulltext (Winter 1988-) [Full Txt.]; Sociol. Abstr.

US/0098-8634
**SYNTHESIS (REDWOOD CITY).**
(SYNTHESIS.). V. 1- 1974-. Periodical. English. Three times a year. $10.00. **NLM** W1 SY66I.

US/1046-171X
**TACD JOURNAL.** ***Title Change.*** [TACD j.]. **Added/Corp** Texas Association for Counseling and Development. **VAT** Texas Association for Counseling and Development Journal. Vol. 12, No. 1 (Spring 1984)-(1992). Periodical. English. sa. Texas Counseling Association, 316 West 12th Street/Suite 402, Aistom TX 78701. **Tel** (512)472-3403, FAX (512)472-3756. **ED** Dr. Riley Harvell (telephone-(817)565-2970). **LC** BF637.C6; T46a. **DD** 158/.3/05. **Ad Acc.** available on microfilm from University Microfilms International (UMI). ***Continues*** *Texas Personnel and Guidance Association. TPGA Journal, 0364-3409.* ***Continued by*** *TCA Journal.*
**Ind/Abst** High. Educ. Abstr. (1984-); Psychol. Abstr. (1974-); PsycINFO (1990-?); PsycLit.

US/0098-6283
**TEACHING OF PSYCHOLOGY.** [Teach. psychol.]. **Added/Corp** American Psychological Association. Division on the Teaching of Psychology. Vol. 1 (Oct. 1974)-. Periodical. English. qt. $115.00 US & Canada; $140.00 other. Lawrence Erlbaum Associates, 365 Broadway, Suite 102, Hillsdale NJ 07642. **Tel** (201)666-4110, (800)926-6579, FAX (201)666-2394. **ED** Charles L Brewer. **LC** BF77; .T43. **DD** 150.7. **Ad Acc. Pr Rev.** available on microfilm and microfiche from University Microfilms International (UMI). Documents available from The Genuine Article. ***Continues*** *Teaching of Psychology Newsletter.*
**Desc:** A resource for teaching methods and as a forum for new ideas.
**Ind/Abst** Acad. Search (July 1993-); Contents Pages Educ.; Curr. Contents Soc. Behav. Sci.; Curr. Index J. Educ.; Educ. Index; INFO-SOUTH Abstr.; Mag. Search; Psychol. Abstr. (1974-); PsycINFO; PsycLit; Res. Alert [Full Cov.]; Soc. Sci. Cit. Index [Full Cov.]; Stud. Women Abstr.; Tech. Educ. Train. Abstr.

US/0887-0217
**TEACHING THINKING & PROBLEM SOLVING.** **VFOAT** Teaching Thinking and Problem Solving. Vol. 7, Issues 1 and 2 (Jan./Feb. 1985)-. Periodical. English. bm. $65.00 US & Canada; $85.00 other. Lawrence Erlbaum Associates, 365 Broadway, Suite 102, Hillsdale NJ 07642. **Tel** (201)666-4110, (800)926-6579, FAX (201)666-2394. **DD** 153. ***Continues*** *Problem Solving.*

NE/0921-0709
**TECHNIQUES IN THE BEHAVIORAL AND NEURAL SCIENCES.** (1987)-. Monographic series. English. ir. Price varies per volume. Elsevier Science Publishers BV, PO Box 211, 1000 AE Amsterdam Netherlands. **Tel** 011 31 20 5803642, FAX 011 31 20 5862696, telex 15682. **NLM** W1; TE197D. **CODEN** TBSCEC.

AG/0325-4437
**TEMAS DE PSICOLOGIA Y PSIQUIATRIA DE LA NINEZ Y ADOLESCENCIA.** **See** Medical Science and Technology-Psychiatry.

US/1062-3981
**TEMPTATION OF SAINT ANTHONY, THE.** [Temptation St. Anthony]. (1991)-. Periodical. English. wk. $10.00 (per year), $1.00 (single issue). Martin Bormann's Cranial Splints, PO Box 8166, Philadelphia PA 19101-8166. **Tel** (215)898-0587. **ED** Mark-Jason Dominus. **DD** 150. **Bk Rev. Circ:** 60,000. available via Internet ((mbCD@radient.cis.Penn.ed)); available on an online database; available on magnetic tape.
**Desc:** Mixed-bag of humor, fiction, bizarre speculation and observation. Emphasis on life as a work of art, philosophy of consciousness, absurdity, surrealism in everyday things.

US/0272-5398
**TENSION CONTROL.** [Tens. control]. **Main/Corp** American Association for the Advancement of Tension Control. (1974)-. English. an. $8.50. American Association of Advancement Tension Control, PO Box 8005, Louisville KY 40208. **Tel** (502)588-6571. **LC** RC489.R45; A44a. **DD** 616.85/22306.

IT/0391-2868
**TERAPIA FAMILIARE : RIVISTA INTERDISCIPLINARE DI RICERCA ED INTERVENTO RELAZIONALES.** **Added/Corp** I.T.F. (Organization). (19??)-. Periodical. Italian. tq. L70000.00 (institutions), L50000.00 (individuals) Italy; L60000.00 Europe; L70000.00 other. APF / ACC Psicoterapia Famiglia, Via Fibreno 10, 00199 Rome Italy. **Tel** 011 39 6 8616860, FAX 011 39 6 8616860. **LC** RC488.5; .T47.
**Ind/Abst** PsycINFO (1977-); PsycLit; Soc. Plann. Policy Dev. Abstr.

US
**TEST CRITIQUES.** Vol. 1 (1984)-. English. an. Price varies per volume. Pro-Ed Inc., 8700 Shoal Creek Boulevard, Austin TX 78757-6897. **Tel** (512)451-3246, FAX (512)451-8542. **ED** Daniel J. Keyser and Richard C. Sweetland. **LC** BF176; .T418. **DD** 150/.28/7.
**Desc:** Noted experts evaluate more than 100 tests in psychology, education, and business. In-depth analysis are valuable for psychologists, teachers, students, personnel specialists, and others. Each review includes practical applications of the tests in clinical and school settings.

US/01612573
**TESTS IN MICROFICHE.** **See** Education-Special Education and Rehabilitation.

US/0749-3185
**TEXAS PSYCHOLOGIST.** [Tex. psychol.]. **Added/Corp** Texas Psychological Association. (19??)-. Periodical. English. qt. $15.00. Texas Psychological Association, 6633 East Highway 290/Suite 305, Austin TX 78723. **Tel** (512)454-2449. **DD** 150.
**Desc:** Promotes access to quality psychological and other mental health services for Texas' residents.

US/0196-0121
**THANATOLOGY ABSTRACTS.** (THANATOLOGY I.E., THANATOLOGY ABSTRACTS.). **VFOAT** Thanatology Abstracts. Vol. 1, No. 1 (1987)-. Periodical. English. sa. $40.00 (paper), $32.00 (diskette) US; $42.25 (paper), $34.25 (diskette) other. Foundation Book & Periodical, 391 Atlantic Avenue, Brooklyn NY 11217. **Tel** (718)270-3725. **ED** Otto Margolis and Robert Stevenson. **DD** 304. **Ad Acc. Circ:** 1,500. available on diskette. ***Continues*** *Thanatology Abstracts (New York, N.Y.), 0196-0121.*
**Desc:** Articles abstracted from many professions dealing with death and dying; psychology, religion, sociology, child development, consumer affairs, anthropology, medicine, law, education, history and more.

UK/0959-3543
**THEORY & PSYCHOLOGY.** **VFOAT** Theory and Psychology. (Feb. 1991)-. Periodical. English. qt. £88.00. Sage Publications Ltd., 6 Bonhill Street, London EC2A 4PU, UK. **Tel** 071 374 0645, FAX 071 374 8741, telex 296207 SAGE G. **ED** Henderikus Stam. **LC** IN PROCESS. **CODEN** THPSEJ. Index available. **Bk Rev. Ad Acc. Acid Free.** Documents available from The Genuine Article.
**Desc:** Fosters theoretical dialogue and innovation within psychology, focusing on the emergent themes at the centre of contemporary psychological debate.
**Ind/Abst** Arts Humanit. Citation Index [Select. Cov.]; Curr. Contents Soc. Behav. Sci.; Except. Hum. Exp.; Res. Alert [Full Cov.]; Soc. Plann. Policy Dev. Abstr.

●UK
**THERAPEUTIC CARE AND EDUCATION : THE JOURNAL OF THE ASSOCIATION OF WORKERS FOR CHILDREN WITH EMOTIONAL AND BEHAVIOURAL DIFFICULTIES.** **Added/Corp** Association of Workers for Children with Emotional and Behavioural Difficulties. Vol. 10, No. 1 (Spring 1992)-. Periodical. English. tq (Mar., June, Oct.). £24.00 (individual), £30.00 (library) UK; £30.00 (surface mail), £35.00 (air mail) other. Therapeutic Care & Education, Longview Lodge Road, Caerleon Newport, Newport Gwent Wales NP6 1QS UK. **Tel** 0633 421209. **NLM** W1; TH133. ***Continues*** *Maladjustment and Therapeutic Education, 0264-4614.*

GW/0344-8967
**THERAPEUTISCHE KONZEPTE DER ANALYTISCHEN PSYCHOLOGIE C.G. JUNG.** [Ther. Konzepte. anal. Psychol. C.G. Jung]. (1978)-. German. ir. Adolph Bonz Verlag, Krahenstrasse 9, W-7013 Oeffingen Germany. **ED** Ursula Eschenbach. **LC** UNC. **DD** 150.19/54/05. **NLM** W1 TH519.

FR
**THERAPIE COMPORTEMENT.** (19??)-. French. $149.00 (institution), $121.00 (individual). Masson Editeur, Box Postale 22, 41353 Vineuil 16 France. **Tel** 011 33 54 438994.

SZ/0250-4952
**THERAPIE FAMILIALE.** [Ther. fam.]. Vol. 1, No. 1 (1980)-. Periodical. French (English; summaries and/or abstracts in English). Four times a year. 73.00F (individuals); 142.00F (institutions). Medecine et Hygiene, Case Postale 456, CH-1211 Geneve 4 Switzerland. **Tel** 011 41 22 3469355, 011 41 22 3469356. **LC** Discard. **NLM** W1 TH644K. **[CCC].**

US
**THESAURUS OF PSYCHOLOGICAL INDEX TERMS.** **Added/Corp** American Psychological Association. 1st Ed. (1974)-. English. ir. $75.00 (latest edition). American Psychological Association, 750 First Street Northeast, Washington DC 20002. **Tel** (800)374-2721, (202)336-5600, (subscriptions - (202)336-5600. **(Subscription address:** American Psychological Association, Order Department, PO Box 2710, Hyattsville MD 20784.**)**

NO/0332-6470
**TIDSSKRIFT FOR NORSK PSYKOLOGFORENING.** [Tidsskr. Nor. psykologforen.]. **VFOAT** Journal of the Norwegian Psychological Association. (1964)-. Periodical. Norwegian. mo. Norsk Psykologforening, Prof. Dahlsgt 18, N-0353 Oslo 3 Norway. **DD** 150. ***Continues*** *Psykologen, 0800-6598.*
**Ind/Abst** PsycINFO (1979-); PsycLit.

NE/0165-1188
**TIJDSCHRIFT VOOR PSYCHOTHERAPIE.** [Tijdschr. psychother.]. (1975)-. Periodical. Dutch. bm. Bohn Stafleu Van Loghum BV, Postbus 246, 3990 GA Houten Netherlands. **Tel** 011 31 3403 95782.
**Ind/Abst** PsycINFO (1977-).

JA/0040-8743
**TOHOKU PSYCHOLOGICA FOLIA.** [Tohoku psychol. folia]. **Added/Corp** Tohoku Daigaku. Vol. 1 (1933)-. Periodical. English (French and German). qt. Tohoku Daigaku Bungakubu Shinrigaku Kenkyoshitsu, Tohoku University, Department of Psychology, Faculty of Arts and Letters, Kawauchi, Sendaishi,, Miyagiken 980 Japan. **LC** BF1; .A2. **DD** 150.5; 159.905. **NLM** W1 TO814. **CODEN** TPSFAD. Documents available from BIOSIS Document Express.
**Ind/Abst** Biol. Abstr.; Life Sci. Collect. (1933-); Psychol. Abstr. (1933-); PsycINFO; PsycLit; Soc. Plann. Policy Dev. Abstr.

US/1058-9864
**TOPICS IN FAMILY PSYCHOLOGY AND COUNSELING.** ***Ceased.*** [Top. fam. psychol. couns.]. **VFOAT** Family Psychology and Counseling; TFPC. Vol. 1, No. 1 (Jan. 1992)-Vol. 1, No. 4 (Oct. 1992). Periodical. English. qt. Aspen Publishers Inc., 7201 McKinney Circle, Frederick MD 21701. **Tel** (800)234-1660, (301)698-7100, FAX (301)251-5784, telex 5106014543. **LC** RC488.5; .T67. **DD** 616.89/156/05. **NLM** W1; TO539MC. **[CCC].**
**Desc:** Each issue covers a single topic of concern that is in step with the challenges family specialists face on a daily basis. Innovative strategies and practical techniques show how to address difficult family problems and case studies, interviews and feature articles give you real-life insight on how these approaches actually work when put to the test with clients.

FR/0040-9375
**TOPIQUE.** (Oct. 1969)-. Periodical. French. Three times a year. 350.00F France; 440.00F other. Dunod Gauthier Villars, 15 rue Gossin, 92543 Montrouge cedex France. **Tel** 011 33 1 46 56 52 66, FAX 011 33 1 46 57 40 69. **(Subscription address:** Centrale des Revues, 11 rue Gossin, 92543 Montrouge Cedex France.**)** **LC** BF173.A2; T6. **DD** 616.89/17/05. **NLM** W1 TO54X. **[CCC].**
**Ind/Abst** PsycINFO (1983-); PsycLit.

IT/0390-6604
**TOTUS HOMO.** **Added/Corp** Istituto Totus Homo. Istituto Psico-Sintesi Scientifica. Vol. 2 (1970)-. Periodical. English (French and Italian). Three times a year. Via Console Marcello 8, 20156 Milan Italy. **LC** BF1; .A22. **NLM** W1 TO82. Each issue contains an index to its own contents (no volume index)--loose.

US/0161-7648
**TOWSON STATE UNIVERSITY JOURNAL OF PSYCHOLOGY.** [Towson State Univ. j. psychol.]. **VFOAT** Journal of Psychology. Vol. 1, No. 1 (Spring 1977)-. Periodical. English. an. **LC** BF1; .T68. **DD** 150/.5.
**Ind/Abst** Psychol. Abstr. (1977-).

US/0362-1537
**TRANSACTIONAL ANALYSIS JOURNAL.** [Trans. anal. j.]. **Added/Corp** International Transactional Analysis Association. Vol. 1, (Jan. 1971)-. Periodical. English. Four times a year (Jan., Apr., July, Oct.). $40.00. International Transaction Analysis, 1772 Vallejo Street, San Francisco CA 94123. **Tel** (415)885-5992, FAX (415)885-5998. **ED** Theodore B. Novey. **LC** RC489.T7; T716. **DD** 616.89/005. **NLM** W1 TR223B. Index available (Oct. issue). **Bk Rev. Ad Acc. Pr Rev. Circ:** 3,600. available on microfilm and microfiche from University Microfilms International (UMI). ***Supersedes*** *Transactional Analysis Bulletin, 0041-1051.*
**Desc:** A theory of personality and a systematic psychotherapy for personal growth and personal change.
**Ind/Abst** Psychol. Abstr. (1974-); PsycINFO; PsycLit.

US/0749-3924
**TRANSITIONS IN MENTAL RETARDATION.** [Transit. ment. retard.]. **Added/Corp** American Association on Mental Deficiency. Northeast Region X. Vol. 1 (1984)-. Monographic series. English. ir. Price varies per volume. Ablex Publishing Corporation, 355 Chestnut Street, Norwood NJ 07648. **Tel** (201)767-8450, (201)767-8455 (Customer Service), FAX (201)767-6717. **ED** James Mulick and Richard Antonak. **LC** HV3006.A2; T73. **DD** 362.3/05. **NLM** W1; TR228Y.
**Desc:** Issues and policies in mental retardation.

FR/0041-1868
**TRAVAIL HUMAIN, LE.** [Trav. hum.]. **Added/Corp** Conservatoire National des Arts et Metiers (France). Vol. 1 (1933)-. Academic Scholarly Publication. French. Four times a year. 400.00F France; 460.00F other. Presses Universitaires de France, Department des Revues, 14 Avenue du Bois de l'Epine, BP 90, 91003 Evry Cedex France. **Tel** (1)60 77 82 05, FAX (1) 60 79 20 45, telex PUF 600 474 F. **ED** J. Leplat Scherrer and S. Bouisset. **LC** T58.A2; T7. **DD** 158.7/05. **NLM** W1 TR271. **CODEN** TRHUAH. **[CCC]. Bk Rev. Pr Rev.** ctrl circ. Documents available from The Genuine Article, BIOSIS Document Express.
**Desc:** Specialists discuss the psychology and physiology of work. Includes bibliographies on security and hygiene of work, personnel recruitment organization of interest to specialists and to general public.
**Ind/Abst** Biol. Abstr.; Curr. Contents Eng. Tech. Appl. Sci.; Curr. Contents Soc. Behav. Sci.; EMBASE; Ergon. Abstr.; LABORDOC; Psychol. Abstr. (1933-); PsycINFO; PsycLit; Res. Alert [Full Cov.]; Saf. Health Work; Soc. Sci. Cit. Index [Full Cov.]; SportSearch.

US/0277-2639
**TUTORIAL ESSAYS IN PSYCHOLOGY.** [Tutor. essays psychol.]. Began with Vol. for 1977. English. bm. John Wiley & Sons, Inc., 605 Third Avenue, New York NY 10158-0012. **Tel** (212)850-6000, (212)850-6645, FAX (212)850-6088, telex 12-7063. **(Subscription address:** John Wiley & Sons / England, Baffins Lane, Chichester, West Sussex PO19 1UD England.**) LC** BF21; .T86. **DD** 150/.5. **NLM** W1 TU986.

US
**TUTORIAL MONOGRAPHS IN COGNITIVE SCIENCE.** (19??)-. English. ir. Price varies per volume. Ablex Publishing Corporation, 355 Chestnut Street, Norwood NJ 07648. **Tel** (201)767-8450, (201)767-8455 (Customer Service), FAX (201)767-6717. **ED** Nigel Shadbolt.
**Desc:** Monographs of tutorial nature on various topics with cognitive science.

US/0743-748X
**TWINS LETTER, THE.** (THE TWINS LETTER : A PUBLICATION OF THE TWINS FOUNDATION.). [Twins lett.]. **Added/Corp** Twins Foundation. Vol. 1, No. 1, 2 (Fall/Winter 1984)-. Periodical. English. qt. comes with membership. The Twins Foundation, PO Box 6043, Providence RI 02940. **Tel** (401)274-8946. **ED** Kay Cassill. **DD** 155. Index available. cum. index. **Circ:** 10,000 (ctrl).
**Desc:** Relating to twins and higher groups of multiples; their lives, achievements, needs, statistics, medical scientific and other new research for and about twins and multiples.

US/8756-4963
**TYPE REPORTER, THE.** [Type report.]. Vol. 1, No. 1 (Summer 1984)-. Periodical. English. Eight times a year. $16.00. Type Reporter, 524 North Paxton, Alexandria VA 22304. **Tel** (703)823-3730, FAX (703)823-2209. **ED** Susan Scanlon (Editor's telephone: (703)764-5370). **DD** 150. **CODEN** TYREE4. **Circ:** 3,000.

SW/0375-4561
**UMEA PSYCHOLOGICAL REPORTS.** (UMEA PSYCHOLOGICAL REPORTS / DEPARTMENT OF PSYCHOLOGY, UNIVERSITY OF UMEA.). [Umea psychol. rep.]. **Added/Corp** Umea Universitet. Psykologiska Institutionen. No. 1 (1968)-. Monographic series. English. qt. **LC** BF11; .U54. **DD** 150/.8. **CODEN** UMPRAO.
**Ind/Abst** Psychol. Abstr. (1973-); Soc. Plann. Policy Dev. Abstr.; Sociol. Abstr.

US
**UNDERSTANDING PEOPLE.** English. mo. $49.00 North America; $59.00 other Paul Sloan. Cromwell-Sloan Publishing Company, 63 Vine Road, Stamford CT 06905-2012. **Tel** (203)323-6839. **Bk Rev.**
**Desc:** A newsletter on psychotherapy.

SA
**UNISA PSYCHOLOGIA. Main/Corp** University of South Africa. V. 1- 1974-. Afrikaans (English). sa. R5.00 South Africa; $4.55 other. University of South Africa, PO Box 392, Pretoria 0001 South Africa. **Tel** 011 27 12 4298468, FAX 011 (27)12 429 3321, telex (59)350068+. **ED** H Shantall. **LC** BF1; .A25. **Bk Rev. Circ:** 4,500 (ctrl).
**Desc:** Presents the main thoughts and activities of psychologists and career opportunities for graduates.

IT
**UOMINI E IDEE.** ***Ceased.*** Periodical. Italian. mo. Corrado Piancastelli, Via Poggio de Mari 16, 80129 Naples Italy. **LC** BF4; .U64.

US/1056-8042
**UP FROM DEPRESSION. See** Health and Personal Fitness.

US
**UPCOMING.** No. 1 1975-. Periodical. English. an. Rational Island Publishers, 719 2nd Avenue North, Seattle WA 98109.

SZ/1016-6262
**VERHALTENSTHERAPIE BASEL. See** Medical Science and Technology-Psychiatry.

RU/0137-0936
**VESTNIK MOSKOVSKOGO UNIVERSITETA SERIA 14 PSIHOLOGIA.** [Vestn. Moskovskogo univ. Ser.14 Psihol.]. (1977)-. Periodical. Russian. qt. Izdatelstvo Moskovskogo Universiteta, K-9 Ulitsa Gertsena 5/7, Moscow Russia. **Tel** (301)881-5973. **UDC** 15.
**Ind/Abst** PsycINFO (1982-).

RU
**VESTNIK MOSKOVSKOGO UNIVERSITETA. SERIIA XIV : PSIKHOLOGIIA. Main/Corp** Moskovskii Gosudarstvennyi Universitet Im. M.V. Lomonosova. (1977)-. Periodical. Russian (summaries and/or abstracts in English). qt. $79.95. Izdatelstvo Moskovskogo Universiteta, K-9 Ulitsa Gertsena 5/7, Moscow Russia. **Tel** (301)881-5973. **(Subscription address:** East View Publications Inc., 3020 Harbor Lane North, Suite 110, Minneapolis MN 55447.**) LC** BF8.R8; M67a.
**Ind/Abst** PsycLit.

CN/1180-3258
**VIE SANS FRONTIERES.** (LA VIE SANS FRONTIERES.). [Vie front.]. **Added/Corp** Institut de Formation et de Reeducation de Montreal. (1990)-. Periodical. French. sa. 3.50Can$ per issue, 6.00Can$ per year. Institut de Formation et de Reeducation de Montreal, 55 Ouest Boulevard Gouin, Montreal, Quebec H3L 1H9 Canada. **DD** 155.2.

CN/0842-1838
**VIES-A-VIES (MONTREAL. 1988).** (VIES-A-VIES : BULLETIN DU SERVICE D'ORIENTATION ET DE CONSULTATION PSYCHOLOGIQUE.). [Vies-a-vies]. **Added/Corp** Universite de Montreal. Service d'Orientation et de Consultation Psychologique. Vol. 1, No 1 (Nov. 1988)-. Bulletin. French. ir (5 issues). 9.24Can$ (includes GST/PST). Universite de Montreal / SOCP, SOCP, CP 6128 Succursale A, Montreal Quebec H3C 3J7 Canada. **Tel** (514)343-6185, FAX (514)343-2270. **DD** 378/.1946/09714281. cum. index. **Pr Rev. Circ:** 8,000 (ctrl).
**Desc:** Written for university students and gives information on psychological realities in a simple manner.

US/1052-2689
**VIOLENCE UPDATE.** ***Ceased.*** (VIOLENCE UPDATE : DEDICATED TO THE CONTINUING EDUCATION OF PROFESSIONALS IN THE FIELD OF INTERPERSONAL VIOLENCE.). [Violence update]. Vol. 1, No. 1 (Sept. 1990)-(Dec. 1994). Periodical. English. mo. Sage Publications Ltd., 6 Bonhill Street, London EC2A 4PU, UK. **Tel** 071 374 0645, FAX 071 374 8741, telex 296207 SAGE G. **DD** 362. **Acid Free.**

US/0892-4996
**VISITOR BEHAVIOR.** [Visit. behav.]. **Added/Corp** Jacksonville State University. Psychology Institute. Anniston Museum of Natural History. Center for Social Design (Jacksonville, Ala.). Vol. 1, No. 1 (April 1986)-. Periodical. English. qt. $20.00 US; $23.00 Canada; $27.00 other. Center for Social Design, PO Box 1111, Jacksonville AL 36265. **Tel** (205)782-5640, FAX (205)782-5640. **ED** Stephen C. Bitgood. **DD** 152. **Bk Rev. Circ:** 500.
**Desc:** Publishes short articles, summaries, and relevant information dealing with visitors to museums, zoos, parks, aquariums, nature centers, and other facilities that share visitation problems.

●UK/1350-6285
**VISUAL COGNITION.** (1994)-. English. qt. $90.00 US; £50.00 Europe; £55.00 other. Lawrence Erlbaum Associates Ltd., 27 Palmeira Mansions, Church Road, Hove East Sussex BN3 2FA England. **Tel** 011 44 273 207411. **(Subscription address:** Turpin Distribution Services Limited, Blackhorse Road, Letchworth, Hertfordshire SG6 1HN, United Kingdom.**) ED** Glyn W. Humphreys.
**Desc:** Publishes research concerned with all aspects of visual cognition. Includes studies of visual object and face recognition, texture and surface perception, perceptual organization, dynamic aspects of vision, visual attention, long-term and short-term visual memory and visual imagery.

US/0749-856X
**VITAL SIGNS (STORRS, CONN.).** (VITAL SIGNS.). [Vital signs]. Periodical. English. qt. $25.00 US; $30.00 other. International Association for Near-Death Studies, PO Box 7767, Philadelphia PA 19101-7767. **ED** Leon Rhodes. **DD** 155. **Bk Rev. Ad Acc. Circ:** 800 (ctrl).
**Desc:** Personal accounts and general discussion of near-death and related experiences, including book reviews, news and notes, etc.

RU/0042-8841
**VOPROSY PSIHOLOGII.** (VOPROSY PSIKHOLOGII.). [Vopr. psihol.]. **Added/Corp** Akademiia Pedagogicheskikh Nauk RSFSR. Akademiia Pedagogicheskikh Nauk SSSR. Vol. 1, (Jan./Feb. 1955)-. Periodical. Russian. bm. $99.95. **(Subscription address:** East View Publications Inc., 3020 Harbor Lane North, Suite 110, Minneapolis MN 55447.**) LC** BF8.R8; V6. **NLM** W1 VO643. **CODEN** VOPSAI. **[CCC].** Index available. **Pr Rev.** Documents available from The Genuine Article.
**Ind/Abst** Curr. Contents Soc. Behav. Sci.; Int. Aerosp. Abstr.; Psychol. Abstr. (1955-); PsycINFO (1955-); PsycLit; Res. Alert [Full Cov.]; Soc. Plann. Policy Dev. Abstr.; Soc. Sci. Cit. Index [Full Cov.].

GW
**WEITERENTWICKLUNG DER PSYCHOANALYSE UND IHRER ANWENDUNGEN. VFOAT** Recent Developments in Psychoanalysis, Theory and Practice. Vol. 5-. Multiple languages (English and German). Vandenhoeck & Ruprecht, Robert Bosch Breite 6, D-37079 Goettingen Germany. **Tel** 011 49 551 695911, FAX 011 49 551 695917, telex 965226 VAN d. **LC** RC500; .F6. **DD** 616.89/17. **NLM** W1 WE24G. ***Continues*** *Fortschritte der Psychoanalyse.*

AT
**WELLNESS : MAXIMUM PHYSICAL & MENTAL HEALTH. See** Health and Personal Fitness.

US/0734-9033
**WHOLE AGAIN RESOURCE GUIDE, THE. See** Sociology.

UK/0738-0860
**WILEY SERIES IN PSYCHOLOGY AND PRODUCTIVITY AT WORK.** [Wiley ser. psychol. prod. work]. **VFOAT** Psychology and Productivity at Work Series. Monographic series. English. ir. Price varies per volume. John Wiley & Sons Ltd., Baffins Lane, Chichester West Sussex PO19 1UD England. **Tel** 0243 779777, FAX 0243 776128 BTG:JWP001, telex 86290 WIBOOKG. **(Subscription address:** North, South and Central America/ John Wiley & Sons, Inc., Subscription Department, 605 Third Avenue, New York, NY 10158-0012, USA; telephone: (212)850-6645; FAX: (212)850-6021**)**

US/0195-4008
**WILEY SERIES ON PERSONALITY PROCESSES.** (19??)-. Monographic series. English. ir. Price varies per volume. John Wiley & Sons Inc / New Jersey, 1 Wiley Drive, Somerset NJ 08875. **Tel** (800)225-5945, (908)469-4400. **[CCC].**

US/1058-773X
**WINNER (NAGS HEAD, N. C.).** (WINNER.). [Winner]. **Added/Corp** Naci Society National. Vol. 1, No. 1 (Fall 1991)-. Periodical. English. qt. $38.97 US; $42.97 Canada. WPI, 6810 Virginia Dare Trail, Nags Head NC 27959. **DD** 158.

UK/0267-3142
**WINNICOTT STUDIES.** (WINNICOTT STUDIES : THE JOURNAL OF THE SQUIGGLE FOUNDATION.). [Winnicott stud.]. **Added/Corp** Squiggle Foundation. No. 1 (Spring 1985)-. Periodical. English. ir. £11.30 (per copy). Karnac H Books Ltd, 118 Finchley Road, London NW3 5HJ England. **Tel** 44 71 584 3303. **NLM** W1; WI652.

US/0270-3149
**WOMEN & THERAPY.** [Women ther.]. **VFOAT** Women and Therapy. Vol. 1, No. 1 (Spring 1982)-. Periodical. English. qt. $175.00 US; $245.00 other. The Haworth Press Inc, 10 Alice Street, Binghamton NY 13904-1580. **Tel** (607)722-5857, (800)3-HAWORTH, FAX (607)722-1424. **ED** Ellen Cole (editor's address: Prescott College, 220 Grove Avenue, Prescott, AZ 86301); Esther D Rothblum (editor's address: John Dewey Hall, University of Vermont, Burlington, VT 05405). **LC** RC451.4.W6; W637. **DD** 616.89/088042. **NLM** W1 WO433V. **CODEN** WOTHDJ. **Bk Rev. Ad Acc. Pr Rev. Acid Free. Circ:** 557. available on microfilm and microfiche from University Microfilms International (UMI). Documents available from BIOSIS Document Express, UMI Article Clearinghouse, Haworth Document Delivery Service.
**Desc:** Explores the unique multidimensional relationship between women and therapy, feminist in orientation. Publishes descriptive, theoretical, clinical, and empirical perspectives on the topic and the therapeutic process.
**Ind/Abst** Abstr. Res. Pastor. Care Couns. (19??-); Altern. Press Index; Biol. Abstr.; Expand. Acad. Index (1992-); Multicult. Educ. Abstr.; Newsp. Period. Abstr. (1992-); Psychol. Abstr. (1982-); PsycINFO; PsycLit; Soc. Work Abstr. [Select. Cov.]; Stud. Women Abstr.; Women Stud. Abstr. (1982-).

UK/0267-8373
**WORK AND STRESS.** [Work stress]. **VFOAT** Work & Stress. Vol. 1, No. 1 (Jan./March 1987)-. Academic Scholarly Publication. English. qt. £99.00 UK; $163.00 other. Taylor & Francis Ltd., Rankine Road, Basingstoke Hampshire, RG24 8PR United Kingdom. **Tel** 011 44 256 840366, FAX 011 44 256 479438, telex 858540. **(Subscription address:** Taylor & Francis Inc., 1900 Frost Road, Suite 101, Bristol PA 19007-1598.**) ED** Tom Cox. **LC** HF5548.85; .W667. **DD** 158.7/05. **NLM** W1; WO8469. **[CCC]. Pr Rev.** available on microfilm and microfiche from University Microfilms International (UMI). Documents available from The Genuine Article.

**Desc:** Presents academic papers relating to stress, health and safety, and associated areas, as well as scholarly articles of concern to the policymakers, managers and trade unionists who have to deal with such issues. The journal is an extensive service which collates news of conferences, seminars and workshops, and introduces news and reviews of people, events, courses, and publications in all aspects of stress at work.
**Ind/Abst** Annals Behav. Med.; Appl. Soc. Sci. Index Abstr.; Contents Pages Manage.; Cumul. Index Nurs. Allied Health Lit.; Curr. Contents Soc. Behav. Sci.; EMBASE; Ergon. Abstr.; HILITES; Int. Labour Doc.; LABORDOC; Psychol. Abstr. (1987-); PsycINFO; PsycLit; Res. Alert [Full Cov.]; Soc. Plann. Policy Dev. Abstr.; Soc. Sci. Cit. Index [Full Cov.].

US/1046-3674
**WORK IN PROGRESS (STONE CENTER FOR DEVELOPMENTAL SERVICES AND STUDIES).** (WORK IN PROGRESS.). [Work prog.]. **Added/Corp** Stone Center for Developmental Services and Studies. (1982)-. Monographic series. English. $2.50 per issue. The Stone Center, Wellesley College, Wellesley MA 02181. **DD** 155.
**Ind/Abst** Soc. Plann. Policy Dev. Abstr.

JA/0285-5313
**YAKUBUTSU, SEISHIN, KODO.** [Yakubutsu, seishin, kodo]. **VFOAT** Japanese Journal of Psychopharmacology. Vol. 1, No. 1 (Oct. 1981)-. Academic Scholarly Publication. Japanese. Japan Soc Psychopharmacology, 1433 Nogawa Miyamaeku, Kwwasaki Kanagawaken Japan. **NLM** W1 YA445N. **CODEN** YSKODB. Documents available from BIOSIS Document Express, CASDDS.
**Ind/Abst** Biol. Abstr.; Chem. Abstr.; CSA Neuro. Abstr.; EMBASE; Index Med.; Life Sci. Collect.

US/0191-0965
**YOGA JOURNAL.** See Health and Personal Fitness.

US/0146-2318
**YOU (NEW YORK. 1976).** (YOU.). [You]. V. 1-Jan. 1976-. Periodical. English. mo. $12.00. Interplay Associates, 515 Madison Avenue, New York NY 10022. **LC** HQ800; .Y64. **DD** 158/.2.

US/1040-7057
**YOUR PERSONAL BEST.** ***Ceased.*** [Your pers. best]. (1989)-(Jan. 1992). Periodical. English. mo. Rodale Press Inc., 400 South 10th Street, Emmaus PA 18098. **Tel** (215)967-5171, (800)666-2503. **DD** 150.

GW
**ZEITSCHRIFT FUER ARBEITS- UND ORGANISATIONSPSYCHOLOGIE.** **Added/Corp** Berufsverband Deutscher Psychologen. Sektion Arbeits- und Betriebspsychologie. **VFOAT** A & O. Heft 1 (1. Quartal 1987)-. Periodical. German (summaries and/or abstracts in English). qt. DM132.00. Verlag fuer Angewandte Psychologie, Rohnsweg 25, Postfache 3751, D 27085 Gottingen Germany. **Tel** 011 49 551 496090, FAX 011 49 551 4960988. **ED** Heinz Schuler, Sigfried Greif. **NLM** W1; ZE234L. **Circ:** 1,800. ***Continues*** *Psychologie und Praxis, 0033-2992.*
**Ind/Abst** PsycLit.

SZ/0170-1789
**ZEITSCHRIFT FUER DIFFERENTIELLE UND DIAGNOSTISCHE PSYCHOLOGIE.** **Added/Corp** Deutsche Gesellschaft fuer Psychologie. (1980)-. Periodical. German (summaries and/or abstracts in English). qt. 118.00F. Verlag Hans Huber Ag Bern, Laenggass Strasse 76, CH 3000 Bern 9 Switzerland. **Tel** 011 41 31 3004500. **ED** M. Amelang, H. Hacker, L.F. Hornke, K. Pawlik, P. Richter, L. Sprung, K.H. Stapf. **NLM** W1; ZE31L. **[CCC]. Circ:** 800.
**Ind/Abst** PsycINFO (1980-); PsycLit.

GW/0049-8637
**ZEITSCHRIFT FUER ENTWICKLUNGSPSYCHOLOGIE UND PADAGOGISCHE PSYCHOLOGIE.** See Education.

GW/0044-2712
**ZEITSCHRIFT FUER EXPERIMENTELLE UND ANGEWANDTE PSYCHOLOGIE.** [Z. exp. angew. Psychol.]. (1953)-. Periodical. German (summaries and/or abstracts in English and French). qt (4 issues). DM178.00. Hogrefe Verlag fuer Psychologie, Rohnsweg 25, D 37085 Goettingen Germany. **Tel** 011 49 551 496090, FAX 011 49 551 4960988. **(Subscription address:** Hogrefe & Huber Publishers, Seattle Office, Box 2487, Kirkland WA 98083.**) ED** A. Friederici, C. Klauer, G. Luer, H. P. Huber, O. Huber. **LC** BF3. **DD** 150/.724. **NLM** W1 ZE347. **CODEN** ZANPAX. **Bk Rev. Ad Acc. Pr Rev. Circ:** 800. Documents available from The Genuine Article.
**Desc:** Covers experimental and applied psychology.
**Ind/Abst** Curr. Contents Soc. Behav. Sci.; Index Med.; Int. Aerosp. Abstr.; Psychol. Abstr. (1953-); PsycINFO (1953-); PsycLit; Res. Alert [Full Cov.]; Soc. Plann. Policy Dev. Abstr.; Soc. Sci. Cit. Index [Full Cov.]; Sociol. Abstr. (?-?).

SZ/1011-6877
**ZEITSCHRIFT FUER GERONTOPSYCHOLOGIE & -PSYCHIATRIE.** See Medical Science and Technology-Geriatrics.

●GW/0943-8149
**ZEITSCHRIFT FUER GESUNDHEITSPSYCHOLOGIE.** (1993)-. German. Four times a year. DM94.00. Hogrefe Verlag fuer Psychologie, Rohnsweg 25, D 37085 Goettingen Germany. **Tel** 011 49 551 496090, FAX 011 49 551 4960988. **ED** Heinz Krohne, Heinz Rueddel, Lothar Schmidt, Ralf Schwarzer, Peter Schwenkmezger. **Circ:** 2,000.

GW/0342-393X
**ZEITSCHRIFT FUER INDIVIDUALPSYCHOLOGIE.** [Z. Individ.psychol.]. (1976)-. Periodical. German. ir. Ernst Reinhardt Verlag, Kemnatenstrasse 46, D 80639 Munich Germany. **Tel** 011 49 89 1783005, FAX 011 49 89 1781827. **UDC** 159.923.
**Ind/Abst** PsycINFO (1984-); PsycLit.

GW/0084-5345
**ZEITSCHRIFT FUER KLINISCHE PSYCHOLOGIE.** (ZEITSCHRIFT FUER KLINISCHE PSYCHOLOGIE, FORSCHUNG UND PRAXIS.). [Z. klin. Psychol.]. **Added/Corp** Berufsverband Deutscher Psychologen. Sektion Klinische Psychologie. Gesellschaft zur Forderung der Verhaltenstherapie. Deutscher Bundesverband der Verhaltenstherapeuten. Gesellschaft fuer Wissenschaftliche Gesprachspsychotherapie (Germany). Vol. 1 (1972)-. Periodical. German (summaries and/or abstracts in English). qt. DM112.00. Hogrefe Verlag fuer Psychologie, Rohnsweg 25, D 37085 Goettingen Germany. **Tel** 011 49 551 496090, FAX 011 49 551 4960988. **ED** Kurt Hahlweg. **NLM** W1 ZE433T. **Bk Rev. Ad Acc. Circ:** 3,000.
**Desc:** Official organ of the Professional Association of German Psychologists, the Society for Scientific Gespraechs-Psychotherapy and the German Society for Behavioral Therapy.
**Ind/Abst** EMBASE; Psychol. Abstr. (1972-); PsycINFO (1972-); PsycLit.

GW/0723-6557
**ZEITSCHRIFT FUER KLINISCHE PSYCHOLOGIE, PSYCHOPATHOLOGIE UND PSYCHOTHERAPIE.** (ZEITSCHRIFT FUER KLINISCHE PSYCHOLOGIE, PSYCHOPATHOLOGIE UND PSYCHOTHERAPIE / IM AUFTRAG DER GORRES-GESELLSCHAFT.). [Z. klin. Psychol., Psychopathol. Psychother.]. **Added/Corp** Gorres-Gesellschaft. Vol. 31, No. 1 (1983)-. Periodical. German (English; summaries and/or abstracts in English). qt. DM100.00 Germany; DM102.00 other. Ferdinand Schoeningh Verlag, Postfach 2540, D 33055 Paderborn Germany. **Tel** 011 49 5251 127665. **NLM** W1 ZE433V. **CODEN** ZKPPET. **[CCC].** Index available. **Bk Rev. Ad Acc. Pr Rev. Circ:** 500 (ctrl). Documents available from The Genuine Article, BIOSIS Document Express. ***Continues*** *Zeitschrift fuer Klinische Psychologie und Psychotherapie.*
**Ind/Abst** Arts Humanit. Citation Index [Select. Cov.]; Biol. Abstr. (1984-); EMBASE; Index Med.; PsycINFO (1971-); PsycLit; Res. Alert [Full Cov.]; Soc. Plann. Policy Dev. Abstr.; Soc. Sci. Cit. Index [Full Cov.].

SZ/1016-264X
**ZEITSCHRIFT FUER NEUROPSYCHOLOGIE.** [Z. Neuropsychol.]. (1990)-. Periodical. German. Twice a year. DM86.00. Verlag Hans Huber Ag Bern, Laenggass Strasse 76, CH 3000 Bern 9 Switzerland. **Tel** 011 41 31 3004500. **ED** Dr. W. Hartje. **UDC** 159.9. **Circ:** 500.

SZ/1010-0652
**ZEITSCHRIFT FUER PAEDAGOGISCHE PSYCHOLOGIE.** (198?)-. Periodical. German (English). qt (March, June, Sept., December). 196.00F (institutions), 123.00F (individuals). Verlag Hans Huber Ag Bern, Laenggass Strasse 76, CH 3000 Bern 9 Switzerland. **Tel** 011 41 31 3004500. **ED** A. Knapp, H. Rost, W. Schneider. **LC** LB1051; .Z42. **DD** 370.15/05. **CODEN** ZPPSE5. **Bk Rev**, (Qty: 12). **Ad Acc**, **Adv Mgr Tel** 0041 31 24 25 33. **Pr Rev. Circ:** 2,400.
**Ind/Abst** Psychol. Abstr. (1987-); PsycINFO (1987-); PsycLit; Soc. Plann. Policy Dev. Abstr.; Spec. Educ. Needs Abstr.

GW/0044-3409
**ZEITSCHRIFT FUER PSYCHOLOGIE MIT ZEITSCHRIFT FUER ANGEWANDTE PSYCHOLOGIE.** [Z. Psychol. Z. angew. Psychol.]. Vol. 168 (1963)-. Periodical. German. qt. $106.00 North America. Johann Ambrosius Barth, Prager Strasse 16 B, D 04103 Leipzig Germany. **Tel** 011 49 341 7137570. **(Subscription address:** Huethig Publishing Inc., 29 Macintosh Drive, Oxford CT 06478.**) Pr Rev. *Continues*** *Zeitschrift fur Psychologie Mit Zeitschrift fur Angewandte Psychologie und Charkaterkunde.*

**Ind/Abst** Index Med.; Life Sci. Collect.; Psychol. Abstr. (1963-); PsycINFO (1929-); PsycLit; Soc. Plann. Policy Dev. Abstr.; Soc. Sci. Cit. Index [Select. Cov.].

SZ/0044-3514
**ZEITSCHRIFT FUER SOZIALPSYCHOLOGIE.** Vol. 1., Issue 1 (1970)-. Periodical. German. qt. 118.00F. Verlag Hans Huber Ag Bern, Laenggass Strasse 76, CH 3000 Bern 9 Switzerland. **Tel** 011 41 31 3004500. **ED** H. Bierhoff, F. Strack, D. Frey, W. Stroebe. **LC** HM251; .Z4. **CODEN** ZSPSDP. **Pr Rev. Circ:** 800. Documents available from The Genuine Article.
**Desc:** Covers research in social psychology, linguistics and political psychology.
**Ind/Abst** Commun. Abstr. (?-?); Curr. Contents Soc. Behav. Sci.; Philos. Index; Psychol. Abstr. (1970-); PsycINFO (1970-); PsycLit; Res. Alert [Full Cov.]; Soc. Plann. Policy Dev. Abstr.; Soc. Sci. Cit. Index [Full Cov.]; Sociol. Abstr. (?-?); Soc. Res. Methodol. Abstr. (1975-).

NE/0169-3395
**ZEITSCHRIFT FUR PSYCHOANALYTISCHE THEORIE UND PRAXIS.** [Z. psychoanal. Theor. Prax.]. **VFOAT** Journal for Psychoanalytical Theory and Practice. (1986)-. Periodical. Multiple languages. sa. Fl162.50 (institutions), Fl140.00 (regular) Netherlands; Fl185.00 (instituions), Fl160.00 (individuals) other. Van Gorcum & Company BV, PO Box 43, NL 9400 AA Assen Netherlands. **Tel** 011 31 5920 46846, FAX 011 31 5920 72064. **UDC** 159.96.
**Ind/Abst** Psychol. Abstr. (1986-); PsycINFO (1986-); PsycLit.

## ABSTRACTING, BIBLIOGRAPHIES AND STATISTICS

US/0360-277X
**BIBLIOGRAPHIC GUIDE TO PSYCHOLOGY.** **Main/Corp** New York Public Library. Research Libraries. (1975)-. English. an. $195.00. GK Hall & Co, 100 Front Street, Riverside NJ 08075. **Tel** (800)257-5755 ext. 2223. **LC** Z7203; .N47a; Z7201; BF121. **DD** 016.15. **NLM** Z 7203 B582. ***Continues*** *Psychology Book Guide.*

GW/0303-5999
**BIBLIOGRAPHIE DER DEUTSCHSPRACHIGEN PSYCHOLOGISCHEN LITERATUR.** No. 1 (1971)-. German. an (Nov.). DM376.00. Vittorio Klostermann, Frauenlobstrasse 22, D 60487 Frankfurt Germany. **Tel** 011 49 69 9708160. **ED** Dambauer. **LC** Z7203; .B52; BF3.

UK/0007-1102
**BRITISH JOURNAL OF MATHEMATICAL & STATISTICAL PSYCHOLOGY, THE.** [Br.j. math. stat. psychol.]. **Added/Corp** British Psychological Society. **VFOAT** British Journal of Mathematical and Statistical Psychology. Vol. 18 (May 1965)-. Statistical Publication. English. Twice a year (May, Nov.). £95.00 Canada & EEC Countries, £176.00 others. British Psychological Society, St. Andrews House, 48 Princess Road, Leicester LE1 7DR England. **Tel** 011 44 533 549568. **(Subscription address:** Turpin Transactions Ltd., Blackhorse Road, Letchworth, Herfordshire SG6 1HN United Kingdom; Telephone: (0462) 672555, FAX: (0462) 480947**) ED** Philip T. Smith. **LC** BF1; .B725. **NLM** W1 BR56. **CODEN** BJMSAX. **[CCC].** Index available (Bound in last issue). cum. index. **Bk Rev. Ad Acc. Pr Rev. Circ:** 770. available on microfilm. Documents available from The Genuine Article. ***Continues*** *British Journal of Statistical Psychology, 0950-561X.*
**Desc:** Published articles relating to any areas of psychology which have a greater mathematical or statistical or other formal aspect to their argument that is usually acceptable to other journals. Articles with clear reference to substantive psychological issues are preferred.
**Ind/Abst** Compumath Citation Index [Full Cov.]; Curr. Contents Soc. Behav. Sci.; Curr. Index Stat.; Health Plan. Adminis.; Index Med.; Linguist. Lang. Behav. Abstr.; Math. Rev.; Psychol. Abstr. (1965-); PsycINFO; PsycLit; PsycScan: Appl. Psych.; Res. Alert [Full Cov.]; Soc. Plann. Policy Dev. Abstr.; Soc. Sci. Cit. Index [Full Cov.]; Sociol. Abstr.; Soc. Res. Methodol. Abstr. (1975-); Stat. Theory Method Abstr. (1968, 1970, 1972, 1974-1977, 1979-1982, 1984); Zentralbl. Math. Ihre Grenzgeb.

XR
**NOVINKY LITERATURY : PSYCHOLOGIE.** 1973-. Periodical. Multiple languages. qt. **(Subscription address:** Artia Pegas Press Ltd., Palac Metro Narodni Trida 25, 11210 Prague 1 Czech Republic.**) LC** Z7203; .N6. ***Continues*** *Novinky Literatury. Spolecenske Vedy. Rada IX: Psychologie.*

●US/1066-9884
**PSYCHOANALYTIC ABSTRACTS.** [Psychoanal. abstr.]. **Added/Corp** American Psychological Association. American Psychological Association. Division of Psychoanalysis. Vol. 7, No. 1 (Mar. 1993)-. Abstracting/Indexing Service. English. qt (Mar., June, Sep., Dec.). $99.00 (nonmember, institution) US. American Psychological Association, 750 First Street Northeast, Washington DC 20002. **Tel** (800)374-2721, (202)336-5600, (subscriptions - (202)336-5600. **DD** 150. **Circ:** 4,200. ***Continues*** *Psycscan. Psychoanalysis, 0889-5236.*

US/0033-2887
**PSYCHOLOGICAL ABSTRACTS.** [Psychol. abstr.]. **Added/Corp** American Psychological Association. Vol. 1 (Jan. 1927)-. Abstracting/Indexing Service. English. mo. $1349.00 (nonmember, institution) US. American Psychological Association, 750 First Street Northeast, Washington DC 20002. **Tel** (800)374-2721, (202)336-5600, (subscriptions - (202)336-5600. **ED** Dennis Auld. **LC** BF1; .P65. **DD** 150/.5. **NLM** Z 7203 P974. (bound in all issues). cum. index. **Circ:** 3,000. available on an online database from OCLC; DATA-STAR; DIALOG; BRS; and DIMDI; available on CD-ROM (As: PsycLit) from SilverPlatter (US); available on microfilm and microfiche from University Microfilms International (UMI).
**Desc:** Provides nonevaluative summaries of journal articles, books, and book chapters from all areas of psychology and related disciplines; reporting advances in journals that individuals may not read on a regular basis and providing subject and author indexes for each month and year.
**Ind/Abst** Ergon. Abstr.; Popul. Index (?-?); Soc. Res. Methodol. Abstr. (1975-).

US
**PSYCINFO.** Abstracting/Indexing Service. English. American Psychological Association, 750 First Street Northeast, Washington DC 20002. **Tel** (800)374-2721, (202)336-5600, (subscriptions - (202)336-5600. available on CD-ROM from CD Plus; (as ClinPSYC) Cambridge Scientific Abstracts; and (as PsycLIT) SilverPlatter (US); available on an online database (as PsychFILE) from Human Resources Information Network.
**Desc:** Online service for Psychological Abstracts providing information products and services that facilitate access to world literature on psychology and related fields. Covers psychology and related disciplines from 1967 on.

US
**PSYCLIT DATABASE.** **Added/Corp** American Psychological Association. **VFOAT** PsycLit; Psyc Lit. (198?)-. Abstracting/Indexing Service. English. qt. $4495.00. Silverplatter Information Inc., 100 River Ridge Drive, Norwood MA 02062. **Tel** (800)343-0064, (617)769-2599, FAX (617)235-1715. **LC** BF1; .P92. available in print (As: Psychological Abstracts).
**Desc:** Contains summaries of the world's serial literature in psychology and related disciplines and is compiled from the PsycINFO database.

US/0891-0685
**PSYCSCAN: APPLIED EXPERIMENTAL AND ENGINEERING PSYCHOLOGY.** **Added/Corp** American Psychological Association. **VFOAT** Applied Experimental & Engineering Psychology; Applied Experimental and Engineering Psychology. Vol. 1, No. 1 (Jan. 1987)-. Abstracting/Indexing Service. English. qt. $66.00 (nonmember, institution) US. American Psychological Association, 750 First Street Northeast, Washington DC 20002. **Tel** (800)374-2721, (202)336-5600, (subscriptions - (202)336-5600. **DD** 150. **NLM** Z 7201; P9745. **Circ:** 2,500.
**Desc:** Gives instant access to current research in computer applications; human factors and ergonomics; transportation and flight; environment; safety and accidents; and working conditions. Approximately 600 new items are added each quarter.

US/0271-7506
**PSYCSCAN. APPLIED PSYCHOLOGY.** [Psycscan, Appl. psychol.]. **Added/Corp** American Psychological Association. **VFOAT** Applied Psychology. Vol. 1, No. 1 (Jan. 1981)-. Abstracting/Indexing Service. English. qt. $66.00 (nonmember, institution) US. American Psychological Association, 750 First Street Northeast, Washington DC 20002. **Tel** (800)374-2721, (202)336-5600, (subscriptions - (202)336-5600. **LC** BF636.A1; P75. **DD** 158/.05. **NLM** Z 7204.A6 P974. **Ad Acc. Circ:** 2,500 (ctrl).
**Desc:** Abstracts approximately 50 subscriber-selected journals on current studies of psychological sciences including applied; accident and safety; environmental; human factors and ergonomics; personnel and guidance; social; consumer and marketing; forensic; management and organization; and psychometrics. 500+ abstracts and citations are included in each quarter.

US/0197-1484
**PSYCSCAN. CLINICAL PSYCHOLOGY.** [Psycscan, Clin. psychol.]. **Added/Corp** American Psychological Association. Vol. 1 (Jan. 1980)-. Abstracting/Indexing Service. English. qt. $66.00 (nonmember, institution) US. American Psychological Association, 750 First Street Northeast, Washington DC 20002. **Tel** (800)374-2721, (202)336-5600, (subscriptions - (202)336-5600. **LC** RC467; .P776. **DD** 616.89/005. **NLM** ZWM 105 P976. **Ad Acc. Circ:** 7,000.
**Desc:** Gives instant access to selected items from over 20 psychological, medical, and therapeutic. Readers are able to scan all the major journals for less than the cost of any single one. They get close to 600 new abstracts and citations each quarter.

US/0197-1492
**PSYCSCAN. DEVELOPMENTAL PSYCHOLOGY.** [Psycscan, Dev. psychol.]. **Added/Corp** American Psychological Association. **VFOAT** Developmental Psychology. Vol. 1, No. 1 (Jan. 1980)-. Abstracting/Indexing Service. English. qt. $66.00 (nonmember, institution) US. American Psychological Association, 750 First Street Northeast, Washington DC 20002. **Tel** (800)374-2721, (202)336-5600, (subscriptions - (202)336-5600. **DD** 155. **NLM** Z 7203 P978. **Ad Acc. Circ:** 3,000 (ctrl).
**Desc:** Provides abstracts from subscriber-selected journals on a wide range of topics including attachment behavior, age and sex differences, self-concept, special education, health care delivery, parental attitudes, residential care, teaching methods, and more--close to 500 abstracts and bibliographic citations from the Psycinfo Database.

US/0730-1928
**PSYCSCAN. LD/MR.** [Psycscan. LD/MR]. **Added/Corp** American Psychological Association. **VFOAT** LD/MR; LD MR; L.D.M.R.; LDMR. **VAT** Psycscan. Learning Disorders, Mental Retardation. Vol. 1, No. 1 (Mar. 1982)-. Abstracting/Indexing Service. English. qt. $66.00 (nonmember, institution) US. American Psychological Association, 750 First Street Northeast, Washington DC 20002. **Tel** (800)374-2721, (202)336-5600, (subscriptions - (202)336-5600. **LC** RC394.L37; P88. **DD** 616.85/88/005. **Ad Acc. Circ:** 8,000 (ctrl).
**Desc:** Gives subscribers all additions to the Psycinfo Database on LD/MR, including research, assessment, treatment, rehabilitation, and educational issues. Provides information on dyslexia; hyperkinesis; psychoneurological, communication, hearing, language and speech disorders; autism; mental retardation; special education; and legal and legislative issues.

●US/1058-6660
**PSYCSCAN. NEUROPSYCHOLOGY.** [PsycSCAN, Neuropsychol.]. **Added/Corp** American Psychological Association. **VFOAT** Neuropsychology. (1992)-. Abstracting/Indexing Service. English. qt. $99.00 (nonmember, institution) US. American Psychological Association, 750 First Street Northeast, Washington DC 20002. **Tel** (800)374-2721, (202)336-5600, (subscriptions - (202)336-5600. **DD** 616. **Circ:** 2,000.
**Desc:** Pulls information from scholarly books and journals covering current research in aspects of the relationship between the brain and behavior. Topics include human experimental cognitive neuropsychology, neurology research, neuropsychopharmacology, neurological aspects of disease and disorders, and neurological assessment-800 abstracts/issue.

US/0889-5236
**PSYCSCAN: PSYCHOANALYSIS.** ***Title Change.*** [Psycscan, Psychoanal.]. **Added/Corp** American Psychological Association. American Psychological Association. Division of Psychoanalysis. **VFOAT** Psychoanalysis. Vol. 1, No. 1 (Jan./June 1986)-(199?). Abstracting/Indexing Service. English. qt. American Psychological Association, 750 First Street Northeast, Washington DC 20002. **Tel** (800)374-2721, (202)336-5600, (subscriptions - (202)336-5600. **(Subscription address:** American Psychological Association, Order Department, PO Box 2710, Hyattsville MD 20784.**)** **DD** 616. **NLM** ZWM 460; P974. **Circ:** 4,000. ***Continued by*** *Psychoanalytic Abstracts, 1066-9884.*
**Desc:** Allows readers to see what's new in their field internationally. This inexpensive research tool brings new ideas from across the world. Subscribers can scan 57 professional journals as well as books for less than the cost of any single one. Close to 500 new abstracts and citations each quarter, selected from the PsycINFO Database.

## PUBLIC ADMINISTRATION

US/0883-413X
**1,000 LARGEST GOVERNMENTS, THE.** [1,000 largest gov.]. **VFOAT** One Thousand Largest Governments. 1983-. English. an. $150.00. Municipal Analysis Services Inc, PO Box 13453, Austin TX 78711-3453. **Tel** (512)327-3328. **ED** Greg Michels. **DD** 330. Index available. cum. index. **Ad Acc. Circ:** 3,000.
**Desc:** Review and comparison of details of each taxing authority of the largest governments in the US.

IT/1121-0788
**A.M. AMMINISTRAZIONE & MANAGEMENT.** ***Title Change.*** [A.M. Ammin. manag.]. **VFOAT** Amministrazione e Management. (1991)-(199?). Periodical. Italian. mo. Maggioli Editore, Casella Postale 290, 47037 Rimini, Italy. **Tel** 011 39 541 628666, FAX 011 39 541 742217. **UDC** 65. Index available. **Bk Rev. Ad Acc. Pr Rev. Circ:** 6,000. ***Continues*** *Administratore E Manager.* ***Merged into*** *Pubblica Amministrazione Oggi.*
**Desc:** Designed in particular for managers operating in public administration.

US
**ABBREVIATED ANNUAL REPORT / U.S. DEPARTMENT OF HEALTH AND HUMAN SERVICES, OFFICE OF INSPECTOR GENERAL.** **Main/Corp** United States. Dept. of Health and Human Services. Office of Inspector General. (19??)-. English. an. **LC** HV85; .U528a. **DD** 353.84/2.

CN/1187-4317
**ACCESS GUIDE TO GOVERNMENT RECORDS AND INFORMATION.** [Access guide gov. rec. inf.]. **Added/Corp** Manitoba. 2nd ed. (Sept. 1991)-. English. be. Government of Manitoba, Winnepeg, Canada. **DD** 354.71270081/9. ***Continues*** *Access Guide (Winnipeg, Man.)., 1187-4333.*

●US/1069-4374
**ACCESSASIA (SEATTLE, WASH.).** (ACCESSASIA : A GUIDE TO SPECIALISTS AND CURRENT RESEARCH.). [AccessAsia]. **Added/Corp** National Bureau of Asian and Soviet Research (U.S.). **VFOAT** Access Asia. (1992)-. English. an. $50.00 (individuals), $75.00 (institutions) US, Canada & Mexico; $70.00 (individuals), $95.00 (institutions) others. National Bureau of Asian Research, 715 Safeco Plaza, Seattle WA 98185. **Tel** (206)632-7370. **LC** H96; .A27. **DD** 950/.025.

AG
**ACCION PARLAMENTARIA.** (1961)-. Periodical. Spanish. mo. $25.00. Redaccion y Administracion / Argentina, Viamonte 749 Piso 10 OF, 1 Buenos Aires 1053 Argentina. **LC** JL2001; .A27. **DD** 320.982.

US/0744-0375
**ACTION (GREENWOOD, IND.).** (ACTION : OFFICIAL PUBLICATION OF MEN FOR MISSIONS INTERNATIONAL.). [Action]. **Added/Corp** Men for Missions International. (19??)-. Periodical. English. Four times a year. Free. OMS International Inc, PO Box A, Greenwood IN 46142-6599. **Tel** (317)881-6751, FAX (317)888-5275. **ED** Ron Mertens and Eleanor Burr. **LC** Discard. **DD** 266. ctrl circ.
**Desc:** Official publication of Men For Missions, a laymen's branch of OMS International.

FR/0150-5726
**ACTIVITES (CHAMBRE DE COMMERCE ET D'INDUSTRIE DE NICE ET DES ALPES-MARITIMES).** (ACTIVITES.). French. Palais Consulaire, 20 Boulevard Carabacel, 06000 Nice France. **LC** HC277.A525; A26.

US/0277-1845
**ACTIVITIES AND SUMMARY REPORT OF THE COMMITTEE ON THE DISTRICT OF COLUMBIA, HOUSE OF REPRESENTATIVES.** ***Title Change.*** **Main/Corp** United States. Congress. House. Committee on the District of Columbia. (19??)-(19??). English. be. US Congress, 515 House Annex 2, Washington DC 20515. **LC** KF31.8; .D573. **DD** 328.73/07652. ***Continued by*** *United States. Congress. House. Committee on the District of Columbia. Activities of the Committee on the District of Columbia, House of Representatives.*

US
**ACTIVITIES OF THE COMMITTEE ON THE DISTRICT OF COLUMBIA, HOUSE OF REPRESENTATIVES.** **Main/Corp** United States. Congress. House. Committee on the District of Columbia. (19??)-. English. be. ***Continues*** *United States. Congress. House. Committee on the District of Columbia. Activities and Summary Report of the Committee on the District of Columbia, House of Representatives, 0277-1845.*

US/0739-3288
**ACTIVITIES OF THE HOUSE COMMITTEE ON GOVERNMENT OPERATIONS.** **Main/Corp** United States. Congress. House. Committee on Government Operations. (19??)-. Government Publication. English. be. Superintendent of Documents, US Government Printing Office, Washington DC 20402. **Tel** (202)275-3328, FAX (202)786-2377. **LC** JK1430.G6; A3. **DD** 328.73/07658. available on microfiche (Vols. for (1979-1980-) distributed to some depository libraries). ***Continues*** *United States. Congress. House. Committee on Government Operations. Activities Report.*

CN/0846-3980
**ACTIVITY REPORT - PUBLIC LEGAL EDUCATION AND INFORMATION SERVICE OF NEW BRUNSWICK.** (ACTIVITY REPORT.). [Act. rep. - Public Leg. Educ. Inf.

Serv. N.B.]. **Main/Corp** Public Legal Education and Information Service of New Brunswick. **VFOAT** Rapport d'Activites. **VAT** Rapport d'Activites - Service Public d'Education et d'Information Juridiques du Nouveau-Brunswick. (1991)-. English (French). **DD** 354.715/10088.

CN/0846-3980
**ACTIVITY REPORT - PUBLIC LEGAL EDUCATION AND INFORMATION SERVICE OF NEW BRUNSWICK.** (RAPPORT D'ACTIVITES.). [Act. rep. - Public Leg. Educ. Inf. Serv. N.B.]. **Main/Corp** Service Public d'Education et d'Information Juridiques du Nouveau-Brunswick. **VFOAT** Activity Report. (1990/1991)-. French (English). **DD** 354.715/10088.

US
**ACTS AND JOINT RESOLUTIONS OF THE GENERAL ASSEMBLY OF THE STATE OF SOUTH CAROLINA.** **Main/Corp** South Carolina. (1776)-. English. an. $60.00. Legislative Printing, 225 Blatt Building, 1105 Pendleton, Columbia SC 29201. **Tel** (803)734-3179. Each issue contains an index to its own contents (no volume index)--loose.

II/0445-6319
**ACTS OF PARLIAMENT.** **Main/Corp** India (Republic). **Added/Corp** India (Republic). Ministry of Law, Justice and Company Affairs. (1???)-. English. an. Price varies. Controller of Publications / Civil Lines, Government of India, Civil Lines, New Delhi 110054 India. **Tel** 3015984, telex 3166415. **(Subscription address:** Prints India, 11 Darya Ganj, New Delhi, 110002 India, (Phone: 011 91 11 3268645))

US
**ACTS OF THE GENERAL ASSEMBLY OF THE COMMONWEALTH OF KENTUCKY.** **Main/Corp** Kentucky. **Added/Corp** Kentucky. General Assembly. (1792)-. Periodical. English. be. $30.00 (two year). Legislative Research Commission, State Capitol/Room 300, Frankfort KY 40601. **Tel** (502)564-8100.

CN/1188-1542
**ACTUALITE GOUVERNEMENTALE / COMMUNICATION-QUEBEC, BAS-SAINT-LAURENT, L'.** [Actual. gouv.]. **Added/Corp** Communication-Quebec (Rimouski, Quebec). (Oct. 1991)-. Periodical. French. mo. **DD** 354.7140081/9.

AT/0814-1231
**ADMIN REVIEW.** [Admin rev.]. **Added/Corp** Administrative Review Council. Australia. (1984)-. Government Publication. English. qt. 15.00Aus$. Australian Government Publishing Service, GPO Box 84, Canberra ACT 2601 Australia. **Tel** 011 61 6 2954411, FAX 011 61 6 2954455. **DD** 342.9406.

PE
**ADMINISTRACION PUBLICA.** **Added/Corp** Peru. Escuela Superior de Administracion Publica. **VFOAT** Revista de la ESAP. No. 1, (May/Aug. 1970)-. Periodical. Spanish. Escuela Superior de Administracion Publica, Apartado No 4963, Miraflores, Lima Peru.

CK
**ADMINISTRACION Y DESARROLLO (1981).** (ADMINISTRACION Y DESARROLLO / DEPARTAMENTO ADMINISTRATIVO DEL SERVICIO CIVIL, ESCUELA SUPERIOR DE ADMINISTRACION PUBLICA.). No. 19 (Dec. 1981)-. Periodical. Spanish. an. $300.00. Asesoria de la Direccion de la Esap, Diagonal 40 No 46A-37 Can Apartado Aereo No 29745, Bogota Colombia. **LC** JA5; .A34. **DD** 350/.0005. cum. index. ***Continues*** *Revista de Administracion y Desarrollo.*
**Ind/Abst** LABORDOC.

US/0364-7986
**ADMINISTRATION & MANAGEMENT.** ***Ceased.*** Began with Oct. 9, 1979-Ceased Jan. 1992. Periodical. English. wk. National Technical Information Service - NTIS, Room 2027S, 5285 Port Royal Road, Springfield VA 22161. **Tel** (703)487-4630, (703)487-4660, (703)487-4650, FAX (703)321-8547, telex 89-9405. ***Continues*** *Administration (United States. National Technical Information Service), 0364-7986.*

US/0095-3997
**ADMINISTRATION & SOCIETY.** [Adm. soc.]. **VAT** Administration and Society. Vol. 6 (May 1974)-. Periodical. English. qt (Feb., May, Aug., Nov.). $176.00. SAGE Periodical Press, 2455 Teller Road, Thousand Oaks CA 91320. **Tel** (805)499-0721, FAX (805)499-0871, telex 100799. **ED** Gary L. Wamsley. **LC** JA3; .J65. **DD** 350/.0005. **[CCC]**. **Pr Rev. Acid Free.** available on microfilm and microfiche from University Microfilms International (UMI). Documents available from The Genuine Article. ***Continues*** *Journal of Comparative Administration.*
**Desc:** Deals with administration, bureaucracy, public organization and public policy, and the impact these have on politics and society.
**Ind/Abst** ABC POL SCI; Acad. Search (Jan. 1994-); Am. Hist. Life (1970-); Bus. ASAP (1992-) [Full Txt.]; Bus. Index (1985-); Curr. Contents Soc. Behav. Sci.; Curr. Index J. Educ.; Educ. Adm. Abstr.; Gen. BusinessFile (1985-); Gen. Period. Index (1985-); Index Period. Artic. Relat. Law (19??-19??); INFO-SOUTH Abstr.; Int. Bibliogr. Sociol.; Int. Polit. Sci. Abstr.; J. Plan. Lit.; Linguist. Lang. Behav. Abstr.; Mag. Search; Middle East Abstr. Index; PAIS Int. Print; Res. Alert [Full Cov.]; Sage Public Adm. Abstr.; Sage Urban Stud. Abstr; School Organ. Manage. Abstr.; Soc. Plann. Policy Dev. Abstr.; Soc. Sci. Cit. Index [Full Cov.]; Sociol. Abstr.; Sociol. Educ. Abstr.; U.S. Polit. Sci. Doc.; Work Relat. Abstr.

IE/0001-8325
**ADMINISTRATION (DUBLIN).** (ADMINISTRATION.). [Administration]. **Added/Corp** Institute of Public Administration (Dublin, Ireland). Vol. 1 (1953)-. Periodical. English. qt. 26.00p UK and Ireland; 31.76p Europe; 37.36p other. Institute of Public Administration, Vergemount Hall Public Department, Dublin 6 Ireland. **Tel** 011 353 1 26977011, FAX 011 353 1 2698644, telex 90533 INPA. **ED** Tony McNavrara. **LC** JA26; .A35. **DD** 350.0005. Index Available, published separately, free-automatically sent. cum. index. **Bk Rev. Ad Acc. Circ:** 1,500. available on microfiche.
**Desc:** Provides a forum for the discussion of law, sociology, public administration, politics, and current affairs.
**Ind/Abst** ABC POL SCI; J. Plan. Lit.; Middle East Abstr. Index; PAIS Int. Print; Sage Public Adm. Abstr. (?-?).

CN/0704-9765
**ADMINISTRATION ET GESTION.** ***Title Change.*** (ADMINISTRATION ET GESTION : SOMMAIRES DE LA DOCUMENTATION COURANTE.). **Added/Corp** Quebec (Province). Ministere des Communications. Bibliotheque Administrative. (Dec. 1973)-(19??). Periodical. French (English). Five times a year. Bibliotheque Administrative, 1056 Conroy R C, Quebec Quebec G1R 5E6 Canada. **Tel** (418)643-5150. **Bk Rev. Ad Acc. Circ:** 1,000 (ctrl). ***Merged into*** *Nouveautes de la Bibliotheque Administrative.*

CN/0576-1409
**ADMINISTRATION FEDERALE DU CANADA, L'.** [Adm. fed. Can.]. 1958-. Periodical. French. an. $10.00 Canada; $12.00 other. Information Canada, 171 Slater Street, Ottawa Ontario K1A 0S9 Canada. **Tel** (819)997-1095. **LC** JL5; .A53. **DD** 354/.71/04.

PP/0304-6028
**ADMINISTRATION FOR DEVELOPMENT.** No. 1- Jan. 1974-. Periodical. English. Administrative College of Papua New Guinea, PO Box 1216, Boroko New Guinea. **LC** JA1; .A35. **DD** 350/.000995.

TR
**ADMINISTRATION REPORT - PORT OF SPAIN, TRINIDAD AND TOBAGO. PUBLIC HEALTH DEPT.** **See** Public Health and Safety.

BG
**ADMINISTRATIVE AFFAIRS IN BANGLADESH.** **Added/Corp** University of Dacca. Centre for Administrative Studies. (1979)-. English. an. TK20.00 Bangladesh; TK5.00 US. Center for Administrative Studies, Room No 4036/Arts Faculty Building, University of Dacca, Dacca-2 Bangladesh. **LC** JQ635; .A75. **DD** 354.549/2/0005.

AT/0813-779X
**ADMINISTRATIVE APPEALS REPORTS.** [Adm. appeals rep.]. **Main/Corp** Australia. Administrative Appeals Tribunal. Vol. 1, Pt. 1 (Aug. 1984)-. Periodical. English. Six times a year. Price varies. The Law Book Company Limited, 44-50 Waterloo Road, North Ryde New South Wales, 2113 Australia. **Tel** 011 61 2 8870177, FAX 011 61 2 8887240, telex ASBOOK 27445. **ED** Matthew Smith.
**Desc:** Provides the fastest reporting of AAT decisions from around the country. Also provides reports of decisions of which have gone on appeal from the AAT to: The Federal Court of Australia and The High Court of Australia.
**Ind/Abst** Aust. Leg. Mon. Dig.

II
**ADMINISTRATIVE CHANGE.** Vol. 1 (June 1973)-. English. sa. $20.00. C-13 Bal Marg Tilak Nagar, Jaipur 302004 India. **Tel** 26 86 45. **(Subscription address:** Prints India, 11 Darya Ganj, New Delhi, 110002 India, (Phone: 011 91 11 3268645)) **LC** JA26; .A37. **DD** 350/.0005.
**Ind/Abst** Geogr. Abstr. Human Geogr.; Int. Dev. Abstr.; Int. Polit. Sci. Abstr.

ET
**ADMINISTRATIVE DIRECTORY OF THE PROVISIONAL MILITARY GOVERNMENT OF SOCIALIST ETHIOPIA.** Directory. English. Institut of Management and Training, Research and Documentation Branch, ATSE Teodros Street, PO Box 51, Addis Ababa Ethiopia. **LC** JQ3757; .A65. **DD** 354/.63/00025. ***Continues*** *Administrative Directory of the Imperial Ethiopian Government.*

US
**ADMINISTRATIVE LAW BULLETIN.** **See** Law.

US
**ADMINISTRATIVE LAW, THIRD SERIES.** **See** Law.

US/0001-8392
**ADMINISTRATIVE SCIENCE QUARTERLY.** [Adm. sci. q.]. **Added/Corp** Cornell University. Graduate School of Business and Public Administration. Vol. 1 (June 1956)-. Periodical. English. qt (4 issues). $90.00 (institution) US; $97.00 (institution) other. Administrative Science Quarterly, 425 Caldwell Hall, Cornell University, Ithaca NY 14853. **Tel** (607)255-5581, FAX (607)255-7524, telex WUI 6713054. **ED** John H. Freeman. **LC** HD28; .A25. **DD** 658.05. **NLM** W1 AD347. **CODEN** ASCQAG. **[CCC]**. Index available (bound in Dec. issue). cum. index. **Bk Rev. Ad Acc. Pr Rev. Circ:** 6,031. available on microfilm and microfiche from University Microfilms International (UMI); available on an online database (Full-Text) from DIALOG. Documents available from The Genuine Article, UMI Article Clearinghouse.
**Desc:** Empirical and theoretical articles that contribute to knowledge of business, governmental, military, health, and other organizations.
**Ind/Abst** ABC POL SCI; ABI/INFORM Glob. Ed.; ABI Inform Ondisc (June 1971-); Acad. Abstr. Full Text Elite (July 1990-); Acad. Abstr. (July 1990-); Acad. Search (July 1990-); Am. Hist. Life (1967-); Anbar Account. Finan. Abstr. [Full Txt.]; Appl. Soc. Sci. Index Abstr.; Bus. Index (1985-); Bus. Period. Index; Commun. Abstr.; Contents Pages Manage.; Cumul. Index Nurs. Allied Health Lit.; Curr. Contents Soc. Behav. Sci.; Curr. Index J. Educ.; Educ. Adm. Abstr. (?-?); Expand. Acad. Index (1984-); Gen. BusinessFile (1985-); Gen. Period. Index (1985-); Health Plan. Adminis.; High. Educ. Abstr. (1965-); Hospit. Health Admin. Index; Hum. Resour. Abstr.; INFO-SOUTH Abstr.; Int. Aerosp. Abstr.; Int. Bibliogr. Sociol.; Int. Polit. Sci. Abstr.; Linguist. Lang. Behav. Abstr.; Mag. Search; Manage. Market. Abstr.; Manage. Bibliogr. Rev.; Manage. Contents; Middle East Abstr. Index; Multicult. Educ. Abstr.; Newsp. Period. Abstr. (1988-); Oper. Prod. Manage. Abstr. [Full Txt.]; Oper. Res./Manag. Sci.; PAIS Int. Print; Person. Manage. Abstr.; Psychol. Abstr. (1956-); PsycINFO; PsycLit; PsycScan: Appl. Psych.; Qual. Control Appl. Stat.; Res. Alert [Full Cov.]; Res. High. Educ. Abstr.; Sage Public Adm. Abstr.; School Organ. Manage. Abstr.; Selec. Coop. Index Manage. Period; Soc. Plann. Policy Dev. Abstr.; Soc. Sci. Source (Jul. 1990-); Soc. Sci. Cit. Index [Full Cov.]; Soc. Sci. Index; Soc. Sci. Index Fulltext (Sept. 1988-) [Full Txt.]; Soc. Work Abstr. [Select. Cov.]; Sociol. Abstr.; Sociol. Educ. Abstr.; UMI ABI/Inform--Bus. Period. Ondisc (Mar. 1987-) [Full Txt.]; U.S. Polit. Sci. Doc.; Wilson Bus. Abstr.; Work Relat. Abstr.

BG/0001-8406
**ADMINISTRATIVE SCIENCE REVIEW.** **Added/Corp** Dacca, Pakistan (City) National Institute of Public Administration. Vol. 1 (March 1967)-. Periodical. English. Four times a year. $18.10. National Institute of Public Administration, Publications Officer, Nilkhet, Dacca 2 Bangladesh. ***Continues*** *Dacca, Pakistan (City) National Institute of Public Administration.*

US
**ADOPTED BUDGET - CITY OF NEW YORK.** **Main/Corp** New York (City). Office of Management and Budget. (1978/79)-. English. an. $20.00 (add $2.50 for postage). CityBooks/ City Publishing Center, Department of General Services, 2208 Municipal Building, 22nd Floor, New York NY 10007. **Tel** (212)669-8245, FAX (212)669-3211. ***Continues*** *Budget of the City of New York.*
**Desc:** Presents the complete budget for the City of New York, as adopted. It is organized in three parts: Expense, Revenue and Capital.

FR
**ADOPTED TEXTS / STANDING CONFERENCE OF LOCAL AND REGIONAL AUTHORITIES OF EUROPE / TEXTES ADOPTES / CONFERENCE PERMANENTE DES POUVOIRS LOCAUX ET REGIONAUX DE L'EUROPE.** **Main/Corp** Standing Conference of Local and Regional Authorities of Europe. **VFOAT** Textes Adoptes. (March 1991)-. English (French). Council of Europe / Group Pact ED, Pharmacopoeia BP 907, 67029 Strasbourg Cedex 01 France. **Tel** 011 33 88 412036, FAX 011 33 88 41277181, telex 880388. ***Continues*** *Standing Conference of Local and Regional Authorities of Europe. Texts Adopted, 0071-2639.*

US/0147-1945
**ADVANCE BUDGETING. A REPORT TO THE CONGRESS.** (ADVANCE BUDGETING; A REPORT TO THE CONGRESS AS REQUIRED BY PUBLIC LAW 93-344.). **Main/Corp** United States. Congressional Budget Office. (19??)-. English. $0.70

# Public Administration

single issue. Congressional Budget Office, 2nd and D Streets SW, Washington DC 20515. **Tel** (202)226-2115. **LC** HJ2051; .U54d. **DD** 353.007/22.

US
**AEI PUBLICATIONS / AMERICAN ENTERPRISE INSTITUTE. Main/Corp** American Enterprise Institute for Public Policy Research. (198?)-. English. ir. American Enterprise Institute / Maryland, 4720 Boston Way, Lanham MD 20706. **Tel** (301)459-3366. **Continues** Publications Catalog / American Enterprise Institute for Public Policy Research.

US
**AFFIRMATIVE ACTION PLAN. PART 1, POLICIES & PROCEDURES / ALASKA DEPT. OF COMMUNITY & REGIONAL AFFAIRS. Main/Corp** Alaska. Dept. of Community and Regional Affairs. **VFOAT** Policies & Procedures. English. an. Alaska Department of Community & Regional Affairs, Pouch B, Juneau AK 99811. **LC** HC107.A47; P6315A. **DD** 353.97980081/8/0681.

UK
**AFRICA GAZETTE.** V. 1- May 10, 1977-. Periodical. English. bw. Africa Gazette, Wheatsheaf House Carmelite Street, London EC4Y 0ax England. **LC** HD3860; .A37. **DD** 350/.711/096.

MR/0007-9588
**AFRICAN ADMINISTRATIVE STUDIES.** [Afr. adm. stud.]. **Added/Corp** Centre Africain de Formation et de Recherches Administratives pour le Developpement, Tangier. No. 13 (Jan. 1975)-. Periodical. English. sa. $10.00 (individuals), $20.00 (institutions) Africa; $20.00 (individuals), $40.00 (institutions) other. CAFRAD, BP 310, Tangier Morocco. **Tel** 011 212 36430, telex 33664. Index available. **Bk Rev. Ad Acc. Circ:** 500. **Continues** Cahiers Africains d'Administration Publique. African Administrative Studies.
**Ind/Abst** Public Aff. Inf. Serv. Bull.

AU
**AGENDEN / AKTIVITATEN 90/91.** German. free. Herrengasse 11-13, 1014 Vienna Austria. **Tel** 53110/2095. Index available. **Circ:** 4,500 (ctrl).

TA
**AGITATOR TADZHIKISTANA. Added/Corp** Kommunisticheskaia Partiia Tadzhkistana. TSentral'nyi Komitet. (1975)-. Periodical. Russian. sm. $14.50. **(Subscription address:** Victor Kamkin, 4956 Boiling Brook Parkway, Rockville MD 20852.**) LC** JQ1089.A55; A8.

PK
**AGTE QADAMU PABULIKESHANI.** (19??)-. Periodical. Sindhi. mo. Rs10.00. **LC** JQ201; .A37.

LE
**AL-AMAL FI KHIDMAT LUBNAN.** No. 1- Festival Year 1977-. Periodical. Multiple languages (Arabic and French). mo. £L10.00 per issue. Al-Amal fi Khidmat Lubnan, PO Box 992, Beirut Lebanon. **LC** JQ1825.L473; K26.

●UA
**AL-MUJTAMA AL-MADANI WA-AL-TAHAWWUL AL-DIMUQRATI FI AL-WATAN AL-ARABI. Added/Corp** Markaz Ibn Khaldun Lil-Dirasat al-Inmaiyah. **VFOAT** Mujtama Al-Madani; Civil Society. (1992)-. Periodical. Arabic (English). Twelve times a year. $40.00 Egypt/$35.00 other. IBN Khaldun Center for Development, PO Box 13, Mokattam Cairo, Egypt. **Tel** 011 20 2 5061617. **LC** JQ1850.A1; M84. **Bk Rev. Ad Acc.** ctrl circ.

US/0892-9084
**ALABAMA COUNTY DATA BOOK.** [Ala. cty. data book]. **Added/Corp** Alabama. Office of State Planning and Federal Programs. Alabama. State Planning Division. (19??)-. English. an (Fall). $10.00. Alabama Department of Economic and Community Affairs, 401 Adams Avenue, c/o R. Garrett Room 500, Montgomery AL 36103. **Tel** (205)242-8672, (205)242-5100, FAX (205)284-8670. **LC** HA221; .A35. **DD** 317.61.
**Ind/Abst** Stat. Ref. Index.

US
**ALABAMA DIRECTORY. Suspended.** (19??)-(19??). Directory. English. Brown Printing Company, PO Box 210219, Montgomery AL 36121. **Tel** (205)277-4700. **LC** JK4530; .A7. **DD** 353.9761/002. **Continues** Alabama Official Directory.

US/0002-4309
**ALABAMA MUNICIPAL JOURNAL, THE. Added/Corp** League of Municipalities (Ala.). (1945)-. Periodical. English. mo. $12.00. Alabama Municipal Journal, PO Box 1270, Montgomery AL 36102. **Tel** (205)262-2566. **ED** Anne Roquemore. **Bk Rev**, (Qty: 1-2). **Ad Acc. Pr Rev. Circ:** 4,300. **Continues** Alabama Local Government Journal.
**Desc:** Devoted exclusively to municipal government, its problems, trends and issues. Legal information, which is staff written, is included monthly. subjects also covered may include records management, legislative news, public safety, etc.
**Ind/Abst** Urban Aff. Abstr.

US
**ALASKA ADMINISTRATIVE CODE : CONTAINING THE PERMANENT AND EMERGENCY REGULATIONS OF THE STATE OF ALASKA, ANNOTATED / PUBLISHED BY THE LIEUTENANT GOVERNOR'S OFFICE [WITH THE STAFFS OF THE ALASKA LEGISLATIVE COUNCIL AND THE LEGISLATIVE AFFAIRS AGENCY]; ANNOTATED, INDEXED AND PRINTED BY THE BOOK PUBLISHING COMPANY. Main/Corp** Alaska. Lieutenant Governor's Office. **Added/Corp** Alaska. Legislative Affairs Agency. Alaska. Legislature. Legislative Council. (19??)-. English. Four times a year. Book Publishing Company, 201 Westlake Avenue North, Seattle WA 98109. **Tel** (206)343-5700. cum. index.

US/0363-4167
**ALASKA MUNICIPAL OFFICIALS DIRECTORY. Added/Corp** Alaska. Dept. of Community and Regional Affairs. Alaska Municipal League. (1976)-. Directory. English. Alaska Department of Community & Regional Affairs, Pouch B, Juneau AK 99811. **LC** JS451.A43; A65. **DD** 354.005/209798. **Continues** Directory of Borough and City Officials, 0361-2910.

CN
**ALBERTA BILLS.** English. ir (weekly when sitting). 50.00Can$. Alberta Bill Legislative Office, 801 Legislative Annex, 9718 107th Street, Edmonton Alberta T5K 1E4 Canada. **Tel** (403)427-2477, FAX (403)427-1623. Index available (published separately).

CN/0002-4775
**ALBERTA GAZETTE.** (THE ALBERTA GAZETTE, PART II.). **Main/Corp** Alberta. Vol. 53, No. 13 (July 15, 1957)-. Periodical. English. Twenty-five times a year (Published on 15th and 30th of each month). 25.00Can$. Alberta Public Affairs Bureau, 11510 Kingsway Avenue, Edmonton Alberta T5G 2Y5 Canada. **Tel** (403)427-4952. **ED** Donna James. **Circ:** 3,800. available on microfilm and microfiche from University Microfilms International (UMI).
**Desc:** Alberta government's vehicle for publication of various public ads, official notices and regulations.

CN/0383-3623
**ALBERTA HANSARD. Main/Corp** Alberta. Legislative Assembly. (1972)-. English. da (during the sessions). 60.00Can$, (individuals and school libraries); 125.00Can$ (institutions); 110.00Can$ (bound hansards). Alberta Bill Legislative Office, 801 Legislative Annex, 9718 107th Street, Edmonton Alberta T5K 1E4 Canada. **Tel** (403)427-2477, FAX (403)427-1623. **ED** Gary Garrison, (403)427-2490. **LC** J112; .H24a. **DD** 328.7123/01. Index available (published separately). **Circ:** 1,400.
**Desc:** The official record of the debates of the legislative assembly of Alberta.

CN/0568-9163
**ALBERTA LIST.** (THE ALBERTA LIST OF OFFICIAL PERSONNEL IN FEDERAL, PROVINCIAL AND MUNICIPAL GOVERNMENTS IN THE PROVINCE OF ALBERTA.). Began with 1954 issue?. English. an. The Alberta List, PO Box 4486, South Edmonton Alberta T6E 4T7 Canada. **DD** 354/.7123/00025.

AT
**ALFRED DEAKIN LECTURE, THE. VFOAT** Deakin Lecture. (1967). Monographic series. English. an. 5.00Aus$. Deakin Lecture Trust, GPO Box 1303L, Melbourne Victoria 3001 Australia. **Tel** 61 3 388 0111, FAX 61 3 388 0100. **Circ:** 1000 (ctrl).

GW
**ALGERIEN ELEKTRIZITATSWIRTSCHAFT / BUNDESSTELLE FUER AUSSENHANDELSINFORMATION.** German. DM2.00. Bundesstelle fuer Aussenhandelsinformation, Agrippastr 87 93, D 50676 Cologne Germany. **Tel** 011 49 221 2057316, FAX 011 49 221 2057212. **LC** HD9685.A5; A44. **DD** 338.4/736362.

US/1059-3799
**ALL-UNIVERSITY GERONTOLOGY CENTER PUBLIC POLICY SERIES. See** Senior Citizens.

●US/1070-3047
**ALTERNATIVES (WASHINGTON, D.C.).** (ALTERNATIVES : NEWSLETTER OF THE CENTER FOR POLICY ALTERNATIVES.). [Alternatives]. **Added/Corp** Center for Policy Alternatives (Washington, D.C.). Vol. 1, No. 1 (May 1993)-. Periodical. English. Ten times a year. $30.00. Center for Policy Alternatives, 1875 Connecticut Avenue Northwest, Suite 710, Washington DC 20009. **Tel** (202)387-6030. **LC** JK2403; .A48. **DD** 352. **Continues** Ways & Means, 0193-4716.

US/1045-3865
**AMERICAN GOVERNANCE.** 1989-. Periodical. English. qt. $20.00. Free Congress Foundation, 717 2nd Street NE, Washington DC 20002.

US/0090-547X
**AMERICAN GOVERNMENT : TEXT. See** Political Science.

US/0003-0066
**AMERICAN MOTOR CARRIER. See** Transportation.

US/0275-0740
**AMERICAN REVIEW OF PUBLIC ADMINISTRATION.** [Am. rev. public adm.]. **Added/Corp** American Society for Public Administration. Greater Kansas City Chapter. Park College. University of Missouri--Columbia. Dept. of Public Administration. University of Missouri--St. Louis. Master of Public Policy Administration Program. L.P. Cookingham Institute of Public Affairs. **VFOAT** A.R.P.A.; ARPA. Vol. 15, No. 1 (Spring 1981)-. Periodical. English. Four times a year. $50.00 (institutions); $22.00 (individuals). L P Cookingham, Institute of Public Affairs, Henry W Block School of Business and Publ Admin, University of Missouri-Kansas City, Kansas City MO 64110. **Tel** (816)276-2342, (816)235-2894, FAX (816)235-2312. **ED** John Clayton, Andrew Glassberg and Michael Diamond. **LC** JK1; .M5. **DD** 350/.0005. **[CCC]. Pr Rev.** available on microfilm and microfiche from University Microfilms International (UMI); available on an online database (file 648/Full-Text) from DIALOG. Documents available from UMI Article Clearinghouse. **Continues** Midwest Review of Public Administration.
**Desc:** Contains articles viewing administrative problems and ideas developing in federal offices away from the Potomac in state or local centers and in many diversified public administration institutions.
**Ind/Abst** ABC POL SCI; ABI/INFORM Glob. Ed.; ABI Inform Ondisc (Oct. 1974-); Bus. ASAP (1990-) [Full Txt.]; Bus. Index (1985-); Gen. BusinessFile (1985-); Gen. Period. Index (1985-); Int. Polit. Sci. Abstr.; J. Plan. Lit.; PAIS Int. Print (1991-); UMI ABI/Inform--Bus. Period. Ondisc (Dec. 1987-) [Full Txt.]; Urban Aff. Abstr. (1981-).

US/0091-1658
**AMERICAN STATISTICS INDEX. See** Public Administration-Abstracting, Bibliographies and Statistics.

IT
**AMMINISTRARE : RIVISTA QUADRIMESTRALE DELL'ISTITUTO PER LA SCIENZA DELL'AMMINISTRAZIONE PUBBLICA. Added/Corp** Istituto per la Scienza dell'Amministrazione Pubblica. (1963)-. Periodical. Italian. Three times a year. L74000.00 Italy; L120000.00 other. Societa Editrice il Mulino, Strada Maggiore 37, 40125 Bologna Italy. **Tel** 011 39 51 256011, FAX 011 39 51 256034.
**Ind/Abst** Soc. Plann. Policy Dev. Abstr.; Sociol. Abstr.

IT/0303-9722
**AMMINISTRAZIONE ITALIANA.** [Amm. ital.]. (1946)-. Periodical. Italian. mo. L210000 Italy; L300000 other. Soc Tipografica Barbieri, Casella Postale 427, 50053 Empoli Italy. **Tel** 011 39 571 920394.

AU
**AMTSBLATT DER STADT WIEN. Main/Corp** Vienna. German. Presse und Informationsdienst, Volksgartenstrasse 3, 1030 Vienna Austria. **LC** JS31.V6; V53A.

RM/1010-5506
**ANALE DE ISTORIE.** [An. ist.]. **Added/Corp** Institutul de Studii Istorice si Social-Politice de pe Linga C.C. al P.C.R. Vol. 15 (1969)-. Romanian (summaries and/or abstracts in French, English, German and Russian). bm (6 issues). $40.00. **(Subscription address:** Rompresfilatelia, PO Box 12 201, Bucharest Romania.**) LC** JN9639.A57; A22. **Bk Rev. Continues** Analele Institutului de Studii Istorice si Social-Politice de pe Linga C.C. al P.C.R.
**Desc:** Review of analysis and debate concerning the history of communist and workers movements in Romania.
**Ind/Abst** Am. Hist. Life (1963-).

UY
**ANALES PARLAMENTARIOS / REPUBLICA ORIENTAL DEL URUGUAY, PALACIO LEGISLATIVO - BIBLIOTECA.** No. 1-. Periodical. Spanish. Republica Oriental del Uruguay, Palacio Legislativo Biblioteca, Montevideo Uruguay. **LC** J251; .H62. **DD** 328.895/01.

US
**ANALYSIS OF FEDERAL R&D FUNDING BY FUNCTION, AN. Added/Corp** United States. National Science Foundation. Division of Science Resources Studies. (1972)-. Government

## Public Administration

Publication. English. an. Superintendent of Documents, US Government Printing Office, Washington DC 20402. **Tel** (202)275-3328, FAX (202)783-2377.

IT/0393-3962
**ANCI NOTIZIE.** [ANCI not.] **VFOAT** Notizie - Associazione Nazionale dei Comuni Italiani; Notizie - ANCI. (1984)-. Periodical. Italian. wk. L63000.00. Societa Editrice Romana SRL, Via Rialto 6, 00136 Rome Italy. **Tel** 011 39 6 39720656, 011 39 6 39720995. **UDC** 352.

IT/0393-3938
**ANCI RIVISTA.** [ANCI riv.]. **VFOAT** Rivista - Associazione Nazionale dei Comuni Italiani; Rivista - ANCI. (1985)-. Periodical. Italian. mo. L156000.00. Societa Editrice Romana SRL, Via Rialto 6, 00136 Rome Italy. **Tel** 011 39 6 39720656, 011 39 6 39720995. **UDC** 352.

CN/0713-6803
**ANJOU (ANJOU, QUEBEC).** (ANJOU ...). [Anjou]. Periodical. French. mo. Free. Hotel de Ville d'Anjou, 7701 Boulevard Louis-H Lafontaine, Anjou Quebec H1K 4B9 Canada. **DD** 352.0714/28.

UK
**ANNOTATED LEGISLATION SERVICE.** **Added/Corp** Butterworths (Firm). (1975)-. Monographic series. English. ir. Price varies per volume. Butterworth Heinemann / Woburn, MA, 225 Wildwood Avenue, Unit B, Woburn MA 01801. **Tel** (800)366-2665, FAX (617)928-2620, telex 880052. **LC** KD135.B8; A56. **Continues** Butterworths Annotated Legislation Service. Statutes Supplement.

CN
**ANNUAIRE ADMINISTRATIF DU QUEBEC.** 1973-. French. an. $5.00. Ministere des Communications, PO Box 1005, Quebec Quebec G1K 7B5 Canada. **Tel** (418)643-5150. **LC** JL241.A1; B67. **DD** 354/.714/0005. **Continues** Bottin Administratif du Quebec.

BE/0066-2461
**ANNUAIRE ADMINISTRATIF ET JUDICIAIRE DE BELGIQUE. ADMINISTRATIEF EN GERECHTELIJK JAARBOEK VOOR BELGIE. VFOAT** Administratif en Gerechtelijk Jaarboek voor Belgie. Vol. 94 (1967/68)-. Dutch (French and German). an. 5913.00F. Etablissements Emile Brylant, 67 rue de la Regence, 1000 Brussels Belgium. **Tel** 011 32 2 5129845. **ED** Johan Van Rillaer. **LC** JN6105; A6. Index available. **Bk Rev. Ad Acc. Circ:** 3,800. **Continues** Annuaire Administratif et Judiciaire de Belgique et de la Capitale du Royaume. Pouvoir Legislatif - Pouvoir Executif - Pouvoir Judiciaire. Institutions Provinciales et Communales.
**Desc:** Addresses public organizations, universities and the legal profession; administrative and legal yearbook of Belgium.

FR
**ANNUAIRE DE L'ADMINISTRATION LOCALE.** (1980)-. French. an. Editions Cujas, 4 6 8 rue de la Maison-Blanche, 75013 Paris France. **LC** JS4801; .A64. **DD** 352.044.

FR
**ANNUAIRE DEPARTEMENTAL PRIVE : ILE DE LA REUNION.** French. Societe les 4 Points Cardinaux France, France. **LC** JS4991.R34; R4. **Continues** Reunion; Annuaire Departmental Prive.

FR/0248-0573
**ANNUAIRE DES COLLECTIVITES LOCALES / C.N.R.S., G.R.A.L.** French. an. 320.00F. Litec Service Abonnements 6 Rue Victor Cousin, 75005 Paris France. **Tel** 011 33 1 46332237, FAX 46.33.50.32. **ED** Y Meny. **LC** JS4801; .A65. **DD** 352.044. ctrl circ.
**Ind/Abst** Int. Polit. Sci. Abstr.

FR
**ANNUAIRE DES SOCIETES ET DES ADMINISTRATEURS.** (1982)-. French. an. DAFSA Documentation, 25 Rue Leblanc, 75510 Paris Cedex 15 France. **Tel** 011 33 1 40605129. **LC** HG4151; .A73. **DD** 338.7/4/02544.

FR
**ANNUAIRE / ETABLISSEMENT PUBLIC REGIONAL DE BRETAGNE. Main/Corp** Brittany (France). Feb. 1983-. French. an. 5 rue Martenot, 35031 Rennes France. **LC** HC277.B7; E83A. **DD** 354.440081/8/09441.

FR
**ANNUAIRE EUROPEEN D'ADMINISTRATION PUBLIQUE.** **Added/Corp** Universite de Droit, d'Economie et des Sciences d'Aix-Marseille. Centre de Recherches Administratives. (1978)-. Periodical. French. an. 511.85F. Centre des Hautes Etudes Touristiques, Immeuble Euroff, 38 Avenue Europe, 13090 Aix-en-Provence France. **Tel** 011 33 42 200973. **LC** JN1; .A55. **DD** 351.004/094. **Circ:** 1,500.
**Desc:** Covers current public administrative issues on a European scale. Composed of studies and chronicles of administrative experience from a European and comparative perspective.
**Ind/Abst** Int. Polit. Sci. Abstr.

GO
**ANNUAIRE NATIONAL OFFICIEL DE LA REPUBLIQUE GABONAISE.** 1973-. French. Agence Havas Gabon, B P 213, Libreville Gabon. **LC** JQ3407.A1; A5. **DD** 916.7/21/034.

II/0376-5563
**ANNUAL ADMINISTRATION REPORT - FOOD AND DRUG ADMINISTRATION, MAHARASHTRA STATE. Main/Corp** Maharashtra, India (State). Food and Drug Administration. (1970/71)-. English. an. Rs0.70. Director - Government Printing and Stationery, Food and Drug Administration, Maharashtra State Director, Bombay India. **LC** HD9672.I53; M3. **DD** 354/.54/7920077. **NLM** W2 JI4.1 M3D5A. **Continues** Maharashtra, India (State). Directorate of Drugs Control Administration. Annual Administration Report.

II
**ANNUAL ADMINISTRATION REPORT FOR THE YEAR ... / TEA BOARD (INDIA). Main/Corp** India. Tea Board. English. an. Tea Board, 14 Biplabi Trailokya Maharaj Sarani, Calcutta-700 001 India. **LC** HD9198.I4; A23. **DD** 354.540082/333. **Continues** India. Central Tea Board. Annual Administration Report.

US
**ANNUAL AUTOMATION REPORT TO THE ARIZONA LEGISLATURE / DATA PROCESSING DIVISION, DEPARTMENT OF ADMINISTRATION, STATE OF ARIZONA. Main/Corp** Arizona. Dept. of Administration. Data Processing Division. English. an. Arizona Department of Administration, 1700 West Washington Street, Phoenix AZ 85007. **LC** JK8249.A8; A75A. **DD** 353.97910071/4.

US/1044-825X
**ANNUAL DIRECTORY OF WORLD LEADERS.** Ceased. [Annu. dir. world lead.]. **VFOAT** Directory of World Leaders. (1988/89)-(Feb. 1992). Directory. English. an. International Academy at Santa Barbara, 800 Garden Street, Suite D, Santa Barbara CA 93101. **Tel** (805)965-5010, FAX (805)965-6071. **LC** JF37; .A63. **DD** 351/.2.
**Desc:** Provides information on the leaders of independent countries.

US/0732-4618
**ANNUAL FINANCIAL REPORT AND REPORT OF OPERATIONS / PUBLIC EMPLOYEES' RETIREMENT SYSTEM, STATE OF CALIFORNIA. Main/Corp** California. Public Employees' Retirement System. **Added/Corp** California. Public Employees' Retirement System. Board of Administration. **VFOAT** PERS Annual Report, 1982-1983; Annual Report, 1984-1986; Annual Financial Report, B.1987-. (1980). English. an. Headquarters Office, Public Employees' Retirement System, 400 P Street, Sacramento CA 95814. **Tel** (916)326-3039. **ED** Jill Thomson-Skeoch. **LC** JK8760.P4; C35a. **DD** 353.9794005/05. ctrl circ. **Continues** Annual Financial Report and Report of Operations of the Board of Administration, State of California, Public Employees' Retirement System.
**Desc:** Contains a report on operations and investments.

US
**ANNUAL FINANCIAL REPORT / EXECUTIVE DEPARTMENT. Main/Corp** Texas. Executive Dept. English. an. Office of the Governor / Oregon, State Capitol, Salem OR 97310. **LC** JK4860.6.E94; T49A. **DD** 353.976471. **Continues** Annual Financial Report of the Executive Department, State of Texas.

US
**ANNUAL FINANCIAL REPORT FOR THE CALENDAR YEAR ENDED DECEMBER 31 ... - PUBLIC EMPLOYEES RETIREMENT SYSTEM OF OHIO. Main/Corp** Public Employees Retirement System of Ohio. English. an. PERS, 277 East Town Street, Columbus OH 43215. **LC** JK5560.P4; A25. **DD** 353.9771005/05. **Continues** Annual Financial Report to the Retirement Board, Public Employees Retirement System of Ohio for the Calendar Year Ended December 31 ..., 0277-6251.

II/0304-6516
**ANNUAL FINANCIAL STATEMENT AND EXPLANATORY MEMORANDUM ON THE BUDGET OF THE PUNJAB GOVERNMENT.** See Public Administration-Public Finance and Taxation.

US
**ANNUAL PLAN FOR THE GOVERNOR'S SPECIAL GRANT / STATE COMPREHENSIVE EMPLOYMENT & TRAINING OFFICE.** See Economics-Labor.

II
**ANNUAL PLAN - GOVERNMENT OF KARNATAKA, PLANNING DEPARTMENT.** See Economics-Economic History, Conditions.

US
**ANNUAL PLANNING INFORMATION. BRIDGEPORT-NORWALK-STAMFORD-VALLEY SERVICE DELIVERY AREA.** **VFOAT** Bridgeport Norwalk Stamford Valley Service Delivery Area. English. an. Free. Office of Research and Information, Employment Security Division, 200 Folly Brook Boulevard, Wethersfield CT 06109. **Tel** (203)566-2120. **ED** Margaret Gagnon and Roger Therrien. **LC** HD5726.A57; C66A. **DD** 331.1/09746/9. **Circ:** 350.
**Desc:** Prepared primarily for use by persons administering the job training partnership act (JTPA) in the Bridgeport, Norwalk, Standford, Valley service delivery area.

US/0748-6278
**ANNUAL PROCUREMENT AND FEDERAL ASSISTANCE REPORT.** Title Change. (ANNUAL PROCUREMENT AND FEDERAL ASSISTANCE REPORT / DEPARTMENT OF ENERGY.). [Annu. procure. fed. assist. rep.]. **Main/Corp** United States. Dept. of Energy. **Added/Corp** United States. Dept. of Energy. Procurement Support Office. (19??)-(19??). English. an. National Technical Information Service - NTIS, Room 2027S, 5285 Port Royal Road, Springfield VA 22161. **Tel** (703)487-4630, (703)487-4660, (703)487-4650, FAX (703)321-8547, telex 89-9405. **LC** HD9502.U5; U523i. **DD** 353.87/05. **Continued by** United States. Dept. of Energy. Annual Procurement and Financial Assistance Report.

AT
**ANNUAL REPORT. Main/Corp** Queensland. Dept. of Industry Development. (19??)-. English. an. Free. Head Office, 11 George Street, Brisbane QLD 4000 Australia. **Tel** FAX 07 2295289. **LC** HC607.Q4; Q4a. **DD** 354.9430082/06. **Circ:** 7,000 (ctrl).
**Desc:** Reports on the financial year activities of the department.

CN/0833-1731
**ANNUAL REPORT.** [Annu. rep. - Minist. Munic. Aff.]. **Main/Corp** Ontario. Ministry of Municipal Affairs. **VFOAT** Rapport Annuel. (1985/86)-. English (French). an. Ministry of Municipal Affairs, 777 Bay Street, Toronto Ontario M5G 2E5 Canada. **Tel** (416)585-7192. **DD** 354.7130686. **Continues in part** Ontario. Ministry of Municipal Affairs and Housing. Annual Report, 0821-9079.

US/0898-3100
**ANNUAL REPORT / ADMINISTRATIVE CONFERENCE OF THE UNITED STATES.** [Annu. rep. - Adm. Conf. U. S.]. **Main/Corp** Administrative Conference of the United States. **VFOAT** ACUS Annual Report. 1983-. English. an. Administrative Conference of the United States, 2120 L Street NW/Suite 500, Washington DC 20037. **Tel** (202)254-7065. **DD** 342. ctrl circ. **Continues** Report / Administrative Conference of the United States, 0898-6320.

US/0082-8610
**ANNUAL REPORT - ADVISORY COMMISSION ON INTERGOVERNMENTAL RELATIONS.** (ANNUAL REPORT.). **Main/Corp** United States. Advisory Commission on Intergovernmental Relations. **VFOAT** Advisory Commission on Intergovernmental Relations, the Year in Review; ACIR, The Year in Review. English. an. Advisory Commission on Intergovernmental Relations Library, 1701 Pennsylvania Avenue NW, Washington DC 20575. **Tel** (202)653-5540. **LC** JK325; .A2. available on microfiche (Vols. for (1978-1980) distributed to depository libraries in microfiche).

US
**ANNUAL REPORT - ALABAMA HISTORICAL COMMISSION. Main/Corp** Alabama Historical Commission. (19??)-. English. an. Alabama Historical Association, 725 Monroe Street, Montgomery AL 36130. **Tel** (205)832-6621. **LC** F321; .A1612a. **DD** 353.97610085/9.

CN/0383-3690
**ANNUAL REPORT - ALBERTA PUBLIC UTILITIES BOARD.** [Annu. rep. - Public Util. Board Alta.]. **Main/Corp** Public Utilities Board for the Province of Alberta. English. an. Free. Alberta Public Utilities Board, 11th Floor, 10055 106 Street, Edmonton Alberta T5J 2Y2 Canada. **Tel** (403)427-4901. **LC** HD9685.C3; A425A. **DD** 354/.7123/0087. **Circ:** 215.

# Public Administration

**US**
**ANNUAL REPORT AND GUIDE TO PROGRAMS / IDAHO DEPARTMENT OF HEALTH AND WELFARE.** See Public Health and Safety.

**US**
**ANNUAL REPORT / BALTIMORE REGIONAL COUNCIL OF GOVERNMENTS.** English. an. Free. Baltimore Regional Council of Governments, 601 N Howard Street, Baltimore MD 21201-4585. **Tel** (301)333-3333, FAX (301)659-1260. **Circ:** 2,000.

**SA**
**ANNUAL REPORT - BLACK RESETTLEMENT BOARD. Main/Corp** South Africa. Black Resettlement Board. **Added/Corp** South Africa. Black Resettlement Board. **VFOAT** Jaarverslag - Raad Vir die Hervestiging van Swartes. (1978/79)-. Afrikaans (English). an. Black Resettlement Board, Private Bag XL, Ferreirasdorp Johannesburg South Africa. **LC** HD991.A1; S64a. **DD** 354.680081/49668. **Continues** South Africa. Bantu Resettlement Board. Annual Report.

**US**
**ANNUAL REPORT - CALIFORNIA. DEPT. OF FAIR EMPLOYMENT AND HOUSING. OFFICE OF PUBLIC INFORMATION AND EDUCATION.** Title Change. **Main/Corp** California. Dept. of Fair Employment and Housing. Office of Public Information and Education. **VFOAT** Annual Report of the California Department of Fair Employment and Housing. English. an. **LC** HD4903.5.U58; C34A. **DD** 353.97940083/3. **Continued by** Annual Report (California. Dept. of Fair Employment and Housing).

CN/1187-2160
**ANNUAL REPORT / CANADIAN CENTRE FOR MANAGEMENT DEVELOPMENT.** [Annu. rep. - Can. Cent. Manage. Dev.]. **Main/Corp** Canadian Centre for Management Development. **VFOAT** Rapport Annuel. **VAT** Rapport Annuel - Centre Ccanadien de Gestion. (1991)-. English (French). **DD** 354.71001. **Continues** The Principal's Report., 0848-4317.

CN/0228-4723
**ANNUAL REPORT / CAPE BRETON DEVELOPMENT CORPORATION.** [Annu. rep. - Cape Breton Dev. Corp.]. **Main/Corp** Cape Breton Development Corporation (Canada). **VFOAT** Rapport Annuel. **VAT** Rapport Annuel - Societe de Developpement du Cap-Breton (Edition Anglaise et Francaise). 1st (1967)-?. English (French). an. Free. Cape Breton Development Corporation, PO Box 2500, Sydney Nova Scotia B1P 6K9 Canada. **Tel** (902)564-2848, FAX (902)564-2805, telex 019-351-32. **LC** HD4010.N6; C36a. **DD** 354.716/9008. **Circ:** 2,000 (ctrl). **Continued in part by** Annual Report ..., 0848-5267.

**AT**
**ANNUAL REPORT / CENTRAL LAND COUNCIL. Main/Corp** Central Land Council (Australia). (19??)-. English. an. Central Land Council, PO Box 3321, Alice Springs Northwest Territory 0870 Australia. **Tel** 011 61 8 9523800. **LC** J905; .L3 subser.; GN666. **DD** 354.940081/49915/005.

US/0360-0076
**ANNUAL REPORT - COMMONWEALTH OF MASSACHUSETTS, OFFICE FOR CHILDREN. Main/Corp** Massachusetts. Office for Children. English. an. Commonwealth of Massachusetts Office for the Children, 120 Boylston Street, Boston MA 02116. **LC** HV883.M4; M37A. **DD** 353.9/744/00847.

US/0882-0341
**ANNUAL REPORT - CONGRESSIONAL AWARD FOUNDATION (U.S.).** (ANNUAL REPORT.). [Annu. rep. - Congr. Award Found. (U.S.)]. **Main/Corp** Congressional Award Foundation (U.S.). English. an. Congressional Award, 701 North Fairfax Street/Suite 300, Alexandria VA 22314. **LC** HN90.V64; C67A. **DD** 361.3/7.

**AT**
**ANNUAL REPORT / CORPORATE AFFAIRS DEPARTMENT, WESTERN AUSTRALIA. Main/Corp** Western Australia. Corporate Affairs Dept. 1985/86-. Corporate Report. English. an. **LC** HD3616.A84; W478A. **DD** 354.9410082. **Continues** Report for the Financial Year ... / The Corporate Affairs Department of Western Australia.

US/0093-6367
**ANNUAL REPORT - DEPARTMENT OF COMMISSIONERS OF THE LAND OFFICE (OKLAHOMA CITY).** (ANNUAL REPORT - DEPARTMENT OF COMMISSIONERS OF THE LAND OFFICE.). **Main/Corp** Oklahoma. Department of Commissioners of the Land Office. **VFOAT** Annual Report - Commissioners of the Land Office. Periodical. English. **LC** LB2827; .O5. **DD** 333. **Continues** Biennial Report - Department of Commissioners of the Land Office.

AT/0816-3073
**ANNUAL REPORT / DEPARTMENT OF INDUSTRY, TECHNOLOGY AND COMMERCE. Main/Corp** Australia. Dept. of Industry, Technology and Commerce. **Added/Corp** Australian Customs Service. Australian Government Publishing Service. (1985)-. Government Publication. English. an. Australian Government Publishing Service, GPO Box 84, Canberra ACT 2601 Australia. **Tel** 011 61 6 2954411, FAX 011 61 6 2954455. **LC** HC601; .A76a. **DD** 354.940082/06.

**AT**
**ANNUAL REPORT / DEPARTMENT OF LANDS ADMINISTRATION. Main/Corp** Western Australia. Dept. of Lands Administration. 1987-. English. an. **LC** HD1039.W47; A33A. **DD** 354.940071/32/06. **Continues** Annual Report / Western Australia. Dept. of Lands and Surveys.

SA/0304-694X
**ANNUAL REPORT - DEPARTMENT OF THE INTERIOR.** (ANNUAL REPORT - DEPARTMENT OF THE INTERIOR (SOUTH AFRICA).). **Main/Corp** South Africa. Dept. of the Interior. **VFOAT** Jaarverslag - Departement Van Binnelandse Sake. 1972-. Afrikaans (Afrikaans and English). 0.75. Government Printer / South Africa, Bosman Street, Private Bag X85, Pretoria 0001 South Africa. **Tel** 011 27 12 3239731 Ext. 262. **LC** JQ1950.I5; S68A.

**US**
**ANNUAL REPORT / ELECTED OFFICIALS' RETIREMENT SYSTEM, STATE OF ARIZONA. Main/Corp** Arizona. Elected Officials' Retirement System. **Added/Corp** Arizona. Public Safety Personnel Retirement System. (June 30, 1982)-. English. an. Elected Officials' Retirement System, 3033 North Central/Room 411, Phoenix AZ 85012. **LC** JK8260.P4; A75a. **DD** 353.9791005.

**AT**
**ANNUAL REPORT FOR THE YEAR ENDED 30TH JUNE ... / ABORIGINAL AFFAIRS PLANNING AUTHORITY. Main/Corp** Western Australia. Aboriginal Affairs Planning Authority. **Added/Corp** Western Australia. Aboriginal Lands Trust. **VFOAT** Annual Report of the Aboriginal Affairs Planning Authority and Aboriginal Lands Trust. (19??)-. English. an. $2.50. Aboriginal Affairs Planning Authority, PO Box 628, West Perth 6005 Western Australia. **Tel** (09)3227044, FAX (09)321 0990, telex 93262. **LC** GN667.W5; W43b. **DD** 354/.941/008484. **Circ:** 1,000 (ctrl). **Desc:** Report on the operations of the Western Australian Government Office of Aboriginal Affairs including the Aboriginal Lands Trust.

**AT**
**ANNUAL REPORT FOR THE YEAR ENDING 30TH JUNE ... / GREAT SOUTHERN DEVELOPMENT AUTHORITY. Main/Corp** Western Australia. Great Southern Development Authority. **VFOAT** Annual Report. English. an. **LC** HC607.W47; W4743A. **DD** 354.9410082/0941/2.

ZA/0514-5562
**ANNUAL REPORT FOR THE YEAR ... / REPUBLIC OF ZAMBIA, MINISTRY OF HOME AFFAIRS. Main/Corp** Zambia. Ministry of Home Affairs. (19??)-. English. an. Zambia Ministry of Home Affairs, Government Printer, Lusaka Zambia. **Tel** 01-215401, telex 2A40290. **LC** WMLC L 83/6430. **DD** 354.

**ZA**
**ANNUAL REPORT FOR THE YEARS ... / REPUBLIC OF ZAMBIA, MINISTRY OF LEGAL AFFAIRS. Main/Corp** Zambia. Ministry of Legal Affairs. English. an. 30. **LC** LAW. **DD** 354.6894008/8.

**IE**
**ANNUAL REPORT / GARDA SIOCHANA COMPLAINTS BOARD. Main/Corp** Ireland. Garda Siochana. Complaints Board. 1987/88-. English. an. Government Publications, 4 5 Harcourt Road, Dublin 2 Ireland. **Tel** 011 353 1 6613111 Ext.4005. **LC** PAR.

**AT**
**ANNUAL REPORT / GOVERNMENT OF WESTERN AUSTRALIA, DEPARTMENT OF COMPUTING & INFORMATION TECHNOLOGY. Main/Corp** Western Australia. Dept. of Computing & Information Technology. **VFOAT** Western Australia Department of Computing and Information Technology Annual Report. (1985)-. Government Publication. English. an. Government of Western Australia / Department of State Services, 32 St George's Terrace, Perth 6000 WA Australia. **LC** HC607.W47; W46a. **DD** 354.9410081/9.

US/0276-9468
**ANNUAL REPORT - ILLINOIS. GENERAL ASSEMBLY. LEGISLATIVE INVESTIGATING COMMITTEE.** (ANNUAL REPORT ... / BY THE ILLINOIS LEGISLATIVE INVESTIGATING COMMISSION.). **Main/Corp** Illinois. General Assembly. Legislative Investigating Commission. Began in 1975. English. an. Legislative Investigating Commission, 300 West Washington Street, Chicago IL 60606. **LC** JK5774.8; .I43B. **DD** 328.773/07452. **Continues** Report of the Illinois Legislative Investigating Commission, 0094-9795.

CN/0823-5864
**ANNUAL REPORT INCLUDING ... OBJECTIVES AND ACTION PLANS - EQUAL OPPORTUNITIES FOR WOMEN.** See Women's Interests.

CN/0826-9904
**ANNUAL REPORT, INFORMATION COMMISSIONER.** [Annu. rep. - Inf. Comm.]. **Main/Corp** Canada. Information Commissioner of Canada. **VFOAT** Rapport Annuel du Commissaire A l'Information. 1983-84-. English (French). an. Free. Information Commissioner of Canada, 112 Kent Street/14th Floor, Ottawa Ontario K1A 1H3 Canada. **Tel** (800)267-0441. **ED** Sharon Cyr. **LC** JL86.S43; C36A. **DD** 354.710081/9/06. Index available. **Bk Rev. Ad Acc. Circ:** 7,000 (ctrl). **Desc:** Report of the specialist ombudsman who investigates complaints under Canada's Access to Information Act. Summaries of all complaints, statistics and organization chart.

NE/0165-1803
**ANNUAL REPORT - INTERNATIONAL INSTITUTE FOR LAND RECLAMATION AND IMPROVEMENT.** (ANNUAL REPORT.). [Annu. rep. - Int. Inst. Land Reclam. Improv.]. **Main/Corp** International Institute for Land Reclamation and Improvement. (1958)-. English. ir. Free on request. International Institute for Land Reclamation and Improvement, PO Box 45, 6700 AA Wageningen Netherlands. **Tel** 011 31 837019100, FAX 11524, telex 75230 NL. **LC** S605; .I5. **DD** 631.6/05. **CODEN** AILRAS.

US/0094-9515
**ANNUAL REPORT - JOINT FEDERAL-STATE LAND USE PLANNING COMMISSION FOR ALASKA.** [Annu. rep. - Jt. Fed.-State Land Use Plan. Comm. Alsk.]. **Main/Corp** Joint Federal-State Land Use Planning Commission for Alaska. 1972-. English. an. Joint Federal-State Land Use Planning Commission for Alaska, 733 West Fourth Avenue, Anchorage AK 99501. **LC** HD243.A3; J64A.

**KE**
**ANNUAL REPORT / KENYA RAILWAYS. Main/Corp** Kenya Railways. English. an. Kenya Railways Corporation, PO Box 30121, Nairobi Kenya. **LC** HE3419; .A35A. **DD** 385/.09676/2. **Continues** Annual Report and Accounts for ... / Kenya Railways Corporation.

**UK**
**ANNUAL REPORT / LAND AUTHORITY FOR WALES. Main/Corp** Great Britain. Land Authority for Wales. (19??)-. English. Land Authority for Wales, Brunel House, Cardiff CF2 1SQ Wales England. **LC** HD609.W3; G73a. **DD** 354.4290082/326/06.

**US**
**ANNUAL REPORT / LEGISLATIVE SERVICE OFFICE - WYOMING. Main/Corp** Wyoming. Legislative Service Office. Began with vol. for 1978. English. an. Legislative Service Office, 213 Capitol Building, Cheyenne WY 82002. **LC** JK7674; .W85A. **DD** 328.787/0761. **Formed by the union of** Annual Report **and** Annual Report.

CN/0837-6840
**ANNUAL REPORT / MANITOBA LOTTERIES FOUNDATION.** [Annu. rep. - Manit. Lotteries Found.]. **Main/Corp** Manitoba Lotteries Foundation. (1983/84)-. English. an. 116 Legislative Building, Winnipeg Manitoba R3C 0V8 Canada. **LC** HG6150.M3; M35A. **DD** 354.71270072/6. **Continues** Annual Report / Manitoba Lotteries and Gaming Control Commission, 0824-8508.

CN/0840-7185
**ANNUAL REPORT / MINISTRY OF CITIZENSHIP.** [Annu. rep. - Minist. Citizsh.]. **Main/Corp** Ontario. Ministry of Citizenship. **VFOAT** Rapport Annuel. **VAT** Rapport Annuel - Ministere des Afaires Civiques. (1988)-. English (French). an. **DD** 354.7130681/4. **Separated from** Ontario. Ministry of Citizenship and Culture. Annual Report., 0823-504X.

# Public Administration

CN/0317-6827
**ANNUAL REPORT - MINISTRY OF GOVERNMENT SERVICES. Main/Corp** Ontario. Ministry of Government Services. (1973)-. English. Ferguson Block, 77 Wellesley Street, Toronto Ontario M7A 1N3 Canada. **LC** JL272; .Z5a. **DD** 354/.713/067.

US/0149-2403
**ANNUAL REPORT - MISSOURI ELECTIONS COMMISSION. Main/Corp** Missouri. Elections Commission. (19??)-. English. an. Missouri Elections Commission, 631 West Main Street, Jefferson City MO 65101. **LC** KFM8220.85.C2; A84. **DD** 353.9/778/091.

UK
**ANNUAL REPORT / NATIONAL GAS CONSUMERS' COUNCIL (GREAT BRITAIN). Main/Corp** National Gas Consumers' Council (Great Britain). English. an. Fred. Gas Consumers Council, Abford House, 15 Wilton Road, London SW1V 1LT England. **Tel** 01-931 0977. **ED** Beverley Parkin. **LC** HD9581.G7; N36A. **DD** 354.410082/042. **Circ:** 15,000. **Continues** National Gas Consumers' Council (Great Britain). Report of the National Gas Consumers' Council for the Year Ended March 31 ... .

AT
**ANNUAL REPORT - NATIONAL TRUST OF AUSTRALIA, W.A. Main/Corp** National Trust of Australia (Western Australia). (19??)-. English. National Trust of Australia -W.A., Old Perth Boys School, 139 Saint Georges Terrace, Perth 6000 Western Australia. **Tel** (09)321-6088. **LC** AS722.N37; A23. **DD** 994. **Bk Rev**. **Ad Acc**. **Circ:** 2,200 (ctrl).
**Desc:** Report of the work of the national trust in Western Australia for the year past.

CN/1183-2614
**ANNUAL REPORT - NEW BRUNSWICK. DEPT. OF INTERGOVERNMENTAL AFFAIRS.** (ANNUAL REPORT / INTERGOVERNMENTAL AFFAIRS). [Annu. rep. - N.B., Dep. Intergov. Aff.]. **Main/Corp** New Brunswick. Dept. of Intergovernmental Affairs. **VFOAT** Rapport Annuel. **VAT** Rapport Annuel - Nouveau-Brunswick. Ministere des Affaires Intergouvernementales. (1989/1990)-. English (French). **DD** 354.715/108/05.

US
**ANNUAL REPORT / NEW MEXICO STATE LAND OFFICE. Main/Corp** New Mexico State Land Office. 71st Fiscal Year (July 1, 1982 to June 30, 1983)-. English. an. Free. New Mexico State Land Office, PO Box 1148, Santa Fe NM 87504. **Tel** (505)827-5760. **LC** HD184.N6; A3. **DD** 353.97890082/3/06. **Circ:** 500 (ctrl). **Continues** New Mexico. Commissioner of Public Lands. Report.
**Desc:** A report which gives departmental updates, beneficiary information, internal reports and information on income generated and earned by the State Land Office.

US
**ANNUAL REPORT ... NEW YORK, NEW JERSEY / PALISADES INTERSTATE PARK COMMISSION. Main/Corp** Palisades Interstate Park Commission. (1981)-. English. an. Palisades Interstate Park Commission, Administrative Building, Bear Mountain NY 10911. ctrl circ. **Continues** Composite Annual Report, New York-New Jersey.

US
**ANNUAL REPORT / NEW YORK STATE ASSEMBLY, STANDING COMMITTEE ON GOVERNMENTAL OPERATIONS. Main/Corp** New York (State). Legislature. Assembly. Standing Committee on Governmental Operations. **Added/Corp** New York (State). Legislature. Assembly. Standing Committee on Governmental Operations. Annual Report of the Standing Committee on Governmental Operations. **VFOAT** Annual Report of the Standing Committee on Governmental Operations; Annual Report of the New York State Assembly Standing Committee on Governmental Operations. (19??)-. English. 839 Legislative Office Building, Albany NY 12248. **LC** KFN5010.8; .G68. **DD** 342.747/066; 347.470266.

US
**ANNUAL REPORT / NEW YORK STATE, OFFICE OF ADVOCATE FOR THE DISABLED. Main/Corp** New York (State). Office of Advocate for the Disabled. (19??)-. Periodical. English. an. New York State Office of Advocate for the Disabled, Agency Building 1/10th Floor, Albany NY 12223. **Tel** (518)473-4129. **ED** Alan Sangiacomo. **LC** HV1555.N7; N5a. **DD** 353.97470084/4/06. **Ad Acc**. **Circ:** 12,000 (ctrl).
**Desc:** Information about the Developmental Disabilities Planning Council in New York State. Contains council initiatives, legislation, grant availability in New York, special projects, etc.

US
**ANNUAL REPORT / NEW YORK'S LOTTERY. Main/Corp** New York (State). Division of the Lottery. **VFOAT** New York's Lottery Annual Report. (1983/84)-. English. Division of the Lottery, Swan Street Building, Empire State Plaza, Albany NY 12223.
**Continues** Report / New York (State). Division of the Lottery.

US/0275-3162
**ANNUAL REPORT - NYS PROJECT FINANCE AGENCY. Main/Corp** New York State Project Finance Agency. 1975-. English. an. New York State Project Finance Agency, 1250 Broadway, New York NY 10001. **LC** HD7303.N7; N47A. **DD** 353.97470081/8/06.

US
**ANNUAL REPORT OF ... / BY THE ILLINOIS LEGISLATIVE INVESTIGATING COMMISSION. Main/Corp** Illinois. General Assembly. Legislative Investigating Commission. (19??)-. English. an. **LC** JK5774.8; .I43b. **DD** 328.773/07452. **Continues** Illinois. General Assembly. Legislative Investigation Commission. Annual Report, 0276-9468.

US/0098-2296
**ANNUAL REPORT OF FEDERAL PREVAILING RATE ADVISORY COMMITTEE. Main/Corp** United States. Federal Prevailing Rate Advisory Committee. 1st (1973)-. Government Publication. English. an. Superintendent of Documents, US Government Printing Office, Washington DC 20402. **Tel** (202)275-3328, **FAX** (202)786-2377. **LC** KF5375; .A834. **DD** 353.001/2.

CN/0227-8073
**ANNUAL REPORT OF THE CHIEF ELECTORAL OFFICER ADMINISTERING THE ELECTION FINANCES AND CONTRIBUTIONS DISCLOSURE ACT.** [Annu. rep. Chief Elect. Off. adm. Elect. financ. contrib. discl. act]. **Main/Corp** Alberta. Chief Electoral Officer. 2nd (1979)-. English. an. Free. Alberta Legislative Assembly, Office of the Chief Electoral Officer, West Chambers Building/Main Floor, 12220 Stony Plain Road, Edmonton Alberta T5N 3Y4 Canada. **Tel** (403)427-7191, FAX (403)422-2900. **DD** 354.712309/1. **Circ:** 1,000 (ctrl). **Continues** Alberta. Office of the Chief Electoral Officer. Report of the Chief Electoral Officer Administering the Election Finances and Contributions Disclosure Act., 0708-6504.
**Desc:** A report covering the administration of the Election Finances and contributions Disclosure Act for the calendar year 1987/1988.

AT
**ANNUAL REPORT OF THE COMMISSIONER OF LAND TAX ON THE OPERATION OF THE ACTS DURING THE YEAR ... / QUEENSLAND. Main/Corp** Queensland. Commissioner of Land Tax. English. an. **LC** WMLC L 83/4851.

CN/0549-9879
**ANNUAL REPORT OF THE COMMISSIONER OF THE NORTHWEST TERRITORIES.** Title Change. **Main/Corp** Northwest Territories. Commissioner. **VFOAT** Rapport Annuel du Commissaire des Territoires du Nord-Ouest. English. an. Canada Department of Information, Ottawa Ontario Canada. **LC** JL461.A1; N67B. **DD** 354.719/20006; 352. **Superseded by** Annual Report of the Government of the Northwest Territories.

US
**ANNUAL REPORT OF THE COMMUNITY RELATIONS SERVICE. Main/Corp** United States. Community Relations Service. (1982)-. Government Publication. English. an. Free on request. US Department of Justice Community Relations Service, 5550 Friendship Boulevard, Room 330, Chevy Chase MD 20815. **Tel** (301)492-5929. **LC** E184.A1; U517.
**Continues** United States. Community Relations Service. Annual Report, 0565-1727.

UK
**ANNUAL REPORT OF THE COUNCIL ON TRIBUNALS FOR THE PERIOD, THE. Main/Corp** Great Britain. Council on Tribunals. (May 29, 1970)-. English. an (Jan.). Price varies. Her Majesty's Stationery Office, 51 Nine Elms Lane, London SW8 5DR England. **Tel** 011 44 71 873 8459, 011 44 71 873 8499, **FAX** 011 44 71 873 8499, 011 44 71 873 8456, telex 297138. **(Subscription address:** Her Majesty's Stationery Office, PO Box 276, Publications Centre, London SW8 5DT England.) **LC** KD4890; .A877. **DD** 343.41/0664; 344.102664. **Continues** Great Britain. Council on Tribunals. Annual Report of the Council on Tribunals for the Year Ended 31st December.

II
**ANNUAL REPORT OF THE DEPARTMENT OF ANIMAL HUSBANDRY AND VETERINARY SERVICES IN KARNATAKA, INDO-DANISH PROJECT HESSARGHATTA AND BANGALORE DAIRY, BANGALORE. Ceased.** See Veterinary Sciences.

RH
**ANNUAL REPORT OF THE DIRECTOR OF WORKS FOR THE YEAR. Main/Corp** Harare (Zimbabwe). Dept. of Works. English. an. Department of Works, Cleveland House, Moffat Street, Harare Zimbabwe. **LC** HD4351; .A37A. **DD** 352.7/096891.

UK
**ANNUAL REPORT OF THE DIRECTOR TO THE BOARD OF GOVERNORS. Main/Corp** Great Britain. Commonwealth Institute. (1958)-. Periodical. English. an. Free. Commonwealth Institute / London, Head of Information, Kensington High Street, London W8 6NQ England. **Tel** 011 44 1 603 4535. **Circ:** 1,500 (ctrl). **Continues** Gt. Brit. Imperial Institute. Annual Report.
**Desc:** Annual report giving a summary of the year's events, activities, future aims, etc.

SE
**ANNUAL REPORT OF THE ELECTRICITY DIVISION FOR THE YEAR ... (SEYCHELLES). Main/Corp** Seychelles. Electricity Division. English. an. **LC** HD9685.S47; S48A. **DD** 354.69/6008722/006.
**Continues** Seychelles. Electricity Dept. Annual Report.

CN/0384-2479
**ANNUAL REPORT OF THE GOVERNMENT OF THE NORTHWEST TERRITORIES. Main/Corp** Northwest Territories. **VFOAT** Rapport Annuel du Gouvernement des Territoires du Nord-Ouest. (1973)-. English (French). an. Bureau of Statistics / Yellow Knife, Government of Northwest Territories, Yellow Knife Northwest Territories, X1A 2L9 Canada. **Tel** (403)873-7653. **LC** JL461.A1; N67A. **DD** 354.719/20006. **Supersedes** Annual Report of the Commissioner of the Northwest Territories, 0549-9879.

ZA
**ANNUAL REPORT OF THE MANAGEMENT SERVICES SECTION FOR THE YEARS ... . Main/Corp** Zambia. Cabinet Office. Management Services Section. (1981)-. English. an. **LC** JQ2829.C55; Z35a. **DD** 354.68940071. **Continues** Zambia. Cabinet Office. Management Services Section. Annual Report.

SA
**ANNUAL REPORT OF THE OILSEED CONTROL BOARD FOR THE PERIOD ... / OILSEED CONTROL BOARD. Main/Corp** South Africa Oilseeds Control Board. 1st- Feb. 1952/Feb. 1953-. English. an.

CN/0708-7217
**ANNUAL REPORT OF THE PARLIAMENTARY COMMISSIONER. OMBUDSMAN.** (ANNUAL REPORT OF THE PARLIAMENTARY COMMISSIONER (OMBUDSMAN) FOR THE CALENDAR YEAR ...). **Main/Corp** Newfoundland. Office of the Parliamentary Commissioner (Ombudsman). (1976)-. English. an. **LC** JL205.A55; O44a. **DD** 328.718/07452. **Continues** Newfoundland. Office of the Parliamentary Commissioner (Ombudsman). Report of the Parliamentary Commissioner (Ombudsman) for the Period ..., 0382-179X.

AT
**ANNUAL REPORT OF THE PIG MEAT PROMOTION ADVISORY COMMITTEE FOR THE YEAR ENDED 30 JUNE ... / DEPARTMENT OF PRIMARY INDUSTRY. Main/Corp** Australia. Pig Meat Promotion Advisory Committee. English. an. $1.00. Pig Meat Promotion Advisory Committee, Department of Primary Industry, Canberra Australian Capitol Territory 2600 Australia. **LC** J905; .L3 subser; HD9435.A8. **DD** 300/.994 S; 354.940082/656649.

US
**ANNUAL REPORT OF THE PRESIDENT ON FEDERAL ADVISORY COMMITTEES. Added/Corp** United States. General Services Administration. **VFOAT** Federal Advisory Committees. 14th (1985)-. English. an. UNIPUB, 4611-F Assembly Drive, Lanham MD 20706-4391. **Tel** (800)274-4888, **FAX** (301)459-0056, telex 28787 GATT CH. **Continues** Federal Advisory Committees ... Annual Report of the President, Covering the Calendar Year ... .

# Public Administration

CN/0827-987X
**ANNUAL REPORT OF THE PRINCE EDWARD ISLAND DEPARTMENT OF COMMUNITY AND CULTURAL AFFAIRS.** (ANNUAL REPORT OF THE PRINCE EDWARD ISLAND DEPARTMENT OF COMMUNITY AND CULTURAL AFFAIRS FOR THE YEAR ENDING DECEMBER 31 ...). [Annu. rep. P.E.I. Dep. Community Cult. Aff.]. **Main/Corp** Prince Edward Island. Dept. of Community and Cultural Affairs. **VFOAT** Annual Report for the Fiscal Year Ended March 31 ... and for Activities to December 31 ... . (1982)-(1986). English. an. PO Box 2000, Charlottetown Prince Edward Island Canada. **LC** JL216.Z3; C656a. **DD** 354.717068. *Continues* Annual Report of the Prince Edward Island Department of Community Affairs for the Year Ending Dec. 31 ..., 0710-4928. *Continued in part by* Annual Report, 0848-5844.

US
**ANNUAL REPORT OF THE PUBLIC EMPLOYEE RETIREMENT SYSTEM OF IDAHO.** *Title Change.* **Main/Corp** Idaho. Public Employee Retirement Board. 1st (Apr. 20, 1965-July 1, 1966)-(19??). English. an. Employee Retirement Board, State House, 820 Washington Street, Boise ID 83712. **LC** JK7560.P4; I3a. **DD** 353.9796001/82/05. *Continued by* PERSI Component Unit Financial Report for the Fiscal Year Ended ... .

PR
**ANNUAL REPORT OF THE PUBLIC SERVICE COMMISSION TO THE HONORABLE GOVERNOR OF PUERTO RICO.** **Main/Corp** Puerto Rico. Public Service Commission. **VFOAT** Annual Report - Public Service Commission. Periodical. English. **LC** HD2768.P7; A34. **DD** 354.

BH
**ANNUAL REPORT OF THE PUBLIC WORKS DEPARTMENT (BELIZE).** (ANNUAL REPORT OF THE PUBLIC WORKS DEPARTMENT.). **Main/Corp** British Honduras. Public Works Department. **VFOAT** Annual Report - British Honduras, Public Works Department. Periodical. English. Government Printer / British Honduras, 1 Church Street, Belize City British Honduras. **LC** HD4019; .A3. **DD** 351.8.

CN/0837-6875
**ANNUAL REPORT OF THE SASKATCHEWAN PORK PRODUCERS MARKETING BOARD.** *See* Food and Food Industry.

US
**ANNUAL REPORT OF THE UTAH LIQUOR CONTROL COMMISSION.** **Main/Corp** Utah. Liquor Control Commission. English. an. Utah Liquor Control Commission, 1625 South 900 West, PO Box 30408, Salt Lake City UT 84125. **LC** HV5079.U8; A3. **DD** 353/97920076/1/05. *Continues* Utah. Liquor Control Commission. Report on Operations.

US/0160-1520
**ANNUAL REPORT - OFFICE OF THE SECRETARY OF STATE.** **Main/Corp** Texas. Secretary of State. (19??)-. English. Secretary of State / Texas, PO Box 13824 Capitol Station, Austin TX 78711. **Tel** (512)463-5561. **LC** J87; .T44aa. **DD** 353.9/764/1.

US
**ANNUAL REPORT - OKLAHOMA PUBLIC EMPLOYEES RETIREMENT SYSTEM.** **Main/Corp** Oklahoma. Public Employees Retirement System. English. an. Oklahoma Public Employees Retirement System, 580 Jim Throphe Building, PO Box 53007, Oklahoma City OK 73132. **LC** JK7160.P4; O37A. **DD** 353.9766005.

CN/0826-7294
**ANNUAL REPORT - OMBUDSMAN. ONTARIO (1984).** (ANNUAL REPORT / THE OMBUDSMAN OF ONTARIO.). [Annu. rep. - Ombudsman, Ont.]. **Main/Corp** Ontario. Office of the Ombudsman. **VFOAT** Rapport Annuel. 11th Ed. (1983/84)-. English. Office of the Ombudsman, 8 Bastion Square, Victoria British Columbia V8W 1H9 Canada. **DD** 354.713009/1/05. *Continues* Ontario. Office of the Ombudsman. Report - The Ombudsman/Ontario., 0704-5204; *Absorbed* Ontario. Office of the Ombudsman. Rapport Annuel.

AT/0726-9943
**ANNUAL REPORT ... ON ACTIVITIES TO 30 JUNE ... / THE AUSTRALIAN BICENTENNIAL AUTHORITY.** **Main/Corp** Australian Bicentennial Authority. **VFOAT** Annual Report. (19??)-. English. an. Australian Bicentennial Authority, 88 George Street, The Rocks Sydney, GPO Box Aus 1988, Sydney New South Wales 2001 Australia. **LC** DU117.14; .A94a. **DD** 354.94085/9.

HK
**ANNUAL REPORT ON THE ACTIVITIES OF THE INDEPENDENT COMMISSION AGAINST CORRUPTION.** **Main/Corp** Hong Kong. Independent Commission Against Corruption. **Added/Corp** Hongkong. Independent Commission Against Corruption. Tsung Tu Te Pai Lien Cheng Chuan Yuan Kung Shu Kung tso Nien Pao. **VFOAT** Tsung Tu Te Pai Lien Cheng Chuan Yuan Kung Shu Kung Tso Nien Pao. (1974)-. Multiple languages (Chinese and English). an. $14.00. The Secretary to the Independent Commission Against Corruption, Hutchinson House/6th Floor, Hong Kong. **(Subscription address:** Government Information Service, Publications Office, 1 Battery Path, Hong Kong Hong Kong.**)** **LC** JQ675.A55; C63. **DD** 354/.51/2500995.

NX/0572-0494
**ANNUAL REPORT ON THE TERRITORY OF NORFOLK ISLAND.** **Main/Corp** Norfolk Island. **Added/Corp** Australia. Department of External Territories. Australia. Department of Territories. **VFOAT** Territory of Norfolk Island Annual Report; Annual Report - Territory of Norfolk Island; Report - Territory of Norfolk Island; Territory of Norfolk Island Report. Government Publication. English. an. 12.65Aus$. Administration of Norfolk Island, Kingston, Norfolk Island 2899. **LC** J912; .R2. **DD** 994; 354.94. **Circ:** 250. *Continues* Norfolk Island. Report of the Administrator.

US/0475-6126
**ANNUAL REPORT - PANAMA CANAL COMPANY, CANAL ZONE GOVERNMENT.** **Main/Corp** Panama Canal Company. **Added/Corp** Canal Zone. **VFOAT** Annual Report - Canal Zone Government. (1952)-. Government Publication. English. ir. Superintendent of Documents, US Government Printing Office, Washington DC 20402. **Tel** (202)275-3328, **FAX** (202)786-2377. **LC** J184.5; .P324. **DD** 338.39; 353.8. *Continues* Annual Report of the Governor of; Annual Report of the Board of Directors the Panama Canal. *Superseded in part by* President's Report to the Board of Directors, 0553-0873.

UK
**ANNUAL REPORT - PARLIAMENTARY COMMISSIONER FOR ADMINISTRATION.** **Main/Corp** Great Britain. Parliament. House of Commons. Parliamentary Commissioner. (19??)-. English. an. £8.90. Her Majesty's Stationery Office, 51 Nine Elms Lane, London SW8 5DR England. **Tel** 011 44 71 873 8459, 011 44 71 873 8499, **FAX** 011 44 71 873 8499, 011 44 71 873 8456, telex 297138. **(Subscription address:** Her Majesty's Stationery Office, PO Box 276, Publications Centre, London SW8 5DT England.**)**

●US
**ANNUAL REPORT PREPARED FOR THE PRESIDENT OF THE UNITED STATES AND THE UNITED STATES CONGRESS.** **Main/Corp** United States. Martin Luther King, Jr., Federal Holiday Commission. (1993)-. Periodical. English. **LC** E185.97.K5; A76. *Continues* Annual Report of the Martin Luther King, Jr. Federal Holiday Commission to Fulfill the King Legacy.

TH
**ANNUAL REPORT / PROVINCIAL ELECTRICITY AUTHORITY.** **Main/Corp** Thailand. Kanfaifa Suan Phumiphak. (19??)-. English. an. **LC** HD9685.T5; T48a. **DD** 354.5930087/22/006.

US/0196-6685
**ANNUAL REPORT - PUBLIC EMPLOYEES' RETIREMENT ASSOCIATION OF NEW MEXICO.** *See* Economics-Labor.

ZA
**ANNUAL REPORT / REPUBLIC OF ZAMBIA, OFFICE OF THE PRIME MINISTER, PROVINCIAL AND LOCAL GOVERNMENT ADMINISTRATION DIVISION, EASTERN PROVINCE.** **Main/Corp** Zambia. Provincial and Local Government Administration Division. Eastern Province. **VFOAT** Eastern Province Annual Report for ... . (1983)-. English. Zambia Government Printer, POB 30136, Lusaka Zambia. **LC** HC915.Z7; E188A. **DD** 354.6894. *Continues* Eastern Province Annual Report.

US
**ANNUAL REPORT / RESIDENTIAL UTILITY CONSUMER UNIT, OFFICE OF CONSUMER SERVICES, MINNESOTA DEPARTMENT OF COMMERCE.** **Main/Corp** Minnesota. Residential Utility Consumer Unit. **Added/Corp** Minnesota. Board of Residential Utility Consumers. (1979)-. English. an. **LC** HD2767.M62; M56a. **DD** 353.97760087.

AT
**ANNUAL REPORT - RURAL RECONSTRUCTION AUTHORITY OF WESTERN AUSTRALIA.** *Title Change.* **Main/Corp** Rural Reconstruction Authority of Western Australia. 1st- 1971/72-. English. Rural Reconstruction Authority of Western Australia, Central Government Buildings, Barrack Street, Perth Western Australia. **LC** HG2051.A82; W34A. **DD** 354/.941/008233. *Continued by* Rural Reconstruction Authority of Western Australia. Annual Report.

CN/0837-9823
**ANNUAL REPORT / SASKATCHEWAN LEGISLATIVE LIBRARY.** [Annu. rep. - Sask., Legis. Libr.]. **Main/Corp** Saskatchewan. Legislative Library. (1983)- Vol. 19 (1993)-. English. Twelve times a year (publish monthly plus an special editions). 127.00Can$. Saskatchewan Chamber Commerce, 1630 Chateau Twr, 1920 Broad Street, Regina Saskatchewan S4P 3V2 Canada. **Tel** (306)352-2672, **FAX** (306)781-7084. **LC** Z736.S28; S28a. **DD** 027.57124.

CN/0702-0724
**ANNUAL REPORT - SECURITIES COMMISSION (EDMONTON).** (ANNUAL REPORT / SECURITIES COMMISSION). **Main/Corp** Alberta Securities Commission. (1973)-. English. an. Free. Alberta Securities Commission, 10025 Jasper Avenue, 21st Floor, Edmonton Alberta T5J 3Z5 Canada. **Tel** (403)427-5201, **FAX** (403)422-0777, telex 037-2701. **LC** KEA318.A72; S4. **DD** 354/.7123/00825.

US
**ANNUAL REPORT / STATE OF NEW MEXICO, REGULATION & LICENSING DEPARTMENT.** **Main/Corp** New Mexico. Regulation and Licensing Dept. (1987)-. English. Department of Regulation and Licensing / New Mexico, Bataan Memorial Building, Santa Fe NM 87503. **LC** HD3630.U7; N64a. **DD** 353.97890082. *Continues* Report to the Governor.

US
**ANNUAL REPORT / SUPPLEMENTAL ANNUITY COLLECTIVE TRUST FUND OF NEW JERSEY.** **Main/Corp** Supplemental Annuity Collective Trust of New Jersey. **Added/Corp** New Jersey. Division of Investment. (1990)-. English. *Continues* Supplemental Annuity Collective Trust of New Jersey. Audited Financial Statements and Other Financial Information.
**Desc:** Focuses on civil service.

US
**ANNUAL REPORT / THE COUNCIL OF STATE GOVERNMENTS.** **Main/Corp** Council of State Governments. (19??)-. English. an. Council of State Governments, PO Box 11910, Iron Works Pike, Lexington KY 40578-1910. **Tel** (800)800-1910, (606)231-1850. **LC** JK2403; .C72a. **DD** 353.9/05.

US
**ANNUAL REPORT ... / THE MARYLAND INDUSTRIAL DEVELOPMENT FINANCING AUTHORITY.** **Main/Corp** Maryland Industrial Development Financing Authority. English. an. Maryland Industrial Development Financing Authority, 217 East Redwood Street, Suite 22, Baltimore MD 21202. **LC** HG3729.U49; M364A. **DD** 353.97520082.

AT
**ANNUAL REPORT / THE PREMIER'S DEPARTMENT.** **Main/Corp** Queensland. Premier's Dept. English. an. **LC** JQ4740; .Q45A. **DD** 354.94304/06.

US/0360-3547
**ANNUAL REPORT - THE STATE OF OKLAHOMA, OFFICE OF COMMUNITY AFFAIRS AND PLANNING.** **Main/Corp** Oklahoma. Office of Community Affairs and Planning. English. an. Oklahoms State Community of Affairs and Planning, 4901 North Lincoln Blvd., Oklahoma City OK 73105. **LC** HN79.O5; O5A. **DD** 353.9/766/008.

CN/0835-5428
**ANNUAL REPORT TO THE LEGISLATIVE ASSEMBLY - PROVINCE OF BRITISH COLUMBIA. OMBUDSMAN.** (ANNUAL REPORT TO THE LEGISLATIVE ASSEMBLY.). [Annu. rep. Legis. Assem. - Prov. B.C., Ombudsman]. **Main/Corp** British Columbia. Office of the Ombudsman. **VFOAT** Ombudsman, Fairness for All in British Columbia; Ombudsman's Annual Report. 1986-. English. an. Office of the Ombudsman, 8 Bastion Square, Victoria British Columbia V8W 1H9 Canada. **LC** JL429.5.O4; B74A. **DD** 354.711009/1. *Continues* Annual Report of the Ombudsman to the Legislative Assembly of British Columbia, 0713-2921.

US/0748-5077
**ANNUAL REPORT TO THE OKLAHOMA TURNPIKE AUTHORITY.** **Main/Corp** Benham Group. **Added/Corp** Oklahoma Turnpike Authority.

(19??)-. English. an. Benham Group, 1200 NW 63rd Street, PO Box 20400, Oklahoma City OK 73156. **LC** HE356.O5; B3. **DD** 388.1/22/09766. ***Continues*** *Benham-Blair & Affiliates. Annual Report to the Oklahoma Turnpike Authority; Oklahoma Turnpike System & Will Rogers Turnpike, 0748-5077.*

US
**ANNUAL REPORT / UNIVERSITY OF OREGON. BUREAU OF GOVERNMENTAL RESEARCH AND SERVICE.** **Main/Corp** University of Oregon. Bureau of Governmental Research and Service. (1987)-. English. **LC** JS303.O7; O57. **DD** 300/.720795/31. ***Continues*** *Biennial Report - Bureau of Governmental Research and Service.*

CN
**ANNUAL REPORT - URBAN AFFAIRS (OTTAWA).** (RAPPORT ANNUEL - AFFAIRES URBAINES.). **Main/Corp** Canada. Urban Affairs Canada. French. an. Information Canada, 171 Slater Street, Ottawa Ontario K1A 0S9 Canada. **Tel** (819)997-1095. **LC** HT169.C3; C3B. **DD** 354/.71/008.

US/0882-7583
**ANNUAL REPORT - UTAH. DEPT. OF NATURAL RESOURCES.** (ANNUAL REPORT / UTAH NATURAL RESOURCES.). [Annu. rep. - Utah, Dept. Nat. Resour.]. **Main/Corp** Utah. Dept. of Natural Resources. (1982/1983)-. English. an. Department of Natural Resources / Utah, 1636 West North Temple, Suite 316, Salt Lake City UT 84116. **Tel** (801)538-7200, FAX (801)538-7315. **ED** Teddie Krause. **LC** HC107.U8; U53a. **DD** 353.97920082/3/06. **Circ:** 1,800 (ctrl). ***Continues*** *Utah. Dept. of Natural Resources and Energy. Annual Report, 0741-5532.*
**Desc:** Fiscal year review of department and eight divisions: oil, gas and mining, parks and recreation, state lands and forestry, Utah energy office, Utah geological and mineral survey, water resources, water rights and wildlife resources.

US
**ANNUAL REPORT / VERMONT LOTTERY.** **Main/Corp** Vermont Lottery Commission. English. an. Vermont Lottery Commission, State Office Building, Montpelier VT 05602. **LC** HG6133.V5; V47A. **DD** 353.97430072/6. ***Continues*** *Annual Report of the Calendar Year Ending December 31 ... .*

AT/0812-566X
**ANNUAL REPORT / VICTORIAN ETHNIC AFFAIRS COMMISSION.** **Main/Corp** Victorian Ethnic Affairs Commission. (198?)-. Government Publication. English. an. Free. Victoria Ethnic Affairs Commission, 232 Victoria Parade, East Melbourne Victoria 3002 Australia. **Tel** (03)412 6700, FAX (03)417 1211. **LC** DU120; .V53a. **DD** 354.9450081/4. **Circ:** 500 (ctrl).
**Desc:** Annual report of activities and finances of the Commission.

US/0360-0246
**ANNUAL REPORT - WEST VIRGINIA GOVERNOR'S HIGHWAY SAFETY ADMINISTRATION.** **Main/Corp** West Virginia. Governor's Highway Safety Administration. English. an. West Virginia Highway Safety Administration, 922 Quarrier Street, Charleston WV 25301. **LC** HE5614.3.W4; W42A. **DD** 353.9/754/00878314.

CN/0848-6719
**ANNUAL REVIEW - ATLANTIC LOTTERY, CANADA.** (ANNUAL REVIEW / THE ATLANTIC LOTTERY CORPORATION INC.). [Annu. rev. - Atl. Loto Can.]. **Main/Corp** Atlantic Loto (Canada). (1989/1990)-. English. **DD** 354.7150072/6. ***Continues*** *Atlantic Loto (Canada) Annual Report., 0703-2919.*

UK
**ANNUAL REVIEW OF GOVERNMENT FUNDED R&D / CABINET OFFICE.** **Main/Corp** Great Britain. Cabinet Office. **VFOAT** R & D. (1983)-. English. an. $55.00 US. Her Majesty's Stationery Office, 51 Nine Elms Lane, London SW8 5DR England. **Tel** 011 44 71 873 8459, 011 44 71 873 8499, FAX 011 44 71 873 8499, 011 44 71 873 8456, telex 297138. **(Subscription address:** Her Majesty's Stationery Office, PO Box 276, Publications Centre, London SW8 5DT England.**)** **LC** Q180.G7; G7145a. **DD** 354.4107.

US/1060-4707
**ANTI-DRUG FUNDING ALERT.** ***Title Change.*** [Anti-drug fund. alert]. **Added/Corp** Government Information Services. **VFOAT** Anti Drug Funding Alert. Issue No. 92-1 (Jan. 1, 1992)-(June 1994). Periodical. English. wk. Government Information Services / Virginia, 4301 North Fairfax Drive, Suite 875, Arlington VA 22203. **Tel** (703)528-1082, FAX (703)528-6060, telex RCA 263591 GIS UR. **DD** 353. ***Continues*** *Grant Alert for the Guide to Federal Funding for Anti-Drug Programs.* ***Continued by*** *Drug & Crime Prevention Funding News, 1076-1519.*

II
**ANUDANOM KI MANGEM (INDIA. DEPT. OF COMPANY AFFAIRS).** **Main/Corp** India (Republic). Dept. of Company Affairs. **VFOAT** Demands for Grants. Multiple languages (Hindi and English). Government of India Press, Minto Road, New Delhi 111054 India. **LC** HD2897; .D4A. **DD** 354/.54/0082.

AT/1037-9630
**ANZLIC NEWS.** (AUSTRALIA NEW ZEALAND LAND INFORMATION COUNCIL.). **VFOAT** Australia New Zealand Land Information Council News. (1991)-. Corporate Report. English. an. Free. Australia New Zealand Land Information Council, PO Box 2, Belconnen ACT 2616 Australia. **Tel** 011 61 6 2014299, FAX 011 61 6 2014366. ***Continues*** *ALICNEWS, 1033-3711.*
**Desc:** Annual report of activities.

US/0146-0579
**AOR REPORTER.** **Main/Corp** California. Legislature. Assembly. Office of Research. **VAT** Assembly Office of Research Reporter. V.1- June 1975-. Periodical. English. qt. Assembly Office of Research Legislature, 1116 Ninth Street, Sacramento CA 95814. **LC** JK8701; .C24A. **DD** 328.794/07/6.

AT/0727-8926
**APAIS. AUSTRALIAN PUBLIC AFFAIRS INFORMATION SERVICE.** **See** Public Administration-Abstracting, Bibliographies and Statistics.

US/0744-1630
**APPEARANCES OF LEADING CHINESE OFFICIALS.** (APPEARANCES OF LEADING CHINESE OFFICIALS DURING ... / NATIONAL FOREIGN ASSESSMENT CENTER.). Began in 1979. English. an. Document Expediting Project, Exchange and Gift Division, Library of Congress, Photoduplication Service, Washington DC 20540. **Tel** (202)287-9527. **LC** JQ1507; .U452A. **DD** 354.51002. ***Continues*** *Appearances and Activities of Leading Chinese Officials During ..., 0193-8681.*

US/0145-0700
**APPEARANCES OF SOVIET LEADERS.** English. an. Document Expediting Project, Exchange and Gift Division, Library of Congress, Photoduplication Service, Washington DC 20540. **Tel** (202)287-9527. **LC** JN6521; .A75. **DD** 354.47002. available on microfiche (Vols. (Jan.-Dec. 1981-) distributed to depository libraries).

US
**APPROPRIATIONS AND LETTERS OF INTENT FOR ... .** English. an. State Legislative Research Council, State Capitol, 500 East Capitol, Pierre SD 57501. **LC** KFS3467; .A243. **DD** 353.97830072/236/05.

US
**APPROPRIATIONS REPORT (MICHIGAN).** **Main/Corp** Michigan. Legislature. Senate. Fiscal Agency. English. an. Senate Fiscal Agency, PO Box 30036, Lansing MI 48909. **Tel** (517)373-2767. **LC** HJ11; .M5148A.

CY
**APS DIPLOMAT.** English. wk. $800.00 (package). Arab Press Service, PO Box 3896, 1B Naxos Str., Nicosia Cyprus. **Tel** 351778.
**Ind/Abst** PTS Newsl. Database [Full Txt.].

US
**APS REVIEW, THE.** **See** Political Science.

GW
**ARBEIT UND BERUF.** **Added/Corp** Bundesanstalt fuer Arbeit (Germany). (19??)-. German. Twelve times a year. DM96.00 Germany; DM112.00 other. Verlag Arbeit und Beruf, Bingstrasse 30, c/o Dr. Walter Lutz, D 90480 Nuernberg Germany. **Tel** 011 49 911 4030355. **ED** Walter Lutz. **LC** HD8443; .A58. **Bk Rev**. **Ad Acc**. **Circ:** 10,000. ***Continues*** *Arbeit, Beruf und Arbeitslosenhilfe.*
**Desc:** Labor administration in general with special regard to the responsibility of the Federal Institute for Labour Administration.
**Ind/Abst** LABORDOC.

GW/0003-9209
**ARCHIV FUER KOMMUNALWISSENSCHAFTEN.** [Arch. Kommunalwiss.]. (1962)-. Periodical. German. sa. DM99.00. W Kohlhammer Verlag GmbH, Postfach 800430, D 70549 Stuttgart Germany. **Tel** 011 49 711 78631, FAX 011 49 711 7863263, telex 7-255820. **ED** Schmidt and Eichstaedt. **LC** JS41; .A75. **[CCC]**. cum. index. **Bk Rev**. **Ad Acc**. ctrl circ.
**Desc:** Urban planning and development, communal politics, law and administration, finances, sociology, social politics, history.
**Ind/Abst** ABC POL SCI; Am. Hist. Life (1970-1971); Int. Bibliogr. Sociol.; Int. Polit. Sci. Abstr.; PAIS Int. Print (1991-).

US
**ARIZONA ADMINISTRATIVE REGISTER.** **Added/Corp** Arizona. Office of Secretary of State. Publications Division. **VFOAT** Register; Administrative Register. Vol. 7, Issue 1 (Jan. 1987)-. Periodical. English. Fifty-two times a year. $276.00. Secretary of State / Publications Division, 1700 West Washington, Suite 706, Phoenix AZ 85007. **Tel** (602)542-4086, FAX (602)542-6172. **ED** Ilene M. Gillen. **LC** KFA2436; .A75. **DD** 348.791/025; 347.910825. Index available. **Circ:** 5,000. ***Continues*** *Arizona Administrative Digest.*
**Desc:** Contains all governor's executive orders, proclamations of general applicability, all notices of proposed rule action, all emergency rule adoptions, governor's appointments to boards and commissions, list of adopted, rejected, and terminated rule numbers.

US/0744-7477
**ARIZONA CAPITOL TIMES.** Vol. 83, Issue 22 (June 2, 1982)-. Periodical. English. Fifty-two times a year. $36.00 (one year), $64.00 (two years). Arizona Capitol Times, PO Box 2260, Phoenix AZ 85002. **Tel** (602)258-7026, FAX (602)258-2504. **ED** Ned Creighton. Index available. cum. index. **Ad Acc**, **Adv Mgr:** Kathy Borders, **Tel** (602)258-7026. **Circ:** 4,500. ***Continues*** *Arizona Legislative Review.*
**Desc:** Emphasis on legislature during legislative session; bill summaries, tracking charts, voting chart, and focus issues on aspects of Arizona state government and political affairs.

US/0098-9746
**ARIZONA DIRECTORY OF STATE REGULATORY AGENCIES FOR BUSINESSES AND OCCUPATIONS.** Directory. English. Office of Economic Planning and Development, Phoenix AZ 85007. **LC** JK8230; .A84. **DD** 353.9/791/091025.

US/0004-1629
**ARIZONA REVIEW.** ***Ceased.*** **See** Business.

US
**ARKANSAS DAILY LEGISLATIVE DIGEST.** English. da. $565.00. Arkansas Legislative Digest Inc, 1401 West 6th Street, Little Rock AR 72201-2901. **Tel** (501)376-2843, FAX (501)374-9256. **ED** Roger Potts. Index available. cum. index. **Circ:** 400 (ctrl). available on an online database.

US
**ARKANSAS REGISTER, THE.** **Added/Corp** Arkansas. Office of Secretary of State. Vol. 1 (Aug. 1977)-. Periodical. English. Twelve times a year. $40.00. Arkansas Register, Secretary of State, State Capitol Building, Room 010, Little Rock AR 72201. **Tel** (501)682-3577, FAX (501)682-1284. **ED** Rick B. Hearne (phone: (501)682-3578) and Tonya D. Springer (phone: (501)682-3577). **LC** KFA3636; .A7. **DD** 348.767/028. Index Available, published separately, free-automatically sent. cum. index. **Circ:** 300 (ctrl).
**Desc:** Publishes rules and regulations of state agencies of Arkansas, opinions of the Attorney General and proclamations of the Governor and the state agencies.

US
**ARKANSAS STATE AGENCIES DIRECTORY.** (199?)-. Directory. English. Heritage Publishing Company, 4200 Heritage Drive, Little Rock AR 72117. **Tel** (501)945-0866. **LC** JK5130; .A74. **DD** 353.9/767/00025. ***Continues*** *Arkansas State Directory.*

US
**ARKANSAS STATE DIRECTORY.** ***Title Change.*** (19??)-(199?). English. an. Heritage Publishing Company, 4200 Heritage Drive, Little Rock AR 72117. **Tel** (501)945-0866. **LC** JK5130; .A74. **DD** 353.9/767/00025. **Ad Acc**. **Circ:** 3,500 (ctrl). ***Continued by*** *Arkansas State Agencies Directory.*
**Desc:** List description, location of government offices.

US
**ARTICLE II : A GUIDE TO THE NORTH CAROLINA LEGISLATURE / NORTH CAROLINA CENTER FOR PUBLIC POLICY RESEARCH.** **Added/Corp** North Carolina Center for Public Policy Research. **VFOAT** Guide to the North Carolina Legislature. (1978)-. English. an (May). $21.50 (two years). North Carolina Center for Public Policy Research, PO Box 430, Raleigh NC 27602. **Tel** (919)832-2839, FAX (919)832-2847.

CN/0711-8031
**ASBESTOS MA VILLE.** (ASBESTOS MA VILLE : BULLETIN MUNICIPAL D'INFORMATION.). **Main/Corp** Asbestos (Quebec). Vol. 1, No. 1 (May 1980)-. Bulletin. French. qt. Asbestos Ma Ville, c/o Directeur des Loisirs, CP 88, Asbestos Quebec J1T 3M9 Canada. **DD** 352.0714/65.

HK
**ASIAN JOURNAL OF PUBLIC ADMINISTRATION / YA-CHOU KUNG KUNG HSING CHENG HSUEH / UNIVERSITY OF HONG KONG, THE.** **Added/Corp** University of Hong Kong. Dept. of Political Science. **VFOAT** Ya-Chou Kung Kung Hsing Cheng

# Public Administration

Hsueh. Vol. 5, No. 1 (June 1983)-. Periodical. English. Twice a year (June & Dec.). HK$25.00 Southeast Asia; HK$ 30.00 others. Asian Journal of Public Administration, University of Hong Kong, Department of Political Science, Pokfulam Road, Hong Kong. **Tel** 011 852 5 8592399, FAX 011 852 5 8583550. **ED** D. Clark and K. Chow. Index available. **Bk Rev**. **Ad Acc**. **Circ**: 7,500. available on microfilm and microfiche from University Microfilms International (UMI). **Continues** Hong Kong Journal of Public Administration.
**Desc:** Seeks to promote the study, research, and dissemination of information on public administration in the Asian region.
**Ind/Abst** Am. Hist. Life (1984-); Hum. Resour. Abstr. (?-?); Int. Polit. Sci. Abstr.; Sage Public Adm. Abstr. (?-?); Sage Urban Stud. Abstr.

II
## ASVASANA SAMITI (VIDHANAPARISHAD) AHAVALA.
**Main/Corp** Maharashtra, India (State). Legislature. Legislative Council. Committee on Government Assurances. Multiple languages (English and Marathi). 2.20. Maharashtra Vidhanamandala Sacivalaya, Legislative Council Secretariat, Napapura India. **LC** JQ620.M263; A25. **Continues** Maharashtra, India (State). Legislature. Legislative Council. Committee on Government Assurances. Report.

UK/0951-8827
## AT PRESS.
[At press]. (198?)-. English. wk. Free. Her Majesty's Stationery Office, 51 Nine Elms Lane, London SW8 5DR England. **Tel** 011 44 71 873 8459, 011 44 71 873 8499, FAX 011 44 71 873 8499, 011 44 71 873 8456, telex 297138. **(Subscription address:** Her Majestys Stationery Offic, PO Box 276 Public Centre, London SW8 5DT England) **Continues** List of Non-Parliamentary Publications Sent for Press Together with Forthcoming Acts of Parliament.

US
## ATTORNEY GENERAL'S ADVISORY COMMITTEE OF UNITED STATES ATTORNEYS ANNUAL REPORT / U.S. DEPARTMENT OF JUSTICE, EXECUTIVE OFFICE FOR UNITED STATES ATTORNEYS, THE.
**Added/Corp** Attorney General's Advisory Committee of United States Attorneys. **VFOAT** Annual Report. (1991)-. English. Attorney General's Advisory Committee of United States, Room 1619, 10 and Constitution Avenue, Washington DC 20530.

CN/0228-1139
## AU COURANT (PUBLIC SERVICE COMMISSION. NATIONAL CAPITAL REGIONAL OFFICE).
(AU COURANT.). **VAT** Au Courant (Commission de la Fonction Publique. Bureau Regional de la Capital Nationale). Periodical. English (French). Public Service Commission of Canada, 300 Laurier Avenue West, Ottawa Ontario K1A 0M7 Canada. **DD** 354.71001/005.
**Ind/Abst** Museum Abstr.

US/0272-3522
## AUDIT OF SAINT LAWRENCE SEAWAY DEVELOPMENT CORPORATION FINANCIAL STATEMENTS.
See Business-Accounting.

US/0148-3870
## AUDIT REPORT, COMMISSION TO CONTROL THE SUPREME COURT BUILDING AT NASHVILLE.
**Main/Corp** Tennessee. Division of State Audit. English. Tennessee Comptroller of the Treasury, Nashville TN 37219. **LC** KFT512; .A87. **DD** 353.9/768/00713.

US/0148-5202
## AUDIT REPORT, DEPARTMENT OF GENERAL SERVICES, MOTOR VEHICLE MANAGEMENT DIVISION.
[Audit rep. Dep. Gen. Serv. Mot. Veh. Manage. Div.]. **Main/Corp** Tennessee. Division of State Audit. (1975)-. English. Tennessee Comptroller of the Treasury, Nashville TN 37219. **LC** JK5288.M7; T45a. **DD** 353.9/768/0087841. **Continues** Audit Report, Division of Motor Vehicle Management, 0148-5210.

US/0148-3862
## AUDIT REPORT, DIVISION OF PRINTING.
**Main/Corp** Tennessee. Division of State Audit. English. Tennessee Comptroller of the Treasury, Nashville TN 37219. **LC** JK5249.P8; T46A. **DD** 353.9/768/007232.

US
## AUDIT REPORT : SECRETARY OF STATE - GEORGIA. DEPT. OF AUDITS AND ACCOUNTS.
**Main/Corp** Georgia. Dept. of Audits and Accounts. English. Georgia Department of Audits, 115 State Capitol, Atlanta GA 30334. **LC** J87; .G44CE.

US/0160-5356
## AUDIT REPORT, STATE OF NEVADA, CLARK COUNTY TAXICAB AUTHORITY.
**Main/Corp** Nevada. Legislative Auditor. English. Legislative Auditor, Legislative Building, Capitol Complex, Carson City NV 89710. **LC** HE5633.N3; N48A. **DD** 353.9/793/00878321.

US/0093-0202
## AUDIT REPORT - STATE OF NEVADA. DEPARTMENT OF ADMINISTRATION. PERSONNEL DIVISION.
(PERSONNEL DIVISION AUDIT REPORT.). **Main/Corp** Nevada. Legislative Counsel Bureau. English. an. Nevada Legislative Counsel Bureau / Carson City, Legislative Building, Carson City NV 89701. **LC** JK8555; .N45A. **DD** 353.9/793/001.

US/0160-5380
## AUDIT REPORT, STATE OF NEVADA, DEPARTMENT OF COMMERCE, HOUSING DIVISION.
**Main/Corp** Nevada. Legislative Auditor. English. an. Legislative Auditor, Legislative Building, Capitol Complex, Carson City NV 89710. **LC** HD7303.N4; N47A. **DD** 353.9/793/00865.

US/0160-5348
## AUDIT REPORT, STATE OF NEVADA, DEPARTMENT OF COMMERCE, REAL ESTATE DIVISION.
**Main/Corp** Nevada. Legislative Auditor. English. Legislative Auditor, Legislative Building, Capitol Complex, Carson City NV 89710. **LC** HD266.N3; N48A. **DD** 353.9/793/008232.

US/0160-533X
## AUDIT REPORT, STATE OF NEVADA, DEPARTMENT OF COMMERCE, REAL ESTATE EDUCATION RESEARCH AND RECOVERY FUND.
**Main/Corp** Nevada. Legislative Auditor. English. an. Legislative Auditor, Legislative Building, Capitol Complex, Carson City NV 89710. **LC** HJ9875; .A23B. **DD** 353.9/793/007232.

US
## AUDIT REPORT, STATE OF NEVADA, OFFICE OF THE GOVERNOR.
**Main/Corp** Nevada. Legislative Auditor. English. an. Legislative Auditor, Legislative Building, Capitol Complex, Carson City NV 89710. **LC** HJ9876; .A25A. **DD** 353.9/793/007232.

US/0092-9239
## AUDIT REPORT - STATE OF NEVADA. PUBLIC SERVICE COMMISSION.
(PUBLIC SERVICE COMMISSION AUDIT REPORT.). **Main/Corp** Nevada. Legislative Counsel Bureau. English. an. Nevada Legislative Counsel Bureau / Carson City, Legislative Building, Carson City NV 89701. **LC** HD2767.N32; N44A. **DD** 353.9/793/008.

US
## AUDIT REPORT. TEXAS BOARD OF LICENSURE FOR NURSING HOME ADMINISTRATORS.
See Medical Science and Technology-Hospital Administration and Medical Centers.

AT/1033-1662
## AUSTPLAN : THE NATIONAL NEWSLETTER OF THE ROYAL AUSTRALIAN PLANNING INSTITUTE, INC.
**Added/Corp** Royal Australian Planning Institute. Vol. 2, No. 1 (Feb. 1982)-. Periodical. English. bm. 45.00Aus$ Australia; 50.00Aus$ (other). Royal Australian Planning Institute Inc, 615 Burwood Road Rapi House, Hawthorn Victoria 3122 Australia. **Tel** 11 61 3 8190728, FAX 011 61 3 8190676. **ED** Diana Marks (Editor's telephone: 011 61 02 419 7121). **Bk Rev**. **Ad Acc**, **Adv Mgr**: Rosalba Drummond. ctrl circ. **Continues** RAPI News.

AT/1033-839X
## AUSTRALIA AND TOMORROWS PACIFIC / FOR AUSTRALIA.
(1989)-. English. ir. 20.00Aus$. Institute of Public Affairs / Australia, 128 36 Jolimont Road, Jolimont Vic 3002 Australia. **Tel** 011 61 3 6547499, FAX 011 61 3 6507627.

AT
## AUSTRALIAN GOVERNMENT GAZETTE.
**Main/Corp** Australia. English. 100.00Aus$ Australia. Government Printer / Australia, PO Box 84, Canberra, Australian Capital Territory, 2600 Australia. **LC** J8; .B8. **DD** 354/.94/0005. **Continues** Commonwealth of Australia Gazette.
**Desc:** The official medium used to notify many government actions and decisions, including appointments to the ministry, the courts, departments and the boards of statutory authorities; laws made and when they come into operation; honours and awards made to citizens; and the letting of government tenders and contracts.

AT/0067-1878
## AUSTRALIAN GOVERNMENT PUBLICATIONS.
(AUSTRALIAN GOVERNMENT PUBLICATIONS. MICROFORM.). [Aust. gov. publ.]. **Added/Corp** National Library of Australia. **VFOAT** AGP; A.G.P. (Sept. 1988)-. English. Four times a year. 50.00Aus$. National Library of Australia, Parkes Place, Canberra ACT, 2600 Australia. **Tel** 011 61 6 2621374, FAX 011 61 6 2731084. **LC** Microfiche (o) 88/422. Index available. cum. index. **Circ**: 500. **Continues** Australian Government Publications (1961), 0067-1878.

AT
## AUSTRALIAN GOVERNMENT PUBLICATIONS. MONTHLY LIST.
**Main/Corp** Australia. Commonwealth Government Printing Office. Publications Branch. (19??)-. Government Publication. English. mo. Free on request. Australian Government Publishing Service, GPO Box 84, Canberra ACT 2601 Australia. **Tel** 011 61 6 2954411, FAX 011 61 6 2954455.

AT/0313-6647
## AUSTRALIAN JOURNAL OF PUBLIC ADMINISTRATION.
[Aust. j. public adm.]. **Added/Corp** Royal Institute of Public Administration. Australian Regional Groups. Royal Institute of Public Administration Australia. Australian Institute of Public Administration. Royal Australian Institute of Public Administration. **VFOAT** AJPA. Vol. 35, (March 1976)-. Periodical. English. Four times a year (Mar., June, Sept., Dec.). 50.00Aus$ Australia; 70.00Aus$ other. Royal Australian Institute of Public Adminsitration Australia, GPO Box 780, Sydney New South Wales 2001 Australia. **Tel** 011 61 2 2285225, 011 61 2 2283705, FAX 011 61 2 2411920. **ED** R. L. Wettenhall and R. D. Scott. **LC** JA26; .P8. **DD** 350/.0005. Index available. **Bk Rev**. **Ad Acc**. **Pr Rev. Circ**: 6,000. Documents available from The Genuine Article, UMI Article Clearinghouse. **Continues** Public Administration (Sydney, N.S.W.), 0033-328x.
**Desc:** Review of issues affecting public administration in Australia.
**Ind/Abst** ABI/INFORM Glob. Ed.; APAIS, Aust. Public Aff. Inf. Ser. (1976-); Appl. Soc. Sci. Index Abstr.; Curr. Contents Soc. Behav. Sci.; Int. Bibliogr. Sociol.; Int. Labour Doc.; Int. Polit. Sci. Abstr.; Res. Alert [Full Cov.]; Sage Public Adm. Abstr.; Sage Urban Stud. Abstr; Soc. Sci. Cit. Index [Full Cov.].

AT/0004-9808
## AUSTRALIAN MUNICIPAL JOURNAL, THE.
Vol. 1- (1921)-. Periodical. English. mo. 42.00Aus$. Municipal Assn of Victoria, 416 St Kilda Road, PO Box 7082 Australia. **Tel** 011 61 03 267 5266.

AT
## AUSTRALIAN RESOURCES GUIDE.
(19??)-. English. Four times a year. 135.00Aus$ Australia; 164.00Aus$ New Zealand, Papua New Guinea; 170.00Aus$ Indonesia, Malaysia, Singapore, 176.00Aus$ Japan, India; 185.00Aus$ US & Canada; 191.00Aus$ Europe. International Public Relations Pty Ltd., 33 Walsh Street, West Melbourne Victoria 3003 Australia. **Tel** 011 61 03 329 9333, FAX 011 61 03 329 7996. **Continues** Guide to Australian Governments.

AU
## AUSZUG AUS DEN TATIGKEITSBERICHTEN DER GRUPPEN UND ABTEILUNGEN DES AMTES DER NO LANDESREGIERUNG, EIN.
Title Change. **Main/Corp** Lower Austria (Austria). **VFOAT** Agenden Aktivitaten. German. an. Herrengasse 11-13, 1014 Vienna Austria. **Tel** 53110/2095. **LC** J314; .R14A. **DD** 354.436/12/0005. **Continued by** Agenden/Aktivitaten 90/91.

US/0163-111X
## AUTOMATIC DATA PROCESSING ACTIVITIES SUMMARY IN THE UNITED STATES GOVERNMENT.
(AUTOMATIC DATA PROCESSING ACTIVITIES SUMMARY IN THE UNITED STATES GOVERNMENT AS OF THE END OF FISCAL YEAR ...). **Added/Corp** United States. General Services Administration. Office of Information Resources Management. United States. Automated Data and Telecommunications Service. (1977)-. English. an. General Services Administration Office of Information Resources Management, Office of Information Resources Management, Eighteenth and F Streets Northwest, Washington DC 20405. **LC** JK468.A8; A34. **DD** 353.007/1. **Continues** Summary of Federal ADP Activities.

IT/0392-2278
## AUTONOMIE LOCALI E SERVIZI SOCIALI.
[Auton. locali serv. soc.]. (1977)-. Periodical. Italian. Three times a year. L70000.00 Italy; L120000.00. Societa Editrice il Mulino, Strada Maggiore 37, 40125 Bologna Italy. **Tel** 011 39 51 256011, FAX 011 39 51 256034. **UDC** 35.

CN/0820-6503
## AVIS MUNICIPAL - VILLE DE CHARNY.
(L'AVIS MUNICIPAL : BULLETIN D'INFORMATION DE LA VILLE DE CHARNY.). [Avis munic. - Ville Charny].

# Public Administration

**Main/Corp** Charny (Quebec). Vol. 1, No. 1 (Sept. 1982)-. Bulletin. French. ir. Free to residents. L'Avis Municipal, 333 20E rue, Charny Quebec G6W 5RG Canada. **Tel** (418)832-4695. **DD** 352.0714/59. Index available. **Circ:** 5,000 (ctrl). *Continues Charny (Quebec). Vos Affaires, 0713-6773.*

IT
### AZIENDA PUBBLICA TEORIA E PROBLEMI DI MANAGEMENT. (19??)-.
Italian. mo. L70000.00 Italy; L105000.00 other. Giuffre Editore SPA, Via Busto Arsizio 40, 20151 Milan Italy. **Tel** 011 398 2 38089200. **ED** G. Rebora. Index available. **Bk Rev. Ad Acc. Circ:** 1,800.
**Desc:** Strives to help developing administrations on an economically sound basis. The journal consists of four sections: essays, case studies, public administration in the world, reviews and bibliographical notices.

AT
### BACKGROUNDER / AUSTRALIA, DEPARTMENT OF FOREIGN AFFAIRS AND TRADE.
**Added/Corp** Australia. Dept. of Foreign Affairs and Trade. (19??)-. Periodical. English. ir (four or six times per year). 80.00Aus$ Australia; 95.00Aus$ other. Institute of Public Affairs / Australia, 128 36 Jolimont Road, Jolimont Vic 3002 Australia. **Tel** 011 61 3 6547499, FAX 011 61 3 6507627. **CODEN** BACKEN. **Bk Rev. Ad Acc. Pr Rev.**

GW/0340-3505
### BADEN-WURTTEMBERGISCHE VERWALTUNGSPRAXIS. (1974)-.
Periodical. German. mo. DM198.00. W Kohlhammer Verlag GmbH, Postfach 800430, D 70549 Stuttgart Germany. **Tel** 011 49 711 78631, FAX 011 49 711 7863263, telex 7-255820. **UDC** 35. **CODEN** 342. **[CCC]**.

US
### BALANCE SHEETS OF THE U.S. ECONOMY.
See Public Administration-Public Finance and Taxation.

US/0739-6279
### BASELINE DATA REPORT.
[Baseline data rep.]. **Added/Corp** International City Management Association. Vol. 15, No. 1 (Jan. 1983)-. Periodical. English. bm. $199.00. International City Management Association, 777 North Capitol Street NE, Suite 500, Washington DC 20002. **Tel** (202)289-4262, (800)745-8780, FAX (202)962-3500. **(Subscription address:** International City Management Association, PO Box 2011, Annapolis Junction MD 20701.**) LC** JS308; .U73. **DD** 352/.0072/0973. Index available. **Circ:** 500 (ctrl). *Continues Urban Data Service Report, 0049-5654.*
**Desc:** Data and text on local government activities and issues such as expenditures, employment, salaries, administrative arrangements and provided services.
**Ind/Abst** PAIS Int. Print; Public Aff. Inf. Serv. Bull.; Stat. Ref. Index; Urban Aff. Abstr.

AT/0726-3406
### BASIC PAPER - PARLIAMENT OF THE COMMONWEALTH OF AUSTRALIA, LEGISLATIVE RESEARCH SERVICE, DEPARTMENT OF THE PARLIAMENTARY LIBRARY.
(BASIC PAPER.). [Basic pap. - Parliam. Commonw. Aust., Legis. Res. Serv., Dep. Parliam. Libr.]. **Added/Corp** Australia. Dept. of the Parliamentary Library. Legislative Research Service. (1981)-. Monographic series. English. ir. Price varies per volume. Legislative Research Service, Department of the Parliamentary Library, Canberra ACT Australia.

GW/0005-6847
### BAUVERWALTUNG.
[Bauverwaltung]. V. 1 (1952)-. Periodical. German. mo. DM168.80. Curt R. Vincentz Verlag, Postfach 6247, D 30062 Hannover Germany. **Tel** 011 49 511 990980, FAX 011 49 511 9909899, telex 923846. **ED** Frank Vincentz. Index available. cum. index. **Bk Rev. Ad Acc. Circ:** 2,010 (ctrl).
**Desc:** Organ of the governmental and local building authorities dealing with their architectural concerns; including typical examples of large public buildings ranging from their project planning up to their completion.
**Ind/Abst** Energy Res. Abstr. (Sept. 1977-).

GW/0522-5337
### BAYERISCHE VERWALTUNGSBLATTER.
See Law.

CN/0823-7662
### BEAU LIEU (SAINTE-PETRONILLE, QUEBEC).
(LE BEAU LIEU.). [Beau lieu]. Mar. 1981-. Periodical. French. mo. Municipalite du Village de Ste-Petronille, 3 Chemin l'Eglise, Ste-Petronille Ile d'Orleans Quebec G0A 4C0 Canada. **DD** 352.0714/48. *Continues Information Municipale.*

SA
### BEDRYFSBEGROTINGS VIR DIE BOEKJARE WAT EINDIG OP ... . Main/Corp
South African Transport Services. **VFOAT** Working Estimates for the Financial Years Ending ... . 1982/83-. Afrikaans (English). an. R4.10. **LC** HE3426; .A43A.

SA
### BEGROTING VAN DIE UITGAWES WAT UIT INKOMSTEREKENING (SOUTH AFRICA).
See Public Administration-Public Finance and Taxation.

GW/0522-6058
### BEHORDENVERZEICHNIS NORDRHEIN-WESTFALEN / LANDSAMT FUER DATENVERARBEITUNG UND STATISTIK NORDRHEIN-WESTFALEN.
**Main/Corp** Landesamt fur Datenverarbeitung und Statistik Nordrhein-Westfalen. German. ir. DM26.00. Landesamt fuer Datenverarbeitung und Statistik Nordrhein-Westfalen, Postfach 101105, 40002 Duesseldorf Germany. **Tel** (0211)944901, FAX (0211)442006, telex 8586654 LDST D. **LC** JN4945.N62; L36A. **DD** 354.43/55/00025. **Circ:** 1,500.
**Desc:** Directory of authorities in the North Rhine-Westphalia region.

BH
### BELIZE TODAY.
**Added/Corp** Belize. Government Information Service. Vol. 1, No. 1 (March 1987)-. Periodical. English. mo. Free on request. Government Information Service / Belize, Belmopan Belize. **Tel** 011 501 8 2659. **ED** M.A. Romero. **LC** HC142; .A28. **DD** 330.97282/005. **Ad Acc. Circ:** 14,000. *Continues New Belize.*
**Desc:** News about government activities.

IO
### BERITA PEKERJAAN UMUM.
V. 6., No. 23/24-. Indonesian. Bagian Hubungan Masyarakat, Departemen Pekerjaan Umun, Jl Pattimura No 20, Kebayoran Baru, Jakarta Selatan, Djakarta Indonesia. **LC** HD4301; .D46C. *Continues Berita Putl.*

US/0897-5728
### BERNAN ASSOCIATES' GOVERNMENT PUBLICATIONS NEWS.
[Bernan Assoc. gov. publ. news]. **Added/Corp** Bernan Associates. **VFOAT** Government Publications News. Vol. 1, Issue 2 (Feb. 10, 1988)-. Periodical. English. Ten times a year. Free. Bernan Associates, 4611-F Assembly Drive, Lanham MD 20706-4391. **Tel** (301)459-7666, (800)274-4447 US, (800)233-0504 CANADA, FAX (301)459-0056, telex 7108260418. **ED** Amy Yeager. **DD** 353. **Circ:** 4,500 (ctrl). *Continues Government Publications News, 0897-571X.*

BE
### BESTUURSMEMORIAAL. Main/Corp
Antwerp (Belgium : Province). (19??)-. Periodical. Dutch. ir. Provinciebestuur Van Antwerpen Grif Koningin, Elisabethlei 22, 2018 Antwerp Belgium. **LC** JS7.N3; A44.

IT
### BIBLIOGRAFIA UMBRA / REGIONE DELL'UMBRA, UFFICIO PER I BENI E SERVIZI BIBLIOTECARI, ARCHIVISTICI, PER LE ATTIVITA DELLO SPETTACOLO SPORT E TEMPO LIBERO.
1 (1982-1983)-. Periodical. Italian. ir. **LC** Z2364.U4; B53; DG975.U5. **DD** 016.945/65/005.

AT/0813-3107
### BIBLIOGRAPHY (AUSTRALIA. PARLIAMENT).
See Public Administration-Abstracting, Bibliographies and Statistics.

US/0732-8222
### BIENNIAL REPORT - ILLINOIS COMMISSION ON ATOMIC ENERGY.
(BIENNIAL REPORT SUBMITTED TO THE GOVERNOR AND THE ... GENERAL ASSEMBLY / THE ILLINOIS COMMISSION ON ATOMIC ENERGY.). [Bienn. rep. - Ill. Comm. At. Energy]. **Main/Corp** Illinois Commission on Atomic Energy. (19??)-. English. be. Illinois Commission on Atomic Energy, 2300 South Dirksen Parkway 320 IL Dot, Springfield IL 62764-4555. **LC** HD9698.U53; I62. **DD** 353.97730082/3. *Continues Illinois Commission on Atomic Energy. Report to the ... Governor of the State of Illinois, the President of the Senate ... of the ... General Assembly from the Illinois Commission on Atomic Energy, 0732-829X.*

US
### BIENNIAL REPORT / LEGISLATIVE POST AUDIT COMMITTEE AND LEGISLATIVE DIVISION OF POST AUDIT.
See Business-Accounting.

US
### BIENNIAL REPORT / NEBRASKA PUBLIC SERVICE COMMISSION.
**Main/Corp** Nebraska. Public Service Commission. (1980/1982)-. English. be. **LC** HE28.N2; P86a. **DD** 353.97820087/005. *Continues Annual Report - Nebraska Public Service Commission, 0098-2083.*

US
### BIENNIAL REPORT OF THE STATE LABORATORIES AND CONSUMER AFFAIRS DEPARTMENT. Main/Corp
North Dakota. State Laboratories Dept. English. be. Box 937, Bismarck ND 58505. **LC** HD9000.9.U6; N95A. **DD** 353.9/784/0077.

US
### BIENNIAL REPORT OF WISCONSIN STATE ELECTIONS BOARD. Main/Corp
Wisconsin. State Elections Board. 1977/78-. Periodical. English. be. State Elections Board, 132 E Wilson Street, Madison WI 53703. **LC** JK1954; .W57A. **DD** 353.9775091. *Continues Annual Report of Wisconsin State Elections Board, 0362-9635.*

US/0092-4938
### BIENNIAL REPORT, OREGON'S SUBMERGED AND SUBMERSIBLE LANDS. Main/Corp
Oregon. Advisory Committee to the State Land Board. English. be. Oregon's Submerged and Submersible Lands, Room 209, State Capitol, Salem OR 97310. **LC** KFO2810.S8; A83. **DD** 346/.795/046918.

US/0099-1600
### BIENNIAL REPORT - STATE OF FLORIDA DEPARTMENT OF STATE.
**Main/Corp** Florida. Department of State. **Added/Corp** Florida. Dept. of State. Annual Report - State of Florida Department of State. (1969)-. English. be. Department of State / Florida, Tallahassee FL 32301. **LC** J87; .F64a. **DD** 353.9/759/3. *Continues Biennial Report - Secretary of State.*

US
### BIENNIAL REPORT / STATE OF MICHIGAN, THE DEPARTMENT OF NATURAL RESOURCES. Main/Corp
Michigan. Dept. of Natural Resources. 25th (1969/70)-. English. be. Michigan Department of Natural Resources, 208 North Capital, Lansing MI 48918. **LC** HC107.M5. **DD** 353.9774/008/232. *Continues Michigan. Dept. of Conservation. Biennial Report.*
**Ind/Abst** Key Word Index Wildl. Res.

US
### BIENNIAL REPORT - STATE OF MINNESOTA DEPARTMENT OF PUBLIC SERVICE. Main/Corp
Minnesota. Dept. of Public Service. English. be. Minnesota Department of Public Service, 211 State Highway Building, St Paul MN 55155. **LC** HE28.M6; A3. **DD** 380.3/09776. *Continues Minnesota. Dept. of Public Service. Report for the Biennium.*

US/0145-8647
### BIENNIAL REPORT - STATE OF WISCONSIN, DEPARTMENT OF REGULATION AND LICENSING. Main/Corp
Wisconsin. Dept. of Regulation and Licensing. English. be. State of Wisconsin, PO Box 7840, Document Sales, Madison WI 53707. **Tel** (608)266-3358. **LC** KFW2725; .A86. **DD** 353.9/775/008243. **Circ:** 300.
**Desc:** Fiscal and administrative report of the state of Wisconsin, Department of Regulation and Licensing.

US/0363-9193
### BIENNIAL REPORT - STATE OF WISCONSIN ETHICS BOARD. See Ethics.

US/0148-9275
### BIENNIAL REPORT TO LEGISLATURE - BUREAU OF PUBLIC LANDS.
(BIENNIAL REPORT TO LEGISLATURE - BUREAU OF PUBLIC LANDS (MAINE).). **Main/Corp** Maine. Bureau of Public Lands. 1st- 1976/77-. English. be. Maine Department of Conservation, State House, Station 22, Augusta ME 04333. **Tel** (207)289-3821. **LC** HD184.M2; B87A.

US
### BIENNIAL REPORT TO THE CONGRESS ON COASTAL ZONE MANAGEMENT.
**Main/Corp** United States. Office of Ocean and Coastal Resource Management. Fiscal Years (1982/1983)-. English. be. Office of Coastal Zone Management, US Department of Commerce, Washington DC 20230. **LC** HT392; .U5586. *Continues National Ocean Survey. Office of Coastal Zone Management. Biennial Report to the Congress on Coastal Zone Management, 0737-5484.*

US
### BIENNIAL REPORT TO THE LEGISLATURE / LEGISLATIVE COMMISSION ON MINNESOTA RESOURCES. Main/Corp
Minnesota. Legislature. Legislative Commission on Minnesota Resources. (1984)-. English. be. Legislative Commission on Minnesota Resources, State Office Building/Room 65, St Paul MN 55155. **Tel** (612)296-2406. **LC** HC107.M6;

# Public Administration

M49145a. **DD** 333.7/09776. ctrl circ. **Continues** Minnesota. Legislature. Legislative Commission on Minnesota Resources. Report to the Legislature.
**Desc:** The report presents the role of the Commission, funding sources, Commission operations and the process utilized in making recommendations for funding natural resource programs.

US/0894-9697
**BILL SHIPP'S GEORGIA.** [Bill Shipp's Ga.]. **VFOAT** Georgia. (1987)-. Newsletter. English. wk (except Christmas week). $195.00. Word Merchants Inc., PO Box 440755, Kennesaw GA 30144. **Tel** (404)422-2543, FAX (404)422-0227. **ED** Bill Shipp. **DD** 320.
**Desc:** Includes information on politics, government and business in Georgia.

UK
**BILLS OF BOTH HOUSES.** (19??)-. English. ir. £13.10. Her Majesty's Stationery Office, 51 Nine Elms Lane, London SW8 5DR England. **Tel** 011 44 71 873 8459, 011 44 71 873 8499, FAX 011 44 71 873 8499, 011 44 71 873 8456, telex 297138. **(Subscription address:** Her Majesty's Stationery Office, PO Box 276, Publications Centre, London SW8 5DT England.**)**

US
**BIOGRAPHIC REGISTER / DEPARTMENT OF STATE, U.S. FOREIGN SERVICE, INTERNATIONAL COOPERATION ADMINISTRATION, U.S. INFORMATION AGENCY, FOREIGN AGRICULTURAL SERVICE, THE.** See Biographies.

UK/0263-9467
**BIRA JOURNAL.** [BIRA j.]. **VFOAT** British Institute of Regulatory Affairs Journal. (1982)-. English. Four times a year. £65.00 (membership). BIRA / British Institute of Regulatory Affairs, 34 Dover Street, London W1X 3RA England. **Tel** 011 44 71 4992797. **Continues** Newsletter of the British Institute of Regulatory Affairs.

US
**BLM FACTS & FIGURES FOR UTAH.** **Main/Corp** United States. Bureau of Land Management. Utah State Office. **VFOAT** B.L.M. Facts and Figures for Utah. **VAT** Bureau of Land Management Facts and Figures for Utah. English. an. Free. US Department of the Interior Bureau of Land Management / Salt Lake City, Utah State Office, PO Box 45155, Salt Lake City UT 84145. **Tel** (801)539-4010, FAX (801)539-4183. **ED** Nelda Elridge. **Circ:** 1,000. **Continues** BLM Facts and Figures for Utah.

US
**BLUE BOOK, THE.** **Main/Corp** Greater Anchorage Area Borough. Information Office. English. 3500 East Tudor Road, Anchorage AK 99507. **LC** HD4606.A5; G7A. **DD** 363.5.

US
**BLUE BOOK - NATIONAL ASSOCIATION OF PARLIAMENTARIANS.** **Main/Corp** National Association of Parliamentarians. English. be. $4.00. National Association of Parliamentarians, 6601 Winchester Avenue, Suite 260, Kansas City MO 64133. **Tel** (816)356-5604. **LC** JF515; .N32A. **DD** 328/.3/06073. **Circ:** 4,195.

US/0896-4998
**BNA ADMINISTRATIVE PRACTICE MANUAL. CURRENT REPORTS.** [BNA adm. pract. man., Curr. rep.]. **VFOAT** BNA Administrative Practice Manual. **VAT** Bureau of National Affairs Administrative Practice Manual. Current Reports. Vol. 1, No. 1 (Oct. 1, 1986)-. Periodical. English. bw. $125.00 (supplement). Bureau of National Affairs Inc., 9435 Key West Avenue, Rockville MD 20850. **Tel** (800)372-1033, (301)258-1033, FAX (301)948-5823. **(Subscription telephone:** FAX (301)948-5823**) ED** Bertram R Cottine. cum. index.
**Desc:** A notification and reference service covering the procedural aspects of administrative proceedings, plus timely and detailed coverage of important related developments.

US/0149-3205
**BOARDS AND COMMISSIONS, STATE OF ALASKA.** **Added/Corp** Alaska. Office of the Governor. (19??)-. English. **LC** JK9530; .B62. **DD** 353.979804/025.

CN/0822-5133
**BOISBRIAND (1983).** (LE BOISBRIAND.). [Boisbriand]. **Main/Corp** Boisbriand (Quebec). May 1983-. Periodical. French. mo. Boisbriand, c/o Hotel de Ville Quebec J7G 2J7 Canada. **DD** 352.0714/24.
**Continues** Boisbriand Express, 0820-0734.

BL
**BOLETIM DOS MUNICIPIOS.** **Main/Corp** FAMEPAR (Organization). Vol. 1 (Oct./Dec. 1972)-. Bulletin. Portuguese. Rua Mariano Torres No 135, Curitiba Brazil. **LC** JS2423.P38; F8a.

BL
**BOLETIM INFORMATIVO.** **Main/Corp** Sao Paulo (Brazil). Secretaria Municipal da Administracao. Bulletin. Portuguese. qt. Secretaria Municipal da Administraco Cao Alameda Santos, 2356, 8O Andar CEP 01418 Sao Paulo Brazil. **LC** JS2425.S36; A17A. **DD** 352.081/61.

UY
**BOLETIN - COMISION DE INTEGRACION ELECTRICA REGIONAL.**
**Title Change. Main/Corp** Comision de Integracion Electrica Regional. (19??)-(19??). Spanish. mo. Comision de Integracion Electrica Regional, Subcomite de Distribucion de Energia Electrica, Boulevar Artigas 996, 1040 Montevideo Uruguay. **Tel** 795359 - 790611, telex CIER UY 920. **LC** HD9685.S6; C65c. Index available. **Bk Rev. Ad Acc. Circ:** 1,400 (ctrl). **Continued by** Boletin de la Cier.
**Desc:** Presents information relative to regional and international energy development. fields of planning engineering operation and management of the electrical utilities as well its financing.

SP/0212-4750
**BOLETIN DE LEGISLACION DE LAS COMUNIDADES AUTONOMAS : BCA.** **Main/Corp** Spain. Cortes Generales. **VFOAT** BCA. 1 (Jan./Feb. 1983)-. Spanish. Seven times a year. 5000ptas Spain; 4700ptas other. Senado / Servicio de Publicaciones, Plaza de la Marina Espanola 8, 28013 Madrid Spain. **Tel** 011 34 1 5381364. **LC** LAW. **DD** 348.46/023; 344.60823. Index available.

MX/0188-4492
**BOLETIN DEL SISTEMA ESTATAL DE DOCUMENTACION DEL ESTADO DE MEXICO.** [Bol. Sist. Estatal Doc. Estado Mex.]. (1988)-. Periodical. Spanish. mo. $10.00. Archivo General del Estado de Mexico, Sotero Prieto Rodriguex, no 208 Apartado Postal No 693, Toluca Mexico. **Tel** 40599, FAX 14-73-26, telex LADA 91-72. **ED** Leopoldo Sarmiento Rea. **DD** 020. Index available. cum. index. **Bk Rev. Ad Acc. Circ:** 1,000.
**Desc:** Information about files, documentation centers, microfilming, serials libraries.

SP
**BOLETIN OFICIAL DEL ESTADO : GACETA DE MADRID.** See Law.

SP
**BOLETIN OFICIAL DEL MINISTERIO DE ECONOMIA Y HACIENDA.** **Main/Corp** Spain. Ministerio de Economia y Hacienda. Spanish. wk. Centro de Publicaciones del Ministerio de Economia y Hacienda, Plaza del Campillo del Mundo Nuevo 3, 28005 Madrid Spain. **Tel** 91/227 14 37. **LC** HJ60; .A187. **DD** 354.460082/06. Index available. cum. index. **Ad Acc. Circ:** 6,200 (ctrl). **Continues** Boletin Oficial / Spain. Ministerio de Hacienda.

IT
**BOLLETINO UFFICIALE DELLA REGIONE : LOMBARDIA. TIPO B. C.** La Tipografica Varese, Via Tonale 49, 21100 Varese Italy. **Tel** 011 39 332 332160.

IT
**BOLLETINO UFFICIALE DELLA REGIONE : MOLISE.** Palazzo Regione / Molise, Via XXIV Maggio 130, 86100 Campobasso Italy.

IT/0300-4422
**BOLLETTINO DELLA DEPUTAZIONE DI STORIA PATRIA PER L'UMBRIA.** [Boll. Deput. stor. patria Umbria]. **Main/Corp** Deputazione di Storia Patria per l'Umbria, Perugia. (1895)-. Periodical. Italian. sa. L40.000. Deputazione di Storia Patria per l'Umbria, Casella Postale 130, 06100 Perugia, Italy. **Tel** 075-5727057. **ED** Giovanni Antonelli. **Bk Rev. Circ:** 500. **Ind/Abst** BHA : Biblio. Hist. Art.

IT
**BOLLETTINO UFFICIALE DELLA REGIONALE : LOMBARDIA. TIPO C.** (19??)-. Italian. ir. L200000.00. La Tipografica Varese, Via Tonale 49, 21100 Varese Italy. **Tel** 011 39 332 332160.

IT
**BOLLETTINO UFFICIALE DELLA REGIONE : AUTONOMA DELLA SARDEGNA.** Buras. Bollettino Ufficiale Del Regione, Autonoma Sardegna, Cagliari Italy.

IT
**BOLLETTINO UFFICIALE DELLA REGIONE : AUTONOMA FRIULI BENEZIA GIULIA.** Amministrazione Bur, Via Carducci N 6, 34133 Trieste Italy.

IT
**BOLLETTINO UFFICIALE DELLA REGIONE : AUTONOMA TRENTINO ALTO ADIGE. PART III.** Italian. wk. L60000. Regione Auto Trentino Alto Adi, Via Gazzoletti, 38100 Trento Italy. **Tel** 011 39 461 237022.

IT
**BOLLETTINO UFFICIALE DELLA REGIONE CALABRIA.** Bollettino Ufficiale Regione Calabria, Via G DA Fiore 86, 88100 Catanzaro Italy. **Tel** 011 39 961 770410.

IT
**BOLLETTINO UFFICIALE DELLA REGIONE : LAZIO.** Italian. ir. 21000000L. Bollettino Ufficiale Regione- Lazio, Via C Colombo 212, 00147 Rome Italy. **Tel** 011 39 6 51681444.

IT
**BOLLETTINO UFFICIALE DELLA REGIONE : LIGURIA.** (19??)-. Periodical. Italian. wk. L200000. Bollettino Ufficiale Regione - Liguria. Via Fiesch 15, Via Fieschi 15, 16121 Genoa Italy. **Tel** 011 39 10 54851.

IT
**BOLLETTINO UFFICIALE DELLA REGIONE : LOMBARDIA. TIPO A.** (19??)-. Italian. ir. L50000.00. La Tipografica Varese, Via Tonale 49, 21100 Varese Italy. **Tel** 011 39 332 332160.

IT
**BOLLETTINO UFFICIALE DELLA REGIONE : MARCHE.** (19??)-. Periodical. Italian. wk. L70000. Bollettino Ufficiale Della Regione Marche, Tesoreria V Gentile Fabriano, 60125 Ancona, Italy. **Tel** 011 39 71 8062288.

IT
**BOLLETTINO UFFICIALE DELLA REGIONE : PIEMONTE.** Regione Piemont, Bollettino Ufficiale, Piazza Castello 165, 10122 Turin Italy.

IT
**BOLLETTINO UFFICIALE REGIONE : BASILICATA.** Regione Basilicata, Bollettino Ufficiale, Via Addone, 85100 Potenza Italy.

IT
**BOLLETTINO UFFICIALE REGIONE : CAMPANIA.** Italian. wk. L100000 (without supplements); L150000 (with supplements). Bollettino Ufficiale Regione Campania, Via S Lucia 81, 80132 Naples Italy. **Tel** 011 39 81 7962580.

IT
**BOLLETTINO UFFICIALE REGIONE. EMILIA ROMAGNA. PART I.** (19??)-. Italian. wk. L35000. Bollettino Ufficiale Regione Emilia Romagna, Viale Silvani 6, 40122 Bologna Italy. **Tel** 011 39 51 284440.

IT
**BOLLETTINO UFFICIALE REGIONE : EMILIA ROMAGNA - PART II.** Bollet Ufficiale Emilia Romagna, Viale Silvani 6, 40122 Bologna Italy.

IT
**BOLLETTINO UFFICIALE REGIONE : EMILIA ROMAGNA - PART III.** Bollet Ufficiale Emilia Romagna, Viale Silvani 6, 40122 Bologna Italy.

IT
**BOLLETTINO UFFICIALE REGIONE : EMILIA ROMAGNA - PART IV.** Bollettino Ufficiale Regione Emilia Romagna, Viale Silvani 6, 40122 Bologna Italy. **Tel** 011 39 51 284440.

IT
**BOLLETTINO UFFICIALE REGIONE : PUGLIA.** Editrice M Liantonio, SS 96, KM 112.400, 70027 Palo Del Colle, Ba Italy.

IT
**BOLLETTINO UFFICIALE REGIONE : TOSCANA.** Bollettino Ufficiale Regione Toscana, Piazza Liberta 15, 50129 Florence Italy.

IT
**BOLLETTINO UFFICIALE REGIONE : UMBRIA. PART 1 & 2.** (19??)-. Italian. L53000; L170000 all four parts. Regione Dell Umbria, Palazzo Donini, Piazza Italia 06100 Perugia Italy. **Tel** 011 39 75 5042598, FAX 011 39 75 5042498. Index available. cum. index. **Bk Rev.** ctrl circ.

IT
**BOLLETTINO UFFICIALE REGIONE : UMBRIA. PART 3.** (19??)-. Italian. L43000; L170000 all four parts. Regione Dell Umbria, Palazzo Donini, Piazza Italia 06100 Perugia Italy. **Tel** 011 39 75 5042598, FAX 011 39 75 5042498.

# Public Administration

IT
**BOLLETTINO UFFICIALE REGIONE : UMBRIA. PART 4.** (19??)-. Italian. L22000; L170000 all four parts. Regione Dell Umbria, Palazzo Donini, Piazza Italia, 06100 Perugia Italy. **Tel** 011 39 75 5042598, FAX 011 39 75 5042498. Index available. cum. index. Bk Rev. ctrl circ.

IT
**BOLLETTINO UFFICIALE REGIONE : VALLE D AOSTA.** (19??)-. Italian. wk. L100000. Regione Autonoma Valle d'Aosta, Aff Gen Legali P Za Deffeyes 1, 11100 Aosta Italy. **Tel** 011 39 165 3031.

IT
**BOLLETTINO UFFICIALE REGIONE : VENETO. TYPE B.** (19??)-. Italian. ir. L250000. La Tipografica SRL, San Polo 2210-A, 30125 Venice, Italy. **Tel** 011 39 41 5241810.

US/0068-0125
**BOOK OF THE STATES, THE.** [Book States]. **Added/Corp** Council of State Governments. American Legislators' Association. Vol. 1 (1935)-. English. be. $85.75. Council of State Governments, PO Box 11910, Iron Works Pike, Lexington KY 40578-1910. **Tel** (800)800-1910, (606)231-1850. **(Subscription address:** Council of State Governments, PO Box 2167, Lexington, KY 40595) **ED** L. E. Purcell. **LC** JK2403; .B6. **DD** 353.9/3/2. **Circ:** 10,000.
**Desc:** Comprehensive reference of indexed information on state government: taxes, education and finance. **Ind/Abst** Stat. Ref. Index.

SW/0283-4529
**BORSMEDDELANDEN.** VFOAT Bors Meddelanden. (1986)-. Swedish. qt. Stadskansliet Kopmansgatan 20, Box 21 31, 404 82 Goteborg Sweden. **LC** JS6285.G59; A13. **Continues** Statistiska Meddelanden Med Delar Av Annat.

FR/1147-1999
**BOTTIN ADMINISTRATIF.** (1989)-. French. an. 1400.00F France; 1180.50F other. Editions Techniques, 141 rue de Javel, 75747 Paris Cedex 15 France. **Tel** 011 33 1 45589100. **ED** Patrice Soulie. **LC** JN2303; .B6. **Continues** Bottin Administratif et Documentaire.

FR
**BOTTIN COMMUNES.** 1978-. French. an. 565.00F France; $95.00 US. Didot Bottin, 28 rue du Docteur Finlay, 75738 Paris Cedex 15 France. **Tel** (1)45 78 61 66, telex 204 286. **LC** DC14; .B63. **Ad Acc.** ctrl circ.

US/0272-4472
**BOUNDARY AND ANNEXATION SURVEY.** Began with 1972. Government Publication. English. be. US Department of Commerce, 14th Street & Constitution Avenue NW, Washington DC 20230. **Tel** (202)482-2000, FAX (202)482-3772. **LC** JS344.A5; U54A. **DD** 352/.006/0973.

UK
**BRIEF OUTLINE OF ACTIVITIES OF THE COMMITTEES OF THE ASSOCIATION.** **Main/Corp** Association of County Councils. English. Eaton House, 66A Eaton Square, Westminister SW1W 9BH England. **LC** JS3260; .A75A. **DD** 352/.0073.

UK
**BRITAIN VOTES : A HANDBOOK OF PARLIAMENTARY ELECTION RESULTS / COMPILED AND EDITED BY F.W.S. CRAIG.** (1977)-. English. ir. £35.00 (Vol. 3); £30.00 (Vol.4 & 5). Gower Publishing Co. Ltd, Gower House, Croft Road, Aldershot, Hampshire GU11 3HR England. **Tel** 011 44 252 331551, FAX 011 44 252 344405, telex 858001. **(Subscription address:** Ashgate Distribution Services, Unite 2-4 Lower Farnham Road, Aldershot GU12 4DY England.**)**
**Desc:** Information on elections.

CN/0007-0505
**BRITISH COLUMBIA GAZETTE MICROFORM, THE.** [B.C. gaz.]. VFOAT British Columbia Gazette. Part I. Periodical. English. Micromedia Limited, 20 Victoria Street, Toronto Ontario M5C 2N8 Canada. **Tel** (416)362-5211, (800)387-2689, FAX (416)362-6161, telex 06524668. **DD** 354.711/0005. available on microfilm from 3M Co. IM Press.

●UK/0968-2481
**BRITISH ELECTIONS AND PARTIES YEARBOOK.** **Added/Corp** Elections, Public Opinion and Parties in Britain (Political Studies Association of the United Kingdom). VFOAT British Elections & Parties Yearbook. (1991)-. English. an (October). $60.00. Frank Cass & Company Ltd, Newbury House, 890-900 Eastern Avenue, Newbury Park, Ilford, Essex IG2 7HH United Kingdom. **Tel** 011 44 81 599 8866, FAX 011 44 81 599 0984, telex 897719. **LC** JN956; .B746. **DD** 324.941/005.

US/0145-7837
**BUDGET AS ADOPTED BY THE BOARD OF COMMISSIONERS.** (BUDGET AS ADOPTED BY THE BOARD OF COMMISSIONERS - METROPOLITAN SANITARY DISTRICT OF GREATER CHICAGO. BOARD OF COMMISSIONERS.). **Main/Corp** Metropolitan Sanitary District of Greater Chicago. Board of Commissioners. English. an. Metropolitan Sanitary District of Greater Chicago, 100 East Erie Street, Chicago IL 60611. **LC** HD4479.C5; M46A. **DD** 352/.93/70977311.

CN/0226-4390
**BUDGET. COMMUNIQUES (QUEBEC).** (BUDGET. COMMUNIQUES.). [Budg., Commun.]. **Main/Corp** Quebec (Province) Ministere des Finances. Direction des Communications. 1979/80-. French. an. Ministere des Finances, 200 Chemin Ste Foy, Quebec Quebec G1R 4X6 Canada. **Tel** (418)691-2233. **DD** 354.7140072/253. **Formed by the union of** Budget. Discours sur le Budget; Communiques **and** Budget. Credits; Communiques.

AT
**BUDGET ESTIMATES / PARLIAMENT OF NEW SOUTH WALES.** **Main/Corp** New South Wales. Parliament. (1982-1983)-. Periodical. English. an. New South Wales Government Printer, Government Printing Office, 390-422 Harris Street, Ultimo New South Wales 2007 Australia. **Tel** (02)552-9717. **Continues in part** Budget Papers / New South Wales. Parliament.

US
**BUDGET ESTIMATES - U.S. NUCLEAR REGULATORY COMMISSION.** **Main/Corp** U.S. Nuclear Regulatory Commission. English. an. US Nuclear Regulatory Commission, Washington DC 20555. **LC** HD9698.U5; U54B. **DD** 353.0087/22. available on microfiche (Vols. for (1982-) distributed to depository libraries).

US/0743-5487
**BUDGET HIGHLIGHTS - UNITED STATES. DEPT. OF ENERGY. OFFICE OF THE CONTROLLER.** (BUDGET HIGHLIGHTS / U.S. DEPARTMENT OF ENERGY.). [Budg. highlights - U.S., Dep. Energy, Off. Control.]. **Main/Corp** United States. Dept. of Energy. Office of the Controller. Government Publication. English. an. US Department of Energy, 1000 Independence Avenue SW, Washington DC 20585. **Tel** (202)586-4073. **LC** HD9502.U5; U523H. **DD** 353.87. available on microfiche (Vols. for 1987- distributed to depository libraries).

BH
**BUDGET / PRESENTED BY THE PRIME MINISTER ... TO THE HOUSE OF REPRESENTATIVE ON, THE.** **Main/Corp** Belize. Prime Minister and Minister of Finance and Defence. English. an. **LC** HJ16.5; .A23A. **DD** 354.72820072/252/05.

US/0193-0362
**BUDGET REQUEST - U.S. CONSUMER PRODUCT SAFETY COMMISSION.** **Main/Corp** United States. Consumer Product Safety Commission. VFOAT CPSC Budget Request. **VAT** Budget Request - United States Consumer Product Safety Commission. Periodical. English. an. United States Consumer Product Safety Commission, 1111 18th Street NW, Washington DC 20207. **LC** HC110.C63; U47B. **DD** 353.007/7.

CN/0712-9661
**BULLETIN - CITE DE COTE SAINT-LUC.** (BULLETIN.). [Bull. - Cite Cote St-Luc]. VFOAT Bulletin; Newsletter. **VAT** Newsletter - Cite de Cote Saint-Luc. Vol. 1, No. 1 (Feb. 1975)-. Bulletin. English (French). Cite de Cote Saint-Luc Quebec H4X 2A6 Canada. **DD** 352.0714/28.

CN/0706-5361
**BULLETIN - CONSEIL DES AFFAIRES FRANCO-ONTARIENNES.** **Main/Corp** Ontario. Council for Franco-Ontarian Affairs. VFOAT Newsletter - Council for Franco-Ontarian Affairs. No. 13- Mar. 1978-. Bulletin. French (English). Council for Franco-Ontarian Affairs, 4th Floor/77 Bloor Street West, Toronto Ontario M7A 2R9 Canada. **Continues** Ontario. Advisory Council for Franco-Ontarian Affairs. Bulletin, 0706-5353.

CN/0712-6808
**BULLETIN DE CHATEAUGUAY, LE.** [Bull. Chateauguay]. **Main/Corp** Chateauguay (Quebec). Bulletin. French (English). qt. Free. Bulletin de Chateauguay, c/o Office of the Town Clerk, 5 Youville Boulevard, Chateauguay Quebec J6J 2P8 Canada. **Tel** (514)692-6701. **DD** 352.0714/33. **Circ:** 13,000.

CN/0316-5140
**BULLETIN D'INFORMATION - UNION DES MUNICIPALITES DE LA PROVINCE DE QUEBEC.** **Main/Corp** Union des Municipalites de la Province de Quebec. V. 1-. Bulletin. French. Union des Municipalites du Quebec, 680 Sherbrooke Street West, Suite 680, Montreal Quebec H3A 2S6 Canada. **Tel** (514)282-7700 49 St-Pierre. **DD** 352/.0006/2714.

FR
**BULLETIN DU SERVICE DE L'ATTACHE D'ARMEMENT A LONDRES.** Bulletin. French. bm (6 issues). 400.00F. Centre de Doc de l'Armement, Srvc Relations Promot Clients, 00460 Armees France. **Tel** 011 33 1 45526048.

LU/0423-7846
**BULLETIN - EUROPEAN PARLIAMENT.** **See** Law-International Law.

FR/0755-2793
**BULLETIN - FRANCE. PARLEMENT (1946- ). ASSEMBLEE NATIONALE.** **Main/Corp** France. Parlement (1946- ). Assemblee Nationale. (1972)-. Bulletin. French. wk (while parliament is in session). Free. Service de la Communication Secretariat General, Palais-Bourbon, 75355 Paris France. **Tel** (1)49 63 6000, FAX (1)40 63 6965, (1)40 635560, telex ASNAL PARIS F 205831. **ED** Pierre Hontebeyrie. **LC** J341; .K974a. **DD** 328.44/01. **Circ:** 7,000 (ctrl).
**Desc:** Presents the activities of the French National Assembly. Analyses texts studied by the Assembly. Information on parliamentary activities with international ramificatons.

GW
**BULLETIN (GERMANY (WEST). PRESSE- UND INFORMATIONSAMT : 1979). ENGLISH.** (BULLETIN.). 1 (June 6, 1979)-. Bulletin. English. Press and Information Office of the Federal Government, 11 Welckerstrasse, W-5300 Bonn 1 Germany. **Continues in part** Bulletin (Germany (West). Presse- und Informationsamt).

CN/0711-7744
**BULLETIN MUNICIPAL - CONSEIL MUNICIPAL DE SAINT-LOUIS-DE-TERREBONNE.** (BULLETIN MUNICIPAL.). [Bull. munic. - Cons. munic. St-Louis-de-Terrebonne]. V. 1, No. 1, (April 30, 1978)-. Bulletin. French. qt. Free. Corporation Municipale de la Paroisse de St-Louis-de-Terrebonne, 4580 Croissant Dauphin, Saint-Louis-de-Terrebonne Quebec J0N 1N0 Canada. **DD** 352.0714/24. ctrl circ.

CN/0820-9278
**BULLETIN MUNICIPAL / OUTREMONT.** [Bull. munic. - Outremont]. **Main/Corp** Outremont (Quebec). VFOAT Bulletin Municipal d'Outremont. No. 91 (April 1981)-. Bulletin. French (English). mo. Free. Hotel de Ville d'Outremont, 510 Avenue Davaar, Outremont Quebec H2V 2B9 Canada. **Tel** (514)274-9451. **DD** 352.0714/281. **Circ:** 10,000. **Continues** Bulletin d'Outremont, 0700-4508.
**Desc:** To provide information to the taxpayers and citizens about municipal projects, by-laws and regulations, safety and public security, corporate finances, etc.

CN/0822-0395
**BULLETIN MUNICIPAL / VILLE DE MONTREAL-NORD.** [Bull. munic. - Ville Montreal-Nord]. **Main/Corp** Montreal-Nord (Quebec). VFOAT Bulletin Municipal de Montreal-Nord. No. 2, (April 1983)-. Bulletin. French. Free to Citizens. Hotel de Ville de Montreal-Nord, 4242 Place de l'Hotel de Ville, Montreal-Nord Quebec H1H 1S5 Canada. **DD** 352.0714/281. **Continues** Montreal-Nord (Quebec). Bulletin Special sur le Budget, 0823-5643.

US/0027-8645
**BULLETIN NATIONAL ASSOCIATION OF REGULATORY UTILITY COMMISSIONERS.** [Bull. - Natl. Assoc. Regul. Util. Comm.]. **Added/Corp** National Association of Regulatory Utility Commissioners. (19??)-. Bulletin. English. Fifty-two times a year. $110.00. National Association of Regulatory Utility Commissioners, 1102 Interstate Commerce Commission Building, PO Box 684, Washington DC 20044. **Tel** (202)898-2200, FAX (202)898-2213. **LC** HD2766.A3; B85. **DD** 363.6/0973. **Continues** Bulletin (National Association of Railroad and Utilities Commissioners).

US/0279-800X
**BULLETIN - NORTH DAKOTA LEAGUE OF CITIES.** (BULLETIN / NORTH DAKOTA LEAGUE OF CITIES.). **Main/Corp** North Dakota League of Cities. **Added/Corp** North Dakota League of Cities. VFOAT North Dakota League of Cities Bulletin. Vol. 37, No. 5 (May 1969)-. Periodical. English. Ten times a year (Jan/Feb. and July/Aug. issues combined). $15.00. North Dakota League of Cities Bulletin, Box 2235, Bismarck ND 58501. **Tel** (701)223-3518, (800)472-2692, FAX (701)223-5174. **ED** Robert E. Johnson. **LC** JS451.N95; L4. **Ad Acc. Circ:** 2,800 (ctrl). **Continues** Bulletin (League of North Dakota Municipalities).
**Desc:** For city officials, government administrators, employees and those interested in such matters.

BE/0378-3693
**BULLETIN OF THE EUROPEAN COMMUNITIES.** (BULLETIN OF THE EUROPEAN COMMUNITIES / ECSC, EEC, [AND] EAEC.). [Bull. Eur. Communities]. **Added/Corp** Commission of the European Communities. **VFOAT** Bulletin EC. Vol. 1, No. 1 (Jan. 1968)-. Bulletin. English. mo (11 times a year). £115.00. Office for Official Publications of the European Communities, 2 Rue Mercier, 2985 Luxembourg Luxembourg. **Tel** 011 352 499281, FAX 011 352 488573. **(Subscription address:** Her Majesty's Stationery Office, PO Box 276, Publications Centre, London SW8 5DT England.**)** **LC** HC241.2; .A212. **DD** 940/.05. **CODEN** BEUCBC. ***Formed by the union of*** *European Coal and Steel Community. High Authority. Bulletin from the European Community for Coal and Steel* ***and*** *European Economic Community. Bulletin of the European Economic Community, 0531-3430;* ***Absorbed*** *Commission of the European Communities. Programme of the Commission.*
**Desc:** Reports on activities of the commission and the other community institutions, including the building of the community, enlargement and external relations, financing community activities, and political and institutional matters.
**Ind/Abst** Chem. Bus. Bull.; Chem. Bus. NewsBase (1985-); Chem. Bus. Update; GeoRef; Int. Packag. Abstr.; LABORDOC; Leis. Recreat. Tour. Abstr.; Maize Abstr.; Nonwovens Abstr.; Pap. Board Abstr.; Rural Dev. Abstr.; World Agric. Econ.; World Text. Abstr.

LU
**BULLETIN OF THE EUROPEAN COMMUNITIES. SUPPLEMENT.** **Added/Corp** Commission of the European Communities. (1968)-. Bulletin. English. ir. Office for Official Publications of the European Communities, 2 Rue Mercier, 2985 Luxembourg Luxembourg. **Tel** 011 352 499281, FAX 011 352 488573. **LC** HC241.2; .A2122. **CODEN** BECSB4. ***Continued by*** *Bulletin of the European Union. Supplement.*
**Ind/Abst** GeoRef (?-?); Middle East Abstr. Index (?-?).

●LU
**BULLETIN OF THE EUROPEAN UNION. SUPPLEMENT.** **Added/Corp** Commission of the European Communities. (1994)-. Monographic series. English. ir. Office for Official Publications of the European Communities, 2 Rue Mercier, 2985 Luxembourg Luxembourg. **Tel** 011 352 499281, FAX 011 352 488573. **LC** HC241.2; .A2122. ***Continues*** *Bulletin of the European Communities. Supplement.*

CN/0708-3912
**BULLETIN - OFFICE DE LA CONSTRUCTION DU QUEBEC.** **Main/Corp** Office de la Construction du Quebec. Periodical. French (English). mo. Office de la Construction du Quebec, 5530 Jean Talon Ouest, Montreal Quebec H3R 2G3 Canada. **Tel** (514)341-7740.

FR
**BULLETIN OFFICIEL.** **Main/Corp** France. Ministere de l'Amenagement du Territoire, de l'Equipement, du Logement et du Tourisme. **Added/Corp** France. Direction des Transports Terrestres. (19??)-. Bulletin. French. Direction des Journaux Officiels, 26 rue Desaix, 75727 Paris Cedex 15 France. **Tel** 011 33 1 40587500. **LC** LAW. **DD** 354/.44/0086.

FR
**BULLETIN OFFICIEL D'ANNONCES DES DOMAINES (FRANCE. MINISTERE DE L'ECONOMIC ET DES FINANCES : 20 JUIN 1981).** (BULLETIN OFFICIEL D'ANNONCES DES DOMAINES / MINISTERE DE L'ECONOMIE ET DES FINANCES.). **Added/Corp** France. Ministere de l'Economie et des Finances. (19??)-. Bulletin. French. sm (24 issues). 98.00F. Direction Generale des Impots, 17 rue Scribe, 75436 Paris Cedex 09 France. **Tel** 011 33 1 42669346. **LC** JN2751; .A35a. **DD** 354.440071/3. ***Continues*** *Bulletin Officiel d'Annonces des Domaines (France. Ministere du Budget).*

FR/0429-2944
**BULLETIN OFFICIEL DES ANNONCES DES MARCHES PUBLICS.** [Bull. off. annonces marches publics]. (1957)-. Periodical. French. wk (52 issues). 305.00F France; 604.00F other. Direction des Journaux Officiels, 26 rue Desaix, 75727 Paris Cedex 15 France. **Tel** 011 33 1 40587500. **UDC** 070.481.

FR
**BULLETIN OFFICIEL DU SECRETARIAT D'ETAT AUX DEPARTEMENTS ET TERRITOIRES D'OUTRE-MER (FRANCE).** **See** Law.

CN/1187-4996
**BULLETIN - ONTARIO. SOCIAL ASSISTANCE REVIEW BOARD.** (BULLETIN / SOCIAL ASSISTANCE REVIEW BOARD.). [Bull. - Ont., Soc. Assist. Rev. Board]. **Main/Corp** Ontario. Social Assistance Review Board. **VFOAT** Bulletin. **VAT** Bulletin - Ontario. Commission de Revision de l'Aide Sociale. Vol. 1:1 (Oct. 1991)-. Bulletin. English (French). sa. **DD** 354.7130084.

CN/0706-0564
**BULLETIN - PUBLIC SERVICE COMMISSION OF CANADA.** **Main/Corp** Public Service Commission of Canada. **VFOAT** Bulletin - Commission de la Fonction Publique du Canada. Began publication in 1967?. Bulletin. English (French).

CN/0226-1014
**BULLETIN ROUTIER; QUEBEC.** [Bull. rout., Que.]. Vol. 5 (April/June 1979)-. Bulletin. French. qt. Ministere des Transports / Canada, 1995 Boulevard Charest-Quest, Edifice Branly 2E Etage, Ste Foy Quebec H1N 2E6 Canada. **DD** 354.7140086/4/0971417. ctrl circ. ***Continues*** *Bulletin Routier.*

US
**BULLETIN (UNITED STATES. OFFICE OF MANAGEMENT AND BUDGET).** (BULLETIN / EXECUTIVE OFFICE OF THE PRESIDENT, OFFICE OF MANAGEMENT AND BUDGET.). Bulletin. English. Office of Management and Budget, Executive Office Building, Washington DC 20503. **Tel** (202)395-3080.

XO
**BULLETIN USTREDNEHO VYBORU NARODNEHO FRONTU SLOVENSKEJ SOCIALISTICKEJ REPUBLIKY.** **Main/Corp** Narodny Front Slovenskej Socialistickej Republiky. Ustredny Vybor. (19??)-. Bulletin. Slovak. Narodneho Frontu Slovenskej Socialistickej Republiky, Sturova 5, Bratislava Slovakia. **LC** JN2199.S44; N37a.

BE/0773-7467
**BULLETIN USUEL DES LOIS ET ARRETES (BRUXELLES).** [Bull. usuel lois arretes Brux.]. (1861)-. Periodical. French. sm (24 issues). 7187.00F Belgium, 7200.00F other. Etablissements Emile Bruylant, 67 rue de la Regence, 1000 Brussels Belgium. **Tel** 011 32 2 5129845. **UDC** 34(493).

CN/0710-3689
**BULLETIN / VILLE DE MONT-LAURIER.** [Bull. - Ville Mont-Laurier]. **Main/Corp** Mont-Laurier (Quebec). Vol. 1, No. 1 (Oct. 1981)-. Bulletin. French. qt. Free. Hotel de Ville, 485 rue Mercier, Mont-Laurier Quebec J9L 3N8 Canada. **DD** 352.0714/225. ctrl circ.

GW/0344-7634
**BUNDESANZEIGER.** [Bundesanzeiger]. **Main/Corp** Germany (West). (1949)-. German. Twenty-six times a year (Publishes Tues.- Sat., except holidays & day after). DM160.00 Germany; DM 275.00 others. Bundesanzeiger Verlagsges GmbH, Postfach 1320, D 53003 Bonn Germany. **Tel** 011 49 228 3820812. **(Subscription address:** Bunddesanzeiger Verlag, Postfach 100534, D 50445 Cologne Germany.**)**
**Ind/Abst** Coal Abstr.

GW
**BUNDESREPUBLIK DEUTSCHLAND STAATSHANDBUCH. LANDESAUSGABE LAND NORDRHEIN-WESTFALEN, DIE.** **VFOAT** Landesausgabe Lane Nordrhein-Westfalen; Land Nordrhein-Westfalen. (Aug. 1981)-. German. Carl Heymanns Verlag KG, Luxemburger Strasse 449, D 50939 Cologne Germany. **Tel** 011 49 221 460100, telex 8 881 888. **LC** JN4945.N62; B86. **DD** 354.43/55/00025. ***Continues*** *Bundesrepublik Deutschland Staatshandbuch. Teilausgabe Land Nordrhein-Westfalen.*

US/0045-3544
**BUREAUCRAT (BEVERLY HILLS), THE.** ***Title Change.*** (THE BUREAUCRAT.). [Bureaucrat]. **Added/Corp** American Society for Public Administration. National Capital Area Chapter. **VFOAT** Journal for Public Managers, the Bureaucrat. Vol. 1 (Spring 1972)-Vol. 20, No. 4 (Winter 1991-92). Periodical. English. qt. The Bureaucrat Inc., 12007 Titian Way, Potomac MD 20854. **Tel** (301)279-9445, FAX (301)251-5872. **ED** Thomas W Novotny. **LC** JK1; .B86. **DD** 353/.0005. **[CCC]**. Index available. **Bk Rev. Ad Acc. Pr Rev. Circ:** 4,000. available on microfilm and microfiche from University Microfilms International (UMI). Documents available from UMI Article Clearinghouse. ***Continued by*** *Public Manager, 1061-7639.*
**Desc:** Dedicated to fostering, developing, and otherwise encouraging the utmost in professionalism and performance by public managers at all levels.
**Ind/Abst** ABC POL SCI; ABI/INFORM Glob. Ed.; ABI Inform Ondisc (Spring 1979-1992); Bus. ASAP [Full Txt.]; Bus. Period. Index; Gen. Period. Index (1985-1992); Hum. Resour. Abstr. (?-?); Int. Polit. Sci. Abstr.; J. Plan. Lit.; Mag. Search; Sage Public Adm. Abstr.; Sage Urban Stud. Abstr (Spring 1979-1992); U.S. Polit. Sci. Doc. (-1992); Urban Aff. Abstr.

IT
**BUSARL : PERUGIA.** Italian. sm. Camera Comm Ind Art Agr / Perugia, V Cacciatori Alpi 40, 06100 Perugia italy. **Tel** 011 39 75 5748230.

IT
**BUSARL : TRIESTE.** Italian. ir. L600000. Camera Comm Ind Art Agr Busarl, Piazza Borsa 14, 34121 Trieste Italy. **Tel** 011 39 40 6701247.

UK
**BUSINESS AND GOVERNMENT.** **See** Business.

SP
**BUTLLETI OFICIAL DEL PARLAMENT DE CATALUNYA.** **Main/Corp** Catalonia (Spain). Parlement. 1A. Legislature, No. 1 (June 12, 1980)-. Catalan (Spanish). sw. 4620ptas. Servei de Publicacions del Parlament de Catalunya, Palau del Parlament Parc de la Ciutadella, Barcelona 08003 Catalonia Spain. **Tel** (93)300-6413, FAX (93)300-8962, telex 97-684. **LC** J409.T3; C43A. **DD** 328.46/7/005. Index available. cum. index. **Circ:** 1,100. available on CD-ROM; available on an online database.
**Desc:** Publishes all the parliamentary papers which enter or leave the house and thus allows to follow all the different processes and successive modifications which a proposal undergoes before eventually being passed.

US/0250-7307
**BY-LAWS, RULES AND REGULATIONS. INTERNATIONAL MONETARY FUND.** (BY-LAWS, RULES AND REGULATIONS.). [By-laws rules regul., Int. Monet. Fund]. **Main/Corp** International Monetary Fund. (1947)-. English (French and Spanish). Free on request. International Monetary Fund, 700 19th Street Northwest, Publishing Unit, Washington DC 20431. **Tel** (202)623-7430, FAX (202)623-7201.

FR
**CABINETS MINISTERIELS.** French. 4114.50F. Soc Gen de Presse et d Edns, 13 Avenue de l Opera, 75001 Paris France. **Tel** 011 33 1 64334905.

BL
**CADERNOS DE ADMINISTRACAO MUNICIPAL / IMAM.** No. 1-. Monographic series. Portuguese. Price varies per volume. Secretaria do Estado do Interior e Justica, rua Paraiba 755, Belo Horizonte Brazil. **LC** JS2423.M5; A14A. **DD** 352/.008/098151.

PO
**CADERNOS MUNICIPAIS.** **Added/Corp** Fundacao Antero de Quental. Vol. 1, (June 1979)-. Periodical. Portuguese. **LC** JS6341; .C3. **DD** 352/.0072/09469.

MR/0007-9588
**CAHIERS AFRICAINS D'ADMINISTRATION PUBLIQUE.** ***Ceased.*** [Cah. afr. adm. publique]. **Added/Corp** African Training and Research Centre in Administration for Development. **VFOAT** Dirasat Ifriqiyah fi Al-Idarah; African Administrative Studies. Vol. 1 (May 1967)-(19??). Periodical. English (French and Arabic). sa. CAFRAD, BP 310, Tangier Morocco. **Tel** 011 212 36430, telex 33664. **LC** JQ1871.A1; C3. Index available. cum. index. **Bk Rev. Ad Acc. Circ:** 750 (ctrl). available in microform.
**Desc:** Aims to contribute to the study of administrative problems concerning economic and social development in Africa.
**Ind/Abst** Int. Bibliogr. Sociol.; Int. Polit. Sci. Abstr.; Leis. Recreat. Tour. Abstr.; Rural Dev. Abstr.; World Agric. Econ.

FR/0753-4418
**CAHIERS DE LA FONCTION PUBLIQUE ET DE L'ADMINISTRATION.** [Cah. fonct. publique adm.]. (1982)-. Periodical. French. mo. 590.00F. Editions Berger-Levrault, BP 50, 54840 Velaine en Haye France. **Tel** 011 33 1 1683916808, FAX 011 33 1 1683232492. **UDC** 35.08.

CG
**CAHIERS ZAIROIS DE LA RECHERCHE ET DU DEVELOPPEMENT.** **See** Political Science.

US/0364-0558
**CALENDARS OF THE UNITED STATES HOUSE OF REPRESENTATIVES AND HISTORY OF LEGISLATION.** [Cal. U. S. House Represent. hist. legis.]. **Main/Corp** United States. Congress. House. (1???)-. Government Publication. English. wk (when House of Representatives is in session). $196.00 domestic. Superintendent of Documents, US Government Printing Office, Washington DC 20402. **Tel** (202)275-3328, FAX (202)786-2377. **LC** J47; .A3. **DD** 328.73.
**Desc:** Presents almost 500 economic indicators in a form convenient for analysts with different approaches to the study of current business conditions and prospects.

US
**CALIFORNIA ACTION SERVICE.** English. Seven times a year. $13.50. League of Women Voters of California, 926 J Street, Suite 1000, Sacramento CA 95814. **Tel** (916)442-7215, FAX (916)442-7362. **ED** Trudy P. Schafer. **Circ:** 400.
**Desc:** News and information on legislation matters.

US
**CALIFORNIA ADMINISTRATIVE CODE.** **Added/Corp** California. Office of Administrative Hearings. **VFOAT** California Administrative Register. (1980)-. English. ir. California Department of General Services Document Section, PO Box 20191, Sacramento CA 95820. **ED** Carolyn A Dyer.

US/0891-2718
**CALIFORNIA, CITIES, TOWNS & COUNTIES.** [Calif. cities towns cty.]. **VFOAT** California, Cities, Towns, and Counties. (1987)-. English. an (March). $75.00. Information Publications, 3790 El Camino Real/Suite 162, Palo Alto CA 94306. **Tel** (415)965-4449. **ED** Edith R. Hornor. **LC** HA261; .C295. **DD** 307/.09794/021. ctrl circ.
**Desc:** Basic one page profiles of all municipalities and counties in California, including demographics and socio-economics characteristic, local officials, elected representatives, crime, school district information, municipal/county finance summary, real property and public library.

US/0738-694X
**CALIFORNIA IN PRINT.** (Mar. 16, 1981)-. Periodical. English. ir (10 to 15 times per year). $75.00. Government Research, 815 North La Brea Avenue, Suite 197, Ingelwood CA 90302. **Tel** (213)678-3851. **ED** Jerry Jeffe.
**Desc:** Lists publications released for public distribution by California state legislature and judicial agencies.

US/0190-969X
**CALIFORNIA JOURNAL ALMANAC OF STATE GOVERNMENT AND POLITICS.** **VFOAT** Almanac of State Government and Politics; California Journal Almanac. 1st Ed. (1975)-. English. be. $37.70. California Journal Press, 1714 Capitol Avenue, Sacramento CA 95814. **Tel** (916)444-2840, FAX (916)444-2339. **LC** JK8701; .C333. **DD** 320.9/794. **Circ:** 6,000.
**Desc:** Statistical and biographical information on California's elected and appointed officials, election data, population, education, finance, legislative districts lobbyists, press and much more.

●US
**CALIFORNIA JOURNAL'S ELECTION WEEKLY.** **See** Political Science.

US/1059-9487
**CALIFORNIA NOTARY BULLETIN.** (CALIFORNIA NOTARY BULLETIN / A PUBLICATION OF THE NATIONAL NOTARY ASSOCIATION.). **Added/Corp** National Notary Association (U.S.). **VFOAT** Notary Bulletin. Vol. 1, No. 1 (Oct. 1991)-. Periodical. English. bm (6 issues). Comes with National Notary Association membership. National Notary Association, 8236 Remmet Ave., PO Box 7184, Canoga Park CA 91304. **Tel** (818)713-4000. ***Continues*** *Notary Viewpoint, 0744-236X.*

US/0742-0927
**CALIFORNIA POLICY CHOICES.** [Calif. policy choices]. **Added/Corp** Sacramento Public Affairs Center. Vol. 1 (1984)-. English. an. $23.70 California; $23.95 others. University Bookstore / Textbooks Department, 840 Childs Way, Los Angeles CA 90007. **Tel** (213)740-8398. **ED** John J. Kirlin and Donald R. Winkler. **LC** JK8701; .C35. **DD** 353.9794/0005. **Circ:** 1,500 (ctrl).
**Desc:** Analyses of policy choices confronting California. Fiscal, welfare, toxics, health, prisons, pensions, demographics, economics, land use, energy, water, juvenile justice and schools have been analyzed.

US/0195-6175
**CALIFORNIA POLITICAL WEEK.** (19??)-. Periodical. English. Forty-Four times a year. $90.00 (one year), $165.00 (two year). California Political Week, PO Box 1468, Beverly Hills CA 90213. **Tel** (310)659-0205, FAX (310)657-4340. **ED** Dick Rosengarten. **Ad Acc. Circ:** 3,000.
**Desc:** News analysis of key public policy issues and analysis of current trends and developments in California and Western U.S.

US
**CALIFORNIA STATE GOVERNMENT DIRECTORY, THE.** **Added/Corp** State Net. (1989)-. Directory. English. qt. $125.00. California Journal Press, 1714 Capitol Avenue, Sacramento CA 95814. **Tel** (916)444-2840, FAX (916)444-2339.

US/0741-2371
**CALIFORNIA'S THE GREEN BOOK.** (CALIFORNIA GREEN BOOK.). [Calif. green book]. **VFOAT** Green Book. (Winter 1989)-. English. Four times a year. $180.00. Green Book California, PO Box 1772, Sacramento CA 95812. **Tel** (916)447-7778. **LC** JK8730; .C38. **DD** 353.9794002. ***Continues*** *California's The Green Book, 0741-2371.*
**Desc:** The most comprehensive and authoritative directory ever published on California government and politics.

AG
**CAMBIOS : MUNICIPIO Y POLITICAS PUBLICAS.** No.1 (1991)-. Periodical. Spanish.

US/0161-9039
**CAMPAIGNER SPECIAL REPORT, THE.** Periodical. English. $1.50. Campaigner Publications Inc, PO Box 9063, McLean VA 22102-0063. **Tel** (703)777-9401. **LC** JK2361; .C35. **DD** 329/.81.

CN/0827-0708
**CANADA: THE STATE OF THE FEDERATION.** (CANADA : THE STATE OF THE FEDERATION / EDITED BY PETER M. LESLIE.). [Can.: state fed.]. **Added/Corp** Queen's University (Kingston, Ont.). Institute of Intergovernmental Relations. **VFOAT** State of the Federation. (1985)-. English. an (Oct., or Nov.). 20.00Can$. Institute of Intergovernmental Relations, Queens University, Kingston Ontario K7L 3N6 Canada. **Tel** (613)547-2619. **(Subscription address:** Renouf Publishing Company Ltd., 1294 Algoma Road, Ottawa Ontario K1B 3WB Canada.) **ED** Douglan Brown and Robert Young. **LC** JL27; .C466. **DD** 321.02/3/0971. **Pr Rev. Circ:** 1,000. ***Continues*** *Year in Review (Kingston, Ont.), 0825-1207.*

●CN/1191-7733
**CANADA WATCH.** [Can. watch]. **Added/Corp** York University (Toronto, Ont.). Centre for Public Law and Public Policy. Robarts Centre for Canadian Studies. Vol. 1, No. 1 (July/Aug. 1992)-. Periodical. English. Eight times a year. 99.00Can$ individuals; 165.00Can$ institutions. Emond Montgomery Publiding Ltd., 58 Shaftesbury Avenue, Toronto Ontario, M4T 1A3 Canada. **Tel** (416)975-3925, FAX (416)975-3924. **LC** IN PROCESS. **DD** 971/.005. **Circ:** 300.

●CN/1189-4709
**CANADIAN FEDERAL GOVERNMENT HANDBOOK.** [Can. fed. gov. handb.]. (1992)-. English. 49.95Can$. Globe & Mail, 444 Front Street West, Toronto Ontario M5V 2S9 Canada. **Tel** (416)585-5000, FAX (416)585-5249. **DD** 354.71/00025. ***Continues*** *Ottawa's Senior Executives Guide, 0826-8355.*

CN/0576-5501
**CANADIAN INTELLIGENCE SERVICE.** Vol. 1 (Jan. 1951)-. Periodical. English. Twelve times a year. 23.36Can$. Canadian Intelligence Service, Bag 78, High River Alberta T0L 1B0 Canada. **Tel** (519)924-2848. **ED** Ron Gostick. **Circ:** 2,400 (ctrl).
**Desc:** A report dealing with defence of freedom and christian values.

CN/0834-1516
**CANADIAN JOURNAL OF PROGRAM EVALUATION, THE.** [Can. j. program eval.]. **Added/Corp** Canadian Evaluation Society. **VFOAT** Revue Canadienne d'Evaluation de Programme. Vol. 1, No. 1 (April 1986)-. Periodical. English (French). Twice a year (Apr. and Oct.). 42.06Can$ (institutions); 60.75Can$ (individuals). Canadian Evaluation Society, 309 James Street, Ottawa Ontario K1R 5M8 Canada. **Tel** (613)230-1007, FAX (613)237-9900. **ED** Bob Segsworth. **DD** 350/.007/6. cum. index. **Bk Rev. Ad Acc, Adv Mgr:** Kathy Jones, **Tel** (613)230-1007. **Pr Rev. Circ:** 1,300.
**Desc:** These articles on all aspects of the theory and practice of evaluation. Including methodology, evaluation standards, implementation of evaluations, reporting and use of studies, and the audit or meta-evaluation of evaluation.

CN/0715-7118
**CANADIAN LEGISLATURES.** [Can. legis.]. **Added/Corp** Ontario. Office of the Assembly. (1981)-. English. an. 65.00Can$. Robert J. Fleming International Research Inc., 344 Davenport Road/Suite 1, Toronto Ontario M5R 1R6 Canada. **Tel** (416)964-2332, FAX (416)362-0089. **ED** Robert J. Fleming. **LC** JL179; .C362. **DD** 328.71/076. **Circ:** 1,500. ***Continues*** *Comparative Study of Administrative Structures of Canadian Legislatures, 0715-7843.*
**Desc:** Study of salaries, allowances, services for elected members of U.S. and Canadian legislatures and administrative arrangements and structures presently in place.

CN/0703-1378
**CANADIAN NEWSLETTER FOR OPEN GOVERNMENT, THE.** [Can. newsl. open gov.]. **VFOAT** Newsletter; Le Bulletin Canadien pour le Droit a l'Information Publique; Bulletin Canadien pour Gouvernement Ouvert. **VAT** Newsletter - Access; Access. V. 1- Nov. 1976-. Newsletter. English (French). Free. Access / Canada, Box 855, Station B, Ottawa K1P 5P9 Canada. **DD** 354/.71/008105. ctrl circ.

CN/0315-6168
**CANADIAN PARLIAMENTARY GUIDE.** (THE CANADIAN PARLIAMENTARY GUIDE. GUIDE PARLEMENTAIRE CANADIEN.). **VFOAT** Guide Parlementaire Canadien. (1909)-. English (French). an. 59.95Can$. Globe & Mail, 444 Front Street West, Toronto Ontario M5V 2S9 Canada. **Tel** (416)585-5000, FAX (416)585-5249. **ED** Pierre G. Normandin. **DD** 328/.71/0025. Index available. **Bk Rev. Circ:** 3,800 (ctrl). ***Continues*** *Canadian Parliamentary Guide and Work of General Reference for the Dominion of Canada, 0315-6168.*
**Desc:** Information on Canadian and provincial parliaments, members with biographies and results of general elections. Also senate, governor general and embassies.

CN/0229-2548
**CANADIAN PARLIAMENTARY REVIEW.** [Can. parliam. rev.]. Vol. 3, No. 4 (Winter 1980/81)-. Periodical. English (French). qt. 20.00Can$. Canadian Parliamentary Association, Canadian Region, PO Box 950, Confederation Building, Ottawa Ontario K1A 0A6 Canada. **Tel** (613)996-1662. **ED** Gary Levy. **LC** JL148; .C33. **DD** 328.71/005. Index available. cum. index. **Bk Rev.** ***Continues*** *Canadian Regional Review, 0707-0837.*
**Desc:** Intended to inform Canadian legislators about activities of their federal and provincial branches, and to promote study of parliamentary institutions in Canada.
**Ind/Abst** Am. Hist. Life (1987-); Can. Index (?-?); Can. Period. Index; PAIS Int. Print (1991-).

CN/0008-4840
**CANADIAN PUBLIC ADMINISTRATION.** [Can. public adm.]. **VFOAT** Administration Publique du Canada. Vol. 1 (March 1958)-. Academic Scholarly Publication. English (French). qt. 80.00Can$ Canada; 85.00Can$ other. Institute of Public Administration of Canada, 150 Eglinton Avenue East, Suite 305, Toronto, Ontario M4P 1E8 Canada. **Tel** (416)932-3666. **ED** Vincent Seymour Wilson. Index available. **Bk Rev. Ad Acc. Pr Rev. Circ:** 4,100. available on microfiche from University Microfilms International (UMI). Documents available from The Genuine Article.
**Desc:** Refereed scholarly journal advancing the study and practice of public administration, especially in Canada. Examination of structures, processes and outcomes of public policy and management related to executive, legislative, judicial and quasi-judicial functions in the municipal, provincial and federal spheres of government.
**Ind/Abst** ABC POL SCI; Acad. Search (Jan. 1994-); Am. Hist. Life (1976-); Appl. Soc. Sci. Index Abstr.; Can. Index; Can. Period. Index; Curr. Contents Soc. Behav. Sci.; Gen. Period. Index (1985-); Hospit. Health Admin. Index; Index Can. Leg. Period. Lit.; INFO-SOUTH Abstr.; Int. Bibliogr. Sociol.; Int. Polit. Sci. Abstr.; Mag. Search; Manage. Contents; PAIS Int. Print (1991-); Res. Alert [Full Cov.]; Sage Public Adm. Abstr.; Soc. Sci. Cit. Index [Full Cov.]; Trade Ind. Index.

CN/0317-0861
**CANADIAN PUBLIC POLICY.** **See** Economics.

CN/0711-7027
**CANAL-ISEP.** [CANAL-ISEP]. **VAT** Canal-Information Scolaire et Professionnelle. No. 1 (81-12)-. Periodical. French. Gouvernement du Quebec, 600 St Amable 4E Etage, Quebec Quebec G1R 4Z1 Canada. **DD** 354.7140085/1/05.

AT/0811-6318
**CANBERRA BULLETIN OF PUBLIC ADMINISTRATION.** (1982)-. Bulletin. English. qt. 60.00Aus$ (Australia); 70.00Aus$ (New Zealand); 90.00Aus$ (other). Australian Institute of Public Administration ACT GRUP, PO Box 329, Belconnen ACT 2616 Australia. **Tel** 61 6 2015113.
**Ind/Abst** APAIS, Aust. Public Aff. Inf. Ser. (1985-).

CN/0844-9228
**CANMET BUSINESS PLAN.** [CANMET bus. plan]. **Main/Corp** Canada Centre for Mineral and Energy Technology. **VAT** Canada Centre for Mineral and Energy Technology Business Plan; Business Plan. (1991)-. Periodical. English (French). Canada Centre For Mineral and Energy Technology, 555 Booth Street, Ottawa Ontario K1A OG1 Canada. **DD** 354.710082/38/05.

US/0147-7749
**CAPITAL IMPROVEMENT PROGRAM (FAIRFAX).** (CAPITAL IMPROVEMENT PROGRAM - FAIRFAX CO., VA.). **Main/Corp** Office of Comprehensive Planning. Fairfax Co., Va. **VFOAT** CIP. Capital Improvement Program for Fairfax County, Virginia. English. an. Office of Comprehensive Planning, 4100 Chain Bridge Road, Fairfax VA 22030. **LC** HD3890.V8; F34A. **DD** 352/.12/09755291.

US/0898-6916
**CAPITAL SOURCE, THE.** [Cap. source]. (1985/86)-. English. Twice a year. $27.44. National Journal Inc., 1501 M Street Northwest, Suite 300, Washington DC 20005. **Tel** (800)356-4838, (202)739-8541, (800)424-2921. **LC** F192.3; .C26. **DD** 975.3/0025.
**Desc:** Divides Washington, D.C., into divisions by government, corporate, professional, and media categories, listing contact names and information for those seeking jobs in the D.C. area.

US
**CAPITOL ADVANTAGE.** ***Title Change.*** (19??)-(19??). English. an (March). Hansan & Group Inc, PO Box 1223, McLean VA 22101. **Tel** (703)734-3266, (800)659-8708, FAX (703)847-0573. ***Continues*** *US Congress Directory.* ***Continued by*** *Congress at Your Fingertips.*

# Public Administration

**Desc:** Directory of Congressional profiles listing Congressmen and Senators and their pictures. Also includes key staff and committee appointments.

US/1064-6957
**CAPITOL CURRENTS.** [Cap. curr.]. **Added/Corp** Michigan Townships Association. (19??)-. Periodical. English. mo. $20.00. Michigan Townships Association, 512 Westshire Drive, Lansing MI 48917-8715. **Tel** (517)321-6467, FAX (517)321-8908. **DD** 340.

US
**CAPITOL NEWSLETTER.** (19??)-. Newsletter. English. Eight times a year (Jan. - April). $20.00 (members of the League of Women Voters); $30.00 other. League of Women Voters of Alabama, 2520 College Street, Montgomery AL 36106. **Tel** (205)244-7477. **ED** Betty Cork. **Circ:** 100. available on microfilm from University Microfilms International (UMI).
**Desc:** Tracking of bills of interest to the League of Women Voters members with description of events occurring in the legislature.

US/0889-4841
**CAPITOL UPDATE.** [Capitol update]. (198?)-. Periodical. English. sm. $50.00. Texas State Directory Press, PO Box 12186 Capitol Station, Austin TX 78711. **Tel** (512)477-5698, (800)388-8075, FAX (512)473-2447. **DD** 342.

US/0502-0166
**CAREERS IN THE UNITED STATES DEPARTMENT OF THE INTERIOR.** See Occupations and Careers.

CN/0825-7345
**CARILLON (CANADA. DEPT. OF VETERANS AFFAIRS).** (CARILLON.). [Carillon]. Vol. 15, No. 8 (Aug./Sept. 1982)-. Periodical. English (French). mo. **DD** 354.710681/2/05. **Continues** Carillon Canada, 0225-8110.

BL
**CARTA, A.** Periodical. Portuguese. $600. Av 9 de Julho 3805, Sao Paulo Brazil. **LC** JL2401; .C36.

BL
**CARTEIRA DE TITULOS, PERFIL DE EMPRESAS / FUNDO DE INVESTIMENTOS DA AMAZONIA, FINAM.** *Title Change.* **Added/Corp** FINAM (Organization : Brazil) Banco da Amazonia. **VFOAT** Perfil de Empresas. No. 8 (Oct. 1980)-(19??). Portuguese. ir. O Fundo, Finam Av Presidente Vargas/800 4 Andar, Belem Para 66000 Brazil. **Continues** Perfis de Empresas Beneficiarias. **Continued by** FINAM (Organization : Brazil). FINAM, Perfil das Empresas.

US
**CASES IN PUBLIC POLICY AND MANAGEMENT.** **Added/Corp** Education for Public Service Clearinghouse Project. Intercollegiate Case Clearing House. (1978)-. English. ir. price varies per volume. Intercollegiate Case Clearing House, Harvard Business School, Soldiers Field, Boston MA 02163.

US/0097-9309
**CATALOG OF STATE ASSISTANCE PROGRAMS.** *Title Change.* (CATALOG OF STATE ASSISTANCE PROGRAMS (MARYLAND).). **Main/Corp** Maryland. Dept. of State Planning. Catalog. English. an. Department of State Planning, State Office Building, Baltimore MD 21201. **Tel** (410)225-4490. **ED** Guy W Hager. **LC** HJ485; .M25A. **DD** 336.1/85. **Circ:** 300 (ctrl). **Continued by** Red Book (Baltimore, MD).
**Desc:** Identifies and describes Maryland state financial assistance and technical service programs.

UK/0951-8835
**CATALOGUE AMENDMENT SERVICE.** [Cat. amend. serv.]. (197?)-. English. wk. Free. Her Majesty's Stationery Office, 51 Nine Elms Lane, London SW8 5DR England. **Tel** 011 44 71 873 8459, 011 44 71 873 8499, FAX 011 44 71 873 8499, 011 44 71 873 8456, telex 297138. **(Subscription address:** Her Majestys Stationery Offic, PO Box 276 Public Centre, London SW8 5DT England)

FR
**CATALOGUE ANNUEL DES LIVRES ET PERIODIQUES.** *Title Change.* **Added/Corp** France. Documentation Francaise. (1990)-(1992). Government Publication. French. Documentation Francaise, 29 Quai Voltaire, 75344 Paris Cedex 7 France. **Tel** 011 33 1 40157000, FAX 011 33 1 40157230, telex 204 826 DOCFRAN. **LC** Z2169; .C383. **Continues** Catalogue des Nouveautes. **Continued by** France. Documentation Francaise. Catalogue des Livres et Periodiques Parus en ... .

●FR
**CATALOGUE DES LIVRES ET PERIODIQUES PARUS EN.** (1992)-. Government Publication. French. Documentation Francaise, 29 Quai Voltaire, 75344 Paris Cedex 7 France.

**Tel** 011 33 1 40157000, FAX 011 33 1 40157230, telex 204 826 DOCFRAN. **Continues** Catalogue Annuel des Livres et Periodiques.

UK
**CATALOGUE OF UNITED KINGDOM OFFICIAL PUBLICATIONS [COMPUTER FILE] : UKOP.** **VFOAT** UKOP. (19??)-. English. qt. £925.00. Chadwyck-Healey Limited, The Quorum Barnwell Road, Cambridge CB5 8SW England. **Tel** 011 44 223 215512, telex 9312102281 CH G. **LC** Z2001.
**Desc:** Catalog of official documents published by HMSO or other official organizations and publications of international organizations distributed by HMSO from 1980 onwards.

US/0737-3007
**CEA CONGRESSIONAL LEDGER.** **VFOAT** Congressional Ledger; C.E.A. Congressional Ledger. **VAT** Congressional Education Associates Congressional Ledger. 1981-. English. an. $5.00. Congressional Education Associates, 302 East Capital Street NE, Washington DC 20002. **LC** JK1051; .C4. **DD** 328.73/0775.

CN/0706-182X
**CEGEP-PRESSE.** [Cegep-presse]. Periodical. French. Department of Manpower & Immigration, 222 Nepean Street Canada. **DD** 354.710083/3.

US
**CENSUS OF SELECTED SERVICE INDUSTRIES.** **Main/Corp** United States. Bureau of the Census. 1972-. Government Publication. English. ir. $12.00 V. 1; $18.00 V. 2, Pt. 1; $19.00 V. 2, Pt. 2; $18.00 V. 2, Pt. 3. US Department of Commerce / Bureau of the Census, Data User Services Division, Customer Services, Washington DC 20233-0800. **Tel** (301)763-4100. **(Subscription address:** Superintendent of Documents, US Government Printing Office, Washington DC 20402.) **Continues** Census of Business.

UK/0072-5722
**CENTRAL OFFICE OF INFORMATION REFERENCE PAMPHLET.** *Ceased.*
**Added/Corp** Great Britain. Central Office of Information. Reference Division. (1944)-(19??). Monographic series. English. ir. Her Majesty's Stationery Office, 51 Nine Elms Lane, London SW8 5DR England. **Tel** 011 44 71 873 8459, 011 44 71 873 8499, FAX 011 44 71 873 8499, 011 44 71 873 8456, telex 297138. **(Subscription address:** Her Majestys Stationery Offic, PO Box 276 Public Centre, London SW8 5DT England) **LC** UNC. **[CCC].**

US
**CHALLENGE II GRANTS.** **VFOAT** Challenge Two Grants; Challenge 2 Grants. 1989-. English. an. National Endowment for the Arts, 1100 Pennsylvania Avenue Northwest, Washington DC 20506. **Tel** (202)682-5400, (202)682-5435.

CN/0228-5037
**CHENE.** (LE CHENE : BULLETIN D'INFORMATION / VILLE DE LACHENAIE.). Bulletin. French. mo. Free. Ville de Lachenaie, 2953 Boul St-Charles, Lachenaie Quebec J6W 3T8 Canada. **DD** 352.0714/416. ctrl circ.

CN/0822-6342
**CHESNAIE.** (LA CHESNAIE : BULLETIN OFFICIEL DE LA MUNICIPALITE DE BEAUMONT.). [Chesnaie]. **Main/Corp** Saint-Etienne-de-Beaumont (Quebec). Bulletin. French. qt. Free to Citizens. Municipalite de Beaumont, 6 Boulevard Mercier, Beaumon Quebec G0R 1C0 Canada. **DD** 352.0714/733. ctrl circ.

US/0162-2951
**CHIEFS OF STATE AND CABINET MEMBERS OF FOREIGN GOVERNMENTS.** (CHIEFS OF STATE AND CABINET MEMBERS OF FOREIGN GOVERNMENTS / NATIONAL FOREIGN ASSESSMENT CENTER.). **Added/Corp** United States. Central Intelligence Agency. National Foreign Assessment Center (U.S.) United States. Central Intelligence Agency. Directorate of Intelligence. (19??)-. Periodical. English. Twelve times a year. $145.00 US; $285.00 other. Documents Expediting Project, Exchange and Gift Division, Library of Congress, Washington DC 20540. **Tel** (202)707-9527. **(Subscription address:** National Technical Information Service, 5285 Port Royal Road, Springfield, VA 22161) **LC** JF37; .U5. **DD** 351.003/13/05. **NLM** JF 37; C533. available on microfiche (Vols. for (1986-) distributed to depository libraries).

US/0250-6114
**CHIEFS OF STATE AND CABINET MINISTERS OF THE AMERICAN REPUBLICS.** **Main/Corp** Organization of American States. General Secretariat. **Added/Corp** Pan American Union. Public Information Office. Pan American Union. Office of Public Relations. Organization of American States. General Secretariat. (1966)-. English. Twice a year. Organization of American States, 19th Street & Constitution Avenue NW, Suite 300, Washington DC 20006. **Tel** (202)458-6256. **LC** F1402; .A228. **DD** 351/.00313/0251812. **Continues** Chiefs of State and Cabinet Ministers of the American Republics.

●US/1060-2917
**CHIEFS OF STATE & CABINET OFFICERS FOR NATIONS OF THE WORLD.** (CHIEFS OF STATE & CABINET OFFICIALS FOR NATIONS OF THE WORLD: YOUR ANNUAL GUIDE TO WORLD LEADERS, U.S. AND FOREIGN AMBASSADORS, AND BUSINESS CONTACTS AROUND THE WORLD.). [Chiefs state cabinet off. nations world]. **VFOAT** Chiefs of State and Cabinet Officials for Nations of the World. (1992)-. English. $125.00. Want Publishing Company, 1511 K Street Northwest, Suite 635, Washington DC 20005. **Tel** (202)783-1887, FAX (202)393-5106. **DD** 350.

CC
**CHIH PU SHENG HUO. CHUNG-CHING.** **VFOAT** Zhibu Shenghuo. Periodical. Chinese. RMBY0.15. Post Office, Chung-Ching Shih, People's Republic of China. **Tel** 3578. **LC** JQ1519.A5; C47572. **DD** 324.251/075.

CC
**CHIH PU SHENG HUO. KUANG-TUNG.** **VFOAT** Zhibushenghuo. Periodical. Chinese. mo. RMBY0.15. Post Office, Kuang-Chou Shih, People's Republic of China. **LC** JQ1519.A5; C475722. **DD** 324.251/075/05.

CC
**CHIH PU SHENG HUO. SSU-CHUAN / CHUNG KUNG SSU-CHUAN SHENG WEI TSU CHIH PU, HSUAN CHUAN PU CHU PAN.** **VFOAT** Zhibushenghuo; SSU-Chuan Chih Pu Sheng Huo. Periodical. Chinese. mo. RMBY0.15. Post Office, Cheng-tu, People's Republic of China. **LC** JQ1519.A5; C475723. **DD** 324.251/075.

US
**CHILD CARE LEGISLATIVE UPDATE.** English. wk (Apr.- Oct. while legislature is in session). $95.00. On the Capitol Doorstep, 926 J Street, Room 1007, Sacramento CA 95814. **Tel** (916)442-5431.

US/0899-0387
**CHILE NEWSLETTER (BERKELEY, CALIF. 1984).** (CHILE NEWSLETTER.). [Chile newsl.]. **Added/Corp** Casa Chile (Berkeley, Calif.). Vol. 1, No. 1 (June 1984)-. Newsletter. English. mo. **DD** 354. **Continues** Casa Chile Update.
**Ind/Abst** Hum. Rights Intern. Rep.

US/0009-4609
**CHINESE LAW AND GOVERNMENT.** See Law.

JA
**CHOSEN MINSHU SHUGI JINMIN KYOWAKOKU SOSHIKIBETSU JINMEIBO.** **VFOAT** North Korea Directory. (1988)-. English (Japanese). an. $50.00 (including airmail postage). Radiopress Inc., R Building, Shinjuku, 33-8 Wakamatsu, Shinjuku-ku Tokyo 162 Japan. **Tel** 011 81 3 5273 2173, FAX 011 81 3 5273 2180. **LC** DS930.9; .C5. **Circ:** 800 (ctrl).
**Desc:** Organization-based directory of North Korean leaders of both central and local political parties, government, military, economic and academic fields.

SZ/0302-2498
**CHRONICLE OF PARLIAMENTARY ELECTIONS.** (CHRONICLE OF PARLIAMENTARY ELECTIONS AND DEVELOPMENTS.). [Chron. parliam. elect.]. **Added/Corp** International Centre for Parliamentary Documentation. Inter-Parliamentary Union. **VFOAT** Chronicle of Parliamentary Elections. Vol. 2 (1967/1968)-. English (French). an. 40.00F. Inter-Parliamentary Union, Place du Petit Saconnex, Ch 1211 Geneva 19 Switzerland. **Tel** 011 41 22 7344150, telex 789784. **LC** JF501; .C47. **DD** 328/.3/05. Index available. **Pr Rev. Circ:** 1,000. **Continues in part** Chronique des Elections Parlementaires.

CN/1188-0856
**CHRONIQUES DU PROTECTEUR DU CITOYEN.** (LES CHRONIQUES DU PROTECTEUR DU CITOYEN.). [Chron. Prot. citoyen]. **Main/Corp** Quebec (Province). Protecteur du Citoyen. (1991)-. Periodical. French. ir. Free. Protecteur du Citoyen, 2875 Boulevard Laurier, 4-E Etage Saint Foy, Quebec G1V 2M2 Canada. **Tel** (418)643-2688. **DD** 354.714009/1. ctrl circ. **Continues** Quebec (Province). Protecteur du Citoyen. Dossier d'Enquete. 0838-5106.

CC
**CHUNG-HUA JEN MIN KUNG HO KUO KUO WU YUAN KUNG PAO.** **Main/Corp** China. Kuo Wu Yuan. **VFOAT** Kuo Wu Yuan Kung Pao; Zhonghua Renmin Gongheguo Gouwuyuan Gongbao. (1954)-. Periodical. Chinese. ir. $34.38. **(Subscription address:** China International Book Trading Corporation, PO Box 399, Library Service Department, Beijing 100044 People's Republic of China.)

CH
**CHUNG KUNG YUAN SHIH TZU LIAO HSUAN CHI. TSUNG HO LEI / CHUNG KUNG YEN CHIU TSA CHIH SHE PIEN YIN.** Periodical. Chinese. qt. $12.00. Chung Kung Yen Chiu Tsa Chih She 64, Lane Chih Cheng Road, Section 1, Taipei Shih-Lin Chu Taiwan. **LC** JQ1519.A5; C48678. **DD** 324.251/075/09.

US/0190-7794
**CIA PUBLICATIONS RELEASED TO THE PUBLIC THROUGH LIBRARY OF CONGRESS DOCEX.** ***Title Change.*** (CIA PUBLICATIONS RELEASED TO THE PUBLIC / DIRECTORATE OF INTELLIGENCE.). [CIA publ. released public Libr. Congr. DOCEX]. **Main/Corp** United States. Central Intelligence Agency. Directorate of Intelligence. **VFOAT** C.I.A. Publications Released to the Public. **VAT** Central Intelligence Agency Publications Released to the Public. (1972-81)-(19??). English. an. Document Expediting Project, Exchange and Gift Division, Library of Congress, Photoduplication Service, Washington DC 20540. **Tel** (202)287-9527. **LC** Z7163; .U56a; JF35. **DD** 016.351/2. ***Continues*** *National Foreign Assessment Center (U.S.). CIA Publications Released to the Public Through Library of Congress DOCEX, 0190-7794.* ***Continued by*** *United States. Central Intelligence Agency. Public Affairs Office. CIA Maps and Publications Released to the Public, 1067-9545.*

AG/0009-6784
**CIENCIAS ADMINISTRATIVAS.** [Cienc. adm.]. **Added/Corp** Universidad Nacional de La Plata. Instituto Superior de Ciencias Administrativas. Universidad Nacional de La Plata. Facultad de Ciencias Economicas. Universidad Nacional de La Plata. Instituto de Investigaciones de Ciencias Administrativas. No. 14 (1963)-. Periodical. Spanish. Three times a year. $30.00 Argentina; $35.00 The Americas; $45.00 Europe; $50.00 other. Facultad de Ciencias Economicas / Argentina, Inst Invest Adm-Calle 53 #419, La Plata Argentina. available on microfilm and microfiche from University Microfilms International (UMI). ***Continues*** *ECA.*
**Ind/Abst** Int. Labour Doc.; Int. Polit. Sci. Abstr.

US/0007-8514
**CIS INDEX TO PUBLICATIONS OF THE UNITED STATES CONGRESS.** **See** Public Administration-Abstracting, Bibliographies and Statistics.

CN/0712-2888
**CITADIN DE LA GARDEUR.** (CITADIN / VILLE DE LE GARDEUR.). **VFOAT** Bulletin d'information de la Ville de le Gardeur. V. 2, No. 8, (Aug. 21, 1978)-. Periodical. French. Citadin Ville de le Gardeur, 1 Montee des Arsenaux, Le Gardeur Quebec J5Z 2C1 Canada. **DD** 352.0714/416. ***Continues*** *Citadin de le Gardeur, 0712-2888.*

US/0009-7535
**CITIES & VILLAGES.** **Added/Corp** Ohio Municipal League. **VAT** Cities and Villages. Vol. 18, No. 2 (Feb. 1970)-. Periodical. English. Eleven times a year. $10.00. Ohio Municipal League, 175 South 3rd Street, Suite 510, Columbus OH 43215-5134. **Tel** (614)221-4349. **ED** William H. Edwards. **DD** 352. **Bk Rev**. **Ad Acc**. **Circ:** 10,000. ***Continues*** *Ohio Cities and Villages.*
**Desc:** Information concerning Ohio municipal government.
**Ind/Abst** Urban Aff. Abstr.

US/0899-6075
**CITIES OF THE UNITED STATES.** [Cities U. S.]. **Added/Corp** Gale Research Inc. Vol. 1 (1988)-. English. be. $275.00. Gale Research Inc., 835 Penobscot Building, Detroit MI 48226. **Tel** (800)877-GALE, (313)961-2242, FAX (313)961-6083, telex TWX 810-221-7086. **ED** Linda Schmittroth. **LC** HT123; .C49677. **DD** 973/.09173/205.
**Desc:** Combines information about some 150 cities from a wide range of sources. For each city, clearly labeled data sections discuss geography and climate, history, population, government, economy, education, health care, recreation, convention facilities, transportation, and communications.

US
**CITIZENS' GUIDE TO LOCAL GOVERNMENT (OLYMPIA, WASH.).** (CITIZENS' GUIDE TO LOCAL GOVERNMENT.). **Added/Corp** Washington State Research Council. (19??)-. English. an. $5.00 (members); $10.00 (non-members). Washington Research Council, 1301 5th Avenue, Suite 2810, Olympia WA 98101-2603. **Tel** (206)467-7088, (800)445-1086, FAX (206)467-6957. **ED** John S. Archee. Index available. **Bk Rev**. **Circ:** 5,000 (ctrl).
**Desc:** Serves as a reference for people who want to monitor and participate in city and county budgeting. Included are statistics on Washington's 45 largest cities and all 39 counties. Statistics include population, property tax collection, revenue, spending and staffing.

US
**CITIZENS LEAGUE RESEARCH INSTITUTE REPORTS.** English. ir. $50.00. Citizens League of Greater Cleveland, 50 Public Square, Suite 843, Cleveland OH 44113. **Tel** (216)241-5340, FAX (216)736-7626. **ED** Janis Purdy. Index available. cum. index.
**Desc:** In depth reports of local and state government operations.

CN/0712-4228
**CITOYEN (CAP-SANTE).** (LE CITOYEN.). [Citoyen]. Vol. 1, No. 1 (Jan. 12, 1976)-. Periodical. French. mo. La Citoyen, 194 Route 138, Cap-Sante Quebec G0A 1L0 Canada. **DD** 352.0714/466.

US/0193-8371
**CITY & TOWN (NORTH LITTLE ROCK, ARK.).** (CITY & TOWN : OFFICIAL PUBLICATION OF THE ARKANSAS MUNICIPAL LEAGUE.). [City town]. **Added/Corp** Arkansas Municipal League. **VFOAT** City and Town. (Sept. 1977)-. Periodical. English. Twelve times a year. $15.00. Arkansas Municipal League, PO Box 38, North Little Rock AR 72115. **Tel** (501)374-3484, FAX (501)374-0541. **ED** John K. Woodruff and Don Zimmerman. **LC** JS303.A8; A74. **DD** 352/.0072/09767. Index available. cum. index. **Bk Rev**. **Ad Acc**, **Adv Mgr:** J. Woodruff. **Circ:** 6,700. available on diskette (8" and 5 1/4"). ***Continues*** *Arkansas Municipalities, 0004-1866.*
**Desc:** Official publication of the Arkansas Municipal League. Discusses urban affairs, municipal government and finance.
**Ind/Abst** Urban Aff. Abstr.

US/0091-9209
**CITY EMPLOYMENT.** (CITY EMPLOYMENT IN ... / DEPARTMENT OF COMMERCE, BUREAU OF THE CENSUS.). 1944-. Government Publication. English. an. US Department of Commerce, 14th Street & Constitution Avenue NW, Washington DC 20230. **Tel** (202)482-2000, FAX (202)482-3772. **LC** HD8011.A1; A3 subser; JS358. **DD** 352/.005/0973.

US/0190-0005
**CITY HALL DIGEST.** **Added/Corp** City Hall Communications. Vol.1, (Nov. 1976)-. Periodical. English. Twelve times a year. $64.00 (one year) $118.00 (two year), $172.00 (three year) US; $69.00 (one year), $128.00 (two year), $187.00 (three year) Canada; $74.00 (one year), $138.00 (two year), $202.00 (three year). City Hall Digest, PO Box 910, Franklin NC 28734-0910. **Tel** (704)369-8528, FAX (704)369-8678. **ED** Raymond L. Bancroft. **Bk Rev**, (Qty: 36).
**Desc:** Covers America's municipal governments, including community development, public safety, management techniques, finance, public relations, environmental programs, and more. Focuses on trends and successful projects by cities.
**Ind/Abst** Urban Aff. Abstr.

CN/0822-790X
**CITY MAGAZINE (WINNIPEG).** (CITY MAGAZINE.). [City mag.]. Vol. 6, No. 1 (Spring 1983)-. Periodical. English. qt. 24.00Can$ (institutions), 18.00Can$ (individuals) Canada; 29.00Can$ (institutions), 23.00Can$ (individuals) other. City Magazine, 1464 Wellington Circle, Winnipeg Manitoba R3N 0B3 Canada. **Tel** (204)489-8145, (204)489-2452. **DD** 307.7/6/0971. ***Continues*** *City Magazine Annual, 0821-5650.*
**Desc:** Canada's national urban magazine; explores urban development, social criticism, trends in architecture and a review of urban literature. Popular forum exploring critical issues and alternatives for living in cities. Thrives on reader's views, comments, articles, poetry, short stories and art.
**Ind/Abst** Can. Index; Can. Period. Index (19??-).

US
**CITY OF BALTIMORE ANNUAL REPORT.** **Main/Corp** Baltimore (MD.). **Added/Corp** Baltimore (Md.) Annual Report. (1975/76)-. Periodical. English. an. City Hall / Baltimore, 100 North Holliday Street, Baltimore MD 21202. **LC** JS571; .B34a. **DD** 352.0752/6.

US
**CITY RECORD.** **Main/Corp** Boston (Mass.). (19??)-. English. wk. $50.00. City Record Office, Room 808A, City Hall, Boston MA 02201. **Tel** (617)725-4186. **ED** Kevin J. Potts. **LC** JS13; .B7i. **DD** 352.0744/61. Index available. cum. index. **Ad Acc**. **Circ:** 1,400.
**Desc:** Publishes municipal news, public notices and all public advertisements of invitations for sealed bids and proposals for all purchase requirements for goods, materials, and services that are estimated to be in excess of two thousand dollars.

US
**CITY RECORD, THE.** **Main/Corp** New York (N.Y.). Vol 1 No. 1 (June 24, 1873)-. Periodical. English. da (Mon.-Fri.). $400.00. CityBooks/ City Publishing Center, Department of General Services, 2208 Municipal Building, 22nd Floor, New York NY 10007. **Tel** (212)669-8245, FAX (212)669-3211. **ED** Virginia Bull. **LC** JS13; .N487. **DD** 352.0747. Index available. cum. index. **Circ:** 3,000 (ctrl).
**Desc:** Publishes proposed and new legislation, along with business opportunities with the city government. Also details proposals for contracts, capital, economics, export development, etc.

US/0196-8327
**CITY RECORD (CLEVELAND), THE.** (THE CITY RECORD.). **Main/Corp** Cleveland (Ohio). Vol. 1 (Jan. 7, 1914)-. English. wk (52 issues per year). $36.00. Cleveland City Record, Room 216/City Hall, Cleveland OH 44114. **Tel** (216)664-2840. **LC** JS13; .C5m. **DD** 352.0771/32. **Circ:** 250.

SP
**CIUDAD Y TERRITORIO.** ***Title Change.*** **Added/Corp** Instituto de Estudios de Administracion Local (Spain). (19??)-(19??). Periodical. Spanish. qt. Ministerio de Obras Publicas y Transportes y Medio Ambiente, Paseo de la Castellana, 67, 28071 Madrid Spain. **Tel** 011 34 1 5977263, 5977266, FAX 011 34 1 5546351. ***Absorbed*** *Estudios Territoriales.* ***Merged with*** *Ciudad y Territorio Estudios Territoriales.*

II/0009-7772
**CIVIC AFFAIRS.** (1953)-. Periodical. English. mo. $15.00. Bhargava Estate, Box 188, Kanpur India. **Tel** 211 685. **(Subscription address:** Prints India, 11 Darya Ganj, New Delhi, 110002 India, (Phone: 011 91 11 3268645)) **ED** S P Mehra. **LC** JS7001; .C5. **DD** 350. **Bk Rev**. **Ad Acc**. **Circ:** 5,000 (ctrl).

CN/0045-7027
**CIVIC AFFAIRS (TORONTO).** (CIVIC AFFAIRS.). Sept. 29, 1948-. Periodical. English. qt. Bureau of Municipal Research, Suite 406, 4 Richmond Street East, Toronto Ontario M5C 1M6 Canada. **LC** JS1789.A1; C58. **DD** 352/.0094/09713541. ***Supersedes*** *Monthly Letter.*

US/0489-8850
**CIVIC CINEMA.** [Civic cine.]. **Main/Corp** South Bend Civic Planning Association. 1949-. English. an. South Bend Civic Planning Association, 403 Lincoln Way West, South Bend IN 46601. **LC** JS1459.S4; S6.

US/0045-7035
**CIVIL AFFAIRS JOURNAL AND NEWSLETTER.** [Civ. aff. j. newsl.]. **Added/Corp** Civil Affairs Association. (19??)-. Newsletter. English. bm. $10.00 (US); $10.80 (other). Civil Affairs Association, 416 Eisner Street, Silver Spring MD 20901. **ED** William Kurylchek. **DD** 355. **Bk Rev**. **Circ:** 3,500. ***Continues*** *Military Government Journal and News Letter.*

II
**CIVIL LIST OF GAZETTED EMPLOYEES UNDER THE GOVERNMENT OF MEGHALAYA, AS ON 1ST JANUARY ... .** **Main/Corp** Meghalaya (India). 1979-. English. Firma KLM Pvt Ltd, 257-B Ganguly Street, Calcutta 700 012 India. **Tel** 011 91 33 274391. **LC** JQ620.M45; A2A. **DD** 354.54/164001/025.

UK
**CIVIL SEVICE YEAR BOOK, THE.** **Added/Corp** Great Britain. Civil Service Dept. Great Britain. Cabinet Office. **VFOAT** Civil Service Yearbook. (1974)-. Government Publication. English. ir. £18.50. Her Majesty's Stationery Office, 51 Nine Elms Lane, London SW8 5DR England. **Tel** 011 44 71 873 8459, 011 44 71 873 8499, FAX 011 44 71 873 8499, 011 44 71 873 8456, telex 297138. **(Subscription address:** PO Box 276, Public Centre, London SW8 5DT England) **LC** JN106; .B8. **DD** 354/.42. ***Continues*** *British Imperial Calendar and Civil Service List.*

US/0092-0142
**CLASSIFICATION AND PAY PLAN - (TALLAHASSEE) DIVISION OF PERSONNEL.** (CLASSIFICATION AND PAY PLAN.). **Main/Corp** Florida. Dept. of Administration. Division of Personnel. English. Florida Department of Administration, 660 Apalachee Parkway, Tallahassee FL 32304. **LC** JK4457; .F54A. **DD** 353.9/759/00103.

US
**CLASSIFICATION PLAN AND SALARY SCHEDULE.** **VFOAT** State of Indiana Salary Schedule. English. an. State Personnel Department, 100 North Senate Avenue, Indianapolis IN 46204. **LC** JK5657; .C57. **DD** 353.9772001/03.

HK/0376-7914
**CLERICAL OFFICERS AND TYPISTS LISTS.** (CLERICAL OFFICERS AND TYPISTS LISTS (HONGKONG)). **Main/Corp** Hong Kong. English. J R Lee, Government Printer, Java Road, Hong Kong Hong Kong. **LC** JQ674; .H65A. **DD** 354/.51/25002.

US/0738-5099
**CM BULLETIN.** [CM bull.]. **Added/Corp** National Classification Management Society (U.S.). **VFOAT** C.M. Bulletin; Bulletin. **VAT** Classification Management Bulletin. (19??)-. English. bm. $25.00. National Classification Management Society, 6116 Roseland Drive, Rockville MD 20852. **Tel** (301)231-9191. **Circ:** 3,000 (ctrl).

# Public Administration

CN/0842-5698
**CODE MUNICIPAL FD DU QUEBEC.** [Code munic. FD Que.]. **Main/Corp** Quebec (Province). **VAT** Code Municipal Formulaires Ducharme du Quebec. (1979)-. Periodical. French. Five times a year. 82.50Can$. Editions Formulaires Ducharme, 1370 EST Chemin Yamaska CP 90, Farnham QUE J2N 2R4 Canada. **Tel** (514)293-4491, FAX (514)293-2923. **DD** 342.714/09/0263.

US
**CODE OF COLORADO REGULATIONS. LIMITED EDITION.** English. Twelve times a year (Regulations published 8 per year/Register published monthly). $1,264.00. The Public Record Corporation, PO Box 18186, 1666 Lafayette Street, Denver CO 80218. **Tel** (303)832-8262, (800)487-8262, FAX (303)861-5821. Index available (Bound in all issues).
**Desc:** Administrative regulations for the state of Colorado, excludes the Department of Social Services.

US
**CODE OF COLORADO REGULATIONS. REGULAR EDITION.** English. Twelve times a year. $1,462.00. The Public Record Corporation, PO Box 18186, 1666 Lafayette Street, Denver CO 80218. **Tel** (303)832-8262, (800)487-8262, FAX (303)861-5821. Index available (Bound in all issues).
**Desc:** Administrative regulations for the state of Colorado.

US
**CODE OF FEDERAL REGULATIONS.** **Added/Corp** United States. Office of the Federal Register. (1949)-. Government Publication. English. ir. $829.00 US; $1,036.25 other. Superintendent of Documents, US Government Printing Office, Washington DC 20402. **Tel** (202)275-3328, FAX (202)786-2377. available on CD-ROM.

US
**CODE OF THE CITY OF DETROIT, MICHIGAN.** **Main/Corp** Detroit. (1???)-. Periodical. English. ir. $30.00. City of Detroit Department of Public Information, 608 City County Building, Detroit MI 48226. **Tel** (313)224-3270.

IT
**CODICE DELLE LEGGI E DEI REGOLAMENTI DELLA REGIONE VENETO.** (19??)-. Italian. sa. 160000.00L. Edizioni Europee Informatica, Via Guido Reni 4, 35134 Padua Italy. **Tel** 011 34 49 861170.

US
**COG NOTES. MONTHLY PROGRESS REPORT.** **Main/Corp** Denver Regional Council of Governments. **VAT** Council of Governments Notes. (19??)-. Periodical. English. mo. Denver Regional Council of Governments, 2480 West 26th Avenue, Suite 200B, Denver CO 80211. **Tel** (303)455-1000. **DD** 352.

US/1060-5045
**COGEL BLUE BOOK.** [COGEL blue book]. **Added/Corp** Council on Governmental Ethics Laws. Council of State Governments. **VFOAT** Blue Book; Campaign Finance, Ethics Lobby Law & Judicial Conduct. **VAT** Council on Governmental Ethics Laws Blue Book. 8th Ed. (1990)-. English. ir. $59.00; Free with Council on Governmental Ethics Laws membership. Council of State Governments, PO Box 11910, Iron Works Pike, Lexington KY 40578-1910. **Tel** (800)800-1910, (606)231-1850. (Subscription address: Council of State Governments, PO Box 2167, Lexington, KY 40595) **LC** KDZ585.A13; C36. **DD** 342.73/078; 347.30278. **Continues** Campaign Finance, Ethics, and Lobby Law Blue Book, 0898-8447.

RM
**COLECTIA DE HOTARIRI ALE CONSILIULUI DE MINISTRI SI ALTE ACTE NORMATIVE.** **Main/Corp** Romania. **Added/Corp** Romania. Consiliul de Ministri. Romania. Consiliul de Stat. Romania. Buletinul Oficial al Republicii Socialiste Romania. Partea I. (Jan. 1/March 31 1969)-. Romanian. qt. (Subscription address: Ilexim Press Department, PO Box 1, 136-1-137, Bucharest, Romania.) **LC** LAW. **Continues in part** Romania. Laws, Etc. (Colectie de Legi, Decrete, Hotariri si Deciziuni).

US/0010-1664
**COLORADO MUNICIPALITIES.** **Added/Corp** Colorado Municipal League. League of Wyoming Municipalities. Vol. 1 (1925)-. Periodical. English. Six times a year (Jan., Mar., May, July, Sept., Nov.). $16.08 Denver; $15.56 Adams, Arapahoe, Boulder, Jefferson & Douglas counties in Colorado; $15.45 others in Colorado; $15.00 others. Colorado Municipal League, 1660 Lincoln, Suite 2100, Denver CO 80264. **Tel** (303)831-6411. **ED** Kay Mariea. **LC** JS39; .C6. **DD** 352.0788. **Ad Acc**. **Circ:** 4,500 (ctrl).
**Desc:** Covers the current interests, activities and concerns of Colorado municipalities and individuals involved in local government.
**Ind/Abst** Urban Aff. Abstr.

US
**COLORADO REGISTER. AIR QUALITY CONTROL COMMISSION.** English. Twelve times a year. $239.00. The Public Record Corporation, PO Box 18186, 1666 Lafayette Street, Denver CO 80218. **Tel** (303)832-8262, (800)487-8262, FAX (303)861-5821.

US
**COLORADO REGISTER. LIMITED EDITION.** English. Twelve times a year. $465.00 Comes with Code of Colorado Regulations Limited Editions. The Public Record Corporation, PO Box 18186, 1666 Lafayette Street, Denver CO 80218. **Tel** (303)832-8262, (800)487-8262, FAX (303)861-5821.

US
**COLORADO REGISTER. REGULAR EDITION.** English. Twelve times a year. $553.00 Comes with Code of Colorado Regulations Regular Edition. The Public Record Corporation, PO Box 18186, 1666 Lafayette Street, Denver CO 80218. **Tel** (303)832-8262, (800)487-8262, FAX (303)861-5821.

AT
**COMMITTEE BULLETIN.** (19??)-. Bulletin. English. mo. 225.00Aus$. Client Solutions Pty Ltd, PO Box 4893, Kingston, Australian Capital Territory, 2604 Australia. **Tel** 011 61 6 2822471, FAX 011 61 67 2822953. **ED** Monica Telesny. Index available in last issue of volume--attached. cum. index. **Ad Acc**. **Circ:** 1,000 (ctrl).
**Desc:** Information on parliamentary committees of Australia.

US/0587-2936
**COMMITTEE REPORTS - LOCAL GOVERNMENT LAW SECTION OF THE AMERICAN BAR ASSOCIATION.** See Law.

UK/0267-2146
**COMMITTEE REPORTS PUBLISHED BY HMSO INDEXED BY CHAIRMAN.** [Comm. rep. publ. HMSO index. chairm.]. **Added/Corp** Great Britain. Her Majesty's Stationery Office. (Jan./Dec. 1984)-. Periodical. English. qt. £8.00. Her Majesty's Stationery Office, 51 Nine Elms Lane, London SW8 5DR England. **Tel** 011 44 71 873 8459, 011 44 71 873 8499, FAX 011 44 71 873 8499, 011 44 71 873 8456, telex 297138. (Subscription address: Her Majestys Stationery Offic, PO Box 276 Public Centre, London SW8 5DT England) **Continues** Index to Chairmen of Committees, 0265-0207.

US/0146-5201
**COMMITTEES AND MEMBER AGENCIES OF THE SOUTHERN LEGISLATIVE CONFERENCE, THE COUNCIL OF STATE GOVERNMENTS.** (COMMITTEES AND MEMBER AGENCIES OF THE SOUTHERN LEGISLATIVE CONFERENCE.). **Main/Corp** Council of State Governments. English. an. Southern Office, 3384 Peachtree Road NE/Room 610, Atlanta GA 30326. **LC** JK2683; .C68A. **DD** 353.9/0006/175.

US/0885-6133
**COMMON GROUND (ARLINGTON, VA.).** (COMMON GROUND : THE JOURNAL OF THE COMMUNITY ASSOCIATIONS INSTITUTE.). [Common ground]. **Added/Corp** Community Associations Institute. (Jan./Feb. 1985)-. Periodical. English. bm (6 issues). Free to members of the Community Association Institute. Community Associations Institute, 1630 Duke Street, Alexandria VA 22314. **Tel** (703)548-8600, FAX (703)684-1581. **DD** 334.
**Ind/Abst** PAIS Int. Print.

AT
**COMMONWEALTH GOVERNMENT DIRECTORY.** (1977)-. Government Publication. English. 160.00Aus$ (four issues), 288.00Aus$ (eight issues), 408.00Aus$ (twelve issues). Australian Government Publishing Service, GPO Box 84, Canberra ACT 2601 Australia. **Tel** 011 61 6 2954411, FAX 011 61 6 2954455. **LC** JQ4021; .C65. **DD** 354/.94/00025. **Supersedes** Australian Government Directory.

UK
**COMMONWEALTH MINISTERS REFERENCE BOOK, THE.** (1989/90)-. English. **LC** JN248; .C5548. **DD** 351/.00025/171241.

AT/0819-7105
**COMMONWEALTH OF AUSTRALIA GAZETTE. GOVERNMENT NOTICES.** [Commonw. Aust. gaz., Gov. not.]. (1987)-. Government Publication. English. wk (50 issues). 290.00Aus$. Australian Government Publishing Service, GPO Box 84, Canberra ACT 2601 Australia. **Tel** 011 61 6 2954411, FAX 011 61 6 2954455. **DD** 342.940853.

AT
**COMMONWEALTH RECORD.** **Title Change.** (1976)-(1987). English. wk. Australian Bureau of Statistics, PO Box 10, Belconnen Australian Capital Territory, 2616 Australia. **Tel** 011 61 6 2527911, FAX 011 61 6 2516009. **Superseded by** Australian Government Weekly Digest.

UK/0952-8083
**COMMONWEALTH YEARBOOK, THE.** **VFOAT** Commonwealth Year Book. 1987-. English. an. £17.50. UNIPUB, 4611-F Assembly Drive, Lanham MD 20706-4391. **Tel** (800)274-4888, FAX (301)459-0056, telex 28787 GATT CH. **LC** JN248; .C5912. **DD** 909/.0971241. **Continues** Year Book of the Commonwealth, 0084-4047.

CN/0707-9133
**COMMUNICATOR (ST. JOHN'S).** (THE COMMUNICATOR.). V. 1- Jan. 1978-. Periodical. English. bm. Newfoundland Association of Public Employees, PO Box 1085, St John's Newfoundland A1C 5M5 Canada. **DD** 354/.718/00173. **Formed by the union of** N A P E News, 0318-1723 **and** N A P E Journal, 0381-6826.

UK/0968-9249
**COMMUNITY CARE MANAGEMENT & PLANNING.** (19??)-. Periodical. English. bm. £102.00 Europe; £106.00 Other (Institutions). Longman Group Ltd., Fourth Avenue, Longman House, Harlow Essex CM19 5SR England. **Tel** 011 44 279 429655, FAX 011 44 279 431059, telex 81259.

US
**COMMUNITY LIVING OF FLORIDA.** (19??)-. Periodical. English. Nine times a year. $32.00 (nonmembers), $24.00 (members). Community Associations Institute, 1630 Duke Street, Alexandria VA 22314. **Tel** (703)548-8600, FAX (703)684-1581. **Ad Acc**, **Adv Mgr:** Jeff Sanderson. **Continues** Condominium Living of Florida.

UK/0140-1084
**COMMUNITY NEWS - WELSH OFFICE OF THE EUROPEAN COMMUNITIES.** [Community news - Welsh Off. Eur. Communities]. **VFOAT** Cymrunewrop. (1976)-. English. bw. Free on request. Office for Official Publications of the European Communities, 2 Rue Mercier, 2985 Luxembourg Luxembourg. **Tel** 011 352 499281, FAX 011 352 488573.

NZ
**COMPENDIUM OF CASE NOTES OF THE OMBUDSMEN.** **Main/Corp** New Zealand. Chief Ombudsman. (1981)-. English. an. Government Printing Office / New Zealand, 10 Mulgrave Street, Wellington New Zealand. **Tel** 011 64 4 4737211, FAX 011 64 4 734943, telex GOVPRINT NZ 31320. **LC** LAW. **DD** 342.931/0667/02646. **Continues in part** Report of the Chief Ombudsman.

US
**COMPENDIUM OF PUBLICLY AVAILABLE REPORTS ON PROCUREMENT AND FINANCIAL ASSISTANCE AWARDS - (DEPT OF ENERGY).** See Energy.

CN/0846-2895
**COMPENSATION FOCUS.** [Compens. focus]. **Added/Corp** Canada. Supply and Services Canada. **VFOAT** Focus Remuneration. Vol. 1, No. 1 (July 1991)-. Periodical. English (French). bm. **DD** 354.71001/2/05.

CN/0846-2895
**COMPENSATION FOCUS.** (FOCUS REMUNERATION.). [Compens. focus]. **Added/Corp** Canada. Approvisionnements et Services Canada. **VFOAT** Compensation Focus. Vol. 1, No 1 (Jul 1991)-. Periodical. French (English). bm. Approvisionnements et Services Canada, Publishing Centre, Ottawa Ontario K1A 0S9 Canada. **DD** 354.71001/2/05.

US/0741-9260
**COMPILATION OF GAO'S WORK ON TAX ADMINISTRATION ACTIVITIES.** **Title Change.** See Business-Accounting.

US
**COMPREHENSIVE ANNUAL, FINANCIAL REPORT.** **Main/Corp** Texas Municipal Retirement System. (Dec. 31, 1987)-. English. Texas Municipal Retirement System, 1200 North Interstate 5, Box 2225, Austin TX 78768. **LC** JS451.T47; T53a. available on microfiche. **Continues** Annual Report/ Texas Municipal Retirement System.

US
**COMPREHENSIVE ANNUAL FINANCIAL REPORT OF THE HIGHWAY PATROLMENS' RETIREMENT FUND FOR THE FISCAL YEAR ENDING JUNE 30 ... - (MINNESOTA).** See Law-Law Enforcement and Criminology.

# Public Administration

BE/0376-7531
**COMPTE RENDU ANALYTIQUE - REPUBLIQUE DU ZAIRE, CONSEIL LEGISLATIF NATIONAL.** **Main/Corp** Zaire. Conseil Legislatif National. No. 36- Oct. 26, 1972-. French. Conseil Legislatif National, rue de Louvain 40 42, 1000 Bruxelles Belgium. **LC** J831; .H25A. **DD** 328.675/1/01. *Continues Compte Rendu Analytique - Republique du Zaire. Assemblee Nationale, 0376-7523.*

FR
**COMPTE RENDU D'ACTIVITE - EDF, DIRECTION DE LA DISTRIBUTION.** **Main/Corp** Electricite de France. Direction de la Distribution. French. EDF/Direction de la Distribution, 2 rue Louis Murat, 75784 Paris Cedex 08 France. **LC** HD9685.F84; E477. **DD** 354/.44/00872.

US
**COMPTROLLER'S REPORT OF COOK COUNTY.** **Main/Corp** Cook Co., Ill. Office of the Comptroller. **VFOAT** Report of the Cook County Comptroller; Report of the County Comptroller; Comptroller's Annual Report. 1912/13-. English. Three times a year. Cook County Office of the Comptroller, Room 500/118 North Clark Street, Chicago IL 60602. *Continues Cook County Comptroller's Report.*

IT/0010-4973
**COMUNI D'EUROPA.** **Added/Corp** Associazione Italiana per il Consiglio dei Comuni d'Europa. (1952)-. Periodical. Italian. mo. L300000 (individuals) Europe; L150000 institutions; L40000 individuals. Aiccre, Piazza di Trevi 86, 00187 Rome Italy. **Tel** 011 39 6 6840461. **DD** 341.18.

IT/0394-8277
**COMUNI D'ITALIA.** [Comuni Italia]. (1964)-. Periodical. Italian. mo. L210000. Maggioli Editore, Casella Postale 290, 47037 Rimini, Italy. **Tel** 011 39 541 628666, FAX 011 39 541 742217. **UDC** 352. Index available. cum. index. **Bk Rev**. **Ad Acc**. **Pr Rev**. **Circ:** 4,000.
**Desc:** Magazine concerned with all issues reguarding both the local government and administration.

AT/0311-9513
**CONFERENCE OF PRESIDING OFFICERS AND CLERKS OF THE PARLIAMENTS OF AUSTRALIA, FIJI, NAURU, PAPUA NEW GUINEA AND WESTERN SAMOA.** (CONFERENCE OF PRESIDING OFFICERS AND CLERKS OF THE PARLIAMENTS OF AUSTRALIA, FIJI, NAURU, PAPUA NEW GUINEA AND WESTERN SAMOA. PROCEEDINGS). **Main/Conf** Conference of Presiding Officers and Clerks of the Parliaments of Australia, Fiji, Nauru, Papua New Guinea and Western Samoa. (1968)-. English. ir. Government Printer / Australia, PO Box 84, Canberra, Australian Capital Territory, 2600 Australia. **LC** J905; .L3 subser; JQ4059. **DD** 328.94/01 S; 328.94/05.

CN/0822-4137
**CONFERENCIER (MONTREAL).** *Ceased.* (LE CONFERENCIER : BULLETIN D'INFORMATION DE LA CONFERENCE DES MAIRES DE LA BANLIEUE DE MONTREAL.). [Conferencier]. Vol. 1, No 1 (Febr. 1980)-Vol. 13, No. 3 (1992). Periodical. French (English; summaries and/or abstracts in English). mo. Conference des Maires de la Banlieue de Montreal, CP 126 Succursale Place Desjardins, Montreal Quebec H5B 1B3 Canada. **DD** 352.0714/27.

FR
**CONGRES.** French. an. 250.00F France; 280.00F other. Club Visu M G Eschard, 23 rue d'Cordonnier, F 19100 Brive Gaillarde France. **Tel** 011 33 55 861618.

DR
**CONGRESISTA, EL.** (19??)-. Periodical. Spanish. mo. Calle Guacanagarix Esq Privada Ensanche Quisqueya, Santo Domingo Dominican Republic. **LC** JL1133; .C65.

US/0195-9840
**CONGRESS AND HEALTH.** See Public Health and Safety.

US
**CONGRESS AT YOUR FINGERTIPS.** (19??)-. English. an (Feb.). $7.50. Hansan & Group Inc, PO Box 1223, McLean VA 22101. **Tel** (703)734-3266, (800)659-8708, FAX (703)847-0573. *Continues Capitol Advantage.*
**Desc:** Directory of Congressional profiles listing Congressmen and Senators and their pictures. Also includes key staff and committee appointments.

US/0193-4627
**CONGRESS IN PRINT.** (CONGRESS IN PRINT : A PUBLICATION OF CONGRESSIONAL QUARTERLY, INC.). (1977)-. Periodical. English. Forty-Five times a year (every Wed. Congress is in session). $198.00. Congressional Quarterly Inc., 1414 22nd Street Northwest, Washington DC 20037. **Tel** (202)887-8500, (800)432-2250 ext. 621, FAX (202)728-1863. *Absorbed Bernan Associates Checklist of Congressional Hearings and Committee Prints.*

II/0376-5776
**CONGRESS MARCHES AHEAD.** Dec. 1, 1969/May 1970-. English. All India Congress Committee, 7 Jantar Mantar Road, New Delhi India. **LC** JQ298.I5; C62. **DD** 329.9/54.

US/0090-8061
**CONGRESSIONAL DISTRICT ATLAS.** See Geography.

US/1064-4679
**CONGRESSIONAL MASTERFILE 2.** See Law.

US/0095-6007
**CONGRESSIONAL QUARTERLY ALMANAC.** [Congr. q. alm.]. Vol. 4 (1948)-. English. an. $215.00. Congressional Quarterly Inc., 1414 22nd Street Northwest, Washington DC 20037. **Tel** (202)887-8500, (800)432-2250 ext. 621, FAX (202)728-1863. [**CCC**]. available on microfilm and microfiche from University Microfilms International (UMI). *Continues Congressional Quarterly.*
**Desc:** Summarizes congressional action in 11 major policy areas from agriculture to defense. Covers every bill that emerges from committee and includes appendices with the text of major presidential messages and Supreme Court decisions, plus studies that analyze the votes of members of Congress.
**Ind/Abst** NEXIS (1975-); Relig. Index One Period. (1949-).

US/0363-7239
**CONGRESSIONAL RECORD (DAILY ED.).** *Ceased.* See Law.

US/0364-7544
**CONGRESSIONAL RECORD INDEX.** See Law.

US
**CONGRESSIONAL RECORD [COMPUTER FILE] : PROCEEDINGS AND DEBATES OF THE ... CONGRESS.** See Law.

US/0589-3178
**CONGRESSIONAL STAFF DIRECTORY.** (1959)-. English. sa (Apr. & Sep.). $138.00. Staff Directories Ltd., PO Box 62, Mount Vernon VA 22121. **Tel** (703)739-0900, FAX (703)739-0234. **ED** Anna L. Brownson. **LC** JK1012; .C65. **DD** 328.738. **NLM** JK 421 C749. **Circ:** 32,000. available on CD-ROM; available on diskette.
**Desc:** Congress, its members, their staffs, its committees and subcommittees and staffs, 9,900 cities and towns with congressmen and districts, 3,200 biographies of key staff.

US/0069-8938
**CONGRESSIONAL STAFF DIRECTORY. ADVANCE LOCATOR FOR CAPITOL HILL.** **VFOAT** C.S.D. Advance Locator; CSD Advance Locator; Advance Locator. (1963)-. Directory. English. an. $26.13 Virginia; $25.00 other. Staff Directories Ltd., PO Box 62, Mount Vernon VA 22121. **Tel** (703)739-0900, FAX (703)739-0234. **ED** Charles B. Brownson and Anna L. Brownson. **DD** 328; 973. **NLM** JK 421 C7494. **Bk Rev**. **Circ:** 30,000. available on CD-ROM; available on diskette.
**Desc:** Covers the US Congress, its members and their staffs, 9,900 cities and towns with congressmen and districts.

US/0191-1422
**CONGRESSIONAL YELLOW BOOK (QUARTERLY ED.).** See Encyclopedias and General Reference Books.

IT
**CONGRESSO (ROME, ITALY).** (IL CONGRESSO.). 1984-. Periodical. Italian. mo. Il Congresso, Piazza della Torretta 36, 00186 Rome Italy. **LC** JN5201; .C66. **DD** 328.45.

US
**CONNECTICUT LEGISLATIVE GUIDE / COMPILED BY OFFICE OF LEGISLATIVE MANAGEMENT.** **Added/Corp** Connecticut. Office of Legislative Management. (19??)-. English. an. $2.00. Legislative Management, Legislative Office, Building #5100, Hartford CT 06106. **Tel** (203) 240-0100. **LC** JK3330; .C67. **DD** 328.746/00202.

IT/0010-6569
**CONSIGLIO DI STATO.** [Cons. stato]. (1953)-. Periodical. Italian. mo. L244000 (Comuni Municipal Administrations), L305000 (other) Italy; L460000 other. Casa Editrice Italedi, Piazza Cavour 19, 00193 Rome Italy. **Tel** 011 39 6 3210803. **UDC** 34. *Continues Raccolta Completa Della Giurisprudenza del Consiglio di Stato.*

US/0747-5764
**CONSOLIDATED FEDERAL FUNDS REPORT. VOLUME II, SUBCOUNTY AREAS.** [Consol. fed. funds rep., Vol. II, Subcty. areas]. **Added/Corp** United States. Bureau of the Census. United States. Office of Management and Budget. **VFOAT** Subcounty Areas. (1983)-. Government Publication. English. an. $24.00. Superintendent of Documents, US Government Printing Office, Washington DC 20402. **Tel** (202)275-3328, FAX (202)786-2377. **LC** HJ275; .C636. **DD** 353.0072.

UK
**CONSOLIDATED INDEX TO GOVERNMENT PUBLICATIONS.** **Main/Corp** Great Britain. Stationery Office. (19??)-. English. Her Majesty's Stationery Office, 51 Nine Elms Lane, London SW8 5DR England. **Tel** 011 44 71 873 8459, 011 44 71 873 8499, FAX 011 44 71 873 8499, 011 44 71 873 8456, telex 297138. (**Subscription address:** Her Majesty's Stationery Office, PO Box 276, Publications Centre, London SW8 5DT England.)

US/0195-5888
**CONSTITUTION, JEFFERSON'S MANUAL, AND RULES OF THE HOUSE OF REPRESENTATIVES OF THE UNITED STATES.** **Main/Corp** United States. Congress. House. **Added/Corp** United States. Constitution. (19??)-. Government Publication. English. be. Superintendent of Documents, US Government Printing Office, Washington DC 20402. **Tel** (202)275-3328, FAX (202)786-2377. **LC** KF4992; .U54. **DD** 328.73/05. *Continues Constitution of the United States, Jefferson's Manual, the Rules of the House of Representatives, and a Digest and Manual of the Rules and Practice of the House of Representatives.*

IT
**CONSULENZA.** L320.000 (one year), L560.00 (two year). Luigi Buffetti Spa, Fosso di'Saute, 00169 Rome Italy. **Tel** 011 39 6 5919910, FAX 011 39 6 5920473, telex 623009.

CN/0820-0084
**CONTACT (ST-ANACLET DE LESSARD).** (CONTACT.). [Contact]. **Added/Corp** Saint-Anaclet-de-Lessard (Quebec). Vol. 1, No. 1 (June 1982)-. Periodical. French. Municipalite de St-Anaclet-de-Lessard Bureau, Municipal 20 rue de la Gare, St-Anaclet-de-Lessard Quebec G0K 1H0 Canada. **DD** 352.0714/771.

CN/0710-6297
**CONTEST AND LOTTERY NEWS.** Vol. 1, No. 1-. Periodical. English. mo. $12.00. Excalibur Publications, Room 111/Central Square Ross Building, York University, 4700 Keele Street, Downsview Ontario M3J 1P3 Canada. **Tel** (416)736-5238. **DD** 790.1/34/0971.

IT/0391-4763
**CONTO RIASSUNTIVO DEL TESORO.** [Conto riass. tesoro]. **VFOAT** Situazione del Bilancio dello Stato e Situazione della Banca d'Italia. (1926)-. Periodical. Italian. mo. L81000.00 Italy; L162000.00 other. Istituto Poligrafico Zecca Stato, Piazza Verdi 10, 00198 Rome Italy. **Tel** 011 39 6 85082307, 011 39 6 85082221. **UDC** 336. **Pr Rev**. *Continues Conto Riassuntivo del Tesoro, Situazione del Bilancio e Indici.*

US/0190-3063
**CONTRACT MANAGEMENT.** See Law.

US/1041-7427
**CONTRACTING INTELLIGENCE.** [Contract. intell.]. **VFOAT** DMS Intelligence. Periodical. English. bw. $375.00. Jane's Information Group, Sentinel House, 163 Brighton Road, Coulsdon Surrey CR3 2NX England. **Tel** 011 44 81 763 1030, FAX 011 44 81 763 1006. **DD** 353. available on an online database (file 587/Full-Text) from DIALOG. *Continues Contracting DMS Intelligence, 0731-0986.*

CN/0703-7384
**CORPUS ADMINISTRATIVE INDEX.** [Corpus adm. index]. (1972)-. Periodical. English. Four times a year. 449.00Can$. Southam Information and Technology Group Inc., 1450 Don Mills Road, Don Mills Ontario M3B 2X7 Canada. **Tel** (416)445-6641, (800)668-2374, FAX (416)442-2261. **DD** 354. 71'00025.

CL
**COSAS.** **VFOAT** VSD. (19??)-. Periodical. Spanish. sm (24 issues). $287.00 North & South America; $375.00 other. Editorial Tiempo Presente Ltda, C 6147 Almirante Pastene 329, Santiago Chile. **Tel** 011 56 2 2352705, FAX 011 56 2 2257799, telex 340905 COSAS CK. **ED** Monica Comandari Kaiser. **LC** AP63; .C627. **DD** 056/.1. **Ad Acc**. **Circ:** 40,000.
**Desc:** Interviews to heads of state, politicians and businessmen.

# Public Administration

**IV**
**COTE D'IVOIRE : ANNUAIRE INTERNATIONAL, LA.** *Title Change.* **VFOAT** La Cote d'Ivoire : International Directory. French. an. **LC** JQ3386.A4; C68. *Continued by Annuaire International, Cote d'Ivoire.*

**US**
**COUNCIL COMMENTS. Main/Corp** Citizens Research Council of Michigan. Vol. 1 1946-. English. ir. Citizens Research Council of Michigan, 625 Shelby Street, Detroit MI 48226-4154. **Tel** (313)961-5377.

**UK**
**COUNCILS, COMMITTEES & BOARDS.** (1970)-. English. ir (Published every 3 to 4 years). £110.00. CBD Research Ltd, 15 Wickham Road, Beckenham Kent BR3 2JS England. **Tel** 011 44 81 6507745, FAX 011 44 81 6500768. **ED** Lindsay Sellar.
**Desc:** A handbook of advisory, consultative, executive and similar bodies in British public life.

**AT**
**COUNCILS WEST.** English. qt. 25.00Aus$. West Australian Municipal Association, PO Box 1544, West Perth 6872 Australia. **Tel** 011 61 09 2212911.

**UK/0264-8822**
**COUNTRYSIDE COMMISSION NEWS.** [Countrys. Comm. news]. (1983)-. Periodical. English. bm (6 issues). Free on request. Countryside Commission News, John Dower House, Crescent Place, Cheltenham GL50 3RA England. **Tel** 011 44 242 521381. **DD** 354.420086305. **[CCC]**.
**Ind/Abst** Museum Abstr.

**US/0739-4330**
**COUNTY AGENTS.** See Agriculture.

**US/1049-7838**
**COUNTY COMMENT.** (COUNTY COMMENT : A PUBLICATION OF THE SOUTH DAKOTA ASSOCIATION OF COUNTY COMMISSIONERS.). [Cty. comment]. **Added/Corp** South Dakota Association of County Commissioners. **VFOAT** SDACC County Comment. Vol. 36, No. 4 (Mar. 1990). Periodical. English. mo. $10.00. South Dakota Association of County Commissioners, 207 East Capital, Suite 203, Pierre SD 57501. **Tel** (605)224-4554. **ED** Susan Comer. **LC** JS39; .S58. **DD** 352/.0073. **Ad Acc.** ctrl circ. *Continues South Dakota Counties, 1049-8397.*

**US/0199-2546**
**COUNTY COMMISSIONER (MONTGOMERY), THE.** (THE COUNTY COMMISSIONER.). **Added/Corp** Association of County Commissions of Alabama. (19??)-. Periodical. English. Six times a year. $10.00. The County Commissioner, 100 North Jackson Street, Montgomery AL 36104. **Tel** (205)263-7594.
**Desc:** News and information on articles of community corrections, state prisoners in the county jail, the prison population, and legislative conference registration and other related fields.

**US/0742-1702**
**COUNTY EXECUTIVE DIRECTORY.**
**Added/Corp** Carroll Publishing Company. (Winter/Spring 1984)-. Directory. English. sa. $150.00. Carroll Publishing Company, 1058 Thomas Jefferson Street Northwest, Washington DC 20007-3832. **Tel** (202)333-8620, FAX (202)337-7020. **ED** Nancy Cahill. **LC** JS414; .C67. **DD** 352/.0052/0973. Index available. **Circ:** 500.
**Desc:** Provides name, title, office address and phone number for more than 27,000 officials in over 3,100 counties.

**US/0193-5593**
**COUNTY GOVERNMENT EMPLOYMENT.** See Economics-Labor.

**US/0743-4197**
**COUNTY INFORMATION SERVICE.** (COUNTY INFORMATION SERVICE / PREPARED THROUGH OFFICE OF THE DIRECTOR, COOPERATIVE EXTENSION SERVICE, COMMUNITY RESOURCE DEVELOPMENT PROJECT, COLORADO STATE UNIVERSITY.). **Added/Corp** Colorado State University. Cooperative Extension Service. (19??)-. English. Four times a year. $40.00. Colorado State University / Agricultural Economics, County Information Service, Fort Collins CO 80523. **Tel** (303)491-8574.
**(Subscription address:** Colorado State University / Department of Agriculture & Economics, County Information Service, Fort Collins CO 80523.)

**US**
**COUNTY OFFICERS / STATE OF ILLINOIS. VFOAT** County Officers. Began with 1979. English. an. Free. State Board of Elections / Illinois, State of Illinois, 1020 South Spring Street, PO Box 4187, Springfield IL 62708. **Tel** (217)782-4141. **ED** Don Schultz. **LC** JS451.I35; C69. **DD** 352/.0052/025773. **Circ:** 2,000. *Continues in part Illinois. State Board of Elections. State and County Officers, 0145-6199.*
**Desc:** Booklet includes listing and title of county elected public officials in each county.

**US/0011-0353**
**COUNTY PROGRESS.** (COUNTY PROGRESS; THE BUSINESS MAGAZINE FOR COUNTY OFFICIALS.). **Added/Corp** County Judges and Commissioners Association of Texas. (1924)-. Periodical. English. Twelve times a year. $17.50. Coursey Publishing Company, PO Box 519, Brownwood TX 76804. **Tel** (915)643-2995, FAX (915)643-2995. **ED** Robert Tindol. **Ad Acc, Adv Mgr:** Pat Coursey. **Circ:** 1,800.
**Desc:** Official publication for the County Judges and Commissioners Association of Texas.

**US/0279-8867**
**COUNTY VIEWPOINT.** (COUNTY VIEWPOINT / KACO.). **Added/Corp** Kentucky Association of Counties. (19??)-. Periodical. English. mo. $6.00. Kentucky Association of Counties, 400 Kings Daughters Drive, Frankfort KY 40601. **Tel** (502)223-7667.

**US**
**COURTHOUSE JOURNAL, THE.**
**Added/Corp** Washington Association of County Officials. Washington State Association of Elected County Officials. Washington State Association of County Officials. (March 1960)-. Periodical. English. mo.

**US/0196-612X**
**CQ GUIDE TO CURRENT AMERICAN GOVERNMENT, THE.** [CQ guide curr. Am. gov.]. **Added/Corp** Congressional Quarterly, Inc. **VFOAT** Current American Government. **VAT** Congressional Quarterly Guide to Current American Government. (1961/62)-. Periodical. English. sa. $16.95. Congressional Quarterly Inc., 1414 22nd Street Northwest, Washington DC 20037. **Tel** (202)887-8500, (800)432-2250 ext. 621, FAX (202)728-1863. **LC** JK1; .C14. **DD** 320; 320.

**US/1058-5931**
**CRA BULLETIN. VAT** Community Reinvestment Act Bulletin. (1991)-. Bulletin. English. mo. $145.00. Community Bulletin, One Penn Plaza, 40th Floor, New York NY 10119.

**UK/0953-8089**
**CRAWFORD'S DIRECTORY OF CITY CONNECTIONS.** [Crawford's dir. city connect.]. (1978)-. Directory. English. Six times a year. £225.00 (with updates); £185.00 (without updates). BBIS Ltd., Riverbank House, Angel Lane, Tonbridge Kent TN9 1SE England. **Tel** 011 44 732 362666. **DD** 332. *Continues Directory of City Connections.*

**IT/0394-6088**
**CROCEVIA MERANO.** (CROCEVIA.). [Crocevia Merano]. (1946)-. Periodical. Italian. mo. L130000 (institutions), L65000 (individuals). Crocevia SRL, Piazza Teatro 21, 39012 Merano Italy. **Tel** 011 473 210443. **(Subscription address:** Maggioli Editore, Casella Postale 290, 47037 Rimini Italy) UDC 351.745.

**IT**
**CRONACHE PARLAMENTARI SICILIANE.** (19??)-. Italian. mo. Free on request. Cronache Parlamentari Pal Normanni, Piazza Parlamento 1, 90134 Palermo Italy. **Tel** 011 39 91 6561111.

**US**
**CSG BACKGROUNDER / COUNCIL OF STATE GOVERNMENTS.** *Ceased.* **VFOAT** Backgrounder. **VAT** Council of State Governments Backgrounder. ( )-(Dec. 1990). Periodical. English. mo. Council of State Governments, PO Box 11910, Iron Works Pike, Lexington KY 40578-1910. **Tel** (800)800-1910, (606)231-1850. **ED** L Edward Purcell. **Bk Rev. Ad Acc.** ctrl circ.
**Desc:** Brief up-to-date special issue reports on current concerns and trends in the states.

**US/0738-646X**
**CSI FEDERAL REGISTER ABSTRACTS (MASTER EDITION).** *Ceased.* (CSI FEDERAL REGISTER ABSTRACTS / CSI.). [CSI Fed. regis. abstr., Master ed.]. **Added/Corp** Capitol Services. **VFOAT** C.S.I. Federal Register Abstracts. **VAT** Capitol Services, Inc. Federal Register Abstracts. Master Edition. (19??)-(19??). English. da. Information Handling Services, 15 Inverness Way East, Englewood CO 80150. **Tel** (800)525-7052, (303)790-0600, FAX (303)397-2599, telex 4322083.
**Desc:** Abstracts of government publications on sessions of congress.

**US/0198-7070**
**CUMULATED INDEX TO THE U.S. DEPARTMENT OF STATE PAPERS RELATING TO THE FOREIGN RELATIONS OF THE UNITED STATES, THE.** [Cumul. index U. S. Dep. State pap. relat. foreign relat. U. S.]. **VAT** Cumulated Index to the United States Department of State Papers Relating to the Foreign Relations of the United States. English. Kraus Reprint and Periodicals, 358 Saw Mill River Road, Millwood NY 10546. **Tel** (914)762-2200, (800)223-8323, FAX (914)762-1195, telex 6818112.

**US**
**CURRENT INFORMATION TECHNOLOGY RESOURCE REQUIREMENTS OF THE FEDERAL GOVERNMENT. Added/Corp** United States. Office of Management and Budget. United States. General Services Administration. United States. Dept. of Commerce. **VFOAT** Current Information Resource Requirements of the Federal Government. (1991)-. Government Publication. English. ir. $29.00. Superintendent of Documents, US Government Printing Office, Washington DC 20402. **Tel** (202)275-3328, FAX (202)786-2377. **LC** JK468.A8; C87. **DD** 353.04/028/5.

**US/0161-5122**
**CURRENT MUNICIPAL PROBLEMS (CUMULATION).** (CURRENT MUNICIPAL PROBLEMS.). V. 1- 1959/76-. Periodical. English. an. Clark Boardman Callaghan, 155 Pfingsten Road, Deerfield IL 60015. **Tel** (800)323-8067. **LC** JS39; .C84. **DD** 352/.008/0973.
**Ind/Abst** Curr. Law Index (1980-); Leg. Resour. Index (1980-?); LegalTrac (1980-1989).

**US**
**D/C : NATIONAL NEWSLETTER FOR STATE ADMINISTERED DEFERRED COMPENSATION PROGRAMS.** See Economics-Labor.

**US**
**DAILY BULLETIN / INSTITUTE OF GOVERNMENT, UNIVERSITY OF NORTH CAROLINA AT CHAPEL HILL.** Began in 1962. Bulletin. English. da (during session). $990.00. State Legislative Building, PO Box 7294, Raleigh NC 27611. **Tel** (919)733-2484. **ED** Joseph S Farrell. **LC** JK4166; .N67. **DD** 328.756/005. Index available. **Circ:** 2,200 (ctrl). *Continues Daily Bulletin (University of North Carolina (1793-1962). Institute of Government).*
**Desc:** Comprehensive record of activities of North Carolina General Assembly while it is in session; digest explanation of each bill introduced; and current status of all bills.

**US/0277-4917**
**DAILY LEGISLATIVE REPORT. Added/Corp** State Capital Information Service, Inc. (1949)-. Periodical. English. da. $520.00. State Capitol Information Service / Illinois, 516 East Monroe Street, Suite 501, Springfield IL 62701. **Tel** (217)782-6295. **ED** Joseph L. Harris.
**Desc:** Issued every day, Illinois General Assembly meets. Includes the digests of all bill introductions, committee hearing schedules, committee and floor actions.

**TS**
**DALIL AL-HUKUMAH WA-AL-QITA AL-AMM FI JUMHURIYAT MISR AL-ARABIYAH.** Arabic. 11 Abd El-Khaliq Tharwat Street, Al-Qahirah United Arab Republic. **LC** JQ3831; .D34.

**US**
**DATA PROCESSING ANNUAL REPORT AND LONG-RANGE PLAN FOR FISCAL YEARS ... / STATE OF LOUISIANA. Main/Corp** Louisiana. Data Processing Coordinating and Advisory Council. 1982-1984-. English. an. $1.66. Louisiana Data Processing, Coordinating and Advisory Council Office of the Governor, 555 St Tammany Street, Baton Rouge LA 70806. **LC** JK4749.A8; L68A. **DD** 353.976630071.

**CN/0542-5492**
**DEBATES AND PROCEEDINGS - LEGISLATIVE ASSEMBLY OF MANITOBA.** [Debates proc. - Legis. Assem. Manit.]. **Main/Corp** Manitoba. Legislative Assembly. Vol. 1 (Oct. 23, 1958)-. Periodical. English. ir (Publishes during daily sessions). 150.00Can$. Queens Printer Statutory Publishing, 200 Vaughn Street, Winnipeg Manitoba R3C 1T5 Canada. **Tel** (204)945-3102. **ED** Suzanne Dion. **LC** J109; .H22. Index available. cum. index. **Bk Rev. Ad Acc. Circ:** 300 (ctrl). available on an online database.
**Desc:** Verbatim record of the legislative assembly, debates, and proceedings.

**CN/0707-8315**
**DEBATES AND PROCEEDINGS - NOVA SCOTIA HOUSE OF ASSEMBLY. Main/Corp** Nova Scotia. House of Assembly. **VAT** Debates and Proceedings of the House of Assembly (Halifax); Official Report of the Debates and Proceedings of the Legislative Council (Halifax). (1???)-. Periodical. English. an. 150.00Can$. Nova Scotia Department of Supplies and Services, PO Box 54, Halifax Nova Scotia B3J 2L4 Canada. **Tel** (902)424-2694.

**SA**
**DEBATES OF PARLIAMENT / REPUBLIC OF SOUTH AFRICA. Main/Corp** South Africa. Parliament. 8th Parliament, 6th Session, No. 1; Feb. 5-12,

1988-. English (Afrikaans). ir. R25.00 South Africa; R28.00 other. House of Assembly / Select Committee on Railway Acounts, Government Printer, Bosman Street, Private Bag X85, Pretoria 0001 South Africa. **Tel** 012-457531. **(Subscription address:** PO Box 571, 8000 Cape Town Republic of South Africa**) ED** B C Culhane and A R G Hendry. **LC** J705; .H27a. Index available. **Circ:** 5,000 (ctrl). ***Formed by the union of*** *South Africa. Parliament. House of Assembly. Debates of the House of Assembly (1985); South Africa. Parliament. House of Delegates. Debates of the House of Delegates* ***and*** *South Africa. Parliament. House of Representatives. Debates of the House of Representatives.*

CN/0709-3616
**DEBATS DE L'ASSEMBLEE LEGISLATIVE DU QUEBEC.** (DEBATS DE L'ASSEMBLEE LEGISLATIVE.). **Main/Corp** Quebec (Province). Assemblee Legislative. 1st Legislature-1867/1868-. Periodical. French. ir. Editeur Officiel du Quebec, 1283 Boul Charest Ouest, Quebec Quebec G1N 2C9 Canada.

SA
**DEBATTE VAN DIE PRESIDENTSRAAD.** **Main/Corp** South Africa. President's Council. **VFOAT** Debates of the President's Council. Periodical. Afrikaans (English). R5.00. The Government Printer, Bosman Street, Private Bag X85, Pretoria 0001 South Africa. **Tel** 012-323-9731, FAX 012-323-0009. **LC** JQ1941; .S65a. ***Continues*** *President's Council.*

SA
**DEBATTE VAN DIE ... SESSIE VAN DIE WETGEWENDE VERGADERING VAN DIE KAVANGO.** **Main/Corp** Kavango (Namibia). Legislative Assembly. Afrikaans. **LC** J812.T3; K37A.

SA
**DEBATTE VAN DIE STAANDE KOMITEE VOOR BEGROTINGSWETSONTWERP.** **Main/Corp** South Africa. Parliament. House of Assembly. Standing Committee on Appropriation Bill. **VFOAT** Debates of the Standing Committee on Appropriation Bill. Afrikaans (English). R8.75. Government Printer / South Africa, Bosman Street, Private Bag X85, Pretoria 0001 South Africa. **Tel** 011 27 12 3239731 Ext. 262. **LC** LAW. **DD** 354.680072/234/05.

CN/0702-9683
**DECISIONS DE LA COMMISSION DES AFFAIRES SOCIALES.** ***Title Change.*** **Main/Corp** Quebec (Province). Commission des Affaires Sociales. **Added/Corp** Quebec (Province). Service de Documentation Juridique Inc. Bureau des Arretistes. Societe Quebecoise d'Information Juridique. **VFOAT** Tables Cumulatives de Concordance et de l'Legislation Citee; Recueil de Jurisprudence. (1975)-(1992). Periodical. French. Periodica Inc, PO Box 444, Outremont Quebec H2V 4R6 Canada. **Tel** (514)274-5468, FAX (514)274-0201. **DD** 344.714/03. ***Continued by*** *Jurisca Decisions de la Commission des Affaire Sociales.*
**Desc:** Indispensable tool for the law practitioner in the area of social security law, for the employer and for employees' associations. It prints in areas such as indemnification of work and auto accident victims, medical records, access, handicapped provisions, etc.

US/0011-7331
**DECISIONS OF THE DEPARTMENT OF THE INTERIOR (MONTHLY).** (DECISIONS OF THE DEPARTMENT OF THE INTERIOR.). [Decis. Dept. Inter.]. **Main/Corp** United States. Dept. of the Interior. (Jan. 1955)-. Government Publication. English. mo. $7.50 domestic; $9.40 other. Superintendent of Documents, US Government Printing Office, Washington DC 20402. **Tel** (202)275-3328, FAX (202)786-2377. **DD** 333.
**Desc:** Decisions by the Department of the Interior on appeals, claims, and acts.

US/0193-5070
**DECISIONS OF THE UNITED STATES DEPARTMENT OF THE INTERIOR.** (DECISIONS OF THE UNITED STATES DEPARTMENT OF THE INTERIOR / UNITED STATES DEPARTMENT OF THE INTERIOR.). **Main/Corp** United States. Dept. of the Interior. Vol. 68 (Jan.-Dec. 1961)-. Government Publication. English. an. Department of the Interior, 1849 C Street Northwest, Washington DC 20240. **Tel** (202)343-3171, FAX (202)208-5048. **LC** PAR. available on microfilm and microfiche from University Microfilms International (UMI). ***Continues*** *Decisions of the Department of the Interior, 0011-7331.*

US
**DEFENSE CONTRACTING AGENCY AUDIT MANUAL.** English. Four times a year (published Jan., Apr., July, and Oct.). $99.00. EZ - Far Systems, 360 Wire Road, York PA 17402. **Tel** 1-800-388-1415, FAX (717)975-2813. **ED** TSA Inc 2 market Plaza Way, Mechanicsburg, Pa 17055 (717)691-5691. **Ad Acc.** ctrl circ. available on CD-ROM (also on Windows).

US
**DELAWARE LEGISLATIVE ROSTER.** **See** Public Administration-Abstracting, Bibliographies and Statistics.

PO
**DEMOCRACIA 76 I.E. SETENTA E SEIS.** Periodical. Portuguese. $12.50 single issue. Partido de Centro Democratico Socical, Largo do Caldas 5, Lisbon Portugal. **LC** JN8651.C45; D45. **DD** 329.9/469.

GW
**DEMOKRATISCHE GEMEINDE.** Periodical. German. mo. DM48.00 (six months). Union-Druckerei und Verlagsanstalt GmbH, Postfach 90 09 07, Theodor-Heuss-Allee 9098, W-6000 Frankfurt 90 Germany. **LC** JS5431; .D35. **DD** 352/.0072/0943.

US
**DEPARTMENT OF REVENUE ANNUAL REPORT (ARIZONA).** **Main/Corp** Arizona. Dept. of Revenue. **VFOAT** Annual Report. 1975-1976-. English. an. Capitol Building, 1700 West Washington, Phoenix AZ 85007. **DD** 351.726. ***Continues*** *Arizona. Dept. of Revenue. Annual Report of the Department of Revenue.*

US
**DEPARTMENT OF STATE PLANNING PUBLICATION.** ***Ceased.*** **Added/Corp** Maryland. Dept. of Budget & Fiscal Planning. Maryland. Dept. of State Planning. (1974)-(1988). English. Department of State Planning, State Office Building, Baltimore MD 21201. **Tel** (410)225-4490. ***Continues*** *Historical Summary of Capital Improvements Authorized by General Assembly.*

CN/0846-0140
**DES MOTS ET DES GENS (SAINT-LAURENT).** ***Title Change.*** (WORDS AND PEOPLE.). [Des mots gens]. **Added/Corp** Saint-Laurent (Ile-de-Montreal, Quebec). **VFOAT** Des Mots et Des Gens. Vol. 1, No. 1 (Mar. 1990)-Vol. 3, No. 5 (Dec. 1992). Periodical. English (French). bm. City of Saint-Laurent, 777 Laurentien Boulevard, Saint-Laurent Quebec H4M 2M7 Canada. **Tel** 744-7305. **DD** 352.0714/28/05. ***Continues*** *Saint-Laurent Journal., 0829-4941.* ***Continued by*** *Saint-Laurent (Saint-Laurent, Quebec), 1197-6241.*

CN/0846-0140
**DES MOTS ET DES GENS (SAINT-LAURENT).** ***Title Change.*** (DES MOTS ET DES GENS.). [Mots gens]. **Added/Corp** Saint-Laurent (Ile-de-Montreal, Quebec). **VFOAT** Words and People. Vol. 1, No. 1 (Mars 1990)- Vol. 3, No. 5 (Dec. 1992). Periodical. French (English). bm. Ville de St-Laurent, 777 Boulevard Laurentien, St-Laurent, Quebec H4M 2M7 Canada. **DD** 352.0714/28/05. ***Continues*** *Le Journal de Saint-Laurent., 0829-4941.* ***Continued by*** *Saint-Laurent (Saint-Laurent, Quebec), 1197-6241.*

CK
**DESPACHOS PUBLICOS.** Spanish. an. Carrera 12 No 15-95 of 307 Apartado A-718, Bogota Colombia. **LC** JL2821; .D48. **DD** 354.861002.

II/0303-8645
**DETAILED DEMAND FOR GRANTS OF FOOD SUPPLIES AND TRANSPORT DEPARTMENT. GOVERNMENT OF JAMMU AND KASHMIR.** (DETAILED DEMAND FOR GRANTS OF FOOD SUPPLIES AND TRANSPORT DEPARTMENT.). **Main/Corp** Jammu and Kashmir. Food Supplies and Transport Dept. English. Ranbir Government Press / Food Supplies, Jammu and Kashmir, Food Supplies and Transport Department, Jammu India. **LC** HD9016.I43; K34A. **DD** 354/.54/600722.

II
**DETAILED ESTIMATES OF REVENUE OF THE PUNJAB GOVERNMENT FOR THE YEAR ... .** **See** Public Administration-Public Finance and Taxation.

US
**DETAILED LISTING OF REAL PROPERTY OWNED BY THE UNITED STATES AND USED BY CIVIL AGENCIES THROUGHOUT THE WORLD AS OF ... .** English. an. **LC** JK1613; .D48. **DD** 353.0071/3.

PH
**DEVELOPMENT ADMINISTRATION JOURNAL.** Vol. 1, No. 1 (1981)-. English. sa. University Research Center, Mindanao State University, PO Box 5594, 9200 Iligan City Philippines. **Circ:** 500 (ctrl).

UK/0957-4115
**DEVELOPMENT JOURNAL (LONDON).** (DEVELOPMENT JOURNAL.). [Dev. j.]. (Feb. 1990)-. Periodical. English. qt. $102.00 US; $110.00 other. Development Journal Ltd, 150 Regent Street/Suite 500, London W1R 5FA England. **Tel** 011 44 71 242 1280. **ED** Irvine Cohen. **LC** IN PROCESS; HG5993; .D48. **NLM** W1; DE997NAJ. **[CCC]. Bk Rev. Ad Acc. Circ:** 5,300 (ctrl).
**Desc:** Leading international journal dealing with Third World development. Primary circulation is to senior government level in developing countries and to policy-making, decision-making and implementation levels in bilateral and multilateral official donor agencies.

II
**DEVELOPMENT POLICY AND ADMINISTRATION REVIEW.** ***Ceased.*** **Added/Corp** HCM State Institute of Public Administration. Vol. 1 (Jan./June 1975)-Vol. 3 (Jan./Feb. 1985). Periodical. English. sa. HCM State Institute of Public Administration, Malviya Hagar, Jaipur 302004 India. **Tel** 64003-6, 365-465 RIPA IN. **ED** M Hasan. **LC** JF1338.A2; D49. **DD** 354/.54/00072. **Bk Rev. Ad Acc. Circ:** 500.
**Desc:** Developmental and administrative issues and policies confronting Third World countries. Review of existing policies and their execution to obtain alternative solutions.
**Ind/Abst** Leis. Recreat. Tour. Abstr.; Rural Dev. Abstr.; World Agric. Econ.

KO
**DIALOGUE (WASHINGTON, D.C.).** (TAIALROGU.). **VFOAT** Dialogue. Periodical. Korean (Korean). qt. United States Information Agency / Teacher Exchange Branch, E/ASX, Washington DC 20547.

UK
**DIARY OF THE CORPORATION OF THE CITY OF GLASGOW & C.** **Main/Corp** Glasgow (Strathclyde). **VFOAT** City of Glasgow Corporation Diary. English. 197 Pollokshawa Road, Glasgow Scotland. **LC** JS4274.A1; G58A. **DD** 352.0414/43.

US/0885-159X
**DICKINSON'S FDA.** ***Title Change.*** [Dickinson's FDA]. **VFOAT** FDA. **VAT** Dickinson's Food and Drug Administration. (1985)-(1994). Periodical. English. Twenty-four times a year. Ferdic Inc., PO Box 367, Las Cruces NM 88004. **Tel** (505)527-8634, FAX (505)527-8858. **ED** James G. Dickinson. **DD** 353. ***Merged with*** *Dickinson's FDA Inspection, 1063-2433* ***to form*** *Dickinson's FDA Review, 1073-4414.*
**Desc:** A newsletter focusing on early drug-device regulatory policy and personnel developments inside the Food and Drug Administration.

US/1063-2433
**DICKINSON'S FDA INSPECTION.** ***Title Change.*** [Dickinson's FDA insp.]. **VFOAT** FDA Inspection; FDA. **VAT** Dickinson's Food and Drug Administration Inspection. Vol. 1, No. 1 (June 1992)-(1994). Periodical. English. sm. Ferdic Inc., PO Box 367, Las Cruces NM 88004. **Tel** (505)527-8634, FAX (505)527-8858. **ED** James G. Dickinson. **DD** 353. ***Merged with*** *Dickinson's FDA, 1073-4414* ***to form*** *Dickinson's FDA Review, 1073-4414.*

●US/1073-4414
**DICKINSON'S FDA REVIEW.** [Dickinson's FDA rev.]. **VFOAT** FDA Review. **VAT** Dickinson's Food and Drug Administration Review. Vol. 1, No. 1 (Jan. 1994)-. Periodical. English. mo. $685.00. Ferdic Inc., PO Box 367, Las Cruces NM 88004. **Tel** (505)527-8634, FAX (505)527-8858. **DD** 353. ***Formed by the union of*** *Dickinson's FDA Inspection, 1063-2433* ***and*** *Dickinson's FDA, 0885-159X.*
**Desc:** Covers FDA policy and intelligence. In-depth insider policy analysis and news with enrollment profiles. Also contains warning letters to companies along with all violations listed. Analysis of current FDI requests for company intelligence, lawsuits, etc.

FR
**DICTIONNAIRE PERMANENT FISCAL.** (19??)-. French. ir. 1650.00F. Editions Legislatives et Admin, 80 82 Avenue de la Marne, 92546 Montrouge Cedex France. **Tel** 011 33 1 40926868. **LC** LAW. **DD** 343.4404/05; 344.403405.

US
**DIGEST OF ADVISORY OPINIONS.** **See** Ethics.

US/0012-2785
**DIGEST OF PUBLIC GENERAL BILLS AND RESOLUTIONS.** ***Ceased.*** **Added/Corp** Library of Congress. Legislative Reference Service. Library of Congress. Congressional Research Service. **VFOAT** CRS Bill Digest. (1967)-Ceased (Jan. 1987). Government Publication. English. ir. Superintendent of Documents, US Government Printing Office, Washington DC 20402. **Tel** (202)275-3328, FAX (202)786-2377. **LC** KF18; .L5. **DD** 348/.73/1. **NLM** Z 6456 D572. available on microfilm and microfiche from University Microfilms International (UMI). ***Continues*** *Digest of Public General Bills and Selected Resolutions with Index, 0090-0125.*

CN/0825-6683
**DIPLOMATIC, CONSULAR, AND OTHER REPRESENTATIVES IN CANADA.** [Dipl. consul. other represent. Can.]. **VFOAT** Representants Diplomatiques, Consulaires, et

Autres au Canada. English (French). be. $4.15 Canada; $5.00 other. Canadian Government Publishing Center, Supply and Services Canada, Hull Quebec K1A 0S9 Canada. **Tel** (613)990-8116, telex 053-4296. **LC** JX1729.A2; A352. **DD** 351.8/92/0971. ***Continues*** *Diplomatic Corps and Consular and Other Representatives in Canada, 0486-4514.*

AT
**DIPLOMATIC LIST AND LIST OF REPRESENTATIVES OF INTERNATIONAL ORGANIZATIONS / DEPARTMENT OF FOREIGN AFFAIRS AND TRADE.** **Added/Corp** Australia. Dept. of Foreign Affairs and Trade. **VFOAT** Diplomatic List. (198?)-. Government Publication. English. Four times a year. 22.00Aus$. Australian Government Publishing Service, GPO Box 84, Canberra ACT 2601 Australia. **Tel** 011 61 6 2954411, FAX 011 61 6 2954455. **LC** JX1875; .A152. **DD** 351.89/2/0994. ***Continues*** *Diplomatic List (Canberra, A.C.T.), 0158-2089.*

II
**DIPLOMATIC LIST (INDIA).** **Main/Corp** India. Protocol Division. English. Rs6.00 India; $2.16 US. Controller of Publications / Civil Lines, Government of India, Civil Lines, New Delhi 110054 India. **Tel** 3015984, telex 3166415. **LC** JX1839; .A165A. **DD** 351/.892.

CN/1181-9367
**DIRECTIONS - B.C. HYDRO.** ***Title Change.*** (DIRECTIONS.). [Dir. - B.C. Hydro]. **Main/Corp** B.C. Hydro. **VAT** Directions - British Columbia Hydro. Vol. 1, No. 1, Fall (1990)-(199?). Periodical. English. Three times a year. British Columbia Hydro Information Center, 970 Burrard Street, Vancouver BC V6Z 1Y3 Canada. **Tel** (604)663-2618. **DD** 354.7110087/22/005. ***Continues in part*** *News (B.C. Hydro)., 0825-0634.* ***Merged with*** *B.C. Hydro. People, 1181-9626* ***and*** *B.C. Hydro. Issues, 1181-6430* ***to form*** *B.C. Hydro. Access Magazine, 1195-0889.*

CN/0848-6859
**DIRECTIONS - PUBLIC SERVICE COMMISSION OF CANADA.** (ORIENTATION.). [Dir. - Public Serv. Comm. Can.]. **Main/Corp** Commission de la Fonction Publique du Canada. **VFOAT** Document des Orientations; Orientations; Directions; Directions Document. (1986/1991)-. French (English). Commission de la Fonction Publique du Canada, Direction Generale de la Formation Linguistique, Ottawa Ontario K1A 0M7 Canada. **DD** 354.71001.

CN/0848-6859
**DIRECTIONS - PUBLIC SERVICE COMMISSION OF CANADA.** (DIRECTIONS.). [Dir. - Public Serv. Comm. Can.]. **Main/Corp** Public Service Commission of Canada. **VFOAT** Directions Document; Orientation; Document des Orientations; Orientations. (1991)-. English (French). Public Service Commission of Canada, 300 Laurier Avenue West, Ottawa Ontario K1A 0M7 Canada. **DD** 354.71001.

CK
**DIRECTORIO DE DESPACHOS PUBLICOS.** Began in 1974. Spanish. $50.00 single issue. Carrera 13 No 10-41 - OF 606, BCO de la Costa Apartado Aereo 718, Bogota Colombia. **LC** JL2821; .D57.

US/1051-5828
**DIRECTORY / MASSACHUSETTS MUNICIPAL ASSOCIATION.** [Dir. - Mass. Munic. Assoc.]. **VFOAT** Massachusetts Municipal Directory. Directory. English. an. $11.00 (members), $20.00 (nonmembers). Massachusetts Municipal Association, 60 Temple Place, Boston MA 02111. **Tel** (800)882-1498. **DD** 352. ***Continues*** *Massachusetts Municipal Directory, 0361-2090.*

US/0090-1989
**DIRECTORY : NORTH DAKOTA CITY OFFICIALS.** Directory. English. $5.00. North Dakota League of Cities, 217 North Third Street, Box 578, Fargo ND 58102. **LC** JS451.N93; D5. **DD** 352.0784. ***Continues*** *Directory of North Dakota Municipal Officials, 0740-6428.*

US/0149-337X
**DIRECTORY OF ADMINISTRATIVE SERVICES.** **VFOAT** American City & County Directory of Administrative Services. (1991)-. Directory. English. $48.00. American City & County, 6255 Barfield Road, Atlanta GA 30328. **[CCC].**

US
**DIRECTORY OF CHINESE OFFICIALS AND ORGANIZATIONS.** **Added/Corp** United States. Central Intelligence Agency. Directorate of Intelligence. (Nov. 1986)-. Directory. English. be. Document Expediting Project, Exchange and Gift Division, Library of Congress, Photoduplication Service, Washington DC 20540. **Tel** (202)287-9527. **LC** JQ1507; .D544. **DD** 354.51002. ***Formed by the union of*** *Directory of Chinese Officials. National Level Organizations; Directory of Chinese Officials. Provincial Organizations, 0733-2025* ***and*** *Directory of Chinese Officials. Scientific and Educational Organizations, 0741-1901.*

US/1046-2686
**DIRECTORY OF CITY POLICY OFFICIALS.** [Dir. city policy off.]. Directory. English. an. $10.00 members, $25.00 nonmembers. National League of Cities Publications Sales, 1301 Pennsylvania Avenue NW, Washington DC 20004. **Tel** (202)626-3000, FAX (202)626-3043. **LC** JS39; .D55. **DD** 352/.0052/0973. **Circ:** 2,000. ***Absorbed*** *Directory of Local Chief Executives.*
**Desc:** Directory of mayors, council members and city managers; lists names, titles, term expiration dates, city hall addresses and phone numbers.

US
**DIRECTORY OF COUNTY OFFICIALS (ANNAPOLIS, MD.).** (DIRECTORY OF COUNTY OFFICIALS.). **Added/Corp** Maryland Association of Counties. (19??)-. Directory. English. Maryland Association of Counties, 169 Conduit Street, Annapolis MD 21401. **LC** JS451.M37; D57. **DD** 352/.0073.

US
**DIRECTORY OF CZECHOSLOVAK OFFICIALS / DIRECTORATE OF INTELLIGENCE.** (May 1985)-. Directory. English. Document Expediting Project, Exchange and Gift Division, Library of Congress, Photoduplication Service, Washington DC 20540. **Tel** (202)287-9527. **LC** JN2217; .D57. **DD** 354.437002. available on microfiche (Vols. for 1986- distributed to depository libraries). ***Continues*** *Directory of Officials of the Czechoslovak Socialist Republic.*

US
**DIRECTORY OF DATA FILES.** **Main/Corp** United States. Bureau of the Census. Oct. 1979-. Government Publication. English. ir. US Department of Commerce / Bureau of the Census, Data User Services Division, Customer Services, Washington DC 20233-0800. **Tel** (301)763-4100. **(Subscription address:** Superintendent of Documents, US Government Printing Office, Washington DC 20402.**)**

US/1058-0158
**DIRECTORY OF DCAA OFFICES.** [Dir. DCAA off.]. **Main/Corp** United States. Defense Contract Audit Agency. **VAT** Directory of Defense Contract Audit Agency Offices. (19??)-. Directory. English. sa. $9.00 domestic; $11.25 other. Superintendent of Documents, US Government Printing Office, Washington DC 20402. **Tel** (202)275-3328, FAX (202)786-2377. **LC** UC267; .U596a. **DD** 355.6/3/02573.
**Desc:** Contains directory and telephone information for Defense Contract Audit Agency headquarters and regional offices, and the Defense Contract Audit Institute.

US/0070-5586
**DIRECTORY OF GOVERNMENT AGENCIES SAFEGUARDING CONSUMER AND ENVIRONMENT.** 1st- Ed.; 1968-. Directory. English. an. Serina Press, 70 Kennedy Street, Alexandria VA 22305. **LC** HC110.C6; D5. **DD** 339.4/7/02573. **NLM** WA 22 AA1 D3.

UA
**DIRECTORY OF GOVERNMENT AND PUBLIC SECTOR IN A.R.E.** Directory. English. Arab Modern House for Foreign Trade, 11 Abd El Khalek Tharwat Street, Cairo Egypt. **LC** HF3886; .A254. **DD** 354.6209/2/025.

US/0736-6183
**DIRECTORY OF GOVERNMENT OFFICIALS. FEDERAL, STATE, COUNTY, CITY, TOWNSHIP AND SPECIAL DISTRICT OFFICIALS IN NORTH DAKOTA.** (DIRECTORY OF GOVERNMENT OFFICIALS ... FEDERAL, STATE, COUNTY, CITY, TOWNSHIP AND SPECIAL DISTRICT OFFICIALS IN NORTH DAKOTA.). **Added/Corp** University of North Dakota. Bureau of Governmental Affairs. (1982)-. Directory. English. an. $15.00. Bureau of Governmental Affairs, University of North Dakota, Box 7176, Grand Forks ND 58202. **Tel** (701)777-3041. **ED** Susan Carlson. **LC** JK6430; .D57. **DD** 353.9784002. **Circ:** 1,100. ***Continues*** *Federal, State, County, City and Special District Officials in North Dakota.*
**Desc:** Addresses, telephone numbers, etc. for all elected and appointed officials in North Dakota.

CN/0084-9944
**DIRECTORY OF GOVERNMENTS IN METROPOLITAN TORONTO.** 1970/71-. Directory. English. be. Bureau of Municipal Research, Suite 406, 4 Richmond Street East, Toronto Ontario M5C 1M6 Canada. **DD** 352.0713/541. ***Supersedes*** *Directory of Municipal Governments.*

●US/1058-2657
**DIRECTORY OF ILLINOIS POLITICAL LEADERS.** [Dir. Ill. polit. lead.]. **Added/Corp** Social Engineering Associates. (1991-1993)-. Directory. English. Social Engineers Association, 343 South Dearborn Street, Chicago IL 60604. **LC** IN PROCESS. **DD** 324.

CN/0845-096X
**DIRECTORY OF INSTITUTIONS - ONTARIO. FREEDOM OF INFORMATION AND PRIVACY BRANCH.** (DIRECTORY OF INSTITUTIONS.). [Dir. inst. - Ont., Freedom Inf. Priv. Branch]. **Added/Corp** Ontario. Freedom of Information and Privacy Branch. (1991)-. Directory. English. **DD** 354.7130081/9. ***Continues in part*** *Directory of institutions (Ontario. Management Board of Cabinet)., 1187-2144.*

US/0363-1842
**DIRECTORY OF IOWA MUNICIPALITIES.** **Added/Corp** League of Iowa Municipalities. (19??)-. English. an. $15.00 (two years). League of Iowa Municipalities, 317 6th Avenue, Suite 1400, Des Moines IA 50309. **Tel** (515)244-7282. **LC** JS451.I85; D56. **DD** 352/.008/025777. **Bk Rev. Ad Acc. Circ:** 3,000.
**Desc:** A directory of elected and appointed officials in Iowa's municipalities.

US/0196-7681
**DIRECTORY OF KANSAS PUBLIC OFFICIALS.** [Dir. Kans. public off.]. **Added/Corp** League of Kansas Municipalities. (19??)-. English. an. League of Kansas Municipalities, 112 West 7th Street, Topeka KS 66603. **Tel** (913)354-9565, FAX (913)354-4186. **ED** Wendy A. Murray. **LC** JK6830; .K2. **DD** 353.9/781/002. **Ad Acc.** ***Continues*** *Kansas Directory of Public Officials.*

US/1051-4988
**DIRECTORY OF LEGISLATIVE LEADERS.** [Dir. legis. lead.]. **Added/Corp** National Conference of State Legislatures. (1986)-. Directory. English. an. $15.00. National Conference of State Legislatures, 1560 Broadway, Suite 700, Denver CO 80202. **Tel** (303)830-2054, FAX (303)863-8003. **LC** JK2679; .D57. **DD** 328.3/3/02573.
**Desc:** Information on state leaders is at your fingertips with this pocket-sized directory. Contains the names of state presiding officers, majority and minority leaders and key staff members. Lists both capitol and district addresses, telephone and fax numbers, as well as interim home or business telephone numbers.

US
**DIRECTORY OF LEGISLATIVE LOBBYISTS / STATE OF KANSAS.** **VFOAT** Legislative Lobbyists. 1980-. Directory. English. Three times a year. Free. Secretary of State / Kansas, Capitol Building/2nd Floor, Topeka KS 66612. **Tel** (913)296-2236. **LC** JK6874.5; .D57. **DD** 328.781/078/025. ***Continues*** *Kansas Legislative Lobbyists.*
**Desc:** Listing of registered lobbyists in the state of Kansas.

US/0415-9675
**DIRECTORY OF MEMBERS, NEW YORK STATE LEGISLATURE, AND MEMBERS OF CONGRESS.** (19??)-. Directory. English. an. NY State Legislature, RD Box 196 E, Albany NY 12203. **LC** JK3430; .D57. **DD** 328.747/0922.

US/0148-7442
**DIRECTORY OF MICHIGAN MUNICIPAL OFFICIALS.** (DIRECTORY OF MICHIGAN MUNICIPAL OFFICIALS, WITH SELECTED LISTING OF STATE & FEDERAL OFFICES.). **Added/Corp** Michigan Municipal League. (19??)-. Directory. English. Ten times a year. $70.00. Michigan Municipal League, PO Box 1487, Ann Arbor MI 48106. **Tel** (313)662-3246. **ED** Judy Campbell. **LC** JS303.M5; M52 subser. **DD** 352/.005/209774. Index available (Bound in December issue). cum. index. **Bk Rev**, (Qty: 20). **Ad Acc. Circ:** 10,000 (ctrl). ***Continues*** *Annual Directory of Michigan Municipal Officials.*
**Desc:** Listing of local government officials.

US/0890-1651
**DIRECTORY OF MINNESOTA CITY OFFICIALS.** [Dir. Minn. city off.]. **Added/Corp** League of Minnesota Cities. **VFOAT** Directory of Minnesota Municipal Officials. (1985)-. Directory. English. Twelve times a year. $20.00. League of Minnesota Cities, 3490 Lexington Avenue North, St Paul MN 55126. **Tel** (612)227-5600, FAX (612)490-0072. **ED** Jean Mehle Goad. **LC** JS451.M65; L35. **DD** 352. Index available (Bound in December issue). **Ad Acc. Circ:** 10,000. ***Continues*** *Directory of Minnesota Municipal Officials.*
**Desc:** List of city officials, city hall addresses and phone numbers, congressional and legislative districts, city hall hours, and council meeting dates and times.

# Public Administration

**US/0540-3820**
**DIRECTORY OF MISSISSIPPI ELECTIVE OFFICIALS.** Directory. English. ir. Secretary of State Mississippi, PO Box 136, Jackson MS 39205. **Tel** (601)359-1350. **LC** JK4630; .A277. **DD** 353.97620022.
**Desc:** A directory of Mississippi state, state districts, county and county districts officials.

**US**
**DIRECTORY OF MISSOURI MUNICIPAL OFFICIALS.** (19??)-. Directory. English. an. $30.00 (prepaid), $35.00 (billed). Missouri Municipal League, 1727 Southridge Drive, Jefferson City MO 65109. **Tel** (314)635-9134.

**US**
**DIRECTORY OF MUNICIPAL AND COUNTY OFFICIALS IN COLORADO / COLORADO MUNICIPAL LEAGUE.** **Added/Corp** Colorado Municipal League. (19??)-. English. an. $35.00. Colorado Municipal League, 1660 Lincoln, Suite 2100, Denver CO 80264. **Tel** (303)831-6411. **Continues** Directory: Municipal and County Officials in Colorado.

**US/0361-6924**
**DIRECTORY OF MUNICIPAL AUTHORITIES IN PENNSYLVANIA.** Directory. English. an. Pennsylvania Department of Community Affairs, Forum Building/Room 311, Harrisburg PA 17120. **LC** HD4606.P4; D57. **DD** 338.7/4. **Continues** Pennsylvania Municipal Authorities Directory.

**US**
**DIRECTORY OF MUNICIPAL OFFICIALS OF NEW MEXICO.** **Added/Corp** New Mexico Municipal League. (19??)-. Directory. English. an (May). $25.00. New Mexico Municipal League, c/o Anita Martinez, PO Box 846, Santa Fe NM 87501. **Tel** (505)982-5573 **LC** JS451.N67; D57. **DD** 352/.008/09789. **Circ:** 1,000.
**Desc:** Lists elected and appointed officials of all incorporated municipalities plus addresses, phone numbers, population, taxes levied, municipal services, and budgeted general fund expenditures.

**US**
**DIRECTORY OF NEW JERSEY MAYORS.** **Added/Corp** New Jersey. Dept. of Community Affairs. (198?)-. Directory. English. (includes one update). New Jersey Department of Community Affairs, Cn 805 Bureau Const. Code Enforcer, Trenton NJ 08625. **Tel** (609)530-8792. **ED** Karen M Schwacha. **LC** JS451.N55; D57. **Circ:** 2,500. **Continues** Directory of Mayors.
**Desc:** A listing of New Jersey mayors.

**US/0095-0920**
**DIRECTORY OF OKLAHOMA.** 1973-. Directory. English. be. $10.00 (add $1.00 for postage). State Library / Oklahoma, 200 Northeast 18th, Oklahoma City OK 73105. **Tel** (405)521-2502. **ED** Patricia Lester. **LC** JK7192; .A36. **DD** 353.9/766/002. Index available. **Ad Acc**. **Circ:** 8,500. available in hardback. **Continues** Directory and Manual of the State ofc Oklahoma.
**Desc:** Contains pictures of senators, house members, judiciary, US congressmen, state emblems, historic sites; also counties, agriculture, election results, state agencies, history, populations, income, maps and general facts.

**US/0099-197X**
**DIRECTORY OF OKLAHOMA'S CITY AND TOWN OFFICIALS.** Directory. English. an. $10.00. Oklahoma Municipa League, 201 NE 23rd Street, Oklahoma City OK 73105. **Tel** (405)528-7560. **LC** JS451.O57; D57. **DD** 352/.008/025766. **Ad Acc**.

**CN/0849-391X**
**DIRECTORY OF OMBUDSMEN AND INTERNATIONAL OMBUDSMAN OFFICES.** [Dir. ombudsmen int. ombudsman off.]. **Added/Corp** International Ombudsman Institute. (Oct. 1990)-. Directory. English. an. International Ombudsman Institute, University of Alberta / Law, Edmonton Alberta T6G 2H5 Canada. **Tel** (403)492-3196. **DD** 351.9/1. **Continues** Directory of Ombudsmen and Listing of International Ombudsman Offices., 0843-1035.

**US**
**DIRECTORY OF PERMITS, STATE OF ALASKA.** **Main/Corp** Alaska. Dept. of Commerce and Economic Development. **VFOAT** Directory of Permits. 1978-. Directory. English. an. $35.00. Book Publishing Company, 201 Westlake Avenue North, Seattle WA 98109. **Tel** (206)343-5700. Each issue contains an index to its own contents (no volume index)--loose.
**Desc:** Inventories information regarding certifications, permits, approvals, plan reviews, licenses and similar government authorizations required for an activity or project.

**US/1057-0578**
**DIRECTORY OF POLITICAL PERIODICALS.** *Title Change.* See Newspapers.

**US**
**DIRECTORY OF REGIONAL COUNCILS IN THE UNITED STATES.** (1989)-. Directory. English. National Association of Regional Councils, 1700 K Street NW, Washington DC 20006. **Tel** (202)457-0710, FAX (202)296-9352. **Continues** Directory of Regional Councils (Washington, D.C. : 1986).

**US**
**DIRECTORY OF SOUTH DAKOTA STATE LICENSES, PERMITS, FEES, AND INFORMATION.** **Added/Corp** South Dakota. Office of the Secretary of State. **VFOAT** Licensing Book; Directory of South Dakota State Licenses, Permits, and Fees; Secretary of State Licensing Book. (1991)-. Directory. English. **LC** HD3630.U7; D625. **DD** 353.9783008.

**US/0742-2830**
**DIRECTORY OF SOVIET OFFICIALS. NATIONAL ORGANIZATIONS.** (DIRECTORY OF SOVIET OFFICIALS. NATIONAL ORGANIZATIONS / NATIONAL FOREIGN ASSESSMENT CENTER.). [Dir. Sov. off., Natl. org.]. **VFOAT** National Organizations. May 1981-. Directory. English. Document Expediting Project, Exchange and Gift Division, Library of Congress, Photoduplication Service, Washington DC 20540. **Tel** (202)287-9527. **LC** JN6521; .D572. **DD** 354.47002. available on microfiche (Vols. for (Aug. 1983-) distributed to depository libraries). **Continues in part** Directory of Soviet Officials, 0734-810X.

**US/0743-5371**
**DIRECTORY OF SOVIET OFFICIALS. REPUBLIC ORGANIZATIONS.** (DIRECTORY OF SOVIET OFFICIALS. REPUBLIC ORGANIZATIONS / NATIONAL FOREIGN ASSESSMENT CENTER.). [Dir. Sov. off., Repub. organ.]. **VFOAT** Republic Organizations. Oct. 1981-. Directory. English. DOCEX Project, Exchange and Gift Division, Library of Congress, Washington DC 20540. **Tel** (202)287-9527. **LC** JN6521; .D573. **DD** 354.47002. **Continues in part** Directory of Soviet Officials, 0734-810X.

**US**
**DIRECTORY OF SOVIET OFFICIALS. SCIENCE AND EDUCATION / DIRECTORATE OF INTELLIGENCE.** **VFOAT** Science and Education. Directory. English. an. Document Expediting Project, Exchange and Gift Division, Library of Congress, Photoduplication Service, Washington DC 20540. **Tel** (202)287-9527. **LC** Q60; .D57. **DD** 506/.047. **NLM** Q 60; D598. **Continues in part** Directory of Soviet Officials, 0734-810X.

**US**
**DIRECTORY OF STATE AGENCIES, COUNCILS OF GOVERNMENTS, UNIVERSITIES AND COLLEGES, TECHNICAL COLLEGES, AND ASSOCIATIONS, A.** **Added/Corp** South Carolina Advisory Commission on Intergovernmental Relations. **VFOAT** Local Government Resources. (1981)-. English. an. South Carolina Advisory Commission on Intergovernmental Relations, 1205 Pendelton Street/Room 474, Columbia SC 29201. **LC** JK4230; .D57. **DD** 353.975704/025.

●**US/1062-0133**
**DIRECTORY OF STATE BAR PUBLIC SERVICE ACTIVITIES AND PROGRAMS.** [Dir. state bar public serv. act. programs]. **Added/Corp** American Bar Association. Public Services Division. **VFOAT** Directory. (1992). English. ir. $20.00. American Bar Association, 750 North Lake Shore Drive, Chicago IL 60611. **Tel** (312)988-5522, (312)988-5241, FAX (312)988-5528, telex 270593. **LC** KF299.P8; D57. **DD** 344.73/03258/025; 347.3043258025.

**US/0440-4947**
**DIRECTORY OF STATE, COUNTY, AND FEDERAL OFFICIALS.** **Added/Corp** Hawaii. Legislature. Legislative Reference Bureau. (1973)-. English. an (March). $2.00. Legislative Reference Bureau - Hawaii, State Capitol, Honolulu HI 96813. **Tel** (800)587-0690, FAX (808)587-0699. **LC** JK9330; .H38a. **DD** 353.9/969/002. **Circ:** 1,300. **Continues** Hawaii. University, Honolulu. Legislative Reference Bureau. Directory of State, County, Federal Officials.
**Desc:** Names, titles, addresses, and telephone numbers of officials in the state, county and federal governments in Hawaii.

**US/1042-4172**
**DIRECTORY OF STATE COURT CLERKS AND COUNTY COURTHOUSES.** [Dir. state court clerks cty. courth.]. (1990)-. Directory. English. an. $69.50 US (except Washington DC, Canada & Mexico); $73.40 (Washington DC, includes 6% sales tax); $82.50 (others). Want Publishing Company, 1511 K Street Northwest, Suite 635, Washington DC 20005. **Tel** (202)783-1887, FAX (202)393-5106. **LC** KF8700.A19; D574. **DD** 347.73/02/025. [CCC].
**Desc:** DIRECTORY OF STATE COURT CLERKS & COUNTY COURTHOUSES allows you easy access to a treasure-trove of vital information, including court documents, land title and property records, and other important records maintained by appellate and trial courts and county courthouses, nationwide.

**US**
**DIRECTORY OF STATE INFORMATION POLICY ORGANIZATIONS / THE COUNCIL OF STATE GOVERNMENTS, [ORGANIZATIONAL PLANNING AND COORDINATING COMMITTEE (OPACC), SUBCOMMITTEE ON INFORMATION POLICY].** **Main/Corp** Council of State Governments. Organizational Planning and Coordinating Committee. Subcommittee on Information Policy. (1991)-. Directory. English. ir. $15.00. Council of State Governments, PO Box 11910, Iron Works Pike, Lexington KY 40578-1910. **Tel** (800)800-1910, (606)231-1850. **LC** Z674.5.U5; C68a. **DD** 351.819/025. **Continues** Council of State Governments. Organizational Planning and Coordinating Committee. Subcommittee on Information Policy. Directory of State Information Resource Commissions, Committees, and Advisory Groups.

**US/0160-0273**
**DIRECTORY OF TENNESSEE COUNTY OFFICIALS.** Sept. 1974-. Directory. English. an. University of Tennessee / 580 Capitol Hill Building, Seventh and Union, Nashville TN 37219. **LC** JS451.T35; D57. **DD** 352/.005/20968. **Continues** Directory, Tennessee County Officials.

**SG/0376-8627**
**DIRECTORY OF THE REPUBLIC OF SENEGAL.** Directory. French. American Embassy / Senegal, Republic of Senegal, Dakar Senegal. **LC** JQ3396.A4; D56. **DD** 916.63/03/5025.

**US/0098-1109**
**DIRECTORY OF U.S. GOVERNMENT AUDIOVISUAL PERSONNEL.** **Added/Corp** National Audiovisual Center. **VFOAT** U.S. Government Audiovisual Personnel. **VAT** Directory of United States Government Audiovisual Personnel. (1970)-. Directory. English. ir. Free. National Audiovisual Center, 8700 Edgeworth Drive, Capitol Heights MD 20743. **Tel** (301)763-1896, (800)788-6282. **LC** JK849; .A24. **DD** 353.008/1. **NLM** JK 849.A24 DI517.

**US/0250-6211**
**DIRECTORY / ORGANIZATION OF AMERICAN STATES.** **Main/Corp** Organization of American States. **VFOAT** OAS Directory of Missions and Heads of State, Government and Senior Government Officials. (Nov. 1963)-. English. ir. $10.00. Organization of American States, 19th Street & Constitution Avenue NW, Suite 300, Washington DC 20006. **Tel** (202)458-6256. **LC** F1402; .A167. **Continues** Organization of American States. Directory of Delegations.

**US**
**DIRECTORY : PROGRAMS IN PUBLIC AFFAIRS AND ADMINISTRATION.** **VFOAT** NASPAA Directory. 1978-. Directory. English. be. $12.50. National Association of Schools of Public Affairs and Administration, 1120 G Street NW/Suite 520, Washington DC 20005. **Tel** (202)628-8965, telex 4972105 NASPAA DC. **ED** Alfred M Zuck. **LC** JF1338.A2; N28A. **DD** 350/.0007/1173. **Continues** Graduate Programs in Public Affairs and Public Administration, 0272-7498.
**Desc:** Directory provides a listing of public affairs and administration programs which are members of the National Association of Schools of Public Affairs and Administration and the degrees offered by these programs.

**IT/0393-1315**
**DIRITTO PROCESSUALE AMMINISTRATIVO.** See Law.

**US**
**DISCIPLINE & GRIEVANCES FOR SUPERVISORS, LOCAL, STATE, AND FEDERAL GOVERNMENT.** **VFOAT** Discipline & Grievances. (198?)-. Periodical. English. mo. $91.92 (US); $111.36 (Canada) (renewals only). Bureau of Business Practice, 24 Rope Ferry Road, Waterford CT 06386. **Tel** (800)243-0876, (203)442-4365, (800)876-9105, FAX (203)443-1123. **Continues** Discipline & Grievance Report.

**FR/0396-5988**
**DISCOURS ET DECLARATIONS DU PRESIDENT DE LA REPUBLIQUE FRANCAISE.** Periodical. French. mo. Documentation Francaise, 29 Quai Voltaire, 75344 Paris Cedex 7 France. **Tel** 011 33 1 40157000, FAX 011 33 1 40157230, telex 204 826 DOCFRAN.

RW
**DISCOURS ET ENTRETIENS - PRESIDENCE DE LA REPUBLIQUE.** **Main/Corp** Rwanda. Presidence. Multiple languages (French and Ruanda). B P 15, Kigali Rwanda. **LC** J816M; .N155A. **DD** 354/.67/571035.

IT
**DISEGNO DI LEGGE.** **Main/Corp** Italy. Parlamento. Senato. Italian. Libreria del Senato Repubblica, Via del Teatro Valle 37, 00186 Rome Italy. **Tel** 011 39 67062505. **LC** J388; .J55. **DD** 342.45/00262.

US/0748-1179
**DISTRICT COUNCIL JOURNAL.** (DISTRICT COUNCIL JOURNAL : AN INDEPENDENT MONTHLY NEWS REPORT OF D.C. GOVERNMENT LEGISLATIVE ACTIVITY.). V. 1, No. 1 (May 1983)-. English. mo. $53.00. Olduvai Publishing, c/o S. Jordan, 611 Pennsylvania Avenue, Suite 243, Washington DC 20003. **Tel** (202)362-2340. **ED** Tom Chorlton. **LC** JK2701; .D57. **DD** 328.753/005. **Bk Rev. Ad Acc. Circ:** 400 (ctrl).
**Desc:** Report on legislative activity of Council of the District of Columbia.

UK/0306-3240
**DISTRICT COUNCILS REVIEW.** **Added/Corp** Rural District Councils Association. Association of District Councils. Vol. 1 (1972)-. Periodical. English. bm (6 issues). £7.50 UK; £10.00 other. Association of District Councils, 26 Chapter Street, London SW1P 4ND England. **Tel** 011 44 71 233 6868.

US/0419-439X
**DISTRICT OF COLUMBIA REGISTER.** **Main/Corp** District of Columbia. Board of Commissioners. (July 19, 1954)-. English. wk. $100.00. DC Treasurer, Room 114/District Building, 14th East Street NW, Washington DC 20004. **Tel** (202)727-5090.

CN/0824-4316
**DOCUMENT DE TRAVAIL - UNIVERSITE D'OTTAWA. FACULTE D'ADMINISTRATION.** **See** Business.

SP/0012-4494
**DOCUMENTACION ADMINISTRATIVA.** [Doc. adm.]. No. 1 (Jan. 1958)-. Periodical. Spanish. qt. Instituto Nacional de Administracion Publica, Rev. Doc. Adm., Jose Maranon 12, 28010 Madrid Spain. **Tel** 011 31 1 44617000. **LC** JA26; .D6. cum. index.
**Ind/Abst** Int. Labour Doc.; Stat. Theory Method Abstr. (1968).

II/0377-7081
**DOCUMENTATION IN PUBLIC ADMINISTRATION.** **Added/Corp** Indian Institute of Public Administration. Vol. 1 (Jan/Mar 1973)-. Periodical. English. qt. $20.00. DIR-Indian Institute of Public Administration, Indraprastha Estate Ring Road, New Delhi 110002 India. **Tel** 011 91 11 3317309. **(Subscription address:** Prints India, 11 Darya Ganj, New Delhi, 110002 India, (Phone: 011 91 11 3268645)) **ED** T. N. Chaturvedi and M. C. Ragavan. **LC** Z7164.A2; D6. **DD** 016.35. **Ad Acc.** ctrl circ.

CN/0712-0451
**DOCUMENTATION TECHNIQUE - COMMISSION DE LA FONCTION PUBLIQUE DU QUEBEC.** (DOCUMENTATION TECHNIQUE.). [Doc. tech. - Comm. fonct. publique Que.]. No. 1, (April 1981)-. Monographic series. French. Price varies per volume. E D F D Etudes et Recherches, 3 rue de Messine, Paris 8E France. **DD** 351.1/005.

LU/0254-1475
**DOCUMENTS - COMMISSION OF THE EUROPEAN COMMUNITIES.** (DOCUMENTS [MICROFORM].). [Doc. - Comm. Eur. Communities]. **Main/Corp** Commission of the European Communities. **VFOAT** COM. (1967)-. Periodical. English. ir. £1615.00. Office for Official Publications of the European Communities, 2 Rue Mercier, 2985 Luxembourg Luxembourg. **Tel** 011 352 499281, FAX 011 352 488573.
**Desc:** Working documents of the European Community (proposals for legislation, broad policy documents and reports on the implementation of EC policy).
**Ind/Abst** Leis. Recreat. Tour. Abstr.; Postharvest News Inf.; Soyabean Abstr.

UK
**DOCUMENTS ON BRITISH POLICY OVERSEAS. SERIES 1.** **Added/Corp** Great Britain. Foreign and Commonwealth Office. (1984)-. Monographic series. English. ir. Price varies per volume. Her Majesty's Stationery Office, 51 Nine Elms Lane, London SW8 5DR England. **Tel** 011 44 71 873 8459, 011 44 71 873 8499, FAX 011 44 71 873 8499, 011 44 71 873 8456, telex 297138. **(Subscription address:** PO Box 276, Public Centre, London SW8 5DT England; telephone: 011 44 71 873 8456**)**

UK/0070-7007
**DOD'S PARLIAMENTARY COMPANION.** (1865)-. English. an (January). £70.00 UK; £80.00 other. Dods Parliamentary Companion, Hurst Green, East Sussex TN19 7PX England. **Tel** 011 44 71 828 7256 580 87264, FAX 011 44 71 828 7269. **ED** Michael Bedford. **LC** JN500; .D7. **[CCC]. Circ:** 5,500. available on microfilm and microfiche from University Microfilms International (UMI). ***Continues** Parliamentary Companion.*
**Desc:** Contains photos and biographies of all 1,854 Lord and members of Parliament in the United Kingdom. It also contains details of all senior officials in government. Eight hundred pages, 250,000 facts and figures.

US
**DOE TELEPHONE DIRECTORY.** **Main/Corp** United States. Dept. of Energy. **VAT** Department of Energy Telephone Directory. Oct. 1977-. Government Publication. English. qt. US Department of Energy, 1000 Independence Avenue SW, Washington DC 20585. **Tel** (202)586-5000, FAX (202)586-4073.

FR/0337-4084
**DOSSIERS DE L'OUTRE-MER : BULLETIN D'INFORMATION DU CENADDOM, LES.** **See** Economics-Economic History, Conditions.

FR/1152-5096
**DOSSIERS ET DEBATS - INSTITUT INTERNATIONAL D'ADMINISTRATION PUBLIQUE.** (DOSSIERS ET DEBATS). [Doss. debats - Inst. int. adm. publique]. (1992)-. Monographic series. French. an. 70.00F. Institut International d'Administration Publique, 2 avenue de l'Observatoire, 75272 Paris Cedex 06 France. **Tel** 44 41 86 15, FAX 44 41 86 19, telex 270229 F. **UDC** 35. ***Continues** Administration.*

FR
**DROIT ADMINISTRATIF.** Periodical. French.
**Desc:** Fundamental legal data on administrative action. Administrative organization. Forms of administrative action, as related to government.

US/8755-3899
**DUKE POLICY NEWS.** [Duke policy news]. Vol. 9, No. 1 (Oct. 1980)-. Periodical. English. qt. Institute of Policy Science and Public Affairs, Duke University, 4875 Duke Station, Durham NC 27706. **Tel** (919)684-6612. **ED** Dee Reid. **DD** 350. **Circ:** 1,500. ***Continues** Policy News.*

CN/0713-8024
**ECHO MUNICIPAL.** (L'ECHO MUNICIPAL / MUNICIPALITE DE L'ANSE ST-JEAN.). [Echo munic.]. Vol. 1, No 2 (Jan. 1981)-. Periodical. French. mo. Free. Municipalite de l'Anse St-Jean, Saint-Jean Quebec G0V 1J0 Canada. **Tel** (418)272-2633. **DD** 352.0714/16. **Circ:** 450 (ctrl). ***Continues** Journal Municipal (Anse Saint-Jean, Quebec), 0713-8032.*

US/1062-645X
**EDI MONTHLY REPORT.** [EDI mon. rep.]. **Added/Corp** Congressional Information Bureau, Inc. **VAT** Electronic Data Interchange Monthly Report. (1988)-. Periodical. English. mo. $250.00 North America, $307.00 other. Congressional Information Bureau, 3030 Clarendon Boulevard, Suite 202, Arlington VA 22201. **Tel** (703)516-4801. **DD** 338. **[CCC]. Ad Acc. Circ:** 1,000 (ctrl).
**Desc:** A factual non-analytical publication reporting on major developments in Global EPI with emphasis on government and congressional acts within the industry.

FR
**EFFECTIFS DES COLLECTIVITES TERRITORIALES AU 31 DECEMBRE, LES.** 1983-. French. an. 60.00F. Institut National de Statistique / Belgium, rue de Louvain, 44, Centre Albert, 8e Etage, 1000 Brussels Belgium. **Tel** 011 32 2 5486211. **LC** JS4888; .E35.

GW
**EINWOHNER-ADRESSBUCH FREIBURG IM BREISGAU.** **VFOAT** Adressbuch Freiberg. (19??)-. German. Rombach, PO Box 1349, 7800 Freiburg Germany. **LC** DD901.F87; A25. **DD** 943/.46. ***Continues** Einwohner-Adressbuch der Stadt Freiberg im Breisgau.*

II
**ELECTION ARCHIVES AND INTERNATIONAL POLITICS.** **VFOAT** International Politics. No. 139-140 (Mar./Apr. 1988)-. Periodical. English. bm. $100.00. **(Subscription address:** Prints India, 11 Darya Ganj, New Delhi, 110002 India, (Phone: 011 91 11 3268645)) ***Continues** Election Archives (New Delhi, India : 1985).*

US
**ELECTION FINANCING FACT BOOK.** **Added/Corp** Washington (State). Public Disclosure Commission. (19??)-. English. $6.00 (add $1.50 for postage). Public Disclosure Commission, 403 Evergreen Plaza, Mail Stop FJ-42, Olympia WA 98504. **ED** Paul Gillie. Index available. **Circ:** 1,000 (ctrl).
**Desc:** Provides detailed information concerning the campaign contributions and expenditures of candidates for office in Washington State. Historical comparisons are also included.

US/0362-6903
**ELECTION RESULTS DATABOOK FOR CUYAHOGA COUNTY.** **Main/Corp** Governmental Research Institute, Cleveland. **VFOAT** Databook, Cuyahoga County Election Results. 1972/74-. English. $3.00. Governmental Research Institute, 502 Ten-Ten Euclid Building, Cleveland OH 44115. **LC** JS451.O39; C84A. **DD** 329/.023/7713104.

US/0363-2571
**ELECTIVE AND APPOINTIVE STATE OFFICERS, STATE OF MICHIGAN.** English. be. Free. Department of Management and Budget, Office Services Division/Publications, 7461 Crowner Drive, Lansing MI 48837. **LC** JK5830; .E44. **DD** 353.9/774/002. **Circ:** 2,500.
**Desc:** A listing of elected and appointed officers in the state of michigan.

UK/0261-3794
**ELECTORAL STUDIES.** [Elect. stud.]. Vol. 1, No. 1 (April 1982)-. Periodical. English. qt. $291.00 The Americas; £195.00 other. Butterworth Heinemann Publishers, Linacre House, Jordan Hill, Oxford OX2 8DP England. **Tel** 011 44 865 310366. **(Subscription address:** Elsevier Science Ltd. Oxford Fulfillment Centre, PO Box 800, Kidlington, Oxford OX5 1DX United Kingdom.**) ED** David Butler (editor's address: Fellow of Nuffield College, Oxford). **LC** JF1001; .E43. **DD** 342/.05. **[CCC].** Index available. **Ad Acc. Pr Rev.** available on microfilm and microfiche from University Microfilms International (UMI). Documents available from The Genuine Article.
**Desc:** An international journal serving the rapidly growing number of scholars concerned with voting, the central act in the democratic process. Political scientists, lawyers, sociologists, game theorists, economists, media students, contemporary historians, and geographers have, over the last forty years focused increasing attention on what causes a nation's voters to act as they do, and on the consequences of their voting.
**Ind/Abst** ABC POL SCI; Am. Hist. Life (1983-); Curr. Contents Soc. Behav. Sci.; Geogr. Abstr. Human Geogr.; Int. Bibliogr. Sociol.; Int. Dev. Abstr.; Int. Polit. Sci. Abstr.; Middle East Abstr. Index; PAIS Int. Print; Res. Alert [Full Cov.]; Soc. Sci. Cit. Index [Full Cov.].

●CN/1194-3750
**ELECTRONIC DISSEMINATION PARTNERSHIPS.** [Electron. dissem. partnersh.]. **Added/Corp** Interdepartmental Working Group on Database Industry Support (Canada). **VFOAT** Partnerships; ED Partnerships. Vol. 1, No. 1 (June 1992)-. Periodical. English. Four times a year (Mar., June, Sept., Dec.). 149.00Can$ Canada; 159.00Can$ US; 179.00Can$ others. Sysnovators Ltd., 17 Taunton Place, Gloucester Ontario K1J 7J7 Canada. **Tel** (613)746-5150, FAX (613)746-9757. **ED** Peter Brandon (phone: (613)746-5150). **DD** 354.710081.

US/1057-834X
**ELECTRONIC PUBLIC INFORMATION NEWSLETTER.** [Electron. public inf. newsl.]. Vol. 1, No. 1 (Oct. 25, 1991)-. Periodical. English. sm. $249.00 regular subscription, $130.00 (libraries, public interest groups). EPIN Publishing, PO Box 21001, Washington DC 20009. **Tel** (301)365-3621, FAX (301)365-3621. **ED** James McDonough. **DD** 350. Index available. **Bk Rev.**
**Desc:** Reports on federal information policies and practices.

IT
**ELEZIONE DELLA CAMERA DEI DEPUTATI / REPUBBLICA ITALIANA, ISTITUTO CENTRALE DI STATISTICA - MINISTERO DELL'INTERNO.** Italian. L11500. Istituto Nazionale Statistica, GBP SEZ4 Via Cesare Balbo 16, 00184 Rome Italy. **Tel** 011 39 6 46735118. **LC** JN5609; .E38. **DD** 324.945/0927.

CN/0849-3308
**EMO OUTLOOK.** (EMO OUTLOOK : THE MANITOBA EMERGENCY MEASURES ORGANIZATION NEWSLETTER.). [EMO outlook]. **Added/Corp** Manitoba Emergency Measures Organization. **VAT** Emergency Measures Organization Outlook. Issue No. 1, Vol. 5 (Summer 1990)-. Newsletter. English. **DD** 363.3/48/097127. ***Continues** EMO (Bulletin)., 0849-3294.*

US/0747-0711
**EMPIRE STATE REPORT (1982).** (EMPIRE STATE REPORT.). [Emp. State rep.]. **VFOAT** E.S.R. Magazine; ESR Magazine; Empire State Report Magazine. Vol. 8, No. 10 (Mar. 1982)-. Periodical. English. Twelve times a year. $35.00 US; $79.20 others. Empire State Report Inc, 4 Central Avenue, 3rd Floor, Albany NY 12210. **Tel** (518)465-5502. **ED** Joseph Laura. **LC** JK3401; .E465. **DD** 974.7/043. **Ad Acc. Circ:** 10,500 (ctrl). available on microfilm and microfiche from University Microfilms International (UMI).
**Desc:** Offers objective reporting on public policy events and issues regarding state, county and local government, as well as business, labor and finance in the state of New York.
**Ind/Abst** PAIS Int. Print (1991-); Urban Aff. Abstr.

US
**EMPLOYEE BENEFITS IN STATE AND LOCAL GOVERNMENTS.** See Economics-Labor.

US/0898-2139
**EMPLOYERS NEGOTIATING SERVICE.** ***Ceased.*** [Empl. negot. serv.]. **Added/Corp** Employee Futures Research, Inc. (Sept. 1983)-(Oct. 1990). Periodical. English. Twenty times a year. Institute for Negotiations Training, PO Box 385, Port Richey FL 34673. **Tel** (813)847-5000. **ED** Eric Rhodes and Richard Neal. **DD** 350. **Bk Rev. Circ:** 500. ***Continues*** *Educators Negotiating Service, 0046-1571.*
**Desc:** Labor relations information for public agencies.

CN/1180-1271
**ENAP, CARREFOUR UNVERSITAIRE DE L'ADMINISTRATION PUBLIQUE, PLAN DE DEVELOPMENT.** [ENAP carrefour univ. adm. publique plan dev.]. **Main/Corp** Ecole Nationale d'Administration Publique (Quebec). **VAT** Ecole Nationale d'Administration Publique, Carrefour Universitaire de l'Administration Publique, Plan de Developpement. (1990)-. Periodical. French. Free. Secretariat General/Ecole Nationale d'Administration Publique, 945 Avenue Wolfe, Ste Foy Quebec G1V 3J9 Canada. **DD** 350/.00071/1714. ***Continues*** *Plan Triennal de Developpement, 0229-5946.*

IT
**ENCICLOPEDIA PER I COMUNI E GLI ALTRI ENTI LOCALI.** (19??)-. Italian. bm (6 issues). L162000.00 Italy; L182000.00 other. Noccioli, Via E Fermi 24, 50019 Sesto Fiorent Fi Italy. **Tel** 011 39 55 310316.

US/0092-8380
**ENCYCLOPEDIA OF GOVERNMENTAL ADVISORY ORGANIZATIONS.** [Encycl. gov. advis. organ.]. **Added/Corp** Gale Research Company. 1st Ed. Issue No. 1 (July 1973)-. English. ir. $505.00. Gale Research Inc., 835 Penobscot Building, Detroit MI 48226. **Tel** (800)877-GALE, (313)961-2242, FAX (313)961-6083, telex TWX 810-221-7086. **ED** Donna Batten. **LC** JK468.C7; E5. **DD** 353.09/3/025. **NLM** JK 468.C7; E56. cum. index. available on magnetic tape; available on diskette.
**Desc:** Contains over 6,500 entries describing the activities and personnel of groups and committees that function to advise the President and various departments and bureaus of the federal government. Also includes information about White House Conferences and other conferences sponsored by the federal government, groups under contract doing studies for the federal government, and congressional committees doing studies of current topical interest.

US/0147-4294
**END OF YEAR REPORT - NORTHWEST FEDERAL REGIONAL COUNCIL.** (END OF YEAR REPORT.). **Main/Corp** United States. Northwest Federal Regional Council. English. an. Northwest Federal Regional Council, 1321-2D Avenue, Seattle WA 98101. **LC** HT392.5P3; U54A.

US/0147-7587
**END OF YEAR REPORT. REGIONAL PROGRAM PLANS ASSESSMENT.** **Main/Corp** United States. Environmental Protection Agency. Office of Planning and Management. **Added/Corp** United States. Environmental Protection Agency. Office of Planning and Management. Regional program plans assessment. (19??)-. English. an. US Environmental Protection Agency, 401 M Street SW, Washington DC 20460. **Tel** (202)755-9163. **LC** TD171; .U56d. **DD** 353.008/232.

BL
**ENDERECOS DOS SENHORES DEPUTADOS E GUIA TELEFONICO DA CAMARA DOS DEPUTADOS.** **Main/Corp** Brazil. Congresso Nacional. Camara dos Deputados. Diretoria Legislativa. Portuguese. Centro de Documentacao e Informacao Coodenacao de Publicacoes Directoria Legislativa, Palacio do Congresso Nacional, 70.000 Brasilia Brazil. **LC** JL2463; .A4A.

FI
**ENERGIATALOUDELLISEEN KOBJAUSTOIMINTAAN VUONNA ... MYONNETTAVAT AVUSTUKSET.** **Main/Corp** Finland. Asuntohallitus. **VFOAT** Energiataloudelliseen Korjaustoimintaan Myonnettavat Avustukset. Finnish. an. **LC** TJ163.4.F5; F54A.

IT
**ENTI PUBBLICI.** (19??)-. Italian. bm (6 issues). L100000 Italy; L150000 other. Nuova Editrice Spada SNC, Via Quirino Majorana 141, 00152 Rome Italy. **Tel** 011 39 6 5581869, 011 39 6 5593471.

CN/0712-967X
**ENTRE NOUS GENS DE BERNIERES.** (ENTRE NOUS GENS DE BERNIERES : BULLETIN D'INFORMATION DE LA CORPORATION MUNICIPALE DE BERNIERES.). [Entre nous gens Bernieres]. Bulletin. French. Free. Entre Nous, c/o Corporation Municipale de Bernieres, 1250 Chemin de la Coop, Bernieres Quebec G0S 1C0 Canada. **DD** 352.0714/59. ctrl circ.

CN/0710-6211
**ENTREFILETS.** [Entrefilets]. Vol. 1, No. 1 (Oct. 1980)-. Periodical. French. mo. Gouvernement du Quebec, 600 St Amable 4E Etage, Quebec Quebec G1R 4Z1 Canada. **DD** 354.710082/362/09714.

UK/0263-774X
**ENVIRONMENT AND PLANNING. C, GOVERNMENT & POLICY.** [Environ. plann. C]. **VFOAT** Government & Policy; Government and Policy. Vol. 1, No. 1 (Jan. 1983)-. Periodical. English. qt (February, May, August and November). £108.00 UK; $180.00 US. Pion Ltd., 207 Brondesbury Park, London NW2 5JN England. **Tel** 011 44 81 459 0066, FAX 011 44 81 451 6454, telex 94016265 PION G. **ED** R. J. Bennett, H. Wolman and P. Knox. **LC** H97; .E65. **DD** 361.6/05. Index available. **Bk Rev. Ad Acc. Pr Rev.** Documents available from The Genuine Article.
**Desc:** Offers a multidisciplinary international approach to the study of theoretical economic, political, legal, fiscal and social issues related to government activities. Covers economics, politics of policy research, and local government policy.
**Ind/Abst** Acad. Search (Jan. 1993-); Curr. Contents Soc. Behav. Sci.; Geogr. Abstr. Human Geogr.; Int. Bibliogr. Sociol.; Int. Dev. Abstr.; J. Plan. Lit.; PAIS Int. Print (1991-); Res. Alert [Full Cov.]; Sage Public Adm. Abstr.; Sage Urban Stud. Abstr; Soc. Sci. Cit. Index [Full Cov.].

CN/1183-4196
**ENVIROSOURCE (HULL. ENGLISH ED.).** (REFERENCE DIRECTORY TO INFORMATION HOLDINGS.). [Envirosource]. **Main/Corp** Canada. Environment Canada. **VFOAT** Envirosource. 1st Ed. (1991)-. English. be. Environment Canada / Emergencies Science Division, Ottawa Ontario K1A 0H3 Canada. **Tel** (819)998-9622. **DD** 354.710082/32/025.

BE/0250-5754
**EP NEWS.** **Added/Corp** European Parliament. **VFOAT** European Parliament EP News. **VAT** European Parliament News. (July 17/20, 1979)-. Periodical. English. mo. Free on request. European Parliament, PO Box 1601, Luxembourg Luxembourg.
**Ind/Abst** Chem. Bus. NewsBase (1988-).

●CN/1192-5019
**EPICENTRE (CHICOUTIMI).** (L'EPICENTRE.). [Epicentre]. **Added/Corp** Regie Regionale de la Sante et des Services Sociaux du Saguenay-Lac-Saint-Jean (Quebec). Vol. 1, No 1 (1992)-. Periodical. French. mo. **DD** 354.7140084. ***Continues*** *Conseil Regional de la Sante et des Services Sociaux, Saguenay-Lac-Saint-Jean (Quebec) Le Centre., 0381-8152.*

BS
**ESTABLISHMENT REGISTER, INDUSTRIAL CLASS.** **Main/Corp** Botswana. English. an. Botswana Government High Court, PO Box 87, Government Printer, Gaborone Botswana. **LC** JQ2760.A691; B68B. **DD** 354.6883001/03. ***Continues*** *Establishment Register - Botswana.*

SA
**ESTIMATE OF THE ADDITIONAL EXPENDITURE TO BE DEFRAYED FROM REVENUE AND LOAN ACCOUNTS.** See Public Administration-Public Finance and Taxation.

KE/0453-5855
**ESTIMATES OF RECURRENT EXPENDITURE OF THE GOVERNMENT OF KENYA.** (ESTIMATES OF RECURRENT EXPENDITURE OF THE GOVERNMENT OF KENYA FOR THE YEAR ENDING 30TH JUNE ...). **Main/Corp** Kenya. **VFOAT** Estimates-Recurrent Expenditure. (196?)-. English. an. Sh235.00 (add Sh65.00 for postage). Government of Kenya, PO Box 30128, Nairobi Kenya. **Tel** NAIROBI 334075. **LC** HJ81.3; .A34a. **DD** 354.676/200722253/05. ***Continues*** *Kenya. Estimates of Expenditure of the Colony and Protectorate of Kenya for the Year Ending 30th June ... .*

NR
**ESTIMATES OF THE GOVERNMENT OF NIGER STATE OF NIGERIA.** **Main/Corp** Niger State (Nigeria). **VFOAT** Niger State Estimates; Government of Niger State of Nigeria Estimates. (19??)-. English. **LC** HJ81P; .N53a. **DD** 354/.669/5. ***Continues*** *Niger State (Nigeria). Estimates of the Military Government of Niger State of Nigeria.*

NR
**ESTIMATES OF THE MILITARY GOVERNMENT OF NIGER STATE OF NIGERIA / NIGER STATE OF NIGERIA.** ***Title Change.*** **Main/Corp** Niger State (Nigeria). **VFOAT** Approved Estimates of the Military Government of Niger State of Nigeria; Niger State Estimates. (1986)-(198?). English. an. **LC** HJ81P; .N53a. **DD** 354/.669/5. ***Continues*** *Niger State (Nigeria). Estimates of the Government of Niger State of Nigeria.* ***Continued by*** *Niger State (Nigeria). Estimates of the Government of Niger State of Nigeria (1990).*

CN
**ESTIMATES. PART III, AUDITOR GENERAL OF CANADA.** **Main/Corp** Canada. **VFOAT** Budget des Depenses. Partie III, Verificateur General du Canada. (19??)-. English (French). Canada Communication Group Publishers, Order Processing, Ottawa Ontario K1A 0S9 Canada. **Tel** (819)956-4800, (819)956-4802. **LC** HJ9921; .Z31d. **DD** 354.710072/32.

CN
**ESTIMATES. PART III, CANADIAN INTERGOVERNMENTAL CONFERENCE SECRETARIAT.** **Main/Corp** Canada. **VFOAT** Budget des Depenses. Partie III, Secretariat des Conferences Intergouvernementales Canadiennes. (19??)-. English (French). $3.00 Canada; $3.60 other. Canada Communication Group Publishers, Order Processing, Ottawa Ontario K1A 0S9 Canada. **Tel** (819)956-4800, (819)956-4802. **LC** JL27; .C25a. **DD** 354.7108.

CN
**ESTIMATES. PART III, CONSUMER AND CORPORATE AFFAIRS EXPENDITURE PLAN.** **Main/Corp** Canada. **VFOAT** Estimates. Part III, Consumer and Corporate Affairs Canada; Budget des Depenses. Partie III, Consommation et Corporations Plan de Depenses; Budget des Depenses. Partie III, Consommation et Corporations Canada. (19??)-. English (French). $6.00 Canada; $7.20 other. Canada Communication Group Publishers, Order Processing, Ottawa Ontario K1A 0S9 Canada. **Tel** (819)956-4800, (819)956-4802. **LC** HC120.C63; C36a. **DD** 354.9710082/042.

CN
**ESTIMATES. PART III, ECONOMIC COUNCIL OF CANADA.** **Main/Corp** Canada. **VFOAT** Budget des Depenses. Partie III, Conseil Economique du Canada. (19??)-. English (French). $3.00 Canada; $3.60 other. Canada Communication Group Publishers, Order Processing, Ottawa Ontario K1A 0S9 Canada. **Tel** (819)956-4800, (819)956-4802. **LC** HC111; .A15a. **DD** 354.710082.

CN
**ESTIMATES. PART III, NATIONAL RESEARCH COUNCIL CANADA.** **Main/Corp** Canada. **VFOAT** Budget des Depenses. Partie III, Conseil National de Recherches du Canada. (19??)-. English (French). $12.00 Canada; $14.40 other. Canada Communication Group Publishers, Order Processing, Ottawa Ontario K1A 0S9 Canada. **Tel** (819)956-4800, (819)956-4802. **LC** Q180.C2; C35a. **DD** 354.710085/5.

CN
**ESTIMATES. PART III, OFFICE OF THE CHIEF ELECTORAL OFFICER.** **VFOAT** Budget des Depenses. Partie III, Bureau du Directeur General des Elections. 1984-85-. English (French). $6.00. Canadian Government Publishing Center, Supply and Services Canada, Hull Quebec K1A 0S9 Canada. **Tel** (613)990-8116, telex 053-4296. **LC** JL193; .C29A. **DD** 354.71008. ***Continues*** *Canada. Estimates. Part III, Chief Electoral Officer.*

CN
**ESTIMATES. PART III, PRIVY COUNCIL OFFICE.** **Main/Corp** Canada. **VFOAT** Budget des Depenses. Partie III, Bureau du Conseil Prive. (19??)-. English (French). $6.00 Canada; $7.20 other. Canada Communication Group Publishers, Order Processing, Ottawa Ontario K1A 0S9 Canada. **Tel** (819)956-4800, (819)956-4802. **LC** JL1; .C24a. **DD** 354.7107/2.

CN
**ESTIMATES. PART III, PUBLIC SERVICE COMMISSION OF CANADA.** **Main/Corp** Canada. **VFOAT** Budget des Depenses. Partie III, Commission de la Fonction Publique du Canada. (19??)-. English (French). $9.00 Canada; $10.80 other. Canada Communication Group Publishers, Order Processing, Ottawa Ontario K1A 0S9 Canada. **Tel** (819)956-4800, (819)956-4802. **LC** JL105; .C33a. **DD** 354.71006.

CN
**ESTIMATES. PART III, PUBLIC SERVICE STAFF RELATIONS BOARD.** See Economics-Labor.

CN
**ESTIMATES. PART III, SUPPLY AND SERVICES CANADA.** **Main/Corp** Canada. **VFOAT** Budget des Depenses. Partie III, Approvisionnements et Services Canada. (19??)-. English (French). $12.00 Canada; $14.40 other. Canada Communication Group Publishers, Order Processing, Ottawa Ontario K1A 0S9 Canada. **Tel** (819)956-4800, (819)956-4802. **LC** JL186; .C32a. **DD** 354.710071.

●CN
**ESTIMATES. PART III, TRANSPORTATION SAFETY BOARD OF CANADA. EXPENDITURE PLAN.**
**Main/Corp** Canada. **VFOAT** Transportation Safety Board of Canada. Estimates; Budget des Depenses. Partie III, Bureau de la Securite des Transports du Canada. Plan de Depenses. (1992)-. English (French). **LC** HE215.A15; C35d. **DD** 354.710087/5/00289. ***Continues*** *Estimates. Part III, Canadian Transportation Accident and Investigation Safety Board. Expenditure Plan.*

BL
**ESTUDOS LEGISLATIVOS.** V. 1- Jan./June 1973-. Periodical. Portuguese. sa. Centro de Documentacao e Informacao Coodenacao de Publicacoes Directoria Legislativa, Palacio do Congresso Nacional, 70.000 Brasilia Brazil. **LC** JL2454; .E84.

US/1068-3526
**ETHICS & LOBBYING.** **See** Ethics.

US/0423-6378
**EUROPE BRIEF NOTES.** ***Ceased.*** **Main/Corp** Europe, Agence Internationale d'Information pour la Presse. **VFOAT** Brief Notes. (19??)-(Jan. 1994). Periodical. English. wk. Agence Europe SA, 32 Rue Philippe II, BP 428, 2014 Luxembourg Luxembourg. **Tel** 011 352 20032. **(Subscription address:** Agence Europe SA, 10 Boulevard St. Lazare, Bte 13, 1210 Brussels Belgium**)**

US/0095-7607
**EUROPEAN PARLIAMENT DIGEST.**
**Main/Corp** European Parliament. Vol. 1 (1973)-. English. Rowman & Littlefield Publishing Inc., 8705 Bollman Place, Savage MD 20763. **Tel** (301)306-0400. **LC** JN32; .E925. **DD** 341.24/2.

●US/1060-9105
**EUROSCOPE INC.** (EUROSCOPE INC.: A WEEKLY REGISTER OF CURRENT EUROPEAN COMMUNITY (EC) LEGISLATION, OFFICIAL INFORMATION AND NOTICES.). [EuroScope Inc.]. Vol. 1, No.1 (Jan. 4-14, 1992)-. English. wk. $300.00. Euroscope Inc., 46679 Winchester Drive, Sterling VA 22170. **Tel** (703)430-5417. **ED** John Baird. **DD** 341. available in Loose-leaf.
**Desc:** Covers legislation regarding the European Community.

US/0098-6798
**EXAMINATION OF FINANCIAL STATEMENTS OF THE PENNSYLVANIA AVENUE DEVELOPMENT CORPORATION.** **Main/Corp** United States. General Accounting Office. English. Comptroller General of the US, 490 l'Enfant Plaza SW, Washington DC 20219. **LC** HT177.D6; U54A. **DD** 353.0081/8/09753.

US/0272-7013
**EXAMINATION OF FISCAL ... PRESIDENTIAL AND VICE PRESIDENTIAL CERTIFIED EXPENDITURES.** 1979-. English. an. US General Accounting Office / District of Columbia, 441 G Street NW, Room 4528, Washington DC 20548. **Tel** (202)275-2812. **LC** JK779; .U55A. **DD** 353.03/1.

FR
**EXECUTION DES DECISIONS DES JURISDICTIONS ADMINISTRATIVES.**
**Added/Corp** France. Conseil d'Etat. Section du Raport et des Eudes. French. ***Continues*** *Jurisprudence du Conseil d'Etat.*

US
**EXECUTIVE ALERT.** English. bm. $50.00 (1 year). National Center Policy Analysis, 12655 North Central Expressway #720, Dallas TX 75243. **Tel** (214)386-6272.

US
**EXECUTIVE BUDGET POLICY ISSUE PAPERS.** **Main/Corp** Wisconsin. State Budget Office. 1977/79-. English. be. State Budget Office / Wisconsin, 1 West Wilson, Madison WI 53702. **LC** JK6001; .W45B. **DD** 309.1/775/04. ***Continues*** *Executive Budget Policy Papers - Wisconsin.*

US/0741-3424
**EXECUTIVE COMPENSATION SURVEY (PRINCETON, N.J.).** **See** Economics-Labor.

US/0149-502X
**EXECUTIVE PERSONNEL IN THE FEDERAL SERVICE.** **Main/Corp** United States. Bureau of Executive Personnel. 1977-. English. an. $1.15. US Civil Service Commission Bureau of Executive Personnel, Washington DC 20402. **LC** JK723.E9; U53A. **DD** 353.001/005. ***Continues*** *Executive Personnel in the Federal Service, 0149-502X.*

MX
**EXPANSION.** (19??)-. Periodical. Spanish. Twenty-five times a year. $$345.00 US and Canada; $392.00 Europe; $453.00 Asia. Grupo Editorial Expansion, Sinaloa 149 P9, Col Roma, 06700 Mexico DF Mexico. **Tel** 011 52 5 2072066, 2072619, FAX 011 52 5 5116351. **ED** Diego Arrazola Menterola. Index available ($5.42 per issue). cum. index. **Ad Acc**, **Adv Mgr:** Elena Bayardo. **Circ:** 27,500 (ctrl).
**Desc:** Geared toward leadership executives in responsible management positions in both business and government in Mexico.

US
**EXTERNAL RESEARCH STUDY.** **Main/Corp** United States. Dept. of State. Office of External Research. (19??)-. Monographic series. English. Price varies per volume. US Department of State / Bureau of Intelligence and Research, 2201 C Street Northwest, Room 6533, Washington DC 20520. **Tel** (202)647-9176.

●US/1062-7715
**EXTRA!, EXTRA! (GREENSBURG, PA.).** (EXTRA!, EXTRA!: A SPECIAL REPORT ON PENNSYLVANIA GOVERNMENT.). (1992)-. English. $2.00 (single issue). Iconoclast Press, PO Box 1826, Greensburg PA 15601-6826.

US/0094-3967
**FAIRFAX COUNTY GOVERNMENT ORGANIZATION MANUAL.** 1974-. English. an. $4.25 single issue. Office of Research and Statistics, 4100 Chain Bridge Road, Fairfax VA 22030. **LC** JS3.V8; F314. **DD** 352.0755/291.

PO
**FAZENDA DO ULTRAMAR.** (19??)-. Periodical. Portuguese. qt. 150$. **LC** JV4263; .F38.

US/0532-7091
**FCL NEWSLETTER.** **Main/Corp** Friends Committee on Legislation of California. **Added/Corp** Friends Committee on Legislation of California. Newsletter. **VAT** Friends Committee on Legislation Newsletter. (196?)-. Newsletter. English. Ten times a year. $18.00 US; $30.00 Canada. Friends Committee on the Legislation of California, 926 J Street/ Suite 707, Sacramento CA 95814. **Tel** (916)443-3734. **ED** Doug Thompson. **Circ:** 3,500 (ctrl). ***Continues*** *Friends Committee on Legislation of California. California Report.*
**Desc:** Legislative report on issues in California legislature and congress. Discusses specific topics including criminal justice, civil liberties, juvenile justice, prison reform, human services, AIDS, peace legislation.

CN/0381-1352
**FCM FORUM (ENGLISH ED.).** (FORUM.). [FCM forum]. **Added/Corp** Federation of Canadian Municipalities. **VAT** Federation of Canadian Municipalities Forum. Vol. 14, No. 1 (Jan./Feb. 1990)-. Periodical. English. bm (Jan., Mar., May, July, Sept., Nov.). $17.00 per year. Federation of Canadian Municipalities, 24 Clarence Street 2nd floor, Ottawa Ontario K1N 5P3 Canada. **Tel** (613)241-5221. **ED** Sheila Keating-Nause. **DD** 352.071/05. **Ad Acc.** ctrl circ. ***Continues*** *FCM Forum., 0381-1352.*
**Ind/Abst** Can. Period. Index (19??-).

US
**FCNL WASHINGTON NEWSLETTER.**
**Main/Corp** Friends Committee on National Legislation, Washington, D.C. **VFOAT** Washington Newsletter. **VAT** Friends Committee on National Legislation Washington Newsletter. (1961)-. Newsletter. English. mo. $25.00. Friends Committee on National Legislation, 245 Second Street NE, Washington DC 20002. **Tel** (202)547-6000, FAX (202)547-6019. **Circ:** 9,500. available on microfilm from University Microfilms International (UMI). ***Continues*** *Washington Newsletter of the Friends Committee on National Legislation.*
**Desc:** Up-to-date news and analysis of legislative actions on issues of concern to Friends.
**Ind/Abst** Hum. Rights Intern. Rep.

US/0362-1332
**FDA CONSUMER.** [FDA consum.]. **Added/Corp** United States. Food and Drug Administration. **VAT** Food and Drug Administration Consumer. Vol. 6, No. 6 (July-Aug. 1972)-. Government Publication. English. mo (combined issues July/Aug. and Dec./Jan.). $15.00 US; $18.75 other. Superintendent of Documents, US Government Printing Office, Washington DC 20402. **Tel** (202)275-3328, FAX (202)786-2377. **LC** HD9000.9.U5; A1735. **DD** 640.73. **NLM** W1 F203E. **CODEN** FDACBH. available on microfilm and microfiche from University Microfilms International (UMI); available on an online database (files 149,647/Full-Text) from DIALOG. Documents available from UMI Article Clearinghouse. ***Continues*** *FDA Papers, 0014-5750.*
**Desc:** Contains information written especially for consumers about Food and Drug Administration regulatory and scientific decisions, and about the safe use of products regulated by FDA.
**Ind/Abst** Acad. Abstr. Full Text Elite (Jan. 1984-) [Full Txt.]; Acad. Abstr. (Jan. 1984-); Acad. Ind. [Computer File] (1984-); Acad. Search (Jan. 1984-); AGRICOLA [Select. Cov.]; BioBusiness; Biol. Dig.; Consum. Health Nutr. Index; Consum. Index Prod. Eval. Inf. Source; Cumul. Index Nurs. Allied Health Lit.; Curr. Lit. Fam. Plan.; Dairy Sci. Abstr.; Expand. Acad. Index (1984-); Foods Adlibra; Gen. Period. Index (1985-); Gen. Sci. Index; Health Index (1989-); Health Period. Database [Full Txt.]; Health Plan. Adminis.; Health Ref. Cent. (Jan. 1989-) [Full Txt.] [Full Cov.]; Health Source (Jan. 1988-) [Full Txt.]; Hospit. Health Admin. Index; INFO-SOUTH Abstr.; Int. Pharm. Abstr. (19??-19??); Mag. Artic. Summar. Elite (Jan. 1984-) [Full Txt.]; Mag. Artic. Summar. Select (Jan. 1984-) [Full Txt.]; Mag. Artic. Summar. CD-ROM (Jan. 1984-); Mag. ASAP Plus [Full Txt.]; Mag. ASAP Sel. [Full Txt.]; Mag. Express (1986-) [Full Txt.]; Mag. Index Plus (1989-); Mag. Index. Sel. (1986-); Mag. Search; Med. Abstr. Newsl.; Newsp. Period. Abstr. (1986-); Nutr. Res. Newsl.; PAIS Int. Print (1991-); Read. Guide Abstr. Select Ed.; Read. Guide Period. Lit.; Resource/One Ondisc; Mag. Index (1978-); TOM Gen. Index (1993-) [Full Txt.]; Vocat. Search (Jan. 1984-) [Full Txt.].

US/0161-7044
**FDA FREEDOM OF INFORMATION LOG.**
**Main/Corp** United States. Food and Drug Administration. **VAT** Food and Drug Administration Freedom of Information Log. (1975)-. Periodical. English. wk. $420.00. FOI Services, 12315 Wilkins Avenue, Rockville MD 20852. **Tel** (301)881-0410, FAX (301)881-0415. **ED** John Carey. **Circ:** 75 (ctrl).
**Desc:** Lists all Freedom of Information requests placed at the Food and Drug Administration.

US/0145-126X
**FDA QUARTERLY ACTIVITIES REPORT.**
**Main/Corp** United States. Food and Drug Administration. Program Information and Analysis Group. **VAT** Food and Drug Administration Quarterly Activities Report. (19??)-. Periodical. English. Four times a year. Free. Health Education & Welfare, 5600 Fisher Lane, Rockville MD 20857. **Tel** (301)443-3160. **NLM** W2; A F686f. available on microfiche (Vols. for (1987-) distributed to depository libraries). Documents available from Documents on Demand.
**Ind/Abst** Am. Stat. Index.

US/8755-9285
**FEDERAL ACQUISITION REPORT.** [Fed. acquis. rep.]. Vol. 1, No. 1 (Sept. 1984)-. Periodical. English. mo (12 issues). $97.00 (one year), $174.00 (two year), $252.00 (three year). Holbrook and Kellogg, 1964 Gallows Road, Suite 200, Vienna VA 22182. **Tel** (703)506-0600, FAX (703)506-1948. **ED** J. Shackford. **DD** 353. Index available. **Bk Rev. Circ:** 2,000.
**Desc:** Rules, regulations, legislation and news of Federal procurement and acquisitions policy and practice.
**Ind/Abst** Int. Aerosp. Abstr.

●US/1074-2727
**FEDERAL ADVISORY DIRECTORY.** [Fed. advis. dir.]. (1994)-. Government Publication. English. an (Dec.). $127.00. Carroll Publishing Company, 1058 Thomas Jefferson Street Northwest, Washington DC 20007-3832. **Tel** (202)333-8620, FAX (202)337-7020. **DD** 351. Index available. available on diskette.
**Desc:** Provides complete contact information for the 20,000 members of Federal advisory committees created by the President, congress and Federal agencies.

US
**FEDERAL AQUISITION REGULATIONS / DISKETTE.** English. Four times a year (Jan., Apr., July, Oct.). $99.00. EZ - Far Systems, 360 Wire Road, York PA 17402. **Tel** 1-800-388-1415, FAX (717)975-2813. **ED** TSA Inc. 2 Market Plaza Way Mechanicsburg, PA 17055 (717)691-5691. **Ad Acc.** ctrl circ. available on CD-ROM.

US
**FEDERAL BUDGET AND THE CITIES - UNITED STATES CONFERENCE OF MAYORS, THE.** **Main/Corp** United States Conference of Mayors. 1st- Oct. 1, 1972/Sept. 30, 1973-. Periodical. English. an. $15.00 US; $16.48 other. US Conference of Mayors, 1620 Eye Street NW, Washington DC 20006. **Tel** (202)293-7330, FAX (202)293-2352. **Circ:** 2,000.
**Desc:** Analyzes annual federal budget proposal of the president to determine impact on urban programs.

US
**FEDERAL CIVIL SERVICE, HISTORY, ORGANIZATION AND ACTIVITIES / OFFICE OF PERSONNEL MANAGEMENT, LIBRARY, THE.** **Main/Corp** United States. Office of Personnel Management. Library. English. Office of Personnel Management, 1900 East Street Northwest, OELR Room 7429, Washington DC 20415. **Tel** (202)632-6256. ***Continues*** *Federal Civil Service, History, Organization, and Activities.*

US/1042-721X
**FEDERAL COMPUTER MARKET REPORT.** **See** Computers-Computer Industry and Industry Directories.

US/0893-052X
**FEDERAL COMPUTER WEEK.** **See** Computers-Computer Systems.

US/1048-4051
**FEDERAL DATA REPORT.** [Fed. data rep.]. (1990)-. Periodical. English. qt. $95.00 US; $119.00 other. DDRI Inc, 510 North Washington Street/Suite 401, Falls Church VA 22046-3537. **Tel** (703)237-0682, FAX (703)532-5447. **DD** 351.
**Desc:** Deals with information about policies, issues, differences of opinion and practice, resolutions, discussions, opinions and news all related to and about digital data, housed in or distributed from the confines of the Government of the United States of America.

US/0360-3512
**FEDERAL DIRECTORY, THE.** 3rd Ed. (1975)-. Directory. English. sa. Consolidated Directories, 1133 15th Street NW, Washington DC 20005. **LC** JK6; .F43. **DD** 353.002. ***Continues*** *Federal Telephone Directory, 0093-674X.*

US/0270-563X
**FEDERAL EXECUTIVE DIRECTORY.** [Fed. exec. dir.]. (March/April 1980)-. Directory. English. bm. $197.00. Carroll Publishing Company, 1058 Thomas Jefferson Street Northwest, Washington DC 20007-3832. **Tel** (202)333-8620, FAX (202)337-7020. **LC** JK6; .F42. **DD** 353.002. ***Continues*** *Federal Executive Telephone Directory, 0363-5384.*
**Desc:** Coverage includes upper and middle management officials in the Executive Office of the President, Cabinet departments and major federal administrative agencies, plus members of Congress with their committee assignments and staff assistants.

●US/1056-7275
**FEDERAL EXECUTIVE DIRECTORY ANNUAL.** [Fed. exec. dir. annu.]. (1992)-. Directory. English. an. $127.00. Carroll Publishing Company, 1058 Thomas Jefferson Street Northwest, Washington DC 20007-3832. **Tel** (202)333-8620, FAX (202)337-7020. **LC** IN PROCESS; JK723.E9; F45. **DD** 353. ***Continues in part*** *Federal/State Executive Directory, 0887-4727.*

US/0278-4580
**FEDERAL FAST FINDER.** ***Title Change.*** (FEDERAL FAST FINDER / WASHINGTON RESEARCHERS.). **Added/Corp** Washington Researchers. (19??)-12 Ed. (1991/1992). English. Washington Researchers, PO Box 19005, 20th Street Station, Washington DC 20036. **Tel** (202)333-3533, (202)333-3499, FAX (202)625-0656. **LC** JK404; .F43. **DD** 353/.00025. ***Merged into*** *Who Knows A Guide to Washington Experts, 0894-8801.*
**Desc:** More than 1,000 government offices are at your fingertips in this book. It is arranged in alphabetical order by key word to make finding federal departments, agencies, boards, and commissions simple.

US
**FEDERAL INFORMATION DISCLOSURE.** (Aug. 1977)-. English. sa. $200.00 (2 volume set), $45.00 (1992 supplement). Shepards McGraw-Hill Inc, 555 Middle Creek Parkway, PO Box 35300, Colorado Springs CO 80935-3530. **Tel** (719)488-3000, FAX (800)525-0053.

US/0083-1816
**FEDERAL INFORMATION PROCESSING STANDARDS PUBLICATION.** (FEDERAL INFORMATION PROCESSING STANDARDS PUBLICATION : FIPS PUB.). **Added/Corp** United States. National Bureau of Standards. **VFOAT** FIPS Pub. (1968)-. English. National Bureau of Standards, Room 120, Voice of Z39, Washington DC 20234. **(Subscription address:** National Technical Information Service, 5285 Port Royal Road, Springfield, VA 22161) **LC** JK468.A8; A3. **DD** 350/.0001/8. **CODEN** FIPPAT.

US/1068-7386
**FEDERAL INFORMATION RESOURCES MANAGEMENT REGULATION AND BULLETINS THROUGH TRANSMITTAL CIRCULAR.** (FEDERAL INFORMATION RESOURCES MANAGEMENT REGULATION AND BULLETINS THROUGH TRANSMITTAL CIRCULAR ... [COMPUTER FILE] : FIRMR ; FEDERAL ACQUISITION REGULATION AND CIRCULARS THROUGH FEDERAL ACQUISITION CIRCULAR ... : FAR.). [Fed. inf. resour. manag. regul. bull. transm. circ.]. **Added/Corp** United States. General Services Administration. United States. Dept. of Defense. National Aeronautics and Space Administration (U.S.). **VFOAT** Federal Acquisition Regulation and Circulars through Federal Acquisition Circular ...; FIRMR; FAR. (Apr. 1, 1991)-. Government Publication. English. qt. $58.00 US; $72.50. Superintendent of Documents, US Government Printing Office, Washington DC 20402. **Tel** (202)275-3328, FAX (202)786-2377. **LC** KF844.7. **DD** 353.
**Desc:** Procurement and contracting regulations for ADP and telecommunications equipment and services to be used in conjunction with general procurement and contracting regulations in the Federal Acquisition Regulations.

US/0898-2821
**FEDERAL LABOR RELATIONS UPDATE.** **See** Economics-Labor.

US/0093-0180
**FEDERAL MOTOR VEHICLE FLEET REPORT FOR THE FISCAL YEAR ENDING ... .** **See** Transportation.

US/0364-6858
**FEDERAL MOTOR VEHICLE SAFETY STANDARDS AND REGULATIONS.** (FEDERAL MOTOR VEHICLE SAFETY STANDARDS AND REGULATIONS, WITH AMENDMENTS AND INTERPRETATIONS.). **Main/Corp** United States. National Highway Traffic Safety Administration. (19??)-. Government Publication. English. ir. $149.00 domestic; $186.25 other. Superintendent of Documents, US Government Printing Office, Washington DC 20402. **Tel** (202)275-3328, FAX (202)786-2377. ***Supersedes*** *Motor Vehicle Safety Standards, with Amendments and Interpretations.*
**Desc:** Contains three sections: procedural rules and regulations; standards; and rulings and additional regulations.

US/0741-5109
**FEDERAL ORGANIZATION SERVICE.** (1976)-. English. ir (updated every 6 weeks). $500.00. Carroll Publishing Company, 1058 Thomas Jefferson Street Northwest, Washington DC 20007-3832. **Tel** (202)333-8620, FAX (202)337-7020. **LC** JK404; .F44. **DD** 353.04/025. ***Continued in part by*** *Defense Organization Service.*
**Desc:** Nearly 140 uniform fold-out organization charts tell you who's who and where in nearly 21,000 departments and offices.

US
**FEDERAL PROCUREMENT DATA SYSTEM. STANDARD REPORT / PREPARED BY FEDERAL PROCUREMENT DATA CENTER.** **Added/Corp** United States. Office of Federal Procurement Policy. Federal Procurement Data Center (U.S.). **VFOAT** Standard Report. (1983)-. Periodical. English. Four times a year. Free. Federal Procurement Data Center, 4040 North Fairfax Drive, Suite 900, Arlington VA 22203. **Tel** (703)235-1326. Documents available from Documents on Demand. ***Formed by the union of*** *Federal Procurement Data System. Quarterly Report of Federal Contract Awards; Federal Procurement Data System. Special Analysis 1, Federal Acquisition Awards Over $10,000 by Type of Contractor; Federal Procurement Data System. Special Analysis 2, Federal Contract Actions Over $10,000 by Product and Service; Federal Procurement Data System. Special Analysis 3, Federal Contract Actions to Minority and Small Disadvantaged Businesses; Federal Procurement Data System. Special Analysis 4, Federal Actions Including Subcontracts with Small Businesses by Executive Department and Agency; Federal Procurement Data System. Combined Special Analyses SA5, Labor Surplus Preference Actions; SA Top 100 Contractors, SA7 R & D Contracting, SA9 Consultant Awards; Federal Procurement Data System. Special Analysis 8, Federal Contract Actions, Various Contracting Operations by Executive Department and Agency; Federal Procurement Data System. Special Analysis 10, Federal Contract Actions Over $10,000, Women Owned Businesses by Executive Department and Agency by State* ***and*** *Federal Procurement Data System. Special Analysis 11, Federal Contract Actions Federal Supply Schedule Orders by Executive Department and Agency by Federal Supply Classification.*
**Ind/Abst** Am. Stat. Index.

US
**FEDERAL PROCUREMENT REGULATIONS.** Periodical. English. $125.00 US; $156.25 other. US General Services Administration, General Services Building, Eighteenth and F Streets NW, Washington DC 20405.
**Desc:** Transmits new or revised Federal Procurement Regulations material prescribed by the Administrator of General Services under the Federal Property and Administrative Services Act of 1949.

US/0278-0488
**FEDERAL PRODUCTIVITY MEASUREMENT.** [Fed. prod. meas.]. English. an. O P M Office of Productivity Programs, Measurement and Analysis Division, 1900 E Street NW, Washington DC 20006. **LC** JK404; .U57A. **DD** 353.001/47/05. ***Continues*** *Measuring Federal Productivity, 0272-460X.*

US
**FEDERAL PROGRAM EXPENDITURES FOR MARYLAND PUBLIC SCHOOLS.** **See** Education.

US
**FEDERAL PROPERTY MANAGEMENT REGULATIONS / DISKETTE.** English. Four times a year (Jan., Apr., July, Oct.). $99.00. EZ - Far Systems, 360 Wire Road, York PA 17402. **Tel** 1-800-388-1415, FAX (717)975-2813. **ED** TSA Inc. 2 Market Plaza Way Mechanicsburg, PA 17055 (717)691-5691. **Ad Acc.** ctrl circ. available on CD-ROM.

CN/0848-5607
**FEDERAL-PROVINCIAL PROGRAMS AND ACTIVITIES, A DESCRIPTIVE INVENTORY.** [Fed.-prov. programs act. descr. inventory]. **Added/Corp** Canada. Federal-Provincial Relations Office. (1987/1988)-. English. an. Free upon request. Federal-Provincial Rel Office, 63 Sparks Suite Room 412, Ottawa Ontario, K1A 0A2 Canada. **Tel** (613)990-3426. **DD** 354.7108/2/05. ***Continues*** *A Descriptive Inventory of Federal-Provincial Programs and Activities., 0707-1639.*

●US
**FEDERAL QUALITY NEWS.** **Added/Corp** Federal Quality Institute (U.S.). (1992)-. Government Publication. English. bm. $13.00 US; $16.25 other. Superintendent of Documents, US Government Printing Office, Washington DC 20402. **Tel** (202)275-3328, FAX (202)786-2377.

US/0498-9791
**FEDERAL REAL AND PERSONAL PROPERTY INVENTORY REPORT (CIVILIAN AND MILITARY) OF THE UNITED STATES GOVERNMENT COVERING ITS PROPERTIES LOCATED IN THE UNITED STATES, IN THE TERRITORIES, AND OVERSEAS.** **Main/Corp** United States. Congress. House. Committee on Government Operation. 1st (1955)-. Government Publication. English. ir. Superintendent of Documents, US Government Printing Office, Washington DC 20402. **Tel** (202)275-3328, FAX (202)786-2377. **LC** JK1661; .A2. **DD** 353.

US/0736-8364
**FEDERAL RECREATION FEE REPORT.** ***Title Change.*** **See** Recreation, Leisure.

US/0742-1729
**FEDERAL REGIONAL EXECUTIVE DIRECTORY.** (Winter/Spring 1984)-. English. sa. $150.00. Carroll Publishing Company, 1058 Thomas Jefferson Street Northwest, Washington DC 20007-3832. **Tel** (202)333-8620, FAX (202)337-7020. **ED** Nancy Cahill. **LC** JK723.E9; F43. **DD** 353.04/025. Index available. **Circ:** 500.
**Desc:** Gives rapid access to the field office personnel of executive branch agencies, including regional maps showing agency service areas.

●US/1061-3153
**FEDERAL REGIONAL YELLOW BOOK.** **See** Encyclopedias and General Reference Books.

US/0097-6326
**FEDERAL REGISTER.** **See** Law.

US/0195-749X
**FEDERAL REGULATORY DIRECTORY.** [Fed. regul. dir.]. **Added/Corp** Congressional Quarterly, Inc. **VFOAT** Congressional Quarterly's Federal Regulatory Directory. (1980)-. English. ir (every 4 years). $119.95. Congressional Quarterly Inc., 1414 22nd Street Northwest, Washington DC 20037. **Tel** (202)887-8500, (800)432-2250 ext. 621, FAX (202)728-1863. **LC** KF5406.A15; F4. **DD** 353/.00025.

●CN/0833-7322
**FEDERAL REGULATORY PLAN.** [Fed. regul. plan]. **Main/Corp** Canada. Treasury Board. Regulatory Affairs. (1992)-. English. an. Free. Privatization & Regulartory Affairs, 155 Queen Street 5th Floor, Heritage Ottawa K1A 1J2, Canada. **DD** 342.71/066/05. ***Continues*** *Canada. Office of Privatization and Regulatory Affairs.; Federal Regulatory Plan., 0833-7322.*

CN/0226-3726
**FEDERAL SCIENCE EXPENDITURES AND PERSONNEL.** [Fed. sci. expend. pers.]. **Main/Corp** Canada. Ministry of State, Science and Technology. 1977/78/1979/80-. English. Ministry of State Science and Technology, 270 Albert Street, Ottawa Ontario K1A 1A1 Canada. **DD** 354.710081/9. ***Continues*** *Canada. Ministry of State, Science and Technology. Federal Science Expenditures and Manpower, 0226-3718.*

US/0735-3324
**FEDERAL STAFF DIRECTORY.** [Fed. staff dir.]. (1982)-. Academic Scholarly Publication. English. sa (2 issues). $138.00. Staff Directories Ltd., PO Box 62, Mount Vernon VA 22121. **Tel** (703)739-0900, FAX (703)739-0234. **ED** Charles B. Brownson and Anna L. Brownson. **LC** JK723.E9; F44. **DD** 353.002. **CODEN** FSDIEM. **Circ:** 12,000. available on CD-ROM. Documents available from CASDDS.
**Desc:** United States government executive branch, with 27,000 key staff by department and agency including building, room, and extension for each inside and out of Washington. 2,000 biographies.
**Ind/Abst** Chem. Abstr. (1989-).

# Public Administration

US/1041-6722
**FEDERAL-STATE-LOCAL GOVERNMENT DIRECTORY, THE.** [Fed.-state-local gov. dir.]. **VFOAT** Federal, State, Local Government Directory. 1988-. Directory. English. be. $59.95 North America; $79.95 other. Braddock Communications, 909 North Washington Street, Suite 310, Alexandria VA 22314-1555. **Tel** (703)549-6500. **ED** Thomas Jacobson and Paul Arnold. **DD** 353. **NLM** JK 6; B798. **Ad Acc. Circ:** 7,500. **Continues** Braddock's Federal-State-Local Government Directory, 0363-6275.
**Desc:** Comprehensive reference to a broad range of government, media, and public policy organizations.

PK
**FEDERAL TAXES ADMINISTRATION REPORT. Main/Corp** Pakistan. Central Board of Revenue. English. Government of Pakistan Central Board of Revenue, Karachi 15 B Pakistan. **LC** LAW. **DD** 354/.549/100724.

US/0898-4298
**FEDERAL UPDATE.** (FEDERAL UPDATE / NATIONAL CONFERENCE OF STATE LEGISLATURES.). [Fed. update]. **Added/Corp** National Conference of State Legislatures. (198?)-. Periodical. English. ir (10-15 issues). $35.00 US; $40.00 Canada. National Conference of State Legislatures, 1560 Broadway, Suite 700, Denver CO 80202. **Tel** (303)830-2054, FAX (303)863-8003. **ED** William Waren and Michael Bird. **DD** 328.
**Desc:** Examines federal issues that affect states and alerts legislators and legislative staff to the need for action.

US/0145-6202
**FEDERAL YELLOW BOOK. See** Encyclopedias and General Reference Books.

US/0736-8151
**FEDERALIST (WASHINGTON, D.C. : 1980), THE. See** History(General)-History of North, South, and Central America.

BE
**FEITEN.** Dutch (French). qt. 500F. Inbel, Kunstlaan 3, B-1040 Brussels Belgium. Index available. cum. index. **Bk Rev. Circ:** 17,000 (ctrl).
**Desc:** Information about the decisions of the Conceil of Ministers on information services of the national government and departments.

CN/0711-396X
**FEUILLET D'INFORMATION DE LA VILLE DE SAINT-LEONARD, LE. Title Change.** [Feuill. inf. ville St.-Leonard]. **Main/Corp** Saint Leonard (Le-de-Montreal, Quebec). Vol. 1, No. 1 (1st Quarterly 1980)-(198?). Periodical. French. qt. La Ville, 8400 Boulevard Lacordaire, Saint-Leonard Quebec H1R 3B1 Canada. **DD** 352.0714/28. ctrl circ. **Continued by** Evenement (Saint-Leonard (Ile-de-Montreal, Quebec), 1183-8612.

NE/0379-3680
**FID DIRECTORY. Main/Corp** International Federation for Information and Documentation. **VAT** Federation Internationale D'Information et de Documentation Directory. (1987/1988)-. Directory. English. be. International Federation for Information and Documentation, PO Box 90402, 2509 LK Hague Netherlands. **Tel** 011 31 70 314095, FAX 011 31 70 834827, telex 34402 KB GV NL. **Continues** FID Directory.

US/0096-3224
**FINANCES OF EMPLOYEE-RETIREMENT SYSTEMS OF STATE AND LOCAL GOVERNMENTS. See** Economics-Labor.

UK/0267-4424
**FINANCIAL ACCOUNTABILITY & MANAGEMENT IN GOVERNMENTS, PUBLIC SERVICES, AND CHARITIES.** [Financ. acc. manage.]. **VFOAT** Financial Accountability & Management; FAM; Financial Accountability and Management in Governments, Public Services, and Charities. Vol. 1, No. 1 (Summer 1985)-. Academic Scholarly Publication. English. Four times a year. £70.00 UK and Europe; $140.00 North America; £90.00; £132.50 (UK and Europe), $280.00 (North America), £151.50 other for combined subscription with Journal of Business Finance & Accounting. Basil Blackwell Publishers Ltd, 108 Cowley Road, Oxford 0X4 1JF England. **Tel** 011 44 865 791100, FAX 011 44 865 791347, telex 837022 OXBOOK G. **(Subscription address:** Blackwell Publishers / UK, Marston Book Services, PO Box 87, Oxford OX2 0DT England.) **ED** John Perrin. **[CCC]. Ad Acc. Circ:** 1,000. available on microfilm and microfiche from University Microfilms International (UMI).
**Desc:** Focuses on central and local governments, public services, charities and other non-for-profit organizations.
**Ind/Abst** Account. Tax Datab. (Summer 1985-) [Full Txt.]; Contents Pages Manage.; Gen. BusinessFile (1992-); PAIS Int. Print (1991-); UMI ABI/Inform--Bus. Period. Ondisc [Full Txt.].

AT
**FINANCIAL ASSISTANCE SCHEMES FOR LOCAL GOVERNMENTS / PREPARED BY RESEARCH SECTION, DEPARTMENT OF LOCAL GOVERNMENT. Added/Corp** Western Australia. Dept. of Local Government. Research Section. (19??)-. English. an. Western Australia Department of Local Government / Research Section, Perth WA Australia. **LC** HJ90.W47; F56. **DD** 354.9410072/53.

CN/0701-4724
**FINANCIAL POST GOVERNMENT & MUNICIPAL SURVEY. Main/Corp** The Financial Post. Began publication in 1927?. Periodical. English. an. Financial Post DataGroup, 333 King Street East, Toronto Ontario M5A 4N2 Canada. **Tel** (800)661-7678, FAX (416)350-6501.

CN/0709-4981
**FINANCIAL PROCEDURES BULLETIN.** [Financ. proced. bull.]. Bulletin. English. Price varies per volume. Publications Centre, 880 Bay Street/5th Floor, Toronto Ontario M7A 1N8 Canada. **DD** 352.1/09713. **Continues** Finance Bulletin / Municipal Budgets and Branch Accounts, Canada, 0709-4973.

CN/0825-7043
**FINANCIAL STATEMENTS & FINANCIAL STATISTICS / CAISSE DE DEPOT ET PLACEMENT DU QUEBEC.** [Financ. statements financ. stat. - Caisse depot place. Que.]. **Main/Corp** Caisse de Depot et Placement du Quebec. **VFOAT** Financial Statements and Financial Statistics - Caisse de Depot et Placement du Quebec; Financial Statements & Financial Statistics, Annual Report. (1983)-. English. an. Free on request. Caisse Depot Placement Quebec, 1981 McGill College, Montreal Quebec H3A 3C7 Canada. **Tel** (514)842-3261. **LC** HD7105.45.C2; C35. **DD** 354.7140072/6. **Separated from** Caisse de Depot et Placement du Quebec Annual Report.

US/0193-2721
**FINANCIAL STATUS OF MAJOR FEDERAL ACQUISITIONS. Main/Corp** United States. General Accounting Office. English. an. Free. US General Accounting Office / District of Columbia, 441 G Street NW, Room 4528, Washington DC 20548. **Tel** (202)275-2812. **LC** HD171.A1; G45. **DD** 353.007/2. **Continues** Financial Status of Major Civil Acquisitions, 0098-7794.

NE/0922-1026
**FINANCIEEL OVERHEIDSMANAGEMENT. Title Change.** (19??)-(1992). Dutch. mo. Infolio BV, Postbus 16500, 2500 BM Den Haag Netherlands. **Tel** 011 31 70 3819900, FAX 011 31 70 3632338. Index available. **Bk Rev. Ad Acc. Circ:** 2,785. **Continued by** Overheidsmanagement, 0928-8503.
**Desc:** Directed to managers who have to deal with finances and informatics, organization at the national and local governmental level.

CN
**FISHERIES DEVELOPMENT ACT, ANNUAL REPORT. See** Fish and Fisheries.

US
**FLORIDA ADMINISTRATIVE CODE SUPPLEMENT SERVICE.** English. $57.93 (single supplements), $83.42 (single volumes). Darby Printing Company, 6215 Purdue Drive, Atlanta GA 30336. **Tel** (404)344-2665, (800)848-2995.

US
**FLORIDA ADMINISTRATIVE CODE; THE OFFICIAL COMPILATION OF RULES AND REGULATIONS OF REGULATORY STATE AGENCIES. Main/Corp** Florida. (19??)-. English. mo. $427.98 (Florida residents, including tax); $355.75 (state agencies); $403.75 (other). Darby Printing Company, 6215 Purdue Drive, Atlanta GA 30336. **Tel** (404)344-2665, (800)848-2995.

US/0098-874X
**FLORIDA ADMINISTRATIVE WEEKLY. See** Law.

US
**FLORIDA DIRECTORY : A GUIDE TO FLORIDA GOVERNMENT, THE. Added/Corp** Florida Communications Network. Vol. 1 (May 1991)-. Directory. English. an (published in Feb.). $61.48 taxable Frorida residents; $58.00 other. Florida Communications Network, PO Box 2099, Gainesville FL 32602. **Tel** (904)336-3805, 591-1172. **ED** John J. Hotaling and Joann Klein. **LC** JK4430; .F63.
**Desc:** This volume is a comprehensive listing of Florida's political leaders. Includes sections on officials in Florida's 67 counties, major cities, state government (legislative, executive and judicial branches) and information on key capital city lobbyists. Florida's Congressional Delegation is also included in this comprehensive reference.

US/0071-5972
**FLORIDA GOVERNMENT SERIES.** No. 1 (1963)-. Monographic series. English. Price varies per volume. Institute of Governmental Research, Florida State University, Tallahassee FL 32303.
**Desc:** No. 1-Florida votes, 1920-1962; selected election statistics, by Annie Mary Hartsfield and Elston E. Roady, No. 2-The impeachment of Circuit Judge Richard Kelly, by Carl D. McMurray.

US/1068-4433
**FLORIDA INSIGHT.** [Fla. insight]. (1989)-. Periodical. English. Twenty-two times a year. $100.70 Florida residents; $95.00 other. Florida Communications Network, PO Box 2099, Gainesville FL 32602. **Tel** (904)336-3805, 591-1172. **DD** 353.

US/0093-4089
**FLORIDA SENATE, THE. Main/Corp** Florida. Legislature. Senate. English. be. Florida Senate, State Capitol Building, Publishers Office, Tallahassee FL 32304. **Tel** (904)487-5270. **ED** Joe Brown. **LC** JK4476; .A22A. **DD** 328.759/07/1. **Circ:** 75,000.
**Desc:** This is a booklet about the Florida Senate, its organization, function and members.

US/0732-0345
**FLRA REPORT OF CASE DECISIONS AND FSIP RELEASES.** (19??)-. Government Publication. English. ir. $173.00 US; $216.25 other. Superintendent of Documents, US Government Printing Office, Washington DC 20402. **Tel** (202)783-3328, FAX (202)786-2377.

IT
**FOGLI ANNUNZI LEGALI.** Italian. L152.000. Editrice La Giuntina, Via Ricasoli 26 - 28, 50122 Florence Italy.
**Desc:** Official communications.

US
**FOOD AND DRUG ADMINISTRATION PUBLIC ADVISORY COMMITTEES : AUTHORITY, STRUCTURE, FUNCTIONS, MEMBERS. Added/Corp** United States. Food and Drug Administration. **VFOAT** Public Advisory Committees. (19??)-. English.

US/0533-1250
**FOOTNOTE (WASHINGTON).** (FOOTNOTE.). **Added/Corp** United States. Dept. of Health, Education, and Welfare. Audit Agency. (1970)-. English. an. US Department of Health and Human Services, 200 Independence Avenue Southwest, Washington DC 20201. **LC** UNC.

US
**FOREIGN ACTIVITY REPORT.** English. qt. $60.00 (nonmembers), $40.00 (members) US and Canada; (add $12.00 postage) other. Securities Industry Association, 120 Broadway/35th Floor, New York NY 10271. **Tel** (212)608-1500, FAX (212)608-1604.
**Desc:** Tracks purchases and sales of US securities by foreign investors.

●CN/1191-3282
**FOREIGN GOVERNMENT AWARDS PROGRAM.** (FOREIGN GOVERNMENT AWARDS PROGRAM / ADMINISTERED BY THE INTERNATIONAL COUNCIL FOR CANADIAN STUDIES.). [Foreign gov. awards program]. **Added/Corp** International Council for Canadian Studies. Canada. External Affairs and International Trade Canada. **VFOAT** Programme de Bourses des Gouvernements Etrangers. (1991/1992)-. English (French). **DD** 378.3. **Continues** Foreign Government Awards., 1191-3274.

AG
**FORMACION POLITICA PARA LA DEMOCRACIA.** (Sept. 6, 1980)-. Periodical. Spanish. wk. Editorial Redaccion S A, Bartolome Mitre 2 Piso, Buenos Aires Argentina. **LC** JL2001; .F67. **DD** 982/.064/05.

DK
**FORSKNINGSSTATISTIK, RESSOURCEFORBRUGET VED FORSKNING OG UDVIKLINGSARBEJDE I DEN OFFENTLIGE SEKTOR. VFOAT** Forskningsstatistik. (1979)-. Danish. ir. Forskningssekretariatet, Holmens Kanal 7, DK-1060 Kbenhavn K Denmark. **Tel** (01)114300. **LC** JF1338.A3; D423.

CN/0704-7177
**FORUM (FEDERATION CANADIENNE DES MUNICIPALITES).** [Forum FCM]. **Added/Corp** Federation Canadienne des Municipalites. **VAT** Forum Federation Canadienne des Municipalites. Vol. 14, No 1 (Jan./Feb. 1990)-. Periodical. French. bm. 17.00Can$. Federation Canadienne Des Municipalites,

# Public Administration

24 Rue Clarence, Ottawa Ontario K1N 5P3. **DD** 352.071/05. *Continues Forum F C M., 0704-7177.* **Ind/Abst** Can. Period. Index (19??-).

FR
**FRANCE MODERNE.** Periodical. French. 25.00. Federation Nationale des Republicans Independants, 195 Bd Saint-Germain (7E), Paris France. **LC** JN3007.F45; F7. **DD** 320.9/44/083.

FR/1157-3783
**FRANCIS BULLETIN SIGNALETIQUE. 528, BIBLIOGRAPHIE INTERNATIONALE DE SCIENCE ADMINISTRATIVE.** See Business-General Management.

CN/0226-5400
**FRANCISATION EN MARCHE.** (LA FRANCISATION EN MARCHE : BULLETIN D'INFORMATION DE L'OFFICE DE LA LANGUE FRANCAISE.). **Added/Corp** Quebec (Province). Office de la Langue Francaise. (Feb. 1981)-. Periodical. French. Four times a year. 12.00Can$. Office de la Langue Francaise, 800 Place Victoria CP 316, Montreal Quebec H4Z 1G8 Canada. **Tel** (514)873-7631. **ED** Charles Soucy and Jean-Yvon Houle. **DD** 354.7140085. *Continues Francisation en Marche (Edition Provinciale), 0226-5400; Bloc-Notes.*
**Desc:** Report on developments in the increasing use of the French language among Quebec businesses.

CN/0835-9733
**FREEDOM OF INFORMATION AND PROTECTION OF INDIVIDUAL PRIVACY. DIRECTORY OF GENERAL RECORDS.** [Freedom inf. prot. indiv. priv., Dir. gen. rec.]. **Main/Corp** Ontario. **Added/Corp** Ontario. Freedom of Information and Privacy Branch. **VFOAT** Directory of General Records; General Records; Directory of Records. No. 1 (1988)-. Directory. English. Ministry of Government Services / Treasurer of Ontario, 50 Grosvenor, Toronto Ontario M7A 1N8 Canada. **Tel** (416)326-5316. **LC** JL269.5.R4; O55b. **DD** 354.7130081/9.

AU
**FREIE ARGUMENTE. Added/Corp** Freiheitliche Partei Osterreichs. Freiheitliches Bildungswerk. (19??)-. Periodical. German. ir. Freiheitliches Bildungswerk, Kolingasse 10/26, 1090 Vienna Austria. **LC** JN2031.F73; F73. **DD** 324.243603.

US/0734-1202
**FROM THE STATE CAPITALS. FEDERAL ACTION AFFECTING THE STATES (NEW HAVEN, CONN.).** (FROM THE STATE CAPITALS. FEDERAL ACTION AFFECTING THE STATES ). [From state cap., Fed. action affect. states]. **VFOAT** Federal Action Affecting the States. (1982)-. Periodical. English. wk. $211.50 (one year); $235.00 (two year) public and institutional libraries; $378.00 (one year); $420.00 (two year) other. Wakeman Walworth Inc., 300 North Washington Street #204, Alexandria VA 22314. **Tel** (703)549-8606. **ED** Emily Novick. **DD** 320. **[CCC].** *Continues From the State Capitals. Federal Action.*
**Desc:** Highlights developments in Washington that impact on states, from block grants and job programs to social security and welfare legislation; also, environmental protection and unemployment.

US/0016-1888
**FROM THE STATE CAPITALS. PUBLIC UTILITIES.** [From state cap., Public util.]. **VFOAT** Public Utilities. (19??)-. Periodical. English. wk. $211.50 (one year), 235.00 (two year) public and institutional libraries; $378.00 (one year), $420.00 (two year) other. Wakeman Walworth Inc., 300 North Washington Street #204, Alexandria VA 22314. **Tel** (703)549-8606. **ED** Emily Novick. **DD** 363. **[CCC].**
**Desc:** New structures for power and telephone rates, allowable profit margins, special taxes, construction surcharges, nuclear plant regulations.

US/1061-9690
**FROM THE STATE CAPITALS. THE OUTLOOK FROM THE STATE CAPITALS.** See Law.

US/0734-0931
**FROM THE STATE CAPITALS. WORKERS' COMPENSATION.** *Title Change.* See Economics-Labor.

US
**GAO'S ... BIENNIAL REPORT ON THE TRANSFER OF EXCESS AND SURPLUS FEDERAL PERSONAL PROPERTY TO NONFEDERAL ORGANIZATIONS.**
**Added/Corp** United States. General Accounting Office. **VFOAT** General Accounting Office's ... Biennial Report on the Transfer of Excess and Surplus Federal Personal Property to Nonfederal Organizations. 3rd (Nov. 9, 1984)-. English. be. *Continues GAO's ... Biennial Report on the Transfers of Federal Personal Property to Grantees and Other eligible Organizations.*

US/8756-6605
**GARDEN STATE REPORT.** [Gard. state rep.]. **VFOAT** GSR; GSR Magazine. Vol. 1, No. 1 (March 1985)-. Periodical. English. mo. $35.00. Garden State Report, 204 Eagle Rock Avenue, Roseland NJ 07068. **Tel** (201)228-7088. **LC** WMLC 90/0639. **DD** 353. **Ad Acc. Circ:** 10,500 (ctrl).
**Desc:** Offers objective reporting on public policy events and issues regarding state, county and local governments, as well as business, labor and finance in the state of New Jersey.

SP
**GASETA MUNICIPAL. Main/Corp** Barcelona (Spain). **VFOAT** Gaseta Municipal de Barcelona. Catalan. tm. 1.500ptas. Placa de Sant Jaume 3A Planta, Barcelona Spain. **Tel** (93)302 4200. **LC** JS31; .B272. **DD** 352.046/72. **Circ:** 2,000 (ctrl). *Continues Barcelona (Spain). Gaseta Municipal de Barcelona.*

CN/0710-1686
**GAZETTE DE QUEBEC.** (LA GAZETTE DE QUEBEC : JOURNAL MUNICIPAL DE LA VILLE DE QUEBEC : SERVICES DES COMMUNICATIONS DE LA VILLE DE QUEBEC.). [Gaz. Que.]. V. 1, No. 1, (Dec. 1980)-. Periodical. French. ir (8 times a year). Free. La Ville de Quebec, Service des Communications, 2 rue des Jardins, Quebec Quebec G1R 4S9 Canada. **Tel** (418)691-6484. **DD** 352.0714/471/05. **Circ:** 85,000.

IT
**GAZZETTA UFFICIALE REGIONE SICILIANA. SERIE SPECIALE CONCORSI.** (19??)-. Italian. L135000. Regione Siciliana Gazzetta Uff, Via Caltanissetta, 90141 Palermo Italy. **Tel** 011 39 91 6964489.

JA
**GEKKAN BOEKI TO SANGYO / HENSHU, TSUSHO SEISAKU KENKYUKAI.** See Economics-Industry and Production.

IO
**GEMA D.P.R.D. TINGKAT I JAWA TENGAH. Main/Corp** Jawa Tengah, Indonesia. Dewan Perwakilan Rakyat Daerah. **VAT** Gema Dewan Perwakilan Rakyat Daerah Tingkat Pertama Jawa Tengah. Periodical. Indonesian. D P R D Tingkat I Jawa Tengah, Jl Letjen Soeprapto No 43, Semarang Indonesia. **LC** JS7191.A1; J38A.

BE
**GEMEENTE.** (19??)-. Dutch. mo (June/July and Aug./Sept. issues combined). $87.56, 2613F. Vereniging Van Belg Sted Gemen, Aarlenstraat 53 Bus 4, 1040 Brussels Belgium. **Tel** 011 32 2 233 21 11, 011 32 2 2332011, **FAX** 011 32 2 231 15 23. **Bk Rev.**
**Desc:** Information on local administration.

GW
**GEMEINDE (VIENNA, AUSTRIA).** (DIE GEMEINDE.). Periodical. German. mo. DM98.00. Israelitische Kultusgemeinde Wien, Bauerfeldgasse 4, 1190 Vienna Austria. **LC** DS101; .G37. **DD** 909/.04924/005. **UDC** 933(436).
**Desc:** Journal for self-government in Schlesuig Holstein.

GW
**GEMEINDESCHLUSSELVERZEICHNIS FUER BAYERN. Main/Corp** Bayerisches Statistisches Landesamt. (19??)-. English. an. DM14.00. Bayerisches Landesamt fuer Statistik und Datenverarbeitung, Neuhauser Str 8, D 80331 Munich Germany. **Tel** 089 2119 205, **FAX** 089 2119 410. **LC** JS5471.B4; A23a. Index available. ctrl circ.

US
**GENERAL ACCOUNTING OFFICE POLICY AND PROCEDURES MANUAL FOR GUIDANCE OF FEDERAL AGENCIES. Main/Corp** United States. General Accounting Office. (19??)-. Government Publication. English. mo. price varies per volume. Superintendent of Documents, US Government Printing Office, Washington DC 20402. **Tel** (202)275-3328, **FAX** (202)786-2377.

US/0098-6534
**GENERAL ASSEMBLY OF GEORGIA, THE. Main/Corp** Georgia. Dept. of Archives and History. English. Department of Archives and History, 330 Capitol Avenue SE, Atlanta GA 30334. **Tel** (404)656-2393, (404)656-2358. **LC** JK4330; .G37A. **DD** 328.758/08/3.

US/0362-9686
**GENERAL REPORT OF THE LEGISLATIVE COUNCIL TO THE LEGISLATURE. Main/Corp** Wisconsin. Legislative Council. English. be. Free. Legislative Council - Wisconsin, North State Capitol/Room 147 North, Madison WI 53702. **LC** JK6074; .A3. **DD** 328.775/07/6. **Circ:** 300. *Continues Report of the Wisconsin Legislative Council.*
**Desc:** Summary of work of Legislative Council study committees and legislation proposed.

CN/0843-5030
**GEO INFO.** [Geo info]. **Added/Corp** Quebec (Province). Conseil Executif. **VFOAT** GEO Info. Vol. 1, No 1 (Feb. 1989)-. Periodical. French. Ten times a year. Free on request. Ministere Des Communications, 1500 B Boulevard Charest, Quest 1 FL, STE-Foy Quebec G1S 2G1 Canada. **Tel** (418)646-3571. **ED** Yves Luc Hudon (phone: (418)643-2915). **DD** 354.7140081/9. **Circ:** 1,100.
**Desc:** An newsletter concerning GIS projects in the Quebec government.

US/1066-0119
**GEORGIA COUNTY GOVERNMENT. Added/Corp** Association County Commissioners of Georgia. (1979)-. English. Twelve times a year. $15.00. Association County Commissioners Georgia, 50 Hurt Plaza, Suite #1000, Atlanta GA 30303. **Tel** (404)522-5022, **FAX** (404)525-2477. **ED** Kay Morgareidge (editor's address: 2445 Garmon Way, Lawrenceville, GA 30244, phone: (404)963-1796). **Ad Acc, Adv Mgr:** John McCurley, **Tel** (404)256-1116. ctrl circ.

US
**GEORGIA DOCLIST : STATE DOCUMENTS ADDED DURING ... / UNIVERSITY OF GEORGIA LIBRARIES, GOVERNMENT DOCUMENTS DEPARTMENT. Added/Corp** University of Georgia. Libraries. Government Documents Dept. **VFOAT** Georgia Doc List. Vol. 1, No 1 (May 1990)-. Periodical. English. mo. Free on request. University of Georgia Libraries, Government Documents Department, Athens GA 30602. **Tel** (706)542-8949. **LC** Z1223.5.G4; G46.

US/1070-7816
**GEORGIA OFFICIAL AND STATISTICAL REGISTER.** [Ga. off. stat. regist.]. **Added/Corp** Georgia. Dept. of Archives and History. (1972)-. Statistical Publication. English. be (Publishes every two years). Department of Archives and History, 330 Capitol Avenue SE, Atlanta GA 30334. **Tel** (404)656-2393, (404)656-2358. **ED** Marian B. Holmes. **LC** JK4330; .A3. **DD** 353.9758/0002/02. Index available. **Circ:** 1,800 (ctrl). *Continues Georgia's Official and Statistical Register, 0090-273X.*
**Desc:** A reference source of the Georgia state government. Includes biographical sketches of Georgia officials in federal and state levels of government, duties of state agencies and last election results.

US
**GEORGIA'S CITIES. Added/Corp** Georgia Municipal Association. Vol. 1, No. 1 (Jan. 1, 1990)-. Periodical. English. mo. $30.00. Georgia Municipal Association, 201 Pryor Street Southwest, Atlanta GA 30303. **Tel** (404)688-0472. **ED** Charles Craig. **LC** JS39; .U72. *Continues Urban Georgia, 0042-0875.*

AU
**GESCHAFTSBERICHT. Main/Corp** Wiener Stadtwerke. (198?)-. German. an. Generaldirektion der Wiener Stadtwerke, Schottenring 30, A-1010 Vienna Austria. **LC** HD4652.V5; W53a. *Continues Verwaltungsbericht - Wiener Stadtwerke.*

JA
**GIKAI SHIRYO. Added/Corp** Okinawa-ken (Japan). Gikai. (19??)-. Periodical. Japanese. Okinawa Kengikai Jimukyoku, 2-14 Senzaki 1, Naha Japan. **LC** JQ1699.O54; G5.

IT
**GIUSTIZIA AMMINISTRATIVA IN EMILIA ROMAGNA.** Italian. Editrice Pragma, Via Brizio 23, 40134 Bologna Italy.

IT
**GIUSTIZIA OGGI.** (19??)-. Italian. Ten times a year. L80000. Sirio Srl, Via Verona 9, 20135 Milan Italy. **Tel** 011 39 2 58321897. *Continues Stato Oggi.*

GW
**GLIEDERUNG DES LANDTAGS RHEINLAND-PFALZ ... WAHLPERIODE. Main/Corp** Rheinland-Palatinate (Germany). Landtag. German. Landtag Rheinland-Pfalz, Deutschhausplatz 12 Postfach 3040, W-6500 Mainz Germany. **LC** JN4945.R45; R53A. **DD** 328.43/43/073.

CK
**GOBIERNOS DEPARTAMENTALES : EJECUCION PRESUPUESTAL.** See Public Administration-Public Finance and Taxation.

UK
**GOSIP.** English. ir. £16.50 (update). Her Majesty's Stationery Office, 51 Nine Elms Lane, London SW8 5DR England. **Tel** 011 44 71 873 8459, 011 44 71 873 8499, **FAX** 011 44 71 873 8499, 011 44 71 873 8456, telex 297138. **(Subscription address:** PO Box 276, Public Centre, London SW8 5DT England)

PL/0860-3081
**GOSPODARKA, ADMINISTRACJA PANSTWOWA.** (July 12, 1986)-. Periodical. Polish. bw. Z1300.00. **(Subscription address:** ARS Polona, PO Box 1001, 00068 Warsaw Poland.**)** **LC** HC10; .R25. ***Continues*** *Rada Narodowa, Gospodarka, Administracja.*

UK/0952-1895
**GOVERNANCE (OXFORD).**
(GOVERNANCE.). [Governance]. Vol. 1, No. 1 (Jan. 1988)-. Periodical. English. Four times a year. $134.00 North America; $149.00 other. Blackwell Publishers, 238 Main Street, Cambridge MA 02142. **Tel** (617)547-7110, (800)835-6770, FAX (617)547-0789. **ED** Colin Campbell and B Guy Peters. **LC** JA1.A1; G68. **DD** 350/.0005. **[CCC]. Bk Rev. Ad Acc. Circ:** 800. available on microfilm and microfiche from University Microfilms International (UMI).
**Desc:** Provides a forum for work in the field of executive politics as practised by elected politicians and career civil servants.
**Ind/Abst** PAIS Int. Print (1991-).

US
**GOVERNING BOARD MONTHLY MINUTES.** English. Twelve times a year. $21.60. St. Johns River Water Management District, PO Box 1429, Palatka FL 32178. **Tel** (904)329-4500.

US/0271-3497
**GOVERNING NORTH DAKOTA.** English. be. Bureau of Governmental Affairs, University of North Dakota, Box 7176, Grand Forks ND 58202. **Tel** (701)777-3041. **ED** Lloyd B Omdahl. **LC** JK6401; .O43A. **DD** 320.4784. **Circ:** 6,000.
**Desc:** Handbook describing government in North Dakota.

US/0894-3842
**GOVERNING (WASHINGTON, D.C.). See** Political Science.

US/0146-8405
**GOVERNMENT AFFAIRS REPORT.** ***Title Change.*** [Gov. aff. rep.]. **Added/Corp** National Parking Association. (1973)-(19??). Periodical. English. Ten times a year. National Parking Association Inc, 1112 16th Street Northwest, Suite 300, Washington DC 20036. **Tel** (202)296-4336, FAX (202)331-8523. ***Merged into*** *Parking.*

UK
**GOVERNMENT AND INDUSTRY.** English. ir. £95.00. Longman Group Ltd., Fourth Avenue, Longman House, Harlow Essex CM19 5SR England. **Tel** 011 44 279 429655, FAX 011 44 279 431059, telex 81259. **(Subscription address:** Fourth Avenue, Harlow Essex CM19 5AA England**)**

UK/0967-3873
**GOVERNMENT AND MUNICIPAL BUYERS GUIDE.** (1935)-. Consumer Publication. English. an. £55.00. Benn Business Information Service Ltd, Riverbank House, Angel Lane, Tonbridge Kent TN9 1SE England. **Tel** 011 44 732 362666, FAX 011 44 732 770483, telex 95454 BBIS. **ED** Maria Atkin.

US/1054-5859
**GOVERNMENT & POLITICS ALERT.** ***Ceased.*** [Gov. polit. alert]. **Added/Corp** Government Research Service. **VFOAT** Government and Politics Alert. Vol. 2, No. 8 (Sept. 1990)-(Sept. 1993). Periodical. English. Six times a year. Government Research Service, 701 Jackson, Suite 304B, Topeka KS 66603. **Tel** (913)232-7720, (800)346-6898, FAX (913)232-1615. **ED** Lynn Hellebust. **LC** IN PROCESS. **DD** 328. **Bk Rev**, (Qty: 240). ***Continues*** *Legislative Information Alert, 1044-9094.*

US/0883-8690
**GOVERNMENT ASSISTANCE ALMANAC.** [Gov. assist. alm.]. (1986)-. English. an (Mar.). $125.00. Omnigraphics Inc., 2500 Penobscot Building, 25th Floor, Detroit MI 48226. **Tel** (313)961-1340, (800)234-1340, FAX (313)961-1383. **ED** J. Robert Dumouchel. **LC** HC110.P63; G69. **DD** 353.0082/025. Index available (bound in all issues).
**Desc:** Describes all 1,013 domestic assistance programs available both financial and non-financial. 3,800 federal addresses, phone numbers. 100 page index. How-to-apply section in introductory chapter.

US/1058-1774
**GOVERNMENT (BOCA RATON, FLA.).**
(GOVERNMENT.). [Government]. **Added/Corp** Social Issues Resources Series, inc. **VFOAT** SirS Global Perspectives, Government. (1991)-. English. $80.00. Social Issues Resources Series Inc, PO Box 2348, Boca Raton FL 33427. **Tel** (800)327-0513, (407)994-0079. **DD** 320.

CN/0840-870X
**GOVERNMENT BUSINESS OPPORTUNITIES. See** Business-Purchasing.

US/0738-4300
**GOVERNMENT COMPUTER NEWS.** [Gov. comput. news]. Vol. 1, No. 1 (Dec. 1982)-. Periodical. English. sm (26 issues). $85.00 US; $123.00 Canada; $115.00 Mexico; $150.00 (surface mail) other. Cahners Publishing Company, 249 West 17th Street, New York NY 10011. **Tel** (212)645-0067, FAX (212)242-6987. **(Subscription address:** Cahners Publishing Company / Colorado, Paid Subscription Service Center, PO Box 7610, Highlands Ranch CO 80126-7610.**)** **DD** 001. **[CCC].** available on microfilm from University Microfilms International (UMI); available on CD-ROM; available on an online database (files 648,675/Full-Text) from DIALOG.
**Desc:** Tells buyers and specifiers what they need to know about new products and services, technology applications and industry and government actions that affect technology in government. Regular sections cover: news, microcomputing, software, communications, systems, DOD computing and government business.
**Ind/Abst** Comput. ASAP [Full Txt.]; Comput. Database [Full Txt.]; Comput. Lit. Index; F&S Index Plus Text, Int. [Select. Cov.]; PROMT; Trade Ind. Index [Full Txt.].

US/0017-2596
**GOVERNMENT CONTRACTOR, THE.** Vol. 1 (Jan. 9, 1959)-. English. wk. $896.00 US; $926.00 other. Federal Publications Inc, 1120 20th Street Northwest, Washington DC 20036. **Tel** (202)337-7000, (800)922-4330, FAX (202)659-2233. **ED** Marvin I. Friedman. **DD** 351.711; 051. ctrl circ.
**Desc:** Analysis of developments in government contracting.

●US/1064-6795
**GOVERNMENT CONTRACTS & SUBCONTRACT LEADS DIRECTORY.**
[Gov. contracts subcontract leads dir.]. **Added/Corp** Government Data Publications (Firm). **VFOAT** Government Contracts and Subcontract Leads Directory. (1992)-. Directory. English. an. $96.75. Government Data Publications / Washington D.C., 1155 Connecticut Avenue Northwest, Washington DC 20036. **Tel** (718)627-0819. **LC** HD3858; .G59. **DD** 381. ***Continues*** *Government Contracts Directory, 0072-5137.*

US/0162-1076
**GOVERNMENT CONTRACTS REPORTS.**
**Added/Corp** United States. Laws, Statutes, etc. Commerce Clearing House. **VFOAT** Government Contracts Reporter. (19??)-. English. wk. $1,530.00 (one year), $1,390.00 (two year). Commerce Clearing House Inc., 4025 West Peterson Avenue, Chicago IL 60646-6085. **Tel** (312)583-8500, FAX (708)940-4600.

US/0145-6598
**GOVERNMENT CONTRACTS SERVICE. See** Law.

CN/0822-8620
**GOVERNMENT DIRECTORY FOR BRITISH COLUMBIA WITH SELECTED FEDERAL CONTACTS.** [Gov. dir. B.C. sel. fed. contacts]. June 1983-. Directory. English. sa. Business Council of British Columbia, 1050 West Pender, Suite 810, Vancouver British Columbia V6E 3S7, Canada. **Tel** (604)684-3384. **DD** 354.711/00025. ctrl circ. ***Continues*** *Departmental and Staff Directory, Government of British Columbia, 0710-2798.*

●US/1062-1466
**GOVERNMENT DIRECTORY OF ADDRESSES AND TELEPHONE NUMBERS, THE.** [Gov. dir. addresses teleph. numbers]. 1st Edition (1992)-. Directory. English. an (July). $150.00. Omnigraphics Inc., 2500 Penobscot Building, 25th Floor, Detroit MI 48226. **Tel** (313)961-1340, (800)234-1340, FAX (313)961-1383. **ED** Laurie Lanzen Harris. **LC** JK6; .G58. **DD** 350/.00025/73. ***Continues*** *Long Distance Book. Vol. 2, Government Directory of Addresses and Telephone Numbers.*

US/1053-282X
**GOVERNMENT DISC. 1, US FEDERAL GOVERNMENT [COMPUTER FILE], THE.**
**VFOAT** US Federal Government. (1991)-. Periodical. English. qt. $350.00. Highlighted Data Inc., 6628 Medhill Place, Falls Church VA 22043. **Tel** (703)516-9211.
**Desc:** Complete CD-ROM directory of the entire US Federal Government: Congress, the executive branch, and the judiciary. This electronic directory is designed for lobbyists, associations, PACs, business leaders, schools, libraries and federal and local officials who need information on the federal government.

US
**GOVERNMENT DOCUMENTS CATALOG SUBSCRIPTION SERVICE [COMPUTER FILE]. Added/Corp** Auto-Graphics, Inc. **VFOAT** GDCS Service. (Dec. 1988)-. Catalog. English. mo (12 issues). $1600.00 (1 regular workstation); $2040.00 (2nd workstation). Auto Graphics Inc., 3201 Temple Avenue, Pomona CA 91768. **Tel** (800)776-6939.
**Desc:** CD-ROM catalog containing available government publications or GPO titles since 1976 on one disc.

US/0017-2626
**GOVERNMENT EXECUTIVE.** [Gov. exec.]. Vol. 1 (March 1969)-. Periodical. English. Twelve times a year. $48.00. Government Executive, 1501 M Street Northwest, Suite 300, Washington DC 20005. **Tel** (202)739-8500. **ED** Timothy B. Clark. **LC** JK1; .G58. **DD** 353. **CODEN** GVEXAW. **[CCC]. Bk Rev. Ad Acc. Circ:** 76,000 (ctrl). available on microfilm and microfiche from University Microfilms International (UMI). Documents available from UMI Article Clearinghouse.
**Desc:** Government marketing, advertising and sales.
**Ind/Abst** ABI/INFORM Glob. Ed.; ABI Inform Ondisc (Sept. 1975-Oct. 1981); Air Univ. Libr. Index Mil. Period. (1987-); Bus. Index (1979-?); PAIS Int. Print (1991-); Sage Public Adm. Abstr. (1974-?); Urban Aff. Abstr. (Sept. 1975-Oct. 1981).

US
**GOVERNMENT FUNDING REPORT.**
(19??)-. English. ir. Grantechs, 3240 North Webster Road, Tucson AZ 85715. **Tel** (602)296-8748. ***Continues*** *Grantechs, 0145-8302.*

PP
**GOVERNMENT GAZETTE. See** Political Science.

MF
**GOVERNMENT GAZETTE OF MAURITIUS, THE. Main/Corp** Mauritius. English. wk. Rs3.00. Mauritius Government Printer, Place D Armes, Government Printing Department, Port Louis Mauritius. **Tel** 08-1783 OR 08 4011. **LC** J8; .B695. **DD** 354/.66/10005. **Circ:** 1,300 (ctrl). ***Continues*** *Government Gazette of the Colony of Mauritius.*

AT
**GOVERNMENT GAZETTE OF THE STATE OF NEW SOUTH WALES.**
**Main/Corp** New South Wales. No. 1, (1832)-. English. Fifty-two times a year. $284.62. NSW Government Printing Office, PO Box 256, Regents Park2143 Australia. **Tel** 011 61 02 7438777, FAX 062 954455. **LC** J8; .B82. **DD** 354.944/0005.

●US
**GOVERNMENT IMAGING. See** Computers.

US
**GOVERNMENT INFORMATION INSIDER.**
**Added/Corp** OMB Watch (Organization : U.S.). **VFOAT** Insider. Vol. 1, No. 1 (June 1990)-. Periodical. English. Six times a year. $75.00 institutions; $35.00 individuals. OMB Watch, 1731 Connecticut Avenue NW, Washington DC 20009. **Tel** (202)234-8494, FAX (202)234-8584. ***Formed by the union of*** *Action alert (OMB Watch (Organization : U.S.))* ***and*** *Monthly review (OMB Watch (Organization : U.S.)).*
**Ind/Abst** PAIS Int. Print.

US/0882-6587
**GOVERNMENT MICROCOMPUTER LETTER. See** Computers-Microcomputers, Personal Computers.

AT
**GOVERNMENT OF NEW SOUTH WALES DIRECTORY OF ADMINISTRATION AND SERVICES, THE.** ***Ceased.*** **VFOAT** New South Wales Government Directory. 1st- Ed.; 1977/78-Ceased 1989. Directory. English. ir. Government of New South Wales, Department of Services, Box 30 Sydney New South Wales 2001 Australia. **LC** JQ4521; .G68. **DD** 354.944/00025.

CN/0701-9599
**GOVERNMENT OF ONTARIO TELEPHONE DIRECTORY. See** Communication-Telecommunications.

US/0364-1260
**GOVERNMENT PAPER SPECIFICATION STANDARDS.** ***Ceased.*** **Main/Corp** United States. Congress. Joint Committee on Printing. **VFOAT** Paper Specification Standards. (1959)-(1993). English. ir (supplements). Superintendent of Documents, US Government Printing Office, Washington DC 20402. **Tel** (202)275-3328, FAX (202)786-2377.
**Desc:** For use in the procurement of paper stock for printing, these standards should be of value and interest to paper manufacturers, printing establishments, and others concerned with paper standards. It contains detailed standard specifications, standards to be used in testing, and definitive color standards for all mimeograph, duplicator, writing, manifold, bond ledger, and index papers.

US/0887-4085
**GOVERNMENT PRIME CONTRACTS MONTHLY.** [Gov. prime contracts mon.]. **Added/Corp** Government Data Publications (Firm). **VFOAT** GDP's Government Prime Contracts Monthly. **VAT** Government Data Publications Government Prime Contracts Monthly. (19??)-. English. Twelve times a year. $72.00. Government Data Publications / New York, GDP Building, 1661 McDonald Avenue, Brooklyn NY 11230. **Tel** (718)627-0819. **ED** Siepfried Lobel. **LC** HD3858;

# Public Administration

.G615. **DD** 338.7/4/02973.
 **Desc:** Lists government contracts. Each listing is complete and contains name and address of awardee, agency, description of material, quantity, contract number and amount.

US/0887-4107
**GOVERNMENT PRODUCTION PRIME CONTRACTORS DIRECTORY.** [Gov. prod. prime contract. dir.]. **Added/Corp** Government Data Publications (Firm). **VFOAT** Directory of Government Production Prime Contractors. (1968)-. Directory. English. an. $15.00. Government Data Publications / New York, GDP Building, 1661 McDonald Avenue, Brooklyn NY 11230. **Tel** (718)627-0819. **LC** HD3861.U6; G684. **DD** 338.7/4/02573.
 **Desc:** This valuable two-part directory lists the names and addresses of organizations which received government production prime contracts. alphabetically by firm name. Directory II is organized in zip code number sequence.

US/0896-0674
**GOVERNMENT PRODUCTIVITY NEWS.** [Gov. prod. news]. Vol. 1, No. 1 (May 1987)-. Periodical. English. Ten times a year (July, & Aug. issue combined). $57.00 US government agencies, universities & non-profit groups, libraries, and individuals; $90.00 US government institutions; $64.00 other. Government Productivity News, PO Box 27435, Austin TX 78755. **Tel** (512)343-1884. **ED** James E. Jarrett. **DD** 658. Index available. cum. index. **Bk Rev**.
 **Desc:** A digest on cost reduction and quality enhancement for all governments. Experiences cites, case histories and academic research is included.

●US/1055-825X
**GOVERNMENT PROGRAMS.** (1993)-. Periodical. English. qt. $29 99. Publishing & Business Consultants, PO Box 75392, Los Angeles CA 90075. **Tel** (213)732-3477, FAX (213)732-9123. **ED** Andeson Napoleon Atia. **Ad Acc.** Full Page (B&W) $5750.00. Half Page (B&W) $3575.00. Full Page (Color) $8750.00 (2 color). Half Page (Color) $5500.00 (2 color). **Circ:** 160,000 total.
 **Desc:** Features articles on grants, as well as special assistance students, business and families with dependents.

US/0737-5255
**GOVERNMENT PROGRAMS AND PROJECTS DIRECTORY. Added/Corp** Gale Research Company. No. 1 (May 1983)-. Directory. English. $135.00. Gale Research Inc., 835 Penobscot Building, Detroit MI 48226. **Tel** (800)877-GALE, (313)961-2242, FAX (313)961-6083, telex TWX 810-221-7086. **ED** Anthony T Kruzas and Kay Gill. **LC** JK404; .G68. **DD** 353.07/8/025. **NLM** JK 404; G721.
 **Desc:** Provides facts and figures on hundreds of programs implemented, managed, and supported by executive departments and independent agencies of the Federal Government.

UK/0969-4110
**GOVERNMENT PROPERTY CONTRACTS BULLETIN.** (19??)-. Periodical. English. mo. £155.00 Europe; £165.00 other (Institutions). Churchill Livingstone, 1-3 Baxter's Place, Leith Walk, Edinburgh EH1 3AF Scotland. **Tel** 011 44 31 556 2424, FAX 011 44 31 558 1278, telex 727511. **(Subscription address:** Maruzen Company Ltd., PO Box 5050, Import & Export Department, Tokyo 100 31 Japan.)

HK
**GOVERNMENT PUBLICATIONS DIRECTORY / CHENG FU KAN WU MU LU. Added/Corp** Hong Kong. Government Services. **VFOAT** Cheng Fu Kan Wu Mu Lu. (Oct. 1976)-. Periodical. English (Chinese) an. Free. Hong Kong Government Information Service, Beaconsfield House, 4 Queens Road, Hong Kong Hong Kong. **Tel** 011 852 8428801 4, telex 61190 HKGIS. **(Subscription address:** Government Information Service, Publications Office, 1 Battery Path, Hong Kong Hong Kong.) **LC** Z3107.H7; G68; J613. **DD** 015/.51/25. **Circ:** 8,000 (ctrl). **Continues** List of Government Publications.
 **Desc:** Lists all saleable government publications which include laws of Hong Kong, maps, trade forms, statistical periodicals and miscellaneous reports.

US/0277-9390
**GOVERNMENT PUBLICATIONS REVIEW (1982).** *Title Change.* See Library and Information Sciences.

US/0161-1127
**GOVERNMENT R & D REPORT.** See Science and Technology.

US/0072-5188
**GOVERNMENT REFERENCE BOOKS.** [Gov. ref. books]. 1st Ed. (1968/69)-. English. be. $67.50. Libraries Unlimited Inc., PO Box 6633, Department 920, Englewood CO 80155. **Tel** (800)237-6124. **ED** Leroy F. Schwarzkopf. **LC** Z1223.Z7; G68. **DD** 015/.73. **NLM** Z 1223.Z7 G721. **Bk Rev. Ad Acc.**
 **Desc:** A single source for government document reference books.

US
**GOVERNMENT RELATIONS NOTE.** See Medical Science and Technology.

US/0733-5156
**GOVERNMENT SALES STRATEGIST.** [Gov. sales strateg.]. Vol. 1, No. 1 (June 1982)-. Periodical. English. Twelve times a year. $77.00 (one year), $131.00 (two year), $185.00 (three year). Newsletter Management Corporation, 10076 Boca Entrada Boulevard, Boca Raton FL 33431. **Tel** (407)241-1800.

US/0738-3096
**GOVERNMENT TENDER REPORT.** (GOVERNMENT TENDER REPORT / ATA.). **Added/Corp** American Trucking Associations. Government Traffic Department. (19??)-. English. da. $325.00. ATA, 1616 P Street NW, Washington DC 20036.

US/0161-1623
**GOVERNMENT TRAINING NEWS.** (197?)-. Periodical. English. mo. $175.00 (one year), $315.00 (two year), $446.00 (three year). Business Publishers Inc., 951 Pershing Drive, Silver Spring MD 20910-4464. **Tel** (301)587-6300, (800)274-0122, FAX (301)585-9075. **(Subscription address:** Government Training News, Subscription Office, PO Box 830350, Birmingham AL 35283-0350.) **ED** Leonard Eiserer.
 **Desc:** A report on training trends and opportunities, cost and effectiveness studies, and over all personnel training, policies at the federal, state and local government levels.

US/0193-4775
**GOVERNMENTAL FLEET MANAGEMENT.** (Sept./Oct. 1979)-. Periodical. English. bm. $14.00 US; $22.50 other. Fleet Technology Inc, PO Box 11130, Antioch Station, Kansas City MO 64119.

US
**GOVERNMENTAL GUIDE. TENNESSEE EDITION. VFOAT** Tennessee Governmental Guide. English. an. Government Guide, PO Drawer 299, Madison TN 37115. **ED** C H Boone. **LC** JK5201.

●US/1074-9845
**GOVERNMENTAL SERVICES NEWSLETTER (ASHLAND, MO.).** (GOVERNMENTAL SERVICES NEWSLETTER.). [Gov. serv. newsl.]. Vol. 1, No. 1 (Sept. 1992)-. Periodical. English. mo. $50.00. Governmental Services / Missouri, PO Box 87, Ashland MO 65010. **Tel** (314)657-7016. **ED** John E. Ballard. **Circ:** 200 (ctrl). **Continues** Governmental Affairs Newsletter, 0148-4664.

AT
**GOVERNMENTS OF AUSTRALIA.** (19??)-. Directory. English. 695.00Aus$ Australia; 730.00Aus$ New Zealand, Papua New Guinea; 738.00Aus$ Indonesia, Malaysia, Singapore, 746.00Aus$ Japan, India; 758.00Aus$ US & Canada; 766.00Aus$ Europe. International Public Relations Pty Ltd., 33 Walsh Street, West Melbourne Victoria 3003 Australia. **Tel** 011 61 03 329 9333, FAX 011 61 03 329 7996. available on an online database.

US
**GOVERNOR'S BIENNIAL REPORT (MONTANA). Main/Corp** Montana. Office of the Governor. English. be. $6.11. Montana Office of the Governor, Helena MT 59601. **LC** J87; .M916A. **DD** 353.9786/0006.

US
**GOVERNOR'S COORDINATION AND APECIAL SERVICES PLAN FOR THE PERIOD OF ... / [PREPARED BY] ILLINOIS DEPARTMENT OF COMMERCE AND COMMUNITY AFFAIRS. Main/Corp** Illinois. Governor. **Added/Corp** Illinois. Dept. of Commerce and Community Affairs. United States. Job Training Partnership Act. (19??)-. English. an. Illinois Department of Commerce & Community Affairs, 620 East Adams Street, Springfield IL 62701. **Tel** (217)782-7500, FAX (217)785-6454. **LC** HD5715.3.I3; I4a. **DD** 353.97730083/3.

US
**GOVERNOR'S LEGISLATIVE MESSAGE AND BUDGET REPORT, THE. Main/Corp** Kansas. Governor. English. an. Topeka Kansas Office of the Governor, Topeka KS 66603. **LC** J87; .K219A. **DD** 353.978103/52.

US
**GOWER FEDERAL SERVICE ROYALTY VALUATION AND MANAGEMENT.** See Earth Sciences-Mineralogy.

US
**GOWER FEDERAL SERVICES PLAN.** See Real Estate.

US/1058-0891
**GPO NEW SALES PUBLICATIONS (1991).** (GPO NEW SALES PUBLICATIONS [MICROFORM].). [GPO new sales publ.]. **Added/Corp** United States. Superintendent of Documents. **VFOAT** Government Printing Office New Sales Publications. (1991)-. Government Publication. English. mo. free. Superintendent of Documents, US Government Printing Office, Washington DC 20402. **Tel** (202)275-3328, FAX (202)786-2377. **DD** 015. **Continues** New Publication PRF Monthly.

US/1058-0824
**GPO SALES PUBLICATIONS REFERENCE FILE.** (GPO SALES PUBLICATIONS REFERENCE FILE [MICROFORM].). [GPO sales publ. ref. file]. **Added/Corp** United States. Government Printing Office. United States. Superintendent of Documents. **VFOAT** Government Printing Office Ssales Publications Reference File. (197?)-. Government Publication. English. bm. $115.00 domestic; $143.75 other. Superintendent of Documents, US Government Printing Office, Washington DC 20402. **Tel** (202)275-3328, FAX (202)786-2377. **DD** 015. **Continues** Publications Reference File.
 **Desc:** A guide to current publications offered for sale by the Superintendent of Documents arranged to GPO stock numbers; International Standard Book Numbers (ISBN); Superintendent of Document classification numbers; and alphabetically.

US/0016-3619
**GRA REPORTER.** (GRA REPORTER / GOVERNMENTAL RESEARCH ASSOCIATION.). [GRA report.]. **Added/Corp** Governmental Research Association (U.S.). **VAT** Governmental Research Association Reporter. Vol. 1 (Jan./Feb. 1949)-. Periodical. English. Four times a year (Mar., June, Sept., Dec.). $40.00 Comes with Governmental Research Association Membership. Governmental Research Association, Samford University, 315 Samford Hall, Birmingham AL 35229. **Tel** (205)870-2482. **ED** Robert E. Norwood (editor's address: P. O. Box 12456, Texas Research League, Austin, TX 78711, telephone: (512)472-3127). **LC** JS302; .G58. **DD** 352. ctrl circ. **Absorbed** Bibliography of Governmental Research, 8755-1365.

●CN/1196-0612
**GRAND BABILLARD, LE.** [Gd. babillard]. **Added/Corp** Saint-Basile-le-Grand (Quebec). Vol. 13, No. 8 (1992)-. Periodical. French. mo. Free. Joliso Bureau du Greffier Hotel de Ville, 204 rue Principale, St-Basile-Le-Grand Quebec J0L 1S0 Canada. **DD** 352.0714/37/05. **Continues** Joliso (Saint-Basile-le-Grand, Quebec)., 0711-4397.

●CN/1193-4077
**GRANDE PRAIRIE CITY DIRECTORY.** [Gd. Prairie city dir.]. **VFOAT** Henderson's Grande Prairie City Directory. (1992)-. Directory. English. $95.00. Henderson Directories, 34 West 2nd Avenue, Vancouver, British Columbia, V5Y 1B3 Canada. **DD** 971.123/1. **Continues** Grande Prairie, Alberta, City Directory., 0715-4127.

US/1054-769X
**GRANT/ACCESS. VFOAT** Grant Access. (1991)-. Periodical. English. bm. $60.00. Jack Wieder, 159 Whitney Street, San Francisco CA 94131.

US
**GRANT$ FOR PUBLIC POLICY AND PUBLIC AFFAIRS.** See Philanthropy.

US
**GRANTS ADMINISTRATION.** (GRANTS ADMINISTRATION; DEPT. STAFF MANUAL.). **VFOAT** Grants Administration Manual. Government Publication. English. US Department of Education, 400 Maryland Avenue SW, Room 4181, Washington DC 20202. **Tel** (202)401-1576, FAX (202)272-5447.
 **Desc:** Serves as a basic reference for those who are operationally engaged in the administrative and financial management of grants, as well as others within the organization who are involved.

US
**GRANTS ADMINISTRATION MANUAL. Main/Corp** United States. Environmental Protection Agency. (19??)-. Government Publication. English. ir. $38.00 domestic; $47.50 other. Superintendent of Documents, US Government Printing Office, Washington DC 20402. **Tel** (202)275-3328, FAX (202)786-2377.
 **Desc:** Designed to provide guidelines on the fiscal and administrative aspects of grant management to all granting agencies of the Department of Health and Human Services. Intended to serve as a basic reference for those who are operationally engaged in the administrative and financial management aspects of grants, as well as those program directors and others within the operating agencies who are involved in the award, review, or other program management aspects of grants.

# Public Administration

US/0889-8871
**GRANTS ADMINISTRATION NEWS.**
[Grants adm. news]. (1981)-. Periodical. English. sm. $200.00. Grants Administration News, 5825 Sky Park Drive, Plano TX 75093. **Tel** (214)447-0519. **DD** 338.

US/0196-4593
**GRANTS FOR RESEARCH ON LAW AND GOVERNMENT IN EDUCATION.** See Education.

●US
**GRANTS-IN-AID APPLICATION AND REFERENCE MATERIALS. Main/Corp** New York State Archives and Records Administration. Local Government Records Bureau. Grants Administration Unit. **VFOAT** New York State Local Government Records Management Improvement Fund; Local Government Records Management Improvement Fund. (1993)-. English. *Formed by the union of* Booklet I : Grant Application Materials *and* Booklet II : Grants-in-Aid Reference Materials.

US/1076-1500
**GRANTSEEKER, THE.** (19??)-. English. mo. $98.00. Government Information Services / Virginia, 4301 North Fairfax Drive, Suite 875, Arlington VA 22203. **Tel** (703)528-1082, FAX (703)528-6060, telex RCA 263591 GIS UR. **ED** Donald B. Hoffman.
 **Desc:** Helps grantseekers and proposal writers improve their writing skills. Takes the guess-work out of how to approach federal and state grant officers.

US
**GRASSROOTS REPORT.** See Law.

UK
**GREAT BRITAIN HOUSE OF COMMONS PARLIAMENTARY PAPERS. MICROFORM. Main/Corp** Great Britain. Parliament. House of Commons. **Added/Corp** Great Britain. Parliament. House of Commons. Parliamentary Papers. **VFOAT** House of Commons Parliamentary Papers; Parliamentary Papers. (1975)-. English. mo. £1500.00 UK; $2,582.78 US. Chadwyck-Healey Limited, The Quorum Barnwell Road, Cambridge CB5 8SW England. **Tel** 011 44 223 215512, telex 9312102281 CH G. **(Subscription address:** Chadwyck Healey Inc. / US Subscriptions, 1101 King Street, Suite 380, Alexandria VA 22314.)

US
**GREATER LOS ANGELES PUBLIC SERVICE GUIDE. VFOAT** Public Service Guide to Los Angeles City, County, State & Federal Offices. (1972/73)-. Periodical. English. ir. $55.00. Public Service Publications, 1523 West Eighth Street, Los Angeles CA 90017. **Tel** (213)484-1088. **ED** Barbara Rosien. **Bk Rev. Ad Acc.**
 **Desc:** Complete listings of government functions & services in Los Angeles, CA; Sacramento, San Francisco & partial Washington, DC.

GH/0379-8658
**GREENHILL JOURNAL OF ADMINISTRATION.** [Greenhill j. adm.]. **Added/Corp** Ghana Institute of Management and Public Administraion. Vol. 1 (April/June 1974)-. Periodical. English. qt. $5.00 Ghana; $11.85 UK; $16.00 other. Ghana Institute of Management & Public Administration, PO Box 50, Greenhill Achimota Ghana. **LC** JA26; .G73. **DD** 350/.0005. *Supersedes* Greenhill Bulletin.
 **Ind/Abst** Int. Polit. Sci. Abstr.

**GSA SUPPLY CATALOG (UNITED STATES. GENERAL SERVICES ADMINISTRATION : 1983).** (GSA SUPPLY CATALOG.). **Added/Corp** United States. General Services Administration. United States. Federal Supply Service. **VFOAT** G.S.A. Supply Catalog. **VAT** General Services Administration Supply Catalog. (Jan. 1983)-. Catalog. English. an. $38.00 domestic; $47.50 other. Superintendent of Documents, US Government Printing Office, Washington DC 20402. **Tel** (202)275-3328, FAX (202)786-2377. *Formed by the union of* GSA Supply Catalog. Furniture; GSA Supply Catalog. Industrial Products; GSA Supply Catalog. Office Products *and* GSA Supply Catalog. Tools.
 **Desc:** Contains a listing of items, office products, industrial products, tools, and furniture, used throughout the Federal Government which are available from GSA supply distribution facilities. Descriptions, prices, units of issue, and other pertinent information for ordering these items are also included.

US/1059-6224
**GUARDIAN (LEXINGTON, KY.), THE.** See Ethics.

AG
**GUIA DEL TERCER MUNDO. VFOAT** Suplemento Anual de Cuadernos del Tercer Mundo. 1976-. Spanish. Technical Press, Paraguay 2028 20. 14, Buenos Aires Argentina. **LC** JF60; .G84.

AG
**GUIA RELACIONES INSTITUCIONALES DEL ESTADO ARGENTINO. VFOAT** Guia Relaciones Institucionales del Estado. (1982)-. Spanish. an. Graform SA Editora, Av Cordoba 669, 120 PA 1054 Argentina. **LC** JL2021; .G84. **DD** 354.8204/025.

IT
**GUIDAZZURRA ALL'AMMINISTRAZIONE PUBBLICA. VFOAT** Guida Azzurra all'Amministrazione Pubblica; Blue Guide to the Italian State; BlueGuide to the Italian State. (199?)-. English. D Anselmi Editore SRL, Via Sommacampagna 9, 00185 Rome Italy. **Tel** 39-6-4463425, FAX 39-6-490356. **LC** JN5201; .G85. **DD** 354.4504/025. *Continues* Guidazzurra all'Amministrazione Italiana.

CN/1183-7705
**GUIDE, AGENCIES, BOARDS & COMMISSIONS, GOVERNMENT OF ONTARIO, A.** [Guide agencies boards comm. Gov. Ont.]. **Main/Corp** Ontario. **Added/Corp** Ontario. Public Appointments Secretariat. **VFOAT** Guide, Aeencies, Boards, and Commissions, Government of Ontario; Agencies, Boards & Commissions; Agencies, Boards, and Commissions. (1991)-. English. **DD** 354.71409.

CN/1183-7713
**GUIDE DES ORGANISMES, CONSEILS ET COMMISSIONS DU GOUVERNEMENT DE L'ONTARIO.** [Guide org. cons. comm. gouv. Ont.]. **Main/Corp** Ontario. **Added/Corp** Ontario. Secretariat des Nominations Publiques. **VFOAT** Organismes, Conseils et Commissions. (1991)-. French. Librairie du Gouvernement de l'Ontario, 880 rue Bay, Toronto Ontario M7A 1N8 Canada. **DD** 354.71409.

GR
**GUIDE. PUBLIC SERVICES, ORGANISATION OF PUBLIC AND PRIVATE LAW, BANKS, DIPLOMATIC CORPS, AIR COMPANIES, CONCISE GUIDE TO THESSALONIKI.** English. .500 Each. Horizon / Greece, Public Relations Organization, 50A Nikis Str, Athens Greece 119. **LC** JN5060.A1; .G84. **DD** 354/.495/002.

US
**GUIDE TO CALIFORNIA GOVERNMENT, A. Added/Corp** League of Women Voters of California. 11th Ed. (1977)-. English. $8.95. League of Women Voters of California, 926 J Street, Suite 1000, Sacramento CA 95814. **Tel** (916)442-7215, FAX (916)442-7362. *Continues* California Voters Handbook.

●US
**GUIDE TO FEDERAL FUNDING FOR ANTI-CRIME PROGRAMS.** (1994)-. English. ir. $107.50. Government Information Services / Virginia, 4301 North Fairfax Drive, Suite 875, Arlington VA 22203. **Tel** (703)528-1082, FAX (703)528-6060, telex RCA 263591 GIS UR. **ED** Elizabeth Basch, Heather Bodell, Charles Edwards.
 **Desc:** Describes over 75 federal programs that provide aid for anti-crime initiatives and activities.

US/0275-8393
**GUIDE TO FEDERAL FUNDING FOR EDUCATION.** See Education.

US/1055-596X
**GUIDE TO FEDERAL FUNDING FOR GOVERNMENTS AND NONPROFITS.** [Guide fed. fund. gov. nonprofits]. **Added/Corp** Government Information Services. (1991)-. English. an (Nov.). $364.90. Government Information Services / Virginia, 4301 North Fairfax Drive, Suite 875, Arlington VA 22203. **Tel** (703)528-1082, FAX (703)528-6060, telex RCA 263591 GIS UR. **ED** Charles Edwards, Heather C. Bodell, Alvin Lin, Elizabeth Basch, Andrea Croker. **LC** HJ275; .F4. **DD** 353.0072/53/05. *Continues* Federal Funding Guide, 0273-4435.

US/0276-9891
**GUIDE TO FEDERAL PROCUREMENT.** English. an. Northeast-Midwest Institute, Center for Regional Policy, 218 D Street Southeast, Washington DC 20003. **Tel** (202)544-5200, FAX (202)544-0043. **LC** JK1673; .G83. **DD** 353.0071/2/024658.

CN/0848-4597
**GUIDE TO FEDERAL PROGRAMS AND SERVICES.** [Guide fed. programs serv.]. **Added/Corp** Canada. Supply and Services Canada. 10th Ed. (1990)-. English. ir. 21.95Can$. Canada Communication Group Publishers, Order Processing, Ottawa Ontario K1A 0S9 Canada. **Tel** (819)956-4800, (819)956-4802. **LC** JL71; .C37a. **DD** 354/.71/00025. *Continues* Index to Federal Programs and Services (Canada. Supply and Services Canada), 0715-7193.

US
**GUIDE TO FLORIDA GOVERNMENT. Added/Corp** Florida. Legislature. House of Representatives. Office of the Clerk. 9th (1978)-. English. an. Office of the Clerk, State of Florida, House of Representatives, State Capital, Tallahassee FL 32301. **Tel** (904)488-1157. **LC** JK4430; .G86. **DD** 353.9759/00025. *Supersedes* Guide to Agencies of the Florida Executive Department.

US/0072-8454
**GUIDE TO GOVERNMENT IN HAWAII. Added/Corp** Hawaii. Legislature. Legislative Reference Bureau. University of Hawaii (Honolulu). Legislative Reference Bureau. 1st Ed. (1961)-. English. ir (Every 3-4 years.). $4.00. Legislative Reference Bureau - Hawaii, State Capitol, Honolulu HI 96813. **Tel** (800)587-0690, FAX (808)587-0699. **LC** JQ6121; .G8. **DD** 353.9. **Circ:** 800. *Continues* University of Hawaii (Honolulu). Legislative Reference Bureau. Directory, Agencies and Officers, Territory of Hawaii.
 **Desc:** Organization, description of departments and agencies of the state, county and federal governments in Hawaii.

US
**GUIDE TO MANAGEMENT IMPROVEMENT PROJECTS IN LOCAL GOVERNMENT, THE. Added/Corp** International City Management Association. Management Information Service. Vol. 1 (Jan. 1977)-. Periodical. English. qt. $65.00. International City Management Association, 777 North Capitol Street NE, Suite 500, Washington DC 20002. **Tel** (202)289-4262, (800)745-8780, FAX (202)962-3500. **(Subscription address:** International City Management Association, PO Box 2011, Annapolis Junction MD 20701.**)**

US/0091-0716
**GUIDE TO NEBRASKA STATE AGENCIES. Added/Corp** Nebraska Publications Clearinghouse. (19??)-. English. be. Nebraska Publications Clearinghouse, 1420 P Street Northeast, Lincoln NE 68508. **Tel** (402)471-2045. **ED** Karen Lusk. **LC** JK6630; .G83. **DD** 353.9/782/04025. ctrl circ.

US/0148-7841
**GUIDE TO SERVICES.** (GUIDE TO SERVICES; AN ANNUAL REPORT - TEXAS. OFFICE OF STATE-FEDERAL RELATIONS.). [Guide Serv.]. **Main/Corp** Texas. Office of State-Federal Relations. English. an. Ideal Publishing Corporation, 2 Park Avenue, New York NY 10016. **LC** JK4801; .T45A. **DD** 353.9/764/92.

UK
**GUIDES TO OFFICIAL PUBLICATIONS.** Vol. 1, (19??)-. Monographic series. English. ir. Price varies per volume. Pergamon Press, An Imprint of Elsevier Science Ltd., The Boulevard, Langford Lane, Kidlington, Oxford OX5 1GB United Kingdom. **Tel** 011 44 865 843000, 011 44 865 843699, FAX 011 44 865 843010. **(Subscription address:** US/ 395 Saw Mill River Road, Elmsford, NY 10523; Can/ 150 Consumers Road/Suite 104, Willowdale Ontario M2J 1P9; Aus-NZ/ POB 544, Potts Point NSW 2011**) ED** J. E. Pemberton.

CN/0833-4641
**GVRD NEWS.** (GVRD NEWS / GREATER VANCOUVER REGIONAL DISTRICT.). [GVRD news]. **Main/Corp** Greater Vancouver (B.C.). **VAT** Greater Vancouver Regional District News. (March/April 1984)-. Periodical. English. bm. Free on request. Greater Vancouver Regional District, 4330 Kingsway, Burnaby BC V5H 4G8 Canada. **Tel** (604)432-6200, FAX (604)432-6251. **ED** Bud Elsie (editor's phone: (604)432-6203). **DD** 352.0711/33. **Circ:** 8,000. *Continues* Greater Vancouver Regional District Newsletter, 0706-7895.
 **Desc:** Activities of the regional government in Greater Vancouver - parks, sewers, water, labour relations, pollution control, planning, etc.

JA
**GYOSEI KANRI KENKYU. Added/Corp** Gyosei Kanri Mondai Kenkyukai. No. 1, (Feb. 2, 1976)-. Periodical. Japanese. qt. Institute of Administrative Management / Tokyo, PO Box 1106, Sunshine 60, 3-1-1 Higashi Ikebulcuro, Toshima-ku, Tokyo 170 Japan. **Tel** 03-981-0441. **LC** JQ1601; .G93. **Bk Rev. Circ:** 1,000.
 **Desc:** Presents research papers on public administration, political science and administrative law. Includes coverage of introduction of administrative reform in local governments.

JA
**GYOSEI KANRICHO NO ARAMASHI. Main/Corp** Japan. Gyosei Kanricho. 1978-. Japanese. Gyosei Kanricho, c/o Chuo Godo Chosa Dai, 4-Gokan 1-1 Kasumigaseki 3 Chiyoda-ku, Tokyo Japan. **LC** JQ1650.G9; J36B.

US/1057-7025
**HALL OF THE STATES MANDATE MONITOR.** [Hall States mandate monit.]. **Added/Corp** National Conference of State Legislatures. (1991)-. Periodical. English. ir (10-12 issues). $35.00 US; $40.00 Canada. National Conference of State

# Public Administration

Legislatures, 1560 Broadway, Suite 700, Denver CO 80202. **Tel** (303)830-2054, FAX (303)863-8003. **ED** Christine Wnuk. **DD** 328.
**Desc:** A complete guide to all congressional bills that impose costly mandates on state and local government. Its "Watch List" will alert you to the most threatening legislation with a summary of bills nearing passage.

US/0438-5047
**HANDBOOK FOR GEORGIA LEGISLATORS.** 1st- Ed.; 1958-. English. University of Georgia Institute of Government, 201 North Milledge Avenue, Athens GA 30602. **Tel** (706)542-2736. **ED** Edwin L Jackson and Mary E Stakes. **LC** JK4330; .H3. **DD** 328.7588.
**Desc:** Handbook describing the powers and duties of the Georgia legislators, and the workings of the Georgia General Assembly.

NR
**HANDBOOK OF BENDEL STATE OF NIGERIA. Main/Corp** Bendel State (Nigeria). **VFOAT** Bendel State of Nigeria Handbook. English. Ministry of Information Social Development and Sports, Benin City Nigeria. **LC** JQ3099.B43; B46A. **DD** 354.669/3/0005.

US/0095-2842
**HANDBOOK OF ILLINOIS GOVERNMENT. See** Political Science.

US
**HANDBOOK OF STATE PROGRAMS FOR LOCAL GOVERNMENTS. Main/Corp** Oregon. Intergovernmental Relations Division. 1978-. English. an. Intergovernmental Relations Division, Executive Department, 306 State Library Building, Salem OR 97310. **LC** JK9035; .O73A. **DD** 309.1/795/04.

US
**HANDBOOK OF THE NEVADA LEGISLATURE. Title Change. Main/Corp** Nevada. Legislature. English. be. Nevada Legislative Counsel Bureau / Carson City, Legislative Building, Carson City NV 89701. **LC** JK8571; .A32. **Continues** Handbook of Nevada Legislature. **Continued by** Nevada Legislative Manual.

US
**HANDY-WHITMAN INDEX OF PUBLIC UTILITY CONSTRUCTION COSTS. BULLETIN, THE. Added/Corp** Whitman, Requardt and Associates, Baltimore. **VFOAT** Public Utility Construction Costs. (1951)-. English. sa. $120.00. Whitman Requardt and Associates, 2315 Saint Paul Street, Baltimore MD 21218. **Tel** (410)235-3450 ext.413.
**Continues** Handy Index of Public Utility Construction Costs.

CJ
**HANSARD OFFICIAL REPORT. Main/Corp** Cayman Islands. Legislative Assembly. (19??)-. English. qt. Cayman Islands Government, Information Services, Tower Building, Government Administration Building, Grand Cayman British West Indies. **Tel** (809)94-98092, FAX 97544, telex 4260 CIGOVT. **LC** J137.5; .H53a. **DD** 354.7292/1/0005. **Circ:** 100 (ctrl).
**Desc:** Verbatim report of the proceedings of the Cayman Islands legislative assembly.

CN/0713-0082
**HANSARD : OFFICIAL REPORT / LEGISLATIVE ASSEMBLY OF THE NORTHWEST TERRITORIES. Main/Corp** Northwest Territories. Legislative Assembly. 4th Session, 9th Assembly (Feb. 1981)-. Periodical. English. ir (daily during legislative session). 85.00Can$ Northwest Territory; 95.00Can$ other. Artisan Press Ltd., Box 1566, Yellowknife, Northwest Territory, X1A 2P2 Canada. **Tel** (403)920-2794, FAX (403)873-8487. **LC** J118; .H26a. **DD** 328.719/202.

CN/0833-0476
**HANSARD OFFICIAL REPORT OF DEBATES.** [Hansard off. rep. debates - Legis. Assem. Ont., Standing Comm. Ombudsman]. **Main/Corp** Ontario. Legislative Assembly. Standing Committee on the Ombudsman. English. Sessional Subscription Service Ministry of Government Services, 5th Floor/880 Bay Street, Toronto Ontario M7A 1N8 Canada. **LC** JL269.5.O4; O55A. **Continues** Hansard Official Report of Debates.

CN/0822-2193
**HANSARD OFFICIAL REPORT OF DEBATES / LEGISLATIVE ASSEMBLY OF ONTARIO, STANDING COMMITTEE ON RESOURCES DEVELOPMENT.**
[Hansard off. rep. debates - Legis. Assemb. Ont., Standing Comm. Resour. Dev.]. **Main/Corp** Ontario. Legislative Assembly. Standing Committee on Resources Development. (June 16, 1983)-. English. ir (Published daily while legistature is in session). 275.00Can$. Crown Publications Inc., 521 Fort Street, Victoria, British Columbia, V8W 1E7 Canada. **Tel** (604)386-4636, FAX (604)386-0221. **LC** J108; .H214f. **DD** 328.713/02.

**Continues** Ontario. Legislative Assembly. Standing Committee on Resources Development. Legislature on Ontario Debates, Official Report (Hansard), 0822-2207.

CN/0822-126X
**HANSARD, OFFICIAL REPORT OF DEBATES / LEGISLATIVE ASSEMBLY OF ONTARIO, STANDING COMMITTEE ON SOCIAL DEVELOPMENT.** [Hansard off. re. debates Legis. Assem. Ont. - Standing Comm. Soc. Dev.]. **Main/Corp** Ontario. Legislative Assembly. Standing Committee on Social Development. No. S-1 (May 16, 1983)-. English. tw. $15.00 per session. Sessional Subscription Service Ministry of Government Services, 5th Floor/880 Bay Street, Toronto Ontario M7A 1N8 Canada. **LC** HN110.O5; O49A. **DD** 361.6/1/09713.
**Continues** Ontario. Legislative Assembly. Standing Committee on Social Development. Legislature on Ontario Debates, Official Report (Hansard).

●US/1071-5401
**HAWVER'S CAPITOL REPORT.**
(HAWVER'S CAPITOL REPORT : REPORTING THE POLITICS & GOVERNMENT OF KANSAS.). [Hawver's capitol rep.]. **VFOAT** Capitol Report. (June 18, 1993)-. Periodical. English. sm. $188.85. Hawver's Capitol Report, 3823 Southwest Wood Valley Drive, Topeka KS 66610. **Tel** (913)266-6222, FAX (913)267-1099. **ED** Martin Hawver. **DD** 328. **Circ:** 400 (ctrl).

US/0193-7928
**HEALTH FUNDS DEVELOPMENT LETTER. See** Medical Science and Technology.

US
**HEALTH INFORMATION RESOURCES IN THE FEDERAL GOVERNMENT / PREPARED BY ODPHP NATIONAL HEALTH INFORMATION CENTER. See** Public Health and Safety.

US
**HEARING CALENDAR.** (19??)-. English. Fifty-two times a year. $20.00. Wisconsin Public Service Commission, PO Box 7854, Madison WI 53707. **Tel** FAX (608)266-3957.

CN/0848-8541
**HEMSON TORONTO LAND USE REPORT.** (THE HEMSON TORONTO LAND USE REPORT : PROCEEDINGS OF THE TORONTO LAND USE COMMITTEE.). [Hemson Tor. land use rep.]. **Added/Corp** Toronto (Ont.). City Council. Land Use Committee. **VFOAT** Toronto Land Use Report. Vol. 6, No. 15 (Sept. 13, 1989)-. Periodical. English. sm (escept July and Aug.). 225.00Can$. Hemson Consulting Ltd, 30 St Patrick Street, Suite 1000, Toronto Ontario, M5T 3A3 Canada. **Tel** 9416)593-5090, FAX (416)595-7144. **DD** 333.77/09713/541. **Continues** Toronto Land Use Report, 0828-167X.

UK
**HER MAJESTY'S CONSULS' LIST.** (1903)-. English. bm (6 issues). £120.00 US. Southern Magazines Ltd., Jewson Complex, Eccleston Road, Maidstone Kent ME15 6ST England. **Tel** 011 44 233 645777.
**(Subscription address:** Data Team Publishing Ltd., Data Team House, Tovil Hill, Maidstone Kent ME15 6OS England.) **LC** JX1784; .A63. **DD** 327.42.

UK
**HER MAJESTY'S INSPECTORATE OF CONSTABULARY ANNUAL REPORT.**
(19??)-. English. an. £11.20. Her Majesty's Stationery Office, 51 Nine Elms Lane, London SW8 5DR England. **Tel** 011 44 71 873 8459, 011 44 71 873 8499, FAX 011 44 71 873 8499, 011 44 71 873 8456, telex 297138. **(Subscription address:** Her Majesty's Stationery Office, PO Box 276, Publications Centre, London SW8 5DT England.)

US/0894-6434
**HERE IS YOUR INDIANA GOVERNMENT.** [Here is your Ind. gov.]. **Added/Corp** Indiana State Chamber of Commerce. Indiana Chamber of Commerce. (1944)-. English. an (Aug.). $9.00 (two years). Indiana Chamber of Commerce, 1 North Capitol, Suite 200, Indianapolis IN 46204. **Tel** (317)264-3110. **ED** Carl Henn Jr. **LC** JK5601; .H47. **DD** 320.9772. Index available.
**Desc:** Book contains complete description of state and local government, budgeting, taxes, courts, school corporations, Constitution of Indiana, plus miscellaneous information and statistics.

TZ
**HIARI / COMMUNITY DEVELOPMENT TRUST FUND. Added/Corp** Community Development Trust Fund of Tanzania. (19??)-. Periodical. English. sa. **LC** WMLC L 83/1972.
**Desc:** Newsletter of the Community Development Trust fund of Tanzania.

US/0747-9743
**HIGHER EDUCATION PUBLIC ADMINISTRATION DIRECTORY, THE.**
[High. educ. public adm. dir.]. Directory. English. Mr. Terry L. Johnson, 1185 Meadow Lane, #107, Concord CA 94520. **LC** JF1338.A2; H5. **DD** 350/.0007/073.

NW/0196-2523
**HIGHLIGHTS (SAIPAN).** (HIGHLIGHTS.). Periodical. English. mo. Public Information Office / Mariana Islands, Trust Territory of the Pacific Islands, Saipan 96950 Mariana Islands.

UK
**HMSO AGENCY CATALOGUE. Main/Corp** Great Britain. Her Majesty's Stationery Office. **VFOAT** Agency Catalogue. (1986/87)-. English. an. £7.55. Her Majesty's Stationery Office, 51 Nine Elms Lane, London SW8 5DR England. **Tel** 011 44 71 873 8459, 011 44 71 873 8499, FAX 011 44 71 873 8499, 011 44 71 873 8456, telex 297138. **(Subscription address:** Her Majesty's Stationery Office, PO Box 276, Publications Centre, London SW8 5DT England.) **LC** Z6464.I6; I62; JX1995. **DD** 016.3412. **Continues** Great Britain. Her Majesty's Stationery Office. International Organisations Catalogue.

UK/0263-7197
**HMSO MONTHLY CATALOGUE. Main/Corp** Great Britain. Her Majesty's Stationery Office. **VFOAT** Monthly Catalogue. **VAT** Her Majesty's Stationery Office Monthly Catalogue. (Feb. 1986)-. Periodical. English. mo. £17.00. Her Majesty's Stationery Office, 51 Nine Elms Lane, London SW8 5DR England. **Tel** 011 44 71 873 8459, 011 44 71 873 8499, FAX 011 44 71 873 8499, 011 44 71 873 8456, telex 297138. **(Subscription address:** Her Majestys Stationery Offic, PO Box 276 Public Centre, London SW8 5DT England) **Continues** Great Britain. Her Majesty's Stationery Office. Government Publications of ... (Monthly).

HK
**HONG KONG ANNUAL DIGEST OF STATISTICS. See** Public Administration-Abstracting, Bibliographies and Statistics.

HK
**HONG KONG GOVERNMENT GAZETTE, THE. Main/Corp** Hong Kong. No. 1 (Sept. 24, 1853)-. Periodical. English (Chinese). wk. HK$1,560 Hong Kong; HK$2570.00 US. Hong Kong Government Information Service, Beaconsfield House, 4 Queens Road, Hong Kong Hong Kong. **Tel** 011 852 8428801 4, telex 61190 HKGIS. **LC** J8; .B55. **DD** 354.51/25/0005. **Bk Rev**. **Ad Acc**. **Circ:** 4,000 (ctrl).
**Desc:** Provides information on latest government legislation, notices, tenders, appointments and various ordinances, regulations and bills of Hong Kong.

HK/0300-418X
**HONG KONG MONTHLY DIGEST OF STATISTICS. See** Public Administration-Abstracting, Bibliographies and Statistics.

CN
**HOOK N' COOK. Main/Corp** Manitoba. Dept. of Renewable Resources and Transportation Services. 1-. Monographic series. English. Price varies per volume. Department of Renewable Resources and Transportation Services, Box 22, 1495 Saint James Street, Winnipeg Manitoba R3H 0W9 Canada.

US/0148-3005
**HOUSE BILL SUMMARIES. Main/Corp** Virginia. General Assembly. House of Delegates. English. Commonwealth of Virginia House Bill Summaries, PO Box 654, Richmond VA 23205. **LC** KFV2407; .G45. **DD** 348/.755/01.

CN/0704-5603
**HOUSE OF COMMONS DEBATES (OTTAWA. DAILY ED.).** (HOUSE OF COMMONS DEBATES, OFFICIAL REPORT / DOMINION OF CANADA.). [House Commons debates (Ott., Dly. ed.)]. **Main/Corp** Canada. Parliament. House of Commons. 21st Parliament, 4th Session, Vol. 1 (1951)-. Periodical. English (French). ir. Canada Communication Group Publishers, Order Processing, Ottawa Ontario K1A 0S9 Canada. **Tel** (819)956-4800, (819)956-4802. **LC** J103; .K2. **DD** 328.71/02. **Continues** Official Report of the Debates of the House of Commons of the Dominion of Canada.

CN/0229-1398
**HOUSE OF COMMONS DEBATES (OTTAWA. RETROSPECTIVE COMPILATION). Title Change.** (HOUSE OF COMMONS DEBATES.). [House Commons debates]. **Main/Corp** Canada. Parliament. House of Commons. **VFOAT** Debats de la Chambre des Communes. (1867/68)-?. Periodical. English (French). Canadian Parlement Chambre of Communes, 180 Wellington Street/Room 435, CRS Ottawa Ontario K1AA 0A6 Canada. **Tel** (613)992-1254. available on microfiche.
**Continued by** Debates of the House of Commons of the Dominion of Canada., 0842-9790.

# Public Administration

US/0091-5939
**HOUSING & DEVELOPMENT REPORTER.** See Housing and Urban Development.

CN/0822-6482
**HOW OTTAWA SPENDS.** [How Ottawa spends]. **Added/Corp** Carleton University. School of Public Administration. (1983)-. Monographic series. English. an. Price varies per volume. Carleton University Press, 160 Paterson HL, Carleton University, Ottawa Ontario, K1S 5B6 Canada. **Tel** (613)788-3740. **(Subscription address:** Oxford University Press / Canada, 70 Wynford Drive, Don Mills ONT M3C 1J9 Canada.) **LC** HJ7662; .H68. **DD** 336.71/05. **Continues** How Ottawa Spends your Tax Dollars, 0711-4990.

US/1044-7784
**HOW TO FIND BUSINESS INTELLIGENCE IN WASHINGTON.** See Business.

CH/0250-8869
**HSIN SHIH / LIEN-HO-KUO CHIAO KO WEN TSU CHIH.** Began with July 1980 issue. Periodical. Chinese. ir. $.095. Science Press, 16 Donghuangchenggen North Street, Beijing 100707, People's Republic of China. **Tel** 011 86 1 4019821, 011 86 1 4010642, FAX 011 86 1 4012180, 011 86 1 4019810, telex 210147. **LC** HD9502.A1; H77. **DD** 333.7/05.

CH
**HSING CHENG YUAN SO SHU KO CHI KUAN ... YEN CHIU FA CHAN CHENG KUO NIEN PAO / HSING CHENG YUAN YEN CHIU FA CHAN KAO HO WEI YUAN HUI PIEN.** Chinese. an. **LC** JQ1530; .H787. **DD** 354.51/24907/8.

UK
**HUME PAPERS ON PUBLIC POLICY.** (19??)-. Periodical. English. qt. £32.00. Edinburgh University Press, 22 George Square, Edinburgh EH8 9LF Scotland. **Tel** 011 44 31 650 6207, FAX 011 44 31 662 0053. **ED** Hector MacQueen. **Ad Acc**, **Adv Mgr:** Kathryn MacLean. **Circ:** 900.
**Desc:** Forum for the publication of research on issues of public policy with special reference to legal and economic aspects.

UK/1350-7516
**HUTHE PAPERS ON PUBLIC POLICY.** (19??)-. English. Four times a year. £68.00 UK & Europe; $116.00 North America; £76.00 other. Edinburgh University Press, 22 George Square, Edinburgh EH8 9LF Scotland. **Tel** 011 44 31 650 6207, FAX 011 44 31 662 0053.

US/1041-5793
**I.D. CHECKING GUIDE. VFOAT** ID Checking Guide. **VAT** I. D. Checking Guide. (1985)-. English. an. $19.95. Drivers License Guide Company, 1492 Oddstad Drive, Redwood City CA 94063. **Tel** (415)369-4849, (800)227-8827. **ED** Liane Strub. **LC** HV8074; .D74. **DD** 929.9. **Bk Rev**. ctrl circ. **Continues** Drivers License Guide, 0276-1696.
**Desc:** Details forms and identification used by government agencies, banks, etc. to check fraud.

IT
**I GOVERNI LOCALI.** (19??)-. Italian. qt. L180000.00. Soc It Studio Problemi Regioni, Via della Scrofa 14, 00186 Rome Italy. **Tel** 011 39 6 6879852.

IS/0334-6056
**ICA INFORMATION.** [ICA inf.]. **VFOAT** International Council for Automatic Data Processing in Government Administration Information. (1969)-. Periodical. English. ir. €15.00. ICA Information, 14 Osgood Gardens Orpington, Kent BR6 6JU England. **Tel** 44 689 57245, FAX 44 689 857245. **ED** Peter Hearson. **UDC** 681.3. **Bk Rev**. Documents available from Ask*IEEE.
**Ind/Abst** INSPEC.

●CN/1187-872X
**ICI BOUCHERVILLE.** [Ici Boucherv.]. **Added/Corp** Boucherville (Quebec). Vol. 1, No 1 (Jan./Febr. 1992)-. Periodical. French. Free. Ville de Boucherville, 500 Riviere-Aux-Pins, Boucherville Quebec J4B 2Z7 Canada. **DD** 352.0714/37. **Continues** Info J4B., 0820-5027.

US/0047-0651
**ICMA NEWSLETTER.** [ICMA newsl.]. **Main/Corp** International City Management Association. **Added/Corp** International City Management Association. Newsletter. **VAT** International City Management Association Newsletter. Vol. 50, No. 13 (July 1969)-. Periodical. English. bw. $115.00. International City Management Association, 777 North Capitol Street NE, Suite 500, Washington DC 20002. **Tel** (202)289-4262, (800)745-8780, FAX (202)962-3500. **(Subscription address:** International City Management Association, PO Box 2011, Annapolis Junction MD 20701.) **ED** Beth Payne. **DD** 352. **Circ:** 7,500. **Continues** City Managers' Newsletter.

**Desc:** Contains legal issues, association news, board information, conference information, member highlights, position vacancies, appointments, applications, and calendar of events.

US
**IDAHO BLUE BOOK. Added/Corp** Idaho. Secretary of State. (1935)-. English. be (Publishes in Fall of every odd year). Free for Idaho libraries; $10.00 other. Idaho State Capital, Room 203, Secretary of State, Boise ID 83720. **Tel** (208)334-2300, FAX (208)334-2282.

US
**IDAHO CITIES. Added/Corp** Association of Idaho Cities. (197?)-. Periodical. English. Twelve times a year. $18.00. Association of Idaho Cities, 3314 Grace Street, Boise ID 83703. **Tel** (208)344-8594, FAX (208)344-8677. **ED** Matt Hanzel. **Ad Acc**. **Pr Rev**. **Circ:** 2,000 (ctrl).
**Desc:** Highlights on cities or issues specifically relating to cities.

US
**IDAHO LEGISLATIVE FISCAL REPORT TO THE JOINT SENATE FINANCE-HOUSE APPROPRIATIONS COMMITTEE : A PUBLICATION OF THE LEGISLATIVE BUDGET OFFICE. Main/Corp** Idaho. Legislature. Legislative Budget Office. English. an. Legislative Budget Office, Statehouse/Room 334, Boise ID 83720. **LC** HJ11; .I248A. **DD** 353.97960072/236/05. ctrl circ. **Continues** Legislative Fiscal Report to the Joint Senate Finance-House Appropriations Committee, 0362-1987.

UK
**IFAC NEWSLETTER. Main/Corp** International Federation of Automatic Control. **VFOAT** Newsletter. **VAT** International Federation of Automatic Control Newsletter. Newsletter. English. bm. Pergamon Press, An Imprint of Elsevier Science Ltd., The Boulevard, Langford Lane, Kidlington, Oxford OX5 1GB United Kingdom. **Tel** 011 44 865 843000, 011 44 865 843699, FAX 011 44 865 843010. **(Subscription address:** US/ 395 Saw Mill River Road, Elmsford, NY 10523; Can/ 150 Consumers Road/Suite 104, Willowdale Ontario M2J 1P9; Aus-NZ/ POB 544, Potts Point NSW 2011) **Continues** Information Bulletin.

II/0536-1761
**IIPA NEWSLETTER. Main/Corp** Indian Institute of Public Administration. Vol. 1 (Feb. 1957)-. Newsletter. English. mo. Rs3.00 India; $1.00 other. DIR-Indian Institute of Public Administration, Indraprastha Estate Ring Road, New Delhi 110002 India. **Tel** 011 91 11 3317309. **ED** Shri T N Chaturvedi. **Ad Acc**. **Circ:** 7,500 (ctrl).
**Desc:** A recorder of national and international news of public administration and allied matters.

US
**IJA REVIEW / THE INSTITUTE OF JUDICIAL ADMINISTRATION. Added/Corp** Institute of Judicial Administration. Vol. 1, No. 1 (Spring 1982)-. Periodical. English. Institute of Judicial Administration, 1 Washington Square Village, New York NY 10012. **Tel** (212)598-7721. **LC** KF8700.A1; I38. **DD** 016.34773/005; 016.347307005.

TU
**ILKE.** (Jan. 1974)-. Periodical. Turkish. mo. 200.00TL. Y Z Bahadnl, P K 1222 Ankara Cad, Babiali Han Kat, Istanbul Turkey. **LC** JQ1801.A1; I58.

US/0019-1949
**ILLINOIS COUNTY AND TOWNSHIP OFFICIAL. Added/Corp** Township Officials of Illinois. Illinois Association of County Officials. Illinois Association of Agricultural Fairs. **VFOAT** Illinois County & Township Official; County & Township Official. (19??)-. Periodical. English. mo (11 issues). $15.00. Illinois County Township Office, PO Box 455 61501, Astoria IL 61501. **Tel** (309)329-2101, FAX (309)329-2133. **ED** George H. Miller. **Ad Acc**, **Adv Mgr:** Bryan E. Smith.

US
**ILLINOIS LEGISLATIVE DIRECTORY. Main/Corp** Illinois. Legislative Council. (1971)-. English. an. $3.14. Center for Business Management, 20 North Wacker Drive, Chicago IL 60606. **Tel** (312)372-7373. **Circ:** 25,000.
**Desc:** Alpha list of members of the Illinois general assembly, office numbers, committee assignments, seating plans and Illinois legislative and congressional districts maps.

US/0442-0713
**ILLINOIS MUNICIPAL PROBLEMS; REPORT OF THE CITIES AND VILLAGES MUNICIPAL PROBLEMS COMMISSION TO THE GENERAL ASSEMBLY OF ILLINOIS. Main/Corp** Illinois. Cities and Villages Municipal Problems Commission. (1959)-. English. be. Cities and Villages Municipal Problems Commission, Springfield IL 62706. **LC** JS3.I29; A23. **DD** 352.0773.

US/0019-2139
**ILLINOIS MUNICIPAL REVIEW.** Periodical. English. mo. $5.00. Illinois Municipal League, PO Box 3387, Springfield IL 62708. **LC** JS39; .I4. **DD** 352/.0072/09773. **Continues** Illinois Municipal Review, to Improve the Quality and Decrease the Cost of Municipal Service.
**Ind/Abst** Urban Aff. Abstr.

US
**ILLINOIS PUBLIC EMPLOYEE RELATIONS REPORT / INSTITUTE OF LABOR AND INDUSTRIAL RELATIONS, UNIVERSITY OF ILLINOIS AT URBANA-CHAMPAIGN, THE. Added/Corp** University of Illinois at Urbana-Champaign. Institute of Labor and Industrial Relations. Vol. 1, No. 1 (Mar. 1984)-. Periodical. English. qt. $35.00 US and Canada; $40.00 other. Chicago Kent College of Law, 565 West Adams Street, Chicago IL 60661. **Tel** (312)906-5190, FAX (312)906-5280. **ED** Scott Schutte and Deborah Buttell. Index available. **Circ:** 700 (ctrl). available on an online database from WESTLAW; and LEXIS.
**Desc:** Provides information for labor and management representatives and others promoting stable labor relations in the public sector of Illinois.

CN/0703-6922
**IMPACT.** Periodical. English. Alberta Union of Provincial Employees, 10975-124 Street, Edmonton Alberta T5M 0J2 Canada. **DD** 331.88/11/35471230005. **Supersedes** Perspective, 0316-5388.

US/0162-1300
**IMPACT JOURNAL. VFOAT** Impact. (19??)-. Periodical. English. Four times a year (Mar., June, Sept., Dec.). $5.00. Al Louis Ripskis, 2605 39th Street Northwest, Suite 303, Washington DC 20007. **Tel** (202)333-4480. **ED** Al Louis Ripskis. **Bk Rev**.
**Desc:** Exposure of waste mismanagement and debate of serious policy issues in federal government and particularly HUD.

IT
**IMPRESA PUBBLICA MUNICIPALIZZAZIONE : RIVISTA BIMESTRALE DELLA CISPEL, CONFEDERAZIONE ITALIANA DEI SERVIZI PUBBLICI DEGLI ENTI LOCALI, L'. Added/Corp** Confederazione Italiana dei Servizi Pubblici Degli Enti Locali. (19??)-. Periodical. Italian. bm. Maggiolo Editore, Casella Postale 290, 47037 Rimini Italy. **Tel** 011 39 541 626760. **Continues** Impresa Pubblica, 0019-3003.

CN/0711-2971
**IN PROCESS (OTTAWA).** (IN PROCESS : AN UP-DATE FROM THE PUBLIC PARTICIPATION GROUP, PROGRAM AND POLICY BRANCH, PLANNING DEPARTMENT.). [In process]. **VFOAT** En Marche. **VAT** En Marche (Ottawa. Edition Anglaise et Francaise). Jan. 3, 1979-. Periodical. English (French). ir (six-eight issues per year). Free. Public Participation Group, Planning Department, Regional Municipality of Ottawa-Carleton, 8th Floor/222 Queen Street, Ottawa Ontario K1P 5Z3 Canada. **Tel** (613)560-2053, FAX (613)560-1380. **ED** Chris Bradshaw. **DD** 352.9/6/0971383. **Circ:** 4,300 (ctrl). **Absorbed** En Marche (Ottawa-Carleton (Ont.). Planning Dept. Public Participation Group.Planning Dept. Public Participation Group).

IE
**INAUGURAL LECTURE SERIES / UNIVERSITY COLLEGE CORK.** Ceased. **Added/Corp** University College, Cork. No. 1 (1983)-(1992). Monographic series. English. Cork University Press, University College, Cork Ireland.

US/0098-6933
**INCORPORATED MUNICIPALITIES, MUNICIPAL OFFICIALS AND STATE STREET AID ALLOCATIONS.** English. an. Department of Transportation and Highway Safety, PO Box 25202, Raleigh NC 27611. **LC** JS451.N85; A3. **DD** 352/.008/09756. **Continues** Incorporated Municipalities, Municipal Officials and State Street Aid Allocations.

IO
**INDEKS PEMILU.** Began in 1977. Indonesian. ir (quinquennial, every five years). Perpustakaan Nasional, Departemen Pendidikan Dan Kebudayaan, Jl Merdeka Selatan #11, Jakarta Pusat Indonesia. **LC** Z7164.R4; I52; JQ778.

US/0743-1236
**INDEPENDENT SECTOR.** (INDEPENDENT SECTOR : IS.). **Main/Corp** Independent Sector (Firm). **VFOAT** IS; I.S. English. an. Independent Sector, 1828 L Street NW, Washington DC 20036. **Tel** (202)223-8100. **LC** HV97.I57; I53A. **DD** 351.7/63/060753.

US
**INDEX, FEDERAL EMPLOYEE APPEALS DECISIONS / MERIT SYSTEMS PROTECTION BOARD.** ***Ceased.*** (Oct. 1981-Mar. 1982)-Ceased (Dec. 1985). English. qt. National Technical Information Service - NTIS, Room 2027S, 5285 Port Royal Road, Springfield VA 22161. **Tel** (703)487-4630, (703)487-4660, (703)487-4650, FAX (703)321-8547, telex 89-9405. ***Continues*** *Index to Appeals of Federal Employees.*

AU
**INDEX KOMMUNALWISSENSCHAFTLICHER LITERATUR: BUCHER.** **Added/Corp** Kommunalwissenschaftliches Dokumentationszentrum (Vienna, Austria). **VFOAT** Index of Publications on Local Government and Urban Studies: Books. No. 1 (May 1970)-. Multiple languages (English and German). sa. Linzer Strasse 452, A 1140 Vienna Austria. **LC** Z7165.A9; I53. **DD** 016.30136/09436.

US/0161-7028
**INDEX OF FDA REGULATORY LETTERS.** **Main/Corp** United States. Food and Drug Administration. **VAT** Index of Food and Drug Administration Regulatory Letters. (1975)-. Periodical. English. wk. $260.00. FOI Services, 12315 Wilkins Avenue, Rockville MD 20852. **Tel** (301)881-0410, FAX (301)881-0415. **ED** John Carey. **Circ:** 75 (ctrl).
**Desc:** Indexes all regulatory letters generated by the Food and Drug Administration.

US/0198-9138
**INDEX OF FEDERAL SPECIFICATIONS, STANDARDS AND COMMERCIAL ITEM DESCRIPTIONS.** [Index Fed. specif. stand. commer. item descr.]. **Added/Corp** United States. Federal Supply Service. (May 1979)-. Government Publication. English. an. Superintendent of Documents, US Government Printing Office, Washington DC 20402. **Tel** (202)275-3328, FAX (202)786-2377. **LC** JK1679; .I53. **DD** 353.0082/1. ***Continues*** *Index of Federal Specifications and Standards.*

US/0891-3129
**INDEX TO COLORADO STATE PUBLICATIONS.** [Index Colo. state publ.]. Vol. 1, No. 1 (Aug. 1982)-. Periodical. English. qt. $30.00. Colorado State Publications Depository and Distribution Center, Colorado State Library, 201 East Colfax Avenue, Denver CO 80203. **Tel** (303)866-6728. **ED** Barbara L Wagner. **LC** Z1223.5.C6; I5; J87.C6. **DD** 015.788/053. Index available. cum. index. **Circ:** 100. available on microfiche.
**Desc:** Lists publications from Colorado governmental units including state-supported colleges and universities.

US/0046-8908
**INDEX TO CURRENT URBAN DOCUMENTS.** Vol. 1, (July/Oct. 1972)-. English. qt. $425.00 (Part 1), $8,950.00 (Part 2, microfiche collection). Greenwood Press Inc., PO Box 5007, Westport CT 06881-5007. **Tel** (203)226-3571, FAX (203)222-1502. **ED** Laura J Kaminsky. **LC** Z7165.U5; I654. **DD** 016.30136/0973. **NLM** Z 1223.Z7 I36. Index available. cum. index.
**Desc:** The only guide to local government publications, annually lists 3,500-4,000 documents and consultants' reports from larger U.S. cities, county and regional planning agencies, authorities and special districts, and civic organizations and other groups involved in local government affairs. Complete bibliographic data are provided in the geographic section of the Index.

US
**INDEX TO PUBLIC ADMINISTRATION SERIES--BIBLIOGRAPHY.** No. P1-P145 (June/Dec. 1978)-. Bibliography. English. $12.00. Vance Bibliographies, PO Box 229, Monticello IL 61856. **Tel** (217)762-3821. **LC** Z7164.A2; I468; JF1351. **DD** 016.35.

II
**INDIAN JOURNAL OF ADMINISTRATIVE SCIENCE.** **Added/Corp** Indian Public Administration Association. **VFOAT** Journal of Administrative Science. Vol. 1, No. 1 (Jan.-June 1990)-. Periodical. English. sa. $60.00. Indian Public Administration Association, Madras, Tamil Nadu, India. **(Subscription address:** Prints India, 11 Darya Ganj, New Delhi, 110002 India, (Phone: 011 91 11 3268645)) **LC** JQ201; .I547. **DD** 354.54/0005.

II/0019-5561
**INDIAN JOURNAL OF PUBLIC ADMINISTRATION, THE.** [Indian j. public adm.]. **Added/Corp** Indian Institute of Public Administration. Vol. 1 (Jan./March 1955)-. Periodical. English. Four times a year (Jan., Apr., July, Oct.). $50.00. DIR-Indian Institute of Public Administration, Indraprastha Estate Ring Road, New Delhi 110002 India. **Tel** 011 91 11 3317309. **(Subscription address:** Prints India, 11 Darya Ganj, New Delhi, 110002 India, (Phone: 011 91 11 3268645)) **LC** JQ201; .I55. Index available. **Bk Rev. Ad Acc. Circ:** 8,000.
**Ind/Abst** ABC POL SCI; Appl. Soc. Sci. Index Abstr.; Int. Bibliogr. Sociol.; Int. Dev. Abstr. (?-?); Int. Labour Doc.; Int. Polit. Sci. Abstr.; Leis. Recreat. Tour. Abstr.; Rural Dev. Abstr.; World Agric. Econ.

US
**INDIANA GENERAL ASSEMBLY LEGISLATIVE DIRECTORY.** **Main/Corp** Indiana. General Assembly. **VFOAT** Legislative Directory. Directory. English. be. $3.00 (per issue). Indiana Chamber of Commerce, 1 North Capitol / Suite 200, Indianapolis IN 46204. **Tel** (317)264-3110. **ED** Jeanne Wiles and Gini Rayman.
**Desc:** Information regarding Indiana legislators, committees, districts, pictures, etc.

●US
**INDIANA LEGISLATIVE SOURCEBOOK.**
**See** Political Science.

US/0099-1023
**INDIANA PUBLIC MANAGEMENT.** V. 1- Spring 1975-. Periodical. English. qt. Indiana Society for Public Administration, 400 East Seventh Street, Bloomington IN 47401. **LC** JK5601; .I48. **DD** 353.9/772/0005.

JA
**INDONESHIA NO GUN-SEI SHIDOSHA ICHIRAN.** **Added/Corp** Tonan Ajia Chosakai. (19??)-. Periodical. Japanese. Tonan Ajia Chosakai, c/o Kotsu Kosha Building, 602 6-4 Marunouchi, 1-chome Chiyoda-ku, Tokyo Japan. **LC** JQ767; .I518.

CN/0715-7592
**INFO-BOURG.** (INFO-BOURG : LE JOURNAL DE LA VILLE DE CHARLESBOURG.). [Info-bourg]. **Main/Corp** Charlesbourg (Quebec). **VFOAT** Journal de la Ville de Charlesbourg. V. 7, No. 9, (Dec. 1982)-. Periodical. French. mo. Free to residents. Infobourg, c/o Bureau d'Information Ville de Charlesbourg, 7575 Boulevard Henri-Bourassa, Charlesbourg Quebec G1H 3E7 Canada. **Tel** (418)622-7500. **DD** 352.0714/47. **Circ:** 29,000. ***Continues*** *Charlesbourg, 0820-0599.*

CN/0383-1272
**INFO LONGUEUIL.** V. 1- July 1975-. Periodical. French (summaries and/or abstracts in English). Le Bureau d'Information de la Ville de Longueuil, 100 Ouest rue Saint-Charles, Longueuil Quebec J4H 1E6 Canada. **DD** 352.0714/37.

CN/0821-2368
**INFO / NORTH YORK.** [Info - North York]. **Main/Corp** North York (Ont.). English. an. Info / Ontario, Public Information Office, City of North York, 5100 Yonge Street, Willowdale Ontario M2N 5V7 Canada. **DD** 352.0713/541.

CN/0712-3949
**INFO-POINTELIERE.** (INFO-POINTELIERE / VILLE DE POINTE-AUX-TREMBLES.). [Info-pointeliere]. **VFOAT** Journal Patme. Vol. 4, No. 1 (June 1980)-. Periodical. French. Free. **DD** 352.0714/28. ***Continues*** *Cite (Pointe-aux-Trembles, Quebec), 0712-3930.*

CN/0714-3885
**INFO-SAINT-BRUNO.** (INFO-SAINT-BRUNO : BULLETIN MUNICIPAL DE LA VILLE DE SAINT-BRUNO-DE-MONTARVILLE.). [Info-St-Bruno]. V. 1, No. 1, (Dec. 1980)-. Bulletin. English (French). Free. City of Saint-Bruno-de-Montarville Information Office, 1585 Montarville Street, Saint-Bruno-de-Montarville Quebec, J3V 3T8 Canada. **DD** 352.0714/37. ctrl circ.

CN/1184-8111
**INFO SOURCE (ED. FRANCAISE).** (INFO SOURCE : SOURCE DE RENSEIGNEMENTS FEDERAUX.). [Info source]. **Main/Corp** Canada. **Added/Corp** Canada. Conseil du Tresor. Pratiques en Matiere de Gestion. (1991)-. French. **LC** KE5325. **DD** 354.710071/4/05. ***Formed by the union of*** *Registre d'Acces. Canada, 0848-4880* ***and*** *Repertoire des Renseignements Personnels. Canada, 0848-4813.*

CN/1184-8103
**INFO SOURCE (ENGLISH ED.).** (INFO SOURCE : SOURCES OF FEDERAL GOVERNMENT INFORMATION.). [Info source]. **Main/Corp** Canada. **Added/Corp** Canada. Treasury Board. Information Management Practices. (1991)-. English. **LC** KE5325. **DD** 354.710071/4/05. ***Formed by the union of*** *Access Register, 0825-107X* ***and*** *Index to Personal Information, 0848-4805.*

CN/1188-7907
**INFO SOURCE. GUIDE TO SOURCES OF FEDERAL GOVERNMENT INFORMATION.** [Info source, Guide sources fed. gov. inf.]. **Main/Corp** Canada. **Added/Corp** Canada. Treasury Board. Information Management Practices. **VFOAT** Guide to Sources of Federal Government Information; Info Source, Guide des Sources de Renseignements Federaux. (1991)-. English. an. 25.35Can$. Canada Communication Group Publishers, Order Processing, Ottawa Ontario K1A 0S9 Canada. **Tel** (819)956-4800, (819)956-4802. **DD** 354.710071/4/05.

SP
**INFORMACION IBERO AMERICANA.** **Added/Corp** Instituto Nacional de Administracion Publica (Spain) Inter-American Municipal Organization. Oficina Tecnica. Federacion Internacional de Antiguos Alumnos del INAP. **VFOAT** Informacion Ibero Americana. Vol. 1 (Oct./Dec. 1988)-. Periodical. Spanish. qt. Istituto Nacional de Administracion Publica, Santa Engracia 7, 28010 Madrid Spain. **Tel** 446-1700. **LC** JS6301; .I48. **DD** 352.046. ***Formed by the union of*** *Cuadernos de Alcala* ***and*** *Boletin de Informacion de la Oficina Tecnica de la OICI, 0210-0975.*

CN/0711-5431
**INFORMATION CIRCULAR / ALBERTA TREASURY, CORPORATE TAX ADMINISTRATION.** [Inf. circ. - Alta. Treas., Corp. Tax Adm.]. **Added/Corp** Alberta. Corporate Tax Administration. (Jan. 1981)-. Periodical. English. ir. Free on request. Tax Information Services, Alberta Treasury Department, 9811 109th Street, Edmonton Alberta T5K 2L5 Canada. **Tel** (403)427-3035. **DD** 354.71230072/44.

US
**INFORMATION DIGEST (U.S. NUCLEAR REGULATORY COMMISSION : POCKET REFERENCE ED.).** (INFORMATION DIGEST.). **VFOAT** Nuclear Regulatory Commission ... Information Digest. 1989-. English. an. US Nuclear Regulatory Commission / Division of Budget and Analysis, Office of the Comptroller, Washington DC 20555.

CN/0826-0613
**INFORMATION LISTING / REGIONAL CLERK'S DEPT.** [Inf. listing - Reg. Clerk's Dep.]. **Main/Corp** Sudbury (Ont. : Regional Municipality). Clerk's Dept. 1979-. English. an. Free. Regional Municipality of Sudbury, Clerk's Department, PO Box 370, Sudbury Ontario P3E 4P2 Canada. **DD** 354.713/00025. ctrl circ.

CN/0710-586X
**INFORMATION MONT-ROLLAND.** [Inf. Mont-Rolland]. **Main/Corp** Mont-Rolland (Quebec). Mar. 1979-. Periodical. French. mo. Information Mont-Rolland, c/o La Corporation Municipale de Mont-Rolland, 245 Morin, Mont-Rolland Quebec J0R 1G0 Canada. **DD** 352.0714/24.

US/0364-9334
**INFORMATION PRACTICES IN WYOMING STATE GOVERNMENT.** **Main/Corp** Wyoming. Office of Information Practices. English. an. Wyoming State Government, Office of Information Practices, Cheyenne WY. **LC** JC599.U52; W97A. **DD** 353.9/787/00714.

CN/0714-508X
**INFORMATION SAINT-CONSTANT.** (INFORMATION SAINT-CONSTANT / VILLE DE SAINT-CONSTANT.). [Info. St-Constant]. Periodical. French. ir. Free. Information Saint-Constant, Hotel de Ville Saint-Constant, 147 rue Saint-Pierre, Saint-Constant Quebec J0L 1X0 Canada. **Tel** (514)638-2010. **DD** 352.0714/34. **Circ:** 5,000. ***Continues*** *Bulletin d'Information (Saint-Constant (Quebec)).*

CN/0821-1094
**INFORMATION U.M.R.C.** (INFORMATION U.M.R.C. / L'UNION DES MUNICIPALITES REGIONALES DE COMTE ET DES MUNICIPALITES LOCALES DU QUEBEC, INC.). [Inf. U.M.R.C.]. **Main/Corp** Union des Municipalites Regionales de Comte et des Municipalites Locales du Quebec. **VAT** Information Union des Municipalites Regionales de Comte et des Municipalites Locales du Quebec, Inc. Vol. 8, No. 1 (Jan. 1983)-. Periodical. French. bm. Free to members. 2795 Boulevard Laurier/Suite 430, Ste Foy Quebec G1V 4M7 Canada. **DD** 352.0714. ***Continues*** *Information U.C.C.Q. (Union des Conseils de Comte et des Municipalites Locales du Quebec), 0701-0621.*

FR
**INFORMATIQUE DANS LES ADMINISTRATIONS FRANCAISES, L'.** 1975-. French. 15.00. Documentation Francaise, 29 Quai Voltaire, 75344 Paris Cedex 7 France. **Tel** 011 33 1 40157000, FAX 011 33 1 40157230, telex 204 826 DOCFRAN. **LC** JN2738.E4; F72A. **DD** 354/.44/00028/54. ***Continues*** *Informatique dans les Administrations Francaises et Son Evolution au Cours des Trois Prochaines Annees.*

FR
**INFORMATIQUE DANS LES ENTREPRISES PUBLIQUES, L'.** French. Documentation Francaise, 29 Quai Voltaire, 75344 Paris Cedex 7 France. **Tel** 011 33 1 40157000, FAX 011 33 1 40157230, telex 204 826 DOCFRAN. **LC** HD4161; .D44A. **DD** 354/.44/008202854. ***Continues*** *Informatique dans les Entreprises Publiques et Son Evolution au Cours des Trois Prochaines Annees.*

PR/0478-8583
**INFORME ANUAL - ESTADO LIBRE ASOCIADO DE PUERTO RICO, COMISION DE SERVICIO PUBLICO.** (INFORME ANUAL - COMISION DE SERVICIO PUBLICO.). **Main/Corp** Puerto Rico. Public Service Commission. **VFOAT** Informe Anual - Comision de Servicio Publico del Estado Libre Asociado de Puerto Rico. Periodical. Spanish. **LC** HD2768.P7; A34. **DD** 354.

UK/0958-4021
**INLOGOV INFORMS.** (1989)-. English. Three times a year. £85.00 UK; £95.00 other; £35.00 (single copies). Institute of Local Government Studies, The University of Birmingham, Edgbaston, Birmingham B15 2TT England. **Tel** 021-414-5004, FAX 021-414-4989, telex 333762 UOBHM G. **(Subscription address:** Technical Communications, 100 High Avenue, Letchworth Herts SG6 3RR England**) ED** Dr. Margaret Hobson and Lesley Grayson, Phone: (021)414 4958. Index available (bound in each issue). **Circ:** 500.
**Desc:** An awareness and briefing series on UK public policy issues, particularly those of concern to local government and other public agencies. Each issue gives systematic and in-depth coverage to a key policy area or topic, providing guidance through official reports, commentaries and analyses. Presented as a commentary, supported by a comprehensive annotated bibliography, each issue combines both reference and practice material.

US/0364-6688
**INSIDE INTERIOR.** No. 1- July 1974-. Periodical. English. bm. Inside Interior, Room 7219/Department of the Interior, Washington DC 20240. ***Supersedes*** *Inside Interior, 0364-6688.*

US/1056-6341
**INSIDE LOBBYING.** [Inside lobby.]. Vol. 1, No. 1 (May 6, 1991)-. Periodical. English. bw. $445.00. Executive Publishing, PO Box 103, Ben Franklin Stn., Washington DC 20044. **DD** 328.

US
**INSIDE THE WHITE HOUSE.** Vol. 7, No. 16 (April 21, 1988)-. Periodical. English. wk. $595.00. Inside Washington Publishers, PO Box 7167, Benjamin Franklin Station, Washington DC 20044. **Tel** (703)416-8500, (800)424-9068. ***Continues*** *Inside the Administration.*

US
**INSIDE WASHINGTON.** English. Madison Books, 4720 Boston Way, Lanham MD 20706. **Tel** (301)459-5308.

US
**INSTITUTE OF PUBLIC SERVICE STATE AND LOCAL GOVENMENT NEWSLETTER.** **Added/Corp** University of Connecticut. Institute of Public Service. Vol. 1, No. 1 (Fall 1989)-. Newsletter. English. sm. Institute of Public Service, University of Connecticut, Storrs CT 06268. ***Continues*** *IPS Local Government Newsletter.*

CN/0837-7111
**INTER-MISSION (QUEBEC).** (INTER-MISSION.). [Inter-mission]. **Added/Corp** Quebec (Province). Ministere de la Main-D'Oeuvre et de la Securite du Revenu. Quebec (Province). Ministere de la Main-D'Oeuvre, de la Securite du Revenu et de la Formation Professionnelle. Vol. 7, No. 9 (Nov. 1984)-. Periodical. French. mo. Inter, Les Editions Intervention, 629 St Jean, Quebec Quebec G1R 1P7 Canada. **Tel** (418)529-9680. **DD** 354.7140683/05. ***Continues*** *L'Inter., 0225-9281.*

CN/0710-7307
**INTER URBA.** (INTER URBA / UNION DES MUNICIPALITES DU QUEBEC.). [Inter urba]. Vol. 1, No. 1 (28 Nov. 1980)-. Periodical. French. Union Des Municipalites Du Quebec, Bureau 301, 315 EST, Boul., Dorchester, Montreal, Quebec H2X 3P3. **DD** 352.0714.

CN/0226-2878
**INTERACTION (INTERGOVERNMENTAL COMMITTEE ON URBAN AND REGIONAL RESEARCH).** (INTERACTION.). [Interaction (Intergov. Comm. Urban Reg. Res.)]. **VFOAT** Interaction. No. 1- Jan. 1976-. Periodical. French (English). bm. Illinois Institute for Environmental Quality, 309 West Washington, Chicago IL 60606.

CN/1184-0552
**INTERFAX (OTTAWA).** (INTERFAX.). [Interfax]. **Main/Corp** National Archives of Canada. **VFOAT** Interfax. Vol. 1, No. 1 (Aug. 1990)-. Periodical. English (French). National Archives of Canada, 395 Wellington/Community Relations, Ottawa Ontario K1A 0N3 Canada. **Tel** (613)996-0394. **DD** 354.710071/46/05.

US/0097-7780
**INTERGOVERNMENTAL AFFAIRS FELLOWSHIP PROGRAM.** (INTERGOVERNMENTAL AFFAIRS FELLOWSHIP PROGRAM, REPORT.). **Main/Corp** United States. Civil Service Commission. Bureau of Training. English. US Civil Service Commission Bureau of Training, General Management Training Center, 1900 E Street NW, Washington DC 20415. **LC** JK723.E9; U54A. **DD** 353.001/5.

US/0362-8507
**INTERGOVERNMENTAL PERSPECTIVE.** Vol. 1, No. 1 (Fall 1975)-. Periodical. English. qt. Free (US); $25.00 (other). Advisory Commission on Intergovernmental Relations, 800 K Street NW, Suite 450 S Building, Washington DC 20575. **Tel** (202)653-5640, FAX (202)653-5429. **ED** Pamela L Reynolds. **LC** JK325; .I57. **DD** 353/.0005. **Circ:** 20,000. available on microfilm and microfiche from University Microfilms International (UMI).
**Ind/Abst** Urban Aff. Abstr.

CN/0226-3351
**INTERIM REPORT - B. C. HYDRO.** [Interim rep. - B.C. Hydro]. **Main/Corp** B.C. Hydro. Began with Sept. 1976? issue. Periodical. English. qt. British Columbia Hydro and Power Authority, 970 Burrard Street, Vancouver British Columbia V6Z 1Y3 Canada. **DD** 354.7110087.

US/0743-2844
**INTERIOR BUDGET IN BRIEF, THE.** **Main/Corp** United States. Dept. of the Interior. Government Publication. English. an. US Department of the Interior, Washington DC 20241. **LC** JK864; .D46A. **DD** 353.3. ***Continues*** *United States. Dept. of the Interior. Budget Highlights.*

GW/0538-6349
**INTERNATIONAL CONGRESS CALENDAR.** 23rd Ed. (1983)-. English. qt. $350.00 (surface mail), $380.00 (air mail). Union of International Associations, Rue Washington 40, 1050 Brussels Belgium. **Tel** 011 32 2 6404109, FAX 011 32 2 646 05 25, telex 65080 INAC B. ***Continues*** *International Congress Calendar.*

UK
**INTERNATIONAL DIRECTORY OF GOVERNMENT, THE.** (1989)-. Directory. English. an (November). $345.00. Europa Publications Ltd, 18 Bedford Square, London WC1B 3JN England. **Tel** 011 44 71 5808236, telex 21540 EUROPA G. **(Subscription address:** Gale Research Co., 835 Penobscot Building, Detroit MI 48226.**) LC** JF1411. **DD** 351.
**Desc:** Lists government ministries, departments, agencies and corporations worldwide.

US/1045-2613
**INTERNATIONAL DIRECTORY OF NUCLEAR CONTRACT SERVICE FIRMS.** [Int. dir. nucl. contract serv. firms]. 1989-. Directory. English. an. $29.95. D P & Son Publishing Company, 31 Sutton Park Road/Suite 467, Poughkeepsie NY 12603. **LC** TK9012; .I56. **DD** 621.48/025.

US/1066-145X
**INTERNATIONAL GAMING & WAGERING BUSINESS.** [Int. gaming wagering bus.]. **VFOAT** International Gaming and Wagering Business; Gaming & Wagering Business. Vol. 11, No. 1, (Jan. 1990)-. Periodical. English. Twelve times a year. $60.00 US; $80.00 Canada; $144.00 others. BMT Publications Inc, Seven Penn Plaza, New York NY 10001. **Tel** (800)223-9638, (212)594-4120. **LC** HV6715; .G295. **DD** 363. ***Continues*** *Gaming & Wagering Business, 8750-8222.*

US/0190-0692
**INTERNATIONAL JOURNAL OF PUBLIC ADMINISTRATION.** [Int. j. public adm.]. (1979)-. Academic Scholarly Publication. English. Twelve times a year. $925.00 US; $967.00 other. Marcel Dekker Inc., 270 Madison Avenue, New York NY 10016. **Tel** (212)696-9000, (800)228-1160, FAX (212)685-4540, telex 421419. **(Subscription address:** Marcel Dekker Inc, PO Box 5017, Monticello NY 12701.**) ED** Jack Rabin and Thomas Vocino. **LC** JA1.A1; I593. **DD** 350/.0005. **CODEN** IJPADR. **[CCC]. Bk Rev. Ad Acc. Pr Rev.** ctrl circ. available on microfiche. Documents available from The Genuine Article, UMI Article Clearinghouse.
**Desc:** This journal is a blind-refereed, scholarly publication which presents a forum for academicians and practitioners in management and administration to share theoretical issues, as well as applications of concepts and theories, with their colleagues in the practitioner community. The journal concentrates primarily on American theory and practice, though matters dealing with comparative and developmental administration are also considered. The 'International Journal of Public Administration' offers readers the broadest array of ideas to be found in any comparable publication.
**Ind/Abst** ABI/INFORM Glob. Ed.; ABI Inform Ondisc (Jan. 1980-); Curr. Contents Soc. Behav. Sci.; Gen. BusinessFile (1992-); Int. Polit. Sci. Abstr.; Res. Alert [Full Cov.]; Sage Public Adm. Abstr.; Sage Urban Stud. Abstr (?-?); Soc. Sci. Cit. Index [Full Cov.]; Soc. Work Abstr. (Summer 1987-?) [Select. Cov.].

UK/0951-3558
**INTERNATIONAL JOURNAL OF PUBLIC SECTOR MANAGEMENT, THE.** **VFOAT** Public Sector Management; IJPSM. Vol. 1, No. 1 (1988)-. Periodical. English. bm. $719.00. MCB University Press, 60 62 Toller Lane, Bradford West Yorkshire BD8 9BX England. **Tel** 011 44 274 499821, FAX 011 44 274 547143, telex 51317 MCBUNI G. **(Subscription address:** MCB University Press / US and Canada Subscriptions, PO Box 10812, Birmingham AL 35201-0812.**) ED** Sue de Verteuil. **LC** HD3840; .I58. **DD** 350.0009/2/05. **[CCC]. Ad Acc.** Documents available from UMI Article Clearinghouse.
**Desc:** Aims to provide a forum for the exchange of new ideas and developments in this ever-changing field. This publication covers the scope of public sector management, tackling each subject in-depth to provide an effective mixture of theory and practical applications.
**Ind/Abst** ABI/INFORM Glob. Ed.; Appl. Soc. Sci. Index Abstr.; Geogr. Abstr. Human Geogr.; Int. Dev. Abstr.; Int. Labour Doc.; LABORDOC; Manage. Market. Abstr.; PAIS Int. Print (1991-?); Rural Dev. Abstr.; World Agric. Econ.

US/1056-5728
**INTERNATIONAL MILITARY REVIEW.** [Int. mil. rev.]. (19??)-. Periodical. English. qt. $26.95. Challenge Publications Inc., 7950 Deering Avenue, Canoga Park CA 91304. **Tel** (818)887-0550. **LC** U1; .I73. **DD** 355/.005.

US/1053-783X
**INTERNATIONAL PUBLIC WORKS REVIEW.** ***Ceased.*** [Int. public works rev.]. **Added/Corp** International Public Works Federation. Vol. 1, No. 1 (Spring 1991)-(19??). Periodical. English. qt. Maxco Publishing Company Inc., 250 Lackawanna Avenue, Little Falls NJ 07424. **Tel** (201)785-0764, FAX (201)785-0447. **DD** 628.

BE/0020-8523
**INTERNATIONAL REVIEW OF ADMINISTRATIVE SCIENCES.** [Int. rev. adm. sci.]. **Added/Corp** International Institute of Administrative Sciences. (1957)-. Periodical. English (French and Spanish; summaries and/or abstracts in English). qt. £125.00. Sage Publications Ltd., 6 Bonhill Street, London EC2A 4PU, UK. **Tel** 071 374 0645, FAX 071 374 8741, telex 296207 SAGE G. **ED** Kenneth Kernaghan. cum. index. **Bk Rev. Ad Acc. Acid Free. *Continues in part*** *Revue Internationale des Sciences Administratives, 0303-965X;* ***Absorbed*** *Progress in Public Administration.*
**Desc:** Articles on comparative public administration. A special section for schools and institutes and a bibliography on recent outstanding publications. Distributed all over the world.
**Ind/Abst** ABC POL SCI; Appl. Soc. Sci. Index Abstr.; Contents Pages Manage.; Int. Bibliogr. Sociol.; Int. Labour Doc.; Int. Polit. Sci. Abstr.; LABORDOC; Middle East Abstr. Index; PAIS Int. Print (1991-?); Peace Res. Abstr. J. (1957-1984).

US/1051-4694
**INTERNATIONAL REVIEW OF COMPARATIVE PUBLIC POLICY.** [Int. rev. comp. public policy]. Vol. 1 (1989)-. Monographic series. English. ir. $73.25. JAI Press Inc., 55 Old Post Road, Suite 2, PO Box 1678, Greenwich CT 06836-1678. **Tel** (203)661-7602, FAX (203)661-0792. **ED** Nicholas Mercuro. **LC** H96; .I57. **DD** 350.

UK/0306-3488
**INTERNATIONAL WHO'S WHO IN COMMUNITY SERVICE.** **See** Biographies.

US
**IOWA CAPITOL COMPLEX TELEPHONE DIRECTORY / STATE OF IOWA, DEPARTMENT OF GENERAL SERVICES, DIVISION OF COMMUNICATIONS.** Directory. English. Core Depository, Des Moines IA 50319. ***Continues*** *Iowa State Government Telephone Directory, Capitol Complex.*
**Desc:** SUMMARY: Telephone directory of the capitol complex. Contains an alphabetical employee listing, a departmental listing and a map of the complex ... .

US/1050-2270
**IOWA INTERLINK.** **Added/Corp** League of Iowa Municipalities. Vol. 1, No. 1 (Aug. 1989)-. Periodical. English. bm. $18.00 (Iowa); $20.00 other. League of Iowa Municipalities, 317 6th Avenue, Suite 1400, Des Moines IA 50309. **Tel** (515)244-7282. **ED** Joy M Newcom. Index available. **Bk Rev. Ad Acc. Circ:** 3,200 (ctrl).
**Desc:** Articles providing city officials information on municipal government. Topics include solid waste management, revenue, current legislation, and administrative rules.

US/0021-0595
**IOWA MUNICIPALITIES.** **Added/Corp** League of Iowa Municipalities. Vol. 15 (Mar. 1960)-. Periodical. English. Six times a year. $18.00 Iowa; $20.00 other. League of Iowa Municipalities, 317 6th Avenue, Suite 1400, Des Moines IA 50309. **Tel** (515)244-7282. **LC** JS303.I55; I554. **Bk Rev. Ad Acc. Circ:** 7,000 (ctrl). ***Continues*** *League of Iowa Municipalities Monthly*

# Public Administration

*Magazine.*
**Desc:** An informative magazine for Iowa's elected and appointed municipal officials.
**Ind/Abst** Urban Aff. Abstr.

US/0741-2924
**IOWA REVIEW QUARTERLY.** Periodical. English. qt. Iowa Office for Planning and Programming, 523 East 12th Street, Des Moines IA 50319. **LC** JK6301; .I66. **DD** 353.977707/2.

US/0360-6260
**IPA INTERGOVERNMENTAL ASSIGNMENT PROGRAM : REPORT, THE. Main/Corp** United States. Civil Service Commission. Bureau of Intergovernmental Personnel Programs. **VAT** Intergovernmental Personnel Act Intergovernmental Assignment Program: Report. English. US Civil Service Commission Bureau of Intergovernmental Personnel Programs, 1900 E Street NW, Washington DC 20415. **LC** JK765; .U55B. **DD** 353.001/4.

IS
**IR VE-EZOR. VFOAT** City and Region. Vol. 1- October 1972-. Periodical. Hebrew (summaries and/or abstracts in English). qt. Misrael Ha-Penim, Box 7499, Tel Aviv Israel. **LC** JS7499.I8; I7.

US/1050-1282
**IRAC JOURNAL.** [IRAC j.]. **VAT** Information Resources Administration Councils Journal. Vol. 1, No. 1 (March 1990)-. Periodical. English. qt. IRAC Journal, 1111 Constitution Avenue NW, Bicentennial Building/10th Floor, Washington DC 20224. **DD** 353.
**Desc:** The purpose of the journal is to provide an open forum for the expression of ideas.

●CN/1188-2999
**IRC PERSPECTIVES.** (IPC PERSPECTIVES / INFORMATION AND PRIVACY COMMISSIONER/ONTARIO.). [IPC perspect.].
**Main/Corp** Information and Privacy Commissioner/Ontario. Vol. 1, Issue 1 (Winter 1992)-. Periodical. English. qt. **DD** 342.713. *Continues Newsletter (Information and Privacy Commissioner/Ontario).*, 0844-8701.

IE
**IRELAND : A PARLIAMENTARY DIRECTORY. Added/Corp** Institute of Public Administration (Dublin, Ireland). (1974)-. Directory. English. an. $87.63. Institute of Public Administration, Vergemount Hall Public Department, Dublin 6 Ireland. **Tel** 011 353 1 26977011, FAX 011 353 1 2698644, telex 90533 INPA. **ED** Jim O'Donnell. **LC** JN1468; .I73. **DD** 328.417/0025. **Bk Rev. Ad Acc. Circ:** 9,000. *Continues Ireland.*
**Desc:** Detailed information on who's who and what's what in Irish life. Covers politics, finance, education, communication, trade, professional and social organizations, major and private companies and statistics.

US
**IRS LETTER RULING SERVICE.** See Business-Accounting.

US/0890-4642
**ISSUE WATCH.** (ISSUE WATCH / THE MUNICIPAL LEAGUE FOUNDATION.). **Added/Corp** Municipal League Foundation (Seattle, Wash.). **VFOAT** IssueWatch. (Winter 1985/1986)-. Periodical. English. Twelve times a year. $50.00. Municipal League Seattle King, 810 3rd Avenue, Suite 604, Seattle WA 98104. **Tel** (206)622-8333. **LC** HT390; .I872. **Circ:** 1,300. *Absorbed in part by Issue Brief (Municipal League Foundation (Seattle, Wash.))*, 0890-4650; *Municipal News*, 0027-352X.

AT
**ISSUES IN LAND INFORMATION MANAGEMENT.** See Economics.

PK
**ISTIQLAL.** Periodical. Urdu. 30.00. Abu Sayyid Anvar, Weekly Istiqlal, Lahaur Pakistan. **LC** JQ201; .I88.

RU/0235-7097
**IZVESTIIA TSK TPSS.** *Ceased.* Vol. 1 (1989)-Ceased with No.8, 1991. Periodical. Russian. mo. **(Subscription address:** Victor Kamkin, 4956 Boiling Brook Parkway, Rockville MD 20852.**) LC** JN6598.K4; I98.

BE
**JAARBOEK (WEST FLANDERS, BELGIUM).** (JAARBOEK / PROVINCIE WEST-VLAANDEREN.). 1988-. Dutch. an. Provincie West-Vlaanderen, Bijlage Brugge Belgium. **LC** DH801.F6; J33.

NE
**JAAROVERZICHT / GEMEENTEARCHIEF AMSTERDAM.** See Genealogy and Heraldry-Archives.

SA
**JAARVERSLAG / DEPARTEMENT VAN MANNEKRAG / ANNUAL REPORT / DEPARTMENT OF MANPOWER. Main/Corp** South Africa. Dept. of Manpower. **VFOAT** Annual Report. (1989)-. Afrikaans (English). an. Department of Manpower / Pretoria, Manpower Building, 215 Schoeman Street, Private Bag X117, 0001 Pretoria South Africa. **Tel** (012)310-6911, FAX (012)320-2059. **LC** HD5842; .A45a. **DD** 354.680083/06. *Continues South Africa. Dept. of Manpower. Report of the Department of Manpower for the Year Ended ... .*

NE
**JAARVERSLAG (NETHERLANDS. RIJKSINKOOPBUREAU).** (JAARVERSLAG / RIJKSINKOOPBUREAU.). Dutch. an. Free. Rijksinkoopbureau, Rechterland 1, Postbus 10200, 8000 GE Zwolle The Netherlands. **Tel** telex 42603 RIB NL. **LC** JN5933; .A23. **Circ:** 10,000.

NE
**JAARVERSLAG VAN DE PERMANENTE COMMISSIE VOOR OVERHEIDSDOCUMENTATIE. Main/Corp** Netherlands (Kingdom, 1815- ). Permanente Commissie voor Overheidsdocumentatie. (19??)-. Dutch. Eleven times a year. F56.00 (latest volume). VNG Uitgeverij, Postbus 30435, 2500 GK Gravenhage Netherlands. **Tel** 011 31 70 3738393, FAX 070-3651826. **LC** JN5853; .N46a.

GW
**JAHRBUCH DER SOZIALDEMOKRATISCHEN PARTEI DEUTSCHLANDS. Main/Corp** Sozialdemokratische Partei Deutschlands. German. te. Vorwaerts Verlag, AM Michaelshof 8-10, W-53 Bonn 2 Germany. **LC** JN3926.S8.

GW
**JAHRBUCH FUER EUROPAISCHE VERWALTUNGSGESCHICHTE : JEV. VFOAT** JEV; Annuaire d'Histoire Administrative Europeenne; Annuario per la Storia Amministrativa Europea; Yearbook of European Administrative History. (1989)-. German (French and Italian; summaries and/or abstracts in English). an. Nomos Verlagsgesellschaft, Postfach 610, D-76484 Baden Baden Germany. **Tel** 011 49 7221 21040. **LC** JN1; .J34. **DD** 350/.00094.

GW
**JAHRBUCH ZUR STAATS- UND VERWALTUNGSWISSENSCHAFT.** Vol. 1 (1987)-. Monographic series. German (English and French). ir. Price varies per volume. Nomos Verlagsgesellschaft, Postfach 610, D-76484 Baden Baden Germany. **Tel** 011 49 7221 21040. **LC** JA14; .J33. **DD** 320/.05.

JA
**JICHI NO UGOKI. Added/Corp** Japan. Jichisho. Japan. Jichisho. Bunsho Kohoka. (19??)-. Japanese. Jichisho Bunsho Kohoka, 1-2 Kasumigaseki 2 chome Chiyoda-ku, Tokyo Japan. **LC** JS7371.A1; J52.

CN/0821-0810
**JIM. JOURNAL INFORMATION MUNICIPALE.** (JIM : JOURNAI INFORMATION MUNICIPALE / VILLE DE DONNACONA.). [JIM, J. inf. munic.]. **Added/Corp** Donnacona (Quebec). **VFOAT** Information Municipale. (1972)-. Periodical. French. mo. Free to citizens. Ville de Donnacona, 138 Avenue Pleau, Donnacona Quebec G0A 1T0 Canada. **DD** 352.0714/466.

CN/0710-5835
**JOHANNAIS.** (LE JOHANNAIS : BULLETIN D'INFORMATION DE LA VILLE DE SAINT-JEAN.). **Main/Corp** Saint-Jean (Saint-Jean, Quebec). Vol. 1, No. 1, (April 1976)-. Periodical. French. qt. Free. Service de l'Information de la Ville, CP 1025 Saint-Jean-sur-Richelieu Quebec J3B 7B2 Canada. **DD** 352.0714/38.

CN/0821-218X
**JONCTION (ASTON JONCTION).** (JONCTION.). [Jonction]. Periodical. French. ir. Free to residents. Jonction, C P 94, Aston-Jonction Quebec G0Z 1A0 Canada. **DD** 352.0714/55.

CN/1183-5699
**JONQUIEROIS (JONQUIERE).** (LE JONQUIEROIS / VILLE DE JONQUIERE.). [Jonquierois]. **Added/Corp** Jonquiere (Quebec). Vol. 1, No 1 Spring (1991)-. Periodical. French. Limited free distribution. Service d'Information de Ville de Jonquiere, CP 2000, Jonquiere Quebec G7X 7W7 Canada. **DD** 352.0714.

CN/1189-0762
**JOURNAL DES DEBATS - QUEBEC (PROVINCE). ASSEMBLEE NATIONALE. COMMISSION D'ETUDE DES QUESTIONS AFFERENTES A L'ACCESSION DU QUEBEC A LA SOUVERAINETE.** (JOURNAL DES DEBATS / ASSEMBLEE NATIONALE, COMMISSION D'ETUDE DES QUESTIONS AFFERENTES A L'ACCESSION DU QUEBEC A LA SOUVERAINETE.). [J. debats - Que. (Prov.), Assem. natl., Comm. etude quest. affer. access. Que. souver.]. **Main/Corp** Quebec (Province). Assemblee Nationale. Commission d'Etude des Questions Afferentes a l'Accession du Quebec a la Souverainete. 1rst Session, 34 Legislature, No 1 (Aug 28, 1991)-. Periodical. French. **DD** 971.4/04/05.

CN/1189-072X
**JOURNAL DES DEBATS - QUEBEC (PROVINCE). ASSEMBLEE NATIONALE. COMMISSION D'ETUDE SUR TOUTE OFFRE D'UN NOUVEAU PARTENARIAT DE NATURE CONSTITUTIONELLE.** (JOURNAL DES DEBATS / ASSEMBLEE NATIONALE, COMMISSION D'ETUDE SUR TOUTE OFFRE D'UN NOUVEAU PARTENARIAT DE NATURE CONSTITUTIONNELLE.). [J. debats - Que. (Prov.), Assem. natl., Comm. etude toute offre nouv. parten. nat. const.]. **Main/Corp** Quebec (Province). Assemblee Nationale. Commission d'Etude sur Toute Offre d'un Nouveau Partenariat de Nature Constitutionnelle. 1rst Session, 34th Legislature, No 1 (Aug. 28, 1991)-. Periodical. French. **DD** 971.4/04/05.

CN/0846-0361
**JOURNAL DES DEBATS - QUEBEC (PROVINCE). ASSEMBLEE NATIONALE. COMMISSION PARLEMENTAIRE SUR L'AVENIR POLITIQUE ET CONSTITUTIONNEL DU QUEBEC.** (JOURNAL DES DEBATS / ASSEMBLEE NATIONALE, COMMISSION SUR L'AVENIR POLITIQUE ET CONSTITUTIONNEL DU QUEBEC.). [J. debats - Que. (Prov.), Assem. natl., Comm. parlem. avenir polit. const. Que.]. **Main/Corp** Quebec (Province). Assemblee Nationale. Commission Parlementaire sur l'Avenir Politique et Constitutionnel du Quebec. No 1 (Nov. 6, 1990)-. Periodical. French. **DD** 971.4/04.

NP
**JOURNAL OF DEVELOPMENT AND ADMINISTRATIVE STUDIES, THE.** See Economics-Industry and Production.

UK/1350-1763
**JOURNAL OF EUROPEAN PUBLIC POLICY.** (19??)-. English. Four times a year. $120.00 (US & Canada); £80.00 (UK); £86.00 (other). Routledge, 11 New Fetter Lane, London EC4P 4EE England. **Tel** 071 583 9855, FAX 071 842 2298. **(Subscription address:** Kinokuniya Company Ltd., 38-1 Sakuragaoka 5, chome Setagaya-ku, Tokyo 156 Japan.**)**

●UK/1352-0237
**JOURNAL OF GOVERNMENT INFORMATION.** [J. gov. inf.]. Vol. 21, No. 1 (Jan./Feb. 1994)-. Periodical. English. bm. $343.00 The Americas; £230.00 other. Pergamon Press, An Imprint of Elsevier Science Ltd., The Boulevard, Langford Lane, Kidlington, Oxford OX5 1GB United Kingdom. **Tel** 011 44 865 843000, 011 44 865 843699, FAX 011 44 865 843010. **(Subscription address:** Elsevier Science Ltd. Oxford Fulfillment Centre, PO Box 800, Kidlington, Oxford OX5 1DX United Kingdom.**) LC** Z7164.G7; G69. **DD** 011. **NLM** Z 7164.G7; G721. available on microfiche from the publisher. Documents available from The Genuine Article, CASDDS. *Continues Government Publications Review (New York, N.Y. : 1982)*, 0277-9390.
**Desc:** Provides a forum for the publication of articles on government information policy, current practice, new developments, and history of distribution, processing, and use of information at all levels of government.
**Ind/Abst** Am. Hist. Life; Chem. Abstr.; Curr. Contents Soc. Behav. Sci.; Libr. Inf. Sci. Abstr.; Libr. Lit.; PAIS Int. Print; Res. Alert; Sci. Abstr.

US/0160-4198
**JOURNAL OF HEALTH AND HUMAN RESOURCES ADMINISTRATION.** See Sociology-Social Services and Welfare.

US/1042-7309
**JOURNAL OF MANAGEMENT SCIENCE & POLICY ANALYSIS.** [J. manag. sci. policy anal.]. **Added/Corp** American Society for Public Administration. Management Science and Policy Analysis Section. **VFOAT** Journal of Management Science and Policy Analysis. Vol. 6, No. 1 (Fall 1988)-. Periodical. English. qt. $25.00 (individuals), $75.00 (institutions). Lonergan Research Institute, 10 St. Mary Street, Suite 500, Toronto ONT M4Y 1P9 Canada. **Tel** (416)922-8374. **LC** JA1; .J56. **DD** 350/.0005. *Continues Management Science and Policy Analysis.*
**Ind/Abst** ABC POL SCI (1990-).

II/0447-9408
**JOURNAL OF PARLIAMENTARY INFORMATION, THE. Added/Corp** India. Parliament. Lok Sabha. Secretariat. Vol. 1 (Apr. 1955)-. Periodical. English. qt. $20.00. Lok Sabha Secretariat, India Parliament House of the People, New Delhi India.

# Public Administration

(Subscription address: Prints India, 11 Darya Ganj, New Delhi, 110002 India, (Phone: 011 91 11 3268645)) LC JQ201; .A32.

US/1053-1858
### JOURNAL OF PUBLIC ADMINISTRATION RESEARCH AND THEORY. (JOURNAL OF PUBLIC ADMINISTRATION RESEARCH AND THEORY : J-PART.). [J. public adm. res. theory]. Added/Corp University of Kansas. Dept. of Public Administration. VFOAT J-PART; J PART. Vol. 1, No. 1 (Jan. 1991)-. Periodical. English. Four times a year. Fl148.50 (individual); Fl250.00 (institution). University of Kansas, 318 Blake Hall, Lawrence KS 66045. Tel (913)843-1235, FAX (913)843-1274. (Subscription address: Transaction Publishers, Rutgers State University, New Brunswick NJ 08903) ED Stuart I Bretschneider. LC JA1; .J62. DD 350/.0005. CODEN JPRTEC. [CCC]. Bk Rev. Ad Acc. Pr Rev. Circ: 500. available on microfilm from University Microfilms International (UMI).
Desc: Dedicated to advancing knowledge of public administration through research and theoretical analysis. The journal publishes reports of empirical work, including both quantitative and qualitative areas of research.
Ind/Abst PAIS Int. Print; Sage Public Adm. Abstr.; Soc. Plann. Policy Dev. Abstr.

US/0743-9156
### JOURNAL OF PUBLIC POLICY & MARKETING. See Business-Marketing.

PK/0047-2751
### JOURNAL OF RURAL DEVELOPMENT AND ADMINISTRATION. Added/Corp Pakistan Academy for Rural Development, Peshawar. Vol. 4 (1964)-. Periodical. English. ir. $20.00. Pakistan Academy of Rural Development, Academy Town Peshawar, Peshawar Pakistan. Tel 011 92 42 402967. LC HC440.5.A1; P4. Continues Academy Quarterly.
Ind/Abst Cot. Trop. Fibr. Abstr. Bibliogr.; Helminthol. Abstr.; Int. Bibliogr. Sociol.; Poult. Abstr.; Protozoolog. Abstr.; Rice Abstr.; Rural Dev. Abstr.; Sug. Indus. Abstr.; Wheat Barley Trit. Abstr.; World Agric. Econ.

US/1059-4329
### JOURNAL OF SUPREME COURT HISTORY. (JOURNAL OF SUPREME COURT HISTORY : YEARBOOK OF THE SUPREME COURT HISTORICAL SOCIETY.). [J. Supreme Court hist.]. Added/Corp Supreme Court Historical Society. (1990)-. English. an. $15.00 (soft cover), $20.00 (bound), free to members. Supreme Court Historical Society, 111 2nd Street NE, Washington DC 20002. Tel (202)543-0400. LC KF8741.A15; S87. DD 347/.73/2609. Continues Supreme Court Historical Society. Yearbook - Supreme Court Historical Society, 0362-5249.
Ind/Abst Am. Hist. Life (1976-); Index Leg. Period.; Leg. Resour. Index.

US
### JOURNAL OF THE HOUSE OF REPRESENTATIVES OF THE ... REGULAR SESSION OF THE GENERAL ASSEMBLY OF THE STATE OF IOWA. Main/Corp Iowa. General Assembly House of Representatives. VFOAT Journal of the House of Representatives of the State of Iowa; Journal of the House of Representatives, of the ... General Assembly of the State of Iowa; Journal of the House of Representatives of the ... Session of the General Assembly of the State of Iowa; Journal of the House of Representatives. 1st Session (1846/47)-. English. an.

US
### JOURNAL OF THE HOUSE OF REPRESENTATIVES OF THE ... SESSION OF THE ... GENERAL ASSEMBLY OF THE STATE OF SOUTH CAROLINA. Main/Corp South Carolina. General Assembly. House of Representatives. (1919)-. English. an (Tues. Wed. & Thurs during sessions meeting). $168.00. Legislative Printing, 225 Blatt Building, 1105 Pendleton, Columbia SC 29201. Tel (803)734-3179. Continues South Carolina. General Assembly. House of Representatives. Journal of the House of Representatives of the State of South Carolina.

II
### JOURNAL OF THE INSTITUTE OF PUBLIC ADMINISTRATION. Added/Corp Lucknow University. Institute of Public Administration. (19??)-. Periodical. English. qt. $25.00. Regional Centre for Urban and Environmental Studies, Lucknow University, Department of Public Administration, Lucknow, India. (Subscription address: Prints India, 11 Darya Ganj, New Delhi, 110002 India, (Phone: 011 91 11 3268645)) LC JA26; .J68.

CN/0319-4973
### JOURNAL OF THE LEGISLATIVE ASSEMBLY OF THE PROVINCE OF PRINCE EDWARD ISLAND. [J. Legis. Assem. prov. P.E.I.]. Main/Corp Prince Edward Island. Legislative Assembly. (Mar. 28, 1894)-. Government Publication. English. an. 30.00Can$. Queen's Printer / Prince Edward Island, PO Box 2000, Charlottetown PEI C1A 7N8 Canada. Tel (902)368-5190. Continues Prince Edward Island. House of Assembly. Journal of the House Assembly of the Province of Prince Edward Island.

US
### JOURNAL OF THE SENATE OF THE GENERAL ASSEMBLY OF THE STATE OF SOUTH CAROLINA. Main/Corp South Carolina. General Assembly. Senate. (1872)-. English. be. Legislative Printing, 225 Blatt Building, 1105 Pendleton, Columbia SC 29201. Tel (803)734-3179. Continues South Carolina. General Assembly. Senate. Journal of the Senate of the State of South Carolina.

II
### JOURNAL OF THE SOCIETY FOR STUDY OF STATE GOVERNMENTS. Main/Corp Society for Study of State Governments. V. 1-Jan./June 1968-. Periodical. English. Kopparti Place Karaunoi, Varanasi 5 India. LC JS7001; .S6. DD 354.50/0005.
Ind/Abst Int. Polit. Sci. Abstr.

FR/0242-6757
### JOURNAL OFFICIEL DE LA REPUBLIQUE FRANCAISE. DEBATS PARLEMENTAIRES, ASSEMBLEE NATIONALE. QUESTIONS ECRITES ET REPONSES DES MINISTRES. (JOURNAL OFFICIEL DE LA REPUBLIQUE FRANCAISE. DEBATS PARLIAMENTAIRES, ASSEMBLEE NATIONALE. QUESTIONS ECRITES REMISES A LA PRESIDENCE DE L'ASSEMBLEE NATIONALE ET RESPONSES DES MINISTRES.). [J. off. Repub. fr., Debats parlem., Assem. natl., Quest. ecrites reponses minist.]. Main/Corp France. Parlement (1946- ). Assemblee Nationale. VFOAT Debats Parlementaires, Assemblee Nationale. Questions Ecrites Remises a la Presidence de l'Assemblee Nnationale et Reponses des Ministres. No. 1 (Jan. 8, 1980)-. Periodical. French. Fifty times a year. 115.00F France; 596.00F others. Direction des Journaux Officiels, 26 rue Desaix, 75727 Paris Cedex 15 France. Tel 011 33 1 40587500. Continues in part France. Parlement (1946- ). Assemblee Nationale. Journal Officiel de la Republique Francaise. Debats Parlementaires: Assemblee Nationale, 0242-6749.

FR/0242-6765
### JOURNAL OFFICIEL DE LA REPUBLIQUE FRANCAISE. DEBATS PARLIAMENTAIRES, ASSEMBLEE NATIONALE. COMPTE RENDU INTEGRAL. [J. off. Repub. fr., Debats parlem., Assem. natl., C. r. integr.]. Main/Corp France. Parlement (1946- ). Assemblee Nationale. VFOAT Debats Parlementaires, Assemblee Nationale. Compte Rendu Integral. No. 1 (Jan. 8, 1980)-. Periodical. French. ir. 116.00F France; 914.00F other. Direction des Journaux Officiels, 26 rue Desaix, 75727 Paris Cedex 15 France. Tel 011 33 1 40587500. Continues in part Journal Officiel de la Republique Francaise. Debats Parlementaires : Assemblee Nationale, 0242-6749.

FR
### JOURNAL OFFICIEL DE LA REPUBLIQUE FRANCAISE DEBATS SENAT COMPTE RENDU. French. 106.00F France; 576.00F other. Direction des Journaux Officiels, 26 rue Desaix, 75727 Paris Cedex 15 France. Tel 011 33 1 40587500.

FR
### JOURNAL OFFICIEL DE LA REPUBLIQUE FRANCAISE DEBATS SENAT QUESTIONS ECRITES. French. 377.00F. Direction des Journaux Officiels, 26 rue Desaix, 75727 Paris Cedex 15 France. Tel 011 33 1 40587500.

UV
### JOURNAL OFFICIEL DU BURKINA FASO. Main/Corp Burkina Faso. French. wk. 18,800.00CFAF. Universite de Ouagadougou Cedres, BP 7021, Ouagadougou Burkina Faso. Tel 307369. LC PAR. Continues Journal Officiel de la Republique de Haute Volta.

AT
### JOURNALS OF THE SENATE / THE PARLIAMENT OF THE COMMONWEALTH OF AUSTRALIA. Main/Corp Australia. Parliament. Senate. No. 1 (Feb. 1967)-. Government Publication. English. ir. 195.00Aus$. Australian Government Publishing Service, GPO Box 84, Canberra ACT 2601 Australia. Tel 011 61 6 2954411, FAX 011 61 6 2954455. Continues in part Australia. Parliament. Records of the Proceedings and the Printed Papers.

CN
### JURISCA DECISIONS DE LA COMMISSION DES AFFAIRS SOCIALES. (19??)-. English. Three times a year. 98.00Can$ Canada; 195.00Can$ others. SOQUIJ Societe Quebecoise Info Juridique, 276 rue Street, Jacques Suite 310, Montreal Quebec H2Y 1N3 Canada. Tel (514)842-8745.
Continues Decisions de la Commission des Affaires Sociales.

NE/0924-4824
### JURISPRUDENTIE VOOR GEMEENTEN. [Jurisprud. gem.]. VFOAT JG. (1990)-. Periodical. Dutch. Ten times a year. Fl120.00. VNG Uitgeverij, Postbus 30435, 2500 GK Gravenhage Netherlands. Tel 011 31 70 3738393, FAX 070-3651826. ED Mr. W G Verkruisen. UDC 34. Index available. Ad Acc. Circ: 600.
Desc: Jurisprudence in the field of municipal governments.

CN/1182-4301
### JUST NEWS. [Just news]. Added/Corp Manitoba. Manitoba Justice. VFOAT Newsletter. Vol. 5, No. 1 (Fall 1989)-. Periodical. English. qt. DD 354.7127008/8. Continues Newsletter (Manitoba. Attorney General)., 1182-4298.
Ind/Abst Hum. Rights Intern. Rep.

●UK/1351-5756
### JUSTICE OF THE PEACE AND LOCAL AND GOVERNMENT LAW. (1993)-. English. wk. £142.00 UK; £151.00 other. Justice of the Peace Limited, Little London, Chichester West Sussex, PO19 1PG England. Tel 011 44 243 787841, FAX 011 44 243 779278.

JA
### KAKUSHOCHO KOHO YOTEI JIKO. Added/Corp Japan. Naikaku Sori Daijin Kanbo. (19??)-. Periodical. Japanese. an. Naikaku Sori Daijin Kanbo, 6-1 Nagatocho 1 Chiyoda-ku, Tokyo Japan. LC JQ1649.P85; K34.

FI
### KANSANEDUSTAJAIN VAALIT. Main/Corp Finland. Tilastokeskus. VFOAT Riksdagsmannavalen; Parliamentary Elections. English (Finnish and Swedish). Tilastokeskus, PL 504, Annankatu 44, 00101 Helsinki Finland. Tel 358-0-17341, FAX 358-0-17342474, telex 1002111 TILASTO SF. LC HA1448; .F4 subser; JN6719.

US/0190-5171
### KANSAS DIRECTORY. 1961-. Directory. English. be. Secretary of State / Kansas, Capitol Building/2nd Floor, Topeka KS 66612. Tel (913)296-2236. ED Nancy R Clark. Continues Directory / State Officers, Boards and Commmissions and Interesting Facts About the State.
Desc: Contains a list of all Kansas congressional and statewide offices, agencies, boards and commission; all legislative, judicial and congressional districts are defined. Kansas population figures, zip code directory and tax information are included.

US/0360-6252
### KANSAS DIRECTORY. SUPPLEMENT. Added/Corp Kansas. Secretary of State. (19??)-. English. Secretary of State / Kansas, Capitol Building/2nd Floor, Topeka KS 66612. Tel (913)296-2236. LC JK6830; .A25 Suppl. DD 353.9/781/04.

US/0022-8613
### KANSAS GOVERNMENT JOURNAL. Added/Corp League of Kansas Municipalities. (Dec. 1937)-. Periodical. English. Twelve times a year. $24.00. League of Kansas Municipalities, 112 West 7th Street, Topeka KS 66603. Tel (913)354-9565, FAX (913)354-4186. ED Paula Freerksen. Index available. cum. index. Ad Acc. Circ: 7,500. Continues Kansas Government Journal and Kansas Municipalities.
Desc: Local, state and federal government issues affecting local governments
Ind/Abst Urban Aff. Abstr.

US
### KANSAS LEGISLATIVE HANDBOOK. Directory. English. an. $145.50. Government Research Service, 701 Jackson, Suite 304B, Topeka KS 66603. Tel (913)232-7720, (800)346-6898, FAX (913)232-1615. ED Lynn Helleburst.
Desc: Provides complete information on legislators including occupation, education, business interests, committee assignments, campaign contributors, governmental experience, and organizational memberships.

US/0744-2254
### KANSAS REGISTER. (KANSAS REGISTER / STATE OF KANSAS.). Added/Corp Kansas. Secretary of State. Vol. 1, No. 1 (Jan. 7, 1982)-. Periodical. English. Fifty-two times a year (Thurs.). $63.54 Kansas residents; $60.00 others. Secretary of State / Kansas, Capitol Building/2nd Floor, Topeka KS 66612. Tel (913)296-2236. ED Nancy R. Reddy. phone: (913)296-3489). LC KFK36; .K36. DD 348.781/01; 347.81081. Index Available, published separately, free-automatically sent. Circ: 1,500.
Desc: Official state paper, contains legal notices;

# Public Administration

contracts for bid; state agency meeting, hearing and public notices; new state laws; legislative bills; administration regulations; attorney general opinions, etc.

CH
**KAO-HSIUNG SHIH CHENG FU ... SHIH CHENG CHI HUA / KAO-HSIUNG SHIH CHENG FU PIEN. Main/Corp** Kao-hsiung Shih (Taiwan). Chinese. an. **LC** JS7366.9.K35; K37A.

US
**KENTUCKY ADMINISTRATIVE REGULATIONS SERVICE : CONTAINING REGULATIONS PROMULGATED BY ADMINISTRATIVE AGENCIES OF THE COMMONWEALTH OF KENTUCKY IN EFFECT AS OF ... . Main/Corp** Kentucky. Legislative Research Commission. **Added/Corp** Kentucky. General Assembly. Legislative Research Commission. **VFOAT** Kentucky Administrative Regulations. (1975)-. English. ir. $120.00; $150.00 combined subscription with Kentucky Administrative Register. Kentucky State Treasurer / Room 64, State Capitol, Frankfort KY 40601. **Tel** (502)564-8100. **ED** Susan C. Harding. **LC** KFK1234.5; .K46. **DD** 348.769/025; 347.690825. **Circ:** 600 (ctrl)

US/0453-5677
**KENTUCKY CITY (1968), THE.** (THE KENTUCKY CITY.). [Ky. city]. Vol 1, No. 1 (June 1968)-. Periodical. English. mo (except Sept.). $11.00. Kentucky League of Cities, 2201 Regency Road, Suite 100, Lexington KY 40503. **Tel** (800)876-4552, FAX (606)278-5766. **ED** Martha McDevitt. **LC** JS39; .K43. **DD** 352.0769. **Ad Acc. Circ:** 4,150 (ctrl). **Continues** Kentucky City Bulletin, 0734-4996.
 **Desc:** Information on city government in Kentucky and articles of general interest on municipal government procedures and administration.
 **Ind/Abst** Urban Aff. Abstr.

US
**KENTUCKY DIRECTORY OF BLACK ELECTED OFFICIALS. Main/Corp** Kentucky Commission on Human Rights. **VFOAT** Directory of Black Elected Officials. 1st- 1969-. Directory. English. ir (every 4 years). Kentucky Commission on Human Rights, 828 Capital Plaza Tower, Frankfort KY 40601. **Tel** (502)564-3550.
 **Desc:** A directory of blacks who hold elective offices in Kentucky. A picture and short biography is included on each official. A brief statistical comparison is made on the number of blacks in current offices and with the number in past years.

US
**KENTUCKY LOCAL OFFICIALS.** English. ir. Kentucky Department of Highways, 501 High Street, Frankfort KY 40622. **Tel** (502)564-3730, FAX (502)564-4809. **LC** JS451.K45; K44.

TU
**KESIN HESAPLAR, BELEDIYELER, IL OZEL IDARELERI. VFOAT** Kesin Hesaplar; Final Accounts; Final Accounts, Municipalities, Special Administrations. (1980/1982)-. English (Turkish). an. **LC** HA1911; .A3 subser; HJ9064. **Continues** Butce ve Kesin Hesaplar.

US/0748-8815
**KETTERING REVIEW.** [Kettering rev.]. **Added/Corp** Charles F. Kettering Foundation. (Winter 1983)-. Periodical. English. Twice a year. $28.95. The Charles F. Kettering Foundation, 200 Commons Road, Dayton OH 45459-2799. **Tel** (513)434-7300, (800)221-3657, FAX (513)439-9804. **ED** Robert J. Kingston. **LC** JK1; .K44. **DD** 361.6/1/05. **Circ:** 15,000 (ctrl).

SJ
**KEY OFFICIALS HANDBOOK. Main/Corp** United States. Embassy (Sudan) Economic Section. English. US Embassy Sudan, Economic Section, Khartoum Sudan. **LC** JQ3981.S82; U55A. **DD** 354/.624/002.

CN/1187-5216
**KEY (VICTORIA).** (THE KEY.). [Key]. **Added/Corp** British Columbia. Ministry of Women's Programs and Government Services and Minister Responsible for Families. No. 1 (Sept. 1991)-. Periodical. English. ir. **DD** 354.7110083/7.

GW
**KGST MITTEILUNGEN / KOMMUNALE GEMEINSCHAFTSSTELLE FUER VERWALTUNGSVEREINFACHUNG.**
**Main/Corp** Kommunale Gemeinschaftsstelle fuer Verwaltungsvereinfachung. **Added/Corp** ommunale Gemeinschaftsstelle fuer Verwaltungsvereinfachung. **VAT** Kommunale Gemeinschaftsstelle fuer Verwaltungsvereinfachung Mitteilungen. Vol. 16. No. 1 (Jan. 10, 1971)-. Periodical. German. Twenty-four times a year. Kommunale Gemeinschaftsstelle, Lindenallee 13 17, Postfach 510720, D 50943 Cologne Germany. **Tel** 011 49 221 376890, FAX 011 49 221 3768959. **ED** Gerhard Banner, Hansjurgen Bals, Jurgen Ostermann and Heinrich Siepmann. **LC** JS5431; .M57. cum. index. **Circ:** 3,000. **Continues** Mitteilungen der Kommunalen Gemeinschaftsstelle fuer Verwaltungsvereinfachung (KGST).
 **Desc:** Reports on management and administration opportunities in education and exchange. Up-date on economic planning at all levels, with special attention given to municipal and social services management.

JA
**KIKAN JICHITAIGAKU KENKYU. VFOAT** Jichitaigaku Kenkyu. Began with issue for May 1979 issue. Periodical. Japanese. qt. ¥1440. Kanagawa-ken Jichisogo Kenkyu Center, 32 Yamashitacho, Naka-ku, Yokohama-shi Japan. **Tel** 045-651-1471, FAX 045-664-5408. **(Subscription address:** 3-6-1-101 Kohinata, Bunkyo-ku Tokyo Japan**) ED** Chihana Murotani. **LC** JS7371.A1; K54. Index available. **Circ:** 2,500.

JA
**KIKAN KOKKAI GIIN. VFOAT** Kokkai Giin. Edition- (No. 1-4); 1979-. Periodical. Japanese. ¥10.000. Ariyama Toredo Sabisu, 13-8 Esakacho 1-chome, Suita 564 Japan. **LC** Z7165.J3; K48; JQ1626.1945.

UK
**KNIGHT'S LOCAL GOVERNMENT AND MAGISTERIAL REPORTS, WITH STATUTES, STATUTORY INSTRUMENTS, & C. Main/Corp** Great Britain. Courts. Vol.1 (1903)-. English. mo. £295.00. Charles Knight & Company Ltd, Tolley House, 2 Addiscombe Road, Croydon Surrey CR9 5AF England. **Tel** 011 44 81 688 4163.

RU/0302-8445
**KNIZHKA PARTIINOGO AKTIVISTA.**
(19??)-. Russian. 0.31rub. Izdatelstvo Polit Lit-ry, A-47 Miussadaia Pl7, Moscow Russia. **LC** JN6598.K7; K515. **Continues** Zapisnaia Knizhka Partinogo Aktivista.

DK
**KOMMUNAL HANDBOGEN.** (199?)-. Danish. **LC** JS6152; .A3a. **Continues** Kommunal Handbogen med Indkbsbogen.
 **Desc:** Journal concerning municipal government in Denmark.

HU
**KOMMUNALIS ELLAS FONTOSABB ADATAI. Added/Corp** Hungary. Kozponti Statisztikai Hivatal. Tarsadalmi Statisztikai Foosztaly. (1985)-. Hungarian. Statisztikai Kiado Vallalat, PO Box 99, H-1033 Budapest 3 Hungary. **Tel** 803-311, telex 22-6699-SKV-H. **LC** HD4652.5; .A29. **Continues in part** Lakas-es Kommunalis Ellatas Fontosobb Adatai.

GW/0450-7169
**KOMMUNALWIRTSCHAFT.**
[Kommunalwirtschaft]. Began in 1912. Academic Scholarly Publication. German. mo. $34.50. Kommunal Verlag, Rosseggerstr 5A, Dusseldorf Germany. **LC** HD4659; .K6. **CODEN** KMLWAB. Documents available from CASDDS.
 **Ind/Abst** Chem. Abstr.; EMBASE; Energy Res. Abstr. (March 1977-).

RU
**KONSULTATSII I OTVETY NA VOPROSY. V POMOSHCH RABOTNIKAM SOVETOV I DEPUTATAM. Added/Corp** Sovety Deputatov Trudiashchikhsia. Vol. 1 (1970)-. Russian. Izdatelstvo Izvestiia, Pl. Pushkina 5, 103798 Moscow Russia. **LC** JS6058; .K59.

NE/0168-9045
**KORT BESTEK.** [Kort bestek]. (1985)-. Periodical. Dutch. Twenty-six times a year. Fl104.50. Samson Bedrijfsinformatie, Postbus 4, 2400 HA Alphen Rij Netherlands. **Tel** 011 31 1 72066633. **(Subscription address:** Intermedia BV, Postbus 4, 2400 MA Alphen Rijn Netherlands.**) UDC** 351. **Continues** Geknipt voor het Raadslid, 0165-1927.

KO
**KUKHOE UIWON CHONGNAM. Main/Corp** Kukhoe Uiwon Tonghoe. Korean. W35. **LC** JQ1727; .K76A.

FI/0786-3624
**KUNNALLINEN VIRKALUETTELO.** Finnish. an. Tilastokeskus, PL 504, Annankatu 44, 00101 Helsinki Finland. **Tel** 358-0-17341, FAX 358-0-17342474, telex 1002111 TILASTO SF. **LC** JS6294.A35; K85.

FI
**KUNNALLISTEN VIRANHALTIJOIDEN JA KUUKAUSIPALKKAISTEN TYONTEKIJOIDEN JA TOIMIHENKILOIDEN PALKAT. Main/Corp** Finland. Tilastokeskus. Finnish. an. Valtion Painatuskeskus, PO Box 516, SF 00101 Helsinki Finland. **Tel** 011 358 0 5660266. **LC** JS6124.A35; F56A.

FI/0356-3669
**KUNNALLISTIETEELLINEN AIKAKAUSKIRJA.** [Kunnallistiet. aikak.]. **VFOAT** Kommunalvetenskaplig Tidskrift. (1973)-. Periodical. Multiple languages. qt. Helsinki Kunnallistieteen Yhdistys, Helsinki Finland. **UDC** 352.
 **Ind/Abst** Selec. Coop. Index Manage. Period.

FI/0784-9370
**KUNTASEKTORIN KUUKAUSIPALKAT / TILASTOKESKUS. Added/Corp** Finland. Tilastokeskus. **VFOAT** Manadsloner for Kommunalanstallda. (19??)-. Finnish (Finnish; summaries and/or abstracts in Swedish). an. Tilastokeskus, PL 504, Annankatu 44, 00101 Helsinki Finland. **Tel** 358-0-17341, FAX 358-0-17342474, telex 1002111 TILASTO SF. **LC** JS6294.A35; K86.

FI
**KUNTIEN JA KUNTAINLIITTOJEN SOSIAALITOIMEN KAYTTOMENOT JA TULOT. VFOAT** Driftsutgifter Och Inkomster for det Kommunala Socialvasendet. Finnish (Swedish). an. Sosiaalihallitus, Suunnittelu Ja Tilastotoimisto, Valtion Painatuskeskus, Pl 516, 00101 Helsinki 10 Finland. **LC** HV315.5; .A468.

CN
**KWIC INDEX TO KNOW YOUR GOVERNMENT.** Ministry of Government Services / Treasurer of Ontario, 50 Grosvenor, Toronto Ontario M7A 1N8 Canada. **Tel** (416)326-5316.

JA
**KYUSHU DENKI NENKAN. Added/Corp** Japan. Fukuoka Tsusho Sangyokyoku. Koeki Jigyobu. (19??)-. Periodical. Japanese. Kyushu Denki Kyokai, c/o Denki Building, 1-82 Watanabe Tori 2-chome Chuo-ku, Fukuoka Japan. **LC** HD9685.J33; K94. **Continues** Kyushu Denki Gasu Nenkan.

US/0272-3689
**LABOR-MANAGEMENT RELATIONS IN STATE AND LOCAL GOVERNMENTS.**
See Economics-Labor.

US
**LABOR MANAGEMENT RELATIONS ISSUES IN STATE AND LOCAL GOVERNMENTS.** See Economics-Labor.

UK
**LABOUR PARTY ANNUAL REPORT.** See Political Science.

CN/0228-4278
**LAND ASSESSMENT/SALES RATIO STUDY AND EQUALIZED ASSESSMENTS. Main/Corp** Alberta. Assessment Equalization Board. (1977)-. English. an. Assessment Equalization Board, 2nd Floor/Jarvis Building, Edmonton Alberta T5K 5H9 Canada. **Tel** 427-8965. **ED** A. Waters and R. Kozack. **LC** HJ4293.A4; A4a. **DD** 336.22/2. **Circ:** 125 (ctrl).
 **Desc:** Contains information prepared for and of interest to property tax assessors, municipal, school and hospital administrators, elected officials and property appraisers operating in Alberta, Canada. Although circulation is limited, it may be found in selected libraries.

AT
**LAND INFORMATION DIRECTORY / SPONSORED BY LAND INFORMATION SYSTEMS ADVISORY COMMITTEE.**
**Added/Corp** Western Australia. Land Information Systems Advisory Committee. (1981)-. Directory. English. Government Computing / Australia, 22 Saint George's Terrace, Perth Western Australia 6000 Australia. **Tel** (09)222 0222, FAX 325 9953, telex AA 96241. **LC** HD1039.W47; L36. **DD** 333.73/13/025941.

GW
**LANDERBERICHTE DES STATISTISCHEN BUNDESAMTES.**
German. Seventy-two issues per year. DM530.00. Metzler Poeschel Verlag Veroeffen, Statist Bundesamt Kernerstr 43, D 70182 Stuttgart Germany. **Tel** 011 49 7071 935350. **(Subscription address:** Metzler Poeschel H Leins GmbH, Holzwiesenstrasse 2, D 72127 Kusterdingen Germany**)**

AU
**LANDESHAUSHALT. Added/Corp** Amt der Salzburger Landesregierung. Landespresseburo. (19??)-. German. ir. Landesverkehrsamt Salzburg, Mozartplatz 1, 5010 Salzburg Austria. **LC** HJ44.S35; L36. **DD** 354.436/30072252/05.

NE/0922-6419
**LANDINRICHTING UTRECHT.**
(LANDINRICHTING.). [Landinrichting Utrecht]. (1988)-. Periodical. Dutch. Eight times a year. Fl75.00 (institution). St Tijdschrift Landinrichting, Postbus 20021, 3502 LA

# Public Administration

Utrecht Netherlands. **Tel** 011 31 30 858722. **UDC** 631.6 + 626.8. **Continues** Cultuurtechnisch Tijdschrift, 0045-9267.

SW/0282-4485
**LANDSTINGSVARLDEN.** [Landstingsvarlden]. (1985)-. Periodical. Swedish. Twenty times a year. Kr170.00. Landstings Varlden, Box 70491, S-107 26 Stockholm Sweden. **UDC** 353. **Continues** Landstingens Tidskrift, 0023-8074.

IO
**LAPORAN - WALIKOTA JAKARTA PUSAT. Main/Corp** Jakarta Pusat, Indonesia. Walikota. Indonesian. Jakarta Pusat, Jln Pegangasaan Barat No 4, Jakarta Indonesia. **LC** JS33.J3; I5A.

IO
**LAPORAN - WALIKOTA JAKARTA TIMUR. Main/Corp** Jakarta Timur (Indonesia). Wali Kota. (197?)-. Indonesian. mo. Jakarta Timur, Jln Raya Jatinegara Timur No 55, Jakarta Indonesia. **LC** JS7206.D5; J34a. **Continues** Jakarta Timur (Indonesia). Wali Kota. Laporan Bulanan Walikota Jakarta Timur.

MY
**LAPURAN TAHUNAN SURUHANJAYA PERKHIDMATAN AWAM NEGERI SABAH. Main/Corp** Sabah. Public Service Commission. Malay. an. Free. Bangunan Wisma Muis, Tingkat 7/Blok B, Peti Surat 10998, 88811 Kota Kinabalu, Sabah Malaysia. **Tel** 088-50511. **LC** HD2768.M35; S25A. **Bk Rev. Circ:** 500 (ctrl).

CN/0704-1217
**LARU STUDIES. VFOAT** Studies LARU. **VAT** Latin American Research Unit Studies. Vol. 1 (Oct. 1976)-. Monographic series. English. Three times a year. Price varies per volume. Latin American Research Unit, PO Box 673, Adelaide Street Post Office, Toronto Ontario Canada. **LC** JL966; .L35. **DD** 980'.005. **Absorbed** Brazilian Studies.
**Ind/Abst** Hum. Rights Intern. Rep.

US
**LAWS OF THE REGENTS, UNIVERSITY OF COLORADO. Main/Corp** University of Colorado, Boulder. Board of Regents. English. an. Secretary of the University and of the Board of Regents, Regent Hall 201 Box 3, University of Colorado, Boulder CO 80309. **Tel** (304)492-8203, FAX (303)492-3107. **ED** Kay Meyer. **LC** LD1155; .A38. **DD** 378.788/63. **Circ:** 150 (ctrl).
**Desc:** Basic policies of the governing board of the University of Colorado.

CN
**LEAFLETS, FOLDERS, ETC. - DEPT. OF HUMAN RESOURCES. Main/Corp** British Columbia. Dept. of Human Resources. Monographic series. English. Price varies per volume. Queen's Printer, 506 Government Street, Victoria British Columbia V8V 4R6 Canada. **Tel** 387-1901.

US/0093-2280
**LEGISLATION AFFECTING SOUTH DAKOTA MUNICIPALITIES. Main/Corp** South Dakota Municipal League. English. an. University of South Dakota Center for Continuing Education, Vermillion SD 57069. **LC** KFS3431.A29; S63. **DD** 342/.783/09.

US
**LEGISLATIVE ALERT.** English. Ten times a year. Free (committee members); $20.00 (non-members). Pennsylvania Institute of CPAS, 208 North Third Street, Suite 200, Harrisburg PA 17101. **Tel** (717) 232-1821, FAX (717) 232-7708.

US
**LEGISLATIVE ALERT. See** Law.

CN/1182-7823
**LEGISLATIVE ASSEMBLY OF ALBERTA.** (LEGISLATIVE ASSEMBLY OF ALBERTA : [FACT SHEET].). [Legis. Assem. Alta.]. **Main/Corp** Alberta. Legislative Assembly. Fact Sheet No. 1 (1990)-. English. **DD** 328.7123/005.

US
**LEGISLATIVE BUDGET BOOK : A PUBLICATION OF THE LEGISLATIVE BUDGET OFFICE / JOINT SENATE FINANCE-HOUSE APPROPRIATIONS COMMITTEE. Main/Corp** Idaho. Legislature. Legislative Budget Office. **VFOAT** Idaho Legislative Budget Book. Fiscal Year 1984-. English. an. Idaho Legislative Budget Office, Room 334/Statehouse, Boise ID 83720. **LC** HJ11; .I243A. **DD** 353.97960072/2/05. ctrl circ.

US/0495-2499
**LEGISLATIVE BUDGET ESTIMATES. See** Public Administration-Public Finance and Taxation.

US/0740-4204
**LEGISLATIVE BULLETIN - ASSOCIATION OF WASHINGTON CITIES. See** Law.

US
**LEGISLATIVE CALENDAR / COMMITTEE ON ENERGY AND COMMERCE. Main/Corp** United States. Congress. House. Committee on Energy and Commerce. 97th Congress, No. 1 (April 10, 1981)-. Periodical. English. an. Committee on Energy and Commerce, Rayburn House Office Building/Room 2125, Washington DC 20515. **LC** KF22; .E554. **DD** 328.73/07652. available on microfiche (Vols. for (1986-) distributed to depository libraries). Documents available from Documents on Demand. **Continues** United States. Congress. House. Committee on Interstate and Foreign Commerce. Legislative Calendar.
**Ind/Abst** CIS Index Publ. U.S. Congr.

US
**LEGISLATIVE CALENDAR / SELECT COMMITTEE ON INTELLIGENCE, UNITED STATES SENATE. Main/Corp** United States. Congress. Senate. Select Committee on Intelligence. Periodical. English. Select Committee on Intelligence, US Senate, US Government Printing Office, Washington DC 20510.

US/0190-5473
**LEGISLATIVE CALENDAR / UNITED STATES HOUSE OF REPRESENTATIVES, COMMITTEE ON BANKING, FINANCE, AND URBAN AFFAIRS. Main/Corp** United States. Congress. House. Committee on Banking, Finance, and Urban Affairs. (197?)-. Government Publication. English. an. Superintendent of Documents, US Government Printing Office, Washington DC 20402. **Tel** (202)275-3328, FAX (202)786-2377. **LC** JK1430.B3; A35. **DD** 328.73/07/65. available on microfiche (Vols. for 1986- distributed to depository libraries). Documents available from Documents on Demand. **Continues** United States. Congress. House. Committee on Banking, Currency and Housing. Legislative Calendar, 0364-9652.
**Ind/Abst** CIS Index Publ. U.S. Congr.

US/0190-5805
**LEGISLATIVE CALENDAR / UNITED STATES HOUSE OF REPRESENTATIVES, COMMITTEE ON RULES. Main/Corp** United States. Congress. House. Committee on Rules. Government Publication. English. an. Superintendent of Documents, US Government Printing Office, Washington DC 20402. **Tel** (202)275-3328, FAX (202)786-2377. **LC** KF22; .R84. **DD** 328.73/07/65. available on microfiche (Vols. for (1986-) distributed to some depository libraries). Documents available from Documents on Demand.
**Ind/Abst** CIS Index Publ. U.S. Congr.

US/0364-4200
**LEGISLATIVE CALENDAR / UNITED STATES HOUSE OF REPRESENTATIVES, COMMITTEE ON VETERAN AFFAIRS. Main/Corp** United States. Congress. House. Committee on Veterans' Affairs. English. an. **LC** JK1430.V4; A34. **DD** 355.115. available on microfiche (Vols. for (99th Congress, 2nd Session) distributed to some depository libraries). Documents available from Documents on Demand.
**Ind/Abst** CIS Index Publ. U.S. Congr.

US/0147-4103
**LEGISLATIVE CALENDAR - UNITED STATES SENATE. COMMITTEE ON AGRICULTURE, NUTRITION, AND FORESTRY.** (LEGISLATIVE CALENDAR / COMMITTEE ON AGRICULTURE, NUTRITION, AND FORESTRY, UNITED STATES SENATE.). **Main/Corp** United States. Congress. Senate. Committee on Agriculture, Nutrition, and Forestry. Began with 95th Congress, 1st Session, (Jan. 4, 1977)-. Government Publication. English. an. Superintendent of Documents, US Government Printing Office, Washington DC 20402. **Tel** (202)275-3328, FAX (202)786-2377. **LC** JK1240.A46; A34. **DD** 328.73/07/65. available on microfiche (Vols. for (1987-) distributed to some depository libraries). Documents available from Documents on Demand. **Continues** United States. Congress. Senate. Committee on Agriculture and Forestry. Legislative Calendar, 0364-4170.
**Ind/Abst** CIS Index Publ. U.S. Congr.

US/0147-6572
**LEGISLATIVE CALENDAR - UNITED STATES SENATE. COMMITTEE ON GOVERNMENTAL AFFAIRS.** (LEGISLATIVE CALENDAR / COMMITTEE ON GOVERNMENTAL AFFAIRS, UNITED STATES SENATE.). **Main/Corp** United States. Congress. Senate. Committee on Governmental Affairs. Began with 95th Congress, 1st Session, (Jan. 4, 1977)-. Government Publication. English. ir. Superintendent of Documents, US Government Printing Office, Washington DC 20402. **Tel** (202)275-3328, FAX (202)786-2377. **LC** JK1240.E8; A34. **DD** 328.73/07/65. available on microfiche (Vols. for (Dec. 31, 1986-) distributed to some depository libraries). Documents available from Documents on Demand. **Continues** United States. Congress. Senate. Committee on Government Operations. Legislative Calendar, 0364-4251.
**Ind/Abst** CIS Index Publ. U.S. Congr.

US
**LEGISLATIVE DIGEST ALASKA.** English. ir (published weekly Jan. through June during Alaska legislative session). $240.00. Alaska Information & Research Service, 3037 South Circle, Anchorage AK 99507. **Tel** (907)349-7711.

US
**LEGISLATIVE INFORMATION SERVICE.** (19??)-. Periodical. English. Nine times a year. $150.00. California Peace Officers Association, 1455 Response Road, Suite 190, Sacramento CA 95815-4501. **Tel** (916)923-1825, FAX (916)263-6090. **ED** Leslie McGill. **Circ:** 120 (ctrl).

US/0362-272X
**LEGISLATIVE MANUAL - GENERAL ASSEMBLY OF SOUTH CAROLINA.** Title Change. [Legis. man. - Gen. Assem. S. C.]. **Main/Corp** South Carolina. General Assembly. (19??)-(198?). English. an. Clerk of the House, South Carolina House of Representatives, PO Box 11867, Columbia SC 29211. **Tel** (803)734-2010. **ED** Sandra K. McKinney. **LC** JK4271; .A4. **DD** 353. **Bk Rev. Ad Acc. Circ:** 15,000 (ctrl). **Continued by** South Carolina. General Assembly. South Carolina Legislative Manual.
**Desc:** Pictures and biographies of members of the General Assembly, judicial system, state officers and Congress, county, state offices and US offices.

US
**LEGISLATIVE MANUAL, STATE OF WASHINGTON. Main/Corp** Washington (State). Legislature. 1989/90-. English. be. Washington State Legislature, Olympia WA 98504. **Tel** (206)786-7500. **Continues** Joint Rules, Rules of the Senate and Rules of the House of the State Legislature of Washington, 0145-1936.

US/0889-4574
**LEGISLATIVE NEWS ALERT.** [Legis. news alert]. **Added/Corp** California Council of Churches. Office for State Affairs. **VFOAT** California Impact. (19??)-. Periodical. English. ir (10-11 issues per year). $10.00. California Council of Churches, Legislative News Alert, 1300 North Street, Sacramento CA 95814. **Tel** (916)442-5447. **DD** 344. **Circ:** 10,000.
**Desc:** Current information on legislation and provides public policy issues facing California in the state capital of Sacramento.

US
**LEGISLATIVE REPORTING SERVICE / COMMERCE CLEARING HOUSE. Added/Corp** Commerce Clearing House. **VFOAT** State legislative Reporting Service. (1972)-. English. ir. $250.00. Illinois State Chamber of Commerce, 20 North Wacker Drive, Chicago IL 60606. **Tel** (312)372-7373. **ED** Linda J Iaun. **Bk Rev. Ad Acc. Circ:** 300 (ctrl).
**Desc:** Summarizes legislative action in the Illinois general assembly on business issues and how member firms are affected.

US
**LEGISLATIVE SYNOPSIS AND DIGEST ... GENERAL ASSEMBLY, STATE OF ILLINOIS. Main/Corp** Illinois. General Assembly. **Added/Corp** Illinois. General Assembly. Senate. Illinois. General Assembly. House of Representatives. Illinois. General Assembly. Legislative Reference Bureau. **VFOAT** Legislative Synopsis and Digest of the ... General Assembly, State of Illinois; Legislative Synopsis and Digest of the ... Session of the ... General Assembly, State of Illinois; Final Legislative Synopsis and Digest ... General Assembly, State of Illinois; Legislative Synopsis and Digest. 53rd (1923)-. English. wk (Published when General Assembly in session). $55.00. Legislative Reference Bureau, Room 112, State House, Springfield IL 62706. **Tel** (217)782-6625. **ED** Kathleen Kenyon. **LC** J87; .I3 date K. Index available. cum. index. **Circ:** 1,800. **Continues** Illinois. General Assembly. Legislative Digest.
**Desc:** Contains a synopsis of each bill and resolution introduced and the action on those bills and resolutions to the date of publication.

US
**LEGISLATOR'S GUIDE, A. VFOAT** Legislative Guide. English. an. Office of Legislature, Room 333/State House, Augusta ME 04333. **LC** JK2830; .L43. **DD** 328.741/002/02.

US
**LEGISTATIVE QUICK REPORT.** English. California School Boards Association, PO Box 1660, West Sacramento CA 95691. **Tel** (916)371-4691.

CN/1183-0050
**LETTRE FISCALE QUEBECOISE.** (LA LETTRE FISCALE QUEBECOISE / UNIVERSITE DE SHERBROOKE, INSTITUT DE RECHERCHE ET D'ENSEIGNEMENT EN FISCALITE.). [Lett. fisc. que.]. **Added/Corp** Universite de Sherbrooke. Institut de Recherche et d'Enseignement pour les Cooperatives. Editeurs Richard De Boo. Vol. 1, No 1 (Dec. 1990/Jan. 1991)-. Periodical. French. mo. Limited free distribution. Richard de Boo Publishers, 81 Curlew Drive, Don Mills Ontario M3A 3P7 Canada. **Tel** (416)445-4940. **DD** 336.2/009714.

UK
**LGC LOCAL GOVERNMENT CHRONICLE.** **VFOAT** Local Government Chronicle. No. 5314 (Jan. 1969)-. Periodical. English. Fifty-two times a year. £71.00 UK and overseas surface mail; £110.00 Europe. Local Governement Chronicle, 33-39 Bowling Green lane, London ECIR ODA England. **Tel** 011 44 071 837 1212, FAX 011 44 071 278 9509. available on microfilm and microfiche from University Microfilms International (UMI). ***Continues** Local Government Chronicle.*
**Ind/Abst** Appl. Soc. Sci. Index Abstr.; Women Manage. Rev. [Full Txt.].

CN/0701-0532
**LIAISON (MONTREAL. 1975).** (LIAISON.). V. 1- Nov. 1975-. Periodical. French. Union des Municipalites du Quebec, 680 Sherbrooke Street West, Suite 680, Montreal Quebec H3A 2S6 Canada. **Tel** (514)282-7700 49 St-Pierre. **DD** 352/.0006/2714.

US/1056-9049
**LICENSEE CONTRACTOR AND VENDOR INSPECTION STATUS REPORT.** [Licens. contract. vend. insp. status rep.]. **Added/Corp** U.S. Nuclear Regulatory Commission. Office of Inspection and Enforcement. U.S. Nuclear Regulatory Commission. Region IV. U.S. Nuclear Regulatory Commission. Division of Reactor Inspection and Safeguards. U.S. Nuclear Regulatory Commission. Division of Reactor Inspection and Licensee Performance. (19??)-. Government Publication. English. qt. $18.00 domestic; $22.50 other. Superintendent of Documents, US Government Printing Office, Washington DC 20402. **Tel** (202)275-3328, FAX (202)786-2377. **DD** 621. available on microfiche (Vols. for (1987-) distributed to depository libraries).
**Desc:** Presents individual reports on violations of NRC standards in nuclear powerplant operations, maintenance, or modifications based on inspections performed by NRC personnel. The reports focus on the quality of vendor products, including hardware, fabrication, licensee-vendor interfaces, environmental qualification of equipment, and equipment problems found during operations or corrective action.

CN/0837-7375
**LIST OF ALBERTA PUBLICATIONS AND LEGISLATION.** ***Title Change.*** [List Alta. publ. legis.]. **Main/Corp** Alberta. Public Affairs Bureau. (1987)-(19??). English. ir. Alberta Statutes Province / Queens Printer, Province Treasury, 11510 Kingsly Avenue, Edmonton Alberta T5G 2Y5 Canada. **Tel** (403)427-4952. **LC** KEA1; .L57. **DD** 016.3497123; 016.347123. ***Continued by** Alberta. Public Affairs Bureau. Table of Alberta Legislation, 0710-8958.*

IR
**LIST OF MEMBERS OF THE DIPLOMATIC CORPS / MINISTRY OF FOREIGN AFFAIRS OF THE ISLAMIC REPUBLIC OF IRAN.** English. **LC** JX1853; .A173. **DD** 351.8/92/0955.

CN/0316-1641
**LIST OF MEMBERS OF THE HOUSE OF COMMONS OF CANADA.** (LIST OF MEMBERS OF THE HOUSE OF COMMONS OF CANADA WITH THEIR RESPECTIVE CONSTITUENCIES AND ADDRESSES.). **Main/Corp** Canada. Parliament. House of Commons. **VFOAT** Liste des Deputes a la Chambre des Communes du Canada Avec Indication de la Circonscription Electorale et de l'Adresse du Depute. Nov. 12, 1953-. Periodical. Multiple languages (French and English). Information Canada, 171 Slater Street, Ottawa Ontario K1A 0S9 Canada. **Tel** (819)997-1095. **DD** 328.71/07/3. ***Continues** List of Members of the House of Commons with Their Constituencies and Post Office Addresses.*

LU/0531-4348
**LIST OF WORKING DOCUMENTS.** **Main/Corp** European Parliament. **Added/Corp** European Parliament. Working Documents. (19??)-. English. ir. Office for Official Publications of the European Communities, 2 Rue Mercier, 2985 Luxembourg Luxembourg. **Tel** 011 352 499281, FAX 011 352 488573. **LC** JN32; .L56. **DD** 341.24/2.

CN/0840-7908
**LISTE BIMESTRIELLE DES PUBLICATIONS DU GOUVERNEMENT DU QUEBEC.** **See** Public Administration-Abstracting, Bibliographies and Statistics.

GW/0723-953X
**LISTE DER DIPLOMATISCHEN MISSIONEN UND ANDEREN VERTRETUNGEN IN BONN.** ***Title Change.*** [Liste dipl. Miss. and. Vertret. Bonn]. **Main/Corp** Germany (West). Auswartiges Amt. (1974)-(19??). German. Three times a year. Stollfuss Verlag GmbH and Company KG, Postfach 2428 Dechenstrasse 7-11, D 53014 Bonn Germany. **Tel** 011 49 228 724222. **LC** JX1795; .A2278. **DD** 354/.43/00892. ***Continues** Liste des Diplomatischen Korps in Bonn. **Continued by** Liste der Diplomatischen Missionen in der Bundesrepublik Deutschland.*

SZ
**LISTE DES MEMBRES DU CORPS CONSULAIRE.** **Main/Corp** Switzerland. Departement des Auswartigen. French. **LC** JX1823; .A165A. **DD** 351.8/92/09494.

TU
**LISTE DES MEMBRES DU CORPS CONSULAIRE, ISTANBUL.** (196?)-. French. **LC** JX1825; .A167. ***Continues** Liste de MM. Les Membres du Corps Consulaire.*

●CN/1187-7154
**LISTE DES RAPPORTS ANNUELS, BIBLIOTHEQUE PRINCIPALE JE.** (LISTE DES RAPPORTS ANNUELS, BIBLIOTHEQUE PRINCIPALE (JE): LIST OF ANNUAL REPORTS, MAIN LIBRARY (JE).). [Liste rapp. annu. bibl. princ. JE]. **Main/Corp** Canada. Secretariat d'Etat du Canada. Bibliotheque Ministerielle. **Added/Corp** Canada. Multiculturalisme et Citoyennete Canada. **VFOAT** List of Annual Reports, Main Library (JE). (1992)-. French (English). Canadian Government Publishing Center, Supply and Services Canada, Hull Quebec K1A 0S9 Canada. **Tel** (613)990-8116, telex 053-4296. **DD** 016.35471/0006.

●CN/1187-7154
**LISTE DES RAPPORTS ANNUELS, BIBLIOTHEQUE PRINCIPALE JE, LIST OF ANNUAL REPORTS, MAIN LIBRARY (JE).** [Liste rapp. annu. bibl. princ. JE]. **Main/Corp** Canada. Dept. of the Secretary of State of Canada. Departmental Library. **Added/Corp** Canada. Multiculturalism and Citizenship Canada. **VFOAT** List of Annual Reports, Main Library (JE). (1992)-. English (French). **DD** 016.35471/0006.

US/1057-5774
**LISTS OF PARTIES EXCLUDED FROM FEDERAL PROCUREMENT OR NONPROCUREMENT PROGRAMS.** (LISTS OF PARTIES EXCLUDED FROM FEDERAL PROCUREMENT OR NONPROCUREMENT PROGRAMS AS OF ....). **Added/Corp** United States. General Services Administration. Office of Acquisition Policy. (June 10, 1988)-. Government Publication. English. mo. $80.00 domestic; $100.00 other. Superintendent of Documents, US Government Printing Office, Washington DC 20402. **Tel** (202)275-3328, FAX (202)786-2377. **DD** 353. ***Continues** Consolidated List of Debarred, Suspended, and Ineligible Contractors as of ...*
**Desc:** Identifies those parties excluded throughout the United States Government (unless otherwise noted) from receiving Federal contracts or federally approved subcontracts and from certain types of Federal financial and nonfinancial assistance and benefits.

AT
**LIVING CITY.** Began with Winter 1967 Issue. Periodical. English. sa. Free. Melbourne & Met Board Works, 625 Little Collins Street, Melbourne Australia. **Tel** 615-4163, telex AA 34220. **ED** Michael Petit. **LC** HT169.A82; M44. **DD** 711/.4/09945. **Circ:** 50,000 (ctrl).
**Desc:** Periodic report of developments in water resource management, parks and waterways developments and other public resource areas under the jurisdiction of the Melbourne and Metropolitan Board of Works.

●CN/1193-4034
**LOBBY DIGEST & PUBLIC AFFAIRS MONTHLY, THE.** [Lobby dig. public aff. mon.]. **Added/Corp** Advocacy Research Centre. **VFOAT** Lobby Digest and Public Affairs Monthly. Issue 33 (July 1992)-. Periodical. English. mo. 199.00Can$. ARC Publications - Advocacy Research Centre Inc., 75 Sparks Street #600, Ottawa Ontario K1P 5A5 Canada. **Tel** (613)230-3029, FAX (613)237-9617. **ED** John Chenier. **DD** 324/.4/0971. **Bk Rev**, (Qty: 12). **Ad Acc. Circ:** 1,000 (ctrl). ***Continues** The Lobby Digest., 1180-2499.*

US/0148-4354
**LOBBYING IN THE FLORIDA HOUSE OF REPRESENTATIVES.** ***Title Change.*** **Main/Corp** Florida. Legislature. House of Representatives. Office of the Clerk. (19??)-(19??). Periodical. English. Florida House of Representatives, Tallahassee FL 32304. **LC** JK4474.5; .F46a. **DD** 328.759/07/38025. ***Continued by** Lobbying in Florida.*

●US/1057-0594
**LOBBYING RESOURCE DIRECTORY.** **Added/Corp** Government Research Service. (1992)-. Directory. English. $45.00. Government Research Service, 701 Jackson, Suite 304B, Topeka KS 66603. **Tel** (913)232-7720, (800)346-6898, FAX (913)232-1615.

CN/1184-0471
**LOBBYISTS REGISTRATION ACT ANNUAL REPORT.** **See** Political Science.

UK/0308-3594
**LOCAL COUNCIL REVIEW.** **Added/Corp** National Association of Local Councils. (1973)-. Periodical. English. bm. $8.00. National Association of Local Councils, c/o Plus Public Relations, Press House, 130A Godinton Road, Ashford Kent TN231LJ. **Tel** 011 44 233 643574, FAX 011 44 233 641816. **ED** Paul Smith. **LC** JS3001; .L58. **DD** 352.041. Index available. **Ad Acc. Circ:** 23,387 (ctrl). ***Continues** Parish Councils Review, 0031-2061.*
**Desc:** Matters of interest to parish, town and community councils in England and Wales.

PK
**LOCAL GOVERNMENT.** **Added/Corp** Pakistan Group for the Study of Local Government. (19??)-. Periodical. English. mo. Rs25.00. Pakistan Group for the Study of Local Government, 14 Japan Mansion Preedy Street, Karachi, Pakistan. **ED** Malik M. Siddig. **LC** JS7091.A1; L6. **DD** 352.0549/1.

●AT/1039-7213
**LOCAL GOVERNMENT AND ENVIRONMENTAL REPORTS OF AUSTRALIA, THE.** **VFOAT** LGERA; Local Government & Environmental Reports of Australia. Vol. 78, Pt. 1 (Apr. 1993)-. English. ir. 195.00Aus$. The Law Book Company Limited, 44-50 Waterloo Road, North Ryde New South Wales, 2113 Australia. **Tel** 011 61 2 8870177, FAX 011 61 2 8887240, telex ASBOOK 27445. ***Continues** Local Government Reports of Australia, 0076-0242.*

AT/1057-1796
**LOCAL GOVERNMENT BULLETIN.** **Added/Corp** Shires Association of New South Wales. Local Government Association of New South Wales. (1976)-. Bulletin. English. Ten times a year. 30.00Aus$. Local Government and Shires Associations of New South Wales, PO Box C364 Clarence Street, Sydney New South Wales 2000 Australia. **Tel** 11 61 2 2997711, FAX 02 262 1049. **ED** C. Barrett. **Circ:** 3800. ***Continues** Bulletin / Local Government Association of New South Wales.*
**Desc:** News and issues relating to local government in Australia.

UK
**LOCAL GOVERNMENT COMPANION.** (197?)-. English. an. £12.00 (one year). Local Government Companion, 18 Lincoln Green, Chichester WS PO19 4DN, England. **Tel** 11 44 243 787272. **ED** E P Craig.
**Desc:** Handy listing of information on all local government councils in England, Scotland, and Wales, including principal address, telephone number, and officers.

CN/0703-7392
**LOCAL GOVERNMENT EMPLOYMENT.** ***Title Change.*** **See** Economics-Labor.

AT/0819-470X
**LOCAL GOVERNMENT FOCUS.** [Local gov. focus]. (1985)-. Periodical. English. Ten times a year (except Jan., Dec.). 30.00Aus$. Eryl Morgan Publications PL., 302 High Street, Northcote VIC 3070 Australia. **Tel** 011 61 3 486121, FAX 011 61 3 4891845. **ED** Corinne Morgan. **DD** 352.0945. **Ad Acc, Adv Mgr:** Marie.

SA/1015-0048
**LOCAL GOVERNMENT IN SOUTHERN AFRICA.** [Local gov. South. Afr.]. **VFOAT** Plaaslike Regering in Suidelike Africa. Academic Scholarly Publication. English (Afrikaans). bm. R28.00 South Africa; R62.00 other. Target Communications, PO Box 3445, 2125 Randburg Transvaal, South Africa. **Tel** 011 27 11 886-4583, 886-4584, 886-4585. **ED** R E Bull and A Van Wyk. **LC** JS7531.A1; L6. **DD** 352.068. **Bk Rev. Ad Acc. Circ:** 3,200 (ctrl). ***Continues** Municipal Administration and Engineering.*
**Desc:** To assist decision makers in local government by publishing in-depth articles on all matters pertaining to their functions including civil defense. Opinions and views from prominent personalities are also published.
**Ind/Abst** EMBASE.

# Public Administration

AT/0819-1212
**LOCAL GOVERNMENT MANAGEMENT.**
[Local gov. manage.]. (1986)-. Periodical. English. Six times a year. 37.50Aus$. Institute of Municipal Management / Victoria, PO Box 409, South Melbourne Victoria 3205, Australia. **Tel** 011 61 3 6965799, FAX 011 61 3 6904217. **DD** 352.094. **Continues** *LGA. Local Government Administration, 0727-7342.*
**Ind/Abst** APAIS, Aust. Public Aff. Inf. Ser.

US/1058-3491
**LOCAL GOVERNMENT MONITOR.** (LOCAL GOVERNMENT MONITOR : IN THE PUBLIC INTEREST OF ASHEVILLE AND BUNCOMBE COUNTY.). [Local gov. monit.]. **VFOAT** Monitor. Vol. 1, No. 1 (Sept. 20, 1991)-. Periodical. English. sm. $25.00. **DD** 320.

UK/0264-2050
**LOCAL GOVERNMENT POLICY MAKING.** [Local gov. policy mak.]. **Added/Corp** Institute of Local Government Studies (Great Britain). (1981)-. Periodical. English. Five times a year. £77.00 Europe; £84.00 Other (Institutions). Longman Group Ltd., Fourth Avenue, Longman House, Harlow Essex CM19 5SR England. **Tel** 011 44 279 429655, FAX 011 44 279 431059, telex 81259. **ED** John Benington and Gerry Stoker. **[CCC].** Index available. **Bk Rev. Ad Acc. Circ:** 700. available on microfilm. **Continues** *Corporate Planning Journal.*
**Ind/Abst** PAIS Int. Print (1991-).

II
**LOCAL GOVERNMENT QUARTERLY.** V. 1- Mar. 1972-. Periodical. English. $4.50. 217 B Dhanmandi Residential Area, Road No 15, Dacca 5 India. **LC** JS7100.A1; L63. **DD** 352.0549/2.

AT/0076-0242
**LOCAL GOVERNMENT REPORTS OF AUSTRALIA, THE.** Title Change. (1956)-(1993). English. The Law Book Company Limited, 44-50 Waterloo Road, North Ryde New South Wales, 2113 Australia. **Tel** 011 61 2 8870177, FAX 011 61 2 8887240, telex ASBOOK 27445. **LC** LAW. **DD** 352.094. Index available. **Continued by** *The Local Government and Environmental Reports of Australia, 1039-7213.*
**Desc:** Reports cases dealing with environmental control, town planning, local government, valuation of land and compensation from the Supreme Courts of the Australian states; includes the authorized reports of the Land and Environment Court of NSW.
**Ind/Abst** Aust. Leg. Mon. Dig.

UK
**LOCAL GOVERNMENT REVIEW.** Title Change. (1971)-(1993). Periodical. English. wk. Barry Rose Law Periodicals Ltd., Little London, Chichester West Sussex PO19 1PG England. **Tel** 011 44 243 787841, 011 44 243 783637, FAX 011 44 243 779174, 011 44 243 779278. **ED** Barry Rose. **LC** K12; .O3. **DD** 352.042. **Bk Rev. Ad Acc. Continues in part** *Justice of the Peace and Local Government Review.* **Continued by** *Local Government Review Reports.*
**Desc:** Oldest weekly journal dealing with a specialist area of local government, including law reports, lands tribunal cases, planning appeal decisions, etc.
**Ind/Abst** Appl. Soc. Sci. Index Abstr. (?-?); J. Plan. Lit. (?-?); Leg. Resour. Index (?-?); LegalTrac (1980-?).

JA/0288-7622
**LOCAL GOVERNMENT REVIEW IN JAPAN.** [Local gov. rev. Jap.]. No. 7 (1979)-. English. an. **LC** JS7371.A1; L63. **DD** 320.8/0952. **Continues** *Local Government Review.*
**Ind/Abst** PAIS Int. Print (1991-?).

AT
**LOCAL GOVERNMENTS OF AUSTRALIA.** (19??)-. Directory. English. 495.00Aus$ Australia; 524.00Aus$ New Zealand, Papua New Guinea; 530.00Aus$ Indonesia, Malaysia, Singapore, 536.00Aus$ Japan, India; 545.00Aus$ US & Canada; 551.00Aus$ Europe. International Public Relations Pty Ltd., 33 Walsh Street, West Melbourne Victoria 3003 Australia. **Tel** 011 61 03 329 9333, FAX 011 61 03 329 7996.

US
**LOCAL ISSUES : A COMPTROLLER OF THE TREASURY PUBLICATION FOR LOCAL GOVERNMENT AND THE PUBLIC.** Vol. 7, No. 6 (Nov. 1987)-. English. qt. Tennessee Division of Local Government, James K Polk State Office Building, 505 Deaderick Street/Suite 1400, Nashville TN 37219. **LC** KFT430.A15; L63. **DD** 342.768/09. **Continues** *Local Government Newsletter (Nashville, Tenn.).*

US/0741-3173
**LOCAL/STATE FUNDING REPORT / GIS, GOVERNMENT INFORMATION SERVICES.** [Local/state fund. rep.]. **Added/Corp** Government Information Services. **VFOAT** Local State Funding Report. Vol. 11, No. 12 (Mar. 28, 1983)-. Periodical. English. wk (Except the last week of August and December). $289.00. Government Information Services / Virginia, 4301 North Fairfax Drive, Suite 875, Arlington VA 22203. **Tel** (703)528-1082, FAX (703)528-6060, telex RCA 263591 GIS UR. **ED** Jeanne M. Williams. **DD** 336. **[CCC].** **Continues in part** *Grant Alert and Local Government Funding Report, 0273-4451.*
**Desc:** Reports on federal and private-sector grant funding for local and state governments and for nonprofit organizations.

FR/0769-2412
**LOCALDOC / GROUPEMENT DE RECHERCHES COORDONNEES SUR L'ADMINISTRATION LOCALE; CENTRE D'ETUDE ET DE RECHERCHE SUR LA VIE LOCALE.** **Added/Corp** Groupement de Recherches Coordonnees sur l'Administration Locale (France) Institut d'Etudes Politiques de Bordeaux. Centre d'Etude et de Recherche sur la Vie Locale. Centre National de la Recherche Scientifique (France). (1985)-. Periodical. French. Four times a year. Editions Techniques, 141 rue de Javel, 75747 Paris Cedex 15 France. **Tel** 011 33 1 45589100.

UK/0023-6349
**LOGA. LOCAL GOVERNMENT ANNOTATIONS.** **VFOAT** Local Government Annotations; Local Government Annotations Service. Vol. 1 (Oct. 1966)-. Periodical. English. mo. London Burough of Havering, Borough Trea Department, Town Hall Romford England.

II/0445-6793
**LOK SABHA. PARLIAMENTARY COMMITTEES. SUMMARY OF WORK.** (PARLIAMENTARY COMMITTEE : SUMMARY OF WORK.). **Main/Corp** India. Parliament. House of the People. English. Lok Sabha Secretariat, India Parliament House of the People, New Delhi India. **LC** JQ257.C6; I52A. **DD** 328.54/07/65.

CN/0824-4596
**LONDON METROBULLETIN.** [Lon. metrobull.]. No. 1 (Mar. 1983)-. Periodical. English. mo. Free. London Metrobulletin, c/o M Emery, PO Box 2214 Station A, London Ontario N6A 4E3 Canada. **DD** 051. ctrl circ. **Continues** *Downtown London Metrobulletin, 0824-4588.*

US/1062-1466
**LONG DISTANCE DIRECTORY OF GOVERNMENT ADDRESSES AND TELEPHONE NUMBERS.** Title Change. (1992)-(199?). Directory. English. Omnigraphics Inc., 2500 Penobscot Building, 25th Floor, Detroit MI 48226. **Tel** (313)961-1340, (800)234-1340, FAX (313)961-1383. **Continues** *Long Distance Book. Vol. 2, Government Directory of Addresses and Telephone Numbers.* **Continued by** *The Government Directory of Addresses & Telephone Numbers.*

●US
**LONG TERM VIEW, THE.** See Political Science.

US
**LOOSELEAF REGULATIONS SYSTEM. SERVICE 5. PROCEDURE AND ADMINISTRATION.** **Main/Corp** United States. Internal Revenue Service. **VFOAT** Procedure and Administration. Periodical. English. ir. Procedure and Administration, US Treasury Department, Internal Revenue Service, Washington DC 20402.
**Desc:** The IRS looseleaf regulation system is a compilation of all regulations issued by the Service, except those relating to alcohol, tobacco, firearms and tax conventions.

CN/0715-8599
**LORRAIN, LE.** [Lorrain]. **VFOAT** Lorrain. Periodical. French (French). mo. Free to residents. Ville de Lorraine, 100 Grande-Cote, Lorraine Quebec J6Z 1L9 Canada. **DD** 352.0714/24.

US/0092-1882
**LOS ANGELES COUNTY ALMANAC.** (LOS ANGELES COUNTY ALMANAC; A GUIDE TO GOVERNMENT.). **Added/Corp** Republican Party. California. Los Angeles Co. Central Committee. 11th Ed. (1972)-. Periodical. English. an. $10.00. Los Angeles County Almanac Program, 2250 West Main Street, Suite 301, Alhambra CA 91081. **Tel** (818)457-9898. **ED** Joe Irvin. **LC** JS451.C29; L94. **DD** 352.0794/93. **Ad Acc. Circ:** 5,600 (ctrl). **Continues** *Los Angeles County Almanac and Buyers' Guide.*
**Desc:** A non-partisan guide to city, county, state and federal government.

●US/1070-2938
**LOS ANGELES LETTER, THE.** (1993)-. Periodical. English. sm. $275.00. The Los Angeles Letter, 1138 S. Hayworth Avenue, Los Angeles CA 90035-2604. **ED** Alex Hartley.
**Desc:** Newsletter focused on Los Angeles County public affairs from the ground up.

CN/0706-196X
**LOTO-LIAISON.** [Loto-liaison]. V. 1- Sept. 1979-. Periodical. French. mo. Bulletin D'Information De Loto-Quebec, 2000 Rue Berri, Montreal Quebec H2L 4N5. **DD** 354.7140072/6.

US/0164-3622
**LOUISIANA MUNICIPAL REVIEW.** V. 1- May/June 1938-. Periodical. English. bm. Louisiana Municipal Association, 5615 Corporate Boulevard/Suite 3B, Baton Rouge LA 70808. **Tel** (504)343-9571. **LC** JS39; .L68. **DD** 352.0763. cum. index.
**Ind/Abst** Urban Aff. Abstr.

US/0084-0793
**LTC PAPER.** **Added/Corp** University of Wisconsin--Madison. Land Tenure Center. **VFOAT** LTC. **VAT** Land Tenure Center Paper. No. 124 (1985)-. Monographic series. English. ir. Price varies per volume. Land Tenure Center, 1300 University Avenue, University of Wisconsin, Madison WI 53706. **Tel** (608)262-3657. **LC** UNC. **Continues** *LTC (Series), 0193-5674.*
**Desc:** Deals with land tenure.
**Ind/Abst** World Agric. Econ.

ZA
**LUSAKA PROVINCE ANNUAL REPORT FOR THE YEAR ... / REPUBLIC OF ZAMBIA, OFFICE OF THE PRIME MINISTER.** **Main/Corp** Zambia. Office of the Prime Minister. 1980-. English. an. K2.50. Zambia Government Printer, POB 30136, Lusaka Zambia. **LC** JQ725.3; .T38A. **DD** 354.6894. **Bk Rev. Ad Acc. Continues** *Zambia. Office of the Cabinet Minister for the Lusaka Province. Lusaka Province Annual Report.*
**Desc:** Consists of two parts. The first part reflects on what happened in the political field outlining party elections. The second part of the report deals with the government wing of the Province.

FI
**MAALAISKUNTIEN JA KUNTAINLIITTOJEN TUNTIPALKKAISTEN TYONTEKIJOIDEN PALKAT.** **Main/Corp** Finland. Tilastokeskus. **VFOAT** Landskommunernas Och Kommunalforbundens Timavlonade Arbetstagares Loner. Multiple languages (Finnish and Swedish). Tilastokeskus, PL 504, Annankatu 44, 00101 Helsinki Finland. **Tel** 358-0-17341, FAX 358-0-17342474, telex 1002111 TILASTO SF. **LC** JS6124; .A35A.

US/0272-8389
**MACHINE MANUAL OF INSTRUCTIONS FOR JUDGES OF ELECTION. PRIMARY ELECTION.** **Main/Corp** Illinois. State Board of Elections. English. State Board of Elections / Illinois, State of Illinois, 1020 South Spring Street, PO Box 4187, Springfield IL 62708. **Tel** (217)782-4141. **LC** JK2023.I3; I38A. **DD** 324.6/09773.

CN/0711-5504
**MAFIA 67.** (MAFIA 67 / ESCADRILLE 67 SHER.). ["Mafia 67"]. **VFOAT** Journal Mafia 67. **VAT** Mafia Soixante-Sept. Vol. 1, No. 1 (Nov. 1981)-. Periodical. French. ir. Free. Mafia 67, Escadron 67, CP 1716, 50 rue Couture, Sherbrooke Quebec J1H 4B4 Canada. **DD** 358.4/12232.

●HU/1216-1993
**MAGYAR KOEZTARSASAG HELYNEVKOENYVE / KOEZPONTI STATISZTIKAI HIVATAL, A.** **Added/Corp** Hungary. Koezponti Statisztikai Hivatal. Helysegnevtar Szerkesztoseg. (Jan. 1992)-. Periodical. Hungarian. Statisztikai Kiado Vallalat, PO Box 99, H-1033 Budapest 3 Hungary. **Tel** 803-311, telex 22-6699-SKV-H. **LC** JS4672.L7; M24. **Continues** *Magyar Koeztarsasag Allamigazgatasi Helynevkoenyve.*

CN/0844-6725
**MAIN ESTIMATES - FINANCIAL MANAGEMENT SECRETARIAT (YELLOWKNIFE. 1987).** (MAIN ESTIMATES / PREPARED BY THE FINANCIAL MANAGEMENT SECRETARIAT UNDER THE DIRECTION OF THE FINANCIAL MANAGEMENT BOARD.). [Main estim. - Financ. Manag. Secr.]. **Main/Corp** Northwest Territories. Financial Management Secretariat. (1987)-. English. Government of Northwest Territories, Department of Information, Yellowknife Northwest Territories, X1A 2L9 Canada. **DD** 354.719/20072/225. **Continues** *Northwest Territories. Financial Management Secretariat. Estimates., 0844-6717.*

CN/0848-5933
**MAIN ESTIMATES, HIGHLIGHTS BY MINISTRY.** (BUDGET DES DEPENSES PRINCIPAL ... . POINTS SAILLANTS, PAR PORTEFEUILLE.). [Main estim., Highlights Minist.]. **Added/Corp** Canada. Conseil du Tresor. **VFOAT** Main Estimates. Highlights by Ministry. (1990)-. French (English). **DD** 354.710072/25.

# Public Administration

**US/0145-9597**
**MAINE REGISTER, STATE YEAR-BOOK AND LEGISLATIVE MANUAL.** (MAINE REGISTER OR STATE YEAR-BOOK AND LEGISLATIVE MANUAL FROM APRIL 1 ... TO APRIL 1 ...). [Maine reg. state year-b. leg. man.]. **VFOAT** Annual Register of Maine; Maine Register. (1888)-. English. an. $115.00. Tower Publishing Company, 588 Saco Road, Standish ME 04084. **Tel** (800)969-8693. **LC** JK2830; .M34. **DD** 974.1/0025. Index available. **Bk Rev. Ad Acc. Circ:** 1,500 (ctrl). *Continues Maine State Year-Book, and Legislative Manual.*
**Desc:** Contains state and local government business and miscellaneous information on the state of Maine.

**US/0025-0791**
**MAINE TOWNSMAN, THE. Added/Corp** Maine Municipal Association. (Jan. 1939)-. Periodical. English. mo. $8.00 (1 year), $15.00 (2 year) members; $15.00 (1 year), $26.00 (2 year) other. Maine Municipal Association, 60 Community Drive, Augusta ME 04330. **Tel** (207)623-8428, FAX (207)626-5947. **ED** Michael Starn. **LC** JS39; .M25. **DD** 352.0741. Index available. **Ad Acc. Circ:** 4,500. *Supersedes Maine Municipal Association. News Bulletin.*
**Desc:** Information about municipal governments in the state of Maine.
**Ind/Abst** Urban Aff. Abstr.

**US**
**MAJOR MATTERS BEFORE THE FEDERAL COMMUNICATIONS COMMISSION.** See Communication.

**MW**
**MALAWI GOVERNMENT GAZETTE, THE. Main/Corp** Malawi. **VFOAT** Government Gazette. Periodical. English. Ministry of Finance / Malawi, Government Printer, Box 37, Zomba Malawi. **LC** LAW. **DD** 354.6897/0005. available on microfilm from New York Public Library. *Continues Gazette / Malawi.*

**US**
**MANAGEMENT IMPROVEMENT AND COST REDUCTION GOALS. Main/Corp** United States. General Services Administration. English. General Services Administration, General Services Building, Eighteenth and F Streets NW, Washington DC 20405. **Tel** (202)655-4000. **LC** JK1672; .M345. **DD** 353.007/1.

**II/0047-570X**
**MANAGEMENT IN GOVERNMENT.**
**Added/Corp** India. Dept. of Administrative Reforms and Public Grievances. India. Dept. of Administrative Reforms. India. Dept. of Personnel & Administrative Reforms. Vol. 1 (April/June 1969)-. Periodical. English. qt. $28.00. Management in Government, Personnel and Administration Reform, Sardar Patel Bhawan Parliament, New Delhi 110001 India. **Tel** 353472. **(Subscription address:** Prints India, 11 Darya Ganj, New Delhi 110002 India.) **ED** Vandana K Jena. **DD** 354.54/0005. **Bk Rev. Circ:** 2,000 (ctrl).
**Desc:** To disseminate, among practising managers and administrators, modern trends and techniques in management and public administration.
**Ind/Abst** Manage. Market. Abstr.

**US/0091-6242**
**MANAGEMENT REPORT - GENERAL SERVICES ADMINISTRATION.**
(MANAGEMENT REPORT.). **Main/Corp** United States. General Services Administration. English. an. US General Services Administration, General Services Building, Eighteenth and F Streets NW, Washington DC 20405. **LC** JK1672; .M35. **DD** 353.007/1.

**US**
**MANAGEMENT SELECTION AND DEVELOPMENT, ANNUAL STATUS REPORT. Main/Corp** Oregon. Governor's Steering Committee for Management Selection and Development. (1972)-. English. an. Management Selection and Development, 240 Cottage Street SE, Salem OR 97310. **LC** JK9060.5.E9; O7A. **DD** 353.9/795/034.

**AT**
**MANAGEMENT SUMMARY (PERTH, W.A.).** See Environmental Issues-Conservation and Natural Resources.

**US**
**MANAGING THE NATION'S PUBLIC LANDS : A PROGRAM REPORT PREPARED PURSUANT TO REQUIREMENTS OF THE FEDERAL LAND POLICY AND MANAGEMENT ACT OF 1976.** See Business-General Management.

**CN/1185-3948**
**MANITOBA CONSTITUTIONAL TASK FORCE.** (MANITOBA CONSTITUTIONAL TASK FORCE : [PROCEEDINGS].). [Manit. Const. Task Force].
**Main/Corp** Manitoba Constitutional Task Force. No. 1 (Jan. 31, 1991)-. English (summaries and/or abstracts in French). da. **DD** 342.71/03.

**CN/0318-1200**
**MANITOBA GOVERNMENT PUBLICATIONS (MONTHLY ED.).**
(MANITOBA GOVERNMENT PUBLICATIONS; MONTHLY CHECKLIST.). [Manit. gov. publ.].
**Added/Corp** Manitoba. Legislative Library. Manitoba. Manitoba Culture, Heritage and Recreation. **VFOAT** Publications du Gouvernement du Manitoba; Manitoba Government Publications for the Month of ..., Monthly Checklist. No. 1 (Jan. 1975)-. Periodical. English (French). mo. 40.00Can$. Legislative Library / Manitoba Government, 200 Vaughan Street, Winnipeg Manitoba R3C 1T5 Canada. **Tel** (204)945-5771, FAX (204)948-2008. **ED** Janina Skawinska. **DD** 015/.7127. **Circ:** 230. *Continues Manitoba. Legislative Assembly. Manitoba Government Publications Received in the Legislative Library.*
**Desc:** Lists all Manitoba government publications received by the Legislative Library of Manitoba in the past month. Gives issuing agency name and price where available.

**US/0094-4106**
**MANPOWER PLANNING DATA (WASHINGTON).** See Business-Personnel Management.

**UK**
**MANUAL DE LA ORGANIZACION DEL GOBIERNO DE CHILE--MICROFORM / DEPARTAMENTO DE ESTUDIOS FINANCIEROS, MINISTERIO DE HACIENDA.** (1957)-. Spanish. 20 Newmarket Road, Cambridge CB5 8DT England.

**US/0196-4585**
**MANUAL FOR THE GENERAL COURT.**
(MANUAL FOR THE GENERAL COURT / STATE OF NEW HAMPSHIRE.). **Added/Corp** New Hampshire. Dept. of State. **VFOAT** NH Manual for the General Court; N.H. Manual for the General Court. (1???)-. English. an (published every two years in odd years). $10.00. Secretary of State / New Hampshire, State House Room 204, Concord NH 03301. **Tel** (603)271-3242. **ED** Karen H. Ladd. **Circ:** 3,400.
**Desc:** News and information on the listing of past elected officials, prior year election results (primary & general) and Governor & council appointed officials.

**US/0098-8103**
**MANUAL OF THE GENERAL ASSEMBLY OF THE STATE OF GEORGIA. Main/Corp** Georgia. Secretary of State. **Added/Corp** Georgia. General Assembly. Georgia. Secretary of State. English. an. Legislative manual. **VFOAT** Legislative Manual; Georgia Legislative Manual. (19??)-. English. an. Secretary of State / Georgia, State Capitol, Room 214, Atlanta GA 30334. **LC** JK4330; .A33. **DD** 328.758/05. *Continues Handbook of the General Assembly of the State of Georgia, 0361-459X.*

**US/0890-3832**
**MANUAL OF THE LEGISLATURE OF NEW JERSEY.** (MANUAL OF THE LEGISLATURE OF NEW JERSEY / STATE OF NEW JERSEY.). [Man. Legis. N. J.]. **Added/Corp** New Jersey. Legislature. **VFOAT** Manual of the ... of the Legislature of New Jersey; Fitzgerald's Legislative Manual, State of New Jersey; New Jersey Legislative Manual. (18??)-. English. an (May). $35.00. New Jersey Legislative Manual, PO Box 2150, Trenton NJ 08607-2150. **Tel** (609)396-2669 ext. 2. **LC** JK3531. **DD** 328.

**US/0363-1184**
**MANUAL OF THE SENATE AND HOUSE OF DELEGATES. Main/Corp** Virginia. General Assembly. English. be. Free. House of Delegates, State Capitol, Richmond VA 23219. **Tel** (804)786-7210. **ED** George A Williams. **LC** JK3930; .A22. **DD** 328/.755/05. **Circ:** 5,000.
**Desc:** Legislative information on Senate and House members, rules, committee assignments, biographies, districts, etc.

**US/0197-4238**
**MANUAL - THE STATE OF RHODE ISLAND AND PROVIDENCE PLANTATIONS.** [Man. - State R. I. Provid. Plant.]. **Main/Corp** Rhode Island. Dept. of State. **VFOAT** State of Rhode Island Manual; Rhode Island Manual. 1975/76-. English. be. Department of State / Rhode Island, 219 State House, Providence RI 02903. **LC** JK3230; .A25. **DD** 320.4745. *Continues Manual, with Rules and Orders, for the Use of the General Assembly of the State of Rhode Island, 0190-5309.*

**IT**
**MANUALE DEL REGISTRO.** (19??)-. Italian. Giuffre Editore SPA, Via Busto Arsizio 40, 20151 Milan Italy. **Tel** 011 398 2 38089200.

**FR/0542-6685**
**MARCHES PUBLICS.** Periodical. French. ir (eight issues per year). Free. Documentation Francaise, 29 Quai Voltaire, 75344 Paris Cedex 7 France. **Tel** 011 33 1 40157000, FAX 011 33 1 40157230, telex 204 826 DOCFRAN. **LC** JN2758; .A28. Index available.

**US/0094-4491**
**MARYLAND MANUAL. VFOAT** Manual, State of Maryland. Periodical. English. be. Hall of Records, PO Box 828, Annapolis MD 21404. **Tel** (410)269-3914. **LC** JK3831. **NLM** JK 3831 M393.
**Desc:** Concerns Maryland government and history.

●**US/1066-2251**
**MARYLAND PROCUREMENT REPORT, THE.** (THE MARYLAND PROCUREMENT REPORT : YOUR INDISPENSIBLE GUIDE TO GOVERNMENTAL PROCUREMENT IN MARYLAND.). (1993)-. Periodical. English. bw. $197.00. B L Bortz, PO Box 65360, Baltimore MD 21209.

●**US/1061-2696**
**MARYLAND REGISTER CONTRACT WEEKLY.** [Md. regist. contract wkly.]. **Added/Corp** Maryland. Division of State Documents. **VFOAT** Contract Weekly. (1992)-. Periodical. English. wk (Tuesdays). $120.00. Maryland Division of State Documents, PO Box 2249, Annapolis MD 21404. **Tel** (410)974-2486. **DD** 351. *Separated from Maryland Register, 0360-2834.*

**US**
**MASSACHUSETTS LEGISLATIVE DIRECTORY / MASSACHUSETTS TAXPAYERS FOUNDATION, INC.**
**Added/Corp** Massachusetts Taxpayers Foundation. (19??)-. English. be. Free on request. Massachusetts Taxpayers Foundation, 24 Province Street, Boston MA 02108. **Tel** (617)720-1000.

**US/0277-1314**
**MASSACHUSETTS POLITICAL ALMANAC, THE. Added/Corp** Almanac Research Services. **VFOAT** Political Almanac, Massachusetts. (1981/82)-. Periodical. English. ir. $40.00 per volume; $65.00 set. Center for Leadership Studies, PO Box 400, Centreville MA 02632. **Tel** (508)775-4323, (800)833-7600, FAX (508)775-7310. **ED** Barbara Talley. **LC** JK3130; .A6. **DD** 353.9744002. Index available. cum. index. **Bk Rev. Ad Acc. Circ:** 2,000. *Continues Almanac: Massachusetts State Officials, 0147-5029.*
**Desc:** Features political and biographical profiles of every member of the Massachusetts Legislature and roll call votes.

**CN/0381-9531**
**MAST. MANITOBA ASSOCIATION OF SCHOOL TRUSTEES.** (M A S T.). [MAST, Manit. Assoc. Sch. Trustees]. **Main/Corp** Manitoba Association of School Trustees. **VAT** Manitoba Association of School Trustees. Vol. 3, No. 2 (Sept. 1976)-. Periodical. English. sa. Free. Manitoba Association of School Trustees, 191 Provencher Boulevard, Winnipeg Manitoba R2H 0G4 Canada. **Tel** (204)233-1595. **ED** Heather L Shepherd. **DD** 370/.97127. **Bk Rev. Ad Acc. Circ:** 2,100 (ctrl).
**Desc:** Articles pertaining to education.

**UN**
**MATERIALY - RESPUBLIKANSKA ONOMASTYCHNA (HIDRONIMICHNA) NARADA. Main/Corp** Respublikans ka Onomastychna (Hidronimichna) Narada. **Added/Corp** Akademiia nauk URSR, Kiev. Instytut Movoznavstva. **VFOAT** Pytannia Hidronimiky. (1965)-. Ukrainian (Russian). an. Izdatelstvo Naukova Dumka / Ukrainian Academy of Sciences, Vladimirskaia Ulitsa 54, 252601 Kiev Ukraine. **Tel** 225-63-66, telex 131376. *Continues Materialy - Respublikanska Narada z Pytan Onomastyky.*

**US**
**MAYOR'S MANAGEMENT REPORT. SUPPLEMENT, THE.** English. $6.00. Sales Office the City Record, Municipal Building/Room 2213, One Centre Street, New York NY 10007. **LC** JS1234.A1; M39. **DD** 352.0747/1.

**US**
**MEDICARE REIBURSEMENT MANUAL FOR CLINICAL LABORATORIES.** See Medical Science and Technology.

**US/0145-2223**
**MEMBERSHIP DIRECTORY - AMERICAN SOCIETY FOR PUBLIC ADMINISTRATION, NATIONAL CAPITAL AREA CHAPTER. Main/Corp** American Society for Public Administration. National Capital Area Chapter. (19??)-. Directory. English. an. Free to members. American Society for Public Administration, 1120 G Street Northwest, Suite 700, Washington DC 20005-3885. **Tel** (202)393-7878, FAX (202)638-4952. **LC** JA28; .A825; .A26. **DD** 350/.0006/273. *Continues Membership Directory - American Society for Public Administration, Washington D.C. Chapter, 0360-0459.*

# Public Administration

**YU**
**MESNE ZAJEDNICE. Main/Corp** Savezni Zavod za Statistiku (Yugoslavia). Serbo-Croatian (Roman). 5.00. Savezni Zavod za Statistiku, Kneza Milosa 20, Belgrad Yugoslavia. **LC** HA1631; .A33 subser; JS6942.

**US**
**METROPOLITAN COUNCIL ... ANNUAL REPORT.** English. 300 Metro Square Building, 7th & Robert Street, St Paul MN 55101.

US/0076-7115
**METROPOLITAN WASHINGTON REGIONAL DIRECTORY.** [Metrop. Wash. reg. dir.]. 1971-. Directory. English. an. Metropolitan Washington Council of Governments, 777 North Capitol Street Northeast, Washington DC 20002-4239. **Tel** (202)962-3256. **LC** JS1512.A3; M4. **DD** 352. *Continues Regional Directory - Metropolitan Washington Council of Governments.*

US/0896-646X
**MICHIGAN COUNTIES.** [Mich. cties.]. **Added/Corp** Michigan Association of Counties. Vol. 6, No. 12 (Jan. 1975)-. Periodical. English. Eleven times a year (Aug./Sept., issues combined). $10.00. Michigan Association of Counties, 935 North Washington Street, Lansing MI 48906. **Tel** (517)372-5374, FAX (517)482-4599. **ED** Maureen Abood. **DD** 352. **Ad Acc. Circ:** 2,000 (ctrl). *Continues Michigan Counties Today.* **Desc:** Gives up-to-date and timely information to county commissioners, elected county officials and others interested in county government on local, state, and federal issues.

US/0091-1933
**MICHIGAN MANUAL. Added/Corp** Michigan. Dept. of State. Michigan. Dept. of Administration. Michigan. Dept. of Management and Budget. Michigan. Legislative Service Bureau. **VFOAT** Red Book. (1960)-. English. be (Jan. in even years). $15.00. Michigan Department of Management and Budget, PO Box 30026, Lansing MI 48909. **Tel** (517)373-5644. **LC** JK5830; .A32. **DD** 353.9/774/0202. Index available. **Circ:** 11,000. *Continues Official Directory and Legislative Manual.* **Desc:** A book of facts and statistics on the State of Michigan.

US/1058-4307
**MICHIGAN MUNICIPAL LIABILITY AND PROPERTY POOL BULLETIN. Added/Corp** Michigan Municipal League. Michigan Municipal Liability and Property Pool. **VFOAT** Personnel Decisions. (1991)-. Bulletin. English. sa. Price varies per volume. Michigan Municipal Liability and Property Pool, Ann Arbor MI.

US/0026-2331
**MICHIGAN MUNICIPAL REVIEW.** [Mich. munic. rev.]. **Added/Corp** Michigan Municipal League. Vol. 1 (Jan. 1928)-. Periodical. English. Ten times a year. $24.00. Michigan Municipal League, PO Box 1487, Ann Arbor MI 48106. **Tel** (313)662-3246. **ED** Joan Hutchison. **LC** JS39; .M12. **DD** 352.0005. Index available. cum. index. **Bk Rev**, (Qty: 50). **Ad Acc, Adv Mgr:** Judi Campbell. **Circ:** 9,600 (ctrl). available on microfilm and microfiche from University Microfilms International (UMI). **Desc:** Publication with information and ideas for local governments in Michigan.
**Ind/Abst** Urban Aff. Abstr.

US/0892-3124
**MICHIGAN REGISTER. See** Law.

**US**
**MICHIGAN REPORT.** English. da (Monday-Friday except holidays). $1,900.00. Gongwer News Service / Michigan, 630 National Tower, Lansing MI 48933. **Tel** (517)489-4327. **ED** Larry Lee.

**US**
**MICHIGAN TOWNSHIP NEWS.** (19??)-. Periodical. English. mo. $12.50 libraries; $25.00 other. Michigan Townships Association, 512 Westshire Drive, Lansing MI 48917. **Tel** (517)321-6467, FAX (517)321-8908. **ED** Katherine H. Gilliland. Index available. **Ad Acc, Adv Mgr:** Daynell McCall, **Tel** (517)321-6467. **Circ:** 9300 (ctrl). **Desc:** Information pertinent to Michigan township government.

CN/0229-7507
**MIM (SAINT-AUGUSTIN-DE-DESMAURES, QUEBEC).** (MIM : MENSUEL D'INFORMATION MUNICIPALE). [MIM, Mens. inf. munic.]. Periodical. French. mo. Free. Municipalite de Saint-Augustin-de-Desmaures, 200 Boul Fossambault, Saint-Augustin-de-Desmaures Quebec G0A 3E0 Canada. **DD** 352.0714/466. ctrl circ. *Continues Trait d'Union (Saint-Augustin-de-Desmaures, Quebec).*

**MINNESOTA ADMINISTRATIVE RULES AND REGULATIONS. Main/Corp** Minnesota. Department of Administration. (19??)-. English. ir.

National Insurance Law Service, 21625 Prairie Street, PO Box 2507, Chatsworth CA 91311. **Tel** (818)998-8830, (800)423-5910.

US/0148-8546
**MINNESOTA CITIES. Added/Corp** League of Minnesota Cities. Vol. 61, No. 10 (Sept. 1976)-. Periodical. English. Twelve times a year. Free on request to members of the League; $18.00 other. League of Minnesota Cities, 3490 Lexington Avenue North, St Paul MN 55126. **Tel** (612)227-5600, FAX (612)490-0072. **ED** Jean Mehle Goad. Index available. **Bk Rev**. **Ad Acc. Circ:** 10,000. *Continues Minnesota Municipalities.* **Desc:** Publication on issues of concern and interest to city officials.
**Ind/Abst** PAIS Int. Print (1991-); Urban Aff. Abstr.

**US**
**MINNESOTA ELECTED OFFICIALS ... .** 1977-. English. be. 180 State Office Building, St Paul MN 55155. **Tel** (612)296-2805. **ED** Joseph Mansky. *Continues Minnesota State, Congressional, Legislative, Judicial, and County Officers.* **Desc:** Contains lists of Minnesota elected officials on statewide and county basis.

**US**
**MINNESOTA ELECTION RESULTS : PRIMARY AND GENERAL ELECTIONS. Main/Corp** Minnesota. Election Division. English. be. Minnesota Election Division, Office of the Secretary of State, 180 State Office Building, St Paul MN 55155. **Tel** (612)296-2805. **ED** Joseph Mansky. **LC** JK6192; .M55A. **DD** 329/.023/77605. **Circ:** 2,000. *Continues Minnesota General Election Results, 0095-6872.* **Desc:** Contains Minnesota election results: federal and state offices.

**US**
**MINNESOTA GOVERNMENT REPORT, THE TWICE-WEEKLY NEWSLETTER ON STATE GOVERNMENT. Added/Corp** Minnesota. Legislature. Vol. 1 (July 3, 1978)-. Newsletter. English. sw (104 issues - published on Tuesdays & Thursdays). $240.00. Minnesota Government Report, PO Box 441, c/o Jean Dawson, Willernie MN 55090. **Tel** (612)429-0423. **ED** Jean L. Dawson. **Circ:** 200 (ctrl). *Continues Capitol Reporter.* **Desc:** A newsletter covering the activities of Minnesota state government, with appellate court opinions.

US/1061-0987
**MINNESOTA GUIDEBOOK TO STATE AGENCY SERVICES.** [Minn. guideb. State agency serv.]. **Added/Corp** Minnesota. Office of the State Registrar. **VFOAT** State Agency Services. 1st Ed., (1977)-. English. an. $18.00. Minnesota Documents, 117 University Avenue, St Paul MN 55155. **Tel** (612)297-3000, (800)657-3757, FAX (612)296-2265. **LC** JK6130; .M47. **DD** 353.9776/0002/02. **Circ:** 10,000. **Desc:** A magazine for the Minnesota residents, business persons, professionals and educators.

US/0741-9449
**MINNESOTA JOURNAL. Added/Corp** Alnes Resources. Citizens League (Minneapolis, Minn.). (Nov. 15, 1983)-. Periodical. English. sm (Except one iss. Aug., Dec.). $40.00. Citizens League, 708 3rd Street, Suite 500, Minneapolis MN 55415-1106. **Tel** (612)338-0791, FAX (612)337-5919. **ED** Stephen Alnes and Jody Haner. **Circ:** 3,200 (ctrl). *Absorbed CL News, 0045-6969.* **Desc:** Analysis and reporting on state, metropolitan, local, and regional government, including public finance, transportation, education, and social services.

**US**
**MINNESOTA LEGISLATIVE MANUAL.** (THE MINNESOTA LEGISLATIVE MANUAL.). **Added/Corp** Minnesota. Secretary of State. (1968)-. English. be. Free. Secretary of State of Minnesota, 180 State Office Building, St Paul MN 55155. **Tel** (612)296-2803. **LC** JK6131. **DD** 328/.776/05. *Continues Legislative Manual (Minnesota. Secretary of State).*

**US**
**MINNESOTA STATE REGISTER, THE. Added/Corp** Minnesota. Dept. of Administration. Print Communications Division. **VFOAT** State Register. Vol. 15, No. 1 (2 July, 1990)-. Periodical. English. wk. $150.00 (one day a week), $195.00 (two days per week). Minnesota Documents, 117 University Avenue, St Paul MN 55155. **Tel** (612)297-3000, (800)657-3757, FAX (612)296-2265. *Continues State Register (Saint Paul, Minn.), 0146-7751.*

**US**
**MINNESOTA VOTER, THE. Added/Corp** League of Women Voters of Minnesota. League of Women Voters of Minnesota. Vol. 1 (Jan. 10, 1921)-. Periodical. English. ir.

**US**
**MINNESOTA'S JOURNAL OF LAW AND POLITICS. See** Law.

**CJ**
**MINUTES : LEGISLATIVE ASSEMBLY OFFICIAL REPORT. Main/Corp** Cayman Islands. Legislative Assembly. English. Legislative Assembly Cayman Islands, Georgetown West Indies. **LC** J137.5; .K44. **DD** 328.7292/1/04. **Desc:** Vols. for Aug. 12/13, 1969, Oct 5, 1971 include special and emergency meetings.

CN/0825-0677
**MINUTES OF PROCEEDINGS AND EVIDENCE OF SUB-COMMITTEE B OF THE SPECIAL COMMITTEE ON EMPLOYMENT OPPORTUNITIES FOR THE '80S. See** Economics-Labor.

CN/0848-7928
**MINUTES OF PROCEEDINGS AND EVIDENCE OF THE SPECIAL COMMITTEE ON SUBJECT MATTER OF BILL C-80 (FIREARMS).** [Minutes proc. evid. Spec. Comm. Subj. Matter Bill C-80 Firearms]. **Main/Corp** Canada. Parlement. Chambre des Communes. Comite Special sur l'Objet du Projet de Loi C-80 (Armes a Feu). **VFOAT** Objet du Projet de Loi C-80 (Armes a Feu); Proces-Verbaux et Temoignages du Comite Special sur l'Objet de Loi C-80 (Armes a Feu). 2nd Session of the 34th Parliament, Issue No. 1 (Nov. 29/Dec. 5, 1990)-. Proceedings. French (English). **DD** 344.71/0533/05.

CN/1187-4430
**MINUTES OF PROCEEDINGS AND EVIDENCE OF THE SPECIAL COMMITTEE ON THE ACT RESPECTING CUSTOMS.** [Minutes proc. evid. Spec. Comm. Act Respect. Cust.]. **Main/Corp** Canada. Parlement. Chambre des Communes. Comite Special Charge de l'Examen de la Loi Concernant les Douanes. **VFOAT** Loi Concernant les Douanes; Proces-Verbaux et Temoignages du Comite Special Charge de l'Examen de la Loi Concernant les Douanes. 34th Parliament, 3rd Session, Issue No. 1 (Oct. 2/Oct. 8, 1991)-. Proceedings. French (English). **DD** 354.710082/7/05.

CN/0710-9733
**MINUTES OF PROCEEDINGS AND EVIDENCE OF THE SPECIAL COMMITTEE ON THE FEDERAL-PROVINCIAL FISCAL ARRANGEMENTS.** [Minutes proc. evid. Spec. Comm. Fed. Prov. Fisc. Arrange.]. **Main/Corp** Canada. Parlement. Chambre des Communes. Comite Special sur les Accords Fiscaux Entre le Gouvernement Federal et les Provinces. **VFOAT** Proces-Verbaux et Temoignages du Comite Special sur les Accords Fiscaux Entre le Gouvernement Federal et les Provinces les Provinces. **VAT** Accords Fiscaux Entre le Gouvernement Federal et les Provinces; Federal-Provincial Fiscal Arrangements. Issue No. 1 (Mar. 23, 1981)-. Proceedings. French (English). Receiver General for Canada / Ottawa, Canada Comm Group Publishing, Ottawa Ontario K1A 0S9 Canada. **Tel** (819)956-4802, (800)661-2868. **DD** 354.710072/52.

CN/0825-0251
**MINUTES OF PROCEEDINGS AND EVIDENCE OF THE SPECIAL JOINT COMMITTEE OF THE SENATE AND OF THE HOUSE OF COMMONS ON SENATE REFORM.** [Minutes proc. evid. Spec. Jt. Comm. Senate House Commons Senate Reform]. **Main/Corp** Canada. Parliament. Special Joint Committee on Senate Reform. **VFOAT** Report of the Special Joint Committee of the Senate and of the House of Commons on Senate Reform; Proces-Verbaux et Temoignages du Comite Mixte Special du Senat et de la Chambre des Communes sur la Reforme du Senat; Senate Reform. Issue No. 1 (April 28/May 31, 1983)-. English (French). Canada Communication Group Publishers, Order Processing, Ottawa Ontario K1A 0S9 Canada. **Tel** (819)956-4800, (819)956-4802. **LC** J103; .J76a. **DD** 328/.3042/0971.

CN/1187-2462
**MINUTES OF PROCEEDINGS AND EVIDENCE OF THE STANDING COMMITTEE ON HOUSE MANAGEMENT.** [Minutes proc. evid. Standing Comm. House Manage.]. **Main/Corp** Canada. Parliament. House of Commons. Standing Committee on House Management. **VFOAT** House Management; Proces-Verbaux et Temoignages du Comite Permanent de la Gestion de la Chambre. Issue no. 1 (May 21, 1991)-. Proceedings. English (French). **DD** 328.71/0765/05.

CN/0713-651X
**MINUTES OF PROCEEDINGS AND EVIDENCE OF THE SUB-COMMITTEE ON DREE PROGRAMMES (QUEBEC) OF THE STANDING COMMITTEE ON REGIONAL DEVELOPMENT.** [Minutes proc. evid. Sub-comm. DREE Programmes (Que.) Standing Comm. Reg.

## Public Administration

Dev.]. **Main/Corp** Canada. Parlement. Chambre des Communes. Sous-Comite des Programmes du Meer (Quebec). **VFOAT** Proces-Verbaux et Temoignages du Sous-Comite des Programmes du Meer (Quebec) du Comite Permanent de l'Expansion Economique Regionale. Economique Regionale. **VAT** DREE Programmes (Quebec); Programmes du Meer (Quebec). Issue No. 1 (June 18, 1981)-. Proceedings. French (English). Receiver General for Canada / Ottawa, Canada Comm Group Publishing, Ottawa Ontario K1A 0S9 Canada. **Tel** (819)956-4802, (800)661-2868. **DD** 354.710082/044.

CN/1187-6514
**MINUTES OF PROCEEDINGS AND EVIDENCE OF THE SUB-COMMITTEE ON NATIONAL SECURITY OF THE STANDING COMMITTEE ON JUSTICE AND THE SOLICITOR GENERAL.** [Minutes proc. evid. Sub-Comm. Natl. Secur. Standing Comm. Justice Solicit. Gen.]. **Main/Corp** Canada. Parlement. Chambre des Communes. Sous-Comite Sur la Securite Nationale. **VFOAT** Proces-Verbaux et Temoignages du Sous-Comite sur la Securite Nationale du Comite Permanent de la Justice et du Solliciteur General. Issue No. 1 (June 18, 1991)-. Proceedings. French (English). **DD** 327.1/271/005.

CN/1187-2470
**MINUTES OF PROCEEDINGS AND EVIDENCE OF THE SUB-COMMITTEE ON PRIVATE MEMBERS BUSINESS OF THE STANDING COMMITTEE ON HOUSE MANAGEMENT.** [Minutes proc. evid. Sub-Comm. Priv. Memb. Bus. Standing Comm. House Manage.]. **Main/Corp** Canada. Parlement. Chambre des Communes. Sous-Comite des Affaires Emanant des Deputes. **VFOAT** Affaires Emanant des Deputes; Proces-Verbaux et Temoignages du Sous-Comite des Affaires Emanant des Deputes du Comite Permanent de la Gestion de la Chambre. No. 1 (May 27, 1991)-. Proceedings. French (English). **DD** 328.71/0731.

CN/1187-2470
**MINUTES OF PROCEEDINGS AND EVIDENCE OF THE SUB-COMMITTEE ON PRIVATE MEMBERS BUSINESS OF THE STANDING COMMITTEE ON HOUSE MANAGEMENT.** [Minutes proc. evid. Sub-Comm. Priv. Memb. Bus. Standing Comm. House Manage.]. **Main/Corp** Canada. Parliament. House of Commons. Sub-Committee on Private Members Business. **VFOAT** Private Members' Business; Proces-Verbaux et Temoignages du Sous-Comite des Affaires Emanant des Deputes du Comite Permanent de la Gestion de la Chambre. Issue No. 1 (May 27, 1991)-. Proceedings. English (French). **DD** 328.71/0731.

CN/1184-1451
**MINUTES OF PROCEEDINGS AND EVIDENCE OF THE SUB-COMMITTEE ON THE STATUS OF WOMEN OF THE STANDING COMMITTEE ON HEALTH AND WELFARE, SOCIAL AFFAIRS, SENIORS AND ON THE STATUS OF WOMEN.** See Women's Interests.

FR
**MINUTES OF PROCEEDINGS - COUNCIL OF EUROPE, PARLIAMENTARY ASSEMBLY.** **Main/Corp** Council of Europe. Parliamentary Assembly. Proceedings. English (French). Council of Europe / Group Pact ED, Pharmacopoeia BP 907, 67029 Strasbourg Cedex 01 France. **Tel** 011 33 88 412036, FAX 011 33 88 41277181, telex 880388. **LC** JN22; .C68B. **DD** 341.24/2.

CN/0229-3285
**MIRABEL-- A VOL D'OISEAU.** [Mirabel, vol oiseau]. Vol. 1, No. 1 (Nov. 1977)-. Periodical. French. ir. Free. Ville de Mirabel, Hotel de Ville, 14111 rue St-Jean Ste-Monique, Mirabel Quebec J0N 1R0 Canada. **DD** 352.0714/25.

US
**MIS REPORT.** **Added/Corp** Management Information Service. International City Management Association. Vol. 16, No. 1 (Jan. 1984)-. Periodical. English. mo. International City Management Association, 777 North Capitol Street NE, Suite 500, Washington DC 20002. **Tel** (202)289-4262, (800)745-8780, FAX (202)962-3500. **LC** JS39; .M28. **DD** 352.073. *Continues Management Information Service Report, 0730-0239.*

US/0026-6337
**MISSISSIPPI MUNICIPALITIES.** [Miss. munic.]. **Added/Corp** Mississippi Municipal Association. Vol. 1 (1955)-. Periodical. English. Eleven times a year (June/July issues combined). $16.00. Mississippi Municipal Association, 200 North State Street, Jackson MS 39201. **Tel** (601)353-5854, FAX (601)353-0435. **ED** Pat Dunne. **LC** JS303.M7; M56. **Bk Rev**. **Ad Acc**. **Circ:** 4,000 (ctrl).
**Desc:** News of primary interest to municipal elected and appointed officials.
**Ind/Abst** Urban Aff. Abstr.

US/0196-4755
**MISSISSIPPI OFFICIAL AND STATISTICAL REGISTER.** See Public Administration-Abstracting, Bibliographies and Statistics.

US/0738-727X
**MISSISSIPPI SUPERVISOR AND CHANCERY CLERK, CIRCUIT CLERK, TAX ASSESSOR & COLLECTOR.** **Added/Corp** Mississippi Association of Supervisors. Mississippi Chancery Clerks Association. Mississippi Circuit Clerks Association. Mississippi Assessors-Collectors Association. **VFOAT** Mississippi Supervisor and Chancery Clerk; Mississippi Supervisor. **VAT** Mississippi Supervisor and Chancery Clerk, Circuit Clerk, Tax Assessor and Collector. (19??)-. Trade Publication. English. Twelve times a year. $30.00 (one year), $55.00 (two years). Mississippi Supervisor and Chancery, PO Box 1314, Jackson MS 39205. **Tel** (601)353-2741. **ED** Clifton Lusk. **Ad Acc**. **Circ:** 1,500 (ctrl).
**Desc:** Trade magazine centered on county government and issues facing county government.

US/0026-6647
**MISSOURI MUNICIPAL REVIEW.** Began in 1936. Periodical. English. mo. $19.12. Missouri Municipal League, 1727 Southridge Drive, Jefferson City MO 65109. **Tel** (314)635-9134. **ED** Diane Peck. **LC** JS39; .M14. **DD** 352.0778. Index available. **Bk Rev**. **Ad Acc**. **Circ:** 5,050 (ctrl).
**Desc:** Contains articles and department coverage of full spectrum municipal administration and operation in Missouri and activities in individual cities.
**Ind/Abst** Ozark Period. Index; Urban Aff. Abstr.

US
**MISSOURI STATE EXECUTIVE BRANCH DIRECTORY.** Directory. English. an. Missouri Office of Administration, State Capitol/Room 125, Jefferson City MO 65102. **LC** JK5430; .M56. **DD** 353.9778/00025.

US
**MN SMALL BUSINESS PROCUREMENT PROGRAM FOR SOCIALLY OR ECONOMICALLY DISADVANTAGED VENDORS F.Y. ... ANNUAL REPORT / DEPARTMENT OF ADMINISTRATION, DIVISION OF PROCUREMENT.** **Main/Corp** Minnesota. Dept. of Administration. Division of Procurement. **VFOAT** M.N. Small Business Procurement Program for Socially or Economically Disadvantaged Vendors F.Y. ... Annual Report; Annual Report on Small Business Procurement Act Fiscal Year ... . **VAT** Minnesota Small Business Procurement Program for Socially or Economically Disadvantaged Vendors F.Y. ... Annual Report. 1982-. English. an. **LC** JK6188.A1; M55A. **DD** 353.97760071/2/05. *Continues Minnesota. Dept. of Administration. Division of Procurement. Annual Report to the Legislature on the Small Business Procurement Act.*

US/0360-7941
**MODERN GOVERNMENT/NATIONAL DEVELOPMENT.** [Mod. gov. natl. dev.]. V. 16, No. 5- June/July 1975-. Periodical. English. mo (nine no. a year). Intercontinental Publications, PO Box 5017, Westport CT 06880. **Tel** (203)226-7463, FAX (203)222-8793. **LC** HD3840; .M6. **DD** 363.5/05. *Continues Modern Government, National Development, 0360-7941.*

FR/0997-7139
**MONDE DU RENSEIGNEMENT 1988, LE.** See Military and Defense.

JA
**MONITA NENPO.** Japanese. an. Naikaku Sori Daijin Kanbo Kohoshitsu Kochogakari, 6-1 Nagata-cho 1 Chiyoda-ku, Tokyo-to 100 Japan. **LC** JQ1601; .M66.

RM
**MONITORUL OFICIAL AL ROMANIEI. PATRTEA 1. PUBLICATII SI ANUNTURI.** **Main/Corp** Romania. **Added/Corp** Romania. Parlament (1990). Adunarea Deputatilor. **VFOAT** Publicatii si Anunturi. (1990)-. Romanian. da. Biroul de Publicitate si Difuzare Pentru Monitorul Oficial al Romaniei, Str. Blanduziei, Number 1, Section 1, Bucuresti, Romania. **LC** IN PROCESS.

US/0738-3207
**MONOGRAPH (MAXWELL GRADUATE SCHOOL OF CITIZENSHIP AND PUBLIC AFFAIRS. METROPOLITAN STUDIES PROGRAM).** (MONOGRAPH.). [Monogr - Maxwell Grad. Sch. Citizship. Public Aff., Metrop. Stud. Program]. **Added/Corp** Maxwell Graduate School of Citizenship and Public Affairs. Metropolitan Studies Program. (19??)-. Monographic series. English. ir. Price varies per volume. Maxwell School, Metropolitan Studies Program, 400 Maxwell Hall, Syracuse NY 13244-1090. **Tel** (315)423-3114. **LC** UNC. **Bk Rev**. **Circ:** 1,600 (ctrl).
**Desc:** Metropolitan Studies Program conducts research on a wide range of public policy issues: domestic, urban and regional studies, international studies, and health and income security.

US/0362-6830
**MONTHLY CATALOG OF UNITED STATES GOVERNMENT PUBLICATIONS.** [Mon. cat. U.S. gov. publ.]. No. 672 (Jan. 1951)-. Catalog. English. mo. $199.00 (domestic); $248.75 (other) $32.00 (domestic; $40.00 (other ) Microfiche. Pierian Press, PO Box 1808, Ann Arbor MI 48106. **Tel** (313)434-5530, (800)678-2435, FAX (313)434-6409. **LC** Z1223. **DD** 015. **NLM** Z 1223 U58M. cum. index. available on microfiche (Vols. for Jan. 1984-). *Continues United States Government Publications Monthly Catalog, 0041-767X.*
**Desc:** Lists publications, both printed and processed, issued during each month. Includes publications sold by the Superintendent of Documents, those for official use, and those sent to Depository Libraries.
**Ind/Abst** MINPROC; Mintec, Min. Technol. Abstr.; Wildl. Rev. (19??-199?).

AT
**MONTHLY SUMMARY OF STATISTICS.** See Public Administration-Abstracting, Bibliographies and Statistics.

AT
**MONTHLY SUMMARY OF STATISTICS, NEW SOUTH WALES.** See Public Administration-Abstracting, Bibliographies and Statistics.

AT/0047-8032
**MONTHLY SUMMARY OF STATISTICS, SOUTH AUSTRALIA.** See Public Administration-Abstracting, Bibliographies and Statistics.

AT
**MONTHLY SUMMARY OF STATISTICS : WESTERN AUSTRALIA.** See Public Administration-Abstracting, Bibliographies and Statistics.

CN/0821-4573
**MONTREALITES.** (MONTREALITES / VILLE DE MONTREAL.). [Montrealites]. V. 1, No. 1, (Dec. 1981)-. Periodical. French. ir. Free. Cidem-Communications Bureau 224, 155 Est rue Notre-Dame, Montreal Quebec H2Y 1B5 Canada. **DD** 352.0714/281. ctrl circ.

PH
**MPWH BULLETIN : OFFICIAL QUARTERLY PUBLICATION OF THE MINISTRY OF PUBLIC WORKS AND HIGHWAYS.** *Suspended.* **Added/Corp** Philippines. Ministry of Public Works and Highways. Vol. 21, No. 1 (June 1982)-(19??). Bulletin. English. qt. Department of Public Works & Highways, DPWH Building, Bonifacio Drive, Port Area, Manila Philippines. **Tel** FAX 40 16 83. **ED** Manuel R. Reyes. **LC** HD4306; .M68. **DD** 354.599086/06. **Circ:** 2,000. *Continues MPW Bulletin.*

US
**MR (UNIVERSITY OF CALIFORNIA, LOS ANGELES. INSTITUTE OF GOVERNMENT AND PUBLIC AFFAIRS).** (MR / INSTITUTE OF GOVERNMENT AND PUBLIC AFFAIRS, UNIVERSITY OF CALIFORNIA.). **Added/Corp** University of California, Los Angeles. Institute of Government and Public Affairs. **VAT** Mimeographed Report. (1963)-. Monographic series. English. Price varies per volume. **LC** AS36.C2; A35.

VE
**MRI INFORMATIVO.** **Main/Corp** Venezuela. Ministerio de Relaciones Interiores. Yearly V. 1- (No. 1- ); March 1976-. Spanish. Ministerio de Relaciones Interiores, Caracas Venezuela. **LC** J257; .R36. **DD** 354./87/305.

US
**MULTI-UNIT AGREEMENTS IN THE FEDERAL GOVERNMENT.** *Title Change.* Periodical. English. an. US Civil Service Commission

Office of Labor-Management Relations, Washington DC 20415. ***Continued by*** *Multi-Unit Agreements in the Federal Service.*

RM
**MUNCA DE PARTID.** ***Ceased.*** **Added/Corp** Partidul Comunist Roman. Comitetul Central. (1957-19??). Periodical. Romanian. mo. **(Subscription address:** Ilexim Press Department, PO Box 1, 136-1-137, Bucharest, Romania.**)** **LC** JN9639.A57; M85.

US
**MUNICIPAL CORPORATIONS.** (19??)-. Periodical. English. $175.00. Michie Company, PO Box 7587, Charlottesville VA 22906-7587. **Tel** (804)972-7600, (800)542-0957, FAX (800)643-1280.

CN/0703-2412
**MUNICIPAL COUNSELLOR.** ***Suspended.*** **Added/Corp** Alberta. Dept. of Municipal Affairs. Vol. 19 (1st Quarter 1975)-. Periodical. English. qt. Free. Alberta Municipal Affairs, 10155 102 Street/18th Floor, City Ctr, Edmonton Alberta T5J 4L4 Canada. **Tel** (403)427-8862. ***Continues*** *Alberta Municipal Counsellor, 0002-4864.*

US/0743-6211
**MUNICIPAL/COUNTY EXECUTIVE DIRECTORY.** ***Title Change.*** [Munic./cty. exec. dir.]. **VFOAT** Municipal County Executive Directory. (1984)-(1991). Directory. English. an. Carroll Publishing Company, 1058 Thomas Jefferson Street Northwest, Washington DC 20007-3832. **Tel** (202)333-8620, FAX (202)337-7020. **ED** Nancy Cahill. **LC** JS363; .M85. **DD** 352. ***Continued by*** *Municipal/County Executive Directory Annual.*
**Desc:** The first and only directories of all federal, state, municipal and county officials. This vital resource provides rapid access to government officials at all levels.

US/0743-6211
**MUNICIPAL/COUNTY EXECUTIVE DIRECTORY ANNUAL.** **VFOAT** County Executive Directory Annual; Municipal County Executive Directory Annual. (1991)-. Government Publication. English. an (June). $127.00. Carroll Publishing Company, 1058 Thomas Jefferson Street Northwest, Washington DC 20007-3832. **Tel** (202)333-8620, FAX (202)337-7020. **LC** JS363; .M85. Index available. available on diskette. ***Continues*** *Municipal/County Executive Directory, 0743-6211.*
**Desc:** Provides names, titles, addresses and phone numbers of key elected, appointed, and career officials in virtually every U.S. municipality, county, borough and parish.

US/0272-4596
**MUNICIPAL DIRECTORY (AUGUSTA).** (MUNICIPAL DIRECTORY - MAINE MUNICIPAL ASSOCIATION.). **Main/Corp** Maine Municipal Association. Directory. English. an. $20.00. Local Government Center, 45 University Drive, PO Box 2268, Augusta ME 04338. **Tel** (207)623-8428, FAX (207)626-5947. **ED** Michael L Starn. **LC** JS451.M25; M34A. **DD** 352/.0052/09741. **Ad Acc. Circ:** 2,000.
**Desc:** Names, addresses, telephone numbers of Maine municipal officials.

CN/0318-0743
**MUNICIPAL DIRECTORY (TORONTO).** (MUNICIPAL DIRECTORY.). [Munic. dir.]. **Added/Corp** Ontario. Dept. of Municipal Affairs. Ontario. Municipal Finance Branch. Ontario. Provincial-Municipal Affairs Secretariat. Ontario. Ministry of Municipal Affairs and Housing. Ontario. Ministry of Municipal Affairs. **VFOAT** Repertoire des Municipalites. (1948)-. Directory. English (French). an. Association of Municipal Clerks and Treasurers of Ontario, 1030 Mississauga ONT 14T 4C2 Ontario. **Tel** (905)564-8025. **DD** 352/.00025/713. ***Absorbed*** *Repertoire des Municipalites (Toronto, Ont.), 1193-4158.*

US/0742-1710
**MUNICIPAL EXECUTIVE DIRECTORY.** **Added/Corp** Carroll Publishing Company. (Winter/Spring 1984)-. Directory. English. sa. $150.00. Carroll Publishing Company, 1058 Thomas Jefferson Street Northwest, Washington DC 20007-3832. **Tel** (202)333-8620, FAX (202)337-7020. **ED** Nancy Cahill. **LC** JS363; .M86. **DD** 352/.0052/0973. Index available. cum. index. **Circ:** 500 (ctrl).
**Desc:** Provides access to government officials in 7,200 cities, towns and villages.

CN/0384-840X
**MUNICIPAL HANDBOOK : THE CITY OF CALGARY.** **Main/Corp** Calgary (Alta.). 1976-. English. an. Public Information Department / Alberta, City of Calgary, PO Box 2100, Calgary Alberta T2P 2M5 Canada. **Tel** (403)268-8844. **DD** 352.07123/3. ***Continues*** *Calgary, Alta. City Clerk's Dept. Municipal Manual, 0381-582X.*
**Desc:** Provides information and statistics about the history of the city of Calgary and the corporation including the duties and functions of the city's government.

US/0739-4918
**MUNICIPAL INSTRUCTORS' SECTION NEWS.** [Munic. Instr. Sect. news]. Periodical. English. qt. ISFSI, 20 Main Street, Ashland MA 01721.

UK/0143-4187
**MUNICIPAL JOURNAL (LONDON. 1970).** (MUNICIPAL JOURNAL.). [Munic. j.]. Vol. 78, No. 25 (June 19, 1970)-. Periodical. English. wk. £59.50. Municipal Engineering Ltd, 32 Vauxhall Bridge Road, London SW1V 2SS England. **Tel** 011 44 71 9736400, telex 262568. **LC** TD1; .M93. **DD** 352.041. ***Continues*** *Municipal and Public Services Journal, 0027-3430;* ***Absorbed*** *Municipal Engineering.*
**Ind/Abst** Curr. Technol. Index; Highw. Res. Abstr.; Libr. Inf. Sci. Abstr.

US/0164-7296
**MUNICIPAL MANAGEMENT.** ***Suspended.*** Vol. 1, Summer 1978-Suspended with Vol. 7, 1985. Periodical. English. qt. $22.50. Center for Public Management, Shalom Saar 999 Asylum Avenue, Hartford CT 06105. **ED** Shalom Saar. **LC** JS39; .M65. **DD** 352/.008/05.
**Desc:** Oriented articles about public management at the local government level.
**Ind/Abst** Urban Aff. Abstr.

AT/1036-2185
**MUNICIPAL MANAGER, QUEENSLAND.** (1991)-. Periodical. English. qt. 100.00Aus$. Institute of Municipal Management / Queensland, 60 Edmondstone Road, Newstead Qld 4006, Australia. **Tel** 011 61 7 854 1156. ***Continues*** *Queensland Institute of Municipal Administration, 0048-6078.*

US/0196-9986
**MUNICIPAL MARYLAND.** [Munic. Md.]. **Added/Corp** Maryland Municipal League. (July 1972)-. Periodical. English. Ten times a year. $21.00. Maryland Municipal League, 1212 West St., % Sharon P. Easton, Annapolis MD 21401. **Tel** (800)492-7121, FAX (410)268-7004. **DD** 352. ***Supersedes*** *Maryland Municipal News, 0025-4304.*
**Desc:** Serves as a medium of exchange of ideas and information on municipal affairs for public officials in Maryland.

US/0027-352X
**MUNICIPAL NEWS (SEATTLE).** ***Title Change.*** (MUNICIPAL NEWS.). **Added/Corp** Municipal League of Seattle and King County. (19??)-(19??). Periodical. English. mo. Municipal League Seattle King, 810 3rd Avenue, Suite 604, Seattle WA 98104. **Tel** (206)622-8333. **ED** Stephen C Forman. **Circ:** 2,000 (ctrl). ***Absorbed by*** *Issue Watch, 0890-4642.*
**Desc:** Information on local public policy and emerging issues analysis with possible solutions. Opportunities for the community to get involved through forums and committee meetings.

CN/0715-6804
**MUNICIPAL OFFICIALS OF MANITOBA.** [Munic. off. Manit.]. **VFOAT** Municipal Officials; Municipal Officials, Manitoba. English. an. $3.50. Department of Municipal Affairs / Manitoba, 1325-405 Broadway, Winnipeg Manitoba R3C 3L6 Canada. **Tel** (204)945-2564. **ED** M Yetman. **LC** JS1721.M3; A15. **DD** 352/.00025/7127. **Circ:** 1,500 (ctrl).
**Desc:** Directory of municipal officials in the Province of Manitoba. Listing of names, addresses, office addresses, telephone, population, and government officials, etc.

US/0090-6875
**MUNICIPAL POLICY STATEMENT - LEAGUE OF ARIZONA CITIES & TOWNS.** (MUNICIPAL POLICY STATEMENT.). **Main/Corp** League of Arizona Cities and Towns. English. an. Municipal Policy Statement, 1820 West Washington Street, Phoenix AZ 85007. **LC** JS303.A6; L4. **DD** 352.0791.

US/0146-8758
**MUNICIPAL PROGRESS.** Periodical. English. mo. $48.00. Educational Service Bureau, 1835 K Street NW, Washington DC 20006. **LC** JS39; .M68. **DD** 352/.008/0973.

US/0028-6257
**MUNICIPAL REPORTER (SANTE FE, N.M.), THE.** (THE MUNICIPAL REPORTER.). **Added/Corp** New Mexico Municipal League. (19??)-. English. mo. $20.00. New Mexico Municipal League, c/o Anita Martinez, PO Box 846, Santa Fe NM 87501. **Tel** (505)982-5573.
**Ind/Abst** Urban Aff. Abstr.

UK/0027-3562
**MUNICIPAL REVIEW & AMA NEWS.** **Added/Corp** Association of Metropolitan Authorities. **VFOAT** Municipal Review and A.M.A. News. Vol. 51/52, No. 610 (Jan. 1981)-. Periodical. English. Ten times a year. £18.00 UK; £36.00 other. Association of Metropolitan Authorities, 35 Great Smith Street, Westminster London SW1P 3BJ England. **Tel** 011 44 71 222 8100, FAX 011 44 71 222 0878. **ED** Peter Smith. **LC** JS3001; .M8. **DD** 352/.00724/0941. Index available. cum. index. **Bk Rev. Ad Acc. Circ:** 7,800. ***Continues*** *Municipal Review, 0027-3562.*
**Ind/Abst** Urban Aff. Abstr.

US/0363-1729
**MUNICIPAL SALARY SURVEY.** (MUNICIPAL SALARY SURVEY - NEW JERSEY. DEPT. OF COMMUNITY AFFAIRS.). **Main/Corp** New Jersey. Dept. of Community Affairs. Municipal Information Service. English. an. New Jersey Department of Community Affairs, Cn 805 Bureau Const. Code Enforcer, Trenton NJ 08625. **Tel** (609)530-8792. **LC** JS451.N57; N47A. **DD** 353.9/749/00123.

US/0542-9676
**MUNICIPAL SALARY SURVEY : BENCH-MARK JOBS.** **See** Economics-Labor.

US/0027-3570
**MUNICIPAL SOUTH.** V. 1- Jan. 1954-. Periodical. English. bm. $6.00, Free to qualified individuals US; $7.00 other. Municipal South Magazine Company, Rt. 2 Box 799, PO Box 1053, Lincolnton NC 38092. **LC** JS39; .M75. **DD** 352.075.

UK/0305-5906
**MUNICIPAL YEAR BOOK AND PUBLIC SERVICES DIRECTORY, THE.** 1973-. Directory. English. an. £110.00. Municipal Engineering Ltd, 32 Vauxhall Bridge Road, London SW1V 2SS England. **Tel** 011 44 71 9736400, telex 262568. **LC** JS3003; .M8. **DD** 352.041. ***Continues*** *Municipal Year Book and Public Utilities Directory.*

US/0077-2186
**MUNICIPAL YEAR BOOK (WASHINGTON), THE.** (THE MUNICIPAL YEAR BOOK.). [Munic. year book]. **Added/Corp** International City Management Association. International City Managers' Association. 1st Ed. (1934)-. English. an. $79.95. International City Management Association, 777 North Capitol Street NE, Suite 500, Washington DC 20002. **Tel** (202)289-4262, (800)745-8780, FAX (202)962-3500. **(Subscription address:** International City Management Association, PO Box 2011, Annapolis Junction MD 20701.**)** **ED** J.B. Yowell. **LC** JS344.C5; A24. **NLM** JS 342 M966. cum. index. ***Continues*** *City Manager Yearbook.*
**Desc:** Source book on trends and developments in American and Canadian cities and counties. Contains data and articles on local government issues such as salaries, city/county profiles, management concerns. Includes a bibliography and comprehensive directories.
**Ind/Abst** Stat. Ref. Index.

US/1054-4062
**MUNICIPAL YELLOW BOOK.** **See** Encyclopedias and General Reference Books.

CN/0713-4800
**MUNICIPALITE (1982).** (MUNICIPALITE.). [Municipalite]. **Added/Corp** Quebec (Province). Ministere des Affaires Municipales. (April/May 1982)-. Periodical. French. Nine times a year. Free on request. Ministere des Affaires Municipales, 20 Ave Chauveau, Quebec Quebec G1R 4J3 Canada. **Tel** (418)643-4224. **DD** 352.0714. ***Continues*** *Nouvelle Revue Municipalite, 0227-3888.*
**Ind/Abst** Point Repere (1983-).

US/0027-3597
**MUNICIPALITY (1916), THE.** (THE MUNICIPALITY / LEAGUE OF WISCONSIN MUNICIPALITIES.). [Municipality]. Vol. 16, No. 1 (Jan. 1916)-. Periodical. English. mo. $18.00. League of Wisconsin Municipalities, 122 West Washington Avenue, Room 301, Madison WI 53703. **Tel** (608)267-2380, FAX (608)267-0645. **ED** Dan Thompson. **DD** 352. Index available in last issue of volume--attached. **Bk Rev. Ad Acc, Adv Mgr:** John O. Kirkpatrick. ctrl circ. ***Continues*** *Wisconsin Municipality (1914).*
**Desc:** Provides information for Wisconsin government officials.
**Ind/Abst** Urban Aff. Abstr.

CN/0319-4167
**MUNICIPALITY OF SHUNIAH.** V. 1- Mar. 1975-. Periodical. English. Free to citizens and property holders of Shuniah. Municipal Offices, 420 Leslie Avenue, Thunder Bay Ontario P7A 1X8 Canada. **DD** 352.0713/12.

II/0027-7584
**NAGARLOK.** **Added/Corp** Centre for Training and Research in Municipal Administration. Vol. 1 (1969)-. Periodical. English. qt. $25.00. DIR-Indian Institute of Public Administration, Indraprastha Estate Ring Road, New Delhi 110002 India. **Tel** 011 91 11 3317309. **(Subscription address:** Prints India, 11 Darya Ganj, New Delhi, 110002 India, (Phone: 011 91 11 3268645)**)** **ED** P K Umashankar and G K Misra. **LC** JS7001; .N34. **DD** 352/.054.

HK
**NAMES OF BUILDINGS (WITH ADDRESSES) / RATING AND VALUATION DEPARTMENT, HONG KONG.** **Added/Corp** Hong Kong. Rating and Valuation Dept. **VFOAT** Names of buildings; Lou Yu Ming Cheng. (19??)-. English (Chinese). ir. HK$75.00. Hong Kong

Government Information Service, Beaconsfield House, 4 Queens Road, Hong Kong Hong Kong. **Tel** 011 852 8428801 4, telex 61190 HKGIS. **LC** DS796.H78; A26.

RU/0236-0918
**NARODNYI DEPUTAT.** ***Title Change.*** **Added/Corp** Soviet Union. Verkhovnyi Sovet. (1990)-(1993). Periodical. Russian. mo. Izdatelstvo Izvestiia, Pl. Pushkina 5, 103798 Moscow Russia. **(Subscription address:** Victor Kamkin, 4956 Boiling Brook Parkway, Rockville MD 20852.**)** **LC** IN PROCESS; JS6058; .S72. ***Continues*** *Sovety Narodnykh Deputatov, 0201-5250.* ***Continued by*** *Rossiikaia Federatsiia.*

US/0891-9291
**NASH & CIBINIC REPORT, THE.** [Nash Cibinic rep.]. **VFOAT** Nash and Cibinic Report. Vol. 1, No. 1 (Jan. 1987)-. Periodical. English. mo. $640.00 US; $670.00 other. Federal Publications Inc, 1120 20th Street Northwest, Washington DC 20036. **Tel** (202)337-7000, (800)922-4330, FAX (202)659-2233. **DD** 351. Index available. cum. index. **Bk Rev.**

US/0735-9691
**NATAT'S REPORTER.** [NATaT's Natl. community rep.]. **Added/Corp** National Association of Towns and Townships (U.S.). **VFOAT** N.A.T.A.T.'S. National Community Reporter. (19??)-. Periodical. English. bm. $18.00 (1 year), $28.00 (2 year) towns and townships; $36.00 (1 year), $60.00 (2 year) other. National Association of Towns and Townships, 1522 K Street NW/Suite 600, Washington DC 20005. **Tel** (202)737-5200, FAX (202)289-7996. **ED** Ronnie Kweller. **Ad Acc. Circ:** 15,000 (ctrl). ***Continues*** *National Community Reporter.*
**Desc:** National news journal devoted to the interests of small-town and rural government.

US/0027-8513
**NATIONAL ALLIANCE.** **See** Economics-Labor.

US/0547-4221
**NATIONAL ASSOCIATION OF SECRETARIES OF STATE HANDBOOK.** [Natl. Assoc. Secret. State handb.]. **Main/Corp** National Association of Secretaries of State. 1st (1958)-. English. ir. $18.00. National Association of Secretaries of State, PO Box 11910, Lexington KY 40578. **LC** JK2403; .N353. **DD** 353. **Pr Rev.** ctrl circ.
**Desc:** Secretary's biography and photographs of past conferences.

US/0027-9013
**NATIONAL CIVIC REVIEW.** [Natl. civic rev.]. **Added/Corp** National Civic League (U.S.). National Municipal League. Vol. 48, No. 1 (Jan. 1959)-. Periodical. English. qt. $30.00. National Civic League, 1445 Market Street, Suite 300, Denver CO 80202. **Tel** (303)571-4343, FAX (303)832-4005. **ED** John Tepper Marlin and David Lampe. **LC** JS39; .N3. **DD** 352. Index available. cum. index. **Bk Rev. Ad Acc. Circ:** 5,000. available on microfilm and microfiche from University Microfilms International (UMI). Documents available from UMI Article Clearinghouse. ***Continues*** *National Municipal Review, 0190-3799.*
**Desc:** Policy journal supplying case studies, insights and programs for government performance measurement and community problem solving.
**Ind/Abst** ABC POL SCI; Am. Hist. Life (1970-); Book Rev. Index; Expand. Acad. Index (1992-); Int. Polit. Sci. Abstr.; J. Plan. Lit.; Newsp. Period. Abstr. (1992-); PAIS Int. Print (1991-); Sage Urban Stud. Abstr (1970-?); U.S. Polit. Sci. Doc.; Urban Aff. Abstr.

US
**NATIONAL DIRECTORY OF HISPANIC ELECTED AND APPOINTED OFFICIALS / CONGRESSIONAL HISPANIC CAUCUS.** 1981-. Directory. English. an. The Caucus, House Annex II Room 557, Washington DC 20515. ctrl circ.

US/0192-4273
**NATIONAL DIRECTORY OF STATE & LOCAL GOVERNMENT TRAINERS.** **VAT** National Directory of State and Local Government Trainers. 1978-. Directory. English. an. Trainer's Resource Service, c/o National Training and Development Service, 5028 Wisconsin Avenue NW, Washington DC 20016. **LC** JK2480.I6; N38. **DD** 350/.15/02573.

AT/1030-6641
**NATIONAL GUIDE TO GOVERNMENT.** **VFOAT** NGTG. 8th Ed. (March/July 1988)-. Periodical. English. Three times a year. 320.00Aus$ Australia; 345.25Aus$ US and Israel. Information Australia Group Pty. Ltd., 45 Flinders Lane, Melbourne Victoria 3000 Australia. **Tel** 11 61 3 6542800. **LC** JQ4021; .N38. **DD** 354.94/00025. Index available. ***Continues*** *National Guide to Government and the Bureaucracy.*

US
**NATIONAL HEALTH POLICY FORUM.** English. Thirty-five times a year. $85.00 others; $250.00 trade associations consultants & health care institutions. National Health Policy Forum, 2021 K Street Northwest, Suite 800, Washington DC 20006. **Tel** (202)872-1390, FAX (202)785-0114. **Circ:** 2,600 (ctrl).
**Desc:** The forum was established to promote the education, communication, and interaction of those federal officials who design legislation or are responsible for its implementation and to assist in filing their needs for objective information from and dialogue with those in the field whether they be consumers, providers, or purchasers.

US
**NATIONAL INDEPENDENT STUDY CENTER FISCAL YEAR ... COURSE CATALOG.** **Main/Corp** National Independent Study Center (U.S.). **VFOAT** Course Catalog. Catalog. English. an. National Independent Study Center, US Civil Service Commission Building, 20 Denver Federal Center, Denver CO 80225.

US
**NATIONAL MUNICIPAL POLICY / AMERICAN MUNICIPAL ASSOCIATION.** **Added/Corp** American Municipal Association. National League of Cities. (1949)-. English. an. $5.00 members, National League of Cities; $10.00 other. National League of Cities, 1301 Pennsylvania Avenue NW, Washington DC 20004. **Tel** (202)626-3150, FAX (202)626-3043. **Circ:** 2,500.
**Desc:** Addresses priorities the federal government could consider in designing policy documents for urban problems.

US/0894-7872
**NATIONAL NOTARY, THE.** **Added/Corp** National Notary Association (U.S.). (19??)-. Periodical. English. bm (6 issues). Comes with National Notary Association membership. National Notary Association, 8236 Remmet Ave., PO Box 7184, Canoga Park CA 91304. **Tel** (818)713-4000. **ED** Charles Faerber. **DD** 347. Index available. **Bk Rev. Ad Acc. Circ:** 62,000 (ctrl).
**Desc:** Contains instructional articles for notaries public, reports on pertinent current events and features regular departments, including "notary adviser."

US/1051-6093
**NATIONAL ORGANIZATIONS OF STATE GOVERNMENT OFFICIALS DIRECTORY.** ***Title Change.*** [Natl. organ. state gov. off. dir.]. **Added/Corp** Council of State Governments. National Conference of State Legislatures. (1984)-(19??). Directory. English. Council of State Governments, PO Box 11910, Iron Works Pike, Lexington KY 40578-1910. **Tel** (800)800-1910, (606)231-1850. **LC** JK2679; .N38. **DD** 353.9/31/06. ***Continued by*** *Organizations of State Government Officials Directory, 1069-5168.*

US/8755-7592
**NATIONAL PARLIAMENTARIAN.** [Natl. parliam.]. **Added/Corp** National Association of Parliamentarians (U.S.). (1938)-. Periodical. English. qt. $8.00. National Association of Parliamentarians, 6601 Winchester Avenue, Suite 260, Kansas City MO 64133. **Tel** (816)356-5604. **DD** 060.

US
**NATIONAL TELEPHONE DIRECTORY / DEPARTMENT OF ENERGY.** **Main/Corp** United States. Dept. for Energy. Office of the Assistant Secretary for Management and Administration. Jan. 1982-. Government Publication. English. an. US Department of Energy, 1000 Independence Avenue SW, Washington DC 20585. **Tel** (202)586-5000, FAX (202)586-4073. ***Continues*** *United States. Dept. of Energy. Directorate of Administration. National Telephone Directory.*

NE/0168-3489
**NATIONALE REKENINGEN / CENTRAAL BUREAU VOOR DE STATISTIEK.** **Added/Corp** Netherlands. Centraal Bureau voor de Statistiek. Netherlands. Centraal Bureau voor de Statistiek. Hoofdafdeling Nationale Rekeningen. **VFOAT** National Accounts. (195?)-. Dutch. an. Fl30.46. Central Bureau of Statistics / Netherlands, Staatsuitgeverij, NL 2500 Hague The Netherlands. **LC** HG186.N4; A32. ***Continues*** *Netherlands. Centraal Bureau Voor de Statistiek. Nationale Jaarrekeningen.*

AU
**NATIONALRAT UND BUNDESRAT AMTLICHES VERZEICHNIS DER MITGLEIDER, AUSSCHUSSE UND KLUBS.** **Main/Corp** Austria. Nationalrat. (19??)-. German. ir. Nationalrat Osterreichische Staatsdruckerei, Vienna Austria. **Tel** (0222)4804/235. **LC** JN2023.A2; A93a. **Circ:** 800. ***Continues*** *Austria. Nationalrat. Nationalrat und Bundesrat Buro, Mitglieder, Ausschusse, Klubs.*
**Desc:** List of Members of both Houses of Parliament (Nationalists and Bundesrat), etc.

US/0164-5935
**NATION'S CITIES WEEKLY.** (NATION'S CITIES WEEKLY / NATIONAL LEAGUE OF CITIES.). [Nation's cities wkly.]. **Added/Corp** National League of Cities. Vol. 1, No. 44 (Dec. 4 1978)-. Periodical. English. Fifty times a year (Mondays). $80.00 (nonmembers), $50.00 (members) US; add $6.00 postage other. National League of Cities, 1301 Pennsylvania Avenue NW, Washington DC 20004. **Tel** (202)626-3150, FAX (202)626-3043. **DD** 352. **Bk Rev. Ad Acc, Adv Mgr:** Al Junge, **Tel** (203)327-4626. **Circ:** 28,000. available on microfilm from University Microfilms International (UMI); available on an online database (files 647,648/Full-Text) from DIALOG. Documents available from UMI Article Clearinghouse, Magazine Collection. ***Formed by the union of*** *Nation's Cities, 0028-0488* ***and*** *City Weekly, 0164-5595.*
**Desc:** Contains news about cities and about legislative developments in Washington, D.C. which will affect cities.
**Ind/Abst** Acad. Search (July 1993-); Bus. Index (1979-?); Gen. Period. Index (1985-); INFO-SOUTH Abstr.; Mag. Index Plus (1989-); Mag. Search; Newsp. Period. Abstr. (1988-); Mag. Index (Dec. 1978-); Trade Ind. ASAP [Full Txt.]; Trade Ind. Index (1981-) [Full Txt.]; Urban Aff. Abstr.

CN/1185-9946
**NATIVE AGENDA, NEWS.** [Native agenda news]. **Added/Corp** Canada. Indian and Northern Affairs Canada. (April/May 1991)-. Periodical. English. mo. **DD** 354.710681/497.

●US/1068-2716
**NCSL LEGISBRIEF.** [NCSL legisbrief]. **Added/Corp** National Conference of State Legislatures. **VFOAT** Legisbrief. **VAT** National Conference of State Legislatures Legisbrief. Vol. 1, No. 1 (1993)-. Periodical. English. wk (48 issues). $79.00 US; $84.00 Canada. National Conference of State Legislatures, 1560 Broadway, Suite 700, Denver CO 80202. **Tel** (303)830-2054, FAX (303)863-8003. **ED** Julie Lays. **DD** 351.
**Desc:** Each issue covers a pressing topic in state government, analyzes successful approaches taken, offers alternative courses of action and offers a better understanding of important developments.

US/0028-1905
**NEBRASKA MUNICIPAL REVIEW.** **Added/Corp** League of Nebraska Municipalities. (19??)-. Periodical. English. mo. $24.00. League of Nebraska Municipalities, 1335 L Street, Lincoln NE 68508. **Tel** (402)476-2829. **ED** Peggy S. Hain. Index available. cum. index. **Ad Acc. Circ:** 3,200 (ctrl).
**Desc:** Issues of interest to local governments.
**Ind/Abst** Urban Aff. Abstr.

NP
**NEPAL RECORDER.** Vol. 1, No. 1 (Mar. 1, 1977)-. Periodical. English. Regmiville Lazimpat, Kathmandu Nepal. **LC** JQ1825.N4; A3. **DD** 354.549/6. ***Continues*** *Nepal Gazette.*
**Desc:** Translations of laws, regulations, orders, notifications, etc.

US
**NEVADA GAMING ABSTRACT / STATE GAMING CONTROL BOARD.** **Added/Corp** Nevada. State Gaming Control Board. Nevada. State Gaming Control Board. Securities and Economic Research Division. (1975)-. English. an. State Gaming Control Board, 1150 East William Street, Carson City NV 89710. **Tel** (702)687-6500. **LC** HD9981.7.N3; N48a. **DD** 338.4/3795/09793.

US/0196-7355
**NEVADA PUBLIC AFFAIRS REVIEW.** **Added/Corp** Nevada Public Affairs Institute. University of Nevada, Reno. Bureau of Governmental Research. (1979)-. Periodical. English. ir (1 or 2 per year). University of Nevada at Reno Center for Applied Research, Reno NV 89557. **Tel** (702)784-6718. **ED** Richard Siegel. **LC** JK8501; .N464. **DD** 320.9793/05. **Circ:** 2,500 (ctrl). ***Continues*** *Nevada Public Affairs Report, 0364-3921.*
**Desc:** Publishes basic and applied research related to public affairs in Nevada and promotes public education on public affairs issues.

US
**NEW DIRECTIONS IN PUBLIC ADMINISTRATION RESEARCH.** ***Ceased.*** Vol. 1, No. 1 (Apr. 1986)-(19??). Periodical. English. Florida Atlantic University, 220 SE 2nd Avenue, Fort Lauderdale FL 33301. **Tel** (305)355-5200.
**Ind/Abst** PAIS Int. Print.

US/0749-016X
**NEW ENGLAND JOURNAL OF PUBLIC POLICY.** (NEW ENGLAND JOURNAL OF PUBLIC POLICY : A JOURNAL OF THE JOHN W. MCCORMACK INSTITUTE OF PUBLIC AFFAIRS, UNIVERSITY OF MASSACHUSETTS AT BOSTON.). [N. Engl. j. public policy]. **Added/Corp** John W. McCormack Institute of Public Affairs. Vol. 1 No. 1 (Winter/Spring 1985)-. Periodical. English. sa. $100.00 (institutions), $20.00 (individuals). New England Journal of Public Policy, University of Massachusetts-Dartmouth, North Dartmouth MA 02747. **Tel** (508)999-8369. **ED** Padraig O'Malley. **LC** WMLC 93/2100; H96; .N4. **DD** 350. **Bk Rev. Ad Acc. Circ:** 2,500.
**Desc:** Provides a medium for practitioners, policy analysts and academics throughout New England to define problems and develop approaches to solving them.

US
**NEW HAMPSHIRE PUBLIC UTILITIES COMMISSION REPORTS.** **Main/Corp** New Hampshire Public Utilities Commission. Vol. 58, 59-60 (1973, 1974-1975)-. English. New Hampshire Public Utilities Commission, 8 Old Suncook Road, Concord NH 03301. **LC** KFN1485; .A556. **DD** 343.742/09. ***Continues in part*** *Reports and Orders -State of New Hampshire Public Utilities Commission.*

US/0545-1671
**NEW HAMPSHIRE REGISTER, STATE YEAR-BOOK AND LEGISLATIVE MANUAL.** (1869)-. English. an. $95.00. Tower Publishing Company, 588 Saco Road, Standish ME 04084. **Tel** (800)969-8693. **ED** Esther Peison. **LC** JK2930; .N4. **Ad Acc. Circ:** 750.
**Desc:** A comprehensive, one volume reference work on the state of New Hampshire.

US/0545-171X
**NEW HAMPSHIRE TOWN & CITY.** **Added/Corp** New Hampshire Municipal Association. **VFOAT** New Hampshire Town and City. (19??)-. Periodical. English. Ten times a year (Monthly with July/Aug. and Nov./Dec. issues combined). $10.00. New Hampshire Municipal Association, PO Box 617, London Road Building 3, Concord NH 03301. **Tel** (603)224-7447. **ED** Jonathan Steiner. Index available. **Bk Rev. Ad Acc. Circ:** 2,700 (ctrl). ***Continues*** *New Hampshire Town and City, 0545-171X.*
**Ind/Abst** Urban Aff. Abstr.

US/0028-5846
**NEW JERSEY MUNICIPALITIES.** **Added/Corp** New Jersey State League of Municipalities. (1917)-. Periodical. English. ir (9 issues). $12.00. State League of Municipalities Trenton NJ 08618, 407 West State Street, Trenton NJ 08618. **Tel** (609)695-3481. **LC** JS39; .N4. Index available (bound in Dec. issue).
**Ind/Abst** Urban Aff. Abstr.

US/8756-2618
**NEW JERSEY POLITICAL ALMANAC.** **Added/Corp** Center for Analysis of Public Issues. (1978)-. English. be (every 2 years). $15.00. Center Analysis Public Issues, 16 Vandeventer Avenue, Princeton NJ 08540. **Tel** (609)924-9750, FAX (609)924-0363. **ED** Neil Upmeyer. **LC** JK3568; .N47. **DD** 328.749/073/05. Index available. **Bk Rev. Circ:** 3,000.
**Desc:** A journal of New Jersey public issues.

US/0300-6069
**NEW JERSEY REGISTER.** **Added/Corp** New Jersey. Division of Administrative Procedure. New Jersey. Office of Administrative Law. Vol. 1, No. 1 (Sept. 25, 1969)-. Periodical. English. sm. $215.00 (first class mail); $125.00 (second class mail). Office Admin Law Publishing, Quakerbridge Plaza,, Building #9 CN049, Trenton NJ 08625. **Tel** (609)588-6500, FAX (609)588-3730. **LC** KFN2240; .A86. **DD** 342.749/06; 347.49026.

US/0195-3192
**NEW JERSEY REPORTER.** **Added/Corp** Center for Analysis of Public Issues. Vol. 9, No. 3, (Sept. 1979)-. Periodical. English. Six times a year (Jan., Mar., May, July, Sept., Nov.). $40.00 (one year); $72.00 (two year); $102.00 (three year). Center Analysis Public Issues, 16 Vandeventer Avenue, Princeton NJ 08540. **Tel** (609)924-9750, FAX (609)924-0363. **ED** Neil Upmeyer. **LC** JK3501; .N48. **DD** 361.6/1/09749. Index available. **Bk Rev**, (Qty: 3). **Circ:** 2,200. ***Continues*** *New Jersey Magazine, 0164-6958.*
**Desc:** A magazine specializing in coverage of New Jersey's public policy and political events and issues.
**Ind/Abst** Phys. Educ. Index.

US/0360-1048
**NEW MEXICO ALMANAC, THE.** 1975-. English. an. $2.00. J R Spencer, 2921 Axtell Street, Clovis NM 88101. **ED** J R Spencer. **LC** JK8030; .N48. **DD** 354/.72.

AT
**NEW SOUTH WALES ACTS PAMPHLETS.** English. ir. 350.00Aus$. NSW Government Information SVC, GPO Box 3896, Sydney NSW 2001 Australia. **Tel** 011 61 2 7437200.

US/1049-4200
**NEW YORK BEIJING DIRECTORY, THE.** ***Suspended.*** **VFOAT** Niu-Yue Pei-Ching Lian Lo Ming Ky. 1983-Suspended 1990. Directory. English. New York City Commission of the United Nations, 2 United Nations Plaza/27th Floor, New York NY 10017. **DD** 382.

US
**NEW YORK LEGISLATIVE SERVICE : REPORT.** **Main/Corp** New York Legislative Service, Inc. (Jan. 1, 1936)-. Periodical. English. Fifty times a year. $800.00. New York Legislative Service Inc, 299 Broadway, New York NY 10007. **Tel** (212)962-2826, FAX (212)962-1420.

US
**NEW YORK STATE CONTRACT REPORTER.** **Added/Corp** New York (State). Division for Small Business. **VFOAT** Contract Reporter. Vol. 1, No. 1 (July 3, 1989)-. Periodical. English. wk. $150.00. New York State Economic Development Department, PO Box 4452, Utica NY 13504. **Tel** (800)724-0973.

US/0737-1314
**NEW YORK STATE DIRECTORY, THE.** [N.Y. State dir.]. (1983)-. Directory. English. an. $137.00. Walker's Western Research, 1650 Borel Place, Suite 130, San Mateo CA 94402. **Tel** (800)258-5737, (415)341-1110, FAX (415)341-2351. **ED** Robert Walsh. **LC** JK3430; .N52. **DD** 353.9747002. Index available.
**Desc:** Detailed reference on New York State Government including executive, legislative and judicial branches, 25 policy areas, pac, lobbyists, chambers, education both on state universities and public schools, private parties in each area.

US/0197-3983
**NEW YORK STATE LEGISLATIVE ANNUAL.** [N.Y. state legis. annu.]. (1946)-. Periodical. English. an. $185.00. New York Legislative Service Inc, 299 Broadway, New York NY 10007. **Tel** (212)962-2826, FAX (212)962-1420. **LC** JK3401; .N48. **DD** 328.747.

US
**NEW YORK STATE MUNICIPAL BULLETIN.** Bulletin. English. Six times a year. $25.00. New York State Conference of Mayors and Municipal Officials, 119 Washington Avenue, Albany NY 12210. **Tel** (518)463-1185. **ED** Patricia Giannola. **LC** JS39. **DD** 352.0747. **Ad Acc. Circ:** 6,500.
**Desc:** Journal for NY State village and city officials. Contains summaries of legislation, conference updates, legal articles, fiscal articles, and features on villages and officials.
**Ind/Abst** Urban Aff. Abstr.

US/0197-2472
**NEW YORK STATE REGISTER, THE.** **Added/Corp** New York (State). Dept. of State. New York (State). Dept. of State. Division of Information Services. **VFOAT** State Register. Vol. 1 (Apr. 11, 1979)-. Periodical. English. wk. $40.00. Department of State / New York, 162 Washington Avenue, Albany NY 12231. **Tel** (518)474-6957. **ED** Maureen L Bigness. **LC** KFN5036; .N48. **DD** 348.747/01. **Circ:** 18,000. ***Supersedes*** *New York State Bulletin.*
**Desc:** Information on rule-making activities on New York state agencies.

NZ
**NEW ZEALAND LOCAL GOVERNMENT.** (19??)-. Periodical. English. mo. 60.00NZ$ New Zealand; 75.00NZ$ other. Trade Publications Ltd., 300 Great South Road Greenlane, Newmarket Auckland New Zealand. **Tel** 011 64 9 9293000. **ED** Chris Black. **LC** JS8331; .N47. **DD** 352.0931. **Bk Rev. Ad Acc. Circ:** 2,500 (ctrl). ***Continues*** *Local Body Review.*
**Desc:** New Zealand's only magazine serving all areas of local (i.e. municipal) government, aimed mainly at senior staff.

US/0197-2316
**NEWS - ADMINISTRATIVE CONFERENCE OF THE UNITED STATES.** **Main/Corp** United States. Administrative Conference. Periodical. English. ir (3-4 times a year). Administrative Conference of the United States, 2120 L Street NW/Suite 500, Washington DC 20037. **Tel** (202)254-7065. **Circ:** 6,000 (ctrl).
**Desc:** News of members, activities and events of the administrative conference of United States.

US/0145-2290
**NEWS DIGEST - INTERNATIONAL INSTITUTE OF MUNICIPAL CLERKS.** **Main/Corp** International Institute of Municipal Clerks. (19??)-. Periodical. English. mo. $15.00. The International Institute of Municipal Clerks, 160 North Altadena Drive, Pasadena CA 91107. **LC** JS42; .I5425. **DD** 352/.008/05. ***Continues*** *IIMC Newsletter.*

US/0042-0271
**NEWS LETTER / THE UNIVERSITY OF VIRGINIA.** [News lett. - Univ. Va.]. **Added/Corp** University of Virginia. School of Rural Social Economics. University of Virginia. Institute of Government. **VFOAT** Newsletter; University of Virginia News Letter; University of Virginia Newsletter. Vol. 1, (Nov. 23, 1918)-. Periodical. English. mo. Center for Public Service, 2015 Ivy Road, Fourth Floor, University of Virginia, Charlottesville VA 22903-1795. **Tel** (804)924-0944. **DD** 378.
**Ind/Abst** PAIS Int. Print.

US
**NEWSLETTER - LAND MANAGEMENT INFORMATION CENTER.** **Main/Corp** Minnesota Land Management Information Center. V. 1- Jan. 1978-. Newsletter. English. mo. State Planning Agency, 300 Centennial Office Building, St Paul MN 55155-1600.

US/0731-1435
**NEWSLETTER - LEAGUE OF OREGON CITIES (1980).** (NEWSLETTER / LEAGUE OF OREGON CITIES.). **Added/Corp** League of Oregon Cities. (June 1980)-. Newsletter. English. mo. $36.00. League of Oregon Cities, PO Box 928, Salem OR 93708. **Tel** (503)588-6550, FAX (503)588-6554. Each issue contains an index to its own contents (no volume index)--loose. **Bk Rev. Ad Acc. Circ:** 2,500 (ctrl). ***Continues in part*** *Information Update for Oregon Cities.*

US
**NEWSROOM DIRECTORY & GUIDE TO THE ILLINOIS ENVIRONMENTAL PROTECTION AGENCY.** **Main/Corp** Illinois Environmental Protection Agency. **VFOAT** Illinois EPA Directory/Guide. 1980-. Directory. English. an. Illinois Environmental Protection Agency, 2200 Churchill Road, Springfield IL 62706. **LC** HC107.I33; E54A. **DD** 353.97730082/321/025. Index available in last issue of volume--attached.

CN/1184-9797
**NEWSTIME - PUBLIC SERVICE ALLIANCE OF CANADA. NATIONAL COMPONENT.** (NEWSTIME / NATIONAL COMPONENT.). [Newstime - Public Serv. Alliance Can., Natl. Compon.]. **Added/Corp** Public Service Alliance of Canada. National Component. (Apr 1991)-. Periodical. English. qt. Free to members. Public Service Alliance of Canada, 233 Gilmour Street, Ottawa Ontario K2P 0P1 Canada. **Tel** (613)560-4211. **DD** 331.88. ***Continues*** *National Component News., 1182-2155.*

NR
**NIGER STATE BUDGET SPEECH.** **Main/Corp** Niger (Nigeria). Ministry of Information. English. Ministry of Information, Malu Road Apapa, Lagos Nigeria. **LC** HJ86.2.N5; N53A. **DD** 354.669/5.

NR
**NIGERIAN JOURNAL OF PUBLIC AFFAIRS, THE.** V. 1- Oct. 1970-. Periodical. English. sa. N30.00 Nigeria; $15.00 or £10.00 other. Ahmadu Bello University, Institute of Administration, PMB 1013, Zaria Nigeria. **Tel** ZARIA 32091/96. **ED** J O Egwurube. **LC** JQ3081.A1. **DD** 354/.669/0005. **Bk Rev. Ad Acc. Circ:** 2,000.
**Desc:** Attempting to expand focus of journal by accepting articles from authors within and outside Nigeria in law, economics, political science, local governments, business, and public administration.

US
**NIMLO MODEL ORDINANCE SERVICE.** **Main/Corp** National Institute of Municipal Law Officers (U.S.). English. National Institute of Municipal Law Officers, 1000 Connecticut Avenue NW/Suite 800, Washington DC 20036. **Tel** (202)466-5424.
**Desc:** A one-volume looseleaf compilation of comprehensive ordinances and annotations dealing with current problems of municipalities.

US
**NIMLO'S CONGRESSIONAL NEWS.** Vol. 1, No. 1 (May 1986)-. Periodical. English. ir. National Institute of Municipal Law Officers, 1000 Connecticut Avenue NW/Suite 800, Washington DC 20036. **Tel** (202)466-5424. ***Continues in part*** *Municipal Law Docket.*
**Desc:** A newsletter devoted to Congressional developments of interest to NIMLO. Coverage of hearings, committee meetings, floor debate and legislative enactments is provided.

US/1073-2268
**NJ VOTER.** **Main/Corp** League of Women Voters of New Jersey. **VFOAT** New Jersey Voter. (19??)-. English. ir (5 issues per year). $6.00. League of Women Voters of New Jersey, 204 West State Street, Trenton NJ 08608. **Tel** (609)394-3303. **ED** Fanny Rowe. **Circ:** 6,000.

DK/0029-1285
**NORDISK ADMINISTRATIVT TIDSSKRIFT.** (NORDISK ADMINISTRATIVT TIDSSKRIFT; UTG. AF DET NORSKE ADMINISTRATIVE FORBUND.). [Nord. adm. tidsskr.]. **Added/Corp** Nordiske Administrative Forbund. Vol. 1 (1920)-. Periodical. Danish (Norwegian and Swedish). Four times a year (Jan., Apr., July, Nov.). kr590.00. Jurist Okonomforbundets Forlag, Gothersgade 133, 1123 Copenhagen Denmark. **Tel** 011 45 1 33142920. **ED** Anne Joker. cum. index. **Bk Rev. Ad Acc. Circ:** 2,000 (ctrl).
**Desc:** For public servants and officials in Scandinavia about the public administration in Denmark, Finland, Iceland, Norway and Sweden.
**Ind/Abst** Am. Hist. Life (1971-1977); Energy Res. Abstr. (1982-); Index Foreign Leg. Per.; Int. Polit. Sci. Abstr.

US
**NORTH CAROLINA.** **See** Business.

US
**NORTH CAROLINA ADMINISTRATIVE CODE. LIST OF RULES AFFECTED / STATE OF NORTH CAROLINA, DEPARTMENT OF JUSTICE.** [NCAC]. Vol. 1, No. 1 (Feb. 2, 1981)-. Periodical. English. mo. North Carolina Department of Justice, PO Box 629, Raleigh NC 27602-0629. available in microform.

US
**NORTH CAROLINA INSIGHT. Added/Corp** North Carolina Center for Public Policy Research. Vol. 6, No. 1 (June 1983)-. Periodical. English. qt. $50.00 US; $70.00 America except US; $75.00 other. North Carolina Center for Public Policy Research, PO Box 430, Raleigh NC 27602. **Tel** (919)832-2839, FAX (919)832-2847. **ED** Michael McLaughlin. Index available. cum. index. **Pr Rev. Circ:** 1,200. ***Continues*** *NC Insight.*
**Desc:** Public policy research or state government operations in North Carolina. A non-government organization which acts as a watchdog on state government.

CN/0225-5898
**NORTHWEST TERRITORIES GAZETTE. PART 1.** (GAZETTE; PART I.). [Northwest Territ. gaz., 1]. **Main/Corp** Northwest Territories. Vol. 1-12 (Oct. 1979)-. Periodical. English (French). sm (24 issues per year). 120.00Can$. Artisan Press Ltd., Box 1566, Yellowknife, Northwest Territory, X1A 2P2 Canada. **Tel** (403)920-2794, FAX (403)873-8487. **DD** 354.719/2/0005. available on microfilm.

CN/0713-2123
**NORTHWEST TERRITORIES GAZETTE; PART II.** [Northwest Territ. gaz., 2]. **Main/Corp** Northwest Territories. V. 1- Oct. 26, 1979-. Periodical. English. bm. Culture and Communications, Government of the Northwest Territories, PO Box 1320, Yellowknife Northwest Territories X1A 2L9 Canada. **DD** 354.719/2/0005. available on microfiche; available on microfilm from Toronto Micromedia.

US/0731-2385
**NOTES - NEW YORK (N.Y.) DEPT. OF RECORDS AND INFORMATION SERVICES.** (NOTES.). Vol. 1, No. 1 (Fall 1982)-. Periodical. English. qt. $10.00 (add $5.00 for airmail outside US). New York City Department of Records & Information Services, New York NY 10007. **Tel** (212)566-0598. **ED** Joan M Nichols. **Circ:** 3,500. ***Continues*** *Notes (Municipal Reference and Research Center (New York, N.Y.)), 0027-3554.*
**Desc:** Newsletter of agency activities in NYC municipal library, archives and records management.
**Ind/Abst** Book Rev. Digest.

AT
**NOTICE PAPER / SENATE & HOUSE OF REPRESENTATIVES.** (19??)-. Government Publication. English. ir. 195.00Aus$. Australian Government Publishing Service, GPO Box 84, Canberra ACT 2601 Australia. **Tel** 011 61 6 2954411, FAX 011 61 6 2954455.

IT
**NOTIZIARIO GIURIDICO REGIONALE. See** Law.

CN/0833-0050
**NOUVEAUTES DE LA BIBLIOTHEQUE ADMINISTRATIVE.** ***Ceased.*** [Nouv. bibl. adm.]. **Main/Corp** Quebec (Province). Ministere des Communications. Bibliotheque Administrative. Vol. 1, No. 1 (Jan. 1987)-(March 1994). Periodical. English (French). Twelve times a year. Les Publications du Quebec, CP 1190, Outremont Quebec H2V 4S7 Canada. **Tel** (514)948-1222, (800)463-2100, FAX (514)278-3030. **DD** 017/.1. ***Formed by the union of*** *Sommaires de la Documentation Courante. Droit., 0824-0558; Sommaires de la Documentation Courante; Communications., 0707-8374; Sommaires de la Documentation Courante; Relations du Travail., 0707-8358* ***and*** *Sommaires de la Documentation Courante; Sciences de l'Education., 0707-8331.*

CN/0844-7535
**NOVA SCOTIA DEPARTMENT OF COMMUNITY SERVICES, THE.** [N.S. Dep. Community Serv.]. **Added/Corp** Nova Scotia. Dept. of Community Services. (1988)-. English. an. Department of Community Services, PO Box 696, Johnston Building, Prince Street, Halifax Nova Scotia B3J 2T7 Canada. **DD** 354.7160684. **Circ:** 1,200 (ctrl). ***Continues*** *Social Services for Nova Scotians, 0833-3491.*

US/1056-9081
**NRC TELEPHONE DIRECTORY.** [NRC teleph. dir.]. **Main/Corp** U.S. Nuclear Regulatory Commission. **VFOAT** Communications Information. **VAT** Nuclear Regulatory Commission Telephone Directory. (198?)-. Directory. English. sa. $16.50. Superintendent of Documents, US Government Printing Office, Washington DC 20402. **Tel** (202)275-3328, FAX (202)786-2377. **DD** 353. ***Continues*** *Telephone Directory (United States Nuclear Regulatory Commission).*

US/1060-4731
**NSI ADVISORY.** [NSI advis.]. **Added/Corp** National Security Institute (Westborough, Mass.). **VFOAT** National Security Institute's Advisory. (198?)-. Periodical. English. Twelve times a year. $298.00. National Security Institute, 57 East Main Street, Suite 217, Westborough MA 01581. **Tel** (508)366-5800. **ED** Dave Marston. **DD** 353.

US
**NTIS ALERT. PROBLEM-SOLVING INFORMATION FOR STATE & LOCAL GOVERNMENTS.** ***Title Change.*** **Added/Corp** United States. National Technical Information Service. **VFOAT** National Technical Information Service AlertProblem-Solving Information for State and Local governments; Problem-Solving Information for State and Local Governments; Problem Solving Information for State and Local Governments. Vol. 92 No. 1 Jan. (1992)-(199?). Periodical. English. wk. National Technical Information Service - NTIS, Room 2027S, 5285 Port Royal Road, Springfield VA 22161. **Tel** (703)487-4630, (703)487-4660, (703)487-4650, FAX (703)321-8547, telex 89-9405. **LC** JK2403; .N74. ***Continues*** *Problem-Solving Information for State & Local Governments, 0364-6459.* ***Merged with*** *NTIS Alert. Urban & Regional Technology & Development* ***to form*** *NTIS Alert. Regional & Urban Planning & Technology.*

US/0888-742X
**NUCLEAR MEDICINE LITERATURE UPDATING AND INDEXING SERVICE, THE.** ***Ceased.*** [Nucl. med. lit. updat. index. serv.]. (Jan. 1986)-(Dec. 1989). Periodical. English. mo. Nuclear Medicine Literature Updating and Indexing Service, 15408 Hannans Way, Rockville MD 20853. **Tel** (301)946-6590. **DD** 616.

US
**NUCLEAR REGULATORY COMMISSION ISSUANCES : OPINIONS AND DECISIONS OF THE NUCLEAR REGULATORY COMMISSION WITH SELECTED ORDERS. Main/Corp** U.S. Nuclear Regulatory Commission. Division of Technical Information and Document Control. Vol. 9 (Jan.-June 1979)-. English. mo (semiannual and quarterly indexes). $132.00 (priority), $102.00 (non-priority), $5.50 (single issues), $37.00 (semiannual index), $1.50 (quarterly index) US; $127.50; $6.88 (single issues), $46.25 (semiannual index), $1.88 (quarterly index). NRC/GPO Sales Program, US Nuclear Regulatory Commission, Washington DC 20555. **LC** HD9698.U5; A332. ***Continues*** *Nuclear Regulatory Commission Issuances (Semiannual).*
**Desc:** Contains opinions, decisions, denials, memorandum and orders of the Commission, the Atomic Safety and Licensing Appeal Board, the Atomic Safety and Licensing Board, and the Administrative Law Judge.

IT
**NUOVA AGENDA DEI COMUNI.** Editrice Caparrini Srl, C So Italia 30, 50123 Florence Italy.

IT/0393-8212
**NUOVO GOVERNO LOCALE, IL.** [Nuovo gov. locale]. **Added/Corp** Milan (Italy : Province). (1983)-. Periodical. Italian. qt. L75000 Italy; L110000 other. Franco Angeli Riviste SRL, Viale Monza 106, 20127 Milan Italy. **Tel** 011 39 2 2827651, 011 39 2 289562.
**Ind/Abst** PAIS Int. Print (1991-).

US/0275-5114
**NYAC NEWS. Main/Corp** New York State Association of Counties. **Added/Corp** New York State Association of Counties. News. **VAT** New York State Association of Counties News. Vol. 2, No. 1, (Jan. 1979)-. Periodical. English. Six times a year (Jan., Mar., May, July, Sept., Nov.). $24.00. New York State Association of Counties, 150 State Street, Albany NY 12207. **Tel** (518)465-1473. **ED** Gay Peter. **Ad Acc. Circ:** 5,000 (ctrl). ***Continues*** *New York State Association of Counties. NYSAC News and Conversationalist.*
**Desc:** This covers the New York State County Government news.

US
**NYSAC COUNTY DIRECTORY. Main/Corp** New York State Association of Counties. **VFOAT** N.Y.S.A.C. County Directory; County Directory. Began with Vol. for 1980. Directory. English. an. $5.00. New York State Association of Counties, 150 State Street, Albany NY 12207. **Tel** (518)465-1473. **LC** JS451.N75; N46A. **DD** 352/.0073. ***Continues*** *Roster - New York State Association of Counties.*

CN/0711-6349
**OCCASIONAL PAPER (INTERNATIONAL OMBUDSMAN INSTITUTE).** (OCCASIONAL PAPER ...). [Occas. pap. - Int. Ombudsman Inst.]. **Added/Corp** International Ombudsman Institute. No. 1 (July 1979)-. Periodical. English (French, Spanish and German). qt. $8.00 U.S. International Ombudsman Institute, University of Alberta / Law, Edmonton Alberta T6G 2H5 Canada. **Tel** (403)492-3196. **ED** Randall E Ivany. **LC** UNC. **DD** 351.9/1. Index available. **Circ:** 200 (ctrl).
**Ind/Abst** Hum. Rights Intern. Rep.

US/0732-507X
**OCCASIONAL PAPER - MAXWELL GRADUATE SCHOOL OF CITIZENSHIP AND PUBLIC AFFAIRS. METROPOLITAN STUDIES PROGRAM.** (OCCASIONAL PAPER / METROPOLITAN STUDIES PROGRAM, MAXWELL SCHOOL, SYRACUSE UNIVERSITY.). [Occas. paper - Maxwell Grad. Sch. Citizsh. Public Aff., Metrop. Stud. Program]. **Added/Corp** Maxwell Graduate School of Citizenship and Public Affairs. Metropolitan Studies Program. No. 1 (Aug. 1971)-. Monographic series. English. ir. Price varies per volume. Metropolitan Studies Program, 400 Maxwell Hall, Syracuse University, Syracuse NY 13244. **Tel** (315)443-3114. **LC** UNC. **DD** 307.7/64/0973. **Bk Rev. Circ:** 1,600 (ctrl).
**Desc:** Conducts research on a wide range of public policy issues including domestic, urban and regional studies, international studies and health and income security.

TU
**ODTU : GELISME DERGISI. See** Economics.

US/0196-4739
**OFF. MAN., STATE MO.** (OFFICIAL MANUAL, STATE OF MISSOURI.). [Off. man. - Mo.]. **Added/Corp** Missouri. Office of the Secretary of State. **VFOAT** Official Manual, Missouri. (1971-1972)-. English. be. Secretary of State / Missouri, State of Missouri, Jefferson City MO 65101. **LC** JK5430; .S74. **DD** 353.9778/00025. ***Continues*** *Official Manual of the State of Missouri, 0196-4739.*

SQ
**OFFICE DIRECTORY - DEPT. OF ESTABLISHMENT & TRAINING. Main/Corp** Swaziland. Dept. of Establishment & Training. **VAT** Office Directory - Department of Establishment and Training. Directory. English. Department of Establishment & Training Office Directory, PO Box 170, Mbabane Swaziland. **LC** JQ2721.A4; S95A. **DD** 354/.68/3002.

NR
**OFFICE DIRECTORY : LAGOS AREA. Main/Corp** Nigeria. Printing Division. Directory. English. 25. Federal Ministry of Information, Malu Road Apapa, Lagos Nigeria. **LC** JQ3087; .N53A. **DD** 354/.669/002.

US/0091-0090
**OFFICIAL CANDIDATES PAMPHLET. See** Political Science.

HK
**OFFICIAL CHINESE CUSTOMS GUIDE / GENERAL OFFICE OF THE CUSTOMS GENERAL ADMINISTRATION OF THE PEOPLE'S REPUBLIC OF CHINA, THE. Added/Corp** China. Hai Kuan Tsung Shu. Pan Kung Shih. **VFOAT** Chinese Customs Guide. (1985/1986)-. English. ir. Sino Hong Kong International, 101 Kings Road, Sing Pao Building 15F, North Point, Hong Kong. **Tel** 011 86 653231. **LC** LAW. **DD** 343.5105/6; 345.10356. Index available. cum. index.
**Desc:** Provides text of new China laws, regulations and other legal materials in chinese and English - side by side. Each selected law, regulation or other document is accompanied with commentary.

US
**OFFICIAL COMPILATION RULES AND REGULATIONS OF THE STATE OF GEORGIA.** English. Twelve times a year. $45.00. Office of the Secretary of State Administrative Process Division, 200 Piedmont Avenue, Floyd Building 816, Atlanta GA 30334. **Tel** (404)656-6710. **ED** George M. Scott. **Circ:** 2,100.
**Desc:** Information on administrative codes for the state of Georgia.

US
**OFFICIAL COMPILATION RULES AND REGULATIONS OF THE STATE OF TENNESSEE; CONTAINING ALL OF THE RULES APPROVED FOR PRINTING BY THE SECRETARY OF STATE, DULY COMPILED, ARRANGED AND NUMBERED AS REQUIRED BY LAW. Main/Corp** Tennessee. State Department. (1975)-. English. mo. $170.00, $20.00 renewals. Tennessee Secretary State Publishers, James K. Polk Building, Suite 500, Nashville TN 37243. **Tel** (615)741-2650, FAX (615)741-1278.

US/0160-9890
**OFFICIAL CONGRESSIONAL DIRECTORY.** (OFFICIAL CONGRESSIONAL DIRECTORY / BY W. H. MICHAEL.). **Main/Corp** United States. Congress. **Added/Corp** United States. Congress. Joint Committee on Printing. **VFOAT** Congressional Directory. 50th Congress, 1st Session (1887)-. Government Publication. English. an. $30.00 (two years). Superintendent of Documents, US Government Printing Office, Washington DC 20402. **Tel** (202)275-3328, FAX (202)786-2377. **(Subscription address:** US Government Bookstore / O'Neil Building, 2023 3rd Avenue North, Birmingham AL 35203.**) LC** JK1011. **DD** 328.73/073/025. **NLM** JK 1011 A1. **CODEN** CODIDS. ***Continues*** *United States. Congress. Congressional Directory.*

LU/0378-5041
**OFFICIAL JOURNAL OF THE EUROPEAN COMMUNITIES: DEBATES OF THE EUROPEAN PARLIAMENT.** [Off. j. Eur. Commun., Debates Eur. Parliam.]. **Added/Corp** European Parliament. **VFOAT** Debates of the European Parliament. No. 157 (Jan. 1973)-. English. mo. £400.00 UK; 425.00p Ireland. Office for Official Publications of the European Communities, 2 Rue Mercier, 2985 Luxembourg Luxembourg. **Tel** 011 352 499281, FAX 011 352 488573. **(Subscription address:** US: UNIPUB, 4611 F Assembly Drive, Lanham, MD 20706) **LC** JN32; .O36. **DD** 341.24/2. available on microfiche.
**Desc:** Consists of 2 related series, the L (legislation) and the C (information and notices), a supplement and an annex. The L series contains all the legislative acts and regulations whose publication is obligatory under the EC treaties, as well as other acts, and the C series covers the complete range of Community information other than legislation. The annex consists of the Debates of the European Parliament.

US/1066-9574
**OFFICIAL POLICY RESOLUTIONS ADOPTED AT THE ANNUAL CONFERENCE OF MAYORS.** (OFFICIAL POLICY RESOLUTIONS ADOPTED AT THE ... ANNUAL CONFERENCE OF MAYORS.). [Off. policy resolut. adopt. annu. Conf. Mayors]. **Main/Corp** United States Conference of Mayors. **VFOAT** Adopted Resolutions. (198?)-. English. an (June). $10.00. US Conference of Mayors, 1620 Eye Street NW, Washington DC 20006. **Tel** (202)293-7330, FAX (202)293-2352. **LC** JS304; .U6. **DD** 320. ***Continues*** *United States Conference of Mayors. Resolutions Adopted ... Annual Conference.*

HK
**OFFICIAL RECORD OF PROCEEDINGS / HONG KONG URBAN COUNCIL.** **Main/Corp** Hong Kong. Urban Council. (19??)-. English (Chinese). mo. Price varies. Hong Kong Government Information Service, Beaconsfield House, 4 Queens Road, Hong Kong Hong Kong. **Tel** 011 852 8428801 4, telex 61190 HKGIS. **LC** HT147.H85; H66a. **DD** 352.94/18/095125. **Circ:** 200 (ctrl).
**Desc:** Official record of proceedings of the Urban Council meeting.

FR/0252-0664
**OFFICIAL REPORT OF DEBATES - COUNCIL OF EUROPE, PARLIAMENTARY ASSEMBLY.** (OFFICIAL REPORT OF DEBATES.). [Off. rep. debates - Counc. Eur., Parliam. Assem.]. **Main/Corp** Council of Europe. Parliamentary Assembly. 26th Session, 2nd Pt. Vol. 2, Sittings 7/15 (Sept. 24-30, 1974)-. English. ir. $26.00 (per volume). Manhattan Publishing Company, PO Box 650, Croton-on-Hudson NY 10520. **Tel** (914)271-5194. **LC** JN22; .A4. **DD** 341.24/2. Index available. ***Continues*** *Council of Europe. Consultative Assembly. Official Report of Debates.*

FR/0252-0540
**OFFICIAL REPORT OF DEBATES / COUNCIL OF EUROPE, STANDING CONFERENCE OF LOCAL AND REGIONAL AUTHORITIES OF EUROPE.** **Main/Corp** Standing Conference of Local and Regional Authorities of Europe. 18th Ordinary Session (Oct. 18-20, 1983)-. English. an. $24.00. Council of Europe / Group Pact ED, Pharmacopoeia BP 907, 67029 Strasbourg Cedex 01 France. **Tel** 011 33 88 412036, FAX 011 33 88 41277181, telex 880388. **LC** JS3000; .E94A. **DD** 352.04. Index available. ***Continues*** *Official Report of Debates / Council of Europe, Conference of Local and Regional Authorities of Europe.*

AT
**OFFICIAL REPORTS OF THE PARLIAMENTARY DEBATES (HANSARD).** **Main/Corp** South Australia. Parliament. (1952)-. English. ir. 250.00Aus$. South Australian Government Printer, 282 Richmond Road, Netley SA 5037 Australia. **Tel** 011 61 8 2921311. **LC** J921; .H2. **DD** 329.942/3/02. Index available. **Circ:** 1,750. ***Continues*** *South Australia. Parliament. Official Reports of the Parliamentary Debates.*
**Desc:** Record of Parliamentary debates of both Houses of the South Australian Parliament (Hansard).

SA
**OFFICIAL SOUTH AFRICAN MUNICIPAL YEARBOOK.** **Added/Corp** South African Association of Municipal Employees. **VFOAT** Amptelike Suid-Afrikaanse Munisipale Jarrboek. (1909)-. English. an. R295.00. Gaffney Group CC, PO Box 812, Northland 2116 South Africa. **LC** JS7531; .A5.

US
**OFFICIALS OF FLORIDA MUNICIPALITIES / FLORIDA LEAGUE OF CITIES.** **Added/Corp** Florida League of Cities. Florida League of Municipalities. (1970)-. English. an (May). $25.00 (government agencies and libraries); $50.00 other. Florida League of Cities, 201 West Park Street, PO Box 1757, Tallahassee FL 32302-1757. **Tel** (904)222-9684, FAX (904)222-3806. **LC** JS451.F65; D57. ***Continues*** *Directory of Officials of Florida Municipalities.*

US/0147-2542
**OHIO DOCUMENTS.** (OHIO DOCUMENTS : A LIST OF PUBLICATIONS OF STATE DEPARTMENTS.). V. 1- Jan./Mar. 1971-. Periodical. English. qt. The State Library of Ohio, 65 South Front Street, Columbus OH 43266. **Tel** (614)644-7051. **ED** Clyde Hordusky. **DD** 015/.771. **Circ:** 600 (ctrl). ***Supersedes*** *Selected Publications of the State of Ohio.*
**Desc:** A list of Ohio publications received by the State Library of Ohio.

US/1063-990X
**OHIO REPORT (COLUMBUS, OHIO).** (OHIO REPORT.). [Ohio rep.]. **Added/Corp** Gongwer News Service, Inc. (19??)-. Periodical. English. da. $2,500.00. Gongwer News Service, 175 South 3rd Street, #230, Columbus OH 43215. **Tel** (614)221-1992, FAX (614)221-0678, (614)221-7844. **ED** Robert J. Drumheller. **DD** 349. Index Available Received separately--bound from publisher. cum. index. ctrl circ. available on an online database.
**Desc:** Provides information pertinent to legislative and state department activities.

US/0890-1007
**OKLAHOMA CONSTITUTION: NEWS FROM THE CAPITOL, THE STATE AND THE NATION, THE.** [Okla. const.]. (1979)-. Periodical. English. qt. $5.00. Oklahoma Constitution, P.O.Box 53482, Oklahoma City OK 73152. **Tel** (405)366-1125. **ED** Steve Byas. **DD** 321. **Bk Rev**, (Qty: 4). **Ad Acc. Circ:** 2,000 (ctrl).
**Desc:** Reports on Oklahoma politics, legislative actions, and related information.

US
**OKLAHOMA LEGISLATIVE DIRECTORY.** **VFOAT** Legislative Directory. (19??)-. Directory. English. be. $60.00. Oklahoma Press Service Inc., 3601 North Lincoln, Oklahoma City OK 73105. **Tel** (405)524-4421, FAX (405)524-2201. **LC** JK7130; .O44. **DD** 328.766/073/025.

CN/0840-612X
**ON BALANCE (VANCOUVER).** **See** Communication.

CN/0380-8831
**ONTARIO COUNCIL BULLETIN.** **Main/Corp** St. John Ambulance. Ontario Council. Jan. 1968-. Bulletin. English. St John Ambulance Association, 46 Wellesley Street East, Toronto Ontario Canada. ***Continues*** *Ontario Provincial Bulletin, 0380-884X.*

CN/0316-1617
**ONTARIO GOVERNMENT PUBLICATIONS MONTHLY CHECKLIST.** (ONTARIO GOVERNMENT PUBLICATIONS MONTHLY CHECKLIST. PUBLICATIONS DU GOUVERNEMENT DE L'ONTARIO LISTE MENSUELLE.). **Added/Corp** Ontario. Ministry of Government Services. Printing Services Branch. **VFOAT** Publications du Gouvernement de l'Ontario Liste Mensuelle. Vol. 1 (May 1971)-. Periodical. English. mo. $14.01. Ministry of Government Services / Treasurer of Ontario, 50 Grosvenor, Toronto Ontario M7A 1N8 Canada. **Tel** (416)326-5316. **DD** 015/.713. Index available.

CN/0841-0798
**ONTARIO PUBLIC SECTOR.** (1988)-. English. an (Apr.). 175.00Can$. Ontario Public Sector, 8278 Manitoba St, Vancouver BC V5X 3A2 Canada. **Tel** (604)482-3100, FAX (604)482-3130. **ED** Glen Edwards. Index available. **Ad Acc, Adv Mgr:** James McGillis, **Tel** (604)482-3104. **Circ:** 5,000 (ctrl).
**Desc:** A directory of official personnel in municipal, provincial, and federal government.

NE
**OPENBAAR BESTUUR.** Dutch. ir. Samson Bedrijfsinformatie, Postbus 4, 2400 HA Alphen Rij Netherlands. **Tel** 011 31 1 72066633. ***Continues*** *Tijdschrift voor Openbaar Bestuur.*

US/0732-0493
**OPERATING BUDGET - TEXAS. STATE PURCHASING AND GENERAL SERVICES COMMISSION.** (OPERATING BUDGET / BY STATE PURCHASING AND GENERAL SERVICES COMMISSION.). **Main/Corp** Texas. State Purchasing and General Services Commission. (19??)-. English. Texas State Purchasing and General Services Commission, Austin TX 78701. **LC** JK4888.A1; T46a. **DD** 353.97640072/236712.

CN/0822-1014
**OPINIONS.** (OPINIONS / OFFICE OF THE AUDITOR GENERAL OF CANADA.). [Opinions]. **Main/Corp** Canada. Office of the Auditor General. Communications Advisory Group. (June/July 1983)-. Periodical. English (French). bm. Office of the Auditor General / Ottawa, 240 Sparks Street, Ottawa Ontario K1A 0G6 Canada. **Tel** (613)995-3766 ext. 6280. **DD** 354.710072/32/05. ***Continues*** *AG, 0713-1410.*

BL
**ORCAMENTO EMPRESAS.** **Main/Corp** Minas Geraid (Brazil). Superintendencia de Orcamento. (19??)-. Portuguese. **LC** HD4095.M55; M56a. **DD** 354.81/51092.

CN/0848-2659
**ORDER PAPER AND NOTICE PAPER.** [Order pap. not. pap.]. **Main/Corp** Canada. Parliament. House of Commons. **VFOAT** Feuilleton et Feuilleton des Avis. 34th Parliament, 1st Session, No. 1/2 (Dec. 13, 1988)-. English (French). da. Queens Printer / Victoria British Columbia, 506 Government Street, Victoria British Columbia V8V 4R6 Canada. **DD** 328.71/05. ***Continues*** *Order Paper and Notices, 0317-8420.*

FR/0377-1962
**ORDERS OF DAY. MINUTES OF PROCEEDINGS - COUNCIL OF EUROPE. PARLIAMENT ASSEMBLY.** (ORDERS OF THE DAY, MINUTES OF PROCEEDINGS.). [Orders day, Minutes proc. - Counc. Eur. Parliam. Assem.]. **Main/Corp** Council of Europe. Parliamentary Assembly. **Added/Corp** Council of Europe. Parliamentary Assembly. Ordres du jour, Proces-Verbaux. **VFOAT** Ordres du Jour, Proces-Verbaux. 26th Session, 2nd Pt. (Sept. 1974)-. Proceedings. Multiple languages (English and French). ir. Manhattan Publishing Company, PO Box 650, Croton-on-Hudson NY 10520. **Tel** (914)271-5194. **LC** JN22; .A3. **DD** 341.24/2. Index available. ***Continues*** *Council of Europe. Consultative Assembly. Orders of the Day, Minutes of Proceedings, 0070-1017.*

HK
**ORDINANCES OF HONG KONG.** **Main/Corp** Hong Kong. Laws, Statutes, etc. (19??)-. Periodical. English. an. Price varies per volume. Hong Kong Government Information Service, Beaconsfield House, 4 Queens Road, Hong Kong Hong Kong. **Tel** 011 852 8428801 4, telex 61190 HKGIS.

US/0196-4577
**OREGON BLUE BOOK.** **Added/Corp** Oregon. Office of the Secretary of State. **VFOAT** Oregon Bluebook. (1933/34)-. Directory. English. be. $10.00. Secretary of State / Oregon, 158 12th Street Northeast, Salem OR 97310. **Tel** (503)378-4144, (503)378-4339, FAX (503)373-7414. **ED** Tom Bryson, Claire Levine and Judy Goard. **LC** JK9031. **Circ:** 25,000. ***Continues*** *Blue Book and Official Directory.*
**Desc:** A reference directory and almanac for facts and figures concerning state government, education, finances, economy and resources, people, history and events in Oregon.

CN/0226-286X
**ORGANIZATION OF THE GOVERNMENT OF ALBERTA.** English. an. Free. Alberta Executive Council, 305 Legislature Building, Edmonton Alberta T5K 2B7 Canada. **Tel** (403)427-9957. **LC** JL331; .O73. **DD** 354.72104. ***Continues*** *Manual of Organization Structure, 0702-9853.*

US/1069-5168
**ORGANIZATIONS OF STATE GOVERNMENT OFFICIALS DIRECTORY.** [Organ. state gov. off. dir.]. **Added/Corp** Council of State Governments. (19??)-. Directory. English. ir (published every 12-18 months). $17.50 (state officials), $25.00 (other) US. Council of State Governments, PO Box 11910, Iron Works Pike, Lexington KY 40578-1910. **Tel** (800)800-1910, (606)231-1850. **(Subscription address:** Council of State Governments, PO Box 2167, Lexington, KY 40595) **LC** JK2679; .N38. **DD** 353.9/31/06. ***Continues*** *National Organizations of State Government Officials Directory, 1051-6093.*

US/1063-9233
**ORGANIZER MAILING, THE.** [Organ. mail.]. **Added/Corp** Organize Training Center. (19??)-. Periodical. English. Four times a year (Jan., Apr., July, Oct.). $45.00 (individual); $55.00 (institutions). Organize Training Center, 442 A Vicksburg, San Francisco CA 94114. **Tel** (415)821-6180, FAX (415)821-1631. **ED** Mike Miller and Tim Sampson. **DD** 307. **Bk Rev**, (Qty: 10). **Circ:** 200 (ctrl).
**Desc:** The Organizer Mailing is a quarterly collection of reprinted articles and documents of interest ot working organizers, leaders, and support of organizing. each issue contains an exciting and informative range of articles and documents on the current activities of community and labor organizations across the country. Articles are sent loose-leaf with a table of contents, so that they may be reprinted by the subscriber for staff meetings, leadership training, staff and leadership education, and organizational mailings.

CN/0702-8210
**OTTAWA LETTER.** [Ott. lett.]. **Added/Corp** C C H Canadian Limited. Vol. 13, No. 1 (Jan. 4, 1977)-. Periodical. English. Fifty-two times a year. CCH Canadian Ltd., 6 Garamond Court, Don Mills Ontario M3C 1Z5 Canada. **Tel** (416)441-2992, FAX (416)441-3418. **DD**

320.9/71/064. ***Continues** View from Ottawa, 0049-6383.*
**Desc:** Provides news and comments on what's going on in Parliament, government departments.

II
**OUTLINE OF ACTIVITIES - GOVERNMENT OF MAHARASHTRA.**
**Main/Corp** Maharashtra (India). English. Government of Maharashtra / Government Central Press, Taredio Bombay 34 WB India. **LC** JQ620.M262; M33A. **DD** 309.2/5/0954792.

NE/0928-8503
**OVERHEIDSMANAGEMENT : VAKBLAD VOOR FINANCIEN AUTOMATISERING EN PERSONEEL 7 ORGANISATIE.** (1992)-. Trade Publication. English. Eleven times a year. Fl105. Vuga Uitgeverij B.V., Postbus 16400, Zeestraat 65, 2500 BK Gravenhage Netherlands. **Tel** 011 31 70 3614011, FAX 011 31 70 3632338. **(Subscription address:** Infolio BV, Postbus 16500, 2500 BM Den Haag Netherlands.**) ED** Gea Boschna. **Bk Rev. Ad Acc. Circ:** 2,700. available with illustrations. ***Continues** Financieel Overheidsmanagement, 0922-1026.*

NZ/0114-6971
**OVERSEAS POSTS.** [Overseas posts]. (1989)-. English. Twice a year. 21.95NZ$. Ministry of External Relations & Trade, Private Bag, Wellington New Zealand. **Tel** 64 9 410 6517, FAX 64 9 410 6329. **DD** 327.202593. **Circ:** 1,950. ***Continues** New Zealand Representatives Overseas, 0110-201X.*
**Desc:** Addresses, contact numbers and names of foreign service staff of New Zealand government offices overseas.

AT
**P S A REPORTER.** (1983)-. Public Service Association of New South Wales, GPO Box 3365, Sydney New South Wales 2001 Australia. **Tel** 02 290 1555, FAX 02 262 1623. **ED** Les Carr. **Circ:** 7,000.
**Desc:** Decisions of industrial reports.

US/1041-6323
**PA TIMES.** (PA TIMES / AMERICAN SOCIETY FOR PUBLIC ADMINISTRATION.). [PA times]. **Added/Corp** American Society for Public Administration. **VFOAT** Public Administration Times. Vol. 10, No. 17 (Sept. 1987)-. Periodical. English. Twelve times a year. $25.00; Comes also with American Society for Public Administration membership. American Society for Public Administration, 1120 G Street Northwest, Suite 700, Washington DC 20005-3885. **Tel** (202)393-7878, FAX (202)638-4952. **DD** 353. ***Continues** Public Administration Times, 0149-8797.*
**Desc:** Reports on current developments in the field of public administration. Also features employment opportunities at all levels of government and within the academic, nonprofit and private sectors.

US/0162-5160
**PA. TOWNSHIP NEWS. Added/Corp** Pennsylvania State Association of Township Supervisors. **VFOAT** Pennsylvania Township News. (1948)-. Periodical. English. mo (12 issues). $27.00. Pennsylvania Township News, 3001 Gettysburg Road, Camp Hill PA 17011. **Tel** (717)763-0930, FAX (717)763-9732. **ED** Ginni Linn. Index available. cum. index. **Ad Acc. Circ:** 12,000. ***Continues** Pennsylvania Township News.*
**Desc:** Concerns local government, and municipal management.

US/1051-4015
**PAIS INTERNATIONAL IN PRINT. See** Social Sciences-Abstracting, Bibliographies and Statistics.

US
**PAIS ON CD-ROM [COMPUTER FILE].** **See** Social Sciences-Abstracting, Bibliographies and Statistics.

●US/1072-0103
**PAIS (PEABODY, MASS.). See** Social Sciences-Abstracting, Bibliographies and Statistics.

PK
**PAKISTAN JOURNAL OF LOCAL GOVERNMENT.** V. 1- June 1974-. Periodical. English. sa. $2.00 per issue. Pakistan Group for the Study of Local Government, 252 Sarwar Shaheed Road, Karachi Pakistan. **LC** JS7091.A1; P34. **DD** 352.0549/1.

NP
**PANCAYATA DARPANA.** Nepali (Nepali). Talima Samagri Utpadana Kendra, Jawalakhel, Lalitapura Nepal. **LC** JQ1825.N45; P34.

US/0196-5786
**PAPERWORK AND RED TAPE.** (PAPERWORK AND RED TAPE; NEW PERSPECTIVES, NEW DIRECTIONS.). **Main/Corp** United States. Office of Management and Budget. June 1978-. English. sa. Office of Management and Budget, Executive Office Building, Washington DC 20503. **Tel** (202)395-3080. **LC** JK468.P34; U55A. **DD** 353.0071/4/06.

US/0033-3352
**PAR. PUBLIC ADMINISTRATION REVIEW POPULATION.** (PUBLIC ADMINISTRATION REVIEW.). [PAR. Public adm. rev.]. **Added/Corp** American Society for Public Administration. **VFOAT** PAR. Vol. 1 (Autumn 1940)-. Periodical. English. bm (6 issues). $80.00 (institution) US. American Society for Public Administration, 1120 G Street Northwest, Suite 700, Washington DC 20005-3885. **Tel** (202)393-7878, FAX (202)638-4952. **ED** David H. Rosenbloom. **LC** JK1; .P85. **DD** 350/.0005. **NLM** W1 PU101K. **[CCC].** Index available in last issue of volume--attached. cum. index. **Bk Rev. Ad Acc. Pr Rev. Circ:** 21,000 (ctrl). available on videocassette; available on microfilm and microfiche from University Microfilms International (UMI); available on an online database (file 15/Full-Text) from DIALOG. Documents available from The Genuine Article, UMI Article Clearinghouse.
**Desc:** Features articles by recognized experts in the field and provides authoritative information, research and theory.
**Ind/Abst** ABC POL SCI; ABI/INFORM Glob. Ed.; ABI Inform Ondisc (Sept. 1971-); Acad. Abstr. Full Text Elite (Sept. 1990-); Acad. Abstr. (Sept. 1990-); Acad. Ind. [Computer File] (1984-); Acad. Search (Sept. 1990-); Am. Hist. Life (1964-1971); Appl. Soc. Sci. Index Abstr.; Book Rev. Index; Bus. Index (1985-); Bus. Period. Index; Comput. Rev.; Curr. Contents Soc. Behav. Sci.; Curr. Index J. Educ.; Curr. Law Index (1980-); Expand. Acad. Index (1984-); Gen. BusinessFile (1985-); Gen. Period. Index (1985-); Hospit. Health Admin. Index; Hum. Resour. Abstr. (?-?); Index Period. Artic. Relat. Law; INFO-SOUTH Abstr.; Int. Aerosp. Abstr.; Int. Bibliogr. Sociol.; Int. Labour Doc.; J. Plan. Lit.; LABORDOC; Leg. Resour. Index (1980-); LegalTrac (1980-); Mag. Search; Middle East Abstr. Index; Newsp. Period. Abstr. (1988-); PAIS Int. Print (1991-); Res. Alert [Full Cov.]; Sage Public Adm. Abstr.; Soc. Sci. Source (Jul. 1990-); Soc. Sci. Cit. Index [Full Cov.]; Soc. Sci. Index; Soc. Sci. Index Fulltext (Nov. 1988-) [Full Txt.]; Soc. Work Abstr. [Select. Cov.]; UMI ABI/Inform--Bus. Period. Ondisc (Jan. 1988-) [Full Txt.]; U.S. Polit. Sci. Doc.; Wilson Bus. Abstr.; Work Relat. Abstr.

NE
**PARLEMENT EN KIEZER: JAARBOEK.** (1911/12)-. Dutch. ir. Martinus Nijhoff Publishers, Subsidiary of Kluwer Academic Publishers, Koraalrood 50, 2718 SC Zoetermeer Netherlands. **Tel** 011 31 79 684400. **LC** JN5873; .A3.

UK/0031-2282
**PARLIAMENTARIAN.** (THE PARLIAMENTARIAN : JOURNAL OF THE PARLIAMENTS OF THE COMMONWEALTH.). [Parliamentarian]. **Added/Corp** Commonwealth Parliamentary Association. General Council. Vol. 47, No. 1 (Jan. 1966)-. Periodical. English. Four times a year (Jan., Apr., July, Oct.). £25.00 UK; £26.00 others. Commonwealth Parliament Association, 7 Millbank, Westminister House 700, London SW1P 3JA England. **Tel** 011 44 71 799 1460. **ED** Andrew Imlach. **LC** IN PROCESS. Index Available, published separately, free-automatically sent. **Bk Rev. Ad Acc.** available on microfilm and microfiche from University Microfilms International (UMI). ***Continues** Journal of the Parliaments of the Commonwealth.*
**Desc:** Parliamentary reports from commonwealth parliaments.
**Ind/Abst** ABC POL SCI; Br. Humanit. Index; Int. Polit. Sci. Abstr.; Middle East Abstr. Index; PAIS Int. Print (1991-).

UK/0031-2290
**PARLIAMENTARY AFFAIRS.** [Parliam. aff.]. **Added/Corp** Hansard Society for Parliamentary Government. Vol. 1 (Winter 1947)-. Periodical. English. qt. £58.00 UK and Europe; $105.00 other. Oxford University Press, Walton Street, Oxford OX2 6DP England. **Tel** 011 44 865 56767, FAX 011 44 865 267773, telex 837330 OXPRES G. **(Subscription address:** Oxford University Press / USA, Journals Marketing Department, Oxford University Press, 2001 Evans Road, Cary NC 27513.**) ED** F. F. Ridley. **LC** JN101; .P3. **DD** 328.42. **[CCC].** Index available. **Pr Rev. Circ:** 1,500. available on microfilm and microfiche from University Microfilms International (UMI). Documents available from The Genuine Article, UMI Article Clearinghouse.
**Desc:** Covers all aspects of government and politics directly or indirectly connected with parliament and parliamentary systems in Britain and throughout the world.
**Ind/Abst** ABC POL SCI; Acad. Abstr. Full Text Elite (Jan. 1992-); Acad. Abstr. (Jan. 1992-); Acad. Search (Jan. 1992-); Am. Hist. Life (1954-); Br. Humanit. Index; Crim. Penol. Police Sci. Abstr.; Curr. Contents Soc. Behav. Sci.; Expand. Acad. Index (1989-); INFO-SOUTH Abstr.; Int. Polit. Sci. Abstr.; Mag. Search; Middle East Abstr. Index; Newsp. Period. Abstr. (1991-); Res. Alert [Full Cov.]; Soc. Plann. Policy Dev. Abstr.; Soc. Sci. Source (Jan. 1992-); Soc. Sci. Cit. Index [Full Cov.]; Soc. Sci. Index; Soc. Sci. Index Fulltext (Oct. 1988-) [Full Txt.]; Sociol. Abstr.

CN/0821-5154
**PARLIAMENTARY ALERT.** [Parliam. alert]. **Added/Corp** Henry & Gray Inc. Canada. Parliament. (1982)-. Periodical. English. Thirty-six times a year. 237.00Can$. ECL Publishing, 155 Queen Street, Suite 1100, Ottawa ONT K1P 6L1 Canada. **Tel** (613)236-9522, FAX (613)234-5210. **DD** 328.71/005.

UK
**PARLIAMENTARY AND EUROPEAN COMMUNITY NEWS BULLETIN.** Bulletin. English. Forty times a year. £95.00 US, Canada, Australia, New Zealand, Far East; £85.00 EEC countries; £75.00 UK; £90.00 other Europe. PMS Publications, 19 Douglas Street, London SW1P 4PA England. **Tel** 011 44 71 2338282, FAX 011 44 71 8219352. **ED** Thomas P McLaughlin.

UK/0309-8826
**PARLIAMENTARY DEBATES (HANSARD). HOUSE OF COMMONS OFFICIAL REPORT.** [Parliam. debates, Hansard, House Commons off. rep.]. **Main/Corp** Great Britain. Parliament. House of Commons. **VFOAT** House of Commons Official Report. (1942)-. English. wk. £1275.00 (daily), £775.00 (weekly). Her Majesty's Stationery Office, 51 Nine Elms Lane, London SW8 5DR England. **Tel** 011 44 71 873 8459, 011 44 71 873 8499, FAX 011 44 71 873 8499, 011 44 71 873 8456, telex 297138. **(Subscription address:** Her Majestys Stationery Offic, PO Box 276 Public Centre, London SW8 5DT England) **LC** J301; .K22. cum. index. ***Continues** Parliamentary Debates. House of Commons Official Report, 0309-9016.*

UK/0309-8834
**PARLIAMENTARY DEBATES (HANSARD). HOUSE OF LORDS OFFICIAL REPORT, THE.** [Parliam. debates, Hansard, House Lords off. rep.]. **Main/Corp** Great Britain. Parliament. House of Lords. **VFOAT** House of Lords Official Report. 5th Ser., Vol. 130 (1943/1944)-. Periodical. English. wk. £615.00 (daily), £310.00 (weekly). Her Majesty's Stationery Office, 51 Nine Elms Lane, London SW8 5DR England. **Tel** 011 44 71 873 8459, 011 44 71 873 8499, FAX 011 44 71 873 8499, 011 44 71 873 8456, telex 297138. **(Subscription address:** Her Majestys Stationery Offic, PO Box 276 Public Centre, London SW8 5DT England) cum. index. ***Continues** Parliamentary Debates, House of Lords Official Report, 0309-9024.*

FJ
**PARLIAMENTARY DEBATES (HANSARD), THE SENATE. Main/Corp** Fiji. Parliament. Senate. English. $0.75. Government of Fiji / Bureau of Statistics, Box 2221, Suva Fiji Islands. **Tel** 011 679 315144. **LC** J961; .H27A. **DD** 328.96/11/02.

NZ
**PARLIAMENTARY DEBATES. HOUSE OF REPRESENTATIVES. Main/Corp** New Zealand. Parliament. 1854/55-. English. qt. $31.53. Government Printing Office / New Zealand, 10 Mulgrave Street, Wellington New Zealand. **Tel** 011 64 4 4737211, FAX 011 64 4 734943, telex GOVPRINT NZ 31320.

AT/0519-6124
**PARLIAMENTARY DEBATES, HOUSE OF REPRESENTATIVES, WEEKLY HANSARD. Main/Corp** Australia. Parliament. House of Representatives. 20th Parliament, 1st Session, 7th Period, Vol. 1 (1953)-. Government Publication. English. wk. 90.00Aus$. Australian Government Publishing Service, GPO Box 84, Canberra ACT 2601 Australia. **Tel** 011 61 6 2954411, FAX 011 61 6 2954455. **LC** J905; .K2. ***Supersedes in part** Australia. Parliament. Parliamentary Debates. Senate and House of Representatives.*
**Ind/Abst** Aust. Educ. Index.

AT/0519-6140
**PARLIAMENTARY DEBATES, SENATE, WEEKLY HANSARD. Main/Corp** Australia. Parliament. Senate. 20th Parliament, 1st Sess., 7th Period (Sept. 8, 1953)-. Government Publication. English. wk. 90.00Aus$. Australian Government Publishing Service, GPO Box 84, Canberra ACT 2601 Australia. **Tel** 011 61 6 2954411, FAX 011 61 6 2954455. **LC** J905; .H25. **DD** 328.94/02. Index Available, published separately, free-automatically sent. ***Supersedes in part** Australia. Parliament. Parliamentary Debates Senate and House of Representatives.*
**Ind/Abst** Aust. Educ. Index.

AT/0155-6290
**PARLIAMENTARY DEBATES SYDNEY.** [Parliam. debatesSyd.]. (1879)-. Periodical. English. wk. Government Printing Office / Australia, PO Box 4050, Sydney NSW 2001 Australia. **DD** _a328.944.
**Ind/Abst** Aust. Educ. Index.

●CN/1188-8652
**PARLIAMENTARY DIRECTORY (OTTAWA. 1992).** (PARLIAMENTARY DIRECTORY.). [Parliam. dir.]. **Added/Corp** Publinet. **VFOAT** Publinet's Parliamentary Directory. (1992)-. Directory. English. $200.00 per volume. Publinet, 130 Slater Street, 11th Floor, Ottawa Ontario K1P 6E2 Canada. **DD** 328.71/0025.

CN/0709-4582
**PARLIAMENTARY GOVERNMENT. See** Political Science.

# Public Administration

UK/0264-2824
**PARLIAMENTARY HISTORY : A YEARBOOK.** [Parliam. hist.]. Vol. 1 (1982)-. English. Three times a year. £59.00 UK & Europe; $112.00 US; £68.00 other. Edinburgh University Press, 22 George Square, Edinburgh EH8 9LF Scotland. **Tel** 011 44 31 650 6207, FAX 011 44 31 662 0053. **ED** Clyve Jones. **LC** JN500; .P29. **DD** 328.41/005. **[CCC].** **Bk Rev.** **Ad Acc,** **Adv Mgr:** Kathryn MacLean. **Circ:** 500. available on microfilm and microfiche from University Microfilms International (UMI).
**Desc:** Research articles and papers of a more general appeal on all aspects of parliamentary history (including the Scottish and Irish parliaments) from the Middle Ages to the twentieth century, covering parliamentary management, political structure, elections and the electorate, architecture and representative art of the various parliaments.
**Ind/Abst** Am. Hist. Life (1982-); Br. Humanit. Index; Romant. Move.

US/0362-8469
**PASSPORT OFFICE WORKLOADS AND ACCOMPLISHMENTS.** **Main/Corp** United States. Passport Office. **Added/Corp** United States. Passport Office. Workloads and Accomplishments. (19??)-. English. an. US Passport Office, 1425 K Street NW Room 338, Washington DC 20524. **LC** KF4794.5; .A853. **DD** 353.008/9.

US/0899-9252
**PATHWAYS (CHESTNUT HILL, MASS.).** (PATHWAYS : A QUARTERLY PUBLICATION OF THE PATHFINDER FUND.). **Added/Corp** Pathfinder Fund. (Summer 1986)-. Periodical. English. qt. Pathfinder Fund, 850 Boylston Street, Chestnut Hill MA 02167. **DD** 351. **NLM** W1; PA963FH. **Continues** Pathpapers, 0738-6265.

US/0161-2964
**PAY STRUCTURE OF THE FEDERAL CIVIL SERVICE.** See Economics-Labor.

●US/1059-2024
**PBC GOVERNMENT PROGRAMS NEWSLETTER.** **VFOAT** Government Programs Newsletter; PBC Government Programs Newsletters. **VAT** Publishing and Business Consultants Government Programs Newsletter. (1992)-. Newsletter. English. qt. Publishing & Business Consultants, PO Box 75392, Los Angeles CA 90075. **Tel** (213)732-3477, FAX (213)732-9123.

US
**PEER ANNUAL REPORT AND CUMULATIVE SUMMARIES OF REPORTS ISSUED THROUGH ... .** English. an. Free. PEER Committee, Mississippi Legislature, PO Box 1204, Jackson MS 39205. **Tel** (601)359-1226. **ED** Ava L Welborn. **LC** JK4674; .P43. **DD** 328.762/07456/05. cum. index.

US
**PENNSYLVANIA REPORT.** Periodical. English. bw. **Continues** Pennsylvania Political Report, 0882-0570.

US/0146-5260
**PENNSYLVANIA STATE EMPLOYES' RETIREMENT SYSTEM.** **Main/Corp** Pennsylvania. State Employes' Retirement Board. (19??)-. English. ir. Pennsylvania State Employees Retirement System, 204 Labor & Industry Building, Harrisburg PA 17120. **LC** JK3660.P; P45a. **DD** 331.2/52/09748.

US/0031-4714
**PENNSYLVANIAN.** **Added/Corp** Associated Institutes of Government of Pennsylvania Universities. Pennsylvania State Association of Boroughs. Vol. 1 (June 1962)-. Periodical. English. mo. $18.00 US; $31.00 other. Local Pennsylvanian, 2941 North Front Street, Harrisburg PA 17110. **Tel** (717)236-9526, FAX (717)236-8164. **ED** Susan Wolfe. **LC** JS39; .P4. **DD** 352/.0009748. Index available. cum. index. **Ad Acc.** **Circ:** 7,000. available on microfilm from University Microfilms International (UMI). **Supersedes** Assessors' Newsletter; Authority; Borough Bulletin; Hub; Pennsylvania League of Cities; Township Commissioner.
**Desc:** Educational and informative needs of local government officials, particularly pertaining to the practical application of new administrative and program development and legislative findings.
**Ind/Abst** Urban Aff. Abstr.

MY
**PENYATA TAHUNAN - SURUHANJAYA PERKHIDMATAN AWAM NEGERI PERAK.** **Main/Corp** Perak. Suruhanjaya Perkhidmatan Awam. Malay. Suruhanjaya Perkhidmatan Awam Negeri Perak, 17 Jalan Douglas, Ipoh Malaysia. **LC** HD2768.M35; P476.

US/0145-7586
**PEOPLE'S REPUBLIC OF CHINA BIOGRAPHICAL APPEARANCES.** **Main/Corp** Harvard University. East Asian Research Center. English. mo. East Asian Research Center, Harvard University, Cambridge MA 02138. **LC** JQ1507; .H37A. **DD** 354/.51/002.

II
**PEOPLES SECTOR.** See Business.

BL
**PERFIL.** **VFOAT** Perfil da Administracao do Estado de Sao Paulo. April 1972-. Portuguese. $25.00. Sociedade Editorial Viscao, rua 7 de Abril 345 30 Andar, Sao Paulo Brazil. **LC** JL2499.S199; P4A.

II
**PERFORMANCE BUDGET - WEST BENGAL STATE ELECTRICITY BOARD.** **Main/Corp** West Bengal State Electricity Board. English. an. West Bengal State Electricity Board, 48/1 Diamond Harbour Road, Calcutta-700 027 India. **LC** HD9685.I44; W478A. **DD** 354.54/1400722253.

CE
**PERFORMANCE REPORT - MINISTRY OF PUBLIC ADMINISTRATION AND HOME AFFAIRS.** **Main/Corp** Sri Lanka. Rajya Paripalana Ha Svadesa Katayutu Amatyamsaya. (19??)-. English. Ministry of Public Administration and Home Affairs, Independence Square, Colombo 7 Ceylon. **LC** JQ656; .Z75a. **DD** 354.549/3/0005.

US/0360-9405
**PERFORMANCE REPORT TO THE LEGISLATURE- LEGISLATIVE BUDGET BOARD.** (PERFORMANCE REPORT TO THE LEGISLATURE.). **Main/Corp** Texas. Legislative Budget Board. 1st- 1975-. English. Box 12666 Capital Station, Austin TX 78711. **LC** JK4835; .T45A. **DD** 353.9/764.

CN/0712-3019
**PERIODICITE.** (PERIODICITE : BULLETIN DE LIAISON DE LA CITE DE DRUMMONDVILLE.). [Periodicite]. Vol. 1, No. 1-. Bulletin. French. ir. Periodicite Hotel de Ville, 413 rue Lindsay, Drummondville Quebec J2B 1G8 Canada. **DD** 352.9714/563.

US
**PERS/ALRA INFORMATION BULLETIN.** See Business-General Management.

CN/0715-5514
**PERSONNEL (OTTAWA).** (PERSONNEL / CANADIAN PUBLIC PERSONNEL MANAGEMENT ASSOCIATION.). [Personnel]. **Main/Corp** Canadian Public Personnel Management Association. Ottawa-Hull Chapter. July 1978-. Periodical. English (French). Free to members. Canadian Public Personnel Management Association, PO Box 2179, Station D, Ottawa Ontario K1P 5W4. **DD** 354.71001/006/071384. **Continues** International Personnel Management Association. Ottawa-Hull Chapter. Personnel, 0715-5514.

CN/0316-5388
**PERSPECTIVE (EDMONTON).** Title Change. (PERSPECTIVE.) July 1974-. Periodical. English. mo. Alberta Union of Provincial Employees, 10975-124 Street, Edmonton Alberta T5M 0J2 Canada. **DD** 354/.7123/00173. **Supersedes** Civil Service Association of Alberta. News, 0316-5396. **Continued by** Impact, 0703-6922.

●CN/1186-7620
**PERSPECTIVE REGIONALE DE DEVELOPPEMENT DE LA MAIN-D'OEUVRE POUR L'ANNEE.** [Perspect. reg. dev. main-d'oeuvre]. **Main/Corp** Quebec (Province). Commission de Formation Professionnelle de la Main-d'Oeuvre. Region de Quebec, Chaudiere-Appalaches et Nord du Quebec. (1992)-. French. **DD** 354.714083.

US
**PERSPECTIVES.** (PERSPECTIVES : A BIENNIAL REPORT OF NEVADA STATE AGENCIES.). English. be. $15.00. Nevada Department of Administration, Planning Office, Capitol Complex, Carson City NV 89710. **Tel** (702)687-4065, FAX (702)687-3983. Index available. **Circ:** 750. **Continues** Catalogue of State Programs - Nevada. State Planning Board.
**Desc:** Biennial report of Nevada state agencies purposes, activities and publications.

US/0743-0388
**PERSPECTIVES (ARLINGTON, VA.).** (PERSPECTIVES.). [Perspectives]. **Added/Corp** Close Up Foundation. (19??)-. English. an. $15.95. Close Up Foundation, 44 Canal Center Plaza, Alexandria VA 22314. **Tel** (800)765-3131, (703)706-3300, FAX (703)892-1118. **ED** Patricia Bandy. **LC** JK1; .P44. **DD** 320.9/73.
**Desc:** A collection of 35 stimulating articles written by the former president Ronald Reagan, members of Congress, respected media professionals, lobbyists and government observers.

●CN/1188-3006
**PERSPECTIVES / COMMISSAIRE A L'INFORMATION ET A LA PROTECTION DE LA VIE PRIVEE/ONTARIO.** [Perspect. - Commis. inf. prot. vie privee/Ont.]. **Main/Corp** Commissaire a l'Information et a la Protection de la Vie Privee/Ontario. Vol. 1, No 1, (Winter 1992)-. Periodical. French. qt. **DD** 342.713. **Continues** Bulletin (Commissaire a l'Information et a la Protection de la Vie Privee/Ontario)., 0840-8041.

FR
**PERSPECTIVES ET REALITES.** Periodical. French. 20.00. 41 rue de la Bienfaisance, 75008 Paris France. **LC** JN2594.2.A3; P47. **DD** 320.4/44/083.

CN/0710-085X
**PETIT RAPPORTEUR DE STONEHAM, TEWKESBURY ET ST-ADOLPHE, LE.** [Petit rapp. Stoneham, Tewkesbury St-Adolphe]. Periodical. French. bm. Free. Corp Municipale des Cantons Unis de Stoneham et Teskesbury, Quebec G0A 4P0 Canada. **DD** 352.0714/47.

PH/0031-7675
**PHILIPPINE JOURNAL OF PUBLIC ADMINISTRATION.** [Philipp. j. public adm.]. **Added/Corp** University of the Philippines. College of Public Administration. University of the Philippines. Institute of Public Administration. University of the Philippines. Graduate School of Public Administration. Vol. 1 (Jan. 1957)-. Periodical. English. qt. $35.00. College of Public Administration, University of the Philippines, PARDEC/SAAC Building, Diliman, PO Box 198, Quezon City 1101 Philippines. **ED** Victoria A Bautista. **LC** JA26; .P5. **DD** 350/.0005. Index available. cum. index. **Bk Rev.** **Circ:** 1,000 (ctrl). available on microfilm and microfiche from University Microfilms International (UMI).
**Desc:** Publishes articles which contribute to the advancement of public administration in general, with particular emphasis on the Philippines, Asia and the Third World.
**Ind/Abst** ABC POL SCI; Am. Hist. Life (1970-1980); Index Philip. Period.; Int. Bibliogr. Sociol.; Int. Polit. Sci. Abstr.; PAIS Int. Print (1991-?); Soc. Plann. Policy Dev. Abstr.; Sociol. Abstr.

●CN/1187-3264
**PLAN - BRITISH COLUMBIA. RESOURCE MANAGEMENT BRANCH.** See Earth Sciences.

US
**PLAN FOR ILLINOIS DEPARTMENT OF REHABILITATION SERVICES.** **Main/Corp** Illinois. Dept. of Rehabilitation Services. **VFOAT** Data Report. English. an. 623 East Adam, PO Box 1587, Springfield IL 62705. **Tel** (217)785-3893. **LC** KHD8243.5A49. **DD** 353.97730083/4.
**Desc:** Human Services Plan prepared annually outlining proposed programs and services for people with disabilities in Illinois for each fiscal year.

BL/0103-4138
**PLANEJAMENTO E POLITICAS PUBLICAS.** **Added/Corp** Instituto de Planejamento Economico e Social. (1989)-. Periodical. Portuguese. Twenty-four times a year. IPEA Servicio Editorial / Instituto de Pesquisa Economica y Aplicada, Av P Antonio Carlos 51-14 Andar, CP 2672, 20020 010 Rio de Janeiro Brazil. **Tel** 011 55 21 2925141. **LC** HC186; .P54. **Ind/Abst** PAIS Int. Print.

UK
**PLANNING.** (1972)-. Newspaper. English. wk (Published on Fridays). £28.00 UK; £35.00 Europe & North America; £50.00 Australia & Japan; £45.00 other. Ambit Publications Ltd, Suite 1 Fullers Court, 40 Lower Quay Street, Gloucester GL1 2LW England. **Tel** 011 44 452 417553, FAX 011 44 452 423430. **ED** Bryan Johnston. Index available. cum. index. **Bk Rev.** **Ad Acc,** **Adv Mgr:** Prue Warne, **Tel** 011 44 384 373421. **Circ:** 5,800.
**Desc:** News and information journal for the whole planning and environment profession. Totally independent.

US
**PLANNING & PUBLIC POLICY.** **VAT** Planning and Public Policy. V. 1 (Winter 1974/75)-. Periodical. English. Three times a year. $5.00. University Illinois at Urbana Champagne, 907 1/2 West Nevada Street, Dept. URP, Urbana IL 61801. **Tel** (217)333-3890, FAX (217)244-1717. **ED** Albert Guttenberg. **Circ:** 5,000 (ctrl).
**Desc:** Urban and regional planning and policy issues.

US/0163-3333
**POCKET DIRECTORY OF THE CALIFORNIA LEGISLATURE.** **Added/Corp** Capitol Enquiry. (1975)-. Directory. English. an. $11.95. Capitol Enquiry, 1228 North Street, Suite 10, Sacramento CA 95814. **Tel** (916)442-1434, FAX (916)442-1260. **ED** Allen E Toon. **Circ:** 20,000.
**Desc:** Contains legislators' capitol and district office

addresses, phone numbers and staff, all committee assignments, basic biographical and district information; also lists state constitutional officers and the California congressional delegation.

US/0032-2318
**POINT OF VIEW (CLEVELAND).** (POINT OF VIEW.). (1968?)-. Periodical. English. ir (21 issues). $50.00. Point of View, PO Box 99530, Cleveland OH 44199. **Tel** (216)321-2757. **ED** Roldo Bartimole. **Circ:** 1,200. available on microfilm and microfiche from University Microfilms International (UMI).
**Desc:** Examines local government, business, and news media and how they inter-relate to make public decisions.

UK/0305-5736
**POLICY AND POLITICS. See** Political Science.

US
**POLICY AND PROCEDURES MANUAL FOR GUIDANCE OF FEDERAL AGENCIES. TITLE 4. CLAIMS. Main/Corp** United States. General Accounting Office. **VFOAT** GAO Manual for Guidance of Federal Agencies. Claims. Periodical. English. US General Accounting Office / District of Columbia, 441 G Street NW, Room 4528, Washington DC 20548. **Tel** (202)275-2812.

US
**POLICY BRIEF / WASHINGTON RESEARCH COUNCIL. Added/Corp** Washington Research Council. (Feb. 19, 1991)-. Periodical. English. Washington Research Council, 1301 5th Avenue, Suite 2810, Olympia WA 98101-2603. **Tel** (206)467-7088, (800)445-1086, FAX (206)467-6957. **LC** JK9201; .P82. ***Continues** Public Policy Brief.*

●US
**POLICY COUNSEL. Added/Corp** Council for National Policy (U.S.). (Spring 1992)-. Periodical. English. Twice a year (Feb., Sept.). $10.00. Council for National Policy, 3030 Clarendon Boulevard, Suite 340, Arlington VA 22201. **Tel** (703)525-8822, FAX (703)525-7237. **ED** Morton Blackwell. **LC** JK1; .P655. **Circ:** 3,000 (ctrl).
**Desc:** Educational lectures on public policy issues.

US
**POLICY FORUM / UNIVERSITY OF ILLINOIS AT URBANA-CHAMPAIGN, INSTITUTE OF GOVERNMENT AND PUBLIC AFFAIRS. Added/Corp** University of Illinois at Urbana-Champaign. Institute of Government and Public Affairs. Vol 1 No. 1 (1988)-. Periodical. English. qt. University of Illinois / Government, Urbana-Champaign Campus, Institute of Government and Public Affairs, 1201 West Nevada Street, Urbana IL 61801. **Tel** (217)333-3340, FAX (217)244-4817. **ED** David Chicoine. **Circ:** 750. ***Continues** Illinois Government Research.*

US/0160-7456
**POLICY POSITIONS. Main/Corp** National Governors' Association. (197?)-. English. Twice a year (Published in the Fall with Winter supplement). $15.00. National Governors Association, 444 North Capitol Street, Suite 267, Washington DC 20001. **Tel** (202)624-5300. **LC** JK2403; .N36a. **DD** 353.9. ***Continues** National Governors' Conference. Policy Positions of the National Governors' Conference, 0361-7262.*

US/0160-7456
**POLICY POSITIONS. WINTER MEETING SUPPLEMENT. Main/Corp** National Governors' Association. English. $2.00. National Governors Association, 444 North Capitol Street, Suite 267, Washington DC 20001. **Tel** (202)624-5300. **LC** JK2403; .N36A SUPPL 2. **DD** 353.9.

US/0196-0369
**POLICY RESEARCH PROJECT REPORT. Main/Corp** Lyndon B. Johnson School of Public Affairs. No. 1-. English. ir. Lyndon B Johnson School of Public Affairs, University of Texas, Austin TX 79112.

US/0190-292X
**POLICY STUDIES JOURNAL. See** Political Science.

US/0278-4416
**POLICY STUDIES REVIEW. See** Political Science.

US/1069-093X
**POLITICAL ARCHIVES OF RUSSIA. *Title Change.* See** Political Science-Socialism, Communism, Anarchism, Utopianism.

NE
**POLITIEK MEMO.** (19??)-. Dutch. an. Libresso BV, Postbus 878, 7400 GA Deventer Netherlands. **Tel** 011 31 5700 47421. **LC** JN5703; .P64.

BW
**POLITINFORMATOR I AGITATOR. Added/Corp** Kamunistychnaia Partyia Belarusi. Tsentralny Kamitet. (1932)-. Periodical. Russian. sm. 0.06rub. Izdatelstvo TSK KP Belorussii, Leninskii Prospekt 77, 220041 Minsk Byelarus. **LC** JN6598.K86; P64.

●NQ
**POPOL-NA. Added/Corp** Fundacion POPOL-NA para la Promocion y el Desarrollo Municipal. **VFOAT** Revista POPOL-NA. Vol. 1, No. 1 (Apr./June 1992)-. Periodical. Spanish. qt. $20.00 Latin America; $25.00 other. Fundacion Popol-Na para la Promocion y el Desarollo Municipal, Apdo., Postal 4611, Plaza Espana, 3 1/2 abajo, Managua Nicaragua. **Tel** 660605, FAX 660133.

US/0032-4515
**POPULAR GOVERNMENT. See** Political Science.

US/0748-2310
**PORTER'S GUIDE TO CONGRESSIONAL ROLL CALL VOTES. HOUSE.** [Porter's guide Congr. roll call votes, House]. **VFOAT** Guide to Congressional Roll Call Votes. House; Porter's Guide. House. (1983)-. English. qt. $250.00. Legislative Information Group Press, 1718 Connecticut Avenue NW/Suite 410, Washington DC 20009. **Tel** (301)270-8939. **ED** Allison I Porter. **LC** JK1319; .P67. **DD** 328.73/0775. Index available. **Bk Rev.** ctrl circ.
**Desc:** Reference books on congressional voting. Includes comprehensive indexes, vote descriptions, and member listings for 1983 and 1984 house and senate sessions.

US
**POSITION-CLASSIFICATION STANDARDS FOR WHITE COLLAR POSITIONS UNDER THE GENERAL SCHEDULE.** Periodical. English. $230.00 US; $287.50 other. US Office of Personnel Management / Office of Classification, 1900 E Street NW/Room 7H29, Washington DC 20415. **Tel** (202)653-5496. **(Subscription address:** Superintendent of Documents, US Government Printing Office, Washington, DC 20402**)** **Circ:** 20,000.
**Desc:** Occupational job evaluation for federal internal personnel management indeterminate - irregular.

IT
**POTERE LOCALE, IL.** (19??)-. Periodical. Italian. sm. L220000. Lega per le Autonomie e I Poteri Locali, Via C Balbo N 43, 00184 Rome Italy. **Tel** 011 39 6 4740041, 011 39 6 484710. **LC** JS5701; .P68. **DD** 352/.0072/0945.

●CN/1183-482X
**POUVOIRS PUBLICS AU QUEBEC.** (REPERTOIRE DESCRIPTIF. LES POUVOIRS PUBLICS AU QUEBEC.). [Pouvoirs publics Que.]. **Added/Corp** Alliance Champlain. **VFOAT** Pouvoirs Publics au Quebec. (Ed. 1991/1992)-. French. be. 24.95Can$. Quebec Dans Le Monde, CP 8503, Sainte-Foy Quebec G1V 4N5 Canada. **Tel** (418)659-5540, FAX (418)659-4143. **DD** 354.714/00025.

II
**PRASHASNIKA. VFOAT** Prasasanika. English (Hindi). qt. Rs40.00 India; $10.00 US. HCM State Institute of Public Administration, Malviya Hagar, Jaipur 302004 India. **Tel** 64003-6, 365-465 RIPA IN. **ED** Pawan Chopra, V K Arora, K K Parnami. **LC** JA26; .P7. **Bk Rev. Circ:** 500.
**Desc:** A multi-disciplinary forum for exchange of ideas, facts and experiences among administrators and academicians concerned with public affairs. It examines issues related to social change, economic development, and administrative processes, and is meant to serve academics and professionals engaged in research in training, public systems and administrative science.

US
**PRELIMINARY DETERMINATION OF EPICENTERS (WEEKLY).** (PRELIMINARY DETERMINATION OF EPICENTERS / U.S. DEPARTMENT OF THE INTERIOR, GEOLOGICAL SURVEY.). **Added/Corp** Geological Survey (U.S.). (19??)-. Government Publication. English. mo. $20.00 domestic; $25.00 other. Superintendent of Documents, US Government Printing Office, Washington DC 20402. **Tel** (202)275-3328, FAX (202)786-2377.
**Desc:** Lists earthquakes recorded throughout the world, during each monthly period by date and time and with preliminary data on location, depth and magnitude. Suited to earth science courses and for statistical studies of seismicity.

ES
**PRESENCIA. Added/Corp** Centro de Investigaciones Tecnologicas y Cientificas (San Salvador, El Salvador). Vol. 1, No. 1 (Apr./June 1988)-. Periodical. Spanish. Centro de Investigaciones Tecnologicas y Cientificas - CENITEC, 85 Av. North, 905 y 15 CP, Col. Escalon, San Salvador, El Salvador. **LC** F1481; .P74. **DD** 972.84/005.
**Ind/Abst** PAIS Int. Print.

FR/0759-2744
**PRESIDENCE DE LA REPUBLIQUE.** [Pres. Repub.]. (1983)-. Periodical. French. ir. 1600.00F. Societe Generale de Presse et d'Editions, 13 Avenue de l'Opera, 75001 Paris France. **Tel** 011 33 1 40151789. **UDC** 354(44).

US/0360-4918
**PRESIDENTIAL STUDIES QUARTERLY.** [Pres. stud. q.]. **Added/Corp** Center for the Study of the Presidency. Vol. 4, No. 2, (Spring 1974)-. Periodical. English. Four times a year. $55.00 (institutions) US; $60.00 other. Center for the Study of the Presidency, 208 East 75th Street, New York NY 10021. **Tel** (212)249-1200, FAX (212)628-9503. **ED** R. Gordon Hoxie. **LC** JK501; .C44. **DD** 353.03/13. **Bk Rev. Ad Acc. Circ:** 12,500 (ctrl). available on microfilm and microfiche from University Microfilms International (UMI). Documents available from UMI Article Clearinghouse. ***Continues** Center House Bulletin.*
**Desc:** Presidency, Congress and major public policy issues including foreign and national security affairs and domestic policies; also decision making and constitutional concerns.
**Ind/Abst** ABC POL SCI; Acad. Abstr. Full Text Elite (Jan. 1992-); Acad. Abstr. (Jan. 1992-); Acad. Search (Jan. 1992-); Am. Hist. Life (1977-); Book Rev. Index; Commun. Abstr.; Expand. Acad. Index (1989-); Index Period. Artic. Relat. Law; INFO-SOUTH Abstr.; Int. Bibliogr. Sociol.; Int. Polit. Sci. Abstr.; Mag. Search; Middle East Abstr. Index; Newsp. Period. Abstr. (1991-); PAIS Int. Print (1991-); Sage Public Adm. Abstr.; Soc. Sci. Source (Jan. 1992-); Soc. Sci. Index; Soc. Sci. Index Fulltext (Fall 1988-) [Full Txt.]; U.S. Polit. Sci. Doc.; West. Hist. Q.

US
**PRESIDENT'S TEAM. *Suspended.*** (19??)-(19??). English. ir. Braddock Publications, 1001 Connecticut Avenue NW, Washington DC 20036. **Tel** (202)296-1317, FAX (202)296-1338. ***Continues** The Executive Bio-Pictorial Directory, 0272-345X.*

SP
**PREVIEW OF THE INSTITUTO NACIONAL DE HIDROCARBUROS ANNUAL REPORT FOR ... . Main/Corp** Instituto Nacional de Hidrocarburos (Spain). Spanish (English). an. Repsol S A, Paseo de la Castellana 89, Madrid 28046 Spain. **Tel** (91)4565300, FAX 4557671, telex 48162 RESOL E. **LC** HD9575.S84; I574B. **DD** 354.460082/388/06. **Circ:** 40,000.

US
**PRIMARY AND GENERAL ELECTION RETURNS - LOUISIANA. Main/Corp** Louisiana. Dept. of State. Nov. 1, 1975 and Dec. 13, 1975-. English. ir. **LC** JK4792; .L68A. **DD** 324.9763. ***Formed by the union of** Primary Election Returns **and** Louisiana. Dept. of State. General Election Returns.*

US/1058-0301
**PRIME CONTRACT AWARDS BY STATE.** [Prime contract awards state]. **Main/Corp** United States. Dept of Defense. **Added/Corp** United States. Dept. of Defense. Washington Headquarters Services. Directorate for Information Operations and Reports. United States. Assistant Secretary of Defense (Comptroller). Directorate for Information Operations and Control. (19??)-. English. sa. $5.00; $2.75 (single issues) US; $6.25; $3.44 (single issues) other. Washington Headquarters Services, Directorate for Information Operations and Reports, Room 3E843/The Pentagon, Washington DC 20301. **LC** UC267; .U598d. **DD** 355. available on microfiche (Vols. for (FY 1981-) distributed to depository libraries).
**Desc:** Reports on a variety of Department of Defense military and civil functions procurements by principal State of performance, with the net value and percent distribution of awards. The net value of awards for the two previous fiscal years for Department of Defense components are given in two tables for comparing the latest quarter associated with the publication. Also includes data on the net value of military procurement actions for the current report year, by Military Department; data on the net value of military procurement actions for the latest fiscal years; and data on the total net value of civil functions procurement actions for the latest fiscal years.

CN/1187-3000
**PRINCE EDWARD ISLAND MUNICIPAL DIRECTORY.** [P.E.I. munic. dir.]. **Added/Corp** Prince Edward Island. Dept. of Community and Cultural Affairs. (1991)-. Directory. English. **LC** JS1721.P72; P75. **DD** 352/.0072/025699. ***Continues** Municipal Directory (Prince Edward Island. Dept. of Community and Cultural Affairs), 0828-0061.*

US/0196-4224
**PRIVATE ACTS OF THE STATE OF TENNESSEE PASSED BY THE GENERAL ASSEMBLY. Main/Corp** Tennessee. 57th (1911)-. English. an (Nov.). $5.00. Secretary of State, c/o Arleen Patton, James K. Polk Building, Suite

500, Nashville TN 32719. **Tel** (615)741-2016. **LC** LAW. **DD** 348/.768/023. cum. index. ***Continues in part*** *Acts of the State of Tennessee.*

AT/1036-9988
**PRIVATISATION REPORT.** (1991)-. Periodical. English. bw. 495.00Aus$ Australia; 518.00Aus$ New Zealand, Papua New Guinea; 522.00Aus$ Indonesia, Malaysia, Singapore, 526.00Aus$ Japan, India; 532.00Aus$ US & Canada; 536.00Aus$ Europe. International Public Relations Pty Ltd., 33 Walsh Street, West Melbourne Victoria 3003 Australia. **Tel** 011 61 03 329 9333, FAX 011 61 03 329 7996.

IT
**PROBLEMI DELLA AMMINISTRAZIONE PUBBLICA.** Italian. qt. L78000.00 Italy; L130000.00 (surface mail), L150000.00 (airmail) other. Societa Editrice il Mulino, Strada Maggiore 37, 40125 Bologna Italy. **Tel** 011 39 51 256011, FAX 011 39 51 256034.

US
**PROCEEDINGS / ANNUAL CONVENTION AND REGULATORY SYMPOSIUM, NATIONAL ASSOCIATION OF REGULATORY UTILITY COMMISSIONERS.** **Main/Corp** National Association of Regulatory Utility Commissioners. Convention and Regulatory Symposium. **VFOAT** N.A.R.U.C. Annual Convention; NARUC Annual Convention. (1974)-. Proceedings. English. an. $49.50. National Association of Regulatory Utility Commissioners, 1102 Interstate Commerce Commission Building, PO Box 684, Washington DC 20044. **Tel** (202)898-2200, FAX (202)898-2213. **ED** Paul Rodgers. **LC** HE2715; .N3. **DD** 363.6/0973. Index available. cum. index. ***Continues*** *National Association of Regulatory Utility Commissioners. Proceedings, Regulatory Symposium, ... Annual Convention.*
**Desc:** NARUC Committee reports, speeches and panel discussions from the annual convention proceedings.

CN/1184-2849
**PROCEEDINGS AT THE OPENING OF THE LEGISLATIVE ASSEMBLY OF THE PROVINCE OF ONTARIO.** [Proc. open. Legis. Assem. Prov. Ont.]. **Main/Corp** Ontario. Legislative Assembly. **VFOAT** Ceremonial pour l'Ouverture de l'Assemblee Legislative de la Province de l'Ontario. 1st Session, 35th Parliament, No. 1 (Nov. 19, 1990)-. Proceedings. English (French). da. **DD** 328.713/01/05.

US/0590-0123
**PROCEEDINGS - COUNTY JUDGES' AND COMMISSIONERS' CONFERENCE.** **Main/Corp** County Judges' and Commissioners' Conference. **Added/Corp** County Judges' and Commissioners' Association of Texas. Conference Proceedings. Texas A and M University, College Station. County Judges' and Commissioners' Conference. Proceedings. (19??)-. Proceedings. English. County Judges and Commissioners Conference, Texas A & M University, Tax Accessor, College Station TX 77843. **DD** 347.9; 352.

US
**PROCEEDINGS - GOVERNOR'S CONFERENCE ON STATE, COUNTY, AND MUNICIPAL RELATIONS.** **Main/Conf** Governor's Conference on State County, and Municipal Relations. **Added/Corp** Massachusetts University. Bureau of Government Research. 10th (1958)-. Proceedings. English. ***Continues*** *Governor's Conference on State-Local Relations. Proceedings.*

US/1061-7485
**PROCEEDINGS OF FLICC FORUMS ON FEDERAL INFORMATION POLICIES.** [Proc. FLICC Forums Fed. Inf. Policies]. **Added/Corp** United States. Federal Library and Information Center Committee. (1991)-. Proceedings. English. an. Free on request. Federal Library and Information Center Committee, Library of Congress, c/o D. Dolan, Washington DC 20540-5100. **Tel** (202)287-5000. **ED** Darlene Dolan, Telephone: (202)707-4828. **DD** 353. **Circ:** 500.

US/0573-2913
**PROCEEDINGS OF THE ANNUAL CONFERENCE FOR MUNICIPAL CLERKS.** **Main/Corp** Conference for Municipal Clerks, Rutgers University. 1st- ; 1958-. Proceedings. English. an. Rutgers University / Government Research, Bureau of Government Research, New Brunswick NJ 08903. **LC** JS304. **DD** 352.073.

US
**PROCEEDINGS OF THE ... ANNUAL CONFERENCES.** **Main/Corp** United States. Office of Government Ethics. Conference. 1st and 2nd (1980-81)-. Proceedings. English. an. Office of Government Ethics, Office of Personnel Management 436H, Washington DC 20415. **LC** JK468.E7; U56A. **DD** 353.009/9.

US/0740-3453
**PROCEEDINGS OF THE ... ANNUAL FINANCIAL MANAGEMENT CONFERENCE, THE.** [Proc. annu. Financ. Manage. Conf.]. **Main/Conf** Financial Management Conference. Began with 3rd (1974) issue. Proceedings. English. an. Joint Financial Management Improvement Program, 666 11th Street NW, Washington DC 20001. **LC** JK404; .A26. **DD** 353.04. ***Continues*** *Federal Management Improvement Conference. Proceedings.*

CN/0576-3851
**PROCEEDINGS OF THE STANDING SENATE COMMITTEE ON NATIONAL FINANCE.** **Main/Corp** Canada. Parliament. Senate. Standing Committee on National Finance. **VFOAT** Deliberations du Comite Senatorial Permanent des Finances Nationales. **VAT** Deliberations du Comite Senatorial Permanent des Finances Nationales (Edition Anglaise et Francaise); National Finance (Ottawa); Finances Nationales (Ottawa). (Feb. 27th, 1969)-. Periodical. English (French). Canada Communication Group Publishers, Order Processing, Ottawa Ontario K1A 0S9 Canada. **Tel** (819)956-4800, (819)956-4802. ***Continues*** *Canada. Parliament. Senate. Standing Committee on Finance. Proceedings of the Standing Senate Committee on Finance.;* ***Absorbed*** *Canada. Parlement. Senat. Comite Permanent des Finances Nationales. Deliberations du Comite Senatorial Permanent des Finances Nationales, Nov. 9, 1976., 0576-3843.*

●CN/1193-5251
**PROCEEDINGS OF THE STANDING SENATE COMMITTEE ON PRIVILEGES, STANDING RULES AND ORDERS.** [Proc. Standing Senate Comm. Privil. Standing Rules Orders]. **Main/Corp** Canada. Parliament. Senate. Committee on Privileges, Standing Rules and Orders. **VFOAT** Privileges, Standing Rules and Orders; Proceedings of the Committee on Privileges, Standing Rules and Orders; Deliberations du Comite Senatorial Permanent des Privileges, du Reglement et de la Procedure. 34th Parliament, 3rd Session, Issue No. 3 (Mar. 26, 1992)-. Proceedings. English (French). **LC** IN PROCESS. **DD** 328.71/05/05. ***Continues*** *Canada. Parliament. Senate. Committee on Standing Rules and Orders. Proceedings of the Committee on Standing Rules and Orders, 1187-2489.*

US
**PROCUREMENT ETHICS DESKTOP REFERENCE.** (1991)-. English. an (Comes with quarterly updates). $169.00. Holbrook and Kellogg, 1964 Gallows Road, Suite 200, Vienna VA 22182. **Tel** (703)506-0600, FAX (703)506-1948.
**Desc:** Covers government purchasing, public contracts and conflicts of interest.

US/0744-6721
**PROFESSIONAL EMPLOYEES IN STATE GOVERNMENT.** (PROFESSIONAL EMPLOYEES IN STATE GOVERNMENT : PEG.). **VFOAT** PEG; P.E.G.; PEG Magazine. Periodical. English. mo. Professional Employees in State Government, 2276 East Reservoir, Springfield IL 62702.

US/0197-8187
**PROGRAM AND RESOURCE DIGEST, THE.** [Program resour. dig.]. **Main/Corp** United States. Dept. of Justice. **Added/Corp** United States. Dept. of Justice. Office of Management and Finance. Program Review and Budget Staff. (1978/79)-. English. an. US Department of Justice, 10th Street & Constitution Avenue NW, Washington DC 20530. **Tel** (202)514-2000, FAX (202)633-4371. **LC** KF5107; .A636. **DD** 353.5.

US/0360-2869
**PROGRAM DIRECTORY - ARKANSAS DEPARTMENT OF PLANNING.** **Main/Corp** Arkansas. Dept. of Planning. Directory. English. Arkansas Department of Planning, 400 Train Station Square, Victory at Markham, Little Rock AK 72201. **LC** HC107.A8; A665A. **DD** 353.9/767/0082.

●CN/1191-3282
**PROGRAMME DE BOURSES DES GOUVERNEMENTS ETRANGERS / ADMINISTRE PAR LE CONSEIL INTERNATIONAL D'ETUDES CANADIENNES.** [Foreign gov. awards program]. **Added/Corp** Conseil International d'Etudes Canadiennes. Canada. Affaires Exterieures et Commerce Exterieur Canada. **VFOAT** Foreign Government Awards Program. (1991/1992)-. French (English). **DD** 378.3. ***Continues*** *Bourses des Gouvernements Etrangers., 1191-3274.*

CN/1185-9954
**PROGRAMME POUR LES AUTOCHTONES, NOUVELLES, LE.** [Programme autoch. nouv.]. **Added/Corp** Canada. Affaires Indiennes et du Nord. (April/May 1991)-. Periodical. French. mo. **DD** 354.710681/497.

HK
**PROGRESS REPORT.** **Main/Corp** Hong Kong. Standing Commission on Civil Service Salaries and Conditions of Service. (19??)-. English. ir. Price varies per volume. Hong Kong Government Information Service, Beaconsfield House, 4 Queens Road, Hong Kong Hong Kong. **Tel** 011 852 8428801 4, telex 61190 HKGIS. **LC** JQ676.Z2; H647a. **DD** 354.51/25001/05.

US/0889-2202
**PROGRESSIVE REVIEW (WASHINGTON, D.C.), THE.** (THE PROGRESSIVE REVIEW.). [Progress. rev.]. No. 245 (Jan./Feb. 1985)-. Periodical. English. Nine times a year. $16.00 one year; $29.00 two year; $41.00 three year US; $26.00 one year; $47.00 two year; $66.00 three year other. Progressive Review, 1739 Connecticut Avenue NW, Washington DC 20009. **Tel** (202)232-5544, FAX (202)234-6222. **ED** Sam Smith. **LC** E876; .P76. **DD** 973/.05. Index available. **Circ:** 1,400. available on microfilm from Bell & Howell. ***Continues*** *Progressive Review & DC Gazette.*
**Desc:** An newsletter of progressive politics.
**Ind/Abst** Hum. Rights Intern. Rep.

US
**PROPERTY HIGHLIGHTS.** **Main/Corp** Wisconsin. Federal Property Program. Highlights No. 78-1- July 1978-. Periodical. English. mo. Federal Property Program, PO Box 650, Middleton WI 53562-0650. ***Continues*** *Property Bulletin.*

US/1071-2194
**PROTOCOL DIGEST.** ***Ceased.*** **See** Military and Defense.

CN/0575-9463
**PROVINCIAL GOVERNMENT ENTERPRISE FINANCE.** (PROVINCIAL GOVERNMENT ENTERPRISE FINANCE / DOMINION BUREAU OF STATISTICS, PUBLIC FINANCE AND TRANSPORTATION DIVISION, GOVERNMENT FINANCE SECTION.). [Prov. gov. enterp. finance]. **Added/Corp** Canada. Dominion Bureau of Statistics. Government Finance Section. Canada. Dominion Bureau of Statistics. Governments Section. Canada. Dominion Bureau of Statistics. Governments Division. Statistics Canada. Governments Division. Statistics Canada. Public Finance Division. Statistics Canada. Public Institutions Division. Statistics Canada. Assets and Liabilities Section. Statistics Canada. Assets and Liabilities and Entreprises Section. **VFOAT** Finance des Entreprises Publiques Provinciales; Finances des Entreprises Publiques Provinciales. (1962)-. English (French). an. 25.00Can$ Canada; $26.50 other. Statistics Canada, Publications Sales & Services, Main Building Room 1710, Ottawa Ontario K1A 0T6 Canada. **Tel** (613)951-5078, (800)267-6677, FAX (613)951-1584, telex 053-3585. **LC** HD4001; .A33. **DD** 354/.71/092. ***Continues*** *Financial Statistics of Provincial Government Entreprises, 0840-271X;* ***Absorbed*** *Finances des Entreprises Publiques Provinciales, 0318-5060.*
**Desc:** An analysis of financial statements of provincial government enterprises, comprising details of assets, liabilities and net worth, surplus, current revenue and expenditure on a comparative basis, by industry and by province; contains a chart on the organization, size and main functions of provincial government enterprises, and an outline of concepts, terminology and classifications.

CN/0711-3943
**PROVINCIAL MEMBERS OF PARLIAMENT (METRO).** [Prov. memb. Parliam., Metro]. 1981 Ed. -. English. Community Information Centre of Metropolitan Toronto, 590 Jarvis Street, Toronto Ontario M4Y 2J4 Canada. **Tel** (416)392-4575, FAX (416)392-4404. **DD** 328.713/0025.

UK/0144-4212
**PSLG. PUBLIC SERVICE & LOCAL GOVERNMENT.** (PUBLIC SERVICE & LOCAL GOVERNMENT : PSLG.). [PSLG. Public serv. local gov.]. **VFOAT** Public Service and Local Government; PSLG; P.S.L.G. (1977)-. Periodical. English. Twelve times a year. £35.00 UK; £50.00 Europe; £70.00 other. EMAP Readerlink, Audit House, 260 Field End Road, Ruislip Middlesex HA4 9LT England. **Tel** 011 44 081 868 4499, FAX 011 44 081 429 3117. **LC** HD4645; .A38. **DD** 363/.0941.
**Ind/Abst** Coal Abstr.

IT/0394-8412
**PUBBLICA AMMINISTRAZIONE OGGI.** [Pubblica ammin. oggi]. (1987)-. Periodical. Italian. mo. L150000. Maggioli Editore, Casella Postale 290, 47037 Rimini, Italy. **Tel** 011 39 541 628666, FAX 011 39 541 742217. **UDC** 352. ***Continues*** *A.M. Amministrazione & Management.*

IT
**PUBBLICO IMPIEGO LOCALE.** Pubblico Impiego Locale, Via San Giacomo 3D, 24100 Bergano Italy.

UK/0271-2075
**PUBLIC ADMINISTRATION AND DEVELOPMENT.** (PUBLIC ADMINISTRATION AND DEVELOPMENT : A JOURNAL OF THE ROYAL

INSTITUTE OF PUBLIC ADMINISTRATION.). [Public adm. dev.]. **Added/Corp** Royal Institute of Public Administration. Vol. 1, No. 1 (Jan./March 1981)-. Periodical. English. Five times a year. $375.00. John Wiley & Sons Ltd., Baffins Lane, Chichester West Sussex PO19 1UD England. **Tel** 0243 779777, FAX 0243 776128 BTG:JWP001, telex 86290 WIBOOKG. **(Subscription address:** John Wiley / Philadelphia, PO Box 7247, Philadelphia PA 19170.**) ED** Paul Collins. **LC** JF60; .P83. **DD** 350.007/8/091724. **CODEN** PADEDR. **[CCC]. Pr Rev. Circ:** 800. available on microfilm and microfiche from University Microfilms International (UMI). Documents available from The Genuine Article. ***Continues*** *Journal of Administration Overseas, 0021-8472.*
**Desc:** Focuses on administrative practice at the local, regional and national levels. It gives special attention to features of administration and development which have an interest and importance beyond a particular government and state, including the management and policy of parastatal organizations or corporations.
**Ind/Abst** ABC POL SCI; Anthropol. Index; Appl. Soc. Sci. Index Abstr.; Commun. Abstr.; Curr. Contents Soc. Behav. Sci.; Geogr. Abstr. Human Geogr.; Int. Bibliogr. Sociol.; Int. Dev. Abstr.; Int. Labour Doc.; Int. Polit. Sci. Abstr.; Irr. Drain. Abstr.; LABORDOC; Leis. Recreat. Tour. Abstr.; Middle East Abstr. Index; PAIS Int. Print; Res. Alert [Full Cov.]; Rice Abstr.; Rural Dev. Abstr.; Sage Public Adm. Abstr.; Soc. Plann. Policy Dev. Abstr.; Soc. Sci. Cit. Index [Full Cov.]; Sociol. Abstr.; Stud. Women Abstr.; Tech. Educ. Train. Abstr.; Urban Aff. Abstr.; World Agric. Econ.

US
**PUBLIC ADMINISTRATION AND PUBLIC POLICY.** (1977?)-. Monographic series. English. ir. Price varies per volume. Marcel Dekker Inc., 270 Madison Avenue, New York NY 10016. **Tel** (212)696-9000, (800)228-1160, FAX (212)685-4540, telex 421419. **(Subscription address:** Marcel Dekker Inc, PO Box 5017, Monticello NY 12701.**) ED** Robert T. Golembiewski.
**Desc:** Covers topics such as personnel management in government and public budgeting.

US/0734-9149
**PUBLIC ADMINISTRATION QUARTERLY.** [Public adm. q.]. **Added/Corp** Southern Public Administration Education Foundation (U.S.). **VFOAT** P.A.Q.; PAQ. Vol. 7, No. 1 (Spring 1983)-. Periodical. English. Four times a year. $30.00 (individuals); $48.00 (institutions). Southern Public Administration Education Foundation, PO Box 632, Randallstown MD 21133. **Tel** (410)665-2137. **ED** Jack Rabin and Thomas Vocino. **LC** JA1; .S68. **DD** 350/.0005. **Bk Rev. Circ:** 1,600. available on microfilm and microfiche from University Microfilms International (UMI). Documents available from Ask*IEEE, UMI Article Clearinghouse. ***Continues*** *Southern Review of Public Administration, 0147-8168.*
**Ind/Abst** ABI/INFORM Glob. Ed.; ABI Inform Ondisc (Spring 1983-); Educ. Adm. Abstr.; INSPEC (Spring 1983-); PAIS Int. Print (1991-); Sage Public Adm. Abstr.; Sage Urban Stud. Abstr; UMI ABI/Inform--Bus. Period. Ondisc (Summer 1987-) [Full Txt.].

US/0149-8797
**PUBLIC ADMINISTRATION TIMES.** ***Title Change.*** [Public adm. times]. V. 1- Jan. 1978-. Periodical. English. Eighteen times a year. American Society for Public Administration, 1120 G Street Northwest, Suite 700, Washington DC 20005-3885. **Tel** (202)393-7878, FAX (202)638-4952. **ED** Daniel R Shingler. **DD** 353. Index available. cum. index. **Bk Rev. Ad Acc. Circ:** 17,000. ***Continues*** *ASPA News & Views, 0360-4233.* ***Continued by*** *PA Times, 1041-6323.*
**Desc:** Reports on timely developments, innovative programs and relevant issues in the field of public service.
**Ind/Abst** Urban Aff. Abstr.

US/0148-4168
**PUBLIC ADMINISTRATION UPDATE.** **VFOAT** PAU. V. 1- Aug. 1977-. Periodical. English. qt. $5.00. Southern Public Administration Education Foundation Inc, PO Box 4434, Montgomery AL 36101. **Tel** (205)288-9055.

US/0735-4703
**PUBLIC ADMINISTRATOR AND THE COURTS, THE.** [Public adm. courts]. Vol. 1, No. 1 (July 1981); V. 1, No. 1 (March 1986)-. Periodical. English. qt. $79.50; $39.50 renewal. Research Publications Inc, 92 Fairway Drive, PO Box 9267, Asheville NC 28815. **Tel** (704)298-8291. **ED** John C Pine. **LC** KF5401.A75; P8. **DD** 342.73/062648; 347.302602648. Index available. cum. index. ctrl circ.
**Desc:** Briefs of selected significant higher court decisions affecting the field of public administration.

US/0033-3395
**PUBLIC AFFAIRS COMMENT.** **Added/Corp** Lyndon B. Johnson School of Public Affairs. University of Texas. Institute of Public Affairs University of Texas at Austin. Institute of Public Affairs. Vol. 1 (Jan. 1955)-. Academic Scholarly Publication. English. qt (4 issues). Free on request. LBJ School of Public Affairs, University of Texas at Austin, Austin TX 78713-7450. **Tel** (512)471-4218. **ED** David C. Warner. **LC** JK4801; .P8. **Circ:** 900 (ctrl).
**Desc:** Articles of current interest in the field of public affairs.
**Ind/Abst** Urban Aff. Abstr.

US/0887-0373
**PUBLIC AFFAIRS QUARTERLY.** **See** Philosophy.

US/0033-3417
**PUBLIC AFFAIRS REPORT.** (PUBLIC AFFAIRS REPORT : BULLETIN OF THE BUREAU OF PUBLIC ADMINISTRATION.). [Public aff. rep.]. **Added/Corp** University of California, Berkeley. Institute of Governmental Studies. University of California, Berkeley. Bureau of Public Administration. Vol. 1, No. 1 (Feb. 1960)-. Periodical. English. ir. Institute of Governmental Studies, University of California, 109 Moses Hall, Berkeley CA 94720. **Tel** (510)642-6722. **ED** Harriet Nathan and Stanley Scott. **LC** JK8701; .P8. **Circ:** 2,700. Documents available from Documents on Demand.
**Ind/Abst** Environ. Abstr.; Hospit. Health Admin. Index; Urban Aff. Abstr.

US/0555-5914
**PUBLIC AFFAIRS (VERMILLION).** (PUBLIC AFFAIRS.). [Public aff.]. **Added/Corp** University of South Dakota. Governmental Research Bureau. Vol. 1 (May 15, 1960)-. Periodical. English. qt. Free on request. University of South Dakota Governmental Research Bureau, Vermillion SD 57069. **Tel** (605)677-5702. **ED** Russell Smith. **LC** JK6501; .P83. **DD** 320/.09783. **Circ:** 2,000.
**Desc:** Articles on public policy issues pertaining to rural areas and South Dakota.
**Ind/Abst** Urban Aff. Abstr.

UK
**PUBLIC AUTHORITIES DIRECTORY.** Directory. English. an. £33.00. LGC Communications, 122 Minories, London EC3N 1NT England. **Tel** 01-623 2530, FAX 01-702 2822, telex 945828 LOGIN. **ED** Heather Bolton. **LC** JS3001; .P83. **DD** 352.041. Index available. **Ad Acc. Circ:** 1,255.
**Desc:** Guide to the public authorities in the United Kingdom concerned with local government and the health and water services.

UK
**PUBLIC BODIES / MANAGEMENT AND PERSONNEL OFFICE.** **Added/Corp** Great Britain. Civil Service Dept. Management and Personnel Office. (1982)-. English. an. £12.00. Her Majesty's Stationery Office, 51 Nine Elms Lane, London SW8 5DR England. **Tel** 011 44 71 873 8459, 011 44 71 873 8499, FAX 011 44 71 873 8499, 011 44 71 873 8456, telex 297138. **(Subscription address:** Her Majesty's Stationery Office, PO Box 276, Publications Centre, London SW8 5DT England.**) LC** JN409; .P8. **DD** 354.4104/05.

JA
**PUBLIC CLEANSING SERVICE IN TOKYO.** **Main/Corp** Tokyo. Seisokyoku. English. Tokyoto Seisokyoku, (Bureau of Public Cleansing, Tokyo Metropolitan Government), 5-1, Marunouchi 3 Chome, Chiyodaku, Tokyoto 100, Japan. **LC** HD4485.J3; T65. **DD** 363.6.

US
**PUBLIC DOCUMENTS OF LOUISIANA (BATON ROUGE, LA : 1981).** (PUBLIC DOCUMENTS OF LOUISIANA.). **Added/Corp** Louisiana State Library. (19??)-. English. sa. State Library of Louisiana, PO Box 131, Baton Rouge LA 70821. **Tel** (504)342-4929. **ED** Grace G. Moore. **LC** Z1223.5.L7; P82; J87.L8. **DD** 015.763/053. Index available. **Circ:** 450 (ctrl).

US/0033-345X
**PUBLIC EMPLOYEE PRESS (NEW YORK).** **See** Economics-Labor.

US/0273-3439
**PUBLIC EMPLOYEES CONFERENCE PROCEEDINGS.** **See** Economics-Labor.

US/0196-4437
**PUBLIC EMPLOYMENT (1965).** (PUBLIC EMPLOYMENT IN ....). **Added/Corp** United States. Bureau of the Census. **VFOAT** Public Employment. (1965)-. Government Publication. English. ir. Superintendent of Documents, US Government Printing Office, Washington DC 20402. **Tel** (202)275-3328, FAX (202)786-2377. **LC** HD8011.A1; A3 subser. **DD** 331.7/6135/0000973; 331.12/5135/0000973. ***Continues*** *State Distribution of Public Employment.*
**Ind/Abst** Predicasts Forecasts.

US/0730-1863
**PUBLIC EXECUTIVE PROJECT BULLETIN.** [Public exec. proj. bull.]. **VFOAT** Management Seminars for Public Executives Bulletin. Bulletin. English. an. Public Executive Project, Graduate School for Public Affairs, State University of New York at Albany, Mohawk Tower/Room 1304, Albany NY 12222. ***Continues*** *Public Executive Project Program, 0730-1855.*

UK
**PUBLIC GENERAL ACTS AND GENERAL SYNOD MEASURES, THE.** **Main/Corp** Great Britain. **Added/Corp** Church of England. General Synod. (1972)-. English. ir. £345.00 (5 volume set). Her Majesty's Stationery Office, 51 Nine Elms Lane, London SW8 5DR England. **Tel** 011 44 71 873 8459, 011 44 71 873 8499, FAX 011 44 71 873 8499, 011 44 71 873 8456, telex 297138. **(Subscription address:** Her Majesty's Stationery Office, PO Box 276, Publications Centre, London SW8 5DT England.**) LC** KD124; .G74. ***Continues*** *Great Britain. Laws, Etc. Public General Acts ... .*

US/0742-5325
**PUBLIC JUSTICE REPORT.** [Public justice rep.]. **Added/Corp** Association for Public Justice (U.S.). Education Fund. **VFOAT** Report. Vol. 1, No. 1 (Oct. 1980)-. English. bm. $12.00 (one year), $20.00 (two year), $25.00 (three year). Center for Public Justice, PO Box 48368, Washington DC 20002. **Tel** (202)546-0489. **ED** James W. Skillen. Index available. cum. index. **Bk Rev. Circ:** 2,500 (ctrl). ***Continues*** *Public Justice Newsletter.*
**Desc:** Commentary and analysis of domestic and international political affairs from a Christian point of view.

US/0033-3611
**PUBLIC MANAGEMENT.** [Public manage.]. **Added/Corp** International City Managers' Association. International City Management Association. **VFOAT** PM. Vol. 8, No. 12 (Dec. 1926)-. Periodical. English. mo. $30.00. International City Management Association, 777 North Capitol Street NE, Suite 500, Washington DC 20002. **Tel** (202)289-4262, (800)745-8780, FAX (202)962-3500. **(Subscription address:** International City Management Association, PO Box 2011, Annapolis Junction MD 20701.**) ED** Beth Payne. **LC** JS344; .C5A2. **DD** 352. **Bk Rev. Ad Acc. Circ:** 14,100. available on microfilm and microfiche from University Microfilms International (UMI). Documents available from UMI Article Clearinghouse, Magazine Collection. ***Continues*** *Public Management.*
**Desc:** Contains solicited and unsolicited feature articles, profiles of public administrators, innovations, letters to the editor, legal news, international subjects and viewpoints.
**Ind/Abst** ABI/INFORM Glob. Ed.; ABI Inform Ondisc (Nov. 1972-July 1976); Acad. Search (July 1993-); Anbar Account. Finan. Abstr. [Full Txt.]; Anbar Mark. Distr. Abstr. [Full Txt.]; Anbar Top Manage. Abstr. [Full Txt.]; Bus. Period. Index; Bus. Source (Jul. 1993-); Expand. Acad. Index (1984-); Gen. Period. Index (1985-); INFO-SOUTH Abstr.; Mag. Index Plus (1989-); Mag. Search; Manage. Contents (1974-); Middle East Abstr. Index; Newsp. Period. Abstr. (1988-); Oper. Prod. Manage. Abstr. [Full Txt.]; PAIS Int. Print (1991-); Person. Train. Abstr. [Full Txt.]; Public Aff. Inf. Serv. Bull.; Sage Public Adm. Abstr.; Sage Urban Stud. Abstr; Soc. Sci. Source (Jul. 1993-); Soc. Sci. Index; Soc. Sci. Index Fulltext (Oct. 1988-) [Full Txt.]; Mag. Index (1977-);(1959-); Urban Aff. Abstr.; Wilson Bus. Abstr.; Women Manage. Rev. [Full Txt.]; Work Relat. Abstr.

●US/1061-7639
**PUBLIC MANAGER (POTOMAC, MD.), THE.** (THE PUBLIC MANAGER.). [Public manag.]. **VFOAT** New Bureaucrat, The Public Manager. Vol. 21, No. 1 (Spring 1992)-. Periodical. English. qt. $48.00 institution. The Bureaucrat Inc., 12007 Titian Way, Potomac MD 20854. **Tel** (301)279-9445, FAX (301)251-5872. **ED** Tom Novotny (Editor's address: PO Box 347, Arlington, VA 22210; telephone: (301)279-9445). **LC** JK1; .B86. **DD** 353/.0005. Index available (free). **Bk Rev. Ad Acc. Pr Rev.** Documents available from UMI Article Clearinghouse. ***Continues*** *Bureaucrat, 0045-3544.*
**Ind/Abst** ABC POL SCI; ABI/INFORM Glob. Ed.; ABI Inform Ondisc (1992-); Acad. Search (July 1993-); Bus. Index (1992-); Bus. Period. Index (1992-); Gen. BusinessFile (1992-); Gen. Period. Index (1992-); Hum. Resour. Abstr. (1992-?); INFO-SOUTH Abstr.; Mag. Search; Sage Public Adm. Abstr. (1992-?); Sage Urban Stud. Abstr (1992-?); U.S. Polit. Sci. Doc. (1992-); Urban Aff. Abstr. (1992-); Wilson Bus. Abstr.

US/0079-7626
**PUBLIC PAPERS OF THE PRESIDENTS OF THE UNITED STATES.** [Public pap. pres. U. S.]. **Main/Corp** United States. President. **Added/Corp** United States. Federal Register Division. United States. Office of the Federal Register. (19??)-. Government Publication. English. an. Must order direct. Superintendent of Documents, US Government Printing Office, Washington DC 20402. **Tel** (202)275-3328, FAX (202)786-2377. **LC** J80; .A283. **DD** 353.03/5. cum. index.

UK
**PUBLIC POLICY AND ADMINISTRATION.** **Added/Corp** Joint University Council for Social and Public Administration. Public Administration Committee. Vol. 1, No. 1 (Spring 1986)-. Periodical. English. Three times a year (Apr., Aug., Dec.). £30.00 (institution), £16.00 (individual) UK and Ireland; £32.00 (institution), £23.00 (individual) other. Joint University Council, RIPA International, Endsleigh House, 22 Bedford Square, London WC1B 3HH England. **Tel** 11 44 71 580 7138, FAX 11 44 81 440 4850, telex 261507. **ED** Grant Jordan. **Pr Rev. Circ:** 300. ***Continues*** *Public*

## Public Administration

Administration Bulletin (London, England).
**Desc:** Articles on public administration, covering both central and local government.

US
### PUBLIC POLICY STUDIES (GREENWICH, CT.). Ceased. (PUBLIC POLICY STUDIES.). Vol. 1 (1984)-Completed Series (1992). Monographic series. English. an. JAI Press Inc., 55 Old Post Road, Suite 2, PO Box 1678, Greenwich CT 06836-1678. **Tel** (203)661-7602, FAX (203)661-0792.

CN/0700-2092
### PUBLIC SECTOR, THE. Vol. 1 (Oct. 10, 1977)-. Periodical. English. wk (50 issues). $497.00 US and Canada; $527.00 other. Public Sector, 9 Antares Drive, Nepean ONT K2E 7V5 Canada. **Tel** (613)521-9886. **DD** 338.971.
**Ind/Abst** ABC POL SCI; Int. Polit. Sci. Abstr.

NZ/0110-5191
### PUBLIC SECTOR (WELLINGTON). (PUBLIC SECTOR : THE PUBLICATION OF THE NEW ZEALAND INSTITUTE OF PUBLIC ADMINISTRATION.). [Public sector]. **Added/Corp** New Zealand Institute of Public Administration. Vol. 1, No. 1 (Winter 1978)-. Periodical. English. Four times a year (Mar., June, Sept., Dec.). 50.00NZ$ New Zealand; 55.00NZ$ other. New Zealand Institute of Public Administration, PO Box 5032, Wellington 1 New Zealand. **Tel** 011 644 3898776. **[CCC]**. *Continues* Public Administration.
**Desc:** News and information on the New Zealand Institute of Public Administration.
**Ind/Abst** ABC POL SCI.

SA/0033-376X
### PUBLIC SERVANT. DIE STAATSAMPTENAAR, THE. Added/Corp Public Servants Association of the Union of South Africa. **VFOAT** Staatsamptenaar. Vol. 1 (1920)-. Afrikaans (English). bm. R9.60. PSA of South Africa, PO Box 40404, Arcadia 0007 South Africa. **Tel** 011 27 12 3234481, FAX 011 27 12 3257434. **ED** J.C. Olivier. **LC** HD8013.S6; P8. **DD** 351.1. **Bk Rev**, (Qty: 12). **Ad Acc, Adv Mgr:** S. Frisby. **Circ:** 100,000.

CN/0842-7259
### PUBLIC SERVICE MANAGEMENT PENSION PLAN, ANNUAL REPORT. (PUBLIC SERVICE MANAGEMENT PENSION PLAN, ANNUAL REPORT FOR THE FISCAL YEAR ENDED MARCH 31, ...). [Public Serv. Manag. Pension Plan annu. rep.]. **Main/Corp** Alberta. Alberta Treasury. (1987)-. English. an. Alberta Pension Administration 108th Street, Edmonton Alberta T5K 2O2 Canada. **DD** 354.7123005. *Continues in part* Alberta. Public Service Management Pension Board. Final Report of the Proceedings of the Public Service Management Pension Board Pursuant to the Public Service Management Pension Act for the Period ..., 0842-7240.

BB
### PUBLIC UTILITIES ACT 1951. Main/Corp Barbados. Public Utilities Board. English. Barbados Public Utilities Board, Barbados Statistical Service, National Insurance Building, Bridgetown Barbados. **LC** HD2768.B37; A3. **DD** 354/.729/810087.

US/0147-359X
### PUBLIC UTILITIES AND TRANSPORTATION NEWSLETTER. Main/Corp Illinois State Bar Association. Section on Public Utilities and Transportation. Newsletter. English. Illinois State Bar Association, 424 South Second, Springfield IL 62701. **Tel** (217)525-1760, FAX (217)525-0712. **LC** KFl1485.A15; I43. **DD** 343/.773/0905.

US
### PUBLIC UTILITY PROPERTY : ASSESSED VALUE OF PUBLIC UTILITY REAL AND PERSONAL PROPERTY, BY COUNTY AND CLASS OF UTILITY. Main/Corp Ohio. Dept. of Taxation. English. Department of Taxation / Ohio, Research and Statistics Section, PO Box 530, Columbus OH 43216. **LC** HD2767.O3; O36A. **DD** 333.33/2.

US/0033-3840
### PUBLIC WORKS. See Engineering.

US/0146-5473
### PUBLIC WORKS NEWS. (1969)-. Periodical. English. Forty-eight times a year. $225.00 (one year), $450.00 (two years), $675.00 (three years). Reynolds Publishing Company, PO Box 578, Glen Echo MD 20768. **Tel** (301)229-2930.

US/0148-5814
### PUBLIC WORKS PROGRESS. Main/Corp Chicago (Ill.). Dept. of Public Works. Periodical. English. qt. Department of Public Works, Room 406/City Hall, Chicago IL 60602. **LC** HD4606.C5; C49A. **DD** 363.5/09773/11.

SP/0213-5760
### PUBLICACIONES OFICIALES. [Publ. of.]. VFOAT Boletin de Novedades. Publicaciones Oficiales. (1986)-. Periodical. Spanish. Three times a year. Servicio Central de Publicaciones, Ministerio de la Presidencia, Fuencarral, 45, 6, 28004 Madrid Spain. **Tel** 011 34 522 81 91. **UDC** 087.7.

US
### PUBLICATION (ILLINOIS. GENERAL ASSEMBLY. LEGISLATIVE COUNCIL). Title Change. (PUBLICATION / ILLINOIS. GENERAL ASSEMBLY.). **Added/Corp** Illinois. General Assembly. Legislative Council. No. 5 (Nov. 1938)-(19??). Monographic series. English. Illinois Legislative Council, 222 S College/3rd Floor, Springfield IL 62704. **LC** JK5774; .A3. **DD** 328.773. *Continues* Illinois. Legislative Council. Research Dept. Research Report. *Continued by* Publication (Illinois. General Assembly. Legislative Research Unit).

US
### PUBLICATION NOTE / U.S. DEPARTMENT OF HEALTH AND HUMAN SERVICES, PUBLIC HEALTH SERVICE, OFFICE OF HEALTH RESEARCH, STATISTICS, AND TECHNOLOGY, NATIONAL CENTER FOR HEALTH STATISTICS. Added/Corp National Center for Health Statistics (U.S.). (Jan./June 1978)-. Periodical. English. qt. Free. National Center for Health Statistics, 6525 Belcrest Road, Hyattsville MD 20782. **Tel** (301)436-8500. Index available. cum. index. ctrl circ. Documents available from Documents on Demand.
**Desc:** Contains lists of reports that have been produced by the National Center for Health Statistics.
**Ind/Abst** Am. Stat. Index.

US
### PUBLICATIONS CATALOG, LOG 1. Main/Corp United States. Dept. of Veterans Affairs. Added/Corp United States. Dept. of Veterans Affairs. Office of Administration. **VFOAT** Publications Catalog; Publications Catalog, LOG One. (July 1990)-. Catalog. English. VA Forms and Publications Depot, 6307 Gravel Avenue, Alexandria VA 22310.

US
### PUBLICATIONS FILED WITH THE STATE RECORDS CENTER FOR THE YEAR ... . English. State Records Center, State Rules and Publications Division/404 Montezuma, Santa Fe NM 87503. **LC** Z1223.5.N56; N48A; J87.N6. **DD** 015.789. *Continues* Publications and Rules Filed.

US
### PUBLICATIONS OF THE NATIONAL INSTITUTE OF JUSTICE. SUPPLEMENT. Main/Corp National Institute of Justice (U.S.). 1980-. English. an. National Institute of Justice, Washington DC 20531. *Continues* Publications of the National Institute of Law Enforcement and Criminal Justice. Supplement, 0198-1455.

US
### PUBLICATIONS OF THE STATE OF ILLINOIS. Main/Corp Illinois. Office of Secretary of State. (195?)-. English. an. Illinois State Library, Centennial Building, Springfield IL 62756. **Tel** (217)782-2994.

SZ
### PUBLICUS (BASEL, SWITZERLAND). (PUBLICUS.). (19??)-. French (German). an (Oct.). 78.00F. Schwabe & Company Ltd., Farnsburgerstrasse 8 PF 254, CH-4132 Muttenz 1 Switzerland. **Tel** 011 41 61 4613001, FAX 01 41 61 4612500. **LC** DQ1; .S28. **Bk Rev.** *Continues* Schweizer Jahrbuch des Offentlichen Lebens.

IT
### QUADERNI BIANCHI. Ceased. Vol. 1, No. 1 (Jan./Feb. 1979)-?. Periodical. Italian. bm. Citta e Societa, Piazza S Ambrogio 21, 20123 Milan Italy. **LC** JN5201; .Q33. **DD** 945.092/7.

US
### QUALIFICATION STANDARDS FOR WHITE COLLAR POSITIONS UNDER THE GENERAL SCHEDULE. Added/Corp United States. Civil Service Commission. Bureau of Policies and Standards. (19??)-. Periodical. English. ir. $93.00 US; $116.25 other. US Civil Service Commission, 1900 E Street Northwest, Room 5354, Washington DC 20415. **Tel** (202)632-5532.

US/0892-4171
### QUALITY CITIES. Added/Corp Florida League of Cities. Vol. 60, No. 7 (Jan. 87)-. Periodical. English. mo (with June/July issue combined). $20.00 nonmembers; $6.00 Florida members; $15.00 other. Florida League of Cities, 201 West Park Street, PO Box 1757, Tallahassee FL 32302-1757. **Tel** (904)222-9684, FAX (904)222-3806. **ED** Cecka R. Trueblood. **LC** JS39; .F55. **DD** 352/.0072/09759. **Ad Acc, Adv Mgr:** Priscilla Dawson, **Tel** (904)222-9684. **Circ:** 5,350. *Continues* Florida Municipal Record, 0015-4164.
**Desc:** Subjects of interest to local government officials in the state of Florida.
**Ind/Abst** Urban Aff. Abstr.

US/1057-9958
### QUARTERLY BULLETIN - UNITED STATES. BUREAU OF ALCOHOL, TOBACCO AND FIREARMS. (QUARTERLY BULLETIN / BUREAU OF ALCOHOL, TOBACCO AND FIREARMS, DEPARTMEMT OF THE TREASURY.). [Q. bull. - U. S., Bur. Alcohol Tob. Firearms]. **Main/Corp** United States. Bureau of Alcohol, Tobacco, and Firearms. **VFOAT** Alcohol, Tobacco and Firearms Quarterly Bulletin. Vol 1 (1983)-. Bulletin. English. qt. $12.00 domestic; $15.00 other. Superintendent of Documents, US Government Printing Office, Washington DC 20402. **Tel** (202)275-3328, FAX (202)786-2377. **DD** 353. *Continues* Alcohol, Tobacco and Firearms Quarterly Bulletin.
**Desc:** Announces all new laws, regulations, codes and rulings or changes relating to alcohol, tobacco and firearms.

US/0499-499X
### QUARTERLY DIGEST OF UNPUBLISHED DECISIONS OF THE COMPTROLLER GENERAL OF THE UNITED STATES : CONTRACTS. Main/Corp United States. General Accounting Office. Office of the General Counsel. V. 1- Sept./Dec. 1957-. Periodical. English. qt. US General Accounting Office / District of Columbia, 441 G Street NW, Room 4528, Washington DC 20548. **Tel** (202)275-2812.

CN/0713-1674
### QUARTERLY JOURNAL - CANADIAN GENERAL STANDARDS BOARD. (QUARTERLY JOURNAL / REVUE TRIMESTRIELLE.). [Q. j. - Can. Gen. Stand. Board]. **Main/Corp** Canadian General Standards Board. **VFOAT** Revue Trimestrielle. **VAT** Revue Trimestrielle - Office des Normes Generales du Canada. Vol. 9, No. 1 (Jan. 1981)-. Periodical. English (French). qt. Free on request. Canada Communication Group Publishers, Order Processing, Ottawa Ontario K1A 0S9 Canada. **Tel** (819)956-4800, (819)956-4802. **DD** 354.710082/1/05. *Continues* Canadian Government Specifications Board. Quarterly Journal., 0384-2096. *Continued in part by* Canadian General Standards Board. Revue Trimestrielle.

II
### QUARTERLY JOURNAL OF THE ALL-INDIA INSTITUTE OF LOCAL SELF-GOVERNMENT, BOMBAY. Added/Corp All-India Institute of Local Self-Government. **VFOAT** Quarterly Journal of the All India Institute of Local Self-Government, Bombay. Vol. 58, No. 1 (Jan.-Mar. 1987)-. Periodical. English. qt. $20.00. All India Institute of Local-Government / Sthanikraj Bhavan, C D Barfiwala Marg, Andheri West Bombay 400 058 India. **Tel** 6206716, telex 78201-ALSG. **(Subscription address:** Prints India, 11 Darya Ganj, New Delhi, 110002 India, (Phone: 011 91 11 3268645)) *Continues* Quarterly Journal of the Local Self-Government Institute (Bombay).

US/0195-4709
### QUARTERLY REPORT - STATE GAMING CONTROL BOARD. Title Change. Main/Corp Nevada. State Gaming Control Board. (19??)-(19??). English. qt. State Gaming Control Board, 1150 East William Street, Carson City NV 89710. **Tel** (702)687-6500. *Merged into* Gaming Revenue Report Quarterly.

US/1049-5452
### QUAYLE QUARTERLY, THE. Ceased. (THE QUAYLE QUARTERLY : A WATCHFUL EYE ON THE VICE PRESIDENCY.). [Quayle q.]. Vol. 1, No. 1 (Winter 1990)-Vol. 3, No. 4 (Winter 1992/1993). Periodical. English. qt. PO Box 8593, Brewster Station, Bridgeport CT 06605. **Tel** (203)333-9399. **ED** Jeffery L Yoder. **LC** E840.8.Q28; Q39. **DD** 973.928/092.
**Desc:** Newsletter about Vice-President Dan Quayle.

CN
### QUEENS PARK UPDATE. English. Twenty-four times a year. 315.65Can$ (GST included). Public Affairs Management, Inc., 1075 Bay Street, Suite 52, Toronto Ontario M5S 2B1 Canada. **Tel** (416)969-9437, FAX (416)969-9512.

AT/0313-3656
### QUEENSLAND GOVERNMENT DIRECTORY. [Queensl. gov. dir.]. (1975)-. Periodical. English. an. 23.75Aus$. Queensland Government / Australia, PO Box 3327, South Brisbane 4101 Australia. **Tel** 011 61 7 2244797. **DD** a354.94304. *Continues* State Directory - State Public Relations Bureau.

PE
### QUEHACER : REVISTA BIMESTRAL DEL CENTRO DE ESTUDIOS Y PROMOCION DEL DESARROLLO-DESCO. Added/Corp Desco. VFOAT Que Hacer. (1979)-. Periodical. Spanish. Six

# Public Administration

times a year. $60.00 Latin America; $80.00 other. Desco Publications, Leon de la Fuente 110, Lima 17 Peru. **Tel** 011 51 14 627193. **LC** F3448.2; .Q44. **DD** 985/.005. **Ind/Abst** PAIS Int. Print.

BE
**QUESTIONS ET REPONSES. Main/Corp**
Belgium. Parlement. Chambre des Representants. **VFOAT** Vragen en Antwoorden. Periodical. Dutch (Dutch and French). ir. 3500F. Moniteur Belge, rue de Louvain 40-42, 1000 Brussels Belgium. **Tel** 011 32 2 5120026. **LC** J393; .K86A. **DD** 328.493/01.

US/0882-3456
**QUORUM REPORT.** (198?)-. Periodical. English. Twenty times a year (Twice a month except July, Aug., Nov., Dec.). $140.00. Quorum Report, 310 Red Bird Lane, Austin TX 78745. **Tel** (512)444-4574, FAX (512)326-2126. **ED** Harvey Kromberg (phone: (512)444-4574). ctrl circ.
**Desc:** News and information on the Texas government and other related fields.

BE
**RAADGEVENDE INTERPARLEMENTAIRE BENELUSRAAD : VERSLAG. VFOAT** Conseil Interparlementaire Consultatif de Benelux : Report. Periodical. Dutch (French). Benelux Parliament, Palais de la Nation, rue de la loi, 1008 Bruscelles Belgium. **Tel** 02/519 83 45. **LC** KJE506; .R33.

IT
**RACCOLTA NORMATIVA REGIONE TOSCANA.** Consiglio Regionale Toscana, Via Cavour 2, 50129 Florence Italy.

CN/0229-8139
**RAPPORT ANNUEL / COMMISSION MUNICIPALE DU QUEBEC.** [Rapp. annu. - Comm. munic. Que.]. **Main/Corp** Commission Municipale du Quebec. Began in 1979. French. an. Editeur Officiel du Quebec, 1283 Boul Charest Ouest, Quebec Quebec G1N 2C9 Canada. **LC** KEQ820.A72; M86. **DD** 352.0714.

CN/0837-7138
**RAPPORT ANNUEL / CONSEIL CONSULTATIF DE L'ENVIRONNEMENT.** [Rapp. annu. - Cons. consult. environ.]. **Main/Corp** Quebec (Province). Conseil Consultatif de l'Environnement. (1986/87)-. French. an. **DD** 354.71409/3. **Continues** Rapport d'Activite / Conseil Consultatif de l'Environnement, 0837-712X.

BE
**RAPPORT ANNUEL / CONSEIL SUPERIEUR DES CLASSES MOYENNES. Main/Corp** Belgium. Conseil Superieur des Classes Moyennes. (19??)-. French (Dutch). an. Hoge Raad voor de Middenstand, Liefdadigheidsstraat 24, 1040 Bruxelles Belgium. **Tel** 02/217.91.43, FAX 02/218.21.44. **LC** HT690.B4; B44a. ctrl circ. **Continues** Belgium. Conseil Superieur des Classes Moyennes. Rapport Annuel du Secretaire General.

FR
**RAPPORT ANNUEL DE LA DATAR, LE. Main/Corp** France. Delegation a l'Amenagement du Territoire et a l'Action Regionale. French. an. 1 Avenue Charles Floquet, 75007 Paris France. **LC** HT395.F7; F73A.

CN/0229-8538
**RAPPORT ANNUEL / INSTITUT NATIONAL DE PRODUCTIVITE.** [Rapp. annu. - Inst. natl. prod.]. **Main/Corp** Quebec (Province). Institut National de Productivite. 1978/1979-. French. an. 51 rue d'Auteuil, Quebec Quebec G1R 4C2 Canada. **DD** 354.7140082.

CN/0715-6219
**RAPPORT ANNUEL / MINISTERE DE L'AGRICULTURE, DES PECHERIES ET DE LA'ALIMENTATION. Main/Corp** Quebec (Province). Ministere de l'Agriculture, des Pecheries et de l'Alimentation. 1979-1980-. French. an. Editeur Officiel du Quebec, 1283 Boul Charest Ouest, Quebec Quebec G1N 2C9 Canada. **LC** HD1790.Q4; Q45A. **DD** 354.7140682/33/06. **Continues** Quebec (Province). Ministere de l'Agriculture. Rapport Annuel, 0383-4484.

CN/1183-868X
**RAPPORT ANNUEL - QUEBEC (PROVINCE). COMITE DE DEONTOLOGIE POLICIERE.** (RAPPORT ANNUEL.). [Rapp. annu. - Que. (Prov.), Comite deontol. polic.]. **Main/Corp** Quebec (Province). Comite de Deontologie Policiere. (1990/1991)-. French. **DD** 354.7140074.

CN/0711-7132
**RAPPORT ANNUEL - REGIE DE L'ELECTRICITE ET DU GAZ.** (RAPPORT ANNUEL / REGIE DE L'ELECTRICITE ET DU GAZ, GOUVERNEMENT DU QUEBEC.). [Rapp. annu. - Regie electr. gaz]. **Main/Corp** Quebec (Province). Electricity and Gas Board. VAT Annual Report - Electricity and Gas Board (Quebec. 1975). 1975/76-. English (French). an. Publication du Quebec, CP1005, Quebec Quebec G1K 7B5 Canada. **Tel** (418)643-5150, (800)463-2100. **DD** 354.7140087/2. **Continues** Quebec. (Province). Electricity and Gas Board. Annual Report.

CN/1187-0893
**RAPPORT ANNUEL / REGIE DES LOTERIES DU QUEBEC.** [Rapp. annu. - Regie loteries Que.]. **Main/Corp** Regie des Loteries du Quebec. (1991)-. French. **LC** HG6149.Q4; R44a. **DD** 354.7140076. **Continues** Rapport Annuel, 0701-9491.

CN/0710-376X
**RAPPORT ANNUEL / REGIE DES PERMIS D'ALCOOL DU QUEBEC.** [Rapp. annu. - Regie permis alcool Que.]. **Main/Corp** Regie des Permis d'Alcool du Quebec. 1980/1981-. French. an. **LC** HV5087.C2; C64A. **DD** 354.7140076/1/06. **Continues** Rapport Annuel - Commission de Controle des Permis d'Alcool du Quebec, 0714-0428.

CN/0713-4711
**RAPPORT ANNUEL - SERVICE DE RECHERCHE EN DEFENSE DES CULTURES.** (RAPPORT ANNUEL.). [Rapp. annu. - Serv. rech. def. cult.]. **Main/Corp** Quebec (Province). Service de Recherche en Defense des Cultures. 1980-. Periodical. French. Free. Publication du Quebec, CP1005, Quebec Quebec G1K 7B5 Canada. **Tel** (418)643-5150, (800)463-2100. **DD** 354.7140082/333042. ctrl circ. **Continues** Repertoire des Travaux de Recherche en Defense des Cultures.

CN/0845-924X
**RAPPORT ANNUEL - SOCIETE DES ALCOOLS DU QUEBEC (1986?).** (RAPPORT ANNUEL.). [Rapp. annu. - Soc. alcools Que.]. **Main/Corp** Societe des Alcools du Quebec. **VFOAT** Rapport Annuel de la Societe des Alcools du Quebec. (198?)-. French. **DD** 354.7140076/1. **Continues** Rapport d'Activite., 0715-8254.

CN/0226-3084
**RAPPORT D'ACTIVITES - OFFICE DE LA CONSTRUCTION DU QUEBEC.** [Rapp. act. - Off. constr. Que.]. **Main/Corp** Quebec (Province) Office de la Construction. 1978-. French. an. Office de la Construction du Quebec, 5530 Jean Talon Ouest, Montreal Quebec H3R 2G3 Canada. **Tel** (514)341-7740. **LC** HD9715.C33. **DD** 354.7140082/42. **Continues** Quebec (Province). Office de la Construction. Rapport Annuel, 0707-3399.

CN/0703-0770
**RAPPORT D'ACTIVITES - OFFICE DES PROFESSIONS DU QUEBEC. Main/Corp** Quebec (Province). Office des Professions. 1973/74-. Periodical. French. Office des Professions du Quebec, 320 rue St Joseph Est, Quebec G1K 8G5 Canada. **LC** HD2429.C3; Q4A. **DD** 354/.714/0083.

CN/0317-7742
**RAPPORT D'ACTIVITIES - SERVICE DE L'HABITATION ET DE L'URBANISME. VILLE DE MONTREAL.** (RAPPORT D'ACTIVITES - VILLE DE MONTREAL, SERVICE DE L'HABITATION ET DE L'URBANISME.). **Main/Corp** Montreal, Quebec. Service de l'Habitation et de l'Urbanisme. 1974-. Periodical. French. Service de l'Habitation et de l'Urbanisme, 330 Est rue St-Paul, Montreal Quebec H2Y 1H2 Canada. **DD** 352/.96/0971481. **Supersedes** Montreal, Quebec. Service de l'Habitation. Rapport des Activites, 0317-7734.

FR
**RAPPORT DU CONSEIL D'ADMINISTRATION. Main/Corp** Etablessment Public pour l'Amenagement de la Region de la Defense. Conseil d'Administration. (19??)-. French. an. Conseil d'Administration, Paris-la Defense, Paris Cedex No 1 France. **LC** HD646; .E8a. **DD** 333.7/7/0944.
**Desc:** Report of the Public Planning Council. Covers budget, plans and projects related to public use of the environment, such as parks, roads, building sites and parking lots.

CN/0821-8129
**RAPPORT DU VERIFICATEUR GENERAL DU CANADA A LA CHAMBRE DES COMMUNES (1979).** (RAPPORT DU VERIFICATEUR GENERAL DU CANADA A LA CHAMBRE DES COMMUNES.). [Rapp. Verif. gen. Can. Chamb. communes]. **Main/Corp** Canada. Bureau du Verificateur General. (1979)-. French (English). an. Free. Office of the Auditor General / Ottawa, 240 Sparks Street, Ottawa Ontario K1A 0G6 Canada. **Tel** (613)995-3766 ext. 6280. **DD** 354.710072/32. **Continues** Canada. Bureau du Verificateur General. Rapport Annuel du Verificateur General a la Chambre des Communes., 0707-3100.

FR
**RAPPORT GENERAL D'ACTIVITE / MINISTERE DE L'AGRICULTURE, DIRECTION DE LA QUALITE. Main/Corp** France. Ministete de l'Agriculture. Direction de la Qualite. Yearly V. 1977-. French. an. 40F. Direction de la Qualite Sous-Direction des Affaires Communes, 44 Bd de Grenelle, 75732 Paris Cedex 15 France. **LC** HD9000.9.F7; A14A. **DD** 354.440077/82.

NP
**RASHTRIYA PANCAYATA NIYAMAVALI. Main/Corp** Nepal. National Panchayat. Nepali (Nepali). an. Rashtriya Pancayata Sacivalaya, Singha Durbar, Kathamadaum India. **LC** JQ1825.N45; N46A.

IT
**RASSEGNA ISTITUZIONALE REGIONE LOMBARDIA.** (19??)-. Italian. wk. L300000. Tesoreria Regione Lombardia Rimb Spese Documenti, V Pirelli 12, 20124 Milan Italy. **Tel** 011 39 2 67654305.

IT
**RASSEGNA TAR.** Italian. Ten times a year. 170000.00L. Rassegna Tar Sas, Via Colsereno 3, 00019 Tivoli Rome Italy. **Tel** 011 39 6 774 293587. **Ad Acc**.

US
**REAL PROPERTY REPORT. Added/Corp** Massachusetts. Division of Capital Planning and Operations. (Aug. 1, 1990)-. English. **LC** IN PROCESS.

FR
**RECEUIL DES LOIS ET DE LA LEGISLATION FINANCIERE.** (1949)-. Government Publication. French (English). mo. $260.00. Recueil Des Lois Et De La Legislation Financiere, De La Republique Arabe Syrienne, Boite Postale 539, Damas Syria. **Tel** 237950 227311, FAX 963 11 542 0510, telex 412829. **ED** Mouna Seriani (editor's address: PO Box 529 Damascus Syria). Index available. **Bk Rev**, (Qty: 12). ctrl circ.
**Desc:** Information on governmental laws and decrees, international agreements, international tenders, and financial instructions.

GW/0344-7871
**RECHT UND POLITIK. See** Law.

US/0882-9217
**RECOMMENDATIONS AND REPORTS / ADMINISTRATIVE CONFERENCE OF THE UNITED STATES.** [Recomm. rep. - Adm. Conf. U. S.]. **Main/Corp** Administrative Conference of the United States. **Added/Corp** Administrative Conference of the United States. Office of the Chairman. (1978)-. English. Administrative Conference of the United States, 2120 L Street NW/Suite 500, Washington DC 20037. **Tel** (202)254-7065. **LC** KF5407; .A615. **DD** 342.73/066; 347.30266. **Continues** Recommendations and Reports of the Administrative Conference of the United States, 0882-9217.

US/0146-9916
**RECOMMENDED SALARIES AND BENEFITS FOR CAREER SERVICE EMPLOYEES. Main/Corp** Florida. Dept. of Administration. Division of Personnel. English. Department of Administration / Florida, Division of Personnel, 660 Apalachee Parkway, Tallahassee FL 32304. **LC** JK4457; .F54B. **DD** 331.2/81/3539759.

FR/0296-6957
**RECUEIL DES ACTES ADMINISTRATIFS - ARDENNES, PREFECTURE. Title Change.** (RECUEIL DES ACTES ADMINISTRATIFS.). [Rcl. actes adm. - Ardennes, Pref.]. **Added/Corp** Ardennes. Prefecture. (1986)-(1993). Periodical. French. mo. Prefecture des Ardennes, 50 Ave d'Arches 08011, Charleville Mezieres France. **UDC** 353.2(443.71). **Continues in part** Recueil des Actes Administratifs de la Prefecture des Ardennes, 0298-6973. **Continued by** Recueil des Actes Administratifs de la Prefecture des Ardennes et des Services Deconcentres de l'Etat, 1252-5367.

●FR/1252-5367
**RECUEIL DES ACTES ADMINISTRATIFS DE LA PREFECTURE DES ARDENNES ET DES SERVICES DECONCENTRES DE L'ETAT. Added/Corp** Ardennes. Prefecture. (1994)-. Periodical. French. mo. Prefecture des Ardennes, 50 Ave d'Arches 08011, Charleville Mezieres France. **UDC** 353.2(443.71). **Continues** Recueil des Actes Administratifs, 0298-6957.

FR/0298-6965
**RECUEIL DES ACTES ADMINISTRATIFS DU DEPARTEMENT DES ARDENNES.** [Rcel. actes adm. dep. Ardennes]. **Added/Corp** Ardennes. Conseil General. (1986)-. Periodical. French. mo. Prefecture des Ardennes, 50 Ave d'Arches 08011,

**Public Administration**

Charleville Mezieres France. **UDC** 353.2(443.71). *Continues in part* Recueil des Actes Administratifs de la Prefecture des Ardennes, 0298-6973.

CN/1180-3533
**RECUEIL DES DECISIONS / COMITES D'APPEL DE LA FONCTION PUBLIQUE.** [Recl. decis. Com. appel fonct. publique]. **Main/Corp** Commission de la Fonction Publique du Quebec. Comites d'Appel de la Fonction Publique. **VFOAT** Recueil des Decisions des Comites d'Appel de la Fonction Publique. (1990)-. Periodical. French. **DD** 354.714001/76/05.

FR
**RECUEIL DES DECISIONS DU CONSEIL D'ETAT, STATUANT AU CONTENTIEUX ET DU TRIBUNAL DES CONFLITS ET DES JUGEMENTS DES TRIBUNAUX ADMINISTRATIFS. Main/Corp** France. Conseil d'Etat. Ser. 1, V. 1-12, 1821-1830; 2. Series., Vol. 1 (1831)-. Periodical. French. bm. 635.00F France; 745.00F other. Dalloz, 35 rue Tournefort, 75240 Paris Cedex 05 France. **Tel** 011 33 1 40515434 or 40515454, FAX 45 87 37 48, telex 206 446 F.
**Desc:** Publishes decisions and judgements of French Council of State, the highest administrative organ, in charge of preparing laws and decrees and of deciding litigation between the administration and individuals.

GW/0341-2512
**REFERATEBLATT ZUR RAUMENTWICKLUNG.** [Referatebl. raumentwickl.]. **Added/Corp** Bundesforschungsanstalt fuer Landeskunde und Raumordnung. (1975)-. Periodical. German. qt. DM72.00, DM25.00 (per issue). Bundesforschungsanstalt Landes, Postfach 200130, D-53131 Bonn 2 Germany. **Tel** 011 49 228 826209. **LC** Z7164.R33; R32; HT390. Index available. **Bk Rev. Circ:** 500 (ctrl). *Continues* Referateblatt zur Raumordnung, 0034-2246.
**Desc:** Annotated bibliography of current literature (mostly in German) on all aspects of spatial planning and research.

CN/0228-3808
**REFERENCE SERIES - EXTERNAL AFFAIRS CANADA.** (REFERENCE SERIES.). [Ref. ser. - Extern. Aff. Can.]. **Added/Corp** Canada. Dept. of External Affairs. (1979)-. Monographic series. English. ir. Price varies per volume. Domestic Information Programs Division, Department of External Affairs, Ottawa Ontario K1A OG2 Canada. **Tel** (613)996-9134. **DD** 971/.005.

FR/0337-7091
**REGARDS SUR L'ACTUALITE.** No. 1 (May 1974)-. French. ir. price varies per volume. Documentation Francaise, 29 Quai Voltaire, 75344 Paris Cedex 7 France. **Tel** 011 33 1 40157000, FAX 011 33 1 40157230, telex 204 826 DOCFRAN. **(Subscription address:** 124 rue Henri Barbusse, 93308 Aubervilliers, Cedex France: phone; 011 33 1 48395600) **LC** JN2301; .R38. **DD** 309.1/44. cum. index.
**Ind/Abst** Int. Bibliogr. Sociol.; PAIS Int. Print.

US/0732-586X
**REGION (WASHINGTON, D.C.), THE. See** Housing and Urban Development.

US/0740-4611
**REGIONAL DIRECTORY - CAPITAL AREA PLANNING COUNCIL.** (REGIONAL DIRECTORY.). **Main/Corp** Capital Area Planning Council. 1976-. Directory. English. Capital Area Planning Council, 2520 Interstate Highway, 35 South/Suite 100, Austin TX 78704. **LC** JS451.T45; R43. **DD** 352/.00025/764. *Continues* Regional Directory for the Capital State Planning Region, 0092-3958.

US/0034-3374
**REGIONAL PLAN NEWS. Title Change.** No. 1- Feb. 17, 1941-. Periodical. English. ir. Regional Planning Association, 1040 Avenue of the Americas, New York NY 10018. **Tel** (212)398-1140. **ED** William B Shore. **Bk Rev. Circ:** 4,000 (ctrl). *Continued by* RPA Bulletin.
**Desc:** Research and analysis of economic development, transportation, open space, social conditions, and land use decisions that affect the New York metropolitan region.

CN/0715-5050
**REGIONAL REFLECTIONS.** [Reg. reflect.]. Periodical. English. an. Free. Clerks Office Region of Peel, 10 Peel Centre Drive, Brampton Ontario L6T 4B9 Canada. **Tel** 791-9400. **ED** Des Phillips-Jamieson. **DD** 917.13/535/005. **Circ:** 9,000 (ctrl).
**Desc:** Magazine-format publication providing an overview of the regional municipality of Peel, emphasizing the government's activities and services.

IT/0393-7437
**REGIONE E GOVERNO LOCALE.** [Reg. gov. locale]. (1980)-. Periodical. Italian. bm (6 issues). L110000. Maggioli Editore, Casella Postale 290, 47037 Rimini, Italy. **Tel** 011 39 541 628666, FAX 011 39 541 742217. **UDC** 353.

US/0270-6245
**REGISTER AND MANUAL - STAGE OF CONNECTICUT.** [Regist. man. - State Conn.]. **Main/Corp** Connecticut. Secretary of the State. **VFOAT** Connecticut State Register and Manual; Register and Manual of the State of Connecticut. (188?)-. English. an (Sept.). $13.60 Connecticut; $13.00 other (soft cover edition). Secretary of the State / Public Division, 30 Trinity Street, Hartford CT 06106. **Tel** (203)566-3606. **LC** JK3331. **DD** 353.9746002/05. Index available (bound in all issues). *Continues* Connecticut State Register and Manual.

US
**REGISTRANTS, LOBBYISTS. VFOAT** Registrants/Lobbyists. English. ir. State Ethics Commission / Maryland, 301 West Preston Street/Room 1515, Baltimore MD 21201. **LC** JK3874.5; .R43. **DD** 328/.38/025752.

●CN/1188-9551
**REGISTRE CANADIEN DES PROPRIETES PATRIMONIALES, ... RAPPORT ANNUEL, LE. Added/Corp** Service Canadien des Parcs. Division de l'Inventaire des Batiments Historiques du Canada. (1992)-. French. **DD** 354.710085/9.

US/0544-4462
**REGULAR MEETING - BOARD OF MISSISSIPPI LEVEE COMMISSIONERS. Main/Corp** Mississippi. Board of Mississippi Levee Commissioners. Periodical. English. sa. Board of Mississippi Levee Commissioners, PO Box 637, Greenville MS 38701. **LC** TC425.M63; M595A. **DD** 353.9/762/0086.

US/0093-0741
**REGULATED ELECTRIC STUDY (JEFFERSON CITY).** (A REGULATED ELECTRIC STUDY.). **Main/Corp** Missouri Public Service Commission. 1962/71-. English. an. $5.50. Missouri Public Service Commission, Jefferson Building, Jefferson City MO 65101. **LC** HD9685.U6; M57A. **DD** 363.6/2/09778.

HK
**REGULATIONS OF HONG KONG / INCLUDING PROCLAMATIONS, ORDERS IN COUNCIL, ETC. FOR THE YEAR ..., THE. Main/Corp** Hong Kong. **VFOAT** Hong Kong Government Gazette. Legal Supplement No. 2. (19??)-. English. an. Price varies per volume. Hong Kong Government Information Service, Beaconsfield House, 4 Queens Road, Hong Kong Hong Kong. **Tel** 011 852 8428801 4, telex 61190 HKGIS.

US/0193-4686
**REGULATORY EYE.** (1979)-. Periodical. English. mo. $297.00. Regulatory Eye, 1625 Eye Street NW/Suite 125, Washington DC 20006. **Tel** (202)296-6997.

US
**REGULATORY MONTHLY MINUTES.** English. Twelve times a year. $18.00. St. Johns River Water Management District, PO Box 1429, Palatka FL 32178. **Tel** (904)329-4500.

US/0275-0902
**REGULATORY WATCHDOG SERVICE. ALERT BULLETIN. VFOAT** Alert Bulletin. (1975)-. Bulletin. English. wk (published Monday). $1,047.00 North America; $1,122 other. Washington Business Information Inc., 1117 North 19th Street, Suite 200, Arlington VA 22209. **Tel** (703)247-3433, (800)426-0416, FAX (703)247-3421. **ED** Nick Wakeman. **[CCC].** *Continues* Product Safety Watchdog Service. Alert Bulletin, 0146-4639.
**Desc:** Bulletin describing and providing documents from CPSC, FDA, congress and other agencies.

BL
**RELACAO DE AUTORIDADES - ASSESSORIA DE RELACOES PUBLICAS. Main/Corp** Goias, Brazil (State). Assessoria de Relacoes Publicas. Portuguese. Assessoria de Relacoes Publicas da Secretaria do Governo, Centro Administrativo 9O. Andar, Goiania Brazil. **LC** JL2499.G55; G64A.

BL/0102-2504
**RELATORIO ANUAL / MINISTERIO DA INDUSTRIA E DO COMERCIO, CONSELHO DE DESENVOLVIMENTO INDUSTRIAL, SECRETARIA EXECUTIVA. Main/Corp** Conselho de Desenvolvimento Industrial (Brazil). Secretaria Executiva. **VFOAT** Relatorio Anual C.D.I.; Relatorio Anual CDI. (1980)-. Portuguese. an. Conselho de Desenvolvimento Industrial, Secretaria Executiva, Setor de Autarquias Sul Quadra 5, Lote 5, Bloco H, Brasilia DF Brazil. **LC** HC186; .C765a. **DD** 354.810082/06. *Continues* Conselho de Desenvolvimento Industrial (Brazil). Relatorio de Atividades (1977).

BL
**RELATORIO DA PRESIDENCIA REFERENTE AOS TRABALHOS DA ... / SENADO FEDERAL.** Portuguese. **LC** JL2461; .R44. **DD** 328.81/04.

BL
**RELATORIO DE ATIVIDADES - SECRETARIA DE ADMINISTRACAO DO ESTADO DO ESPIRITO SANTO. Main/Corp** Espirito Santo (Brazil : State). Secretaria de Administracao. Portuguese. Secretaria de Administracao, Av Jeronimo Monteiro 103, Vitoria Brazil. **LC** J208.E8; R26.

BL
**RELATORIO DE ATIVIDADES - SECRETARIA DE ESTADO DE ADMINISTRACAO. Main/Corp** Para (Brazil : State). Secretaria de Estado de Administracao. Portuguese. Rua Manoel Barata No 50 - 10O. Andar Sala 1006 66.000, Belem Brazil. **LC** JL2499.P33; P39B.

CN/0709-9495
**RENCONTRE (QUEBEC. EDITION ANGLAISE).** (RENCONTRE.). [Rencontre (Que., Ed, angl.)]. **Added/Corp** SAGMAI. Vol. 1 (Sept. 1979)-. Periodical. English. Four times a year. Free. Secretaire Auxiliaire Affaires Autochtones, 875 Grande-Allee Estate, Quebec Quebec G1R 4Y8 Canada. **Tel** (418)643-3166. **DD** 354.7140081/497. **Bk Rev. Circ:** 34,500.
**Desc:** Information on the Government du Quebec and on organizations which may be of particular interest.

CN/0709-9487
**RENCONTRE (QUEBEC. EDITION FRANCAISE).** (RENCONTRE.). [Rencontre (Que., Ed. fr.)]. **Added/Corp** SAGMAI. Vol. 1 (Sept. 1979)-. Periodical. French (English). qt. Free on request. Secretaire Auxiliaire Affaires Autochtones, 875 Grande-Allee Estate, Quebec Quebec G1R 4Y8 Canada. **Tel** (418)643-3166. **DD** 354.7140081/497. **Bk Rev. Circ:** 35,500.
**Desc:** Information on and for aboriginal peoples and on government Quebec programs related to them.

GW
**RENTENVERSICHERUNG IM BEITRITTSGEBIET. Added/Corp** Bundesversicherungsanstalt fuer Angestellte, Dezernat fuer Presse- und Offentlichkeitsarbeit. (1991)-. German. Bundesversicherungsanstalt fuer Angestellte, Dezernat fur Presse und Offentlichkeitsarbeit, Postfach, 1000 Berlin 88 Germany. **LC** KKA3272.2; .R46.

CN/0846-9709
**REPERTOIRE ... DES FICHIERS DES MINISTERES ET ORGANISMES DU GOUVERNEMENT DU QUEBEC.** [Repert., fich. minist. org. gouv. Que.]. **Added/Corp** Quebec (Province). Commission d'Acces a l'Information. (198?)-. French. an. $39.95. Les Publications du Quebec, CP 1190, Outremont Quebec H2V 4S7 Canada. **Tel** (514)948-1222, (800)463-2100, FAX (514)278-3030. **LC** JL249.5.R4; R46. **DD** 354.7140071/4.

CN/1183-5486
**REPERTOIRE DES INSTITUTIONS - ONTARIO. DIRECTION DE L'ACCES A L'INFORMATION ET DE LA PROTECTION DE LA VIE PRIVEE.** (REPERTOIRE DES INSTITUTIONS.). [Repert. inst. - Ont., Dir. acces inf. prot. vie privee]. **Added/Corp** Ontario. Direction de l'Acces a l'Information et de la Protection de la Vie Privee. (1991)-. French. Direction de l'Acces a l'Information et de la Protection de la Vie Privee, Ontario Canada. **DD** 354.7130081/9. *Continues in part* Reportoire [SIC] des Institutions., 1187-2144.

CN/0079-869X
**REPERTOIRE DES MUNICIPALITES DU QUEBEC.** [Repert. munic.]. French. an. Edifice G, 29E Etage 1039, De la Chevrotiere, Quebec Quebec G1R 9Z9 Canada. **LC** JS1721.Q4; R46. **DD** 352/.008/09714.

CN
**REPERTOIRE DES MUNICIPALITES ET DES COMMISSIONS SCOLAIRES.** 1973-. French. $3.00. Section Repertoire et Recensements Hotel du Gouvernement, Editeur Officiel du Quebec, Quebec Quebec Canada. **LC** JS4.Q4; R46. **DD** 352/.0072/09714.

CN/1182-7556
**REPERTOIRE DES USINES QUEBECOISES DE PLACAGES, DE CONTRE-PLAQUES ET DE PANNEAUX AGGLOMERES A BASE DE BOIS / MINISTERE DE L'ENERGIE ET DES RESSOURCES, DIRECTION DU DEVELOPPEMENT INDUSTRIEL.** [Reper. usines que. placages contre-plaques panneaux agglom.

# Public Administration

base bois]. **Added/Corp** Quebec (Province). Direction du Developpement Industriel. (1990)-. Periodical. French. **DD** 338.4/767483/025714.

FR/0240-4729
**REPERTOIRE MENSUEL DU MINISTERE DE L'INTERIEUR. Main/Corp** France. Ministere de l'Interieur. (19??)-. French. mo. 260.00F. S A des Publications Periodiques de l'Impr Paul Dupont, 38 rue Croix-des-Petits-Champs, Paris 1ER France. **Tel** 1 4360687. **ED** P. Dupont. **LC** J341; .R29. Index available. cum. index. **Bk Rev**. **Ad Acc**. **Circ:** 15,000. *Continues Bulletin Officiel du Ministere de l'Interieur.*

FR
**REPERTOIRE PERMANENT DE L'ADMINISTRATION FRANCAISE.** Feb. 15, 1945-. French. an. Documentation Francaise, 29 Quai Voltaire, 75344 Paris Cedex 7 France. **Tel** 011 33 1 40157000, FAX 011 33 1 40157230, telex 204 826 DOCFRAN. **LC** JN2304.

CN/1184-2326
**REPERTOIRE TELEPHONIQUE - QUEBEC (PROVINCE). MINISTERE DES AFFAIRES CULTURELLES.** (REPERTOIRE TELEPHONIQUE / MINISTERE DES AFFAIRES CULTURELLES.). [Repert. teleph. - Que. (Prov.), Minist. aff. cult.]. **Main/Corp** Quebec (Province). Ministere des Affaires Culturelles. (Sept. 1990)-. French. **DD** 354.7140085/025.

IT
**REPERTORIO DELLE DECISIONI DELLA CORTE COSTITUZIONALE. Main/Corp** Italy. Corte Costituzionale. **VFOAT** Repertorio Corte Costituzionale; Giurisprudenza Costituzionale. (1967)-. Italian. an. Giuffre Editore SPA, Via Busto Arsizio 40, 20151 Milan Italy. **Tel** 011 398 2 38089200. **LC** KKH2066; .I8. cum. index.

II
**REPORT AND PROCEEDINGS OF THE COMMITTEE - TAMIL NADU. LEGISLATURE. Main/Corp** Tamil Nadu. Legislature. Legislative Assembly. Committee of Privileges. Proceedings. Multiple languages (English and Tamil). Legislative Assembly Department, Fort St George 9, Madras India. **DD** 328.54/82/0747. *Continues Madras (State). Legislature. Legislative Assembly. Committee on Privileges. Report and Proceedings.*

MF
**REPORT AND STATEMENT OF ACCOUNT / THE MAURITIUS SUGAR SYNDICATE. Main/Corp** Mauritius Sugar Syndicate. English. The Mauritius Sugar Syndicate, Plantation House, Place d'Armes, Port Louis Mauritius. **LC** HD9118.M45; M38A. **DD** 354.69/820082333.

CN/0708-9864
**REPORT - ASSOCIATION FOR REPORT ON CONFEDERATION.** (REPORT; THE MAGAZINE OF PUBLIC AFFAIRS.). V. 2, No. 5- Apr. 1979-. Periodical. English. mo. $7.00 students, $10.00 Canada; $13.00 other. Association for Report on Confederation, PO 1681, Station H, Montreal Quebec H3G 2N6 Canada. **DD** 320.9/71. *Continues Report on Confederation, 0704-612X.*

US
**REPORT BY THE U. S. GENERAL ACCOUNTING OFFICE.** See Business-Accounting.

CN
**REPORT - CANADA LAND INVENTORY. Main/Corp** Canada Land Inventory. **VFOAT** Rapport - Inventaire des Terres du Canada; CLI Report. No. 1- 1965-. Monographic series. English (French). Price varies per volume.

II
**REPORT - COMMITTEE ON GOVERNMENT ASSURANCES.** See Insurance.

MY
**REPORT - DEPARTMENT OF PERSONNEL AND ADMINISTRATIVE REFORMS (ADMINISTRATIVE REFORMS). Main/Corp** India (Republic). Dept. of Personnel and Administrative Reforms (Administrative Reforms). 1972/73-. English. Government of India / Malaysia, PO Box 1023, Kuala Lumpar 1002 Malaysia. **LC** JQ231; .A27. **DD** 354/.54/001. *Continues India (Republic). Dept. of Administrative Reforms. Report.*

US/0428-6383
**REPORT - FLORIDA. LEGISLATURE. JOINT INTERIM COMMITTEE ON MENTAL HEALTH. Main/Corp** Florida. Legislature. Joint Interim Committee on Mental Health. Vol. 1 (1957)-. English. Florida Legislature, 111 West Madison Street, Room 716, Tallahassee FL 32399. **Tel** (904)922-0647. **DD** 131.3.

SA
**REPORT FOR THE FINANCIAL YEAR ENDING 30 SEPTEMBER ... / WHEAT BOARD. Main/Corp** South Africa. Wheat Board. **VFOAT** Annual Report for the ... Season. English. an. R2.00. Wheat Board, PO Box 908, Pretoria South Africa. **LC** HD9049.W3; S6. **DD** 354.680082/61311/06. *Continues South Africa. Wheat Board. Annual Report.*

BS
**REPORT FOR THE PERIOD ... / REPUBLIC OF BOTSWANA, MINISTRY OF LOCAL GOVERNMENT AND LANDS, DEPARTMENT OF SURVEYS AND LANDS. Main/Corp** Botswana. Dept. of Surveys and Lands. English. an. **LC** TA528.B67; B67A. **DD** 354.68830081/9.

US
**REPORT FROM STATE CIRCLE.** English. ir. $20.00. League of Women Voters of Maryland, 200 Duke of Gloucester Street, Annapolis MD 21401. **Tel** (410) 269-0232.

UK
**REPORT FROM THE COMMITTEE OF PUBLIC ACCOUNTS TOGETHER WITH THE PROCEEDINGS OF THE COMMITTEE AND THE MINUTES OF EVIDENCE TAKEN BY THE COMMITTEE OF PUBLIC ACCOUNTS ON. Main/Corp** Great Britain. Parliament. House of Commons. Committee of Public Accounts. Proceedings. English. ir. **LC** HJ40; .A65A. **DD** 354.410072/31.

II
**REPORT - GOVERNMENT OF INDIA, MINISTRY OF INDUSTRY AND CIVIL SUPPLIES. Main/Corp** India. Ministry of Industry and Civil Supplies. (1974/75)-. English. an. Government of India / Ministry of Industry and Civil Supply, Civil Lines Delhi 110054 India. **LC** HC431; .A352a. **DD** 354/.54/0082.

US
**REPORT (HAWAII. LEGISLATURE. LEGISLATIVE REFERENCE BUREAU).** (REPORT - STATE OF HAWAII, LEGISLATIVE REFERENCE BUREAU.). English. ir. Free. Legislative Reference Bureau - Hawaii, State Capitol, Honolulu HI 96813. **Tel** (800)587-0690, FAX (808)587-0699. **LC** KFH20; .H38. **DD** 027.6/5. **Circ:** 400-600. *Continues Hawaii. University, Honolulu. Legislative Reference Bureau. Report.*

US
**REPORT / IDAHO. PUBLIC UTILITIES COMMISSION. Main/Corp** Idaho Public Utilities Commission. English. an. Idaho Public Utilities Commission, Boise ID 83720-6000. **Tel** (208)334-0339, FAX (208)334-3762. **ED** Gary Richardson. **LC** KFI285; .A85. **DD** 343/.796/0902646. cum. index. **Pr Rev**. **Circ:** 600. **Desc:** General overview of regulated utilities, summaries of all cases considered, rate histories, maps of utilities services and their areas.

II
**REPORT / INDIA. PLANNING COMMISSION. Main/Corp** India. Planning Commission. 1977/78-. English. an. Government of India / Planning Commission, New Delhi India. **LC** HC435; .A37. **DD** 354.540082/05. *Continues Review of Important Activities and Studies, 0537-0329.*

II
**REPORT - JAMMU AND KASHMIR. LEGISLATIVE ASSEMBLY. COMMITTEE ON PUBLIC UNDERTAKINGS. Main/Corp** Jammu and Kashmir Legislature. Legislative Assembly. Committee on Public Undertakings. English. Jammu & Kashmir Legislative Assembly Committee on Public Undertakings, Jammu India. **LC** HD4295.K3; A27. **DD** 354/.54/600825.

II/0448-2433
**REPORT - JAMMU AND KASHMIR LEGISLATIVE COUNCIL, COMMITTEE ON PRIVILEGES.** [Rep.-Jammu Kashmir Legis. Counc., Comm. Privil.]. **Main/Corp** Jammu and Kashmir. Legislature. Legislative Council. Committee on Privileges. English. Jammu and Kashmir Legislative Council Secretariat, Committee on Privileges, Spinagar India. **LC** JQ620.K35; J35B. **DD** 328.54/6/0747.

II/0537-0280
**REPORT - JOINT COMMITTEE ON OFFICES OF PROFIT. Main/Corp** India (Republic). Parliament. Joint Committee on Offices of Profit. (19??)-. English. Lok Sabha Secretariat, India Parliament House of the People, New Delhi India. **LC** JQ229.C56; A3.

II
**REPORT - KARNATAKA LEGISLATIVE ASSEMBLY, COMMITTEE OF PRIVILEGES. Main/Corp** Karnataka, India. Legislature. Legislative Assembly. Committee of Privileges. English. Karnataka Legislative Secretariat, Vidhana Soudha, Bangalore 560001 India. **LC** JQ620.M75; A27; JQ620.K296. **DD** 328.54/87/0747. *Continues Mysore. Legislature. Legislative Assembly. Committee of Privileges. Report.*

US
**REPORT OF EXAMINATION, PUBLIC EMPLOYEES' PENSION FUNDS. Main/Corp** Illinois. Dept. of Insurance. English. be. Illinois Department of Insurance, 320 West Washington Street, Springfield IL 62767. **Tel** (217)782-4515, FAX (217)782-5020. **LC** JK5760.P4; A28. **DD** 353.9773005. *Continues Report of Examination, Public Employees' Pension Funds.*

US
**REPORT OF SOUTH DAKOTA'S PROFESSIONAL AND OCCUPATIONAL LICENSING BOARDS AND COMMISSIONS. Main/Corp** South Dakota. Dept. of Commerce and Consumer Affairs. English. an. South Dakota Department of Commerce and Consumer Affairs, State Capitol, 500 East Capitol, Pierre SD 57501. **LC** HD3630.U7; S65A. **DD** 353.97830082/4046/06.

ZA
**REPORT OF THE AUDITOR-GENERAL FOR ... ON THE ACCOUNTS OF PARASTATAL BODIES. Main/Corp** Zambia. Auditor-General. **VFOAT** Report of the Auditor-General for ... on the Accounts of Parastatal Bodies, Presented to the National Assembly. 1979-. English. an. **LC** HJ9929.Z35; Z33B. **DD** 354.68940072/32.

SA
**REPORT OF THE AUDITOR-GENERAL ON THE ACCOUNTS OF THE DECIDUOUS FRUIT BOARD AND THE SOUTH AFRICAN PLANT IMPROVEMENT ORGANISATION. VERSLAG VAN DIE OUDITEUR-GENERAAL VOR DIE REKENINGEN VAN DIE SAGTEVRUGTERAAD EN DIE SUID-AFRIKAANSE PLANT-VERBETERINGSORGANISASIE. Main/Corp** South Africa. Deciduous Fruit Board. **Added/Corp** South Africa. Dept. of the Auditor-General. South Africa. Office of the Auditor-General. **VFOAT** Verslag van die Ouditeur-Generaal vor die Rekeningen van die Sagtevrugteraad en die Suid-Afrikaanse Plant-Verbeteringsorganisasie. (1975)-. Afrikaans (English). R2.05. Government Printer / South Africa, Bosman Street, Private Bag X85, Pretoria 0001 South Africa. **Tel** 011 27 12 3239731 Ext. 262. **LC** HD9257.S7; S65c. **DD** 354/.68/008233. *Continues South Africa. Deciduous Fruit Board. Report of the Controller and Auditor-General on the Accounts of the Deciduous Fruit Board and the Balance Sheet.*

SA
**REPORT OF THE AUDITOR-GENERAL ON THE ACCOUNTS OF THE OILSEEDS BOARD FOR THE FINANCIAL YEAR ... . VFOAT** Verslag van die Ouditeur-Generaal oor die Rekenings van die Oliesaderaad vir die Boekjaar / .. Afrikaans (English). an. R1.30. Government Printer / South Africa, Bosman Street, Private Bag X85, Pretoria 0001 South Africa. **Tel** 011 27 12 3239731 Ext. 262. **LC** HD9490.S6; S65A. **DD** 354.680082/333. *Continues Verslag van die Ouditeur-Generaal oor die Rekenings van die Oliesadebeerraad.*

# Public Administration

CN/0708-3998
**REPORT OF THE CHIEF ELECTORAL OFFICER ON THE ... GENERAL ENUMERATION. Main/Corp** Alberta. Chief Electoral Officer. Began with 1978. English. an. Free. Alberta Legislative Assembly, Office of the Chief Electoral Officer, West Chambers Building/Main Floor, 12220 Stony Plain Road, Edmonton Alberta T5N 3Y4 Canada. **Tel** (403)427-7191, FAX (403)422-2900. **LC** JL338; .A42B. **DD** 324.97123. **Circ:** 1,500 (ctrl).
**Desc:** Poll by poll results of the 1989 General Election for the province of Alberta, as well as a financial summary of its costs.

AT/0480-970X
**REPORT OF THE CO-ORDINATOR-GENERAL OF PUBLIC WORKS, QUEENSLAND. Main/Corp** Queensland. Department of the Co-Ordinator General of Public Works. **VFOAT** Report - Co-Ordinator-General of Public Works. Periodical. English. Government Printer / Queensland, Box 680 GPO, 102 George Street, Brisbane Queensland 4001 Australia. **DD** 354.

ZA
**REPORT OF THE COMMITTEE ON GOVERNMENT ASSURANCES FOR THE ... SESSION OF THE ... NATIONAL ASSEMBLY, APPOINTED ON ... / REPUBLIC OF ZAMBIA. Main/Corp** Zambia. National Assembly. Committee on Government Assurances. 2nd Session, 4th National Assembly (1980)-. English. an. K1.80. Zambia Government Printer, POB 30136, Lusaka Zambia. **LC** JQ2854; .Z35A. **DD** 328.6894/07456.
**Desc:** Report of the Committee on Government Assurances; scrutinizes the assurances, promises and undertakings of ministers given periodically on the floor of the house. Comments on delays in implementation and the equality of the action taken.

RH
**REPORT OF THE CONTROLLER OF WORKS. Main/Corp** Rhodesia, Southern. Dept. of Works. (19??)-. English. **LC** HD4350.R45; R47a. **DD** 354/.689/10086.

SA
**REPORT OF THE DEPARTMENT OF PLURAL RELATIONS AND DEVELOPMENT. Main/Corp** South Africa. Dept. of Plural Relations and Development. **VFOAT** Verslag van die Departement van Plurale Betrekkinge en Ontwikkeling. Afrikaans (English). R10.55. The Government Printer, Bosman Street, Private Bag X85, Pretoria 0001 South Africa. **Tel** 012-323-9731, FAX 012-323-0009. **LC** DT763.6; .S672A. **DD** 354.680081/4/96.

HK
**REPORT OF THE DIRECTOR OF AUDIT ON THE RESULTS OF VALUE FOR MONEY AUDITS. Main/Corp** Hong Kong. Audit Dept. (198?)-. English. an. HK$70.00. Hong Kong Government Information Service, Beaconsfield House, 4 Queens Road, Hong Kong Hong Kong. **Tel** 011 852 8428801 4, telex 61190 HKGIS. **Continues** Hong Kong. Audit Dept. Report and Certificate of the Director of Audit on the Accounts of the Hong Kong Government.

US
**REPORT OF THE DIVISION OF PUBLIC UTILITY CONTROL (CONNECTICUT). Main/Corp** Connecticut. Division of Public Utility Control. 1978/79-. English. an. Division of Public Utility Control, Department of Business Regulation, 165 Capitol Avenue, State Office Building, Hartford CT 06115. **LC** HD2767.C8; C66. **DD** 363.6/09746.

UK
**REPORT OF THE GAMING BOARD FOR GREAT BRITAIN. Added/Corp** Gaming Board for Great Britain. (1975)-. Periodical. English. an. £6.60. Her Majesty's Stationery Office, 51 Nine Elms Lane, London SW8 5DR England. **Tel** 011 44 71 873 8459, 011 44 71 873 8499, FAX 011 44 71 873 8499, 011 44 71 873 8456, telex 297138. **(Subscription address:** Her Majesty's Stationery Office, PO Box 276, Publications Centre, London SW8 5DT England.**)**

NZ
**REPORT OF THE GOVERNMENT COMPUTING SERVICE FOR THE YEAR ENDED 31 MARCH - NEW ZEALAND. Main/Corp** New Zealand. Government Computing Service. (1986)-. English. **LC** JQ5829.A8; N495a. **DD** 354.93104/028/5.

NZ
**REPORT OF THE JOHNSONVILLE LICENSING TRUST FOR THE YEAR ENDED 31 MARCH ... . Main/Corp** Johnsonville Licensing Trust (N.Z.). English. an. $0.75. **LC** HD9368.N47; J634A. **DD** 352.94/26.

US
**REPORT OF THE MASSACHUSETTS COMMISSION ON INDIAN AFFAIRS. Main/Corp** Massachusetts. Commission on Indian Affairs. 1975-. English. an. Room 1401/Saltonstall Building, 100 Cambridge Street, Boston MA 02202. **LC** E78.M4; M514A. **DD** 353.9/744/008484.

US
**REPORT OF THE MISSISSIPPI RIVER PARKWAY COMMISSION OF MINNESOTA. Main/Corp** Mississippi River Parkway Commission of Minnesota. English. be. 130 State Office Building, St Paul MN 55101. **Tel** (612)224-9903. **ED** John F Edman. **LC** HE356.M6; M57A. **DD** 353.97760086/42/06.
**Desc:** Annual report of 1983-1984.

US/0094-7326
**REPORT OF THE NEW MEXICO VETERANS' SERVICE COMMISSION. Main/Corp** New Mexico. Veterans' Service Commission. (19??)-. English. an. Free. Veterans' Service Commission, 408 Galisteo Street, Box 2324, Santa Fe NM 87503. **Tel** (505)827-6300, FAX (505)827-6300. **LC** UB358.N6; N47a. **DD** 353.9/789/00848. **Circ:** 100. available with charts.

NZ
**REPORT OF THE OAMARU LICENSING TRUST FOR THE YEAR ENDED. Main/Corp** Oamaru Licensing Trust (N.Z.). English. an. LC HV5682; .O215. **DD** 354.9310076/1/05. **Continues** Report Presented to the House of Representatives.

US
**REPORT OF THE OFFICE OF THE PUBLIC COUNSEL, STATE OF MISSOURI. Main/Corp** Missouri. Office of the Public Counsel. (Sept. 1974/Dec. 1976)-. Periodical. English. be. Free on request. Office of the Public Counsel, PO Box 7800, Jefferson City MO 65102. **Tel** (314)751-4857.

US/0073-1137
**REPORT OF THE OMBUDSMAN. Main/Corp** Hawaii. Office of the Ombudsman. No. 1 (1969/70)-. Government Publication. English. an. Free on request. Office of the Ombudsman, Kekuanaoa Building, 4th Floor, 465 South King Street, Honolulu HI 96813. **Tel** (808)587-0770. **ED** Yen L. Lew. **LC** JK9349.O4; H37a. **DD** 353.9/969/0091. ctrl circ.

US/0098-1338
**REPORT OF THE PLANNING DIVISION, STATE DEPARTMENT OF FINANCE. Main/Corp** Arizona. State Dept. of Finance. Planning Division. English. an. Arizona Department of Finance, 1700 West Washington, Phoenix AZ 85007. **LC** JK1651.A7; A27A. **DD** 353.9/791/00862.

CN/0225-2376
**REPORT OF THE PRESIDENT / NATURAL SCIENCES AND ENGINEERING RESEARCH COUNCIL CANADA.** [Rep. Pres. - Nat. Sci. Eng. Res. Counc. Can.]. **Main/Corp** Natural Sciences and Engineering Research Council Canada. **VFOAT** Rapport du Président. (1978/1979)-. English (French). an. Natural Sciences & Engineering Research Council, 200 Kent Street, Ottawa Ontario K1A 1H5 Canada. **Tel** (613)995-5992. **LC** Q180.C2; N36a. **DD** 354.710085/5.

MF
**REPORT OF THE PUBLIC AND POLICE SERVICE COMMISSIONS. Main/Corp** Mauritius. Public Service Commission. **Added/Corp** Mauritius. Police Service Commission. (198?)-. English. Mauritius Government Printer, Place D Armes, Government Printing Department, Port Louis Mauritius. **Tel** 08-1783 OR 08 4011. **Continues** Mauritius. Public Service Commission. Report of the Public Service Commission.

MF
**REPORT OF THE PUBLIC SERVICE COMMISSION. Title Change. Main/Corp** Mauritius. Public Service Commission. (19??)-(198?). English. Mauritius Government Printer, Place D Armes, Government Printing Department, Port Louis Mauritius. **Tel** 08-1783 OR 08 4011. **LC** JQ3172; .A35a. **DD** 354/.69/82001. **Continued by** Mauritius. Public Service Commission. Report of the Public and Police Service Commissions.

US
**REPORT OF THE SECRETARY OF DEFENSE TO THE PRESIDENT AND THE CONGRESS. Main/Corp** United States. Dept. of Defense. **VFOAT** Annual Report to the President and the Congress. (1990)-. Government Publication. English. an. Superintendent of Documents, US Government Printing Office, Washington DC 20402. **Tel** (202)275-3328, FAX (202)786-2377. **LC** UA23.2; .D47b. **DD** 353.6/05. **Continues** Report of Secretary of Defense ... to the Congress on the FY ... Budget, FY ... Authorization Request, and FY ... Defense Programs, 0191-6513.

US/0145-1928
**REPORT OF THE SECRETARY OF THE COMMONWEALTH TO THE GOVERNOR AND GENERAL ASSEMBLY OF VIRGINIA.** [Rep. Secr. Commonw. Gov. Gen. Assem. Va.]. **Main/Corp** Virginia. Secretary of the Commonwealth. (1925)-. Periodical. English. an (Jan.). $23.00. Secretary Commonwealth of Virginia, PO Box 1 - D, Richmond VA 23201. **Tel** (804)786-2441. **DD** 351. **Continues** Virginia. Secretary of the Commonwealth. Biennial Report of the Secretary of the Commonwealth to the Governor and General Assembly of Virginia.

CN
**REPORT OF THE SELECT STANDING COMMITTEE ON PUBLIC ACCOUNTS AND PRINTING, TOGETHER WITH MINUTES AND VERBATIM REPORT OF PROCEEDINGS. Main/Corp** Saskatchewan. Legislative Assembly. Select Standing Committee on Public Accounts and Printing. **VFOAT** Report and Minutes. V. 1- 1968-. Proceedings. English. Legislative Assembly Office, Legislative Building, Regina Saskatchewan Canada.

NL
**REPORT OF THE SOUTH PACIFIC CONFERENCE AND PROCEEDINGS OF THE SOUTH PACIFIC COMMISSION. Main/Corp** South Pacific Conference. **Added/Corp** South Pacific Commission. **VFOAT** Rapport de la Conference du Pacifique Sud et Compte Rendu de la Commission du Pacific Sud. Proceedings. Multiple languages (English and French). South Pacific Commission, PO Box D5, Noumea Cedex New Caledonia. **Tel** (687)26 20 00, FAX (687)26 38 18. **LC** DU1; .S58. **DD** 990.62. **Continues** Proceedings - South Pacific Commission.

CN/0706-0890
**REPORT OF THE STANDING COMMISSION ON REFORM OF THE ELECTORAL DISTRICTS. Title Change.** [Rep. Standing Comm. Reform Elect. Dist.]. **Main/Corp** Quebec (Province) National Assembly. Standing Commission on Reform of the Electoral Districts. **VAT** Report - Standing Commission on Reform of the Electoral Districts. (1972)-(19??). Periodical. English. Directeur General des Elections, 3460 de la Perade Sainte-Foy G1X 3Y5 Canada. **DD** 328.714/073454. **Continued by** Electoral Map of Quebec, Report, 0226-5141.

US
**REPORT OF THE STATE BUDGET AND CONTROL BOARD, DIVISION OF SINKING FUNDS AND PROPERTY. Main/Corp** South Carolina. State Budget and Control Board. Division of Sinking Funds and Property. **VFOAT** Report. English. **Continues** Report of the Commissioners of the State Sinking Fund to the General Assembly of South Carolina.
**Desc:** Includes the reports of the Division of Office Supplies and Printing and the Division of Purchasing.

AT
**REPORT OF THE STATE CO-ORDINATION COUNCIL. Main/Corp** State Co-Ordination Council (Victoria). (19??)-. English. **LC** JQ5301; .S7b. **DD** 354.94504.

AT
**REPORT OF THE STATE EMPLOYEES RETIREMENT BENEFITS BOARD FOR THE YEAR ENDED 30 JUNE ... . Main/Corp** Victoria. State Employees Retirement Benefits Board. English. an. 2.00Aus$ Australia; $1.00 US. State Employees Retirement Benefits Board, 35 Spring Street, Melbourne 3000 Australia. **Tel** (613)614-7566, FAX 62-7038. **LC** JQ5349.S2; V53A. **DD** 354.945005. **Circ:** 1,000 (ctrl).
**Desc:** Report to the Parliament of Victoria, Australia on the administration of the state employees retirement benefits board.

US
**REPORT OF THE UTAH CONSTITUTIONAL REVISION COMMISSION. Main/Corp** Utah. Constitutional Revision Commission. 1978-. Periodical. English. qt. Office of Legislative Research, State Capitol Salt Lake City UT 84114. **LC** KFU401 1895; .A183. **DD** 342.792/03/05. **Continues** Utah. Constitutional Revision Commission. Interim Report.

US
**REPORT ON ACTIVITIES OF THE COUNTY GOVERNMENT DURING THE FISCAL YEAR, A. Main/Corp** Montgomery Co., Md. Office of Information. **VFOAT** Annual Report on

# Public Administration

Activities of the Government of Montgomery County. English. an. Montgomery County Government / Office of Information, County Office Building, Rockville MD 20850. **LC** JS451.M39; M667A. **DD** 352.0752/84. **Continues** *Annual Report - Montgomery County, Md.*

US/0361-0314
### REPORT ON FRINGE BENEFITS AND RELATED PRACTICES AFFECTING GENERAL EMPLOYEES OF CITIES.
**Main/Corp** New York (State). Public Employment Relations Board. English. Public Employment Relations Board, 80 Wolf Road, Albany NY 12205-2604. **Tel** (518)457-2676. **LC** JS3.N7; P76A. **DD** 352/.005/1234097471.

US
### REPORT ON LEGISLATIVE ACTIVITIES OF THE COMMITTEE ON LABOR AND HUMAN RESOURCES, UNITED STATES SENATE DURING THE ... CONGRESS ... : PURSUANT TO SECTION 136 OF THE LEGISLATIVE REORGANIZATION ACT OF 1946, AS AMENDED BY THE LEGISLATIVE REORGANIZATION ACT OF 1970.
**See** Public Health and Safety.

US
### REPORT ON MANDATES AND MEASURES AFFECTING LOCAL GOVERNMENT FISCAL CAPACITY / FLORIDA ADVISORY COUNCIL ON INTERGOVERNMENTAL RELATIONS.
*Title Change.* **Added/Corp** Florida Advisory Council on Intergovernmental Relations. (19??)-(1992). English. an. Florida Advisory Council on Intergovernmental Relations, Lewis State Bank Building/Suite 400, Tallahassee FL 32304. **LC** KFF488; .A877. **DD** 353.97590072/53. *Continued by Intergovernmental Impact Report.*

US
### REPORT ON OFFICE OF THE LIEUTENANT GOVERNOR - CONNECTICUT.
**Main/Corp** Connecticut. Auditors of Public Accounts. English. an. Connecticut Auditors of Public Accounts, State Capitol, Hartford CT 06106. **LC** JK3353.L5; C66A. **DD** 353.974603/18.

US
### REPORT ON STATE COMPTROLLER-RETIREMENT DIVISION. CONNECTICUT MUNICIPAL EMPLOYEES' RETIREMENT AND SOCIAL SECURITY SYSTEMS, FISCAL YEAR ENDED JUNE 30 ... .
**Added/Corp** Connecticut. Auditors of Public Accounts. Connecticut. Office of the State Comptroller. Retirement Division. **VFOAT** Connecticut Municipal Employees' Retirement and Social Security Systems, Fiscal Year Ended June 30 ...; Auditors' Report, State Comptroller-Retirement Division; Connecticut Municipal Employees' Retirement and Social Security Systems for the Fiscal Year Ended June 30 ... . (1981)-. English. an. Connecticut Auditors of Public Accounts, State Capitol, Hartford CT 06106. **LC** JS451.C87; R46. **DD** 352/.0055/09746. **Continues** *Connecticut. Office of the State Comptroller. Retirement Division. Report on State Comptroller-Retirement Division. Connecticut Municipal Employees' Retirement Fund, Fiscal Year Ended June 30 ...;* **Absorbed in part** *Connecticut. Office of the State Comptroller. Retirement Division. Report on State Comptroller-Retirement Division. State and Municipal Employees' Social Security Funds, Fiscal Year Ended June 30 ... .*

US
### REPORT ON STATE ELECTIONS COMMISSION - CONNECTICUT.
**Main/Corp** Connecticut. Auditors of Public Accounts. Periodical. English. Connecticut Auditors of Public Accounts, State Capitol, Hartford CT 06106. **LC** JK1954; .C66A. **DD** 353.9/746/008.

US
### REPORT ON THE FISCAL ... PAY INCREASE UNDER THE FEDERAL STATUTORY PAY SYSTEMS : ANNUAL REPORT OF THE ADVISORY COMMITTEE ON FEDERAL PAY.
**Main/Corp** United States Advisory Committee on Federal Pay. English. an. Advisory Committee on Federal Pay, 1730 K Street NW, Washington DC 20006. **Circ:** 1,000. **Desc:** Report includes federal pay statistics, historical tables and discussion of recent pay events.

HK
### REPORT ON THE PAY LEVEL SURVEY, THE.
**Main/Corp** Hong Kong. Standing Commission on Civil Service Salaries and Conditions of Service. (1986)-. Government Publication. English. ir. Hong Kong Government Information Service, Beaconsfield House, 4 Queens Road, Hong Kong Hong Kong. **Tel** 011 852 8428801 4, telex 61190 HKGIS. **LC** JQ676.Z2; H647b. **DD** 354.51/2500123.

KE
### REPORT ON THE WORKING OF THE PUBLIC SERVICE COMMISSION OF KENYA.
**Main/Corp** Kenya. Public Service Commission. Began in 1963. English. 1/50. Kenya Public Service Commission, PO Box 30095, Nairobi Kenya. **LC** JQ2947.A65; A56A. **DD** 354/.676/2006.

AT
### REPORT - PIPELINE AUTHORITY.
**Main/Corp** Pipeline Authority. 1973/74-. English. an. $0.40. The Pipeline Authority, 39 London Circuit, Canberra City Australian Capital Territory Australia. **Tel** (062)435222, FAX (062)497043. **(Subscription address:** GPO Box 1950, Canberra Australian Capital Territory Australia) **LC** J905; .L3 subser; HD9580.A8. **DD** 328.94/01 S; 354/.94/008232. **Circ:** 2,000.

SA
### REPORT - SOUTH AFRICA. DRY BEAN BOARD.
**Main/Corp** South Africa. Dry Bean Board. **VFOAT** Verslag. Multiple languages (English and Afrikaans). Arcadia Telegrams Boneraad, 45 Hamilton Street, PO Box 678, Pretoria South Africa. **LC** HD9235.B42; S65. **DD** 354/.68/008233.

US
### REPORT / SPECIAL JOINT COMMITTEE OF THE GENERAL ASSEMBLY TO REVIEW RETIREMENT COST-OF-LIVING SUPPLEMENTS AND FUNDING SOURCES.
**Main/Corp** Pennsylvania. General Assembly. Special Joint Committee to Review Retirement Cost-of-Living Supplements and Funding Sources. 1981-82-. English. be. Joint State Government Commission, Room 108/Finance Building, Harrisburg PA 17120. **LC** JK3660.P4; P43A. **DD** 353.9748005/05.

II
### REPORT - TAMIL NADU LEGISLATIVE ASSEMBLY COMMITTEE ON PUBLIC UNDERTAKINGS.
**Main/Corp** Tamil Nadu. Legislature. Legislative Assembly. Committee on Public Undertakings. 1st (1973/74)-. English. Legislative Assembly Department, Fort St George 9, Madras India. **LC** HD4295.T35; T35a. **DD** 354/.54/820086.

CN
### REPORT - TASK FORCE HYDRO.
**Main/Corp** Ontario. Task Force Hydro. No. 1- 1972-. Monographic series. English. Price varies per volume. Ontario Government Bookstore, 880 Bay Street, Toronto Ontario M7A 1N8 Canada.

US
### REPORT/TECHNICAL STUDY : REPORTED LOBBYING EXPENDITURES.
**Main/Corp** Washington (State). Public Disclosure Commission. English. Public Disclosure Commission, 403 Evergreen Plaza, Mail Stop FJ-42, Olympia WA 98504. **LC** JK9274.5; .W37A. **DD** 322.4/3/09797.

US/0739-3989
### REPORT TO CONGRESS, ADMINISTRATION OF THE WILD FREE-ROAMING HORSE AND BURRO ACT.
**VFOAT** Administration of the Wild Free-Roaming Horse and Burro Act. Government Publication. English. US Department of the Interior Bureau of Land Management, 1849 C Street NW, Room 5660, Washington DC 20240. **Tel** (202)208-3801, FAX (202)208-5902. **LC** SF360.3.U6; R46. **DD** 353.0082/328. available on microfiche (Vols. for (1982-) distributed to depository libraries). **Continues** *Report to Congress by the Secretary of the Interior and the Secretary of Agriculture on Administration of the Wild Free-Roaming Horse and Burro Act,* Public Law 92-195, 0739-4071.

US
### REPORT TO THE GOVERNOR.
English. an. Free. Virginia Department of Agriculture & Consumer Services, 1100 Bank Street, Washington Building, Suite 210, Richmond VA 23219. **Tel** (804)786-2373, FAX (804)371-7679. **ED** B.J. Altschul. **Circ:** 1,000. **Desc:** Review of current programs and policy recommendations to the Governor by the Virginia Board of Agriculture and Consumer Services and the Virginia Department of Agriculture and Consumer Services.

US/0882-679X
### REPORT TO THE GOVERNORS.
[Rep. gov. - Counc. State Plan. Agencies]. **VFOAT** CSPA State Scanning Network. 1985, No. 1-. Periodical. English. qt. Council of State Policy and Planning Agencies, 400 North Capitol Street NW/Suite 291, Washington DC 20001. **Tel** (202)624-5386. **DD** 353. ctrl circ. **Desc:** Emerging state policy issues in executive brief format. Content derived from process involving network of gubernatorial level policy teams and national experts.

UK
### REPORT TO THE HEADS OF GOVERNMENT BY THE COMMONWEALTH SECRETARY-GENERAL.
**Main/Corp** Commonwealth Secretariat. **VFOAT** Report of the Commonwealth Secretary-General. English. Commonwealth Secretariat / London, Marlborough House, Pall Mall, London SW1Y 5HX England. **Tel** 44 71 8393411, telex 27678. **LC** JN248; .C592A. **DD** 320.9/171/241.

US
### REPORT TO THE JOINT STANDING COMMITTEE ON PUBLIC UTILITIES, MAINE LEGISLATURE.
**Main/Corp** Maine. Public Utilities Commission. English. an. Public Utilities Commission, 242 State Street, State House Station 18, Augusta ME 04333. **LC** HD2767.M2; M346A. **DD** 363.6/09741.

NL
### REPORT TO THE SOUTH PACIFIC COMMISSION.
(REPORT OF THE SOUTH PACIFIC COMMISSION TO THE GOVERNMENTS OF AUSTRALIA, FRANCE, THE NETHERLANDS, NEW ZEALAND, THE UNITED KINGDOM, THE UNITED STATES OF AMERICA.). **Main/Corp** South Pacific Commission. **VFOAT** Progress in the Pacific; Progress in the South Pacific; South Pacific Report; Annual Report of the South Pacific Commission. 1948-. English. PO Box D 5, Noumea Cedex New Caledonia. **LC** DU1; .S584.

AT
### REPORT UPON THE OPERATIONS OF THE SUB-DEPARTMENTS OF NATIVE AFFAIRS, EVENTIDE (SANDGATE), EVENTIDE (CHARTERS TOWERS), EVENTIDE (ROCKHAMPTON), INSTITUTION FOR INEBRIATES (MARBURG), AND QUEENSLAND INDUSTRIAL INSTITUTION FOR THE BLIND (SOUTH BRISBANE).
**See** Sociology-Social Services and Welfare.

II
### REPORT / WESTERN PREMIERS' TASK FORCE ON CONSTITUTIONAL TRENDS.
**Main/Corp** Western Premiers' Task Force on Constitutional Trends. Began in 1977. English. an. The Task Force, Parliament Building, Victoria British Columbia V8V 1X4 Canada. **LC** KE4275; .W474. **DD** 342.71/042/05; 347.1024205.

US/0092-4873
### REPORTER - AMERICAN PUBLIC WORKS ASSOCIATION.
(THE APWA REPORTER.). **Main/Corp** American Public Works Association. V. 29- Jan. 1962-. Periodical. English. mo. $5.00. American Public Works Association, 1313 East 60th Street, Chicago IL 60637. **Tel** (312)667-2200. **LC** TA23. **DD** 363.5/0973. **CODEN** APRPE3. **Continues** *American Public Works Association. Newsletter.* **Ind/Abst** Ei Page One; Highw. Res. Abstr.

CN/0710-815X
### REPORTER (SUPPLY AND SERVICES CANADA).
(REPORTER.). [Reporter]. **Main/Corp** Canada. Supply and Services Canada. **VFOAT** Reporter. **VAT** Reporter (Approvisionnements et Services Canada). Vol. 1, No. 1 (Apr. 1976)-. Periodical. English (French). ir. Canada Communication Group Publishers, Order Processing, Ottawa Ontario K1A 0S9 Canada. **Tel** (819)956-4800, (819)956-4802. **DD** 354.710671/2/05. **Continues** *Intendant.*

II
### REPORTS AND SUMMARIES OF DISCUSSIONS / INTERNATIONAL SOCIAL SECURITY ASSOCIATION, COMMITTEE ON PROVIDENT FUNDS.
**See** Insurance.

US
### REPORTS / NEW YORK STATE, PUBLIC SERVICE COMMISSION.
**Main/Corp** New York (State). Public Service Commission. V. 2 (1962)-. English. Public Service Commission / New York, Empire State Plaza, Agency Building 3, Albany NY 12223. **Tel** (518)474-2532. **LC** KFN5455. **DD** 342/.747/0902646.

NZ
### REPORTS ON NIUE AND THE TOKELAU ISLANDS.
**Main/Corp** New Zealand. Maori and Island Affairs Dept. English. an. Price varies. Government Printing Office / New Zealand, 10 Mulgrave Street, Wellington New Zealand. **Tel** 011 64 4 4737211, FAX 011 64 4 734943, telex GOVPRINT NZ 31320. **LC** DU430.N5; N48A. **DD** 996/.12. **Continues** *Reports on Niue and the Tokelau Islands.*

## Public Administration

MM
**REPORTS ON THE WORKING OF GOVERNMENT DEPARTMENTS FOR THE YEAR ... .** **Main/Corp** Malta. Information Division. English. an. **LC** JN1586; .M32A. **DD** 354.45/8504/05. *Continues Malta. Dept. of Information. Report on the Working of Government Departments.*

US
**REPRESENTABLE COMPENSATION PLAN - OREGON. EXECUTIVE DEPT. PERSONNEL DIVISION. OPERATIONS AND DEVELOPMENT UNIT.** **Main/Corp** Oregon. Executive Dept. Personnel Division Operations and Development Unit. English. Operations and Development Unit, Personnel Division, Executive Department, 155 Cottage Street NE, Salem OR 97310. **LC** JK9057; .A32. **DD** 353.9795001/23. *Continues Executive Dept. Personnel Division. Compensation Plan.*

US/0738-193X
**REPUBLICANS ABROAD.** [Repub. abroad]. Periodical. English. qt. Republicans Abroad, c/o Republican National Committee, 310 1st Street Southeast, Washington DC 20003. **LC** JK2351; .R45. **DD** 324.2734/05.

US/0092-617X
**RES PUBLICA (CLAREMONT). See** Political Science.

SW
**RESEARCH ACTIVITIES / SWEDISH NATIONAL INDUSTRIAL BOARD.** **Main/Corp** Sweden. Statens Industriverk. English. an. Statens Industriverk, 117 86 Stockholm Sweden. **Tel** 46 8 7449000, FAX 46 8 7440980. **LC** T177.S4; S92A. **DD** 607/.20485.

US
**RESEARCH IN PUBLIC ADMINISTRATION.** Vol. 1 (1991)-. English. ir. $73.25. JAI Press Inc., 55 Old Post Road, Suite 2, PO Box 1678, Greenwich CT 06836-1678. **Tel** (203)661-7602, FAX (203)661-0792. **ED** James L. Perry. **LC** JA1; .R374; JA1; .R37.

UK
**RESEARCH MEMORANDUM.** **Main/Corp** University of Birmingham. Centre for Urban and Regional Studies. No. 1- 1967-. Monographic series. English. Price varies per volume.

US/0092-5500
**RESEARCH MEMORANDUM - MUNICIPAL RESEARCH AND SERVICES CENTER OF WASHINGTON (SEATTLE).** (RESEARCH MEMORANDUM.). **Main/Corp** Municipal Research and Services Center of Washington. English. Municipal Research Coun, 10517 NE 38th Pl, Kirkland WA 98033-7926. **LC** JS451.W25; M85A. **DD** 352/.008/09797.

US
**RESEARCH MONITOR.** V. 1- Jan. 1978-. Periodical. English. wk. $495.00. National Information Service, 1754 Church Street NW, Washington DC 20036. **Tel** (202)234-5149. **ED** Dale Hudelson. **Circ:** 100.
**Desc:** A news and reference service including a directory of all federal programs supporting extramural research and development and a weekly newsletter on policy and budget developments of federal research programs.

US
**RESEARCH MONITOR; PROFILES.** **Added/Corp** National Information Service. No. 1 (1978)-. Periodical. English. ir. $350.00 Comes with Research Monitor Service. Research Monitor, 1754B Church Street Northwest, Washington DC 20036. **Tel** (202)234-6630.

US
**RESEARCH PROGRAM PROSPECTUS / APPALACHIAN REGIONAL COMMISSION.** **Main/Corp** Appalachian Regional Commission. **VFOAT** Research Program. English. an. Appalachian Regional Commission, 1666 Connecticut Avenue Northwest, Washington DC 20235. **Tel** (202)673-7968, FAX (202)673-7930.

FR
**RESOLUTION - PARLIAMENTARY ASSEMBLY OF THE COUNCIL OF EUROPE.** **Main/Corp** Council of Europe. Parliamentary Assembly. Multiple languages (English and French). Council of Europe / Group Pact ED, Pharmacopoeia BP 907, 67029 Strasbourg Cedex 01 France. **Tel** 011 33 88 412036, FAX 011 33 88 41277181, telex 880388. **LC** JN22; .C68A. **DD** 341.24/2. *Continues Council of Europe. Consultation Assembly. Resolution.*

US/0160-9882
**RETAIL PRICES AND INDEXES OF FUELS AND UTILITIES.** July 1971-. Government Publication. English. bm. US Department of Labor / Bureau of Labor Statistics, 441 G Street NW, Washington DC 20212. **Tel** (202)606-7800, FAX (202)606-7797. *Continues Retail Prices and Indexes of Fuels and Electricity.*

US/0034-6179
**RETIREMENT LIFE.** **Added/Corp** National Association of Retired Federal Employees. Vol. 1 (1922)-. Periodical. English. mo. $25.00. National Association Retired Federal Employees, 1533 New Hampshire Northwest, Washington DC 20036. **Tel** (202)234-0832. **LC** JK791; .A7.

II
**REVIEW - ANDHRA PRADESH, INDIA. LEGISLATURE. LEGISLATIVE COUNCIL.** **Main/Corp** Andhra Pradesh, India. Legislature. Legislative Council. English. India Legislature, Legislative Council Hyderabad, Andhra Pradesh, Hyderabad India. **LC** J601.A4; J85. **DD** 328.54/84/04.

UK
**REVIEW OF PARLIAMENT AND PARLIAMENTARY DIGEST.** Began with Oct. 20, 1972 issue. Periodical. English. wk. **LC** JN101; .R35. **DD** 328.42/03.

UK/0143-0556
**REVIEW OF SECURITY AND THE STATE.** [Rev. secur. state]. **VFOAT** Security and The State; Security & The State. 1978-. English. an. $10.00. Julian Friedmann Books Ltd, 15 Catherine Street, London WC2B 5JZ England. **LC** DA592; .R48. **DD** 320.941.

US/0738-842X
**REVIEW OF THE UNITED STATES SYNTHETIC FUELS CORPORATIONS FINANCIAL STATEMENTS.** (REVIEW OF THE UNITED STATES SYNTHETIC FUELS CORPORATION'S FINANCIAL STATEMENTS FOR THE YEAR ENDED SEPTEMBER 30 ...). English. an. US G A O Document Handling and Information Services Facility, PO Box 6015, Gaithersburg MD 20760. **LC** HD9502.5.S964; S977. **DD** 353.09/2.

CN
**REVISED STATUTES OF SASKATCHEWAN.** English. ir. 60.00Can$. Office of the Queens Printer / Saskatchewan, 1874 Scarth Street, Eighth Floor, Regina Saskatchewan S4P 3V7 Canada. **Tel** (306)787-6894.

CK/0120-4289
**REVISTA / CAMARA DE COMERCIO DE BOGOTA.** [Rev. - Camara Comer. Bogota]. **Added/Corp** Camara de Comercio de Bogota. **VFOAT** Revista Camara de Comercio de Bogota. Vol. 1, No. 1 (Dec. 1970)-. Periodical. Spanish. Four times a year (Mar., June, Sept., Dec.). $60.00. Camara de Comercio de Bogota, Apartado Aereo 29824, Bogota, Colombia. **Tel** 011 57 1 2819900.
**Ind/Abst** PAIS Int. Print.

CR
**REVISTA CENTROAMERICANA DE ADMINISTRACION PUBLICA.** **Added/Corp** Instituto Centroamericano de Administracion Publica. No. 1 (July/Dec. 1981)-. Periodical. Spanish. ir. Instituto Centroamericano Administration, Apartado 10025, San Jose 1000 Costa Rica. **Tel** 011 506 341011, 011 506 254616. **LC** JL1401.A1; R48. **DD** 354.728/0005.

BL
**REVISTA DE ADMINISTRACAO MUNICIPAL.** **Added/Corp** Instituto Brasileiro de Administracao Municipal. (1961)-. Periodical. Portuguese. qt. $40.00. Largo Ibarn, 1 50. Andar Botafogo ZC 02, 20000 Rio de Janeiro Brazil. **Tel** (021)266-6622, telex (021)22638 INBM. **ED** Francois E.J. de Bremaeker. **LC** JS41; .R37. Index available. **Bk Rev. Ad Acc. Circ:** 3,000 (ctrl). *Continues Noticias Municipais.*

BL
**REVISTA DE ADMINISTRACAO PARA O DESENVOLVIMENTO.** Periodical. Portuguese. INAD, Caixa Postal 1817, Recife Brazil. **LC** JA5; .R483. **DD** 350/.0005.

BL/0034-7612
**REVISTA DE ADMINISTRACAO PUBLICA (RIO DE JANEIRO).** (REVISTA DE ADMINISTRACAO PUBLICA.). **Added/Corp** Rio de Janeiro. Escola Brasileira de Administracao Publica. (1967)-. Periodical. Portuguese. qt. $60.00. Fundacao Getulio Vargas, Praia de Botafogo, 190 6 Andar, 22253-900 Rio de Janeiro RJ Brazil. **Tel** 011 5521 551 0698, FAX 011 5521 551 1596, 011 5521 551 5755. **ED** Ana Maria G. Marquesini. **LC** JA5; .R486. **Bk Rev. Circ:** 1,700.
**Desc:** A prospective view of the administrative questions and similar issues, with a critical analysis of public administration theories and practices.

SP
**REVISTA DE ADMINISTRACION GALEGA.** Periodical. Spanish. sa. Revista de Administracion Galega, Asociacion de Funcionarios para a Normalizacion Linguistica de Galicia, Apartado de Correos 114, Santiago de Compostela Spain. **LC** JA84.S7; R48. **DD** 320.446/1/05.

MX/0482-5209
**REVISTA DE ADMINISTRACION PUBLICA. Ceased.** Spanish. qt. Instituto Nacional de Administracion Publica, A.C., Km. 14.5 Carretera Mexico-Toluca, Col. Palo Alto Delegacion Cuajimalpa, 05110 Mexico D.F. Mexico. **Tel** FAX 570-05-32. Index available. **Bk Rev. Ad Acc. Circ:** 1,000.
**Desc:** An institution dedicated to the teaching, investigation and diffusion of the administrative sciences.
**Ind/Abst** ABC POL SCI.

SP/0034-7639
**REVISTA DE ADMINISTRACION PUBLICA (MADRID, SPAIN).** (REVISTA DE ADMINISTRACION PUBLICA.). [Rev. adm. publica]. (1950)-. Periodical. Spanish. Three times a year. $61.00. Centro de Estudios Constitucionales, Calle Fuencarial 45 6A, 28071 Madrid Spain. **Tel** 011 34 1 5325069, 011 34 1 5316430. **LC** K19; .D2. **DD** 354.46/0005. cum. index.
**Ind/Abst** ABC POL SCI; Index Foreign Leg. Per.; Int. Bibliogr. Sociol.; PAIS Int. Print.

PN
**REVISTA FACULTAD DE ADMINISTRACION PUBLICA Y COMERCIO.** **Main/Corp** Panama (City). Universidad. Facultad de Administracion Publica y Comercio. (19??)-. Periodical. Spanish. qt. **LC** JF1338.P33; A3.

MX
**REVISTA LATINOAMERICANA DE ADMINISTRACION PUBLICA.** Spanish. Instituto Nacional de Administracion / MexicoPublica, Barranca del Muerto 210 P B, Mexico Mexico. **LC** JA5; .R54.

MX
**REVISTA SINDICAL.** **Added/Corp** Congreso Permanente de Unidad Sindical de los Trabajadores de America Latina. No. 1 (July 1979)-. Periodical. Spanish. qt. Congreso Permanente de Unidad Sindical de los Trabajodores de America Latina, Apartado Postal 32-269, Mexico 1 DF Mexico.

CK/0120-033X
**REVISTA UNIVERSIDAD EAFIT.** **Added/Corp** Universidad EAFIT. **VFOAT** Revista Universidad E.A.F.I.T.; Temas Administrativos y de Ingenieria; Revista Universidad Eafit--Temas Administrativos y de Ingenieria. No. 49 (Jan./March 1983)-. Periodical. Spanish. Four times a year. 12,000Col$ Colombia; $30.00 other. Revista Universidad EAFIT, Carrera 49 No. 7S-50, Apartado Aereo 3300, Medellin Columbia. **Tel** 574 2660500, FAX 574 2664284. **ED** Jorge E. Devia. **LC** HD28; .T44. **DD** 350/.0009861. Index available. cum. index. **Bk Rev. Ad Acc. Circ:** 1,000. *Continues Temas Administrativos.*
**Desc:** University journal providing the diffusion of the intellectual product of the professionals of the EAFIT University.

VE
**REVISTA VENEZOLANA DE CIENCIA POLITICA. See** Political Science.

VE
**REVISTA VENEZOLANA DE DESARROLLO ADMINISTRATIVO.** **Added/Corp** Centro Venezolano de Estudios de la Administracion Publica. No. 1 (Jan. 1982)-. Periodical. Spanish. Three times a year. $15.00. Ediciones Funacademus, Revista Venezolana de Desarrollo Administrativo, Av Andres Bello Edificio Vam, Torre Oeste Mezzanina Caracas.

FR/0035-0672
**REVUE ADMINISTRATIVE, LA.** (LA REVUE ADMINISTRATIVE, REVUE BIMESTRIELLE DE L'ADMINISTRATION MODERNE.). [Rev. adm.]. Vol. 1 (Jan./Feb. 1948)-. Periodical. French. bm. 795.00F. Revue Administrative Bureau, 203 2 rue de Viarmes, 75001 Paris France. **Tel** 011 33 1 42362390. **ED** Francois Monnier. **LC** JA11; .R37. **DD** 351.05. Index available in last issue of volume--attached. **Bk Rev,** (Qty: 6). **Ad Acc. Circ:** 35,000 (ctrl).
**Desc:** Covers administrative law, public administration, and general management for all countries.
**Ind/Abst** Index Foreign Leg. Per.; Int. Polit. Sci. Abstr.; PAIS Int. Print.

CN/0848-6727
**REVUE ANNUELLE - LOTO ATLANTIQUE, CANADA.** (REVUE ANNUELLE / LA SOCIETE DES LOTERIES DE L'ATLANTIQUE INC.). [Rev. annu. - Loto Atl. Can.]. **Main/Corp** Loto Atlantique (Canada). (1989/1990). French. **DD** 354.7150072/6. *Continues Loto Atlantique (Canada) Rapport Annuel - Loto Atlantique., 0703-2927.*

# Public Administration

FR/0181-0855
**REVUE DU SCOM.** [Rev. S.C.O.M.]. **Main/Corp** France. Service Central d'Organisation et Methodes. No. 71, (Jan./Mars 1979)-. Periodical. French. qt. Imprimerie Nationale / France, BP 514, 59505 Douai Cedex France. **Tel** 011 33 27 937090. *Continues Bulletin O.et M.*

FR/0152-7401
**REVUE FRANCAISE D'ADMINISTRATION PUBLIQUE.** [Rev. fr. adm. publique]. No. 1 (Jan./March 1977)-. Periodical. French. qt. 265.00F France; 327.00F (surface mail), 375.00F (airmail) other. Documentation Francaise, 29 Quai Voltaire, 75344 Paris Cedex 7 France. **Tel** 011 33 1 40157000, FAX 011 33 1 40157230, telex 204 826 DOCFRAN. **LC** JS41; .R45. **DD** 352/.0072/05. available in microform. *Continues Bulletin de l'Institut International d'Administration Publique, 0020-2355.*
**Desc:** News and commentary on public administration.
**Ind/Abst** ABC POL SCI; Int. Bibliogr. Sociol.; Int. Polit. Sci. Abstr.; Selec. Coop. Index Manage. Period.

GO/1016-2410
**REVUE GABONAISE D'POLITIQUES, ECONOMIQUES, ET JURIDIQUES.** [Rev. gabon. etud. polit. econ. jurid.]. French. 500.00. Compagnie Generale de Diffusion de la Culture Immeuble Branly, BP 14, 201 Libreville Gabon. **LC** JQ3407.A1; R48. **DD** 320.967/21.

RM
**REVUE - LA COMMISSION NATIONALE DE LA REPUBLIQUE SOCIALISTE DE ROUMANIE. JOURNAL - THE NATIONAL COMMISSION OF THE SOCIALIST REPUBLIC OF ROMANIA.** **Main/Corp** Comisia Nationala a Republicii Socialiste Romania Pentru UNESCO. **Added/Corp** Comisia Nationala a Republicii Socialiste Romania Pentru UNESCO. Journal. **VFOAT** Journal - The National Commission of the Socialist Republic of Romania; Revue UNESCO. (19??)-. English (French). qt. Journal - The National, 47 Chaussee Kisseleff, R-71268 Bucarest Romania. **LC** AS4.U825; R82a. **DD** 082. *Continues Comisia Nationala a Republicii Socialiste Romania Pentru UNESCO. Bulletin de la Commission Nationale de la Republique Socialiste de Roumanie pour l'Unesco.*

CN/0317-5510
**REVUE MUNICIPALE. ANNUAIRE (MONTREAL).** (LA REVUE MUNICIPALE. ANNUAIRE.). (1975)-. Periodical. French. Communications Vero Inc, 1600 Henri Bourassa Boulevard, Montreal Quebec H3M 3E2 Canada. **Tel** (514)332-8376, FAX (541)332-2666. **DD** 338.4/7/6025714.

CN/0035-3728
**REVUE MUNICIPALE (MONTREAL).** (LA REVUE MUNICIPALE.). [Rev. munic.]. **VFOAT** Revue Municipale du Canada; Revue Municipale du Quebec. Vol. 1 (June 1923)-. Periodical. French (English). mo (10 issues per year). 32.00Can$ (1 year), 50.00Can$ (2 year) Canada; 65.00Can$ (2 year) US; 40.00Can$ (1 year) other. Communications Vero Inc, 1600 Henri Bourassa Boulevard, Montreal Quebec H3M 3E2 Canada. **Tel** (514)332-8376, FAX (541)332-2666. **ED** Jean-Guy Thibault. **Ad Acc. Circ:** 12,000 (ctrl). *Absorbed Cites et Villes, 0009-7500.*
**Desc:** Articles about cities and the municipal government.
**Ind/Abst** Environ.; Point Repere (1983-).

CN/0229-2556
**REVUE PARLEMENTAIRE CANADIENNE.** [Rev. parlem. can.]. **Added/Corp** Association des Parlementaires du Commonwealth. Conseil de la Region Canadienne. Vol. 3 No. 4 (Winter 1981)-. Periodical. French. qt. 20.00Can$. Canadian Parliamentary Association, Canadian Region, PO Box 950, Confederation Building, Ottawa Ontario K1A 0A6 Canada. **Tel** (613)996-1662. **ED** Gary Levy. **DD** 328.71/005. Index available. **Bk Rev.** *Continues Revue de la Region Canadienne., 0707-0845.*
**Desc:** Articles about parliamentary offers by legislators, staff, professors and others interested in legislative institutions.
**Ind/Abst** Can. Period. Index.

CN/0849-567X
**RICH VIVONE'S INSIGHT INTO GOVERNMENT.** (INSIGHT INTO GOVERNMENT.). [Rich Vivone's insight gov.]. **Added/Corp** Rich Vivone and Associates. **VFOAT** Insight Into Government. (Aug. 1986)-. Periodical. English. wk (except in July and Aug.). 260.00Can$. Rich Vivone & Associates, 11208-66 Street, Edmonton Alberta T5B 1H3 Canada. **Tel** (403)479-7084, FAX (403)474-0277. **ED** Rich Vivone. **DD** 328.7123/005.

TZ
**RIPOTI YA UTEKELEZAJI WA MPANGO WA MAENDELEO / SERIKALI YA MAPINDUZI YA ZANZIBAR, WIZARA YA HABARI, UTAMADUNI, NA MICHEZO.** **Main/Corp** Zanzibar. Wizara Ya Habari, Utamaduni, Na Michezo. Swahili. an. Idara Ya Mipango Na Uendeshaji Wizara Ya Habari Utamaduni Na Michezo, S L P 772, Zanzibar Tanzania. **LC** JQ2961.A69; P859A.

RU
**RITM PERESTROIKI.** See Political Science.

IT
**RIVISTA AMMINISTRATIVA DELLA REPUBBLICA ITALIANA.** Vol. 3 (1852)-. Periodical. Italian. Ten times a year. L220000 Italy; L270000 other. Rivista Amministrativa Della Repubblica Italiana, Via B Tortolini 34, 00197 Rome Italy. **Tel** 011 39 6 8070155. **LC** JF1354.A2; R4. *Continues Rivista Amministrativa Del Regno.*
**Desc:** News and information on court decisions.

IT/0394-8439
**RIVISTA DEL PERSONALE DELL'ENTE LOCALE.** [Riv. pers. Ente Locale]. (1987)-. Periodical. Italian. Six times a year. L185000.00. Maggioli Editore, Casella Postale 290, 47037 Rimini, Italy. **Tel** 011 39 541 628666, FAX 011 39 541 742217. **UDC** 352.

IT/0391-190X
**RIVISTA TRIMESTRALE DI SCIENZA DELLA AMMINISTRAZIONE.** (Jan./March 1972)-. Periodical. Italian. qt. L120000 Italy; L160000 other. Franco Angeli Editore Riviste, Via le Monza 106, 20127 Milan Italy. **Tel** 011 39 2 2827651 or, 289562, FAX 011 39 2 258004, telex 051-511650. **ED** Giorgio Freddi. **LC** JA18; .T4. *Continues Scienza e la Tecnica della Organizzazione Nella Pubblica Amministrazione.*

●US
**ROBINSONS REDBOOK. A NATIVE AMERICAN GUIDE TO WASHINGTON D.C.** (1992)-. English. ir. $150.00 (latest edition). Native American Directory, PO Box 39003, Washington DC 20016. **Tel** (312)380-2700.

US
**ROCKEFELLER INSTITUTE BULLETIN.** **Added/Corp** Nelson A. Rockefeller Institute of Government. **VFOAT** Bulletin. (1991)-. English. Rockefeller Institute, 411 State Street, Albany NY 12203. **Tel** (518)443-5522, FAX (518)443-5788. **LC** WMLC 91/1933.

CN/0712-2993
**ROSEMERE-NOUVELLES.** (ROSEMERE NEWS.). [Rosemere-nouv.]. Vol. 1, No. 1 Mar. 1979-. Periodical. English (French). mo. Free. Rosemere News, Town of Rosemere, 100 Charbonneau, Rosemere Quebec J7A 3W1 Canada. **DD** 352.0714/24. ctrl circ.

●RU
**ROSSIISKAIA FEDERATSIIA.** **Added/Corp** Russia (Federation). Sovet Ministrov. (1993)-. Periodical. Russian. mo. Izdatelstvo Izvestiia, Pl. Pushkina 5, 103798 Moscow Russia. **LC** DK510.763; .R67. *Continues Narodnyi Deputat, 0236-0918.*

US
**ROSTER AND LIST OF COMMITTEES OF THE GENERAL ASSEMBLY OF MARYLAND.** **Main/Corp** Maryland. General Assembly. English. Maryland General Assembly, Printing Division, Annapolis MD 21404. **LC** JK3830; .M37A. **DD** 328.752/073/025.

US/0093-9951
**ROSTER OF BLACK ELECTED OFFICIALS IN THE SOUTH.** English. ir. Voter Education Project, 604 Beckwith Street SW, Atlanta GA 30314-4113. **Tel** (404)522-7495. **LC** JK1929.A2; R67. **DD** 353.9/75/002.

CN
**ROYAL GAZETTE.** See Law.

CN/0703-8623
**ROYAL GAZETTE. NEW BRUNSWICK.** (THE ROYAL GAZETTE [MICROFORM] / NEW BRUNSWICK.). **Main/Corp** New Brunswick. **VFOAT** Gazette Royale; New Brunswick Royal Gazete. (1976)-. Periodical. English (French). sa. Micromedia Limited, 20 Victoria Street, Toronto Ontario M5C 2N8 Canada. **Tel** (416)362-5211, (800)387-2689, FAX (416)362-6161, telex 06524668. **DD** 354.715/0005.

TH
**ROYAL THAI GOVERNMENT GAZETTE.** **Main/Corp** Thailand. **Added/Corp** Thailand. Laws, Statutes, etc. Thailand. Ratchakitchanubeksa English. No. 1 (Dec. 1946)-. English. ir. $250.00. Nibondh & Company Ltd, PO Box 402, Bangkok Thailand. **DD** 349.59302.

US
**RULES AND DIRECTORY.** **Main/Corp** Kansas. Legislature. House of Representatives. Directory. English. Kansas Legislature, House of Representatives, Topeka KS 66612. **LC** JK6878; .A15. **DD** 328.7815.

US/0747-4784
**RURAL ELECTRIC NEWSLETTER.** **VFOAT** RE. Newsletter. English. ir (weekly Feb-Sept, then bi-weekly Oct-Jan). $26.00. National Rural Electric Cooperative Association, 1800 Massachusetts Avenue Northwest, Washington DC 20036. **Tel** (202)857-9500, FAX (202)857-4863. **ED** J C Brown. **Bk Rev. Ad Acc. Circ:** 23,000.
**Desc:** Edited for managers and employees of rural electric utilities. Technical information news and opinions that strengthen skills and provide a background of regulatory, legislative and utility developments.

CN/0226-658X
**RURAL UTILITIES NEWSLETTER.** [Rural util. newsl.]. V. 1- Feb. 1980-. Newsletter. English. qt. Alberta Utilities, 12323 Stoney Plaine Road/7th Floor, Edmonton Alberta T5N 3Y9 Canada. **DD** 354.71230087. *Supersedes Rural Gas Newsletter, 0704-4097.*

●US/1069-1081
**RUSSIAN GOVERNMENT TODAY.** (RUSSIAN GOVERNMENT TODAY / [EDITORIAL CONTENT BY THE INTERNATIONAL CENTER].). [Russ. gov. today]. **Added/Corp** International Center (Washington, D.C.). (Spring 1993)-. Government Publication. English. sa (April and Oct). $195.00. Carroll Publishing Company, 1058 Thomas Jefferson Street Northwest, Washington DC 20007-3832. **Tel** (202)333-8620, FAX (202)337-7020. **LC** JN6691.A1; R87. **DD** 320.947. available on diskette.
**Desc:** Gives access to over 13,000 Russian leaders, including officials of the Russian Parliament (complete with voting scores), the Administration of the President, ministries and agencies, local and regional governments in the 86 administrative jurisdictions, associations and foundations, independent banks, commodity exchanges and brokers.

US/0486-8161
**SACRAMENTO NEWSLETTER, THE.** See Law.

US/0094-6958
**SAGE PUBLIC ADMINISTRATION ABSTRACTS.** See Public Administration-Abstracting, Bibliographies and Statistics.

US/0275-5297
**SAGE YEARBOOKS IN POLITICS AND PUBLIC POLICY.** See Political Science.

CN/0712-7308
**SAINT-HUBERT, NOTRE VILLE.** *Title Change.* (NOTRE VILLE / SAINT-HUBERT.). [St.-Hubert, notre ville]. **Main/Corp** Saint-Hubert (Quebec). **VFOAT** Saint-Hubert Notre Ville. Vol. 1, No. 1 (June 1981)-(19??). Periodical. French. qt. Service d'Information / Ville Saint-Hubert, 5900 Boulevard Cousineau, Saint-Hubert Quebec J3Y 7K8 Canada. **DD** 352.0714/37. *Formed by the union of Ingo Loisir (Saint-Hubert, Quebec : 1980), 0712-7286 and Saint-Hubert (Quebec). Entre-Nous, 0712-7294. Continued by Info-Loisir (Saint-Hubert, Quebec : 1984)., 0831-1366.*

CN/0829-4941
**SAINT-LAURENT JOURNAL.** *Title Change.* [J. St.-Laurent]. **VFOAT** Journal de Saint-Laurent. (Sept. 1985)-?. Periodical. English (French). Six times a year. City of Saint-Laurent, 777 Laurentien Boulevard, Saint-Laurent Quebec H4M 2M7 Canada. **Tel** 744-7305. **DD** 352.0714/28. *Continues Bulletin Saint-Laurent, 0710-961X. Continued by Words and People, 0846-0140.*
**Desc:** City news, public administration informations and leisure activities.

SA/0036-0767
**SAIPA.** (SAIPA; TYDSKRIF VIR PUBLIEKE ADMINISTRASIE. JOURNAL FOR PUBLIC ADMINISTRATION.). [SAIPA]. **Added/Corp** South African Institute for Public Administration. **VFOAT** Tydskrif vir Publieke Administrasie; Journal for Public Administration. Vol. 1 No. 1 (Jan. 1965)-. Periodical. Afrikaans (English). qt (Mar., June, Sep., Dec.). R25.00 South Africa; $22.00 other. South African Institute of Public Administration, PO Box 2752, Pretoria South Africa. **Tel** 011 27 12 2022851, 011 27 12 2022871, FAX 011 27 12 3265362. **ED** A Viljoen. **LC** JA26; .S23. Index available. **Bk Rev. Ad Acc. Circ:** 2,300 (ctrl).
**Desc:** Covers all aspects of public administration including municipal and international administration and public affairs, mainly South African but also other countries.
**Ind/Abst** ABC POL SCI; Int. Polit. Sci. Abstr.

II
**SAJJANAGADA.** Periodical. Marathi (Marathi). 10.00. Srisamartha Seva Mandala, Srisamartha Sadan, 179 Somwar Peth, Satara City India. **LC** BL1245.S26; A57.

US/0099-0477
**SALARY PLAN, STATE OF NORTH CAROLINA.** **Main/Corp** North Carolina. Office of State Personnel. English. an. North Carolina Office of State Personnel, 116 West Jones Street, Raleigh NC 27609. **LC** JK4157; .N65A. **DD** 353.9/756/0012.

# Public Administration

US/0738-4467
**SAMPAN.** Added/Corp Chinese American Civic Association (Boston, Mass.). **VFOAT** Shan Pan Yueh Kan. (19??)-. Periodical. English. sm (except Jan. and Feb.). Sampan, 90 Tyler Street, Boston MA 02111. **Tel** (617)426-8673.

PK
**SANGAT.** (19??)-. Periodical. Urdu (Urdu). wk. Rs25.00. Gajyan Baloch, General Manager Sangat, Rustamji Lane, Jinah Road, Koitah Pakistan. **LC** JQ201; .S25.

JA
**SANGIIN GIIN SENKYO NO KIROKU.** **Main/Corp** Tokyo, Japan. Senkyo Kanri Iinkai. (19??)-. Japanese. Senkyo Kanri Iinkai, 13 Yurakucho 2-chome Chiyoda-ku, Tokyo Japan. **LC** JQ1693.T58; T6a.

JA
**SANGYO KOZO NO CHOKI BIJON.** See Economics-Industry and Production.

IT/0393-4101
**SANITA PUBBLICA.** [Sanita pubbl.]. (1981)-. Periodical. Italian. Twelve times a year. L128000 Italy; L230000 others. Maggioli Editore, Casella Postale 290, 47037 Rimini, Italy. **Tel** 011 39 541 628666, FAX 011 39 541 742217. **NLM** WA 33.1; GI8 S2.

CN/0036-4894
**SASKATCHEWAN GAZETTE.** (THE SASKATCHEWAN GAZETTE [MICROFORM].). [Sask. gaz.]. **Main/Corp** Saskatchewan. **VFOAT** Regulations Under the Regulations Act; Revised Regulations of Saskatchewan; Regulations of Saskatchewan. Vol. 1, No. 1 (Sept. 15, 1905)-. Periodical. English. Fifty-two times a year. Micromedia Limited, 20 Victoria Street, Toronto Ontario M5C 2N8 Canada. **Tel** (416)362-5211, (800)387-2689, FAX (416)362-6161, telex 06524668. **DD** 354.7124/0005. available in microform from Micromedia Limited.

CN/0036-4894
**SASKATCHEWAN GAZETTE, THE.** [Sask. gaz.]. **Main/Corp** Saskatchewan. **VFOAT** Regulations Under the Regulations Act; Revised Regulations of Saskatchewan; Regulations of Saskatchewan. (Sept. 15, 1905)-. Periodical. English. wk. 133.05Can$. Office of the Queens Printer / Saskatchewan, 1874 Scarth Street, Eighth Floor, Regina Saskatchewan S4P 3V7 Canada. **Tel** (306)787-6894. **CODEN** SAGAEU. available on microfilm.

CN/0581-8435
**SASKATCHEWAN MUNICIPAL DIRECTORY.** [Sask. munic. dir.]. **Added/Corp** Saskatchewan. Dept. of Municipal Affairs. Saskatchewan. Saskatchewan Municipal Affairs. Saskatchewan. Saskatchewan Urban Affairs. Saskatchewan. Saskatchewan Rural Development. (1958)-. Directory. English. an. 10.00Can$. Saskatchewan Urban Affairs, 1855 Victoria Avenue, Regina Saskatchewan S4P S4P Canada. **Tel** (306)787-2664. **ED** Irene Rau. **LC** JS1721.S3; S34. **DD** 352/.00025/7124. **Circ:** 5,500. Continues Municipal Directory., 0318-143X.
**Desc:** Listing of municipal offices, officials and populations in Saskatchewan.

US/0363-9401
**SCA, STATE & COUNTY ADMINISTRATOR.** **VFOAT** State & County Administrator. **VAT** State County Administrator, State and County Administrator. V. 1- Jan./Feb. 1976-. Periodical. English. bm. $10.00. Security World Publishing, 2629 So La Cienega Blvd., Los Angeles CA 90034. **LC** JK2403; .S18. **DD** 353.9/05.

US
**SCAG: A RECORD OF ACCOMPLISHMENT.** **Main/Corp** Southern California Association of Governments. (19??)-. Periodical. English. an. Southern California Association of Governments, 818 West 7th Street, 12th Floor, Los Angeles CA 90017. **Tel** (213)236-1800. **LC** JS303.C2; S64a. **DD** 352/.0094/097949.

AT/0314-1543
**SCHOOL AND COMMUNITY NEWS CANBERRA.** See Education.

GW
**SCHRIFTENREIHE DES DEUTSCHEN STADTE- UND GEMEINDEBUNDES.** **Main/Corp** Deutscher Stadte-und Gemeindebund. Vol. 18 (1974)-. Monographic series. German. ir. Price varies per volume. Verlag Otto Schwartz & Company, Annastrasse 7, D 37075 Goettingen Germany. **Tel** 011 49 551 31051, 011 49 551 31052, FAX 011 49 551 372812. Continues Deutscher Stadtebund. Schriftenreihe, 0418-9590.

UK/0302-3427
**SCIENCE & PUBLIC POLICY.** [Sci. public pol.]. **Added/Corp** Science Policy Foundation. **VAT** Science and Public Policy. Vol. 1 (Jan. 1974)-. Periodical. English. bm. £114.00. Beech Tree Publishing, 10 Waterford Close, Guildford Surrey GU1 2EP England. **Tel** +44 483 67497, FAX +44 0483 67497. **(Subscription address:** World-Wide Subscription Services, Unit 4, Gibbs Reed Farm Pashley Road, Ticehurst TN5 7HE England.**) LC** Q179.9; .S32. **DD** 301.24/3. **NLM** W1 SC683K. **[CCC].** Index Available in first issue of next volume--loose--separately paged. **Bk Rev. Ad Acc.** Documents available from Documents on Demand. Supersedes Science Policy.
**Desc:** Interactions of science, technology, policy, economic development, sociology, business, Third World, hi-tech, R&D, tech assessment, hi-technology, research and development, technology assessment, articles, books, news, teaching, diary, briefings, research centre profiles.
**Ind/Abst** Asia.-Pac. Econ. Lit.; Coal Abstr.; Curr. Lit. Sci. Sci.; EMBASE; Environ. Abstr.; Geogr. Abstr. Human Geogr.; GeoRef; Int. Dev. Abstr.; LABORDOC; Soc. Plann. Policy Dev. Abstr.; Sociol. Abstr.

UK/0305-6562
**SCOTLANDS REGIONS.** (19??)-. English. an. £19.50 UK; £23.00 Canada and Europe; £25.50 other. WM Culross & Son Ltd, Queen Street, Coupar Angus, Perthshire PH13 9DF Scotland. **Tel** 011 44 828 27266, FAX 011 44 828 27146. **ED** Robert Benzies. **LC** JS4101; .C6. **DD** 352.0411. **Bk Rev. Ad Acc. Circ:** 1,300. Continues County & Municipal Year Book for Scotland.

CN/0383-7262
**SCRIBE (VAL-DAVID).** (LE SCRIBE.). **Added/Corp** Corporation des Secretaires Municipaux du Quebec. Vol. 1 (Mar. 1975)-. Periodical. French. Four times a year. 20.00Can$. Corp Secretaires Municipaux Quebec, 580 Grande Allee Est, Bur 225, Quebec Quebec GR1 2K2 Canada. **Tel** (418)647-4518. **DD** 352/.0006/2714.

US/0162-2838
**SEC NO-ACTION LETTERS INDEX AND SUMMARIES.** **Added/Corp** Washington Service Bureau. **VFOAT** No-Action Letters Index and Summaries. **VAT** Securities and Exchange Commission No-Action Letters Index and Summaries. (19??)-. Periodical. English. wk (52 issues). $1325.00 Washington, D.C. residents (tax included); $1250.00 other. Washington Service Bureau Inc., 655 15th Street Northwest, Suite 270, Washington DC 20005. **Tel** (800)955-5219, (202)508-0600. **ED** Susan Kavanagh. **LC** KF1068.32; .S43. **DD** 346.73/092; 347.30692. **[CCC].** Index available (bound in all issues). cum. index. **Circ:** 450. available on microfiche.
**Desc:** Abstracts of every no-action and interpretative letter made public by the Securities and Exchange Commission.

US/1061-0340
**SECRECY & GOVERNMENT BULLETIN.** [Secrecy gov. bull.]. **Added/Corp** Federation of American Scientists. **VFOAT** Secrecy and Government Bulletin. Issue No. 1 (July 1991)-. Periodical. English. mo. $20.00. Federation of American Scientists, 307 Massachusetts Avenue Northeast, Washington DC 20002. **Tel** (202)546-3300. **LC** JK468.S4; S43. **DD** 323.

MY
**SECRETARY-GENERAL'S REPORT.** **Main/Corp** Malaysian Chinese Association. General Assembly. **VFOAT** Report; Ma Hua Kung Hui Tai Piao Ta Hui Chang Nien Hui I. English (Chinese). Malaysian-Chinese Association, General Assembly, Kuala Lumpur Malaysia. **LC** JQ719.A8. **DD** 329.9/595.

MX
**SECTOR ELECTRICO.** Periodical. Spanish. mo. Departamento de Informacion Comision Federal de Electricidad, Rio Atoyac No 97 Mexico. **LC** HD9685.M63; M488. **DD** 363.6/2.

II/0582-3730
**SECULAR DEMOCRACY.** (1968)-. Periodical. English. an. **(Subscription address:** Prints India, 11 Darya Ganj, New Delhi 110002 India.**) LC** JQ201; .S43.

JA
**SEIFU KANKOBUTSU TO SOGO MOKUROKU.** Japanese. an. ¥350. Zenkoku Kampo Hambai Kyodo Kumiai, 2-4 Toranomon 2 Minato-ku, Tokyo 105 Japan. **Tel** (03)459-8881, FAX (03)294-4673. **LC** Z3305; .S434; JQ1601.

JA
**SEIFU KOHO YOTEI JIKO.** **Added/Corp** Japan. Naikaku Sori Daijin Kanbo. (19??)-. Periodical. Japanese. Naikaku Sori Daijinkambo Kohoshitsu, 6-1 Nagata-cho 1-chome, Chiyoda-ku 100 Tokyo Japan. **LC** JQ1649.P85; S42.

JA
**SEIKAN YORAN.** Began in 1982. Japanese. ¥2000. Seisaku Jihosa 4 Goban-cho Chiyoda-ku, Tokyo-to 102 Japan. **LC** JQ1621; .S46.

JA
**SEISAKU SHIRYO.** **Main/Corp** Nihon Shakaito (1945-). **Added/Corp** Gekkan Shakaito. Gogai. Nihon ShakaitÃo (1945- ). Seisaku Shingikai. No. 1 (May 1974)-. Japanese. ¥800. Nihon Shakaito Seisaku Shingikai, c/o Shugiin Daiichi Kaikan Nagatocho 2-chome, Chiyoda-ku, Tokyo Japan. **LC** JQ1698.S5; A25.

US
**SELECTED STATE DEPARTMENT PUBLICATIONS / UNITED STATES DEPARTMENT OF STATE, BUREAU OF PUBLIC AFFAIRS.** **Main/Corp** United States. Dept. of State. Bureau of Public Affairs. Began with June 1980. English. Three times a year. US Department of State / Bureau of Public Affairs, Washington DC 20520. Continues United States. Dept. of State. Bureau of Public Affairs. Recent Releases.

US/0148-2653
**SELF DETERMINATION QUARTERLY JOURNAL, THE.** V. 1- Mar. 1977-. Periodical. English. qt. Self Determination, PO Box 126, San Jose CA 95052. **Tel** (408)984-8134. **LC** JK8701; .S45. **DD** 3220.9/794/05.

US
**SEMIANNUAL REPORT TO THE CONGRESS / OFFICE OF INSPECTOR GENERAL.** **Main/Corp** United States. General Services Administration. Office of Inspector General. English. sa. General Services Administration / Office of Inspector General, Eighteenth and F Streets Northwest, Washington DC 20405. **LC** JK1672; .U53F. **DD** 353.0071/05.

US/0361-1310
**SEMSCOPE, THE.** [SEMscope]. **VFOAT** SEM Scope. **VAT** Southeast Michigan Scope. Periodical. English. ir. Free. Southeast Michigan Council of Governments, 1900 Edison Plaza, Detroit MI 48226. **Tel** (313)961-4266, FAX (313)961-4869. **ED** Alma Simmons. **DD** 352. **Circ:** 11,800 (ctrl). Continues COG Camera.
**Desc:** Southeast Michigan Council of Governments is a short and long-range planning organization for housing, economic development, population, transportation, environment, public safety in southeast Michigan.

MY
**SENARAI PERJAWATAN DI KEMENERIAN-KEMENTERIAN DAN JABATAN-JABATAN DALAM ANGGARAN PERBELANJAAN PERSEKUTUAN.** **Main/Corp** Malaysia. **Added/Corp** Malaysia. Jabatan Percetakan Negara. **VFOAT** Senarai Perjawatan Persekutuan. Malay. **LC** JQ716; .M34a. Continues Anggaran Perbelanjaan Mengurus.

US/0271-4280
**SENATE ISSUES YEARBOOK.** English. an. $3.50. Conservative Caucus Research Analysis and Education Foundation, 450 Maple Avenue East, Vienna VA 22180. **LC** JK1161; .S45. **DD** 328.73/0775.

JA
**SENKYO NO AYUMI.** Japanese. Yokohama-shi Senkyo Kanri Iinkai Jimukyoku, 1 Minato-cho 1 Naka-ku, Yokohama-shi 231 Japan. **LC** JQ1693.Y64; S46.

IO/0302-8879
**SERI PMST.** [Seri PMST]. **Main/Corp** Indonesia. Direktorat Pembangunan Masyarakat Suku-Suku Terasing. **VAT** Seri Pembangunan Masyarakat Suku-Suku Terasing. Indonesian. Department Social, JL IR H Juanda, Jakarta Indonesia. **LC** HN710.Z9; C622A.

SZ
**SERIES "REPORTS AND DOCUMENTS" / INTER-PARLIAMENTARY UNION.** **Main/Corp** Inter-Parliamentary Union. **Added/Corp** Inter-parliamentary Union. **VFOAT** Series Reports and Documents; Rapports et Documents; Reports and Documents. (19??)-. Monographic series. French (English). ir. Price varies per volume. Inter-Parliamentary Union, Place du Petit Saconnex, Ch 1211 Geneva 19 Switzerland. **Tel** 011 41 22 7344150, telex 789784. **LC** JF8; .I54a. **DD** 320.3.

●CN/1193-2724
**SERVICE QUALITY B.C. UPDATE.** [Serv. Qual. B.C. update]. **Added/Corp** Service Quality B.C. SQ Coordinators Council (B.C.). (1992)-. Periodical. English. **DD** 354.711001.

CN
**SERVING YOU IN BOTH OFFICIAL LANGUAGES / TREASURY BOARD OF CANADA.** **VFOAT** A Votre Service dans les Deux Langues Officielles. Began in 1982. English (French). **LC** JL71; .S47. **DD** 354.71/00025.

IT
**SERVIZI SOCIALI.** Italian. Two issues per month. L40.000. Centro Studi Form Soc Zancan, Via Patriarcato #41, 35139 Padua Italy. **(Subscription address:** Centrostudi E Formazione Sociale, Fondazione "E, Zancan" Via Patriarcaro 41, 35139 Padova Italy**) ED** Fondazione Zancan. Index available. **Bk Rev. Pr Rev.** ctrl circ.

4685

# Public Administration

**US**
**SESSION REPORT / STATE PLANNING AND COMMUNITY AFFAIRS COMMITTEE.** **Main/Corp** Georgia. General Assembly. House of Representatives. State Planning and Community Affairs Committee. English. an. State Planning and Community Affairs Committee, 142-C State Capitol, Atlanta GA 30334. **LC** KFG15; .G45. **DD** 328.758/077.

US/1049-8176
**SESSION WEEKLY.** (THE SESSION WEEKLY / MINNESOTA HOUSE OF REPRESENTATIVES.). [Sess. wkly.]. **Added/Corp** Minnesota. Legislature. House of Representatives. Vol. 1, No. 1 (Mar. 5-9 1984)-. Periodical. English. ir (published weekly during the legislative session)). Free on request. Public Information Office, 175 State Office Building, St. Paul MN 55155. **Tel** (612)296-2146. **DD** 342. **Continues** Session Monthly.

**CE**
**SESSIONAL PAPER - SRI LANKA.** **Main/Corp** Sri Lanka. **VFOAT** Sasi Vartava. Monographic series. English (table of contents in Sinhalese). Price varies per volume. Government Publications Bureau, PO Box 500, Colombo Sri Lanka.

**XV**
**SESTAVA ORGANOV SAMOUPRAVNIH INTERESNIH SKUPNOSTI / ZAVOD SR SLOVENIJE ZA STATISTIKO.** Slovenian. Zavod Sr Slovenije za Statistiko, Vozarski Pot 12, Ljubljana Slovenia. **LC** JS6949.S6; A17.

**JA**
**SHINKEN KAWARABAN (SHUSATSUBAN).** (SHINKEN KAWARABAN.). 1 (75-Winter/76-Summer)-. Periodical. Japanese. an. ¥1000 single issue. Asahi Shinbun Rodo Kumiai Honbu Shinbun Kenkyu Iinkai Asahi Shinbun Nai, 3-2 Tsukiji 5 Chuo-ku, Tokyo-to 104 Japan. **LC** JC599.J3; S56.

**AT**
**SHIRE & MUNICIPAL RECORD, THE.** Ceased. Vol. 1 (1909)-(19??). Periodical. English. mo. The Law Book Company Limited, 44-50 Waterloo Road, North Ryde New South Wales, 2113 Australia. **Tel** 011 61 2 8870177, FAX 011 61 2 8887240, telex ASBOOK 27445. **ED** E Stuckey.
**Desc:** Discusses law policy and administration at the local government level.
**Ind/Abst** Aust. Leg. Mon. Dig. (-19??).

**JA**
**SHOKUIN JIMU HANDOBUKKU.** **Added/Corp** Kitakyushu-Shi (Japan). Kikakukyoku. Kitakyushu-Shi (Japan). Kikakukyoku. Jimu Kanribu. Gyosei Kanrika. (1974)-. Periodical. Japanese. Kitakyushu-shi Kikakukyoku, Jimi Kanribu Gyosri, 1-ban 1-go Kokuraku Jonai, Kitakyushu Japan. **LC** JS7374.A1; S5.

**JA**
**SHOTOKUZEIHO SOCHIHO SANRIN SHOTOKU JOTO SHOTOKU KIHON TSUTATSU.** **Main/Corp** Japan. Kokuzeicho. **Added/Corp** Nozei Kyokai Rengokai. **VFOAT** Shotokuzeiho Sochiho Kihon Tsutatsu. (19??)-. Periodical. Japanese. ¥22.00. Nozei Kyokai Rengokai, 14-1 Minami Ogicho Kita-ku 530, Osaka Japan. **LC** LAW.

**JA**
**SHUCHO.** **Added/Corp** Zenkoku Chosonkai. (19??)-. Japanese. Zenkoku Chosonkai, 1-11-35 Nagata-cho Chiyoda-ku, Tokyo Japan. **LC** JS7371.A1; S55.

**US**
**SIA WASHINGTON REPORT.** See Law.

**IO**
**SIARAN UMUM - DEPARTEMEN PENERANGAN R.I.** **Main/Corp** Indonesia. Departemen Penerangan. Indonesian. Direktorat Publikasi, Jl Merdeka Barat 7, Jakarta Indonesia. **LC** JQ761.A1; I53A.

CN/0713-682X
**SILLERY VOUS INFORME.** [Sillery vous inf.]. Periodical. French. Free. Sillery Vous Informe, Ville de Sillery, 1445 Avenue Maguire, Sillery Quebec G1T 1Z2 Canada. **DD** 352.0714/47.

**SI**
**SINGAPORE GOVERNMENT DIRECTORY.** Directory. English. $8.00. Publicity Division, Ministry of Culture, Singapore 0617 Singapore. **LC** JQ745.S5; A35. **DD** 354/.595/2002. **Continues** Singapore. Directory of Istana Negara, Judicial, Cabinet, Legislative Assembly, Public Service Commission, Audit, Ministeries, Industrial Arbitration Court, Statutory Boards, Advisory Committees, Universities, Polytechnic, Commonwealth Representatives and Foreign Consuls.

**RU**
**SIRENA : PROLETARSKII DVUKHNEDELNIK.** **Added/Corp** Voronezhskii Gorodskoi Ispolnitelnyi Komitet Sovetov Rabochikh i Krasnoarmeiskikh Deputatov. (1918)-. Russian. Twenty-four times a year. $109.95. (Subscription address: East View Publications Inc., 3020 Harbor Lane North, Suite 110, Minneapolis MN 55447.) **LC** WMLC 6013/91.

**LU**
**SITTINGS - EUROPEAN PARLIAMENT, THE.** **Main/Corp** European Parliament. Vol. 1, Jan. 1975-. English. European Parliament, PO Box 1601, Luxembourg Luxembourg. **LC** JN32; .S57. **DD** 341.24/2.

US/0892-5917
**SITUATION REPORT - SECURITY AND INTELLIGENCE FOUNDATION (WASHINGTON, D.C.).** (SITUATION REPORT / SECURITY AND INTELLIGENCE FOUNDATION.). [Situat. rep. - Secur. Intell. Found. (Wash. D.C.)]. **Added/Corp** Security and Intelligence Foundation (Washington, D.C.). (198?)-. Periodical. English. ir. $50.00. Security and Intelligence Foundation, 1010 Vermont Avenue NW/Suite 516, Washington DC 20005. **Tel** (202)393-0883. **DD** 355. **Continues** Situation Report (Security and Intelligence Fund).

**US**
**SIX-YEAR CAPITAL IMPROVEMENT PROGRAM, THE.** Title Change. See Transportation.

**UK**
**SOCIAL AUDIT.** Title Change. Vol 1 (Summer 1973)-(19??). Periodical. English. qt. Social Audit Ltd, BOx 111, London NW1 8XG England. **LC** JC507; .S63. **DD** 659.2.

US/1063-7516
**SOCIAL LIST OF WASHINGTON, D.C. AND SOCIAL PRECEDENCE IN WASHINGTON, THE.** [Soc. list Wash. D.C. soc. preced. Wash.]. (19??)-. English. an (Oct.). $105.00 Maryland; $110.25 other. Social List of Washington DC, PO Box 29, Kensington MD 20895. **Tel** (301)949-7544, FAX (301)949-6190. **DD** 920. **Ad Acc, Adv Mgr:** P. Murray, **Tel** (301)949-4445. ctrl circ. **Continues** Social List of Washington and Social Precedence in Washington, 0583-6824.

UK/0144-5596
**SOCIAL POLICY & ADMINISTRATION.** [Soc. policy adm.]. **VAT** Social Policy and Administration. Vol. 13 (Spring 1979)-. Academic Scholarly Publication. English. Four times a year. £100.00 UK and Europe; $201.00 North America; £129.50 other. Basil Blackwell Publishers Ltd, 108 Cowley Road, Oxford OX4 1JF England. **Tel** 011 44 865 791100, FAX 011 44 865 791347, telex 837022 OXBOOK G. (Subscription address: Blackwell Publishers / UK, Marston Book Services, PO Box 87, Oxford OX2 0DT England.) **ED** R.A.B. Leaper. **LC** H1; .S5. **DD** 361/.005. **NLM** W1 SO122T. **[CCC]. Pr Rev.** available on microfilm from University Microfilms International (UMI). Documents available from The Genuine Article. **Continues** Social and Economic Administration, 0037-7643.
**Desc:** Articles on policy and current provision in social services, health care, social security, employment and housing in Britain and other countries.
**Ind/Abst** Appl. Soc. Sci. Index Abstr.; Crim. Penol. Police Sci. Abstr.; Curr. Contents Soc. Behav. Sci.; Int. Bibliogr. Sociol.; J. Plan. Lit.; PAIS Int. Print; Res. Alert [Full Cov.]; Soc. Plann. Policy Dev. Abstr.; Soc. Sci. Cit. Index [Full Cov.]; Sociol. Abstr.; Stud. Women Abstr.; Trop. Dis. Bull.

**SO**
**SOMALI JOURNAL OF RANGE SCIENCE : PUBLICATION OF THE DEPARTMENT OF BOTANY AND RANGE SCIENCE, FACULTY OF AGRICULTURE, SOMALI NATIONAL UNIVERSITY.** See Agriculture-Livestock and Poultry.

CN/1186-723X
**SOURCE (EDMONTON).** (THE SOURCE : INFORMATION ON THE GOVERNMENT MARKET.). [Source]. **Added/Corp** Alberta. Procurement Division. No. 1 (Spring 1991)-. Periodical. English. sa. **DD** 354.71230071.

CN/0841-2227
**SOURCES-ENAP.** [Sources-ENAP]. **Added/Corp** Ecole Nationale d'Administration Publique (Quebec). **VAT** Sources-Ecole Nationale d'Administration Publique (Quebec). Vol. 4, No 5 (Sept./Oct. 1988)-. Periodical. French. bm. 10,00 $ par annee. 945 Ave World, Sainte-Foy Quebec G1V 3J9 Canada. **DD** 350/.0005. **Continues** Sources (Sainte-Foy, Quebec)., 0831-0459.

SA/0038-254X
**SOUTH AFRICAN PANORAMA.** Vol. 1 (1956)-. Monographic series. English. ir. Price varies per volume. Bureau of Information, Private Bag X745, Pretoria 0001 South Africa. (Subscription address: Information Services for South Africa, 425 Park Avenue, 12th Floor, New York NY 10021.) available on microfilm and microfiche from University Microfilms International (UMI).

**US**
**SOUTH CAROLINA LEGISLATIVE MANUAL / GENERAL ASSEMBLY OF SOUTH CAROLINA.** **Main/Corp** South Carolina. General Assembly. (1987?)-. English. an. $5.00. Clerk of the House, South Carolina House of Representatives, PO Box 11867, Columbia SC 29211. **Tel** (803)734-2010. **ED** Sandra K. McKinney. **LC** JK4271; .A4. **Continues** South Carolina. General Assembly. Legislative Manual.

●**US**
**SOUTH CAROLINA POLICY FORUM : A REVIEW OF PUBLIC AFFAIRS IN SOUTH CAROLINA, THE.** **Added/Corp** University of South Carolina. Institute of Public Affairs. Vol. 3, No. 1 (Winter 1992)-. Periodical. English. qt. $19.75. Institute of Public Affairs / South Carolina, University of South Carolina, Columbia SC 29208. **Tel** (803)777-8157, FAX (803)777-4575. **ED** Charlie Tyer. **LC** JK4201; .S69. **DD** 353.9757/0005. **Bk Rev**, (Qty: 4). **Circ:** 800. **Continues** South Carolina Forum, 1055-2901.

**US**
**SOUTH CAROLINA STATE DEVELOPMENT BOARD NEWS.** **Added/Corp** South Carolina. State Development Board. Vol. 1, No. 1 (Oct./Dec. l976)-. Periodical. English. qt.

US/0300-6182
**SOUTH DAKOTA MUNICIPALITIES.** **Added/Corp** South Dakota Municipal League. (1947)-. Periodical. English. Twelve times a year. $20.00. South Dakota Municipalities, 214 East Capitol, Pierre SD 57501. **Tel** (605)224-8654, FAX (605)224-8655. **ED** Marla Gienger. **Ad Acc, Adv Mgr:** M. Gienger. **Circ:** 3,000 (ctrl). **Continues** League of South Dakota Municipalities. Bulletin - League of South Dakota Municipalities.
**Desc:** Local government news and information.
**Ind/Abst** Urban Aff. Abstr.

US/0361-7130
**SOUTHERN CITY.** **Added/Corp** North Carolina League of Municipalities. Vol. 1 (1949)-. Periodical. English. Twelve times a year. $6.00. North Carolina League of Municipalities, Margot Christensen, PO Box 3069, Raleigh NC 27602. **Tel** (919)834-1311. **ED** Margot F. Christensen. **Ad Acc. Circ:** 6,200 (ctrl). **Continues** Southern City (Raleigh, N.C. : 1940).
**Desc:** Issues and topics concerning municipal Government in North Carolina.
**Ind/Abst** Urban Aff. Abstr.

**US**
**SOUTHERN LIBERTARIAN MESSENGER, THE.** **Added/Corp** Quality Education, Inc. (May 1972)-. Periodical. English. mo. $6.00 US; $8.00 Canada; $9.00 other. Southern Libertarian Messenger, Rt. 10 Box 52-A, Florence SC 29501. **ED** John T. Harllee. **Circ:** 450.

**US**
**SPECIAL DATA ISSUE / ICMA.** **Added/Corp** International City Management Association. **VFOAT** ICMA Special Data Issue. No. 1 (1987)-. Monographic series. English. ir. $29.75. International City Management Association, 777 North Capitol Street NE, Suite 500, Washington DC 20002. **Tel** (202)289-4262, (800)745-8780, FAX (202)962-3500.

US/0065-9932
**SPECIAL REPORT - AMERICAN PUBLIC WORKS ASSOCIATION.** [Spec. rep. - Am. Public Works Assoc.]. **Main/Corp** American Public Works Association. **VFOAT** APWA Special Report. No. 22 (1957)-. Monographic series. English. ir. Price varies per volume. American Public Works Association, 106 West 11th Street, Suite 1800, Kansas City MO 64105. **Tel** (816)472-6100. **ED** Kenneth Bauder. **CODEN** SRAADG. Documents available from Article Express International. **Continues** American Public Works Association. Public Works Engineers' Special Report.
**Desc:** Research reports of the American Public Works Association.
**Ind/Abst** Bioeng. Abstr.; Ei Page One; Eng. Index Annu.; GeoRef.

●US/1067-8530
**SPECTRUM (LEXINGTON, KY.).** (SPECTRUM: THE JOURNAL OF STATE GOVERNMENT.). [Spectrum]. **Added/Corp** Council of State Governments. Vol. 65, No. 3 (Summer 1992)-. Periodical. English. qt (4 issues) $45.00 US; $50.00 other. Council of State Governments, PO Box 11910, Iron Works Pike, Lexington KY 40578-1910. **Tel** (800)800-1910, (606)231-1850. (Subscription address: Council of State Governments, PO Box 2167, Lexington, KY 40595) **LC** JK2403; .S7. **DD** 328.73. Index available (free). **Continues** Journal of State Government, 1043-2248.

**Ind/Abst** Acad. Search (June 1992-); Soc. Sci. Cit. Index [Full Cov.]; Soc. Sci. Index Fulltext (1992-) [Full Txt.]; UMI ABI/Inform--Bus. Period. Ondisc (Nov. 1987-) [Full Txt.].

RU
**SSSR, ADMINISTRATIVNO-TERRITORIALNOE DELENIE SOIUZNYKH RESPUBLIK.**
**Added/Corp** Soviet Union. Verkhovny Sovet. Prezidium. Informatsionno-Statisticheski Otdel. Soviet Union. Verkhovnyi Sovet. Prezidium. Otdel po Voprasam Raboty Sovetov. (19??)-. Russian.

GW
**STAATS-ZEITUNG; STAATSANZEIGER FUER RHEINLANDJ-PFALZ (MICROFICHE).** (STAATS-ZEITUNG; STAATSANZEIGER FUER RHEINLAND-PFALZ.). **Main/Corp** Rhineland-Palatinate. **Added/Corp** Rhineland-Palatinate. Laws, Statutes, etc. Vol. 1 (May 1950)-. Periodical. German. wk. $105.00. German News Company Inc, 220 East 86th Street, New York NY 10028. **Tel** (212)288-5500. **LC** Microfilm 05511J; J7; .G24.

NE/0169-5037
**STAATSCOURANT.** (NEDERLANDSE STAATSCOURANT.). [Staatscourant]. (1985)-. Periodical. Dutch. da. Fl290.95. SDU Uitgeverij, Postbus 20014, Christoffel Plan, 2500 EA Den Haag Netherlands. **Tel** 011 31 70 3789911. **ED** J M Spendel. **UDC** 342 (054). Index available. cum. index. **Bk Rev**. **Ad Acc**. **Circ:** 14,000. available in microform. ***Continues*** *Uitspraken van de Raad voor de Luchtvaart, 0921-7487; Uitspraken van de Nederlandse Marine-Raad, 0921-7495.*
**Desc:** Governmental regulations and policy.

SA
**STAATSKOERANT. GOVERNMENT GAZETTE.** **Main/Corp** South Africa. **Added/Corp** South Africa. Government Gazette. **VFOAT** Government Gazette. Vol. 1 (May 31, 1961)-. Periodical. English (Afrikaans). R273.60. Staatsdrukkery Government Printing Works, Bosmanstraat/Bosman Street, Private Bag X85, Pretoria 0001 South Africa. **Tel** 012 323-9731, FAX 012 323-0009. ***Supersedes*** *South Africa. Government Gazette.*

GW/0038-9048
**STAEDTETAG (1948), DER.** (DER STAEDTETAG.). [Staedtetag]. **Added/Corp** Deutscher Staedtetag. Vol. 1 (July/Aug. 1948)-. Academic Scholarly Publication. German. Twelve times a year. DM209.00. Deutscher Gemeindeverlag, Postfach 400263, D 50832 Cologne Germany. **Tel** 011 49 2234 106214. **LC** JS41; .S78. **[CCC]**. ***Supersedes*** *Gemeindetag.*
**Desc:** Concerns municipal administration management.
**Ind/Abst** Coal Abstr.; EMBASE; Energy Res. Abstr. (Oct. 1972-); Geogr. Abstr. Human Geogr.; Int. Dev. Abstr.

HK
**STAFF BIOGRAPHIES, HONG KONG GOVERNMENT / COMPILED IN THE GOVERNMENT SECRETARIAT / HSIANG-KANG CHENG FU KUNG WU YUAN CHIEN CHIEH / PU CHENG SSU SHU PIEN.** **Main/Corp** Hong Kong. Government Secretariat. **VFOAT** Hsiang-Kang Cheng fu Kung wu uan Chien Chieh; Hong Kong Government Staff Biographies. (19??)-. Government Publication. English (Chinese). be. Hong Kong Government Information Service, Beaconsfield House, 4 Queens Road, Hong Kong Hong Kong. **Tel** 011 852 8428801 4, telex 61190 HKGIS. **LC** JQ674; .H67a. **DD** 354.5125/002; B. ***Continues*** *Hong Kong. Colonial Secretariat. Staff Biographies, Hong Kong Government.*

HK
**STAFF LIST, HONG KONG GOVERNMENT.** **Main/Corp** Hong Kong. Government Secretariat. **Added/Corp** Hong Kong. Government Secretariat. Hsiang-Kang Cheng fu Chih Yuan ming ts∞e. **VFOAT** Hsiang-Kang Cheng fu Chih Yuan Ming Tse. (1976)-. English. an. HK$286.00 Hong Kong; $38.10 other. Hong Kong Government Information Service, Beaconsfield House, 4 Queens Road, Hong Kong Hong Kong. **Tel** 011 852 8428801 4, telex 61190 HKGIS. **(Subscription address:** Government Information Service, Publications Office, 1 Battery Path, Hong Kong Hong Kong.**)** **LC** JQ674; .A3. **DD** 354/.51/25002. **Circ:** 400. ***Continues*** *Staff List, Hong Kong Government.*
**Desc:** Includes the names of all officers in ranks, their salaries and the master pay scale.

NR
**STAFF LIST - MID-WESTERN STATE, NIGERIA. MINISTRY OF ESTABLISHMENTS.** **Main/Corp** Mid-Western State, Nigeria. Ministry of Establishments. English. Nigeria Ministry of Establishments, Benin City Nigeria. **LC** JQ3099.M54; A3. **DD** 331.2/81/3546693.

NR
**STAFF LIST - SOUTH-EASTERN STATE OF NIGERIA.** **Main/Corp** South-Eastern State, Nigeria. English. 75/-. Cabinet Office, Government Printer, Calabar Nigeria. **LC** JQ3099.S6; S6B. **DD** 354/.669/4002.

US
**STANDARD AND OPTIONAL FORMS FACSIMILE HANDBOOK.** **Added/Corp** United States. National Archives and Records Service. Office of Records Management. (19??)-. Government Publication. English. an (supplements). $109.00 US; $136.25 other. Superintendent of Documents, US Government Printing Office, Washington DC 20402. **Tel** (202)275-3328, FAX (202)786-2377.
**Desc:** Consists of facsimiles of each Standard and Optional Form authorized for government-wide use, and data necessary for the management and use of these forms.

US/0049-206X
**STANDARD-BEARER, THE.** V. 1- ; 1967-. Periodical. English. Three times a year. National Accreditation Council, New York NY 10016.

US/1057-9990
**STANDARDIZED REGULATIONS.** (STANDARDIZED REGULATIONS : GOVERNMENT CIVILLIANS FOREIGN AREAS / DEPARTMENT OF STATE.). [Stand. regul.]. **Main/Corp** United States. Dept. of State. **VFOAT** Section 920, Post Classification and Payment Tables, and Amendments to the Standardized Regulations (Government Civilians, Foreign Areas). (19??)-. Government Publication. English. mo. $52.00 US; $65.00 other. Superintendent of Documents, US Government Printing Office, Washington DC 20402. **Tel** (202)275-3328, FAX (202)786-2377. **DD** 353.
**Desc:** Presents information on standardized regulations pertaining to civilian employees working in foreign areas. Also announces changes and updates to current regulations as well as new regulations.

NO/0803-0103
**STAT & STYRING.** [Stat styr.]. **VFOAT** Stat og Styring. (1991)-. Periodical. Norwegian. bm. Kr450.00, $79.00. Scandinavian University Press, PO Box 2959 Toeyen, N 0608 Oslo 6 Norway. **Tel** 011 47 2 2575400, FAX 011 47 2 2575353, telex 71896 UROR N. **(Subscription address:** Scandinavian University Press, 200 Meacham Ave., Elmont NY 11003.**)** **ED** Bjorn Talen. **DD** 658.
**Desc:** Norwegian journal on government and leadership, published in cooperation with the Directorate of Organization and Management.

US/0191-9423
**STATE ADMINISTRATIVE OFFICIALS CLASSIFIED BY FUNCTIONS.** [State adm. off. classif. funct.]. **Added/Corp** Council of State Governments. **VFOAT** State Administrative Officials Classified by Function. (1967)-. English. be. $30.00. Council of State Governments, PO Box 11910, Iron Works Pike, Lexington KY 40578-1910. **Tel** (800)800-1910, (606)231-1850. **ED** L. E. Purceep. **LC** JK2403; .B6 Suppl 2. **DD** 353.9/32. **NLM** JK 2403; S7973. **Circ:** 10,000. ***Continues*** *Administrative Officials Classified by Functions, 0191-9458.*
**Desc:** Lists thousands of administrators in more than 130 areas of state government.

US
**STATE AND LOCAL DOCUMENTS INDEX [MICROFORM] / BOSTON PUBLIC LIBRARY.** **Added/Corp** Boston Public Library. (Mar. 1990)-. English.

US/0160-323X
**STATE & LOCAL GOVERNMENT REVIEW.** [State local gov. rev.]. **Added/Corp** University of Georgia. Institute of Government. Carl Vinson Institute of Government. **VFOAT** State and Local Government Review. **VAT** State and Local Government Review. Vol. 8 (Jan. 1976)-. Periodical. English. Three times a year (Spring & Fall & Winter). $14.00 (individual), $20.00 (institutions) one year; $26.00 (individual), $38.00 (institutions) two years; $36.00 (individual), $54.00 (institutions) three years. University of Georgia Institute of Government, 201 North Milledge Avenue, Athens GA 30602. **Tel** (706)542-2736. **ED** Dr. Richard W. Campbell. **LC** JK2403; .S684. **DD** 353.9. **Circ:** 800 (ctrl). ***Continues*** *Georgia Government Review, 0016-8289.*
**Desc:** A journal of current research and viewpoints in state and local government.
**Ind/Abst** ABC POL SCI; PAIS Int. Print; Sage Public Adm. Abstr.; Sage Urban Stud. Abstr; U.S. Polit. Sci. Doc.; Urban Aff. Abstr.

●US
**STATE & LOCAL LAW NEWS.** **Added/Corp** American Bar Association. Section of Urban, State, and Local Government Law. **VFOAT** State and Local Law News. Vol. 17, No. 2 (Winter 1994)-. Periodical. English. qt. American Bar Association, 750 North Lake Shore Drive, Chicago IL 60611. **Tel** (312)988-5522, (312)988-5241, FAX (312)988-5528, telex 270593. **LC** KF5300; .S7. **DD** 342.73/09/05. ***Continues*** *Urban, State and Local Law Newsletter, 0195-7686.*

US/0147-0566
**STATE COASTAL ZONE MANAGEMENT ACTIVITIES.** **Main/Corp** United States. Office of Coastal Zone Management. Government Publication. English. an. US Department of Commerce, 14th Street & Constitution Avenue NW, Washington DC 20230. **Tel** (202)482-2000, FAX (202)482-3772. **LC** HT392; .U558A. **DD** 353.008/232.

US/0081-4474
**STATE CONSTITUTIONAL CONVENTION STUDIES.** **Main/Corp** National Municipal League. (1969)-. Monographic series. English. ir. Price varies per volume. National Civic League, 1445 Market Street, Suite 300, Denver CO 80202. **Tel** (303)571-4343, FAX (303)832-4005.

US/0585-1173
**STATE DIRECTORY OF KENTUCKY.** [State dir. Ky.]. (1965)-. Directory. English. an (Feburary). $16.00. Directories Inc, PO Box 187, Pewee Valley KY 40056. **Tel** (502)241-8256. **ED** Mary McKay Wright. **LC** JK5330; .S8. **DD** 353.9/769/002. **Circ:** 4,500 (ctrl).
**Desc:** City, county and state elected and appointed officials, including practicing attorneys, news media, school superintendents, courts, judicial, and vital statistics.

US/0099-0175
**STATE DIRECTORY OF PUBLIC OFFICIALS IN GEORGIA, THE.** V. 1- 1975-. Directory. English. an. $10.00. PO Box 125, Richmond Hill GA 31324. **LC** JK4330; .S73. **DD** 353.9/758/002.

US/0191-9466
**STATE ELECTIVE OFFICIALS AND THE LEGISLATURES (1977).** (STATE ELECTIVE OFFICIALS AND THE LEGISLATURES.). **Added/Corp** Council of State Governments. **VFOAT** State Elective Officials & the Legislatures. (1977)-. English. be (every odd year). $35.00. Council of State Governments, PO Box 11910, Iron Works Pike, Lexington KY 40578-1910. **Tel** (800)800-1910, (606)231-1850. **ED** L. E. Purceep. **LC** JK2403; .S69. **DD** 353.9/3/2. **NLM** JK 2403; S7974. **Circ:** 10,000. ***Continues*** *Selected State Officials and the Legislatures, 0191-944X.*
**Desc:** Names, parties, addresses, and districts of state legislators.

US/0276-7163
**STATE EXECUTIVE DIRECTORY.** [State exec. dir.]. (Spring/Summer 1980)-. Directory. English. Three times a year. $160.00. Carroll Publishing Company, 1058 Thomas Jefferson Street Northwest, Washington DC 20007-3832. **Tel** (202)333-8620, FAX (202)337-7020. **ED** Nancy Cahill. **LC** JK2482.E94; S76. **DD** 353.9/32. Index available. cum. index. **Circ:** 1,000 (ctrl).
**Desc:** Current alphabetic name and organizational directory of 37,000 state executive branch officials, with subject index, fully cross-referenced.

●US/1056-7011
**STATE EXECUTIVE DIRECTORY ANNUAL.** [State exec. dir. annu.]. (1992)-. Directory. English. an. $127.00. Carroll Publishing Company, 1058 Thomas Jefferson Street Northwest, Washington DC 20007-3832. **Tel** (202)333-8620, FAX (202)337-7020. **LC** JK2482.E94; S77. **DD** 353.9/32/025. ***Continues in part*** *Federal/state Executive Directory, 0887-4727.*

US/0039-0119
**STATE GOVERNMENT NEWS.** [State gov.]. **Added/Corp** Council of State Governments. Vol. 1 (July 1958)-. Periodical. English. mo. $39.00 US; $45.00 other. Council of State Governments, PO Box 11910, Iron Works Pike, Lexington KY 40578-1910. **Tel** (800)800-1910, (606)231-1850. **(Subscription address:** Council of State Governments, PO Box 2167, Lexington, KY 40595**)** **ED** Elaine S. Knapp. **LC** JK2403; .S75. **Bk Rev**. **Ad Acc**. **Circ:** 13,000 (ctrl). available on microfilm and microfiche from University Microfilms International (UMI). Documents available from Documents on Demand. ***Absorbed*** *Legislative Session Sheet, 0193-3833.*
**Desc:** News from all branches of state government for all 50 states. Covers new state laws, trends, court decisions, administrative actions and federal state relations.
**Ind/Abst** Energy Inf. Abstr.; Environ. Abstr.; Index Period. Artic. Relat. Law; PAIS Int. Print; Urban Aff. Abstr.

US/0190-6623
**STATE GOVERNMENT RESEARCH CHECKLIST.** (STATE GOVERNMENT RESEARCH CHECKLIST / THE COUNCIL OF STATE GOVERNMENTS.). **Added/Corp** Council of State Governments. **VFOAT** Legislative Research Checklist; Research Checklist. (Feb. 1979)-. English. bm (6 issues). $20.00 US; $25.00 other. Council of State Governments, PO Box 11910, Iron Works Pike, Lexington KY 40578-1910. **Tel** (800)800-1910, (606)231-1850. **(Subscription address:** Council of State Governments, PO Box 2167, Lexington, KY 40595**)** ***Continues*** *Legislative Research Checklist (Chicago, Ill. : 1959), 0024-0486.*

US/1070-7719
**STATE HOUSE WATCH.** [State house watch]. **Added/Corp** Massachusetts Human Services Coalition, Inc. (1983)-. Periodical. English. Twenty-one times a year. $60.00 (members); $120.00 (other). Massachusetts Human Services Coalition Inc., 37 Temple Place, 3rd Floor, Boston MA 02111. **Tel** (617) 482-6119, FAX (617) 695-1295. **ED** Donna Southwell. **DD** 353. **Ad Acc. Circ:** 650.
**Desc:** Reports on current legislative action regarding human services. Provides a forum for advocates of particular human services to voice concerns and promote solutions. Also rates the Representatives and Senators on their votes on key human service issues at the end of the legislative year.

●US/1066-842X
**STATE IRM ORGANIZATIONAL STRUCTURES.** (STATE IRM ORGANIZATIONAL STRUCTURES : .... NASIRE BIENNIAL REPORT.). [State IRM organ. struct.]. **Added/Corp** National Association of State Information Resource Executives. **VFOAT** NASIRE Biennial Report; State Information Resource Management Organizational Structures. (1992)-. English. be (Spring). $50.00. Council of State Governments, PO Box 11910, Iron Works Pike, Lexington KY 40578-1910. **Tel** (800)800-1910, (606)231-1850. **(Subscription address:** Council of State Governments, PO Box 2167, Lexington, KY 40595**)** **DD** 353.93/819. ***Continues*** *State Information Resource Management, Structure, and Activities, 1062-6131.*
**Desc:** Information on state governments, information resources management, and management information systems.

US/0195-6639
**STATE LEGISLATIVE LEADERSHIP, COMMITTEES, AND STAFF.** **Added/Corp** Council of State Governments. (1979)-. English. be (every odd year). $30.00. Council of State Governments, PO Box 11910, Iron Works Pike, Lexington KY 40578-1910. **Tel** (800)800-1910, (606)231-1850. **(Subscription address:** Council of State Governments, 3560 Iron Works Pike, Lexington, KY 40578**)** **LC** JK2495; .S688; JS308; .C6. **DD** 353.9 S; 328.73/0025. **NLM** JK 2495; S797. ***Continues*** *Principal Legislative Staff Offices.*

US/0735-8733
**STATE LEGISLATIVE REPORT.** **Added/Corp** National Conference of State Legislatures. (19??)-. Monographic series. English. ir (15-25 issues). $5.00 individual issue. National Conference of State Legislatures, 1560 Broadway, Suite 700, Denver CO 80202. **Tel** (303)830-2054, FAX (303)863-8003. **LC** KF85; .S745. **DD** 342.73/00262; 347.3020262.
**Desc:** Provides a fast, yet thorough briefing on topics of state legislative concern. A quick reference on specific state policies in the area of fiscal policy, education, health, labor, HIV/AIDS and more.

US/0898-7297
**STATE LEGISLATIVE SOURCEBOOK.** [State legis. sourceb.]. **Added/Corp** Government Research Service. (1986)-. English. an (Dec.). $155.00. Government Research Service, 701 Jackson, Suite 304B, Topeka KS 66603. **Tel** (913)232-7720, (800)346-6898, FAX (913)232-1615. **ED** Lynn Hellebust. **LC** JK2495; .S689. **DD** 328.73/005.
**Desc:** Comprehensive guide to legislative information in all 50 states. Each state section includes entries identifying sources of information on that state's legislative organization and procedure, individual legislators, bill status information, copies of bills, interim study period and lobbying information.

US/0147-6041
**STATE LEGISLATURES.** [State legis.]. **Added/Corp** National Conference of State Legislatures. (June/July 1975)-. Periodical. English. Twelve times a year. $49.00 US; $55.00 Canada. National Conference of State Legislatures, 1560 Broadway, Suite 700, Denver CO 80202. **Tel** (303)830-2054, FAX (303)863-8003. **ED** Karen Hansen. **LC** JK2403; .S76. **DD** 328.73/005. **[CCC]. Circ:** 13,500. Documents available from UMI Article Clearinghouse. ***Continues*** *State Legislatures Today, 0196-1640.*
**Desc:** Provides unbiased insight on state issues and politics. In each issue you receive commentary and analysis on significant past, current and future legislation.
**Ind/Abst** Educ. Adm. Abstr. (?-?); Expand. Acad. Index (1992-); Hum. Resour. Abstr. (?-?); Newsp. Period. Abstr. (1992-); PAIS Int. Print; Sage Public Adm. Abstr.; Urban Aff. Abstr.

US/0898-8374
**STATE MUNICIPAL LEAGUE DIRECTORY.** [State munic. leag. dir.]. Directory. English. an. National League of Cities, 1301 Pennsylvania Avenue NW, Washington DC 20004. **Tel** (202)626-3150, FAX (202)626-3043. **DD** 352.

US
**STATE OF DELAWARE DEFERRED COMPENSATION COUNCIL'S ANNUAL REPORT FOR THE FISCAL YEAR ENDED JUNE 30 ... .** **Main/Corp** Delaware. Deferred Compensation Council. **Added/Corp** Delaware. Deferred Compensation Council Annual Report. **VFOAT** Annual Report. (19??)-. English. an. **LC** JK3757; .D44a. **DD** 353.975100123/05.

US
**STATE OF FLORIDA BUDGET RECOMMENDATIONS.** **Main/Corp** Florida. Office of the Governor. **VFOAT** Framework for Fiscal Responsibility; Budget Recommendations. (1991)-. English. be. Office of the Governor / Florida, The Capitol, Tallahassee FL 32301. **LC** HJ2053.F6; F57A. **DD** 353.97590072/256/05. ***Continues*** *Budget Recommendations / Florida. Office of the Governor.*

US
**STATE OF GEORGIA ... OFFICIAL DIRECTORY OF UNITED STATES CONGRESSMEN, STATE AND COUNTY OFFICERS / OFFICE OF SECRETARY OF STATE.** **Added/Corp** Georgia. Secretary of State. **VFOAT** Official Directory of United States Congressmen, State and County Officers; Georgia Official Directory. (1991)-. Directory. English. Max Cleveland, Secretary of State, Electronics Division, 110 State Capitol, Atlanta GA 30334-1505. **LC** JK4330; .U54. ***Continues*** *Georgia Official Directory of United States Congressmen, State and County Officers.*

US/0146-4914
**STATE OF MONTANA OFFICE OF THE SUPERINTENDENT OF PUBLIC INSTRUCTION AND BOARD OF PUBLIC EDUCATION : REPORT ON AUDIT.** **Main/Corp** Montana. Office of the Legislative Auditor. English. an. Office of the Legislative Auditor, State Capitol, Helena MT 59601. **LC** LB2826.M9; M66A. **DD** 379/.152/09786.

US/0743-7447
**STATE OF MUNICIPAL SERVICES, THE.** **Added/Corp** Citizens Budget Commission (New York, N.Y.). **VFOAT** State of Municipal Services in New York City. (19??)-. English. an. 110 East 42nd Street, New York NY 10017. **LC** HD4606.N5; S73. **DD** 352.7/09747/1.

US
**STATE OF NEVADA, DEPARTMENT OF CONSERVATION AND NATURAL RESOURCES, DIVISION OF STATE PARKS AUDIT REPORT.** **Main/Corp** Nevada. Legislative Auditor. English. Legislative Auditor, Legislative Building, Capitol Complex, Carson City NV 89710. **LC** SB482.N3; N46A. **DD** 353.97930072/32. ***Continues*** *Audit Report - State of Nevada. Department of Conservation and Natural Resources. Division of State Parks, 0093-6596.*

US
**STATE OF NEW MEXICO OFFICIAL RETURNS ... GENERAL AND PRIMARY RETURNS.** **Main/Corp** New Mexico. Secretary of State. (19??)-. English. be. New Mexico Office of the Secretary of State, Executive Legislative Building, Santa Fe NM 87501. **LC** JK8092; .N48a. **DD** 324.9789/053.

US
**STATE OF THE UNION ADDRESS.** **Main/Corp** United States. President. English. ir. US Congress, 515 House Annex 2, Washington DC 20515.

US/0743-5916
**STATE PLAN FOR DEVELOPMENTAL DISABILITIES (HARRISBURG, PA.).** (STATE PLAN FOR DEVELOPMENTAL DISABILITIES.). **Main/Corp** Pennsylvania Developmental Disabilities Planning Council. (19??)-. English. Pennsylvania Developmental Disabilities Planning Council, Room 569/Forum Building, Commonwealth Avenue, Harrisburg PA 17120. **LC** HV3006.P4; P43a. **DD** 353.97480084/4. ***Continues*** *Pennsylvania State Plan, Developmental Disabilities Services and Facilities Construction Act of 1970, 0193-1423.*

US/8750-6637
**STATE POLICY REPORTS.** (STATE POLICY REPORTS : SPR.). [State policy rep.]. **VFOAT** SPR. Vol. 1, No. 1 (Jan. 3, 1983)-. Periodical. English. bw. $405.00 (full service), $340.00 (limited service). State Policy Research Inc., 182 West Royal Forest Boulevard, Columbus OH 43214-2029. **Tel** (614)447-9443, FAX (614)447-2077. **(Subscription address:** State Policy Research, Subscription Office, PO Box 11806, Birmingham AL 35202-1806.**)** **ED** Harold A. Hovey. **DD** 350. Index available (free). **Bk Rev**. ctrl circ.
**Desc:** Journal covering wide range of state government policy issues, featuring expert analysis of revenue and spending topics.

●US/1057-0586
**STATE REFERENCE PUBLICATIONS.** [State ref. publ.]. **Added/Corp** Government Research Service. (1992)-. English. an (June). $64.00. Government Research Service, 701 Jackson, Suite 304B, Topeka KS 66603. **Tel** (913)232-7720, (800)346-6898, FAX (913)232-1615. **ED** Lynn Hellebust. **LC** Z7165.U5; S679; JK2408. **DD** 016.3539.
**Desc:** State blue books and other state reference publications. This provides complete up-to-date information on how to obtain such publications.

US
**STATE REGULATORY PERMITS INVENTORY / THE GOVERNOR'S DEVELOPMENT OFFICE.** 1980-. English. an. The Governor's Development Office, John W McCormack Building, One Ashburton Place, Room 2101, Boston MA 02108. **LC** JK3130; .S73. **DD** 353.974409/1/025.

AT/0158-1996
**STATE REPORTS, WESTERN AUSTRALIA.** [State rep. West. Aust.]. (1980)-. Periodical. English. qt. **DD** 348.941043.
**Ind/Abst** Aust. Leg. Mon. Dig.

US/0506-7588
**STATE SERIES.** **Main/Corp** Vermont. University. Government Research Center. No. 1 (1959)-. English. University of Vermont Government Research Center, Burlington VT 05401. **DD** 350.

UK
**STATE SERVICE.** **Added/Corp** Institution of Professional Civil Servants, London. (1926)-. Periodical. English. mo. Institute of Professional Civil Service, 3-7 Northumberland Street, London WC-2 England. ***Continues*** *State Technology.*

US
**STATE TREASURER'S ANNUAL REPORT.** English. North Carolina Department of State Treasurer, 325 North Salisbury Street, Raleigh NC 27611.

●US/1075-5209
**STATE TRENDS FORECASTS.** [State trends forecasts]. **Added/Corp** Council of State Governments. **VFOAT** Forecasts; State Trends and Forecasts; State Trends & Forecasts. Vol. 1, No. 1 (Dec. 1992)-. English. tq (3 issues). $15.00. Council of State Governments, PO Box 11910, Iron Works Pike, Lexington KY 40578-1910. **Tel** (800)800-1910, (606)231-1850. **(Subscription address:** Council of State Governments, PO Box 2167, Lexington, KY 40595**)** **DD** 351.

US/0278-1859
**STATE (WASHINGTON, D.C.).** (STATE / UNITED STATES DEPARTMENT OF STATE.). [State]. **Added/Corp** United States. Dept. of State. No. 230 (Jan. 1981)-. Government Publication. English. mo (except Aug./Sept. combined). $19.00 US; $23.75 other. Superintendent of Documents, US Government Printing Office, Washington DC 20402. **Tel** (202)275-3328, FAX (202)786-2377. **LC** JX1; .U542. **DD** 353.008/92. available on microfilm and microfiche from University Microfilms International (UMI). ***Continues*** *Newsletter (United States. Dept. of State), 0041-7629.*
**Desc:** Published to acquaint the State Department's officers and employees, at home and abroad, with developments of interest which may affect operations or personnel.

US/0899-2207
**STATE YELLOW BOOK.** **See** Encyclopedias and General Reference Books.

US/0091-1402
**STATEHOUSE OBSERVER, THE.** Periodical. English. mo. Nebraska Department of Personnel, Room 1319/State Capitol Building, Lincoln NE 68509. **LC** JK6655; .S8. **DD** 331.7/61/3539782.

US
**STATEVIEW.** **See** Law.

US/0361-7475
**STATISTICAL ABSTRACT - NEW YORK STATE DEPARTMENT OF STATE.** **See** Public Administration-Abstracting, Bibliographies and Statistics.

IT
**STATO CIVILE ITALIANO.** Sepel Sas, Via Sopra Castello 11, 400061 Minerbio Bo Italy.

IT
**STATO OGGI.** ***Title Change.*** (19??)-(19??). Italian. Sirio Srl, Via Verona 9, 20135 Milan Italy. **Tel** 011 39 2 58321897. ***Continued by*** *Giustizia Oggi.*

US
**STATUS OF MAJOR ACQUISITIONS AS OF ... .** **See** Business-Purchasing.

CN/0382-1293
**STATUS REPORT - COUNTY RESTRUCTURING STUDIES PROGRAM.** (COUNTY RESTRUCTURING STUDIES PROGRAM : STATUS REPORT.). **Main/Corp** Ontario. Ministry of Treasury, Economics and Intergovernmental Affairs. Local Government Organization Branch. 1-. English. Local Government Organization Branch, Ministry of

# Public Administration

Treasury Economics and Intergovernmental Affairs, Forest Building, North Queen's Park, Toronto Ontario Canada. **LC** JS4.O7; M54A. **DD** 352/.0073/09713.

UK
### STATUTORY INSTRUMENTS. Main/Corp
Great Britain. (1952)-. English. an. £32.50. Her Majesty's Stationery Office, 51 Nine Elms Lane, London SW8 5DR England. **Tel** 011 44 71 873 8459, 011 44 71 873 8499, FAX 011 44 71 873 8499, 011 44 71 873 8456, telex 297138. **(Subscription address:** Her Majestys Stationery Offic, PO Box 276 Public Centre, London SW8 5DT England) **Continues** Great Britain. Laws, Statutes, etc. Statutory Instruments Other Than Those of a Local, Personal or Temporary Character.
**Ind/Abst** Food Sci. Technol. Abstr.

AT
### STATUTORY RULES MADE DURING THE YEAR / OFFICE OF THE PARLIAMENTARY COUNSEL. Main/Corp
Tasmania. Office of the Parliamentary Counsel. **VFOAT** Statutory Rules. English. an. Government Printer / Parliamentary Counsel, Hobart 7000 Australia.
**Continues** Statutory Rules.

US/0092-4687
### STATUTORY SALARIES, MISSOURI STATE OFFICIALS. Main/Corp
Missouri. General Assembly. Committee on State Fiscal Affairs. English. General Assembly, State Capitol/Room 132, Jefferson City MO 65101. **LC** JK5457; .M57A.

NO
### STORTINGET I NAVN OG TALL. Main/Corp
Norway. Stortinget. (1981)-. Norwegian. ir. Scandinavian University Press, PO Box 2959 Toeyen, N 0608 Oslo 6 Norway. **Tel** 011 47 2 2575400, FAX 011 47 2 2575353, telex 71896 UROR N. **(Subscription address:** Scandinavian University Press, 200 Meacham Ave., Elmont NY 11003.) **LC** JN7543; .S8. **Continues** Norway. Stortinget. Stortinget.

GW
### STRASSEN, BRUCKEN UND PARKEINRICHTUNGEN. Main/Corp
North Rhine-Westphalia (Germany). Landesamt fur Datenverarbeitung und Statistik. German. 9.50. Landesamt fuer Datenverarbeitung und Statistik Nordrhein-Westfalen, Postfach 101105, 40002 Duesseldorf Germany. **Tel** (0211)944901, FAX (0211)442006, telex 8586654 LDST D. **LC** HA1320.N6; A32 subser HE363.G33.

●CN/1184-616X
### STRATEGIC PLAN - CANADA MORTGAGE AND HOUSING CORPORATION. (PLAN STRATEGIQUE.).
[Strateg. plan - Can. Mort. Hous. Corp.]. **Main/Corp** Societe Canadienne d'Hypotheques et de Logement. **VFOAT** Strategic Plan. (1992)-. French (English). **DD** 354.710086/05.

US
### STUDIES ON DEVELOPMENT PROBLEMS IN COUNTRIES OF WESTERN ASIA. Ceased. Main/Corp
United Nations. Economic Commission for Western Asia. **Added/Corp** United Nations. Economic Commission for Western Asia. (1974)-(19??). Government Publication. English. an. United Nations Publications, 2 United Nations Plaza, Room DC2 0853, Department 007C, New York NY 10017. **Tel** (212)963-8303, (800)253-9646. **LC** JX1977; .A2 subser; HC410.7. **DD** 300/.8 S; 338.956. **Continues** Studies on Development Problems in Selected Countries of the Middle East.
**Desc:** Issues carry also United Nations publication sales number

US/0070-1157
### SUGGESTED STATE LEGISLATION (1965). See Law.

US/0193-2926
### SUMMARIES OF CONCLUSIONS AND RECOMMENDATIONS ON THE OPERATIONS OF CIVIL DEPARTMENTS AND AGENCIES.
(SUMMARIES OF CONCLUSIONS AND RECOMMENDATIONS ON THE OPERATIONS OF CIVIL DEPARTMENTS AND AGENCIES : REPORT TO THE HOUSE AND SENATE COMMITTEES ON APPROPRIATIONS BY THE COMPTROLLER GENERAL OF THE UNITED STATES.). **Main/Corp** United States. General Accounting Office. English. an. US General Accounting Office / District of Columbia, 441 G Street NW, Room 4528, Washington DC 20548. **Tel** (202)275-2812. **LC** JK671; .G45A. **DD** 353.04/05.

AT
### SUMMARY OF ACTIVITIES / COMMONWEALTH OF AUSTRALIA, DEPARTMENT OF NATIONAL DEVELOPMENT. Main/Corp
Australia. Dept. of National Development. (19??)-. English. ir. **LC** WMLC L 83/3023.

US/0090-1520
### SUMMARY OF GENERAL LEGISLATION (TALLAHASSEE).
(SUMMARY OF GENERAL LEGISLATION.). **Main/Corp** Florida. Legislature. Joint Legislative Management Committee. English. Florida Legislature, 111 West Madison Street, Room 716, Tallahassee FL 32399. **Tel** (904)922-0647. **LC** KFF15; .L45. **DD** 348/.73/1.

US
### SUMMARY OF LEGISLATION APPROVED BY THE ... SESSION OF THE ... IOWA GENERAL ASSEMBLY MEETING IN THE YEAR ... . Main/Corp
Iowa. Legislative Service Bureau. Began publication with 1969 issue?. English. an. Iowa Legislative Service Bureau, Des Moines IA 50309.

US/0278-4815
### SUMMARY OF PROCEEDINGS : ANNUAL MEETING OF THE SOUTHERN GOVERNORS' ASSOCIATION. Main/Corp
Southern Governors' Association (U.S.). Meeting. Proceedings. English. an. Southern Governors' Association, Suite 610/3384 Peachtree Road NE, Atlanta GA 30326. **LC** JK2403; .S6. **DD** 353.97503/13/06. **Continues** Southern Governors' Conference. Meeting. Summary of Proceedings.

US
### SUMMARY OF ... REDUCTIONS IN LOCAL GOVERNMENT FISCAL ASSISTANCE.
1983-84-. Periodical. English. an. Joint Publications, State Capitol, Box 942849, Sacramento CA 94249-0001. **Tel** (916)445-4874. **Continues** Reductions in Local Government Fiscal Relief.

US
### SUMMARY OF SELECTED IPA PRODUCTS. Main/Corp
United States. Civil Service Commission. Bureau of Intergovernmental Personnel Programs. **VFOAT** Selected IPA Products. **VAT** Summary of Selected Intergovernmental Personnel Act Products; Selected Intergovernmental Personnel Act Products. English. US Civil Service Commission Bureau of Intergovernmental Personnel Programs, 1900 E Street NW, Washington DC 20415.

AT/1033-3665
### SUMMARY OF STATISTICS - AUSTRALIAN BUREAU OF STATISTICS. VICTORIAN OFFICE. See
Public Administration-Abstracting, Bibliographies and Statistics.

CN/0710-5134
### SUMMARY PROCEEDINGS OF THE ANNUAL CONFERENCE - FEDERATION OF CANADIAN MUNICIPALITIES.
(SUMMARY PROCEEDINGS OF THE ... ANNUAL CONFERENCE.). [Summ. proc. annu. conf. - Fed. Can. Munic.]. **Main/Corp** Federation of Canadian Municipalities. Conference. **VAT** Summary Proceedings of the Annual Conference of the Federation of Canadian Municipalities. 43rd (June 8/11, 1980)-. Proceedings. English. an. Federation of Canadian Municipalities, 24 Clarence Street 2nd floor, Ottawa Ontario K1N 5P3 Canada. **Tel** (613)241-5221. **DD** 352.071. **Continues** Federation of Canadian Municipalities. Conference. Proceedings of the Annual Conference, 0708-9511.

US/0730-983X
### SUPPLEMENT TO ORGANIZATION OF FEDERAL EXECUTIVE DEPARTMENTS AND AGENCIES. (SUPPLEMENT TO ...
ORGANIZATION OF FEDERAL EXECUTIVE DEPARTMENTS AND AGENCIES / PREPARED BY THE OFFICE OF THE FEDERAL REGISTER, NATIONAL ARCHIVES AND RECORDS SERVICE, GENERAL SERVICES ADMINISTRATION FOR THE COMMITTEE ON GOVERNMENTAL AFFAIRS, UNITED STATES SENATE.). **Added/Corp** United States. Office of the Federal Register. United States. Congress. Senate. Committee on Governmental Affairs. **VFOAT** Agencies and Functions of the Federal Government Established, Continued, Abolished, Transferred, of Changed in Name by Legislative or Executive Action During Calendar Year ... . (1977)-. English. an. Iowa Department of Corrections, 523 East 12th Street, Capitol Annex, Des Moines IA 50319. **Tel** (515)281-4811, FAX (515)281-7345. **LC** JK646; .A3 suppl. **DD** 353.04/05. available on microfiche (Vols. for (1982)-) distributed to some depository libraries).

●CN/1189-0630
### SUPPLEMENTARY INFORMATION FOR LEGISLATIVE REVIEW ... EXPENDITURE ESTIMATES/ DEPARTMENT OF CULTURE, HERITAGE AND CITIZENSHIP.
[Suppl. inf. legis. rev. expend. estim. - Manit., Manit. Cult. Herit. Citiz.]. **Main/Corp** Manitoba. Manitoba Culture, Heritage and Citizenship. **VFOAT** Supplementary Information for Legislative Review, ... Departmental Expenditure Estimates. (1992)-. English. **DD** 354.71270685.
**Continues** Supplementary Information for Legislative Review, ... Estimates., 0849-3499.

●CN/1189-0770
### SUPPLEMENTARY INFORMATION FOR LEGISLATIVE REVIEW, EXPENDITURE ESTIMATES - MANITOBA., CIVIL SERVICE COMMISSION. EMPLOYEE BENEFITS AND OTHER PAYMENTS.
(.SUPPLEMENTARY INFORMATION FOR LEGISLATIVE REVIEW, EXPENDITURE ESTIMATES.). [Suppl. inf. legis. rev. expend. estim. - Manit., Civ. Serv. Comm., Empl. Benefits Other Paym.]. **Main/Corp** Manitoba. Civil Service Commission. Employee Benefits and Other Payments. (1992)-. English. **DD** 354.7127001.

US
### SURVEY OF FINANCIAL REPORTING AND ACCOUNTING DEVELOPMENTS IN THE PUBLIC UTILITY INDUSTRY, A. See
Business-Accounting.

US
### SURVEY OF FLORIDA'S LOCAL RETIREMENT SYSTEMS : REPORT TO THE FLORIDA LEGISLATURE, THE.
**VFOAT** Florida's Local Retirement Systems; Survey, Florida's Local Retirement Systems. English. an.
**Continues** The Survey of Local Retirement Systems : Report to the Legislature.

US/0190-5163
### SURVEY OF GRANT-MAKING FOUNDATIONS WITH ASSETS OF OVER $1,000,000 OR GRANTS OF OVER $200,000.
**VAT** Survey of Grant Making Foundations with Assets of Over One Million Dollars or Grants of Over Two Hundred Thousand Dollars. English. Public Service Materials Center / New York, 355 Lexington Avenue, New York NY 10017.

US/0093-7150
### SURVEY OF INCOME OF CIVIL SERVICE ANNUITANTS (WASHINGTON). (SURVEY OF INCOME OF CIVIL SERVICE ANNUITANTS.).
**Main/Corp** United States. Civil Service Commission. English. Iowa Department of Corrections, 523 East 12th Street, Capitol Annex, Des Moines IA 50319. **Tel** (515)281-4811, FAX (515)281-7345. **LC** JK791; .U555A. **DD** 353.005.

NE
### SZW NIEUWS.
Dutch. bw (26 issues). Fl37.00. SDU Uitgeverij, Postbus 20014, Christoffel Plan, 2500 EA Den Haag Netherlands. **Tel** 011 31 70 3789911.

FR
### TABLE DES DEBATS DU SENAT. TABLE DES MATIERES / ETABLIE PAR LE SERVICE DES ARCHIVES DU SENAT. Title Change. Main/Corp
France. Parlement (1946-). Senta. Service des Archives. **Added/Corp** France. Parlement (1946-). Senat. Debats du Senat. **VFOAT** Table des Debats du Senat. (Matieres). (19??)-(19??). French. Journaux Officiels, 26 rue Desaix, 75727 Paris Cedex 15 France. **Tel** 40 58 77 27. **LC** J341; .J25a Suppl. **DD** 328.44/02/016. **Continued by** France. Parlement (1946-). Senat. Service des Archives. Table des Debats du Senat. Table Thematiques.

FR
### TABLE DES DEBATS DU SENAT. TABLE NOMINATIVE / ETABLIE PAR LE SERVICE DES ARCHIVES DU SENAT.
**Main/Corp** France. Parlement (1946- ). Senta. Service des Archives. **VFOAT** Table des Debats du Senta. (Nominative). French. 17F each issue. Journaux Officiels, 26 rue Desaix, 75727 Paris Cedex 15 France. **Tel** 40 58 77 27. **LC** J341; .J25A SUPPL. 2. **DD** 328.44/02/016.

UK/0264-7133
### TABLE (LONDON. 1953). (THE TABLE : BEING THE JOURNAL OF THE SOCIETY OF CLERKS-AT-THE-TABLE IN COMMONWEALTH PARLIAMENTS.).
[Table]. **Main/Corp** Society of Clerks-at-the-Table in Commonwealth Parliaments. **Added/Corp** Society of Clerks-at-the-Table in Commonwealth Parliaments. Vol. 22 (1953)-. English. an. Society of Clerks Commonwealth, c/o B. P. Keith, House of Parliament, London SWI England. **Tel** (01)219-3152, FAX (01)219-5979. **ED** B. P. Keith. Index available. cum. index. **Bk Rev. Circ:** 1,000 (ctrl). **Continues** Journal of the Society of Clerks-at-the-Table in Empire Parliaments.
**Desc:** News of the parliamentary, constitutional, legal, administrative and historical questions of the British Commonwealth.

UK
### TABLE OF GOVERNMENT ORDERS.
**Main/Corp** Great Britain. Statue Law Committee. (1966)-. English. an. Her Majesty's Stationery Office, 51 Nine Elms Lane, London SW8 5DR England. **Tel** 011 44 71 873 8459, 011 44 71 873 8499, FAX 011 44 71 873 8499,

011 44 71 873 8456, telex 297138. **(Subscription address:** PO Box 276, Public Centre, London SW8 5DT England)

FR
**TABLES DES QUESTIONS ET DES REPONSES DES MINISTRES PUBLIEES DU ... / ETABLIES PAR LE SERVICE DES IMPRESSIONS, DE LA DOCUMENTATION PARLEMENTAIRE ET DE L'INFORMATIQUE.** **Added/Corp** France. Parlement (1946- ). Senat. Service des Impressions, de la Documentation Parlementaire et de l'Informatique. France. Parlement (1946). Senat. Debats du Senat. **VFOAT** Tables des Questions Ecrites et des Questions Orales et Reponses des Ministres Publiees du ...; Tables des Questions Ecrites et Orales du Senat. (19??)-. French. ir. Journaux Officiels, 26 rue Desaix, 75727 Paris Cedex 15 France. **Tel** 40 58 77 27. **LC** J341; .J25a Suppl. 3. **DD** 328.44/02/016.

CC
**TANG SHIH TZU LIAO TSUNG KAN.** **VFOAT** Tang Shih Tzu Liao. Periodical. Chinese. RMBY0.55. Hsin Hua Shu Tien / Shang-Hai Fa Hsing So, Shanghai, People's Republic of China. **LC** JQ1519.A5; T2553. **DD** 324.251/075/09.

CH
**TANG SHIH YEN CHIU TZU LIAO / CHUNG-KUO KO MING PO WU KUAN TANG SHIH YEN CHIU SHIH PIEN.** Periodical. Chinese. NT$1.76. Ssu-Chuan Sheng Hsin Hua Shu Tien, Cheng-tu, People's Republic of China. **LC** JQ1519.A5; T2556. **DD** 324.251075/09.

US
**TAUBMAN CENTER ANNUAL REPORT, THE.** **Added/Corp** Taubman Center for State and Local Government. (1991)-. English. John F Kennedy School of Government, Harvard University, 79 Johnn F Kennedy Street, Cambridge MA 02138.

UK/0144-7394
**TEACHING PUBLIC ADMINISTRATION : TPA.** **Added/Corp** Joint University Council for Social and Public Administration. Public Administration Committee. University of Manchester. Dept. of Administrative Studies. Politics Association (Great Britain). **VFOAT** TPA. (197?)-. Periodical. English. sa. £13.50 (individuals); £16.50 (institutions) UK; £20.00 (institutions) other. University of Manchester / Institute of Development, Policy Management, Crawford House Precinct Centre, Oxford Road, Manchester M13 9Q5 England. **Tel** 011 44 61 273-6241. **ED** Lloyd Edmonds. **Bk Rev. Ad Acc. Circ:** 200.
**Ind/Abst** Br. Educ. Index; Sage Public Adm. Abstr. (?-?).

CN/0020-2991
**TECHNICAL BULLETIN - INSTITUTE OF MUNICIPAL ASSESSORS OF ONTARIO.** [Tech. bull. - Inst. Munic. Assess. Ont.]. **Main/Corp** Institute of Municipal Assessors of Ontario. No. 1 (1965)-. Bulletin. English. ir. Institute of Municipal Assessors of Ontario, 180 Yorkland Boulevard 2, Willowdale Ontario M2J 1R5 Canada. **DD** 352/.131.

US/0548-3646
**TECHNICAL REPORT - BUREAU OF GOVERNMENTAL RESEARCH, UNIVERSITY OF NEVADA.** **Main/Corp** University of Nevada, Reno. Bureau of Governmental Research. No. 1- 1965-. Periodical. English. University of Nevada Bureau of Governmental Research, Box 8037 University Station, Reno NV 89507. **LC** JK8501; .N45. **DD** 353.9.

IT
**TECNOLOGIE DEI SERVIZI PUBBLICI.** Italian. mo. L80.000 Italy; $139.00 other. Stammer Spa, Via della Liberazione 1, 20068 Peschiera Borromeo, Italy. **Tel** 011 39 2 55302606, FAX 011 39 2 55302700, telex 321083. **ED** Girolamo Bellina. **Bk Rev. Ad Acc. Pr Rev. Circ:** 9,100 (ctrl).
**Desc:** Information on public administration, health, safety, utilities, fire prevention, ecology, housing and urban development, conservation and natural resources.

US
**TELEPHONE DIRECTORY, CENTRAL OFFICE AND NATIONAL CAPITAL REGION.** **Main/Corp** United States. General Services Administration. (1980)-. Directory. English. an. General Services Administration, General Services Building, Eighteenth and F Streets NW, Washington DC 20405. **Tel** (202)655-4000. ***Continues in part*** *United States. General Services Administration. Telephone Directory, Central Office, National Capital Region, and Region 3.*

US
**TELEPHONE DIRECTORY CENTRAL OFFICE AND REGION 3.** **Main/Corp** United States. General Services Administration. **VFOAT** Telephone Directory - General Services Administration: Central Office and Region 3. (19??)-. Directory. English. US General Services Administration / Automated Data and Telecommunication, General Services Building, Eighteenth and F Streets NW, Washington DC 20405.
**Desc:** Contains alphabetical and organizational listings.

CN/0701-7510
**TELEPHONE DIRECTORY. GOVERNMENT OF ALBERTA AND THE LEGISLATIVE ASSEMBLY OF ALBERTA.** (TELEPHONE DIRECTORY.). April 1977-. Directory. English. an. Alberta Public Affairs Bureau, 11510 Kingsway Avenue, Edmonton Alberta T5G 2Y5 Canada. **Tel** (403)427-4952. **DD** 354.7123/00025. ***Continues*** *Government of Alberta Telephone Directory.*

CN/0710-8265
**TELEPHONE DIRECTORY (GREATER VANCOUVER AND AREA EDITION).** (TELEPHONE DIRECTORY.). **VFOAT** Telephone Directory for Greater Vancouver and Area. Oct. 1981 Ed. -. Directory. English. Government of British Columbia / Victoria, Parliament Buildings, Victoria British Columbia V8V 1X4 Canada. **DD** 354.711/00025.

CN/0318-0255
**TELEPHONE DIRECTORY. MANITOBA GOVERNMENT.** (MANITOBA GOVERNMENT TELEPHONE DIRECTORY.). **VFOAT** Telephone Directory - Manitoba Government. (1974)-. Directory. English. an. 5.00Can$. Queens Printer Statutory Publishing, 200 Vaughn Street, Winnipeg Manitoba R3C 1T5 Canada. **Tel** (204)945-3102. **DD** 354/.7127/00025.

●CN/1196-054X
**TELEPHONE DIRECTORY, OTTAWA-HULL.** [Teleph. dir., Ott.-Hull]. **Added/Corp** Canada Government Telecommunications Agency. **VFOAT** Telephone Directory, Ottawa Hull; Telephone Directory, Ottawa; Annuaire Telephonique, Ottawa-Hull. (Apr. 1993)-. Periodical. English (French). sa. Canada Communication Group Publishers, Order Processing, Ottawa Ontario K1A 0S9 Canada. **Tel** (819)956-4800, (819)956-4802. **DD** 354.7100025/713/83. ***Continues*** *Telephone Directory, National Capital Region.*

US
**TELEPHONE DIRECTORY / UNITED STATES DEPARTMENT OF STATE.** **Main/Corp** United States. Dept. of State. (Spring 1980)-. Periodical. English. an. $16.00 US; $17.50 other. US Department of State, 2201 C Street NW, Room 5819, Washington DC 20520. **Tel** (202)647-9859. ***Continues*** *Telephone Directory. Department of State, International Development Cooperation Agency, Agency for International Development, Arms Control and Disarmament Agency, Overseas Private Investment Corporation, Board for International Broadcasting.*

US/0364-5746
**TENNESSEE BLUE BOOK.** **Added/Corp** Tennessee. Dept. of State. (19??)-. English. be. Free on request. Tennessee Secretary State Publishers, James K. Polk Building, Suite 500, Nashville TN 37243. **Tel** (615)741-2650, FAX (615)741-1278. **ED** Sherwin Clift. **LC** JK5230; .T4. **DD** 353.9768. Index available.

US
**TENNESSEE GOVERNMENT OFFICIALS DIRECOTRY UPDATE SERVICE.** English. an. $37.00. M. Lee Smith Publishers and Printers, 162 4th Avenue North, PO Box 198867, Nashville TN 37219. **Tel** (615)242-7395, (800)274-6774, FAX (615)256-6601.

US/0892-5380
**TENNESSEE PUBLIC WORKS.** **Added/Corp** American Public Works Association. Tennessee Chapter. Executive Committee. Vol. 1, No. 1 (May 1983)- Vol. 11 (May, 1993)-. Periodical. English. Seven times a year. $21.00. Images Publications, PO Box 474, Loudon TN 37774. **Tel** (615)458-3560. **ED** Judy McGill. **LC** HD3890.T2; T46. **DD** 363/.09768. **Ad Acc. Circ:** 2,300.
**Desc:** Education and state news for Tennessee city and county managers, mayors and public works directors.

US/0040-3415
**TENNESSEE TOWN & CITY.** **Added/Corp** Tennessee Municipal League. University of Tennessee, Knoxville. Municipal Technical Advisory Service. Tennessee. University. Municipal Technical Advisory Service. **VFOAT** Tennessee Town and City. (1950)-. Periodical. English. Twenty-three times a year (Twice monthly except one issue in June). $6.00 members; $10.00 other. Tennessee Municipal League, 226 Capitol Building, Nashville TN 37129. **Tel** (615)255-6416, FAX (615)255-4752. **ED** Beverly Bruninga. **LC** JS39; .T38. **Ad Acc. Circ:** 5,000 (ctrl).
**Desc:** Municipal government affairs.
**Ind/Abst** Urban Aff. Abstr.

JA
**TENNOSEI KENKYU.** Vol. 1- ; 1980-. Periodical. Japanese. JCS Shuppan, c/o Nitto Building, 42 Kanda Jimbocho 1-chome, Chiyoda-ku Tokyo Japan. **LC** JQ1601; .T46.

FR/0991-2428
**TERRITOIRES PARIS. 1988.** (TERRITOIRES.). (1988)-. Periodical. French. Ten times a year. 440.74F France; 450.00F EEU; 520.00F other Europe; 575.00F other. Adels, 108 110 rue St. Maur, 75011 Paris France. **Tel** 011 33 1 43 554005. **UDC** 352. ***Continues*** *Correspondance Municipale, 0223-5951.*

AT
**TERRITORY OF NORFOLK ISLAND; REPORT.** **Main/Corp** Australia. Dept. of Territories. (19??)-. English. an (Dec.). 14.50Aus$. Norfolk Island Administrations, Chief Administrator Officer of, Norfolk Island, South Pacific 2899 Australia. **Tel** 011 61 672 32001. **LC** J905; .L3 subser; HC607.N56. **DD** 309.1/948.

IT
**TEST : AUTONOMIE.** (19??)-. Italian. mo (11 issues). L80000.00. Editoriale Test Srl, L Go Fontanella Borghese 77, 00186 Rome Italy. **Tel** 011 39 6 6876407.

US/0362-4781
**TEXAS REGISTER.** [Tex. regist.]. **Main/Corp** Texas. Secretary of State. (19??)-. Periodical. English. sw (100 times per year). $95.00 (print), $90.00 (electronic). Secretary of State / Texas, PO Box 13824 Capitol Station, Austin TX 78711. **Tel** (512)463-5561. **ED** Dan Procter. **LC** KFT1236; .S4. **DD** 348/.764/025. Index available. cum. index. **Circ:** 5,000 (ctrl).
**Desc:** Publishes regulations, open meetings, governor appointments. Attorney General opinions, and other general information submitted by state agencies.

US/0363-7530
**TEXAS STATE DIRECTORY.** (19??)-. Directory. English. an. $26.95. Texas State Directory Press, PO Box 12186 Capitol Station, Austin TX 78711. **Tel** (512)477-5698, (800)388-8075, FAX (512)473-2447. **ED** Scott Sayers. **LC** JK4830; .T4. **DD** 328.764. Index available. cum. index. **Bk Rev. Ad Acc. Circ:** 12,000 (ctrl).
**Desc:** Publishes Texas savings and loan directory, Texas legislative handbook, and Texas legislative manual.

●US
**TEXAS STATE PUBLICATIONS.** (TEXAS STATE PUBLICATIONS DEPOSITORY PROGRAM.). (1993)-. English. Twelve times a year. Free. Texas State Library Clearinghouse, PO Box 12927, Capitol Station, Austin TX 78711. **Tel** (512)463-5435, FAX (512)463-5436. ***Continues*** *Texas State Publications Clearinghouse. Texas State Publications.*

US
**TEXAS STATE PUBLICATIONS.** ***Title Change.*** **Main/Corp** Texas State Publications Clearinghouse. **Added/Corp** Texas State Library. **VFOAT** News from the Texas State Publications Clearinghouse. (Feb. 1989)-(1992). Periodical. English. Twelve times a year. Texas State Library Clearinghouse, PO Box 12927, Capitol Station, Austin TX 78711. **Tel** (512)463-5435, FAX (512)463-5436. **LC** Z1223.5.T47; T47b; J87.T4. cum. index. ***Continues*** *Texas State Publications Clearinghouse. Texas State Documents.* ***Continued by*** *Texas State Publications Depository Progrmam. Texas State Publications.*

FR/0377-6093
**TEXTS ADOPTED BY THE ASSEMBLY - COUNCIL OF EUROPE. PARLIAMENTARY ASSEMBLY.** (TEXTS ADOPTED BY THE ASSEMBLY.). [Texts adopt. by Assemb. - Counc. Eur., Parliam. Assemb.]. **Main/Corp** Council of Europe. Parliamentary Assembly. **Added/Corp** Council of Europe. Parliamentary Assembly. Textes Adoptes Par l'Assemblee. **VFOAT** Textes Adoptes par l'Assemblee. 26th Session, 2nd Pt.(Sept. 1974)-. Multiple languages (English and French). ir. Manhattan Publishing Company, PO Box 650, Croton-on-Hudson NY 10520. **Tel** (914)271-5194. **LC** JN22; .A43. **DD** 341.24/2. Index available. ***Continues*** *Council of Europe. Consultative Assembly. Texts Adopted by the Assembly.*

●US/1063-3340
**THINK TANK DIRECTORY.** (THINK TANK DIRECTORY : A GUIDE TO INDEPENDENT NONPROFIT PUBLIC POLICY RESEARCH ORGANIZATIONS.). **Added/Corp** Government Research Service. (1992)-. Directory. English. an (July). $85.00. Government Research Service, 701 Jackson, Suite 304B, Topeka KS 66603. **Tel** (913)232-7720, (800)346-6898, FAX (913)232-1615.
**Desc:** This magazine has a major impact on public policy in this country. The men and women who staff these organizations are constantly quoted in the news media and their comments and studies have tremendous influence on policy makers.

BE
**TIJDSCHRIFT VOOR BESTUURSWETENSCHAPPEN EN PUBLEKRECHT.** Academic Scholarly Publication. Dutch. mo. 3300F Belgium; 3700F other. TBP - Tijdschrift voor Bestuurswetenschappen, G Mercatorlaan 28,

B-1780 Wemmel Belgium. **Tel** 011 02 269 41 09, FAX 011 02 270 13 19. Index available. cum. index. **Bk Rev. Ad Acc. Circ:** 2,000.

US/1054-2914
**TITLE LIST OF DOCUMENTS MADE PUBLICLY AVAILABLE.** [Title list doc. made publicly available]. **Added/Corp** U.S. Nuclear Regulatory Commission. Division of Technical Information and Document Control. U.S. Nuclear Regulatory Commission. Division of Publications Services. U.S. Nuclear Regulatory Commission. Division of Freedom of Information and Publications Services. Vol. 1, No. 1 (Jan. 1979)-. Government Publication. English. mo. $66.00 US; $82.50 other. Superintendent of Documents, US Government Printing Office, Washington DC 20402. **Tel** (202)275-3328, FAX (202)786-2377. **LC** Z5162.R42; T57; TK9152. **DD** 016.62148/35/0973. ***Formed by the union of*** *U.S. Nuclear Regulatory Commission Publications. U.S. Nuclear Regulatory Commission* ***and*** *Power Reactor Docket Information. U.S. Nuclear Regulatory Commission, 0363-5856.*
**Desc:** Contains descriptions of the information received and generated by the Nuclear Regulatory Commission. Includes docketed material associated with civilian nuclear power plants and other uses of radioactive materials and non-docketed material received and generated by the Commission pertinent to its role as a regulatory agency. Docketed refers to the system by which the Commission maintains its regulatory records.

US/1040-6565
**TML TEXAS TOWN & CITY. Added/Corp** Texas Municipal League. **VFOAT** TML Texas Town and City. **VAT** Texas Municipal League Texas Town & City. Vol. 71, No. 9 (Sept. 1984)-. Periodical. English. mo. Texas Municipal League, 211 East Seventh, Suite 1020, Austin TX 78701. **Tel** (512)478-6601. ***Continues*** *Texas Town & City, 0040-473X.*

JA/0040-893X
**TOKYO METROPOLITAN NEWS : A QUARTERLY JOURNAL OF THE TOKYO METROPOLITAN GOVERNMENT. Added/Corp** Tokyo (Japan). Kokusaibu. Gaijika. Vol. 41, No. 2 (Summer 1991)-. Periodical. English (French, Chinese and Korean). Four times a year. Free on request. Tokyo Metropolitan Government / Liaison and Protocol Section, 8-1 Nishi-Shinjuku 2-chome, Shinjuku-ku Tokyo 163-01, Japan. **Tel** 03-5388-3172. **ED** Makoto Inaishi. **LC** DS896; .T64. **Circ:** 2,500 (ctrl). ***Continues*** *Tokyo Municipal News, 0040-893X.*
**Desc:** Articles and a graphic view on metropolitan Tokyo's government administrative and international exchange activities.
**Ind/Abst** PAIS Int. Print (?-?).

JA
**TOKYO-TO KOBUNSHOKAN NENPO. Main/Corp** Tokyo-to Kobunshokan. Periodical. Japanese. an. Tokyo-to Kobunshokan, 13-17 Kaigan 1 Minato-ku, Tokyo-to Japan. **LC** CD2187.T64; T65A.

JA
**TOKYO TOGIKAI GIIN SENKYO NO KIROKU. Main/Corp** Tokyo. Senkyo Kanri Iinkai. (19??)-. Periodical. Japanese. Senkyo Kanri Iinkai, 13 Yurakucho 2-chome Chiyoda-ku, Tokyo Japan. **LC** JS7385.T63; A87a.

JA
**TOSEI. Main/Corp** Tokyo (Japan). (1973)-. Japanese. Tokyo-To Kohoshitsu, 5-1 Marunouchi Chiyoda-ku 100, Tokyo Japan. **LC** JS7385.T6; A152a. ***Continues*** *Tokyo. Tokyo Tosei Gaiyo.*

UK/0040-9960
**TOWN & COUNTRY PLANNING.** (TOWN AND COUNTRY PLANNING : THE QUARTERLY REVIEW OF THE TOWN AND COUNTRY PLANNING ASSOCIATION.). [Town ctry. plann.]. **Added/Corp** Town and Country Planning Association (Great Britain) Garden Cities and Town Planning Association (Great Britain). **VFOAT** Town & Country Planning. (1932)-. Periodical. English. mo (except July/Aug.). £51.00 UK; £63.00 other. Town & Country Planning Association, 17 Carlton House Terrace, London SW1Y 5AS England. **Tel** 011 44 1 930 8903. **ED** David Boyle. **LC** NA9000; .T5. Index available. **Bk Rev. Ad Acc. Circ:** 4,000 (ctrl). available on microfilm and microfiche from University Microfilms International (UMI). ***Continues*** *Garden Cities and Town Planning.*
**Desc:** The magazine of the Town and Country Planning Association concerned with planning and the environment worldwide.
**Ind/Abst** Appl. Soc. Sci. Index Abstr.; Archit. Period. Index (1970-); Art Index; Br. Humanit. Index; Coal Abstr.; Ecol. Abstr. (?-?); Geogr. Abstr. Human Geogr.; Int. Dev. Abstr.; J. Plan. Lit.; Life Sci. Collect.

US/0732-4049
**TOWN HALL JOURNAL. Added/Corp** Town Hall (Los Angeles, Calif.). Vol. 30, No. 43 (Oct. 22, 1968)-. Periodical. English. Fifty-two times a year. $80.00. Town Hall of California, 523 West 6th Street, Suite 232, Los Angeles CA 90014. **Tel** (310)628-8141. ***Continues*** *Town Hall of California, 0732-4057.*

US
**TOWN TOPICS. Added/Corp** Town and County Officers Training School of the State of New York. Vol. 1, No. 1 (Apr. 1991)-. Periodical. English. bm. Town and Country Training School of the State of New York, 90 State Street, Albany NY 12207. ***Formed by the union of*** *Miscellaneous Topics; Justice Court Topics; Highway Topics; Assessors Topics; Town and County Topics* ***and*** *Town Clerks, Tax Receivers & Collectors topics.*

US
**TRADE POLICY AGENDA AND ... ANNUAL REPORT OF THE PRESIDENT OF THE UNITED STATES ON THE TRADE AGREEMENTS PROGRAM.** English. Office of the US Trade Representative, 600 17th Street NW, Washington DC 20506.

UK/0957-0004
**TRAINING TOMORROW.** (19??)-. English. Nine times a year. $769.00. MCB University Press, 60 62 Toller Lane, Bradford West Yorkshire BD8 9BX England. **Tel** 011 44 274 499821, FAX 011 44 274 547143, telex 51317 MCBUNI G. **(Subscription address:** MCB University Press / US and Canada Subscriptions, PO Box 10812, Birmingham AL 35201-0812.**) ED** Margaret Reid. **LC** WMLC 93/1267. **Bk Rev. Ad Acc. Circ:** 3,000 (ctrl).
**Desc:** Publishes informative and objective articles on every aspect of government training schemes.

CN/0225-2627
**TRAIT D'UNION (OTTAWA).** (TRAIT D'UNION.). [Trait d'union]. V. 1- Aug. 1977-. Periodical. French. Commission de la Fonction Publique du Canada, Direction Generale de la Formation Linguistique, Ottawa Ontario K1A 0M7 Canada. **DD** 354.71001/5/05.

CN/0820-7720
**TRAIT D'UNION (ROUYN).** (LE TRAIT D'UNION : BULLETIN MUNICIPAL DE ROUYN.). [Trait union]. **Main/Corp** Rouyn (Quebec). Vol. 1, No. 1 (Oct. 82)-. Bulletin. French. ir (4 times a year). Free for former Rouyn-Noranda citizens. Ville de Rouyn-Noranda, C P 220, Quebec J9X 5C3 Canada. **Tel** (819)762-1721. **DD** 352.0714/212. **Bk Rev. Circ:** 11,000 (ctrl).
**Desc:** Municipal information: bylaw, municipal finance, investment (public and private), urbanism.

SZ
**TRAKTANDUM MAGAZIN.** (1988)-. Periodical. German. qt. Verlag Steiner und Gruninger, AG Haus Zum Adler, 8226 Schleitheim Germany. ***Continues in part*** *Traktandum.*

SZ
**TRAKTANDUM PERSONLICH. VFOAT** Traktandum. Vol. 7, Nr. 1 (Feb. 22, 1988)-. German. bm. Verlag Steiner und Gruninger, AG Haus Zum Adler, 8226 Schleitheim Germany. ***Continues in part*** *Traktandum.*

●CN/1191-4254
**TRANSCRIPT OF SELECT COMMITTEE ON THE CONSTITUTION (FRENCH EDITION).** [Transcr. Sel. Commit. Const.]. **Main/Corp** Nouveau-Brunswick. Assemblee Legislative. Comite Special de la Constitution. 1st Meeting (Feb. 19, 1992)-. Periodical. French (English). **DD** 342.71/03.

US/0278-2804
**TRANSITIONS (CINCINNATI, OHIO).** **See** Transportation.

US
**TRANSLATION - BUREAU OF RECLAMATION. Main/Corp** United States. Bureau of Reclamation. Monographic series. English. Price varies per volume.

BE/0020-6059
**TRANSNATIONAL ASSOCIATIONS. Added/Corp** Union of International Associations. **VFOAT** Associations Transnationales. No 1 (Jan/Feb 1986)-. Periodical. English (French). Six times a year. $55.50 surface mail; $67.00 airmail. Union of International Associations, Rue Washington 40, 1050 Brussels Belgium. **Tel** 011 32 2 6404109, FAX 011 32 2 646 05 25, telex 65080 INAC B. **ED** J. Raeymaeckers. **LC** AS1; .I57. **DD** 060. **[CCC]**. Index available. **Bk Rev. *Continues*** *International Transnational Associations, 0250-4928.*
**Ind/Abst** Hum. Rights Intern. Rep. (19??-); PAIS Int. Print (19??-); World Agric. Econ. (19??-).

UK
**TREASURY AND CIVIL SERVICE COMMITTEE.** (19??)-. English. an. Her Majesty's Stationery Office, 51 Nine Elms Lane, London SW8 5DR England. **Tel** 011 44 71 873 8459, 011 44 71 873 8499, FAX 011 44 71 873 8499, 011 44 71 873 8456, telex 297138. **(Subscription address:** Her Majesty's Stationery Office, PO Box 276, Publications Centre, London SW8 5DT England.**)**

US
**TREASURY DEPARTMENT TELEPHONE DIRECTORY. Main/Corp** United States. Treasury Dept. (1977)-. Government Publication. English. tq. $14.00 US; $17.50 other. Superintendent of Documents, US Government Printing Office, Washington DC 20402. **Tel** (202)275-3328, FAX (202)786-2377. ***Continues*** *Treasury Telephone Directory.*

●CN/1191-4750
**TRENT-SEVERN WATERWAY, MANAGEMENT PLANNING.** [Trent-Severn Waterw. manag. plan.]. **Added/Corp** Canadian Parks Service. No. 1 (Spring 1992)-. Periodical. English. qt. **DD** 333.78.

FR/0996-8407
**TRESORERIE PARIS.** (TRESORERIE.). [Tresor. Paris]. **VFOAT** Revue Europeenne de Tresorerie (Paris). (1989)-. Periodical. French. Ten times a year. 783.55F France; 1000.00F other. Finway, 22 Rue Chauchat, F-75009 Paris France. **Tel** 011 33 1 40220674. **UDC** 336.71. ***Continues*** *Revue Europeenne de Tresorerie.*

US/0272-2623
**TRIENNIAL ASSESSMENT OF THE TENNESSEE VALLEY AUTHORITY. Main/Corp** United States. General Accounting Office. Fiscal years 1977-1979-. English. te. US General Accounting Office / District of Columbia, 441 G Street NW, Room 4528, Washington DC 20548. **Tel** (202)275-2812. **LC** HN79.A135; U53A. **DD** 353.0082/3/09768. available on microfiche (Vols. for 1977/1979- distributed to depository libraries). ***Continues*** *Examination of Financial Statements, Tennessee Valley Authority, 0565-5803.*

CN/0849-1127
**TRIFLUVIEN (TROIS-RIVIERES. 1990).** (LE TRIFLUVIEN.). [Trifluvien]. **Added/Corp** Trois-Rivieres (Quebec). Vol. 1, No 1 (Jan. 1990)-. Periodical. French. Three times a year. Limited free distribution. La Ville de Trois-Rivieres, CP 368, Trois-Rivieres, Quebec G9A 5H3 Canada. **DD** 971.4/451/005. ***Continues*** *Bulletin Municipal (Trois-Rivieres, Quebec)., 0849-1119.*

US
**TRL ANALYZES DEVELOPMENTS IN TEXAS STATE AND LOCAL GOVERNMENT. Main/Corp** Texas Research League. **VAT** Texas Research League Analyzes Developments in Texas State and Local Government. Periodical. English. PO Box 12456, Austin TX 78711.

TU/0251-2955
**TURKISH PUBLIC ADMINISTRATION ANNUAL.** [Turk. public adm. annu.]. No. 1- 1974-. English. 1 No 1u Cadde Yucetepe, Ankara Turkey. **LC** JQ1801.A1; T87. **DD** 354/.561/0005.
**Ind/Abst** Int. Labour Doc.

IT
**TUTTOPARLAMENTO.** (19??)-. Italian. wk. L330000. C Ed Et, Via Vittorio Fantini 61, 00128 Rome Italy. **Tel** 011 39 6 5081269.

US/0895-545X
**U.S. AGRICULTURAL POLICY GUIDE.** (U.S. AGRICULTURAL POLICY GUIDE / WORLD PERSPECTIVES.). [U. S. agric. policy guide]. **Added/Corp** World Perspectives (Firm). **VFOAT** US Agricultural Policy Guide. **VAT** United States Agricultural Policy Guide. (Fall 1987)-. English. an. $140.00. World Perspectives Inc., 1150 18th Street Northwest, Suite 275, Washington DC 20036. **Tel** (202)785-3345, FAX (202)659-6891, telex 89490 WPINEWS. **LC** HD1751; .U18. **DD** 338.1/873. **Bk Rev. Circ:** 500.
**Desc:** A comprehensive reference guide to U.S. agricultural policy and policy-makers. Clear and up-to-date analyses of the policy process, policy-makers, key committees and lobbyists, as well as the relationship between congress, the administration and the private sector. Includes an easy reference glossary of terms.

US/1052-5238
**U.S. & FOREIGN DIPLOMATIC CONTACTS.** [U. S. foreign dipl. contacts]. **VFOAT** U.S. and Foreign Diplomatic Contacts; Albertsen's U.S. and Foreign Diplomatic Contacts; Albertsen's U.S. & Foreign Diplomatic Contacts. **VAT** United States and Foreign Diplomatic Contacts. (1991)-. Periodical. English. $10.00. Albertsen's, Box 339, Nevada City CA 95959. **Tel** (916)292-3655, FAX (916)477-0915. **DD** 327.

US/0196-7614
**U.S. CONGRESS HANDBOOK, THE.** [U. S. Congr. handb.]. **VFOAT** Congress Handbook. **VAT** United States Congress Handbook. (1974)-. English. an. $9.95, $8.95 (spiral edition). Congress Handbook, PO Box 566, McLean VA 22101. **Tel** (703)356-3572. **ED** Barbara Pullen. **LC** JK1012; .U55. **DD** 328.73/0025. **Bk Rev. Ad Acc. Circ:** 100,000.
**Desc:** Features how congress is organized and operates with members pictures, biographies, addresses, telephone numbers, committee assignments key staff aides listed alphabetically and by state and much more.

# Public Administration

US/0735-6021
**U.S. CONGRESSMAN JACK BRINKLEY REPORTS FROM WASHINGTON.** VFOAT Jack Brinkley Reports from Washington; Reports From Washington. Periodical. English. 2470 Rayburn House Office Building, Washington DC 20515.

US
**U.S. CUSTOMS DIRECTORY.** Main/Corp United States. Customs Service. Directory. English. Customs Service, 1301 Constitution Avenue NW, Washington DC 20229.

US
**U.S.D. REPORT ON ENROLLMENTS AND GENERAL FUND BUDGET PER PUPIL.** See Education.

US/0193-1040
**U.S. DEPARTMENT OF ENERGY BUDGET TO CONGRESS : BUDGET HIGHLIGHTS.** Main/Corp United States. Dept. of Energy. VFOAT Budget Highlights. VAT United States Department of Energy Budget to Congress: Budget Highlights. Government Publication. English. an. US Department of Energy, 1000 Independence Avenue SW, Washington DC 20585. **Tel** (202)586-5000, FAX (202)586-4073. **LC** HD9502.U5; U523B. **DD** 353.87.

US/1058-0018
**U.S. DEPARTMENT OF STATE INDEXES OF LIVING COSTS ABROAD, QUARTERS ALLOWANCES, AND HARDSHIP DIFFERENTIALS.** See Population Studies.

US
**U. S. GOVERNMENT RESEARCH AND DEVELOPMENT REPORTS. GOVERNMENT-WIDE INDEX TO FEDERAL RESEARCH AND DEVELOPMENT REPORTS.** English.

US/1049-2119
**U.S. MAYOR.** [U.S. mayor]. **Added/Corp** United States Conference of Mayors. VFOAT US Mayor. VAT United States Mayor. Vol. 56, Issue 24 (Nov. 14, 1989)-. Periodical. English. sm. $35.00. US Conference of Mayors, 1620 Eye Street NW, Washington DC 20006. **Tel** (202)293-7330, FAX (202)293-2352. **LC** JS39; .U6. **DD** 352/.0072/0973. **Continues** Mayor.

HU/0302-9778
**UGYVITEL ES INFORMACIO AZ ALLAMIGAZGATASBAN.** [Ugyvitel inf. allamigazgatasban]. Periodical. Hungarian. Lapkiado Vallalat, Lenin Korut 9-11, 1073 Budapest 7, Hungary. **Tel** 222-408. **LC** JF1525.A8; U33. **CODEN** UIALD8. Documents available from Ask*IEEE.
**Ind/Abst** INSPEC (1980-).

UK
**UK OFFSHORE LEGISLATION GUIDE.** English. Six times a year (Includes 4 newsletters & 2 supplements). £225.00 UK; £250.00 others. Tolley Publishing Company Ltd, Tolley House, 2 Addiscombe Road, Croydon, Surrey CR9 5AF United Kingdom. **Tel** 011 44 81 6869141, FAX 011 44 81 6863155, 011 44 81 7600588.
**Desc:** Accurate summary of the legislation which governs the exploration for, and exploitation of, oil and gas reserves on the UK continental shelf.

IS
**UNDZER SHTIME.** Added/Corp Yisroeldike Komunistishe Opozitsye. VFOAT Our Voice. (19??)-. Periodical. Yiddish. mo. AKI, POB 12133, Tel-Aviv 61121 Israel. **LC** JQ1825.P3; A39.

US/1063-0813
**UNICAMERAL UPDATE.** (UNICAMERAL UPDATE : A PUBLICATION OF THE NEBRASKA LEGISLATURE.). **Main/Corp** Nebraska. Legislature. **Added/Corp** Nebraska. Legislature. Unicameral Information Service. Vol. 1, No. 1 (Jan. 31-Feb. 4, 1977)-. Periodical. English. ir (weekly during legislative sessions). Free on Request. Office of Clerk of Legislature, State Capitol Building, #2018 Rosie, Linclon NE 68509. **Tel** (402)417-2321. **ED** Judy Meyer (phone: (402)471-2788). **DD** 328. **Circ:** 11,000 (ctrl).
**Desc:** Coverage of Nebraska Legislature - introduction of bills, public hearings on bills, legislative on bills, legislative floor debate of bills.

US
**UNITED NATIONS PUBLICATIONS.** **Main/Corp** United Nations. Department of Public Information. -. Government Publication. English. United Nations Publications, 2 United Nations Plaza, Room DC2 0853, Department 007C, New York NY 10017. **Tel** (212)963-8303, (800)253-9646.

US
**UNITED STATES CODE CONGRESSIONAL AND ADMINISTRATIVE NEWS.** Main/Corp United States. **Added/Corp** United States. Congress. United States. President. VFOAT US Code Congressional and Administrative News; Congressional and Administrative News; U.S. Code Congressional & Administrative News; Congressional & Administrative News. (1952)-. Periodical. English. ir. West Publishing Company, 610 Opperman Drive, PO Box 64526, Eagan MN 55123-1308. **Tel** (612)687-5618, (800)328-9352, FAX (612)687-5388, (800)562-2329. **Continues** United States Code Congressional Service.

US
**UNITED STATES DEPARTMENT OF HOUSING AND URBAN DEVELOPMENT ANNUAL REPORT / U.S. DEPARTMENT OF HOUSING AND URBAN DEVELOPMENT, THE.** Main/Corp United States. Dept. of Housing and Urban Development. Government Publication. English. US Department of Housing and Urban Development, 451 Seventh Street SW, Washington DC 20401. **Tel** (202)708-0980, FAX (202)708-0299. **LC** HT167.2; .A3. **DD** 353.85/06. **Continues** Annual Report.

US/0730-1332
**UNITED STATES DIRECTORY OF FEDERAL REGIONAL STRUCTURE.** [U.S. dir. fed. reg. struct.]. 1979-. Directory. English. an. $8.75. National Archives and Records Administration, Eighth Street and Pennsylvania Avenue NW, Washington DC 20408. **Tel** (202)523-3220. **LC** JK404. **DD** 353/.00025. **NLM** JK 404 U58.

US/0884-1063
**UNITED STATES GOVERNMENT ANNUAL REPORT.** [U. S. gov. annu. rep.]. **Added/Corp** United States. Dept. of the Treasury. Financial Management Service. VFOAT Annual Report of the United States Government for the Fiscal Year Ended September 30 ... . (1984)-. Government Publication. English. an. $23.50. Bernan Associates, 4611-F Assembly Drive, Lanham MD 20706-4391. **Tel** (301)459-7666, (800)274-4447 US, (800)233-0504 CANADA, FAX (301)459-0056, telex 7108260418. **ED** Arlene Johnson. **LC** HJ10; .A6. **DD** 353.0072/05. **Circ:** 2,500. **Continues** Treasury Combined Statement of Receipts, Expenditures, and Balances of the United States Government for the Fiscal Year Ended ..., 0191-2062.
**Desc:** Presents an overview of the government's cash basis financial position and results of operation.

US/0362-6792
**UNITED STATES GOVERNMENT GRANTS UNDER THE FULBRIGHT-HAYS ACT : UNIVERSITY LECTURING, ADVANCED RESEARCH.** **Main/Corp** Conference Board of the Associated Research Councils. Committee on International Exchange of Persons. English. Committee on International Exchange of Persons, 11 Dupont Circle NW, Washington DC 20036.

US/0092-1904
**UNITED STATES GOVERNMENT MANUAL (1974).** (THE UNITED STATES GOVERNMENT MANUAL.). [U. S. gov. man.]. **Main/Corp** United States. Office of the Federal Register. **Added/Corp** United States. Office of the Federal Register. (1973/1974)-. English. an. $33.75. Claitors Law Books, 3165 South Acadian, Baton Rouge LA 70808. **Tel** (504)344-0476, (800)274-1403. **(Subscription address:** Claitors Law Books, PO Box 3333, Baton Rouge, LA 70821) **LC** JK421; .A3. **DD** 353. **NLM** JK 421 U57. available on microfilm and microfiche from University Microfilms International (UMI). **Continues** United States Government Organization Manual (1964), 0083-1174.

US/0276-7457
**UNITED STATES GOVERNMENT ... TELEPHONE DIRECTORY. REGION 1.** Directory. English. General Services Administration, General Services Building, Eighteenth and F Streets NW, Washington DC 20405. **Tel** (202)655-4000. **LC** JK7.5.N36; U54. **DD** 353.9/32/0974.

US
**UNITED STATES GOVERNMENT TELEPHONE DIRECTORY. UTAH.** Directory. English. General Services Administration / Automated Data and Telecommunications, Region 8, Denver CO 80225.

US
**UNITED STATES NUCLEAR REGULATORY COMMISSION STAFF PRACTICE AND PROCEDURE DIGEST.** Ceased. **Main/Corp** U.S. Nuclear Regulatory Commission. Office of the Executive Legal Director. (Dec. 1977)-(1992). Periodical. English. qt. $40.00. National Technical Information Service - NTIS, Room 2027S, 5285 Port Royal Road, Springfield VA 22161. **Tel** (703)487-4630, (703)487-4660, (703)487-4650, FAX (703)321-8547, telex 89-9405.

US
**UNITED STATES SENATE TELEPHONE DIRECTORY.** Main/Corp United States. Congress. Senate. VFOAT Senate Telephone Directory. (May 1983)-. English. an. $19.50. Superintendent of Documents, US Government Printing Office, Washington DC 20402. **Tel** (202)275-3328, FAX (202)786-2377. **Continues** United States. Congress. Senate. Telephone Directory.

CN/1183-5206
**UNITY DEBATE, THE.** Ceased. [Unity debate]. **Added/Corp** Publinet. Vol. 1, No. 1 (Mar. 12, 1991)-(1992). Periodical. English. wk. Publinet, 130 Slater Street, 11th Floor, Ottawa Ontario K1P 6E2 Canada. **DD** 320.971/05.

II
**UNIVERSITY STUDIES IN PUBLIC ADMINISTRATION.** English. University of Rajasthan Department of Public Administration, Jaipur 4 India. **LC** JF1338.U54; U53. **DD** 350/.0007/11544.

US
**UPDATE / CONGRESSIONAL CAUCUS FOR WOMEN'S ISSUES.** Added/Corp Congressional Caucus for Women's Issues. Vol. 2, No. 10 (July 19, 1982)-. Periodical. English. ir. Free on request. Women's Research Education Institute, 1700 18th Street Northwest, Suite 400, Washington DC 20009. **Tel** (202)328-7070, FAX (202)328-3514. **ED** Azar Kattan. **Bk Rev.** ctrl circ. **Continues** Update (Congresswomen's Caucus).

US/0276-8909
**UPDATE (WASHINGTON, D.C. 1976).** (UPDATE.). 76-1- Oct. 29, 1976-. Government Publication. English. wk. US Department of the Interior / Office of Public Affairs, Room 7224, Washington DC 20240.

CN/0709-9444
**URBA.** [Urba]. **Added/Corp** Union des Municipalites de la Province de Quebec. Vol. 1 (Dec. 1979)-. Periodical. French. Ten times a year (July/Aug. & Dec./Jan. issues combined). 45.00Can$. Union des Municipalites du Quebec, 680 Sherbrooke Street West, Suite 680, Montreal Quebec H3A 2S6 Canada. **Tel** (514)282-7700 49 St-Pierre. **DD** 352.0714. **Ad Acc, Adv Mgr:** Pierre Christiane. **Circ:** 8,000.

US/0300-6859
**URBAN AFFAIRS ABSTRACTS.** See Public Administration-Abstracting, Bibliographies and Statistics.

CN/1187-6212
**URBAN CENTRE, THE.** [Urban cent.]. **Added/Corp** University of Toronto. Centre for Urban and Community Studies. (1989-). Periodical. English. ir. Free on request. Centre for Urban and Community Studies, 455 Spadina Avenue, Room 426, Toronto Ontario M5S 2G8 Canada. **Tel** (416)978-2072. **DD** 307.76. **Continues** The Urban Centre Newsletter., 1187-6204.

US/0195-7686
**URBAN, STATE AND LOCAL LAW NEWSLETTER.** Title Change. See Law.

US
**US CHAMBER WATCH.** English. mo. 49.50 (members), 65.00 (nonmembers). US Chamber of Commerce, 1615 H Street NW, Washington DC 20062. **Tel** (800)638-6582, (800)352-1450, FAX (202)887-3430.

US/1051-7693
**US DEPARTMENT OF STATE DISPATCH.** (US DEPARTMENT OF STATE DISPATCH / BUREAU OF PUBLIC AFFAIRS.). [U. S. Depart. State dispatch]. **Added/Corp** United States. Dept. of State. Bureau of Public Affairs. United States. Dept. of State. Office of Public Communication. VFOAT Dispatch. Vol. 1, No. 1 (Sept. 3, 1990)-. Government Publication. English. wk (semi-annual and annual indexes). $91.00 US; $113.75 other. Superintendent of Documents, US Government Printing Office, Washington DC 20402. **Tel** (202)275-3328, FAX (202)786-2377. **LC** JX232; .U83. **DD** 327.73. available on microfilm and microfiche from University Microfilms International (UMI); available on an online database (file 647/Full-Text) from DIALOG. Documents available from UMI Article Clearinghouse. **Continues** Department of State Bulletin, 0041-7610; **Absorbed** Current Treaty Actions.
**Ind/Abst** Acad. Abstr. Full Text Elite (Sept. 1990-) [Full Txt.]; Acad. Ind. [Computer File] (1990-); Acad. Search (Sept. 1990-); Expand. Acad. Index (1990-); Gen. Period. Index (1990-); INFO-SOUTH Abstr. (19??-); Mag. Artic. Summar. Elite (Sept. 1990-) [Full Txt.]; Mag. Artic. Summar. Select (19??-) [Full Txt.]; Mag. Artic. Summar. CD-ROM (Sept. 1990-); Mag. ASAP Plus (19??-) [Full Txt.]; Mag. ASAP Sel. (19??-) [Full Txt.]; Mag. Express (1989-) [Full Txt.]; Mag. Index Plus (1990-); Mag. Index. Sel. (1990-); Newsp. Period. Abstr. (1990-); Read. Guide Abstr. Select Ed. (19??-); Read. Guide Period. Lit.

(19??-); Resource/One Ondisc (19??-); Mag. Index (Sept. 1990-); TOM Gen. Index (1993-) [Full Txt.]; Vocat. Search (Sept. 1990-) [Full Txt.].

UK/0957-1787
**UTILITIES POLICY.** (UTILITIES POLICY : STRATEGY, PERFORMANCE, REGULATION.). [Util. policy] Vol. 1, No. 1 (Oct. 1990)-. Periodical. English. Five times a year. $261.00 The Americas; £175.00 other. Butterworth Heinemann Publishers, Linacre House, Jordan Hill, Oxford OX2 8DP England. **Tel** 011 44 865 310366. **(Subscription address:** Elsevier Science Ltd. Oxford Fulfilment Centre, PO Box 800, Kidlington, Oxford OX5 1DX United Kingdom.**) LC** HD2766.A3; U8. **DD** 363.6/0973/05. **CODEN** UPOLEQ. available on microfilm and microfiche from University Microfilms International (UMI).
**Ind/Abst** Energy Inf. Abstr.; Int. Dev. Abstr.

●US
**UTILITY REGULATORY POLICY IN THE UNITED STATES AND CANADA : COMPILATION ... OF THE NATIONAL ASSOCIATION OF REGULATORY UTILITY COMMISSIONERS. Added/Corp** National Association of Regulatory Utility Commissioners. **VFOAT** Compilation of Utility Regulatory Policy; NARUC Compilation of Utility Regulatory Policy. (1991/1992)-. English. **LC** HD2766; .N273. **Continues in part** National Association of Regulatory Utility Commissioners. Annual Report on Utility and Carrier Regulation of the National Association of Regulatory Utility Commissioners.

UK/0958-0336
**VACHER'S EUROPEAN COMPANION & CONSULTANTS' REGISTER.** (VACHER'S EUROPEAN COMPANION.). [Vacher's Eur. companion consult. regist.]. **VFOAT** Vacher's European Companion and Consultants' Register; Vacher's European Companion (198?). (198?)-. English. qt. £38.00 UK; £47.00 other Europe; £54.00 other. Vachers Publications, 113 High Street Berkhamsted, Herts HP4 2DJ England. **Tel** 011 44 0442 876135, FAX 0442 870148. **Ad Acc.** ctrl circ. available on microfilm from University Microfilms International (UMI). **Continues** Vacher's European Companion (1972).
**Desc:** A diplomatic, political and commercial reference book for Europe.
**Ind/Abst** Museum Abstr.; World Ceram. Abstr.

UK/0958-0328
**VACHER'S PARLIAMENTARY COMPANION. VFOAT** Parliamentary Companion. (1832)-. English. qt. £26.00 UK; £35.00 Europe; £42.00 other. Vachers Publications, 113 High Street Berkhamsted, Herts HP4 2DJ England. **Tel** 011 44 0442 876135, FAX 0442 870148. **LC** JN500; .V2. available on microfilm from University Microfilms International (UMI).
**Desc:** Containing lists of the House of Lords and House of Commons.
**Ind/Abst** Museum Abstr. (19??-).

FI/0430-5094
**VALTION VIRALLISJULKAISUT. Main/Corp** Finland. Eduskunta. Kirjasto. **Added/Corp** Eduskunnan Kirjasto (Finland). **VFOAT** Statens Officiella Publikationer; Government Publications in Finland. (1961)-. Finnish. an. $6.41. Academic Bookstore Akateeminen, Postilokero 23, FIN-00371 Helsinki Finland. **Tel** 011 358 0 12141. **NLM** Z 2520; V215.

FI
**VALTION VIRKAMIESTEN PALKAT MARRASKUUSSA. Main/Corp** Finland. Tilastokeskus. Finnish. 3.00. Tilastokeskus, PL 504, Annankatu 44, 00101 Helsinki Finland. **Tel** 358-0-17341, FAX 358-0-17342474, telex 1002111 TILASTO SF. **LC** JN6712.Z2; F54A.

US/0147-6971
**VALUE OF PUBLIC UTILITY REAL AND PERSONAL PROPERTY BY COUNTY.** [Value public util. real pers. prop. cty.]. **Main/Corp** Ohio. Dept. of Taxation. English. an. Department of Taxation / Ohio, Research and Statistics Section, PO Box 530, Columbus OH 43216. **LC** HD2765; .O34A. **DD** 333.3/36.

US/0149-0303
**VEHICLE REGISTRATION AND MOTOR FUEL TAXES, AMOUNTS DISTRIBUTED TO LOCAL GOVERNMENTS, BY COUNTY. Main/Corp** Ohio. Dept. of Taxation. English. PO Box 530, Columbus OH 43216. **LC** HJ5359; .O36B.

IT
**VENETO SICUREZZA SOCIALE. Suspended.** (19??)-(Dec. 1990). Italian. Regione Veneto Abb Inserzioni, Lista Spagna 168, 30122 Venice Italy. **Tel** 011 39 41 792630.

CN
**VERBATIM REPORT. Main/Corp** Newfoundland. House of Assembly. English. Three times a year. University of Maine / English Building, 303 English / Math Building, Orono ME 04473. **Tel** (207)581-7307. **LC** J125; .H25. **DD** 328.718/04.
**Ind/Abst** MLA Int. Bibl. Books Artic. Mod. Lang. Lit.

US/1056-6996
**VERMONT GOVERNMENT DIRECTORY.** [Vt. gov. dir.]. (1991)-. English. an. $21.95. Putney Press, PO Box 935, Brattleboro VT 05302. **Tel** (802)257-7505, FAX (802)254-7630. **DD** 351.

US/0363-3225
**VERMONT LEGISLATIVE DIRECTORY AND STATE MANUAL.** (VERMONT LEGISLATIVE DIRECTORY AND STATE MANUAL / PREPARED PURSUANT TO LAW BY ... SECRETARY OF STATE.). **Main/Corp** Vermont. Office of Secretary of State. **VFOAT** Vermont Legislative Directory. (1951)-. English. be. Vermont Department of Libraries, State Office Building, 109 State Street, Montpelier VT 05602. **Tel** (802)828-3265. **ED** Virginia Ashley. **LC** JK3031. **DD** 328.743/0025. cum. index. **Circ:** 2,000. **Continues** Vermont Legislative Directory.

US/0083-5781
**VERMONT YEAR BOOK. See** Business.

SA
**VERSLAE VAN DIE GEKOSE KOMITEE VOOR STAATSGROND. Main/Corp** South Africa. Parliament. House of Assembly. Select Committee on State-Owned Land. **VFOAT** Reports of the Select Committee on State-Owned Land. Afrikaans (English). House of Assembly, Government Printer, Bosman Street, Private Bag X85, Pretoria 0001 South Africa. **LC** HD991; .A3A.

SA
**VERSLAG DEUR DIE VOORSITTER OOR DIE RAAD SE BEDRYWIGHEDE. Main/Corp** Cape Division, Cape of Good Hope. Divisional Council. **Added/Corp** Cape Division, Cape of Good Hope. Divisional Council. **VFOAT** Report by the Chairman on the Council's Activities. (1976)-. Multiple languages (Afrikaans and English). **LC** JS7565.C26; C36.

SA
**VERSLAG VAN DIE OUDITEUR-GENERAAL OOR DIE REKENINGS VAN DIE SYBOKHAARRAAD. REPORT OF THE AUDITOR-GENERAL ON THE ACCOUNTS OF THE MOHAIR BOARD. Main/Corp** South Africa. Controller and Auditor-General. **Added/Corp** South Africa. Dept. of the Auditor-General. Report of the Auditor-General on the Accounts of the Mohair Board. **VFOAT** Report of the Auditor-General on the Accounts of the Mohair Board. (1976)-. Afrikaans (English). an. Government Printer / South Africa, Bosman Street, Private Bag X85, Pretoria 0001 South Africa. **Tel** 011 27 12 3239731 Ext. 262. **LC** HD9907.S6; S53a. **DD** 354.680072/32. **Continues** Report of the Controller and Auditor-General on the Accounts of the Mohair Board.

SA
**VERSLAG VIR DIE TYDPERK. DEPARTEMENT VAN JUSTISIE VAN DIE REPUBLIEK VAN SUID-AFRIKA. Main/Corp** South Africa. Dept. of Justice. **VFOAT** Report for the Period ... . Afrikaans (English). an. R9.10. Government Printer / South Africa, Bosman Street, Private Bag X85, Pretoria 0001 South Africa. **Tel** 011 27 12 3239731 Ext. 262. **LC** J705; .R63. **DD** 354.68065/05. **Continues** Annual Report / South Africa. Dept. of Justice.

GW/0042-4498
**VERWALTUNG (BERLIN), DIE.** (DIE VERWALTUNG.). [Verwaltung]. Vol. 1 (1968)-. Periodical. German. qt. DM158.30 Germany; DM162.40 other. Duncker und Humblot Verlag, Postfach 410329, D-12113 Berlin Germany. **Tel** 011 49 30 79000612, 011 49 30 79000613. **LC** JA44; .V46. **DD** 350'.0005. **[CCC].**
**Ind/Abst** ABC POL SCI; Int. Polit. Sci. Abstr.

GW
**VERWALTUNG UND FORTBILDUNG.** 1973-. Periodical. German. qt. DM49.60. Carl Heymanns Verlag KG, Luxemburger Strasse 449, D 50939 Cologne Germany. **Tel** 011 49 221 460100, telex 8 881 888. **LC** JF1338.A2; V47. **DD** 350/.0007. **Bk Rev**. **Ad Acc**. **Circ:** 1,500 (ctrl).
**Desc:** Treatises on problems within the administrative complexity and the professional advanced training within it.

AT
**VICTORIA GOVERNMENT GAZETTE. Added/Corp** Victoria. (1???)-. English. wk. 107.00Aus$. Victorian Government Printing Office, PO Box 203, North Melbourne Victoria 3051 Australia. **Tel** 011 61 3 320 0217. **LC** J8; .B88. **Circ:** 1,700 (ctrl).
**Desc:** Serves as the official government reference source to legislation that has come into effect. It has other sections such as contracts accepted by government, etc.

AT/0158-1589
**VICTORIAN GOVERNMENT DIRECTORY. Added/Corp** Victoria. Dept. of the Premier. (19??)-. Directory. English. an. Law Printer, PO Box 292, South Melbourne VIC 3205 Australia. **Tel** 011 61 3 2424600. **LC** JQ5321; .V52. **DD** 354.945002.

AT
**VICTORIAN GOVERNMENT PUBLICATIONS RECEIVED BY THE STATE LIBRARY OF VICTORIA. Added/Corp** Library Council of Victoria. (1976)-. English. mo. 50.00Aus$. Library Council of Victoria, Public Libraries Division, 328 Swanston Street, Melbourne Victoria 3000 Australia. **Tel** 03-6699840, FAX 03-6631480, telex AA38104. **LC** Z4379; .V68; J931. **DD** 015.945. Index available. cum. index. **Circ:** 165.
**Desc:** A bibliography of Victorian State Government Publications.

II
**VIDESA MANTRALAYA KI ANUDANOM KI MANGEM. Main/Corp** India. Ministry of External Affairs. **VFOAT** Demands for Grants of Ministry of External Affairs. Multiple languages (English and Hindi). an. Ministry of External Affairs / India, Minto Road, New Delhi India. **LC** JQ250.I48; I56A. **Continues** India (Republic). Ministry of External Affairs. Demands for Grants.

FR/0042-5400
**VIE COMMUNALE ET DEPARTEMENTALE, LA.** Vol. 1, No. 1 (Dec. 1923)-. French. mo (11 issues). 308.52F France; 322.00F other. Vie Communale et Departementale, 35 rue Marbeuf, 75008 Paris France. **Tel** 011 33 1 43592741.

CN/0712-3248
**VIE MUNICIPALE A JONQUIERE, LA.** [Vie munic. Jonquiere]. **Main/Corp** Jonquiere (Quebec). Mar. 1978-. French. an. Free. Service d'Information de Ville de Jonquiere, CP 2000, Jonquiere Quebec G7X 7W7 Canada. **DD** 352.0714/16.

US/0277-4844
**VIEW FROM SPRINGFIELD.** (19??)-. Periodical. English. wk ((Thursday)). $60.00. State Capitol Information Service / Illinois, 516 East Monroe Street, Suite 501, Springfield IL 62701. **Tel** (217)782-6295. **ED** Joseph L. Harris.
**Desc:** Features news about hearings, investigations, appointments, Governor's actions, Supreme Court and Attorney General opinions and political developments in Illinois.

VI
**VIRGIN ISLANDS GOVERNMENT DOCUMENTS: A QUARTERLY CHECKLIST. Main/Corp** Virgin Islands of the United States. Bureau of Libraries, Museums and Archaeological Services. Began with: Vol. 1, Winter 1977. English. qt. Department of Conservation & Cultural Affairs, Bureau of Libraries, St Thomas Virgin Islands. **LC** Z1561.V8; V59A; J166. **DD** 015/.729/722.

US
**VIRGINIA MUNICIPAL LEAGUE DIRECTORY.** 1981-. Directory. English. an. $20.00. Virginia Municipal League, PO Box 12164, Richmond VA 23241. **Tel** (804)649-8471. **Continues** Directory of Virginia Governmental Officials.

US
**VIRGINIA REGISTER OF REGULATIONS, THE. See** Law.

US/0732-9156
**VIRGINIA REVIEW.** (VIRGINIA REVIEW / VIRGINIA ASSOCIATION OF COUNTIES.). **Added/Corp** Virginia Association of Counties. Vol. 59, No. 9 (Sept./Oct. 1981)-. Periodical. English. bm. $14.00. County Publications, PO Box 860, Chester VA 23831. **Tel** (804)748-6351, (800)827-3834, FAX (804)796-6931. **ED** Alyson L. Taylor-White. **LC** JS39; .V5. **DD** 352.0755. **Bk Rev**, (Qty: 8-10). **Ad Acc**, **Adv Mgr:** Roger Habeck. **Circ:** 5,000 (ctrl). **Continues** Virginia Municipal Review, 0042-6660.

US/0042-6784
**VIRGINIA TOWN & CITY. Added/Corp** Virginia Municipal League. **VAT** Virginia Town and City. Vol. 1 (Jan. 1966)-. Periodical. English. mo. $8.00. Virginia Municipal League, PO Box 12164, Richmond VA 23241. **Tel** (804)649-8471. **ED** Christine A Everson. **LC** JS39; .V55. Index available. **Bk Rev**. **Ad Acc**. **Circ:** 4,500 (ctrl). **Continues** Virginia Municipal Review, 0042-6660.
**Desc:** Articles addressing local government issues, management, and activities of the Virginia Municipal League.
**Ind/Abst** Urban Aff. Abstr.

US/0896-9469
**VITAL STATISTICS ON CONGRESS.** [Vital stat. Congr.]. **Added/Corp** American Enterprise Institute for Public Policy Research. (1980)-. English. be (every two years). $39.95. Congressional Quarterly Inc., 1414

## Public Administration

22nd Street Northwest, Washington DC 20037. **Tel** (202)887-8500, (800)432-2250 ext. 621, FAX (202)728-1863. **LC** JK1041; .V58. **DD** 328.73/0021.

US/0883-573X
**VOICE (EAST LANSING, MICH.).** See Education.

●CN/1191-4742
**VOIE NAVIGABLE TRENT-SEVERN, PLANIFICATION DE GESTION.** [Voie navig. Trent-Severn planif. gest.]. **Added/Corp** Service Canadien des Parcs. Spirng (1992)-. Periodical. French. qt. **DD** 333.78.

CN/0704-7770
**VOIX DE L'A.M.S.A, LA.** [Voix A.M.S.A.]. **VAT** Voix de l'Alliance Municipale de Sainte-Adele. V. 1, No. 1 (Jan. 1978)-. Periodical. French. bm. Free. Alliance Municipale de Ste-Adele, CP 1166, Ste-Adele Quebec J0R 1L0 Canada. **DD** 352.0714/24.

XV
**VOLITVE.** **Main/Corp** Zavod sr Slovenije za Statistiko. 1974-. Slovenian. Zavod Sr Slovenije za Statistiko, Vozarski Pot 12, Ljubljana Slovenia. **LC** JN9679.S6; A32A. **Continues** Volitve v Predstavniska Telesa.

BW
**VOPROSY ISTORII KPSS. NEKOTORYE VOPROSY ORGANIZATORSKOI I IDEOLOGICHESKOI DEIATELNOSTI KPSS, NA MATERIALAKH BELORUSSKOI SSR.** Russian. Ul Kirova 24, Minsk Byelarus. **LC** JN6598.K86; V66.

CN/0713-6714
**VOS AFFAIRES MUNICIPALES.** [Vos aff. munic.]. Periodical. French. Three times a year. Free. Vos Affaires Municipales, Hotel de Ville, CP 489, Thetford-Mines Quebec G6G 5T3 Canada. **Tel** (418)335-2981, FAX (418)335-7980. **ED** Nilte de Shilford. **DD** 352.0714/575. Index available. ctrl circ.

AT
**VOTES AND PROCEEDINGS OF THE HOUSE OF REPRESENTATIVES.** **Main/Corp** Australia. Parliament. House of Representatives. 26th Parliament (1968)-. Government Publication. English. ir. 195.00Aus$. Australian Government Publishing Service, GPO Box 84, Canberra ACT 2601 Australia. **Tel** 011 61 6 2954411, FAX 011 61 6 2954455. **Continues in part** Australia. Parliament. Records of the Proceedings and Printed Papers.

CN/0319-3020
**VOTES AND PROCEEDINGS OF THE LEGISLATIVE ASSEMBLY OF MANITOBA.** [Votes proc. Legis. Assem. Manit.]. **Main/Corp** Manitoba. Legislative Assembly. **VAT** Votes and Proceedings - Legislative Assembly of Manitoba. Proceedings. English. ir. 16.00Can$. Queens Printer Statutory Publishing, 200 Vaughn Street, Winnipeg Manitoba R3C 1T5 Canada. **Tel** (204)945-3102. ctrl circ.
 **Desc:** Minutes and record of vote of the legislative assembly.

CN/0384-224X
**VOTES AND PROCEEDINGS (OTTAWA).** (VOTES AND PROCEEDINGS - HOUSE OF COMMONS.). **Main/Corp** Canada. Parliament. House of Commons. **VFOAT** Proces-Verbaux - Chambre des Communes. (19???)-. Periodical. English (French). da. Canada Communication Group Publishers, Order Processing, Ottawa Ontario K1A 0S9 Canada. **Tel** (819)956-4800, (819)956-4802. **Absorbed** Canada. Parlement. Chambre des Communes. Proces-Verbaux de la Chambre des Communes du Canada., 0384-2223.

US/0090-4465
**VRA BULLETIN BOARD.** **Main/Corp** United States. Dept. of Health, Education, and Welfare. Vocational Rehabilitation Administration. (19??)-. Bulletin. English. mo. Vocational Rehabilitation Administration, 330 Independence Avenue, Washington DC 20201. **LC** HD7256U5; A314. **DD** 362.8/5. **Continues** OVR Bulletin Board.

US/0163-8300
**W-MEMO.** (W-MEMO / AMERICAN PUBLIC WELFARE ASSOCIATION.). **Added/Corp** American Public Welfare Association. **VFOAT** W Memo. Memorandum W-17 (Dec. 31, 1988); Vol. 1, No. 1 (Feb. 22, 1989)-. Periodical. English. Ten times a year. $75.00 (non-members), $65.00 (members) US; $75.00 (members), $85.00 (non-members) others. American Public Welfare Association, 810 First Street Northeast, Suite 500, Washington DC 20002. **Tel** (202)682-0100, FAX (202)289-6555. **ED** Bard Shollenberger. Index available. **Circ:** 800.
 **Desc:** Up-to-minute detailed information and analysis of agency action affecting human service programs.

GW
**WAS UND WIE.** No. 1 (1973)-. German. 0.30M single issue. AM Marx-Engels-Platz 102, Berlin Germany. **LC** JN3971.5.A98; S565.

US/0195-5233
**WASHINGTON ACTION REPORTER.** **Added/Corp** Veterans of Foreign Wars of the United States. Vol. 1, No. 1 (Oct. 1986)-. Periodical. English. mo. Free on request. Veterans of Foreign Wars, 200 Maryland Avenue Northeast, Washington DC 20002. **Tel** (202)543-2239.

US/0192-5342
**WASHINGTON D. C. METROPOLITAN AREA FOUNDATION DIRECTORY, THE.** Directory. English. Community Foundation of Greater Washington Inc, 1002 Wisconsin Avenue Northwest, Washington DC 20007. **Tel** (202)338-8993. **LC** AS911.A2; W37. **DD** 001.4/4/025753.

US/0887-8064
**WASHINGTON INFORMATION DIRECTORY.** [Wash. inf. dir.]. **Added/Corp** Congressional Quarterly, Inc. **VFOAT** Congressional Quarterly's Washington Information Directory. (1976)-. Directory. English. an (July). $94.95. Congressional Quarterly Inc., 1414 22nd Street Northwest, Washington DC 20037. **Tel** (202)887-8500, (800)432-2250 ext. 621, FAX (202)728-1863. **LC** F192.3; .W33. **DD** 975.3/0025. **NLM** F 192.3 W318B.
 **Desc:** Lists thousands of names, addresses and phone numbers throughout the government and private sector sources of information.

US
**WASHINGTON MUNICIPAL SALARIES AND FRINGE BENEFITS.** See Economics-Labor.

US
**WASHINGTON POLICY CHOICES / INSTITUTE FOR PUBLIC POLICY AND MANAGEMENT, UNIVERSITY OF WASHINGTON.** **Added/Corp** University of Washington. Institute for Public Policy and Management. Vol. 1, Issue 1 (Spring 1991)-. Periodical. English. qt. **LC** HN79.W2; W37.

US/0737-3503
**WASHINGTON REPORT (INTERSTATE CONFERENCE ON WATER PROBLEMS).** **Suspended.** (WASHINGTON REPORT / INTERSTATE CONFERENCE ON WATER PROBLEMS, ICWP.). [Washington rep. - Interstate Conf. Water Probl.]. Periodical. English. ICWP, 955 L'Enfant Plaza SW/6th Floor, Washington DC 20024.

US/0149-2578
**WASHINGTON SOCIAL LEGISLATION BULLETIN.** **Added/Corp** Social Legislation Information Service. **VFOAT** Social Legislation Bulletin. Vol. 24, Issue 33 (May 1976)-. Periodical. English. sm (24 issues). $65.00. Child Welfare League of America, 440 1st Street Northwest, Suite 310, Washington DC 20001. **Tel** (202)638-2952, FAX (202)638-4004. **NLM** W1 WA639. available on microfilm and microfiche from University Microfilms International (UMI). **Continues** Washington Bulletin.
 **Desc:** Reports on federal social legislation and the activities of federal agencies in health, education, welfare, housing, employment, and other social welfare conditions affecting childrens the elderly, the handicapped, and juvenile delinquents.

US/0092-380X
**WASHINGTON STATE.** [Wash. State]. V. 1- Oct. 1973-. English. Office of Program Planning & Fiscal Management, Information Services Division, House Office Building, Olympia WA 98504. **LC** JK9230; .W36. **DD** 353.9/797.

US
**WASHINGTON STATE BIENNIAL REPORT ON STATE AGENCIES.** **Added/Corp** Washington (State). Office of Financial Management. **VFOAT** Biennial Report on State Agencies. (1989/1991)-. English. be. Office of Financial Management, Insurance Building AQ-44, Olympia WA 98504. **Tel** (206)456-4775. **LC** JK9201; .B53. **Continues** Biennial Report, Agencies of the State of Washington.

US/0164-6389
**WASHINGTON STATE REGISTER.** **Added/Corp** Washington (State). Office of the Code Reviser. **VFOAT** WSR. (1978)-. English. sm (24 issues). $188.82 Washington State; $175.00 other. Washington State Register, Code Revisers Office, Legislative Building, Olympia WA 98504. **Tel** (206)753-6804. **ED** Susan J. Brooks. **LC** KFW34.A2; W37. **DD** 348.797/025; 347.970825. Index available. cum. index. **Circ:** 700. **Continues** Washington Administrative Code Bulletin.
 **Desc:** Full text of proposed, emergency and permanent rules of state agencies, and other state government information.

US/0736-3850
**WASHINGTON STATE YEARBOOK.** [Wash. State yearb.]. **Added/Corp** Washington (State). Office of the Governor. Washington (State). Office of the Secretary of State. **VFOAT** Washington State Year Book. (1983)-. English. an. Information Press, PO Box 1422, Eugene OR 97440. **Tel** (503)689-0188. **LC** JK9230; .W38. **DD** 320.9797/05.

US/0892-9548
**WATER JOURNAL.** See Water Resources.

US/0193-4716
**WAYS & MEANS (WASHINGTON, D.C.).** **Title Change.** (WAYS & MEANS.). [Ways & means]. **Added/Corp** Conference on Alternative State and Local Policies (U.S.) Conference on Alternative State and Local Public Policies (U.S.) National Center for Policy Alternatives. Center for Policy Alternatives (Washington, D.C.). **VFOAT** Ways and Means. (19??)-Vol. 16, No. 1 (Winter 1993). Periodical. English. bm. Ways & Means Conference on Alternative State and Local Public Policies, 1901 Q Street NW, Washington DC 20009. **DD** 352. **Continued by** Alternatives (Washington, D.C.), 1070-3047.

CN/0706-4659
**WEEKLY CHECKLIST OF CANADIAN GOVERNMENT PUBLICATIONS.** **Added/Corp** Canadian Government Publishing Centre. Canada Communication Group. Publishing. **VFOAT** Liste Hebdomadaire des Publications du Gouvernement Canadien; Liste Hebdomadaire des Publications du Gouvernement du Canada. (Nov. 17, 1978)-. Periodical. English (French). wk. 60.00Can$ Canada; 72.00Can$ other. Canada Communication Group Publishers, Order Processing, Ottawa Ontario K1A 0S9 Canada. **Tel** (819)956-4800, (819)956-4802. **Continues** Daily Checklist of Canadian Government Publications, 0700-2904.

US/0197-8403
**WEEKLY CONGRESSIONAL MONITOR, THE.** [Wkly. congr. monit.]. **Added/Corp** Washington Monitor. Vol. 1 (Sept. 19, 1977)-. Periodical. English. Forty times a year. $498.00. Congressional Quarterly Inc., 1414 22nd Street Northwest, Washington DC 20037. **Tel** (202)887-8500, (800)432-2250 ext. 621, FAX (202)728-1863.

UK
**WEEKLY INFORMATION BULLETIN - HOUSE OF COMMONS.** **Main/Corp** Great Britain. Parliament. House of Commons. (19??)-. Bulletin. English. wk. £88.80. Her Majesty's Stationery Office, 51 Nine Elms Lane, London SW8 5DR England. **Tel** 011 44 71 873 8459, 011 44 71 873 8499, FAX 011 44 71 873 8499, 011 44 71 873 8456, telex 297138. **(Subscription address:** Her Majestys Stationery Offic, PO Box 276 Public Centre, London SW8 5DT England) **ED** D. Inns. **LC** J301; .K856a. **DD** 328.41/07/205.
 **Desc:** Provides the most comprehensive and cost-effective way for individuals and organizations to keep up with events in Parliament.

US
**WEEKLY LIST OF MONTANA STATE PUBLICATIONS RECEIVED BY MONTANA STATE LIBRARY.** **Main/Corp** Montana. State Library, Helena. English. wk. Montana State Library, 1515 East 6th Avenue, Helena MT 59620. **Tel** 444-5349, FAX 444-5612. **LC** Z1223.5.M9; M66A; J87.M9. **DD** 015.786. **Pr Rev. Circ:** 50.

CN/0836-4397
**WEST VANCOUVER REPORT.** See Housing and Urban Development.

US
**WEST VIRGINIA BLUE BOOK.** **Added/Corp** West Virginia. Legislature. Senate. Vol. 1 (1916)-. English. an. Free on request. West Virginia Blue Book, Clerk of Senate, State Capitol, Charleston WV 25305. **Tel** (304)357-7800. **ED** Todd C. Willis. **Circ:** 20,000 (ctrl).
 **Desc:** General information and statistics on federal state and local government in West Virginia.

US/0363-356X
**WESTCHESTER PLANNING.** V. 1- Summer 1973-. Periodical. English. qt. Westchester County Department of Planning, 910 County Office Building, White Plains NY 10601.

US/0279-5337
**WESTERN CITY (SACRAMENTO, CALIF. : 1976).** (WESTERN CITY.). [West. city]. **Added/Corp** League of California Cities. Vol. 52, No. 9 (Sept. 1976)-. Periodical. English. mo. $34.00 one year; $55.00 two year. League of California Cities, 1400 K Street, Sacramento CA 95814. **Tel** (916)444-5790, FAX (916)444-5129. **ED** Victoria Clark. **LC** TD1; .W44. **DD** 363/.0978. Index available (Bound in 12th issue). Bk Rev. **Ad Acc, Adv Mgr:** J. Flagg. **Circ:** 10,000 (ctrl). **Continues** Western City Magazine, 0043-356X.
 **Desc:** A magazine to keep California city leaders up to date on theoretical and practical developments in city

# Public Administration

administration. **Ind/Abst** Am. Hist. Life; Calif. Period. Index (19??-); Calif. Period. Microfi. (19??-); Urban Aff. Abstr.

US/0279-0602
**WESTERN PLANNER, THE. Added/Corp** Wyoming Planning Association. Montana Association of Planners. North Dakota Planning Association. Vol. 1, No. 1 (Jan./Feb. 1980)-. Periodical. English. Eight times a year. $24.00. Western Planning Resources, Inc., 200 Pronghorn, Casper WY 82601. **Tel** (307)266-2524. **ED** Steve Klutz (editor's address: 632 South David, Casper, WY 82601, phone: (307)266-2524 or FAX: (307)235-5604). **Bk Rev. Ad Acc. Circ:** 1,400 (ctrl).
**Desc:** A journal of information and ideas for community planners, their boards and constituents, and the elected officials they serve.

CN/1184-017X
**WESTMOUNT BULLETIN (1990).** (WESTMOUNT bull.). [Westmount bull.].
**Added/Corp** Westmount (Quebec). **VFOAT** Westmount-Bulletin. Vol. 1, No. 1 (May/June 1990)-. Bulletin. English (French). Limited free distribution. Westmount City Hall, 4333 Sherbrooke Street West, Montreal Quebec H3Z 1E2 Canada. **DD** 352.0714/28/05.

CN/1184-017X
**WESTMOUNT BULLETIN (1990).** (WESTMOUNT-BULLETIN.). [Westmount bull.].
**Added/Corp** Westmount (Quebec). **VFOAT** Westmount Bulletin; Bulletin de Westmount. Vol. 1, No 1 (May/June 1990)-. Bulletin. French (English). Limited free distribution. Hotel de Ville Westmount, 4333 Ouest Rue Sherbrooke, Westmount, Quebec H3Z 1E2 Canada. **DD** 352.0714/28/05.

CN/0703-5926
**WHITE LIST OF CUSTOMS OFFICERS IN CANADA, THE. Added/Corp** Canadian Importers Association. (1976)-. English. an. Canadian Importers Association, 210 Dundas Street West, Suite 700, Toronto Ontario M5Q 2E8 Canada. **Tel** (416)595-5333, FAX (416)595-8226. **DD** 354/.71/007246002571.

●UK
**WHITEHALL COMPANION, THE.** (1992)-. English. an. £139.50. Dods Publishing & Research Ltd, 31-A Saint James's Square, London WC1Y 4JR England. **Tel** 011 44 71 9306640, FAX 011 44 71 9309166.

US/0894-8801
**WHO KNOWS, A GUIDE TO WASHINGTON EXPERTS. Title Change.** (WHO KNOWS, A GUIDE TO WASHINGTON EXPERTS / BY WASHINGTON RESEARCHERS PUBLISHING.). [Who knows guide Wash.]. 8th Edition (1986)-(1993). Monographic series. English. ir (Publishes every eighteen months). Washington Researchers, PO Box 19005, 20th Street Station, Washington DC 20036. **Tel** (202)333-3533, (202)333-3499, FAX (202)625-0656. **LC** JK6; .W37a. **DD** 353.04/025. **NLM** JK 6; R432. Index available. **Continues** Researcher's Guide to Washington Experts, 0740-087X. **Continued by** Who Knows What, a Guide to Experts.
**Desc:** Gives the names and direct telephone numbers for experts on 12,000 topics of interest to the business researcher.

●US
**WHO KNOWS WHAT, A GUIDE TO EXPERTS / BY WASHINGTON RESEARCHERS, LTD. Added/Corp** Washington Researchers. (1994)-. Monographic series. English. ir. $20.00. Washington Researchers, PO Box 19005, 20th Street Station, Washington DC 20036. **Tel** (202)333-3533, (202)333-3499, FAX (202)625-0656. **LC** JK6; .W37a. **DD** 353.04/025. **Continues** Who Knows, a Guide to Washington Experts, 0894-8801.

US
**WHO'S WHAT IN FLORIDA GOVERNMENT. Added/Corp** Florida Chamber of Commerce. (19??)-. English. an (Feb.). $7.49 Florida residents (includes 7% tax); $7.00 others. Florida Chamber of Commerce, PO Box 11309, Tallahassee FL 32302. **Tel** 800/940-3034, FAX (904)425-1260. **ED** Gary Cliett (phone: (904)425-1242). **Circ:** 8,000.
**Desc:** Lists Florida's legislators with their pictures, along with Florida's congressmen, governor, Supreme Court justices, members of the Cabinet and the departments they manage.

US/0000-0205
**WHO'S WHO IN AMERICAN POLITICS. See** Biographies.

AT
**WHO'S WHO IN FEDERAL GOVERNMENT DIRECTORY. Directory.** English. Eleven times a year (not published in January). 155.00Aus$. Commerce Management, PO Box E162, Queen Victoria Terrace, ACT 2600 Australia. **Tel** 011 61 6 2951961, FAX 011 61 6 2590170.

US/0882-0260
**WHO'S WHO IN FEDERAL GOVERNMENT PRIME CONTRACTORS. See** Biographies.

US
**WISCONSIN ADMINISTRATIVE CODE; ADMINISTRATIVE RULES OF STATE AGENCIES PUBLISHED PURSANT TO CHAP. 227 WISCONSIN STATUTES.**
**Main/Corp** Wisconsin. English. ir. Price ranges from $5.00 to $630.00 depending upon material and service ordered. Wisconsin Department of Administration, 101 South Webster Street, PO Box 7864, Madison WI 53702. **Tel** (608)266-1651.
**Desc:** Consists of seventeen loose-leaf binders containing all 'administrative rules' of state agencies.

US
**WISCONSIN BLUE BOOK, THE.**
**Added/Corp** Wisconsin. Dept. of State. Legislative Manual of the State of Wisconsin. Wisconsin. Bureau of Labor and Industrial Statistics. Blue Book of the State of Wisconsin. Wisconsin. Industrial Commission. Wisconsin. State Printing Board. Wisconsin. Legislative Reference Library. Wisconsin. Legislative Reference Bureau. Wisconsin. Blue Book of the State of Wisconsin. **VFOAT** State of Wisconsin Blue Book. (1862)-. English. be. $6.55. Wisconsin Department of Administration, 101 South Webster Street, PO Box 7864, Madison WI 53702. **Tel** (608)266-1651. **LC** JK6031.

US/0749-6818
**WISCONSIN COUNTIES. Added/Corp** Wisconsin Counties Association. Wisconsin County Boards Association. Vol. 1 (July 1938)-. Periodical. English. mo. $21.50. Wisconsin Counties Association, 802 West Broadway, Suite 308, Madison WI 53713. **Tel** (608)266-6480. **ED** Mark M. Rogacki. Index available. **Ad Acc. Circ:** 3,500 (ctrl).
**Desc:** Directed to elected county officials. Topics covered include: insurance, roads, job training, economic development, law enforcement, social services, legislative action and laws affecting counties.

US/1043-0490
**WISCONSIN LAWYER.** (WISCONSIN LAWYER : OFFICIAL PUBLICATION OF THE STATEBAR OF WISCONSIN.). [Wis. lawyer]. Vol. 62, No. 1 (Jan. 1989)-. Periodical. English. mo. $42.00 US; $63.00 other. State Bar of Wisconsin, 402 West Wilson Street, Madison WI 53703. **Tel** (608)257-3838. **ED** Joyce R Hastings. **LC** KF200; .W57. **DD** 349.73/09775/05. Index available. **Bk Rev. Ad Acc. Pr Rev. Circ:** 15,000 (ctrl). available on microfilm and microfiche from University Microfilms International (UMI); available on audiocassette. **Continues** Wisconsin Bar Bulletin, 0043-6380.
**Desc:** Recent law changes and legal articles of interest to Wisconsin Bar Association members.
**Ind/Abst** Fed. Tax Artic.; Highw. Res. Abstr.; Index Leg. Period.; Leg. Resour. Index; LegalTrac (1989-).

US/0277-3325
**WORK YEARS AND PERSONNEL COSTS, EXECUTIVE BRANCH, UNITED STATES GOVERNMENT. See** Economics-Labor.

CN/0701-3086
**WORKING PAPER - FACULTY OF ADMINISTRATION, UNIVERSITY OF OTTAWA. See** Business.

US/0894-1521
**WORLDWIDE GOVERNMENT DIRECTORY, WITH INTERNATIONAL ORGANIZATIONS.** [Worldw. gov. dir. int. organ.].
**Added/Corp** National Standards Association (U.S.). **VFOAT** Worldwide Government Directory. (1987/1988)-. Directory. English. an. $347.00. Belmont Publications, 7979 Old Georgetown Road, Bethesda MS 20814. **Tel** (301)718-8770. **(Subscription address:** US & Canada: Gale Research Co., 835 Penobscot Building, Detroit, MI 48226) **LC** JF37; .L345. **DD** 351/.2/025. **NLM** JF 37; L222. **Continues** Lambert's Worldwide Government Directory, with Inter-Governmental Organizations, 0276-900X.
**Desc:** Provides the names and addresses of foreign officials and government agencies operating in more than 190 countries around the world.

●US/1065-1098
**WORLDWIDE GOVERNMENT REPORT.** [Worldw. gov. rep.]. Vol. 1, No. 1 (July 1992)-. Periodical. English. mo. $295.00 US. Belmont Publications, 7979 Old Georgetown Road, Bethesda MS 20814. **Tel** (301)718-8770. **DD** 909.

US/0146-700X
**WYOMING OFFICIAL DIRECTORY.**
**Main/Corp** Wyoming. Secretary of State's Office. **VFOAT** Wyoming Official Directory and ... Election Returns. (1976)-. Directory. English. an. $10.00. Secretary of State of Wyoming, State Capital Building, Cheyenne WY 82002. **Tel** (307)777-7378, FAX (307)777-5339. **ED** Dawn Hill. **LC** JK7630; .A33. **DD** 353.9/787/002. Index available. **Circ:** 7,500 (ctrl). **Continues** Wyoming. Secretary of State. Wyoming Official Directory and Election Returns, 0363-8421.
**Desc:** Listing of all Wyoming state and county officials, including all state boards and commissions and their members.

UK
**YEAR BOOK - ASSOCIATION OF COUNTY COUNCILS. Main/Corp** Association of County Councils. (197?)-. English. an. Association of County Councils, Eaton House, 66A Eaton Square, London SW1W 9BH England. **Tel** 011 44 71 235 1200. **Circ:** 3,000. **Continues** Year Book - County Councils Association.
**Desc:** Details the association's aims and constitution; information on member counties, association committees and other national and local organizations.

US
**YEAR BOOK / CALIFORNIA COMMUNITY FOUNDATION. Main/Corp** California Community Foundation. **VFOAT** Yearbook. (1981)-. Periodical. English. an. California Community Foundation, 1151 West 6th Street, Los Angeles CA 90017. **Continues** Report - California Community Foundation.

US/0547-521X
**YEARBOOK OF THE NATIONAL CONFERENCE OF STATE LEGISLATIVE LEADERS. Main/Corp** National Conference of State Legislative Leaders. **VFOAT** State Legislature: Winds of Change. Began with issue for 1966. English. an. National Conference of State Legislative Leaders, 5215 North Ironwood Road, Milwaukee WI 53217. **LC** JS301; .N32. **DD** 328.73.

CH
**YEN KAO YUEH KAN.** Periodical. Chinese. mo. $300.00. Yu Ying She, 63 Chung-Ching South Road, Sec 1, Taipei Shih Taiwan. **LC** JQ1521.A1; Y46. **DD** 354.51/249/0005.

II/0044-0515
**YOJANA. Added/Corp** India. Planning Commission. India. Ministry of Information and Broadcasting. Vol. 1 (1957)-. Periodical. English. Twenty-six times a year. $20.00. Ministry of Information and Broadcasting, Government of India, Patiala House, New Delhi 110 001 India. **Tel** 387983. **(Subscription address:** Prints India, 11 Darya Ganj, New Delhi 110002 India.) **LC** DS401; .A366.
**Ind/Abst** AgBiotech News Inf.; Curr. Lit. Sci. Sci.; Indian Geosci. Abstr.; Int. Dev. Abstr. (?-?); Rural Dev. Abstr.; World Agric. Econ.

●RU
**ZAKONNOST. See** Law-Law Enforcement and Criminology.

NE
**ZEGGENSCHAP.** Welboombladen BV, OZ Voorburgwal 103, 1012 EM Amsterdam Netherlands. **Tel** 011 31 20 6267811.

GW/0044-2348
**ZEITSCHRIFT FUER AUSLAENDISCHES OEFFENTLICHES RECHT UND VOELKERRECHT. See** Law-International Law.

GW/0179-4051
**ZEITSCHRIFT FUER GESETZGEBUNG : ZG. Ceased. See** Law.

GW/0340-1758
**ZEITSCHRIFT FUER PARLAMENTSFRAGEN.** [Z. Parlamentsfragen].
**Added/Corp** Deutsche Vereinigung fuer Parlamentsfragen. Vol. 1 (June 1970)-. Periodical. German. qt. DM47.60 Germany; DM62.60 other. Westdeutscher Verlag GmbH, Postfach 5829, D 65048 Wiesbaden Germany. **Tel** 011 49 611 160220. **(Subscription address:** VVA Bertelsmann Dist GmbH, Postfach 7600, D 33310 Guetersloh Germany) **LC** JN3971.A7; Z4. **[CCC]. Ad Acc. Circ:** 2,400.
**Ind/Abst** Energy Res. Abstr. (March 1979-)(Mar. 1979-); Int. Bibliogr. Sociol.; Int. Polit. Sci. Abstr.

GW
**ZEITUNG FUER KOMMUNALE WIRTSCHAFT.** (19??)-. Periodical. German. mo. DM58.34 Germany; DM69.85 other (print). Sigillum Verlag GmbH, Brohler Strasse 13, 50968 Cologne Germany. **Tel** 011 49 221 37700, FAX 011 49 221 3770 266. **LC** Microfilm 03030 HD; HD4421. **Bk Rev,** (Qty: 20). **Ad Acc, Adv Mgr Tel** 49 89 4376045. **Circ:** 21,000 (ctrl).

BU
**ZEMIA I KHORA : SPISANIE NA BULGARSKIIA ZEMEDELSKI NARODEN SUIUZ. Added/Corp** Bulgarski Zemedelski Naroden Suiuz. (1991)-. Periodical.

Bulgarian. Suiuz Na Iuristite v Bulgaria, Ul Zhdanov No, 1000 Sofia Bulgaria. **LC** JN9609.A8; Z69. ***Continues*** *Zemia i Progres.*

RH
**ZIMBABWE GOVERNMENT GAZETTE.** (19??)-. English. K420.00. Zimbabwe Government Printing, PO Box 8062, Causeway Harare Zimbabwe. **Tel** 011 263 4 706161.

GW
**ZIVILDIENST, DER. Added/Corp** Germany (Federal Republic, 1949- ). Bundesamt fuer den Zivildienst. (19??)-. Periodical. German. ir (ten issues per year). DM8.00. Bundesamt fur den Zivildenst, Sibille-Hartmann-Strasse 2-6, 5000 Koln 1 Germany. **Tel** 02 21 3 67 31. **ED** Heinz-Joerge Beckmann. **LC** HD4875.G4; Z58. **Bk Rev**.
**Desc:** Published for those engaged in the West German civil service, but of general interest to the serious reader. Contains articles on ecology, industry, international relations, arts and education.

XR
**ZPRAVA O SPOLECNE SCHUZI SNEMOVNY LIDU A SNEMOVNY NARODU / FEDERALNI SHROMAZDENI CESKOLOVENSKE SOCIALISTICKE REPUBLIKY. Main/Corp** Czechoslovakia. Federalni Shromazdeni. 1st electorial period, 6th session (Dec. 20-21, 1970) 1970)-. Czech. ir. Kancel AR Federalniho Shromazdeni, Vinohradska 1, 110 02 Prague Czech Republic. **LC** J338; .H453A. ***Continues*** *Tesnopisecka Zprava o Spolecne Schuzi Snemovny Lidu a Snemovny Narodu.*

---

## ABSTRACTING, BIBLIOGRAPHIES AND STATISTICS

---

YU
**AKTIVNOST MESNIH ZAJEDNICA. Main/Corp** Savezni Zavod Za Statistiku (Yugoslavia). Serbo-Croatian (Roman). 5.00. Savezni Zavod za Statistiku, Kneza Milosa 20, Belgrad Yugoslavia. **LC** HA1631; .A33 subser; JS6942.

US/0091-1658
**AMERICAN STATISTICS INDEX.** [Am. stat. index]. **Added/Corp** Congressional Information Service. **VFOAT** ASI. (1973)-. Abstracting/Indexing Service. English. Twelve times a year. Congressional Information Service Inc, 4520 East-West Highway, Suite 800, Bethesda MD 20814-3389. **Tel** (800)638-8380, (301)654-1550, FAX (301)654-4033, telex 292386 CIS UR. **ED** Daniel Coyle. **LC** Z7554.U5; A46. **DD** 016.3173. **NLM** Z 7554.U5 A512. available on CD-ROM.
**Desc:** A comprehensive guide and index to US Government statistical publications.
**Ind/Abst** Middle East Abstr. Index; Popul. Index (?-?).

CN
**ANNUAL REPORT OF MUNICIPAL STATISTICS. Main/Corp** Nova Scotia. Dept. of Municipal Affairs. 1st- 1936-. English. an. Free. Department of Municipal Affairs / Nova Scotia, Community Planning, Provincial Building, PO Box 216, Halifax Nova Scotia B3J 2M4 Canada. **ED** Melissa T Raymond. **LC** TS4.N6. **DD** 352.0716. **Circ:** 800 (ctrl).
**Desc:** Summaries of audited financial statements for Nova Scotia's local governments as well as census information, list of officials with mailing addresses, area and road mileage figures.

UK/0307-1146
**ANNUAL REPORT / THE ELECTRICITY COUNCIL.** [Annu. rep. - Electr. Counc.]. **Main/Corp** Electricity Council. **VFOAT** Electricity Council Annual Report. (1973)-. English. an. Electricity Association Services Ltd, 30 Millbank, London SW1P 4RD England. **Tel** 011 44 71 834 2333. ***Continues in part*** *Report and Accounts / Electricity Council, 0072-615X.*

US
**ANNUAL STATISTICS OF GAS COMPANIES. VFOAT** Statistics of Gas Companies. (1984)-. English. an. Washington Utilities and Transportation Commission, 1300 Evergreen Drive South, Chandler Plaza, Olympia WA 98504. **LC** HD9581.U52; W377A. ***Continues*** *Statistics of Gas Companies.*

AT/0727-8926
**APAIS. AUSTRALIAN PUBLIC AFFAIRS INFORMATION SERVICE.** (APAIS : AUSTRALIAN PUBLIC AFFAIRS INFORMATION SERVICE : A SUBJECT INDEX TO CURRENT LITERATURE.). [APAIS, Aust. public aff. inf. ser.]. **Added/Corp** National Library of Australia. Commonwealth National Library (Australia). **VFOAT** APAIS; Australian Public Affairs Information Service. No. 1 (July 1945)-. Abstracting/Indexing Service. English. Twelve times a year. 185.00Aus$. National Library of Australia, Parkes Place, Canberra ACT, 2600 Australia. **Tel** 011 61 6 2621374, FAX 011 61 6 2731084. **LC** Z7165.A8; A8. **DD** 015.94.
**Desc:** A current subject index to Australian periodical and newspaper articles, scholarly journals, conference papers and books falling within the scope of the social sciences and the humanities.
**Ind/Abst** Annu. Bibliogr. Engl. Lang. Lit.

SW/0065-020X
**ARSBOK FOR SVERIGES KOMMUNER. VFOAT** Statistical Yearbook of Administrative Districts of Sweden. Vol. 1- ; 1918-. Swedish. an. Kr240.00. SCB Statistiska Centralbyran, 11581 Stockholm Sweden. **(Subscription address:** Statistiska Centralbyan, Distributionen, 70189 Orebro, Sweden**) LC** JS7; .S85. **DD** 352.0485. **Circ:** 2,500 (ctrl).
**Desc:** Yearbook contains 26 tables of local taxation statistics, with certain information regarding each municipality, city council and parish.

●AT/1039-6594
**AUSTRALIAN CAPITAL TERRITORY IN FOCUS. Added/Corp** Australian Bureau of Statistics. (1993)-. English. Australian Bureau of Statistics, PO Box 10, Belconnen Australian Capital Territory, 2616 Australia. **Tel** 011 61 6 2527911, FAX 011 61 6 2516009. **LC** HA3008.A9; A25. ***Continues*** *Australian Capital Territory Statistical Summary, 0067-1754.*
**Desc:** Information for the Australian Capital Territory on climate, demography, health, welfare, education, and more.

AT/1033-3010
**AUSTRALIAN NATIONAL ACCOUNTS. CAPITAL STOCK.** [Aust. natl. acc., Cap. stock.]. **Added/Corp** Australian Bureau of Statistics. (1989)-. English. an. 21.40Aus$. Australian Bureau of Statistics, PO Box 10, Belconnen Australian Capital Territory, 2616 Australia. **Tel** 011 61 6 2527911, FAX 011 61 6 2516009. **DD** 339.394021. ***Continues*** *Australian National Accounts. Estimates of Capital Stock, 0819-7431.*
**Desc:** Estimates of consumption of fixed capital, gross and net capital stock and gross fixed capital expenditure, at both current and average prices.

AT/1038-4286
**AUSTRALIAN NATIONAL ACCOUNTS FINANCIAL ACCOUNTS.** (1991)-. English. qt. 50.00Aus$. Australian Bureau of Statistics, PO Box 10, Belconnen Australian Capital Territory, 2616 Australia. **Tel** 011 61 6 2527911, FAX 011 61 6 2516009. ***Continues*** *Australian National Accounts. Flow of Funds Developmental Estimates, 1034-0475.*
**Desc:** Contains information about the level of financial assets and liabilities of each sector of the economy, as well as information about financial transactions between the sectors.

AT
**AUSTRALIAN NATIONAL ACCOUNTS; INPUT-OUTPUT TABLES. Main/Corp** Australian Bureau of Statistics. (19??)-. English. Three times a year. 50.00Aus$. Australian Bureau of Statistics, PO Box 10, Belconnen Australian Capital Territory, 2616 Australia. **Tel** 011 61 6 2527911, FAX 011 61 6 2516009.
**Desc:** Shows input by industry and output by commodity group; industry by industry flow matrices; direct and total requirement coefficient matrices.

AT/0067-1983
**AUSTRALIAN NATIONAL ACCOUNTS : NATIONAL INCOME AND EXPENDITURE.** [Aust. natl. acc. Natl. income expend.]. **Added/Corp** Australian Bureau of Statistics. (1972/1973)-. English. an. 32.00Aus$. Australian Bureau of Statistics, PO Box 10, Belconnen Australian Capital Territory, 2616 Australia. **Tel** 011 61 6 2527911, FAX 011 61 6 2516009. **LC** HC610.I5; A92a. **DD** 332.1. ***Continues*** *Australian National Accounts. National Income and Expenditure, 0067-1983.*
**Desc:** Detailed presentation of national accounts, with tables grouped under the following headings: summary tables, income components of gross domestic product, corporate trading enterprises, financial enterprises, etc.

AT
**AUSTRALIAN NATIONAL ACCOUNTS. STATE ACCOUNTS. Added/Corp** Australian Bureau of Statistics. (1985/1986)-. English. an. 21.40Aus$. Australian Bureau of Statistics, PO Box 10, Belconnen Australian Capital Territory, 2616 Australia. **Tel** 011 61 6 2527911, FAX 011 61 6 2516009.
**Desc:** Dissections for the last 12 years of various national accounting aggregates by State and Territory including household income, private final consumption expenditure, farm income, gross domestic product at market prices, and more.

AT
**BALANCE OF PAYMENTS, AUSTRALIA. Added/Corp** Australian Bureau of Statistics. (1977/1978)-. English. mo. 16.30Aus$. Australian Bureau of Statistics, PO Box 10, Belconnen Australian Capital Territory, 2616 Australia. **Tel** 011 61 6 2527911, FAX 011 61 6 2516009. ***Continues*** *Australian Bureau of Statistics. Balance of Payments.*
**Desc:** Provides estimates of the principal balance of payments aggregates and balances for 15 months, including preliminary estimates for the latest month.

AT/0819-6001
**BALANCE OF PAYMENTS, AUSTRALIA. REGIONAL SERIES ON MICROFICHE.** (BALANCE OF PAYMENTS, AUSTRALIA.). [Balance paym. Aust., Reg. ser. microfiche]. **Added/Corp** Australian Bureau of Statistics. (1985)-. English. an. Price varies. Australian Bureau of Statistics, PO Box 10, Belconnen Australian Capital Territory, 2616 Australia. **Tel** 011 61 6 2527911, FAX 011 61 6 2516009. **DD** 382.170994.
**Desc:** Estimates of the balance of payments dissected into the greatest level of country and regional detail available.

DK/0067-6543
**BIBLIOGRAFI OVER DANMARKS OFFENTLIGE PUBLIKATIONER.** Vol. 1 1948-. Danish. an. kr221.31. Dansk Bibliotekscenter AS, Tempovej 7 11, DK-2750 Ballerup Denmark. **Tel** 011 45 42 974000. **NLM** Z 2569 D411B. **Circ:** 400 (ctrl).
**Desc:** List of publications from the Danish government and from the cities of Copenhagen and Aarhus.

US/0360-280X
**BIBLIOGRAPHIC GUIDE TO GOVERNMENT PUBLICATIONS - FOREIGN. Main/Corp** New York Public Library. Research Libraries. 1975-. English. an. GK Hall & Co, 100 Front Street, Riverside NJ 08075. **Tel** (800)257-5755 ext. 2223. **ED** G.K. Hall. **LC** Z7164.G7; N54 1972 SUPPL; J9.5. **DD** 011.
**Desc:** Lists materials cataloged by the research libraries of the NYPL, with additional entries from LC MARC tapes. Listed are: parliamentary debates and papers, treaties, censuses, and correspondence on foreign relations.

US/0741-4994
**BIBLIOGRAPHIC SERIES / PROFESSIONAL SERVICES DEPARTMENT, INTERNATIONAL ASSOCIATION OF ASSESSING OFFICERS.** [Bibliogr. ser. - Int. Assoc. Assess. Off., Res. Tech. Serv. Dep.]. Monographic series. English. ir. Price varies per volume. Professional Services Department, International Association of Assessing Officers, 1313 East 60th Street, Chicago IL 60637-9990. **Tel** (312)947-2054. **(Subscription address:** prepaid orders: International Association of Assessing Officers, 1313 East 60th Street, Chicago IL 60680-1874**) ED** Robert Clatanoff.
**Desc:** Bibliographies on topics of interest to government policy makers, assessing officials, and others on property tax related matters.

AT/0813-3107
**BIBLIOGRAPHY (AUSTRALIA. PARLIAMENT).** (BIBLIOGRAPHY / PARLIAMENT OF THE COMMONWEALTH OF AUSTRALIA.). **Added/Corp** Australia. Dept. of the Parliamentary Library. Reader Services and Reference Section. No. 1 (1984)-. Monographic series. English. ir. Price varies per volume. Library Reference and Information Service / Reader Services and Reference Section, Department of the Parliamentary Library, Canberra ACT Australia.

BL
**BOLETIM ESTATISTICO ANUAL - COMPANHIA DE ELETRICIDADE DE CEARA. Main/Corp** Companhia de Eletricidade de Cera. Bulletin. Portuguese. Diretoria da Area Economico-Financeira, Av Barao de Studart 2917 Aldeota, Fortaleza Brazil. **LC** HD9685.B83; C563.

BL
**BOLETIM ESTATISTICO - COMPANHIA PAULISTA DE FORCA E LUZ. Main/Corp** Companhia Paulista de Forca e Luz. Bulletin. Portuguese. Companhia Paulista de Forca e Luz, Avenida Angelica 2565, Sao Paulo Brazil. **LC** HD9685.B83; P483B.

DR
**BOLETIN ESTADISTICO (DOMINICAN REPUBLIC. SECRETARIA DE ESTADO DE FINANZAS, DEPARTAMENTO DE ESTUDIOS ECONOMICOS).** (BOLETIN ESTADISTICO.). Yearly V. 1, No. 2 (April/June 1980)-. Spanish. an. $10.00 US. Centro Dominicano de Promocion de Exportaciones, Plaza de la Independencia, Santo Domingo Republica Dominicana. **LC** HJ26; .A33. **DD** 336.7293. ***Continues*** *Boletin Estadistico (Dominican Republic. Secretaria de Estado de Finanzas).*

SA
**BUDGET : STATISTICAL SURVEY. Main/Corp** South Africa. **VFOAT** Begroting: Statistiese Oorsig. Statistical Publication. Multiple languages (English and Afrikaans). an. Government Printer / South Africa, Bosman Street, Private Bag X85, Pretoria 0001 South Africa. **Tel** 011 27 12 3239731 Ext. 262. **LC** HC517.S7; A155. **DD** 354/.68/00722.

SA/0034-5024
**BULLETIN VAN STATISTIEK / REPUBLIEK VAN SUID-AFRIKA, SENTRALE STATISTIEKDIENS.**
**Added/Corp** South Africa. Central Statistical Services. **VFOAT** Bulletin of Statistics. (19??)-. Bulletin. Afrikaans (English). qt. R80.00 South Africa; R88.00 other. Staatsdrukkery Government Printing Works, Bosmanstraat/Bosman Street, Private Bag X85, Pretoria 0001 South Africa. **Tel** 012 323-9731, FAX 012 323-0009. **LC** HA1991; .B86a. **DD** 316.8. ***Continues*** *Bulletin van Statistiek (South Africa. Dept. of Statistics).*

CN/0318-675X
**CANADIAN GOVERNMENT PUBLICATIONS: CATALOGUE.**
**Added/Corp** Canada. Dept. of Public Printing and Stationery. Information Canada Canada. Publishing Centre. **VFOAT** Publications du Gouvernement Canadien: Catalogue. (1???)-. English (French). ir. Canada Communication Group Publishers, Order Processing, Ottawa Ontario K1A 0S9 Canada. **Tel** (819)956-4800, (819)956-4802. **LC** Z1373; .C22; J103. **DD** 015/.71.

UK/0263-2985
**CAPITAL EXPENDITURE AND DEBT FINANCING STATISTICS / CIPFA, STATISTICAL INFORMATION SERVICE.**
1981-82-. Statistical Publication. English. an. £15.00. The Director CIPFA/Statistical Information Service, 1 Buckingham Place, London SW1E 6HS England. **LC** HJ9431; .C46A. **DD** 336.3/431/41. ***Continues*** *Return of Outstanding Debt as at 31st March ... .*

US
**CHECKLIST : PUBLICATIONS OF CONNECTICUT STATE AGENCIES.** No. 1-July 1964-. English. Connecticut State Library, 231 Capital Avenue, Hartford CT 06115. **LC** Z1223.5.C8; C44; J87.C8. **DD** 015.746.

US/0741-2878
**CIS FEDERAL REGISTER INDEX.** [CIS fed. reg. index]. **Added/Corp** Congressional Information Service. **VFOAT** C.I.S. Federal Register Index; Federal Register Index. Issue No. 1984-1 (Jan. 3-6, 1984)-. English. wk. Congressional Information Service Inc, 4520 East-West Highway, Suite 800, Bethesda MD 20814-3389. **Tel** (800)638-8380, (301)654-1550, FAX (301)654-4033, telex 292386 CIS UR. **LC** KF70; .A2 Suppl. **DD** 353/.0005. **NLM** KF 70.A2; F2921.
**Desc:** Itemization of material published in the Daily Federal Register.

US/0007-8514
**CIS INDEX TO PUBLICATIONS OF THE UNITED STATES CONGRESS.** [CIS/index publ. U. S. Congr.]. **Main/Corp** Congressional Information Service. **Added/Corp** Congressional Information Service. Index to Publications of the United States Congress. **VFOAT** Index to Publications of the United States Congress; CIS Index; CIS/Index. **VAT** Congressional Information Service Index to Publications of the United States Congress. Vol. 1 (Jan. 1970)-. Abstracting/Indexing Service. English. mo. Price varies. Congressional Information Service Inc, 4520 East-West Highway, Suite 800, Bethesda MD 20814-3389. **Tel** (800)638-8380, (301)654-1550, FAX (301)654-4033, telex 292386 CIS UR. **ED** Aaron Lerner. **DD** 348. **NLM** Z 1223.A2 C14. available on CD-ROM; available on an online database from DIALOG.
**Desc:** Indexes and abstracts to information published by congressional committees.
**Ind/Abst** Middle East Abstr. Index.

AT/0157-2067
**COMPENDIUM OF LOCAL GOVERNMENT AREA STATISTICS / AUSTRALIAN BUREAU OF STATISTICS, TASMANIAN OFFICE.** **Added/Corp** Australian Bureau of Statistics. Tasmanian Office. (19??)-. English. an. 8.20Aus$. Australian Bureau of Statistics, PO Box 10, Belconnen Australian Capital Territory, 2616 Australia. **Tel** 011 61 6 2527911, FAX 011 61 6 2516009. **LC** HA3113; .A323a. **DD** 319.46. ***Continues*** *Compendium of Municipal Statistics.*
**Desc:** Most recent principal statistics available for local government areas, statistical divisions and subdivisions including population by sex, building activity, local government area, and more.

TI
**CONGRESS OF MICRONESIA BIBLIOGRAPHY.** **Main/Corp** Pacific Islands (Trust Territory). Congress of Micronesia. Library. No. 1-. Bibliography. English. Capitol Hill, Saipan Mariana Islands, 96950 Trust Territory of the Pacific Islands. **LC** Z7165.P27; P3A; JQ6451.A1. **DD** 015/.96/5.

CN/0576-0119
**CORPORATION TAXATION STATISTICS (OTTAWA).** ***Title Change.*** (CORPORATION TAXATION STATISTICS / DOMINION BUREAU OF STATISTICS, CORPORATION AND LABOUR UNIONS RETURNS DIVISION.). [Corp. tax. stat.]. **Main/Corp** Canada. Statistics Canada. Business Finance Division. **Added/Corp** Canada. Dominion Bureau of Statistics. Corporations and Labour Unions Returns Division. Statistics Canada. Corporations and Labour Unions Returns Division. Statistics Canada. Business Finance Division. Statistics Canada. Industrial Organization and Finance Division. **VFOAT** Statistique Fiscale des Societes. (1965)-(19??). English (French). an. Statistics Canada, Publications Sales & Services, Main Building Room 1710, Ottawa Ontario K1A 0T6 Canada. **Tel** (613)951-5078, (800)267-6677, FAX (613)951-1584, telex 053-3585. **LC** HJ4662.A7; A24. **DD** 336.2/43/0971. ***Continues in part*** *Taxation Statistics., 0700-1665.* ***Continued by*** *Annual Financial and Taxation Statistics for Enterprises.*
**Desc:** Taxation of corporation income, indicating the industries earning the income on which income tax is based, the province in which that income is earned and a reconciliation of corporation profit with taxable income and with taxes, including a general review and analysis of the data presented for the reference year.

UK/0263-743X
**DAILY LIST / HMSO BOOKS.** **Added/Corp** Great Britain. Her Majesty's Stationery Office. List No. 203 (21 Oct. 1985)-. Periodical. English. da. Free (first copy), £85.00 (extra copy) daily; Free (first copy), £50.00 (extra copy) weekly. Her Majesty's Stationery Office, 51 Nine Elms Lane, London SW8 5DR England. **Tel** 011 44 71 873 8459, 011 44 71 873 8499, FAX 011 44 71 873 8499, 011 44 71 873 8455, telex 297138. **(Subscription address:** Her Majestys Stationery Offic, PO Box 276 Public Centre, London SW8 5DT England**)** **LC** Z2009; .G774; J301. **DD** 015.41/053. ***Continues*** *Daily List of Government Publications from Her Majesty's Stationery Office.*

CN/0827-0465
**DAILY / STATISTICS CANADA, THE.** [Dly. - Stat. Can.]. **Added/Corp** Statistics Canada. (Apr. 1, 1985)-. Periodical. English. da. 175.00Can$ Canada; $210.00 US; $245.00 other. Statistics Canada, Publications Sales & Services, Main Building Room 1710, Ottawa Ontario K1A 0T6 Canada. **Tel** (613)951-5078, (800)267-6677, FAX (613)951-1584, telex 053-3585. **LC** HC111; .D34. **DD** 330.971/005. ***Continues*** *Statistics Canada Daily, 0380-612X.*
**Desc:** Vehicle for official release of statistical data and publications produced by Statistics Canada. Provides highlights of newly released data with source information for more detailed facts.

US
**DELAWARE LEGISLATIVE ROSTER.**
English. ir. $10.00. Delaware Chamber of Commerce, 1 Commerce Center, Suite 200, Wilmington DE 19801. **Tel** (302)655-7221.

YU
**DELEGACIJE OSNOVNIH SAMOUPRAVNIH ORGANIZACIJA I ZAJEDNICA I SKUPSTINE DRUSTVENO-POLITICKIH ZAJEDNICA.**
**Main/Corp** Savezni Zavod za Statistiku (Yugoslavia). **VFOAT** Delegations of Basic Self-Managing Organizations and of Communities and Assemblies of Socio-Political Communities. Serbo-Croatian (Roman). $30.00. Savezni Zavod za Statistiku, Kneza Milosa 20, Belgrad Yugoslavia. **LC** HA1631; .A33 subser; JN9670.

GR/0256-3592
**DELTION STATISTIKE DEMASION OIKONOMIKON.** **Main/Corp** Greece. Ethnike Statistike Hyperesia. **VFOAT** Statistical Bulletin of Finance. V. 16, 1st Quarter of 1974. Periodical. Greek, Modern (English). qt. Dr400.00 Greece; $16.00 US. National Statistical Service of Greece, 14 Lycourgou Street, GR 10166 Athens Greece. **Tel** 3244-746, telex 216-734 ESYE GR. **Circ:** 1,000. ***Continues*** *Meniaien Deltion Statistikes Demasion Oikonomikon; Monthly Statistical Bulletin of Public Finance.*
**Desc:** Includes data on public finance, state revenue and expenditures, investments, etc.

US
**DICTIONARY CATALOG OF OFFICIAL PUBLICATIONS OF THE STATE OF NEW YORK.** Dec. 18, 1973/Sept. 24, 1976-. Catalog. English. qt. $8.00 US; $12.50 other. New York State Library, Documents Gift & Exchange Section, Empire State Plaza, Albany NY 12230. **Tel** (518)474-5953. **LC** Z1223.5.N57; D5; J87.N7. **DD** 015/.747. Index available. cum. index. ctrl circ.
**Desc:** Includes information from the checklist of official publications of the State of New York.

AT/1035-3062
**DIRECTORY OF MINISTERIAL ADVISERS AND ASSISTANTS.** [Dir. minist. advis. assist.]. (1990)-. Periodical. English. Four times a year. 295.00Aus$ Australia; 312.00Aus$ New Zealand, Papua New Guinea; 314.00Aus$ Indonesia, Malaysia, Singapore; 316.00Aus$ Japan, India; 319.00Aus$ US & Canada; 321.00Aus$ Europe. International Public Relations Pty Ltd., 33 Walsh Street, West Melbourne Victoria 3003 Australia. **Tel** 011 61 03 329 9333, FAX 011 61 03 329 7996. **DD** 354.9404025.

US
**DIRECTORY OF THE STATE AND COUNTY OFFICIALS OF NORTH CAROLINA.** **Added/Corp** North Carolina. Secretary of State. (19??)-. Directory. English. an. $9.53 North Carolina; $9.05 other. Secretary of State Publishing Division, 300 North Salisbury Street, Raleigh NC 27603-5909. **Tel** (919)733-7355. **ED** John L. Cheney Jr. **Circ:** 15,000. available on diskette. ***Continues*** *Directory of the State and County Officials of North Carolina and Members of the General Assembly.*
**Desc:** Listing of public officials in state and county governments in North Carolina with addresses and phone numbers.

CN/0380-0229
**ELECTRIC POWER STATISTICS (OTTAWA. MONTHLY ED.).** (ELECTRIC POWER STATISTICS / PREPARED IN THE TRANSPORTATION AND PUBLIC UTILITIES SECTION.). [Electr. power stat.]. **Added/Corp** Canada. Dominion Bureau of Statistics. Transportation and Public Utilities Section. Canada. Dominion Bureau of Statistics. Public Utilities Section. Canada. Dominion Bureau of Statistics. Industry Division. Canada. Dominion Bureau of Statistics. Manufacturing and Primary Industries Division. Statistics Canada. Manufacturing and Primary Industries Division. Statistics Canada. Industry Division. **VFOAT** Statistique de l'Energie Electrique. Vol. 25, No. 1 (Jan. 1957)-. Periodical. English (French). mo. 110.00Can$ Canada; $132.00 US; $154.00 other. Statistics Canada, Publications Sales & Services, Main Building Room 1710, Ottawa Ontario K1A 0T6 Canada. **Tel** (613)951-5078, (800)267-6677, FAX (613)951-1584, telex 053-3585. **LC** HD9685.C18; A34. **DD** 338.4/762131/0971. ***Continues*** *Central Electric Stations (Monthly).*

LU
**EUROPE IN FIGURES.** **Added/Corp** Statistical Office of the European Communities. (1988)-. English. an. £11.80 UK; 12.80p Ireland. Office for Official Publications of the European Communities, 2 Rue Mercier, 2985 Luxembourg Luxembourg. **Tel** 011 352 499281, FAX 011 352 488573. **(Subscription address:** US: UNIPUB, 4611 F Assembly Drive, Lanham, MD 20706**)** **LC** HC241.2; .E81297. **DD** 314/.05.
**Desc:** A new and original way of presenting statistics on life in Europe. Covers all the aspects of interest to the present and future citizens of Europe.

LU/0255-3953
**EUROSTAT, GENERAL GOVERNMENT ACCOUNTS AND STATISTICS.** (GENERAL GOVERNMENT ACCOUNTS AND STATISTICS.). [EUROSTAT, Gen. gov. acc. stat.]. **Added/Corp** Statistical Office of the European Communities. **VFOAT** Comptes et Statistiques des Administrations Publiques. (1970/1977)-. Dutch (Danish, Dutch, English, French, German and Italian). an. £17.80 UK; 19.30p Ireland. Office for Official Publications of the European Communities, 2 Rue Mercier, 2985 Luxembourg Luxembourg. **Tel** 011 352 499281, FAX 011 352 488573. **LC** HC240.9.I5; G46. **DD** 339.34. ***Continues in part*** *Nationalregnskaber, Ens Arbog.*
**Desc:** Shows the total of general transactions broken down by sub-sector, together with an analysis of the revenue and expenditure of the sector.

US
**FEDERAL STATISTICAL SOURCE : WHERE TO FIND AGENCY EXPERTS & PERSONNEL / BY WILLIAM R. EVINGER.** 29th Ed. (1991)-. Statistical Publication. English. $37.50. Oryx Press, 4041 North Central Avenue, #700, Phoenix AZ 85012-3397. **Tel** (800)279-ORYX, (602)265-2651, FAX (602)265-6250, (800)279-4663, (800)279-6799. **(Subscription address:** Eurospan Ltd., Journals and Serials Division, 3 Henrietta Street, Covent Garden, London WC2E 8LU England.**)** **ED** William R. Evinger. ***Continues*** *Federal Statistical Directory, 8755-3279.*
**Desc:** Direct route to the more than 4,000 individuals throughout the federal government who assemble and disseminate statistical information.

JA/0289-1522
**FINANCIAL STATISTICS OF JAPAN.**
[Financ. stat. Jpn.]. **Added/Corp** Japan. Okurasho. Daijin Kanbo. Chosa Kikakuka. Okurasho Zaisei Kinyu Kenkyujo (Japan). (1983)-. English. an (Aug.). Free. Ministry of Finance Research and Planning Division, Minister's Secretariat, 1-1 Kasumigaseki 3-chome Chiyoda-ku, Tokyo 100 Japan. **LC** HG41; .J2. **DD** 332/.0952. ***Continues*** *Japan. Okurasho. Daijin Kanbo. Quarterly Bulletin of Financial Statistics, 0447-4740.*

US/0363-2113
**FINANCIAL STATISTICS OF THE MAJOR PRIVATELY OWNED UTILITIES IN NEW YORK STATE.** **Main/Corp** New York (State). Dept. of Public Service. **Added/Corp** New York (State). Dept. of Public Service. New York (State). Dept. of Public Service. Office of Accounting and Tariff Analysis. New York (State). Dept. of Public Service. Office of Accounting and Utility Finance. New York (State). Dept. of Public Service. Office of Accounting and Finance. New

York (State). Dept. of Public Service. Accounting Systems Section. **VFOAT** Financial Statistics of the Major Privately Owned Utilities Within New York State. (19??)-. English. an. $8.00. Department of Public Service, Empire State Plaza, Agency Building 3, Albany NY 12223. **Tel** (518)474-8053. **LC** HD2767.N7; N48a. **DD** 338.7/61/363609747.
**Desc:** Tabulation of detailed financial and services data and associated analysis by unit of output.

US
**FLOW OF FUNDS SUMMARY STATISTICS / BOARD OF GOVERNORS OF THE FEDERAL RESERVE SYSTEM.**
**Added/Corp** Board of Governors of the Federal Reserve System (U.S.). (19??)-. Periodical. English. qt. $5.00. Board of Governors of the Federal Reserve System, Mail Stop 127, Washington DC 20551. **Tel** (202)452-3244 or 3245.

NO
**FYLKESTINGSVALGET. COUNTY COUNCIL ELECTIONS.** **Main/Corp** Norway. Statistisk Sentralbyra. **Added/Corp** Norway. Statistisk Sentralbyra. County Council Elections. **VFOAT** County Council Elections. (1975)-. Norwegian (English). **LC** HA1501; subser.; JS6218.S7.

AT/1031-7104
**GOVERNMENT FINANCE STATISTICS, AUSTRALIA.** [Gov. finance stat. Aust.]. **Added/Corp** Australian Bureau of Statistics. (1990)-. English. an. 20.40Aus$. Australian Bureau of Statistics, PO Box 10, Belconnen Australian Capital Territory, 2616 Australia. **Tel** 011 61 6 2527911, FAX 011 61 6 2516009. **DD** 336.9405. ***Formed by the union of*** *Commonwealth Government Finance, Australia, 0725-3427* ***and*** *State and Local Government Finance, Australia, 0158-9946.*
**Desc:** Provides details of the consolidated financial transactions of the non-financial public sector for all levels of government compiled in accordance with standards promulgated by the International Monetary Fund and the United Nations.

US/0250-7374
**GOVERNMENT FINANCE STATISTICS YEARBOOK.** [Gov. finance stat. yearb., Int. Monet. Fund]. **Added/Corp** International Monetary Fund. Government Finance Statistics Division. Vol. 1 (1977)-. English (French and Spanish). an. $54.00. International Monetary Fund, 700 19th Street Northwest, Publishing Unit, Washington DC 20431. **Tel** (202)623-7430, FAX (202)623-7201. **LC** HJ101; .G68. **DD** 336/.0212. **CODEN** GFSYEV. available on magnetic tape.
**Desc:** Provides information on units of government, government accounts, enterprises and financial institutions that governments own and control and national sources of data on government operations. Detailed statistical tables are presented on central government revenue, grants, expenditure, lending, financing and debt.

CN/0709-0412
**GOVERNMENT OF CANADA PUBLICATIONS. QUARTERLY CATALOGUE.** (GOVERNMENT OF CANADA PUBLICATIONS, QUARTERLY CATALOGUE / ISSUED BY THE CANADIAN GOVERNMENT PUBLISHING CENTRE.). [Gov. Can. publ., Q. cat.]. **Added/Corp** Canadian Government Publishing Centre. Canada Communication Group. Publishing. **VFOAT** Publications du Gouvernement du Canada. (Jan./March 1979)-. English (French). qt. 88.00Can$ Canada; 114.40Can$ other. Canada Communication Group Publishers, Order Processing, Ottawa Ontario K1A 0S9 Canada. **Tel** (819)956-4800, (819)956-4802. **LC** Z1373; .G68; J103. **DD** 015.71/053. **NLM** Z 1373; C212ca. ***Continues*** *Canadian Government Publications, 0008-3690.*
**Ind/Abst** Popul. Index (?-?).

US
**GPO MONTHLY CATALOG [COMPUTER FILE].** **Added/Corp** United States. Superintendent of Documents. OCLC. **VFOAT** Monthly Catalog. (Feb. 1990)-. Catalog. English. bm. OCLC Asia Pacific Services, 6565 Frantz Road, Dublin OH 43017. **Tel** (800)848-5878, (614)764-6394 or 6000, FAX (614)764-6096.
**Desc:** System requirements: OCLC workstation or IBM PS/2, XT, AT or compatible; 640K RAM; hard disk drive; CD-ROM drive; MS-DOS extensions version 2.0 or higher; OCLC Search CD450 software.

FR
**GUIDE DES GUIDES, LE.** French. an. 19 rue de Constantine, 75007 Paris France. **LC** Z2169; .G85; J341.R1. **DD** 015.44/053.

FR
**GUIDE STATISTIQUE DE LA FISCALITE DIRECTE LOCALE / MINISTERE DE L'INTERIEUR ET DE LA DECENTRALISATION, DIRECTION GENERALE LOCALES, MISSION D'ETUDES ET DESTATISTIQUES.** French. an. Documentation Francaise, 29 Quai Voltaire, 75344 Paris Cedex 7 France. **Tel** 011 33 1 40157000, FAX 011 33 1 40157230, telex 204 826 DOCFRAN. **LC** HJ9047; .A484.
**Desc:** Fiscal policy for departments.

HK
**HONG KONG ANNUAL DIGEST OF STATISTICS.** **Added/Corp** Hong Kong. Census and Statistics Dept. (1978)-. English. an. 98.00HK$. Hong Kong Government Information Service, Beaconsfield House, 4 Queens Road, Hong Kong Hong Kong. **Tel** 011 852 8428801 4, telex 61190 HKGIS. **(Subscription address:** Government Information Service, Publications Office, 1 Battery Path, Hong Kong Hong Kong.**)** **LC** HA1950.H6; A2. **DD** 315.1/25. **Circ:** 900 (ctrl).
**Desc:** Comprehensive collection of data from government departments and data from major census and surveys.

HK/0300-418X
**HONG KONG MONTHLY DIGEST OF STATISTICS.** **Main/Corp** Hong Kong. Census and Statistics Dept. **Added/Corp** Hong Kong. Census and Statistics Dept. Digest of Statistics. (1970)-. English. mo. HK$576.00. Hong Kong Government Information Service, Beaconsfield House, 4 Queens Road, Hong Kong Hong Kong. **Tel** 011 852 8428801 4, telex 61190 HKGIS. **(Subscription address:** Government Information Service, Publications Office, 1 Battery Path, Hong Kong Hong Kong.**)** **LC** HA1950.H6; A23. **DD** 315.12/5. **Bk Rev. Ad Acc. Circ:** 2,300 (ctrl).
**Desc:** Contains main data series from all government departments and up-to-date statistical information on the social and economic characteristics of Hong Kong.

CN/0843-6142
**INDEX TO STATISTICS CANADA SURVEYS AND QUESTIONNAIRES.** [Index Stat. Can. surv. quest.]. **Added/Corp** Statistics Canada. Standards Division. **VFOAT** Index des Enquetes et Questionnaires de Statistique Canada. (1988)-. English (French). an. 28.00Can$ Canada; $34.00 US; $40.00 other. Statistics Canada, Publications Sales & Services, Main Building Room 1710, Ottawa Ontario K1A 0T6 Canada. **Tel** (613)951-5078, (800)267-6677, FAX (613)951-1584, telex 053-3585. **LC** Z7554.C2; I54; HA741. **DD** 001.4/222/0971. ***Continues*** *Index to the Inventory of Statistics Canada Questionnaires on Microfiche, 0713-9349.*

CN/0380-0547
**INFOMAT (ENGLISH ED.).** (INFOMAT, A WEEKLY REVIEW.). [Infomat]. **Added/Corp** Statistics Canada. (June 27, 1986)-. Periodical. English. wk. 130.00Can$ Canada; $156.00 US; $182.00 other. Statistics Canada, Publications Sales & Services, Main Building Room 1710, Ottawa Ontario K1A 0T6 Canada. **Tel** (613)951-5078, (800)267-6677, FAX (613)951-1584, telex 053-3585. **LC** HC111; .A543. **DD** 354.710081/9. ***Continues*** *Infomat, Weekly Bulletin, 0380-0547.*
**Desc:** This weekly review highlights major Statistics Canada reports, reference papers and other releases.

UK
**INLAND REVENUE STATISTICS.**
**Added/Corp** Great Britain. Board of Inland Revenue. Great Britain. Board of Inland Revenue. Statistics Division. (1973)-. English. ir. Her Majesty's Stationery Office, 51 Nine Elms Lane, London SW8 5DR England. **Tel** 011 44 71 873 8459, 011 44 71 873 8499, FAX 011 44 71 873 8499, 011 44 71 873 8456, telex 297138. **(Subscription address:** Her Majesty's Stationery Office, PO Box 276, Publications Centre, London SW8 5DT England.**)** ***Continues*** *Great Britain. Board of Inland Revenue. Statistics. Statistics;* ***Absorbed*** *Great Britain. Board of Inland Revenue. Survey of Personal Incomes.*

XN
**IZBORI NA DELEGACII I DELEGATI ZA SOBORITE NA SOBRANIJATA.** **Main/Corp** Macedonia (Republic). Republicki Zavod za Statistika. (19??)-. Macedonian. 50.00Din. Republicki Zavod za Statistika, Maksim Gorki 26, Skopje Macedonia. **LC** HA1; .M22 subser; JS6949.M3.

SW/0023-3056
**KOMMUNAL LITTERATUR.** Periodical. Swedish. bm. Kr220.00 Sweden; $26.62 US. Bibliotekstjanst AB, Box 200, S-221 00 Lund Sweden. **Tel** 011 46 46 180000. **ED** Siu Rehnstann. **LC** Z7164.L8; K648; JS6255. Index available. cum. index. **Circ:** 1,300 (ctrl). available on an online database.

NO
**KOMMUNEVALGET.** **Main/Corp** Norway. Statistisk Sentralbyra. **VFOAT** Municipal Elections. Multiple languages (English and Norwegian). 8.00. **LC** HA1501; subser; JS6218.S7.

YU
**KOMUNALNI FONDOVI U GRADSKIM NASELJIMA.** **Main/Corp** Savenzi Zavod za Statistiku (Yugoslavia). Serbo-Croatian (Roman). 4.00. Savezni Zavod za Statistiku, Kneza Milosa 20, Belgrad Yugoslavia. **LC** HA1631; .A33 subser; HD2768.Y85.

US/0889-4574
**LEGISLATIVE NEWS ALERT.** **See** Public Administration.

CN/0840-7908
**LISTE BIMESTRIELLE DES PUBLICATIONS DU GOUVERNEMENT DU QUEBEC.** **Main/Corp** Quebec (Province). Ministere des Communications. Bibliotheque Administrative. Vol. 8, No 1 (Jan.-Feb. 1988)-. French (English). bm. 35.00Can$. Les Publications du Quebec, CP 1190, Outremont Quebec H2V 4S7 Canada. **Tel** (514)948-1222, (800)463-2100, FAX (514)278-3030. **LC** Z1373.5.Q4; L57; J107. ***Continues*** *Liste Mensuelle des Publications du Gouvernement du Quebec, 0714-5993.*

NZ
**LOCAL AUTHORITY ELECTION STATISTICS.** 1977-. English. **LC** JS8348.5; .L6. ***Continues*** *Local Authority Elections.*

NZ
**LOCAL AUTHORITY STATISTICS / NEW ZEALAND.** 1962-63-. Periodical. English. an. 15.40Z$. Government Printing Office / New Zealand, 10 Mulgrave Street, Wellington New Zealand. **Tel** 011 64 4 4737211, FAX 011 64 4 734943, telex GOVPRINT NZ 31320. ***Continues*** *Report on the Local Authority Statistics of New Zealand.*
**Desc:** Transactions of individual local authorities in such areas as transport, water supply, airports, libraries, real estate, and refuse, drainage and sewerage.

US/0092-9212
**MICHIGAN STATE EMPLOYEES' RETIREMENT SYSTEM.** (MICHIGAN STATE EMPLOYEES' RETIREMENT SYSTEM FINANCIAL AND STATISTICAL REPORT.). **Main/Corp** Michigan. Dept. of Administration. Statistical Publication. English. an. Michigan Department of Administration, Stevens T Mason Building/2nd Floor West Wing, Lansing MI 48913. **LC** JK5860.P4; M5A. **DD** 353.9/774/005.

US/0196-4755
**MISSISSIPPI OFFICIAL AND STATISTICAL REGISTER.** **Added/Corp** Mississippi. Secretary of State. **VFOAT** Official and Statistical Register. (1952)-. Statistical Publication. English. ir (every four years). Free. Secretary of State Mississippi, PO Box 136, Jackson MS 39205. **Tel** (601)359-1350. **LC** J87; .M74a. **DD** 353.9762002. ***Continues*** *Mississippi Blue Book.*

US
**MONTHLY GAS UTILITY STATISTICAL REPORT.** **Main/Corp** American Gas Association. (1974)-. Statistical Publication. English. mo. American Gas Association / Virginia, 1515 Wilson Boulevard, Arlington VA 22209. **Tel** (703)841-8400, (703)841-8559, FAX (703)841-8697.

AT
**MONTHLY SUMMARY OF STATISTICS.**
**Main/Corp** Australian Bureau of Statistics. Queensland Office. (19??)-. English. mo. 9.70Aus$. Australian Bureau of Statistics, PO Box 10, Belconnen Australian Capital Territory, 2616 Australia. **Tel** 011 61 6 2527911, FAX 011 61 6 2516009. **LC** HA3071; .A25. **DD** 319.43. ***Continues*** *Australian Bureau of Statistics. Queensland Office. Queensland Statistics.*
**Desc:** Summary of up-to-date statistics on a wide range of subjects.

AT
**MONTHLY SUMMARY OF STATISTICS, NEW SOUTH WALES.** **Main/Corp** Australian Bureau of Statistics. New South Wales Office. No. 551 (Sept. 1979)-. English. mo. 14.30Aus$. Australian Bureau of Statistics, PO Box 10, Belconnen Australian Capital Territory, 2616 Australia. **Tel** 011 61 6 2527911, FAX 011 61 6 2516009. **LC** HA3011; .A18. **DD** 330.9944/00212. ***Continues*** *Australian Bureau of Statistics. New South Wales Office. New South Wales Monthly Summary of Business Statistics, 0028-680X.*
**Desc:** Covers population and vital statistics, employment and unemployment, wages and prices, production, building, finance, trade, transport and welfare.

AT/0047-8032
**MONTHLY SUMMARY OF STATISTICS, SOUTH AUSTRALIA.** **Main/Corp** Australian Bureau of Statistics. South Australian Office. (19??)-. English. mo. 10.00Aus$. Australian Bureau of Statistics, PO Box 10, Belconnen Australian Capital Territory, 2616 Australia. **Tel** 011 61 6 2527911, FAX 011 61 6 2516009. **LC** HA3091; .B86a. **DD** 319.42/3. ***Continues*** *Australia. Commonwealth Bureau of Census and Statistics. South Australian Office. Monthly Summary of Statistics.*
**Desc:** Current major statistical series on population, vital statistics, employment, unemployment, industrial disputes, earnings, production of selected items, and more.

# Public Administration —Abstracting, Bibliographies and Statistics

AT
**MONTHLY SUMMARY OF STATISTICS : WESTERN AUSTRALIA. Added/Corp** Australian Bureau of Statistics. Western Australian Office. (1958)-. English. mo. 11.00Aus$. Australian Bureau of Statistics, PO Box 10, Belconnen Australian Capital Territory, 2616 Australia. **Tel** 011 61 6 2527911, FAX 011 61 6 2516009. **ED** Robin Dalby. **LC** HA3159; .B87a. **DD** 319.41. **Circ:** 950. **Continues** Monthly Statistical Summary, Western Australia.
**Desc:** Presents indicators of business activity, population statistics, employment and and vital statistics: employment and unemployment, wages and prices, production and building, finance, trade and transport.

II/0303-8505
**NAGALAND BUDGET. SOME FACTS AND CHARTS.** (NAGALAND BUDGET / SOME FACTS AND CHARTS.). **Main/Corp** Nagaland (India). Directorate of Economics and Statistics. (19??)-. English. an. Free. Directorate of Economics and Statistics / Nagaland, Nagaland Kohima India. **Tel** 2556. **LC** HJ66.N25; B125a. **DD** 354/.54/16500722. **Circ:** 500 (ctrl).
**Desc:** Contains state governments budgetary receipts and disbursements during current financial year.

JA/0449-5314
**NEWS BULLETIN. Main/Corp** Japan. Sorifu. Tokeikyoku. (1967)-. Bulletin. English. qt. Free. Statistics Bureau / Management and Coordination Agency, 19-1 Wakamatsu-cho, Shinjuku-ku, 162 Tokyo Japan. **LC** HA37; .J344a. **DD** 354/.52/0081.

CN/0708-1596
**NEWSPAPERS AND PERIODICALS CURRENTLY RECEIVED BY THE LIBRARY OF PARLIAMENT INCLUDING THE READING ROOM OF THE HOUSE OF COMMONS. Main/Corp** Canada. Library of Parliament. VFOAT Journaux et Revues Recus par la Bibliotheque du Parlement y Compris la Salle de Lectures de la Chambre des Communes. Periodical. English (French). Library of Parliament / Information & Technical Services Branch, Ottawa Ontario K1A 0A9 Canada. **Tel** (613)996-3121. **DD** 016.05.

US
**NORTH CAROLINA MANUAL. Main/Corp** North Carolina. Secretary of State. English. be (Fall of every odd year). $15.77 North Carolina; $15.01 other. Secretary of State Publishing Division, 300 North Salisbury Street, Raleigh NC 27603-5909. **Tel** (919)733-7355. **ED** John L. Cheney Jr. **Circ:** 500.
**Desc:** Current information on North Carolina state government by branch.

US/8756-632X
**NRRI QUARTERLY BULLETIN.** (NRRI QUARTERLY BULLETIN ARTICLES AND ABSTRACTS FOR STATE REGULATORY AGENCY COMMISSIONERS AND STAFF.). [NRRI q. bull.]. **Added/Corp** National Regulatory Research Institute (Ohio State University). (19??)-. English. Four times a year (Mar., June, Sept., Dec.). $120.00. National Regulatory Research Institute, 1080 Carmack Road, Columbus OH 43210. **Tel** (614)292-9404, FAX (614)292-7196. **ED** Fran Sevel. **LC** WMLC 93/1437. **DD** 343. Index available. **Circ:** 1,200 (ctrl).
**Desc:** Articles and abstracts on state actions and issues in regulation of electric, gas, telecommunications and water utilities.

US
**OFFICIAL RETURNS OF THE PRIMARY AND GENERAL ELECTIONS / STATE OF WEST VIRGINIA.** English. sa. $5.00. Office of the Secretary of State, Capitol Building/Room 157, Charleston WV 25305. **Tel** (304)345-4000. **LC** JK4092; .O36. **DD** 324.9754/043. **Circ:** 750. **Formed by the union of** Official Returns of the General Election **and** Official Returns of the Primary Election.
**Desc:** The most complete comparative analysis of election statistics ever published in West Virginia.

CN/0382-2834
**ONTARIO HYDRO STATISTICAL YEARBOOK (1973).** (STATISTICAL YEARBOOK.). **Main/Corp** Ontario Hydro. **Added/Corp** Ontario Hydro. Annual Report. (19??)-. Statistical Publication. English. an. Free. Ontario Hydro, 700 University Avenue, Toronto Ontario M5G 1X6 Canada. **Tel** (416)592-5111. **LC** HD9685.C3; O87a. **DD** 363.6/09713. **Circ:** 1,300.

US/0098-3225
**OPERATING REVENUE AND EXPENSE STATISTICS CLASS A AND B PRIVATE GAS UTILITIES IN WISCONSIN. Main/Corp** Public Service Commission of Wisconsin. Accounts and Finance Division. English. Wisconsin Public Service Commission, PO Box 7854, Madison WI 53707. **Tel** FAX (608)266-3957. **LC** HD2767.W6; A37 ; HD9581.U5 U52. **DD** 363.6/09775 S; 338.4/3.

US
**OREGON PERSONAL INCOME TAX ANNUAL STATISTICS. Added/Corp** Oregon. Dept. of Revenue. Research Section. (1984)-. English. an. $5.00. Department of Revenue / Oregon, State Office Building, Salem OR 97310. **Tel** (503)378-3359. **LC** HJ4655.O65; O76. **DD** 336.24/2/09795021. cum. index.
**Pr Rev. Continues in part** Analysis of Oregon.
**Desc:** Statistical information on Oregon's income taxes.

US/0145-4269
**OREGON PROPERTY TAX STATISTICS.** [Or. prop. tax stat.]. **Main/Corp** Oregon. Dept. of Revenue. Research and Special Services Division. 1975-. English. an. $5.00. Department of Revenue / Oregon, State Office Building, Salem OR 97310. **Tel** (503)378-3359. **LC** HJ4121.O7; A24. **DD** 336.2/2/09795. **Circ:** 220. **Continues** Oregon. Dept. of Revenue. Research and Special Services Division. Summary of Assessment and Tax Rolls.
**Desc:** Statistics on Oregon assessed values and property tax levies are presented for fiscal year 1987-1988.

GW
**PERSONAL IM OEFFENTLICHEN DIENST.** German. an. DM9.30. Niedersachsisches Landesverwaltungsamt, Postfach 107, 3000 Hannover Germany. **Tel** (0511)108-9466. **LC** HA1248.L69; S73 subser. **DD** 354.43/59001. **Bk Rev. Circ:** 200.
**Desc:** Data about the administrative staff in Lower-Saxony.

UK/0260-8642
**PLANNING AND DEVELOPMENT STATISTICS ... ACTUALS / CIPFA, STATISTICAL INFORMATION SERVICE.** Statistical Publication. English. an. £10.00. Chartered Institute of Public Finance and Accountancy, 2 3 Robert Street, London WC2N 6BH England. **Tel** 011 44 1 895 8823. **LC** HD601.A1; P55. **DD** 352.94/18/0942.

US
**PROPERTY TAX STATISTICAL REPORT FROM THE OFFICE OF STATE TAX COMMISSIONER ... ON ... PROPERTY TAXES LEVIED AND PROPERTY VALUATION.** Statistical Publication. English. North Dakota Tax Department, State Capitol, Bismarck ND 58505. **LC** HJ4121.N9; T39A. **DD** 336.22/09784. **Continues** Statistical Report (North Dakota. Tax Dept.).

US/0099-2410
**PUBLIC DOCUMENTS (BATON ROUGE, LA.).** (PUBLIC DOCUMENTS.). No. 12, (Jan./June 1954)-. English. sa. Free. Louisiana State Library, PO Box 131, Baton Rouge LA 70821. **LC** Z1223.5.L7; A32; J87.L8. **DD** 015.763. **NLM** W2 AL6 D85P. Index available. cum. index. **Circ:** 1,000 (ctrl). **Continues** Semi-Annual List of the Public Documents of Louisiana.

AT/1031-7112
**PUBLIC SECTOR DEBT, AUSTRALIA.** [Public sect. debt Aust.]. **Added/Corp** Australian Bureau of Statistics. (1987)-. English. an. 10.70Aus$. Australian Bureau of Statistics, PO Box 10, Belconnen Australian Capital Territory, 2616 Australia. **Tel** 011 61 6 2527911, FAX 011 61 6 2516009. **DD** 336.343394021.
**Desc:** Statistics on the financial assets and liabilities of the Australian non-financial public sector.

US/0147-7641
**PUBLICATIONS OF THE INSTITUTE OF GOVERNMENT. CUMULATIVE SUPPLEMENT. Main/Corp** University of North Carolina at Chapel Hill. Institute of Government. English. be. Free. University of North Carolina at Chapel Hill Institute of Government, CB 3330, Knapp Building, Chapel Hill NC 27599-3330. **Tel** (919)966-4119, FAX (919)962-0654. **LC** Z7165.U6; N733 SUPPL; JK4101. **DD** 016.3209/756. **Circ:** 250.

US/0749-9183
**QUARTERLY STATISTICAL REPORT - EDISON ELECTRIC INSTITUTE. STATISTICAL DEPT.** (QUARTERLY STATISTICAL REPORT.). [Q. stat. rep. - Edison Electr. Instit., Stat. Dep.]. **Added/Corp** Edison Electric Institute. Statistical Dept. (1982)-. Statistical Publication. qt. Edison Electric Institute, 701 Pennsylvania Avenue Northwest, Washington DC 20004. **Tel** (202)508-5607, (202)508-5610, FAX (202)508-5030. **DD** 333. **Continues** Total Electric Utility Industry in the United States, including Alaska and Hawaii.

CN/1193-0721
**QUEEN'S PARK DIRECTORY.** [Queen's Park dir.]. **Added/Corp** Public Affairs Management Inc. (Fall 1989)-. Directory. English. an. 190.00Can$ (includes GST). Public Affairs Management, Inc., 1075 Bay Street, Suite 52, Toronto Ontario M5S 2B1 Canada. **Tel** (416)969-9437, FAX (416)969-9512. **DD** 354.713/00025.

CN/0380-6103
**QUOTIDIEN DE STATISTIQUE CANADA.** (LE QUOTIDIEN / STATISTIQUE CANADA.). [Quotid. Stat. Can.]. **Added/Corp** Statistics Canada. (April 1985)-. Periodical. French. da. 175.00Can$ Canada; $210.00 US ; $245.00 other. Statistics Canada, Publications Sales & Services, Main Building Room 1710, Ottawa Ontario K1A 0T6 Canada. **Tel** (613)951-5078, (800)267-6677, FAX (613)951-1584, telex 053-3585. **DD** 317.1/05. **Continues** Le Quotidien de Statistique Canada, 0380-6103.

UK/0142-5137
**RATE SUPPORT GRANT STATISTICS / SOCIETY OF COUNTY TREASURERS. Added/Corp** Society of County Treasurers. (1979)-. English. £2.50. K Hyde Honorary Treasurer, County Hall, Truro TR1 3AY England. **LC** HJ1023; .R37. **DD** 336.1/85.

BL
**RELATORIO ESTATISTICO DE INFORMACOES ECONOMICO-TRIBUTARIAS / GOVERNO DO ESTADO DE MINAS GERAIS, SECRETARIA DE ESTADO DA FAZENDA, DIRECTORIA DA RECEITA ESTADUAL, CENTRO DE INFORMACOES ECONOMICO-FISCAIS.** (19??)-. Portuguese. an. **LC** HJ5715.B8; R39. **DD** 336.2/713/098151.

SW
**RIKSREVISIONSVERKETS TAXERINGSSTATISTISKA UNDERSOKNING TAXERINGSARET ... .** Swedish. an. Liber Distribution, Prenumberationsorder, Forlagsorder 162 89, Stockholm Sweden. **LC** HC380.I5; S74 subser; HJ4743.

US/0094-6958
**SAGE PUBLIC ADMINISTRATION ABSTRACTS.** [Sage public admin. abstr.]. **Added/Corp** Sage Publications, Inc. Vol. 1 (April 1974)-. Abstracting/Indexing Service. English. qt (Jan., Apr., July, Oct.). $295.00. SAGE Periodical Press, 2455 Teller Road, Thousand Oaks CA 91320. **Tel** (805)499-0721, FAX (805)499-0871, telex 100799. **LC** JA1; .S27. **DD** 350/.008. **Bk Rev. Acid Free. Circ:** 500. available on microfilm and microfiche from University Microfilms International (UMI).
**Desc:** Publishes abstracts covering recent literature (plus related citations) on all aspects of public administration. Entries are drawn from books, articles, pamphlets, government publications, significant speeches, legislative research studies and other fugitive material.

GW
**SCHULDEN DES LANDES, DER GEMEINDEN, GEMEINDEVERBANDE UND ZWECKVERBANDE AM ..., DIE.** (19??)-. German. an. Hessisches Statistisches Landesamt, Postfach 3205, Rheinstrasse 35/37, 6200 Wiesbaden 1 Germany. **Tel** (06121)368.0, telex 6121850 HSLD. **LC** HA1320; .H529 subser.; HJ48.H47. **DD** 314.3/41 S; 336.43. **Continues** Schulden des Landes, der Gemeinden und Gemeindeverbande.

JA
**SEIFU KANKOBUTSU SHIMBUN.** Japanese. an. ¥2000. Okurasho Insatukyoku, 2-4, Toranomon 2 chome, Minatoku, Tokyoto 105 Japan. **LC** Z3305; .S4272; J674.

LU
**SKATTESTATISTIK.** VFOAT Steuerstatistik; Tax Statistics. 1968/73-. English (French, German and Italian). Centre Europeen, Boite Postale 1907, Luxembourg Luxembourg. **LC** HJ2599.5; .S56A. **DD** 336.2/0094.

US/0361-7475
**STATISTICAL ABSTRACT - NEW YORK STATE DEPARTMENT OF STATE. Main/Corp** New York (State). Dept. of State. (19??)-. Academic Scholarly Publication. English. an. **LC** J87; .N74ac. **DD** 353.9/747/1. Documents available from CASDDS.
**Ind/Abst** Chem. Abstr.

II
**STATISTICAL ABSTRACT OF PUBLIC FINANCE OF HARYANA STATE. Main/Corp** Haryana. Economic and Statistical Organisation. (1969/70)-. Statistical Publication. English. **LC** HJ1320.H3; A3. **DD** 336.54/558.

US
**STATISTICAL DIGEST - LEGISLATIVE BUDGET AND FINANCE COMMITTEE. Main/Corp** Pennsylvania. General Assembly. Legislative Budget and Finance Committee. 1978/79-. Statistical Publication. English. an. Legislative Budget and Finance Committee Senate, PO Box 80, Main Capitol Building, Harrisburg PA 17120. **LC** HJ11; .P4498A. **DD**

353.97480072/23/05. ***Continues*** *Selected Financial and Related Statistical Facts of the Commonwealth of Pennsylvania.*

US
**STATISTICAL REPORT (MICHIGAN. LEGISLATURE. SENATE. FISCAL AGENCY).** (STATISTICAL REPORT / SENATE FISCAL AGENCY.). **VFOAT** Senate Fiscal Agency ... Statistical Report. Statistical Publication. English. Senate Fiscal Agency, PO Box 30036, Lansing MI 48909. **Tel** (517)373-2767. **LC** HJ11; .M517. **DD** 336.774. **Circ:** 500 (ctrl).

US/0362-4315
**STATISTICAL SERVICES OF THE UNITED STATES GOVERNMENT.** **Main/Corp** United States. Office of Management and Budget. Statistical Policy Division. (19??)-. Statistical Publication. English. ir. Superintendent of Documents, US Government Printing Office, Washington DC 20402. **Tel** (202)275-3328, FAX (202)786-2377. **LC** HA37; .U176a. **DD** 001.4/22/0973. ***Continues*** *Statistical Services of the United States Government, 0362-4315.*

US/0361-3607
**STATISTICAL YEAR BOOK OF THE ELECTRIC UTILITY INDUSTRY.** (STATISTICAL YEAR BOOK OF THE ELECTRIC UTILITY INDUSTRY FOR ...). [Stat. year b. electr. util. ind.]. **Added/Corp** Edison Electric Institute. **VFOAT** EEI Statistical Year Book. (1960)-. Statistical Publication. English. an. $65.00 nonmembers, $52.00 members. Edison Electric Institute, 701 Pennsylvania Avenue Northwest, Washington DC 20004. **Tel** (202)508-5607, (202)508-5610, FAX (202)508-5030. **(Subscription address:** Edison Electric Institute, PO Box 2800, Kearneysville WV 25430.**)** **LC** HD9685.U4; E33. **DD** 338.4/736362. ***Continues*** *Electric Utility Industry in the United States.*
**Desc:** Operational and financial aspects of the total electric utility industry. Provides data on national and state statistics on topics such as installed capacity, electric generation and electric supply, sales, revenue and customers by class of service.

US/0740-5790
**STATISTICAL YEARBOOK OF MUNICIPAL FINANCE.** ***Suspended.*** (STATISTICAL YEARBOOK OF MUNICIPAL FINANCE / PUBLIC SECURITIES ASSOCIATION.). [Stat. yearb. munic. finance]. (1979)-?. Statistical Publication. English. an. $61.50. Public Securities Association, 40 Broad St, 12th Floor, New York NY 10004. **Tel** (212)809-7000, (212)440-9430, FAX (212) 797-3895, (212) 742-1549. ***Continues*** *Statistical Yearbook: Municipal Securities Data Base.*

CN/0838-4223
**STATISTICS CANADA CATALOGUE (1988).** (STATISTICS CANADA CATALOGUE.). [Stat. Can. cat.]. **Main/Corp** Statistics Canada. Library Services Division. **Added/Corp** Statistics Canada. Library. (1987/1988)-. English (French). an. 15.00Can$ Canada; $18.00 US; $21.00 other. Statistics Canada, Publications Sales & Services, Main Building Room 1710, Ottawa Ontario K1A 0T6 Canada. **Tel** (613)951-5078, (800)267-6677, FAX (613)951-1584, telex 053-3585. **LC** Z7554.C2; S7c; HA741. **DD** 016.3171. **Circ:** 4,500. ***Continues*** *Statistics Canada. Communications Division. Current Publications Index, 0832-8331.*
**Desc:** Lists publications available for sale from Publication Sales; maps and mapping services available from Geography Division; and publicly available microdata files.

US/0147-4626
**STATISTICS FOR MUNICIPAL AUTHORITIES IN PENNSYLVANIA.** English. an. Pennsylvania Department of Community Affairs, Forum Building/Room 311, Harrisburg PA 17120. **LC** HD4606.P4; S73. **DD** 336.748.

US/0160-9920
**STATISTICS OF INCOME. CORPORATION INCOME TAX RETURNS.** (STATISTICS OF INCOME. CORPORATION INCOME TAX RETURNS / PREPARED UNDER THE DIRECTION OF THE COMMISSIONER OF INTERNAL REVENUE BY THE STATISTICS DIVISION.). **Added/Corp** United States. Internal Revenue Service. Statistics Division. United States. Internal Revenue Service. Corporation Statistics Branch. United States. Internal Revenue Service. **VFOAT** Corporation Income Tax Returns. (1954)-. English. ir. Superintendent of Documents, US Government Printing Office, Washington DC 20402. **Tel** (202)275-3328, FAX (202)786-2377. **LC** HJ4653.C7; A3. **DD** 336.243. cum. index. ***Continues in part*** *Statistics of Income for ... / U.S. Treasury Department, Bureau of Internal Revenue.*

US
**STATISTICS OF INCOME : INCOME TAX RETURNS.** **Main/Corp** New Jersey. Division of Taxation. Research and Statistics Section. 1976-. English. an. Department of Treasury Divison of Taxation, Trenton NJ 08625. **LC** HJ11; .N553B. **DD** 336.24/2/09749.

US
**STATISTICS OF INCOME. INDIVIDUAL INCOME TAX RETURNS.** **Added/Corp** United States. Internal Revenue Service. United States. Internal Revenue Service. Statistics Division. **VFOAT** Individual Income Tax Returns. (1954)-. Government Publication. English. ir. Superintendent of Documents, US Government Printing Office, Washington DC 20402. **Tel** (202)275-3328, FAX (202)786-2377. **LC** HJ4652; .A2425. **DD** 336.24/2/0973. cum. index. ***Continues in part*** *Statistics of Income for ... .*

US/0734-1709
**STATISTICS OF INCOME. PARTNERSHIP RETURNS (1977).** (STATISTICS OF INCOME. PARTNERSHIP RETURNS.). **VFOAT** Partnership Returns. 1977-. English. ir. Department of Justics, Constitution Avenue and Tenth Street NW, Washington DC 20530. **Tel** (202)633-2000. **LC** HJ4653.C7; S68. **DD** 336.2/07. ***Continues*** *Statistics of Income. Business Income Tax Returns, Sole Proprietorships, Partnerships.*

US/0730-0743
**STATISTICS OF INCOME. SOI BULLETIN.** (STATISTICS OF INCOME. SOI BULLETIN / DEPARTMENT OF THE TREASURY, INTERNAL REVENUE SERVICE.). [Stat. income, SOI bull.]. **Added/Corp** United States. Internal Revenue Service. **VFOAT** SOI Bulletin; Statistics of Income. S.O.I. Bulletin; S.O.I. Bulletin. Vol. 1, No. 1 (1981)-. Bulletin. English. qt. $25.00 US; $31.25 other. Superintendent of Documents, US Government Printing Office, Washington DC 20402. **Tel** (202)275-3328, FAX (202)786-2377. **LC** HJ4653.S7; S73. **DD** 336.2/00973. Documents available from UMI Article Clearinghouse. ***Formed by the union of*** *Preliminary Statistics of Income. Individual Income Tax Returns; Statistics of Income, Preliminary. Business Income Tax Returns, Sole Proprietorships, Partnerships* ***and*** *Statistics of Income, Preliminary. Corporation.*
**Desc:** Provides information and statistics on income, assets and expenses of individuals and businesses, as compiled from Federal tax returns.
**Ind/Abst** Newsp. Period. Abstr. (1992-); PAIS Int. Print.

US/0744-0030
**STATISTICS OF INCOME. SOLE PROPRIETORSHIP RETURNS.** **VFOAT** Sole Proprietorship Returns. English. an. Department of the Treasury / Pennsylvania Avenue, Fifteenth Street and Pennsylvania Avenue NW, Washington DC 20220. **Tel** (202)566-2969. **LC** HJ4653.C7; U54A. **DD** 336.2/07. ***Continues in part*** *Statistics of Income. Business Income Tax Returns, Sole Proprietorships, Partnerships.*

US
**STATISTICS OF INCOME. SUPPLEMENTAL REPORT. INTERNATIONAL INCOME AND TAXES. DOMESTIC INTERNATIONAL SALES CORPORATION RETURNS.** **Main/Corp** United States. Internal Revenue Service. **VFOAT** International Income and Taxes. Domestic International Sales Corporation Returns; Domestic International Sales Corporation Returns. English. Internal Revenue Service, 1111 Constitution Avenue NW, Washington DC 20224.

CN/0702-0988
**STATISTICS RELATING TO REGIONAL AND MUNICIPAL GOVERNMENTS IN BRITISH COLUMBIA.** [Stat. relat. reg. munic. gov. B.C.]. English. an. Free. Ministry of Municipal Affairs, Recreation and Culture, Parliament Building, Victoria British Columbia V8V 1X4 Canada. **Tel** (604)387-4063, FAX (604)356-1873. **LC** HJ9014.B7; D46A. **DD** 317.11. **Circ:** 1,600 (ctrl).

NE
**STATISTIEK DER GEMEENTEBEGROTINGEN / CENTRAAL BUREAU VOOR DE STATISTIEK, HOOFDAFDELING FINANCIELE STATISTIEKEN.** **Added/Corp** Netherlands. Centraal Bureau voor de Statistiek. Hoofdafdeling Financiele Statistieken. **VFOAT** Statistics of the Municipal Budgets. (1983)-. Dutch. an. 12.10. Staatsuitgeverij, Christoffel Plantijnstraat 1, 2515 TZ'S Gravenhage Netherlands. **Tel** 070/78-95-70. **LC** HJ9054; .A32. ***Continues*** *Statistiek der Gemeentefinancien Begrotingen.*

NE/0168-3837
**STATISTIEK DER PROVINCIALE FINANCIEN / CENTRAAL BUREAU VOOR DE STATISTIEK.** **VFOAT** Statistics of the Provincial Finances of the Netherlands; Statistics of Income and Expenditure Accounts of the Dutch Provinces. Dutch. be. Fl15.00. Centraal Bureau voor de Statistiek, AFD ALG Zaken, Postbus 959, 2270 AZ Voorburg Netherlands. **Tel** 011 31 70 3373800, FAX 011 31 038 7429, telex 32692 CBS NL. **LC** HJ54; .A17.

NE/0168-5163
**STATISTIEK VAN DE ELEKTRICITEITS--VOORZIENING IN NEDERLAND / CENTRAAL BUREAU VOOR DE STATISTIEK, HOOFDAFDELING STATISTIEKEN VAN INDUSTRIE EN BOUWNIJVERHEID.** **VFOAT** Statistics on Electricity-Supply in the Netherlands. Dutch. an. Fl12.45. Centraal Bureau voor de Statistiek, AFD ALG Zaken, Postbus 959, 2270 AZ Voorburg Netherlands. **Tel** 011 31 70 3373800, FAX 011 31 038 7429, telex 32692 CBS NL. **LC** HD9685.N2; A34.

IO/0126-4397
**STATISTIK KEUANGAN DESA JAWA DAN MADURA.** **VFOAT** Village Government Financial Statistics, Java and Madura. 1977/1978-. English (Indonesian). an. Rp6,000 Indonesia; $4.80 US. Central Bureau of Statistics / Indonesia, c/o Dr. Sutomo, 8 Jalan, PO Box 3, Jakarta Indonesia. **Tel** 372808 374908 Ext.342. **LC** HJ9575; .S7. **DD** 336/.014/598. ctrl circ. ***Continues in part*** *Statistik Keuangan Pemerintahan Desa.*

IO
**STATISTIK KEUANGAN DESA. SULAWESI-MALUKU-BALI-NUSATENGGARA.** **VFOAT** Village Government Financial Statistics. Sulawesi-Maluku-Bali and Nusatenggara. English (Indonesian). an. Rp6,000 Indonesia; $4.80 US. Central Bureau of Statistics / Indonesia, c/o Dr. Sutomo, 8 Jalan, PO Box 3, Jakarta Indonesia. **Tel** 372808 374908 Ext.342. **LC** HJ9575; .S82. **DD** 336/.014/598. ctrl circ. ***Continues in part*** *Statistik Keuangan Pemerintahan Desa.*

GR
**STATISTIKE EPETERIS DEMOSION OIKONOMIKON.** **VFOAT** Statistical Yearbook of Public Finance. Multiple languages (English and Greek, Modern). National Statistical Service of Greece, 14 Lycourgou Street, GR 10166 Athens Greece. **Tel** 3244-746, telex 216-734 ESYE GR. **LC** HJ50; .A7A. **DD** 336.495.

FR
**STATISTIQUES DE RECETTES PUBLIQUES DES PAYS MEMBRES DE L'OCDE: UNE CLASSIFICATION NORMALISEE.** **Main/Corp** Organisation for Economic Co-Operation and Development. **Added/Corp** Organisation for Economic Co-Operation and Development. Revenue Statistics of OECD Member Countries: a Standardized Classification. **VFOAT** Revenue Statistics of OECD Member Countries : A Standardized Classification. **VAT** Statistiques de Recettes Publiques des Pays Membres de l'Organisation de Cooperation et de Developpement Economiques. (1965)-. French (English). an (published in Nov.). $54.00. OECD Publications and Information Center, 2 rue Andre-Pascal, 75775 Paris Cedex 16 France. **Tel** 011 33 1 45248167, US:(202)785-6323, FAX 011 33 1 45248500 OR 45248176, telex 620 160 OCDE. **(Subscription address:** OECD Publications Center, 2001 L Street, Suite 700, Washington DC 20036.**)** **LC** HJ2279; .O75a. **DD** 336.2/009171/3.
**Desc:** Presents data on national, state, local and social security tax revenues, with analysis of tax levels and structures, comparative tables and detailed country tables.

FR
**STATISTIQUES DES COMPTES POUR L'EXERCICE ... DES COMMUNES, DES DEPARTEMENTS, DES REGIONS ET DES ETABLISSEMENTS PUBLICS LOCAUX.** **VFOAT** Communes, les Departements, les Regions, les Etablissements Publics Locaux. French. an. 93 rue de Rivoli, Paris 1Er France. **LC** HJ9779.F7; S76. **DD** 336/.014/44. ***Continues*** *Statistiques des Comptes des Communes, des Departements et de Leurs Etablissements Publics.*

CN/0705-579X
**STATISTIQUES FINANCIERES DU GOUVERNEMENT DU QUEBEC.** ***Title Change.*** [Stat. financ. Gouv. Que.]. **Main/Corp** Bureau de la Statistique du Quebec. Service des Finances, des Gouvernements et des Institutions a But Non Lucratif. Began with Vol. for (1976/77)-Vol. for (1981/82). French. an. Statistique Quebec, 117 rue Saint Andre, Quebec Quebec G1K 3Y3 Canada. **Tel** (514)283-2642. **LC** HJ13; .B87A. **DD** 354.7140072. ***Continues*** *Statistiques Financieres du Gouvernement du Quebec, 0705-579X.* ***Continued by*** *Statistiques Financieres de l'Administration Publique Provinciale.*

DK/0108-545X
**STATISTISKE EFTERRETNINGER. NATIONALREGNSKAB, OFFENTLIGE FINANSER, BETALINGSBALANCE.** **VFOAT** Nationalregnskab, Offentlige Finanser, Betalingsbalancer. Vol. 1 (1983)-. Monographic series.

Danish. Price varies per volume. Danmarks Statistik, Sejrgade 11, DK-2100 Copenhagen Denmark. **Tel** 011 45 3 9173917, FAX 011 45 31 18 48 01, telex 1 62 36. **LC** HJ56; .A197. ***Continues in part*** *Danmarks Statistik. Statistiske Efterretninger.*
**Desc:** Statistics on national accounts, public finance, local government budgets and accounts, personal taxation, advance assessment of incomes, real property taxation, taxes and duties, customs and excise duties, balance of payments and foreign debt.

US/0730-3440
**STATUS, PROGRESS, AND PROBLEMS IN FEDERAL AGENCY ACCOUNTING.** English. an. US General Accounting Office / District of Columbia, 441 G Street NW, Room 4528, Washington DC 20548. **Tel** (202)275-2812. **LC** HJ9801; .S73. **DD** 353.0072/31.

NO
**STRUKTURTALL FOR KOMMUNENES KONOMI.** **Main/Corp** Norway. Statistisk Sentralbyra. **VFOAT** Structural Data from the Municipal Accounts. Norwegian. **LC** HA1501 ; HJ9159 subser.

NR/0331-0434
**SUMMARY OF CURRENT INCOME TAX STATISTICS.** (A SUMMARY OF CURRENT INCOME TAX STATISTICS.). **Main/Corp** Western State, Nigeria. Ministry of Economic Planning and Reconstruction. Statistics Division. (19??)-. English. an. $3.00. Ministry of Economic Planning and Reconstruction, Statistics Division, Ibadan Nigeria. **Tel** 022-400262. **LC** HJ4794.N5; W48a. **DD** 336.2/42/09669. **Circ:** 500.

AT/1033-3665
**SUMMARY OF STATISTICS - AUSTRALIAN BUREAU OF STATISTICS. VICTORIAN OFFICE.** (SUMMARY OF STATISTICS.). [Summ. stat. - Aust. Bur. Stat. Vic. Off.]. **Added/Corp** Australian Bureau of Statistics. Victorian Office. **VFOAT** Summary of Statistics, Victoria. (1989)-. English. an. 9.00Aus$. Australian Bureau of Statistics, PO Box 10, Belconnen Australian Capital Territory, 2616 Australia. **Tel** 011 61 6 2527911, FAX 011 61 6 2516009. **DD** 319.4505. ***Continues*** *Victorian Pocket Year Book, 0067-1207.*
**Desc:** Compact tables covering most fields of statistics collected by the ABS relating to Victoria.

AT
**TAXATION REVENUE, AUSTRALIA.** **Main/Corp** Australian Bureau of Statistics. (1978)-. English. an. 16.30Aus$. Australian Bureau of Statistics, PO Box 10, Belconnen Australian Capital Territory, 2616 Australia. **Tel** 011 61 6 2527911, FAX 011 61 6 2516009. **LC** HJ90; .A33a. **DD** 336.2/00994. ***Continues*** *Australian Bureau of Statistics. Public Authority Finance, Taxation.*
**Desc:** Provides details of the revenue from taxation of Commonwealth, State and local authorities in Australia compiled in accordance with standards promulgated by the International Monetary Fund and the United Nations.

CN/0700-1665
**TAXATION STATISTICS (OTTAWA).** (TAXATION STATISTICS - CANADA.). **Main/Corp** Canada. Taxation. 1946-. Periodical. English (French). an. Price per Volume varies. Department of National Revenue Taxation, 875 Heron Road, Ottawa Ontario K1A 0L8 Canada. **LC** HJ4661; .A26. **DD** 336.2/00971. ***Absorbed*** *Statistique Fiscale, 0576-4092.* ***Continued in part by*** *Corporation Taxation Statistics, 0576-0119; Corporation Financial Statistics, 0575-8262.*

PP
**TAXATION STATISTICS (PORT MORESBY, PAPUA NEW GUINEA).** (TAXATION STATISTICS.). English. an. k2.00 (surface mail), k4.00 (airmail). National Statistical Office, PO Wards Strip NCO, Papua New Guinea. **Tel** 011 675 27182 271172, FAX 011 657 255057, telex FINANCE NE 22312. **LC** HJ4819.8; .A36. **DD** 336.24/0995/3021.

US/0300-6859
**URBAN AFFAIRS ABSTRACTS.** **Added/Corp** National League of Cities. United States Conference of Mayors. (August 1971)-. Abstracting/Indexing Service. English. mo. $250.00 (members), $300.00 (non-members) US; $350.00 other. Urban Research Institute, University of Louisville, Louisville KY 40292. **Tel** (502)588-6626, FAX (502)588-7386. **ED** Dennis K. Rosser. **LC** HT123; .U7. **DD** 301.36/0973. Index available. cum. index. **Circ:** 300. available on an online database.
**Desc:** Provides original abstracts and subject area access to substantive articles.

AT/0067-1223
**VICTORIAN YEAR-BOOK.** **Added/Corp** Australia. Commonwealth Bureau of Census and Statistics. Victorian Office. Australian Bureau of Statistics. Victorian Office. **VFOAT** Victorian Year Book. (1873)-. English. an (April). 31.00Aus$ (softcover); 37.70Aus$ (hardcover). Australian Bureau of Statistics, PO Box 10, Belconnen Australian Capital Territory, 2616 Australia. **Tel** 011 61 6 2527911, FAX 011 61 6 2516009. **NLM** W2 KA8.1 V6. **Bk Rev. Ad Acc. Circ:** 2,000.
**Desc:** Contains statistical information about Victoria's government, history, commerce, business etc.

US/0511-4187
**WEEKLY COMPILATION OF PRESIDENTIAL DOCUMENTS.** [Wkly. compil. pres. doc.]. **Added/Corp** United States. Office of the Federal Register. Vol. 1, No. 1 (Aug. 2, 1965)-. Government Publication. English. wk (With quarterly, semiannual, and annual indexes). $65.00 US; $81.25 other. Superintendent of Documents, US Government Printing Office, Washington DC 20402. **Tel** (202)275-3328, FAX (202)786-2377. **LC** J80; .A284. **DD** 353. **NLM** Z 1223.P7 W394. available on microfilm and microfiche from University Microfilms International (UMI). Documents available from UMI Article Clearinghouse.
**Desc:** Transcripts of the President's news conferences, messages to Congress, public speeches and statements, and other presidential materials released by the White House. Carries an index of contents and a cumulative index to prior issues. Separate indexes are published quarterly, semiannually and annually. Other finding aids include lists of laws approved by the President and of nominations submitted to the Senate, and a check-list of White House releases.
**Ind/Abst** Expand. Acad. Index (1992-); Middle East Abstr. Index (19??-); Newsp. Period. Abstr. (1992-); PAIS Int. Print (19??-).

---

## CIVIL SERVICE

---

US/0270-7578
**ACHIEVEMENTS (WASHINGTON).** (ACHIEVEMENTS : A REPORT ON THE FEDERAL INCENTIVE AWARDS PROGRAM.). **Added/Corp** United States. Office of Personnel Management. Incentive Awards Branch. United States. Office of Personnel Management. Incentive Awards Division. (1978)-. English. an. US Office of Personnel Management, 1900 E Street Northwest, Washington DC 20415. **Tel** (202)632-6256. **ED** Lewis Thatcher. **LC** JK768.3; .U52a. **DD** 353.006/05. **Circ:** 5,000 (ctrl). ***Continues*** *United States. Office of Personnel Management. Incentive Awards Branch. Progress Through Achievements, 0193-3361.*
**Desc:** Statistical summary of cash and honorary incentive awards granted to Federal employees.

US/0361-9036
**AFFIRMATIVE ACTION REPORT - TEXAS. EQUAL EMPLOYMENT OPPORTUNITY OFFICE.** **Main/Corp** Texas. Equal Employment Opportunity Office. 1973/74-. English. PO Box 12428, Capital Station TX 78711. **LC** JK4860.5.M5; T48A. **DD** 331.2.

US/1041-5335
**AFGE GOVERNMENT STANDARD.** [AFGE gov. stand.]. **Added/Corp** American Federation of Government Employees. **VFOAT** AFGE, The Government Standard; Standard; Government Standard. **VAT** American Federation of Government Employees Government Standard. (198?)-. Periodical. English. Twelve times a year (8 issues and 4 agendas). Free to Libraries; $3.50 others. American Federation of Government Employees, 80 F Street Northwest, Washington DC 20001. **Tel** (202)737-8700. **DD** 353. ***Continues*** *Government Standard, 0017-2669.*

US
**ANNUAL PROGRESS REPORT ... / GOVERNOR'S OFFICE OF INTERGOVERNMENTAL PERSONNEL (MISSISSIPPI).** **Main/Corp** Mississippi. Governor's Office of Intergovernmental Personnel. English. an. Office of Intergovernmental Personnel, Walter Sillers Building, Jackson MS 39201. **LC** JK4655; .M57A. **DD** 353.9762001.

US
**ANNUAL REPORT - MICHIGAN DEPARTMENT OF CIVIL SERVICE.** **Main/Corp** Michigan. Dept. of Civil Service. (1965)-. English. an. Department of Civil Service / Lansing, Lewis Class Building, 320 South Walnut Street, Box 30002, Lansing MI 48909. **LC** JK5855; .M54a. **DD** 353.9774006/05. ***Continues*** *Annual Report - State of Michigan, Civil Service Commission.*

SA
**ANNUAL REPORT OF THE GAZANKULU PUBLIC SERVICE COMMISSION, GAZANKULU GOVERNMENT.** **Main/Corp** Gazankulu (South Africa). Public Service Commission. English.

AT
**ANNUAL REPORT - PUBLIC SERVICE BOARD (AUSTRALIA).** ***Suspended.*** **Main/Corp** Australia. Public Service Board. Suspended. English. an. $2.84. Government Printing Office / Australia, PO Box 4050, Sydney NSW 2001 Australia. **LC** JQ4045; .A21. **DD** 354.94006/05. ***Continues*** *Report on the Public Service of the Commonwealth by the Public Service Board.*

AT/0312-5688
**ANNUAL REPORT - PUBLIC SERVICE BOARD (PERTH).** ***Title Change.*** (ANNUAL REPORT - PUBLIC SERVICE BOARD (WESTERN AUSTRALIA).). [Annu. rep. - Public Ser. Board (Perth)]. **Main/Corp** Western Australia. Public Service Board. (1941)-(19??). English. **LC** JQ5545; .A28a. **DD** 354/.941/006. ***Continued by*** *Annual Report.*

AT
**ANNUAL REPORT / PUBLIC SERVICE COMMISSION OF WESTERN AUSTRALIA.** **Main/Corp** Public Service Commission of Western Australia. (19??)-. English. **LC** JQ5545; .A28a. **DD** 354/.941/006. ***Continues*** *Western Australia Public Service Board. Annual Report - Public Service Board, 0312-5688.*

US
**ANNUAL REPORT - SECRETARY OF STATE, MERIT COMMISSION.** **Main/Corp** Illinois. Merit Commission. (19??)-. English. an. Secretary of State / Illinois, 490 Centennial Building, Springfield IL 62756. **LC** JK5755; .I42a. **DD** 353.9773006/06.

US
**ANNUAL REPORT TO CONGRESS ON THE FEDERAL EQUAL OPPORTUNITY RECRUITMENT PROGRAM.** ***Title Change.*** **Main/Corp** United States. Office of Personnel Management. **VFOAT** Annual Report to Congress on the Implementation of the Federal Equal Opportunity Recruitment Program. (198?)-(199?). English. US Office of Personnel Management / Office of Affirmative Employment Programs, 1900 E Street NW, Washington DC 20415. **LC** JK766.4; .U54a. **DD** 353.001/04. ***Continues*** *United States. Office of Personnel Management. Office of Affirmative Employment Programs.; Report to Congress, Annual Report on Implementation of the Federal Equal Opportunity Recruitment Program.* ***Continued by*** *United States. Office of Personnel Management. Federal Equal Opportunity Recruitment Program (FEORP), Report to Congress.*

US
**ANNUAL REPORT - VIRGINIA DEPARTMENT OF PERSONNEL AND TRAINING.** **Main/Corp** Virginia. Dept. of Personnel and Training. (1979)-. English. an. Office of Communications Department of Personnel and Training, 320 State Finance Building, Richmond VA 23219. **LC** JK3955; .V56a. **DD** 353.9755001/06.

US
**ASSOCIATION ADVOCATE / STATE OF NEVADA EMPLOYEES ASSOCIATION.** Vol. 21, No. 20 (Nov. 1, 1990)-. Periodical. English. SNEA, PO Box 1016, Carson City NV 89702. ***Continues*** *S.N.E.A. News.*

US/8756-7156
**BIENNIAL REPORT OF EMPLOYMENT BY GEOGRAPHIC AREA.** **Added/Corp** United States. Office of Personnel Management. Office of Workforce Information. (Dec. 31, 1982)-. English. be. US Office of Personnel Management / Personal Systems and Oversight Group, Office of Workforce Information, 1900 E Street NW/Room 7494, Washington DC 20415. **Tel** (202)632-5417. **(Subscription address:** National Technical Information Service, US Department of Commerce, 5285 Port Royal Road, Springfield, VA 22161) **ED** Christine E Steele. **LC** JK639; .B53. **DD** 353.006 S; 353.001. ctrl circ. ***Continues*** *Annual Report of Employment by Geographic Area, 0148-8597.*
**Desc:** Federal civilian employment distributions by state, county, metropolitan area, US territory, foreign country, agency, pay system category, work schedule for states, and citizenship for overseas.

US/0540-1887
**BIENNIAL REPORT - STATE OF MINNESOTA, DEPARTMENT OF CIVIL SERVICE.** **Main/Corp** Minnesota. Dept. of Civil Service. Periodical. English. be. 215 Administration Building, St Paul MN 55155. **LC** JK6155; .M53A. **DD** 354/.7127/001.

US
**BIENNIAL REPORT - STATE OF WISCONSIN, DEPARTMENT OF EMPLOYMENT RELATIONS.** **Main/Corp** Wisconsin. Dept. of Employment Relations. 1977/79-. English. be. Wisconsin Department of Employment Relations, 137 East Wilson Street, Madison WI 53702. **LC** JK6035; .W57A. **DD** 353.9775001/7/06.

# Public Administration —Civil Service

US
**BIENNIAL REPORT - STATE OF WISCONSIN, PERSONNEL COMMISSION.** Main/Corp Wisconsin. Personnel Commission. 1977/79-. English. be. Wisconsin Personnel Commission, 121 East Wilson Street, 2nd Floor, Madison WI 53702. LC KFW2835.15; .A863. DD 353.9775001/06.

BL
**BOLETIM DO SERVIDOR.** Main/Corp Minas Gerais (Brazil). Secretaria de Estado de Administracao. Bulletin. Portuguese. Secretaria de Estado de Administracao, rua da Bahia 1.148 - 4 Andar, Belo Horizonte Brazil. DD 354/.81/5001005.

IT/0300-4422
**BOLLETTINO DELLA DEPUTAZIONE DI STORIA PATRIA PER L'UMBRIA.** See Public Administration.

FR/0249-6046
**BULLETIN OFFICIEL DES SERVICES DU PREMIER MINISTRE.** Main/Corp France. Premier Ministre. (19??)-. Bulletin. French. ir. 180.00F. Direction des Journaux Officiels, 26 rue Desaix, 75727 Paris Cedex 15 France. Tel 011 33 1 40587500. LC KJV5030.A15; F73. DD 342.44/068; 344.40268.

NR
**BUREAUCRAT, THE.** Added/Corp Bendel State (Nigeria). Public Service. Mid-Western State (Nigeria). Public Service. Vol. 1 (Jan./Mar. 1973)-. Periodical. English. qt. $3.00 US, $4.00 Canada. Mr S E Okotie, Business Manager, The Bureaucrat, c/o Ministry of Finance, Accounting Division, Benin City Nigeria. LC JQ3092.Z1; B85. DD 354.669/3006/05.
Ind/Abst Bus. Index (1985-1992); Bus. Period. Index; Gen. BusinessFile (1985-1992).

US
**CALIFORNIA ROSTER OF FEDERAL STATE COUNTY & CITY OFFICIALS.** English (French). ir. $14.00. Secearatary of State, 1230 J Street, Suite 209, Sacramento CA 95814. Tel (916)445-3085.

CK/0120-193X
**CARTA ADMINISTRATIVA.** Added/Corp Colombia. Departamento Administrativo del Servicio Civil. (1968)-. Periodical. Spanish. bm. LC JL2845; .C37. DD 354.861001/05.

US/0009-7543
**CITIZEN (DENVER), THE.** (THE CITIZEN.). Added/Corp Colorado Association of Public Employees. (19??)-. Periodical. English. Twelve times a year. $12.00. Citizen / Denver, 1390 Logan Street, Denver CO 80203. Tel (303)832-1001. ED Phil Christie (editor's phone: (800)245-2273 or (303)832-1001). Ad Acc. Circ: 10,000 (ctrl).
Desc: Newspaper for state employees and officials pertaining to state employment issues in Colorado.
Ind/Abst Curr. Thoughts Trends.

US
**CITY EMPLOYMENT.** 1966-. Government Publication. English. an. US Department of Commerce / Bureau of the Census, Data User Services Division, Customer Services, Washington DC 20233-0800. Tel (301)763-4100. (Subscription address: Superintendent of Documents, US Government Printing Office, Washington DC 20402.)
Ind/Abst Predicasts Forecasts.

NR/0331-085X
**CIVIL SERVANT, THE.** V. 1- Dec. 1971-. Periodical. English. mo. 2/6. Nigeria Civil Service Union, Western State Branch, PO Box 1640, Ibadan Nigeria. LC JQ3092.Z1; C58. DD 331.88/11/3546690005.

US/0272-006X
**CIVIL SERVICE COURT DIGEST, THE.** [Civil serv. court dig.]. V. 1- Jan. 1980-. Periodical. English. mo. $20.00. The Civil Service Court Digest NY 10023. LC KF5390.A59; C58. DD 342.73/068/02643.

PH/0300-3620
**CIVIL SERVICE REPORTER (QUEZON CITY).** (CIVIL SERVICE REPORTER.). Main/Corp Philippines. Civil Service Commission. Began in 1956. Periodical. English. mo. Civil Service Commission / Phillipines, Finance Building, Rizal Park Manila Philippines. LC JQ1412; .P47A. DD 354/.599/006.

US/0731-4450
**DECISIONS OF THE UNITED STATES MERIT SYSTEMS PROTECTION BOARD.** Main/Corp United States. Merit Systems Protection Board. Vol. 1 (Jan. 11, 1979-Mar. 19, 1980)-. English. ir. Merit Systems Protection Board, 1120 Vermont Avenue NW, Washington DC 20419. Tel (202)653-7124. LC KF5336; .A615. DD 342.73/068/02646; 347.3026802646. cum. index.

US/0419-2699
**DIRECTORY OF GEORGIA MUNICIPAL OFFICIALS.** Added/Corp Georgia Municipal Association. (19??)-. Directory. English. $15.00. Georgia Municipal Association, 201 Pryor Street Southwest, Atlanta GA 30303. Tel (404)688-0472. LC JS303.G4; D57. DD 352/.005/209758.

US/0415-9659
**DIRECTORY OF MARYLAND MUNICIPAL OFFICIALS.** Added/Corp Maryland Municipal League. (1952)-. Directory. English. Maryland Municipal League, 1212 West St., % Sharon P. Easton, Annapolis MD 21401. Tel (800)492-7121, FAX (410)268-7004. LC JS451.M33; D5. DD 352/.005/209752.

US/1058-0859
**EMPLOYMENT AND TRENDS AS OF ... .** VFOAT Employment and Trends. (May 1986)-. Periodical. English. bm. $15.95, $6.95 (microfiche). US Office of Personnel Management / Personnel Systems and Oversight Group, Personnel Systems and Oversight Group, Office of Workforce Information, 1900 E Street NW, Washington DC 20415. Tel (202)632-4917. (Subscription address: Superintendent of Documents, US Government Printing Office, Washington, DC 20402) ED Anne Yu Ni. LC JK671; .E47. available on microfiche. Continues Monthly Release.
Desc: Federal civilian employment, payroll and turnover distributions by agency, tenure, pay system category, work schedule, major geographic area, competitive/excepted SES service, employment ceiling and turnover category.

US/0362-5788
**EMPLOYMENT OF DISABLED AND VIETNAM ERA VETERANS IN THE FEDERAL GOVERNMENT.** Main/Corp United States. Civil Service Commission. Jan./June 1975-. Periodical. English. sa. $1.60. Civil Service Commission / US, 1900 East Street/Room 5-F10, Washington DC 20415. Tel (202)632-5532. LC UB357; .U48A. DD 353.001/3243.

US/0363-9371
**FED LETTER, THE.** Began in 1975. Periodical. English. sm. $24.00. L A Holley, Box 188, Bainbridge Island WA 98110. LC KF5336.A15; F15. DD 342/.73/085.

US/0279-2230
**FEDERAL CAREER OPPORTUNITIES.** [Fed. career oppor.]. Added/Corp Federal Research Service. Vol. 7, No. 20 (Sept. 24/Oct. 7, 1980)-. Periodical. English. bw (26 issues). $175.00. Federal Research Service Inc, PO Box 1059, 243 Church Street Northwest, Vienna VA 22183. Tel (703)281-0200. ED J. A. Mcardle. Continues Civil Service Career Opportunities.
Desc: Provides specialized information for potential & current federal employees. Each issue offers informative articles related to Federal employment and current vacancies in all professional and technical fields nation-wide and overseas.

US/0014-9071
**FEDERAL EMPLOYEE, THE.** [Fed. empl.]. Added/Corp National Federation of Federal Employees. Vol. 1 (July 1916)-. Periodical. English. mo (10 issues per year). $15.00. National Federation of Federal Employees, 1016 16th Street NW, Washington DC 20036. Tel (202)862-4400. ED James M Pierce Jr. LC HD8008.A1; F4. DD 331.7/61/353. Circ: 62,000.
Desc: News of interest to federal employees, including legislative affairs and union activities.

US/0071-4127
**FEDERAL EMPLOYEES ALMANAC.** [Fed. empl. alm.]. (1954)-. English. an. $7.95. Federal Employees News Digest, PO Box 98122, Washington DC 20090. Tel (703)648-9551, (800)544-0155. ED Joseph Young and Don Mace. LC JK671; .F385. DD 353.001. Bk Rev. Circ: 160,000 (ctrl).
Desc: Contains benefits and job rights of federal and postal employees and retirees, plus listings of government unions and professional organizations, key committees of Congress, etc.

US/1065-0970
**FEDERAL EMPLOYEES NEWS DIGEST.** [Fed. empl. news dig.]. VFOAT News Digest. Vol. 41, No. 12 (Oct. 21, 1991)-. Periodical. English. wk. $49.00. Federal Employees News Digest, PO Box 98122, Washington DC 20090. Tel (703)648-9551, (800)544-0155. LC HD8008.A1; F43. DD 385/.0973. Continues Weekly Federal Employees' News Digest, 0430-1692.

●US/1066-8764
**FEDERAL EQUAL OPPORTUNITY ... DESK BOOK.** [Fed. equal oppor. desk book]. Added/Corp LRP Publications. VFOAT Equal Opportunity Desk Book. (1992)-. Periodical. English. an. $59.00. LRP Publications, 747 Dresher Road, PO Box 980, Horsham PA 19044-0980. Tel (800)341-7874, (215)784-0860, FAX (215)784-9639, (215)784-0870. DD 344.
Desc: Compiles the previous year's significant decisions of the US Equal Employment Opportunity Commission (EEOC) and federal courts on matters of workplace discrimination in the federal government.

US
**FEDERAL EQUAL OPPORTUNITY RECRUITMENT PROGRAM (FEORP), REPORT TO CONGRESS.** Main/Corp United States. Office of Personnel Management. VFOAT Annual Report to Congress on the Implementation of the Federal Equal Opportunity Recruitment Program (FEORP). (199?)-. English. US Office of Personnel Management / Office of Affirmative Employment Programs, 1900 E Street NW, Washington DC 20415. LC JK766.4; .U54a. DD 353.001/04. Continues United States. Office of Personnel Management. Annual Report to Congress on the Federal Equal Opportunity Recruitment Program.

US
**FEDERAL HOSPITAL PHONE BOOK.** See Medical Science and Technology-Physicians and Medical Personnel.

US/0746-035X
**FEDERAL MERIT SYSTEMS REPORTER.** [Fed. merit syst. report.]. VFOAT FMSR. (1979)-. Periodical. English. wk (50 issues). $785.00. LRP Publications, 747 Dresher Road, PO Box 980, Horsham PA 19044-0980. Tel (800)341-7874, (215)784-0860, FAX (215)784-9639, (215)784-0870. (Subscription address: LRP Publications, PO Box 980, Horsham PA 19044.) LC KF5336; .A614. DD 344.73/01; 347.3041. Bk Rev. Ad Acc.
Desc: Full-text reporter of MSPB and court decisions. Includes abstracts, full-text, many access points, cite tracker, statute tracker, citator, articles, and parallel database.

US/0888-269X
**FEDERAL PAY AND BENEFITS REPORTER.** [Fed. pay benefits report.]. Added/Corp Labor Relations Press. VFOAT FPBR. (198?)-. Periodical. English. mo. $550.00. LRP Publications, 747 Dresher Road, PO Box 980, Horsham PA 19044-0980. Tel (800)341-7874, (215)784-0860, FAX (215)784-9639, (215)784-0870. (Subscription address: LRP Publications, PO Box 980, Horsham PA 19044.) LC KF5370; .A554. DD 342.73/0686; 347.302686.
Desc: A full-text subscription service reporting all decisions rendered under the General Accounting Office's authority to review legal entitlements of federal employees (travel, leave, relocation and compensation). All cases indexed, headnoted and summarized. Includes analysis of issues and developments.

US/0163-7665
**FEDERAL PERSONNEL GUIDE.** [Fed. pers. guide]. (1979)-. English. an. $9.95. Key Communications, PO Box 42578, Washington DC 20015. Tel (301)656-0450, (301)656-2923, FAX (301)656-4554. ED Kenneth D. Whitehead. LC JK671; .F43. DD 353.006/02/02. [CCC]. Ad Acc. Circ: 50,000.
Desc: The most complete reference book on pay, benefits, employment, retirement, health care, insurance, policies, and many more subjects of vital importance and interest to all federal employees.

US
**FEDERAL PERSONNEL INDEX.** English. an. $97.00 (postage included). LRP Publications, 747 Dresher Road, PO Box 980, Horsham PA 19044-0980. Tel (800)341-7874, (215)784-0860, FAX (215)784-9639, (215)784-0870.
Desc: Comprehensive index providing effective cross-referencing to the many subjects found in the Federal Personnel Manual, including grade and pay retention, position classification, and personnel policies, procedures, and standards.

US
**FEDERAL PERSONNEL MANUAL.** Periodical. English. US Civil Service Commission, 1900 E Street Northwest, Room 5354, Washington DC 20415. Tel (202)632-5532.

US
**FEDERAL PERSONNEL MANUAL SYSTEM. FPM SUPPLEMENT 271-1. DEVELOPMENT OF QUALIFICATION STANDARDS.** VFOAT Development of Qualification Standards. Periodical. English. US Civil Service Commission, 1900 E Street Northwest, Room 5354, Washington DC 20415. Tel (202)632-5532.

US
**FEDERAL PERSONNEL MANUAL SYSTEM. FPM SUPPLEMENT 271-2. TESTS AND OTHER APPLICANT APPRAISAL PROCEDURES.** VFOAT Tests and Other Applicant Appraisal Procedures. Periodical. English. US Civil Service Commission, 1900 E Street Northwest, Room 5354, Washington DC 20415. Tel (202)632-5532.

# Public Administration — Civil Service

**US**
**FEDERAL PERSONNEL MANUAL SYSTEM. FPM SUPPLEMENT 293-31. BASIC PERSONNEL RECORDS AND FILES SYSTEM.** VFOAT Basic Personnel Records and Files System. Periodical. English. ir. $65.00 US; $81.25 other. US Civil Service Commission, 1900 E Street Northwest, Room 5354, Washington DC 20415. **Tel** (202)632-5532.

**US**
**FEDERAL PERSONNEL MANUAL SYSTEM. FPM SUPPLEMENT 305-1. EMPLOYMENT UNDER THE EXECUTIVE ASSIGNMENT SYSTEM.** VFOAT Employment Under the Executive Assignment System. Periodical. English. US Civil Service Commission, 1900 E Street Northwest, Room 5354, Washington DC 20415. **Tel** (202)632-5532.

**US**
**FEDERAL PERSONNEL MANUAL SYSTEM. FPM SUPPLEMENT 330-1. EXAMINING PRACTICES.** VFOAT Examining Practices. Periodical. English. US Civil Service Commission, 1900 E Street Northwest, Room 5354, Washington DC 20415. **Tel** (202)632-5532.

**US**
**FEDERAL PERSONNEL MANUAL SYSTEM. FPM SUPPLEMENT 339-31. REVIEWING AND ACTING ON MEDICAL INFORMATION.** VFOAT Reviewing and Acting on Medical Information. Periodical. English. US Civil Service Commission, 1900 E Street Northwest, Room 5354, Washington DC 20415. **Tel** (202)632-5532.

**US**
**FEDERAL PERSONNEL MANUAL SYSTEM. FPM SUPPLEMENT 512-1. JOB GRADING SYSTEM FOR TRADES AND LABOR OCCUPATIONS.** Added/Corp United States. Civil Service Commission. VFOAT Job Grading System for Trades and Labor Occupations. (19??)-. Government Publication. English. ir (3 parts). $69.00 US; $86.25 other. Superintendent of Documents, US Government Printing Office, Washington DC 20402. **Tel** (202)275-3328, FAX (202)786-2377.
**Desc:** Contains basic information relating to the subscription service, a description of the Individual Job Standards, and occupational definitions.

**US**
**FEDERAL PERSONNEL MANUAL SYSTEM. FPM SUPPLEMENT 532-1. FEDERAL WAGE SYSTEM.** Added/Corp United States. Civil Service Commission. VFOAT Federal Wage System. (19??)-. Government Publication. English. ir. $94.00 domestic; $117.50 other. Superintendent of Documents, US Government Printing Office, Washington DC 20402. **Tel** (202)275-3328, FAX (202)786-2377.

**US**
**FEDERAL PERSONNEL MANUAL SYSTEM. FPM SUPPLEMENT 532-2. FEDERAL WAGE SYSTEM, NON-APPROPRIATED EMPLOYEES.** VFOAT Federal Wage System, Non-Appropriated Employees. Periodical. English. ir. $91.00 US; $113.75 other. US Civil Service Commission, 1900 E Street Northwest, Room 5354, Washington DC 20415. **Tel** (202)632-5532.

**US**
**FEDERAL PERSONNEL MANUAL SYSTEM. FPM SUPPLEMENT 711-1. LABOR-MANAGEMENT RELATIONS PROGRAMS PROVISIONS AND TECHNICAL GUIDE.** VFOAT Labor-Management Relations Programs Provisions and Technical Guide. English. US Civil Service Commission, 1900 E Street Northwest, Room 5354, Washington DC 20415. **Tel** (202)632-5532.

**US**
**FEDERAL PERSONNEL MANUAL SYSTEM. FPM SUPPLEMENT 711-2. LABOR-MANAGEMENT CASE FINDER.** VFOAT Labor-Management Case Finder. Periodical. English. US Civil Service Commission, 1900 E Street Northwest, Room 5354, Washington DC 20415. **Tel** (202)632-5532.

**US**
**FEDERAL PERSONNEL MANUAL SYSTEM. FPM SUPPLEMENT 731-1. DETERMINING SUITABILITY FOR FEDERAL EMPLOYMENT.** VFOAT Determining Suitability for Federal Employment. Periodical. English. US Civil Service Commission, 1900 E Street Northwest, Room 5354, Washington DC 20415. **Tel** (202)632-5532.

**US**
**FEDERAL PERSONNEL MANUAL SYSTEM. FPM SUPPLEMENT 752-1. ADVERSE ACTIONS BY AGENCIES.** Added/Corp United States. Civil Service Commission. VFOAT Adverse Actions by Agencies. (19??)-. Periodical. English. US Civil Service Commission, 1900 E Street Northwest, Room 5354, Washington DC 20415. **Tel** (202)632-5532.

**US**
**FEDERAL PERSONNEL MANUAL SYSTEM. FPM SUPPLEMENT 792-1. OCCUPATIONAL HEALTH SERVICES FOR FEDERAL CIVILIAN EMPLOYEES.** VFOAT Occupational Health Services for Federal Civilian Employees. Periodical. English. US Civil Service Commission, 1900 E Street Northwest, Room 5354, Washington DC 20415. **Tel** (202)632-5532.

**US**
**FEDERAL PERSONNEL MANUAL SYSTEM. FPM SUPPLEMENT 831-1. RETIREMENT.** VFOAT Retirement. Periodical. English. US Civil Service Commission, 1900 E Street Northwest, Room 5354, Washington DC 20415. **Tel** (202)632-5532.

**US**
**FEDERAL PERSONNEL MANUAL SYSTEM. FPM SUPPLEMENT 870-1. LIFE INSURANCE.** Added/Corp United States. Civil Service Commission. VFOAT Life Insurance. (19??)-. Government Publication. English. ir. $209.00 US; $261.25 other. Superintendent of Documents, US Government Printing Office, Washington DC 20402. **Tel** (202)275-3328, FAX (202)786-2377.

**US**
**FEDERAL PERSONNEL MANUAL SYSTEM. FPM SUPPLEMENT 890-1. FEDERAL EMPLOYEES HEALTH BENEFITS.** Added/Corp United States. Civil Service Commission. VFOAT Federal Employees Health Benefits. (19??)-. Government Publication. English. ir. $296.00 US; $370.00 other. Superintendent of Documents, US Government Printing Office, Washington DC 20402. **Tel** (202)275-3328, FAX (202)786-2377.

**US**
**FEDERAL PERSONNEL MANUAL SYSTEM. FPM SUPPLEMENT 910-1. NATIONAL EMERGENCY READINESS OF FEDERAL PERSONNEL MANAGEMENT.** VFOAT National Emergency Readiness of Federal Personnel Management. Periodical. English. US Civil Service Commission, 1900 E Street Northwest, Room 5354, Washington DC 20415. **Tel** (202)632-5532.

**US**
**FEDERAL PERSONNEL MANUAL SYSTEM. FPM SUPPLEMENT 990-1. CIVIL SERVICE LAWS, EXECUTIVE ORDERS, RULES AND REGULATIONS.** Added/Corp United States. Civil Service Commission. VFOAT Civil Service Laws, Executive Orders, Rules and Regulations. (19??)-. Government Publication. English. ir. Superintendent of Documents, US Government Printing Office, Washington DC 20402. **Tel** (202)275-3328, FAX (202)786-2377.

**US**
**FEDERAL PERSONNEL MANUAL SYSTEM. FPM SUPPLEMENT 990-2. HOURS OF DUTY, PAY, AND LEAVE, ANNOTATED.** Added/Corp United States. Civil Service Commission. VFOAT Hours of Duty, Pay, and Leave, Annotated. (19??)-. Government Publication. English. ir. $89.00 US; $111.25 other. Superintendent of Documents, US Government Printing Office, Washington DC 20402. **Tel** (202)275-3328, FAX (202)786-2377.

**US**
**FEDERAL PERSONNEL MANUAL SYSTEM. FPM SUPPLEMENT 990-3. NATIONAL EMERGENCY STANDBY REGULATIONS (PERSONNEL AND MANPOWER).** (FEDERAL PERSONNEL MANUAL SYSTEM. FPM SUPPLEMENT 990-3. NATIONAL EMERGENCY STANDBY REGULATIONS (PERSONNEL AND EMERGENCY STANDBY REGULATIONS (PERSONNEL AND MANPOWER)).). VFOAT National Emergency Standby Regulations (Personnel and Manpower). Periodical. English. US Civil Service Commission, 1900 E Street Northwest, Room 5354, Washington DC 20415. **Tel** (202)632-5532.

US/1053-4652
**FEDERAL STAFFING DIGEST.** (FEDERAL STAFFING DIGEST / U.S. OFFICE OF PERSONNEL MANAGEMENT.). [Fed. staff. dig.]. Added/Corp United States. Office of Personnel Management. Career Entry & Employee Development Group. VFOAT Staffing Digest. (1989)-. Government Publication. English. qt. $8.50 domestic; $10.65 other. Superintendent of Documents, US Government Printing Office, Washington DC 20402. **Tel** (202)275-3328, FAX (202)786-2377. **DD** 353.
*Continues Recruiting Highlights.*
**Desc:** Describes current activities and programs in the area of recruiting, college recruiting, and affirmative employment.

US/0014-9233
**FEDERAL TIMES.** Added/Corp Army Times Publishing Company. (1965)-. Periodical. English. wk. $48.00 (one year), $88.00 (two years). Army Times Publishing Company, 6883 Commercial Drive, Springfield VA 22159. **Tel** (800)368-5718, (703)750-8099. **ED** Marianne Lester. **LC** UNC. **[CCC]**. **Bk Rev**. **Ad Acc**. **Pr Rev. Circ:** 30,000 (ctrl). available on microfilm and microfiche from University Microfilms International (UMI).
**Desc:** An independent weekly career journal for federal employees.

●**US**
**FEHB GUIDE. OPEN SEASON FOR FEDERAL CIVILIAN EMPLOYEES / FEDERAL EMPLOYEES HEALTH BENEFITS PROGRAM.** See Insurance.

●**US**
**FEHB GUIDE. OPEN SEASON FOR FEDERAL CIVILIAN EMPLOYEES / FEDERAL EMPLOYEES HEALTH BENEFITS PROGRAM (LARGE PRINT EDITION).** See Insurance.

●**US**
**FEHB GUIDE. OPEN SEASON FOR FEDERAL CIVILIAN EMPLOYEES IN POSITIONS OUTSIDE THE CONTINENTAL UNITED STATES / FEDERAL EMPLOYEES HEALTH BENEFITS PROGRAM.** See Insurance.

●**US**
**FEHB GUIDE. OPEN SEASON FOR INDIVIDUALS ELIGIBLE TO ENROLL FOR TEMPORARY CONTINUATION OF COVERAGE, COVERAGE UNDER THE SPOUSE EQUITY LAW OR SIMILAR STATUTES PROVIDING COVERAGE TO FORMER SPOUSES / FEDERAL EMPLOYEES HEALTH BENEFITS PROGRAM.** See Insurance.

●**US**
**FEHB GUIDE. OPEN SEASON FOR INDIVIDUALS RECEIVING COMPENSATION FROM THE OFFICE OF WORKERS' COMPENSATION PROGRAMS (OWCP).** See Insurance.

●**US**
**FEHB GUIDE. OPEN SEASON FOR RETIREMENT SYSTEMS PARTICIPATING IN THE FEDERAL EMPLOYEES HEALTH BENEFITS PROGRAM.** See Insurance.

●**US**
**FEHB GUIDE. OPEN SEASON FOR UNITED STATES POSTAL SERVICE EMPLOYEES / FEDERAL EMPLOYEES HEALTH BENEFITS PROGRAM.** See Insurance.

US/1061-9674
**FROM THE STATE CAPITALS. EMPLOYEE POLICY FOR THE PRIVATE & PUBLIC SECTORS.** [From state cap., Empl. policy priv. public sect.]. VFOAT Employee Policy for the Private & Public Sectors; Employee Policy. Vol. 45, No. 19 (Oct. 7, 1991)-. Periodical. English. wk. $211.50 (one year), $378.00 (two year) public and institutional libraries; $235.00 (one year), $420.00 (two year) other. Wakeman Walworth Inc., 300 North Washington Street #204, Alexandria VA 22314. **Tel** (703)549-8606. **DD** 351.
*Formed by the union of* From the State Capitals. Public Employee Policy, 0741-3521 *and* From the State Capitals. Labor Relations, 0734-1105.

US/0017-260X
**GOVERNMENT EMPLOYEE RELATIONS REPORT.** **Added/Corp** Bureau of National Affairs (Washington, D.C.). Vol. 1, No. 1 (Sept. 16, 1983)-. Periodical. English. wk. $832.00 (includes supplements). Bureau of National Affairs Inc., 9435 Key West Avenue, Rockville MD 20850. **Tel** (800)372-1033, (301)258-1033, FAX (301)948-5823. **(Subscription address:** 9435 Key West Avenue, Rockville MD 20850; telephone: FAX (301)948-5823**)** **ED** Anthony A Harris. **LC** HD8008.A1; B8. **DD** 353.001/7/05. **[CCC].**
**Desc:** A notification service that covers federal, state and municipal government employee relations.

US/0148-7949
**GOVERNMENT MANAGER, THE.** ***Ceased.*** [Gov. manager]. **Added/Corp** Bureau of National Affairs (Washington, D.C.). No. 1 (Jan. 5, 1973)-No. 548 (Dec. 1993). Periodical. English. bw. Bureau of National Affairs Inc., 9435 Key West Avenue, Rockville MD 20850. **Tel** (800)372-1033, (301)258-1033, FAX (301)948-5823. **(Subscription address:** 9435 Key West Avenue, Rockville MD 20850; telephone: FAX (301)948-8523**)** **ED** Anthony A Harris. **[CCC].**
**Desc:** Covers developments in public sector human resource management.

US/0097-868X
**GOVERNMENTAL FINANCES AND EMPLOYMENT AT A GLANCE.** **See** Public Administration-Public Finance and Taxation.

US/0095-6171
**GRANT AWARDS - UNITED STATES CIVIL SERVICE COMMISSION, BUREAU OF INTERGOVERNMENTAL PERSONNEL PROGRAMS.** **Main/Corp** United States. Civil Service Commission. Bureau of Intergovernmental Personnel Programs. English. US Civil Service Commission Bureau of Intergovernmental Personnel Programs, 1900 E Street NW, Washington DC 20415. **LC** HJ275; .U525A. **DD** 336.1/85.

US/0360-5019
**INTERAGENCY TRAINING CATALOG OF COURSES.** **Main/Corp** United States. Office of Personnel Management. 1979-81-. Catalog. English. be. $2.50. Office of Personnel Management, 1900 East Street Northwest, OELR Room 7429, Washington DC 20415. **Tel** (202)632-6256. **ED** Ernestine Blakcuore. **LC** JK639; JK718. **DD** 658/.07/15. ctrl circ. ***Continues*** *Interagency Training Catalog of Courses, 0360-5019.*
**Desc:** A listing of in-service training courses available from the US Office of Personnel Management.

US
**INTERAGENCY TRAINING PROGRAMS CATALOG.** **Main/Corp** United States Civil Service Commission. Bureau of Training. **VFOAT** Catalog of Interagency Training Programs. (1971/72)-. Catalog. English. an. $1.50. US Civil Service Commission Bureau of Training, General Management Training Center, 1900 E Street NW, Washington DC 20415. **LC** JK718; .A33. **DD** 353/.001/505. ***Continues*** *Interagency Training Programs.*

AU
**JAHRBUCH ... DER GEWERKSCHAFT OFFENTLICHER DIENST.** German. an. Gewerkschaft Offentlicher Dienst, Teinfaltstrasse 7, 1010 Wien 1 Germany. **LC** HD8013.A9; G4. **DD** 354.436002/05. ***Continues*** *Jahrbuch (Gewerkschaft der Offentlich Bediensteten).*

US
**JOB PATTERNS FOR MINORITIES AND WOMEN IN STATE AND LOCAL GOVERNMENT / U.S. EQUAL EMPLOYMENT OPPORTUNITY COMMISSION.** **Added/Corp** United States. Equal Employment Opportunity Commission. (198?)-. English. US Equal Employment Opportunity Commission, 2401 E Street NW, Washington DC 20506. **Tel** (202)634-6930. **LC** JK2480.M5; M56. **DD** 353.9/3104/021. ***Continues*** *Minorities and Women in State and Local Government (Washington, D.C. : 1985).*

UK
**JOURNAL OF H.M. CUSTOMS AND EXCISE, THE.** **Main/Corp** Customs and Excise Federation. Began publication in 1910. Periodical. English. sm. **LC** HD8013.G7. **DD** 351.1.

UK/0957-8978
**JOURNAL : PAPER OF THE NATIONAL UNION OF CIVIL AND PUBLIC SERVANTS.** **Added/Corp** National Union of Civil and Public Servants. (19??)-. Periodical. English. Twelve times a year (Jan.). £15.00 UK; £25.00 other. National Union of Civil Public Servants, 5 13 Great Suffolk Street, London SE1 0NS England. **Tel** 011 44 71 9603036, FAX 071 620 2707. **ED** Nick Wright. **LC** HD8005.2.G7; J68a. **DD** 331.88/0941/05. **Ad Acc, Adv Mgr:** G. Ellis, **Tel** 071 928 9671. **Circ:** 132,000 (ctrl). ***Continues*** *Opinion.*

JA
**KIKAN JINJI GYOSEI.** **Added/Corp** Nihon Jinji Gyosei Kenkyujo. **VFOAT** Jinji Gyosei. No. 1 (1976)-. Periodical. Japanese. ¥800. Gakuyo Shobo, 7-5 Fujimi 1 Chiyoda-ku, Tokyo 102 Japan. **LC** JQ1601; .K5.

KO
**KOSI WOLBO.** **Added/Corp** Taemyong Kosi Yonguhoe (Korea). (19??)-. Periodical. Korean. mo. Taemyong Kosi Yonguhoe, 6 Chongjin-dong Chongno-ku, Seoul Korea. **LC** JQ1726.Z13; E8762.

KO
**KUKKA KOSI.** (19??)-. Periodical. Korean. mo. Popchisa, 10-26 Jongam-dong, Seongbuk-ku, Seoul South Korea. **LC** JQ1726.Z13; E8763.

MY
**LAPURAN TAHUNAN - SURUHANJAYA PERKHIDMATAN AWAM NEGERI SABAH.** **Main/Corp** Sabah. Suruhanjaya Perkhidmatan Awam Negeri. 1972-. Malay. ***Continues*** *Annual Report of the Sabah State Public Service Commission, 0304-7938.*

US/0732-4537
**LEGAL NEWSLETTER (SPRINGFIELD, ILL.).** (LEGAL NEWSLETTER / DEPARTMENT OF PERSONNEL.). **Added/Corp** Illinois. Dept. of Personnel. (June 1980)-. Newsletter. English. mo. Illinois Department of Personnel, 501 Stratton Building, Springfield IL 62506. **LC** KFI1635; .A84. **DD** 342.773/068; 347.730268.

UK/0263-4678
**MANAGEMENT IN GOVERNMENT (LONDON, ENGLAND).** (MANAGEMENT IN GOVERNMENT.). [Manage. gov.]. V. 37, No. 1 (Feb. 1982)-. Periodical. English. qt. £7.72. Her Majesty's Stationery Office, 51 Nine Elms Lane, London SW8 5DR England. **Tel** 011 44 71 873 8459, 011 44 71 873 8499, FAX 011 44 71 873 8499, 011 44 71 873 8456, telex 297138. **(Subscription address:** PO Box 276, Public Centre, London SW8 5DT England**)** **LC** JA8; .O15. **DD** 350/.0005. **CODEN** MAGOD5. available on microfilm and microfiche from University Microfilms International (UMI). Documents available from Ask*IEEE. ***Continues*** *Management Services in Government, 0307-8558.*
**Ind/Abst** INSPEC (Feb. 1982-); World Text. Abstr.

JA
**NINMEN KANKEI HOREISHU / HENSHU NIHON JINJI GYOSEI KENKYUJO.** **Main/Corp** Japan. Japanese. Okurasho Insatukyoku, 2-4, Toranomon 2 chome, Minatoku, Tokyoto 105 Japan. **LC** LAW.

UK
**OPINION.** ***Title Change.*** **Added/Corp** Society of Civil Servants. Vol. 52, No. 616 (March 1975)-(19??). English. mo. National Union of Civil Public Servants, 5 13 Great Suffolk Street, London SE1 0NS England. **Tel** 011 44 71 9603036, FAX 071 620 2707. **LC** HD8013.G7; C5. **DD** 354/.41/006062. ***Continues*** *Civil Service Opinion.* ***Continued by*** *Journal : Paper of the National Union of Civil and Public Servants, 0957-8978.*

US/0197-6885
**PAMPHLET - OFFICE OF PERSONNEL MANAGEMENT.** (PAMPHLET.). **VFOAT** SM. (1979)-. Monographic series. English. Price varies per volume. Office of Personnel Management, 1900 East Street Northwest, OELR Room 7429, Washington DC 20415. **Tel** (202)632-6256. **LC** JK639; .A42. **DD** 353.006. ***Continues*** *Pamphlet (United States Civil Service Commission).*

US/1046-2082
**PED FORUM.** (PED FORUM : THE QUARTERLY NEWSLETTER OF THE AFL-CIO PUBLIC EMPLOYEE DEPARTMENT.). [PED forum]. **Added/Corp** AFL-CIO. Public Employee Dept. **VAT** Public Employee Department Forum. Vol. 1 No. 1 (Summer 1985)-. Newsletter. English. qt. $2.00. Public Employee Department AFL-CIO, 815 16th Street NW/Room 308, Washington DC 20006. **Tel** (202)393-2820. **ED** Laura Ginsburg. **DD** 331. **Bk Rev. Circ:** 3,500. ***Continues*** *In Public Service, 0161-9330.*

US
**PERSI COMPONENT UNIT FINANCIAL REPORT FOR THE FISCAL YEAR ENDED ... .** **Main/Corp** Idaho. Public Employee Retirement Board. **VFOAT** Component Unit Financial Report for the Fiscal Year Ended ... . **VAT** Public Employee Retirement System of Idaho Component Unit Financial Report for the Fiscal Year Ended ... . (June 30, 1991)-. English. ***Continues*** *Annual Report of the Public Employee Retirement System of Idaho.*

GW/0175-9299
**PERSONALRAT, DER.** (19??)-. Periodical. German. mo. DM114.00 Germany; DM126.00 other. Bund Verlag GmbH, Postfach 900840, D 51118 Cologne Germany. **Tel** 011 49 2203 934758. **LC** KK5932.A13; P47.

US/0031-5753
**PERSONNEL LITERATURE.** [Pers. lit.]. **Added/Corp** United States. Office of Personnel Management. Library. United States Civil Service Commission. Library. Vol. 1 (1941)-. Government Publication. English. mo (annual index). $22.00 domestic; $27.50 other. Superintendent of Documents, US Government Printing Office, Washington DC 20402. **Tel** (202)275-3328, FAX (202)786-2377. **LC** Z7164.C81; U45683; HF5549.A2. **DD** 016.3501. **NLM** Z 7164.C81 P467. Index available in last issue of volume--attached. available on microfilm and microfiche from University Microfilms International (UMI).
**Desc:** Includes selected books, pamphlets, and other publications received in the Library of the Office of Personnel Management during the previous month. Periodical articles, unpublished dissertations, and microfilms are also listed.

US/0498-935X
**PERSONNEL MANAGEMENT SERIES (WASHINGTON).** (PERSONNEL MANAGEMENT SERIES.). No. 1- 1951-. Monographic series. English. Price varies per volume. United States Civil Service Commission, 1900 East Street NW, Washington DC 20415. **LC** JK765. **DD** 351.

US
**PERSONNEL MANAGEMENT TRAINING CENTER COURSE CATALOGUE.** **Main/Corp** United States. Civil Service Commission. Personnel Management Training Center. English. US Civil Service Commission Bureau of Training, General Management Training Center, 1900 E Street NW, Washington DC 20415.

US
**PERSONNEL NEWS.** **Main/Corp** Chicago (Ill.). Dept. of Personnel. Vol. 1, No. 1 (Aug. 1981)-. English. Twelve times a year. $55.00 one year; $92.00 two year. Personnel News, 4701 Patrick Henry Drive, Suite 1301, Santa Clara CA 95054. **Tel** (408)988-8991, FAX (408)727-2118. **ED** Judy Sims (phone: (408)988-8991). **LC** JS714.A35; C48a. **DD** 352/.0051/0977311. cum. index. **Ad Acc, Adv Mgr:** Ken Whelan, **Tel** (408)988-8991. **Circ:** 40,000 (ctrl).
**Desc:** Offers informative, entertaining and pragmatic articles useful on the job. Concise format, easy to read. Covers all facts of personnel, employment, benefits, safety, security, compensation, labor law, seminars, service awards, relocation, EEO/AAP, training executive search, temporary help, consulting assistance, placement and communications.

US/0148-6977
**PERSONNEL RESEARCH AND DEVELOPMENT CENTER OF THE U. S. CIVIL SERVICE COMMISSION, THE.** **Main/Corp** United States. Civil Service Commission. Personnel Research and Development Center. **VAT** Personnel Research and Development Center of the United States Civil Service Commission. English. Personnel Research and Development Center, US Civil Service Commission, 1900 East Street NW, Washington DC 20415.

FR
**PSI-INFO / PUBLIC SERVICES INTERNATIONAL.** **Added/Corp** Public Services International. **VFOAT** PSI Info; Info. **VAT** Public Services International Info. (1990)-. Periodical. English. mo. ***Continues*** *Info (Feltham, Middlesex).*

UK/0033-3298
**PUBLIC ADMINISTRATION (LONDON).** (PUBLIC ADMINISTRATION.). [Public adm.]. Vol. 4, No. 1 (Jan. 1926)-. Academic Scholarly Publication. English. Four times a year. £89.00 UK and Europe; $163.00 North America; £105.00 other. Basil Blackwell Publishers Ltd, 108 Cowley Road, Oxford 0X4 1JF England. **Tel** 011 44 865 791100, FAX 011 44 865 791347, telex 837022 OXBOOK G. **(Subscription address:** Blackwell Publishers / UK, Marston Book Services, PO Box 87, Oxford OX2 0DT England.**)** **ED** Rod Rhodes, Christopher Pollitt. **CODEN** PUADDD. **[CCC].** cum. index. **Bk Rev. Ad Acc. Pr Rev. Circ:** 4,400. available on microfilm and microfiche from University Microfilms International (UMI). Documents available from The Genuine Article, Ask*IEEE, UMI Article Clearinghouse. ***Continues*** *Journal of Public Administration (London, England).*
**Desc:** Essential reading for anyone with an interest in the public sector. Includes insights into the policy making process and the actual workings of the public sector.
**Ind/Abst** ABC POL SCI; Acad. Abstr. Full Text Elite (Jan. 1992-); Acad. Abstr. (Jan. 1992-); Acad. Search (Jan. 1992-); Am. Hist. Life (1955-); Br. Humanit. Index; Bus. ASAP (1992-) [Full Txt.]; Bus. Index (1985-); Contents Pages Manage.; Curr. Contents Soc. Behav. Sci.; Expand. Acad. Index (1984-); Gen. BusinessFile (1985-); Gen. Period. Index (1985-); Geogr. Abstr. Human Geogr.; INFO-SOUTH Abstr.; INSPEC (1984-1985); Int. Bibliogr. Sociol.; J. Plan. Lit.; Mag. Search; Newsp. Period. Abstr. (1991-); PAIS Int. Print (1991-); Res. Alert [Full Cov.]; Sage Public Adm. Abstr.; Soc. Sci. Source (Jan. 1992-); Soc. Sci. Cit. Index [Full Cov.]; Soc. Sci. Index; Soc. Sci.

Index Fulltext (Winter 1988-) [Full Txt.]; Soc. Work Abstr. (?-?); Sociol. Educ. Abstr.; Stud. Women Abstr.; Women Manage. Rev. [Full Txt.].

SI
**PUBLIC EMPLOYEE, THE.** **Added/Corp** Amalgamated Union of Public Employees. (19??)-. Periodical. English. mo. Free on request. Amalgamated Union of Public Employees, 295 Upper Paya Lebar, Singapore 1953 Singapore. **Tel** 011 65 2 808033. **Ind/Abst** Work Relat. Abstr.

US
**PUBLIC EMPLOYEE BENEFIT PLANS.** **Added/Corp** International Foundation of Employee Benefit Plans. (1989)-. English. $28.00, ($20.00 for Foundation members). International Foundation of Employee Benefit Plans, PO Box 69, 18700 West Bluemound Road, Brookfield WI 53008-0069. **Tel** (414)786-6700. **LC** JK791; .P8a. ***Continues*** *Public Employees Conference. Public Employee Benefit Plans.*

US/1062-5992
**PUBLIC EMPLOYEE MAGAZINE, THE.** ***Title Change.*** (THE PUBLIC EMPLOYEE MAGAZINE / AFSCME.). [Public empl. mag.]. **Added/Corp** AFSCME. **VFOAT** Public Employee. Vol. 56, No. 2 (Feb./Mar. 1991)-Vol. 57, No. 8 (Nov./Dec. 1992). Periodical. English. bm. American Federal of State, County and Municipal Employees, AFSCME, 1625 L Street NW, Washington DC 20036-5687. **LC** HD8008.A1; A53. **DD** 351.10973. ***Continues*** *Public Employee (Mount Morris, Ill.), 0161-7494.* ***Continued by*** *AFSCME Public Employee, 1072-9992.*

US
**PUBLIC EMPLOYEE RELATIONS LIBRARY.** **Added/Corp** International Personnel Management Association. Public Personnel Association. No. 1 (1968)-. Monographic series. English. ir. $12.00 (members), $14.00 (nonmembers). International Personnel Management Association, 1617 Duke Street, Alexandria VA 22314. **Tel** (703)549-7100, FAX (703)684-0948. **Bk Rev**.

US/1044-8039
**PUBLIC PRODUCTIVITY & MANAGEMENT REVIEW.** [Public Prod. Manage. Rev.]. **Added/Corp** American Society for Public Administration. Management Science and Policy Analysis Section. National Center for Public Productivity (U.S.). **VFOAT** Public Productivity and Management Review. Vol. 13, No. 1 (Fall 1989)-. Periodical. English. qt. $88.00 institutions; $56.00 individuals. Jossey Bass Inc., 350 Sansome Street, San Francisco CA 94104. **Tel** (415)433-1767, FAX (415)433-0499. **LC** JF1411; .P8. **DD** 350.1/47/05. available on microfilm and microfiche from University Microfilms International (UMI); available on an online database (file 15/Full-Text) from DIALOG. Documents available from UMI Article Clearinghouse. ***Continues*** *Public Productivity Review, 0361-6681.* **Ind/Abst** ABI/INFORM Glob. Ed.; ABI Inform Ondisc (March 1981-); Acad. Search (July 1993-); Bus. Period. Index; Bus. Source (Jul. 1993-); Cumul. Index Nurs. Allied Health Lit.; Gen. BusinessFile; INFO-SOUTH Abstr.; Int. Labour Doc.; LABORDOC; Mag. Search; Manage. Contents; PAIS Int. Print (1991-); UMI ABI/Inform--Bus. Period. Ondisc (Winter 1987-) [Full Txt.]; Wilson Bus. Abstr.

CN/1188-0619
**PUBLIC SECTOR EMPLOYMENT AND REMUNERATION / STATISTICS CANADA, PUBLIC INSTITUTIONS DIVISION, EMPLOYMENT SECTION.** **Added/Corp** Statistics Canada. Employment Section. **VFOAT** Emploi et Remuneration dans le Secteur Public. (19??)-. English (French). an. 42.00Can$ Canada; $51.00 US; $59.00 other. Statistics Canada, Publications Sales & Services, Main Building Room 1710, Ottawa Ontario K1A 0T6 Canada. **Tel** (613)951-5078, (800)267-6677, FAX (613)951-1584, telex 053-3585. **LC** JL106; .P83. **DD** 354.71004/021.

CN/1183-1081
**PUBLIC SECTOR MANAGEMENT (TORONTO).** (PUBLIC SECTOR MANAGEMENT / MANAGEMENT ET SECTEUR PUBLIC.). [Public sect. manage.]. **Added/Corp** Institute of Public Administration of Canada. **VFOAT** Management et Secteur Public. (Fall 1990)-. Periodical. English (French). Four times a year. 20.00Can$ Canada; 25.00Can$ others. Institute of Public Administration of Canada, 150 Eglinton Avenue East, Suite 305, Toronto, Ontario M4P 1E8 Canada. **Tel** (416)932-3666. **LC** JL1; .P8. **DD** 354.71/0005. ***Continues*** *Institute of Public Administration of Canada. Bulletin - Institute of Public Administration of Canada., 0380-3988.*

UK/0308-0803
**PUBLISHED BY CSD.** (PUBLISHED BY CSD : A SUBJECT GUIDE TO THE LITERATURE ISSUED BY THE CIVIL SERVICE DEPARTMENT.). **Main/Corp** Great Britain. Civil Service Dept. **VFOAT** Subject Guide to the Literature Issued by the Civil Service Department. 1968/73-. English. an. Central Management Library, Civil Service Department, London SW1A 2AZ England. **LC** Z7165.G8; G68A; JN301. **DD** 016.354/41/001.

US
**REPORT - FLORIDA. STATE PERSONNEL BOARD.** **Main/Corp** Florida. State Personnel Board. **Added/Corp** Florida. Merit System Council. (1956/58)-. Periodical. English. be. ***Continues*** *Merit System Council.*

US
**REPORT OF IPA GRANT ACTIVITY.** **Main/Corp** United States. Civil Service Commission. Bureau of Intergovernmental Personnel Programs. Periodical. English. qt. US Civil Service Commission Bureau of Intergovernmental Personnel Programs, 1900 E Street NW, Washington DC 20415.

NR
**REPORT OF THE BENDEL STATE PUBLIC SERVICE COMMISSION.** **Main/Corp** Bendel (Nigeria). Public Service Commission. English. 50. Public Service Commission / Nigeria, P M B 1066, Benin City Bendel State of Nigeria. **LC** JQ3099.B434; B45A. **DD** 354.669/3006.

NR
**REPORT OF THE PUBLIC SERVICE COMMISSION.** **Main/Corp** Oyo, Nigeria (State). Public Service Commission. (19??)-. Periodical. English. an. N50.00. Oyo State of Nigeria, Government Printer, Ibadan Nigeria. **LC** JQ3099.O924; O93a. **DD** 354/.669/2.

II
**REPORT - STAFF SELECTION COMMISSION.** **Main/Corp** India. Staff Selection Commission. English. Lok Nayak Bhavan, Kha Market, New Delhi 110003 India. **LC** JQ247; .I565A. **DD** 354.54001/3.

US/0148-5520
**REQUESTS FOR INTERPRETATIONS AND POLICY STATEMENTS.** **Main/Corp** United States. Federal Labor Relations Council. English. US Federal Labor Relations Council, 1900 E Street NW, Washington DC 20415. **LC** KF5365; .A84. **DD** 353.001/7.

US/0734-371X
**REVIEW OF PUBLIC PERSONNEL ADMINISTRATION.** [Rev. public pers. adm.]. **Added/Corp** University of South Carolina. Bureau of Governmental Research and Service. **VFOAT** Public Personnel Administration. Vol. 1, No. 1 (Fall 1980)-. Periodical. English. qt. $40.00 (one year), $72.00 (two years) US; $56.00 (one year), $101.00 (two years) other. University of South Carolina Institute of Public Affairs, Gambrell Hall, Columbia SC 29208. **Tel** (803)777-8156. **ED** Steven W Hays and Nicholas Larich (editor's address: Washington State University, Division of Governmental Studies, Pullman WA 99164-4870; editor's phone: (509)335-3329). **LC** JK765; .R48. **DD** 353.001/05. Index available (bound in fourth issue). **Bk Rev**, (Qty: 10-12). **Ad Acc, Adv Mgr:** P Whitheld, **Tel** (803)777-8157. **Pr Rev. Circ:** 1,200. available on microfilm from University Microfilms International (UMI); available on an online database (file 15/Full-Text) from DIALOG. Documents available from UMI Article Clearinghouse.
**Desc:** Examines the function of personnel administration and labor relations in public organizations. Emphasizes specific personnel policies and programs and employee relations.
**Ind/Abst** ABC POL SCI; ABI/INFORM Glob. Ed.; ABI Inform Ondisc (Fall 1980-); Gen. BusinessFile (1992-); PAIS Int. Print; Person. Manage. Abstr.; Sage Public Adm. Abstr. (Fall 1980-?); UMI ABI/Inform--Bus. Period. Ondisc (Fall 1987-) [Full Txt.].

US
**SALARY ORDINANCE OF THE COUNTY OF LOS ANGELES.** **Main/Corp** Los Angeles Co., Calif. (19??)-. Periodical. English. an. 222 North Grand Avenue, Los Angeles CA 90012.

IE/0332-2688
**SEIRBHIS PHOIBLI : JOURNAL OF THE DEPARTMENT OF THE PUBLIC SERVICE.** V. 1, No. 1 (Bealtaine 1980)-. Periodical. English. qt. 1.50p single issue. Government Publications, 4 5 Harcourt Road, Dublin 2 Ireland. **Tel** 011 353 1 6613111 Ext.4005. **ED** Mary Dowling. **LC** JN1448; .S44. **DD** 354.417006. Index available. cum. index. **Ad Acc. Circ:** 3,000.

US
**SEPARATIONS, STATE SERVICE.** **Main/Corp** New Jersey. Dept. of Civil Service. 1960/61-. English. Department of Civil Service / Trenton, Trenton NJ 08625. **LC** JK3558; .N48A. **DD** 353.9749001/8.

II/0304-100X
**SERVICES LAW CASES.** [Serv. law cases]. Jan. 1974-. English. Rs30.00. International Law Book Company Gate, Delhi-6 India. **LC** LAW. **DD** 342/.54/068.

US
**SPBR REVIEW.** **Main/Corp** Ohio. State Personnel Board of Review. Periodical. English. SPBR Review, 30 East Broad Street/28th Floor, Columbus OH 43215. **LC** KFO435; .A867. **DD** 353.9771001/05.

CN/1187-7316
**SPECIAL NOTICE - ONTARIO MUNICIPAL EMPLOYEES RETIREMENT BOARD.** (SPECIAL NOTICE / OMERS.). [Spec. not. - Ont. Munic. Empl. Retire. Board]. **Added/Corp** Ontario Municipal Employees Retirement Board. No. 1 (Feb 12 1991)-. Periodical. English. **DD** 352/.0055/09713.

US/0733-480X
**STATUS OF EQUAL EMPLOYMENT OPPORTUNITY PROGRAM (WASHINGTON, D.C. : 1970).** (STATUS OF EQUAL EMPLOYMENT OPPORTUNITY PROGRAM / FEDERAL AVIATION ADMINISTRATION.). [Status equal employ. oppor. program]. **Main/Corp** United States. Federal Aviation Administration. Office of Civil Rights. Internal Program Division. Began with 1970. Government Publication. English. an. US Department of Transportation / Federal Aviation Administration, 800 Independence Avenue Southwest, Washington DC 20591. **Tel** (202)367-3484, FAX (202)367-3505. **LC** HE9803.A1; U55A. **DD** 331.11/43.

US
**SUMMARY OF DECISIONS / WASHINGTON STATE PERSONNEL APPEALS BOARD.** **Main/Corp** Washington (State) Personnel Appeals Board. **VFOAT** Summaries for Personnel Appeals Board. Vol. 1 (June 30, 1982)-. English. **LC** KFW435.A59; W37. **DD** 342.797/0686; 347.9702686.

US/0278-5803
**VETERANS READJUSTMENT APPOINTMENTS IN THE FEDERAL GOVERNMENT.** (VETERANS READJUSTMENT APPOINTMENTS IN THE FEDERAL GOVERNMENT : A REPORT PREPARED BY THE OFFICE OF PERSONNEL MANAGEMENT SUBMITTED TO THE COMMITTEE ON VETERANS' AFFAIRS, U.S. HOUSE OF REPRESENTATIVES.). English. sa. US House of Representatives / Office of Personnel Management, Washington DC. **LC** UB357; .V44. **DD** 353.001/3243/05.

CN/0838-7176
**VOICES (TORONTO, ONT.).** (VOICES.). [Voices]. Vol. 1, No. 1 (Nov. 1987)-. Periodical. English. Free. Ontario Public Service Employees Union, 1901 Yonge Street, Toronto Ontario M4S 2Z5 Canada. **Tel** (416)482-7423, FAX (416)482-1493. **DD** 354.713001.

US
**WEST VIRGINIA CIVIL SERVICE SYSTEM; ANNUAL REPORT.** **Main/Corp** West Virginia. Civil Service Commission. 1st- 1961/62-. English. an. **LC** JK4055.

US/0149-2837
**WHITE HOUSE FELLOWSHIPS, THE.** **Main/Corp** President's Commission on White House Fellowships (U.S.). Began with 1975/76. English. an. US President's Commission on White House Fellowships, 712 Jackson Place NW, Washington DC 20503. **Tel** (202)395-4522. **LC** JK718; .A37. ***Continues*** *White House Fellows.*
**Desc:** Information on those assigned to Cabinet level agencies federal agencies, Presidential assistants and Vice Presidents through the White House Fellowships program.

●UK/0965-3783
**WORLD DIRECTORY OF DIPLOMATIC REPRESENTATION.** (1992)-. English. an. $375.00. Europa Publications Ltd, 18 Bedford Square, London WC1B 3JN England. **Tel** 011 44 71 5808236, telex 21540 EUROPA G. **(Subscription address:** Gale Research Co., 835 Penobscot Building, Detroit MI 48226.) **LC** JX1625; .W67. **DD** 351.89/2/025.
**Desc:** Comprehensive guide to over 7,000 embassies, high commissions and consulates world-wide. A vast range of personnel is covered. Includes permanent missions to International Organizations. Lists even the most recently established states.

## PARKS AND RECREATION

US
**AMERICA'S GREAT OUTDOORS : NEWSLETTER FOR THE NATIONAL RECREATION STRATEGY.** See Forestry.

AT
**ANNUAL REPORT FOR YEAR ENDING 30 JUNE ... CONSERVATION COMMISSION OF THE NORTHERN TERRITORY.** See Environmental Issues-Conservation and Natural Resources.

CN/0847-4516
**ANNUAL REPORT - MINISTRY OF PARKS (VICTORIA).** (ANNUAL REPORT.). [Annu. rep. - Minist. Parks]. **Main/Corp** British Columbia.

Ministry of Parks. (1988/1989)-. English. Ministry of Parks, Public Information, 3rd Floor/4000 Seymour Place, Victoria British Columbia V8V 1X5 Canada. **Tel** (604)387-4609, FAX (604)387-5757. **LC** SB484.C2; B75a. **DD** 354.7110086/32. ***Continues in part*** *Annual Report / British Columbia. Ministry of Environment and Parks, 0838-1933.*

CN/0711-2815
**ANNUAL REPORT / RECREATION, PARKS AND WILDLIFE FOUNDATION.** [Annu. rep. - Recreat., Parks Wildl. Found.]. **Main/Corp** Alberta. Recreation, Parks and Wildlife Foundation. English. an. Parks and Wildlife Foundation, PO Box 4732, Edmonton Alta T6E 5G6. **LC** GV56.A4; A44A. **DD** 354.7123/0086/35.

US/0362-6377
**ANNUAL STATEMENT, CONCESSIONS IN THE CALIFORNIA STATE PARK SYSTEM.** **VFOAT** Annual Statement in the California State Park System, Concessions. English. an. Department of Parks and Recreation, PO Box 2390, Sacramento CA 95811. **Tel** (916)322-7000. **LC** SB482.C2; A595. **DD** 338.4/3333783/09794.

AT/0311-8223
**AUSTRALIAN PARKS AND RECREATION.** [Aust. parks recreat.]. **Added/Corp** Australian Institute of Parks and Recreation. **VFOAT** Australian Parks & Recreation. (197?)-. Periodical. English. Four times a year (Mar., June, Sept., Dec.). 35.00Aus$ Australia; 45.00Aus$ others. Royal Australian Institute of Parks and Recreation, PO Box 603, Dickson Australian Capital Territory, 2602 Australia. **Tel** 011 61 6 2414371, FAX 011 61 6 2415817. **ED** Ian Frencham. Index available. **Bk Rev**. **Ad Acc**, **Adv Mgr:** Eva Smith. **Circ:** 1,800 (ctrl). ***Continues*** *Australian Parks.*
**Desc:** Professional journal dealing with all aspects of parks and recreation, sporting facilities, recreation planning, horticulture and arboreta, and leisure pursuits.
**Ind/Abst** For. Prod. Abstr.; For. Abstr.; Geogr. Abstr. Phys. Geogr.; Geogr. Abstr. Human Geogr.; Leis. Recreat. Tour. Abstr.; Rural Dev. Abstr.; SPORT Discus; SportSearch; World Agric. Econ.

CN/0840-6189
**BOREALIS (TORONTO).** (BOREALIS.). [Borealis]. **Added/Corp** Canadian Parks and Wilderness Society. Vol. 1, No. 1 (Fall 1988)-. Periodical. English. qt. 41.12Can$. Canadian Parks and Wilderness Society, 160 Bloor Street East/Suite 1150, Toronto Ontario M4W 1B9 Canada. **Tel** (416)972-0868. **ED** David Dodge. **DD** 333.78/0971. **Ad Acc**. **Circ:** 7,500. available on microfilm and microfiche from Micromedia Limited. ***Continues*** *Park News, 0553-3066.*
**Ind/Abst** Can. Index.

US/0733-5326
**CALIFORNIA PARKS & RECREATION.** **VAT** California Parks and Recreation. (197?)-. Periodical. English. qt. $20.00 US; $22.00 Canada; $25.00 other; $35.00 combined with Leisure Lines. California Park Recreation Society, 3031 F Street, Suite 202, Sacramento CA 95814. **Tel** (916)446-2777. **ED** Norma Minas. **Bk Rev**. **Ad Acc**. **Circ:** 4,000 (ctrl). ***Continues*** *California Park and Recreation Magazine.*
**Desc:** Magazine and professional journal of primary interest to park and recreation professionals.

US
**COMPADRES DE SANTO ANTONIO MISSIONS NATIONAL PARK NEWSLETTER, LOS.** Newsletter. English. ir. $100.00 (institution/business membership), $50.00 (individual/family membership). Los Compadres Santo Antonio Mission National Park, 6539 Jose Drive, San Antonio TX 78214. **Tel** (512)922-3218.

US
**CONGRESS HIGHLIGHTS.** **Main/Conf** Congress for Recreation and Parks. (Oct. 1-6, 1972)-. English. National Recreation and Park Association, 2775 South Quincy Street, Suite 300, Arlington VA 22206. **Tel** (703)820-4940, (703)578-5564, FAX (703)671-6772. ***Continues*** *Highlights / Congress for Recreation and Parks, 0092-0975.*

US/0360-4667
**COUNTY RECREATION & PARK SERVICES STUDY (NORTH CAROLINA).** **Main/Corp** North Carolina. Recreation Division. **VAT** County Recreation and Park Services Study. English. 436 North Harrington Street, Raleigh NC 27603. **LC** GV54.N8; N68A. **DD** 338.4/7/3015709756.

SA
**CUSTOS.** **Added/Corp** South Africa. National Parks Board of Trustees. Vol. 1 (Dec. 1971)-. Periodical. Multiple languages (Afrikaans and English). mo. R40.00 South Africa; R70.00 other. National Parks Board of Trustees, PO Box 787, Pretoria 0001 South Africa. **Tel** 011 27 012 3439770, FAX 011 27 012 3430907, telex 321324 SA. **ED** Susan Van Dor Morwe. **LC** SB484.S5; C87. **DD** 333.7/8/0968. **Bk Rev**. **Ad Acc**. **Circ:** 30,000.
**Desc:** National parks and wildlife magazine.

US
**DESIGN / U.S. DEPARTMENT OF THE INTERIOR, HERITAGE CONSERVATION AND RECREATION SERVICE.** **Added/Corp** United States. National Park Service. United States. Heritage Conservation and Recreation Service. Park Practice Program (U.S.) National Recreation and Park Association. National Conference on State Parks. National Society for Park Resources (U.S.). (1971)-. Periodical. English. qt. $35.00. National Recreation and Park Association, 2775 South Quincy Street, Suite 300, Arlington VA 22206. **Tel** (703)820-4940, (703)578-5564, FAX (703)671-6772. ***Continues*** *Park Practice Design.*
**Ind/Abst** SPORT Discus.

US
**EXPERIENCE THE WILLAMETTE NATIONAL FOREST.** **See** Forestry.

US
**FACILITIES DIRECTORY.** **Added/Corp** Texas. Parks and Wildlife Dept. (19??)-. English. ir. Texas Parks & Wildlife, 4200 Smith School Road, Austin TX 78744. **Tel** (512)707-0032. **LC** GV54.T59; F3. **DD** 790/.025/764.

US
**FEDERAL PARKS AND RECREATION.** English. bw. $167.00 (one year), $301.00 (two year), $451.00 (three year). Resources Publishing Company, 1010 Vermont Avenue Northwest, Suite 708, Washington DC 20005. **Tel** (202)638-7529, FAX (202)393-2075. **ED** James B Coffin. **Circ:** 1,400 (ctrl).

US/0749-2804
**FROM THE STATE CAPITALS. PARKS AND RECREATION TRENDS, (NEW HAVEN, CONN.).** ***Title Change.*** (FROM THE STATE CAPITALS. PARKS AND RECREATION TRENDS.). [From state cap., Parks recreat. trends]. **VFOAT** Parks and Recreation Trends. (19??)-(199?). Periodical. English. mo. Wakeman Walworth Inc., 300 North Washington Street #204, Alexandria VA 22314. **Tel** (703)549-8606. **ED** Emily Novick. **DD** 333. ***Continues*** *From the State Capitals. Parks and Recreation;* ***Absorbed*** *From the State Capitals. Fish and Game Regulation, 0734-1067.* ***Absorbed by*** *From the State Capitals. Economic Devleopment.*
**Desc:** What states and municipalities are doing in conservation, land management and development, financial assistance, special taxes and fees, as well as parks and recreation personnel.

US/0732-4715
**GEORGE WRIGHT FORUM, THE.** **See** Environmental Issues-Conservation and Natural Resources.

●CN/1191-4734
**GEORGIAN BAY ISLANDS NATIONAL PARK, MANAGEMENT PLANNING.** [Georgian Bay Isl. Natl. Park manag. plan.]. **Added/Corp** Canadian Parks Service. (Mar. 1992)-. Periodical. English. **DD** 333.78.

US
**GRIST (WASHINGTON, D.C.).** (GRIST / U.S. DEPT. OF THE INTERIOR, HERITAGE CONSERVATION AND RECREATION SERVICE.). **Added/Corp** United States. Heritage Conservation and Recreation Service. Park Practice Program (U.S.) United States. National Park Service. National Conference on State Parks. National Society for Park Resources (U.S.) National Recreation and Park Association. **VFOAT** Park Practice Grist. Vol. 14, No. 1 (Jan./Feb. 1970)-. Periodical. English. qt. $30.00. National Recreation and Park Association, 2775 South Quincy Street, Suite 300, Arlington VA 22206. **Tel** (703)820-4940, (703)578-5564, FAX (703)671-6772. **ED** Kathleen A. Pleasant. **LC** SB482.A4; G74. **DD** 333.78/0973.
**Ind/Abst** SPORT Discus; SportSearch.

US/8756-310X
**HELPING OUT IN THE OUTDOORS.** [Help. out outdoors]. **Added/Corp** Northwest Trails Association. American Hiking Society. (198?)-. Periodical. English. an. $5.00 US; $13.00 other. The American Hiking Society, PO Box 20160, Washington DC 20041. **Tel** (703)385-3252, FAX (703)754-9008. **DD** 331. **Circ:** 11,000.
**Desc:** A directory of internships and volunteer jobs in state and national parks and forests and other lands open to the public in the United States.

US/0149-662X
**IDAHO STATE PARKS AND RECREATION.** [Ida. State parks recreat.]. **Main/Corp** Idaho. Dept. of Parks and Recreation. English. an. State House, 2263 Warm Springs Avenue, Boise ID 83720. **LC** GV191.42.I2; I3A. **DD** 353.9/796/00863.

UK/1012-7720
**IFPRA BULLETIN.** [IFPRA bull.]. **VFOAT** International Federation of Park and Recreation Administration Bulletin. (1988)-. Periodical. English. qt.
**Ind/Abst** Leis. Recreat. Tour. Abstr.

US/0019-2155
**ILLINOIS PARKS & RECREATION.** **VAT** Illinois Parks and Recreation. V. 26, No. 5- Sept./Oct. 1970-. Periodical. English. bm. $20.00 US; $30.00 other; $15.00 US; $25.00 other (libraries and schools). Illinois Association of Park Districts, 211 East Monroe Street, Springfield IL 62701. **Tel** (217)523-4554, FAX (217)523-4273. **ED** Mildred K Wallace. Index available. **Bk Rev**. **Ad Acc**. **Circ:** 4,000. ***Formed by the union of*** *Illinois Parks* ***and*** *Illinois Park and Recreation Quarterly.*
**Desc:** Reflects current trends, problems, solutions, programs and services affecting parks, recreation, conservation and the leisure field.

US
**INDEX/ PARK PRACTICE PROGRAM.** **Added/Corp** Park Practice Program (U.S.). (198?)-. English. an. Free to subscribers of Trends, Grist and Design. National Recreation and Park Association, 2775 South Quincy Street, Suite 300, Arlington VA 22206. **Tel** (703)820-4940, (703)578-5564, FAX (703)671-6772. **LC** Z6905; .I5; SB481. **DD** 016.36368. Index available. ***Continues*** *Park Practice Program Index.*

CN/0831-9103
**INTERCOMM - INTERPRETATION CANADA. ONTARIO SECTION.** (INTERCOMM.). [InterComm - Interpret. Can., Ont. Sect.]. **Added/Corp** Interpretation Canada. Ontario Section. (Jan./Feb. 1985)-. Periodical. English. bm. Interpretation Canada Ontario Section, PO Box 160, Aylmer Quebec J9H 5E5 Canada. **DD** 363.6/8/060713. ***Continues*** *ICOS (Newsletter), 0831-909X.*

●CN/1193-2562
**JOURNAL LE MACAREUX.** [J. macareux]. **Added/Corp** Canadian Parks Service. **VFOAT** Mingan Archipelago; Macareux Magazine. (1992)-. Periodical. English (French). **DD** 333.78. ***Continues*** *Macareux (Canadian Parks Service)., 1193-2554.*

●CN/1193-2562
**JOURNAL LE MACAREUX (FRENCH EDITION).** [J. macareux]. **Added/Corp** Service Canadien des Parcs. **VFOAT** Archipel-de-Mingan; Macareux Magazine. (1992)-. Periodical. French (English). **DD** 333.78. ***Continues*** *Macareux (Service Canadien des Parcs)., 1193-2554.*

US/0735-1968
**JOURNAL OF PARK AND RECREATION ADMINISTRATION.** [J. park recreat. admi]. **Added/Corp** American Academy for Park and Recreation Administration. Vol. 1, No. 1 (Jan. 1983)-. Periodical. English. Four times a year (Mar., June, Sept., Dec.). $35.00 (individuals); $40.00 (institutions). Saganore Publishing, 302 West Hill, Champaign IL 61824-0647. **Tel** (800)327-5557, FAX (217)359-5975. **ED** Brain Moore. **LC** GV181.5; .J68. **DD** 790/.06/9. Index available. **Bk Rev**. **Circ:** 1,000 (ctrl).
**Desc:** The journal provides a forum for the analysis of management and organization of the delivery of park, recreation, and leisure services.
**Ind/Abst** Leis. Recreat. Tour. Abstr.; Phys. Educ. Index; SPORT Discus.

US/1052-3774
**LEGACY (FORT COLLINS, COLO.).** (LEGACY : THE JOURNAL OF THE NATIONAL ASSOCIATION FOR INTERPRETATION.). [Legacy]. **Added/Corp** National Association for Interpretation (U.S.). Vol. 1, No. 1 (Aug./Sept. 1990)-. Periodical. English. Six times a year (Feb., Apr., June, Aug., Oct., Dec.). $45.00 US & Canada, $65.00 other, (non-members); $65.00 regular, $165.00 institutional, (membership). National Association for Interpretation, PO Box 1892, Fort Collins CO 80522. **Tel** (303)491-6434, FAX (303)491-2255. **ED** Dr. Alan Leftridge, (phone : (707)826-4306). **LC** SB481.A1; .L43. **DD** 574. **Bk Rev**. **Ad Acc**, **Adv Mgr:** Ted Wood, **Tel** (406)442-6597. **Pr Rev**. **Circ:** 3,100. ***Continues*** *Journal of Interpretation.*

US/1062-6719
**LEGAL ISSUES IN RECREATION ADMINISTRATION.** (LEGAL ISSUES IN RECREATION ADMINISTRATION / SPONSORED BY GEORGE MASON UNIVERSITY, CENTER FOR RECREATION RESOURCES POLICY, NATIONAL RECREATION AND PARK ASSOCIATION.). [Legal issues recreat. adm.]. **Added/Corp** George Mason University. Center for Recreation Resources Policy. National Recreation and Park Association. **VFOAT** LIRA. (1991)-. Periodical. English. qt. $100.00, (non-member), $50.00 (member). National Recreation and Park Association, 2775 South Quincy Street, Suite 300, Arlington VA 22206. **Tel** (703)820-4940, (703)578-5564, FAX (703)671-6772. **DD** 333.
**Ind/Abst** SPORT Discus.

US/0733-5377
**LEISURE LINES (SACRAMENTO, CALIF.).** (LEISURE LINES.). **Added/Corp** California Park and Recreation Society. **VFOAT** Leisurelines. (19??)-. Periodical. English. Twelve times a year. $15.00. California Park Recreation Society, 3031 F Street, Suite 202, Sacramento CA 95814. **Tel** (916)446-2777. **ED**

Norma Minas. **Bk Rev. Ad Acc. Circ:** 5,000.
**Desc:** In-house newsletter for park and recreation professionals.

●CN/1189-4873
**LEISURE WATCH CANADA.** [Leis. watch Can.]. **Added/Corp** Canadian Parks/Recreation Association. Rethink Group (Calgary, Alta.). Vol. 1, No. 1 (Feb. 1992)-. Periodical. English. bm. 50.00Can$. Canadian Parks/Recreation Association, 1600 James Naismith Drive, Gloucester Ontario K1B 5N4 Canada. **Tel** (613)748-5651, FAX (613)748-5706. **DD** 790/.01/35. ctrl circ.

US/0889-9444
**MANAGEMENT STRATEGY.** [Manage. strategy]. **Added/Corp** Management Learning Laboratories (U.S.). (1977)-. Periodical. English. Four times a year (Mar., June, Sept., Dec.). $20.00 US; $25.00 other. Sagamore Publishing, 302 West Hill, Champaign IL 61824-0647. **Tel** (800)327-5557, FAX (217)359-5975. **ED** Brain Moore. **DD** 363. **Circ:** 5300.
**Desc:** Contains management tips for leisure service professionals

●CN/1189-4407
**MANITOBA PARKS AND WILDERNESS.** [Manit. Parks Wilderness]. **Added/Corp** Canadian Parks and Wilderness Society. Manitoba Chapter. (1992)-. Periodical. English. qt. Free (members), $8.00 (non-members). Canadian Parks and Wilderness Society, 160 Bloor Street East/Suite 1150, Toronto Ontario M4W 1B9 Canada. **Tel** (416)972-0868. **DD** 333.78/097127.

US/0360-6716
**MUNICIPAL RECREATION & PARK SERVICES STUDY. Main/Corp** North Carolina. Recreation Division. **VAT** Municipal Recreation and Park Services Study. English. 436 North Harrington Street, Raleigh NC 27603. **LC** GV54.N8; N68B. **DD** 353.9/756/0085.

US/0895-819X
**NATIONAL ASSOCIATION FOR OLMSTED PARKS.** (NATIONAL ASSOCIATION FOR OLMSTED PARKS : [NEWSLETTER].). [Natl. Assoc. Olmsted Parks]. **Added/Corp** National Association for Olmsted Parks (U.S.). Vol. 1, No. 1 (Fall/Winter 1980/81)-. Periodical. English. Three times a year (Feb., July, Sept.). $12.00. National Association for Olmsted Parks, 7315 Disconsin Avenue, Suite 504E, Bethesda MD 20814. **Tel** (202)362-9511. **ED** Susan L. Klaus. **DD** 363. Index available. cum. index. **Bk Rev. Ad Acc. Circ:** 1,000 (ctrl).
**Desc:** Discussion of Olmsted landscape activities.

US
**NATIONAL JOB BULLETIN. See** Occupations and Careers.

US/0734-7960
**NATIONAL PARK GUIDE (NEW YORK, N.Y.).** (NATIONAL PARK GUIDE / BY MICHAEL FROME.). [Natl. park guide]. **Added/Corp** Allstate Motor Club. Prentice-Hall, Inc. Trade Division. **VFOAT** Allstate Motor Club National Park Guide. (1971)-. English. an. Price varies. Macmillan Publishing Co. / Indiana, 201 West 103rd Street, Indianapolis IN 46290. **Tel** (800)428-5331, (800)858-7674. **(Subscription address:** Simon and Schuster, 200 Old Tappan Road, Old Tappan NJ 07675.) **ED** Michael Frome. **LC** E160; .F73. **DD** 917.304/928. **Bk Rev. Ad Acc. Circ:** 35,000. ***Continues*** *Frome, Michael. Rand McNally National Park Guide.*
**Desc:** The guide to your trip to our nation's national parks. Covers all national parks, plus about 300 other areas in the national park service.

JA
**NATIONAL PARKS.** Japanese. mo. $78.00. Kokuritsu Koen Kyokai, (National Parks Assoc. of Japan), 8-1, Toranomon 2 Chome, Minatoku, Tokyoto 105, Japan. **(Subscription address:** Maruzen Company Ltd., PO Box 5050, Import & Export Department, Tokyo 100 31 Japan.)
**Ind/Abst** Gen. Period. Index (1985-); TOM Gen. Index (1993-) [Full Txt.].

UK/0265-0460
**NATIONAL PARKS TODAY.** [Natl. parks today]. (1983)-. Periodical. English. qt. **DD** 719.320942. ***Continues*** *National Park News.*
**Ind/Abst** Leis. Recreat. Tour. Abstr.; Museum Abstr.

US/0276-8186
**NATIONAL PARKS (WASHINGTON, D.C.).** (NATIONAL PARKS : THE MAGAZINE OF THE NATIONAL PARKS & CONSERVATION ASSOCIATION.). [Natl. parks]. **Added/Corp** National Parks and Conservation Association. Vol. 55, No. 1 (Jan. 1981)-. Periodical. English. bm (6 issues). $22.00. National Parks & Conservation Association, 1776 Massachusetts Avenue Northwest, Washington DC 20036. **Tel** (202)223-6722, (800)628-7275, FAX (202)659-0650. **ED** Michele Strutin. **LC** SB482.A4; N377. **DD** 333.78/3/0973. Index available. cum. index. **Bk Rev. Ad Acc. Circ:** 150,000. available on microfilm and microfiche from University Microfilms International (UMI); available on microfilm from Information Access Company. Documents available from BIOSIS Document Express, UMI Article Clearinghouse, Documents on Demand, Magazine Collection. ***Continues*** *National Parks & Conservation Magazine, 0027-9870.*
**Desc:** The journal reports about the environment of national parks or problems of national administration.
**Ind/Abst** ASTIS Curr. Aware. Bull. (1981-); Acad. Abstr. Full Text Elite (Jan. 1984-); Acad. Abstr. (Jan. 1984-); Acad. Ind. [Computer File] (1984-); Acad. Search (Jan. 1984-); Am. Hist. Life; ASTIS Bibliogr. (1981-); Biol. Abstr.; Biol. Dig.; Book Rev. Index; Energy Inf. Abstr.; Environ. Abstr.; Environ. Period. Bibliogr.; Expand. Acad. Index (1984-); Gen. Sci. Index (1992-); Geol. Abstr.; GeoRef; Hist. Source (Jan. 1984-); INFO-SOUTH Abstr.; Mag. Artic. Summar. Elite (Jan. 1984-); Mag. Artic. Summar. Select (Jan. 1984-); Mag. Artic. Summar. CD-ROM (Jan. 1984-); Mag. Index Plus (1989-); Mag. Index. Sel. (1986-); Mag. Search; Mid. Search (Jan. 1984-); Newsp. Period. Abstr. (1988-); Read. Guide Abstr. Select Ed.; Read. Guide Period. Lit.; SportSearch; Mag. Index (Jan. 1981-); Vocat. Search (Jan. 1984-); Wildl. Rev.

US
**NEW ORLEANS JAZZ STUDY NEWSLETTER / NATIONAL PARK SERVICE/DENVER SERVICE CENTER. Added/Corp** United States. National Park Service. Denver Service Center. United States. Preservation of Jazz Advisory Commission. No. 1 (Aug. 1991)-. Newsletter. English. National Park Service / Denver, Denver Service Center-TCE, 12795 West Alameda Parkway, PO Box 25287, Denver CO 80225-0287.

●CN/1189-4512
**NEW PARKS NORTH.** [New parks north]. **Added/Corp** Northwest Territories. Dept. of Economic Development and Tourism. Canadian Parks Service. Vol. 1, No. 1 (1992)-. English. **DD** 333.78.

CN/1186-799X
**NORTHERN YUKON NATIONAL PARK.** [North. Yukon Natl. Park]. **Main/Corp** Canadian Parks Service. **VFOAT** Newsletter; Parc-National Du-Nord-Du-Yukon. **VAT** Newsletter - Northern Yukon National Park. No. 1 (June 1991)-. Periodical. English (French). Three times a year. **DD** 333.78.

CN/1186-799X
**NORTHERN YUKON NATIONAL PARK.** (PARC-NATIONAL DU-NORD-DU-YUKON.). [North. Yukon Natl. Park]. **Main/Corp** Service Canadien des Parcs. **VFOAT** Bulletin; Northern Yukon National Park. **VAT** Newsletter - Northern Yukon National Park; Bulletin - Parc-National du-Nord-du-Yukon. (Jun 1991)-. Periodical. French (English). Three times a year. **DD** 333.78.

US/0030-7068
**OUTDOOR INDIANA. Added/Corp** Indiana. Dept. of Natural Resources. Indiana. Dept. of Conservation. (Feb. 1934)-. Periodical. English. Six times a year (Jan., Mar., May., July, Sept., Nov.). $10.00 Indiana, $9.52 other. Department of Natural Resources / Indiana, 402 West Washington Street W160, Indianapolis IN 46204. **Tel** (317)232-4004 Jeff Myers, FAX (317)232-8036. **ED** Don Henkel (phone: (317)232-4200). **LC** HC107.I6; A474. Index available. cum. index. **Bk Rev**, (Qty: 1-3). **Circ:** 20,000.
**Desc:** Reporting on Indiana's natural resources: state parks, fish and wildlife, flora and fauna, state history. Extensive use of nature photography.

●CN/1191-4726
**PARC NATIONAL DES ILES-DE-LA-BAIE-GEORGIENNE, PLAN DE GESTION.** [Parc natl. Iles-Baie-Georgienne plan gest.]. **Added/Corp** Service Canadien des Parcs. (Mar 1992)-. Periodical. French. **DD** 333.78.

●CN/1191-470X
**PARC NATIONAL DES ILES-DU-SAINT-LAURENT, PLAN DE GESTION.** [Parc natl. Iles-St.-Laurent plan gest.]. **Added/Corp** Service Canadien des Parcs. (1992)-. Periodical. French. **DD** 333.78.

US/1057-204X
**PARK & GROUNDS MANAGEMENT.** [Park grounds manage.]. **VFOAT** Park and Grounds Management; Park/Grounds Management. Vol. 44, No. 1 (Jan. 1991)-. Periodical. English. mo (June/July and Nov./Dec. issues combined). $22.00 US; $27.00 Canada; $35.00 other. Madisen Publishing Co., PO Box 1936, Appleton WI 54913-1936. **Tel** (414)733-2301. **ED** Erik Madison Jr. **LC** SB481.A1; P34. **DD** 635.9. Index available (Dec.). **Bk Rev. Ad Acc, Adv Mgr:** Hooper Jones, **Tel** (708)486-1021. **Circ:** 13,000 (ctrl). ***Continues*** *Park Maintenance and Grounds Management, 0192-2505.*
**Desc:** Magazine for park and grounds managers, workers form colleges, public/ private parks and school districts.

SA/0258-2457
**PARKS AND. GROUNDS.** [Parks grounds]. (1977)-. Periodical. English. bm. R46.93 So Africa; R87.00 other. Avonwold Publishing Company Pty Limited, PO Box 52068, Saxonwold 2132, South Africa. **Tel** 11 27 11 7881610.

US/0031-2215
**PARKS & RECREATION (ARLINGTON, VA.).** (PARKS & RECREATION.). [Parks recreat.]. **Added/Corp** National Recreation and Park Association. **VAT** Parks and Recreation. Vol. 1 (Jan. 1966)-. Periodical. English. mo. $25.00 (individuals), $30.00 (institutions) US; $31.00 (individuals), $36.00 (institutions) other. National Recreation and Park Association, 2775 South Quincy Street, Suite 300, Arlington VA 22206. **Tel** (703)820-4940, (703)578-5564, FAX (703)671-6772. **LC** SB481.A1; P35. **DD** 790. available on microfilm and microfiche from University Microfilms International (UMI). Documents available from UMI Article Clearinghouse, Magazine Collection. ***Formed by the union of*** *Parks & Recreation; Recreation (New York, N.Y. : 1931), 0162-6590; American Recreation Journal* ***and*** *Planning and Civic Comment, 0569-7263.*
**Ind/Abst** Acad. Search (July 1993-); Avery Index Archit. Period. Suppl. Colum. Univ. (1989/90-); Book Rev. Index; Curr. Index J. Educ.; For. Abstr.; Gen. Period. Index (1985-); INFO-SOUTH Abstr.; J. Plan. Lit.; Leis. Recreat. Tour. Abstr.; Mag. Index Plus (1989-); Mag. Search; Newsp. Period. Abstr. (1988-); Phys. Educ. Index; Read. Guide Period. Lit.; SPORT Discus; SportSearch (May 1987-); Mag. Index (1977-); Urban Aff. Abstr.

NZ/0114-8087
**PARKS & RECREATION AUCKLAND.** (PARKS & RECREATION.). [Parks recreat.Auckl.]. (1989)-. Periodical. English. qt. **DD** _a790.06893. ***Continues*** *New Zealand Parks & Recreation, 0110-4497.*
**Ind/Abst** Leis. Recreat. Tour. Abstr.

UK/0954-3880
**PARKS, GOLF COURSES & SPORTS GROUNDS (1975).** (PARKS, GOLF COURSES & SPORTS GROUNDS.). **VFOAT** Parks, Golf Courses and Sports Grounds. (1975)-. English. mo. MGS Publishing Ltd., 172 London Road, Guildford Surr GU1 1XR England. **Tel** 011 44 483 306304. ***Continues*** *Parks & Sports Grounds, 0031-224X.*
**Ind/Abst** Agric. Eng. Abstr. (1991-); Archit. Period. Index (1978-1983); SPORT Discus.

SP/0213-4489
**PARQUES Y JARDINES.** [Parq. jard.]. No. 14 (Jan. 1975)-. Periodical. Spanish. Three times a year.
**Ind/Abst** AGRICOLA; Archit. Period. Index (June 1978).

US/0742-793X
**PENNSYLVANIA RECREATION & PARKS. Added/Corp** Pennsylvania Recreation and Park Society. Pennsylvania Recreation and Park Society. Bi-annual report. **VFOAT** Pennsylvania Recreation and Parks. (19??)-. Periodical. English. qt. $10.00 US; $11.00 other. Penn Recreation and Park Society, 723 South Antherton Street, State College PA 16801. **Tel** (814)234-4272, FAX (814)234-5276. **ED** Vanyla S. Tierney. **Ad Acc, Adv Mgr:** Marcie Lynch. **Circ:** 1,500 (ctrl).
**Desc:** Information on a range of topics related to recreation, parks, and conservation focused toward the interests of professional society members.

US
**PENNSYLVANIA STATE PARKS / PENNSYLVANIA DEPARTMENT OF ENVIRONMENTAL RESOURCES, BUREAU OF STATE PARKS, ENVIRONMENTAL EDUCATION AND INTERPRETIVE SECTION. Added/Corp** Pennsylvania. Bureau of State Parks. Environmental Education and Interpretive Section. **VFOAT** State Parks. Vol. 1, No. 1 (Winter 1991)-. Periodical. English. qt. Pennsylvania State Parks Magazine, PO Box 8551, Harrisburg PA 17105-8551. **LC** SB482.P4; P46.

US
**PROGRAMMERS INFORMATION NETWORK.** (19??)-. Periodical. English. Four times a year. $18.00 (members), $30.00 (nonmembers). National Recreation and Park Association, 2775 South Quincy Street, Suite 300, Arlington VA 22206. **Tel** (703)820-4940, (703)578-5564, FAX (703)671-6772.

US/0473-2014
**PROGRESS REPORT - OREGON STATE PARKS AND RECREATION DIVISION. Main/Corp** Oregon. State Parks and Recreation Division. (1959)-. Periodical. English. Oregon State Parks and Recreation Division, Salem OR 97310. **LC** SB482.O7; A3. **DD** 333.7. ***Continues*** *Report - Oregon State Park Division.*

US
**PROPOSED BUDGET FOR THE MARYLAND-NATIONAL CAPITAL PARK AND PLANNING COMMISSION. MONTGOMERY COUNTY PROGRAMS, A. Main/Corp** Maryland-National Capital Park and Planning Commission. **VFOAT** Montgomery County

## Public Administration — Parks and Recreation

Programs; Montgomery County; Proposed Budget. Montgomery County. English. Maryland-National Capital Park and Planning Commission, 6609 Riggs Road, Hyattsville MD 20782. **LC** F187.M7; M36B. **DD** 352.7/32/0975284.

US/0733-8309
**RAND MCNALLY CAMPGROUND & TRAILER PARK GUIDE, EASTERN.** *Title Change.* [Rand McNally campground trailer park guide, East.]. **Added/Corp** Rand McNally and Company. **VFOAT** Rand McNally Campground and Trailer Park Guide, Eastern; Campground & Trailer Park Guide, Eastern; Campground and Trailer Park Guide, Eastern. (19??)-(19??). English. an. Rand McNally & Company, PO Box 32, Skokie IL 60076. **Tel** (708)673-0813, (800)444-4062. **ED** Mary Niles. **LC** GV191.35; .R36. **DD** 647/.9473. **Bk Rev**. **Ad Acc**. **Circ:** 260,000. *Continues Rand McNally Eastern Campgrounds & Trailer Parks, 0194-4177. Continued by Rand McNally RV Park and Campground Directory, U.S.A., Canada, Mexico.*
**Desc:** About 10,000 public and private campground listings in chart form, park name, address, phone, directions, number of sites, fees, etc. The directory preferred by Americas campers.

US
**RANGER.** (19??)-. English. Four times a year (Feb., Apr., July, Sept.). $30.00. Association National Park Rangers, PO Box 307, Gansevoort NY 12831. **Tel** (518) 793-3140. **ED** Teresa Ford (editor's address: 265 Mt. Vernon Club Road, Golden, CO 80401, phone: (303)526-1380). **Bk Rev**, (Qty: 4). **Ad Acc**. **Circ:** 1,700.

CN/0710-6025
**RECREACTION (VANIER).** *Ceased.* (RECREACTION.). [RecreAction]. **Added/Corp** Canadian Parks/Recreation Association. No. 1 (1980)-No. 4 (1992). Periodical. English (French). CP/RA National Office, 1600 Prom James Naismith Drive, Gloucester Ontario K1B 5N4 Canada. **DD** 790./06/071.

US/0148-2882
**RECREATION AND PARK EDUCATION CURRICULUM CATALOG.** **Added/Corp** Society of Park and Recreation Educators. **VFOAT** Curriculum Catalog. (19??)-. Catalog. English. be. $17.50. National Recreation and Park Association, 2775 South Quincy Street, Suite 300, Arlington VA 22206. **Tel** (703)820-4940, (703)578-5564, FAX (703)671-6772. **LC** GV181.35; .R4. **DD** 375/.79/00973.

US/0743-5649
**RECREATION AND PARKS LAW REPORTER.** See Law.

US
**REPORTS AND RECOMMENDATIONS ... / KENTUCKY. STATE PARK COMMISSION.** **Main/Corp** Kentucky. State Park Commission. Periodical. English. be. **LC** SB482.K4.

CN/0846-3948
**ROUGE VALLEY, PARK FORUM.** [Rouge Val. park forum]. **Main/Corp** Rouge Valley Park Project (Ont.). **VFOAT** Park Forum; Rouge Valley, Info-Parc. Vol. 1, No. 1 (Summer 1991)-. Periodical. English (French). **DD** 333.78.

US/0893-8210
**SPORTS, PARKS & RECREATION LAW REPORTER, THE.** See Law.

●CN/1191-4718
**ST. LAWRENCE ISLANDS NATIONAL PARK, MANAGEMENT PLAN REVIEW.** [St. Lawrence Isl. Natl. Park manag. plan rev.]. **Added/Corp** Canadian Parks Service. (1992)-. Periodical. English. **DD** 333.78.

●US/1056-8514
**STATE PARK AND RECREATION UPDATE.** [State park recreat. update]. **Added/Corp** Southwest Missouri State University. Center for Leisure Studies. **VFOAT** State Park and Recreation Update Magazine. (June 1991)-. Periodical. English. Twice a year. $30.00. Southwest Missouri State University, 901 South National Avenue, Springfield MO 65804-0089. **Tel** (417)836-4455. **ED** Steve Illum. **LC** GV191.4; .S72. **DD** 796.5/0973/05. Index available ($3.00). cum. index.

US/0362-6563
**STEWARDSHIP REPORT, A.** **Main/Corp** California. Dept. of Parks and Recreation. 1973/74-. English. ir. Department of Parks and Recreation, PO Box 2390, Sacramento CA 95811. **Tel** (916)322-7000. **ED** Bruce Kennedy. **LC** SB482.C2; C24A. **DD** 333.7/8/09794. *Continues California State Park System, A Stewardship Report.*

US/0040-4586
**TEXAS PARKS & WILDLIFE.** **Added/Corp** Texas. Parks and Wildlife Dept. **VFOAT** Texas Parks and Wildlife. **VAT** Texas Parks and Wildlife. Vol. 23, No. 4 (April 1965)-. Periodical. English. mo. $10.50 (private/public schools K-12); $12.95 (other). Texas Parks & Wildlife, 4200 Smith School Road, Austin TX 78744.

**Tel** (512)707-0032. **ED** David Baxter. **LC** SK1; .T45. Index available (free). **Ad Acc**. **Circ:** 142,000. *Continues Texas Game and Fish.*
**Desc:** Fishing, hunting, state park info, articles, wildlife, wild flowers.
**Ind/Abst** Fish Rev.; Key Word Index Wildl. Res.; Wildl. Rev.

US
**TRENDS (PARK PRACTICE PROGRAM (U.S.)).** (TRENDS / PARK PRACTICE.). **Added/Corp** United States. National Park Service. United States. Heritage Conservation and Recreation Service. Park Practice Program (U.S.) National Recreation and Park Association. National Conference on State Parks. National Society for Park Resources (U.S.). Vol. 6 I.E. Vol. 7, No. 2 (Apr. 1970)-. Periodical. English. Four times a year. $35.00. National Recreation and Park Association, 2775 South Quincy Street, Suite 300, Arlington VA 22206. **Tel** (703)820-4940, (703)578-5564, FAX (703)671-6772. **ED** Kathleen A Pleasant. **Circ:** 1,700. *Continues Trends in Parks & Recreation.*
**Ind/Abst** SPORT Discus; SportSearch.

CN/0848-7324
**VISIONS (VICTORIA).** (VISIONS : BC PARKS NEWSLETTER.). [Visions]. **Added/Corp** British Columbia. Parks and Outdoor Recreation Division. Vol. 1, No. 1 (Mar. 1990)-. Newsletter. English. **DD** 363.6/8/09711.

CN/1183-6830
**WARBLER (TORONTO).** (THE WARBLER : A NEWSLETTER ABOUT PLANNING BLACKSTONE HARBOUR (MASSAUGA WILDLANDS) PROVINCIAL PARK.). [Warbler]. **Added/Corp** Ontario. Ministry of Natural Resources. (Spring, 1991)-. Newsletter. English. sa. Ministry of Natural Resources / Ontario, Whitney Block, Parliament Buildings, Toronto Ontario M7A 1W3 Canada. **DD** 333.78.

## PUBLIC FINANCE AND TAXATION

US/0363-2997
**1040 PREPARATION.** **VAT** One Thousand and Forty Preparation; Ten Forty Preparation. (1976)-. English. an (Jan.). $41.50. Commerce Clearing House Inc., 4025 West Peterson Avenue, Chicago IL 60646-6085. **Tel** (312)583-8500, FAX (708)940-4600. **ED** Sidney Kess, Ben Eisenberg and Barbara Weltman. **LC** KF6369.A1; K48. **DD** 343/.73/052. *Continues Kess, Sidney. Practical Guide to Individual Income Tax Return Preparation.*
**Desc:** An easy-to-use guide for the beginner, or refresher for the part-time tax preparer on the basics of preparing individual tax returns.

US
**1040NR FORMS AND INSTRUCTIONS.** **Main/Corp** United States. Internal Revenue Service. (1991)-. English. Internal Revenue Service / Richmond, Eastern Distribution Center, PO Box 85074, Richmond VA 23261-5074.

US/0163-1241
**ABINGDON CLERGY INCOME TAX GUIDE.** 6th- Ed.; 1978-. English. an. $7.50 (paper), $37.50 (ten-copy prepack: NET, ICN). Abingdon Press, PO Box 801, Nashville TN 37202. **Tel** (615)749-6451, (800)251-3320. **LC** KF6369.8.C5; C54. **DD** 343/.73/052. *Continues Clergy's Federal Income Tax Guide, 0090-9866.*
**Desc:** An easy to use guide that offers clergy of all denominations accurate information when filing federal income tax forms.

US/0734-8606
**ABINGDON CLERGY TAX RECORD BOOK.** **VFOAT** Clergy Tax Record Book. English. an. Abingdon Press, PO Box 801, Nashville TN 37202. **Tel** (615)749-6451, (800)251-3320.

IE
**ABSTRACT ACCOUNT - CENTRAL FUND (IRELAND).** **Main/Corp** Ireland (Eire). Central Fund. English. an. Government Publications, 4 5 Harcourt Road, Dublin 2 Ireland. **Tel** 011 353 1 6613111 Ext.4005. **LC** HJ42; .D47A. **DD** 354./417/00722. **Circ:** 1,000.

ZA
**ACCOUNTS FOR THE YEAR ENDED 31ST DECEMBER ... : AUDITOR-GENERAL'S REPORT / REPUBLIC OF ZAMBIA, THE COUNCIL OF LEGAL EDUCATION.** **Main/Corp** Council of Legal Education (Zambia). English. an. K0.20. Auditor-General, PO Box 217377, Lusaka Zambia. **LC** LAW. **DD** 354.6894008/8.

NN
**ACCOUNTS - NEW HEBRIDES CONDOMINIUM. COMPTES - CONDOMINIUM DES NOUVELLES-HEBRIDES.** **Main/Corp** New Hebrides. Condominium Treasurer. **VFOAT** Comptes - Condominium des Nouvelles-Hebrides. (19??)-. Multiple languages (English and French). **LC** HJ99.N4; A33a. **DD** 354/.93/40071.

HK
**ACCOUNTS OF HONG KONG AND ANNUAL REPORT OF THE ACCOUNTANT GENERAL.** **Main/Corp** Hong Kong. Treasury. **VFOAT** Annual Departmental Report with the Accounts of Hong Kong. English. **LC** HJ68; .H616. **DD** 354/.51/25007231. *Continues Hong Kong. Treasury. Departmental Report by the Accountant General.*

US/1052-1674
**ACQUISITION ISSUES.** [Acquis. issues]. (Apr. 1991)-. Periodical. English. mo. $299.00 (one year), $565.00 (two year). Holbrook and Kellogg, 1964 Gallows Road, Suite 200, Vienna VA 22182. **Tel** (703)506-0600, FAX (703)506-1948. **ED** John Shackford. **LC** KF842; .A25. **DD** 346.73/023; 347.30623.
**Desc:** Monthly newsletter written by top government contracts attorneys, brings in-depth legal analysis and practical guidance on business issues affecting government contractors today.

US
**ADOPTED BUDGET - CITY OF NEW YORK.** See Public Administration.

US/0147-1945
**ADVANCE BUDGETING. A REPORT TO THE CONGRESS.** See Public Administration.

US
**ADVANCED UNDERWRITING SERVICE.** (19??)-. English. ir (includes 7 binders plus monthly updates). $429.00 (includes postage). Dearborn Financial Publishing, Inc., 520 North Dearborn Street, Chicago IL 60610-4354. **Tel** (312)836-4400, (800)252-0866, FAX (312)836-1021. (**Subscription address:** Dearborn Financial Publishing, Inc., Subscription Office, PO Box 830350, Birmingham AL 35283-0350.)

US/1058-7497
**ADVANCES IN TAXATION.** [Adv. tax]. Vol. 1 (1987)-. Periodical. English. an. $73.25. JAI Press Inc., 55 Old Post Road, Suite 2, PO Box 1678, Greenwich CT 06836-1678. **Tel** (203)661-7602, FAX (203)661-0792. **ED** Jerrold J. Stern. **LC** HJ2240; .A37. **DD** 336.2/00973. Documents available from UMI Article Clearinghouse.
**Desc:** Aimed at a range of tax academicians, and therefore, research in all subject areas will be considered. Such areas may include the current federal income tax system, and possible alternatives to the systems such as comprehensive based, flat-rate income tax, a consumption base/cash flow tax, or a value-added tax.
**Ind/Abst** ABI/INFORM Glob. Ed.

NE
**AFRICAN TAX SYSTEMS.** (1970)-. English. ir (4 binders updated 4 times a year). $860.00. International Bureau of Fiscal Documentation - IBFD Publications, PO Box 20237, 1000 HE Amsterdam The Netherlands. **Tel** 011 31 20-6267726, FAX 011 31 20-6228658, telex 13217 INTAX NL. Index available. cum. index. **Circ:** 500.
**Desc:** Detailed, practical guides to the tax and foreign investment legislation of Anglophone and Francophone Africa.

●US
**AGENCY BUDGET DETAIL.** **Main/Corp** North Dakota. (1991-1993)-. English. be. **LC** HJ11; .N935a. **DD** 353.97840072/256/05. *Continues Executive Budget.*

US/1044-4130
**AKRON TAX JOURNAL.** [Akron tax j.]. **Added/Corp** University of Akron. School of Law. Vol. 1 (1983)-. Periodical. English. an (Feb.). $12.00. Akron Law Review, School of Law, University of Akron, Akron OH 44325. **Tel** (216)972-7335. **ED** Gregory N. Longworth. **LC** K1; .K78. **DD** 343.7304; 347.3034. **Circ:** 200.
**Desc:** Articles on current tax issues.
**Ind/Abst** Index Leg. Period.; Leg. Resour. Index; LegalTrac (1989-).

NO/0332-8422
**AKTUELLE SKATTETALL.** **Added/Corp** Norway. Statistisk Sentralbyra. **VFOAT** Current Tax Data. (19??)-. English (Norwegian). an. Kr20.00 Norway; $3.00 US. Central Bureau of Statistics / Norway, PO Box 8131 DEP, N-0033 Oslo 1 Norway. **Tel** 011 47 2 2864964, FAX 011 47 2 864973. **LC** HJ3997.A2; A47; HA1503; .A45 subser. **Bk Rev**. **Circ:** 850.
**Desc:** Tax rates in Norway.

US/0250-1571
**AL-TAMWIL WA-AL-TANMIYAH.** [Tamwil wa al-tanmiyya]. Began in March 1980. Periodical. Arabic. qt. Free. Finance and Development, International Monetary Fund Building, Washington DC 20431. **Tel**

# Public Administration — Public Finance and Taxation

(202)623-8308. **ED** Shuja Nawaz. **LC** HC59.8; .T35. Index available. cum. index. **Bk Rev**. **Circ:** 8,500 (ctrl). available on microfilm; available on microfiche; available on CD-ROM; available in microform.
**Desc:** Contains work and policies of International Monetary Fund and the World Bank and issues in International Monetary ad development economics.

US/0733-2912
**ALASKA BUDGET IN BRIEF.** **Main/Corp** Alaska. Division of Budget & Management. FY 1982-. English. an. Alaska Division of Budget & Management, Office of the Governor, Juneau AK. **LC** HJ11; .A4443C. **DD** 353.97980072/253/05.

US/0191-3689
**ALI-ABA CONFERENCE. CONFERENCE ON FEDERAL INCOME TAX SIMPLIFICATION: PAPERS.** See Law.

US/0191-8249
**ALI-ABA COURSE OF STUDY. ABA SECTION OF TAXATION, ADVANCED STUDY SESSIONS, ESTATE AND INCOME TAX PLANNING FOR EXECUTIVES AND SMALL BUSINESS OWNERS : MATERIALS.** See Law-Estate Planning.

US
**ALI-ABA COURSE OF STUDY. ADVANCED TAX PLANNING FOR THE CLOSELY HELD BUSINESS : MATERIALS.** See Law-Corporate Law.

US/0191-2623
**ALI-ABA COURSE OF STUDY. DOMESTIC TAXATION OF HARD MINERALS : MATERIALS.** See Law.

US/0190-3888
**ALI-ABA COURSE OF STUDY MATERIALS. PRACTICE AND PROCEDURE IN FEDERAL TAX CONTROVERSIES: TAX COURT AND ELSEWHERE.** See Law.

US/0191-2380
**ALI-ABA COURSE OF STUDY : STATE AND LOCAL TAXATION AND FINANCE : MATERIALS.** See Law.

US/1055-2480
**ALI-ABA TAX COURSE MATERIALS JOURNAL.** **Added/Corp** American Law Institue. America Bar Association. **VAT** American Law Institue, America Bar Association Tax Course Materials Journal. (1991)-. Periodical. English. bm. $30.00. American Law Institute, 4025 Chestnut Street, Philadelphia PA 19104-3099. **Tel** (215)243-1661, (800)253-6397, FAX (215)243-1664.

US/0148-9976
**ALL STATES TAX HANDBOOK.** **Added/Corp** Prentice-Hall, inc. (19??)-. English. an (Jan.). $30.00. Research Institute of America, 117 East Stevens Avenue, Valhalla NY 10595. **Tel** (800)431-9025. **LC** KF6750; .A93. **DD** 343/.73/043.

UK
**ALLIED DUNBAR TAX GUIDE / BY W.I. SINCLAIR.** **Added/Corp** Allied Dunbar (Firm : Great Britain). **VFOAT** Tax Guide. (1986)-. Periodical. English. an. $19.99. Longman Group Ltd., Fourth Avenue, Longman House, Harlow Essex CM19 5SR England. **Tel** 011 44 279 429655, FAX 011 44 279 431059, telex 81259. **ED** Walter Sinclair. **LC** KD5429.A1; S55. **DD** 343.4104; 344.1034. **Continues** Allied Hambro Tax Guide.
**Desc:** A clear and concise guide to every aspect of UK taxation including many useful tax saving hints.

US
**AMERICAN FEDERAL TAX REPORTS.** **Added/Corp** Prentice-Hall, inc. 2nd Series Vol. 1 (1924)-. Periodical. English. sa. Maxwell Macmillan Professional Business Division, 910 Sylvan Avenue, Englewood Cliffs NJ 07632-3310. **Tel** (800)431-9025. **(Subscription address:** Prentice Hall Inc, PO Box 801, Englewood Cliffs NJ 07632.) **LC** KF6280.A2; A5. **DD** 336.202673. cum. index.

US/0739-7569
**AMERICAN JOURNAL OF TAX POLICY, THE.** [Am. j. tax policy]. **Added/Corp** American College of Tax Counsel. Vol. 1 (Spring 1982)-. Periodical. English. sa. $26.00. University of Alabama School of Law, PO Box 870382, Tuscaloosa AL 35487. **Tel** (205)348-1175. **LC** K1; .M4457. **DD** 343.7304/05; 347.303405. available on microfilm.
**Ind/Abst** Curr. Law Index (1984-); Fed. Tax Artic.; Index Leg. Period.; Leg. Resour. Index (1984-); LegalTrac (1982-).

GW
**AMTSBLATT DES BAYERISCHEN STAATSMINISTERIUMS DER FINANZEN.** **Main/Corp** Bavaria. Staatsministerium der Finanzen. German. 16.00. Staatsministerium der Finanzen, Germany. **LC** HJ49.B4; A26A.

US
**ANALYSIS OF GOVERNOR'S RECOMMENDED ... BUDGET.** **VFOAT** LFO Analysis of Governor's Recommended ... Budget. (1991)-. English. be. Oregon Legislative Fiscal Office, H178 State Capitol, Salem OR 97310. **Continues** Analysis of the Governor's ... Budget Recommendations.

US/0739-3059
**ANALYSIS OF MARYLAND SALES AND USE TAX ... REVENUES COLLECTED IN MONTGOMERY COUNTY / MONTGOMERY COUNTY GOVERNMENT, DEPARTMENT OF FINANCE.** English. an. Montgomery County Government / Department of Finance, 101 Monroe Street, Rockville MD 20850. **LC** HJ5715.U6; M36. **DD** 336.2/71. **Continues** Maryland Sales and Use Tax Revenues Collected in Montgomery County Compared with Collections Statewide and in other Major Subdivisions, 0276-4008.

US/0747-5187
**ANALYSIS OF THE PRESIDENT'S BUDGETARY PROPOSALS, AN.** **Ceased.** (AN ANALYSIS OF THE PRESIDENT'S BUDGETARY PROPOSALS FOR FISCAL YEAR ... / THE CONGRESS OF THE UNITED STATES, CONGRESSIONAL BUDGET OFFICE.). [Anal. Pres. budg. propos.]. **Main/Corp** United States. Congressional Budget Office. (1978/1979)-(19??). English. an. Congressional Budget Office, 2nd and D Streets SW, Washington DC 20515. **Tel** (202)226-2115. **LC** HJ9; .U55A. **DD** 353.0072/2/05.

US/0147-6637
**ANALYSIS - TEXAS. COMPTROLLER'S OFFICE.** (ANALYSIS - COMPTROLLER OF PUBLIC ACCOUNTS.). [Anal. - Tex., Comptrol. Off.]. **Main/Corp** Texas. Comptroller's Office. Periodical. English. Comptroller of Public Accounts, Division of Planning and Research, 111 East 17th Street, Austin TX 78774. **LC** HJ11; .T44423B. **DD** 353.9/764/00723.

II/0570-0329
**ANDHRA PRADESH BUDGET IN BRIEF.** **Main/Corp** Andhra Pradesh (India). English. an. Government Central Press, Hyderabad India. **LC** HJ66.A485; B117. **DD** 354.54/840072253/05.

SZ
**ANGGARAN HASIL DAN PERBELANJAAN BAGI TAHUN ... (MICROFORM).** **Main/Corp** Sarawak. **VFOAT** Estimates of Revenue and Expenditure for the Year ... . 1972-. English (Malay). an. **Continues** Sarawak. Estimates of Revenue and Expenditure for the Year ... .

PK
**ANNUAL BUDGET STATEMENT OF PAKISTAN RAILWAYS.** See Transportation-Railroads.

US/0360-5647
**ANNUAL BUDGET TO CONTINUE CURRENT PROGRAMS.** (ANNUAL BUDGET TO CONTINUE CURRENT PROGRAMS- ARIZONA). **Main/Corp** Arizona. (19??)-. English. an. **LC** HJ11; .A6415a. **DD** 353.9/791/00722.

US
**ANNUAL CAPITAL INVESTMENT BUDGET - COLORADO. OFFICE OF STATE PLANNING AND BUDGETING.** See Business-Investments.

US
**ANNUAL CASH REPORT / TEXAS COMPTROLLER OF PUBLIC ACCOUNTS.** **Main/Corp** Texas. Comptroller's Office. **VFOAT** Summary of Financial Information; Revenue and Expenditures of State Funds; Annual Cash Report of the State of Texas. (1989)-. English. an. Texas Comptroller of Public Accounts, 111 East 17th Street, Austin TX 78774. **LC** HJ11; .T44423a. **DD** 353.97640072/31. **Continues** Annual Financial Report of the State of Texas, 0145-3688.

US/0095-3016
**ANNUAL ECONOMIC REPORT - WISCONSIN DEPARTMENT OF REVENUE.** **Main/Corp** Wisconsin. Dept. of Revenue. English. an. Department of Revenue / Wisconsin, PO Box 8933, 125 West Webster Street, Madison WI 53708. **Tel** (608)266-8661. **LC** HJ11; .W6543A. **DD** 330.9/775/04.

US
**ANNUAL FINANCIAL REPORT FOR YEAR ENDING AUG. 31 ... - TEXAS. ATTORNEY-GENERAL'S OFFICE.** **Main/Corp** Texas. Attorney-General's Office. English. an. Attorney General, PO Box 12548, Austin TX 78711. **LC** KFT1627.5.A8; A832. **DD** 353.97640072/31.

US/0361-1019
**ANNUAL FINANCIAL REPORT OF THE DIRECTOR OF ADMINISTRATIVE SERVICES.** **Title Change.** (ANNUAL FINANCIAL REPORT OF THE DIRECTOR OF ADMINISTRATIVE SERVICES - OHIO. DEPT. OF ADMINISTRATIVE SERVICES.). **Main/Corp** Ohio. Dept. of Administrative Services. English. an. Columbus Department of Administrative Services, 30 East Broad Street, Columbus OH 43215. **LC** HJ11; .O343A. **DD** 353.9/771/00722.

US
**ANNUAL FINANCIAL REPORT, STATE OWNED TOLL BRIDGES.** See Transportation.

US
**ANNUAL FINANCIAL REPORT / TEXAS ANIMAL HEALTH COMMISSION.** **Main/Corp** Texas Animal Health Commission. English. an. Texas Animal Health Commission, Sam Houston State Office Building, PO Box 12966, Austin TX 78711. **Tel** (512)475-4111. **LC** SF624.T4; T48A. **DD** 353.97640082/336.

US
**ANNUAL FINANCIAL REPORT / TEXAS DEPARTMENT OF HEALTH.** See Public Health and Safety.

II/0304-6516
**ANNUAL FINANCIAL STATEMENT AND EXPLANATORY MEMORANDUM ON THE BUDGET OF THE PUNJAB GOVERNMENT.** **Main/Corp** Punjab (India). (19??)-. English (Panjabi). an. Rs27.30. Government of Punjab / Chandigarh, Economic & Statistical Organization, Chandigarh India. **LC** HJ66.P73; B13a. **DD** 354/.54/55200722. **Supersedes** Memorandum Explanatory of the Budget.

II
**ANNUAL FINANCIAL STATEMENT (BUDGET) OF THE GOVERNMENT OF GUJARAT FOR THE YEAR ... .** **Main/Corp** Gujarat (India). **VFOAT** Gujarata Sarakaranum ... Na Varshanum Varshika Nanakiya Patraka (Andajapatra). (1979/80)-. English (Gujarati). an. **LC** HJ66.G8; B16. **DD** 354.54/75007231. **Continues** Gujarata Sarakaranum Nanakiya Patraka.

US
**ANNUAL FISCAL REPORT YEAR ENDING JUNE 30 ... / STATE OF NEBRASKA.** **Main/Corp** Nebraska. Accounting Division. **VFOAT** State of Nebraska Annual Fiscal Report. English. an. Department of Administrative Services, State Capitol Building, Lincoln NE 68509. **Tel** (402)471-2581. **ED** Donald Herz. **LC** HJ11; .N2197A. **DD** 353.97820072/31/05. **Circ:** 500. **Continues** Annual Fiscal Report (Cash Basis) State of Nebraska.
**Desc:** Comprehensive Financial Report for the State of Nebraska.

UK
**ANNUAL INDEX TO THE FINANCIAL TIMES.** **Added/Corp** Financial Times Business Information Ltd. (1981)-. English. an. Financial Times Business Information Ltd., Tower House, Southampton Street, London WC2E 7HA England. **Tel** 011 44 71 353 1040. **(Subscription address:** Research Publications Inc. / Microfilm, 12 Lunar Drive Drawer AB, Woodbridge CT 06525.) **LC** HG11; .A56. **DD** 332/.0941.

CN/0382-2486
**ANNUAL NORTHERN EXPENDITURE PLAN.** [Annu. north. expend. plan]. **Main/Corp** Canada. Indian and Northern Affairs Canada. **VFOAT** Programme Annuel des Depenses dans le Nord. (1985/86)-. English. an. Canada Advisory Committee on Northern Development, Department of Indian Affairs, Publishing Division, Ottawa Ontario K1A 0H4 Canada. **LC** HJ13; .A18113A. **DD** 354.710072/2253/09719. **Separated from** Government Activities in the North, 0575-7681; **Absorbed** Canada. Indian and Northern Affairs Canada. Programme Annuel des Depenses dans le Nord., 0382-2494.

US
**ANNUAL REPORT - ADVISORY COUNCIL ON INTERGOVERNMENTAL RELATIONS.** **Main/Corp** Florida Advisory Council on Intergovernmental Relations. (1977/1978)-. English. an. Florida Advisory Council on Intergovernmental Relations, Lewis State Bank Building/Suite 400, Tallahassee FL 32304. **LC** HJ370; .F56a. **DD** 353.9/759/00725.

# Public Administration — Public Finance and Taxation

**US**
**ANNUAL REPORT AND AUDITED FINANCIAL STATEMENTS AS OF ... .** **Main/Corp** Puerto Rico Municipal Finance Agency. **VFOAT** Audited Financial Statements. English. an. free. Government Development Bank for Puerto Rico, PO Box 42001, San Juan PR 00940. **Tel** (809)722-2525, FAX (809)268-5496. **ED** Meniemil Rodriguez. **Circ:** 13,000 (ctrl).
**Desc:** Describes GDB's performance for a particular fiscal year. Includes a summary of priorities and economic activity for that period

**US**
**ANNUAL REPORT - AUDITOR OF STATE.** *Title Change.* **Main/Corp** Ohio. Auditor of State. **Added/Corp** Ohio. Auditor of State. Public Relations Office. Ohio. Auditor of State. Public Information Office. **VFOAT** State of Ohio Annual Report. (1972)-(19??). English. an. **LC** HJ11; .O32. **DD** 336.771. *Continues* Annual Report of the State of Ohio for the Fiscal Year ... . *Continued by* Annual Report (1991).

**US/0360-6627**
**ANNUAL REPORT, BOND PAYMENT FUND.** (ANNUAL REPORT - BOND PAYMENT FUND, CITY OF AKRON, OHIO.). [Annu. rep. Bond Paym. Fund]. **Main/Corp** Akron, Ohio. Dept. of Finance. English. an. Ohio Department of Finance, Akron OH 44328.

**US**
**ANNUAL REPORT / COMMISSIONER OF INTERNAL REVENUE AND THE CHIEF COUNSEL FOR THE INTERNAL REVENUE SERVICE.** **Main/Corp** United States. Internal Revenue Service. **Added/Corp** United States. Internal Revenue Service. Office of the Chief Counsel. Annual Report. (1981)-. Government Publication. English. an. Superintendent of Documents, US Government Printing Office, Washington DC 20402. **Tel** (202)275-3328, FAX (202)786-2377. **LC** HJ10; .R73a. **DD** 353.0072/4/006. available on microfiche (Vols. for (1982-) distributed to depository libraries). *Formed by the union of* Annual Report of the Commissioner of Internal Revenue *and* United States. Internal Revenue Service. Chief Counsel, Annual Report.

**US**
**ANNUAL REPORT / COMMONWEALTH OF MASSACHUSETTS, DEPARTMENT OF REVENUE.** **Main/Corp** Massachusetts. Dept. of Revenue. English. an. Department of Revenue / Massachusetts, Leverett Saltonstall Building, 100 Cambridge Street, Boston MA 02204. **LC** HJ11; M4525A. **DD** 353.97440072/6/06.

**DK**
**ANNUAL REPORT - DENMARK. STATENS REGNSKABSDIREKTORAT.** **Main/Corp** Denmark. Statens Regnskabsdirektorat. English. an. Danish State Accounting Directorate, Statens Regnskabsdirektorat, Borgergade 18, Postboks 2193, 1017 Kbenhavn K Denmark. **LC** HJ56; .A63A. **DD** 354.4890072/31/05.

**US/0093-7207**
**ANNUAL REPORT - DEPARTMENT OF REVENUE AND TAXATION. AD VALOREM TAX DIVISION (CHEYENNE).** (ANNUAL REPORT - DEPARTMENT OF REVENUE AND TAXATION, AD VALOREM TAX DIVISION (WYOMING).). **Main/Corp** Wyoming. Ad Valorem Tax Division. 1973-. English. an. Department of Revenue and Taxation / Wyoming, Herschler Building, Cheyenne WY 82002-0110. **Tel** (307)777-5236. **LC** HJ4285; .A25A. **DD** 336.2/2/09787. *Continues* Biennial Report of the State Board of Equalization of the State of Wyoming, Ad Valorem Tax Department.

**US**
**ANNUAL REPORT, FISCAL YEAR ENDED JUNE 30 ... / STATE OF OKLAHOMA, STATE AUDITOR AND INSPECTOR.** **Main/Corp** Oklahoma. Office of the Auditor and Inspector. English. an. **LC** HJ11; .O526A. **DD** 353.97660072/32.

**US**
**ANNUAL REPORT FOR THE FISCAL YEAR ... TO THE GOVERNOR AND LEGISLATURE OF THE STATE OF WASHINGTON.** **Main/Corp** Washington (State). Office of the State Treasurer. **VFOAT** Annual Financial Report; Annual Report of the Treasurer, State of Washington. (July 1984-June 1985)-. English. **LC** HJ11; .W16b. **DD** 353.97970072/05. *Continues* Annual Financial Report for the Fiscal Year... to the Governor and Legislature of the State of Washington.

**AT**
**ANNUAL REPORT FOR ... / WESTERN AUSTRALIA, LEGISLATIVE ASSEMBLY, PUBLIC ACCOUNTS AND EXPENDITURE REVIEW COMMITTEE.** **Main/Corp** Western Australia. Parliament. Legislative Assembly. Public Accounts and Expenditure Review Committee. (July 30, 1986/June 30, 1987)-. English. an. Public Accounts and Expenditure Review Committee, Parliament House, Perth Western Australia 6000 Australia. **LC** HJ90.W47; W48A. **DD** 336.94/05. *Continues* Annual Report / Western Australia. Parliament. Legislative Assembly.

**NE**
**ANNUAL REPORT. INTERNATIONAL BUREAU OF FISCAL DOCUMENTATION.** **Main/Corp** International Bureau of Fiscal Documentation. (1953)-. Periodical. English. ir. Free. International Bureau of Fiscal Documentation - IBFD Publications, PO Box 20237, 1000 HE Amsterdam The Netherlands. **Tel** 011 31 20-6267726, FAX 011 31 20-6228658, telex 13217 INTAX NL. **(Subscription address:** IBFD / International Bureau of Fiscal Documentation USA, Inc., 24 Hudson Street, Kinderhook NY 12106.) **ED** H. A. Sherman, CA, FCA, ATII (Canada).
**Desc:** Developments and new trends in the international tax world.

**US/0588-4519**
**ANNUAL REPORT - LEGISLATIVE AUDIT COMMITTEE. (COLORADO).** **Main/Corp** Colorado. General Assembly. Legislative Audit Committee. (1965)-. English. an. **LC** HJ11; .C6276a. **DD** 353.97880072/32/06. *Continued in part by* Colorado. Office of State Auditor. Annual Report.

**CN**
**ANNUAL REPORT OF THE AUDITOR GENERAL OF BRITISH COLUMBIA TO THE LEGISLATIVE ASSEMBLY.** *Title Change.* **Main/Corp** British Columbia. Office of the Auditor General. (19??)-(19??). English. Office of the Auditor General / Victoria, 756 Fort Street, Victoria British Columbia V8V 1X4 Canada. **LC** HJ13; .B56a. **DD** 354.7110072/32/06. *Continues* British Columbia. Office of the Auditor General. Report of the Auditor General for the Year Ended 31 March ..., 0708-5222. *Continued by* British Columbia. Office of the Aditor General. Report to the Legislative Assembly of British Columbia on the ... Public Accounts, 1193-2430.

**US**
**ANNUAL REPORT OF THE AUDITOR GENERAL / STATE OF ARIZONA.** **Main/Corp** Arizona. Office of the Auditor General. (19??)-. English. an. Free. Arizona Auditor General, 2700 North Central 700, Phoenix AZ 85004. **Tel** (602)255-4385. **LC** HJ11; .A623. **DD** 353.97910072/32/05.

**AT**
**ANNUAL REPORT OF THE AUDITOR-GENERAL UPON THE BOOKS AND ACCOUNTS OF THE BRISBANE CITY COUNCIL.** **Main/Corp** Brisbane City Council. English. an. **LC** HJ9779.A8; B74A. **DD** 352.1/72/099431. *Continues in part* Brisbane City Council. Annual Report.

**US/0147-0507**
**ANNUAL REPORT OF THE LEGISLATIVE BUDGET AND FINANCE COMMITTEE FOR THE REGULAR SESSION OF THE GENERAL ASSEMBLY OF THE COMMONWEALTH OF PENNSYLVANIA.** *Title Change.* **Main/Corp** Pennsylvania. General Assembly. Legislative Budget and Finance Committee. English. an. Legislative Budget and Finance Committee Senate, PO Box 80, Main Capitol Building, Harrisburg PA 17120. **LC** JK3671; .P45A. **DD** 328.748/07/65. *Continued by* Annual Report of the General Assembly (Pennsylavnia. General Assembly. Legislative Budget and Finance Committee).

**US/0093-660X**
**ANNUAL REPORT OF THE OFFICE OF REVENUE SHARING (WASHINGTON).** *Ceased.* (ANNUAL REPORT OF THE OFFICE OF REVENUE SHARING.). **Main/Corp** United States. Office of Revenue Sharing. (1974)-(19??). English. an. **(Subscription address:** Superintendent of Documents, US Government Printing Office, Washington DC 20402**)** **LC** HJ275; .U574A. **DD** 353.007/25.

**US/0196-6103**
**ANNUAL REPORT OF THE OHIO DEPARTMENT OF TAXATION.** [Annu. rep. Ohio Dep. Tax.]. **Main/Corp** Ohio. Dept. of Taxation. 1940-. English. an. Department of Taxation / Ohio, Research and Statistics Section, PO Box 530, Columbus OH 43216. **LC** HJ11; .O36. **DD** 336.2. *Continues* Annual Report of the Tax Commission of Ohio.

**AT**
**ANNUAL REPORT OF THE PUBLIC TRUSTEE OF QUEENSLAND FOR THE FINANCIAL YEAR ENDED 30TH JUNE.** **Main/Corp** Queensland. Public Trust Office. (1989)-. English. an. Public Trust Office, 444 Queen Street, Brisbane Australia. **LC** HG4490.A8; Q43A. **DD** 354.943008. *Continues* Financial Statements of the Public Trustee of Queensland for the Financial Year Ended ... .

**US**
**ANNUAL REPORT OF THE STATE OF CALIFORNIA FOR THE FISCAL YEAR ENDED JUNE 30 ... .** **Main/Corp** California. Office of State Controller. **VFOAT** State of California Annual Report. 1978-. English. an. Free. Grey Davis State Controller, Division of Accounting, PO Box 942850, Sacramento CA 94250-5875. **Tel** (916)445-4181. **LC** HJ11; .C218E. **DD** 353.97940072/31/05. Index available. **Circ:** 2,000. *Continues* Annual Report of the State Controller, State of California, for the Fiscal Year Ended June 30 ... .
**Desc:** Reports statements of financial condition and operations for all funds administered by the state of California Government.

**US**
**ANNUAL REPORT OF THE STATE TREASURER FOR THE PERIOD JANUARY 1 ... TO DECEMBER 31 ... / DEPARTMENT OF TREASURY.** **Main/Corp** Oregon. Dept. of Treasury. English. an. **LC** HJ11; .O687A. **DD** 353.97950072/06.

**US/0148-6519**
**ANNUAL REPORT OF THE TREASURER (STATE OF NEW HAMPSHIRE).** (ANNUAL REPORT OF THE TREASURER.). **Main/Corp** New Hampshire. Treasury Dept. (1939)-. English. an. Treasury Department / New Hampshire, State House, Concord NH 03301. **LC** HJ11; .N4. **DD** 353.9/742/0072. *Continues* New Hampshire. Treasury Dept. Report of the State Treasurer for the Fiscal Year Ending ... .

**US**
**ANNUAL REPORT ON DEPOSITORY ACTIVITIES, FY ... / OFFICE OF THE DISTRICT OF COLUMBIA AUDITOR.** **Main/Corp** District of Columbia. Office of the Auditor. 1978-. English. an. **LC** HJ3835.W18; D57A. **DD** 352.1/4.

**UK**
**ANNUAL REPORT / PUBLIC FINANCE FOUNDATION.** **Main/Corp** Public Finance Foundation (Great Britain). (19??)-. English. an. Comes with Public Finance Foundation Review. Chartered Institute of Public Finance and Accountancy, 2 3 Robert Street, London WC2N 6BH England. **Tel** 011 44 1 895 8823.

**US/0091-0686**
**ANNUAL REPORT - STATE INVESTMENT COUNCIL. STATE OF NEBRASKA.** (ANNUAL REPORT.). **Main/Corp** Nebraska. State Investment Council. English. an. Nebraska State Investment Council, 941 O Street/#107 Terminal Building, Lincoln NE 68508-3626. **LC** HJ3835.N2; A28. **DD** 353.97820072/6.

**US/0095-3865**
**ANNUAL REPORT - STATE OF ALASKA, LEGISLATIVE BUDGET AND AUDIT COMMITTEE.** **Main/Corp** Alaska. Legislature. Budget and Audit Committee. English. an. Legislative Budget and Audit Committee, Juneau AK 99801. **LC** HJ11; .A42. **DD** 353.9/798/007232. *Continues* Alaska. Legislature. Audit Committee. Annual Report.

**US/0099-1627**
**ANNUAL REPORT - STATE OF OHIO, LEGISLATIVE BUDGET OFFICE OF THE LEGISLATIVE SERVICE COMMISSION, LEGISLATIVE BUDGET COMMITTEE.** (ANNUAL REPORT - STATE OF OHIO, LEGISLATIVE BUDGET COMMITTEE.). **Main/Corp** Ohio. Legislative Budget Committee. (1974)-. English. an. Legislative Budget Committee - Ohio, 40 South Third Street, Columbus OH 43215. **LC** HJ9889; .A25a. **DD** 353.9/771/00722.

**US**
**ANNUAL REPORT - TAXATION & REVENUE DEPARTMENT, PROPERTY TAX DIVISION.** **Main/Corp** New Mexico. Property Tax Division. 1978-. English. an. Taxation & Revenue Department / New Mexico, Property Tax Division, Manuel Lujan Sr Building, Santa Fe NM 87509. **LC** HJ4121.N6; P75A. **DD** 353.97890072/42/06. *Continues* Annual Report - Property Tax Department, 0360-2958.

**US**
**ANNUAL REPORT TO CONGRESS ON TRUTH IN LENDING.** **Main/Corp** Board of Governors of the Federal Reserve System (U.S.). 1st (1969)-. English. an. Free upon request. Board of Governors of the Federal Reserve System, Mail Stop 127, Washington DC 20551. **Tel** (202)452-3244 or 3245.

# Public Administration — Public Finance and Taxation

**US**
**ANNUAL REPORT TO THE GENERAL ASSEMBLY / LEGISLATIVE BUDGET AND FINANCE COMMITTEE.** **Main/Corp** Pennsylvania. General Assembly. Legislative Budget and Finance Committee. English. Legislative Budget and Finance Committee Senate, PO Box 80, Main Capitol Building, Harrisburg PA 17120. *Continues Annual Report of the Legislative Budget and Finance Committee for the Regular Session of the General Assembly of the Commonwealth of Pennsylvania, 0147-0507.*

**US**
**ANNUAL REPORT TO THE LEGISLATURE / LEGISLATIVE COMMISSION ON EXPENDITURE.** **Main/Corp** New York (State). Legislature. Legislative Commission on Expenditure Review. 1983-. English. an. Free. Legislative Committee on Expenditure Review, 111 Washington Avenue, Albany NY 12210. **Tel** (518)455-7410. Index available. **Circ:** 400. *Continues Report to the Legislature / New York (State). Legislature. Legislative Commission on Expenditure Review.*
**Desc:** The commission makes reviews of state programs and expenditures to evaluate program efficiency, effectiveness, and program achievement measured against legislative intent.

**US/0739-6058**
**ANNUAL REPORT - UNITED STATES. DEPT. OF THE TREASURY. OFFICE OF THE INSPECTOR GENERAL.** (ANNUAL REPORT / OFFICE OF INSPECTOR GENERAL, DEPARTMENT OF THE TREASURY.). **Main/Corp** United States. Dept. of the Treasury. Office of Inspector General. **VFOAT** Department of the Treasury Annual Report to the Secretary on Program Integrity. 1980-. English. an. Department of the Treasury / Pennsylvania Avenue, Fifteenth Street and Pennsylvania Avenue NW, Washington DC 20220. **Tel** (202)566-2969. **LC** HJ10; .A458A. **DD** 353.2. available on microfiche (Vols. for (1986-) distributed to depository libraries). *Continues United States. Dept. of the Treasury. Office of Inspector General. Annual Report of the Inspector General for Fiscal Year ... .*

**HK**
**ANNUAL SUMMARY BY THE COMMISSIONER OF RATING AND VALUATION (HONGKONG).** **Main/Corp** Hong Kong. Rating and Valuation Dept. English. an. Rating and Valuation Department, Hennessy Centre, 500 Hennessy Road, Causeway Bay Hong Kong. **Tel** 5-8957614. **LC** HJ4403.H85; H66A. **DD** 336.2/2/095125.

**SW**
**ANSLAGSFRAMSTALLNING FOR BUDGETARET ... / STATENS RAD FOR BYGGNADSFORSKNING.** Swedish. an. Statens Rad for Byggnadsforskning, St Goransgatan 66, 112 30 Stockholm Sweden. **LC** TH89; .A68.

**US/1060-4707**
**ANTI-DRUG FUNDING ALERT.** *Title Change.* See Public Administration.

**IE**
**APPROPRIATION ACCOUNTS.** **Main/Corp** Ireland. Office of the Comptroller and Auditor General. **VFOAT** Accounts of the Public Services. (19??)-. Government Publication. English. an. £11.00. Office of the Comptroller and Auditor General, Dublin Castle, Dublin 2 Ireland. **Tel** 6793122, FAX 6793288. **LC** HJ42; .C3. **DD** 354.4170072/236/05. Index available. **Circ:** 1,500. available on diskette. *Continues Ireland. Exchequer and Audit Dept. Appropriations Accounts.*

**II**
**APPROPRIATION ACCOUNTS, GOVERNMENT OF ORISSA.** **Main/Corp** India. Comptroller and Auditor-General. English. an. Rs4.00. Comptroller and Auditor-General, Madhupatna 3 India. **LC** HJ66.043C4. **DD** 336.3/9/095413.

**TZ**
**APPROPRIATION ACCOUNTS, REVENUE STATEMENTS, ACCOUNTS OF THE FUNDS AND OTHER PUBLIC ACCOUNTS OF TANZANIA, THE.** **Main/Corp** Tanzania. 1964/65-. English. The Government Printer / Tanzania, Dar es Salaam Tanzania. **LC** HJ9929.T3; T3A. **DD** 354/.678/007231.

**US**
**APPROPRIATIONS REPORT / COMMITTEE ON STATE FISCAL AFFAIRS.** **Main/Corp** Missouri. General Assembly. Committee on State Fiscal Affairs. English. an. Committee on State Fiscal Affairs, Room 132/State Capitol, Jefferson City MO 65101. **LC** HJ11; .M852A. **DD** 353.97780072/236/05. *Continues Missouri. General Assembly. Committee on State Fiscal Affairs. Appropriation Summary.*

**US**
**APPROPRIATIONS REPORT / KANSAS LEGISLATIVE RESEARCH DEPARTMENT.** **Main/Corp** Kansas. Legislature. Legislative Research Dept. Began with 1975/76 issue. English. an. Legislative Research Department, Statehouse/Room 545-N, Topeka KS 66612. **LC** HJ11; .K238A. **DD** 353.97810072/236/05.

**NR/0331-1619**
**APPROVED ESTIMATES OF ANAMBRA STATE OF NIGERIA.** **Main/Corp** Anambra State (Nigeria). **VFOAT** Recurrent Estimates of the Government of Anambra State of Nigeria; Estimates of Anambra State of Nigeria. Began with 1976/77. English. an. Government Printer / Kaduna, Private Mail Bag 2020, Kaduna Nigeria. **LC** HJ86.2.A86; A5A. **DD** 354.669/4.
**Desc:** Vols. for 1979-1980 include Budget speech, delivered by the Military Administrator of Anambra State.

**BM**
**APPROVED ESTIMATES OF REVENUE AND EXPENDITURE.** **Main/Corp** Bermuda Islands. English. **LC** HJ28.B4; A32A. **DD** 354/.729/900722.

**NR/0189-9023**
**APPROVED REVENUE, RECURRENT AND CAPITAL ESTIMATES (NIGERIA).** **Main/Corp** Nigeria. **VFOAT** Approved Budget ... Fiscal Year. (1983)-. English. an. N5.00. **LC** HJ81P; .A315. **DD** 354.6690072/225/05. *Continues Revenue, Recurrent and Capital Estimates of the Government of the Federal Republic of Nigeria, 0331-468X.*

**SI/0217-6661**
**APTIRC BULLETIN.** **Added/Corp** Asian-Pacific Tax and Investment Research Centre. **VFOAT** APTIRC Tax and Investment News. **VAT** Asian Pacific Tax and Investment Research Centre Bulletin. Vol. 9, No. 1 (Jan. 1991)-. Bulletin. English. mo. 416.67Sing$. Asian Pacific Tax Investment Research Center, 2 Nassim Road, Singapore 1025 Singapore. **Tel** 011 65 2351954. **LC** K4456.2; .A84. **DD** 343.052/46/091823; 342.35246091823. *Continues Asian-Pacific Tax and Investment Bulletin.*

**US**
**ARKANSAS PERSONAL INCOME HANDBOOK.** Oct. 1978-. English. an. University of Arkansas / Industrial Research, Industrial Research Extension Center, PO Box 3017, Little Rock AR 72203. **LC** HC107.A83; I5134. **DD** 339.3767.

**US**
**ARKANSAS STATE AND COUNTY ECONOMIC DATA.** **Added/Corp** Arkansas Industrial Development Commission. University of Arkansas at Little Rock. Industrial Research and Extension Center. University of Arkansas at Little Rock. Research and Public Service. (Oct. 1984)-. English. Industrial Research and Extension Center, University of Arkansas, PO Box 3017, Little Rock AR 72203. *Continues State and County Economic Data for Arkansas.*

**US/0732-491X**
**ARNOLD G. RUDOFF'S TAX SHELTER DIRECTORY.** See Business-Investments.

**US/0884-2221**
**ARREARAGE TABLES OF AMOUNTS DUE AND UNPAID 90 DAYS OR MORE ON FOREIGN CREDITS OF THE UNITED STATES GOVERNMENT (1979).** (ARREARAGE TABLES OF AMOUNTS DUE AND UNPAID 90 DAYS OR MORE ON FOREIGN CREDITS OF THE UNITED STATES GOVERNMENT.). [Arrear. tables amounts due unpaid 90 days more foreign credits U.S. gov. (1979)]. **Added/Corp** United States. Dept. of the Treasury. Office of the Assistant Secretary for International Affairs. **VFOAT** Amounts Due and Unpaid 90 Days or More on Foreign Credits of the United States Government. **VAT** Arrearage Tables of Amounts Due and Unpaid Ninety Days or More on Foreign Credits of the United States Government. (1979)-. English. qt. Department of the Treasury / Pennsylvania Avenue, Fifteenth Street and Pennsylvania Avenue NW, Washington DC 20220. **Tel** (202)566-2969. **LC** HJ8085; .U54b. **DD** 336.3/4/0973021. **Circ:** 200. available on microfiche; available on microfilm. *Continues United States. Dept. of the Treasury. Office of the Assistant Secretary for International Affairs. Amounts Due and Unpaid 90 Days or More on Foreign Credits of the United States Government.*
**Desc:** Tables present a record of foreign indebtedness to the United States Government with principal emphasis on amounts due and unpaid 90 days or more. Includes various summaries of the data by program and country, as well as detail of long-term credit arrearages.

**BL**
**ARRECADACAO DOS TRIBUTOS FEDERAIS / MINISTERIO DA FAZENDA, SECRETARIA DA RECEITA FEDERAL, CENTRO DE INFORMACOES ECONOMICO-FISCAIS.** Vol. 1 (1974)-. Portuguese. an. Centro de Informacoes Economico-Foscais, Esplanada Dos Ministerios Bloco 5-9O Andar 70.000, Brasilia DF Brasil. **LC** HJ32; .A32. **DD** 336.2/00981.

**SW**
**ARSBOK - RIKSSKATTEVERKET.** **Main/Corp** Sweden. Riksskatteverket. (1971)-. Swedish. Liberforlag, 171 94 Solna, Stockholm Sweden. **LC** HJ59; .R7a.

**NP**
**ARTHIKA VARSHA KO KARYAKRAMA VIVARANA.** **Main/Corp** Nepal. Ministry of Finance. Nepali. Sri Panc Ko Sarakare Artha Mantralaya, Singha Durbar, Kathamadaum India. **LC** HJ2169.N46; A3A.

**NE**
**ASIA-PACIFIC TAX BULLETIN.** (19??)-. English. mo. $175.00. International Bureau of Fiscal Documentation - IBFD Publications, PO Box 20237, 1000 HE Amsterdam The Netherlands. **Tel** 011 31 20-6267726, FAX 011 31 20-6228658, telex 13217 INTAX NL. (Subscription address: IBFD / International Bureau of Fiscal Documentation USA, Inc., 24 Hudson Street, Kinderhook NY 12106.)
**Desc:** In-depth articles on taxation and investment, taxation news, and documentation.

**US**
**ASIAN TAX AFFAIRS.** Periodical. English. qt. $15.00. Surrey and Morse, 655 15th Street NW, Washington DC 20005-5701. **DD** 343.504; 34.034.

**AT**
**ASIATRADE.** See Economics-International Economics.

**US/0090-6352**
**ASSESSMENT AND VALUATION LEGAL REPORTER.** *Title Change.* [Assess. valuat. leg. report.]. **Added/Corp** International Association of Assessing Officers. Vol. 1 (July 1971)-Vol. 18 (Nov. 199?). English. mo. International Association of Assessing Officers, 130 East Randolph Street, Suite 850, Chicago IL 60601. **Tel** (312)819-6100. **ED** Annie Aubrey. **LC** KF6759.5.A59; A8. **DD** 343/.73/042. Index available. cum. index. **Bk Rev. Ad Acc. Circ:** 700 (ctrl). *Merged with IAAO Update, 0892-7154 and Assessment Digest, 0731-0277 Property Tax Journal, 0731-0285 to form Assessment Journal, 1073-8568.*
**Desc:** Summaries of court decisions dealing with questions of valuation, property taxation, etc.

**US/0731-0277**
**ASSESSMENT DIGEST.** *Title Change.* [Assess. dig.]. **Added/Corp** International Association of Assessing Officers. Vol. 1 (Jan./Feb. 1979)-(199?). Periodical. English. bm. International Association of Assessing Officers, 130 East Randolph Street, Suite 850, Chicago IL 60601. **Tel** (312)819-6100. **ED** Annie Aubrey. **Bk Rev. Ad Acc. Circ:** 8,500 (ctrl). *Continues International Assessor. Merged with IAAO Update, 0892-7154 and Property Tax Journal, 0731-0285 Assessment and Valuation Legal Reporter, 0090-6352 to form Assessment Journal, 1073-8568.*
**Desc:** Magazine of news on issues in valuation and property taxation as well as association announcements, etc.
**Ind/Abst** Urban Aff. Abstr.

●**US/1073-8568**
**ASSESSMENT JOURNAL.** [Assess. j.]. **Added/Corp** International Association of Assessing Officers. Vol. 1, No. 1 (Jan./Feb. 1994)-. Periodical. English. Six times a year. Free to members; $150.00 other. International Association of Assessing Officers, 130 East Randolph Street, Suite 850, Chicago IL 60601. **Tel** (312)819-6100. **DD** 336. *Formed by the union of Assessment Digest, 0731-0277 and IAAO Update, 0892-7154 Property Tax Journal, 0731-0285 Assessment and Valuation Legal Reporter, 0090-6352.*

**US**
**ASSESSMENT OF THE COMMONWEALTH.** **Main/Corp** Virginia. Dept. of Planning and Budget. Economic Research Section. (19??)-. English. ir. Commonwealth of Virginia, Department of Planning and Budget, Economic Reasearch Section, Richmond VA 23219. **LC** HJ11; .V8447a. **DD** 336.755.

**US**
**ASSESSMENT/SALES RATIO STUDY.** **Main/Corp** New Mexico. Property Tax Division. English. Taxation & Revenue Department / New Mexico, Property Tax Division, Manuel Lujan Sr Building, Santa Fe NM 87509. **LC** HJ4247; .A33A. **DD** 336.22/2.

# Public Administration — Public Finance and Taxation

BL
**ASSESSOR, O. Main/Corp** Pernambuco, Brazil (State). Assessoria de Comunicacao Fazendaria. Periodical. Portuguese. Secretaria da Fazenda, Assessoria de Comunicacao Fazendaira Pernambuco, rua do Imperador Pedro II, S/N 80 Andar, 5000 Recife Brazil. **LC** HJ32; .P368A.

UK/0958-367X
**AUDIT BRIEFING.** [Audit brief]. (1989)-. Periodical. English. mo. £75.00. Tolley Publishing Company Ltd, Tolley House, 2 Addiscombe Road, Croydon, Surrey CR9 5AF United Kingdom. **Tel** 011 44 81 6869141, **FAX** 011 44 81 6863155, 011 44 81 7600588. **DD** 657.450941.

US/0095-5817
**AUDIT OF NEW YORK STATE AGENCIES. See** Business-Accounting.

US
**AUDIT REPORT, DEPARTMENT OF ARKANSAS NATURAL AND CULTURAL HERITAGE, ARKANSAS TERRITORIAL CAPITOL RESTORATION COMMISSION. Main/Corp** Arkansas. General Assembly. Division of Legislative Audit. 1974/75-. English. an. **LC** HJ9823; .A238A. **DD** 353.9/767/008232. *Continues* Audit Report. Department of Parks and Tourism, Monuments and Historical Sites Division, Arkansas Territorial Capitol Restoration, 0146-5503.

US/0148-0464
**AUDIT REPORT, DEPARTMENT OF INSURANCE, TENNESSEE BOARD OF BARBER EXAMINERS. Main/Corp** Tennessee. Division of State Audit. English. Tennessee Comptroller of the Treasury, Nashville TN 37219. **LC** HJ5366; .T45A. **DD** 353.9/768/008.

US/0146-5503
**AUDIT REPORT, DEPARTMENT OF PARKS AND TOURISM, MONUMENTS AND HISTORICAL SITES DIVISION, ARKANSAS TERRITORIAL CAPITOL RESTORATION. Main/Corp** Arkansas. General Assembly. Division of Legislative Audit. English. an. Arkansas Legislative Joint Auditing Committee, 1401 West 6th Street, Little Rock AR 72201-2901. **LC** HJ9823; .A238A. **DD** 353.9/767/008232.

II
**AUDIT REPORT, GOVERNMENT OF ORISSA. Main/Corp** India (Republic). Comptroller and Auditor-General. English. an. Rs6.00. Orissa Government Press, Madhupatna 3, Cuttack India. **LC** HJ9927.I4; A296. **DD** 354/.54/130072.

JA
**AUDIT REPORT ON FINAL ACCOUNTS FOR FISCAL ..., THE.** *Title Change.* **Main/Corp** Japan. **Added/Corp** Japan. Kaikei Kensain. (19??)-(198?). English. an. **LC** HJ77; .A55a. **DD** 354.520072/32/05. *Continued by* Japan. Kaikei Kensain. Audit Report for Fiscal ... .

US
**AUDIT REPORT, STATE COMPTROLLER OF PUBLIC ACCOUNTS, AUSTIN, TEXAS, YEAR ENDED AUGUST 31 ... . Main/Corp** Texas. Comptroller's Office. English. an. **LC** HJ11; .T437. **DD** 353.97640072/32/05.

US/0160-5755
**AUDIT REPORT, STATE OF NEVADA DEPARTMENT OF GENERAL SERVICES, PURCHASING DIVISION, DONATED COMMODITIES REVOLVING FUND. Main/Corp** Nevada. Legislature. Legislative Auditor. (19??)-. English. an. Legislative Auditor, Legislative Building, Capitol Complex, Carson City NV 89710. **LC** HJ9875; .A23c. **DD** 353.9/793/007232.

AT
**AUDITOR-GENERAL'S REPORT TO THE LEGISLATIVE ASSEMBLY ON HIS AUDIT OF THE TREASURER'S ANNUAL STATEMENT FOR THE FINANCIAL YEAR ENDED 30TH JUNE ..., THE. Main/Corp** Queensland. Auditor-General's Dept. **VFOAT** Auditor-General's Report on the Treasurer's Annual Statement for the Financial Year Ended 30th June ... . English. an. **LC** HJ9931.Q43; Q43B. **DD** 354.9430072/32/05. *Continues* Queensland. Auditor-General's Dept. Auditor-General's Annual Report upon the Treasurer's Annual Statement, 0312-6374.

US
**AUDITOR'S ANNUAL REPORT OF EL PASO COUNTY, TEXAS. Main/Corp** El Paso Co., Tex. Auditor's Office. (1926)-. English.

CN/0845-0722
**AUDITOR'S REPORT AND FINANCIAL STATEMENTS FOR THE YEAR ENDED DECEMBER 31 ... .** [Annu. financ. rep. - Brandon Univ., Pension Fund]. **Main/Corp** Brandon University. Retirement Plan. **VFOAT** Annual Financial Report for the Year Ended December 31 ... . (1985)-. English. an. Brandon University Retirement Plan, Brandon Manitoba R7A 6A9 Canada. **DD** 658.3/253. *Continues* Auditor's Report and Financial Statements for the Year Ended December 31 ..., 0225-9931.

AT
**AUSTRALASIAN TAX REPORTS.** Vol. 1 (1970)-. English. ir. 438.00Aus$ (includes bound volumes and advance parts issued every two weeks). Butterworths Pty Ltd, 271-273 Lane Cove Road, PO Box 345, North Ryde NSW 2113 Australia. **Tel** 011 61 2 3354444, **FAX** 011 61 2 3354655. **DD** 343/.9/052. *Supersedes* Australian and New Zealand Income Tax Reports.
**Desc:** Brings together significant tax cases decided in the Courts and Administrative Appeals Tribunals. Cases relate to income tax, stamp duty, payroll tax, land tax, sales tax, and other taxes and imposts.
**Ind/Abst** Aust. Leg. Mon. Dig.

AT/0310-7817
**AUSTRALIAN FEDERAL TAX REPORTER.** [Aust. fed. tax rep.]. (1971)-. Periodical. English. wk. 1855.00Aus$. CCH Australia Ltd, PO Box 230, North Ryde New South Wales, 2113 Australia. **Tel** 011 61 02 888 2555, **FAX** 011 61 02 888 7324. **DD** 336.240994. **[CCC]**.

AT
**AUSTRALIAN INCOME TAX GUIDE.** 22nd Ed. (1977)-. English. ir. 625.00Aus$. CCH Australia Ltd, PO Box 230, North Ryde New South Wales, 2113 Australia. **Tel** 011 61 02 888 2555, **FAX** 011 61 02 888 7324. Each issue contains an index to its own contents (no volume index)--loose. **Circ:** 6,500. *Continues* Guide to Australian Income Tax.
**Desc:** Explanations and fast, accurate answers on all aspects of Australian income tax laws.

AT/0810-5499
**AUSTRALIAN INCOME TAX LEGISLATION IN 2 VOLUMES. 2. REGULATIONS, RATING ACTS, INTERNATIONAL AGREEMENTS, OTHER LEGISLATION.** [Aust. income tax legis. 2 vol., 2, Regul. rating acts int. agreem. other legis.]. (1982)-. Periodical. English. an. 580.00Aus$. CCH Australia Ltd, PO Box 230, North Ryde New South Wales, 2113 Australia. **Tel** 011 61 02 888 2555, **FAX** 011 61 02 888 7324. **DD** 343.94052. *Continues* Australian Income Tax Assessment Act.
**Desc:** Provides a summary of amendments made during the year, comprehensive indexes covering all legislation, detailed history notes of substantive amendments for the last seven years, and more.

AT
**AUSTRALIAN MASTER TAX GUIDE. Added/Corp** CCH Australia Limited. (19??)-. English. an. 44.90Aus$. CCH Australia Ltd, PO Box 230, North Ryde New South Wales, 2113 Australia. **Tel** 011 61 02 888 2555, **FAX** 011 61 02 888 7324. **DD** 343/.94/052. available on CD-ROM.
**Desc:** Provides information on significant income tax and fringe benefits tax developments.

AT/1033-3010
**AUSTRALIAN NATIONAL ACCOUNTS. CAPITAL STOCK. See** Public Administration-Abstracting, Bibliographies and Statistics.

AT/1038-4286
**AUSTRALIAN NATIONAL ACCOUNTS FINANCIAL ACCOUNTS. See** Public Administration-Abstracting, Bibliographies and Statistics.

AT
**AUSTRALIAN NATIONAL ACCOUNTS; INPUT-OUTPUT TABLES. See** Public Administration-Abstracting, Bibliographies and Statistics.

AT/0067-1983
**AUSTRALIAN NATIONAL ACCOUNTS : NATIONAL INCOME AND EXPENDITURE. See** Public Administration-Abstracting, Bibliographies and Statistics.

AT
**AUSTRALIAN NATIONAL ACCOUNTS. STATE ACCOUNTS. See** Public Administration-Abstracting, Bibliographies and Statistics.

AT/0726-5859
**AUSTRALIAN TAX CASES. Main/Corp** Commerce Clearing House Australia Limited. **Added/Corp** CCH Australia Limited. (1969)-. English. bw. 900.00Aus$. CCH Australia Ltd, PO Box 230, North Ryde New South Wales, 2113 Australia. **Tel** 011 61 02 888 2555, **FAX** 011 61 02 888 7324. cum. index.
**Desc:** Covers tax decisions of federal and state courts, and administrative appeals tribunals. Each case is preceded by a headnote written by the CCH tax editors which outline the facts, the decision and the reasons for the decision.
**Ind/Abst** Aust. Leg. Mon. Dig.

AT/0812-695X
**AUSTRALIAN TAX FORUM.** [Aust. tax forum.]. **Added/Corp** Monash University. Faculty of Law. Monash University. Centre of Policy Studies. Vol. 1, No. 1 (March 1984)-. Periodical. English. qt. $67.00 (libraries), $47.00 (individuals). The Australian Tax Research Foundation, 8th Level, 17 Castlereagh Street, Sydney NSW 2000, Australia. **Tel** 61 2 2324044, **FAX** 61 2 2216310. **ED** Craene Cooper. **LC** HJ1511; .A97. **Circ:** 1,000. available on an online database (file 485/Full-Text) from DIALOG; and University Microfilms International (UMI).
**Desc:** A journal of taxation policy, law and reform.
**Ind/Abst** Account. Index, Suppl. (1984-); Account. Tax Datab. (1984-) [Full Txt.]; Econ. Lit. Index; J. Econ. Lit.; Leg. Resour. Index; LegalTrac (1984-); PAIS Int. Print.

US/0092-6876
**AUTOMATIC TAXFINDER AND TAX PREPARER'S HANDBOOK. VFOAT** Taxfinder; Tax Preparer's Handbook. English. Recordkeeper Tax Publications, Inc., 48 West 21st Street, New York NY 10010. **LC** KF6370; .A9. **DD** 343/.73/052.

IT
**AZIENDO & FISCO.** (19??)-. Periodical. Italian. sm. L320000 Italy; L640000 other. IPSOA Editore SRL, Casella Postale 12055, Mastrangelo, 20120 Milan Italy. **Tel** 011 39 2 82476248.

CN/0068-161X
**B. C. MUNICIPAL YEAR BOOK.** (1949)-. Periodical. English. an. $7.74. Journal of Commerce Ltd., Box 82230, North Burnaby British Columbia V5C 6E7 Canada. **Tel** (604)433-8164, **FAX** 433-9549. **ED** Cindy Ring. **LC** HJ8514.B72; B18. **DD** 336.711. *Continues* Red Book of British Columbia Municipal and Corporate Finance, 0317-4557.
**Desc:** B.C. Municipal Yearbook contains detailed municipal government data plus information on the British Columbia, Canada, Provincial Government, school districts, regional districts, industrial parks, development regions, boards & commissions, assessment authorities, finance authorities and a municipal suppliers directory.

US/0190-7174
**BACKGROUND PAPER - CONGRESS OF THE UNITED STATES, CONGRESSIONAL BUDGET OFFICE.** (BACKGROUND PAPER.). Monographic series. English. Price varies per volume. Congressional Budget Office, 2nd and D Streets SW, Washington DC 20515. **Tel** (202)226-2115.

TZ
**BACKGROUND TO THE BUDGET; AN ECONOMIC SURVEY.** *Title Change.* **Main/Corp** Tanzania. Periodical. English. **LC** HC557.T3. *Continued by* Annual Economic Survey (Dar es Salaam, Tanzania : 1968).

AT
**BALANCE OF PAYMENTS, AUSTRALIA. See** Public Administration-Abstracting, Bibliographies and Statistics.

AT/0819-6001
**BALANCE OF PAYMENTS, AUSTRALIA. REGIONAL SERIES ON MICROFICHE. See** Public Administration-Abstracting, Bibliographies and Statistics.

US
**BALANCE SHEET - STATE TREASURER OF THE STATE OF OKLAHOMA. Main/Corp** Oklahoma. State Treasurer. Periodical. English. Oklahoma State Treasurer, Oklahoma City OK 73105. **LC** HJ11; .O512A. **DD** 353.9/766/00722.

US
**BALANCE SHEETS OF THE U.S. ECONOMY.** (19??)-. Periodical. English. sa (2 issues per year). $5.00, Free to libraries and education institutions. Board of Governors of the Federal Reserve System, Mail Stop 127, Washington DC 20551. **Tel** (202)452-3244 or 3245.

BL
**BALANCO GERAL / GOVERNO PARANA, SECRETARIA DE ESTADO DAS FINANCAS, COORDENACAO DA ADMINISTRACAO FINANCEIRA DO ESTADO. Main/Corp** Parana (Brazil : State). Coordenacao da Administracao Financeira do Estado. (19??)-. Portuguese. **LC** HJ32.P348; P37a. **DD** 354.81/6200722253/05.

# Public Administration —Public Finance and Taxation

US
**BALDWIN'S OHIO TAX LAW AND RULES.** See Law.

US/0739-1234
**BALDWIN'S OHIO TAX SERVICE.** See Law.

AQ
**BARBUDA COUNCIL ESTIMATES.** **Main/Corp** Antigua and Barbuda. Barbuda Council. **VFOAT** Estimates. (19??)-. English. an. Barbuda Council, St. John's Antigua & Barbuda. **LC** HJ28.33; .A23a. **DD** 354.729740072/225/05.

US
**BASIS AND RATES OF TAXES FOR FISCAL YEAR ... .** **Main/Corp** South Carolina Tax Commission. Research Section. 1970-. English. an. **LC** KFS2270; .A872. **DD** 343.75704/2/05; 347.57034205.

NE
**BEGROTING DER INKOMSTEN EN UITGAVEN VAN DE PROVINCIE NOORD-BRABANT.** **Main/Corp** North Brabant (Netherlands). (19??)-. Dutch. **LC** HJ9054; .B7a.

NE
**BEGROTING. TOELICHTING.** **Main/Corp** North Holland (Netherlands). **VFOAT** Toelichting. (19??)-. Dutch. an. **LC** HJ54; .H64a. **Continues** North Holland (Netherlands). Begroting: Memorie Van Toelichting.

SA
**BEGROTING VAN DIE UITGAWES WAT UIT INKOMSTEREKENING (SOUTH AFRICA).** **Added/Corp** South Africa. Estimate of the Expenditure to be Defrayed from Revenue Account. **VFOAT** Estimate of the Expenditure to be Defrayed from Revenue Account. Afrikaans (English). an. R4.00. Government Printer / South Africa, Bosman Street, Private Bag X85, Pretoria 0001 South Africa. **Tel** 011 27 12 3239731 Ext. 262. **LC** HJ80A; .A3145. **DD** 354/.68/00722.

SA
**BEGROTING VAN INKOMSTE.** **Main/Corp** South Africa. **VFOAT** Estimate of Revenue. Afrikaans (English). R1.20. Government Printer / South Africa, Bosman Street, Private Bag X85, Pretoria 0001 South Africa. **Tel** 011 27 12 3239731 Ext. 262. **LC** HJ80A; .A318B.

NE/0077-670X
**BELASTINGDRUK IN NEDERLAND.** **VFOAT** Burden of Taxes in the Netherlands. Dutch. an. Centraal Bureau voor de Statistiek, AFD ALG Zaken, Postbus 959, 2270 AZ Voorburg Netherlands. **Tel** 011 31 70 3373800, FAX 011 31 038 7429, telex 32692 CBS NL. **LC** HJ54; .A62. **DD** 336.2/009492. **Continues** Overzicht van Den Belastingdruk in Nederland.

NE
**BELEIDSNOTA VAN GEDEPUTEERDE STATEN.** **Main/Corp** South Holland (Netherlands). (19??)-. Dutch. **LC** HJ2128.5.H64; H64a.

US/0270-5206
**BENDER'S DICTIONARY OF 1040 DEDUCTIONS.** See Law.

US
**BENDER'S FEDERAL TAX WEEK. Title Change.** **Added/Corp** Matthew Bender (Firm). **VFOAT** Federal Tax Week. No. 18 (May 3, 1989)-No. 25 (July 1, 1993). English. wk. Matthew Bender & Company Inc., 1275 Broadway, Albany NY 12204. **Tel** (800)833-9844, (518)487-3000. **Continues** U.S. Tax Week, 0041-8129. **Continued by** CCH Federal Tax Weekly.

US
**BENDER'S TAX RETURN MANUAL FOR ... .** **VFOAT** Tax Return Manual. English. an. $38.00. Matthew Bender & Company Inc., 1275 Broadway, Albany NY 12204. **Tel** (800)833-9844, (518)487-3000. **ED** E D Fiore. **Continues** Bender's Tax Guide. Tax Return Manual.

GW/0340-7918
**BETRIEBS-BERATER.** (DER BETRIEBS-BERATER; ZEHNTAGDIENST FUER WIRTSCHAFTS-, STEUER-, ARBEITS- UND SOZIALRECHT.). [Betr.-berat.]. (June 1946)-. Periodical. German. Thirty-five times a year. DM480.60 Germany; DM560.60 other. Verlag Recht und Wirtschaft GmbH, Postfach 105960, D 69049 Heidelberg Germany. **Tel** 011 49 6221 9061. [CCC].
**Ind/Abst** Energy Res. Abstr. (Aug. 1977-).

US
**BIENNIAL REPORT - DEPARTMENT OF REVENUE (WISCONSIN).** **Main/Corp** Wisconsin. Dept. of Revenue. English. be. Department of Revenue / Wisconsin, PO Box 8933, 125 South Webster Street, Madison WI 53708. **Tel** (608)266-8661. **LC** HJ11; .W6543B. **DD** 353.97750072/06.

US
**BIENNIAL REPORT FROM THE OFFICE OF STATE TAX COMMISSIONER ... TO THE GOVERNOR AND THE OFFICE OF MANAGEMENT AND BUDGET, STATE OF NORTH DAKOTA.** **Main/Corp** North Dakota. Tax Dept. 35th (July 1, 1979 to June 30, 1981)-. English. be. Tax Department, State Capitol, Bismarck ND 58505. **LC** HJ11; .N956A. **DD** 353.97840072/4/006. **Continues** Biennial Report of the Tax Commissioner of the State of North Dakota to the Governor and Department of Accounts and Purchases.

US
**BIENNIAL REPORT OF EXAMINING AND LICENSING BOARDS / BOARD OF ASSESSORS.** **Main/Corp** Minnesota. Board of Assessors. (19??)-. English. Board of Assessors, 2nd Floor Centennial Office Building, St Paul MN 55146. **LC** HJ11; .M662a. **DD** 353.97760082/43. **Continues** Minnesota. State Board of Accessors. Biennial Report of Examining and Licensing Boards.

US
**BIENNIAL REPORT OF THE AUDITOR OF ACCOUNTS TO THE GENERAL ASSEMBLY OF VERMONT.** **Main/Corp** Vermont. Office of Auditor of Accounts. English. be. Vermont Office of the Auditor of Accounts, Montpelier VT 05602. **LC** HJ11; .V535A. **DD** 353.97430072/32.

US
**BIENNIAL REPORT OF THE COMMISSIONER OF REVENUE SUBMITTING AN EQUALIZATION AND PROPORTIONMENT UPON THE SEVERAL CITIES AND TOWNS OF THE AMOUNT OF PROPERTY AND THE PROPORTION OF EVERY ONE THOUSAND DOLLARS OF STATE AND COUNTY TAX WHICH SHOULD BE ASSESSED UPON EACH CITY AND TOWN.** **Main/Corp** Massachusetts. Dept. of Revenue. (19??)-. English. be. Department of Revenue / Massachusetts, Leverett Saltonstall Building, 100 Cambridge Street, Boston MA 02204. **LC** J87; .M4 date g subser; HJ4121.M39. **DD** 300/.9744 S; 336.22/2.

US
**BIENNIAL REPORT OF THE LEGISLATIVE AUDITOR (NEVADA).** **Main/Corp** Nevada. Legislative Auditor. English. be. Legislative Auditor, Legislative Building, Capitol Complex, Carson City NV 89710. **LC** HJ11; .N334. **DD** 353.9/793/007232. **Continues** Nevada. Legislative Auditor. Report.

US
**BIENNIAL REPORT ... OF THE LEGISLATIVE FINANCE COMMITTEE - NEW MEXICO.** 1968/70-. English. be. Legislative Finance Committee, State of New Mexico, State Capitol, Santa Fe NM 87503. **Continues** New Mexico. Legislature. Finance Committee. Report and Recommendations.

US
**BIENNIAL REPORT OF THE TREASURER OF STATE OF THE STATE OF ARKANSAS FOR THE BIENNIAL PERIOD BEGINNING JULY 1 ... AND ENDING JUNE 30 ... .** **Main/Corp** Arkansas. Treasurer of State. **VFOAT** Biennial Report for the Period Beginning July 1 ... and Ending June 30 ...; Biennial Report. English. be. **LC** HJ11; .A79A. **DD** 353.97670072/31.

US/0095-0645
**BIENNIAL REPORT - STATE OF MINNESOTA, DEPARTMENT OF REVENUE.** (BIENNIAL REPORT - MINNESOTA, DEPARTMENT OF REVENUE.). **Main/Corp** Minnesota. Dept. of Revenue. 17th- 1970/72-. English. be. Department of Revenue / Minnesota, 10 River Park Plaza, St Paul MN 55146. **LC** HJ11; .M65. **DD** 353.9/776/007232. **Continues** Report to the Governor and the Legislature for the ... Biennium.

US/0364-5495
**BIENNIAL REPORT - STATE OF WISCONSIN, INVESTMENT BOARD.** **Main/Corp** Wisconsin. Investment Board. English. be. Investment Board, 121 E Wilson Street, Madison WI 53703. **LC** HJ3835.W5; W57A. **DD** 353.9/775/0072.

US/0363-5317
**BIENNIAL REPORT - TENNESSEE DEPARTMENT OF REVENUE.** **Main/Corp** Tennessee. Dept. of Revenue. English. be. Andrew Jackson State Office Building, Nashville TN 37219. **LC** HJ11; .T235. **DD** 353.97680072/6/06. **Continues** Tennessee. Dept. of Revenue. Biennial Report for the Fiscal Years ... .

US/0741-4900
**BK SPECIAL REPORT.** [BK spec. rep.]. VAT Blackman, Kallick Special Report. 1-. Periodical. English. an. Blackman Kallick & Company, 300 SOuth Riverside Plaza, Chicago IL 60606. **Tel** (312)207-1040. **ED** E Blackman.
**Desc:** Lists over 22 different books for the average reader that deal with taxes and tax laws.

FR
**BLOC NOTES DE L'OBSERVATOIRE ECONOMIQUE DE PARIS (MONTHLY).** (BLOC NOTES DE L'OBSERVATOIRE ECONOMIQUE DE PARIS.). French. Eleven times a year. 135.00F France; 155.00F other. Observatoire Economique de Paris, 195 rue de Bercy, Tour Gamma A, 75582 Paris Cedex 12 France. **Tel** 43 41 71 41, FAX 43 42 58 43, telex 230541. **ED** Guy Stehle. **LC** HA37; .F632. Index available.

US/0887-154X
**BLUE SKY PRACTICE FOR PUBLIC AND PRIVATE OFFERINGS.** See Law.

US/0145-6520
**BOARD OF TAX APPEALS DECISIONS.** **Main/Corp** Ohio. Board of Tax Appeals. 1974-. English. Banks-Baldwin Law Publishing Company, PO Box 1974, University Center, Cleveland OH 44106. **Tel** (216)721-7373. **LC** KFO470; .A552. **DD** 343/.771/040269.

BL
**BOLETIM INFORMATIVO DA SECAO DE DOCUMENTACAO.** **Main/Corp** Brazil. Ministerio de Fazenda. Delegacia no Rio de Janeiro. Secao de Cocumentacao. Bulletin. Portuguese. Av Presidente Antonio Carlos, 375 12. Andar Ala, Rio de Janeiro Brazil. **LC** Z1007; .B727A; HJ925. **Continues** Boletim Informativo do Setor de Documentacao.

BL
**BOLETIM INFORMATIVO DA SECRETARIA DE FAZENDA.** **Main/Corp** Mato Grosso (Brazil : State). Secretaria de Fazenda. Bulletin. Portuguese. Secretaria de Fazenda Gabinete, Brazil. **LC** HJ32; .M56B.

AG
**BOLETIN DE DERECHO FISCAL.** Periodical. Spanish. mo. Ediciones Contabilidad Moderna, Parana 717 719, CP 1017 Buenos Aires Argentina. **Tel** 011 54 1 469342. **LC** LAW. **DD** 343/.82/0405.

DR
**BOLETIN DE LA CAMARA DE CUENTAS Y DEL TRIBUNAL SUPERIOR ADMINISTRATIVO.** **Main/Corp** Dominican Republic. Camara de Cuentas. Periodical. Spanish. an. Free. Camara de Cuentas, Avenida Independencia No 658, Santo Domingo Dominican Republic. **Tel** (809)565-5555, FAX (809)566-2902. **LC** KGQ4550.A49; D65. **DD** 343.7293/03/0269; 347. 2930330269. Index available. cum. index. **Bk Rev. Circ:** 400 (ctrl). **Continues** Boletin Oficial (Dominican Republic. Camara de Cuentas).
**Desc:** Texts of special laws and case verdicts about public finance claims.

DR
**BOLETIN ESTADISTICO (DOMINICAN REPUBLIC. SECRETARIA DE ESTADO DE FINANZAS, DEPARTAMENTO DE ESTUDIOS ECONOMICOS).** See Public Administration-Abstracting, Bibliographies and Statistics.

IT/0006-6893
**BOLLETTINO TRIBUTARIO D'INFORMAZIONI.** See Law.

US/0741-8477
**BOSTON UNIVERSITY JOURNAL OF TAX LAW. Ceased.** See Law.

CN/0827-2794
**BRIAN COSTELLO ON MONEY MANAGEMENT.** [Brian Costello money manage.]. June 1984-. Periodical. English. Free. Stoddart Publishing, 30 Lesmill Road, Don Mills Ontario M3B 2T6 Canada. **DD** 332.024/00971. ctrl circ.

US/0149-2020
**BRIEF OUTLINE OF THE OKLAHOMA REVENUE SYSTEM, A.** **Main/Corp** Oklahoma. Tax Commission. (19??)-. English. an. Oklahoma Tax Commission, 2501 Lincoln Boulevard, Oklahoma City OK 73194. **LC** HJ11; .O552. **DD** 353.9/76600724.

UK
**BRITISH INTERNATIONAL TAX AGREEMENTS.** (19??)-. English. ir. Comes with British Tax Reporter. Her Majesty's Stationery Office, 51 Nine Elms Lane, London SW8 5DR England. **Tel** 011 44 71 873 8459, 011 44 71 873 8499, FAX 011 44 71 873 8499, 011 44 71 873 8456, telex 297138. **(Subscription address:** Her Majesty's Stationery Office, PO Box 276, Publications Centre, London SW8 5DT England.**)**

UK
**BRITISH TAX ENCYCLOPEDIA.** English. ir. £625.00. Sweet & Maxwell Ltd., South Quay Plaza, 183 Marsh Wall, London E14 9FT England. **Tel** 011 44 264 342899, FAX 011 44 264 342723, telex 929089 ITPINF G.

US
**BRITISH TAX GUIDE.** **Main/Corp** Commerce Clearing House. (1962)-. Periodical. English. Twenty-six times a year. £282.00. CCH Editions Ltd., Telford Road, Bicester, Oxfordshire OX6 OXD England. **Tel** 011 44 86 925 3300.

UK/0141-2876
**BRITISH TAX REPORT.** [Br. tax rep.]. Periodical. English. mo. Institute for International Research / New York, 95 Madison Avenue, New York NY 10016.

UK/0007-1870
**BRITISH TAX REVIEW.** [Br. tax rev.]. (June 1956)-. Periodical. English. Six times a year. £95.00 Europe; £100.00 other. Sweet & Maxwell Ltd., South Quay Plaza, 183 Marsh Wall, London E14 9FT England. **Tel** 011 44 264 342899, FAX 011 44 264 342723, telex 929089 ITPINF G. **LC** K2; .R55. **DD** 343.4104/05; 344.103405. cum. index. available on microfilm and microfiche from University Microfilms International (UMI). **Ind/Abst** Account. Tax Datab. (1974-); Aust. Leg. Mon. Dig.; Contents Recent Econ. J.; Curr. Law Index (1980-); Index Leg. Period.; Leg. Resour. Index (1980-); LegalTrac (1980-); Leis. Recreat. Tour. Abstr.; PAIS Int. Print (1991-); Rural Dev. Abstr.; World Agric. Econ.

UK
**BRITISH VALUE ADDED TAX REPORTER.** (19??)-. Periodical. English. ir (once every three weeks). £387.00. CCH Editions Ltd., Telford Road, Bicester, Oxfordshire OX6 OXD England. **Tel** 011 44 86 925 3300.

CN/0828-5365
**BRUNSWICK TAX REPORT, THE.** [Brunswick tax rep.]. Began with issue for Mar. 1984 V. 5, No. 3). Periodical. English. mo. $95.00. Brunswick Publishing, 595 Bay Street/Suite 1200, Toronto Ontario M5H 2C2 Canada. **Tel** (416)593-0155. **DD** 343.7104. ***Continues*** *Gage/MacMillan Tax Report, 0228-4170.*

●SA
**BUDGET.** **Main/Corp** Johannesburg (South Africa). **Added/Corp** Johannesburg (South Africa). Management Committee. (1992)-. English. **LC** WMLC 91/1560. ***Continues*** *Budget Address of the Chairman of the Management Committee (Johannesburg, South Africa)).*

II/0448-2352
**BUDGET.** **Main/Corp** Jammu and Kashmir (India). English. Jammu and Kishmer, Ranbir Government Press, Jammu India. **LC** HJ67.K3.

HK
**BUDGET, THE.** **Main/Corp** Hong Kong. Financial Secretary. English (Chinese). an. HK$23.00 Hong Kong; $3.10 US. Hong Kong Government Printer, Beaconsfield House, Queens Road, Victoria Hong Kong. **LC** HJ77.75; .A25A. **DD** 354.51/250072256/05. **Circ:** 800.
**Desc:** Speeches by the Financial Secretary, concluding the second reading of the appropriation bill.

CN/0706-0335
**BUDGET. ADDITIONAL INFORMATION : ESTIMATES.** **Main/Corp** Quebec (Province). Conseil du Tresor. **VAT** Gouvernement du Quebec. Budget. Additional Information. Estimate. French (English). an. 5.00Can$. Ministere des Finances, 200 Chemin Ste Foy, Quebec Quebec G1R 4X6 Canada. **Tel** (418)691-2233. **LC** HJ13; .Q185C. **DD** 354.7140072/225/05. **Circ:** 11,000. ***Formed by the union of*** *Quebec (Province). Ministere des Finances. Direction des Communications. Supplementary Information. Budget Speech, 0026-4471* ***and*** *Quebec (Province). Conseil du Tresor. Notes Explicatives.*
**Desc:** Economic situation of Quebec; direction to be taken; measures affecting individuals; reforms; tax expenditures; fiscal measures; financial framework; fiscal and budgetary measures; medium-term outlook on the Quebec financial position; fiscal arrangements.

AQ
**BUDGET ADDRESS.** **Main/Corp** Antigua and Barbuda. Ministry of Finance. **VFOAT** Budget Speech. (1988)-. English. **LC** HJ28.3.A84; A58a. **DD** 354.729740072/256/05. ***Continues*** *Budget Speech of the ... Minister of Finance to the House of Representatives of Antigua and Barbuda.*

US
**BUDGET AMENDMENT REPORT.** **Main/Corp** Montana. Office of the Governor. English. Montana Office of the Governor, Helena MT 59601. **LC** HJ11; .M9457A. **DD** 353.9/786/00722.

US
**BUDGET ANALYSES OF STATE AGENCIES : REPORT OF THE LEGISLATIVE FINANCE COMMITTEE TO THE ... LEGISLATURE.** **Main/Corp** New Mexico. Legislature. Finance Committee. English. an. State Capitol, Santa Fe NM 87503. **LC** HJ11; .N6482A. **DD** 353.97890072/2/05. ***Continues*** *New Mexico. Legislature. Finance Committee. Budget Analyses, Selected State Agencies, 0145-5966.*

●US
**BUDGET ANALYSIS FOR SFY ... / STATE OF NEW YORK, LEGISLATIVE COMMISSION ON STATE-LOCAL RELATIONS.** **Added/Corp** New York (State). Legislature. Legislative Commission on State-Local Relations. **VFOAT** Working Paper. (1991/1992)-. English.

US/0896-3584
**BUDGET AND THE REGION, THE.** [Budg. reg.]. **Added/Corp** Northeast-Midwest Institute (U.S.) Northeast-Midwest Senate Coalition (U.S.) Northeast-Midwest Congressional Coalition (U.S.). (1985)-. Periodical. English. an. The Northeast-Midwest Institute, 218 D Street Southeast, Washington DC 20003. **Tel** (202)544-5200. **DD** 351. **Bk Rev. Circ:** 500.
**Desc:** Regional perspective on the president's budget request.

CN/0839-8429
**BUDGET. BUDGET SPEECH AND ADDITIONAL INFORMATION.** [Budg., Budg. speech addit. inf.]. **Main/Corp** Quebec (Province). Ministere des Finances. **VFOAT** Budget Speech and Additional Information. (1986/1987)-. English. Editeur Officiel du Quebec, 1283 Boul Charest Ouest, Quebec Quebec G1N 2C9 Canada. **LC** HJ13; .Q195e. **DD** 354.7140072/256/05. ***Formed by the union of*** *Budget. Budget Speech, 0226-4374* ***and*** *Budget. Additional Information, 0839-8410.*

LU
**BUDGET DE L'ETAT - MINISTERE DES FINANCES.** **Main/Corp** Luxemburg. Ministere Des Finances. French. an. **LC** HJ54.5; .A25A. **DD** 354.493/50072252/05. ***Continues*** *Budget de l'Etat - Luxembourg. Ministere du Budget.*

CN/0848-6220
**BUDGET DES DEPENSES PRINCIPAL DE LA PROVINCE DU MANITOBA.** (BUDGET DES DEPENSES PRINCIPAL DE LA PROVINCE DU MANITOBA POUR L'EXERCICE SE TERMINANT LE 31 MARS ... DEPOSE POUR ADOPTION LORS DE LA ... DE LA ...). [Budg. depenses princ. prov. Manit.]. **Main/Corp** Manitoba. **Added/Corp** Manitoba. Finances Manitoba. (1990)-. French. **DD** 354.71270072/2253/021. ***Continues*** *Manitoba. Budget Detaille des Depenses de la Province du Manitoba pour l'Exercice se Terminant le 31 Mars ... Depose pour Adoption lors de la ... de la ..., 0848-6212.*

TG
**BUDGET D'INVESTISSEMENT ET D'EQUIPEMENT.** **Main/Corp** Togo. Ministere du Plan, du Developpement Industriel et de la Reforme Administrative. French. an. 3,000.00CFAF Togo; $10.00 US. Direction Generale du Plan et du Developpement, BP No 1667, Lome Togo. **Tel** 21 37 51, telex 5380 MIPLAN TO. **LC** HJ86T; .A27A. **DD** 354.66/81007222534/05. available in microform.
**Desc:** Presents investment/equipment budget information; sets the amount of public funds to apply in all sectors of the national program of economics and social development; reports on programs and projects realized in each sector; supplies figures concerning budgetary projections for future years.

CN/0839-8445
**BUDGET. DISCOURS SUR LE BUDGET ET RENSEIGNEMENTS SUPPLEMENTAIRES.** [Budg., Discours budg. renseign. suppl.]. **Main/Corp** Quebec (Province). Ministere des Finances. 1986/87-. French. an. Ministere des Finances, 200 Chemin Ste Foy, Quebec Quebec G1R 4X6 Canada. **Tel** (418)691-2233. **DD** 354.7140072/23/05. ***Formed by the union of*** *Budget. Discours sur le Budget / Quebec (Province). Ministere des Finances, 0226-4382* ***and*** *Budget. Renseignements Supplementaires / Quebec (Province). Ministere des Finances.*

CN/0705-3401
**BUDGET: ESTIMATES (QUEBEC).** (BUDGET. ESTIMATES.). [Budg., Estim.]. **Main/Corp** Quebec (Province). Conseil du Tresor. 1978/79-. English. an. Editeur Officiel du Quebec, 1283 Boul Charest Ouest, Quebec Quebec G1N 2C9 Canada. **LC** HJ13; .Q195K. **DD** 354.7140072/2253/05. ***Continues*** *Quebec (Province). Ministere des Finances. Credits. Estimates.*

II/0536-9290
**BUDGET / GOVERNMENT OF INDIA, MINISTRY OF FINANCE.** **Main/Corp** India (Republic). Ministry of Finance. (19??)-. English. Government of India Press, Minto Road, New Delhi 111054 India. **LC** HJ65; .B155.

UK
**BUDGET - GREATER LONDON COUNCIL.** **Main/Corp** Greater London Council. English. Greater London Council, The County Hall, London SE1 7PB England. **Tel** (01)633-7139. **LC** HJ9041.L7; B4A. **DD** 352/.12/09421.
**Desc:** Vols. for (1974-75) include its projections for (1975-79).

US
**BUDGET IN BRIEF.** **Main/Corp** Ohio. Office of the Governor. **Added/Corp** Ohio. General Assembly. (19??)-. English. be. Office of the Governor / Ohio, 77 South High Street, 30th Floor, Columbus OH 43266. **Tel** (614)644-0813, FAX (614)466-9354. **LC** HJ11; .O346a. **DD** 353.97710072/253/05.

II
**BUDGET IN BRIEF - MANIPUR (INDIA). DEPT. OF STATISTICS.** **Main/Corp** Manipur (India). Dept. of Statistics. English. Department of Statistics / India, Imphal Manipur India. **LC** HJ66.M53; B14A. **DD** 354/.54/1700722.

US
**BUDGET IN BRIEF / STATE OF GEORGIA.** **Main/Corp** Georgia. Office of Planning and Budget. **VFOAT** Georgia's Budget in Brief. English. an. Georgia Office of Planning and Budget, 270 Washington Street Southwest, Room 611, Atlanta GA 30334. **Tel** (404)656-3820. **LC** HJ11; .G445B. **DD** 353.97580072/253. ***Continues*** *Budget in Brief / Georgia. Budget Bureau.*

US/0272-8435
**BUDGET IN BRIEF / U.S. DEPARTMENT OF ENERGY.** [Budg. brief]. **Main/Corp** United States. Dept. of Energy. Office of the Controller. English. an. DOE, Office of the Controller, Washington DC 20585 20585. **LC** HD9502.U5; U523E. **DD** 353.87.

IE
**BUDGET IRELAND.** (BUDGET.). **Main/Corp** Ireland. (19??)-. English. an. Government Publications, 4 5 Harcourt Road, Dublin 2 Ireland. **Tel** 011 353 1 6613111 Ext.4005. **LC** HJ43.5; .A24a. **DD** 354.4170072/2/05. **Circ:** 2,000.

US/0090-242X
**BUDGET - LOS ANGELES.** (BUDGET.). **Main/Corp** Los Angeles (Calif.). Office of the Mayor. (19??)-. Periodical. English. wk. $29.00 local edition except Ohio; $25.00 local within Ohio; $25.00 national. The Budget / SugarCreek, PO Box 249, 134 North Factory Street, Sugarcreek OH 44681. **Tel** (216)852-4634, FAX (216)852-4421. **ED** George R Smith (national edition) and Jerry Dudek (local edition). **LC** HJ9013; .L6e42. **DD** 352/.12/0979494. **Ad Acc, Adv Mgr:** V Baab. **Circ:** 18,000.
**Desc:** The daily happenings of the Amish-Mennonite Communities through-out the Americas.

US
**BUDGET MESSAGE.** **Main/Corp** Delaware. Governor. 1981-. English. an. Legislative Hall, Dover DE 19901. **LC** HJ11; .D3432B. **DD** 353.97510072/256/05. ***Continues*** *Delaware. Governor. Budget Message for Fiscal Year.*

AT
**BUDGET MONITOR.** English. Four times a year (Feb., June, Aug., Nov.). 300.00Aus$ universities & libraries; 200.00Aus$ individuals; 650.00Aus$ others. Access Economics Pty. Ltd., PO Box E347, Queen Victoria Terrace, Barton ACT 2600 Australia. **Tel** 011 61 6 2731222, FAX 011 61 6 2731223. ctrl circ.
**Desc:** An analysis of state budgets and federal budget prospects with detailed economic forecasts and estimates of the federal budget starting point on unchanged policies.

US/0163-2000
**BUDGET OF THE UNITED STATES GOVERNMENT.** **Main/Corp** United States. Office of Management and Budget. **VFOAT** Budget of the U.S. Government. (1971/1972)-. English. an. $22.00. Claitors Law Books, 3165 South Acadian, Baton Rouge LA 70808. **Tel** (504)344-0476, (800)274-1403. **LC** HJ2051; .A59. **DD** 353.007/22. **NLM** HJ 2051 A59. available on microfilm and microfiche from University Microfilms International (UMI). ***Continues*** *United States. Bureau of the Budget. Budget of the United States Government, 0163-2000;* ***Absorbed*** *United States. Office of Management and Budget. United States Budget in Brief; United States. Office of Management and Budget. Budget of the United States Government (Dept. Ed.). Appendix; United States. Office of Management and Budget. Special*

**Public Administration —Public Finance and Taxation**

Analyses, Budget of the United States Government; United States. Office of Management and Budget. Historical Tables, Budget of the United States Government; Management of the United States Government **and** United States. Office of Management and Budget. Major Policy Initiatives.
**Ind/Abst** F&S Index Plus Text, Int. [Select. Cov.]; Predicasts Forecasts.

US
**BUDGET PREPARATION MANUAL.**
**Main/Corp** Arkansas. Dept. of Finance and Administration. Office of Budget. Periodical. English. be. Office of Budget, PO Box 3278, Little Rock AR 72203. **LC** HJ11; .A842B. **DD** 353.9/767/00722.

•US
**BUDGET PRESENTATION TO THE GENERAL ASSEMBLY OF THE COMMONWEALTH OF PENNSYLVANIA - UNIVERSITY OF PITTSBURGH.**
**Main/Corp** University of Pittsburgh. (1992)-. English. University of Pittsburgh / Commonwealth of Pennsylvania, Budget Presentation to the General Assembly, Pittsburgh PA.

US/0161-4770
**BUDGET PROPOSED FOR THE DEPARTMENT OF LABOR AND RELATED AGENCIES, THE. See**
Economics-Labor.

CN/0711-8651
**BUDGET. RENSEIGNEMENTS SUPPLEMENTAIRES : IMPOTS. Main/Corp**
Quebec (Province). Ministere des Finances. Direction Generale des Etudes Economiques et Fiscales. French. an. Ministere des Finances, 200 Chemin Ste Foy, Quebec Quebec G1R 4X6 Canada. **Tel** (418)691-2233. **LC** HJ13; .Q195H. **DD** 354.7140072/225/05.

CN/0707-9230
**BUDGET. RENSEIGNEMENTS SUPPLEMENTAIRES : REFORME DE LA FISCALITE MUNICIPALE. Main/Corp** Quebec (Province). Ministere des Finances. **VFOAT** Reforme de la Fiscalite Municipale. French. Editeur Officiel du Quebec, 1283 Boul Charest Ouest, Quebec Quebec G1N 2C9 Canada. **LC** HJ9014.Q39; Q4A. **DD** 352.1/3/09714.

US/0146-907X
**BUDGET REVISIONS - EXECUTIVE OFFICE OF THE PRESIDENT, OFFICE OF MANAGEMENT AND BUDGET.**
(BUDGET REVISIONS.). **Main/Corp** United States. Office of Management and Budget. **VFOAT** Additional Details on Budget Savings. English. Congressional Budget Office, 2nd and D Streets SW, Washington DC 20515. **Tel** (202)226-2115. **LC** HJ2051; .U56A. **DD** 353.007/22.

MY
**BUDGET SPEECH AND TAX PROPOSALS. Main/Corp** Malaysia. Kenentarian Kewangan. English. an. Malaysian Law Publishers, Room 201/2nd Floor, Lee Yan Lian Building, Jalan Tun Perak, Kuala Lumpur Malaysia. **DD** 354.5950072/2.

GD
**BUDGET SPEECH DELIVERED BY THE MINISTER FOR FINANCE ... IN THE HOUSE OF REPRESENTATIVES ON. Title Change. Main/Corp** Grenada. Ministry of Finance. (1988-1992). English. an. **LC** HJ28.5.G7; G73a. **DD** 354.7298450072/256/05. **Continues** Grenada. Prime Minister.; Budget Speech of the ... Prime Minister and Minister of Finance ... to the House of Representatives on ... . **Continued by** Grenada. Ministry of Finance.; Budget Speech of the ... Minister of Finance to the House of Representatives.

II
**BUDGET SPEECH - MEGHALAYA (INDIA). Main/Corp** Meghalaya (India). English. an. Assam Government Press / Government of Meghalaya, Shillong India. **LC** HJ66.M55; B13. **DD** 354/.54/16400722.

NR
**BUDGET SPEECH - MILITARY ADMINISTRATOR, IMO STATE OF NIGERIA. Main/Corp** Imo State (Nigeria). Military Administrator. Began in 1979. English. Imo State of Nigeria, Military Administrator, Owerri Nigeria. **LC** HJ81P; .I455A. **DD** 354.669/4.

MF
**BUDGET SPEECH - MINISTER OF FINANCE. Main/Corp** Mauritius. Ministry of Finance. (19??)-. English. an. **LC** HJ82.M3; A276a. **DD** 354/69/8200722.

NR
**BUDGET SPEECH OF HIS EXCELLENCY THE MILITARY GOVERNOR. Main/Corp**
North Central State, Nigeria. Military Governor's Office. Multiple languages (English and Hausa). North Central State Nigeria, Military Governors Office, Kaduna Nigeria. **LC** HJ81P.N67; A3. **DD** 354/.669/5.

AT
**BUDGET SPEECH / PRESENTED BY THE TREASURER OF VICTORIA ON THE OCCASION OF THE BUDGET. Main/Corp**
Victoria. Treasury Dept. (19??)-. English. an. Government Printer / Treasury Department, PO Box 203, North Melbourne Victoria, 3051 Australia. **LC** HJ90.V53; V54e. **DD** 354.9450072/2/05.

US/0147-2984
**BUDGET - STATE OF NORTH CAROLINA, THE. Main/Corp** North Carolina. Division of State Budget. 1977/79-. English. be. North Carolina Division of State Budget, Department of Administration, Raleigh NC 27609. **LC** HJ11; .N847A. **DD** 353.9/756/00722. **Continues** Budget - State of North Carolina, 0147-2984.

SA
**BUDGET : STATISTICAL SURVEY. See**
Public Administration-Abstracting, Bibliographies and Statistics.

AT
**BUDGET SUMMARY AND PROGRAM BUDGET EXPENDITURES / PRESENTED BY THE TREASURER OF VICTORIA FOR THE INFORMATION OF HONOURABLE MEMBERS ON THE OCCASION OF THE BUDGET. Main/Corp** Victoria. Treasury Dept. (198?)-. English. an. Government Printer / Treasury Department, PO Box 203, North Melbourne Victoria, 3051 Australia. **LC** HJ90.V53; V54h. **DD** 354.9450072/2/05.

BG
**BUDGET SUMMARY STATEMENTS. Main/Corp** Bangladesh. Artha Bibhaga. (1990)-. English. an. Ministry of Finance / Bangladesh, Finance Division, Dacca Bangladesh. **Continues** Budget Summary Statements / Bangladesh. Artha Mantranalaya.

US
**BUDGET. SUPPLEMENT (VIRGINIA. GOVERNOR). Main/Corp** Virginia. Governor. English. Commonwealth of Virginia / Virginia Governor, State Office Building, Richmond VA 23219. **LC** HJ11; V8467A; SUPPL. **DD** 353.97550072/252/05.

TI
**BUDGET TUNISIEN, LE.** French. an. Dar El Amal d'Edition de Diffusion de Presse et Publicite, rue 2 Mars 1934, La Kasbah Tunis Tunisia. **LC** HJ2179.5.Z7; B82. **DD** 354.61/100722/05.

CN/0227-9142
**BUDGET / VILLE DE MONTREAL.**
**Main/Corp** Montreal (Quebec). **VAT** Budget - City of Montreal. English. **LC** HJ9014.Q4; M682A. **DD** 352.1/252/09714281. **Continues in part** Montreal (Quebec). City Council. Budget.

HT
**BULLETIN ANNUEL - ADMINISTRATION GENERALE DES CONTRIBUTIONS (HAITI (REPUBLIC)). Main/Corp** Haiti. Administration Generale des Contributions. 1976/77-. Bulletin. French. an. Department des Finances et des Affaires Economiques, Port-au-Prince Haiti. **LC** HJ25; .R25A. **DD** 336.2/0097294.

BE
**BULLETIN DE DOCUMENTATION - BELGIQUE, MINISTERE DES FINANCES.**
**Main/Corp** Belgium. Ministere des Finances. (19??)-. Bulletin. French (Dutch). Six times a year. 2,500F. Ministere des Finances, Service d'Etudes et de Documentation, Tour Finances C A E, bte 30, Bd du Jardin Botanique 1010 Bruxelles Belgium. **Tel** 011 02 210 21 11, FAX 011 02 210 39 46. **ED** S. Vandendriessche. **LC** HJ53; .A184a. **DD** 354/.493/0072. Index available. **Circ**: 1,000 (ctrl).
**Desc**: Contains statistics over the publics finances (receipts and expenditures of the State, operations of the Treasury, financing of the public debt. Normally contains one or several different completed studies.

BE/0777-2238
**BULLETIN DE DOCUMENTATION - MINISTERE DES FINANCES, SERVICE D'ETUDES ET DE DOCUMENTATION.**
(BULLETIN DE DOCUMENTATION (BELGIUM. MINISTERE DES FINANCES).). [Bull. doc. - Minist. finances Serv. etud. doc.]. **Main/Corp** Belgium. Ministere des Finances. Service d'Etudes et de Documentation. (19??)-. Bulletin. French. mo. 2700F. Administratie der Directe, Belastingen, 1010 Brussels Belgium. **Tel** 011 32 2 5371418. **LC** HJ53; .A18.

CN/1183-6474
**BULLETIN DE RENSEIGNEMENTS, LA TAXE DE VENTE AU DETAIL / DIRECTION DE LA TAXE DE VENTE AU DETAIL.** [Bull. renseign. taxe vente detail]. **Added/Corp** Ontario. Direction de la Taxe de Vente au Detail. No 1/91 (Mar 1991)-. Bulletin. French. **DD** 343.71305. **Continues** Bulletin d'Information; Retail Sales Tax Act (Loi sur la Ttaxe de Vente au Detail)., 0226-3033.

FR/0242-5912
**BULLETIN FISCAL FRANCIS LEFEBVRE.** [Bull. fisc. Francis Lefebvre]. Vol. 1/81 (Jan. 1981)-. Bulletin. French. mo. 315F. Editions Francis Lefebvre, 5 rue Jacques Bingen, F-75854 Paris Cedex 17 France. **Tel** (1)47 63 12 60, FAX 46 22 72 66, telex 649 470 F. Index available. **Formed by the union of** Bulletin de Documentation Pratique des Impots Directs et des Droits d'Enregistrement, 0242-5556 **and** Bulletin de Documentation Pratique des Taxes sur le Chiffre d'Affaires et des Contributions Indirectes, 0242-5564.

NE/0007-4624
**BULLETIN FOR INTERNATIONAL FISCAL DOCUMENTATION.** (BULLETIN FOR INTERNATIONAL FISCAL DOCUMENTATION : OFFICIAL ORGAN OF THE INT. FISCAL ASSOCIATION, I.F.A..). [Bull. int. fisc. doc.]. **Added/Corp** International Bureau of Fiscal Documentation. International Fiscal Association. **VFOAT** Bulletin de Documentation Fiscale Internationale. (1946/1947)-. Bulletin. English (French). mo. $315.00. International Bureau of Fiscal Documentation - IBFD Publications, PO Box 20237, 1000 HE Amsterdam The Netherlands. **Tel** 011 31 20-6267726, FAX 011 31 20-6228658, telex 13217 INTAX NL. **ED** S. M. C. Lyons and D. E. Reid. **LC** HJ101; .I65. **DD** 336.05. **Bk Rev**. **Ad Acc**. **Circ**: 2,500 (ctrl).
**Desc**: Journal on taxation around the world. Articles contributed by leading local tax experts, bibliography, conference diary, and International Fiscale Documentation (IFA) news.
**Ind/Abst** Contents Recent Econ. J.; Econ. Lit. Index; Fed. Tax Artic.; Index Foreign Leg. Per.; Index Period. Artic. Relat. Law; J. Econ. Lit.; Middle East Abstr. Index; PAIS Int. Print.

BE
**BULLETIN TRIMESTRIEL. Title Change.**
**Main/Corp** Credit Communal de Belgique. (1947)-(19??). Bulletin. French. qt. Credit Communal de Belgique, Boulevard Pachaco 44, 1000 Brussels, Belgium. **Continued by** Bulletin du Credit Communal.
**Ind/Abst** PAIS Int. Print.

US
**BULLETIN (WISCONSIN. BUREAU OF LOCAL FINANCIAL ASSISTANCE).**
(BULLETIN - BUREAU OF LOCAL FINANCIAL ASSISTANCE.). **Main/Corp** Wisconsin. Bureau of Local Financial Assistance. No. 56 (1977)-. Bulletin. English. Department of Revenue / Wisconsin, PO Box 8933, 125 South Webster Street, Madison WI 53708. **Tel** (608)266-8661. **LC** HJ9011.W6; B85A. **DD** 352.1/09775. **Continues** Bulletin (Wisconsin. Bureau of Local Fiscal Information and Analysis), 0094-7644.

AU
**BUNDESRECHNUNGSABSCHLUSS.**
**Main/Corp** Austria. Rechnungshof. (19??)-. Periodical. German. ir. Springer-Verlag Wien, Sachsenplatz 4 6, PO Box 89, A-1201 Vienna Austria. **Tel** 011 43 1 3302415. (**Subscription address**: Springer Verlag New York Inc. / for North America, 44 Hartz Way, Secaucus NJ 07096.) **LC** HJ44; .B6.

GW
**BUNDESSTEUERBLATT. Added/Corp**
Germany (West). Bundesministerium der Finanzen. Germany (West). Bundesministerium fuer Wirtschaft und Finanzen. Vol. 1 (Jan. 1951)-. Periodical. German. ir. DM62.80. Stollfuss Verlag Bonn GmbH, Postfach 2428, Dechenstr 7, D 53014 Bonn Germany. **Tel** 011 49 228 724257.

AU
**BUNDESVORANSCHLAG. Main/Corp**
Austria. Bundesministerium fur Finanzen. (198?)-. German. ir. Osterreichische Staatsdruckere, Postfach 129, A 1037 Vienna Austria. **Tel** 011 43 1 797890. **LC** HJ44; .A24a. **Continues** Bundeshaushalt.

CN/0846-0620
**BUSINESS PLAN (VICTORIA).** (BUSINESS PLAN / CORPORATE SERVICES DIVISION.). [Bus. plan]. **Main/Corp** British Columbia. Ministry of Social Services and Housing. **Added/Corp** British Columbia. Ministry of Social Services and Housing. Corporate Services Division. (1991)-. English. **DD** 354.7110084/05.

US/0146-0587
**BUSINESS TAX INTERPRETATIONS.** Vol. 4, No. 2 (Feb. 1976)-. Periodical. English. mo. $60.00. Alexander Hamilton Institute Inc, 70 Hilltop Road,

# Public Administration — Public Finance and Taxation

Ramsey NJ 07446-1119. **Tel** (201)825-8161, FAX (201)825-8696. **LC** KF6457; .H3. **DD** 343/.73/06705. *Continues* Hagendorf, Stanley. AD&D.

TU
**BUTCE GELIRLERI YLLG. Main/Corp** Turkey. Gelirler Umum Mudurlugu. **VFOAT** Budget Revenues Yearbook. Multiple languages (English and Turkish). **LC** HJ75; .C14. **Supersedes** Devlet Gelirleri Bulteni.

UK
**BUTTERWORTH'S BUDGET TAX TABLES.** English. an. £4.95. Butterworth & Co. Ltd. / Kent, England, Borough Green, Sevenoaks Kent TN15 8PH England. **Tel** 011 44 732-884567, FAX 011 44 732-885996.
**Desc:** Contains details and explanations of the budget proposals, set out under distinctive headings. Tables are given for both unchanged and new rates and allowances, and the operative date for each change is clearly shown.

UK
**BUTTERWORTHS ORANGE TAX HANDBOOK.** See Law.

UK
**BUTTERWORTH'S UK TAX GUIDE.** See Law.

UK
**BUTTERWORTHS YELLOW TAX HANDBOOK.** See Law.

US/0730-6202
**CABLE TV TAX LETTER.** See Communication-Broadcasting.

US/1041-9454
**CABOT'S MUTUAL FUND NAVIGATOR.** [Cabot's mutual fund navig.]. **VFOAT** Mutual Fund Navigator. (Oct. 1988)-. Periodical. English. Twelve times a year. $86.00. Cabot Heritage Corporation, PO Box 3044, Salem MA 01970. **Tel** (617)745-5532, FAX (508)745-1283. **ED** Timothy Lutts. **DD** 332.
**Desc:** Contains sound advise on investing in well-managed no-load mutual funds, using long-term market timing to increase profits and reduce risk.

BL
**CADERNO DE PESQUISAS TRIBUTARIAS.** See Law.

NE
**CAHIERS DE DROIT FISCAL INTERNATIONAL. VFOAT** Schriften zum Internationalen Steuerrecht; Studies on International Fiscal Law. (1939)-. Monographic series. French (English, German and Spanish). an. Price varies per volume. Kluwer Law and Taxation Publishers, Staverenstraat 32015, PO Box 23, 7400 GA Deventer Netherlands. **Tel** 011 31 5700 47261. **LC** HJ1905; .C3. **DD** 336.082.
**Ind/Abst** Index Foreign Leg. Per.

US
**CAL-TAX LETTER.** (19??)-. Periodical. English. wk. $275.00 non-members; $225.00 members of the California Taxpayers Association. California Taxpayers Association, 921 11th Street, Suite 800, Sacramento CA 95814. **Tel** (916)441-0490. **ED** Dave R. Doerr.

US/0008-0543
**CAL-TAX NEWS. Added/Corp** California Taxpayers' Association. **VAT** Cal Tax News. Vol. 1 (1960)-. Periodical. English. Twenty-two times a year (twice monthly except July and Dec.). $55.00. California Taxpayers Association, 921 11th Street, Suite 800, Sacramento CA 95814. **Tel** (916)441-0490. **ED** Ron Roach. cum. index.
**Ind/Abst** Calif. Period. Index; Calif. Period. Microfi.

US/0146-1826
**CALIFORNIA PROPERTY TAX CONFERENCE. Main/Corp** California Property Tax Conference. (19??)-. English. an. Stanford University, 1000 Welch Road, Palo Alto CA 94304. **Tel** (415)723-7049. **LC** HJ4121.C2; C34a. **DD** 336.2/2/09794.

US
**CALIFORNIA PUBLIC FINANCE.** (19??)-. English. ir (48 issues). $495.00. American Banker, Concourse Level, 1 State Street Plaza, New York NY 10004. **Tel** (212)803-8200, (800)221-1809. **(Subscription address:** American Banker Newsletter Division, PO Box 28315, Washington DC 20038**)** available on an online database (files 16,636/Full-Text) from DIALOG.
**Ind/Abst** PROMT [Full Txt.]; PTS Newsl. Database [Full Txt.].

US
**CALIFORNIA TAX LAWYER.** (19??)-. English. Three times a year. $45.00. State Bar of California, 555 Franklin Street, San Francisco CA 94102. **Tel** (415)561-8200, FAX (415)561-8228. **ED** Lisa Loeffler (editor's address: 2049 Century Park East, Suite 1800, Los Angeles, Ca 90067, phone: (310)551-0012). **Bk Rev**, (Qty: 3). **Ad Acc**. **Circ**: 3,800.

**Desc:** Features current developments, section activities and other helpful information on issues relating to federal, state and local tax laws.
**Ind/Abst** Fed. Tax Artic.

CN/0317-2821
**CANADA. TAX APPEAL BOARD CASES. INDEX. SUPPLEMENT.** See Law.

US/1044-3223
**CANADA-U.S. OUTLOOK.** *Title Change.* [Can.-U. S. outlook]. **Added/Corp** National Planning Association. **VFOAT** Canada, U.S. Outlook. **VAT** Canada-United States Outlook. Vol. 1, No. 1 (July 1989)-Vol. 3, No. 4 (May 1993). Monographic series. English. qt. National Planning Association, 1424 16th Street Northwest, Suite 700, Washington DC 20036. **Tel** (202)265-7685. **LC** E183.8.C2; C337. **DD** 327.71073/05. *Continued by* North American Outlook (Washington, D.C.), 1071-5584.
**Ind/Abst** PAIS Int. Print.

CN/0318-8817
**CANADIAN BALANCE OF INTERNATIONAL PAYMENTS, THE. Main/Corp** Statistics Canada. Balance of Payments Division. **VFOAT** Balance Canadienne des Paiements Internationaux.; System of National Accounts; Balance Canadienne des Paiements Internationaux. (1971)-. English (French). an. 50.00Can$ Canada; $60.00 US; $70.00 other. Statistics Canada, Publications Sales & Services, Main Building Room 1710, Ottawa Ontario K1A 0T6 Canada. **Tel** (613)951-5078, (800)267-6677, FAX (613)951-1584, telex 053-3585. **LC** HG3883.C3; C35. **DD** 382.1/7/0971. *Continues* Statistics Canada. Balance of Payments Section. Canadian Balance of International Payments., 0318-8817.

CN/0823-6089
**CANADIAN FARMTAX.** [Can. farmtax]. 1983-. English. an. $1.50 per vol. CCH Canadian Ltd., 6 Garamond Court, Don Mills Ontario M3C 1Z5 Canada. **Tel** (416)441-2992, FAX (416)441-3418. **DD** 343.7105/2.

CN/0316-1331
**CANADIAN MASTER TAX GUIDE. Added/Corp** CCH Canadian Limited. (1945)-. Periodical. English. ir. Commerce Clearing House Inc., 4025 West Peterson Avenue, Chicago IL 60646-6085. **Tel** (312)583-8500, FAX (708)940-4600. **DD** 343/.71/.052.

CN/0838-0961
**CANADIAN PETROLEUM TAX JOURNAL.** See Petroleum and Natural Gas.

CN/0382-7585
**CANADIAN POCKETAX (ENGLISH EDITION).** (CANADIAN POCKETAX.). 1953-. English. an. CCH Canadian Ltd., 6 Garamond Court, Don Mills Ontario M3C 1Z5 Canada. **Tel** (416)441-2992, FAX (416)441-3418. **DD** 343/.71/.052.

AT
**CANADIAN SALES TAX REPORTS.** English. ir. Commerce Clearing House Inc., 4025 West Peterson Avenue, Chicago IL 60646-6085. **Tel** (312)583-8500, FAX (708)940-4600.

US/0160-4708
**CANADIAN TAX AND TRADE BRIEFS. Main/Corp** Arthur Andersen & Co. English. Arthur Andersen & Company / Chicago, 33 West Monroe Street, Chicago IL 60603. **Tel** (312)580-0033. **LC** KE5662; .A52. **DD** 343/.71/0405.

CN/0229-8031
**CANADIAN TAX DIGEST (ANNUAL EDITION).** (CANADIAN TAX DIGEST.). [Can. tax dig.]. 1979 Ed.-. English. an. $125.00. CB Media Ltd., 70 the Esplanade 2nd Floor, Toronto Ontario M5E 1R2 Canada. **Tel** (416)364-4266. **ED** Morris C Kaiser. **DD** 336.24/0971.

CN/0008-5111
**CANADIAN TAX JOURNAL.** [Can. tax j.]. **Added/Corp** Canadian Tax Foundation. **VFOAT** Revue Fiscale Canadienne. Vol. 1; Jan./Feb. 1953-. Periodical. Multiple languages (English and French; summaries and/or abstracts in French). bm. 75.00Can$. Canadian Tax Foundation, 1 Queen Street East, Suite 1800, Toronto Ontario M5C 2Y2 Canada. **Tel** (416)863-9784. *Supersedes* Tax Bulletin, 0576-6222.
**Ind/Abst** Account. Tax Datab. (1974-); Account. Art.; Can. Legal Lit.; Can. Period. Index (1964); Fed. Tax Artic.; Index Leg. Period.; Int. Exec.; J. Plan. Lit.; Leg. Resour. Index (1980-); LegalTrac (1980-).

CN/0319-2431
**CANADIAN TAX NEWS.** See Law.

CN/0008-512X
**CANADIAN TAX PAPERS. Added/Corp** Canadian Tax Foundation. No. 1 (1951)-. Monographic series. English. ir. Price varies per volume. Canadian Tax Foundation, 1 Queen Street East, Suite 1800, Toronto Ontario M5C 2Y2 Canada. **Tel** (416)863-9784. **DD** 336.2/00971.

CN/0225-0608
**CANADIAN TAXPAYER.** (THE CANADIAN TAXPAYER.). [Can. taxpayer]. (Feb. 6, 1979)-. Periodical. English. Twenty-four times a year. 295.00Can$. Carswell / Canada, 2075 Kennedy Road, Scarborough Ontario M1T 3V4 Canada. **Tel** (416)609-3800, (800)387-5164. **DD** 343.7105/2.

US/0883-0622
**CANADIAN TREASURY SERVICES.** (CANADIAN TREASURY SERVICES / GREENWICH RESEARCH ASSOCIATES.). [Can. treas. serv.]. **Added/Corp** Greenwich Research Associates. (19??)-. English. an. Greenwich Research Associates Inc, Office Park 8, Greenwich CT 06830. **LC** HG1616.C87; C36. **DD** 332.1/7/0971.

●US
**CAPITAL BUDGET. Main/Corp** New Mexico. Governor. **Added/Corp** New Mexico. State Budget Division. **VFOAT** State of New Mexico Capital Budget. 80th fiscal year (1991/92)-. English. New Mexico Department of Finance & Administration, Bataan Memorial Building, Room 180, Santa Fe NM 87503. **Tel** (505)827-4985, FAX (505)827-4948. *Continues* Capital Project Recommendations for the State of New Mexico.

US/0363-0870
**CAPITAL BUDGET AND SIX YEAR IMPROVEMENT PROGRAM. Main/Corp** Alaska. Dept. of Administration. (1975)-. English. **LC** HJ2053.A4; A37a. **DD** 353.9/798/00722.

US
**CAPITAL BUDGET (GEORGIA). Main/Corp** Georgia. Office of Planning and Budget. **VFOAT** Georgia' Capital Budget Report. English. an. Georgia Office of Planning and Budget, 270 Washington Street Southwest, Room 611, Atlanta GA 30334. **Tel** (404)656-3820. **LC** HJ11; .G446B. **DD** 353.97580072/22534.

UK/0263-2985
**CAPITAL EXPENDITURE AND DEBT FINANCING STATISTICS / CIPFA, STATISTICAL INFORMATION SERVICE.** See Public Administration-Abstracting, Bibliographies and Statistics.

●US/1065-8114
**CAPITAL IDEAS / FROM THE NATIONAL TAXPAYERS UNION FOUNDATION.** [Cap. ideas]. **Added/Corp** National Taxpayers Union Foundation. Vol. 1, No. 1 (Sept./Oct. 1992)-. Periodical. English. mo. $15.00. National Taxpayers Union Federation, 325 Pennsylvania Avenue Southeast, Washington DC 20003. **Tel** (202)543-1300. **DD** 336.

●US
**CAPITAL IMPROVEMENT PROGRAM, FISCAL YEARS ... / STATE OF MARYLAND, DEPARTMENT OF STATE PLANNING. Added/Corp** Maryland. Dept. of State Planning. **VFOAT** State of Maryland Capital Improvement Program, Fiscal Years ... . (1989-1993)-. English. Department of State Planning, State Office Building, Baltimore MD 21201. **Tel** (410)225-4490. **LC** HJ11; .M3424a. **DD** 353.97520072/22534/05. *Continues* Department Projections of Capital Needs for the Five Year Cal Period ... .

US/0149-1059
**CAPITAL IMPROVEMENTS PROGRAM FOR CHICAGO. Main/Corp** Chicago (Ill.). Dept. of Development and Planning. English. an. Department of Development and Planning, Room 1000/City Hall, Chicago IL 60602. **LC** HD4606.C5; C5A. **DD** 352/.12/0977311. *Continues* Joint Capital Improvements Program for Chicago.

US
**CAPITAL OUTLAY BUDGET (LOUISIANA). Main/Corp** Louisiana. Office of the Governor. Division of Administration. English. an. Office of the Governor / Louisiana, Division of Administration, State Capitol Building, Box 44095, Baton Rouge LA 70804. **LC** HJ11; .L646A. **DD** 353.97630072/22534/05.

US/0146-8952
**CAPITAL PROJECTS.** (CAPITAL PROJECTS (MARYLAND).). **Main/Corp** Maryland. Dept. of State Planning. English. Department of State Planning, State Office Building, Baltimore MD 21201. **Tel** (410)225-4490. **LC** HJ11; .M348A. **DD** 353.9/752/00722.

UK
**CAPITAL TAX PLANNING.** (19??)-. English. Twelve times a year. $223.00 US & Canada; £145.00 others. Longman Group Ltd., Fourth Avenue, Longman House, Harlow Essex CM19 5SR England. **Tel** 011 44 279 429655, FAX 011 44 279 431059, telex 81259.

UK
**CAPITAL TAXES : A QUARTERLY COMMENTARY. Added/Corp** Sweet & Maxwell. (19??)-. Periodical. English. qt. £80.00. Sweet & Maxwell Ltd., South Quay Plaza, 183 Marsh Wall, London E14

# Public Administration —Public Finance and Taxation

9FT England. **Tel** 011 44 264 342899, FAX 011 44 264 342723, telex 929089 ITPINF G. **LC** KD5532.A13; C37. **DD** 343.4105/45; 344.10354.

UK/0964-9204
**CAPITAL TAXES NEWS AND REPORTS.** *Title Change.* [Cap. taxes news rep.]. (199?)-(199?). Periodical. English. mo. Longman Group Ltd., Fourth Avenue, Longman House, Harlow Essex CM19 5SR England. **Tel** 011 44 279 429655, FAX 011 44 279 431059, telex 81259. **(Subscription address:** PO Box 11318, Birmingham, AL 35202) **DD** 344.1035. available on microfilm and microfiche from University Microfilms International (UMI). *Continues* CTT News & Reports, 0264-7834. *Continued by* Capital Tax Planning.

CK
**CARTA FINANCIERA - ANIF.** Main/Corp Asociacion Nacional de Instituciones Financireras. Periodical. Spanish. bm. Bogota Anif Etc, Asociacion Nacionel de Instituciones Financireras, Cale 35 No 4-8A Apartado Aero 29765, Bogota Colombia. **LC** HG185.C6; A87A.

US
**CATALOG OF CALIFORNIA STATE FUNDING SOURCES / CALIFORNIA STATE LIBRARY.** Added/Corp California State Library. California State Library. Foundation. (1991)-. Catalog. English. ir. California State Library Foundation, 1225 8th Street, Suite 345, Sacramento CA 95814. **Tel** (916)447-6331. **LC** HJ321; .C37. **DD** 353.97940072/53/025. *Continues* Catalog of California State Grants Assistance.

US/0097-9309
**CATALOG OF STATE ASSISTANCE PROGRAMS.** *Title Change.* **See** Public Administration.

AT/1031-8364
**CCH JOURNAL OF ASIAN PACIFIC TAXATION, THE.** [CCH j. Asian Pac. tax.]. (1988)-. Periodical. English. Six times a year. CCH Australia Ltd, PO Box 230, North Ryde New South Wales, 2113 Australia. **Tel** 011 61 02 888 2555, FAX 011 61 02 888 7324. **(Subscription address:** Commerce Clearing House Inc., 4025 West Peterson Avenue, Chicago IL 60646.) **DD** 336.20099.
**Desc:** Tax and investment matters are comprehensively covered by tax professionals from the region, with a strong emphasis on practical implications.
**Ind/Abst** Account. Art.

AT/1032-1810
**CCH JOURNAL OF AUSTRALIAN TAXATION, THE.** [CCH j. Aust. tax.]. (1989)-. Periodical. English. bm. 285.00Aus$. CCH Australia Ltd, PO Box 230, North Ryde New South Wales, 2113 Australia. **Tel** 011 61 02 888 2555, FAX 011 61 02 888 7324. **DD** 336.200994.
**Desc:** Devoted solely to Australian tax issues. Provides a forum where Australia's top tax professionals come together to analyze and discuss complex tax issues.
**Ind/Abst** Account. Art.

US
**CENSUS OF LOCAL GOVERNMENTS / DEPARTMENT OF VETERAN AND COMMUNITY AFFAIRS.** English. an. 2571 Executive Center Circle East, Tallahassee FL 32301. **LC** HJ9218; .C45. **DD** 336/.014/759.

NE
**CENTRAL AND EAST EUROPEAN TAX DIRECTORY.** (1992)-. English. an. $135.00 subscriptions, $165.00 single copy. International Bureau of Fiscal Documentation - IBFD Publications, PO Box 20237, 1000 HE Amsterdam The Netherlands. **Tel** 011 31 20-6267726, FAX 011 31 20-6228658, telex 13217 INTAX NL.
**Desc:** News on the latest taxation developments. Also articles on relevant new laws.

SJ
**CENTRAL BUDGET PROPOSALS - DEMOCRATIC REPUBLIC OF SUDAN, MINISTRY OF FINANCE & NATIONAL ECONOMY.** Main/Corp Sudan. Wizarat Al-Maliyag Wa-Al-Iqtisad. English. Ministry of Finance and National Economy, PO Box 2092, Khartoum Sudan. **LC** HJ80.6; .A28A. **DD** 354.6240072/252/05.

US
**CERTIFICATION OF AVERAGE RATIOS AND COMMON LEVEL RANGE FOR USE IN THE TAX YEAR ... / STATE OF NEW JERSEY, DEPARTMENT OF THE TREASURY, DIVISION OF TAXATION.** Main/Corp New Jersey. Division of Taxation. Began in 1979. English. an. **LC** HJ4245; .A35B. **DD** 336.22/2.

US/0362-2517
**CERTIFICATION OF CONSTITUTIONAL LIMITATION ON THE BONDED DEBT OF THE STATE OF WASHINGTON.** Main/Corp Washington (State). Office of the State Treasurer. English. an. Office of the State Treasurer, Legislative Building, Olympia WA 98504. **LC** HJ11; .W16A. **DD** 336.3/4/09797.

US/0272-6017
**CHANGING PUBLIC ATTITUDES ON GOVERNMENTS AND TAXES.** [Chang. public attitudes gov. taxes]. English. an. Advisory Commission on Intergovernmental Relations Library, 1701 Pennsylvania Avenue NW, Washington DC 20575. **Tel** (202)653-5540. **LC** HJ275; .U52B. **DD** 336.73.

US/0737-2094
**CHAPTER 1 HANDBOOK.** (CHAPTER 1 HANDBOOK / EDUCATION FUNDING RESEARCH COUNCIL.). [Chapter 1 handb.]. **Added/Corp** Education Funding Research Council. **VFOAT** Chapter One Handbook; Update; Handbook Update; Chapter I Handbook. Vol. 4, No. 1 (Dec. 27, 1982)-. English. qt. $195.50. Education Funding Research Council, 4301 North Fairfax Drive, Suite 875, Arlington VA 22203. **Tel** (703)528-1082. **ED** Charles E. Edwards. *Continues* Title I Handbook Update, 0275-0759.
**Desc:** Complete reference source on federal government's largest program of financial aid to educationally and economically disadvantaged children.

US/0193-1660
**CHARACTERISTICS OF FHA SINGLE-FAMILY MORTGAGES, SELECTED SECTIONS OF NATIONAL HOUSING ACT.** VFOAT Characteristics of F.H.A. Single-Family Mortgages, Selected Sections of National Housing Act. English. an. US Department of Housing and Urban Development Federal Housing Commissioner, 451 Seventh Street SW, Room 9100, Washington DC 20410. **Tel** (202)708-3600, FAX (202)755-2580. **LC** HG2040.5.U5; A17B. **DD** 332.7/22/0973. available on microfiche (Vols. for (1977-) distributed to depository libraries).

US
**CHARITABLE GIFT PLANNING NEWS.** VFOAT Charitable Gift Planning. Vol. 1, No. 1 (Feb. 1983)-. Newsletter. English. Twelve times a year. $132.00 one year. Charitable Gift Planning News, PO Box 214373, Dallas TX 75221. **Tel** (214)978-3326, FAX (415)788-1466. **ED** Lynda S. Moerschbaecher, Jerry Mc Coy and Terry Simmons. **LC** KF6388.A15; C48. **DD** 343.73005/232; 347.3035232. Index available. cum. index. **Circ:** 500.
**Desc:** For planned giving news and views, including case and ruling updates as well as an editorial column on a topic of common interest. Designed for professional and technical planned giving officers and advisers.

US
**CHARITABLE GIVING TAX SERVICE.** (19??)-. English. $360.00 (3 volume set including updates). R & R Newkirk, 8695 South Archer, #10, Willow Springs IL 60480. **Tel** (312)836-4400, (800)252-0866, FAX (312)836-1021.

US/1061-9461
**CHARITABLE GIVING TECHNIQUES.** (CHARITABLE GIVING TECHNIQUES : ALI-ABA COURSE OF STUDY MATERIALS.). [Charit. giv. tech.]. **Added/Corp** American Law Institute-American Bar Association Committee on Continuing Professional Education. American Bar Association. Section of Taxation. American Bar Association. Section of Real Property, Probate and Trust Law. VFOAT ALI-ABA Course of Study Materials. (June 7-8, 1990)-. English. ALI-ABA, 4025 Chestnut Street, Philadelphia PA 19104. **DD** 343.

US/0360-2508
**CHART BOOK OF GOVERNMENTAL DATA: ORGANIZATION, FINANCES AND EMPLOYMENT.** Main/Corp United States. Bureau of the Census. (19??)-. Government Publication. English. US Department of Commerce, 14th Street & Constitution Avenue NW, Washington DC 20230. **Tel** (202)482-2000, FAX (202)482-3772. **LC** HJ257.2; .U54b. **DD** 336.73. *Continues* United States. Bureau of the Census. Chart Book on Governmental Finances and Employment.

UK
**CHARTAC TAXATION MANUAL.** *Title Change.* (19??)-(1992). English. sa. Gee & Company Limited, 183 Marsh Wall, South Quay Plaza, London E14 9FS England. **Tel** 011 44 71 538 5386, FAX 071 538 8623. *Continued by* Taxation Manual.

US
**CHECKLISTS AND ILLUSTRATIVE FINANCIAL STATEMENTS FOR COLLEGES AND UNIVERSITIES.** **See** Education-Higher Education.

JA
**CHIHO ZAISEI.** Added/Corp Chiho Zaimu Kyokai. (19??)-. Periodical. Japanese. mo. $126.00. Chiho Zaimu Kyokai, 4-3 Hirakawacho 2-chome chiyoda-ku, Tokyo 102 Japan. **LC** HJ9570; .C43.

KO
**CHOSE SINBO.** VFOAT Tax News. (1987)-. Periodical. Korean. sw. Chusik Hoesa Chugan Semu, 12 Susong-Dong Chongno-ku, Seoul 110 Korea. **LC** HJ77.5; .A13. *Continues* Chugan semu.

GW
**CHRONIK DER FINANZ- UND WAHRUNGSPOLITIK.** Main/Corp Germany (West). Bundesministerium der Finanzen. German. an. Bundesministerium der Finanzen, Rheindorfer Strasse 108, W-5300 Bonn 1 Germany. **LC** HJ48; .A13. **DD** 336.43.

CC
**CHUNG-KUO SHUI WU.** Added/Corp Chung-kuo Shui Wu Hsueh Hui. (19??)-. Periodical. Chinese. mo. $56.75. **(Subscription address:** China Books & Periodicals Inc., 2929 24th Street, San Francisco CA 94110.) **LC** HJ3631; .A2. **DD** 354.510072/4.

US
**CIS LAW REPRINTS. TAX SERIES : THE SUPREME COURT OF THE UNITED STATES PETITIONS AND BRIEFS.** VFOAT Tax Series. Vol. 17, No. 1 (1984/85)-. English. ir. Congressional Information Service Inc, 4520 East-West Highway, Suite 800, Bethesda MD 20814-3389. **Tel** (800)638-8380, (301)654-1550, FAX (301)654-4033, telex 292386 CIS UR. *Continues* BNA's Law Reprints. Tax Series.

US/1055-7814
**CITIZEN PARTICIPATION (CLEVELAND, OHIO).** (CITIZEN PARTICIPATION.). **Added/Corp** Citizens League of Greater Cleveland. No. 1 (Feb. 1991)-. Periodical. English. bm. $30.00. Citizens League of Greater Cleveland, 50 Public Square, Suite 843, Cleveland OH 44113. **Tel** (216)241-5340, FAX (216)736-7626. **ED** Janis Purdy. **Circ:** 3,000. *Formed by the union of* Greater Cleveland (Cleveland, Ohio : 1987), 1040-9122 *and* Governmental Review.
**Desc:** Reports on current issues involving local and state government operations.

US/0885-940X
**CITY & STATE (CHICAGO, ILL.).** *Title Change.* (CITY & STATE.). [City state]. **Added/Corp** Crain Communications Inc. VFOAT City and State; Crain's City & State; Crain's City and State. Vol. 1, No. 1 (Apr. 16, 1984)-(Jan. 1994). Periodical. English. sm. Crain Communications Inc., 1400 Woodbridge, Detroit MI 48207. **Tel** (313)446-6000, (800)992-9970. **LC** HJ275; .C56. **DD** 336.73/05. **[CCC]**. available on microfilm and microfiche from University Microfilms International (UMI); available on an online database (file 16/Full-Text) from DIALOG. *Merged into* Governing.
**Ind/Abst** PAIS Int. Print; PROMT [Full Txt.].

US
**CITY FISCAL CONDITIONS IN ... (WASHINGTON, D.C. : 1986).** (CITY FISCAL CONDITIONS IN ...). **Added/Corp** National League of Cities. (1986)-. English. an. $30.00 (nonmembers), $20.00 (members). National League of Cities, 1301 Pennsylvania Avenue NW, Washington DC 20004. **Tel** (202)626-3150, FAX (202)626-3043. **ED** William Barnes. **LC** HJ9011; .A13. **DD** 336/.014/73. **Circ:** 700. *Continues* City Fiscal Conditions and Outlook for Fiscal ... .
**Desc:** Reviews financial conditions and trends in the nation's cities.

US/0082-9439
**CITY GOVERNMENT FINANCES.** (CITY GOVERNMENT FINANCES IN ...). **Added/Corp** United States. Bureau of the Census. (1965)-. Government Publication. English. an. $16.00. Superintendent of Documents, US Government Printing Office, Washington DC 20402. **Tel** (202)275-3328, FAX (202)786-2377. **ED** Vance Kane. **LC** HJ9011; .A4b. **DD** 336.73. *Continues in part* City Finances.
**Desc:** National and size-group totals of municipal government finances. Statistics are supplied for each of the cities and selected townships having 50,000 inhabitants or more.
**Ind/Abst** Predicasts Forecasts.

US
**CITY OF CHICAGO ... BUDGET RECOMMENDATIONS / AS SUBMITTED TO THE CITY COUNCIL.** Main/Corp Chicago (Ill.). Mayor. **Added/Corp** Chicago (Ill.). Mayor. Budget Recommendations for the Year. VFOAT Budget Recommendations. (19??)-. English. an. **LC** HJ9013.C5; B3b. **DD** 352.1/225/0977311.

# Public Administration — Public Finance and Taxation

US/0361-0578
**CITY OF ROCHESTER BUDGET.**
(BUDGET.). **Main/Corp** University of Rochester. English. an. University of Rochester / NY, 500 Joseph C Wilson Boulevard, Rochester NY 14627.

LU
**CODE FISCAL LUXEMBOURGEOIS. MISE A JOUR.** Monographic series. French. ir. Price varies per volume. Editions Imprimerie St. Paul, 2 Rue Christophe Plantin, L 2988 Luxembourg Luxembourg. **Tel** 011 352 4993313.

FR
**CODE GENERAL DES IMPOTS ET ANNEXES AVEC ANNOTATIONS ET RENVOIS.** **See** Business-Commerce.

US
**CODE OF FEDERAL REGULATIONS. 26, INTERNAL REVENUE.** **See** Law.

US
**CODE OF FEDERAL REGULATIONS. 31, MONEY AND FINANCE, TREASURY.** **See** Law.

US
**CODE OF FEDERAL REGULATIONS. 48, FEDERAL ACQUISITION REGULATIONS SYSTEM.** **Added/Corp** United States. Office of the Federal Register. **VFOAT** Federal Acquisition Regulations System; CFR. 48, Federal Acquisition Regulations System. (19??)-. English. an. Superintendent of Documents, US Government Printing Office, Washington DC 20402. **Tel** (202)275-3328, **FAX** (202)786-2377.
**Ind/Abst** Int. Aerosp. Abstr.

US
**COLLEGE GRADUATES APPOINTED BY IRS.** **Main/Corp** United States. Internal Revenue Service. (19??)-. Periodical. English. Internal Revenue Service, 1111 Constitution Avenue NW, Washington DC 20224. **LC** HJ5018; .U545a. **DD** 353.007/24.

US
**COLLEGE OF WILLIAM & MARY ANNUAL TAX CONFERENCE : [PAPERS].** **Added/Corp** Marshall-Wythe School of Law. **VFOAT** Annual Tax Conference; College of William and Mary Annual Tax Conference. 32nd (1986)-. English. Marshall Wythe School of Law, College of William and Mary, PO Box 8795, Williamsburg VA 23187. **Tel** (804)221-3279. **Continues** Tax Conference (Marshall-Wythe School of Law). Tax Conference : [Papers].
**Ind/Abst** Fed. Tax Artic.

US
**COLORADO TAX PROFILE STUDY.**
English. an. Free. Colorado Legislative Council, Colorado Legislature, State Capitol Building, Denver CO 80211. **Tel** (303)866-3521. **LC** KFC1820; .L4 subser; HJ2396. **DD** 328.788/04 S 336.2/009788. **Circ:** 400.

US
**COLORADO TAXPAYER REPORT, A.**
**Added/Corp** Colorado Public Expenditure Council. Vol. 1, No. 1, (1955)-. Periodical. English. Colorado Public Expenditure Council, 1410 Grant A301, Denver CO 80203. **Tel** (303)832-8888.

CN/1183-3343
**COMMENTAIRE SUR LA TPS.**
(COMMENTAIRE SUR LA TPS / RICHTER.). [Comment. TPS]. **Added/Corp** Richter, Usher & Vineberg (Firme). **VFOAT** Commentaire sur la Taxe sur les Produits et les Services. (Sept. 1990)-. Periodical. French. Limited free distribution. Richter, Usher, and Vineberg, 2 Place Alexis Nihon, Montreal, Quebec H3Z 3C2 Canada. **DD** 343.7105/52/05.

PH
**COMMISSION ON AUDIT JOURNAL.**
Periodical. English. qt. 20.00. Commission on Audit, Don Mariano Marcos Avenue, Quezon City Metro Manila Philippines. **LC** HJ9927.P3; P43. **DD** 354.5990072/32/05. **Continues** Philippine Commission on Audit Journal.

AT
**COMMONWEALTH TAXATION BOARD OF REVIEW DECISIONS. NEW SERIES.** **See** Law.

LU
**COMMUNITY BUDGET : THE FACTS AND FIGURES, THE.** **Main/Corp** Commission of the European Communities. (1988)-. English. an. £7.90 UK; 8.50p Ireland. Office for Official Publications of the European Communities, 2 Rue Mercier, 2985 Luxembourg Luxembourg. **Tel** 011 352 499281, **FAX** 011 352 488573. **LC** HJ2094.5; .C65a. **DD** 354.1/722252/05.

US/0737-3392
**COMPARATIVE REPORT OF LOCAL GOVERNMENT REVENUES AND EXPENDITURES, YEAR ENDED JUNE 30, ... .** **Added/Corp** Virginia. Auditor of Public Accounts. 1981-. English. an. Auditor of Public Accounts / Virginia, PO Box 1295, Richmond VA 23210. **LC** HJ9011.V8; C65. **DD** 352.1/72/09755. **Formed by the union of** Report of Auditor of Public Accounts of Commonwealth of Virginia on Comparative Cost of City Government Year Ended June 30, ..., 0364-488X **and** Report of Auditor of Public Accounts of Commonwealth of Virginia on Comparative Cost of County Government.

AG
**COMPENDIO TEORICO Y PRACTICO - ALALC.** **See** Business-Commerce.

US/0741-9260
**COMPILATION OF GAO'S WORK ON TAX ADMINISTRATION ACTIVITIES.** *Title Change.* **See** Business-Accounting.

US/0743-2224
**COMPLETE BOOK OF TAX DEDUCTIONS.** *Ceased.* (1985)-(1993). English. an. Harper Collins Publishers, Keystone Industrial Park, Scranton PA 18512. **Tel** (800)242-7737, (800)233-4727, **FAX** (800)822-4090. **ED** Robert S. Holzman. **LC** HJ4653.D4; T34. **DD** 343.7305/2305; 347.30352305. **Continues** Take It Off, 0193-3094.

US/0090-7219
**COMPLETE INCOME TAX GUIDE, THE.**
English. an. $1.75. Universal Publishing and Distributing Corporation, 235 East 45 Street, New York NY 10017. **ED** A C Strasburger. **LC** KF6369.6; .C65. **DD** 343/.73/052.

US
**COMPREHENSIVE ANNUAL FINANCIAL REPORT / CITY OF PHILADELPHIA, PENNSYLVANIA.**
English. an. City of Philadelphia, City Hall, Philadelphia PA 19107. **LC** HJ9013.P6; B18. **DD** 352.1/71. **Continues** Philadelphia (PA.). Office of the Director of Finance. Comprehensive Annual Report of the Directory of Finance.

US
**COMPREHENSIVE ANNUAL FINANCIAL REPORT, COUNTY OF LOS ANGELES.** **Main/Corp** Los Angeles County (Calif.). Auditor-Controller. **VFOAT** County of Los Angeles Comprehensive Annual Financial Report. (19??)-. English. an. Department of Auditor-Controller, 525 Hall of Administration, Los Angeles CA 90012. **LC** HJ9012.C2; L773a. **DD** 352.1/71.

US
**COMPREHENSIVE ANNUAL FINANCIAL REPORT FOR THE FISCAL YEAR ENDED JUNE 30 ... / STATE OF UTAH.** **VFOAT** State of Utah Comprehensive Annual Financial Report for the Fiscal Year Ended June 30 ... . English. an. Utah Department of Finance, State Archives and Records Services, Salt Lake City UT 84114. **ED** Lynn Vellinga. **LC** HJ11; .U828A. **DD** 353.97920072/32. **Circ:** 1,000.
**Desc:** Financial report for the State of Utah including statistical and demographic information.

US
**COMPREHENSIVE ANNUAL FINANCIAL REPORT FOR THE YEAR ENDED ... - COMPTROLLER'S OFFICE, COMPTROLLER OF THE TREASURY OF MARYLAND.** **Main/Corp** Maryland. Comptroller's Office. 1982-. English. an. State Treasury Building, PO Box 466, Annapolis MD 21404. **LC** HJ11; .M334B. **DD** 353.97520072/31. **Continues** Annual Report of the Comptroller of the State of Maryland.

US
**COMPREHENSIVE ANNUAL FINANCIAL REPORT FOR THE YEAR ENDED JUNE 30, ... (MINNESOTA).**
**Main/Corp** Minnesota. Dept. of Finance. 1983-. English. an. Minnesota Department of Finance, 658 Cedar Street, 400 Centennial Building, St Paul MN 55155. **Tel** (612)296-9721, **FAX** (612)296-8685. **LC** HJ11; .M616A. **DD** 353.97760072/31. **Continues** Minnesota. Dept. of Finance. Annual Financial Report.

US
**COMPREHENSIVE ANNUAL FINANCIAL REPORT MONTGOMERY COUNTY, MARYLAND.** **Main/Corp** Montgomery County (Md.). Dept. of Finance. **VFOAT** Annual Financial Report. Fiscal Year 1983-. English. an. Department of Finance / Rockville, 101 Monroe Street, Rockville MD 20850. **LC** HJ9012.M3; M63. **DD** 352.1/71. **Continues** Montgomery County (MD.). Dept. of Finance. Annual Financial Report.

US
**COMPREHENSIVE ANNUAL FINANCIAL REPORT OF THE COMPTROLLER FOR THE YEAR ENDED JUNE 30 ... - NEW YORK STATE.**
**Main/Corp** New York (N.Y.). Office of the Comptroller. English. an. Free. Comptroller's Press Office, Alfred E Smith State Office Building, Albany NY 12236. **Tel** (518)474-4015, telex 5184738940. **LC** HJ9013; .N5D. **DD** 352.1/71. **Continues** Comprehensive Annual Report of the Comptroller for the Fiscal Year Ended June 30 ... .
**Desc:** Presents the financial position and results of operations of New York State as measured by the financial activities of its various funds.

US
**COMPREHENSIVE ANNUAL FINANCIAL REPORT, STATE OF MISSOURI.** **Main/Corp** Missouri. Office of Administration. Division of Accounting. (June 30, 1982)-. English. an. Free on request. Missouri Accounting Division, PO Box 809, Jefferson City MO 65102. **LC** HJ11; .M814a. **DD** 353.97780072/31. **Circ:** 800 (ctrl). **Continues** Missouri. Office of Administration. Division of Accounting. Report, Financial Status, State of Missouri.

US
**COMPTROLLER GENERAL'S ANNUAL REPORT.** **Main/Corp** United States. General Accounting Office. **VFOAT** Annual Report; GAO Annual Report. **VAT** General Accounting Office Annual Report. (1986)-. English. Free (1st copy), $1.25 (subsequent copies). US General Accounting Office / District of Columbia, 441 G Street NW, Room 4528, Washington DC 20548. **Tel** (202)275-2812. **LC** HJ10.2; .U55a. **DD** 353.0072/32. **Continues in part** GAO Annual Report.

US/0361-7203
**COMPUTER LAW AND TAX REPORT.**
**See** Law.

US
**CONFERENCE ON TAX PLANNING FOR 501(C)(3) ORGANIZATIONS : [PROCEEDINGS] / NEW YORK UNIVERSITY.** **Added/Corp** New York University. 17th (1989)-. English. an. $87.00. Matthew Bender & Company Inc., 1275 Broadway, Albany NY 12204. **Tel** (800)833-9844, (518)487-3000. **Continues** Conference on Tax Planning for the Charitable Sector. Conference on Tax Planning for the Charitable Sector : [Proceedings].
**Ind/Abst** Leg. Resour. Index.

CN/0823-8669
**CONSCIENCE CANADA NEWSLETTER.**
**Added/Corp** Conscience Canada. Peace Tax Fund Committee. No. 16 (Winter 1983/1984)-. Periodical. English. Four times a year (Mar., May, Sept., Dec.). $15.00. Conscience Canada Inc., PO Box 8601, Victoria Center Post, Victoria British Columbia, V8W 3S2 Canada. **Tel** (604)384-5532. **ED** Edith Adamson. **DD** 261.8/73. **Bk Rev.** **Ad Acc.** **Circ:** 1,400. **Continues** Taxes for Peace, Not War, 0229-5377.
**Desc:** News, letters and articles about conscientious objection to war taxes and the direction of such taxes to peace.

CG
**CONSEILLER COMPTABLE, LE.** **VFOAT** Revue Zairoise de la Comptabilite. No. 1/2- 1974-. Periodical. French. $40.00. Secretariat General de la Comptabilite, 17 Avenue du Port, Building KDL ler Etage, BP 308, Kinshasa Congo Zaire. **LC** HJ9703; .C65. **DD** 354/.675/1007231.

US
**CONSERVATION ASSESSMENT PROGRAM, GRANT APPLICATION AND INFORMATION.** **See** Museums and Galleries.

II
**CONSOLIDATED FINANCE AND REVENUE ACCOUNTS OF ZILLA PARISHADS AND PANCHAYAT SAMITIS IN THE STATE OF MAHARASHTRA.** **Main/Corp** Maharashtra, India (State). Rural Development Dept. English. Rural Development Department, Government of Maharashtra, Bombay India. **LC** HJ9927.I4; M38A. **DD** 354.54/792007231/05.

AT
**CONSOLIDATED REVENUE FUND : SUMMARY OF ESTIMATED EXPENDITURE (INCLUDING EXPENDITURE RESERVED BY LAW) AND ESTIMATED REVENUE.** **Main/Corp** Tasmania. Dept. of the Treasury. **VFOAT** Summary of Estimated Expenditure (Including Expenditure Reserved by Law) Estimated Revenue. (19??)-. English. Tasmania Department of the Treasury, Hobart Tasmania Australia. **LC** HJ94; .C213. **DD** 354/.946/00722.

# Public Administration —Public Finance and Taxation

US/0148-009X
**CONSOLIDATED TAX RETURNS.**
**Added/Corp** Practising Law Institute. (19??)-. Periodical. English. ir. $155.00. Warren Gorham & Lamont Inc., Park Square Building, 31 St. James Avenue, Boston MA 02116-4112. **Tel** (617)423-2020, (800)950-1207, FAX (617)423-2026. **LC** KF6499.C58; C6. **DD** 343/.73/052.

CN/1184-1869
**CONSOMMATION (MONTREAL).** (CONSOMMATION.). [Consommation]. **Added/Corp** ACEF du Centre de Montreal. Vol. 1, No 1 (Nov./Dec. 1990)-. Periodical. French. Five times a year. 28.04Can$ (institutions), 9.35Can$ (individuals). ACEF / Assoc Coop d'Econ Familiale, 1215 rue de la Visitation, Montreal Quebec H2L 3B5 Canada. **Tel** (514)598-7288. **DD** 381.3/4/0971405. *Continues S'en Sortir., 0226-9058.*
**Ind/Abst** Selec. Coop. Index Manage. Period.

●CN
**CONSULTATIONS PREBUDGETAIRES/ COMITE PERMANENT DES FINANCES ET DES AFFAIRES ECONOMIQUES.**
**Main/Corp** Ontario. Assemblee Legislative. Comite Permanent des Finances et des Affaires Economiques. **VFOAT** Pre-Budget Consultation. (1992)-. Periodical. French (English). CNA Memo, Suite 306/40 East Avenue St-Clair, Toronto Ontario M4T 1M9 Canada. **DD** 354.7130072/223.

US/0162-6779
**CONTINGENT FOREIGN LIABILITIES OF THE UNITED STATES GOVERNMENT.** (CONTINGENT FOREIGN LIABILITIES OF THE UNITED STATES GOVERNMENT / U.S. TREASURY DEPT., OFFICE OF THE ASSISTANT SECRETARY FOR INTERNATIONAL AFFAIRS.). [Conting. foreign liabil. U. S. Gov.]. **Added/Corp** United States. Dept. of the Treasury. Office of the Assistant Secretary for Economic Policy. United States. Dept. of the Treasury. Office of the Assistant Secretary for International Affairs. (19??)-. Periodical. English. Three times a year. Department of the Treasury / Pennsylvania Avenue, Fifteenth Street and Pennsylvania Avenue NW, Washington DC 20220. **Tel** (202)566-2969. **LC** HJ8119; .U57a. **DD** 336.3/4/0973. **Circ**: 200. available on microfiche (National Technical Information Service); available on microfilm (Congressional Research Service and Depository Library System).
**Desc:** Tables of contingent liabilities of the United States Government on its contracts of foreign insurance and guarantee. Includes summaries by program and program within country for both official and private obligors, as well as detail on individual contracts exceeding one million dollars.

US/0160-4732
**CORPORATE AND PERSONAL TAXATION IN THE ARAB WORLD.** See Law-Corporate Law.

US/0731-4604
**CORPORATE CAPITAL TRANSACTIONS ALERT.** (CORPORATE CAPITAL TRANSACTIONS ALERT : TAXATION, REGULATION, PLANNING / RESEARCH INSTITUTE OF AMERICA, INC.). Vol. 1, No. 1 (Nov. 1980)-. Corporate Report. English. mo. $72.00. Research Institute of America, 117 East Stevens Avenue, Valhalla NY 10595. **Tel** (800)431-9025. **LC** KF1428.A15; .C67.

CN/0070-0282
**CORPORATE MANAGEMENT TAX CONFERENCE.** [Corp. Manage. Tax Conf.]. **Main/Corp** Corporate Management Tax Conference. **Added/Corp** Canadian Tax Foundation. (1965)-. Periodical. English. an. 47.50Can$. Canadian Tax Foundation, 1 Queen Street East, Suite 1800, Toronto Ontario M5C 2Y2 Canada. **Tel** (416)863-9784. **LC** LAW. **DD** 336.2/43/0971. *Continues International Corporate Tax Conference. Conference: Papers, 0837-7502.*
**Ind/Abst** Account. Tax Datab. (1991-); Curr. Law Index (1980-); Leg. Resour. Index (1980-); LegalTrac (1980-).

US/0742-7824
**CORPORATE, PARTNERSHIP, ESTATE AND GIFT TAXATION.** [Corp. partnersh. estate gift tax.]. 1985 Ed.-. English. an. $28.95. Dame Publications, 7800 Bissonnet/Suite 415, Houston TX 77074. **Tel** (713)995-1000. **LC** KF6335; .C6. **DD** 332.

●US/1188-7834
**CORPORATE TAX PLANNING.** [Corp. tax plan.]. No. 1 (1992)-. Periodical. English. ir. $155.00. Little Brown & Company, 34 Beacon Street, Boston MA 02108. **Tel** (617)227-0730, (800)759-0190. **DD** 343.7106/7.

CN/0824-314X
**CORPORATE TAX RETURN HANDBOOK.** *Ceased.* [Corp. tax return handb.]. **Added/Corp** Canadian Institute of Chartered Accountants. (1980)-(1993 ed.). English. an. Canadian Institute of Chartered Accountants, 277 Wellington Street West, Toronto Ontario M5V 3H2 Canada. **Tel** (416)977-3222, FAX (416)204-3415. **ED** Harvey J. Graham. **DD** 343.7106/7. **Circ**: 7,000.
**Desc:** A practical guide to completing federal or provincial corporate tax returns.

NE
**CORPORATE TAXATION FOR LATIN AMERICA.** *Title Change.* (1970)-?. Periodical. English. qt. International Bureau of Fiscal Documentation - IBFD Publications, PO Box 20237, 1000 HE Amsterdam The Netherlands. **Tel** 011 31 20-6267726, FAX 011 31 20-6228658, telex 13217 INTAX NL. *Continued by Taxation in Latin America.*

US
**CORPORATE TAXES, A WORLDWIDE SUMMARY.** **Added/Corp** Price, Waterhouse Center for Transnational Taxation. **VFOAT** Corporate Taxes. (Oct. 1980)-. English. an. free. Price Waterhouse & Company, 1177 Avenue of the Americas, New York NY 10020. **Tel** (212)596-7000. *Continues Corporate Taxes in 80 Countries, 0733-6187.*

US
**CORPORATION FRANCHISE TAX. NUMBER OF CORPORATIONS AND REPORTED TAX LIABILITY BY TAX BASE (COLUMBUS, OHIO: 1981).** (CORPORATION FRANCHISE TAX. NUMBER OF CORPORATIONS AND REPORTED TAX LIABILITY BY TAX BASE / OHIO DEPARTMENT OF TAXATION.). **VFOAT** Number of Corporations and Reported Tax Liability by Tax Base. Tax Year 1980-. English. an. Department of Taxation / Ohio, Research and Statistics Section, PO Box 530, Columbus OH 43216. **LC** HJ4655.O33; C66. **DD** 336.24/3/09771. *Continues Corporate Franchise Tax. Number of Corporations and Reported Tax Liability by Tax Base.*

US
**CORPORATION FRANCHISE TAX. NUMBER OF MANUFACTURING CORPORATIONS AND REPORTED TAX LIABILITY BY TAX BASE / OHIO DEPARTMENT OF TAXATION.** **VFOAT** Number of Manufacturing Corporations and Reported Tax Liability by Tax Base. English. Department of Taxation / Ohio, Research and Statistics Section, PO Box 530, Columbus OH 43216. **LC** HJ4655.O33; C67. **DD** 336.24/3/09771.

US/0147-1619
**CORPORATION LAW AND TAX REPORT (1975).** *Ceased.* See Law-Corporate Law.

CN/0576-0119
**CORPORATION TAXATION STATISTICS (OTTAWA).** *Title Change.* See Public Administration-Abstracting, Bibliographies and Statistics.

US/0093-0768
**COUNTY ASSESSMENT STATUS REPORT (SALEM).** (COUNTY ASSESSMENT STATUS REPORT (OREGON).). **Main/Corp** Oregon. Dept. of Revenue. English. an. Department of Revenue / Oregon, State Office Building, Salem OR 97310. **Tel** (503)378-3359. **LC** HJ4259; .A25A. **DD** 336.2/2/09795.

US/0098-678X
**COUNTY GOVERNMENT FINANCES.** (COUNTY GOVERNMENT FINANCES IN ...). **Added/Corp** United States. Bureau of the Census. **VFOAT** County Government Finances. (1972/73)-. Government Publication. English. an. $8.00. Superintendent of Documents, US Government Printing Office, Washington DC 20402. **Tel** (202)275-3328, FAX (202)786-2377. **LC** HJ9011; .A4c. **DD** 336.73.
**Ind/Abst** Predicasts Forecasts.

US/0090-2829
**COUNTY OF ALLEGHENY BUDGET FOR OPERATING DEPARTMENTS, THE.** **Main/Corp** Allegheny Co., Pa. County Controller. English. Allegheny County, Office of the Controller, Pittsburgh PA 15219. **LC** HJ9012.P4; A44. **DD** 352/.12/0974885.

US
**COUNTY UNDIVIDED LOCAL GOVERNMENT REVENUE ASSISTANCE FUNDS. AMOUNTS DISTRIBUTED WITHIN COUNTIES BY COUNTY BUDGET COMMISSIONS, BY SUBDIVISION OR SUBDIVISION CLASS, CALENDAR YEAR ... / OHIO DEPARTMENT OF TAXATION.** **Added/Corp** Ohio. Tax Analysis & Local Government Distributions. **VFOAT** Amounts Distributed Within Counties by County Budget Commissions, by Subdivision or Subdivision Class, Calendar Year ... . (1990)-. English. Tax Analysis & Local Government Distributions, PO Box 530, Columbus OH 43266-0030. **DD** 352.13/09771. *Continues County Undivided Local Government Funds. Amounts Distributed Within Counties by County Budget Commissioners, by Source and Subdivision.*

UK
**CRONER'S REFERENCE BOOK FOR VALUE ADDED TAX.** (19??)-. Periodical. English. mo. £145.60. Croner Publ Ltd, Croner House, London Road, Kingston upon Thames, Surrey KT2 6SR England. **Tel** 011 44 81 5473333, FAX 081 547-2637. Index available (Free).

SP
**CRONICA TRIBUTARIA / MINISTERIO DE HACIENDA, INSTITUTO ESTUDIOS FISCALES.** Periodical. Spanish. qt. 400 ptas. Servicio de Publicaciones del Ministerio de Hacienda, Rey Francisco 21, Madrid 8 Spain. **LC** K3; .R575.

US/0499-6453
**CUMULATIVE LIST OF ORGANIZATIONS DESCRIBED IN SECTION 170 (C) OF THE INTERNAL REVENUE CODE OF 1954.** **Added/Corp** United States. Internal Revenue Service. **VFOAT** Cumulative List of Organizations Described in Section 170 (c) of the Internal Revenue Code of 1986. **VAT** Cumulative List of Organizations Described in Section One Hundred and Seventy C of the Internal Revenue Code of Nineteen Hundred and Fifty-Four. (19??)-. Government Publication. English. an (3 cumulative quarterly supplemets). $48.00 domestic; $60.00 other. Superintendent of Documents, US Government Printing Office, Washington DC 20402. **Tel** (202)275-3328, FAX (202)786-2377. **LC** HJ4653.D4; A3.
**Desc:** Lists contributions of organizations which are deductible under Section 170(c) of the Internal Revenue Code of 1986.

CN/0317-9664
**CURRENT ESTIMATES - CITY OF WINNIPEG.** (CURRENT ESTIMATES.). **Main/Corp** Winnipeg, (Man.). **VFOAT** Current Estimates and Capital Estimates. **VAT** Current Estimates and Capital Estimates - City of Winnipeg (1965); Estimates - City of Winnipeg. English. an. Free. City of Winnipeg Budget Bureau, Manitoba R3B 1B9 Canada. **DD** 336.7127/4. ctrl circ.

UK
**CURRENT TAX INTELLIGENCE.** **Added/Corp** Sweet & Maxwell. (19??)-. English. **LC** KD5352; .C87. **DD** 343.4104; 344.1034.

II
**CURRENT TAX REPORTER. Main/Corp** India. Supreme Court. V. 1- Jan./July 1972-. Periodical. English. mo. Rs25.00. India Supreme Court, 861 Chopasani Road, Sardarpura Jodhpur India. **DD** 343/.54/040264.

US/0897-1609
**CUSTOMS TODAY.** (CUSTOMS TODAY / DEPARTMENT OF THE TREASURY/U.S. CUSTOMS SERVICE.). [Cust. today]. **Added/Corp** U.S. Customs Service. (19??)-. Periodical. English. qt. Customs Today, US Customs Service, Room 6311, Washington DC 20229. **Tel** (202)566-9102. **LC** HJ6622; .A58. **DD** 336.2/6/0973.

US/0092-6884
**DAILY TAX REPORT (WASHINGTON).** See Law.

CN/1184-0323
**DAVID INGRAM'S THE ULTIMATE YEAR ROUND TAX GUIDE.** [David Ingram's ultim. year round tax guide]. **VFOAT** Ultimate Tax Book; Ultimate Year Round Tax Guide. 17th Ed. (1991)-. English. $14.95 per volume. Hancock Hse Publishers, 19313 Zero Avenue, Surrey British Columbia V3S 5J9 Canada. **DD** 343.7105/2/05. *Continues Ultimate Tax Book., 1184-0315.*

GW
**DDZ. DER DEUTSCHE ZOLLBEAMTE.** **VFOAT** Der Deutsche Zollbeamte. German. mo. DM48.00 Germany; DM36.00 US. Bund der Deutschen Zollbeamten. **Tel** (0228)230031/32. **ED** Richard Muller, Dietrich Halbig, Herbert Bar, Heinz Schulze and Horst Rohl. **LC** HJ6920; .A34. Index available. cum. index. **Bk Rev. Ad Acc. Circ**: 33,000 (ctrl).
**Desc:** Official organ of the Federal German Customs Personnel Union. Including special supplements concerning customs, laws and regulations.

US
**DECISIONS OF THE COMPTROLLER GENERAL OF THE UNITED STATES.** *Ceased.* **Main/Corp** United States. General Accounting Office. **Added/Corp** United States. General Accounting Office. Office of the General Counsel. (July 1921)-Vol. 71, (Sept. 1993). Government Publication. English. mo. Superintendent of Documents, US Government Printing Office, Washington DC 20402. **Tel** (202)275-3328, FAX (202)786-2377.
**Desc:** Each issue contains decisions of the Comptroller General on financial matters arising in the Federal Service.

## Public Administration — Public Finance and Taxation

US
**DECISIONS - WISCONSIN TAX APPEALS COMMISSION. Main/Corp** Wisconsin Tax Appeals Commission. **Added/Corp** Commerce Clearing House. **VFOAT** Decisions - Wisconsin Board of Tax Appeals. Vol. 7 (1967/1969)-. English. $70.00. Wisconsin Department of Administration, 101 South Webster Street, PO Box 7864, Madison WI 53702. **Tel** (608)266-1651. **Continues** Wisconsin. Board of Tax Appeals. Decisions - Wisconsin Board of Tax Appeals.

BL
**DECISOES DE TRIBUNAIS FISCAIS : IMPOSTO DE RENDA.** Portuguese. Editora Resenha Tributaria Ltda, rua Quatinga 12, Sao Paulo Brazil. **LC** LAW.

CK
**DECRETO DEL PRESUPUESTO GENERAL DE LA NACION.** *Title Change.* **Main/Corp** Colombia. Direccion General del Presupuesto. **Added/Corp** Colombia. Direccion General del Presupuesto. **VFOAT** Presupuesto General de la Nacion. (19??)-(1992). Spanish. **Continues** Ley de Presupuesto Nacional. **Continued by** Colombia. Direccion General del Presupuesto. Ley de Presupuesto Nacional de la Nacion (1993).

GR
**DELTIO PHOROLOGIKES NOMOTHESIAS.** Periodical. Greek, Modern. sm. 6.000. Hodos Akademias 71-73, Athens 106 78 Greece. **Continues** Deltion Phorologikes Nomothesias.

GR/0256-3592
**DELTION STATISTIKE DEMASION OIKONOMIKON. See** Public Administration-Abstracting, Bibliographies and Statistics.

CN/1184-9347
**DEPARTMENT OF INDUSTRY, TRADE AND TOURISM AND LOTTERIES FUNDED PROGRAMS, FITNESS AND SPORT DIRECTORATES, SUPPLEMENTARY INFORMATION FOR LEGISLATIVE REVIEW, ... EXPENDITURE ESTIMATES.** [Dep. Ind. Trade Tour. lotteries funded programs Fit. Sport Dir. suppl. inf. legis. rev. expend. estim.]. **Main/Corp** Manitoba. Manitoba Industry, Trade and Tourism. **VFOAT** Supplementary Information for Legislative Review, ... Departmental Expenditure Estimates. (1991)-. English. **DD** 354.71270682. **Continues** Supplementary Information for Legislative Review, ... Expenditure Estimates., 0848-3876.

CN/1184-7999
**DEPARTMENTAL EXPENDITURE ESTIMATES SUPPLEMENT GUIDELINES.** *Ceased.* [Dep. expend. estim. suppl. guidel.]. **Added/Corp** Manitoba. Comptrollier's Division. (1992)-(1992). English. Manitoba Department of Finance, 204 Legislative Building, Winnipeg Manitoba R3C 0V8 Canada. **DD** 354.7127062/05. **Continues** Estimates Supplement Guidelines, 1184-7980.

CN/1183-4420
**DEPECHE-TPS : BULLETIN MENSUEL DE TPS CANADA-QUEBEC.** [Depeche-TPS]. **VFOAT** Depeche-TPS; TPS Canada-Quebec. **VAT** Depeche-Taxe sur les Produits et Services. No. 1 (Mar 1991)-. Bulletin. French. mo. Les Publications Dacfo, Inc., CP 845 Tour de la Bourse, Montreal Quebec H4Z 1K2 Canada. **DD** 343.7105/52/05.

US
**DEPRECIATION : FOR USE IN PREPARING ... RETURNS. Added/Corp** United States. Internal Revenue Service. (1979)-. Government Publication. English. Superintendent of Documents, US Government Printing Office, Washington DC 20402. **Tel** (202)275-3328, FAX (202)786-2377. **Continues** United States. Internal Revenue Service. Tax Information on Depreciation.

BL
**DESEMPENHO DAS FINANCAS PUBLICAS DE PERNAMBUCO. Main/Corp** Pernambuco (Brazil). Diretoria Geral das Financas. Financas. Portuguese. Rua Imperador S/N, 8 Andar, 50.000 Recife Brazil. **LC** HJ9388.A2; P476.

II/0376-821X
**DETAILED CIVIL BUDGET ESTIMATES. GOVERNMENT OF WEST BENGAL.** (DETAILED CIVIL BUDGET ESTIMATES FOR THE YEAR ... ). **Main/Corp** West Bengal (India). Finance Dept. (19??)-. English. an. West Bengal Government Press / Finance Department, Alipore West Bengal India. **LC** HJ66.B353; B224. **DD** 354/.54/140072225/05. **Continues** West Bengal (India). Finance Dept. Civil Budget Estimate.

II/0303-8653
**DETAILED DEMAND FOR GRANTS OF EDUCATION DEPARTMENT. GOVERNMENT OF JAMMU AND KASHMIR. See** Education.

II/0376-8260
**DETAILED DEMAND FOR GRANTS OF HOUSING AND URBAN DEVELOPMENT DEPARTMENT. See** Housing and Urban Development.

II/0303-8629
**DETAILED DEMAND FOR GRANTS OF INDUSTRIES & COMMERCE DEPARTMENT. GOVERNMENT OF JAMMU AND KASHMIR. See** Business-Commerce.

II/0376-8279
**DETAILED DEMAND FOR GRANTS OF LABOUR AND SOCIAL WELFARE DEPARTMENT.** *Title Change.* **See** Economics-Labor.

II/0303-8637
**DETAILED DEMAND FOR GRANTS OF LADAKH AFFAIR DEPARTMENT. GOVERNMENT OF JAMMU AND KASHMIR. See** Economics.

II/0376-8295
**DETAILED DEMAND FOR GRANTS OF PLANNING DEPARTMENT.** *Title Change.* **See** Economics.

II
**DETAILED DEMAND FOR GRANTS OF REVENUE DEPARTMENT FOR ... . Main/Corp** Jammu and Kashmir (India). Revenue Dept. **VFOAT** Tafsili Mutalabati Zar Mahkamahyi Umuri Mal Babat Sal ... . (1990)-. English (Urdu). an. Ranbir Government Press / Revenue Relief, Jammu and Kashmir, Revenue Relief and Rehabilitation Department, Jammu India. **Continues** Detailed Demand for Grants of Revenue, Relief, and Employment Department for ... .

II/0303-948X
**DETAILED DEMAND FOR GRANTS OF WORKS DEPARTMENT. GOVERNMENT OF JAMMU AND KASHMIR.** (DETAILED DEMAND FOR GRANTS OF WORKS DEPARTMENT.). **Main/Corp** Jammu and Kashmir. Public Works Dept. (19??)-. English. Ranbir Government Press / Works Department, Jammu and Kashmir, Works Department, Jammu India. **LC** HD4295.K3; J35a. **DD** 354/.54/0086.

II
**DETAILED ESTIMATES OF REVENUE OF THE PUNJAB GOVERNMENT FOR THE YEAR ... . Main/Corp** Punjab (India). 1977-78-. English. **LC** HJ66.P73; C14A. **DD** 354/.02/54552. **Continues** Demands for Grants of the Punjab Government with Detailed Estimates of Revenue and Expenditure.

II/0570-0345
**DETAILED IRRIGATION BUDGET. Main/Corp** Andhra Pradesh (India). (19??)-. English. an. Government Central Press, Hyderabad India. **LC** HD1741.I3; A53. **DD** 354.548400722.

GW/0724-5637
**DEUTSCHE STEUER-ZEITUNG.** (19??)-. Periodical. German. sm. DM324.00. Stollfuss Verlag GmbH and Company KG, Postfach 2428 Dechenstrasse 7-11, D 53014 Bonn Germany. **Tel** 011 49 228 724222. **LC** HJ2670; .D39. **[CCC].**

GW/0012-1347
**DEUTSCHES STEUERRECHT.** [Dtsch. Steuerr.]. **VFOAT** DSTR. Deutsches Steuerrecht. (1962)-. Periodical. German. wk. DM315.80 Germany ;DM339.20 other. CH Beck Verlagsbuchhandlung, D 80791 Munich Germany. **Tel** 011 49 89 381891.

UK
**DHSS OFFICIAL TAX CONTRIBUTIONS.** English. an. £145.00 England; £155.00 other. Longman Group Ltd., Fourth Avenue, Longman House, Harlow Essex CM19 5SR England. **Tel** 011 44 279 429655, FAX 011 44 279 431059, telex 81259. **(Subscription address:** Fourth Avenue, Harlow Essex CM19 5AA England)

AG
**DIGESTO NOTARIAL. Main/Corp** Argentine Republic. **Added/Corp** Colegio de Escribanos de la Provincia de Buenos Aires. **VFOAT** Boletin de Legislacion. (1968/69)-. Spanish. Colegio de Escribanos, Alsina 2280 Piso 3, 1090 Buenos Aires Argentina. **Tel** 011 54 1 489056, 8010081.

US
**DIGESTS OF DECISIONS OF THE COMPTROLLER GENERAL OF THE UNITED STATES. Main/Corp** United States. General Accounting Office. Office of General Counsel. Vol. 1, No. 1 (October 1989)-. Periodical. English. mo. $18.00, $3.00 (single issue), $8.50 (index) US; $22.50, $3.75 (single issue), $10.63 (index) other. US General Accounting Office / District of Columbia, 441 G Street NW, Room 4528, Washington DC 20548. **Tel** (202)275-2812. **Continues** Digests of Unpublished Decisions of the Comptroller General of the United States, 0011-7323.

US/0093-8823
**DIRECT LEVIES ON GAMING IN NEVADA.** (DIRECT LEVIES ON GAMING IN NEVADA; ANALYSIS OF THE RATES AND STRUCTURE BY ALL LEVELS OF GOVERNMENT.). **Main/Corp** Nevada. State Gaming Control Board. Economic Research Unit. (19??)-. English. an. State Gaming Control Board, 1150 East William Street, Carson City NV 89710. **Tel** (702)687-6500. **LC** HJ5352; .N48a. **DD** 336.2/78/795.

II
**DIRECT TAXES BULLETIN.** *Ceased.* **Main/Corp** India (Republic). Directorate of Inspection (Research, Statistics and Publication). Bulletin. English. Government of India / Ministry of Urban Development, Department of Publication, Civil Lines, Delhi 110054 India.

US/0148-1762
**DIRECTORY OF MEMBERS - MUNICIPAL FINANCE OFFICERS ASSOCIATION. Main/Corp** Municipal Finance Officers Association of the United States and Canada. (19??)-. English. an. Municipal Finance Officers Association, 180 North Michigan Avenue/Suite 800, Chicago IL 60601. **LC** HJ9145; .M86a. **DD** 336/.014/06273.

BL
**DIREITO TRIBUTARIO. See** Law.

BL
**DIREITO TRIBUTARIO ATUAL.** Vol. 1-. Periodical. Portuguese. $18.00. Editora Resenha Tributaria Ltda, rua Quatinga 12, Sao Paulo Brazil. **LC** KHD4582; .D57. **DD** 344.8104/05; 348.104405.

US
**DISTRIBUTION REPORT OF INTANGIBLE PERSONAL PROPERTY TAX COLLECTIONS AND SPECIAL ALLOCATIONS. Main/Corp** North Carolina. Intangibles Tax Section. **VFOAT** Distribution Report of Intangible Personal Property Tax and Special Allocations. (198?)-. English. an. Department of Revenue / North Carolina, Intangibles Tax Division, Raleigh NC 27611. **LC** HJ5907.N8; A34. **DD** 336.2/3/09756. available on microfiche. **Continues** Distribution Report of Intangible Personal Property Tax Collections, 0090-1946.

IE
**DISTRICT COUNCILS SUMMARY OF STATEMENTS OF ACCOUNTS - (NORTHERN IRELAND). Main/Corp** Northern Ireland. Dept. of the Environment. English. an. £0.45. Department of the Environment / Ireland, 80 Chichester Street, Belfast BT1 4JY Northern Ireland. **LC** HJ9042.2; A3A. **DD** 336.416.

CN/0046-0419
**DIVIDEND RECORD.** *Title Change.* **Added/Corp** Financial Post Corporation Service. **VFOAT** Dividend Record and Investors' Diary. (1???)-(1???). Periodical. English. mo. Financial Post DataGroup, 333 King Street East, Toronto Ontario M5A 4N2 Canada. **Tel** (800)661-7678, FAX (416)350-6501. **ED** D Jones. ctrl circ. **Continued by** Financial Post Investment Report Service Annual Dividend Record.
**Desc:** A permanent, year-end record of all dividends paid and/or declared on all Canadian public companies.

AG
**DIVULGACION IMPOSITIVA.** Vol. 1 (Oct. 1942)-. Periodical. Spanish. mo. **LC** HJ2501; .D5. **DD** 336.205.
**Desc:** Information on taxation.

CL/0417-7371
**DIVULGACION TRIBUTARIA.** Periodical. English. Edificio Congresso Bandera, 550 Plso 7 of 76, Santiago de Chile.

US
**DOING BUSINESS IN THE EUROPEAN COMMUNITY. See** Law.

US/0745-9092
**DOLLARS & SENSE (WASHINGTON, D.C. 1979).** (DOLLARS & SENSE.). [Dollars sense]. **Added/Corp** National Taxpayers Union (U.S.). **VFOAT** Dollars and Sense. (19??)-. Periodical. English. mo (10

# Public Administration —Public Finance and Taxation

issues - Dec./Jan. and July/Aug. issues combined). $15.00. National Taxpayers Union Federation, 325 Pennsylvania Avenue Southeast, Washington DC 20003. **Tel** (202)543-1300. **ED** Peter Sepp. **DD** 336. **Bk Rev**, (Qty: 5).

CN/0046-0567
**DOMINION TAX CASES.** Began publication with V. 1, 1920/40. English. an. CCH Canadian Ltd., 6 Garamond Court, Don Mills Ontario M3C 1Z5 Canada. **Tel** (416)441-2992, **FAX** (416)441-3418. **DD** 343/.71/0402643.
 **Desc:** Decisions of the Supreme Court of Canada, the Federal Court and the Tax Review Board on federal tax questions.

UK/0962-3582
**DRUG TARIFF.** [Drug tariff]. (1990)-. Periodical. English. £41.25. Her Majesty's Stationery Office, 51 Nine Elms Lane, London SW8 5DR England. **Tel** 011 44 71 873 8459, 011 44 71 873 8499, **FAX** 011 44 71 873 8499, 011 44 71 873 8456, telex 297138. **(Subscription address:** Her Majestys Stationery Offic, PO Box 276 Public Centre, London SW8 5DT England) **DD** 615.1.

US/0894-1742
**DTEXPERT.** *Suspended.* [DTExpert]. **VFOAT** DTE Expert. Vol. 1, No. 1 (Jan./Feb. 1986)-Suspended with Vol. 5, No. 4. Periodical. English. bm. $120.00. Divorce Taxation Education Inc, 1710 Rhode Island Avenue NW/#600, Washington DC 20036. **LC** KF6333.A15; D84. **DD** 343.7305/2042/0240653.

NE
**EC CORPORATE TAX LAW.** See Law-Corporate Law.

US
**ECLECTIC BUDGET. Added/Corp** Central Alabama Regional Planning and Development Commission. **VFOAT** Annual Budget ... Eclectic, Alabama. (19??)-. English. an. Town of Eclectic Town Hall, Eclectic AL 36024. **LC** HJ9193.E27; E27. **DD** 352.1/225/0976152.

IT
**ECONOMIA DELLE SCELTE PUBBLICHE / JOURNAL OF PUBLIC FINANCE AND PUBLIC CHOICE. VFOAT** Journal of Public Finance and Public Choice; SP; S.P. Vol. 1 No. 1 (Jan./April 1983)-. Periodical. Italian (English). Three times a year. L50000.00 (institutions); L30000.00 (individuals). Tibergraph Editrice SRL, Via G Sorel Z Industr Nord, 06011 Citta Castello Italy. **Tel** 011 39 75 8511444.
 **Ind/Abst** Econ. Lit. Index (19??-); J. Econ. Lit.; PAIS Int. Print.

●CN
**ECONOMIC AND FISCAL REFERENCE TABLES. Added/Corp** Canada. Dept. of Finance. (Aug. 1993)-. English. ir. Distribution Centre / Department of Finance, 300 Laurier Avenue West, Ottawa Ontario K1A 0G5 Canada. **Tel** (613)995-2855, **FAX** (613)996-0518. *Continues* Economic Reference Tables.
 **Desc:** Provides data on the main economic, fiscal and financial aggregates over the past few decades.

II
**ECONOMIC AND FUNCTIONAL CLASSIFICATION OF THE MANIPUR GOVERNMENT BUDGET, AN. Main/Corp** Manipur (India). Dept. of Statistics. (19??)-. English. mo. Department of Statistics / India, Imphal Manipur India. **LC** HJ66.M53; B14b. **DD** 354/.54/1700722.

US/0884-4852
**ECONOMIC POLICY ISSUES.** *Ceased.* (ECONOMIC POLICY ISSUES / ECONOMIC POLICY RESEARCH, THE CONFERENCE BOARD.). [Econ. policy issues]. **Added/Corp** Conference Board. Economic Policy Research. No. 1 (1981)-?. English. Conference Board, 845 Third Avenue, New York NY 10022. **Tel** (212)759-0900 ext. 582, (800)872-6273, **FAX** (212)980-7014. **LC** HJ2051; .N28. **DD** 338.973/005. *Continues* Federal Budget. Its Impact on the Economy, 0430-1609.

US/0196-5980
**ECONOMIC REPORT OF THE GOVERNOR (LANSING).** See Economics.

AT
**ECONOMIC ROUND-UP / AUSTRALIA, THE TREASURY. Added/Corp** Australia. Treasury. (Apr. 1988)-. Government Publication. English. Four times a year. 40.00Aus$. Australian Government Publishing Service, GPO Box 84, Canberra ACT 2601 Australia. **Tel** 011 61 6 2954411, **FAX** 011 61 6 2954455. **LC** HC601; .A344. **DD** 330.994/005. *Continues* Round-Up (Canberra, Australia), 0815-1881.

PR
**ECONOMY AND FINANCES, PUERTO RICO.** See Economics.

UK/0954-6154
**EDI UPDATE LONDON.** [EDI Update Lond.]. (1988)-. Periodical. English. mo. £494.00. Eurostudy Publishing Co. Ltd., 36 38 Willesden Lane, London N26 7SW England. **Tel** 011 44 71 6374383. **(Subscription address:** IBC Subscription Services, IBC House, Vickers Drive Weybridge, Surrey KT13 0XS England.) **DD** 384.3. **Bk Rev**, (Qty: 10-20). **Circ:** 1,000 (ctrl). available on an online database.

SA
**EHOKOLOLONINGOMWA LYOMTYEKINDJAYI LYOOLEKENENGA EPANGELO LYOWAMBO NODHOMALELO GIILONGO MOWAMBO MOLWEENDO LWOMUMVO GWEMBO ... .** *Title Change.* **Main/Corp** South Africa. Dept. of the Auditor-General. **VFOAT** Ehokololoningomwa LyOmutyekindjai Leelekenenga Epangelo LOwambo Nodomalelo Oilongo MOwambo Moshitukulwa Lomudu Wembo ...; Report of the Auditor-General on the Accounts of the Owambo Government and of the Tribal Authorities in Owambo for the Financial Year ... (1976)-(19??). Afrikaans (English, Kuanyama and Ndonga). Pretoria Government Printer, Department of Water Affairs, Private Bag X85, Pretoria 0001 South Africa. **LC** HJ9080A.A55; O887. **DD** 354/.68/8. *Continues* South Africa. Dept. of the Controller and Auditor-General. Ehokololoningomwa LyOmukondoloii Nomtyekindjayi Koolekenenga DhEpangelo LyOwambo Nodhomaleloshilongo Moshitopolwa Molweendo Lwomumvo Gwembo ... . *Continued by* South Africa. Office of the Auditor-General. Report of the Auditor-General on the Accounts of the Representative Authority of the Ovambos and of the Tribal Authorities in Ovambo for the Financial Year ... .

GR
**EISEGETIKE EKTHESE OIKONOMIKOU ETOUS ... HYPOURGOU OIKONOMIKON. Main/Corp** Greece. Hypourgeion Ton Oikonomikon. **VFOAT** Proypologismos Oikonomikou Etous ... . Greek, Modern. an. **LC** HJ50; .A25A. *Continues* Eisegetike Ekthesis ... Hypourgou Ton Oikonomikon Epi Tou Proypologismou Oikon. Etous ... .

SP
**EJECUCION DE PRESUPUESTOS DE AYUNTAMIENTOS Y CONCEJOS DE NAVARRA.** (1984)-. Spanish. an. Gobierno de Navarra, Navas de Tolosa 21, 31002 Pamplona Spain. **Tel** 34 948 107121, **FAX** 34 948 227673. **LC** HJ9060.A55; N384.

CN/0713-049X
**ENTRE GENS D'ICI.** See Education.

US/0735-5394
**ENVIRONMENTAL FINANCE.** (ENVIRONMENTAL FINANCE/ FINANCIAL MANAGEMENT ASSISTANCE PROGRAM.). [Environ. financ.]. **Added/Corp** Government Finance Research Center (U.S.) Municipal Finance Officers Association of the United States and Canada. United States. Financial Management Assistance Program. Periodical. English. qt. Government Finance Resource Center, Municipal Finance Offices, Washington DC. available in microform from University Microfilms International (UMI).

●US/1065-7312
**ERNEST & YOUNG NEW YORK, NEW JERSEY, CONNECTICUT STATE TAX GUIDE, THE. VFOAT** Ernest and Young New York, New Jersey, Connecticut State Tax guide; New York, New Jersey, Connecticut State Tax Guide. (1992)-. English. John Wiley & Sons, Inc., 605 Third Avenue, New York NY 10158-0012. **Tel** (212)850-6000, (212)850-6645, **FAX** (212)850-6088, telex 12-7063. **(Subscription address:** John Wiley & Sons / England, Baffins Lane, Chichester, West Sussex PO19 1UD England.**)**

●US/1059-809X
**ERNST & YOUNG TAX GUIDE, THE.** [Ernst Young tax guide]. **VFOAT** Ernst and Young Tax Guide. (1992)-. English. John Wiley & Sons, Inc., 605 Third Avenue, New York NY 10158-0012. **Tel** (212)850-6000, (212)850-6645, **FAX** (212)850-6088, telex 12-7063. **(Subscription address:** John Wiley & Sons / England, Baffins Lane, Chichester, West Sussex PO19 1UD England.**) LC** KF6369.6; .A77. **DD** 343. *Continues* Ernst & Young's Arthur Young Tax Guide, 1057-9508.

US/1058-6342
**ERNST & YOUNG'S TAX-SAVING STRATEGIES / ERNST & YOUNG.** [Ernst Young's tax-sav. strategies]. **Added/Corp** Ernst & Young. **VFOAT** Ernst and Young's Tax-Saving Strategies; Ernst & Young Tax Saving Strategies; Ernst and Young's Tax Saving Strategies; Tax-Saving Strategies; Tax Saving Strategies. (1991)-. English. John Wiley & Sons, Inc., 605 Third Avenue, New York NY 10158-0012. **Tel** (212)850-6000, (212)850-6645, **FAX** (212)850-6088, telex 12-7063. **(Subscription address:** John Wiley & Sons / England, Baffins Lane, Chichester, West Sussex PO19 1UD England.**) DD** 343.

US/0195-1238
**ESTATE PLANNING & TAXATION COORDINATOR.** See Law-Estate Planning.

BL
**ESTATISTICA BASICA DE ARRECADACAO. Added/Corp** Coordenacao do Sistema de Informacoes Economico-Fiscais (Brazil). Vol. 1, No. 1 (Jan. 1980)-. Periodical. Portuguese. mo. Ministerio da Fazenda Secretaria da Receita Federal Coordenacao do Sistema de Informacoes, Economico-Fiscais Esplanada dos Ministerios Bl P Anexo Ala A, 3O. Andar 70.079 Brasilia DF Brazil. **LC** HJ32; .A395. **DD** 336.2/00981. *Continues* Estatisticas Tributarias Basicas (Coordenacao do Sistema de Informacaoes Economico-Fiscais (Brazil)).

II
**ESTIMATE OF EXPENDITURE IN RESPECT OF WHICH A VOTE-ON-ACCOUNT IS REQUIRED. Main/Corp** Meghalaya (India). April 1972-. English. Assam Government Press / Government of Meghalaya, Shillong India. **LC** HJ66.M55; C18. **DD** 354/.54/1600722.

SA
**ESTIMATE OF THE ADDITIONAL EXPENDITURE TO BE DEFRAYED FROM REVENUE AND LOAN ACCOUNTS. Main/Corp** South Africa. Treasury. **VFOAT** Begroting van die Addisionele Uitgawes Wat Uit Inkomste- en Leningsrekenings. Multiple languages (Afrikaans and English). R0.30. Government Printer / South Africa, Bosman Street, Private Bag X85, Pretoria 0001 South Africa. **Tel** 011 27 12 3239731 Ext. 262. **LC** HJ80A; .A37. **DD** 354/.68/007224.

SA
**ESTIMATE OF THE ADDITIONAL EXPENDITURE TO BE DEFRAYED FROM STATE REVENUE ACCOUNT. BEGROTING VAN DIE ADDISIONALE UITGAWES WAT UIT STAATSINKOMSTEREKENING. Main/Corp** South Africa. **VFOAT** Begroting van die Addisionale Uitgawes Wat Uit Staatsinkomsterekening. (1977/78)-. Afrikaans (English). R2.60. The Government Printer, Bosman Street, Private Bag X85, Pretoria 0001 South Africa. **Tel** 012-323-9731, **FAX** 012-323-0009. **LC** HJ80A; .A3154a. *Continues in part* South Africa. Estimate of the Additional Expenditure to be Defrayed from State Revenue and South West Africa Accounts.

CN
**ESTIMATES, HIGHLIGHTS - TREASURY BOARD. Main/Corp** Quebec (Province). Treasury Board. **VFOAT** Credits, Faits Saillants - Conseil du Tresor; Highlights on the Estimates - Treasury Board; Faits Saillants des Credits - Conseil du Tresor. 1973/74-. Multiple languages (English and French). Gouvernement du Quebec, 600 St Amable 4E Etage, Quebec Quebec G1R 4Z1 Canada. **LC** HJ13; .Q198A. **DD** 354/.714/00722.

TZ
**ESTIMATES OF CAPITAL EXPENDITURE OF THE EAST AFRICAN COMMUNITY. Main/Corp** East African Community. 1976/77-. English. Finance & Administration Secretariat, PO Box 3081, Arusha Tanzania. **LC** HJ81; .A315A. **DD** 354/.67/00722. *Supersedes in part* East African Community. Estimates of Expenditure of the East African Community.

CN
**ESTIMATES OF EXPENDITURE (ALBERTA. TREASURY DEPT.). Main/Corp** Alberta. Treasury Dept. 1976/77-. English. an. Alberta Treasury Department, 9515 107th Street, Terrace Building, Edmonton Alberta Canada. **Tel** (403)427-3035.

CN
**ESTIMATES OF EXPENDITURE : CAPITAL ACCOUNT AND SUMMARY OF AMOUNTS TO BE VOTED (ALBERTA). Main/Corp** Alberta. English. Alberta Statutes Province / Queens Printer, Province Treasury, 11510 Kingsly Avenue, Edmonton Alberta T5G 2Y5 Canada. **Tel** (403)427-4952. **LC** HJ13; .A715a. **DD** 336.3/9/097123.

RH
**ESTIMATES OF EXPENDITURE FOR THE YEAR ENDING JUNE 30 - ZIMBABWE. Main/Corp** Zimbabwe. English. an. Began with Vol. for 1979/80. English. an. $2.10. Zimbabwe Government Printing, PO Box 8062, Causeway Harare Zimbabwe. **Tel** 011 263 4 706161. **LC** HJ82.4; .A37A. **DD** 354.68910072/2253/05.

CN
**ESTIMATES OF EXPENDITURE : INCOME ACCOUNT. Main/Corp** Alberta. English. Alberta Statutes Province / Queens Printer, Province

# Public Administration —Public Finance and Taxation

Treasury, 11510 Kingsly Avenue, Edmonton Alberta T5G 2Y5 Canada. **Tel** (403)427-4952. **LC** HJ13; .A715B. **DD** 336.3/9/097123.

CN/0713-0872
**ESTIMATES OF EXPENDITURE. SUPPLEMENTARY INFORMATION. RECONCILIATION OF HISTORICAL DATA.** (ESTIMATES OF EXPENDITURE : SUPPLEMENTARY INFORMATION.). [Estim. expend., Suppl. inf., Reconcil. hist. data]. **Main/Corp** Alberta. Treasury Dept. 1976/77-. English. an. Alberta Treasury Department, 9515 107th Street, Terrace Building, Edmonton Alberta Canada. **Tel** (403)427-3035. **LC** HJ13; .A715F. **DD** 354/.7123/00722.

TR
**ESTIMATES OF EXPENDITURE (TRINIDAD AND TOBAGO).** **Main/Corp** Trinidad and Tobago. English. Government Printer / Trinidad and Tobago, Trinidad and Tobago. **LC** HJ27; .T363. **DD** 336.3/9/0972983.

SA
**ESTIMATES OF INCOME & EXPENDITURE.** **Main/Corp** Cape Town. City Treasurer's Dept. English. City Treasurer's Department, Electricity House, Cape Town South Africa. **LC** HJ9080C.C3; C14B. **DD** 352/.12/09687.
**Desc:** Vols. for 1976- include revised estimates for the preceding year.

SA
**ESTIMATES OF PROVINCIAL REVENUE TO BE COLLECTED AND EXPENDITURE TO BE DEFRAYED FROM THE PROVINCIAL REVENUE FUND DURING THE YEAR ... / REPUBLIC OF SOUTH AFRICA, PROVINCE OF THE CAPE OF GOOD HOPE.** **Main/Corp** Cape of Good Hope (South Africa). **VFOAT** Begroting van Provinsiale Inkomste Wat Ingerorder Moet Word en Uitgawes Wat Uit die Provinsiale Inkomstefonds Bestry Moet Word Gedurende die Jaar ... . Afrikaans (English). an. **LC** HJ82.1.C36; C36A. **DD** 354.6870072/6/05.

TZ
**ESTIMATES OF RECURRENT EXPENDITURE OF THE EAST AFRICAN COMMUNITY.** **Main/Corp** East African Community. 1976/77-. English. Finance & Administration Secretariat, PO Box 3081, Arusha Tanzania. **LC** HJ81; .A315C.
**Supersedes in part** East African Community. Estimates of Expenditure of the East African Community.

KE/0453-5855
**ESTIMATES OF RECURRENT EXPENDITURE OF THE GOVERNMENT OF KENYA.** **See** Public Administration.

BS
**ESTIMATES OF RECURRENT REVENUE AND EXPENDITURE.** **Main/Corp** Botswana. (19??)-. English. 2.00. Government Printer / Botswana Government, Private Bag 0081, Gaberone Republic of Botswana. **Tel** 09267-315551. **LC** HJ80N; .A334. **DD** 354/.68/100722.

AM
**ESTIMATES OF RECURRENT REVENUE, EXPENDITURE & LOCAL CONTRIBUTION TO CAPITAL BUDGET / GOVERNMENT OF ANGUILLA.** **Added/Corp** Anguilla. (1989)-. English. **LC** HJ28.3.A83; A54a. **DD** 354.72973. **Continues** Estimates of Recurrent Revenue and Expenditures.

BS
**ESTIMATES OF REVENUE AND EXPENDITURE.** **Main/Corp** Botswana. (19??)-. English. Government Printer / Botswana Government, Private Bag 0081, Gaberone Republic of Botswana. **Tel** 09267-315551. **LC** HJ80N; .A23. **DD** 354/.68/100722.
**Continues** Bechuanaland (Protectorate). Estimates of Revenue and Expenditure.

NR
**ESTIMATES OF THE GOVERNMENT - KANO. NIGERIA (STATE).** **Main/Corp** Kano. Nigeria (State). 1968/69-. English. -/15/-. Government Printer / Kaduna, Private Mail Bag 2020, Kaduna Nigeria. **LC** HJ81P.K36; A25. **DD** 354/.669/5. **Supersedes in part** Estimates of the Government of Northern Nigeria, 0549-9208.

CN/0383-4786
**ESTIMATES OF THE GOVERNMENT OF NOVA SCOTIA.** **Main/Corp** Nova Scotia. Dept. of Finance. (1975/1976)-. English. an. Free on request. Nova Scotia Government Bookstore, PO Box 637, Halifax NS B3J 2T3 Canada. **Tel** (902)424-7580. **LC** HJ13; .N83. **DD** 354/.716/00722. **Supersedes** Nova Scotia. Dept. of Finance and Economics. Estimates of Revenue and Expenditure for Public Service of Nova Scotia., 0383-4794.

AT
**ESTIMATES OF THE PROBABLE WAYS AND MEANS AND EXPENDITURE OF THE GOVERNMENT OF QUEENSLAND.** **Main/Corp** Queensland. **VFOAT** Estimates of Receipts and Expenditures. (19??)-. English. Government Printer / Queensland, Box 680 GPO, 102 George Street, Brisbane Queensland 4001 Australia. **LC** HJ92; .C325. **DD** 336.3/9/09943.

CN
**ESTIMATES. PART I, THE GOVERNMENT EXPENDITURE PLAN.** **Main/Corp** Canada. **VFOAT** Government Expenditure Plan; Plan de Depenses du Gouvernement; Budget des Depenses. Partie I, Plan de Depenses du Gouvernement. (19??)-. English (French). Canada Communication Group Publishers, Order Processing, Ottawa Ontario K1A 0S9 Canada. **Tel** (819)956-4800, (819)956-4802. **LC** HJ13; .A126b. **DD** 354.710072/2253/05.

CN
**ESTIMATES. PART III, AUDITOR GENERAL OF CANADA.** **See** Public Administration.

CN
**ESTIMATES. PART III, DEPARTMENT OF FINANCE CANADA.** **Main/Corp** Canada. **VFOAT** Budget des Depenses. Partie III, Ministere des Finances Canada. (19??)-. English (French). $9.00 Canada; $10.80 other. Canada Communication Group Publishers, Order Processing, Ottawa Ontario K1A 0S9 Canada. **Tel** (819)956-4800, (819)956-4802. **LC** HJ13; .A124a. **DD** 354.710072.

●CN
**ESTIMATES. PART III, DEPARTMENT OF FOREIGN AFFAIRS AND INTERNATIONAL TRADE.** **Main/Corp** Canada. **VFOAT** Budget des Depenses. Partie III, Le Ministere des Affaires Etrangeres et du Commerce International. (1995)-. English (French). an. Canadian Government Publishing Center, Supply and Services Canada, Hull Quebec K1A 0S9 Canada. **Tel** (613)990-8116, telex 053-4296. **Continues in part** Canada. Estimates. Part III, External Affairs and International Trade Canada. Expenditure plan.

CN
**ESTIMATES. PART III, EXTERNAL AFFAIRS AND INTERNATIONAL TRADE CANADA. EXPENDITURE PLAN.** **Title Change.** **Main/Corp** Canada. **VFOAT** External Affairs and International Trade Canada. Estimates; Budget des Depenses. Partie III, Plan de Depenses. (1991)-(1994). English (French). ir. Canadian Government Publishing Center, Supply and Services Canada, Hull Quebec K1A 0S9 Canada. **Tel** (613)990-8116, telex 053-4296. **LC** JX1730; .A24a. **DD** 354.710089. **Continues** Estimates. Part III, External Affairs. **Continued in part by** Canada. Part III, Department of Foreign Affairs and International Trade.

CN
**ESTIMATES. PART III, REVENUE CANADA, CUSTOMS AND EXCISE.** **Main/Corp** Canada. **VFOAT** Budget des Depenses. Partie III, Revenue Canada, Douanes et Accise. (19??)-. English (French). $6.00 Canada; $7.20 other. Canada Communication Group Publishers, Order Processing, Ottawa Ontario K1A 0S9 Canada. **Tel** (819)956-4800, (819)956-4802. **LC** HJ5731.C2; C36a. **DD** 354.710072/46.

CN
**ESTIMATES. PART III, REVENUE CANADA, TAXATION.** **Main/Corp** Canada. **VFOAT** Budget des Depenses. Partie III, Revenue Canada, Impot. (19??)-. English (French). $6.00 Canada; $7.20 other. Canada Communication Group Publishers, Order Processing, Ottawa Ontario K1A 0S9 Canada. **Tel** (819)956-4800, (819)956-4802. **LC** HJ13; .A126a. **DD** 354.710072/4/005.

CN
**ESTIMATES. PART III, TAX REVIEW BOARD.** **See** Law.

CN/0712-4597
**ESTIMATES - PROVINCE OF BRITISH COLUMBIA.** (ESTIMATES.). [Estim. - Prov. B.C.]. **Main/Corp** British Columbia. (1983)-. English. an. Queen's Printer, 506 Government Street, Victoria British Columbia V8V 4R6 Canada. **Tel** 387-1901. **LC** HJ13; .B382a. **DD** 354.7110072/25/05. **Continues** Estimates of Revenue and Expenditure, 0707-3046.

UK/0141-1047
**EUROPEAN & MIDDLE EAST TAX REPORT, THE.** [Europ. Middle East tax rep.]. **VAT** European and Middle East Tax Report. Periodical. English. bw. Institute for International Research / England, 57 61 Mortimer Street, London W1N 7TD England. **DD** 336.2. **[CCC]. Continues** European Tax Report.

NE/0925-9759
**EUROPEAN TAX HANDBOOK.** **Added/Corp** International Bureau of Fiscal Documentation. (1990)-. English. an. $160.00 subscription, $200.00 for single copy. International Bureau of Fiscal Documentation - IBFD Publications, PO Box 20237, 1000 HE Amsterdam The Netherlands. **Tel** 011 31 20-6267726, FAX 011 31 20-6228658, telex 13217 INTAX NL. **(Subscription address:** IBFD / International Bureau of Fiscal Documentation USA, Inc., 24 Hudson Street, Kinderhook NY 12106.) **LC** KJC7101.3; .E94. **DD** 343.404; 344.034.
**Desc:** Gives details of corporate and individual taxation in over thirty major European countries, plus EC information.

NE/0014-3138
**EUROPEAN TAXATION.** [Euro. tax.]. **Added/Corp** International Bureau of Fiscal Documentation. Vol. 1 (Jan. 1961)-. Periodical. English. Eleven times a year (Aug./Sept. issues combined). $570.00; Also comes with International Bureau of Fiscal Documentation membership. International Bureau of Fiscal Documentation - IBFD Publications, PO Box 20237, 1000 HE Amsterdam The Netherlands. **Tel** 011 31 20-6267726, FAX 011 31 20-6228658, telex 13217 INTAX NL. **(Subscription address:** IBFD / International Bureau of Fiscal Documentation USA, Inc., 24 Hudson Street, Kinderhook NY 12106.) **ED** C. S. Bobbett. **LC** LAW. cum. index. **Bk Rev**. **Ad Acc**. **Circ:** 2,000 (ctrl). available on microfiche. Documents available from UMI Article Clearinghouse.
**Desc:** A journal of articles examining tax systems of Europe and analyzing trends and implications. Contains case notes, rulings and decisions, and also European communities tax developments.
**Ind/Abst** ABI/INFORM Glob. Ed.; Index Foreign Leg. Per.; Selec. Coop. Index Manage. Period.

NE/0531-4577
**EUROPEAN TAXATION. SUPPLEMENTARY SERVICE.** **Added/Corp** International Bureau of Fiscal Documentation, Amsterdam. **VFOAT** Supplementary Service to European Taxation. No. 1- (Jan. 1963)-. Periodical. English. mo. $1,660.00. International Bureau of Fiscal Documentation - IBFD Publications, PO Box 20237, 1000 HE Amsterdam The Netherlands. **Tel** 011 31 20-6267726, FAX 011 31 20-6228658, telex 13217 INTAX NL. **ED** W. A. Cornello. **Bk Rev**. **Ad Acc**. ctrl circ.
**Desc:** Covers corporate/individual taxation, tax treaties, EC tax directives, OECD model conventions; includes a worldwide bibliography of new tax documents and publications.

LU/0255-3953
**EUROSTAT, GENERAL GOVERNMENT ACCOUNTS AND STATISTICS.** **See** Public Administration-Abstracting, Bibliographies and Statistics.

US/0749-2529
**EVALUATING TAX SHELTER OFFERINGS.** English. Practising Law Institute, 810 Seventh Avenue, New York NY 10019-5818. **Tel** (212)765-5700, FAX (212)581-4670 general correspondence, (212)265-4742 orders and billing inquiries. **LC** KF6297.5.Z9; E95. **DD** 343.7305/23; 347.303523.

US/0094-5609
**EXAMINATION OF FINANCIAL STATEMENTS, INTER-AMERICAN FOUNDATION.** **Main/Corp** United States. General Accounting Office. English. 441 G Street NW, Washington DC 20548. **LC** HC125; .U588C. **DD** 658.1/5.

●US
**EXECUTIVE BUDGET AND FINANCIAL PLAN / TRIBOROUGH BRIDGE AND TUNNEL AUTHORITY.** **Main/Corp** Triborough Bridge and Tunnel Authority. (1993)-. English. **Continues** Triborough Bridge and Tunnel Authority. Financial Plan and ...Executive Budget.

US
**EXECUTIVE BUDGET / COMMONWEALTH OF VIRGINIA.** **Main/Corp** Virginia. Dept. of Planning and Budget. English. Department of Planning and Budget, 9th Street Office Building, Box 1422, Richmond VA 23211. **LC** HJ11; .V842. **DD** 353.97550072/256/05. **Continues** Virginia. Governor. Budget.

US/0738-3258
**EXECUTIVE BUDGET - DISTRICT OF COLUMBIA.** (EXECUTIVE BUDGET.). **Main/Corp** District of Columbia. English. an. **LC** HJ9013.W2; E34A. **DD** 352.1/256/05.

# Public Administration —Public Finance and Taxation

**US**
**EXECUTIVE BUDGET FOR FISCAL YEAR ... / STATE OF IDAHO. Main/Corp** Idaho. Office of the Governor. English. an. Office of the Governor / Ohio, 77 South High Street, 30th Floor, Columbus OH 43266. **Tel** (614)644-0813, FAX (614)466-9354. **LC** HJ11; .I249A. **DD** 353.97960072/22/05. *Continues Executive Program: Executive Budget.*

**US**
**EXECUTIVE BUDGET MESSAGE / STATE OF WISCONSIN. Main/Corp** Wisconsin. Governor. **VFOAT** Budget Message. English. be. **LC** HJ2053.W6; W57B. **DD** 353.97750072/256/05.

**US**
**EXECUTIVE BUDGET / STATE OF ARIZONA. Main/Corp** Arizona. Governor. (1969)-. English. an. Arizona Governors Office, Phoenix AZ 85007. **LC** HJ11; .A643. **DD** 359.9/791/00722. *Continues Arizona. Office of State Auditor. Budget Requests.*
**Desc:** Information on the executive budget for the state of Arizona.

**US**
**EXECUTIVE BUDGET / STATE OF NEBRASKA ; SUBMITTED TO THE ... SESSION OF THE LEGISLATURE BY ... GOVERNOR ; PREPARED BY ... TAX COMMISSIONER AND BUDGET DIRECTOR. Main/Corp** Nebraska. Governor. **Added/Corp** Nebraska. Tax Commissioner. (19??)-. English. an. **LC** HJ11; .N24. **DD** 353.97820072/256/05.

**US**
**EXECUTIVE CAPITAL BUDGET AND CAPITAL PROGRAM - NEW YORK CITY. Main/Corp** New York (N.Y.) Mayor. English. $6.00. The City Record Sales Office, 2213 Municipal Building, New York NY 10007. **LC** HJ9013; .N5E574. **DD** 352/.12/097471. *Continues New York (City). Executive Capital Budget.*

**US/0090-841X**
**EXECUTIVE CAPITAL CONSTRUCTION BUDGET. Main/Corp** Nebraska. Governor. (19??)-. English. Nebraska Governor, Department of Administrative Services, State Capitol Building, Lincoln NE 68509. **LC** JK1651.N2; A23. **DD** 353.9/782/00712.

**US/0273-7612**
**EXECUTIVE COMPENSATION & TAXATION COORDINATOR. See** Law.

**US/1063-0481**
**EXECUTIVE'S TAX REPORT.** (EXECUTIVE'S TAX REPORT / PRENTICE HALL.). [Exec. tax rep.]. **Added/Corp** Prentice-Hall, inc. (19??)-. Periodical. English. wk. $210.36 (US); $255.60 (Canada). Bureau of Business Practice, 24 Rope Ferry Road, Waterford CT 06386. **Tel** (800)243-0876, (203)442-4365, (800)876-9105, FAX (203)443-1123. **LC** KF6289.A1; E9. **DD** 343/.73/0405. *Continues Executives Tax Report & What's Happening in Taxation, 0423-8990.*

**US/0899-3831**
**EXEMPT ORGANIZATION TAX REVIEW, THE.** [Exempt organ. tax rev.]. Vol. 1, No. 1 (Mar. 1988)-. Periodical. English. mo. $549.00 (includes annual index). Tax Analysts, 6830 North Fairfax Drive, Arlington VA 22213. **Tel** (703)533-4400, (800)955-3444.
**(Subscription address:** Exempt Organization Tax Review, 6830 North Fairfax Avenue, Arlington, VA 22213; telephone: (800)955-2444, (703)533-4400) **LC** KF6449.A15; E93. **DD** 343.7306/68/05; 347.30366805. **[CCC]**. Index available.

**US/0197-2529**
**EXPENDITURES OF GENERAL REVENUE SHARING AND ANTIRECESSION FISCAL ASSISTANCE FUNDS.** 1976/77-. Government Publication. English. an. US Department of Commerce / Bureau of the Census, Data User Services Division, Customer Services, Washington DC 20233-0800. **Tel** (301)763-4100. **(Subscription address:** Superintendent of Documents, US Government Printing Office, Washington DC 20402.) **LC** JK2403; .A35 subser; HJ275. **DD** 300/.973 S; 336.1/85. *Continues Reported Uses of General Revenue Sharing Funds, 0197-2391.*

**US**
**EXPIRING LEGISLATION WITH BUDGETARY IMPACT / COMMITTEE ON THE BUDGET, U.S. HOUSE OF REPRESENTATIVES. Added/Corp** United States. Congress. House. Committee on the Budget. (19??)-. English. Congressional Budget Office, 2nd and D Streets SW, Washington DC 20515. **Tel** (202)226-2115. **LC** KF6221.A55; C6614. **DD** 343.73/03.

**PK/0304-0933**
**EXPLANATORY MEMORANDUM ON THE BUDGET (ISLAMABAD).** (EXPLANATORY MEMORANDUM ON THE BUDGET.). **Main/Corp** Pakistan. Finance Division. English. Government of Pakistan / Finance Division, Islamabad ICP Pakistan. **LC** HJ67.5; .B35. **DD** 354/.549/100722. *Continues Explanatory Memorandum on the Budget and Economic Survey.*

**II**
**EXPLANATORY MEMORANDUM ON THE BUDGET OF THE GOVERNMENT OF NAGALAND FOR ... . Main/Corp** Nagaland (India). English. **LC** HJ65.N33; N33D. **DD** 354.54/165007231.

**II/0511-5280**
**EXPLANATORY MEMORANDUM ON THE BUDGET OF THE GOVERNMENT OF WEST BENGAL. Main/Corp** West Bengal (India). Finance Dept. English. an. Superintendent Government Printer, West Bengal Government Press, West Bengal India. **LC** HJ66.B353; B23. **DD** 354.54/140072255/05.

**CY**
**EXPLANATORY NOTE ON THE ... BUDGET / MINISTRY OF FINANCE, CYPRUS, AN. Main/Corp** Cyprus. Hypourgeion Oikonomikon. English. an. **LC** HJ64.2; .A24A. **DD** 354.56450072/255.

**US**
**EXPORT TAX REPORT.** English. mo. $195.00. Corporate Tax Press, 104 Crandon Boulevard, Suite 300, Key Biscayne FL 33149. **Tel** (305)361-0500.
**Ind/Abst** Fed. Tax Artic.

**US/0071-3678**
**FACTS AND FIGURES ON GOVERNMENT FINANCE.** [Facts fig. gov. finance]. **Added/Corp** Tax Foundation. (1943)-. Periodical. English. an. $60.00. Tax Foundation Inc., 1250 H Street Northwest, Suite 750, Washington DC 20005. **Tel** (202)783-2760, FAX (202)942-7675. **ED** E.M. Watters. **DD** 336.73. *Continues Facts & Figures on War Finance.*
**Desc:** Current and historical data on revenue expenditures, debt, and tax rates of federal, state, and local government, and related factors.
**Ind/Abst** Stat. Ref. Index.

**IT**
**FALLIMENTO E FISCO.** (19??)-. Periodical. Italian. an. IPSOA Editore SRL, Casella Postale 12055, Mastrangelo, 20120 Milan Italy. **Tel** 011 39 2 82476248. Index available (Included). cum. index. **Circ:** 6,000 (ctrl).
**Desc:** Covers failure and taxation.

**US**
**FAMILY TAX PLANNING.** English. ir. Matthew Bender & Company Inc., 1275 Broadway, Albany NY 12204. **Tel** (800)833-9844, (518)487-3000.

**AT**
**FARM TAXATION.** English. an (July). 19.00Aus$ Australia; 21.00Aus$ others. Department of Primary Industries / Queensland Australia, GPO Box 46, Brisbane Queensland 4001 Australia. **Tel** 011 61 7 2393111, FAX 011 61 7 2212490, telex AA41620.
**Desc:** Gives producers, accountants, students, and prospective investors an understanding of tax provisions affecting the rural sector.

**US/0731-4612**
**FARMERS FEDERAL TAX ALERT. See** Agriculture.

**US**
**FEDERAL AID TO ILLINOIS STATE AGENCIES.** English. an. Illinois Commission on Intergovernmental Cooperation, 721 Stratton Office Building, Springfield IL 62706. **LC** HJ400; .F42. **DD** 336.1/85.

**US**
**FEDERAL BUDGET AND THE CITIES - UNITED STATES CONFERENCE OF MAYORS, THE. See** Public Administration.

**US/0363-5422**
**FEDERAL BUDGET; FOCUS AND PERSPECTIVES, THE. Main/Corp** Tax Foundation. (19??)-. English. Tax Foundation Inc., 1250 H Street Northwest, Suite 750, Washington DC 20005. **Tel** (202)783-2760, FAX (202)942-7675. **LC** HJ2051; .T33a. **DD** 353.007/22.

**US/0734-2454**
**FEDERAL CIVIL RIGHTS ENFORCEMENT BUDGET, THE. See** Political Science-Civil Rights.

**CN/0713-7257**
**FEDERAL CORPORATE TAX RETURN, THE.** [Fed. corp. tax return]. 11th Ed. (1982)-. English. an. CCH Canadian Ltd., 6 Garamond Court, Don Mills Ontario M3C 1Z5 Canada. **Tel** (416)441-2992, FAX (416)441-3418. **DD** 343.7106/7. *Continues Preparation of Federal Corporate Tax Return, 0702-7168.*

**US/0414-0141**
**FEDERAL EXCISE TAX REPORTS. Main/Corp** Commerce Clearing House. **VFOAT** Federal Excise Tax Reporter. (19??)-. English. wk. $325.00. Commerce Clearing House Inc., 4025 West Peterson Avenue, Chicago IL 60646-6085. **Tel** (312)583-8500, FAX (708)940-4600. **ED** A. E. Schechter. **DD** 336.5.
**Desc:** Sets out federal excise tax laws, regulations, decisions, rulings and explanation.

**US/0092-0126**
**FEDERAL FINANCIAL MANAGEMENT DIRECTORY.** *Title Change.* Directory. English. an. Superintendent of Documents, US Government Printing Office, Washington DC 20402. **Tel** (202)275-3328, FAX (202)786-2377. **LC** JK723.E9; F4. **DD** 353.007/2/025. *Continued by Directory (United States. Joint Financial Management Improvement Program).*

**CN/0575-8521**
**FEDERAL GOVERNMENT FINANCE.** (FEDERAL GOVERNMENT FINANCE, REVENUE AND EXPENDITURE, ASSETS AND LIABILITIES / STATISTICS CANADA, GOVERNMENTS DIVISION, FEDERAL GOVERNMENTS SECTION / FINANCES DE L'ADMINISTRATION PUBLIQUE FEDERALE, RECETTES ET DEPENSES, ACTIF ET PASSIF / STATISTIQUE CANADA, DIVISION DES ADMINISTRATIONS PUBLIQUES, SECTION DE L'ADMINISTRATION PUBLIQUE FEDERALE.). [Fed. gov. finance]. **Added/Corp** Statistics Canada. Federal Government Section. Statistics Canada. Consolidated and Federal Government Section. Statistics Canada. Public Institutions Division. Statistics Canada. Revenue and Expenditure Section. **VFOAT** Finances de l'Administration Publique Federale, Recettes et Depenses, Actif et passif; Finances de l'Administration Publique Federale, Revenus et Depenses, Actif et passif; Finances Publiques Federales, Revenus et Depenses, Actif et passif; Finances Publiques Federales, Recettes et Depenses, Actif et Passif. (1969)-. English (French). an. 26.00Can$. Statistics Canada, Publications Sales & Services, Main Building Room 1710, Ottawa Ontario K1A 0T6 Canada. **Tel** (613)951-5078, (800)267-6677, FAX (613)951-1584, telex 053-3585. **LC** HJ13; .A374. **DD** 336.71. *Formed by the union of Federal Government Finance, Revenue and Expenditure, Direct and Indirect Debt. and Finances de l'Administration Publique Federale, Revenus et Depenses, Dette Directe et Indirecte.*

**US/0361-1582**
**FEDERAL GRANT-IN-AID ACTIVITY IN FLORIDA : A SUMMARY REPORT. Main/Corp** Florida. Bureau of Intergovernmental Relations. 1973/74-. English. an. $2.22. Florida Department of Administration, 660 Apalachee Parkway, Tallahassee FL 32304. **LC** HJ370; .F57A. **DD** 336.1/85.

**US/0093-8300**
**FEDERAL GRANT-IN-AID PROGRAMS (PHOENIX).** (FEDERAL GRANT-IN-AID PROGRAMS.). **Main/Corp** Arizona. Dept. of Administration. Finance Division. 1973/74-. English. an. Arizona Department of Administration, 1700 West Washington Street, Phoenix AZ 85007. **LC** HJ300; .A3. **DD** 336.1/85. *Continues Federal Grant-In-Aid Programs.*

**US/0195-2617**
**FEDERAL GRANTS MANAGEMENT HANDBOOK. Added/Corp** Grants Management Advisory Service. (1978)-. English. mo. $246.00. Thompson Publishing Group, 7711 Anderson Road, Tampa FL 33634. **Tel** (800)677-3789, (813)282-8607. **[CCC]**. *Continues Federal Grants Reporter.*

**US**
**FEDERAL INCOME, GIFT, AND ESTATE TAXATION, BY JACOB RABKIN AND MARK H. JOHNSON. Added/Corp** United States Laws, Statutes, etc. Internal Revenue Code. (19??)-. English. Twelve times a year. $730.00. Matthew Bender & Company Inc., 1275 Broadway, Albany NY 12204. **Tel** (800)833-9844, (518)487-3000. **ED** Alan Prigal. **LC** KF6335; .R284. **DD** 343/.73/052.
**Desc:** News and information about income tax and includes the Internal Revenue code.

**US/0195-4768**
**FEDERAL INCOME TAX (ENGLEWOOD CLIFFS), THE.** (THE FEDERAL INCOME TAX : ITS SOURCES AND APPLICATIONS.). (1968)-. English. an. Prentice-Hall Law and Business, 270 Sylvan Avenue, Englewood Cliffs NJ 07632. **Tel** (800)223-0231, (201)894-8538, FAX (201)894-8666. **LC** KF6369; .M28. **DD** 343.7305/2.

# Public Administration —Public Finance and Taxation

US/0196-1349
**FEDERAL INCOME TAX GUIDE.** 1979-.
English. an. Ace Books, 1120 Avenue of the Americas, New York NY 10036. **LC** KF6369.6; .F43. **DD** 343.7305/2044. Index available in last issue of volume--attached.

US/0278-1875
**FEDERAL INCOME TAX PROCEDURES.** (19??)-. English. an. Prentice-Hall Law and Business, 270 Sylvan Avenue, Englewood Cliffs NJ 07632. **Tel** (800)223-0231, (201)894-8538, FAX (201)894-8666. **ED** D. Bandy and R.G. Swad. **LC** KF6369.3; .F37. **DD** 343.7305/2044; 347.3052044.

US/1043-7371
**FEDERAL INCOME TAX REGULATIONS (1986).** (FEDERAL INCOME TAX REGULATIONS.). [Fed. income tax regul.]. **Main/Corp** United States. Dept. of the Treasury. **Added/Corp** Prentice-Hall, Inc. Information Services Division. United States. Internal Revenue Service. **VFOAT** Federal Regulations. (Jan. 15, 1986)-. English. sa. Research Institute of America, 117 East Stevens Avenue, Valhalla NY 10595. **Tel** (800)431-9025. **LC** KF6356.99; .F43. **DD** 343.7305/2; 347.30352. **Continues** United States. Dept. of the Treasury. Federal Regulations.

US/0191-2364
**FEDERAL INCOME TAX (RESTON, VA.).** (FEDERAL INCOME TAX / CHARLES B. EDELSON, MBA, CPA.). (19??)-. English. an. $12.95. Reston Times, 1760 Reston Avenue, Reston VA 22090. **Tel** (703)437-5400. **LC** KF6369.6; .F425. **DD** 343/.7305/2044; 347.3052044.

US/1071-0825
**FEDERAL INCOME TAXATION.** [Fed. income tax.]. (1990)-. English. an. $47.50 (latest chapter). Little Brown & Company, 34 Beacon Street, Boston MA 02108. **Tel** (617)227-0730, (800)759-0190. **LC** KF6369.A1; B68. **DD** 343/.73/052. **Continues** Bower, James B. Income Tax Procedure, 0091-2816.

US
**FEDERAL INCOME TAXATION OF CORPORATIONS AND SHAREHOLDERS; FORMS. Main/Corp** Bittker, Boris I. (1975)-. English. ir. $215.00 US; $279.50 other. Warren Gorham & Lamont Inc., Park Square Building, 31 St. James Avenue, Boston MA 02116-4112. **Tel** (617)423-2020, (800)950-1207, FAX (617)423-2026.

US
**FEDERAL INCOME TAXATION OF CORPORATIONS. SUPPLEMENT.** English. an. $62.50. American Law Institute, 4025 Chestnut Street, Philadelphia PA 19104-3099. **Tel** (215)243-1661, (800)253-6397, FAX (215)243-1664.

US
**FEDERAL INCOME TAXATION OF DEBT INSTRUMENTS.** (19??)-. English. an. $119.35. Prentice-Hall Law and Business, 270 Sylvan Avenue, Englewood Cliffs NJ 07632. **Tel** (800)223-0231, (201)894-8538, FAX (201)894-8666.

US/0148-4109
**FEDERAL RESEARCH REPORT.** (19??)-. Periodical. English. wk. $270.00. Business Publishers Inc., 951 Pershing Drive, Silver Spring MD 20910-4464. **Tel** (301)587-6300, (800)274-0122, FAX (301)585-9075. **ED** Leonard Eiserer.
**Desc:** Focus is on federal grant opportunities in areas such as education, environment, energy, medicine, science, and similar disciplines, primarily for institutions of higher education and research and development firms.

CN/0832-0705
**FEDERAL SALES TAX. Ceased.** [Can. commod. tax news fed. sales tax]. **VFOAT** Canadian Commodity Tax News; Canadian Commodity Tax News, Federal Sales Tax. Vol. 1, No. 1 (June 1985)-Ceased (1991). Periodical. English. ir. Canadian Institute of Chartered Accountants, 277 Wellington Street West, Toronto Ontario M5V 3H2 Canada. **Tel** (416)977-3222, FAX (416)204-3415. **DD** 343.7105/52/05.

US
**FEDERAL TAX ARTICLES: INCOME, ESTATE, GIFT, EXCISE, EMPLOYMENT TAXES. Main/Corp** Commerce Clearing House. **VFOAT** CCH Federal Tax Articles. (1967)-. Abstracting/Indexing Service. English. ir. $470.00. Commerce Clearing House Inc., 4025 West Peterson Avenue, Chicago IL 60646-6085. **Tel** (312)583-8500, FAX (708)940-4600. **ED** A. E. Schechter.
**Desc:** Describes articles from tax, law, accounting, business and other journals, code-arranges and indexes them, tells where to get the full story.

US/0735-9918
**FEDERAL TAX COMPLIANCE PLANNING.** [Fed. tax compliance plann.]. **Added/Corp** Institute for Business Planning, Inc. **VFOAT** Federal Tax Compliance Planning Manual. Vol. 1, No. 1 (Jan. 31, 1983)-. English. an. $138.00. Maxwell Macmillan Professional Business Division, 910 Sylvan Avenue, Englewood Cliffs NJ 07632-3310. **Tel** (800)431-9025. **LC** KF6296.A8; F43. **DD** 343.7304; 347.3034.

US/0738-8632
**FEDERAL TAX COORDINATOR 2D.** (FEDERAL TAX COORDINATOR 2D / PREPARED BY RESEARCH INSTITUTE OF AMERICA.). [Fed. tax coord. 2d]. **Added/Corp** Research Institute of America, Inc. United States. Internal Revenue Service. Internal Revenue Bulletin. **VAT** Federal Tax Coordinator Second. (1977)-. English. Research Institute of America, 117 East Stevens Avenue, Valhalla NY 10595. **Tel** (800)431-9025. **[CCC].** available on CD-ROM. **Continues** Tax Coordinator, 0039-999X.

US
**FEDERAL TAX COORDINATOR 2D. LISTING OF CURRENT TAX ARTICLES.** See Law.

US/0163-996X
**FEDERAL TAX COORDINATOR 2D. WEEKLY ALERT.** (FEDERAL TAX COORDINATOR 2D. WEEKLY ALERT / RIA.). [Fed. tax coord. 2d, Wkly. alert]. **Added/Corp** Research Institute of America, Inc. **VFOAT** Weekly Alert. (19??)-. English. wk. Research Institute of America, 117 East Stevens Avenue, Valhalla NY 10595. **Tel** (800)431-9025. **ED** James E. Cheeks. **Continues** Tax Coordinator. Bi-Weekly Alert.
**Desc:** Newsletter analyzing every significant federal tax development as it happens.

US/0737-8718
**FEDERAL TAX COURSE (STUDENTS ED.).** See Law.

US/0888-0522
**FEDERAL TAX MANUAL. Added/Corp** Commerce Clearing House. **VFOAT** CCH Federal Tax Manual. (1986)-. English. ir. must order direct. Commerce Clearing House Inc., 4025 West Peterson Avenue, Chicago IL 60646-6085. **Tel** (312)583-8500, FAX (708)940-4600. **ED** A. E. Schechter. **LC** KF6365; .F4195. **DD** 343.7305/2; 347.30352. Index available. **Continues** Federal Tax Compliance Manual, 0748-1462.
**Desc:** One volume coverage of basic tax rules affecting individuals and businesses. Numerous fact-filled pages and scores of filled-in forms and practical examples simplify tax return preparation.

US/0194-1798
**FEDERAL TAX VALUATION DIGEST.** [Fed. tax valuat. dig.] (1979)-. English. an. $165.00 US; $214.50 other. Warren Gorham & Lamont Inc., Park Square Building, 31 St. James Avenue, Boston MA 02116-4112. **Tel** (617)423-2020, (800)950-1207, FAX (617)423-2026. **LC** KF6450.A59; F43. **DD** 346.73/065; 347.30665. **Continues** Corporate Security Values as Determined by the Tax Court.

US/0742-7816
**FEDERAL TAXATION (HOUSTON, TEX.).** (FEDERAL TAXATION.). [Fed. tax.]. (1984)-. English. an (Aug.). Irwin Professional Publishing, 1333 Burr Ridge Parkway, Burr Ridge Parkway IL 60521. **Tel** (800)634-3966, (708)789-5480. **LC** KF6289; .F42. **DD** 343.7304; 347.3034.
**Desc:** A college textbook that covers the United States Tax Code.

US
**FEDERAL TAXATION OF LIFE INSURANCE COMPANIES.** See Insurance.

US
**FEDERAL TAXATION OF MUNICIPAL BONDS DESKBOOK.** (19??)-. English. an. $65.00. Prentice-Hall Law and Business, 270 Sylvan Avenue, Englewood Cliffs NJ 07632. **Tel** (800)223-0231, (201)894-8538, FAX (201)894-8666.

US
**FEDERAL TAXATION OF OIL AND GAS TRANSACTIONS.** English. ir. Matthew Bender & Company Inc., 1275 Broadway, Albany NY 12204. **Tel** (800)833-9844, (518)487-3000.

US
**FEDERAL TAXES. Macmillan Publishing Company, 866 3rd Avenue, New York NY 10022. Tel** (212)702-2000, (800)257-5755.

UK
**FEDERAL TAXES. Title Change.** (19??)-(Aug. 1992). English. wk. Research Institute of America, 117 East Stevens Avenue, Valhalla NY 10595. **Tel** (800)431-9025. **Continued by** United States Tax Reporter.

US
**FEDERAL TAXES CITATOR.** Macmillan Publishing Company, 866 3rd Avenue, New York NY 10022. **Tel** (212)702-2000, (800)257-5755.

US/0736-0975
**FIDUCIARY TAX RETURN GUIDE.**
**Added/Corp** Research Institute of America, inc. Vol. 1, (1977)-. English. an. $8.50. Research Institute of America, 117 East Stevens Avenue, Valhalla NY 10595. **Tel** (800)431-9025. **LC** KF6443.Z9; F5. **DD** 343.7305/32; 347.303532.

US
**FINAL BUDGET / COUNTY OF LOS ANGELES. Main/Corp** Los Angeles County (Calif.). Board of Supervisors. **VFOAT** Final County Budget. (1987/1988)-. English. an. **LC** HJ9012.C2; L773b. **DD** 352.1/252/097949305. **Continues** Los Angeles County (Calif.). Auditor-Controller. County Budget.

NO
**FINAL BUDGET PROPOSAL / ROYAL NORWEGIAN MINISTRY OF FINANCE. Main/Corp** Norway. Finans- og Tolldepartementet. (19??)-. English. **LC** HJ58; .A32a. **DD** 354.4810072/252/05.
**Ind/Abst** F&S Index Plus Text, Int. [Select. Cov.].

US
**FINAL BUDGET SUMMARY / STATE OF CALIFORNIA. Main/Corp** California. English. an. $1.00. Bill Room, State Capitol, Sacramento CA 95814. **LC** KFC842; .A243. **DD** 353.97940072/253.

BL
**FINANCAS E ORCAMENTO.** Periodical. Portuguese. Tribunal de Contas do Estado de Goias, Praca Civica No 332, Goiania Brazil. **LC** HJ32; .G56.

BL
**FINANCAS PUBLICAS MUNICIPAIS. Main/Corp** Sao Paulo (Brazil). Secretaria das Financas. Periodical. Portuguese. bm. Secretaria das Financas, rua Florencio de Abreu 84, Sao Paulo CEP 01030 Brazil. **LC** HJ9032.S26; A17A.

AT
**FINANCE. Main/Corp** Victoria. Treasury Dept. **Added/Corp** Victoria. Audit Office. (1864)-. English. an. Government Printer / Treasury Department, PO Box 203, North Melbourne Victoria, 3051 Australia. **LC** HJ95; .A3. **DD** 354.9450072/31.
**Ind/Abst** Econ. Lit. Index (19??-); J. Econ. Lit.

II
**FINANCE ACCOUNTS, GOVERNMENT OF ORISSA. Main/Corp** India (Republic). Comptroller and Auditor-General. English. an. Orissa Government Press, Madhupatna 3, Cuttack India. **LC** HJ9927.I4; I55A. **DD** 354/.54/1300723.

UK
**FINANCE ACTS.** (19??)-. English. ir. £30.50. Her Majesty's Stationery Office, 51 Nine Elms Lane, London SW8 5DR England. **Tel** 011 44 71 873 8459, 011 44 71 873 8499, FAX 011 44 71 873 8499, 011 44 71 873 8456, telex 297138. **(Subscription address:** Her Majesty's Stationery Office, PO Box 276, Publications Centre, London SW8 5DT England.)

MY
**FINANCE AND DEVELOPMENT.** See Economics.

UK
**FINANCE AND GENERAL STATISTICS. Added/Corp** Chartered Institute of Public Finance and Accountancy. Statistical Information Service. **VFOAT** Finance, General, and Rating Statistics; Finance, General & Rating Statistics. (1982/1983)-. English. an. Chartered Institute of Public Finance and Accountancy, 2 3 Robert Street, London WC2N 6BH England. **Tel** 011 44 1 895 8823. **LC** HJ9423; .C47a. **DD** 336/.014/41. **Continues** Chartered Institute of Public Finance and Accountancy. Statistical Information Service. Financial, General & Rating Statistics.

UK
**FINANCE BILLS. COMMONS & LORDS.** (19??)-. English. ir. £29.45. Her Majesty's Stationery Office, 51 Nine Elms Lane, London SW8 5DR England. **Tel** 011 44 71 873 8459, 011 44 71 873 8499, FAX 011 44 71 873 8499, 011 44 71 873 8456, telex 297138. **(Subscription address:** Her Majesty's Stationery Office, PO Box 276, Publications Centre, London SW8 5DT England.)

UK
**FINANCE BILLS. ORIGINALS & AMENDMENTS.** (19??)-. English. ir. £29.45. Her Majesty's Stationery Office, 51 Nine Elms Lane, London SW8 5DR England. **Tel** 011 44 71 873 8459, 011 44 71 873 8499, FAX 011 44 71 873 8499, 011 44 71 873 8456, telex 297138. **(Subscription address:** Her Majesty's Stationery Office, PO Box 276, Publications Centre, London SW8 5DT England.)

UK
**FINANCE DIRECTOR'S REVIEW.** English. mo. £125.00. Tolley Publishing Company Ltd, Tolley

## Public Administration —Public Finance and Taxation

House, 2 Addiscombe Road, Croydon, Surrey CR9 5AF United Kingdom. **Tel** 011 44 81 6869141, FAX 011 44 81 6863155, 011 44 81 7600588.

FR/0752-6180
**FINANCE (PARIS).** (FINANCE : REVUE DE L'ASSOCIATION FRANÇAISE DE FINANCE.). [Finance]. **Added/Corp** Association Française de Finance. Vol. 3, No. 1 (April 1982)-. Periodical. English (French). sa. 570.00F France; 705.00F other. Presses Universitaires de France, Department des Revues, 14 Avenue du Bois de l'Epine, BP 90, 91003 Evry Cedex France. **Tel** (1)60 77 82 05, FAX (1) 60 79 20 45, telex PUF 600 474 F. **Continues** Revue de l'Association Française de Finance, 0248-0167.

US
**FINANCE QUARTERLY BULLETIN.** **Added/Corp** New York (N.Y.). Dept. of Finance. Vol. 1 (Spring 1989)-. Bulletin. English. qt. $40.00. New York City Department of Finance, 345 Adams Street, First Floor, Brooklyn NY 11201. **Tel** (212)669-4868. **ED** Joseph Dunn. cum. index. **Pr Rev. Circ:** 700 (ctrl). **Continues** Department of Finance Bulletin.

UK
**FINANCE STANDING COMMITTEE DEBATES.** (19??)-. English. ir. £7.50. Her Majesty's Stationery Office, 51 Nine Elms Lane, London SW8 5DR England. **Tel** 011 44 71 873 8459, 011 44 71 873 8499, FAX 011 44 71 873 8499, 011 44 71 873 8456, telex 297138. (**Subscription address:** Her Majesty's Stationery Office, PO Box 276, Publications Centre, London SW8 5DT England.)

FR
**FINANCES DES DEPARTEMENTS, LES.** 10th Ed. (Exercise 1980)-. French. an. Documentation Francaise, 29 Quai Voltaire, 75344 Paris Cedex 7 France. **Tel** 011 33 1 40157000, FAX 011 33 1 40157230, telex 204 826 DOCFRAN. **LC** HJ9047; .A49. **DD** 336/.014/44. **Continues** Statistiques Departementales.

US/0196-9226
**FINANCIAL ASSISTANCE BY GEOGRAPHIC AREA. REGION I, BOSTON, MASS.** (FINANCIAL ASSISTANCE BY GEOGRAPHIC AREA. REGION I, BOSTON, MASS. / U.S. DEPARTMENT OF HEALTH AND HUMAN SERVICES.). **VAT** Financial Assistance By Geographic Area. Region One, Boston, Massachusetts. English. an. Division of Financial Operations and Fiscal Procedures, Department of Health and Human Services, 739 D1 Humphrey Building, 200 Independence Avenue SW, Washington DC 20201. **LC** HC107.A113; P638. **DD** 336.1/85. **NLM** W2; AN25 U5f. available on microfiche (Vols. for (1983-) distributed to depository libraries).

US/0192-4613
**FINANCIAL ASSISTANCE BY GEOGRAPHIC AREA. REGION II, NEW YORK, N.Y.** (FINANCIAL ASSISTANCE BY GEOGRAPHIC AREA. REGION II, NEW YORK, N.Y. / U.S. DEPARTMENT OF HEALTH AND HUMAN SERVICES.). **VAT** Financial Assistance By Geographic Area. Region Two, New York, New York. English. an. Division of Financial Operations and Fiscal Procedures, Department of Health and Human Services, 739 D1 Humphrey Building, 200 Independence Avenue SW, Washington DC 20201. **LC** HC107.N73; P638. **DD** 336.1/85. **NLM** W2; A F7dk. available on microfiche (Vols. for (1983-) distributed to depository libraries).

US/0192-4982
**FINANCIAL ASSISTANCE BY GEOGRAPHIC AREA. REGION III, PHILADELPHIA, PENNA.** (FINANCIAL ASSISTANCE BY GEOGRAPHIC AREA. REGION III, PHILADELPHIA, PENNA. / U.S. DEPARTMENT OF HEALTH AND HUMAN SERVICES.). **VAT** Financial Assistance By Geographic Area. Region Three, Philadelphia, Pennsylvania. English. an. US Department of Health and Human Services, 200 Independence Avenue Southwest, Washington DC 20201. **LC** HC107.A12; U54A. **DD** 336.1/85. **NLM** W2; A F7dkj. available on microfiche (Vols. for (1981-) distributed to depository libraries).

US/0192-6586
**FINANCIAL ASSISTANCE BY GEOGRAPHIC AREA. REGION IX, SAN FRANCISCO, CALIFORNIA.** (FINANCIAL ASSISTANCE BY GEOGRAPHIC AREA. REGION IX, SAN FRANCISCO, CALIFORNIA / U.S. DEPARTMENT OF HEALTH AND HUMAN SERVICES.). **VAT** Financial Assistance by Geographic Area. Region Nine, San Francisco, California. English. an. Division of Financial Operations and Fiscal Procedures, Department of Health and Human Services, 739 D1 Humphrey Building, 200 Independence Avenue SW, Washington DC 20201. **LC** HC110.P63; U485A. **DD** 336.1/85. **NLM** W2; A F7ek. available on microfiche (Vols. for (1981-) distributed to depository libraries).

US/0192-4966
**FINANCIAL ASSISTANCE BY GEOGRAPHIC AREA. REGION V, CHICAGO, ILLINOIS.** (FINANCIAL ASSISTANCE BY GEOGRAPHIC AREA. REGION V, CHICAGO, ILLINOIS / U.S. DEPARTMENT OF HEALTH AND HUMAN SERVICES.). **VAT** Financial Assistance by Geographical Area. Region Five, Chicago, Illinois. English. an. Division of Financial Operations and Fiscal Procedures, Department of Health and Human Services, 739 D1 Humphrey Building, 200 Independence Avenue SW, Washington DC 20201. **LC** HC107.A14; F56. **DD** 336.1/85. **NLM** W2; A F7dq. available on microfiche (Vols. for (1983-) distributed to depository libraries).

US/0192-5598
**FINANCIAL ASSISTANCE BY GEOGRAPHIC AREA. REGION VI, DALLAS, TEXAS.** **VAT** Financial Assistance By Geographic Area. Region Six, Dallas, Texas. English. an. Division of Financial Operations and Fiscal Procedures, Department of Health and Human Services, 739 D1 Humphrey Building, 200 Independence Avenue SW, Washington DC 20201. **LC** HC107.A17; U54A. **DD** 336.1/85. **NLM** W2; A F7dt. available on microfiche (Vols. for (1981-) distributed to depository libraries).

US/0192-8074
**FINANCIAL ASSISTANCE BY GEOGRAPHIC AREA. REGION VII, KANSAS CITY, MISSOURI.** (FINANCIAL ASSISTANCE BY GEOGRAPHIC AREA. REGION VII, KANSAS CITY, MISSOURI / U.S. DEPARTMENT OF HEALTH AND HUMAN SERVICES.). **Added/Corp** United States. Dept. of Health and Human Services. United States. Dept. of Health and Human Services. Deputy Assistant Secretary, Finance. United States. Dept. of Health, Education, and Welfare. Office of the Assistant Secretary, Comptroller. **VAT** Financial Assistance By Geographic Area. Region Seven, Kansas City, Missouri. (19??)-. English. an. US Department of Health and Human Services, 200 Independence Avenue Southwest, Washington DC 20201. **LC** HC107.A1723; P638. **DD** 336.1/85. **NLM** W2; A F7dw.

US/0192-6578
**FINANCIAL ASSISTANCE BY GEOGRAPHIC AREA. REGION VIII, DENVER, COLORADO.** **VAT** Financial Assistance by Geographic Area. Region Eight, Denver, Colorado. English. an. Division of Financial Operations and Fiscal Procedures, Department of Health and Human Services, 739 D1 Humphrey Building, 200 Independence Avenue SW, Washington DC 20201. **LC** HC107.A1713; P638. **DD** 336.1/85. **NLM** W2; A F7dz. available on microfiche (Vols. for (1981-) distributed to depository libraries).

US/0192-6608
**FINANCIAL ASSISTANCE BY GEOGRAPHIC AREA. REGION X, SEATTLE, WASHINGTON.** **VAT** Financial Assistance by Geographic Area. Region Ten, Seattle, Washington. English. an. Division of Financial Operations and Fiscal Procedures, Department of Health and Human Services, 739 D1 Humphrey Building, 200 Independence Avenue SW, Washington DC 20201. **LC** HC107.A1453; P638. **DD** 336.1/85. **NLM** W2; A F7ep. available on microfiche (Vols. for (1981-) distributed to depository libraries).

US
**FINANCIAL CONNECTION, THE.** **Added/Corp** United States. Dept. of the Treasury. Financial Management Service. Vol. 1, Issue 1 (Summer 1991)-. Periodical. English. qt. Department of Treasury Financial Management Service, Washington DC 20226. **Tel** (202)566-2000.

US/0270-5605
**FINANCIAL FACTS ON WYOMING TAXING UNITS.** 1978/79-. English. an. Dain Bosworth Inc, 100 Dain Tower, Minneapolis MN 55402. **LC** HJ9341; .F56. **DD** 336/.014/787.

●US/1065-6456
**FINANCIAL OFFICER'S TAX & MANAGEMENT REPORT.** See Business-General Management.

US
**FINANCIAL PLAN AND ... EXECUTIVE BUDGET / TRIBOROUGH BRIDGE AND TUNNEL AUTHORITY.** Title Change. **Main/Corp** Triborough Bridge and Tunnel Authority. **VFOAT** Executive Budget. (1992)-(1992). English. **Continues** Triborough Bridge and Tunnel Authority. Budget and ... Financial Plan. **Continued by** Triborough Bridge and Tunnel Authority. Executive Budget and Financial Plan.

US
**FINANCIAL PLAN STATUS REPORT / OFFICE OF THE STATE DEPUTY COMPTROLLER FOR THE CITY OF NEW YORK.** **Main/Corp** New York (State). Office of the State Deputy Comptroller for the City of New York. (Mar 1991)-. Periodical. English. mo.

US/0146-7328
**FINANCIAL PLANNING GUIDE FOR MILITARY PERSONNEL.** See Military and Defense.

●US
**FINANCIAL PROJECTIONS AND CAPITAL PLAN.** **Added/Corp** New York (State). Governor. (1993)-. English. **Formed by the union of** Five-Year Governmental Funds Projections **and** Five-Year Capital Plan.

LU
**FINANCIAL REPORT - COMMISSION OF THE EUROPEAN COMMUNITIES.** **Main/Corp** Commission of the European Communities. English. European Communities Commission, Case Postale 1003, Luxembourg Luxembourg. **Tel** (352)48 80 41, FAX (352)48 80 40, telex 2181. **LC** HJ2094.5; .C65B. **DD** 354.1/0422.

CN/0710-8435
**FINANCIAL REPORT - MANITOBA DEPARTMENT OF FINANCE.** (FINANCIAL REPORT.). [Financ. rep. - Manit. Dep. Finance]. **Main/Corp** Manitoba. Dept. of Finance. 1979-80-. English. an. Manitoba Department of Finance, 204 Legislative Building, Winnipeg Manitoba R3C 0V8 Canada. **LC** HJ13; .M74A. **DD** 354.7127072/31.

US
**FINANCIAL REPORT OF THE MISSOURI DEPARTMENT OF REVENUE.** **Main/Corp** Missouri. Dept. of Revenue. (1987)-. English. an. **LC** HJ11; .M844A. **DD** 353.97780072/31. **Continues** Annual Combined Financial Report.

US
**FINANCIAL REPORT - STATE INVESTMENT COUNCIL.** **Main/Corp** State of New Mexico State Investment Council. English. mo. Jose A Garcia, State Investment Officer, PO Box 966, Santa Fe NM 87503. **LC** HJ3835.N58; N48A. **DD** 353.97890072/31.

US
**FINANCIAL REPORT / STATE OF NEW MEXICO, OFFICE OF STATE TREASURER.** **Main/Corp** New Mexico. Office of State Treasurer. **VFOAT** Annual Financial Report for the Year ... . English. an. New Mexico State Treasurer, PO Box 608, Santa Fe NM 87503. **LC** HJ11; .N615A. **DD** 353.97890072/31.

CN/0848-5194
**FINANCIAL RESULTS - GOVERNMENT OF CANADA.** (FINANCIAL RESULTS FOR THE FISCAL YEAR ...). [Financ. results - Gov. Can.]. **Main/Corp** Canada. **VFOAT** Monthly Statements of Financial Transactions ...; Resultats Financiers de l'Exercice ... . (1990)-. Periodical. English (French). mo. **DD** 354.710072.

US
**FINANCIAL STATEMENT.** **Main/Corp** Waseca County, Minnesota. Auditor. (1???)-. English. qt. $126.04.

UK
**FINANCIAL STATEMENT AND BUDGET REPORT.** **Main/Corp** Great Britain. Treasury. (19??)-. English. an. Her Majesty's Stationery Office, 51 Nine Elms Lane, London SW8 5DR England. **Tel** 011 44 71 873 8459, 011 44 71 873 8499, FAX 011 44 71 873 8499, 011 44 71 873 8456, telex 297138. (**Subscription address:** Her Majesty's Stationery Office, PO Box 276, Publications Centre, London SW8 5DT England.)

IE
**FINANCIAL STATEMENT - DEPARTMENT OF FINANCE (NORTHERN IRELAND).** **Main/Corp** Northern Ireland. Dept. of Finance. English. Government Publications, 4 5 Harcourt Road, Dublin 2 Ireland. **Tel** 011 353 1 6613111 Ext.4005. **LC** HJ42.2; .C56. **DD** 354/.416/00722. **Continues** Northern Ireland. Ministry of Finance. Financial Statement.

CN/0825-7043
**FINANCIAL STATEMENTS & FINANCIAL STATISTICS / CAISSE DE DEPOT ET PLACEMENT DU QUEBEC.** See Public Administration.

# Public Administration —Public Finance and Taxation

SA
**FINANCIAL STATEMENTS - CITY TREASURER.** **Main/Corp** Durban, Natal. City Treasurer. **VFOAT** Finansiele State - Stadstesourier. Multiple languages (Afrikaans and English). Durban Museum, PO Box 4085, Durban 4000 South Africa. **LC** HJ9080E.D8; A17A. **DD** 352/.17/09684.

IT
**FINANCIAL STATEMENTS / CONSORZIO DI CREDITO PER LE OPERE PUBBLICHE.** **Main/Corp** Consorzio di Credito per le Opere Pubbliche. 61st Financial Year (1980)-. English. Consorzio di Credito per le Opere Pubbliche, Via Quintino Selle 2, Rome Italy. **LC** HD4186; .C62a. **DD** 354.450072/53/06. **Continues** Consorzio di Credito per le Opere Pubbliche.; Report and Accounts.

CN
**FINANCIAL STATEMENTS OF QUEBEC GOVERNMENT ENTERPRISES.** **Main/Corp** Quebec (Province) Dept. of Finance. 1971/72-. English (French). an.

US
**FINANCIAL STATEMENTS, STATE OF COLORADO, STATE CONTROLLER.** **Main/Corp** Colorado. Division of Accounts and Control. Began in 1976/77. English. an. Division of Accounts & Control, Department of Administration, 1525 Sherman Street/Room 707, Denver CO 80203. **LC** HJ11; .C627B. **DD** 353.97880072/32/05.

JA/0289-1522
**FINANCIAL STATISTICS OF JAPAN.** See Public Administration-Abstracting, Bibliographies and Statistics.

CN/0226-6458
**FINANCIAL SUMMARY AND BUDGETARY REVIEW.** (FINANCIAL SUMMARY AND BUDGETARY REVIEW (ALBERTA).). [Financ. summ. budg. rev.]. **Main/Corp** Alberta. Alberta Treasury. 1978/79-. English. an. Alberta Treasury, 407 Legislative Building, Edmonton Alberta T5K 2B6 Canada. **LC** HJ13; .A74B. **DD** 354.71230072/252/05; 336.7123.

US
**FINANCIAL SUMMARY - DELAWARE. OFFICE OF THE GOVERNOR.** **Main/Corp** Delaware. Office of the Governor. English. an. Executive Department Office of the Budget, Townsend Building, Dover DE 19901. **Tel** (302)736-4204. **LC** HJ11; .D3432A. **DD** 353.97510072/253. **Continues** Governor's Budget Summary.

UK
**FINANCIAL TIMES TAX NEWSLETTER.** (19??)-. Periodical. English. mo. $121.70 UK & Europe; $190.00 other. Financial Times England, 8 16 Great New Street, London EC4A 3BN England. **Tel** 011 44 71 353 0305, 353 1040, FAX 011 44 353 0846. **LC** HJ2240; .F55. **DD** 336.2/005.

US/0250-6157
**FINANCIAMIENTO DEL DESARROLLO.** **Main/Corp** Organization of American States. Development Financing Program. Began with July 1977 issue. Periodical. Spanish. sa. Secretaria General / Washington, DC, Organizacion de los Estados Americanos, Departmento de Publicaciones, Washington DC 20006. **LC** HJ799.53; .O73C. **Continues in part** Financiamiento del Desarrollo, 0250-6157.

FR
**FINANCING AND EXTERNAL DEBT OF DEVELOPING COUNTRIES.** **Added/Corp** Organisation for Economic Co-Operation and Development. Development Co-Operation Directorate. (1985)-. English. an. $43.00. OECD Publications and Information Center, 2 rue Andre-Pascal, 75775 Paris Cedex 16 France. **Tel** 011 33 1 45248167, US:(202)785-6323, FAX 011 33 1 45248500 OR 45248176, telex 620 160 OCDE. (Subscription address: OECD Publications Center, 2001 L Street, Suite 700, Washington DC 20036.) **LC** HJ8899; .F545. **DD** 336.3/435/091724. **Continues** External Debt of Developing Countries.
**Desc:** Presents information on financial resource flows to developing countries and their external indebtness.

US
**FINANCING LOCAL GOVERNMENT.** **Added/Corp** Government Information Services. Vol. 1, No. 1 (June 30, 1988)-. Periodical. English. bw. $157.00. Government Information Services / Virginia, 4301 North Fairfax Drive, Suite 875, Arlington VA 22203. **Tel** (703)528-1082, FAX (703)528-6060, telex RCA 263591 GIS UR. **ED** Donald Hoffman. **LC** HJ9011; .A3. **Absorbed** Privatization Report.
**Desc:** Shows proven techniques that other governments have used to expand their revenue base through innovative tax levies, user fees and portfolio management. Reports on innovative taxing efforts around the nation are supplemented with articles on unique money-saving ways to deliver essential services. Provides news about activities in Washington that is of interest to small to mid-size local governments.

●RU
**FINANSY.** (1992)-. Periodical. Russian. mo. $99.95. (Subscription address: East View Publications Inc., 3020 Harbor Lane North, Suite 110, Minneapolis MN 55447.) **LC** HJ109.R8; F5. **Continues** Finansy SSSR, 0130-576X.

AU/1017-5695
**FINANZ JOURNAL.** [Finanz J.]. (Feb. 1965)-. Periodical. German. mo. S270.00. Grenz-Verlag, Flossgasse 6, A-1025 Vienna 2 Austria. **LC** K6; .I62. **DD** 343/.436/0305.

GW/0340-9007
**FINANZ-RUNDSCHAU. Title Change.** (1946)-(19??). Periodical. German. bw. Otto Schmidt KG, Postfach 511026, Ulmenallee 96-98, W-5000 Koeln 51 Germany. **Tel** 02 21/37 30 21, telex 8 883 831. **ED** Otto Schmidt Verlag. Index available. **Bk Rev. Ad Acc. Circ:** 3,150. **Continued by** Finanz-Rundschau fur Einkommensteuer und Korperschaftsteuer, 0176-7771.

GW/0015-2218
**FINANZARCHIV.** (FINANZ-ARCHIV : ZEITSCHRIFT FUER DAS GESAMTE FINANZWESEN.). [Finanzarchiv]. Vol. 1-48 (1884-1931). New Series Vol. 1 (1932)-. German (English). qt. DM258.00. JCB Mohr / Paul Siebeck, Postfach 2040, D 72010 Tuebingen Germany. **Tel** 011 49 7071 9230, FAX 011 49 7071 51104, telex 7/262872 mohr d. **ED** Norbert Andel and Fritz Neumark. **LC** HJ105; .F4. **[CCC].** cum. index. **Bk Rev. Ad Acc. Circ:** 1,200.
**Desc:** Special emphasis is on West German and foreign fiscal and tax policy.
**Ind/Abst** J. Econ. Lit. (1968-1982); PAIS Int. Print (1991-).

GW/0072-1883
**FINANZEN UND STEUEREN. REIHE 2 : STEUERHAUSHALT VON BUND, LANDERN UND GEMEINDEN.** **Main/Corp** Germany (West). Statistisches Bundesamt. **VFOAT** Steuerhaushalt Von Bund, Landern und Gemeinden. German. W Kohlhammer Verlag GMBH, Postfach 800430, D70549 Stuttgart Germany. **Tel** 011 49 711 78631.

GW
**FINANZEN UND STEUERN. REIHE 5: SCHULDEN DER OFFENTLICHEN HAUSHALTE.** **Main/Corp** Germany (West). Statistisches Bundesamt. **Added/Corp** Germany (West). Statistisches Bundesamt. Schulden der Offentlichen Haushalte. (1976)-. German. ir. 7.50. W Kohlhammer Verlag GMBH, Postfach 800430, D70549 Stuttgart Germany. **Tel** 011 49 711 78631. **LC** HJ48; .D153a. **DD** 336.3/4/0943. **Continues** Finanzen und Steuern. Reihe 3: Schulden und Vermogen von Bund, Landern und Gemeinden. I. Schulden.

GW
**FINANZEN UND STEUERN. REIHE 7.S.1, WIRTSCHAFTLICHE GLIEDERUNG DER EINKOMMEN- UND KORPERSCHAFTSTEUERPFLICHTIGEN.** **VFOAT** Wirtschaftliche Gliederung der Einkommen- und Fachserie 14. German. ir. DM14.60. W Kohlhammer Verlag GmbH, Postfach 800430, D 70549 Stuttgart Germany. **Tel** 011 49 711 78631, FAX 011 49 711 7863263, telex 7-255820. **LC** HJ4719; .A18.

GW
**FINANZPLAN DES BUNDES, DER.** **Main/Corp** Germany (West). Bundesministerium der Finanze. German. an. Bundesministerium der Finanzen, Rheindorfer Strasse 108, W-5300 Bonn 1 Germany. **LC** HJ1120; .G43A.

●SZ
**FINANZPLAN DES KANTONS BERN.** **Main/Corp** Bern (Switzerland : Canton). **Added/Corp** Bern (Switzerland : Canton). Grosser Rat. Tagblatt des Grossen Rates. **VFOAT** Plan Financier du Canton de Berne. (1990-1993)-. German (French). **LC** HJ62.B4; B47a.

GW
**FINANZPLANUNG VON BERLIN.** **Main/Corp** Berlin (Germany : West). Senator fur Finanzen. German. Senator fur Finanzen, Nurnberger Str 53-55, 1 Berlin 30 Germany. **LC** HJ9484.B4; A22. **DD** 336.43/1554. **Continues** Finanzplanung des Landes Berlin.

GW
**FINANZWIRTSCHAFT : ZEITSCHRIFT FUR DAS FINANZ-, PREIS- UND KREDITWESEN DER DDR.** (1990)-. Periodical. German. Twelve times a year. DM151.20 Germany; DM180.00 others. Verlag die Wirtschaft Berlin, Am Friedrichshain 22, D 10407 Berlin Germany. **Tel** 011 49 30 42870. **LC** HJ1150.A2; S63. **Continues** Sozialistische Finanzwirtschaft.

MW
**FIRST REPORT OF THE PUBLIC ACCOUNTS COMMITTEE TO THE NATIONAL ASSEMBLY, THE.** **Main/Corp** Malawi. Select Committee on Public Accounts. English. Government Printer / Malawi, Office of President and Cabinet, PO Box 37, Zomba Malawi. **LC** HJ9929.M34; M34B. **DD** 354.68970072/31.

US
**FISCAL ACCOUNTABILITY ACT; SUMMARY REPORT TO THE GENERAL ASSEMBLY.** **Main/Corp** South Carolina. Legislative Audit Council. (1976)-. Periodical. English.

US
**FISCAL GUIDELINES FOR FEDERAL AND STATE AIDED GRANTS.** See Education.

US/0197-288X
**FISCAL LETTER, THE.** **Added/Corp** National Conference of State Legislatures. Vol. 1 (Oct. 1978)-. Periodical. English. bm. $35.00 US; $40.00 Canada. National Conference of State Legislatures, 1560 Broadway, Suite 700, Denver CO 80202. **Tel** (303)830-2054, FAX (303)863-8003. **ED** Judy Zelio. cum. index. **Bk Rev. Circ:** 1,800.
**Desc:** Reports on current and emerging state fiscal issues. Prepared by and for state fiscal experts, it gives a national perspective on state issues.
**Ind/Abst** Urban Aff. Abstr.

US
**FISCAL REPORT FOR THE FISCAL PERIOD ENDED JUNE 30 ... / COMMONWEALTH OF PENNSYLVANIA, OFFICE OF THE AUDITOR GENERAL.** **Main/Corp** Pennsylvania. Office of the Auditor General. **VFOAT** Fiscal Report; Auditor General's Report--Pennsylvania; Report of the Auditor General--Pennsylvania. (1962)-. English. an. Commonwealth of Pennsylvania Office of the Auditor General, Harrisburg PA 17120. **LC** HJ11; .P44. **DD** 353.97480072/32/05. **Continues** Pennsylvania. Office of the Auditor General. Biennial Report for the Two Years Ended May 31 ... .

UK/0143-5671
**FISCAL STUDIES.** [Fisc. stud.]. **Added/Corp** Institute for Fiscal Studies (Great Britain). Vol. 1, No. 1 (Nov. 1979)-. Periodical. English. qt. £60.00 (institutions), £40.00 (individuals) UK; £77.50 (institutions), £49.50 (individuals) other. World Wide Subscription Services, Unit 4, Gibbs Reed Farm, East Sussex TN5 7HE England. **Tel** (0580)200657, FAX (0580)200616. **[CCC].** Index available. cum. index. **Ad Acc. Circ:** 1,720. available on microfilm and microfiche from University Microfilms International (UMI). Documents available from UMI Article Clearinghouse.
**Ind/Abst** ABI/INFORM Glob. Ed.; ABI Inform Ondisc (Nov. 1984-); Contents Pages Manage.; Econ. Lit. Index; Gen. BusinessFile (1992-); J. Econ. Lit.

US
**FISCAL SUMMARY OF ... / VERMONT DEPARTMENT OF FINANCE AND MANAGEMENT.** **Main/Corp** Vermont. Dept. of Finance and Management. (1987)-. English. **LC** HJ11; .V514c. **Continues** Fiscal Summary of ... / Vermont.

US/0198-6562
**FISCAL SURVEY OF THE STATES.** [Fisc. surv. States]. **Main/Corp** National Association of State Budget Officers. **Added/Corp** National Governors' Association. Center for Policy Research. (1977)-. English. Twice a year. $30.50. National Governors Association, 444 North Capitol Street, Suite 267, Washington DC 20001. **Tel** (202)624-5300. (Subscription address: NGA Publications, PO Box 421, Annapolis Junction, MD 20701; telephone: (301)498-3738) **LC** HJ275; .N32a. **DD** 336.73.

US
**FISCAL YEAR BUDGET ESTIMATES - FEDERAL AVIATION ADMINISTRATION.** **Main/Corp** United States. Federal Aviation Administration. Government Publication. English. US Department of Transportation / Federal Aviation Administration, 800 Independence Avenue Southwest, Washington DC 20591. **Tel** (202)367-3484, FAX (202)367-3505.

●US
**FISCAL YEAR ESTIMATED TAX ON UNRELATED BUSINESS TAXABLE INCOME FOR TAX-EXEMPT ORGANIZATIONS (WORKSHEET).** **Added/Corp** United States. Internal Revenue Service. (1992/1993)-. English. Eastern Area Distribution Center, PO Box 85074, Richmond VA 23261-5074.

# Public Administration —Public Finance and Taxation

CN/0319-2423
**FISCALITE AU CANADA, LA.** V. 1- May 1973-. Periodical. French. mo. $40.00 with self-binder. Carswell / Canada, 2075 Kennedy Road, Scarborough Ontario M1T 3V4 Canada. **Tel** (416)609-3800, (800)387-5164.

FR
**FISCALITE EUROPEENNE.** (19??)-. French. Four times a year. Cahiers Fiscaux Europeens, 51 Avenue Reine Victoria, 06000 Nice France. **Tel** 011 33 93 810326.

FR/0750-8662
**FISCALITE IMMOBILIERE.** [Fisc. immobil.]. (1973)-. French. ir. 1740.00F. Editions Techniques, 141 rue de Javel, 75747 Paris Cedex 15 France. **Tel** 011 33 1 45589100. **UDC** 336.2.

GW/0015-2862
**FISCHERS TARIF-NACHRICHTEN FUER EISENBAHN UND KRAFTWAGEN.** (19??)-. Periodical. German. mo. DM74.25. Verkehrs Verlag J Fischer, Postfach 140265, D 40072 Dusseldorf Germany. **Tel** 011 49 211 991930. **UDC** 656.1.03.

BL
**FISCOMAT.** VFOAT Revista Fiscomat. (19??)-. Portuguese. Fiscomat. Caixa Postal 879, Campo Grande Brazil. **LC** LAW. **DD** 343.8104/05; 348.103405.

CN/0848-6913
**FISHING INCOME TAX GUIDE.** [Fish. income tax guide]. **Added/Corp** Canada. Taxation. (1989)-. English. Revenue Canada Taxation, 875 Heron Road, Ottawa Ontario K1A 0L8 Canada. **Tel** (613)957-3508, FAX (613)941-0914. **DD** 343.7105/26. **Continues** Fisherman's Income Tax Guide., 0710-8885.

US/0146-7034
**FLORIDA AD VALOREM VALUATIONS AND TAX DATA.** **Main/Corp** Florida. Dept. of Revenue. English. Florida Department of Revenue, Tax Research, 137 Carlton Building, Tallahassee FL 32399. **Tel** (904)488-5630. **LC** HJ4121.F6; D46B. **DD** 336.2/2/09759.

US
**FLORIDA GOVERNOR ... BIENNIAL BUDGET RECOMMENDATION AMENDMENT.** **Main/Corp** Florida. Office of the Governor. VFOAT Biennial Budget Recommendation. Amendment. English. se. Office of the Governor / Florida, The Capitol, Tallahassee FL 32301. **LC** HJ2053.F6; F572A. **DD** 353.97590072/256/05.

●US/1066-3487
**FLORIDA TAX REVIEW.** [Fla. tax rev.]. **Added/Corp** University of Florida. College of Law. Graduate Tax Program. Vol. 1, No. 1 (Oct. 1992)-. Periodical. English. ir (12-14 issues per year). $125.00. Tax Analysts, 6830 North Fairfax Drive, Arlington VA 22213. **Tel** (703)533-4400, (800)955-3444. **(Subscription address:** Exempt Organization Tax Review, 6830 North Fairfax Avenue, Arlington, VA 22213; telephone: (800)955-2444, (703)533-4400) **LC** K6; .L673. **DD** 343.75904/05; 347.5903405.

US
**FLORIDA'S FISCAL ANALYSIS.** **Added/Corp** Florida. Legislature. House of Representatives. Committee on Appropriations. Florida. Legislature. Senate. Committee on Appropriations. VFOAT Fiscal Analysis. (1991)-. English. **LC** HJ11; .F643. **DD** 353.97590072/236. **Continues** Florida's Fiscal Analysis in Brief.

US
**FLORIDA'S FISCAL ANALYSIS. EXECUTIVE SUMMARY.** **Added/Corp** Florida. Legislature. House of Representatives. Committee on Appropriations. Florida. Legislature. Senate. Committee on Appropriations. VFOAT Fiscal Analysis. Executive Summary; Executive Summary. (1991)-. English. **LC** HJ11; .F648. **DD** 336.759/05.

●US
**FLOW OF FUNDS ACCOUNTS, FLOWS AND OUTSTANDINGS.** **Added/Corp** Board of Governors of the Federal Reserve System (U.S.). (1992)-. Periodical. English. qt. Formed by the union of Flow of Funds Accounts. Financial Assets and Liabilities Year-End and Flow of Funds Accounts. Seasonally Adjusted Flows.

US
**FLOW OF FUNDS SUMMARY STATISTICS / BOARD OF GOVERNORS OF THE FEDERAL RESERVE SYSTEM.** See Public Administration-Abstracting, Bibliographies and Statistics.

BL
**FONTES DE FINANCIAMENTO PARA O SETOR PUBLICO ESTADUAL.** **Main/Corp** Parana (Brazil : State). Coordenadoria de Orcamento e Programaco. 1.- Ed.; 1978-. Portuguese. Palacio Castello Branco, Centro Civico, Curtiba Brazil. **LC** HJ32; .P348B.

NE
**FOREIGN-RELATED TAX LAWS AND REGULATIONS OF THE PEOPLE'S REPUBLIC OF CHINA.** (1992)-. English. sa. $430.00. International Bureau of Fiscal Documentation - IBFD Publications, PO Box 20237, 1000 HE Amsterdam The Netherlands. **Tel** 011 31 20-6267726, FAX 011 31 20-6228658, telex 13217 INTAX NL. **(Subscription address:** IBFD / International Bureau of Fiscal Documentation USA, Inc., 24 Hudson Street, Kinderhook NY 12106.**)**
**Desc:** Unique translation of laws, regulations and rulings, fully approved by the Chinese government.

SW
**FORFATTNINGAR OM UPPBORD M.M.** **Main/Corp** Sweden. Swedish. Kr235.00. Allmanna Forlaget Kundtjanst, S-162 89 Stockholm Sweden. **Tel** 8-7399630. **LC** LAW. **DD** 343/.485/042.

MX
**FORUM HACENDARIO.** Periodical. Spanish. qt. Gobierno del Estado de Mexico, Imprenta Madero Avena 102, Zona 13 Mexico. **LC** HJ805.M4; F67.

●US/1055-4998
**FOUNDATION REPORTER (1990).** (FOUNDATION REPORTER.). [Found. rep.]. **Added/Corp** Taft Group (Rockville, Md.). VFOAT Taft Foundation Reporter. 23rd ed. (1992)-. English. $327.00. Taft Group, 835 Penobscott Building, Customer Service, Detroit MI 48226. **Tel** (800)877-8238, FAX (313)961-6083. **Continues** Taft Foundation Reporter, 0730-6237.

IE
**FRAMEWORK FOR ... BUDGET.** **Main/Corp** Ireland. English. Government Publications, 4 5 Harcourt Road, Dublin 2 Ireland. **Tel** 011 353 1 6613111 Ext.4005. **LC** HJ43.5; .A194A. **DD** 336.417.

SW
**FRAN RIKSDAG & I.E. OCH DEPARTEMENT.** **Main/Corp** Sweden. Riksdagen. V. 1- Jan. 22, 1976-. Swedish. Kr78.75. Sveavagen, 166 9 Tr, 113 46 Stockholm Sweden. **LC** J406; .H84A.

US/0749-2820
**FROM THE STATE CAPITALS. TAXATION AND REVENUE POLICIES.** [From state cap., Tax. revenue policies]. VFOAT Taxation and Revenue Policies. (1984)-. Periodical. English. wk. $292.00 (one year), $378.00 (two year) public and institutional libraries; $235.00 (one year), $420.00 (two year) other. Wakeman Walworth Inc., 300 North Washington Street #204, Alexandria VA 22314. **Tel** (703)549-8606. **ED** Emily Novick. **DD** 336. **Continues** From the State Capitals. Taxation and Revenue, 0741-3556.
**Desc:** Covers revenue-raising other than property taxes: sales, excise, business, inheritance, bank, capital gains taxes, lotteries.

US/0734-1121
**FROM THE STATE CAPITALS. TAXES-PROPERTY (NEW HAVEN, CONN.).** (FROM THE STATE CAPITALS. TAXES--PROPERTY.). [From state cap., Taxes--prop.]. VFOAT Taxes - Property. (1982)-. Periodical. English. wk. $292.50 (one year), 325.00 (two year) public and institutional libraries; $526.50 (one year), 858.00 (two year) other. Wakeman Walworth Inc., 300 North Washington Street #204, Alexandria VA 22314. **Tel** (703)549-8606. **DD** 336. **[CCC]**. **Continues** From the State Capitals. Taxes-Property Report; **Absorbed** From the State Capitals. School Financing, 0734-0907.
**Desc:** Reassessment programs, exemptions, incentives and collection methods.

JA
**FUKUOKA KOKUZEIKYOKU TOKEISHO.** **Main/Corp** Japan. Fukuoka Kokuzeikyoku. (19??)-. Periodical. Japanese. Fukuoka Kokuzeikyoku, 11-1 Hakataeki Higashi, 2-chome Hakata-ku, Fukuoka Japan. **LC** HJ77.Z5; K95a. **Continues** Zeimu Tokeisho.

●CN/1189-4296
**FUNDING OF EDUCATION IN ALBERTA, A SCHOOL FINANCE BROCHURE, THE.** See Education.

SP/0212-6591
**GACETA FISCAL : REVISTA MENSUAL DE ORIENTACION JURIDICO-TRIBUTARIA.** VFOAT Revista Mensual de Orientacion Juridico-Tributaria. (198?)-. Periodical. Spanish. Eleven times a year (monthly except Aug.). 30024ptas Spain; 42187ptas other. Gaceta Fiscal SA, Plaza de las Cortes 4-1, 28014 Madrid Spain. **Tel** 011 34 1 4292169. **LC** K7; .A25. **DD** 343.46/03/05; 344.603305.

IO
**GALANG / LEMBAGA STUDI PEMBANGUNAN.** V. 1, No. 1-. Periodical. Indonesian. Lembaga Studi Pembangunan, Gedung Arthaloka Lantai 17, JL Jenderal Sudirman 2, Jakarta Indonesia. **LC** HJ2348.5; .G35.

US
**GAMING REVENUE REPORT QUARTERLY.** (19??)-. English. Four times a year. $20.00. State Gaming Control Board, 1150 East William Street, Carson City NV 89710. **Tel** (702)687-6500. **Absorbed** Quarterly Report - State Gaming Control Board, 0195-4709.

UK
**GAMMIE & DE SOUZA LAND TAXATION UPDATES.** (1985)-. English. £210.00 Europe; £220.00 other. Sweet & Maxwell Ltd., South Quay Plaza, 183 Marsh Wall, London E14 9FT England. **Tel** 011 44 264 342899, FAX 011 44 264 342723, telex 929089 ITPINF G.

US
**GASOHOL TAX EXEMPTIONS.** 1st (1981)-. English. an. Department of Revenue / Washington, Olympia WA 98504. **LC** HD9399.U53; W23. **DD** 336.2/78662669.

SZ/0256-0119
**GATT FOCUS (ENGLISH ED.).** See Business-Commerce.

GW
**GEMEINDEERGEBNISSE DER FINANZSTATISTIK ... AUSGEWAHLTE EINNAHME UND AUSGABEARTEN, STEUERKRAFTZAHLEN, HEBESATZE, SCHULDENSTAND UND PERSONALSTAND.** VFOAT Gemeindeergebnisse der Finanzstatistik. German. Niedersachsisches Landesverwaltungsamt, Postfach 107, 3000 Hannover Germany. **Tel** (0511)108-9466. **LC** HJ9493.5.L6; G45. **Continues** Gemeindeergebnisse der Finanzstatistik ... Steuerkraft, Hebesatze, Steuereinnahmen, Allgemeine Finanzzuweisungen, Kreisumlageausgabe, Schuldenstand und Personalstand.

AT
**GENERAL LOAN AND CAPITAL WORKS FUND, ESTIMATES OF EXPENDITURE FOR THE YEAR ENDING 30TH JUNE ... .** **Main/Corp** Western Australia. (19??)-. English. an. **LC** HJ96; .C18a. **DD** 336.3/9/09941. **Continues** Western Australia. General Loan Fund, Estimates of Expenditure.

US/1051-6964
**GFOA NEWSLETTER.** [GFOA newsl.]. **Added/Corp** Government Finance Officers Association. Vol. 65, No. 7 (April 13, 1990)-. Newsletter. English. sm. Government Finance Officers Association, 180 North Michigan Avenue, Suite 800, Chicago IL 60601-7476. **Tel** (312)977-9700, FAX (312)977-4806. **DD** 352. **Continues** Newsletter / Government Finance Officers Association, 1047-0247.

IT
**GIURISPRUDENZA DELLE IMPOSTE : RASSEGNA DELLE DECISIONI DI MASSIMA DELLA CORTE DI CASSAZIONE E DELLA COMMISSIONE CENTRALE DELLE IMPOSTE ... / ASSOCIAZIONE FRA LE SOCIETA ITALIANE PER AZIONI.** See Law.

CK
**GOBIERNOS DEPARTAMENTALES : EJECUCION PRESUPUESTAL.** **Main/Corp** Colombia. Contraloria General de la Republica. Division de Control Interno y Analisis Financiero. 1st. Semester 1971-. Spanish. Contraloria General de la Republica, Carrera Calle 8, Bogota Colombia. **LC** HJ34; .B15. **DD** 354/.861/00722.

NZ/0112-9392
**GOODS AND SERVICES TAX LEGISLATION.** [Goods serv. tax legis.]. VFOAT New Zealand Goods & Services Tax Legislation. (1986)-. English. an. 585.00Aus$. CCH Australia Ltd, PO Box 230, North Ryde New South Wales, 2113 Australia. **Tel** 011 61 02 888 2555, FAX 011 61 02 888 7324. **DD** 343.931055.
**Desc:** A reference source for those who need accurate and up-to-date information about developments in the field of goods and services tax.

RU
**GOSUDARSTVENNYI BIUDZHET SSSR.** **Added/Corp** Soviet Union. Ministerstvo Finansov. Soviet Union. Svodnyi Otdel Gosudarstvennogo Biudzheta.

(19??)-. Russian. an. Izdatelstvo Finansy I Statistika, Ulitsa Chernyshvskogo 7, K-142, 101000 Moscow Russia. **LC** HJ2130; .S68.

CN
**GOUVERNEMENT DU QUEBEC : PUBLIC ACCOUNTS.** **Main/Corp** Quebec (Province). Ministere des Finances. English. an. Editeur Officiel du Quebec, 1283 Boul Charest Ouest, Quebec Quebec G1N 2C9 Canada. **LC** HJ9921.Z9; Q834A. **DD** 354.7140072/31.

US/1057-0675
**GOVERNING FLORIDA.** (GOVERNING FLORIDA : ANALYSIS OF GOVERNMENT AND POLITICS IN THE SUNSHINE STATE.). [Gov. Fla.]. **Added/Corp** Florida State University. College of Social Sciences. Vol. 1, No. 1 (Winter 1990)-. Periodical. English. qt. Policy Sciences Program, Florida State University, Tallahassee FL 32306. **Tel** (904)644-3848. **LC** JK4001; .G68. **DD** 975.9/063/05. ***Formed by the union of*** *Florida Policy Review* ***and*** *Florida Public Opinion.*

US/0883-1483
**GOVERNMENT ACCOUNTANTS JOURNAL, THE.** **See** Business-Accounting.

CN/0842-4810
**GOVERNMENT ESTIMATES.** [Gov. estim.]. **Main/Corp** Alberta. (1985/86)-. English. an. Alberta Treasury, 407 Legislative Building, Edmonton Alberta T5K 2B6 Canada. **LC** HJ13.A715H. **DD** 354.71230072/2253/05. ***Continues*** *Estimates of Expenditure ... Government Estimates, 0828-1092.*

US/0883-7856
**GOVERNMENT FINANCE REVIEW.** [Gov. finance rev.]. **Added/Corp** Government Finance Officers Association. Vol. 1 No. 1 (April 1985)-. Periodical. English. bm. $50.00. Government Finance Officers Association, 180 North Michigan Avenue, Suite 800, Chicago IL 60601-7476. **Tel** (312)977-9700, FAX (312)977-4806. **ED** Barbara Weiss and Karen Utterback. **LC** HJ9103; .M782. **DD** 336.73. Index available. **Bk Rev. Ad Acc. Circ:** 13,000. Documents available from UMI Article Clearinghouse. ***Formed by the union of*** *Governmental Finance, 0091-4835* ***and*** *Government Financial Management Resources in Review, 0272-6823.*
**Ind/Abst** ABC POL SCI; ABI/INFORM Glob. Ed.; ABI Inform Ondisc (May 1972-); Acad. Search (July 1993-); Account. Tax Datab. (May 1972-); Account. Art.; Bus. ASAP (1992-) [Full Txt.]; Bus. Index (1985-); Bus. Period. Index; Bus. Source (Jul. 1993-); Gen. BusinessFile (1985-); Gen. Period. Index (1985-); INFO-SOUTH Abstr.; J. Plan. Lit.; Mag. Search; PAIS Int. Print; Sage Public Adm. Abstr.; Sage Race Relat. Abstr.; Sage Urban Stud. Abstr; Urban Aff. Abstr.; Wilson Bus. Abstr.

AT/1031-7104
**GOVERNMENT FINANCE STATISTICS, AUSTRALIA.** **See** Public Administration-Abstracting, Bibliographies and Statistics.

PP
**GOVERNMENT FINANCE STATISTICS / NATIONAL STATISTICAL OFFICE.** Statistical Publication. English. ir. k3.00 Papua New Guinea; k3.50 (surface mail); k5.00 (airmail) other. National Statistical Office, PO Wards Strip NCO, Papua New Guinea. **Tel** 011 675 27182 271172, FAX 011 657 255057, telex FINANCE NE 22312. **LC** HJ98.4; .A15. **DD** 336.953/05.

US/0250-7374
**GOVERNMENT FINANCE STATISTICS YEARBOOK.** **See** Public Administration-Abstracting, Bibliographies and Statistics.

US
**GOVERNMENT FINANCES IN .... .** **Added/Corp** United States. Bureau of the Census. (1985/86)-. Government Publication. English. an. Superintendent of Documents, US Government Printing Office, Washington DC 20402. **Tel** (202)275-3328, FAX (202)786-2377. ***Continues*** *Governmental Finances in ..., 0095-3741.*
**Ind/Abst** Predicasts Forecasts.

DK
**GOVERNMENT FINANCES IN DENMARK.** **Main/Corp** Denmark. English. Ministry of Finance / Denmark, Department of the Budget, Christiansborg Slotsplads 1, Dk-1218 Copenhagen K Denmark. **LC** HJ56; .A194A. **DD** 336.489.

AT
**GOVERNMENT FINANCIAL ESTIMATES: AUSTRALIA.** **Main/Corp** Australian Bureau of Statistics. (1980)-. English. an (Nov.). 30.00Aus$. Australian Bureau of Statistics, PO Box 10, Belconnen Australian Capital Territory, 2616 Australia. **Tel** 011 61 6 2527911, FAX 011 61 6 2516009. **LC** HJ90; .A53a. **DD** 354.940072/225/05. ***Continues*** *Australian Bureau of Statistics. Public Authority Finance, Public Authority Estimates.*
**Desc:** Shows state government budget estimates and similar forward estimates for state authorities outside the budget sectors and local authorities; compiled in accordance with national accounting concepts.

US/0199-1744
**GOVERNMENT FINANCIAL MANAGEMENT TOPICS.** (19??)-. Periodical. English. mo. Association of Government Accountants, 2200 Mount Vernon Avenue, Alexandria VA 22301. **Tel** (703)684-6931.

US
**GOVERNMENTAL FINANCE.** **Main/Corp** United States. Bureau of the Census. May 1965-. Government Publication. English. an. US Department of Commerce / Bureau of the Census, Data User Services Division, Customer Services, Washington DC 20233-0800. **Tel** (301)763-4100. **(Subscription address:** Superintendent of Documents, US Government Printing Office, Washington DC 20402.**)** ***Continues*** *Governmental Finances in the United States.*

US/0097-868X
**GOVERNMENTAL FINANCES AND EMPLOYMENT AT A GLANCE.** **Main/Corp** United States. Bureau of the Census. Government Publication. English. US Department of Commerce / Bureau of the Census, Data User Services Division, Customer Services, Washington DC 20233-0800. **Tel** (301)763-4100. **(Subscription address:** Superintendent of Documents, US Government Printing Office, Washington DC 20402.**)** **LC** HJ257.2; .U45C. **DD** 336.73.

UK
**GOVERNMENT'S EXPENDITURE PLANS / PRESENTED TO PARLIAMENT BY THE CHANCELLOR OF THE EXCHEQUER BY COMMAND OF HER MAJESTY, THE.** **Main/Corp** Great Britain. Treasury. (19??)-. Government Publication. English. an. £175.00. Her Majesty's Stationery Office, 51 Nine Elms Lane, London SW8 5DR England. **Tel** 011 44 71 873 8459, 011 44 71 873 8499, FAX 011 44 71 873 8499, 011 44 71 873 8456, telex 297138. **(Subscription address:** Her Majesty's Stationery Office, PO Box 276, Publications Centre, London SW8 5DT England.**)** **LC** HJ2096; G7a. **DD** 336.3/9/0941.

US/0883-3753
**GOVERNMENTS OF ALABAMA.** [Gov. Ala.]. 1983-. English. an. $150.00. Municipal Analysis Services Inc, PO Box 13453, Austin TX 78711-3453. **Tel** (512)327-3328. **ED** Greg Michels. **DD** 330. Index available. cum. index. **Bk Rev. Ad Acc. Circ:** 3,000.
**Desc:** Review and comparison of 650 details of each taxing authority in the state of Alabama.

US/0883-3761
**GOVERNMENTS OF ARKANSAS.** [Gov. Ark.]. **Added/Corp** Municipal Analysis Services. (1983)-. Periodical. English. an. $150.00 (one year), $250.00 (two year). Municipal Analysis Services Inc, PO Box 13453, Austin TX 78711-3453. **Tel** (512)327-3328. **ED** Greg Michels. **DD** 330. Index available. cum. index. **Bk Rev. Ad Acc. Circ:** 3,000.
**Desc:** Review and comparison of details of each taxing authority in the state of Arkansas.

US/0883-377X
**GOVERNMENTS OF CALIFORNIA.** [Gov. Calif.]. 1983-. English. an. $150.00. Municipal Analysis Services Inc, PO Box 13453, Austin TX 78711-3453. **Tel** (512)327-3328. **ED** Greg Michels. **DD** 330. Index available. cum. index. **Ad Acc. Circ:** 3,000.
**Desc:** Review and comparison of 650 details of each taxing authority in the state of California.

US/0883-3788
**GOVERNMENTS OF COLORADO.** [Gov. Colo.]. 1983-. English. an. $150.00. Municipal Analysis Services Inc, PO Box 13453, Austin TX 78711-3453. **Tel** (512)327-3328. **ED** Greg Michels. **DD** 330. Index available. cum. index. **Ad Acc. Circ:** 3,000.
**Desc:** Review and comparison of 650 details of each taxing authority of the state of Colorado.

US/0883-3796
**GOVERNMENTS OF CONNECTICUT.** [Gov. Conn.]. 1983-. English. an. $150.00. Municipal Analysis Services Inc, PO Box 13453, Austin TX 78711-3453. **Tel** (512)327-3328. **ED** Greg Michels. **DD** 330. Index available. cum. index. **Ad Acc. Circ:** 3,000.
**Desc:** Review and comparison of 650 details of each taxing authority in the state of Connecticut.

US/0883-380X
**GOVERNMENTS OF FLORIDA.** [Gov. Fla.]. **Added/Corp** Municipal Analysis Services, Inc. (1983)-. English. an (Feb.). $150.00 one year. Municipal Analysis Services Inc, PO Box 13453, Austin TX 78711-3453. **Tel** (512)327-3328. **ED** Greg Michels. **DD** 330. Index available. cum. index. **Ad Acc. Circ:** 3,000.
**Desc:** Review and comparison of 650 details of each taxing authority in the state of Florida.

US/0883-3818
**GOVERNMENTS OF GEORGIA.** [Gov. Ga.]. 1983-. English. an. $150.00. Municipal Analysis Services Inc, PO Box 13453, Austin TX 78711-3453. **Tel** (512)327-3328. **ED** Greg Michels. **DD** 330. Index available. cum. index. **Bk Rev. Ad Acc. Circ:** 3,000.
**Desc:** Review and comparison of 650 details of each taxing authority in the state of Georgia.

US/0883-3826
**GOVERNMENTS OF ILLINOIS.** [Gov. Ill.]. 1983-. English. an. $150.00. Municipal Analysis Services Inc, PO Box 13453, Austin TX 78711-3453. **Tel** (512)327-3328. **ED** Greg Michels. **DD** 330. Index available. cum. index. **Bk Rev. Ad Acc. Circ:** 3,000 (ctrl).
**Desc:** Review and comparison of 650 details of each taxing authority in the state of Illinois.

US/0883-3834
**GOVERNMENTS OF INDIANA.** [Gov. Indiana]. 1983-. English. an. $150.00. Municipal Analysis Services Inc, PO Box 13453, Austin TX 78711-3453. **Tel** (512)327-3328. **ED** Greg Michels. **DD** 330. Index available. cum. index. **Bk Rev. Ad Acc. Circ:** 3,000.
**Desc:** Review and comparison of 650 details of each taxing authority in the state of Indiana.

US/0883-3842
**GOVERNMENTS OF IOWA.** [Gov. Iowa]. 1983-. English. an. $150.00. Municipal Analysis Services Inc, PO Box 13453, Austin TX 78711-3453. **Tel** (512)327-3328. **ED** Greg Michels. **DD** 330. Index available. cum. index. **Bk Rev. Ad Acc. Circ:** 3,000.
**Desc:** Review and comparison of 650 details of each taxing authority in the state of Iowa.

US/0883-3850
**GOVERNMENTS OF KANSAS.** [Gov. Kans.]. 1983-. English. an. $150.00. Municipal Analysis Services Inc, PO Box 13453, Austin TX 78711-3453. **Tel** (512)327-3328. **ED** Greg Michels. **DD** 330. Index available. cum. index. **Bk Rev. Ad Acc. Circ:** 3,000.
**Desc:** Review and comparison of 650 details of each taxing authority in the state of Kansas.

US/0883-3869
**GOVERNMENTS OF KENTUCKY.** [Gov. Ky.]. 1983-. English. an. $150.00. Municipal Analysis Services Inc, PO Box 13453, Austin TX 78711-3453. **Tel** (512)327-3328. **DD** 330. Index available. cum. index. **Ad Acc. Circ:** 3,000.
**Desc:** Review and comparison of 650 details of each taxing authority in the state of Kentucky.

US/0883-3877
**GOVERNMENTS OF LOUISIANA.** [Gov. La.]. 1983-. English. an. $150.00. Municipal Analysis Services Inc, PO Box 13453, Austin TX 78711-3453. **Tel** (512)327-3328. **ED** Greg Michels. **DD** 330. Index available. cum. index. **Ad Acc. Circ:** 3,000.
**Desc:** Review and comparison of 650 details of each taxing authority in the state of Louisiana.

US/0883-3885
**GOVERNMENTS OF MAINE.** [Gov. Maine]. 1983-. English. an. $150.00. Municipal Analysis Services Inc, PO Box 13453, Austin TX 78711-3453. **Tel** (512)327-3328. **ED** Greg Michels. **DD** 330. Index available. cum. index. **Ad Acc. Circ:** 3,000.
**Desc:** Review and comparison of 650 details of each taxing authority in the state of Maine.

US/0883-3893
**GOVERNMENTS OF MASSACHUSETTS.** [Gov. Mass.]. 1983-. English. an. $150.00. Municipal Analysis Services Inc, PO Box 13453, Austin TX 78711-3453. **Tel** (512)327-3328. **ED** Greg Michels. **DD** 330. Index available. cum. index. **Ad Acc. Circ:** 3,000.
**Desc:** Review and comparison of 650 details of each taxing authority in the state of Massachusetts.

US/0883-3907
**GOVERNMENTS OF MICHIGAN.** [Gov. Mich.]. 1983-. English. an. $150.00. Municipal Analysis Services Inc, PO Box 13453, Austin TX 78711-3453. **Tel** (512)327-3328. **ED** Greg Michels. **DD** 330. Index available. cum. index. **Ad Acc. Circ:** 3,000.
**Desc:** Review and comparison of 650 details of each taxing authority in the state of Michigan.

US/0883-3915
**GOVERNMENTS OF MINNESOTA.** [Gov. Minn.]. 1983-. English. an. $150.00. Municipal Analysis Services Inc, PO Box 13453, Austin TX 78711-3453. **Tel** (512)327-3328. **ED** Greg Michels. **DD** 330. Index available. cum. index. **Ad Acc. Circ:** 3,000.
**Desc:** Review and comparison of 650 details of each taxing authority in the state of Minnesota.

US/0883-3923
**GOVERNMENTS OF MISSISSIPPI.** [Gov. Miss.]. 1983-. English. an. $150.00. Municipal Analysis Services Inc, PO Box 13453, Austin TX 78711-3453. **Tel** (512)327-3328. **ED** Greg Michels. **DD** 330. Index available. cum. index. **Ad Acc. Circ:** 3,000.
**Desc:** Review and comparison of 650 details of each taxing authority in the state of Mississippi.

US/0883-3931
**GOVERNMENTS OF MISSOURI.** (GOVERNMENTS OF MISSOURI : ANNUAL FINANCIAL AND EMPLOYEE ANALYSIS.). [Gov. Mo.]. **Added/Corp**

# Public Administration —Public Finance and Taxation

Municipal Analysis Services. (1983)-. English. an (Feb.). $150.00. Municipal Analysis Services Inc, PO Box 13453, Austin TX 78711-3453. **Tel** (512)327-3328. **ED** Greg Michels. **DD** 330. **Ad Acc. Circ:** 3,000.
**Desc:** Review and comparison of 650 details of each taxing authority in the state of Missouri.

US/0883-3958
## GOVERNMENTS OF NEW JERSEY. [Gov. N.J.]. 1983-. English. an. $150.00. Municipal Analysis Services Inc, PO Box 13453, Austin TX 78711-3453. **Tel** (512)327-3328. **ED** Greg Michels. **DD** 330. Index available. cum. index. **Ad Acc. Circ:** 3,000.
**Desc:** Review and comparison of 650 details of each taxing authority in the state of New Jersey.

US/0883-3966
## GOVERNMENTS OF NEW YORK. [Gov. N.Y.]. 1983-. English. an. $150.00. Municipal Analysis Services Inc, PO Box 13453, Austin TX 78711-3453. **Tel** (512)327-3328. **ED** Greg Michels. **DD** 330. Index available. cum. index. **Ad Acc. Circ:** 3,000.
**Desc:** Review and comparison of 650 details of each taxing authority in the state of New York

US/0883-3974
## GOVERNMENTS OF NORTH DAKOTA. [Gov. N.D.]. 1983-. English. an. $150.00. Municipal Analysis Services Inc, PO Box 13453, Austin TX 78711-3453. **Tel** (512)327-3328. **ED** Greg Michels. **DD** 330. Index available. cum. index. **Ad Acc. Circ:** 3,000.
**Desc:** Review and comparison of 650 details of each taxing authority in the state of North Dakota.

US/0883-3982
## GOVERNMENTS OF OHIO. [Gov. Ohio]. 1983-. English. an. $150.00. Municipal Analysis Services Inc, PO Box 13453, Austin TX 78711-3453. **Tel** (512)327-3328. **ED** Greg Michels. **DD** 330. Index available. cum. index. **Ad Acc. Circ:** 3,000.
**Desc:** Review and comparison of 650 details of each taxing authority in the state of Ohio.

US/0883-3990
## GOVERNMENTS OF OKLAHOMA. [Gov. Okla.]. 1983-. English. an. $150.00. Municipal Analysis Services Inc, PO Box 13453, Austin TX 78711-3453. **Tel** (512)327-3328. **ED** Greg Michels. **DD** 330. Index available. cum. index. **Ad Acc. Circ:** 3,000.
**Desc:** Review and comparison of 650 details of each taxing authority in the state of Oklahoma.

US/0883-4008
## GOVERNMENTS OF PENNSYLVANIA. [Gov. Pa.]. **Added/Corp** Municipal Analysis Services. (1983)-. English. an. $150.00. Municipal Analysis Services Inc, PO Box 13453, Austin TX 78711-3453. **Tel** (512)327-3328. **ED** Greg Michels. **DD** 330. Index available. cum. index. **Ad Acc. Circ:** 3,000.
**Desc:** Review and comparison of 650 details of each taxing authority in the state of Pennsylvania.

US/0883-4016
## GOVERNMENTS OF SOUTH DAKOTA. [Gov. S.D.]. 1983-. English. an. $150.00. Municipal Analysis Services Inc, PO Box 13453, Austin TX 78711-3453. **Tel** (512)327-3328. **ED** Greg Michels. **DD** 330. Index available. cum. index. **Ad Acc. Circ:** 3,000.
**Desc:** Review and comparison of 650 details of each taxing authority in the state of South Dakota.

US/0883-4024
## GOVERNMENTS OF TENNESSEE. [Gov. Tenn.]. 1983-. English. an. $150.00. Municipal Analysis Services Inc, PO Box 13453, Austin TX 78711-3453. **Tel** (512)327-3328. **ED** Greg Michels. **DD** 330. Index available. cum. index. **Ad Acc. Circ:** 3,000.
**Desc:** Review and comparison of 650 details of each taxing authority in the state of Tennessee.

US/0883-4032
## GOVERNMENTS OF TEXAS. [Gov. Tex.]. 1983-. English. an. $150.00. Municipal Analysis Services Inc, PO Box 13453, Austin TX 78711-3453. **Tel** (512)327-3328. **ED** Greg Michels. **LC** HJ9011.T4; G68. **DD** 336/.014/764. Index available. cum. index. **Ad Acc. Circ:** 3,000.
**Desc:** Review and comparison of 650 details of each taxing authority in the state of Texas.

US/0883-4091
## GOVERNMENTS OF THE CAROLINAS. [Gov. Carol.]. 1983-. English. an. $150.00. Municipal Analysis Services Inc, PO Box 13453, Austin TX 78711-3453. **Tel** (512)327-3328. **ED** Greg Michels. **DD** 330. Index available. cum. index. **Ad Acc. Circ:** 3,000.
**Desc:** Review and comparison of 650 details of each taxing authority in the Carolinas.

US/0883-4121
## GOVERNMENTS OF THE NORTHEAST. [Gov. Northeast]. 1983-. English. an. $150.00. Municipal Analysis Services Inc, PO Box 13453, Austin TX 78711-3453. **Tel** (512)327-3328. **ED** Greg Michels. **DD** 330. Index available. cum. index. **Ad Acc. Circ:** 3,000.
**Desc:** Review and comparison of 650 details of each taxing authority in the Northeast.

US/0883-4105
## GOVERNMENTS OF THE NORTHWEST. [Gov. Northwest]. 1983-. English. an. $150.00. Municipal Analysis Services Inc, PO Box 13453, Austin TX 78711-3453. **Tel** (512)327-3328. **ED** Greg Michels. **DD** 330. Index available. cum. index. **Ad Acc. Circ:** 3,000.
**Desc:** Review and comparison of 650 details of each taxing authority in the Northwest.

US/0883-4113
## GOVERNMENTS OF THE WEST. [Gov. West]. 1983-. English. an. $150.00. Municipal Analysis Services Inc, PO Box 13453, Austin TX 78711-3453. **Tel** (512)327-3328. **ED** Greg Michels. **DD** 330. Index available. cum. index. **Ad Acc. Circ:** 3,000.
**Desc:** Review and comparison of 650 details of each taxing authority in the West.

US/0883-4040
## GOVERNMENTS OF VERMONT. (GOVERNMENTS OF VERMONT / MUNICIPAL ANALYSIS SERVICES, INC.). [Gov. Vt.]. **Added/Corp** Municipal Analysis Services. (1983)-. English. an. $150.00. Municipal Analysis Services Inc, PO Box 13453, Austin TX 78711-3453. **Tel** (512)327-3328. **ED** Greg Michels. **DD** 330. Index available. cum. index. **Ad Acc. Circ:** 3,000.
**Desc:** Review and comparison of 650 details of each taxing authority in the state of Vermont.

US/0883-4059
## GOVERNMENTS OF VIRGINIA. [Gov. Va.]. 1983-. English. an. $150.00. Municipal Analysis Services Inc, PO Box 13453, Austin TX 78711-3453. **Tel** (512)327-3328. **ED** Greg Michels. **DD** 330. Index available. cum. index. **Ad Acc. Circ:** 3,000.
**Desc:** Review and comparison of 650 details of each taxing authority in the state of Virginia.

US/0883-4067
## GOVERNMENTS OF WASHINGTON. [Gov. Wash.]. 1983-. English. an. $150.00. Municipal Analysis Services Inc, PO Box 13453, Austin TX 78711-3453. **Tel** (512)327-3328. **ED** Greg Michels. **DD** 330. Index available. cum. index. **Ad Acc. Circ:** 3,000.
**Desc:** Review and comparison of 650 details of each taxing authority of the state of Washington.

US/0883-4075
## GOVERNMENTS OF WEST VIRGINIA. [Gov. W. Va.]. 1983-. English. an. $150.00. Municipal Analysis Services Inc, PO Box 13453, Austin TX 78711-3453. **Tel** (512)327-3328. **ED** Greg Michels. **DD** 330. Index available. cum. index. **Ad Acc. Circ:** 3,000.
**Desc:** Review and comparison of 650 details of each taxing authority in the state of West Virginia.

US/0883-4083
## GOVERNMENTS OF WISCONSIN. [Gov. Wis.]. **Added/Corp** Municipal Analysis Services, Inc. (1983)-. English. an. $150.00. Municipal Analysis Services Inc, PO Box 13453, Austin TX 78711-3453. **Tel** (512)327-3328. **ED** Greg Michels. **LC** HJ9011.W6; G68. **DD** 336/.014775. Index available. cum. index. **Ad Acc. Circ:** 3,000.
**Desc:** Review and comparison of 650 details of each taxing authority in Wisconsin.

US
## GOVERNMENTS QUARTERLY REPORT. GT, PRELIMINARY QUARTERLY SUMMARY OF STATE TAX REVENUE. **VFOAT** Preliminary Quarterly Summary of State Tax Revenue. Began with Jan./March 1975. Government Publication. English. qt. Included in Subscription to Quarterly Summary of State and Local Tax Revenue. US Department of Commerce, 14th Street & Constitution Avenue NW, Washington DC 20230. **Tel** (202)482-2000, FAX (202)482-3772. Documents available from Documents on Demand.
**Ind/Abst** Am. Stat. Index.

US
## GOVERNOR'S BUDGET. **Main/Corp** Colorado. Governor. **Added/Corp** Colorado. Office of State Planning and Budgeting. English. Executive Chambers, 136 State Capitol, Denver CO 80203. **Continues** Executive Budget Recommendations.

US
## GOVERNOR'S BUDGET - CALIFORNIA. **Main/Corp** California. Governor. 1971/72-. English. an. **LC** HJ11; .C23425A. **DD** 353.97940072/252/05. **Formed by the union of** Capitol Outlay Budget Submitted to the California Legislature **and** Support and Local Assistance Budget Submitted to the California Legislature.

US
## GOVERNOR'S ... BUDGET IN-BRIEF. **Main/Corp** Connecticut. Governor. **VFOAT** Governor's ... Budget in Brief. English. **LC** HJ11; .C8465B. **DD** 353.97460072/256/05.

●US
## GOVERNOR'S BUDGET REPORT, PREPARED BY THE DIVISION OF THE BUDGET, THE. **Main/Corp** Kansas. Division of the Budget. **Added/Corp** Kansas. Governor. (1992)-. English. **Continues** State of Kansas Budget.

US
## GOVERNOR'S BUDGET REPORT - SOUTH DAKOTA. **Title Change. Main/Corp** South Dakota. Governor. July 1, 1967 to June 30, 1969-. English. an. South Dakota Executive Office, 500 East Capitol, Pierre SD 57501. **LC** HJ11; .S8445A. **DD** 353.97830072/22/05. **Continued by** State of South Dakota Governor's Budget.

US
## GOVERNOR'S LEGISLATIVE MESSAGE AND BUDGET REPORT, THE. **See** Public Administration.

●US
## GOVERNOR'S PROPOSED ... OPERATING BUDGET SUPPORTING DATA, STATEWIDE SUMMARY TABLES. **Main/Corp** Washington (State). Governor. **Added/Corp** Washington (State). Office of Financial Management. **VFOAT** Budget Summaries; Operating Budget Supporting Data, Statewide Summary Tables. (1995)-. English. be. **LC** IN PROCESS. **Continues** Washington (State). Governor. Governor's Proposed Supporting Data and ... Operating Budget.

US
## GOVERNOR'S PROPOSED SUPPORTING DATA AND ... OPERATING BUDGET. **Title Change. Main/Corp** Washington (State). Governor. **Added/Corp** Washington (State). Office of Financial Management. **VFOAT** Supporting Data and ... Operating Budget. (1993)-(1993). English. be. **LC** HJ11; .W246. **Continues** Washington (State). Governor. Current Law Operating Budget. **Continued by** Washington (State). Governor. Governor's Proposed ... Operating Budget Supporting Data, Statewide Summary Tables.

US
## GOVERNOR'S STATE OF THE STATE MESSAGE AND BUDGET SUMMARY. **Main/Corp** North Carolina. Division of State Budget. 1977/79-. English. North Carolina Department of Administration, 431 North Sailsbury Street, Raleigh NC 27603. **Tel** (919)733-3514, (919)733-1110. **LC** HJ11; .N848A. **DD** 353.9/756/00722. **Continues** State of North Carolina Budget Summary.

US/0893-9128
## GRANT PROPOSAL NEWS. [Grant propos. news]. Periodical. English. sm. $170.00. Grants Administration News, 5825 Sky Park Drive, Plano TX 75093. **Tel** (214)447-0519. **ED** R T Grant. **DD** 001. **Circ:** 200 (ctrl).

US/1055-596X
## GRANT UPDATE! FOR GUIDE TO FEDERAL FUNDING FOR GOVERNMENTS & NONPROFITS. [Grant update, Guide fed. fund gov. nonprofits]. **VFOAT** Grant Update. Vol. 13, No. 1 (Jan. 1991)-. Periodical. English. mo. Government Information Services / Virginia, 4301 North Fairfax Drive, Suite 875, Arlington VA 22203. **Tel** (703)528-1082, FAX (703)528-6060, telex RCA 263591 GIS UR. **DD** 353. **Continues** Grant Update!.

UK
## GREATER LONDON COUNCIL, INNER LONDON EDUCATION AUTHORITY REPORT ON ACCOUNTS. **Main/Corp** Greater London Council. **VFOAT** Greater London Council Report on Accounts. English. Greater London Council, The County Hall, London SE1 7PB England. **Tel** (01)633-7139. **LC** HJ9438.L5; G72C. **DD** 352.1/71/09421.

II
## GRHA VIBHAGANUM ANDAJAPATRA. BUDGET ESTIMATES OF HOME DEPARTMENT. **Title Change. Main/Corp** Gujarat (India). Home Dept. **Added/Corp** Gujarat (India). Home Dept. Budget Estimates of Home Department. **VFOAT** Budget Estimates of Home Department. (19??)-(19??). Multiple languages (English and Gujarati). an. **LC** HJ66.G8; B195a. **DD** 354/.54/75008. **Continued by** Budget Estimates of Home Department for ... .

SW
## GTM, GENERALTULLSTYRELSENS MEDDELANDEN. **Main/Corp** Sweden. Generaltullstyrelsen. Periodical. Swedish. ir. 55.00. Liber Distribution, Prenumerationsorder, Forlagsorder 162 89, Stockholm Sweden. **LC** HJ6981; .A2752A.

# Public Administration — Public Finance and Taxation

AG
**GUIA PRACTICA DEL EXPORTADOR E IMPORTADOR Y PARA TODO HOMBRE DE NEGOCIOS. SUPLEMENTO.** See Business-Commerce.

FR
**GUIDE BUDGETAIRE COMMUNAL, DEPARTEMENTAL ET REGIONAL.** **Added/Corp** France. Bureau des Budgets Locaux. **VFOAT** Guide Budgetaire. French. 60.00F. Documentation Francaise, 29 Quai Voltaire, 75344 Paris Cedex 7 France. **Tel** 011 33 1 40157000, FAX 011 33 1 40157230, telex 204 826 DOCFRAN. **LC** HJ9047; .A483. **DD** 352.1/2/0944. *Continues Guide Budgetaire Communal et Departemental.*

FR
**GUIDE DES RATIOS DES COMMUNES DE PLUS DE 10 000 HABITANTS / MINISTERE DE L'INTERIEUR, DIRECTION GENERALE DES COLLECTIVITES LOCALES, MISSION D'ETUDES ET DE STATISTIQUES.** Began with 1973 Vol. French. an. 30F. Documentation Francaise, 29 Quai Voltaire, 75344 Paris Cedex 7 France. **Tel** 011 33 1 40157000, FAX 011 33 1 40157230, telex 204 826 DOCFRAN. **LC** HJ9047; .A485. **DD** 336/.014/44. *Continues Methode d'Analyse Financiere des Budgets Communaux par les Ratios et les Indices.*

CN/0710-8915
**GUIDE D'IMPOT SUR LE REVENU DES AGRICULTEURS.** [Guide impot revenu agric.]. French. an. Revenue Canada Impot, 875 Heron Road, Ottawa Ontario K1A 0L8 Canada. **DD** 336.2/7863/0971. *Continues in part Impot (Canada). Guide d'Impot des Agriculteurs et Pecheurs, 0700-1649.*

FR
**GUIDE STATISTIQUE DE LA FISCALITE DIRECTE LOCALE / MINISTERE DE L'INTERIEUR ET DE LA DECENTRALISATION, DIRECTION GENERALE LOCALES, MISSION D'ETUDES ET DESTATISTIQUES.** See Public Administration-Abstracting, Bibliographies and Statistics.

US/0278-5064
**GUIDE TO FEDERAL ASSISTANCE. NEWSLETTER, THE.** [Guide fed. assist., Newsl.]. (1966)-. Newsletter. English. Twelve times a year. $450.00 first class mail; $425.00 surface mail. Wellborn Associates Inc., PO Box 11369, Rock Hill SC 29731. **Tel** (803)324-8626, FAX (803)324-8626. **ED** Jennifer M. Wellborn. **DD** 353. Index available. ctrl circ. *Continues Guide to Federal Assistance for Education.*
**Desc:** Describes the funding programs administered by all Federal departments and agencies. They range from agriculture to White House Fellows and include research, training, curriculum development, model programs and student financial aid.

US
**GUIDE TO INCOME TAX PREPARATION.** **Added/Corp** Consumers Reports Books. Consumers Union of United States. **VFOAT** Consumer Reports Books Guide to Income Tax Preparation. (1988)-. English. Consumer Reports Books, 9180 Le Saint Drive, Fairfield OH 45014. **Tel** (800)272-0722.

JA/0072-8551
**GUIDE TO JAPANESE TAXES.** (1965)-. Periodical. Multiple languages (English). an. $110.00. **(Subscription address:** Maruzen Company Ltd., PO Box 5050, Import & Export Department, Tokyo 100 31 Japan.**)** **ED** Taizo Hayashi.

US
**GUIDE TO PROGRAMS / NATIONAL SCIENCE FOUNDATION.** See Science and Technology.

US
**GUIDE TO TAXATION, PUBLIC FINANCE AND RELATED LITERATURE.** V. 1-. English. an. 1156 15th Street NW, Washington DC 20005. **LC** Z7165.U5. **DD** 016.33673.

●US/1064-7732
**GUIDE TO TEXAS FRANCHISE TAX.** See Law.

●NE
**GUIDE TO THE EUROPEAN VAT DIRECTIVES: COMMENTARY ON THE VALUE ADDED TAX OF THE EUROPEAN COMMUNITY.** (1993)-. English. Four times a year. $860.00. International Bureau of Fiscal Documentation - IBFD Publications, PO Box 20237, 1000 HE Amsterdam The Netherlands. **Tel** 011 31 20-6267726, FAX 011 31 20-6228658, telex 13217 INTAX NL. **(Subscription address:** IBFD / International Bureau of Fiscal Documentation USA, Inc., 24 Hudson Street, Kinderhook NY 12106.**)**
**Desc:** Provides comprehensive coverage of all aspects of the European Community's Directives on VAT.

US/0730-9511
**GUIDE TO THE FEDERAL BUDGET, THE.** (THE GUIDE TO THE FEDERAL BUDGET / STANLEY E. COLLENDER.). [Guide fed. budg.]. **Added/Corp** Urban Institute. Northeast-Midwest Institute (U.S.). **VFOAT** New Guide to the Federal Budget. (1983)-. English. an. $23.50. University Press of America, 4720 A Boston Way, Lanham MD 20706. **Tel** (301)459-3366, (800)462-6420. **LC** HJ2051; .G84. **DD** 353.0072/252/05.

US/0278-3576
**GUIDE TO U.S. TAXES FOR CITIZENS ABROAD.** **VFOAT** U.S. Expatriate Tax Guide. **VAT** Guide to United States Taxes for Citizens Abroad. Jan. 1978-. English. an. Ernst & Whinney International Operations, Citicorp Center, 153 East 53rd Street, New York NY 10022. **Tel** (212)888-9100. **ED** Robert H Sharpenberg. **LC** KF6445.Z9; G8. **DD** 343.7305/248/05; 347.303524805. **Circ:** 10,000 (ctrl). *Continues Guide to U.S. Taxes for U.S. Citizens Abroad, 0190-6879.*
**Desc:** Easy explanation of United States taxation of United States citizens overseas. Useful for personnel managers and international employees.

US/0093-8637
**GUIDEBOOK TO FLORIDA TAXES.** **Added/Corp** Commerce Clearing House. (19??)-. English. ir. Commerce Clearing House Inc., 4025 West Peterson Avenue, Chicago IL 60646-6085. **Tel** (312)583-8500, FAX (708)940-4600. **ED** A. E. Schechter. **LC** KFF470.A73; G8. **DD** 343/.759/0405.
**Desc:** Covers taxes within the state and includes the latest changes in tax laws.

US/0072-8888
**GUIDEBOOK TO NEW JERSEY TAXES.** **Main/Corp** Commerce Clearing House. (1969)-. English. an. Commerce Clearing House Inc., 4025 West Peterson Avenue, Chicago IL 60646-6085. **Tel** (312)583-8500, FAX (708)940-4600. **ED** A.E. Schechter. **LC** KFN5860.Z9; G8. **DD** 343.

US/0072-8896
**GUIDEBOOK TO NEW YORK TAXES.** [Guideb. N. Y. taxes]. **Added/Corp** Commerce Clearing House. (1965)-. English. an. $74.00 (quizzer and guidebook). Commerce Clearing House Inc., 4025 West Peterson Avenue, Chicago IL 60646-6085. **Tel** (312)583-8500, FAX (708)940-4600. **ED** A. E. Schechter. **LC** KFN5860.Z9; G8. **DD** 340. Each issue contains an index to its own contents (no volume index)--loose.
**Desc:** Prepared for use with New York Guidebook. This easy-to-use quizzer covers taxation within New York. Includes the latest changes in tax laws.

US/0091-4010
**GUIDEBOOK TO OHIO TAXES.** **Added/Corp** Commerce Clearing House. (19??)-. English. ir. $15.00. Arthur Andersen & Company, Special Project, Birmingham AL 35201. **ED** A. E. Schechter. **LC** KFO470.A73; G8. **DD** 343/.771/04.
**Desc:** Covers taxes within the state and includes the latest 1985 changes in tax laws down to press time.

US/0072-890X
**GUIDEBOOK TO PENNSYLVANIA TAXES.** **Main/Corp** Commerce Clearing House. (1965)-. English. an. $15.00. Commerce Clearing House Inc., 4025 West Peterson Avenue, Chicago IL 60646-6085. **Tel** (312)583-8500, FAX (708)940-4600. **ED** A. E. Schechter. **LC** KFP470.Z9; C6.
**Desc:** Covers taxes within the state and includes the latest changes in tax laws.

US/0093-8645
**GUIDEBOOK TO WISCONSIN TAXES.** **Added/Corp** Commerce Clearing House. (19??)-. Periodical. English. $15.00. Commerce Clearing House Inc., 4025 West Peterson Avenue, Chicago IL 60646-6085. **Tel** (312)583-8500, FAX (708)940-4600. **ED** A.E. Schechter. **LC** KFW2870.A73; G8. **DD** 343/.775/0405.
**Desc:** Covers taxes within the state and includes the latest 1985 changes in tax laws down to press time.

●NR
**GUIDELINES FOR THE ROLLING PLAN.** **Main/Corp** Nigeria. **Added/Corp** Nigeria. Ministry of Budget and Planning. Planning Office. Nigeria. National Rolling Plan. **VFOAT** Guidelines for the National Rolling Plan. (1990/1992)-. English. **LC** HC1055.A1; N48a. **DD** 338.9669/005.

NE/0072-8926
**GUIDES TO EUROPEAN TAXATION.** *Ceased.* (19??)-(199?). English. International Bureau of Fiscal Documentation - IBFD Publications, PO Box 20237, 1000 HE Amsterdam The Netherlands. **Tel** 011 31 20-6267726, FAX 011 31 20-6228658, telex 13217 INTAX NL.
**Desc:** Series of five (separately available) looseleaf volumes, designed as practical sources of reference to assist the international business executive and his financial and legal advisors in evaluating the tax aspects of doing business or contemplating new investments in Europe.

US/1054-9846
**H & R BLOCK ... INCOME TAX GUIDE.** [H&R Block income tax guide]. **Added/Corp** H & R Block. **VFOAT** H and R Block ... Income Tax Guide; H&R Block Income Tax Guide; A.Income tax guide. (1990)-. Periodical. English. an. $13.99. Prentice-Hall General Reference and Travel, 200 Old Tappan Road, Old Tappan NJ 07675. **Tel** (800)922-0579. **(Subscription address:** Simon and Schuster, 200 Old Tappan Road, Old Tappan NJ 07675.**)** **LC** KF6369.6; .H2. **DD** 343.7305/2; 347.30352. *Continues H & R Block ... Income Tax Workbook (1988).*

SP
**HACIENDA PUBLICA ESPANOLA.** Periodical. Spanish. **LC** HJ1244.
**Ind/Abst** PAIS Int. Print (1991-?).

CC
**HAI KUAN TUNG CHI.** **Added/Corp** China. Hai Kuan Tsung Shu. **VFOAT** Hai Kuan Tung Chi. (19??)-. Periodical. Chinese. qt. RMBY1.00. Hai Kuan Tung Chi Fa Hsing Tsu, Beijing, People's Republic of China. **Tel** 668981. **ED** Peng Yan-Sheng. **LC** HJ7071; .A17. **DD** 354.510072/46/05.
**Desc:** Statistical figures of China's imports and exports which are the actual shipment into or out of the territory of China.

NE
**HANDBOOK ON THE 1989 DOUBLE TAXATION CONVENTION BETWEEN THE FEDERAL REPUBLIC OF GERMANY AND THE UNITED STATES OF AMERICA.** (19??)-. English. Twice a year. $575.00. International Bureau of Fiscal Documentation - IBFD Publications, PO Box 20237, 1000 HE Amsterdam The Netherlands. **Tel** 011 31 20-6267726, FAX 011 31 20-6228658, telex 13217 INTAX NL. **(Subscription address:** IBFD / International Bureau of Fiscal Documentation USA, Inc., 24 Hudson Street, Kinderhook NY 12106.**)**

US/1066-0925
**HARMONIZED TARIFF SCHEDULE OF THE UNITED STATES.** (HARMONIZED TARIFF SCHEDULE OF THE UNITED STATES / UNITED STATES INTERNATIONAL TRADE COMMISSION.). [Harmon. tariff sched. U.S.]. **Main/Corp** United States. **Added/Corp** United States International Trade Commission. Office of Tariff Affairs and Trade Agreements. **VFOAT** HTS. 1st Ed. (1987)-. Government Publication. English. $66.00 domestic (priority); $82.50 other. Superintendent of Documents, US Government Printing Office, Washington DC 20402. **Tel** (202)275-3328, FAX (202)786-2377. **LC** KF6654.599; .U55. **DD** 343.7305/6; 347.30356. *Continues United States. Tariff Act of 1930. Title I, Tariff Schedules of the United States.*
**Desc:** Contains the legal text of the Schedules, as amended and modified, together with annotations prescribing statistical information to be supplied on customs forms.

UK
**HARRISONS INLAND REVENUE.** English. ir. £285.00. Longman Group Ltd., Fourth Avenue, Longman House, Harlow Essex CM19 5SR England. **Tel** 011 44 279 429655, FAX 011 44 279 431059, telex 81259.

UK
**HARRISON'S INLAND REVENUE. INDEX TO TAX CASES.** English. £220.00. Longman Group Ltd., Fourth Avenue, Longman House, Harlow Essex CM19 5SR England. **Tel** 011 44 279 429655, FAX 011 44 279 431059, telex 81259. **(Subscription address:** PO Box 11318, Birmingham AL 35202**)**

II
**HARYANA BUDGET AT A GLANCE.** **Main/Corp** Haryana. Finance Dept. English. Government of Haryana, Finance Department, Chandigarh India. **LC** HJ66.H3. **DD** 354.54/55.

●US
**HBJ MILLER COMPREHENSIVE GOVERNMENTAL GAAP GUIDE.** **Added/Corp** Harcourt Brace Jovanovich. **VFOAT** Harcourt Brace Jovanovich Miller Comprehensive Governmental Generally Accepted Accounting Principles guide; Comprehensive Governmental GAAP Guide; GAAP Guide; Miller Comprehensive Governmental GAAP Guide; Miller Comprehensive GAAP Guide. (1992)-. English. **LC** HJ9801; .M54. *Continues Miller Comprehensive Governmental GAAP Guide, 0891-6918.*
**Desc:** Concerns public finance and accounting.

# Public Administration — Public Finance and Taxation

CN/0824-667X
**HENRY B. ZIMMER'S INCOME TAX PROBLEMS WITH DETAILED SOLUTIONS.** [Henry B. Zimmer's income tax probl. detail. solut.]. (1984)-. English. an. $22.00. Henry B Zimmer's Income Tax Problems with Detailed Solutions, c/o Cantax Seminars, 475-15055 5th Street SW, Calgary Alberta T2R 1K3 Canada. **DD** 336.24/0971. *Continues Income Tax Problems with Detailed Solutions and Notes, 0715-3090.*

CN/0824-6378
**HENRY B. ZIMMER'S PROBLEMS & QUESTIONS IN CANADIAN TAXATION.** See Law.

US/0148-2947
**HIGH INCOME TAX RETURNS. Main/Corp** United States. Office of Tax Analysis. 1974/75-. English. an. $1.15. US Treasury Department, Office of Tax Analysis, Washington DC 20402. **LC** HJ4652; .A476A. **DD** 336.2/42/0973.

JA
**HIROSHIMA KOKUZEIKYOKU TOKEISHO. Main/Corp** Japan. Hiroshima Kokuzeikyoku. (19??)-. Periodical. Japanese. Hiroshima Kokuzeikyoku, 6-30 Kami Hatchobori, Hiroshima Japan. **LC** HJ77.Z5; C474.

UK/0262-0421
**HM CUSTOM AND EXCISE TARIFF AMENDMENT.** [HM Custom. Excise tariff amend.]. (1960)-. English. ir (three volumes with monthly updates). £120.00. Her Majesty's Stationery Office, 51 Nine Elms Lane, London SW8 5DR England. **Tel** 011 44 71 873 8459, 011 44 71 873 8499, FAX 011 44 71 873 8499, 011 44 71 873 8456, telex 297138. **(Subscription address:** Her Majestys Stationery Offic, PO Box 276 Public Centre, London SW8 5DT England)
**Desc:** Comprises three volumes: Volume 1 - General Information, Volume 2 - Schedule of duty and trade statistical descriptions, codes and rates, and Volume 3 - Customs freight procedures.

UK
**HM CUSTOMS AND EXCISE NEWS RELEASES.** English. sw. $60.00. HM Customs and Excise, c/o Central Office of Information, PO Box 48, London SE1 7DL England. **Tel** 011 44 1 620 1313.

UK
**HM CUSTOMS & EXCISE.VAT GUIDE.** English. qt. Longman Group Ltd., Fourth Avenue, Longman House, Harlow Essex CM19 5SR England. **Tel** 011 44 279 429655, FAX 011 44 279 431059, telex 81259. **(Subscription address:** Fourth Avenue, Harlow Essex CM19 5AA England)

US
**HYPOTHETICAL U.S. TAX TABLES FOR U.S. CITIZENS ABROAD.** English. Ernst & Whinney International Operations, Citicorp Center, 153 East 53rd Street, New York NY 10022. **Tel** (212)888-9100. **ED** Robert H Sharfenberg. **Circ:** 5,000 (ctrl).
**Desc:** Used to prepare tax equalization calculations and estimating tax costs of expatriate (international) employees.

US/0733-5687
**IAFP FINANCIAL PLANNING UPDATE.** (IAFP FINANCIAL PLANNING UPDATE / INTERNATIONAL ASSOCIATION OF FINANCIAL PLANNERS, INC.). **Added/Corp** International Association of Financial Planners. **VFOAT** Financial Planning Update; I.A.F.P. Financial Planning Guide. **VAT** International Association of Financial Planners Financial Planning Update. (19??)-. Periodical. English. mo. Comes with International Association for Financial Planning membership. International Association of Financial Planning, 2 Concourse Parkway, Suite 800, Atlanta GA 30328. **Tel** (404)395-1605.

UK
**ICAEW TAXATION SERVICE.** English. ir. £275.00. Gee & Company Limited, 183 Marsh Wall, South Quay Plaza, London E14 9FS England. **Tel** 011 44 71 538 5386, FAX 071 538 8623.

●US
**ILLINOIS STATE BUDGET DETAIL. Main/Corp** Illinois. Governor. **VFOAT** State Budget Detail. Fiscal year (1992)-. English. Office of the Governor / Illinois, State House, Room 108, Springfield IL 62706. **LC** HJ2053.I3; I4c. **DD** 353.97730072/252/05.

US/0360-9340
**ILLINOIS STATE BUDGET IN BRIEF. Main/Corp** Illinois. Office of the Governor. English. Office of the Governor / Illinois, State House, Room 108, Springfield IL 62706. **LC** HJ11; .I3483A. **DD** 353.9/773/00722.

US/8755-7770
**ILLINOIS TAX CLIMATE, THE.** English. be. Taxpayers' Federation of Illinois, Suite 506, Jefferson Building, 525 West Jefferson Street, Springfield IL 62702. **LC** HJ2403; .I23. **DD** 336.2/009773.

US
**ILLINOIS TAX RATE AND LEVY MANUAL / OFFICE OF COMMUNITY SERVICES DEPARTMENT OF LOCAL GOVERNMENT AFFAIRS.** English. Office of Local Management Services, Department of Commerce and Community Services, 222 South College Street, Springfield IL 62706. **LC** HJ9228; .I37A. **DD** 343.77304/3/05; 347.73034305.

UK/0308-1958
**IMPACT OF TAX CHANGES ON INCOME DISTRIBUTION, THE.** 1971-. Periodical. English. an. **LC** HJ2621; .B76.

BL
**IMPOSTO DE RENDA APLICADO, PESSOA JURIDICA.** Portuguese. Editora Resenha Tributaria Ltda, rua Quatinga 12, Sao Paulo Brazil. **LC** LAW.

BL
**IMPOSTO DE RENDA PESSOA JURIDICA. Main/Corp** Brazil. Secretaria da Receita Federal. Coordenacao do Sistema de Informacoes Economico-Fiscais. Vol. 4- 1976-. Portuguese. Esplanada dos Ministerios, Bloco 6 - 5 Andar, CEP 70053, Brasilia DF Brazil. **Tel** 011 55 61 2257479, telex 011 55 61 1012 MNIC-BR. *Continues Imposto de Renda Pessoa Juridica.*

BL
**IMPOSTO FISCAL.** (19??)-. Periodical. Portuguese. sm. Publicacoes Associadas Paulista Ltda, Caixa Postal 30.560, CEP 01039 Sao Paulo Brazil. **LC** KHD4582; .I47. **DD** 343.8104/05; 348.103405. *Continues Revista Imposto Fiscal.*

FR
**IMPOTS EN FRANCE, LES.** (1969)-. Periodical. French. an. Editions Francis Lefebvre, 5 rue Jacques Bingen, F-75854 Paris Cedex 17 France. **Tel** (1)47 63 12 60, FAX 46 22 72 66, telex 649 470 F.

IT
**IMPRESA PUBBLICA : CIVILITA POSTINDUSTRIALE.** *Ceased.* (19??)-(1994). Italian. Ten times a year. Euroitalia Srl, Via della Scrofa 39, 00186 Rome Italy. **Tel** 011 39 6 68300831.

CK/0120-0550
**IMPUESTO A LA RENTA; REGIMEN LEGAL TRIBUTARIO. Main/Corp** Colombia. **VFOAT** Regimen Legal Tributario. (19??)-. Spanish. $60.00. Editores y Distribuidores Asociados Ltda, Avenida Jimenez No 4-49, Apartado Aereo 14965, Bogota Colombia. **LC** LAW.

AG
**IMPUESTOS : BOLETIN INFORMATIVO MENSUAL AL SERVICIO DE LOS CONTRIBUYENTES. Main/Corp** LEY (Firm). (1942)-. Periodical. Spanish. Twelve times a year. La Ley SA, Tucuman 1471, 1050 Buenos Aires Argentina. **Tel** 011 54 1 495481, 011 54 1 495489. **LC** KHA4582; .I47.

US/0896-4556
**INCENTIVE TAXATION.** [Incent. tax]. **Added/Corp** Center for the Study of Economics. (1975)-. Periodical. English. Eight times a year (Jan., Mar., May, July, Sept., Oct., Nov., Dec.). $13.00. Incentive Taxation, 2000 Century Plaza Suite 238, Columbia MD 21044. **Tel** (410)740-1177, FAX (410)740-3279. **ED** Steven Cord. **DD** 336. **Circ:** 4500. *Continues Tax-Free New Towns.*

CN/0317-9060
**INCOME TAX ACT.** (CANADIAN INCOME TAX ACT ... WITH INCOME TAX REGULATIONS.). **Main/Corp** Canada. **Added/Corp** C C H Canadian Limited. **VFOAT** Canadian Income Tax Act with Regulations; Canadian Income Tax Act. 35th Ed. (1966)-. Periodical. English. an. 20.95Can$. CCH Canadian Ltd., 6 Garamond Court, Don Mills Ontario M3C 1Z5 Canada. **Tel** (416)441-2992, FAX (416)441-3418. **DD** 343/.71/05202633. *Continues Income Tax Act. Canadian Income Tax Act.*
**Desc:** Texts of federal income tax law, regulations, rulings.

CN/1187-7502
**INCOME TAX ACT AND REGULATIONS, DEPARTMENT OF FINANCE TECHNICAL NOTES.** (INCOME TAX ACT AND REGULATIONS, DEPARTMENT OF FINANCE TECHNICAL NOTES : A CONSOLIDATION OF TECHNICAL NOTES AND OTHER INCOME TAX COMMENTARY FROM THE DEPARTMENT OF FINANCE / COMPILED, EDITED AND ANNOTATED BY DAVID M. SHERMAN.). [Income Tax Act regul. Dep. Finance tech. notes]. **Added/Corp** Canada. Dept. of Finance. **VFOAT** Income Tax Act, Department of Finance Technical Notes. 3rd ed. (1991)-. English. $80.00 per vol. Thomson Professional Publishing Canada, 2075 Kennedy Road, Scarborough Ontario M1T 3V4. **DD** 343.7105/2. *Continues Income Tax Act, Department of Finance Technical Notes., 0847-351X.*

CN/0527-7884
**INCOME TAX ACT ... ANNOTATED.** See Law.

CN
**INCOME TAX AND FAMILY LAW HANDBOOK.** See Law-Family Law.

CN/1193-3879
**INCOME TAX BULLETINS, CIRCULARS, RULINGS.** [Income tax bull. circ. rulings]. **Added/Corp** CCH Canadian Limited. **VFOAT** Income Tax. (1991)-. Bulletin. English. Revenue Canada Taxation, 875 Heron Road, Ottawa Ontario K1A 0L8 Canada. **Tel** (613)957-3508, FAX (613)941-0914. **DD** 343.7105/2/05. *Continues Income Tax Interpretation Bulletins, Information Circulars, Rulings., 0841-6141.*

US/0091-2816
**INCOME TAX PROCEDURE.** *Title Change.* (1965)-(19??). English. an. South-Western Publishing Company, 5101 Madison Road, College University Department, Cincinnati OH 45227. **Tel** (513)271-8811. **LC** KF6369.A1; B68. **DD** 343/.73/052. Index available. *Continues Niswonger, C. Rollin (Clifford Rollin), 1907- Income Tax Procedure. Continued by Federal Income Taxation.*
**Desc:** Update of current income tax procedures and forms for personal income taxes, partnerships, s-corporations and c-corporations.

II/0019-3453
**INCOME TAX REPORTS, THE.** -. Periodical. English. Fifty-two times a year. $50.00 (surface mail); $96.49 (airmail). Company Law Institute of India, 88 Thyagaraya Road, T Nagar Madras 600017 India. **Tel** 011 91 11 442047.

CN/0704-2930
**INCOME TAX RULING.** (INCOME TAX RULING. DECISION EN MATIERE D'IMPOT SUR LE REVENU.). **Main/Corp** Canada. Taxation. **VFOAT** Decision en Matiere d'Impot sur le Revenu. Vol. 1 (June 24, 1974)-. Periodical. English (French). an. 20.00Can$. Revenue Canada Taxation, 875 Heron Road, Ottawa Ontario K1A 0L8 Canada. **Tel** (613)957-3508, FAX (613)941-0914.

US
**INCOME TAX TECHNIQUES.** *Ceased.* Vol. 4-?. English. ir. Matthew Bender & Company Inc., 1275 Broadway, Albany NY 12204. **Tel** (800)833-9844, (518)487-3000. **ED** J K Lasser. *Continues Estate Tax Techniques.*

UK/0019-3451
**INCOMES DATA REPORT. Added/Corp** Incomes Data Services. (May 1966)-. Periodical. English. sm. £242.00. Incomes Data Services, 193 St John Street, London EC1V 4LS England. **Tel** 011 44 71 250 3434, FAX 011 44 71 608 0949. **ED** Alastair Hatchett. cum. index.
**Desc:** Provides a factual record of the news on pay bargaining and developments in pay. Reports on claims, negotiations and settlements at company and industry levels in both public and private sectors. **Ind/Abst** Contents Pages Manage.

CN/0319-5953
**INCORPORATION AND INCOME TAX IN CANADA.** 1st Ed.- ; 1960-. Periodical. English. CCH Canadian Ltd., 6 Garamond Court, Don Mills Ontario M3C 1Z5 Canada. **Tel** (416)441-2992, FAX (416)441-3418. **DD** 336.2/43/0971. *Continues Incorporation and Income Tax in Canada, 0319-5953.*

US
**INDEX FOR FISCAL YEAR APPROPRIATIONS. Main/Corp** Missouri. Office of Administration. Division of Accounting. English. Office of Administration / Missouri, Division of Budget and Planning, PO Box 809, Jefferson City MO 65102. **LC** HJ11; .M814B. **DD** 353.97780072/236/016.

US/0149-6166
**INDEX TO FEDERAL TAX ARTICLES. SUPPLEMENT.** [Index fed. tax artic.]. (1977)-. English. qt. $425.00 US; $552.50 other. Warren Gorham & Lamont Inc., Park Square Building, 31 St. James Avenue, Boston MA 02116-4112. **Tel** (617)423-2020, (800)950-1207, FAX (617)423-2026.

US
**INDIANA COMPREHENSIVE ANNUAL FINANCIAL REPORT FOR THE FISCAL YEAR ENDED ... . Main/Corp** Indiana. Auditor of State's Office. **VFOAT** Comprehensive Annual Financial Report for the Fiscal Year Ended ...; Annual Report of the Auditor of State of Indiana for the Fiscal Year Ending ... . (1989)-. English. an. Auditor of the State of Indiana, 240 State House, Indianapolis IN 46204. **LC** HJ11; .I62. **DD** 353.9/772/007232. *Continues Indiana.*

*Auditor's Office. Annual Report of the Auditor of State, 0362-3041.*
**Desc:** Provides a detailed statement of revenue received, refunded and transferred and a statement of appropriations, allotments and expenditures.

US/0742-7832
**INDIVIDUAL TAXATION.** [Individ. tax.]. (1985)-. English. an. $28.95. Irwin Professional Publishing, 1333 Burr Ridge Parkway, Burr Ridge Parkway IL 60521. **Tel** (800)634-3966, (708)789-5480. **LC** KF6369; .I53. **DD** 343.7305/2; 347.30352.

US
**INDIVIDUALS' FILLED-IN TAX RETURN FORMS.** **Added/Corp** Commerce Clearing House. (19??)-. English. an. $11.50. Commerce Clearing House Inc., 4025 West Peterson Avenue, Chicago IL 60646-6085. **Tel** (312)583-8500, FAX (708)940-4600. **LC** KF6369.6; .I5. **DD** 343.7305/2044; 347.30352044. Index available (topical index). ***Continues*** *Explanation [of] Individual Federal Income Tax Return.*
**Desc:** Shows step-by-step preparation of tax return forms 1040 EZ, 1040A and 1040, Schedule C and other schedules in reporting income and deductions for individuals- all filled in by CCH's tax law editors. Includes worksheets and checklists of deductible and nondeductible items.

CN/0709-860X
**INFORMATION BULLETIN - CORPORATIONS TAX BRANCH.** [Inf. bull. - Corp. Tax Br.]. **Main/Corp** Ontario. Corporations Tax Branch. No. 1-77- Mar. 21, 1977-. Bulletin. English. Free. Corporations Tax Branch, Ministry of Revenue, PO Box 622, 33 King Street West, Oshawa Ontario L1H 8H6 Canada. **DD** 336.24/3/0971. ctrl circ.

US
**INFORMATION FOR PERSONS WITH HANDICAPS OR DISABILITIES : FOR USE IN PREPARING ... RETURNS.** ***Title Change.*** **See** Physically Impaired.

PN
**INFORMATIVO - CENTRO INTERAMERICANO DE ADMINISTRADORES TRIBUTARIOS.** **Main/Corp** Inter-American Center of Tax Administrators. **VFOAT** Newsletter - Inter-American Center of Tax Administrators. Periodical. English (Spanish). $10.00. Inter-American Center of Tax Administrators, Apartado 215 1, Panama Panama. **LC** HJ3231; .I58A. **DD** 350/.724/0097.

PR
**INFORME ANUAL DEL TESORERO DE PUERTO RICO.** ***Title Change.*** **Main/Corp** Puerto Rico. Dept. of Finance. (19??)-(195?). Spanish. **LC** HJ24; .A185. ***Continued by*** *Annual Report of the Secretary of the Treasury of Puerto Rico. Spanish. Informe Anual del Secretario de Hacienda para el ano Fiscal que Termino ...*

VE/0506-631X
**INFORME - DISTRITO FEDERAL (VENEZUELA). CONTRALORIA MUNICIPAL.** ***Title Change.*** **Main/Corp** Distrito Federal (Venezuela). Contraloria Municipal. Spanish. an. **LC** HJ39; .F43. **DD** 336.877. ***Continued by*** *Contraloria Municipal Sus Actividades en ... Informe (Distrito Federal (Venezuela).*

PE
**INFORME TRIBUTARIO.** Vol. 1, No. 1 (June 1991)-. Periodical. Spanish. mo.

SA
**INGXELO YOMLAWULI NOMPHICOTHI-ZINCWADI JIKELELE KWIIAKHAWUNTI ZORHULUMENTE WASECISKEI KUNYE NOOGUNYAZIWE ABANGEZANTSI KULOO MMANDLA.** **Main/Corp** South Africa. Dept. of the Controller and Auditor-General. **Added/Corp** South Africa. Dept. of the Controller and Auditor-General Report of the Controller and Auditor-General on the Accounts of the Ciskeian Government and of the Lower Authorities in the Area. **VFOAT** Report of the Controller and Auditor-General on the Accounts of the Ciskeian Government and of the Lower Authorities in the Area. (19??)-. Afrikaans (English and Xhosa). R2.00. The Government Printer, Bosman Street, Private Bag X85, Pretoria 0001 South Africa. **Tel** 012-323-9731, FAX 012-323-0009. **LC** HJ9929.S6; A3. ***Continues*** *Ingxelo Yo- Mlawuli No-Mpicothi-Zincwadi Jikelele Zeeakhawunti Zikagunyaziwe Wamazwana Asecikei Kunye Noo- Gunyaziew Abangezantsi Kummandla Wakhe.*

UK
**INLAND REVENUE OF OFFICIAL TAX GUIDES.** English. qt. £120.00. Longman Group Ltd., Fourth Avenue, Longman House, Harlow Essex CM19 5SR England. **Tel** 011 44 279 429655, FAX 011 44 279 431059, telex 81259. **(Subscription address:** PO Box 11318, Birmingham, AL 35202**)**

UK
**INLAND REVENUE PRACTICES & CONCESSIONS.** English. £135.00. Longman Group Ltd., Fourth Avenue, Longman House, Harlow Essex CM19 5SR England. **Tel** 011 44 279 429655, FAX 011 44 279 431059, telex 81259. **(Subscription address:** Fourth Avenue, Harlow Essex CM19 5AA England**)**
**Desc:** Complete coverage of UK Inland Revenue's interpretation of tax legislation.

UK
**INLAND REVENUE STATISTICS.** **See** Public Administration-Abstracting, Bibliographies and Statistics.

UK
**INLAND REVENUE TAX CASE LEAFLETS.** English. ir. £54.00. Her Majesty's Stationery Office, 51 Nine Elms Lane, London SW8 5DR England. **Tel** 011 44 71 873 8459, 011 44 71 873 8499, FAX 011 44 71 873 8499, 011 44 71 873 8456, telex 297138. **(Subscription address:** Her Majestys Stationery Offic, PO Box 276 Public Centre, London SW8 5DT England**)**

US
**INSIDE NEW YORK TAXES.** Vol. 1, No. 1 (Nov. 1988)-. Periodical. English. Twelve times a year. $120.00 (one year), $205.00 (two years). Corporate Tax Publishers, PO Box 261, Leonia NJ 07605. **Tel** (201)461-6619.
**Desc:** Developments in New York State and City taxation.

US
**INSTITUTE ON FEDERAL TAXATION.** **Main/Corp** New York University. Division of General Education. **VFOAT** New York University Institute on Federal Taxation. No. 1 (1942)-. Monographic series. English. an. Price varies per volume. Matthew Bender & Company Inc., 1275 Broadway, Albany NY 12204. **Tel** (800)833-9844, (518)487-3000. cum. index.
**Ind/Abst** Curr. Law Index (1980-); Index Leg. Period.; Leg. Resour. Index (1980-); LegalTrac (1980-).

US
**INSTRUCTIONS FOR FORM W-2, WAGE AND TAX STATEMENT.** **Main/Corp** United States. Internal Revenue Service. **VFOAT** Wage and Tax Statement. (1991)-. English. Forms Distribution Center, PO Box 25866, Richmond VA 23289. ***Continues*** *Instructions for Forms W-2 and W-2P.*

US
**INSURANCE & TAX NEWS.** ***Ceased.*** (19??)-(March 1994). English. Twenty-six times a year. Bureau of Business Practice, 24 Rope Ferry Road, Waterford CT 06386. **Tel** (800)243-0876, (203)442-4365, (800)876-9105, FAX (203)443-1123.

●US
**INTER-ARTS. GRANTS TO PRESENTING ORGANIZATIONS, SERVICES TO PRESENTING ORGANIZATIONS, SPECIAL TOURING INITIATIVES: APPLICATION GUIDELINES.** **See** The Arts.

US
**INTERIM REPORT OF THE ASSESSMENT COORDINATION DIVISION.** **Main/Corp** Arkansas. Division of Assessment Coordination. English. be. Assessment Coordination Division, 2020 West 3rd, Little Rock AR 72205. **LC** HJ4121.A8; D57A. **DD** 353.9/767/0072401.

US
**INTERNAL CONTROL REPORT TO THE STATE LEGISLATURE.** **Main/Corp** Minnesota. Office of the Legislative Auditor. Financial Audits Division. English. an. Office of the Legislative Auditor, Financial Audits Division, Veterans Service Building, St Paul MN 55155. **LC** HJ11; .M6214A. **DD** 353.9776007/2/05.

US/0020-5761
**INTERNAL REVENUE BULLETIN.** [Intern. revenue bull.]. **Main/Corp** United States. Internal Revenue Service. (1953)-. Government Publication. English. wk. $123.00 domestic; $153.75 other. Superintendent of Documents, US Government Printing Office, Washington DC 20402. **Tel** (202)275-3328, FAX (202)786-2377. **DD** 336.2. available on microfilm from University Microfilms International (UMI). ***Continues*** *United States. Bureau of Internal Revenue. Internal Revenue Bulletin, 0020-5761.*
**Desc:** Announces official Internal Revenue Service rulings, Treasury Decisions, Executive Orders, legislation, and court decisions pertaining to internal revenue matters.

US/0163-7177
**INTERNAL REVENUE CODE.** **Main/Corp** United States. **VFOAT** U.S. Code Congressional and Administrative News. (1954)-. English. an. West Publishing Company, 610 Opperman Drive, PO Box 64526, Eagan MN 55123-1308. **Tel** (612)687-5618, (800)328-9352, FAX (612)687-5388, (800)562-2329. **(Subscription telephone:** (612)228-2500**)** **LC** KF6276.526.A19; I57. **DD** 343/.73/0402632.

US/0364-0620
**INTERNAL REVENUE CUMULATIVE BULLETIN.** [Intern. revenue cumul. bull.]. **Main/Corp** United States. Internal Revenue Service. **VFOAT** Cumulative Bulletin. (1969)-. Periodical. English. ir. $40.00. Claitors Law Books, 3165 South Acadian, Baton Rouge LA 70808. **Tel** (504)344-0476, (800)274-1403. **(Subscription address:** Claitors Law Books and Publ. Division, PO Box 261333, Baton Rouge LA 70826.**)** **LC** KF6282.A2; I495. **DD** 343.7304/02646; 347.304402646. Index available ($78.00). cum. index. **Circ:** 15,000. available on microfilm and microfiche from University Microfilms International (UMI). ***Continues*** *United States. Internal Revenue Service. Internal Revenue Bulletin. Cumulative Bulletin, 0145-6040.*
**Desc:** Revenue rulings of the Internal Revenue Service (IRS). Used for official interpretations of tax situations by the IRS.

US
**INTERNAL REVENUE MANUAL; AUDIT.** **Main/Corp** Commerce Clearing House. Vol. 1 (1977)-. Periodical. English. ir. $560.00. Commerce Clearing House Inc., 4025 West Peterson Avenue, Chicago IL 60646-6085. **Tel** (312)583-8500, FAX (708)940-4600. **ED** A. E. Schechter. ***Continues in part*** *Commerce Clearing House. Internal Revenue Manual.*
**Desc:** Reproduces IRS tax audit provisions and procedures.

NE
**INTERNATIONAL GUIDE TO MERGERS AND ACQUISITIONS.** (1992)-. English. sa. $745.00. International Bureau of Fiscal Documentation - IBFD Publications, PO Box 20237, 1000 HE Amsterdam The Netherlands. **Tel** 011 31 20-6267726, FAX 011 31 20-6228658, telex 13217 INTAX NL. **(Subscription address:** IBFD / International Bureau of Fiscal Documentation USA, Inc., 24 Hudson Street, Kinderhook NY 12106.**)**
**Desc:** Complete details of tax regulations, legislation and practice and full outline of company law.

NE
**INTERNATIONAL GUIDE TO PARTNERSHIPS, THE.** (19??)-. English. Twice a year. $690.00. International Bureau of Fiscal Documentation - IBFD Publications, PO Box 20237, 1000 HE Amsterdam The Netherlands. **Tel** 011 31 20-6267726, FAX 011 31 20-6228658, telex 13217 INTAX NL. **(Subscription address:** IBFD / International Bureau of Fiscal Documentation USA, Inc., 24 Hudson Street, Kinderhook NY 12106.**)**
**Desc:** Guide to company and tax law applying to partnerships.

US/1041-2743
**INTERNATIONAL JOURNAL OF FINANCE, THE.** [Int. j. finance]. Vol. 1, No. 1 (1988 Autumn)-. Periodical. English. sa (June and Dec.). $50.00 (individuals), $100.00 (institutions). Suffolk University, c/o Professor D. Ghosh, 8 Ashburton Place, Department of Finance, Boston MA 02108. **Tel** (617)573-8754. **DD** 332.

CN/0047-0724
**INTERNATIONAL JOURNAL OF GOVERNMENT AUDITING.** [Int. j. gov. audit.]. **Added/Corp** International Organization of Supreme Audit Institutions. **VFOAT** Journal International des Institutions Superieures de Controle; Revista Internacional de Entidades Fiscalizadoras Superiores. Vol. 1 (Sept. 1971)-. Periodical. English (French and Spanish). qt. $5.00. International Journal of Government Auditing, PO Box 50009, Washington DC 20004. **Tel** (202)275-4707, FAX (202)275-4021, telex 7108229273. **ED** Donald R Drach. **LC** HJ9701; .I55. **DD** 350/.7232. **CODEN** IJGADG. **[CCC].** Index available. **Bk Rev**. **Ad Acc**. available on microfilm and microfiche from University Microfilms International (UMI); available on an online database (files 15,485/Full-Text) from DIALOG. Documents available from UMI Article Clearinghouse.
**Desc:** Dedicated to the advancement of government auditing procedures and techniques. Opinions and beliefs expressed are those of editors or individual contributors and do not necessarily reflect the views or policies of the organization.
**Ind/Abst** ABI/INFORM Glob. Ed.; ABI Inform Ondisc (Jan. 1974-); Account. Tax Datab. (Jan. 1974-) [Full Txt.]; Anbar Account. Finan. Abstr. [Full Txt.]; Anbar Mark. Distr. Abstr. [Full Txt.]; Anbar Top Manage. Abstr. [Full Txt.]; Bus. Index (1979-?); Manage. Bibliogr. Rev.; Middle East Abstr. Index; Oper. Prod. Manage. Abstr. [Full Txt.]; Person. Train. Abstr. [Full Txt.]; UMI ABI/Inform--Bus. Period. Ondisc (Jan. 1988-) [Full Txt.]; Women Manage. Rev. [Full Txt.].

US/0074-896X
**INTERNATIONAL TAX AGREEMENTS.** **Added/Corp** United Nations. Dept. of Economic Affairs. Fiscal Division. United Nations. Dept. of Economic and Social Affairs. Fiscal and Financial Branch. **VFOAT** World Guide to International Tax Agreements. Vol. 1 (1948)-. Government Publication. English. an. $10.00. United Nations Publications, 2 United Nations Plaza, Room DC2 0853, Department 007C, New York NY 10017. **Tel** (212)963-8303, (800)253-9646. **LC** JX1977; .A2. **DD** 336.294.
**Desc:** Loose-leaf series on the status of international taxation agreements on income and fortune, moveable capital, commercial and industrial and agricultural enterprises; or maritime and air transport enterprises.

US/0741-4269
**INTERNATIONAL TAX & BUSINESS LAWYER.** See Law-International Law.

NE/0927-5940
**INTERNATIONAL TAX AND PUBLIC FINANCE.** English. Three times a year. $265.00. Kluwer Academic Publishers / Massachusetts, PO Box 358, Accord Station, Hingham MA 02018. **Tel** (617)871-6600. **ED** Jack Mintz and Michael Keen. **Pr Rev. Acid Free.**
**Desc:** Will serve as an outlet for, and seek to stimulate, first-rate research on both theoretical and empirical aspects of tax policy, broadly interpreted to include expenditure and financial policies. A special emphasis will be on open economy issues: the coordination of policies across jusrisdictions, jurisdictions instance, or the effects of taxation on capital and trade flows.

UK/0306-6045
**INTERNATIONAL TAX-FREE TRADER & DUTY-FREE WORLD.** [Int. tax-free trader duty-free world]. **VFOAT** International Tax Free Trader and Duty-Free World; International Tax-Free Trader; International Tax Free Trader. (19??)-. Periodical. English. Ten times a year. £96.00 UK; £115.00, $211.00 other. Argus Press Group, Queensway House, 2 Queensway Redhill, Surrey RH1 1QS England. **Tel** 011 44 737 768611, 011 44 737 761685, FAX 011 44 737 760510, telex 948669 TOPJNL G.
**Desc:** Widely regarded as the original and most authoritative source of information on the world's duty-free industry.

UK/0263-5488
**INTERNATIONAL TAX-FREE TRADER. BUYERS GUIDE & DIRECTORY.** [Int. tax-free trader. Buy. guide dir.]. (1982)-. Periodical. English. an. £88.00 UK; £97.00, $164.00 other. Argus Press Group, Queensway House, 2 Queensway Redhill, Surrey RH1 1QS England. **Tel** 011 44 737 768611, 011 44 737 761685, FAX 011 44 737 760510, telex 948669 TOPJNL G. **DD** 380.1025.

NE
**INTERNATIONAL TAX GLOSSARY.** (19??)-. English. $55.00. International Bureau of Fiscal Documentation - IBFD Publications, PO Box 20237, 1000 HE Amsterdam The Netherlands. **Tel** 011 31 20-6267726, FAX 011 31 20-6228658, telex 13217 INTAX NL. **(Subscription address:** IBFD / International Bureau of Fiscal Documentation USA, Inc., 24 Hudson Street, Kinderhook NY 12106.**)**
**Desc:** Extensive glossary and lexicon of English and significant non-English international tax terms, including brief description.

AT/1034-8506
**INTERNATIONAL TAX HANDBOOK / HORWATH INTERNATIONAL.** **Added/Corp** Horwath International. (1990)-. English. **LC** K4471.2; .I57.

US/0097-7314
**INTERNATIONAL TAX JOURNAL, THE.** [Int. tax j.]. Vol. 1 (Fall 1974)-. Periodical. English. Four times a year (Mar., June, Sept., Dec.). $156.00 US. Aspen Publishers Inc., 7201 McKinney Circle, Frederick MD 21701. **Tel** (800)234-1660, (301)698-7100, FAX (301)251-5784, telex 5106014543. **(Subscription address:** Aspen Publishers Inc., PO Box 990, Frederick MD 21701.**) ED** Scott Spector. **LC** HJ2240; .I68. **DD** 368.2/005. **[CCC]. Circ:** 1,800 (ctrl). Documents available from UMI Article Clearinghouse.
**Desc:** Devoted to transnational taxation problems and opportunities, and regularly keeps you current on the broad range of topics impacting from day-to-day operations.
**Ind/Abst** ABI/INFORM Glob. Ed.; ABI Inform Ondisc (June 1979-); Account. Tax Datab. (1974-); Account. Art.; Bus. Index (1985-); Curr. Law Index (1980-); Fed. Tax Artic.; Gen. BusinessFile (1985-); Leg. Resour. Index (1980-); LegalTrac (1980-); PAIS Int. Print; Trade Ind. Index (1981-).

UK/0958-7594
**INTERNATIONAL TAX REVIEW.** Vol. 1, No. 1 (Nov. 1989)-. Periodical. English. Ten times a year. £315.00 UK; $570.00 US. Euromoney Publications PLC, Nestor House, Playhouse Yard, London EC4Z 5EX England. **Tel** 011 44 71 779 8888, FAX 011 44 71 779 8617, telex 290700 EUROMON G. **(Subscription address:** Euromoney Publications Plc, Perrymount Road Haywards Heath, West Sussex RH16 3DH England.**) LC** K4456.2; .I6. **DD** 343/.04; 342.34.
**Desc:** For the international tax practitioner. Covers techniques for creating tax-efficient corporate structures, financial instruments and M&A transactions on a cross-border basis around the world. Special reports on what's happening in Brussels, with bilateral treaty negotiations and within the tax profession .

US/8755-1551
**INTERNATIONAL TAX SUMMARIES.** (INTERNATIONAL TAX SUMMARIES / COOPERS & LYBRAND INTERNATIONAL TAX NETWORK.). [Int. tax summ.]. **Added/Corp** Coopers & Lybrand. (1982)-. English. an. John Wiley & Sons, Inc., 605 Third Avenue, New York NY 10158-0012. **Tel** (212)850-6000, (212)850-6645, FAX (212)850-6088, telex 12-7063. **(Subscription address:** John Wiley & Sons / England, Baffins Lane, Chichester, West Sussex PO19 1UD England.**) LC** K4505.4; .I54. **DD** 343.04; 342.3.

UK
**INTERNATIONAL TAX SYSTEMS AND PLANNING TECHNIQUES.** English. Three times a year. £125.00 UK; £130.00 other. Longman Group Ltd., Fourth Avenue, Longman House, Harlow Essex CM19 5SR England. **Tel** 011 44 279 429655, FAX 011 44 279 431059, telex 81259. **(Subscription address:** PO Box 11318, Birmingham, AL 35202**)**

IE
**INTERNATIONAL TAX TREATIES SERVICE.** English. In-Depth Publishing Ltd, Alton House, Herbert Street, Dublin 2 Ireland.

UK
**INTERNATIONAL TAX TREATIES SERVICE.** English. ir. £200.00. In-Depth Company, PO Box 2680, 216 Blythe Road, London W14 0ZN, England. **Tel** 011 44 71 3027100, FAX 011 44 71 6028221.

US/0883-4601
**INTERNATIONAL TREASURY SERVICES.** (INTERNATIONAL TREASURY SERVICES / GREENWICH RESEARCH ASSOCIATES.). [Int. treas. serv.]. **Added/Corp** Greenwich Research Associates. (19??)-. English. an. Greenwich Research Associates Inc, Office Park 8, Greenwich CT 06830. **LC** HG4027.5; .I583. **DD** 658.1/599/05.

NE/0925-0832
**INTERNATIONAL VAT MONITOR.** **Added/Corp** International Bureau of Fiscal Documentation. **VFOAT** VAT Monitor. **VAT** International Value Added Tax Monitor. Vol. 1 (Jan. 1990)-. Periodical. English. bm. $450.00. International Bureau of Fiscal Documentation - IBFD Publications, PO Box 20237, 1000 HE Amsterdam The Netherlands. **Tel** 011 31 20-6267726, FAX 011 31 20-6228658, telex 13217 INTAX NL. **(Subscription address:** IBFD / International Bureau of Fiscal Documentation USA, Inc., 24 Hudson Street, Kinderhook NY 12106.**) LC** HJ5711; .I57. **DD** 336.2/714/05.
**Desc:** Includes major subject articles, news column discussing global and case law on VAT and other indirect taxes, case reviews and discussions, bibliography (latest books and articles), conference diary, and EC developments.

CN/0822-3726
**INTERPRETATION REVENU QUEBEC.** [Interpret. Revenu Que.]. (1982)-. Periodical. French (English). mo. 77.00Can$ French edition; 72.00Can$ English edition. Les Publications du Quebec, CP 1190, Outremont Quebec H2V 4S7 Canada. **Tel** (514)948-1222, (800)463-2100, FAX (514)278-3030. **DD** 343.71405202638.

US/0731-5651
**INTERSTATE TAX REPORT.** (INTERSTATE TAX REPORT : ITR.). **VFOAT** ITR; I.T.R. Vol. 1, No. 1 (Apr. 1981)-. Periodical. English. Twelve times a year. $175.00 (includes binder), $165.00 (without binder). Interstate Tax Corporation, 193 East Avenue, Norwalk CT 06855. **Tel** (203)854-0704. **LC** KF6763.A15; I55. **DD** 343.7305/267/05; 347.303526705.

NE/0165-2826
**INTERTAX.** (INTERTAX : BULLETIN OF THE CONFEDERATION FISCALE EUROPEENNE (CFE).). [Intertax]. **VFOAT** Bulletin of the Confederation Fiscale Europeenne; European Tax Review; Europaische Steuer-Zeitung; Fiscalite du Marche Commun. (1973)-. Bulletin. English (summaries and/or abstracts in German and French). mo. $250.00. Kluwer Law and Taxation Publishers (Mass.), 675 Massachusetts Avenue, Cambridge MA 02139. **Tel** (617) 354-0140. **ED** Fred C de Hosson. **[CCC]. Bk Rev. Ad Acc. Circ:** 1,500 (ctrl). ***Continues*** *Europaische Steuer-Zeitung.*
**Desc:** Provides information on international aspects of taxation, both in the direct taxes and topical reviews of developments in Europe.
**Ind/Abst** Index Foreign Leg. Per.

US
**INTRO TO COMPUTERIZED TAX PLANNING WITH AATAXCOM TO ACCOMPANY WEST'S FEDERAL TAXATION [COMPUTER FILE].** **Added/Corp** West Publishing Company. Arthur Andersen & Co. **VFOAT** Introduction to Computerized Tax Planning with AATAXCOM. 1988-. English. an. West Publishing Company, 610 Opperman Drive, PO Box 64526, Eagan MN 55123-1308. **Tel** (612)687-5618, (800)328-9352, FAX (612)687-5388, (800)562-2329. **(Subscription telephone:** FAX (612)688-3570**) LC** KF242.T38; I58. **DD** 343.7305/2/028553.
**Desc:** System requirements: IBM PC and compatibles, at least 320K, DOS, 102 disk drives or hard disk, monochrome or color monitor.

CN/0821-5340
**INTRODUCTION TO FEDERAL INCOME TAXATION IN CANADA.** (INTRODUCTION TO FEDERAL INCOME TAXATION IN CANADA / BY ROBERT E. BEAM, STANLEY N. LAIKEN.). [Introd. fed. income tax. Can.]. **Added/Corp** CCH Canadian Limited. (1981)-. English. an. 49.95Can$. Introduction to Federal Income Taxation in Canada, CCH Canadian, 6 Garamond Court, Don Mills Ontario M3C 1Z5 Canada. **Tel** (416)441-2992, FAX (416)441-3418. **ED** R E Beam and S N Laiken. **LC** KE5759; .B4. **DD** 343.7105/2; 347.10352.
**Desc:** Designed for those seeking to develop a general understanding of federal income tax law. Includes references to CCH's Canada Income Tax Guide and Canadian Master Tax Guide as primary texts. With its fact situations or sample problems demonstrating the application of the provisions of the Income Tax Act to realistic situations.

●US/1070-8502
**INTRODUCTION TO FEDERAL INCOME TAXES, AN.** (1994)-. English. $25.00. Prentice-Hall General Reference and Travel, 200 Old Tappan Road, Old Tappan NJ 07675. **Tel** (800)922-0579.

US/0731-7905
**INTRODUCTION TO FEDERAL TAXATION (ENGLEWOOD CLIFFS, N.J.).** (INTRODUCTION TO FEDERAL TAXATION / WILLIAM L. RABY, VICTOR H. TIDWELL.). (1981)-. English. an. Prentice-Hall Law and Business, 270 Sylvan Avenue, Englewood Cliffs NJ 07632. **Tel** (800)223-0231, (201)894-8538, FAX (201)894-8666. **LC** HJ2381; .I56. **DD** 343.7304/05; 347.303405.

US/1046-8803
**INVESTMENT & TAX SHELTER BLUE BOOK.** [Investm. tax shelter blue book]. **VFOAT** Investment and Tax Shelter Blue Book. 1988-. English. sa. $95.00. Securities Investigations Inc, PO Box 888, Mill Hill Road, Woodstock NY 12498. **Tel** (914)679-2300. **DD** 332. Index available. cum. index. ***Continues*** *Tax Shelter Blue Book, 0749-6206.*

NE
**INVESTMENT AND TAXATION IN THE PEOPLE'S REPUBLIC OF CHINA.** (19??)-. English. Twice a year. $260.00. International Bureau of Fiscal Documentation - IBFD Publications, PO Box 20237, 1000 HE Amsterdam The Netherlands. **Tel** 011 31 20-6267726, FAX 011 31 20-6228658, telex 13217 INTAX NL.
**Desc:** Offers a comprehensive and detailed description of one of the world's least known tax systems as well as a complete collection of laws and regulations.

US/0148-8082
**IOWA ELDERLY AND DISABLED PROPERTY TAX RELIEF REPORT.** **Main/Corp** Iowa. Dept. of Revenue. Research & Statistics Division. **VFOAT** Elderly and Disabled Property Tax Relief Report. English. an. Research and Statistics Division, Lucas State Office Building, Des Moines IA 50319. **LC** HJ4121.I7; D46A. **DD** 336.2/2/09777.

US
**IOWA INDIVIDUAL INCOME TAX ANNUAL REPORT.** **Added/Corp** Iowa. Dept. of Revenue. Research & Management Services Division. Iowa. Dept. of Revenue & Finance. Information & Management Services Division. (1981)-. English. Iowa Department of Revenue, Research and Statistics Division, Hoover State Office Building, Des Moines IA 50319. **LC** HJ4655.I77; A56. **DD** 336.24/09777/05. ***Continues*** *Individual Income Tax Annual Statistical Report.*

AT/1030-4177
**IPA REVIEW (1986).** (IPA REVIEW.). [IPA rev.]. **Added/Corp** Institute of Public Affairs (Melbourne, Vic.). **VFOAT** Institute of Public Affairs Review. Vol. 40, No. 3 (Spring 1986)-. Periodical. English. qt. 40.00Aus$. Institute of Public Affairs / Australia, 128 36 Jolimont Road, Jolimont Vic 3002 Australia. **Tel** 011 61 3 6547499, FAX 011 61 3 6507627. **ED** Ken Baker. **LC** HB1; .I6. **DD** 330/.05. **Bk Rev. Ad Acc. Circ:** 17,000. ***Continues*** *Review (Institute of Public Affairs (Melbourne, Vic.)), 1030-4169.*
**Desc:** Major vehicle for the publication of free enterprise

opinion in Australia.
**Ind/Abst** APAIS, Aust. Public Aff. Inf. Ser.; Aust. Educ. Index.

BL
**IPI: ARRECADACAO SETORIAL.** **VAT** Imposto Sobre Produtos Industrializados: Arrecadacao Setorial. Began with Vol. for 1974. Portuguese. Esplanada dos Ministerios, Bloco 6 - 5 Andar, CEP 70053, Brasilia DF Brazil. **Tel** 011 55 61 2257479, telex 011 55 61 1012 MNIC-BR. **LC** HJ5715.B8; I16.

CN/1186-8643
**IPSCO INC. / MIDLAND WALWYN RESEARCH.** [IPSCO Inc.]. **Added/Corp** Midland Walwyn Capital. Research Dept. Midland Walwyn Capital. **VFOAT** Interporvincial Steel and Pipe Incorporated. (Apr. 23, 1991)-. Periodical. English. Limited free distribution to selected clients of Midland Walwyn Capital. Midland Walwyn Capital, Suite 1600, 121 King Street West, Toronto Ontario M5H 3W6 Canada. **DD** 336.2.

US/0148-1940
**IRS LETTER RULINGS.** [IRS lett. ruling]. **Main/Corp** Commerce Clearing House. **VAT** Internal Revenue Service Letter Rulings. (19??)-. Periodical. English. wk. $1275.00. Commerce Clearing House Inc., 4025 West Peterson Avenue, Chicago IL 60646-6085. **Tel** (312)583-8500, FAX (708)940-4600. **ED** A. E. Schechter. **LC** KF6282.A2; C65. **DD** 343/.73/0402646.
**Desc:** Provides thousands of private letter rulings in full text. Applies IRS thinking to specific tax payer situations.

US/1053-1173
**IRS PRACTICE ALERT.** ***Ceased.*** [IRS pract. alert]. (1987)-(1993). Periodical. English. mo. Warren Gorham & Lamont Inc., Park Square Building, 31 St. James Avenue, Boston MA 02116-4112. **Tel** (617)423-2020, (800)950-1207, FAX (617)423-2026. **ED** Lois A Ferraro. **LC** KF6300.A15; I79. **DD** 343.7304; 347.3034. **Circ:** 2,000 (ctrl). ***Continues*** *Practical Accountant Alert.*
**Desc:** Provides thorough analysis and practical guidance of the latest IRS policies and procedures. Offers answers to practitioners' most frequent tax practice questions.

US/0194-8210
**IRS PRACTICE AND PROCEDURES.** **Added/Corp** Tax Report Clearinghouse. **VAT** Internal Revenue Service Practice and Procedures. (197?)-. Periodical. English. Twelve times a year. $77.00. Mark A Stephens Ltd, 10018 Colesville Road, Silver Spring MD 20901. **Tel** (301)593-0443. **ED** Lavaughn T Davis. **Circ:** 86.
**Desc:** Procedures for individuals, corporations and employee retirement plans in dealing with the Internal Revenue Service.

●US
**IRS PROCEDURAL FORMS AND ANALYSIS.** **VFOAT** Procedural Forms and Analysis. (1992)-. English. ir. $125.00. Warren Gorham & Lamont Inc., Park Square Building, 31 St. James Avenue, Boston MA 02116-4112. **Tel** (617)423-2020, (800)950-1207, FAX (617)423-2026. **LC** KF6300; .I77. **DD** 343.7304; 347.3034. ***Continues*** *IRS Practice and Procedure Manual, 1046-7866.*

US/1063-4932
**IRS TAX PRACTICE INSIDER, THE.** ***Title Change.*** [IRS tax pract. insid.]. **VAT** Internal Revenue Service Tax Practice Insider. Vol. 1, No. 1 (June 1991)-(1993). Periodical. English. mo. $170.00. Tax Analysts, 6830 North Fairfax Drive, Arlington VA 22213. **Tel** (703)533-4400, (800)955-3444. **DD** 343. ***Merged with*** *Tax-Related Documents, 1062-9106* ***to form*** *Tax Practice & Controversies, 1074-5858.*

US/1066-6303
**IRS TECHNICAL ADVICE MEMORANDUMS AND IRS LETTER RULINGS.** [IRS tech. advice memo. IRS lett. rulings]. **Added/Corp** United States. Internal Revenue Service. Tax Analysts (Firm : U.S.). **VFOAT** Technical Advice Memorandums and IRS Letter Rulings; IRS Technical Advice Memorandums & Letter Rulings; IRS Technical Advice Memorandums and Letter Rulings. (198?)-. Periodical. English. wk (52 issues). $149.00. Tax Analysts, 6830 North Fairfax Drive, Arlington VA 22213. **Tel** (703)533-4400, (800)955-3444. **LC** KF6301.A33; I77. **DD** 343.7304/05; 347.303405. Index available (free).

US/0146-8928
**ISSUES - EXECUTIVE OFFICE OF THE PRESIDENT, OFFICE OF MANAGEMENT AND BUDGET.** **Main/Corp** United States. Office of Management and Budget. 1977/78-. English. $8.90. Executive Office of the President Office of Management & Budget, Washington DC 20503. **LC** HJ2051; .U56B. **DD** 353.007/22.

FR
**ISSUES IN INTERNATIONAL TAXATION.** **Added/Corp** Organisation for Economic Co-Operation and Development. No. 1 (1987)-. Monographic series. English. ir. Price varies per volume. OECD Publications and Information Center, 2 rue Andre-Pascal, 75775 Paris Cedex 16 France. **Tel** 011 33 1 45248167, US:(202)785-6323, FAX 011 33 1 45248500 OR 45248176, telex 620 160 OCDE. **(Subscription address:** OECD Publications Center, 2001 L Street, Suite 700, Washington DC 20036.**)**

US/0198-7232
**IT'S YOUR BUSINESS (ROCKVILLE CENTER).** **See** Law.

US/1056-3121
**J.K. LASSER'S MONTHLY TAX LETTER.** [J.K. Lasser's mon. tax lett.]. **Added/Corp** J.K. Lasser Tax Institute. **VFOAT** Monthly Tax Letter; J. K. Lasser's Mmonthly Tax Letter. Vol. 1, No. 1 (Aug. 1991)-. Periodical. English. mo. $24.00; $35.95 combined subscription with Your Income Tax. JK Lasser Tax Institute, 15 Columbus Circle, 16th Floor, New York NY 10023. **Tel** (212)373-8786. **DD** 343. ***Continues*** *J.K. Lasser's Monthly Tax Service, 0895-3147.*

NE
**JAARVERSLAG - NEDERLANDSE FINANCIERINGS-MAATSCHAPPIJ VOOR ONTWIKKELINGSLANDEN.** **Main/Corp** Nederlandse Financierings-Maatschappij Voor Ontwikkelingslanden. **VFOAT** Annual Report. Dutch. Theo Mann-Bouwmeesterlaan 3, Postbus 96909, 2509 JH Den Haag Netherlands. **LC** HC60; .N427B. **DD** 332.1/53.

GW
**JAHRESBERICHT.** **Added/Corp** Bavaria (Germany). Oberster Rechnungshof. German. **LC** HJ9925.G3; B467. ***Continues*** *Bericht des Bayerischen Obersten Rechnungshof ... zur Haushalts- und Wirtschaftsfuhrung mit Bemerkungen zur Haushaltsrechnung.*

GW/0075-2886
**JAHRESFACHKATALOG: RECHT, WIRTSCHAFT, STEUERN.** **See** Law.

JA
**JITSUMU ZEIHO ROPPO. HOREI / OKURASHO SHUZEIKYOKU SOMUKA KANSHU.** **Main/Corp** Japan. **VFOAT** Zeiho Roppo. Japanese. ¥4000. Shin Nihon Hoki Shuppan, 6 Ichigaya Sadohara-cho, Shinjuku-ku, Tokyo-to Japan.

US/0094-0593
**JOURNAL OF CORPORATE TAXATION, THE.** [J. corp. tax.]. Vol. 1 (Spring 1974)-. Periodical. English. qt. $147.25 US; $225.95 other. Warren Gorham & Lamont Inc., Park Square Building, 31 St. James Avenue, Boston MA 02116-4112. **Tel** (617)423-2020, (800)950-1207, FAX (617)423-2026. **ED** Gersham Goldstein and Joel D. Kuntz. **LC** K10; .O8587. **DD** 336.2/43/0973. **[CCC]. Pr Rev.** available on microfilm and microfiche from University Microfilms International (UMI). Documents available from The Genuine Article, UMI Article Clearinghouse.
**Desc:** Provides analysis and guidance for practitioners who must stay on top of all the latest developments and their planning implications.
**Ind/Abst** ABI/INFORM Glob. Ed.; ABI Inform Ondisc (Spring 1974-); Acad. Search (Jan. 1994-); Account. Tax Datab. (Spring 1974-); Account. Art.; Bowne Dig. Corp. Sec. Lawyers; Bus. Index (1985-); Bus. Period. Index; Bus. Source (Jul. 1993-); Curr. Contents Soc. Behav. Sci.; Curr. Law Index (1980-); Fed. Tax Artic.; Gen. BusinessFile (1985-); Gen. Period. Index (1985-); Index Leg. Period.; INFO-SOUTH Abstr.; Leg. Resour. Index (1980-); LegalTrac (1980-); Mag. Search; PAIS Int. Print (1991-?); Res. Alert [Full Cov.]; Soc. Sci. Cit. Index [Full Cov.]; Trade Ind. Index (1981-?); Wilson Bus. Abstr.

US/1065-1853
**JOURNAL OF FINANCIAL & STRATEGIC DECISIONS.** [J. financ. strateg. decis.]. **Added/Corp** Institute of Financial and Strategic Decisions. **VFOAT** Journal of Financial and Strategic Decisions; JFSD. (198?)-. Periodical. English. Three times a year (Spring, Fall and Winter). $35.00. Institute Finance Strategic Decision Making, PO Box 23080 A, Econmonic & Finance, Johnson City TN 37614. **Tel** (615)929-4202. **ED** Sharon Garrison, (phone: (615)929-5936). **DD** 332. **Pr Rev.** ***Continues*** *Journal of Financial & Strategic Decision making.*

US/1049-6378
**JOURNAL OF INTERNATIONAL TAXATION.** [J. int. tax.]. **Added/Corp** Warren, Gorham & Lamont, Inc. **VFOAT** International Taxation. (1990)-. Periodical. English. bm. $279.25 US; $388.45 other. Warren Gorham & Lamont Inc., Park Square Building, 31 St. James Avenue, Boston MA 02116-4112. **Tel** (617)423-2020, (800)950-1207, FAX (617)423-2026. **LC** K4464.A13; J68. **DD** 343/.04; 342.34. **[CCC].** available on microfilm and microfiche.
**Ind/Abst** Account. Art.; Am. Bibliogr. Slavic East Europ. Stud.; Fed. Tax Artic.

US/1054-8394
**JOURNAL OF MULTISTATE TAXATION, THE.** **Added/Corp** Warren, Gorham & Lamont, Inc. **VFOAT** Multistate Taxation. Began in (1991)-. Periodical. English. bm. $216.25 US; $310.45 other. Warren Gorham & Lamont Inc., Park Square Building, 31 St. James Avenue, Boston MA 02116-4112. **Tel** (617)423-2020, (800)950-1207, FAX (617)423-2026. **LC** KF6750.A15; J68. **DD** 343.7304/05; 347.303405. **[CCC].**
**Ind/Abst** Account. Tax Datab. (May 1992-); Account. Art.

US/1052-1496
**JOURNAL OF NEW YORK TAXATION.** ***Ceased.*** [J. N. Y. tax.]. **VFOAT** New York Taxation. Vol. 1, No. 1 (Fall 1990)-(19??). Periodical. English. qt. Faulkner & Gray Inc., 11 Penn Plaza, 17th Floor, New York NY 10001. **Tel** (212)967-7000, (800)535-8403. **LC** K10; .O8825. **DD** 343.74704/05; 347.4703405. available in microform from University Microfilms International (UMI); available on an online database (file 485/Full-Text) from DIALOG.

●US/1078-1161
**JOURNAL OF OFFSHORE FINANCE AND TAX.** **See** Business-Banking and Finance.

US/0749-4513
**JOURNAL OF PARTNERSHIP TAXATION.** **Added/Corp** Warren, Gorham & Lamont, Inc. Vol. 1, No. 1 (Spring 1984)-. Periodical. English. qt. $147.25 US and Canada; $225.95 other. Warren Gorham & Lamont Inc., Park Square Building, 31 St. James Avenue, Boston MA 02116-4112. **Tel** (617)423-2020, (800)950-1207, FAX (617)423-2026. **LC** K10; .O8827. **DD** 343.7306/62/05; 347.30366205. available on microfilm and microfiche from University Microfilms International (UMI). Documents available from UMI Article Clearinghouse.
**Desc:** Provides articles and regular columns covering trends and developments in the partnership tax area. Its articles also highlight and analyze alternative ways to capitalize on planning opportunities and avoid tax pitfalls.
**Ind/Abst** ABI/INFORM Glob. Ed.; ABI Inform Ondisc (Summer 1985-); Account. Tax Datab. (Summer 1985-); Account. Art.; Bowne Dig. Corp. Sec. Lawyers; Fed. Tax Artic.; Gen. BusinessFile (1992-).

US
**JOURNAL OF PROPERTY TAX MANAGEMENT.** (1990)-. Periodical. English. qt. $142.00 US. Panel Publishers, A Division of Aspen Publishers, Inc., 7201 McKinney Circle, PO Box 990, Frederick MD 21705-9727. **Tel** (800)638-8437. **(Subscription address:** Aspen Publishers Inc., PO Box 990, Frederick MD 21701.**) ED** James T. Collins, JD and Sheree L. Nelson, CPA. **LC** K10; .O8839. ***Continues*** *Journal of Property Taxation, 1041-4797.*
**Ind/Abst** Account. Art.

US/1041-4797
**JOURNAL OF PROPERTY TAXATION.** ***Title Change.*** [J. prop. tax.]. **VFOAT** Property Taxation. Vol. 1, No. 1 (Winter 1988)-(1989?). Periodical. English. qt. Panel Publishers, A Division of Aspen Publishers, Inc., 7201 McKinney Circle, PO Box 990, Frederick MD 21705-9727. **Tel** (800)638-8437. **LC** K10; .O8839. **DD** 343.7305/4/05; 347.3035405. ***Continued by*** *Journal of Property Tax Management.*

NE/0047-2727
**JOURNAL OF PUBLIC ECONOMICS.** [J. public econ.]. (April 1972)-. Periodical. English. Nine times a year (3 vols.). 1170.00F. Elsevier Sequoia SA, PO Box 564, CH-1001 Lausanne 1 Switzerland. **Tel** 011 41 21 3207381. **ED** A.B. Atkinson and N.H. Stern. **LC** HJ101; .J68. **DD** 336/.005. **CODEN** JPBEBK. **[CCC]. Pr Rev.** available on microfilm and microfiche from University Microfilms International (UMI). Documents available from The Genuine Article, UMI Article Clearinghouse.
**Desc:** Encourages original contributions to the problems of public sector economics, with particular emphasis on the application of modern economic theory and methods of quantitative analysis.
**Ind/Abst** ABI/INFORM Glob. Ed.; ABI Inform Ondisc (Feb. 1981-); Acad. Search (July 1993-); Appl. Soc. Sci. Index Abstr.; Bus. Index (1985-); Bus. Source (Jul. 1993-); Contents Recent Econ. J.; Curr. Contents Soc. Behav. Sci.; Econ. Lit. Index; Educ. Adm. Abstr. (?-?); Gen. BusinessFile (1985-); Gen. Period. Index (1985-); Hum. Resour. Abstr. (?-?); Index Period. Artic. Relat. Law (19??-19??); INFO-SOUTH Abstr.; J. Econ. Lit.; J. Plan. Lit.; Mag. Search; Middle East Abstr. Index; PAIS Int. Print; Res. Alert [Full Cov.]; Rural Dev. Abstr.; Sage Public Adm. Abstr.; Sage Urban Stud. Abstr; Soc. Sci. Cit. Index [Full Cov.]; World Agric. Econ.

US/0093-5107
**JOURNAL OF REAL ESTATE TAXATION.** (THE JOURNAL OF REAL ESTATE TAXATION.). [J. real estate tax.]. (Fall 1973)-. Periodical. English. qt. $147.25 US; $225.95 other. Warren Gorham & Lamont Inc., Park Square Building, 31 St. James Avenue, Boston MA 02116-4112. **Tel** (617)423-2020, (800)950-1207, FAX (617)423-2026. **ED** Lester B. Snyder. **LC** HJ4181.A1; J68. **DD** 336.2/2/0973. **[CCC]. Pr Rev.** available on microfilm and microfiche from University Microfilms International (UMI). Documents available from The Genuine Article, UMI Article Clearinghouse.
**Desc:** Provides coverage of all aspects of real estate tax planning. Delivers guidance on how to structure clients'

transactions to increase after-tax profits, and advice on dealing effectively with capital gains, forms of ownership, and land development.
**Ind/Abst** ABI/INFORM Glob. Ed.; ABI Inform Ondisc (Fall 1974-); Account. Tax Datab. (Fall 1974-); Account. Art.; Curr. Law Index (1980-); Fed. Tax Artic.; Gen. BusinessFile (1992-); Index Leg. Period.; Leg. Resour. Index (1980-); LegalTrac (1980-); Res. Alert [Full Cov.]; Soc. Sci. Cit. Index [Full Cov.].

US/1045-1471
**JOURNAL OF S CORPORATION TAXATION.** [J. S corp. tax.]. **VFOAT** S Corporation Taxation. Vol. 1, No. 1 (Summer 1989)-. Periodical. English. qt. $147.25 US; $225.95 other. Warren Gorham & Lamont Inc., Park Square Building, 31 St. James Avenue, Boston MA 02116-4112. **Tel** (617)423-2020, (800)950-1207, FAX (617)423-2026. **LC** K10; .O893. **DD** 343.7306/7/05; 347.3036705. **[CCC].**
**Ind/Abst** Account. Tax Datab. (1989-); Account. Art.; Fed. Tax Artic.

US/0744-6713
**JOURNAL OF STATE TAXATION.** [J. state tax.]. Vol. 1, No. 1 (Spring 1982)-. Periodical. English. qt. $148.00 US. Panel Publishers, A Division of Aspen Publishers, Inc., 7201 McKinney Circle, PO Box 990, Frederick MD 21705-9727. **Tel** (800)638-8437. **(Subscription address:** Aspen Publishers Inc., PO Box 990, Frederick MD 21701.**) ED** James T. Collins, JD. **LC** K10; .O8954. **DD** 343.04/3; 342.343. **[CCC]. Circ:** 2,000 (ctrl).
**Desc:** Devoted exclusively to the growing challenges of the state tax field. Special departments monitor important cases, and pertinent articles in professional literature.
**Ind/Abst** Account. Tax Datab. (1986-); Account. Art.; Curr. Law Index (1984-); Leg. Resour. Index (1984-); LegalTrac (1984-); PAIS Int. Print (1991-).

US/0022-4863
**JOURNAL OF TAXATION, THE.** [J. tax.]. **VFOAT** Taxation. Vol. 1, No. 1 (June 1954)-. Periodical. English. mo. $178.75 US and Canada; $264.95 other. Warren Gorham & Lamont Inc., Park Square Building, 31 St. James Avenue, Boston MA 02116-4112. **Tel** (617)423-2020, (800)950-1207, FAX (617)423-2026. **LC** HJ2360; .J6. **DD** 336.205. **CODEN** JOTAAM. **[CCC]. Pr Rev.** available on microfilm and microfiche from University Microfilms International (UMI). Documents available from The Genuine Article, UMI Article Clearinghouse.
**Desc:** Coverage of every key tax development. Contains analysis of every important court decision, revenue ruling and administrative and legislative development, as well as advice on daily tax problems.
**Ind/Abst** ABI/INFORM Glob. Ed.; ABI Inform Ondisc (Sept. 1971-); Acad. Search (Jan. 1994-); Account. Tax Datab. (Sept. 1971-); Account. Art.; Bus. Index (1985-); Bus. Period. Index; Cumul. Index Nurs. Allied Health Lit.; Curr. Contents Soc. Behav. Sci.; Curr. Law Index (1980-); Expand. Acad. Index (1992-); Fed. Tax Artic.; Gen. BusinessFile (1985-); Gen. Period. Index (1985-); Index Leg. Period.; INFO-SOUTH Abstr.; Law Office Inf. Serv.; Leg. Resour. Index (1980-); LegalTrac (1980-); Mag. Search; Newsp. Period. Abstr. (1992-); PAIS Int. Print (1991-?); Res. Alert [Full Cov.]; Soc. Sci. Cit. Index [Full Cov.]; Trade Ind. Index (1981-?); Wilson Bus. Abstr.

US/8755-6049
**JOURNAL OF TAXATION DIGEST, THE.** ***Title Change.*** [J. tax. dig.]. (1981)-(1992). English. an. Warren Gorham & Lamont Inc., Park Square Building, 31 St. James Avenue, Boston MA 02116-4112. **Tel** (617)423-2020, (800)950-1207, FAX (617)423-2026. **LC** KF6271; .J68. **DD** 343.7304; 347.3034. **[CCC].** ***Continued by*** *WGL Tax Journal Digest, 8755-6049.*

US/1043-0539
**JOURNAL OF TAXATION OF EXEMPT ORGANIZATIONS, THE.** [J. tax. exempt organ.]. Vol. 1, No. 1 (Spring 1989)-. Periodical. English. bm. $168.25 US and Canda; $251.95 other. Warren Gorham & Lamont Inc., Park Square Building, 31 St. James Avenue, Boston MA 02116-4112. **Tel** (617)423-2020, (800)950-1207, FAX (617)423-2026. **ED** Robert J. Murdich. **LC** KF6449.A15; J66. **DD** 343.7305/266/05; 347.303526605. **Bk Rev. Ad Acc. Circ:** 1,500 (ctrl). available on microfilm and microfiche from University Microfilms International (UMI); available on an online database (file 485/Full-Text) from DIALOG.
**Ind/Abst** Account. Tax Datab. (1989-) [Full Txt.]; Account. Art.

US/0198-9073
**JOURNAL OF THE AMERICAN TAXATION ASSOCIATION, THE.** (THE JOURNAL OF THE AMERICAN TAXATION ASSOCIATION : A PUBLICATION OF THE TAX SECTION OF THE AMERICAN ACCOUNTING ASSOCIATION.). [J. Am. Tax. Assoc.]. **Added/Corp** American Taxation Association. American Accounting Association. Tax Section. (1979)-. Periodical. English. sa (Spring and Fall). $20.00. American Accounting Association, 5717 Bessie Drive, Sarasota FL 34233-2399. **Tel** (813)921-7747, FAX (813)923-4093. **ED** Jane O. Burns. **LC** HF5681.T3; J68. **DD** 657/.46/0973. **Bk Rev. Ad Acc. Circ:** 1,300. available on microfilm and microfiche from University Microfilms International (UMI).
**Desc:** The editorial policy and instructions for submitting a manuscript to the journal are included in the front pages of each issue.
**Ind/Abst** Account. Tax Datab. (1979-); Account. Art.; Fed. Tax Artic.; J. Plan. Lit.

SA
**JUTA'S SOUTH AFRICAN AND RHODESIAN INCOME TAX SERVICE : INCOME TAX TABLES AND COMPUTATIONS FOR REPUBLIC OF SOUTH AFRICA, SOUTH WEST AFRICA, UNITED KINGDOM, RHODESIA.** **VFOAT** Income Tax Tables and Computations for Republic of South Africa, South West Africa, United Kingdom, Rhodesia. English. Juta Subscription Services, PO Box 14373, Kenwyn 7790 South Africa. **Tel** 011 27 21 7975101, FAX (021)761-5010, telex 523072 SA. **DD** 343/.68/052. ***Continues*** *Juta's South African Income Tax Service. Income Tax Tables, Rates, Rebates and Computations for Republic of South Africa, South West Africa, Federation of Rhodesia and Nyasaland, United Kingdom.*

JA
**KANAZAWA KOKUZEIKYOKU TOKEISHO.** **Main/Corp** Japan. Kanazawa Kokuzeikyoku. (19??)-. Periodical. Japanese. Kanazawa Kokuzei Kysku, c/o Godo Chosa 920, Kanawa Japan. **LC** HJ77.Z5; C454a.

FI
**KANSANTALOUS.** **VFOAT** Nationalrakenskaper; National Accounts. Finnish (Swedish and English). ir. Fmk855.00 Finland; Fmk827.00 other. Central Statistical Office, PO Box 504, SF-00101 Helsinki Finland. **Tel** 358-0-17347, 1002111 TILASTO SF, FAX 358-0-17342279.

US
**KANSAS ANNUAL FINANCIAL REPORT FOR PERIOD JULY 1, ... TO JUNE 30, ... / STATE OF KANSAS, DEPARTMENT OF ADMINISTRATION, DIVISION OF ACCOUNTS AND REPORTS.** **Main/Corp** Kansas. Dept. of Administration. Division of Accounts and Reports. **VFOAT** Financial Report. (1988/89)-. English. an. Kansas Department of Administration, Division of Accounts and Reports, 900 Jackson, 251 Landon Street, Topeka KS 66612-1220. **Tel** (913)296-2311. ***Continues in part*** *Financial Report for Period July 1, ... to June 30, ... / State of Kansas, Department of Administration, Division of Accounts and Reports.*

JA
**KANTO SHIN-ETSU KOKUZEIKYOKU TOKEISHO.** **Main/Corp** Japan. Kanto Shin-Etsu Kokuzeikyoku. No. 19 (1966)-. Periodical. Japanese. Otemachi Godo Chosha, 3-2 Otemachi 1 Chiyoda-ku 100, Tokyo Japan. **LC** HJ77.Z5; K364. ***Continues*** *Zeimu Tokeisho.*

US/0095-1498
**KENTUCKY LOCAL DEBT REPORT.** **Main/Corp** Kentucky. Dept. for Local Government. (19??)-. English. ir. Free. Kentucky Department of Finance and Administration, State Capitol Annex, Room 318, Frankfort KY 40601. ***Continues*** *Kentucky. Office for Local Government. Kentucky Local Debt Report.*

US/0162-7511
**KESS TAX PRACTICE REPORT.** ***Ceased.*** (19?? )-(1985). English. mo. Warren Gorham & Lamont Inc., Park Square Building, 31 St. James Avenue, Boston MA 02116-4112. **Tel** (617)423-2020, (800)950-1207, FAX (617)423-2026.

IO
**KEUANGAN NEGARA.** Vol. 1- July 1957-. Periodical. Indonesian. Kementerian Kenangan, Lapangan Banteng Timur 2, Djakarta Indonesia. **LC** HJ1344; .K46.

UK
**KEY TO INCOME TAX.** **VFOAT** Taxation, Key to Income Tax. English. an. Taxation Publishing Company, 98 Park Street, London W1Y 4BR England. **LC** KD5429.3; .K49. **DD** 343.4105/2/05; 344.1035205. ***Continues*** *Taxation, Key to Income Tax and Surtax.*

II
**KEY TO THE BUDGET DOCUMENTS.** **Main/Corp** India (Republic). Dept. of Economic Affairs. Budget Division. (19??)-. English. **LC** HJ65; .B153. **DD** 354/.54/00722.

DK
**KILDESKATTELEKSIKON.** **Main/Corp** Fllesradet for Danske Tjenestemands- Og Funktionrorganisationer. Danish. 13.00. FTF, Vesterport Trommesalen 2 3, 1614 V Kbenhavn Denmark.

US/0023-1762
**KIPLINGER TAX LETTER, THE.** **Added/Corp** Kiplinger Washington Agency, Inc. Kiplinger Washington Editors, Inc. (1925)-. Periodical. English. bw (26 issues). $54.00 (one year), $100.00 (two year). Kiplinger Washington Editors, 1729 H Street Northwest, Washington DC 20006. **Tel** (202)887-6400, (800)544-0155, FAX (202)331-1206. **(Subscription address:** Kiplinger Washington Editors, 3401 East West Highway, c/o Rick Topolski, Editors Park MD 20782.**) ED** S. Ivins. **LC** HJ9; .K56. **DD** 343.7305/05; 347.303505. **Circ:** 114,000.
**Desc:** News focusing on tax issues and problems associated with personal or business financial management.

US
**KIPLINGER'S SURE WAYS TO CUT YOUR TAXES.** (19??)-. Periodical. English. an. $13.95. Kiplinger Washington Editors, 1729 H Street Northwest, Washington DC 20006. **Tel** (202)887-6400, (800)544-0155, FAX (202)331-1206.

JA
**KOGAKU SHOTOKUSHA MEIBO; KANTO-BAN.** **Added/Corp** Tokyo Shoko Risachi. (19??)-. Periodical. Japanese. ¥27000. Tokyo Shoko Risachi, c/o Shinichi Building, 9-6 Shinbashi 1-chome Minato-ku 105, Tokyo Japan. **LC** HJ4773.K35; K63.

GR
**KOINONIKOS PROYPOLOGISMOS ETOUS ... / HYPOURGEIO HYGEIAS, PRONOIAS, KAI KOINONIKON ASPHALISEON, GENIKE GRAMMATEIA KOINONIKON ASPHALISEON, D/NSE EPITHEORESES.** **See** Sociology-Social Services and Welfare.

JA
**KOKYO JIGYO TO YOSAN / KENSETSUSHO KOKYO JIGYO YOSAN KENKYUKAI HEN.** **Added/Corp** Kensetsusho Kokyo Jigyo Yosan Kenkyukai (Japan). (19??)-. Periodical. Japanese. ¥2800. Taisei Shuppansha, 1-7-11 Hanegi 1, Setagaya-ku, Tokyo-to Japan. **LC** HJ7909; .K65 .

DK/0901-0319
**KOMMUNALE TAL FRA INDENRIGSMINISTERIET ... SKN.** **VFOAT** Skn. Danish. **LC** HJ9056; .A23.

SW/0347-7290
**KOMMUNERNAS FINANSER.** **Main/Corp** Sweden. Statistiska Centralbyran. **VFOAT** Local Government Finance. 1918/21-. Swedish (English). an. Kr140.00. SCB Statistiska Centralbyran, 11581 Stockholm Sweden. **LC** HA1521; .F44; HJ9523. **DD** 336/.014/485. Index available.

FI
**KULTTUURIN JULKINEN RAHOITUS.** **VFOAT** Public Financing of Cultural Activities. (1987)-. Finnish (summaries and/or abstracts in English). Tilastokeskus, PL 504, Annankatu 44, 00101 Helsinki Finland. **Tel** 358-0-17341, FAX 358-0-17342474, telex 1002111 TILASTO SF.

JA
**KUMAMOTO KOKUZEIKYOKU TOKEISHO.** **Main/Corp** Japan. Kumamoto Kokuzeikyoku. (1967)-. Periodical. Japanese. Kumamoto Kokuzeikyoku, c/o Kumamoto Godo Chosha 1-2 Ninomaru, Kumamoto 860 Japan. **LC** HJ77.Z5; K97a. ***Continues*** *Zeimu Tokeisho.*

FI
**KUNNALLISTALOUDEN ENNAKKOTILASTO.** **VFOAT** Kommunalhushallningens Forhandsstatistk. 1972-. Multiple languages (Finnish and Swedish). Tilastokeskus, PL 504, Annankatu 44, 00101 Helsinki Finland. **Tel** 358-0-17341, FAX 358-0-17342474, telex 1002111 TILASTO SF. **LC** HJ9055.3; .A25A.

FI
**KUNTAINLIITTOJEN TALOUS.** **Main/Corp** Finland. Tilastokeskus. **VFOAT** Kommunalforbundens Ekonomi. Finnish (Swedish). Tilastokeskus, PL 504, Annankatu 44, 00101 Helsinki Finland. **Tel** 358-0-17341, FAX 358-0-17342474, telex 1002111 TILASTO SF. **LC** HJ9055.3; .A22A.

FI
**KUNTIEN TALOUS: KUNNITTAISET TIEDOT. KOMMUNERNAS EKONOMI: UPPGIFTER ENLIGT KOMMUN.** **Main/Corp** Finland. Tilastokeskus. **Added/Corp** Finland. Tilastokeskus. Kommunernas Ekonomi: Uppgifter Enlight Kommun. **VFOAT** Kommunernas Ekonomi : Uppgifter Enligt Kommun. (19??)-. Multiple languages (Finnish and Swedish). ir. Tilastokeskus, PL 504, Annankatu 44, 00101 Helsinki Finland. **Tel** 358-0-17341, FAX 358-0-17342474, telex 1002111 TILASTO SF. **LC** HJ9055.3; .A22b.

FR
**LAMY FISCAL.** **See** Law.

# Public Administration — Public Finance and Taxation

IO
**LAPORAN TRIWULAN - DIREKTORAT JENDERAL PAJAK.** Main/Corp Indonesia. Direktorat Jenderal Pajak. 1972/73-. Indonesian. **LC** HK69; .R127. *Continues* Indonesia. Direktorat Djenderal Padjak. Laporan.

US/0745-4449
**LATAX REPORT.** [Latax rep.]. Added/Corp Los Angeles Taxpayers Association. **VAT** Los Angeles Taxpayers Association Report. (19??)-. Periodical. English. sm. $25.00. Los Angeles Taxpayers Association, 1052 West 6th Street, Suite 600, Los Angeles CA 90017. **Tel** (213) 482-5214. **Circ:** 700.
Desc: Focus is on actions of local governments within Los Angeles County.

US
**LEGISLATIVE ASSEMBLY REPORT ON APPROPRIATIONS AND ESTIMATED REVENUES.** Main/Corp North Dakota. Legislative Assembly. Legislative Council. English. be. Legislative Council - Alaska, State Capitol, Juneau AK 99811. **Tel** (406)444-3064. **LC** HJ11; .N9394A. **DD** 353.9/784/00722. *Continues* Final Report on Appropriations and Estimated Revenues.

US/0495-2499
**LEGISLATIVE BUDGET ESTIMATES.** [Legis. budg. estim.]. Main/Corp Texas. Legislative Budget Board. (19??)-. English. be. Legislative Budget Board, Box 12666 Capitol Station, Austin TX 78711. **LC** HJ2053.T4; A3. **DD** 353.9/764/00722.

US/0147-3638
**LEGISLATIVE CALENDAR / UNITED STATES HOUSE OF REPRESENTATIVES, COMMITTEE ON THE BUDGET.** Main/Corp United States. Congress. House. Committee on the Budget. English. an. Congressional Budget Office, 2nd and D Streets SW, Washington DC 20515. **Tel** (202)226-2115. **LC** KF22; .B83. **DD** 328.73/07/5. available on microfiche (Vols. for (99th Congress-) distributed to some depository libraries). Documents available from Documents on Demand.
Ind/Abst CIS Index Publ. U.S. Congr.

US/0278-1352
**LEGISLATOR'S HANDBOOK (DETROIT, MICH.), THE.** (THE LEGISLATOR'S HANDBOOK.). English. be. Citizens Research Council of Michigan, 625 Shelby Street, Detroit MI 48226-4154. **Tel** (313)961-5377. **LC** HJ505; .L43. **DD** 336.774.

•US
**LET'S GO: THE BUDGET GUIDE TO WASHINGTON, D.C./ WRITTEN BY HARVARD STUDENT AGENCIES, INC.** Added/Corp Harvard Student Agencies. **VFOAT** Budget Guide to Washington D.C. 1st Ed. (1992)-. English. St. Martin's Press, 175 Fifth Avenue, New York NY 10010. **Tel** (800)221-7945, (212)982-3900, FAX (212)777-6359.

VE
**LEY DE PRESUPUESTO PARA EL EJERCICIO FISCAL.** Main/Corp Venezuela. Spanish. an. **LC** HJ39.

DK/0106-5408
**LIGNINGSVEJLEDNINGEN. SELSKABER / STATSSKATTEDIREKTORATET, LIGNINGSAFDELINGEN, SELSKABSSKATTEKONTORET.** Main/Corp Denmark. Statsskattedirektoratet. Danish. Statsskattedirektoratet Ligningsafdelingen, Meldahlsgade 5, 1613 Kbenhavn V Denmark.

FI
**LIIKEVAIHTOVEROVELVOLLISET YRITYKSET.** Main/Corp Finland. Tilastokeskus. **VFOAT** Omsattningsskattskyldiga Foretag. Multiple languages (Finnish and Swedish). Tilastokeskus, PL 504, Annankatu 44, 00101 Helsinki Finland. **Tel** 358-0-17341, FAX 358-0-17342474, telex 1002111 TILASTO SF. **LC** HJ5715.F5; F56B.

US
**LIST OF APPROPRIATIONS : MADE BY THE REGULAR SESSION OF THE ... GENERAL ASSEMBLY AND THE ... SPECIAL SESSION THEREOF FOR THE BIENNIUM.** Main/Corp Indiana. State Budget Agency. Added/Corp Indiana. General Assembly. (June 30, 1991)-. English. be. **LC** HJ11; .I643c. *Continues* State of Indiana Budget Report for the Biennium ... as passed by the ... Session of the General Assembly and the ... Special Session.

US/0277-0776
**LIST OF PUBLICATIONS - UNITED STATES. CONGRESSIONAL BUDGET OFFICE.** (LIST OF PUBLICATIONS.). Main/Corp United States. Congressional Budget Office. Spring 1979-. English. an. Congressional Budget Office, 2nd and D Streets SW, Washington DC 20515. **Tel** (202)226-2115. **LC** Z7164.F5; U465A; HJ2052. **DD** 016.3530072/2. *Continues* Congressional Budget Office List of Publications, 0277-0776.

CN/0821-0772
**LISTE TEMOIN SUR LA PLANIFICATION FISCALE.** French (English). an. Free. Liste Temoin sur la Planification Fiscale, Coopers & Lybrand, 1170 Peel Street, Montreal Quebec H3B 4T2 Canada. **DD** 343.7105/23. ctrl circ.

AT
**LOCAL GOVERNMENT FINANCE, NEW SOUTH WALES.** Added/Corp Australian Bureau of Statistics. New South Wales Office. (1977)-. English. an. Price varies. Australian Bureau of Statistics, PO Box 10, Belconnen Australian Capital Territory, 2616 Australia. **Tel** 011 61 6 2527911, FAX 011 61 6 2516009. **LC** HA3011; .A22. **DD** 336/.014/944. *Continues* Local Government, New South Wales.
Desc: Summary tables of financial data for Sydney statistical division, Newcastle and Wollongong statistical districts and rest of State classified according to type of services provided.

CN/0703-2749
**LOCAL GOVERNMENT FINANCE REVENUE AND EXPENDITURE ASSETS AND LIABILITIES ACTUAL.** Suspended. [Local gov. finance, Revenue expend. assets liabil. actual]. **VFOAT** Finances des Administrations Publiques Locales, Recettes et Depenses, Actif et Passif, Chiffres Reels. (1967)-. English (French). an. 26.00Can$ Canada; $31.00 other. Statistics Canada, Publications Sales & Services, Main Building Room 1710, Ottawa Ontario K1A 0T6 Canada. **Tel** (613)951-5078, (800)267-6677, FAX (613)951-1584, telex 053-3585. **LC** HJ9014; .A365. **DD** 336/.014/71. Absorbed Finances des Administrations Locales, Recettes et Depenses, Actif et Passif, Chiffres Reels, 0703-2730; *Continues* Municipal Government Finance. Revenue and Expenditure, Assets and Liabilities, Actual, 0575-9153.

US
**LOOSELEAF REGULATIONS SYSTEM. SERVICE 1. INCOME TAX.** Main/Corp United States. Internal Revenue Service. **VFOAT** Income Tax. Periodical. English. ir. Income Tax, US Treasury Department, Internal Revenue Service, Washington DC 20402.
Desc: The IRS Looseleaf regulation system is a compilation of all regulations issued by the Service, except those relating to alcohol, tobacco, firearms and tax conventions.

US
**LOOSELEAF REGULATIONS SYSTEM. SERVICE 2. ESTATE AND GIFT TAX.** Main/Corp United States. Internal Revenue Service. **VFOAT** Estate and Gift Tax. Periodical. English. ir. Estate and Gift Tax, US Treasury Department, Internal Revenue Service, Washington DC 20402.
Desc: The IRS regulation system is a compilation of all regulations issued by the Service, except those relating to alcohol, tobacco, firearms and tax conventions.

US
**LOOSELEAF REGULATIONS SYSTEM. SERVICE 3. EMPLOYMENT TAX.** Main/Corp United States. Internal Revenue Service. **VFOAT** Employment Tax. (1???)-. Periodical. English. Homemaker's, 2300 Yonge Street/Suite 401, Toronto Ontario M4P 1E4 Canada. **Tel** (416)482-8260.
Desc: The IRS looseleaf regulation system is a compilation of all regulations issued by the Service, except those relating to alcohol, tobacco, firearms and tax conventions.

US/0098-9177
**LOTTERY WORLD.** V. 1- Apr. 1975-. English. Automatic Totalisators Inc, Circulation, 100 Bellevue Road, Newark DE 19713. **LC** HG6126; .L68. **DD** 338.4/7/79501.

US
**LOW-INCOME HOUSING TAX CREDIT HANDBOOK.** Added/Corp Clark Boardman Company. Clark Boardman Callaghan. **VFOAT** Low Income Housing Tax Credit Handbook. (1990)-. English. Clark Boardman Callaghan, 155 Pfingsten Road, Deerfield IL 60015. **Tel** (800)323-8067. **LC** IN PROCESS; KF6397.A1; L69.

US/0899-563X
**LRC NEWSBRIEFS.** [LRC newsbr.]. Added/Corp Lutheran Resources Commission. Lutheran Resources Commission-Washington. **VFOAT** Newsbriefs. **VAT** Lutheran Resources Commission Newsbriefs. 1987 Series, No. 10 (October 30, 1987)-. Periodical. English. mo. $60.00. Lutheran Resources Commission, Five Thomas Circle NW, Washington DC 20005. **Tel** (202)667-9844. **DD** 001. *Continues* LRC-W Newsbriefs, 0889-5562.

US/0557-4447
**LUSK'S MONTGOMERY COUNTY, MARYLAND, ASSESSMENT DIRECTORY.** See Real Estate.

II
**MADHYA PRADESH BUDGET IN BRIEF.** Main/Corp Madhya Pradesh (India). Directorate of Economics and Statistics. **VFOAT** MP Budget in Brief. English. an. Directorate of Economics and Statistics / Bhopal, Bhopal India. **LC** HJ66.M26; B25. **DD** 354.54/30072253.

CN/0844-6695
**MAIN ESTIMATES - BUDGET BUREAU.** (MAIN ESTIMATES.). [Main estim. - Budg. Bur.]. Main/Corp Yukon Territory. Budget Bureau. (1990)-. English. an. **DD** 354.719/10072225. *Continues* Operation and Maintenance Estimates. Yukon Territory. Budget Bureau, 0842-5019; Absorbed Capital Estimates. Yukon Territory. Budget Bureau., 0842-5000.

CN/0704-1748
**MAIN ESTIMATES OF CURRENT EXPENDITURE OF THE PROVINCE OF MANITOBA.** Main/Corp Manitoba. Dept. of Finance. 1978-. Periodical. English. Manitoba Department of Finance, 204 Legislative Building, Winnipeg Manitoba R3C 0V8 Canada. *Continues in part* Manitoba. Dept. of Finance. Main and Supplementary Estimates of Current Expenditure and Revenue of the Province of Manitoba, 0318-3394.

US/1055-5498
**MAJOR TAX PLANNING.** [Major tax plann.]. Main/Corp Tax Institute, University of Southern California. Added/Corp University of Southern California. School of Law. Gould School of Law. **VFOAT** Major Tax Planning. 1956-. English. ir. $136.00. Matthew Bender & Company Inc., 1275 Broadway, Albany NY 12204. **Tel** (800)833-9844, (518)487-3000. **LC** KF6289; .T3. **DD** 343.7304/05; 347.303405. cum. index. *Continues* Major Tax Problems, 1055-5501.
Ind/Abst Curr. Law Index (1985-); Index Leg. Period.; Leg. Resour. Index (1985-); LegalTrac (1985-).

US
**MANHATTAN LAND USE DIRECTORY.** Added/Corp Real Estate Data, Inc. **VFOAT** Manhattan, New York Land Use Directory. Vol. 1 (1983)-. Directory. English. ir. Real Estate Data Inc, 475 Fifth Avenue, Suite 1901, New York NY 10017. **Tel** (212)532-2705. **LC** HJ9289.N4; M23. **DD** 336.22/2.

CN/0317-0306
**MANITOBA AND SASKATCHEWAN SUCCESSION DUTY AND GIFT TAX LEGISLATION.** Main/Corp Manitoba. 2d- Ed.; 1974-. Periodical. English. CCH Canadian Ltd., 6 Garamond Court, Don Mills Ontario M3C 1Z5 Canada. **Tel** (416)441-2992, FAX (416)441-3418. **DD** 343/.7127/05302632. *Continues* Manitoba and Saskatchewan Succession Duty and Gift Tax Acts, 0317-0314.
Desc: Provides information on inheritance and transfer tax, gifts, and donations.

CL
**MANUAL DE CONSULTAS TRIBUTARIAS / ASSOCIACION NACIONAL DE INSPECTORES DE IMPUESTOS INTERNOS.** See Law.

CN/0824-3158
**MANUEL POUR LA PREPARATION DES DECLARATIONS D'IMPOT DES CORPORATIONS.** [Man. prep. declar. impot corp.]. French. an. 24.75Can$ Canada; $18.70 US. Manuel pour la Preparation des Declarations d'Impot des Corporations, a/s Institut Canadien des Comptables Agrees, 150 Ouest rue Bloor, Toronto Ontario M5S 2Y2 Canada. **Tel** (416)962-1242, telex 06-22835. **ED** Harvey J Graham. **DD** 343.7106/7. **Circ:** 1,000.

US/0272-0868
**MARK SKOUSEN'S FORECASTS & STRATEGIES ON INFLATION, TAXES AND GOVERNMENT CONTROLS.** **VFOAT** Forecasts & Strategies. **VAT** Mark Skousen's Forecasts and Strategies on Inflation, Taxes and Government Controls. (Sept. 1980)-. Periodical. English. Twelve times a year. $99.95. Phillips Business Information, Inc., 1201 Seven Locks Road, Potomac MD 20854. **Tel** (301)424-3338, (800)777-5006, FAX (301)309-3847. (Subscription address: Phillips Publishing Inc., 7811 Montrose Road, Potomac MD 20854.) [CCC].
*Supersedes* Price Controls Alert, 0199-9893.

SJ
**MASHRU AL-MIZANIYAH AL-AMMAH WA-MIZANIYAT AL-TANMIYAH LIL-AM AL-MALI ... .** Main/Corp Sudan. Wizarat Al-Maliyah Wa-Al-Iqtisad. Arabic. **LC** HJ80.6; .A28B.

# Public Administration — Public Finance and Taxation

US/0732-0825
**MASSACHUSETTS APPELLATE TAX BOARD REPORTER.** [Mass. Appell. Tax Board report.]. Added/Corp Appellate Tax Board of the Commonwealth of Massachusetts. Butterworth Legal Publishers. Vol. 1, No. 1 (1982)-. Periodical. English. Four times a year. $85.00. Butterworth Heinemann / Woburn, MA, 225 Wildwood Avenue, Unit B, Woburn MA 01801. **Tel** (800)366-2665, FAX (617)928-2620, telex 880052. **LC** KFM2870; .A5575. **DD** 343.74404/02646; 347.4403402646.

US/1046-3216
**MASSACHUSETTS PRIMER / MASSACHUSETTS TAXPAYERS FOUNDATION, INC, A.** [Mass. prim.]. (1980)-. English. be. Massachusetts Taxpayers Foundation Inc, 24 Province Street, Boston MA 02108. **DD** 343. *Continues* Massachusetts Tax Primer, 0362-868X.

US
**MAYOR'S MANAGEMENT REPORT, THE.** English. sa. $15.00 (add $2.00 for postage). CityBooks/ City Publishing Center, Department of General Services, 2208 Municipal Building, 22nd Floor, New York NY 10007. **Tel** (212)669-8245, FAX (212)669-3211. **LC** JS1234.A1; M38. **DD** 352.0747/1.
**Desc:** Shows city agencies' performance, funding and personnel figures.

NE/0005-8335
**MBB : BELASTINGBESCHOUWINGEN.** **VFOAT** Belastingbeschouwingen; Maandblaad Belastingbeschouwingen; M.B.B. (19??)-. Periodical. Dutch (English). Eleven times a year. Fl179.25 Belgium; Fl210.00 Netherlands; Fl225.00 other. BV Belastingbeschouwingen, Van Der Borchlaan 1, 4835 KM Breda Netherlands. **Tel** 011 31 76 612356, FAX 011 31 76 100153. **ED** H.P.A.M. van Arendonk. **LC** K13; .A317. Index available. **Bk Rev**. **Ad Acc**. ctrl circ. *Continues* Belastingbeschouwingen.
**Desc:** Articles about taxation. Gives summaries of Dutch sentences of the fiscal courts and short information about international tax law and EC tax developments.

DK
**MEDDELELSER FRA STATSSKATTEDIREKTORATET OG LIGNINGSRADET.** Main/Corp Denmark. Statsskattedirektoratet. Danish. Meldahlsgade 5, 1613 Kbenhavn Denmark.

US/0895-4550
**MEDIA MERGERS & ACQUISITIONS.** See Business.

US/0538-446X
**MEMBERSHIP DIRECTORY - INTERNATIONAL ASSOCIATION OF ASSESSING OFFICERS (1977).** (MEMBERSHIP DIRECTORY - INTERNATIONAL ASSOCIATION OF ASSESSING OFFICERS.). [Membsh. dir. - Int. Assoc. Assess. Off.]. Main/Corp International Association of Assessing Officers. **VFOAT** Members Only. (1977)-. English. ir. International Association of Assessing Officers, 130 East Randolph Street, Suite 850, Chicago IL 60601. **Tel** (312)819-6100. **ED** Annie Aubrey. *Continues* IAAO Membership Directory.

US/0737-4267
**MEMBERSHIP DIRECTORY - INTERNATIONAL ASSOCIATION OF ASSESSING OFFICERS. PERSONAL PROPERTY SECTION.** (MEMBERSHIP DIRECTORY / PERSONAL PROPERTY SECTION.). Main/Corp International Association of Assessing Officers. Personal Property Section. (19??)-. English. an. International Association of Assessing Officers, 130 East Randolph Street, Suite 850, Chicago IL 60601. **Tel** (312)819-6100. **ED** Stuart W. Miller. **LC** HD1387; .I5a. **DD** 350.72/431/02573. **Circ:** 650 (ctrl).

CN/0846-1023
**MEMBERSHIP ROSTER / CANADIAN PETROLEUM TAX SOCIETY.** [Membsh. roster - Can. Pet. Tax Soc.]. Main/Corp Canadian Petroleum Tax Society. (1990)-. English. Canadian Petroleum Tax Society, PO Box 2562, Station M, Calgary Alberta T2P 3K8 Canada. **Tel** (403)268-3083. **DD** 343.7105/58228/02571.

US/0521-8098
**MEMORANDUM FROM TAX MANAGEMENT.** Added/Corp Tax Management Inc. **VFOAT** Tax Management Memorandum, B. English. bw. Tax Management Inc / Washington DC, 1231 25th Street NW, Washington DC 20037. **Tel** (202)452-4556, (800)372-1033, FAX (202)452-4096, telex 285656 BNAI WSH. **LC** KF6272; .M46. **DD** 343.7305/05; 347.303505. available on microfilm from University Microfilms International (UMI).

II
**MEMORANDUM ON THE BUDGET ESTIMATES WITH DEMANDS FOR GRANTS AND ANNUAL FINANCIAL STATEMENT.** Main/Corp Meghalaya (India). English. an. Assam Government Press / Finance Department Meghalaya, Shillong Meghalaya India. **LC** HJ66.M55; B15. **DD** 354/.54/16400722.

US
**MESSAGE OF THE CITY MANAGER TO THE CITY COUNCIL SUBMITTING THE EXECUTIVE BUDGET.** Main/Corp Kansas City, Mo. City Manager. (19??)-. English. City Manager, City Hall, Kansas City KS 66101. **LC** HJ9013; .K5e3. **DD** 352/.12/09778411.

US
**MICHIGAN LODGING.** See Business-Accounting.

US/0899-2460
**MICHIGAN TAX LAWYER.** See Law.

●US
**MID-SESSION REVIEW : THE PRESIDENT'S BUDGET AND ECONOMIC GROWTH AGENDA OF THE ... BUDGET / EXECUTIVE OFFICE OF THE PRESIDENT, OFFICE OF MANAGEMENT AND BUDGET.** Main/Corp United States. Office of Management and Budget. **VFOAT** Mid Session Review. (July 24, 1992)-. English. Executive Office of the President Office of Management & Budget, Washington DC 20503. **LC** HJ2052.A2; U551. *Continues* United States. Office of Management and Budget.; Mid-Session Review of the ... Budget.

US
**MILLAGE COMPARISON FOR ... .** Assessment Coordination Division, 2020 West 3rd, Little Rock AR 72205.

JA
**MINAMI KYUSHU ZAIMUKYOKU YORAN.** Main/Corp Japan. Minami Kyushu Zaimukyoku. (19??)-. Periodical. Japanese. Minami Kyushu Zaimukyoku, 1-2 Ninomaru 860, Kumamoto Japan. **LC** HJ77.Z5; K974a.

US
**MINNESOTA CORPORATION INCOME TAX.** 1977-. English. an. Minnesota Department of Revenue, Centennial Office Building, St Paul MN 55145. **LC** HJ4655.M57; M56; HJ4655.M567. **DD** 336.24/09776 S; 336.24/3/09776. *Continues* Minnesota State Corporation Income Tax.

US
**MINNESOTA STATE INDIVIDUAL INCOME TAX, THE.** 1976-. English. an. Free in US. Minnesota Department of Revenue Research Division, Mail Station 2230, St Paul MN 55146-2230. **LC** HJ4655.M58; I6 subser. **DD** 336.24/09776 S; 336.24/2/09776. ctrl circ. *Continues* Minnesota Individual Income Tax, 0363-4906.

US/0734-7707
**MINNESOTA TAX COURT DECISIONS.** [Minn. tax court decis.]. Added/Corp Minnesota. Tax Court. **VFOAT** Tax Court Decisions. Vol. 1, No. 1 (Nov. 1, 1982)-. English. ir. Minnesota Documents, 117 University Avenue, St Paul MN 55155. **Tel** (612)297-3000, (800)657-3757, FAX (612)296-2265. **LC** KFM5870; .A515. **DD** 343.77604/02643; 347.7603402643.
**Desc:** Information on the Department of Commerce tax court and property decisions.

US
**MINNESOTA TAX GUIDE.** Main/Corp Minnesota. Dept. of Economic Development. English. Minnesota Department of Trade & Economic Development, 150 East Kellogg Boulevard, American Center Building, Room 900, St Paul MN 55101. **Tel** (612)296-6424, FAX (612)296-1290. **LC** HJ2415; .M48A. **DD** 343.77604/05; 347.7603405.

US/0734-7537
**MINNESOTA TAX JOURNAL.** Ceased. [Minn. tax j.]. **VFOAT** Tax Journal. Vol. 1, No. 1 (Dec. 1982)-Ceased Vol. 16, 1986. Periodical. English. qt. Butterworth Heinemann / Woburn, MA, 225 Wildwood Avenue, Unit B, Woburn MA 01801. **Tel** (800)366-2665, FAX (617)928-2620, telex 880052. **LC** KFM5870.A15; M56. **DD** 343.77604/05; 347.7603405.

CN/1187-4430
**MINUTES OF PROCEEDINGS AND EVIDENCE OF THE SPECIAL COMMITTEE ON THE ACT RESPECTING CUSTOMS.** [Minutes proc. evid. Spec. Comm. Act Respect. Cust.]. Main/Corp Canada. Parliament. House of Commons. Special Committee on the Act Respecting Customs. **VFOAT** Act Respecting Customs; Proces-Verbaux et Temoignages du Comite Special Charge de l'Examen de la Loi Concernant les Douanes. Issue No. 1 (Oct. 2/Oct. 8, 1991)-. Proceedings. English (French). **DD** 354.710082/7/05.

●US/1065-125X
**MONEY INCOME TAX HANDBOOK, THE.** (THE MONEY ... INCOME TAX HANDBOOK / MARY L. SPROUSE WITH THE EDITORS OF MONEY MAGAZINE.). (1993)-. English. $13.99. Warner Books Inc, 666 Fifth Avenue, New York NY 10103. *Continues* Sprouse's Income Tax Handbook, 0899-9107.

US
**MONTANA SUPPLEMENTAL FINANCIAL SCHEDULES.** Main/Corp Montana. Dept. of Administration. Accounting Division. **VFOAT** Supplemental Financial Schedules. (19??)-. English. Montana Department of Administration, Director's Office, Mitchell Building, Helena MT 59601. **LC** HJ11; .M9143b. **DD** 353.97860072/31.

US
**MONTANA TAXATION.** Main/Corp Montana Taxpayer's Association. (19??)-. English. an. $21.00. Montana Tax Foundation, PO Box 4909, Helena MT 59601. **Tel** (406)442-2130.

US
**MONTANA TAXATION.** Added/Corp Montana Tax Foundation. (1981)-. Periodical. English. *Continues* Montana Property Tax.

US/0027-0385
**MONTHLY DIGEST OF TAX ARTICLES, THE.** **VFOAT** Digest of Tax Articles. (Oct. 1950)-. Periodical. English. Twelve times a year. $48.00 US; $80.00 other. Newkirk Products Inc., 15 Corporate Circle, Albany NY 12203. **Tel** (518)452-1000, FAX (518)452-1475. **ED** James H. Blake. **LC** LAW. **DD** 336.205. **[CCC].** Index available (September). **Circ:** 10,000 (ctrl).
**Desc:** Tax and legal publication.

US/0364-1015
**MONTHLY STATEMENT OF THE PUBLIC DEBT OF THE UNITED STATES.** [Mon. statement public debt U. S.]. Added/Corp United States. Bureau of the Public Debt. United States. Dept. of the Treasury. (19??)-. Government Publication. English. mo. $37.00 domestic; $46.25 other. Superintendent of Documents, US Government Printing Office, Washington DC 20402. **Tel** (202)275-3328, FAX (202)786-2377. **DD** 336. Documents available from Documents on Demand. *Continues* Monthly Statement of the Public Debt of the United States, 0364-1015.
**Ind/Abst** Am. Stat. Index.

UK/0951-8223
**MOORES & ROWLAND'S ORANGE TAX GUIDE.** [Moores Rowland's orange tax guide]. **VFOAT** Moores and Rowland's Orange Tax Guide. (1987)-. English. an. £30.95. Butterworth & Co. Ltd. / Kent, England, Borough Green, Sevenoaks Kent TN15 8PH England. **Tel** 011 44 732-884567, FAX 011 44 732-885996. **ED** John Jeffrey-Cook. **DD** 344.103405. *Continues in part* Moores & Rowland's Tax Guide, 0267-8829.
**Desc:** Provides a clear, succinct commentary on Inheritance Tax, National Insurance Contributions, Stamp Duty and VAT.

UK/0951-8231
**MOORES & ROWLAND'S YELLOW TAX GUIDE.** [Moores Rowland's yellow tax guide]. **VFOAT** Moores and Rowland's Yellow Tax Guide. (1987)-. English. an. £30.95. Butterworth & Co. Ltd. / Kent, England, Borough Green, Sevenoaks Kent TN15 8PH England. **Tel** 011 44 732-884567, FAX 011 44 732-885996. **ED** John Jeffrey-Cook. **DD** 344.103405. *Continues in part* Moores & Rowland's Tax Guide, 0267-8829.
**Desc:** Provides a clear, succinct commentary on income tax, corporation tax and capital gains tax.

UK
**MOORE'S AND ROWLAND'S YELLOW TAX GUIDE.** English. an. £27.95. Butterworth & Co. Ltd. / Kent, England, Borough Green, Sevenoaks Kent TN15 8PH England. **Tel** 011 44 732-884567, FAX 011 44 732-885996.

US
**MOTOR FUEL TAXES, AMOUNTS DISTRIBUTED TO CITIES, AND TO ALL LOCAL GOVERNMENTS BY COUNTY, CALENDAR YEAR ... / OHIO DEPARTMENT OF TAXATION.** English. an. Department of Taxation / Ohio, Research and Statistics Section, PO Box 530, Columbus OH 43216. **LC** HD6579.G5; U5725. **DD** 336.2/7866553827/09771.

US/0364-250X
**MSA TAX CORRESPONDENT.** Main/Corp Management Services Associates, Austin, Tex. **VFOAT** Tax Correspondent. **VAT** Management Services

Associates Tax Correspondent. English. Management Service Associates, PO Box 3750, Austin TX 78764. **LC** HJ4121.T4; M35A. **DD** 336.2/009764.

US/0730-9171
**MULTI-LEVEL MARKETING TAX AND FINANCIAL NEWSLETTER / MLM. See** Business-Marketing.

US/1051-1555
**MULTISTATE CORPORATE TAX GUIDE.** [Multistate corp. tax guide]. **VFOAT** Multi State Corporate Tax Guide; Mid Year Updates. (1990)-. English. sa (2 main volumes per year plus monthly updates). $212.00. Aspen Publishers Inc., 7201 McKinney Circle, Frederick MD 21701. **Tel** (800)234-1660, (301)698-7100, FAX (301)251-5784, telex 5106014543. **(Subscription address:** Aspen Publishers Inc., PO Box 990, Frederick MD 21701.**) LC** HD2753.U6; M85. **DD** 343.7305/267/05; 347.303526705. ***Continues*** *Multistate Corporate Tax Almanac, 0747-718X.*

US
**MULTISTATE PART-YEAR NONRESIDENT RETURN GUIDE.** (19??)-. Periodical. English. mo. Commerce Clearing House Inc., 4025 West Peterson Avenue, Chicago IL 60646-6085. **Tel** (312)583-8500, FAX (708)940-4600. **ED** Daniel Newquist. Index available. cum. index.
**Desc:** Covers the personal income tax laws of all 40 states that have income taxes, plus New York City and the District of Columbia. Provides information to prepare and file income tax returns of clients regardless of their residence or investment location.

US/0892-4678
**MULTISTATE TAX ANALYST. VFOAT** MTA. Vol. 1, No. 1 (March 1986)-. Periodical. English. Twelve times a year. $205.00 (one year), $345.00 (two year). Corporate Tax Publishers, PO Box 261, Leonia NJ 07605. **Tel** (201)461-6619. **ED** Michael Fishbein. **LC** KF6755.A59; M85. **DD** 343.7305/267; 347.3035267. Index available. **Bk Rev. Circ:** 1,200.
**Desc:** Contains analysis of recent developments in state taxation of significance to large corporations.

US
**MULTISTATE TAX COMMISSION REVIEW. Added/Corp** Multistate Tax Commission. **VFOAT** Review. Vol. 1, No. 1 (Nov. 1981)-. Periodical. English. Four times a year. Free to government agencies and libraries; $35.00 other. Multistate Tax Commission, 444 North Capital Street NW, Suite 425, Washington DC 20001. **Tel** (202)624-8699, FAX (202)624-8819. **ED** Eugene Corrigan. **Bk Rev. Circ:** 3,000. ***Continues*** *Multistate Tax Newsletter.*

US/0199-6134
**MUNICIPAL FINANCE JOURNAL.** [Munic. finance j.]. Vol. 1, Winter (Jan. 1980)-. Periodical. English. qt. $156.00 US. Panel Publishers, A Division of Aspen Publishers, Inc., 7201 McKinney Circle, PO Box 990, Frederick MD 21705-9727. **Tel** (800)638-8437. **(Subscription address:** Aspen Publishers Inc., PO Box 990, Frederick MD 21701.**) ED** W. Bartley Hildreth. **LC** HJ9103; .M79. **DD** 352.1/0973. **[CCC]. Bk Rev. Ad Acc. Circ:** 1,500 (ctrl).
**Desc:** Covers municipal bonds and finance. Give timely analysis and creative ideas for raising capital at both the state and local level.
**Ind/Abst** Account. Tax Datab. (1986-); PAIS Int. Print (1991-); Urban Aff. Abstr.

SA
**MUVHIGO WA MULAULI NA MUTOLAMUVHALELANO MUHULU NGA HA MBALELANO DZA MUVHUSO WA VENDA NA WA MBALELANO DZA MIVHUSO MITUKU VHUPONI HAWO DZA NWAHA. Main/Corp** South Africa. Controller and Auditor-General. **VFOAT** Report of the Controller and Auditor-General on the Accounts of the Venda Government and of the Accounts of Lower Authorities in the Area. Afrikaans (English and Venda). R2.00. The Government Printer, Bosman Street, Private Bag X85, Pretoria 0001 South Africa. **Tel** 012-323-9731, FAX 012-323-0009. **LC** HJ9588.A2; V47A.

US
**N T A-T I A BOOKSHELF. Main/Corp** National Tax Association-Tax Institute of America and Fund for Public Policy Research. (1970)-. Periodical. English.

II/0303-8505
**NAGALAND BUDGET. SOME FACTS AND CHARTS. See** Public Administration-Abstracting, Bibliographies and Statistics.

US/0363-4965
**NASBO NEWSLETTER. Main/Corp** National Association of State Budget Officers. Newsletter. English. qt. PO Box 11910, Lexington KY 40578. **LC** HJ2050.A2; N37A. **DD** 353.007/22. ***Continues*** *National Association of State Budget Officers. Quarterly Newsletter.*

LU
**NATIONAL ACCOUNTS ESA, AGGREGATES. Main/Corp** Statistical Office of the European Communities. **Added/Corp** Statistical Office of the European Communities. Comptes Nationaux SEC. Agregats. Statistical Office of the European Communities. Nationale Rekeningen ESER. Totalen. **VFOAT** Comptes Nationaux, SEC Agregats; Nationale Rekeningen, ESER Totalen. (1960/74)-. English (Dutch and French). ir. $7.50. Office for Official Publications of the European Communities, 2 Rue Mercier, 2985 Luxembourg Luxembourg. **Tel** 011 352 499281, FAX 011 352 488573. **(Subscription address:** Moniteur Belge Belg Staatsbald, rue de Louvain 40-42, 1000 Brussels Belgium.**) LC** HC240.9.I5; S7a. **DD** 339.34. ***Continues*** *Nationalregnskaber, ENS Totaler.*
**Desc:** Results of the principal aggregates of the national accounts drawn up according to ESA (European system of integrated national accounts).

CN/0825-9216
**NATIONAL BALANCE SHEET ACCOUNTS.** (NATIONAL BALANCE SHEET ACCOUNTS / STATISTICS CANADA, INTERNATIONAL AND FINANCIAL ECONOMICS DIVISION, FINANCIAL FLOWS SECTION.). [Natl. balance sheet acc.]. **Added/Corp** Statistics Canada. Financial Flows Section. Statistics Canada. National Accounts and Environment Division. **VFOAT** Comptes du Bilan National; Financial Flow and National Balance Sheet Accounts; Comptes des Flux Financiers et Bilan National. (1961/1984)-. English (French). an. 40.00Can$ Canada; $48.00 US; $56.00 other. Statistics Canada, Publications Sales & Services, Main Building Room 1710, Ottawa Ontario K1A 0T6 Canada. **Tel** (613)951-5078, (800)267-6677, FAX (613)951-1584, telex 053-3585. **LC** HC120.I5; N37. **DD** 339.2/6/0971.
**Desc:** Provides data for national and sectoral wealth and net worth in the form of annual balance sheets for the total economy and its component sectors.

NO
**NATIONAL BUDGET, THE. Main/Corp** Norway. **Added/Corp** Norway. Finans- og Tolldepartementet. (1986)-. English. **LC** HJ58; .A26 subser. ***Continues*** *Norway. Finans- og Tolldepartementet. Nasjonalbudsjettet.*
**Ind/Abst** F&S Index Plus Text, Int. [Select. Cov.]; Predicasts Forecasts.

FI
**NATIONAL BUDGET FOR FINLAND. Main/Corp** Finland. Kansantalousosasto. (19??)-. Finnish. an. Free on request. Ministry of Finance / Finland, Economics Department, PO Box 295, 00171 Helsinki Finland. **Tel** 011 90 160 3178. **LC** HJ55.3; .B15a. **DD** 354/.471/00722.
**Ind/Abst** F&S Index Plus Text, Int. [Select. Cov.]; Predicasts Forecasts.

US/0271-9150
**NATIONAL CONSULTOR. See** Business-Accounting.

CN/0077-4529
**NATIONAL FINANCES, THE.** 1st- Ed.; 1954/55-. English. an. Canadian Tax Foundation, 1 Queen Street East, Suite 1800, Toronto Ontario M5C 2Y2 Canada. **Tel** (416)863-9784. **LC** HJ2055; .C33. **DD** 336.71.
**Desc:** An analysis of the revenues and expenditures of the Government of Canada.

AT/1031-2765
**NATIONAL INCOME AND EXPENDITURE CANBERRA. Added/Corp** Australian Bureau of Statistics. (1986)-. English. an. 10.00Aus$. Australian Bureau of Statistics, PO Box 10, Belconnen Australian Capital Territory, 2616 Australia. **Tel** 011 61 6 2527911, FAX 011 61 6 2516009. **DD** 339.394.
**Desc:** Commonwealth budget related paper containing annual estimates of major national accounting aggregates.

●NR
**NATIONAL ROLLING PLAN. Main/Corp** Nigeria. **Added/Corp** Nigeria. Ministry of Budget and Planning. Planning Office. 1st (1990/1992)-. English. **LC** HC1055.A1; N48b. **DD** 338.9669/005.

US/0028-0283
**NATIONAL TAX JOURNAL.** [Natl. tax j.]. **Added/Corp** National Tax Association. National Tax Association-Tax Institute of America. Vol. 1 (Mar. 1948)-. Periodical. English. qt. $80.00 US; $85.00 other. National Tax Association - Tax Institute of America, 5310 East Main Street, Suite 104, Columbus OH 43213. **Tel** (614)864-1221, FAX (614)235-6804. **ED** Joel B. Slemrod. **LC** HJ2240; .N3135. **DD** 336.205. **CODEN** NTXJAC. Index available. cum. index. **Pr Rev. Circ:** 3,600 (ctrl). available on microfilm and microfiche from University Microfilms International (UMI); available on an online database (file 648/Full-Text) from DIALOG. Documents available from The Genuine Article, UMI Article Clearinghouse. ***Supersedes*** *Bulletin of the National Tax Association.*
**Desc:** Articles deal with topics of current interest in the fields of taxation, public finances and economics.
**Ind/Abst** ABI/INFORM Glob. Ed.; ABI Inform Ondisc (June 1971-); Acad. Search (July 1993-); Account. Tax Datab. (Jun. 1971-); Account. Art.; Bus. ASAP (1992-) [Full Txt.]; Bus. Index (1985-); Bus. Period. Index; Bus. Source (Jul. 1993-); Contents Recent Econ. J.; Curr. Contents Soc. Behav. Sci.; Curr. Law Index (1980-); Econ. Lit. Index; Expand. Acad. Index (1992-); Fed. Tax Artic.; Gen. BusinessFile (1985-); Gen. Period. Index (1985-); INFO-SOUTH Abstr.; Int. Polit. Sci. Abstr.; J. Econ. Lit.; Law Office Inf. Serv.; Leg. Resour. Index (1980-); LegalTrac (1980-); Mag. Search; Newsp. Period. Abstr. (1992-); PAIS Int. Print (1991-); Res. Alert [Full Cov.]; Soc. Sci. Cit. Index [Full Cov.]; SportSearch; Trade Ind. Index (1981-?); UMI ABI/Inform--Bus. Period. Ondisc (Mar. 1987-) [Full Txt.]; Urban Aff. Abstr.; Wilson Bus. Abstr.

NE
**NEDERLANDSE JURISPRUDENTIE INZAKE INTERNATIONAAL BELASTINGRECHT: DIRECTE BELASTINGEN VAN INTERNATIONAAL OPERERENDE ONDERNEMINGEN.** (19??)-. English. Twice a year. $110.00. International Bureau of Fiscal Documentation - IBFD Publications, PO Box 20237, 1000 HE Amsterdam The Netherlands. **Tel** 011 31 20-6267726, FAX 011 31 20-6228658, telex 13217 INTAX NL. **(Subscription address:** IBFD / International Bureau of Fiscal Documentation USA, Inc., 24 Hudson Street, Kinderhook NY 12106.**)**

MX/0028-2456
**NEGOCIOS Y BANCOS : REVISTA PARA EL EJECUTIVO. See** Business-Banking and Finance.

US
**NEVADA LEGISLATURE FINAL REPORT: CONTINGENCY FUND, LEGISLATIVE FUND, THE. Main/Corp** Nevada. Legislative Commission. (1975)-. English. an. Legislative Commission, Legislative Building, Capitol Complex, Carson City NV 89710. **LC** HJ9777.N3; N47a. **DD** 328.793/07/6.

II/0441-7119
**NEW EXPENDITURE. Main/Corp** Haryana. English. Government Press, Ring Road, Chandigarh India. **LC** HJ2154.H35. **DD** 352/.17/0954558.

II
**NEW EXPENDITURE FOR THE YEAR. Main/Corp** Punjab (India). Finance Dept. (19??)-. English. **LC** HJ66.P73; A37. **DD** 354.54/55/00722.

US/0147-2844
**NEW JERSEY TAX HANDBOOK. Added/Corp** Prentice-Hall, Inc. (1977)-. English. $7.50. Prentice-Hall Law and Business, 270 Sylvan Avenue, Englewood Cliffs NJ 07632. **Tel** (800)223-0231, (201)894-8538, FAX (201)894-8666. **LC** KFN2270; .N48. **DD** 343/.748/04.

US
**NEW MEXICO LOCAL GOVERNMENTS AND THE PROPERTY TAX.** English. an. New Mexico Department of Finance & Administration, Bataan Memorial Building, Room 180, Santa Fe NM 87503. **Tel** (505)827-4985, FAX (505)827-4948. **LC** HJ4121.N6; N48. **DD** 336.22/09789.

US/0737-5891
**NEW YORK STATE TAX MONITOR. See** Law.

US/0898-9117
**NEW YORK TAX CASES (BUFFALO, N.Y.).** (NEW YORK TAX CASES.). [N. Y. tax cases]. **Added/Corp** William S. Hein & Company. (1988)-. Periodical. English. mo. $490.00. William S. Hein & Company Inc., 1285 Main Street, Buffalo NY 14209. **Tel** (716)882-2600, (800)828-7571, FAX (716)883-8100, telex 91-209 WM S HEIN BUF. **ED** Edited by Paul R Comeau and Arthur R Rosen. **LC** KFN5860; .A516. **DD** 343.74704/0264; 347.470340264. **Pr Rev.**
**Desc:** Contains Case Digest and Highlights, Topical Index, and Case Table to locate the case you need by name. The only timely hard copy source containing a complete and comprehensive compilation of all decisions.

US
**NEW YORK TAX LAW. See** Law.

NZ/0545-7572
**NEW ZEALAND CURRENT TAXATION.** (1957)-. Periodical. English. sm. Butterworth Ltd. / New Zealand, 33 35 Cumberland Place, Wellington New Zealand. **(Subscription address:** Butterworth Heinemann Publishers, 225 Wildwood Avenue, Unit B, Woburn MA 01801.**) [CCC].**

AT
**NEW ZEALAND DUTIES TAX GUIDE.** English. qt. 371.00Aus$. CCH Australia Ltd, PO Box 230, North Ryde New South Wales, 2113 Australia. **Tel** 011 61

# Public Administration —Public Finance and Taxation

02 888 2555, FAX 011 61 02 888 7324.
**Desc:** Guide to the laws governing stamp, estate and other duties in New Zealand.

US
**NEWSLETTER (BUDGET AND PROGRAM (FIRM)).** (NEWSLETTER / BUDGET AND PROGRAM.). **Added/Corp** Budget and Program (Firm). **VFOAT** Budget and Program Newsletter. Vol. 1, No. 1 (Sept. 1975)-. Periodical. English. wk. $172.00. Budget and Program Newsletter, PO Box 6269, Washington DC 20015. **Tel** (202)628-3860.

US/1066-1018
**NON-PROFIT LEGAL & TAX LETTER.** [Non-profit leg. tax lett.]. **Added/Corp** Organization Management, Inc. **VFOAT** Non Profit Legal and Tax Letter. Vol. 19, No. 12 (Aug. 30, 1991)-. Periodical. English. Eighteen times a year. $195.00. Organization Management Inc., 13231 Pleasantview Lane, Fairfax VA 22033. **Tel** (703)968-7039, FAX (703)818-0259. **ED** Ed Coleman, George Webster and Hugh Webster (editors' address: Webster, Chamberlain & Bean, 1747 Pennsylvania Avenue, Washington, DC 20006; phone: (202)835-0243). **DD** 343. *Formed by the union of Non-Profit Organization Tax Letter, 0550-8401 and Membership Organizations Newsletter, 1051-7391.*
**Desc:** Up-to-date information for non-profit organizations and their professional advisors on legal and tax issues affecting the tax-exempt sector.

US
**NON-PROFIT TAX LETTER.** English. Twenty-four times a year. $134.28 (US); $162.48 (Canada). Bureau of Business Practice, 24 Rope Ferry Road, Waterford CT 06386. **Tel** (800)243-0876, (203)442-4365, (800)876-9105, FAX (203)443-1123.

US/1056-4594
**NONPROFIT INSIGHTS.** [Nonprofit insights]. (1991)-. Periodical. English. bw. $249.00 (one year), $475.00 (two year). Whitaker Newsletter, PO Box 340, 313 South Avenue, Suite 202, Fanwood NJ 07023-0340. **Tel** (201)889-6336, FAX (201)889-6339. **(Subscription address:** Whitaker Newsletters, PO Box 192, Fanwood NJ 07923.) **ED** Fred Rossi. **DD** 343. **Bk Rev**. *Continues Tax Exempt News, 0194-228X.*
**Desc:** Summarizes new developments affecting the nonprofit community, including colleges and universities, religious organizations, and nonprofit associations which make charitable contributions.

GW
**NORDRHEIN-WESTFALEN. FINANZMINISTER. MITTEILUNGSBLATT.** German. mo. Finanzminister, Jaegerhofstr 6 Germany. **Tel** 0211 4972 533, FAX 0211 4972 300, telex 172114101. **Circ:** 39,000 (ctrl).
**Desc:** Information leaflet for finance administration staff.

●US/1071-5584
**NORTH AMERICAN OUTLOOK.** **Added/Corp** National Planning Association. (1993)-. Periodical. English. Four times a year. $35.00. National Planning Association, 1424 16th Street Northwest, Suite 700, Washington DC 20036. **Tel** (202)265-7685. *Continues Canada-U.S. Outlook, 1044-3223.*

US
**NOTEBOOK (WASHINGTON RESEARCH COUNCIL).** (NOTEBOOK.). **VFOAT** WRC Notebook; Washington Research Council Notebook. Vol. 1, No. 1 (Aug. 1986)-. Periodical. English. mo. $100.00. Washington Research Council, 1301 5th Avenue, Suite 2810, Olympia WA 98101-2603. **Tel** (206)467-7088, (800)445-1086, FAX (206)467-6957. ctrl circ.

●FR
**NOTES BLEUES DE BERCY / MINISTERE DE L'ECONOMIE ET DES FINANCES, MINISTERE DU BUDGET, LES.** **Added/Corp** France. Ministere de l'Economie et des Finances. France. Ministere du Budget. (Oct. 1992)-. Periodical. French. Twenty-six times a year. 419.20F France; 535.00F others. Sevpo Notes Bleues, 139 rue de Bercy, F-75572 Paris Cedex 12 France. **Tel** 011 33 1 40248815. *Formed by the union of Notes Bleues and Notes Bleues (Quarterly).*

CN/0706-4624
**NOUVELLES FISCALES DU QUEBEC.** **Title Change.** [Nouv. fisc. Que.]. **Added/Corp** Quebec (Province). Ministere du Revenu. **VFOAT** Quebec Tax News. Vol. 10 (Dec. 1976)-(19??)-. Periodical. French (French and English). mo. Quebec Ministere du Revenu, 3800 rue Marly, Sainte-Foy Quebec G1X 4A5 Canada. **Tel** (418)652-6822. *Formed by the union of Nouvelles Fiscales sur les Impots, 0317-4441 and Nouvelles Fiscales sur les Taxes de Vente, 0706-4616. Continued by Novelles Fiscales, 1192-1722.*

US
**NTA FORUM : PERSPECTIVES, IDEAS AND NEWS FROM THE NATIONAL TAX ASSOCIATION.** **Added/Corp** National Tax Association. **VAT** National Tax Association Forum. (19??)-. Periodical. English. qt. Free to members of the National Tax Association; $100.00 membership. National Tax Association - Tax Institute of America, 5310 East Main Street, Suite 104, Columbus OH 43213. **Tel** (614)864-1221, FAX (614)235-6804.

US/0091-0783
**NTA-TIA BOOKSHELF.** [N.T.A.-T.I.A. bookshelf]. No. 86- Dec. 1970-. English. $5.00 per copy. 457 Nassau Street, Princeton NJ 08540. **LC** Z7164.F5; T25; HJ2279. **DD** 016.336. *Continues Tax Institute Bookshelf, 0040-0033.*

AU
**OFFENTLICHE SEKTOR, DER.** **Added/Corp** Arbeitsgemeinschaft fuer Finanzwissenschaftliche Forschung und Information. (Dec. 1975)-. Periodical. German. ir. **LC** HJ105; .O33. **DD** 336/.005.

US/0364-2267
**OFFICIAL SUMMARY OF SECURITY TRANSACTIONS AND HOLDINGS.** [Offic. summ. secur. trans. hold.]. **Added/Corp** United States. Securities and Exchange Commission. (1936)-. Government Publication. English. mo. $92.00 domestic; $115.00 other. Superintendent of Documents, US Government Printing Office, Washington DC 20402. **Tel** (202)275-3328, FAX (202)786-2377. **DD** 332. Documents available from Documents on Demand. *Continues Official Summary of Stock Transactions and Holdings of Officers, Directors, and Principal Stockholders.*
**Desc:** Made up of securities holdings figures showing owners, relationships to issues, amounts of securities bought or sold by each owner, their individual holdings at the end of the reported month, and types of securities.
**Ind/Abst** Am. Stat. Index.

UK
**OFFSHORE TAX PLANNING REVIEW.** (1990)-. English. Three times a year (Feb., June, Oct.). £125.00 UK; £135.00 other. Key Haven Publications Ltd, 139 Upper Richmond Road, London W15 2TN England. **Tel** 011 44 081-780-2522, FAX 022 44 081 780 1693. **ED** Robert Venables and David Ewart. cum. index. **Bk Rev**. **Ad Acc**.
**Desc:** News and information on articles of offshore tax planning and non - resident trusts.

US/1071-4243
**OHIO TAX REVIEW.** [Ohio tax rev.]. **Added/Corp** Capital University. Law & Graduate Center. Office of Graduate Studies. Capital University. Graduate Tax Programs. **VFOAT** Capitol University Ohio Tax Review. Vol. 1, No. 1 (Jan. 1987)-. Periodical. English. Four times a year (Jan., Apr., July, Oct.). $50.00. Ohio Tax Review, Capital University, Law Graduate Center, Columbus OH 43215. **Tel** (614)445-886. **LC** KFO470.A15; O37. **DD** 343.77104; 347.71034. cum. index. **Pr Rev**. **Circ:** 500.

US/0731-4620
**OIL & GAS TAX ALERT / THE RESEARCH INSTITUTE OF AMERICA.** **Added/Corp** Research Institute of America, inc. **VFOAT** Oil and Gas Tax Alert. (19??)-. Periodical. English. mo. $150.00. Research Institute of America, 117 East Stevens Avenue, Valhalla NY 10595. **Tel** (800)431-9025. **ED** James E. Cheek. **LC** HD9560.8.U5; O54. **DD** 343.7305/585333823.05; 347.303558533382305. [**CCC**].
**Desc:** Focuses on the special needs of tax professionals serving clients with oil and gas interests.

UK
**OIL TAXATION ACTS.** **See** Petroleum and Natural Gas.

CN/0381-2332
**ONTARIO BUDGET.** **Main/Corp** Ontario. Ministry of Treasury and Economics. 1982-. English. an. Ontario Government Bookstore, 880 Bay Street, Toronto Ontario M7A 1N8 Canada. **LC** HJ13; .O212A. **DD** 354.7130072/252/05. *Continues Ontario Budget, 0381-2332.*

CN/0383-5863
**ONTARIO FINANCES.** [Ont. financ.]. **Main/Corp** Ontario. Taxation and Fiscal Policy Branch. **Added/Corp** Ontario. Taxation and Fiscal Policy Branch. (197?)-. Periodical. English. qt. free on request. Ontario Ministry of Treasury Economics and Intergovernmental Affairs, 1 Frost Building South/5th Floor, Toronto Ontario M7A 1Y7 Canada. **Tel** (416)965-7171.

●CN/1188-2867
**ONTARIO FISCAL OUTLOOK.** [Ont. fisc. outlook]. **Added/Corp** Ontario. Ministry of Treasury and Economics. (Jan. 1992)-. Periodical. English. Ontario Ministry of Treasury Economics and Intergovernmental Affairs, 1 Frost Building South/5th Floor, Toronto Ontario M7A 1Y7 Canada. **Tel** (416)965-7171. **DD** 330.9713/005.

CN
**OPERATING BUDGET AS ADOPTED BY THE METROPOLITAN COUNCIL ON ... .** **Main/Corp** Metropolitan Toronto (Ont.). Apr. 29, 1983-. English. an. Department of Management Services / Ontario, Municipality of Metropolitan Toronto, 401 Bay Street/Suite 2700, Toronto Ontario M5H 2Y4 Canada. **LC** HJ9014.O6; T59. **DD** 352.1/252/09713541. *Continues Operation Budget - Metropolitan Toronto.*

US
**OPERATING REPORT, NEW YORK STATE COMPTROLLER : THE TAXPAYERS' WATCHDOG.** **Main/Corp** New York (State). Comptroller's Office. **VFOAT** Operating Report. English. Comptroller's Press Office, Alfred E Smith State Office Building, Albany NY 12236. **Tel** (518)474-4015, telex 5184738940.

US
**OPERATIONS BUDGET / STATE OF UTAH.** **Main/Corp** Utah. State Budget Office. **VFOAT** Governor's Operations Budget. English. an. Utah State Budget Office, 104B State Capitol Building, Salt Lake City UT 84114. **LC** HJ11; .U848B. **DD** 353.97920072/256.

BL
**ORCAMENTO DA UNIAO. PROJETO DE LEI / SECRETARIA DE PLANEJAMENTO DA PRESIDENCIA DA REPUBLICA, SECRETARIA DE ORCAMENTO E FINANCAS.** **Main/Corp** Brazil. Secretaria de Orcamento e Financas. Portuguese. an. Free. SEDN, W3 Norte Q 516 Ed Sof, 70.770 Brasilia DF Brazil. **Tel** 274-2177, telex 4321. **Circ:** 3,600. *Continues Brazil. Secretaria de Orcamento e Financas. Projeto de Lei Orcamentaria Anual.*
**Desc:** Estimates the receipts and determines the expenses of the Brazilian Confederation.

BL
**ORCAMENTO DO ESTADO.** **Main/Corp** Mato Grosso (Brazil : State). Coordenadoria de Planejamento e Orcamentacao. Portuguese. an. **LC** HJ32; .M554A. **DD** 354.81/720072252/05. *Continues Mato Grosso (Brazil : State). Departamento de Orcamento e Administracao Geral. Orcamento do Estado.*

MH
**ORCAMENTO GERAL PARA O ANO ECONOMICO DE ... / REPUBLICA PORTUGUESA, GOVERNO DE MACAU, SERVICOS DE FINANCAS.** **Main/Corp** Macao. Direccao dos Servicos de Financas. **VFOAT** Orcamento. Portuguese. an. **LC** HJ72.M3; A27A. **DD** 354.51/260072252/05. *Continues Macao. Reparticao Provincial Dos Servicos de Financas. Orcamento Geral Para O Ano Economico.*

BL
**ORCAMENTO PROGRAMA DE ... / GOVERNO DO ESTADO DE SAO PAULO, SECRETARIA DE ECONOMIA E PLANEJAMENTO.** **Main/Corp** Sao Paulo (Brazil : State). Secretaria de Economia e Planejamento. **VFOAT** Orcamento-Programa de ... . 1979-. Portuguese. an. **LC** HJ32; .S46B. **DD** 354.81/610072252/05. *Continues Orcamento Programa Anual.*

BL
**ORCAMENTO-PROGRAMA ... E ORCAMENTO PLURIANUAL DE INVESTIMENTOS / GOVERNO DO ESTADO DE PERNAMBUCO, SECRETARIA DE PLANEJAMENTO, COORDENADORIA DE ORCAMENTO.** **Main/Corp** Pernambuco (Brazil). Coordenadoria de Orcamento. Portuguese. an. **LC** HJ32; .P372B. **DD** 354.81/340072252/05.
**Desc:** Includes investment budget for report year and subsequent two years.

US
**OREGON ECONOMIC AND REVENUE FORECAST.** **Added/Corp** Oregon. Executive Dept. Oregon. Budget and Management Division. Vol. 2, No. 2 (June 1982)-. English. Four times a year. $20.00. Budget & Management Division, 155 College Avenue, Executive Dept, Salem OR 97310. **Tel** (503)378-3106. **LC** HJ11; .O716. **DD** 338.5/443/09795. *Formed by the union of Oregon Economic Forecast and Oregon Revenue Forecast.*

US
**OREGON INDIVIDUAL INCOME TAX: PUBLICATION 17 1/2/OREGON DEPARTMENT OF REVENUE.** **Added/Corp** Oregon. Dept. of Revenue. **VFOAT** Publication 17 1/2. (1979)-. English. an. $5.00. Department of Revenue / Oregon, State Office Building, Salem OR 97310. **Tel** (503)378-3359. **LC** KFO2875.Z9; O74. **DD** 343.79505/2; 347.950352. **Circ:** 7,000.

# Public Administration — Public Finance and Taxation

**Desc:** Supplements Oregon income tax instruction booklet and federal Publication 17. Also summarizes new laws.

US
### OREGON PERSONAL INCOME TAX ANNUAL STATISTICS. See Public Administration-Abstracting, Bibliographies and Statistics.

US/0145-4269
### OREGON PROPERTY TAX STATISTICS.
See Public Administration-Abstracting, Bibliographies and Statistics.

US
### OREGON RATIO AND ASSESSMENT ROLL DATA FOR LOCALLY ASSESSED PROPERTY. VFOAT Ratio and Assessment Roll Data for Locally Assessed Property. 1980-. English. an. Department of Revenue / Oregon, State Office Building, Salem OR 97310. **Tel** (503)378-3359. **LC** HJ4121.O7; P76A. **DD** 336.22/2. *Continues* Oregon Ratio and Assessment Data for Locally Assessed Property.

US/0739-1374
### ORGANIZATIONS EXEMPT FROM LIMITED SALES AND USE TAX. English. Bob Bullock, Comptroller of Public Accounts, Austin TX 78774. **LC** HJ5715.U6; T46A. **DD** 338.7/09764. *Continues* List of Organizations Exempt from Limited Sales and Use Tax.

JA
### OSAKA ZEIKAN. Main/Corp Japan. Zeikan, Osaka. (19??)-. Japanese. Kowan Godo Chosha, 10-3 Chikka 4, Minato-ku 552 Osaka Japan. **LC** HJ7276.Z7; O85a.

IT
### OSSERVATORIO FINANZIARIO REGIONALE / ISTITUTO DI STUDI SULLE REGIONI - C.N.R. 1 (Ed. 1982)-. Italian. sa. L28.000. Franco Angeli Editore Riviste, Via le Monza 106, 20127 Milan Italy. **Tel** 011 39 2 2827651 or, 289562, FAX 011 39 2 258004, telex 051-511650. **LC** HJ9051; .A54. **DD** 336/.014/45.

AU
### OSTERREICHISCHE ZOLL UND STEUER NACHRICHTEN. (1957)-. German. sm. S720.00. Grenz-Verlag, Flossgasse 6, A-1025 Vienna 2 Austria. **LC** HF2081; .O85. **DD** 336.2/009436.

JA
### OUTLINE OF JAPANESE TAXES, AN.
**Main/Corp** Japan. Okurasho. Shuzeikyoku. **Added/Corp** Japan. Okurasho. Shuzeikyoku. Outline of National Tax in Japan. (1953)-. English. Government Publications Service Center, 2-1, 1-chome Kasumigaseki, Chiyoda-ku, Tokyo 100 Japan. **LC** HJ2986; .A3. **DD** 336.2/00952.

US
### OVERALL REAL PROPERTY TAXES.
**Added/Corp** New York (State). Dept. of Audit and Control. New York (State). Bureau of Municipal Research and Statistics. (1989)-. English. New York State Office of the State Comptroller, Albany NY 12236. **Tel** (518)474-4015. *Continues* Overall Real Property Tax Rates, Local Governments in New York State.

DK
### OVERSIGT OVER FINANSLOVFORSLAGET FOR ... BILAG.
**Added/Corp** Denmark. Budgetdepartementet. (19??)-. Danish. an. Finansministeriet Budgetdepartementet, Christiansborg Slotsplads 1, DK-1218 Kbenhavn K Denmark. **LC** HJ56; .A273.

US/0160-9912
### PACKAGE X. (PACKAGE X : INFORMATIONAL COPIES OF FEDERAL TAX FORMS.). **Main/Corp** United States. Internal Revenue Service. **VFOAT** Package 10. VAT Package Ten. English. an. Department of Treasury, 15th Street and Pennsylvania Avenue NW, Washington DC 20220. **Tel** (202)566-2000. **LC** KF6289.A355. **DD** 343.7305/2044; 347.30352044.

PK/0078-7892
### PAKISTAN -- BASIC FACTS. VFOAT Pakistan Basic Facts. 1st Ed.-. English. an. NGM Communication, PO Box 2627, Karachi 75900 Pakistan. **Tel** 011 92 21 428625. **LC** HC440.5.A1; P26. **DD** 330.9549/1/005.

US
### PANEL STUDY OF INCOME DYNAMICS: PROCEDURES AND TAPE CODES, A.
**Added/Corp** University of Michigan. Survey Research Center. (1973)-. English. ir. Price varies per volume. ICPSR Inter University Consortium for Political and Social Research, University of Michigan, PO Box 1248, Ann Arbor MI 48106. **Tel** (313)764-2570. **ED** James N. Morgan and Greg J. Duncan.
**Desc:** Volumes of documentation, procedures and tape codes for a major continuing study of family dynamics.

US
### PAPERS AND PROCEEDINGS, IDAHO STATE TAX INSTITUTE. **Main/Corp** Idaho State Tax Institute. **Added/Corp** Idaho State University. Idaho Society of Certified Public Accountants. Idaho Law Foundation. (19??)-. Proceedings. English. an. $5.00. Idaho State Tax Institute, Student Union Building, Idaho State University, Pocatello ID 83209. **LC** KFI470.A75; I3. **DD** 343/.73/04.

US/1052-8806
### PARTNERSHIP FEDERAL AND STATE INCOME TAX REPORTING. [Partnersh. fed. state income tax report.]. **Added/Corp** Warren, Gorham & Lamont, Inc. (1991)-. English. ir. Warren Gorham & Lamont Inc., Park Square Building, 31 St. James Avenue, Boston MA 02116-4112. **Tel** (617)423-2020, (800)950-1207, FAX (617)423-2026. **ED** Michael N. Jennings and Daniel R. Bolar. **DD** 343.

●US/1061-978X
### PASTOR'S TAX & MONEY. See Religion and Theology.

US/0191-9660
### PAY LESS TAX LEGALLY. (19??)-. English. an. New American Library, 120 Woodbine Street, Bergenfield NJ 07621. **Tel** (201)387-0600. **LC** KF6369.6; .S74. **DD** 343/.73/052.

●US/1065-6529
### PAYROLL CURRENTLY. (PAYROLL CURRENTLY : THE BIWEEKLY TAXATION PUBLICATION BY THE AMERICAN PAYROLL ASSOCIATION.). [Payr. curr.]. **Added/Corp** American Payroll Association. (1992)-. Periodical. English. Twenty-six times a year. $247.00. API Fund for Payroll Education, 30 East 33rd Street, 5th Floor, New York NY 10016. **Tel** (212)686-2030. **DD** 341.

US/1059-2032
### PBC FEDERAL TAX GUIDE. *Title Change.*
**VFOAT** Federal Tax Guide. VAT Publishing and Business Consultants Federal Tax Guide. (1992)-(199?). English. Publishing & Business Consultants, PO Box 75392, Los Angeles CA 90075. **Tel** (213)732-3477, FAX (213)732-9123. *Continued by* Tax Magazine.

●US/1059-1974
### PBC TAX BRIEFS. VFOAT Tax Briefs. VAT Publishing and Business Consultants Tax Briefs. (1992)-. English. qt. Publishing & Business Consultants, PO Box 75392, Los Angeles CA 90075. **Tel** (213)732-3477, FAX (213)732-9123.

SA
### PEGO YA MOHLAKISI-MOGOLO KA DITSHUPAMOLATO TSA MMUSO WA LEBOWA LE YA DITSHUPAMOLATO TSA DIPUSWANA TIKOLOGONG MO NGWAGATSHELETENG. **Main/Corp** South Africa. Controller and Auditor-General. **VFOAT** Verslag van die Ouditeur-Generaal oor die Rekenings van die Lebowaregering en van die Rekenings van Laer Owerhede in die Gebied; Report of the Auditor-General on the Accounts of the Lebowa Government and of the Accounts of Lower Authorities in the Area. Afrikaans (English and Northern Sotho). an. R3.00. Government Printer / South Africa, Bosman Street, Private Bag X85, Pretoria 0001 South Africa. **Tel** 011 27 12 3239731 Ext. 262. **LC** HJ9080A.A55; L47A.

IO
### PEMERIKSA. No. 1 (June 1980)-. Periodical. Indonesian. mo. Badan Pemeriksa Keuangan, Jl Jend Gatot Subroto, Jakarta Pusat Indonesia. **LC** HJ9927.I5; P45.

US
### PENNSYLVANIA TAX COMPENDIUM.
**Main/Corp** Pennsylvania. Dept. of Revenue. 1982-83 Fiscal Year-. English. Department of Revenue / Pennsylvania, PO Box 1671, Harrisburg PA 17127. **LC** HJ11; .P464A. **DD** 353.97480072/6/05. *Continues* Compendium of Revenues Collected by the Commonwealth of Pennsylvania.

US
### PENNSYLVANIA TAX HANDBOOK. See Law.

CN/1180-1565
### PENSION COMMISSION OF ONTARIO BULLETIN, THE. [Pension Comm. Ont. bull.]. **Added/Corp** Pension Commission of Ontario. **VFOAT** PCO Bulletin. Vol. 1, Issue 1 (Feb. 1990)-. Bulletin. English. qt. **DD** 354.7130083/5.

CN/1183-1634
### PENSION TAX REPORTS. (PENSION TAX REPORTS : PTR.). [Pension tax rep.]. **Added/Corp** Deloitte & Touche. National Pension Tax Coordinator. Price Waterhouse (Firm). Pension Services Group. **VFOAT** PTR. VAT Pension & Tax Reports. Vol. 1, No. 1 (Sept. 1, 1990)-. Periodical. English. Twenty-four times a year. 395.00Can$. Hybrid Press, PO Box 589, Orleans, Ontario K1C 1S9 Canada. **Tel** (613)824-8988. **DD** 336.24/28/0971.

US
### PERFORMANCE AUDIT. English. Twenty times a year. Legislative Budget Committee - Washington, Legislative Building, Olympia WA 98504. **Tel** (206)753-5796. **LC** HJ11; .W2453. **DD** 353.9/797/007232. Circ: 150 (ctrl) *Continues* Washington (State). Legislative. Budget Committee. Report.

II
### PERFORMANCE BUDGET: IRRIGATION AND POWER DEPARTMENT. **Main/Corp** Maharashtra (India). English. an. Central Board of Irrigation Power, Maalcha Marg Chanakyapuri, New Delhi 110021 India. **LC** HJ66.M5; C12A. **DD** 354/.54/792008232.

II
### PERFORMANCE BUDGET OF PORTS AND FISHERIES DEPARTMENT (FISHERIES). **Main/Corp** Gujarat (India). Ports and Fisheries Dept. 1982-83-. English. an. $1.75. **LC** HJ65.G83; G84A. **DD** 354.54/7500722253. *Continues* Gujarat (India). Agriculture, Forests, and Co-Operation Dept. Performance Budget of Agriculture, Forests, and Co-Operation Department. Fisheries.

II
### PERFORMANCE BUDGET OF REVENUE DEPARTMENT - GUJARAT, INDIA (STATE). **Main/Corp** Gujarat, India (State) Revenue Dept. English. Rs2.55. The Government Press, Vadodara India. **LC** HJ4400.G83; G83A. **DD** 354.54/7500722253.

II
### PERFORMANCE REVIEW. **Added/Corp** State Trading Corporation of India, Ltd. **VFOAT** State Trading Corporation Performance Review; STC Performance Review. English. State Trading Corporation of India Ltd, Chandralok 36 Janpath, New Delhi 110001 India. **LC** HD4293; .S75a. **DD** 354.540082/6. *Continues* STC ... Performance Review.

US
### PERMANENT FUND DIVIDENDS. COMMUNITY PROFILE / STATE OF ALASKA, DEPARTMENT OF REVENUE.
English. Department of Revenue / Alaska, Research Section, Pouch SA, Juneau AK 99811. **LC** HJ7553; .A43. **DD** 353.97980072/6.

CN/0226-7403
### PERMIS ACCORDES AUX COMPAGNIES ETRANGERES. *Title Change.* [Permis accord. cie. etrang.]. **Added/Corp** Quebec (Province). Ministere des Consommateurs, Cooperatives et Institutions Financieres. Service des Compagnies. Quebec (Province). Ministere des Consommateurs, Cooperatives et Institutions Financieres. Direction des Compagnies. Quebec (Province). Ministere des Institutions Financieres et Cooperatives. Direction des Compagnies. (19??)-?. French. an. Editeur Officiel du Quebec, 1283 Boul Charest Ouest, Quebec Quebec G1N 2C9 Canada. **LC** HJ5376.Q42; Q4a. **DD** 338.7/09714. *Continues* Etat des Permis Accordes aux Compagnies Etrangeres, 0229-9283. *Continued by* Etat Annuel des Permis Accordes aux Compagnies Etrangeres, 0837-7219.

US
### PERSI COMPONENT UNIT FINANCIAL REPORT FOR THE FISCAL YEAR ENDED ... . See Public Administration-Civil Service.

US/0091-5661
### PERSONAL INCOME TAX IN OREGON, THE. *Title Change.* **Main/Corp** Oregon. Dept. of Revenue. Research and Special Services Division. English. Department of Revenue / Oregon, State Office Building, Salem OR 97310. **Tel** (503)378-3359. **LC** HJ4655.O65; O74A. **DD** 336.2/42/09795. *Continued by* Oregon Personal Income Tax Statistics.

US
### PERSONAL INCOME TAX. INCOME TAX RETURNS BY COUNTY / OHIO DEPARTMENT OF TAXATION. English. Department of Taxation / Ohio, Research and Statistics Section, PO Box 530, Columbus OH 43216. **LC** HJ4655.O33; P48. **DD** 336.24/2/09771.

US
### PERSONAL INCOME TAX. INCOME TAX RETURNS BY INCOME CLASS / OHIO DEPARTMENT OF TAXATION.
English. Department of Taxation / Ohio, Research and Statistics Section, PO Box 530, Columbus OH 43216. **LC** HJ4655.O33; P49. **DD** 336.24/2/09771.

# Public Administration — Public Finance and Taxation

US/0743-3921
**PERSONAL TAX & FINANCIAL PLANNING GUIDE.** VFOAT Personal Tax and Financial Planning Guide; A.A.I.I. Tax Guide; AAII Tax Guide. English. an. American Association of Individual Investors, 625 North Michigan Avenue/Suite 1900, Chicago IL 60611. **Tel** (312)280-0170. **LC** KF6296.A15; P47. **DD** 343.7305/2/05; 347.3035205.

US
**PERSONAL TAXATION ABROAD.** English. Four times a year. $170.00. Organization Resources Counselors, Inc., 1211 Avenue of the Americas, Rock Center, New York NY 10036. **Tel** (212)790-9220, (212)719-3400. **ED** Nancy Carter, (212)852-0313. ctrl circ.
 **Ind/Abst** Account. Art.; Fed. Tax Artic.

NE
**PERSONELE VERMOGENSVERDELING ... REGIONALE GEGEVENS / CENTRAAL BUREAU VOOR DE STATISTIEK, HOOFDAFDELING STATISTIEKEN VAN INKOMEN EN CONSUMPTIE, DE.** VFOAT Distribution of Personal Property ... Regional Data. 1977-. Dutch. **LC** HC329.I5; N46C. **Continues** Vermogensverdeling ... Regionale Gegevens.

●CN/1188-2875
**PERSPECTIVES BUDGETAIRES DE L'ONTARIO.** [Perspect. budg. Ont.]. **Added/Corp** Ontario. Ministere du Tresor et de l'Economie. (Jan. 1992)-. French. **DD** 330.9713/005.

US/0740-0624
**PERSPECTIVES ON LOCAL PUBLIC FINANCE AND PUBLIC POLICY.** [Perspect. local public financ. public policy]. Vol. 1 (1983)-. Periodical. English. an. $73.25. JAI Press Inc., 55 Old Post Road, Suite 2, PO Box 1678, Greenwich CT 06836-1678. **Tel** (203)661-7602, FAX (203)661-0792. **LC** HJ9103; .P47. **DD** 336/.014/73.

GR
**PHOROLOGIKE ENEMEROSIS.** Main/Corp Greece. Greek, Modern. mo. 3 Es Septembriou 22 Orophos, 5 Graph 6, Athens Greece. **LC** LAW.

GR
**PHOROLOGIKE EPITHEORESIS.** Periodical. Greek, Modern. 500.00. Ekdosis Panelleniou Henoseos Ephoriakon Hypalleloun, Akadimias 76, Athens Greece. **LC** K16; .H6.

FR
**PLAN DE LA CAISSE DES DEPOTS, LE.** Main/Corp Caisse des Depots et Consignations (France). (1987)-. French. Caisse des Depots et Consignations, 56 rue de Lille, 75356 Paris Cedex 07 France. **LC** HJ1072; .C36a.

UK/0260-8642
**PLANNING AND DEVELOPMENT STATISTICS ... ACTUALS / CIPFA, STATISTICAL INFORMATION SERVICE.** **See** Public Administration-Abstracting, Bibliographies and Statistics.

BL
**PLANO OPERATIVO ANUAL / GOVERNO DO ESTADO DE SERGIPE, SECRETARIA DO PLANEJAMENTO.** Main/Corp Sergipe (Brazil). Secretaria do Planejamento. Portuguese. an. Governo de Estado De Sergipe, Secretaria Do Planejamento, Aracaju Brazil. **LC** HJ32.S5; S4A. **DD** 354.81/410072225/05.

US
**POCKET GUIDE TO EUROPEAN INDIVIDUAL TAXES.** Main/Corp Arthur Andersen & Co. VFOAT European Individual Taxes. 1st- Ed.; 1972-. English. Arthur Andersen & Company / Texas, 711 Louisiana Street/Suite 1300, Houston TX 77002. **Tel** (713)237-2469.

CN/0821-4697
**POCKETAX QUEBECOIS.** [Pocketax que.]. 1983-. French. an. CCH Canadian Ltd., 6 Garamond Court, Don Mills Ontario M3C 1Z5 Canada. **Tel** (416)441-2992, FAX (416)441-3418. **DD** 336.24/2/09714.

●US
**POPULI / UNITED NATIONS POPULATION FUND.** Main/Corp United Nations Population Fund (UNFPA). **Added/Corp** United Nations Population Fund (UNFPA). VFOAT Populi. (1992)-. Periodical. English. **Continues** Populi (Eng. Edition).

UK
**POTTER AND MONROES TAX PLANNING WITH PRECEDENTS.** (1988)-. English. Sweet & Maxwell Ltd., South Quay Plaza, 183 Marsh Wall, London E14 9FT England. **Tel** 011 44 264 342899, FAX 011 44 264 342723, telex 929089 ITPINFG.

US/0890-4898
**PRACTICAL TAX LAWYER, THE.** See Law.

UK
**PRACTICAL TAX PLANNING AND PRECEDENTS.** English. £150.00. Longman Group Ltd., Fourth Avenue, Longman House, Harlow Essex CM19 5SR England. **Tel** 011 44 279 429655, FAX 011 44 279 431059, telex 81259. **(Subscription address:** Fourth Avenue, Harlow Essex CM19 5AA England)
 **Desc:** Tax planning advice per whole range of business and personal taxation in the UK.

US/1050-9928
**PRACTITIONERS GUIDE TO SUCCESSFUL TAX PRACTICE.** [Pract. guide success. tax pract.]. (1991)-. Periodical. English. an. $125.00. Practitioners Publishing Company, PO Box 901007, Fort Worth TX 76101-0966. **Tel** (800)323-8724, (817)332-3709.

●CN/1193-1701
**PRACTITIONER'S INCOME TAX ACT, THE.** [Pract. Income Tax Act]. 2nd Ed. (Mar. 1992)-. English. Thomson Professional Publishing Canada, 2075 Kennedy Road, Scarborough Ontario M1T 3V4. **DD** 343.7105/2.

US/0191-233X
**PRENTICE-HALL 1040 HANDBOOK.** Ceased. (PRENTICE-HALL 1040 HANDBOOK; HOW TO PREPARE INCOME TAX RETURNS.). Main/Corp Prentice-Hall, Inc. VAT Prentice-Hall Ten Forty Handbook. (1979)-(Nov. 1993). English. an. Research Institute of America, 117 East Stevens Avenue, Valhalla NY 10595. **Tel** (800)431-9025. **LC** KF6369.6; .P69. **DD** 343/.73/052.

US/1050-0170
**PRENTICE HALL'S FEDERAL TAXATION. COMPREHENSIVE VOLUME.** [Prentice Hall's fed. tax., Compr.]. VFOAT Comprehensive Volume. (1991)-. English. an. $44.00. Prentice-Hall General Reference and Travel, 200 Old Tappan Road, Old Tappan NJ 07675. **Tel** (800)922-0579. **LC** KF6289; .P77. **DD** 343.7304/05.

US/1050-0162
**PRENTICE HALL'S FEDERAL TAXATION. COMPREHENSIVE VOLUME (COMPLIMENTARY INSTRUCTOR'S COPY).** (PRENTICE HALL'S FEDERAL TAXATION. COMPREHENSIVE VOLUME.). [Prentice Hall's fed. tax., Compr.]. VFOAT Comphehensive Volume. (1991)-. English. an. Complimentary to Adopters. Prentice-Hall General Reference and Travel, 200 Old Tappan Road, Old Tappan NJ 07675. **Tel** (800)922-0579. **LC** KF6289; .P773. **DD** 343.7304/05.

US/0898-2635
**PRENTICE HALL'S FEDERAL TAXATION. CORPORATIONS, PARTNERSHIPS, ESTATES, AND TRUSTS.** [Prentice Hall's fed. tax., Corp. partn. estates trusts]. **Added/Corp** Prentice-Hall, inc. VFOAT Federal Taxation. Corporations, Partnerships, Estates, and Trusts. (1989)-. English. an. $64.00. Macmillan Publishing Co. / Indiana, 201 West 103rd Street, Indianapolis IN 46290. **Tel** (800)428-5331, (800)858-7674. **LC** KF6335; .P74. **DD** 336.24/3/0973.

US/1049-8435
**PRENTICE HALL'S FEDERAL TAXATION. CORPORATIONS, PARTNERSHIPS, ESTATES, AND TRUSTS (ANNOTATED INSTRUCTOR'S ED.).** (PRENTICE HALL'S FEDERAL TAXATION. CORPORATIONS, PARTNERSHIPS, ESTATES, AND TRUSTS.). [Prentice Hall's fed. tax., Corp. partn. estates trusts]. **Added/Corp** Prentice-Hall, Inc. VFOAT Federal Taxation. Corporations, Partnerships, Estates, and Trusts; Corporations, Partnerships, Estates & Trusts; Prentice Hall's Federal Taxation. (1991)-. English. an. $64.00. Macmillan Publishing Company, 100 Front Street, Box 500, Riverside NJ 08075-7500. **Tel** (800)257-5755, (609)461-6500, FAX (609)461-7070. **DD** 336.

US/0898-2627
**PRENTICE HALL'S FEDERAL TAXATION. INDIVIDUALS.** [Prentice Hall's fed. tax., Individ.]. VFOAT Federal Taxation. Individuals. (1989)-. English. an. Prentice-Hall General Reference and Travel, 200 Old Tappan Road, Old Tappan NJ 07675. **Tel** (800)922-0579. **LC** KF6369; .P74. **DD** 336.24/2/0973.

US/1049-8044
**PRENTICE HALL'S FEDERAL TAXATION. INDIVIDUALS (ANNOTATED INSTRUCTOR'S ED.).** (PRENTICE HALL'S FEDERAL TAXATION. INDIVIDUALS.). [Prentice Hall's fed. tax., Individ.]. **Added/Corp** Prentice-Hall, Inc. VFOAT Federal Taxation. Individuals. (1991)-. Monographic series. English. an. Price varies per volume. Macmillan Publishing Company, 100 Front Street, Box 500, Riverside NJ 08075-7500. **Tel** (800)257-5755, (609)461-6500, FAX (609)461-7070. **DD** 336.

CN/0713-8946
**PREPARING YOUR CORPORATE TAX RETURNS.** (PREPARING YOUR CORPORATE TAX RETURNS / W. GORDON WILLIAMSON AND A. CRAIG LAHMER.). [Prep. your corp. tax returns]. **Added/Corp** CCH Canadian Limited. (1981)-. English. an. $16.50 each volume. CCH Canadian Ltd., 6 Garamond Court, Don Mills Ontario M3C 1Z5 Canada. **Tel** (416)441-2992, FAX (416)441-3418. **DD** 343.7106/7.

CN/0588-6589
**PREPARING YOUR INCOME TAX RETURNS : CANADA AND PROVINCES.** **Added/Corp** CCH Canadian Limited. 1st Ed. (1966)-. Periodical. English. an. CCH Canadian Ltd., 6 Garamond Court, Don Mills Ontario M3C 1Z5 Canada. **Tel** (416)441-2992, FAX (416)441-3418. **LC** KE5759.2; .P74. **DD** 343.705/2044; 347.0352044.
 **Desc:** Explains Canadian federal income tax for individuals. Emphasizes legitimate tax savings and takes the reader through the T1 Individual Tax Return form step by step.

FR
**PRESENTATION FONCTIONNELLE DU BUDGET DE L'ETAT.** Main/Corp France. French. Imprimerie Nationale / France, BP 514, 59505 Douai Cedex France. **Tel** 011 33 27 937090. **LC** HJ47; .A225. **DD** 354/.44/00722.

BL
**PRESTACAO DE CONTAS.** Main/Corp Santa Catarina (Brazil : State). Governor. Portuguese. Governador, Florianopolis Brazil. **LC** HJ32; .S37A. **DD** 354/.81/6. **Continues** Prestacao de Contas do Governo do Estado.

BL
**PRESTACAO DE CONTAS DA GESTACAO DO EXERCICIO DE ... .** Main/Corp Rio de Janeiro (Brazil : State). Inspetoria Geral de Financas. VFOAT Prestacao de Contas. Portuguese. **LC** HJ32; .R497A. **DD** 354.81/530072310212.

SP/0210-5977
**PRESUPUESTO Y GASTO PUBLICO.** **Added/Corp** Instituto de Estudios Fiscales (Spain). (19??)-. Periodical. Spanish. Three times a year. $39.03. Servicio de Publicaciones del Min de Economia y Hacienda, Plaza Campillo, Mundo Nuevo 3, 28005 Madrid, Spain. **Tel** 011 34 1 527-1437, 583-5665. **LC** HJ7; .P74.

AG
**PRESUPUESTOS PROVINCIALES Y PRESUPUESTO NACIONAL DISTRIBUIDO FOR PROVINCIAS.** Main/Corp Argentine Republic. Direccion Nacional de Programacion e Investigacion. **Added/Corp** Argentina. Direccion Nacional de Programacion e Investigacion. Argentina. Direccion Nacional de Programacion Presupuestaria. (19??)-. Periodical. Spanish. Inst Nacional Estadist Censos Arg, Av Pte Julio a Roca 609 Piso 9, 1067 Buenos Aires Argentina. **Tel** 011 54 1 9529860. **LC** HJ30; .A368.

CN
**PREVISIONS BUDGETAIRES DES MUNICIPALITES.** **Added/Corp** Quebec (Province). Ministere des Affaires Municipales. (1989)-. French. **LC** HJ9014.Q39; B86a. **Continues** Analyse Budgetaire des Municipalites du Quebec, 0079-8436.

US/1056-7690
**PRICE WATERHOUSE INVESTOR'S TAX ADVISER (POCKET BOOKS), THE.** (THE PRICE WATERHOUSE INVESTOR'S TAX ADVISER.). [Price Waterhouse investor's tax advis.]. **Added/Corp** Price Waterhouse (Firm). VFOAT Investor's Tax Adviser. (1990/1991 Ed.)-. English. $5.50. Pocket Books, 1230 Avenue of the Americas, New York NY 10020. **DD** 343.

IT
**PROCEDURE REVISIONE FISCALE IMPOSTA VALORE AGGIUNTO.** See Law.

IT
**PROCEDURE REVISIONE FISCALE REDDITO IMPRESA.** (19??)-. Periodical. Italian. sa. L72600. IPSOA Editore SRL, Casella Postale 12055, Mastrangelo, 20120 Milan Italy. **Tel** 011 39 2 82476248. Index available (Included). cum. index. **Circ:** 3,600 (ctrl)

# Public Administration — Public Finance and Taxation

**US**
**PROCEEDINGS OF NEW YORK UNIVERSITY ... ANNUAL INSTITUTE ON FEDERAL TAXATION. Main/Corp** New York University. Institute on Federal Taxation. **Added/Corp** New York University. Division of General Education. **VFOAT** New York University ... Annual Institute on Federal Taxation; Lectures, Discussions, Questions and Answers in a Nine-Day Conference Conducted by the Division of General Education, New York Universtiy; N.Y.U. Institute on Federal Taxation. 1st (1942)-. Proceedings. English. Fred B. Rothman & Company, 10368 West Centennial Road, Littleton CO 80127. **Tel** (800)457-1986, (303)979-5657, FAX (303)978-1457, telex 87669.
**Ind/Abst** Fed. Tax Artic.

**US/1066-8608**
**PROCEEDINGS OF THE ... ANNUAL CONFERENCE ON TAXATION HELD UNDER THE AUSPICES OF THE NATIONAL TAX ASSOCIATION-TAX INSTITUTE OF AMERICA.** [Proc. annu. conf. tax. held auspices Natl. Tax Assoc.-Tax Inst. Am.]. **Main/Corp** National Tax Association-Tax Institute of America. 66th (Sept. 9-13, 1973)-. Proceedings. English. an. $25.00. National Tax Association - Tax Institute of America, 5310 East Main Street, Suite 104, Columbus OH 43213. **Tel** (614)864-1221, FAX (614)235-6804. **ED** Frederick D. Stocker. **DD** 336. Index available. **Bk Rev. Ad Acc. Circ:** 2,000. *Continues National Tax Association. Proceedings of the ... Annual Conference.*
**Desc:** Compilation of papers given at the Annual Conference on Taxation covering the theory and practice of federal, state, and local taxation.

**US/0740-3453**
**PROCEEDINGS OF THE ... ANNUAL FINANCIAL MANAGEMENT CONFERENCE, THE. See** Public Administration.

**US**
**PROCEEDINGS OF THE ... ANNUAL INSTITUTE ON STATE AND LOCAL TAXATION AND CONFERENCE ON PROPERTY TAXATION. Main/Conf** Institute on State and Local Taxation. 1983-. Proceedings. English. an. **LC** KF6730.A75; I57.

**US**
**PROCEEDINGS OF THE CONFERENCE ON ASSISTANCE TO LOCAL GOVERNMENT. Main/Conf** Conference on Assistance to Local Government. Proceedings. English. ir. Rutgers University / Government Research, Bureau of Government Research, New Brunswick NJ 08903. **LC** HJ9145; .C58. **DD** 350/.725.

**US/0195-8917**
**PROCEEDINGS OF THE CONGRESS OF THE INTERNATIONAL INSTITUTE OF PUBLIC FINANCE.** [Proc. Congres. Int. Inst. Public Financ.]. **Main/Corp** International Institute of Public Finance. (19??)-. Proceedings. English (French and German). an. $40.00. Wayne State University Press, 4809 Woodward Avenue, The Leonard N. Simons Building, Detroit MI 48201-1309. **Tel** (313)577-6119, (313)577-6120, FAX (313)577-6131. **ED** Karl Roskamp. **Bk Rev. Circ:** 1,100 (ctrl).
**Desc:** Collection of papers delivered at annual proceedings of the International Institute of Public Finance; titles reflect specific focus on each volume.

**US**
**PROFESSIONAL EDITION OF J.K. LASSER'S YOUR INCOME TAX, THE. Added/Corp** J.K. Lasser Tax Institute. **VFOAT** J.K. Lasser's Your Income Tax; Your Income Tax. (1961)-. English. an. $40.00. JK Lasser Tax Institute, 15 Columbus Circle, 16th Floor, New York NY 10023. **Tel** (212)373-8786.

**CN**
**PROGRAM PERFORMANCE MEASUREMENT. VFOAT** La Mesure de la Performance des Programmes; Mesure de la Performance des Programmes. English (French). Distribution Centre, Office of the Comptroller General, Ottawa Ontario K1A 0R5 Canada. **LC** HJ13; .A18117.

**AT**
**PROGRAM STATEMENTS / WESTERN AUSTRALIA. Main/Corp** Western Australia. (1991)-. English. **LC** HJ90.W47; W46d. **DD** 354.9410072/05.

**GW/0175-8438**
**PROGRAMM-BUDGET. Main/Corp** Arbeitsgemeinschaft der Grossforschungseinrichtungen (Germany). **VFOAT** Programmbudget. German. Arbeitsgemeinschaft der Grossforschungseinrichtungen, Ahr-Strasse 45 Wissenschaftszentrum, W-5300 Bonn-Bad Godesberg Germany. **LC** Q180.G4; A8A.

**CN/0382-2494**
**PROGRAMME ANNUEL DES DEPENSES DANS LE NORD. Main/Corp** Canada. Advisory Committee on Northern Development. 1975/76-. French. an. Information Canada, 171 Slater Street, Ottawa Ontario K1A 0S9 Canada. **Tel** (819)997-1095. **LC** HJ13; .A13B.

**UK**
**PROGRAMME BUDGET. Main/Corp** Greater London Council. (1974)-. English. £2.00. Greater London Council, The County Hall, London SE1 7PB England. **Tel** (01)633-7139. **LC** HJ9438.L5; G72a. **DD** 352/.12/09421.

**NG**
**PROGRAMME DES INVESTISSEMENTS DE L'ETAT ... ET BUDGET D'INVESTISSEMENT ... . Main/Corp** Niger. Ministere du plan et de la Planification Regionale. (1991)-. French. an. *Continues Programme des Investissements de l'Etat ... et Budget d'Investissement.*

**US/0194-2824**
**PROGRESS IN IMPROVING PROGRAM AND BUDGET INFORMATION FOR CONGRESSIONAL USE.** English. an. US General Accounting Office / District of Columbia, 441 G Street NW, Room 4528, Washington DC 20548. **Tel** (202)275-2812. **LC** HJ2052; .U56A. **DD** 353.007/22.

**IT**
**PRONTUARIO CONTRIBUTI PIROLA.** Vol. 1, No. 1 (Jan. 1984)-. Periodical. Italian. qt. L100.000. Pirola Editore, CP 10444, Via Parabiago 19, 20151 Milan Italy. **Tel** 011 39 2 3022888. **LC** KKH3585.A13; P76. **Circ:** 13,000.

**US**
**PROPERTY TAX DATA, NEW JERSEY TAXING DISTRICTS, TAX RATES, TAX LEVIES, ASSESSMENT RATIOS. Main/Corp** New Jersey State Chamber of Commerce. Dept. of Governmental and Economic Research. English. 54 Park Place, Newark NJ 07102. **LC** HJ4245; .A3A. **DD** 336.2/2/09749. *Continues Property Tax Rates, Assessment Ratios and Tax Levies, New Jersey Taxing Districts.*

**US/0731-0285**
**PROPERTY TAX JOURNAL.** *Title Change.* [Prop. tax j.]. Vol. 1, No. 1 (Mar. 1982)-(1997?). Academic Scholarly Publication. English. qt. International Association of Assessing Officers, 130 East Randolph Street, Suite 850, Chicago IL 60601. **Tel** (312)819-6100. **ED** Annie Aubrey. **LC** HJ4101; .P76. **DD** 350.72/421/05. Index available. cum. index. **Bk Rev. Ad Acc. Circ:** 1,300 (ctrl). available on microfilm and microfiche from University Microfilms International (UMI). Documents available from UMI Article Clearinghouse. *Continues Assessors Journal, 0004-5071. Merged with IAAO Update, 0892-7154 and Assessment Digest, 0731-0277 Assessment and Valuation Legal Reporter, 0090-6352 to form Assessment Journal, 1073-8568.*
**Desc:** Scholarly investigations of property taxation, valuation, and related areas.
**Ind/Abst** ABI/INFORM Glob. Ed.; ABI Inform Ondisc (March 1985-); Account. Tax Datab. (Mar. 1985-); Index Period. Artic. Relat. Law; J. Plan. Lit.; PAIS Int. Print (1991-); Urban Aff. Abstr.

**US/0744-6926**
**PROPERTY TAX REPORT.** (PROPERTY TAX REPORT / INSTITUTE OF PROPERTY TAXATION.). Periodical. English. mo. Institute of Property Taxation, Suite 412, 499 South Capitol Street SW, Washington DC 20003.

**US**
**PROPERTY TAX STATISTICAL REPORT FROM THE OFFICE OF STATE TAX COMMISSIONER ... ON ... PROPERTY TAXES LEVIED AND PROPERTY VALUATION. See** Public Administration-Abstracting, Bibliographies and Statistics.

**US**
**PROPERTY TAX STATISTICS. Added/Corp** Washington (State). Dept. of Revenue. (1989)-. English. Washington State Department of Revenue, Olympia WA 98504. **LC** HJ4121.W2; D46c. **DD** 336.22/09797/021. *Continues Property Tax Collections and Levies Due.*

**US**
**PROPERTY TAXES.** Macmillan Publishing Company, 866 3rd Avenue, New York NY 10022. **Tel** (212)702-2000, (800)257-5755.

**US**
**PROPERTY VALUATION REPORT. Added/Corp** Iowa. Property Tax Division. (1973)-. English. an. Department of Revenue / Iowa, Hoover State Office Building, Des Moines IA 50319. **LC** HJ4121.I7; P77. **DD** 33.33/2/09777. *Continues Taxable Values of Real, Personal Property, Including Moneys and Credits and Public Utilities.*

**US**
**PROPOSED BIENNIAL BUDGET PRESENTED BY GOVERNOR TO LEGISLATURE. Main/Corp** Minnesota. Office of the Governor. English. be. Minnesota Office of the Governor, St Paul MN 55155. **LC** HJ11; .M6425A. **DD** 353.9/776/00722.

**US**
**PROPOSED BUDGET FOR THE MARYLAND-NATIONAL CAPITAL PARK AND PLANNING COMMISSION. MONTGOMERY COUNTY PROGRAMS, A. See** Public Administration-Parks and Recreation.

**CN/0229-5253**
**PROVINCE OF BRITISH COLUMBIA BUDGET.** (BUDGET / PROVINCE OF BRITISH COLUMBIA.). [Prov. B.C. budg.]. **Main/Corp** British Columbia. **VAT** Budget - Province of British Columbia. March 1981-. English. an. Government of British Columbia / Victoria, Parliament Buildings, Victoria British Columbia V8V 1X4 Canada. **DD** 354.7110072/252. *Continues British Columbia Budget, 0382-1986.*

**CN/0317-946X**
**PROVINCIAL AND MUNICIPAL FINANCES. Main/Corp** Canadian Tax Foundation. 5th- Ed.; 1971-. English. be. 15.75Can$ Canada. Canadian Tax Foundation, 1 Queen Street East, Suite 1800, Toronto Ontario M5C 2Y2 Canada. **Tel** (416)863-9784. **ED** L Amalia. **LC** HJ795.A1; C3. **DD** 336.71. **Circ:** 10,000,000. *Formed by the union of Provincial Finances, 0068-9823 and Local Finance, 0459-6609.*
**Desc:** A review of the revenues and expenditures of provincial and municipal governments in Canada; statistical tables throughout.

**CN/0706-3083**
**PROVINCIAL ECONOMIC ACCOUNTS.** (PROVINCIAL ECONOMIC ACCOUNTS, EXPERIMENTAL DATA / STATISTICS CANADA, GROSS NATIONAL PRODUCT DIVISION.). [Prov. econ. acc.]. **Added/Corp** Statistics Canada. Gross National Product Division. Statistics Canada. Income and Expenditure Accounts Divison. **VFOAT** Comptes Economiques Provinciaux, Donnees au Stade Experimental. (1967/1982)-. English (French). an. 80.00Can$ Canada; $96.00 US; $112.00 other. Statistics Canada, Publications Sales & Services, Main Building Room 1710, Ottawa Ontario K1A 0T6 Canada. **Tel** (613)951-5078, (800)267-6677, FAX (613)951-1584, telex 053-3585. **DD** 336.71. cum. index. **Circ:** 600.

**CN/0383-5855**
**PROVINCIAL FINANCIAL ASSISTANCE TO MUNICIPALITIES, BOARDS AND COMMISSIONS.** [Prov. financ. assist. munic. boards comm.]. 1975-. English. an. Government Bookstore, 880 Bay Street, Toronto Ontario M7A 1N8 Canada. **LC** HJ795.O6; P76. **DD** 354.7130072/53. *Continues Provincial Assistance to Municipalities, Boards and Commissions, 0383-5847.*

**CN/0712-8762**
**PROVINCIAL GROSS DOMESTIC PRODUCT BY INDUSTRY.** (PROVINCIAL GROSS DOMESTIC PRODUCT BY INDUSTRY / STATISTICS CANADA, INDUSTRY PRODUCT DIVISION.). [Prov. gross domest. prod. ind.]. **Added/Corp** Statistics Canada. Industry Product Division. Statistics Canada. Industry Measures and Analysis Division. Statistics Canada. Input-Output Division. Statistics Canada. Provincial Industry Measures Section. **VFOAT** Produit Interieur Brut Provincial par Industrie. (1979)-. English (French). an. 50.00Can$ Canada; $60.00 US; $70.00 other. Statistics Canada, Publications Sales & Services, Main Building Room 1710, Ottawa Ontario K1A 0T6 Canada. **Tel** (613)951-5078, (800)267-6677, FAX (613)951-1584, telex 053-3585. **LC** HC120.I52; C36a. **DD** 339.371. *Continues Survey of Production, 0068-7227.*
**Desc:** Presents current price estimates of provincial gross domestic product at factor cost (GDP) for goods-producing industries, plus education, hospitals and accommodation and food services.

**SA**
**PROVINSIALE OUDITEUR SE VERSLAG VOOR DIE MIDDELEREKENINGS EN DIE FINANSIEREKENINGS, DIE. Main/Corp** Natal. Audit Office. **VFOAT** The Provincial Auditor's Report on the Appropriation Accounts and the Finance Accounts. Multiple languages (Afrikaans and English). R10.85. **LC** HJ9929.S6; N38A. *Continues Natal. Audit Office. Finance Accounts (Including Trust, Housing Loan and Village Water Supply Accounts) Teachers' Pension and Provident Funds Accounts and Appropriation Accounts ... with the Provincial Auditor's Reports Thereon.*

PL/0867-7514
**PRZEGLAD PODATKOWY.** (1991)-. Periodical. Polish. mo. $102.00. **(Subscription address:** ARS Polona, PO Box 1001, 00068 Warsaw Poland.**) UDC** 438.

CN/0317-4999
**PUBLIC ACCOUNTS: ALBERTA.**
**Main/Corp** Alberta. Treasury Dept. (19??)-. English. an. Alberta Treasury Department, 9515 107th Street, Terrace Building, Edmonton Alberta Canada. **Tel** (403)427-3035. **LC** HJ9921.Z9; A53a. **DD** 354/.7123/007232.

CN/0706-2710
**PUBLIC ACCOUNTS (REGINA).** (PUBLIC ACCOUNTS.). [Public acc.]. **Main/Corp** Saskatchewan. **VAT** Province of Saskatchewan. Public Accounts; Public Accounts of the Province of Saskatchewan. Periodical. English. an. Saskatchewan Department of Finance, Legislative Building, Regina Saskatchewan S4S 0B3 Canada.

US/0275-1100
**PUBLIC BUDGETING & FINANCE.** [Public budg. finance]. **VFOAT** Public Budgeting and Finance. Vol. 1, No. 1 (Spring 1981)-. Periodical. English. Four times a year. Fl148.50 (individual), Fl223.00 (institution). Transaction Publishers / Rutgers State University, New Brunswick NJ 08903. **Tel** (908)932-2280 Ext. 105, FAX (908)932-3138. **ED** Naomi Caiden, John L Mikesell. **LC** HJ2052.A2; P8. **DD** 353.0072/2/05. **[CCC]. Bk Rev. Ad Acc. Circ:** 3,300. available on labels; available on microfilm and microfiche from University Microfilms International (UMI). Documents available from UMI Article Clearinghouse.
**Desc:** The fundamental journal of theory and practice in financial management and budgeting at all levels of public sector government. The official journal of the American Association for Budget and Program Analysis and the Section on Budgeting and Financial Management of the American Society for Public Administration.
**Ind/Abst** ABI/INFORM Glob. Ed.; ABI Inform Ondisc (Spring 1985-); Account. Tax Datab. (Spring 1985-) [Full Txt.]; Contents Recent Econ. J.; Contents Pages Manage.; Econ. Lit. Index; Educ. Adm. Abstr.; Gen. BusinessFile (1992-); Int. Polit. Sci. Abstr.; J. Econ. Lit.; PAIS Int. Print (1991-); Sage Public Adm. Abstr.; Sage Urban Stud. Abstr; Urban Aff. Abstr.

US/1042-4741
**PUBLIC BUDGETING AND FINANCIAL MANAGEMENT.** [Public budg. financ. manage.]. Vol. 1, No. 1 (1989)-. Periodical. English. Three times a year. $275.00 US; $285.00 other. Marcel Dekker Inc., 270 Madison Avenue, New York NY 10016. **Tel** (212)696-9000, (800)228-1160, FAX (212)685-4540, telex 421419. **(Subscription address:** Marcel Dekker Inc, PO Box 5017, Monticello NY 12701.**) ED** Jack Rabin. **LC** HJ101; .P78. **DD** 350.72/05. **CODEN** PBFMEZ. **[CCC].**
**Desc:** Contains high-quality original papers, review articles, and special topical volumes that address significant developments and new research in the field. Opens a vital dialogue of communication between public administration worldwide.
**Ind/Abst** Int. Abstr. Oper. Res. [Select. Cov.]; PAIS Int. Print (1991-).

AT
**PUBLIC FINANCE. Main/Corp** Australian Bureau of Statistics. South Australian Office. 1976/77-. English. Australian Bureau of Statistics, PO Box 10, Belconnen Australian Capital Territory, 2616 Australia. **Tel** 011 61 6 2527911, FAX 011 61 6 2516009. **LC** HJ90.S68; A87A. **DD** 336.02/9423.
**Ind/Abst** Appl. Soc. Sci. Index Abstr.

NE/0033-3476
**PUBLIC FINANCE.** [Public. financ.]. **VFOAT** Finances Publiques. (1950)-. Periodical. English (French and German; summaries and/or abstracts in French and German). Three times a year. DM230.00 (institutions); DM190.00 (individuals). Public Finance Professor, Goethestrasse 13, D 61462 Koenigstein Germany. **Tel** 011 49 6174 23370. **ED** Dieter Biehl, Alan T. Peacock, Max Frank, Andre Middelhoek. Index Available, published separately, free-automatically sent. cum. index. **Bk Rev. Ad Acc. Pr Rev.** available on microfilm and microfiche from University Microfilms International (UMI). Documents available from The Genuine Article. ***Continues** Openbare Financien.*
**Desc:** Deals with public finance and related issues both from a theoretical and applied point of view.
**Ind/Abst** Curr. Contents Soc. Behav. Sci.; Econ. Lit. Index (199?-); J. Econ. Lit.; J. Plan. Lit.; Leis. Recreat. Tour. Abstr.; PAIS Int. Print (1991-?); Res. Alert [Full Cov.]; Soc. Sci. Cit. Index [Full Cov.].

UK/0305-9014
**PUBLIC FINANCE AND ACCOUNTANCY.** ***Title Change.*** [Public finance account.]. **Added/Corp** Chartered Institute of Public Finance and Accountancy. Vol. 1 (1974)-(19??). Periodical. English. wk. FSF Ltd, 3 Robert Street, London WC2N 6BH England. **Tel** 011 44 71 895 8823. **LC** HJ9701; .P8. **DD** 657/.835/00941. Documents available from Ask*IEEE. ***Continued by** Public Finance.*
**Ind/Abst** Acad. Search (July 1993-Oct. 1993); Account. Tax Datab. (1974-); Anbar Account. Finan. Abstr. [Full Txt.]; Anbar Mark. Distr. Abstr. [Full Txt.]; Anbar Top Manage. Abstr. [Full Txt.]; Bus. Index (1985-); Bus. Source (Jul. 1993-); Gen. BusinessFile (1985-); Gen. Period. Index (1985-); Health Serv. Abstr.; INFO-SOUTH Abstr.; INSPEC (July 1983-); Mag. Search; Manage. Bibliogr. Rev.; Oper. Prod. Manage. Abstr. [Full Txt.]; Person. Train. Abstr. [Full Txt.]; Women Manage. Rev. [Full Txt.].

AT
**PUBLIC FINANCE: GOVERNMENT AUTHORITIES. Main/Corp** Australian Bureau of Statistics. Queensland Office. (1975)-. English. an. Australian Bureau Statistics / Tasmanian Office, Commonwealth Government Centre, 188 Collins Street, Hobart GPO Box 66A, Hobart Tasmania 7001 Australia. **Tel** (002)205889. **LC** HJ92; .R13a. **DD** 336.943.

UK
**PUBLIC FINANCE (LONDON, ENGLAND).** (PUBLIC FINANCE.). (19??)-. English. wk. £88.50. FSF Ltd, 3 Robert Street, London WC2N 6BH England. **Tel** 011 44 71 895 8823. ***Continues** Public Finance and Accountancy.*
**Ind/Abst** Acad. Search (Oct. 1993-).

US/0048-5853
**PUBLIC FINANCE QUARTERLY.** [Public finan. q.]. **VFOAT** PFQ. Vol. 1 (Jan. 1973)-. Periodical. English. qt (Jan., Apr., July, Oct.). $197.00. SAGE Periodical Press, 2455 Teller Road, Thousand Oaks CA 91320. **Tel** (805)499-0721, FAX (805)499-0871, telex 100799. **ED** J. Ronnie Davis (University of New Orleans-Lakefront). **LC** HJ101; .P83. **DD** 336/.005. **CODEN** PFQADD. **[CCC]. Pr Rev. Acid Free.** available on microfilm and microfiche from University Microfilms International (UMI); available on an online database (file 648/Full-Text) from DIALOG. Documents available from The Genuine Article, UMI Article Clearinghouse.
**Desc:** Studies the theory, policy and institutions related to the allocation, distribution and stabilization functions within the public sector of the economy.
**Ind/Abst** ABI/INFORM Glob. Ed.; ABI Inform Ondisc (Oct. 1975-); Acad. Search (Jan. 1994-); Account. Tax Datab. (Oct. 1975-); Bus. ASAP (1990-) [Full Txt.]; Bus. Index (1986-); Contents Recent Econ. J.; Curr. Contents Soc. Behav. Sci.; Econ. Lit. Index; Educ. Adm. Abstr.; Gen. BusinessFile (1986-); Gen. Period. Index (1986-); INFO-SOUTH Abstr.; J. Econ. Lit.; J. Plan. Lit.; Mag. Search; Middle East Abstr. Index; PAIS Int. Print (1991-); Res. Alert [Full Cov.]; Sage Public Adm. Abstr.; Sage Urban Stud. Abstr; Soc. Sci. Cit. Index [Full Cov.]; UMI ABI/Inform--Bus. Period. Ondisc (Jul. 1988-) [Full Txt.]; U.S. Polit. Sci. Doc.

US/0736-7848
**PUBLIC FUND DIGEST.** [Public fund dig.]. **Added/Corp** International Consortium on Governmental Financial Management. Vol. 1, No. 1 (1982)-. Periodical. English. an. $35.00 (organizations); $65.00 (educators); $130.00 (individuals) Includes International Consortium on Governmental Financial Management Membership. International Consortium on Governmental Financial Management, PO Box 8665, Silver Spring MD 20907. **Tel** (301)681-3836. **ED** James Hamilton. **LC** HJ101; .P834. **DD** 350.72/05. **Bk Rev. Ad Acc. Circ:** 1,500.
**Desc:** Articles reprinted or summarized from worldwide sources relating to modern techniques of governmental financial management. Some original articles published when they are of widespread international interest.

US/1042-1912
**PUBLIC GAMING INTERNATIONAL.** [Public gaming int.]. **Added/Corp** Public Gaming Research Institute. **VFOAT** Public Gaming. Vol. 15, No. 4 (April 1987)-. Periodical. English. Twelve times a year. $85.00. Public Gaming Research Institute, 15825 Shady Grove Road, Suite 130, Rockville MD 20850. **Tel** (301)330-7600. **LC** HG6111; .P83. **DD** 336.1/7/05. ***Formed by the union of** Public Gaming, 0270-2827; International Gaming **and** Lottery Journal.*

UK
**PUBLIC INCOME & EXPENDITURE.**
**Main/Corp** Northern Ireland. Dept. of Finance. **VAT** Public Income and Expenditure. (19??)-. English. an. **LC** HJ42.2; .C25b. **DD** 336.416. ***Continues** Northern Ireland. Ministry of Finance. Public Income and Expenditure, Northern Ireland.*

UK/0954-0962
**PUBLIC MONEY & MANAGEMENT.**
**VFOAT** Public Money and Management. Vol. 8, No. 1 & 2 (Spring/Summer 1988)-. Academic Scholarly Publication. English. Four times a year. £120.00 UK and Europe; $212.00 North America; £137.00 other. Basil Blackwell Publishers Ltd, 108 Cowley Road, Oxford 0X4 1JF England. **Tel** 011 44 865 791100, FAX 011 44 865 791347, telex 837022 OXBOOK G. **(Subscription address:** Blackwell Publishers / UK, Marston Book Services, PO Box 87, Oxford OX2 0DT England.**) ED** Sue Richards and Mike Connolly. **LC** HC251; .P8. **DD** 336.41. **[CCC].** Index available. **Bk Rev. Ad Acc. Circ:** 2,600. available on microfilm and microfiche from University Microfilms International (UMI); available on an online database (files 15,485/Full-Text) from DIALOG. ***Continues** Public Money, 0261-1252.*
**Desc:** Features articles, research reports, reviews of developments in the public services and independent statements of view.
**Ind/Abst** Account. Tax Datab. (Winter 1991-) [Full Txt.]; Contents Pages Manage.; PAIS Int. Print (1991-); Soc. Sci. Cit. Index [Full Cov.].

LB/0377-3167
**PUBLIC SECTOR ACCOUNTS OF LIBERIA. Main/Corp** Liberia. Ministry of Planning and Economic Affairs. English. Ministry of Planning and Economic Affairs, Monrovia Liberia West Africa. **Tel** 222082. **LC** HJ89.L5; A315. **DD** 336.666/2. ***Continues** Public Sector Accounts of Liberia, 0377-3167.*

AT/1031-7112
**PUBLIC SECTOR DEBT, AUSTRALIA.**
**See** Public Administration-Abstracting, Bibliographies and Statistics.

US
**PUBLIC WORKS FINANCING.** (19??)-. Periodical. English. Eleven times a year. Comes with Public Works Financing International. PW Financing, c/o Bill Reinhardt, 154 Harrison Avenue, Westfield NJ 07090. **Tel** (908)654-0397, FAX (908)654-0436. **ED** William Reinhardt. Index available. cum. index. **Ad Acc. Circ:** 2,000 (ctrl).
**Desc:** News, features, case studies, and legislation trends in the innovative financing of public purpose infrastructure facilities worldwide.

US/0590-6598
**PUBLICATIONS - COMMITTEE ON TAXATION, RESOURCES AND ECONOMIC DEVELOPMENT. Main/Corp** Committee on Taxation, Resources and Economic Development. 1-. Monographic series. English. Price varies per volume. University of Wisconsin Press, Journal Division, 114 North Murray Street, Madison WI 53715. **Tel** (608)262-4952, FAX (608)262-8909.

US/0735-7893
**PUERTO RICO TAXES.** (PUERTO RICO TAXES / PRENTICE-HALL.). [P.R. taxes]. **Added/Corp** Prentice-Hall, Inc. Vol. 1, No. 1 (Jan. 31, 1983)-. Periodical. English. ir. $445.00. Research Institute of America, 117 East Stevens Avenue, Valhalla NY 10595. **Tel** (800)431-9025.

BL
**QUADROS DE DETALHAMENTO DAS DESPESAS / GOVERNO DO ESTADO DO RIO DE JANEIRO. Main/Corp** Rio de Janeiro (Brazil : State). **VFOAT** Orcamento. Quadros de Detalhamento das Despesas. (1991)-. Portuguese. ***Continues** Orcamento. Quadros de Detalhamento das Despesas.*

US
**QUARTERLY ECONOMIC REPORT.**
(QUARTERLY ECONOMIC REPORT, STATE OF SOUTH CAROLINA.). **Main/Corp** South Carolina. State Budget and Control Board. Division of Research and Statistical Services. (Spring 1980)-. English. qt. Board of Economic Advisors, Edgar A Brown Building/Suite 535, 1205 Pendleton Street, Columbia SC 29201. **Tel** (803)734-1510, FAX (803)734-1530.

CN/0849-3596
**QUARTERLY STATEMENTS OF FINANCIAL OPERATIONS ENDING ... .**
[Q. statements financ. oper.]. **Main/Corp** Canada. **VFOAT** Etats Trimestriels des Operations Financieres se Terminant ... . (June 30, 1990)-. Periodical. English (French). ir. free. Financial Distribution Center, 300 Laurie Avenue West Esplanade Lau, Ottowa, Ontario K1A 0R5 Canada. **Tel** (613)995-2855. **DD** 354.710072/31/05.

US/1057-9699
**QUARTERLY SUMMARY OF FEDERAL, STATE, AND LOCAL TAX REVENUE.** [Q. summ. fed. state local tax revenue]. **VFOAT** Quarterly Tax Report. (April-June 1989)-. Government Publication. English. qt. $7.00 US; $8.75 other. Superintendent of Documents, US Government Printing Office, Washington DC 20402. **Tel** (202)275-3328, FAX (202)786-2377. **DD** 336. ***Continues** Governments Quarterly Report. GT, Quarterly Summary of Federal, State, and Local Tax Revenue, 8756-3606.*

CN
**QUEBEC SALES TAX WITH RELATED TAXES. Main/Corp** Quebec (Province). English. CCH Canadian Ltd., 6 Garamond Court, Don Mills Ontario M3C 1Z5 Canada. **Tel** (416)441-2992, FAX (416)441-3418. **LC** KEQ1029.A29; Q4. **DD** 343.71405/52. ***Supersedes in part** Ontario and Quebec Sales Tax with Related Taxes, 0380-5190.*

LU
**RAPID REPORTS. ECONOMY AND FINANCE / EUROSTAT. Added/Corp** Statistical Office of the European Communities. **VFOAT** Economy and Finance. (19??)-. Periodical. English. ir. ECU 206.00 (complete set). Office for Official Publications of the European Communities, 2 Rue Mercier, 2985 Luxembourg Luxembourg. **Tel** 011 352 499281, FAX 011 352 488573.

# Public Administration —Public Finance and Taxation

**SA**
**RAPORTA ZOMUKONAKONI NOMUTARELI-NTONI KOMBINGA ZOYIVARO YEPANGERO LYAKAVANGO KUMWE NEZI ZOMAPANGERO GORUDI MOSIRONGO ZOMUMVHO.** **Main/Corp** South Africa. Dept. of the Controller and Auditor-General. **Added/Corp** South Africa. Dept. of the Controller and Auditor-General Report of the Controller and Auditor-General on the Accounts of the Kavango Government and of the Tribal Authorities in the Area. **VFOAT** Report of the Controller and Auditor-General on the Accounts of the Kavango Government and of the Tribal Authorities in the Area. (19??)-. Afrikaans (English and Niger-Kordofanian). R2.00. The Government Printer, Bosman Street, Private Bag X85, Pretoria 0001 South Africa. **Tel** 012-323-9731, FAX 012-323-0009. **LC** HJ80A; .K36a. **Continues** Raporta Zomu Konakoni Nomutareli-Ntoni Kombinga Zoyivaro Yondango Zeturopoveta Zakavango Neyi Yepangero Lyorudi.

**FR**
**RAPPORT ANNUEL - CONSEIL NATIONAL DU CREDIT.** **Main/Corp** Conseil National du Credit (France). (19??)-. French. an. 15.00F. Brochure pas en Vente a l'Imprimerie Nationale, 27 39 rue de la Convention, 75732 Paris Cedex 15 France. **LC** HJ47; .A17a subser; HG973.

**FR**
**RAPPORT AU PRESIDENT DE LA REPUBLIQUE.** **Main/Corp** France. Conseil des Impots. French. 15F. Conseil des Impots, 26 rue Desaix, 75732 Cedex 15 France. **LC** HJ47; .A118A. **DD** 336.2/00944.

**FR**
**RAPPORT AU PRESIDENT DE LA REPUBLIQUE DU CONSEIL DES IMPOTS.** Journal Officiel de la Republique Francaise, 26 rue Desaix, 75727 Paris Cedex 15 France.

**FR**
**RAPPORT - CONSEIL DE DIRECTION DU FONDS DE DEVELOPPEMENT ECONOMIQUE ET SOCIAL.** **Main/Corp** Fonds de Developpement Economique et Social. Conseil de Direction. French. 15.00F. Ministere de l'Economie et des Finances, Service d'Edition et de Vente des Publications Officielles, 39 rue de la Convention, CCP 9060.06, Paris France. **LC** HJ47; .A17A subser; HC276.2.

**MQ**
**RAPPORT DE PRESENTATION ET EXPOSE DES MOTIFS DE LA DECISION MODIFICATIVE ... / REPUBLIQUE FRANCAISE, DEPARTEMENT DE LA MARTINIQUE. CONSEIL GENERAL.** **Main/Corp** Martinique. Conseil General. French. **LC** HJ29.7; .A256A.

**IT**
**RASSEGNA TRIBUTARIA : RT.** **VFOAT** RT; R.T. Periodical. Italian. ir. 110.000. Editoriale Tributaria Italiana, Viale Mazzini 25, 00195 Rome Italy. **Tel** 011 39 6 87130300. **DD** 343.4504/02648; 344.503402648.

UK/0142-5137
**RATE SUPPORT GRANT STATISTICS / SOCIETY OF COUNTY TREASURERS.** See Public Administration-Abstracting, Bibliographies and Statistics.

**UK**
**RATING AND VALUATION REPORTER.** See Law.

**UK**
**READERS PAYE : PII HANDBOOK.** English. ir. £97.00. Longman Group Ltd., Fourth Avenue, Longman House, Harlow Essex CM19 5SR England. **Tel** 011 44 279 429655, FAX 011 44 279 431059, telex 81259. **(Subscription address:** Fourth Avenue, Harlow Essex CM19 5AA England)
**Desc:** Comprehensive review of UK payroll taxation legislation.

US/0732-0701
**REAL ESTATE AND PUBLIC UTILITY PROPERTY TAXES.** See Real Estate.

US/0095-3032
**REAL ESTATE ASSESSMENT/SALES RATIO STUDY.** See Real Estate.

US/0735-0678
**REAL ESTATE FINANCING REPORT.** See Real Estate.

US/8756-3835
**REAL ESTATE TAX DIGEST (ALBANY, N.Y.), THE.** See Real Estate.

US/0899-0670
**RECENT TITLES IN LAW FOR THE SUBJECT SPECIALIST. TAXATION AND ESTATE PLANNING.** [Recent titles law subj. spec., Tax. estate plan.]. **VFOAT** Taxation and Estate Planning. Vol. 5, No. 1 (Jan.-March 1988)-. Periodical. English. qt. $85.00. Ward & Associates, 317 South Division, Suite 66, Ann Arbor MI 48104. **Tel** (313)665-3520, FAX (313)665-7880. **DD** 016. **Continues** National Legal Bibliography. Subject Area List. Taxation and Estate Planning, 8755-8130.

**AU**
**RECHNUNGSABSCHLUSS DES LANDES VORARLBERG.** **Main/Corp** Vorarlberg (Austria). (19??)-. German. **LC** HJ45.V6; A32.

US/0733-530X
**RECREATION VEHICLE FINANCING.** **Added/Corp** Recreation Vehicle Industry Association (U.S.). (19??)-. English. an. $6.00. Recreation Vehicle Industry Association, PO Box 2999, 1896 Preston WH Dr., Reston VA 22090-0999. **Tel** (703)620-6003. **LC** HD9710.37.U6; R43. **DD** 338.4/3629226/0973. **Circ:** 8,500.
**Desc:** Part of the ongoing program of the RVIA Finance Committee to achieve closer liaison and better understanding of the mutual needs of the lending communities, the RV industry and the RV consumer.

CN/0712-6565
**RECUEIL FISCAL. PROBLEMES ET SOLUTIONS.** (RECUEIL FISCAL. PROBLEMES ET SOLUTIONS / PREPARE PAR RENE HUOT.). [Recl. fisc., Probl. solut.]. French (English). an. 15.00Can$. Recueil Fiscal Problemes Et Solutions Tome I, c/o Thourene Ltee, CP 14, Ste-Julie Quebec J0L 2C0 Canada. **Tel** (514)649-5367. **ED** Thourene Ltee. **DD** 336.24/0971. Index available. **Bk Rev. Circ:** 4,000 (ctrl).
**Desc:** Canadian income tax problems and solutions.

●CN/1193-3836
**REGLES BUDGETAIRES DU MINISTRE DES TRANSPORTS CONCERNANT LE TRANSPORT DES ELEVES.** (REGLES BUDGETAIRES DU MINISTRE DES TRANSPORTS CONCERNANT LE TRANSPORT DES ELEVES POUR L'ANNEE SCOLAIRE ..). [Regles budg. minist. Transp. concern. transp. elev.]. **Added/Corp** Quebec (Province). Ministere des Transports. (1992/1993)-. French. **DD** 371.8/72/0681.

●CN
**REGLES BUDGETAIRES POUR L'ANNEE SCOLAIRE ..., COMMISSION SCOLAIRE DU LITTORAL.** See Education.

●CN
**REGLES BUDGETAIRES POUR L'ANNEE SCOLAIRE ..., COMMISSION SCOLAIRE KATIVIK.** See Education.

●CN
**REGLES BUDGETAIRES POUR L'ANNEE SCOLAIRE ..., ECOLE DES NASKAPIS.** See Education.

**BL**
**RELATORIO DAS ATIVIDADES ADMINISTRATIVAS DA INSPETORIA-GERAL DE FINANCAS DO MINISTERIO DA FAZENDA.** **Main/Corp** Brazil. Ministerio da Fazenda. Inspetoria-Geral de Financas. Portuguese. an. A Inspetoria-Geral, AV Almirante Baroso 81, 4 Andar Rio de Janeiro Brazil. **LC** HJ32; .A5685. **DD** 354.810072/31/05. **Continues** Brazil. Ministerio da Fazenda. Inspetoria-Geral de Financas. Relatorio das Atividades.

**BL**
**RELATORIO ESTATISTICO DE INFORMACOES ECONOMICO-TRIBUTARIAS / GOVERNO DO ESTADO DE MINAS GERAIS, SECRETARIA DE ESTADO DA FAZENDA, DIRECTORIA DA RECEITA ESTADUAL, CENTRO DE INFORMACOES ECONOMICO-FISCAIS.**
See Public Administration-Abstracting, Bibliographies and Statistics.

**BL**
**RENDA E CIRCULACAO.** (19??)-. Periodical. Portuguese. ir. Renda E Circulacao, rua Mexico 98 S/712 Centro, Rio de Janeiro Brazil. **LC** KHD4582; .R46. **DD** 343.8104/05; 348.103405.

**BL**
**RENDAS ADUANEIRAS.** Began in 1973. Portuguese. an. Ministerio da Fazenda, Bloco 5 90 and 70000, Brasilia DF Brazil. **LC** HJ6851; .A2. **DD** 382.7/0981.

**IT**
**REPERTORIO 4 CODICI TRIBUTARI.** See Law.

**UK**
**REPORT AND ACCOUNTS - SUTTON HOUSING TRUST.** **Main/Corp** Sutton Housing Trust. (1973)-. Corporate Report. English. an. Free. Sutton Housing Trust, Sutton Court, Herfordshire HP23 5BB England. **Tel** 0442 891100, FAX 0442 828433. **ED** Michael Morris. **LC** HD7333.A3; S87a. **DD** 301.5/4. **Continues** Sutton Dwellings Trust. Report and Accounts.

**AM**
**REPORT AND STATEMENTS OF ACCOUNTS OF THE ACCOUNTANT GENERAL FOR THE YEAR ENDED 31ST DECEMBER ... .** **Main/Corp** Anguilla. Accountant General. **VFOAT** Report of the Accountant General on the Accounts for the Year ... . English. **LC** HJ28.3.A83; A535A. **DD** 354.7297/3.

**II**
**REPORT - ANDHRA PRADESH (INDIA). LEGISLATURE. ESTIMATES COMMITTEE.** **Main/Corp** Andhra Pradesh (India). Legislature. Legislative Assembly. Estimates Committee. English. Legislative Assembly, Andhra Pradesh India. **LC** HJ66.A485; B25A. **DD** 354/.54/8400722.

**SQ**
**REPORT BY THE AUDITOR GENERAL FOR THE PERIOD ... / KINGDOM OF SWAZILAND.** **Main/Corp** Swaziland. **Added/Corp** Swaziland. Audit Dept. (Apr. 1st 1976/Mar. 31st 1979)-. English. Audit Department, PO Box 98, Mbabane Swaziland. **LC** HJ9929.S95; S9a. **DD** 354.681/3007232/05. **Continues** Swaziland. Report by the Auditor General, Swaziland, on the Audit of the Accounts of Swaziland.

**AT**
**REPORT : EXPENDITURE FROM THE CONSOLIDATED REVENUE FUND.** **Main/Corp** Australia. Parliament. Joint Committee of Public Accounts. English. Government Printer / Australia, PO Box 84, Canberra, Australian Capital Territory, 2600 Australia. **LC** J905; .L3 subser; HJ90. **DD** 328.94/01 S; 354/.94/00722.

US/0742-5317
**REPORT - FEDERAL BAR ASSOCIATION. SECTION OF TAXATION.** See Law.

**AT**
**REPORT FROM THE PUBLIC ACCOUNTS COMMITTEE UPON UNPAID ACCOUNTS.** **Main/Corp** Victoria, Australia. Committee of Public Accounts. (19??)-. English. $0.20. Melbourne Government Printer, 232 Victoria Parade, East Melbourne 3002 Australia. **Tel** 03 628 5777, FAX 03 628 5631. **LC** HJ95; .R2a. **DD** 336.3/432/09944.

**II**
**REPORT, GOVERNMENT OF NAGALAND.** **Main/Corp** India (Republic). Comptroller and Auditor-General. (1970)-. English. Government of Nagaland, Government Press, India Comptroller & Auditor General, Kohima Nagaland India. **LC** HJ9927.I4; A295. **DD** 354/.54/61600723. **Continues** India. Comptroller and Auditor-General. Audit Report, Government of Nagaland.

**II**
**REPORT, GOVERNMENT OF TAMIL NADU.** **Title Change. Main/Corp** India. Comptroller and Auditor-General. 1969/70-. English. an. **LC** HJ9927.I4; A365. **DD** 354/.54/8200723. **Continues** Audit Report, Government of Tamil Nadu. **Superseded by** Report of the Comptroller and Auditor General of India, Government of Tamil Nadu: Civil; Report of the Comptroller and Auditor General of India, Government of Tamil Nadu: Revenue Receipts.

**II**
**REPORT, GOVERNMENT OF THE UNION TERRITORY OF GOA, DAMAN, AND DIU.** **Main/Corp** India (Republic). Comptroller and Auditor-General. 1969/70-. English. an. Rs2.00. Government of Nagaland, Government Press, India Comptroller & Auditor General, Kohima Nagaland India. **LC** HJ9927.I4; A3. **DD** 354/.54/7990072. **Continues** Audit Report, Government of the Union Territory of Goa, Daman, and Diu.

**II**
**REPORT, GOVERNMENT OF THE UNION TERRITORY OF PONDICHERRY.** **Main/Corp** India (Republic). Comptroller and Auditor-General. 1969/70-. English. an. Government Press Director, Comptroller and Auditor General,

# Public Administration — Public Finance and Taxation

Pondicherry India. **LC** HJ9927.I4; A315. **DD** 354/.54/8600723. **Continues** Audit Report, Government of the Union Territory of Pondicherry.

US
**REPORT - KENTUCKY. DEPT. OF REVENUE.** **Main/Corp** Kentucky. Dept. of Revenue. (1917)-. English. Department of Revenue / Kentucky, New Capitol Annex, Frankfort KY 40620. **LC** HJ11; .K45. **DD** 336.2061769.

US
**REPORT OF DATA FROM FA-1 FORMS - NEW JERSEY. DIVISION OF TAXATION. LOCAL PROPERTY AND PUBLIC UTILITY BRANCH.** **Main/Corp** New Jersey. Division of Taxation. Local Property and Public Utility Branch. English. Division of Taxation, West State and Willow Streets, Trenton NJ 08625. **LC** HJ4245; .A35A. **DD** 336.2/2/09749.

FJ
**REPORT OF E.D.P. BRANCH, MINISTRY OF FINANCE FOR THE YEAR ... .** **Main/Corp** Fiji. Ministry of Finance. E.D.P. Branch. **Added/Corp** Fiji. Ministry of Finance. E.D.P. Branch. Report of EDP Branch, Ministry of Finance for the Year ... . **VFOAT** Report of EDP Branch, Ministry of Finance for the Year ... . (19??)-. English. **LC** J961; .H835 subser; HJ99.3. **DD** 300/.996/11; 354.96/10072/02854.

US
**REPORT OF FUNDS GRANTED TO DELAWARE DURING FISCAL YEAR ... BY STATE AGENCY AND BY FEDERAL PROGRAM (OMB NUMBER).** English. an. **LC** HJ11; .D334. **DD** 353.97510072/52.

US/0147-975X
**REPORT OF OUTSTANDING INDEBTEDNESS OF COUNTIES, CITIES, VILLAGES, TOWNSHIPS, SCHOOLS, SPECIAL DISTRICTS, AUTHORITIES, STATE BONDS.** **Main/Corp** Michigan. Municipal Finance Commission. English. an. Municipal Finance Commission, Treasury Buildings/First Floor, Lansing MI 48922. **LC** HJ8364; .M5A. **DD** 336.3/4/09774.

CN/0316-3571
**REPORT OF PROCEEDINGS OF THE TAX CONFERENCE CONVENED BY THE CANADIAN TAX FOUNDATION.** (REPORT OF PROCEEDINGS OF THE ... ANNUAL TAX CONFERENCE CONVENED BY THE CANADIAN TAX FOUNDATION.). [Rep. proc. tax. conf. conv. Can. Tax Found.]. **Main/Corp** Canadian Tax Foundation. **VFOAT** Report os Proceedings of the ... Tax Conference Convened by the Canadian Tax Foundation. (1947)-. Periodical. English. an. 180.00Can$. Canadian Tax Foundation, 1 Queen Street East, Suite 1800, Toronto Ontario M5C 2Y2 Canada. **Tel** (416)863-9784. **LC** HJ2449; .C3. **DD** 336.2/00971. **Continues** Report of the ... Tax Conference Convened by the Canadian Tax Foundation.
**Ind/Abst** Can. Legal Lit.; Leg. Resour. Index (1980-); LegalTrac.

CN/0228-314X
**REPORT OF THE AUDITOR GENERAL (EDMONTON).** (REPORT OF THE AUDITOR GENERAL - ALBERTA. OFFICE OF THE AUDITOR GENERAL.). [Rep. Audit. Gen.]. **Main/Corp** Alberta. Office of the Auditor General. 1979-. Periodical. English. Alberta Legislative Assembly, Office of the Chief Electoral Officer, West Chambers Building/Main Floor, 12220 Stony Plain Road, Edmonton Alberta T5N 3Y4 Canada. **Tel** (403)427-7191, (403)422-2900. **LC** HJ9921.Z9; A52A. **DD** 354.71230072/32.

CN/0318-8124
**REPORT OF THE AUDITOR GENERAL OF PRINCE EDWARD ISLAND TO THE LEGISLATIVE ASSEMBLY.** **Main/Corp** Prince Edward Island. Office of the Auditor General. English. an. Office of the Auditor General Province of Prince Edward Island, PO Box 2000, Charlottetown Prince Edward Island C1A 7N8 Canada. **Tel** (902)368-4520, FAX (902)892-3420. **LC** HJ13; .P37A. **DD** 354.7170072/32/05. **Circ:** 300 (ctrl).

SA
**REPORT OF THE AUDITOR-GENERAL ON THE ACCOUNTS OF THE REPRESENTATIVE AUTHORITY OF THE OVAMBOS AND OF THE TRIBAL AUTHORITIES IN OVAMBO FOR THE FINANCIAL YEAR ... .** **Main/Corp** South Africa. Office of the Auditor-General. (19??)-. English. Controller and Auditor-General, The Government Printer, Bosman Street, Privat Bag X85, Pretoria 0001 South Africa. **LC** HJ83.3.O94; S66a. **DD** 354.6881. **Continues** South Africa. Dept. of the Auditor-General. Ehokololoningomwa LyOmtyekindjayi Lyoolekenenga Epangelo LyOwambo Nodhomalelo Giilongo MOwambo Molweendo Lwomumvo Gwembo ... .

TR
**REPORT OF THE AUDITOR GENERAL ON THE ACCOUNTS OF TRINIDAD AND TOBAGO.** **Main/Corp** Trinidad and Tobago. Auditor General's Dept. English. an. $1.80. Government Printery / Trinidad, 110 Henry Street, Port of Spain Trinidad. **LC** HJ9923.T753; T75A. **DD** 354/.729/83007232.

GL
**REPORT OF THE AUDITOR GENERAL ON THE PUBLIC ACCOUNTS OF THE GOVERNMENT OF GUYANA FOR THE FINANCIAL YEAR ENDED 31ST DECEMBER ... / GUYANA.** **Main/Corp** Guyana. Auditor General. 1970-. English. an. **LC** HJ9923.G83; G89A. **DD** 354.88/1007232/05. **Continues** Public Accounts of the Government of Guyana Together with the Report Thereon by the Directory of Public Audit.

PP
**REPORT OF THE AUDITOR GENERAL ON THE PUBLIC ACCOUNTS ... / PAPUA NEW GUINEA.** **Main/Corp** Papua New Guinea. Auditor-General's Office. **VFOAT** Auditor General's Report; Auditor-General's Report. English. an. Auditor General's Office, PO Box 2042, Konedobu Papua New Guinea. **LC** HJ98.4; .A362A. **DD** 354.95/3007232/05.

ZA
**REPORT OF THE AUDITOR GENERAL ON THE ZANZIBAR SSTATE ENTERPRISES FOR THE PERIOD ENDED 31ST DECEMBER.** **Added/Corp** Zanzibar. Auditor General. (1980)-. English. an. **LC** HJ9929.T3; R46. **DD** 354.678/1092.

CN/0382-1420
**REPORT OF THE AUDITOR GENERAL TO THE LEGISLATIVE ASSEMBLY (FREDERICTON).** (REPORT OF THE AUDITOR GENERAL TO THE LEGISLATIVE ASSEMBLY - NEW BRUNSWICK.). **Main/Corp** New Brunswick. Office of the Auditor-General. **VFOAT** Rapport du Verificateur General a l'Assemblee Legislative. English (French). an. Free. Office of the Auditor-General, PO Box 758, Fredericton New Brunswick E3B 5B4 Canada. **Tel** (506)453-2243. **LC** HJ9921.Z9; N425A. **DD** 354/.715/007232. **Circ:** 500.
**Desc:** Report on the work of the auditor general in auditing the accounts and records of the Province of New Brunswick and its agencies.

US
**REPORT OF THE AUDITOR OF PUBLIC ACCOUNTS. AUDIT EXAMINATION OF THE GRAYSON COUNTY FISCAL COURT.** **Main/Corp** Grayson County (KY.). Fiscal Court. **VFOAT** Audit Examination of the Grayson County Fiscal Court. an. Auditor of Public Accounts / Kentucky, Commonwealth of Kentucky, Capitol Annex/Suite 168, Frankfort KY 40601. **LC** HJ11; .K426A. **DD** 352.1/72/09769842.

US
**REPORT OF THE AUDITOR OF PUBLIC ACCOUNTS. AUDIT EXAMINATIONS OF THE CUMBERLAND COUNTY FISCAL COURT, FISCAL YEAR ENDED JUNE 30 ... CUMBERLAND COUNTY CLERK, CALENDAR YEAR ... .** **Main/Corp** Cumberland County (KY.). Fiscal Court. **Added/Corp** Cumberland County (Ky.). County Clerk. Kentucky. Auditor of Public Accounts. **VFOAT** Audit Examinations of the Cumberland County Fiscal Court, Fiscal Year Ended June 30 ... Cumberland County Clerk, Calendar Year ... . (19??)-. English. an. Commonwealth of Kentucky Auditor of Public Accounts, Room 168/Capitol Annex, Frankfort KY 40601. **LC** HJ11; .K425a. **DD** 352.1/72/09769683.

US/0091-8229
**REPORT OF THE COMMISSION ON TAXATION AND PRODUCTION OF IRON ORE AND OTHER MINERALS.** (REPORT SUBMITTED TO THE MINNESOTA LEGISLATURE.). **Main/Corp** Minnesota. Legislature. Commission on Taxation and Production of Iron Ore and Other Minerals. (19??)-. English. ir. Minnesota Legislature, 180 State Capital, St Paul MN 55101. **LC** HD9510.8.U5; M53. **DD** 336.2/71. **Continues** Report Submitted to the MInnesota Legislature.

UK
**REPORT OF THE COMMISSIONERS OF HIS MAJESTY'S INLAND REVENUE.** **Main/Corp** Great Britain. Board of Inland Revenue. (18??)-. English. ir. £13.90. Her Majesty's Stationery Office, 51 Nine Elms Lane, London SW8 5DR England. **Tel** 011 44 71 873 8459, 011 44 71 873 8499, FAX 011 44 71 873 8499, 011 44 71 873 8456, telex 297138. (Subscription address: Her Majesty's Stationery Office, PO Box 276, Publications Centre, London SW8 5DT England.) **LC** HJ40; .R7. **DD** 336.2.

II
**REPORT OF THE COMMITTEE ON PUBLIC ACCOUNTS.** **Main/Corp** West Bengal (India). Legislature. Legislative Assembly. Committee on Public Accounts. English. West Bengal Legislative Assembly Secretariat, Assembly House, Calcutta India. **LC** HJ9927.I4; W45A. **DD** 354.54/14007231/05.

II
**REPORT OF THE COMPTROLLER AND AUDITOR GENERAL OF INDIA FOR THE YEAR ... (COMMERCIAL), GOVERNMENT OF RAJASTHAN.** **VFOAT** Report of the Comptroller and Auditor General of India, Govt. of Rajasthan (Commercial). English. an. **LC** HJ9769.I52; R37. **DD** 354.54/4007232/05.

II
**REPORT OF THE COMPTROLLER AND AUDITOR GENERAL OF INDIA FOR THE YEAR ..., (REVENUE RECEIPTS) GOVERNMENT OF RAJASTHAN.** **Main/Corp** India. Comptroller and Auditor-General. English. an. **LC** HJ65.R33; C64B. **DD** 354.54/400726/050.

II
**REPORT OF THE COMPTROLLER AND AUDITOR-GENERAL OF INDIA. GOVERNMENT OF GUJARAT.** **Main/Corp** India (Republic). Comptroller and Auditor-General. English. an. **LC** HJ9927.I4; A288. **DD** 354.54/75007232/05. **Continues** Audit Report, Government of Gujarat.

II
**REPORT OF THE COMPTROLLER AND AUDITOR GENERAL OF INDIA, GOVERNMENT OF KERALA, CIVIL.** **Main/Corp** India (Republic). Comptroller and Auditor-General. 1972/73-. English. an. **LC** HJ9927.I4; I55I. **Supersedes in part** Report, Government of Kerala.

II
**REPORT OF THE COMPTROLLER AND AUDITOR GENERAL OF INDIA GOVERNMENT OF TAMIL NADU : CIVIL.** **Main/Corp** India. Comptroller and Auditor-General. (1973)-. English. an. **LC** HJ9927.I4; I55G. **DD** 354/.54/82007232. **Supersedes in part** Report, Government of Tamil Nadu.

II
**REPORT OF THE COMPTROLLER AND AUDITOR GENERAL OF INDIA, GOVERNMENT OF TAMIL NADU : REVENUE RECEIPTS.** **Main/Corp** India. Comptroller and Auditor-General. (1973)-. English. an. **LC** HJ2934.T3; I53A. **DD** 354/.54/82007232. **Supersedes in part** Report, Government of Tamil Nadu.

II
**REPORT OF THE COMPTROLLER AND AUDITOR-GENERAL OF INDIA (REVENUE RECEIPTS).** **Main/Corp** India. Comptroller and Auditor-General. English. **LC** HJ65.M33; I53B. **DD** 354.54/3007232/05. **Supersedes in part** Government of Madhya Pradesh: Report of the Comptroller and Auditor General.

US/0146-7387
**REPORT OF THE COMPTROLLER TO THE GOVERNOR OF VIRGINIA.** **Main/Corp** Virginia. Dept. of Accounts. English. an. Commonwealth of Virginia Department of Accounts, PO Box 6N, Richmond VA 23215. **LC** HJ11; .V834. **DD** 353.9/755/0072. **Continues** Virginia. Dept. of Finance. Division of Accounts and Control. Report of Comptroller.

SA
**REPORT OF THE CONTROLLER AND AUDITOR-GENERAL ON THE ACCOUNTS OF THE ADMINISTRATION OF COLOURED AFFAIRS.** **Main/Corp** South Africa. Dept. of the Controller and Audtor-General. **Added/Corp** South Africa. Dept. of the Controller and Auditor-General. Verslag van die Kontroleur en Ouditeur-Generaal oor die Rekeninge van die Administrasie van Kleurlingsake. **VFOAT** Verslag van die Kontroleur on Ouditeur-Generaal van die Administrasie van Kleurlingsake. 1st (1969/1970)-. Multiple languages (Afrikaans and English). an. R1.55. Government Printer / South Africa, Bosman Street, Private Bag X85, Pretoria 0001 South Africa. **Tel** 011 27 12 3239731 Ext. 262. **LC** DT763; .A255. **DD** 354/.68/00723205.

# Public Administration — Public Finance and Taxation

**AT**
**REPORT OF THE CONTROLLER FOR THE PERIOD ENDED 30 JUNE / DEPARTMENT OF THE TREASURY, ROYAL AUSTRALIAN MINT.** Main/Corp Royal Australian Mint. VFOAT Annual Report. 1st (1965)-. English. an. LC WMLC L 83/6592.

**MF**
**REPORT OF THE DIRECTOR OF AUDIT ON THE ACCOUNTS OF MAURITIUS FOR THE YEAR ENDED 30 JUNE ... .** Main/Corp Mauritius. Audit Dept. English. an. Rs30.00. LC HJ9929.M38; M38A. DD 354.69/82007232/05. *Continues* Mauritius. Audit Dept. Report of the Directory of Audit.

**US**
**REPORT OF THE MARYLAND BOARD OF REVENUE ESTIMATES ON ESTIMATED MARYLAND REVENUES.** Main/Corp Maryland. Board of Revenue Estimates. (19??)-. English. an. Free. Board of Revenue Estimates, State Treasury Building, PO Box 466, Annapolis MD 21404. Tel (410)269-3881. ED Robert D. Rader. LC HJ2412.A65; A25. DD 353.97520072/6/05. Circ: 500 (ctrl). *Continues* Maryland. Board of Revenue Estimates. Report on Estimated Maryland Revenues.
**Desc:** Contains estimates of state revenues for two fiscal years based upon current laws and administrative practices.

**ZA**
**REPORT OF THE PUBLIC ACCOUNTS COMMITTEE.** Main/Corp Zambia. Public Accounts Committee. English. an. K9.50 Zambia; $5.50 US. Zambia Government Printer, POB 30136, Lusaka Zambia. LC HJ9929.Z35; Z36A. DD 354/.689/4007231. Bk Rev. Circ: 500.
**Desc:** Aims for the continuous checking of financial records in accordance with existing programs in order to arrest irregularities at an early stage to allow remedial action to be taken.

**US/0095-3199**
**REPORT OF THE STATE AUDITOR OF MINNESOTA ON THE REVENUES, EXPENDITURES, AND DEBT OF THE CITIES AND VILLAGES IN MINNESOTA.** *Title Change.* Main/Corp Minnesota. State Auditor. 1972/73-1973/74. English. an. LC HJ9777.M55; M55A. DD 352/.1/09776. *Continued by* Report of the State Auditor of Minnesota on the Revenues, Expenditures, and Debt of the Cities in Minnesota.

**US**
**REPORT OF THE STATE COMMISSION ON EMINENT DOMAIN AND REAL PROPERTY TAX ASSESSMENT REVIEW.** See Real Estate.

**CN/0846-3336**
**REPORT OF THE STEERING COMMITTEE TO THE STANDING COMMMITTEE ON PUBLIC ACCOUNTS.** [Rep. Steer. Comm. Standing Comm. Public Acc.]. Main/Corp Nova Scotia. House of Assembly. Standing Committee on Public Accounts. Steering Committee. 55th General Assembly, 2nd session (May, 1991)-. English. The Steering Committee. DD 354.7160072/32/05.

**US**
**REPORT OF THE TREASURER OF STATE - IOWA. DEPT. OF TREASURER OF STATE.** Main/Corp Iowa. Dept. of Treasurer of State. 1914/16-. English. be. Iowa Treasurer of the State, Des Moines IA 50304. LC HJ11; .I814A. DD 353.97770072/31. *Continues* Biennial Report of the Treasurer of State to the Governor of Iowa.

**US/0091-8695**
**REPORT ON FEDERAL FUNDS RECEIVED IN IOWA.** Main/Corp Iowa. Office for Planning and Programming. English. an. Office for Planning and Programming, 523 East 12th Street, Des Moines IA 50319. LC HJ430; .A3. DD 336.1/85/09777. *Continues* Report on Federal Grants-in-Aid in Iowa.

**US**
**REPORT ON STATE COMPTROLLER - CONNECTICUT.** Main/Corp Connecticut. Auditors of Public Accounts. English. Auditors of Public Accounts, State Capitol, Hartford CT 06106. LC HJ11; .C824A. DD 353.97460072/32.

**US**
**REPORT ON STATE COMPTROLLER. SPECIAL APPROPRIATIONS ADMINISTERED BY STATE COMPTROLLER, FISCAL YEAR ENDED JUNE 30 ... .** VFOAT Special Appropriations Administered by State Comptroller, Fiscal Year Ended June 30 ... . English. LC HJ9830; .R46. DD 353.97460072/32/05.

**II**
**REPORT ON THE APPROPRIATION ACCOUNTS OF THE GOVERNMENT OF PUNJAB AND THE REPORTS OF THE COMPTROLLER AND AUDITOR GENERAL OF INDIA.** Main/Corp Punjab, India (State). Legislature. Legislative Assembly. Public Accounts Committee. English. India Legislature, Legislative Council Hyderabad, Andhra Pradesh, Hyderabad India. LC HJ9927.I42; P8. DD 354.54/55200723/05.

**SY**
**REPORT ON THE ... SYRIA'S BUDGET.** Main/Corp Syria. English. an. $55.00 (airmail) US. Office Arabe de Presse et de Documentation, 67 Place Chahbandar, BP 3550, Damascus Syria. Tel 459166 (operator assisted requested), telex 411613 OFA SY. LC HJ64.25; .A295B. DD 354.56910072/255/05. Index available. cum. index. Circ: 200 (ctrl).

**II/0440-8411**
**REPORT - PUBLIC ACCOUNTS COMMITTEE.** Main/Corp Himachal Pradesh, India. Legislative Assembly. Public Accounts Committee. 1st-1964/65-. English. Himachal Pradesh Vidhan Sabha Secretariat, Legislative Assembly, Public Accounts Committee, Simla India. LC HJ9927.I4. DD 354.54/52/0072.

**US**
**REPORT / STATE OF NEBRASKA, INVESTMENT COUNCIL.** Main/Corp Nebraska. Investment Council. (19??)-. English. an. Nebraska Investment Council, 941 O Street/#107 Terminal Building, Lincoln NE 68508-3626. LC HJ3835.N2; A28. DD 353.97820072/6. *Continues* Nebraska. State Investment Council. Annual Report.

**CN/1193-2430**
**REPORT TO THE LEGISLATIVE ASSEMBLY OF BRITISH COLUMBIA ON THE PUBLIC ACCOUNTS.** (REPORT TO THE LEGISLATIVE ASSEMBLY OF BRITISH COLUMBIA ON THE ... PUBLIC ACCOUNTS / AUDITOR GENERAL.). [Rep. Legis. Assem. B.C. public acc.]. Main/Corp British Columbia. Office of the Auditor General. Added/Corp British Columbia. Legislative Assembly. (1991)-. English. an. LC HJ13; .B56a. DD 354.7110072/32/05. *Continues* British Columbia. Office of the Auditor General.; Annual Report of the Auditor General of British Columbia to the Legislative Assembly.

**US/0898-7491**
**REPORT TO THE SENATE AND HOUSE COMMITTEES ON THE BUDGET, A.** See Economics.

**US**
**REPORT TO THE STATE BOARD OF EQUALIZATION.** Main/Corp Tennessee. Division of Property Assessment. English. Division of Property Assessments, Nashville TN 37219. LC HJ11; T265A. DD 353.9/768/007242.

**US**
**REPORT TO THE STOCKHOLDERS.** Main/Corp Wyoming. State Auditor. English. Wyoming State Auditor, State Capitol Building, Cheyenne WY 82002. LC HJ11; .W833A. DD 353.97870072/32/05.

**US**
**REPORTS AND TESTIMONY / UNITED STATES GENERAL ACCOUNTING OFFICE, OFFICE OF PUBLIC AFFAIRS.** Added/Corp United States. General Accounting Office. Office of Public Affairs. (Oct. 1989)-. Periodical. English. mo. Free on request. US General Accounting Office / District of Columbia, 441 G Street NW, Room 4528, Washington DC 20548. Tel (202)275-2812. (Subscription address: Supt. of Documents General Accounting Office, PO Box 6015, Gaithersburg, MD 20877) available on an online database (file 636/Full-Text) from DIALOG. *Continues* Reports Issued in ... .
**Ind/Abst** PTS Newsl. Database [Full Txt.].

**UK**
**REPORTS OF TAX CASES.** Added/Corp Great Britain. Board of Inland Revenue. Incorporated Council of Law Reporting for England and Wales. VFOAT Tax Cases Reported Under the Direction of the Board of Inland Revenue (With Notes of Argument Supplied by the Incorporated Council of Law Reporting); Tax Cases Reports. Vol. 2 (1883-1890)-. Periodical. English. mo. £42.00. Her Majesty's Stationery Office, 51 Nine Elms Lane, London SW8 5DR England. Tel 011 44 71 873 8459, 011 44 71 873 8499, FAX 011 44 71 873 8499, 011 44 71 873 8456, telex 297138. (Subscription address: Her Majesty's Stationery Office, PO Box 276, Publications Centre, London SW8 5DT England.) *Continues* Reports of Tax Cases Under the Act 37 Vict. 37 Cap. 16 and Under the Taxes Management Act.

**US/8755-6294**
**REPORTS OF THE UNITED STATES TAX COURT.** See Law.

**US/0040-0017**
**REPORTS - UNITED STATES. TAX COURT.** See Law.

**US/0884-0741**
**RESEARCH IN GOVERNMENTAL AND NONPROFIT ACCOUNTING.** [Res. gov. non-profit account.]. Vol. 1 (1985)-. English. an. $73.25. JAI Press Inc., 55 Old Post Road, Suite 2, PO Box 1678, Greenwich CT 06836-1678. Tel (203)661-7602, FAX (203)661-0792. ED James L. Chan. LC HJ9701; .R47. DD 657/.835/005.

**US/0163-9994**
**RESEARCH INSTITUTE LAWYERS TAX ALERT, THE.** See Law.

**US**
**RESEARCH INSTITUTE MASTER FEDERAL TAX MANUAL WITH FEDERAL TAX COORDINATOR 2D REFERENCES.** *Title Change.* See Law.

**US**
**RESEARCH REPORT - FEDERATION OF TAX ADMINISTRATORS.** Main/Corp Federation of Tax Administrators. English. Federation of Tax Administrators, 444 North Capital Street Northwest, Suite 334, Washington DC 20001. Tel (202)624-5890. LC HJ2360. DD 336.2072.

**US**
**RETAIL SALES AND USE TAX REPORT.** English. an. Free. Department of Revenue and Finance / Iowa, 1300 East Walnut Street, Hoover State Office Building, Des Moines IA 50319. Tel (515)281-3024, FAX (515)242-6040. LC HJ11; .I853A. DD 353.97770072/47. Circ: 450. available on microfiche (from Congressional Infromation Service). *Continues* Retail Sales and Use Tax.

**UK**
**RETIREMENT PLANNING.** (19??)-. English. an. Chiltern Publishing, 18 Burgess Wood Road, Beaconsfield Bucks HP9 1EQ England. Tel 011 44 494 673062, FAX 011 44 494 678914.
**Desc:** Handbook of personal taxation for individuals, businesses and consultants.

**UK**
**RETURN OF OUTSTANDING DEBT (ENGLAND AND WALES).** Main/Corp Chartered Institute of Public Finance and Accountancy. 919??)-. English. an. £2.00 single issue. Chartered Institute of Public Finance and Accountancy, 2 3 Robert Street, London WC2N 6BH England. Tel 011 44 1 895 8823. LC HJ9431; .C46a. DD 336.3/431/41.

**US/0160-0818**
**REVENEWS.** Main/Corp United States. Office of Revenue Sharing. VAT Revenue News. Periodical. English. Department of the Treasury Office of Revenue Sharing, Fifteenth Street and Pennsylvania Avenue NW, Washington DC 20220.

**FR**
**REVENU FRANCAIS.** French. mo. 264.00F France; (add 60.00F postage) other. Revenu Francais, 1 Bis Av de la Republique, 75011 Paris France. Tel 011 33 1 43553999.

**US**
**REVENUE.** Main/Corp Illinois. Dept. of Revenue. VFOAT Annual Report. (1978)-. English. an. Free. Illinois Department of Revenue Public Information Office, 101 West Jefferson Street, Springfield IL 62794. Tel (217)785-2602. LC HJ11; .I352a. DD 336.2/009773. *Continues* Illinois. Dept. of Revenue. Report to Taxpayers, 0146-3004.

**US**
**REVENUE COMPARISON WITH FY ... AND FY ... ESTIMATES.** Main/Corp Montgomery County (MD.). Dept. of Finance. Office of the Director. VFOAT Revenue Comparison with F.Y. ... and F.Y. Estimates. English. Department of Finance / Rockville, 101 Monroe Street, Rockville MD 20850. LC HJ9012.M3; M632A. DD 352.1/252/0975284.

**UK**
**REVENUE ESTIMATES - GREATER LONDON COUNCIL.** Main/Corp Greater London Council. 1965/66-. English. an. £0.05. Greater London Council, The County Hall, London SE1 7PB England. Tel (01)633-7139. LC HJ9041.L7; C24. DD 336/.02/421.
**Desc:** Vols. for 1965/66-1967/68-1972/73 include the estimates of the Inner London Education Authority.

**AT/1034-7747**
**REVENUE LAW JOURNAL.** [Revenue law j.]. Added/Corp Bond University (Gold Coast, Qld.). Taxation & Corporate Research Centre. Vol. 1, No. 1

# Public Administration — Public Finance and Taxation

(Mar. 1990)-. Periodical. English. sa. 90.00Aus$ Australia; 98.00Aus$ other. Bond University, Gold Coast Law School, Queensland 4229 Australia. **Tel** 011 61 75 925011, FAX 011 61 75 952246. **LC** K18; .E935. **DD** 343.9404; 349.4034.
**Ind/Abst** Aust. Leg. Mon. Dig.

US/0147-3344
**REVENUE NEWS.** (REVENUE NEWS. AN ANNUAL SUPPLEMENT.). **Main/Corp** Alaska. Dept. of Revenue. Research & Analysis Section. English. an. Department of Revenue / Alaska, Research Section, Pouch SA, Juneau AK 99811. **LC** HJ11; .A4535A. **DD** 336/.02/798.

US
**REVENUE REPORT - MAINE. Main/Corp** Maine. Bureau of Taxation. Periodical. English. Bureau of Taxation, State Office Building, Augusta ME 04333. **LC** HJ11; .M263B. **DD** 353.9/741/00724.

HK
**REVIEW / CUSTOMS AND EXCISE DEPARTMENT. Main/Corp** Hong Kong. Customs and Excise Dept. (19??)-. English. **LC** HJ7085.A5; H66a. **DD** 354.51/25007246/06.

US/0147-9229
**REVIEW OF TAXATION OF INDIVIDUALS, THE. Ceased.** See Law-Estate Planning.

NO
**REVISED NATIONAL BUDGET / ROYAL NORWEGIAN MINISTRY OF FINANCE, THE. Main/Corp** Norway. Finans- Og Tolldepartementet. **VFOAT** Norwegian Economy. (198?)-. English. **LC** J405; .H5 subser.; HJ58.A2. **DD** 300/.9481 S; 354.4810072/252/05. **Continues** Norway. Finans- Og Tolldepartementet. Revised National Budget of Norway.
**Ind/Abst** Predicasts Forecasts.

BL
**REVISTA ABOP. Main/Corp** Associacao Brasileira de Orcamento Publico. **VAT** Revista Associacao Brasileira de Orcamento Publico. V. 1- May/Aug. 1975-. Periodical. Portuguese. Associacao Brasileira de Orcamento Publico SCS, Edificio Palacio do Commercio, Salas 801/4 CX Postal, 040162 Brasilia Brazil. **LC** HJ2079; .A88A.

BL
**REVISTA DA PROCURADORIA FISCAL. Main/Corp** Pernambuco (Brazil). Procuradoria Fiscal do Estado. (1978)-. Periodical. Portuguese. sa. Procuradoria Fiscal do Estado, Secretaria da Fazenda de Pernambuco, rua do Imperador Pedro II S/N, 4 Andar 50.000 Recife Pe Brazil. **DD** 354.81/3400724.

VE
**REVISTA DE CONTROL FISCAL.** Yearly V. 16, No. 76 (Jan./Feb./March 1975)-. Periodical. Spanish. qt. Contraloria General de la Republica, Carrera Calle 8, Bogota Colombia. **LC** HJ9703; .V45. **DD** 336.87.
**Continues** Control Fiscal y Tecnificacion Administrativa.

SP
**REVISTA DE DERECHO FINANCIERO Y DE HACIENDA PUBLICA.** See Law.

BL
**REVISTA DE ECONOMIA E FINANCAS. Added/Corp** Instituto de Economia e Financas da Bahia. Vol. 1, No. 1 (1940)-. Portuguese. sa. **LC** WMLC 91/4587.

SP
**REVISTA DE HACIENDA LOCAL.** (19??)-. Periodical. Spanish. Three times a year. 9500ptas Spain; 10500ptas other. Edersa Editoriales de Derecho, Reunidas SA Valverde 32 1, 28004 Madrid Spain. **Tel** 011 34 1 5210246, 011 34 1 5229849. **Continues** Revista de Hacienda Autonomica y Local, 0212-4610.

PE
**REVISTA DE JURISPRUDENCIA FISCAL.** See Law.

MX
**REVISTA DEL TRIBUNAL FISCAL DEL ESTADO DE MEXICO. Main/Corp** Mexico (State). Tribunal Fiscal. Periodical. Spanish. Three times a year. **LC** K13; .E4. **DD** 343.725204; 347.252034.

MX
**REVISTA DIFUSION FISCAL.** Periodical. Spanish. mo. $200.00. **LC** HJ3375; .C73. **DD** 336.2/00972. **Continues** Difusion Fiscal.

BL
**REVISTA DO TRIBUNAL DE CONTAS DO DISTRITO FEDERAL. Main/Corp** Distrito Federal (Brazil). Tribunal de Contas. Portuguese. Praca Do Buriti 70000, Brasilia Brazil. **LC** K4; .I83.

BL
**REVISTA DO TRIBUNAL DE CONTAS DO ESTADO DE SAO PAULO: JURISPRUDENCIA E INSTRUCOES. Main/Corp** Sao Paulo, Brazil (State). Tribunal de Contas. (1973)-. Portuguese. sa. Tribunal de Contas, Avenida Rangel Pestana No 315 - 120. Andar, Sao Paulo 01017 Brazil. **Continues** Sao Paulo, Brazil (State). Tribunal de Contas. Jurisprudencia E Instrucoes.

AG
**REVISTA DO TRIBUNAL DE CONTAS DO MUNICIPIO DO RIO DE JANEIRO.** See Law.

UY
**REVISTA TRIBUTARIA.** See Law.

FR
**REVUE DE DROIT DES AFFAIRES INTERNATIONALES. INTERNATIONAL BUSINESS LAW JOURNAL.** See Law-International Law.

FR/0035-2713
**REVUE DU TRESOR, LA.** See Business-Accounting.

UK/1105-1590
**REVUE EUROPEENNE DE DROIT PUBLIC.** See Law-Constitutional Law.

FR/0294-0833
**REVUE FRANCAISE DE FINANCES PUBLIQUES.** Vol. 1 (1983)-. Periodical. French. qt. 451.00F France; 480.00F other. Editions Juridiques Associees, 26 rue Vercingetorix, 75014 Paris France. **Tel** 011 33 1 43350167. **LC** WMLC 93/4394.

FR
**REVUE FRANCAISE DE L'AUDIT INTERNE.** French. Five times a year. 473.93F France. Institut Francais des Auditeurs et Consultants Internes, 8 rue Jean Goujon, F-75008 Paris France.
**Desc:** Promotion of internal auditing.

BE
**REVUE GENERALE DE FISCALITE.** See Law.

SW
**RIKSREVISIONSVERKETS TAXERINGSSTATISTISKA UNDERSOKNING TAXERINGSARET ... .** See Public Administration-Abstracting, Bibliographies and Statistics.

PL/0079-2640
**ROCZNIK STATYSTYCZNY FINANSOW. Title Change. Main/Corp** Poland. Gowny Urzad Statystyczny. (1945/67)-(19??). Polish. an. Zaklad Wydawnictw Statystycznych, Al Niepodleglosci 208, 00-925 Warszawa Poland. **Tel** 253241, telex 814581A GUS. **LC** HJ55.7; .R17. **Circ:** 1,000 (ctrl). **Continued by** Roczniki Statystyczne. Finanse.
**Desc:** Financial yearbook of Poland.

US/1054-6812
**SALES & USE TAX ALERT.** (SALES & USE TAX ALERT : THE MONTHLY ADVISOR ON LAW, REGULATION, COMPLIANCE, AND TACTICS.). [Sales use tax alert]. **Added/Corp** Sales Tax Institute. **VFOAT** Sales and Use Tax Alert. Vol. 1, No. 1 (Jan. 1991)-. Periodical. English. mo. $189.00. State Taxation Institute, PO Box 81143, Atlanta GA 30366. **Tel** (404)457-1000, FAX (404)936-0149. **DD** 343.

US/0095-1056
**SALES RATIO STUDY; RESIDENTIAL AND COMMERCIAL PROPERTIES. Main/Corp** Colorado. Division of Property Taxation. English. $5.00. State Capitol Annex, Denver CO 80203. **LC** HJ4121.C55; C6B. **DD** 336.2/2/09788.

II
**SALES TAX AFFAIRS.** Periodical. English. 45.00. Kamla Kuj, D-74 Anand Niketan, New Delhi 110021 India. **DD** 343/.54/055.

US
**SALES TAX TOTALS BY KIND FOR ... / STATE OF FLORIDA, DEPARTMENT OF REVENUE. Added/Corp** Florida. Dept. of Revenue. **VFOAT** Sales Tax Totals by Kind for ...; Sales Tax Totals by Category for ...; Tourist Development Tax Totals by Kind for ...; Tourist Development Tax Totals by County for ... . (19??)-. English. mo. Free on request. Florida Department of Revenue, Tax Research, 137 Carlton Building, Tallahassee FL 32399. **Tel** (904)488-5050. **LC** HJ5715.U6; S24. **DD** 336.2/713/09759.

JA
**SAPPORO KOKUZEIKYOKU TOKEISHO. Main/Corp** Japan. Sapporo Kokuzeikyoku. (19??)-. Periodical. Japanese. Sapporo Kokuzeikyoku, Odori Nishi 10-chome Chuo-ku, Sapporo Japan. **LC** HJ77.Z5; H644a.

II/0440-8233
**SCHEDULE OF NEW EXPENDITURE, NON-PLAN. Main/Corp** Himachal Pradesh, India. Finance Dept. English. Government of Himachal, Pradesh India. **LC** HJ66.H5. **DD** 354.54/52/00722.

GW
**SCHULDEN DES LANDES, DER GEMEINDEN, GEMEINDEVERBANDE UND ZWECKVERBANDE AM ..., DIE.** See Public Administration-Abstracting, Bibliographies and Statistics.

GW
**SCHULDEN DES LANDES, DER GEMEINDEN, SAMTGEMEINDEN UND LANDKREISE. Main/Corp** Niedersachsisches Landesverwaltungsamt. German. qt. DM28.20. Niedersachsisches Landesverwaltungsamt, Postfach 107, 3000 Hannover Germany. **Tel** (0511)108-9466. **LC** HJ49.S33; D14A. **DD** 336.43/59. **Bk Rev. Circ:** 450.
**Desc:** Burden of debts: federal, state, district, community.

US/0277-2361
**SECTION OF TAXATION NEWSLETTER / ABA.** See Law.

NE
**SELECTED BIBLIOGRAPHY ON INCOME TAX ADMINISTRATION IN DEVELOPED AND DEVELOPING COUNTRIES.** (19??)-. Bibliography. English. International Bureau of Fiscal Documentation - IBFD Publications, PO Box 20237, 1000 HE Amsterdam The Netherlands. **Tel** 011 31 20-6267726, FAX 011 31 20-6228658, telex 13217 INTAX NL. **(Subscription address:** IBFD / International Bureau of Fiscal Documentation USA, Inc., 24 Hudson Street, Kinderhook NY 12106.**)**
**Desc:** Comprehensive compilation of articles, books, conference papers and other material on income tax administration.

US
**SELECTED DATA ON FEDERAL R & D FUNDING BY BUDGET FUNCTION. Added/Corp** National Science Foundation (U.S.). Division of Science Resources Studies. **VFOAT** Selected Data on Federal R and D Funding by Budget Function. **VAT** Selected Data on Federal Research and Development Funding by Budget Function. Fiscal Years (1990-92)-. English. National Science Foundation, 1800 G Street Northwest, Washington DC 20550. **Tel** (202)357-9859, (202)357-9498. **Continues** Federal R & D Funding by Budget Function.

NE
**SELECTED MONOGRAPHS ON TAXATION. Added/Corp** Harvard University. International Tax Program. International Bureau of Fiscal Documentation. (1974)-. Monographic series. English. ir. Price varies per volume. International Bureau of Fiscal Documentation - IBFD Publications, PO Box 20237, 1000 HE Amsterdam The Netherlands. **Tel** 011 31 20-6267726, FAX 011 31 20-6228658, telex 13217 INTAX NL. **(Subscription address:** IBFD / International Bureau of Fiscal Documentation USA, Inc., 24 Hudson Street, Kinderhook NY 12106.**) Bk Rev. Ad Acc.** ctrl circ.

US/1052-7443
**SELLER'S GUIDE TO GOVERNMENT PURCHASING.** [Seller's guide gov. purch.]. **VFOAT** Guide to Government Purchasing. 1st Ed (1991)-. English. be. $135.95. Gale Research Inc., 835 Penobscot Building, Detroit MI 48226. **Tel** (800)877-GALE, (313)961-2242, FAX (313)961-6083, telex TWX 810-221-7086. **LC** JK1673; .S45. **DD** 353.0071/2/025.
**Continues** Government Procurement Sourcebook.

FR
**SESSION BUDGETAIRE / GRAND CONSEIL DE L'AFRIQUE EQUATORIALE FRANCAISE. Main/Corp** French Equatorial Africa. Grand Conseil. (19??)-. French. **LC** HJ83.8; .A14a.

US/0272-8362
**SETTING MUNICIPAL PRIORITIES.** 1980-. English. an. $25.00 paper-bound; $60.00 cloth-bound. Allanheld Osmun and Company Publishers Inc, 4720 Boston Way, Lanham MD 20706. **LC** HJ9289.N4; S48. **DD** 352.1/09747/1.
**Ind/Abst** Int. Polit. Sci. Abstr.

US/0732-7714
**SHEPARD'S FEDERAL TAX CITATIONS.** See Law.

US/0730-4714
**SHEPARD'S FEDERAL TAX LOCATOR. Ceased.** See Law.

# Public Administration — Public Finance and Taxation

US
**SHEPARD'S ... TAX DICTIONARY.** VFOAT Tax Dictionary. (1991)-. English. an. $38.00. Shepards McGraw-Hill Inc, 555 Middle Creek Parkway, PO Box 35300, Colorado Springs CO 80935-3530. **Tel** (719)488-3000, FAX (800)525-0053. **ED** Richard Westin. **LC** KF6287; .S54. **DD** 343.7304/03; 347.303403.

JA
**SHOTOKUZEI HOREI SHU.** Main/Corp Japan. Added/Corp Japan. Laws, Statutes, etc. Shotokuzeiho. Japan. Sozei Tokubetsu Sochi Ho. Japan. Kokuzei Tsusoku Ho. Zeimu Keiri Kyokai. (19??)-. Periodical. Japanese. ¥2000. Zeimu Keiri Kyokai, 5-13 Shimo Ochiai 2-chome Shinjuku-ku, Tokyo 161 Japan.

CH/0559-9407
**SHUI WU HSUN KAN.** (SHUI WU HSUN KAN / TAX AFFAIRS.). VFOAT Shui Wu; Tax Affairs. (Oct. 10, 1951)-. Periodical. Chinese. ir. $110.00. Shui Wu Hsun Kan Tsa Chih She, 63 Hang-Chou S Road/1 Sec, Taipei Taiwan. **LC** HJ2996; .S53. **DD** 336.2/00951/249. cum. index.

US/0146-9002
**SIGNIFICANT FEATURES OF FISCAL FEDERALISM.** [Signif. featur. fisc. fed.]. Added/Corp United States. Advisory Commission on Intergovernmental Relations. (1976)-. English. an. $20.00 (Vol. I); $22.50 (Vol II). Advisory Commission on Intergovernmental Relations. 800 K Street NW, Suite 450 S Building, Washington DC 20575. **Tel** (202)653-5640, FAX (202)653-5429. **ED** Michael Lawson. **LC** HJ275; .U52a. **DD** 336.1/85/0973.
**Desc:** A compendium of statistical information on state and local revenues and expenditures; federal intergovernmental assistance, and major trends in intergovernmental finance and relations.

UK
**SIMON'S TAX CASES.** (Jan. 12, 1973)-. English. an. £55.00. Butterworth & Co. Ltd. / Kent, England, Borough Green, Sevenoaks Kent TN15 8PH England. **Tel** 011 44 732-884567, FAX 011 44 732-885996. **LC** KD5355.A2; S552. **DD** 343/.41/040264.
**Ind/Abst** Aust. Leg. Mon. Dig.

UK
**SIMON'S TAX INTELLIGENCE.** VFOAT Simon's Weekly Tax Service. (Jan. 12, 1973)-. English. wk. £142.00. Butterworth & Co. Ltd. / Kent, England, Borough Green, Sevenoaks Kent TN15 8PH England. **Tel** 011 44 732-884567, FAX 011 44 732-885996. **LC** KD5355.A1; S55. **DD** 343/.41/04.
**Desc:** Contains full coverage of all developments in tax law and practice notified during the previous week.

UK
**SIMON'S TAXES.** See Law.

GO
**SITUATION ECONOMIQUE, FINANCIERE ET SOCIALE DE LA REPUBLIQUE GABONAISE.** Main/Corp Gabon. Direction de la Statistique et des Etudes Economiques. French. Direction de la Statistique et des Etudes Economiques, BP 2081, Libreville Gabon. **LC** HC547.G3; A2. **DD** 330.967/2104. *Continues* Situation Economique, Financiere et Sociale de la Republique Gabonaise.

CN/0822-9589
**SIX, CINQ ET APRES : INNOVATIONS DANS L'ECONOMIE MUNICIPALE.** [Six cinq apres, innov. econ. munic.]. VFOAT Innovations dans l'Economie Municipale; Innovations. VAT Innovations (Ottawa. Ed. Francaise). Vol. 1, No 1 (June 1983)-. Periodical. French. Free. Federation Canadienne Des Municipalites, 24 Rue Clarence, Ottawa Ontario K1N 5P3. **DD** 352.1/0971.

CN/0822-9597
**SIX, FIVE AND COUNTING : INNOVATIONS IN MUNICIPAL ECONOMY.** [Six five count., innov. munic. econ.]. VFOAT Innovations in Municipal Economy; Innovations. VAT Innovations (Ottawa. English Ed.) Vol. 1, No. 1 (June 1983)-. Periodical. English. Free. Federation of Canadian Municipalities, 24 Clarence Street 2nd floor, Ottawa Ontario K1N 5P3 Canada. **Tel** (613)241-5221. **DD** 352.1/0971.

DK/0105-1164
**SKATTER OG AFGIFTER.** VFOAT Taxes and Duties. Danish (English). an. kr68.85. Danmarks Statistik, Sejrgade 11, DK-2100 Copenhagen Denmark. **Tel** 011 45 3 9173917, FAX 011 45 31 18 48 01, telex 1 62 36. **LC** HJ4369; .S56. *Formed by the union of Personbeskatningen I Indkomstaret ..., 0105-1164 and Ejendoms- Og Selskabsbeskatningen I Skattearet ... .*

LU
**SKATTESTATISTIK.** See Public Administration-Abstracting, Bibliographies and Statistics.

NO
**SKATTESTATISTIKK: KOMMUNER OG HANDELSDISTRIKTER.** Main/Corp Norway. Statistisk Sentralbyra. Added/Corp Norway. Statistisk Sentralbyra. Tax Statistics: Municipalities and Trade Districts. VFOAT Tax Statistics Municipalities and Trade Districts. (19??)-. Multiple languages (English and Norwegian). 9.00. **LC** HA1501; subser; HJ9058.

US/0276-5322
**SMALL BUSINESS TAX REVIEW, THE.** (19??)-. Periodical. English. Twelve times a year. A N Group, PO Box 895, Melville NY 11747. **Tel** (516)549-4090. **ED** Steven A. Hopfenmuller. **LC** KF6491.A15; S63. **DD** 343.7306/8; 347.30368. ctrl circ.
**Desc:** Coverage of tax issues and developments affecting small businesses. Contains a brief review of the month's tax news, analyses of law changes and tax tips.

US/0732-5525
**SMALL BUSINESS TAX SAVER.** Vol. 1, No. 1 (Sept. 1982)-. Periodical. English. mo. $72.00. Enterprise Publishing Inc, 725 North Market Street, Wilmington DE 19801.

BP
**SOLOMON ISLANDS ... RECURRENT ESTIMATE.** Main/Corp Solomon Islands. Ministry of Finance. VFOAT Recurrent Estimate. (19??)-. English. British Solomon Islands Protectorate, Prime Minister, PO Box 718, Honiara British Solomon Islands. **LC** HJ98.5; .A27a. **DD** 354.95930072/225/05.

US/0494-8203
**SOURCE REFERENCES FOR FACTS AND FIGURES ON GOVERNMENT FINANCE.** Main/Corp Tax Foundation. English. be. Tax Foundation Inc., 1250 H Street Northwest, Suite 750, Washington DC 20005. **Tel** (202)783-2760, FAX (202)942-7675.

SA/0038-2752
**SOUTH AFRICAN TAX CASES, INCLUDING DECISIONS OF THE SUPREME COURT OF SOUTH AFRICA, THE HIGH COURT OF ZIMBABWE AND THE SPECIAL COURTS FOR HEARING INCOME TAX APPEALS.** See Law.

SA/0038-2779
**SOUTH AFRICAN TREASURER, THE.** Added/Corp Institute of Municipal Treasurers and Accountants, South Africa. (1929)-. Periodical. English (Afrikaans). mo. R52.63. Institute of Municipal Treasurers, PO Box 3565, Braamfontein 2017 South Africa. **Tel** 011 27 11 4037613, FAX 011 27 11 4031754. **ED** J.R.J. Bosch. **LC** HJ9103; .S67. **DD** 352.1. Index available. **Ad Acc.** Circ: 1,500 (ctrl).
**Desc:** Specializing in the finance of local and related authorities.

US
**SOUTH CAROLINA STATE BUDGET FOR THE FISCAL YEAR ENDING ... .** *Title Change.* Main/Corp South Carolina. Budget Commission. English. *Continues* South Carolina State Budget. *Continued by* South Carolina State Budget.

US/0038-3260
**SOUTH DAKOTA BUSINESS REVIEW.** [South Dakota bus. rev.]. Added/Corp University of South Dakota. Business Research Bureau. Vol. 1 (May 1942)-. Periodical. English. qt. Free on request. University of South Dakota Business Research Bureau, 414 East Clark, Vermillion SD 57069. **Tel** (605)677-5287, FAX (605)677-5427. **ED** Donald W. Lewis. **LC** HC107.S8; S63. **DD** 330.9783. **CODEN** SDBRA5. Circ: 1,300 (ctrl). available on microfilm and microfiche from University Microfilms International (UMI); available on an online database (file 648/Full-Text) from DIALOG. Documents available from UMI Article Clearinghouse.
**Desc:** State tax information and articles by the University teaching staff.
**Ind/Abst** ABI/INFORM Glob. Ed.; ABI Inform Ondisc (Feb. 1979-); Acad. Search (July 1993-); Bus. ASAP (1990-) [Full Txt.]; Bus. Index (1985-); Bus. Source (Jul. 1993-); Gen. BusinessFile (1985-); Gen. Period. Index (1985-); INFO-SOUTH Abstr.; PAIS Int. Print; Stat. Ref. Index; Trade Ind. ASAP [Full Txt.]; Trade Ind. Index [Full Txt.]; UMI ABI/Inform--Bus. Period. Ondisc (Dec. 1987-) [Full Txt.].

US
**SOUTH DAKOTA DEPARTMENT OF SOCIAL SERVICES - PRE-EXPENDITURE REPORT FOR TITLE XX SOCIAL SERVICES BLOCK GRANT.** English. an. Free. Department of Social Services / South Dakota, State Office Building, 700 Governors Drive, Pierre SD 57501. **Tel** (605)773-4855. ctrl circ.
**Desc:** The publication is a detailed summary of the projected Title XX expenditures for the next fiscal year.

JA
**SOZEI TO ZAISEI NO ARAMASHI.** Main/Corp Japan. Fukuoka Kokuzeikyoku. (19??)-. Periodical. Japanese. Fukuoka Kokuzeikyoku, 11-1 Hakataeki Higashi 2 Hakata-ku 812, Fukuoka Japan. **LC** HJ9077.A55; K94a.

JA
**SOZEIHO KENKYU.** Added/Corp Sozeiho Gakkai. VFOAT Japan Tax Law Review. Vol. 1 (1973)-. Periodical. Japanese (table of contents in English). Yuhikaku Publishing Company Ltd., 2-17 Kanda Jinbocho, Chiyoda-ku, Tokyo 101 Japan. **Tel** 03 2641311. **LC** K23; .O93.

US/0196-9161
**SPECIAL BULLETIN - MUNICIPAL FINANCE OFFICERS ASSOCIATION OF THE UNITED STATES AND CANADA.** [Spec. bull. - Munic. Financ. Off. Assoc. U. S. Can.]. Main/Corp Municipal Finance Officers Association of the United States and Canada. Bulletin. English. Price varies per volume. Municipal Finance Officers Association, 180 North Michigan Avenue/Suite 800, Chicago IL 60601. **LC** HJ9103; .M82. **DD** 336.73.
**Desc:** Vols. include the annual indexes to the Municipal finance newsletter.

US
**SPECIAL ENROLLMENT EXAMINATION. QUESTIONS AND ANSWERS.** English. an. Department of the Treasury Internal Revenue Service, Fifteenth Street and Pennsylvania Avenue NW, Washington DC 20220.

US
**SPECIAL REPORT ON MUNICIPAL AFFAIRS FOR LOCAL FISCAL YEARS ENDED IN ... .** Main/Corp New York (State). Dept. of Audit and Control. VFOAT Comptroller's Special Report on Municipal Affairs. 1980-. English. an. Free. Bureau of Municipal Research and Statistics, Division of Municipal Affairs, New York State Office of the State Comptroller, Governor Alfred E Smith, State Office Building, Albany NY 12236. **Tel** (518)474-3687. **ED** Joseph D Hilton. **LC** HJ9011.N7; A3. **DD** 352.1/71/09747. Circ: 4,000 (ctrl). *Continues* New York (State). Office of the State Comptroller. Special Report on Municipal Affairs by the State Comptroller.
**Desc:** Contains comprehensive financial statistics of New York State local government for the latest available fiscal year. Included are statistical tables on revenues, expenditures and debt for each municipality, school district, fire district, joint activity, and special purpose unit in the State, with tables showing trends in local government statistics.

US/0194-8237
**SPIDELL'S CALIFORNIA TAXLETTER.** See Law.

GW
**STAATS- UND GEMEINDEFINANZEN IM RECHNUNGSJAHR, DIE.** German. an. DM12.00. Hessisches Statistisches Landesamt, Postfach 3205, Rheinstrasse 35/37, 6200 Wiesbaden 1 Germany. **Tel** (06121)368.0, telex 6121850 HSLD. **LC** HA1320; .H529 subser; HJ48.H47.

US
**STANDARD FEDERAL TAX REPORTER.** Added/Corp Commerce Clearing House. United States. Dept. of the Treasury. United States. Tax Court. VFOAT Standard Federal Tax Reports. (1945)-. Periodical. English. ir. Commerce Clearing House Inc., 4025 West Peterson Avenue, Chicago IL 60646-6085. **Tel** (312)583-8500, FAX (708)940-4600. **ED** A.E. Schechter. **LC** KF6285; .C67. **DD** 343.7304; 347.3034. Index Available, published separately, free-automatically sent. *Continues* Standard Federal Tax Service.

US/1066-1972
**STANLEY & KILCULLEN'S FEDERAL INCOME TAX LAW.** See Law.

CE
**STATE ACCOUNTS OF THE REPUBLIC OF SRI LANKA FOR THE YEAR ... .** Main/Corp Sri Lanka. VFOAT State Accounts of the Democratic Socialist Republic of Sri Lanka for the Financial Year ... . English. an. 44.00. Government Publications Bureau, PO Box 500, Colombo Sri Lanka. **LC** J611; .H62 subser; HJ64.85. **DD** 300/.9549/3; 354.549/30072252/05.

US/0363-3381
**STATE AGENCY EXPENDITURES BY COUNTY.** Main/Corp Texas. Governor's Budget Office. 1972/73-. English. an. Office of the Governor / Austin, PO Box 12428, Austin TX 78711. **Tel** (512)463-1919. **LC** HJ11; .T44425B. **DD** 336.3/9/09764.

US
**STATE AID TO LOCAL GOVERNMENT.** Added/Corp New York (State). Division of Municipal Affairs. Bureau of Statistical Services. New York (State). Bureau of Municipal Research and Statistics. New York

# Public Administration — Public Finance and Taxation

(State). Division of Municipal Affairs. Research and Statistics Section. New York (State). Dept. of Audit and Control. (Aug. 23, 1951)-. English. an. $27.50. NASBO, 400 North Capitol Street, Northwest Suite 295, Washington DC 20001. **Tel** (202)624-5382. **LC** HJ9011.N7; A33. **DD** 336.39; 336.18.

US/0195-7392
**STATE AND LOCAL GRANT AWARDS.** **Main/Corp** United States. Environmental Protection Agency. Grants Administration Division. Oct.-Mar. FY 1977-. Periodical. English. sa. US Environmental Protection Agency / Grants Administration Division, 401 M Street SW, Washington DC 20460. **LC** HC110.E5; U55B. **DD** 353.0072/52. *Continues in part* Awards Register, Grants Assistance Programs, 0161-6277.

US
**STATE AND LOCAL TAX PERFORMANCE.** **Added/Corp** Southern Regional Education Board. (1978)-. English. an. Southern Regional Educational Board, 592 10th Street NW, Atlanta GA 30318. **Tel** (404)875-9211. **ED** Compilers: 1978- K.E. Quindry and N. Schoening. *Continues* Southern Regional Education Board. State and Local Tax Ability and Effort.

US
**STATE AND LOCAL TAXES; REPORT BULLETIN.** **Main/Corp** Prentice-Hall, Inc. (1???)-. Periodical. English. an. $340.00. Research Institute of America, 117 East Stevens Avenue, Valhalla NY 10595. **Tel** (800)431-9025.

US
**STATE AND MUNICIPAL SALES AND USE TAX COLLECTION REPORTS.** **Main/Corp** Oklahoma Tax Commission. **VFOAT** Oklahoma State & Municipal Sales & Use Taxes. English. an. Oklahoma Tax Commission, 2501 Lincoln Boulevard, Oklahoma City OK 73194. **LC** HJ5715.U6; O342A. **DD** 336.2/71. *Continues* State & Municipal Sales Tax Reports.

US
**STATE AUDITOR'S OFFICE ANNUAL REPORT, FISCAL YEAR ENDED JUNE 30 ... (MASSACHUSETTS), THE.** **Main/Corp** Massachusetts. State Auditor's Office. **VFOAT** Annual Report, Fiscal Year Ended June 30 ... . English. an. **LC** HJ11; .M42. **DD** 353.97440072/32/06. *Continues* Massachusetts. Dept. of the State Auditor. Annual Report.

US/0742-0498
**STATE BUDGET & TAX NEWS.** [State budg. tax news]. **VFOAT** State Budget and Tax News. Vol. 1, No. 1 (Aug. 19, 1982)-. Periodical. English. bw. $215.00. State Policy Research Inc., 182 West Royal Forest Boulevard, Columbus OH 43214-2029. **Tel** (614)447-9443, FAX (614)447-2077. **(Subscription address:** State Policy Research, Subscription Office, PO Box 11806, Birmingham AL 35202-1806.**) DD** 353.
**Desc:** Provides nationwide coverage of tax issues, supplying continuous updates on tax, spending and borrowing policies from all 50 states.

US/0093-5247
**STATE BUDGET - OFFICE OF FISCAL ANALYSIS (HARTFORD).** (THE STATE BUDGET FOR THE FISCAL YEAR - CONNECTICUT.). **Main/Corp** Connecticut. General Assembly. Office of Fiscal Analysis. English. an. Connecticut General Assembly, State Capital, Hartford CT 06115. **LC** HJ11; .C84616A. **DD** 353.9/746/00722.

US/0272-7862
**STATE BUDGET TRENDS.** (STATE BUDGET TRENDS - MASSACHUSETTS TAXPAYERS FOUNDATION.). **Main/Corp** Massachusetts Taxpayers Foundation. English. an. Massachusetts Taxpayers Foundation, 24 Province Street, Boston MA 02108. **Tel** (617)720-1000. **ED** Lou Starrow, Susanne Tempkins. **LC** HJ2053.M4; M37A. **DD** 353.97440072/2/05. **Circ:** 2,000.
**Desc:** Analysis of Massachusetts Governor's proposed budget.

US
**STATE FORMULA AIDS AND ENTITLEMENTS FOR ELEMENTARY AND SECONDARY EDUCATION IN NEW YORK STATE ... .** **See** Education.

US/0090-5895
**STATE GOVERNMENT FINANCES.** (STATE GOVERNMENT FINANCES IN ...). [State gov. financ.]. **Added/Corp** United States. Bureau of the Census. (1966)-. Government Publication. English. an. $14.95. Superintendent of Documents, US Government Printing Office, Washington DC 20402. **Tel** (202)275-3328, FAX (202)786-2377. **(Subscription address:** US Government Bookstore / O'Neil Building, 2023 3rd Avenue North, Birmingham AL 35203.**) LC** HJ275; .S7. **DD** 336.73. **NLM** W2; A B9sf. *Continues* Compendium of State Government Finances in ... .
**Ind/Abst** Predicasts Forecasts.

US/0270-0808
**STATE GOVERNMENT TAX COLLECTIONS IN ... .** **Added/Corp** United States. Bureau of the Census. (1977)-. Government Publication. English. an. $13.00 (per copy). US Department of Commerce / Bureau of the Census, Data User Services Division, Customer Services, Washington DC 20233-0800. **Tel** (301)763-4100. **(Subscription address:** US Government Bookstore / O'Neil Building, 2023 3rd Avenue North, Birmingham AL 35203.**) LC** HJ2385; .U6a. **DD** 336.2/00973. *Continues* State Tax Collections, 0095-4152.
**Ind/Abst** Predicasts Forecasts.

US
**STATE INHERITANCE TAXES.** Macmillan Publishing Company, 866 3rd Avenue, New York NY 10022. **Tel** (212)702-2000, (800)257-5755.

US
**STATE LOCAL GOVERNMENT FUND, AMOUNTS DISTRIBUTED DIRECTLY TO MUNICIPALITIES LEVYING INCOME TAXES AND BASIS FOR DISTRIBUTION, BY MUNICIPALITY.** **Main/Corp** Ohio. Dept. of Taxation. English. an. Department of Taxation / Ohio, Research and Statistics Section, PO Box 530, Columbus OH 43216. **LC** HJ11; .O354B. **DD** 336.2/4/09771.

US
**STATE LOCAL GOVERNMENT FUND, AMOUNTS DISTRIBUTED TO COUNTIES AND BASIS FOR DISTRIBUTION, BY COUNTY.** **Main/Corp** Ohio. Dept. of Taxation. English. an. Department of Taxation / Ohio, Research and Statistics Section, PO Box 530, Columbus OH 43216. **LC** HJ11; .O354A. **DD** 336.2/009771.

US
**STATE OF ARKANSAS ... BIENNIAL BUDGET.** **Main/Corp** Arkansas. Dept. of Finance and Administration. Office of Budget. **VFOAT** Biennial Budget. 1983-85-. English. be. **LC** HJ11; .A842C. **DD** 353.97670072/252/05. *Continues* Arkansas State Budget.

US/0146-7409
**STATE OF FLORIDA: LOCAL GOVERNMENT FINANCIAL REPORT.** **Main/Corp** Florida. Dept. of Banking and Finance. (1973/1974)-. English. an (July). Free. Florida Department of Banking & Finance, State Capitol, Tallahassee FL 32399. **Tel** (904)488-0370, FAX (904)488-9818. **LC** HJ9011.F6; B86a. **DD** 353.9/759/00722. *Continues* Florida. Bureau of Local Government Finance Annual Local Government Financial Report, State of Florida, 0094-8551.

US/0091-3588
**STATE OF IOWA SCHOLARSHIPS, TUITION GRANTS, MEDICAL TUITION LOANS : BIENNIUM REPORT.** **See** Education.

US
**STATE OF MINNESOTA FINANCES.** **Main/Corp** Minnesota Legislature. Office of the Legislative Auditor. Financial Audits Division. 1984-1985 Biennium-. English. be. **LC** HJ11; .M6214b. **DD** 353.97760072/32. *Continues* Report to the State Legislature on the Statewide Audit.

US/0148-6306
**STATE OF MONTANA, BOARD OF EXAMINERS, REPORT ON EXAMINATION OF FINANCIAL STATEMENTS.** **Main/Corp** Montana. Office of the Legislative Auditor. **VFOAT** Report on Examination of Financial Statements. English. State Capitol, Santa Fe NM 87503. **LC** JK1651.M9; A26A. **DD** 353.9/786/007232.

US/0146-7271
**STATE OF MONTANA OFFICES OF THE GOVERNOR AND LIEUTENANT GOVERNOR : REPORT ON AUDIT.** **Main/Corp** Montana. Office of the Legislative Auditor. English. an. Office of the Legislative Auditor, State Capitol, Helena MT 59601. **LC** HJ9871; .A23. **DD** 353.9/786/007232.

US/0149-2179
**STATE OF NEVADA, COMPUTER ACQUISITION SINKING FUND, AUDIT REPORT.** (AUDIT REPORT, STATE OF NEVADA, COMPUTER ACQUISITION SINKING FUND.). [State Nev. Comput. Acquis. Sinking Fund audit rep.]. **Main/Corp** Nevada. Legislative Auditor. English. Legislative Auditor, Legislative Building, Capitol Complex, Carson City NV 89710. **LC** JK8549.A8; N48A. **DD** 353.9/793/00712.

US/0149-2160
**STATE OF NEVADA, CONSOLIDATED BOND AND INTEREST REDEMPTION FUND, AUDIT REPORT.** (AUDIT REPORT, STATE OF NEVADA, CONSOLIDATED BOND AND INTEREST REDEMPTION FUND.). [State Nev., Consol. Bond Interest Redempt. Fund audit rep.]. **Main/Corp** Nevada. Legislative Auditor. English. Legislative Auditor, Legislative Building, Capitol Complex, Carson City NV 89710. **LC** HJ8391; .N48A. **DD** 353.9/793/0072.

US/0094-517X
**STATE OF NEVADA REVENUE SHARING TRUST FUND AUDIT REPORT.** **Main/Corp** Nevada. Legislative Auditor. English. an. Legislative Commission, Legislative Building, Capitol Complex, Carson City NV 89710. **LC** HJ9875; .A23A. **DD** 353.9/793/007232.

●US
**STATE OF NEW YORK EXECUTIVE BUDGET, AGENCY PRESENTATIONS.** **Main/Corp** New York (State). Governor. **VFOAT** Executive Budget, Agency Presentations. (1991/1992)-. English. *Continues* State of New York Executive Budget.

●US
**STATE OF NEW YORK EXECUTIVE BUDGET ... ANNUAL MESSAGE.** **Main/Corp** New York (State). Governor. **VFOAT** Annual Message; Message of the Governor. (1992)-. English. *Continues* State of New York Annual Budget Message.

US
**STATE OF NEW YORK EXECUTIVE BUDGET BRIEFING BOOK.** **Main/Corp** New York (State). Governor. **VFOAT** Executive Budget Briefing Book. (1989/1990)-. English. *Continues* New York (State). Governor. Executive Budget Briefing Book.

US
**STATE OF OKLAHOMA EXECUTIVE BUDGET.** **Main/Corp** Oklahoma. Governor. **VFOAT** Executive Budget. English. an. Executive Department Division of the Budget, 309 State Capitol Building, Oklahoma City OK 73105. **LC** HJ11; .O545. **DD** 353.97660072/22/05. *Continues* Oklahoma. Governor. Budget.

US
**STATE OF RHODE ISLAND AND PROVIDENCE PLANTATIONS, BUDGET IN BRIEF.** **Main/Corp** Rhode Island. Governor. English. Rhode Island Governor, Providence RI 02903. **LC** HJ11; .R444A. **DD** 353.97450072/253/05.

US
**STATE OF SOUTH DAKOTA GOVERNOR'S BUDGET.** **Main/Corp** South Dakota. Governor. English. State Capitol / South Dakota, 500 East Capitol, Pierre SD 57501. **LC** HJ11; .S8445A. **DD** 353.97830072/256/05. *Continues* South Dakota. Governor's Budget Report.

US
**STATE OF UTAH BIENNIAL CAPITAL BUDGET ... .** **Main/Corp** Utah. Office of Planning and Budget. **VFOAT** Biennial Capital Budget ... . English. be. Georgia Office of Planning and Budget, 270 Washington Street Southwest, Room 611, Atlanta GA 30334. **Tel** (404)656-3820. **LC** HJ2053.U8; U76A. **DD** 353.97920072/22534/05.

US/0360-2311
**STATE PAYMENTS TO LOCAL GOVERNMENT.** (STATE PAYMENTS TO LOCAL GOVERNMENTS - OKLAHOMA TAX COMMISSION.). **Main/Corp** Oklahoma Tax Commission. 1968/69-. English. an. Oklahoma Tax Commission, 2501 Lincoln Boulevard, Oklahoma City OK 73194. **LC** HJ640; .O37A. **DD** 336.1/85. *Supersedes* Payments to Local Units of Government.

US/0362-1367
**STATE SALES TAX COLLECTIONS REPORT.** **Main/Corp** Oklahoma Tax Commission. **Added/Corp** Oklahoma Tax Commission Oklahoma Sales Tax. **VFOAT** Oklahoma Sales Tax. (19??)-. English. an. Oklahoma Tax Commission, 2501 Lincoln Boulevard, Oklahoma City OK 73194. **LC** HJ5715.U6; O34. **DD** 336.2/71. *Continues* Oklahoma Tax Commission. Oklahoma Sales Tax Including Operations of the Use Tax. Statistical Report.

US
**STATE TAX NEWS.** **Added/Corp** New Jersey. Division of Taxation. (19??)-. Periodical. English. bm. Free. New Jersey Division of Taxation, 50 Barrich Street, CN 269 K. Munn, Trenton NJ 08646. **Tel** (609)292-6400. **LC** HJ2422; .S75. **DD** 336.2/009749. **Circ:** 13,000 (ctrl).
**Desc:** Newsletter of New Jersey tax items of interest.

## Public Administration —Public Finance and Taxation

●US/1060-491X
**STATE TAX NOTES (MICROFICHE).** (STATE TAX NOTES MICROFICHE DATABASE.). [State tax notes]. **Added/Corp** Tax Analysts (Firm : U.S.). (1991)-. Periodical. English. wk. $699.00. Tax Analysts, 6830 North Fairfax Drive, Arlington VA 22213. **Tel** (703)533-4400, (800)955-3444. **DD** 343. available in hardback.

US/1057-8404
**STATE TAX NOTES (PRINT).** (STATE TAX NOTES.). [State tax notes]. **Added/Corp** Tax Analysts (Firm : U.S.). Vol. 1, No. 1 (Sept. 2, 1991)-. Periodical. English. wk (52 issues). $749.00. Tax Analysts, 6830 North Fairfax Drive, Arlington VA 22213. **Tel** (703)533-4400, (800)955-3444. **LC** KF6750; .S735. **DD** 343.7304/05; 347.303405. **[CCC]**. available on microfiche.
 **Desc:** Covers state and local tax developments. Tax professionals report from all 50 states.
 **Ind/Abst** Account. Art.

US
**STATE TREASURER'S ANNUAL REPORT (COLORADO).** **Main/Corp** Colorado. Dept. of the Treasury. English. an. Colorado Department of the Treasury, 140 State Capitol, Denver CO 80203. **LC** HJ11; .C613. **DD** 353.97880072. *Continues* Annual Report of Treasurer of the State of Colorado.

US
**STATEMENT.** **Added/Corp** Texas. Property Tax Division. Vol. 14, No. 3 Sept. (1991)-. English. mo. **LC** KFT1691.P7; A137. **DD** 343.76405/4/05; 347.64035405. *Continues* Statement (Texas. State Property Tax Board).

US/0275-9373
**STATEMENT OF FOREIGN CURRENCIES PURCHASED WITH DOLLARS.** English. sa. Department of the Treasury Fiscal Service, Bureau of Government, Fifteenth Street and Pennsylvania Avenue Northwest, Washington DC 20220. **LC** HJ2052.A2; S74. **DD** 353.0072/31.

AT
**STATEMENT OF PUBLIC ACCOUNTS PREPARED BY THE TREASURER.** **Main/Corp** Tasmania. Dept. of the Treasury. (18??)-. English. ir. **LC** HJ94; .A14.

IE
**STATEMENT OF SUMS REQUIRED ON ACCOUNT.** **Main/Corp** Northern Ireland. Dept. of Finance. English. an. Her Majesty's Stationery Office / Belfast, 80 Chichester Street, Belfast BT1 4JY Northern Ireland. **LC** HJ42.2; .C154A. **DD** 354/.416/00722.

US/0146-9797
**STATEMENT OF TAX POLICY.** **Added/Corp** American Institute of Certified Public Accountants. (19??)-. Monographic series. English. ir. Price varies per volume. American Institute of Certified Public Accountants, Harborside Financial Center, 201 Plaza 3, Jersey City NJ 07311. **Tel** (201)938-3333, (800)862-4272.

WS
**STATEMENT ON THE ... SUPPLEMENTARY ESTIMATES / BY THE MINISTER OF FINANCE.** Periodical. English. ir. **LC** HJ99.6; .A23. **DD** 354.96140072/243/05.

II
**STATEMENT SHOWING THE SUPPLEMENTARY GRANTS.** **Main/Corp** Goa, Daman, and Diu (India). English. an. Government Printer Press, General Statistics Department, Panjim India. **LC** HJ66.G6; C15. **DD** 354/.54/799007224.

FI
**STATENS INKOMSTER OCH UTGIFTER LANSVIS.** 1978-. Finnish. be. Valtion Painatuskeskus, PO Box 516, SF 00101 Helsinki Finland. **Tel** 011 358 0 5660266. **LC** HC337.F5; A36 subser; HJ55.3.

US
**STATISTICAL DIGEST - LEGISLATIVE BUDGET AND FINANCE COMMITTEE.** *See* Public Administration-Abstracting, Bibliographies and Statistics.

US
**STATISTICAL REPORT (MICHIGAN. LEGISLATURE. SENATE. FISCAL AGENCY).** *See* Public Administration-Abstracting, Bibliographies and Statistics.

US/0740-5790
**STATISTICAL YEARBOOK OF MUNICIPAL FINANCE.** *Suspended.* *See* Public Administration-Abstracting, Bibliographies and Statistics.

IT/0075-1820
**STATISTICHE DEI BILANCI DELLE AMMINISTRAZIONI REGIONALI, PROVINCIALI E COMUNALI.** (19??)-. Italian. an. L990000 Italy; L11200000 other. Istituto Nazionale Statistica, GBP SEZ4 Via Cesare Balbo 16, 00184 Rome Italy. **Tel** 011 39 6 46735118. **LC** HJ9497; .S68.

US/0147-4626
**STATISTICS FOR MUNICIPAL AUTHORITIES IN PENNSYLVANIA.** *See* Public Administration-Abstracting, Bibliographies and Statistics.

US/0160-9920
**STATISTICS OF INCOME. CORPORATION INCOME TAX RETURNS.** *See* Public Administration-Abstracting, Bibliographies and Statistics.

US
**STATISTICS OF INCOME : INCOME TAX RETURNS.** *See* Public Administration-Abstracting, Bibliographies and Statistics.

US
**STATISTICS OF INCOME. INDIVIDUAL INCOME TAX RETURNS.** *See* Public Administration-Abstracting, Bibliographies and Statistics.

US/0734-1709
**STATISTICS OF INCOME. PARTNERSHIP RETURNS (1977).** *See* Public Administration-Abstracting, Bibliographies and Statistics.

US/0730-0743
**STATISTICS OF INCOME. SOI BULLETIN.** *See* Public Administration-Abstracting, Bibliographies and Statistics.

US/0744-0030
**STATISTICS OF INCOME. SOLE PROPRIETORSHIP RETURNS.** *See* Public Administration-Abstracting, Bibliographies and Statistics.

US
**STATISTICS OF INCOME. SUPPLEMENTAL REPORT. INTERNATIONAL INCOME AND TAXES. DOMESTIC INTERNATIONAL SALES CORPORATION RETURNS.** *See* Public Administration-Abstracting, Bibliographies and Statistics.

FR
**STATISTICS ON EXTERNAL INDEBTEDNESS (PARIS, FRANCE : 1985).** (STATISTICS ON EXTERNAL INDEBTEDNESS : THE DEBT AND OTHER EXTERNAL LIABILITIES OF DEVELOPING, CMEA, AND CERTAIN OTHER COUNTRIES AND TERRITORIES / ORGANISATION OR ECONOMIC CO-OPERATION AND DEVELOPMENT.). **Added/Corp** Organisation for Economic Co-operation and Development. (19??)-. English. an. OECD Publications and Information Center, 2 rue Andre-Pascal, 75775 Paris Cedex 16 France. **Tel** 011 33 1 45248167, US:(202)785-6323, FAX 011 33 1 45248500 OR 45248176, telex 620 160 OCDE. available on diskette (from OECD Data Dissemination and Reception Unit).

CN/0702-0988
**STATISTICS RELATING TO REGIONAL AND MUNICIPAL GOVERNMENTS IN BRITISH COLUMBIA.** *See* Public Administration-Abstracting, Bibliographies and Statistics.

NE
**STATISTIEK DER GEMEENTEBEGROTINGEN / CENTRAAL BUREAU VOOR DE STATISTISTIEK, HOOFDAFDELING FINANCIELE STATISTIEKEN.** *See* Public Administration-Abstracting, Bibliographies and Statistics.

NE/0168-3837
**STATISTIEK DER PROVINCIALE FINANCIEN / CENTRAAL BUREAU VOOR DE STATISTIEK.** *See* Public Administration-Abstracting, Bibliographies and Statistics.

IO/0126-4397
**STATISTIK KEUANGAN DESA JAWA DAN MADURA.** *See* Public Administration-Abstracting, Bibliographies and Statistics.

IO
**STATISTIK KEUANGAN DESA. SULAWESI-MALUKU-BALI-NUSATENGGARA.** *See* Public Administration-Abstracting, Bibliographies and Statistics.

GR
**STATISTIKE DEMOSION OIKONOMIKON.** **Main/Corp** Ethnike Statistike Hyperesia Tes Helladas. **VFOAT** Public Finance Statistics. Greek, Modern (English). an. Dr100.00 Greek; $4.00 US. National Statistical Service of Greece, 14 Lycourgou Street, GR 10166 Athens Greece. **Tel** 3244-746, telex 216-734 ESYE GR. **LC** HJ50; .C16A. **Circ:** 1,000.

GR
**STATISTIKE EPETERIS DEMOSION OIKONOMIKON.** *See* Public Administration-Abstracting, Bibliographies and Statistics.

FR
**STATISTIQUES DES COMPTES POUR L'EXERCICE ... DES COMMUNES, DES DEPARTEMENTS, DES REGIONS ET DES ETABLISSEMENTS PUBLICS LOCAUX.** *See* Public Administration-Abstracting, Bibliographies and Statistics.

CN/0705-579X
**STATISTIQUES FINANCIERES DU GOUVERNEMENT DU QUEBEC.** *Title Change.* *See* Public Administration-Abstracting, Bibliographies and Statistics.

DK/0108-545X
**STATISTISKE EFTERRETNINGER. NATIONALREGNSKAB, OFFENTLIGE FINANSER, BETALINGSBALANCE.** *See* Public Administration-Abstracting, Bibliographies and Statistics.

US/0198-6716
**STATUS OF ACTIVE FOREIGN CREDITS OF THE U.S. GOVT.: FOREIGN CREDITS BY U.S. GOVT. AGENCIES.** (STATUS OF ACTIVE FOREIGN CREDITS OF THE U.S. GOV'T., FOREIGN CREDITS BY U.S. GOV'T. AGENCIES / U.S. TREASURY DEPARTMENT, OFFICE OF THE ASSISTANT SECRETARY FOR INTERNATIONAL AFFAIRS.). [Status act. foreign credits U.S. Gov't: foreign credits U.S. Gov't agencies]. **VFOAT** Active Foreign Credits of the U.S. Government. **VAT** Status of Active Foreign Credits of the United States Government: Foreign Credits by United States Government Agencies. Periodical. English. Three times a year. Department of the Treasury / Pennsylvania Avenue, Fifteenth Street and Pennsylvania Avenue NW, Washington DC 20220. **Tel** (202)566-2969. **LC** HJ8085; .U54A. **DD** 336.3/4/0973. **Circ:** 300. available on microfiche (from National Technical Information Service). *Continues* Foreign Credits by the United States Government.
 **Desc:** Presents the status of loans and credits to foreigners by the United States Government as of specified dates.

US/0730-3440
**STATUS, PROGRESS, AND PROBLEMS IN FEDERAL AGENCY ACCOUNTING.** *See* Public Administration-Abstracting, Bibliographies and Statistics.

US/0364-8281
**STATUS REPORT: CAPITAL IMPROVEMENT PROGRAM, BOND FUND SUMMARY.** **Main/Corp** Hawaii. Planning Division. (19??)-. English. **LC** HJ11; .H346. **DD** 336.969.

CN/1186-8619
**STELCO INC.** (STELCO INC.- MIDLAND WALWYN RESEARCH.). [Stelco Inc.]. **Added/Corp** Midland Walwyn Capital. Research Dept. Midland Walwyn Capital. (Apr. 26, 1991)-. Periodical. English. Limited free distribution to selected clients of Midland Walwyn Capital. Midland Walwyn Capital, Suite 1600, 121 King Street West, Toronto Ontario M5H 3W6 Canada. **DD** 336.2.

US/1055-3622
**STEP-BY-STEP GUIDE TO LOWERING YOUR INCOME TAX 50-90%, THE.** **VFOAT** Step by Step Guide to Lowering Your Income Tax 50-90%. (1991)-. English. $29.95. B&M Publishing, PO Box 291142, Tampa FL 33687.

GW
**STEUER UND WIRTSCHAFT.** (Dec. 1921)-. Periodical. German. qt. DM232.10 Germany; DM253.00 other. Verlag Dr. Otto Schmidt KG, Postfach 511026, D 50946 Cologne Germany. **Tel** 011 49 221 93738450. **ED** Klaus Tipke. **LC** HJ2670; .S75. **DD** 336.205. Index available. cum. index. **Bk Rev**. **Ad Acc**: **Circ:** 1,600.

AU
**STEUERAUFKOMMEN DER GEMEINDEN NIEDEROSTERREICHS, DAS.** **Main/Corp** Austria, Lower. Landesamtsdirektion. Pressedienst, Statistik. German. be. Amt der Niederosterreichischen, Landesregierung Pressedienst Statistik, Herrengasse 11-13, 1014 Vienna Austria. **Tel**

# Public Administration — Public Finance and Taxation

02236/84986. **(Subscription address:** Amt der No Landesregierung, Abt R/2, Sachgegiet Statistik, 2344 Ma Enzersdorf, Sudstadtzentrum 4/4) **LC** HJ9448.A2; A8A. ctrl circ. available in hardback. **Continues** *Steueraufkommen der Gemeinden.*
 **Desc:** Statistics and tax reciepts of all communities of lower Austria.

SZ
### STEUERBELASTUNG IN DER SCHWEIZ.
**VFOAT** Charge Fiscale en Suisse; Kantonshauptorte, Kantonsziffern; Chefs-Lieux des Cantons, Nombres Cantonaux. (1983)-. German (French). an. **Continues in part** *Steuerbelastung in der Schweiz.*

GW
### STEUERBERATER RECHTSHANDBUCH / DEUTSCHER STEUERBERATERVERBAND E.V.
**Added/Corp** Deutscher Steuerberaterverband. (1989)-. German. be. Stollfuss Verlag GmbH and Company KG, Postfach 2428 Dechenstrasse 7-11, D 53014 Bonn Germany. **Tel** 011 49 228 724222. **LC** KK160.F56; S74.

AU
### STEUEREINNAHMEN DER GEMEINDEN IM JAHR ... / HERAUSGEBER, VERBINDUNGSSTELLE DER BUNDESLANDER BEIM AMT DER NIEDEROSTERREICHISCHEN LANDESREGIERUNG. Added/Corp
Verbindungsstelle der Bundeslander Beim Amt der Niederosterreichischen Landesregierung. (19??)-. German. be. Verbindungsstelle der Bundeslaender beim Amt der Noelandesregierung, Schenkenstrasse 4, 1014 Vienna Austria. **Tel** 011 43 222 5353761, **FAX** 011 43 222 5356079. **LC** HJ9447; .S73. **DD** 336.2/014436/021.
 **Desc:** Contains all the taxes for the Austrian Communes.

US/0081-5624
### STOCK VALUES AND DIVIDENDS FOR TAX PURPOSES. See Business-Investments.

NO
### STRUKTURTALL FOR KOMMUNENES KONOMI. See Public Administration-Abstracting, Bibliographies and Statistics.

US
### STUDY OF PROPERTY VALUATIONS FOR THE TAX YEAR ... . Added/Corp West
Virginia. Dept. of Tax & Revenue. **VFOAT** Tax Year ... Study of Property Values. (1990)-. English. **LC** HJ4121.W4; T38a. **DD** 336.2/2/0954. **Continues** *West Virginia. Dept. of Tax & Revenue. Study of Property Valuations as They Relate to Levies Laid for the Support of Schools in West Virginia for the Tax Year ... .*

SA
### SUIDWES-AFRIKA REKENING : BEGROTING VAN INKOMSTE EN UITGAWES. Main/Corp South Africa. Added/Corp
South Africa. South West Africa account: Estimate of revenue and expenditure. **VFOAT** South West Africa Account: Estimate of Revenue and Expenditure. Afrikaans (English). **LC** HJ83.3; .A24a.

NR/0331-0434
### SUMMARY OF CURRENT INCOME TAX STATISTICS. See Public Administration-Abstracting, Bibliographies and Statistics.

US
### SUMMARY OF FISCAL YEAR ... APPROPRIATIONS. English. an. Committee on
Appropriations, Republican Staff, Illinois House of Representatives, 300 State Capitol Building, Springfield IL 62706. **LC** HJ11; .I3196. **DD** 353.97730072/236/05.

●US
### SUMMARY OF REVENUE PROPOSALS IN THE PRESIDENT'S ... BUDGET / PREPARED BY THE STAFF OF THE JOINT COMMITTEE ON TAXATION.
**Added/Corp** United States. Congress. Joint Committee on Taxation. Fiscal year (1993)-. English. Superintendent of Docs, US Government Printing Office, Washington DC 20402. **Continues** *Summary of Revenue Provisions in the President's Fiscal Year ... Budget Proposal.*

US
### SUMMARY OF STATE REGULATIONS AND LAWS AFFECTING GENERAL CONTRACTORS. Added/Corp American
Insurance Association. (19??)-. Periodical. English. be. American Insurance Association, 85 John Street, New York NY 10038. **LC** KF1950.Z95; S95. **DD** 343.73/078624; 347.30378624. **Continues** *Summary of State Regulations and Taxes Affecting General Contractors, 0733-3617.*

US
### SUMMARY OF TAX EXEMPTION DEVICES / DIVISION OF RESEARCH AND ANALYSIS, DEPARTMENT OF REVENUE. Main/Corp Wisconsin. Dept. of Revenue.
Division of Research and Analysis. **Added/Corp** Wisconsin. Division of State Executive Budget and Planning. State of Wisconsin ... Biennial Budget. 1981/83-. 4th (1981/1983)-. English. be. Department of Revenue / Wisconsin, PO Box 8933, 125 South Webster Street, Madison WI 53708. **Tel** (608)266-8661. **LC** HJ2337.U6; W57a. **DD** 336.2/06/09775. **Continues** *Wisconsin. Dept. of Revenue. State Tax Analysis Section. Summary of Tax Exemption Devices.*

US/0272-9318
### SUMMARY OF TAXES IN ARKANSAS, A.
**Main/Corp** University of Arkansas, Fayetteville. Industrial Research and Extension Center. English. Industrial Research and Extension Center, University of Arkansas, PO Box 3017, Little Rock AR 72203. **LC** HC107.A8; A66 subser; HJ2394. **DD** 338.09767 S; 336.2/009767.

US
### SUMMARY OF THE ANNUAL FINANCIAL REPORT, STATE OF TEXAS.
**Added/Corp** Texas. Comptroller's Office. (19??)-. English. an. Comptroller of Public Accounts, Division of Planning and Research, 111 East 17th Street, Austin TX 78774. **LC** HJ715; .S84. **DD** 353.97640072/31/05.

US
### SUMMARY OF TOTAL REVENUES COLLECTED BY THE SALES AND USE TAX SECTION FOR THE MONTH OF FISCAL YEAR ... / ARIZONA DEPARTMENT OF REVENUE. English. an.
**LC** HJ5715.U6; A86A. **DD** 336.2/71. **Continues** *Arizona. Sales and Use Tax Division. Summary of Total Revenues Collected by the Sales and Use Tax Division, 0148-9070.*

US
### SUMMARY REPORT, INDIVIDUAL INCOME TAX RETURNS FILED. Main/Corp
Maryland. Income Tax Division. (19??)-. Periodical. English. an. State Income Tax Building, Annapolis MD 21401. **Tel** (410)974-3885. **LC** HJ4655.M316; M35a. **DD** 336.2/42/09752. **Circ:** 600 (ctrl). **Continues** *Maryland. Income Tax Division. Summary Report, Resident Individual Income Tax Returns Filed for the Year ... .*
 **Desc:** A journal of statistics from Maryland individual income tax returns.

BL
### SUMULA TRIBUTARIA TRABALHISTA (SEMIMONTHLY). See Law-Labor Law.

AT/0729-3828
### SUPERFUNDS. (1962)-. Periodical. English. Eleven
times a year. 88.00Aus$. ASFA, 31 Queen Street, 9th Floor, Melbourne Victoria 3000 Australia. **Tel** 011 61 3 6294817. Index available (Mar.).
 **Ind/Abst** APAIS, Aust. Public Aff. Inf. Ser. (1973-).

US
### SUPPLEMENTAL FINANCIAL DATA FOR THE FISCAL YEAR ENDED JUNE 30 ... / STATE OF MARYLAND. Main/Corp
Maryland. Comptroller's Office. **VFOAT** Supplemental Financial Data of the Comptroller of the State of Maryland. English. Maryland Comptroller of the Treasury, Annapolis MD 21401. **LC** HJ11; .M334A. **DD** 353.97520072/05.

US
### SUPPLEMENTAL GENERAL APPROPRIATIONS AND LEGISLATIVE INTENT FOR THE ... BIENNIUM. Main/Corp
Florida. Legislature. Senate. Ways and Means Committee. English. be. Senate Committee on Ways and Means, State Capitol Building, Publishing Office, Tallahassee FL 32304. **LC** HJ11; .F645A. **DD** 353.97590072/248/05.

AT
### SUPPLEMENTARY BUDGET INFORMATION / WESTERN AUSTRALIA.
**Main/Corp** Western Australia. (19??)-. English. ir. Government Printer / Parliament House, Harvest Terra, Perth Western Australia, 6000 Australia. **LC** HJ90.W47; W46c. **DD** 354.9410072/243/05.

PK
### SUPPLEMENTARY BUDGET STATEMENT OF PAKISTAN RAILWAYS. See Transportation-Railroads.

SA
### SUPPLEMENTARY ESTIMATE OF THE EXPENDITURE TO BE DEFRAYED FROM REVENUE, LOAN AND SOUTH-WEST AFRICA ACCOUNTS.
**Main/Corp** South Africa. **VFOAT** Supplementere Begroting van die Uitgawes wat uit Inkomste-, Lenings en Suidwes-Afrikarekenings. Multiple languages (Afrikaans and English). $0.80. **LC** HJ80A; .A317. **DD** 354/.68/007224.

PK
### SUPPLEMENTARY STATEMENT OF EXPENDITURE. Main/Corp Sind (Pakistan).
Finance Dept. English. Karachi Finance Department, Karachi Pakistan. **LC** HJ2154.5.Z9; S55A. **DD** 354/.549/1800722.

SW
### SWEDISH BUDGET, THE. Main/Corp Sweden.
Ekonomidepartementet. 16th- Ed.; 1978/79-. Swedish (English). an. Finansdepartementet, 103 33 Stockholm Sweden. **Tel** 08-7631000, telex 11741 FINANS S. **LC** HJ2139; .S94A. **DD** 354/.485/00722. **Continues** *Swedish Budget.*
 **Ind/Abst** F&S Index Plus Text, Int. [Select. Cov.]; Predicasts Forecasts.

SY
### SYRIA'S BUDGET. Main/Corp Syria. English. an.
$90.00. Office Arabe de Presse et de Documentation, 67 Place Chahbandar, BP 3550, Damascus Syria. **Tel** 459166 (operator assisted requested), telex 411613 OFA SY. **LC** HJ64.25; .A295A. **DD** 354.56910072/225/05. Index available. cum. index. **Circ:** 200 (ctrl).

JA
### TAKAMATSU KOKUZEIKYOKU TOKEISHO. Main/Corp Japan. Takamatsu
Kokuzeikyoku. (19??)-. Periodical. Japanese. Takamatsu Kokuzeikyoku, 10 Tenjinmae 2-chome, Takamatsu Japan. **LC** HJ77.Z5; S544a.

US
### TANGIBLE PERSONAL PROPERTY TAXES. TAXES LEVIED BY TYPE OF GOVERNMENTAL UNIT AND VALUE OF PROPERTY, BY COUNTY, CALENDAR YEAR ... OHIO DEPARTMENT OF TAXATION. English. Department of Taxation / Ohio,
Research and Statistics Section, PO Box 530, Columbus OH 43216. **LC** HJ4591.O3; T36. **DD** 336.2/3/09771021.

US/0039-9949
### TAX ADMINISTRATORS NEWS.
**Added/Corp** Federation of Tax Administrators (U.S.). Vol. 1 (Oct. 1937)-. Periodical. English. mo. $35.00. Federal Tax Administrators, 444 North Capitol Street NW, Suite 334, Washington DC 20001. **Tel** (202)624-5890. **LC** HJ2360; .T2. **DD** 336.205. Index available. cum. index (in Dec. issue).

US/0039-9957
### TAX ADVISER, THE. [Tax advis.]. Added/Corp
American Institute of Certified Public Accountants. Vol. 1 (Jan. 1970)-. Periodical. English. mo. $98.00 US and US Possessions; $123.00 other. American Institute of Certified Public Accountants, Harborside Financial Center, 201 Plaza 3, Jersey City NJ 07311. **Tel** (201)938-3333, (800)862-4272. **ED** Nicholas Fiore. **LC** K24; .A84. **DD** 343/.73/0405. **CODEN** TAADDJ. **[CCC]**. **Bk Rev**. **Ad Acc**. **Circ:** 25,000 (ctrl). available on microfilm and microfiche from University Microfilms International (UMI). Documents available from UMI Article Clearinghouse.
 **Desc:** A magazine of tax planning, trends and techniques.
 **Ind/Abst** ABI/INFORM Glob. Ed.; ABI Inform Ondisc (Aug. 1975-); Acad. Search (July 1993-); Account. Tax Datab. (1974-) [Full Txt.]; Account. Art.; Bus. Index (1985-); Bus. Source (Jul. 1993-); Curr. Law Index (1980-); Fed. Tax Artic.; Gen. BusinessFile (1985-); Gen. Period. Index (1985-); Index Leg. Period.; Index Period. Artic. Relat. Law; INFO-SOUTH Abstr.; Law Office Inf. Serv.; Leg. Resour. Index (1980-); LegalTrac (1980-); Mag. Search; Trade Ind. Index (1981-?); UMI ABI/Inform--Bus. Period. Ondisc (Jan. 1990-) [Full Txt.].

Il/0039-9965
### TAX AFFAIRS. See Law.

US/0196-8882
### TAX ALERT FOR MANAGEMENT. [Tax alert
manage.]. **Main/Corp** Research Institute of America, Inc. English. wk. Research Institute of America, 117 East Stevens Avenue, Valhalla NY 10595. **Tel** (800)431-9025. **LC** KF6272; .R46. **DD** 343.7304/05; 347.303405.

US/0889-3055
### TAX ANALYSTS' DAILY TAX HIGHLIGHTS & DOCUMENTS. Added/Corp
Tax Analysts (Firm : U.S.). **VFOAT** Daily Tax Highlights & Documents; Daily Tax Highlights and Documents; Highlights and Documents; Highlights & Documents. (1988)-. English. Five issues per week (published Mon.-Fri.). $1999.00. Tax Analysts, 6830 North Fairfax Drive, Arlington VA 22213. **Tel** (703)533-4400, (800)955-3444. **LC** KF6272; .T36. **DD** 343.7304/05; 347.303405. **[CCC]**. **Continues** *Daily Tax Highlights & Documents.*

# Public Administration —Public Finance and Taxation

US
### TAX & INVESTMENT PROFILE.
GERMANY. Added/Corp Touche Ross & Co. VFOAT Tax and Investment Profile. Germany; Germany. (19??)-. English. Touche Ross and Company, 1900 M Street NW, Washington DC 20036.

CN/0820-0653
### TAX & TARIFF BULLETIN. [Tax & tariff bull.].
Added/Corp Canadian Construction Association. VFOAT Taxes & Tariffs Bulletin. VAT Tax and Tariff Bulletin. No. 2/82 (May 1982)-. Bulletin. English. Four times a year. $39.82. Canadian Construction Association, 85 Albert Street/2nd Floor, Ottawa Ontario K1P 6A4 Canada. Tel (613)236-9455, FAX (613)236-9526, telex 053-4436. DD 336.2/7869/00971. Continues Taxes & Tariffs Bulletin, 0319-7476.

US/0193-5771
### TAX ANGLES. (197?)-. Periodical. English. Twelve times a year. $66.00 (one year); $120.00 (two years). American Tax Institute, 200 West 57th Street, New York NY 10019. Tel (212)399-1086. ED Elliot Beier. Circ: 2,000.
Desc: News and information on articles of tax-saving ideas, strategies, and techniques.

UK
### TAX ASPECTS OF INTERNATIONAL TREASURY PLANNING. English. Longman Group Ltd., Fourth Avenue, Longman House, Harlow Essex CM19 5SR England. Tel 011 44 279 429655, FAX 011 44 279 431059, telex 81259. (Subscription address: Fourth Avenue, Harlow Essex CM19 5AA England)

US/0733-2254
### TAX AVOIDANCE DIGEST. Title Change. [Tax avoid. dig.]. Vol. 2, No. 7 (July 1982)-. Periodical. English. Twelve times a year. Tax Avoidance Digest, 7910 Woodmont Avenue/#1200, Bethesda MD 20814-3015. Tel (301)951-3800. ED Robert C. Carlson. DD 343. Circ: 60,000. Continues Tax Digest. Continued by Tax Wise Money, 1070-0269.
Desc: Digest of all the best legal methods for reducing taxes, in layman's language.

FR
### TAX/BENEFIT POSITION OF PRODUCTION WORKERS, THE.
Added/Corp Organisation for Economic Co-Operation and Development. VFOAT Tax Benefit Position of Production Workers; Situation des Ouvriers Au Regard de l'Impot et des Transferts Sociaux. (1983)-. English (French). an (published in Dec.). $45.00. OECD Publications and Information Center, 2 rue Andre-Pascal, 75775 Paris Cedex 16 France. Tel 011 33 1 45248167, US:(202)785-6323, FAX 011 33 1 45248500 OR 45248176, telex 620 160 OCDE. (Subscription address: OECD Publications Center, 2001 L Street, Suite 700, Washington DC 20036.) LC HC79.I5; T35. DD 336.24/05. Continues Tax/Benefit Position of a Typical Worker in OECD Member Countries.

CN/0846-1112
### TAX BREAKS. [Tax breaks]. Added/Corp Deloitte & Touche. (Sept./Oct. 1990)-. Periodical. English. bm. Limited free distribution. Deloitte & Touche, Suite 1000, 95 Wellington Street West, Toronto, Ontario M5J 2P4 Canada. DD 343.7105.

US
### TAX BULLETIN. Bulletin. Macmillan Publishing Company, 866 3rd Avenue, New York NY 10022. Tel (212)702-2000, (800)257-5755.

US
### TAX COLLECTORS MANUAL. Main/Corp
Pennsylvania. Dept. of Community Affairs. Information Services Center. English. Pennsylvania Department of Community Affairs, Forum Building/Room 311, Harrisburg PA 17120. LC KFP471; .A83. DD 343.74804/2.
Continues Manual for Pennsylvania Tax Collectors.

US/0270-0077
### TAX COMPANION, THE. 1977-. English. an. $11.95 (1987 edition) plus $3.90 postage. Longman Financial Services Publishing, Division of Longman Financial Services Institute Inc, 500 North Dearborn, c/o Longman, Chicago IL 60610-4975. Tel (312)836-0466. LC KF1164.3; .T27. DD 343.7304/05. Index available. Circ: 30,000. Continues Tax Handbook.
Desc: Up-to-the-minute source of information and analysis needed to earn a tax advantage for you and your clients.

II
### TAX CONSULTANT. 1- July 1969-. Periodical. English. Unique Printing Press, 103 Sharda Chambers, New Marine Lines Bombay India. ED S K Agarwal. LC K24. DD 336.2/00954.

US
### TAX COURT. Macmillan Publishing Company, 866 3rd Avenue, New York NY 10022. Tel (212)702-2000, (800)257-5755.

US
### TAX DIGEST (CORAL GABLES, FLA.).
See Law.

UK
### TAX DIGEST (LONDON, ENGLAND). See Law.

US/0888-1243
### TAX DIRECTORY, THE. [Tax dir.]. (Fall 1985)-. Directory. English. qt (published within seasons). $299.00. Tax Analysts, 6830 North Fairfax Drive, Arlington VA 22213. Tel (703)533-4400, (800)955-3444. LC HJ9; .T39. DD 351.72/4/002573. [CCC].
Desc: Two volume set containing US and international government officials and private sector tax professionals.

US/0040-0025
### TAX EXECUTIVE, THE. [Tax exec.].
Added/Corp Tax Executives Institute (U.S.). Vol. 1 (1949)-. Periodical. English. Six times a year (Feb., Apr., June, Aug., Oct., Dec.). $105.00 US & Canada & Latin America; $130.00 others. Tax Executives Institute Inc, 1001 Pennsylvania Avenue Northwest, Suite 320, Washington DC 20004-2505. Tel (202)638-5601, FAX (202)638-5607. (Subscription address: PO Box 96129, Washington, DC 20090-6129) ED Timothy J. McCormally. LC K24; .A9. DD 336.20973. Index available. Bk Rev. Ad Acc. Pr Rev. Circ: 5,000. available on microfilm and microfiche from University Microfilms International (UMI); available on CD-ROM; available on an online database (file 648/Full-Text) from DIALOG. Documents available from UMI Article Clearinghouse.
Desc: Concerns corporate taxation.
Ind/Abst ABI/INFORM Glob. Ed.; ABI Inform Ondisc (Jan. 1975-); Acad. Search (July 1993-); Account. Tax Datab. (Jan. 1975-) [Full Txt.]; Account. Art.; Bus. ASAP (1990-) [Full Txt.]; Bus. Index (1985-); Bus. Source (Jul. 1993-); Curr. Law Index (1980-); Fed. Tax Artic.; Gen. BusinessFile (1985-); Gen. Period. Index (1985-); Index Period. Artic. Relat. Law; INFO-SOUTH Abstr.; Leg. Resour. Index (1980-); LegalTrac (1980-); Mag. Search; PAIS Int. Print.

US/1043-0873
### TAX EXEMPT FINANCING. See Law.

US/0194-228X
### TAX EXEMPT NEWS. Title Change. [Tax exempt news]. (197?)-(19??). Periodical. English. bw. Tax Exempt News, 655 15th Street NW/Suite 300, Washington DC 20005. Tel (202)639-4004. ED Jennifer Fisch. DD 343. [CCC]. Bk Rev. Circ: 1,000 (ctrl). Continued by Nonprofit Insights, 1056-4594.
Desc: Summarizes new developments affecting the nonprofit community, including colleges and universities, religious organizations, nonprofit associations and corporations which make charitable contributions. Provides information on new legislation and Internal Revenue Service regulation as well as trends in the Treasury and colleges.

US
### TAX EXEMPTIONS (OLYMPIA, WASH.).
See Law.

US
### TAX EXPENDITURE BUDGET FOR THE STATE OF MINNESOTA, FISCAL YEARS. VFOAT Minnesota Tax Expenditure Budget. 1989-. English. be. Department of Revenue / Minnesota, 10 River Park Plaza, St Paul MN 55146. LC HJ11; .M658. DD 353.97760072/2252. Continues Tax Expenditure Budget.

UK
### TAX FACT BOOK. English. Gee & Company Limited, 183 Marsh Wall, South Quay Plaza, London E14 9FS England. Tel 011 44 71 538 5386, FAX 071 538 8623.

CN/0821-0780
### TAX FACTS AND FIGURES (MONTREAL). (TAX FACTS AND FIGURES.). [Tax facts fig.]. Added/Corp Coopers & Lybrand (Firm). (1977)-. English (French). an. Free. Coopers and Lybrand, 29th floor, 385 Bourke Street, Melbourne 3000 Asutralia. Tel 011 61 03 606 4500. DD 343.7105/2/05. ctrl circ.

US/0739-6619
### TAX FACTS ON INVESTMENTS. See Business-Investments.

US/1069-711X
### TAX FEATURES. (TAX FEATURES / TAX FOUNDATION.). [Tax featur.]. Added/Corp Tax Foundation. (19??)-. Periodical. English. Eleven times a year. Free College University & Public Libraries; $50.00 others. Tax Foundation Inc., 1250 H Street NW/Suite 750, Washington DC 20005. Tel (202)783-2760, FAX (202)942-7675. DD 336. Continues Tax Foundation's Tax Features, 0883-1335.

UK
### TAX FILE. English. wk. £193.00 UK; £222.00 other. Denewood Ltd., Unit 5 Orchard Ind. Est. Pk. Wood, Maidstone Kent ME159XT England. Tel 011 44 622 757032.

US/0736-6469
### TAX FOUNDATION'S LIBRARY BULLETIN. See Library and Information Sciences.

US/0883-1335
### TAX FOUNDATION'S TAX FEATURES.
Title Change. [Tax Found. Tax Features]. Added/Corp Tax Foundation. (19??)-(1992). Periodical. English. Eleven times a year (Dec/Jan. issue combined). Tax Foundation Inc., 1250 H Street Northwest, Suite 750, Washington DC 20005. Tel (202)783-2760, FAX (202)942-7675. ED Stephen Gold. DD 336. ctrl circ. Continued by Tax Features Tax Foundation, 1069-711X.

US/0883-1335
### TAX FOUNDATION'S TAX FEATURES.
Title Change. [Tax Found. tax features]. Added/Corp Tax Foundation. VFOAT Tax Features; Monthly Tax Features. Vol. 28, No. 7 (Aug./Sept. 1984)-(19??). Periodical. English. mo. Tax Foundation Inc., 1250 H Street Northwest, Suite 750, Washington DC 20005. Tel (202)783-2760, FAX (202)942-7675. ED William J Wilson. DD 336. ctrl circ. available on microfilm and microfiche from University Microfilms International (UMI). Continues Tax Foundation's Monthly Tax Features (Washington, D.C.). Continued by Tax Features, 1069-711X.
Desc: Short feature articles on fiscal topics of current interest, including public finance and analysis of federal, state, and local government.
Ind/Abst Stat. Ref. Index.

US
### TAX FREE INCOME BULLETIN.
Added/Corp Tax Reports Newsletter Associates. VFOAT Tax Free; Tax-Free Income Bulletin. (19??)-. Periodical. English. mo. $177.00. Newsletter Management Corporation, 10076 Boca Entrada Boulevard, Boca Raton FL 33431. Tel (407)241-1800. LC KF6297.5.A15; T39. DD 343.7305/23; 347.303523. Continues Tax Shelter Insider, 0270-7977.

US/0190-7522
### TAX GUIDE FOR COLLEGE TEACHERS AND OTHER COLLEGE PERSONNEL.
Main/Corp Academic Information Service, Inc. Added/Corp Academic Information Service, Inc. (197?)-. English. an. $29.85. Academic Information Service, PO Box 929, College Park MD 20740. Tel (202)347-0079. LC KF6369.8.E3; T37. DD 343.7305/2/024372; 347.3035204372. Continues Academic Information Service, Inc. Tax Guide for College Teachers and Other School Personnel., 0734-2357.

US/0146-8235
### TAX GUIDE FOR ENGINEERS. (1977)-. English. ir. $31.95. Academic Information Service, PO Box 929, College Park MD 20740. Tel (202)347-0079. LC KF6369.8.E54; A25. DD 343/.73/052.

US
### TAX GUIDE FOR INDIVIDUALS WITH INCOME FROM U.S. POSSESSIONS : FOR USE IN PREPARING ... RETURNS.
Added/Corp United States. Internal Revenue Service. (1990)-. English. Eastern Area Distribution Center, PO Box 85074, Richmond VA 23261-5074. Continues Tax Guide for Individuals in U.S. Possessions.

US/0083-1484
### TAX GUIDE FOR SMALL BUSINESS / DEPARTMENT OF THE TREASURY, INTERNAL REVENUE SERVICE. Began with 1956. English. an. Internal Revenue Service, 1111 Constitution Avenue NW, Washington DC 20224. LC KF6491.A73; I5. DD 336.2.

US
### TAX GUIDE FOR U.S. CITIZENS ABROAD / DEPARTMENT OF THE TREASURY, INTERNAL REVENUE SERVICE. Added/Corp United States. Internal Revenue Service. (19??)-. Government Publication. English. ir. $11.40. Superintendent of Documents, US Government Printing Office, Washington DC 20402. Tel (202)275-3328, FAX (202)786-2377.

US/1045-8484
### TAX GUIDE (NEW YORK, N.Y.). (TAX GUIDE.). [Tax guide]. VFOAT Research Institute Tax Guide. English. an. Research Institute of America, 117 East Stevens Avenue, Valhalla NY 10595. Tel (800)431-9025. DD 343.

US/0195-6531
### TAX GUIDE. WEEKLY ALERT. [Tax guide, Wkly. alert]. Main/Corp Research Institute of America, Inc. VFOAT Weekly Alert. Periodical. English. wk. $148.00. Research Institute of America, 117 East Stevens Avenue, Valhalla NY 10595. Tel (800)431-9025. LC KF6272; .R47. DD 343.7304/05.

US/0143-9677
### TAX HAVEN & SHELTER REPORT. NORTH AMERICAN EDITION. (TAX HAVEN & SHELTER REPORT.). [Tax haven shelter rep., North

Am. ed.]. **Added/Corp** Institute for International Research. **VAT** Tax Haven and Shelter Report. North American Edition. (1980)-. Periodical. English. mo. Inst for Intl Research, 57 61 Mortimer Street, London W1N 7TD England.

UK
**TAX HAVEN ENCYCLOPEDIA.** (19??)-. English. ir. Butterworth & Co. Ltd. / Kent, England, Borough Green, Sevenoaks Kent TN15 8PH England. **Tel** 011 44 732-884567, FAX 011 44 732-885996.

US/0279-4446
**TAX HOTLINE.** (198?)-. Periodical. English. mo. $59.00. Tax Hotline, 330 West 42nd Street, New York NY 10036. **Tel** (212)239-9000. **ED** David Ellis.
**Desc:** The report for people who want to keep on top of every tax break the law allows, including how to make the most of the new tax reform opportunities.

US/0279-2109
**TAX IDEAS.** [Tax ideas]. **Main/Corp** Prentice-Hall, Incorporated. **Added/Corp** Prentice-Hall, Inc. Maxwell Macmillan (Firm). (19??)-. English. ir. $264.00. Warren Gorham & Lamont Inc., Park Square Building, 31 St. James Avenue, Boston MA 02116-4112. **Tel** (617)423-2020, (800)950-1207, FAX (617)423-2026. **DD** 343.
**Ind/Abst** Fed. Tax Artic.

CN/0713-7192
**TAX INFORMATION BULLETIN.** [Tax inf. bull.]. **Added/Corp** Ontario. Ministry of Revenue. Vol. 1 (Feb. 1981)-. Bulletin. English. Ministry of Revenue, Queens Park, Toronto Ontario M7A 1X8 Canada. **DD** 336.2/09713.

UK/0954-7274
**TAX JOURNAL, THE.** (198?)-. Periodical. English. wk. £99.00. Butterworth & Co. Ltd. / Kent, England, Borough Green, Sevenoaks Kent TN15 8PH England. **Tel** 011 44 732-884567, FAX 011 44 732-885996. **ED** Christopher Reece. **LC** K24; .A915. **DD** 343.4104/05; 344.103405.
**Desc:** Carries the latest news, analysis, and developments in the tax business.

US/0892-4430
**TAX LAW ANTHOLOGY.** ***Ceased.*** **See** Law.

US/0040-0041
**TAX LAW REVIEW.** **See** Law.

US
**TAX LAWS OF THE WORLD. CLASS B.** (19??)-. English. Twenty-six times a year. Comes with Foreign Tax Law Publishers membership; $1350.00 (membership). Foreign Tax Law Publishers Inc., PO Box 2189, Ormond Beach FL 32175-2189. **Tel** (904)253-5785, FAX (904)257-3003. **ED** S. Yanaura. Index available. **Pr Rev.** ctrl circ.
**Desc:** Includes income tax and profits tax laws, VAT Laws, corporation tax laws and net wealth, estate, import, and other miscellaneous taxes in some monographs.

US/0040-005X
**TAX LAWYER : BULLETIN OF THE SECTION OF TAXATION, AMERICAN BAR ASSOCIATION, THE.** **See** Law.

US
**TAX LEVY AUTHORIZATIONS AND LIMITATIONS.** **Added/Corp** Minnesota. Local Government Aids & Analysis Division. (1979)-. English. an. Centennial Office Building, St Paul MN 55155. **LC** KFM5890; .A457. **DD** 343.77604/3/02638; 347.760343026638. ***Continues*** *Tax Levy Authorizations and Limitations for Cities, Counties, Towns, School Districts, and Special Taxing Districts in Minnesota.*

US/8755-0369
**TAX LITERATURE REPORT.** ***Ceased.*** **See** Law.

US
**TAX MAGAZINE.** (199?)-. Periodical. English. qt. $29.99. Publishing & Business Consultants, PO Box 75392, Los Angeles CA 90075. **Tel** (213)732-3477, FAX (213)732-9123. **ED** Andeson Napoleon Atia. **Ad Acc.** Full Page (B&W) $5750.00. Half Page (B&W) $3575.00. Full Page (Color) $8750.00 (2 color). Half Page (Color) $5500.00 (2 color). **Circ:** 165,000 total. ***Continues*** *PBC Federal Tax Guide.*
**Desc:** Features articles on business and personal deductions, accounting, promotional expenses and investments.

US/8756-1360
**TAX MANAGEMENT FINANCIAL PLANNING JOURNAL.** [Tax Manage. financ. plan. j.]. **Added/Corp** Tax Management Inc. **VFOAT** Financial Planning Journal. Vol. 1, No. 1 Jan. (1985)-. Periodical. English. mo. $300.00. Bureau of National Affairs Inc., 9435 Key West Avenue, Rockville MD 20850. **Tel** (800)372-1033, (301)258-1033, FAX (301)948-5823. **(Subscription telephone:** FAX (301)948-5823**)** **ED** Glenn Davis. **LC** KF6296.A15; T37. **DD** 343.7304/05; 347.303405. **[CCC].** available on microfilm and microfiche from University Microfilms International (UMI).
**Desc:** Provides coverage on the state of financial planning today, including new legislative, regulatory and economic developments.
**Ind/Abst** Account. Tax Datab. (1985-) [Full Txt.]; Leg. Resour. Index; LegalTrac (1980-).

US
**TAX MANAGEMENT FOREIGN INCOME PORTFOLIOS.** Tax Management Inc / Washington DC, 1231 25th Street NW, Washington DC 20037. **Tel** (202)452-4556, (800)372-1033, FAX (202)452-4096, telex 285656 BNAI WSH.

UK/0143-7941
**TAX MANAGEMENT INTERNATIONAL FORUM, THE.** **Added/Corp** Tax Management International (Firm). Vol. 1, No. 1 (1980)-. Periodical. English. qt. £192.00 UK; $330.00 other. BNA International Inc., Herron, HSE Dean 10 Farrar Street, 6th Floor, London SW1H 0DL England. **Tel** (44) 71 222 8831, FAX (44) 71 222 0294, telex 262570 BNA LONG. **ED** Linda Omahoney. **LC** K4456.2; .T39. **DD** 343.04/05; 342.3405. **[CCC].** available on an online database (file 485/Full-Text) from DIALOG; and Finsbury Data Services.
**Desc:** A comparative discussion of international tax law problems by distinguished practitioners in major industrial countries.

US/0090-4600
**TAX MANAGEMENT INTERNATIONAL JOURNAL.** **See** Business-General Management.

UK
**TAX MANAGEMENT INTERNATIONAL PORTFOLIOS.** Tax Management Inc / England, 17 Dartmouth Street, London SW1H 9BL England.

UK
**TAX MANAGEMENT INTERNATIONAL PROGRAM.** (19??)-. Periodical. English. ir. £684.00. BNA International Inc., Herron, HSE Dean 10 Farrar Street, 6th Floor, London SW1H 0DL England. **Tel** (44) 71 222 8831, FAX (44) 71 222 0294, telex 262570 BNA LONG.

US
**TAX MANAGEMENT IRS FORMS.** Tax Management Inc / Washington DC, 1231 25th Street NW, Washington DC 20037. **Tel** (202)452-4556, (800)372-1033, FAX (202)452-4096, telex 285656 BNAI WSH.

US/0148-8295
**TAX MANAGEMENT MEMORANDUM.** **Added/Corp** Tax Management Inc. (19??)-. Periodical. English. ir. $268.00. Bureau of National Affairs Inc., 9435 Key West Avenue, Rockville MD 20850. **Tel** (800)372-1033, (301)258-1033, FAX (301)948-5823. **(Subscription address:** 9435 Key West Avenue, Rockville MD 20850; telephone: FAX (301)948-5823**)** **ED** Glenn David. **[CCC].** cum. index. available on microfilm and microfiche from University Microfilms International (UMI); available on an online database (file 485/Full-Text) from DIALOG.
**Desc:** Contains an analysis of a current important tax development which has been closely examined and discussed by Tax Management's advisory board.
**Ind/Abst** Account. Tax Datab. (Jul. 1992-) [Full Txt.]; Leg. Resour. Index; LegalTrac (1984-).

US/0738-5285
**TAX MANAGEMENT, PRIMARY SOURCES.** [Tax manage. prim. sources]. **Added/Corp** Tax Management Inc. (19??)-. Periodical. English. ir. $1,000.00. Bureau of National Affairs Inc., 9435 Key West Avenue, Rockville MD 20850. **Tel** (800)372-1033, (301)258-1033, FAX (301)948-5823. **ED** Glenn Davis. **[CCC].** Index available.
**Desc:** Legislative history of IRC sections as affected by Tax Reform Act of 1986 and subsequent legislation.

US
**TAX MANAGEMENT U.S. INCOME.** Tax Management Inc / Washington DC, 1231 25th Street NW, Washington DC 20037. **Tel** (202)452-4556, (800)372-1033, FAX (202)452-4096, telex 285656 BNAI WSH.

US/0887-2562
**TAX MANAGEMENT WASHINGTON TAX REVIEW.** [Tax Manage. Wash. tax rev.]. **Added/Corp** Tax Management Inc. **VFOAT** Washington Tax Review. Vol. 10, No. 2 Feb. (1984)-. Periodical. English. mo. $173.00. Bureau of National Affairs Inc., 9435 Key West Avenue, Rockville MD 20850. **Tel** (800)372-1033, (301)258-1033, FAX (301)948-5823. **(Subscription address:** 9435 Key West Avenue, Rockville MD 20850; telephone: FAX (301)948-5823**)** **ED** Glenn Davis. **LC** KF6272; .W37. **DD** 343.7304/05; 347.303405. available on microfilm and microfiche from University Microfilms International (UMI). ***Continues*** *Washington Tax Review, 0737-5875.*
**Desc:** An analysis of tax legislative developments: including BNA's Advisory Board Outlook, summaries of recent tax legislation and analyses by tax practitioners of current issues.

US/0884-6057
**TAX MANAGEMENT WEEKLY REPORT.** [Tax Manage. wkly. rep.]. **Added/Corp** Tax Management Inc. Vol. 4, No. 36 (Sept. 9, 1985)-. English. ir. $2335.00 (renewals only). Bureau of National Affairs Inc., 9435 Key West Avenue, Rockville MD 20850. **Tel** (800)372-1033, (301)258-1033, FAX (301)948-5823. **ED** Glenn Davis. **LC** KF6272; .B55. **DD** 343.7304/05; 347.303405. **[CCC].** ***Continues*** *BNA's Weekly Tax Report, 0733-0405.*
**Desc:** Reports developments affecting taxation and the tax aspects of accounting. Covers summaries of federal cases including the U.S. Tax Court, synopses of IRS general counsel and technical advice memoranda, analysis of noteworthy IRS revenue rulings, procedures and private letter rulings, and status reports of Treasury Department actions on pending regulations.

CN/0712-6921
**TAX MEMO (PRICE WATERHOUSE (FIRM)).** (TAX MEMO / PRICE WATERHOUSE.). [Tax memo- Price Waterhouse]. Oct. 1981-. Periodical. English. mo. Free. Tax Memo, c/o Price Waterhouse Centre, Toronto Ontario M5K 1G1 Canada. **DD** 336.2/00971. ctrl circ. ***Continues*** *Tax Bulletin (Price Waterhouse & Company), 0712-6913.*

CE/0377-600X
**TAX MONTHLY, THE.** V. 1 (Feb. 1974)-. Periodical. English. mo. Rs2.50 single issue. Income Tax Payers Association of Ceylon, 54 3/2 Australia Building 1, Colombo Ceylon Sri Lanka. **LC** LAW. **DD** 343/.5493/0405.
**Ind/Abst** Index Philip. Period.

US/0196-1950
**TAX MONTHLY FOR ASSOCIATIONS.** (197?)-. Periodical. English. mo. $115.00 one year; $198.00 two year, for associations; $121.90 Washington; $115.00 other for organizations. Harmon Curran Gallagher & Spielberg, 2001 South Street Northwest, Suite 430, Washington DC 20009. **Tel** (202)328-3500, FAX (202)328-6918. **ED** Robert R. Statham.
**Desc:** Tax news for associations and Chamber of Commerce.

US
**TAX NEWS.** **Added/Corp** California. Franchise Tax Board. (19??)-. English. bm (Jan., Mar., May, July, Sept., Nov.). $12.00. Franchise Tax Board, PO Box 520, Rancho Cordova CA 95741-0520. **Tel** (816)292-7607. **ED** Patricia Huberty. Index available (available in Jan. issue). **Circ:** 23,500.

NE/0040-0076
**TAX NEWS SERVICE.** **See** Law.

US
**TAX NOTES.** **Main/Corp** Ernst & Whinney. Aug. 1979-. Periodical. English. bm. Tax Analysts, 6830 North Fairfax Drive, Arlington VA 22213. **Tel** (703)533-4400, (800)955-3444. ***Continues*** *Tax Notes.*

US/0270-5494
**TAX NOTES (ARLINGTON).** (TAX NOTES.). [Tax notes]. **Added/Corp** Tax Analysts and Advocates. Taxation With Representation Fund. Tax Analysts (Firm : U.S.) Taxation With Representation--Research (Firm). Vol. 1, No. 1 (Sept. 18, 1972)-. Periodical. English. wk (4 volumes per year). $1499.00. Tax Analysts, 6830 North Fairfax Drive, Arlington VA 22213. **Tel** (703)533-4400, (800)955-3444. **ED** R. Eliot Rosen. **LC** KF6272; .T39. **DD** 343.7304/05; 347.303405. **[CCC].** Index available (free). **Ad Acc.** **Circ:** 3,200 (ctrl). available on microfiche.
**Desc:** In-depth investigative articles cover tax developments as well as congressional hearings. Also included are summaries of weekly letter rulings from IRS, treasury letters, and regulations. Tax items from the Congressional Record appear when Congress is in session.
**Ind/Abst** Bus. Index (1985-); Fed. Tax Artic.; Gen. BusinessFile (1985-); Leg. Resour. Index; LegalTrac (1980-); Urban Aff. Abstr.

CN/0715-8556
**TAX NOTES (EDMONTON).** (TAX NOTES.). [Tax notes]. Sept. 1982-. Periodical. English. Tax Information Services, Alberta Treasury Department, 9811 109th Street, Edmonton Alberta T5K 2L5 Canada. **Tel** (403)427-3035. **DD** 343.712304/05.

US/1048-3306
**TAX NOTES INTERNATIONAL.** [Tax notes int.]. **Added/Corp** Tax Analysts (Firm : U.S.). Vol. 1, No. 1 (July 1989)-. Periodical. English. wk (52 issues). $749.00. Tax Analysts, 6830 North Fairfax Drive, Arlington VA 22213. **Tel** (703)533-4400, (800)955-3444. **LC** PAR. **DD** 341. **[CCC].** ***Continues*** *Taxes International, 0142-6877.*
**Ind/Abst** Account. Art.; Leg. Resour. Index; LegalTrac (1990-).

UK
**TAX ON PROPERTY.** **See** Real Estate.

US/1055-2456
**TAX PENALTIES : THE COMPLETE GUIDE TO PENALTIES UNDER THE INTERNAL REVENUE SERVICE.** (1991)-. English. $49.95 (paper), $89.95 (cloth). Financial Sourcebooks, PO Box 313, Naperville IL 60566. **Tel** (708)961-2161. **DD** 343.

CN/0821-0764
**TAX PLANNING CHECKLIST. See** Law.

CN/0841-6621
**TAX PLANNING GUIDE.** [Tax plan. guide]. **Added/Corp** Laventhol & Horwath (Firm) CCH Canadian Limited. (1987/88)-. English. CCH Canadian Ltd., 6 Garamond Court, Don Mills Ontario M3C 1Z5 Canada. **Tel** (416)441-2992, FAX (416)441-3418. **DD** 343.7104. ***Continues*** *Year-End Tax Planning Guide (Don Mills, Ont.), 0824-5886.*

US/0040-0092
**TAX PLANNING IDEAS.** Periodical. English. bm. $174.00. Subscription Service Center, IBP Plaza, Englewood Cliffs NJ 07632. **LC** KF6296.A15; T38.

UK
**TAX PLANNING INTERNATIONAL.** Vol. 3, No. 6 (June 1976)-. Periodical. English. mo. £420.00 UK; $745.00 other. BNA International Inc., Herron, HSE Dean 10 Farrar Street, 6th Floor, London SW1H 0DL England. **Tel** (44) 71 222 8831, FAX (44) 71 222 0294, telex 262570 BNA LONG. **ED** Zigurds Kronbergs. **LC** K4464.A13; T38. **DD** 343.04/05. Index available. cum. index. **Bk Rev.** ***Continues*** *Tax Haven Review.*
**Desc:** Written by tax practitioners worldwide and provides updates on tax developments and opportunities.

UK/0309-7900
**TAX PLANNING INTERNATIONAL REVIEW.** **Added/Corp** Tax Management International (Firm) BNA International Inc. Vol. 8 No. 1 (Jan. 1981)-. Periodical. English. mo. $695.00 US and Canada; £384.00 other. BNA International Inc., Herron, HSE Dean 10 Farrar Street, 6th Floor, London SW1H 0DL England. **Tel** (44) 71 222 8831, FAX (44) 71 222 0294, telex 262570 BNA LONG. **ED** Sondra Beecroft and Kenneth H. Skilling. **LC** K4464.A13; T38. **DD** 343.04/05; 342.3405. ***Continues*** *Tax Planning International, 0309-7900.*
**Desc:** Journal of international tax planning developments and opportunities, including country surveys and tax treaty developments.
**Ind/Abst** Account. Tax Datab. (1988-).

US/0091-1178
**TAX PRACTICE AND PROCEDURE.** (IBP TAX PRACTICE AND PROCEDURE.). **Main/Corp** Institute for Business Planning, Inc. **VFOAT** Tax Practice and Procedure. (19??)-. English. mo. Thomas Gamound, 142 West Scotland Drive, Irving TX 75062. **Tel** (214)259-3809. **LC** KF6289.A1; I56. **DD** 343/.73/0405.

UK/0269-3720
**TAX PRACTITIONER'S DIARY.** [Tax pract. diary]. (19??)-. English. an. £16.00. Butterworth & Co. Ltd. / Kent, England, Borough Green, Sevenoaks Kent TN15 8PH England. **Tel** 011 44 732-884567, FAX 011 44 732-885996. **DD** 336.2.
**Desc:** Covers a period of over 15 months, commencing in September. Income tax, corporation tax, CGT, VAT and stamp duties are all summarised.

US/0279-7046
**TAX PREPARERS LIABILITY SERVICE. See** Law.

CN/0227-1265
**TAX PRINCIPLES TO REMEMBER.** [Tax princ. remember]. 1972-. English. an. $30.00. Canadian Institute of Chartered Accountants, 277 Wellington Street West, Toronto Ontario M5V 3H2 Canada. **Tel** (416)977-3222, FAX (416)204-3415. **ED** G M Colley and E J Newman. **LC** HJ4661.A2; T39. **DD** 336.24/0971.

CN/0827-3677
**TAX PROFILE (DON MILLS, ONT.).** (TAX PROFILE.). [Tax profile]. **Added/Corp** CCH Canadian Limited. Vol. 1, No. 1 (July 1984)-. Periodical. English. mo. CCH Canadian Ltd., 6 Garamond Court, Don Mills Ontario M3C 1Z5 Canada. **Tel** (416)441-2992, FAX (416)441-3418. **LC** KE5662; .T4. **DD** 343.7104/05; 347.103405. ctrl circ.
**Desc:** Commenting on items of interest regarding federal income tax and other federal and provincial taxes.

US
**TAX RATES IN VIRGINIA TOWNS.** **Main/Corp** Virginia Municipal League. English. $5.00. Virginia Municipal League, PO Box 12164, Richmond VA 23241. **Tel** (804)649-8471. **LC** JS303.V8; L315 subser; HJ9330. **DD** 320.4/755 S; 336.755.

US
**TAX RATES IN VIRGINIA'S CITIES, COUNTIES, AND SELECTED TOWNS.** **VFOAT** Tax Rates in Virginia. 1982-. Periodical. English. an. $9.50 (add $1.50 postage) (single copy). Virginia Municipal League, PO Box 12164, Richmond VA 23241. **Tel** (804)649-8471. **ED** Albert W Spengler. **LC** HJ9011.V8; T39. **DD** 336.2/014/755. **Circ:** 250 (ctrl). ***Formed by the union of*** *Tax Rates in Virginia Counties* ***and*** *Tax Rates in Virginia Cities and Selected Counties.*
**Desc:** A compilation and analysis of tax rates in Virginia for the 1986 tax year.

US/1062-9106
**TAX-RELATED DOCUMENTS.** ***Title Change.*** [Tax-relat. doc.]. **Added/Corp** Tax Analysts (Firm : U.S.). **VFOAT** Tax Related Documents. Vol. 7, No. 3 (Apr. 20, 1992)-(1993). Periodical. English. wk. Tax Analysts, 6830 North Fairfax Drive, Arlington VA 22213. **Tel** (703)533-4400, (800)955-3444. **DD** 343. ***Continues*** *Tax-Related Administrative Documents, 1060-9865.* ***Merged with*** *IRS Tax Practice Insider, 1063-4932* ***to form*** *Tax Practice & Controversies, 1074-5858.*

NZ/0110-0246
**TAX REPORTS, NEW ZEALAND. See** Law.

US/1059-0390
**TAX RETURN PREPARER'S GUIDE.** [Tax return prep. guide]. **Added/Corp** Prentice Hall Tax and Professional Practice (Firm). **VFOAT** Prentice Hall ... Tax Return Preparer's Guide. (1991)-. English. Prentice-Hall Law and Business, 270 Sylvan Avenue, Englewood Cliffs NJ 07632. **Tel** (800)223-0231, (201)894-8538, FAX (201)894-8666. **LC** KF6369.3; .T394. **DD** 343.7305/2; 347.30352.

US/1059-6356
**TAX RETURN PREPARER'S LETTER.** (TAX RETURN PREPARER'S LETTER / PRENTICE HALL.). [Tax return prep. lett.]. **Added/Corp** Prentice Hall Tax and Professional Practice (Firm) Prentice-Hall, Inc. (198?)-. Periodical. English. Twenty-six times a year. $108.36 US; $131.40 Canada. Bureau of Business Practice, 24 Rope Ferry Road, Waterford CT 06386. **Tel** (800)243-0876, (203)442-4365, (800)876-9105, FAX (203)443-1123. **DD** 343.

US
**TAX SERVICE FOR "C" CORPORATIONS.** **VFOAT** Monthly Report. Vol. 1, No. 1 (Dec. 1991)-. Periodical. English. Twelve times a year. $350.00. Mark A Stephens Ltd, 10018 Colesville Road, Silver Spring MD 20901. **Tel** (301)593-0443.

US/0742-888X
**TAX SHELTER ANALYST. See** Law.

US/0895-7266
**TAX SHOP 1040.** (TAX SHOP 1040 [COMPUTER FILE].). (1987)-. Periodical. English. an. Erin Softward Inc, 42 West Market Street, Blairsville PA 15717. **DD** 336.

US
**TAX TECHNIQUES FOR FOUNDATIONS AND OTHER EXEMPT ORGANIZATIONS.** ***Ceased.*** English. ir. Matthew Bender & Company Inc., 1275 Broadway, Albany NY 12204. **Tel** (800)833-9844, (518)487-3000.

CN/1187-4589
**TAX TIPS - DOANE, RAYMOND, PANNELL.** (TAX TIPS.). [Tax tips - Doane Raymond Pannell]. **Added/Corp** Doane, Raymond, Pannell (Firm). (1991)-. English. Doane, Raymond, Pannell, Box 12517, 20th Floor Oceanic Plaza, 1066 West Hastings Street, Vancouver British Columbia V6E 3X1 Canada. **DD** 343.7105. ***Continues*** *Tax Tips (Pannell, Kerr, MacGillivray (Firm)), 0836-5814.*

NE
**TAX TREATMENT OF CROSS-BORDER DONATIONS: INCLUDING THE TAX STATUS OF CHARITIES AND FOUNDATIONS, THE.** (19??)-. English. an. $145.00. International Bureau of Fiscal Documentation - IBFD Publications, PO Box 20237, 1000 HE Amsterdam The Netherlands. **Tel** 011 31 20-6267726, FAX 011 31 20-6228658, telex 13217 INTAX NL. **(Subscription address:** IBFD / International Bureau of Fiscal Documentation USA, Inc., 24 Hudson Street, Kinderhook NY 12106.**)**
**Desc:** Study of the treatment of charitable non-governmental organizations in over twenty-five countries.

NE
**TAX TREATMENT OF TRANSFER PRICING, THE.** (19??)-. English. qt (two updates per year). $1,115.00. International Bureau of Fiscal Documentation - IBFD Publications, PO Box 20237, 1000 HE Amsterdam The Netherlands. **Tel** 011 31 20-6267726, FAX 011 31 20-6228658, telex 13217 INTAX NL. **ED** Hubert Hamaekers, Maurice H. Collins and Wilhelmina A. Comello. **Circ:** 600.
**Desc:** In-depth country surveys of transfer pricing, with an introduction to corporate taxation, the arm's length principle, methods of price adjustment, specific transactions and sectors, rules in tax treaties, exchange of information, text of relevant documents, including the OECD reports of 1979 and 1984.

US/0746-0384
**TAX UPDATE FOR BUSINESS OWNERS.** [Tax update bus. own.]. Periodical. English. mo. $72.00 (one year), $126.00 (two year), $171.00 (three year). Tax Update for Business Owners, 81 Montgomery Street, Scarsdale NY 10583. **Tel** (914)472-0366. **ED** John L Springer and Karen Sanders. **[CCC].** Index available. cum. index. **Circ:** 30,000.
**Desc:** Publication containing tax guidance for owners of small businesses.

US/0163-9978
**TAX YEAR IN REVIEW, THE. See** Business-Accounting.

US
**TAXABLE AND NONTAXABLE INCOME : FOR USE IN PREPARING ... RETURNS.** **Added/Corp** United States. Internal Revenue Service. (19??)-. English.

US/0095-2753
**TAXABLE SALES IN CALIFORNIA. SALES AND USE TAX (ANNUAL).** (TAXABLE SALES IN CALIFORNIA (SALES AND USE TAX); ANNUAL REPORT.). **Main/Corp** California. State Board of Equalization. (1972)-. English. an. Free. State Board of Equalization, Box 942879, Sacramento CA 94279-0001. **Tel** (916)445-0840. **LC** HJ5715.U6; C276a. **DD** 336.2/71/09794. **Circ:** 5,000. ***Continues*** *Trade Outlets and Taxable Retail Sales in California, 0068-581X.*
**Desc:** Analysis of business transactions subject to California's sales and use tax. Dollar volume of taxable sales listed by city, county and type of business.

US/0095-7798
**TAXABLE SALES IN VIRGINIA COUNTIES & CITIES BASED ON RETAIL SALES TAX REVENUES.** **Main/Corp** Virginia. Dept. of Taxation. **VAT** Taxable Sales in Virginia Counties and Cities Based on Retail Sales Tax Revenues. English. an. Department of Taxation / Virginia, Richmond VA 23215. **LC** HJ11; .V856A. **DD** 336.2/71.

UK/0040-0149
**TAXATION.** Vol. 1 (Oct. 1 1927)-. Periodical. English. wk. £99.00 Europe & UK; £144.00 North America & Asia; £138.00 Mid East & North Africa; £151.00 other. Tolley Publishing Company Ltd, Tolley House, 2 Addiscombe Road, Croydon, Surrey CR9 5AF United Kingdom. **Tel** 011 44 81 6869141, FAX 011 44 81 6863155, 011 44 81 7600588. **ED** Craig McLellan, Circulation Manager. **LC** HJ2600; .T3. **DD** 343.4104; 344.1034. Index available. cum. index. **Bk Rev. Ad Acc. Circ:** 12,000.
**Desc:** Contains leading articles on current technical issues and topical comment written by tax professionals. Also contains regular reviews of tax software.
**Ind/Abst** Curr. Law Index (1980-); Leg. Resour. Index (1980-).

NE
**TAXATION AND INVESTMENT IN CANADA.** (19??)-. English. Twice a year. $230.00. International Bureau of Fiscal Documentation - IBFD Publications, PO Box 20237, 1000 HE Amsterdam The Netherlands. **Tel** 011 31 20-6267726, FAX 011 31 20-6228658, telex 13217 INTAX NL. **(Subscription address:** IBFD / International Bureau of Fiscal Documentation USA, Inc., 24 Hudson Street, Kinderhook NY 12106.**)**
**Desc:** Looseleaf treatise explaining and analyzing the tax systems of Canada.

NE
**TAXATION AND INVESTMENT IN CENTRAL AND EAST EUROPEAN COUNTRIES.** (1992)-. English. Three times a year. $915.00. International Bureau of Fiscal Documentation - IBFD Publications, PO Box 20237, 1000 HE Amsterdam The Netherlands. **Tel** 011 31 20-6267726, FAX 011 31 20-6228658, telex 13217 INTAX NL. **(Subscription address:** IBFD / International Bureau of Fiscal Documentation USA, Inc., 24 Hudson Street, Kinderhook NY 12106.**)**

NE
**TAXATION & INVESTMENT IN MEXICO.** (19??)-. English. an. $230.00. International Bureau of Fiscal Documentation - IBFD Publications, PO Box 20237, 1000 HE Amsterdam The Netherlands. **Tel** 011 31 20-6267726, FAX 011 31 20-6228658, telex 13217 INTAX NL. **(Subscription address:** IBFD / International Bureau of Fiscal Documentation USA, Inc., 24 Hudson Street, Kinderhook NY 12106.**)**
**Desc:** Covers laws, treaties and practices affecting business and investment; gives full details of taxation and tax treaties.

NE
**TAXATION AND INVESTMENT IN SOUTH AFRICA.** (19??)-. English. an. $260.00. International Bureau of Fiscal Documentation - IBFD Publications, PO Box 20237, 1000 HE Amsterdam The Netherlands. **Tel** 011 31 20-6267726, FAX 011 31 20-6228658, telex 13217 INTAX NL. **(Subscription address:** IBFD / International Bureau of Fiscal Documentation USA, Inc., 24 Hudson Street, Kinderhook NY 12106.**)**
**Desc:** Provides a detailed account of taxation and investment, and includes background information and coverage of all taxes.

NE
**TAXATION AND INVESTMENT IN THE CARIBBEAN.** (1992)-. English. sa. $860.00. International Bureau of Fiscal Documentation - IBFD Publications, PO Box 20237, 1000 HE Amsterdam The

Netherlands. **Tel** 011 31 20-6267726, FAX 011 31 20-6228658, telex 13217 INTAX NL.
**Desc:** Covers tax systems, company law, investment, exchange control and regional cooperation, and tax treaties.

US/1049-9830
**TAXATION AND MERGERS & ACQUISITIONS.** ***Ceased.*** [Tax. mergers acquis.]. **VFOAT** Taxation of Mergers and Acquisitions. Vol. 1, No. 1 May (1990)-(199?). Periodical. English. mo. Faulkner & Gray Inc., 11 Penn Plaza, 17th Floor, New York NY 10001. **Tel** (212)967-7000, (800)535-8403. **LC** KF6499.M4; A137. **DD** 343.7305/267/05; 347.303526705. available on microfilm and microfiche from University Microfilms International (UMI); available on an online database (file 485/Full-Text) from DIALOG.
**Ind/Abst** Account. Tax Datab. (Jan. 1991-Jun. 1992) [Full Txt.].

CN/0384-9201
**TAXATION (DON MILLS).** (TAXATION.). **Added/Corp** Life Underwriters Association of Canada. (1976)-. English (French). ir. price varies. Life Underwriters Association of Canada, 41 Lesmill Road, Don Mills Ontario M3B 2T3 Canada. **Tel** (416)444-5251, (800)563-5822, FAX (416)444-8031. **ED** Karl Keilhack. **LC** KE5974; .L54. **DD** 343.7105/3; 347.10353. Index available. **Bk Rev. Circ:** 22,000. ***Continues*** *Life Insurance and Taxation.*
**Desc:** Life insurance-related topics to aid life insurance agents. Articles relate to: taxation of life insurance, annuities, employee benefits.

US/0040-0165
**TAXATION FOR ACCOUNTANTS. See** Business-Accounting.

US/0161-178X
**TAXATION FOR LAWYERS. See** Law.

US
**TAXATION IN AUSTRALIA.** English.
**Ind/Abst** Account. Tax Datab. (1989-); Account. Art.; APAIS, Aust. Public Aff. Inf. Ser. (1982-); Aust. Leg. Mon. Dig.

NE
**TAXATION IN LATIN AMERICA. Main/Corp** International Bureau of Fiscal Documentation. (19??)-. English. ir (3 binders updated 4 times a year). $860.00. International Bureau of Fiscal Documentation - IBFD Publications, PO Box 20237, 1000 HE Amsterdam The Netherlands. **Tel** 011 31 20-6267726, FAX 011 31 20-6228658, telex 13217 INTAX NL. ***Continues*** *Corporate Taxation in Latin America.*
**Desc:** A detailed, practical reference guide to the tax and foreign investment legislation of the Spanish and Portuguese speaking countries of the western hemisphere, including the full texts (in English) of relevant tax treaties.

NE
**TAXATION IN LATIN AMERICA. SUPPLEMENT. Main/Corp** International Bureau of Fiscal Documentation. No. 66 (March 1987)-. English. qt. $860.00 (includes three binders and four supplements). International Bureau of Fiscal Documentation - IBFD Publications, PO Box 20237, 1000 HE Amsterdam The Netherlands. **Tel** 011 31 20-6267726, FAX 011 31 20-6228658, telex 13217 INTAX NL. **(Subscription address:** IBFD / International Bureau of Fiscal Documentation USA, Inc., 24 Hudson Street, Kinderhook NY 12106.**)** ***Continues*** *Corporate Taxation in Latin America.*

UK/0954-7053
**TAXATION INTERNATIONAL.** (19??)-. Periodical. English. mo. £135.00 p.a. Tolley Publishing Company Ltd, Tolley House, 2 Addiscombe Road, Croydon, Surrey CR9 5AF United Kingdom. **Tel** 011 44 81 6869141, FAX 011 44 81 6863155, 011 44 81 7600588. **LC** K4456.2; .T395. **DD** 343.04/05.
**Desc:** This concise service combines up to minute news and information with facts and figures on the latest developments in taxation around the world.

UK
**TAXATION MANUAL.** English. ir. £95.00. Gee & Company Limited, 183 Marsh Wall, South Quay Plaza, London E14 9FS England. **Tel** 011 44 71 538 5386, FAX 071 538 8623. **(Subscription address:** Professional Publishing Ltd., So Quay Plaza, 183 Marsh Wall, Lindon E14 9FS England, telephone: 011 44 71 5385386**)**

NE
**TAXATION OF COMPANIES IN EUROPE.** (19??)-. English. bm. $1,545.00. International Bureau of Fiscal Documentation - IBFD Publications, PO Box 20237, 1000 HE Amsterdam The Netherlands. **Tel** 011 31 20-6267726, FAX 011 31 20-6228658, telex 13217 INTAX NL. **(Subscription address:** IBFD / International Bureau of Fiscal Documentation USA, Inc., 24 Hudson Street, Kinderhook NY 12106.**)**
**Desc:** Comparative survey systematically examining the practical aspects of taxation at every stage in the life of a company in each of the twelve EC countries as well as Austria, Cyprus, Finland, Norway, Sweden, Switzerland and Turkey.

US
**TAXATION OF ESTATES, GIFTS, AND TRUSTS : CASES AND MATERIALS. Added/Corp** Commerce Clearing House. **VFOAT** Cases and Materials. Taxation of Estates, Gifts, and Trusts. (199?)-. English. an. $56.50. Commerce Clearing House Inc., 4025 West Peterson Avenue, Chicago IL 60646-6085. **Tel** (312)583-8500, FAX (708)940-4600. ***Continues*** *Study of Federal Tax Law. Taxation of Estates, Gifts, and Trusts.*

NE
**TAXATION OF INDIVIDUALS IN EUROPE.** (1992)-. English. sa. $800.00. International Bureau of Fiscal Documentation - IBFD Publications, PO Box 20237, 1000 HE Amsterdam The Netherlands. **Tel** 011 31 20-6267726, FAX 011 31 20-6228658, telex 13217 INTAX NL.
**Desc:** Country-by-country survey, analyzing the taxation of resident and non-resident individuals in Austria, Belgium, Denmark, Finland, Germany, Greece, Ireland, Italy, Norway, Portugal, Spain, Sweden and the United Kingdom.

US
**TAXATION OF MINING OPERATIONS.** English. Matthew Bender & Company Inc., 1275 Broadway, Albany NY 12204. **Tel** (800)833-9844, (518)487-3000. cum. index.

NE
**TAXATION OF PATENT ROYALTIES, DIVIDENDS, INTEREST IN EUROPE. Main/Corp** International Bureau of Fiscal Documentation, Amsterdam. (19??)-. English. Three times a year. $515.00. International Bureau of Fiscal Documentation - IBFD Publications, PO Box 20237, 1000 HE Amsterdam The Netherlands. **Tel** 011 31 20-6267726, FAX 011 31 20-6228658, telex 13217 INTAX NL. **(Subscription address:** IBFD / International Bureau of Fiscal Documentation USA, Inc., 24 Hudson Street, Kinderhook NY 12106.**) ED** B. P. Dik. **Bk Rev. Ad Acc.** ctrl circ.
**Desc:** Guide to all withholding taxes on corporate cross-border payments in 18 West European countries.

●NE
**TAXATION OF PERMANENT ESTABLISHMENTS, THE.** (1993)-. English. Twice a year. $690.00. International Bureau of Fiscal Documentation - IBFD Publications, PO Box 20237, 1000 HE Amsterdam The Netherlands. **Tel** 011 31 20-6267726, FAX 011 31 20-6228658, telex 13217 INTAX NL. **(Subscription address:** IBFD / International Bureau of Fiscal Documentation USA, Inc., 24 Hudson Street, Kinderhook NY 12106.**)**
**Desc:** Offers a systematic analysis of their role in international tax law and their possible impact on international business.

NE
**TAXATION OF PRIVATE INVESTMENT INCOME.** (19??)-. Periodical. English. Three times a year. $515.00 on diskette. International Bureau of Fiscal Documentation - IBFD Publications, PO Box 20237, 1000 HE Amsterdam The Netherlands. **Tel** 011 31 20-6267726, FAX 011 31 20-6228658, telex 13217 INTAX NL. **(Subscription address:** IBFD / International Bureau of Fiscal Documentation USA, Inc., 24 Hudson Street, Kinderhook NY 12106.**) Bk Rev. Ad Acc.** ctrl circ. available on diskette (as The Taxation of Private Investment Income in OECD Countries).
**Desc:** Presents comparative analysis, including tables of effective tax burdens on dividends and interest received by individuals in 17 Western European countries and the United States.

AT
**TAXATION REVENUE, AUSTRALIA. See** Public Administration-Abstracting, Bibliographies and Statistics.

PP
**TAXATION STATISTICS (PORT MORESBY, PAPUA NEW GUINEA). See** Public Administration-Abstracting, Bibliographies and Statistics.

CN/0840-5735
**TAXATION TODAY (WINNIPEG).** (TAXATION TODAY.). [Tax. today]. **Added/Corp** U & R Tax Services. (198?)-. Periodical. English. mo (10 issues). 100.00Can$ (one year), 180.00Can$ (two year), 255.00Can$ (three year). U&R Tax Services, 1345 Pembina Highway, Winnipeg Manitoba R3T 2B6, Canada. **Tel** (204)949-3636, (800)665-5144, FAX (204)284-8954. **DD** 343.7105/2/05. ***Continues*** *Canadian Income Tax Update., 0844-1405.*

NE
**TAXES AND INVESTMENT IN ASIA AND THE PACIFIC.** (1992)-. English. mo. $1,660. International Bureau of Fiscal Documentation - IBFD Publications, PO Box 20237, 1000 HE Amsterdam The Netherlands. **Tel** 011 31 20-6267726, FAX 011 31 20-6228658, telex 13217 INTAX NL. **(Subscription address:** IBFD / International Bureau of Fiscal Documentation USA, Inc., 24 Hudson Street, Kinderhook NY 12106.**)**
**Desc:** Practical guide providing an in-depth country-by-country survey of tax and foreign investment legislation.

NE
**TAXES AND INVESTMENT IN THE MIDDLE EAST.** (19??)-. English. ir (2 binders updated 4 times a year). $630.00. International Bureau of Fiscal Documentation - IBFD Publications, PO Box 20237, 1000 HE Amsterdam The Netherlands. **Tel** 011 31 20-6267726, FAX 011 31 20-6228658, telex 13217 INTAX NL. **LC** LAW. **DD** 346.56/066.
**Desc:** Practical guide to the complex network of legal, administrative, economic and tax measures related to trade and investment within, with and between the Arab countries of the Middle East and Iran.

NE
**TAXES AND INVESTMENT IN THE MIDDLE EAST. SUPPLEMENT. See** Law-Corporate Law.

II/0304-1964
**TAXES AND PLANNING.** Periodical. English. mo. $9.00. Malpani, 11-E Kalpana, Tilanknagar, Sardar Patel Road-4, Bombay India. **LC** LAW. **DD** 343/.54/0405.

US/0040-0181
**TAXES (CHICAGO, ILL.).** (TAXES.). [Taxes]. Vol. 17, No. 1 (Jan. 1939)-. Periodical. English. mo. $140.00. Commerce Clearing House Inc., 4025 West Peterson Avenue, Chicago IL 60646-6085. **Tel** (312)583-8500, FAX (708)940-4600. **ED** Jerry Nestor. **LC** KF6272; .T394. **DD** 343.7304/05; 347.303405. **Circ:** 12,000. available on microfilm and microfiche from University Microfilms International (UMI). ***Continues*** *Tax Magazine, 8755-2221.*
**Desc:** Publishes authoritative articles on legal, accounting and economic aspects of federal and state taxes.
**Ind/Abst** Acad. Search (July 1993-); Account. Tax Datab. (1974-); Account. Art.; Bus. Index (1985-); Bus. Period. Index; Bus. Source (Jul. 1993-); Fed. Tax Artic.; Gen. BusinessFile (1985-); Gen. Period. Index (1985-); Index Leg. Period.; INFO-SOUTH Abstr.; Leg. Resour. Index; Mag. Search; PAIS Int. Print (?-?); SportSearch; Wilson Bus. Abstr.

US
**TAXES (MADISON, WIS.).** (TAXES.). English. an. $1.40. Wisconsin Taxpayers Alliance, 335 West Wilson Street, Madison WI 53703-3694. **Tel** (608)255-4581. **ED** Rindert Kiemel. **Circ:** 47,000.
**Desc:** Contains information on all federal, state and local taxes paid by Wisconsin Taxpayers. Includes federal and state income tax guides.

US/1048-2121
**TAXLINE (CINCINNATI, OHIO).** (TAXLINE.). [Taxline]. **Added/Corp** National Underwriter Company. **VFOAT** National Underwriter Taxline. Vol. 89, No. 3 Mar. (1989)-. Periodical. English. Twelve times a year. $48.00 one year; $70.00 two years. National Underwriter Company, 505 Gest Street, Cincinnati OH 45203-0874. **Tel** (513)721-2140, (800)543-0874. **LC** KF6352; .T39. **DD** 343.7305/05; 347.303505. available on microfilm and microfiche from University Microfilms International (UMI). ***Continues*** *Editors' Report.*
**Desc:** Tax information on legislation, cases, public and private rulings and regulations, concentrating on tax laws relevant to insurance, annuities, employee benefits, business planning, estate planning, and social security.
**Ind/Abst** Account. Tax Datab. (May 1992-) [Full Txt.].

AT
**TAXPAYER. Added/Corp** Taxpayers' Association of New South Wales. (19??)-. Periodical. English. sm. 0.30Aus$ each copy. Niche Publishing Pty Ltd., 165 Fitzroy Street, St. Kilda West 3182 Australia. **Tel** 011 61 3 5255566, FAX 011 61 3 5255627. **LC** HJ4811; .T28. **DD** 336.2/4/0994. ***Supersedes*** *Taxpayers Bulletin.*

CN
**TAXPAYER, THE.** English. Six times a year (also supplements). 55.00Can$. Canadian Taxpayers Federation, #105 - 438 Victoria Avenue East, Regina Saskatchewan SN4 ON7 Canada. **Tel** (306)352-7199.

AT
**TAXPAYER: ANNUAL TAXATION SUMMARY. Added/Corp** Australian Taxpayers' Associations. **VFOAT** Annual Taxation Summary. (19??)-. Periodical. English. an. $36.95. Taxpayers Association of New South Wales, Level 29, Australia Square, 264 George Street, Sydney NSW 2000 Australia. **Tel** 02 241 3299, FAX 02 251 7138. **ED** Peter McDonald. **LC** HJ3106; .T34. **DD** 343/.94.04. Index available. cum. index. **Circ:** 15,000 (ctrl).
**Desc:** Provides information on Australian income tax law.

US/0734-5755
**TAXPAYERS NEWS (HARTFORD, CONN.).** (TAXPAYERS NEWS / CPEC.). Periodical. English. Connecticut Public Expenditure Council, 21 Lewis Street, Hartford CT 06103. **LC** HJ340; .C23. **DD** 336.746. ***Continues*** *CPEC Taxpayer News.*

US/0734-2349
**TAXWISE GIVING.** **VAT** Tax Wise Giving. (1962)-. English. Twelve times a year. $155.00. Taxwise Giving, PO Box 299, 13 Arcadia Road, Old Greenwich CT 06870. **Tel** (800)243-9122, (203)637-4553, FAX (203)637-4572. **ED** Conrad Teitell. Index available (free). **Circ:** 1,400.
**Desc:** A newsletter which alerts development officers and advisors to proposed changes in the law, regulations and revenue rulings that would affect charitable gifts.

US
**TC MEMORANDUM DECISIONS : CONTAINING THE FULL TEXT OF ALL MEMORANDUM DECISIONS OF THE TAX COURT OF THE UNITED STATES RENDERED DURING ... .** **Main/Corp** United States. Tax Court. **Added/Corp** Prentice-Hall, Inc. Maxwell Macmillan (Firm) Research Institute of America, Inc. **VFOAT** T.C. Memorandum Decisions. Vol. 12 (1943)-. English. ir. Maxwell Macmillan Professional Business Division, 910 Sylvan Avenue, Englewood Cliffs NJ 07632-3310. **Tel** (800)431-9025. **(Subscription address:** Prentice Hall, PO Box 801, Englewood, NJ 07632**)** ***Continues*** *United States. Board of Tax Appeals. BTA-TC Memorandum Decisions.*

US
**TC REPORTED DECISIONS; CONTAINING THE FULL TEXT OF ALL REPORTED DECISIONS OF THE TAX COURT OF THE UNITED STATES.** **Main/Corp** United States. Tax Court. **Added/Corp** Prentice-Hall, Inc., New York. **VFOAT** Tax Court Service. Reported Decisions. (19??)-. Periodical. English. wk. Prentice-Hall Law and Business, 270 Sylvan Avenue, Englewood Cliffs NJ 07632. **Tel** (800)223-0231, (201)894-8538, FAX (201)894-8666. **DD** 336.2.

US/0742-0757
**TENNESSEE TAX GUIDE.** (TENNESSEE TAX GUIDE : A COMPREHENSIVE SURVEY OF MAJOR TENNESSEE STATE AND LOCAL TAXES / BY BRADFORD N. FORRISTER.). (1982)-. English. an. $12.95. M. Lee Smith Publishers and Printers, 162 4th Avenue North, PO Box 198867, Nashville TN 37219. **Tel** (615)242-7395, (800)274-6774, FAX (615)256-6601. **ED** Bradford N. Forrister. **LC** HJ11; .T257. **DD** 343.76804; 347.68034. **Circ:** 3,500 (ctrl).
**Desc:** A description of Tennessee State and local taxes.

IT
**TESTO UNICO IMPOSTE DIRETTE.** **See** Law.

US
**TEXAS TAX GUIDE UPDATES.** (19??)-. English. qt. $50.00. Agency Rules Service, PO Box 9366, Austin TX 78766. **Tel** (512)454-3786. **ED** Nita Yeck.

DK
**TOLDVAESENET.** **Main/Corp** Denmark. Direktoratet for Toldvaesenet. (19??)-. Danish. Straudgade 29, 1401 Kobenhavn K Denmark. **LC** HJ6971; .A17.

UK
**TOLLEY'S CAPITAL GAINS TAX / DAVID G. YOUNG, DAVID R. HARRIS.** **See** Law.

UK
**TOLLEY'S CORPORATION TAX.** **Main/Corp** Tolley Publishing Company. English. an (September). £21.95. Tolley Publishing Company Ltd, Tolley House, 2 Addiscombe Road, Croydon, Surrey CR9 5AF United Kingdom. **Tel** 011 44 81 6869141, FAX 011 44 81 6863155, 011 44 81 7600588. **ED** Glyn Saunders and Alan Dolton. **LC** KD5509.Z9; T64. **DD** 343.4106/7; 344.10367.
**Desc:** Covers new tax deduction arrangements, Building Society share provisions, and new, revised corporation tax rate structure.

UK/0305-893X
**TOLLEY'S INCOME TAX.** [Tolley income tax]. (197?)-. English. (September). £25.95. Tolley Publishing Company Ltd, Tolley House, 2 Addiscombe Road, Croydon, Surrey CR9 5AF United Kingdom. **Tel** 011 44 81 6869141, FAX 011 44 81 6863155, 011 44 81 7600588. **ED** Glyn Saunders and David Smailes. **LC** KD5429; .T64. **DD** 343/.41/052. ***Continues*** *Tolley's Income Tax Chart-Manual.*
**Desc:** Covers controversial new benefits-in-kind provisions, mortgage interest relief charges and additional relief for trading losses.

UK
**TOLLEY'S INHERITANCE TAX.** English. an. £19.95. Tolley Publishing Company Ltd, Tolley House, 2 Addiscombe Road, Croydon, Surrey CR9 5AF United Kingdom. **Tel** 011 44 81 6869141, FAX 011 44 81 6863155, 011 44 81 7600588. **ED** Patrick Noakes and Stephen Savory.
**Desc:** Covers the increase in level of nil rate band and details of relevant new cases.

UK
**TOLLEY'S OFFICIAL TAX STATEMENTS.** (19??)-. English. an (November). £32.95. Tolley Publishing Company Ltd, Tolley House, 2 Addiscombe Road, Croydon, Surrey CR9 5AF United Kingdom. **Tel** 011 44 81 6869141, FAX 011 44 81 6863155, 011 44 81 7600588. **ED** John Boulding.
**Desc:** Contains the full text of all Inland Revenue Extra-Statutory Concessions and Statements of Practice together with important Press Releases and CCAB/ICAEW Statements.

UK
**TOLLEY'S PRACTICAL TAX.** English. sm. £105.00. Tolley Publishing Company Ltd, Tolley House, 2 Addiscombe Road, Croydon, Surrey CR9 5AF United Kingdom. **Tel** 011 44 81 6869141, FAX 011 44 81 6863155, 011 44 81 7600588.
**Desc:** Concentrates solely on taxation matters for the busy accountant and taxation practitioner. Covers all UK taxes, both direct and indirect, news of changes in law and practice, and brief summaries of all relavent cases with expert analysis. Also reports on IR Statements of Practice, Extra-Statutory Concessions, Statutory Instruments and Parliamentary written answers.

UK
**TOLLEY'S PROPERTY TAXES.** (19??)-. English. an (October). £32.95. Tolley Publishing Company Ltd, Tolley House, 2 Addiscombe Road, Croydon, Surrey CR9 5AF United Kingdom. **Tel** 011 44 81 6869141, FAX 011 44 81 6863155, 011 44 81 7600588. **ED** Robert W Maas.
**Desc:** A guide to the taxation provisions relating to land transactions. Includes expert advice on both the application and effect of taxes on property. Contains practical planning ideas and numerous worked examples. Also provides information on recent developments in case law.

UK
**TOLLEY'S STAMP DUTIES & STAMP DUTY RESERVE TAX.** (19??)-. English. an. £16.95. Tolley Publishing Company Ltd, Tolley House, 2 Addiscombe Road, Croydon, Surrey CR9 5AF United Kingdom. **Tel** 011 44 81 6869141, FAX 011 44 81 6863155, 011 44 81 7600588.

UK
**TOLLEY'S TAX CASES.** **See** Law.

UK
**TOLLEY'S TAX COMPUTATIONS.** English. £28.95. Tolley Publishing Company Ltd, Tolley House, 2 Addiscombe Road, Croydon, Surrey CR9 5AF United Kingdom. **Tel** 011 44 81 6869141, FAX 011 44 81 6863155, 011 44 81 7600588. **ED** David Smailes, Stephen Savory and Robert Wareham.
**Desc:** Covers the main UK taxes. Provides detailed explanatory notes for further clarification. Contains over 460 worked examples.

UK
**TOLLEY'S TAX DATA.** **Added/Corp** Tolley Publishing Company. **VFOAT** Tax Data. (1982)-. Periodical. English. an. £13.95. Tolley Publishing Company Ltd, Tolley House, 2 Addiscombe Road, Croydon, Surrey CR9 5AF United Kingdom. **Tel** 011 44 81 6869141, FAX 011 44 81 6863155, 011 44 81 7600588. **ED** Alan Dolton and Nicholas Bowen. **LC** HJ2621; .T638. **DD** 343.4104/205; 344.1034205.
**Desc:** Covers rates, allowances and exemptions on all the main taxes in the United Kingdom, including inheritance tax.

UK
**TOLLEY'S TAX PLANNING.** English. an (December). £60.00 (two volumes). Tolley Publishing Company Ltd, Tolley House, 2 Addiscombe Road, Croydon, Surrey CR9 5AF United Kingdom. **Tel** 011 44 81 6869141, FAX 011 44 81 6863155, 011 44 81 7600588. **ED** Glyn Saunders, MA.
**Desc:** Contains clear explanation and practical taxation strategies across the whole range of financial decision-making required of individuals, partnerships and corporate bodies. Provides important new material on deceased estates, EC Directives, termination payments and interest relief.

UK
**TOLLEY'S TAX TABLES.** (19??)-. English. an (March). £8.95. Tolley Publishing Company Ltd, Tolley House, 2 Addiscombe Road, Croydon, Surrey CR9 5AF United Kingdom. **Tel** 011 44 81 6869141, FAX 011 44 81 6863155, 011 44 81 7600588. **ED** Paul C Baker and Peter Diggles. **LC** HJ2621; .T64. **DD** 336.2/00942.
**Desc:** Brings together the results of time-consuming computations in easy to read tables. Includes the main taxes plus social security, take home pay, statutory sick pay and charitable covenants. Contains a useful summary of the 1991 Budget Proposals and details of the National Insurance contributions for 1991-92.

UK
**TOLLEY'S TAXATION IN THE CHANNEL ISLANDS AND ISLE OF MAN.** **VFOAT** Taxation in the Channel Islands and Isle of Man. (1977)-. English. an (November). £19.95. Tolley Publishing Company Ltd, Tolley House, 2 Addiscombe Road, Croydon, Surrey CR9 5AF United Kingdom. **Tel** 011 44 81 6869141, FAX 011 44 81 6863155, 011 44 81 7600588. **ED** John Boulding. **LC** KDG162; .L56. **DD** 343.423/404. ***Continues*** *Tolley's Taxation in the Channel Islands and Isle of Man.*
**Desc:** Provides a complete overview of the taxation structure and company law of these tax havens. Includes tax rates and allowances for at least six years. Also gives details of the various provisions of the Isle of Man Income Tax Bill 1991.

UK
**TOLLEY'S TAXATION IN THE REPUBLIC OF IRELAND / BY NIGEL A.D. LAMBERT LLM, BARRISTER & ERIC L. HARVEY, FCA AITI.** **See** Law.

UK
**TOLLEY'S TRADING IN EUROPE.** **See** Business-Commerce.

UK
**TOLLEY'S VALUE ADDED TAX.** English. £22.95. Tolley Publishing Company Ltd, Tolley House, 2 Addiscombe Road, Croydon, Surrey CR9 5AF United Kingdom. **Tel** 011 44 81 6869141, FAX 011 44 81 6863155, 011 44 81 7600588. **ED** Robert Wareham and Nicholas Bowen.
**Desc:** Covers changes in bad debt relief, serious misdeclaration penalties and registration thresholds. Customs and excise notices and leaflets are also included.

UK
**TOLLEY'S VAT CASES.** English. an (April). £49.95. Tolley Publishing Company Ltd, Tolley House, 2 Addiscombe Road, Croydon, Surrey CR9 5AF United Kingdom. **Tel** 011 44 81 6869141, FAX 011 44 81 6863155, 011 44 81 7600588. **ED** Alan Dolton and Hugh Mainprice.
**Desc:** Concise, expert summaries of more than 5,300 VAT tribunal decisions and court cases. Contains expanded coverage of decisions of the European Court of Justice and full reference to legislation, statutory instruments and Customs and Excise notices and leaflets.

UK
**TOLLEY'S VAT PLANNING.** (19??)-. English. an (November). £29.95. Tolley Publishing Company Ltd, Tolley House, 2 Addiscombe Road, Croydon, Surrey CR9 5AF United Kingdom. **Tel** 011 44 81 6869141, FAX 011 44 81 6863155, 011 44 81 7600588.
**Desc:** Comprehensive, practical advice on achieving the optimum tax position presented in readable style. Contains all the changes made by relevant legislation and cases. Each chapter is written by a practising expert.

BS
**TOWN COUNCILS ESTIMATES OF REVENUE AND EXPENDITURE, RECURRENT BUDGET.** ***Ceased.*** **Main/Corp** Botswana. (19??)-Ceased (19??). English. **LC** HJ9080N.; A25b. **DD** 352/.12/09681. ***Continues*** *Town Councils Estimates of Expenditure and Income, Recurrent Budget and Capital Budgets.*

US
**TOWN, VILLAGE AND CITY TAXES.** **VFOAT** Town, Village & City Taxes. (1968)-. English. an. Department of Revenue / Wisconsin, PO Box 8933, 125 South Webster Street, Madison WI 53708. **Tel** (608)266-8661. **Circ:** 500 (ctrl). ***Formed by the union of*** *Town Taxes* ***and*** *Village and City Taxes.*
**Desc:** A listing of the various property taxes levied in each town, village, and city in Wisconsin. Resources provided and expended is a listing of revenues and expenses for each town, village, city and county in Wisconsin.

CN/1183-0042
**TPS ET LES TAXES A LA CONSOMMATION, LA.** [TPS taxes consomm.]. **Added/Corp** Editeurs Richard De Boo. **VAT** Taxe sur les Produits et Services et les Taxes a la Consommation. Vol. 1, No. 1 (Dec. 1990/Jan. 1991)-. Periodical. English. ir. 175.00Can$ per year. Richard de Boo Publishers, 81 Curlew Drive, Don Mills Ontario M3A 3P7 Canada. **Tel** (416)445-4940. **DD** 343.7105/52.

UK
**TRADE FINANCE REVIEW.** (19??)-. English. mo. $580.00. Euromoney Publications PLC, Nestor House, Playhouse Yard, London EC4Z 5EX England. **Tel** 011 44 71 779 8888, FAX 011 44 71 779 8617, telex 290700 EUROMON G.

●CN/1189-4210
**TRANSCRIPT OF STANDING COMMITTEE ON PUBLIC ACCOUNTS.** [Transcr. Standing Comm. Public Acc.]. **Main/Corp** New Brunswick. Legislative Assembly. Standing Committee on Public Accounts. 1st Meeting (Mar. 10, 1992)-. Periodical. English. **DD** 354.715/100723.

# Public Administration — Public Finance and Taxation

US/0733-0030
**TRAVEL AND ENTERTAINMENT, BUSINESS OR PLEASURE?.** [Travel entertain. bus. pleas.]. (19??)-. English. an (May). $6.50. Commerce Clearing House Inc., 4025 West Peterson Avenue, Chicago IL 60646-6085. **Tel** (312)583-8500, FAX (708)940-4600. **ED** A. E. Schechter. **LC** KF6395.T7; T7. **DD** 343.7305/23; 347.303523.
**Desc:** Helps distinguish between travel and entertainment expenses that qualify as legitimate business deductions and those that do not.

UK/0960-8532
**TREASURY BULLETIN. Ceased.** (1990)-Vol. 4, No. 2, (1993). Bulletin. English. Three times a year. Her Majesty's Stationery Office, 51 Nine Elms Lane, London SW8 5DR England. **Tel** 011 44 71 873 8459, 011 44 71 873 8499, FAX 011 44 71 873 8499, 011 44 71 873 8456, telex 297138. **(Subscription address:** Her Majestys Stationery Offic, PO Box 276 Public Centre, London SW8 5DT England)

DR
**TRIBUTACION. See** Law.

US
**TRUST ADMINISTRATION AND TAXATION.** (19??)-. English. ir. Price varies. Matthew Bender & Company Inc., 1275 Broadway, Albany NY 12204. **Tel** (800)833-9844, (518)487-3000.

FM
**TRUST TERRITORY BUDGET PLAN. Main/Corp** Pacific Islands (Trust Territory). Congress of Micronesia. Joint Committee on Program and Budget Planning. English. Congress of Micronesia Saipan, Capitol Hill, Saipan 96950 Trust Territory of the Pacific States. **LC** HJ99.M3; A23A. **DD** 354/.96/500722.
**Desc:** Vols. for 1976 include supplemental request for previous year.

CC
**TSAI CHENG.** (19??)-. Periodical. Chinese. mo. $20.65. **(Subscription address:** China International Book Trading Corporation, PO Box 399, Library Service Department, Beijing 100044 People's Republic of China.) **LC** HJ1401; .T77. **DD** 336.51. **Absorbed** Jen Min Shui Wu.

US
**TSAI CHENG NIEN CHIEN.** Began with Vol. for 1935. Chinese. Center for Chinese Research Materials / Washington DC, Association of Research Libraries, 1527 New Hampshire Avenue, Washington DC 20036. **LC** HJ76; .A17. **DD** 336.51.

CC
**TSAI CHENG YEN CHIU. VFOAT** Cai Zheng Yan Jiu. Periodical. Chinese. bm. 0.50. Pei-Ching Pao Kan Fa Hsing Chu, Beijing, People's Republic of China. **Tel** 483531. **LC** HJ77.6; .A17. **DD** 336.51.

CC
**TSAI MAO CHING CHI. Added/Corp** Chung-kuo She Hui Ko Hsueh Yuan. Tsai Mao Wu Tzu Ching Chi Yen Chiu So. **VFOAT** Finance and Trade Economics. (January 1981)-. Periodical. Chinese. Twelve times a year. $38.88. **(Subscription address:** China International Book Trading Corporation, PO Box 399, Library Service Department, Beijing 100044 People's Republic of China.) **LC** HJ1401; .T796. **DD** 336.51/05.

UK/0950-3234
**TURKEY MONITOR. Title Change.** [Turk. monit.]. (1986)-(1993). Periodical. English. mo. The Economist Intelligence Unit, 40 Duke Street, London W1A 1DW England. **Tel** 011 44 71 8301000. **(Subscription address:** US: Economist Intelligence Unit, 111 West 57th Street, New York, NY 10019; Europe: Economist Intelligence Unit, PO Box 154, Dartford Kent DA1 1QB England) **ED** Stephen Harris. **DD** 330.9561038. **Bk Rev**. **Circ:** 400 (ctrl). **Absorbed by** Business Middle East.
**Desc:** Provides guidance and analysis on the meaning and practical effects of the UK financial services regulatory system. Contains news on official announcements and procedures by every SRO and all the main RPBs. Clarifies compliance regulations and includes international aspects.

●US
**TWO YEAR BUDGET/ CITY OF PALO ALTO. Main/Corp** Palo Alto (Calif.). City Manager. **Added/Corp** Palo Alto (Calif.). City Council. (1992)-. English. be. **Continues** Annual Budget/ City of Palo Alto.

US/0095-8069
**U.S. BUDGET RECOMMENDATIONS. Main/Corp** Nebraska. State Office of Planning and Programming. (19??)-. English. Office of Planning and Programming, PO Box 94601, Lincoln NE 68509. **LC** HJ2051; .N37a. **DD** 353.007/22.

US
**U.S. CUSTOM HOUSE GUIDE. VFOAT** US Custom House Guide; Custom House Guide. (1988)-. English. an. $399.00 US; $419.00 Canada; $449.00 other. North American Publishing Company, 401 North Broad Street, Philadelphia PA 19108. **Tel** (215)238-5300, (800)777-8074, FAX (215)238-5283. **LC** KF6652; .O35. **Continues** Official U.S. Custom House Guide, 0891-1517.

US/0277-402X
**U.S. TAX CASES.** [U. S. tax cases]. **Main/Corp** Commerce Clearing House. **Added/Corp** United States. Courts. United States. Dept. of the Treasury. United States. Tax Court. **VFOAT** US Tax Cases; United States Tax Cases. **VAT** United States Tax Cases. Vol. 35 (1936)-. Periodical. English. sa. $29.50. Commerce Clearing House Inc., 4025 West Peterson Avenue, Chicago IL 60646-6085. **Tel** (312)583-8500, FAX (708)940-4600. **ED** A.E. Schechter. **LC** KF6280.A2; C63. **DD** 343/.73/0402643.
**Desc:** 1935-42 decisions originally reported currently in the Standard federal tax service, and 1941-42 also in the Federal estate and gift tax service, and in the federal excise tax.

DK/0905-7544
**UDGIFTSANALYSER. Added/Corp** Denmark. Budgetdepartementet. **VFOAT** Udgifts Analyser. (1990)-. Danish. Finansministeriet Budgetdepartementet, Christiansborg Slotsplads 1, DK-1218 Kbenhavn K Denmark. **LC** HJ56; .A24a. **Continues** Redegrelse om den Offentlige Sektor, 0904-3098.

US
**UNDERSTANDING TAXES. FARM SUPPLEMENT ... EDITION. Added/Corp** United States. Internal Revenue Service. **VFOAT** Farm Supplement ... Edition. (197?)-. English. an. **Continues** Understanding Taxes. Farm Edition, Student Text.

UK/0963-8156
**UNITED KINGDOM OIL AND GAS. See** Petroleum and Natural Gas.

US
**UNITED STATES AIR FORCE STATISTICAL DIGEST (ABRIDGED) FISCAL YEAR ... ESTIMATE / PREPARED BY DEPUTY ASSISTANT SECRETARY (COST AND ECONOMICS), ASSISTANT SECRETARY OF THE AIR FORCE (FINANCIAL MANAGEMENT AND COMPTROLLER OF THE AIR FORCE). See** Military and Defense.

US/0083-0534
**UNITED STATES EXCISE TAX GUIDE. Main/Corp** Commerce Clearing House. (19??)-. English. an (June). $22.50. Commerce Clearing House Inc., 4025 West Peterson Avenue, Chicago IL 60646-6085. **Tel** (312)583-8500, FAX (708)940-4600. **ED** A. E. Schechter. **DD** 336.2.
**Desc:** Thoroughly examines all excise taxes. Fully reflects changes brought about by the Revenue Reconciliation Act of 1993, including the repeal of the luxury taxes on aircraft, boats, jewelry and furs.

US
**UNITED STATES GENERALIZED SYSTEM OF PREFERENCES, CARIBBEAN BASIN INITIATIVE. Added/Corp** Organization of American States. Dept. of Economic Affairs. Organization of American States. Executive Secretariat for Economic and Social Affairs. (1984)-. English. General Secretariat of the Organization of American States, 1889 F Street NW, Washington DC 20006. **Tel** (202)789-6284. **LC** KF6708.P7; A138. **DD** 343.7305/6/02636; 347.3035602636. **Continues** United States Generalized System of Preferences.

●US
**UNITED STATES TAX REPORTER.** (Aug. 1992)-. English. Research Institute of America, 117 East Stevens Avenue, Valhalla NY 10595. **Tel** (800)431-9025. **(Subscription address:** Research Institute of America, 910 Sylvan Avenue, Englewood NJ 07632.) **Continues** Federal Taxes.

US
**UPDATED OHIO EXPENDITURES.** English. Governmental Research Institute, 502 Ten-Ten Euclid Building, Cleveland OH 44115. **LC** HJ11; .O348. **DD** 336.3/9/09771.

US/0275-1119
**UPDATES AND SUPPLEMENTS TO ACCOMPANY WEST'S FEDERAL TAXATION. VFOAT** West's Federal Taxation. Updates and Supplements. No. 1 (Jan. 15, 1981)-. English. bw. West Publishing Company, 610 Opperman Drive, PO Box 64526, Eagan MN 55123-1308. **Tel** (612)687-5618, (800)328-9352, FAX (612)687-5388, (800)562-2329. **(Subscription telephone:** FAX (612)688-3570) **LC** KF6335; .W47 SUPPL. **DD** 343.7304; 347.3034.

US/0083-1700
**US MASTER TAX GUIDE.** [U. S. master tax guide]. **Added/Corp** Commerce Clearing House. **VFOAT** Master Tax Guide. (1943)-. English. an. $21.00. Commerce Clearing House Inc., 4025 West Peterson Avenue, Chicago IL 60646-6085. **Tel** (312)583-8500, FAX (708)940-4600. **LC** KF6272.5; .C59. **DD** 343. **Continues** United States Master Tax Guide.
**Desc:** Explains the basic rules affecting personal and business income tax.

US
**UTAH TAXPAYER.** (19??)-. English. mo. $25.00. Utah Taxpayer Association, 1578 West 1700 S Street, Suite 105, Salt Lake City UT 84104. **Tel** (801)972-8814.

FI/0784-9745
**VALTION MENOT LAANEITTAIN. VFOAT** Statens Utgifter Lansvis. Finnish (Swedish). an. Tilastokeskus, PL 504, Annankatu 44, 00101 Helsinki Finland. **Tel** 358-0-17341, FAX 358-0-17342474, telex 1002111 TILASTO SF. **LC** HJ55.3; .A298.

NE
**VALUE ADDED TAXATION IN EUROPE.** (1973)-. English. Three times a year. $915.00. International Bureau of Fiscal Documentation - IBFD Publications, PO Box 20237, 1000 HE Amsterdam The Netherlands. **Tel** 011 31 20-6267726, FAX 011 31 20-6228658, telex 13217 INTAX NL. **(Subscription address:** IBFD / International Bureau of Fiscal Documentation USA, Inc., 24 Hudson Street, Kinderhook NY 12106.)
**Desc:** A comparative survey of the system of value added taxation in the twelve EC countries, Austria, Cyprus, Hungary, Norway, Sweden and Turkey.

NE
**VALUE ADDED TAXATION IN EUROPE. SUPPLEMENT.** (19??)-. English. qt. $915.00 (includes three binders and four supplements). International Bureau of Fiscal Documentation - IBFD Publications, PO Box 20237, 1000 HE Amsterdam The Netherlands. **Tel** 011 31 20-6267726, FAX 011 31 20-6228658, telex 13217 INTAX NL.

US/0147-6971
**VALUE OF PUBLIC UTILITY REAL AND PERSONAL PROPERTY BY COUNTY. See** Public Administration.

●UK/0964-5985
**VAT PLANNING.** [VAT plan.]. **VFOAT** Value Added Tax Planning. (1991)-. Periodical. English. mo. £165.00. Butterworth & Co. Ltd. / Kent, England, Borough Green, Sevenoaks Kent TN15 8PH England. **Tel** 011 44 732-884567, FAX 011 44 732-885996. **ED** Alan Buckett. **DD** 336.27140941. **Continues in part** Customs Duty Planning.
**Desc:** Designed to keep tax practitioners up to date with all new and proposed developments in the complex areas of VAT and customs duties.

UK
**VAT TRIBUNALS REPORTS. VFOAT** Value Added Tax Tribunals Reports. (19??)-. English. ir. Her Majesty's Stationery Office, 51 Nine Elms Lane, London SW8 5DR England. **Tel** 011 44 71 873 8459, 011 44 71 873 8499, FAX 011 44 71 873 8499, 011 44 71 873 8456, telex 297138. **(Subscription address:** Her Majesty's Stationery Office, PO Box 276, Publications Centre, London SW8 5DT England.)

FI
**VEROHALLINNON KASIKIRJA: MAATILATALOUDEN VEROTUS. Main/Corp** Finland. Verohallitus. (19??)-. Finnish. **LC** LAW.

FI
**VEROHALLITUKSEN YHTENAISTAMISOHJEET VUODELTA ... TOIMITETTAVAA VEROTUSIA VARTEN. Main/Corp** Finland. Verohallitus. **VFOAT** Verohallituksen Yhtenaistamisohjeet. Finnish. an. **LC** LAW.

SA
**VERSLAG VAN DIE OUDITEUR-GENERAAL OOR DIE REKENINGS VAN DIE ONTWIKKELINGSRAAD SUID-ORANJE-VRYSTAAT-GEBIED VIR DIE BOEKJAAR ... / REPORT OF THE AUDITOR-GENERAL ON THE ACCOUNTS OF THE SOUTHERN ORANGE FREE STATE AREA DEVELOPMENT BOARD FOR THE FINANCIAL YEAR ... . Added/Corp** South Africa. Office of the Auditor-General. South Africa. Southern Orange Free State Development Board. **VFOAT** Report of the Auditor-General on the Accounts of the Southern Orange Free State Area Development Board for the Financial Year ... . (1984)-(198?). Afrikaans (English). Government Printer / South Africa, Bosman Street, Private Bag X85, Pretoria 0001 South Africa. **Tel** 011 27 12 3239731 Ext. 262. **LC** HJ9082.3.A55; O728. **DD** 354.6850082/05. **Continues** South Africa. Dept. of the

# Public Administration —Public Finance and Taxation

*Auditor-General. Verslag van die Ouditeur-Generaal oor die Administrasieraad, Suid-Oranje-Vrystaatgebied.*

**SA**
**VERSLAG VAN DIE OUDITEUR-GENERAAL OOR DIE REKENINGS VAN DIE RAAD VIR INMAAKVRUGTE VIR DIE BOEKJAAR ... .** See Food and Food Industry.

**SA**
**VERSLAG VAN DIE OUDITEUR-GENERAAL VOOR DIE SUIDWES-AFRIKAREKENING WAT DEEL UITMAAK VAN DIE STAATSINKOMSTEFONDS VAN DIE REPUBLIEK VAN SUID-AFRIKA. Main/Corp** South Africa. Dept. of the Auditor-General. **VFOAT** Report of the Auditor-General on the South West Africa Account Which Forms Part of the State Revenue Fund of the Republic of South Africa. Afrikaans (English). R11.45. Government Printer / South Africa, Bosman Street, Private Bag X85, Pretoria 0001 South Africa. **Tel** 011 27 12 3239731 Ext. 262. **LC** HJ83.3; .A17A.

**II**
**VINIYOJANA LEKHE, UTTARA PRADESA SARAKARA. Main/Corp** India. Comptroller and Auditor-General. Hindi (Hindi). **LC** HJ9927.I4; I55Y.

VI/0735-9926
**VIRGIN ISLANDS OF THE UNITED STATES. GOVERNOR. BUDGET.** (THE VIRGIN ISLANDS EXECUTIVE BUDGET.). **Main/Corp** Virgin Islands of the United States. Governor. English. an. Office of the Governor / Virgin Islands, Charlotte Amalie, St Thomas Virgin Islands. **LC** HJ29; .A22. **DD** 354.7297/220072256/05. *Continues Budget / Virgin Islands of the United States. Governor.*

US/0099-2186
**VIRGINIA ASSESSMENT/SALES RATIO STUDY. Main/Corp** Virginia. Dept. of Taxation. English. an. Department of Taxation / Virginia, Richmond VA 23215. **LC** HJ4277; .A5A. **DD** 336.2/2/09755.

**US**
**VIRGINIA, LOCAL TAXES ON MANUFACTURERS. Added/Corp** Virginia. Dept. of Economic Development. **VFOAT** Local Taxes on Manufacturers. English. Governor's Office, Division of Industrial Development, State Office Building, Richmond VA 23219. **LC** HJ9330; .V5a. **DD** 336.24/3/09755. *Continues Local Taxes on Manufacturers in Virginia.*

US/0735-9004
**VIRGINIA TAX REVIEW.** See Law.

US/0889-3543
**VOICE (FRANKLIN, WIS.), THE.** See Medical Science and Technology-Hospital Administration and Medical Centers.

**US**
**VOLUNTEER HAPPENINGS. Added/Corp** United States. Internal Revenue Service. 20th Anniversary Revue (1990)-. English. Internal Revenue Service, 1111 Constitution Avenue NW, Washington DC 20224. *Continues Volunteer Guidelines.*

**UK**
**WAKEFORD MANUAL EMPLOYEE TAXATION.** (19??)-. English. Three times a year. Price varies per issue. Butterworth & Co. Ltd. / Kent, England, Borough Green, Sevenoaks Kent TN15 8PH England. **Tel** 011 44 732-884567, FAX 011 44 732-885996.

CN/1184-7468
**WARD'S TAX LAW AND PLANNING. INFORMATION CIRCULARS AND RULINGS.** [Ward's tax law plan., Inf. circ. rulings]. **Added/Corp** Davies, Ward & Beck (Firm). **VFOAT** Information Circulars and Rulings; Ward's Information Circulars and Rulings. (1990)-. English. Carswell / Canada, 2075 Kennedy Road, Scarborough Ontario M1T 3V4 Canada. **Tel** (416)609-3800, (800)387-5164. **DD** 343.7105/2.

CN/1184-745X
**WARD'S TAX LAW AND PLANNING. INTERPRETATION BULLETINS.** [Ward's tax law plan., Interpret. bull.]. **VFOAT** Interpretation Bulletins; Ward's Interpretation Bulletins. (1991)-. English. Carswell / Canada, 2075 Kennedy Road, Scarborough Ontario M1T 3V4 Canada. **Tel** (416)609-3800, (800)387-5164. **DD** 343.7105/2.

CN/1184-1494
**WARD'S TAX TREATIES.** [Ward's tax treaties]. **VFOAT** Ward's Tax Law and Planning. Tax Treaties. (1991)-. English. an. Carswell / Canada, 2075 Kennedy Road, Scarborough Ontario M1T 3V4 Canada. **Tel** (416)609-3800, (800)387-5164. **DD** 341.4/844/026471.

**IO**
**WARTA BEA CUKA. VFOAT** WBC. Indonesian. Public Relations Direktorat Jendral Bea Dan Cukai, Jalan Jendral A Yani By Pass, Jakarta Indonesia. **LC** HJ69; .R1274A.

**US**
**WASHINGTON STATE RESOURCE DIRECTORY FOR LOCAL JURISDICTIONS. Added/Corp** Washington (State). Planning and Community Affairs Agency. Local Government Services Division. (19??)-. Directory. English. 400 Capitol Center Building, Olympia WA 98504. **LC** HJ755; .W37. **DD** 336.1/85.

US/0749-8071
**WEALTH FORMULA, THE.** Vol. 3, No. 10 (Oct. 1984)-. Periodical. English. mo $77.00. Wealth Formula, 10076 Boca Entrade Boulevard, PO Box 307, Boca Raton FL 33431-0907. **Tel** (407)483-2600. **ED** Mark M Ford. **DD** 332. *Continues Financial Planning Strategist, 0731-9177.*

US/0271-6119
**WELCOME TO THE TAX REVOLT.** 1980/81-. English. $20.00. Bill Greenes Tycoon Class, PO Box 280664, San Francisco CA 94128-0664. **LC** KF6297.Z9; G7. **DD** 343.7304.

**SA**
**WERKLIKE EN VERWAGTE KAPITAALBESTEDING VAN DIE OPENBARE SEKTOR. VFOAT** Actual and Anticipated Capital Expenditure of the Public Sector. Afrikaans. Government Printer / South Africa, Bosman Street, Private Bag X85, Pretoria 0001 South Africa. **Tel** 011 27 12 3239731 Ext. 262. *Continues Verwagte Kapitaalbesteding van die Openbare Sektor.*

**US**
**WEST GERMANY. Ceased. Added/Corp** Ernst & Whinney. (19??)-(19??). English. **LC** HC281; .W47. *Continues West Germany (Ernst & Ernst).*

US/1043-3961
**WEST-TAX PREPARER TO ACCOMPANY WEST'S FEDERAL TAXATION.** (WEST-TAX PREPARER ... TO ACCOMPANY WEST'S FEDERAL TAXATION [COMPUTER FILE].). **Added/Corp** West Publishing Company. **VFOAT** Student Manual to Accompany West-Tax Preparer. **VAT** West Tax Preparer ... To Accompany West's Federal Taxation. (19??)-. English. West Publishing Company, 610 Opperman Drive, PO Box 64526, Eagan MN 55123-1308. **Tel** (612)687-5618, (800)328-9352, FAX (612)687-5388, (800)562-2329. **LC** KF6289; .W472. **DD** 343.7305/2; 347.30352. **Desc:** System requirements: IBM PC, XT, AT, or compatible system, Texas Instrument Professional Computer, NCR or DEC Rainbow Personal Computer, 128K or available memory, MS-DOS or PC-DOS. Available on 5 1/4" diskettes.

US/0008-106X
**WESTERN FINANCIAL JOURNAL. VFOAT** California-Western Financial Journal. V. 3, No. 7- July 1970-. Periodical. English. mo. $18.00. California Western Financial Journal, PO Box 76974, Los Angeles CA 90005. *Continues California Financial Journal, 0575-5662.*

US/0734-9904
**WESTERN TAX.** See Law.

US/8755-0083
**WESTERN TAX REVIEW.** [West. tax rev.]. **Added/Corp** Western Tax Association. **VFOAT** WTR. Vol. 1, No. 1 (June 1979)-. Periodical. English. sa. $50.00. Western Washington University / College of Business and Economics, c/o R. Singleton, Billingham WA 98225-9072. **Tel** (206)650-3896, FAX (206)650-4844. **ED** Ron Singleton. **LC** HJ9; .W47. **DD** 343. **Bk Rev. Pr Rev. Circ:** 200 (ctrl). **Desc:** Government taxes, budgets, deficits, fiscal policy and efficiency.

**II**
**WESTERN TIMES ANNUAL.** English. an. 65.00. Mobel Book Merchant D-6 Ojas Apts, S M Road, Ambawadi Ahmedabad 380015 India. **LC** HG187.I4; W47. **DD** 336.54/75.

US/0749-1034
**WEST'S FEDERAL TAX MANUAL WITH WESTLAW.** See Law.

US/0277-5158
**WEST'S FEDERAL TAX SYSTEM.** See Law.

US/0741-5184
**WEST'S FEDERAL TAXATION. COMPREHENSIVE VOLUME.** [West's fed. tax., Compr. vol.]. **VFOAT** Comprehensive Volume. 1983 Annual Ed.-. English. an. West Publishing Company, 610 Opperman Drive, PO Box 64526, Eagan MN 55123-1308. **Tel** (612)687-5618, (800)328-9352, FAX (612)687-5388, (800)562-2329. **(Subscription telephone:** FAX (612)688-3570) **LC** KF6289; .W47. **DD** 343.7305/2; 347.30352.

US/0270-5265
**WEST'S FEDERAL TAXATION. CORPORATIONS, PARTNERSHIPS, ESTATES AND TRUSTS.** [West's Fed. tax., Corp. partnersh. estates trusts]. **VFOAT** Corporations, Partnerships, Estates and Trusts. English. an. West Publishing Company, 610 Opperman Drive, PO Box 64526, Eagan MN 55123-1308. **Tel** (612)687-5618, (800)328-9352, FAX (612)687-5388, (800)562-2329. **(Subscription telephone:** FAX (612)688-3570) **LC** KF6335; .W47. **DD** 343.7305/2044; 347/30352044.

US/0741-532X
**WEST'S FEDERAL TAXATION. FEDERAL TAX FORMS. VFOAT** Federal Tax Forms. English. West Publishing Company, 610 Opperman Drive, PO Box 64526, Eagan MN 55123-1308. **Tel** (612)687-5618, (800)328-9352, FAX (612)687-5388, (800)562-2329. **(Subscription telephone:** FAX (612)688-3570) **LC** KF6335.A65; W47. **DD** 343.7305/2044; 347.30352044.

US/0272-0329
**WEST'S FEDERAL TAXATION. INDIVIDUAL INCOME TAXES.** [West's Fed. tax., Individ. income taxes]. **Added/Corp** West Publishing Company. **VFOAT** Individual Income Taxes. (19??)-. English. ir. West Publishing Company, 610 Opperman Drive, PO Box 64526, Eagan MN 55123-1308. **Tel** (612)687-5618, (800)328-9352, FAX (612)687-5388, (800)562-2329. **LC** KF6369; .W47. **DD** 343.7305/2.

US/1068-8943
**WEST'S FEDERAL TAXATION. INDIVIDUAL PRACTICE SETS.** (WEST'S FEDERAL TAXATION. INDIVIDUAL PRACTICE SETS / PREPARED BY JOHN B. BARRACK). [West's fed. tax., Individ. pract. sets]. **Added/Corp** West Publishing Co. **VFOAT** Individual Practice Sets. (199?)-. English. West Publishing Company, 610 Opperman Drive, PO Box 64526, Eagan MN 55123-1308. **Tel** (612)687-5618, (800)328-9352, FAX (612)687-5388, (800)562-2329. **LC** KF6369,3; W47. **DD** 343.7305/2/0269; 347.303520269. *Continues in part West's Federal Taxation. Practice Sets, 0749-1476.*

●**US**
**WEST'S TAX LAW DICTIONARY.** See Law.

US/0898-9516
**WG & L TAX PLANNING ANNUAL.** [WG & L tax plan. annu.]. **Added/Corp** Warren, Gorham & Lamont, Inc. **VFOAT** WG and L Tax Planning Annual; Tax Planning Annual. **VAT** Warren, Gorham & Lamont Tax Planning Annual. (1989)-. English. an. $98.00. Warren Gorham & Lamont Inc., Park Square Building, 31 St. James Avenue, Boston MA 02116-4112. **Tel** (617)423-2020, (800)950-1207, FAX (617)423-2026. **LC** KF6297.Z9; W45. **DD** 343.7304; 347.3034. Index available. **Pr Rev.**

US/1056-6554
**WG&L TAX PLANNING CHECKLISTS. VFOAT** Tax Planning Checklists. **VAT** Warren, Gorham & Lamont, Tax Planning Checklists. (1991)-. English. ir (1 issue). $105.00 US and Canada; $136.50 other. Warren Gorham & Lamont Inc., Park Square Building, 31 St. James Avenue, Boston MA 02116-4112. **Tel** (617)423-2020, (800)950-1207, FAX (617)423-2026.

●**US**/1075-0223
**WGL TAX JOURNAL DIGEST, THE.** [WGL tax j. dig.]. **Added/Corp** Warren Gorham Lamont. **VFOAT** Warren Gorham Lamont Tax Journal Digest; Tax Journal Digest. **VAT** Warren Gorham Lamont tax journal digest. (1993)-. English. an. $51.00 US and Canada; $66.30. Warren Gorham & Lamont Inc., Park Square Building, 31 St. James Avenue, Boston MA 02116-4112. **Tel** (617)423-2020, (800)950-1207, FAX (617)423-2026. **LC** KF6271; J68. **DD** 343.7304; 347.3034. *Continues Journal of Taxation Digest, 8755-6049.*

**UK**
**WHILLAN'S TAX TABLES.** English. an. £2.95. Butterworth & Co. Ltd. / Kent, England, Borough Green, Sevenoaks Kent TN15 8PH England. **Tel** 011 44 732-884567, FAX 011 44 732-885996. **ED** Sheila Parrington. **Desc:** Covers all aspects of taxation and includes foreign exchange rates, NI benefits, personal reliefs and stamp duties.

**UK**
**WHITEMAN AND WHEATCROFT ON INCOME TAX. Ceased.** (1971)- Out of Print (Feb. 1994). English. ir. Sweet & Maxwell Ltd., South Quay Plaza, 183 Marsh Wall, London E14 9FT England. **Tel** 011 44 264 342899, FAX 011 44 264 342743, telex 929089 ITPINF G. **LC** KD5429. **DD** 343.4105/2.

**UK**
**WHITEMAN ON CAPITAL GAINS TAX. Ceased.** (19??)-(Feb. 1994). English. ir. Sweet & Maxwell

Ltd., South Quay Plaza, 183 Marsh Wall, London E14 9FT England. **Tel** 011 44 264 342899, FAX 011 44 264 342723, telex 929089 ITPINF G.

AT/1035-2015
**WHO AUDITS AUSTRALIA? (1987).** See Business-Accounting.

US
**WISCONSIN TAX BULLETIN. Added/Corp** Wisconsin. Income, Sales, and Excise Tax Division. (1976)-. Bulletin. English. qt. $7.00. Wisconsin Department of Administration / Document Sales, PO Box 7840, 202 South Thornton Avenue, Madison WI 53707. **Tel** (608)266-3358.

US/0043-6720
**WISCONSIN TAXPAYER, THE. Added/Corp** Wisconsin Taxpayers Alliance. (Jan. 1933)-. Periodical. English. ir. $7.00 (one year); $16.00 (three years) includes Annual Copy of Taxes. Wisconsin Taxpayers Alliance, 335 West Wilson Street, Madison WI 53703-3694. **Tel** (608)255-4581. **ED** James R. Morgan and Rindert Kiemel. **LC** HJ2441; .W46. **DD** 336.775. **Circ:** 12,000.
**Desc:** Presents authoritative current interest information on Wisconsin government and taxation. Contains helpful charts, graphs and tables. Summarizes current attorney general opinions.

US/0363-4795
**WORLD MILITARY AND SOCIAL EXPENDITURES.** See Military and Defense-Abstracting, Bibliographies and Statistics.

UK
**WORLD TAX REPORT.** Periodical. English. mo. £242.00. Financial Times Business Information Ltd., Tower House, Southampton Street, London WC2E 7HA England. **Tel** 011 44 71 353 1040. **ED** Clive Wolman. **LC** K4456.2; .W67. **DD** 343.04/05, 342.3405. **Bk Rev** available on an online database (file 636/Full-Text) from DIALOG.
**Desc:** A survey of world developments in taxation.
**Ind/Abst** PTS Newsl. Database [Full Txt.].

US/0272-2739
**WRITE-OFF.** [Write-off]. **VFOAT** Write Off. Vol. 1 (Nov. 1980)-. Periodical. English. mo. $126.72. Propub Inc., PO Box 102, 49 Van Syckel Lane, Wyckoff NJ 07481. **Tel** (201)891-6430. **DD** 336.

US
**WYOMING STATE BUDGET. SUPPLEMENT. Main/Corp** Wyoming. Governor. English. be. Wyoming Governors Office, 213 State Capitol, Cheyenne WY 82002. **LC** HJ11; .W843A SUPPL. **DD** 353.9/787/00722.

JA
**YAKUIN NO HOSHU SHOYO NENSHU. Main/Corp** Seikei Kenkyujo. (19??)-. Japanese. an. ¥16000. Seikei Kenkyujo / Wako 15 Building 8, Wako 15 Building 8, Nihonbashi Honcho, 1-chome Chuo-ku, Tokyo 103 Japan. **LC** HJ4965.5.J3; S44d.

II
**YEAR-BOOK AND DIGEST, THE.** 1979-. English. an. Taxation Publishers Private Ltd, 174 Jor Bagh, New Delhi 110003 India. **DD** 343.5404/02638; 345.403402638. **Continues** Taxation's Year Book and Digest.

NE/0377-6662
**YEARBOOK - IFA.** (YEARBOOK - INTERNATIONAL FISCAL ASSOCIATION.). **Main/Corp** International Fiscal Association. English. General Secretariat, PO Box 1738, Burg Oudlaan 50, 3016 Rotterdam Netherlands. **DD** 341.7/5. **Continues** Annual of the International Fiscal Association.

IS
**YEDA LE-MEDA.** Periodical. Hebrew. Rayonot BM, POB 26051, Tel Aviv Israel.

JA
**YORAN - HOKKAIDO ZAIMUKYOKU. Main/Corp** Japan. Hokkaido Zaimukyoku. (19??)-. Periodical. Japanese. Hokkaido Zaimukyoku, Nishi 4-chome Kita 3-jo chuo-ku, Sapporo 060 Japan. **LC** HJ9077.A55; H644.

JA
**YOSAN JIMU TEIYO. Added/Corp** Okura Zaimu Kyokai. (19??)-. Periodical. Japanese. ¥43. Okura Zaimu Kyokai, 2-30 Sambancho Chiyoda-ku, Tokyo Japan. **LC** HJ2986; .Y67.

JA
**YOSETSU SHOTOKUZEIHO.** (1970)-. Periodical. Japanese. ¥2100. Zeimu Keiri Kyokai, 5-13 Shimo Ochiai 2-chome Shinjuku-ku, Tokyo 161 Japan. **LC** LAW.

CN/0317-8951
**YOUR CANADA PENSION PLAN. Added/Corp** C C H Canadian Limited. (1965)-. English (French). an. 4.95Can$. CCH Canadian Ltd., 6 Garamond Court, Don Mills Ontario M3C 1Z5 Canada. **Tel** (416)441-2992, FAX (416)441-3418. **DD** 368.4/3/00971.

US
**YOUR FEDERAL INCOME TAX FOR INDIVIDUALS / DEPARTMENT OF THE TREASURY, INTERNAL REVENUE SERVICE. Added/Corp** United States. Internal Revenue Service. (1943)-. English. an. Department of the Treasury Internal Revenue Service, Fifteenth Street and Pennsylvania Avenue NW, Washington DC 20220.

US
**YOUR INCOME TAX.** English. an. $14.00; $35.95 combined subscription with Lasser's Monthly Tax Letter. JK Lasser Tax Institute, 15 Columbus Circle, 16th Floor, New York NY 10023. **Tel** (212)373-8786.

AT
**YOUR MONEY WEEKLY.** English. wk. 325.00Au$$. Ian Huntley Publishers Pty Limited, PO Box 99, Cremorne NSW, 2090 Australia. **Tel** 11 61 2 9535788. **ED** Jan Huntley. ctrl circ.
**Desc:** The Australian Sharemarket, review of Australian companies, advice on stocks.

JA
**ZAISEI SHOROPPO. Main/Corp** Japan. **Added/Corp** Gakuyo Shobo. Japan. Okurasho. Shukeikyoku. Hokika. Zaisei Kaikei Horei Kenkyukai. (19??)-. Periodical. Japanese. an. ¥1800. Gakuyo Shobo, 7-5 Fujimi 1 Chiyoda-ku, Tokyo 102 Japan.

JA
**ZAISEI TO JICHI. Added/Corp** Okura Zaimu Shiryo Chosakai. (1978)-. Periodical. Japanese. U. ¥13500. Okura Zaimu Shiryo Chosakai, c/o Kato Building, 3-15 Kanda Nishikicho, Chiyoda-ku 101, Tokyo Japan. **LC** HJ1424; .Z34. **Continues** Zaisei to Chiho Jichi.

JA/0494-8262
**ZEIHOGAKU. Added/Corp** Nihon Zeiho Gakkai. **VFOAT** Tax jurisprudence; Steuerrechtswissenschaft; Zei-Ho-Gaku. (1951)-. Periodical. Japanese (table of contents in English and German). mo. $229.00.
**(Subscription address:** Japan Publications Trading Company, Ltd., PO Box 5030, Tokyo International, Tokyo 100-31 Japan.**)**

GW
**ZEITSCHRIFT FUER ZOLLE + VERBRAUCHSTEUERN : ZFZ. VFOAT** ZfZ; Zeitschrift fuer Zolle und Verbrauchsteuern. (19??)-. German. mo. DM39.80. Stollfuss Verlag GmbH and Company KG, Postfach 2428 Dechenstrasse 7-11, D 53014 Bonn Germany. **Tel** 011 49 228 724222. **LC** HJ2670; .Z4. **DD** 333.2/6/0943. **Continues** Zeitschrift fuer Zolle und Verbrauchsteuern.

CN/0842-3946
**ZIMMER'S QUICK & EASY COMPUTER TAX PROGRAM.** (ZIMMER'S QUICK & EASY COMPUTER TAX PROGRAM [COMPUTER FILE] : PREPARING YOUR CANADIAN ... PERSONAL INCOME TAX RETURN.). [Zimmer's quick easy comput. tax program]. **VFOAT** Preparing Your Canadian ... Personal Income Tax Return. **VAT** Zimmer's Quick and Easy Computer Tax Program. (1986)-. English. $39.95 per volume. Zimmer's Quick & Easy Computer Tax Program, 68 Pumpmeadow Crescent South West, Calgary Alberta T2V 5A4 Canada. **DD** 343.7105/2044/0285.

# PUBLIC UTILITIES

US/0894-5020
**ADVANCE RELEASE OF DATA FOR THE ... STATISTICAL YEARBOOK OF THE ELECTRIC UTILITY INDUSTRY.** [Adv. release data Stat. yearb. electr. util. ind.]. **Added/Corp** Edison Electric Institute. **VFOAT** Advance Release of Data for the ... Statistical Year Book of the Electric Utility Industry. (19??)-. Statistical Publication. English. Edison Electric Institute, 701 Pennsylvania Avenue Northwest, Washington DC 20004. **Tel** (202)508-5607, (202)508-5610, FAX (202)508-5030. **DD** 338.
**Ind/Abst** F&S Index Plus Text, Int. [Select. Cov.]; Predicasts Forecasts.

US/0895-1713
**ANNUAL DIGEST OF PUBLIC UTILITIES REPORTS.** [Annu. dig. public util. rep.]. **Added/Corp** Public Utilities Reports, Inc. **VFOAT** Public Utilities Reports, Annual. (1934)-. English. an. $125.00. Public Utilities Reports, 2111 Wilson Boulevard, Suite 200, Arlington VA 22201. **Tel** (703)243-7000, (800)368-5001, FAX (703)527-5829. **LC** KF2085.A2; P82. **DD** 351.
**Continues** Digest of Public Utilities Reports, 0272-7463.

MY
**ANNUAL REPORT. Main/Corp** Sarawak Electricity Supply Corporation. English. an. **LC** HD9865.S36; S3. **DD** 354.595/4008722/006. **Continues** Report / Sarawak Electricity Supply Corporation.

CN/0836-1509
**ANNUAL REPORT - ALBERTA TRANSPORTATION AND UTILITIES.** See Transportation.

US
**ANNUAL REPORT FOR ... / NEW YORK POWER AUTHORITY. Main/Corp** New York Power Authority. English. an (March). Power Authority of the State of New York, 1633 Broadway, New York NY 10019. **Tel** (212)468-6401, FAX (212)468-6259. **Pr Rev. Circ:** 20,000 (ctrl). **Continues** Annual Report - Power Authority of the State of New York, 0275-0864.

MY
**ANNUAL REPORT - KUCHING WATER BOARD. Main/Corp** Kuching Water Board. English. **LC** TD313.S32; K84. **DD** 354/.595/400871.

AT
**ANNUAL REPORT - METROPOLITAN WATER BOARD.** See Water Resources.

CN/0382-2826
**ANNUAL REPORT / ONTARIO HYDRO.** See Engineering-Electricity, Electrical Engineering, Electronics.

US/0272-4529
**ANNUAL REPORT, PUBLIC WATER SUPPLIES FOR THE STATE OF OKLAHOMA, NORTHWEST DISTRICT.** See Environmental Issues-Pollution and Waste Management.

US/1064-0959
**ANNUAL REPORT, SECTION OF PUBLIC UTILITY, COMMUNICATIONS AND TRANSPORTATION LAW.** [Annu. rep. Sect. Public Util. Commun. Transp. Law]. **Main/Corp** American Bar Association. Section of Public Utility, Communications and Transportation Law. (19??)-. English. an. $10.00. American Bar Association, 750 North Lake Shore Drive, Chicago IL 60611. **Tel** (312)988-5522, (312)988-5241, FAX (312)988-5528, telex 270593. **LC** KF325.184; .A4. **DD** 343/.73/09. **Continues** American Bar Association. Section of Public Utility Law. Annual Report, 0887-9281.

US/0191-1457
**ANNUAL REPORT - STATE OF ARKANSAS, PUBLIC SERVICE COMMISSION. Main/Corp** Arkansas. Public Service Commission. English. an. $5.00. Public Service Commission of Arkansas, PO Box C-400, Little Rock AR 72203. **Supersedes** Annual Report - State of Arkansas, Department of Public Utilities, 0197-0097.

UK/0307-1146
**ANNUAL REPORT / THE ELECTRICITY COUNCIL.** See Public Administration-Abstracting, Bibliographies and Statistics.

CN/0460-9581
**ANNUAL REPORT - THE MANITOBA HYDRO-ELECTRIC BOARD. Main/Corp** Manitoba Hydro. **VAT** Manitoba Hydro-Electric Board Annual Report. (1952)-. English. an. Free. Manitoba Hydro, Box 815, Winnipeg Manitoba R3C 2P4 Canada. **Tel** (204)474-3311, FAX (204)475-9044. **LC** HD9685.C3; M3. ctrl circ.

AT/1031-5225
**ANNUAL REPORT / WATER AUTHORITY OF WESTERN AUSTRALIA.** See Water Resources.

US
**ANNUAL REPORT / WATER WORKS AND SEWER BOARD OF THE CITY OF BIRMINGHAM.** See Water Resources.

US
**ANNUAL STATISTICS OF ELECTRIC COMPANIES.** 1985-. English. an. Washington Utilities and Transportation Commission, 1300 Evergreen Drive South, Chandler Plaza, Olympia WA 98504. **LC** HD9685.U6; W197. **DD** 363.6/2/0973021. **Continues** Statistics of Electric Companies, 0093-5042.

US
**ANNUAL STATISTICS OF GAS COMPANIES.** See Public Administration-Abstracting, Bibliographies and Statistics.

●CN/1199-1801
**AREAS SERVED BY NATURAL GAS.** [Areas served nat. gas]. **Added/Corp** Canadian Gas

Association. Economics and Statistical Dept. Canadian Gas Association. (199?)-. English. be (May). $30.00 members; $60.00 nonmembers. Canadian Gas Association, 243 Consumers Road / Suite 1200, North York Ontario M2J 5E3 Canada. **Tel** (416)498-1994, FAX (416)498-7465. **DD** 333.8/233/0971. ***Continues*** *Areas Served by Gas in Canada., 0849-5416.*
**Desc:** Lists distributors and areas served by natural gas, population, number of customers or meters in each area.

US
**AUDITED ANNUAL FINANCIAL REPORT / PUBLIC UTILITY COMMISSION OF TEXAS. Main/Corp** Texas. Public Utility Commission. (August 31, 1983)-. English. Public Utility Commission of Texas, 7800 Shoal Creek Boulevard/Suite 400 N, Austin TX 78757. **Tel** (512)458-0100. **LC** HD2767.T4; T48c. **DD** 353.97640087/005. ***Continues*** *Audited Annual Report / Public Utility Commission of Texas.*

US/0271-5422
**AWWA SEMINAR PROCEEDINGS.** [AWWA semin. proc.]. **Added/Corp** American Water Works Association. **VAT** American Water Works Association Seminar Proceedings. (19??)-. Proceedings. English. an. Price varies. American Water Works Association / Colorado, 6666 West Quincy Avenue, Denver CO 80235. **Tel** (303)794-7711, (303)794-7310 (editorial), FAX (303)794-7310 (editorial), (303)795-1989 (marketing).
**Ind/Abst** GeoRef.

GW/0937-3756
**BBR : WASSER UND ROHRBAU. See** Water Resources.

US
**BIENNIAL REPORT OF THE DEPARTMENT OF PUBLIC SERVICE / STATE OF VERMONT. Main/Corp** Vermont. Public Service Dept. (June 1984)-. English. be. Vermont Department of Public Services, Montpelier VT 05602. **LC** HD2767.V5; V46a. **DD** 363.6/09743. ***Continues*** *Vermont. Public Service Dept. Biennial Report of the Public Service Department.*

BL
**BOLETIM ESTATISTICO ANUAL - COMPANHIA DE ELETRICIDADE DE CEARA. See** Public Administration-Abstracting, Bibliographies and Statistics.

BL
**BOLETIM ESTATISTICO - COMPANHIA PAULISTA DE FORCA E LUZ. See** Public Administration-Abstracting, Bibliographies and Statistics.

UY
**BOLETIN DE LA CIER. VFOAT** Boletin CIER; Boletin de la Comision de Integracion Electrica Regional; Boletin Comision de Integracion Electrica Regional. Periodical. Spanish. mo. Comision de Integracion Electrica Regional, Subcomite de Distribucion de Energia Electrica, Boulevar Artigas 996, 1040 Montevideo Uruguay. **Tel** 795359 - 790611, telex CIER UY 920. **LC** HD9685.S6; C65c. ***Continues*** *Boletin - Comision de Integracion Electrica Regional.*

BE
**BULLETIN MENSUEL DE L'ENERGIE ELECTRIQUE. VFOAT** Maandelijks Bulletin van de Electrische Energie. Bulletin. Multiple languages (Dutch and French). **LC** HD9685.B4; B44A.

CN/0316-3547
**CANADIAN GAS FACTS. Added/Corp** Canadian Gas Association. Statistical Dept. Canadian Gas Association. (1965)-. English. an (Sept.). $30.00 members; $60.00 nonmembers. Canadian Gas Association, 243 Consumers Road / Suite 1200, North York Ontario M2J 5E3 Canada. **Tel** (416)498-1994, FAX (416)498-7465. **LC** HD9581.C3; C33. **DD** 333.8/2. Index available. **Circ:** 2,000 (ctrl). ***Absorbed*** *Canadian Residential Heating Survey, 0830-8578.* ***Continued in part by*** *Canadian Residential Heating Survey (1990), 1184-177X.*
**Desc:** Comprehensive statistics illustrating growth of the natural gas industry in Canada.

CN/1194-2967
**CANADIAN GAS RATES.** (1962)-. English. an (also periodic updates). $30.00 members; $60.00 nonmembers. Canadian Gas Association, 243 Consumers Road / Suite 1200, North York Ontario M2J 5E3 Canada. **Tel** (416)498-1994, FAX (416)498-7465.
**Desc:** Rate structures of Canadian gas utilities' franchise areas.

CN
**CGA DOMESTIC DEMAND FORECAST.** (19??)-. English. an (Dec.). $40.00 members; $80.00 nonmembers. Canadian Gas Association, 243 Consumers Road / Suite 1200, North York Ontario M2J 5E3 Canada. **Tel** (416)498-1994, FAX (416)498-7465.
**Desc:** Covers natural gas demand, by province and sector in Canada for the next ten years.

CN/0829-772X
**CIVIC PUBLIC WORKS. *Title Change.*** [Civic public works]. **VFOAT** Public Works Reference Manual & Buyers Guide. Vol. 30, No. 5 (May 1978)-(19??). Periodical. English. Nine times a year. MacLean Hunter Ltd. Business Publishers / Canada, Box 9100, Station A, Toronto ONT M5W 1A5 Canada. **Tel** (416)946-8420, (800)567-0444. **(Subscription address:** Indas, 35 Riviera Drive, Building 17, Markham Ontario L3R 8N4 Canada.**) ED** Clifford J. Allum. **LC** JS1701; .C5. **DD** 352/.0072/0971. **[CCC]. Bk Rev. Ad Acc. Circ:** 13,500 (ctrl). available on microfilm from University Microfilms International (UMI). ***Absorbed*** *Wastes Handling, 0315-1921;* ***Continues*** *Civic, 0315-1972.* ***Merged into*** *Heavy Construction News.*
**Desc:** Covers every aspect of the environment, including water supply, sewage treatment, with comprehensive and informative articles on highways, transportation, solid waste management, parks, public safety, public utilities, office equipment and systems.
**Ind/Abst** Can. Bus. Index.

US/0738-2332
**CLEARING UP.** (CLEARING UP / CLEARINGHOUSE SERVICE.). [Clear. up]. **Added/Corp** Information Resources (Firm). Clearinghouse Service. NewsData Corporation. No. 1 (Apr. 1982)-. Periodical. English. wk. $1500.00. Newsdata Corporation, PO Box 900928, Queen Anne Station, Seattle WA 98109. **Tel** (206)285-4848, FAX (206)281-8035.

US/0883-2781
**COLLAGE (CAMP HILL, PA.).** (COLLAGE / AMERICAN SOCIETY OF UTILITY INVESTORS.). [Collage]. **Added/Corp** American Society of Utility Investors. Vol. 1, No. 1 (Summer 1981)-. Periodical. English. sa. $15.00. American Society of Utility Investors, Box 342, New Cumberland PA 17070. **Tel** (717)774-2556. **ED** James R Spang. **LC** HD9685.U4; C64. **DD** 338.4/736362/0971. **Ad Acc. Circ:** 7,500 (ctrl).
**Desc:** This journal is financially oriented in subject matter, and features articles dealing with business and the free market.

US
**COLORADO COUNTRY LIFE. Added/Corp** Colorado Rural Electric Association. (19??)-. Periodical. English. mo. $11.95. Colorado Rural Electric Association, 1313 West 46th Avenue, Denver CO 80211. **Tel** (303)455-2700, FAX (303)455-2807. **ED** Frank McCrea. **Ad Acc. Circ:** 86,000.
**Desc:** Information on the problems and conditions in rural utilities. Other content is of general interest.
**Ind/Abst** Energy Res. Abstr. (May 1978-).

US/1064-0886
**DA&DSM MONITOR.** (DA & DSM MONITOR : THE MONTHLY TECHNOLOGY NEWSLETTER ON DISTRIBUTION AUTOMATION AND DEMAND SIDE MANAGEMENT.). [DA&DSM monit.]. **Added/Corp** Eureka Information Services Group. **VFOAT** DA&DSM Monitor; DA and DSM Monitor; DA/DSM Monitor. **VAT** Distribution Automation and Demand Side Management Monitor. (1990)-. Newsletter. English. Twelve times a year. $230.00 US; $243.00 Canada and Mexico; $268.00 other. PennWell Publishing Company, 1421 South Sheridan, PO Box 1260, Tulsa OK 74101. **Tel** (918)835-3161, (800)331-4463, FAX (918)831-9497. **(Subscription address:** DA/DSM Monitor, PO Box 2750, Tulsa OK 74101.**) ED** Susan Borowitz. **DD** 621. Index available ($20.00).
**Desc:** Information on electric utilities and power distribution, specifically distribution automation and demand-side management.

US
**DECISIONS OF THE PUBLIC UTILITIES COMMISSION OF THE STATE OF CALIFORNIA. Main/Corp** California Public Utilities Commission. **VFOAT** Opinions and Orders of the Public Utilities Commission of California. Vol. 47 (Nov. 15, 1946 to Apr. 6, 1948)-Vol. 84 (May 2, 1978 to Dec. 12, 1978)-. English. an. $50.00 (per volume) US. Public Utilities Commission of the State of California, California State Building, San Francisco CA 94102. **LC** HD2767.C2; A34. **DD** 353.97940087. ***Continues*** *Railroad Commission of the State of California. Decisions of the Railroad Commission of the State of California.*

US
**DEMAND SIDE MONTHLY.** (1990)-. English. mo. $245.00. Cogen Publications, PO Box 2303, Falls Church VA 22042. **Tel** (703)641-0613. **ED** Glen Lovin. **Ad Acc.**
**Desc:** Demand side management of electric utilities; information on conservation and efficiency in the electric utilities field.

JA
**DENRYOKU JUKYU NO GAIYO.** Vol. 23, 1973-. Japanese. an. ¥870. Shigen Enerugicho Koeki Jigyobu, (Public Utilities Dept., Agency of Natural Resources & Energy), 2-14, Irifune 2 Chome, Chuoku, Tokyoto 104 Japan. **(Subscription address:** Maruzen Company Ltd., PO Box 5050, Import & Export Department, Tokyo 100 31 Japan.**) LC** HD9685.J3; A25. ***Continues*** *Denryoku Jukyu No Gaiyo.*

US/0360-6899
**DIRECTORY - AMERICAN PUBLIC WORKS ASSOCIATION. Main/Corp** American Public Works Association. (1970)-. English. an. $52.00 (two years). American Public Works Association, 106 West 11th Street, Suite 1800, Kansas City MO 64105. **Tel** (816)472-6100. **LC** TD1; .A28. **DD** 363.5/06/273. ***Continues*** *Yearbook - American Public Works Association, 0096-025X.*

CN/0704-7878
**DIRECTORY - AMERICAN WATER WORKS ASSOCIATION, ONTARIO SECTION. See** Water Resources.

CN/0229-1142
**DIRECTORY / CANADIAN GAS ASSOCIATION.** [Dir. - Can. Gas Assoc.]. **Main/Corp** Canadian Gas Association. (1980/1981)-. English. an. Available to members only - not for sale as individual subscription. Canadian Gas Association, 243 Consumers Road / Suite 1200, North York Ontario M2J 5E3 Canada. **Tel** (416)498-1994, FAX (416)498-7465. **DD** 363.6/3/02571. ctrl circ. ***Continues*** *Canadian Gas Utilities Directory, 0576-5269.*

CN/1193-1345
**DIRECTORY OF NATURAL GAS COMPANY OPERATIONS. *Title Change.*** (DIRECTORY OF NATURAL GAS COMPANY OPERATIONS / PREPARED BY THE ECONOMICS AND STATISTICS DEPARTMENT, CANADIAN GAS ASSOCIATION.). [Dir. nat. gas co. oper.]. **Added/Corp** Canadian Gas Association. Economics and Statistical Dept. (1991)-(199?). English. Canadian Gas Association, 243 Consumers Road / Suite 1200, North York Ontario M2J 5E3 Canada. **Tel** (416)498-1994, FAX (416)498-7465. **DD** 363.6/3/02571. ***Continues*** *Canadian Gas Association. Economics/Statistics Dept. Directory of Gas Distribution, Transmission and Production Companies., 0840-9455.* ***Continued by*** *Natural Gas Utility Directory.*

IT
**ECONOMIA E DIRITTO DEL TERZIARIO. Added/Corp** Cassa di Risparmio di Genova e Imperia. (1989)-. Periodical. Italian. Three times a year. L75000 Italy; L110000 other. Franco Angeli Riviste SRL, Viale Monza 106, 20127 Milan Italy. **Tel** 011 39 2 2827651, 011 39 2 289562. **LC** K5; .C645. **DD** 343.45/07; 344.5037.

●US/1058-2479
**EL & P U.S. ELECTRIC UTILITY INDUSTRY DIRECTORY.** (EL&P U.S. ELECTRIC UTILITY INDUSTRY DIRECTORY.). [EL & P U.S. electr. util. ind. dir.]. **VFOAT** EL and P US Electric Utility Industry Directory; EL&P U.S. Electric Utility Industry Directory; EL and P U.S. Electric Utility Industry Directory; U.S. Electric Utility Industry Directory; US Electric Utility Industry Directory; Electric Utility Industry Directory. **VAT** Electric Light and Power United States Electric Utility Industry Directory. (1992)-. Directory. English. an. $195.00 US and Canada; $270.00 other. PennWell Publishing Company, 1421 South Sheridan, PO Box 1260, Tulsa OK 74101. **Tel** (918)835-3161, (800)331-4463, FAX (918)831-9497. **(Subscription address:** PennWell Books, PO Box 21288, Tulsa OK 74121.**) LC** HD9685.U4; E357. **DD** 333.79/32/02573.
**Desc:** Information on the electric utility industry. Organized by company name, each listing will include such information as utility name, address, phone, fax, telex, and cable number. Also includes type of utility or organization (investor-owned, municipal, rural electric or electric cooperative, federal power agency, publicly owned utility, independent power producer, power pool, or state/federal regulatory agency), executives, financial information, description, regulatory information, and generating stations.

US
**ELECTRIC GENERATION AND TRANSMISSION FACILITIES IN OHIO, SITE INFORMATION / COMPILED ... BY THE PUBLIC UTILITIES COMMISSION OF OHIO, DIVISION OF FORECASTING AND THE OHIO POWER SITING BOARD. Added/Corp** Public Utilities Commission of Ohio. Forecasting Division. Ohio Power Siting Board. **VFOAT** Site Information. (1990)-. English. ***Continues*** *Site Information.*

CN/0380-0229
**ELECTRIC POWER STATISTICS (OTTAWA. MONTHLY ED.). See** Public Administration-Abstracting, Bibliographies and Statistics.

US
**ELECTRIC RATE BOOK.** English. an. $550.00 (trade). Casazza Schultz and Associates Inc, 1901 North Fort Myer Drive, Arlington VA 22209. **Tel** (703)841-9644, FAX 841-9649. **Pr Rev. Circ:** 200.
**Desc:** Abstracts of electric rates of over 120 investor-owned utilities in the United States covering 93% of consumers.

US/0894-3788
**ELECTRIC UTILITY BUSINESS.** [Electr. util. bus.]. **Added/Corp** Electric Utility Consultants. (1987)-. Periodical. English. wk. $495.00 (one year), $950.00 (two year). Electric Utility Consultants, PO Box 4474, Englewood CO 80155. **Tel** (303)770-8800, FAX (303)741-0849. **ED** L.C. Mrig. **DD** 338.

●US/1065-8696
**ELECTRIC UTILITY WEEK'S DEMAND-SIDE REPORT.** [Electr. util. week's demand-side rep.]. **VFOAT** Electric Utility Week's Demand Side Report; Demand Side Report; Demand-Side Report. (Sept. 3, 1992)-. Periodical. English. bw. $445.00. McGraw Hill Publishing Company, Inc., 1221 Avenue of the Americas, New York NY 10020. **Tel** (212)512-6410, (800)525-5003, FAX (212)512-6111. **DD** 333.

US/1058-4218
**ELECTRICAL DESIGN AND INSTALLATION.** ***Suspended.*** (ELECTRICAL DESIGN AND INSTALLATION : EDI.). [Electr. des. install.]. **VFOAT** EDI. Vol. 1, No 1 (Sept/Oct 1990)-(Dec 1991). Periodical. English. mo. $25.00 (U.S., non-professionals). McPartland Publishing Company, PO Box 1506, Englewood Cliffs NJ 07632. **DD** 696.

US/0092-2501
**ELECTRICAL WORLD DIRECTORY OF ELECTRIC UTILITIES IN LATIN AMERICA, BERMUDA AND THE CARIBBEAN ISLANDS.** **VFOAT** Directory of Electric Utilities in Latin America, Bermuda and the Caribbean Islands. (19??)-. Directory. English. McGraw Hill Publishing Company, Inc., 1221 Avenue of the Americas, New York NY 10020. **Tel** (212)512-6410, (800)525-5003, FAX (212)512-6111. **LC** HD9685.S6; E4. **DD** 363.6/2/02572.

US/1040-6190
**ELECTRICITY JOURNAL, THE.** [Electr. j.]. Vol. 1, No. 1 (July 1988)-. Periodical. English. Ten times a year (JanFeb. and Aug.Sept. combined). $125.00 Public Schools & Libraries; $275.00 Regulatory & Governmental Agencies; $395.00 other. The Electricity Journal, 1501 Western Avenue, Suite 100, Seattle WA 98101. **Tel** (206)382-0195, FAX (206)382-0098. **ED** Robert O. Marritz. **LC** HD9685.U4; E415. **DD** 363.6/2/0973. **CODEN** ELEJE4. Index available. cum. index. **Bk Rev**, (Qty: 3). **Circ:** 1,700 (ctrl). available on CD-ROM; available on an online database.
**Desc:** Magazine of electric policy, regulation, DSM IRP transmissions, and fiber optics.
**Ind/Abst** Energy Inf. Abstr.; PAIS Int. Print (1991-).

US/1046-3186
**ELECTRICITY SUPPLY & DEMAND FOR ... THE REGIONAL RELIABILITY COUNCILS OF THE NORTH AMERICAN ELECTRIC RELIABILITY COUNCIL.** [Electr. supply demand]. **VFOAT** Electricity Supply and Demand; Annual Data Summary; Electricity Supply & Demand for ... . (1986)-. English. an. Free. North American Electric Reliability Council, 101 College Road East, Princeton NJ 08540-6601. **Tel** (609)452-8060. **DD** 333. **Circ:** 5,000. ***Continues*** *Electric Power Supply and Demand, 0737-1845.*
**Desc:** Aggregations of electric utility ten-year projections of electricity supply and demand by regions.
**Ind/Abst** F&S Index Plus Text, Int. [Select. Cov.]; Predicasts Forecasts.

US/0430-4845
**FINANCIAL STATISTICS OF PUBLIC UTILITIES.** (FINANCIAL STATISTICS OF PUBLIC UTILITIES : ELECTRIC AND GAS OPERATING COMPANIES.). **Added/Corp** C.A. Turner & Associates. C.A. Turner Utility Reports (Firm). **VFOAT** Financial Statistics of Public Utilities: Electric Companies, Natural Gas Companies, Telephone Companies, Water Companies; Public Utilities. (1943)-. English. an (Published in July). $205.00. CA Turner Utility Reports, PO Box 1050, Morestown NJ 08057. **Tel** (609)234-9200 Ext. 400, FAX (609)234-8371. **ED** Robert Webb. **LC** HD9685.U4; F514. **DD** 338.4/3363/60973. **Circ:** 275 (ctrl). ***Absorbed*** *Financial Statistics of Telephone and Water Companies, 0430-4853.*
**Desc:** Financial and statistical data on electric and gas public utilities.

US
**FINANCIAL STATISTICS OF SELECTED PUBLICLY OWNED ELECTRIC UTILITIES.** Government Publication. an. $24.00. Superintendent of Documents, US Government Printing Office, Washington DC 20402. **Tel** (202)275-3328, FAX (202)786-2377.

US/0363-2113
**FINANCIAL STATISTICS OF THE MAJOR PRIVATELY OWNED UTILITIES IN NEW YORK STATE.** **See** Public Administration-Abstracting, Bibliographies and Statistics.

●US/1074-6099
**FORTNIGHTLY : THE NORTH AMERICAN UTILITIES BUSINESS MAGAZINE.** (Oct. 1, 1993)-. Periodical. English. ir (22 issues). $119.00 US; $178.00 other. Public Utilities Reports Inc., 2111 Wilson Boulevard, Suite 200, Arlington VA 22201. **Tel** (703)243-7000, (800)368-5001, FAX (703)527-5829. **(Subscription address:** Public Utilities Reports Inc., PO Box 1110, Pearl River NY 10965.**)** ***Continues*** *Public Utilities Fortnightly, 0033-3808.*
**Ind/Abst** Acad. Search (Oct. 1993-); Vocat. Search (Oct. 1993-).

●US
**GAS UTILITY REPORT.** (1994)-. Newsletter. English. bw. $575.00 US and Canada; $600.00 other. McGraw Hill Publishing Company, Inc., 1221 Avenue of the Americas, New York NY 10020. **Tel** (212)512-6410, (800)525-5003, FAX (212)512-6111.

AT
**GENERAL REPORT / THE PARLIAMENT OF THE COMMONWEALTH OF AUSTRALIA, PARLIAMENTARY STANDING COMMITTEE ON PUBLIC WORKS.** **Main/Corp** Australia. Parliament. Standing Committee on Public Works. (19??)-. English. an. Government Printer / Victoria, PO Box 203, North Melbourne Victoria, 3051 Australia. **LC** J905; .L3 subser.; TA121. **DD** 328.94/07657.

●US/1065-870X
**INDEPENDENT POWER MARKETS QUARTERLY.** [Indep. power mark. q.]. (1992)-. Periodical. English. qt. $625.00. McGraw Hill Publishing Company, Inc., 1221 Avenue of the Americas, New York NY 10020. **Tel** (212)512-6410, (800)525-5003, FAX (212)512-6111. **LC** HD9685.U4; I52. **DD** 333.79/323/097305. ***Continues*** *Independent Power Report's Avoided-Cost Quarterly, 1059-3039.*

US/0743-3492
**INDEX TO ELECTRIC UTILITY WEEK.** [Index Electr. util. week]. **Added/Corp** National Energy Researchers (Firm). (1983)-. Periodical. English. qt. National Energy Researchers, PO Box 35286, Houston TX 77235. **Tel** (713)723-1921. cum. index. ***Continues*** *Index to Electrical Week.*

US/1046-8544
**INTERSTATE SECURITIES TELEPHONE AND ELECTRIC UTILITIES ATLAS, THE.** [Interstate Secur. teleph. electr. util. atlas]. **Added/Corp** Interstate Securities Corporation. **VFOAT** Interstate Securities Telephone & Electric Utilities Atlas. 7th Ed. (1984)-. English. an. $10.00. Interstate Securities Corporation, 2700 NCNB Plaza, Charlotte NC 28280. **Tel** (704)379-9000. **LC** HD9685.U4; I56. **DD** 338.7/613636/02573. ***Continues*** *Interstate Securities Corporation. Interstate Securities Electric Utilities Atlas, 0275-7400.*

NE/0257-6333
**IRC NEWSLETTER.** **See** Public Health and Safety.

US/0025-0805
**JOURNAL - MAINE WATER UTILITIES ASSOCIATION.** **Main/Corp** Maine Water Utilities Association. (1924)-. Periodical. English. bm. Comes with membership to Maine Water Utilities Association. Maine Water Utilities Association, 225 Douglass Street, Portland ME 04104. **ED** J. Ronald Caron. **LC** TD201; .M3. **DD** 628.1062741. **Ad Acc. Circ:** 400.

US/0028-4939
**JOURNAL OF THE NEW ENGLAND WATER WORKS ASSOCIATION.** [J. N. Engl. Water Works Assoc.]. **Main/Corp** New England Water Works Association. **VFOAT** Journal of New England Water Works Association. Vol. 1 (1886)-. Academic Scholarly Publication. English. qt (Mar., June, Sept., Dec.). $20.00 US; $28.00 other. New England Water Works Association, 42 Dilla Street/#A, Milford MA 01757. **Tel** (508)478-6996, FAX (508)634-8643. **ED** Peter C. Karalekas Jr. **LC** TD201; .N53. **CODEN** JNEWA6. Index available. cum. index. **Bk Rev**. **Ad Acc. Circ:** 2,900 (ctrl). available on microfilm and microfiche from University Microfilms International (UMI). Documents available from Article Express International, BIOSIS Document Express, CASDDS. ***Supersedes*** *New England Water Works Association. Transactions.*
**Desc:** Includes papers by leading authorities in the water works industry. Is an internationally recognized source of information of the design, operation, maintenance, and management of water utilities.
**Ind/Abst** Bioeng. Abstr.; Biol. Abstr.; Chem. Abstr.; Ei Page One; EMBASE; Eng. Index Annu. [Select. Cov.]; Fluid Abstr., Civil Eng.; Fluid Abstr. Proc. Eng.; FLUIDEX (1973-1990); GeoRef; Pollut. Abstr. Indexes.

YU
**KOMUNALNI FONDOVI U GRADSKIM NASELJIMA.** **See** Public Administration-Abstracting, Bibliographies and Statistics.

US/1053-9379
**MCGRAW-HILL'S UTILITY ENVIRONMENT REPORT.** [McGraw-Hill's util. environ. rep.]. **Added/Corp** McGraw-Hill, Inc. **VFOAT** Utility Environment Report. (Oct. 19, 1990)-. Newsletter. English. Twenty-six times a year. $825.00 US, Canada & Mexico; $875.00 others. McGraw Hill Publishing Company, Inc., 1221 Avenue of the Americas, New York NY 10020. **Tel** (212)512-6410, (800)525-5003, FAX (212)512-6111. **(Subscription address:** McGraw Hill Management Information Center, 1221 Avenue of the Americas, 36th Floor, New York NY 10020.**)** **LC** TD195.E4; M39. **DD** 363.73/1.

●CN
**NATURAL GAS UTILITY DIRECTORY.** (199?)-. Directory. English. an (June). $40.00 members; $80.00 nonmembers. Canadian Gas Association, 243 Consumers Road / Suite 1200, North York Ontario M2J 5E3 Canada. **Tel** (416)498-1994, FAX (416)498-7465. ***Continues*** *Directory of Natural Gas Company Operations, 1193-1345.*
**Desc:** Directory on diskette listing Canadian natural gas distribution and transmission companies, executive officers and senior personnel. Also includes company sales, customers, daily demand, storage capacities, areas serviced by natural gas and length of pipeline network for each company.

US/0362-8833
**NRECA--APPA LEGAL REPORTING SERVICE.** **See** Law.

US/8756-632X
**NRRI QUARTERLY BULLETIN.** **See** Public Administration-Abstracting, Bibliographies and Statistics.

US
**OKLAHOMA UTILITIES DIRECTORY.** Directory. English. Oklahoma Department of Commerce, 6601 North Broadway Ext, Oklahoma City OK 73116. **Tel** (405)843-9770, FAX (405)841-5199, telex 350352. **LC** HD2767.O5; O38. **DD** 363.6/025/766.

CN/0382-2834
**ONTARIO HYDRO STATISTICAL YEARBOOK (1973).** **See** Public Administration-Abstracting, Bibliographies and Statistics.

US/0098-3225
**OPERATING REVENUE AND EXPENSE STATISTICS CLASS A AND B PRIVATE GAS UTILITIES IN WISCONSIN.** **See** Public Administration-Abstracting, Bibliographies and Statistics.

US/0733-4915
**P.U.R. ANALYSIS OF INVESTOR-OWNED ELECTRIC AND GAS UTILITIES, THE.** (THE P.U.R. ... ANALYSIS OF INVESTOR-OWNED ELECTRIC AND GAS UTILITIES / CONCEIVED AND PREPARED IN COLLABORATION WITH THE UTILITIES CONSULTING GROUP.). [P.U.R. anal. investor-owned elec. gas util.]. **Added/Corp** Utilities Consulting Group. Public Utilities Reports, Inc. **VFOAT** PUR ... Analysis of Investor-Owned Electric and Gas Utilities. **VAT** Public Utilities Reports Analysis of Investor-Owned Electric and Gas Utilities. (1982)-. English. an. $225.00. Public Utilities Reports Inc., 2111 Wilson Boulevard, Suite 200, Arlington VA 22201. **Tel** (703)243-7000, (800)368-5001, FAX (703)527-5829. **ED** Susan M Johnson. **LC** HD9685.U4; P2. **DD** 338.7/6136362. **Circ:** 800.
**Desc:** Analysis provides information concerning over 200 investor-owned electric and gas utility companies. Management, financial statements and operating information given.

US/0896-1069
**PIPELINE & UTILITIES CONSTRUCTION.** **See** Engineering-Mechanical Engineering and Machinery.

US
**POWER SOURCE.** **See** Energy.

US/0360-814X
**PROCEEDINGS AWWA ANNUAL CONFERENCE.** [Proc. AWWA annu. conf.]. **Main/Corp** American Water Works Association. Conference. **VFOAT** Annual Conference Proceedings. **VAT** Proceedings, American Water Works Association Annual Conference; Proceedings American Water Works Annual Conference. 95th (June 9-12, 1975)-. Academic Scholarly Publication. English. an. $72.50 (AWWA members), $91.50 (nonmembers). The American Water Works Association, 6666 West Quincy Avenue, Denver CO 80235. **Tel** (303)794-7711. **LC** TD201; .A592A. **DD** 363.6/1. **CODEN** PWACDO. Index available. **Circ:** 500. Documents available from Article Express International, CASDDS.
**Desc:** Scientific and management papers pertaining to water-supply and water quality issues and innovations.
**Ind/Abst** Chem. Abstr.; Eng. Index Annu.; GeoRef.

US
**PROCEEDINGS OF THE ... ANNUAL IOWA STATE REGULATORY CONFERENCE.** **Added/Corp** Iowa State University. Business and Engineering Extension. Iowa State University. Industrial Engineering Dept. **VFOAT** Proceedings of the ... Regulatory Conference. 27th (May 17-19, 1988)-. Proceedings. English. ***Continues*** *Proceedings of the ... Annual Iowa State Regulatory Conference on Public Utility Valuation and the Rate Making Process.*

US/0033-3654
**PUBLIC POWER.** [Public power]. **Added/Corp** American Public Power Association. (Dec. 10, 1942)-. Periodical. English. Six times a year. $50.00 US; $60.00 other. American Public Power Association, 2301 M Street NW, Washington DC 20037. **Tel** (202)467-2900, FAX (202)467-2910. **ED** Jeanne Wickline LaBella. **LC** HD9685.U4; P75. **DD** 338.4/736362. Index available. **Bk Rev. Ad Acc. Circ:** 12,000 (ctrl). Documents available from Documents on Demand.
**Desc:** Articles and pictures about local publicly owned electric systems, including annual directory and annual report on public power innovation.
**Ind/Abst** Coal Abstr.; Energy Inf. Abstr.; Energy Res. Abstr. (May 1974-); Environ. Abstr.; Stat. Ref. Index.

US/0747-3613
**PUBLIC POWER WEEKLY.** [Public power wkly.]. **Added/Corp** American Public Power Association. (198?)-. Periodical. English. Fifty-one times per year. Free to members; $400.00 other. American Public Power Association, 2301 M Street NW, Washington DC 20037. **Tel** (202)467-2900, FAX (202)467-2910. **LC** HD9685.U4; P76. **DD** 363.6/2/0973. ***Continues*** *Public Power Weekly Newsletter, 0195-7325.*

US/0033-3808
**PUBLIC UTILITIES FORTNIGHTLY.** ***Title Change.*** [Public util. fortn.]. Vol. 3, No. 2 (Jan. 24, 1929)-Vol. 131, No. 17 (Sept. 1993). Periodical. English. Twenty-two times a year. Public Utilities Reports Inc., 2111 Wilson Boulevard, Suite 200, Arlington VA 22201. **Tel** (703)243-7000, (800)368-5001, FAX (703)527-5829. **(Subscription address:** Public Utilites Reports, PO Box 1110, Pearl River, NY 10965) **ED** David Wagman. **LC** K16; .U23. **DD** 343.73/09/05; 347.303905. **CODEN** PUFNAV. **[CCC].** Index available. **Ad Acc. Circ:** 7,600. available on microfilm and microfiche from University Microfilms International (UMI); available on an online database (files 15,648/Full-Text) from DIALOG. Documents available from Ask*IEEE, UMI Article Clearinghouse, Documents on Demand. ***Continues*** *Public Utilities Reports Fortnightly.* ***Continued by*** *Fortnightly (Arlington, Va.).*
**Desc:** Includes feature articles by outstanding utility professionals, regulators, and legislators in which they discuss current problems and explore discernible trends within the utility industry. Regular columns include financial news and comments on the performance of utility companies, report on legislature developments in Washington and highlight recent regulatory actions throughout the states.
**Ind/Abst** ABI/INFORM Glob. Ed.; ABI Inform Ondisc (Feb. 1972-); Acad. Search (Jan. 1993-Sept. 1993); Account. Art.; Bus. ASAP (1990-) [Full Txt.]; Bus. Index (1985-); Bus. Period. Index; Coal Abstr.; Curr. Law Index (1980-); Energy Inf. Abstr.; Energy Res. Abstr.; Environ. Abstr.; Fed. Tax Artic.; Gas Abstr.; Gen. BusinessFile (1985-); Gen. Period. Index (1985-); GeoRef; INFO-SOUTH Abstr.; INSPEC (Jan. 1984-); Leg. Resour. Index (1980-); LegalTrac (1980-); Mag. Search; PAIS Int. Print (1991-); Trade Ind. ASAP [Full Txt.]; Trade Ind. Index (1981-) [Full Txt.]; UMI ABI/Inform--Bus. Period. Ondisc (Jan. 1987-) [Full Txt.]; Vocat. Search (Jan. 1993-Sept. 1993); Wilson Bus. Abstr.

US/0095-5086
**PUBLIC UTILITIES LAW ANTHOLOGY.** **See** Law.

US/0196-7843
**PUBLIC UTILITIES REPORTS.** [Public util. rep.]. **Added/Corp** Public Utilities Reports, Inc. (1915)-. English. ir (8 volumes with Annual Digest). $1095.00. Public Utilities Reports Inc., 2111 Wilson Boulevard, Suite 200, Arlington VA 22201. **Tel** (703)243-7000, (800)368-5001, FAX (703)527-5829. **(Subscription address:** Public Utilities Reports Inc., PO Box 1110, Pearl River NY 10965.**)** **LC** KF2085.A2; P8. **DD** 343/.73/090264. Each issue contains an index to its own contents (no volume index)--loose.

US
**PUBLIC UTILITIES REPORTS ADVANCE SHEETS.** (PUR ADVANCE SHEETS.). (19??)-. English. Twenty-six times a year. $595.00. Public Utilities Reports Inc., 2111 Wilson Boulevard, Suite 200, Arlington VA 22201. **Tel** (703)243-7000, (800)368-5001, FAX (703)527-5829.

US
**PUBLIC UTILITIES REPORTS UTILITY WEEKLY.** (PUR UTILITY WEEKLY.). (19??)-. English. Fifty-two times a year. $459.00 US and Canada; $595.00 other. Public Utilities Reports Inc., 2111 Wilson Boulevard, Suite 200, Arlington VA 22201. **Tel** (703)243-7000, (800)368-5001, FAX (703)527-5829. **ED** Lori A. Burkhart. ***Continues*** *PUR Executive Information Service.*

US/0896-5927
**PUC BULLETIN.** [PUC bull.]. **Main/Corp** Texas. Public Utility Commission. **VFOAT** Bulletin. **VAT** Public Utility Commission Bulletin. Vol. 12, No. 4 (Dec. 1986)-. Bulletin. English. mo. $50.00 (plus tax). State Treasurer, Accounting Division, Public Utility Commission, 7800 Shoal Creek Boulevard, Austin TX 78757. **LC** KFT1485; .A557. **DD** 343.764/09/0262; 347.640390262. ***Continues*** *Bulletin (Texas Public Utility Commission).*

US
**PUR LETTER.** ***Title Change.*** (19??)-(19??). English. Fifty-two times a year. Public Utilities Reports Inc., 2111 Wilson Boulevard, Suite 200, Arlington VA 22201. **Tel** (703)243-7000, (800)368-5001, FAX (703)527-5829. **ED** Lori A. Burkhart. ***Continues*** *PUR Executive Information Service.* ***Continued by*** *PUR Utility Letter.*
**Desc:** Utility issues are covered, mostly from a regulatory viewpoint, at state and federal levels. Commission decisions, court actions, Capital Hill meetings affecting energy and telecommunications industry are included.

US/0886-7178
**PURPA LINES.** ***Title Change.*** **See** Energy.

US/1047-8272
**PURTI RESEARCH SUMMARIES.** [PURTI res. summ.]. **Added/Corp** Public Utility Research and Training Institute (University of Wyoming). **VAT** Public Utility Research and Training Institute Research Summaries. (1989)-. Periodical. English. Three times a year (Mar., July, Nov.). $150.00. Public Utilities Research and Training Institute, PO Box 3275, Laramie WY 82071-3275. **Tel** (307)766-5506, FAX (307)766-4028. **ED** Curtis Crameer and John Tschirhart. **LC** HD2771; .P87. **DD** 363.2/0973/05. **Circ:** 130.

US/0749-9183
**QUARTERLY STATISTICAL REPORT - EDISON ELECTRIC INSTITUTE. STATISTICAL DEPT.** **See** Public Administration-Abstracting, Bibliographies and Statistics.

US/0898-3933
**RELIABILITY ASSESSMENT.** **See** Engineering-Electricity, Electrical Engineering, Electronics.

UK/0528-4082
**REPORT AND ACCOUNTS - CENTRAL ELECTRICITY GENERATING BOARD (LONDON).** **See** Business.

HK
**REPORT OF THE PUBLIC WORKS SUBCOMMITTEE OF FINANCE COMMITTEE APPOINTED TO REVIEW THE PUBLIC WORKS PROGRAMME.** **Main/Corp** Hong Kong. Legislative Council. Finance Committee. Public Works Subcommittee. Began with Vol. for 1953/54. English. HK$200.00 Hong Kong; $26.70 US. J R Lee, Government Printer, Java Road, Hong Kong Hong Kong. **LC** HD4331.H6; L43A. **DD** 354/.51/250086. **Circ:** 100.
**Desc:** A review of the Public Works Programme carried out in Hong Kong with analyses and recommendations.

CN/0845-0919
**REPORT ON GREAT LAKES WATER QUALITY : REPORT TO THE INTERNATIONAL JOINT COMMISSION / GREAT LAKES WATER QUALITY BOARD.** **See** Water Resources.

US/0145-2215
**REPORT - SPECIAL STUDIES SECTION, FIELD OPERATIONS DIVISION, TEXAS WATER QUALITY BOARD.** **Main/Corp** Texas. Water Quality Board. Field Operations Division. Special Studies Section. English. Texas Water Quality Board, PO Box 13087, Austin TX 78711. **LC** TD224.T4; T4216B. **DD** 363.6/1/09764.

US/1073-6646
**STATE DIRECTORY OF NEW ELECTRIC POWER PLANTS.** [State dir. new electr. power plants]. **Added/Corp** Utility Data Institute. **VFOAT** State Directory. (Feb. 1991)-. English. an (Feb.). $145.00 US; $155.00 Canada. Utility Data Institute, Inc., 1700 K Street Northwest, Suite 400, Washington DC 20006. **Tel** (800)246-3660, (202)466-3660. **LC** TK1194; .S73. **DD** 333.79/3211/0973.

US/0361-3607
**STATISTICAL YEAR BOOK OF THE ELECTRIC UTILITY INDUSTRY.** **See** Public Administration-Abstracting, Bibliographies and Statistics.

NE/0168-5163
**STATISTIEK VAN DE ELEKTRICITEITS--VOORZIENING IN NEDERLAND / CENTRAAL BUREAU VOOR DE STATISTIEK, HOOFDAFDELING STATISTIEKEN VAN INDUSTRIE EN BOUWNIJVERHEID.** **See** Public Administration-Abstracting, Bibliographies and Statistics.

●CN/0825-6667
**SUMMARY OF ECONOMIC AND LOAD FORECASTS.** (SUMMARY OF ECONOMIC AND LOAD FORECASTS / PREPARED AND ISSUED BY STRATEGIC PLANNING UNIT, CORPORATE PLANNING.). [Summ. econ. load forecasts]. **Added/Corp** B.C. Hydro. Strategic Planning. (1995)-. English. British Columbia Hydro Information Center, 970 Burrard Street, Vancouver BC V6Z 1Y3 Canada. **Tel** (604)663-2618. **LC** HD9685.C4; B157. **DD** 333.79/3213. ***Continues*** *Summary of Projections of Electric and Gas Gross Load Requirements.*
**Desc:** Information on electric power consumption and electric utilities.

US/1060-4944
**TAX COURT PETITIONS.** (TAX COURT PETITIONS [MICROFORM].). [Tax court petitions]. (Dec. 1991)-. Periodical. English. wk. $349.00. Tax Analysts, 6830 North Fairfax Drive, Arlington VA 22213. **Tel** (703)533-4400, (800)955-3444. **DD** 343.

US/0744-7981
**TEXAS PUBLIC UTILITY NEWS.** (TEXAS PUBLIC UTILITY NEWS : A PUBLICATION OF RESEARCH & PLANNING CONSULTANTS, INC.). [Tex. public util. news]. **Added/Corp** Research and Planning Consultants (Austin, Tex.). (19??)-. Periodical. English. sm. $621.00 Texas; $575.00 other. RPC Publications, 7600 Chevy Chase Drive, Building 2, Austin TX 78752. **Tel** (512)371-8100. **ED** Bonnie Sonnek. **DD** 363. Index available. **Circ:** 120 (ctrl). ***Continues*** *Patton Utility News, 0164-3355.*
**Desc:** Covers public utility issues including gas, electric and water rates, civil and state court action and final orders by PUC, RRC and TWC.

US
**UDI WHO'S WHO IN COGENERATION & INDEPENDENT POWER.** **Added/Corp** Utility Data Institute. **VFOAT** Who's Who in Cogeneration & Independent Power; Utility Data Institute Who's Who in Cogeneration & Independent Power. 1st Ed. (1991)-. English. $150.00. Utility Data Institute, Inc., 1700 K Street Northwest, Suite 400, Washington DC 20006. **Tel** (800)246-3660, (202)466-3660. **LC** HD9685.U4; U84. available on diskette.

UK
**UK ELECTRICITY / ELECTRICITY ASSOCIATION.** **Added/Corp** Electricity Association (Great Britain). (1991)-. English. **LC** WMLC 91/4463. ***Continues*** *Annual Report and Accounts.*

CN/0821-056X
**UPDATE, MARKET FORECAST, ELECTRIC ENERGY REQUIREMENTS IN YUKON.** [Update, mark. forecast, electric energy requir. Yukon]. 1981/'82/2001/'02-. English. an. Northern Canada Power Commission, PO Box 5700 Station L, Edmonton Alberta T6C 4J8 Canada. **DD** 333.79/3212/097191. ***Continues*** *Market Forecast, Electric Energy Requirements in the Yukon Territory, 0821-0551.*

UK/0960-2356
**UTILITIES LAW REVIEW.** **See** Law.

US/0889-4248
**UTILITY COMMUNICATOR'S EXCHANGE.** [Util. commun. exch.]. **VFOAT** Exchange. (19??)-. Periodical. English. mo. $250.00 (over 2,000 customers), $187.00 (1,000 to 2,000 customers), $125.00 (50,000 to 100,000 customers), $98.00 other. Utility Communicators Exchange, PO Box 337, Central City IA 52214. **ED** Kathy Staskal. **DD** 380. Index available (Sent with Jan. issue). cum. index. **Ad Acc, Adv Mgr:** Kathy Staskal, **Tel** (319)438-6101.
**Desc:** Professional journal with articles of interest to utility communicators (gas and electric), in advertising, PR, environment, DSM, marketing, and economic development.

●US/1064-5373
**UTILITY FORECASTER, THE.** [Util. forecast.]. (1992)-. Periodical. English. mo. $87.00 (one year), $174.00 (two year). KCI Communications Inc, 1101 King Street, Suite 400, Alexandria VA 22314. **Tel** (703)548-2400, (800)832-2330, FAX (703)683-6974. **DD** 332.

US/0890-2984
**UTILITY REPORTER (SCHENECTADY, N.Y.).** (UTILITY REPORTER.). (19??)-. English. mo. $269.00. Infoteam Inc., PO Box 15640, Plantation FL

33318. **Tel** (305)473-9560. **DD** 338. **[CCC]**.
**Ind/Abst** PROMT (19??-) [Full Txt.]; PTS Newsl. Database (19??-) [Full Txt.].

●US
**UTILITY WORKERS' LIGHT. Added/Corp** Utility Workers Union of America. **VFOAT** Light. Vol. 37, No. 3 (Mar. 1992)-. Periodical. English. mo. Utility Workers Union of America AFL-CIO, 815 Sixteenth Street NW, Washington DC 20006. **Tel** (202)347-8105. **Continues** Light.

# PUBLIC HEALTH AND SAFETY

US
**A P C O PUBLIC SAFETY COMMUNICATIONS.** Periodical. English. mo. $30.00. Association of Public Communications, PO Box 669, 105 1/2 Canal Street, New Smyrna Beach FL 32070. **Tel** (904)427-3461. **ED** Bob Buttgen. **Ad Acc. Circ:** 6,000 (ctrl).
**Desc:** Articles detailing the latest news of public safety communications for law enforcement, fire, 9-1-1 centers, forestry and conservation. Two-way radios, microwave, data transmission.

GW/0178-0999
**A + S AKTUELL.** [A S aktuell]. **VFOAT** A und S Aktuell; Arbeit und Sozialpolitik Aktuell; A + S. Arbeit und Sozialpolitik Aktuell. (19??)-. Periodical. German. Four times a year. DM643.08. Giesel Verlag Publizitaet GmbH, Postfatch 120161, D 30907 Isernhagen Germany. **Tel** 011 49 511 7304146, FAX 011 49 511 7304157, telex 511889. **UDC** 304.

US/0363-3837
**ABSTRACTS OF CONTRIBUTED PAPERS - MEDICAL CARE SECTION.** See Medical Science and Technology.

UK/0260-5511
**ABSTRACTS ON HYGIENE AND COMMUNICABLE DISEASES.** See Public Health and Safety-Abstracting, Bibliographies and Statistics.

US/0360-6090
**ACCELERATION AND PASSING ABILITY.** See Transportation.

UK/0001-4575
**ACCIDENT ANALYSIS AND PREVENTION.** [Accident anal. prev.]. Vol. 1 (July 1969)-. Periodical. English. bm (1 volume). $656.00 The Americas; £440.00 other. Pergamon Press, An Imprint of Elsevier Science Ltd., The Boulevard, Langford Lane, Kidlington, Oxford OX5 1GB United Kingdom. **Tel** 011 44 865 843000, 011 44 865 843699, FAX 011 44 865 843010. **(Subscription address:** Elsevier Science Ltd. Oxford Fulfillment Centre, PO Box 800, Kidlington, Oxford OX5 1DX United Kingdom.) **ED** Frank A. Haight (editor's address: Transportation Science, University of California, Irvine CA 92717). **LC** HV675.A1; A3. **DD** 614.8/05. **NLM** W1 AC69K. **CODEN** AAPVB5. **[CCC]**. **Pr Rev.** available on microfilm and microfiche from University Microfilms International (UMI); and Microfilms International Marketing Corp. Documents available from Article Express International, The Genuine Article, BIOSIS Document Express.
**Desc:** Provides wide coverage of the general areas relating to accidental injury and damage, including the pre-injury and immediate post-injury phases. Published papers deal with medical, legal, educational, behavioral, theoretical or empirical aspects of transportation accidents, as well as with accidents at other sites.
**Ind/Abst** Bioeng. Abstr.; Biol. Abstr.; Crim. Penol. Police Sci. Abstr.; Curr. Contents Soc. Behav. Sci.; Ei Page One; EMBASE; Eng. Index Annu.; Ergon. Abstr.; Health Saf. Sci. Abstr.; Health Plan. Adminis.; Highw. Res. Abstr.; Index Med. (Vol. 17, No. 1, 1985-); Pollut. Abstr. Indexes; Psychol. Abstr. (1969-); PsycINFO; PsycLit; PsycScan: Appl. Psych.; Res. Alert [Full Cov.]; Risk Abstr.; Saf. Health Work; Soc. Sci. Cit. Index [Full Cov.].

US
**ACCIDENT AND HEALTH BUSINESS.** **VFOAT** Summary of Accident and Health Insurance Business in North Carolina. English. an. North Carolina Department of Insurance, PO Box 26387, Raleigh NC 27611. **Tel** (919)733-7343. **LC** HG9338.N8; A27. **DD** 368.3/8/009756.

US/0895-7142
**ACCIDENT AND SAFETY ADVISORY : ASA. Ceased.** [Accid. saf. advis.]. **VFOAT** ASA. Periodical. English. mo. A.S.A., 106 Brushy Hill Road, Newtown CT 06470. **ED** Fred Ryder. **DD** 620.
**Desc:** The safety engineer explains technical aspects of accidents to lawyers, claims personnel, safety educators and corporate executives.

US/0148-6039
**ACCIDENT FACTS (CHICAGO).** (ACCIDENT FACTS.). **Added/Corp** National Safety Council. National Safety Council. Statistics Committee. National Safety Council. Statistics Dept. National Safety Council. Statistics Division. (1921)-. English. an. $26.25. National Safety Council, 1121 Spring Lake Drive, Itasca IL 60143. **Tel** (800)621-7615, (708)775-2294, FAX (708)285-0797. **LC** HA217; .A4. **DD** 312/.4/0973.
**Ind/Abst** Predicasts Forecasts; Stat. Ref. Index.

CN/0316-7283
**ACCIDENT FATALITIES, CANADA.** **Added/Corp** Canada Safety Council. Statistics Canada. Vital Statistics Section. (1969)-. Periodical. English (French). an. 8.25Can$. Canada Safety Council, 2750 Stevenage Drive Unit 6, Ottawa Ontario K1G 3N2 Canada. **Tel** (613)739-1535, FAX (613)739-1566. **DD** 312/.27. **Circ:** 300. **Continues** Accident Facts, Canada, 0547-891X.

US/0163-4674
**ACCIDENT/INCIDENT BULLETIN.** [Accid. incid. bull.]. **VAT** Accident Incident Bulletin. Began with No. 14 (1975). Bulletin. English. an. US Department of Transportation / Federal Railroad Administration, 400 Seventh Street SW, Washington DC 20590. **Tel** (202)366-0881, FAX (202)366-7009. **LC** HE1780; .A2. **DD** 312/.44/0973. **Continues** United States. Federal Railroad Administration. Office of Safety. Accident Bulletin, 0092-1645.

US
**ACCIDENT PREVENTION (ARLINGTON, VA.).** See Aeronautics, Astronautics.

US/0094-5927
**ACCIDENTAL POISONING IN WISCONSIN.** [Accid. poisoning Wis.]. **Main/Corp** Wisconsin. Division of Health. English. Wisconsin. Division of Health / Wisconsin, Box 309, Madison WI 53701. **LC** RA11965.W6; W57A. **DD** 312/.4.

US/0065-082X
**ACCIDENTS IN NORTH AMERICAN MOUNTAINEERING.** See Recreation, Leisure-Outdoor Life.

US
**ACQUIRED IMMUNE DEFICIENCY SYNDROME ... (REPORTED COSTS).** Aug. 1986-. English. New Jersey Department of Health, John Fitch Plaza, CN-360, Trenton NJ 08625. **Tel** (609)292-7837, FAX (609)984-5474.

AT/1321-1609
**ACTIVE AND HEALTHY QUARTERLY.** (19??)-. English. Four times a year. 31.00Aus$ Australia; 38.00Aus$ others. ACHPER, 214 Port Road, PO Box 304, Hindmarsh 5007 South Australia. **Tel** 011 61 (08)340 3388, FAX 011 61 (08)340 3399. **Continues** M/C Health and Fitness Newsletter.

●FR/1243-275X
**ACTUALITE ET DOSSIER EN SANTE PUBLIQUE.** (1992)-. Periodical. French. qt (Mar., June, Sept., Dec.). Free on request. Haut Comite de la Sante Publique, 2 rue Auguste Comte, 92170 Vanves France. **Tel** 011 33 1 46 62 42 80, FAX 011 33 1 46 62 42 55. **ED** Segolene Chappellon. **UDC** 354.84/.85(44). **Continues** HCSP Actualite.

CN/0711-169X
**ACTUALITES PREVENTION.** [Actual. prev.]. Vol. 1, No. 1 (Autumn 1979)-. Periodical. French. qt. Free. Actualite Prevention Health Marketing Systems, CP 490 Succursale A, Scarborough Ontario M1K 2N0 Canada. **DD** 614/.05. ctrl circ.

US
**ADAMHA ADVISORY COMMITTEES.** **Added/Corp** United States. Alcohol, Drug Abuse, and Mental Health Administration. **VAT** Alcohol, Drug Abuse, and Mental Health Administration Advisory Committees. (19??)-. English. **LC** RA11; .B15b. **Continues** ADAMHA Public Advisory Committes.

US
**ADDITIONS TO STATE MENTAL HEALTH FACILITIES, FISCAL YEAR ... .** 1978/79-. English. an. Mis and Data Services Division, Department of Mental Health/Retardation, PO Box 1797, Richmond VA 23214. **LC** RA790.65.V54; A33. **DD** 362.2/09755.

US/0894-587X
**ADMINISTRATION AND POLICY IN MENTAL HEALTH.** See Sociology-Social Services and Welfare.

TR
**ADMINISTRATION REPORT - PORT OF SPAIN, TRINIDAD AND TOBAGO. PUBLIC HEALTH DEPT. Main/Corp** Port of Spain, Trinidad and Tobago. Public Health Dept. English. an. Trinidad & Tobago Public Health Department, Government Printing Office, Port of Spain Trinidad & Tobago. **LC** RA194.T7; P67A. **DD** 362.1/09729/83.

US/0731-2199
**ADVANCES IN HEALTH ECONOMICS AND HEALTH SERVICES RESEARCH.** [Adv. health econ. health serv. res.]. Vol. 2 (1981)-. English. ir. $73.25. JAI Press Inc., 55 Old Post Road, Suite 2, PO Box 1678, Greenwich CT 06836-1678. **Tel** (203)661-7602, FAX (203)661-0792. **ED** Richard M. Scheffler and Louis F. Rossiter. **LC** RA410.A1; R48. **DD** 338.4/73621. **NLM** W1 AD621T. **[CCC]**. **Continues** Research in Health Economics, 0197-0690.
**Ind/Abst** Health Plan. Adminis.; Hospit. Health Admin. Index.

US/0890-4073
**ADVANCES IN HEALTH EDUCATION.** [Adv. health educ.]. **VFOAT** Advances in Health Education, Current Research. Vol. 1 (1988)-. English. an. $37.50. AMS Press Inc., 56 East 13th Street, New York NY 10003. **Tel** (212)777-4700, FAX (212)995-5413, telex 710 581 2302. **ED** James H. Humphrey. **LC** RA440.A1; A28. **DD** 613/.07. **NLM** W1; AD621TL.
**Desc:** Reports original research investigating issues related to human health and health education. Contains contributions from both experienced and up-and-coming researchers and educators in the field. The research topics addressed range from a broad review of research issues and methods in health education to more specific discussions of behavioral risk indicators and health education in the workplace.

US/0896-1255
**ADVANCES IN HEALTH EDUCATION AND PROMOTION.** [Adv. health educ. promot.]. Vol. 1 (1986)-. Monographic series. English. ir. Price varies per volume. Jessica Kingsley Publishers, 118 Pentonville Road, London N1 9JN England. **Tel** 011 44 71 833 2307, FAX 011 44 71 837 2917. **(Subscription address:** Taylor & Francis Inc., 1900 Frost Road, Suite 101, Bristol PA 19007-1598.) **LC** RA440.A1; A3. **DD** 607/.1. **NLM** W1; AD621U.

US
**ADVANCES IN RISK ANALYSIS.** See Public Health and Safety-Abstracting, Bibliographies and Statistics.

US/0891-7450
**AFB ACTION.** (AFB ACTION / ASSOCIATION FOR FITNESS IN BUSINESS.). [AFB action]. **Added/Corp** Association for Fitness in Business (U.S.). **VFOAT** Action; AFB. **VAT** Association for Fitness in Business Action. (19??)-. Periodical. English. Six times a year. $130.00 (professional general); $250.00 (company); $350.00 (associate). Comes with subscription to Association for Fitness in Business membership. Association for Fitness in Business, 200 Marott Center, 342 Mass Avenue, Indianapolis IN 46204. **Tel** (317)636-6621. **Absorbed** AAFDBI Fitprints.
**Ind/Abst** SportSearch (May 1987-).

US/0731-3446
**AFFIRMATIVE ACTION PLAN - MAINE. DEPT. OF MENTAL HEALTH AND CORRECTIONS.** (AFFIRMATIVE ACTION PLAN / DEPARTMENT OF MENTAL HEALTH AND CORRECTIONS.). **Main/Corp** Maine. Dept. of Mental Health and Corrections. English. an. Maine Department of Mental Health and Corrections22, State Office Building, Augusta ME 04333. **LC** RA790.65.M3; M34B. **DD** 353.97410084.

US
**AFFIRMATIVE ACTION PLAN / OKLAHOMA HEALTH PLANNING COMMISSION. Main/Corp** Oklahoma Health Planning Commission. (19??)-. English. an. Oklahoma Health Planning Commission, 1000 Northeast 10th Street, Oklahoma City OK 73117. **Tel** (405)271-5600. **LC** RA134; .O49a. **DD** 353.97660077/068/3.

US
**AFFIRMATIVE ACTION PROGRAM - ILLINOIS DEPT. OF MENTAL HEALTH AND DEVELOPMENTAL DISABILITIES. Main/Corp** Illinois Dept. of Mental Health and Developmental Disabilities. English. an. Illinois Department of Mental Health, 401 State Building, Springfield IL 62706. **LC** RA790.65.I4; I43B. **DD** 353.9/773/001.

UK
**AFRICA HEALTH MARKETLETTER.** **VFOAT** AHML. (1987)-. Newsletter. English. Ten times a year. £225.00. FSG Communications (U.K.), Vine House, Fair Green Reach, Cambridge CB5 0JD England. **Tel** 011 44 638 743633, FAX 011 44 638 743998, telex 9312102384 AH G. **ED** Bryan Pgarson. **NLM** W1; AF513F.
**Desc:** Provides economic, financial and development news affecting the health care sector in Africa.

FR
**AFRIQUE MEDECINE ET SANTE.** ***Ceased.*** No. 1 (May 1986)-No. 65 (April 1992). Periodical. French. mo. SAPEF, 11 rue de Teheran, 75008 Paris France. **Tel** 33/1/45697476, FAX 33/1/45632248, telex 641916F. **ED** Therese Lethu. **NLM** W1; AF628H. **Bk Rev. Ad Acc. Circ:** 7,200.
**Desc:** Medical and pharmaceutical information for French speaking Africa.

CF/0250-8621
**AFRO TECHNICAL PAPERS.** [AFRO tech. pap.]. **Added/Corp** World Health Organization. Regional Office for Africa. No. 1, (1970)-. Monographic series. English (French). ir. Price varies per volume. World Health Organization / Congo, BP 6, Regional Office for Africa, Brazzaville Congo. **LC** UNC. **NLM** W1 AI1545.
**Desc:** Covers public health problems in Africa.
**Ind/Abst** Curr. Titl. Dent.; Leis. Recreat. Tour. Abstr.; Rural Dev. Abstr.; World Agric. Econ.

KE/0378-4851
**AFYA (NAIROBI).** **See** Medical Science and Technology.

CN/0843-4700
**AGENCY INSIGHT.** (AGENCY INSIGHT / ALBERTA PUBLIC SAFETY SERVICES.). [Agency insight]. **Added/Corp** Alberta Public Safety Services. **VAT** Insight - Alberta Public Safety Services. Vol. 1, No. 1 (Mar. 1989)-. Periodical. English. Three times a year. 20.00Can$. Alberta Public Safety Services, 10320 146th Street, Edmonton Alberta T5A 3N2 Canada. **Tel** (403)427-2772. **DD** 363.1/097123. ***Formed by the union of*** *H.o.t.line (Alberta Disaster Services. Transportation of Dangerous Goods Control)., 0319-9746* ***and*** *News and Notes - Alberta Disaster Services., 0702-3138.*

JA/0515-7803
**AICHI-KEN EISEI KENKYUSHOHO.** [Aichi-Ken Eisei Kenkyushoho]. **VFOAT** Reports of the Aichi Institute of Public Health. (1949)-. Japanese. ir. Aichiken Eisei Kenkyujo, (Aichi Prefectural Institution of Public Health), 7-6 Nagare, Tsujimachi, Kitaku,, Nagoyashi, Aichiken 462 Japan. **CODEN** AKEKAK. Documents available from CASDDS.
**Ind/Abst** Chem. Abstr.

US/0887-3852
**AIDS & PUBLIC POLICY JOURNAL.** **See** Medical Science and Technology-Allergy and Immunology.

US/0893-7613
**AIDS CRISIS, THE.** **See** Medical Science and Technology-Allergy and Immunology.

US/0895-8882
**AIDS EDUCATION.** ***Title Change.*** **See** Medical Science and Technology-Allergy and Immunology.

US/0899-9546
**AIDS EDUCATION AND PREVENTION.** [AIDS educ. prev.]. **Added/Corp** International Society for AIDS Education. **VAT** Acquired Immune Deficiency Syndrome Education and Prevention. Vol. 1, No. 1 (Spring 1989)-. Periodical. English. Six times a year. $115.00 (institutions); $145.00 other. Guilford Publications Inc., 72 Spring Street, New York NY 10012. **Tel** (212)431-9800, (800)365-7006, FAX (212)966-6708. **(Subscription address:** Turpin Distribution Services Limited, Blackhorse Road, Letchworth, Hertfordshire SG6 1HN, United Kingdom.**)** **ED** Francisco S. Sy (editor's address: AIDS Education and Prevention, University of South Carolina, School of Public Health, Columbia, SC 29208). **LC** RA644.A25; A359. **DD** 614.5/993. **NLM** W1; AI696CHN. **CODEN** AEPREO. **[CCC].** Index available. cum. index. **Bk Rev. Ad Acc. Pr Rev. Circ:** 1,700. available on microfilm and microfiche from University Microfilms International (UMI). Documents available from The Genuine Article.
**Desc:** Provides professionals who deal with AIDS with the state-of-the-art information they need. High-caliber original contributions highlighting existing and theoretical models of AIDS education and prevention.
**Ind/Abst** Abstr. Res. Pastor. Care Couns. (19??-); Cumul. Index Nurs. Allied Health Lit.; Curr. Contents Soc. Behav. Sci.; EMBASE; Health Saf. Sci. Abstr.; Health Plan. Adminis.; Index Med. (1989-); Linguist. Lang. Behav. Abstr.; Physic. Medline Plus; Psychol. Abstr. (1989-); PsycINFO (1990-); Res. Alert [Full Cov.]; Risk Abstr.; Soc. Plann. Policy Dev. Abstr.; Soc. Sci. Cit. Index [Full Cov.]; Soc. Work Abstr. [Select. Cov.]; Sociol. Abstr.; Trop. Dis. Bull.

NE/1013-7785
**AIDS HEALTH PROMOTION, EXCHANGE.** **See** Medical Science and Technology-Allergy and Immunology.

US/0891-7426
**AIDS INFORMATION EXCHANGE.** (AIDS INFORMATION EXCHANGE / THE UNITED STATES CONFERENCE OF MAYORS.). [AIDS inf. exch.]. **Added/Corp** United States Conference of Mayors. United States. Dept. of Health and Human Services. **VAT** Acquired Immunodeficiency Syndrome Information Exchange. (June 1984)-. Periodical. English. bm. Free to mayors and local health departments; $50.00 other. US Conference of Mayors, 1620 Eye Street NW, Washington DC 20006. **Tel** (202)293-7330, FAX (202)293-2352. **DD** 616. **NLM** W1; AI696D.

US/0893-1526
**AIDS LITERATURE & NEWS REVIEW.** **See** Medical Science and Technology-Allergy and Immunology.

US
**AIDS REFERENCE AND RESEARCH COLLECTION.** **See** Medical Science and Technology-Allergy and Immunology.

US
**AIDS SURVEILLANCE QUARTERLY UPDATE FOR CASES REPORTED THROUGH... .** **Added/Corp** New York (State). Bureau of Communicable Disease Control (1982- ). (Mar 1991)-. Periodical. English. qt. ***Continues*** *AIDS Surveillance Monthly Update.*

US/1053-9093
**AIDS UPDATE (ALBANY, N.Y.).** ***Ceased.*** **See** Medical Science and Technology-Allergy and Immunology.

US/1059-8847
**AIDSMONTHLY (BUSINESS AND FINANCE ED.).** ***Title Change.*** **See** Sociology-Social Services and Welfare.

●US/1065-4038
**ALABAMA HEALTH CARE IN PERSPECTIVE.** [Ala. health care perspect.]. **Added/Corp** Morgan Quitno Corporation. 1st Ed. (1993)-. English. $18.00. Morgan Quitno Corporation, PO Box 1656, 512 East 9th Street, Lawrence KS 66044. **Tel** (800)457-0742, (913)841-3534, FAX (913)841-3534. **DD** 362.
**Desc:** Reports on the state's data and rank for each of the categories featured in Health Care State Rankings.

US/0891-1665
**ALABAMA SHPA MONTHLY REVIEW.** **Added/Corp** Alabama State Health Planning Agency. **VAT** Alabama State Health Planning Agency Monthly Review. (19??)-. Periodical. English. mo (12 issues per year). $70.00. State Health Planning Agency, 121 6th Street, North Montgomery, Montgomery AL 36104. **Tel** (205)261-4103. **ED** Jim Sanders and Katrina Grant. **Circ:** 500.
**Desc:** Status of projects or applications for certificates of need.

US/0145-6857
**ALABAMA'S HEALTH.** **Added/Corp** Alabama. Dept. of Public Health. Bureau of Primary Prevention. Alabama. Dept. of Public Health. Division of Primary Prevention. (19??)-. Periodical. English. Twelve times a year. Free. Alabama Department of Public Health, 206 State Office Building, Room 381, Montgomery AL 36111. **Tel** (205)242-5052, FAX (205)240-3387. **ED** Arrol Sheehan. **Circ:** 1,200 (ctrl).
**Desc:** An interdepartmental publication. Distribution is restricted to health related organizations. activities, accomplishments and a calendar of events.

●US/1065-4046
**ALASKA HEALTH CARE IN PERSPECTIVE.** [Ala. health care perspect.]. **Added/Corp** Morgan Quitno Corporation. 1st Ed. (1993)-. English. $18.00. Morgan Quitno Corporation, PO Box 1656, 512 East 9th Street, Lawrence KS 66044. **Tel** (800)457-0742, (913)841-3534, FAX (913)841-3534. **DD** 362.
**Desc:** Reports on the state's data and rank for each of the categories featured in Health Care State Rankings.

CN/1182-4867
**ALBERTA COORDINATED HOME CARE PROGRAM DIRECTORY.** [Alta. Coord. Home Care Program dir.]. **Main/Corp** Alberta Coordinated Home Care Program. **Added/Corp** Alberta. Alberta Health. **VAT** Directory - Alberta Coordinated Home Care Program. (May 1990)-. Directory. English. **DD** 362.1/4/0257123. ***Continues*** *Alberta Coordinated Home Care Program. Program Directory., 1182-4875.*

CN/0848-399X
**ALBERTA HEALTH AND SOCIAL SERVICE EDUCATION PROGRAMS INVENTORY.** **See** Sociology-Social Services and Welfare.

SP/0300-5755
**ALIMENTARIA.** [Alimentaria]. (1964)-. Trade Publication. Spanish (English and French). Ten times a year. 12000.00ptas Spain; 19500.00ptas Europe; 21500.00ptas America; 24500.00ptas other. Eypasa, Sandoval 12 I J, 28010 Madrid Spain. **Tel** 011 34 1 4469659. **ED** Carlos Barros. **CODEN** ALMNEC. **[CCC].** Index available. cum. index. **Bk Rev. Ad Acc. Circ:** 5,000 (ctrl). Documents available from BIOSIS Document Express, CASDDS.
**Desc:** Trade journal offering articles on food preparation, preservation and biological properties. Also covers legal aspects of the food industry and marketing, as well as transportation technology.
**Ind/Abst** AGRICOLA; Anim. Breed. Abstr.; Biodeter. Abstr. (19??-19??); Biol. Abstr. (1986-); Chem. Abstr. (1986-); Dairy Sci. Abstr.; Field Crop Abstr.; Food Sci. Technol. Abstr.; Helminthol. Abstr.; Hortic. Abstr.; Index Vet.; Nutr. Abstr. Rev., Ser. B, Live Feeds and Feed.; Nutr. Abstr. Rev., Ser. A, Hum. Exp.; Postharvest News Inf.; Rev. Med. Vet. Mycology; Seed Abstr.; Soyabean Abstr.; Sug. Indus. Abstr.

US/0148-5067
**ALLIED HEALTH EDUCATION PROGRAMS IN JUNIOR AND SENIOR COLLEGES. HEALTH PLANNERS EDITION.** **Added/Corp** U.S. Bureau of Health Manpower. Manpower Analysis Branch. (1973)-. Government Publication. English. ir. $18.50. Superintendent of Documents, US Government Printing Office, Washington DC 20402. **Tel** (202)275-3328, FAX (202)786-2377. **NLM** W 22 AA1 A34. ***Formed by the union of*** *Allied Health Education Programs in Junior Colleges* ***and*** *Allied Health Education Programs in Senior Colleges, 0090-3442.*
**Desc:** Provides information about degree and non-degree educational programs in the United States and Puerto Rico. Includes programs for supportive personnel in public health and special education.

US/0275-7699
**ALLIED HEALTH TRENDS.** [Allied heal. trends]. Periodical. English. ir. $40.00. American Society of Allied Health Professionals, 1730 M Street Northwest, Suite 500, Washington DC 20036. **Tel** (202)293-4848, FAX (202)293-4852. **Ad Acc.**

US/0747-9263
**ALTERNATIVE DESIGNS.** [Altern. des.]. Began with Vol. 1, No. 1 (June 1983). Periodical. English. mo. $90.00. Pracon Inc, 10390 Democracy Lane, Fairfax VA 22030. **NLM** W1; AL987C. ***Continues*** *Blueprint for Healthcare Program Development.*

US/0002-9262
**AMERICAN JOURNAL OF EPIDEMIOLOGY.** **See** Medical Science and Technology-Epidemiology.

US/0890-1171
**AMERICAN JOURNAL OF HEALTH PROMOTION.** (AMERICAN JOURNAL OF HEALTH PROMOTION : AJHP.). [Am. j. health promot.]. **VFOAT** AJHP. Vol. 1 No. 1 (1986)-. Periodical. English. Six times a year. $59.95 US; $64.95 Canada & Mexico; $78.95 other. American Journal of Health Promotion, 1812 South Rochester Road, Suite 200, Rochester Hills MI 48307. **Tel** (313)650-9600, FAX (312)650-9602. **LC** WMLC 93/1376. **DD** 613. **NLM** W1; AM452HF. **CODEN** AJHPED. Index available (bound in first issue). cum. index. **Bk Rev**, (Qty: 12). **Ad Acc, Adv Mgr:** David Revels, **Tel** (810)650-9600. **Pr Rev. Circ:** 6,000 (ctrl).
**Desc:** This journal is defined as "the science and art of helping people change their lifestyle to move toward a state of optimal health." It is to provide a forum for the exchange of ideas among the diverse disciplines which promote health.
**Ind/Abst** Abstr. Soc. Gerontol.; Abstr. Res. Pastor. Care Couns. (19??-); Cumul. Index Nurs. Allied Health Lit.; EMBASE; Health Plan. Adminis.; Hospit. Health Admin. Index (1986-); Hum. Resour. Abstr. (?-?); Phys. Educ. Index (1987-); Psychol. Abstr. (1986-); PsycINFO (1990-); Sage Fam. Stud. Abstr.; SPORT Discus.

US/0090-0036
**AMERICAN JOURNAL OF PUBLIC HEALTH (1971).** (AMERICAN JOURNAL OF PUBLIC HEALTH.). [Am. j. publ. health]. **Added/Corp** American Public Health Association. **VFOAT** JPH; J.P.H.; Journal of Public Health; AJPH. Vol. 61, No. 1 (Jan. 1971)-. Academic Scholarly Publication. English. mo. $160.00 (institutions), $100.00 (individuals) US; $200.00 (institutions), $140.00 (individuals) other. American Public Health Association, 1015 15th Street Northwest, Washington DC 20005. **Tel** (202)789-5666. **(Subscription address:** American Public Health Association, Publication Sales, Department 5037, Washington, DC, 20061-5037**)** **ED** Michel A. Ibrahim. **LC** RA421; .A395. **NLM** W1 AM521C. **CODEN** AJHEAAJPEA. **[CCC].** Index available. cum. index. **Bk Rev. Ad Acc. Pr Rev. Circ:** 35,000. available on microfilm and microfiche from University Microfilms International (UMI). Documents available from The Genuine Article, BIOSIS Document Express, UMI Article Clearinghouse, CASDDS, Documents on Demand. ***Continues in part*** *American Journal of Public Health and the Nation's Health, 0002-9572.*
**Desc:** Publishes authoritative articles in general and specialized areas of the science, art and practice of public health, including environmental health, maternal and child health, health promotion, epidemiology, health administration, occupational health, health education, international health, and statistics.
**Ind/Abst** Abr. Index Med.; Abstr. Soc. Gerontol.; Acad. Abstr. Full Text Elite (July 1990-); Acad. Abstr. (July 1990-); Acad. Ind. [Computer File] (1987-); Acad. Search (July 1990-); AGRICOLA [Select. Cov.]; Agric. Eng. Abstr. (1991-); Am. Bibliogr. Slavic East Europ. Stud.; Annals Behav. Med.; Appl. Soc. Sci. Index Abstr.; Biocont. News

Inf. (1991-); Biodeter. Abstr. (1991-); Biol. Abstr.; Biol. Dig.; Chem. Abstr. (1971-1983); Coal Abstr.; Commun. Abstr.; Crim. Justice Abstr.; Cumul. Index Nurs. Allied Health Lit.; Curr. Aware. Biol. Sci., CABS; Curr. Contents Clin. Med.; Curr. Contents Life Sci.; Curr. Contents Soc. Behav. Sci.; Curr. Index J. Educ.; Curr. Lit. Fam. Plan.; Curr. Titl. Dent.; Dairy Sci. Abstr.; Dent. Abstr. (-1991); Dev. Med. Child Neurol.; EMBASE; Energy Res. Abstr. (Jan. 1981-); Environ. Abstr.; Environ. Period. Bibliogr.; Expand. Acad. Index (1988-); Food Sci. Technol. Abstr.; Gen. Sci. Index; Gen. Sci. Source (Jul. 1990-); Health Saf. Sci. Abstr.; Health Devices Alerts; Health Index (1989-); Health Period. Database; Health Plan. Adminis.; Health Ref. Cent. (Jan. 1989-) [Full Txt.] [Full Cov.]; Health Source (Jul. 1990-); Helminthol. Abstr.; Highw. Res. Abstr.; Hospit. Health Admin. Index; Hospit. Manage. Rev.; Index Med.; Index Vet.; INFO-SOUTH Abstr.; INIS Atomindex [Micro.]; Int. Pharm. Abstr.; Irr. Drain. Abstr.; J. Plan. Lit.; Leis. Recreat. Tour. Abstr.; Mag. Search; Med. Abstr. Newsl.; Multicult. Educ. Abstr.; Newsp. Period. Abstr. (1988-); Nutr. Abstr. Rev., Ser. B, Live Feeds and Feed.; Nutr. Abstr. Rev., Ser. A, Hum. Exp.; Nutr. Res. Newsl.; Life Sci. Collect.; Phys. Educ. Index; Physic. Medline Plus; Pollut. Abstr. Indexes; Popul. Index; Potato Abstr.; Protozoolog. Abstr.; Ref. Upd. Deluxe Ed.; Res. Alert [Full Cov.]; Res. High. Educ. Abstr.; Rev. Agric. Entomol.; Rev. Med. Vet. Entomol.; Rev. Med. Vet. Mycology; Risk Abstr.; Rural Dev. Abstr.; Sage Fam. Stud. Abstr.; Sci. Cit. Index; SCISEARCH; Soc. Sci. Source (Jul. 1990-); Soc. Sci. Cit. Index [Full Cov.]; Soc. Sci. Index; Soc. Sci. Index Fulltext (Oct. 1988-) [Full Txt.]; Soc. Work Abstr. (?-?); Spec. Educ. Needs Abstr.; SportSearch; Stud. Women Abstr.; Tech. Educ. Train. Abstr.; Vet. Bull.; Trop. Dis. Bull.; Virol. AIDS Abstr.; Vocat. Search (July 1990-); World Agric. Econ.

US
**AMERICA'S HEALTH.** ***Ceased.*** Vol. 1 (1978)-?. Periodical. English. qt. Pfizer Inc, 235 East 43rd Street, New York NY 10017.

BL
**ANAIS DA CONFERENCIA NACIONAL DE SAUDE.** **Added/Corp** Brazil. Ministerio da Saude. (19??)-. Portuguese. be (every two years). Free on request. Centre Documentacao Ministerio de Saude, Bloco G Terreo, 70058 Brasilia DF Brazil. **LC** RA463; .C66a. **Circ:** 5,000 (ctrl).

US
**ANALYSIS OF RESEARCH PUBLICATIONS SUPPORTED BY NIH AND NHLBI.** **Main/Corp** National Institutes of Health (U.S.). **VFOAT** Analysis of Research Publications Supported by NIH. NIH and NHLBI; Analysis of Research Publications Supported by the National Institute of Health. National Heart, Lung, and Blood Institute. (1976)-. Periodical. English. National Institutes of Health / Program Evaluation Branch, Office of Program Planning and Evaluation, 9000 Rockville Pike, Bethesda MD 20014.

US
**ANALYSIS OF RESEARCH PUBLICATIONS SUPPORTED BY NIH AND NIAID.** **Main/Corp** National Institutes of Health (U.S.). **VFOAT** Analysis of Research Publications Supported by NIH. NIH and NIAID; Analysis of Research Publications Supported by the National Institutes of Health. National Institute of Allergy and Infectious Diseases. 1970-1976-. English. National Institutes of Health / Program Evaluation Branch, Office of Program Planning and Evaluation, 9000 Rockville Pike, Bethesda MD 20014.

AT
**ANIMAL QUARANTINE.** ***Ceased.*** (1972)-(19??). Periodical. English. Australia Department of Health, PO Box 100, Woden ACT 2606 Australia. **Tel** 011 61 6 2398711.
**Ind/Abst** Index Vet.; Vet. Bull.

MG/0253-6390
**ANNALES DE L'UNIVERSITE DE MADAGASCAR. BIOLOGIE, CLINIQUE, SANTE PUBLIQUE.** **See** Biology.

IT
**ANNALI DELLA SANITA PUBBLICA.** **Added/Corp** Italy. Alto Commissariato per l'Igiene e la Sanita Pubblica. Italy. Ministero Della Sanita. Vol. 9 (1948)-. Periodical. Italian. Six times a year. L72000 Italy; L96000 others. Istituto Poligrafico Zecca Stato, Piazza Verdi 10, 00198 Rome Italy. **Tel** 011 39 6 85082307, 011 39 6 85082221. **LC** RA421; .A64. **NLM** W1 AN484. ***Supersedes*** *Notiziario dell'Amministrazione Sanitaria.*

IT/0021-2571
**ANNALI DELL'ISTITUTO SUPERIORE DI SANITA.** [Ann. Ist. super. sanita]. **Added/Corp** Istituto Superiore di Sanita (Italy). Vol. 1 (1965)-. Periodical. Italian (English and German). qt. L75000 Italy; L90000 other. Istituto Poligrafico Zecca Stato, Piazza Verdi 10, 00198 Rome Italy. **Tel** 011 39 6 85082307, 011 39 6 85082221. **LC** R61; .I78. **NLM** W1 AN486G. **CODEN** AISSAW. Documents available from BIOSIS Document Express, Ask*IEEE, CASDDS. ***Continues*** *Rendiconti - Istituto Superiore di Sanita.*

**Ind/Abst** Anal. Abstr.; Biol. Abstr.; Chem. Abstr.; Dairy Sci. Abstr.; EMBASE; Food Sci. Technol. Abstr.; Health Plan. Adminis.; Helminthol. Abstr.; Index Med.; Index Vet.; INSPEC (1980-); Irr. Drain. Abstr.; Nutr. Abstr. Rev., Ser. B, Live Feeds and Feed.; Nutr. Abstr. Rev., Ser. A, Hum. Exp.; Protozoolog. Abstr.; Rev. Med. Vet. Entomol.; Vet. Bull.; Trop. Dis. Bull.

FR
**ANNUAIRE / ASSOCIATION GENERALE DES HUGIENISTES ET TECHNICIENS MUNICIPAUX.** **Main/Corp** Association Generale des Hygienistes et Techniciens Municipaux (France). French. an. 75.00F. Association Generale des Hygienistes et Techniciens Municipaux, 9 rue de Phalsbourg, 75017 Paris France. **Tel** (1)227-3891, FAX (1)43.80.65.90. **LC** RA713; .A9. **DD** 362.1/0944. **Ad Acc. Circ:** 1,500. ***Continues*** *Association Generale des Hygienistes et Techniciens Municipaux (France). Annuaire des Membres.*

US
**ANNUAL FINANCIAL REPORT / TEXAS DEPARTMENT OF HEALTH.** **Main/Corp** Texas. Dept. of Health. **Added/Corp** Texas. Dept. of Health. Financial Report. (19??)-. English. Texas Department of Health, 1100 West 49th Street, Austin TX 78756-3180. **Tel** (512)458-7550, FAX (512)458-7407. **LC** RA157; .D45b. **DD** 353.97640084/1. ***Continues*** *Texas. Dept. of Health. Audit Report.*

US
**ANNUAL IMPLEMENTATION PLAN FOR NORTHERN INDIANA, AN.** **Main/Corp** Northern Indiana Health Systems Agency. Periodical. English. an. Northern Indiana Health Systems Agency, PO Box 1372, South Bend IN 46624-1372.

US
**ANNUAL IMPLEMENTATION PLAN / HEALTH POLICY COUNCIL.** **Main/Corp** Health Policy Council (Vt.). (19??)-. Periodical. English. ***Continues*** *Vermont Health Policy Corporation. Annual Implementation Plan, 0273-2203.*

US/0273-2203
**ANNUAL IMPLEMENTATION PLAN (WATERBURY).** ***Title Change.*** (ANNUAL IMPLEMENTATION PLAN.). **Main/Corp** Vermont. Health Policy Corporation. (19??)-(198?). English. an. 103 South Main Street, Waterbury VT 05676. **LC** RA395.A4; V58a. **DD** 362.1/09743. ***Continued by*** *Vermont. Health Policy Council. Annual Implementation Plan.*

US/0276-6922
**ANNUAL PLAN ... OF THE ILLINOIS DEPARTMENT OF MENTAL HEALTH AND DEVELOPMENTAL DISABILITIES.** **Main/Corp** Illinois. Dept. of Mental Health and Developmental Disabilities. 1979-1982-. English. an. Illinois Department of Mental Health and Developmental Disabilities / Chicago, 100 West Randolph 6-400, Chicago IL 60601-3278. **LC** RA790.65.I4; I43C. **DD** 362.2/09773. **NLM** W2 AI3 D37A. **Circ:** 2,000 (ctrl).

US
**ANNUAL REPORT / ALABAMA DEPARTMENT OF PUBLIC HEALTH.** **Main/Corp** Alabama. Dept. of Public Health. English. an. Alabama Department of Public Health, 206 State Office Building, Room 381, Montgomery AL 36111. **Tel** (205)242-5052, FAX (205)240-3387. **LC** RA446.5.A3; A43A. **DD** 353.97610077/05.

CN/1185-2984
**ANNUAL REPORT / ALBERTA HEALTH.** [Annu. rep. - Alta. Health]. **Main/Corp** Alberta. Alberta Health. (1989)-. English. **LC** RA983.A4; A4218. **DD** 354.71230084/.045; 362.1/1/097123. ***Continues*** *Alberta. Alberta Hospitals & Medical Care. Annual Report - Alberta Hospitals & Medical Care., 0227-7883.*

US
**ANNUAL REPORT AND GUIDE TO PROGRAMS / IDAHO DEPARTMENT OF HEALTH AND WELFARE.** **Main/Corp** Idaho. Dept. of Health and Welfare. **VFOAT** Annual Report and Guide to ... Programs. (19??)-. English. **LC** HV86; .I217. **DD** 353.9/796/008405. ***Continues*** *Idaho. Dept. of Health and Welfare. Annual Report - Department of Health and Welfare.*

SA
**ANNUAL REPORT / BOPHUTHATSWANA, DEPARTMENT OF HEALTH AND SOCIAL SERVICES.** **Main/Corp** Bophuthatswana (South Africa). Dept. of Health and Social Services. English. **LC** RA352.S75; B66a. **DD** 354.682/9400841. ***Continues*** *Annual Report.*

US/0271-339X
**ANNUAL REPORT - CITY OF CHICAGO/HSA.** **Main/Corp** City of Chicago/HSA. **VAT** Annual Report - City of Chicago, Health Systems Agency. 1977/78-. English. an. City of Chicago Health Systems Agency, 180 North Lasalle Street, Suite 700, Chicago IL 60601. **LC** RA55.C56; H43A. **DD** 352.94/41/0977311.

US
**ANNUAL REPORT / COMMONWEALTH OF VIRGINIA, DES, DEPARTMENT OF EMERGENCY SERVICES.** **Main/Corp** Virginia. Dept. of Emergency Services. (1984/1985)-. English. Virginia Office of Emergency & Energy Service, Richmond VA 23219. **LC** HV555.U62; V53a. **DD** 353.97550075/4/06. ***Continues*** *Annual Report.*

CN/0820-9979
**ANNUAL REPORT - DEPARTMENT OF HEALTH AND SOCIAL SERVICES (CHARLOTTETOWN).** (ANNUAL REPORT.). [Annu. rep. - Dep. Health Soc. Serv.]. **Main/Corp** Prince Edward Island. Dept. of Health and Social Services. 1st (1980/1981)-. English. an. **LC** RA185.P8. **DD** 354.7170684/06. **NLM** W2; DC2.1 P9D4a. ***Formed by the union of*** *Prince Edward Island. Dept. of Social Services. Annual Report, 0701-5291* ***and*** *Prince Edward Island. Dept. of Health. Annual Report of the Department of Health, 0317-4530.*

US
**ANNUAL REPORT / DEPARTMENT OF MENTAL HEALTH.** **Main/Corp** Ohio. Dept. of Mental Health. (1981)-. English. an. Ohio Department of Mental Health, Office of Program Evaluation and Research, State Office Tower/Room 1340J, 30 East Broad Street, Columbus OH 43266-0414. **Tel** (614)466-8651, FAX (614)466-9928. **LC** RA790.65.O3; O45b. **DD** 353.97710084/2/06. **NLM** W2; AO3 D47f. ***Continues*** *Ohio. Dept. of Mental Health and Mental Retardation. Annual Financial and Statistical Report, 0094-6508.*

PP/0377-9203
**ANNUAL REPORT - DEPARTMENT OF PUBLIC HEALTH.** (ANNUAL REPORT.). **Main/Corp** Papua-New Guinea (Ter.) Dept. of Public Health. **VFOAT** Annual Report - Dept. of Public Health. Papua-New Guinea. Periodical. English. **NLM** W2 LP2 D4A.

US
**ANNUAL REPORT - DIVISION OF MENTAL HYGIENE AND MENTAL RETARDATION.** **Main/Corp** Nevada. Division of Mental Hygiene and Mental Retardation. (19??)-. English. **LC** RA790.65.N3; N45a. **DD** 353.9/793/00842.

UK/0144-7084
**ANNUAL REPORT / EASTERN HEALTH AND SOCIAL SERVICES BOARD, NORTHERN IRELAND.** **Main/Corp** Northern Ireland. Eastern Health and Social Services Board. (19??)-. English. Eastern Health and Social Services Board, 65 University Street, Belfast BT7 1HN Northern Ireland. **LC** RA246; .N67a. **DD** 354.4160084/094165.

US
**ANNUAL REPORT - EPIDEMIOLOGY & DISEASE CONTROL STUDY SECTION, NATIONAL INSTITUTES OF HEALTH.** **See** Medical Science and Technology-Epidemiology.

SA
**ANNUAL REPORT FOR PERIOD ... / DEVELOPMENT AND SERVICES BOARD (NATAL).** **Main/Corp** Natal (South Africa). Development and Services Board. **VFOAT** Jaarverslag vir die Tydperk ... . Afrikaans (English). an. **LC** RA352.S75; N3A. **DD** 362.1/09684. ***Continues*** *Natal (South Africa). Development and Services Board. Annual Report of the Medical Officer of Health.*

●CN/1193-3003
**ANNUAL REPORT FOR THE FISCAL YEAR ENDING ... / NOVA SCOTIA PROVINCIAL HEALTH COUNCIL.** [Annu. rep. - N.S. Prov. Health Counc.]. **Main/Corp** Nova Scotia Provincial Health Council. (Mar 31 1992)-. English. **DD** 354.7160084.

CN
**ANNUAL REPORT FOR THE YEAR ENDING MARCH 31 ... / SASKATCHEWAN HEALTH.** **Main/Corp** Saskatchewan. Saskatchewan Health. **VFOAT** Annual Report. English. an. Saskatchewan Health, T C Douglas Building, 3475 Albert Street, Regina Saskatchewan S4S 6X6 Canada. **LC** RA185.S3; B1. **DD** 362.1/097124. ***Continues*** *Saskatchewa. Annual Report for the Department of Health.*

UK
**ANNUAL REPORT - GREATER LONDON COUNCIL. DEPT. OF PUBLIC HEALTH ENGINEERING.** **Main/Corp** Greater London Council. Dept. of Public Health Engineering. English. an. **LC** TD64.L8; G74A. **DD** 352/.4/09421.

# Public Health and Safety

CN/0838-3693
**ANNUAL REPORT - HEALTH AND COMMUNITY SERVICES. NEW BRUNSWICK.** (ANNUAL REPORT / HEALTH AND COMMUNITY SERVICES, NEW BRUNSWICK.). [Annu. rep. - Health Community Serv., N.B.]. **Main/Corp** New Brunswick. Dept. of Health and Community Services. **VFOAT** Rapport Annuel. **VAT** Rapport Annuel - Sante et Services Communautaires. Nouveau--Brunswick. (1986/87)-. English (French). an. Health and Community Services, New Brunswick, Canada. **LC** RA450.N5; N48a. **DD** 354.7150684/05. *Formed by the union of Annual Report / New Brunswick. Dept. of Health, 0711-8376 and Annual Report - New Brunswick Social Services, 0708-4242.*

US
**ANNUAL REPORT, HIGHWAY SAFETY IMPROVEMENT PROGRAMS IN VIRGINIA / PREPARED BY THE DIVISION OF TRAFFIC AND SAFETY FOR THE VIRGINIA DEPARTMENT OF HIGHWAYS AND TRANSPORTATION.** **Added/Corp** Virginia. Division of Traffic & Safety. Virginia. Dept. of Highways and Transportation. **VFOAT** Annual Report, Highway Safety Improvement Programs. (19??)-. English. an. Virginia Department of Transportation, 1401 East Broad Street, Richmond VA 23219. **Tel** (804)786-4243, FAX (804)786-6250. **LC** HE5614.3.V8; A55. **DD** 363.1/256/09755. ctrl circ.

US
**ANNUAL REPORT - IOWA DEPARTMENT OF PUBLIC SAFETY.** **Main/Corp** Iowa. Dept. of Public Safety. 1978-. English. Department of Public Safety / Iowa, Administration Division, Des Moines IA 50319. **LC** HV7571.I8; D46A.

US
**ANNUAL REPORT - LIPID METABOLISM ADVISORY COMMITTEE, NATIONAL INSTITUTES OF HEALTH.** **Main/Corp** National Heart, Lung, and Blood Institute. Lipid Metabolism Advisory Committee. 1975/76-. English. an. National Heart Lung and Blood Institute, Division of Heart and Vascular Diseases, Devices and Technology Branch, 9000 Rockville Pike, Bethesda MD 20014. *Continues Annual Report - Lipid Metabolism Advisory Committee, National Institutes of Health.*

NZ
**ANNUAL REPORT / MANAGEMENT SERVICES AND RESEARCH UNIT, DEPARTMENT OF HEALTH (NEW ZEALAND).** **Main/Corp** New Zealand. Dept. of Health. Management Services and Research Unit. English. an. New Zealand Department of Health Management Services and Research Unit, PO Box 5013, Wellington New Zealand. **LC** RA373; .N48A. **DD** 354.9310084/1.

US/0730-1286
**ANNUAL REPORT / MARCH OF DIMES BIRTH DEFECTS FOUNDATION.** See Medical Science and Technology.

CN/1183-997X
**ANNUAL REPORT / MENTAL HEALTH COMMISSION OF NEW BRUNSWICK.** [Annu. rep. - Ment. Health Comm. N.B.]. **Main/Corp** Commission de la Sante Mentale du Nouveau-Bunswick. **VFOAT** Rapport Annuel. **VAT** Rapport Annuel - Commission de la Sante Mentale du Nouveau-Brunswick. (Mar. 31 1991)-. French (English). **DD** 354.715/100842.

CN/1183-997X
**ANNUAL REPORT / MENTAL HEALTH COMMISSION OF NEW BRUNSWICK.** [Annu. rep. - Ment. Health Comm. N.B.]. **Main/Corp** Mental Health Commission of New Brunswick. **VFOAT** Rapport Annuel. **VAT** Rapport Annuel - Commission de la Sante Mentale du Nouveau-Brunswick. (Mar 31, 1991)-. English (French). **DD** 354.715/100842.

US/0270-3300
**ANNUAL REPORT - MENTAL HYGIENE ADMINISTRATION.** (ANNUAL REPORT - MENTAL HYGIENE ADMINISTRATION (MARYLAND).). **Main/Corp** Maryland. Mental Hygiene Administration. **VFOAT** Mental Hygiene Administration Annual Report. 1st- 1978-. English. an. US Department of Health and Human Services National Institutes of Health, 9000 Rockville Pike, Bethesda MD 20892. **Tel** (301)496-9291, FAX (301)496-2443. **NLM** W2 AM3 M5A. *Supersedes Annual Report - State of Maryland, Department of Mental Hygiene, 0461-1861.*

CN/0706-4810
**ANNUAL REPORT - MINISTRY OF HEALTH (VICTORIA).** (ANNUAL REPORT - MINISTRY OF HEALTH (BRITISH COLUMBIA).). **Main/Corp** British Columbia. Ministry of Health. **VFOAT** Ministry of Health Annual Report. **VAT** Ministry of Health Annual Report (Victoria). 1977-. English. an. **LC** RA185.B7; D46A. **DD** 354.7110077. **NLM** W2 DC2.1 B8D4A. *Continues British Columbia. Dept. of Health. Annual Report, 0701-5372.*

US
**ANNUAL REPORT - MISSISSIPPI HEALTH CARE COMMISSION. Ceased.** **Main/Corp** Mississippi Health Care Commission. July 1, 1979-June 30, 1980-Ceased (June 1986). English. an. Mississippi Department of Health, PO Box 1700, Jackson MS 39215. **Tel** (601)960-7634, FAX (601)960-7948. **LC** RA395.A4; M75. **DD** 353.97620084/105. **NLM** W2; AM7 H4a. *Continues Mississippi. State Health Planning and Development Agency. Annual Report.*

US
**ANNUAL REPORT / MISSISSIPPI, STATE DEPARTMENT OF HEALTH.** **Main/Corp** Mississippi. State Dept. of Health. English. an. Free. Office of Public Relations, Mississippi State, Department of Health, PO Box 1700, Jackson MS 39205. **Tel** (601)960-7667. **ED** Nancy Kay Sullivan. **LC** RA94; .M57A. **DD** 353.97620084/1. **NLM** W2; AM7 S7b. **Circ:** 3,000 (ctrl).
**Desc:** A general interest magazine with news features and photographs depicting public health in Mississippi.

US
**ANNUAL REPORT - NATIONAL BLOOD RESOURCE PROGRAM ADVISORY COMMITTEE, NATIONAL INSTITUTES OF HEALTH.** **Main/Corp** National Heart and Lung Institute. National Blood Resource Program Advisory Committee. English. an. National Heart Lung and Blood Institute, Division of Heart and Vascular Diseases, Devices and Technology Branch, 9000 Rockville Pike, Bethesda MD 20014.

PL/0208-595X
**ANNUAL REPORT - NATIONAL INSTITUTE OF HYGIENE.** [Annu. rep. - Natl. Inst. Hyg.]. **Added/Corp** Panstwowy Zakad Higieny. (1978)-. Periodical. English. **NLM** W 20.5 A614. *Continues Annual Report - State Institute of Hygiene, 0208-5887.*
**Desc:** Consists of abstracts of research carried out at the Institute of Hygiene.

US
**ANNUAL REPORT - NORTHERN INDIANA HEALTH SYSTEMS AGENCY.** **Main/Corp** Northern Indiana Health Systems Agency. (197?)-. English. 900 East Colfax Avenue, South Bend IN 46617.

US
**ANNUAL REPORT OF THE ACTIVITIES OF THE ALABAMA DEPT. OF PUBLIC HEALTH.** **Main/Corp** Alabama. Dept. of Public Health. English. an. Alabama Department of Public Health, 206 State Office Building, Room 381, Montgomery AL 36111. **Tel** (205)242-5052, FAX (205)240-3387. **LC** RA15; .D46A. **DD** 353.9/761/007705. **Bk Rev. Ad Acc. Circ:** 1,000 (ctrl). *Continues Activities Report - Alabama Dept. of Public Health.*
**Desc:** Describes the activities of the various bureaus of the Alabama Department of Public Health, including statistics and graphs of services rendered.

CN
**ANNUAL REPORT OF THE ALBERTA HEALTH DISCIPLINES BOARD FOR THE PERIOD OF JANUARY 1 ... TO DECEMBER 31.** **Main/Corp** Alberta Health Disciplines Board. (1984)-. English. an. Alberta Health Occupations Board, 8th Floor/7th Street Plaza South, 10030-107 Street, Edmonton Alberta T5J 3E4 Canada. **LC** RA185.A5; A34A. **DD** 354.71230084/1. *Continues Annual Report of the Alberta Health Occupations Board for the Period of January 1 ... to December 31 ... .*

US/0098-4205
**ANNUAL REPORT OF THE INDIANA DEPARTMENT OF MENTAL HEALTH, THE.** **Main/Corp** Indiana. Dept. of Mental Health. English. an. 117 East Washington Street, Indianapolis IN 46202. **Tel** (317)232-7800. **LC** RA790.65.I5; I54A. **DD** 353.9/772/0084205.

CN
**ANNUAL REPORT OF THE MENTAL HEALTH DIVISION OF THE DEPARTMENT OF HEALTH OF THE PROVINCE OF ONTARIO.** **Main/Corp** Ontario. Mental Health Division. English. an. Ontario Mental Health Foundation, 365 Bloor Street East, Toronto Ontario M4W 3L4 Canada. **LC** RC448; .O495. **DD** 362.2/09713. *Continues Ontario. Hospitals Division. Annual Report of the Hospitals Division, Department of Health Upon the Ontario Mental Hospitals and Mental Health Services of the Province of Ontario.*

US
**ANNUAL REPORT OF THE STATE DEPARTMENT OF HEALTH OF NEW YORK.** *Title Change.* **Main/Corp** New York (State). Dept. of Health. **VFOAT** Annual Report of the Department of Health for the Year Ending December 31 ... . 22nd (1901)-(19??). English. an. New York State Health Department, Empire State Plaza Tower Building, Room 1408, Albany NY 12237. **Tel** (518)474-2011, FAX (518)474-4471. **LC** RA121; .B1. **NLM** W2 AN6 D3A. *Continues Annual Report of the State Board of Health of New York, 0275-3367; Absorbed Marriage Statistics, New York State (Exclusive of New York City) ... with Introductory Analysis of Marriage Statistics ... . Continued in part by Annual Statistical Report of the Department of Health for the Year Ending December 31 ... and Annual Report.*

US
**ANNUAL REPORT ON MONITORING AND IMPLEMENTATION OF THE INDIANA PLAN FOR HEALTH. Ceased.** **Added/Corp** Indiana Statewide Health Coordinating Council. Indiana Plan for Health, 1982-1987. Indiana Statewide Health Coordinating Council. Indiana Plan for Health, 1986-1991. Indiana State Board of Health. Health Planning and Development Bureau. Indiana State Board of Health. Bureau of Policy Development. (1983)-(199?). English. an. Indiana State Board of Health, 1330 West Michigan Street, Indianapolis IN 46206. **Tel** (317)633-0109. **LC** RA395.A4; I643. **DD** 353.97720084/1. **Circ:** 150. *Continued by Monitoring and Implementation of the Indiana Plan for Health.*
**Desc:** Report issued by the Indiana State Board of Health.

US/0147-9016
**ANNUAL REPORT - PARKLAWN COMPUTER CENTER.** [Annu. rep. Parklawn Comput. Cent.]. **Main/Corp** Parklawn Computer Center (U.S.). (1976)-. English. an. **LC** RA409.5; .P29a. **DD** 353.008/41.

CN/0833-7659
**ANNUAL REPORT - PUBLIC SAFETY SERVICES (ALBERTA).** [Annu. rep. - Alta. Public Saf. Serv.]. **Main/Corp** Alberta Public Safety Services. 1984/85-. English. an. Alberta Public Safety Services, 10320 146th Street, Edmonton Alberta T5A 3N2 Canada. **Tel** (403)427-2772. **LC** HV555.C3; A7A. **DD** 354.71230075/06. **Circ:** 400 (ctrl). *Continues Annual Report - Alberta Disaster Services, 0703-0797.*
**Desc:** Report for the fiscal year ending March 31, 1986.

US/0731-244X
**ANNUAL REPORT - RHODE ISLAND. DEPT. OF HEALTH (1979).** (ANNUAL REPORT ... / DEPARTMENT OF HEALTH.). [Annu. rep. - R. I., Dep. Health]. **Main/Corp** Rhode Island. Dept. of Health. 1978-1979-. English. an. **DD** 753. **NLM** W2 AR4 D3A. *Continues Department of Health, State of Rhode Island, 0731-7042.*

US/0556-8471
**ANNUAL REPORT - RHODE ISLAND GOVERNOR'S COUNCIL ON MENTAL HEALTH.** **Main/Corp** Rhode Island. Governor's Council on Mental Health. (19??)-. English. an. Governor's Council on Mental Health, 333 Grotto Avenue, Providence RI 02906. **LC** RA790.65.R4; R464a. **DD** 353.9/745/00842.

CN/0839-8658
**ANNUAL REPORT / SASKATCHEWAN ENVIRONMENT AND PUBLIC SAFETY.** [Annu. rep. - Sask. Environ. Public Saf.]. **Main/Corp** Saskatchewan. Saskatchewan Environment and Public Safety. 1986/87-. English. an. Saskatchewan Environment and Public Safety, 1855 Victoria Avenue/5th Floor, Regina Saskatchewan S4P 3V5 Canada. **LC** HC117.S3; S333A. **DD** 354.71240082/321/06. *Continues Annual Report / Saskatchewan. Saskatchewan Environment, 0710-6718.*

CN/0715-9714
**ANNUAL REPORT / SASKATCHEWAN HEALTH RESEARCH BOARD.** *Title Change.* [Annu. rep. - Sask. Health Res. Board]. **Main/Corp** Saskatchewan Health Research Board. (1980)-(199?). English. an. Saskatchewan Health Research Board, 2302 Arlington Avenue, Saskatoon, Sask S7J 3L3. **LC** R854.C3; S27a. **DD** 354.71240084/1042. *Continued by Saskatchewan. Health Services Utilization and Research Commission. Annual Report, Period Ending March 31, ..., 1197-5385.*

CN/1191-0313
**ANNUAL REPORT / SASKATOON HEALTH SERVICES AUTHORITY.** [Annu. rep. - Saskat. Health Serv. Auth.]. **Main/Corp** Saskatoon Health Services Authority. (1991)-. English. **DD** 354.7124/250841/05.

US
**ANNUAL REPORT, SOUTH DAKOTA GOVERNOR'S TRAFFIC SAFETY PROGRAM.** See Transportation-Roads and Traffic.

US/0090-3795
**ANNUAL REPORT - STATE OF NEBRASKA. DEPARTMENT OF HEALTH.** (ANNUAL REPORT - NEBRASKA. DEPT. OF HEALTH.). [Annu. rep. - State of Neb. Dep. Health]. **Main/Corp** Nebraska. Dept. of Health. English. an. Nebraska State Department of Health, PO Box 95007, Lincoln NE 68509. **Tel** (402)471-2133, FAX (402)471-0383. **LC** RA447.N2; N4A. **DD** 353.9/782/0077.

CN
**ANNUAL REPORT: TUBERCULOSIS CONTROL IN THE PROVINCE OF NEW BRUNSWICK.** **Main/Corp** New Brunswick. Division of Tuberculosis Control. **Added/Corp** New Brunswick. Division of Tuberculosis Control. Tuberculosis Control in the Province of New Brunswick. (19??)-. English. an. Free. Miller Unit, Kentville Hospital Association, Kentville Nova Scotia Canada. **Tel** (902)678-3251. **DD** 614.5/42/09715.

US/0163-7525
**ANNUAL REVIEW OF PUBLIC HEALTH.** [Annu. rev. public health]. Vol. 1 (1980)-. Academic Scholarly Publication. English. an (May). $52.00 US; $57.00 other. Annual Reviews Inc., 4139 El Camino Way, PO Box 10139, Palo Alto CA 94303-0139. **Tel** (415)493-4400, (800)523-8635, FAX (415)855-9815. **ED** Gilbert Omenn. **LC** RA421; .A66. **DD** 362.1/05. **NLM** W1 AN7796K. **CODEN** AREHDT. **[CCC].** Index available. cum. index. **Pr Rev.** ctrl circ. available on microfilm and microfiche from University Microfilms International (UMI). Documents available from The Genuine Article, BIOSIS Document Express, CASDDS.
**Desc:** Comprehensive, thorough coverage of latest advances in public health, written by acknowledged experts in the field. Extensive literature citations included.
**Ind/Abst** AGRICOLA [Select. Cov.]; Biol. Abstr. (1985-); Chem. Abstr. (1980-1982); Cumul. Index Nurs. Allied Health Lit.; Curr. Contents Clin. Med.; Curr. Contents Soc. Behav. Sci.; EMBASE; Health Plan. Adminis.; Helminthol. Abstr.; Hospit. Health Admin. Index; Index Med. (1980-); Index Period. Artic. Relat. Law (19??-19??); Int. Bibliogr. Sociol.; Nutr. Abstr. Rev., Ser. A, Hum. Exp.; Life Sci. Collect.; Pollut. Abstr. Indexes; Protozoolog. Abstr.; Ref. Upd. Deluxe Ed.; Res. Alert [Full Cov.]; Rev. Med. Vet. Entomol.; Risk Abstr. (19??-19??); SCISEARCH; Soc. Sci. Cit. Index [Full Cov.]; SportSearch; Trop. Dis. Bull.

US
**ANNUAL WORK PLAN ... FOR THE OFFICE OF HEALTH PROTECTION, COLORADO DEPARTMENT OF HEALTH.** **Main/Corp** Colorado. Office of Health Protection. English. an. **LC** RA31; .C64A. **DD** 353.97880077.

US/0095-3385
**ANNUAL WORK PROGRAM - WASHINGTON TRAFFIC SAFETY COMMISSION.** **Main/Corp** Washington (State). Traffic Safety Commission. English. an. Washington Traffic Safety Commission, PO Box 1399, 1000 South Cherry, Edit Centerline, Olympia WA 98504. **Tel** (206)753-6197. **LC** HE5614.3.W2; W39A. **DD** 614.8/62/09797.

BE/0778-7383
**ANPI MAGAZINE.** See Fire Prevention.

EC
**ANUARIO DE ESTADISTICAS VITALES. NACIMIENTOS Y DEFUNCIONES.** **VFOAT** Nacimientos y Defunciones. (1985)-. Statistical Publication. Spanish. an. $24.10 (1987 edition), $19.00 (1985 edition), $15.00 (1984 edition). Instituto Nacional de Estadistica y Censos, Avda 10 de Agosto 229, Quito Ecuador. **Tel** 51.95.97/51.93.20, telex 21421 INFEC ED. **LC** HA1021; .E53. ***Continues*** *Encuesta Anual de Estadisticas Vitales. Nacimientos y Defunciones.*

US/0001-2165
**APCO BULLETIN, THE.** [APCO bull.]. **Added/Corp** Associated Public-Safety Communications Officers. **VFOAT** Journal of Public-Safety Communications. **VAT** Associated Public Safety Communications Officers Bulletin. (19??)-. Bulletin. English. mo. $50.00. Association of Public Safety Communications Officers, 2040 S Ridgewood Ave, Suite 104, South Daytona FL 32119-2257. **Tel** (904)322-2500. **ED** Alan Chase. **DD** 363. Index available. cum. index. **Ad Acc. Pr Rev. Circ:** 9,750 (ctrl). available on microfilm; available on microfiche; available on CD-ROM; available on an online database.
**Desc:** News and features on public safety communications, from law enforcement and fire departments, civil defense, 9-1-1- centers. Stories on power supplies, antennas, and recording devices.

US
**APCO REPORTS.** English. Twelve times a year. $24.00 (members) Association Public Safety Commission Officers; $60.00 (non-members). Association of Public Safety Communications Officers, 2040 S Ridgewood Ave, Suite 104, South Daytona FL 32119-2257. **Tel** (904)322-2500.

US
**APLASTIC ANEMIA FOUNDATION OF AMERICAN NEWSLETTER.** Newsletter. English. qt. Free. APlastic Anemia Foundation of America, PO Box 22689, Baltimore MD 21203. **Tel** (410)955-0247. **ED** Lynn H Rauch. **Circ:** 4,500 (ctrl).
**Desc:** Devoted to issues of interest to patient and families as well as physicians.

NE/0924-4107
**APOTHEEK IN PRAKTIJK.** ***Ceased.*** See Pharmacy and Pharmacology.

US/0003-9896
**ARCHIVES OF ENVIRONMENTAL HEALTH.** [Arch. environ. health]. **Added/Corp** American Medical Association. American Academy of Occupational Medicine. Society for Occupational and Environmental Health. **VFOAT** Environmental Health. Vol. 1 (July 1960)-. Academic Scholarly Publication. English. bm. $112.00. Heldref Publications, 1319 Eighteenth Street Northwest, Washington DC 20036-1802. **Tel** (202)296-6267, (800)365-9753, FAX (202)296-5149. **ED** Philippe Grandjean and Kaye H. Kilburn. **LC** RC963; .A22. **DD** 616.9/8. **NLM** W1 AR455. **CODEN** AEHLAU. **[CCC]. Ad Acc. Pr Rev. Circ:** 3,100. available on microfilm and microfiche from University Microfilms International (UMI); available on an online database (file 149/Full-Text) from DIALOG. Documents available from The Genuine Article, BIOSIS Document Express, CASDDS, Documents on Demand. ***Supersedes*** *A.M.A. Archives of Industrial Health, 0567-3933.*
**Desc:** Provides documentation of the effects of environmental agents on human health. Brings together the latest research from fields of epidemiology, toxicology, biostatistics, and biochemistry.
**Ind/Abst** Abr. Index Med.; Acoust. Abstr.; AGRICOLA [Select. Cov.]; Air Pollut. Titles; Biol. Agric. Index; Biol. Abstr.; Chem. Abstr.; Chem. Hazards Ind.; Coal Abstr.; Curr. Aware. Biol. Sci., CABS; Curr. Contents, Agric. Biol. Environ. Sci.; Curr. Contents Life Sci.; Dairy Sci. Abstr.; EMBASE; Energy Inf. Abstr.; Energy Res. Abstr.; Environ. Abstr.; Environ. Period. Bibliogr.; For. Prod. Abstr.; Gas Abstr. (?-?); GeoRef; Guide Soc. Sci. Relig.; Health Saf. Sci. Abstr.; Health Index (1989-); Health Period. Database [Full Txt.]; Health Plan. Adminis.; Health Ref. Cent. (Jan. 1989-) [Full Txt.] [Full Cov.]; Index Med.; Index Vet.; Ind. Hyg. Dig.; INIS Atomindex [Micro.]; Int. Aerosp. Abstr.; Lab. Hazards Bull.; Leadscan; Lit. Pat. Abstr., Oilfield Chem. (1972-); Lit. Abstr., Catal. Catal.; Lit. Abstr., Health Environ.; Lit. Abstr., Pet. Refin. Petrochem.; Lit. Abstr., Pet. Substit.; Lit. Abstr., Transp. Storage; Nematol. Abstr.; Nutr. Abstr. Rev., Ser. B, Live Feeds and Feed.; Nutr. Abstr. Rev., Ser. A, Hum. Exp.; Nutr. Res. Newsl.; Life Sci. Collect.; PESTDOC; Pollut. Abstr. Indexes; Poult. Abstr.; Protozoolog. Abstr.; Ref. Upd. Deluxe Ed.; Res. Alert [Full Cov.]; Rev. Agric. Entomol.; Rev. Med. Vet. Entomol.; Rev. Med. Vet. Mycology; Rev. Plant Pathol.; Rice Abstr.; Risk Abstr.; Saf. Health Work; Sci. Cit. Index; SCISEARCH; Soc. Sci. Cit. Index [Select. Cov.]; Vet. Bull.; Toxicol. Abstr.; Trop. Dis. Bull.; Weed Abstr.; World Ceram. Abstr.

BE
**ARCHIVES OF PUBLIC HEALTH / ARCHIVES BELGES DE SANTE PUBLIQUE.** **Added/Corp** Belgium. Ministere de la Sante Publique et de l'Environnement. **VFOAT** Archives Belges de Sante Publique. Vol. 48, No. 1/2 (1990)-. Periodical. French (Dutch; summaries and/or abstracts in English). Eleven times a year. Price varies. Institut Hygiene en Epidemiologie, Bibliotheek, J Wijtsmanstraat 4, 1050 Bruxelles Belgium. **Tel** 011 32 2 6425111. **NLM** W1; AR481R. ***Continues*** *Archives Belges (Brussels, Belgium).*

US/0882-0171
**ARDELL WELLNESS REPORT, THE.** [Ardell wellness rep.]. (19??)-. Periodical. English. Four times a year (Feb., May, Aug., Nov.). $200.00 (institutions), $28.00 (individuals). Ardell Wellness Report, 9901 Lake Georgia, Orlando FL 32817. **Tel** (407)823-2453, FAX (407)823-2099. **ED** Donald B. Ardell (editor's address: The Wellness Institute, University of Central Florida, Orlando FL 32816, telephone: (407)823-2453). **DD** 613. **Bk Rev**, (Qty: 6). **Circ:** 10,000.
**Desc:** The Wellness Report is provocative, insightful, funny and timely. It contains commentaries on health care reform, evaluates and reports on prevention and offers wellness-oriented critiques of the news.
**Ind/Abst** Acad. Abstr. Full Text Elite (Jan. 1992-) [Full Txt.]; Acad. Abstr. (Jan. 1992-); Acad. Search (Jan. 1992-); Health Source (Jan. 1992-); Mag. Artic. Summar. Elite (Jan. 1992-) [Full Txt.]; Mag. Artic. Summar. CD-ROM (Jan. 1992-); Mag. Search.

US/0162-6922
**ARIZONA COMPREHENSIVE BEHAVIORAL HEALTH PLAN.** 1977/82-. Periodical. English. Arizona Department of Health Services, 1740 West Adams Street, Phoenix AZ 85007. **Tel** (602)542-1025, FAX (602)642-1062. **NLM** W2 AA7 D6A. ***Formed by the union of*** *Arizona. Dept. of Health Services. Mental Health Plan* ***and*** *Arizona. Dept. of Health Services. State Alcohol and Drug Abuse Plan.*

●US/1065-4054
**ARIZONA HEALTH CARE IN PERSPECTIVE.** [Ariz. health care perspect.]. **Added/Corp** Morgan Quitno Corporation. 1st Ed. (1993)-. English. $18.00. Morgan Quitno Corporation, PO Box 1656, 512 East 9th Street, Lawrence KS 66044. **Tel** (800)457-0742, (913)841-3534, FAX (913)841-3534. **DD** 362.
**Desc:** Reports on the state's data and rank for each of the categories featured in Health Care State Rankings.

US
**ARIZONA PUBLIC SAFETY SURVEY.** English. an. Classification and Compensation Division, City of Phoenix Personnel Department, 10 North Third Avenue, Phoenix AZ 85003. **LC** HV8145.A7; A77. **DD** 331.2/813632/09791.

US
**ARIZONA STATE PLAN FOR CONSTRUCTION OF MENTAL HEALTH CENTERS.** ***Title Change.*** **Main/Corp** Arizona. Division of Mental Health and Mental Retardation. (19??)-(19??). English. an. Arizona Department of Health Services, 1740 West Adams Street, Phoenix AZ 85007. **Tel** (602)542-1025, FAX (602)642-1062. **LC** RA790.65.A6; A75. **DD** 353/97910084/2. ***Continued by*** *Arizona State Plan for Construction of Mental Health Centers.*

●US/1065-4062
**ARKANSAS HEALTH CARE IN PERSPECTIVE.** [Ark. health care perspect.]. **Added/Corp** Morgan Quitno Corporation. 1st Ed. (1993)-. English. $18.00. Morgan Quitno Corporation, PO Box 1656, 512 East 9th Street, Lawrence KS 66044. **Tel** (800)457-0742, (913)841-3534, FAX (913)841-3534. **DD** 362.
**Desc:** Reports on the state's data and rank for each of the categories featured in Health Care State Rankings.

US
**ARKANSAS MENTAL HEALTH SERVICES [BIENNIAL REPORT].** **Main/Corp** Arkansas Mental Health Services. (19??)-. English. be. Department of Social and Rehabilitation Services / Arkansas, 4313 West Markham Street, Little Rock AR 72201. **LC** RA790.65.A8; A76a. **DD** 353.9/767/00842. **NLM** W2 AA8 M4A. ***Continues*** *Arkansas State Hospital. Biennial Report of the Arkansas State Hospital for the Period July 1 ... to June ... .*

US/0893-858X
**ASBESTOS ABATEMENT REPORT.** ***Title Change.*** [Asbestos abat. rep.]. **Added/Corp** Buraff Publications. Bureau of National Affairs (Washington, D.C.). Vol. 1, No. 1 (1987)-(1993). Periodical. English. bw. Business Publishers Inc., 951 Pershing Drive, Silver Spring MD 20910-4464. **Tel** (301)587-6300, (800)274-0122, FAX (301)585-9075. **ED** Corby Anderson. **DD** 363. **[CCC].** available on an online database (file 636/Full-Text) from DIALOG. ***Continues*** *Asbestos Control Report, 0893-4533.* ***Absorbed by*** *Asbestos & Lead Abatement Report, 1068-2643.*
**Desc:** Covers developments in asbestos control.

●US/1068-2643
**ASBESTOS & LEAD ABATEMENT REPORT.** [Asbestos lead abat. rep.]. **VFOAT** Asbestos and Lead Abatement Report. Vol. 6, No. 4 (Feb. 12, 1993)-. Periodical. English. bw (26 issues). $507.00. Business Publishers Inc., 951 Pershing Drive, Silver Spring MD 20910-4464. **Tel** (301)587-6300, (800)274-0122, FAX (301)585-9075. **DD** 363. ***Continues*** *Asbestos Abatement Report, 0893-858X.*

US/1048-907X
**ASH SMOKING AND HEALTH REVIEW.** [Smok. health rev.]. **Added/Corp** Action on Smoking and Health (Organization). **VFOAT** ASH Smoking and Health Review; ASH Review. Vol. 11, No. 1 (Jan./Feb. 1981)-. Periodical. English. bm. $15.00. Action on Smoking and Health / US, PO Box 19556, 2000 H Street Northwest, Washington DC 20006. **Tel** (202)659-4310. **ED** John F. Banzhaf. **DD** 613. **NLM** W1; SM558S. **Bk Rev. Circ:** 30,000. ***Continues*** *ASH Newsletter, 0748-9374.*
**Desc:** Covers the protection of nonsmokers' rights.

TH/1010-5395
**ASIA-PACIFIC JOURNAL OF PUBLIC HEALTH : ASIA-PACIFIC ACADEMIC CONSORTIUM FOR PUBLIC HEALTH.** [Asia-Pac. j. public health]. **Added/Corp** Asia-Pacific Academic Consortium for Public Health. **VFOAT** Asia Pacific Journal of Public Health. Vol. 1, No. 1 (1987)-. Periodical. English. qt. $20.00. APACPH Office Fac. Public Health, 420 1 Rasuithi Road Phyatmai, Bangkok 10400 Thailand. **Tel** 66-2-247-9669, FAX 246-5227, telex 84770 UNIMAHITH. **(Subscription address:** Mahidol University, Faculty of Public Health, 420/1 Rajvithi Road,

# Public Health and Safety

3rd Floor, 5th Building, Phyathai, Bangkok 10400 Thailand) **NLM** W1; AS139BJ. Index available. cum. index. **Bk Rev. Ad Acc. Circ:** 2,000 (ctrl). available on CD-ROM; available on diskette.
**Ind/Abst** Health Plan. Adminis.; Index Med. (Vol. 1, No. 1, 1987)-; Trop. Dis. Bull.

●US/1072-0367
**ASIAN AMERICAN AND PACIFIC ISLANDER JOURNAL OF HEALTH.** [Asian Am. Pac. Isl. j. health]. Vol. 1, No. 1 (Summer 1993)-. Periodical. English. qt. $60.00. Asian American and Pacific Islander Journal of Health, 5525 Corey Swirl Drive, Dublin OH 43017-3057. **Tel** (614)766-5219, FAX (614)766-5219. **ED** Moon S. Chen, Jr. **DD** 362. **NLM** W1; AS139BT. Index available. **Bk Rev**, (Qty: 4). **Ad Acc. Pr Rev. Circ:** 200.
**Desc:** Dedicated to presenting an empirical, scholarly perspective of the health of Asian Pacific Islander Americans and Asian Indians.

BE
**ASPECTS TECHNIQUES DE LA SECURITE ROUTIERE.** See Transportation-Roads and Traffic.

CN/0715-4690
**AU NATUREL (MONTREAL).** (AU NATUREL : BULLETIN DE LA FEDERATION QUEBECOISE DE NATURISME.). [Au nat.]. Vol. 1, No. 1 (Summer 1982)-. Bulletin. French. qt. $3.00 (per issue). Au Naturel, c/o Federation Quebecoise de Naturisme, Porte 3-37, 1415 Est rue Jarry, Montreal Quebec H2E 2Z7 Canada. **Tel** (514)252-3014. **ED** Michel Vals, Michel Michaud. **DD** 613/.194/05. **Bk Rev. Ad Acc. Circ:** 4,000. Continues Information Naturistes Quebecoises, 0715-4682.
**Desc:** Published by the federation quebecoise de naturisme (Federation of Quebec naturists) whose aims are to development of naturism Quebec.

AT/0810-7491
**AUSTRALIAN HEALTH CARE SYSTEM, THE. Added/Corp** University of New South Wales. School of Health Administration. (1979)-. English. an. 35.00Aus$. University of New South Wales, PO Box 1, Kensington New South Wales, 2033 Australia. **Tel** 011 61 2 697-3362, FAX 011 61 2 662-6616. **LC** RA421; .A94 subser.; RA407.5.A8. **DD** 362.1/0994. **NLM** W1; AU697 no.37 etc.

AT/1035-7319
**AUSTRALIAN JOURNAL OF PUBLIC HEALTH. Added/Corp** Public Health Association of Australia. Vol. 15, No. 1 (Mar. 1991)-. Periodical. English. Four times a year (Mar., June, Oct., Dec.). 185.00Aus$ (institutions), 120.00Aus$ (individuals). Public Health Association of Australia, GPO Box 2204, Canberra Australian Capital Territory 2601 Australia. **Tel** 011/61/6/2852373, FAX 011/61/6/2825438. **ED** Charles Kerr. **NLM** W1; AU618R. **CODEN** AJPHET. Index available. **Bk Rev. Ad Acc, Adv Mgr:** Rhana Pike. **Pr Rev. Circ:** 2,000. available on microfilm and microfiche from University Microfilms International (UMI). Documents available from The Genuine Article, UMI Article Clearinghouse. Continues Community Health Studies, 0314-9021.
**Desc:** Concerned with public health issues. Reports of finished research projects are the staple diet of the journal. Methodological notes and brief research reports from time to time. Research reported includes formal epidemiological inquiries into the correlates and causes of diseases and health-related behavior, analyses of public policy affecting health and disease, and detailed studies of the cultures and social structures in which health and illness are produced and defined.
**Ind/Abst** ABI/INFORM Glob. Ed.; APAIS, Aust. Public Aff. Inf. Ser. (1991-); Curr. Contents Soc. Behav. Sci.; EMBASE; Health Plan. Adminis.; Index Med.; Res. Alert [Full Cov.]; Soc. Sci. Cit. Index [Full Cov.].

AT/1034-4608
**AUSTRALIAN PRODUCT LIABILITY REPORTER.** [Aust. prod. liabil. report.]. (1989)-. Periodical. English. Ten times a year. 345.00Aus$ (Australia); 366.00Aus$ (New Zealand); 369.00Aus$ (Fiji, Indonesia, & Malaysia); 372.30Aus$ (India & Japan); 377.00Aus$ (US & Israel); 379.00Aus$ (other). International Business Communications Pty Ltd, Level 11 55 63 Elizabeth Street, Sydney, Australia. **Tel** 011 61 2 2216199. **ED** Peter Cashman, Ellen Beerworth, Neil Francey, John Goldring and David Harland. **DD** 344.94042. Index available. **Pr Rev**.
**Desc:** A review of legal and regulatory developments in product liability, toxics and related areas.

AT/1032-6138
**AUSTRALIA'S HEALTH / AUSTRALIAN INSTITUTE OF HEALTH. Added/Corp** Australian Institute of Health. Australian Institute of Health and Welfare. 1st (1988)-. English. ir. Australian Government Publishing Service, GPO Box 84, Canberra ACT 2601 Australia. **Tel** 011 61 6 2954411, FAX 011 61 6 2954455. **LC** RA371; .A94. **DD** 362.1/0994/05. **NLM** W2; KA8 A91. Index available. **Pr Rev. Circ:** 1,000.

US/0277-1764
**AVIATION SAFETY (RIVERSIDE, CONN.).** See Aeronautics, Astronautics.

US
**AWARE. Added/Corp** United States. National Weather Service. United States. National Oceanic and Atmospheric Administration. (Jan. 1990)-. Periodical. English. qt. US Department of Commerce / National Weather Service, 1325 East-West Highway, Room 18130, Silver Spring MD 20912. **Tel** (301)713-0689, FAX (301)713-0610. Continues Disaster Preparedness Report.

US/0742-471X
**AWARE (DARBY, PA.).** (AWARE.). [Aware]. Periodical. English. bm. $5.00 Donation. Mercy Catholic Medical Center, Lansdowne Avenue & Baily Road, Darby PA 19023. **DD** 613.

US/0161-2212
**BALANCED PERSPECTIVE ON : THE HEALTH OF KANSANS. Main/Corp** Kansas. Dept. of Health and Environment. **VFOAT** Health of Kansas. 1976/77-. English. an. Free from issuing agency. Kansas Department of Health and Environment, Office of Research and Analysis, 109 Southwest 9th Street, Suite 400A, Topeka KS 66612-2219. **Tel** (913)296-0632. **LC** RA67; .S7A. **DD** 362.1/09781.
**Desc:** Discusses priorities of health problems in Kansas. Topics include the balance between health promotion and illness care, medical care costs, care of the aged, rural health services, etc.

SZ/0512-3003
**BASIC DOCUMENTS. Main/Corp** World Health Organization. (1951)-. English (Arabic, Chinese, French, Russian and Spanish). 15.00F. World Health Organization, Distribution and Sales, 20 Avenue Appia, CH-1211 Geneva 27 Switzerland. **Tel** 011 41 22 7912111, FAX 011 41 22 7880401. **LC** RA8; .A275. **DD** 614.0611.
**Desc:** Contains essential documents of the World Health Organization.

●CN/1189-4199
**BC HEALTH AND DISEASE SURVEILLANCE.** [BC health dis. surveill.]. **Added/Corp** British Columbia. Office of the Provincial Health Officer. **VAT** British Columbia Health and Disease Surveillance. Vol. 1, No. 1 (Jan. 6, 1992)-. Periodical. English. wk. **DD** 614.4. Continues Disease Surveillance., 0846-121X.

●US/1063-8490
**BEHAVORIAL HEALTHCARE TOMORROW.** [Behav. healthc. tomorrow]. Vol. 1, No. 1 (Nov./Dec. 1992)-. Periodical. English. bm (6 issues). $58.00. CentraLink, 1110 Mar West Street, Suite E, Tiburon CA 94920-1879. **Tel** (415)435-9821, FAX (415)435-9092. **ED** Michael A. Freeman, MD, DMH (editor-in-chief) and Adam B. Richmond (associate editor). **DD** 362. **NLM** W1; BE13I. **Ad Acc, Adv Mgr:** Nancy E. Bechtel.
**Desc:** The national dialogue journal on mental health and addiction treatment benefits and services in the era of managed care.

UK
**BEST PRACTICE IN HEALTH CARE COMMISSIONING.** (19??)-. Periodical. English. sa. £52.00 Europe; £55.00 Other (Institutions). Longman Group Ltd., Fourth Avenue, Longman House, Harlow Essex CM19 5SR England. **Tel** 011 44 279 429655, FAX 011 44 279 431059, telex 81259.

NE/0168-9908
**BETER.** [Beter]. (1983)-. Periodical. Dutch. bm. FL29.80. UGN, POB 75, 8080 AB Tilburg Netherlands. **UDC** 61.

GW/0932-2361
**BGA SCHRIFTEN.** [BGA-Schr.]. **Added/Corp** Germany (West). Bundesgesundheitsamt. (1983)-. Monographic series. German. MMV Medizin Verlag, Postfach 801246, Neumarkter Street 18, W-8000 Muenchen 80 F R Germany. **Tel** 011/49/89/9269070, FAX 089/48189-633, telex 522053. **LC** UNC. **NLM** W1; BG57. **CODEN** BGASEB. Documents available from CASDDS.
**Ind/Abst** Chem. Abstr.

US
**BIENNIAL REPORT / COMMONWEALTH OF VIRGINIA, DEPARTMENT OF HEALTH REGULATORY BOARDS. Title Change. Main/Corp** Virginia. Dept. of Health Regulatory Boards. (1980)-(198?)-. English. be. Virginia Department of Health Regulatory Boards, Virginia Commission of Health Regulatory Boards, Seabord Building/ Suite 453, 3600 West Broad Street, Richmond VA 23230. **LC** RA396.A4; V73a. **DD** 353.97550084/1. **NLM** W2; AV8 D3b. Continued by Virginia. Dept. of Health Professions. Report of the Department of Health Professions, Commonwealth of Virginia for the ... Biennium.

US
**BIENNIAL REPORT - MINNESOTA DEPARTMENT OF HEALTH. Main/Corp** Minnesota. Dept. of Health. English. be. Minnesota Department of Health, 717 Southeast Delaware Street, Minneapolis MN 55440. **Tel** (612)623-5000. **LC** RA91; .S8A. **DD** 362.1/09776. **NLM** W2 AM6 D4B. Continues Biennial Report - Minnesota State Board of Health.

US
**BIENNIAL REPORT OF EXAMINING AND LICENSING BOARDS / ADVISORY COMMITTEE OF EXAMINERS IN MORTUARY SCIENCE (MINNESOTA). Main/Corp** Minnesota. Advisory Committee of Examiners in Mortuary Science. English. be. 717 Delaware Street SE, Minneapolis MN 55440. **Tel** (612)623-5491. **ED** David F Schwietz. **LC** RA623.A3; M65A. **DD** 353.9776007/72.

US
**BIENNIAL REPORT OF EXAMINING AND LICENSING BOARDS - MINNESOTA. BOARD OF EXAMINERS FOR NURSING HOME ADMINISTRATORS. Main/Corp** Minnesota. Board of Examiners for Nursing Home Administrators. English. be. Minnesota Board of Medical Examiners, 2700 University Avenue West #106, St Paul MN 55114-1080. **LC** RA997.5.M6; M56A. **DD** 353.9/776/008243.

UA
**BIENNIAL REPORT OF THE REGIONAL DIRECTOR TO THE ... SESSION OF THE REGIONAL COMMITTEE / WORLD HEALTH ORGANIZATION, REGIONAL OFFICE FOR THE EASTERN MEDITERRANEAN. VFOAT** Biennial Report of the WHO Regional Director for the Eastern Mediterranean. (June 1979)-. English. be. **LC** RA541.N36; B54. **DD** 362.1/0956.

US
**BIENNIAL REPORT - TEXAS DEPARTMENT OF HEALTH. Main/Corp** Texas. Dept. of Health. 1977/79-. English. be. Texas Department of Health, 1100 West 49th Street, Austin TX 78756-3180. **Tel** (512)458-7550, FAX (512)458-7407. **LC** RA157; .D46A. **DD** 353.97640084/1/06. Continues Biennial Report - Texas Department of Health Resources, 0163-1667.

BE/0778-4910
**BIOMEDICAL & HEALTH RESEARCH.** See Medical Science and Technology-Biotechnology.

SP
**BIS BUTLLETI D'INFORMACIO SANITARIA.** Spanish. bm. Fundacion Rafael Campalans, Rossello 239 3/1, 08008 Barcelona Spain.

US/1042-329X
**BLACK HEALTH.** [Black health]. (1988)-. Periodical. English. Four times a year. $15.00 US; $30.00 other. Altier Maynard Communications, 59 Oakwood Drive, Madison CT 06443. **Tel** (203)421-3494, FAX (203)421-3250. **LC** RA448.N4; B522. **DD** 362. **Ad Acc. Pr Rev. Circ:** 26,000 (ctrl).
**Desc:** Health articles of interest to black people.
**Ind/Abst** Acad. Abstr. Full Text Elite (Jan. 1992-); Acad. Abstr. (Jan. 1992-); Acad. Search (Jan. 1992-); Health Source (Jan. 1992-); INFO-SOUTH Abstr.; Mag. Search.

●US/1065-3104
**BNA CALIFORNIA SAFETY & HEALTH REPORT.** [BNA Calif. saf. health rep.]. **Added/Corp** Bureau of National Affairs (Washington, D.C.). **VFOAT** BNA California Safety and Health Report. **VAT** Bureau of National Affairs California Safety & Health Report. Vol. 1, No. 1 (Oct. 26, 1992)-. Periodical. English. bw. $411.00. Bureau of National Affairs Inc., 9435 Key West Avenue, Rockville MD 20850. **Tel** (800)372-1033, (301)258-1033, FAX (301)948-5823. **LC** KFC584.A15; B63. **DD** 344. [CCC].

●US/1064-2137
**BNA'S HEALTH LAW REPORTER.** See Law.

●US/1065-8076
**BNA'S STATE ENVIRONMENT & SAFETY REGULATORY MONITORING REPORT.** See Environmental Issues.

US/0190-5481
**BOATING SAFETY TRAINING MANUAL.** (BOATING SAFETY TRAINING MANUAL / DEPARTMENT OF TRANSPORTATION, COAST GUARD.). English. an. G-BEL-3 U S Coast Guard, Washington DC 20593. **LC** KF2558.P5; A813. **DD** 623.88/8.

## Public Health and Safety

US/8756-8551
**BODY-MIND NETWORKS.** [Body-mind netw.]. **VFOAT** Body Mind Networks; Networks. Began in 1984. Periodical. English. $20.00. Networks Main Office, 4139 Chestnut Street, Philadelphia PA 19104. **LC** RA773; .N45. **DD** 613/.05. *Continues Networks (Philadelphia, PA.), 8756-8543.*

US/0030-0632
**BOLETIN DE LA OFICINA SANITARIA PANAMERICANA.** [Bol. Of. Sanit. Panam.]. **Main/Corp** Pan American Sanitary Bureau. Vol. 2, No. 7 (July 1923)-. Periodical. Spanish (summaries and/or abstracts in Portuguese and English). mo. $28.00 (surface mail). Pan American Health Organization, 525 23rd Street Northwest, Office District Sales, Washington DC 20037. **Tel** (202)293-8130, FAX (202)338-0869. **ED** Egla Blouin. **NLM** W1 BO243A. **CODEN** BOSPA8. Index available. cum. index. **Bk Rev. Pr Rev. Circ:** 16,000 (ctrl). Documents available from BIOSIS Document Express. *Continues Boletin Panamericano de Sanidad.*
**Desc:** Principal organ of scientific information of the Pan American Health Organization. Includes original papers on preventive medicine, public health, and other subjects connected with PAHO's activities, summaries of important reports and events in the health field, reviews of recent books and publications, and a list of health authorities of the Organization's member governments.
**Ind/Abst** Biocont. News Inf. (1991-); Biol. Abstr.; Dairy Sci. Abstr.; Geogr. Abstr. Human Geogr.; Helminthol. Abstr.; Index Med.; Index Vet.; Int. Dev. Abstr.; Nutr. Abstr. Rev., Ser. A, Hum. Exp.; Protozoolog. Abstr.; Rev. Agric. Entomol.; Saf. Health Work; Trop. Dis. Bull.

CL
**BOLETIN DEL INSTITUTO DE SALUD PUBLICA DE CHILE.** **Added/Corp** Instituto de Salud Publica de Chile. (19??)-. Periodical. Spanish (summaries and/or abstracts in English). sa.
**Ind/Abst** Trop. Dis. Bull.

SP/0214-3852
**BOLETIN EPIDEMIOLOGICO DE CASTILLA Y LEON.** [Bol. epidemiol. Castilla Leon]. (1985)-. Periodical. Spanish. wk. free. Junta de Castilla-Leon, Consejeria de Bienestar Social, Avenida deburgos S N, 47071 Valladolid Spain. **Tel** 34 83 34 3899. **(Subscription address:** Direccion General de Salud Publica, Avenida de Burbos S U, 47071 Salladolid Spain) **UDC** 614.4. Index available. **Circ:** 5,500.

SP/0212-9183
**BOLETIN OFICIAL DEL MINISTERIO DE SANIDAD Y CONSUMO.** See Consumer Interests.

US/0095-1854
**BRAKES.** [Brakes]. **Main/Corp** United States. National Highway Traffic Safety Administration. English. National Transportation Safety Board, 800 Independence Avenue SW, Washington DC 20594. **Tel** (202)382-6600. **LC** TL242; .C65 subser. **DD** 629.2/08 S; 629.2/46. *Continues Brakes, 0095-1854.*

GW/0340-8019
**BRANDSCHUTZ (AUSGABE RHEINLAND-PFALZ).** (BRANDSCHUTZ.). [Brandschutz]. May 1947-. Periodical. German. mo. DM92.00. W Kohlhammer Verlag GMBH, Postfach 800430, D70549 Stuttgart Germany. **Tel** 011 49 711 78631. **UDC** 614.841.3.
**Desc:** Journal for the entire field of fire fighting equipment and rescue service.
**Ind/Abst** Coal Abstr.; Int. Civil Eng. Abstr.; Saf. Health Work; Soft. Abstr. Eng.

●US/1065-710X
**BREATHE! (LA QUINTA, CALIF.).** (BREATHE! : OFFICIAL PUBLICATION OF THE SMOKE FREE TRAVEL COUNCIL.). [Breathe!]. **Added/Corp** Smoke Free Travel Council. (1992)-. Periodical. English. qt. $24.00. Smoke Free Travel Council, 78-365 Highway 111, Suite 361, La Quinta CA 92253. **DD** 910.

US/1054-6995
**BRIEFINGS ON JCAHO.** (BRIEFINGS ON JCAHO : ALTERNATIVE PERSPECTIVES ON ACCREDITATION.). [Brief. JCAHO]. **Added/Corp** Joint Commission on Accreditation of Healthcare Organizations. **VAT** Briefings on Joint Commission on Accreditation of Healthcare Organizations. Vol. 1, No. 10 (Nov. 1990)-. Periodical. English. mo. $292.00 (one year), $492.00 (two year). Medical Records Briefing, PO Box 1168, Marblehead MA 01945. **Tel** (617)639-1872. **DD** 610.
**Ind/Abst** Hospit. Manage. Rev. (19??-).

●US/1076-6014
**BRIEFINGS ON LONG-TERM CARE REGULATIONS.** [Brief. long-term care regul.]. **Added/Corp** Opus Communications. **VFOAT** Briefings on Long Term Care Regulations. (1993)-. Periodical. English. mo. $147.00. Medical Records Briefing, PO Box 1168, Marblehead MA 01945. **Tel** (617)639-1872. **DD** 362.

US/0362-8884
**BRIEFS OF ACCIDENTS INVOLVING AMATEUR-HOME BUILT AIRCRAFT, U.S. GENERAL AVIATION.** See Aeronautics, Astronautics.

US/0091-1399
**BRIEFS OF AIRCRAFT ACCIDENTS INVOLVING TURBINE POWERED AIRCRAFT, U.S. GENERAL AVIATION.** See Aeronautics, Astronautics.

US/0360-7127
**BRIEFS OF FATAL ACCIDENTS INVOLVING WEATHER AS A CAUSE-FACTOR, U.S. GENERAL AVIATION.** See Aeronautics, Astronautics.

US/1042-1386
**BROWN UNIVERSITY LONG-TERM CARE LETTER, THE.** *Title Change.* [Brown Univ. long-term care lett.]. **Added/Corp** Brown University. **VFOAT** Brown University Long Term Care Letter; Long-Term Care Letter; Long Term Care Letter. Vol. 1, No. 1 (Nov. 1988)-(19??). Periodical. English. mo. Manisses Communications Group Inc., PO Box 3357, Providence RI 02906-0757. **Tel** (401)831-6020, (800)333-7771, FAX (401)861-6370. **ED** Vincent Mor. **DD** 362. **NLM** W1; BR91K. **[CCC].** *Continued by Brown University Long Term Care Quality Letter.*
**Desc:** Report for health care professionals working in long term care facilities.
**Ind/Abst** Health Index (1989-); Health Period. Database [Full Txt.]; Health Ref. Cent. (Jan. 1989-) [Full Txt.] [Full Cov.].

US
**BROWN UNIVERSITY LONG TERM CARE QUALITY LETTER.** (19??)-. Periodical. English. Twenty-four times a year. $317.00 (institutions), $249.00 (individuals) US; $332.00 (institutions), $265.00 (individuals) Canada; $347.00 (institutions), $275.00 (individuals) other. Manisses Communications Group Inc., PO Box 3357, Providence RI 02906-0757. **Tel** (401)831-6020, (800)333-7771, FAX (401)861-6370. Index available. available on an online database (file 149/Full-Text) from DIALOG. *Continues Brown University Long Term Care Letter.*

US/0898-8323
**BROWN UNIVERSITY STD UPDATE, THE.** *Title Change.* [Brown Univ. STD update]. **Added/Corp** Brown University. **VAT** Brown University Sexually Transmitted Diseases Update. (1987)-(19??). Periodical. English. mo. Manisses Communications Group Inc., PO Box 3357, Providence RI 02906-0757. **Tel** (401)831-6020, (800)333-7771, FAX (401)861-6370. **DD** 616. Index available. cum. index. **Bk Rev. Circ:** 700. *Absorbed by CDC AIDS Weekly.*
**Desc:** A report for health care professionals on AIDS and other sexually transmitted diseases.
**Ind/Abst** Health Index (1989-); Health Period. Database; Health Ref. Cent. (Jan. 1989-) [Full Cov.].

US/0090-1156
**BRUCELLOSIS SURVEILLANCE (ANNUAL SUMMARY).** *Ceased.* (BRUCELLOSIS SURVEILLANCE ANNUAL SUMMARY / CENTER FOR DISEASE CONTROL.). **VFOAT** Brucellosis Surveillance. (1971)-Ceased (1978). English. an. Centers for Disease Control, 1600 Clifton Road NE, Atlanta GA 30333. **Tel** (404)639-3311, FAX (404)639-3296. **LC** RA644.B7; C45A. **DD** 312/.39/5700973. **NLM** W2 A C7CT. *Continues Zoonosis Surveillance. Brucellosis, 0091-0341.*

US/0896-2642
**BUENA SALUD.** [Buena salud]. **Added/Corp** Interamerican College of Physicians & Surgeons. (19??)-?. Periodical. Spanish. mo. $1.75 per issue. Buena Salud, 299 Madison Avenue, New York NY 10017. **Tel** (212)687-5584. **ED** Frank Calderon. **DD** 613. **Ad Acc.** *Continued in part by BuenaSalud (National ed.), 1053-5543; BuenaSalud (Puerto Rico ed.), 1053-5551.*
**Desc:** Focuses on the health needs of Hispanic Americans.

US/1042-7708
**BULLETIN - ASSOCIATION FOR THE ADVANCEMENT OF AUTOMOTIVE MEDICINE.** See Transportation-Roads and Traffic.

LE/0253-9349
**BULLETIN / CROIX-ROUGE LIBANAISE.** [Bull. - Croix-Rouge liban.]. **Main/Corp** Croix-Rouge Libanaise. Bulletin. French. mo. La Croix-Rouge, 95 Est, Rue Wellesley, Toronto Ontario M4Y 1H6. **NLM** W1 RE156UQT.

FR/1011-7903
**BULLETIN DE L'UNION INTERNATIONALE CONTRE LA TUBERCULOSE ET LES MALADIES RESPIRATOIRES.** *Ceased.* See Medical Science and Technology-Respiratory System.

BE/0304-9450
**BULLETIN DU MINISTERE DE LA SANTE PUBLIQUE ET DE LA FAMILLE.** **Main/Corp** Belgium. Ministere de la Sante Publique et de la Famille. Bulletin. French. qt. 200F. CCP 26, Bruxelles 392 Belgium. **LC** RA254; .M56A. **DD** 614/.09493. **NLM** W2 GB4 M6B. *Supersedes Bulletin de la Sante Publique, 0378-4673.*
**Ind/Abst** Trop. Dis. Bull.

CN/0712-4775
**BULLETIN / HEALTH SCIENCES ASSOCIATION OF ALBERTA.** See Economics-Labor.

US
**BULLETIN - NATIONAL INSTITUTES OF HEALTH (U.S.).** **Main/Corp** National Institutes of Health (U.S.). Bulletin. English. **LC** RA421. available on microfilm from University Microfilms International (UMI).

IQ/0007-4845
**BULLETIN OF ENDEMIC DISEASES.** [Bull. endemic dis.]. **Added/Corp** Iraq. Institute of Endemic Diseases. Vol. 1 (July 1954)-. Periodical. English. sa. $15.00. Institute of Endemic Diseases, Ministry of Health, Baghdad Iraq. **DD** 616.9. **NLM** W1 BU757. Documents available from BIOSIS Document Express.
**Ind/Abst** Biocont. News Inf. (1991-); Biol. Abstr.; Dairy Sci. Abstr.; EMBASE; Health Plan. Adminis.; Index Vet.; Protozoolog. Abstr.; Rev. Med. Vet. Entomol.; Trop. Dis. Bull.

UA/0379-7988
**BULLETIN OF THE HIGH INSTITUTE OF PUBLIC HEALTH, THE.** Began in 1971. Bulletin. English (Arabic and French). Dar Al-Hoda, 1008 Street Behind Gamal ABD-EL-Nasser Street, Miamy Alexandria Egypt. **LC** RA421; .B94. **DD** 362.1/0962. **NLM** W1 BU848.

US/0301-5750
**BULLETIN OF THE PAN AMERICAN HEALTH ORGANIZATION.** [Bull. Pan Am. Health Organ.]. **Main/Corp** Pan American Sanitary Bureau. **Added/Corp** Pan American Health Organization. Pan American Sanitary Bureau. Boletin de la Oficina Sanitaria Panamericana. **VFOAT** PAHO Bulletin. Vol. 7, No. 3, (1973)-. Academic Scholarly Publication. English. qt. $26.00 US and Canada; $20.00 the Americas; 52.00F (surface mail), 82.00F (airmail) other. Pan American Health Organization, 525 23rd Street Northwest, Office District Sales, Washington DC 20037. **Tel** (202)293-8130, FAX (202)338-0869. **(Subscription address:** Her Majesty's Stationery Office, PO Box 276, Publications Centre, London SW8 5DT England.) **ED** Donna Reynolds. **LC** RA10; .P254. **DD** 362.1/09181. **NLM** W1 BU884D. Index available. **Bk Rev. Circ:** 6,000 (ctrl). available on an online database from MEDLINE. Documents available from Documents on Demand. *Continues Boletin de la Oficina Sanitaria Panamericana. English Edition, 0085-4638.*
**Desc:** Medical research, preventative and social medicine, health systems, administration, health, manpower, common diseases, veterinary, public health, environmental health, maternal and child health, food and nutrition, health technology and chronical diseases.
**Ind/Abst** Biocont. News Inf. (1991-); EMBASE; Environ. Abstr.; Food Sci. Technol. Abstr.; Health Saf. Sci. Abstr.; Helminthol. Abstr. (1991-); Index Med.; Index Vet.; Int. Nurs. Index; Int. Pharm. Abstr.; Leis. Recreat. Tour. Abstr.; Nutr. Abstr. Rev., Ser. B, Live Feeds and Feed.; Nutr. Abstr. Rev., Ser. A, Hum. Exp.; Nutr. Res. Newsl.; Life Sci. Collect. (1985-); Pollut. Abstr. Indexes; Protozoolog. Abstr.; Rev. Med. Vet. Entomol.; Saf. Health Work; Soc. Plann. Policy Dev. Abstr.; Vet. Bull.; Trop. Dis. Bull.

SZ/0042-9686
**BULLETIN OF THE WORLD HEALTH ORGANIZATION.** See Medical Science and Technology.

CN/0715-366X
**BULLETIN - ONTARIO DIVISION. CANADIAN RED CROSS SOCIETY.** (BULLETIN.). [Bull. - Ont. Div., Can. Red Cross Soc.]. **Added/Corp** Canadian Red Cross Society. Ontario Division. (Feb./Mar. 1976)-. Periodical. English. ir. Canadian Red Cross Society, Blood Programme, 95 Wellesley Street East, Toronto Ont. M4Y 1H6. **DD** 363.1/005. *Continues Canadian Red Cross Society. Ontario Division. News Bulletin, 0045-5288.*

IO/0303-3236
**BULLETIN PENELITIAN KESEHATAN.** [Bull. penelitian kesehatan]. **Added/Corp** Lembaga Research Kesehatan Nasional. Badan Penelitian dan Pengembangan Kesehatan. **VFOAT** Health Studies in

Indonesia. Vol. 1, No. 1 (1973)-. Academic Scholarly Publication. English (summaries and/or abstracts in Indonesian). **NLM** W1 BU899P.
**Ind/Abst** EMBASE; Trop. Dis. Bull.

GW/0007-5914
**BUNDESGESUNDHEITSBLATT.** [Bundesgesundheitsblatt]. **Added/Corp** Germany (West). Bundesgesundheitsamt. Jan. (1958)-. Academic Scholarly Publication. German. sm. DM138.00. Carl Heymanns Verlag KG, Luxemburger Strasse 449, D 50939 Cologne Germany. **Tel** 011 49 221 460100, telex 8 881 888. **ED** Gunther Beitzke and Dieter Briggemauu. **NLM** W2 GG4 B7B. **Bk Rev. Ad Acc. Circ:** 2,500 (ctrl).
**Desc:** Statements and treatises on juvenile law and juvenile aid in court justice-adolescents and family.
**Ind/Abst** Dairy Sci. Abstr.; EMBASE; Energy Res. Abstr.; Food Sci. Technol. Abstr.; Index Vet.; Int. Packag. Abstr.; Nutr. Abstr. Rev., Ser. A, Hum. Exp.; Saf. Health Work; Vet. Bull.

US/0739-9413
**BUSINESS AND HEALTH.** See Business.

US/0360-7208
**BUSINESS, HEALTH AND EDUCATIONAL DISCIPLINES.** See Business.

JA
**BYOIN NEMPO. Main/Corp** Kokuritsu Kyoto Byoin. (19??)-. Periodical. Japanese. Kokuritsu Kyoto Byoin, Fushimi-ku 612, Kyoto Japan. **LC** RA990.J6; K9444a. **NLM** WX 2 JJ3 K2K2B.

CN/0227-3748
**C H R A RECORDER.** [CHRA rec.]. **Main/Corp** Canadian Health Record Association. **VAT** Canadian Health Record Association Recorder; Recorder (Oshawa). Dec. 1976-. Periodical. English (French). Free to members. Canadian Health Record Association, 187 King Street East, Oshawa Ontario L1H 1C3 Canada. **Tel** (416)728-9743. **DD** 651.5/04261/0971. ***Continues*** *CAMRL Recorder, 0316-0637.*

US/0526-6742
**C.O.A. BULLETIN. Main/Corp** Commissioned Officers Association of the United States Public Health Service. **Added/Corp** Commissioned Officers Association of the United States Public Health Service. Bulletin. **VAT** Commissioned Officers Association Bulletin. (19??)-. Periodical. English. ir (9 issues). Free to those affiliated with public health services; $15.00 other. Commissioned Officers Association USPHS Inc., 2111 Wilson Boulevard, Suite 321, Arlington VA 22201. **Tel** (703)243-1301. **NLM** W1 C541.

CN/0703-5624
**C P H A HEALTH DIGEST. Main/Corp** Canadian Public Health Association. **VAT** Canadian Public Health Association Health Digest. Vol. 1 (Feb. 1977)-. Periodical. English (French). qt. $10.00 per year. Free to members. Canadian Public Health Association, 1565 Carling Avenue/Suite 400, Ottawa Ontario K1Z 8R1 Canada. **Tel** (613)725-3769, FAX (613)725-9826. **ED** Karen Devine. **DD** 614/.0971. **Bk Rev. Ad Acc. Circ:** 4,000 (ctrl). ***Supersedes*** *Canadian Public Health Association. C P H A Newsletter., 0703-5594.*

BL/0102-311X
**CADERNOS DE SAUDE PUBLICA / MINISTERIO DA SAUDE, FUNDACAO OSWALDO CRUZ, ESCOLA NACIONAL DE SAUDE PUBLICA. Added/Corp** Escola Nacional de Saude Publica (Brazil). (198?)-. Periodical. Portuguese. Four times a year. $10.00. Fundacao Oswaldo Cruz, Escola Nacional de Saude Publica, Rio De Janeiro Brazil. **LC** RA421; .C25. **DD** 614. **NLM** W1; CA109F.
**Ind/Abst** Linguist. Lang. Behav. Abstr.; Soc. Plann. Policy Dev. Abstr.; Sociol. Abstr.; Trop. Dis. Bull.

FR/0007-9952
**CAHIERS DE NOTES DOCUMENTAIRES.** [Cah. notes doc.]. **Added/Corp** Institut National de Recherche et de Securite. (19??)-. Academic Scholarly Publication. French (summaries and/or abstracts in French and English). qt. 400.00F France; 460.00F other. Institut National de Recherche & Securite, 4 rue Andre Boulle, 94942 Creteil Cedex 09 France. **Tel** 011 33 1 42070606. **CODEN** CNDIBJ. Documents available from BIOSIS Document Express, CASDDS.
**Ind/Abst** Biol. Abstr. (1986-); Chem. Abstr.; Chem. Hazards Ind.; Lab. Hazards Bull.; Saf. Health Work.

FR/0007-9995
**CAHIERS DE SOCIOLOGIE ET DE DEMOGRAPHIE MEDICALES.** (1961)-. Periodical. French. qt. 303.62F France; 330.00F other. Centre Sociologie et de Demographie Medicales, 60 Bld de Latour Maubourg, 75007 Paris France. **Tel** 011 33 1 45557377, FAX (1)45 55 8794. **UDC** 61:30. Index available.
**Ind/Abst** Health Plan. Adminis.; Index Med.; Trop. Dis. Bull.

US/0273-6896
**CAHPERD JOURNAL TIMES. Main/Corp** California Association for Health, Physical Education, Recreation, and Dance. **VFOAT** CAHPERD Journal/Times. **VAT** California Association for Health, Physical Education, Recreation, and Dance Journal Times. (19??)-. Periodical. English. mo (8 issues Oct.-May). $20.00 libraries; $75.00 institutions. California Association for Health, Physical Education, Recreation and Dance, 1501 El Camino, Suite 3, Sacramento CA 95815-2742. **Tel** (916)922-3596. **ED** Phyllis A. Blatz. available on microfilm and microfiche from University Microfilms International (UMI). ***Continues*** *CAHPER Journal Times, 0194-8261.*
**Ind/Abst** SPORT Discus; SportSearch (May 1987-).

●US/1065-4070
**CALIFORNIA HEALTH CARE IN PERSPECTIVE.** [Calif. health care perspect.]. **Added/Corp** Morgan Quitno Corporation. 1st Ed. (1993)-. English. $18.00. Morgan Quitno Corporation, PO Box 1656, 512 East 9th Street, Lawrence KS 66044. **Tel** (800)457-0742, (913)841-3534, FAX (913)841-3534. **DD** 362.
**Desc:** Reports on the state's data and rank for each of the categories featured in Health Care State Rankings.

US/0191-9806
**CALIFORNIA STATE PLAN FOR COMMUNITY MENTAL HEALTH CENTERS. Main/Corp** California. Dept. of Mental Health. Grants Section. 1978/79-. English. an. California Department of Mental Health, Office of Prevention, 2340 Irving Street/Suite 108, San Francisco CA 94122. **LC** RA790.65.C2; C2635A. **DD** 354.9/794/00842. **NLM** W2 AC2 B943C. ***Continues*** *California State Plan for Community Mental Health Centers, 0191-9806.*

US
**CAMPUS SAFETY NEWSLETTER / NATIONAL SAFETY COUNCIL. Added/Corp** National Safety Council. **VFOAT** Campus Safety. (19??)-. Newsletter. English. Six times a year. $19.00 (one year), $33.00 (two year). National Safety Council, 1121 Spring Lake Drive, Itasca IL 60143. **Tel** (800)621-7615, (708)775-2294, FAX (708)285-0797.

US/0885-3398
**CAMPUS SAFETY REPORT NEWSLETTER.** [Campus saf. rep. newsl.]. **VFOAT** CSR. Vol. 1, No. 1 (Dec. 1985)-. Periodical. English. Twelve times a year. $36.00. University of Tennessee / Department of Public Safety, 1208 B Helena Drive, Chattanooga TN 37343. **Tel** (615)875-4534. **ED** Charles Goodroe. **DD** 371. Index available. cum. index. **Bk Rev. Ad Acc. Circ:** 200 (ctrl).
**Desc:** Provides information dealing with police techniques, safety, and health for college/university campus safety departments.

US/1055-4319
**CAMPUS SECURITY REPORT.** [Campus secur. rep.]. (1990)-. Periodical. English. mo. $199.00 (one year), $349.00 (two year). Rusting Publications, PO Box 190, Port Washington NY 11050. **Tel** (516)883-1440. **ED** Robert Rusting. **LC** LB2866; .C65. **DD** 363. Index available. cum. index. **Bk Rev**, (Qty: 12). **Circ:** 700. ***Continues*** *College Security Report.*
**Desc:** Newsletter on security and safety management on campus

●CN/1188-4169
**CANADA COMMUNICABLE DISEASE REPORT.** [Can. commun. dis. rep.]. **Added/Corp** Canada. Sante et Bien-Etre Social Canada. **VFOAT** Releve des Maladies Transmissibles au Canada. Vol. 18, No. 1 (Jan. 17, 1992)-. Periodical. French (English). sm. **DD** 614.4. ***Continues*** *Canada. Services Epidemiologiques.; Canada Diseases Weekly Report., 0382-232X.*

●CN/1188-4169
**CANADA COMMUNICABLE DISEASE REPORT.** (CANADA COMMUNICABLE DISEASE REPORT / RELEVE DES MALADIES TRANSMISSIBLES AU CANADA.). [Can. commun. dis. rep.]. **Added/Corp** Canada. Health and Welfare Canada. **VFOAT** Releve des Maladies Transmissibles au Canada. Vol. 18, No. 1 (Jan. 17, 1992)-. Periodical. English (French). Twenty-four times a year. 75.00Can$. Canada Communication Group Publishers, Order Processing, Ottawa Ontario K1A 0S9 Canada. **Tel** (819)956-4800, (819)956-4802. **DD** 614.4. **NLM** W1; CA467. ***Continues*** *Laboratory Centre for Disease Control (Canada). Bureau of Epidemiology. Canada Diseases Weekly Report, 0382-232X.*
**Ind/Abst** Index Med. (1992-).

CN/0008-2791
**CANADA'S MENTAL HEALTH. *Suspended.*** [Can. ment. health]. (1953)-Suspended with (March 1991). Periodical. English. qt. $4.26. Statistics Canada, Publications Sales & Services, Main Building Room 1710, Ottawa Ontario K1A 0T6 Canada. **Tel** (613)951-5078, (800)267-6677, FAX (613)951-1584, telex 053-3585. **NLM** W1 CA492. **CODEN** CAMHA3.
**Desc:** Directed to mental health professionals and interested lay persons to foster the promotion of mental health and the prevention of mental disorders.
**Ind/Abst** Appl. Soc. Sci. Index Abstr.; Can. Index; Can. Period. Index; Cumul. Index Nurs. Allied Health Lit.; Health Plan. Adminis.; Health Serv. Abstr.; Hospit. Health Admin. Index; Middle East Abstr. Index; PAIS Int. Print (1991-); Psychol. Abstr. (1965-); PsycINFO; PsycLit; Soc. Work Abstr. [Select. Cov.].

CN/0847-947X
**CANADIAN EMERGENCY NEWS.** [Can. emerg. news]. **VFOAT** Emergency News. Vol. 12, No. 1 (Jan./Feb. 1989)-. Periodical. English. bm. 45.00Can$ (one year), 65.00Can$ (two year). Pendragon Publishing Ltd., PO Box 54087, 2640 52nd Street Northeast, Calgary Alberta T1Y 6S6 Canada. **Tel** (403)248-0755, FAX (403)248-7856. **(Subscription address:** Canadian Emergency News, PO Box 54087, Calgary Alberta T1Y 6S6 Canada; telephone: (403)248-0755) **ED** Lyle Blumhagen. **DD** 363.3/48/0971. **Bk Rev**, (Qty: varies). **Ad Acc, Adv Mgr Tel** (800)567-0911. **Pr Rev. Circ:** 4,000 (ctrl). Documents available. ***Continues*** *Canadian Emergency Services News., 0706-9278.*
**Desc:** Emergency responses professionals gives information on emergency medicine, firefightings, search and rescues that serves in Canada.

CN/1183-5702
**CANADIAN JOURNAL OF INFECTION CONTROL : THE OFFICIAL JOURNAL OF THE COMMUNITY & HOSPITAL INFECTION CONTROL ASSOCIATION-CANADA, THE. Added/Corp** CHICA-Canada. **VFOAT** Revue Canadienne de Prevention des Infections. Vol. 6, No. 1 (Spring 1991)-. Periodical. English (French). qt. 24.00Can$ (institution), 20.00Can$ (individual) Canada; $24.00 (institution), $20.00 (individual) US; 45.00Can$ (institution), 35.00Can$ (individual) other. Pulsus Group Inc., 2902 South Sheridan Way, Oakville Ontario L6J 7L6 Canada. **Tel** (416)829-4770, FAX (416)829-4799. **NLM** W1; CA594EE. ***Continues*** *Infection Control Canada, 0833-076X.*
**Ind/Abst** Cumul. Index Nurs. Allied Health Lit.

US/0008-4263
**CANADIAN JOURNAL OF PUBLIC HEALTH.** (CANADIAN JOURNAL OF PUBLIC HEALTH [MICROFORM].). [Can. j. public health]. **Added/Corp** Canadian Public Health Association. **VFOAT** Revue Canadienne d'Hygiene Publique; Revue Canadienne de Sante Publique. Vol. 34, No. 1 (Jan. 1943)-. Periodical. English (French). ir. $20.40 (microfiche). University Microfilms International, 300 North Zeeb Road, Ann Arbor MI 48106-1346. **Tel** (313)761-4700, (800)521-0600 Exts. 2490, 2491, FAX (313)973-1540. **[CCC]. *Continues*** *Canadian Public Health Journal, 0319-2652.*

CN/0008-4263
**CANADIAN JOURNAL OF PUBLIC HEALTH.** (CANADIAN JOURNAL OF PUBLIC HEALTH. REVUE CANADIENNE DE SANTE PUBLIQUE). [Can. j. public health]. **Added/Corp** Canadian Public Health Association. **VFOAT** Revue Canadienne de Sante Publique; Revue Canadienne d'Hygiene Publique. Vol. 34 (Jan. 1943)-. Academic Scholarly Publication. English (French). bm. 75.00Can$ Canada; 90.00Can$ US; 115.00Can$ other. Canadian Public Health Association, 1565 Carling Avenue/Suite 400, Ottawa Ontario K1Z 8R1 Canada. **Tel** (613)725-3769, FAX (613)725-9826. **ED** J. M. Last. **NLM** W1 CA605. **CODEN** CJPEA4. **[CCC].** cum. index. **Bk Rev. Ad Acc. Pr Rev. Circ:** 4,000 (ctrl). available on microfilm and microfiche from University Microfilms International (UMI). Documents available from The Genuine Article, BIOSIS Document Express, CASDDS. ***Continues*** *Canadian Public Health Journal, 0319-2652.*
**Desc:** Original articles only which are of interest to public health officers, nurses, doctors and public health researchers.
**Ind/Abst** ASTIS Curr. Aware. Bull. (1978-); ASTIS Bibliogr. (1978-); Biol. Abstr.; Biol. Dig.; Can. Index (?-?); Can. Period. Index (19??-); Chem. Abstr.; Cumul. Index Nurs. Allied Health Lit.; Curr. Contents Soc. Behav. Sci.; Dairy Sci. Abstr.; Dev. Med. Child Neurol.; EMBASE; Food Sci. Technol. Abstr.; Health Plan. Adminis.; Helminthol. Abstr. (1991-); Index Med.; Index Vet.; INIS Atomindex [Micro.]; Nutr. Res. Newsl.; Life Sci. Collect.; Pollut. Abstr. Indexes; Protozoolog. Abstr.; Res. Alert [Full Cov.]; Rev. Med. Vet. Entomol.; Rev. Med. Vet. Mycology; Rev. Plant Pathol.; Risk Abstr.; Soc. Sci. Cit. Index [Full Cov.]; SPORT Discus; SportSearch; Vet. Bull.; Trop. Dis. Bull.; Virol. AIDS Abstr.

CN/1185-9814
**CANADIAN JOURNAL OF QUALITY IN HEALTH CARE, THE.** [Can. j. qual. health care]. **Added/Corp** Canadian Association for Quality Assurance in Health Care. Vol. 9, No. 1 (Nov. 1991)-. Periodical. English. qt. Comes with Canadian Association for Quality in Health Care membership. Canadian Association for Quality Assurance in Health Care, c/o BB&C Publishing, Suite 409, 1 Eva Road, Etobicoke Ontario M9C 4Z5 Canada. **Tel** (905)626-0102. **DD** 362.1. ***Continues*** *The Canadian Journal of Quality Assurance., 0847-9445.*

US/1059-9010
**CANCERMONTHLY (EDUCATION AND HEALTHCARE ED.).** ***Title Change.*** (CANCERMONTHLY.). [Cancermonthly]. **VFOAT** Cancer Monthly. (Jan. 1992)-(19??). Periodical. English. mo. Cancer Weekly, PO Box 830409, Birmingham AL 35283-0409. **Tel** (800)633-4931, (205)995-1567. **DD** 362. ***Merged into*** *Cancer Weekly.*

UK/0300-5909
**CARE IN THE HOME.** [Care home]. (1972)-. Periodical. English. qt. £7.00 UK; £8.05 other. Royal Society for the Prevention of Accidents, Cannon House, Priory Queensway, Birmingham B4 6BS England. **Tel** 011 44 21 200 2461, FAX 021 200 1254. ***Absorbed*** *Home Safety Journal.*
**Ind/Abst** Acad. Abstr. Full Text Elite (Jan. 1992-); Acad. Abstr. (Jan. 1992-); Acad. Search (Jan. 1992-Dec. 1993); Health Source (Jan. 1992-); INFO-SOUTH Abstr.; Mag. Search; Vocat. Search (Jan. 1992-).

US/1046-0748
**CASE MANAGEMENT RESOURCE GUIDE: A DIRECTORY OF HOMECARE, REHABILITATION, MENTAL HEALTH AND LONG TERM CARE SERVICES.** (1990)-. Directory. English. $225.00. Center for Consumer Healthcare Information, PO Box 16067, Irvine CA 92713. **Tel** (714)752-2335. **LC** RA645.35; .C37. **DD** 362. **NLM** W 22; AA1 C3.
**Desc:** Contains entries on homecare providers, rehabilitation, psychiatric and addiction treatment programs, eldercare services, specialty referral centers, and patient support organizations.

US/0748-5093
**CATALOG OF UNIVERSITY PRESENTATIONS.** (CATALOG OF UNIVERSITY PRESENTATIONS / NATIONAL CENTER FOR HEALTH STATISTICS.). [Cat. univ. present.]. **Main/Corp** National Center for Health Statistics (U.S.). Catalog. English. an. National Center for Health Statistics, 6525 Belcrest Road, Hyattsville MD 20782. **Tel** (301)436-8500. **LC** RA407.3; .N28A. **DD** 016.3621/0973/021. available on microfiche (Vols. for (1986-1987-) distributed to depository libraries).

US
**CDC HIV : AIDS PREVENTION NEWSLETTER.** **See** Medical Science and Technology-Communicable Diseases.

US
**CDP FILE [COMPUTER FILE] / NATIONAL CENTER FOR CHRONIC DISEASE PREVENTION AND HEALTH PROMOTION.** **Added/Corp** National Center for Chronic Disease Prevention and Health Promotion (U.S.). **VFOAT** Chronic Disease Prevention File; Centers for Disease Control CD-ROM. NCCDPHP CD-ROM No.1 Oct. (1991)-. Periodical. English. sa. Technical Information Services Branch, National Center for Chronic Disease Prevention and Health Promotion, 1600 Clifton Road, Rhodes Building-Mail Stop K-13, Atlanta GA 30333.

CS/0009-0689
**CESKOSLOVENSKE ZDRAVOTNICTVI.** ***Ceased.*** [Cesk. zdrav.]. Vol. 1 (1953)-(1991). Periodical. Czech (Russian). mo. **(Subscription address:** Artia Pegas Press Ltd., Palac Metro Narodni Trida 25, 11210 Prague 1 Czech Republic.**)** **NLM** W1 CE9155. **[CCC].** Index Available in first issue of next volume--attached.
**Ind/Abst** Coal Abstr.; Health Plan. Adminis.; Index Med.; Saf. Health Work.

CN/0822-8426
**CHAC INFO.** (CHAC INFO : QUARTERLY NEWSLETTER OF THE CATHOLIC HEALTH ASSOCIATION OF CANADA.). [CHAC info]. **Added/Corp** Catholic Health Association of Canada. **VFOAT** Info Accs. **VAT** Catholic Health Association of Canada Info; Info Association Catholique Canadienne de la Sante. Vol. 1, No. 1 (Mar. 1983)-. Periodical. English (French). Four times a year. 40.00Can$ Canada; $45.00Can$ others (individuals); 200.00Can$ (associate); 750.00Can$ (corporate) Comes with Catholic Health Association of Canada membership. Catholic Health Association of Canada, 1247 Killborn Place, Ottawa Ontario K1H 6K9 Canada. **Tel** (613)731-7148, FAX (613)731-7797. **ED** Freda Froser. **DD** 362.1/06/071. **Ad Acc.** ***Separated from*** *Catholic Health Association of Canada. C.H.A.C. Review., 0226-5923.*

US/0196-3813
**CHAN. CONSUMER HEALTH ACTION NETWORK.** **See** Consumer Interests.

US/1063-0538
**CHECK-UP (SAN DIEGO, CALIF.).** ***Title Change.*** (CHECK-UP: A CHRONICLE OF CALIFORNIA HEALTH PROFESSION REGULATION.). **Added/Corp** University of San Diego. Center for Public Interest Law. **VFOAT** Check Up. (1992)-(19??). Periodical. English. qt. Center for Public Interest Law, 5998 Alcala Park, University of San Diego, San Diego CA 92110. **Tel** (619)260-4806. ***Merged into*** *California Regulatory Law Reporter.*

US
**CHECKLISTS AND ILLUSTRATIVE FINANCIAL STATEMENTS FOR HEALTH CARE PROVIDERS.** **See** Business-Accounting.

JA/0386-6742
**CHIBA-KEN EISEI KENKYUJO KENKYU HOKOKU.** [Chiba-ken Eisei Kenkyujo kenkyu hokoku]. **VFOAT** Bulletin of the Public Health Laboratory of Chiba Prefecture. Academic Scholarly Publication. Japanese (Japanese). an. Chiba-Ken Eisei Kenkyujo, 666-2 Nitona-cho, Chiba-shi 280 Japan. **LC** RA532.C45; C45. **CODEN** CEKHDO. Documents available from CASDDS.
**Ind/Abst** Chem. Abstr.

US/1064-4849
**CHILD HEALTH ALERT.** [Child health alert]. Vol. 1, No. 1 (April 1983)-. Periodical. English. mo. $29.00 (1 year), $52.00 (2 year) US; $33.00 (1 year), $60.00 (2 year) Canada and Mexico; $46.00 (1 year), $69.00 (2 year) other. Child Health Alert, PO Box 338, Newton Highlands MA 02161. **Tel** (617)237-3310. **ED** Paula Mitchell, Allen Mitchell and Fred Mandell. **DD** 613. available on an online database (file 149/Full-Text) from DIALOG.
**Desc:** A survey of current developments affecting child health. Covers a small number of topics in considerable depth. Articles on topics such as minor head trauma in children, cholesterol, superabsorbent diapers, and SIDS-are based upon analysis and interpretation of relevant articles in the professional literature.
**Ind/Abst** Acad. Abstr. Full Text Elite (Jan. 1992-); Acad. Abstr. (Jan. 1992-); Acad. Search (Jan. 1992-); Consum. Health Nutr. Index; Health Index (1989-); Health Period. Database [Full Txt.]; Health Ref. Cent. (Jan. 1989-) [Full Cov.]; Health Source (Jan. 1992-); Mag. Search.

US/0147-1260
**CHILD PROTECTION REPORT.** [Child prot. rep.]. (197?)-. Periodical. English. bw. $221.00. Business Publishers Inc., 951 Pershing Drive, Silver Spring MD 20910-4464. **Tel** (301)587-6300, (800)274-0122, FAX (301)585-9075. **ED** William E. Howard. **DD** 362. **NLM** W1 CH668I. **[CCC].** **Bk Rev.** **Circ:** 1,000 (ctrl).
**Desc:** An independent news service for professionals working with children and youth.

AT/1033-7660
**CHILD SAFETY LIBRARY NEWS.** ***Title Change.*** [Child Saf. Libr. news]. (1989)-(1992). Periodical. English. qt. Child Safety Library, Royal Childrens Hospital, Flem Road, Parkville 3052 Australia. **Tel** 011 61 3 3455522, FAX 011 61 3 3455789. **DD** 016.6136083. ***Continued by*** *Child Safety News, 1039-7477.*

●AT
**CHILD SAFETY NEWS.** (1993)-. Bulletin. English. Four times a year (Mar., June, Sept., Dec.). 30.00Aus$. Child Safety Library, Royal Childrens Hospital, Flem Road, Parkville 3052 Australia. **Tel** 011 61 3 3455522, FAX 011 61 3 3455789. **ED** Jan Shield (phone: (03)345-5085). **Bk Rev**, (Qty: 10). **Circ:** 200. ***Continues*** *Child Safety Library News.*
**Desc:** Current awareness bulletin of literature on childhood injury prevention and related topics.

UK/0957-4107
**CHILD SAFETY REVIEW.** [Child saf. rev.]. (1989)-. Periodical. English. sa. £15.00 UK; £22.50 other. Child Accident Prevention Trust, 18 20 Farringdon Lane, 4th Floor, London EC1R 3AU England. **Tel** 011 44 71 608-3828, FAX 011 44 71 608-3674. **DD** 613.69. **Bk Rev**, (Qty: 15-20). **Pr Rev.** **Circ:** 500 (ctrl).
**Desc:** News and developments in child accident prevention. Feature articles, conference reports, and new publications.

JA
**CHOSA GEPPO.** **Main/Corp** Kokuritsu Eisei Shikenjo. (19??)-. Periodical. Japanese. Kokuritsu Eisei Shikenjo Fosoku Toshokan, 1-18 Kamiyoga Setagaya-ku, Tokyo 158 Japan. **LC** RA421; .K64a.

CN/0228-8699
**CHRONIC DISEASES IN CANADA.** **See** Medical Science and Technology.

●US/1062-1245
**CITIZENS HEALTH ALERT.** **Added/Corp** Citizens for Health. (1992)-. Periodical. English. $15.00. Citizens for Health, PO Box 368, Tacoma WA 98401.

US/0896-2359
**CIVIC HEALTH OCCASIONAL PAPER.** **See** Medical Science and Technology-Allergy and Immunology.

US
**CLINICAL ELECTIVES FOR MEDICAL AND DENTAL STUDENTS AT THE NATIONAL INSTITUTES OF HEALTH.** **Main/Corp** National Institutes of Health (U.S.). English. an. US Department of Health and Human Services, 200 Independence Avenue Southwest, Washington DC 20201. ***Continues*** *Clinical Electives for Medical Students at the National Institutes of Health.*

US/0888-7950
**CLINICAL LABORATORY MANAGEMENT REVIEW.** [Clin. lab. manage. rev.]. **Added/Corp** Clinical Laboratory Management Association. Vol. 1, No. 1 (Jan./Feb. 1987)-. Periodical. English. bm. $66.00 (individual), $92.00 (institutional) US and Canada; $96.00 (individual), $122.00 (institutional) other. Williams & Wilkins Company, 428 East Preston Street, Baltimore MD 21202-3993. **Tel** (410)528-4000, (800)638-6423, FAX (410)528-8596, telex 87669. **(Subscription address:** Williams & Wilkins, PO Box 64380, Baltimore MD 21264.**)** **DD** 658. **NLM** W1; CL726DF. **Ad Acc.** Documents available from Quick Copies.
**Desc:** Provides balanced coverage of financial management, new equipment, medical information systems, operational issues, marketing, personnel management, regulatory issues, and a broad range of topics in health care.
**Ind/Abst** EMBASE; Health Plan. Adminis.; Hospit. Health Admin. Index (Vol 3 No 1, 1989-).

CN/1189-0657
**CLIPBOARD.** [Clipboard]. **Added/Corp** Nova Scotia Association of Health Organizations. **VFOAT** Clip Board. Vol. 1, No. 1 (Jan. 19, 1991)-. Periodical. English. mo. Limited free distribution. Nova Scotia Association of Health Organizations, 5164 Fenwick Street, Halifax Nova Scotia B3H 1P9 Canada. **DD** 362.1/06/0716.

TU/0010-0161
**COCUK SAGLIGI VE HASTALIKLARI DERGISI.** [Cocuk saglg ve hastalklar derg.]. **Added/Corp** Hacettepe Universitesi Cocuk Saglg. Hacettepe Tp Merkezi Cocuk Hastanesi. Hacettepe Tp Merkezi. Cocuk Saglg B.S.A. Enstitusu. (1958)-. Periodical. Turkish. qt. Turkish and International Children's Center, PO Box 66Samanparzari, 06240 Ankara Turkey. **Tel** 011 90 4 3242326. **NLM** W1 CO103H. **CODEN** CSHDAO. Documents available from BIOSIS Document Express.
**Ind/Abst** Biol. Abstr.

FR
**CODE DE LA SANTE PUBLIQUE.** French. 293.60F (updates). Editions Tissot Sa, BP 93, F 74003 Annecy Cedex France. **Tel** 011 33 50 231823.

US
**CODE OF FEDERAL REGULATIONS. 42, PUBLIC HEALTH.** **See** Law.

●US/1061-8767
**COLLEGIATE JOURNAL, THE.** [Coll. j.]. (1992)-. Periodical. English. mo. $30.00. The Collegiate Journal, Inc., 2660 Mountain View Circle, Emmaus PA 18049. **DD** 613.

IT/1120-639X
**COLLETTIVITA CONVIVENZE.** [Colletiv. Conviv.]. (1979)-. Periodical. Italian. mo (10 issues per year). L90000 Italy; L155000 other. Unisco SRL, Via a Pestalozza 31, 20131 Milan Italy. **Tel** 011 39 2 236-1556, FAX 011 39 2 26680526. **UDC** 64.022. Index available. **Bk Rev.** **Ad Acc.** **Circ:** 24,500.
**Desc:** Covers the designing and management of health and social assistance to institutions.

●US/1065-4089
**COLORADO HEALTH CARE IN PERSPECTIVE.** [Colo. health care perspect.]. **Added/Corp** Morgan Quitno Corporation. 1st Ed. (1993)-. English. $18.00. Morgan Quitno Corporation, PO Box 1656, 512 East 9th Street, Lawrence KS 66044. **Tel** (800)457-0742, (913)841-3534, FAX (913)841-3534. **DD** 362.
**Desc:** Reports on the state's data and rank for each of the categories featured in Health Care State Rankings.

UK/0953-1084
**COMMISSION OF THE EUROPEAN COMMUNITIES HEALTH SERVICES RESEARCH SERIES.** [Comm. Eur. Communities health serv. res. ser.]. **Added/Corp** Commission of the European Communities. **VFOAT** Health Services Research Series. No. 1 (1986)-. Monographic series. English. ir. Price varies per volume. Oxford University Press, Walton Street, Oxford OX2 6DP England. **Tel** 011 44 865 56767, FAX 011 44 865 267773, telex 837330 OXPRES G. **(Subscription address:** Oxford University Press / USA, Journals Marketing Department, Oxford University Press, 2001 Evans Road, Cary NC 27513.**)** **NLM** W1; CO395.

US
**COMMISSIONED CORPS BULLETIN.** **Main/Corp** United States. Public Health Service. Commissioned Corps. Bulletin. English. mo. Public Health Service, Office of the Surgeon General, Rockville MD 20857.

US
**COMMUNICABLE DISEASE NEWSLETTER.** (1974)-. Newsletter. English. bw. New York State Health Department, Empire State Plaza Tower Building, Room 1408, Albany NY 12237. **Tel** (518)474-2011, FAX (518)474-4471.

US
**COMMUNICATING FOR HEALTH SERIES.** **Added/Corp** Pan American Health Organization. No. 1 (1991)-. Monographic series. English. ir. Pan American Health Organization, 525 23rd Street Northwest, Office District Sales, Washington DC 20037. **Tel** (202)293-8130, FAX (202)338-0869. **NLM** W1; CO427VJ.

US
**COMMUNIQUE (RICHMOND, VA).** **See** Dentistry.

AT/0312-6579
**COMMUNITY HEALTH BULLETIN.** **Added/Corp** Australia. Dept. of Health. Australia. Hospitals and Health Services Commission. No. 1 (July/Sept. 1975)-. Periodical. English. qt. **NLM** W1 CO4288H.

US/1052-6552
**COMMUNITY HEALTH FUNDING REPORT.** **See** Sociology-Social Services and Welfare.

US/0191-3972
**COMMUNITY HEALTH INSTITUTE CLEARINGHOUSE NEWS, THE.** Periodical. English. National Association of Community Health Centers, 1625 I Street NW/Suite 403, Washington DC 20006. **NLM** W1 CO429CI. ***Continues*** *Newsletter Supplement - National Association of Community Health Centers, Inc, 0191-3980.*

US/0069-7850
**COMMUNITY MENTAL HEALTH JOURNAL. MONOGRAPH SERIES.** ***Ceased.*** No. 1 (1965)-(19??). Monographic series. English. ir. Human Sciences Press, PO Box 735, 233 Spring Street, New York NY 10013. **Tel** (212)620-8000, FAX (212)807-1047, telex 23421139. **DD** 131.3.

BE
**COMMUNITY'S RESEARCH AND DEVELOPMENT PROGRAMME ON DECOMMISSIONING OF NUCLEAR POWER PLANTS. ANNUAL PROGRESS REPORT, THE.** **Main/Corp** Commission of the European Communities. Directorate-General for Science, Research, and Development. **VFOAT** Annual Progress Report. English. an. **LC** TK9152.2; .C66A. **DD** 363.1/799.

US/0192-270X
**COMPREHENSIVE ENVIRONMENT, HEALTH, AND SAFETY PROGRAM REPORT.** **Main/Corp** United States. Dept. of Energy. Assistant Secretary for Environment. Office of Program Coordination. English. an. $5.25. National Technical Information Service - NTIS, Room 2027S, 5285 Port Royal Road, Springfield VA 22161. **Tel** (703)487-4630, (703)487-4660, (703)487-4650, FAX (703)321-8547, telex 89-9405. **LC** TD195.E49; U54A. **DD** 614.7.

US/0588-9715
**CONCEPTS FOR TRAFFIC SAFETY.** **See** Transportation-Roads and Traffic.

CN/0229-2661
**CONCERN (NEW WESTMINSTER).** (CONCERN : A PAPER FOR PEOPLE WHO CARE ABOUT PEOPLE.). [Concern]. Vol. 1, No. 1-. Periodical. English. qt. Food for the Hungry/Canada, 210 6th Street, New Westminster British Columbia V3L 3H2 Canada. **DD** 363.8/575/05.
**Ind/Abst** Health Devices Alerts.

CN/0700-6659
**CONGRES ANNUEL - CONSEIL CANADIEN DA LA SECURITE.** **Main/Corp** Conseil Canadien de la Securite. Periodical. French. an. 6.50Can$. Conseil Canadien de la Securite, 1765 Boulevard Saint Laurent, Ottawa Ontario K1G 3V4 Canada. **Tel** (613)521-6881, FAX (613)521-0097. **DD** 614.8/05. **Circ:** 200,000. ***Supersedes*** *Canada Safety Council Conference.*
**Desc:** For safety education in the home, traffic and recreational environments.

US/0195-9840
**CONGRESS AND HEALTH.** **Added/Corp** National Health Council (U.S.). (Feb. 1976)-. English. ir. $25.00. National Health Council Inc., 1730 M Street Northwest, Suite 500, Washington DC 20036. **Tel** (202)785-3910. **ED** T.L. Schmidt. **LC** JK1083; .C58. **DD** 328.73/002/02. **NLM** W1 CO595.
**Desc:** Resource document on the 99th Congress and its involvement in the health field. Describes legislative process and lists all key individuals involved.

●US/1065-4097
**CONNECTICUT HEALTH CARE IN PERSPECTIVE.** [Conn. health care perspect.]. **Added/Corp** Morgan Quitno Corporation. 1st Ed. (1993)-. English. $18.00. Morgan Quitno Corporation, PO Box 1656, 512 East 9th Street, Lawrence KS 66044. **Tel** (800)457-0742, (913)841-3534, FAX (913)841-3534. **DD** 362.
**Desc:** Reports on the state's data and rank for each of the categories featured in Health Care State Rankings.

US/0732-2658
**CONSOLIDATED PLAN. APPENDICES / MISSOURI DEPARTMENT OF MENTAL HEALTH.** [Consol. plan, Append. - Mo., Dept. Ment. Health]. **Main/Corp** Missouri. Dept. of Mental Health. English. te. Missouri Department of Mental Health, 2002 Missouri Boulevard, Jefferson City MO 65101. **LC** RA790.65.M8; M57B SUPPL. **DD** 353.97780084/2.

US/0732-264X
**CONSOLIDATED PLAN / MISSOURI DEPARTMENT OF MENTAL HEALTH.** [Consol. plan - Mo., Dept. Ment. Health]. **Main/Corp** Missouri. Dept. of Mental Health. English. te. Missouri Department of Mental Health, 2002 Missouri Boulevard, Jefferson City MO 65101. **LC** RA790.65.M8; M57B. **DD** 353.97780084/2.

US/1050-4060
**CONSTRUCTION INJURY LIABILITY MONTHLY.** **See** Building and Construction.

US/0736-010X
**CONSUMER HEALTH.** [Consum. health]. (1983)-. Periodical. English. Ten times a year. $19.50. Medical Second Opinion Inc, 156 Algonquin Parkway, Whippany NJ 07981. **Tel** (201)884-5050. **ED** Suzanne Gallagher. **Pr Rev.** ctrl circ.

●US/1058-0387
**CONSUMER HEALTH SAFETY DIGEST.** **VFOAT** Health Safety Digest. (1992)-. Periodical. English. qt. Medical Second Opinion Inc, 156 Algonquin Parkway, Whippany NJ 07981. **Tel** (201)884-5050.

US/0147-3360
**CONSUMER PRODUCT HAZARD INDEX.** **Main/Corp** United States. Consumer Product Safety Commission. English. 5401 Westbard Avenue, Washington DC 20207. **LC** HV676.A1; U53A. **DD** 614.8/53/0973.

US/1044-3193
**CONSUMER REPORTS HEALTH LETTER.** ***Title Change.*** [Consum. Rep. health lett.]. **Added/Corp** Consumers Union of United States. **VFOAT** Health Letter. Vol. 1, No. 1 (Sept. 1989)-(19??). Periodical. English. mo. Consumer Reports Health Letter, 101 Truman Avenue, Yonkers NY 80322-2148. **Tel** (800)288-7898. **ED** Michael Leff. **DD** 613. **NLM** W1; CO755T. **CODEN** CRHLEB. **Circ:** 50,000. available on an online database (files 149,646,647/Full-Text) from DIALOG. ***Continued by*** *Consumer Reports on Health, 1058-0832.*
**Ind/Abst** Cumul. Index Nurs. Allied Health Lit.; Health Devices Alerts; Health Index (1990-1991); Health Period. Database [Full Txt.]; Health Ref. Cent. (Jan. 1990-) [Full Txt.] [Full Cov.]; INFO-SOUTH Abstr.

FR
**CONTACT SANTE.** (19??)-. French. mo. 100.00F. Maison Regionale de Promotion de la Sante, Immeuble Perinor, 4/6 rue Jeanne Maillotte, 59110 la Madeleine France. **Tel** 011 33 2074 85 23, FAX 011 33 20 5559 17.

●US/1061-866X
**CONTAMINATION ALERT.** [Contam. alert]. Issue No. 1 (June 1992)-. Periodical. English. mo. $299.00 US. Interpharm Press, Inc., 1358 Busch Parkway, Buffalo Grove IL 60089. **DD** 362.

US/0882-4479
**CONTEMPORARY HEALTH JOURNAL.** [Contemp. health j.]. **VFOAT** CHJ. Vol. 1, No. 1 (March 1983)-. Periodical. English. mo. CHJ Enterprises, PO Box 443, Racine WI 53401-0443. **DD** 614.

US
**CONTEMPORARY PUBLIC HEALTH ISSUES.** **See** Medical Science and Technology-Forensic Medicine, Medical Jurisprudence.

●CN/1191-3959
**CORONER (SAINTE-FOY).** (LE CORONER.). [Coroner]. **Added/Corp** Association des Coroners du Quebec. (1992)-. Periodical. French. qt. Free for members. Association des Coroners du Quebec, Bureau 380, 2590 Boulevard Laurier, Sainte-Foy Quebec G1V 4M6 Canada. **DD** 614. ***Continues*** *Prescriptions (Sainte-Foy, Quebec)., 1188-2247.*

US/1061-172X
**CORPORATE HEALTH PROMOTION TODAY.** ***Ceased.*** [Corp. health promot. today]. **Added/Corp** International Health Awareness Center, Inc. **VFOAT** Health Promotion Today; Health Promotion. Vol. 1, No. 1 (1992)- Vol. 1, No. 5 (Sept. 1992). Periodical. English. mo. IHAC, 350 East Michigan Avenue, Suite 301, Kalamazoo MI 49007-3851. **DD** 613.

UK/0958-1596
**CRITICAL PUBLIC HEALTH.** [Crit. public health]. **VFOAT** CPH (London). (1990)-. Periodical. English. qt. £22.00 UK; $47.00 other. Multilingual Matters Ltd., Frankfurt Lodge, Clevedon Hall, Clevedon Avon, BS21 7SJ England. **Tel** 011 44 275 876519, FAX 011 44 275 343096. **DD** 362.10941. **Bk Rev. Pr Rev. Circ:** 750. ***Continues*** *Radical Community Medicine, 0265-0851.*
**Desc:** A quarterly journal on political and economical issues relating to and affecting public health and health services. Aims to change health policy and practice.
**Ind/Abst** Trop. Dis. Bull.

IT
**CRP NOTIZIE.** ***Suspended.*** (19??)-(1990). Italian. Centro Regionale Prevenzione, Via Marconi 69, 40122 Bologna Italy.

XR/0514-2431
**CSSR ZDRAVOTNICTVI.** [CSSR zdrav.]. **Added/Corp** Czechoslovakia. Ministerstvo Zdravotnictvi. Czech Socialist Republic (Czechoslovakia). Ustav pro Zdravotnickou Statistiku. Slovak Socialist Republic (Czechoslovakia). Ustav Zdravotnickej Statistiky. Czech Socialist Republic (Czechoslovakia). Ustav Zdravotnickych Informaci a Statistiky. Slovak Socialist Republic (Czechoslovakia). Ustav Zdravotnickych Informacii a Statistiky. **VFOAT** Zdravotnictvi CSSR. (1965)-. Czech. an. **LC** RA299.C95; A33. **NLM** W2 GC8 M6Z. ***Continues*** *Zdravotnictvi CSSR.*

SP
**CUADERNOS DE LA CONSEJERIA DE TRABAJO Y SEGURIDAD SOCIAL DE SANTA CRUZ DE TENERIFE.** Spanish. Three times a year. Gobierno Canario, Consejeria de Trabajo, Sanidad y Seguridad Social, Rambla General Franco 53, 38006 Santa Cruz de Tenerife Spain.

US/0893-5165
**CURRENT CONTENTS. HEALTH SERVICES ADMINISTRATION.** ***Ceased.*** [Curr. contents, Health serv. adm.]. **Added/Corp** Institute for Scientific Information. American Hospital Association. **VFOAT** CC/Health Services; CC/HSA; Health Services Administration. (1989)-(Dec. 1989). Academic Scholarly Publication. English. mo. Institute for Scientific Information, 3501 Market Street, Philadelphia PA 19104. **Tel** (215)386-0100, (800)523-1850, FAX (215)386-6362, telex 84-5305. **(Subscription address:** Institute for Scientific Information, PO Box 71416, Chicago, IL 60694) **DD** 362. **NLM** ZW 84.1; C976.

US/0891-4591
**CURRENT ESTIMATES FROM THE NATIONAL HEALTH INTERVIEW SURVEY, UNITED STATES.** [Curr. estim. Natl. Health Interview Surv. U. S.]. **Added/Corp** National Health Interview Survey (U.S.) National Center for Health Statistics (U.S.). **VFOAT** Current Estimates from the National Health Interview Survey. (1979)-. English. an. $21.00. Superintendent of Documents, US Government Printing Office, Washington DC 20402. **Tel** (202)275-3328, FAX (202)786-2377. **LC** RA407.3; .A346 subser. **DD** 312. available on microfiche. ***Continues*** *Current Estimates from the Health Interview Survey, United States, 0502-2673.*

US/0199-820X
**CURRENT HEALTH 1.** [Curr. health 1]. **VAT** Current Health One. (197?)-. Periodical. English. Nine times a year. $26.95. Weekly Reader Corporation, 3001 Cindel Drive, Delran NJ 08370. **Tel** (609)786-1000, (800)446-3355, FAX (609)786-3360. Index available (bound in May issue). available on microfilm and microfiche from University Microfilms International (UMI). ***Separated from*** *Current Health.*
**Ind/Abst** Child. Mag. Guide (1981-); Health Source (Jul. 1989-); Mag. Artic. Summar. Elite (July 1989-); Mag. Artic. Summar. Select (July 1989-); Mag. Artic. Summar. CD-ROM (July 1989-); Mag. Search; Mid. Search (Jul. 1989-); Prim. Search (Jul. 1989-); Mag. Index; TOM Gen. Index (1985-?).

US/0163-156X
**CURRENT HEALTH 2.** [Curr. health 2]. **VFOAT** Current Health Two. (19??)-. Periodical. English. Nine times a year. $26.95; (includes Human Sexuality supplement). Weekly Reader Corporation, 3001 Cindel Drive, Delran NJ 08370. **Tel** (609)786-1000, (800)446-3355, FAX (609)786-3360. Index available (bound in May issue). available on microfilm and microfiche from University Microfilms International (UMI); available on an online database (files 149,647/Full-Text) from DIALOG. Documents available from UMI Article Clearinghouse, Magazine Collection. ***Separated from*** *Current Health.*
**Ind/Abst** Acad. Abstr. Full Text Elite (Jan. 1984-); Acad. Abstr. (Jan. 1984-); Acad. Ind. [Computer File] (1986-); Expand. Acad. Index (1986-); Gen. Period. Index (1986-); Health Index (1992-); Health Ref. Cent. (1987-) [Select. Cov.]; Health Source (Jan. 1984-); Mag. Artic. Summar. Elite (Jan. 1984-); Mag. Artic. Summar. Select (Jan.

# Public Health and Safety

1984-)]; Mag. Artic. Summar. CD-ROM (Jan. 1984-); Mag. ASAP Plus [Full Txt.]; Mag. ASAP Sel. [Full Txt.]; Mag. Express (1988-) [Full Txt.]; Mag. Index Plus (1989-); Mag. Index Sel. Microfiche (1986-) [Full Txt.]; Mag. Index. Sel. (1986-); Mag. Search; Mid. Search (Jan. 1984-); Newsp. Period. Abstr. (1988-); Prim. Search (Jan. 1984-); Read. Guide Abstr. Select Ed.; Read. Guide Period. Lit.; Resource/One Ondisc; Mag. Index (1977-); TOM Gen. Index (1986-) [Full Txt.].

●US/1076-7762
**CURRENT ISSUES IN PUBLIC HEALTH.** (1995-). Periodical. English. Six times a year. $59.95 (individuals); $119.95 (institutions). Current Science, 20 North 3rd Street, Philadelphia PA 19106. **Tel** (215)574-2266, (800)552-5866, FAX (215)574-2270.

UK/0898-5871
**CURRENT TOPICS IN AIDS. See** Medical Science and Technology-Allergy and Immunology.

CN/0823-3918
**CUSSCO NEWSLETTER.** (CUSSCO NEWSLETTER / COLLEGE, UNIVERSITY AND SCHOOL SAFETY COUNCIL OF ONTARIO.). [CUSSCO newsl.]. **Added/Corp** College, University and School Safety Council of Ontario. Ontario. Workers' Compensation Board. Safety Education Division. **VAT** College, University and School Safety Council of Ontario Newsletter. Vol. 1, No. 1 (July/Aug. 1983)-. Newsletter. English. bm. Free to Education Institutions. Workers Compensation Board, Occupational Health and Safety Education Authority, 80 Bloor Street West, Toronto Ontario M5S 2V1 Canada. **Tel** (416)927-4873. **ED** Ronald M. Angus. **DD** 371.7/7/09713. **Bk Rev. Ad Acc. Circ:** 1,800.
**Desc:** Occupational health and safety information for educational workplaces in Ontario.

CN/0256-3223
**DANGEROUS GOODS REGULATIONS.** (DANGEROUS GOODS REGULATIONS / IATA.). [Daner. goods regul.]. **Main/Corp** International Air Transport Association. **VFOAT** IATA Dangerous Goods Regulations. **VAT** International Air Transport Association Dangerous Goods Regulations. (Jan. 1983)-. Periodical. English (Spanish, German and French). an. $73.00. International Air Transport Association / Montreal, 2000 Peel Street, Room 3050, Montreal Quebec H3A 2R4 Canada. **Tel** (514)844-6311 ext. 232, FAX (514)844-5286, telex 05-267627. **DD** 363.1/77. **Continues** International Air Transport Association. Restricted Articles Regulations.
**Desc:** Advise how materials can be carried by air safely in accordance with national and international laws.

GW/0172-3723
**DATEN DES GESUNDHEITSWESENS. See** Public Health and Safety-Abstracting, Bibliographies and Statistics.

KE/0379-5071
**DEFENDER (NAIROBI).** (THE DEFENDER.). **Added/Corp** African Medical and Research Foundation. Health Education Dept. (Oct. 1968)-. Periodical. English (Swahili). Four times a year (Apr., June, Sept., Dec.). Free in East Africa; $10.00 rest of Africa; $15.00 Asia; $20.00 others. African Medical Research & Educatie Foundation, PO Box 30125, Nairobi Kenya. **Tel** 501301, FAX 506112. **ED** William Okedi. **NLM** W1 DE114. **Circ:** 15,000.
**Desc:** Ideas in the area of family health, sex education, chronic illness, first aid, personal hygiene, and environmental health.

●US/1065-4100
**DELAWARE HEALTH CARE IN PERSPECTIVE.** [Del. health care perspect.]. **Added/Corp** Morgan Quinto Corporation. (1993-). English. $18.00. Morgan Quinto Corporation, PO Box 1656, 512 East 9th Street, Lawrence KS 66044. **Tel** (800)457-0742, (913)841-3534, FAX (913)841-3534. **DD** 362.
**Desc:** Reports on the state's data and rank for each of the categories featured in Health Care State Rankings.

UK/0260-0862
**DEVELOPMENTS IN ENVIRONMENTAL CONTROL AND PUBLIC HEALTH.** [Dev. environ. control public health]. 1-. Academic Scholarly Publication. English. ir. $51.00. Elsevier Science Publishers BV, PO Box 211, 1000 AE Amsterdam Netherlands. **Tel** 011 31 20 5803642, FAX 011 31 20 5862696, telex 15682. **ED** A Porteous. **NLM** W1 DE997VWF. **CODEN** DCPHDC. Documents available from CASDDS.
**Ind/Abst** Chem. Abstr. (1979-1981); GeoRef.

●NE
**DEVELOPMENTS IN HEALTH ECONOMICS AND PUBLIC POLICY.** Vol. 1 (1992)-. Monographic series. English. ir. Price varies per volume. Kluwer Academic Publishers, Postbus 322, 3300 AH Dordrecht, The Netherlands. **Tel** 011 (31) 78 524400, FAX 011 31 78 183273, telex 20083. (**Subscription address:** Kluwer Academic Publishers / US Subscriptions, PO Box 253, Accord Station, Hingham MA 02018.) **NLM** W1; DE997VZE.

US/1063-9977
**DEVELOPMENTS IN MENTAL HEALTH LAW. See** Law.

FR/0396-8014
**DEVELOPPEMENT ET SANTE.** [Dev. sante]. (1976)-. Periodical. French. bm. 195.89F France; 200.00F other. John Libbey Eurotext Ltd, 6 rue Blanche, Isabelle Trope, 92120 Montrouge France. **Tel** 011 33 1 47358552. **UDC** 61.

CN/1181-7720
**DIARY / CANADIANS FOR HEALTH RESEARCH.** [Diary - Can. Health Res.]. **Added/Corp** Canadians for Health Research. Vol. 2, No. 4 (Dec. 1988)-. Periodical. English. qt. 25.00Can$. Canadians for Health Research, PO Box 126, Westmount Quebec H3Z 2T1 Canada. **Tel** (514)398-7478, FAX (514)398-8361. **DD** 619/.05. **Continues** Newsletter (Canadians for Health Research)., 1181-7712.

US
**DICKINSON'S FDA INSPECTION.** (19??)-. English. mo. $395.00 US and Canada; $455.00 other. Ferdic Inc., PO Box 367, Las Cruces NM 88004. **Tel** (505)527-8634, FAX (505)527-8858. **ED** James G. Dickinson.

IT/0012-2653
**DIFESA SOCIALE. Added/Corp** Istituto Italiano d'Igiene, Previdenza ed Assistenza Sociale, Rome. Istituto Nazionale Fascista della Previdenza Sociale. Istituto Italiano di Medicina Sociale. Vol. 1 (Jan. 1922)-. Periodical. Italian. Six times a year. Istituto Italiano Medicina, Sociale Via Ps Mancini 28, 00195 Rome Italy. **Tel** 011 39 6 3200642, 011 39 6 3202493. **NLM** W1 DI518. **CODEN** DISOAJ. cum. index. Documents available from BIOSIS Document Express.
**Ind/Abst** Biol. Abstr.; Saf. Health Work.

US
**DIGEST - TEXAS. DEPT. OF PUBLIC SAFETY. DIVISION OF DISASTER EMERGENCY SERVICES, THE. Main/Corp** Texas. Dept. of Public Safety. Division of Disaster Emergency Services. Periodical. English. bm. Department of Public Safety / Texas, PO Box 4087, 5805 North Lamar Boulevard, Austin TX 78773. **Tel** (512)465-2138.

US/0883-5330
**DIRECTORY OF BIOMEDICAL AND HEALTH CARE GRANTS. See** Medical Science and Technology.

US/0744-0804
**DIRECTORY OF FEDERAL HEALTH/MEDICINE GRANTS AND CONTRACTS PROGRAMS. See** Medical Science and Technology.

US/0197-0704
**DIRECTORY OF FULL-TIME COUNTY AND URBAN HEALTH DEPARTMENTS, A.** [Dir. full-time cty. urban health dep.]. **Added/Corp** Illinois. Dept. of Public Health. (19??)-. English. qt. Office of Health Services and Local Health Administration, Department of Public Health, Springfield IL 62761. **NLM** WA 22 AI3 D7.

US/0361-9516
**DIRECTORY OF MENTAL HEALTH AND ALCOHOLISM PROGRAMS IN MARYLAND. Added/Corp** Maryland. Planning and Community Mental Health Services. (19??)-. Directory. English. Maryland Department of Health and Mental Hygiene, 201 West Preston Street, Baltimore MD 21201. **Tel** (410)225-6500. **LC** RA790.65.M33; D56. **DD** 362.2/04/25025752.

US/0361-8455
**DIRECTORY OF MENTAL HEALTH SERVICES IN ILLINOIS.** **Ceased. Added/Corp** Illinois. Dept. of Mental Health and Developmental Disabilities. (19??)-?. Directory. English. Illinois Department of Mental Health, 401 State Office Building, Springfield IL 62706. **LC** RA790.65.I4; D56. **DD** 362.2/025773.

US/0095-4888
**DIRECTORY OF MINNESOTA'S AREA MENTAL HEALTH, MENTAL RETARDATION, INEBRIETY PROGRAMS.** 1973-. Directory. English. 658 Cedar Street, St Paul MN 55155. **LC** RA790.65.M53; A25. **DD** 362.2/025/776. **Continues** Directory of Minnesota's Area Mental Health - Mental Retardation Programs.

US/0070-6000
**DIRECTORY OF ON-GOING RESEARCH IN SMOKING AND HEALTH.** (DIRECTORY, ON-GOING RESEARCH IN SMOKING AND HEALTH / OFFICE ON SMOKING AND HEALTH.). **VFOAT** On-Going Research in Smoking and Health. 8th Ed. (1980)-. Directory. English. be. US Department of Health and Human Services, 200 Independence Avenue Southwest, Washington DC 20201. **LC** RA1242.T6; D57. **DD** 615.9/52374. **NLM** QV 22.1; D598. available on microfiche (Vols. for (1984-1985)-) distributed to depository libraries.
**Continues** Directory of On-Going Research in Smoking and Health, 0070-6000.

US/0149-8304
**DIRECTORY OF-- PERSONNEL RESPONSIBLE FOR RADIOLOGICAL HEALTH PROGRAMS. Added/Corp** United States. Bureau of Radiological Health. National Center for Devices and Radiological Health (U.S.). (Jan. 1969)-. English. an (Jan.). $30.00. Conference Radiation Control, 205 Capital Avenue, Frankfort KY 40601. **Tel** (502)227-4543. **LC** RA569; .D57. **DD** 363.1/79. **NLM** WN 22 AA1 D5.

US/0162-9387
**DIRECTORY OF PRECEPTORSHIP PROGRAMS IN THE HEALTH PROFESSIONS, A. Added/Corp** National Health Council (U.S.). Manpower Distribution Project. United States. Health Resources Administration. Bureau of Health Manpower. (1975)-. English. an. National Health Council, Manpower Distribution Project, 1740 Broadway, New york NY 10019. **NLM** W 22 AA1 D67.

US/0270-9953
**DIRECTORY OF RURAL HEALTH CARE PROGRAMS.** [Dir. rural health care programs]. 1979-. Directory. English. US Department of Health and Human Services National Institutes of Health, 9000 Rockville Pike, Bethesda MD 20892. **Tel** (301)496-9291, FAX (301)496-2443. **NLM** WA 22 AA1 D65.

US
**DIRECTORY OF SERVICES, ARKANSAS MENTAL HEALTH SERVICES. VFOAT** Mental Health Services in Arkansas, Directory. Directory. English. an. Mental Health Services, 4313 West Markham Street, Little Rock AR 72201. **LC** RA790.65.A8; D57. **DD** 362.2/025/767. Index Available in last issue of each volume--loose separately paged.

IT/0416-024X
**DIRITTO SANITARIO MODERNO.** [Dir. sanit. mod.]. (1953)-. Periodical. Italian. qt. L100000 Italy; $100.00 other. Edizioni Luigi Pozzi Srl, Via Panama 68, 00198 Rome Italy. **Tel** (06)8553548, FAX (06)8554105. **UDC** 614. Index available.

US/0251-4494
**DISASTER PREPAREDNESS IN THE AMERICAS. AMERICAN SANITARY BUREAU.** [Disaster prep. Am.]. **Added/Corp** Pan American Sanitary Bureau. Pan American Health Organization. Emergency Preparedness and Disaster Relief Coordination Office. Pan American Health Organization. Emergency Preparedness and Disaster Relief Coordination Program. (19??)-. Periodical. English (Spanish). qt. Free. Pan American Health Organization, 525 23rd Street Northwest, Office District Sales, Washington DC 20037. **Tel** (202)293-8130, FAX (202)338-0869. **ED** Liz Stonaker. **NLM** W1; DI732. **Bk Rev**, (Qty: 12). **Circ:** 18,000 (ctrl). Documents available from Documents on Demand.
**Desc:** Contains articles on current topics related to emergency preparedness and disaster relief coordination; news from international organizations and member countries in the Americas; reviews current publications and audiovisual material on the subject.
**Ind/Abst** Environ. Abstr.

US
**DISCHARGES FROM STATE MENTAL HEALTH FACILITIES FISCAL YEAR ... / PREPARED BY DATA SERVICES DIVISION, DEPARTMENT OF MENTAL HEALTH/RETARDATION. Added/Corp** Virginia. Dept. of Mental Health and Mental Retardation. Data Services Division. Virginia. Dept. of Mental Health and Mental Retardation. MIS and Data Services Division. (1979)-. English. an. MIS and Data Services Division, Department of Mental Health and Mental Retardation, PO Box 1797, Richmond VA 23214. **LC** RC445.V78; D58. **DD** 362.2/0422/0973.

US
**DISEASE CONTROL NEWSLETTER.** (19??)-. Newsletter. English. mo (10 issues). Free on request. Minnesota Department of Health, 717 Southeast Delaware Street, Minneapolis MN 55440. **Tel** (612)623-5000.

US
**DISPATCH MONTHLY.** English. Twelve times a year. $20.00 (individuals); $25.00 (institutions). Dispatch Specialists, 2945 David Lane, Medford OR 97504. **Tel** (503)535-3724, FAX (503)535-1114. **ED** Alan Burton. **Circ:** 6,000.
**Desc:** News and information for public safety and 911 center dispatchers, supervisors, and management.

US/0883-6698
**DNI JOURNAL.** [DNI j.]. **VAT** Disabled Naturists International Journal. Periodical. English. qt. $5.00 US; $10.00 other. Disabled Naturists International, PO Box 268, Cokedale CO 81032. **DD** 613. ***Continues*** *DNSIG Newsletter.*

US/1043-8165
**DR. FOX'S NEW HEALTH JOURNAL.** [Dr. Fox's new health j.]. **VFOAT** New Health Journal; Drs. Fox New Health Journal. (Jan. 1978)-. Periodical. English. sm. $15.00 (libraries), $30.00 (individuals) North America; $20.00 (libraries), $35.00 (individuals) other. Barry Fox, 6433 Topanga Canyon Boulevard/Suite 580, Canoga Park CA 91303. **ED** Barry Fox. **DD** 613. **Bk Rev. Ad Acc. Circ:** 5,000.

US
**DRAFT HEALTH SYSTEMS PLAN FOR SOUTH CAROLINA HEALTH SERVICE AREA III. Main/Corp** Pee Dee Regional Health Systems Agency, Inc. **VFOAT** Health Systems Plan. No. 2- ; 1978-. English. an. PO Box 5959, Florence SC 29502.

US/0363-0811
**DRINKING AND DRUG PRACTICES SURVEYOR, THE.** ***Suspended.*** **See** Drug Abuse and Alcoholism.

●US/1076-1519
**DRUG & CRIME PREVENTION FUNDING NEWS.** (June 1994)-. English. wk. $239.00. Government Information Services / Virginia, 4301 North Fairfax Drive, Suite 875, Arlington VA 22203. **Tel** (703)528-1082, FAX (703)528-6060, telex RCA 263591 GIS UR. **ED** Stephanie Neuben. ***Continues*** *Anti-Drug Funding Alert, 1060-4707.*
**Desc:** Covers developments affecting federal aid for anti-drug programs and law enforcement.

FI/0783-6201
**EAST AFRICAN NEWSLETTER ON OCCUPATIONAL HEALTH AND SAFETY.** [East Afr. newsl. occupat. health saf]. (1987)-. Newsletter. Multiple languages. ir. **UDC** 613.6. **Ind/Abst** LABORDOC; Trop. Dis. Bull.

US/0891-6977
**EATING DISORDERS DIGEST.** [Eating disord. dig.]. (May 1986)-. Periodical. English. Twelve times a year. $20.00. Center Publishing, 5625 Government Street, Baton Rouge LA 70806. **Tel** (504)924-4313. **DD** 613.

SZ
**EDUCATION AND TRAINING.** (19??)-. English. $176.00. World Health Organization, Distribution and Sales, 20 Avenue Appia, CH-1211 Geneva 27 Switzerland. **Tel** 011 41 22 7912111, FAX 011 41 22 7880401.

US
**EDUCATOR'S INTERNATIONAL GUIDE TO FREE & LOW COST HEALTH AUDIO-VISUAL TEACHING AIDS. VFOAT** International Guide to Free & Low Cost Health Audio-Visual Teaching Aids; Guide to Free & Low Cost Health Audio-Visual Teaching Aids; Free & Low Cost Health Audio-Visual Teaching Aids; Health Audio-Visual Teaching Aids. English. be. Shugar Publishing Inc., 32 Mill Road, West Hampton Beach NY 11978. **Tel** (516)288-4404, FAX (516)288-4435. **ED** James Hazlett. **Bk Rev. Ad Acc. Circ:** 250,000 (ctrl).
**Desc:** Offers frank, practical, up-to-date information that diabetics need to better understand their diabetes. Features clear, lively, fact-filled articles by leading physicians, pharmacists and educators in the diabetes health care field.

IT
**EDUCAZIONE SANITARIA E PROMOZIONE DELLA SALUTE. Added/Corp** Universita di Perugia. Centro Sperimentale per l'Educazione Sanitaria. Vol. 11, No. 1 (Mar. 1988)-. Periodical. Italian (summaries and/or abstracts in English). Four times a year. L100000 (institutions), L70000 (individuals). Il Pensiero Scientifico Editore s.r.l., Via Bradano 3C, 00199 Rome Italy. **Tel** 011 39 6 86207158, 86207159, 86207168, 86207169, FAX 011 39 6 86207160. **ED** M.A. Modolo. **NLM** W1; ED89H. **Bk Rev. Ad Acc, Adv Mgr:** Dott Dalla, **Tel** 06-86207165. Full Page (B&W) L1.300.000. **Circ:** 1,300. ***Continues*** *Educazione Sanitaria e Medicina Preventiva, 0391-6200.*

HU
**EGESZSEGNEVELES. EDUCATIO SANITARIA. Added/Corp** Hungary. Egeszseguegyi Felvilagositasi Koezpont. **VFOAT** Egeszsegneveles. Educatio Sanitaria. (19??)-. Periodical. Hungarian (Hungarian). bm. $29.50 US. Ifsusagi Lap es Konyvkiado Vallalat, Revay U, 16, 1374, Budapest, Hungary. **Tel** 361-113-7038. **(Subscription address:** Kultura, PO Box 149, H-1389, Budapest 62 Hungary) **ED** Simon Tamas. **LC** RA440.3.H9; E35. Index available. cum. index. **Bk Rev. Ad Acc. Circ:** 4,300 (ctrl). ***Continues*** *Egeszseguegyi Felvilagositas.*
**Desc:** Deals with the history, research, theory, methods, organization and experiences of health education in Hungary.

JA
**EISEI GYOSEI GYOMU HOKOKU. Main/Corp** Japan. Koseisho. Daijin Kambo. Tokei Johobu. 1973-. Japanese. Koseisho Daijin Kanbo Tokei Johobu, (Statistics & Information Dept., Minister's Secretariat, Ministry of Health & Welfare), 7-3, Ichigaya Honmuracho, Shinjukuku, Tokyoto 162 Japan. **LC** RA531; .J27C. **NLM** W2 JJ3 K8EI. ***Continues*** *Eisei Gyosei Gyomu Hokoku.*

JA/0077-4715
**EISEI SHIKENJO HOKOKU.** [Eisei Shikenjo hokoku]. **Main/Corp** Kokuritsu Eisei Shikenjo. **Added/Corp** Kokuritsu Eisei Shikenjo. Bulletin of National Institute of Hygienic Sciences. Kokuritsu Eisei Shikenjo. Bulletin of the National Hygienic Laboratory. **VFOAT** Bulletin of National Institute of Hygienic Sciences; Bulletin of the National Hygienic Laboratory. No. 67 (1949)-. Academic Scholarly Publication. Japanese (summaries and/or abstracts in English). an (Nov.). Kokuritsu Eisei Shikenjo, 18-1 Kami Yoga 1-chome, Setagaya-ku 158, Tokyo Japan. **Tel** 03 3700 1141 454, FAX 03 3700 7592. **LC** RA421; .T64a. **NLM** W1 EI573. **CODEN** ESKHA5. Documents available from CASDDS. ***Continues*** *Tokyo Eisei Shikenjo. Eisei Shikenjo Iho.*
**Ind/Abst** AGRICOLA; Biodeter. Abstr.; Chem. Abstr.; Cot. Trop. Fibr. Abstr. Bibliogr.; CSA Neuro. Abstr. (?-?); EMBASE [Select. Cov.]; Food Sci. Technol. Abstr.; Index Med.; Int. Packag. Abstr.; Nematol. Abstr.; Nutr. Abstr. Rev., Ser. B, Live Feeds and Feed.; Nutr. Abstr. Rev., Ser. A, Hum. Exp.; Life Sci. Collect.; Postharvest News Inf.; Rev. Med. Vet. Mycology.

US/0275-2204
**ELECTRON MICROSCOPY AND X-RAY APPLICATIONS TO ENVIRONMENTAL AND OCCUPATIONAL HEALTH ANALYSIS. See** Medical Science and Technology-Radiology.

US/0162-5942
**EMERGENCY.** [Emergency]. Vol. 10, No. 2 (Feb. 1978)-. Periodical. English. mo. $21.95 (one year), $35.95 (two year), $42.95 (three year). Hare Publications Inc, 6300 Yarrow Drive, Carlsbad CA 92009. **Tel** (619)438-2511, (800)854-2706, FAX (619)931-5809, telex 697127. **ED** Laura Gilbert. **LC** RA995.A1; E46. **DD** 616/.025/05. **NLM** W1 EM661Q. cum. index. **Bk Rev. Ad Acc. Circ:** 29,000. available on microfilm and microfiche from University Microfilms International (UMI). ***Continues*** *Emergency Product News, 0098-2180.*
**Desc:** Designed to meet the needs and interests of various providers of pre-hospital emergency medical care.
**Ind/Abst** Cumul. Index Nurs. Allied Health Lit.; Health Plan. Adminis.; Hospit. Health Admin. Index (Vol. 18, No. 1, 1986-Vol. 21, No. 12, 1989).

US
**EMERGENCY BIOLOGICS LOCATIONS ... WASHINGTON STATE / DEPARTMENT OF HEALTH, DIVISION OF HEALTH INFORMATION, COMMUNICABLE DISEASE EPIDEMIOLOGY SECTION. See** Biology.

●US/1066-0348
**EMERGENCY SERVICES SOURCEBOOK.** [Emerg. serv. sourceb.]. (1993)-. English. be. $99.95. Specialized Publication Services Inc, PO Box 1915, Madison Square Station, New York NY 10159. **LC** TH9123; .F53. **DD** 628.9/2. ***Continues*** *Fire/Emergency Services Sourcebook, 1045-3385.*
**Desc:** Information on fire extinction.

●US/1062-5526
**EMF HEALTH & SAFETY DIGEST. Added/Corp** Interdisciplinary Environmental Associates, Inc. **VFOAT** EMF Health and Safety Digest; Health & Safety Digest; Health and Safety Digest. (1992)-. Periodical. English. mo. $350.00. EMF Health & Safety Digest, PO Box 14501, University Station, Minneapolis MN 55414. **NLM** W1; EM661M. ***Continues*** *Transmission/Distribution Health & Safety Report, 0737-5743.*

CN/1182-9745
**ENVIRONMENT & PUBLIC SAFETY TODAY.** [Environ. public. saf. today]. **Added/Corp** Saskatchewan. Saskatchewan Environment and Public Safety. **VAT** Environment and Public Safety Today. Vol. 1, No. 1 (Jan. 1991)-. Periodical. English. mo. Saskatchewan Environment and Public Safety, 1855 Victoria Avenue/5th Floor, Regina Saskatchewan 54P 3V5 Canada. **DD** 333.7/097124.

US/1053-9190
**ENVIRONMENT, HEALTH & SAFETY MANAGEMENT.** [Environ. health saf. manage.]. **VFOAT** Environment, Health, and Safety Management; EHS Management. Vol. 1, No. 1 (Oct. 15, 1990)-. Periodical. English. bw (25 issues per year.). $397.00 US, Canada and Mexico; $447.00 other. EHS Management, PO Box 1269, Wainscott NY 11975. **Tel** (516)324-3508, FAX (516)329-1209. **LC** RA565.A1; E12. **DD** 363.7/005.

UK/0160-4120
**ENVIRONMENT INTERNATIONAL. See** Environmental Issues.

US/1047-336X
**ENVIRONMENTAL CONTRACTOR MAGAZINE. See** Building and Construction.

SZ
**ENVIRONMENTAL HEALTH AND CHEMICAL SAFETY.** (19??)-. English. ir. $264.00. World Health Organization, Distribution and Sales, 20 Avenue Appia, CH-1211 Geneva 27 Switzerland. **Tel** 011 41 22 7912111, FAX 011 41 22 7880401.

US/0897-6422
**ENVIRONMENTAL HEALTH BULLETIN (WASHINGTON, D.C.).** ***Ceased.*** (ENVIRONMENTAL HEALTH BULLETIN.). [Environ. health bull.]. **VFOAT** EH Bulletin. Vol. 3, No. 1 (Jan./Feb. 1988)-?. Bulletin. English. mo. Environmental Health Bulletin, 1220 L Street NW, Washington DC 20005. **DD** 363.

SZ/0250-863X
**ENVIRONMENTAL HEALTH CRITERIA.** [Environ. health criter.]. **Added/Corp** United Nations Environment Programme. World Health Organization. International Labour Organisation. Commission of the European Communities. International Program on Chemical Safety. (1976)-. Academic Scholarly Publication. English (French). ir (approximately 15 reports). $176.00 Surface Mail; $208.00 (airmail) Europe; $224.00 (airmail) other. World Health Organization, Distribution and Sales, 20 Avenue Appia, CH-1211 Geneva 27 Switzerland. **Tel** 011 41 22 7912111, FAX 011 41 22 7880401. **LC** RA1190; .E58. **DD** 363.1/7. **NLM** W1 EN983. **CODEN** EHCRDN. Documents available from CASDDS, Documents on Demand.
**Desc:** Serves as a review of virtually everything ever written about a selected chemical, environmental pollutant or method for testing toxicity and carcinogenicity. Features as many as 1,000 references; concentrates on points of inconsistency or consensus in the literature that can be used to develop a more precise understanding of health hazards and how to prevent them.
**Ind/Abst** Chem. Abstr. (1976-1983); Chem. Hazards Ind.; Dairy Sci. Abstr.; EMBASE; Environ. Abstr.; Food Sci. Technol. Abstr.; Helminthol. Abstr. (1991-); Index Vet.; Lab. Hazards Bull.; Nematol. Abstr.; Nutr. Abstr. Rev., Ser. B, Live Feeds and Feed.; Nutr. Abstr. Rev., Ser. A, Hum. Exp.; Postharvest News Inf.; Rev. Agric. Entomol.; Rev. Med. Vet. Entomol.; Vet. Bull.; Trop. Dis. Bull.

US/0091-6765
**ENVIRONMENTAL HEALTH PERSPECTIVES.** (ENVIRONMENTAL HEALTH PERSPECTIVES : EHP.). [Environ. health perspect.]. **Added/Corp** National Institute of Environmental Health Sciences. National Institutes of Health (U.S.). **VFOAT** EHP. No. 1 (Apr. 1972)-. Academic Scholarly Publication. English. mo. $36.00 US; $45.00 other. Superintendent of Documents, US Government Printing Office, Washington DC 20402. **Tel** (202)275-3328, FAX (202)786-2377. **LC** RA565.A1; E13. **DD** 614.7/05. **NLM** W1 EN984AB. **CODEN** EVHPAZ. cum. index. **Pr Rev.** available on microfilm and microfiche from University Microfilms International (UMI). Documents available from The Genuine Article, BIOSIS Document Express, CASDDS, Documents on Demand.
**Desc:** Published to research findings of environmental health significance and inform the scientific community of potential health hazards that are associated with particular elements in the environment. Contains conference and workshop proceedings, perspective statements on selected problem areas, toxicologic information summaries, overviews of areas on environmental health, and reviews on specific environmental problems and agents.
**Ind/Abst** AGRICOLA [Select. Cov.]; Biol. Abstr.; Chem. Abstr.; Chem. Hazards Ind.; Coal Abstr.; CSA Neuro. Abstr. (?-?); Curr. Aware. Biol. Sci., CABS; Curr. Contents, Agric. Biol. Environ. Sci.; Curr. Contents Life Sci.; Dairy Sci. Abstr.; EMBASE; Energy Res. Abstr. (April 1976-); Environ. Abstr.; Environ. Period. Bibliogr.; Food Sci. Technol. Abstr.; Health Saf. Sci. Abstr.; Health Plan. Adminis.; Index Med.; Ind. Hyg. Dig. (19??-); INIS Atomindex [Micro.]; Lab. Hazards Bull.; Leadscan; Middle East Abstr. Index; Nutr. Abstr. Rev., Ser. B, Live Feeds and Feed.; Nutr. Abstr. Rev., Ser. A, Hum. Exp.; Nutr. Res. Newsl.; Pollut. Abstr. Indexes; Protozoolog. Abstr.; Ref. Upd. Deluxe Ed.; Res. Alert [Full Cov.]; Rev. Med. Vet. Mycology; Rev. Plant Pathol.; Risk Abstr.; Saf. Health Work; Sci. Cit. Index; SCISEARCH; Soc. Sci. Cit. Index [Select. Cov.]; Soils Fert.; SportSearch; Trop. Dis. Bull.

CN/0319-6771
**ENVIRONMENTAL HEALTH REVIEW. Added/Corp** Canadian Institute of Public Health Inspectors. Vol. 15 (Spring 1971)-. Periodical. English. qt.

26.17Can$ Canada; 35.00Can$ other. Canadian Institute of Public Health Inspectors, Box 1280 Station A, Burlington Ontario L7R 2H0 Canada. **Tel** (905)828-5794. **ED** A. Amalfa. **NLM** W1 EN984AC. cum. index. **Bk Rev. Ad Acc. Circ:** 1,500 (ctrl). ***Continues*** *Canadian Sanitarian, 0527-9747.*
**Desc:** Topics of public health concerns; includes disease control, pollution, food poisoning, swimming pools, water and wastewater and occupational health.
**Ind/Abst** Biol. Dig.

CN
**ENVIRONMENTAL MANAGERS' SAFETY GUIDE.** an. 120.00Can$. Southam Information and Technology Group Inc., 1450 Don Mills Road, Don Mills Ontario M3B 2X7 Canada. **Tel** (416)445-6641, (800)668-2374, FAX (416)442-2261.

UK/0267-5994
**EPC PUBLICATION.** [EPC publ.]. **Added/Corp** EPC (Research Center). **VAT** Evaluation and Planning Centre Publication. No. 1 (Summer 1984)-. Monographic series. English. **NLM** W1; EP393K.
**Ind/Abst** Trop. Dis. Bull.

FR
**EPIDEMIOLOGIE ET SANTE ANIMALE : BULLETIN DE L'ASSOCIATION POUR L'ETUDE DE L'EPIDEMIOLOGIE DES MALADIES ANIMALES. Added/Corp** Association pour l'Etude de l'Epidemiologie des Maladies Animales. No 1 (1982)-. Bulletin. French. sa.
**Ind/Abst** Index Vet.; Pig News Inf.; Small Anim. Abstr. Bibliogr.; Vet. Bull.

US/0744-0898
**EPIDEMIOLOGY MONITOR, THE.** [Epidemiol. monit.]. (1980)-. Periodical. English. Eleven times a year (except Aug.). $55.00. The Epidemiology Monitor, 2560 Whisper Wind Court, Roswell GA 30076. **Tel** (404)594-1613, FAX (404)594-0997. **ED** Roger Bernier. **DD** 614. **CODEN** EPMOEJ. **Bk Rev. Ad Acc. Circ:** 2,000 (ctrl).
**Desc:** News and information for epidemiologists, public health officials, preventive medicine and community health departments.
**Ind/Abst** BioBusiness (1989-).

SP/0212-0283
**ESCUELA MEDICA.** [Esc. med.]. (1970)-. Periodical. Spanish. qt. Colegio Oficial de Medicos de Caceres, Santa Joaquina Vedruna 5, 10001 Caceres Spain. **UDC** 61.

US
**ESTABLISHMENT AND PRODUCTS LICENSED UNDER SECTION 351 OF THE PUBLIC HEALTH SERVICES ACT / U.S. DEPARTMENT OF HEALTH AND HUMAN SERVICES, PUBLIC HEALTH SERVICE, FOOD AND DRUG ADMINISTRATION.** Began with 1971. English. an. 800 Rockville Pike, Bethesda MD 20205. **LC** RM270; .E85. **DD** 615/.39/029. **NLM** QV 22 AA1 B6. ***Continues*** *Biological Products.*

CN
**ESTIMATES. PART III, HEALTH AND WELFARE CANADA. Main/Corp** Canada. **VFOAT** Budget des Depenses. Partie III, Sante et Bien-Etre Social Canada. (19??)-. English (French). $12.00 Canada; $14.40 other. Canada Communication Group Publishers, Order Processing, Ottawa Ontario K1A 0S9 Canada. **Tel** (819)956-4800, (819)956-4802. **LC** RA184; .C3b. **DD** 354.710084/1.

US/8756-5943
**ETA SIGMA GAMMAN, THE. *Title Change.*** [Eta Sigma Gamman]. **Added/Corp** Eta Sigma Gamma. Vol. 1, No. 1 (Spring 1969)-Vol. 23, No. 2 (Spring 1992). Periodical. English. sa. ETA Sigma Gamma, Ball State University, Muncie IN 47306. **Tel** (317)285-5961. **ED** Denise Amschler. **Bk Rev. Circ:** 2,500. ***Continued by*** *Health Educator.*
**Desc:** Publishes articles dealing with a broad range of health-related topics of interest to students, school health educators, public health professionals, and those in related areas.
**Ind/Abst** Curr. Index J. Educ.

ET
**ETHIOPIAN JOURNAL OF HEALTH DEVELOPMENT, THE. Added/Corp** National Health Development Network--Ethiopia. **VFOAT** Yaltyopya Tena Lemat Mashet. (July 1984)-. Periodical. English. sa. **LC** RA755.E8; E84. **DD** 362.1/0963/05.
**Ind/Abst** Protozoolog. Abstr.

SW/1101-1262
**EUROPEAN JOURNAL OF PUBLIC HEALTH.** Vol. 1, No. 1 (1991)-. Periodical. English. qt. £80.00 UK; $130.00 other. Oxford University Press, Walton Street, Oxford OX2 6DP England. **Tel** 011 44 865 56767, FAX 011 44 865 267773, telex 837330 OXPRES G. **(Subscription address:** Oxford University Press / USA, Journals Marketing Department, Oxford University Press, 2001 Evans Road, Cary NC 27513.**) ED** P. G. Svensson. **NLM** W1; EU72ECL.
**Desc:** A multidisciplinary journal publishing papers on epidemiology health services research, management and administration, ethics and law, health economics, information sciences, social and behavioral sciences and environmental health. European aspects are given priority. Target readership: policymakers, health managers, legal experts, health professionals, students and public health practitioners.

UK
**EUROSAFETY.** (19??)-. Periodical. English. qt. £60.00 UK; £70.00 other. Eclipse Publications Ltd, 18 20 Highbury Place, London N5 1QP England. **Tel** 011 44 71 354 5858.

NE
**EXCERPTA MEDICA. SECTION 17. PUBLIC HEALTH, SOCIAL MEDICINE AND EPIDEMIOLOGY. See** Medical Science and Technology-Abstracting, Bibliographies and Statistics.

US/1071-8680
**EXECUTIVE HEALTH'S GOOD HEALTH REPORT. See** Health and Personal Fitness.

US
**FACTS. See** Transportation-Roads and Traffic.

US/0196-6294
**FACTS AT YOUR FINGERTIPS. Added/Corp** National Center for Health Statistics (U.S.). 3rd Ed. (Fall 1978)-. English. US Department of Health and Human Services, 200 Independence Avenue Southwest, Washington DC 20201. **NLM** ZWA 900 AA F14. ***Continues*** *Facts at Your Fingertips, Almost, 0196-6278.*

CN/0315-954X
**FAMILLE AVERTIE.** Vol. 1 (Fall 1974)-. Periodical. French (English). qt. $7.95. Canada Safety Council, 2750 Stevenage Drive Unit 6, Ottawa Ontario K1G 3N2 Canada. **Tel** (613)739-1535, FAX (613)739-1566. **ED** Heather Totten (613)739-1535. **DD** 614.8/05. Index available. **Circ:** 100,000.

TG
**FAMILLE ET DEVELOPPEMENT.** (19??)-. Periodical. French. Four times a year. 25.00CFAF. ASAFED / Famille et Developpement, rue des Hydrocarbures, BP 3907 Lome Togo. **Tel** 011 228 216316, FAX 011 228 216316, telex 5131 TG. **LC** HQ691; .F35. **DD** 614/.096. **Ad Acc, Adv Mgr:** K. Attigno. **Circ:** 40,000.
**Desc:** It highlights problems of health, education, and development in Africa.
**Ind/Abst** Hum. Rights Intern. Rep.

US/0160-6379
**FAMILY & COMMUNITY HEALTH.** [Fam. commun. health]. **VAT** Family and Community Health. Vol. 1 (Apr. 1978)-. Periodical. English. qt. $104.00 US. Aspen Publishers Inc., 7201 McKinney Circle, Frederick MD 21701. **Tel** (800)234-1660, (301)698-7100, FAX (301)251-5784, telex 5106014543. **(Subscription address:** Aspen Publishers Inc., PO Box 990, Frederick MD 21701.**) ED** Jeanette Lancaster, RN PhD. **LC** RA421; .F35. **DD** 362.1. **NLM** W1 FA432BK. **[CCC]. Pr Rev.** available on microfilm and microfiche from University Microfilms International (UMI).
**Desc:** The primary objective is to unite health care practitioners, regardless of area of practice, in a common goal: to teach the essentials of self-care, family and community health care, and health promotion and maintenance.
**Ind/Abst** Abstr. Res. Pastor. Care Couns. (19??-); AGRICOLA; Cumul. Index Nurs. Allied Health Lit.; Hospit. Health Admin. Index (1978-1990); Nurs. Abstr.; Nutr. Res. Newsl.; Psychol. Abstr. (1982-); PsycINFO; PsycLit; Sage Fam. Stud. Abstr. (?-?); Soc. Plann. Policy Dev. Abstr.

US
**FAMILY CAREGIVER APPLICATIONS SERIES.** Vol. 1 (1991)-. Monographic series. English. Price varies per volume. SAGE Periodical Press, 2455 Teller Road, Thousand Oaks CA 91320. **Tel** (805)499-0721, FAX (805)499-0871, telex 100799. **NLM** W1; FA432CK. **Acid Free.**

US/0749-3118
**FAMILY SAFETY AND HEALTH (CANADIAN ED.).** (FAMILY SAFETY AND HEALTH.). [Fam. saf. health]. **Added/Corp** National Safety Council. Vol. 42, No. 4 (Winter 1983-84)-. Periodical. English. Four times a year. $19.00. National Safety Council, 1121 Spring Lake Drive, Itasca IL 60143. **Tel** (800)621-7615, (708)775-2294, FAX (708)285-0797. **DD** 613. ***Continues*** *Family Safety (Canadian Edition), 0749-3231.*

US/0749-310X
**FAMILY SAFETY AND HEALTH (U.S. ED.).** (FAMILY SAFETY AND HEALTH.). **Added/Corp** National Safety Council. **VFOAT** Family Safety & Health. Vol. 42, No. 4, (Winter 1983/1984)-. Periodical. English. Four times a year. $19.00. National Safety Council, 1121 Spring Lake Drive, Itasca IL 60143. **Tel** (800)621-7615, (708)775-2294, FAX (708)285-0797. **ED** Beverlee A. Burke. **LC** TX150; .F2. **DD** 613. **NLM** W1 FA454K. **Circ:** 2,500,000. available on microfilm and microfiche from University Microfilms International (UMI). ***Continues*** *Family Safety, 0014-7397.*
**Desc:** Promotes off-the-job safety and health.
**Ind/Abst** Acad. Abstr. Full Text Elite (Jan. 1992-); Acad. Abstr. (Jan. 1992-); Acad. Search (Jan. 1992-); Health Source (Jan. 1992-); INFO-SOUTH Abstr.; Mag. Search.

●UK/1354-5299
**FAR EAST FOCUS.** (April 1994)-. English. ir (20 issues). $1,750.00. Nicholas Hall & Company, 35 Alexandra Street, Southend-on-Sea, Essex SS1 1BW England. **Tel** 011 44 702 433422, FAX 011 44 702 430787.
**Desc:** Covers the consumer health care market in China and Japan.

●US/1059-6836
**FAXON HEALTH INFORMATION CATALOG.** (1992)-. Catalog. English. Free. Faxon Press, PO Box 9102, Boston MA 02132.

US/1057-9397
**FDA ENFORCEMENT REPORT. See** Drug Abuse and Alcoholism.

US/1042-2781
**FDC REPORTS. HEALTH NEWS DAILY.** [FDC rep., Health news dly.]. **Added/Corp** F-D-C Reports, Inc. **VFOAT** Health News Daily; F-D-C Reports Health News Daily. Vol. 1, No. 1 (Jan. 18, 1989)-. Government Publication. English. da. $1,250.00. FDC Reports Inc., 5550 Friendship Boulevard/Suite 1, Chevy Chase MD 20815. **Tel** (301)657-9830. **DD** 362. **NLM** W1; FD410J. **[CCC]. *Continues*** *Healthdaily, 1043-0512.*
**Desc:** A specialized daily information service of executives and decision-makers in the health industries. It draws on the resources of the combined staffs of all F-D-C's publications, putting 35 reporters and editors to work keeping constant track of a broad range of events affecting the health fields.

US/0364-6858
**FEDERAL MOTOR VEHICLE SAFETY STANDARDS AND REGULATIONS. See** Transportation.

FR
**FICHIER PERMANENT DES CORPS ET GRADES ES ETS SANITAIRES ET SOCIAUX.** (19??)-. French. 590.00F. Editions de l' Ensp, Avenue du Professeur Leon Bernard, 35043 Rennes Cedex France. **Tel** 011 33 99 282964, FAX 011 33 9954 2284.

US/0362-7187
**FINANCIAL REPORT - DEPARTMENT OF HEALTH & SOCIAL SERVICES, DIVISION OF HEALTH.** (FINANCIAL REPORT - DIVISION OF HEALTH.). **Main/Corp** Wisconsin. Division of Health. **VAT** Financial Report - Department of Health and Social Services, Division of Health. English. an. Department of Health & Social Services / Wisconsin, 1 West Wilson Street, PO Box 309, Madison WI 53701. **LC** RA177; .D57A. **DD** 353.9/775/0077.

US
**FINANCIAL REPORT, OHIO'S LOCAL HEALTH DEPARTMENT / PREPARED BY GRANTS MANAGEMENT UNIT, BUREAU OF ADMINISTRATIVE SERVICES, OHIO DEPARTMENT OF HEALTH.** English. an. Ohio Department of Health, 246 North High Street, Columbus OH 43266. **Tel** (614)466-2253, FAX (614)644-8526. **LC** RA410.54.O3; F56. **DD** 353.97710072/236841. ***Continues*** *Financial Report of Ohio Local Health Departments.*

US/0164-6397
**FIRE AND POLICE PERSONNEL REPORTER.** (FIRE AND POLICE PERSONNEL REPORTER : A MONTHLY PUBLICATION OF THE PUBLIC SAFETY PERSONNEL RESEARCH INSTITUTE.). **Added/Corp** Public Safety Personnel Research Institute (South San Francisco, Calif.). (19??)-. Periodical. English. mo. $168.00. Public Safety Personnel Res In, 5519 North Cumberland, Suite 1008, Chicago IL 60656-1471. **Tel** (312)763-2800, FAX (312)763-3225. **ED** Wayne W. Schmidt (phone: (312)763-5259). **LC** HV8138; .F455. **DD** 350.74/0973. Index available. cum. index. **Circ:** 1,300. ***Continues*** *Fire Department Personnel Reporter.*
**Desc:** Contains information on disciplinary problems, contested terminations, wrongful dismissal and labor problems in police, fire sheriff and corrections services.
**Ind/Abst** Crim. Justice Period. Index (-1989).

●US/1065-4119
**FLORIDA HEALTH CARE IN PERSPECTIVE.** [Fla. health care perspect.]. **Added/Corp** Morgan Quitno Corporation. 1st Ed. (1993)-. English. $18.00. Morgan Quitno Corporation, PO Box 1656, 512 East 9th Street, Lawrence KS 66044. **Tel** (800)457-0742, (913)841-3534, FAX (913)841-3534. **DD**

# Public Health and Safety

362.
**Desc:** Reports on the state's data and rank for each of the categories featured in Health Care State Rankings.

US/0430-7739
**FLORIDA J.O.H.P.E.R.** (FLORIDA JOHPER. JOURNAL OF HEALTH, PHYSICAL EDUCATION AND RECREATION.). [Fla. JOHPER]. **Added/Corp** Florida Association for Health, Physical Education, and Recreation. **VFOAT** Journal of Health, Physical Education and Recreation; Florida JOHPER. Vol. 1 (Aug. 1963)-. Periodical. English. qt. Florida Association for Health Physical Education & Recreation, JOHFERD 304, Florida Gymnasium of Florida, Gainesville FL 32601. **DD** 371.7.
**Ind/Abst** Phys. Educ. Index; SPORT Discus; SportSearch.

US/0897-4624
**FLORIDA JOURNAL OF ENVIRONMENTAL HEALTH.** See Environmental Issues.

US/1045-9758
**FLORIDA JOURNAL OF PUBLIC HEALTH.** [Fla. j. public health]. **VFOAT** FPHA Journal; Florida Public Health Association Journal. Periodical. English. Three times a year. Florida Mental Health Institute, 13301 Bruce B Downs Boulevard, Tampa FL 33612-3899. **LC** RA447.F6. **DD** 362.1/09759. **NLM** W1; FL79T.
**Ind/Abst** Environ. Period. Bibliogr. (?-?); Index Vet.; Trop. Dis. Bull.

US/0092-007X
**FLORIDA SUMMARY OF ACCIDENT DATA.** See Transportation-Roads and Traffic.

US
**FLORIDA VITAL STATISTICS. HRS DISTRICT SUPPLEMENT.** English. an. free (first copy), $6.51 (additional). Office of Vital Statistics, Public Health Statistics Section, PO Box 210, Jacksonville FL 32231-0042. **Tel** (904)359-6960, FAX (904)359-6997. **LC** HA311; .F56. **DD** 312/.09759. **Circ:** 1,000.
**Desc:** Vital statistics data for births, deaths, fetal deaths, marriages and dissolutions for state of Florida, counties and districts.

US/0732-8389
**FLOWER ESSENCE JOURNAL, THE.** [Flower essence j.]. Periodical. English. an. Flower Essence Society, PO Box 459, Nevada City CA 95959. **Continues** Flower Essence Quarterly, 0273-7868.

US/0271-3152
**FOCUS ON HEALTH (NEW YORK, N.Y.).** (FOCUS ON HEALTH : ISSUES AND EVENTS OF ... FROM THE NEW YORK TIMES INFORMATION BANK.). [Focus health]. Began in 1978. English. an. Arno Press, 3 Park Avenue, New York NY 10016. **Tel** (212)725-2050. **LC** R101.F63A. **DD** 610/.5. **NLM** ZWA 100 F625.

US/0270-4072
**FOODBORNE DISEASE SURVEILLANCE. ANNUAL SUMMARY.** (FOODBORNE DISEASE SURVEILLANCE, ANNUAL SUMMARY / CENTERS FOR DISEASE CONTROL.). [Foodborne dis. surveill., Annu. summ.]. **Added/Corp** Center for Disease Control. Centers for Disease Control (U.S.). **VFOAT** Foodborne Disease Surveillance; Foodborne Disease Outbreaks, Annual Summary. (1978)-. English. an. Free. Centers for Disease Control, 1600 Clifton Road NE, Atlanta GA 30333. **Tel** (404)639-3311, FAX (404)639-3296. **(Subscription address:** CDC Distribution / Georgia, c/o G. Dixon, Mail Stop A 2, Atlanta GA 30333.) **LC** RC143; .C45a. **DD** 615.9/54/0973. **NLM** W2 A C2FA. available on microfiche (Vols. for 1978 Rev. - (1981) distributed to depository libraries). **Continues in part** Foodborne & Waterborne Disease Surveillance, 0737-1241.

US
**FOREIGN TRAVEL & IMMUNIZATION GUIDE.** See Travel and Tourism.

CN/0710-0663
**FORESIGHT (TORONTO).** (FORESIGHT / CANADIAN DRIVER AND SAFETY EDUCATION ASSOCIATION.). [Foresight]. **Added/Corp** Canadian Driver and Safety Educators Association. Vol. 1, No. 1 (Spring 1981)-. Periodical. English. qt. Free to members. Foresight, 175 College Street, Toronto Ontario M5T 1P8 Canada. **DD** 629.28/3/07071.
**Desc:** Information on traffic safety and automobile driver education.

IT
**FORO MONDIALE DELLA SANITA.** Italian. ir. Tecnindustria Srl, Dr Ragno Edi, Via Crescenzio 43, 00193 Rome Italy. **Tel** 011 39 6 6875657.

GW/0170-5431
**FORSCHUNGSPROGRAMM - BUNDESANSTALT FUR STRASSENWESEN, BEREICH UNFALLFORSCHUNG.** See Transportation-Roads and Traffic.

SZ/0251-8716
**FORUM MONDIAL DE LA SANTE.** [Forum mond. sante]. (1980)-. Periodical. French. Four times a year. $60.00. World Health Organization, Distribution and Sales, 20 Avenue Appia, CH-1211 Geneva 27 Switzerland. **Tel** 011 41 22 7912111, FAX 011 41 22 7880401. **UDC** 614. **CODEN** NU054.
**Ind/Abst** LABORDOC.

US/0196-4909
**FORWARD PLAN FOR THE HEALTH SERVICES ADMINISTRATION.** **Main/Corp** United States. Health Services Administration. **VFOAT** Forward Plan. 1976/80-. English. an. US Department of Health & Human Services / Public Health Service, 200 Independence Avenue SW, Room 716G, Washington DC 20201. **Tel** (202)690-6867, FAX (202)690-6274. **NLM** W2 A H6F.

US/0272-5622
**FOUNDATION ONE.** [Found. one]. Periodical. English. qt. $15.00. International Foundation for Biosocial Development and Human Health, 6 Lomond Avenue, Spring Valley NY 10977. **Tel** (914)624-8516. **ED** Ivana Podvalova. **NLM** W1 FO985. **Bk Rev.** **Ad Acc.** **Pr Rev.** **Circ:** 5,000 (ctrl). available on videocassette; available on audiocassette.
**Desc:** Devoted to biopsychosocial health, pastoral medicine, international health, biology, health communications, and traditional cultures.

US/0016-1810
**FROM THE STATE CAPITALS. MOTOR VEHICLE REGULATION.** See Transportation-Automobiles.

US/0734-1156
**FROM THE STATE CAPITALS. PUBLIC HEALTH (1982).** (FROM THE STATE CAPITALS. PUBLIC HEALTH.). [From state cap., Public health]. **VFOAT** Public Health. (1982)-. Periodical. English. mo. $211.50 (one year), $235.00 (two year) public and institutional libraries; $378.00 (one year), $420.00 (two year). Wakeman Walworth Inc., 300 North Washington Street #204, Alexandria VA 22314. **Tel** (703)549-8606. **DD** 362. **[CCC]. Continues** From the State Capitals. Public Health Trends From State Capitals.

US/1061-9704
**FROM THE STATE CAPITALS. PUBLIC SAFETY & JUSTICE POLICIES.** See Law-Law Enforcement and Criminology.

US/0898-5758
**FSF CABIN CREW SAFETY BULLETIN.** See Aeronautics, Astronautics.

US/0898-5723
**FSF HUMAN FACTORS BULLETIN & AVIATION MEDICINE.** See Aeronautics, Astronautics.

US/1072-0758
**FSIS FOOD SAFETY REVIEW.** See Food and Food Industry.

JA/0388-6166
**FUKUOKA-SHI EISEI SHIKENJO HO.** See Environmental Issues-Pollution and Waste Management.

SP/0213-9111
**GACETA SANITARIA.** [Gac. sanit.]. Vol. 1, No. 1 (July/Aug. 1987)-. Periodical. Spanish. bm. 4900ptas. Masson SA / Spain, Juan Bravo 46, Madrid Spain. **Tel** 011 34 1 4021212. **(Subscription address:** DIPSA, Calle Florida 6-8, 08120 Llagosta, Barcelona Spain) **NLM** W1; GA356G. **[CCC]. Continues** Gaseta Sanitaria de Barcelona.
**Ind/Abst** Index Med. (1987-); Indice Med. Esp.; Trop. Dis. Bull.

RU/0869-8902
**GARMONIIA.** **Added/Corp** Soviet Union. Ministerstvo Zdravookhraneniia. (1991)-. Periodical. Russian. Four times a year. $26.00. Izdatelstvo Meditsina / Russian Academy of Medical Sciences, Ulitsa Solyanka 14, 109801 Moscow Russia. **Tel** 011 95 297-05-04. **(Subscription address:** Victor Kamkin, 4956 Boiling Brook Parkway, Rockville MD 20852.)

NE
**GEDRAGSTHERAPIE.** Dutch. qt. Intermedia BV, Postbus 4, 2400 M Alphen Rijn Netherlands. **Tel** 011 31 1720 66855.
**Ind/Abst** PsycINFO (1982-); PsycLit.

GW
**GEFAHRGUT-BEAUFTRAGTE, DER.** German. mo. KO Storck & Co Verlag & Druck, Stahltwiete 7, D 22761 Hamburg Germany. **Tel** 011 49 40 8500071.

GW/0932-4712
**GEFAHRLICHE ARBEITSSTOFFE.** (19??)-. Monographic series. German. ir. Price varies per volume. Bundesanstalt fuer Arbeitsschutz, Postfach 170202, D44061 Dortmund Germany. **Tel** 011 49 231 9071 306, FAX 011 49 0231 9071 454, telex 822 153 BAU D. Index available. **Circ:** 60,000.
**Desc:** Information about dangerous substances workers might come in contact with.

UK/0266-4348
**GENITOURINARY MEDICINE.** [Genitourin. med.]. **Added/Corp** British Medical Association. Medical Society for the Study of Venereal Diseases (Great Britain). Vol. 61, No. 1 (Feb. 1985)-. Academic Scholarly Publication. English. bm. £136.00. BMJ / British Medical Journal Publishing Group, British Medical Association House, Tavistock Square, London WC1H 9JR England. **Tel** 011 44 71 3874499, FAX 011 44 71 383 6402, telex 290034 HBJ MN. **(Subscription address:** Box 560B, Kennebunkport, ME 04046) **ED** A. Mindel. **NLM** W1; GE334. **CODEN** GEMEE2. **[CCC]**. Index available. cum. index. **Bk Rev.** **Ad Acc.** **Pr Rev.** available on microfilm and microfiche from University Microfilms International (UMI). Documents available from The Genuine Article, BIOSIS Document Express, CASDDS, ADONIS. **Continues** British Journal of Venereal Diseases, 0007-134X.
**Desc:** Papers on medical disorders of the genitourinary system, sexually transmittable diseases, diagnosis, microbiology, the treatment of pelvic inflammatory disease, immunology of genitourinary diseases, the role of viruses in the aetiology of genital malignancy and AIDS.
**Ind/Abst** ADONIS; Biol. Abstr. (1985-); Chem. Abstr.; Curr. Aware. Biol. Sci., CABS; Curr. Contents Clin. Med.; Curr. Contents Life Sci.; EMBASE; Health Plan. Adminis.; Index Med. (Feb. 1985-); Microbiol. Abstr. Sect. B; Microbiol. Abstr. Sect. A; Microbiol. Abstr. Sect. C; PESTDOC; Protozoolog. Abstr.; Ref. Upd. Deluxe Ed.; Res. Alert [Full Cov.]; Rev. Med. Vet. Entomol.; Rev. Med. Vet. Mycology; Sci. Cit. Index; SCISEARCH; Soc. Sci. Cit. Index [Select. Cov.]; Trop. Dis. Bull.; Virol. AIDS Abstr.

US
**GEOCHEMISTRY AND THE ENVIRONMENT.** See Environmental Issues.

●US/1065-4127
**GEORGIA HEALTH CARE IN PERSPECTIVE.** [Ga. health care perspect.]. **Added/Corp** Morgan Quinto Corporation. 1st Ed. (1993)-. English. $18.00. Morgan Quinto Corporation, PO Box 1656, 512 East 9th Street, Lawrence KS 66044. **Tel** (800)457-0742, (913)841-3534, FAX (913)841-3534. **DD** 362.
**Desc:** Reports on the state's data and rank for each of the categories featured in Health Care State Rankings.

●GW/0941-3790
**GESUNDHEITSWESEN, DAS.** **Added/Corp** Bundesverband der Arzte des Offentlichen Gesundheitsdienstes (Germany). Vol. 54, No. 1 (Jan. 1992)-. Periodical. German (summaries and/or abstracts in English). mo. $178.00. Georg Thieme Verlag Stuttgart, Postfach 301120, D 70451 Stuttgart Germany. **Tel** 011 49 711 89310, FAX 011 49 711 8931298, telex 7 252 275 GTVD. **(Subscription address:** Thieme Medical Publishers Inc., 381 Park Avenue South, New York NY 10016.) **NLM** W1; GE943O. **Continues** Offentliche Gesundheitswesen, 0029-8573.
**Ind/Abst** Index Med. (1992-).

GW
**GESUNDHEITSWESEN DER BUNDESREPUBLIK DEUTSCHLAND, DAS.** **VFOAT** Public Health in the Federal Republic of Germany; Statistical Atlas on Public Health in the Federal Republic of Germany. V. 1- 1963-. German (English and French).

NE/0921-8343
**GGD-NIEWS (GRAVENHAGE).** (GGD NIEUWS.). **VFOAT** Gemeentelijke Gezondheids Dienst-Nieuws ('S-Gravenhage). (1988)-. Periodical. Dutch. Ten times a year. Fl85.00. St GGD Uitgeverij, Postbus 237, 3400 AE Ijsselstein Netherlands. **Tel** 011 31 3408 87930. **UDC** 613.

US/0897-3059
**GHAA'S NATIONAL DIRECTORY OF HMOS.** [GHAA's Natl. dir. HMOs]. **Added/Corp** Group Health Association of America. **VFOAT** National Directory of HMOS. (1986)-. Directory. English. an. $102.50. Group Health Association of America, Department 0612, Washington DC 20073. **Tel** (202)778-3247, FAX (202)331-7487. **DD** 338. **NLM** W 22; AA1 G4. **Circ:** 700. **Continues** Directory of the Nation's HMOS.

IT/1120-7892
**GIAIDS. GIORNALE ITALIANO DELL' AIDS.** See Medical Science and Technology-Allergy and Immunology.

JA/0385-1575
**GIFU-KEN EISEI KENKYUJOHO.** (GIFU-KEN EISEI KENKYUJO HO.). [Gifu-ken Eisei Kenkyujoho]. **Added/Corp** Gifu-Ken Eisei Kenkyujo. **VFOAT** Report of Gifu Prefectural Institute of Public Health; Gifu Kenjo Ho. (1956)-. Japanese. an. Gifuken Eisei Kenkyujo, (Gifu Prefectural Research Inst. of Public Health), 6-3, Noishiki 4 Chome, Gifushi, Gifuken 500 Japan. **NLM** W1; GI114GE. **CODEN** GEKHDY. Documents available from CASDDS.
**Ind/Abst** Chem. Abstr.

JA
**GIFU-KEN SEISHIN EISEI SENTA SHOHO.** **Main/Corp** Gifu-ken Seishin Eisei Senta. No. 1- 1971-. Japanese. Gifu-ken Gifu Sofo Chosha, Gifu-shi Japan. **LC** RA790.7.J3; G53A.

UN/0301-2468
**GIGIENA NASELENIH MISC.** (GIGIENA NASELENNYKH MEST.). [Gig. nasel. misc']. Vol. 12- 1973-. Ukrainian. an. **NLM** W1 GI134HB. ***Continues*** *Hihiena Naselenykh Mists', 0301-2468.*

IT/0017-0321
**GIORNALE DI MALATTIE INFETTIVE E PARASSITARIE.** [G. mal. infett. parassit.]. **Added/Corp** Societa Italiana Per lo Studio Delle Malattie Infettive e Parassitarie. Vol. 1 (Jan./Feb. 1949)-. Periodical. Italian (English). mo. L145600 Italy; L250000 other. Giornale di Malattie Infettive e Parassitarie, Via G B Grassi 74, 20157 Milan Italy. **Tel** 011 39 2 35799452. **ED** Francesco Colonnello. **NLM** W1 GI615. Index available. **Bk Rev**. **Ad Acc**. **Circ:** 1,250 (ctrl).
**Desc:** Includes unpublished writings dealing with clinical, biological and experimental studies concerning infectious and parasitical diseases, and the proceedings of the society's national conferences and of its chapters' regional meetings.
**Ind/Abst** Dairy Sci. Abstr.; EMBASE; Helminthol. Abstr. (19??-19??); Index Vet.; Life Sci. Collect.; Protozoolog. Abstr.; Rev. Med. Vet. Entomol.; Rev. Med. Vet. Mycology; Small Anim. Abstr. Bibliogr.; Trop. Dis. Bull.

•US/1063-8423
**GLOBAL ACCESS TO STD DIAGNOSTICS.** **See** Medical Science and Technology-Communicable Diseases.

NO
**GLOBE.** **See** Drug Abuse and Alcoholism.

US/0147-7811
**GOAL ATTAINMENT REVIEW.** English. an. Program Evaluation Resource Center, 501 Park Avenue South, Minneapolis MN 55415. **LC** RA790.A1; G57. **DD** 362.2.

KO/0023-401X
**GONJUN BOGEN JABJI.** (KONGJUNG POGON CHAPCHI. THE KOREAN JOURNAL OF PUBLIC HEALTH.). [Gonjun bogen jabji]. **Added/Corp** Soul Taehakkyo. Pogon Taehagwon. **VFOAT** Korean Journal of Public Health. (1964)-. Periodical. Korean (summaries and/or abstracts in English). sa. **LC** RA421; .K664. **NLM** W1 KO585. **CODEN** KOPOAL.
**Ind/Abst** Protozoolog. Abstr.

US
**GRANT APPLICATION FOR CONTINUATION OF FULL DESIGNATION.** **Main/Corp** Montana Health Systems Agency. English. Montana Health Systems Agency Inc, PO Box 1277, Helena MT 59624-1277. **LC** RA395.A4; M953. **DD** 353.97860084/1.

US
**GRANT$ FOR PUBLIC HEALTH AND DISEASES.** **See** Philanthropy.

US/0732-9385
**GREEN SHEET - UNITED STATES. DEPT. OF HEALTH AND HUMAN SERVICES, THE.** (THE GREEN SHEET : NEWS ABOUT THE U.S. DEPARTMENT OF HEALTH AND HUMAN SERVICES.). Periodical. English. da. US Department of Health and Human Services, 200 Independence Avenue Southwest, Washington DC 20201. **ED** Ronald D Steele. ctrl circ.

UK
**GUIDE TO HEALTH SERVICES OF THE WORLD.** English. ir. £9.50. Intl Hospital Federation, 4 Abbots Place, London NW6 4NP England. **Tel** 011 44 71 3727181, FAX (071)328-7433. **(Subscription address:** International Hospital Federation Ï4 Abbots Place ÏLindon NW6 4NP England**)**
**Desc:** Provides a basic overview of the health services of 60 nations. Contains information on how systems are financed, organized and administered.

SW
**HAELSA OCH SJUKVAARDSKONSUMTION.** **Main/Corp** Sweden. Statistiska Centralbyran. **Added/Corp** Sweden. Statististiska Centralbyran. Health and Medical Care Utilization. **VFOAT** Health and Medical Care Utilization. (1974)-. Swedish (English and Swedish). SCB Statistiska Centralbyran, 11581 Stockholm Sweden. **LC** RA407.5.S8; S95a.

SW
**HALSOUPPLYSNING.** **Main/Corp** Sweden. Socialstyrelsen. Namnden for Halsoupplysning. Swedish. Socialstyrelsens Namnd for Halsoupplysning, 106 30 Stockholm Sweden. **LC** RA440.3.S8; S94A.

BL/0017-7512
**HANSENIASE: RESUMOS E NOTICIAS. HANSENIASIS: ABSTRACTS AND NEWS.** [Hansen.; res. not./abs. news.]. **Added/Corp** Sao Paulo, Brazil (State). Instituto de Saude. Instituto de Saude, Sao Paulo, Brazil. Biblioteca. **VFOAT** Hanseniasis : Abstracts and News. (1970)-. Portuguese (English). sa. Instituto de Saude - Biblioteca, Caixa Postal 8027, 01000 Sao Paulo Brazil. **NLM** ZWC 335 H249. ***Absorbed*** *Hansenologia.*

IO/0216-9053
**HASIL-HASIL RAPAT KERDJA KESEHATAN NASIONAL.** [Hasil-hasil rapat kerdja kesehatan Nas.]. **Main/Conf** Rapat Kerdja Kesehatan Nasional. **Added/Corp** Indonesia. Departemen Kesehatan. Bagian Penerbitan & Perpustakaan. (1900)-. Indonesian. **NLM** W1 HA716.

•US/1065-4135
**HAWAII HEALTH CARE IN PERSPECTIVE.** [Hawaii health care perspect.]. **Added/Corp** Morgan Quitno Corporation. 1st Ed. (1993)-. English. $18.00. Morgan Quitno Corporation, PO Box 1656, 512 East 9th Street, Lawrence KS 66044. **Tel** (800)457-0742, (913)841-3534, FAX (913)841-3534. **DD** 362.
**Desc:** Reports on the state's data and rank for each of the categories featured in Health Care State Rankings.

US/0888-6849
**HAZ-MAT TECHNOLOGY.** [Haz-mat technol.]. **VFOAT** Haz Mat Technology. (Jan. 1986)-. Periodical. English. Six times a year. $20.00 US; $28.00 Canada; $50.00 other. Teaberry Associates, 21 Saw Mill Road, RR 21, Medford NJ 08055. **Tel** (609)983-2619, FAX (609)983-7523. **ED** James Mackenzie. **DD** 604. Index available. cum. index. **Bk Rev**. **Ad Acc**. **Circ:** 500.
**Desc:** Published for emergency services personnel regarding basic procedures and the advanced technology needed for the effective response to and control of all hazardous materials incidents.

US/0891-3072
**HAZCHEM ALERT.** [Hazchem alert]. **VFOAT** Vis Hazchem Alert. Vol. 1, No. 1 (Jan. 31, 1986)-. Periodical. English. mo. $190.00 US and Canada; $230.00 other. NDS Information Consultants, 23 Virginia Drive, Middletown CT 06457. **Tel** (203)344-1880, FAX (203)344-1880. **ED** Judith A. Douville. **DD** 363. **CODEN** HAALEE. **Ad Acc**. **Circ:** 100.
**Desc:** Provides critical worldwide news on hazardous chemicals and potential risk substances. Drawing from over 100 global sources, it delivers up to minute news on toxicology, industrial hygiene, occupational health and safety, environmental compliance, R & D, government research, and much more.

•US/1064-4237
**HEALING (SACRAMENTO, CALIF.).** (HEALING.). [Healing]. **Added/Corp** Health Communication Research Institute. Vol. 1, No. 1 (Winter 1992)- Vol. 2 (Jan. 1993)-. Periodical. English. Four times a year (Jan., Apr., July, Oct.). $30.00 one year; $55.00 two year; $75.00 three year. Health Communication Research Institute, 1050 Fulton Avenue, Suite 105, Sacramento CA 95825. **Tel** (916)483-1583, FAX (916)483-1584. **ED** Marlene M. von Friedericks Fitzwater. **DD** 610. cum. index. **Bk Rev**. **Ad Acc**. **Circ:** 6,000 (ctrl).

US/0278-2715
**HEALTH AFFAIRS (MILLWOOD, VA.).** (HEALTH AFFAIRS.). [Health aff.]. **Added/Corp** Project Hope. Vol. 1, No. 1 (Winter 1981)-. Periodical. English. qt. $45.00 (individuals), $75.00 (institutions) US; $70.00 (individuals), $100.00 (institutions) other. Health Affairs, 7500 Old Georgetown Road, Suite 600, Bethesda MD 20814. **Tel** (301)656-7401, FAX (301)654-2845. **(Subscription address:** Health Affairs, PO Box 8015, Syracuse NY 13217-7982**) ED** John K Iglehart. **LC** RA410.A1; H36. **DD** 338.4/73621. **NLM** W1 HE209. Index available. cum. index. **Bk Rev**. **Pr Rev**. **Circ:** 9,000. available on microfilm and microfiche from University Microfilms International (UMI). Documents available from The Genuine Article, UMI Article Clearinghouse.
**Desc:** A multidisciplinary journal dedicated to the serious explanation of major domestic health policy issues.
**Ind/Abst** ABI/INFORM Glob. Ed.; ABI Inform Ondisc (Spring 1987-); Biostatistica (19??-19??); Cumul. Index Nurs. Allied Health Lit. (1981-); Curr. Contents Soc. Behav. Sci.; EMBASE; Health Plan. Adminis.; Health Serv. Abstr.; Hospit. Health Admin. Index; Hospit. Manage. Rev.; Hum. Resour. Abstr.; Index Med.; Index Period. Artic. Relat. Law; Int. Nurs. Index; Int. Pharm. Abstr.; Manage. Contents (1981-); PAIS Int. Print (1991-); Public Aff. Inf. Serv. Bull.; Res. Alert [Full Cov.]; Sage Fam. Stud. Abstr. (?-?); Soc. Sci. Cit. Index [Full Cov.].

US/8755-4763
**HEALTH ALERT (PASADENA, CALIF.).** ***Suspended.*** (HEALTH ALERT.). [Health alert]. Vol. 1 No. 1 (Sept. 1984)-Suspended with Vol. 1, No. 11. Periodical. English. mo. $78.00. Health Alert Publications, 180 South Lake Avenue/Suite 235, Pasadena CA 91101. **DD** 613.
**Ind/Abst** Index Philip. Period. (-199?).

US/0893-6242
**HEALTH & ENVIRONMENT DIGEST.** [Health environ. dig.]. **Added/Corp** Health and Environment Network. Freshwater Foundation. Bush Foundation. **VFOAT** Health and Environment Digest. Vol. 1, No. 1 (Feb. 1987)-. Periodical. English. mo (11 issues). $90.00 (libraries, government agencies, and individuals), $115.00 (private enterprise) US; $98.00 (libraries, government agencies, and individuals), $123.00 (private enterprise) Canada and Mexico; $90.00 (libraries, government agencies, and individuals), $130.00 (private enterprise) other. Health & Environment Digest, 725 County Road 6, Wayzata MN 55391. **Tel** (612)449-0092, FAX (612)449-0592. **ED** Timothy D. Burkhardt. **LC** RA565.A1; H43. **DD** 363.7/005. **NLM** W1; HE25D. **CODEN** HENDEF. Index available. cum. index. **Pr Rev**. **Circ:** 1,250. Documents available from Documents on Demand.
**Desc:** Information on public health issues related to air, land and water quality.
**Ind/Abst** Biol. Dig.; Environ. Abstr.; Health Saf. Sci. Abstr.

US/1048-8405
**HEALTH & FITNESS MAGAZINE FOR HEALTHY, SOUND LIVING : HF.** [Health fit. mag. healthy sound living]. **VFOAT** Health and Fitness Magazine for Healthy, Sound Living; HF; Health & Fitness Magazine. No. 6 (1989)-. Periodical. English. qt. $2.95 (single issue) US; $3.75 (single issue) Canada. Fell Publishers Inc, 2131 Hollywood Boulevard/Suite 204, Hollywood FL 33020. **Tel** (305)925-5242. **DD** 613. **Ad Acc**. **Circ:** 50,000. ***Continues*** *Fell's Health Series.*
**Desc:** Special interest articles on health topics.
**Ind/Abst** Acad. Search (Jan. 1992-).

US
**HEALTH AND HEALTH INSURANCE : THE PUBLIC'S VIEW.** **See** Insurance.

UK/0140-2986
**HEALTH AND HYGIENE (LONDON).** (HEALTH AND HYGIENE.). [Health hyg.]. **Added/Corp** Royal Institute of Public Health and Hygiene (Great Britain). Vol. 1, (July/Sept. 1977)-. Academic Scholarly Publication. English. Four times a year (Jan., Apr., July, Oct.). £35.00 EEC countries; £39.00 others. Royal Institute of Public Health and Hygiene, 28 Portland Place, London W1N 4DE England. **Tel** 44-71-5802731. **ED** Dr. A. M. B. Golding. **LC** RA421; .H412. **NLM** W1; HE25ZH. **CODEN** HEHYDD. Index available. **Bk Rev**, (Qty: 20-25). **Ad Acc, Adv Mgr:** Riphh, **Tel** (071)580 2731. **Pr Rev**. **Circ:** 2,500 (ctrl). available on microfilm and microfiche from University Microfilms International (UMI). Documents available from BIOSIS Document Express.
**Desc:** Publishes papers on all aspects of public health and hygiene, presented in an informal and informative style.
**Ind/Abst** Biol. Abstr. (1985-); EMBASE; Health Serv. Abstr.; Helminthol. Abstr. (1991-); Index Vet.; Protozoolog. Abstr.; Rev. Med. Vet. Entomol.; Trop. Dis. Bull.

•US/1061-6446
**HEALTH AND MEDICINE.** **VFOAT** New Book of Knowledge, Health and Medicine. (1992)-. Periodical. English. Grolier Electronic Publishing, Sherman Turnpike, Danbury CT 06816. **Tel** (203)797-3500, FAX (203)797-3835.

CN/0831-8530
**HEALTH & NUTRITION UPDATE.** ***Title Change.*** **See** Nutrition and Dietetics.

SZ/0253-6803
**HEALTH AND POPULATION. PERSPECTIVES AND ISSUES.** ***Ceased.*** (HEALTH AND POPULATION. PERSPECTIVE AND ISSUES : JOURNAL OF NATIONAL INSTITUTE OF HEALTH AND FAMILY WELFARE.). [Health popul., Perspect. issues]. **Added/Corp** National Institute of Health and Family Welfare (India). **VFOAT** Health and Population. Vol. 1, No. 1 (Jan./Mar. 1978)-(19??). Academic Scholarly Publication. English. qt. National Institute of Health and Family, New Mehrauli Road, Munirka, New Delhi 110 067 India. **Tel** 665482. **LC** RA529; .H4. **DD** 362.1/0954. **NLM** W1 HE263D. **Bk Rev**. **Circ:** 800. ***Formed by the union of*** *NIHAE Bulletin, 0378-6196* ***and*** *Journal of Population Research, 0377-0478.*
**Desc:** Deals with health problems and issues.
**Ind/Abst** Curr. Lit. Sci. Sci.; EMBASE; Popul. Index; Trop. Dis. Bull. (-19??).

NE
**HEALTH & SAFETY CASE LAW INDEX.** **See** Law.

UK
**HEALTH AND SAFETY COMMISSION NEWSLETTER.** **VFOAT** Newsletter of the Health and Safety Commission. (19??)-. Newsletter. English. Six times a year. £10.00. HSE Books, PO Box 1999, Sudbury Suffolk C010 6FS England. **Tel** 011 44 0787 881165. **Bk Rev**, (Qty: 60). **Circ:** 60,000.
**Desc:** Each issue takes an in-depth look at real incidents and accidents, the European scene and how it affects UK business, legislation and new codes of practice and guidance on a wide range of industrial processes and hazards.
**Ind/Abst** Eng. Mater. Abstr.; Int. Packag. Abstr.; Trop. Dis. Bull.; World Surf. Coat. Abstr.

UK
**HEALTH AND SAFETY EXECUTIVE GUIDANCE NOTES. CHEMICAL SAFETY.** (19??)-. English. ir. Price varies. Health & Safety Executive, Room 414 St Hughs House Stanley, Btle Merseyside L20 3QY England. **Tel** 011 44 51 951 4000, FAX 011 44 51 922 5394, telex 628235. **(Subscription address:** HSE Books, PO Box 1999, Sudbury Suffolk CO10 6FS England.**)**

UK
**HEALTH AND SAFETY EXECUTIVE GUIDANCE NOTES. ENVIRONMENTAL HYGIENE.** (19??)-. English. ir. Health & Safety Executive, Room 414 St Hughs House Stanley, Btle Merseyside L20 3QY England. **Tel** 011 44 51 951 4000, FAX 011 44 51 922 5394, telex 628235.

UK
**HEALTH AND SAFETY EXECUTIVE GUIDANCE NOTES. GENERAL SERIES.** (19??)-. English. ir. Health & Safety Executive, Room 414 St Hughs House Stanley, Btle Merseyside L20 3QY England. **Tel** 011 44 51 951 4000, FAX 011 44 51 922 5394, telex 628235.

UK
**HEALTH AND SAFETY EXECUTIVE GUIDANCE NOTES. MEDICAL SERIES.** (19??)-. English. ir. Health & Safety Executive, Room 414 St Hughs House Stanley, Btle Merseyside L20 3QY England. **Tel** 011 44 51 951 4000, FAX 011 44 51 922 5394, telex 628235.

UK
**HEALTH AND SAFETY EXECUTIVE GUIDANCE NOTES. PLANT AND MACHINERY.** (19??)-. English. ir. Health & Safety Executive, Room 414 St Hughs House Stanley, Btle Merseyside L20 3QY England. **Tel** 011 44 51 951 4000, FAX 011 44 51 922 5394, telex 628235.

UK
**HEALTH AND SAFETY EXECUTIVE GUIDANCE NOTES. WORKPLACE AIR & BIOLOGICAL MONITORING DATABASE.** English. an. £200.00. Health & Safety Executive, Room 414 St Hughs House Stanley, Btle Merseyside L20 3QY England. **Tel** 011 44 51 951 4000, FAX 011 44 51 922 5394, telex 628235. **(Subscription address:** HSE Books, PO Box 1999, Sudbury Suffolk CO10 6FS England**)**

UK
**HEALTH AND SAFETY FACTBOOK.** (19??)-. Consumer Publication. English. Twice a year. £100.00 UK; £110.00 other. GEE Publishing Limited, South Quay Plaza, 183 Marsh Wall, London E14 9FS England. **Tel** 011 44 71 538 5368. **(Subscription address:** Professional Publishing Ltd., South Quay Plaza, 183 March Wall, London E14 9FS United Kingdom.**)**

●UK/1352-5611
**HEALTH AND SAFETY MANAGER.** (1994)-. Periodical. English. mo (10 issues and 3 updates). £168.50. Croner Publ Ltd, Croner House, London Road, Kingston upon Thames, Surrey KT2 6SR England. **Tel** 011 44 81 5473333, FAX 081 547-2637.

UK
**HEALTH & SAFETY. MICROFILE.** (1980)-. Trade Publication. English. £835.00. Barbour Index Plc, New Lodge Drift Road, Windsor Berkshire, SL4 4RQ England. **Tel** 011 44 3 448 84121, FAX 011 44 3 448 84845. **ED** Vic Quayle. Index available (Hard copy index used with microfiche). cum. index. **Pr Rev. Circ:** 3,500 (ctrl).

US/0892-9351
**HEALTH AND SAFETY SCIENCE ABSTRACTS.** **See** Public Health and Safety-Abstracting, Bibliographies and Statistics.

UK
**HEALTH & SAFETY SPECIFIER.** (19??)-. English. bm. £15.00 UK; £18.00 Europe; £25.00 other. Portland Communications Ltd, 32 Portland Street, Cheltenham Gloschester, GL52 2PB England. **Tel** 011 44 242 236336, FAX 011 44 242 222331. **ED** D. Constantine. **Ad Acc**, **Adv Mgr:** Debbie Preece, **Tel** 011 44 242 581480. ***Continues*** *Caution Magazine.*
**Desc:** Covers environmental products, provides equipment reviews and articles that relate to commercial health and safety.

US/1054-2957
**HEALTH AND SEXUALITY.** [Health sex.]. **Added/Corp** Association of Reproductive Health Professionals. **VFOAT** Health & Sexuality. Vol. 1, No. 1 (Fall 1990)-. Periodical. English. Four times a year. $100.00 physicians; $60.00 others Comes with Association of Reproductive Health Professionals membership. Association of Reproductive and Health Professionals (ARHP), 2401 Pennsylvania Avenue Northwest, Suite 350, Washington DC 20037. **Tel** (202)466-3825. **LC** RA788; .H4. **DD** 613.9/05.
**Ind/Abst** Curr. Lit. Fam. Plan.

AT
**HEALTH AND WELFARE ESTABLISHMENTS / QUEENSLAND.** **See** Public Health and Safety-Abstracting, Bibliographies and Statistics.

US/1055-3517
**HEALTH BENEFITS LETTER.** ***Ceased.*** [Health benefits lett.]. Vol. 1, No. 1 (Feb. 14, 1991)-(April 1994). Periodical. English. Twenty-four times a year. Capitol Publications, 1101 King Street, Suite 444, Alexandria VA 22314. **Tel** (703)683-4100, (800)655-5597. **(Subscription address:** Capitol Publications, PO Box 1453, Alexandria, VA 22313**) DD** 362.
**Desc:** Detailed coverage of state, federal and private sector health care reform activities, including mandated benefits, insurance reform, universal health proposals, managed care regulations, tax and solvency issues, and cost containment efforts. Features descriptive tables and charts.

UK
**HEALTH BUILDING LIBRARY BULLETIN.** Bulletin. English. £7.50. Department of Health and Social Security Library, PO Box 21, Stanmore, Middlesex HA7 1AY England. **Tel** 011 44 71 9722000, 9728161.

UK/0374-8014
**HEALTH BULLETIN (EDINBURGH).** (HEALTH BULLETIN.). [Health bull.]. (1941)-. Bulletin. English. bm (6 issues). £6.00. Scottish Home & Health Department, St Andrews House, Edinburgh Scottland EH1 3DE, United Kingdom. **Tel** (031)556-8501 ext. 2618. **NLM** W2 FS2 D4H. **CODEN** HBHSA5. Index available (bound in first issue). cum. index. **Bk Rev. Circ:** 15,000 (ctrl). Documents available from BIOSIS Document Express.
**Ind/Abst** Biol. Abstr.; Cumul. Index Nurs. Allied Health Lit.; EMBASE; Index Med.; Trop. Dis. Bull.

AT/0311-9254
**HEALTH BULLETIN (MELBOURNE).** (HEALTH BULLETIN.). **Added/Corp** Victoria. Commission of Public Health. Victoria. Dept. of Health. No. 77/78 (Jan./June 1944)-. Periodical. English. sa. Victoria Department of Health / Commission of Public Health, Melbourne Victoria Australia. **NLM** W1 HE292.
**Ind/Abst** Appl. Soc. Sci. Index Abstr.; Cumul. Index Nurs. Allied Health Lit.; Health Serv. Abstr.; Nutr. Abstr. Rev., Ser. B, Live Feeds and Feed.; Nutr. Abstr. Rev., Ser. A, Hum. Exp.

US/0017-8934
**HEALTH BULLETIN (RALEIGH), THE.** (THE HEALTH BULLETIN.). [Health bull.]. **Added/Corp** North Carolina. Board of Health. (Sept. 1913)-. Bulletin. English. mo. **NLM** W2 AN8 B26H. ***Continues*** *North Carolina. Board of Health. Bulletin of the North Carolina State Board of Health.*
**Ind/Abst** Cumul. Index Nurs. Allied Health Lit.; Health Plan. Adminis.

US
**HEALTH BUSINESS NEWSLETTER.** (19??)-. Newsletter. English. Fifty times a year. $595.00. Faulkner & Gray Inc., 11 Penn Plaza, 17th Floor, New York NY 10001. **Tel** (212)967-7000, (800)535-8403.

AT/0046-7006
**HEALTH (CANBERRA).** ***Ceased.*** (HEALTH : JOURNAL OF THE COMMONWEALTH DEPARTMENT OF HEALTH.). [Health]. (19??)-(19??). Periodical. English. qt. **NLM** W1 HE165.
**Ind/Abst** Energy Res. Abstr. (1981-).

US/1050-9976
**HEALTH CARE 500, THE.** ***Title Change.*** [Health care 500]. **VFOAT** Health Care Five Hundred. (1991)-(1992). English. Faulkner & Gray Inc., 11 Penn Plaza, 17th Floor, New York NY 10001. **Tel** (212)967-7000, (800)535-8403. **LC** RA393; .H37. **DD** 362.1/0973. **NLM** WA 22; AA1 H42. ***Continued by*** *Health Care 1000.*

●US/1070-9150
**HEALTH CARE 1000, THE.** (THE HEALTH CARE 1000 : LEADERS OF TODAY, TOMORROW AND BEYOND.). [Health care 1000]. **VFOAT** Health Care One Thousand. (1994)-. Periodical. English. an (Oct.). $179.95. Faulkner & Gray Inc., 11 Penn Plaza, 17th Floor, New York NY 10001. **Tel** (212)967-7000, (800)535-8403. **LC** RA393; .H37. **DD** 362.1/0973. ***Continues*** *Health Care 500, 1050-9976.*

●UK/1065-3058
**HEALTH CARE ANALYSIS.** **See** Medical Science and Technology.

●US/1063-5335
**HEALTH CARE BILLER, THE.** [Health care biller]. **VFOAT** HCB. Vol. 1, No. 1 (Apr. 1992)-. Periodical. English. mo. $197.00. Aspen Publishers Inc., 7201 McKinney Circle, Frederick MD 21701. **Tel** (800)234-1660, (301)698-7100, FAX (301)251-5784, telex 5106014543. **DD** 658.

US/0889-5465
**HEALTH CARE COMPENSATION & BENEFITS ADVISOR.** ***Ceased.*** [Health care compens. benefits advis.]. **VFOAT** Health Care Compensation and Benefits Advisor. Vol. 1, No. 1 (March 1987)-Ceased (June 1987). Periodical. English. mo. Aspen Publishers Inc., 7201 McKinney Circle, Frederick MD 21701. **Tel** (800)234-1660, (301)698-7100, FAX (301)251-5784, telex 5106014543. **DD** 658.

US/0886-2095
**HEALTH CARE COMPETITION WEEK.** ***Title Change.*** [Health care compet. week]. **VFOAT** HCCW. Vol. 1, No. 1 (1984)-(19??). Periodical. English. sm. Capitol Publications, 1101 King Street, Suite 444, Alexandria VA 22314. **Tel** (703)683-4100, (800)655-5597. **(Subscription address:** Capitol Publications, PO Box 1453, Alexandria VA 22313.**) DD** 362. **NLM** W1; HE298T. **[CCC].** available on an online database (files 16,636/Full-Text) from DIALOG. ***Absorbed*** *Washington Actions on Health, 0194-5416.* ***Continued by*** *Healthcare Systems Strategy Report.*
**Ind/Abst** Hospit. Manage. Rev.; PROMT [Full Txt.]; PTS Newsl. Database [Full Txt.].

US/0739-8034
**HEALTH CARE COSTS.** (HEALTH CARE COSTS / DRI.). [Health care costs]. **Added/Corp** Data Resources, Inc. DRI/McGraw-Hill. Vol. 1, No. 1 (May 1981)-. Periodical. English. Four times a year. $875.00. DRI McGraw Hill, 24 Hartwell Avenue, Lexington MA 02173. **Tel** (617)863-5100. **LC** RA410.53; .H414446. **DD** 338.4/33621/097305. **NLM** W1; HE298TM.

US/0160-7006
**HEALTH CARE EDUCATION.** Vol. 6, No. 2 (April 1977)-. Periodical. English. bm. $18.00. Reinhardt/Keymer Publishing Company, 60 East 42nd Street, New York NY 10017. **NLM** W1 HE299E. available on microfilm and microfiche from University Microfilms International (UMI). ***Continues*** *In-Service Training and Education, 0090-2225.*

US/1060-2909
**HEALTH CARE FEDERAL REGISTER ALERT.** ***Ceased.*** [Health care fed. regist. alert]. **VFOAT** Health Care Federal Register. (1991)-(Sept. 1994). Periodical. English. wk. LRP Publications, 747 Dresher Road, PO Box 980, Horsham PA 19044-0980. **Tel** (800)341-7874, (215)784-0860, FAX (215)784-9639, (215)784-0870. **ED** Kenneth Kahn. **DD** 353. available in Loose-leaf.
**Desc:** Provides health care law practitioners with all relevant information published in the Federal Register. Each update includes a table of contents listing all of the applicable Federal Register releases copied for the week.

US/1060-0434
**HEALTH CARE REGISTRAR, THE.** ***Title Change.*** [Heal. care regist.]. **Added/Corp** Zimmerman & Associates (Hales Corners, Wis.). (Oct. 1991)-(199?). Periodical. English. mo. Zimmerman & Associates, PO Box 407, 5307 South 92nd Street, Hales Corners WI 53130. **Tel** (414)425-2189. **DD** 658. ***Continued by*** *Health Care Registration.*

●US
**HEALTH CARE REGISTRATION.** (1994)-. English. mo. $227.00. Aspen Publishers Inc., 7201 McKinney Circle, Frederick MD 21701. **Tel** (800)234-1660, (301)698-7100, FAX (301)251-5784, telex 5106014543. ***Continues*** *Health Care Registrar, 1060-0434.*

US/1044-4076
**HEALTH CARE STANDARDS.** (HEALTH CARE STANDARDS : OFFICIAL DIRECTORY.). [Health care stand.]. **VFOAT** Healthcare Standards; Health Care Standards Directory. (1990)-. Directory. English. an. $285.00. ECRI Emergency Care Research Institute, 5200 Butler Pike, Plymouth Meeting PA 19462. **Tel** (215)825-6000, FAX (215)834-1275, telex 510-660-8023. **LC** RA399.A3; H43. **DD** 362.1/021873. **NLM** W 22; AA1 H42. **[CCC].**
**Desc:** A concise newsletter that features abstracts of important standards and guidelines, notice of anticipated changes, authoritative answers to questions from readers, and editorial analyses of key standards that affect the quality of health care.

●US/1065-1403
**HEALTH CARE STATE RANKINGS.** [Health care state rank.]. **Added/Corp** Morgan Quitno Corporation. 1st Edition (1993)-. English. an. $43.95. Morgan Quitno Corporation, PO Box 1656, 512 East 9th Street, Lawrence KS 66044. **Tel** (800)457-0742, (913)841-3534, FAX (913)841-3534. **LC** RA407.3; .H423. **DD** 362.1/0973. **NLM** W1; HE3014.
**Desc:** Contains a collection of state information for health care.

US/1041-0236
**HEALTH COMMUNICATION.** [Health commun.]. Vol. 1, No. 1 (1986)-. Periodical. English. qt. $180.00 US & Canada; $205.00 other. Lawrence Erlbaum Associates, 365 Broadway, Suite 102, Hillsdale NJ 07642. **Tel** (201)666-4110, (800)926-6579, FAX (201)666-2394. **ED** Teresa L Thompson. **LC** WMLC 93/1307; R118; .H4. **DD** 362. **NLM** W1; HE313B. **CODEN** HECOER.
**Desc:** An interdisciplinary journal that will publish scholarly research on the relationship between communication processes and health.
**Ind/Abst** Psychol. Abstr. (1989-); PsycINFO; PsycLit; Soc. Plann. Policy Dev. Abstr.

US/0894-4172
**HEALTH CONFIDENTIAL.** [Health confid.]. Vol. 1, No. 1 (May 1987)-. Periodical. English. mo. $49.00. Boardroom Reports Inc., 330 West 42nd Street, 14th Floor, New York NY 10036. **Tel** (212)239-9000. **(Subscription address:** Neodata, PO Box 2606, Boulder, CO 80322**)** **DD** 614.
**Desc:** The authoritative new report that brings you health secrets of America. What doctors, hospitals, and dentists don't tell you. Exercise, nutrition, weight reduction, medication, and surgery. Straight from the researchers who are creating tomorrow's health care today. Inside information that can help you feel better and live longer.
**Ind/Abst** Acad. Abstr. Full Text Elite (Jan. 1992-); Acad. Abstr. (Jan. 1992-); Acad. Search (Jan. 1992-); Health Source (Jan. 1992-); INFO-SOUTH Abstr.; Mag. Search.

US/0895-9986
**HEALTH CONSCIOUSNESS (OVIEDO, FLA.).** (HEALTH CONSCIOUSNESS : HC.). [Health conscious.]. (19??)-. Periodical. English. bm (Jan., Mar., May, July, Sept., Nov.). $18.00. Health Consciousness, PO Box 550, Oviedo FL 32765. **Tel** (407)365-6681, FAX (407)365-1834. **ED** Roy Kupsinel. **LC** WMLC 93/1072. **DD** 613. **Bk Rev**, (Qty: 30-40). **Ad Acc**, **Adv Mgr:** John Zielinski.
**Desc:** Presents a truthful look at health and healing from around the globe.

US/0098-311X
**HEALTH CONSEQUENCES OF SMOKING, THE.** (THE HEALTH CONSEQUENCES OF SMOKING : A PUBLIC HEALTH SERVICE REVIEW.). **Added/Corp** United States. Public Health Service. Office of the Surgeon General. United States. Office of the Assistant Secretary for Health. United States. Health Services and Mental Health Administration. National Clearinghouse for Smoking and Health. United States. Public Health Service. Center for Health Promotion and Education (U.S.). Office on Smoking and Health. **VFOAT** Health Consequences of Smoking for Women; Health Consequences of Involuntary Smoking; Reducing the Health Consequences of Ssmoking; The Health Benefits of Smoking Cessation. (1967)-. English. an. Office on Smoking and Health, 5600 Fishers Lane, Room 1-58, Rockville MD 20857. **Tel** (301)443-1575. **LC** RA1242.T6; U474. **DD** 615.9/52379. **NLM** W1 HE313G. ***Continues*** *Smoking and Health.*

US/0735-0848
**HEALTH DATA INVENTORY.** [Health data inventory]. **Added/Corp** United States. Dept. of Health and Human Services. (19??)-. English. an. US Department of Health and Human Services, 200 Independence Avenue Southwest, Washington DC 20201. **LC** RA445; .H3375. **DD** 362.1/072073. available on microfiche (Vols. for 1982- distributed to depository libraries).

US/8755-240X
**HEALTH DATA SUMMARIES FOR CALIFORNIA COUNTIES.** [Health data summ. Calif. cty.]. **Added/Corp** California. Center for Health Statistics. (1980)-. English. an (July). $7.50. California Health & Welfare, 714 P Street, room 1494, Sacramento CA 95814. **Tel** (916)445-1010. **LC** RA407.4.C2; H43. **DD** 362.1/09794.

US
**HEALTH DEVELOPMENT IN AFRICA.** **Added/Corp** World Health Organization. Regional Office for Africa. (1980)-. Monographic series. English. ir. Free. World Health Organization / Congo, BP 6, Regional Office for Africa, Brazzaville Congo.

US/8756-8713
**HEALTH DEVICES INSPECTION AND PREVENTIVE MAINTENANCE SYSTEM.** **Added/Corp** Emergency Care Research Institute. 1st Ed. (April 1984)-. English. ir. $695.00 (non-member), $495.00 (member). ECRI Emergency Care Research Institute, 5200 Butler Pike, Plymouth Meeting PA 19462. **Tel** (215)825-6000, FAX (215)834-1275, telex 510-660-8023. **ED** R. Mosenkis. **DD** 363. **[CCC].**

●US/1057-9230
**HEALTH ECONOMICS.** [Health econ.]. (1992)-. Periodical. English. Six times a year. $225.00. John Wiley & Sons, Inc., 605 Third Avenue, New York NY 10158-0012. **Tel** (212)850-6000, (212)850-6645, FAX (212)850-6088, telex 12-7063. **(Subscription address:** John Wiley & Sons / England, Baffins Lane, Chichester, West Sussex PO19 1UD England.**)** **ED** Alan Maynard and John Hutton. **LC** RA410.A1; .H385. **DD** 338.4/33621. **NLM** W1; HE318LW. **CODEN** HEECEZ. **[CCC]. Bk Rev**.
**Desc:** Articles on all aspects of health economics: theoretical contributions, empirical studies, economic evaluations and analyses of health policy from the economic perspective. Its scope will include the determinants of health and its definition and valuation, as well as the demand for and supply of health care; planning and market mechanisms for achieving equilibrium; micro-economic evaluation of individual prodedures and treatments; and evaluation for the performance of health care systems in terms of equity and allocative efficiency.

US/0270-0603
**HEALTH EDUCATION BULLETIN.** [Health educ. bull.]. **Added/Corp** National Clearinghouse for Family Planning Information. (Jan. 1978)-. Bulletin. English. National Clearing House for Family Planning Information, PO Box 2225, Rockville MD 20852. **NLM** W1 HE321G.
**Ind/Abst** Curr. Lit. Fam. Plan. (19??-199?).

US/0195-8402
**HEALTH EDUCATION QUARTERLY.** [Health educ. q.]. **Added/Corp** Society for Public Health Education. Vol. 7 (Spring 1980)-. Academic Scholarly Publication. English. Four times a year. $262.00. SAGE Periodical Press, 2455 Teller Road, Thousand Oaks CA 91320. **Tel** (805)499-0721, FAX (805)499-0871, telex 100799. **ED** Noreen M. Clark. **LC** RA440.A1; S63. **DD** 613/.07/1. **NLM** W1 HE325H. **CODEN** HEQUDC. **[CCC]. Ad Acc**. **Pr Rev. Circ:** 2,000. available on microfilm and microfiche from University Microfilms International (UMI). Documents available from The Genuine Article. ***Continues*** *Health Education Monographs, 0073-1455.*
**Desc:** The journal discusses the promotion of public health elevating the quality of health education, improving medical practice and stimulating research. Its focus is on providing both academics and public health and medical care practitioners with topics of practical and theoretical importance, as well as the adaptation of health care services to meet consumer needs.
**Ind/Abst** AGRICOLA [Select. Cov.]; Appl. Soc. Sci. Index Abstr.; Contents Pages Educ.; Cumul. Index Nurs. Allied Health Lit.; Curr. Contents Soc. Behav. Sci.; Curr. Index J. Educ.; Educ. Index (1992-); EMBASE; Energy Res. Abstr. (Aug. 1982-); Health Plan. Adminis.; Index Med.; Nutr. Res. Newsl.; Phys. Educ. Index; Psychol. Abstr. (1980-); PsycINFO; PsycLit; Res. Alert [Full Cov.]; Risk Abstr.; Soc. Plann. Policy Dev. Abstr.; Soc. Sci. Cit. Index [Full Cov.]; Sociol. Abstr.

US/0193-7138
**HEALTH EDUCATION REPORT (OJAI).** (HEALTH EDUCATION REPORT.). V. 1- Nov./Dec. 1973-. Periodical. English. bm. $9.00. Daniel Sullivan, PO Box 728, Ojai CA 93023.

US/0193-5232
**HEALTH EDUCATION REPORTS.** **VFOAT** HE Reports. Vol. 1 (Feb. 9, 1979)-. Periodical. English. sm. $198.00. Feistritzer Publications, 4401A Connecticut Avenue Northwest, Suite 212, Washington DC 20008. **Tel** (202)362-3444, FAX (202)362-3493. **ED** Lawrence O'Rourke. **NLM** W1 HE325M. Index available. cum. index. **Circ:** 670 (ctrl).
**Ind/Abst** Health Plan. Adminis.

UK/0268-1153
**HEALTH EDUCATION RESEARCH.** [Health educ. res.]. Vol. 1, No. 1 (April 1986)-. Periodical. English. qt. £115.00 UK and Europe; $185.00 other. Oxford University Press, Walton Street, Oxford OX2 6DP England. **Tel** 011 44 865 56767, FAX 011 44 865 267773, telex 837330 OXPRES G. **(Subscription address:** Oxford University Press / USA, Journals Marketing Department, Oxford University Press, 2001 Evans Road, Cary NC 27513.**)** **ED** Keith Tones. **NLM** W1; HE325P. **CODEN** HRTPE2. **[CCC].** Index available. cum. index. **Bk Rev**. **Ad Acc**. available on microfilm and microfiche from University Microfilms International (UMI). Documents available from The Genuine Article, BIOSIS Document Express.
**Desc:** Papers covering policy, evaluation and research, communications, correspondence and book reviews. News and views sections covering topical development.
**Ind/Abst** Appl. Soc. Sci. Index Abstr.; Biol. Abstr. (1986-); Br. Educ. Index; Cumul. Index Nurs. Allied Health Lit.; Curr. Contents Soc. Behav. Sci.; Educ. Technol. Abstr.; EMBASE; Health Saf. Sci. Abstr.; Psychol. Abstr. (1986-); PsycINFO (1990-); PsycLit; Res. Alert [Full Cov.]; Soc. Sci. Cit. Index [Full Cov.]; Stud. Women Abstr.; Tech. Educ. Train. Abstr.

UK
**HEALTH EDUCATION SUBSCRIPTION SERVICE.** **See** Education.

●US
**HEALTH EDUCATOR : JOURNAL OF ETA SIGMA GAMMA.** **Added/Corp** Eta Sigma Gamma. **VFOAT** Journal of Eta Sigma Gamma. Vol. 24, No. 1 (Fall 1992)-. Periodical. English. Twice a year. $20.00. ETA Sigma Gamma, Ball State University, Muncie IN 47306. **Tel** (317)285-5961. **LC** RA773; .E8. ***Continues*** *Eta Sigma Gamman, 8756-5943.*

US
**HEALTH EFFECTS ASSESSMENT SUMMARY TABLES.** **Added/Corp** United States. Environmental Protection Agency. Office of Research and Development. United States. Environmental Protection Agency. Office of Emergency and Remedial Response. (1991 Fical Year)-. English. US Environmental Protection Agency, 401 M Street SW, Washington DC 20460. **Tel** (202)755-9163. **(Subscription address:** National Technical Information Service, 5285 Port Royal Road, Springfield, VA 22161**)** ***Continues*** *Health Effects Assessment Summary Tables ... Quarter ... .*

US/0899-6210
**HEALTH FACILITIES MANAGEMENT.** [Health facil. manage.]. **Added/Corp** American Society for Hospital Engineering. Vol. 1, No. 1 (Sept. 1988)-. Periodical. English. mo. $30.00 US; $50.00 other. American Hospital Publishing Inc., (A Subsidiary of the American Hospital Association), PO Box 92683, Chicago IL 60675. **Tel** (312)440-6836, (800)621-6902, FAX (312)951-8491. **ED** Frank G Sabatino. **LC** RA971; .H414. **DD** 658. **NLM** W1; HE335PJ. **Ad Acc. Circ:** 40,000. available on microfilm and microfiche from University Microfilms International (UMI).
**Desc:** Edited for professionals who buy and specify products used and maintenance of the nation's health care facilities.
**Ind/Abst** Health Plan. Adminis.; Hospit. Health Admin. Index (1988-).

US/0738-811X
**HEALTH FACTS.** [Health facts]. **Added/Corp** Center for Medical Consumers and Health Care Information (U.S.) Consumer Action Now (Organization). Council on Environmental Alternatives. Center for Medical Consumers Inc. **VFOAT** HealthFacts. Vol. 1, No. 1 (1977)-. Periodical. English. mo. $21.00 US; $24.00 Canada and Mexico; $32.00 other. Center for Medical Consumers, 237 Thompson Street, New York NY 10012. **Tel** (212)674-7105, FAX (212)674-7100. **ED** Maryann Napoli. **NLM** W1; HE333. Index available. cum. index. **Bk Rev**, (Qty: on occasion). **Circ:** 11,000. available on an online database (file 149/Full-Text) from DIALOG. Documents available from UMI Article Clearinghouse, Magazine Collection.
**Desc:** Explores issues of appropriate medical treatment, non-medical alternatives, and medical practices that do not reflect research findings.
**Ind/Abst** Acad. Abstr. Full Text Elite (Jan. 1992-); Acad. Abstr. (Jan. 1992-); Acad. Search (Jan. 1992-); Consum. Health Nutr. Index; Cumul. Index Nurs. Allied Health Lit.; Gen. Period. Index (1992-); Health Index (1989-); Health Period. Database [Full Txt.]; Health Ref. Cent. (Jan. 1989-) [Full Txt.] [Full Cov.]; Health Source (Jan. 1992-); INFO-SOUTH Abstr.; Mag. Artic. Summar. Elite (Jan. 1992-) [Full Txt.]; Mag. Artic. Summar. CD-ROM (Jan. 1992-); Mag. Index Plus (1992-); Mag. Search; Newsp. Period. Abstr. (1992-).

II/0970-8685
**HEALTH FOR THE MILLIONS.** (1975)-. Periodical. English. bm. $25.00. Voluntary Health Assn of India, 40 Institutional Area, New Dehli 110016 India. **Tel** 91 11 668071, FAX 91 11 676377. **UDC** 613. **Bk Rev**. **Circ:** 3,500.
**Desc:** Aimed at generating action oriented debates on health and developmental issues particularly with references to policies and implementations.
**Ind/Abst** Trop. Dis. Bull.

AT/1030-6072
**HEALTH FORUM.** [Health forum]. (1987)-. Periodical. English. Five times a year. 70.00Aus$ (institutional libraries); 40.00Aus$ (individuals). Consumers' Health Forum of Australia Inc., PO Box 52, Lyons ACT 2606 Australia. **Tel** 011 61 6 2810811, FAX 011 61 6 2810959. **ED** Lisa Neill. **DD** 362.0994. Index available. **Bk Rev**, (Qty: 20). **Ad Acc**. **Circ:** 800. ***Continues*** *Newsletter - Comsumers' Health Forum of Australia, 0819-7539.*
**Desc:** Journal of The Consumers' Health Forum of Australia Inc. (CHF), a national non-government health policy and consumer advocacy organization which represents consumers on health issues.

US/0749-4742
**HEALTH FREEDOM NEWS (MONROVIA, CALIF.).** (HEALTH FREEDOM NEWS : THE JOURNAL OF THE NATIONAL HEALTH FEDERATION / NHF.). [Health freedom news]. **Added/Corp** National Health Federation. Vol. 1, No. 1 (June 1982)-. Periodical. English. Ten times a year. $36.00 US; $48.00 other. National Health Federation, PO Box 688, Monrovia CA 91016. **Tel** (818)357-2181, FAX

(818)303-0642. **ED** M Salaman and K Donsbach. **DD** 363. **NLM** W1; HE337M. ***Continues*** *National Health Federation's Public Scrutiny, 0743-5053.*

US/0194-2352
**HEALTH GRANTS & CONTRACTS WEEKLY.** **VAT** Health Grants and Contracts Weekly. (197?)-. Periodical. English. wk. $339.00. Capitol Publications, 1101 King Street, Suite 444, Alexandria VA 22314. **Tel** (703)683-4100, (800)655-5597. **(Subscription address:** Capitol Publications, PO Box 1453, Alexandria, VA 22313**)** **ED** Bob Zuckerman. **[CCC].**
**Desc:** Timely and comprehensive record of all health related federal grants and contracts, plus profiles of key funding agencies, legislative and regulatory updates, conference calendars, etc.

US/0278-5323
**HEALTH GROUPS IN WASHINGTON : A DIRECTORY.** [Health groups Wash., dir.]. Began with: 3rd Ed. (1977). Directory. English. ir. $10.00 (nonmembers). National Health Council Inc, 350 Fifth Avenue/Room 1118, New York NY 10018. **Tel** (212)268-8900. **LC** PAR. **NLM** W 22 AD6 H434. ***Continues*** *Private Health Organizations' Government Relations Directory.*
**Desc:** Directory of national health organizations in the Greater Washington, DC area.

US/0278-4653
**HEALTH (GUILFORD, CONN.).** (HEALTH.). [Health]. **VFOAT** Annual Editions. Health. (1982)-. English. an. $12.95. Dushkin Publishing Group Inc., Sluice Dock, Guilford CT 06437. **Tel** (203)453-4351, (800)243-6532, FAX (203)453-6000. **ED** Richard Yarian. **LC** RA773; .A66. **DD** 613/.05. ***Continues*** *Readings in Health, 0360-9766.*
**Desc:** Presents a sampling of quality articles that represent current thinking on a variety of health issues, and serves as a tool for developing critical thinking skills.

NZ
**HEALTH IN NEW ZEALAND.** English. Health Magazine / New Zealand, PO Box 5013, Wellington New Zealand. **Tel** 736014. **LC** RA555; .H4. **DD** 614/.09931.

US/0148-7450
**HEALTH IN THE UNITED STATES.**
**Main/Corp** National Center for Health Statistics (U.S.). English. 5600 Fishers Lane, Rockville MD 20852. **LC** RA407.3; .U57B. **DD** 362.1/0973.

US/0146-2768
**HEALTH IN WISCONSIN.** V. 22-. Periodical. English. ir. Department of Health & Social Services / Wisconsin, 1 West Wilson Street, PO Box 309, Madison WI 53701. **LC** RA177. **DD** 362.1/09775. **NLM** W1 HE35K. ***Continues*** *Wisconsin's Health, 0043-6747.*

US
**HEALTH INDEX [COMPUTER FILE].** **See** Health and Personal Fitness-Abstracting, Bibliographies and Statistics.

KE
**HEALTH INFORMATION BULLETIN / HEALTH INFORMATION SYSTEM, MINISTRY OF HEALTH, GOVERNMENT OF KENYA.** Bulletin. English. Health Information System, PO Box 20781, Nairobi Kenya. **LC** RA407.5.K45; H4. **DD** 614.4/26762/021.

US
**HEALTH INFORMATION RESOURCES IN THE FEDERAL GOVERNMENT / PREPARED BY ODPHP NATIONAL HEALTH INFORMATION CENTER.**
**Added/Corp** ODPHP National Health Information Center (U.S.) United States. Office of Disease Prevention and Health Promotion. 4th Ed. (1987)-. English. ***Continues*** *National Health Information Clearinghouse (U.S.). Health Information Resources in the Federal Government.*

US/0017-9019
**HEALTH INSURANCE UNDERWRITER, THE.** **See** Insurance.

US/0884-0717
**HEALTH IS WEALTH.** [Health is wealth]. No. 1 (1986)-. Periodical. English. bm. $12.00. Christian Health Research Institute for Spiritual Truth, PO Box 888, Captain Cook HI 96704. **DD** 613.

US/0145-336X
**HEALTH ISSUES ON CAPITOL HILL.** Vol. 1 (Jan. 1976)-. English. mo. $19.00 US; $20.90 other. Health Issues on Capitol Hill, PO Box 2936, Washington DC 20013. **NLM** W1 HE373.

US/0549-804X
**HEALTH LAW BULLETIN.** **See** Law.

●US/1063-4061
**HEALTH LAW WEEK.** **See** Law.

US/0145-4129
**HEALTH LAWYERS NEWS REPORT.** **See** Law.

US
**HEALTH LETTER / AMERICAN HEALTH FOUNDATION.** **Added/Corp** American Health Foundation. Vol. 1, No. 1 (Jan./Feb. 1986)-. Periodical. English. bm. $15.00. American Health Foundation, 1 Dana Road, Valhalla NY 10595. **Tel** (914)592-2600, FAX (914)592-6317. **NLM** W1; HE4124G.
**Ind/Abst** SPORT Discus.

US/1078-2907
**HEALTH LETTER ON THE CDC.** (19??)-. English. wk (48 issues). $129.00 US, Canada and Mexico; $179.00 other. CW Henderson, PO Box 5528, Atlanta GA 30307-0528. **Tel** (404)377-8895, FAX (404)378-5411. **(Subscription address:** CW Henderson, Subscription Office, PO Box 830409, Birmingham AL 35283-0409.**)**
**Desc:** Concentrates on the accomplishments and contributions of the US Centers for Disease Control and Prevention. Reports first-hand on the CDC's front line involvement with epidemics and threats to public health.

US/0739-4217
**HEALTH LETTER (SAN ANTONIO, TEX.), THE.** ***Ceased.*** (THE HEALTH LETTER.). [Health lett.]. Vol. 1, No. 1 (1972)-(May 1994). Periodical. English. sm. North American Syndicate, 235 East 45th Street, New York NY 10017. **Tel** (714)751-9211. **(Subscription address:** Starr Fulfillment 900 Haddon Avenue 326, Collingswood NJ 08108 (800) 443-8199**)** **ED** Michael Woyton (editors telephone (212) 455-4168. **DD** 614. **Circ:** 11,000 (ctrl).
**Ind/Abst** Health Period. Database; SportSearch; Mag. Index.

US/0740-7262
**HEALTH LITERATURE REVIEW.** (HEALTH LITERATURE REVIEW : HLR.). [Health lit. rev.]. **VFOAT** HLR. Vol. 1, No. 1 (1983)-. Periodical. English. Eight times a year. $280.00. True to Form Press, PO Box 308, Wenham MA 01904. **NLM** ZWB 100; H433.

US/0894-4679
**HEALTH MANAGER'S UPDATE.** ***Title Change.*** [Health manager's update]. **Added/Corp** McGraw-Hill's Healthcare Information Center. **VFOAT** McGraw-Hill's Health Managers's Update. Vol. 1, No. 1 (June 17, 1987)-(1993). Periodical. English. bw. McGraw Hill Healthcare Information Center, 1120 Vermont Avenue NW/Suite 1200, Washington DC 20005. **Tel** (202)686-7900. **DD** 362. **NLM** W1; HE413QJ. available on an online database (file 636/Full-Text) from DIALOG. ***Continues*** *Medicare Medicaid Information, 0193-2152.* ***Continued by*** *Managed Care Update.*

US/0735-9683
**HEALTH MARKETING QUARTERLY.** **See** Medical Science and Technology.

NZ
**HEALTH (NEW ZEALAND).** (HEALTH.). **Added/Corp** New Zealand. Dept. of Health. (19??)-. Periodical. English. Four times a year. Free. Health Magazine / New Zealand, PO Box 5013, Wellington New Zealand. **Tel** 736014. **NLM** W1 HE181.

US/1065-1810
**HEALTH NEWS DIGEST (MARLBOROUGH, MASS.).** ***Ceased.*** (HEALTH NEWS DIGEST.). (1992)-(199?). Periodical. English. mo. B.E.A. Inc., 102 Pleasant Hill Road, Marlborough MA 07152.

US/0899-4137
**HEALTH OF AMERICA'S CHILDREN, THE.** [Health Am. child.]. English. an. $9.95 (plus postage). Children's Defense Fund, 122 C Street NW, Washington DC 20001. **Tel** (202)628-8787. **ED** Kay Johnson and Sara Rosenbaum. **LC** RJ102; .H43. **DD** 362.1/9892/000973.
**Desc:** Analysis of the current status of maternal and infant health, including: national, state, and large city infant mortality rates, low-birthweight rates, American women's access to prenatal care, child bearing among teenagers and unmarried women, and the nation's progress on reaching the Surgeon General's objectives for maternal and infant health.

US/0276-606X
**HEALTH OF KANSANS CHART BOOK, THE.** Began with Vol. for 1978. English. an. Free. Research and Analysis Section / Health, Department of Health and Environment, Bureau of Registration and Health Statistics, Topeka KS 66620. **LC** RA407.4 .K3; H4. **DD** 362.1/09781.
**Desc:** The chart book is divided into four sections-Health status, Life style, Environment, and Health systems.

NZ/0301-0384
**HEALTH OF THE PEOPLE, THE.** [Health people]. (1972)-. Periodical. English. ***Formed by the union of*** *Occupational Health. New Zealand, 0048-1378* ***and*** *Community Health (Auckland, N.Z.).*
**Ind/Abst** Health Plan. Adminis.

US/0017-9051
**HEALTH/PAC BULLETIN.** [Health/PAC bull.]. **Main/Corp** Health/PAC. **VFOAT** Health PAC Bulletin. **VAT** Health/Policy Advisory Center Bulletin. (June 1968)-. Bulletin. English. qt. $35.00 individual; $45.00 institution. Health Policy Advisory Center, 853 Broadway, Suite 1607, New York NY 10007. **Tel** (212)614-1660. **ED** Nancy McKenzie, Ellen Bilofsky, Rod Sorge. **LC** RA418; .H394A. **DD** 362.1/0973/05. **NLM** W1 HE468. **[CCC].** Index available. cum. index. **Bk Rev. Ad Acc. Circ:** 1300 (ctrl). available on microfilm and microfiche from University Microfilms International (UMI).
**Desc:** The bulletin analyzes health policy and its effect on all United States residents toward the goal of affordable, appropriate, quality health care for everyone.
**Ind/Abst** Altern. Press Index; Health Plan. Adminis.; Hospit. Health Admin. Index; PAIS Int. Print (1991-?); Sage Race Relat. Abstr.

US/0164-7598
**HEALTH PATHWAYS.** **Added/Corp** Health Professions Career Opportunity Program (Calif.). (197?)-. Periodical. English. Ten times a year. Free. Sierra Health Foundation, 11211 Gold Country Boulevard, Suite 101, Rancho Cordova CA 95670.
**Ind/Abst** Chicano Index.

US
**HEALTH PERIODICALS DATABASE [ONLINE DATABASE].** **See** Health and Personal Fitness-Abstracting, Bibliographies and Statistics.

CN/0837-7251
**HEALTH PERSONNEL IN CANADA.** [Health pers. Can.]. **VFOAT** Le Personnel de la Sante au Canada. 1986-. English (French). an. Health and Welfare Canada, Headquarters Brooke Claxton Building, Ottawa Ontario K1A 0K9 Canada. **DD** 610.69/0971/021. ***Continues*** *Canada Health Manpower Inventory, 0381-2561.*

UK/0268-1080
**HEALTH POLICY AND PLANNING.** [Health policy plan.]. **Added/Corp** London School of Hygiene and Tropical Medicine. Vol. 1, No. 1 (March 1986)-. Periodical. English. qt. £95.00 UK and Europe; $170.00 other. Oxford University Press, Walton Street, Oxford OX2 6DP England. **Tel** 011 44 865 56767, FAX 011 44 865 267773, telex 837330 OXPRES G. **(Subscription address:** Oxford University Press / USA, Journals Marketing Department, Oxford University Press, 2001 Evans Road, Cary NC 27513.**)** **ED** P. Vaughan and G. Walt. **LC** RA441.5; .H46. **DD** 362.1/09172/4. **NLM** W1; HE474G. **[CCC]. Bk Rev. Ad Acc. Pr Rev. Circ:** 500. available on microfilm and microfiche from University Microfilms International (UMI). Documents available from The Genuine Article.
**Desc:** Concerned with issues in health policy planning, management and evaluation, particularly in the developing world.
**Ind/Abst** Appl. Soc. Sci. Index Abstr.; Curr. Contents Soc. Behav. Sci.; Dairy Sci. Abstr.; EMBASE; Health Plan. Adminis.; Hospit. Health Admin. Index (1986-); Int. Bibliogr. Sociol.; Nutr. Abstr. Rev., Ser. A, Hum. Exp.; PAIS Int. Print; Protozoolog. Abstr.; Res. Alert [Full Cov.]; Rural Dev. Abstr.; Soc. Plann. Policy Dev. Abstr.; Soc. Sci. Cit. Index [Full Cov.]; Trop. Dis. Bull.

US/1056-2389
**HEALTH POLICY ANNUAL.** [Health policy annu.]. **Added/Corp** Association of Academic Health Centers (U.S.). (1991)-. English. Association of Academic Health Centers, 1400 16th Street Northwest, Suite 410, Washington DC 20036. **Tel** (202)265-9600, FAX (202)265-7514. **DD** 362. **NLM** W1; HE474L.

US/0733-9143
**HEALTH POLICY (NEW YORK, N.Y.).** (HEALTH POLICY.). [Health policy]. Vol. 1 (1981)-. Monographic series. English. ir. Price varies per volume. Marcel Dekker Inc., 270 Madison Avenue, New York NY 10016. **Tel** (212)696-9000, (800)228-1160, FAX (212)685-4540, telex 421419. **(Subscription address:** Marcel Dekker Inc, PO Box 5017, Monticello NY 12701.**)** **LC** UNC. **NLM** W1 HE473S. Documents available from The Genuine Article.
**Desc:** Explores issues and presents information relevant in health care and health care systems.
**Ind/Abst** Appl. Soc. Sci. Index Abstr.; Curr. Contents Soc. Behav. Sci.; Res. Alert [Full Cov.]; Soc. Sci. Cit. Index [Full Cov.].

US/0732-7439
**HEALTH POLICY WEEK.** ***Title Change.*** (HEALTH POLICY WEEK : HPW.). **VFOAT** HPW; H.P.W. (1982)-(1992). Periodical. English. Forty-eight times a year. United Communications Group, 11300 Rockville Pike, Suite 1100, Rockville MD 20852. **Tel** (301)816-8950 ext. 223, FAX (301)816-8945. **ED** Burt Schorr. **NLM** W1; HE475H. ***Continues*** *Morris Report on Federal Health Policy, 0277-3902.* ***Continued by*** *Health Care Reform Week, 1067-2214.*
**Desc:** Probes the plans of Washington and state policymakers each week, telling health care executives how key trends and events in health care financing and regulation will make them or cost them money. Gives in-depth guidance and proven tactics for making the right strategic planning decisions and boosting institutional

profit lines.
**Ind/Abst** Health Plan. Adminis.; Hospit. Health Admin. Index (1989-).

●CN/1195-6747
**HEALTH PROMOTION IN CANADA.**
**Added/Corp** Canada. Health Promotion Directorate. Vol. 32, No. 1 (Summer/Fall 1993)-. Periodical. English. Four times a year. Free. Health Services & Promotion Branch, Health Promotion Directorate, Ottawa Ontario K1A 1BA Canada. **Tel** (613)954-8842. **DD** 613/.07/071. ***Continues*** *Health Promotion (Ottawa, Ont.), 0833-7594.*
**Ind/Abst** Can. Educ. Index; Can. Period. Index.

UK/0957-4824
**HEALTH PROMOTION INTERNATIONAL.** **Added/Corp** World Health Organization. Vol. 5, No. 1 (1990)-. Periodical. English. qt. £95.00 UK and Europe; $170.00 other. Oxford University Press, Walton Street, Oxford OX2 6DP England. **Tel** 011 44 865 56767, FAX 011 44 865 267773, telex 837330 OXPRES G. **(Subscription address:** Oxford University Press / USA, Journals Marketing Department, Oxford University Press, 2001 Evans Road, Cary NC 27513.**) ED** J. Catford. **LC** RA427.8; .H49. **DD** 362.1/05. **NLM** W1; HE487P. **CODEN** HPINET. **[CCC].** Index available. **Bk Rev. Ad Acc. Pr Rev. Circ:** 750. available on microfilm and microfiche from University Microfilms International (UMI). ***Continues*** *Health Promotion (Oxford, England), 0268-1099.*
**Desc:** An international journal of health research in all areas of health promotion/ primary care, publishing both clinical and theoretical papers.
**Ind/Abst** EMBASE; Soc. Plann. Policy Dev. Abstr.; Trop. Dis. Bull.

US/0882-0252
**HEALTH PROMOTION NEWSLETTER.**
[Health promot. newsl.]. V. 1, No. 1-. Newsletter. English. mo. $18.00. Health Promotion Publications, 2952 Mesquite Drive, Riverside CA 92503. **DD** 613. available on microfilm and microfiche from University Microfilms International (UMI).

CN/0833-7594
**HEALTH PROMOTION (OTTAWA).** ***Title Change.*** (HEALTH PROMOTION.). [Health promot.]. **Added/Corp** Canada. Health Promotion Directorate. Vol. 24, No. 2 (Fall 1985)-Vol. 31, no. 3/4 (Spring 1993). Periodical. English. qt. Health Services & Promotion Branch, Health Promotion Directorate, Ottawa Ontario K1A 1BA Canada. **Tel** (613)954-8842. **LC** RA440.3.C2; H4. **DD** 613/.07/1071. ***Continues*** *Health Education (Ottawa, Ont.), 0017-8950.* ***Continued by*** *Health Promotion in Canada (Ottawa, Ont.), 1195-6747.*
**Ind/Abst** Can. Period. Index (19??-).

●US/1060-5517
**HEALTH PROMOTION PRACTITIONER.**
(HEALTH PROMOTION PRACTITIONER: PRACTICAL SOLUTIONS FOR HEALTH ENHANCEMENT PROGRAMMING.). [Health promot. pract.]. **Added/Corp** Health Enhancement Services. Vol. 1, No. 1 (Apr. 1992)-. Periodical. English. mo. $79.00 US; $89.00 Canada. Health Enhancement Services, 802 East Ashman, Midland MI 48640. **Tel** 800 326-2317, FAX (517)839-0025. **ED** Dean Witherspoon. **DD** 362. **NLM** W1; HE487R. Index available. **Bk Rev**, (Qty: 12). **Pr Rev. Circ:** 1,800 (ctrl).
**Desc:** A monthly "how-to" newsletter for individuals and organizations responsible for worksite health promotion. This monthly idea source provides practical, insightful, useable information that can be applied to any organization interested in improving the health and productivity of its workforce.

CN/1188-6250
**HEALTH QUEST.** [Health quest]. **Added/Corp** Memorial University of Newfoundland. Faculty of Medicine. Vol. 1, No. 1 (Oct. 1991)-. Periodical. English. qt. Limited free distribution. Memorial University of Newfoundland / Health Sciences Centre, c/o R. B. Fredericksen, St John's Newfoundland A1B 3W6 Canada. **DD** 610.

CN/0840-6529
**HEALTH REPORTS / RAPPORT SUR LA SANTE / STATISTIQUE CANADA, DIVISION DE LA SANTE. STATISTICS CANADA, HEALTH DIVISION.** **Added/Corp** Statistics Canada. Health Division. **VFOAT** Rapport sur la Sante. (Mar. 1988)-. Periodical. English (French). qt. 112.00Can$ Canada; $135.00 US; $157.00 other. Statistics Canada, Publications Sales & Services, Main Building Room 1710, Ottawa Ontario K1A 0T6 Canada. **Tel** (613)951-5078, (800)267-6677, FAX (613)951-1584, telex 053-3585.
**Ind/Abst** Health Plan. Adminis.; Popul. Index.

CN/1180-3096
**HEALTH REPORTS. SUPPLEMENT. DEATHS.** **See** Public Health and Safety-Abstracting, Bibliographies and Statistics.

US/0161-6765
**HEALTH, SAFETY & EDUCATION.** **VAT** Health, Safety and Education. (Jan. 1977)-. English. Twelve times a year. $240.75 Ohio (includes 7% tax); $225.00 others. Predicasts Inc., A Ziff Communications Company, 11001 Cedar Avenue, Cleveland OH 44106. **Tel** (800)321-6388, (216)795-3000, FAX (216)229-9944, telex 985 604. **(Subscription address:** Information Access Company, PO Box 61000, Department 1851, San Francisco, CA 94161; Phone: (800)321-6388**) NLM** ZW 1 M4894. ***Continues*** *Health & Education, 0361-9885.*

UK
**HEALTH, SAFETY AND ENVIRONMENT BULLETIN.** (19??)-. Bulletin. English. mo. £190.00 UK; £208.00 other. Eclipse Publications Ltd, 18 20 Highbury Place, London N5 1QP England. **Tel** 011 44 71 354 5858. **(Subscription address:** Industrial Relations Services, 18 20 Highbury Place, London N5 1QP England.**)** ***Continues*** *Health and Safety Bulletin, 0142-9086.*

●US/1059-938X
**HEALTH (SAN FRANCISCO, CALIF.).**
(HEALTH.). [Health]. Vol. 6, No. 1 (Feb./Mar. 1992)-. Periodical. English. Seven times a year. $18.00. Hippocrates Inc., 301 Howard Street, 18th Floor, San Francisco CA 94105. **Tel** (415)512-9100, (800)274-2522. **(Subscription address:** Neodata / Colorado, PO Box 2606, Boulder Boulder CO 80322.**) LC** RA773; .H254. **DD** 613. **NLM** W1; HE178. Documents available from UMI Article Clearinghouse. ***Formed by the union of*** *In Health, 0279-3547* ***and*** *Health (Family Media, Inc.), 1047-0549.*
**Ind/Abst** Acad. Abstr. (Jan. 1992-); Acad. Search (Jan. 1992-); Gen. Period. Index (1992-); Gen. Sci. Index (1992-); Health Period. Database [Full Txt.]; Health Source (Jan. 1992-); Mag. Artic. Summar. Elite (Jan. 1992-); Mag. ASAP Plus; Mag. Index Plus (1992-); Mag. Index. Sel. (?-?); Newsp. Period. Abstr. (1989-); TOM Gen. Index (1992-) [Full Txt.].

US/0883-8216
**HEALTH SCIENCE (1985).** (HEALTH SCIENCE.). [Health sci.]. **Added/Corp** American Natural Hygiene Society. Vol. 8, No. 3 (May/June 1985)-. Periodical. English. bm (6 issues). Comes as part of American Natural Hygiene Society membership. American Natural Hygiene Society, PO Box 30630, Tampa FL 33630. **Tel** (813)855-6607. **ED** James Michael Lennon. **DD** 613. **Bk Rev. Ad Acc. Circ:** 4,500 (ctrl). ***Continues*** *Vegetarian Health Science, 8750-1643.*
**Desc:** Covers the subject of natural hygiene, living in harmony with nature.

US/0278-7318
**HEALTH SCIENCES AUDIOVISUALS.**
***Ceased.*** (HEALTH SCIENCES AUDIOVISUALS MICROFORM.). [Health sci. audiov.]. **Main/Corp** National Library of Medicine (U.S.). (Fall 1983)-Ceased (Dec. 1988). English. qt. National Library of Medicine, 8600 Rockville Pike, Bethesda MD 20894. **Tel** (301)496-6308. **DD** 610. **NLM** W 18 N28015h (P).
**Desc:** Contains citations to all audiovisuals cataloged by the National Library of Medicine from 1975 through December 1988, except cataloging-in-publication titles and titles which have been withdrawn from NLM's collection.

US/0731-5945
**HEALTH SCIENCES VIDEOLOG, THE.**
[Health sci. videolog]. (1981)-. Periodical. English. $49.50. Norton Publishers Inc., 145 East 49th Street, New York NY 10017. **NLM** WA 18 V652. ***Continues*** *Videolog, Programs for the Health Sciences, 0195-7295.*

UK/0952-2271
**HEALTH SERVICE JOURNAL, THE.**
[Health serv. j.]. Vol. 96 No. 4989 (Mar. 6, 1986)-. Periodical. English. wk (Thursday). £69.50 UK; $160.00 US & Canada; £169.00 other. Macmillan Magazines Ltd., Houndmills, Basingstoke, Hampshire RG21 2XS England. **Tel** 011 44 256 29242, FAX 011 44 256 812358, telex 858493. **ED** Rob MacLachlan. **LC** RA427; .H65. **DD** 362.1/068. **NLM** W1; HE54W. **CODEN** HSJOEO. **[CCC].** Index available. **Bk Rev. Ad Acc. Circ:** 11,752. available on microfilm and microfiche from University Microfilms International (UMI). Documents available from Ask*IEEE. ***Continues*** *Health and Social Service Journal, 0300-8347.*
**Desc:** Management of service delivering health care to the public.
**Ind/Abst** Appl. Soc. Sci. Index Abstr.; Health Serv. Abstr.; Hospit. Health Admin. Index (1986-); Infomat Int. Bus.; INSPEC (1986); Sage Race Relat. Abstr.; Trop. Dis. Bull.

US/0160-4961
**HEALTH SERVICES ADMINISTRATION EDUCATION.** **Added/Corp** Association of University Programs in Health Administration. (1979)-. English. be. $20.45 US; $23.95 North and South America; $26.95 Europe; $29.95 other. Association of University Programs in Health Administration, 1911 North Fort Myer Drive, Suite 503, Arlington VA 22209. **Tel** (703)524-5500, FAX (703)525-4791. **ED** Gary L Filerman and Donna Royston. **LC** RA440.7.U6; H43. **DD** 362.1/068. **NLM** W 22.1 H434. **Circ:** 1,500 (ctrl).
**Desc:** A descriptive directory of college programs in health administration at the bachelor's, master's and doctoral level.
**Ind/Abst** Hospit. Health Admin. Index.

XR
**HEALTH SERVICES IN CZECHOSLOVAKIA.** English. Institute for Health Information and Statistics, Prague 10 Vinohrady, T R W Piecka 98 Czech Republic. **LC** RA407.5.C95; H4. **DD** 362.1/09437.

UK/1011-5153
**HEALTH SERVICES INTERNATIONAL.**
[Health serv. int.]. **VFOAT** Services de Sante dans le Monde; Servicios de Salud en el Mundo. (1988)-. Periodical. English (French and Spanish). qt. £26.00. International Hospital Federation, 4 Abbots Place, London NW6 4NP England. **Tel** 011 44 71 372-7181, FAX 011 44 71 328-7433. **ED** Errol Pickering. **Bk Rev. Ad Acc. Circ:** 2,000 (ctrl).
**Desc:** Consists of summaries of health care trends worldwide, reforms in national health systems, innovations and developments in management. Features a lead article on a current topic, news of IHF events, short reviews, biographical profiles and conference dates. Aim is to provide practising managers and other health professionals with information that is both quick and easy to read.

●US/1063-9810
**HEALTH SOURCE (PEABODY, MASS.).**
**See** Health and Personal Fitness-Abstracting, Bibliographies and Statistics.

US/0737-7568
**HEALTH SPECTRUM.** [Health spectr.]. Vol. 1, No. 1 (Summer 1983)-. Periodical. English. qt. McKesson Corporation, 1 Post Street/Suite 3275, San Francisco CA 94104. ***Continues*** *Professional Nutritionist, 0033-0159.*
**Ind/Abst** AGRICOLA.

US
**HEALTH SYSTEMS AGENCIES, STATE HEALTH PLANNING AND DEVELOPMENT AGENCIES, AND STATEWIDE HEALTH COORDINATING COUNCILS.** Feb. 1, 1979-. English. ir. Bureau of Health Planning Information Office, Room 6-22/Center Building, 3700 East-West Highway, Hyattsville MD 20782. **NLM** WA 22; AA1 D7. ***Continues*** *Directory, Health Systems Agencies, State Health Planning and Development Agencies, Statewide Health Coordinating Councils, 0273-3943.*

US/0892-7677
**HEALTH SYSTEMS PLAN (HOUSTON, TEX.).** **See** Law.

US
**HEALTH TIPS.** English. five issues per month. Must order direct. California Medical Association, PO Box 7690, San Francisco CA 94120-5179. **Tel** (415)541-0900, FAX (415)882-5116. available on an online database (file 149/Full-Text) from DIALOG.
**Ind/Abst** Acad. Abstr. Full Text Elite (Jan. 1992-); Acad. Abstr. (Jan. 1992-); Acad. Search (Jan. 1992-); Consum. Health Nutr. Index; Health Index (1989-); Health Period. Database [Full Txt.]; Health Ref. Cent. (Jan. 1989-) [Full Txt.] [Full Cov.]; Health Source (Jan. 1992-); Mag. Search.

●AT/1036-4005
**HEALTH TRANSITION REVIEW : THE CULTURAL, SOCIAL, AND BEHAVIOURAL DETERMINANTS OF HEALTH.** **Added/Corp** Health Transition Centre. Vol. 1, No. 1 (Apr. 1991)-. Periodical. English. Twice a year (Apr., Oct.). Free. Health Transition Centre, NCEPH Australia National University, GPO Box 4, Canberra ACT 2601 Australia. **Tel** 011 61 6 2495626, FAX 011 61 6 2490740. **NLM** W1; HE5995H.
**Ind/Abst** Popul. Index.

UK/0017-9132
**HEALTH TRENDS.** [Health trends]. **Added/Corp** Great Britain. Dept. of Health and Social Security. Great Britain. Welsh Office. (19??)-. Periodical. English. qt. £11.90. Her Majesty's Stationery Office, 51 Nine Elms Lane, London SW8 5DR England. **Tel** 011 44 71 873 8459, 011 44 71 873 8499, FAX 011 44 71 873 8499, 011 44 71 873 8456, telex 297138. **(Subscription address:** Her Majestys Stationery Offic, PO Box 276 Public Centre, London SW8 5DT England**) ED** J L Hunt. **LC** RA485; .H37. **DD** 362.1/0941. **NLM** W1 HE5996. **CODEN** HETBAT. **Circ:** 72,000. Documents available from BIOSIS Document Express. ***Continues*** *Monthly Bulletin of the Ministry of Health & The Public Health Laboratory Service.*
**Desc:** A review for the medical profession on subjects relevant to the management of the British national health service including statistics and epidemiological studies.
**Ind/Abst** Appl. Soc. Sci. Index Abstr.; Biol. Abstr.; Dev. Med. Child Neurol.; EMBASE; Health Plan. Adminis.; Hospit. Health Admin. Index; Trop. Dis. Bull.

US/0361-4468
**HEALTH, UNITED STATES.** **Added/Corp** National Center for Health Statistics (U.S.) National Center for Health Services Research. **VFOAT** Health, United States ... with Prevention Profile; Health, United

States ... and Prevention Profile. 1st Report, (1975)-. Government Publication. English. an. Superintendent of Documents, US Government Printing Office, Washington DC 20402. **Tel** (202)275-3328, FAX (202)786-2377. **LC** RA407.3; .U57a. **DD** 362.1/0973. **NLM** W2 A N1479H.
**Ind/Abst** AGRICOLA; Predicasts Forecasts.

US/0147-0353
**HEALTH VALUES.** [Health values]. Vol. 1 (Jan./Feb. 1977)-. Periodical. English. bm. $55.00 (one year), $90.00 (two year), $125.00 (three year) individual; $80.00 (one year), $125.00 (two year), $165.00 (three year) institutional; $10.00 (mail charge for Canada), $30.00 (foreign mail charge). PNG Publications, PO Box 4593, Star City WV 26504-4593. **Tel** (304)293-4699, FAX (304)293-4693. **ED** Elbert D Glover. **LC** RA421; .H4184. **DD** 613/.05. **NLM** W1 HE602. Index available. **Bk Rev**, (Qty: 18 /yr). **Ad Acc**, **Adv Mgr:** P Glover. **Circ:** 2,000 (ctrl). available on microfilm and microfiche from University Microfilms International (UMI).
**Desc:** Articles concerning and supporting the ideas and philosophies of high level wellness.
**Ind/Abst** AGRICOLA; Consum. Health Nutr. Index (?-?); Cumul. Index Nurs. Allied Health Lit.; Curr. Index J. Educ.; Health Plan. Adminis.; Hospit. Health Admin. Index; Hum. Resour. Abstr. (?-?); Nutr. Res. Newsl.; Phys. Educ. Index; Psychoanal. Abstr.; Psychol. Abstr. (1990-); PsycINFO; PsycLit; PsycScan: Appl. Exp. Eng. Psych.; PsycScan: LD/MR; PsycScan: Neuropsych.; Sage Fam. Stud. Abstr.; Soc. Plann. Policy Dev. Abstr.

●CN/1189-475X
**HEALTH VISION.** [Health vis.]. **Main/Corp** Alberta. Alberta Health. Vol. 1, Issue 1 (Apr. 1992)-. Periodical. English. **DD** 362.1.

UK/0017-9140
**HEALTH VISITOR : THE JOURNAL OF THE HEALTH VISITORS' ASSOCIATION.** **See** Medical Science and Technology-Nursing.

US/1051-9726
**HEALTH WATCH (LOUISVILLE, KY.).** (HEALTH WATCH.). [Health watch]. **VFOAT** Health Watch. (Apr. 1991)-. Periodical. English. Six times a year. $14.95. Health Watch Magazine, 455 South 4th Avenue, Suite 1515, Louisville KY 40202. **Tel** (502)589-2824. **ED** Mollie Vento. **DD** 613. **Ad Acc.**
**Desc:** The magazine for health and money conscious consumers. Shows how to receive better health care, understand procedures and how to save money.

CN/0845-8251
**HEALTH WATCH (TORONTO).** (HEALTH WATCH.). [Health watch]. Vol. 1, No. 1 (May/June 1989)-. Periodical. English. Four times a year. 12.95Can$. Telemedia Publishing Inc., 555 West 12th Avenue, Suite 300, North York Ontario V5Z 4L4 Canada. **Tel** (604)877-7732. **(Subscription address:** Indas, 35 Riviera Drive, Building 17, Markham ONT L3R 8N4 Canada**)** **DD** 613/.05.

US/0888-7330
**HEALTH WORLD.** [Health world]. Vol. 1, No. 1 (Fall 1986)-. Periodical. English. Six times a year. $12.00 US; $35.00 others. Health World, 1675 Rollins Road, Suite B 3, Burlingame CA 94010. **Tel** (415)697-8038, FAX (415)697-7937. **ED** Abhay Kumar Pati, Monica Valerio and Jeff Kravitz. **DD** 613. Index available. cum. index. **Bk Rev**. **Ad Acc. Circ:** 70,000 (ctrl). ***Continues** Holistic Health, 0882-8148.*
**Desc:** An educational journal dealing with vitamins, minerals, natural therapy, and new approaches to the treatment of many problematic diseases, such as candida, AIDS, hepatitis, and cancer.
**Ind/Abst** Consum. Health Nutr. Index (?-?).

US/0895-108X
**HEALTHACTION MANAGERS.** ***Ceased.*** [HealthAction managers]. **VFOAT** Health Action Managers. (Sept. 1987)-Ceased (Oct. 1991). Periodical. English. sm. Kelly Communications / Charlottesville, 410 East Water Street, Suite 500, Charlottesville VA 22901. **DD** 362.

US/8756-4513
**HEALTHCARE ADVERTISING REVIEW.** **See** Business-Advertising and Public Relations.

US/1055-5250
**HEALTHCARE ENVIRONMENTAL MANAGEMENT SYSTEM.** (1991)-. Periodical. English. mo. $695.00. ECRI Emergency Care Research Institute, 5200 Butler Pike, Plymouth Meeting PA 19462. **Tel** (215)825-6000, FAX (215)834-1275, telex 510-660-8023.

US/1050-575X
**HEALTHCARE HAZARDOUS MATERIALS MANAGEMENT.** (HEALTHCARE HAZARDOUS MATERIALS MANAGEMENT : HHMM.). [Healthc. hazard. mater. manage.]. **Added/Corp** ECRI (Organization). **VFOAT** HHMM. Vol. 3, No. 10 (July 1990)-. Periodical. English. Twelve times a year. $225.00. ECRI Emergency Care Research Institute, 5200 Butler Pike, Plymouth Meeting PA 19462. **Tel** (215)825-6000, FAX (215)834-1275, telex 510-660-8023. **DD** 363. **NLM** W1; HE608RCC. **[CCC]. Pr Rev.** ctrl circ. ***Continues** Hospital Hazardous Materials Management, 0895-7169.*
**Desc:** Occupational health and safety and environmental compliance in healthcare facilities.
**Ind/Abst** Hospit. Health Admin. Index (1990-).

US/1058-028X
**HEALTHCARE ISSUES & TRENDS.** [Healthc. issues trends]. **VFOAT** Healthcare Issues and Trends. Vol. 1, No. 1 (Fall 1991)-. Periodical. English. qt. $450.00. Scott-Levin Associates, 60 Blacksmith Road, Newtown PA 18940. **Tel** (215)860-0440, FAX (215)860-5477. **DD** 362. ***Continues** Managed Healthcare, Issues and Trends, 1040-0176.*

US/8755-9153
**HEALTHCARE MARKET RESEARCH, REPORTS, STUDIES, & SURVEYS. VFOAT** Health Care Market Research, Reports, Studies, & Surveys; Healthcare Market Research. English. an. Find/SVP, 625 Avenue of Americas, New York NY 10011. **Tel** (212)645-4500. **LC** HD9994.A1; H43. **DD** 380.1/45681761/05.

US/0891-5016
**HEALTHCARE MARKETING ABSTRACTS.** **See** Business-Marketing.

US
**HEALTHCARE SYSTEMS STRATEGY REPORT.** (19??)-. Periodical. English. sm. $438.00. Capitol Publications, 1101 King Street, Suite 444, Alexandria VA 22314. **Tel** (703)683-4100, (800)655-5597. **(Subscription address:** Capitol Publications, PO Box 1453, Alexandria VA 22313.**)** **ED** Terry Rudd. ***Continues** Health Care Competition Week, 0886-2095.*

US/8756-453X
**HEALTHLINES (ANN ARBOR, MICH.).** (HEALTHLINES / FITNESS RESEARCH CENTER, THE UNIVERSITY OF MICHIGAN.). [Healthlines]. **Added/Corp** University of Michigan. Fitness Research Center. **VFOAT** Health Lines. (198?)-. Periodical. English. mo. $15.00. Fitness Research Center, 401 Washtenaw Avenue, University of Michigan, Ann Arbor MI 48109. **Tel** (313)763-2462. **ED** Marilyn P. Edington. **DD** 613. **Bk Rev**, (Qty: 12). **Circ:** 15,000.
**Desc:** A newsletter that focuses on self-responsibility and preventive health behavior as vital components of a healthy lifestyle.

US/1048-5562
**HEALTHLINES (WACO, TEX.).** (HEALTHLINES.). [Healthlines]. (19??)-. Periodical. English. mo. $24.00 (one year), $42.00 (two year). Scott Publishing, 420 5th Avenue South, Suite D, Edmonds WA 98020. **Tel** (206)775-8777, (800)888-7853, FAX (206)775-8250. **ED** Diane McReynolds. **DD** 613. **Bk Rev**, (Qty: 5). **Circ:** 3 million (ctrl).

US/0745-4538
**HEALTHMARKETING.** ***Title Change.*** [HealthMarketing]. **VFOAT** Health Marketing. Vol. 1, Issue No. 1 (Nov.-Dec. 1982)-(19??). Periodical. English. bm. Mages Publishing Company, PO Box 381453, Germantown TN 38183. **Tel** (901)755-0776. **NLM** W1; HE614H. **CODEN** HEAMEB. ***Continues** Hospital Management Communications, 0274-5429. **Continued by** HealthService Leader, 1070-0978.*
**Ind/Abst** Hospit. Health Admin. Index.

●US/1070-0978
**HEALTHSERVICE LEADER, THE.** [HealthServ. lead.]. **VFOAT** Health Service Leader. (June 1993)-. Periodical. English. Four times a year. $97.00. Mages Publishing Company, PO Box 381453, Germantown TN 38183. **Tel** (901)755-0776. **DD** 338. **NLM** W1; HE615J. ***Continues** HealthMarketing, 0745-4538.*

CN/0226-1510
**HEALTHSHARING.** ***Ceased.*** [Healthsharing]. **Added/Corp** Chinese Library Association. Vol. 1 (Nov. 1979)-Vol. 14, No. 2 (Dec. 1993). Periodical. English (summaries and/or abstracts in French). qt. Women Healthsharing, 14 Skey Lane, Toronto Ontario M6J 3S4, Canada. **Tel** (416)532-0812, FAX (416)588-6638. **ED** Hazelle Palmer. **DD** 613/.04244/05. **Bk Rev**, (Qty: 4-6). **Ad Acc**, **Adv Mgr:** Lisa Huncar, **Tel** (416)532-0812. **Circ:** 5,000.
**Desc:** Canadian magazine for vital information on women's physical, mental and social health, from a feminist perspective. Provides current information, practical advice and insights on a wide range of health concerns as they affect women: sexuality, reproductive health, nutrition, the environment, violence, occupational health and safety, and more. Each issue includes news, letters, reviews and resources.
**Ind/Abst** Altern. Press Index; Can. Index; Can. Period. Index; Stud. Women Abstr.

US/0890-2259
**HEALTHWEEK.** ***Ceased.*** [HealthWeek]. **VFOAT** Health Week. (1987)-(Jan. 1992). Periodical. English. bw. Hutchins & Associates, 1865 East Valley Parkway/Suite 206, Escondido CA 92027. **NLM** W1; HE619B. **CODEN** HEAWE7. **[CCC].** available on an online database (file 16/Full-Text) from DIALOG.
**Desc:** The newspaper for America's health industry.
**Ind/Abst** BioBusiness; F&S Index Plus Text, Int. [Full Txt.] [Select. Cov.]; Health Devices Alerts; Hospit. Manage. Rev. (19??-1992); Int. Pharm. Abstr.; PROMT [Full Txt.].

UK/0955-5358
**HEALTHY CITIES.** [Heal. cities]. (1988)-. Periodical. English. Four times a year (Mar., June, Sept., Dec.). £12.00 UK; £16.00 other. University of Liverpool / Department of Public Health, PO Box 147, Liverpool L69 3BX England. **Tel** 011 44 51 7945581, FAX 011 44 51 7945588. **(Subscription address:** John Aston, University of Liverpool, PO Box 147, Department of Public Health, Liverpool L69 3BX England**)** **ED** Dr. Nigel Bruce. **DD** 613.0941. **Circ:** 300.

CN/1183-4331
**HEALTHY EXCHANGE (OTTAWA).** (HEALTHY EXCHANGE.). [Healthy exch.]. **Added/Corp** CUSO. Health Support Service. **VFOAT** Echo Sante. Vol. 1, No. 1 (Apr. 1991)-. Periodical. English (French). ir. Limited free distribution. Cuso Forum, 135 Rideau Street, Ottawa Ontario K1N 9K7 Canada. **Tel** (613)563-1242. **DD** 362.1.

CN/1191-0054
**HEALTHY INTERCHANGE.** (A HEALTHY INTERCHANGE / WELLNESS CONNECTION.). [Healthy interchange]. **Main/Corp** Sask Tel. Wellness Connection. (198?)-. Periodical. English. sa. **DD** 613.6.

US/0884-2094
**HEALTHY PEOPLE.** [Heal. people]. Vol. 1, No. 1-. Periodical. English. mo. $18.00. Health Management Communications, Harwood Building/Room 319, Scarsdale NY 10583. **Tel** (914)681-1373. **ED** Gilbeart H Collings. **DD** 614. **Pr Rev.**
**Desc:** Articles on general health and health care utilization for consumers, including nutrition, fitness, stress, self-care, sleep, mental health, personal health management, work and health. Deals with the health care system, alcohol and substance abuse, evaluating health information, and safety.

●US/1075-0169
**HEALTHY WEIGHT JOURNAL.** **See** Nutrition and Dietetics.

US/0897-5949
**HEART HEALTH DIGEST.** ***Ceased.*** [Heart health dig.]. (Summer 1988)-Ceased ?. Periodical. English. qt. Voyager Press, PO Box 1068, Norristown PA 19404. **DD** 613.

US
**HELPER (AMERICAN SOCIAL HEALTH ASSOCIATION).** (THE HELPER : A PROGRAM SERVICE OF THE AMERICAN SOCIAL HEALTH ASSOCIATION.). Vol. 1, No. 1 (July 1979)-. Periodical. English (Spanish). qt. $25.00. Herpes Resource Center, PO Box 100, Palo Alto CA 94302. **Tel** (415)321-5134. **ED** Alice Robinson. Index available. **Bk Rev**. **Ad Acc. Circ:** 35,000 (ctrl).
**Desc:** To inform the public about all aspects of herpes simplex virus disease using current, factual information.

UK/0018-0696
**HERE'S HEALTH (WEST BYFLEET).** [Here's health West Byfleet]. (1956)-. Consumer Publication. English. mo. £21.60 UK; £31.20 other. Tower Publishing, Tower House, Sovereign Park, Market Harborough, Leicester LE16 9EF England. **Tel** 011 44 858 468888. **(Subscription address:** EMAP Consumer Publications, Tower House, Sovereign Park, Market Harbor, Leicester, LE16 9EF England.**)** **[CCC].** ***Absorbed** New Health (Teddington. 1983), 0269-9400.*

US/1045-6058
**HIDA MANUFACTURERS DIRECTORY.** [HIDA manuf. dir.]. **Added/Corp** Health Industry Distributors Association (U.S.). **VAT** Health Industry Distributors Association Manufacturers Directory. 30th Ed. (1989)-. Periodical. English. an. $85.00. McKnight Medical Communications Inc, 1419 Lake Cook Road, Suite 110, Deerfield IL 60015. **Tel** (708)647-0259, (800)451-7838. **LC** HD9994.U5; H53. **DD** 338.7/681761/029473. **NLM** W 22; AA1 H53o. ***Continues** Directory of Health Care Manufacturers, Products and Supplies, 0888-2797.*

CN/0848-7804
**HIGHLIGHT (VICTORIA).** (HIGHLIGHT, THE MINISTRY OF HEALTH'S NEWSLETTER FOR WOMEN'S PROGRAMS.). [Highlight]. **Added/Corp** British Columbia. Women's Programs. Vol. 1, No. 1 (May 14, 1990)-. Newsletter. English. qt. **DD** 354.7110081/3/05.

US/0161-0325
**HIGHWAY & VEHICLE SAFETY REPORT.** **See** Transportation-Roads and Traffic.

US/0738-5277
**HIGHWAY SAFETY LITERATURE (1973).** **See** Transportation-Roads and Traffic.

US
**HIGHWAY SAFETY PLAN / OTSC.** **See** Transportation-Roads and Traffic.

US
**HIGHWAY SAFETY PLAN - WASHINGTON (STATE). TRAFFIC SAFETY COMMISSION.** **See** Transportation-Roads and Traffic.

US/0741-8191
**HIMA DIRECTORY.** [HIMA dir.]. **Added/Corp** Health Industry Manufacturers Association. **VFOAT** H.I.M.A. Directory. **VAT** Health Industry Manufacturers Association Directory. (19??)-. English. be. Health Industry Manufacturers Association, 1030 15th Street NW, Washington DC 20005. **LC** HD9994.U5; H55. **DD** 338.7/681761/02573. ctrl circ.

US
**HIV/AIDS UPDATE / PENNSYLVANIA DEPARTMENT OF HEALTH, BUREAU OF HIV/AIDS.** **Added/Corp** Pennsylvania. Bureau of HIV/AIDS. **VFOAT** HIV AIDS Update; Human Immunodeficiency Viruses, Acquired Immune Deficiency Syndrome Update. (Feb. 1991)-. Periodical. English. mo. Bureau of HIV / AIDS, Room 913, H & W Building, PO Box 90, Harrisburg PA 17108. **LC** RA644.A25; H58. ***Continues*** *AIDS Update (Harrisburg, Pa.).*

US
**HIV HOTLINE.** Vol. 1, No. 1 (Aug. 1991)-. Periodical. English. $47.00. D & H Health Care Corp, 10 East Ridge Road, Sandia Park NM 87047. **Tel** (800)852-7392, (505)271-2159. **NLM** W1; HI921.

US/0278-1247
**HMO EXECUTIVE SALARY SURVEY.** **See** Economics-Labor.

UK
**HMSO ENVIRONMENTAL HYGIENE SERIES.** (19??)-. Monographic series. English. ir. Price varies per volume. Her Majesty's Stationery Office, 51 Nine Elms Lane, London SW8 5DR England. **Tel** 011 44 71 873 8459, 011 44 71 873 8499, FAX 011 44 71 873 8499, 011 44 71 873 8456, telex 297138. **(Subscription address:** Her Majesty's Stationery Office, PO Box 276, Publications Centre, London SW8 5DT England.**)**

US/0882-1976
**HMTC UPDATE.** (HMTC UPDATE / HAZARDOUS MATERIALS TECHNICAL CENTER.). [HMTC update]. **VFOAT** Update. **VAT** Hazardous Materials Technical Center Update. Periodical. English. bm. $50.00. HMTC, PO Box 8168, Rockville MD 20856. **Tel** (800)638-8958. **DD** 363. **Circ:** 4,000.
**Desc:** Provides information for the proper management of hazardous materials and hazardous wastes.

JA
**HOKENJO UNEI HOKOKU.** **Main/Corp** Japan. Koseisho. Tokei Johobu. 1973-. Japanese. Koseisho Daijin Kanbo Tokei Johobu, (Statistics & Information Dept., Minister's Secretariat, Ministry of Health & Welfare), 7-3, Ichigaya Honmuracho, Shinjukuku, Tokyo 162 Japan. **LC** RA531; .J27E. **NLM** W2; JJ3 K82s. ***Continues*** *Hokenjo Unei Hokoku.*

JA
**HOKKAIDORITSU SEISHIN EISEI SENTA NEMPO.** **Main/Corp** Hokkaidoritsu Seishin Eisei Senta. Japanese. an. Hokkaidoritsu Seishin Eisei Senta, Kita 6-ben 34-go, Hondori 16-chome, Shiroishi-ku 003, Sapporo-shi Japan. **LC** RA790.7.J3; H64A.

JA/0386-3530
**HOKURIKU KOSHU EISEI GAKKAISHI.** [Hokuriku Koshu Eisei Gakkaishi]. **Added/Corp** Hokuriku Koshu Eisei Gakkai. **VFOAT** Hokuriku Journal of Public Health. (1974)-. Periodical. Japanese. Hokuriku Koshu Eisei Gakkai, (Hokuriku Soc. of Public Health), Kanazawa Daigaku Igakubu Koshu, Eiseigaku Kyoshitsu, 13-1,, Takaramachi, Kanazawashi, Ishikawaken 920 Japan. **CODEN** HKEGDK. Documents available from CASDDS.
**Ind/Abst** Chem. Abstr.

US/0277-7401
**HOME CARE SERVICES IN NEW YORK STATE.** [Home care serv. N. Y. State]. English. an. Bureau of Home and Health Care Services, Office of Health Systems Management, Room 1970/Empire State Plaza, Tower Building, Albany NY 12237.

CN/0841-1883
**HOME HEALTH CARE.** (HOME HEALTH CARE : THE CANADIAN JOURNAL OF HOME CARE & REHABILITATION.). [Home health care]. Vol. 1, No. 1 (Fall 1988)-. Periodical. English. Six times a year. Home Health Care Publisher Inc, 26 Dorchester Avenue, Toronto Ont M8Z 4W3 Canada. **DD** 362.1/4/0971.

●US/1074-4541
**HOME HEALTH CARE REIMBURSEMENT REPORT.** [Home health care reimburse. rep.]. **Added/Corp** Zimmerman & Associates (Hales Corners, Wis.). Vol. 1, No. 1 (Nov. 1993)-. Periodical. English. mo. $197.00. Aspen Publishers Inc., 7201 McKinney Circle, Frederick MD 21701. **Tel** (800)234-1660, (301)698-7100, FAX (301)251-5784, telex 5106014543. **DD** 362.

US
**HOME HEALTH LINE.** Vol. 1 (1976)-. Periodical. English. Forty-eight times a year. $418.95 Maryland non-exempt; $399.00 other. Home Health Line, PO Box 250, Port Republic MD 20676. **Tel** (410)535-4103.

US/0883-0835
**HOMEHEALTH MAGAZINE.** [HomeHealth mag.]. **VFOAT** Homehealth; Home Health Magazine; Home Health. Vol. 1, No. 1 (Jan./Feb. 1985)-. Periodical. English. bm. $12.00. Sherman-Lank Communications, 10524 Detrick Avenue, Kensington MD 20895. **ED** Matthew J. Roberts. **DD** 362. **Bk Rev. Ad Acc. Circ:** 20,000.
**Desc:** A publication for consumers of health care products and services. Articles focus on the concerns of persons with minor or severe health problems.

US/1050-0111
**HOPE BOLETIN DE SALUD.** [Hope bol. salud]. **Added/Corp** Hope Heart Institute. Vol. 10, No. 1 (1990)-. Periodical. Spanish. qt. $15.00. International Health Awareness Center, 5197 Beach Side Drive, Minnetonka MN 55343. **Tel** (616)343-0770. **DD** 613.

US/0891-3374
**HOPE HEALTH LETTER.** [Hope health lett.]. **Added/Corp** Bob Hope International Heart Research Institute (Seattle, Wash.). **VFOAT** BHIHRI. Vol. 6, No. 6 (July 1986)-. Periodical. English. mo. $19.80. International Health Awareness Center, 5197 Beach Side Drive, Minnetonka MN 55343. **Tel** (616)343-0770. **DD** 613. ***Continues*** *Hope Newsletter (Seattle, Wash.).*
**Desc:** Contains short but informative news items on a wide variety of medical topics. Emphasis is placed on preventive medicine and health maintenance-seat belt use, diet and nutrition, exercise, smoking cessation, stress management, second opinions and generic drugs.
**Ind/Abst** Acad. Abstr. Full Text Elite (Jan. 1992-); Acad. Abstr. (Jan. 1992-); Acad. Search (Jan. 1992-); Consum. Health Nutr. Index (?-?); Health Source (Jan. 1992-); INFO-SOUTH Abstr.; Mag. Search.

US
**HOPE NEWS.** V. 1- May 1963-. Periodical. English. qt. **NLM** W1 HO587P.
**Ind/Abst** Trop. Dis. Bull.

US/0276-2323
**HOSPITAL SAFETY INFORMATION SERVICE.** **See** Medical Science and Technology-Hospital Administration and Medical Centers.

UK
**HSC NEWSLETTER.** (19??)-. Newsletter. English. Six times a year. £10.00. Health & Safety Executive, Room 414 St Hughs House Stanley, Btle Merseyside L20 3QY England. **Tel** 011 44 51 951 4000, FAX 011 44 51 922 5394, telex 628235.
**Desc:** Provides an inexpensive service to employers, employees and all those involved in health and safety at work. Regular features include: new health and safety legislation, details of the guidance material, news items of subjects of national and international interest in the health and safety field. Description of accidents and how they could have been prevented.

US
**HSE LANGUAGE SERVICES BULLETIN.** Bulletin. English. an. £5.00. Language Services, Health and Safety Executive, Harpur Hill Derbyshire, Buxton SK17 9JN England.
**Desc:** Quarterly index of complete HSE translations.

US/1045-2729
**HUMAN ECOLOGY & ENERGY BALANCING SCIENTIST, THE.** [Hum. ecol. energy balanc. sci.]. **VFOAT** Human Ecology and Energy Balancing Scientist. Vol. 2, No. 4 (April 1989)-. Periodical. English. qt. $14.95. Human Ecology Balancing Sciences Inc, PO Box 1134, Setauket NY 11733. **DD** 613. ***Continues*** *Human Ecology Balancing Scientist, 0896-7164.*

FR/0751-7149
**HYGIE.** ***Title Change.*** [Hygie]. **Added/Corp** International Union for Health Education. (1982)-(1993). Academic Scholarly Publication. English (French and Spanish). qt. Hygie CO Institute Sante Et Dev, 15 21 Rue De L Ecole De Med, 75270 Paris Cedex 06 France. **Tel** 11 33 1 43269082, FAX 11 33 1 43293315. **ED** Anne Bunde-Birouste. **NLM** W1; HY353. cum. index. **Bk Rev. Ad Acc. Pr Rev. Circ:** 2,000 (ctrl). available on microfilm and microfiche from University Microfilms International (UMI). ***Continues*** *International Journal of Health Education.* ***Continued by*** *Promotion & Education.*
**Desc:** Field and research activities, interviews and reports. Includes a round-up on a particular health education theme, and international news on meetings and events.
**Ind/Abst** Br. Educ. Index (?-?); Cumul. Index Nurs. Allied Health Lit. (?-?); EMBASE (?-?); Index Med. (?-?); Nutr. Res. Newsl. (?-?); Trop. Dis. Bull. (?-?).

AT/0819-9558
**IAAH NEWSLETTER.** [IAAH newsl.]. **VFOAT** International Association of Adolescent Health Newsletter. (1987)-. Newsletter. English. Four times a year. 20.00Aus$ Australia; $15.00 other. International Association of Adolescent Health, Centre for Adolescent Health, William Buchlaud House, 2 Gatehouse Street, Parkville VIC 3052 Australia. **Tel** 011 61 3 345 5800, FAX 011 61 3 345 6502. **ED** John Court. **DD** 362.79605. **Bk Rev. Circ:** 400.
**Desc:** Provides extracts and reports from international publications relevant to adolescent health. Lists forthcoming activities, conferences and training opportunities in adolescent health.

AU/0074-1892
**IAEA SAFETY SERIES.** (SAFETY SERIES / INTERNATIONAL ATOMIC ENERGY AGENCY.). [IAEA Saf. ser.]. **Added/Corp** International Atomic Energy Agency. No. 1 (1958)-. Monographic series. English (Chinese, French, Russian and Spanish). ir. Price varies per volume. International Atomic Energy Agency / IAEA, Wagramerstrasse 5, PO Box 100, A-1400 Vienna Austria. **Tel** 011 43 1 2360 ext. 2530, FAX 011 43 1 234564. **(Subscription address:** UNIPUB, 4611 F Assembly Drive, Lanham MD 20706.**)** **LC** HD7269.A6; I4. **DD** 363.1/79 #2. **NLM** W1 SA125M. **CODEN** SSAEAW.
**Desc:** Series covering nuclear engineering and radiation protection.
**Ind/Abst** GeoRef.

DK
**IATROGENICS : SAFETY IN HEALTH CARE.** ***Title Change.*** (19??)-(19??). Academic Scholarly Publication. English. qt. Elsevier Science Publishers BV, PO Box 211, 1000 AE Amsterdam Netherlands. **Tel** 011 31 20 5803642, FAX 011 31 20 5862696, telex 15682. ***Absorbed by*** *The International Journal of Risk and Safety in Medicine.*
**Desc:** Official journal of the International Society for the Prevention of Iatrogenic Complications.

JA/0386-1112
**IATSS RESEARCH.** **See** Transportation-Roads and Traffic.

JA
**IBARAKI-KEN EISEI KENKYUJO NEMPO.** **Main/Corp** Ibaraki-Ken Eisei Kenkyujo. (19??)-. Japanese. Ibarakiken Eisei Kenkyujo, (Ibaraki Prefectural Inst. of Public Health), 4-1, Atagocho, Mitoshi, Ibarakiken 310 Japan. **LC** RA532.I2; I2a. **CODEN** IEKND6. Documents available from CASDDS.
**Ind/Abst** Chem. Abstr.

US/0272-5916
**IDAHO DEPARTMENT OF HEALTH & WELFARE ANNUAL REPORT.** **Main/Corp** Idaho. Department of Health and Welfare. **VAT** Idaho Department of Health and Welfare Annual Report. English. **NLM** W2 AI2 D28I.

●US/1065-4143
**IDAHO HEALTH CARE IN PERSPECTIVE.** [Ida. health care perspect.]. **Added/Corp** Morgan Quitno Corporation. 1st Ed. (1993)-. English. $18.00. Morgan Quitno Corporation, PO Box 1656, 512 East 9th Street, Lawrence KS 66044. **Tel** (800)457-0742, (913)841-3534, FAX (913)841-3534. **DD** 362.
**Desc:** Reports on the state's data and rank for each of the categories featured in Health Care State Rankings.

GW/0932-5034
**IDIS-LITERATURLISTE. SOZIALMEDIZIN / IDIS.** **Added/Corp** Institut fuer Dokumentation und Information Ueber Sozialmedizin und Offentliches Gesundheitswesen. **VFOAT** IDIS Literaturliste. Sozialmedizin; Sozialmedizin. (1988)-. Monographic series. German (English). Eight times a year. Price varies per volume. Instiutt fur Dokumentation und Information Uber Sozialmedizin und Oeffentliches Gesundheitswesen, Westerfeldstr 35-37, Postfach 20 10 12, W-4800 Bielefeld 1 Germany. **Tel** 49 0521 86035, FAX 49 0521 870050. **ED** Christiane Kelm-Kirkmorfeld and Barbara Zitzmann. **NLM** ZWA 31; I19. Index available. cum. index. **Bk Rev.** ctrl circ.

IT/0019-1639
**IGIENE E SANITA PUBBLICA.** [Ig. sanita pubblica]. **Added/Corp** Associazione dei medici provinciali italiani. (1945)-. Academic Scholarly Publication. Italian (English, French and German). bm. L110000 Italy; L165000 other. Igiene e Sanita Pubblica, Via Stamira 7, 00162 Rome Italy. **Tel** (06)442.40.948, FAX (06)442.40.948. **ED** Gaetano del Vecchio. **NLM** W1 IG445. **CODEN** ISPRA2. **[CCC].** Index available. **Bk Rev. Ad Acc.** available on microfilm. Documents available from BIOSIS Document Express, CASDDS.
**Desc:** Original articles, unedited and experimental, that concern hygiene and public health. Original, unedited contributions on microbiology, parasitology, immunology, statistics, and infectious diseases.
**Ind/Abst** Biol. Abstr.; Chem. Abstr. (1945-1983); Trop. Dis. Bull.

IT/0019-1655
**IGIENE MODERNA.** [Ig. mod.]. Vol. 1, (Jan. 1908)-. Periodical. Italian (English and Spanish). Twelve times a year. $180.00. Igiene Moderna Amministrazione, Via R Zandonai 11, 00194 Rome Italy. **Tel** 011 39 6 3279593, FAX 011 39 6 3290343, telex 611330. **ED** Dr. Giovanni Fadda. **NLM** W1 IG585. **CODEN** IGMPAX. **Bk**

**Rev. Ad Acc.** Documents available from BIOSIS Document Express, CASDDS.
**Ind/Abst** Biodeter. Abstr. (1991-); Biol. Abstr.; Chem. Abstr.; Dairy Sci. Abstr.; Food Sci. Technol. Abstr.; Health Saf. Sci. Abstr.; Microbiol. Abstr. Sect. B; Microbiol. Abstr. Sect. A; Nutr. Abstr. Rev., Ser. B, Live Feeds and Feed.; Nutr. Abstr. Rev., Ser. A, Hum. Exp.; Life Sci. Collect.; Pollut. Abstr. Indexes; Rev. Agric. Entomol.; Rev. Med. Vet. Mycology; Saf. Health Work; Trop. Dis. Bull.; Virol. AIDS Abstr.

US/0892-1318
**IHPS REPORT.** (IHPS REPORT / THE INSTITUTE FOR HEALTH POLICY STUDIES, UNIVERSITY OF CALIFORNIA, SAN FRANCISCO.). [IHPS rep.]. **Main/Corp** University of California, San Francisco. Institute for Health Policy Studies. **Added/Corp** University of California, San Francisco. Institute for Health Policy Studies. **VFOAT** I.H.P.S. Report. **VAT** Institute for Health Policy Studies Report. (July 1981)-. Periodical. English. sa. Free. Institute for Health Policy Studies, 1326 Third Avenue, San Francisco CA 94143. **Tel** (415)476-4921. **LC** Discard. **DD** 362.

●US/1065-4151
**ILLINOIS HEALTH CARE IN PERSPECTIVE.** [Ill. health care perspect.]. **Added/Corp** Morgan Quitno Corporation. 1st Ed. (1993)-. English. $18.00. Morgan Quitno Corporation, PO Box 1656, 512 East 9th Street, Lawrence KS 66044. **Tel** (800)457-0742, (913)841-3534, FAX (913)841-3534. **DD** 362.
**Desc:** Reports on the state's data and rank for each of the categories featured in Health Care State Rankings.

US
**ILLINOIS TRAFFIC ACCIDENT FACTS AND STATISTICS.** **See** Transportation-Roads and Traffic.

US/1054-8866
**IMMUNIZATION ALERT, THE.** (THE IMMUNIZATION ALERT [COMPUTER FILE] : INTERNATIONAL HEALTH DATABASE.). [Immun. alert]. **VFOAT** Immunization Alert International Health Database. (19??)-. Periodical. English. wk. $750.00 (weekly), $300.00 (monthly). Immunization Alert, 93 Timber Drive, Storrs CT 06268. **Tel** (203)487-0611. **DD** 614.
**Desc:** System requirements: IBM PC's or compatibles. Issued on 5 1/4" or 3 1/2" diskettes.

US
**INDIAN HEALTH PROGRAM OF THE U.S. PUBLIC HEALTH SERVICE, THE.** **Main/Corp** United States. Health Services and Mental Health Administration. (19??)-. Government Publication. English. ir. Superintendent of Documents, US Government Printing Office, Washington DC 20402. **Tel** (202)275-3328, FAX (202)786-2377. **LC** RA448.5.I5; U54b. **DD** 362.

II/0970-1346
**INDIAN JOURNAL OF COMMUNITY GUIDANCE SERVICE.** ***Title Change.*** [Indian j. community guidance serv.]. Vol. 1, No. 1 (Jan. 1984)-(19??). Periodical. English. tq. Dr M Rajamanickam, No 3, K V Reddy Road, Annamalainagar 609002 India. **LC** RA790.7.I5; I53. **NLM** W1; IN207C. ***Continued by*** *Journal of Community Guidance and Research.*

II/0378-6323
**INDIAN JOURNAL OF DERMATOLOGY, VENEREOLOGY AND LEPROLOGY.** **See** Medical Science and Technology-Dermatology.

II/0254-9395
**INDIAN JOURNAL OF LEPROSY.** [Indian j. lepr.]. **Added/Corp** Hind Kusht Nivaran Sangh. Vol. 56, No. 1 (Jan.-March 1984)-. Periodical. English. qt. $22.00. Hind Kusht Nivaran Sangh, 1 Red Cross Road, New Delhi 110001 India. **Tel** 606608. **(Subscription address:** Prints India, 11 Darya Ganj, New Delhi 110002 India.**) ED** Dv Dharmemdra. **LC** RC154.7.I6; L4. **DD** 616.9/98. **NLM** W1; IN211R. Index available. **Bk Rev. Ad Acc. Circ:** 1,500. Documents available from BIOSIS Document Express. ***Continues*** *Leprosy in India, 0024-1024.*
**Desc:** Publishes research articles, abstracts from current literature, reviews, reports on leprosy and allied subjects of medicine.
**Ind/Abst** Biol. Abstr.; EMBASE; Index Med.; Indian Sci. Abstr.; Microbiol. Abstr. Sect. B; Trop. Dis. Bull.

II/0019-557X
**INDIAN JOURNAL OF PUBLIC HEALTH.** [Indian j. public health]. **Added/Corp** Indian Public Health Association. (Jan. 1957)-. Periodical. English. qt. $20.00. Indian Public Health Association, 110 Chittaranjan Avenue, Calcutta India. **(Subscription address:** Prints India, 11 Darya Ganj, New Delhi, 110002 India, (Phone: 011 91 11 3268645)**) ED** A K Chakraborty. **LC** RA421; .I37. **NLM** W1 IN229. **CODEN** IPBHAH. **Bk Rev. Ad Acc. Circ:** 2500. Documents available from BIOSIS Document Express, CASDDS.
**Ind/Abst** Biol. Abstr.; Chem. Abstr.; Helminthol. Abstr.; Index Med.; Index Vet.; Nutr. Abstr. Rev., Ser. A, Hum. Exp.; Protozoolog. Abstr.; Rev. Med. Vet. Entomol.; Rural Dev. Abstr.; Vet. Bull.

II/0253-7184
**INDIAN JOURNAL OF SEXUALLY TRANSMITTED DISEASES.** [Indian j. sex. transm. dis.]. **Added/Corp** Indian Association for the Study of Sexually Transmitted Diseases. Vol. 1, No. 1 (1980)-. Periodical. English. sa. $20.00. Indian Association for the Study of Sexually Transmitted Diseases, Lady Harding Medical College, New Delhi 110001 India. **(Subscription address:** Prints India, 11 Darya Ganj, New Delhi, 110002 India, (Phone: 011 91 11 3268645)**) NLM** W1 IN234P.
**Ind/Abst** EMBASE [Select. Cov.].

●US/1065-416X
**INDIANA HEALTH CARE IN PERSPECTIVE.** [Indiana health care perspect.]. **Added/Corp** Morgan Quitno Corporation. 1st Ed. (1993)-. English. $18.00. Morgan Quitno Corporation, PO Box 1656, 512 East 9th Street, Lawrence KS 66044. **Tel** (800)457-0742, (913)841-3534, FAX (913)841-3534. **DD** 362.
**Desc:** Reports on the state's data and rank for each of the categories featured in Health Care State Rankings.

US/0019-6754
**INDIANA STATE BOARD OF HEALTH BULLETIN, THE.** **VFOAT** Bulletin; I.S.B.H. Bulletin; ISBH Bulletin. Bulletin. English. qt. Free. Indiana State Board of Health, 1330 West Michigan Street, Indianapolis IN 46206. **Tel** (317)633-0109. **ED** Woodrow A Myers. **LC** RA61. **DD** 353.97720077. **NLM** W2 AI6 S6M. **Bk Rev. Ad Acc. Circ:** 15,000 (ctrl). ***Continues*** *Monthly Bulletin (Indiana State Board of Health).*
**Desc:** Magazine on wide range of public health related subjects.

BO/0253-5521
**INDICE BOLIVIANO DE CIENCIAS DE LA SALUD.** (INDICE BOLIVIANO DE CIENCIAS DE LA SALUD / UNIVERSIDAD MAYOR DE SAN ANDRES, CENTRO NACIONAL DE DOCUMENTACION CIENTIFICA Y TECNOLOGICA.). [Indice boliv. cienc. salud]. 1977/78-. Spanish. Universidad Mayor de San Andres, Centro Nacional de Documentation Cientifica y Tecnologica, Casilla 3283, La Paz Bolivia. **NLM** ZW 1 I3886.

CN/0712-2063
**INDORAIR.** [Indorair]. Vol. 3 I.E. V. 2, No. 3 (Fall 1976)-. Periodical. English. qt. Non Smokers Rights Association, Canada. **Tel** (416)595-1538. **DD** 363.1/95/09713. ***Continues*** *Non-Smokers' Rights Association Newsletter, 0712-2071.*

SP
**INFANCIA Y SOCIEDAD.** Spanish. bm. 1800ptas. Centro de Publicaciones, Min. Trabajo, Agustin de Bethencourt 11, 28071 Madrid Spain. **Tel** 011 34 1 5543400. **(Subscription address:** Ministerio de Asunto Sociales, Centro de Publicaciones, Alonso Cano 20, 28003 Madrid Spain**)**
**Desc:** Covers all aspects of child health, education and welfare.

US
**INFECTION CONTROL BULLETIN.** (19??)-. Bulletin. English. Twelve times a year. $42.00. Infection Control Educational, 16961 Cumberland, Yorba Linda CA 92686. **Tel** (714)524-2261.

US/1071-6580
**INFECTION CONTROL IN LONG-TERM CARE FACILITIES NEWSLETTER.** [Infect. control long-term care facil. newsl.]. **Added/Corp** Association for Practitioners in Infection Control. **VFOAT** Infection Control in Long Term Care Facilities Newsletter. (1989)-. Periodical. English. ir. $39.95. Pelmar Publishers, 2 Computer Drive West, Box 15015, Albany NY 12212. **Tel** (201)469-4400 Ext. 2497. **DD** 614.

US/1040-791X
**INFECTIOUS DISEASE REPORT.** (1990)-. Periodical. English. Three times a year. $52.50. Mosby Year Book Inc., 11830 Westline Industrial Drive, St Louis MO 63146. **Tel** (800)325-4177, (314)872-8370, FAX (314)432-1380, telex 44-2402.

US/0741-7462
**INFECTIOUS DISEASES CAPSULE & COMMENT.** **VFOAT** Infectious Diseases Capsule and Comment. Vol. 1, No. 1 (Feb. 1982)-. Periodical. English. mo. Free. Hospital Practice, 10 Astor Place/7th Floor, New York NY 10003-6903. **Tel** (212)477-2727. ctrl circ.

UK/0261-0590
**INFORMATION BULLETIN - ASH.** [Inf. bull. - ASH]. **VFOAT** Information Bulletin - Action on Smoking and Health. (1978)-. English. Twenty-four times a year. £50.00 (corporate subscribers), £15.00 (individuals) UK; £60.00 (corporate subscribers), £25.00 (individuals) other. Action on Smoking and Health / UK, 109 Gloucester Place, Lindon W1H 3PH England. **Tel** 071-935-3519, FAX 071-935-3463. **DD** _a613.8505. Index available. cum. index (Every six months, Free). ctrl circ.
**Desc:** Provides a brief but detailed overview of smoking-related news from the national and local press, medical journals, and trade. It also provides notice of books and papers of interest professionals, educators and information service providers concerned with tobacco use.

US
**INFORMATION GUIDE - ARIZONA DEPARTMENT OF HEALTH SERVICES.** **Main/Corp** Arizona. Bureau of Vital Records and Information Services. Research and Statistical Analysis. 1979-. English. Bureau of Vital Records and Information Services, Arizona Department of Health Services, 1740 West Adams Street, Phoenix AZ 85007. **LC** RA21; .D46A. **DD** 353.97910084/1042. ***Continues*** *Information Guide - Arizona Department of Health Services, 0161-6722.*

UK
**INFORMATION TECHNOLOGY IN HEALTH CARE.** English. Longman Group Ltd., Fourth Avenue, Longman House, Harlow Essex CM19 5SR England. **Tel** 011 44 279 429655, FAX 011 44 279 431059, telex 81259. **(Subscription address:** Fourth Avenue, Harlow Essex CM19 5AA England**)**

PE/0253-8326
**INFORME ANUAL DE ACTIVIDADES - SERVICIO ESPECIAL DE SALUD PUBLICA.** (INFORME ANUAL DE ACTIVIDADES / REPUBLICA DEL PERU, SERVICIO ESPECIAL DE SALUD PUBLICA.). [Inf. anu. act. - Serv. espec. salud publica]. **Main/Corp** Peru. Servicio Especial de Salud Publica. Began in 1960. Spanish. an. **NLM** W2 DP6 S5I.

IT/0302-7775
**INGEGNERIA AMBIENTALE INQUINAMENTO E DEPURAZIONE.** Academic Scholarly Publication. Italian. mo. $47.52. Inst di Ingegneria Sanitario, Piazza Leonarda de Vinvi 32, 20133 Milan Italy. **CODEN** IGEABH. Documents available from CASDDS.
**Ind/Abst** Chem. Abstr.; Health Saf. Sci. Abstr.

●UK
**INJURY PREVENTION.** (Feb. 1995)-. English. qt. £100.00. BMJ / British Medical Journal Publishing Group, British Medical Association House, Tavistock Square, London WC1H 9JR England. **Tel** 011 44 71 3874499, FAX 011 44 71 383 6402, telex 290034 HBJ MN.

US
**INJURY PREVENTION NETWORK NEWSLETTER.** **Added/Corp** Injury Prevention Network. Trauma Foundation. Vol. 2, No. 1 (Spring 1985)-. Newsletter. English. Twice a year (With double issues twice a year). $20.00. Trauma Foundation, Building One Room 311, San Francisco CA 94110. **Tel** (415)821-8209, FAX (415)282-2563. **ED** Liz McLoughlin. **NLM** W1; IN454D. **Ad Acc. Circ:** 2,000 (ctrl). ***Continues*** *Council on Injury Control Quarterly Newsletter.*

SI/0129-6078
**INSIGHT (SINGAPORE).** (INSIGHT : OFFICIAL PUBLICATION OF THE SINGAPORE ASSOCIATION FOR MENTAL HEALTH.). [Insight]. **Added/Corp** Singapore Association for Mental Health. (1978)-. English. **NLM** W1 IN458J.

NE
**INSTELLINGEN.** Dutch. mo. Koggeschip Vakbladen BV, Postbus 1198, 1000 BD Amsterdam Netherlands. **Tel** 011 31 20 6916666.

US/1048-0501
**INTERACTIVE HEALTHCARE NEWSLETTER.** (INTERACTIVE HEALTHCARE NEWSLETTER : COVERING VIDEODISC, CD-ROM AND RELATED TECHNOLOGIES.). [Interact. healthc. newsl.]. **VFOAT** Interactive Health Care Newsletter; IHN. Vol. 5, No. 6 (Nov./Dec. 1989)-. Newsletter. English. mo. $70.00. Stewart Publishing Inc., 6471 Merritt Court, Alexandria VA 22312. **Tel** (703)354-8155. **DD** 610. ***Continues*** *MedicalDisc Reporter, 0882-4665.*

US/0195-9549
**INTERCHANGE (PHILADELPHIA).** (INTERCHANGE.). V. 1- Fall 1978-. Periodical. English. National Health Care Management Center, The University of Pennsylvania, 3641 Locust Walk CE, Philadelphia PA 19104. **NLM** W1 IN669M.

US/0020-5419
**INTERFACE (BETHESDA).** **See** Computers.

US/0161-0120
**INTERFACE (SOCIETY FOR ENVIRONMENTAL GEOCHEMISTRY AND HEALTH).** **See** Environmental Issues-Pollution and Waste Management.

US/1051-0087
**INTERGOVERNMENTAL AIDS REPORTS.** (INTERGOVERNMENTAL AIDS REPORTS / THE GEORGE WASHINGTON UNIVERSITY INTERGOVERNMENTAL HEALTH POLICY PROJECT.). [Intergov. AIDS rep.]. **Added/Corp** George Washington University. Intergovernmental Health Policy Project. George Washington University. AIDS Policy Center. Intergovernmental AIDS Resource Network. (1989)-. Periodical. English. Ten times a year. $97.00 (non-profit) Universities & Government employees; $147.00 other. Intergovernmental Health Policy Project, 2021 K Street NW, Suite 800, Washington DC 20006. **Tel** (202)872-1445, FAX (202)785-0114. **LC** RC607.A26; I54. **DD** 362.1/969792/0097305. **NLM** W1; IN685W. **Circ:** 1,000. ***Continues** State AIDS Reports.*
**Desc:** This publication features state legislative trends, policy research finding, innovative programs, and strategies related to HIV/AIDS.

FR/1016-8699
**INTERNATIONAL CHILD HEALTH.** [Int. child health]. Vol. 1, No. 1 (July 1990)-. Periodical. English. qt. $48.00. International Pediatric Association, Chateau Longchamp Bois, Boulogne 75016 Paris France. **DD** 362. **NLM** W1; IN728.
**Desc:** Current issues in child health and welfare in the world, including medical, social, economic, administrative, educational, legal aspects, with special emphasis on problems in developing countries.

SZ/0020-6563
**INTERNATIONAL DIGEST OF HEALTH LEGISLATION.** **See** Law.

●UK/0960-9784
**INTERNATIONAL FOOD SAFETY NEWS.** **See** Food and Food Industry.

UK
**INTERNATIONAL H&E / HEALTH & EFFICIENCY.** **VFOAT** International Health & Efficiency; International H & E; International Health and Efficiency. English (French and German). mo. £24.30 UK; $45.00 North America. Peenhill Ltd, 28 Charles Square, Pitfield Street, London N1 6HT England. **Tel** 071 253 4037, FAX 071 253 0539. **ED** Jane Hendy-Smith and Kate Sturdy. **Circ:** 100,000.
**Desc:** Naturist news and information. Articles on health, travel, human behavior, with naturist bias, naturist/nudist lifestyle.

US/0731-7220
**INTERNATIONAL HEALTH NEWS.** ***Ceased.*** [Int. health news]. Vol. 3, No. 1 (Feb. 1982)-Vol. 9 (Nov./Dec. 1988). Periodical. English. bm. National Council of International Health, 1701 K Street NW/Suite 600, Washington DC 20006. ***Continues** NCIH Newsletter.*
**Ind/Abst** Trop. Dis. Bull.

US/0731-6615
**INTERNATIONAL HEALTH PLANNING SERIES.** [Int. health plann. ser.]. Began with: 1, 1979. English. US Department of Health & Human Services National Center for Health Statistics, 6525 Belcrest Road, Room 1140, Hyattsville MD 20782. **Tel** (301)436-7016, FAX (301)436-4258. **NLM** W1 IN764F.

UK/0952-6862
**INTERNATIONAL JOURNAL OF HEALTH CARE QUALITY ASSURANCE.** **VFOAT** Health Care Quality Assurance. (1988)-. Periodical. English. Seven times a year. $829.00. MCB University Press, 60 62 Toller Lane, Bradford West Yorkshire BD8 9BX England. **Tel** 011 44 274 499821, FAX 011 44 274 547143, telex 51317 MCBUNI G. **(Subscription address:** MCB University Press / US and Canada Subscriptions, PO Box 10812, Birmingham AL 35201-0812.**) ED** Robin Gourlay and Barbara Morris. **NLM** W1; IN766UL. **[CCC]. Ad Acc.** Documents available from UMI Article Clearinghouse.
**Desc:** Seeks to provide an essential source of up-to-date information and comment. It will become an invaluable forum of debate for everyone involved with the concepts and practise of quality assurance as it relates to health care.
**Ind/Abst** ABI/INFORM Glob. Ed.; Hospit. Health Admin. Index.

UK/0749-6753
**INTERNATIONAL JOURNAL OF HEALTH PLANNING & MANAGEMENT, THE.** [Int. j. health plann. manage.]. **VFOAT** Health Planning and Management. Vol. 1, No. 1 Nov. (1985)-. Periodical. English. Four times a year. $475.00. John Wiley & Sons Ltd., Baffins Lane, Chichester West Sussex PO19 1UD England. **Tel** 0243 779777, FAX 0243 776128 BTG:JWP001, telex 86290 WIBOOKG. **(Subscription address:** John Wiley / Philadelphia, PO Box 7247, Philadelphia PA 19170.**) ED** Kenneth Lee. **DD** 362. **NLM** W1; IN767R. **CODEN** IJHMEO. **[CCC].** Index available. cum. index. **Bk Rev. Ad Acc. Circ:** 2,000. available on microfilm and microfiche from University Microfilms International (UMI).
**Desc:** Discusses major issues in health planning and management systems and practices. Overall the intention is to maintain a sound balance between practice and theory from a variety of schools of thought.
**Ind/Abst** EMBASE; Geogr. Abstr. Human Geogr.; Health Plan. Adminis.; Health Serv. Abstr.; Int. Dev. Abstr.; Soc. Plann. Policy Dev. Abstr.; Trop. Dis. Bull.

NE/0924-2287
**INTERNATIONAL JOURNAL OF HEALTH SCIENCES.** Vol. 1, No. 1 (March 1990)-. Periodical. English. qt. $89.57. Van Gorcum & Company BV, PO Box 43, NL 9400 AA Assen Netherlands. **Tel** 011 31 5920 46846, FAX 011 31 5920 72064. **ED** Prof W A Van der Meuvel. **NLM** W1; IN767W. **Bk Rev. Ad Acc. Circ:** 500 (ctrl).
**Ind/Abst** Abstr. Anthropol. (19??-).

US/0020-7314
**INTERNATIONAL JOURNAL OF HEALTH SERVICES.** [Int. j. health serv.]. Vol. 1 (Feb. 1971)-. Academic Scholarly Publication. English. qt. $119.00. Baywood Publishing Company Inc., 26 Austin Avenue, PO Box 337, Amityville NY 11701. **Tel** (516)691-1270, (800)638-7819, FAX (516)691-1770. **ED** Vicente Navarro. **LC** RA421; .I49. **DD** 362.1/05. **NLM** W1 IN768. **CODEN** IJUSC3. cum. index. **Pr Rev.** Documents available from The Genuine Article, BIOSIS Document Express.
**Desc:** A multidisciplinary publication devoted to health and social policy, political economy, sociology, history and philosophy, ethics and law.
**Ind/Abst** Appl. Soc. Sci. Index Abstr.; Biol. Abstr.; Chicano Index; Cumul. Index Nurs. Allied Health Lit.; Curr. Contents Soc. Behav. Sci.; EMBASE; Energy Res. Abstr. (Aug. 1981-); Geogr. Abstr. Human Geogr.; Health Saf. Sci. Abstr.; Health Plan. Adminis.; Hospit. Health Admin. Index; Index Med.; INIS Atomindex [Micro.]; Int. Dev. Abstr.; Int. Pharm. Abstr.; PAIS Int. Print (1991-); Res. Alert [Full Cov.]; Soc. Plann. Policy Dev. Abstr.; Soc. Sci. Cit. Index [Full Cov.]; Sociol. Abstr.; Trop. Dis. Bull.

US/0148-916X
**INTERNATIONAL JOURNAL OF LEPROSY AND OTHER MYCOBACTERIAL DISEASES.** [Int. j. lepr. other mycobact. dis.]. **Added/Corp** International Leprosy Association. Leonard Wood Memorial for the Eradication of Leprosy. Vol. 34- (Jan./Mar. 1966)-. Academic Scholarly Publication. English (French and Spanish). qt (March, June, Sept., Dec.). $100.00 US; $150.00 airmail delivery. International Journal of Leprosy, One Alm Way, Greenville SC 29601. **Tel** (803)271-7040, FAX (803)271-7062. **ED** Robert C Hastings. **NLM** W1; IN769PT. cum. index. **Bk Rev. Pr Rev. Acid Free.** ctrl circ. available on microfilm and microfiche from University Microfilms International (UMI). Documents available from The Genuine Article, CASDDS. ***Continues** International Journal of Leprosy, 0020-7349.*
**Desc:** Provides a source of reliable information on leprosy and other mycobacterial diseases through the publication of high quality original articles and editorial reviews, selected abstracts of articles published in current media journals, and of news and notes of the leprosy world. It is the house organ of the International Leprosy Association and an indispensable resource for clinicians, program managers and investigators.
**Ind/Abst** Chem. Abstr.; EMBASE; Immunol. Abstr.; Index Med. (1966-); Microbiol. Abstr. Sect. B (19??-19??); Life Sci. Collect. (1966-); Ref. Upd. Deluxe Ed.; Res. Alert [Full Cov.]; Sci. Cit. Index; SCISEARCH; Soc. Sci. Cit. Index [Select. Cov.].

US/8755-5328
**INTERNATIONAL PERSPECTIVES IN PUBLIC HEALTH.** [Int. perspect. public health]. **Added/Corp** Ministry of Concern for Public Health (U.S.) Institute of Concern for Public Health (Canada) Int'l. Inst. of Concern for Public Health. **VFOAT** IPPH. Vol. 1, Issue 1 (Spring 1984)-. Periodical. English. an (4 issues per volume). $25.00 US & Canada; $30.00 other. Ministry of Concern for Public Health, 5495 Main Street, Suite 147, Buffalo NY 14221. **Tel** FAX (416)533-7879. **ED** Rosalie Bertell. **DD** 614. **NLM** W1; IN827JT. **Ad Acc. Circ:** 300.
**Desc:** Environmental health, including health problems related to military production and weapon testing and ways of preventing further problems.

US/0272-684X
**INTERNATIONAL QUARTERLY OF COMMUNITY HEALTH EDUCATION.** [Int. q. community health educ.]. Vol. 1 No. 1 (1981)-. Periodical. English. qt. $118.00. Baywood Publishing Company Inc., 26 Austin Avenue, PO Box 337, Amityville NY 11701. **Tel** (516)691-1270, (800)638-7819, FAX (516)691-1770. **ED** George P Cernada. **LC** RA440.A1; I58. **DD** 613/.07/1. **NLM** W1 IN827Z. cum. index. **Bk Rev.**
**Desc:** Committed to publishing applied research, policy and case studies dealing with community health education and its relationship to social change. Stresses systematic application of social science and health education theory and methodology to public health problems and consumer-directed approaches to control of preventive and curative health services.
**Ind/Abst** Abstr. Anthropol. (19??-); Multicult. Educ. Abstr.; Nutr. Res. Newsl.; Psychoanal. Abstr.; PsycScan: Appl. Exp. Eng. Psych.; PsycScan: LD/MR; PsycScan: Neuropsych.; Soc. Plann. Policy Dev. Abstr.; Sociol. Abstr.; Stud. Women Abstr.; Tech. Educ. Train. Abstr.

US
**INTERNATIONAL RESCUER NEWSLETTER.** Newsletter. English. International Rescue and First Aid Association, 8 Jackson Place, Caldwell NJ 07006.

US
**INTERNATIONAL RESEARCH AND DEMONSTRATION PROJECTS. AN ANNOTATED LISTING.** **VFOAT** Social and Rehabilitation International Research and Demonstration Projects. Periodical. English. an. Social Rehabilitation Service, Washington DC 20202.
**Desc:** Research and demonstration projects approved under the Agricultural Trade, development and assistance act as amended, P.L. 480.

SZ
**INTERNATIONAL TRAVEL AND HEALTH.** **Added/Corp** World Health Organization. (Jan. 1, 1989)-. English. an. $16.50. World Health Organization, Distribution and Sales, 20 Avenue Appia, CH-1211 Geneva 27 Switzerland. **Tel** 011 41 22 7912111, FAX 011 41 22 7880401. **LC** RA638; .C46. **DD** 614.4/7. **NLM** QW 539; V112. ***Continues** Vaccination Certificate Requirements and Health Advice for International Travel, 0257-912X.*
**Desc:** Issues authoritative advice on the medical and personal precautions needed to protect the health of travellers; it presents the latest information on country-specific health risks and the vaccinations that are either recommended by WHO or required for entry into any of 199 countries and territories.

US/1058-1294
**INTERSTUDY COMPETITIVE EDGE, THE.** (THE INTERSTUDY COMPETITIVE EDGE : BIANNUAL REPORT OF THE MANAGED HEALTH CARE INDUSTRY.). [Interstudy compet. edge]. **Added/Corp** InterStudy (Center). **VFOAT** Competitive Edge. Vol. 1, No. 1 (1991)-. Periodical. English. sa (Summer & Winter). $270.00. Interstudy, PO Box 4366, St. Paul MN 55104. **Tel** (612)858-9291. **LC** RA413.5.U5; N34. **DD** 362.1/0425. **NLM** W1; IN982P. ***Continues** InterStudy Edge.*

NE/0168-4604
**INTRAMURALE GEZONDHEIDSZORG / CENTRAAL BUREAU VOOR DE STATISTIK, HOOFDAFDELING GEZINDHEIDSSTATISTIEKEN.** **VFOAT** Intramural Health Care. 1981-. Dutch (summaries and/or abstracts in English). an. Fl18.25. Centraal Bureau voor de Statistiek, AFD ALG Zaken, Postbus 959, 2270 AZ Voorburg Netherlands. **Tel** 011 31 70 3373800, FAX 011 31 038 7429, telex 32692 CBS NL. **LC** RA407.5.N37; I57. ***Continues** Intramurale Gezondheidszorg in Nederland.*

●US/1065-4178
**IOWA HEALTH CARE IN PERSPECTIVE.** [Iowa health care perspect.]. **Added/Corp** Morgan Quitno Corporation. 1st Ed. (1993)-. English. $18.00. Morgan Quitno Corporation, PO Box 1656, 512 East 9th Street, Lawrence KS 66044. **Tel** (800)457-0742, (913)841-3534, FAX (913)841-3534. **DD** 362.
**Desc:** Reports on the state's data and rank for each of the categories featured in Health Care State Rankings.

IR/0304-4556
**IRANIAN JOURNAL OF PUBLIC HEALTH.** [Nsry bhdst yrn]. **VFOAT** Nashriyan-i Bihdasht-i Iran. Periodical. English (Persian; summaries and/or abstracts in French). qt. $25.00. Iranian Public Health Association, Ghodes Avenue Number 43, PO Box 1310, Tehera Iran. **NLM** W1 IR329. **CODEN** IJPHCD. Documents available from CASDDS.
**Ind/Abst** Biodeter. Abstr. (1991-); Chem. Abstr. (1972-1982); EMBASE; Index Vet.; Nutr. Abstr. Rev., Ser. B, Live Feeds and Feed.; Nutr. Abstr. Rev., Ser. A, Hum. Exp.; Protozoolog. Abstr.; Rev. Agric. Entomol.; Rev. Med. Vet. Entomol.; Rev. Med. Vet. Mycology; Trop. Dis. Bull.

NE/0257-6333
**IRC NEWSLETTER.** [IRC newsl.]. **VFOAT** International Reference Centre Newsletter. (1???)-. Newsletter. English. **CODEN** NU054.
**Ind/Abst** Trop. Dis. Bull.

JA
**ISHIKAWA-KEN EISEI KOGAI KENKYUJO NEMPO.** **Main/Corp** Ishikawa-ken Eisei Kogai Kenkyujo. Japanese. an. Ishikawa-Ken Eisei Kogai Kenkyujo, 251 Minma 2-chome, Kanazawa-shi 921 Japan. **LC** RA566.5.J3; I84A.

US/0195-5551
**ISSUE PAPER / UNIVERSITY OF PENNSYLVANIA, NATIONAL HEALTH CARE MANAGEMENT CENTER.** **Added/Corp** University of Pennsylvania. National Health Care Management Center. No. 1, (Feb. 1979)-. Monographic series. English. ir. Price varies per volume. **NLM** W1 IS6672.

JA
**IWATE-KEN EISEI KENKYUJO NENPO.** **Added/Corp** Iwate-ken Eisei Kenkyujo. **VFOAT** Annual Report of the Iwate Prefectural Institute of Public Health. (1952)-. Academic Scholarly Publication. Japanese. an. Iwate-Ken Eisei Kenkyujo, 15-ban 25 go Uchimaru, Morioka-shi 020 Japan. **LC** RA532.I9; I93. **CODEN** IKENDI. Documents available from CASDDS.
**Ind/Abst** Chem. Abstr.

JA
**JIGYO YORAN - KOKURITSU KOSHU EISEIIN.** **Main/Corp** Kokuritsu KÂoshÂu Eiseiin (Japan). (1978)-. Japanese. an. Koseisho Kokuritsu Koshu Eiseiin, (Institute of Health Ministry of Health and Welfare), 6-1 Shiroganedai 4-chome, Minatoku Tokyoto 108 Japan. **LC** RA532.T64; K64b.

BL
**JORNAL DA ABES.** **Added/Corp** Associacao Brasileira de Engenharia Sanitaria e Ambiental. (197?)-. Periodical. Portuguese. Twelve times a year. $350.00 Comes with Associacao Brasileira de Engenharia Sanitaria e Ambiental membership. Associacao Brasileira de Engenharia Sanitaria e Ambiental, Avenue Beira Mar 216, 13 Andar, 20021 Rio de Janeiro RJ Brazil. **Tel** 011 55 21 2103221. Index Available Supplement or subseries--indexed in parent journal index.

CN/0044-6203
**JOURNAL - ADDICTION RESEARCH FOUNDATION, THE.** [J. - Addict. Res. Found.]. **Main/Corp** Addiction Research Foundation of Ontario. **Added/Corp** Addiction Research Foundation of Ontario. Ontario. Addiction Research Foundation. Vol. 1 (June 1972)-. Periodical. English. mo (except combined Jan./Feb. and July/Aug.). 15.00Can$ Canada; 19.00Can$ other. Addiction Research Foundation, 33 Russell Street, Toronto Ontario M5S 2S1 Canada. **Tel** (416)595-6000, FAX (416)595-5017. **ED** Anne MacLennan. **NLM** W1 JO222P. Index available. **Bk Rev. Ad Acc. Circ:** 24,000. available on microfiche.
**Desc:** News publication for professionals in addictions and related health, enforcement, research, and education fields.
**Ind/Abst** Can. Index (?-?); Can. Period. Index (19??-).

CN/0705-0003
**JOURNAL DE L'A. I. H. P. Q, LE.** **Main/Corp** Association des Inspecteurs en Hygiene Publique du Quebec. **VAT** Journal de l'Association des Inspecteurs en Hygiene Publique du Quebec. V. 17- May 1976-. Periodical. French. Association des Inspecteurs en Hygiene Publique du Quebec, CP 39 Succursale N, Montreal Quebec H2X 3M2 Canada. **DD** 614/.09714. ***Continues*** *Journal de l'A.I.S.P.Q., 0315-4300.*

●US
**JOURNAL FOR HEALTHCARE QUALITY: PROMOTING EXCELLENCE IN HEALTHCARE.** **Added/Corp** National Association for Healthcare Quality (U.S.). **VFOAT** JHQ. Vol. 14, No. 1 (Jan./Feb. 1991)-. Periodical. English. bm. ***Continues*** *Journal of Quality Assurance.*

II/0019-5138
**JOURNAL OF COMMUNICABLE DISEASES.** (THE JOURNAL OF COMMUNICABLE DISEASES.). [J. commun. dis.]. **Added/Corp** Indian Society for Malaria and other Communicable Diseases. (1969)-. Academic Scholarly Publication. English. qt. $50.00. Indian Society for Malaria and Communicable Diseases, 22 Alipur Road, Delhi 6 India. **(Subscription address:** Prints India, 11 Darya Ganj, New Delhi, 110002 India, (Phone: 011 91 11 3268645)) **NLM** W1 JO593E. **CODEN** JCDSBF. Documents available from BIOSIS Document Express. ***Continues*** *Bulletin of the Indian Society for Malaria & Other Communicable Diseases, 0537-2526.*
**Ind/Abst** Biocont. News Inf.; Biol. Abstr.; EMBASE; Helminthol. Abstr. (19??-19??); Index Med.; Index Vet.; Protozoolog. Abstr.; Rev. Med. Vet. Entomol.; Rev. Med. Vet. Mycology; Rural Dev. Abstr.; Small Anim. Abstr. Bibliogr.; Vet. Bull.; Trop. Dis. Bull.

US/0094-5145
**JOURNAL OF COMMUNITY HEALTH.** [J. commun. health]. **Added/Corp** Association of Teachers of Preventive Medicine. Vol. 1 (Fall 1975)-. Academic Scholarly Publication. English. bm. $255.00 US; $300.00 other. Human Sciences Press, PO Box 735, 233 Spring Street, New York NY 10013. **Tel** (212)620-8000, FAX (212)807-1047, telex 23421139. **(Subscription address:** Eurospan Ltd., Journals and Serials Division, 3 Henrietta Street, Covent Garden, London WC2E 8LU England.**) ED** Pascal James Imperato. **LC** RA421; .J86. **DD** 362.1/2/05. **NLM** W1 JO593Q. **CODEN** JCMHB. **[CCC].** available on microfilm and microfiche from University Microfilms International (UMI). Documents available from UMI Article Clearinghouse.
**Desc:** Devotes itself to original articles on the practice, teaching and research of community health, and encompasses the areas of preventative medicine, new forms of health manpower, analysis of environmental factors, delivery of health care services and the study of health maintenance and health insurance programs.
**Ind/Abst** Acad. Abstr. Full Text Elite (July 1990-); Acad. Abstr. (July 1990-); Acad. Ind. [Computer File] (1987-); Acad. Search (July 1990-); AGRICOLA; Crim. Justice Abstr.; Cumul. Index Nurs. Allied Health Lit.; EMBASE; Energy Res. Abstr. (Jan. 1982-); Expand. Acad. Index (1987-); Gen. Sci. Index; Gen. Sci. Source (Jul. 1990-); Health Saf. Sci. Abstr.; Health Ref. Cent. (1987-) [Select. Cov.]; Health Source (Jul. 1990-); Hum. Resour. Abstr. (?-?); Index Med.; INFO-SOUTH Abstr.; Mag. Search; Newsp. Period. Abstr. (1987-); Nurs. Abstr.; Nutr. Abstr. Rev., Ser. A, Hum. Exp.; PAIS Int. Print; Life Sci. Collect.; Pollut. Abstr. Indexes; Sage Urban Stud. Abstr (?-?); Soc. Plann. Policy Dev. Abstr.; Soc. Sci. Source (Jul. 1990-); Soc. Sci. Index Fulltext (Fall 1988-) [Full Txt.]; Soc. Work Abstr. [Select. Cov.]; Sociol. Abstr.; Trop. Dis. Bull.

SA
**JOURNAL OF COMPREHENSIVE HEALTH IN SOUTH AFRICA.** (19??)-. English. Four times a year. R87.72 South Africa; R150.00 other. Chasa, PO Box 29375, 0132 Sunnyside South Africa. **Tel** 011 27 12 3238793.

US/0022-0892
**JOURNAL OF ENVIRONMENTAL HEALTH.** **See** Environmental Issues.

UK/0143-005X
**JOURNAL OF EPIDEMIOLOGY AND COMMUNITY HEALTH (1979).** **See** Medical Science and Technology-Epidemiology.

US/0146-9428
**JOURNAL OF FOOD QUALITY.** **See** Food and Food Industry.

US/0149-6085
**JOURNAL OF FOOD SAFETY.** **See** Food and Food Industry.

NE/0304-3894
**JOURNAL OF HAZARDOUS MATERIALS.** **See** Environmental Issues-Pollution and Waste Management.

US/0735-6722
**JOURNAL OF HEALTH ADMINISTRATION EDUCATION, THE.** [J. health admin. educ.]. **Added/Corp** Association of University Programs in Health Administration. Vol. 1, No. 1 (Winter 1983)-. Periodical. English (Spanish). Four times a year. $65.00, US, Canada, & Mexico; $70.00 others; $130.00 Comes with Association of University Programs in Health Administration membership. Association of University Programs in Health Administration - AUPHA, 1911 North Fort Myer Drive, Suite 503, Arlington VA 22209. **Tel** (703)524-5500, FAX (703)525-4791. **ED** Donna Royston. **LC** RA440.6; .J68. **DD** 362.1/068. Index available. **Pr Rev. Circ:** 1,650 (ctrl).
**Desc:** An international journal of management development for health services, including topics of interest to educators and practitioners involved in the education of health managers.
**Ind/Abst** Hospit. Health Admin. Index; Hospit. Manage. Rev.

US/0160-4198
**JOURNAL OF HEALTH AND HUMAN RESOURCES ADMINISTRATION.** **See** Sociology-Social Services and Welfare.

●UK/1353-8292
**JOURNAL OF HEALTH AND PLACE.** (1995)-. English. Four times a year. $179.00 The Americas; £120.00 other. Butterworth Heinemann Publishers, Linacre House, Jordan Hill, Oxford OX2 8DP England. **Tel** 011 44 865 310366. **(Subscription address:** Elsevier Science Ltd. Oxford Fulfillment Centre, PO Box 800, Kidlington, Oxford OX5 1DX United Kingdom.**)**

UK/0954-576X
**JOURNAL OF HEALTH AND SAFETY, THE.** [J. heal. saf.]. **Added/Corp** British Health and Safety Society. (1988)-. Periodical. English. ir. £7.50. Aston University, British Health and Safety Unit, Birmingham B4 7ET England. **Tel** (021)359-3611. **DD** 363.110941. ***Formed by the union of*** *Newsletter - British Health and Safety Society, 0268-0572* ***and*** *Reviews Bulletin - British Health and Safety Society, 0268-0580.*
**Ind/Abst** Chem. Hazards Ind.; Lab. Hazards Bull.

US/0022-1465
**JOURNAL OF HEALTH AND SOCIAL BEHAVIOR.** [J. health soc. behav.]. **Added/Corp** American Sociological Association. **VFOAT** Journal of Health and Social Behavior. Vol. 8, No. 1 (Mar. 1967)-. Academic Scholarly Publication. English. qt (4 issues). $80.00 (institutions), $40.00 (individuals) US; $88.00 (institutions), $48.00 (individuals) other. American Sociological Association, 1722 North Street Northwest, Washington DC 20036-2981. **Tel** (202)833-3410, FAX (202)785-0146. **ED** Eugene Gallagher. **LC** R11; .J687. **NLM** W1 JO67BG. **CODEN** JHSBA5. Index available. **Ad Acc. Pr Rev. Circ:** 5,000. available on microfilm and microfiche from University Microfilms International (UMI). Documents available from The Genuine Article, BIOSIS Document Express, UMI Article Clearinghouse. ***Continues*** *Journal of Health and Human Behavior, 0095-9006.*
**Desc:** Reports of empirical studies, theoretical analyses and synthesizing reviews that employ a sociological perspective to clarify aspects of social life bearing on human health and illness, both physical and mental.
**Ind/Abst** Abstr. Anthropol.; Acad. Abstr. Full Text Elite (Jan. 1992-); Acad. Abstr. (Jan. 1992-); Acad. Search (Jan. 1992-); Appl. Soc. Sci. Index Abstr.; Biol. Abstr.; Crim. Justice Abstr.; Cumul. Index Nurs. Allied Health Lit.; Curr. Contents Soc. Behav. Sci.; EMBASE; Expand. Acad. Index (1989-); Health Source (Jan. 1992-); High. Educ. Abstr. (1968-19??); Hospit. Health Admin. Index; Hospit. Manage. Rev.; Index Med.; INFO-SOUTH Abstr.; Mag. Search; Med. Abstr. Newsl.; Middle East Abstr. Index; Multicult. Educ. Abstr.; Newsp. Period. Abstr. (1991-); Psychol. Abstr. (1967-); PsycINFO; PsycLit; Res. Alert [Full Cov.]; Soc. Plann. Policy Dev. Abstr.; Soc. Sci. Source (Jan. 1992-); Soc. Sci. Cit. Index [Full Cov.]; Soc. Sci. Index; Soc. Sci. Index Fulltext (Sept. 1988-) [Full Txt.]; Soc. Work Abstr. [Select. Cov.]; Sociol. Abstr. [Full Cov.]; Sociol. Educ. Abstr.; Spec. Educ. Needs Abstr.; Stud. Women Abstr.; Trop. Dis. Bull.; Women Stud. Abstr.

US/0897-7186
**JOURNAL OF HEALTH & SOCIAL POLICY.** [J. health soc. policy]. **VFOAT** Journal of Health and Social Policy; Health & Social Policy; Health and Social Policy. Vol. 1, No. 1 (1989)-. Periodical. English. qt (4 issues). $120.00 US; $168.00 other. The Haworth Press Inc, 10 Alice Street, Binghamton NY 13904-1580. **Tel** (607)722-5857, (800)3-HAWORTH, FAX (607)722-1424. **ED** Marvin D. Feit (editor's address: Department of Social Work, University of Akron, 222 Exchange Building, Akron, OH 44325-8001); Stanley F. Battle (editor's address: 16 Quail Run Lane, Bloomfield, CT 06002). **LC** RA418; .J68. **DD** 362.1/05. **NLM** W1; JO67BGC. **CODEN** JHSPEH. **Bk Rev. Ad Acc. Pr Rev. Acid Free. Circ:** 115. available on microfilm and microfiche from University Microfilms International (UMI). Documents available from Haworth Document Delivery Service.
**Desc:** A journal in which health and social policy issues, concerns, and questions are addressed by a diverse group of multidisciplinary authors achieving a blend of conceptual and practical considerations. Professionals in the health care and social work fields gain special insight into policy formulation and implementation through the journal's unique approach of featuring articles written by policy makers as well as by representatives of the affected populations.
**Ind/Abst** EMBASE; Geogr. Abstr. Human Geogr.; Health Plan. Adminis.; J. Plan. Lit.; PAIS Int. Print (1991-); Psychoanal. Abstr.; Psychol. Abstr. (1989-); PsycScan: Appl. Exp. Eng. Psych.; PsycScan: LD/MR; PsycScan: Neuropsych.; Soc. Plann. Policy Dev. Abstr.; Soc. Work Abstr. [Select. Cov.]; World Agric. Econ.

US/1057-5073
**JOURNAL OF HEALTH CARE BENEFITS.** **See** Insurance.

US/1049-2089
**JOURNAL OF HEALTH CARE FOR THE POOR AND UNDERSERVED.** **Added/Corp** Meharry Medical College. Institute on Health Care for the Poor and Underserved. **VFOAT** Journal of Health Care for the Poor & Underserved. Vol. 1, No. 1 (Summer 1990)-. Periodical. English. qt. $84.00. SAGE Periodical Press, 2455 Teller Road, Thousand Oaks CA 91320. **Tel** (805)499-0721, FAX (805)499-0871, telex 100799. **ED** Kirk Johnson. **DD** 362. **NLM** W1; JO67BGL. **CODEN** JHCUEK. Index available. **Bk Rev. Pr Rev. Acid Free. Circ:** 2000 (ctrl). available on microfilm and microfiche from University Microfilms International (UMI).
**Desc:** Explores health care problems and solution of the poor, the elderly, rural and inner-city residents, the uninsured and the underinsured. Each issue reveals research findings, explores successful programs, makes policy recommendations, and offers innovative strategies.
**Ind/Abst** Abstr. Res. Pastor. Care Couns.; Cumul. Index Nurs. Allied Health Lit.; Curr. Index J. Educ.; Curr. Lit. Fam. Plan.; Health Plan. Adminis.; Health Serv. Abstr.; Hospit. Health Admin. Index (Summer 1990-); Hum. Resour. Abstr.; Index Med. (Summer 1990-); Psychoanal. Abstr.; Psychol. Abstr. (1990-); PsycINFO; PsycScan: Appl. Exp. Eng. Psych.; PsycScan: LD/MR; PsycScan: Neuropsych.; Soc. Plann. Policy Dev. Abstr.; Soc. Work Abstr. [Select. Cov.]; Sociol. Abstr.

US/0737-3252
**JOURNAL OF HEALTH CARE MARKETING.** **See** Business-Marketing.

US/1055-6699
**JOURNAL OF HEALTH EDUCATION. ASSOCIATION FOR THE ADVANCEMENT OF HEALTH EDUCATION.** [J. health educ.]. **Added/Corp** Association for the Advancement of Health Education (U.S.) American Alliance for Health, Physical Education, Recreation, and Dance. **VFOAT** Health Education. (1991)-. Periodical. English. Six times a year. $70.00. American Alliance for Health, Physical Education, Recreation, and Dance / AAHPERD, 1900 Association Drive, Reston VA 22091. **Tel** (703)476-3493, (800)321-0789. **LC** IN PROCESS. **DD** 371. **NLM** W1; JO67BIG. Index available (bound in Nov. issue). cum.

index. **Bk Rev. Ad Acc. Pr Rev.** ctrl circ. available on microfilm. ***Continues*** *Health Education (Washington, D.C.), 0097-0050.*
**Desc:** Journal on health education for educators.
**Ind/Abst** Acad. Abstr. Full Text Elite (Jan. 1992-); Acad. Abstr. (Jan. 1992-); Acad. Search (Jan. 1992-); Contents Pages Educ.; Cumul. Index Nurs. Allied Health Lit. (1991-); Curr. Index J. Educ. (1991-); Educ. Index (1991-); Health Source (Jan. 1992-); Hospit. Health Admin. Index (1991-); INFO-SOUTH Abstr.; Int. Nurs. Index (1991-).

●US/1060-5657
**JOURNAL OF HEALTH INFORMATION MANAGEMENT RESEARCH, THE.**
**Added/Corp** American Health Information Management Association. **VFOAT** Health Information Management Research. (1992)-. Periodical. English. sa. $25.00 (US); $45.00 (other). American Health Information Management Association, Order Unit, PO Box 97349, Chicago IL 60690-7349. **Tel** (312) 787-2672, FAX (312) 787-5926, (312) 787-9793. **NLM** W1; JO67BIN.

●US/1069-837X
**JOURNAL OF HIV/AIDS PREVENTION & EDUCATION FOR ADOLESCENTS & CHILDREN.** **VFOAT** Journal of HIV AIDS Prevention and Education for Adolescents and Children; Journal of HIV/AIDS Prevention and Education for Adolescents and Children. **VAT** Journal of Human Immunodeficiency Virus/Acquired Immune Deficiency Syndrome Prevention & Education for Adolescents & Children. Vol. 1, No. 1 (1994)-. Periodical. English. Four times a year. $60.00 US; $84.00 other. The Haworth Press Inc, 10 Alice Street, Binghamton NY 13904-1580. **Tel** (607)722-5857, (800)3-HAWORTH, FAX (607)722-1424. Documents available from Haworth Document Delivery Service.

XR/0022-1732
**JOURNAL OF HYGIENE, EPIDEMIOLOGY, MICROBIOLOGY, AND IMMUNOLOGY.** [J. hyg. epidemiol. microbiol. immunol.]. **Added/Corp** Institute of Epidemiology and Microbiology (Prague, Czechoslovakia). (1957)-. Academic Scholarly Publication. English (German and French). qt. $192.00. **(Subscription address:** Karger Libri AG, Petersgraben 31, CH-4009 Basel 11 Switzerland; telephone: 011 41 61 3061500 or FAX: 011 41 61 3061234**) LC** RA421; .J9. **NLM** W1; JO674L. **CODEN** JHEMA2. Documents available from BIOSIS Document Express, CASDDS.
**Ind/Abst** AGRICOLA; Biodeter. Abstr.; Biol. Abstr.; Chem. Abstr.; Chem. Hazards Ind.; Coal Abstr.; Dairy Sci. Abstr.; EMBASE [Select. Cov.]; Health Saf. Sci. Abstr.; Helminthol. Abstr.; Immunol. Abstr.; Index Med.; Lab. Hazards Bull.; Microbiol. Abstr. Sect. B; Microbiol. Abstr. Sect. A; Microbiol. Abstr. Sect. C; Nutr. Abstr. Rev., Ser. A, Hum. Exp.; Nutr. Res. Newsl.; Life Sci. Collect.; PESTDOC; Pollut. Abstr. Indexes; Potato Abstr.; Protozoolog. Abstr.; Rev. Med. Vet. Entomol.; Rev. Med. Vet. Mycology; Rev. Plant Pathol.; Saf. Health Work; Soils Fert.; Trop. Dis. Bull.; Virol. AIDS Abstr.

US/0740-2279
**JOURNAL OF LATIN COMMUNITY HEALTH, THE.** [J. Lat. community health]. Vol. 1, No. 1 (Fall, 1982)-. Periodical. English. sa. $12.00. Journal of Latin Community Health Inc, Box 273, 107 Avenue Louis Pasteur, Boston MA 02115. **LC** RA448.5.H57; J68. **DD** 362.1/08968073.

US/0883-7589
**JOURNAL OF MARKETING FOR MENTAL HEALTH.** ***Title Change.*** [J. mark. ment. health]. Vol. 1, No. 1 (Fall/Winter 1986)-(19??). Periodical. English. be. The Haworth Press Inc, 10 Alice Street, Binghamton NY 13904-1580. **Tel** (607)722-5857, (800)3-HAWORTH, FAX (607)722-1424. **ED** William J Winston (editor's address: Professional Services Marketing Group, 1044 Masonic Avenue, Albany CA 94706). **DD** 362. **NLM** W1; JO748DF. **Bk Rev. Ad Acc. Circ:** 498. available on microfilm and microfiche from University Microfilms International (UMI). Documents available from Haworth Document Delivery Service. ***Continued by*** *Journal for Nonprofit & Public Sector Marketing.*
**Desc:** Provides an outlet for in-depth papers by leading marketing professionals and consultants as well as educators, practitioners, and administrators who are involved in marketing roles of any type for either institution-based or private- office-based mental health services.
**Ind/Abst** Health Plan. Adminis.; Hospit. Health Admin. Index (1986-); Hospit. Manage. Rev. (19??-19??); Hum. Resour. Abstr. (?-?); Soc. Work Abstr. [Select. Cov.].

US/0022-2585
**JOURNAL OF MEDICAL ENTOMOLOGY.**
**See** Zoology-Entomology.

UK
**JOURNAL OF MEDICAL SCREENING.**
**See** Medical Science and Technology.

IT
**JOURNAL OF PREVENTIVE MEDICINE AND HYGIENE.** Vol. 30, No. 1/2 (Jan./June 1989)-. Periodical. English (summaries and/or abstracts in Italian). Four times a year. L50000.00 Italy; $70.00 other. Medical Systems SPA, V Rio Torbido 40, 16165 Genoa Italy. **Tel** 011 39 10 83401. **NLM** W1; JO844E. **CODEN** JPMHEJ. ***Continues*** *Giornale di Igiene e Medicina Preventiva, 0017-0313.*

US/0278-095X
**JOURNAL OF PRIMARY PREVENTION, THE.** [J. prim. prev.]. **Added/Corp** National Association of Prevention Professionals (U.S.). Vol. 2, No. 1 (Fall 1981)-. Periodical. English. qt. £41.00 (individuals), £170.00 (institutions) UK; $215.00 US; $250.00 other. Human Sciences Press, PO Box 735, 233 Spring Street, New York NY 10013. **Tel** (212)620-8000, FAX (212)807-1047, telex 23421139. **(Subscription address:** Europspan Ltd., Journals and Serials Division, 3 Henrietta Street, Covent Garden, London WC2E 8LU England.**) ED** Thomas Gullotta. **LC** RA790.A1; J68. **DD** 362.2/05. **NLM** W1 JO841H. **CODEN** JPPRDT. **[CCC].** available on microfilm and microfiche from University Microfilms International (UMI). Documents available from BIOSIS Document Express. ***Continues*** *Journal of Prevention, 0163-514X.*
**Desc:** An invaluable journal presenting significant theoretical, empirical and methodological research in all major areas of preventative intervention in human services prevention. With the purpose of developing prevention as a scientific and professional speciality, this periodical serves as an important forum for the open exchange of innovative programs and and concepts.
**Ind/Abst** Biol. Abstr. (1987-); EMBASE; Psychol. Abstr. (1981-); PsycINFO; PsycLit; Soc. Plann. Policy Dev. Abstr.; Sociol. Abstr.

UK/0957-4832
**JOURNAL OF PUBLIC HEALTH MEDICINE.** **See** Medical Science and Technology.

US/0197-5897
**JOURNAL OF PUBLIC HEALTH POLICY.** [J. public health policy]. Vol. 1 (Mar. 1980)-. Periodical. English. qt. $110.00 US; $120.00 other. Journal of Public Health Policy, 208 Meadowood Drive, South Burlington VT 05403. **Tel** (802)658-0136, FAX (802)862-4011. **ED** Milton Terris. **LC** RA421; .J92. **DD** 614/.05. **NLM** W1 JO859UH. **CODEN** JPPODK. Index available. cum. index. **Bk Rev. Ad Acc. Circ:** 1,800. Documents available from BIOSIS Document Express, Documents on Demand.
**Desc:** Covers all aspects of public health policy, including prevention, medical care, and the physical and social environment.
**Ind/Abst** Biol. Abstr.; Cumul. Index Nurs. Allied Health Lit.; EMBASE; Environ. Abstr.; Environ. Period. Bibliogr.; Health Plan. Adminis.; Health Serv. Abstr.; Hospit. Health Admin. Index; Hospit. Manage. Rev. (19??-19??); Index Med.; Nutr. Res. Newsl.; PAIS Int. Print (1991-); Soc. Plann. Policy Dev. Abstr.; Sociol. Abstr.; Trop. Dis. Bull.

US/1058-8663
**JOURNAL OF PUBLIC SAFETY COMPUTING, THE.** ***Ceased.*** [J. public saf. comput.]. **Added/Corp** Public Safety Research Corporation. **VFOAT** JPSC. (Oct. 1991)-(19??). Periodical. English. mo. Public Safety Research Corporation, 300 Main Avenue, Aliquippa PA 15001. **LC** HV7936.A8; J68. **DD** 363.2/0285.

US/0890-765X
**JOURNAL OF RURAL HEALTH, THE.** (THE JOURNAL OF RURAL HEALTH : OFFICIAL JOURNAL OF THE AMERICAN HEALTH ASSOCIATION AND THE NATIONAL RURAL HEALTH CARE ASSOCIATION.). [J. rural health]. **VFOAT** JRH. Vol. 1, No. 1 (Jan. 1985)-. Periodical. English. qt. $90.00 institutions, $35.00 individuals. National Rural Health Association, 301 E Armour Blvd, Suite 420, Kansas City MO 64111. **Tel** (816)756-3140, FAX (816)756-3144. **ED** Thomas C Ricketts. **LC** RA771.A1. **DD** 362.1/0425. **NLM** W1; JO871N. Index available. **Bk Rev. Ad Acc, Adv Mgr:** Steve Levine, **Tel** (816)649-1681. **Pr Rev. Circ:** 2,000. ***Continues*** *American Journal of Rural Health, 0278-9388.*
**Desc:** Research focusing on health issues and services in rural areas.
**Ind/Abst** AGRICOLA [Full Cov.]; EMBASE; Health Plan. Adminis.; Hospit. Health Admin. Index (1986-).

US/0022-4391
**JOURNAL OF SCHOOL HEALTH, THE.** [J. sch. health]. **Added/Corp** American Association of School Physicians. American School Health Association. **VFOAT** JOSH. The Journal of School Health. Vol. 7 (Jan. 1937)-. Periodical. English. mo (except June and July). $100.00 US; $110.00 other. American School Health Association, 7263 State Route 43, PO Box 708, Kent OH 44240. **Tel** (216)678-1601, FAX (216)678-4526. **ED** R Morgan Pigg Jr. **LC** LB3401; .J7. **DD** 371.7/05. **NLM** W1 JO873S. **CODEN** JSHEA2. Index available (bound in Dec. issue). cum. index. **Bk Rev. Ad Acc. Pr Rev. Circ:** 7,500. available on microfilm and microfiche from University Microfilms International (UMI). Documents available from The Genuine Article, BIOSIS Document Express, UMI Article Clearinghouse. ***Continues*** *School Physicians' Bulletin.*
**Desc:** Articles on current trends, research and developments on the physical and mental health of school-age children.
**Ind/Abst** Acad. Ind. [Computer File] (1987-); AGRICOLA [Select. Cov.]; Biol. Abstr.; Chicano Index; Contents Pages Educ.; Cumul. Index Nurs. Allied Health Lit.; Curr. Contents Soc. Behav. Sci.; Curr. Index J. Educ.; Curr. Lit. Fam. Plan.; Educ. Index; Energy Res. Abstr. (March 1982-); Expand. Acad. Index (1987-); Health Index (1989-); Health Period. Database [Full Txt.]; Health Ref. Cent. (Jan. 1989-) [Full Txt.] [Full Cov.]; Index Med.; Int. Nurs. Index; Med. Rev. Dig.; Multicult. Educ. Abstr.; Newsp. Period. Abstr. (1989-); Nutr. Res. Newsl.; Phys. Educ. Index; Psychol. Abstr. (1956-); PsycINFO (?-?); PsycLit; Res. Alert [Full Cov.]; Res. High. Educ. Abstr.; Soc. Sci. Cit. Index [Full Cov.]; Spec. Educ. Needs Abstr.; SPORT Discus; SportSearch (May 1987-); Stud. Women Abstr.; Tech. Educ. Train. Abstr.; Women Stud. Abstr.

US/0898-4131
**JOURNAL OF THE ASSOCIATION OF FOOD AND DRUG OFFICIALS.** [J. Assoc. Food Drug Of.]. **Added/Corp** Association of Food and Drug Officials. Association of Food and Drug Officials. Proceedings. Vol. 51, No. 4 (Oct. 1987)-. Periodical. English. Four times a year. $73.00 US & Canada; $88.00 other. Association of Food and Drug Officials, PO Box 3425, York PA 17402. **Tel** (717)757-2888, FAX (717)755-8089. **ED** Kenneth Silver. **LC** HD90000.9.U5; A617. **DD** 363.1/92/006073. **NLM** W1; JO912EU. **Circ:** 800 (ctrl). Documents available from Documents on Demand. ***Continues*** *Quarterly Bulletin (Association of Food and Drug Officials), 0195-4865.*
**Desc:** International non-profit organization of individuals concerned with development and enforcement of uniform food, drug and other consumer protection laws.
**Ind/Abst** Environ. Abstr.; Food Sci. Technol. Abstr.; Foods Adlibra; Nutr. Res. Newsl.

UK/0004-5780
**JOURNAL OF THE ASSOCIATION OF PUBLIC ANALYSTS.** ***Ceased.*** [J. Assoc. Public Anal.]. **Main/Corp** Association of Public Analysts (Great Britain). **VFOAT** J.A.P.A. Vol. 1 (Quarter 1963)-Vol 27 ( ). Academic Scholarly Publication. English. qt. Academic Press Ltd., A Division of Harcourt Brace & Company Ltd., 24-28 Oval Road, London NW1 7DX England. **Tel** 071 267 4466, FAX 071 482 2293, 071 485 4752, telex 25775 ACPRES G. **(Subscription address:** Harcourt Brace Jovanovich Limited, Footscray High Street, Sidcup, Kent DA14 5HP UK, (Phone: 081-300-3322)**) ED** M C Finniear. **LC** TX501; .A723. **NLM** W1 JO912P. **CODEN** JPANA7. **[CCC].** Documents available from CASDDS.
**Desc:** The medium for publication of scientific papers relating to all aspects of the work of the public analysts. Ensures the safety, correct description, and satisfactory composition of food, fertilizers, and animal feeding-stuffs.
**Ind/Abst** AGRICOLA; Anal. Abstr.; Chem. Abstr.; Chem. Hazards Ind.; Dairy Sci. Abstr.; Field Crop Abstr.; Food Sci. Technol. Abstr.; Hortic. Abstr.; Lab. Hazards Bull.; Life Sci. Collect.; Potato Abstr.; SCISEARCH; Soils Fert.

UA/0013-2446
**JOURNAL OF THE EGYPTIAN PUBLIC HEALTH ASSOCIATION, THE.** [J. Egypt. Pub. Health Assoc.]. Periodical. Multiple languages (Arabic). tq (3 issues). $60.00. Shousha Building, Block A 31, Sharia 26, Cairo Egypt. **Tel** 011 20 2 755728. **NLM** W1 JO92F. **CODEN** JEGPAY. Documents available from BIOSIS Document Express, CASDDS.
**Ind/Abst** Biol. Abstr.; Chem. Abstr.; EMBASE; Index Med.

US/1055-355X
**JOURNAL OF THE FLORIDA MOSQUITO CONTROL ASSOCIATION.** [J. Fla. Mosq. Control Assoc.]. **Added/Corp** Florida Mosquito Control Association. (1990)-. Periodical. English. sa (published July and Nov.). $20.00. Florida Mosquito Control Association, PO Box 11876, Jacksonville FL 32211. **Tel** (904)743-4482, FAX (604)743-6879. **LC** RA640; .J693. **DD** 614.4/323/09759. **CODEN** JFMCE2. **Ad Acc. Circ:** 375. ***Continues*** *Journal of the Florida Anti-mosquito Association, 0743-1554.*

UK/0307-3289
**JOURNAL OF THE INSTITUTE OF HEALTH EDUCATION.** [J. Inst. Health Educ.]. (1962)-. Periodical. English. Four times a year. £20.00. Journal of the Institute of Health Education, 9 Elmbridge Drive Hale Barns, Cheshire WA15 0JE England. **Tel** 011 44 61 980 8696, FAX 011 44 61 980 7446. **ED** A.S. Blinkhom (Editor's Address: Manchester University Dental Hospital, Higher Cambridge Street, Manchester, M15 6FH England). Index available. **Bk Rev. Ad Acc, Adv Mgr:** P. Davies. **Circ:** 1,000 (ctrl).
**Ind/Abst** Br. Educ. Index; Trop. Dis. Bull.

NP
**JOURNAL OF THE NEPAL MEDICAL ASSOCIATION : JNMA.** **Added/Corp** Nepal Medical Association. **VFOAT** JNMA. (1963)-. Periodical. English. qt. $24.00. Nepal Medical Association, Kathmandu, Nepal. **(Subscription address:** Prints India, 11 Darya Ganj, New Delhi 110002 India.**)**

UK/0264-0325
**JOURNAL OF THE ROYAL SOCIETY OF HEALTH.** [J. R. Soc. Health]. **Added/Corp** Royal Society of Health (Great Britain). **VFOAT** JRSH; J.R.S.H. Vol. 103, No. 1 (Feb. 1983)-. Academic Scholarly

# Public Health and Safety

Publication. English. Six times a year (Feb., Apr., June, Aug., Oct., Dec.). £113.00. Royal Society of Health House, 38A St Georges Drive, London SW1V 4BH England. **Tel** 011 44 71 630 0121. **ED** T. F. West. **NLM** W1 JO951G. Index available. **Bk Rev. Ad Acc. Circ:** 15,000. available on microfilm and microfiche from University Microfilms International (UMI). Documents available from The Genuine Article, BIOSIS Document Express, CASDDS. *Continues* Royal Society of Health Journal, 0035-9130.
**Desc:** All matters related to the protection and preservation of health and the advancement of health related sciences.
**Ind/Abst** Appl. Soc. Sci. Index Abstr.; Archit. Period. Index; Biol. Abstr.; Chem. Abstr.; Cumul. Index Nurs. Allied Health Lit.; Curr. Contents Soc. Behav. Sci.; Curr. Technol. Index; EMBASE; Food Sci. Technol. Abstr.; Highw. Res. Abstr.; Index Med.; Index Vet.; Nutr. Abstr. Rev., Ser. A, Hum. Exp.; Nutr. Res. Newsl.; Poult. Abstr.; Res. Alert [Full Cov.]; Rev. Med. Vet. Entomol.; Rice Abstr.; Small Anim. Abstr. Bibliogr.; Soc. Sci. Cit. Index [Full Cov.]; Soc. Work Abstr. [Select. Cov.]; SportSearch; Trop. Dis. Bull.

US/1043-1721
**JOURNAL OF THE SOCIETY FOR HEALTH SYSTEMS.** [J. Soc. Health Syst.]. **Added/Corp** Society for Health Systems. Institute of Industrial Engineers (1981)-. Vol. 1, No. 1 (May 1989)-. Periodical. English. Four times a year (Mar., June, Sept., Dec.). $60.00. Institute of Industrial Engineers, 25 Technology Park-Atlanta, Norcross GA 30092. **Tel** (404)449-0460, FAX (404)263-8532. **ED** Donald P. Snider. **LC** RA399.A1; J68. **DD** 362.1/05. **NLM** W1; JO954M. **[CCC]**.
**Ind/Abst** Health Plan. Adminis.; Index Med. (May 1989-).

HK/0379-3176
**JOURNAL OF THE SOCIETY OF COMMUNITY MEDICINE HONG KONG.** **VFOAT** Journal of Society of Community Medicine Hong Kong. (197?)-. English.
**Ind/Abst** Trop. Dis. Bull.

SW/0345-5564
**JOURNAL OF TRAFFIC MEDICINE.** See Medical Science and Technology.

JA/0387-821X
**JOURNAL OF UOEH.** [J. UOEH]. **Added/Corp** Sangyo Ika Daigaku (Kitakyushu-shi, Japan). **VFOAT** Journal of University of Occupational and Environmental Health; Journal of U.O.E.H.; Sangyo Ika Daigaku Zasshi. No. 1 (March 1, 1979)-. Academic Scholarly Publication. English (Japanese). qt. $48.00. Sangyo Ikadaigaku Gakkai Uoeh, 1-1 Iseigaoka Yahatanish, Kitakyushu 807 Japan. **Tel** 093 603 1611. **NLM** W1 SA649D. **CODEN** JOUOD4. Documents available from BIOSIS Document Express, CASDDS.
**Ind/Abst** Biol. Abstr.; Chem. Abstr.; EMBASE; Index Med.; SEA Abstr.; Trop. Dis. Bull.

JA/0289-7512
**KAGOSHIMA-KEN EISEI KENKYUJOHO (1983).** (KAGOSHIMA-KEN EISEI KENKYUJOHO.). [Kagoshima-ken Eisei Kenkyujoho]. **Added/Corp** Kagoshima-Ken Eisei Kenkyujo. **VFOAT** Report of Kagoshima Prefectural Institute of Public Health. (1983)-. Japanese. an. Kagoshimaken Eisei Kenkyujo, (Kagoshima Prefectural Inst. of Public Health), 1-24, Shiroyamacho, Kagoshimashi, Kagoshimaken 890 Japan. **CODEN** KAEKEU. Documents available from CASDDS. *Continues* Kagoshima-Ken Kogai Eisei Kenkyujo Ho, 0388-2012.
**Ind/Abst** Chem. Abstr.

JA/0303-0350
**KANAGAWA-KEN EISEI KENKYUJO KENKYU HKOKU.** [Kanagawa-ken Eisei Kenkyujo kenkyu hokoku]. **VFOAT** Bulletin of the Kamagawa Prefectural Public Health Laboratories. (Oct. 1971)-. Periodical. Japanese (summaries and/or abstracts in English). an. Kanagawa-ken Eisei Kenkyujo, 52-2 Nakaocho Asahi-ku, Yokohama-shi 241 Japan. **LC** RA532.K36. **NLM** W1 KA429M. **CODEN** KEKHB8. Documents available from CASDDS.
**Ind/Abst** Chem. Abstr.

●US/1065-4186
**KANSAS HEALTH CARE IN PERSPECTIVE.** [Kans. health care perspect.]. **Added/Corp** Morgan Quitno Corporation. 1st Ed. (1993)-. English. $18.00. Morgan Quitno Corporation, PO Box 1656, 512 East 9th Street, Lawrence KS 66044. **Tel** (800)457-0742, (913)841-3534, FAX (913)841-3534. **DD** 362.
**Desc:** Reports on the state's data and rank for each of the categories featured in Health Care State Rankings.

JA/0387-5911
**KANSENSHOGAKU ZASSHI.** [Kansenshogaku zasshi]. **VFOAT** The Journal of the Japanese Association for Infectious Diseases; Journal of the Japanese Association for Infectious Diseases. (1970)-. Academic Scholarly Publication. Japanese (Japanese). mo. $280.00. (**Subscription address:** Kyowa Book Company Inc., 1 38 Kanda Jinbocho Chiyoda-ku, Tokyo 101 Japan.) **CODEN** KSSZAT.

Documents available from CASDDS. *Continues* Nihon Densenbyo Gakkai Zasshi.
**Ind/Abst** Chem. Abstr. (1970-1985); Helminthol. Abstr.; Index Med.; Protozoolog. Abstr.

JA
**KENENKEN DAYORI / HENSHU, KENENKEN KAKURITSU O MEZASU HITOBITO NO KAI JIMUKYOKU.** No. 1 (Aug. 1979)-. Periodical. Japanese. ¥2000. Aki Shobo, 9 Kanda Jinbocho 2 Chiyoda-ku, Tokyo-to 101 Japan. **LC** HV5770.J3; K46.

●US/1065-4194
**KENTUCKY HEALTH CARE IN PERSPECTIVE.** [Ky. health care perspect.]. **Added/Corp** Morgan Quitno Corporation. 1st Ed. (1993)-. English. $18.00. Morgan Quitno Corporation, PO Box 1656, 512 East 9th Street, Lawrence KS 66044. **Tel** (800)457-0742, (913)841-3534, FAX (913)841-3534. **DD** 362.
**Desc:** Reports on the state's data and rank for each of the categories featured in Health Care State Rankings.

IO/0126-0979
**KESEHATAN MASYARAKAT.** *Title Change.* **VFOAT** Journal of Public Health. Periodical. Multiple languages (English and Indonesian). Bagian Penerbitan Dan Perpustakaan, Birov Department, Indonesia. **LC** RA317. **NLM** W1 KE758C. *Continues* Kesehatan Masjarakat. *Continued by* Majalah Kesehatan Masyarakat.

UK
**KEY POPULATION AND VITAL STATISTICS. LOCAL AND HEALTH AUTHORITY AREAS / OFFICE OF POPULATION CENSUSES AND SURVEYS.** See Population Studies.

JA
**KITSUENSHITSU.** **VFOAT** Smoking Room. Week 1-. Japanese. Nihon Senbai Kosha Eigyo Honbu Hanbai Sokushinka, 2-1 Toranomon 2 Minato-ku, Tokyo-to Japan. **LC** GT3020; .K525.

UK
**KNIGHTS ENVIRONMENT & PUBLIC HEALTH ACTS.** English. qt. £195.00. Charles Knight & Company Ltd, Tolley House, 2 Addiscombe Road, Croydon Surrey CR9 5AF England. **Tel** 011 44 81 688 4163.

JA
**KOKURITSU EISEI SHIKENJO YORAN.** **Main/Corp** Kokuritsu Eisei Shikenjo. **VFOAT** National Institute of Hygienic Sciences. Japanese (Japanese). Kokuritsu Eisei Shikenjo, 18-1 Kami Yoga 1-chome, Setagaya-ku 158, Tokyo Japan. **Tel** 03 3700 1141 454, FAX 03 3700 7592. **LC** RA428.3.K64; K64A.

JA
**KOKURITSU KOSHU EISEIIN NEMPO.** **Main/Corp** Kokuritsu Koshu Eiseiin (Japan). (1948)-. Periodical. Japanese. an. Koseisho Kokuritsu Koshu Eiseiin, (Institute of Health Ministry of Health and Welfare), 6-1 Shiroganedai 4-chome, Minatoku Tokyo 108 Japan. **LC** RA440.6; .K63a.

JA
**KOKURITSU YOBO EISEI KENKYUJO NEMPO.** **Main/Corp** Kokuritsu Yobo Eisei Kenkyujo (Japan). **VFOAT** Nempo. (1947)-. Japanese. Kokuritsu Yobo Eisei Kenkyujo, 10-35 Kami Osaki 2-chome Shinaga-ku, Tokyo 141 Japan. **LC** RA421; .K66A. **NLM** W1 KO308.

KO
**KONGANG SAENGHWAL.** **VFOAT** Health Life. V. 1- (Dec. 1982)-. Periodical. Korean. mo. W27.500. Chusik Hoesa Kongang Saenghwal, Seoul 150-04 Korea. **LC** RA773; .K66.

KO
**KONGANG SIDAE.** V. 1- (1983. 12)-. Periodical. Korean. mo. W3,000. Kongang Sidaesa, 51-3 Nonhyon-dong Kangnam-ku, Seoul Korea. **LC** RA773; .K68.

JA/0916-6823
**KOSHU EISEI KENKYU.** **Added/Corp** Kokuritsu Koshu Eiseiin (Japan). **VFOAT** Bulletin of the Institute of Public Health. (1991)-. Periodical. Japanese (English). qt. **LC** RA421; .K65a. *Continues* Koshu Eiseiin Kenkyu Hokoku, 0020-3106.
**Ind/Abst** Trop. Dis. Bull.

JA
**KOSHU EISEI NI KANSURU KENKYU HOKOKU.** **Added/Corp** Tokyo (Japan) Tokyo, Japan. Eiseikyoku. Somubu. Hokenjo Kanrika. (19??)-. Periodical. Japanese. an. Tokyoto Eiseikyoku Somubu, (General Affairs Division,, Bureau of Public Health,, Tokyo Metropolitan Government), 5-1 Marunouchi 3 chome, Chiyodaku Tokyo 100 Japan. **LC** RA421; .K67. **NLM** W1 KO623L.

NE/0075-6954
**KOSTEN EN FINANCIERING VAN DE GEZONDHEIDSZORG / CENTRAAL BUREAU VOOR DE STATISTIEK, HOOFDAFDELING GEZONDHEIDSSTATISTIEKEN.** **VFOAT** Cost and Financing of Health Care. Dutch (summaries and/or abstracts in English). an. FI14.40. Centraal Bureau voor de Statistiek, AFD ALG Zaken, Postbus 959, 2270 AZ Voorburg Netherlands. **Tel** 011 31 70 3373800, FAX 011 31 038 7429, telex 32692 CBS NL. **LC** RA412.5.N4; A3. *Continues* Netherlands. Centraal Bureau Voor de Statistiek. Kosten en Financiering van de Gezondheidszorg in Nederland.

GW/0720-3373
**KRANKENHAUS-HYGIENE + INFEKTIONSVERHUTUNG.** [Krankenh.hyg. Infekt.verhut.]. **VFOAT** Krankenhaus-Hygiene und Infektionsverhutung. Began with: 1 (Feb. 1979). Academic Scholarly Publication. German. bm. DM96.00. Verlag fuer Medizin VFM, Postfach 105767, Fritz Frey Str 21, W6900 Heidelberg 1 Germany. **Tel** 011 49 06221/406248, FAX 011 49 06221/400727, telex 461 683 HVVFMD. **ED** Gerhard Schmidt-Burbach and Burkhard Wille. **NLM** W1 KR257M. Index available. cum. index. **Bk Rev. Ad Acc. Circ:** 5,000.
**Desc:** Specialist periodical for hygiene, prevention of infection and hospital hygiene.
**Ind/Abst** EMBASE.

JA
**KUMAMOTO-KEN EISEI KOGAI KENKYUJO HO.** **Main/Corp** Kumamoto-ken Eisei Kogai Kenkyujo. 1971/72-. Japanese. Kumamoto-Ken Eisei Kogai Kenkyujo, 4-33 Minami-Sendanbatamachi, Kumamoto 860 Japan. **LC** RA565.A1; K85A.

IO
**KUMPULAN PIDATO MENTERI KESEHATAN RI.** **VFOAT** Kumpulan Pidato Menteri Kesahatan Republik Indonesia. English (Indonesian). an. Departemen Kesahatan Republik Indonesia, J1 Prapatan No 10, Jakarta Indonesia. **LC** RA317; .K85.

NE
**KWARTAALSCHRIFT / RIJKS PSYCHOLOGISCHE DIENST.** Periodical. Dutch. qt. **LC** RA790.7.N4; K87.
**Ind/Abst** Crim. Penol. Police Sci. Abstr.

JA/0389-5041
**KYOTO-FU EISEI KENKYUJO NENPO.** [Kyoto-fu Eisei Kenkyujo nenpo]. **Main/Corp** Kyoto-Fu Eisei Kenkyujo. **Added/Corp** Kyoto-Fu Kogai Kenkyujo. Kyoto-Fu Kogai Kenkyujo. Kyoto-Fu Eisei Kenkyujo Nempo. **VFOAT** Kyoto-Fu Kogai Kenkyujo Nenpo; Annual Report of Kyoto Prefectural Institute of Public Health; Annual report of Kyoto Prefectural Institute of Environmental Disruption. (19??)-. Japanese. Kyoto-fu Eisei Kenkyujo, Higashi Oji 5-Jo Noboru, Higashiyama-ku, Kyoto-shi Japan. **LC** RA532.K96; K95a. **CODEN** KEKNDS. Documents available from CASDDS.
**Ind/Abst** Chem. Abstr.

US
**LAHEY CLINIC HEALTH LETTER.** English. $18.00 US; $24.00 other. Lahey Clinic Foundation, 41 Mall Road, Box 541, Burlington MA 01805. **Tel** (617)273-5100.

US/0277-9196
**LAURISTON S. TAYLOR LECTURES IN RADIATION PROTECTION AND MEASUREMENTS.** [Lauriston S. Taylor lect. radiat. prot. meas.]. **Added/Corp** National Council on Radiation Protection and Measurements. **VFOAT** Lauriston S. Taylor Lecture Series in Radiation Protection and Measurements. Lecture No. 1 (Mar. 17, 1977)-. Monographic series. English. ir. Price varies per volume. National Council of Radiation Protection Publications, 7910 Woodmont Avenue, Suite 800, Bethesda MD 20814. **Tel** (301)657-2652, (800)229-2652. **LC** UNC. **NLM** W1 LA826. **Ad Acc. Pr Rev.** ctrl circ.

US/0890-5037
**LAW AND MENTAL HEALTH.** *Ceased.* See Law.

US/1059-4930
**LEAD DETECTION & ABATEMENT REPORT.** *Title Change.* [Lead detect. abat. rep.]. **VFOAT** Lead Detection and Abatement Report. Vol. 1, No. 1 (Nov. 1991)-(199?). English. mo. IAQ Publications, 2 Wisconsin Circle, Suite 430, Chevy Chase MD 20815. **Tel** (301)913-0115, (800)394-0115, FAX (301)913-0119. **LC** TD196.L4; L38. **DD** 363.17/91. *Continued by* Lead Poisoning Report, 1075-0665.

●US/1075-0665
**LEAD POISONING REPORT.** Vol. 3, No. 8 (June 1994)-. Periodical. English. mo. $325.00. IAQ Publications, 2 Wisconsin Circle, Suite 430, Chevy Chase MD 20815. **Tel** (301)913-0115, (800)394-0115, FAX (301)913-0119. **DD** 615. *Continues* Lead Detection & Abatement Report, 1059-4930.

# Public Health and Safety

UK
**LEGIONNAIRES DISEASE UPDATE SERVICE.** (19??)-. English. qt. $110.00. CAB International Centre, Wallingford, Oxon OX10 8DE United Kingdom. **Tel** 44 491 832111, FAX 44 491 833508, telex 847964 (COMAGG G).

US/0739-7690
**LEGISLATIVE STATUS REPORT (NATIONAL ASSOCIATION OF COMMUNITY HEALTH CENTERS).** See Law.

IT
**LEGISLAZIONE PER LA SICUREZZA E L IGIENE DEL LAVORO.** Istituto Poligrafico Zecca Stato, Piazza Verdi 10, 00198 Rome Italy. **Tel** 011 39 6 85082307, 011 39 6 85082221.

CN/0382-7682
**LEPROSY RELIEF CANADA INC.** (THE LEPROSY RELIEF (CANADA) INC.; INFORMATION BULLETIN.). **Main/Corp** Leprosy Relief (Canada). Bulletin. English. Leprosy Relief Canada, PO Box 1672/Station B, Montreal Quebec H3B 3L3 Canada. **DD** 362.1/9/699805. **Continues** Help for the Leper, 0382-7674.

US
**LEPTOSPIROSIS SURVEILLANCE, ANNUAL SUMMARY (1977).** (LEPTOSPIROSIS SURVEILLANCE, ANNUAL SUMMARY.). **VFOAT** Letospirosis Surveillance. English. ir. Centers for Disease Control, 1600 Clifton Road NE, Atlanta GA 30333. **Tel** (404)639-3311, FAX (404)639-3296. **Continues** Leptospirosis, Annual Summary, 0091-0295.

FR/1148-9480
**LETTRE - EUROSANTE, LA.** (LA LETTRE.). **VFOAT** Lettre Eurosante (Versailles). (1989)-. Periodical. French. Six times a year. 1300.00F. Eurosante, 12 rue de Noailles, 78011 Versailles France. **Tel** 33 1 39505206. **ED** Diane Spama (editor's phone: 33 1 40509645). **UDC** 61. Index available. ctrl circ.
**Desc:** Health systems in Europe and reforms.

US/0277-545X
**LIFE STYLES HEALTH SERIES.** [Life styles health ser.]. **Added/Corp** University of North Carolina at Chapel Hill. Institute for Research in Social Science. No. 1, (1975)-. Monographic series. English. ir. Price varies per volume. Institute for Research in Social Science / University of North Carolina at Chapel Hill, 026A Manning Hall, Chapel Hill NC 27514. **Tel** (919)962-3061. **NLM** W1 LI407H.

CN/0712-2462
**LIFELINE (SORRENTO).** (LIFELINE.). [Lifeline]. (1980)-. Periodical. English. bm. $13.00. Lifeline Publications, PO Box 206, Sorrento BC V2E 2W0. **DD** 363.3/5.

CN/0711-4257
**LIFELINES SASKATCHEWAN (1981).** (LIFELINES SASKATCHEWAN.). [Lifelines Saskatchewan]. **Main/Corp** Royal Life Saving Society Canada. Saskatchewan Branch. Vol. 6, No. 12 (June 1981)-. Periodical. English. qt. Royal Life Saving Society Canada / Saskatchewan Branch, Saskatchewan Branch, 2205 Victoria Avenue, Regina Saskatchewan S4P 0S4 Canada. **Tel** (306)780-9200, FAX (306)525-4009. **ED** Ron Thomson. **DD** 363.1/4. **Continues** Royal Life Saving Society Canada. Saskatchewan Branch. Lifelines, 0706-7933.

US/0735-8407
**LINK LINE.** See Education.

US/0894-3036
**LINKS (NEW YORK, N.Y.).** Suspended. (LINKS / CENTRAL AMERICA HEALTH RIGHTS NETWORK.). [Links]. **Added/Corp** National Central America Health Rights Network (U.S.) Central America Health Rights Network (U.S.). (1984)-(19??). Periodical. English. qt. Central America Health Rights Network, PO Box 202, New York NY 10276. **Tel** (212)732-4790. **LC** WMLC 93/4081. **DD** 972. **Circ:** 3500.
**Ind/Abst** Hum. Rights Intern. Rep.

●CN/1200-2275
**LIVING SAFETY.** [Living saf.]. **Added/Corp** Canada Safety Council. (1992)-. Periodical. English (French). Four times a year. $7.95. Canada Safety Council, 2750 Stevenage Drive Unit 6, Ottawa Ontario K1G 3N2 Canada. **Tel** (613)739-1535, FAX (613)739-1566. Index available. cum. index. **Ad Acc. Circ:** 300,000 (ctrl). **Continues** Living Safety for the Canadian Family, 0714-5896.

CN/0714-5896
**LIVING SAFETY FOR THE CANADIAN FAMILY.** Title Change. [Living saf. Can. fam.]. **Added/Corp** Canada Safety Council. **VFOAT** Living Safety. Spring (1983)-Vol. 10, no. 2 (Summer 1992). Periodical. English (French). Four times a year. Canada Safety Council, 2750 Stevenage Drive Unit 6, Ottawa Ontario K1G 3N2 Canada. **Tel** (613)739-1535, FAX (613)739-1566. **DD** 363.1/005. Index available. cum. index. **Ad Acc. Circ:** 300,000 (ctrl). **Continued by** Living Safely, 1200-2275.

US/0146-1516
**LOCAL HEALTH DEPARTMENTS IN OREGON.** [Local health dep. Or.] (19??)-. English. Oregon State Health Division, Vital Statistics Section, Portland OR 97201. **Tel** (503)229-5897. **LC** RA447.07; L63. **DD** 362.1/2/09795. **NLM** W2 AO7 L8Y. **Continues** Tabulation of Local Health Services, Annual Summary, 0362-4080.

US/0896-7032
**LOOKING FORWARD (SEATTLE, WASH.).** (LOOKING FORWARD / THE HOPE HEART INSTITUTE.). [Look. forw.]. **Added/Corp** Hope Heart Institute. (1988)-. Periodical. English. qt. $15.00. International Health Awareness Center, 5197 Beach Side Drive, Minnetonka MN 55343. **Tel** (616)343-0770. **DD** 613.

●US/1065-4208
**LOUISIANA HEALTH CARE IN PERSPECTIVE.** [La. health care perspect.]. **Added/Corp** Morgan Quitno Corporation. 1st Ed. (1993)-. English. $18.00. Morgan Quitno Corporation, PO Box 1656, 512 East 9th Street, Lawrence KS 66044. **Tel** (800)457-0742, (913)841-3534, FAX (913)841-3534. **DD** 362.
**Desc:** Reports on the state's data and rank for each of the categories featured in Health Care State Rankings.

US/0162-8461
**LOUISIANA STATE PLAN FOR COMPREHENSIVE MENTAL HEALTH SERVICES.** **Main/Corp** Louisiana. Office of Mental Health. English. an. Louisiana Department of Health and Human Resources, Office of Mental Health, 655 North 5th Street, Room 303, Baton Rouge LA 70804. **LC** RA790.65.L8; L68A. **DD** 362.2/09763.

AT
**M/C HEALTH AND FITNESS NEWSLETTER.** Title Change. **Added/Corp** New York (State). Governor's Office of Employee Relations. Division of Management/Confidential Affairs. Vol. 1, No. 1 (Dec. 1984)-(19??). Periodical. English. bm. ACHPER, 214 Port Road, PO Box 304, Hindmarsh 5007 South Australia. **Tel** 011 61 (08)340 3388, FAX 011 61 (08)340 3399. **Bk Rev. Ad Acc. Merged into** Active and Healthy Quarterly.

NE
**MAANDBERICHT GEZONDHEIDSSTATISTIEK.** **VFOAT** Monthly Bulletin of Health Statistics. (Jan. 1982)-. Dutch. mo. SDU Uitgeverij, Postbus 20014, Christoffel Plan, 2500 EA Den Haag Netherlands. **Tel** 011 31 70 3789911. **LC** RA407.5.N37; M32.

NE/0024-8711
**MAANDSTATISTIEK VAN BEVOLKING EN VOLKSGEZONDHEID.** **Main/Corp** Netherlands. Centraal Bureau voor de Statistiek. **Added/Corp** Netherlands. Centraal Bureau voor de Statistiek. Monthly Bulletin of Vital and Health Statistics and Migration. Netherlands. Centraal Bureau voor de Statistiek Monthly Bulletin of Population and Health Statistics. **VFOAT** Monthly Bulletin of Vital and Health Statistics and Migration; Monthly Bulletin of Population and Health Statistics. (19??)-. Dutch. mo. Centraal Bureau voor de Statistiek, AFD ALG Zaken, Postbus 959, 2270 AZ Voorburg Netherlands. **Tel** 011 31 70 3373800, FAX 011 31 038 7429, telex 32692 CBS NL.
**Ind/Abst** Popul. Index.

●US/1065-4216
**MAINE HEALTH CARE IN PERSPECTIVE.** [Maine health care perspect.]. **Added/Corp** Morgan Quitno Corporation. 1st Ed. (1993)-. English. $18.00. Morgan Quitno Corporation, PO Box 1656, 512 East 9th Street, Lawrence KS 66044. **Tel** (800)457-0742, (913)841-3534, FAX (913)841-3534. **DD** 362.
**Desc:** Reports on the state's data and rank for each of the categories featured in Health Care State Rankings.

US/0147-2585
**MAINE MENTAL HEALTH PLAN.** **Main/Corp** Maine. Dept. of Mental Health and Corrections. English. Maine Department of Mental Health and Corrections22, State Office Building, Augusta ME 04333. **LC** RA790.65.M3; M34A. **DD** 362.2/09741.

IO/0126-0979
**MAJALAH KESEHATAN MASYARAKAT.** **Added/Corp** Indonesia. Departemen Kesehatan. **VFOAT** Journal of Public Health. Periodical. Indonesian (English; summaries and/or abstracts in English). Bagian Penerbitan Dan Perpustakaan, Birov Department, Indonesia. **LC** RA317; .K47. **Continues** Kesehatan Masyarakat.

UA
**MAJALLAT AL-KHADAMAT AL-SIHHIYAH LI-IQLIM SHARQ AL-BAHR AL-MUTAWASSIT.** See Medical Science and Technology.

CN/0228-8702
**MALADIES CHRONIQUES AU CANADA.** See Medical Science and Technology.

US
**MALARIA SURVEILLANCE : ANNUAL SUMMARY / NATIONAL COMMUNICABLE DISEASE CENTER.** See Medical Science and Technology-Communicable Diseases.

US
**MANAGED CARE UPDATE.** Title Change. (19??)-(19??). English. sm (24 issues per year). Faulkner & Gray Inc., 11 Penn Plaza, 17th Floor, New York NY 10001. **Tel** (212)967-7000, (800)535-8403. **Continues** Health Managers Update, 0894-4679. **Merged into** Health Alliance Alert, 1075-024X.

US/1060-1392
**MANAGED HEALTHCARE.** **VFOAT** Managed Health Care. (19??)-. Periodical. English. mo. Advanstar Communications Inc., 131 West First Street, Duluth MN 55802. **Tel** (218)723-9477, (800)346-0085. (**Subscription address:** Advanstar Communications / New Jersey, PO Box 7683, Riverton NJ 08077.) **LC** RA413.5.U5; M364. **DD** 362.1/0425. [CCC]. **Continues** Managed Healthcare News.

US/1060-1392
**MANAGED HEALTHCARE NEWS.** Title Change. (1991)-(199?). English. Twelve times a year. Advanstar Communications Inc., 131 West First Street, Duluth MN 55802. **Tel** (218)723-9477, (800)346-0085. **NLM** W1; MA57KE. [CCC]. available on an online database (file 16/Full-Text) from DIALOG. **Continued by** Managed Healthcare.
**Desc:** Directed towards healthcare benefits managers, managed healthcare organizations, and providers of healthcare services, who need current news and information regarding trends and issues in employee health care programs.

US/0897-7607
**MANAGING FOR HEALTH.** Ceased. [Manag. health]. Vol. 1, No. 1 (1987)-Ceased ?. Periodical. English. qt. Business and Health Inc, 1290 Wall Street W, Lyndhurst NJ 07071. **Tel** (201)438-1000. **DD** 658.

●US/1065-4224
**MARYLAND HEALTH CARE IN PERSPECTIVE.** [Md. health care perspect.]. **Added/Corp** Morgan Quitno Corporation. 1st Ed. (1993)-. English. $18.00. Morgan Quitno Corporation, PO Box 1656, 512 East 9th Street, Lawrence KS 66044. **Tel** (800)457-0742, (913)841-3534, FAX (913)841-3534. **DD** 362.
**Desc:** Reports on the state's data and rank for each of the categories featured in Health Care State Rankings.

●US/1065-4232
**MASSACHUSETTS HEALTH CARE IN PERSPECTIVE.** [Mass. health care perspect.]. **Added/Corp** Morgan Quitno Corporation. 1st Ed. (1993)-. English. $18.00. Morgan Quitno Corporation, PO Box 1656, 512 East 9th Street, Lawrence KS 66044. **Tel** (800)457-0742, (913)841-3534, FAX (913)841-3534. **DD** 362.
**Desc:** Reports on the state's data and rank for each of the categories featured in Health Care State Rankings.

KG
**MATERIALY KRAEVOI EPIDEMIOLOGII I GIGIENY.** See Medical Science and Technology-Epidemiology.

US/0891-9232
**MATURE HEALTH.** Ceased. [Mature health]. V. 1, No. 1 (Nov./Dec. 1986)-?. Periodical. English. bm. Mature Health, PO Box 499, Sanford MI 48657. **Tel** (517)687-5555. **DD** 362. **Bk Rev. Ad Acc. Circ:** 50,000 (ctrl).
**Desc:** A health magazine for the 50+ adult written primarily by health care professionals with an editorial emphasis on credibility of depth.
**Ind/Abst** Consum. Health Nutr. Index (Jan. 1990-199?); Health Index (1989-1990); Health Ref. Cent. (Jan. 1989-) [Full Txt.] [Full Cov.].

US/0741-6245
**MAYO CLINIC HEALTH LETTER (ENGLISH ED.).** (MAYO CLINIC HEALTH LETTER.). [Mayo Clinic health lett.]. **Added/Corp** Mayo Clinic. Vol. 1, No. 1, (Sept. 1983)-. Periodical. English. mo. Free on request, Minnesota public libraries; $24.00 other US; $31.00 Canada and Mexico; $39.00 other. Mayo Clinic, 200 First Street Southwest, Rochester MN 55905. **Tel** (800)633-4567. (**Subscription address:** Neodata / Colorado, PO Box 2606, Boulder Boulder CO 80322.) **DD** 362. **NLM** W1; MA997UH. **CODEN**

MCHLEG. Documents available from UMI Article Clearinghouse.
**Ind/Abst** Acad. Abstr. Full Text Elite (Jan. 1992-); Acad. Abstr. (Jan. 1992-); Acad. Search (Jan. 1992-); Consum. Health Nutr. Index (Jan. 1990); Cumul. Index Nurs. Allied Health Lit.; Foods Adlibra; Gen. Period. Index (1988-); Health Index (1989-); Health Period. Database; Health Ref. Cent. (Jan. 1989-) [Full Cov.]; Health Source (Jan. 1992-); INFO-SOUTH Abstr.; Mag. Artic. Summar. Elite (Jan. 1992-); Mag. Artic. Summar. CD-ROM (Jan. 1992-); Mag. Index Plus (1989-); Mag. Index. Sel. (1988-); Mag. Search; Newsp. Period. Abstr. (1988-); Mag. Index (1988-).

GW/0933-9914
**MAYO CLINIC HEALTH LETTER (GERMAN ED.).** (MAYO CLINIC HEALTH LETTER.). [Mayo Clinic health lett.]. **Added/Corp** Mayo Clinic. (19??)-. Periodical. German. mo. DM120.00 Germany; DM138.00 Europe; DM150.00 other. Mayo Clinic Health Letter Verlags SVC, Postfach 111629, W 2000 Hamburg 11 Germany. **Tel** 011 49 40 41181.

US
**MAYORS OF AMERICA'S PRINCIPAL CITIES, THE.** **Added/Corp** United States Conference of Mayors. National League of Cities. (19??)-. English. sa. $16.00 (members), $32.00 (nonmembers). US Conference of Mayors, 1620 Eye Street NW, Washington DC 20006. **Tel** (202)293-7330, FAX (202)293-2352.

US/0888-9805
**MCGRAW-HILL'S HEALTH BUSINESS.** ***Title Change.*** [McGraw-Hill's health bus.]. **Added/Corp** McGraw-Hill's Healthcare Information Center. **VFOAT** Health-Business; McGraw-Hill's Health-Business; Health Business. Vol. 1, No. 1 (July 15, 1986)-(19??). Periodical. English. wk (50 no. a year). McGraw Hill Publishing Company, Inc., 1221 Avenue of the Americas, New York NY 10020. **Tel** (212)512-6410, (800)525-5003, FAX (212)512-6111. **ED** John Reichard. **DD** 362. **NLM** W1; MC998E. Index available. **Bk Rev**. ctrl circ. Documents available from UMI Article Clearinghouse. ***Continued by*** *Health Business, 1062-6107.*
**Desc:** Information and interpretation about significant developments affecting all aspects of the business of health care, including providers, suppliers, manufacturers, and insurers.
**Ind/Abst** Pharm. News Index.

US/0198-6899
**MEASLES SURVEILLANCE REPORT.** (MEASLES SURVEILLANCE REPORT / CENTERS FOR DISEASE CONTROL.). **VFOAT** Measles Surveillance. Began with No. 1, Aug. 1966. English. ir. US Department of Health and Human Services, 200 Independence Avenue Southwest, Washington DC 20201. **LC** RA644.M5; C43. **DD** 614.5/23/0973. **NLM** W2 A C2G.

UK/0308-7050
**MEAT HYGIENIST, THE.** **See** Food and Food Industry.

FR/0765-9547
**MEDECINE SCOLAIRE ET UNIVERSITAIRE.** [Med. sc. univ.]. **VFOAT** School and University Medicine. Periodical. French (table of contents in English and French). Assn Francaise Hygiene Medecin, 53 rue Truffaut, 75017 Paris France. **Tel** 42 29 50 30. **NLM** W1; ME148W.

US/0740-1892
**MEDIA PROFILES. THE HEALTH SCIENCES EDITION.** [Media profiles, Health sci. ed.]. **VFOAT** Health Sciences Edition; Media Profiles. Health Sciences. (1983)-. Periodical. English. qt. $475.00 US; $495.00 Canada; $515.00 other. Olympic Media Information, Vandewater Road, PO Box 190, West Park NY 12493. **Tel** (914)384-6563. **ED** Walt Carroll. **LC** RA440.55; .M4. **DD** 016.61. **NLM** WA 18 M489. Index available. cum. index. **Bk Rev**. ctrl circ. ***Continues*** *Hospital/Health Care Training Media Profiles, 0095-0580.*
**Desc:** Critical reviews of film, video, and other audiovisual media for education and health sciences professionals and patient education.

US/0363-0366
**MEDICAL AND HEALTH ANNUAL.** **See** Encyclopedias and General Reference Books.

US/0749-9973
**MEDICAL AND HEALTH INFORMATION DIRECTORY.** **See** Medical Science and Technology.

US/0146-8022
**MEDICAL AND HEALTHCARE MARKETPLACE GUIDE, THE.** [Med. healthcare mark. guide]. **Added/Corp** International Bio-Medical Information Service. (1975)-. Periodical. English. an. $595.00. Investment Dealers Digest Inc., Two World Trade Center, 18th Floor, New York NY 10048. **Tel** (212)227-1200, FAX (212)432-1039. **LC** HD9994.U5; M42. **DD** 338.7/6136211/0973. **NLM** W 22 AA1 M45. **[CCC].** ***Continues*** *Medical and Healthcare Stock Market Guide, 0097-4870.*

HK
**MEDICAL CHINA. NEWSFILE / CHUNG-KUO I HSUEH. NEWSFILE.** ***Suspended.*** **See** Medical Science and Technology.

US/1060-3131
**MEDICAL EXECUTIVE COMMITTEE REPORTER, THE.** [Med. Exec. Comm. report.]. **Added/Corp** National Health Foundation (U.S.). (1986)-. Periodical. English. bm. $110.00 (one year), $200.00 (two year), $250.00 (three year). National Health Foundation, 201 North Figucroa Street, Los Angeles CA 90012. **DD** 362.
**Ind/Abst** Hospit. Manage. Rev. (19??-).

UK
**MEDICINE AND GLOBAL SURVIVAL.** (19??)-. English. £80.00. BMJ / British Medical Journal Publishing Group, British Medical Association House, Tavistock Square, London WC1H 9JR England. **Tel** 011 44 71 3874499, FAX 011 44 71 383 6402, telex 290034 HBJ MN.

RU/0025-8318
**MEDITSINSKAIA GAZETA.** **Added/Corp** Soviet Union. Ministerstvo Zdravookhraneniia. Professionalnyi Soiuz Meditsinskikh Rabotnikov (Soviet Union). Tsentralnyi Komitet. Russian S.F.S.R. Ministerstvo Zdravookhraneniia. (1922)-. Periodical. Russian. ir (104 issues per year). $169.95. **(Subscription address:** East View Publications Inc., 3020 Harbor Lane North, Suite 110, Minneapolis MN 55447.**)** **NLM** W1 ME7951. **CODEN** MEGZAT. ***Continues*** *Meditsinskii Rabotnik.*
**Ind/Abst** Curr. Dig. Post Sov. Press.

UK/0264-5947
**MEMBERS DIRECTORY / THE INSTITUTION OF ENVIRONMENTAL HEALTH OFFICERS.** [Memb. dir. - Inst. Environ. Health Officers]. **Main/Corp** Institution of Environmental Health Officers (London, England). Began in 1981?. Directory. English. £56.00. Institution of Environmental Health Officers, Chadwick House, Rushworth Street, London SE1 ORB England. **Tel** (01)928-6006. **ED** A M Tanner. **NLM** WA 22 FA1 I4M. **Bk Rev. Ad Acc. Circ:** 7,500 (ctrl).
**Desc:** Covers all areas of public health, housing, food hygiene, air and water pollution, health and safety, legislation, book reviews, etc.

US/1057-7114
**MEMORIAL'S SENIOR HEALTH UPDATE.** (MEMORIAL'S SENIOR HEALTH UPDATE : SENIOR SERVICES AT MEMORIAL HOSPITAL OF SOUTH BEND.). **Added/Corp** Memorial Hospital (South Bend, Ind.). Issue 1 (Oct. 1, 1991)-. Periodical. English. mo. Free. Memorial Senior Services, Memorial Hospital of South Bend, 615 North Michigan Street, South Bend IN 46601-9986.

SP
**MENORES : REVISTA DE LA DIRECCION GENERAL DE PROTECCION JURIDICA DEL MENOR.** **Added/Corp** Spain. Direccion General de Proteccion Juridica del Menor. (19??)-. Periodical. Spanish. bm. 1800ptas. Ministerio Asuntos Sociales Publicaciones, Alonso Cano 20, 28003 Madrid Spain. **Tel** 011 34 1 3477353, 011 34 1 3477351. **LC** K13; .E359. **DD** 346.4601/35/05; 344.60613505.

US
**MENTAL HEALTH ANNUAL REPORT / DEPARTMENT OF HEALTH AND SOCIAL SERVICES, DIVISION OF MENTAL HEALTH AND DEVELOPMENTAL DISABILITIES.** FY 1980-. English. an. Free. Alaska Division of Mental Health and Developmental Disabilities, Department of Health and Social Services, Pouch H-04, Juneau AK 99811. **Tel** (907)465-3370. **ED** Vincent A Van Der Hyde. **LC** RA790.65.A4; M46. **DD** 362.2/09798. **Circ:** 200. ***Separated from*** *Analysis of Patient and Program Characteristics; Community Mental Health Client and Services Summary.*
**Desc:** Trend analysis and statistical data for current fiscal year on admissions, discharges, open-cases and case loads at community Mental Health Centers and state psychiatric hospitals.

US/0190-1672
**MENTAL HEALTH AUDIT CRITERIA SERIES.** **Added/Corp** InterQual. (1978)-. Monographic series. English. ir. Price varies per volume. Interqual, 740 North Rush Street, Chicago IL 60611. **NLM** W1 ME924F.

US/0272-9962
**MENTAL HEALTH (BOCA RATON).** (MENTAL HEALTH.). V. 1, Article 1-. English. an. Social Issues Resources Series Inc, PO Box 2348, Boca Raton FL 33427. **Tel** (800)327-0513, (407)994-0079. **ED** E C Goldstein. **LC** RA790.A1; M2263. **DD** 362.2.
**Desc:** Interdisciplinary resource material consisting of reprinted articles from popular and professional journals, newspapers, magazines and government documents.

AT/0310-5776
**MENTAL HEALTH IN AUSTRALIA (1973).** (MENTAL HEALTH IN AUSTRALIA.). [Ment. health Aust.]. **Added/Corp** Australian National Association for Mental Health. Vol. 1 (Aug. 1973)-. Periodical. English. Twice a year (July & Dec.). 25.00Aus$. Australia National Association of Mental Health, Tweedie Place, Richmond Victoria 3121 Australia. **Tel** 011 61 3 4270373, FAX 011 61 3 4271294. **ED** Graham Burrows (editor's address: Department of Psychiatry, Austin Hospital, Heidelberg, Victoria 3084 Australia, phone: 011 61 3 496 5665). **NLM** W1 ME9258. cum. index. **Bk Rev. Circ:** 1,000 (ctrl). ***Supersedes*** *Mental Health in Australia, 0025-9667.*
**Desc:** Original articles which describe research or reported opinions of interest on matters relating to mental health.
**Ind/Abst** APAIS, Aust. Public Aff. Inf. Ser. (1980-); Psychol. Abstr. (1974-); PsycINFO; PsycLit.

US/0889-017X
**MENTAL HEALTH LAW NEWS.** **See** Law.

CN/0827-2700
**MENTAL HEALTH NEWS BULLETIN.** (MENTAL HEALTH NEWS BULLETIN / GUELPH-WELLINGTON.). [Ment. health news bull.]. **VAT** Guelph/Wellington Mental Health News Bulletin. Began publication with Spring 1979 issue. Bulletin. English. qt. Free to members. Canadian Mental Health Association Guelph-Wellington Branch, 15 Yarmouth Street, PO Box 932, Guelph Ontario N1H 6M6 Canada. **DD** 362.2/09713/43.

US/0743-9113
**MENTAL HEALTH PLAN (AUGUSTA, ME.).** (MENTAL HEALTH PLAN / STATE OF MAINE, DEPARTMENT OF MENTAL HEALTH AND MENTAL RETARDATION.). [Ment. health plan]. **Main/Corp** Maine. Dept. of Mental Health and Mental Retardation. **VFOAT** Maine Mental Health Plan. 1982-83-. English. an. Maine Department of Mental Health and Corrections22, State Office Building, Augusta ME 04333. **LC** RA790.65.M3; M35A. **DD** 362.2/0425/09741.

US/0083-2154
**MENTAL HEALTH PROGRAM REPORTS.** **Main/Corp** National Institute of Mental Health (U.S.). (1967)-. English. an. National Institute of Mental Health / Program Analysis and Reports Branch, Office of Program Planning and Evaluation, 5600 Fishers Lane, Rockville MD 20852. **NLM** W1 ME9269.

●US/1065-7525
**MENTAL HEALTH RAP.** **See** Sociology-Social Services and Welfare.

US/0191-6750
**MENTAL HEALTH REPORTS.** [Ment. heal. rep.]. (1977)-. Periodical. English. bw. $325.00. Business Publishers Inc., 951 Pershing Drive, Silver Spring MD 20910-4464. **Tel** (301)587-6300, (800)274-0122, FAX (301)585-9075. **ED** Joyce Barrett. **NLM** W1 ME927E. **[CCC]. Circ:** 900 (ctrl).
**Desc:** Key developments affecting the mentally ill. Covers congress, federal agencies, state programs, community MH centers, medicare for psychiatric services, SSDI, grants, contracts, trends and innovations.

US/0276-6884
**MENTAL HEALTH SERVICE SYSTEM REPORTS. SERIES AN, EPIDEMIOLOGY.** **See** Medical Science and Technology-Epidemiology.

US/0733-9852
**MENTAL HEALTH SERVICE SYSTEM REPORTS. SERIES EN, MENTAL HEALTH ECONOMICS.** [Ment. health serv. syst. rep., Ser EN, Ment. health econ.]. **VFOAT** Mental Health Economics. No. 1-. English. US Department of Health and Human Services National Institutes of Health, 9000 Rockville Pike, Bethesda MD 20892. **Tel** (301)496-9291, FAX (301)496-2443. **NLM** W1 ME928EU.

US/0279-4136
**MENTAL HEALTH SPECIAL INTEREST SECTION NEWSLETTER.** [Mental Health Spec. Interest Sect. newsl.]. **Added/Corp** American Occupational Therapy Association. Mental Health Special Interest Section. (19??)-. Newsletter. English. qt. $20.00. American Occupational Therapy Association, 1383 Piccard Drive, PO Box 1725, Rockville MD 20849. **Tel** (301)948-9626, FAX (301)948-5512. **ED** Virginia Dickie. **Bk Rev. Circ:** 3,700 (ctrl). ***Continues*** *Newsletter - Mental Health Specialty Section, American Occupational Therapy Association, 0194-6382.*
**Desc:** Mental health issues relevant to occupational therapy.

US/0361-9311
**MENTAL HEALTH STATISTICAL NOTE.** [Ment. health stat. note]. **Added/Corp** National Institute of

Mental Health (U.S.). Division of Biometry and Epidemiology. Survey and Reports Branch. National Institute of Mental Health (U.S.). Division of Biometry and Applied Sciences. Survey and Reports Branch. (1976)-. Statistical Publication. English. ir. Free on request. National Institute of Mental Health, 9000 Rockville Pike, Rockville MD 20892. **Tel** (301)496-9291. **LC** RC443; .U54b. **DD** 362.2/1/0973021. **NLM** W2 A N205PS. ***Continues*** *Statistical Note (National Institute of Mental Health (U.S.). Division of Biometry and Epidemiology. Survey and Reports Branch).*
**Ind/Abst** Index Med.; Psychol. Abstr. (1985-); PsycINFO; PsycLit.

US
**MENTAL HEALTH SYSTEM DESCRIPTION AND BUDGET REQUESTS FOR THE STATE OF OKLAHOMA / OKLAHOMA STATE DEPARTMENT OF MENTAL HEALTH.** **Added/Corp** Oklahoma. Dept. of Mental Health. (19??)-. English. Oklahoma Department of Mental Health, PO Box 54277 Capitol Station, 408-A North Wanul Street, Oklahoma City OK 73105. **LC** RA790.65.O5; M43. **DD** 353.97660084/206.

US/0195-766X
**MENTAL HEALTH YEARBOOK/DIRECTORY, THE.** **VAT** Mental Health Yearbook Directory. 1979/80-. English. Van Nostrand Reinhold Company Inc., 115 5th Avenue, New York NY 10003. **Tel** (212)254-3232, FAX (212)673-1239, telex 272562. **ED** J Norback. **LC** RA790.6; .M465. **DD** 362.2/025/73. **NLM** WM 22 AA1 M62.

US/0364-2518
**MERGE.** **See** Transportation-Roads and Traffic.

US
**MH, MARYLAND'S HEALTH.** V. 1- Jan./Feb. 1971-. Periodical. English. qt. Public Information Services, Maryland State Department of Health and Mental Hygiene, 301 West Preston Street, Baltimore MD 21201. **LC** RA81; .M15. **DD** 362.1/09752. **NLM** W2 AM3 S72M. ***Supersedes*** *Maryland's Health.*

US/0746-0368
**MICHIGAN HEALTH & SAFETY DIGEST.** [Mich. health saf. dig.]. **VFOAT** Michigan Health and Safety Digest. (198?)-. English. mo. $70.00. Pathfinder Associates, PO Box 5240, North Muskegon MI 49445. **Tel** (616)744-8462. **ED** Ronald E. Hauxwell.
**Desc:** A summary of Michigan and national occupational safety and health news and cases.

●US/1065-4240
**MICHIGAN HEALTH CARE IN PERSPECTIVE.** [Mich. health care perspect.]. **Added/Corp** Morgan Quitno Corporation. 1st Ed. (1993)-. English. $18.00. Morgan Quitno Corporation, PO Box 1656, 512 East 9th Street, Lawrence KS 66044. **Tel** (800)457-0742, (913)841-3534, FAX (913)841-3534. **DD** 362.
**Desc:** Reports on the state's data and rank for each of the categories featured in Health Care State Rankings.

US
**MICHIGAN HIV REPORT / DEPARTMENT OF PUBLIC HEALTH.** **Added/Corp** Michigan. Dept. of Public Health. Michigan. Special Office on AIDS Prevention. (Nov./Dec. 1991)-. Periodical. English. bm. Special Office on AIDS Prevention, Division of Disease Control, Bureau of Infectious Disease Control, Michigan Department of Public Health, PO Box 30195, Lansing MI 48909. ***Continues*** *Michigan HIV/AIDS Report.*

US/0097-8744
**MICHIGAN SCHOOL BUS ACCIDENTS.** **See** Transportation.

US/0145-1340
**MIGRANT HEALTH PROJECTS.** (MIGRANT HEALTH PROJECTS; SUMMARY OF PROJECT DATA.). **Main/Corp** United States. Health Services Administration. Bureau of Community Health Services. Division of Monitoring and Analysis. 1975-. Periodical. English. qt. US Department of Health and Human Services National Institutes of Health, 9000 Rockville Pike, Bethesda MD 20892. **Tel** (301)496-9291, FAX (301)496-2443. **LC** RA448.5.M5; U54A. **DD** 362.8/5. **NLM** W2 A H64M.

FR/0335-7198
**MIGRATIONS SANTE.** [Migr. sante]. (1974)-. Periodical. French. Three times a year. 150.00F France; 200.00F other. Migrations Sante, 23 Rue du Louvre, 75001 Paris France. **Tel** 011 33 1 42 33 24 74, FAX 011 33 1 42 33 29 73. **UDC** 61. **Bk Rev. Pr Rev.**
**Desc:** Articles, bibliographies, and interviews on the social, cultural, and psychological health of migrants.

US/0887-378X
**MILBANK QUARTERLY, THE.** [Milbank q.]. Vol. 64, No. 1 (1986)-. Periodical. English. qt. $77.00 North America; $92.00 other. Blackwell Publishers, 238 Main Street, Cambridge MA 02142. **Tel** (617)547-7110, (800)835-6770, FAX (617)547-0789. **(Subscription address:** outside North America/ Cambridge University Press, Journal Fulfillment Department, The Edinburgh Building, Cambridge CB2 2RU England; telephone: 11-44-223-312-393; FAX: 11-44-223-325-959) **ED** Ronald Bayer. **LC** RA418.3.U6. **DD** 362.1/0973. **NLM** W1; MI483P. **CODEN** MIQUES. **[CCC]**. available on microfilm and microfiche from University Microfilms International (UMI); available on an online database (files 149,648/Full-Text) from DIALOG. Documents available from The Genuine Article, UMI Article Clearinghouse. ***Continues*** *Milbank Memorial Fund Quarterly. Health and Society, 0160-1997.*
**Desc:** Covers the broad fields of public health and social welfare. Offers an in-depth approach to all aspects of healthcare policy and has earned a high regard throughout the academic and health-care communities. Topics covered include economics and health care, law and ethics in health care, and issues in hospital administration.
**Ind/Abst** Abstr. Soc. Gerontol.; Acad. Abstr. Full Text Elite (July 1990-); Acad. Abstr. (July 1990-); Acad. Ind. [Computer File] (1988-); Acad. Search (July 1990-); Appl. Soc. Sci. Index Abstr.; Bus. ASAP (1990-) [Full Txt.]; Bus. Index (1988-); Bus. Period. Index; Curr. Contents Soc. Behav. Sci.; Expand. Acad. Index (1988-); Gen. BusinessFile (1988-); Gen. Period. Index (1988-); Health Index (1989-); Health Period. Database [Full Txt.]; Health Plan. Adminis.; Health Ref. Cent. (Jan. 1989-) [Full Cov.]; Health Source (Jul. 1990-); Hospit. Health Admin. Index (1986-); Hospit. Manage. Rev.; Hum. Resour. Abstr.; Index Med. (1986-); INFO-SOUTH Abstr.; Int. Bibliogr. Sociol.; Mag. Search; Newsp. Period. Abstr. (1989-); PAIS Int. Print (1991-); Psychol. Abstr. (1988-); PsycINFO (1990-); PsycLit; Res. Alert [Full Cov.]; Sage Fam. Stud. Abstr.; Soc. Plann. Policy Dev. Abstr.; Soc. Sci. Source (Jul. 1990-); Soc. Sci. Cit. Index [Full Cov.]; Soc. Sci. Index; Soc. Sci. Index Fulltext (1987-) [Full Txt.]; Soc. Work Abstr. [Select. Cov.]; Trop. Dis. Bull.

UK
**MILLER PRODUCT LIABILITY SAFETY ENCYCLOPEDIA.** **See** Law.

US/0093-2558
**MINNESOTA ALCOHOL PROGRAMS FOR HIGHWAY SAFETY.** **Main/Corp** Minnesota. Highway Safety and Research Station. 1972-. English. 210 State Highway Building, St Paul MN 55155. **LC** HE5620.D7; M55A. **DD** 614.8/62.

●US/1065-4259
**MINNESOTA HEALTH CARE IN PERSPECTIVE.** [Minn. health care perspect.]. **Added/Corp** Morgan Quitno Corporation. (1993)-. English. $18.00. Morgan Quitno Corporation, PO Box 1656, 512 East 9th Street, Lawrence KS 66044. **Tel** (800)457-0742, (913)841-3534, FAX (913)841-3534. **DD** 362.
**Desc:** Reports on the state's data and rank for each of the categories featured in Health Care State Rankings.

US/0094-5641
**MINNESOTA HEALTH STATISTICS.** **See** Public Health and Safety-Abstracting, Bibliographies and Statistics.

US
**MINNESOTA MEDICAL ASSISTANCE (TITLE XIX) FOR FISCAL YEAR ... .** **See** Sociology-Social Services and Welfare.

CN/1187-4406
**MINUTES OF PROCEEDINGS AND EVIDENCE OF THE SUB-COMMITTEE ON HEALTH ISSUES OF THE STANDING COMMITTEE ON HEALTH AND WELFARE, SOCIAL AFFAIRS, SENIORS AND THE STATUS OF WOMEN.** [Minutes proc. evid. Sub-Comm. Health Issues Standing Comm. Health Welf. Soc. Aff. Sr. Status Women]. **Main/Corp** Canada. Parliament. House of Commons. Sub-Committee on Health Issues. **VFOAT** Health Issues; Proces-Verbaux et Temoignages du Sous-Comite des Questions de Sante du Cornite Permanent de la Sante et du Bien-Etre Social, des Affaires Sociales, du Troisieme Age et de la Condition Feminine. 34th Parliament, 3rd Session, Issue No. 1 (June 18/Oct. 3, 1991)-. Proceedings. English (French). **DD** 362.1/042/0971.

CN/1187-4406
**MINUTES OF PROCEEDINGS AND EVIDENCE OF THE SUB-COMMITTEE ON HEALTH ISSUES OF THE STANDING COMMITTEE ON HEALTH AND WELFARE, SOCIAL AFFAIRS, SENIORS AND THE STATUS OF WOMEN.** [Minutes proc. evid. Sub-Comm. Health Issues Standing Comm. Health Welf. Soc. Aff. Sr. Status Women]. **Main/Corp** Canada. Parlement. Chambre des Communes. Sous-Comite des Questions de Sante. **VFOAT** Questions de Sante; Proces-Verbaux et Temoignages du Sous-Comite des Questions de Sante du Comite Permanent de la Sante et du Bien-Etre Social, des Affaires Sociales, du Troisieme Age et de la Condition Feminine. Issue no. 1 (June 18/Oct. 3, 1991)-. Proceedings. French (English). **DD** 362.1/042/0971.

●US/1065-4267
**MISSISSIPPI HEALTH CARE IN PERSPECTIVE.** [Miss. health care perspect.]. **Added/Corp** Morgan Quitno Corporation. 1st Ed. (1993)-. English. $18.00. Morgan Quitno Corporation, PO Box 1656, 512 East 9th Street, Lawrence KS 66044. **Tel** (800)457-0742, (913)841-3534, FAX (913)841-3534. **DD** 362.
**Desc:** Reports on the state's data and rank for each of the categories featured in Health Care State Rankings.

US
**MISSISSIPPI'S HEALTH.** Periodical. English.

US/0094-0429
**MISSOURI C.H.P. IN RETROSPECT.** **Main/Corp** Missouri. Governor's Advisory Council on Comprehensive Health Planning. (1972)-. Periodical. English. Office of Comprehensive Health Planning, 303 Missouri Boulevard, Jefferson City MO 65101. **LC** RA395.A4; M852a. **DD** 362.1/09778.

●US/1065-4275
**MISSOURI HEALTH CARE IN PERSPECTIVE.** [Mo. health care perspect.]. **Added/Corp** Morgan Quitno Corporation. 1st Ed. (1993)-. English. $18.00. Morgan Quitno Corporation, PO Box 1656, 512 East 9th Street, Lawrence KS 66044. **Tel** (800)457-0742, (913)841-3534, FAX (913)841-3534. **DD** 362.
**Desc:** Reports on the state's data and rank for each of the categories featured in Health Care State Rankings.

US
**MISSOURI HOME HEALTH AGENCY PROFILES.** English. an. $17.50. Missouri Department of Health, Financial Services, PO Box 570, Jefferson City MO 65102. **Tel** (314)751-6279, (314)751-6400. **LC** RA64.36.M8; M59.
**Desc:** Contains summary and agency-specific information for each licensed home health agency in the state.

US
**MISSOURI STATE HEALTH PLAN.** **Main/Corp** Missouri. Statewide Health Coordinating Council. **VFOAT** State Health Plan. 1978-. English. an. Missouri State Health Planning and Development Agency, Broadway State Office Building, Jefferson City MO 65101. **LC** RA395.A4; M87. **DD** 362.1/09778.

AT/0157-5503
**MONOGRAPH SERIES (AUSTRALIA. DEPT. OF HEALTH. POLICY AND PLANNING DIVISION).** (MONOGRAPH SERIES / POLICY AND PLANNING DIVISION, COMMONWEALTH DEPARTMENT OF HEALTH.). [Monogr. ser. - Policy Plann. Div., Commonw. Dep. Health]. **Added/Corp** Australia. Dept. of Health. Policy and Planning Division. No. 1 (Apr. 1978)-. Monographic series. English. ir. Price varies per volume. Commonwealth Department of Health / Policy and Planning Division, PO Box 100, Woden ACT 2606 Australia. **NLM** W1 MO559Q.

UK/0300-5666
**MONOGRAPH SERIES (GREAT BRITAIN. PUBLIC HEALTH LABORATORY SERVICE).** ***Ceased.*** (MONOGRAPH SERIES / PUBLIC HEALTH LABORATORY SERVICE.). [Monogr. ser. - Public Health Lab. Serv.]. **Added/Corp** Great Britain. Public Health Laboratory Service. (1972)-?. Monographic series. English. ir. Public Health Laboratory Service Treasurer, 61 Colindale Avenue, Supplies Dept, London NW9 5DF England. **NLM** W1 PU47L.
**Ind/Abst** Life Sci. Collect.; Trop. Dis. Bull.

●US/1065-4283
**MONTANA HEALTH CARE IN PERSPECTIVE.** [Mont. health care perspect.]. **Added/Corp** Morgan Quitno Corporation. 1st Ed. (1993)-. English. $18.00. Morgan Quitno Corporation, PO Box 1656, 512 East 9th Street, Lawrence KS 66044. **Tel** (800)457-0742, (913)841-3534, FAX (913)841-3534. **DD** 362.
**Desc:** Reports on the state's data and rank for each of the categories featured in Health Care State Rankings.

US
**MONTANA STATE HEALTH PLAN.** **Main/Corp** Montana. Statewide Health Coordinating Council. 1979/80-. English. an. Montana Department of Health & Environmental Sciences, 1400 Broadway, Cogswell Building, Room C108, Helena MT 59620. **Tel** (406)444-2544, FAX (406)444-2606. **LC** RA395.A4; M96. **DD** 362.1/09786.

US/0090-7456
**MONTHLY STATISTICAL SUMMARY REPORT - STATE OF OHIO, DEPARTMENT OF MENTAL HEALTH AND MENTAL RETARDATION, DIVISION OF BUSINESS ADMINISTRATION, BUREAU OF STATISTICS.** **See** Public Health and Safety-Abstracting, Bibliographies and Statistics.

US/0149-2195
**MORBIDITY AND MORTALITY WEEKLY REPORT.** (MORBIDITY AND MORTALITY WEEKLY REPORT : MMWR / CENTER FOR DISEASE CONTROL.). [Morb. mort. wkly. rep.]. **Added/Corp** Center for Disease Control. Centers for Disease Control (U.S.) Massachusetts Medical Society. **VFOAT** MMWR. Vol. 25, No. 10 (March 19, 1976)-. Periodical. English. wk (with an annual report and supplements). $85.00 (first class), $59.00 (regular class) US, Canada, and Mexico; $105.00 other. MMS Publications, CSPO Box 9120, Waltham MA 02254. **Tel** (800)843-6356. **ED** Michael B. Gregg. **LC** RA407.3; .A37. **DD** 614.4/273. **NLM** W2 A N25M. Index available. **Circ:** 43,000. available on CD-ROM from Maxwell Electronic Publishing; available on microfilm and microfiche from University Microfilms International (UMI); available on an online database (file 149/Full-Text) from DIALOG. Documents available from UMI Article Clearinghouse, Documents on Demand. ***Continues** Morbidity and Mortality (Washington, D.C. : 1952), 0091-0031.*
**Desc:** Provides analysis and statistics on the occurrence of disease and death due to all causes in the United States.
**Ind/Abst** Am. Stat. Index; Cumul. Index Nurs. Allied Health Lit.; Curr. Lit. Fam. Plan.; Dent. Abstr. (1992-); Environ. Abstr.; Expand. Acad. Index (1992-); Food Sci. Technol. Abstr.; Foods Adlibra; Health Devices Alerts; Health Index (1989-); Health Period. Database [Full Txt.]; Health Ref. Cent. (Jan. 1989-) [Full Txt.] [Full Cov.]; Index Med.; Index Vet.; Int. Pharm. Abstr. (19??-19??); J. Watch; Mod. Med.; NAPRALERT; Newsp. Period. Abstr. (1992-); Nutr. Abstr. Rev., Ser. A, Hum. Exp.; Physic. Medline Plus; Poult. Abstr.; Protozoolog. Abstr.; Rev. Med. Vet. Entomol.; Trop. Dis. Bull.

US/0892-3787
**MORBIDITY AND MORTALITY WEEKLY REPORT. CDC SURVEILLANCE SUMMARIES.** (MORBIDITY AND MORTALITY WEEKLY REPORT. CDC SURVEILLANCE SUMMARIES : MMWR. CDC SURVEILLANCE SUMMARIES / CENTERS FOR DISEASE CONTROL.). [Morb. mortal. wkly. rep., CDC surveill. summ.]. **Added/Corp** Centers for Disease Control (U.S.) Centers for Disease Control (U.S.). Epidemiology Program Office. **VFOAT** CDC Surveillance Summaries; MMWR. CDC Ssurveillance Summaries. Vol. 32, No. 3SS (Aug. 1983)-. Government Publication. English. qt. $110.00 US; $137.00 other. Superintendent of Documents, US Government Printing Office, Washington DC 20402. **Tel** (202)275-3328, FAX (202)786-2377. **LC** RA407.3; .M55. **DD** 614.4/273/021. **NLM** W2; A C7cma. available on microfilm and microfiche from University Microfilms International (UMI). ***Continues** MMWR. Surveillance Summaries.*
**Desc:** Provides analysis and statistics on the occurrence of disease and death due to all causes in the United States.

TH/0857-0817
**MOSQUITO BORNE DISEASES BULLETIN.** (MOSQUITO BORNE DISEASES BULLETIN : MBD / MUSEUM AND REFERENCE CENTRE, SEAMEO-TROPMED NATIONAL CENTRE OF THAILAND.). [Mosq. borne dis. bull.]. **Added/Corp** SEAMEO-TROPMED National Centre of Thailand. Museum and Reference Centre. **VFOAT** MBD. Vol. 1, No. 1 (July/Sept. 1984)-. Bulletin. English. qt. Free on request. MRC Tropmed Faculty of Tropical Medicine, Mahidol Univ, 420 6 Rajvithi, Bangkok 10400 Thailand. **NLM** W1; MO9394. **CODEN** MBDBER. Documents available from BIOSIS Document Express.
**Ind/Abst** Biocont. News Inf. (1991-); Biol. Abstr. (1991-); Helminthol. Abstr. (1991-); Nematol. Abstr.; Protozoolog. Abstr.; Rev. Med. Vet. Entomol.; Rice Abstr.; SEA Abstr.; Trop. Dis. Bull.

NZ/0550-5089
**MOTOR ACCIDENTS IN NEW ZEALAND.** **See** Transportation.

US/0194-9411
**MOTOR CRASH ESTIMATING GUIDE.** **See** Transportation-Automobiles.

CN
**MOTOR VEHICLE TRAFFIC ACCIDENTS.** ***Ceased.*** **See** Transportation-Roads and Traffic.

GW/0170-5792
**MOTORIK.** **Added/Corp** Aktionskreis Psychomotorik. Vol. 1, (1978)-. Periodical. German. Four times a year (Mar., June., Sep., Dec.). DM52.00 Germany; DM57.60 other. Verlag Karl Hofmann, Postfach 1360, D-73603 Schorndorf Germany. **Tel** 011 49 7181 4020. **[CCC]. Bk Rev. Ad Acc. Circ:** 3,500 (ctrl).
**Desc:** Journal about the movement process, particularly at disabled persons.
**Ind/Abst** SportSearch (May 1987-).

GW/0027-2957
**MULL UND ABFALL.** [Mull Abfall]. (1968)-. Academic Scholarly Publication. German. mo. DM196.80. Erich Schmidt Verlag GmbH, Postfach 304240, D 10724 Berlin Germany. **Tel** 011 49 30 25008525. **UDC** 628.4. **[CCC].** Documents available from CASDDS.
**Ind/Abst** Chem. Abstr.

US/0734-9998
**MUTUAL AID.** (MUTUAL AID : THE EMS MANAGEMENT NEWSLETTER.). **Added/Corp** EMS Management Institute. (198?)-. Newsletter. English. bm. Mutual Aid Newsletter, PO Box 102, Sterling VA 22170. **Tel** (703)450-6097. **ED** Joseph V. Saitta. **Bk Rev. Ad Acc. Circ:** 1,000 (ctrl).
**Desc:** A review of current public safety issues with emphasis on management.

GW/0173-0452
**MVP-BERICHTE.** (MVP BERICHTE / MAX-VON-PETTENKOFER-INSTITUT DES BUNDESGESUNDHEITSAMTES.). [MvP-Ber.]. **Added/Corp** Max-von-Pettenkofer-Institut des Bundesgesundheitsamtes. **VAT** Max-Von-Pettenkofer Berichte. (1978)-. Academic Scholarly Publication. German. ir. Price varies per volume. Dietrich Reimer Verlag, Unter Den Eichen 57, D-12203 Berlin Germany. **Tel** 011 49 30 8314081, FAX 011 49 30 831623. **LC** UNC. **NLM** W1 MV993. **CODEN** MVBEDT. Documents available from CASDDS.
**Ind/Abst** Chem. Abstr. (1978-1982).

KO
**NA HAKHOE CHI.** **VFOAT** Korean Leprosy Bulletin. Periodical. English (Korean). Taehan Na Hakhoe, 1 2-ka Myong-dong, Chung-ku, Seoul South Korea. **LC** RC154.A1; N3.

JA/0387-9070
**NAGANO-KEN EISEI KOGAI KENKYUJO KENKYU HOKOKU.** [Nagano-ken Eisei Kogai Kenkyujo kenkyu hokoku]. **Added/Corp** Nagano-ken Eisei Kogai Kenkyujo. **VFOAT** Bulletin of the Nagano Research Institute for Health and Pollution. (1979)-. Academic Scholarly Publication. Japanese. Naganoken Eisei Kogai Kenkyujo, (Nagano Research Inst. for Health & Pollution), 1978, Komemura, Amori, Naganoshi, Naganoken 380, Japan. **CODEN** NKEHDL. Documents available from CASDDS. ***Continues** Nagano-ken Eisei Kogai Kenkyujo Chosa Kenkyu Hokoku.*
**Ind/Abst** Chem. Abstr.

JA
**NAGASAKI-KEN EISEI KOGAI KENKYUJO HO.** [Nagasaki-ken Eisei Kogai Kenkyujo ho]. **Added/Corp** Nagasaki-ken Eisei Kogai Kenkyujo. **VFOAT** Annual Report of Nagasaki Prefectural Institute of Public Health and Environmental Sciences. (19??)-. Academic Scholarly Publication. Japanese (summaries and/or abstracts in English). Nagasakiken Eisei Kogai Kenkyujo, (Nagasaki Prefectural Inst. of Public Health & Environmental Sciences), 9-5, Nameishimachi 1 Chome, Nagasakishi, Nagasakiken 852, Japan. **LC** RA532.N34; N34. **CODEN** NKHODN. Documents available from CASDDS.
**Ind/Abst** Chem. Abstr.

JA
**NAGOYA-SHI EISEI KENKYUJO HO.** [Nagoya-shi Eisei Kenkyujo ho]. **Main/Corp** Nagoya-shi Eisei Kenkyujo. **VFOAT** Annual Report of Nagoya City Health Research Institute. Began in 1951. Academic Scholarly Publication. Japanese (English). an. Free. Nagoya-Shi Eisei Kenkyujo, 1-11 Hagiyama-cho Mizuho-ku, Nagoya Japan. **Tel** 052-841-1511, FAX 052-841-1514. **ED** Akinobu Tsuyama. **LC** RA421; .N217A. **CODEN** NEKSD8. **Circ:** 380 (ctrl). Documents available from CASDDS.
**Ind/Abst** Chem. Abstr.

●US/1064-6078
**NAHE (WESTWOOD, MASS.).** (NAHE : THE NEWSLETTER FOR ALLIED HEALTH EDUCATORS.). [NAHE]. **Added/Corp** Allied Health Education Services. **VFOAT** Newsletter for Allied Health Educators. Vol. 1, No. 1 (May 1992)-. Newsletter. English. Three times a year. $40.00. Allied Health Education Services, 48 Lyons Drive, Westwood MA 02090. **DD** 370.

US
**NATIONAL DIRECTORY OF AIDS CARE.** 1st Ed. (1990/1991)-. Directory. English. $80.00. The National Directory for AIDS Care, 4903 Calle de Caring NE, Albuquerque NM 87111-2962. **ED** Helenmae Hammrich and Jeanette Dunn. **LC** RC607.A26; N38. **NLM** W 22; AA1 N272. **Bk Rev. Ad Acc. Pr Rev.** available on labels.
**Desc:** The authoritative reference for all health care providers, service organizations, agencies and the consumer. First of its kind with 14,000 resources. Comprehensive; up-to-date, national, state, county alphabetical listings; crucial referral directory; easy to read format; timely listings of: home health care, testing sites, community-based agencies, health departments, research, education, medical services, national organizations.

US/0361-7904
**NATIONAL DIRECTORY OF SAFETY CONSULTANTS.** 3rd Ed.; 1974-. Directory. English. sa. $25.00. American Society of Safety Engineers, 1800 East Oakton Street, Des Plaines IL 60018. **Tel** (312)692-4121. **ED** Renee S Schleicher. **LC** T55.A1; N33. **DD** 338.4/7/614802573. **NLM** WA 22 AA1 N23. **Circ:** 2,000.
**Desc:** Qualifications/credentials of about 500 safety and health consultants available to work with lawyers and corporate executives.

US
**NATIONAL EMERGENCY TRAINING & INFORMATION GUIDE.** English. sa. $35.00. Emergency Response Institute, 4537 Fox Hall Drive NE, Olympia WA 98516. **Tel** (206)493-7785, FAX (206)493-0949. **ED** Patrick LaValla. **Circ:** 2000.

US/0147-2771
**NATIONAL HEALTH DIRECTORY.** (1977)-. English. an (May). $103.00. Aspen Publishers Inc., 7201 McKinney Circle, Frederick MD 21701. **Tel** (800)234-1660, (301)698-7100, FAX (301)251-5784, telex 5106014543. **(Subscription address:** Aspen Publishers Inc., PO Box 990, Frederick MD 21701.**) LC** RA7.5; .N37. **DD** 353.008/41/02573. **NLM** WA 22 AA1 N32.
**Desc:** Covers public health administration, government agencies, and delivery of health care.

US
**NATIONAL HEALTH INTERVIEW SURVEY [COMPUTER FILE] / U.S. DEPARTMENT OF HEALTH AND HUMAN SERVICES, PUBLIC HEALTH SERVICE, CENTERS FOR DISEASE CONTROL.** **Added/Corp** National Health Interview Survey (U.S.) National Center for Health Statistics (U.S.). (1987)-. English. National Center for Health Statistics, 6525 Belcrest Road, Hyattsville MD 20782. **Tel** (301)436-8500.
**Desc:** System requirements: IBM compatible 80286 based PC; 640K or more; MS-DOS 3.0 or higher; 5MB of free space on hard disk drive; CD-ROM reader; MS-DOS CD-ROM extensions 2.0 or higher.

US
**NATIONAL HEALTH POLICY FORUM.** **See** Public Administration.

US/0278-6834
**NATIONAL INSTITUTES OF HEALTH RESEARCH PLAN.** [Natl. Inst. Health res. plan]. **Main/Corp** National Institutes of Health (U.S.). **VFOAT** NIH Research Plan. Began in 1980-1982. English. an. US Department of Health and Human Services National Institutes of Health, 9000 Rockville Pike, Bethesda MD 20892. **Tel** (301)496-9291, FAX (301)496-2443. **NLM** W2 A N2058N.

US/0094-761X
**NATIONAL TRANSPORTATION SAFETY BOARD DECISIONS.** **See** Transportation.

US/0741-9147
**NATIONAL WOMEN'S HEALTH REPORT.** [Natl. women's health rep.]. **Added/Corp** National Women's Health Resource Center (U.S.). Vol. 1, No. 1 (Jan. 1984)-. Periodical. English. bm. $50.00 (institutions), $25.00 (individuals) US; $55.00 other. National Women's Health Resource Center, 2400 M Street NW, Suite 325, Washington DC 20037. **Tel** (202)293-6045, FAX (202)293-7256. **NLM** W1; NA782L. **Bk Rev**, (Qty: 12/yr). **Circ:** 15,000 (ctrl).
**Desc:** Disseminates comprehensive and objective information about women's health, offering individuals the information they need to make informed decisions about their health care, including unbiased information on preventive care, nutrition, medical research, legislation and more.
**Ind/Abst** Cumul. Index Nurs. Allied Health Lit.

US/0028-0496
**NATION'S HEALTH (1971), THE.** (THE NATION'S HEALTH : THE OFFICIAL NEWSPAPER OF THE AMERICAN PUBLIC HEALTH ASSOCIATION.). [Nation's health]. Vol. 1, (Jan. 1971)-. Periodical. English. ir (11 issues). $15.00 US and territories; $18.00 other. American Public Health Association, 1015 15th Street Northwest, Washington DC 20005. **Tel** (202)789-5666. **ED** Kathryn Foxhall. **LC** RA421. **DD** 362.1/0973. **NLM** W1 NA796. **[CCC]. Bk Rev. Ad Acc. Circ:** 32,000. available on microfilm and microfiche from University Microfilms International (UMI); available on an online database (file 149/Full-Text) from DIALOG. ***Continues in part** American Journal of Public Health and the Nation's Health, 0002-9522.*
**Desc:** Health policy, APHA business, environmental health, nutrition, occupational health, safety, congress, federal agencies, and health statistics.
**Ind/Abst** Acad. Abstr. Full Text Elite (Jan. 1992-); Acad.

Abstr. (Jan. 1992-); Acad. Search (Jan. 1992-); Biol. Dig.; Energy Res. Abstr. (Jan. 1981-); Health Index (1989-); Health Period. Database; Health Ref. Cent. (Jan. 1989-) [Full Txt.] [Full Cov.]; Health Source (Jan. 1992-); INFO-SOUTH Abstr.; Mag. Search.

US/0083-209X
**NCRP REPORT.** [NCRP rep.]. **Added/Corp** National Council on Radiation Protection and Measurements. National Council on Radiation Protection and Measurements. Report. **VAT** National Council on Radiation Protection and Measurements Report. No. 32 (1967)-. Academic Scholarly Publication. English. ir. Price varies per volume. National Council on Radiation Protection and Measurements Report, 7910 Woodmont Avenue, Suite 800, Bethesda MD 20814. **Tel** (301)657-2652, (800)229-2652. **LC** UNC. **CODEN** NCRDBG. **Pr Rev. Circ:** 20,000. Documents available from BIOSIS Document Express. ***Continues*** *NCRP Report, 0083-209X.*
**Desc:** Presents scientific information and recommendations about protection against radiation, and radiation measurements, quantities and units especially those concerned with radiation protection.
**Ind/Abst** Biol. Abstr.; EMBASE; GeoRef.

●US/1065-4291
**NEBRASKA HEALTH CARE IN PERSPECTIVE.** [Neb. health care perspect.]. **Added/Corp** Morgan Quitno Corporation. 1st Ed. (1993)-. English. $18.00. Morgan Quitno Corporation, PO Box 1656, 512 East 9th Street, Lawrence KS 66044. **Tel** (800)457-0742, (913)841-3534, FAX (913)841-3534. **DD** 362.
**Desc:** Reports on the state's data and rank for each of the categories featured in Health Care State Rankings.

US
**NEBRASKA HEALTH MANPOWER REPORTS : PHYSICIAN'S ASSISTANTS.** **Main/Corp** Nebraska. Division of Health Data and Statistical Research. English. an. 301 Centennial Mall South, PO Box 95007, Lincoln NE 68509. **LC** R697.P45; N42A. **NLM** W2; AN1 D34ndc.

US/0161-4533
**NEIGHBORHOOD HEALTH CENTERS : SUMMARY OF PROJECT DATA. REPORT.** **Main/Corp** United States. Health Services Administration. Bureau of Community Health Service. Division of Monitoring and Analysis. No. 9- 4th Quarter 1974-. Periodical. English. qt. US Health Services Administration, Rockville MD 20852. **LC** RA445; .U53A. **DD** 362.1. ***Continues*** *Comprehensive Health Service Projects. Summary of Project Data. CHSP Report, 0161-4525.*

US
**NEISS DATA HIGHLIGHTS : NATIONAL ELECTRONIC INJURY SURVEILLANCE SYSTEM.** **Added/Corp** U.S. Consumer Product Safety Commission. Directorate for Hazard Identification and Analysis. U.S. Consumer Product Safety Commission. Directorate for Epidemiology. **VAT** National Electronic Injury Surveillance System Data Highlights. (Mar./May 1977)-. Periodical. English. an. Free on request. US Consumer Product Safety Commission, 5401 West Bard Avenue, Room 625, Washington DC 20207. **Tel** (301)504-0424. **LC** HV676.A1; N43. **DD** 363.1/02/097305. **Circ:** 3,000 (ctrl). Documents available from Documents on Demand. ***Continues*** *Neiss News, 0364-6475.*
**Desc:** Provides national estimates of products under the jurisdiction of Consumer Product Safety Commission treated in hospital emergency departments.
**Ind/Abst** Am. Stat. Index.

HU/0369-3805
**NEPEGESZSEGUGY.** [Nepegeszsegugy]. **Added/Corp** Hungary. Egeszsegugy-Miniszterium. Hungary. Belugy-Miniszterium. Hungary. Nepjoleti Miniszterium. **VFOAT** Vengerskoe Zdravookhranenie; People's Health. (1920)-. Periodical. Hungarian (summaries and/or abstracts in English, French, German and Russian). bm. $18.00. **(Subscription address:** Kultura, PO Box 149, H 1389 Budapest 62 Hungary.**)** **NLM** W1 NE204.
**Ind/Abst** Trop. Dis. Bull.

US/8755-867X
**NETWORK NEWS - NATIONAL WOMEN'S HEALTH NETWORK (U.S.).** (NETWORK NEWS : THE NEWSLETTER OF THE NATIONAL WOMEN'S HEALTH NETWORK.). [Netw. news - Natl. Women's Health Netw. (U.S.)]. Vol. 7, No. 4 (July/Aug. 1982)-. Newsletter. English. bm. $25.00 individuals, $50.00 groups or organizations. National Women's Health Network, 1324 G Street NW, Washington DC 20005. **Tel** (202)543-9222. **ED** Gretchen Bloom. **DD** 362. **Bk Rev.** ***Continues*** *National Women's Health Network News, 0277-0385.*
**Desc:** We are a non-profit, consumer advocacy organization devoted exclusively to women's health issues. We monitor federal health legislation and run a public education service on women's health issues.
**Ind/Abst** Consum. Health Nutr. Index; Health Period. Database [Full Txt.]; Health Ref. Cent. (Jan. 1989-) [Full Txt.] [Full Cov.].

US/0270-3637
**NETWORK (RESEARCH TRIANGLE PARK).** **See** Birth Control.

US
**NEVADA HEALTH.** (19??)-. Periodical. English. Free on request. Nevada State Division of Health, Capitol Complex, Carson City NV 89710.

●US/1065-4305
**NEVADA HEALTH CARE IN PERSPECTIVE.** [Nev. health care perspect.]. **Added/Corp** Morgan Quitno Corporation. 1st Ed. (1993)-. English. $18.00. Morgan Quitno Corporation, PO Box 1656, 512 East 9th Street, Lawrence KS 66044. **Tel** (800)457-0742, (913)841-3534, FAX (913)841-3534. **DD** 362.
**Desc:** Reports on the state's data and rank for each of the categories featured in Health Care State Rankings.

US/0146-1451
**NEW DIMENSIONS IN MENTAL HEALTH.** **Added/Corp** National Institute of Mental Health (U.S.). (June 1976)-. Monographic series. English. Price varies per volume. US Department of Health & Human Services / Alcohol Drug Abuse & Mental Health Administration, 5600 Fishers Lane, Rockville MD 20857. **Tel** (301)443-3783, FAX (301)443-1719. **NLM** W1 NE372N. ***Continues in part*** *Memo from the Director - National Institute of Mental Health.*

●US/1065-4313
**NEW HAMPSHIRE HEAALTH CARE IN PERSPECTIVE.** [N.H. heaalth care perspect.]. **Added/Corp** Morgan Quitno Corporation. 1st Ed. (1993)-. English. $18.00. Morgan Quitno Corporation, PO Box 1656, 512 East 9th Street, Lawrence KS 66044. **Tel** (800)457-0742, (913)841-3534, FAX (913)841-3534. **DD** 362.
**Desc:** Reports on the state's data and rank for each of the categories featured in Health Care State Rankings.

●US/1065-4526
**NEW JERSEY HEALTH CARE IN PERSPECTIVE.** [N.J. health care perspect.]. **Added/Corp** Morgan Quitno Corporation. 1st Ed. (1993)-. English. $18.00. Morgan Quitno Corporation, PO Box 1656, 512 East 9th Street, Lawrence KS 66044. **Tel** (800)457-0742, (913)841-3534, FAX (913)841-3534. **DD** 362.
**Desc:** Reports on the state's data and rank for each of the categories featured in Health Care State Rankings.

●US/1065-4321
**NEW MEXICO HEALTH CARE IN PERSPECTIVE.** [N.M. health care perspect.]. **Added/Corp** Morgan Quitno Corporation. 1st Ed. (1993)-. English. $18.00. Morgan Quitno Corporation, PO Box 1656, 512 East 9th Street, Lawrence KS 66044. **Tel** (800)457-0742, (913)841-3534, FAX (913)841-3534. **DD** 362.
**Desc:** Reports on the state's data and rank for each of the categories featured in Health Care State Rankings.

US/8756-260X
**NEW RESEARCH IN MENTAL HEALTH.** [New res. ment. health]. **Added/Corp** Ohio. Division of Mental Health and Forensic Services. Office of Program Evaluation and Research. Ohio. Division of Mental Health. Office of Program Evaluation and Research. (1975)-. Periodical. English. be. free. Ohio Department of Mental Health, Office of Program Evaluation and Research, State Office Tower/Room 1340J, 30 East Broad Street, Columbus OH 43266-0414. **Tel** (614)466-8651, FAX (614)466-9928. **ED** Dee Roth. **LC** RA790.65.O3; N48. **DD** 362.2/05. **Circ:** 5,000.
**Desc:** Articles concerning completed or in-progress research projects in the field of mental health.

US/1048-2911
**NEW SOLUTIONS.** (NEW SOLUTIONS : A JOURNAL OF ENVIRONMENTAL AND OCCUPATIONAL HEALTH POLICY.). [New solut.]. **Added/Corp** Alice Hamilton Memorial Library. Oil, Chemical, and Atomic Workers International Union. **VFOAT** NS. (1990)-. Periodical. English. qt. $40.00 (individuals & non-profit institutions); $60.00 (others). Oil Chem Atomic Workers Intl, PO Box 281200, Lakewood CO 80228-8200. **Tel** (303)987-2229, FAX (303)987-1967. **LC** RA566.3; .N49. **DD** 616.9/803. **NLM** W1; NE496. **CODEN** NESLES. Documents available from Documents on Demand.
**Ind/Abst** Altern. Press Index (199?-); Environ. Abstr.; Environ. Period. Bibliogr.; PAIS Int. Print (1991).

●US/1065-433X
**NEW YORK HEALTH CARE IN PERSPECTIVE.** (1993)-. English. $18.00. Morgan Quitno Corporation, PO Box 1656, 512 East 9th Street, Lawrence KS 66044. **Tel** (800)457-0742, (913)841-3534, FAX (913)841-3534.
**Desc:** Reports on the state's data and rank for each of the categories featured in Health Care State Rankings.

NZ/0114-3727
**NEW ZEALAND HEALTH & HOSPITAL.** **See** Medical Science and Technology-Hospital Administration and Medical Centers.

NZ/0111-6304
**NEW ZEALAND HEALTH REVIEW.** (NEW ZEALAND HEALTH REVIEW : JOURNAL OF THE COLLEGE OF COMMUNITY MEDICINE, THE NZ INSTITUTE OF HEALTH ADMINISTRATORS AND THE NZ NURSES ASSOCIATION.). [N.Z. health rev.]. **Added/Corp** NZ Nurses Association. NZ Institute of Health Administrators. College of Community Medicine (N.Z.). (198?)-. Periodical. English. qt. $10.00. New Zealand Health Review, PO Box 10-245, The Terrace, Wellington New Zealand. **NLM** W1 NE9729. Documents available from UMI Article Clearinghouse.
**Desc:** Information on health resources and services and the delivery of health care.
**Ind/Abst** ABI/INFORM Glob. Ed.

NZ/0112-0212
**NEW ZEALAND JOURNAL OF ENVIRONMENTAL HEALTH.** [N.Z. j. environ. health]. (1982)-. Periodical. English. Four times a year. 22.50NZ$. New Zealand Institute of Environmental Health, 161 West Street, Invercargill New Zealand. **Tel** 011 64 3 2170199, 2181959, FAX 011 64 3 2144655. **ED** Rodney Giddens (editor's address: 348 Ngatai Road, Tauranga, New Zealand; phone: 07 5761344). **DD** 614. **Ad Acc.** ***Continues*** *New Zealand Environmental Health Inspector, 0110-4969.*

US
**NEWS.** **Main/Corp** United States-Mexico Border Health Association. **Added/Corp** Pan American Health Association. **VFOAT** Noticia - Asociacion Fronteriza Mexicano-Estaounidense de Salud. (19??)-. Periodical. English. ir (3 to 4 per year). comes with membership. US Mexico Border Health Association, PAHO Field Office, 6006 North Mesa/Suite 600, El Paso TX 79912. **Tel** (915)581-6645.

US
**NEWS & FEATURES FROM NIH.** ***Title Change.*** **Added/Corp** National Institutes of Health (U.S.). **VFOAT** News and Features from NIH. (19??)-(199?). English. mo. National Institute of Health, 9000 Rockville Pike, Building 31/Room 2B-03, Bethesda MD 20892. **Tel** (301)496-9291. ***Continued by*** *NIH News & Features.*

MY
**NEWS: HEALTH ACTION INTERNATIONAL, HAI.** English. bm. $20.00 (1 year), $36.00 (2 year), $48.00 (3 year) non-profit groups and individuals in industrialized countries; $10.00 (1 year), $18.00 (2 year), $24.00 (3 year) non-profit groups and indivuals in third world countries; $50.00 (one year), $90.00 (2 year), $120.00 (3 year) other. International Organ of Consumers Unions, PO Box 1045, 10830 Penang Malaysia. **Tel** 011 60 4 371396, FAX 011 60 4 366506.
**Ind/Abst** Trop. Dis. Bull.

US
**NEWSBANK : HEALTH.** 1970-. Periodical. English. mo. Newsbank Inc, 58 Pine Street, New Canaan CT 06840. **Tel** (800)243-7694, (800)762-8182, FAX (203)966-6254. **LC** RA445. cum. index.

BE
**NEWSLETTER BIOCHEMICAL AND HEALTH RESEARCH.** **See** Biology-Biochemistry.

UK/0950-2424
**NEWSLETTER - CENTRE FOR HEALTH ECONOMICS.** (NEWSLETTER.). [Newsl. - Cent. Health Econ.]. **VFOAT** Centre for Health Economics Newsletter. (1986)-. Newsletter. English. sa. **DD** 338.47362105.
**Ind/Abst** Trop. Dis. Bull.

US/1049-2364
**NEWSLETTER - MACRO SYSTEMS. INSTITUTE FOR RESOURCE DEVELOPMENT. DEMOGRAPHIC AND HEALTH SURVEYS.** (NEWSLETTER / DEMOGRAPHIC AND HEALTH SURVEYS.). [Newsl. - Macro Syst., Inst. Resour. Dev., Demogr. Health Surv.]. **Added/Corp** Macro Systems. Institute for Resource Development. Demographic and Health Surveys. **VFOAT** DHS Newsletter; DHS/Macro Systems. (198?)-. Newsletter. English. sa. Free on request. IRD MACRO, 8850 Stanford Boulevard, Suite 4000, Columbia MD 21045. **Tel** (301)290-2955, (301)290-2800. **DD** 001. Documents available from Documents on Demand. ***Continues*** *Newsletter (Institute for Resource Development/Westinghouse (Columbia, Md.). Demographic and Health Surveys).*
**Ind/Abst** Environ. Abstr.; Trop. Dis. Bull.

CN/0226-2789
**NEWSLETTER - MINISTRY OF HEALTH (VICTORIA).** (NEWSLETTER - MINISTRY OF HEALTH.). [Newsl. - Minist. Health (Victoria)]. **Main/Corp** British Columbia. Ministry of Health. Nov. 1- Nov. 1978-. Newsletter. English. Ministry of Health / Victoria, 1515 Blanshard Street, Victoria British Columbia V8W 3C8 Canada. **Tel** 387-2749. **DD** 354.7110677.

SW/0348-7598
**NEWSLETTER - NATIONAL BOARD OF OCCUPATIONAL SAFETY AND HEALTH.** **Added/Corp** Sweden. Arbetarskyddsstyrelsen. No. 1 (1976)-. Periodical. English. bm. Free on request. National Board of Occupational Safety and Health, International Secretariat, S 17184 Solna Sweden. **Tel** 46 8 7309000. **NLM** W1 NE998L.
**Ind/Abst** Chem. Hazards Ind.; Ergon. Abstr.; Int. Labour Doc.; Lab. Hazards Bull.

US
**NIH ADVISORY COMMITTEES.** **Main/Corp** National Institutes of Health (U.S.). Committee Management Staff. (Oct. 1987)-. English. sa. US Department of Health and Human Services National Institutes of Health, 9000 Rockville Pike, Bethesda MD 20892. **Tel** (301)496-9291, FAX (301)496-2443. **LC** RA11; .D32A. **DD** 362.1/025/73. **NLM** WA 22; AA1 N13. available on microfiche (Vols. for Oct. 1987- distributed to depository libraries). ***Continues** NIH Public Advisory Groups, 0566-8301.*

US/8756-601X
**NIH ALMANAC.** (NIH ALMANAC / PREPARED BY THE DIVISION OF PUBLIC INFORMATION.). [NIH alm.]. **Main/Corp** National Institutes of Health (U.S.). Division of Public Information. **Added/Corp** National Institutes of Health (U.S.). Editorial Operations Branch. (1978)-. English. an. Free on request. National Institute of Health, 9000 Rockville Pike, Building 31/Room 2B-03, Bethesda MD 20892. **Tel** (301)496-9291. **LC** RA11; .D293. **DD** 353.0077/05. **NLM** W2 A N221. ***Continues** National Institutes of Health Almanac, 0565-789X.*

US/8755-4674
**NIH DATA BOOK.** **See** Medical Science and Technology.

US
**NIH HEALTHLINE : CONSUMER HEALTH INFORMATION FROM THE NATIONAL INSTITUTES OF HEALTH.** **Added/Corp** National Institutes of Health (U.S.) National Institutes of Health (U.S.). Office of Communications. **VFOAT** National Institutes of Health Healthline. (Oct. 1991)-. Periodical. English. National Institutes of Health, 9000 Rockville Pike, Bethesda MD 20014. **Tel** (301)496-6975. ***Continues** Healthline (Bethesda, Md.).*

US/0737-6863
**NIH PUBLICATION.** [NIH publ.]. **Added/Corp** National Institutes of Health (U.S.). **VFOAT** N.I.H. Publication. **VAT** National Institutes of Health Publication. (19??)-. Academic Scholarly Publication. English. bm. National Institute of Mental Health, 9000 Rockville Pike, Rockville MD 20892. **Tel** (301)496-9291. **CODEN** DPNSDO. Documents available from CASDDS.
**Ind/Abst** Chem. Abstr.

US/1057-5871
**NIH RECORD, THE.** [NIH rec.]. **Added/Corp** National Institutes of Health (U.S.). **VFOAT** N.I.H. Record; Record. **VAT** National Institutes of Health Record. (1949)-. Government Publication. English. bw. $45.00 domestic; $56.25 other. Superintendent of Documents, US Government Printing Office, Washington DC 20402. **Tel** (202)275-3328, FAX (202)786-2377. **LC** RA11; .D15. **DD** 614. **NLM** W1 N137. ctrl circ.
**Desc:** A National Institute of Health publication covering current health news and events within the Institute, and general information of interest for NIH and Department of Health and Human Services employees, and the public.

NO/0332-5652
**NIPH ANNALS.** ***Suspended.*** [NIPH ann.]. **Added/Corp** Statens institutt for folkehelse. **VAT** National Institute of Public Health Annals. Vol. 1 (Jan. 1978)-Suspended Vol. 16. Academic Scholarly Publication. English. sa. National Institute of Public Health, Geitmyrsveien 75, 0462 Oslo 4 Norway. **Tel** 011 47 22 042200, FAX 011 2 353605. **ED** S. Erichsen. **NLM** W1 N139T. **CODEN** NIAND5. **Pr Rev. Circ:** 900. Documents available from BIOSIS Document Express, CASDDS.
**Ind/Abst** Biol. Abstr.; Chem. Abstr.; EMBASE [Select. Cov.]; Index Med.; Life Sci. Collect.; Trop. Dis. Bull.

JA/0021-5082
**NIPPON EISEIGAKU ZASSHI.** (NIHON EISEIGAKU ZASSHI.). [Nippon eiseigaku zasshi]. **Added/Corp** Nihon Eisei Gakkai. **VFOAT** Japanese Journal of Hygiene. Vol. 1 (Aug. 1946)-. Academic Scholarly Publication. Japanese. bm. $92.00. Nihon Eisei Gakkai, (Japanese Soc. for Hygiene), Kyoto Daigaku Igakubu, Eiseigaku Kyoshitsu, Yoshida Konoecho, Sakyoku, Kyotoshi, Kyotofu 606, Japan. **(Subscription address:** Kyowa Book Company Inc., 1-38 Kanda Jinbo-Cho, Chiyoda-Ku Tokyo 101, Japan**)** **NLM** W1 NI889M. **CODEN** NEZAAQ. Documents available from BIOSIS Document Express, CASDDS.
**Ind/Abst** Biol. Abstr.; Chem. Abstr.; EMBASE; Index Med.; Saf. Health Work.

JA/0546-1766
**NIPPON KOSHU EISEI ZASSHI.** **Added/Corp** Nippon Koshu Eisei Gakkai. Nippon Koshu Eisei Kyokai. **VFOAT** Japanese Journal of Public Health; Nihon Koshu Eisei Zasshi. (1954)-. Academic Scholarly Publication. Japanese (English; summaries and/or abstracts in English). mo. $144.00. **(Subscription address:** Kyowa Book Company Inc., 1-38 Kanda Jinbo-Cho, Chiyoda-Ku, Tokyo 101, Japan (Phone: 03-3293-0727)**)** **NLM** W1 NI92T. **CODEN** NKEZA4. Documents available from CASDDS.
**Ind/Abst** Chem. Abstr.

●US/1065-4348
**NORTH CAROLINA HEALTH CARE IN PERSPECTIVE.** [N.C. health care perspect.]. **Added/Corp** Morgan Quitno Corporation. 1st Ed. (1993)-. English. $18.00. Morgan Quitno Corporation, PO Box 1656, 512 East 9th Street, Lawrence KS 66044. **Tel** (800)457-0742, (913)841-3534, FAX (913)841-3534. **DD** 362.
**Desc:** Reports on the state's data and rank for each of the categories featured in Health Care State Rankings.

US/0098-5783
**NORTH CAROLINA LOCAL HEALTH DEPARTMENTS : BUDGETARY, ECONOMIC, AND OTHER PERTINENT DATA.** **Main/Corp** North Carolina. Division of Health Services. Office of Local Administration. English. PO Box 2091, Raleigh NC 27602. **Tel** (919)733-3421. **LC** RA124; .D57B. **DD** 353.9/756/00841.

●US/1065-4356
**NORTH DAKOTA HEALTH CARE IN PERSPECTIVE.** [N.D. health care perspect.]. **Added/Corp** Morgan Quitno Corporation. 1st Ed. (1993)-. English. $18.00. Morgan Quitno Corporation, PO Box 1656, 512 East 9th Street, Lawrence KS 66044. **Tel** (800)457-0742, (913)841-3534, FAX (913)841-3534. **DD** 362.
**Desc:** Reports on the state's data and rank for each of the categories featured in Health Care State Rankings.

US/0361-8099
**NORTH DAKOTA HIGHWAY SAFETY IMPROVEMENT PROGRAM, ANNUAL REPORT.** **See** Transportation-Roads and Traffic.

US
**NORTH DAKOTA VEHICULAR CRASH FACTS.** **See** Transportation-Roads and Traffic.

UK
**NOSTRUM.** qt. Free. Scottish Development Agency, 120 Bothwell Street, Glasgow G2 7JP Scotland.
**Desc:** Pertains to the Scottish health care and biotechnology industry.
**Ind/Abst** Abstr. BioCommer.

●US
**NTIS ALERT. HEALTH CARE / PREPARED BY THE NATIONAL TECHNICAL INFORMATION SERVICE, U.S. DEPARTMENT OF COMMERCE, TECHNOLOGY ADMINISTRATION.** **Added/Corp** United States. National Technical Information Service. **VFOAT** Health Care. Vol. 92, No. 01 (Jan. 7, 1992)-. Periodical. English. Twenty-four times a year. $145.00 US; $210.00 other. National Technical Information Service - NTIS, Room 2027S, 5285 Port Royal Road, Springfield VA 22161. **Tel** (703)487-4630, (703)487-4660, (703)487-4650, FAX (703)321-8547, telex 89-9405. **NLM** ZWA 540; AA1 H4. ***Continues** Health Care (Springfield, Va.), 1048-6917.*
**Desc:** Provides information on agency administrative and financial management, community and population characteristics, data and information systems, environmental and occupational factors, health care assessment, and more.

CN/0702-8504
**NUDISTES DU QUEBEC.** Vol. 1 (Apr 1976)-. Periodical. French. bw. 0.50Can$ per no. Enterprises Jemapro, CP 135, Succursale Ste-Therese De, Blainville Quebec J7E 4J1. **DD** 613.1/94/05.

●CN/1199-7699
**NUTRITION & MENTAL HEALTH.** **See** Nutrition and Dietetics.

NE
**NVS NIEUWS.** Dutch (English). Five times a year. Fl50.00. Ned Ver Voor Stralingshygiene, Mekelweg 15, 2629 JB Delft The Netherlands. **Tel** 015-783764. **ED** W F Passchier, J Visses, L Vliet and W Zwaard. **Bk Rev. Ad Acc. Circ:** 500 (ctrl).
**Desc:** Information about health physics and radiological protection.

US
**NY-PENN NEWS.** **Added/Corp** NY-Penn Health Systems Agency. **VAT** NY Penn News; New York Penn News. (19??)-. Periodical. English. Twelve times a year. $5.00 (individuals); $10.00 (institutions); $7.50 (health professionals). New York Penn Health Systems Agency, 306 Press Building, 19 Chennago Street, Binghamton NY 13902. **Tel** (607)722-3445.

US/1044-1522
**OBESITY & HEALTH.** ***Title Change.* See** Nutrition and Dietetics.

CN/0705-0577
**OBJECTIF PREVENTION (MONTREAL).** (OBJECTIF PREVENTION.). **Added/Corp** Association des Hopitaux de la Province de Quebec. Service Prevention. Vol. 1 (Nov. 1977)-. Periodical. French. Four times a year. 35.00Can$ Canada; 25.00Can$ Quebec; 75.00Can$ other. Association Sante Securite du Travail, 801 Sherbrooke East 12th Floor, Montreal Quebec H2L 1K7 Canada. **Tel** (514)524-6871, (800)361-4528. **DD** 614.7/93/05. **Ad Acc, Adv Mgr:** Claude Gallant. **Circ:** 7000 (ctrl). ***Supersedes** Vie, 0380-9234.*

●US/1064-265X
**O'CONNOR REPORT (SEATTLE, WASH.).** (O'CONNOR REPORT :). [O'Connor rep.]. Vol. 2, No. 2 (Mar. 1992)-. Periodical. English. Twelve times a year. $95.00. O'Conner Communications, 911 Western Avenue, Suite 330, Seattle WA 98104. **Tel** (206)467-9075. **ED** Kathleen O'Connor. **DD** 362. cum. index. **Circ:** 1,500 (ctrl). ***Continues** Health Forum, 1064-2641.*
**Desc:** This newsletter from policy officials, to business coalitions, journalists and health care opinion leaders. We are a neutral interpreter in a special interest field.

UK
**OFFICE HEALTH AND SAFETY.** (19??)-. Periodical. English. ir. £155.20. Croner Publ Ltd, Croner House, London Road, Kingston upon Thames, Surrey KT2 6SR England. **Tel** 011 44 81 5473333, FAX 081 547-2637.

US/1056-3369
**OFFICIAL USSR MINISTRY OF HEALTH DIRECTORY OF HEALTH RESOURCES, THE.** (1991)-. Directory. English. $495.00. Health & Sciences Communications, 1090 Vermont Avenue NW, Suite 700, Washington DC 20005.

UK/0305-6031
**OHE BRIEFING.** [OHE brief.]. **VFOAT** Office of Health Economics Briefing. (1974)-. English. Office of Health Economics, 12 Whitehall, London SW1A 2DY England. **Tel** 44 71 9309203.
**Ind/Abst** Trop. Dis. Bull.

UK
**OHE INFORMATION SHEET.** **Main/Corp** Office of Health Economics (London, England). Periodical. English. Office of Health Economics, 12 Whitehall, London SW1A 2DY England. **Tel** 44 71 9309203.

●US/1065-4364
**OHIO HEALTH CARE IN PERSPECTIVE.** [Ohio health care perspect.]. **Added/Corp** Morgan Quitno Corporation. 1st Ed. (1993)-. English. $18.00. Morgan Quitno Corporation, PO Box 1656, 512 East 9th Street, Lawrence KS 66044. **Tel** (800)457-0742, (913)841-3534, FAX (913)841-3534. **DD** 362.
**Desc:** Reports on the state's data and rank for each of the categories featured in Health Care State Rankings.

●US/1065-4372
**OKLAHOMA HEALTH CARE IN PERSPECTIVE.** [Okla. health care perspect.]. **Added/Corp** Morgan Quitno Corporation. 1st Ed. (1993)-. English. $18.00. Morgan Quitno Corporation, PO Box 1656, 512 East 9th Street, Lawrence KS 66044. **Tel** (800)457-0742, (913)841-3534, FAX (913)841-3534. **DD** 362.
**Desc:** Reports on the state's data and rank for each of the categories featured in Health Care State Rankings.

US/0098-5651
**OKLAHOMA HEALTH STATISTICS.** **See** Public Health and Safety-Abstracting, Bibliographies and Statistics.

US/0740-7343
**OKLAHOMA TRIENNIAL STATE HEALTH PLAN.** (OKLAHOMA TRIENNIAL STATE HEALTH PLAN / OKLAHOMA STATE HEALTH COORDINATING COUNCIL.). [Okla. trienn. state health plan]. English. te. Oklahoma Health Planning Commission, 1000 Northeast 10th Street, Oklahoma City OK 73117. **Tel** (405)271-5600. **LC** RA395.A4; O54. **DD** 362.1/09766. ***Continues** Oklahoma State Health Plan, 0740-7351.*

US
**OMEGA 3 NEWS.** English. qt. $20.00. Massachusetts General Hospital, Department of

Preventive Medicine, Boston MA 02114. **Tel** (617)726-5908. ***Continues*** *N 3 News.*
**Ind/Abst** Foods Adlibra.

UK/0072-6087
**ON THE STATE OF THE PUBLIC HEALTH (1963).** (ON THE STATE OF THE PUBLIC HEALTH; THE ANNUAL REPORT OF THE CHIEF MEDICAL OFFICER.). [On state public health]. **Main/Corp** Great Britain. Dept. of Health and Social Security. **Added/Corp** Great Britain. Dept. of Health and Social Security. Annual Report of the Chief Medical Officer. (1968)-. English. an. £5.95. Her Majesty's Stationery Office, 51 Nine Elms Lane, London SW8 5DR England. **Tel** 011 44 71 873 8459, 011 44 71 873 8499, FAX 011 44 71 873 8499, 011 44 71 873 8456, telex 297138. **(Subscription address:** Her Majesty's Stationery Office, PO Box 276, Publications Centre, London SW8 5DT England.**) LC** RA241; .B132. **DD** 614/.0942. **[CCC]**. ***Continues*** *Great Britain. Ministry of Health. On the State of the Public Health.*

CN/0710-345X
**ONTARIO BRANCH NEWS.** (ONTARIO BRANCH NEWS / CANADIAN INSTITUTE OF PUBLIC HEALTH INSPECTORS, ONTARIO BRANCH INC.). [Ont. Branch news]. Vol. 1, No. 1 (1980)-. Periodical. English. qt. Free to members, $4.00 Canada; $10.00 other. Ontario Branch News/Editor, PO Box 687, Clinton Ontario N0M 1L0 Canada. **Tel** (519)482-3416, FAX (519)482-7231. **ED** Klaus Seeger. **DD** 614/.06/0713. Index available. cum. index. **Bk Rev. Ad Acc. Circ:** 1,000 (ctrl). ***Continues*** *Canadian Institute of Public Health Inspectors. Ontario Branch. Newsletter, 0383-0497.*
**Desc:** Discusses environmental and public health and defines roles for the public health professional. Covers legal matters, communicable diseases, methods of health inspection, recreational and occupational health issues and results of liaisons with government ministers.

UK/0265-511X
**OPENMIND (LONDON. 1983).** (OPENMIND.). [OpenMind]. **Added/Corp** MIND (Mental Health Association). **VFOAT** Open Mind. No. 1 (Feb./Mar. 1983)-. Periodical. English. Six times a year. £12.00 (individuals) members, £15.00 (institutions) members UK; £16.00 (individuals) non-members, £19.00 (institutions) non-members UK; £25.00 others. Mind Publications / Granta House, 15 19 Broadway Stratford, London E15 4BQ England. **Tel** 011 44 81 519 2122. **NLM** W1; OP134. ***Continues*** *Mind Out.*
**Ind/Abst** Appl. Soc. Sci. Index Abstr.

●US/1065-4380
**OREGON HEALTH CARE IN PERSPECTIVE.** [Or. health care perspect.]. **Added/Corp** Morgan Quitno Corporation. 1st Ed. (1993)-. English. $18.00. Morgan Quitno Corporation, PO Box 1656, 512 East 9th Street, Lawrence KS 66044. **Tel** (800)457-0742, (913)841-3534, FAX (913)841-3534. **DD** 362.
**Desc:** Reports on the state's data and rank for each of the categories featured in Health Care State Rankings.

US/1056-6767
**OREGON HEALTH FORUM.** [Or. health forum]. Vol. 1, No. 1 (May 1991)-. Periodical. English. mo. $198.00 institutions; $98.00 individuals. Oregon Health Forum, PO Box 2942, Portland OR 97208. **Tel** (503)643-3986, (503)627-9404, FAX (503)641-7266. **ED** Diane S. Lund (editor's address and telephone: 325 Northwest 21st Street, Suite 104, Portland, OR 97208; (503)226-7870). **DD** 613. **NLM** W1; OR528M. **Circ:** 2,500 (ctrl).
**Desc:** Covers health policy in the Pacific Northwest.

JA/0285-5801
**OSAKA SHIRITSU KANKYO KAGAKY KENKYUJO HOKOKU. CHOSA KENKYU NENPO.** [Osaka Shiritsu Kankyo Kagaku Kenkyujo hokoku, Chosa kenkyu nenpo]. **Added/Corp** Osaka Shiritsu Kankyo Kagaku Kenkyujo. **VFOAT** Annual Report of Osaka City Institute of Public Health and Environmental Sciences. (19??)-. Japanese. an. **CODEN** AOISDR. Documents available from CASDDS.
**Ind/Abst** Chem. Abstr.

FR
**OSTEO.** (19??)-. French. bm. F330.00 France; F360.00 other. Atman Club, Allee Hibiscus Chemin Camouyer, 06330 Roquefort Pins France. **Tel** 011 33 1 93771778. ***Continues*** *Osteopathie, 1167-380X.*

FR/0753-6019
**OSTEOPATHIE : THERAPIES MANUELLES.** ***Title Change.*** (19??)-(19??). French. Three times a year. Atman Club, Allee Hibiscus Chemin Camouyer, 06330 Roquefort Pins France. **Tel** 011 33 1 93771778. Index available. **Bk Rev. Ad Acc.** ctrl circ. ***Absorbed by*** *Osteo.*

US/0278-5811
**OUT HEALTH.** **VFOAT** Out Magazine's Quarterly Guide to Health in Gay Life. Vol. 1, No. 1 (Winter 1981)-. Periodical. English. qt. $10.00. Out Enterprises, 1522 14th Street NW, Washington DC 20005.

US
**OVERVIEW / STATE OF WASHINGTON, DEPARTMENT OF SOCIAL & HEALTH SERVICES, AN.** ***Title Change.*** **Main/Corp** Washington (State). Dept. of Social and Health Services. Periodical. English. mo. Office of Public Affairs / Olympia, Department of Social & Health Services, OB-44Q, Olympia WA 98504. **Tel** (206)753-2745. ***Continues*** *Washington (State). Dept. of Social and Health Services. Overview of Social and Health Services.* ***Continued by*** *Connections (Olympia, Wash.).*

US/0254-3419
**PAHODOC.** ***Ceased.*** [PAHODOC]. Vol. 1, No. 1 (June 1979)-Vol. 8, No. 12 (?). English. Pan American Health Organization, 525 23rd Street Northwest, Office District Sales, Washington DC 20037. **Tel** (202)293-8130, FAX (202)338-0869. **LC** Z6673; RA425. **DD** 016.3621. **NLM** ZWA 4 P101.

US/0251-4729
**PAI BOLETIN INFORMATIVO.** (PAI BOLETIN INFORMATIVO / PROGRAMA AMPLIADO DE IMMUNIZACION EN LAS AMERICAS.). **VAT** Programa Ampliado de Inmunizacion Boletin Informativo. Periodical. Spanish (English). bm. Free. Programa Ampliado de Inmunizacion OPS, 525 23rd Street NW, Washington DC 20037. **Tel** (202)861-3248. **ED** Ciro de Quadros. **Bk Rev. Circ:** 10,000 (ctrl).

PK
**PAKISTAN JOURNAL OF COMMUNITY MEDICINE : THE OFFICIAL JOURNAL OF THE PUBLIC HEALTH ASSOCIATION OF PAKISTAN, THE.** Vol. 4, No. 3-4 (July-Dec. 1987)-. Periodical. English. qt. $35.00. Public Health Association of Pakistan, 14-F Gulberg 11, Lahore Pakistan. **NLM** W1; PA35GE. ***Continues*** *Community Medicine (Lahore, Pakistan : 1978).*

US/1052-9985
**PARKING SECURITY REPORT.** (PARKING SECURITY REPORT : THE NEWSLETTER OF PUBLIC SAFETY, CRIME PREVENTION, ASSET PROTECTION, LIABILITY AVOIDANCE.). [Parking secur. rep.]. Vol. 1, No. 1 (Apr. 1990)-. Newsletter. English. mo. $169.00 (one year), $298.00 (two year). Rusting Publications, PO Box 190, Port Washington NY 11050. **Tel** (516)883-1440. **ED** Robert Rusting. **LC** TL175; .P384. **DD** 363.2/87. cum. index. **Bk Rev. Circ:** 400.
**Desc:** Security and safety management in parking lots.

US/0278-8209
**PATIENT EDUCATION NEWSLETTER.** [Patient educ. newsl.]. **Added/Corp** University of Alabama in Birmingham. Dept. of Family Practice. Vol. 4 No. 6 (Dec. 1981)-. Newsletter. English. bm. $20.00. UAB School of Public Health, 720 20th Street, Birmingham AL 35294. **Tel** (205)934-7178. **ED** Edward E Bartlett. **Ad Acc. Circ:** 2,300 (ctrl). ***Continues*** *Physician's Patient Education Newsletter.*
**Desc:** Newsletter for health professionals on patient education developments.
**Ind/Abst** Health Plan. Adminis.; Hospit. Health Admin. Index (1983-1985).

●US/1059-2067
**PBC COMPREHENSIVE HEALTH BRIEFS.** **VFOAT** Comprehensive Health Briefs. **VAT** Publishing and Business Consultants Comprehensive Health Briefs. (1992)-. Newsletter. English. qt. Publishing & Business Consultants, PO Box 75392, Los Angeles CA 90075. **Tel** (213)732-3477, FAX (213)732-9123.

●US/1065-4399
**PENNSYLVANIA HEALTH CARE IN PERSPECTIVE.** [Pa. health care perspect.]. **Added/Corp** Morgan Quitno Corporation. 1st Ed. (1993)-. English. $18.00. Morgan Quitno Corporation, PO Box 1656, 512 East 9th Street, Lawrence KS 66044. **Tel** (800)457-0742, (913)841-3534, FAX (913)841-3534. **DD** 362.
**Desc:** Reports on the state's data and rank for each of the categories featured in Health Care State Rankings.

US/0146-6593
**PEOPLE (RENO).** (PEOPLE.). **VFOAT** This Magazine is About People. Periodical. English. qt. Navada Division of Mental Hygiene and Mental Retardation, 4600 Kietzke Lane, Suite 108, Reno NV 89502. **LC** RA790.65.N3; P46. **DD** 362.2/05.

II
**PERFORMANCE BUDGET OF HEALTH AND FAMILY WELFARE DEPARTMENT.** **Main/Corp** Gujarat (India). Health and Family Welfare Dept. English. an. Rs2.95. The Government Press, Vadodara India. **LC** RA312.G8; H42A. **DD** 354.54/7500841.

●US/1065-6642
**PERFORMING ARTS HEALTH NEWS.** [Perform. arts health news]. **Added/Corp** Performing Arts Health Information Services. Performing Arts Health Network. Vol. 1, No. 1 (Sept./Oct. 1992)-. Periodical. English. Ten times a year. $69.00 (institutions). Performing Arts Health Network, PO Box 566, Radion City Station, New York NY 10101. **DD** 613.

●US/1061-4125
**PERSONAL HEALTH REPORTER.** (1992)-. English. ir. $95.00. Gale Research Inc., 835 Penobscot Building, Detroit MI 48226. **Tel** (800)877-GALE, (313)961-2242, FAX (313)961-6083, telex TWX 810-221-7086.

US/0094-4483
**PERSPECTIVES - CENTER FOR HEALTH ADMINISTRATION STUDIES, UNIVERSITY OF CHICAGO.** A9- 1971-. Periodical. English. ir. University of Chicago Center for Health Administration Studies, Chicago IL 60637. **Tel** (312)962-7104. **NLM** W1 PE8705K. ***Continues*** *Health Administration Perspectives, 0577-702X.*
**Ind/Abst** Health Plan. Adminis.

US
**PHI : PLANNING FOR HEALTH ISSUES.** **Added/Corp** Health Planning and Resource Development Association of the Central Ohio River Valley. **VFOAT** Planning for Health Issues; PHI Magazine. Vol. 1, No. 1 (Spring 1980)-. Periodical. English. Four times a year (Jan., Apr., July, Oct.). $10.00. Planning for Health Issues, 35 East 7th Street, Suite 608, Cincinnati OH 45202. **Tel** (513)621-2434.

US/0090-2896
**PHYSICAL CONDITION REPORT OF COMMERCIAL DRIVERS INVOLVED IN ACCIDENTS.** **See** Transportation.

KO
**POGON YONGAM.** **Added/Corp** Pogon Sinbo (Chu). (1984)-. Korean. Pogon Sinbosa 90-4, 3-ka Chongpa-dong Yongsan-ku, Seoul Korea. **LC** RA395.K8; P65. **NLM** W1; PO16.

US/0734-6611
**POLIOMYELITIS SURVEILLANCE (1978).** (POLIOMYELITIS SURVEILLANCE.). [Polio. surveill.]. **VFOAT** Poliomyelitis Surveillance Summary. Summary 1977-1978-. English. an. Centers for Disease Control, 1600 Clifton Road NE, Atlanta GA 30333. **Tel** (404)639-3311, FAX (404)639-3296. **LC** RA644.P9; P64. **DD** 614.5/49. **NLM** W2 A C7CNA. ***Continues*** *Neurotropic Diseases Surveillance. Poliomyelitis.*

UK/0958-5737
**POSITIVE HEALTH.** [Posit. health]. (?986)-. Periodical. English. qt. £20.00 (institutions), £12.00 (individuals). Institute for Health Promotion/UWCM, Fynnon-Las, Ilex Close, Ty Glass Avenue, Llanishen Cardiff, CF4 5DZ Wales. **Tel** 44 222 472472, FAX 44 222 480851. **ED** Jenny Sanders (editor's phone: 44 222 752222). **DD** 613. **Bk Rev. Ad Acc. Circ:** 700 (ctrl).
**Desc:** International news on health promotion and projects in action. Perspectives on health and working towards "Health for all 2,000"

●US
**POSITIVE LIVING.** **Added/Corp** AIDS Project Los Angeles. Vol. 1, No. 1 (Jan. 1992)-. Periodical. English. Twelve times a year. $12.00. AIDS Project Los Angeles, 6721 Romaine Street, Los Angeles CA 90038-2425. **Tel** (213)962-1600 ext. 534. **LC** RA644.A25; P6.

US/0149-3744
**POST ROCK.** V. 9- (No. 32- ); Summer/Fall 1975-. Periodical. English. qt. Free. Kansas Bureau of Health and Environmental Education, Education Building 740, Forbes Air Force Base, Topeka KS 66620. **LC** RA447.K2; C65. **DD** 614/.09781. ***Continues*** *Community Health.*
**Desc:** Contains articles on issues pertinent to the health and environment of Kansas.

PL/0032-5449
**POSTEPY HIGIENY I MEDYCYNY DOSWIADCZALNEJ.** [Postepy hig. med. dosw.]. **Added/Corp** Panstwowy Zakad Higieny (Poland) Instytut Immunologii i Terapii Doswiadczalnej (Polska Ademia Nauk). Vol. 1 (1949)-. Academic Scholarly Publication. Polish. bm. $81.00. **(Subscription address:** ARS Polona, PO Box 1001, 00068 Warsaw Poland.**) NLM** W1 PO941. **CODEN** PHMDAD. Documents available from BIOSIS Document Express, CASDDS. ***Absorbed*** *Postepy Wiedzy Medycznej, 0477-7891.*
**Ind/Abst** Biol. Abstr.; Chem. Abstr.; Index Med.; Life Sci. Collect.

US/0892-1857
**PRAEGER MONOGRAPHS IN INFECTIOUS DISEASE.** [Praeger monogr. infect. dis.]. **VFOAT** MID. Vol. 1-. Monographic series. English. Price varies per volume. Praeger, Publishing Division of Greenwood Press, PO Box 5007, Westport CT 06881. **Tel** (203)226-3571. **ED** David Schlossberg. **DD** 616. **NLM** W1; PR224C.

GW/0170-2602
**PRAVENTION.** **Added/Corp** Landeszentrale fuer Gesundheitsforderung Baden-Wurttemberg. Institut fuer Dokumentation und Information uber Sozialmedizin und

Offentliches Gesundheitswesen. Dezernat Gesundheitserziehung. Landeszentrale fuer Gesundheitserziehung in Rheinland-Pfalz. (1978)-. Periodical. German (summaries and/or abstracts in English and French). qt. DM24.00. Idis Oeffentl Gesundheitswesen, Postfach 201012, D33548 Bielefeld F R Germany. **Tel** 011 49 521 86033. **NLM** W1 PR204.

BL
**PRAXIS.** Feb. 1980-. Periodical. Portuguese (Portuguese). Centro de Estudos Margarida Terapia Ocupacional, rua Corcovado 74 Jardim Botanico, Rio de Janeiro Brazil. **LC** RA790.A1; P7. ***Supersedes*** *Abertura.*

CN/0317-5987
**PREVENTION AU CANADA, LA.** [Prev. Can.]. March 1969-. Periodical. French (English). bm. Conseil Canadien de la Securite, 1765 Boulevard Saint Laurent, Ottawa Ontario K1G 3V4 Canada. **Tel** (613)521-6881, FAX (613)521-0097. **ED** Particia Janzen. **DD** 614.8/05. ***Supersedes*** *Nouvelles de Securite Routiere, 0319-3373.*

US/0032-8006
**PREVENTION (EMMAUS).** (PREVENTION.). [Prevention]. **VFOAT** Prevention Magazine. Vol. 1, No. 1 (June 1950)-. Periodical. English. Twelve times a year. $19.97 US; $36.97 other. Rodale Press Inc., 400 South 10th Street, Emmaus PA 18098. **Tel** (215)967-5171, (800)666-2503. **ED** Robert Rodale and Mark Bricklin. **LC** RA421; .P68. **DD** 613.05. **NLM** W1 PR496. **CODEN** PRVEAT. **[CCC]**. Index available. cum. index. **Ad Acc. Circ:** 2,850,000. available on microfilm and microfiche from University Microfilms International (UMI). Documents available from UMI Article Clearinghouse, CASDDS.
**Desc:** Presents practical, useful information on health, nutrition, fitness and psychology. All articles are based on the latest research published in professional journals, as well as interviews with leading medical authorities.
**Ind/Abst** Abr. Read. Guide Period. Lit.; Acad. Abstr. Full Text Elite (Jan. 1989-) [Full Txt.]; Acad. Abstr. (Jan. 1989-); Acad. Search (Jan. 1989-); AGRICOLA; Chem. Abstr.; Consum. Health Nutr. Index (Jan. 1990); Foods Adlibra; Gen. Period. Index (1985-); Gen. Sci. Index; Health Index (1989-); Health Period. Database [Full Txt.]; Health Ref. Cent. (Jan. 1989-) [Full Txt.] [Full Cov.]; Health Source (Jan. 1989-) [Full Txt.]; INFO-SOUTH Abstr.; Mag. Artic. Summar. Elite (Jan. 1989-) [Full Txt.]; Mag. Artic. Summar. Select (Jan. 1989-) [Full Txt.]; Mag. Artic. Summar. CD-ROM (Jan. 1989-); Mag. ASAP Plus [Full Txt.]; Mag. ASAP Sel. [Full Txt.]; Mag. Index Plus (1989-); Mag. Index. Sel. (1986-); Mag. Search; Mid. Search (Jan. 1989-); Newsp. Period. Abstr. (1986-); Read. Guide Abstr. Select Ed.; Read. Guide Period. Lit.; Mag. Index (1977-); Vocat. Search (Jan. 1989-) [Full Txt.].

US/0270-3114
**PREVENTION IN HUMAN SERVICES. See** Public Health and Safety-Abstracting, Bibliographies and Statistics.

CN/0711-1681
**PREVENTION PREVIEW.** [Prev. preview]. Vol. 1, No. 1 (Fall 1979)-. Periodical. English. qt. Free. Prevention Preview, Health Marketing Systems, PO Box 490, Station A, Scarborough Ontario M1K 2N0 Canada. **DD** 614/.05. ctrl circ.

FR/0247-6800
**PREVENTION SANTE.** (1981)-. Periodical. French. mo. 137.12F France; 185.00F other. EDI 7, 6 rue Ancelle, 92525 Neuilly Sur Seine, Cedex France. **Tel** 011 33 1 40886000. **UDC** 614.

US/0091-7435
**PREVENTIVE MEDICINE (1972). See** Medical Science and Technology.

CN/0710-0671
**PREVOYANCE.** (PREVOYANCE / L'ASSOCIATION CANADIENNE DES MONITEURS EN CONDUITE AUTOMOBILE ET SECURITE ROUTIERE.). [Prevoyance]. Vol. 1, No. 1 Spring 1981-. Periodical. French. qt. Free to members. Prevoyance, 175 rue College, Toronto Ontario M5T 1P8 Canada. **DD** 629.28/3/07071.

LU
**PRI REVIEW. INTERNATIONAL ROAD SAFETY.** French (English and German). Three times a year. 1,350F Belgium; $40.00 US. PRI, 75 rue de Mamer BP 40, L-8001 Bertrange Luxembourg. **Tel** 011 352 318341. **(Subscription address:** PRI, B.p 40, L-8005 Luxembourg - Bertrange) **ED** Leon Nilles. Index available. cum. index. **Ad Acc. Circ:** 1,000 (ctrl).
**Desc:** Information on road safety.

US/0743-5088
**PRIDE INSTITUTE JOURNAL OF LONG TERM HOME HEALTH CARE.** [Pride Inst. j. long term home health care]. **Added/Corp** PRIDE Institute. **VFOAT** Journal of Long Term Home Health Care. Vol. 1, No. 1 (Summer 1982)-. Periodical. English. qt. $39.00 (individuals, 1 year), $69.00 (individuals, 2 year), $74.00 (institutions, 1 year), $129.00 (institutions, 2 year) US; $44.00 (individuals, 1 year), $79.00 (individuals, 2 year), $85.00 (institutions, 1 year), $149.00 (institutions, 2 year) other. Springer Publishing Company, 536 Broadway, New York NY 10012-3955. **Tel** (212)431-4370, FAX (212)941-7842. **ED** Ann Berson. **NLM** W1 PR516H. cum. index.
**Desc:** Publishes articles of practical and theoretical interest and seeks to inform practitioners of relevant work being done by their peers throughout the country and world.
**Ind/Abst** Abstr. Soc. Gerontol.; Hospit. Health Admin. Index; Int. Nurs. Index; Psychol. Abstr. (1986-); PsycINFO; PsycLit; Soc. Work Abstr. (Summer 1987-) [Select. Cov.].

US
**PRIORITY HEALTH PROBLEMS OF MICHIGAN. Main/Corp** Michigan. Dept. of Public Health. English. an. Michigan Department of Public Health, 3423 North Logan Street, PO Box 30195, Lansing MI 48909. **Tel** (517)335-8216, FAX (517)335-8560. **LC** RA87; .D46B. **DD** 362.1/09774.

NE/0168-1796
**PRIORITY ISSUES IN MENTAL HEALTH : A BOOK SERIES PUBLISHED UNDER THE AUSPICES OF THE WORLD FEDERATION FOR MENTAL HEALTH.** ***Ceased.*** [Prior. issues ment. health]. **Added/Corp** World Federation for Mental Health. Vol. 1 (1981)-(19??). Monographic series. English. ir. Kluwer Academic Publishers, Postbus 322, 3300 AH Dordrecht, The Netherlands. **Tel** 011 (31) 78 524400, FAX 011 31 78 183273, telex 20083. **NLM** W1 PR524R.

BU/0323-9179
**PROBLEMI NA HIGIENATA.** (PROBLEMI NA KHIGIENATA.). [Probl. hig.]. Vol. 1 (1975)-. Academic Scholarly Publication. Bulgarian. Six times a year. Izdatelstvo Medicina i Fizkult, PL Slavejkov 11, 1000 Sofia Bulgaria. **NLM** W1 PR572EK. **CODEN** PRKHDK. Documents available from CASDDS.
**Ind/Abst** Chem. Abstr.; EMBASE; Index Med.; Saf. Health Work.

●RU/0869-866X
**PROBLEMY SOTSIALNOI GIGIENY I ISTORIIA MEDITSINY / NII SOTSIALNOI GIGIENY, EKONOMIKI I UPRAVLENIIA ZDRAVOOKHRANENIEM IM N.A. SEMASHKO RAMN, AO ASSOTSIATSIIA 'MEDITSINSKAIA LITERATURA.'.** (1994)-. Russian (English). Izdatelstvo Meditsina / Russian Academy of Medical Sciences, Ulitsa Solyanka 14, 109801 Moscow Russia. **Tel** 011 95 297-05-04. Index available. **Bk Rev.** ***Continues*** *Sovetskoe Zdravookhranenie, 0038-5239.*
**Ind/Abst** Biol. Abstr.; CIS Abstr.; Index Med.; Int. Aerosp. Abstr.; Int. Labour Doc.; Int. Nurs. Index; Saf. Health Work; Trop. Dis. Bull.

US
**PROCEEDINGS ... ANNUAL GROUP HEALTH INSTITUTE / GROUP HEALTH ASSOCIATION OF AMERICA. Main/Corp** Group Health Institute. **Added/Corp** Group Health Association of America. Group Health Federation of America. Cooperative Health Federation of America. (1950)-. Proceedings. English. an (Jun.). $35.00. Group Health Association of America, Department 0612, Washington DC 20073. **Tel** (202)778-3247, FAX (202)331-7487.

CN/0319-2644
**PROCEEDINGS OF THE ANNUAL MEETING OF THE CANADIAN PUBLIC HEALTH ASSOCIATION. Main/Corp** Canadian Public Health Association. **VFOAT** Travaux de l'Assemblee Generale de l'Association Canadienne d'Hygiene Publique. (1974)-. Proceedings. Multiple languages (English and French). Canadian Public Health Association, 1565 Carling Avenue/Suite 400, Ottawa Ontario K1Z 8R1 Canada. **Tel** (613)725-3769, FAX (613)725-9826. **DD** 614/.05.

US/0195-7740
**PROCEEDINGS OF THE ... ANNUAL MEETING OF THE NATIONAL COUNCIL ON RADIATION PROTECTION AND MEASUREMENTS. See** Medical Science and Technology-Radiology.

US/0162-0657
**PROCEEDINGS OF THE ANNUAL SEMINAR OF THE CALIFORNIA COMMUNITY HEALTH INSTITUTE. Main/Conf** California Community Health Seminar. **Main/Corp** California Community Health Institute. Seminar. 1st- 1974-. Proceedings. English. an. **NLM** W3 C11.

US/0195-976X
**PROCEEDINGS OF THE HEALTH POLICY FORUM. Main/Conf** Health Policy Forum. No. 1-. Proceedings. English. Price varies per volume. United Hospital Fund of New York, 3 East 54th Street, New York NY 10022. **Tel** (212)645-2500. **ED** Sally J Rogers. **NLM** W3 HE375.
**Desc:** Deals with foreign medical graduates in New York City and hospital closures in New York City and the problems of such closures and the responsibility for the provision for patients, doctors, etc.
**Ind/Abst** Health Plan. Adminis.

US/0193-306X
**PROCEEDINGS OF THE INTERNATIONAL CONFERENCE ON FIRE SAFETY. See** Fire Prevention.

US/0092-7732
**PRODUCT SAFETY & LIABILITY REPORTER.** [Prod. saf. liabil. report.]. **Added/Corp** Bureau of National Affairs (Washington, D.C.). **VFOAT** Product Safety and Liability Reporter; Product Safety & Liability Reporter Current Report. Vol. 1 (Jan. 5, 1973)-. Periodical. English. wk. $955.00 (full service). Bureau of National Affairs Inc., 9435 Key West Avenue, Rockville MD 20850. **Tel** (800)372-1033, (301)258-1033, FAX (301)948-5823. **ED** William Harris Frank. **LC** KF3945.A73; P7. **DD** 344/.73/042. **[CCC]. Circ:** 1,206.
**Desc:** A weekly notification and reference service providing comprehensive coverage of current administrative, legislative, judicial, and industry developments relating to product safety and product liability.

US/0094-5463
**PRODUCT SAFETY & THE LAW. See** Law.

US/0091-8954
**PRODUCT SAFETY UP TO DATE. Main/Corp** National Safety Council. (19??)-. English. Six times a year. $19.00 (one year), $34.00 (two year). National Safety Council, 1121 Spring Lake Drive, Itasca IL 60143. **Tel** (800)621-7615, (708)775-2294, FAX (708)285-0797. **LC** TS175; .N37a. **DD** 658.5/6.

US/0196-0407
**PROFESSIONAL STANDARDS REVIEW ORGANIZATIONS.** (PROFESSIONAL STANDARDS REVIEW ORGANIZATION; PROGRAM EVALUATION.). **Main/Corp** United States. Health Care Financing Administration. Office of Policy, Planning, and Research. 1978-. English. an. Health Care Financing Administration, 6325 Security Boulevard, Room 700, Baltimore MD 21207. **Tel** (410)966-3000, FAX (410)966-5267. **NLM** W2; A H614P. ***Continues*** *Professional Standards Review Organizations, 0196-0407.*

US/1046-7785
**PROFESSIONALS AND THEIR ADDICTIONS.** [Prof. their addict.]. (1989)-. English. an. Charter Peachford Hospital, Publications Department, 2151 Peachford Road, Atlanta GA 30338. **DD** 362.

CN/0836-1576
**PROFIL (TROIS-RIVIERES).** (PROFIL : UN REGARD AVERTI SUR LA SANTE.). [Profil]. **Added/Corp** Centre Hospitalier Ste-Marie (Trois-Rivieres, Quebec). Departement de Sante Communautaire. Centre Hospitalier Regional de la Mauricie. Departement de Sante Communautaire. Hopital Ste-Croix (Drummondville, Quebec). Departement de Sante Communautaire. Vol. 1, No 1 (Apr. 1988)-. Periodical. French. Ten times a year. 20.00Can$ two years. Department Sante Comm. Profil 04, 3350 Boulevard Royal, Trois-Rivieres G9A 5ZA Canada. **Tel** (819)378-9813, FAX (819)378-6600. **DD** 614/.09714/45.

US/1040-7480
**PROFILES IN HEALTHCARE MARKETING. See** Business-Marketing.

IT/0393-8018
**PROGETTO CARE ITALIA.** [Progetto CARE Ital.]. (1985)-. Periodical. Italian. qt. L30000.00 (regular subscribers); L100000.00 (sustaining subscribers). Care Italia, Via R Cadorna 29, 00187 Rome Italy. **Tel** 011 39 6 462427. **UDC** 362.54(73-87).

US/0192-9747
**PROGRAM BUDGET STATEMENT. Main/Corp** Michigan. Dept. of Public Health. (19??)-. English. an. Michigan Department of Public Health, 3423 North Logan Street, PO Box 30195, Lansing MI 48909. **Tel** (517)335-8216, FAX (517)335-8560. **LC** RA87; .D46a. **DD** 353.9/774/00841.

US/0731-8073
**PROGRAM EVALUATION IN THE HEALTH FIELDS.** [Program eval. health fields]. Vol. 1 (1969)-. Monographic series. English. ir. Price varies per volume. Human Sciences Press, PO Box 735, 233 Spring Street, New York NY 10013. **Tel** (212)620-8000, FAX (212)807-1047, telex 23421139. **ED** H. C. Schulberg, A. Sheldon, and F. Baker. **NLM** W1 PR632H.

US/1042-363X
**PROGRESS IN AIDS PATHOLOGY.** [Prog. AIDS pathol.]. **VAT** Progress in Acquired Immune Deficiency Syndrome Pathology. Vol. 1 (1989)-. English. an. $115.00 (institutions), $95.00 (individuals). Field & Wood, 1405 Locust Street, Philadelphia PA 19102. **Tel**

(215)824-4010. **DD** 616. **NLM** W1; PR666ER. Index available. cum. index.
**Ind/Abst** Health Plan. Adminis.; Index Med. (1989-).

US/0731-7050
**PROGRESS REPORT - HEALTH AND SAFETY RESEARCH DIVISION.** (HEALTH AND SAFETY RESEARCH DIVISION PROGRESS REPORT FOR THE PERIOD ...). [Health Saf. Res. Div. prog. rep.]. **VFOAT** Progress Report. Began with: 1977/78. English. an. National Technical Information Service - NTIS, Room 2027S, 5285 Port Royal Road, Springfield VA 22161. **Tel** (703)487-4630, (703)487-4660, (703)487-4650, FAX (703)321-8547, telex 89-9405. **NLM** W1 HE264J.

●FR/0751-7149
**PROMOTION AND EDUCATION.** [Hygie]. **Added/Corp** International Union for Health Education. (1993)-. Periodical. English (French and Spanish). qt. $45.00 (one year), $75.00 (two year), $105.00 (three year). International Union Health Promotion & Education, 2 rue Auguste Comte IMM Berry, 92170 Vanves France. **Tel** 011 33 1 46450059. **ED** Anne Bunde-Birouste. cum. index. **Bk Rev.** **Ad Acc.** **Pr Rev.** **Circ:** 2,000 (ctrl). available on microfilm and microfiche from University Microfilms International (UMI). ***Continues*** *Hygie.*
**Desc:** Field and research activities, interviews and reports. Includes a round-up on a particular health education theme, and international news on meetings and events.

US/1012-9685
**PROPOSED PROGRAM AND BUDGET ESTIMATES - PAN AMERICAN HEALTH ORGANIZATION.** (PROPOSED PROGRAM AND BUDGET ESTIMATES.). [Propos. program budg. estim. - Pan Am. Health Organ.]. **Main/Corp** Pan American Health Organization. **Added/Corp** Pan American Sanitary Bureau. (1959)-. English. an. Pan American Health Organization, 525 23rd Street Northwest, Office District Sales, Washington DC 20037. **Tel** (202)293-8130, FAX (202)338-0869. **NLM** W2 MP2 P92PE. ***Continues*** *Pan American Sanitary Organization. Proposed Program and Budget Estimates, 1012-9685.*

US/0195-573X
**PSITTACOSIS SURVEILLANCE.** (PSITTACOSIS SURVEILLANCE, ANNUAL SUMMARY / CENTER FOR DISEASE CONTROL.). **VFOAT** Center for Disease Control Psittacosis Surveillance. 1975-1977-. English. an. Centers for Disease Control, 1600 Clifton Road NE, Atlanta GA 30333. **Tel** (404)639-3311, FAX (404)639-3296. **LC** RA644.P95; C46A. **DD** 614.5/66/0973. **NLM** W2 A C7CZA. ***Continues*** *Zoonosis Surveillance. Psittacosis, Annual Summary, 0271-7816.*

SZ/0887-0446
**PSYCHOLOGY & HEALTH.** [Psychol. health]. **VFOAT** Psychology and Health. Vol. 1, No. 1 (1987)-. Periodical. English. ir. Price varies. Harwood Academic Publishers, PO Box 90, Reading RG1 8JL England. **Tel** 011 44 734 560080. **(Subscription address:** Harwood Academic Publishers, PO Box 786, Cooper Station, New York NY 10276.) **LC** R726.7; .P79. **DD** 150. **NLM** W1; PS746J. **CODEN** PSHEE4. **[CCC].** ***Continues*** *Health Psychology, 0278-6133.*
**Ind/Abst** Annals Behav. Med.; Cumul. Index Nurs. Allied Health Lit.; Curr. Contents Soc. Behav. Sci.; Psychol. Abstr. (1987-); PsycINFO; PsycLit; Soc. Sci. Cit. Index [Full Cov.].

US/0147-4251
**PUBLIC ADVISORY COMMITTEES, AUTHORITY, STRUCTURE, FUNCTIONS, MEMBERS.** **Main/Corp** United States. Food and Drug Administration. (19??)-. English. US Food and Drug Administration / FDA, 5600 Fishers Lane, Room 14-71, Rockville MD 20857. **Tel** (301)443-2410, FAX (301)443-0755. **LC** RA401.A3; U53a. **DD** 353.008/41.

SZ
**PUBLIC HEALTH.** (19??)-. English (French). ir. $282.00. World Health Organization, Distribution and Sales, 20 Avenue Appia, CH-1211 Geneva 27 Switzerland. **Tel** 011 41 22 7912111, FAX 011 41 22 7880401.

US/0895-8157
**PUBLIC HEALTH COMMENTS.** [Public health comments]. **Added/Corp** Public Health Information Services (Detroit, Mich.). (1987)-. Periodical. English. mo. $72.00; $96.00 (libraries). Public Health Information Services Inc, 11661 Charter Oak Court, Reston VA 22090. **Tel** (703)709-0020, FAX (703)709-0089. **ED** Terence E Carroll. **DD** 362. **Circ:** 450. ***Continues*** *Monday Comments.*
**Desc:** Reports on and discusses public health and medical issues of current interest. The cost and quality of medical care, HMO's, AIDS, the social costs of the arms race, are some of the subjects covered.

UK/0033-3506
**PUBLIC HEALTH (LONDON).** (PUBLIC HEALTH.). [Public health]. **Added/Corp** Society of Community Medicine. Society of Medical Officers of Health. Transactions. (1888)-. Academic Scholarly Publication. English. bm. £130.00 UK and EEC; £140.00 (surface mail), £168.00 (airmail) other. Macmillan Magazines Ltd., Houndmills, Basingstoke, Hampshire RG21 2XS England. **Tel** 011 44 256 29242, FAX 011 44 256 812358, telex 858493. **ED** M. W. Beaver. **NLM** W1 PU309. **CODEN** PUHEAE. **[CCC].** Index available. **Bk Rev.** **Ad Acc.** **Pr Rev.** **Circ:** 2,000. available on microfilm and microfiche from University Microfilms International (UMI). Documents available from The Genuine Article, BIOSIS Document Express, CASDDS. ***Supersedes*** *Society of Medical Officers of Health. Transactions.*
**Desc:** Provides international coverage of preventive medicine, epidemiology, social and community medicine. A typical issue will include: child health, communicable disease control, health service provision and management, allocation of scarce resources, epidemiology and a wide range of other topics.
**Ind/Abst** Appl. Soc. Sci. Index Abstr.; Biol. Abstr.; Chem. Abstr.; Curr. Aware. Biol. Sci., CABS; Curr. Contents Clin. Med.; Curr. Contents Soc. Behav. Sci.; Dev. Med. Child Neurol.; EMBASE; Health Serv. Abstr.; Helminthol. Abstr. (19??-19??); Index Med.; Nutr. Res. Newsl.; Life Sci. Collect.; Protozoolog. Abstr.; Res. Alert [Full Cov.]; Saf. Health Work; Soc. Sci. Cit. Index [Full Cov.]; Trop. Dis. Bull.

US/1060-7714
**PUBLIC HEALTH MACROVIEW.** [Public health macroview]. **Added/Corp** Public Health Foundation (U.S.). Vol. 1, No. 1, Jan./Feb. (1988)-. Periodical. English. bm. Free. Public Health Foundation, 1220 L Street NW/Suite 350, Washington DC 20005. **Tel** (202)898-5600. **DD** 614.

UK
**PUBLIC HEALTH NEWS.** (19??)-. English. mo. $162.00. CAB International Centre, Wallingford, Oxon OX10 8DE United Kingdom. **Tel** 44 491 832111, FAX 44 491 833508, telex 847964 (COMAGG G).

US/0033-3549
**PUBLIC HEALTH REPORTS (1974).** (PUBLIC HEALTH REPORTS. [MICROFILM EDITION].). **Added/Corp** United States. Health Resources Administration. United States. Public Health Service. Vol. 89, No. 4 (July/Aug. 1974)-. Periodical. English. Health Resources Administration, Office of the Administrator, DMS Committee Management Branch, 5600 Fishers Lane, Rockville MD 20857. **LC** Microfilm (o) 89/2524. available in print; available on an online database (file 149/Full-Text) from DIALOG. Documents available from UMI Article Clearinghouse. ***Continues*** *T.Health Services Reports (United States. Health Services Administration), 0090-2918.*
**Ind/Abst** INFO-SOUTH Abstr.; Mag. Search; Newsp. Period. Abstr. (1991-); PESTDOC; Protozoolog. Abstr.

US/0033-3549
**PUBLIC HEALTH REPORTS (1974).** (PUBLIC HEALTH REPORTS.). [Public health rep.]. **Added/Corp** United States. Health Resources Administration. United States. Public Health Service. Vol. 89, No. 4 (July/Aug. 1974)-. Academic Scholarly Publication. English. bm (6 issues). $13.00 US; $16.25 other. Superintendent of Documents, US Government Printing Office, Washington DC 20402. **Tel** (202)275-3328, FAX (202)786-2377. **LC** RA11; .B17. **DD** 614/.0973. **NLM** W1 PU545. available on microfilm and microfiche from University Microfilms International (UMI); available on an online database (file 149/Full-Text) from DIALOG. Documents available from The Genuine Article, UMI Article Clearinghouse, Documents on Demand. ***Continues*** *Health Services Reports, 0090-2918.*
**Desc:** Consists principally of scholarly articles on public health, disease prevention, health promotion, medical care, community medicine, and the delivery of health services.
**Ind/Abst** Abr. Index Med.; Acad. Abstr. Full Text Elite (Nov. 1990-) [Full Txt.]; Acad. Abstr. (Nov. 1990-); Acad. Ind. [Computer File] (1988-); Acad. Search (Nov. 1990-); AGRICOLA [Select. Cov.]; Air Pollut. Titles; Am. Stat. Index; Biodeter. Abstr.; Biol. Dig.; Chicano Index; Cumul. Index Nurs. Allied Health Lit.; Curr. Contents Clin. Med.; Curr. Contents Soc. Behav. Sci.; Curr. Lit. Fam. Plan.; Curr. Titl. Dent.; Dairy Sci. Abstr.; Dent. Abstr. (19??-19??); Dev. Med. Child Neurol.; EMBASE; Energy Res. Abstr.; Expand. Acad. Index (1988-); Gen. Period. Index (1989-); Gen. Sci. Index; Gen. Sci. Source (Jul. 1990-); Health Saf. Sci. Abstr.; Health Index (1989-); Health Period. Database [Full Txt.]; Health Ref. Cent. (Jan. 1989-) [Full Txt.] [Full Cov.]; Health Source (Jul. 1990-) [Full Txt.]; Hospit. Manage. Rev.; Index Med.; Ind. Hyg. Dig.; INFO-SOUTH Abstr.; Int. Pharm. Abstr. (19??-19??); Mag. Artic. Summar. Elite (Nov. 1990-) [Full Txt.]; Mag. Artic. Summar. Select (July 1990); Mag. Artic. Summar. CD-ROM (Nov. 1990-); Mag. ASAP Plus; Mag. Index Plus (1992-); Mag. Search; Middle East Abstr. Index; Newsp. Period. Abstr. (1991-); Nutr. Abstr. Rev., Ser. A, Hum. Exp.; Nutr. Res. Newsl.; PAIS Int. Print (1991-); PESTDOC; Physic. Medline Plus; Popul. Index; Protozoolog. Abstr.; Res. Alert [Full Cov.]; Risk Abstr.; Sage Fam. Stud. Abstr.; Sci. Cit. Index; SCISEARCH; Soc. Sci. Source (Jul. 1990-) [Full Txt.]; Soc. Sci. Cit. Index [Full Cov.]; Soc. Sci. Index; Soc. Sci. Index Fulltext (July 1988-) [Full Txt.]; Soc. Work Abstr. (Spring, Summer 1987-) [Select. Cov.]; SPORT Discus; SportSearch; Stat. Theory Method Abstr. (1959-1963); Trop. Dis. Bull.; Virol. AIDS Abstr.

IS/0301-0422
**PUBLIC HEALTH REVIEWS.** [Public health rev.]. Vol. 1 (1972)-. Periodical. English. qt. $100.00. Technosdar Ltd, International Scientific Publishers, 5 Levontin Street, POB 31684, Tel Aviv 61316 Israel. **Tel** 011 972 3 5607418, FAX 011 972 3 614932, telex 341667. **ED** Sigmund Geller. **NLM** W1 PU547. **CODEN** PBHRAM. Index available. **Ad Acc.** **Circ:** 1,000 (ctrl). available on microfilm from University Microfilms International (UMI). Documents available from BIOSIS Document Express.
**Desc:** Publishes reviews on topics in public health which bring together, evaluate, and provide a synthesis of studies to date. Also publishes guest editorials, abstracts, and proceedings of symposia.
**Ind/Abst** Biol. Abstr.; Cumul. Index Nurs. Allied Health Lit.; Curr. Contents Soc. Behav. Sci.; EMBASE; Food Sci. Technol. Abstr.; Health Plan. Adminis.; Hospit. Health Admin. Index; Index Med.; Nutr. Res. Newsl.

US/1060-7706
**PUBLIC HEALTH UPDATE (WASHINGTON, D.C.).** (PUBLIC HEALTH UPDATE / PUBLIC HEALTH FOUNDATION.). [Public health update]. **Added/Corp** Public Health Foundtion (U.S.). Vol. 1, No. 1 (Jan. 1991)-. Periodical. English. mo. Free. Public Health Foundation, 1220 L Street NW/Suite 350, Washington DC 20005. **Tel** (202)898-5600. **DD** 362.

US
**PUBLICATIONS OF THE NATIONAL INSTITUTE OF MENTAL HEALTH.** Periodical. English. qt. National Clearinghouse for Mental Health Information, Public Inquiries Section, 5600 Fishers Lane, Rockville MD 20857.

FI/0357-3346
**PUBLICATIONS OF THE UNIVERSITY OF KUOPIO. COMMUNITY HEALTH. SERIES ORIGINAL REPORTS.** **VFOAT** Community Health. Series Original Reports. Monographic series. English. Price varies per volume. **NLM** W1 PU736U.

US/1047-4773
**QA REVIEW.** ***Ceased.*** (QA REVIEW: QUALITY ASSURANCE NEWS AND VIEWS.). [QA rev.]. **VAT** Quality Assurance Review. Vol. 1, No. 1 (Aug. 1989)-(1992). Periodical. English. bm. American Medical Association, 515 North State Street, Chicago IL 60610. **Tel** (312)464-5000, (800)262-2350, FAX (312)464-5831. **DD** 362. **NLM** W1; Q52.
**Ind/Abst** Hospit. Health Admin. Index (Aug. 1989-19??); Hospit. Manage. Rev. (19??-19??).

IT/0393-9529
**QUADERNI DI SANITA PUBBLICA.** (1978)-. Periodical. Italian. bm. L45000.00. Centro Informazione Sanitaria, Via San Siro 1, 20149 Milan Italy. **Tel** 011 39 2 4694542. **UDC** 361.

US/1049-7323
**QUALITATIVE HEALTH RESEARCH.** [Qual. health res.]. (1991)-. Periodical. English. qt (Feb., May, Aug., Nov.). $128.00. SAGE Periodical Press, 2455 Teller Road, Thousand Oaks CA 91320. **Tel** (805)499-0721, FAX (805)499-0871, telex 100799. **ED** Janice M. Morse (Pennsylvania State University). **LC** RA440.85; .O35. **DD** 362.1/05. **NLM** W1; QU158IH. **CODEN** QHREEM. **Acid Free.**
**Desc:** Provides an interdisciplinary forum to enhance health care and further the development and understanding of qualitative research in health care settings.
**Ind/Abst** Cumul. Index Nurs. Allied Health Lit.; Hum. Resour. Abstr.; Sage Fam. Stud. Abstr.; Soc. Plann. Policy Dev. Abstr.

UK/1040-6166
**QUALITY ASSURANCE IN HEALTH CARE.** ***Title Change.*** (QUALITY ASSURANCE IN HEALTH CARE : THE OFFICIAL JOURNAL OF THE INTERNATIONAL SOCIETY FOR QUALITY ASSURANCE IN HEALTH CARE / ISQA.). [Qual. assur. health care]. **Added/Corp** International Society for Quality Assurance in Health Care. Vol. 1, No. 1 (1989)-(199?). Periodical. English. qt (1 volume). Pergamon Press, An Imprint of Elsevier Science Ltd., The Boulevard, Langford Lane, Kidlington, Oxford OX5 1GB United Kingdom. **Tel** 011 44 865 843000, 011 44 865 843699, FAX 011 44 865 843010. **ED** P. Reizenstein. **LC** RA399.A1; Q32. **DD** 362.1/068/5. **NLM** W1; QU154C. **CODEN** QAHCEJ. **[CCC].** available on microfilm and microfiche from University Microfilms International (UMI). ***Continued by*** *International Journal for Quality in Health Care, 1353-4505.*
**Desc:** Publishes papers in all disciplines related to the quality of health care, including health services research, health care evaluation, technology assessment, health economy, utilization review and nursing care research.
**Ind/Abst** Health Plan. Adminis.; Index Med. (1989-).

US
**QUALITY IN HEALTHCARE MANAGEMENT.** **See** Medical Science and Technology.

# Public Health and Safety

US/0889-9495
**RADIANCE (OAKLAND, CALIF.).** See Beauty and Cosmetics.

AT/0729-7963
**RADIATION PROTECTION IN AUSTRALIA.** [Radiat. prot. Aust.]. (1980)-. Periodical. English. Four times a year (Jan., Apr., July, Oct.). 54.00Aus$. Australian Radiation Protection Society, CPO Box 128, Rosanna 3084 Australia. **Tel** 011 61 3 4332211, FAX 011 61 3 4321835. **ED** Dr. Colin Ray. **DD** 363.17906094. Index available. **Bk Rev**. **Ad Acc**. **Pr Rev**. **Circ**: 300 (ctrl).
 **Desc**: Scientific articles, conferences papers, technical notes and letters on all aspects of radiation safety and radiation health.

FR/0033-8451
**RADIOPROTECTION.** [Radioprotection]. **Added/Corp** Societe Francaise de Radioprotection. (1966)-. Academic Scholarly Publication. French. qt. 950.00F. Les Editions de Physique, 7 Avenue du Hoggar, Z.I. de Courtaboeuf - BP 112, 91944 les Ulis Cedex A France. **Tel** 011 33 1 69 07 36 88, FAX 011 33 1 69 28 84 91, telex EDITPHY 692321F. **LC** RA569; .R34. **NLM** W1 RA363. **CODEN** RAPRBA. **[CCC]**. **Pr Rev**. Documents available from The Genuine Article, CASDDS.
 **Ind/Abst** Chem. Abstr. (19??-); Curr. Contents Eng. Tech. Appl. Sci. (19??-); EMBASE (19??-); Energy Res. Abstr. (19??-); Res. Alert (19??-) [Select. Cov.]; Saf. Health Work (1972-).

IT/1120-1762
**RAGIUSAN. RASSEGNA GIURIDICA DELLA SANITA.** See Law.

US/0148-0200
**RAILROAD ACCIDENT REPORT. BRIEF FORMAT.** See Transportation-Railroads.

CN/0837-5496
**RAPPORT ANNUEL - CONSEIL REGIONAL DE LA SANTE ET DES SERVICES SOCIAUX DE L'OUTAOUAIS.** (RAPPORT ANNUEL.). [Rapp. annu. - Cons. reg. sante serv. sociaux Outaouais]. **Main/Corp** Conseil Regional de la Sante et des Services Sociaux de l'Outaouais (Quebec). 1985/1986. French. Conseil de la Sante et des Services Sociaux de l Outaousis, Le Region 04 364 Des Forges Trois-Rivieres, Quebec G9A 2HI Canada. **LC** RA185.Q2; C67a. **DD** 354.714/2200841. **Continues** Rapport Annuel / Conseil de la Sante et des Services Sociaux de l'Outaouais, 0710-2569.

RE
**RAPPORT ANNUEL / DIRECTION DEPARTEMENTALE DES AFFAIRES SANITAIRES ET SOCIALES.** **Main/Corp** Reunion. Direction Departementale des Affaires Sanitaires et Sociales. French. an. DDASS Route du Campus Universitaire, le Chaudron 97490, Ste-Clotilde Reunion. **LC** RA363.R4; R48A. **DD** 354.69/810084.

CN/0824-8567
**RAPPORT ANNUEL DU CURATEUR PUBLIC (1977).** (RAPPORT ANNUEL DU CURATEUR PUBLIC.). **Main/Corp** Quebec (Province). Curatelle Publique. 1977-. French. an. Editeur Officiel du Quebec, 1283 Boul Charest Ouest, Quebec Quebec G1N 2C9 Canada. **LC** RA790.7.C2; Q44A. **DD** 354.714004/2. **Continues** Rapport Annuel -Curatelle Publique du Quebec, 0824-8559.

RW
**RAPPORT ANNUEL - MINISTERE DE LA SANTE PUBLIQUE.** **Title Change**. **Main/Corp** Rwanda. Ministere de la Sante Publique. French. **LC** RA352.R95; M56A. **DD** 354.67/5710077. **Continued by** Trapport ... Annuel (Rwanda Ministere de la Sante Publique et des Affaires Sociales. Rwanda).

BE
**RAPPORT D'ACTIVITE - INSTITUT D'HYGIENE ET D'EPIDEMIOLOGIE.** **Main/Corp** Institut d'Hygiene et d'Epidemiologie (Belgium). French. Institut d'Hygiene et d Epidemiologie, 14 rue Juliette Wytsman, Bruxelles Belgium. **LC** RA428.3.I57; I57A. **DD** 610/.7/20493.

CN/1189-3087
**RAPPORT D'ACTIVITES / CENTRE QUEBECOIS DE COORDINATION SUR LE SIDA.** [Rapp. act. - Cent. que. coord. sida]. **Main/Corp** Centre Quebecois de Coordination sur le Sida. (1991)-. French. **DD** 362.1/969792/0060714.

IT
**RASSEGNA AMMINISTRATIVA DELLA SANITA.** (19??)-. Italian. Four times a year. L90000. Rassegna Amministrativa Sanita, Via Azuni 9, 00196 Rome Italy. **Tel** 011 39 6 3202891.

IT/0033-9601
**RASSEGNA DI SERVIZIO SOCIALE.** (19??)-. Italian. Four times a year. L45000 Italy; L50000 other. EISS Ente Italiano Servizio Sociale, Sociale Ferdinando Baldelli 41, 00146 Rome Italy. **Tel** 011 39 6 5410603, 011 39 6 5402762, FAX 011 39 2 5402762. **Bk Rev**, (Qty: 25.yr). **Circ**: 1500 (ctrl).

UK/0144-1256
**RECENT ADVANCES IN COMMUNITY MEDICINE.** [Recent adv. community med.]. No. 1 (1978)-. English. ir. Churchill Livingstone, 1-3 Baxter's Place, Leith Walk, Edinburgh EH1 3AF Scotland. **Tel** 011 44 31 556 2424, FAX 011 44 31 558 1278, telex 727511. **(Subscription address**: US/ Churchill Livingstone, Fulfillment Office, PO Box 11318, Birmingham, AL 35202**)** **ED** A. E. Bennett & Alwyn Smith. **NLM** W1 RE105UE. **CODEN** RCOMD6. Documents available from BIOSIS Document Express.
 **Desc**: Covers community medicine and health services.
 **Ind/Abst** Biol. Abstr.

FR
**RECHERCHE ET SANTE.** French. qt. 58.77F. Fondation Recherche Medicale, 54 rue de Varenne, 75007 Paris France. **Tel** 011 33 1 45492070.

US
**REFORMING THE HEALTH CARE SYSTEM : STATE PROFILES / SUSAN OEHME RAETZMAN.** **Added/Corp** Public Policy Institute (American Association of Retired Persons). **VFOAT** State Health Profiles. (1990)-. Periodical. English. Health Team Public Policy Institute, American Association of Retired Persons, 601 E Street NW, Washington DC 20049. **LC** RA407.3; .R43.

FR
**REGIME DISCIPLINAIRE DES AGENTS DES ETABLISSEMENTS SANITAIRES ET SOCIAUX PUBLICS.** (19??)-. French. 650.00F. Association Developpement du Droit Hospitalier, BP 229, 44146 Chateaubriant Cedex France. **Tel** 011 33 1 1640558800.

MZ/0254-0282
**RELATORIO - DIRECCAO PROVINCIAL DOS SERVICOS DE SAUDE E ASSISTENCIA.** [Relat. - Dir. prov. Serv. saude assist.]. **Main/Corp** Mozambique. Direccao dos Servicos de Saude e Assistencia. Seccao de Estatistica. 1964-. Portuguese. an. **LC** WMLC L 83/9432. **NLM** W2 HM7 D45R. **Formed by the union of** Relatorio Anual da Direccao dos Servicos de Saude e Higiene, 0254-0266 **and** Estatistica dos Servicos de Saude.

IT
**RELAZIONE DELLA CORTE DEI CONTI AL PARLAMENTO SULLA GESTIONE FINANZIARIA DEGLI ENTI SOTTOPOSTI A CONTROLLO IN APPLICAZIONE DELLA LEGGE 21 MARZO 1958, N. 259.** See Law.

CN/0318-6067
**REPERTOIRE DES ETABLISSEMENTS DE SANTE ET DE SERVICES SOCIAUX.** **Added/Corp** Quebec (Province). Ministere des Affaires Sociales. (1974)-. French. an. Ministere des Affaires Sociales, 1075 Chemin Ste Foy, Quebec Ontario G1S 2M1 Canada. **DD** 362/.0025/714.

US
**REPORT - FLORIDA. DEPARTMENT OF HEALTH AND REHABILITATIVE SERVICES. DIVISION OF MENTAL HEALTH.** **Main/Corp** Florida. Department of Health and Rehabilitative Services. Division of Mental Health. (19??)-. English.

US/0428-6383
**REPORT - FLORIDA. LEGISLATURE. JOINT INTERIM COMMITTEE ON MENTAL HEALTH.** See Public Administration.

UK/0436-3779
**REPORT - GREAT BRITAIN. COMMITTEE ON SAFETY OF DRUGS.** **Main/Corp** Great Britain. Committee on Safety of Drugs. (1964)-. English. **DD** 615.

US
**REPORT - KENTUCKY. DEPT OF HEALTH.** **Main/Corp** Kentucky. Dept of Health. English. qt. Kentucky Department of Health, Frankfort KY 40601. **LC** RA71; .B25. **DD** 614.061769.

IE
**REPORT - NATIONAL HEALTH COUNCIL.** **Main/Corp** Ireland (Eire). National Health Council. English. ir. 25p. Government Publications, 4 5 Harcourt Road, Dublin 2 Ireland. **Tel** 011 353 1 6613111 Ext.4005. **LC** RA273; .N38A. **DD** 362.1/09417. **Circ**: 1,000.

NZ
**REPORT - NEW ZEALAND. DEPT. OF HEALTH.** **Title Change**. **Main/Corp** New Zealand. Dept. of Health. (19??)-(1969). English. an. **LC** RA372.N6; A3. **DD** 614.09931. **Continued by** Public Health.

US/0193-0494
**REPORT OF THE ADMINISTRATOR / ALCOHOL, DRUG ABUSE, AND MENTAL HEALTH ADMINISTRATION.** See Drug Abuse and Alcoholism.

US/0276-8321
**REPORT OF THE ADMINISTRATOR - UNITED STATES. HEALTH SERVICES ADMINISTRATION.** (REPORT OF THE ADMINISTRATOR / HEALTH SERVICES ADMINISTRATION.). [Rep. adm. - U.S., Health Serv. Adm.]. **Main/Corp** United States. Health Services Administration. English. an. US Department of Health & Human Services / Public Health Service, 200 Independence Avenue SW, Room 716G, Washington DC 20201. **Tel** (202)690-6867, FAX (202)690-6274. **LC** RA412.5.U6; U54A. **DD** 353.0084/1/06. **NLM** W2 A H635R.

US
**REPORT OF THE DEPARTMENT OF HEALTH PROFESSIONS, COMMONWEALTH OF VIRGINIA FOR THE ... BIENNIUM.** **Main/Corp** Virginia. Dept. of Health Professions. **VFOAT** Report of the Department of Health Professions; Biennial Report of the Department of Health Professions. (1990)-. English. be. Virginia Department of Health Regulatory Boards, Virginia Commission of Health Regulatory Boards, Seaboard Building/ Suite 453, 3600 West Broad Street, Richmond VA 23230. **LC** RA396.A4; V73a. **DD** 353.97550084/1. **Continues** Virginia. Dept. of Health Regulatory Boards. Biennial Report.

US/0193-7340
**REPORT OF THE DIRECTOR, NATIONAL HEART, LUNG, AND BLOOD INSTITUTE.** **Main/Corp** National Heart, Lung, and Blood Institute. **VFOAT** Report of the Director of the National Heart, Lung, and Blood Institute. Began with 4th (1977). English. an. US Department of Health and Human Services National Institutes of Health, 9000 Rockville Pike, Bethesda MD 20892. **Tel** (301)496-9291, FAX (301)496-2443. **LC** RA645.H4; N365A. **DD** 353.0084/1. **NLM** W2 A N163A. available on microfiche (Vols. for (1984-) distributed to depository libraries). **Continues** Report of the Director of the National Heart and Lung Institute, 0145-6679.

AT
**REPORT OF THE DIRECTOR OF MENTAL HEALTH SERVICES.** **Main/Corp** Western Australia. Mental Health Services. **VFOAT** Annual Report of the Director of Mental Health Services. (19??)-. English. **LC** RA790.7.A8; W47b. **DD** 354/.941/00842. **NLM** W2 KA8.1 W5M5R.

US/0731-6194
**REPORT OF THE JOINT LEGISLATIVE COMMITTEE ON MOTOR VEHICLES, HIGHWAY AND TRAFFIC SAFETY TO THE LEGISLATURE OF THE STATE OF NEW YORK.** **Title Change**. See Transportation.

CN/0707-1973
**REPORT OF THE SASKATCHEWAN SAFETY COUNCIL PUBLIC OPINION POLL, A.** **Main/Corp** Saskatchewan Safety Council. **VFOAT** Traffic Safety Public Opinion Poll. **VAT** Traffic Safety Public Opinion Poll (1976). 1976-. English. an. Saskatchewan Safety Council, 348 Victoria Avenue, Regina Saskatchewan S4N 0P6 Canada. **DD** 301.15/43/614862097124. **Continues** Saskatchewan Safety Council. Report of the Traffic Safety Public Opinion Poll, 0707-7645.

US
**REPORT ON ALTERNATIVE RESIDENTIAL MODEL (ARM) RATES.** **Added/Corp** California. Dept. of Developmental Services. (1991)-. English. **Continues** Residential Rates Proposal Alternative Residential Model (ARM).

US
**REPORT ON LEGISLATIVE ACTIVITIES OF THE COMMITTEE ON LABOR AND HUMAN RESOURCES, UNITED STATES SENATE DURING THE ... CONGRESS ... : PURSUANT TO SECTION 136 OF THE LEGISLATIVE REORGANIZATION ACT OF 1946, AS AMENDED BY THE LEGISLATIVE REORGANIZATION ACT OF 1970.** **Main/Corp** United States. Congress. Senate. Committee on Labor and Human Resources. (198?)-. English. be. **LC** KF30.8; .L342. **DD** 344.73; 347.304. ***Continues*** *United States. Congress. Senate. Committee on Labor and Human Resources. Legislative Review Activity, 0730-2649.*
**Desc:** Concentrates on social legislation, public health, social welfare, and research.

SZ
**REPORT ON THE WORLD HEALTH SITUATION.** **Added/Corp** World Health Organization. **VFOAT** World Health Situation. 6th (1973/1977)-. English. ir. Price varies per volume. World Health Organization, Distribution and Sales, 20 Avenue Appia, CH-1211 Geneva 27 Switzerland. **Tel** 011 41 22 7912111, FAX 011 41 22 7880401. ***Continues*** *World Health Organization. Report on the World Health Situation.*

US/0145-7306
**REPORT TO THE GOVERNOR - NEW YORK STATE FACILITIES DEVELOPMENT CORPORATION.** **Main/Corp** Facilities Development Corporation (N.Y.). 1974-. English. an. New York State Facilities Development Corporation, 44 Holland Avenue, Albany NY 12208. **LC** RA790.65.N7; M45A. **DD** 362.2/09747. ***Continues*** *Report to the Governor - New York State Health and Mental Hygiene Facilities Improvement Corporation, 0094-2545.*

US
**REPORT TO THE PEOPLE.** **See** Transportation-Roads and Traffic.

US/0273-5202
**REPORTED MORBIDITY AND MORTALITY IN TEXAS, ANNUAL SUMMARY.** V. 1- 1978-. English. an. Texas Department of Health, 1100 West 49th Street, Austin TX 78756-3180. **Tel** (512)458-7550, FAX (512)458-7407. **LC** RA643.6.T4. **DD** 312/.39/09764. **NLM** W2; AT4 B65r.

US/0034-477X
**REPORTER - NEW JERSEY ASSOCIATION FOR HEALTH, PHYSICAL EDUCATION AND RECREATION, THE.** (NEW JERSEY ASSOCIATION FOR HEALTH, PHYSICAL EDUCATION AND RECREATION REPORTER.). **Main/Corp** New Jersey Association for Health, Physical Education and Recreation. (19??)-. Periodical. English. Twice a year. $15.00. New Jersey Association for Health, Physical Education and Recreation, PO Box 353, c/o Sandra D. Wilbur, Villas NJ 08251. **Tel** (609)886-1762. **ED** Virginia Overdorf. **Ad Acc. Circ:** 1,000 (ctrl).

UK/0300-8045
**REPORTS ON HEALTH AND SOCIAL SUBJECTS.** (REPORTS ON HEALTH AND SOCIAL SUBJECTS / DEPARTMENT OF HEALTH AND SOCIAL SECURITY.). [Rep. health soc. subj.]. **Added/Corp** Great Britain. Dept. of Health and Social Security. Great Britain. Dept. of Health. **VFOAT** Report on Health and Social Subjects. (1972)-. Monographic series. English. ir. Price varies per volume. Her Majesty's Stationery Office, 51 Nine Elms Lane, London SW8 5DR England. **Tel** 011 44 71 873 8459, 011 44 71 873 8499, FAX 011 44 71 873 8499, 011 44 71 873 8456, telex 297138. **(Subscription address:** Her Majesty's Stationery Office, PO Box 276, Publications Centre, London SW8 5DT England.**) LC** UNC. **NLM** W1 RE212VM. ***Continues*** *Reports on Public Health and Medical Subjects) Great Britain. Dept. of Health and Social Security).*
**Ind/Abst** Index Med.

US/1073-9998
**RESCUE-EMS MAGAZINE.** (1991)-. English. bm. $15.00; $25.00 combined subscription with Firefighters News. Lifesaving Communications, PO Box 100, Nassau DE 19969. **Tel** (302)645-5600, FAX (302)645-8747. **ED** Steve Stevenson. **Ad Acc, Adv Mgr:** Al Frazier. **Circ:** 30,000 (ctrl). ***Continues*** *Rescue News.*
**Desc:** Management information and skills for rescue, EMS, and patient transport leadership including legal; vehicle operations, and maintenance; rescue and extriction skills; administrative systems; quality assurance; EMS continuing education; association/organization news; new products; calendar; new vehicle listing.

US/1041-0651
**RESCUE MAGAZINE.** [Rescue mag.]. **VFOAT** Rescue. (1988)-. Periodical. English. bm. $12.97. Mosby Year Book Inc., 11830 Westline Industrial Drive, St Louis MO 63146. **Tel** (800)325-4177, (314)872-8370, FAX (314)432-1380, telex 44-2402. **(Subscription address:** JEMS Communications, PO Box 2789, Carlsbad CA 92018.**) ED** Lee Reeder. **DD** 363.
**Desc:** The magazine for the people of rescue, rescuers and EMT's who care for the sick and injured who locate those in peril and extricate them.

SZ
**RESOLUTIONS AND DECISIONS, ANNEXES / WORLD HEALTH ORGANIZATION, EXECUTIVE BOARD.** **Main/Corp** World Health Organization. Executive Board. 73rd Session (Jan. 1984)-. English. $16.20. World Health Organization, Distribution and Sales, 20 Avenue Appia, CH-1211 Geneva 27 Switzerland. **Tel** 011 41 22 7912111, FAX 011 41 22 7880401. **LC** RA8.A4; E92a. **DD** 341.7/65. ***Continues in part*** *World Health Organization. Executive Board. Resolutions and Decisions, Annexes, Summary Records.*
**Desc:** Records the texts, resolutions, and decisions adopted by the Executive Board of the World Health Organization.

US/0190-3527
**RESOURCE DIRECTORY, HEALTH INFORMATION SHARING PROJECT.** **VFOAT** Health Information Sharing Project Resource Directory. 1978-. Directory. English. Syracuse University / Information Studies, School of Information Studies, Syracuse NY. **NLM** W 22 AN6 R434.

US
**RESOURCE [SOUND RECORDING]: A MONTHLY AUDIO DIGEST OF CURRENT ISSUES IN HEALTH CARE RISK MANAGEMENT/ PRODUCED BY THE RISK MANAGEMENT FOUNDATION OF THE HARVARD MEDICAL INSTITUTIONS.** **Added/Corp** Risk Management Foundation. (Aug. 1985)-. Periodical. English. mo. $75.00; $150.00 combined subscription with Forum. Risk Management Foundation, 840 Memorial Drive, Cambridge MA 02139. **Tel** (617)495-5100, FAX (617)495-9711. **ED** Tom Augello. **NLM** W1; RE246Y. Index available. cum. index.
**Desc:** Monthly updates on health care risk management news and trends.

US/0360-7933
**RESOURCES FOR HEALTH R & D REPORT.** **VAT** Resources for Health Research and Development Report. No. 21-. English. US Department of Health and Human Services National Institutes of Health, 9000 Rockville Pike, Bethesda MD 20892. **Tel** (301)496-9291, FAX (301)496-2443. **LC** R854.U5; R49. **DD** 610/.7/2073. **NLM** W2 A N213R. ***Continues*** *Resources for Biomedical Research, 0163-3481.*

US/0732-2933
**RESPONSE (SOLANA BEACH, CALIF.).** (RESPONSE : OFFICIAL JOURNAL OF THE NATIONAL ASSOCIATION FOR SEARCH AND RESCUE.). [Response]. **Added/Corp** National Association for Search and Rescue (U.S.). Vol. 1, No. 1 (Winter 1982)-. Periodical. English. qt. $11.95 (one year), $19.95 (two year). National Association for Search and Rescue, PO Box 3709, Fairfax VA 22038. **Tel** (703)352-1349. **ED** Rick Minerd. **LC** TL553.8; .R47. **DD** 363.3/48/05. **Bk Rev. Ad Acc. Circ:** 10,000.
**Desc:** Magazine of search and rescue management. Discusses rescue techniques, equipment, disaster management, missions, etc.

CU/0253-1151
**REVISTA CUBANA DE HIGIENE Y EPIDEMIOLOGIA.** **See** Medical Science and Technology-Epidemiology.

CU/0864-3466
**REVISTA CUBANA DE SALUD PUBLICA.** **Added/Corp** Centro Nacional de Informacion de Ciencias Medicas. Vol. 14, No. 2 (April-June 1988)-. Spanish (Spanish; summaries and/or abstracts in English and French). Twice a year. 33.19Cub$ South America; 35.93Cub$ North America; 38.30Cub$ others. Ediciones Cubanas, Obispo 527, Altos ESQ Bernaza, CP 10100 Havana Cuba. **Tel** 011 632980, 631942, FAX 011 631011, telex 512337, 6540. **LC** RA456.C7; R48. **DD** 362.1/097291/05. ***Continues*** *Revista Cubana de Administracion de Salud.*
**Ind/Abst** Trop. Dis. Bull.

BL/0304-2138
**REVISTA DA FUNDACAO SESP.** [Rev. Fund. SESP]. **Main/Corp** Fundacao Servicos de Saude Publica. **VAT** Revista da Fundacao Servicos de Saude Publica. Vol. 17, No. 2 (1972)-. Periodical. Portuguese (summaries and/or abstracts in English). sa. Fundacao Servicos de Saude Publica, Av Rio Branco 251, Caixa Postal 1530, Guanabara Rio de Janeiro Brazil. **LC** RA463; .F85a. **NLM** W1 RE37V. **CODEN** RFSEAK. Documents available from BIOSIS Document Express, CASDDS. ***Continues*** *Revista do Servico Especial de Saude Publica, 0100-0101.*
**Ind/Abst** Biol. Abstr. (-1985); Chem. Abstr.

RM/0303-8440
**REVISTA DE IGIENA, BACTERIOLOGIE, VIRUSOLOGIE, PARAZITOLOGIE, EPIDEMIOLOGIE, PNEUMOFTIZIOLOGIE. SERIA : IGIENA.** [Rev. ig., bacteriol., virusol., parazitol., epidemiol., pneumoftiziol., Ser. ig.]. **Added/Corp** Societatea de Igiena. **VFOAT** Igiena. Vol. 23, No. 7 (July/Sept. 1974)-. Periodical. Romanian (summaries and/or abstracts in English, French, German and Russian). Four times a year. $20.00. Uniunea Societatilor de Stiinte Medicale din Romania, Str. Progresului Nr. 10, Bucurest Romania. **(Subscription address:** Orion Press SRL, SPL Independentei 202-A, Bucharest 6 Romania.**) NLM** W1 RE402AN. **CODEN** RABIDH. Documents available from BIOSIS Document Express, CASDDS. ***Continues*** *Igiena, 0019-1620.*
**Desc:** Review of hygiene and public health.
**Ind/Abst** Biol. Abstr.; Chem. Abstr.; Coal Abstr.; Saf. Health Work.

CK/0120-386X
**REVISTA DE LA FACULTAD NACIONAL DE SALUD PUBLICA.** **Added/Corp** Universidad de Antioquia. Colombia. Ministerio de Salud Publica. Facultad Nacional de Salud Publica (Colombia). **VFOAT** Revista Facultad Nacional de Salud Publica. Vol. 7, No. 1-2 (Jan.-June- July-Dec., 1981)-. Periodical. Spanish. Twice a year. 2,000Col$; $25.00 other. Universidad de Antioquia / Departamento de Publicaciones, Apartado 1226, Medellin Colombia. **Tel** 11 57 4 2631311, 011 57 4 2630011, FAX 11 57 4 2638282. **ED** Alberto Vasco U. **NLM** W1; RE409VH. **Circ:** 1,000 (ctrl). ***Continues*** *Revista de la Escuela Nacional de Salud Publica, 0120-0607.*

PE/1018-6212
**REVISTA DE LA SANIDAD DE LA POLICIA NACIONAL DEL PERU.** (1989)-. Spanish. Direccion de Instruccion, Capacitation e Investigacion Med., PO Box 1683, Av. Arequipa 4898, Miraflores, Lima, Peru. **Tel** (14)453140. ***Continues*** *Revista de la Sanidad de las Fuerzas Policiales, 0254-3435.*
**Ind/Abst** EMBASE [Select. Cov.].

SP/0034-8732
**REVISTA DE PREVENCION.** (REVISTA DE PREVENCION / ASOCIACION PARA LA PREVENCION DE ACCIDENTES.). [Rev. Prev.]. **Added/Corp** Asociacion Para la Prevencion de Accidentes (Spain). No. 1 (1962)-. Periodical. Spanish. qt. $22.00. Asociacion Para la Prevencion de Accidentes, Echaide 4 Apdo 527, San Sebastian Spain.

CU/0253-570X
**REVISTA DE SALUD ANIMAL.** [Rev. salud anim.]. Vol. 1, No. 1 (1979)-. Academic Scholarly Publication. Spanish. Three times a year. 31.14Cub$ North and South America; 39.52Cub$ other. Ediciones Cubanas, Obispo 527, Altos ESQ Bernaza, CP 10100 Havana Cuba. **Tel** 011 632980, 631942, FAX 011 631011, telex 512337, 6540. **CODEN** RSANDH. Documents available from BIOSIS Document Express, CASDDS.
**Ind/Abst** Agrofor. Abstr. (1991-); Anim. Breed. Abstr.; Biol. Abstr.; Chem. Abstr.; Dairy Sci. Abstr.; Food Sci. Technol. Abstr.; For. Abstr.; Helminthol. Abstr.; Index Vet.; Nutr. Abstr. Rev., Ser. B, Live Feeds and Feed.; Pig News Inf.; Poult. Abstr.; Protozoolog. Abstr.; Rev. Agric. Entomol.; Rev. Med. Vet. Entomol.; Rev. Med. Vet. Mycology; Rice Abstr.; Vet. Bull.

SP
**REVISTA DE SALUD PUBLICA DE CASTILLA Y LEON.** Spanish. Junta de Castilla y Leon, Consejeria de Cultura y Bienestar Social, Avda. de Burgos 5, 47071 Vallodolid Spain.
**Ind/Abst** Indice Med. Esp.

SP/0034-8899
**REVISTA DE SANIDAD E HIGIENE PUBLICA.** [Rev. sanid. hig. publica]. Vol. 7, No. 1, (Jan. 1932)-. Periodical. Spanish (summaries and/or abstracts in French and English). Six times a year. Free. Ministerio de Sanidad y Consumo, Paseo del Prado 18 20, 28071 Madrid Spain. **Tel** 011 34 1 420-2227, 420-2051. **NLM** W1 RE49. ***Continues*** *Boletin Tecnico de la Direccion General de Salud Publica y Sanidad Veterinaria.*
**Ind/Abst** Index Med.; Index Vet.; Indice Med. Esp.

BL/0034-8910
**REVISTA DE SAUDE PUBLICA.** [Rev. saude publica]. Vol. 1 (1967)-. Academic Scholarly Publication. Portuguese (summaries and/or abstracts in English). Six times a year. $40.00 (institutions), $28.00 (individuals). Faculdade de Saude Publica USP, Av Dr Arnaldo 715, 01255 Sao Paulo, SP Brazil. **Tel** 11 55 11 2803233. **ED** Oswaldo Paulo Forattini. **NLM** W1 RE498. **CODEN** RSPUB9. Index available in last issue of volume--attached. **Bk Rev. Pr Rev. Circ:** 1,400 (ctrl). Documents available from The Genuine Article,

CASDDS. **Supersedes** *Arquivos da Faculdade de Higiene e Saude Publica da Universidade de Sao Paulo.*
**Ind/Abst** Biodeter. Abstr.; Chem. Abstr. (1967-1983); Curr. Contents Soc. Behav. Sci.; Dairy Sci. Abstr.; EMBASE [Select. Cov.]; Index Med.; Index Vet.; Nutr. Abstr. Rev., Ser. A, Hum. Exp.; Life Sci. Collect.; Res. Alert [Full Cov.]; Rev. Agric. Entomol.; Rev. Med. Vet. Entomol.; Soc. Sci. Cit. Index [Full Cov.]; Vet. Bull.; Trop. Dis. Bull.

EC
**REVISTA DEL INSTITUTO JUAN CESAR GARCIA.** **Added/Corp** Instituto Juan Cesar Garcia. Vol. 1, No. 1 (Enero de 1991)-. Periodical. Spanish. sa.

BL/0073-9855
**REVISTA DO INSTITUTO ADOLFO LUTZ.** [Rev. Inst. Adolfo Lutz]. **Main/Corp** Sao Paulo, Brazil (City). Instituto Adolfo Lutz. Vol. 1 (July 1941)-. Academic Scholarly Publication. Portuguese (summaries and/or abstracts in English). sa. Free to governments and cultural institutions. Biblioteca do Instituto Adolfo Lutz, Av. Dr. Arnaldo 335, Caixa Postal 7027, 01246-902 Sao Paulo, SP Brazil. **Tel** 8530111. **ED** Carlos Jose Linardi. **LC** R25; .S28. **DD** 610/.5. **NLM** W1 RE521. **CODEN** RIALA6. Index available. cum. index. **Circ:** 1,200 (ctrl). Documents available from BIOSIS Document Express, CASDDS.
**Desc:** Publishes original papers on research in the field of public health: food, drugs, cosmetics, and disinfectant analysis; human pathology; clinical analysis; medical biology.
**Ind/Abst** Abstr. Hyg. Commun. Dis.; AGRICOLA; Agrindex; Anal. Abstr.; Biol. Abstr.; Chem. Abstr.; Dairy Sci. Abstr.; EMBASE; Food Sci. Technol. Abstr.; Helminthol. Abstr. (1991-); Index Med.; Microbiol. Abstr. Sect. B; Microbiol. Abstr. Sect. A; Microbiol. Abstr. Sect. C; Life Sci. Collect.; Protozoolog. Abstr.; Rev. Med. Vet. Entomol.; Soyabean Abstr.; Toxicol. Abstr.; Trop. Dis. Bull.; Virol. AIDS Abstr.; Virol. Abstr.

MX
**REVISTA LATINOAMERICANA DE SALUD.** 1-. Periodical. Spanish. $20.00. Editorial Nueva Imagen, Apartado Postal 600, Mexico 1 DF Mexico. **LC** RA450.5; 0.R48. **DD** 362.1/098.

CR/0034-9909
**REVISTA MEDICA DE COSTA RICA.** **See** Medical Science and Technology.

MZ
**REVISTA MEDICA DE MOCAMBIQUE.** **See** Medical Science and Technology.

PO/0870-9025
**REVISTA PORTUGUESA DE SAUDE PUBLICA / ESCOLA NACIONAL DE SAUDE PUBLICA.** **Added/Corp** Escola Nacional de Saude Publica (Portugal). (1983)-. Periodical. Portuguese (English; summaries and/or abstracts in French). qt. $45.00. Escola Nacional Saude Publica, Av Padre Cruz 5, Lisbon Portugal. **NLM** W1; RE718E.
**Ind/Abst** Soc. Plann. Policy Dev. Abstr.; Trop. Dis. Bull.

CN/1191-9191
**REVUE ALERTE.** (LA REVUE ALERTE / SERVICE NATIONAL DES SAUVETEURS.). [Rev. alerte]. **Added/Corp** Service National des Sauveteurs. Vol. 43 (1991)-. Periodical. French. qt. Service National des Sauveteurs, 1415 East rue Jarry, Montreal Quebec H2E 2Z7 Canada. **Tel** 252-3100. **DD** 797.2. **Continues** *Alerte., 0704-6340.*

FR/0245-9469
**REVUE DE DROIT SANITAIRE ET SOCIAL.** [Rev. droit sanit. soc.]. No. 61, (Jan./March 1980)-. Periodical. French. qt. 570.00F France; 665.00F other. Dalloz, 35 rue Tournefort, 75240 Paris Cedex 05 France. **Tel** 011 33 1 40515434 or 40515454, FAX 45 87 37 48, telex 206 446 F. **ED** Elie Alfandari. **NLM** W1 RE778EE. **Continues** *Revue Trimestrielle de Droit Sanitaire et Social.*
**Desc:** Analyses and comments on the most significant of recent texts, projects and judicial decisions in the field. Covers public health, pharmacy products, hospitals and social protection systems such as social security, unemployed and handicapped topics.

US/0398-7620
**REVUE D'EPIDEMIOLOGIE ET DE SANTE PUBLIQUE.** **See** Medical Science and Technology-Epidemiology.

SZ
**REVUE INTERNATIONALE DE PROTECTION CIVILE.** **Added/Corp** International Civil Defence Organization. **VFOAT** International Civil Defence Journal; Majallah Al-Dawliyah Lil-Himayah Al-Madaniyah; Revue de l'OIPC. **VAT** Revue de l'Organisation Internationale de Protection Civile. (Jan./Feb./March 1988)-. Periodical. Arabic (English, French and Spanish). qt. 50.00F Europe; 70.00F other. Organisation Internationale de Protection Civile, 10-12 Chemin de Surveille, 1213 Petit-Lancy Switzerland. **Tel** 011 32 22 7934433, FAX 011 32 22 7934428, telex 423786. **LC** UA926.A1; R48. **DD** 363.3/5/05.

US
**RHODE ISLAND ANNUAL HIGHWAY SAFETY REPORT.** **VFOAT** Annual Highway Safety Report; Highway Safety Report; Rhode Island Highway Safety Report. English. an. Rhode Island Department of Transportation, Planning Division, State Office Building, Smith Street, Providence RI 02903. **LC** HE5614.3.R4; R48. **DD** 363.1/256/09745. **Continues** *Rhode Island Highway Safety Report.*

●US/1065-4402
**RHODE ISLAND HEALTH CARE IN PERSPECTIVE.** [R.I. health care perspect.]. **Added/Corp** Morgan Quitno Corporation. 1st Ed. (1993)-. English. $18.00. Morgan Quitno Corporation, PO Box 1656, 512 East 9th Street, Lawrence KS 66044. **Tel** (800)457-0742, (913)841-3534, FAX (913)841-3534. **DD** 362.
**Desc:** Reports on the state's data and rank for each of the categories featured in Health Care State Rankings.

CN/0824-3336
**RISK ABSTRACTS.** **See** Public Health and Safety-Abstracting, Bibliographies and Statistics.

US/0272-4332
**RISK ANALYSIS.** (RISK ANALYSIS : AN OFFICIAL PUBLICATION OF THE SOCIETY FOR RISK ANALYSIS.). [Risk anal.]. **Added/Corp** Society for Risk Analysis. Vol. 1, No. 1 (March 1981)-. Periodical. English. Six times a year. $355.00 US; $415.00 other. Plenum Press, 233 Spring Street, New York NY 10013-1578. **Tel** (212)620-8000, (800)221-9369, FAX (212)463-0742, (212)807-1047, telex 23/421139. **ED** Curtis Travis. **LC** T174.5; .R55. **DD** 658.4/03. **NLM** W1 RI285D. **CODEN** RIANDF. **[CCC]**. Index available. **Pr Rev.** available on microfilm and microfiche from University Microfilms International (UMI). Documents available from Article Express International, The Genuine Article, Ask*IEEE, Documents on Demand.
**Desc:** Provides a focal point for new developments in risk analysis for scientists from a wide range of disciplines. Covers topics of interest to researchers, deals with health risk engineering, math and theoretical aspects of risks.
**Ind/Abst** Bioeng. Abstr.; Chem. Hazards Ind.; Curr. Contents Soc. Behav. Sci.; Ei Page One; EMBASE; Energy Inf. Abstr.; Energy Res. Abstr. (May 1982-); Eng. Index Annu.; Environ. Abstr.; Ergon. Abstr.; Geogr. Abstr. Phys. Geogr.; Geogr. Abstr. Human Geogr.; GeoRef; Health Saf. Sci. Abstr.; Index Med. (1985-); INSPEC (March 1981-); Ins. Period. Index (?-199?); Int. Dev. Abstr.; Lab. Hazards Bull.; PAIS Int. Print; Life Sci. Collect. (1985-); Pollut. Abstr. Indexes; Psychol. Abstr. (1985-); PsycINFO (1990-); PsycLit; Res. Alert [Full Cov.]; Rev. Med. Vet. Mycology; Risk Abstr.; Sage Public Adm. Abstr. (?-?); Sage Urban Stud. Abstr; Soc. Plann. Policy Dev. Abstr.; Soc. Sci. Cit. Index [Full Cov.].

US/1047-0484
**RISK, ISSUES IN HEALTH & SAFETY.** ***Title Change.*** [Risk issues health saf.]. **Added/Corp** Franklin Pierce Law Center. **VFOAT** Risk, Issues in Health and Safety. Vol. 1, No. 1 (Winter 1990)-(1993). Periodical. English. Four times a year. Franklin Pierce Law Center, 2 White Street, Concord NH 03301. **Tel** (603)228-1541, FAX (603)224-3342, (603)228-0388. **ED** Thomas G. Field, Jr. **LC** K22; .I462. **DD** 344.73/04; 347.3044. **NLM** W1; RI285F. **CODEN** RIHSEW. Index available in last issue of volume--attached. **Bk Rev.** **Pr Rev.** Documents available from Documents on Demand. **Continued by** *Risk (Concord, N.H.), 1073-8673.*
**Desc:** Explores basic policy issues related to public and private efforts to manage science and technology for net reduction in the probability, severity and aversive quality of health and safety impacts on individuals and institutions.
**Ind/Abst** Environ. Abstr.; Environ. Period. Bibliogr.; Index Leg. Period. (1992-); Leg. Resour. Index; LegalTrac (1990-); PAIS Int. Print; Risk Abstr.

IT
**RIVISTA DELL'INFERMIERE.** **See** Medical Science and Technology-Hospital Administration and Medical Centers.

IT/0035-6921
**RIVISTA ITALIANA D'IGIENE.** [Riv. ital. ig.]. (1941)-. Academic Scholarly Publication. Italian. bm. L100000.00 Italy; L120000.00 other. Nistri Lichi Editore, Via XXIV Maggio 28, 56123 Pisa Italy. **Tel** 011 39 50 563371, FAX 011 39 50 562726. **ED** G Armani. **LC** RA421; .R54. **NLM** W1 RI771. **CODEN** RIIGAV. Index available. **Bk Rev**, (Qty: 8). **Circ:** 500. Documents available from CASDDS.
**Ind/Abst** Biodeter. Abstr.; Chem. Abstr.; Dairy Sci. Abstr.; EMBASE; Index Vet.; Nutr. Abstr. Rev., Ser. A, Hum. Exp.; Pig News Inf.; Saf. Health Work; Vet. Bull.; Trop. Dis. Bull.

CN/0317-8196
**ROAD SAFETY ANNUAL REPORT.** **See** Transportation-Roads and Traffic.

NZ
**ROAD TRAFFIC SAFETY RESEARCH COUNCIL REPORT.** **See** Transportation-Roads and Traffic.

SA
**ROBOT.** **See** Transportation-Roads and Traffic.

PL
**ROCZNIK STATYSTYCZNY OCHRONY ZDROWIA (POLAND. GOWNY URZAD STATYSTYCZNY : 1974).** ***Title Change.*** (ROCZNIK STATYSTYCZNY OCHRONY ZDROWIA / GOWNY URZAD STATYSTYCZNY.). **Added/Corp** Poland. Gowny Urzad Statystyczny. (1974)-(198?). Polish. ir (every five years). Zaklad Wydawnictw Statystycznych, Al Niepodleglosci 208, 00-925 Warszawa Poland. **Tel** 253241, telex 814581A GUS. **LC** RA523.P7; R62. ctrl circ. **Continues** *Poland. Gowny Urzad Statystyczny. Ochrona Zdrowia.* **Continued by** *Roczniki Statystyczne. Ochrona Zdrowia.*
**Desc:** Yearbook of the polish health statistics.

PL/0035-7715
**ROCZNIKI PANSTWOWEGO ZAKADU HIGIENY.** [Rocz. panstw. zak. hig.]. (1950)-. Periodical. Polish (summaries and/or abstracts in English and Russian). bm. Price on Request. Panstwowe Wydawn Naukowe, Miodowa 10, PO Box 391, 00251 Warsaw Poland. **NLM** W1; RO221W. **CODEN** RPZHAW. Documents available from CASDDS.
**Ind/Abst** AGRICOLA; Biodeter. Abstr.; Chem. Abstr.; EMBASE [Select. Cov.]; Field Crop Abstr.; Food Sci. Technol. Abstr.; Hortic. Abstr.; Index Med.; Index Vet.; Life Sci. Collect.; Potato Abstr.; Rev. Med. Vet. Mycology; Vet. Bull.; Trop. Dis. Bull.

UK/0143-3377
**ROSPA BULLETIN.** [RoSPA bull.]. **VFOAT** Royal Society for the Prevention of Accidents Bulletin. (1979)-. Periodical. English. mo. £16.00 (members), £20.00 (nonmembers) UK; £20.00 (members), £23.00 (nonmembers) other. Royal Society of the Prevention of Accidents, Cannon House, Priory Queensway, Birmingham B4 6BS England. **Tel** 011 44 21 200 2461. **DD** 363.110941. **Continues** *OS & H Bulletin, 0309-1155.*
**Ind/Abst** Chem. Hazards Ind.; Lab. Hazards Bull.

US/0272-0515
**ROUNDTABLE REPORT.** ***Ceased.*** (ROUNDTABLE REPORT / WOMEN AND HEALTH ROUNDTABLE.). **Main/Corp** Women and Health Roundtable. English. Women & Health Roundtable Report, 1718 Connecticut AVenue/Suite 310, Washington DC 20009.

UK
**ROYAL LIFE SAVING SOCIETY LIFESAVER UK, THE.** English. £10.00 (libraries), £20.00 (individuals). Royal Life Saving Society UK, Mountbatten House, Studley Warwickshire B80 7NN England. **ED** Sandra Caldwell. **Ad Acc.** **Circ:** 8,000 (ctrl).

US
**RUBELLA SURVEILLANCE / CENTER FOR DISEASE CONTROL.** **Added/Corp** Center for Disease Control. National Communicable Disease Center (U.S.). (19??)-. English. an. free. Centers for Disease Control, 1600 Clifton Road NE, Atlanta GA 30333. **Tel** (404)639-3311, FAX (404)639-3296. **(Subscription address:** CDC Distribution, Attention G Dixon, Mail Stop A 22, Atlanta GA 30333.**)** **DD** 616.9.

IO/0485-6015
**RUMAH TANGGA DAN KESEHATAN.** (19??)-. Periodical. Indonesian.

GW/0340-1219
**RUNDSCHAU FUER FLEISCHBESCHAUER, TRICHINENSCHAUER UND GEFLUGELFLEISCHKONTROLLEURE.** Vol. 26, No. 4, Apr. (1974)-. Periodical. German. mo. Verlag M & H Schaper GmbH & Co, Postfach 16 42, D 31046 Alfeld Leine Germany. **Tel** 011 49 5181 80090. **NLM** W1 RU684. **Continues** *Rundschau fur Fleischbeschauer und Trichinenschauer, 0340-126X.*
**Desc:** Includes colored inserts as diagnostic aids, issued quarterly, June 1974- .

US
**RURAL HEALTH NEWS.** (19??)-. English. Four times a year. $7.00. New Mexico Health Resources, PO Box 27650, Albuquerque NM 87125. **Tel** (505)242-0633. **Circ:** 3,000-5,000.
**Desc:** Addresses the problems of rural health care delivery.

US/0161-7680
**RYAN ADVISORY FOR HEALTH SERVICES GOVERNING BOARDS, THE.** **Added/Corp** Ryan Advisors Inc. Vol. 5, No. 4 (Apr. 1977)-. Periodical. English. Six times a year. $59.00. Advisory Newsletter Group Inc., PO Box 90833, Washington DC 20090. **Tel** (301)772-2277. **NLM** W1 RY33. **Continues** *Ryan Advisory for Hospital Governing Boards, 0196-9242.*

US/0898-8749
**SAFE DRIVER.** **See** Transportation-Automobiles.

# Public Health and Safety

UK/0958-479X
**SAFETY & HEALTH PRACTITIONER.** [Saf. health pract.]. **VFOAT** Safety and Health Practitioner. (1989)-. Periodical. English. mo. £45.00 UK; £53.00 other. Paramount Publishing Ltd, 17 21 Shenley Road, Borehamwood, Herts WD6 IRT England. **Tel** 011 44 81 207-5599, FAX 011 44 81 207-2598. **DD** 363.110941. **Bk Rev.** Index available. **Ad Acc. Continues** Safety Practitioner, 0265-4792.
**Desc:** All aspects of occupational safety and health.
**Ind/Abst** Infomat Int. Bus.

US/1041-9489
**SAFETY BRIEF.** [Saf. brief]. **Added/Corp** Triodyne. (1981)-. Periodical. English. ir. Free. Triodyne Incorporated, 5950 West Touhy Avenue, Sharon Meyer, Niles IL 60714. **Tel** (708)677-4730, FAX (708)647-2047. **DD** 620.

US
**SAFETY EFFECTIVENESS EVALUATION : REPORT NO. NTSB-SEE.** **Main/Corp** United States. National Transportation Safety Board. **Added/Corp** United States. National Transportation Safety Board. Report No. NTSB-SEE. **VFOAT** Report No. NTSB-SEE. (1900)-. Periodical. English. National Transportation Safety Board, 800 Independence Avenue SW, Washington DC 20594. **Tel** (202)382-6600.

UK
**SAFETY MANAGEMENT LONDON.** (SAFETY MANAGEMENT.). [Saf. manag. Lond.]. (1987)-. English. mo (except combined July/Aug.). £32.00 (1 year), £64.00 (2 year) UK; £40.00 (1 year), £79.00 (2 year) other Europe; £50.00 (1 year), £100.00 (2 year) other. British Safety Council, National Safety Center, Chancellors Road, London W6 9RS England. **Tel** 011 44 81 7411231 Ext 228, FAX 011 44 81 7410835. **ED** Bob Jarvis, 081-741-1231 Ext 233. **Bk Rev**, (Qty: 20). **Ad Acc, Adv Mgr:** Bill Bateman, **Tel** 0676-23435. **Circ:** 23,734 (ctrl). **Continues** Safety & Risk Management, 0267-8624.
**Desc:** Covers workplace safety, wellness, maintenance problems, law, new regulations, loss control, product liability and company insurance.
**Ind/Abst** Chem. Hazards Ind.; Lab. Hazards Bull.

US/0740-1426
**SAFETY MANAGEMENT NEWSLETTER.** **VAT** Saf. Manage. Newsl. (19??)-. Newsletter. English. mo. $287.00. Merritt Company, 1661 Ninth Street, PO Box 955, Santa Monica CA 90406. **Tel** (310)450-7234, (800)638-7597, FAX (310)396-4563.

US
**SAFETY RECOMMENDATIONS / NATIONAL TRANSPORTATION SAFETY BOARD.** **Main/Corp** United States. National Transportation Safety Board. English. mo. National Technical Information Service – NTIS, Room 2027S, 5285 Port Royal Road, Springfield VA 22161. **Tel** (703)487-4630, (703)487-4660, (703)487-4650, FAX (703)321-8547, telex 89-9405.

US/0146-7026
**SAFETY RELATED RECALL CAMPAIGNS FOR MTOR VEHICLES AND MOTOR VEHICLE EQUIPMENT, INCLUDING TIRES: DETAILED REPORTS.** **See** Transportation-Automobiles.

US/0147-3743
**SAFETY SADISTICS.** **Suspended. Main/Corp** Arizona. Office of Highway Safety. **VFOAT** Arizona Safety Sadistics. (197?)-Vol. 5, No. 1 (1979). Periodical. English. qt. Arizona Department of Transportation Office of Highway Safety, 1655 West Jackson, Phoenix AZ 85007. **LC** HE5614.3.A6; A74A. **DD** 614.8/62/09791. **Continues** Arizona Safety Sad-istics, 0044-8869.

CN/0704-4739
**SAFETY UPDATE.** **Added/Corp** Ontario Safety League. Vol. 1 (Apr. 1979)-. Periodical. English. qt. Free. Ontario Safety League, 21 Four Seasons Drive, Suite 100, Etobiocoke Ontario M9B 6J8 Canada. **DD** 363.1/09713. ctrl circ. **Supersedes** Ontario Safety League. News, 0700-9844.

US/0739-7283
**SAGE ANNUAL REVIEWS OF COMMUNITY MENTAL HEALTH.** [Sage annu. rev. commun. ment. health]. **VFOAT** Annual Reviews of Community Mental Health. Vol. 1-. Monographic series. English. an. Price varies per volume. SAGE Periodical Press, 2455 Teller Road, Thousand Oaks CA 91320. **Tel** (805)499-0721, FAX (805)499-0871, telex 100799. **ED** Richard H Price and John Monahan. **DD** 362.2/2/05. **NLM** W1 SA125TC. **Acid Free.**

JA
**SAITAMA-KEN EISEI KENKYUJO HO.** **Main/Corp** Saitama-ken Eisei Kenkyujo. **VFOAT** Report of the Saitama Institute of Public Health. Japanese (Japanese). Saitama-ken Eisei Kenkyujo, 639-1 Kami Okubo Higashi, Urawa 338 Japan. **LC** RA421; .S13A.

US/0191-5789
**SALUBRITAS (ENGLISH EDITION).** **Ceased.** (SALUBRITAS.). Vol. 1 (1977)-Vol. 9 (1986). Periodical. English. qt. American Public Health Association, 1015 15th Street Northwest, Washington DC 20005. **Tel** (202)789-5666. **NLM** W1 SA352. **Bk Rev.** **Circ:** 2,500.
**Desc:** Information exchange on primary health care in developing countries including articles on "How to ...", family planning, health education, immunizations, conferences, training publications, etc.

IT/0391-223X
**SALUTE UMANA, LA.** [Salute umana]. Periodical. Italian. Delta Editrice, Via Bach 6, 06080 San Sisto Italy. **Tel** 075 798040. **NLM** W1 SA412.

FR
**SANTE DE L'ECOLIER.** (19??)-. French. qt. 177.00F. La Sante de l'Ecolier, 23 rue de Lorraine, 16800 Soyaux France. **Tel** 011 33 45 953927.

FR
**SANTE DE L'HOMME, LA.** **Added/Corp** Centre d'Education Sanitaire (France) Centre Interdepartemental d'Education Sanitaire (France) Centre Interdepartemental d'Education Sanitaire, Demographique et Sociale (France) Centre Interdepartemental d'Education sanitaire, Demographique et Sociale (France). Direction Departementale de la Sante a Paris. Centre National de l'Education Sanitaire, Demographique et Sociale (France) Comite Francais d'Education Pour la Sante. (19??)-. Periodical. French. bm. 98.00F France; 175.00F other. Comite Francais d'Educ Sante, 2 rue Auguste Comte BP 47, 92170 Vanves France. **Tel** 011 33 1 46454500. **LC** RA421; .S42. **NLM** W1 SA826.

SZ/0250-9326
**SANTE DU MONDE.** [Sante monde]. (1957)-. Periodical. French (English, Spanish, Portuguese, Arabic, German and Russian). bm. $25.00. World Health Organization, Distribution and Sales, 20 Avenue Appia, CH-1211 Geneva 27 Switzerland. **Tel** 011 41 22 7912111, FAX 011 41 22 7880401. **UDC** 61. **CODEN** NU054. cum. index. **Circ:** 30,000.
**Desc:** Designed to increase awareness of health problems and what can be done about them.

FR/0397-0329
**SANTE MAGAZINE.** (1976)-. Periodical. French. mo. 190.00F France; 210.00F other. Sante Magazine, 7 Boulevard de Courbevoie, 92521 Neuilly S Seine France. **Tel** 011 33 1 47476488. **UDC** 61.

CN/0707-2910
**SANTE MENTALE AU CANADA.** [Sante ment. Can.]. **Added/Corp** Canada. Health Services and Promotion Branch. Vol. 26, No. 4 (Dec. 1978)-. Periodical. French. qt. Free in Canada. **Continues** Hygiene Mentale au Canada., 0701-9602.
**Ind/Abst** Can. Period. Index (1983-); Point Repere.

RM/0048-9107
**SANTE PUBLIQUE, LA.** [Sante publique]. (1958)-. Periodical. French (English and German; summaries and/or abstracts in English). Four times a year. 530.00F France; 730.00F other. Presses Universitaires Nancy, 42 avenue de la Liberation, 54001 Nancy Cedex France. **Tel** 011 33 83 935830, FAX 011 33 83 935839. **ED** J.P. Deschamps. **NLM** W1 SA832.
**Ind/Abst** EMBASE; Index Med.; Saf. Health Work.

●BL/0104-1290
**SAUDE E SOCIEDADE.** (1992)-. Portuguese. sa. Universidade de Sao Paulo / Faculdade de Saude Publica, Av. Dr. Arnoldo 715, 01246-904 Sao Paulo SP Brazil.

FR
**SAUVETAGE : REVUE DE LA SOCIETE NATIONALE DE SAUVETAGE EN MER.** (19??)-. French. an. 80.00F. Societe Nationale de Sauvetage en Mer, Rue de Chaillot 9, F 75116 Paris France.

US/1055-8969
**SCHIFF REPORT, THE.** (THE SCHIFF REPORT : A PUBLICATION FOR THE INTERNATIONAL HEALTH INDUSTRY.). [Schiff rep.]. (1988)-. Periodical. English. mo. $175.00 US; $195.00 other. Schiff & Company, 1129 Bloomfield Avenue, West Caldwell NJ 07006. **Tel** (201)227-1830, (800)255-0734, FAX (201)227-5330. **ED** Mary Ann Weinberg. **DD** 338. **Ad Acc. Circ:** 16,000.

US
**SCHOOL SAFETY : NATIONAL SCHOOL SAFETY CENTER NEWSJOURNAL.** **See** Education.

US
**SCHOOL SAFETY WORLD NEWSLETTER / SCHOOL AND COLLEGE DEPARTMENT, NATIONAL SAFETY COUNCIL.** **Added/Corp** National Safety Council. School and College Dept. Vol. 1, No. 1 (Winter 1973)-. Newsletter. English. Four times a year. $19.00.

National Safety Council, 1121 Spring Lake Drive, Itasca IL 60143. **Tel** (800)621-7615, (708)775-2294, FAX (708)285-0797.

GW/0172-2131
**SCHRIFTENREIHE DER AKADEMIE FUR OEFFENTLICHES GESUNDHEITSWESEN IN DUSSELDORF.** [Schriftenr. Akad. Off. Gesundheitswes. Dusseld.] V. 1-. Monographic series. English (German). Price varies per volume. **NLM** W1 SC326F.

GW/0932-478X
**SCHRIFTENREIHE DER BUNDESANSTALT FEUR ARBEITSSCHUTZ. REGELWERKE.** [Schr.reihe Bundesanst. Arb.schutz, Regelw.]. (1987)-. Monographic series. German. ir. Price varies per volume. Bundesanstalt fuer Arbeitsschutz, Postfach 170202, D44061 Dortmund Germany. **Tel** 011 49 231 9071 306, FAX 011 49 0231 9071 454, telex 822 153 BAU D. **UDC** 331.823. Index available. **Circ:** 60,000. **Continues** Schriftenreihe Regelwerke Arbeitsschutz, 0173-2013.
**Desc:** Rules and regulations concerning working conditions.

GW/0932-481X
**SCHRIFTENREIHE DER BUNDESANSTALT FEUR ARBEITSSCHUTZ. SONDERSCHRIFT.** [Schr.reihe Bundesanst. Arb.schutz, Sonderschr.]. (1985)-. Monographic series. German (summaries and/or abstracts in English). ir. Price varies per volume. Bundesanstalt fuer Arbeitsschutz, Postfach 170202, D44061 Dortmund Germany. **Tel** 011 49 231 9071 306, FAX 011 49 0231 9071 454, telex 822 153 BAU D. **UDC** 331.823. Index available. **Circ:** 60,000. **Continues** Sonderschrift - Bundesanstalt feur Arbeitsschutz, 0932-4976.
**Desc:** Various subjects in public health and safety.

GW/0932-3856
**SCHRIFTENREIHE DER BUNDESANSTALT FUER ARBEITSSCHUTZ. FORSCHUNG.** [Schr.reihe Bundesanst. Arb.schutz, Forsch.]. (1985)-. Monographic series. German. ir. Price varies per volume. Bundesanstalt fuer Arbeitsschutz, Postfach 170202, D44061 Dortmund Germany. **Tel** 011 49 231 9071 306, FAX 011 49 0231 9071 454, telex 822 153 BAU D. **UDC** 331.45. Index available. **Circ:** 60,000. **Continues** Forschungsbericht - Bundesanstalt fuer Arbeitsschutz, 0932-3813.
**Desc:** Covers research in occupational safety and health.

GW/0932-4836
**SCHRIFTENREIHE DER BUNDESANSTALT FUER ARBEITSSCHUTZ. FORSCHUNGSANWENDUNG.** **Added/Corp** Bundesanstalt fuer Arbeitsschutz (Germany). **VFOAT** Forschungsanwendung; Schriftenreihe Forschungsanwendung. (198?)-. Monographic series. German. ir. Price varies per volume. Bundesanstalt fuer Arbeitsschutz, Postfach 170202, D44061 Dortmund Germany. **Tel** 011 49 231 9071 306, FAX 011 49 0231 9071 454, telex 822 153 BAU D. **NLM** W1; SC329AB. Index available. **Circ:** 60,000.
**Desc:** Practical uses of research regarding working conditions.

GW/0932-4828
**SCHRIFTENREIHE DER BUNDESANSTALT F...UR ARBEITSSCHUTZ. TAGUNGSBERICHT.** (TAGUNGSBERICHTE.). [Schr.reihe Bundesanst. Arb.schutz, Tag.ber.]. (1984)-. Monographic series. German. ir. Price varies per volume. Bundesanstalt fuer Arbeitsschutz, Postfach 170202, D44061 Dortmund Germany. **Tel** 011 49 231 9071 306, FAX 011 49 0231 9071 454, telex 822 153 BAU D. **UDC** 331.823. Index available. **Circ:** 60,000. **Continues** Schriftenreihe Arbeitsschutz, 0341-9819.
**Desc:** Reports on conferences of public health and safety, including all lectures.

US
**SCHS STUDIES.** No. 8 (Aug. 1980)-. English. Free. PO Box 2091, Raleigh NC 27602. **Tel** (919)733-3421. **ED** Charles J Rothwell. **LC** RA407.4.N8; P48. **DD** 362.1/09756. **NLM** W2; AN8 P9p. **Circ:** 500. **Continues** PHSB Studies.
**Desc:** Studies on health topics of current interest are presented in newsletter form.

FR/0294-0337
**SCIENCES SOCIALES ET SANTE.** [Sci. soc. sante]. **Added/Corp** Association pour le Developpement des Sciences Sociales de la Sante. (Dec. 1982)-. Periodical. French (summaries and/or abstracts in English and Spanish). qt. 529.00F (institutions), 333.00F (individuals) France; 590.00F (institutions), 390.00F (individuals) other. John Libbey Eurotext Ltd, 6 rue

Blanche, Isabelle Trope, 92120 Montrouge France. **Tel** 011 33 1 47358552. **NLM** W1; SC79R.
**Ind/Abst** PAIS Int. Print.

JA/1013-834X
**SEAMIC INFORMATION RETRIEVAL ON CURRENT LITERATURE. SERIES A: TYPHOID AND PARA-TYPHOID FEVERS, AND SALMONELLA FOOD POISONING.** [SEAMIC inf. retr. curr. lit., Ser. A: Typhoid para-typhoid fevers salmonella food poisoning]. **Added/Corp** National Library of Medicine (U.S.) Nihon Kagaku Gijutsu Joho Senta. Nihon Kokusai Iryodan. Tonan Ajia Iryo Joho Senta. **VFOAT** Typhoid and Para-Typhoid Fevers, and Salmonella Food Poisoning. No. 3 (Mar. 1979)-. Periodical. English. Southeast Asian Medical Information Center, International Medical Foundation of Japan, No 6 Toyo-Kaiji Building, 7-2 Shinbashi 4-chome, Minato-ku 105, Tokyo Japan. **Tel** (03)432-2888, telex IMFJ J34484. **NLM** ZWC 260 S106. ***Continues*** *SEAMIC Information Retrieval on Current Literature. Series A: Typhoid Fever & Salmonellosis.*
**Desc:** Based on the US National Library of Medicine's MEDLARS data file, in cooperation with the Japan Information Center of Science and Technology.

JA/0254-2870
**SEAMIC INFORMATION RETRIEVAL ON CURRENT LITERATURE. SERIES F: HEALTH STATUS INDICATORS.** [SEAMIC inf. retr. curr. lit., Ser. F, Health status indic.]. **Added/Corp** MEDLARS. National Library of Medicine (U.S.) Nihon Kagaku Gijutsu Joho Senta. Southeast Asian Medical Information Center (International Medical Foundation of Japan). **VFOAT** Health Status Indicators. **VAT** Southeast Asian Medical Information Center Information Retrieval on Current Literature. Series F, Health Status Indicators. No. 1 (Jan. 1980)-. English. Southeast Asian Medical Information Center, International Medical Foundation of Japan, No 6 Toyo-Kaiji Building, 7-2 Shinbashi 4-chome, Minato-ku 105, Tokyo Japan. **Tel** (03)432-2888, telex IMFJ J34484. **NLM** ZWA 900.1 S104.

JA
**SEAMIC INFORMATION RETRIEVAL ON CURRENT LITERATURE. SERIES H, ENTEROTOXIGENIC COLI.** **Added/Corp** Nihon Kokusai Iryodan. Tonan Ajia Iryo Joho Senta. Nihon Kagaku Gijutsu Joho Senta. MEDLARS. National Library of Medicine (U.S.). No. 1 (Dec. 1980)-. English. Southeast Asian Medical Information Center, International Medical Foundation of Japan, No 6 Toyo-Kaiji Building, 7-2 Shinbashi 4-chome, Minato-ku 105, Tokyo Japan. **Tel** (03)432-2888, telex IMFJ J34484. **NLM** ZWC 260 S106H.

JA/1012-8638
**SEAMIC INFORMATION RETRIEVAL ON CURRENT LITERATURE. SERIES I, CAMPYLOBACTER.** [SEAMIC inf. retriev. curr. lit., Ser. I. Campylobacter]. **Added/Corp** Southeast Asian Medical Information Center (International Medical Foundation of Japan) MEDLARS. Nihon Kagaku Gijutsu Joho Senta. **VAT** Southeast Asian Medical Information Center Information Retrieval on Current Literature. Series I, Campylobacter. No. 1 (1980)-. English. Southeast Asian Medical Information Center, International Medical Foundation of Japan, No 6 Toyo-Kaiji Building, 7-2 Shinbashi 4-chome, Minato-ku 105, Tokyo Japan. **Tel** (03)432-2888, telex IMFJ J34484. **NLM** ZQW 154 S438.

JA/1012-8646
**SEAMIC INFORMATION RETRIEVAL ON CURRENT LITERATURE. SERIES J, VIRAL DIARRHEA.** [SEAMIC inf. retriev. curr. lit., Ser. J Viral diarrhea]. **Added/Corp** Southeast Asian Medical Information Center (International Medical Foundation of Japan) International Medical Foundation of Japan. National Library of Medicine (U.S.). **VFOAT** S.E.A.M.I.C. Information Retrieval on Current Literature. Series J, Viral Diarrhea; Viral Diarrhea; Series J. **VAT** Southeast Asian Medical Information Center Information Retrieval on Current Literature. Series J, Viral Diarrhea. No. 1 (Dec. 1981)-. Periodical. English. Southeast Asian Medical Information Center, International Medical Foundation of Japan, No 6 Toyo-Kaiji Building, 7-2 Shinbashi 4-chome, Minato-ku 105, Tokyo Japan. **Tel** (03)432-2888, telex IMFJ J34484. **NLM** ZWI 407 S438.

JA/1012-8654
**SEAMIC INFORMATION RETRIEVAL ON CURRENT LITERATURE. SERIES K, DYSENTERY, BACILLARY.** [SEAMIC inf. retriev. curr. lit., Ser. K Dysent. bacill.]. **Added/Corp** Southeast Asian Medical Information Center (International Medical Foundation of Japan) International Medical Foundation of Japan. National Library of Medicine (U.S.). **VFOAT** S.E.A.M.I.C Information Retrieval on Current Literature. Series K, Dysentery, Bacillary; Series K; Dysentery, Bacillary. No. 1 (Dec. 1981)-. Periodical. English. Southeast Asian Medical Information Center, International Medical Foundation of Japan, No 6 Toyo-Kaiji Building, 7-2 Shinbashi 4-chome, Minato-ku 105, Tokyo Japan. **Tel** (03)432-2888, telex IMFJ J34484. **NLM** ZWC 282 S438.

JA/0254-8720
**SEAMIC INFORMATION RETRIEVAL ON CURRENT LITERATURE. SERIES L. VENEREAL DISEASE, GONORRHEA.** (SEAMIC INFORMATION RETRIEVAL ON CURRENT LITERATURE. SERIES L. VENEREAL DISEASE.). [SEAMIC inf. retr. curr. lit., Ser. L, Vener. dis. gonorrhea]. **Added/Corp** Southeast Asian Medical Information Center (International Medical Foundation of Japan) International Medical Foundation of Japan. National Library of Medicine (U.S.). **VFOAT** Venereal Disease; Venereal Disease, Gonorrhea. No. 1 (Dec. 1981)-. Monographic series. English. Price varies per volume. Southeast Asian Medical Information Center, International Medical Foundation of Japan, No 6 Toyo-Kaiji Building, 7-2 Shinbashi 4-chome, Minato-ku 105, Tokyo Japan. **Tel** (03)432-2888, telex IMFJ J34484. **NLM** ZWC 140 S438.

JA/1010-5441
**SEAMIC INFORMATION RETRIEVAL ON CURRENT LITERATURE. SERIES M, MALARIA.** [SEAMIC inf. retr. curr. lit., Ser. M, Malaria]. **Added/Corp** Southeast Asian Medical Information Center (International Medical Foundation of Japan) International Medical Foundation of Japan. National Library of Medicine (U.S.). **VFOAT** S.E.A.M.I.C. Information Retrieval on Current Literature. Series M, Malaria; Series M; Malaria. No. 1 (Dec. 1981)-. Periodical. English. Southeast Asian Medical Information Center, International Medical Foundation of Japan, No 6 Toyo-Kaiji Building, 7-2 Shinbashi 4-chome, Minato-ku 105, Tokyo Japan. **Tel** (03)432-2888, telex IMFJ J34484. **NLM** ZWC 750 S438.

US/0092-5136
**SEARCH AND RESCUE MAGAZINE.** [Search rescue mag.]. (1975)-. Periodical. English. qt. $28.80. Search & Rescue Magazine, PO Box 701, Newbury Park CA 91319. **Tel** (805)499-2219. **ED** Dottie Kelley. **LC** TL553.8; .S42. **DD** 614.8. Index available. **Bk Rev. Ad Acc.** ctrl circ.
**Desc:** Describes happenings in the search and rescue world.

US/1047-4609
**SEASONS (OAKLAND, CALIF.).** (SEASONS : THE NATIONAL NATIVE AMERICAN AIDS PREVENTION CENTER QUARTERLY.). [Seasons]. **Added/Corp** National Native American AIDS Prevention Center. (Winter 1989)-. Periodical. English. Three times a year. Free (US only). National Native American / AIDS Prevention Center, 3515 Grand Avenue / Suite 200, Oakland CA 94610. **Tel** (510)444-2051, FAX (510)444-1593. **ED** Andrea Green Rush. **DD** 362. **Circ:** 3,000. available on microfiche from ERIC. ***Continues*** *AIDS in Indian Country.*
**Desc:** Documents the impact of HIV/AIDS on the Native American community. It includes features and columns by Native Americans with HIV, and profiles successful prevention and care strategies in Native communities.

US/0748-9528
**SECOND OPINION (SAN FRANCISCO, CALIF.).** ***Title Change.*** (SECOND OPINION / THE COALITION FOR THE MEDICAL RIGHTS OF WOMEN.). **Added/Corp** Coalition for the Medical Rights of Women (California). **VFOAT** 2nd Opinion. (19??)-. Periodical. English. mo. CMRW, 2845 24th Street, San Francisco CA 94110. **Tel** (415)826)4401. **DD** 362. **Bk Rev. Circ:** 1,500 (ctrl). ***Continued by*** *CDRR News.*
**Desc:** Gives our members the latest news on health care issues that affect women and children: sexually transmitted diseases, PMS, toxic shock syndrome, osteoporosis, hazards from cleaning, endometriosis, and perinatal health.
**Ind/Abst** Consum. Health Nutr. Index (Jan. 1990).

JA/0582-4176
**SEIKATSU EISEI.** [Seikatsu eisei]. **Added/Corp** Osaka Seikatsu Eisei Kyokai. **VFOAT** Journal of Urban Living and Health Association. (1955)-. Periodical. Japanese. bm. Osaka Seikatsu Eisei Kyokai, (Urban Living & Health Assoc.), Osaka Shiritsu Kankyo Kagaku, Kenkyujo, 8-34, Tojocho, Tennojiku, Osakashi, Osakafu 543 Japan. **CODEN** SEEIAY. Documents available from CASDDS.
**Ind/Abst** Chem. Abstr.

JA/0454-2010
**SEISHIN EISEI SHIRYO.** [Seishin eisei shiryo]. **VFOAT** Annual Report on Mental Health. No. 1- ; 1953-. Japanese. Kokuritsu Seishin Eisei Kenkyujo, 7-3 Konodai 1, 272 Ichikawa Japan. **LC** RA790.A1. **CODEN** SESHAX.
**Ind/Abst** Psychol. Abstr. (1967-).

●US
**SELECTED REPORTABLE DISEASES BY HEALTH JURISDICTION.** **See** Medical Science and Technology-Communicable Diseases.

US/1044-548X
**SENIOR HEALTH CARE.** ***Ceased.*** [Sr. health care]. (1989)-(1989). Periodical. English. qt. Mary Ann Liebert Inc., 1651 Third Avenue, New York NY 10128. **Tel** (212)289-2300, (800)M-LIEBERT, FAX (212)289-4697. **DD** 362. ***Continues*** *Senior Health Care News, 0898-3593.*

US/1044-209X
**SENIOR HEALTH DIGEST.** (1989)-. Periodical. English. bm. $30.00. DCE Publications Inc, PO Box 496, Des Moines IA 50302.

US
**SERENITY'S NEW LIFE.** Serenity Health Organization Inc, Box 1408, Ansonia Street, New York NY 10023.

US
**SEXUAL ABUSE.** English. ir. $19.95. Learning Publications Inc, PO Box 1326, Holmes Beach FL 34218-1326. **Tel** (813)778-6651, FAX (813)778-6818.
**Desc:** Deals with the causes, consequences and treatment of incestuous and pedophilic acts.

US/0148-5717
**SEXUALLY TRANSMITTED DISEASES.** [Sex. transm. dis.]. **Added/Corp** American Venereal Disease Association. Vol. 4 (Jan./Mar. 1977)-. Periodical. English. bm. $135.00 (individuals), $187.00 (institutions) US; $145.00 (individuals), $225.00 (institutions) other. J.B. Lippincott Company, 227 East Washington Square, Philadelphia PA 19106-3780. **Tel** (215)238-4200 or 4454, FAX (215)238-4227. **(Subscription address:** J.B. Lippincott, PO Box 350, Hagerstown MD 21740.) **ED** William M. McCormack. **LC** RC201.A1; A764a. **DD** 616.9/51/005. **NLM** W1 SE99U. **CODEN** STRDDM. **[CCC]. Ad Acc. Pr Rev. Circ:** 2,073. available on microfilm and microfiche from University Microfilms International (UMI). Documents available from The Genuine Article, BIOSIS Document Express. ***Continues*** *Journal of the American Venereal Disease Association, 0095-148X.*
**Desc:** Disseminates information on all human sexually transmitted diseases.
**Ind/Abst** Biol. Abstr.; Cumul. Index Nurs. Allied Health Lit.; Curr. Contents Clin. Med.; Curr. Contents Life Sci.; Curr. Lit. Fam. Plan.; EMBASE; Health Index (1989-); Health Period. Database; Health Ref. Cent. (Jan. 1989-) [Full Cov.]; Index Med.; Med. Abstr. Newsl.; Mod. Med.; Life Sci. Collect.; PESTDOC; Protozoolog. Abstr.; Ref. Upd. Deluxe Ed.; Res. Alert [Full Cov.]; Risk Abstr.; Sci. Cit. Index; SCISEARCH; Soc. Sci. Cit. Index [Select. Cov.]; Trop. Dis. Bull.

CN/0711-8929
**SEXUALLY TRANSMITTED DISEASES IN CANADA.** (SEXUALLY TRANSMITTED DISEASES IN CANADA / BUREAU OF EPIDEMIOLOGY, L.C.D.C., HEALTH PROTECTION BRANCH, DEPARTMENT OF NATIONAL HEALTH AND WELFARE.). [Sex. transm. dis. Can.]. **VFOAT** Sexually Transmitted Diseases Canada. 1976-. English (French). an. Free. Bureau of Communicable Disease Epidemiology, Laboratory Centre for Disease Control, Room 240, Tunney's Pasture, Ottawa Ontario K1A 0L2 Canada. **Tel** (613)957-1785. **ED** M J Todd and A G Jessamine. **DD** 312/.3951/00971. **Circ:** 2,000. ***Continues*** *Sexually Transmitted Disease in Canada, 0711-8910.*
**Desc:** Includes information on gonorrhea, syphilis, herpes, AIDS, pelvic inflammatory disease and ectopic pregnancy.

US/0890-3131
**SHAPE (SEATTLE, WASH.).** (SHAPE.). [Shape]. Periodical. English. mo. $18.00. Corporate Fitness Programs Inc, 320 Northeast 97th Street, Suite B, Seattle WA 98115. **Tel** (206)522-0571. **DD** 613.

HK
**SHENG HUO YU CHIEN KANG.** **Added/Corp** Ta Kuang Chu Pan She. **VFOAT** Life and Health. (August 1976)-. Periodical. Chinese (English). bm. $2.00 single issue. Ta Kuang Chu Pan She, 64 Marble Road, Hsiang-Kang Hong Kong. **LC** RA773; .S44.

JA
**SHIGA KENRITSU EISEI KANKYO SENTA SHOHO.** [Shiga Kenritsu Eisei Kankyo Senta shoho]. **Main/Corp** Shiga Kenritsu Eisei Kankyo Senta. **VFOAT** Report of the Shiga Prefectural Institute of Public Health and Environmental Science. Began in 1977. Academic Scholarly Publication. Japanese. an. Shiga Kenritsu Eisei Kankyo Senta, 13-45 Gotenhama, Otsu-shi 520 Japan. **LC** RA566.5.J3; S52A. **CODEN** SEKSDT. Documents available from CASDDS. ***Formed by the union of*** *Shiga Kenritsu Eisei Kenkyujo Ho. Shiga Kenritsu Eisei Kenkyujo* ***and*** *Shiga-ken Kankyo Senta Shoho. Shiga-ken Kankyo Senta.*
**Ind/Abst** Chem. Abstr.

JA
**SHOKUHIN EISEI KANKEI JIGYO HOKOKU.** **Main/Corp** Tokyo. Eiseikyoku. Kankyo Eiseibu. **Added/Corp** Tokyo (Japan). Eiseikyoku. (1952)-. Periodical. Japanese. an. Tokyoto Eiseikyoku Kankyo Eiseibu, (Environmental Sanitation Division,, Bureau of Public Health, Tokyo Metropolitan Government), 5-1 Marunouchi 3 chome, Chiyodaku Tokyoto 100 Japan. **LC** RA601; .T64a.

JA/0559-8974
**SHOKUHIN EISEI KENKYU.** (SHOKUHIN EISEI KENKYU. FOOD SANITATION RESEARCH.). [Shokuhin eisei kenkyu]. **Added/Corp** Nihon Shokuhin Eisei Kyokai. **VFOAT** Food Sanitation Research. (19??)-. Academic Scholarly Publication. Japanese (Japanese). Twelve times a year. $132.00. Nihon Shokuhin Eisei Kyokai, 6-1 Jingumae 2 Shibuya-ku, Tokyo 150 Japan. **(Subscription address:** Kyowa Book Company Inc., 1 38 Kanda Jinbocho Chiyoda-ku, Tokyo 101 Japan.**) LC** RA601; .S443. **NLM** W1 SH514. **CODEN** SHEKAR. Documents available from CASDDS.
**Ind/Abst** Chem. Abstr.; Curr. Biotechnol.

JA/0015-6426
**SHOKUHIN EISEIGAKU ZASSHI.** [Shokuhin eiseigaku zasshi]. **Added/Corp** Nihon Shokuhin Eisei Gakkai. **VFOAT** Journal of the Food Hygienic Society of Japan. (1960)-. Academic Scholarly Publication. Japanese (English and Japanese). bm. $304.00. Nihon Shokuhin Eisei Gakkai, c/o Shokuhin Eisei Senta, 6-1 Hingumae 1, Shibuya-ku Tokyo-to 150 Japan. **(Subscription address:** Kyowa Book Company Inc., 1-38 Kanda Jinbo-Cho, Chiyoda-Ku Tokyo 101, Japan**) LC** RA601; .S4455. **NLM** W1 SH514K. **CODEN** SKEZAP. **Pr Rev.** Documents available from The Genuine Article, BIOSIS Document Express, CASDDS.
**Ind/Abst** AGRICOLA; Anal. Abstr.; BioBusiness; Biol. Abstr.; Chem. Abstr.; CSA Neuro. Abstr. (?-?); Curr. Contents, Agric. Biol. Environ. Sci.; EMBASE [Select. Cov.]; Food Sci. Technol. Abstr.; Maize Abstr.; Nutr. Abstr. Rev., Ser. A, Hum. Exp.; Life Sci. Collect.; Postharvest News Inf.; Poult. Abstr.; Protozoolog. Abstr.; Res. Alert [Select. Cov.]; Rev. Agric. Entomol.; Rev. Med. Vet. Entomol.; SCISEARCH; Soyabean Abstr.; Sug. Indus. Abstr.; Weed Abstr.; Wheat Barley Trit. Abstr.

IT
**SICUREZZA NOTIZIE.** (19??)-. Italian. Five times a year. Free on request. Ctro Sicurezza Applicata Organ, C So M D Azeglio 42, 10125 Turin Italy. **Tel** 011 39 11 6508737.

CN/0037-4911
**SIGNAL (MONTREAL).** (SIGNAL.). **VFOAT** Signal. V. 1- Nov. 1974-. Periodical. English (French). Qeubec Safety League, 5576 Upper Lachine Road, Montreal Quebec H4A 2A7. **DD** 614.8/05. ***Supersedes*** *Le Signal, 0037-4911.*

SI/0129-7457
**SINGAPORE COMMUNITY HEALTH BULLETIN, THE.** [Singap. community health bull.]. **Added/Corp** Singapore. Ministry of Health. Singapore. Ministry of the Environment. No. 19 (July 1978)-. Academic Scholarly Publication. English. an. Free. Ministry of Health / Singapore, Train and Health Education, Hyderabad Road, 0511 Singapore. **NLM** W1 SI519J. ***Continues*** *Singapore Public Health Bulletin, 0304-4378.*
**Ind/Abst** EMBASE.

US/0890-6076
**SKI PATROL MAGAZINE.** (SKI PATROL MAGAZINE : THE OFFICIAL PUBLICATION OF THE NATIONAL SKI PATROL.). [Ski patrol mag.]. **Added/Corp** National Ski Patrol System (U.S.). (198?)-. Periodical. English. qt. $20.00 US; $30.00 other. National Ski Patrol System Inc, 133 South Van Gordon Street, Suite 101, Lakewood CO 80228. **Tel** (303)988-1111, FAX (303)988-3005. **DD** 363.

●US/1076-4488
**SMALL BUSINESS HEALTH REFORM WATCH.** (1994)-. Periodical. English. mo. $196.00. Aspen Publishers Inc., 7201 McKinney Circle, Frederick MD 21701. **Tel** (800)234-1660, (301)698-7100, FAX (301)251-5784, telex 5106014543. **(Subscription address:** Aspen Publishers Inc., PO Box 990, Frederick MD 21701.**)**

US/0081-0363
**SMOKING AND HEALTH BULLETIN.** [Smok. health bull.]. **Added/Corp** National Clearinghouse for Smoking and Health. United States. Office on Smoking and Health. (Feb./March 1970)-. Periodical. English. qt. Free. Technical Information Center, Office on Smoking and Health, Park Building Room 116/5600 Fishers Lane, Rockville MD 20857. **Tel** (301)443-1690. **LC** RA1242.T6; S58. **DD** 615.9/52379. **NLM** ZQV 137 S666. Index available. cum. index. **Circ:** 7,000. available on an online database. Documents available from Documents on Demand. ***Continues*** *Smoking and Health Bibliographical Bulletin.*
**Desc:** Health effects of cigarettes, smokeless tobacco, and passive smoking. Legislation, policy and agriculture covered selectively.
**Ind/Abst** Am. Stat. Index.

SW/0037-7619
**SOCIALNYTT.** ***Title Change.*** **Added/Corp** Sweden. Socialstyrelsen. (Jan. 1968)-(19??). Periodical. Swedish. mo. Socialnytt, Liber Foerlag, 16289 Stockholm Sweden. **LC** HN571; .S67. **NLM** W1 SO139K. ***Continues*** *Sociala Meddelanden.* ***Merged with*** *Vigor (Stockholm, Sweden)* ***to form*** *Val & Ve.*

IT/0391-5913
**SOCIETA E SALUTE.** ***Suspended.*** (1976)-Vol. 62 (1990). Monographic series. Italian. ir. Price varies per volume. Il Pensiero Scientifico Editore s.r.l., Via Bradano 3C, 00199 Rome Italy. **Tel** 011 39 6 86207158, 86207159, 86207168, 86207169, FAX 011 39 6 86207160. **ED** G Berlinguer and A Seppilli. **LC** UNC. **NLM** W1 SO3315.

US/0198-7399
**SOCIOECONOMIC ISSUES OF HEALTH.** [Socioecon. issues health]. **Added/Corp** Center for Health Services Research and Development (American Medical Association). (1979)-. English. an. American Medical Association, 515 North State Street, Chicago IL 60610. **Tel** (312)464-5000, (800)262-2350, FAX (312)464-5831. **LC** RA410.53; .R44. **DD** 338.4/33621/0973. **NLM** W1 SO878MH. ***Continues*** *Reference Data on Socioeconomic Issues of Health, 0092-8836.*
**Ind/Abst** Health Plan. Adminis.

FR/0998-0113
**SOCIOLOGIE SANTE.** **Added/Corp** Centre Aquitain de Recherche sur les Problemes de Sante. **VFOAT** Sociologie de la Sante. (19??)-. Periodical. French (summaries and/or abstracts in English). sa. 160.00F France; 210.00F other. Revue Sociologie Sante, MSHA Esplanade des Antilles, 33405 Talence Cedex France. **Tel** 011 33 56 846800. **LC** RA418.3.F8; S66. **DD** 362.1/0944/05.

UK/0141-9889
**SOCIOLOGY OF HEALTH & ILLNESS.** **See** Sociology.

US/1050-0219
**SOLUTIONS FOR BETTER HEALTH.** ***Suspended.*** **See** Social Sciences.

GW
**SONDERHEFT.** **Main/Corp** Landesarbeitsgemeinschaft zur Bekampfund der Geschlechtskrankheiten und fur Geschlechtserziehung Nordrhein-Westfalen. Monographic series. German. Price varies per volume. Koln-Sulz, Zulpicher Strasse 337, Koln Germany. **LC** RA644.V4; L36A.

KO
**SONGSIM CHUNGANG YUJI CHAEDAN YONBO.** **VFOAT** Annual Report. English (Korean). an. Songsim Chungang Yuji Chaedan, 94-195 Yongdungpo-dong Yongdungpo-ku, Seoul South Korea. **LC** RA990.K64; S467.

●US/1065-4410
**SOUTH CAROLINA HEALTH CARE IN PERSPECTIVE.** [S.C. health care perspect.]. **Added/Corp** Morgan Quitno Corporation. 1st Ed. (1993)-. English. $18.00. Morgan Quitno Corporation, PO Box 1656, 512 East 9th Street, Lawrence KS 66044. **Tel** (800)457-0742, (913)841-3534, FAX (913)841-3534. **DD** 362.
**Desc:** Reports on the state's data and rank for each of the categories featured in Health Care State Rankings.

●US/1065-4429
**SOUTH DAKOTA HEALTH CARE IN PERSPECTIVE.** [S.D. health care perspect.]. **Added/Corp** Morgan Quitno Corporation. 1st Ed. (1993)-. English. $18.00. Morgan Quitno Corporation, PO Box 1656, 512 East 9th Street, Lawrence KS 66044. **Tel** (800)457-0742, (913)841-3534, FAX (913)841-3534. **DD** 362.
**Desc:** Reports on the state's data and rank for each of the categories featured in Health Care State Rankings.

TH/0038-3619
**SOUTHEAST ASIAN JOURNAL OF TROPICAL MEDICINE AND PUBLIC HEALTH, THE.** [Southeast Asian j. trop. med. public health]. V. 1- March 1970-. Academic Scholarly Publication. English. qt. $36.00. Seameo-Tropmed Project, 420/6 Rajvithi Road, Bangkok 10400 Thailand. **Tel** 66-2-2457193, FAX 66-2-2468340. **ED** Tranakchit Harinasuta, Chev Kidson. **NLM** W1 SO924P. **CODEN** SJTMAK. Index available. cum. index. **Bk Rev. Ad Acc. Circ:** 1,000 (ctrl). available on microfilm and microfiche from University Microfilms International (UMI). Documents available from BIOSIS Document Express, CASDDS.
**Desc:** Tropical diseases, parasitology, entomology, nutritional disorders, public health, infectious diseases, immunology, clinical trials, case reports, SEAMEO symposia proceedings, technical meetings, etc.
**Ind/Abst** AgBiotech News Inf.; AGRICOLA; Biocont. News Inf. (1991-); Biol. Abstr.; Chem. Abstr.; Dairy Sci. Abstr.; EMBASE [Select. Cov.]; Food Sci. Technol. Abstr.; Genet. Abstr.; Helminthol. Abstr. (19??-19??); Immunol. Abstr.; Index Med.; Microbiol. Abstr. Sect. B; Microbiol. Abstr. Sect. C; Life Sci. Collect.; Philip. Sci. Technol. Abstr.; Pig News Inf.; Protozoolog. Abstr.; Rev. Med. Vet. Entomol.; Rice Abstr.; Trop. Dis. Bull.; Virol. AIDS Abstr.

RU/0038-5239
**SOVETSKOE ZDRAVOOKHRANENIE.** (SOVETSKOE ZDRAVOOKHRANENIE / MINISTERSTVO ZDRAVOOKHRANENIIA SSSR.). [Sov. zdravookhran.]. **Added/Corp** Soviet Union. Ministerstvo Zdravookhraneniia. (1942)-(199?). Academic Scholarly Publication. Russian (summaries and/or abstracts in English; table of contents in English). mo. Izdatelstvo Meditsina / Russian Academy of Medical Sciences, Ulitsa Solyanka 14, 109801 Moscow Russia. **Tel** 011 95 297-05-04. **NLM** W1 SO993. **CODEN** SOZDAO. Index available. **Bk Rev.** available in microform. Documents available from BIOSIS Document Express, CASDDS. ***Continues*** *Bolnichnoe Delo.* ***Continued by*** *Problemy Sotsialnoi Gigieny i Istoriia Meditsiny, 0869-866X.*
**Ind/Abst** Biol. Abstr. (1986-?); Chem. Abstr. (?-1973); CIS Abstr.; Index Med.; Int. Aerosp. Abstr.; Int. Labour Doc.; Int. Nurs. Index; Saf. Health Work; Trop. Dis. Bull.

SZ/0303-8408
**SOZIAL- UND PRAEVENTIVMEDIZIN.** (SOZIAL- UND PRAEVENTIVMEDIZIN / MEDECINE SOCIALE ET PREVENTIVE.). [Soz.- Praeventivmed.]. **Added/Corp** Schweizerische Gesellschaft fuer Sozial- und Praeventivmedizin. Deutsche Gesellschaft fuer Sozialmedizin und Praevention. **VFOAT** Medecine Sociale et Preventive. Vol. 19 (Jan./Feb. 1974)-. Academic Scholarly Publication. Multiple languages (English, French and German; summaries and/or abstracts in English, French and German). bm. 229.80F Switzerland; 241.30F other. Birkhaeuser Verlag Ag, Klosterberg 23, PO Box 133, CH-4010 Basel Switzerland. **Tel** 011 41 61 2717400, FAX 011 41 0 61 2717666, telex 963475 birk ch. **(Subscription address:** Birkhauser Verlag AG, PO Box 151, CH 4106 Therwil Switzerland; Phone: 011 41 61 7217740**) ED** Fred Paccaud. **NLM** W1 SO999B. **CODEN** SZPMAA. **Bk Rev. Ad Acc. Circ:** 1,000. Documents available from The Genuine Article, CASDDS. ***Continues*** *Praeventivmedizin, 0301-0988.*
**Desc:** Publishes original scientific papers and review articles in the field of epidemiology, preventive medicine, health services research, environmental health, medical sociology and industrial hygiene. Also includes communications, book reviews and letters to the Editor.
**Ind/Abst** Chem. Abstr.; Curr. Contents Clin. Med.; EMBASE; Index Med.; Life Sci. Collect.; Res. Alert [Select. Cov.]; Saf. Health Work; Soc. Sci. Cit. Index [Select. Cov.]; SportSearch; Trop. Dis. Bull.

US/1047-272X
**SPECIAL REPORT ON HEALTH.** ***Title Change.*** [Spec. rep. health]. **VFOAT** Special Report. (Nov. 1988-Jan. 1989)-(199?). Periodical. English. qt. Whittle Communications, 333 Main Avenue, Knoxville TN 37902. **Tel** (615)595-5000, FAX (615)595-5877. **LC** RA773; .S66. **DD** 613/.05. ***Merged with*** *Special Report, Fiction, 1047-2886; Special Report on Family, 1047-2878; Special Report on Living, 1047-0123; Special Report on Personalities, 1047-286X* ***and*** *Special Report on Sports, 1047-2851* ***to form*** *Special Report (Whittle Communications), 1059-5201.*

MX/0185-2264
**SPM. SALUD PUBLICA DE MEXICO.** [SPM. Salud publica Mex.]. **Added/Corp** Centro Nacional de Informacion y Documentacion en Salud. Mexico. Secretaria de Salubridad y Asistencia. **VFOAT** Salud Publica de Mexico. Vol. 18, No. 3 (May/June. 1976)-. Academic Scholarly Publication. Spanish. bm. $50.00 Latin America; $70.00 other. Inst Nacional Salud Publica, Av Universidad 655 Ahuacatitla, 62508 Cuernavaca Morelo Mexico. **Tel** 011 52 73 110111 ext. 2281. **ED** Hemann Bellinghausen, Octavio Gomez. **NLM** W1 SA368. **Circ:** 5,000. ***Continues*** *Salud Publica de Mexico, (OCoLC) 1764947.*
**Desc:** Covers public health in Mexico, endocrinology, etc.
**Ind/Abst** Biodeter. Abstr. (1991-); Dairy Sci. Abstr.; EMBASE; Helminthol. Abstr. (1991-); Index Med.; Nutr. Abstr. Rev., Ser. A, Hum. Exp.; Protozoolog. Abstr.; Rev. Med. Vet. Entomol.; Rural Dev. Abstr.; Soc. Sci. Cit. Index [Full Cov.]; Trop. Dis. Bull.

US/0895-755X
**SPOTLIGHT ON AIDS.** **See** Medical Science and Technology-Allergy and Immunology.

US
**ST. RAPHAEL'S BETTER HEALTH.** (19??)-. English. bm. $15.00. Hospital of St. Raphael, 1450 Chapel Street, New Haven CT 06511. **Tel** (203)789-3912.

US/8755-3554
**STANDARD METHODS FOR THE EXAMINATION OF DAIRY PRODUCTS (1967).** (STANDARD METHODS FOR THE EXAMINATION OF DAIRY PRODUCTS.). [Stand. methods exam. dairy prod.]. **Main/Corp** American Public Health Association. 12th Ed. (1967)-. English. in. $55.00 (hardcover), $45.00 (softcover) nonmembers; $38.50 (hardcover), $31.50 (softcover) members. American Public Health Association, 1015 15th Street Northwest, Washington DC 20005. **Tel** (202)789-5666. **ED** Robert T. Marshall. **LC** SF253; .A55. **DD** 637/.028/7. ***Continues*** *Standard Methods for the Examination of Dairy Products, Microbiological and Chemical.*
**Desc:** Contains important updated industry standards in an easy to read, easy to find format, complete with tables figures and index.

# Public Health and Safety

US/0049-2116
**STAR, THE.** V. 1- Sept. 1941-. Periodical. English. bm. $2.00. Star / Louisiana, Box 325, Carville LA 70721. **Tel** (504)642-5559. available on microfilm and microfiche from University Microfilms International (UMI). **Supersedes** Star. **Ind/Abst** EMBASE.

US
**STATE ADM REPORTS : ALCOHOLISM, DRUG ABUSE & MENTAL HEALTH / INTERGOVERNMENTAL HEALTH POLICY PROJECT. See** Drug Abuse and Alcoholism.

US
**STATE HEALTH NOTES. Added/Corp** National Conference of State Legislatures. George Washington University. Intergovernmental Health Policy Project. (Jan. 1979)-. Periodical. English. Twice a year. $95.00 Public officials, non-profit, & universities; $195.00 other. Intergovernmental Health Policy Project, 2021 K Street NW, Suite 800, Washington DC 20006. **Tel** (202)872-1445, FAX (202)785-0114. **NLM** W1; ST314GD. **Circ**: 1,5000.
**Desc**: This publication identifies and analyzes important health policy trends and innovations within state government.

US/0735-0880
**STATE HEALTH PLAN (LITTLE ROCK, ARK.).** (STATE HEALTH PLAN ...). [State health plan]. **Main/Corp** Arkansas State Health Planning and Development Agency. 1979-. English. an. Arkansas State Health Planning & Development Agency, 4815 West Markham, Little Rock AR 72201. **LC** RA24; .A74A. **DD** 353.97670084/1.

US/0146-017X
**STATE LEGISLATION ON SMOKING AND HEALTH.** 1975-. English. an. Centers for Disease Control, 1600 Clifton Road NE, Atlanta GA 30333. **Tel** (404)639-3311, FAX (404)639-3296. **LC** KF3812.Z95; S7. **DD** 344.73/046342/05. **NLM** W2 A N1486S.

US/0741-0573
**STATE MEDICAL FACILITIES PLAN (RALEIGH, N.C.).** (STATE MEDICAL FACILITIES PLAN.). **Main/Corp** North Carolina. Dept. of Human Resources. Division of Facility Services. 1979-1980-. English. an. Division of Facility Services, 1330 St Mary's Street, Raleigh NC 27605. **LC** RA981.N82; N67B. **DD** 362.1/109756. **Continues** North Carolina State Medical Facilities Plan.

US/0097-000X
**STATE OF COLORADO ANNUAL HIGHWAY SAFETY WORK PROGRAM. See** Transportation-Roads and Traffic.

US/0193-4260
**STATE PLAN FOR COMPREHENSIVE MENTAL HEALTH SERVICES : ANNUAL REVIEW AND PROGRESS REPORTS FOR THE STATE OF OKLAHOMA. Main/Corp** Oklahoma. Dept. of Mental Health. English. an. Oklahoma Department of Mental Health, PO Box 54277 Capitol Station, 408-A North Wanul Street, Oklahoma City OK 73105. **LC** RA790.65.O5; O43A. **DD** 362.2/09766.

US
**STATE PLAN PROGRESS REPORT FOR FISCAL YEAR ... / SOUTH CAROLINA STATE DEPARTMENT OF MENTAL HEALTH. Main/Corp** South Carolina. State Dept. of Mental Health. 1979-80-. English. an. South Carolina State Department of Mental Health, 2414 Bull Street, PO Box 485, Columbia SC 29202. **LC** RA790.65.S6; S692A. **DD** 362.2/09757.

US
**STATE PLAN / SOUTH CAROLINA STATE DEPT OF MENTAL HEALTH. Main/Corp** South Carolina. State Dept. of Mental Health. English. an. South Carolina State Department of Mental Health, 2414 Bull Street, PO Box 485, Columbia SC 29202. **LC** RA790.65.S6; S692B. **DD** 362.2/09757.

IT/1121-1008
**STATISTICHE DALLA SANITA. Added/Corp** Istituto Nazionale di Statistica (Italy). No. 1 (1985)-. Italian. Istituto Nazionale Statistica, GBP SEZ4 Via Cesare Balbo 16, 00184 Rome Italy. **Tel** 011 39 6 46735118. **LC** RA407.5.I8; S74. **DD** 614.4/245/021. **Continues in part** Statistiche Sanitarie.

US/0895-9579
**STAYING WELL SCHOOL NEWS.** Ceased. **See** Education.

●US/1067-9537
**STRATEGIES & SOLUTIONS.** (STRATEGIES & SOLUTIONS : THE JOURNAL OF MANAGED MENTAL HEALTH CARE.). [Strat. solut.]. **VFOAT** Strategies and Solutions. Vol. 1, No. 1 (Oct. 1992)-. Periodical. English. mo (Sept., thru Aug.). $99.00 (individuals); $180.00 (institutions). Strategies & Solutions, 9100 West Bloomington Freeway, #100, Bloomington MN 55431. **Tel** (612)881-1082, telex (612)881-0955. **ED** Kim Baranko. **DD** 362. cum. index. **Bk Rev**, (Qty: 2). **Ad Acc, Adv Mgr**: Kim Branko, **Tel** (612)881-1082. **Circ**: 6,500.
**Desc**: A journal on how managed mental health care has grown in the last three years.

US/0891-849X
**STUDIES IN HEALTH AND HUMAN SERVICES.** [Stud. health hum. serv.]. Vol. 1 (1983)-. Monographic series. English. ir. Price varies per volume. Edwin Mellen Press, PO Box 450, Lewiston NY 14092. **Tel** (716)754-2788. **DD** 362. **NLM** W1; ST92D.

UK/0263-8630
**STUDIES IN LAW AND PRACTICE FOR HEALTH SERVICE MANAGEMENT. See** Law.

CN/0714-0169
**STUDY - ROYAL COMMISSION ON MATTERS OF HEALTH AND SAFETY ARISING FROM THE USE OF ASBESTOS IN ONTARIO.** (STUDY.). **Added/Corp** Royal Commission on Matters of Health and Safety Arising from the Use of Asbestos in Ontario. **VFOAT** Study Series. **VAT** Study Series - Royal Commission on Matters of Health and Safety Arising from the Use of Asbestos in Ontario. (1981)-. Periodical. English. **DD** 363.17/75/09713.

US/0094-7741
**SUMMARY OF GRANTS AND CONTRACTS ACTIVE ON ... .** [Summ. grants contracts]. **Main/Corp** National Center for Health Services Research. Began with June 30, 1974. English. an. US Department of Health and Human Services, 200 Independence Avenue Southwest, Washington DC 20201. **LC** RA440.6; .N33A. **DD** 362.1/07/2073. available on microfiche (Vols. for (1977-1978, 1980-1983) distributed to depository libraries). **Continues** Summary of Grants and Contracts Administered by the National Center for Health Services Research and Development, 0094-7741.

UK
**SUMMARY OF HEALTH AND PERSONAL SOCIAL SERVICES ACCOUNTS. Main/Corp** Northern Ireland. Dept. of Health and Social Services. English. **LC** RA247.N6; N67A. **DD** 354/.416/00841. **Continues** Northern Ireland. Dept. of Health and Social Services. Summary of Health Services Accounts.

US
**SUMMARY OF RECEIPTS, DISBURSEMENTS, AND BALANCES. Main/Corp** Florida. Division of Health. English. PO Box 210, Jacksonville FL 32201. **LC** RA44; .B55a. **DD** 353.9/759/00841.

US/0748-2949
**SUMMARY OF SAFETY MANAGEMENT AUDITS.** (SUMMARY OF SAFETY MANAGEMENT AUDITS / U.S. DEPARTMENT OF TRANSPORTATION, FEDERAL HIGHWAY ADMINISTRATION.). [Summ. saf. manage. audits]. English. an. US Department of Transportation - Federal Highway Administration, 400 Seventh Street Southwest, Washington DC 20590. **Tel** (202)366-0660. **LC** HE5623.A216. **DD** 363.1/259.

US
**SUMMARY STATEMENTS OF NIEHS-SUPPORTED RESEARCH PROJECTS. VFOAT** Summary Statements of N.I.E.H.S.-Supported Research Projects. **VAT** Summary Statements of National Institute of Environmental Health Sciences-Supported Research Projects. English. an. National Institute of Environmental Health Sciences, PO Box 12233, Research Triangle Park NC 27711. **Tel** (202)245-6296. **NLM** WA 22 AA1 S956.

DK
**SUNDHEDSTILSTANDEN I KBENHAVN; STADSLGENS ARSBERETNING. Main/Corp** Copenhagen. Stadslgeembedet. **VFOAT** State of Health in Copenhagen. Multiple languages (Danish and English). an. **LC** RA258.C6; A3. **Continues** Arsberetning Angaende Sundhedstilstanden I Kbenhavn.

US/0194-8717
**SUPERVISOR'S SAFETY CLINIC. Added/Corp** Bureau of Business Practice. (19??)-. Periodical. English. sm. $45.72 US; $56.04 Canada. Bureau of Business Practice, 24 Rope Ferry Road, Waterford CT 06386. **Tel** (800)243-0876, (203)442-4365, (800)876-9105, FAX (203)443-1123. **ED** Laurie Beth Roberts.

PL/0137-8686
**SUZBA ZDROWIA.** (1949)-. Periodical. Polish. wk. $65.00. **(Subscription address**: ARS Polona, PO Box 1001, 00068 Warsaw Poland.) UDC 614.2.

US
**TAKING CARE. Added/Corp** Center for Consumer Health Education. (1978)-. English. mo. $21.24. Center for Consumer Health Education, 1850 Centennial Park Drive/520, Reston VA 22091. **Tel** (703)391-1900. **ED** George Pfeiffer. **Bk Rev**. **Ad Acc**. **Circ**: 450,000 (ctrl).

CN/0712-3094
**TALLYBOARD. See** Forestry.

US/1042-3036
**TAN MAGAZINE. See** Beauty and Cosmetics.

JO
**TARIQ AL-SALAMAH / AL-JAMIYAH AL-URDUNIYAH LIL-WIQAYAH MIN HAWADITH AL-TURUQ. See** Transportation.

AT
**TECHNICAL AND FURTHER EDUCATION. HEALTH AND COMMUNITY CARE. Main/Corp** Western Australia. Technical Education Division. **VFOAT** Health and Community Care. (19??)-. English. ir. Nelson Wadsworth, PO Box 4725, Melbourne Victoria, 3001 Australia. **Tel** 03 329-5199. **LC** WMLC L 83/1796.

US/0882-4584
**TECHNOLOGY ASSESSMENT AND RESEARCH PROGRAM FOR OFFSHORE MINERALS OPERATIONS. See** Environmental Issues-Pollution and Waste Management.

IT/0392-8144
**TECNICA SANITARIA E MEDICINA DI COMUNITA : ORGANO UFFICIALE DELL'ASSOCIAZIONE NAZIONALE UFFICIALI SANITARI, MEDICI IGIENISTI. Added/Corp** Associazione Nazionale Ufficiali Sanitari, Medici Igienisti. 15, No. 2 (Mar.-Apr. 1977)-. Periodical. Italian (summaries and/or abstracts in English). bm. **NLM** W1; TE222C. **Continues** Tecnica Sanitaria.

IT
**TECNOLOGIE DEI SERVIZI PUBBLICI. See** Public Administration.

US
**TELEPHONE AND SERVICE DIRECTORY / NATIONAL INSTITUTES OF HEALTH. Main/Corp** National Institutes of Health (U.S.). **VFOAT** NIH Telephone and Service Directory. (19??)-. Directory. English. sa. $43.00. Superintendent of Documents, US Government Printing Office, Washington DC 20402. **Tel** (202)275-3328, FAX (202)786-2377.

US/0898-6967
**TENNESSEE COMMUNICABLE DISEASE BULLETIN.** (TENNESSEE COMMUNICABLE DISEASE BULLETIN / TENNESSEE DEPARTMENT OF HEALTH & ENVIRONMENT.). [Tenn. commun. dis. bull.]. **Added/Corp** Tennessee. Dept. of Health and Environment. (19??)-. Periodical. English. mo. Free on request. Tennessee Department of Health & Environment, 100 9th Avenue North, 3rd Floor, Nashville TN 37219. **Tel** (615)741-7247. **DD** 614.

●US/1065-4437
**TENNESSEE HEALTH CARE IN PERSPECTIVE.** [Tenn. health care perspect.]. **Added/Corp** Morgan Quitno Corporation. 1st Ed. (1993)-. English. $18.00. Morgan Quitno Corporation, PO Box 1656, 512 East 9th Street, Lawrence KS 66044. **Tel** (800)457-0742, (913)841-3534, FAX (913)841-3534. **DD** 362.
**Desc**: Reports on the state's data and rank for each of the categories featured in Health Care State Rankings.

FI
**TERVEYDENHUOLLON LAITOKSET JA VIRANOMAISET. VFOAT** Halsovardens Inrattningar Och Myndigheter. Finnish (Swedish). Government Printing Centre, PO Box 516, SF-00101 Helsinki 10 Finland. **LC** RA7.8.F5; T47. **Continues** Terveydenhuollon Organisaatio, 0357-1343.

FI/0303-2442
**TERVEYDENHUOLTO. Main/Corp** Finland. Laakintohallitus. **VFOAT** Halsovard; Health Services. 1971/77-. Finnish (Swedish; summaries and/or abstracts in English). an. Valtion Painatuskeskus, PO Box 516, SF 00101 Helsinki Finland. **Tel** 011 358 0 5660266. **LC** HA1448; RA299.F5. **DD** 362.1/09471. **NLM** W2 GF5 L2Y. **Continues** Yleinen Terveyden- Ja Sairaanhoito.
**Desc**: Serves also as annual report of the National Board of Health.

US
**TEXAS COMPENDIUM OF HEALTH RELATED DATA.** **Main/Corp** Texas. Bureau of State Health Planning & Resource Development. 1979-. English. an. Texas Department of Health, 1100 West 49th Street, Austin TX 78756-3180. **Tel** (512)458-7550, FAX (512)458-7407. **LC** RA7.6.T4; T48A. **DD** 362.1/09764.

●US/1063-8202
**TEXAS EMS MAGAZINE.** [Tex. EMS mag.]. **Added/Corp** Texas. Dept. of Health. Bureau of Emergency Management. **VAT** Texas Emergency Medical Services Magazine. (1992)-. Periodical. English. mo. $20.00 (two years), $30.00 (four years). Texas Department of Health, 1100 West 49th Street, Austin TX 78756-3180. **Tel** (512)458-7550, FAX (512)458-7407. **ED** Alana S Mallard. **DD** 362. **Bk Rev. Circ:** 7,500. ***Continues*** *Texas EMS Messenger, 1048-8235.*
**Desc:** Covers pre-hospital medicine, state regulations and services, clinical care, local news, and information on jobs.

US/1048-8235
**TEXAS EMS MESSENGER.** ***Title Change.*** [Tex. EMS messenger]. **Added/Corp** Texas. Dept. of Health. Bureau of Emergency Management. Texas. Dept. of Health. Division of Emergency Medical Services. **VAT** Texas Emergency Medical Services Messenger. (1989)-(19??). Periodical. English. mo. Texas Department of Health, 1100 West 49th Street, Austin TX 78756-3180. **Tel** (512)458-7550, FAX (512)458-7407. **DD** 362. ***Continues*** *EMS Messenger, 0164-8977.* ***Continued by*** *Texas EMS Magazine, 1063-8202.*

●US/1065-4445
**TEXAS HEALTH CARE IN PERSPECTIVE.** [Tex. health care perspect.]. **Added/Corp** Morgan Quitno Corporation. 1st Ed. (1993)-. English. $18.00. Morgan Quitno Corporation, PO Box 1656, 512 East 9th Street, Lawrence KS 66044. **Tel** (800)457-0742, (913)841-3534, FAX (913)841-3534. **DD** 362.
**Desc:** Reports on the state's data and rank for each of the categories featured in Health Care State Rankings.

US/0266-0806
**TEXAS HEALTH LAW REPORTER.** ***Ceased.*** **See** Law.

US/8750-9474
**TEXAS PREVENTABLE DISEASE NEWS.** ***Title Change.*** [Tex. prev. dis. news]. **Added/Corp** Texas. Bureau of Epidemiology. Texas. Dept. of Health. **VFOAT** Preventable Disease News. (June 26, 1982)-(199?). Periodical. English. wk. Texas Department of Health, 1100 West 49th Street, Austin TX 78756-3180. **Tel** (512)458-7550, FAX (512)458-7407. **ED** Penny Herndon. **DD** 616. Index available. **Circ:** 4,000. ***Continues*** *Texas Morbidity This Week.* ***Continued by*** *Disease Prevention News, 1068-7920.*
**Desc:** Technical publication for health care providers in Texas. Provides current topics related to the epidemiology of infectious, occupational, and chronic disease.

US/0364-4642
**TEXAS STATE PLAN FOR CONSTRUCTION OF COMMUNITY MENTAL HEALTH CENTERS.** **Main/Corp** Texas. Dept. of Mental Health and Mental Retardation. English. an. Texas Department of Mental Health, PO Box 12668 Capitol Station, Austin TX 78711. **LC** RA790.65.T4; T48A. **DD** 362.2/2/09764.

US
**TEXAS WORKERS COMPENSATION & SAFETY REPORTER.** **See** Economics-Labor.

IT/0394-025X
**THERAPY OF INFECTIOUS DISEASES.** [Ther. infect. dis.]. (1986)-. Periodical. Multiple languages. qt.
**Ind/Abst** EMBASE [Select. Cov.]; Helminthol. Abstr. (1991-); Protozoolog. Abstr.; Virol. AIDS Abstr.

UK/0266-9056
**THS HEALTH SUMMARY.** [THS health summ.]. **VFOAT** Times Health Supplement Health Summary. (1984)-. Periodical. English. an. **DD** 362.1068.
**Ind/Abst** Trop. Dis. Bull.

US
**TIE-LINES.** (19??)-. English. Four times a year. $35.00 (institutions), $12.00 (individuals). Information Exchange Young Adult Chronic Patients, 20 Squandron Boulevard 400, New City NY 10956. **Tel** (914)634-0050.

NE/0920-0517
**TIJDSCHRIFT VOOR SOCIALE GEZONDHEIDSZORG : TSG : 14-DAAGS BLAD VAN DE ALGEMENE NEDERLANDSE VERENIGING VOOR SOCIALE GEZONDHEIDSZORG.** **Added/Corp** Algemene Nederlandse Vereniging voor Sociale Gezondheidszorg. (1983)-. Periodical. Dutch (summaries and/or abstracts in English). Eight times a year. Fl198.75. ADM TSG St Journals Publishers Health Science, Maliebaan94, 3581 CX Utrecht Netherlands. **Tel** 011 31 30 364388. **NLM** W1; TI788D. available on microfilm from University Microfilms International (UMI). ***Continues*** *Tijdschrift voor Sociale Geneeskunde, 0040-7607.*
**Ind/Abst** Ergon. Abstr. (?-?); Highw. Res. Abstr.

NE/0921-5832
**TIJDSCHRIFT VOOR VERZORGENDEN.** No. 1 (Jan. 1988)-. Periodical. Dutch. mo. Fl52.00 Netherlands; Fl63.00 other. Uitgeversmaatschappij de Tijdstroom BV, Noorderwal 38, Postbus 14, 7240 BA Lochem Netherlands. **Tel** 011 31 5730 53651, FAX 011 31 5730 56724. **NLM** W1; TI792EG. ***Continues*** *Tijdschrift voor Bejaarden- Kraam- en Ziekenversorging, 0049-3880.*
**Ind/Abst** Int. Nurs. Index (1988-).

US/0095-2001
**TIRES.** **Main/Corp** United States. National Highway Traffic Safety Administration. (1972)-. English. National Transportation Safety Board, 800 Independence Avenue SW, Washington DC 20594. **Tel** (202)382-6600. **LC** TL242; .C65 subser. **DD** 629.2/08 S; 629.2/48. available on microfilm from University Microfilms International (UMI). ***Continues*** *Tires, 0095-2001.*

US/0882-522X
**TO YOUR GOOD HEALTH.** Vol. 1, No. 1 (Jan. 1985)-. Periodical. English. bm. Sirius B Publishing Company, PO Box 428, Toledo OR 97391.

US/0891-1304
**TO YOUR HEALTH.** [To your health]. 1986-. Periodical. English. bm. $25.00 US; $31.00 Canada. Cornell Publishing and Communications, 330 Garfield Avenue, Eau Claire WI 54701. **Tel** (715)834-6046. **ED** Dixie Cornell. **DD** 613. Index available. cum. index. **Circ:** 5,000.
**Desc:** Health and safety information for employees. Includes information on emotional health, first aid, nutrition, fitness, child care and substance abuse topics.

●US/1064-8577
**TOBACCO & HEALTH.** **See** Tobacco.

●UK/0964-4563
**TOBACCO CONTROL.** Vol 1, No 1 (Mar. 1992)-. Periodical. English (summaries and/or abstracts in Chinese, French and Spanish). qt. £108.00. BMJ / British Medical Journal Publishing Group, British Medical Association House, Tavistock Square, London WC1H 9JR England. **Tel** 011 44 71 3874499, FAX 011 44 71 383 6402, telex 290034 HBJ MN. **ED** Ronald M. Davis. **NLM** W1; TO13.
**Desc:** This journal aims to study the nature and extent of tobacco use worldwide, the effects of tobacco use on health, the economy, the environment and society, the efforts of the health community and health advocates to prevent and control tobacco use, and the activities of the tobacco industry and its allies to promote tobacco use.

US/0164-498X
**TODAY IN HEALTH PLANNING.** **Added/Corp** American Health Planning Association. Vol. 1, No. 1 (Jan. 22, 1979)-. Periodical. English. ir. $70.00. Rhode Island Department of Health, Room 408 William Waters, Providence RI 02908. **Tel** (401)277-2901. **ED** James W. O'Donnell. **NLM** W1; TO149. **Circ:** 800 (ctrl).

CN/0821-6819
**TODAY'S HEALTH (TORONTO).** ***Title Change.*** (TODAY'S HEALTH.). [Today's health]. Vol. 1, No. 1 (Feb./Mar. 1983)-. Periodical. English. bm. Thomson Healthcare, 1120 Birchmount Road, Suite 200, Scarborough Ontario M1K 5G4 Canada. **Tel** (905)750-8900. **DD** 613/.05. **Bk Rev. Ad Acc. Circ:** 45,000 (ctrl). ***Continued by*** *Today's Health Report.*
**Ind/Abst** Can. Index (?-?).

JA/0082-4771
**TOKYO TORITSU EISEI KENKYUJO KENKYU NENPO.** [Tokyo Toritsu Eisei Kenkyujo kenkyu nenpo]. **VFOAT** Annual Report of Tokyo Metropolitan Research Laboratory of Public Health. Vol. 21 (1969)-. Academic Scholarly Publication. Japanese (summaries and/or abstracts in English). an. Tokyo Toritsu Eisei Kenkyujo, (Tokyo Metropolitan Research Lab. of Public Health), 24-1, Hyakunincho 3 Chome, Shinjukuku, Tokyoto 160, Japan. **CODEN** TRENAF. Documents available from CASDDS. ***Continues*** *Nenpo (tokyo Toritsu Eisei Kenkyujo).*
**Ind/Abst** Biodeter. Abstr.; Chem. Abstr.; Hortic. Abstr.; Index Vet.; Rev. Med. Vet. Entomol.; Seed Abstr.

NE/0166-2082
**TOPICS IN ENVIRONMENTAL HEALTH.** [Top. environ. health]. Vol. 1A (1978)-. Academic Scholarly Publication. English. ir. Price varies per volume. Elsevier Science Publishers BV, PO Box 211, 1000 AE Amsterdam Netherlands. **Tel** 011 31 20 5803642, FAX 011 31 20 5862696, telex 15682. **LC** UNC. **NLM** W1 TO539LM. **CODEN** TEHEDH. **Pr Rev.** Documents available from CASDDS.
**Ind/Abst** AGRICOLA; Chem. Abstr.; Life Sci. Collect.

●US/1065-0989
**TOPICS IN HEALTH INFORMATION MANAGEMENT.** [Top. health inf. manag.]. **VFOAT** THIM. Vol. 13, No. 1 (Aug. 1992)-. Periodical. English. qt. $92.00 US and Canada. Aspen Publishers Inc., 7201 McKinney Circle, Frederick MD 21701. **Tel** (800)234-1660, (301)698-7100, FAX (301)251-5784, telex 5106014543. **(Subscription address:** Aspen Publishers Inc., PO Box 990, Frederick MD 21701.**)** **DD** 651. **NLM** W1; TO539MO. **[CCC].** ***Continues*** *Topics in Health Record Management, 0270-5230.*
**Ind/Abst** Hospit. Health Admin. Index (1992-).

KO
**TORO KYOTONG.** **See** Transportation-Roads and Traffic.

CN/0824-507X
**TOT TALK.** [Tot talk]. Periodical. English. ir. Alberta Safety Council, 10526 Jasper Avenue, Edmonton Alberta T5J 1Z7 Canada. **DD** 363.1/3/088054. Index available. **Bk Rev. Ad Acc.** ctrl circ.

US
**TOTAL AIDS CASES, UTAH AND UNITED STATES.** **Added/Corp** Utah. Bureau of Epidemiology. **VAT** Total Acquired Immune Deficiency Syndrome Cases, Utah and United States. (Feb. 1990)-. English. mo. Utah Department of Health, Center for Health Information, PO Box 16700, Salt Lake City UT 84116-0700. **LC** IN PROCESS.

US
**TOTAL COMPLIANCE.** English. mo. $95.00 1 year; $171.00 2 year; $228.00 3 year. Safety Kleen Corp., 777 Big Timber, Elgin IL 60123. **Tel** 800-669-5740, ext. 2497, FAX (708)468-8515. **ED** Michael Fraser (704)468-2479 1000 N. Randall Road Elgin, Il 60123. Index available. cum. index. **Circ:** 10,000.
**Desc:** A partnership in compliance between Safet-Kleen and its customers.

US/0274-6743
**TOTAL HEALTH.** [Total health]. Vol. 2 (Mar./Apr. 1980)-. Periodical. English. bm. $13.00 (US); $15.00 (Canada); $25.00 (other). Trio Publications Co, 6001 Topanga Canyon Boulevard, Woodland Hills CA 92367. **Tel** (818)887-6484. **ED** Robert L Smith and Sue Newton. **DD** 613. **Bk Rev. Ad Acc. Circ:** 91,000 (ctrl). available on an online database (file 149/Full-Text) from DIALOG. ***Continues*** *Trio, 0196-2191.*
**Desc:** Dedicated to preventive health care. Covers nutrition, food preparation, exercise, fitness, skin and body care, and mental health, with practical tips on care of the body, mind and spirit.
**Ind/Abst** Acad. Abstr. Full Text Elite (Jan. 1992-); Acad. Abstr. (Jan. 1992-); Acad. Search (Jan. 1992-); Health Index (1989-); Health Period. Database [Full Txt.]; Health Ref. Cent. (Jan. 1989-) [Full Txt.] [Full Cov.]; Health Source (Jan. 1992-); INFO-SOUTH Abstr.; Mag. Search.

US/0041-0721
**TRAFFIC SAFETY (CHICAGO, ILL.).** **See** Transportation-Roads and Traffic.

US/0884-612X
**TRANSAFETY REPORTER.** [Transafety report.]. (Jan. 1983)-. Periodical. English. mo. $147.00 (one year), $247.00 (two year). TranSafety Inc, PO Box 10735, Burke VA 22009. **Tel** (703)644-0050. **DD** 363.
**Desc:** Road safety newsletter covering accident litigation, safety research, city, state, and federal efforts to improve road safety. For attorneys, engineers, highway officials, etc.

US/0737-5743
**TRANSMISSION/DISTRIBUTION HEALTH & SAFETY REPORT.** ***Title Change.*** **See** Engineering-Electricity, Electrical Engineering, Electronics.

US
**TRICHINOSIS SURVEILLANCE, ANNUAL SUMMARY.** **VFOAT** Trichinosis Surveillance. Began with 1966. English. an. Centers for Disease Control, 1600 Clifton Road NE, Atlanta GA 30333. **Tel** (404)639-3311, FAX (404)639-3296. **LC** WMCL 90/0298. **DD** 614.5/62/0973.

TU
**TURK HIJIYEN VE DENEYSEL BIYOLOJI DERGISI.** **See** Medical Science and Technology.

US/0160-676X
**U.S. FACILITIES AND PROGRAMS FOR CHILDREN WITH SEVERE MENTAL ILLNESSES : DIRECTORY.** **See** Medical Science and Technology-Pediatrics.

US/0278-6435
**UNDERSTANDING HEALTH.** (1991)-. Periodical. English. mo. Health Awareness Publications Inc, PO Box 519, East Syracuse NY 13057.

MX
**UNIDAD DE PROMOCION VOLUNTARIA DEL IMSS : REVISTA.** **See** Sociology-Social Services and Welfare.

US/1043-9250
**UNITED SENIORS HEALTH REPORT.** **See** Senior Citizens.

US/0748-9234
**UNIVERSITY OF CALIFORNIA, BERKELEY, WELLNESS LETTER.** [Univ. Calif. Berkeley wellness lett.]. **Added/Corp** University of California, Berkeley. School of Public Health. **VFOAT** Wellness Letter; University of California at Berkeley Wellness Letter. Vol. 1, Issue 1 (Oct. 1984)-. Periodical. English. mo (12 issues). $24.00. Health Letter Associates, 632 Broadway, 11th Floor, New York NY 10012. **Tel** (212)505-2255 ext. 100. **LC** RA773; .U54. **DD** 613/.05. **CODEN** UCWLE9. **[CCC]. Bk Rev.** available on an online database (file 149/Full-Text) from DIALOG. Documents available from UMI Article Clearinghouse.
**Desc:** Contains health blurbs or brief articles. Includes comments on health and medicine concerning such topics as diet and hygiene.
**Ind/Abst** Acad. Abstr. Full Text Elite (Jan. 1992-); Acad. Abstr. (Jan. 1992-); Acad. Ind. [Computer File] (1992-); Acad. Search (Jan. 1992-); Consum. Health Nutr. Index (Jan. 1990); Cumul. Index Nurs. Allied Health Lit.; Expand. Acad. Index (1992-); Foods Adlibra; Gen. Period. Index (1992-); Health Index (1989-); Health Period. Database [Full Txt.]; Health Ref. Cent. (Jan. 1989-) [Full Txt.] [Full Cov.]; Health Source (Jan. 1992-); INFO-SOUTH Abstr.; Mag. Artic. Summar. Elite (Jan. 1992-); Mag. Artic. Summar. CD-ROM (Jan. 1992-); Mag. ASAP Plus [Full Txt.]; Mag. Index Plus (1992-); Mag. Search; Newsp. Period. Abstr. (1992-).

AT
**UNIVERSITY OF CALIFORNIA, BERKELEY, WELLNESS LETTER. / AUSTRALIA.** English. mo. 40.00Aus$. Jericho Publishing Pty Ltd, PO Box 572, Wahroonga NSW 2076 Australia. **Tel** 011 61 02 489 7427.

US/1042-203X
**UNIVERSITY OF TEXAS LIFETIME HEALTH LETTER, THE.** [Univ. Tex. lifetime health lett.]. **Added/Corp** University of Texas Health Science Center at Houston. **VFOAT** Lifetime Health Letter. Vol. 1, No. 1 (Feb. 1989)-. Periodical. English. mo. $24.00. University of Texas Health Science Center, PO Box 20036, Houston TX 77225. **Tel** (713)792-4278. **DD** 613.
**Ind/Abst** Consum. Health Nutr. Index.

US
**URBAN PRACTICE.** (198?)-. English. ir. Urban Health, PO Box 42409, Atlanta GA 30311. **Tel** (404)762-7668. ***Continues*** *Urban Health.*

●US/1065-4453
**UTAH HEALTH CARE IN PERSPECTIVE.** [Utah health care perspect.]. **Added/Corp** Morgan Quitno Corporation. 1st Ed. (1993)-. English. $18.00. Morgan Quitno Corporation, PO Box 1656, 512 East 9th Street, Lawrence KS 66044. **Tel** (800)457-0742, (913)841-3534, FAX (913)841-3534. **DD** 362.
**Desc:** Reports on the state's data and rank for each of the categories featured in Health Care State Rankings.

US
**UTAH STATE PLAN FOR HEALTH SERVICES.** **Main/Corp** Utah. State Division of Health. English. Division of Health / Utah, 44 Medical Drive, Salt Lake City UT 84113. **LC** RA161; .S8A. **DD** 362.1/09792.

SW
**VAL & VE : SOCIALSTYRELSENS TIDNING.** **See** Sociology-Social Services and Welfare.

SW/0347-0911
**VARDFACKET.** [Vardfacket]. **Added/Corp** Svenska Halso Och Sjunvardens Tjanstemannaforbund. (1977)-. Periodical. Swedish. ir. Svenska Halso Och Sjukvardens Tjanstemannaforbund, Box 3207, 103 64 Stockholm Sweden. **Tel** 011 46 8 147700. **NLM** W1 VA125. ***Supersedes*** *Tidskrift for Sveriges Sjukskoterskor, 0037-6027.*
**Ind/Abst** Int. Nurs. Index (19??-).

US
**VD NEWS.** **VAT** Venereal Disease News. V. 1- 1976-. English. qt. American Social Health Association, PO Box 13827, Research Triangle Park NC 27709. available on microfilm and microfiche from University Microfilms International (UMI). ***Supersedes*** *Social Health News.*

US/0742-938X
**VDT NEWS.** [VDT news]. **VFOAT** V.D.T. News. **VAT** Video Display Terminal News. Vol. 1, No. 1, (Jan./Feb. 1984)-. Periodical. English. bm. $127.00 (1 year), $225.00 (2 year), $325.00 (3 year) US; $150.00 (1 year), $265.00 (2 year), $385.00 (3 year) other. Slesin, PO Box 1799 Grand Central Station, New York NY 10163. **Tel** (212)517-2800. **ED** Louis Slesin. **DD** 363. **Bk Rev. Ad Acc, Adv Mgr:** Barbara Gerson. **Circ:** 1,000.
**Desc:** Containing health and safety research, legislation, litigation, resources, meetings, international news, and more.

US/0271-1591
**VEGETARIAN VOICE.** [Veg. voice]. **Added/Corp** North American Vegetarian Society. (1974)-. Periodical. English. qt. $12.00 (Comes with North American Vegetarian Society membership). North American Vegetarian Society, PO Box 72, Dolgeville NY 13329. **Tel** (518)568-7970. **ED** Jennie Collura. **Bk Rev. Ad Acc. Circ:** 3,000 (ctrl).
**Desc:** Information about vegetarianism, animal rights, health, recipes, and related topics.

GW/0042-4021
**VERKEHRSMEDIZIN UND IHRE GRENZGEBIETE.** [Verkehrsmed. ihre Grenzgeb.]. **VFOAT** Medicine du Trafic et ses Domaines FrontieresaMedicina v Transportnom dele i ee Smeznye Oblasti. (1954)-. Periodical. German. bm. DM32.40, $22.78. Transpress Verlagsgesellschaft, Postfach 02, D 13161 Berlin Germany. **Tel** 011 49 30 478050. **UDC** 61+656.
**Ind/Abst** Ergon. Abstr. (19??-).

●US/1065-4461
**VERMONT HEALTH CARE IN PERSPECTIVE.** [Vt. health care perspect.]. **Added/Corp** Morgan Quitno Corporation. 1st Ed. (1993)-. English. $18.00. Morgan Quitno Corporation, PO Box 1656, 512 East 9th Street, Lawrence KS 66044. **Tel** (800)457-0742, (913)841-3534, FAX (913)841-3534. **DD** 362.
**Desc:** Reports on the state's data and rank for each of the categories featured in Health Care State Rankings.

NE
**VERSLAG VAN DE DELEGATIE VAN HET KONINKRIJK DER NEDERLANDEN NAAR DE WERELDGEZONDHEIDSVERGADERING.** **Main/Corp** Netherlands. Delegatie naar de Wereldgezondheidsvergadering. (19??)-. Multiple languages (Dutch and English). Staatsuitgeverij, Christoffel Plantijnstraat 1, 2515 TZ'S Gravenhage Netherlands. **Tel** 070/78-95-70. **LC** RA8; .N4a.

US/0195-7295
**VIDEOLOG : PROGRAMS FOR THE HEALTH SCIENCES, THE.** ***Title Change.*** 1979-. English. Video Forum / New York, Division of Jeffrey Norton Publ, 145 East 49th Street, New York NY 10017. **Tel** (212)753-1783. **LC** R835; .H4. **DD** 016.61. **NLM** WA 18 V652. ***Continues*** *Health Sciences Video Directory, 0363-0781.* ***Continued by*** *Health Sciences Videolog, 0731-5945.*
**Desc:** Summary: Fully annotated entries on each program and series. Covers medicine, dentistry, nursing, allied health professions, psychology, public health, hospital, administration, and title.

FR/0042-5524
**VIE ET SANTE DAMMARIE-LES-LYS.** (VIE ET SANTE.). (1923)-. Periodical. French. Eleven times a year. 279.00F France; 349.00F other. Societe Diffusion Vie et Sante, 60 Avenue Emile-Zola, 77192 Dammarie les Lys Cedex France. **Tel** 011 33 1 64 39 38 26, FAX 011 33 1 64 87 00 66, telex 690587F. **UDC** 613.
**Ind/Abst** Point Repere (1979-).

IT
**VIGILANZA IGIENICO SANITARIA.** (19??)-. Italian. Six times a year. L70000 Italy; L140000 other (includes membership). Unione Nazional Personale Ispettivo Italia, Via Fiorentina 392, 56023 Navacchio Pi Italy. **Tel** 011 39 50 772850.

●US/1065-447X
**VIRGINIA HEALTH CARE IN PERSPECTIVE.** [Va. health care perspect.]. **Added/Corp** Morgan Quitno Corporation. 1st Ed. (1993)-. English. $18.00. Morgan Quitno Corporation, PO Box 1656, 512 East 9th Street, Lawrence KS 66044. **Tel** (800)457-0742, (913)841-3534, FAX (913)841-3534. **DD** 362.
**Desc:** Reports on the state's data and rank for each of the categories featured in Health Care State Rankings.

CN/1185-5940
**VISIONS / CANADIAN MENTAL HEALTH ASSOCIATION, B.C. DIVISION.** [Visions]. **Added/Corp** Canadian Mental Health Association. B.C. Division. (May 1991)-. Periodical. English. qt. Limited free distribution. Canadian Mental Health Association, 10050 112th Street, 9th Floor, Edmonton Alberta T5K 2J1 Canada. **Tel** (403)482-6091. **DD** 362.2/06/0711.

CN/0826-2756
**VITA SANA.** ***Ceased.*** [Vitasana]. **VFOAT** Vitasana Magazine. Vol. 1, No. 1, (Jan./Feb. 1984)-(1992). Periodical. Italian. mo. Vita Sana, Suite 405, 1017 Wilson Avenue, Downsview Ontario M3K 1Z1. **DD** 613/.05.

US/0083-2014
**VITAL AND HEALTH STATISTICS. SERIES 1: PROGRAMS AND COLLECTION PROCEDURES.** [Vital health stat., Ser.1, Programs collect. proced.]. **Added/Corp** National Center for Health Statistics (U.S.). **VFOAT** Programs and Collection Procedures. (1963)-. Monographic series. English. ir. Free. National Center for Health Statistics, 6525 Belcrest Road, Hyattsville MD 20782. **Tel** (301)436-8500. **LC** RA409; .U44. **DD** 614.4/2/0723. **NLM** W2 A N148VA. ***Supersedes*** *Health Statistics. Series A.*
**Ind/Abst** Energy Res. Abstr. (Aug. 1982-); Index Med. (19??-).

US/0083-2057
**VITAL AND HEALTH STATISTICS. SERIES 2, DATA EVALUATION AND METHODS RESEARCH.** [Vital health stat., Ser. 2, Data eval. methods res.]. **Added/Corp** National Center for Health Statistics (U.S.) United States. Public Health Service. **VFOAT** Data Evaluation and Methods Research. (1963)-. Monographic series. English. ir. Free. National Center for Health Statistics, 6525 Belcrest Road, Hyattsville MD 20782. **Tel** (301)436-8500. **NLM** W2 A; N148vb. **CODEN** VHSBA. ***Continues*** *Health Statistics from the U.S. National Health Survey. Series D.*
**Ind/Abst** Index Med. (19??-); Popul. Index (19??-).

US/0886-4691
**VITAL & HEALTH STATISTICS. SERIES 3, ANALYTICAL AND EPIDEMIOLOGICAL STUDIES.** [Vital health stat., Ser. 3, Anal. epidemiol. stud.]. **Added/Corp** National Center for Health Statistics (U.S.). **VFOAT** Vital and Health Statistics. Series 3, Analytical and Epidemiological Studies; Analytical and Epidemiological Studies. (1983)-. Monographic series. English. ir. Free. National Center for Health Statistics, 6525 Belcrest Road, Hyattsville MD 20782. **Tel** (301)436-8500. **DD** 614. **NLM** W2; A N148vc. ***Continues*** *Vital and Health Statistics. Series 3, Analytical Studies, 0083-2065.*
**Ind/Abst** Energy Res. Abstr. (Aug. 1982-); Index Med. (19??-).

US/0892-8959
**VITAL & HEALTH STATISTICS. SERIES 5, COMPARATIVE INTERNATIONAL VITAL AND HEALTH STATISTICS REPORTS.** [Vital health stat., Ser. 5, Comp. int. vital health stat. rep.]. **Added/Corp** National Center for Health Statistics (U.S.). **VFOAT** Comparative International Vital and Health Statistics Reports; Vital and Health Statistics. Series 5, Comparative International Vital and Health Statistics Reports. (1984)-. Monographic series. English. ir. Free. National Center for Health Statistics, 6525 Belcrest Road, Hyattsville MD 20782. **Tel** (301)436-8500. **LC** UNC. **DD** 312. **NLM** W2; A N148ve.
**Ind/Abst** Energy Res. Abstr. (1984-); Health Plan. Adminis. (19??-).

US/0083-1972
**VITAL AND HEALTH STATISTICS. SERIES 10, DATA FROM THE NATIONAL HEALTH SURVEY.** [Vital health stat., Ser. 10, Data Natl. Health Surv.]. **Added/Corp** United States. Public Health Service. National Center for Health Statistics (U.S.). **VFOAT** Data From the National Health Survey. (1963)-. Monographic series. English. ir. Free. National Center for Health Statistics, 6525 Belcrest Road, Hyattsville MD 20782. **Tel** (301)436-8500. **NLM** W2 A; N148vj. ***Supersedes*** *Health Statistics From the U.S. National Health Survey. Series B; Health Statistics From the U.S. National Health Survey. Series C.*
**Ind/Abst** Energy Res. Abstr. (Aug. 1982-); Index Med. (19??-).

US/0083-1980
**VITAL AND HEALTH STATISTICS. SERIES 11, DATA FROM THE NATIONAL HEALTH SURVEY.** [Vital health stat., Ser. 11, Data Natl. Health Surv.]. **Added/Corp** National Center for Health Statistics (U.S.) United States. Public Health Service. **VFOAT** Data from the National Health Survey. (1964)-. Monographic series. English. ir. Free on request. National Center for Health Statistics, 6525 Belcrest Road, Hyattsville MD 20782. **Tel** (301)436-8500. **LC** RA407.3; .A347. **NLM** W2 A; N148vk. **CODEN** VHSKAS.
**Ind/Abst** Energy Res. Abstr. (Aug. 1982-); Index Med.

US/0083-2006
**VITAL AND HEALTH STATISTICS. SERIES 13, DATA FROM THE NATIONAL HEALTH SURVEY.** **Added/Corp** National Center for Health Statistics (U.S.). **VFOAT** Data from the National Health Survey; Data from the National Vital Statistics System; Vital & Health Statistics. Series 13, Data on Health Resources Utilization; Data on Health Resources Utilization; Vital & Health Statistics. Series 13, Data from the National Health Survey; Vital and Health Statistics. Series 13, Data the National Vital Statistics System No. 2. (1967)-. Monographic series. English. ir. Free. National Center for Health Statistics, 6525 Belcrest

Road, Hyattsville MD 20782. **Tel** (301)436-8500. **LC** RA407.3; .A349. **DD** 362.1/1/0973. ***Continues*** *Vital and Health Statistics. Series 13: Data from the Hospital Discharge Survey. National Center for Health Statistics;* ***Absorbed*** *Vital and Health Statistics. Series 12, Data from the National Health Survey, 0083-1964.*
**Ind/Abst** Energy Res. Abstr. (Aug. 1982-).

US
**VITAL & HEALTH STATISTICS. SERIES 14, DATA FROM THE NATIONAL HEALTH SURVEY.** **Added/Corp** National Center for Health Statistics (U.S.). **VFOAT** Vital and Health Statistics. N.Series 14, P.Data From The National Health Survey; Data From The National Health Survey; Vital and Health Statistics. N.Series 14, P.Data on Health Resources--Manpower and facilities. No. 27 (1982)-. Monographic series. English. ir. Price varies per volume. National Center for Health Statistics, 6525 Belcrest Road, Hyattsville MD 20782. **Tel** (301)436-8500. **NLM** W2; A N148vn. ***Continues*** *Vital & Health Statistics. Series 14, Data from the National Inventory of Family Planning Services.*
**Ind/Abst** Index Med. (1982-).

US/0895-4925
**VITAL & HEALTH STATISTICS. SERIES 15, DATA FROM THE NATIONAL HEALTH SURVEY.** [Vital health stat., Ser. 15 Data Natl. Health Surv.]. **Added/Corp** National Center for Health Statistics (U.S.) National Health Survey (U.S.). **VFOAT** Data From the National Health Survey; Vital and Health Statistics. Data From Special Surveys. No. 1, (1981)-. Monographic series. English. ir. Price varies per volume. National Center for Health Statistics, 6525 Belcrest Road, Hyattsville MD 20782. **Tel** (301)436-8500. **DD** 362. **NLM** W2; A N148vp.

US
**VITAL AND HEALTH STATISTICS. SERIES 16, COMPILATIONS OF ADVANCE DATA FROM VITAL AND HEALTH STATISTICS.** **Added/Corp** National Center for Health Statistics (U.S.). **VFOAT** Compilations of Advance Data from Vital and Health Statistics. No. 1 (1989)-. Monographic series. English. ir. Free. National Center for Health Statistics, 6525 Belcrest Road, Hyattsville MD 20782. **Tel** (301)436-8500.
**Ind/Abst** Index Med. (19??-).

US/0083-2022
**VITAL AND HEALTH STATISTICS. SERIES 20, DATA FROM THE NATIONAL VITAL STATISTICS SYSTEM.** **Added/Corp** National Center for Health Statistics (U.S.). **VFOAT** Data From the National Vital Statistics System. (1965)-. English. ir. Free on request to libraries. National Center for Health Statistics, 6525 Belcrest Road, Hyattsville MD 20782. **Tel** (301)436-8500. **NLM** W2; A N148vt. ***Supersedes in part*** *Vital Statistics-Special Reports.*

US
**VITAL AND HEALTH STATISTICS. SERIES 24, COMPILATIONS OF DATA ON NATALITY, MORTALITY, MARRIAGE, DIVORCE, AND INDUCED TERMINATIONS OF PREGNANCY.** **Added/Corp** National Center for Health Statistics (U.S.). **VFOAT** Compilations of Data on Natality, Mortality, Marriage, Divorce, and Induced Terminations of Pregnancy. No. 1 (1989)-. Monographic series. English. ir. Price varies per volume. National Center for Health Statistics, 6525 Belcrest Road, Hyattsville MD 20782. **Tel** (301)436-8500.
**Ind/Abst** Index Med.

SP/0042-7578
**VIVIR.** [Vivir]. **VFOAT** Consejos Para Vivir Con Salud; Vivir Con Salud. (1953)-. Periodical. Spanish. Eight times a year. $38.00 US; $33.00 other. Cedel, PO Box 5326, Barcelona Spain. **Tel** 011 34 3 215 6039. **UDC** 613. Index available. **Bk Rev. Ad Acc. Pr Rev. Circ:** 6,000.
**Desc:** Articles on natural medicine, health and ecology.

SP
**VIVIR CON SALUD.** Spanish. Federacion Naturista- Vegetariana, Apdo 5326, 08080 Barcelona Spain.

AT/0312-1267
**VOLUME OF PAPERS - ANNUAL CONFERENCE AUSTRALIAN INSTITUTE OF HEALTH SURVEYORS SOUTH AUSTRALIAN DIVISION.** (ANNUAL CONFERENCE; VOLUME OF PAPERS - AUSTRALIAN INSTITUTE OF HEALTH SURVEYORS, SOUTH AUSTRALIAN DIVISION.). [Vol. pap. - Annu. Conf. Aust. Inst. Health Surv. South Aust. Div.]. **Added/Corp** Australian Institute of Health Surveyors. South Australian Division. **VFOAT** SA Health Surveyors Conference. (Oct. 1974)-. Periodical. English. **NLM** W1 AN748W.

US
**VOLUNTEER UPDATE.** **Added/Corp** Whitman-Walker Clinic. Vol. 7 (1991)-. Periodical. English. mo. **NLM** W1; VO355. ***Continues*** *WWC Newsletter.*

JA/0915-3179
**WAKAYAMA-KEN EISEI KOGAI KENKYU SENTA NENPO.** **See** Environmental Issues.

IO/0377-6549
**WARTA KESEHATAN.** (WARTA DINAS KESEHATAN.). **Main/Corp** Jakarta Raya (Indonesia). Dinas Kesehatan. No. 5- August 1972-. Periodical. Indonesian. mo. Dinas Kesehatan, Jl Kesehatan No 100, Jakarta Indonesia. **LC** RA318.J34; D55A. **NLM** W1 WA287. ***Continues*** *Warta Kesehatan, 0377-6549.*

US/0899-1405
**WARY CANARY, THE.** **See** Environmental Issues.

●US/1065-4488
**WASHINGTON HEALTH CARE IN PERSPECTIVE.** [Wash. health care perspect.]. **Added/Corp** Morgan Quitno Corporation. 1st Ed. (1993)-. English. $18.00. Morgan Quitno Corporation, PO Box 1656, 512 East 9th Street, Lawrence KS 66044. **Tel** (800)457-0742, (913)841-3534, FAX (913)841-3534. **DD** 362.
**Desc:** Reports on the state's data and rank for each of the categories featured in Health Care State Rankings.

US/0164-1514
**WASHINGTON HEALTH RECORD.** [Wash. heal. rec.]. (1978)-. Periodical. English. wk (50 issues). $195.00. Faulkner & Gray Inc., 11 Penn Plaza, 17th Floor, New York NY 10001. **Tel** (212)967-7000, (800)535-8403. **ED** Susan Namovicz. **NLM** W1 WA603. **Circ:** 300.
**Desc:** Calendar of regulations, legislation, publications, meetings, developments and happenings in the health field.

US/0043-0900
**WASHINGTON'S HEALTH.** **Added/Corp** Washington (State) Dept. of Health. Vol. 1, (Aug. 1956)-. Periodical. English. mo (Except during legislative session). $95.00. Washington Health, 1107 Northeast 45th Street, Suite 400, Seattle WA 98105. **Tel** (206)464-6143. **NLM** W1 WA689. ***Absorbed*** *Annual Report - State of Washington, Department of Health, 0193-0893.* ***Continued in part by*** *Report to the People - Washington State Department of Health, 0511-2168.*

US
**WATER SAFETY JOURNAL.** (19??)-. English. qt (4 issues). $4.00; Also comes with National Water Safety Congress membership. Water Safety Congress, 96 Sheila Drive, Oxford MS 38655. **Tel** (601)234-1828, FAX (601)234-1828. ***Continues*** *National Water Safety Congress Journal.*

SZ/0049-8114
**WEEKLY EPIDEMIOLOGICAL RECORD.** **See** Medical Science and Technology-Communicable Diseases.

US/0896-4696
**WEIGHT WATCHERS WOMEN'S HEALTH AND FITNESS NEWS.** ***Ceased.*** [Weight Watchers women's health fit. news]. **VFOAT** Women's Health and Fitness News. Vol. 1, No. 1 (Sept. 1986)-(April 1991). English. mo. Weight Watchers Magazine, 360 Lexington Avenue, 11th Floor, New York NY 10017. **Tel** (212)370-0644.
**Ind/Abst** Consum. Health Nutr. Index (Jan. 1990-199?).

US
**WELLNESS DIGEST, THE.** Periodical. English. mo. $36.00. Medical Concepts Publ Company, PO Box 3000, Princeton NJ 08540.

US
**WELLNESS ENCYCLOPEDIA OF FOOD AND NUTRITION.** English. ir. $24.96 (subscribers of University of California Berkeley Newsletter); $29.95 newstand. Health Letter Associates, 632 Broadway, 11th Floor, New York NY 10012. **Tel** (212)505-2255 ext. 100.

US/0739-4411
**WELLNESS JOURNAL, THE.** ***Ceased.*** -Ceased March 1984. Periodical. English. mo. Wellness Journal, PO Box 19095, Minneapolis MN 55419. ***Continues*** *Minnesota Wellness Journal.*

US/1062-1156
**WELLNESS MANAGEMENT.** [Wellness manag.]. **Added/Corp** National Wellness Association. Vol. 1, No. 1 (June 1985)-. Periodical. English. Four times a year (Jan., Mar., June, Sept.,). $135.00 institutions, $58.00 individuals. National Wellness Institute, 1045 Clark Street, Suite 210, Stevens Point WI 54481-2962. **Tel** (715)342-2969, FAX (715)342-2979. **ED** Linda R. Chapin, D.D.S., M.S. **DD** 613. **Circ:** 2,500 (ctrl).
**Desc:** Published as a service to the members of the National Wellness Association (NWA) with the purpose of providing information on recent developments, resources, programming, research, events, and educational opportunities in the wellness and health promotion field as well as to serve as a networking tool for NWA members.

US
**WELLNESS MEDIA.** ***Ceased.*** **VFOAT** Wellness Media Index; NICEM Wellness Media Index; NICEM Wellness Media. **VAT** National Information Center for Educational Media Wellness Media Index; National Information Center for Educational Media Wellness Media. 1st Ed. (1986)-?. English. Access Innovations Inc, PO Box 40130, Albuquerque NM 87196. **Tel** (505)265-3591. **(Subscription address:** Plexus Publishing Inc., 143 Old Marlton Pike, Medford, NJ 08055**)** **LC** R835; .W4. Index available in last issue of volume--attached.

US/0748-1764
**WELLNESS PERSPECTIVES.** [Wellness perspect.]. **Added/Corp** Organization of Wellness Networks. University of Nebraska--Lincoln. Dept. of Human Development and the Family. University of Alabama. College of Education. Vol. 1, No. 1 (Winter 1984)-. Periodical. English. Four times a year. $15.00 individuals; $20.00 institutions. University of Alabama, PO Box 870312, Tuscaloosa AL 35487. **Tel** (205)348-2956, FAX (205)348-7568. **ED** James M. Eddy and Elbert D. Glover. **LC** RA773; .W444. **DD** 613. **Bk Rev**, (Qty: 1-2). **Ad Acc. Pr Rev. Circ:** 1,000.
**Desc:** Intended for researchers and practitioners in the myriad professional and academic fields that relate to health promotion and wellness, including intervention, policy, corporate culture, social support and environment support components.
**Ind/Abst** Acad. Abstr. Full Text Elite (Jan. 1992-); Acad. Abstr. (Jan. 1992-); Acad. Search (Jan. 1992-); Health Source (Jan. 1992-); INFO-SOUTH Abstr.; Mag. Search.

CN/0225-4255
**WEST COAST LIFELINER.** [West Coast lifeliner]. **Main/Corp** Royal Life Saving Society Canada. B.C. & Yukon Branch. Periodical. English. Free. Royal Life Saving Society, Canada B C & Yukon Branch, 100-1200 Hornby Street, Vancouver British Columbia V6Z 2E2 Canada. **DD** 363.1/4. ctrl circ.

●US/1065-4496
**WEST VIRGINIA HEALTH CARE IN PERSPECTIVE.** [W. Va. health care perspect.]. **Added/Corp** Morgan Quitno Corporation. 1st Ed. (1993)-. English. $18.00. Morgan Quitno Corporation, PO Box 1656, 512 East 9th Street, Lawrence KS 66044. **Tel** (800)457-0742, (913)841-3534, FAX (913)841-3534. **DD** 362.
**Desc:** Reports on the state's data and rank for each of the categories featured in Health Care State Rankings.

DK/0378-2255
**WHO REGIONAL PUBLICATIONS. EUROPEAN SERIES.** [WHO reg. publ., Eur. ser.]. **VFOAT** Regional Publications Series; European Series. **VAT** World Health Organization Regional Publications. European Series. (1976)-. Monographic series. English. ir. $10.80. World Health Organization / Denmark, Scherfigsvej 8, 2100 Copenhagen 0 Denmark. **Tel** 011 45 39171717. **(Subscription address:** World Health Organization, 49 Sheridan Avenue, Albany NY 12210.**)** **NLM** W1 W156. **CODEN** WRPSDJ. Documents available from BIOSIS Document Express.
**Ind/Abst** Biol. Abstr. (1988-); EMBASE; Health Plan. Adminis.; Index Med. (1988-); Trop. Dis. Bull.

US/0888-2061
**WHOLE LIFE.** [Whole life]. **VFOAT** Whole Life Magazine. No. 1 (Apr. 1986)-. Periodical. English. ir. $20.00 US; $30.00 other. Whole Life Magazine, PO Box 205B, New York NY 10159. **Tel** (212)353-3395. **ED** Marc Medaff. **DD** 613. Index available. cum. index. **Bk Rev. Ad Acc. Circ:** 60,000 (ctrl). available in microform. ***Continues*** *Whole Life New York.*
**Desc:** Focuses on personal health and natural living.
**Ind/Abst** Altern. Press Index (-199?); Health Ref. Cent. (Jan. 1989-) [Full Cov.].

UK
**WHO'S WHO IN THE EMERGENCY & RESCUE SERVICES.** English. an. £15.00 UK; $29.00 US. Lincoln Publications, 28 Centre Point House, St Giles Street, London WC2H 8LW England. **Tel** 071-240 5562, FAX 071-497 2811. **ED** Derek V Tofts. **Bk Rev. Ad Acc. Circ:** 2,000.
**Desc:** The only Directory specifically for all the UK Emergency and Rescue Services. The contents includes a Directory of Public Fire Brigades, Ambulance Service, Police, Civil Defence, giving the names of Chief Officers, Headquarters address, areas covered, equipment and vehicles statistics, etc.

US/0148-7728
**WISCONSIN ANNUAL HIGHWAY SAFETY WORK PROGRAM.** **See** Transportation-Roads and Traffic.

●US/1065-450X
**WISCONSIN HEALTH CARE IN PERSPECTIVE.** [Wis. health care perspect.]. **Added/Corp** Morgan Quitno Corporation. 1st Ed. (1993)-. English. $18.00. Morgan Quitno Corporation, PO Box

1656, 512 East 9th Street, Lawrence KS 66044. **Tel** (800)457-0742, (913)841-3534, FAX (913)841-3534. **DD** 362.
**Desc:** Reports on the state's data and rank for each of the categories featured in Health Care State Rankings.

US/0742-1052
**WN TRENDS, HEALTH CARE AND MANAGEMENT.** [WN trends, health care manage.]. **VFOAT** W.N. Trends, Health Care and Management; Trends, Health Care and Management; WN Trends and Health Care and Management. Vol. 1, No. 1 (Jan. 1984)-. Periodical. English. mo. $240.00. Wenz-Neely Company, 1009 South 4th Street, Louisville KY 40203. **LC** RA410.A1; W58. **DD** 362.1/068.

US/1047-2800
**WOMEN'S HEALTH ADVISER POSTER.** **See** Women's Interests.

US/0890-9695
**WOMENWISE.** [WomenWise]. **Added/Corp** New Hampshire Feminist Health Center. **VFOAT** Women Wise. Vol. 1, No. 1 (Winter 1978)-. Periodical. English. Four times a year. $10.00 (individuals); $20.00 (institutions). Womenwise, 38 South Main Street, Concord NH 03301. **Tel** (603)225-2739. **ED** Michelle Duford. **DD** 362. Index available (Free). **Bk Rev. Ad Acc. Circ:** 2,500 (ctrl). available on microfilm.
**Desc:** Women's health information and resources.

US/1051-9815
**WORK : A JOURNAL OF PREVENTION, ASSESSMENT, AND REHABILITATION.** Vol. 1, No. 1 (Fall 1990)-. Periodical. English. qt. $95.00 (institution), $60.00 (individual) US and Canada; $110.00 (institution), $75.00 (individual) other. Butterworth Heinemann / Woburn, MA, 225 Wildwood Avenue, Unit B, Woburn MA 01801. **Tel** (800)366-2665, FAX (617)928-2620, telex 880052. **DD** 613. **NLM** W1; WO8463. **[CCC].**

BG/0254-959X
**WORKING PAPER (INTERNATIONAL CENTRE FOR DIARRHOEAL DISEASE RESEARCH, BANGLADESH).** (WORKING PAPER / INTERNATIONAL CENTRE FOR DIARRHOEAL DISEASE RESEARCH, BANGLADESH.). [Work. pap. - Int. Cent. Diarrh. Dis. Res. Bangladesh]. Began in 1979. Monographic series. English. Price varies per volume. **NLM** W1 WO848D. ***Continues** Working Paper (Cholera Research Laboratory).*
**Ind/Abst** Popul. Index (?-?).

UK/0141-2647
**WORKING PAPER SERIES - HEALTH SERVICES MANAGEMENT UNIT. DEPARTMENT OF SOCIAL ADMINISTRATION. UNIVERSITY OF MANCHESTER.** (WORKING PAPER SERIES.). [Work pap. ser. - Health Serv. Manage. Unit, Dep. Soc. Adm., Univ. Manch.]. **Added/Corp** University of Manchester. Health Services Management Unit. No. 1 (1978)-. Monographic series. English. ir. Price varies per volume. University of Manchester / Department of Social Administration, Health Services Management Unit, Manchester M13 9PL England. **LC** UNC. **NLM** W1 WO848M.

US/1053-492X
**WORKSITE WELLNESS WORKS.** **See** Nutrition and Dietetics.

US/0890-4480
**WORLD BOOK HEALTH & MEDICAL ANNUAL, THE.** **See** Medical Science and Technology.

SZ/0043-8502
**WORLD HEALTH.** (WORLD HEALTH : THE MAGAZINE OF THE WORLD HEALTH ORGANIZATION.). [World health]. **Added/Corp** World Health Organization. (1957)-. Periodical. English (French, German, Russian, Spanish, Arabic and Faroese). bm. $25.00 Surface Mail; $43.00 (airmail) Europe; $54.00 (airmail) other. World Health Organization, Distribution and Sales, 20 Avenue Appia, CH-1211 Geneva 27 Switzerland. **Tel** 011 41 22 7912111, FAX 011 41 22 7880401. **ED** John Bland. **NLM** W2 MW6 W9W. cum. index. available on an online database from DIALOG; available on microfilm and microfiche from University Microfilms International (UMI). Documents available from BIOSIS Document Express, UMI Article Clearinghouse, Documents on Demand. ***Continues** WHO Newsletter.*
**Desc:** Illustrates the human side of efforts to improve world health. Designed to increase public awareness of health problems and what can be done to prevent them. Global in its scope, it encourages readers to be more conscious of the role that good health plays both in their own lives and at the community level in different parts of the world.
**Ind/Abst** Acad. Abstr. Full Text Elite (April 1989-); Acad. Abstr. (Apr. 1989-); Acad. Search (Apr. 1989-); Appl. Soc. Sci. Index Abstr.; Biol. Abstr.; Biol. Dig.; Cumul. Index Nurs. Allied Health Lit.; Environ. Abstr.; Gen. Period. Index (1985-); Geogr. Abstr. Human Geogr.; Health Index (1989-); Health Period. Database [Full Txt.]; Health Ref. Cent. (Jan. 1989-) [Full Cov.]; Health Source (Jan. 1989-); Hum. Rights Intern. Rep.; INFO-SOUTH Abstr.; Int. Aerosp. Abstr.; Int. Dev. Abstr.; Int. Pharm. Abstr.; Mag. Artic. Summar. Elite (Apr. 1989-); Mag. Artic. Summar. Select (Jan. 1989-); Mag. Artic. Summar. CD-ROM (Apr. 1989-); Mag. ASAP Plus [Full Txt.]; Mag. ASAP Sel. [Full Txt.]; Mag. Express (1988-) [Full Txt.]; Mag. Index Plus (1989-); Mag. Index. Sel. (1986-); Mag. Search; Middle East Abstr. Index; Mid. Search (Jan. 1989-); NAPRALERT; Newsp. Period. Abstr. (1988-); Nutr. Res. Newsl.; Point Repere (1979-); Read. Guide Abstr. Select Ed.; Read. Guide Period. Lit.; Resource/One Ondisc; Mag. Index (1977-); Trop. Dis. Bull.; Vocat. Search (Apr. 1989-).

SZ/0251-2432
**WORLD HEALTH FORUM.** [World health forum]. **Added/Corp** World Health Organization. Vol. 1 (1980)-. Periodical. English (Arabic, Chinese, French, Russian and Spanish). qt. $60.00 Surface Mail; $76.00 (airmail) Europe; $88.00 (airmail) other. World Health Organization, Distribution and Sales, 20 Avenue Appia, CH-1211 Geneva 27 Switzerland. **Tel** 011 41 22 7912111, FAX 011 41 22 7880401. **LC** RA441; .W67. **DD** 362.1/05. **NLM** W1 WO873. **CODEN** WHFODN. Index available. available on microfilm and microfiche from University Microfilms International (UMI). Documents available from BIOSIS Document Express, Documents on Demand.
**Desc:** A record of ideas, arguments and experiences contributed by health professionals the world over. Individual issues, which may feature as many as 30 communications, are edited to reflect the latest thinking about public health policy and practice around the world. Priority is given to practical information that can bring the processes of health thinking and planning closer to real conditions in the field.
**Ind/Abst** Abstr. Anthropol.; Appl. Soc. Sci. Index Abstr.; Biol. Abstr.; Curr. Titl. Dent.; Ecol. Abstr. (?-?); EMBASE; Environ. Abstr.; Environ. Period. Bibliogr. (?-?); Geogr. Abstr. Human Geogr.; Health Plan. Adminis.; Helminthol. Abstr. (19??-19??); Index Med. (v9n1,1988-); Index Vet.; Ind. Hyg. Dig.; Int. Dev. Abstr.; Int. Nurs. Index; Int. Pharm. Abstr.; LABORDOC; Maize Abstr.; NAPRALERT; Nutr. Abstr. Rev., Ser. B, Live Feeds and Feed.; Nutr. Abstr. Rev., Ser. A, Hum. Exp.; Nutr. Res. Newsl.; PAIS Int. Print; Life Sci. Collect.; Protozoolog. Abstr.; Ref. Upd. Deluxe Ed.; Rev. Agric. Entomol.; Rural Dev. Abstr.; Soc. Work Abstr. [Select. Cov.]; Trop. Dis. Bull.

SZ/0512-3054
**WORLD HEALTH ORGANIZATION TECHNICAL REPORT SERIES.** (TECHNICAL REPORT SERIES / WORLD HEALTH ORGANIZATION.). [W.H.O. tech. rep. ser.]. **Main/Corp** World Health Organization. **Added/Corp** World Health Organization. **VFOAT** WHO Technical Report Series. No. 1 (1950)-. Academic Scholarly Publication. English (French, Spanish and Arabic). ir (approximately 15 reports). $106.00 Surface Mail; $138.00 (airmail) Europe; $155.00 (airmail) other. World Health Organization, Distribution and Sales, 20 Avenue Appia, CH-1211 Geneva 27 Switzerland. **Tel** 011 41 22 7912111, FAX 011 41 22 7880401. **LC** RA8; .A25. **NLM** W2 MW6 W9T. **CODEN** WHOTAC. Index available. cum. index. **Pr Rev.** Documents available from The Genuine Article, BIOSIS Document Express.
**Desc:** Highly concentrated reports summarizing current technical knowledge on a given disease, health risk, medical technology or research approach. Topics are selected as representing either a major health problem or an area where research advances have been especially rapid. It is a consensus report reflecting the opinions and experiences of international groups of experts.
**Ind/Abst** Biol. Abstr.; EMBASE; Helminthol. Abstr. (1991-); Index Med.; Int. Pharm. Abstr. (199?-); Nutr. Abstr. Rev.. Ser. A, Hum. Exp.; Life Sci. Collect.; Protozoolog. Abstr.; Res. Alert [Full Cov.]; Rev. Med. Vet. Entomol.; Rural Dev. Abstr.; Sci. Cit. Index; SCISEARCH; Soc. Sci. Cit. Index [Select. Cov.]; Trop. Dis. Bull.

CN/0380-4712
**WORLD OF ASP.** **Main/Corp** American Self-Protection Association. V. 1- Nov./Dec. 1975-. Periodical. English. bm. S Fraser, PO Box 302, Kingston NC B0P 1R0.

US/0161-7672
**WORLD SMOKING & HEALTH.** **See** Tobacco.

UK
**WRAP.** (19??)-. English. Twelve times a year. £13.50. Royal Society for the Prevention of Accidents, Cannon House, Priory Queensway, Birmingham B4 6BS England. **Tel** 011 44 21 200 2461, FAX 021 200 1254. **ED** Jacqui Heath. **Bk Rev. Ad Acc.**
**Desc:** Health and safety issues.

●US/1065-4518
**WYOMING HEALTH CARE IN PERSPECTIVE.** [Wyo. health care perspect.]. **Added/Corp** Morgan Quitno Corporation. 1st Ed. (1993)-. English. $18.00. Morgan Quitno Corporation, PO Box 1656, 512 East 9th Street, Lawrence KS 66044. **Tel** (800)457-0742, (913)841-3534, FAX (913)841-3534. **DD** 362.
**Desc:** Reports on the state's data and rank for each of the categories featured in Health Care State Rankings.

JA/0513-4706
**YAMAGATA-KEN EISEI KENKYUJO HO.** [Yamagata-ken Eisei Kenkyujo ho]. **Added/Corp** Yamagata-Ken Eisei Kenkyujo. **VFOAT** Report of the Yamagata Prefectural Institute of Public Health. (1960)-. Japanese. Yamagataken Eisei Kenkyujo, (Yamagata Prefectural Inst. of Public Health), 6-6, Tokamachi 1 Chome, Yamagatashi, Yamagataken 990, Japan. **CODEN** YEKHAP. Documents available from CASDDS.
**Ind/Abst** Chem. Abstr.

JA
**YAMAGUCHI-KEN EISEI KENKYUJO NEMPO.** **Main/Corp** Yamaguchi-ken Eisei Kenkyujo. Japanese. an. Yamaguchiken Kankyo Hokenbu, (Environmental Protection & Public Health Bureau, Yamaguchi Prefectural Govt.), 1-1, Takimachi, Yamaguchishi, Yamaguchiken 753 Japan. **LC** RA532.Y35; Y36A.

JA/0915-437X
**YAMANASHI-KEN EISEI KOGAI KENKYUJO NENPO.** [Yamanashi-ken Eisei Kogai Kenkyujo nenpo]. **Main/Corp** Yamanashi-Ken Eisei Kogai Kenkyujo. **VFOAT** Annual Report of the Yamanashi Institute for Public Health. (1975)-. Japanese. Yamanashiken Eisei Kogai Kenkyujo, (Yamanashi Inst. for Public Health), 7-31, Fujimi 1 Chome, Kofushi, Yamanashiken 400, Japan. **LC** IN PROCESS. **CODEN** YKKNDK. Documents available from CASDDS. ***Continues** Yamanashi Kenritsu Eisei Kogai Kenkyujo. Yamanashi Kenritsu Eisei Kogai Kenkyujo Nenpo.*
**Ind/Abst** Chem. Abstr.

US/1050-995X
**YEAR BOOK OF HEALTH CARE MANAGEMENT.** [Year book health care manage.]. **VFOAT** Yearbook of Health Care Management; Year Book of Healthcare Management. (1991)-. English. an. $59.95. Mosby Year Book Inc., 11830 Westline Industrial Drive, St Louis MO 63146. **Tel** (800)325-4177, (314)872-8370, FAX (314)432-1380, telex 44-2402. **LC** RA971; .Y43. **DD** 362.1/068. **NLM** W1; YE199CE.

SZ/0510-8675
**YELLOW-FEVER VACCINATING CENTRES FOR INTERNATIONAL TRAVEL.** **Main/Corp** World Health Organization. **Added/Corp** World Health Organization. Centres de Vaccination Contre la Fievre Jaune pour les Voyages Internationaux. **VFOAT** Centres de Vaccination Contre la Fievre Jaune pour les Voyages Internationaux. (19??)-. English (French). World Health Organization, Distribution and Sales, 20 Avenue Appia, CH-1211 Geneva 27 Switzerland. **Tel** 011 41 22 7912111, FAX 011 41 22 7880401. **LC** RA644.Y4; W58. **DD** 614.5/41. **NLM** WC 22; MW6 W9c.

JA
**YORAN - KOKURITSU KOSHU EISEIIN.** **Main/Corp** Kokuritsu Koshu Eiseiin, Tokyo. (19??)-. Periodical. Japanese. an. Koseisho Kokuritsu Koshu Eiseiin, (Institute of Health Ministry of Health and Welfare), 6-1 Shiroganedai 4-chome, Minatoku Tokyoto 108 Japan. **LC** RA532.T64; K64a.

US/0279-9324
**YOUR HEALTH & FITNESS.** [Your health fitness]. **VFOAT** Your Health and Fitness. Vol. 6, No. 5 (Oct./Nov. 1984). Periodical. English. bm. $21.00. General Learning Corporation, 60 Revere Drive, PO Box 3060, Northbrook IL 60065. **Tel** (800)323-5471, (708)564-4070. **LC** RA773; .Y66. **DD** 613/.05. **Bk Rev. Ad Acc.** ***Continues** Current Health and Fitness, 0279-5752. **Continued in part by** Your Health & Safety, 8750-8842.*
**Desc:** A custom publication that promotes health care cost containment and wellness issues to employees and their families.

US/8750-8842
**YOUR HEALTH & SAFETY.** [Your health saf.]. **VFOAT** Your Health and Safety. Vol. 6, No. 6 (Dec. 1984/Jan. 1985)-. Periodical. English. Six times a year. $17.70. General Learning Corporation, 60 Revere Drive, PO Box 3060, Northbrook IL 60065. **Tel** (800)323-5471, (708)564-4070. available on microfilm and microfiche from University Microfilms International (UMI). ***Continues in part** Your Health & Fitness, 0279-9324.*

MV/0513-8728
**ZDRAVOOHRANENIE (KISINEV).** ***Title Change.*** (ZDRAVOOHRANENIE.). [Zdravoohranenie]. **Added/Corp** Moldavian S.S.R. Ministerul Okrotirii Senetetsii. (1958)-(19??). Periodical. Russian. bm. **LC** R91; .Z27. **NLM** W1 ZD852. **CODEN** ZDVKAP. Documents available from BIOSIS Document Express, CASDDS. ***Continued by** Meditsinskii Kurer.*
**Ind/Abst** Biol. Abstr.; Chem. Abstr. (1965-1990).

KZ/0372-8277
**ZDRAVOOKHRANENIE KAZAKHSTANA.** **Added/Corp** Kazakh S.S.R. Ministerstvo Zdravookhraneniia. (Apr. 1941)-. Periodical. Russian. mo. Izdatelstvo TSK Kompartii Kazakhstana, Ulitsa M. Gorkogo 50, Alma-Ata 480044 Kazakhstan. **(Subscription address:** Victor Kamkin, 4956 Boiling

Brook Parkway, Rockville MD 20852.) **NLM** W1 ZD853. **CODEN** ZDKAA8. available on microfilm. Documents available from CASDDS.
**Ind/Abst** Chem. Abstr.

KG
**ZDRAVOOKHRANENIE KYRGYZSTANA / MINISTERSTVO ZDRAVOOKHRANENIIA RESPUBLIKI KYRGYZSTAN.** **Added/Corp** Kyrgyzstan. Ministerstvo Zdravookhraneniia. (1991)-. Academic Scholarly Publication. Russian. bm. **(Subscription address:** Victor Kamkin, 4956 Boiling Brook Parkway, Rockville MD 20852.) **LC** RA421; .Z314. Documents available from CASDDS. ***Continues*** *Zdravookhranenie Kirgizii, 0490-1177.*
**Ind/Abst** Chem. Abstr.

RU/0044-197X
**ZDRAVOOKHRANENIE ROSSIJSKOJ FEDERACII.** (ZDRAVOOKHRANENIE ROSSIISKOI FEDERATSII.). [Zdravookhran. Ross. Fed.]. **Added/Corp** Russian S.F.S.R. Ministerstvo Zdravookhraneniia. (1957)-. Periodical. Russian. mo. $99.95. Izdatelstvo Meditsina / Russian Academy of Medical Sciences, Ulitsa Solyanka 14, 109801 Moscow Russia. **Tel** 011 95 297-05-04. **(Subscription address:** East View Publications Inc., 3020 Harbor Lane North, Suite 110, Minneapolis MN 55447.) **NLM** W1; ZD854.
**Ind/Abst** Int. Aerosp. Abstr.

TK/0513-8736
**ZDRAVOOKHRANENIE TURKMENISTANA / ORGAN MINISTERSTVA ZDRAVOOKHRANENIIA TSSR.** **Added/Corp** Turkmen S.S.R. Saglygy Saklaiysh Ministrligi. (1957)-. Academic Scholarly Publication. Russian. Six times a year. $109.95. **(Subscription address:** East View Publications Inc., 3020 Harbor Lane North, Suite 110, Minneapolis MN 55447.) **NLM** W1 ZD8547. **CODEN** ZDTUAB. Documents available from CASDDS.
**Ind/Abst** Chem. Abstr.

XR
**ZDRAVOTNICKE AKTUALITY.** Czech. **(Subscription address:** Artia Pegas Press Ltd., Palac Metro Narodni Trida 25, 11210 Prague 1 Czech Republic.)
**Ind/Abst** Index Med.

PL
**ZDROWIE.** ***Title Change.*** **Added/Corp** Polskie Towarzystwo Higieniczne. (Aug. 1885)-(193?). Periodical. Polish. sm. **(Subscription address:** ARS Polona, PO Box 1001, 00068 Warsaw Poland.) **NLM** W1; ZD935. ***Continued by*** *Zdrowie Publiczne, 0044-2011.*

PL/0044-2011
**ZDROWIE PUBLICZNE.** (ZDROWIE PUBLICZNE / POLSKIE TOWARZYSTWO HIGJENICZNE.). [Zdr. publ.]. **Added/Corp** Polskie Towarzystwo Higieniczne. Panstwowa Szkoa Higieny (Poland) Poland. Ministerstwo Zdrowia i Opieki Spoecznej. **VFOAT** Zdravookhranenie; Public Health. Vol. 49, No. 1 (Aug. 1934)-. Periodical. Polish (summaries and/or abstracts in English and Russian). mo. Price on Request. **(Subscription address:** ARS Polona, PO Box 1001, 00068 Warsaw Poland.) **LC** RA421; .Z4. **NLM** W1; ZD935. ***Continues*** *Zdrowie (Warsaw, Poland : 1885).*

GW/0049-8610
**ZEITSCHRIFT FUER DIE GESAMTE HYGIENE UND IHRE GRENZGEBIETE.** ***Ceased.*** [Z. gesamte Hyg. ihre Grenzgeb.]. Vol. 1 (Oct. 1955)-Vol. 37 (March 1991). Academic Scholarly Publication. German (summaries and/or abstracts in English and Russian). mo. VCH Publishers Inc, 220 East 23rd Street, New York NY 10010. **Tel** (212)683-8333, , FAX (212)481-0897. **(Subscription address:** 303 NW 12th Avenue, Deerfield Beach FL 33442; telephone: (305)428-5566) **LC** RA421. **NLM** W1 ZE265. **CODEN** ZHYGAM. **[CCC]**. Documents available from CASDDS.
**Ind/Abst** Anal. Abstr.; Anim. Breed. Abstr.; Chem. Abstr.; Chem. Hazards Ind.; Coal Abstr.; Dairy Sci. Abstr.; EMBASE; Index Med.; Lab. Hazards Bull.; Life Sci. Collect.; Poult. Abstr.; Protozoolog. Abstr.; Rev. Med. Vet. Entomol.; Rev. Med. Vet. Mycology; Saf. Health Work; SportSearch; Trop. Dis. Bull.

GW/0044-3654
**ZEITSCHRIFT FUR VERKEHRSSICHERHET.** **See** Transportation-Roads and Traffic.

GW/0934-8859
**ZENTRALBLATT FUER HYGIENE UND UMWELTMEDIZIN.** [Zent.bl. Hyg. Umweltmed.]. **VFOAT** International Journal of Hygiene and Environmental Medicine. Vol. 188, No. 1-2 (May 1989)-. Academic Scholarly Publication. German (English). Six times a year. DM984.00 Germany; DM1008.00 other. Gustav Fischer Verlag Stuttgart, Postfach 720143, Wollgrasweg 49, D 70577 Stuttgart Germany. **Tel** 011 49 711 458030, FAX 0711-4580334, telex 2627-7111488. **(Subscription address:** VCH Publishers Inc., 303 Northwest 12th Avenue, Journals Department, Deerfield FL 33442.) **LC** QR46; .Z453. **DD** 616.9/8/005. **NLM** W1; ZE778NH. **CODEN** ZHUMEOZAOMDC. **[CCC]**. Documents available from The Genuine Article, BIOSIS Document Express, CASDDS. ***Continues*** *Zentralblatt fur Bakteriologie, Mikrobiologie und Hygiene. Serie B. Umwelthygiene, Krankenhaushygiene, Arbeitshygiene, Praventive Medizin, 0932-6073.*
**Ind/Abst** Biodeter. Abstr.; Biol. Abstr. (1990-); Chem. Abstr.; Curr. Contents Life Sci.; Food Sci. Technol. Abstr.; Health Plan. Adminis.; Helminthol. Abstr. (1991-); Index Med. (May 1989-); Nutr. Abstr. Rev., Ser. A, Hum. Exp.; PESTDOC; Pollut. Abstr. Indexes; Protozoolog. Abstr.; Res. Alert [Full Cov.]; Rev. Med. Vet. Mycology; Sci. Cit. Index; SCISEARCH; Soc. Sci. Cit. Index [Select. Cov.]; Trop. Dis. Bull.

CC/0254-5098
**ZHONGHUA FANGSHE YIXUE YU FANGHU ZAZHI.** **See** Medical Science and Technology-Radiology.

PL
**ZYCIE I ZDROWIE.** (1974)-. Polish. bw. $21.00. **(Subscription address:** ARS Polona, PO Box 1001, 00068 Warsaw Poland.) **LC** RA421; .Z94.

---

## ABSTRACTING, BIBLIOGRAPHIES AND STATISTICS

---

UK/0260-5511
**ABSTRACTS ON HYGIENE AND COMMUNICABLE DISEASES.** [Abstr. hyg. commun. dis.]. **Added/Corp** Great Britain. Bureau of Hygiene and Tropical Diseases. Vol. 56, No. 1 (Jan. 1981)-. Abstracting/Indexing Service. English. mo. $381.00 North America. CAB International Centre, Wallingford, Oxon OX10 8DE United Kingdom. **Tel** 44 491 832111, FAX 44 491 833508, telex 847964 (COMAGG G). **ED** D W Fitzsimons. **LC** RA421; .L618. **DD** 610/.5. **NLM** ZWA 100 B936. Index available. cum. index. **Bk Rev**. **Ad Acc. Circ:** 1,000. available on microfilm and microfiche from University Microfilms International (UMI). ***Continues*** *Abstracts on Hygiene, 0001-3692.*
**Desc:** Concentrates on key papers on public health and disease with emphasis on developed countries but of global relevance. Topics covered include environmental health, occupational health, community medicine, chronic diseases and communicable diseases.
**Ind/Abst** Biodeter. Abstr.; Dairy Sci. Abstr.; Ergon. Abstr.; Index Vet.; Rev. Med. Vet. Mycology; Rev. Plant Pathol.; Vet. Bull.; World Text. Abstr.

US/0147-3956
**ADVANCE DATA FROM VITAL AND HEALTH STATISTICS OF THE NATIONAL CENTER FOR HEALTH STATISTICS.** (ADVANCE DATA FROM VITAL & HEALTH STATISTICS OF THE NATIONAL CENTER FOR HEALTH STATISTICS / U.S. DEPARTMENT OF HEALTH, EDUCATION, AND WELFARE, PUBLIC HEALTH SERVICE, OFFICE OF HEALTH RESEARCH, STATISTICS, AND TECHNOLOGY.). [Adv. data vital health stat. Natl. Cent. Health Stat.]. **Added/Corp** National Center for Health Statistics (U.S.) United States. Public Health Service. Office of Health Research, Statistics, and Technology. **VFOAT** NCHS Advance Data; Advance Data From Vital and Health Statistics of the Centers for Disease Control/National Center for Health Statistics; Advance Data From the Centers for Disease Control/National Center for Health Statistics; Advance Data From Vital and Health Statistics of the Centers for Disease Control and Prevention/National Center for Health Statistics; Advance Data. No. 1, Oct. 18 (1976)-. Monographic series. English. ir. Free. National Center for Health Statistics, 6525 Belcrest Road, Hyattsville MD 20782. **Tel** (301)436-8500. **LC** RA407.3; .U57c. **DD** 362.1/6/0973. **NLM** W2 A N148A. **CODEN** NADADR. Documents available from BIOSIS Document Express, Documents on Demand.
**Desc:** Information on health surveys and vital statistics.
**Ind/Abst** AGRICOLA [Select. Cov.]; Am. Stat. Index (1986-); Biol. Abstr.; EMBASE; Health Plan. Adminis.; Hospit. Health Admin. Index; Popul. Index.

US
**ADVANCES IN RISK ANALYSIS.** **Added/Corp** Society for Risk Analysis. Vol. 1 (1983)-. Monographic series. English. ir. Price varies per volume. Plenum Press, 233 Spring Street, New York NY 10013-1578. **Tel** (212)620-8000, (800)221-9369, FAX (212)463-0742, (212)807-1047, telex 23/421139.

CN/0708-7233
**ANNUAL STATISTICS / MANITOBA HEALTH SERVICES COMMISSION.** Began in 1976. English. an. Manitoba Health Services Commission, Box 925, 599 Empress Street, Winnipeg Manitoba R3C 2T6 Canada. **LC** RA410.9.C2; S73. **DD** 362.1/097127/021. ***Continues*** *Statistical Supplement to the Annual Report of the Manitoba Health Services Commission, 0383-3933.*

US
**ARIZONA HEALTH STATUS AND VITAL STATISTICS.** **Added/Corp** Arizona. Dept. of Health Services. Office of Planning and Budget Development. Arizona. Office of Planning and Health Status Monitoring. **VFOAT** Health Status and Vital Statistics. (1984)-. English. Arizona Department of Health Services, 1740 West Adams Street, Phoenix AZ 85007. **Tel** (602)542-1025, FAX (602)642-1062. **LC** RA407.4.A7; A2. **DD** 614.4/2791/021. ***Continues*** *Arizona Vital Statistics (Phoenix, Ariz. : 1983).*

US
**BASIC BIBLIOGRAPHIES FOR EDUCATORS IN HEALTH.** Nov. 1969-. English. ir. Continuing Educ Comm Soc Pub, 2131 Univ Avenue, Acheson Bldg, Berkeley CA 94704.

GW/0176-2575
**BIBLIOGRAPHIE PADAGOGIK. REIHE B, BUCHER.** **VFOAT** Bucher; Educational Bibliography. Reihe B, Books; Books. (1982)-. German (German). an. K.G. Saur Verlag KG, A Reed Reference Publishing Company, Part of Reed International PLC, Ortlerstrasse 8, D 81373 Munich Germany. **Tel** 011 49 89 769020, FAX 011 49 89 76902150, telex 5212067-SAUR-D. **LC** Z5813; .B425; LB14.6. ***Continues in part*** *Bibliographie Padagogik, 0523-2678.*

US/0882-8989
**BIBLIOGRAPHY OF PUBLICATIONS RESULTING FROM NCHSR EXTRAMURAL RESEARCH.** (BIBLIOGRAPHY OF PUBLICATIONS RESULTING FROM NCHSR EXTRAMURAL RESEARCH / NATIONAL CENTER FOR HEALTH SERVICES RESEARCH.). [Bibliogr. publ. resulting NCHSR extramur. res.]. **VAT** Bibliography of Publications Resulting from National Center for Health Services Research Extramural Research. Bibliography. English. US Department of Health and Human Services, 200 Independence Avenue Southwest, Washington DC 20201. **LC** Z6673.6.U6; B52; RA440.85. **DD** 016.3621/0973.

US
**BIOGRAPHICAL DIRECTORY OF THE AMERICAN PUBLIC HEALTH ASSOCIATION.** **Main/Corp** American Public Health Association. (1979)-. Directory. English. ir. $54.50 US and Canada. R R Bowker, A Reed Reference Publishing Company, Part of Reed International PLC, PO Box 31, 121 Chanlon Drive, New Providence NJ 07974. **Tel** (908)464-6800, (800)521-8110, FAX (908)665-6688, telex 138-755. **LC** RA424.4; .A472a. **DD** 614/.092/2; B.

FR/0335-7414
**BULLETIN BIBLIOGRAPHIQUE.** No. 714- Jan. 12, 1973-. Bulletin. French. **NLM** Z 7164.S66 B936. ***Continues*** *Bulletin Bibliographique Hebdomadaire, 0335-7406.*

US
**CALIFORNIA CHILDREN SERVICES INFORMATION AND STATISTICS FOR FISCAL YEARS ... .** English. California Department of Health Services, B A Myers Director, 714 P Street, Room 1494, Sacramento CA 95814. **Tel** (916)445-1010. **LC** RJ102.5.C2; C36. **DD** 362.1/9892/0009794.

US/0278-4912
**CATALOG OF PUBLICATIONS OF THE NATIONAL CENTER FOR HEALTH STATISTICS.** **Main/Corp** National Center for Health Statistics (U.S.). 1980-. Catalog. English. an. National Center for Health Statistics, 6525 Belcrest Road, Hyattsville MD 20782. **Tel** (301)436-8500. **LC** Z7553.M43; N35A; RA407.3. **DD** 016.3621/0973/021. ***Continues*** *Current Listing and Topical Index to the Vital and Health Statistics Series, 0092-7287.*

US/0145-1294
**CUMULATED ANNOTATIONS / CLEARINGHOUSE ON HEALTH INDEXES.** **Added/Corp** Clearinghouse on Health Indexes (U.S.) National Center for Health Statistics (U.S.). (Oct. 1973/Dec. 1974)-. English. an. National Center for Health Statistics, 6525 Belcrest Road, Hyattsville MD 20782. **Tel** (301)436-8500. **LC** Z6673; .C83; RA407. **DD** 016.3621. **NLM** ZWA 4 C971.

GW/0172-3723
**DATEN DES GESUNDHEITSWESENS.** **Main/Corp** Germany (West). Bundesministerium fuer Jugend, Familie und Gesundheit. **Added/Corp** Germany (West). Bundesministerium fuer Jugend, Familie und Gesundheit. Germany (West). Bundesministerium fuer Jugend, Familie, Frauen und Gesundheit. Aug. (1977)-. Statistical Publication. German. an. DM57.00. Der Bundesminister fuer Gesundheil, 53708 Bonn Germany. **Tel** 011 49 947 4900. **LC** RA407.5.G4; G45b. **Bk Rev**, (Qty: 12). **Acid Free. Circ:** 3,000 (ctrl).
**Desc:** A collection of German health statistics.

AT/0814-8155
**DEATHS, TASMANIA.** See Population Studies-Abstracting, Bibliographies and Statistics.

US
**FILM AND PAMPHLET CATALOG.**
**Main/Corp** Kansas. Bureau of Health Education. Catalog. English. Kansas Department of Health and Environment, Office of Research and Analysis, 109 Southwest 9th Street, Suite 400A, Topeka KS 66612-2219. **Tel** (913)296-0632. **LC** RA440.5; .K3. **DD** 016.61. ***Continues*** *Film and Pamphlet Catalog.*

GW
**GESUNDHEITSWESEN IN NORDRHEIN-WESTFALEN, DAS.**
**Main/Corp** North Rhine-Westphalia (Germany). Landesamt fur Datenverarbeitung und Statistik. German. an. DM22.50. Landesamt fuer Datenverarbeitung und Statistik Nordrhein-Westfalen, Postfach 101105, 40002 Duesseldorf Germany. **Tel** (0211)944901, FAX (0211)442006, telex 8586654 LDST D. **LC** HA1320.N6; A32 subser; RA407.5.G. **Circ:** 300.
**Desc:** Statistical returns on public health.

US/0892-9351
**HEALTH AND SAFETY SCIENCE ABSTRACTS.** [Health saf. sci. abstr.]. **Added/Corp** Cambridge Scientific Abstracts, Inc. University of Southern California. Institute of Safety and Systems Management. Vol. 14, No. 1 (Feb. 1987)-. Abstracting/Indexing Service. English. qt (plus annual index). $695.00 US; $745.00 other. Cambridge Scientific Abstracts, 7200 Wisconsin Avenue, #601, Bethesda MD 20814-4823. **Tel** (301)961-6750, (800)843-7751, FAX (301)961-6720. **ED** Roberta Gorinson. **LC** HD7260; .S339. **DD** 614. **NLM** ZWA 485; S128. Index available. cum. index. available on an online database from Pollution and Toxicology Database; available on CD-ROM (POLTOX) from Cambridge Scientific Abstracts; available on microfiche; available on magnetic tape; available via Internet (to the current year's abstracts and five-year backfiles) from Cambridge Scientific Abstracts. ***Continues*** *Safety Science Abstracts Journal, 0160-1342.*
**Desc:** Abstracts journal articles dealing with industrial, occupational, transportation, aviation, and aerospace. Also deals with environmental and ecological and medical safety.

AT
**HEALTH AND WELFARE ESTABLISHMENTS / QUEENSLAND.**
**Added/Corp** Australian Bureau of Statistics. Queensland Office. **VFOAT** Health and Welfare Establishments, Queensland. (1977/1978)-. English. an. 14.00Aus$. Australian Bureau of Statistics, PO Box 10, Belconnen Australian Capital Territory, 2616 Australia. **Tel** 011 61 6 2527911, FAX 011 61 6 2516009. **NLM** W2; KA8.1.Q3 A2h.
**Desc:** Types of residential health and welfare establishments: number, size, activities, income, operating expenditure, staff and staff/patient ratios, nature of treatment by condition, and more.

US/0883-3699
**HEALTH CARE EXPENDITURES IN KANSAS.** 1966-1976-. English. an. Kansas Department of Health and Environment, Office of Research and Analysis, 109 Southwest 9th Street, Suite 400A, Topeka KS 66612-2219. **Tel** (913)296-0632. **LC** RA410.54.K2; H43. **DD** 338.4/33621/0981021.
**Desc:** Estimated total expenditures are examined both in terms of the types of services which are purchased and the sources of the funds used to purchase them.

CN/1180-3096
**HEALTH REPORTS. SUPPLEMENT. DEATHS.** (HEALTH REPORTS. SUPPLEMENT. DEATHS / STATISTICS CANADA, CANADIAN CENTRE FOR HEALTH INFORMATION.). [Health rep., Suppl., Deaths]. **Added/Corp** Canadian Centre for Health Information. **VFOAT** Deaths; Deces; Rapports sur la Sante. Deces. (1988)-. English (French). an. 20.00Can$ Canada; $24.00 US; $28.00 other. Statistics Canada, Publications Sales & Services, Main Building Room 1710, Ottawa Ontario K1A 0T6 Canada. **Tel** (613)951-5078, (800)267-6677, FAX (613)951-1584, telex 053-3585. **LC** HB1359; .H4. **DD** 304.6/4/0971021. ***Continues in part*** *Births and Deaths, Vital Statistics, Volume I., 0825-2971.*

IE
**HEALTH STATISTICS (DUBLIN, IRELAND).** (HEALTH STATISTICS.). English. an. 40p. Government Publications, 4 5 Harcourt Road, Dublin 2 Ireland. **Tel** 011 353 1 6613111 Ext.4005. **LC** RA273; .H4. **DD** 614.4/2417/021. **Circ:** 1,000.

DK/0900-7962
**HEALTH STATISTICS IN THE NORDIC COUNTRIES / HELSESTATISTIKK I DE NORDISKE LAND / NOMESKO.** **Added/Corp** NOMESCO. **VFOAT** Helsestatistikk i de Nordiske Land; Helsestatistik for de Nordiske Lande. (1978)-. English (Norwegian). an. Kr200.00. Nordic Medical Statistical Committee (NOMESCO), Nordisk Statistisk Sekretariat, Sejrogade 11, DK-2100 Kobenhavn 0 Denmark. **Tel** 45 39 17 39 91, FAX 45 31 18 48 01. **ED** Johannes Nielsen. **LC** RA407.5.S34; H4. **DD** 362.1/0948. **NLM** W2; GA1 N8h. **Circ:** 1,200. available on microfilm from CIS / Congressional Information Service, Inc. Documents available.
**Desc:** Provides health statistical data collected from the Nordic countries, with tables and definitions in English. Also gives description of organization of health services and patient's payment.

US/0147-0949
**HEALTH STATISTICS PLAN.** **Main/Corp** United States. Dept. of Health, Education, and Welfare. (19??)-. English. an. US Department of Health and Human Services, 200 Independence Avenue Southwest, Washington DC 20201. **LC** RA407.3; .U53a. **DD** 353.008/41. **NLM** W2 A H3H.

NZ/0548-9938
**HOSPITAL AND SELECTED MORBIDITY DATA.** [Hosp. sel. morb. data]. **Main/Corp** National Health Statistics Centre (N.Z.). 1971-. English. an. 17.00NZ$. National Health Statistics, PO Box 5013, Wellington New Zealand. **Tel** 844-167, telex NZ 3571. **LC** RA407.5.N4. **DD** 312/.3/09931. **NLM** W2 KN4 D4HB. **Ad Acc. Circ:** 450 (ctrl). ***Continues in part*** *Medical Statistics Report, 0112-3548.*
**Desc:** Statistics of causes of admission (morbidity) into New Zealand hospitals. Includes length of stay and number of operations.

NZ
**INDEX OF STATISTICS PUBLISHED BY THE DEPARTMENT OF HEALTH / NATIONAL HEALTH STATISTICS CENTRE, DEPARTMENT OF HEALTH (NEW ZEALAND).** **Main/Corp** National Health Statistics Centre (N.Z.). English. The Chief Health Statistician of the National Health Statistics Centre, PO Box 6314, Wellington New Zealand. **Tel** 844-167, telex 3571. **LC** Z7553.M43; N37A; RA407.5.N4. **DD** 312/.09931. **Ad Acc.** ctrl circ.

US/0278-6877
**MENTAL HEALTH SERVICE SYSTEM REPORTS. SERIES CN, MENTAL HEALTH NATIONAL STATISTICS.** (MENTAL HEALTH SERVICE SYSTEM REPORTS. SERIES CN, MENTAL HEALTH NATIONAL STATISTICS / U.S. DEPARTMENT OF HEALTH AND HUMAN SERVICES, PUBLIC HEALTH SERVICE, ALCOHOL, DRUG ABUSE, AND MENTAL HEALTH ADMINISTRATION.). [Ment. health serv. syst. rep., Ser. CN, ment. health natl. stat.]. **VFOAT** Mental Health National Statistics. No. 1-. Monographic series. English. Price varies per volume. National Institute of Mental Health, 9000 Rockville Pike, Rockville MD 20892. **Tel** (301)496-9291. **NLM** W1 ME928EN.

US/0196-562X
**MENTAL HEALTH STATISTICS (JEFFERSON CITY).** (MENTAL HEALTH STATISTICS.). **Main/Corp** Missouri. Dept. of Mental Health. 1975/76-. English. an. Missouri Department of Mental Health, 2002 Missouri Boulevard, Jefferson City MO 65101. **LC** RA790.65.M8. **DD** 362.2/09778. **NLM** W2 AM8 D35M.

US/0098-4949
**METHODOLOGY REPORTS.** (MENTAL HEALTH STATISTICS SERIES.). English. National Institute of Mental Health, 9000 Rockville Pike, Rockville MD 20892. **Tel** (301)496-9291. **LC** RA790.6; .M45. **DD** 362.2/0973.

US/0539-7413
**MICHIGAN HEALTH STATISTICS.**
**Main/Corp** Center for Health Statistics (Michigan). **Added/Corp** Michigan. Division of Disease Control, Records and Statistics. Center for Health Statistics (Michigan). **VFOAT** Annual Statistical Report. (1951)-. English. an. $11.00. Center for Health Statistics / Michigan, 3500 North Logan Street, Lansing MI 48909. **Tel** (517)335-8705. **LC** RA407.4.M5; A32. **DD** 312/.09774. ***Continues*** *Michigan Public Health Statistics.*

US/0094-5641
**MINNESOTA HEALTH STATISTICS.**
**Added/Corp** Minnesota Center for Health Statistics. Minnesota. Health Statistics Section. (1972)-. English. an. Free. Minnesota Department of Health, 717 Southeast Delaware Street, Minneapolis MN 55440. **Tel** (612)623-5000. **LC** RA407.4.M6; M55a. **DD** 362.1/09776/021. **NLM** W2 AM6 S6MI. available on microfiche (from Minnesota State Document Depository System). ***Continues*** *Minnesota Vital Statistics.*

US/0090-7456
**MONTHLY STATISTICAL SUMMARY REPORT - STATE OF OHIO, DEPARTMENT OF MENTAL HEALTH AND MENTAL RETARDATION, DIVISION OF BUSINESS ADMINISTRATION, BUREAU OF STATISTICS.** (MONTHLY STATISTICAL SUMMARY REPORT - STATE OF OHIO, DEPARTMENT OF MENTAL HEALTH AND MENTAL RETARDATION.). **Main/Corp** Ohio. Dept. of Mental Health and Mental Retardation. Bureau of Statistics. (May 1972)-. Statistical Publication. English. Twelve times a year. Free. Ohio Mental Health & Mental Retardation Department, Department of Statistics Bureau, Columbus OH 43215. **Tel** (614)466-2596. **NLM** W2 AO3 D48m. ***Continues*** *Monthly Statistical Summary Report - State of Ohio, Department of Mental Hygiene and Correction, Division of Business, Bureau of Statistics, 0090-7464.*

US/0449-7732
**MONTHLY SUMMARY OF VITAL STATISTICS.** **Main/Corp** Kansas. Bureau of Registration and Health Statistics. V. 1- Jan. 1979-. English. mo. Kansas Department of Health and Environment, Office of Research and Analysis, 109 Southwest 9th Street, Suite 400A, Topeka KS 66612-2219. **Tel** (913)296-0632. ***Continues*** *Monthly Summary of Vital Statistics, 0449-7732.*

US
**NATIONAL COMMITTEE ON VITAL AND HEALTH STATISTICS : [SUMMARY REPORT], THE.** **Main/Corp** United States. National Committee on Vital and Health Statistics. **Added/Corp** National Center for Health Statistics (U.S.). Fiscal Years 1979 and 1980-. English. National Center for Health Statistics, 6525 Belcrest Road, Hyattsville MD 20782. **Tel** (301)436-8500. **LC** HA37; .U1758a. **DD** 362.1/0973/021. **NLM** W2 A N149A. ***Continues*** *Annual Report of the United States National Committee on Vital and Health Statistics.*

PK
**NATIONAL HEALTH SURVEY / FEDERAL BUREAU OF STATISTICS, STATISTICS DIVISION, GOVERNMENT OF PAKISTAN.** (1982/83)-. English. Rs30.00. NGM Communication, PO Box 2627, Karachi 75900 Pakistan. **Tel** 011 92 21 428625. **LC** RA407.5.P2; N38. **DD** 362.1/09549/1021.

US/0027-6650
**NIH PUBLICATIONS LIST.** (NIH PUBLICATIONS LIST / NATIONAL INSTITUTES OF HEALTH, OFFICE OF COMMUNICATIONS, OD, DIVISION OF PUBLIC INFORMATION, EDITORIAL OPERATIONS BRANCH.). **Main/Corp** National Institutes of Health (U.S.). Editorial Operations Branch. **VFOAT** N.I.H. Publications List. **VAT** National Institutes of Health Publications List. Began with July 1974. English. an. NIH Office of the Director, Division of Public Information, Editorial Operations Branch, Bethesda MD 20014. **LC** Z6660; .U5A; RA11. **DD** 016.61. ***Continues*** *NIH Publications List, 0027-6650.*

US/0098-5651
**OKLAHOMA HEALTH STATISTICS.** [Okla. health stat.]. **Main/Corp** Oklahoma. Public Health Statistics Division. (19??)-. English. an. Free. Oklahoma State Department of Health, 1000 Northeast 10th Street, Oklahoma City OK 73117. **Tel** (405)271-4200, (405)271-5600, FAX (405)271-7339. **LC** RA407.4.O6; O36a. **DD** 312/.09766. ***Continues*** *Oklahoma. State Dept. of Health. Public Health Statistics, State of Oklahoma, 0099-118X.*

US
**OREGON VITAL STATISTICS REPORT FOR CALENDAR YEAR.** **VFOAT** Oregon Vital Statistics. 1985-. English. an. Oregon State Health Division, Vital Statistics Section, Portland OR 97201. **Tel** (503)229-5897. **LC** RA407.4.O7; O75A. **DD** 304.6/09795/021. **Circ:** 1,000. ***Continues*** *Oregon Public Health Statistics Report for Calendar Year ... .*

II
**POCKET BOOK OF HEALTH STATISTICS.** **Main/Corp** India (Republic). Central Bureau of Health Intelligence. English. Central Bureau of Health Intelligence, Directorate General of Health Services, Nirman Bhavan, New Delhi 110011 India. **Tel** 3019544. **LC** RA407.5.I4; I5A. **DD** 312./0954.

US/0270-3114
**PREVENTION IN HUMAN SERVICES.**
[Prev. hum. serv.]. Vol. 1 No. 1 (Fall 1981)-. Abstracting/Indexing Service. English. sa. $165.00 US; $231.00 other. The Haworth Press Inc, 10 Alice Street, Binghamton NY 13904-1580. **Tel** (607)722-5857, (800)3-HAWORTH, FAX (607)722-1424. **ED** Robert Hess (editor's address: Bureau of Mental Health, 450 West

State, Boise, ID 83720). **LC** RA421; .P683. **DD** 362.1. **NLM** W1 PR497. **CODEN** PHSEDF. **Bk Rev. Ad Acc. Pr Rev. Acid Free. Circ:** 233. available on microfilm and microfiche from University Microfilms International (UMI). Documents available from BIOSIS Document Express, Haworth Document Delivery Service. ***Continues*** *Community Mental Health Review, 0363-1605.*
**Desc:** Devoted entirely to the application of the philosophy of prevention in mental health and other human services.
**Ind/Abst** Abstr. Res. Pastor. Care Couns. (19??-); Biol. Abstr.; Child Dev. Abstr. Bibliogr.; EMBASE; Hospit. Health Admin. Index (1988-); Psychol. Abstr. (1981-); PsycINFO; PsycLit; Ref. Z.; Soc. Plann. Policy Dev. Abstr.; Soc. Work Abstr. [Select. Cov.]; Sociol. Abstr.

US/0148-5555
**PUBLIC HEALTH STATISTICS (NEW ORLEANS).** (PUBLIC HEALTH STATISTICS.). **Main/Corp** Louisiana. Office of Public Health Statistics. Periodical. English. qt. E H Atkins Statistical Officer, PO Box 60630, New Orleans LA 70160. **LC** RA74; .B125. **DD** 312/.09763. **NLM** W2 AL6 D41L. ***Continues*** *Public Health Statistics, 0148-5555.*

NZ
**PUBLICATIONS INDEX / NATIONAL HEALTH STATISTICS CENTRE. Main/Corp** National Health Statistics Centre (N.Z.). English. be. 5.00NZ$ New Zealand; $10.00 US. The Chief Health Statistician of the National Health Statistics Centre, PO Box 6314, Wellington New Zealand. **Tel** 844-167, telex 3571. **LC** Z6673.6.N45; N38A; RA373. **DD** 016.3621/09931/021. Index available. **Ad Acc. Circ:** 400 (ctrl).
**Desc:** A comprehensive list of data published by the Department of Health in alphabetical order by subject area.

US/0098-812X
**PUBLICATIONS REPORT - NATIONAL CENTER FOR HEALTH SERVICES RESEARCH AND DEVELOPMENT. Main/Corp** National Center for Health Services Research and Development. No. 1 (1970)-. English. an. National Center for Health Services, Rockville MD 20852. **LC** Z6675.E2; N37a; RA395.A3. **DD** 362.1/0973. **NLM** ZWA 100 N277P.

US
**REPORT OF MEDICAL ASSISTANCE & COUNTY INDIGENT STATISTICS. VFOAT** Report of Medical Assistance and County Indigent Statistics; Medical Assistance. FY 1979-80-. English. an. Free. Bureau of Cost Management, Division of Health Care Financing and Standards, PO Box 2500, Salt Lake City UT 84110. **Tel** (801)533-7329. **LC** HD7102.U5; U88. **DD** 362.1/04252/09792. **Circ:** 500. ***Continues*** *Utah Report of Medicaid Statistics, 0193-4252.*
**Desc:** Expenditure and program analysis of public medical assistance programs in Utah.

US/0147-5614
**REPORT OF VITAL STATISTICS FOR OHIO. Main/Corp** Ohio. Division of Vital Statistics. **VFOAT** Vital Statistics. English. an. Ohio Department of Health, 246 North High Street, Columbus OH 43266. **Tel** (614)466-2253, FAX (614)644-8526. **LC** HA571; .A52. **DD** 312/.09771. ***Continues*** *Ohio. Dept. of Health. Report of Vital Statistics.*

CN/0824-3336
**RISK ABSTRACTS.** [Risk abstr.]. **Added/Corp** University of Waterloo. Institute for Risk Research. Vol. 1, No. 1 (Jan. 1984)-. Abstracting/Indexing Service. English. qt (4 issues). $225.00 US; $235.00 other. Cambridge Scientific Abstracts, 7200 Wisconsin Avenue, #601, Bethesda MD 20814-4823. **Tel** (301)961-6750, (800)843-7751, FAX (301)961-6720. **ED** N. C. Lind. **LC** HD61; .R554. **DD** 368/.005. Index available. cum. index. **Bk Rev. Circ:** 250. available on magnetic tape; available via Internet (to the current year's abstracts and five-year backfiles) from Cambridge Scientific Abstracts.
**Desc:** Deals with risks from technology, industry, and other sources, to health and the environment, including social and psychological aspects of risk.

JA
**SEAMIC HEALTH STATISTICS. See** Population Studies-Abstracting, Bibliographies and Statistics.

FR
**SOLIDARITE, SANTE. ETUDES STATISTIQUES / MINISTERE DES AFFAIRES SOCIALES ET DE LA SOLIDARITE NATIONALE. Added/Corp** France. Ministere des Affaires Sociales et de la Solidarite Nationale. Service des Statistiques, des Etudes et des Systemes d'Information. Nos. 1-2 (Jan./Feb., April 1984)-. Periodical. French. qt. $58.00. Masson Editeur, Box Postale 22, 41353 Vineuil 16 France. **Tel** 011 33 54 438994. **(Subscription address:** 7A Boulevard de Perolles, CH-1701 Fribourg Switzerland**) LC** RA407.5.F7; B85. **DD** 362.1/0944/021. **NLM** W2; GF7 M5sc. ***Formed by the union of*** *Sante, Securite Sociale, 0338-3423* ***and*** *Economie et Sante.*

US/0147-6807
**STATISTICAL AND ACCOUNTING REPORT.** [Stat. account. rep.]. **Main/Corp** Maryland. Dept. of Health and Mental Hygiene. Laboratories Administration. **VFOAT** Report of Statistical and Cost Accounting of Laboratory Examinations for the Laboratories Administration; Statistical and Accounting Report of Laboratories Examinations, Laboratories Administration. (1973)-. Statistical Publication. English. an. Maryland Department of Health and Mental Hygiene, 201 West Preston Street, Baltimore MD 21201. **Tel** (410)225-6500. **LC** RA4283.M37; M37A. **DD** 353.9/752/007231. ***Continues*** *Statistical and Cost Accounting Report / Maryland Dept. of Health and Mental Hygiene. Laboratories and Research Administration, 0161-2255.*

●US
**STATISTICAL NEWS. Main/Corp** Pennsylvania. State Center for Health Statistics and Research. **Added/Corp** Pennsylvania. Dept. of Health. Vol.16, No.5 (Sept. 1993)-. Statistical Publication. English. bm. Health Data Center, Pennsylvania Department of Health, PO Box 90, Harrisburg PA 17108. **Tel** (717)783-2548. ***Continues*** *Statistical News from The Health Data Center.*

US/0098-2725
**SUMMARY OF GENERAL STATISTICS.** ***Title Change.*** **Main/Corp** Virginia. Dept. of Mental Health and Mental Retardation. (19??)-(199?). Statistical Publication. English. Virginia Department of Mental Health and Mental Retardation, PO Box 1797, Richmond VA 23214. **LC** RC445; .V7415a. **DD** 362.2. ***Continued by*** *Annual Statistical Report (Richmond, Va.).*

US/0161-2557
**UNITED STATES UNDERWATER FATALITY STATISTICS.** English. an. US Department of Commerce / National Oceanic & Atmospheric Administration NOAA, 6010 Executive Boulevard, Washington Science Center, Building 5, Rockville MD 20852. **Tel** (202)482-6090, FAX (202)482-3154. **LC** RC1220.D5; S33. **DD** 614.8/1.

GW
**VERZEICHNIS DER WISSENSCHAFTLICHEN VEROFFENTLICHUNGEN. Main/Corp** Germany (West). Bundesgesundheitsamt. Institut fur Wasser-, Boden- und Lufthygiene, Forschungsstatte fur Allgemeine Hygiene und Gesundheitstechnik. German. **LC** Z6673; .B418A.

CN/0707-7548
**VITAL STATISTICS ANNUAL REVIEW. Main/Corp** Alberta. Vital Statistics Division. 1975/76-. English. an. Alberta Bureau of Vital Statistics, 21st Floor Park Square 10001, Edmonton Alberta T5J 3B6 Canada. **LC** RA185.A5; A3. **DD** 312/.097123. ***Continues*** *Annual Report of the Department of Health Including Vital Statistics Division, 0702-9500.*

SZ/0250-3794
**WORLD HEALTH STATISTICS ANNUAL. Added/Corp** World Health Organization. **VFOAT** Annuaire de Statistiques Sanitaires Mondiales. (1962)-. English (French). an. $90.00 (last edition published). World Health Organization, Distribution and Sales, 20 Avenue Appia, CH-1211 Geneva 27 Switzerland. **Tel** 011 41 22 7912111, FAX 011 41 22 7880401. **LC** RA651; .A485. **DD** 312/.2/05. **NLM** W2 MW6 W9S. ***Continues*** *Statistiques Epidemiologiques et Demographiques Annuelles.*
**Desc:** Complete source of vital statistics, life tables and changing morbidity rates presented for virtually every country in the world.

SZ/0379-8070
**WORLD HEALTH STATISTICS QUARTERLY.** [World health stat. q.]. **Main/Corp** World Health Organization. **Added/Corp** World Health Organization. Rapport Trimestriel de Statistiques Sanitaires Mondiales. **VFOAT** Rapport Trimestriel de Statistiques Sanitaires Mondiales. Vol. 31 (1978)-. English (French). qt. $88.00 Surface Mail; $97.00 (airmail) Europe; $103.00 (airmail) other. World Health Organization, Distribution and Sales, 20 Avenue Appia, CH-1211 Geneva 27 Switzerland. **Tel** 011 41 22 7912111, FAX 011 41 22 7880401. **LC** RA651; .W65. **DD** 312/.3/05. **NLM** W2 MW6 W9RA. **CODEN** WHSQDQ. Documents available from BIOSIS Document Express, Documents on Demand. ***Continues*** *World Health Statistics Report, 0043-8510.*
**Desc:** Provides health guidance based on what can be learned when statistical data, drawn from global sources are submitted to appropriate analysis. Each issue focuses on a selected theme or topic of current public health interest. Analysis may concentrate on a particular disease, risk factor, socioeconomic indicator, or risk group as evaluated at country, regional or global levels.
**Ind/Abst** Biol. Abstr. (1986-); EMBASE; Environ. Abstr.; Index Med.; Popul. Index; Trop. Dis. Bull.

## PUBLISHING

CN/0700-3579
**A C P NEWSLETTER. Main/Corp** Association of Canadian Publishers. Vol. 4, No. 3 (April 1976)-. Newsletter. English. Association of Canadian Publishers, 3rd Floor, 70 the Esplanade, Toronto Ontario M5E 1R2. **DD** 070.5/0971.

CN/0705-6621
**A C P NOTEBOOK. Main/Corp** Association of Canadian Publishers. **VAT** Association of Canadian Publishers Notebook. No. 10 (March 1978)-. Periodical. English. mo. Free. 70 The Esplanade/3rd Floor, Toronto Ontario M5E 1R2 Canada. **ED** Hamish Cameron. **DD** 070.5/0971. ctrl circ. ***Continues*** *Association of Canadian Publishers Notebook, 0705-6613.*
**Desc:** Newsletter of the Association Canadian Publishers.

US/0160-6999
**AADE EDITORS' JOURNAL.** [AADE ed. j.]. **Added/Corp** American Association of Dental Editors. **VFOAT** AADE Journal. **VAT** American Association of Dental Editors Editors' Journal. Vol. 1, (1974)-. Periodical. English. Four times a year (Mar., June, Sept., Dec.). $25.00. American Association of Dental Editors, 1100 Lake Street, Suite 240, Oak Park IL 60301. **Tel** (708)445-0320, FAX 708445-0321. **ED** Joanna Carey (phone: (708)445-0322). **NLM** W1 A102BJ. **Circ:** 325 (ctrl). ***Formed by the union of*** *Bulletin - American Association of Dental Editors, 0569-2555* ***and*** *Transactions - American Association of Dental Editors.*
**Desc:** News of members, and articles on all aspects of editing and publishing.
**Ind/Abst** Index Dent. Lit.

US/1070-700X
**ABAA NEWSLETTER, THE.** [ABAA newsl.]. **Added/Corp** Antiquarian Booksellers Association of America. **VAT** Antiquarian Booksellers Association of America Newsletter. Vol. 1, No. 1 (Nov. 1989)-. Periodical. English. Four times a year. $20.00 US; $25.00 Canada & Mexico; $32.00 others. Antiquarian Booksellers Association AM, 50 Rockefeller Plaza, New York NY 10020. **Tel** (212)757-9395. **ED** R. Rulon-Miller, (editor's address: 400 Summit Avenue, St Paul, MN 55102, phone: (612)290-0700). **LC** IN PROCESS. **DD** 380.

UK/0306-0322
**AFRICAN BOOK PUBLISHING RECORD, THE.** [Afr. book publ. rec.]. Vol. 1 (Jan. 1975)-. Periodical. English (French). qt. $165.00. Bowker Saur Ltd., A Reed Reference Publishing Company, Part of Reed International PLC, 59-60 Grosvenor Street, London WIX 9DA England. **Tel** 011 44 71 4935841, FAX 011 44 71 4991590. **(Subscription address:** World-Wide Subscription Services, Unit 4, Gibbs Reed Farm Pashley Road, Ticehurst TN5 7HE England.**) LC** Z465.7; .A35. **DD** 070.5/73/096. **[CCC].** Index available. cum. index. **Bk Rev. Ad Acc. Circ:** 1,000.
**Desc:** Provides bibliographic coverage of new and forthcoming African publications in English and French and significant new titles in the African languages. Provides a buying and acquisitions tool for librarians and booksellers, and serves as a medium of communication between the African book trade activities and developments.
**Ind/Abst** Ethnoarts Index (19??-); MLA Int. Bibl. Books Artic. Mod. Lang. Lit. (19??-).

●UK
**AFRICAN PUBLISHERS NETWORKING DIRECTORY AND NAMES & NUMBERS. VFOAT** African Publishers Networking Directory. (1993/1994)-. Directory. English (French). **LC** Z465.5; .A56.

US/1043-2094
**AGAINST THE GRAIN (CHARLESTON, S.C.). See** Library and Information Sciences.

US/1040-449X
**AGGS NEWS VIEWS.** [AGGS news views]. **VFOAT** News Views. **VAT** American Gloxinia and Gesneriad Society News Views. Vol. 1, No. 1 (Autumn 1988)-. Periodical. English. qt. $10.00 (society members), $14.00 (non-members). American Gloxinia and Gesneriad Society, 128 West 58th Street, New York NY 10019. **Tel** (413)323-6661. **DD** 070.

LY
**AL-NASHIR AL-ARABI. Added/Corp** Ittihad Al-Nashirin Al-Arab. **VFOAT** Arab Publisher. (1983)-. Periodical. Arabic. PO Box 4607, Tarabulus Libya. **Tel** 37581. **ED** Khalifa Telisi. **LC** Z464.A65; N38. **Bk Rev. Ad Acc.**

UK
**ALBION.** **See** Printing Industry.

CN/0824-5908
**AL'MANAKH VYDAVNYTSTVA "TRYZUB".** [Alm. vidav. Trizub]. **VFOAT** Almanac of Trident Press. (1976)-. Ukrainian (English). an. 30.00Can$ Canada; 36.00Can$ other. Trident Press Ltd., 842 Main Street, Winnipeg Manitoba R2W 3N8 Canada. **Tel** (204)589-5871, FAX (204)586-3618. **(Subscription address:** PO Box 3626, Station B, Winnipeg Manitoba R2W 3N8 Canada**) ED** P. Danyluk, Y. Mokriy and R. Romanovich. **DD** 057/.91. **Bk Rev**. **Ad Acc. Circ:** 4,100 (ctrl). available on diskette. ***Continues*** *Kalendar-Al'Manakh Vydavnytstva Tryzub, 0319-5678.*
**Desc:** General interest - special days or events in the Ukrainian community in Canada and abroad.

US/0002-7707
**AMERICAN BOOK PUBLISHING RECORD.** (AMERICAN BOOK PUBLISHING RECORD. ABPR CUMULATIVE.). [Am. book publ. rec.]. **Added/Corp** R.R. Bowker Company. Data Services Division. R.R. Bowker Company. Publications Systems Dept. **VFOAT** ABPR Cumulative. (1984)-. English. an. Price varies per volume. R R Bowker, A Reed Reference Publishing Company, Part of Reed International PLC, PO Box 31, 121 Chanlon Drive, New Providence NJ 07974. **Tel** (908)464-6800, (800)521-8110, FAX (908)665-6688, telex 138-755. **LC** Z1201; .A52. **DD** 015.73. **[CCC].** ***Continues*** *American Book Publishing Record. BPR Cumulative, 0002-7707.*
**Desc:** Contains more than 490,000 cataloged entries for books published or distributed in the US which are arranged in Dewey sequence, with separate sections for adult and juvenile fiction.

US/0002-7707
**AMERICAN BOOK PUBLISHING RECORD.** [Am. book publ. rec.]. **Added/Corp** R.R. Bowker Company. **VFOAT** BPR; ABPR. Vol. 1 (Feb. 1960)-. Periodical. English. mo. $225.00 US; $250.00 other. R R Bowker, A Reed Reference Publishing Company, Part of Reed International PLC, PO Box 31, 121 Chanlon Drive, New Providence NJ 07974. **Tel** (908)464-6800, (800)521-8110, FAX (908)665-6688, telex 138-755. **LC** Z1219; .A515. **DD** 015. **NLM** Z 1219 A512. **[CCC].** available on microfilm and microfiche from University Microfilms International (UMI).
**Ind/Abst** Abstr. Bull. Inst. Pap. Sci. Tech.; Annu. Bibliogr. Engl. Lang. Lit.

US/1054-7479
**AMERICAN PERIODICALS : A JOURNAL OF HISTORY, CRITICISM, AND BIBLIOGRAPHY.** [Am. period.]. **Added/Corp** University of North Texas. Dept. of English. Research Society for American Periodicals. Vol. 1, No. 1 (Fall 1991)- Vol. 3 (1993)-. Bibliography. English. an (Fall). $15.00 one year; $28.00 two year. University of North Texas Press, PO Box 13856, Denton TX 76203. **Tel** (817)565-2124, FAX (817)369-8770. **ED** James T. and F. Tanner P.O. Box 5096, Denton, TX 76203-5096, (817)565-2134. **LC** PN4877; .A485. **DD** 051. **Bk Rev**, (Qty: 6-10). **Ad Acc, Adv Mgr:** Jane Tanner, **Tel** (817)565-2124. **Circ:** 500.
**Ind/Abst** Am. Hist. Life (1991-).

CN/0844-465X
**ANNUAIRE DES EDITEURS.** [Annu. ed.]. **Added/Corp** Association des Editeurs Canadiens. Association Nationale des Editeurs de Livres. Association des Editeurs de p,eriodiques culturels Quebecois. Societe de Developpement des Periodiques Culturels Quebecois. Association Quebecoise des Presses Universitaires. Societe des Editeurs de Manuels Scolaires du Quebec. (1988)-. French. 10,00 $ le v. **DD** 070.5/025/71. ***Continues*** *Societe de Developpement du Livre et du Periodique. Annuaire, 0820-019X.*
**Desc:** Covers publishers, publishing, and published editions.

US/0276-5349
**ANNUAL REPORT / ASSOCIATION OF AMERICAN PUBLISHERS.** [Annu. rep. - Assoc. Am. Publ.]. **Main/Corp** Association of American Publishers. English. an. Association of American Publishers, Inc., 1 Park Avenue, New York NY 10016. **LC** Z477; .A87A. **DD** 070.5/0973.

GW/0066-4596
**ANSCHRIFTEN DEUTSCHER VERLAGE, BUNDESREPUBLIK DEUTSCHLAND, DDR UND AUS DEM DEUTSCHSPRACHIGEN RAUM OSTERREICH, SCHWEIZ, SOWIE ANSCHRIFTEN WEITERER AUSLANDISCHER VERLAG MIT DEUTSCHEN AUSLIEFERUNGEN.** ***Title Change.*** **VFOAT** Anschriften Deutscher Verlage. (19??). German. Verlag der Schillerbuchhandlung, Hans Banger OHG, Guldenbachstrabe 1, D 50935 Cologne Germany. **Tel** 011 49 221 431641. **LC** Z317; .A57. **DD** 070.5/025/43. ***Continues*** *Anschriften deutscher Verlage und auslËandische Verlage mit deutschen Auslieferungen.* ***Continued by*** *Deutschsprachige Verlage, Deutschland, Osterreich, Schweiz, Sowie Anschriften Weiterer Auslandischer Verlage mit Deutschen Auslieferungen.*

US/1055-2545
**ASSOCIATION PUBLISHING.** [Assoc. publ.]. (1990)-. Periodical. English. mo. $45.95. Elbaum Publishing Corporation, 619 Alexander Road, Princeton NJ 08540. **Tel** (609)987-8868. **DD** 070.
**Ind/Abst** Int. Aerosp. Abstr.

●US/1062-0036
**AT RANDOM.** [At Random]. **Added/Corp** Random House (Firm). Vol. 1, No. 1 (Winter 1992)-. Periodical. English. tq. Free. Random House inc., 400 Hahn Road, Westminster MD 21157. **Tel** (800)726-0600, (800)733-3000, FAX (800)659-2436. **ED** Helen Morris. **LC** Z473.R33; A87. **DD** 070.5/09747/1. **Bk Rev**. **Ad Acc. Circ:** 100,000 (ctrl).
**Desc:** Includes news from the publishing industry and interviews with authors.

AT
**AUSTRALIAN BOOK SCENE.** **Added/Corp** D.W. Thorpe Pty. (19??)-. English. D. W. Thorpe, A Reed Reference Publishing Company, A Subsidiary of Reed International Books Australia, 18 Salmon Street, Port Melbourne, Victoria 3207 Australia. **Tel** 011 61 3 6451511, FAX 011 61 3 6453981, telex 39476. **LC** Z533.7; .I33 Suppl. **DD** 070.5/0994.

CN/0713-0171
**AUTHOR'S NEWS.** [Author's news]. No. 1 (Mar. 1981)-. Periodical. English. mo. $9.00. Author's News, 4340 Coldfall Road, Richmond BC V7C 1P8 Canada. **DD** 808/.02/05.

●US
**BACON'S MAGAZINE DIRECTORY.** 41st Ed. (1993)-. Directory. English. **LC** Z286.P4; B32. ***Continues in part*** *Bacon's Publicity Checker, 0162-3125.*
**Desc:** Directory of American and Canadian periodicals.

●US
**BACON'S NEWSPAPER DIRECTORY.** 41st Ed. (1993)-. Directory. English. **LC** Z286.N48; B32. ***Continues in part*** *Bacon's Publicity Checker, 0162-3125.*
**Desc:** Directory of American and Canadian newspapers.

US/0739-6694
**BEGINNING (IOWA CITY, IOWA).** (BEGINNING.). [Beginning]. Vol. 1, No. 1 & 2 (Spring/Summer 1983)-. Periodical. English. qt. $8.00 individuals, $10.00 institutions. Community Writers Association, PO Box 3071, Iowa City IA 52244.

SW/0430-8417
**BIBLIS.** **See** Publishing-Books and Bookmaking.

US/0747-5438
**BNA ONLINE.** **See** Computers-Online Computing and Information.

NE/0167-4765
**BOEKBLAD.** **Added/Corp** Vereeniging ter Bevordering van de Belangen des Boekhandels (Amsterdam, Netherlands). Volume 147, No. 40 (Oct. 3, 1980)-. Periodical. Dutch. wk. Fl366.98 Netherlands; Fl554.72 other. WYT Uitgeefgroeup, Postbus 6438, 3000 AG Rotterdam Netherlands. **Tel** 011 31 10 4762566, 4255944. **LC** Z2435; .N68. ***Continues*** *Nieuwsblad voor den Boekhandel.*

CN/0381-7261
**BOOK NEWS FOR BOOKSELLERS AND LIBRARIANS.** No. 1- Oct. 1975-. Periodical. English. qt. McGraw Hill Publishing Company, Inc., 1221 Avenue of the Americas, New York NY 10020. **Tel** (212)512-6410, (800)525-5003, FAX (212)512-6111. **DD** 070.5/0971.

CN/1181-6635
**BOOK PUBLISHING (OTTAWA).** (BOOK PUBLISHING / STATISTICS CANADA, EDUCATION, CULTURE AND TOURISM DIVISION.). [Book publ.]. **Added/Corp** Statistics Canada. Education, Culture and Tourism Division. **VFOAT** Edition du Livre. (1988/1989)-. English (French). an. 20.00Can$ Canada; $24.00 US; $28.00 other. Statistics Canada, Publications Sales & Services, Main Building Room 1710, Ottawa Ontario K1A 0T6 Canada. **Tel** (613)951-5078, (800)267-6677, FAX (613)951-1584, telex 053-3585. **DD** 338.4/70705/0971. ***Continues*** *Book Publishing in Canada., 1180-3320.*
**Desc:** Contains data on book publishing and on exclusive distribution of books provided by firms having attained a certain level of revenues.

CN/0836-8619
**BOOK TRADE IN CANADA, WITH WHO'S WHERE, THE.** [Book trade Can. who's where]. **VFOAT** Industrie du Livre au Canada, Avec ou Trouver Qui. 1985-. Periodical. English (French). an. 45.00Can$ Canada; 45.00Can$ US. Ampersand Communications Services Inc, 2766 Sheffield Road, Ottawa Ontario K1B 3V9 Canada. **Tel** (613)749-9998. **ED** Eunice Thorne and Ed Matheson. **DD** 070.5/025/71. **Circ:** 2,500. ***Continues*** *Book Trade in Canada, 0700-5296.*
**Desc:** Standard reference on the book publishing industry in Canada.

IE/0376-6039
**BOOKS IRELAND.** [Books Irel.]. No. 1- Mar. 1976-. English (Irish). mo (except Jan. and Aug.). $22.50 (surface), $40.50 (airmail). Books Ireland, 11 Newgrove Avenue, Dublin 4 Ireland. **Tel** 011 353 1 2692185. **ED** Jeremy Addis. **LC** Z331.7; .B66. **DD** 658.8/09/07057309415. Index available. cum. index. **Bk Rev**. **Ad Acc. Circ:** 5,000.
**Desc:** Ireland's leading magazine of book reviews and news about publishing in Ireland. Available in US from Irish Books and Media.
**Ind/Abst** Libr. Inf. Sci. Abstr.

SZ
**BORSENBLATT FUR DEN DEUTSCHEN BUCHHANDEL.** ***Ceased.*** (1834)-(19??). Periodical. German. ir. Deutscher Judo Verband, Redaktion Ippon Segewaldweg 40, D 12557 Berlin Germany. **Tel** 011 49 711 210770, telex 051 678.

CN/0826-9335
**BRAUCH REPORT ON ELECTRONIC PUBLISHING, THE.** [Brauch rep. electron. pub.]. **VFOAT** Brauch Report. Vol. 1, Issue 1 (March/April 1985)-. Periodical. English. ir. $595.00. Brauch Report on Electronic Publishing, PO Box 1010, Markham Ontario L3P 4C7 Canada. **DD** 070.5/028/54.

BE
**BREPOLS PUBLISHERS NEWSLETTER.** **Main/Corp** Brepols (Firm). Issue 1 (Spring 1981)-. Newsletter. English. ir. Free. Brepols Publishers, Steenweg OP Tielen 68, B-2300 Turnhout Belgium. **Tel** 011 32 14 402500. ctrl circ.

UK
**BRITISH BOOK TRADE DIRECTORY, THE.** (1933)-. Directory. English. J. Whitaker & Sons Ltd, 12 Dyott Street, London WC1A 1DF England. **Tel** 011 44 71 8368911, FAX 011 44 71 836 2909. **LC** Z327; .B85. **DD** 655.505.
**Desc:** Contains section Trade associations.

GW/0007-2761
**BUCH DER ZEIT.** Began publication in 1959. Periodical. German (English). mo. Free. World Amateur Boxing Magazine Editor's Office, P.O.Box 0141, 10321 Berlin/GERMANY. **Tel** (049.30)423 5932, (049.30)423 6766, FAX (049.30)423 5943. **DD** 015. **Bk Rev**. **Ad Acc. Circ:** 12,000 (ctrl). ***Supersedes*** *Deutscher Buch-Kurier.*
**Desc:** An illustrated selection of the most important publications, editors' articles regarding the publishing programme and the authors.

BU
**BULGARSKI KNIGOPIS.** **See** Publishing-Abstracting, Bibliographies and Statistics.

US
**BUSINESS PUBLISHER.** **See** Business.

US/1060-2208
**BUSINESS PUBLISHING (CAROL STREAM, ILL.).** ***Title Change.*** (BUSINESS PUBLISHING.). [Bus. publ.]. Vol. 8, No. 1 (Jan. 1992)-Vol. 9, No. 1 (Jan. 1993). Periodical. English. mo. Hitchcock Publishing Company, 191 South Gary Avenue, Carol Stream IL 60188. **Tel** (708)665-1000. **LC** IN PROCESS; Z286.D47; P47. **DD** 070. **[CCC].** available on microfilm and microfiche from University Microfilms International (UMI). ***Continues*** *Personal Publishing, 0884-951X.* ***Absorbed by*** *Publish!, 0897-6007.*
**Ind/Abst** Abstr. Bull. Inst. Pap. Sci. Tech.

US/0732-6599
**BUY BOOKS WHERE, SELL BOOKS WHERE.** (BUY BOOKS WHERE - SELL BOOKS WHERE / COMPILED BY RUTH E. ROBINSON AND DARYUSH FARUDI.). [Buy books where, sell books where]. (1978)-. Monographic series. English. ir. Price varies per volume. Ruth E. Robinson Books, Route 7 Box 162A, Morgantown WV 26505. **Tel** (304)594-3140. **ED** Ruth E. Robinson and Daryush Farudi. **LC** Z475; .R63. **DD** 070.5/025/73. **Bk Rev**. **Ad Acc**. **Pr Rev**.
**Desc:** A directory of out-of-print booksellers and their author/subject specialties by author/subject and geographic location of bookseller.

US
**CABELL'S DIRECTORY OF PUBLISHING OPPORTUNITIES IN BUSINESS AND ECONOMICS.** **VFOAT** Directory of Publishing Opportunities in Business and Economics. 3rd Ed. (1985)-. Directory. English. ir. $69.95 US; $89.95 (surface mail), $119.95 (air mail) other. Cabell Publishing Company, PO Box 5428, Beaumont TX 77726-7173. **Tel** (409)898-0575. **ED** David W. E. Cabell. cum. index. ***Continues*** *Cabell's Directory of Publishing Opportunities in Business, Administration and Economics.*
**Desc:** Provides current review guidelines on over 200 journals in business and economics.

# Publishing

US
**CABELL'S DIRECTORY OF PUBLISHING OPPORTUNITIES IN EDUCATION.** VFOAT Directory of Publishing Opportunities in Education. 1st Ed. (1984)-. Directory. English. ir. $69.95 US; $89.95 (surface mail), $119.95 (air mail) other. Cabell Publishing Company, PO Box 5428, Beaumont TX 77726-7173. **Tel** (409)898-0575. **ED** David W. E. Cabell. cum. index.
**Desc:** Provides the current review guidelines on over 200 journals in education.

US/1058-2096
**CALIFORNIA AND HAWAII PUBLISHING MARKET PLACE.** [Calif. Hawaii publ. mark. place]. VFOAT Publishing Market Place. (19??)-. Periodical. English. LC PN161; .C32. **DD** 070.5/2/0979405. **Continues** California Publishing Marketplace.

US/0008-1434
**CALIFORNIA PUBLISHER.** [Calif. publ.]. **Added/Corp** California Newspaper Publishers Association. (19??)-. Periodical. English. mo. $15.00. California Newspaper Publishers Association, 1311 I Street/Suite 200, Sacramento CA 95814-2912. **Tel** (916)443-5991, FAX (916)443-6447. **ED** Jackie Nava. **LC** PN4700; .C34. **DD** 071.94. **Ad Acc. Circ:** 1,800. Documents available from UMI Article Clearinghouse.
**Ind/Abst** ABI/INFORM Glob. Ed.; ABI Inform Ondisc (March 1975-Dec. 1977).

US
**CALIFORNIA PUBLISHING MARKETPLACE.** *Title Change.* VFOAT California Publishing Market Place. (1990)-(199?). English. be. Writers Connection, 1601 Saratoga Sunnyvale/Suite 180, Cupertino CA 95014. **Tel** (408)973-0227. *Continued by California and Hawaii Publishing Market Place, 1058-2096.*

CN/0008-4859
**CANADIAN PUBLISHERS' DIRECTORY.** (Fall 1965)-. Directory. English. sa. Free to subscribers of Quill & Quire. Quill & Quire, 70 The Esplanade, 4th Floor, Toronto Ontario M5E 1R2 Canada. **Tel** (416)360-0044, (416)946-0406.

US/0736-9077
**CAPELL'S CIRCULATION REPORT.** (198?)-. Periodical. English. Twenty times a year. $295.00 US; $335.00 other. Capell's Circulation Report, 60 East 42nd Street #3810, New York NY 10165. **Tel** (212)697-5753, FAX (212)949-7294. **ED** Dan Capell. **[CCC]**. Index available (Jan. and July issues). cum. index. **Circ:** 300.
**Desc:** Newsletter serving the magazine publishing industry.

US/0740-3119
**CATALOG AGE.** *See* Business-Advertising and Public Relations.

US/0730-9937
**CATALOG MARKETER, THE.** (THE CATALOG MARKETER / MAXWELL SROGE PUBLISHING, INC.) [Cat. mark.]. (198?)-. Catalog. English. Twenty-four times a year. $189.00. Maxwell Sroge Publications Inc., 522 Forest Avenue, Evanston IL 60202. **Tel** (313)819-1890, FAX (312)819-0411. **ED** Ann Meyer.
**Desc:** Offers cost-saving, money-making practical ideas on all aspects of catalog creation and production in every issue. Easy to read with departments such as: news, merchandising, the bottom line, high tech, creative ideas, advertising, legal advisor, photography, etc.

IT
**CATALOGO DEGLI EDITORI ITALIANI / ASSOCIAZIONE ITALIANA EDITORI.** (1988)-. Italian. Editrice Bibliografica, Viale Vittoria Veneto 24, 20124 Milan Italy. **Tel** 011 39 2 29006965, FAX 011 39 2 654624. **LC** Z342; .E32. **DD** 381/.45002/02545. *Continues* Editori Italiani.

CN/0316-1560
**CATALOGUE DE L'EDITEUR OFFICIEL DU QUEBEC.** **Main/Corp** Editeur Officiel du Quebec. (1976)-. English (French). ir. Ministere des Communications, PO Box 1005, Quebec Quebec G1K 7B5 Canada. **Tel** (418)643-5150. **LC** Z1373.5.Q4; E35A; J107. **DD** 015.714/053. *Continues* Catalogue de l'Editeur Officiel du Quebec, 0316-1560.

US/0008-8129
**CATHOLIC JOURNALIST.** *See* Journalism.

US/0164-5609
**CBE VIEWS.** *See* Biology.

CH
**CHU PAN JEN / CHUNG-HUA MIN KUO TU SHU CHU PAN SHIH YEH HSIEH HUI.** **Added/Corp** Chung-Hua Min Kuo Tu Shu Chu Pan Shih Yeh Hsieh Hui. (Mar 30, 1991)-. Periodical. Chinese. qt. **LC** Z464.T4; C47. *Continues* Chu Pan Chih Yu.

CH
**CHU PAN SHIH LIAO.** VFOAT Chuban Shiliao. 1-. Periodical. Chinese. NT$0.60. Hsin Hua Shu Tien / Shang-Hai Fa Hsing So, Shanghai, People's Republic of China. **LC** Z462.7; .C54. **DD** 079/.51.

US/1051-8983
**CIRCULATION IDEA SERVICE.** [Circ. idea serv.]. (19??)-. Periodical. English. Twelve times a year. $180.00 non-daily newspapers; $198.00 (circulation 10,000-24,999), $228.00 (circulation 25,000-49,999), $255.00 (circulation 50,000+) daily newspapers. RCAnderson Associates Inc., PO Drawer 300, Pittsford NY 14534. **Tel** (716)248-5385, FAX (716)248-9551. **DD** 070. Index available.
**Desc:** A reference volume of ideas and programs, successful sales promotions, commentary by industry professionals, material for carrier newsletters and bulletins, camera-ready art, etc.

IT/0413-4028
**COLLANA DI STUDI SULLA PUBBLICITA.** 1- 1957-. Periodical. Italian. Via Giovanni Pascoli 55, 20133 Milan Italy.

US/1055-9701
**COLOR PUBLISHING.** [Color pub.]. Vol. 1, No. 1 (Spring 1991)-. Periodical. English. Six times a year. $24.95 US; $29.95 Canada; $39.95 other. PennWell Publishing Company, 1421 South Sheridan, PO Box 1260, Tulsa OK 74101. **Tel** (918)835-3161, (800)331-4463, FAX (918)831-9497. **(Subscription address:** Color Publishing, Publishing Services, PO Box 3093, Tulsa OK 74101-9616.) ED Frank Romano (editor's phone: (603)898-2822). **LC** Z48; .C65. **DD** 686.2/3042. **[CCC]**. **Ad Acc, Adv Mgr:** Robert Holton, **Tel** (508)692-2157. **Pr Rev. Circ:** 25,000.
**Desc:** Designed to satisfy the need for a comprehensive source of information in the evolving market for color systems and imaging services.

FR
**COMMERCE EXTERIEUR DU LIVRE POUR L'ANNEE ... D'APRES LES STATISTIQUES DOUANIERES, LE.** **Added/Corp** Syndicat National de l'Edition (France). Bureau d'Information et de Liaison Pour l'Exportation. VFOAT Commerce Exterieur du Livre. (19??)-. French. an. Cercle de la Librairie, 35 rue Gregoire de Tours, F-75279 Paris Cedex 06 France. **Tel** 011 33 1 43291000, FAX 011 33 1 43296895, telex LIFRAN 270 838. **LC** Z309; .C59. **DD** 338.8/2616862/0944021.

US/0737-0334
**COMPUTER BOOK REVIEW.** *See* Computers.

US/8756-7911
**COMPUTERITER.** *See* Computers-Microcomputers, Personal Computers.

US/1049-3190
**COPY EDITOR.** [Copy ed.]. Vol. 1, No. 1 (April/May 1990)-. Periodical. English. bm. $69.00 (one year); $118.00 (two year) US; $74.00 (one year), $128.00 (two year) Canada; $78.00 (one year), $136.00 (two year) other. Copy Editor, PO Box 604, Ansonia Station, New York NY 10023-0604. **Tel** (212)757-2645. **ED** Mary Beth Protomastro. **LC** PN4784.C75; C66. **DD** 070. **CODEN** CPDIE2. Index available. cum. index. **Bk Rev.**

US/1064-4482
**COSMEP NEWSLETTER (1981).** (COSMEP NEWSLETTER.). [COSMEP newsl.]. **Added/Corp** Committee of Small Magazine Editors and Publishers (U.S.). **VAT** Committee of Small Magazine Editors and Publishers Newsletter. Vol. 12, No. 6 (March 1981)-. Newsletter. English. mo. $60.00 North America; $70.00 other. COSMEP Inc, PO Box 420703, San Francisco CA 94142. **Tel** (415)922-9490, FAX (415)922-5566. **ED** Richard Morris. **DD** 070. **Bk Rev**, (Qty: 20): **Circ:** 2,000.
*Continues* Independent Publisher.
**Desc:** For small book and periodical publishers.

US/0007-8905
**CPH COMMENTATOR.** **Main/Corp** Concordia Publishing House. Periodical. English. qt. Concordia Publishing House, 3558 South Jefferson Avenue, St Louis MO 63118. **Tel** (314)268-1000, (800)325-3381, FAX (314)268-1329.

FR/0398-8074
**CURIOSPRESS INTERNATIONAL.** No. 1- 1974-. Multiple languages (French, English, German, Spanish and Italian). Pierre Birukoff, c/o Infos A1 International, BP 127, 75563 Cedex France. **LC** Z282; .C87. **DD** 011.

SP
**DELIBROS : REVISTA PROFESIONAL DEL LIBRO.** (198?)-. Spanish. Eleven times a year. $48.11 Canary Islands; $49.60 Spain; $87.75 other. BBR Action, GOYA 115, 28009 Madrid Spain. **Tel** 011 34 1 3090352. **LC** Z2685; .D45. **DD** 015.46/34.

UK/0957-3178
**DESKTOP PUBLISHING COMMENTARY.** [Deskt. publ. comment.]. (1989)-. Periodical. English. Ten times a year. £165.00 UK & Europe; $312.00 US; £195.00 other. Pira International, Randalls Road, Leatherhead, Surrey KT22 7RU England. **Tel** 011 44 372 376161, FAX 011 44 372 377526. **ED** Alan Aitken. **DD** 070.50285416. *Formed by the union of* Desktop Publisher, 0269-5847 *and* Pira DTP Commentary.
**Desc:** Feature articles on all aspects of desktop publishing, conference reports and new product updates.

US/1040-8932
**DESKTOP PUBLISHING DIGEST.** [Deskt. publ. dig.]. Vol. 1, No. 1 (May 1988)-. Periodical. English. mo. $45.00. Creative Ink Inc, 14573 Grand Avenue South, Burnsville MN 55337. **DD** 070.

GW/0939-0553
**DEUTSCHE NATIONALBIBLIOGRAPHIE UND BIBLIOGRAPHIE DER IM AUSLAND ERSCHIENENEN DEUTSCHSPRACHIGEN VEROFFENTLICHUNGEN. REIHE C, KARTEN, VIERTELJAHRLICHES VERZEICHNIS / BEARBEITER UND HERAUSGEBER, DIE DEUTSCHE BIBLIOTHEK.** **Added/Corp** Deutsche Bibliothek (Frankfurt am Main, Germany). VFOAT Karten, Vierteljahrliches Verzeichnis. (Mar 1991)-. Periodical. German. qt. Buchhandler Vereinigung GmbH, Grosser Hirschgraben 17-21, D 60311 Frankfurt 1 Germany. **Tel** 011 49 69 1306243, telex 413573 BUCH VOL. **LC** Z2221; .F7522. *Continues* Deutsche Bibliographie. Wochentliches Verzeichnis. Reihe C, Beilage, Karten, 0170-107X.

GW/0940-2721
**DEUTSCHE NATIONALBIBLIOGRAPHIE UND BIBLIOGRAPHIE DER IM AUSLAND ERSCHIENENEN DEUTSCHSPRACHIGEN VEROFFENTLICHUNGEN. REIHE D, MONOGRAPHIEN UND PERIODIKA -- HALBJAHRESVERZEICHNIS.** **Added/Corp** Deutsche Bibliothek (Frankfurt am Main, Germany). VFOAT Deutsche Nationalbibliographie. Reihe D, Monographien und Periodika -- Halbjahresverzeichnis; Monographien und Periodika -- Halbjahresverzeichnis; Halbjahres-Verzeichnis. Jan/Jun (1991)-. German (Multiple languages). sa. Buchhandler Vereinigung GmbH, Grosser Hirschgraben 17-21, D 60311 Frankfurt 1 Germany. **Tel** 011 49 69 1306243, telex 413573 BUCH VOL. **LC** Z2221; .F73. *Continues* Deutsche Bibliogrphie. Halbjahres-Verzeichnis, 0532-5854.

US/0884-0881
**DIGITAL PUBLISHING.** Periodical. English. Ten times a year. $24.00. Lee Douglas Publications, 9607 Gayton Road, Suite 201, Richmond VA 23233. **Tel** (804)741-6704, FAX (804)750-2399. **ED** Richard A Bowers.
**Desc:** Regular features will include news, new products, people, special interviews and regular columns on standards and the business of publishing. Will contain important category reviews, as well as features on the issues and trends facing publishers trying to make tough decisions about new markets and new products.

US/0739-3024
**DIRECTORY / ASSOCIATION OF AMERICAN UNIVERSITY PRESSES.** [Dir. - Assoc. Am. Univ. Presses]. **Main/Corp** Association of American University Presses. VFOAT AAUP Directory. (195?)-. Directory. English. an (October). $14.95. Association of American University Presses Inc, Publications Department, 584 Broadway, Suite 410, New York NY 10012. **Tel** (212)941-6610, FAX (212)941-6618. **LC** Z475; .A88. **DD** 070.5/94.
**Desc:** Directory of members and affiliates of the association of American University Presses.

US
**DIRECTORY OF ALTERNATIVE AND RADICAL PUBLICATIONS.** (19??)-. English. an. $4.00. Alternative Press Centre, PO Box 33109, Baltimore MD 21218. **Tel** (410)243-2471, FAX (410)235-5325. **ED** Bill Wilson.
**Desc:** A listing of alternative periodicals, includes title, subscription information and general subject area.

US/1053-4210
**DIRECTORY OF DIRECTORY PUBLISHERS.** [Dir. dir. publ.]. (1990)-. Directory. English. an. $125.00. Morgan-Rand Publications Inc, 1800 Byberry Road 800, Huntingdon Valley PA 19006. **Tel** (215)938-5511, FAX (215)938-0402. **ED** John Krol. **LC** Z5771; .D55. **DD** 070.
**Desc:** Provides key facts on more than 7,000 directory publishers worlwide, including listings of each publisher's titles and their markets.

US/1057-1337
**DIRECTORY OF ELECTRONIC JOURNALS, NEWSLETTERS, AND ACADEMIC DISCUSSION LISTS.** [Dir. electron. j. newsl. acad. discuss. lists]. **Added/Corp** Association of Research Libraries. Office of Scientific and Academic Publishing. 1st Ed. (July 1991)-. Directory. English. ir. $12.50 (members), $25.00 (non-members). Office of Research Libraries, Office of Scientific and Academic Publishing, 1527 New Hampshire Avenue, Northwest, Washington DC 20036. **ED** Ann Okerson. **LC** Z286.E43; D57. **DD** 016.

JA
**DIRECTORY OF JAPANESE PUBLISHING INDUSTRY.** (1970)-. Directory. English. be. Free. Publishers Association for Cultural Exchange, 1-2-1 Saragaku-cho Chiyoda-ku, Tokyo 101 Japan. **Tel** (03) 3291-5685, FAX (03) 3233-3645. **ED** Hiroyasu Ochiai. ***Continues*** *Guide to Publishers and Related Industries in Japan.*

CN/0711-3056
**DIRECTORY OF MEMBERS / ASSOCIATION OF CANADIAN UNIVERSITY PRESSES.** [Dir. memb. - Assoc. Can. Univ. Presses]. **Main/Corp** Association of Canadian University Presses. **VFOAT** Repertoire des Membres. **VAT** Repertoire des Membres - Association des Presses Universitaires Canadiennes. 1980-. Directory. English (French). an. Free. Secretary of the Association of Canadian University Presses, c/o Pontificial Institute of Mediaeval Studies, 59 Queen's Part Cres E, Toronto Ontario M5S 2C4 Canada. **Tel** (416)926-7143. **DD** 070.5/94. **Circ:** 400.
**Desc:** Directory of Canadian University Presses.

II
**DIRECTORY OF MEMBERS - FEDERATION OF INDIAN PUBLISHERS.** **Main/Corp** Federation of Indian Publishers. Directory. English. an. Federation of Indian Publishers, 18/1-C Institutional Area Jnu Road, New Delhi 110067 India. **Tel** 654847. **ED** Prabha Naresh. **LC** Z455; .F4A. **DD** 070.5/025/54. **Ad Acc. Circ:** 500 (ctrl).
**Desc:** Contains names, addresses and subjects of specialisation of major publishers and also details of the Executive Committee members of the Federation.

CN/0226-9031
**DIRECTORY OF MEMBERS - FREELANCE EDITORS' ASSOCIATION OF CANADA.** (DIRECTORY OF MEMBERS.). [Dir. memb. - Freelance Ed. Assoc. Can.]. **Main/Corp** Freelance Editors' Association of Canada. **VFOAT** Repertoire des Membres; FEAC Directory; APRC Repertoire. **VAT** FEAC Directory; Freelance Editors' Association of Canada Directory. (1979)-. Directory. English (French). an. 10.00Can$ Canada; $10.00 US. Freelance Editors' Association of Canada, 34 Ross Street/Suite 200, Toronto Ontario M5T 1Z9 Canada. **Tel** (416)593-4692. **ED** Shaun Oakey. **DD** 808/.02/02571. **Circ:** 3,500 (ctrl).
**Desc:** Indexed list of current association members, divided geographically, showing areas of editorial and production expertise and experience.

CN/0833-9821
**DIRECTORY OF MEMBERS - PERIODICAL WRITERS ASSOCIATION OF CANADA.** **See** Journalism.

US/1062-8010
**DIRECTORY OF PUBLICATIONS RESOURCES.** (1991)-. English. be. $18.00 US and Canada; $19.00 other. Editorial Experts Inc. / EEI, 66 Canal Center Plaza, Suite 200, Alexandria VA 22314. **Tel** (703)683-0683, FAX (703)683-4915. **LC** PN162; .D57. **DD** 070.4/1/02573. ***Continues*** *Directory of Editorial Resources, 0731-4426.*
**Desc:** Desk reference for publications professionals focusing on reference books, software programs, training opportunities, professional organizations, etc.

●UK
**DIRECTORY OF PUBLISHING. CONTINENTAL EUROPE.** **Added/Corp** Cassell Ltd. Publishers' Association. Federation of European Publishers. **VFOAT** Continental Europe. (1992)-. Directory. English. an. £70.00. Cassell PLC / London, Villiers House, 41-47 Strand, London WC2N 5JE England. **Tel** 011 44 71 8394900, FAX 011 44 71 8391804. **ED** Steve Cook. **LC** Z291; .D57. **DD** 070.5/025/4. **Circ:** 2,000.
**Desc:** Listings for publishers in continental Europe, highlighting those involved in international manufacturing, co-publishing, righst deals, and foreign language editions.

UK
**DIRECTORY OF PUBLISHING IN SCOTLAND.** (1989)-. Directory. English.

●UK
**DIRECTORY OF PUBLISHING. UNITED KINGDOM, COMMONWEALTH AND OVERSEAS.** **Added/Corp** Cassell Ltd. Publishers' Association. **VFOAT** Cassell & the Publishers Association Directory of Publishing. United Kingdom, Commonwealth and overseas; Cassell and the Publishers Association Directory of Publishing. United Kingdom, Commonwealth and overseas; United Kingdom, Commonwealth and Overseas. (1992)-. Directory. English. an. $78.00. Cassell PLC / London, Villiers House, 41-47 Strand, London WC2N 5JE England. **Tel** 011 44 71 8394900, FAX 011 44 71 8391804. **LC** Z327; .C37. **DD** 070.5/025/41. Index available. ***Continues*** *Cassell & the Publishers Association Directory of Publishing, 0268-0394.*

US/0277-1519
**DIRECTORY OF SMALL PRESS & MAGAZINE EDITORS & PUBLISHERS, THE.** [Dir. small press mag. ed. publ.]. **VFOAT** Directory of Small Press and Magazine Editors and Publishers. 11th Ed. (1980-81)-. Directory. English. an. $23.95. Dustbooks, PO Box 100, Paradise CA 95969. **Tel** (916)877-6110. **ED** Len Fulton. **LC** PN4820; .D57. **DD** 070.4/1/025. **Ad Acc. Circ:** 2,500. ***Continues*** *Directory of Small Magazine Press Editors and Publishers, 0095-6414.*
**Desc:** Lists small press editors and publishers by name alphabetically with press or magazine with which they are associated.

US
**DIRECTORY STRATEGIES.** (1992)-. Directory. English. Nine times a year. $99.00. Directory Publishing Resources, Box 19107, George Mason Station, Alexandria VA 22320.
**Desc:** Dedicated to the practical aspects of directory publishing. Information relevant to doing your job - how to protect your copyrights post-Feist, recession-beating strategies, how to improve questionnaire response, and tips for better circulation and advertising sales.

US
**DIRECTORY WORLD.** (1989)-. English. mo. $84.00 (one year), $151.00 (two year). Simba Information Inc., 213 Danbury Road, Wilton CT 06897-7430. **Tel** (203)834-0033 ext. 133, FAX (203)884-1771. **(Subscription address:** Simba Information Inc., PO Box 7430, Wilton CT 06897.)

US
**DIRECTORY WORLD.** Directory. English. ir. $96.00. Communications Trends Inc., 2 East Avenue, Suite 201, Larchmont NY 10538. **Tel** (914)833-0600, FAX (914)833-0558.
**Desc:** Lively, independent magazine covering the issues of strategy, planning and operations that most directly affect the future of directory publishers. Aimed at top executives in the yellow and white pages industry, including decisionmakers at RBOCs and independent publishers, production and planning managers.

US/0196-7134
**DOCUMENTARY EDITING.** **See** Journalism.

GW
**DOKUMENTATION DEUTSCHSPRACHIGER VERLAGE.** No. 1 (August 1962)-. Periodical. German. Three times a year. DM64.00. Gunter Olzog Verlag GmbH, Thierschstrabe 11, 8 Munchen 22 Germany.

US/0741-6547
**DUNN REPORT, ELECTRONIC PUBLISHING & PREPRESS SYSTEMS NEWS & VIEWS.** **Added/Corp** Dunn Technology. **VFOAT** Dunn Report, Electronic Publishing and Prepress Systems News and Views; Dunn Report, Electronic Publishing & Prepress Systems; Electronic Publishing & Prepress Systems; Electronic Publishing and Prepress Systems; Dunn Report on Electronic Publishing and Prepress Systems; Dunn Report on EP2S. Vol. 1, No. 2 (Oct. 1983)-. Periodical. English. Twelve times a year. $295.00 US; $310.00 Canada; $330.00 other. Dunn Technology, 1855 East Vista Way #1, Vista CA 92084. **Tel** (619)758-9460, FAX (619)758-5401. **ED** S. Thomas Dunn. **[CCC].** ctrl circ. ***Continues*** *Dunn Report on Electronic Publishing & Prepress System News & Views.*
**Ind/Abst** Graph. Arts Bull. Inst. Pap. Sci. Technol. (Jan. 1989); Print. Abstr.

FR/0245-1875
**EDITEURS ET DIFFUSEURS DE LANGUE FRANCAISE, LES.** **Added/Corp** Cercle de la Librairie (France). **VFOAT** Repertoire International des Editeurs et Diffuseurs de Langue Francaise. (1970)-. French. an. 460.00F. Cercle de la Librairie, 35 rue Gregoire de Tours, F-75279 Paris Cedex 06 France. **Tel** 011 33 1 43291000, FAX 011 33 1 43296895, telex LIFRAN 270 838. **LC** Z282; .R46. **DD** 015.44. ***Continues*** *Repertoire International des Editeurs et Diffuseurs de Langue Francaise.*
**Desc:** Listing of main publishers in the French and Francophone edition.

US/0883-3532
**EDITING HISTORY.** [Ed. hist.]. **Added/Corp** Conference for History Journals. Vol. 1, No. 1 (June 1984)-. Periodical. English. ir (2 or 3 per year). comes with membership. Virginia Historical Society, PO Box 7311, Richmond VA 23221-0311. **Tel** (804)358-4901, FAX (804)355-2399. **ED** R.V. Schnucker. **DD** 905. **Bk Rev. Ad Acc. Circ:** 200 (ctrl).
**Desc:** For history editors, covering all aspects of publishing.

US/0013-094X
**EDITOR & PUBLISHER.** [Ed. publ.]. **VFOAT** E & P. **VAT** Editor and Publisher. Vol. 1-14, No. 40 (June 29, 1901)-(March 13, 1915)-. Periodical. English. wk. $50.00 US & Canada; $110.00 other. Editor & Publisher Company, 11 West 19th Street, New York NY 10011. **Tel** (212)675-4380. **ED** Robert U. Brown. **LC** PN4700; .E4. **DD** 070.4. **Ad Acc. Circ:** 30,000 (ctrl). available on microfilm and microfiche from University Microfilms International (UMI); available on an online database (file 648/Full-Text) from DIALOG. Documents available from UMI Article Clearinghouse. ***Absorbed*** *Journalist; Advertising **and** Fourth Estate.*
**Desc:** Newsmagazine reporting to the newspaper industry, its suppliers, advertisers and advertising agencies.
**Ind/Abst** ABI/INFORM Glob. Ed.; ABI Inform Ondisc (March 1975-Dec. 1977); Abstr. Bull. Inst. Pap. Sci. Tech.; Abstr. Graphic Arts Tech. Found. (1984); Acad. Ind. [Computer File] (1992-); Acad. Search (July 1993-); Bus. ASAP (1990-) [Full Txt.]; Bus. Index (1985-); Bus. Period. Index; Expand. Acad. Index (1984-); F&S Index Plus Text, Int. [Select. Cov.]; Fed. Tax Artic.; Gen. BusinessFile (1985-); Gen. Period. Index (1985-); Graph. Arts Bull. Inst. Pap. Sci. Technol. (Jan. 1989-July 1989, Sept. 1989-Dec. 1989); INFO-SOUTH Abstr.; Infobank (Jan. 1969-); Mag. Search; Newsp. Period. Abstr. (1986-); Print. Abstr.; PROMT; Topicator; Trade Ind. ASAP [Full Txt.]; Trade Ind. Index (1981-) [Full Txt.]; UMI ABI/Inform--Bus. Period. Ondisc [Full Txt.]; Vocat. Search (July 1993-); Wilson Bus. Abstr.

IT
**EDITORE, L'.** (1978)-. Periodical. Italian. mo (11 issues per year). L60000 Italy; L80000 others. Gutenberg 2000 Srl., C S Massimo D Azeglio 60, 10126 Turin Italy. **Tel** 011 39 11 6504430. **LC** Z344; .E34. **DD** 070.5/0945.

US/0193-7383
**EDITORIAL EYE, THE.** (1978)-. Periodical. English. mo. $87.00 US; $92.00 Canada; $96.00 other. Editorial Experts Inc. / EEI, 66 Canal Center Plaza, Suite 200, Alexandria VA 22314. **Tel** (703)683-0683, FAX (703)683-4915. **ED** Linda Jorgensen. **CODEN** EDEYDQ. **[CCC].** Index available (included in Jan. issue). **Bk Rev,** (Qty: 1). **Circ:** 2,300. ***Absorbed in part*** *Freelancer's Newsletter, 0016-0636.*
**Desc:** Newsletter for publications professionals. Focuses on editorial standards and practices. Covers writing, editing, proofreading, grammar style and usage.

US
**EDITOR'S DIGEST.** English. qt. $15.00 US; $17.00 Canada; $20.00 other. Quadriga Publishing, Suite 311, 1613 Chelsea Road, San Marino CA 91108. **Tel** (818)355-6847. **ED** W M Reinshagen. **Bk Rev. Ad Acc. Circ:** 200. ***Continues*** *Trellis (San Marino).*
**Desc:** Information on magazine editing.

UK/0894-3982
**ELECTRONIC PUBLISHING.** [Electron. publ.]. Vol. 1 (1988)-. Periodical. English. Four times a year (Jan., Apr., July, Oct.). $315.00. John Wiley & Sons Ltd., Baffins Lane, Chichester West Sussex PO19 1UD England. **Tel** 0243 779777, FAX 0243 776128 BTG:JWP001, telex 86290 WIBOOKG. **(Subscription address:** John Wiley / Philadelphia, PO Box 7247, Philadelphia PA 19170.) **ED** D. F. Brailsford and R. Furuta. **LC** Z286.E43; E432. **DD** 070.5/025. **CODEN** EPODEU. **[CCC]. Pr Rev.** available on microfilm and microfiche from University Microfilms International (UMI). Documents available from Ask*IEEE.
**Desc:** Publishes refereed papers on all aspects of electronic publishing. A broad interpretation of the topic is taken that encompasses areas such as structured editors, authoring tools, hypermedia, document bases, production or concordances and indexes, document display on workstations, electronic documents over networks, integration of text and illustrations, typeface design and imaging hardware.
**Ind/Abst** Abstr. Bull. Inst. Pap. Sci. Tech.; Abstr. Hum. Comput. Interact.; ACM Guide Comput. Lit.; Comput. Lit. Index; Comput. Rev.; HILITES; INSPEC (Jan. 1988-); Libr. Inf. Sci. Abstr.

UK/0954-3244
**EPJOURNAL.** **VFOAT** EP Journal. (Feb. 1984)-. English. mo. £260.00; £200.00 (libraries). Electronic Publ Services Ltd, 104A St John Street, London EC1M 4EH England. **Tel** 071-490-1185, FAX 071-490-4706.

UK
**EUROCAT - COMPLETE CATALOGUE OF EC PUBLICATIONS AND DOCUMENTS.** (19??)-. English. an. £450.00, $789.00. Chadwyck-Healey Limited, The Quorum Barnwell Road, Cambridge CB5 8SW England. **Tel** 011

44 223 215512, telex 9312102281 CH G. **(Subscription address:** Chadwyck Healey Inc. / US Subscriptions, 1101 King Street, Suite 380, Alexandria VA 22314.**)**

UK/0958-3866
**EUROPEAN BOOKSELLER. See** Publishing-Books and Bookmaking.

UK/0309-4715
**EUROPEAN SCIENCE EDITING : BULLETIN OF THE EUROPEAN ASSOCIATION OF SCIENCE EDITORS. Added/Corp** European Association of Science Editors. No. 27 (Jan. 1986)-. Periodical. English. Three times a year (Jan., May, Sept.). $50.00 US and Canada. European Association Science Editors, 49 Rossendale Way, London NW1 0XB England. **Tel** 011 44 71 3889668, FAX 011 44 71 3833092. **(Subscription address:** European Science Editing / North America Subscriptions, PO Box 1897, Lawrence KS 66044-8897.**) LC** Z286.S4; E18. **DD** 070.5/72. Index available. **Bk Rev**, (Qty: 1-9). **Ad Acc**. **Pr Rev. Circ:** 1,000. ***Continues** Earth & Life Science Editing.*
**Desc:** Contains articles, meeting reports, new developments, correspondence and bibliography of items for editors.

IT
**EUROSTAMPA.** (19??)-. Italian. Eurostampa, Via Tomacelli #103, 00100 Rome Italy.

US/0147-0310
**EXHIBITS DIRECTORY - ASSOCIATION OF AMERICAN PUBLISHERS. Main/Corp** Association of American Publishers. **Added/Corp** Association of American Publishers. National, State, Regional Exhibits Directory. **VFOAT** National, State, Regional Exhibits Directory. (196?)-. Directory. English. an. Association of American Publishers Inc., 220 East 23rd Street/2nd Floor, New York NY 10010. **Tel** (212)689-8920. **ED** Ray George. **Ad Acc. Circ:** 700. ***Continues** Joint Directory of Exhibit Opportunities. National, State and Region.*
**Desc:** Directory of educational, library, and technical associations at which publishers may exhibit their books.

US/0046-4333
**FOLIO : THE MAGAZINE FOR MAGAZINE MANAGEMENT.** [Folio mag. mag. manage.]. (1972)-. Periodical. English. Twenty-four times a year. $96.00 US; $116.00 Canada & Mexico; $199.00 other. Cowles Business Media Inc., 6 River Bend Center, 911 Hope Street, Stamford CT 06907. **Tel** (203)358-9900, (800)775-3777, FAX (203)357-9014. **(Subscription address:** Hanson Publishing Group, Box 4294, Stamford, CT 06907**) ED** Sean Callahan. **LC** PN4734; .F65. **DD** 658/.91/070572. **Ad Acc. Circ:** 10,000. available on microfilm and microfiche from University Microfilms International (UMI); available on an online database (files 15,648/Full-Text) from DIALOG. Documents available from UMI Article Clearinghouse.
**Desc:** Contains articles on all aspects of magazine management and protection.
**Ind/Abst** ABI/INFORM Glob. Ed.; ABI Inform Ondisc (Nov. 1988-); Abstr. Bull. Inst. Pap. Sci. Tech.; Abstr. Graphic Arts Tech. Found. (1984); Acad. Search (July 1993-); Bus. ASAP (1990-) [Full Txt.]; Bus. Index (1985-); Bus. Period. Index; Bus. Source (Jul. 1993-); Expand. Acad. Index (1992-); Gen. BusinessFile (1985-); Gen. Period. Index (1985-); INFO-SOUTH Abstr.; Mag. Search; Mark. Advert. Ref. Serv.; Newsp. Period. Abstr. (1992-); Topicator; Trade Ind. ASAP [Full Txt.]; Trade Ind. Index [Full Txt.]; UMI ABI/Inform--Bus. Period. Ondisc (Nov. 1988-) [Full Txt.]; Wilson Bus. Abstr.

US/1053-4563
**FOLIO'S PUBLISHING NEWS. *Ceased.*** [Folio's pub. news]. **VFOAT** Publishing News. (199?)-Ceased in (1993). Periodical. English. mo. Cowles Business Media Inc., 6 River Bend Center, 911 Hope Street, Stamford CT 06907. **Tel** (203)358-9900, (800)775-3777, FAX (203)357-9014. **ED** Sean Callahan and Anne Russell. **LC** Z286.P4; P816. **Ad Acc, Adv Mgr:** Shirley Sax, **Tel** (203)358-9900. **Circ:** 20,000 (ctrl). available on microfilm and microfiche from University Microfilms International (UMI); available on an online database (file 648/Full-Text) from DIALOG. ***Continues** Publishing News (Stamford, Ct.), 1043-8688.*
**Desc:** News and news analysis concerning magazine publishing. Also, industry people and company profiles.
**Ind/Abst** F&S Index Plus Text, Int. [Select. Cov.]; Mark. Advert. Ref. Serv.; PROMT; Trade Ind. ASAP [Full Txt.]; Trade Ind. Index [Full Txt.].

US/1049-6394
**GALACTIC CENTRAL PUBLISHER CHECKLISTS. VFOAT** Galactic Central. (1990)-. Monographic series. English. ir. $20.00. Borgo Press, PO Box 2845, San Bernardino CA 92406. **Tel** (714)884-5813, (714)885-1161.
**Desc:** Guides and indexes to science fiction publishing houses.

US/0433-163X
**GANNETTEER. See** Journalism.

IT
**GIORNALE DELLA LIBRERIA. Added/Corp** Associazione Italiana Editori. Associazione Editoriale Libreria Italiana. Federazione Nazionale Fascista Degli Industriali Editori. (192?)-. Periodical. Italian. Eleven times a year (Except Aug.). L88000.00 Italy; L85500.00 Libraries in Italy; L146000.00 others. Editrice Bibliografica, Viale Vittoria Veneto 24, 20124 Milan Italy. **Tel** 011 39 2 29006965, FAX 011 39 2 654624. **ED** Carlo Enrico Rivolta. Index available. **Bk Rev. Ad Acc. Circ:** 5,000. ***Continues** Giornale Della Libreria, Della Tipografia, Edelle Arti e Industrie Affini.*
**Desc:** Covers book publishing and marketing. Three sections: publishers, booksellers, librarians. Lists the books of the month - about 1,800.

BE/0773-591X
**GRAFISCH NIEUWS.** [Graf. nieuws]. (1951)-. Periodical. Dutch. Twenty-two times a year. 2000F. Keesing Uitgevers, Keesinglaan 2 20, 2100 Antwerp Deurne, Belgium. **Tel** 011 32 3 3243890, FAX 011 32 3 324 3898, telex 32507. **ED** Alain Vermeire. **Bk Rev. Ad Acc, Adv Mgr:** Kris Mortier. Full Page (Color) $1720.00. Half Page (Color) $1220.00. **Circ:** 7,300 (ctrl).

DK
**GRAFISKE FAG, DE. See** Printing Industry.

BL
**GUIA DAS EDITORAS BRASILEIRAS.** 1978-. Portuguese. Sindicato Nacional dos Editores de Livros, Av Rio Branco 37-150 Andar, 20.000 Rio de Janeiro Brazil. **LC** Z521.5; .G8. **DD** 070.5/025/81.

US/0749-1255
**HOTLINE - NEWSLETTER ASSOCIATION OF AMERICA. See** Journalism.

CH
**HSIN SHU YUEH KAN.** First published in Oct. 1983. Periodical. Chinese. mo. $15.00. Yu Chen Shu Pao She 6, 230 Lane Yen Ping S Road, Taipei Shih Taiwan. **LC** Z464.T357; H77. **DD** 079/.51249.

US
**HUDSON'S SUBSCRIPTION NEWSLETTER DIRECTORY.** Directory. English. $128.00 US, $140.00 others. Newsletter Clearinghouse, PO Box 311, Rhinebeck NY 12572. **Tel** (914)876-2081, FAX (914)876-2561. **ED** Joan W Artz. Index available. ***Continues** Hudson's Newsletter Directory.*
**Desc:** Lists new newsletters and reveals changes in titles, addresses, phone and fax numbers. Every listing in the directory is verified.

US
**HUENEFELD REPORT.** English. Twenty-six times a year (every other Monday). $88.00 (1 year), $145.00 (2 year). Huenefeld Company, Inc, Box 665, Bedford MA 01730. **Tel** (617)275-1070, FAX (617)275-1713.
**Desc:** For managers and planners in modest-sized book publishing houses.

CN/0711-3269
**HUMBER MAGAZINE WORLD.** [Humber mag. world]. Spring 1980-. Periodical. English. qt. Free to Canadian editors publishers and freelance writers, others $2.00 per issue. Humber College of Applied Arts and Technology, PO Box 1900, Rexdale Ontario M9W 5L7 Canada. **DD** 070.5/72/05.

NO/0333-3620
**IASP NEWSLETTER (INTERNATIONAL ASSOCIATION OF SCHOLARLY PUBLISHERS).** (IASP NEWSLETTER.). **Added/Corp** International Association of Scholarly Publishers. **VAT** International Association of Scholarly Publishers Newsletter. (19??)-. Newsletter. English. Six times a year. $60.00. Aarhus University Press, Aarhus University, Building 170, DK-8000 Aarhus C Denmark. **Tel** 011 45 86 197033, FAX 011 45 86 198433, telex 16600. **ED** Tonnes Bekker-Nielsen. **LC** Z286.S37; I17. **DD** 070.5/94. **[CCC]. Bk Rev. Circ:** 550.

US/0197-0178
**IDP REPORT. See** Computers-Data Base Management.

US/0743-2925
**ILLINOIS SMALL PRESS DIRECTORY. *Ceased.*** (1984)-?. Directory. English. an. Red Herring Press, 1209 West Oregon Street, Urbana IL 61801. **LC** Z231.5.L5; I44. **DD** 070.5/025/773.

US/0886-3121
**IN-PLANT REPRODUCTIONS & ELECTRONIC PUBLISHING. *Title Change.*** (IN-PLANT REPRODUCTIONS & ELECTRONIC PUBLISHING MICROFORM.). [In-plant reprod. electron. publ.]. **VFOAT** In-Plant Reproductions and Electronic Publishing; In Plant Reproductions & Electronic Publishing. Vol. 35, No. 11 (Nov. 1985)-(19??). Periodical. English. North American Publishing Company, 401 North Broad Street, Philadelphia PA 19108. **Tel** (215)238-5300, (800)777-8074, FAX (215)238-5283. available on microfilm and microfiche from University Microfilms International (UMI). ***Continues** In-Plant Reproductions, 0198-9065. **Continued by** In-Plant Reproductions, 1043-1942.*
**Ind/Abst** Abstr. Bull. Inst. Pap. Sci. Tech.; Graph. Arts Bull. Inst. Pap. Sci. Technol. (Feb. 1989); Print. Abstr.

US/1067-5132
**IN PRINT (TRENTON, N.J.).** (IN PRINT : THE MONTHLY NEWSLETTER OF THE NEW JERSEY PRESS ASSOCIATION.). [In print]. **Added/Corp** New Jersey Press Association. **VFOAT** Inprint. Vol. 1 No. 1 (Jan. 1990)-. Newsletter. English. mo. **DD** 070. ***Continues** Jersey Publisher, 0021-5961.*
**Desc:** Looks at the press and newspaper publishing.

US/1056-3504
**INCITE INFORMATION.** No. 13 (July/Aug. 1991)-. Periodical. English. bm. $10.00. Incite Information, PO Box 326, Arlington VA 22210. ***Continues** Big Forehead Express, 1049-978X.*

II/0019-6223
**INDIAN PUBLISHER AND BOOKSELLER, THE. Added/Corp** Federation of Publishers and Booksellers Associations in India. **VFOAT** Pustaka-Vyavasayi Patrika; Bharatiya Pustaka Prakasaka Aura Vikreta. Vol. 1 (Nov. 1950)-. Periodical. English. Twelve times a year. $4.00 (latest edition). Indian Publisher and Bookseller, Popular Book Depot, Bombay 7 India. **LC** Z457; .I5.

US/0019-6711
**INDIANA PUBLISHER, THE. Added/Corp** Hoosier State Press Association. (19??)-. Periodical. English. mo. $5.00. Hoosier State Press Association Inc, 1542 Consolidate Building, 115 North Penn, Indianapolis IN 46204. **Tel** (317)637-3966. **ED** Grace A Falvey, 115 N Penn #300, Indianapolis, IN 46204 (phone# (317)637-3966). **LC** PN4700; .I39. **Ad Acc.** ctrl circ. ***Absorbed** Confidential bulletin (Hoosier State Press Association).*

US
**INFORMATION EXPRESS / NATIONAL STANDARDS ASSOCIATION, INC.** Began in 1983. Periodical. English. mo. Information Handling Services, 15 Inverness Way East, Englewood CO 80150. **Tel** (800)525-7052, (303)790-0600, FAX (303)397-2599, telex 4322083.

US
**INFORMATION INDUSTRY FACTBOOK : THE INFORMATION INDUSTRY'S ANNUAL REPORT. *Ceased.*** (19??)-(19??). English. an. Digital Information Group, 51 Bank Street, Stamford CT 06901. **Tel** (800)255-0942, FAX (203)977-8310.
**Desc:** A compendium of trends and statistics about the business of publishing information.

US/1058-4730
**INFORMATION PUBLISHING. See** Journalism.

US/1052-0120
**INSIDER'S GUIDE TO BOOK EDITORS AND PUBLISHERS, THE. *Title Change.*** [Insid. guide book ed. publ.]. **VFOAT** Guide to Book Editors and Publishers; Book Editors and Publishers. (1991-1992). English. Prima Publishing & Communication, PO Box 1260JHB, Rocklin CA 95677. **ED** Jeff Herman. **LC** Z475; .I57. **DD** 070.5/2025/7. ***Continued by** Insider's Guide to Book Editors, Publishers, and Literary Agents, 1064-5667.*

FR
**INTERNATIONAL DIRECTORY OF SCHOLARLY PUBLISHERS. Added/Corp** Unesco. International Association of Scholarly Publishers. (1977)-. English. ir. UNESCO / France, 31 rue Francois Bonvin, 75732 Paris Cedex 15 France. **Tel** 011 33 1 45684564, 011 33 1 45684565, FAX 011 33 1 42733007, telex 204461 Paris. **LC** Z286.S37; I572. **DD** 070.5/94/025.

US/0074-6827
**INTERNATIONAL LITERARY MARKET PLACE. See** Publishing-Abstracting, Bibliographies and Statistics.

TH/0125-4111
**ISDS-SEA BULLETIN. VFOAT** I.S.D.S.-S.E.A. Bulletin. Vol. 1, No. 1 (1980)-. Bulletin. English (Thai, Indonesian, Malay, Tamil, Chinese and Tagalog). an. Free. ISDS-SEA Regional Centre, National Library of Thailand, Samsen Road, Bangkok 10300 Thailand. **Tel** 2815212, telex 84189 DEPFIAR TH. **ED** Songvit Kaeosri. **LC** Z6957; .I82; PN4832. **DD** 015.59/034. Index available. **Circ:** 1,000. available on a computer list.
**Desc:** The bulletin is a list of serials published in five member countries of Indonesia, Malaysia, Philippines, Singapore and Thailand. Contains data received within March of previous year and February of present year.

RU
**IZDATELSKOE DELO; BIBLIOGRAFICHESKAIA INFORMATSIIA.** **Added/Corp** Gosudarstvennyi Komitet SSSR po Delam Izdatelstv, Poligrafii i Knizhnoi Torgovli. Vsesoiuznaia Knizhnaia Palata. Tsentralnoe Biuro Nauchno-Tekhnicheskoi Informatsii i Tekhnko-Ekonomicheskikh Issledovanii po Poligraficheskoi Promyshlennosti, Izdatelskomu Delu i Knozhnoi Torgovle. (1973)-. Periodical. Russian (Multiple languages). mo. 0.06 rub (single issue). Izdatelstvo Kniga, 50 Gorky Ulitsa, 125047 Moscow Russia. **LC** Z279; .I95. ***Supersedes in part*** *Izdatelskoe Delo, Knigovedenie, Knizhnaia Torgovlia i Gosudarstvennaia Bibliografiia.*

JA
**JAPAN PUBLISHERS DIRECTORY.** 1st Ed. (1987)-. Directory. English. Intercontinental Marketing Corporation, IPO Box 5056, Tokyo 100-31 Japan. **Tel** 011 81 3 3661 7458, FAX 011 81 3 3661 9646.
**Desc:** The largest and most complete listing ever attempted of commercial publishers and other organizations.

US/0021-5961
**JERSEY PUBLISHER.** ***Title Change.*** [Jersey publ.]. **Added/Corp** New Jersey Press Association. (19??)-(19??). Periodical. English. mo. New Jersey Press, Association of Rutgers University, 206 West State Street, Trenton NJ 08608. **DD** 070. ***Continued by*** *In Print (Trenton, N.J.), 1067-5132.*

●CN
**JOURNAL OF SCHOLARLY PUBLISHING.** **VFOAT** Scholarly Publishing. Vol. 25, No. 3 (Apr. 1994)-. Periodical. English. qt. $53.00. University of Toronto Press, 5201 Dufferin Street, Downsview Ontario M3H 5T8 Canada. **Tel** (416)667-7781, (416)667-7782, FAX (416)667-7803. **LC** Z286.S37; S33. ***Continues*** *Scholarly Publishing, 0036-634X.*
**Desc:** A journal for authors as well as publishers, it is the only international quarterly devoted to the writing, publication, and use of serious nonfiction. For 23 years, its editors have offered a unique blend of philosophical analysis and practical advice that has attracted readers around the world.

RU
**KATALOG KNIG IZDATELSTVA NAUKA.** **Main/Corp** Izdatelstvo Nauka. (1967)-. Russian. te. Izdatelstvo Nauka / Akademiia Nauk, Publishing House of the Russian Academy of Sciences, Leninskii Porspekt 14, 117901 Moscow Russia. **Tel** 011 95 954-21-53, FAX 011 95 938-21-44, telex 411964. **LC** Z2493; .I9b. ***Continues*** *Katalog Knig Izdatelstva Akademii Nauk SSSR.*

US/0453-4867
**KEMBLE OCCASIONAL, THE.** ***Ceased.*** **See** Printing Industry.

RU
**KNIGI GLAVNOI REDAKTSII VOSTOCHNOI LITERATURY IZDATELSTVA NAUKA.** **Main/Corp** Izdatelstvo Nauka. Glavnaia Redaktsiia Vostochnoi Literatury. **Added/Corp** Akademiia Nauk SSSR. (1966)-. Russian. ir. Izdatelstvo Nauka / Akademiia Nauk, Publishing House of the Russian Academy of Sciences, Leninskii Porspekt 14, 117901 Moscow Russia. **Tel** 011 95 954-21-53, FAX 011 95 938-21-44, telex 411964. **LC** Z2493; .I9a.

XO
**KNIZNY MAGAZIN.** Czech. 24.00. Zdruzeni Slvenskych Vdavatelstiev a Podnikov, Knizneho Obchodu Vo Vydavatelstve Obzor, Ul Cs Armady 29 A, Bratislava Slovakia. **LC** Z301.7; .K5.

PL/0137-2998
**KWARTALNIK HISTORII PRASY POLSKIEJ.** [Kwart. hist. prasy pol.]. **Added/Corp** Polska Akademia Nauk. Pracownia Historii Czasopismiennictwa Polskiego XIX i XX Wieku. Vol. 16 (1977)-. Periodical. Polish. qt. $48.00. **(Subscription address:** ARS Polona, PO Box 1001, 00068 Warsaw Poland.**)** **LC** PN5355.P6; R58. ***Continues*** *Rocznik Historii Czasopismiennictwa Polskiego.*
**Ind/Abst** Am. Hist. Life (1989-).

US/1056-0327
**LAUGHING BEAR NEWSLETTER.** [Laugh. bear newsl.]. Newsletter. English. mo. $8.00 US; $10.00 North America; $17.50 other. Laughing Bear Press, PO Box 36159, Denver CO 80236-0159. **Tel** (303)989-5614. **ED** Tom Person. **DD** 070. **[CCC].** Index available. **Bk Rev. Ad Acc. Circ:** 150.
**Desc:** Small press information and how-to reviews of small press publications and resources for the small press publisher and writer.

UK/0953-1513
**LEARNED PUBLISHING.** (LEARNED PUBLISHING : JOURNAL OF THE ASSOCIATION OF LEARNED AND PROFESSIONAL SOCIETY PUBLISHERS.). [Learn. publ.]. **Added/Corp** Association of Learned and Professional Society Publishers. (198?)-. Periodical. English. qt. £60.00 UK; $110.00 US. The Association of Learned and Professional Society Publishers, 48 Kelsey Lane Bechenham, Kent BR3 3NE England. **Tel** 011 44 81 6580459. **(Subscription address:** Turpin Distribution Services Limited, Blackhorse Road, Letchworth, Hertfordshire SG6 1HN, United Kingdom.**)** **ED** H.K. Bell. **LC** Z286.S37; L4. **DD** 070.5/94/05. Index available. **Circ:** 300. ***Continues*** *Bulletin of ALPSP.*

US/0149-1695
**LEGAL BRIEFS FOR EDITORS, PUBLISHERS, AND WRITERS.** **See** Law.

US/1056-196X
**LEGAL PUBLISHER, THE.** (THE LEGAL PUBLISHER [COMPUTER FILE].). [Legal publ.]. Vol. 1, No. 1 (1991)-. Newsletter. English. mo (11 issues). $149.00. JK Publisher, PO Box 71020, Milwaukee WI 53211. **Tel** (414)332-1625, FAX (414)962-0084. **ED** John Kenney. **DD** 070.
**Ind/Abst** PTS Newsl. Database [Full Txt.].

FR
**LETTRE (PARIS, 1957).** ***Suspended.*** (1957)-. French. mo. 200.00F. Lettre, 68 rue de Babylone, 75007 Paris France. **Tel** 011 31 1 45515713.

FR
**LIVRES.** French. Agent Comptable du CNDP, BP 107-05, 75224 Paris Cedex 05 France.

CN/0836-7078
**LIVRES DISPONIBLES CANADIENS DE LANGUE FRANCAISE.** [Livres dispon. can. langue fr.]. **Added/Corp** Bibliodata (Firme). **VFOAT** Canadian French Books in Print. (September 1987)-. Periodical. French. qt. 270.00Can$ Canada; 295.00Can$ other. Periodica Inc, PO Box 444, Outremont Quebec H2V 4R6 Canada. **Tel** (514)274-5468, FAX (514)274-0201. ***Continues*** *Liste des Livres Disponibles de Langue Francaise des Auteurs et des Editeurs Canadiens.*

FR/0294-0027
**LIVRES DU MOIS, LES.** [Livres mois]. (Jan. 1982)-. Periodical. French. mo. Editions Professionnelles du Livre, BP 180, 75263 Paris Cedex 06 France. **Tel** 011 33 1 44412800, FAX 011 33 1 44412864. ***Formed by the union of*** *Livres du Mois (Edition Avec Prix Cession de Base), 0223-498X; Livres du Mois (Edition Destinee a l'Etranger), 0223-5005* ***and*** *Livres du Mois (Edition sans Prix), 0223-4998.*
**Ind/Abst** Annu. Bibliogr. Engl. Lang. Lit.

US/0047-4959
**LOCUS (CAMBRIDGE, MASS.).** **See** Literature.

US/0744-3102
**MAGAZINE & BOOKSELLER.** [Mag. books.]. **VFOAT** Magazine and Bookseller; M&B. Vol. 37, No. 2 (Feb. 1982)-. Periodical. English. Twelve times a year. $49.00. North American Publishing Company, 401 North Broad Street, Philadelphia PA 19108. **Tel** (215)238-5300, (800)777-8074, FAX (215)238-5283. **ED** Michele Marini. **LC** Z284; .M27. **DD** 338.8/260705. **Bk Rev. Ad Acc.** available on microfilm from University Microfilms International (UMI). ***Continues*** *Marketing Bestsellers, 0164-9876;* ***Absorbed*** *Profitways.*

US/0882-049X
**MAGAZINE DESIGN & PRODUCTION.** ***Title Change.*** **See** Journalism.

US/0899-7039
**MAGAZINE ISSUES.** [MagazineIssues]. **VFOAT** MagazineIssues. Vol. 7, No. 3 (June 1988)-. Periodical. English. qt. $20.00 US; $25.00 Canada. Feredonna Communications, Drawer 23010, Knoxville TN 37933. **Tel** (615)584-1918. **ED** Michael Scott Wart (editor's address: Drawer 9808, Knoxville TN 37940). **LC** Z286.P4; P82. **DD** 070.5/72. **Ad Acc. Circ:** 10,000 (ctrl). ***Continues*** *Publishing Trade, 0730-6741.*
**Desc:** Addresses the problems and opportunities faced by publishers in all areas of magazine management.

CN/1184-1516
**MAGAZINE MARKETS & FEES.** ***Title Change.*** [Mag. mark. fees]. **Added/Corp** Periodical Writers Association of Canada. **VFOAT** Magazine Markets and Fees. (1990)-(199?). English. be. Periodical Writers Association of Canada, 24 Ryerson Avenue, Toronto Ontario M5T 2P3 Canada. **Tel** (416)868-6914, (416)504-1645, FAX (416)860-0826. **DD** 015.71/034. ***Continues*** *Fees Survey., 0829-0865.* ***Continued by*** *Who Pays What, 1193-6665.*

US/8756-3827
**MAGAZINE PEOPLE.** [Mag. people]. '84-. English. an. $50.00. MIN Publishing Inc, 145 East 49th Street, New York NY 10017. **Tel** (212)751-2670. **ED** William E Barlow. **LC** Z479; .M34. **DD** 070.5/025/73.
**Desc:** A who's who of magazine publishing.

US/0889-8502
**MAGAZINES CAREER DIRECTORY.** [Mag. career dir.]. **Added/Corp** Career Press Inc. Visible Ink Press. 2nd Ed. (1987)-. Directory. English. be. $29.95 (hardcover), $17.95 (softcover). Gale Research Inc., 835 Penobscot Building, Detroit MI 48226. **Tel** (800)877-GALE, (313)961-2242, FAX (313)961-6083, telex TWX 810-221-7086. **LC** PN4797; .M23. **DD** 070.5/72/02373. ***Continues*** *Magazine Publishing Career Directory, 0882-827X.*
**Desc:** Discusses some of the industry's varied career paths including art, editor, sales, and business management.

US/0895-2124
**MAGAZINEWEEK (FRAMINGHAM, MASS.).** ***Ceased.*** (MAGAZINEWEEK.). [MagazineWeek]. **VFOAT** Magazine Week. (1987)-(1993). Periodical. English. wk (except for the first week in Jan. and August, the second week in July and December). Cowles Business Media Inc., 6 River Bend Center, 911 Hope Street, Stamford CT 06907. **Tel** (203)358-9900, (800)775-3777, FAX (203)357-9014. **(Subscription address:** PO Box 504, Mount Morris IL 61054; telephone: (800)435-0715**)** **ED** Gary Hoenig. **DD** 070. **Ad Acc. Circ:** 1,500.
**Desc:** The magazine publishing industry's weekly publication of record. Each issue offers up-to-date news, thought provoking analysis and an ongoing chronical of the world's leading magazine publishing companies, the people who run them, and the factors that affect them.

US/0272-5541
**MASSON TODAY.** **Main/Corp** Masson Publishing USA. V. 1-. Periodical. English. qt. Masson SA, Avenue Beauregard 12, CH-1701 Fribourg Switzerland. **Tel** 011 41 37 249585, FAX 011 41 37 247559, telex 942658 SEMI CH. **(Subscription address:** 7A Boulevard de Perolles, CH-1701 Fribourg Switzerland**)**

CN/0832-512X
**MASTHEAD (MISSISSAUGA).** (MASTHEAD.). [Masthead]. Vol. 1, No. 1 (Oct. 1987)-. Periodical. English. Ten times a year (Except January & July). 34.24Can$ Canada; 42.00Can$ others. North Island Publishing, 1606 Sedlescomb Drive, Unit 8, Ontario L4X 1M6 Canada. **Tel** (905)625-7070. **ED** Doug Bennet. **DD** 070.5/72/0971. **Ad Acc. Circ:** 5,000 (ctrl).
**Desc:** The Canadian magazine about magazines.

GW/0170-4184
**MEDIA DATEN ZEITUNGEN, ANZEIGENBLATTER.** **VFOAT** Media Daten Handbuch der Deutschen Werbetrager; Media Daten Zeitungen. (198?)-. Periodical. German. ir (7 issues per year). DM706.00 Germany; DM736.00 other. Media Daten Verlagsgesellschaf GmbH, Postfach 4260, D-65032 Wiesbaden Germany. **Tel** 011 49 6123 7000, FAX 011 49 6123 700122. **LC** Z6941; .M42; PN5219.G3. **DD** 015.43035. ctrl circ. ***Continues in part*** *Media Daten: Zeitungen, Radio + [i.e. und] TV.*
**Desc:** Information on publishers, publishing, newspapers, and advertising.

DK/0076-5821
**MEDIA SCANDINAVIA.** **Added/Corp** Danske Reklamebureauers Brancheforening. (1967)-. Danish (English). an. Kr590.00. Danish Association of Advertising Agencies, Badstuestrede 20, 1209 Kobenhavn N Denmark. **Tel** 011 45 33 134444. **ED** Borge O. Madsen. **LC** Z6941; .M4. **Ad Acc. Circ:** 2,100. ***Continues*** *Media.*
**Desc:** Covering all Scandinavian countries. Information on newspapers, magazines, tradepapers, etc. Data on readerships rates circulations and production details.

US/0270-9864
**MEMORANDUM - AMERICAN NEWSPAPER PUBLISHERS ASSOCIATION.** [Memo. - Am. Newsp. Publ. Assoc.]. **Main/Corp** American Newspaper Publishers Association. Began with Mar. 1976 issue. Periodical. English. $100.00. American Newspaper Publishers Association, PO Box 17407, Dulles International Airport, Washington DC 20041. **Tel** (703)648-1000. **ED** James E Donahue. **LC** Z675.N37; A45A. **DD** 026/.071/3. **Bk Rev. Ad Acc. Circ:** 10,000 (ctrl). ***Continues*** *American Newspaper Publishers Association. Library Bulletin, 0402-0170.*
**Desc:** Journal of the American Newspapers Association, content includes press freedom, government affairs, circulation, advertising, labor and personnel, telecommunications, newsprint, promotion, education, news editorial, production technologies, and readerships.

CN/0708-790X
**MICROLOG NEWSLETTER.** [Microlog newsl.]. June 1979-. Newsletter. English. mo. Free with subscription to Microlog Index. Micromedia Limited, 20 Victoria Street, Toronto Ontario M5C 2N8 Canada. **Tel** (416)362-5211, (800)387-2689, FAX (416)362-6161, telex 06524668. **DD** 070.5/0971.

US/0889-9533
**MICROPUBLISHING REPORT.** [MicroPubl. rep.]. **VFOAT** Micro Publishing Report; Publishing Report. (1985)-. Periodical. English. mo. $295.00 North America; $320.00 other. Micropublishing Report, 21150 Hawthorne Boulevard/Suite 104, Torrance CA 90503. **Tel** (310)371-5787, FAX (650)256-2485. **ED** James Cavuoto. **DD** 070. ctrl circ.
**Desc:** Industry newsletter targeted at vendors of

electronic publishing and computer graphics hardware and software. Articles offer competitive insight into key technical and marketing trends in the industry.

US/0026-6671
**MISSOURI PRESS NEWS.** [Mo. press news]. **Added/Corp** Missouri Press Association. (1938)-. Periodical. English. Twelve times a year. $10.00. Missouri Press Association, 802 Locust, Columbia MO 65201. **Tel** (314)449-4167, FAX (314)874-5894. **ED** Kent Ford. **Ad Acc. Circ:** 1,500 (ctrl). Documents available from UMI Article Clearinghouse.
**Desc:** The Missouri Press Association for newspaper publishers, editors, printers, advertising and circulation managers and allied graphic arts trade.
**Ind/Abst** ABI/INFORM Glob. Ed.; ABI Inform Ondisc (March 1975-Nov. 1977).

UK
**MONDE. INDEX ANALYTIQUE, LE. VFOAT** Index Analytique. (1944-1945)-. French. mo. £407.00. Research Publications Ltd., PO Box 45, Reading RG1 8HF England. **Tel** 011 44 734 583247, 011 44 734 583248, FAX 011 44 734 591325, telex 848336 RPLG. **LC** AI21; .M58. **DD** 074/.36. cum. index.

US/0748-8173
**MONTHLY REPORT - ASSOCIATION OF AMERICAN PUBLISHERS.** (MONTHLY REPORT : A NEWSBULLETIN FOR MEMBERS OF THE ASSOCIATION OF AMERICAN PUBLISHERS / AAP.). [Mon. rep. - Assoc. Am. Publ.]. Vol. 1, No. 1 (Sept. 1984)-. Periodical. English. mo. AAP, 1718 Connecticut Avenue NW, Washington DC 20009. **Tel** (202)232-3335, FAX (202)745-0694. **ED** Judith Platt. **DD** 070. **Circ:** 2,300 (ctrl). ***Formed by the union of*** *AAP Capital Letter, 0162-3303; Trade Voices; AAP International News and Notes; Paperback Publishing Division Information Bulletin; AAP School Division Newsletter; Higher Education Division Information Bulletin; AAP Professional and Scholarly Division Newsletter* ***and*** *School Higher Education Trade Voices Paperback Publishing News and Notes.*
**Desc:** Reports on issues of concern to the American book publishing industry and the activities of its trade association.

US/0890-9512
**MORGAN REPORT ON DIRECTORY PUBLISHING.** [Morgan rep. dir. publ.]. **VFOAT** Morgan Report. (1???)-. Periodical. English. mo. $145.00. Morgan-Rand Publications Inc., 1800 Byberry Road 800, Huntingdon Valley PA 19006. **Tel** (215)938-5511, FAX (215)988-0402. **ED** Marie Weakley. **DD** 659. **[CCC].** Index available. **Ad Acc, Adv Mgr:** Mr. Wolden, **Tel** (609)259-1695. **Circ:** 1,000. available on an online database (file 636/Full-Text) from DIALOG; and NEWSNET.
**Desc:** Covers developments in directory publishing and yellow pages industry including new publications, mergers, trends, etc.
**Ind/Abst** PTS Newsl. Database [Full Txt.].

US/0739-5272
**MOTHEROOT JOURNAL.** ***Suspended.*** **See** Publishing-Books and Bookmaking.

PL
**NASZE PROBLEMY.** Periodical. Polish. 40.00 single issue. Warszawskii Wydawn Prasowe RSW Prasa-Ksiazka-Ruch, Ul Wiejska 12, Warszawa Poland. **LC** PN4705; .N37.

US/0897-4764
**NATIONAL ASSOCIATION OF DESKTOP PUBLISHERS FORUM, THE.** [Deskt. publ. forum]. **Added/Corp** National Association of Desktop Publishers (U.S.). Vol. 1 (1988)-. Periodical. English. bm. $95.00 membership. National Association of Desktop Publishers, 462 Old Boston Street, Topsfield MA 01983. **Tel** (800)874-4113, (508)887-7900, FAX (508)887-6117. **DD** 070.

US
**NATIONAL ASSOCIATION OF DESKTOP PUBLISHERS JOURNAL.** (1990)-. English. mo. $48.00. National Association of Desktop Publishers, 462 Old Boston Street, Topsfield MA 01983. **Tel** (800)874-4113, (508)887-7900, FAX (508)887-6117. ***Continues*** *Journal / National Association of Desktop Publishers, 0897-6503.*

US/0147-7528
**NATIONAL NEWSPAPER ASSOCIATION DIRECTORY.** **Main/Corp** National Newspaper Association. Directory. English. $2.00. National Newspaper Association, 1627 K Street NW, Suite 400, Washington, DC 20006. **Tel** (202)466-7200, FAX (202)331-1403. **LC** JK1010; .N37A. **DD** 070/.06/273. Index available. **Bk Rev.** ctrl circ.
**Desc:** Covers the news of the newspaper industry.

BU
**NATSIONALNA BIBLIOGRAFIIA NA REPUBLIKA BULGARIIA. SERIIA 1, BULGARSKI KNIGOPIS. KNIGI, NOTNI, GRAFICHESKI I KARTOGRAFSKI IZDANIIA.** **See** Publishing-Abstracting, Bibliographies and Statistics.

BU
**NATSIONALNA BIBLIOGRAFIIA NA REPUBLIKA BULGARIIA. SERIIA 2, BULGARSKI KNIGOPIS. SLUZHEBNI IZDANIIA I DISERTATSII.** **See** Publishing-Abstracting, Bibliographies and Statistics.

BU
**NATSIONALNA BIBLIOGRAFIIA NA REPUBLIKA BULGARIIA. SERIIA 5, LETOPIS NA STATIITE OT BULGARSKITE SPISANIIA I SBORNITSI.** **Added/Corp** Narodna Biblioteka "Sv. sv. Kiril i Metodii.". **VFOAT** Letopis na Statiite ot Bulgarskite Spisaniia i Sbornitsi; Bulgarian National Bibliography. Articles from Bulgarian Journals and Collections. (1991)-. Periodical. Bulgarian. bw. Narodna Biblioteka Sv.sv. Kiril i Metodij, 88 V. Levski Boulevard, 1504 Sofia Bulgaria. **Tel** 011 359 2 882811, FAX 011 359 2 881600, telex 22432. **LC** AI15; .L375. ***Continues*** *Natsionalna Bibliografiia na NR Bulgariia. Seriia 5, Letopis na Statiite ot Bulgarskite Spisaniia i Sbornitsi, 0324-0398.*

CN/0709-0641
**NEW BOOK NEWS FROM QUEBEC.** V. 1-Oct. 1978-. Periodical. English. mo. Free. Societe de Promotion du Livre Inc, 445 rue St Francois Xavier Street/Suite 40, Montreal Quebec H2Y 2T1 Canada. **Tel** (514)845-9183. **DD** 028.1/05.

US/0271-8197
**NEW PAGES.** [New pages]. (1980)-. Periodical. English. Three times a year. $12.00 three years. New Pages Press, 4426 South Balsay Road, Grand Blanc MI 48439. **Tel** (313)743-8055, FAX (313)743-2730. **ED** Casey Hill and Grant Burns. **LC** Z477; .N38. **DD** 070.5/0973. **Bk Rev. Ad Acc.**
**Desc:** Reviews books, periodicals and audio-visual material from independent publishers.
**Ind/Abst** Altern. Press Index (-199?); Book Rev. Index (1984-Oct. 1990).

PL/0028-6486
**NEW POLISH PUBLICATIONS.** ***Ceased.*** **VFOAT** Nouvelles Publications Polonaises; Polnische Neuerscheinungen; Polskie Izdaniia. ( )-(1990). Periodical. English. mo. **(Subscription address:** ARS Polona, PO Box 1001, 00068 Warsaw Poland.**)** **LC** Z2521; .N45. **DD** 015.438.

AT/0157-7662
**NEW ZEALAND BOOKS IN PRINT / NEW ZEALAND BOOK PUBLISHERS ASSOCIATION.** **See** Publishing-Abstracting, Bibliographies and Statistics.

CN/1183-4609
**NEWS / CANADIAN CENTRE FOR STUDIES IN PUBLISHING.** [News - Can. Cent. Stud. Publ.]. **Added/Corp** Canadian Centre for Studies in Publishing. **VFOAT** Canadian Centre for Studies in Publishing News. Issue 1 (Apr. 1991)-. Periodical. English. Three times a year. Free. Canadian Centre for Studies in Publishing, Simon Fraser University at Harbour Centre, 515 West Hastings Street, Vancouver British Columbia V6B 5K3 Canada. **DD** 070.5/0971.

US/0095-2680
**NEWS PREVIEWS.** (1974)-. Periodical. English. Twelve times a year. Free on request. Springer-Verlag New York Inc., 175 5th Avenue, New York NY 10010. **Tel** (212)460-1500, telex 232 235 SPB UR. **(Subscription address:** Springer Verlag New York Inc. / for North America, 44 Hartz Way, Secaucus NJ 07096.**)**
**Desc:** Announcement of new titles available from Springer-Verlag.

CN/1184-7379
**NEWSLETTER (CANADIAN MAGAZINE PUBLISHERS ASSOCIATION).** [Newsl. - Can. Mag. Publ. Assoc.]. **Added/Corp** Canadian Magazine Publishers Association. (1989)-. Newsletter. English (French). Six times a year. 15.00Can$. Canadian Magazine Publishers Association, 2 Stewart Street, Toronto Ontario M5V 1H6 Canada. **Tel** (416)362-2546, FAX (416)362-2547. **ED** Cindy Goldrick and Kathleen Hickey. **DD** 051/.06/071. **Bk Rev. Circ:** 500 (ctrl). ***Continues*** *CPPA Newsletter., 0826-9572.*
**Desc:** Practical information and news of interest to the Canadian consumer magazine industry.

CN/0825-7752
**NEWSLETTER / CANADIAN TELEBOOK AGENCY.** [Newsl. - Can. Telebook Agency]. **Added/Corp** Canadian Telebook Agency. 4 (Spring 1983)-. Newsletter. English. qt. Free to members. Canadian Telebook Agency, Suite 209/31 Wellesley Street, Toronto Ontario M4Y 1G7 Canada. **DD** 070.5/028/54. ***Continues*** *Information Newsletter (Canadian Telebook Agency), 0823-1893.*

US
**NEWSLETTER DESIGN.** Newsletter. English. mo. $95.00 US; $107.00 other. Newsletter Clearinghouse, PO Box 311, Rhinebeck NY 12572. **Tel** (914)876-2081, FAX (914)876-2561. **ED** Howard Penn Hudson.

CN/1185-5088
**NEWSLETTER TRENDS.** [Newsl. trends]. Vol. 1, No. 3 (Mar. 1991)-. Periodical. English. mo. $95.00. Sterling Communications Inc., Suite 104, 1920 Ellesmere Road, Scarborough Ontario M1H 2W7 Canada. **Tel** (416)512-2218. **ED** Barbara A. Fanson. **DD** 070.1/75. **Ad Acc, Adv Mgr:** same as editor. ***Continues*** *Trends (Scarborough, Ont.)., 1183-1855.*

US/0899-0425
**NEWSLETTERS IN PRINT.** [Newsl. print]. **Added/Corp** Gale Research Inc. 4th Ed. (1988/1989)-. English. an. $185.00. Gale Research Inc., 835 Penobscot Building, Detroit MI 48226. **Tel** (800)877-GALE, (313)961-2242, FAX (313)961-6083, telex TWX 810-221-7086. **ED** Shawn Brennan. **LC** Z6941; .N3; PN4888.N48. **DD** 071/.3/025. available on magnetic tape; available on diskette; available on an online database (File Option NIP) from HRIN; and (File 469) DIALOG. ***Continues*** *Newsletters Directory, 0893-7656.*
**Desc:** Provides detailed entries for over 12,000 sources of authoritative information on a wide range of high-interest topics.

US/0889-4590
**NEWSPAPER FINANCIAL EXECUTIVE JOURNAL.** **See** Journalism.

US/0739-5329
**NEWSPAPER RESEARCH JOURNAL.** [Newsp. res. j.]. **Added/Corp** Association for Education in Journalism and Mass Communication. Newspaper Division. Association for Education in Journalism. Newspaper Division. **VFOAT** NRJ. (Nov. 1979)-. Periodical. English. Four times a year. $40.00 (institutions), $20.00 (individuals), $30.00 (newspaper & media organizations). Newspaper Research Journal, EW Scripps School of Journalism, Ohio University, Athens OH 45701-2979. **Tel** (614)593-2471, FAX (614)593-2592. **ED** Ralph S. Izard. **LC** PN4700; .N515. **DD** 070/.05. Index available (included in subscription price). **Bk Rev. Pr Rev. Circ:** 1,500 (ctrl). available on microfilm and microfiche from University Microfilms International (UMI). Documents available from UMI Article Clearinghouse.
**Desc:** Practical research and commentary of interest to the newspaper industry on topics including advertising, circulation, management, ownership, reporting, legal and writing.
**Ind/Abst** Commun. Abstr.; Expand. Acad. Index (1992-); Newsp. Period. Abstr. (1989-).

GW
**NEWSPAPER TECHNIQUES (DARMSTADT, GERMANY).** (NEWSPAPER TECHNIQUES.). **Added/Corp** INCA-FIEJ Research Association. **VFOAT** IFRA Newspaper Techniques. (19??)-. Newsletter. English (German and French). mo (11 issues). DM377.50. International Research Association Newspaper Technology, Washingtonplatz 1, D 64287 Darmstadt Germany. **Tel** 011 49 6151 700561, FAX 011 49 6151 784542, telex 0419273. **ED** George B. Smith. **LC** Z119; .N44. **DD** 070.5/72/05. Index available. **Bk Rev. Ad Acc. Circ:** 4,880 (ctrl).
**Desc:** Technical magazine dealing with developments in the newspaper industry and the news media on an international basis.
**Ind/Abst** Abstr. Bull. Inst. Pap. Sci. Tech.; Abstr. Graphic Arts Tech. Found. (1979, 1984); Graph. Arts Bull. Inst. Pap. Sci. Technol. (Feb. 1989-March 1989, May 1989-July 1989, Sept. 1989, Dec. 1989); Print. Abstr.

US/0730-224X
**NEWSREAL.** **VFOAT** News Real. (19??)-. Periodical. English. Twelve times a year. $8.00. Newsreal, PO Box 40323, Tucson AZ 85717. **Tel** (602)887-3982. available on microfilm from Bell & Howell. ***Continues*** *Tucson's Mountain Newsreal.*

UK
**NEWSTIME (LONDON, ENGLAND).** ***Ceased.*** (NEWSTIME.). ( )-(Sept. 1988). Periodical. English. mo. Newspaper Society, 6 Carmelite Street, London EC4Y 0BL England. **Tel** 01 583 3311, FAX 01 353 7179, telex 265 871 MONREF Q. **ED** Gary Cullum. **LC** PN4701; .N43. **DD** 070/.05. **Bk Rev. Ad Acc. Circ:** 2,500 (ctrl).
**Desc:** Journal of the Newspaper Society; covers matters concerning newspaper publishing and management, law, technology, sales and advertising.
**Ind/Abst** Print. Abstr.

US/1049-1872
**NIE INFORMATION SERVICE.** [NIE inf. serv.]. **VAT** Newspaper in Education Information Service. (19??)-. Periodical. English. Twelve times a year. $140.00 US; $152.00 Canada; $175.00 other. RCAnderson

Associates Inc., PO Drawer 300, Pittsford NY 14534. **Tel** (716)248-5385, FAX (716)248-9551. **DD** 070. Index available.

CN/0820-8255
**NIGOG +, LE.** [Nigog +]. **VAT** Nigog Plus. Feb. 1983. Periodical. French. qt. Free. Association des Editeurs de Periodiques Culturels Quebecois, C P 786 Succursale Place d'Armes, Montreal Quebec H2Y 3J2 Canada. **Tel** (514)523-7724. **DD** 070.5/72/060714. **Circ:** 450.
**Desc:** Liaison and informative bulletin for periodicals that are members of the Association of Publishers of Cultural Periodicals in Quebec.

JA
**NIHON SHUPPANJIN SOKAN.** (1976)-. Japanese. Bunka Tsushinsha, 1-12 Yushima 4-chome Bunkyo-ku, Tokyo 113 Japan. **LC** Z463.5; .N55.

US/0897-9812
**NOVEL & SHORT STORY WRITER'S MARKET. See** Literature.

US/0743-9792
**OFFICIAL PRICE GUIDE TO PAPERBACKS & MAGAZINES, THE. See** Hobbies.

US/0896-9841
**OPTICAL PUBLISHING DIRECTORY, THE.** ***Title Change.*** [Opt. publ. dir.]. (1987)-(1992). Directory. English. an. Learned Information Inc., 143 Old Marlton Pike, Medford NJ 08055-8750. **Tel** (609)654-6266, FAX (609)654-4309. **LC** Z286.E43; O67. **DD** 070.5/0285. **CODEN** OPDIEW. ***Continues*** *Optical/Electronic Publishing Directory, 0893-0317.* ***Continued by*** *CD-ROM Finder.*
**Desc:** An objective unbiased view of the state-of-the-marketplace for anyone involved in the optical publishing area. Over 84 products from vendors are detailed. Semi-annual updates ensure coverage of new products, applications and trends.

US/0745-6379
**OREGON PUBLISHER.** [Or. publ.]. **Added/Corp** Oregon Newspaper Publishers Association. (1932)-. Periodical. English. Twelve times a year. $7.50. Oregon Newspaper Publishers Association, 2130 5th Street SW / Suite 2, Portland OR 97201.

US/0193-7391
**OUTPUT MODE.** (July 1979)-. Periodical. English. mo. $24.00. Padre Productions Inc, Box 1275, San Luis Obispo CA 93406. **Tel** (805)543-5404.

UK
**PALAUY DULCET ANTONIO MANUAL DEL LIBRERO HISPANO AMERICANO.** Spanish. £25.00. Dolphin Book Co Ltd, Tredwr Llangranog Llandyssul, Dyfed SA44 6BA Wales. **Tel** 404 02 3978.

NR
**PAN AFRICAN BOOK WORLD.** Vol. 1, No. 1 (Aug. 1981)-. Periodical. English. Fourth Dimension Publishers, 179 Zik Avenue Enugu, Anambra State Nigeria. **LC** Z465; .P36. **DD** 070.5/096.

US/0896-8209
**PC PUBLISHING.** ***Title Change.*** [PC publ.]. **VAT** Personal Computer Publishing. Periodical. English. mo. PC Publishing, 950 Lee Street, Des Plaines IL 60016. **Tel** (312)296-0770. **ED** Robert Mueller. **DD** 004. **[CCC]. Bk Rev. Ad Acc. Circ:** 50,000 (ctrl). ***Continued by*** *PC Publishing and Presentations, 1056-540X.*
**Desc:** Desktop publishing/presentation graphics for IBM and compatible PC users.
**Ind/Abst** Comput. Rev. Index (Dec. 1987-); Graph. Arts Bull. Inst. Pap. Sci. Technol. (Jan. 1989-March 1989, May 1989-June 1989, Aug. 1989, Oct. 1989, Dec. 1989).

CN/0847-1231
**PERIODICAL PUBLISHING.** (PERIODICAL PUBLISHING / STATISTICS CANADA, EDUCATION, CULTURE AND TOURISM DIVISION.). [Period. publ.]. **Added/Corp** Statistics Canada. Education, Culture and Tourism Division. **VFOAT** Edition du Periodique. (1987/1988)-. English (French). an. 20.00Can$ Canada; $24.00 US; $28.00 other. Statistics Canada, Publications Sales & Services, Main Building Room 1710, Ottawa Ontario K1A 0T6 Canada. **Tel** (613)951-5078, (800)267-6677, FAX (613)951-1584, telex 053-3585. **LC** Z484; .C85. **DD** 070.5/72/0971021. ***Continues*** *Culture Statistics, Periodical Publishing, Preliminary Statistics., 0831-7267.*
**Desc:** Provides details on all aspects of the Periodical Publishing Survey including highlights and methodology.

SP
**PERIODICOS Y REVISTAS ESPANOLAS E HISPANOAMERICANAS.** (19??)-. Spanish (English, French and German). ir. $250.00. Libros de Espana y America, 170 23 83rd Avenue, Jamaica Hills NY 11432. **Tel** (718)291-9891, FAX (718)291-9830. **Bk Rev. Ad Acc.**
**Desc:** Comprehensive directory of all periodical publications in Spanish, worldwide.

US/0030-8196
**PNPA PRESS.** [PNPA press]. **Added/Corp** Pennsylvania Newspaper Publisher's Association. **VAT** Pennsylvania Newspaper Publisher's Association Press. (1929)-. Periodical. English. mo (10 issues). $17.75. PA Newspaper Publication Association, 2717 North Front Avenue, Harrisburg PA 17110. **Tel** (717)234-4067. **ED** M. Diane McCormick. **Bk Rev. Ad Acc. Circ:** 900. Documents available from UMI Article Clearinghouse. ***Continues*** *PNPA Press Bulletin.*
**Desc:** Edited for the newspaper and publishing industry of Pennsylvania. Comment on journalism, advertising circulation, marketing, personnel etc.
**Ind/Abst** ABI/INFORM Glob. Ed.; ABI Inform Ondisc (Jan. 1975-Dec. 1977).

US/0272-0671
**POLICY PUBLISHERS AND ASSOCIATIONS DIRECTORY.** ***Ceased.*** **See** Social Sciences.

US/1042-0304
**PRE- (PRAIRIE VILLAGE, KAN.).** (PRE-.). [Pre-]. Vol. 1, No. 1 (Jan. 1989)-. Periodical. English. qt. $45.00 US; $58.00 Canada; $150.00 other. Cowles Business Media Inc., 6 River Bend Center, 911 Hope Street, Stamford CT 06907. **Tel** (203)358-9900, (800)775-3777, FAX (203)357-9014. **ED** Maureen Waters. **LC** Z286.E43; P73. **DD** 070. **Bk Rev. Ad Acc. Circ:** 40,000 (ctrl).
**Desc:** Targeted toward users and buyers of electronic design and pre-press systems and services. Editorial will cover news, trends, products and services in the industry.
**Ind/Abst** Abstr. Bull. Inst. Pap. Sci. Tech.; Graph. Arts Bull. Inst. Pap. Sci. Technol. (Dec. 1989-).

US/0194-3243
**PRESSTIME.** [Presstime]. **VAT** Press Time. Vol. 1 (Oct. 1979)-. Periodical. English. mo. $100.00 US; $135.00 other. Newspaper Association of America, 11600 Sunrise Valley Drive, Reston VA 22091. **Tel** (703)648-1286. **LC** PN4700; .P74. **DD** 070/.05. Index available. **Ad Acc. Circ:** 15,000 (ctrl).
**Desc:** A journal of the American Newspaper Publishers Association which covers all aspects of the newspaper business.
**Ind/Abst** Abstr. Bull. Inst. Pap. Sci. Tech.; Abstr. Graphic Arts Tech. Found. (1984); Graph. Arts Bull. Inst. Pap. Sci. Technol. (Feb. 1989-March 1989, May 1989-July 1989, Oct. 1989, Dec. 1989); Print. Abstr.; Stat. Ref. Index; World Publ. Monit.

US/1058-4749
**PRINT PUBLISHING FOR THE SCHOOL MARKET.** [Print publ. sch. mark.]. **Added/Corp** Simba Information Inc. 1st Ed. (1991)-. English. be (every two years). $1501.00. Simba Information Inc., 213 Danbury Road, Wilton CT 06897-7430. **Tel** (203)834-0033 ext. 133, FAX (203)884-1771. **LC** Z286.T48; P75. **DD** 381/.45002/0973.

US/0032-860X
**PRINTING IMPRESSIONS. See** Printing Industry.

CN/0575-9412
**PRINTING, PUBLISHING AND ALLIED INDUSTRIES. See** Printing Industry.

UK/0032-9878
**PRODUCTION JOURNAL.** [Prod. j.]. **Added/Corp** Newspaper Society (London, England). (19??)-. Periodical. English. Ten times a year. £25.00. The Newspaper Society, Bloomsbury House, Bloomsbury Square, 74-77 Great Russell Street, London WC1B 3DA England. **Tel** 11 44 71 636 701439, FAX 11 44 71 631 5119, telex 265871. **ED** Gary Cullum. **DD** 070. **Bk Rev. Ad Acc, Adv Mgr:** Terry Gunter, **Tel** 071 404 1501. **Circ:** 3,000. Documents available from UMI Article Clearinghouse, Ask*IEEE.
**Desc:** All matters connected with newspaper publishing.
**Ind/Abst** ABI/INFORM Glob. Ed.; ABI Inform Ondisc (Jan. 1975-April 1977); Abstr. Bull. Inst. Pap. Sci. Tech.; Abstr. Graphic Arts Tech. Found. (1979); Graph. Arts Bull. Inst. Pap. Sci. Technol. (March 1989, Sept. 1989, Nov. 1989); INSPEC; Print. Abstr.

●US/1066-0674
**PROFESSIONAL PUBLISHING UPDATE.** [Prof. pub. update]. (1993)-. Periodical. English. bm. W.B. Saunders Company, A Subsidiary of Harcourt Brace Jovanovich, Inc., The Curtis Center/Suite 300, Independence Square West, Philadelphia PA 19106-3399. **Tel** (215)238-7800 or, 5587, FAX (215)238-7883, telex 173146. **(Subscription address:** W. B. Saunders Company / North America Subscriptions, c/o Periodicals, 6277 Sea Harbour Drive, 4th Floor, Orlando FL 32887.) **DD** 070.

BE
**PUB NEWSLETTER.** (19??)-. Newsletter. French (Dutch). ir (85 times a year). 15455.00F. Kluwer Business, Excelsiorlaan 18, 1930 Zaventem Belgium. **Tel** 011 32 2 7191592. **ED** Bernard Lefeure. **Ad Acc. Circ:** 300.

US/8756-4084
**PUBFAX.** ***Ceased.*** [PUBFAX]. **VFOAT** Pub Fax. Vol. 1, No. 1 (Feb. 1985)-?. Periodical. English. mo. PubFax, 316 President Street, Brooklyn NY 11231. **DD** 070.

US/0885-6370
**PUBLICATION DESIGN ANNUAL. See** The Arts-Graphic Arts.

●US/1063-1739
**PUBLICITY AND MEDIA RESOURCES FOR BOOK PUBLISHERS. Added/Corp** Association of American University Presses. (1993)-. English. $189.00. Morgan-Rand Publications Inc., 1800 Byberry Road 800, Huntingdon Valley PA 19006. **Tel** (215)938-5511, FAX (215)988-0402.

UK/0269-3003
**PUBLISHER (HODDESDON, ENGLAND).** (THE PUBLISHER.). [Publisher]. Periodical. English. mo. $76.22 UK; $127.02 other. Macro Publishing Ltd., Conbar House, Mead Lane, Hertford SG13 7AS England. **Tel** 011 44 992 584233. **CODEN** PUBLE9. Documents available from Ask*IEEE.
**Ind/Abst** INSPEC (1985-).

CN/0380-8025
**PUBLISHER (OTTAWA).** ***Ceased.*** (PUBLISHER.). [Publisher]. **Added/Corp** Canadian Community Newspapers Association. (April 1973)-(1???). Trade Publication. English. mo. Canadian Community Newspapers Association, 90 Eglanton Avenue E Suite 206, Toronto ONT M4P 2Y3 Canada. **Tel** (416)482-1090. **ED** Maureen de Jong. **Ad Acc. Circ:** 1,200 (ctrl). ***Supersedes*** *Canadian Community Publisher, 0045-4583.*
**Desc:** A trade journal of the Canadian Community Newspapers Association.
**Ind/Abst** Print. Abstr.

US/0048-5942
**PUBLISHERS' AUXILIARY.** [Publ. aux.]. **Added/Corp** National Newspaper Association. Western Newspaper Union. (1865)-. Periodical. English. bw. $55.00 (US); $90.00 (other). National Newspaper Association, 1627 K Street NW, Suite 400, Washington, DC 20006. **Tel** (202)466-7200, FAX (202)331-1403. **ED** Chuck Holahan. **LC** PN4700; .P8. Index available. **Bk Rev. Ad Acc. Circ:** 8,000 (ctrl). available on microfilm. Documents available from UMI Article Clearinghouse.
**Desc:** The newspaper industry's oldest newspaper. Covers news and features of interest to publishers, editors and other key employees.
**Ind/Abst** ABI/INFORM Glob. Ed.; ABI Inform Ondisc (April 1975-Jan. 1977); Graph. Arts Bull. Inst. Pap. Sci. Technol. (Jan. 1989-Feb. 1989, May 1989, July 1989, Nov. 1989).

US/0735-665X
**PUBLISHERS' CATALOGS ANNUAL.** ***Ceased.*** (PUBLISHERS' CATALOGS ANNUAL [MICROFORM].). [Publ. cat. annu.]. (1979)-Ceased (19??). English. an. Chadwyck-Healey Limited, The Quorum Barnwell Road, Cambridge CB5 8SW England. **Tel** 011 44 223 215512, telex 9312102281 CH G.

US/0742-0501
**PUBLISHERS DIRECTORY.** [Pub. dir.]. **Added/Corp** Gale Research Company. 5th Ed. (1984)-. Directory. English. an. $275.00. Gale Research Inc., 835 Penobscot Building, Detroit MI 48226. **Tel** (800)877-GALE, (313)961-2242, FAX (313)961-6083, telex TWX 810-221-7086. **ED** Wendy Van de Sande. **LC** Z475; .B65. **DD** 070.5/025/73. **NLM** Z 475; B724. available on magnetic tape; available on diskette. ***Continues*** *Book Publishers Directory, 0196-0903.*
**Desc:** Source of detailed information on 19,000 U.S. and Canadian publishers covers all major publishing firms as well as small, independent presses and 600 distributors. Provides the most recent address, telephone number, date founded, ISBN prefix, principle personnel, a description of the aims of the organization, subjects covered in the firm's publications, discount and returns policy, and a list of representative titles.

US/0741-5966
**PUBLISHERS IDEA EXCHANGE.** (19??)-. English. mo. $122.50. Publishers Idea Exchange, 111 East Grand, Monticello IA 52310. **Tel** (319)465-5300.

II
**PUBLISHER'S MONTHLY.** (1959)-. Periodical. English (Hindi). Twelve times a year. Rs100.00. S. Chand & Company Ltd., PO Box 5733, Ram Nagar, New Delhi 110055 India. **Tel** 011 91 11 772080, FAX 011 91 11 7777446, telex 3161310. **ED** Shashi Kanta. **LC** Z284; .P8. **Bk Rev. Ad Acc. Circ:** 8,000 (ctrl).
**Desc:** Articles concerning educational topics, list of books published during the month, outstanding books of some particular subject beneficial to university students.

US/0887-316X
**PUBLISHER'S MULTINATIONAL DIRECT.** (PUBLISHER'S MULTINATIONAL DIRECT: PMD.). [Publ. multinatl. direct]. **VFOAT** PMD. Vol. 1, No. 1 (April 1986)-. Periodical. English. mo. $195.00 US, Mexico, and Canada; $225.00 other. Direct International

Inc, 1501 3rd Avenue, New York NY 10028. **Tel** (212)861-4188, FAX (212)988-3537, telex 237818SVP. **ED** Alfred M. Goodloe. **DD** 070.
**Desc:** An insider's monthly newsletter to help increase direct to customer sales of your publications in multinational markets. Covers news, ideas, tips on multinational lists, copy, offers, tests, licensing deals, agency representation, and more.

UK/0953-7899
**PUBLISHERS REPORTS.** [Publ. rep.]. (1988)-. Periodical. English. mo. £155.00. Outdoors Illustrated Inc, PO Box 845, Bath Avon, BA1 3TW England. **Tel** 011 44 225 443194, FAX 011 44 225 443195. **ED** F. Russell Cobb. **DD** 338.7610705. Index available. **Bk Rev. Ad Acc.**
**Desc:** Covers news, analysis and market surveys on international publishing.

US/0898-7076
**PUBLISHING & DISTRIBUTION FAX-SPEED NEWS FROM AMERICA : PDN.** [Publ. distrib. fax-speed news Am.]. **VFOAT** Publishing and Distribution Fax-Speed News from America; PDN. **VAT** Publishing & Distribution News. 1988-. Periodical. English. wk. $500.00 (by telefax) US; $750.00 (by telefax), $650.00 (by airmail). Roy Britton Associates, PO Box 421, Bedford NY 10506. **Tel** (914)234-7331, FAX (914)234-6591. **ED** Roy Britton. **DD** 071.
**Desc:** Timely information on U.S. publishing matters for senior management overseas.

US/1048-3055
**PUBLISHING & PRODUCTION EXECUTIVE.** [Publ. prod. exec.]. **VFOAT** Publishing and Production Executive. Vol. 3 No. 6 (Nov. 1989)-. Periodical. English. Twelve times a year. $38.00. North American Publishing Company, 401 North Broad Street, Philadelphia PA 19108. **Tel** (215)238-5300, (800)777-8074, FAX (215)238-5283. **LC** Z284.; .P86. **DD** 380. available on microfilm from University Microfilms International (UMI). ***Continues** Publishing Technology, 1040-9440.*
**Desc:** For manufacturing and fulfillment professionals in publishing. Editorial focus is on equipment, production techniques, computer hardware and software and related products and services. Issues contain management and purchasing tips, profiles of industry leaders and corporate trendsetters, manufacturing and fulfillment ideas and more.
**Ind/Abst** Abstr. Bull. Inst. Pap. Sci. Tech.; F&S Index Plus Text, Int. [Select. Cov.]; PROMT.

US/0190-048X
**PUBLISHING EDUCATION NEWSLETTER.** V. 1- Jan. 1979-. Newsletter. English. qt. Free to AAP members, $10.00 nonmembers. Education for Publishing Program, Association of American Publishers, 1 Park Avenue, New York NY 10016.

UK/0309-2445
**PUBLISHING HISTORY.** [Publ. hist.]. (1977)-. Academic Scholarly Publication. English. sa. $110.00 (institutions), $50.00 (individuals). Chadwyck-Healey Limited, The Quorum Barnwell Road, Cambridge CB5 8SW England. **Tel** 011 44 223 215512, telex 9312102281 CH G. **(Subscription address:** Chadwyck Healey Inc. / US Subscriptions, 1101 King Street, Suite 380, Alexandria VA 22314.**) ED** Michael Turner. **LC** Z280; .P8. **DD** 658.8/09/0705730941. **[CCC].** cum. index. **Ad Acc. Circ:** 800. available on microfiche. Documents available from The Genuine Article.
**Desc:** A scholarly journal devoted to the social, economic and literary history of book, newspaper and magazine publishing.
**Ind/Abst** Am. Hist. Life (1982-); Arts Humanit. Citation Index (19??-19??) [Full Cov.]; Br. Humanit. Index (1982-); Child. Lit. Abstr. (19??-); Curr. Contents Arts Humanit. (19??-); MLA Int. Bibl. Books Artic. Mod. Lang. Lit. (19??-); Res. Alert (19??-) [Full Cov.].

UK
**PUBLISHING NEWS.** English. Gradegate Ltd, 43 Museum Street, London WC1A 1ZY England.

US/0894-282X
**PUBLISHING NOTES.** [Publ. notes]. **Added/Corp** Graphic Arts Support Services. (198?)-. Newsletter. English. mo. $170.00. Graphic Arts Support Services Inc, 17 Center Street, Wayland MA 01778. **Tel** (617)653-7732. **DD** 070.

US/0741-6148
**PUBLISHING RESEARCH QUARTERLY.** **Added/Corp** Transaction Periodicals Consortium. (1991)-. Periodical. English. Four times a year. Fl167.00 (individual), Fl279.00 (institution). Transaction Publishers / Rutgers State University, New Brunswick NJ 08903. **Tel** (908)932-2280 Ext. 105, FAX (908)932-3138. **ED** Beth Luey. **[CCC]. Circ:** 1,100. available on labels. ***Continues** Book Research Quarterly, 0741-6148.*
**Desc:** Significant research and analysis on or about the full range of the publishing environment, the distribution and marketing of books and journals, and the social, political, economic and technological conditions that shape the publishing process from editorial decision making to order processing. The official journal of the International Association for Publishing Education.
**Ind/Abst** Child. Lit. Abstr. (19??-); PAIS Int. Print (1991-); Soc. Plann. Policy Dev. Abstr.

●UK/1351-0177
**PUBLISHING TECHNOLOGY REVIEW.** (1994)-. English. Ten times a year. £175.00 UK & Europe; $320.00 US; £200.00 other. Pira International, Randalls Road, Leatherhead, Surrey KT22 7RU England. **Tel** 011 44 372 376161, FAX 011 44 372 377526.

US/1061-6780
**PUBLISHING TRENDS & TRENDSETTERS.** [Publ. trends trendsetters]. **VFOAT** Publishing Trends and Trendsetters. No. 135 (Jan. 1991)-. Periodical. English. Ten times a year. $245.00. Oxbridge Communications Inc., 150 5th Avenue, Room 302, New York NY 10011. **Tel** (212)741-0231, FAX (212)633-2938. **ED** Jim Mann. **LC** Z479; .M43. **DD** 070.5. ***Continues** Media Management Monograph, 0192-7663.*
**Desc:** Takes you behind the doors of the executive suites of publishers all over the country, and probes for the success secrets of the trendsetters who are the acknowledged masters of their fields.

US/0735-6854
**QUALIS.** (QUALIS : THE YEARBOOK OF HUNTER PUBLISHING COMPANY.). 1981-. English. Hunter Publishing Company, PO Box 5867, Winston Salem NC 27113. **LC** Z286.Y43; Q34. **DD** 070.5/09756/67.

IT
**RASSEGNA STAMPA ACRI.** (19??)-. Italian. da (5 days per week). L1900000 (1st copy). Ace Acri, Via Lovanio 11, 00198 Rome, Italy. **Tel** 011 39 6 85354395.

FR/0257-2222
**REGISTRE DE L'ISDS (ED. SUR MICROFICHE).** (REGISTRE DE L'ISDS [MICROFORM].). [Reg. ISDS]. **Main/Corp** International Centre for the Registration of Serial Publications. **VFOAT** ISDS Register. Vol. 1, No. 1 (1986)-. French (English). qt (plus cumulative indexes). 1700.00F. ISSN International Centre, 20 rue Bachaumont, F-75002 Paris France. **Tel** 011 33 1 42367381, FAX 011 33 1 40263243, telex SERIALS 219847F. Index available. available on magnetic tape; available on CD-ROM.
**Desc:** Provides a comprehensive list of ISSN, key titles and records of the serials processed by the ISDS network. Lists more than 80,000 new and amended records per year.

CN/0823-969X
**REPERTOIRE DE LA LECTURE FRANCOPHONE, LE.** [Repert. lect. francoph.]. Vol. 1, No. 1 (Nov. 1983)-. Periodical. French. Services De Presse, 9756 Boul. St. Laurent, Montreal Quebec H3L 2N3 Canada. **DD** 015.71/0241.

CN/0826-5631
**REPERTOIRE DES EDITEURS ET DE LEURS DISTRIBUTEURS.** [Repert. ed. distrib.]. **Added/Corp** Association des Libraires du Quebec. (Nov 1983)-. Periodical. French. qt. Repertoire des Editeurs et de Leurs Distributeurs, 1839 rue Plessis App 4, Montreal Quebec H2L 2X9 Canada. **DD** 070.5/025/714. ***Continues** Repertoire des Editeurs et de Leurs Distributeurs a l'Usage Exclusif des Libraires., 0228-0264.*

IT/0036-5955
**SCHEDARIO.** [Schedario]. (1952)-. Periodical. Italian. Three times a year. L45000.00 Italy; L56000.00 other. Giunti Editore, Via Bolognese 165, 50139 Florence Italy. **Tel** 011 39 55 6679267, FAX 011 39 55 268312, telex 571438. **UDC** 087.5.

CN/0036-634X
**SCHOLARLY PUBLISHING.** ***Title Change.*** [Sch. publ.]. Vol. 1 (Oct. 1969)-(199?). Periodical. English. qt (Jan., Apr., July, Oct.). University of Toronto Press, 5201 Dufferin Street, Downsview Ontario M3H 5T8 Canada. **Tel** (416)667-7781, (416)667-7782, FAX (416)667-7803. **ED** Hamish Cameron. **LC** Z286.S37; S33. **DD** 655.4. **[CCC].** Index available. cum. index. **Bk Rev. Ad Acc. Pr Rev. Circ:** 2,200 (ctrl). available on microfilm and microfiche from University Microfilms International (UMI). Documents available from The Genuine Article. ***Continued by** Journal of Scholarly Publishing.*
**Desc:** A journal for authors as well as publishers, it is the only international quarterly devoted to the writing, publication, and use of serious nonfiction. For 23 years, its editors have offered a unique blend of philosophical analysis and practical advice that has attracted readers around the world.
**Ind/Abst** Abstr. Engl. Stud.; ACM Guide Comput. Lit.; Am. Hist. Life (1969-); Annu. Bibliogr. Engl. Lang. Lit.; Arts Humanit. Citation Index [Full Cov.]; Can. Index; Comput. Rev.; Curr. Contents Arts Humanit.; Curr. Contents Soc. Behav. Sci.; High. Educ. Abstr. (1988-); Index Period. Artic. Relat. Law (19??-19??); Inf. Instruc. Technol.; Libr. Inf. Sci. Abstr.; Libr. Lit.; MLA Int. Bibl. Books Artic. Mod. Lang. Lit.; Res. Alert [Full Cov.]; Soc. Plann. Policy Dev. Abstr.; Soc. Sci. Cit. Index [Full Cov.].

GR
**SCHOLIASTIS.** Greek, Modern. mo. George Pitouropoulos, Tim Filimonos 13, Athens 115 21 Greece. **Tel** 6461380 OR 6469827.

US/0195-5365
**SCIENCE FICTION CHRONICLE.** **See** Literature.

UK/0954-8769
**SCOTTISH BOOK COLLECTOR.** (Aug. 1987)-. Periodical. English. Six times a year. £10.00 UK; £13.50 Europe; £15.00 US and Canada; £16.00 other. Scottish Book Collector, 11A Forth Street, Edinburgh EH1 3LE Scotland. **Tel** 011 44 31 2284837. **ED** Jennie Renton. **Bk Rev. Ad Acc.**
**Desc:** Scottish literature and history. Contains interviews and profiles of Scottish writers, publishing history, bibliography and book crafts, and reviews.

US/0091-6226
**SELF-PUBLISHING WRITER, THE.** V. 1- Oct. 1972-. Periodical. English. qt. $7.50. S S Morril, 547 Howard Street, San Francisco CA 94105. **LC** Z285.5; .S43. **DD** 051.

US/0883-1467
**SESAME (MEDFORD, OR.).** (SESAME.). [Sesame]. Vol. 1, No. 1 (April 1985)-. Periodical. English. mo. $26.00. Windyridge Press, PO Box 327, Medford OR 97501. **Tel** (503)772-5399. **ED** Gene Olsen. **DD** 808. **Bk Rev. Circ:** 100.
**Desc:** Instruction and marketing advice for professional writers. Most phases of writing and publishing covered.

US/0889-9762
**SEYBOLD REPORT ON PUBLISHING SYSTEMS, THE.** [Seybold rep. publ. syst.]. Vol. 11, No. 9 (Jan. 18, 1982)-. Periodical. English. Twenty-two times a year. $395.00 US; $413.00 other. Seybold Publications Inc., 428 West Baltimore Pike, PO Box 644, Media PA 19063. **Tel** (610)565-2480, (800)325-3830, FAX (610)565-4659, or 3261, telex 4991494. **ED** Jonathan Seybold. **LC** Z286.E43; S49. **DD** 070.5/028/5416. **[CCC].** Index available. available on an online database (file 675/Full-Text) from DIALOG. Documents available from Ask*IEEE. ***Continues** Seybold Report, 0364-5517. **Continued in part by** Seybold Report on Desktop Publishing, 0889-9762.*
**Desc:** Covers, typesetting equipment, page make-up facilities, and related electronic pre-press systems for the printing and publishing market.
**Ind/Abst** Abstr. Bull. Inst. Pap. Sci. Tech.; Abstr. Graphic Arts Tech. Found. (1984); Comput. ASAP [Full Txt.]; Comput. Database [Full Txt.]; Graph. Arts Bull. Inst. Pap. Sci. Technol. (Jan. 1989-Feb. 1989, April 1989, Aug. 1989-Oct. 1989); INSPEC (Jan. 1985-); Print. Abstr.; World Publ. Monit.

IT/1120-253X
**SFOGLIALIBRO.** [Sfoglialibro]. (1988)-. Periodical. Italian. Six times a year (Feb., Apr., June, Sept., Oct., Dec.). L70000.00 Italy; L120000.00 others. Editrice Bibliografica, Viale Vittoria Veneto 24, 20124 Milan Italy. **Tel** 011 39 2 29006965, FAX 011 39 2 654624. **UDC** 37.

US
**SHARP NEWS.** **See** Publishing-Abstracting, Bibliographies and Statistics.

●UK/0963-0171
**SHEPPARD'S BOOK DEALERS IN EUROPE.** **See** Publishing-Books and Bookmaking.

NE
**SHORT BOOK REVIEWS / INTERNATIONAL STATISTICAL INSTITUTE.** **See** Publishing-Abstracting, Bibliographies and Statistics.

CN/1183-5559
**SIGNATURE (TORONTO).** (SIGNATURE/ ASSOCIATION OF CANADIAN PUBLISHERS.). [Signatureb]. **Added/Corp** Association of Canadian Publishers. Vol. 1, No. 1 (Jan./Feb. 1991)-. Periodical. English. bm. Limited free distribution. Association of Canadian Publishers, 3rd Floor, 70 the Esplanade, Toronto Ontario M5E 1R2. **DD** 338.4.

CN/0708-515X
**SIGNATURE (VANCOUVER).** (SIGNATURE.). 1- Apr. 1979-. Periodical. English. Three times a year. Free. Association of Book Publishers of British Columbia, 1622 West 7th Avenue, Vancouver British Columbia V6J 1S5 Canada. **DD** 338.4/7/070509711. ctrl circ.

UK
**SMALL PRESS YEARBOOK.** 1989-. English. an.

US/1059-5341
**SOUTHWEST PUBLISHING MARKET PLACE : A COMPREHENSIVE DIRECTORY OF MARKETS, RESOURCES, AND OPPORTUNITIES FOR WRITERS.** [Southwest publ. mark. place]. **VFOAT** Publishing Market Place; Southwest Publishing

Marketplace. (1991)-. Directory. English. Writers Connection, 1601 Saratoga Sunnyvale/Suite 180, Cupertino CA 95014. **Tel** (408)973-0227. **DD** 070.

US/0895-254X
**SPECIALTY BOOKSELLERS DIRECTORY.** [Spec. books. dir.]. (1987)-. Directory. English. Twice a year. $19.95. Ad-lib Publications, 51 North Fifth Street, Box 1102, Fairfield IA 52556-1102. **Tel** (515)472-6617, FAX (515)472-3186. **ED** John Kremer. **DD** 070. Index available. **Ad Acc. Circ:** 2,000. available on diskette.
**Desc:** A directory of 2,100 specialty booksellers.

US
**STET. TRICKS OF THE TRADE FOR WRITERS AND EDITORS.** (19??)-. Trade Publication. English. ir. $17.95 US; $20.95 other. Editorial Experts Inc. / EEI, 66 Canal Center Plaza, Suite 200, Alexandria VA 22314. **Tel** (703)683-0683, FAX (703)683-4915.

NE
**STM INFORMATION BOOKLET. Main/Corp** International Group of Scientific, Technical, and Medical Publishers. **VFOAT** STM Membership List. English. an. Secretariat, Keizersgracht 462, 1016GE Amsterdam The Netherlands. **LC** Z286.S4; I59A. **DD** 070.5/025. ctrl circ.

US/1045-2273
**SUBMISSION SOURCEBOOK FOR CREATIVE CLASSROOM PUBLISHING, THE. See** Education.

US/0892-6581
**SUCCESSFUL MAGAZINE PUBLISHING.** (SUCCESSFUL MAGAZINE PUBLISHING : THE JOURNAL OF THE SMALL MAGAZINE PUBLISHERS GROUP.). [Success. mag. publ.]. **Added/Corp** Small Magazine Publishers Group. **VFOAT** Magazine Publishing. (198?)-. Periodical. English. bm. $10.00 members, $15.00 nonmembers. Lighthouse Communications Inc, 233 West Central Street, Natick MA 01760. **Tel** (508)650-1001, FAX (508)650-4648. **LC** Z231.5.L5; S92. **DD** 070.

UK/0968-0349
**TAGLINE (OLNEY).** [TAGline Olney]. (1992)-. Newsletter. English. mo (10 issues). Free to members of CVU. Ventura Publisher Users Ltd., 49 Olney Road, Emberton, Olney, Bucks, MK46 5BU England. **Tel** 581028 (UK), 353 706 3912 (outside UK). **ED** Dr. Kathy Lang. **Bk Rev. Ad Acc, Adv Mgr:** Leigh Foster, **Tel** 01234 241454. ***Continues*** *VPU News.*
**Desc:** Newsletter of Corel Ventura Users. Packed with news, reviews, hints and tips, and answers to members' questions.

US/0894-9581
**TELEPUBLISHING REPORT. *Suspended.*** (Sept. 1987)-(1993). Periodical. English. bm. $240.00. Telepublishing Report, 2 Vernon Street/Suite 639, Framingham MA 01701. **LC** Z286.E43; T45. **DD** 686.2/2544536.
**Desc:** Focused on networks and electronic publishing. Defined as the sending of composed pages to remote output devices, including laser printers or typesetters.

JA
**TENKANKI NI ARU SHUPPANGYOKAI. Added/Corp** Marunouchi Risachi Senta. Vol. 4 (1974)-. Japanese. ¥40000. Marunouchi Risachi Senta, c/o Nihon Building, 6-2 Otemachi, 2-chome Chiyoda-ku, Tokyo 100 Japan. **LC** Z463.5; .S53. ***Continues*** *Shuppansha Chosaroku.*

UK/0307-661X
**TLS. TIMES LITERARY SUPPLEMENT.** (TLS, THE TIMES LITERARY SUPPLEMENT.). [TLS. Times lit. suppl.]. **VFOAT** Times Literary Supplement. (Jan. 2, 1969)-. Periodical. English. Fifty-two times a year. $120.00. News International Newspapers Ltd., PO Box 495 Virginia Street, London E1 9XU England. **Tel** 011 44 71 7823000. **ED** Jeremy Treglown. **LC** AP4; .T45. **DD** 072/.1. Documents available from The Genuine Article, UMI Article Clearinghouse. ***Continues*** *Times Literary Supplement, 0040-7895.*
**Desc:** Literary supplement with comprehensive weekly selection of new and forthcoming books received by TLS. Comprised of books that have been printed and are available to booksellers. Provides full hardback and paperback publication details, including date, price and ISBN. Coverage of world literature, including history, politics, the arts, etc.
**Ind/Abst** Acad. Abstr. Full Text Elite (Aug. 1990-); Acad. Abstr. (Aug. 1990-); Acad. Ind. [Computer File] (1987-1991); Acad. Search (Aug. 1990-); Am. Hist. Life (1954-1959); Annu. Bibliogr. Engl. Lang. Lit.; Arts Humanit. Citation Index [Full Cov.]; BHA : Biblio. Hist. Art; Book Rev. Digest; Book Rev. Index; Br. Humanit. Index; Child. Lit. Abstr. (19??-); Curr. Contents Arts Humanit.; Expand. Acad. Index (1991-); Humanit. Index; Humanit. Source (Jul. 1990-); Index Book Rev. Relig.; INFO-SOUTH Abstr.; Mag. Search; Middle East Abstr. Index; MLA Int. Bibl. Books Artic. Mod. Lang. Lit.; Newsp. Period. Abstr. (1990-); Peace Res. Abstr. J.; Res. Alert [Full Cov.]; Romant. Move.; Sci. Fict. Fantasy Book Rev. Index; Soc. Sci. Cit. Index [Select. Cov.].

US/0194-9802
**TPA MESSENGER. Main/Corp** Texas Press Association. Vol. 54, No. 6 (June 1979)-. Periodical. English. mo. $6.00. Texas Press Messenger, 718 West 5th Avenue, Austin TX 78701. **Tel** (512)477-6755. **ED** Lyndell Williams (Editor-in-Chief) and Ed Sterling (Managing Editor). **Bk Rev.** (Qty: 4). **Photos. Ad Acc, Adv Mgr:** Ed Sterling. Full Page (B&W) $442.00. Half Page (B&W) $221.00. Full Page (Color) $742.00. Half Page (Color) $521.00. **Pub. Size:** Tabloid. **Circ:** 105 (free), 733 (paid) (ctrl). available in microform from Southwest Micropublishing International. ***Continues*** *Texas Press Messenger, 0040-4624.*
**Desc:** News of and about newspaper publishers, staff members, newspaper industry, education and profession.

CN/1183-1855
**TRENDS (SCARBOROUGH).** (TRENDS.). [Trends]. Vol 1, No. 1 (Jan. 1991)-. Newsletter. English. mo. $85.00 per year. Sterling Communications Inc., Suite 104, 1920 Ellesmere Road, Scarborough Ontario M1H 2W7 Canada. **Tel** (416)512-2218. **DD** 070.1/75.
**Desc:** Contains information in a "how to" format. Covers writing, design, and publication in a newsletter.

IT
**TUTTOLIBRI.** (19??)-. Periodical. Italian. ir (supplement to La Stampa newspaper). La Stampa, Via Marenco 32, 10126 Turin Italy. **Tel** 011 39 11 65681. **LC** Z1035.4; .T88. **DD** 055/.1.

US
**UK PUBLISHERS DIRECTORY.** (March 1993)-. Directory. English. $88.00. Gale Research Inc., 835 Penobscot Building, Detroit MI 48226. **Tel** (800)877-GALE, (313)961-2242, FAX (313)961-6083, telex TWX 810-221-7086.
**Desc:** Covers approximately 2,000 publishers and imprints based in England, Northern Ireland, Scotland and Wales. Publishers of all sizes are included.

JM
**UNIVERSITY OF THE WEST INDIES PUBLISHERS' ASSOCIATION NEWSLETTER. VFOAT** Newsletter; UMI Publishers' Association Newsletter. Vol. 3, No. 4 (July/Aug. 1989)-. Newsletter. English. bm. UWIPA, PO Box 42, Mona, Kingston 7 Jamaica. **Tel** (809)927-1201. ***Continues*** *Newsletter (University of the West Indies Publishers' Association).*
**Desc:** Reaches over 1000 publishers, academics, book stores and libraries throughout the Caribbean.

CN/1180-3401
**UPDATE - INTERNATIONAL ASSOCIATION FOR PUBLISHING EDUCATION.** (UPDATE / IAPE.). [Update - Int. Assoc. Publ. Educ.]. **Added/Corp** International Association for Publishing Education. **VAT** IAPE Update. Issue 1 (Jan. 1991)-. Periodical. English. sa. Free to members. International Association for Publishing Education, c/o Canadian Centre for Studies in Publishing, Simon Fraser University, Harbour Centre, 515 West Hastings Street, Vancouver British Columbia V6B 5K3 Canada. **DD** 070/.07.

●GW
**VERZEICHNIS DER VEROFFENTLICHUNGEN / STATISTISCHES BUNDESAMT. Main/Corp** Germany. Statistisches Bundesamt. (1991/92)-. German. **LC** Z7554.G3; A25. **DD** 016.3143. ***Continues*** *Germany (West). Statistisches Bundesamt. Veroffentlichungsverzeichnis.*
**Desc:** Specifically focuses on government publications.

US/0362-997X
**VIKING COLLEGE CATALOG. Main/Corp** Viking Press, Inc., New York. (19??)-. Catalog. English. ir. Viking Press, 40 West 23rd Street, New York NY 10010. **LC** Z473.V5; V5a. **DD** 017/.8/097471.

CN/0823-6127
**VIREO.** [Vireo]. No. 1 (Spring 1981)-. Periodical. French. qt. Free. Centre Vireo, 2215 rue Marie-Victorin, Sillery Quebec G1T 1J6 Canada. **DD** 015.714.

UK
**WHITAKER'S PUBLISHERS IN THE UNITED KINGDOM AND THEIR ADDRESSES. Added/Corp** J. Whitaker & Sons. **VFOAT** Publishers in the United Kingdom and Their Addresses. (March 1982)-. English. an. £9.95 UK; £12.50 other. J. Whitaker & Sons Ltd, 12 Dyott Street, London WC1A 1DF England. **Tel** 011 44 71 8368911, FAX 011 44 71 836 2909. **LC** Z327; .P82. **DD** 070.5/025/41. ***Continues*** *Publishers in the United Kingdom and Their Addresses.*

CN/1193-6665
**WHO PAYS WHAT.** (WHO PAYS WHAT / PWAC, PERIODICAL WRITERS ASSOCIATION OF CANADA.). [Who pays what]. **Added/Corp** Periodical Writers Association of Canada. (199?)-. English. be. $15.00 per vol. Periodical Writers Association of Canada, 24 Ryerson Avenue, Toronto Ontario M5T 2P3 Canada. **Tel** (416)868-6914, (416)504-1645, FAX (416)860-0826. **DD** 015.71/034. ***Continues*** *Magazine Markets & Fees., 1184-1516.*

GW
**WHO'S WHO AT THE FRANKFURT BOOK FAIR. See** Publishing-Books and Bookmaking.

UK/0960-653X
**WORLD PUBLISHING MONITOR. See** Publishing-Abstracting, Bibliographies and Statistics.

UK
**WRITER'S HANDBOOK (LONDON, ENGLAND).** (THE WRITER'S HANDBOOK.). 1988-. English. an. H. Holt, Macmillan Journals, Houndmills, Basingstoke Hants RG21 2XS United Kingdom. **Tel** (0256)29242, FAX (0256)479476, telex 858493.

US/0084-2729
**WRITER'S MARKET, THE.** [Writ. mark.]. (1922)-. English. an. $29.95. Writer's Digest Books, 1507 Dana Avenue, Cincinnati OH 45207. **Tel** (513)531-2222, (800)289-0963, FAX (513)531-4744. **ED** Mark Kissling. **LC** PN161; .W83. **DD** 808/.025/0977178. Index available. **Circ:** 160,000.
**Desc:** Contains up-to-date information on 4,000 buyers of freelance materials, as well as listings of workshops, contests and awards. Also contains helpful articles and interviews with top professionals.

US/1053-833X
**WRITER'S N.W.** [Writ. N.W.]. **VFOAT** Writer's NW; WNW. **VAT** Writer's Northwest. Vol. 4, No. 1 (Spring 1989)-. Periodical. English. qt. $10.00 US; $12.00 Canada. Blue Heron Publishing, 24450 Northwest Hansen Road, Hillsboro OR 97124. **Tel** (503)621-3911, FAX (503)621-9826. **DD** 070. ***Continues*** *Writer's Northwest Newsletter, 0895-898X.*

US/0896-7946
**WRITER'S NORTHWEST HANDBOOK.** [Writ. northwest handb.]. (1986)-. English. be. $21.45 US; $24.45 Canada. Blue Heron Publishing, 24450 Northwest Hansen Road, Hillsboro OR 97124. **Tel** (503)621-3911, FAX (503)621-9826. **ED** Linny Stovall and Dennis Stovall. **LC** PN147; .W69. **DD** 070.5/025/795. **Ad Acc. Circ:** 15,000.
**Desc:** Publishing guide to Northwest with 2,600 markets, 500 resources, 40 how-to articles and interviews.

US/0890-0981
**WYSIWYG. *Suspended.*** [WYSIWYG]. (1985)-?. Periodical. English. mo. $215.00 US; $225.00 Canada. New Leaf Press, 518 Channing Avenue, Palo Alto CA 94301. **DD** 070.

US
**YELLOW PAGES AND DIRECTORY REPORT.** (Sept. 1985)-. English. bw. $499.00 (one year), $898.00 (two year). Simba Information Inc., 213 Danbury Road, Wilton CT 06897-7430. **Tel** (203)834-0033 ext. 133, FAX (203)884-1771. **(Subscription address:** Simba Information Inc., PO Box 7430, Wilton CT 06897.**)**

US
**YELLOW PAGES AND DIRECTORY REPORT.** Directory. English. ir. $480.00. Communications Trends Inc., 2 East Avenue, Suite 201, Larchmont NY 10538. **Tel** (914)833-0600, FAX (914)833-0558.
**Desc:** Newsletter covering directory publishing, advertising, printing and competition with other media. Regular features include a monthly roundup of major releases from the Bell publishers; news of independent/competitive books; and coverage of new national yellow pages accounts.

US
**YELLOW PAGES INDUSTRY SOURCEBOOK.** English. an. $300.00. Communications Trends Inc., 2 East Avenue, Suite 201, Larchmont NY 10538. **Tel** (914)833-0600, FAX (914)833-0558.
**Desc:** The key reference provides you with every important fact and figure about every important participant in the yellow pages industry. Company listings, descriptions, addresses, phone numbers, names of officers, company revenues and print runs, key customers and national accounts.

US
**YELLOW PAGES MARKET FORECAST.** English. Communications Trends Inc., 2 East Avenue, Suite 201, Larchmont NY 10538. **Tel** (914)833-0600, FAX (914)833-0558. **LC** HF6146.T4; Y45. **DD** 384.6/4.

CC/1001-8859
**ZHONGGUO CHUBAN NIANJIAN / CHINA PUBLISHING YEARBOOK. Added/Corp** Chung-kuo chu pan Kung tso che Hsieh hui. **VFOAT** Zhongguo Chuban Nianjian; China Publishers

Yearbook. (1980)-. Chinese. an. RMBY38.00. China Book Publishing House, 7A Xi Rong Xian Hu Tong, Xi Cheng District, Beijing 100031, People's Republic of China. **Tel** 6059534. **ED** Fang Houshu. **DD** 070.5. **Ad Acc. Circ:** 5,000.
**Desc:** Co-sponsored by the Publishing Association of China, this directory contains information on the developments in China's publishing industry.

## ABSTRACTING, BIBLIOGRAPHIES AND STATISTICS

US/0065-759X
**AMERICAN BOOK TRADE DIRECTORY.** (1915)-. Directory. English. an. $225.00. R R Bowker, A Reed Reference Publishing Company, Part of Reed International PLC, PO Box 31, 121 Chanlon Drive, New Providence NJ 07974. **Tel** (908)464-6800, (800)521-8110, FAX (908)665-6688, telex 138-755. **LC** Z475; .A5. **[CCC]**. Index available. available on magnetic tape and CD-ROM.
**Desc:** Captures listings for more than 27,000 retail, antiquarian and foreign-language book dealers, plus over 1,400 book and magazine wholesalers, distributors and jobbers.

UK/0968-7513
**ANNUAL REGISTER OF BOOK VALUES. EARLY PRINTED BOOKS.** ***Title Change.*** **VFOAT** Early Printed Books; ARBV. Early Printed Books. (1993)-(1993). English. ir. Ross Burnet, PO Box 2, Uralla New South Wales 2358, Australia. **Tel** 011 067 784682, FAX 011 067 784516. **LC** Z1012; .I63. **DD** 011/.44. ***Continues*** *International Rare Book Prices. Early Printed Books.* ***Continued by*** *Annual Register of Book Values. Children's Books.*

GW/0723-3590
**BIBLIOGRAPHIE DER BUCH- UND BIBLIOTHEKSGESCHICHTE : BBB.** **VFOAT** BBB; B.B.B. V. 1 (1980/81)-. German. an. **LC** Z4; .B54. **DD** 016.002.

US/0006-7326
**BOOK REVIEW DIGEST. CD-ROM.** English. qt. $1095.00. H W Wilson Company, 950 University Avenue, Bronx NY 10452. **Tel** (800)367-6770, (718)588-8400, FAX (718)590-1617, telex 4990003 HWILSON. **ED** Martha T Mooney. cum. index. ctrl circ. available on diskette from WILSONSEARCH; available on magnetic tape from WILSONTAPE; available in print; available on an online database from WILSONLINE.
**Desc:** Provides excerpts and citations from book reviews from an international list of over 98 periodicals and journals.

US/0524-0581
**BOOK REVIEW INDEX.** [Book rev. index]. **Added/Corp** Gale Research Company. Vol. 1 (Jan. 1965)-. Abstracting/Indexing Service. English. bm. $210.00. Gale Research Inc., 835 Penobscot Building, Detroit MI 48226. **Tel** (800)877-GALE, (313)961-2242, FAX (313)961-6083, telex TWX 810-221-7086. **ED** Neil E. Walker and Beverly Baer. **LC** Z1035.A1; B6. **NLM** Z 1035.A1 B724. **Circ:** 3,000. available on diskette; available on magnetic tape; available on CD-ROM; available on an online database (File 137) from DIALOG.
**Desc:** Provides quick access to reviews of books, periodicals, and books on tape representing a wide range of popular, academic and professional interests.

US
**BOOKLIST'S GUIDE TO THE YEAR'S BEST BOOKS : DEFINITIVE REVIEWS OF OVER 1,000 FICTION AND NONFICTION TITLES IN ALL FIELDS.** ***Ceased.*** **VFOAT** Guide to the Year's Best Books.; Year's Best Books. (1992)-(1992 ed.). Periodical. English. Triumph Books, 644 South Clark Street, Suite 2000, Chicago IL 60605. **Tel** (312)939-3330. **LC** Z1035.A1; B56. **DD** 028.1. ***Continues*** *Book Buyer's Advisor.*

US/0147-0787
**BOOKS AT BROWN.** [Books Brown]. **Added/Corp** Brown University. Library. Friends. Vol. 1 (June 1938)-. Periodical. English. an (Apr.). Brown University / Books at Brown, PO Box A, Providence RI 02912. **Tel** (401)863-1518, (401)863-2146. **ED** John H. Stanley. **LC** Z733.P958; B6. **DD** 027.7745. **Circ:** 800 (ctrl).
**Desc:** Prints articles and bibliographic essays from research based on the collections of Brown University Library. Also considers profiles of book collectors, articles on book collecting, fine printing, and graphic arts.
**Ind/Abst** MLA Int. Bibl. Books Artic. Mod. Lang. Lit.

FI/0006-7490
**BOOKS FROM FINLAND.** [Books Finl.]. **Added/Corp** Suomen Kustannusyhdistys. Suomen Kirjastoseura. Helsingin Yliopisto. Kirjasto. Vol. 1 (1967)-. Periodical. English. Four times a year. Fmk150.00. Academic Bookstore Akateeminen, Postilokero 23, FIN-00371 Helsinki Finland. **Tel** 011 358 0 12141. **LC** Z2520; .B65. **DD** 015/.471.
**Ind/Abst** MLA Int. Bibl. Books Artic. Mod. Lang. Lit.

CN/0829-4976
**BOOKS--NOTED FOR YOU.** [Books noted you.]. **VFOAT** International Corner. No. 54 (Mar. 1977)-. Periodical. English (French). mo. Free. George Bonavia, PO Box 826 Station B, Ottawa Ontario K1P 5P9 Canada. **Tel** (613)521-5285. **ED** George Bonavia. **DD** 028.1/05. Index available. **Bk Rev**. ctrl circ. ***Continues*** *The International Corner, 0316-6260.*
**Desc:** Reviews books of interest to ethnic groups. Covers culture, travel, history and ethno-cultural affairs.

UK/0006-7539
**BOOKSELLER (LONDON).** (THE BOOKSELLER.). [Bookseller]. No. 1455 (Oct. 6, 1933)-. Periodical. English. wk. £108.00 UK; £129.00 other. J. Whitaker & Sons Ltd, 12 Dyott Street, London WC1A 1DF England. **Tel** 011 44 71 8368911, FAX 011 44 71 836 2909. **[CCC]**. Index available. **Bk Rev**. **Ad Acc**. available on microfilm and microfiche from University Microfilms International (UMI). ***Continues*** *Publisher and Bookseller.*
**Desc:** Covers a spectrum of topics and events that are of important to the bookselling and publishing industry. Book previews, index of new books and features.
**Ind/Abst** Child. Lit. Abstr. (19??-); LABORDOC; Libr. Inf. Sci. Abstr.; Print. Abstr.; World Ceram. Abstr.

BU
**BULGARSKI KNIGOPIS.** **Added/Corp** Sofia. Narodna Biblioteka. (1969)-. Bibliography. Bulgarian. sm. 220.00lv ($48.00) First Series; 180.00lv ($29.00) Second Series. Narodna Biblioteka Sv.sv. Kiril i Metodij, 88 V. Levski Boulevard, 1504 Sofia Bulgaria. **Tel** 011 359 2 882811, FAX 011 359 2 881600, telex 22432. **(Subscription address:** Hemus Foreign Trade Organization, 6 Tzar Osvoboditel Boulevard, 1000 Sofia Bulgaria.**) ED** Gergana Vanchurova. **LC** Z2893; .B847. Index available. cum. index. **Bk Rev**. **Ad Acc, Adv Mgr:** Asen Georgiev, **Tel** 011 359 2 882811 Ext. 376. Full Page (B&W) $50.00. Half Page (B&W) $25.00. **Circ:** 700 (ctrl).

CN/0380-6286
**CAMPUS BOOK STORES.** [Campus book stores]. **Added/Corp** Canada. Dominion Bureau of Statistics. Merchandising and Services Division. Statistics Canada. Merchandising and Services Division. Statistics Canada. Retail Trade Section. **VFOAT** Campus Bookstores; Librairies de Campus. (1969)-. English (French). an. 24.00Can$ Canada; $29.00 US; $34.00 other. Statistics Canada, Publications Sales & Services, Main Building Room 1710, Ottawa Ontario K1A 0T6 Canada. **Tel** (613)951-5078, (800)267-6677, FAX (613)951-1584, telex 053-3585. **LC** Z487; .A3. **DD** 381/.450705/0971.

CN/0315-1999
**CANADIAN BOOKS IN PRINT. SUBJECT INDEX.** [Can. books print, Subj. index]. **VFOAT** Canadian Books in Print. Subject Guide. (1975)-. English (French). an. $130.00. University of Toronto Press, 5201 Dufferin Street, Downsview Ontario M3H 5T8 Canada. **Tel** (416)667-7781, (416)667-7782, FAX (416)667-7803. **ED** Marian Butler. **LC** Z1365; .S9. **DD** 015'.71. ***Continues*** *Subject Guide to Canadian Books in Print, 0318-8493.*
**Desc:** Designed to provide subject access to Canadian books. Lists some 35,000 titles in 700 subject categories.

CN
**CANADIAN LITERARY PERIODICALS INDEX.** English. an. 185.00Can$. Reference Press, PO Box 70, Teeswater Ontario N0G 2S0 Canada. **Tel** (519)392-6634. Index available (published first quarter of the following year).
**Desc:** Indexes more than 100 Canadian literary journals, selected general interest magazines, newspapers and scholarly publications, as well as the contents of anthologies of poetry, short fiction and criticism published during the indexing year.

CC/0578-073X
**CHUAN KUO HSIN SHU MU.** **Added/Corp** Wen Hua pu Chu Pan Shih yeh Kuan li Chu Pan Pen tu Shu Kuan (China) China. Chu Pan Tsung Shu. Tu Shu Chi Kan Ssu. China Chu Pan Tsung Shu. Tu Shu Kuan. China. Wen Hua pu. Chu Pan Shih Yeh Kuan li Chu. Tu Shu Kuan. **VFOAT** Quan-Guo Xinshumu. (1950)-. Periodical. Chinese. mo. $40.68. **(Subscription address:** China International Book Trading Corporation, PO Box 399, Library Service Department, Beijing 100044 People's Republic of China.**) DD** 016. available on an online database, CD-ROM, magnetic tape, and microfilm from University Microfilms International (UMI).

US/0011-300X
**CUMULATIVE BOOK INDEX. CD-ROM.**
**See** Literature-Abstracting, Bibliographies and Statistics.

JA
**CURRENT JAPANESE PERIODICALS FOR ... .** **Added/Corp** Nihon Shuppan Boeki Kabushiki Kaisha. (19??)-. English. an. Free on request. **(Subscription address:** Japan Publications Trading Company, Ltd., PO Box 5030, Tokyo International, Tokyo 100-31 Japan.**)**

NE/0013-9955
**ERASMUS.** (ERASMUS : SPECULUM SCIENTIARUM; INTERNATIONAL BULLETIN OF CONTEMPORARY SCHOLARSHIP; BULLETIN INTERNAIONAL DE LA SCIENCE CONTEMPORAINE.). Vol. 1, No. 1 (1947)-. Bulletin. English (French and German). sm. **LC** Z1007; .E9. **DD** 010.5. cum. index.
**Ind/Abst** BHA : Biblio. Hist. Art.

GW
**FACHLITERATUR ZUM BUCH- UND BIBLIOTHEKSWESEN.** **VFOAT** Literature About the Book and Librarianship; International Bibliography of the Book Trade and Librarianship. English (German). $95.00. Gale Research Inc., 835 Penobscot Building, Detroit MI 48226. **Tel** (800)877-GALE, (313)961-2242, FAX (313)961-6083, telex TWX 810-221-7086. **LC** Z279; .F3. **DD** 016.0705. ***Continues*** *Fachliteratur fur den Autor, Bibliothekar, Buchhandler, Dokumentar, Literaturingenieur und Verleger.*

US/1066-5471
**FIRSTS (LOS ANGELES, CALIF.).** (FIRSTS : COLLECTING MODERN FIRST EDITIONS.). [Firsts]. Vol. 1, No. 1 (Jan. 1991)-. Periodical. English. mo. $35.00. The Lucerne Group, 575 North Lucerne Boulevard, Los Angeles CA 90004. **ED** Kathryn Smiley. **LC** Z1033.F53; F58. **DD** 094/.4075. Index available (Bound in Dec. issue). **Bk Rev**, (Qty: 24). **Ad Acc. Circ:** 5,000.
**Desc:** Magazine for book enthusiasts and collectors of modern first editions.

GW/0170-9348
**INTERNATIONAL BOOKS IN PRINT.** (1979)-. English. ir. Price varies per volume. KG Saur Inc., PO Box 31, New Providence NJ 07974. **Tel** (800)521-8110, (908)665-3576, FAX (908)771-7792. **ED** Archie Rugh. **LC** Z2005; .I57. **DD** 018/.4. **NLM** Z 2005 I61. **Ad Acc**. available on CD-ROM from R.R. Bowker.
**Desc:** Listing of English-language titles published out of US and UK. Includes over 140,000 title entries and 140,000 cross references from over 5,000 publishers. Also two-part author/ title lists and subject guide.

US/0074-6827
**INTERNATIONAL LITERARY MARKET PLACE.** [Int. lit. marketpl.]. **Added/Corp** R.R. Bowker Company. **VFOAT** ILMP. (1972)-. English. an (published in Sept. of prior year). $179.95. R R Bowker, A Reed Reference Publishing Company, Part of Reed International PLC, PO Box 31, 121 Chanlon Drive, New Providence NJ 07974. **Tel** (908)464-6800, (800)521-8110, FAX (908)665-6688, telex 138-755. **DD** 070. **NLM** Z 282 I63. **[CCC]**. available on CD-ROM from R.R. Bowker. ***Continues*** *International Literary Market Place. European Edition, 0538-8562.*
**Desc:** Profiles of more than 15,500 book related concerns include book trade organizations, trade reference books and agents, publishers, literary agents, book manufacturers, book clubs, major booksellers and libraries, literary associations, suppliers, periodicals and prizes and translation agencies.

●US/1064-5470
**JOURNAL SUBSCRIPTION CATALOG / THE ASSOCIATION OF AMERICAN UNIVERSITY PRESSES.** **Added/Corp** Association of American University Presses. **VFOAT** AAUP Journal Subscription Catalog. (1992)-. Catalog. English. Free (libraries). Association of American University Presses Inc, Publications Department, 584 Broadway, Suite 410, New York NY 10012. **Tel** (212)941-6610, FAX (212)941-6618.

US/0000-1155
**LITERARY MARKET PLACE (1988).** (LITERARY MARKET PLACE : LMP.). [Lit. mark. place]. **Added/Corp** R.R. Bowker Company. **VFOAT** LMP. (1989)-. English. an. $165.00. R R Bowker, A Reed Reference Publishing Company, Part of Reed International PLC, PO Box 31, 121 Chanlon Drive, New Providence NJ 07974. **Tel** (908)464-6800, (800)521-8110, FAX (908)665-6688, telex 138-755. **LC** PN161; .L5. **DD** 070.5/025/73. available on magnetic tape and CD-ROM. ***Continues*** *Literary Market Place with Names & Numbers, 0161-2905.*
**Desc:** Tracks the latest developments in publishing with over 15,500 essential publishing, printing, sales, and media services, and puts their 20,000 personnel right at your fingertips. More than 3,000 major publishers (and hundreds of small presses) to some 100 typing and word processing services.

US/0163-3058
**MAGILL'S LITERARY ANNUAL.** 1977-. English. an. $74.00. Salem Press Inc, 580 Sylvan Avenue, Englewood Cliffs NJ 07632. **Tel** (201)871-3700, (800)221-1592, FAX (201)871-8668, telex 138881. **ED** F N Magill. **LC** Z1219; .M33. **DD** 028.1. ***Continues*** *Masterplots Annual.* ***Continued in part by*** *Magill's History Annual, 0740-4344.*
**Desc:** Essay reviews of 200 noteworthy books - fiction, poetry, drama, biography, autobiography, diaries, memoirs - during the preceding calendar year. Provides an update to both Masterplots and Survey of Contemporary Literature.

US/0362-0999
**MICROFORM MARKET PLACE.** **VFOAT** MMP, Microform Market Place. (1974/75)-. English. be. $75.00. K.G. Saur Verlag KG, A Reed Reference Publishing Company, Part of Reed International PLC, Ortlerstrasse 8, D 81373 Munich Germany. **Tel** 011 49 89 769020, FAX 011 49 89 76902150, telex 5212067-SAUR-D. **(Subscription address:** Reed Reference Publishing Company / New Jersey, 131 Chanlaon Road, PO Box 31, New Providence NJ 07974.**)** **ED** Barbara Hopkinson. **LC** Z286.M5; M53. **DD** 070.5/7. **NLM** Z 286.M5 M619. **Bk Rev**. **Ad Acc**. **Circ:** 1,000.
**Desc:** Source for information on microform publishing. Main entries furnish publisher name, address, telephone, fax and telex numbers, ISBN prefix, key personnel, and major microform programs and microformats offered.

BU
**NATSIONALNA BIBLIOGRAFIIA NA REPUBLIKA BULGARIIA. SERIIA 1, BULGARSKI KNIGOPIS. KNIGI, NOTNI, GRAFICHESKI I KARTOGRAFSKI IZDANIIA.** **Added/Corp** Narodna Biblioteka "Sv. sv. Kiril i Metodij.". **VFOAT** Bulgarski Knigopis. Knigi, Notni, Graficheski i Kartografski Izdaniia; Bulgarian National Bibliography. Books, Music, Prints, Maps. (1991)-. Bibliography. Bulgarian. sm. 220.00lv ($48.00). Narodna Biblioteka Sv.sv. Kiril i Metodij, 88 V. Levski Boulevard, 1504 Sofia Bulgaria. **Tel** 011 359 2 882811, FAX 011 359 2 881600, telex 22432. **(Subscription address:** Hemus Foreign Trade Organization, 6 Tzar Osvoboditel Boulevard, 1000 Sofia Bulgaria.**)** **LC** Z2893; .N37. ***Continues*** *Natsionalna Bibliografiia na NR Bulgariia. Seriia 1, Bulgarski Knigopis. Knigi, Notni, Graficheski i Kartografski Izdeniia.*

BU
**NATSIONALNA BIBLIOGRAFIIA NA REPUBLIKA BULGARIIA. SERIIA 2, BULGARSKI KNIGOPIS. SLUZHEBNI IZDANIIA I DISERTATSII.** **Added/Corp** Narodna Biblioteka "Sv. sv. Kiril i Metodij.". **VFOAT** Bulgarski Knigopis; Bulgarian National Bibliography. Official Publications and Dissertations. (1991)-. Bibliography. Bulgarian. mo. 180.00lv ($29.00). Narodna Biblioteka Sv.sv. Kiril i Metodij, 88 V. Levski Boulevard, 1504 Sofia Bulgaria. **Tel** 011 359 2 882811, FAX 011 359 2 881600, telex 22432. **(Subscription address:** Hemus Foreign Trade Organization, 6 Tzar Osvoboditel Boulevard, 1000 Sofia Bulgaria.**)** **ED** S. Penheva. **LC** Z2893; .N372. **Circ:** 500. ***Continues*** *Natsionalna Bbliografiia na NR Bulgariia. Seriiia 2, BEulgarski knigopis; sluzhebni izdaniiia i disertatsii.*

AT/0157-7662
**NEW ZEALAND BOOKS IN PRINT / NEW ZEALAND BOOK PUBLISHERS ASSOCIATION.** **Added/Corp** Book Publishers Association of New Zealand. (196?)-. English. an. $70.00. D. W. Thorpe, A Reed Reference Publishing Company, A Subsidiary of Reed International Books Australia, 18 Salmon Street, Port Melbourne, Victoria 3207 Australia. **Tel** 011 61 3 6451511, FAX 011 61 3 6453981, telex 39476. **ED** Maria Watt. **[CCC]**. **Ad Acc**. **Circ:** 4,000. ***Continues*** *List of New Zealand Books in Print.*
**Desc:** Lists all New Zealand books in print by title, author, subject classification with full details, as well as other New Zealand book trade information.

US/0031-1235
**PAPERBOUND BOOKS IN PRINT.** **Added/Corp** R.R. Bowker Company. (Mar. 1971)-. English. sa (Spring and Fall). $389.00. R R Bowker, A Reed Reference Publishing Company, Part of Reed International PLC, PO Box 31, 121 Chanlon Drive, New Providence NJ 07974. **Tel** (908)464-6800, (800)521-8110, FAX (908)665-6688, telex 138-755. **LC** Z1033.P3; P33. **DD** 011. **[CCC]**. available on magnetic tape, an online database, and CD-ROM.
**Desc:** Arranges more than 471,000 titles alphabetically by author, title, and subject that are available in paperback.

US/1054-1985
**PROGRESSIVE PERIODICALS DIRECTORY.** [Progress. period. dir.]. **Added/Corp** Progressive Education (Organization). (1989)-. Directory. English. ir. $18.00. Progressive Education, PO Box 120574, Nashville TN 37212. **Tel** (615)327-2565. **ED** Craig T. Canan. **LC** Z6951; .U13; PN4877. **DD** 051/.025. **Ad Acc**. **Circ:** 1,500. ***Continues*** *U.S. Progressive Periodicals Directory, 0743-4138.*
**Desc:** Reviews and details on some 600 national social concerns magazines, newsletters and newspapers. The directory serves primarily as a resource book of periodical publications. The only comprehensive directory reviewing national social justice periodicals.

US/0000-0671
**PUBLISHERS, DISTRIBUTORS, & WHOLESALERS OF THE UNITED STATES.** [Publ. distrib. wholes. U. S.]. **Added/Corp** R.R. Bowker Company. Dept. of Bibliography. R.R. Bowker Company. Publications Systems Dept. R.R. Bowker Company. Database Publishing Group. **VFOAT** Publishers, Distributors, and Wholesalers of the United States; Publishers, Distributors, and Wholesalers of the U.S.; Publishers, Distributors, & Wholesalers of the U.S. 3rd Ed. (1981)-. English. an. $175.00. R R Bowker, A Reed Reference Publishing Company, Part of Reed International PLC, PO Box 31, 121 Chanlon Drive, New Providence NJ 07974. **Tel** (908)464-6800, (800)521-8110, FAX (908)665-6688, telex 138-755. **LC** Z475; .P86. **DD** 070.5/025/73. **NLM** Z 475 P976. **[CCC]**. available on magnetic tape, an online database, and CD-ROM. ***Continues*** *Publishers and Distributors of the United States, 0000-0620.*
**Desc:** A directory of publishers, distributors, associations, wholesalers, software producers and manufacturers. Listing editorial and ordering addresses, and an ISBN publisher prefix index.

GW
**PUBLISHERS' INTERNATIONAL ISBN DIRECTORY / INTERNATIONAL ISBN AGENCY, BERLIN.** **Added/Corp** International ISBN Agency. 16th Ed. (1989/90)-. English. an. $325.00. K.G. Saur Verlag KG, A Reed Reference Publishing Company, Part of Reed International PLC, Ortlerstrasse 8, D 81373 Munich Germany. **Tel** 011 49 89 769020, FAX 011 49 89 76902150, telex 5212067-SAUR-D. **LC** Z282; .P7946. **CODEN** PIIDE4. ***Formed by the union of*** *Internationales ISBN-Verlagsverzeichnis, 0720-2768* ***and*** *Publishers' Publishers' International Directory with ISBN Index.*
**Desc:** Provides comprehensive listings and includes coverage of publishers in Eastern Europe and the former Soviet Union.

US/0079-7855
**PUBLISHERS' TRADE LIST ANNUAL, THE.** **Added/Corp** R.R. Bowker Company. (1874)-. English. an. $265.00 (3 volume set). R R Bowker, A Reed Reference Publishing Company, Part of Reed International PLC, PO Box 31, 121 Chanlon Drive, New Providence NJ 07974. **Tel** (908)464-6800, (800)521-8110, FAX (908)665-6688, telex 138-755. **ED** Margaret Spier. **LC** Z1215; .P97. **DD** 015.73. **[CCC]**. Index available. **Ad Acc**. ***Continues*** *Uniform Trade List Annual.*
**Desc:** A buying and reference guide to books and related products. Helpful indexes include all publisher catalogs in 75 subject areas.

RM
**ROMANIAN BOOKS IN FOREIGN LANGUAGES.** **Added/Corp** Centrala Cartii. (19??)-. English (French, German and Russian). qt. Centrala Editoriala, 1 Piata Sctnteii, 79715 Bucharest Romania. **Tel** 173306. **LC** Z2921; .R65. **DD** 015/.498. **Circ:** 24,000.
**Desc:** Includes a selection of annotated works issued by all Romanian publishing houses, information about the activity of publishing houses, lists of books available for export, etc.

US
**SHARP NEWS.** (19??)-. English. Four times a year. $15.00 Comes with Society for the History of Authorship Reading & Publishing membership. Society of Authorship, Reading & Publishing, Drew University Library, c/o L. Connors, Madison NJ 07940. **Tel** (201)408-3474, FAX (201)408-3993. **ED** Jonathan Rose. **Acid Free. Circ:** 560.
**Desc:** Reports news of interest to scholars of book history, including conferences, research notes, lectures, and recent publications.

NE
**SHORT BOOK REVIEWS / INTERNATIONAL STATISTICAL INSTITUTE.** **Added/Corp** International Statistical Institute. Vol. 1, No. 1 (Apr. 1981)-. Statistical Publication. English. Three times a year. $28.75. International Statistical Institute, 428 Prinses Beatrixlaan, 2270 AZ Voorburg Netherlands. **Tel** 011 31 70 3375737, FAX 011 31 70 3860025, telex 32260 ISI NL. **ED** A.M. Herzberg. **Bk Rev**. ***Continues in part*** *International Statistical Review, 0306-7734.*
**Desc:** Provides a rapid book review service for statisticians covering books on statistics and related subjects published throughout the world. Each review includes bibliographical information, the table of contents, the intended readership and a short critical evaluation. Includes book reviews, list of books received, collected papers, tables and proceedings, and new journals.
**Ind/Abst** Stat. Theory Method Abstr.

CN/1180-548X
**STATISTICS CANADA PUBLICATIONS LIST.** (STATISTICS CANADA PUBLICATIONS LIST / STATISTICS CANADA, LIBRARY SERVICES DIVISION.). [Stat. Can. publ. list]. **Added/Corp** Statistics Canada. Library Services Division. (1990)-. English. an. Free. Statistics Canada, Publications Sales & Services, Main Building Room 1710, Ottawa Ontario K1A 0T6 Canada. **Tel** (613)951-5078, (800)267-6677, FAX (613)951-1584, telex 053-3585. **LC** Z7554.C2; S73; HA37.C2. **DD** 016.3171.
**Desc:** List includes over 500 titles with their content description and prices.

GW/0067-8899
**VERZEICHNIS LEIFERBARER BUCHER. EERGANZUNGSBAND.** (Spring 1972/73)-. German. ir. $200.00. K.G. Saur Verlag KG, A Reed Reference Publishing Company, Part of Reed International PLC, Ortlerstrasse 8, D 81373 Munich Germany. **Tel** 011 49 89 769020, FAX 011 49 89 76902150, telex 5212067-SAUR-D. **(Subscription address:** Reed Reference Publishing Company / New Jersey, 131 Chanlaon Road, PO Box 31, New Providence NJ 07974.**)**
**Desc:** Authors, titles, keywords. Listing of all available German-language books. Cross references. Available from Gale.

UK/0960-653X
**WORLD PUBLISHING MONITOR.** [World publ. monit.]. **Added/Corp** Pira (Association) International Electronic Publishing Research Centre. Vol. 1, No. 1 (Jan. 1991)-. Abstracting/Indexing Service. English. mo. $824.00 US; £515.00 other. Pira International, Randalls Road, Leatherhead, Surrey KT22 7RU England. **Tel** 011 44 372 376161, FAX 011 44 372 377526. **LC** Z286.E43; W68. **DD** 070. **CODEN** WPMOED. **Bk Rev**. **Pr Rev**. available on CD-ROM from DIALOG; available on microfilm and microfiche from University Microfilms International (UMI); available on an online database. Documents available. ***Continues*** *Electronic Publishing Abstracts, 0739-2907.*
**Desc:** Computing and publishing information, company and market information, technical papers, conference papers and products.

## BOOKS AND BOOKMAKING

US/0001-0340
**AB BOOKMAN'S WEEKLY.** (AB BOOKMAN'S WEEKLY : FOR THE SPECIALIST BOOK WORLD.). [AB bookm. wkly.]. **VFOAT** Bookman's Weekly; AB. **VAT** Antiquarian Bookman Bookman's Weekly. Vol. 39, No. 23-24 (June 5-12, 1967)-. Periodical. English. Forty-eight times a year. $80.00 US, $75.00 others (surface mail); $225.00 Asia, Africa, Australia, USSR & Japan, $175.00 others (airmail). AB Bookmans Publications Inc, PO Box AB, Clifton NJ 07015. **Tel** (201)772-0020, FAX (201)772-9281. **ED** Jacob L. Chernofsky. **LC** Z999.A1; A5. Index available in last issue of volume--attached. cum. index. **Circ:** 10,000. available on an online database. ***Continues*** *Antiquarian Bookman.*
**Desc:** The connecting link between the library world and the specialist and antiquarian book trade, and has continually sought to focus on those areas of librarianship that concern books.
**Ind/Abst** Art Archaeol. Tech. Abstr.; Book Rev. Index; Child. Lit. Abstr. (19??-); Index Period. Artic. Relat. Law; Libr. Lit.

US/0065-0005
**AB BOOKMAN'S YEARBOOK.** **VFOAT** A.B. Bookman's Yearbook; Bookman's Yearbook. **VAT** Antiquarian Bookman Bookman's Yearbook. Began in (1954)-. English. sa. $25.00. AB Bookmans Publications Inc, PO Box AB, Clifton NJ 07015. **Tel** (201)772-0020, FAX (201)772-9281. **ED** Jacob L Chernofsky. **LC** Z990; .A18. **DD** 010.58. cum. index. **Ad Acc**. **Circ:** 10,000.

US
**ABA NEWSWIRE.** ***Title Change.*** **Main/Corp** American Booksellers Association. (1973)-(19??). Periodical. English. wk. American Booksellers Association, 828 South Broadway, Tarrytown NY 10591. **Tel** (914)591-2665, FAX (914)631-8391. ***Continued by*** *Book Selling this Week.*

JA/0916-7838
**ABD. ASIAN/PACIFIC BOOK DEVELOPMENT.** [ABD, Asian/Pac. book dev.]. **VFOAT** Asian Pacific Book Development. (1989)-. Periodical. English. Four times a year. $40.00 (one year), $100.00 (three years) Comes with Asian Cultural Centre for Unesco membership. Asia/Pacific Cultural Centre for UNESCO (ACCU), Japan Publishers Building, No. 6 Fukuromachi, Shinjuku-ku Tokyo, 162 Japan. **Tel** 011 81 3 3269 4435, FAX 011 81 3 3269 4510. ***Continues*** *Asian/Pacific Book Development Newsletter, 0388-5593.*
**Desc:** This magazine is for book development providing up-to-date news and articles sent by the correspondents of the region.

US
**ABSTRACTS OF PAPERS PRESENTED AT THE ... ANNUAL MEETING ... / THE AMERICAN INSTITUTE FOR CONSERVATION OF HISTORIC AND ARTISTIC WORKS.** **See** The Arts-Art.

BU/0205-0838
**ABV.** (1991)-. Periodical. Bulgarian. wk. **LC** Z2893; .A282. ***Continues*** *ABV.*
**Ind/Abst** Annu. Bibliogr. Engl. Lang. Lit.

US/0894-993X
**ACADEMIC LIBRARY BOOK REVIEW.** [Acad. libr. book rev.]. **VFOAT** LBR; L.B.R. Vol. 1, No. 2

(March 1985)- Vol. 8 (Dec. 1992)-. Periodical. English. Six times a year (Feb., Apr., June, Aug., Oct., Dec.). $36.00 one year; $66.00 two year. Academic Library Book Review, 290 Broadway, Suite 354, Lynbrook NY 11563. **Tel** (516)593-1195, FAX (516)596-2911. **ED** Hannah Merker and Barbara Fiegas. **LC** Z1039.C65; A22. **DD** 028. Index available. **Bk Rev**. **Ad Acc. Circ:** 2,400 (ctrl).
**Desc:** Journal aimed toward collection development librarians, acquisition specialists, book selectors and intends to provide them with an honest evaluation of the latest titles.

US/0567-6487
**ACADEMIC REVIEWER, THE. See** Education-Higher Education.

GW/0065-2032
**ADRESSBUCH DES DEUTSCHSPRACHIGEN BUCHHANDEL.** (ADRESSBUCH FUER DEN DEUTSCHSPRACHIGEN BUCHHANDEL.). [Adressb. deutschspr. Buchhand.]. **Added/Corp** Buchhandler-Vereinigung. (1977-1978)-. Monographic series. German. an. Price varies per volume. Buchhandler Vereinigung GmbH, Grosser Hirschgraben 17-21, D 60311 Frankfurt 1 Germany. **Tel** 011 49 69 1306243, telex 413573 BUCH VOL. **LC** Z317; .A26. **NLM** Z 317 A243. **Ad Acc. Circ:** 4,500. ***Continues*** *Adressbuch des Deutschsprachigen Buchhandels, 0065-2032.*

II
**ADVENT, THE.** (1???)-. Periodical. English. Four times a year. Hindustan Book Agency, 17 UB Jawahar Nagar, Delhi 7 India.

UK
**AFRICAN BOOK WORLD & PRESS: DIRECTORY, THE. VFOAT** Repertoire du Livre et de la Presse en Afrique. **VAT** African Book World and Press: A Directory. (1977)-. English (French). ir. $135.00. K.G. Saur Verlag KG, A Reed Reference Publishing Company, Part of Reed International PLC, Ortlerstrasse 8, D 81373 Munich Germany. **Tel** 011 49 89 769020, FAX 011 49 89 76902150, telex 5212067-SAUR-D. **ED** Hanz M. Zell. **LC** Z857.A1; A37. **DD** 021/.0025/6.
**Desc:** Furnishes details on a variety of institutions and enterprises concerned with the book trade and press in Africa.

SU
**ALAM AL-KUTUB. VFOAT** World of Books. Journal 1 (May 1980)-. Periodical. Arabic. qt. 6500 riyals. Dar Thaqif, PO Box 1590, Al-Riyad Al-Mamlakah Al-Arabiyah Al-Saudiyah, Al-Taif Saudi Arabia. **ED** Yahya M Saati. **LC** Z1007; .A4.
**Desc:** Devoted to Arabic book indexing as well as foreign publications. It's essential field is to introduce the books in a review or a bibliographic form to academic or public libraries within the Arab and the Islamic world, hence serving as a selection and acquisition tool.

HK
**ALL ASIA REVIEW.** Vol. 2, No. 2 (Sept./Oct. 1990)-. Periodical. English. sa. Geoghegan Publishing Ltd., GPO Box 13311, Hong Kong. **Tel** 011 852 8949250. ***Continues*** *All Asia Review of Books.*

SW
**ALLT OM BOCKER.** (19??)-. Periodical. Swedish. bm (6 issues). Kr315.00 Sweden. Progek Prospar, Box 31003, S 400-32 Goteborg Sweden. **Tel** 011 46 31 243425.
**Ind/Abst** Annu. Bibliogr. Engl. Lang. Lit.

US/0196-5654
**AMERICAN BOOK COLLECTOR (1980). See** Hobbies.

US/0091-9357
**AMERICAN BOOK PRICES CURRENT.** Vol. 1, (1895)-. English. an (Jan.). $140.90. Bancroft Parkman Inc, PO Box 1236, Old Litchfield Road, Washington CT 06793. **Tel** (203)868-7408, FAX (203)868-0080. **ED** Katharine Kyes Leab. **LC** Z1000; .A51. **DD** 018/.3. **NLM** Z 1000 A512. Index available. cum. index. **Ad Acc. Circ:** 3,000. available on CD-ROM.

US/0148-5903
**AMERICAN BOOKSELLER (NEW YORK. 1977).** (AMERICAN BOOKSELLER.). [Am. books.]. **Added/Corp** American Booksellers Association. (1977)-. Periodical. English. Twelve times a year. Free (members); $49.95 (non-members). American Booksellers Association, 828 South Broadway, Tarrytown NY 10591. **Tel** (914)591-2665, FAX (914)631-8391. **ED** Dan Cullen. **LC** Z477; .A58. **DD** 658.8/09/0705730973. Index available. **Ad Acc. Circ:** 9,500 (ctrl).
**Desc:** This magazine emphasizes the business of retail bookselling through how-to articles, bookstore profiles, interviews with industry figures.

CN/0003-200X
**AMPHORA. Added/Corp** Alcuin Society. Vol. 1 (1967)-. Periodical. English. qt. 35.00Can$. Alcuin Society, PO Box 3216, Vancouver British Columbia V6B 3X8 Canada. **Tel** (604)888-9049, FAX (604)888-9049. **LC** Z990; .A55. **DD** 020/.75. **Ad Acc. Circ:** 200. ***Supersedes*** *Alcuin Society. Notes from the Alcuin Society., 0568-935X.*

**Desc:** Items of interest to members who are fond of fine books and with various crafts which produce fine books.
**Ind/Abst** BHA : Biblio. Hist. Art; Br. Archaeol. Bibliogr.

JA
**ANNOTATED CATALOGUE OF BOOKS PUBLISHED IN JAPAN. Added/Corp** Shuppan Bunka Kokusai Koryu-Kai. No. 2 (1975/76)-. Catalog. English. an. Free. Publishers Association for Cultural Exchange, 1-2-1 Saragaku-cho Chiyoda-ku, Tokyo 101 Japan. **Tel** (03) 3291-5685, FAX (03) 3233-3645. **ED** Hisashi Sakanishi. **LC** Z3301; .A53. **DD** 015/.52. ***Continues*** *Annotated Catalogue of 270 Books Published in Japan.*

BE
**ANNUAIRE DU CENTENAIRE / CERCLE BELGE DE LA LIBRAIRIE. Added/Corp** Cercle Belge de la Librairie. (19??)-. French. an. Cercle Belge de la Librairie, rue du Luxembourg 5/Boite 1, 1040 Brussles Belgium. **LC** Z354; .A56.

●UK/0968-7521
**ANNUAL REGISTER OF BOOK VALUES. MODERN FIRST EDITIONS. VFOAT** Modern First Editions; ARBV. Modern First Editions. (1993)-. English. Ross Burnet, PO Box 2, Uralla New South Wales 2358, Australia. **Tel** 011 067 784682, FAX 011 067 784516. **LC** Z1029; .I55. ***Continues*** *International Rare Book Prices. Modern First Editions.*

US/0098-7379
**ANNUAL REVIEW OF ENGLISH BOOKS ON ASIA.** 1974-. English. an. Brigham Young University Press / Print Services, 205 VPB, Provo UT 84602. **LC** Z3001; .A7; DS5. **DD** 016.95.

●UK
**ANTIQUARIAN BOOK MONTHLY. VFOAT** Antiquarian Book. Vol. 20, No. 2 (Feb. 1993)-. Periodical. English. mo. £28.00 UK; £36.00 Europe; £44.00 US, Canada, South Africa, Singapore and Thailand; £46.00 Australia, New Zealand and Japan. Antiquarian Book Monthly, 1 Park Parade, Park Road, Farnham Royal Bucks SL2 3AU England. **Tel** 011 44 753 645999, FAX 011 44 753 645255. **LC** Z990; .A57. Index available. cum. index. **Bk Rev**, (Qty: 40-50). **Ad Acc, Adv Mgr:** Jan Richford, **Tel** same as publisher. **Acid Free. Circ:** 3,000 (ctrl). ***Continues*** *Antiquarian Book Monthly Review, 0306-7475.*

UK/0306-7475
**ANTIQUARIAN BOOK MONTHLY REVIEW. *Title Change.* VFOAT** ABMR. Vol. 1-20, No. 1 (Feb. 1974)-(Jan. 1993). Periodical. English. mo. ABMR Publishing Ltd, G Bullingdon House, 174 B Cowley, Oxford OX4 1UE England. **Tel** (0865)794704, FAX (0865)794582. **ED** John A Kinnane. **LC** Z990; .A57. **DD** 002/.075. Index available. cum. index. **Bk Rev. Ad Acc. Circ:** 3,000. ***Continued by*** *Antiquarian Book Monthly.*
**Desc:** Articles, reports and reviews of interest to book collectors, booksellers and libraries, modern and antiquarian.

US/0197-0364
**ANTIQUARIAN TRADE LIST ANNUAL. *Ceased.*** (ANTIQUARIAN TRADE LIST ANNUAL: (ALTA).). [Antiq. trade list annu.]. **VFOAT** ATLA. (1980)-(19??). English. ir. Pergamon Press, An Imprint of Elsevier Science Ltd., The Boulevard, Langford Lane, Kidlington, Oxford OX5 1GB United Kingdom. **Tel** 011 44 865 843000, 011 44 865 843699, FAX 011 44 865 843010. **(Subscription address:** Pergamon Press, 660 White Plains Road, Tarrytown, NY 10591; telephone: (914)524-9200) **LC** Microfiche (w)82-2. **DD** 017/.8. available on microfiche.
**Desc:** A three ring binder which is arranged in three parts: antiquarian list (printed); specialties index (printed); and microfiches.

US/0890-1341
**ARAB BOOK WORLD.** [Arab book world]. Vol. 1, No. 1 (July 1981)-. Periodical. English. qt. International Crescent Publ Co, 12021 Nieta Drive, Garden Grove CA 92640. **LC** IN PROCESS. **DD** 909.

GW/0066-6327
**ARCHIV FUER GESCHICHTE DES BUCHWESENS.** [Arch. Gesch. Buchwes.]. **Added/Corp** Borsenverein des Deutschen Buchhandels. Historische Kommission. Vol. 1 (1956)-. Periodical. German. bm. DM380.00. Buchhandler Vereinigung GmbH, Grosser Hirschgraben 17-21, D 60311 Frankfurt 1 Germany. **Tel** 011 49 69 1306243, telex 413573 BUCH VOL. **LC** Z4; .A7. **DD** 070.5/73. cum. index. ***Supersedes*** *Archiv fur Geschichte des Deutschen Buchhandels.*
**Desc:** Interdisciplinary organ concerning all media; historical problems of books.
**Ind/Abst** Annu. Bibliogr. Engl. Lang. Lit.; BHA : Biblio. Hist. Art; MLA Int. Bibl. Books Artic. Mod. Lang. Lit.

FR
**ARGUS DE L'AUTOGRAPHE & DU MANUSCRIT : REPERTOIRE BIBLIOGRAPHIQUE, L'. VFOAT** Repertoire Bibliographique; Argus de l'Autographe et du Manuscrit. **VAT** Argus de l'Autographe et du Manuscrit. (July. 1986-1987)-. Bibliography. French. an (Fall). Cercle de la Librairie, 35 rue Gregoire de Tours, 75279 Paris Cedex 06 France. **Tel** 011 33 1 44412800. **LC** Z1000; .A72. **DD** 017/.3/0944. ***Separated from*** *Repertoire Bibliographique (Paris, France).*

FR
**ARGUS DU LIVRE DE COLLECTION.** (19??)-. French. an. 1023.13F. Cercle de la Librairie, 35 rue Gregoire de Tours, 75279 Paris Cedex 06 France. **Tel** 011 33 1 44412800. ***Continues*** *Repertoire Bibliographique.*

YU
**ARHEOGRAFSKI PRILOZI. Added/Corp** Narodna Biblioteka SR Srbije. Arheografsko Odeljenje. (1979)-. Periodical. Serbo-Croatian (Cyrillic). Narodna Biblioteka Srbije, Arheografsko Odeljenje, Skerliceva 1, 11 000 Belgrad Yugoslavia. **LC** Z115.5.S45; A73.

FR
**ART ET METIERS DU LIVRE.** Vol. 83, No. 45, (Nov. 1973)-. Periodical. French. Six times a year. 685.00F France; 940.00F other. Editions Filigranes, 55 Bis rue de Lyon, 75012 Paris France. **Tel** 011 33 1 43401088. **ED** R. Baschet. Index available. **Bk Rev. Ad Acc. Circ:** 4,600. ***Continues*** *Reliure-Brochure-Dorure.*
**Desc:** Handicraft bookbinding and all subjects concerned with art books.
**Ind/Abst** Art Archaeol. Tech. Abstr.

JA
**ASIAN BOOK DEVELOPMENT NEWSLETTER. Added/Corp** Asian Cultural Centre for Unesco. Vol. 10 (July 1978)-. Newsletter. English. qt. Asian Cultural Centre for UNESCO, Book Publishers Building, No 6 Fukuromachi Shinjuku-ku, Tokyo Japan. **LC** Z448.7; .Y85a. **DD** 070.5/73/095. ***Continues*** *Newsletter - Tokyo Book Development Centre.*

II/0004-4547
**ASIAN BOOKS NEWSLETTER.** Vol. 1 (Apr. 1966)-. Newsletter. English. mo. $48.00. K K Roy Private Ltd, PO Box 10210, 55 Gariahat Road, Calcutta 700019 India. **Tel** 91 33-474872, 91 33-475069. **Circ:** 1,900. available on microfilm from University Microfilms International (UMI).
**Desc:** Bibliographic listings of material published in all Asian countries.

●CN/1192-3652
**ATLANTIC BOOKS TODAY.** [Atl. books today]. **Added/Corp** Atlantic Provinces Book Review Society. No. 1 (Fall 1992)-. Periodical. English. qt. Atlantic Provinces Book Review Society, 2085 Mainland Street, 2nd Floor, Halifax, Nova Scotia B3K 2Z8 Canada. **DD** 028.1/09715. ***Continues*** *Atlantic Provinces Book Review, 0316-5981.*
**Ind/Abst** Can. Period. Index.

GW
**AUKTION. See** The Arts-Graphic Arts.

US
**AUSTIN BOOKWORKERS.** (Spring 1990)-. Periodical. English. qt.

AT
**AUSTRALIAN BOOK AUCTION RECORDS / COMPILED BY MARGARET WOODHOUSE.** Vol. 1 (1969/70)-. Periodical. English. be. price varies per volume. Australian Book Aution Record, PO Box 64, Curtin Australian Capital Territory 2611 Australia. **Tel** 011 61 6 2812745. **LC** Z1000; .A9. **DD** 017/.3.

AT/1034-0785
**AUSTRALIAN BOOK COLLECTOR.** (1989)-. Periodical. English. Eleven times a year (Except Jan.). 44.00Aus$ Australia; 62.00Aus$ US & Canada; 70.00Aus$ Europe; 56.00Aus$ New Zealand. Ross Burnet, PO Box 2, Uralla New South Wales 2358, Australia. **Tel** 011 067 784682, FAX 011 067 784516. **ED** Ross Burnet. **Bk Rev**, (Qty: 20). **Ad Acc. Circ:** 500 (ctrl).
**Desc:** News, feature articles, book reviews, books wanted, books for sale most anything about books.

AT
**AUSTRALIAN BOOKS ; A SELECT LIST. Added/Corp** National Library of Australia. (1933)-. Periodical. English. an. National Library of Australia, Parkes Place, Canberra ACT, 2600 Australia. **Tel** 011 61 6 2621374, FAX 011 61 6 2731084.
**Desc:** A current reference and selective reading list of works dealing with Australia or of Australian authorship.

AT
**AUSTRALIAN BOOKSELLER & PUBLISHER. Added/Corp** D.W. Thorpe Pty. Vol. 51, (1971)-. Trade Publication. English. mo (with combined Dec./Jan.). 49.00Aus$ Australia; 81.00Aus$ New Zealand and Asia; 104.00Aus$ US and Canada; 115.00Aus$ UK and Europe. D. W. Thorpe, A Reed Reference Publishing Company, A Subsidiary of Reed International Books Australia, 18 Salmon Street, Port Melbourne, Victoria 3207 Australia. **Tel** 011 61 3 6451511, FAX 011 61 3 6453981, telex 39476. **ED** John

## Publishing —Books and Bookmaking

Nieuwgnituizen. **LC** Z533.7; .I33. **DD** 070.5/0994. Index available. cum. index. **Ad Acc**. **Pr Rev. Circ:** 9,000 (ctrl). **Continues** Ideas: Book Trade Journal.
 **Desc:** Monthly trade journal for publishers, booksellers, and librarians.
 **Ind/Abst** Child. Lit. Abstr. (19??-).

UK
**AVERAGE PRICES OF USA ACADEMIC BOOKS.** **Added/Corp** Loughborough University of Technology. Centre for Library and Information Management. Library Management Research Unit (Great Britain) Loughborough University of Technology. Library and Information Statistics Unit. (July/Dec. 1984)-(Jan./June 1986)-. Periodical. English. Twice a year. £7.50. Library History Group, Department of Library Studies, Loughborough University, Leicester LE11 3TU England. **Tel** 011 44 509 263171.

MX
**AZTECA : BOLETIN BIBLIOGRAFICO INTERNACIONAL / FONDO DE CULTURA ECONOMICA.** **Added/Corp** Fondo de Cultura Economica (Mexico). (1990)-. Periodical. Spanish. mo.

GW
**BA, BESPRECHUNGEN/ANNOTATIONEN.**
**VFOAT** Besprechungen/Annotationen. Periodical. German. Einkaufszentrale fur Offentliche Bibliotheken GmbH, Postfach 96, Bismarckstrasse 3. **LC** Z1035.A1; B18.

PK
**BAI.** **Main/Corp** National Book Centre of Pakistan. 1-1965-. Periodical. Bengali (Bengali). **LC** Z459.7.

UK/0307-8647
**BAR QUARTERLY.** **VAT** Book-Auction Records Quarterly. Vol. 73 (Jan. 1976)-. Periodical. English. qt. £35.00. Dawson UK Ltd, Cannon House, Folkestone Kent CT19 5EE England. **Tel** 011 44 303-850101, FAX 011 44 303-850440, telex 96392. **ED** Wendy Y Heath. **LC** Z1000; .B18. **DD** 017/.3. Index available. cum. index. **Ad Acc**.
 **Desc:** A priced and annotated record of international book auctions.

FR/0763-7063
**BEAUX LIVRES.** [Beaux livres]. (1984)-. French. an. 151.78F. Cercle de la Librairie, 35 rue Gregoire de Tours, F-75279 Paris Cedex 06 France. **Tel** 011 33 1 43291000, FAX 011 33 1 43296895, telex LIFRAN 270 838. **LC** Z2165; .B58ET; AY16. **Continues** Livres d'Entrennes, 0245-8691.
 **Desc:** Presentation of new year book gifts in color and glossy paper.

FR
**BEAUX LIVRES DE L'ANNEE, LES.** 1973-. French. Office of Promotion de L'Edition Francaise, 35 zue Giegoire-de-Tours, 75279 Cedex 06 Paris France. **LC** Z1033.F5; B4. **DD** 011. ctrl circ. **Continues** Cinquante Beaux Livres de l'Annee.

US/1049-0035
**BEFORE AND AFTER.** [Before After]. **VFOAT** Before and After. Vol. 1, No. 1 (1990)-. Periodical. English. bm. $36.00 US; $40.00 Canada; $54.00 other. PAGELAB, 1830 Sierra Gardens #30, Roseville CA 95661. **Tel** (916)784-3880, FAX (916)784-3995. **ED** Gaye A. McWade. **DD** 070. ctrl circ.

US/0882-0708
**BEST BOOKS FOR YOUNG ADULTS.**
[Best books for young adults]. **Main/Corp** American Library Association. Young Adult Services Division. (19??)-. Periodical. English. an. $25.00 (nonmember), $22.50 (member). American Library Association, 50 East Huron Street, Chicago IL 60611. **Tel** (312)944-6780, (800)545-2433, FAX (312)944-2641. **(Subscription address:** American Library Association, Subscription Department, 434 West Downer, Aurora IL 60506-9936.) **DD** 028.

PL/0867-0218
**BESTSELLER BODZ.** (BESTSELLER.). (1990)-. Periodical. Polish. mo. Price on Request. **(Subscription address:** ARS Polona, PO Box 1001, 00068 Warsaw Poland.) **UDC** 884. **CODEN** 008.

IT/0006-0941
**BIBLIOFILIA (FLORENCE, ITALY).** (LA BIBLIOFILIA.). [Bibliofilia]. Vol. 1, (April 1889)-. Periodical. Italian. Three times a year. L90000 Italy; L112000 other. Casa Editrice Leo S. Olschki, Viuzzo del Pozzetto, Casella Postale 66, 50126 Florence Italy. **Tel** 011 39 55 6530684, FAX 011 39 55 6530214. **LC** Z1007; .B56. cum. index.
 **Ind/Abst** BHA : Biblio. Hist. Art; MLA Int. Bibl. Books Artic. Mod. Lang. Lit.

UK
**BIBLIOGRAPHICAL SERIES OF SUPPLEMENTS TO BRITISH BOOK NEWS ON WRITERS AND THEIR WORK.**
(1950)-. Periodical. English. Pergamon Press, An Imprint of Elsevier Science Ltd., The Boulevard, Langford Lane, Kidlington, Oxford OX5 1GB United Kingdom. **Tel** 011 44 865 843000, 011 44 865 843699, FAX 011 44 865 843010.

AT/0045-1940
**BIBLIONEWS AND AUSTRALIAN NOTES AND QUERIES.** **Added/Corp** Book Collectors' Society of Australia. Vol. 1 (Jan. 1966)-. Periodical. English. Four times a year (Mar., June, Sept., Dec.). 20.00Aus$ Australia; 25.00Aus$ other. Book Collectors Society of Australia, 16 Edwin Street South, Croydon NSW 2132 Australia. **Tel** 011 61 2 7988984, FAX 011 61 2 7988984. **DD** 001. Index available. cum. index. **Bk Rev**. **Ad Acc**. **Circ:** 400. **Continues** Biblionews.
 **Desc:** For members of the Book Collectors' Society of Australia. Articles, reviews, notes and queries.
 **Ind/Abst** Annu. Bibliogr. Engl. Lang. Lit.; Aust. Educ. Index.

FR
**BIBLIOPHILE, LE.** No. 1 (Jan. 1975)-. Periodical. French. mo.

SW/0430-8417
**BIBLIS.** **Added/Corp** Foreningen for Bokhantverk. (1957)-. Swedish. an. **LC** Z119.5; .B5.
 **Ind/Abst** BHA : Biblio. Hist. Art.

GW/0342-3573
**BINDEREPORT.** [Bindereport]. **VFOAT** Allgemeiner Anzeiger fuer Buchbindereien. (May 12, 1977)-. Periodical. German. Twelve times a year. DM158.00 Germany; DM180.00 other. Schluetersche Verlag Druckerei, Postfach 5440, D-30054 Hannover Germany. **Tel** 011 49 511 85500, FAX 011 49 511 1236400, telex 923978. **ED** Eberhard Furch. **[CCC]**. **Bk Rev**. **Ad Acc**. ctrl circ. **Continues** Allgemeiner Anzeiger fuer Buchbindereien.
 **Desc:** Manufacturing process of books, printing process in trade industry and publishing industry.
 **Ind/Abst** Print. Abstr.

NE
**BINDERIFEN / CENTRAL BUREAU VOOR DE STATISTIEK, HOOFDAFDELING STATISTIEKEN VAN INDUSTRIE EN BOUWNIJVERHEID.**
**VFOAT** Binderies. Dutch (summaries and/or abstracts in English). an. Fl7.00. Centraal Bureau voor de Statistiek, AFD ALG Zaken, Postbus 959, 2270 AZ Voorburg Netherlands. **Tel** 011 31 70 3373800, FAX 011 31 038 7429, telex 32040 CBS NL. **LC** Z270.N43; N47A. **DD** 686.3/09492. **Continues** Netherlands. Central Bureau Voor de Statistiek. Produktiestatistieken: Binderijen.

●US/1066-940X
**BLACK AUTHORS BOOKS IN PRINT.**
(1994)-. English. $19.95. Grace Publishing Company, Box 80047, Rochester Hills MI 48308-0047. **Tel** (313)650-9450.

NO
**BOK OG SAMFUNN (OSLO, NORWAY : 1981).** (BOK OG SAMFUNN.). Vol. 1, No. 1 (Jan. 12, 1981)-. Periodical. Norwegian. bw (thirty-six issues yearly). Norwegian Booksellers Association, Ovre Vollgate 15, 0158 Oslo 1 Norway. **Tel** 011 47 2 410 760. **Bk Rev**. **Ad Acc**. **Circ:** 2,500. **Formed by the union of** Bok Og Samfunn A-Utgave and Bok Og Samfunn B-Utgave.

PL/0867-2806
**BOKSER WARSZAWA.** (BOKSER.). [Bokser Warsz.]. (1990)-. Periodical. Polish. mo. Price on Request. **(Subscription address:** ARS Polona, PO Box 1001, 00068 Warsaw Poland.) **UDC** 196.8. **Continues** Boks (Warszawa), 0137-8007.

SW/0006-5846
**BOKVAENNEN.** See Literature.

CK/0120-1204
**BOLETIN BIBLIOGRAFICO (REGIONAL CENTER FOR BOOK PROMOTION IN LATIN AMERICA AND THE CARIBBEAN).** (BOLETIN BIBLIOGRAFICO / CENTRO REGIONAL PARA EL FOMENTO DEL LIBRO EN AMERICA LATINA Y EL CARIBE.). Vol. 5, No. 2-4 (April/Dec. 1978)-. Spanish. qt. $12.00 US; $13.50 Europe; $14.00 Asia. Cerlalc, Calle 70 #9 52, Bogota 2 Colombia. **Tel** 2554614, telex CERLACO 44637. **ED** Oscar Delgado Sanchez. **LC** Z1601; .U5A. **DD** 016.98. **Ad Acc**. **Circ:** 5,000. **Continues** Boletin Bibliografico CERLAL.

US/0740-8439
**BOOK - AMERICAN ANTIQUARIAN SOCIETY, THE.** (THE BOOK : NEWSLETTER OF THE PROGRAM IN THE HISTORY OF THE BOOK IN AMERICAN CULTURE.). [Book - Am. Antiq. Soc.].
**Added/Corp** American Antiquarian Society. American Antiquarian Society. Program in the History of the Book in American Culture. No. 1 (Nov. 1983)-. Periodical. English. Four times a year. Free. American Antiquarian Society, 185 Salisbury Street, Worcester MA 01609. **Tel** (508)752-5813, (508)755-5221. **ED** David D. Hall and John B. Hench. **Bk Rev**. **Circ:** 2,100 (ctrl).

UK
**BOOK AND MAGAZINE COLLECTOR.**
See Hobbies.

US/0887-8978
**BOOK & PAPER GROUP ANNUAL, THE.**
See The Arts-Art.

RU
**BOOK AS ART (MOSCOW, R.S.F.S.R.).**
(BOOK AS ART.). **Added/Corp** Vsesoiuznoe Aentstvo po Atorskim Pavam. (19??)-. Periodical. English. qt. **LC** Z165; .B68. **DD** 686/.0947.

NE
**BOOK AUCTION.** **Main/Corp** Van Gendt Book Auctions BV. **VFOAT** Print Auction. English. ir. Van Gendt Book Auctions B V, 96-98 Keizersgracht, 1015 CV Amsterdam Netherlands.

UK/0068-0095
**BOOK AUCTION RECORDS.** **VFOAT** Book-Auction Records. (1903)-. English. an. £95.00. Dawson UK Ltd, Cannon House, Folkestone Kent CT19 5EE England. **Tel** 011 44 303-850101, FAX 011 44 303-850440, telex 96392. **ED** Wendy Heath. **LC** Z1000; .B65. **DD** 017.3. **NLM** Z 1000 B723. cum. index. **Ad Acc**. **Continues** Sale Records.
 **Desc:** A list of books sold at international auctions and the prices realized.

UK/0006-7237
**BOOK COLLECTOR, THE.** [Book collect.]. Vol. 1 (Spring 1952)-. Periodical. English. qt (Mar., June, Sept., Dec.). $60.00. The Collector Limited, 20 Maple Grove, London NW9 8QY England. **Tel** 011 44 81 2005004, FAX 011 44 81 2005004. **ED** Nicolas J. Barker. **LC** Z990; .B6. **DD** 020/.75. Index available. cum. index. **Bk Rev**. **Ad Acc**. Documents available from The Genuine Article. **Supersedes** Book Handbook.
 **Desc:** Articles on antiquarian books and bibliography.
 **Ind/Abst** Abstr. Engl. Stud.; Annu. Bibliogr. Engl. Lang. Lit.; ARTBibliogr. Mod.; Arts Humanit. Citation Index [Full Cov.]; BHA : Biblio. Hist. Art; Biblio. Hist. Index; Br. Humanit. Index; Curr. Contents Arts Humanit.; Libr. Lit.; MLA Int. Bibl. Books Artic. Mod. Lang. Lit.; Res. Alert [Full Cov.]; Romant. Move.

US/0160-970X
**BOOK INDUSTRY TRENDS.** [Book ind. trends]. **Added/Corp** Book Industry Study Group. (1977)-. English. an (Sept.). $125.00 (members), $450.00 (non-members) Comes with Book Industry Study Group membership. Book Industry Study Group, 160 5th Avenue, New York NY 10010. **Tel** (212)929-1393, FAX (212)989-7542. **LC** Z477; .D47. **DD** 658.8/09/0705730973. **[CCC]**.

US/1055-4742
**BOOK LINKS.** [Book links]. Vol. 1, No. 1 (Sept. 1991)-. Periodical. English. Six times a year. $16.95 US; $20.00 Canada and Mexico; $25.00 other. American Library Association, 50 East Huron Street, Chicago IL 60611. **Tel** (312)944-6780, (800)545-2433, FAX (312)944-2641. **(Subscription address:** American Library Association, Subscription Department, 434 West Downer, Aurora IL 60506-9936.) **LC** Z1037; .B7218. **DD** 015/.73062.
 **Desc:** Magazine that connects books, libraries, and classrooms.

US/1040-6344
**BOOK/LOS ANGELES, THE.** [Book Los Angel.]. **VFOAT** The Book Los Angeles. 1988-. Periodical. English. Three times a year. Kahn & Partners, 14624 Round Valley Drive, Sherman Oaks CA 91403. **DD** 051.

US/0891-8813
**BOOK MARKETING UPDATE.** [Book mark. update]. Vol. 1 (Dec. 1986)-. Periodical. English. mo (10 issues). $60.00 US; $66.00 Canada; $72.00 other. Open Horizons, PO Box 205, Fairfield IA 52556. **Tel** (515)472-6130, FAX (515)472-1560. **ED** John Kremer. **DD** 070. **[CCC]**. Index available (Index published on disk). cum. index. **Bk Rev**, (Qty: 50). **Ad Acc**, **Adv Mgr:** Bob Sanny. **Circ:** 3,000.
 **Desc:** Each issue lists names, addresses, and buyers of key book marketing contacts. Also features media contacts as well as show you how to write effective news releases, how to create background fact sheets that sell your books, and how to book radio and TV interviews.

UK
**BOOK MARKETS IN THE AMERICAS, ASIA, AFRICA & AUSTRALASIA.**
1979/1980-. English. Euromonitor Publications Ltd., 87-88 Turnmill Street, London EC1M 5QU England. **Tel** 011 44 71 2518024, FAX 011 44 71 6083149, telex 21120. **LC** Z284; .B59. **DD** 0705/0212.

UK
**BOOK MARKETS IN WESTERN EUROPE.** 1st Ed.; 1978/79-. English. an. £95.00. Euromonitor Publications Ltd., 87-88 Turnmill Street,

London EC1M 5QU England. **Tel** 011 44 71 2518024, FAX 011 44 71 6083149, telex 21120. **LC** Z291; .B6. **DD** 070.5/094.

US/0161-5556
**BOOK-MART (DECATUR), THE.** (THE BOOK-MART.). [Book-mart]. **VAT** Book Mart. (19??)-. Periodical. English. mo. $4.00 (3rd class mail), $8.50 (1st class mail). Americana Books, 144 South Second Street, Decatur IN 46733.

UK
**BOOK PRODUCTION (BENN PUBLICATIONS LTD.).** (BOOK PRODUCTION.). (19??)-. Periodical. English. sa. Printing World, 25 New Street Square, London EC4A 3JA England. **LC** Z119; .B83 Suppl. **DD** 070.5/05. **Bk Rev. Ad Acc.** ctrl circ.

US/0882-8261
**BOOK PUBLISHING CAREER DIRECTORY.** [Book publ. career dir.]. **Added/Corp** Career Publishing Corp. (New York, N.Y.) Career Press Inc. (1986)-. Directory. English. $29.95 (hardcover), $17.95 (softcover). Gale Research Inc., 835 Penobscot Building, Detroit MI 48226. **Tel** (800)877-GALE, (313)961-2242, FAX (313)961-6083, telex TWX 810-221-7086. **LC** Z477; .B63. **DD** 070.5/023/73.
**Desc:** Covers working for a university press, independent publishing, religious book publishing, book clubs, electronic publishing, marketing, sales, publicity and more.

UK
**BOOK REPORT.** See Business-Marketing.

US
**BOOK REPORT.** English. **(Subscription address:** Book Report Subscription Department, 5701 North High Street, Suite 1, Worthington, OH 43085-3963**)**
**Ind/Abst** Child. Lit. Abstr. (19??-).

II
**BOOK REVIEW, THE.** V. 1- Jan. 1976-. English. bm. Rs12.00 India; $12.00 US; £5.00 UK. Perspective Publications, F-24 Bhagat Singh Market, New Delhi 110001 India. **Tel** 344772/353519. **ED** Chandra Chari. **LC** Z1035.A1; B59. **DD** 028.1/0954. Index available. cum. index. **Bk Rev. Ad Acc. Circ:** 1,200.
**Desc:** Seeks to focus attention on important publications, both in India and other countries in various subjects of general and specialized interest, through reviews by scholars and well-known cities.

US/0524-0581
**BOOK REVIEW INDEX.** See Publishing-Abstracting, Bibliographies and Statistics.

US/1056-635X
**BOOK RIGHTS REPORT.** [Book rights rep.]. Vol. 91, No. 2 (Feb. 1991)-. Periodical. English. bm. Bookmarket, 4156 Elm Avenue, Brookfield IL 60513. **DD** 070. ***Continues*** *Bookfinder (Brookfield, Ill.).*

US/0145-627X
**BOOK TALK (ALBUQUERQUE).** (BOOK TALK.). **Added/Corp** New Mexico Book League. Vol. 1 (1972)-. English. Five times a year (Jan., Mar., June, Sept., Nov.). $10.00. New Mexico Book League, 8632 Horacio Place NE, Albuquerque NM 87111. **Tel** (505)299-8940, FAX (505)294-8032. **ED** Carol A. Myers. **Bk Rev**, (Qty: 125). **Ad Acc. Circ:** 500 (ctrl).
**Desc:** Articles and book listings of interest to libraries, booksellers and collectors interested in southwestern United States.

CN/0836-8619
**BOOK TRADE IN CANADA, WITH WHO'S WHERE, THE.** See Publishing.

II
**BOOK WORLD.** 1978-. English. an. Rs20.00. Bookworld Publications, Kitab Mahal Chaura Rasta, Jaipur 302003 India. **LC** Z284; .B63. **DD** 658.8/09/070573.
**Ind/Abst** Annu. Bibliogr. Engl. Lang. Lit.

US/0006-7369
**BOOK WORLD (WASHINGTON).** (BOOK WORLD.). [Book world]. **VFOAT** Chicago Tribune Book World. Vol. 1 (Sept. 10, 1967)-. Periodical. English. Fifty-two times a year. $26.00. The Washington Post Company, 1150 15th Street Northwest, Washington DC 20071. **Tel** (202)334-5950. available on microfilm from University Microfilms International (UMI). ***Formed by the union of*** *Books Today* ***and*** *Book Week, 0524-059X.*
**Ind/Abst** Am. Bibliogr. Slavic East Europ. Stud. (19??-19??); Annu. Bibliogr. Engl. Lang. Lit.; Book Rev. Index.

UK
**BOOKBINDER : JOURNAL OF THE SOCIETY OF BOOKBINDERS AND BOOK RESTORERS.** **Main/Corp** Society of Bookbinders and Book Restorers. **VFOAT** Journal of the Society of Bookbinders and Book Restorers. (1987)-. English. an (Dec.). £27.00 UK, £37.00 others (full membership); £50.00 (institutional) UK; £55.00 (institutional) others Comes with Society of Bookbinders membership. Society of Bookbinders, Lower Hammonds Farm, Ripley Lane, West Horsley Surrey KT24 GJP England. **Tel** 011 41 48653175.

UK/0260-0315
**BOOKMARK (EDINBURGH, LOTHIAN).** (BOOKMARK.). (19??)-. English. ir. £3.00 UK; £5.00 others. Bookmark, Moray House College of Education, English Dept, Holyrood Road, Edinburgh EH8 8AQ Scotland.

US/0747-847X
**BOOKNOTES (PORTLAND, ORE.).** (BOOKNOTES.). **VFOAT** Book Notes. July 1984-. Periodical. English. mo. $35.00. Interpub, 82644 Howe Lane, Creswell OR 97426.

UK/0264-3693
**BOOKPLATE JOURNAL, THE.** [Bookpl. j.]. **Added/Corp** Bookplate Society (Great Britain). Vol. 1, No. 1 (March 1983)-. Periodical. English. Twice a year (Mar., & Sept.). $50.00. Bookplate Society, 125 Brampton Road, Carlisle Cumbria, CA3 9AP England. **Tel** 011 44 0228 402630. **ED** Brian North Lee. Index available (Every 4 yrs.). cum. index. **Circ:** 300 (ctrl).
**Desc:** This articles contains information on bookplates. It features comments, artists, and reviews on the bookplates.

US
**BOOKPRESS, THE.** Vol. 1, No. 1 (Sept. 1991)-. Periodical. English. Nine times a year. $10.00. The Bookery, 215 North Cayuga, Ithaca NY 14850. **Tel** (607)273-5055. **ED** Jack Goldman. **Bk Rev. Ad Acc. Circ:** 14,000.

RU/0201-8500
**BOOKS AND ART IN THE USSR.** **Added/Corp** Vsesoiuznoe Agentstvo po Avtorskim Pravam. (1979)-. Periodical. English (French, German, Spanish and Russian). qt. $19.00. **(Subscription address:** Victor Kamkin, 4956 Boiling Brook Parkway, Rockville MD 20852.**)** **LC** Z2491; .B645. **DD** 015.47.
**Desc:** Articles about the activities of soviet scholars, writers, playwrights, artists and composers, and informing the reader about business and creative ties between cultural figures in different countries.

US/0890-0841
**BOOKS & RELIGION.** ***Ceased.*** See Religion and Theology.

UK/0268-6538
**BOOKS AT BOSTON SPA. MICROFORM.** **Main/Corp** British Library. Document Supply Centre. (Jan. 7, 1987)-. Periodical. English. an. £153.00 UK; £158.00 other. British Library / Publications Sale Unit, Boston Spa, Wetherby, West Yorkshire LS23 7BQ England. **Tel** 011 44 937 546546 546543, FAX 011 44 937 546333, telex 557381.

US/1040-0362
**BOOKS BY BLACK WOMEN.** Periodical. English. qt. $30.00 North America; $40.00 other. Jacqueline M Sellers, 9226 Edwards Way/Suite 1107, Hyattsville MD 20783-3414. **Tel** (301)445-0014. **ED** Jacqueline M Sellers. Index available. cum. index. **Bk Rev. Ad Acc.**
**Desc:** Literary reviews of books written by women of African descent.

US/0882-5343
**BOOKS FOR CHILDREN WASHINGTON, D.C.).** ***Ceased.*** (BOOKS FOR CHILDREN.). [Books child.]. **Added/Corp** Children's Literature Center (Library of Congress). No. 1 (1985)-(19??). English. an. Library of Congress / Cataloging Distribution Service, Washington DC 20541-5017. **Tel** (800)255-3666, (202)707-6100, FAX (202)707-1334. **ED** Margaret N. Coughlan. **LC** Z1037; .C542; PN1009.A1. **DD** 011/.62. ***Continues*** *Children's Books (Washington, D.C.), 0069-3464.*

II
**BOOKS FROM INDIA.** English. **LC** Z3203; .B73. ***Continues*** *Books India.*

IS/0578-932X
**BOOKS FROM ISRAEL.** ***Ceased.*** **Main/Corp** Israel Export Institute. Book and Printing Center. English. an. Israel Book & Printing Center, 29 Hamered Street, PO Box 29732, 68125 Tel Aviv Israel. **Tel** (03)630-830. **Bk Rev. Ad Acc. Circ:** 2,500 (ctrl). ***Continues*** *Catalogue of Selected Books from Israel for the International Book Trade.*
**Desc:** A review of books published in Israel in the current year. Short annotations with relevant information about books. Covers all subject areas.

CN/0713-4460
**BOOKS IN ARABIC (1980).** (BOOKS IN ARABIC : RECENT ACQUISITIONS.). [Books Arab.]. **Main/Corp** Metropolitan Toronto Library Board. **VFOAT** Lughah Al-Arabiyyah. Vol. 1, No. 1 (Aug. 1980)-. Periodical. English. Free. Metropolitan Toronto Library Board, 789 Yonge Street, Toronto Ontario M4W 2G8 Canada. **Tel** (416)393-7134, telex 06-22232. **DD** 017/.12927. ctrl circ. ***Continues*** *Metropolitan Toronto Library Board. Languages Co-Ordinator. Arabic, 0713-4452.*

CN/0705-8209
**BOOKS IN ARMENIAN.** **Main/Corp** Metropolitan Toronto Library Board. Languages Co-Ordinator. Periodical. English. qt. Free. Metropolitan Toronto Library Board, 789 Yonge Street, Toronto Ontario M4W 2G8 Canada. **Tel** (416)393-7134, telex 06-22232. **ED** Jaswinder Gundara. **DD** 016.891/992. **Bk Rev. Ad Acc. Circ:** 307 (ctrl). ***Supersedes*** *Books in Armenian.*
**Desc:** A list of multilanguage acquisitions in the Public Library Systems of Metropolitan Toronto.

CN/0713-5335
**BOOKS IN BENGALI (1980).** (BOOKS IN BENGALI : RECENT ACQUISITIONS.). [Books Bengali]. **Main/Corp** Metropolitan Toronto Library Board. Vol. 1, No. 1 (Aug. 1980)-. Periodical. English. Free. Metropolitan Toronto Library Board, 789 Yonge Street, Toronto Ontario M4W 2G8 Canada. **Tel** (416)393-7134, telex 06-22232. **DD** 017/.129144. ctrl circ. ***Continues*** *Metropolitan Toronto Library Board. Languages Co-Ordinator. Bengali, 0713-5327.*

CN/0045-2564
**BOOKS IN CANADA.** [Books Can.]. Vol. 1 (July 1971)-. Periodical. English. Nine times a year (Jun., Jul., and Aug. combined in one issue). 21.48Can$ (one year), 40.00Can$ (two year) individuals Canada; 28.02 (one year), 54.19Can$ (two year) institutions Canada; 13.50Can$ additional postage US; 24.00Can$ additional postage other. Canadian Review of Books Ltd, 130 Spadina Avenue, Suite 603, Toronto Ontario M5V 2L4 Canada. **Tel** (416)601-9880, FAX (416)601-9883. **ED** Paul Stuewe. **LC** Z1369; .B73. **DD** 028.1/0971. **Bk Rev. Ad Acc. Circ:** 10,000. available on microfilm (from McLaren Micropublishing).
**Desc:** National review magazine with emphasis on Canadian writing and related cultural fields. Informed criticism, interviews, profiles of Canadian authors, feature articles on the state of the arts and in-depth reports on the literary scene at home and abroad presented by many of the country's known writers and critics. More than 400 books reviewed each year, regular columns.
**Ind/Abst** Book Rev. Digest; Book Rev. Index; Can. Index (?-?); Can. Period. Index.

CN/0713-4495
**BOOKS IN CHINESE (1980).** (BOOKS IN CHINESE : RECENT ACQUISITIONS.). [Books Chin.]. **Main/Corp** Metropolitan Toronto Library Board. Vol. 1, No. 1 (Aug. 1980)-. Periodical. English (Chinese). Free. Metropolitan Toronto Library Board, 789 Yonge Street, Toronto Ontario M4W 2G8 Canada. **Tel** (416)393-7134, telex 06-22232. **DD** 017/.12951. ctrl circ. ***Continues*** *Metropolitan Toronto Library Board. Languages Co-Ordinator. Chinese, 0713-4487.*

CN/0713-4568
**BOOKS IN CROATIAN.** (BOOKS IN CROATIAN-SERBIAN : RECENT ACQUISITIONS.). [Books Croat. Serb.]. **Main/Corp** Metropolitan Toronto Library Board. Vol. 1, No. 1 (Aug. 1980)-. Periodical. English. Free. Metropolitan Toronto Library Board, 789 Yonge Street, Toronto Ontario M4W 2G8 Canada. **Tel** (416)393-7134, telex 06-22232. **DD** 017/.129182. ctrl circ. ***Continues*** *Metropolitan Toronto Library Board. Languages Co-Ordinator. Croatian Serbian, 0713-455X.*

CN/0705-2332
**BOOKS IN DANISH.** **Main/Corp** Metropolitan Toronto Library Board. Languages Co-Ordinator. Periodical. English. qt. Languages Co-Ordinator of the Metropolitan Toronto Library Board, 214 College Street, Toronto Ontario M5T 1R4 Canada. **DD** 016.8398/1. ***Supersedes*** *Books in Danish.*

CN/0713-4533
**BOOKS IN DUTCH (1980).** (BOOKS IN DUTCH : RECENT ACQUISITIONS.). [Books Dutch]. **Main/Corp** Metropolitan Toronto Library Board. **VFOAT** Nederlands. Vol. 1, No. 1 (Aug. 1980)-. Periodical. English. qt. Free. Metropolitan Toronto Library Board, 789 Yonge Street, Toronto Ontario M4W 2G8 Canada. **Tel** (416)393-7134, telex 06-22232. **ED** Jaswinder Gundara. **DD** 018/.123931. **Bk Rev. Ad Acc. Circ:** 307 (ctrl). ***Continues*** *Metropolitan Toronto Library Board. Languages Co-Ordinator. Dutch, 0713-4525.*
**Desc:** A list of multi-language acquisitions in the public library system of Metropolitan Toronto.

CN/0714-2129
**BOOKS IN ESTONIAN (1980).** (BOOKS IN ESTONIAN : RECENT ACQUISITIONS.). [Books Est.]. **Main/Corp** Metropolitan Toronto Library Board. **VFOAT** Esti Keel. Vol. 1, No. 1 (Aug. 1980)-. Periodical. English. Metropolitan Toronto Library Board, 789 Yonge Street, Toronto Ontario M4W 2G8 Canada. **Tel** (416)393-7134, telex 06-22232. **DD** 017/.1294545. ctrl circ. ***Continues*** *Metropolitan Toronto Library Board. Languages Co-Ordinator. Estonian, 0714-2110.*

CN/0714-2382
**BOOKS IN FINNISH (1980).** (BOOKS IN FINNISH : RECENT ACQUISITIONS.). [Books Finn.]. **Main/Corp** Metropolitan Toronto Library Board. **VFOAT** Suomenkieli. Vol. 1, No. 1 (Aug. 1980)-. Periodical. English. qt. Free. Metropolitan Toronto Library Board, 789

Yonge Street, Toronto Ontario M4W 2G8 Canada. **Tel** (416)393-7134, telex 06-22232. **ED** Jaswinder Gundara. **DD** 018/.1294541. **Bk Rev. Ad Acc. Circ:** 307 (ctrl). ***Continues*** *Metropolitan Toronto Library Board. Languages Co-Ordinator. Finnish, 0714-2374.*
**Desc:** A list of multi-language acquisitions in the public library systems of Metropolitan Toronto.

CN/0714-2420
**BOOKS IN FRISIAN (1980).** (BOOKS IN FRISIAN : RECENT ACQUISITIONS.). **Main/Corp** Metropolitan Toronto Library Board. Vol. 1, No. 1 (Aug. 1980)-. Periodical. English. Metropolitan Toronto Library Board, 789 Yonge Street, Toronto Ontario M4W 2G8 Canada. **Tel** (416)393-7134, telex 06-22232. **DD** 018/12392. ctrl circ. ***Continues*** *Metropolitan Toronto Library Board. Languages Co-Ordinator. Frisian, 0714-2412.*

CN/0714-2455
**BOOKS IN GERMAN (1980).** (BOOKS IN GERMAN : RECENT ACQUISITIONS.). [Books Ger.]. **Main/Corp** Metropolitan Toronto Library Board. **VFOAT** Deutsch. Vol. 1, No. 1 (Aug. 1980)-. Periodical. English. Free. Metropolitan Toronto Library Board, 789 Yonge Street, Toronto Ontario M4W 2G8 Canada. **Tel** (416)393-7134, telex 06-22232. **DD** 018/.1231. ctrl circ. ***Continues*** *Metropolitan Toronto Library Board. Languages Co-Ordinator. German, 0714-2447.*

CN/0714-2471
**BOOKS IN GREEK (1980).** (BOOKS IN GREEK : RECENT ACQUISITIONS.). [Books Greek]. **Main/Corp** Metropolitan Toronto Library Board. **VFOAT** Ellinika. Vol. 1, No. 1 (Aug. 1980)-. Periodical. English. Free. Metropolitan Toronto Library Board, 789 Yonge Street, Toronto Ontario M4W 2G8 Canada. **Tel** (416)393-7134, telex 06-22232. **DD** 018/.1289. ctrl circ. ***Continues*** *Metropolitan Toronto Library Board. Languages Co-Ordinator. Greek, 0714-2463.*

CN/0714-2501
**BOOKS IN GUJARATI.** (BOOKS IN GUJARATI : RECENT ACQUISITIONS.). [Books Gujarati]. **Main/Corp** Metropolitan Toronto Library Board. **VFOAT** Gajarati. Vol. 1, No. 1 (Aug. 1980)-. Periodical. English. Free. Metropolitan Toronto Library Board, 789 Yonge Street, Toronto Ontario M4W 2G8 Canada. **Tel** (416)393-7134, telex 06-22232. **DD** 017/.1291471. ctrl circ. ***Continues*** *Metropolitan Toronto Library Board. Languages Co-Ordinator. Gujarati, 0714-2498.*

CN/0714-2528
**BOOKS IN HINDI (1980).** (BOOKS IN HINDI : RECENT ACQUISITIONS.). [Books Hindi]. **Main/Corp** Metropolitan Toronto Library Board. Vol 1, No. 1 (Aug. 1980)-. Periodical. English. Free. Metropolitan Toronto Library Board, 789 Yonge Street, Toronto Ontario M4W 2G8 Canada. **Tel** (416)393-7134, telex 06-22232. **DD** 017/.1291431. ctrl circ. ***Continues*** *Metropolitan Toronto Library Board. Languages Co-Ordinator. Hindi, 0714-251X.*

CN/0714-2544
**BOOKS IN HUNGARIAN (1980).** (BOOKS IN HUNGARIAN : RECENT ACQUISITIONS.). [Books Hung.]. **Main/Corp** Metropolitan Toronto Library Board. **VFOAT** Magyar. Vol. 1, No. 1 (Aug. 1980)-. English. qt. Free. Metropolitan Toronto Library Board, 789 Yonge Street, Toronto Ontario M4W 2G8 Canada. **Tel** (416)393-7134, telex 06-22232. **ED** Jaswinder Gundara. **DD** 018/.1294511. **Bk Rev. Ad Acc. Circ:** 307 (ctrl). ***Continues*** *Metropolitan Toronto Library Board. Languages Co-Ordinator. Hungarian, 0714-2536.*
**Desc:** A list of multi-language acquisitions in the public library systems of Metropolitan Toronto.

CN/0714-2609
**BOOKS IN ITALIAN.** (BOOKS IN ITALIAN : RECENT ACQUISITIONS.). [Books Ital.]. **Main/Corp** Metropolitan Toronto Library Board. **VFOAT** Italianio. Vol. 1, No. 1 (Aug. 1980)-. English. Free. Metropolitan Toronto Library Board, 789 Yonge Street, Toronto Ontario M4W 2G8 Canada. **Tel** (416)393-7134, telex 06-22232. **DD** 018/.1251. ctrl circ. ***Continues*** *Metropolitan Toronto Library Board. Languages Co-Ordinator. Italian, 0714-2595.*

CN/0705-6486
**BOOKS IN JAPANESE. Main/Corp** Metropolitan Toronto Library Board. Languages Co-Ordinator. Periodical. English. qt. Languages Co-Ordinator of the Metropolitan Toronto Library Board, 214 College Street, Toronto Ontario M5T 1R4 Canada. **DD** 016.8956. ***Continues*** *Books in Japanese.*

CN/0705-8225
**BOOKS IN LITHUANIAN. Main/Corp** Metropolitan Toronto Library Board. Languages Co-Ordinator. Periodical. English. qt. Free. Metropolitan Toronto Library Board, 789 Yonge Street, Toronto Ontario M4W 2G8 Canada. **Tel** (416)393-7134, telex 06-22232. **ED** Jaswinder Gundara. **DD** 016.891/92. **Bk Rev. Ad Acc. Circ:** 307 (ctrl). ***Supersedes*** *Books in Lithuanian.*
**Desc:** A list of multilanguage acquisitions in the Public Library Systems of Metropolitan Toronto.

CN/0317-2406
**BOOKS IN MARATHI. Main/Corp** Metropolitan Toronto Library Board. Languages Co-Ordinator. Periodical. English. qt. Free. Metropolitan Toronto Library Board, 789 Yonge Street, Toronto Ontario M4W 2G8 Canada. **Tel** (416)393-7134, telex 06-22232. **ED** Jaswinder Gundara. **DD** 016.891/46. **Bk Rev. Ad Acc. Circ:** 307 (ctrl). ***Supersedes*** *Books in Marathi.*
**Desc:** A list of multilanguage acquisitions in the Public Library Systems of Metropolitan Toronto.

CN/0714-282X
**BOOKS IN PANJABI (1980).** (BOOKS IN PANJABI : RECENT ACQUISITIONS.). [Books Panjabi]. **Main/Corp** Metropolitan Toronto Library Board. Vol. 1, No. 1 (Aug. 1980)-. Periodical. English. Free. Metropolitan Toronto Library Board, 789 Yonge Street, Toronto Ontario M4W 2G8 Canada. **Tel** (416)393-7134, telex 06-22232. **DD** 017/.129142. ctrl circ. ***Continues*** *Metropolitan Toronto Library Board. Languages Co-Ordinator. Panjabi, 0714-2811.*

CN/0227-2741
**BOOKS IN PERSIAN (1980).** (BOOKS IN PERSIAN : RECENT ACQUISITIONS.). **Main/Corp** Metropolitan Toronto Library Board. **VFOAT** Farsi. Vol. 1, No. 1 (Aug. 1980)-. Periodical. English. qt. Free. Metropolitan Toronto Library Board, 789 Yonge Street, Toronto Ontario M4W 2G8 Canada. **Tel** (416)393-7134, telex 06-22232. **ED** Jaswinder Gundara. **DD** 017/.129155. **Bk Rev. Ad Acc. Circ:** 307 (ctrl). ***Continues*** *Metropolitan Toronto Library Board. Languages Co-Ordinator. Persian, 0714-2757.*
**Desc:** A list of multi-language acquisitions in the Metropolitan Toronto Library systems.

CN/0714-2773
**BOOKS IN POLISH (1980).** (BOOKS IN POLISH : RECENT ACQUISITIONS.). [Books Pol]. **Main/Corp** Metropolitan Toronto Library Board. **VFOAT** Jezyk Polski. Vol. 1, No. 1 (Aug. 1980)-. Periodical. English. qt. Free. Metropolitan Toronto Library Board, 789 Yonge Street, Toronto Ontario M4W 2G8 Canada. **Tel** (416)393-7134, telex 06-22232. **ED** Jaswinder Gundara. **DD** 018/.1291851. **Bk Rev. Ad Acc. Circ:** 307 (ctrl). ***Continues*** *Metropolitan Toronto Library Board. Languages Co-Ordinator. Polish, 0714-2765.*
**Desc:** A list of multi-language acquisitions in the public library systems of Metropolitan Toronto.

CN/0714-279X
**BOOKS IN PORTUGUESE (1980).** (BOOKS IN PORTUGUESE : RECENT ACQUISITIONS.). [Books Portug.]. **Main/Corp** Metropolitan Toronto Library Board. **VFOAT** Portuguese. Vol. 1, No. 1 (1980)-. Periodical. English. Free. Metropolitan Toronto Library Board, 789 Yonge Street, Toronto Ontario M4W 2G8 Canada. **Tel** (416)393-7134, telex 06-22232. **DD** 018/.1269. ctrl circ. ***Continues*** *Metropolitan Toronto Library Board. Languages Co-Ordinator. Portuguese, 0714-2781.*

UK/0143-1285
**BOOKS IN SCOTLAND.** No. 1 (Spring-Summer 1978)-. Periodical. English. qt. £9.95. Ramsay Head Press Publishers, 15 Gloucester Place, Edinburgh EH3 6EE Scotland. **Tel** 031-225 5666. **ED** Norman Wilson. **Bk Rev. Ad Acc. Circ:** 3,000.
**Desc:** Covers books in general, new books by Scottish writers and books about Scotland. Also, articles on contemporary writing and authors' who's who.

US/0000-0906
**BOOKS IN SERIES.** (BOOKS IN SERIES / [PREPARED BY R.R. BOWKER COMPANY'S DEPARTMENT OF BIBLIOGRAPHY IN COLLABORATION WITH THE PUBLICATION SYSTEMS DEPARTMENT].). [Books ser.]. **Added/Corp** R.R. Bowker Company. R.R. Bowker Company. Dept. of Bibliography. R.R. Bowker Company. Publication Systems Dept. R.R. Bowker Company. Data Services Division. 3rd Ed. (1980)-. Bibliography. English. an. $199.95. R R Bowker, A Reed Reference Publishing Company, Part of Reed International PLC, PO Box 31, 121 Chanlon Drive, New Providence NJ 07974. **Tel** (908)464-6800, (800)521-8110, FAX (908)665-6688, telex 138-755. **LC** Z1215; .B65; Z1033.S5. **DD** 011/.34. **NLM** Z 1033.S5 B724. available on CD-ROM and an online database. ***Continues*** *Books in Series in the United States, 0000-0515.*
**Desc:** Five indexes offer convenient access to full information on all original, reprinted, in-print, and out-of-print books published or distributed in the US.

CN/0713-5998
**BOOKS IN SPANISH (1980).** (BOOKS IN SPANISH : RECENT ACQUISITIONS.). [Books Span.]. **Main/Corp** Metropolitan Toronto Library Board. Vol. 1, No. 1 (Aug. 1980)-. Periodical. English. Free. Metropolitan Toronto Library Board, 789 Yonge Street, Toronto Ontario M4W 2G8 Canada. **Tel** (416)393-7134, telex 06-22232. **DD** 018/.1261. ctrl circ. ***Continues*** *Metropolitan Toronto Library Board. Languages Co-Ordinator. Spanish, 0713-598X.*

CN/0824-5592
**BOOKS IN TAGALOG (1980).** (BOOKS IN TAGALOG : RECENT ACQUISITIONS.). [Books Tagalog]. **Main/Corp** Metropolitan Toronto Library Board. Periodical. English. Free. Metropolitan Toronto Library Board, 789 Yonge Street, Toronto Ontario M4W 2G8 Canada. **Tel** (416)393-7134, telex 06-22232. **DD** 017/.1299211. ctrl circ. ***Continues*** *Tagalog, 0714-2994.*

CN/0714-2927
**BOOKS IN UKRAINIAN (1980).** (BOOKS IN UKRAINIAN : RECENT ACQUISITIONS.). [Books Ukr.]. **Main/Corp** Metropolitan Toronto Library Board. Vol. 1, No. 1 (Aug. 1980)-. Periodical. English. Free. Metropolitan Toronto Library Board, 789 Yonge Street, Toronto Ontario M4W 2G8 Canada. **Tel** (416)393-7134, telex 06-22232. **DD** 017/.1291791. ctrl circ. ***Continues*** *Metropolitan Toronto Library Board. Languages Co-Ordinator. Ukrainian, 0714-2919.*

CN/0714-296X
**BOOKS IN URDU (1980).** (BOOKS IN URDU : RECENT ACQUISITIONS.). [Books Urdu]. **Main/Corp** Metropolitan Toronto Library Board. Vol. 1, No. 1 (Aug. 1980)-. Periodical. English. Free. Metropolitan Toronto Library Board, 789 Yonge Street, Toronto Ontario M4W 2G8 Canada. **Tel** (416)393-7134, telex 06-22232. **DD** 017/.1291439. ctrl circ. ***Continues*** *Metropolitan Toronto Library Board. Languages Co-Ordinator. Urdu, 0714-2951.*

CN/0227-2776
**BOOKS IN VIETNAMESE (1980).** (BOOKS IN VIETNAMESE : RECENT ACQUISITIONS.). **Main/Corp** Metropolitan Toronto Library Board. Vol. 1, No. 1 (Aug. 1980)-. Periodical. English. Free. Metropolitan Toronto Library Board, 789 Yonge Street, Toronto Ontario M4W 2G8 Canada. **Tel** (416)393-7134, telex 06-22232. **DD** 018/.1295922. ctrl circ. ***Continues*** *Metropolitan Toronto Library Board. Languages Co-Ordinator. Vietnamese, 0714-2854.*

CN/0705-8268
**BOOKS IN YIDDISH. Main/Corp** Metropolitan Toronto Library Board. Vol. 1, No. 1 (Aug. 1980)-. Periodical. English. Free. Metropolitan Toronto Library Board, 789 Yonge Street, Toronto Ontario M4W 2G8 Canada. **Tel** (416)393-7134, telex 06-22232. **DD** 017/.1237. ctrl circ. ***Continues*** *Metropolitan Toronto Library Board. Languages Co-Ordinator. Books in Yiddish, 0705-8268.*

UK
**BOOKS (LONDON, ENGLAND : 1944).** (BOOKS : THE JOURNAL OF THE NATIONAL BOOK LEAGUE.). No. 183 (Nov. 1944)-. Periodical. English. ***Continues*** *News Sheet.*

UK/0952-987X
**BOOKS (LONDON,1987).** ***Title Change.*** (BOOKS.). [Books (Lond.,1987)]. No. 1 (Apr. 1987)-No. 24 (Mar. 1989)/Vol. 3 No. 1 (Apr. 1989)/Vol. 6 No. 6 (Nov./Dec. 1992). Periodical. English. mo. 43 Museum Street, London WC1A 1LY England. **LC** Z2005; .B62. **DD** 028.1/0941. ***Continues*** *Books and Bookmen, 0006-744X.* ***Continued by*** *Books Magazine.*
**Ind/Abst** Book Rev. Index (1987-); Child. Lit. Abstr. (19??-).

●UK/0952-987X
**BOOKS MAGAZINE.** Vol. 7, No. 1 (Jan./Feb. 1993)-. Periodical. English. Six times a year. £9.00 UK & Eire; £15.00 others. Publishing News Ltd., Books Subscription Accounts, 43 Museum Street, London WC1 1AY England. **Tel** 011 44 71 4040304. ***Continues*** *Books (London, England : 1987).*

CN/0707-6924
**BOOKS NOW. See** Literature.

US/0736-9034
**BOOKS ON DEMAND: AUTHOR GUIDE. INTERNATIONAL ED.** (BOOKS ON DEMAND; AUTHOR GUIDE.). [Books demand, author guide]. **Added/Corp** University Microfilms International. (1983)-. English. ir. University Microfilms International, 300 North Zeeb Road, Ann Arbor MI 48106-1346. **Tel** (313)761-4700, (800)521-0600 Exts. 2490, 2491, FAX (313)973-1540.

US/0000-0736
**BOOKS OUT-OF-PRINT.** [Books out-of-print]. **Added/Corp** R.R. Bowker Company. **VFOAT** Books Out of Print. (1983)-. English. an. $110.00. R R Bowker, A Reed Reference Publishing Company, Part of Reed International PLC, PO Box 31, 121 Chanlon Drive, New Providence NJ 07974. **Tel** (908)464-6800, (800)521-8110, FAX (908)665-6688, telex 138-755. **LC** Z1000.5; .B67. **DD** 015. **NLM** Z 1000.5; B7243. available on CD-ROM from R.R. Bowker.

US
**BOOKSELLING THIS WEEK.** (19??)-. English. Forty-eight times a year. $30.00 (members), $50.00 (non-members). American Booksellers Association, 828 South Broadway, Tarrytown NY 10591. **Tel** (914)591-2665, FAX (914)631-8391. ***Continues*** *ABA Newswire.*

US/0092-6264
**BOOKSTORE JOURNAL REVIEWS. Added/Corp** Christian Booksellers Association. Vol. 1 (Fall 1973)-. Periodical. English. Three times a year. C B A Service Corporation, 2620 Venetucci Boulevard, Box 200, Colorado Springs CO 80901. **LC** Z286.R4; B6. **DD** 028.1.

UK/0307-854X
**BOOKTALK.** ***Ceased.*** [Booktalk]. (197?)-(1993). English. Four times a year (Jan., June, Sept., Dec.). Booktalk, 804 South Hoyt, Lakewood CO 80226. **Tel** (303)986-3258. **ED** Ron Rich. Index available (In Dec.). cum. index. **Bk Rev**, (Qty: 300).
**Desc:** A service to teachers and parents who want to find the most exciting new books for boys and girls.

US
**BOOKTALKER, THE.** ***Title Change.*** **VFOAT** Book Talker. Vol. 1, No. 1 (Sept. 1989)-(199?). Periodical. English. bm. H W Wilson Company, 950 University Avenue, Bronx NY 10452. **Tel** (800)367-6770, (718)588-8400, FAX (718)590-1617, telex 4990003 HWILSON. **LC** Z716.3; .B6. ***Continued by*** *New Booktalker, 1064-7511.*

US/0896-4521
**BOOKWATCH (SAN FRANCISCO, CALIF.), THE.** (THE BOOKWATCH : A PUBLICATION OF THE MIDWEST BOOK REVIEW.). [Bookwatch]. **Added/Corp** Midwest Book Review (Firm). **VFOAT** Book Watch. (Mar. 1986)-. Periodical. English. qt. $12.00. The Bookwatch, 166 Mirimar Avenue, San Francisco CA 94112. **DD** 028. ***Formed by the union of*** *Midwest Bookwatch* ***and*** *Children's Bookwatch.*

US/1057-6355
**BOOKWAYS (AUSTIN, TEX.).** ***Ceased.*** (BOOKWAYS.). [Bookways]. **Added/Corp** W. Thomas Taylor (Firm). No. 1 (Oct. 1991)-(Apr. 1995). Periodical. English. Four times a year (Jan., Apr., July, Oct.). Bookways, 1906 Miriam Avenue, Austin TX 78722. **Tel** (512)478-7414, FAX (512)478-5508. **ED** W. Thomas Tylor, (phone: (512)478-7628). **LC** Z119; .B73. **DD** 016.09/4. **Bk Rev**, (Qty: 50-70). **Ad Acc**, **Adv Mgr:** A. Prewett, **Tel** (512)478-7414. **Circ:** 1,100.
**Desc:** Dedicated to providing comprehensive coverage of the book arts community, its contents are colored by a broad spectrum of topics and issues.

US/0163-1128
**BOOKWOMAN, THE.** Periodical. English. Three times a year. Free to members; $8.00 US; $12.00 other. Women's National Book Association Inc, 160 Fifth Avenue, New York NY 10010. **ED** Nancy M Lutz. **Bk Rev. Ad Acc. Circ:** 1,000 (ctrl).
**Desc:** Contains regular columns written by the president, the book review editor, and a correspondent from each chapter, and major articles about news or developments of special interest to book people.

GW
**BORSENBLATT FUR DEN DEUTSCHEN BUCHHANDEL. FRANKFURTER AUSGABE. SONDERNUMMER.** Vol. 1- ; 1945-. Periodical. German. sw. DM622.80. Buchhandler Vereinigung GmbH, Grosser Hirschgraben 17-21, D 60311 Frankfurt 1 Germany. **Tel** 011 49 69 1306243, telex 413573 BUCH VOL. Index available. **Ad Acc. Circ:** 10,500.

US/0145-9457
**BP REPORT ON THE BUSINESS OF BOOK PUBLISHING.** **VFOAT** BP Report; Report on the Business of Book Publishing. (1975)-. Periodical. English. Fifty times a year. $456.00 (one year), $821.00 (two year). Simba Information Inc., 213 Danbury Road, Wilton CT 06897-7430. **Tel** (203)834-0033 ext. 133, FAX (203)884-1771. **(Subscription address:** Simba Information Inc., PO Box 7430, Wilton CT 06897.**) ED** Morilynn Mcgeehon. **[CCC].** ***Absorbed*** *International Publishing Newsletter.*
**Desc:** Newsletter on business of book publishing. Covers financial, personnel, product and general news about book publishing.
**Ind/Abst** PROMT [Full Txt.]; PTS Newsl. Database [Full Txt.].

US/0006-873X
**BRAILLE BOOK REVIEW.** **See** Physically Impaired.

US/0277-5247
**BRAILLE BOOKS.** [Braille books]. **Main/Corp** Library of Congress. National Library Service for the Blind and Physically Handicapped. 1980-1981-. English. be. National Library Service for the Blind and Physically Handicapped, Library of Congress, 1291 Taylor Street Northwest, Washington DC 20542. **Tel** (800)424-8567, (202)707-5100, (800)424-9100. **LC** Z5346.Z9; U62A; HV1721. **DD** 011/.63. ***Continues*** *Press Braille, Adult, 0079-502X.*

UK/0007-0343
**BRITISH BOOK NEWS.** ***Ceased.*** [Br. book news]. No. 15 (May 1941)-(1993). Academic Scholarly Publication. English. Twelve times a year. Basil Blackwell Publishers Ltd, 108 Cowley Road, Oxford 0X4 1JF England. **Tel** 011 44 865 791100, FAX 011 44 865 791347, telex 837022 OXBOOK G. **(Subscription address:** Marston Book Services, PO Box 87, Oxford OX2 0DT England**) LC** Z1035; .B838. **DD** 016. available on microfilm and microfiche from University Microfilms International (UMI). ***Continues*** *Selection of Recent Books Published in Great Britain.*
**Ind/Abst** Br. Humanit. Index; Child. Lit. Abstr. (19??-); Libr. Inf. Sci. Abstr.; Middle East Abstr. Index.

UK/0268-2400
**BRITISH BULLETIN OF PUBLICATIONS ON LATIN AMERICA, THE CARIBBEAN, PORTUGAL AND SPAIN / CANNING HOUSE, HISPANIC AAN LUSO-BRAZILIAN COUNCIL.** No. 59 (Oct. 1978)-. Bulletin. English. sa. $24.74. World Wide Subscription Services, Unit 4, Gibbs Reed Farm, East Sussex TN5 7HE England. **Tel** (0580)200657, FAX (0580)200616. **ED** Noel Treacy. **LC** Z1601.B7; F1408. **DD** 016.909/097561. **Bk Rev. Circ:** 1,000 (ctrl). ***Continues*** *British Bulletin of Publications on Latin America, The West Indies, Portugal and Spain.*
**Desc:** Informs readers of recently published books in English on the countries included in the title.

AU/0003-6277
**BUCH.** **Added/Corp** Hauptverband des Osterreichischen Buchhandels. **VFOAT** B; Anzeiger des Osterreichischen Buchhandels. No. 24 (Dec. 1990)-. Periodical. German. sm. Hauptverband des Oesterreichischen Buchhandels, Grunangergrasse 4, 1010 Vienna 1 Austria. **Tel** 512-15-35. ***Continues*** *Anzeiger des Osterreichischen Buchhandels.*

SZ
**BUCHERPICK.** German (German). ir. 3.00 Single Issue. **LC** Z1035.3; .B95. **DD** 028/.1.

HU/1215-735X
**BUDAPEST REVIEW OF BOOKS.** Vol. 1, No. 1 (Winter 1991)-. English. qt. $18.00 (individuals), $21.00 (institutions) Europe; $27.00 (institutions), $24.00 (individuals) other. Budapest Review of Books, Babhori U 10, 1054 Budapest, Hungary. **Tel** 011 36 1 1755089.
**Desc:** Features review essays, book reviews and notices of rigorous and sometimes biting criticism about new approaches in the humanities.
**Ind/Abst** Am. Hist. Life (1991-).

GW/0007-3059
**BUECHERSCHIFF; DIE DEUTSCHE BUECHERZEITUNG.** (May 1951)-. Periodical. German. bm. DM12.00. Verlag Buecherschiff, Kaiserstrasse 186, 7140 Ludwigsburg Germany. **ED** Helmut Bode. Index available. **Bk Rev. Ad Acc. Circ:** 22,000. available with illustrations.

BU/0324-0509
**BULGARIAN ACADEMIC BOOKS.** **Added/Corp** Bulgarska Akademiia na Naukite. (1969)-. Academic Scholarly Publication. English. an. Free on request. Bulgarska Akademiia na Naukite, 7 Noemvri 1, Sofia Bulgaria. **ED** Maria Gercheva. **LC** Z5055.B9; S594a. **DD** 015/.4977. **Ad Acc. Circ:** 4,500.

CN/0700-5083
**BULLETIN D'INFORMATION - FOIRE INTERNATIONALE DU LIVRE DE MONTREAL.** **Main/Corp** Montreal International Book Fair. **VFOAT** Newsletter - Montreal International Book Fair. No. 1- Dec. 1, 1975-. Bulletin. English (French). Montreal International Book Fair, 436 Sherbrooke Street East, Montreal Quebec H2L 1J6 Canada. **DD** 338.4/7/07050740114281.

CM
**BULLETIN OF INFORMATION - REGIONAL CENTRE FOR BOOK PROMOTION IN AFRICA.** **Main/Corp** Regional Centre for Book Promotion in Africa. **VFOAT** Bulletin d'Information - Centre Regional de Promotion du Livre en Afrique. V. 1- Jan./Mar. 1978-. Bulletin. English (French). Regional Centre for Book Promotion in Africa, PO Box 1646, Yaounde Cameroon. **LC** Z465.7; .C46A. **DD** 658.8/09/070573096.

US/0146-7182
**BUTT.** V. 1-. Periodical. English. qt. $5.00. Len Andersen, 156 Pleasant Street, Arlington MA 02174.

CN/0228-6556
**CAHIERS DE BIBLIOLOGIE.** 1-. Periodical. French. $4.00 per number. Librairie Jean Gagnon, 498 rue d'Aiguillon/CP 653 HV, Quebec Quebec G1R 4S2 Canada. **DD** 010.

CN/0380-6286
**CAMPUS BOOK STORES.** **See** Publishing-Abstracting, Bibliographies and Statistics.

CN/0711-7299
**CANADA BOOK AUCTIONS RECORDS.** [Can. book auctions rec.]. **Added/Corp** Canada Book Auctions. Vol. 6 (1980)-. English. be. $27.09. Canada Book Auctions, 35 Front Street East, Toronto Ontario M5E 1B3 Canada. **DD** 018/.3. ***Continues*** *Montreal Book Auction Records, 0226-0107.*

CN/0068-8398
**CANADIAN BOOKS IN PRINT. AUTHOR AND TITLE INDEX.** [Can. books print, Author title index]. (1975)-. English (French; summaries and/or abstracts in French). an. $150.00. University of Toronto Press, 5201 Dufferin Street, Downsview Ontario M3H 5T8 Canada. **Tel** (416)667-7781, (416)667-7782, FAX (416)667-7803. **ED** Marian Butler. **LC** Z1365; .C2196. **DD** 015/.71. available on microfiche. ***Continues*** *Canadian Books in Print, 0068-8398.*
**Desc:** Reference and buying guide to English-language Canadian books currently in print.

CN/0315-1999
**CANADIAN BOOKS IN PRINT. SUBJECT INDEX.** **See** Publishing-Abstracting, Bibliographies and Statistics.

CN/0225-2392
**CANADIAN BOOKSELLER (TORONTO).** (THE CANADIAN BOOKSELLER.). [Can. books. (Toronto)]. **Added/Corp** Canadian Booksellers Association. (Jan. 1979)-. Periodical. English. Ten times a year. 35.00Can$ (members), 70.00Can$ (nonmembers) Canada; 65.00Can$ (members), 100.00Can$ (nonmembers) other. Canadian Booksellers Association, 301 Donlands Avenue, Toronto Ontario M4J 3R8 Canada. **Tel** (416)467-7883. **ED** Gillian O'Reilly. **DD** 658.8/0907057/0971. **[CCC]. Ad Acc. Circ:** 1,300 (ctrl). ***Continues*** *Net 30, 0225-6622.*
**Desc:** Journal of the Canadian retail book trade.

CN/0228-8753
**CANADIAN ISBN PUBLISHER'S DIRECTORY.** (CANADIAN ISBN PUBLISHERS' DIRECTORY / CANADIAN ISBN AGENCY / REPERTOIRE DES PREFIXES ISBN DES EDITEURS CANADIENS / AGENCE CANADIENNE DE L'ISBN.). [Can. ISBN publ. dir.]. **Added/Corp** Canadian ISBN Agency. **VFOAT** Repertoire des Prefixes ISBN des Editeurs Canadiens. **VAT** Canadian International Standard Book Number Publisher's Directory. (Jan. 1981)-. Directory. English (French). an. 53.50Can$ Canada; 64.20Can$ other. National Library of Canada, 395 Wellington Street, Ottawa Ontario K1A 0N4 Canada. **Tel** (613)995-7969, (613)995-7969, (819)994-6881, FAX (613)991-9871. **LC** Z485; .C36. **DD** 070.5/025/71. available on audiocassette; available in braille; available in large print.
**Desc:** Lists Canadian publishers, their addresses and ISBN publisher prefixes assigned.

US/0363-9029
**CASSETTE BOOKS.** **Main/Corp** Library of Congress. National Library Service for the Blind and Physically Handicapped. (1978)-. English. an. National Library Service for the Blind and Physically Handicapped, Library of Congress, 1291 Taylor Street Northwest, Washington DC 20542. **Tel** (800)424-8567, (202)707-5100, (800)424-9100. **LC** Z5347; .U59b; HV1721. **DD** 011. ***Continues*** *Library of Congress. Division for the Blind and Physically Handicapped. Cassette Books, 0363-9029.*

US/8756-7083
**CATALOGUE - LAURENCE WITTEN RARE BOOKS.** [Cat. - Laurence Written Rare Books]. **Main/Corp** Laurence Witten Rare Books. English. ir. Laurence Witten Rare Books, PO Box 490, Southport CT 06490. **Tel** (203)255-3474. **DD** 018. ctrl circ. ***Continues*** *Laurence Witten. Catalogue.*

JA
**CATALOGUE OF RARE BOOKS.** **Main/Corp** Meisei Daigaku. Toshokan. No. 1- 1974-. Japanese (Japanese). Meisei University Library, 1-1 Hodokubo 2-chome, Hino-shi Tokyo 191 Japan. **LC** Z1029; .M45A.

US
**CCBC : COOPERATIVE CHILDREN'S BOOK CENTER CIRCULAR.** **Main/Corp** Cooperative Children's Book Center, Madison, Wis. **VFOAT** Cooperative Children's Book Center Circular. V. 1, No. 1-. Periodical. English. Cooperative Children's Book Center, 4290 Helen C White Hall, 600 Park Street, Madison WI 53706.
**Desc:** A cooperative program of the Wiconsin Dept. of Public Instruction, Division for Library Services (Free Library Commission, 1964-5) and UW-Madison, School of Education and UW-Madison ... .

UK
**CHILDREN'S BOOKS HISTORY SOCIETY NEWSLETTER.** Newsletter. English. John Coles, 15 Rushfield Road, Liss, Hampshire GU33 7LW United Kingdom.
**Ind/Abst** Child. Lit. Abstr. (19??-).

IE/0791-2641
**CHILDREN'S BOOKS IN IRELAND.** (1989)-. English. Children's Literature Association of Ireland, The Library, Church of Ireland College of Education, 96 Upper Rathmines Road, Rathmines Dublin 6, Ireland.
**Ind/Abst** Child. Lit. Abstr. (19??-).

UK/0577-781X
**CHILDREN'S BOOKS IN PRINT (LONDON, ENGLAND).** (CHILDREN'S BOOKS IN PRINT.). **VFOAT** Whitaker Children's Books in Print. Began in 1969. English. an. £39.00. J. Whitaker & Sons Ltd, 12 Dyott Street, London WC1A 1DF England. **Tel** 011

44 71 8368911, FAX 011 44 71 836 2909. **ED** Edward Heron. **LC** Z1037; .C543. **DD** 028.52. **Ad Acc.**
**Desc:** Listing of over 24,000 children's books in print with alphabetical and classified sections of titles published or distributed in UK plus directory of publishers and distributors.

CC/0578-073X
**CHUAN KUO HSIN SHU MU.** **See** Publishing-Abstracting, Bibliographies and Statistics.

KO/0009-6245
**CHULPAN MUNHWA.** **VFOAT** Korean Books Journal; Korean Publishers Association Journal. Periodical. Korean. mo. W1000. Korean Publishers Association, 105-2 Sagan-dong Chongno-ku, Seoul 110-190 Korea. **Tel** (02)735-2701, FAX (02)738-5414. **ED** Lee Doo-young. **LC** Z464.K67; C48. Index available. **Bk Rev.** **Ad Acc. Circ:** 3,000 (ctrl).
**Desc:** A periodical of the Korean Publishers Association; emphasizes the interpretation, study and data of books.

UK
**CLEANING AND CARING FOR BOOKS.** English. £6.00. Richard Joseph Publishers Ltd, Unit 2 Monks Walk, Farnham, Surrey GU9 8HT England. **Tel** 11 44 252 734347, FAX 11 44 252 734307.

UK
**COLE'S REGISTER OF BRITISH ANTIQUARIAN & SECONDHAND BOOKDEALERS.** **VFOAT** British Antiquarian & Secondhand Bookdealers; British Antiquarian and Secondhand Bookdealers; A.Register of British antiquarian & secondhand bookdealers. **VAT** Cole's Register of British Antiquarian and Secondhand Bookdealers Active in Britain. (1988)-. Periodical. English. an. £22.00. Clique, Ltd., 7 Pulleyn Drive, York YO2 2DY England. **Tel** 011 44 904 631752, FAX 011 44 904 651325. **LC** Z327; .C63. **DD** 381/.45002/02541. ***Continues*** *Cole's Register of Antiquarian and Second-Hand Bookdealers Active in Britain, 0268-3407.*

US/0000-1120
**COMPLETE DIRECTORY OF LARGE PRINT BOOKS & SERIALS, THE.** [Complete dir. large print books ser.]. **Added/Corp** R.R. Bowker Company. **VFOAT** Complete Directory of Large Print Books and Serials; Large Print Books & Serials; Large Print Books and Serials. (1988)-. Directory. English. an (Feb.). $149.95. R R Bowker, A Reed Reference Publishing Company, Part of Reed International PLC, PO Box 31, 121 Chanlon Drive, New Providence NJ 07974. **Tel** (908)464-6800, (800)521-8110, FAX (908)665-6688, telex 138-755. **LC** Z5348; .L37; HV1731. **DD** 011/.63. **[CCC].** available on microfiche and CD-ROM; available on magnetic tape and an online database. ***Continues*** *Large Type Books in Print, 0163-3198.*
**Desc:** Covers the large print field like no other resource. Information on more than 8,950 titles.

US/0162-7929
**CONCORDIA COMMENTATOR.** (19??)-. Periodical. English. qt. Free. Concordia Publishing House, 3558 South Jefferson Avenue, St Louis MO 63118. **Tel** (314)268-1000, (800)325-3381, FAX (314)268-1329.

US
**CONSERVATIONEWS.** **Added/Corp** Arizona Paper and Photograph Conservation Group. **VFOAT** Conservation News. Vol. 1, No. 1 (May 1981)-. Periodical. English. Four times a year. $15.00. University of Arizona Main Library, Central Reference, Tucson AZ 85716. **Tel** (602)621-4869. **ED** Amy Rule, Peter Steere, Roger Myer. **Bk Rev**, (Qty: 4-10). **Circ:** 150 (ctrl).

US/0010-8669
**CORANTO (LOS ANGELES, CALIF.).** ***Ceased.*** (CORANTO.). [Coranto]. **Added/Corp** University of Southern California. Friends of the Libraries. Vol. 1 (1963)-(19??). Academic Scholarly Publication. English. sa. USC Fine Arts Press, University of Southern California, Research Annex, 3716 South Hope Street, Los Angeles CA 90007. **Tel** (310)743-3939. **ED** Gerald W Lange. **LC** AP2; .C758. **DD** 051. Index available. cum. index. **Circ:** 2,000.
**Desc:** Scholarly articles relating to the variate world of the book: history and contemporary surveys of its literary, artistic, and bibliographic nature. Special focus on the collections of the USC libraries.
**Ind/Abst** Abstr. Engl. Stud.; Annu. Bibliogr. Engl. Lang. Lit.; MLA Int. Bibl. Books Artic. Mod. Lang. Lit.

NE
**DEUTSCHE BUCHER.** (1974)-. Periodical. German. Four times a year (Mar., June, Sept., Dec.). F85.00. Editions Rodopi BV, Keizersgracht 302-304, 1016 Ex Amsterdam Netherlands. **Tel** 011 31 20 6227507, FAX 011 31 20 380948. **DD** 015. ***Supersedes*** *Duitse Boek, 0046-080X.*

US
**DIRECTORIES AND ASSOCIATIONS OF THE BOOK TRADE AND LIBRARIANSHIP.** **VFOAT** Adressbucher und Verbande des Buch- und Bibliothekswesens. Periodical. English. Gale Research Inc., 835 Penobscot Building, Detroit MI 48226. **Tel** (800)877-GALE, (313)961-2242, FAX (313)961-6083, telex TWX 810-221-7086. ***Continues*** *Bibliographie der Bibliotheksadressbucher.*

AT
**DIRECTORY OF MEMBERS - AUSTRALIAN BOOK PUBLISHERS ASSOCIATION.** Directory. English. an. 20.00Aus$. Australian Book Publishers Association, Suite 60, 89 Jones Street, Ultimo NSW 2007 Australia. **Tel** (02)281 9788, FAX (02)281 1073. **ED** Susan Blackwell. **Ad Acc. Circ:** 2,000.
**Desc:** A listing of publishing houses, key personnel in various departments of the companies, and types of books in which each publisher specializes.

●UK
**DIRECTORY OF PUBLISHING. CONTINENTAL EUROPE.** **See** Publishing.

IT/0070-6906
**DOCUMENTI SULLE ARTI DEL LIBRO.** **Added/Corp** Cartiera Ventura, Milan. (1962)-. Italian. ir. L200000. Edizioni Polifilo, Via Borgonuovo 2, 20121 Milan Italy. **Tel** 011 39 2 6551549. **LC** Z4; .D6. **DD** 002.

UK
**ECONOMIC SURVEY.** **Main/Corp** Booksellers Association of Great Britain and Ireland. (19??)-. English. an. Economic Survey / UK, 154 Buckingham Palace Road, London SW1W 9TZ England. **Tel** (01)730-8214, FAX (01)730-4105. **LC** Z329; B66a. **DD** 658.8/09/0705730941. ctrl circ.
**Desc:** Analysis of statistics gathered from selected booksellers, presented in table and text form.

IT/1120-1819
**EDIZIONI PER LA CONSERVAZIONE.** **VFOAT** Conservazione. Vol. 1, No. 1 (Jan. 1989)-. Periodical. Italian (English). Six times a year. L75000. Semar Editore, 29/29A via della Reginella, I-00186 Rome Italy. **Tel** 39 6 6876523, FAX 39 6 68308601. **ED** Luciano Sahlan Momo. **LC** WMLC 93/1743. Index available. cum. index. **Bk Rev**, (Qty: 25-30). **Ad Acc. Circ:** 5,000.
**Desc:** Deals with the conservation of the environment and culture from west philosophical, symbolic, ethical & historical point of view.

●US/1063-8938
**END PAPERS (ARLINGTON, VA.).** (END PAPERS : A GUIDE TO SELLERS OF USED & ANTIQUARIAN BOOKS IN MARYLAND, VIRGINIA & WASHINGTON DC.). (1992)-. English. qt. $20.00. End Papers, PO Box 10154, Arlington VA 22210.

UK
**EUROMONITOR BOOK READERSHIP SURVEY, THE.** English. an. Euromonitor Publications Ltd., 87-88 Turnmill Street, London EC1M 5QU England. **Tel** 011 44 71 2518024, FAX 011 44 71 6083149, telex 21120. ***Continues*** *Book Readership Survey.*

UK/0958-3866
**EUROPEAN BOOKSELLER.** [Eur. books.]. (1990)-. Periodical. English. bm. £66.00 UK & Europe; £78.00 North America, Africa, & Middle East; £95.00 other. European Bookseller Ltd, 3 Queen Square, London WC1N 3AR England. **Tel** 011 44 71 837-1357, FAX 011 44 71 485-2268, telex 896217. **ED** Jonathan Reuvid (editor's telephone: 01 485 5994). **DD** 381.45002094. **Circ:** 7,000.
**Desc:** Contains comprehensive access for publishers, both large and small, to English-language booksellers throughout Europe in preparation for the integrated European Community in 1992.
**Ind/Abst** Int. Labour Doc.

UK
**EUROPEAN CHRISTIAN BOOKSELLER.** English. Nuprint Ltd., Station Road, Harpenden, Herts AL5 4SE United Kingdom.
**Ind/Abst** Child. Lit. Abstr. (19??-).

UK
**EXETER WORKING PAPERS IN BRITISH BOOK TRADE HISTORY. SPECIAL SERIES.** Vol. 1 (1987)-. Monographic series. English. ir. Price varies per volume. J Maxted, No 10, Leighdene Close, Exeter Devon EX2 4PN England. **ED** Ian Maxted. **Circ:** 100.
**Desc:** Occassional publications containing items of interest to book made historians.

IE
**FACSIMILES IN COLLOTYPE OF IRISH MANUSCRIPTS.** **Main/Corp** Ireland (Eire). Irish Manuscripts Commission. (1931)-. English. Government Publications, 4 5 Harcourt Road, Dublin 2 Ireland. **Tel** 011 353 1 6613111 Ext.4005. **LC** Z115IR; .I68. **DD** 091.

UK
**FEDERATION OF CHILDREN'S BOOK GROUPS YEARBOOK.** **Main/Corp** Federation of Children's Book Groups (Great Britain). English. an. **LC** Z1037.A1; F4A. **DD** 028.5.

UK/0015-5772
**FOLIO, THE.** **Added/Corp** Folio Society, Ltd., London. Vol. 1 (Sept./Oct. 1947)-. Periodical. English. ir. Folio Society Ltd, 202 Great Suffolk Street, London SE1 1PR England. **LC** Z990; .F6. **DD** 655.405.
**Ind/Abst** Child. Lit. Abstr. (19??-).

US/0748-4615
**FOREIGN LANGUAGE BOOKS.** **See** Physically Impaired.

●US/1066-2979
**FROM THE OLDE BOOKSHELF.** (1993)-. Periodical. English. mo. $2.50 (single issue). A Wilson, 10707 Lee Avenue, Number 2, Cleveland OH 44106.

FR/0753-5015
**GAZETTE DU LIVRE MEDIEVAL.** (Autumn 1982)-. Periodical. French. sa. 160.00F. CNRS Cemat, 7 Rue Guy Moquet, BP 8, F 94801 Villejuif CDX France. **ED** Dennis Muzerelle. cum. index. **Circ:** 500.

US/0146-616X
**GENEALOGICAL & LOCAL HISTORY BOOKS IN PRINT.** **VFOAT** Genealogical and Local History Books in Print. **VAT** Genealogical and Local History Books in Print. Vol. 2 (1976)-. English. ir. $27.00 soft cover, $34.35 hard cover (latest edition). Genealogical Res. Directory, 3324 Carail Way, Glendale CA 91206. **Tel** (818)790-2642. **ED** Netti Schriener-Vantis. **LC** Z5313.U5; G45; CS47. **DD** 016.929/1/0973. **Ad Acc. Circ:** 15,000. ***Continues*** *Genealogical Books in Print, 0147-426X.*
**Desc:** A bibliography of over 30,000 books and microforms valuable to those tracing their ancestry, with full ordering information for each.

UK
**GOOD BOOK GUIDE.** English. bm. Braithwaite & Taylor Ltd, PO Box 400, Havelock Terrace, London SW8 4AU England. **Tel** +15.00 UK, +17.00 EUROPE, +19.00 OTHER.

BL
**GUIA DAS LIVRARIAS E PONTOS DE VENDA DE LIVROS NO BRASIL.** 1.- Ed.; 1976-. Portuguese. Sindicato Nacional dos Editores de Livros, Av Rio Branco 37-150 Andar, 20.000 Rio de Janeiro Brazil. **LC** Z521.5; .G84.

US/0434-9245
**GUILD OF BOOK WORKERS JOURNAL.** [Guild Book Work. j.]. **Main/Corp** Guild of Book Workers. **Added/Corp** Guild of Book Workers. Journal. Guild of Book Workers. Exhibition of Hand Bookbinding, Casemaking, Restoration, Calligraphy & Illumination. **VFOAT** Journal of the Guild of Book Workers. Vol. 1 (Fall 1962)-. Periodical. English. ir. $40.00 Comes with Guild Books Workers membership. Guild of Book Workers, 521 Fifth Avenue, New York NY 10175. **Tel** (212)757-6454. **ED** Dennis Moser. **LC** Z1008; .G9. **DD** 686.3/05. cum. index. **Bk Rev. Ad Acc. Circ:** 900 (ctrl).
**Desc:** History of book arts, related subjects, modern practices, and reviews of exhibitions.
**Ind/Abst** Art Archaeol. Tech. Abstr.

GW/0073-1684
**HEIDELBERGER TASCHENBUCHER.** [Heidelb. Taschenb.]. (1964)-. Monographic series. German. ir. Price varies per volume. Springer-Verlag GmbH & Company KG, Heidelberger Platz 3, D 14197 Berlin Germany. **Tel** 011 49 30 8207223, FAX 011 49 30 8214091, telex 183 319 SPBLN D. **(Subscription address:** Springer Verlag New York Inc. / for North America, 44 Hartz Way, Secaucus NJ 07096.**) CODEN** HDTSAB. Documents available from BIOSIS Document Express.
**Ind/Abst** Biol. Abstr.; GeoRef; Math. Rev.

II
**HINDI PRACARAKA PATRIKA.** V. 1- Jan. 1973-. Periodical. Hindi (Hindi). 6.00. Hindi Pracaraka Samsthana, PO Box 106 Pisachmochan, 221001 Varanasi India. **LC** Z457; .H5.

US/0894-2358
**HISPANIC BOOKS BULLETIN.** (HISPANIC BOOKS BULLETIN : H.B.B.). [Hisp. books bull.]. **VFOAT** H.B.B.; HBB. Vol. 1, No. 1 (June 1987)-. Leighdene English (Spanish). sa. $15.00 (US); $20.00 (Canada); $25.00 (other). Hispanic Books Distributors Inc, 1665 West Grant Road, Tucson AZ 85745. **Tel** (602)882-9484, (800)634-2124, FAX (602)882-7696. **ED** Arnulfo D Trejo and Annette M Trejo. **DD** 011. **Bk Rev. Ad Acc. Circ:** 5,000 (ctrl).
**Desc:** Provides bibliographical information and annotations of the latest titles available through HBD, as well as articles of interest to professionals in the publishing and library worlds.

UK
**HMSO BOOKS IN PRINT. [MICROFICHE].** (19??)-. English. bm. £97.75 UK; £102.75 other. Her Majesty's Stationery Office, 51 Nine Elms Lane, London SW8 5DR England. **Tel** 011 44 71 873 8459, 011 44 71 873 8499, FAX 011 44 71 873 8499,

011 44 71 873 8456, telex 297138. **(Subscription address:** Her Majesty's Stationery Office, PO Box 276, Publications Centre, London SW8 5DT England.**)**

US/0887-5499
**HUNGRY MIND REVIEW.** [Hungry mind rev.]. No. 1 (Spring 1986)-. Periodical. English. Four times a year (Mar., May, Sept., Nov.). $13.00 (one year); $22.00 (two years). Hungry Mind Review, 1648 Grand Avenue, St. Paul MN 55105. **Tel** (612)699-2610, FAX (612)699-0970. **ED** Bart Schneider. **DD** 028.1/05. **Bk Rev**, (Qty: 250). **Ad Acc, Adv Mgr:** Philip Patrick. **Pr Rev. Circ:** 55,000.
**Desc:** Geared for the iconoclastic and wide-ranging reader. We leave the bestsellers to the bigger book reviews and concentrate with unbiased, strong-voiced reviews on important books that may otherwise be given cursory notice.
**Ind/Abst** Book Rev. Index.

IT
**I GRANDI LIBRI.** (1983)-. Monographic series. Italian. Price varies per volume.

GW/0073-5620
**IMPRIMATUR (MUNCHEN).** (IMPRIMATUR; EIN JAHRBUCH FUER BUCHERFREUNDE.). **Added/Corp** Gesellschaft der Bucherfreunde zu Hamburg. Essener Bibliophilen-Abend. Vol. 1-12, (1930-55); New Series 1 (1956)-. English. ir. DM150.00. Gesellschaft der Bibliophilen, 2 Theresienstrasse 60, D 80333 Munchen Germany. **Tel** 011 49 89 283682. **LC** Z1008; .I34. **DD** 655.058.
**Ind/Abst** BHA : Biblio. Hist. Art; MLA Int. Bibl. Books Artic. Mod. Lang. Lit.

II/0019-4433
**INDIAN BOOK INDUSTRY.** Vol. 1 (Oct. 1969)-. Periodical. English. mo. $35.00. Sterling Publishers Pvt Ltd, L-10 Green Park Extension, New Delhi 110016 India. **Tel** 011 91 11 660904, FAX 011 91 11 6886646, telex 031-65625 COMD IN. **(Subscription address:** Prints India, 11 Darya Ganj, New Delhi 110002 India.**)** **ED** O P Ghai and R K Kakar. **LC** Z457; .I48. **DD** 338.47/655/00954. **Bk Rev. Ad Acc. Circ:** 2,000.
**Desc:** Links the activities of publishers, booksellers, librarians, scholars, research bodies, universities and other trades and industries connected with the production and distribution of books.

II
**INDIAN BOOK REVIEW.** Jan. 1981-. Tamil. mo. Rs30.00 India; Rs72.00 other. Kalaikathir, 6/48 Avanashi Road, Coimbatore 641 037 South India. **Tel** 25454, 25455, 24011. **ED** D Padmanaban. **LC** Z1035.A1; I638. **DD** 028.1. **Bk Rev. Ad Acc. Circ:** 10,000.
**Desc:** Disseminate the knowledge of science among the Tamil-knowing public.

II/0019-6223
**INDIAN PUBLISHER AND BOOKSELLER, THE.** See Publishing.

IT
**INDICE DEI LIBRI DEL MESE, L'.** Vol. 1, No. 1 (Oct. 1984)-. Periodical. Italian. Eleven times a year. 90.000L. Via Grazioli Lante 15A, 00195 Rome Italy. **LC** Z1035.4; .I53. **DD** 028.1/0945.

IT
**INFORMAZIONE BIBLIOGRAFICA, L'.** **Added/Corp** Consorzio Provinciale per la Pubblica Lettura (Bologna, Italy). (Jan./Mar. 1975)-. Periodical. Italian. qt. L70000.00 Italy; L120000.00 (surface mail), L140000.00 (airmail) other. Societa Editrice il Mulino, Strada Maggiore 37, 40125 Bologna Italy. **Tel** 011 39 51 256011, FAX 011 39 51 256034.

US/0741-9953
**INTERNATIONAL BOOK COLLECTORS ALMANAC/NEWSLETTER.** [Int. book collect. alm.]. Vol. 1, Issue 1 (Feb. 1984)-. Periodical. English. mo (ten issues a year). $36.00. Pegasus Publishing Inc., PO box 1350, Vashon Island WA 98070. **DD** 002.

GW
**INTERNATIONAL BOOK TRADE DIRECTORY : EUROPE, AUSTRALIA, OCEANIA, LATIN AMERICA, AFRICA AND ASIA / INTERNATIONALES BUCHHANDELSADRESSBUCH : EUROPA, AUSTRALIAN, OZEANIEN, LATEINAMERIKA, AFRIKA UND ASIEN.** **VFOAT** Internationales Buchhandelsadressbuch. 2nd Ed. (1989)-. English (German). K.G. Saur Verlag KG, A Reed Reference Publishing Company, Part of Reed International PLC, Ortlerstrasse 8, D 81373 Munich Germany. **Tel** 011 49 89 769020, FAX 011 49 89 76902150, telex 5212067-SAUR-D. **(Subscription address:** Reed Reference Publishing Company / New Jersey, 131 Chanlaon Road, PO Box 31, New Providence NJ 07974.**)** **LC** Z282; .I563. **DD** 381/.45002/025. ***Continues*** *Internationales Buchhandelsadressbuch, 0344-6190; International Directory of Booksellers, 0161-6617* ***and*** *International Book Trade Directory.*

US/0020-6180
**INTERNATIONAL BOOKBINDER / OFFICIAL JOURNAL OF THE INTERNATIONAL BROTHERHOOD OF BOOKBINDERS OF NORTH AMERICA, THE.** **Added/Corp** International Brotherhood of Bookbinders of North America. (1???)-. Periodical. English. mo.

UK
**INTERNATIONAL DIRECTORY OF BOOK COLLECTORS.** (1976/1977)-. English. ir. $25.00. Trigon Press, 117 Kent House Road, Beckenham BR3 1JJ England. **Tel** (01)778-0534. **ED** Roger and Judith Sheppard. **LC** Z987; .I57. **DD** 020/.75/025. Index available. **Bk Rev. Ad Acc. Circ:** 1,500.

UK
**INTERNATIONAL RARE BOOK PRICES.** ***Title Change.*** (INTERNATIONAL RARE BOOK PRICES. THE ARTS & ARCHITECTURE.). **VFOAT** Arts & Architecture; Arts and Architecture; IRBP. Arts & Architecture. **VAT** International Rare Book Prices. The Arts and Architecture. (198?)-(1992). English. an. Sppon River Press, PO Box 3635, Peoria IL 61614. **LC** Z5937; .I57. **DD** 017/.8/05. ***Continued by*** *Annual Register of Book Prices. Arts & Architecture.*

UK
**INTERNATIONAL RARE BOOK PRICES. EARLY PRINTED BOOKS.** ***Title Change.*** **VFOAT** Early Printed Books; IRBP. Early Printed Books. **VAT** IRBP. (1987)-(1992). English. an. Ross Burnet, PO Box 2, Uralla New South Wales 2358, Australia. **Tel** 011 067 784682, FAX 011 067 784516. **LC** Z1012; .I63. **DD** 011/.44. ***Continued by*** *Annual Register of Book Values. Early Printed Books, 0968-7513.*

UK
**INTERNATIONAL RARE BOOK PRICES. MODERN FIRST EDITIONS.** ***Title Change.*** **VFOAT** Modern First Editions; IRBP. Modern First Editions. **VAT** IRBP. (1987)-(1992). English. an. Ross Burnet, PO Box 2, Uralla New South Wales 2358, Australia. **Tel** 011 067 784682, FAX 011 067 784516. **LC** Z1029; .I55; PN701. **DD** 011/.44. ***Continued by*** *Annual Register of Book Values. Modern First Editions, 0968-7521.*

UK
**INTERNATIONAL RARE BOOK PRICES. VOYAGES, TRAVEL & EXPLORATION.** ***Title Change.*** **VFOAT** Voyages, Travel & Exploration; Voyages, Travel and Exploration; IRBP. Voyages Travel & Exploration. (1987)-Vol. 1 (1992). English. an. Ross Burnet, PO Box 2, Uralla New South Wales 2358, Australia. **Tel** 011 067 784682, FAX 011 067 784516. **ED** Michael Cole. **LC** Z6011; .I594; G156. **DD** 016.9109. ***Continued by*** *Annual Register of Book Values. Voyages, Travel & Exploration, 0968-7548.*

IE
**IRISH BOOKS IN PRINT & LEABHAIR GAEILGE I GCLO.** **VFOAT** Irish Books in Print and Leabhair Gaeilge i Gclo. (1984)-. English (Irish). ir. S & J Cleary, Ballymerrigan House, Wicklow Ireland. **LC** Z2031; .I75. **DD** 016.9415.

IS
**ISRAEL BOOK TRADE DIRECTORY.** 5th Ed. (1975)-. English. be. Free on request. Publishers and Printers of Israel, PO Box 50084, Tel Aviv 61500 Israel. **Tel** 03-630-830. **LC** Z449.5; .P8. **DD** 070.5/0885/5694. **Ad Acc. Circ:** 3,000. ***Continues*** *Publishers and Printers of Israel, 0079-7820.*
**Desc:** Publication listing Israeli publishers and printing services with a special emphasis on Israeli export in this area. Each listing has a comprehensive description.

GW/0937-261X
**JAHRBUCH / BORSENVEREIN DES DEUTSCHEN BUCHHANDELS E.V.** **Added/Corp** Borsenverein des Deutschen Buchhandels. (1989)-. German. an. price varies per volume. Buchhandler Vereinigung GmbH, Grosser Hirschgraben 17-21, D 60311 Frankfurt 1 Germany. **Tel** 011 49 69 1306243, telex 413573 BUCH VOL. **LC** Z313; .B886. ***Continues*** *Buch und Buchhandel in Zahlen, 0068-3051.*

JA/0910-7908
**JAPAN ENGLISH PUBLICATIONS IN PRINT.** 1st Ed. (1985/1987)-. English. ir. Y27,000 Japan; $270.00 US. Intercontinental Marketing Corporation, IPO Box 5056, Tokyo 100-31 Japan. **Tel** 011 81 3 3661 7458, FAX 011 81 3 3661 9646. **LC** Z3301; .J35. **DD** 015.52034. ***Formed by the union of*** *Japan English Magazine Directory* ***and*** *Japan English Books in Print.*
**Desc:** Lists all books, monographs and substantial booklets. Also lists all annuals, magazines and other periodicals that are published wholly or partly in English in Japan.

CN/0826-1067
**JOURNAL OF RARE OLD BOOKS, THE.** [J. rare old books]. No. 1 (1984)-. Periodical. English (French). $5.50 per volume. Journal of Rare Old Books, PO Box 9542, Sainte-Foy Quebec G1V 4B8 Canada. **DD** 002/.075.

RU
**KNIZHNAIA TORGOVLIA. BIBLIOGRAFICHESKAIA INFORMATSIIA; NOVOSTI LITERATURY.** **Added/Corp** Gosudarstvennyi Komitet Soveta Ministrov SSSR po Delam Izdatelstv, Poligrafii i Knizhnoi Torgovli. Vsesoiuznaia Knizhnaia Palata. Tsentralnoe Biuro Nauchno-Tekhnicheskoi Informatsii i Tekhniko-Ekonomicheskikh Issledovannii po Poligraficheskoi Promyshlennosti, Izdatelskomu Delu, Knigovedeniiu i Knizhnoi Torgovle. Vol. 1 (1973)-. Multiple languages (Russian and Multiple languages). bm. 0.05rub (single issue). Izdatelstvo Kniga, 50 Gorky Ulitsa, 125047 Moscow Russia. **LC** Z279; .K55. ***Supersedes in part*** *Izdatelskoe Delo, Knigovedenie, Knizhnaia Torgovlia I Gosudarstvennaia Bibliografiia.*

RU/0320-1244
**KNIZHNAIA TORGOVLIA. OPYT, PROBLEMY, ISSLEDOVANIIA.** (19??)-. Periodical. Russian. Izdatelstvo Kniga, 50 Gorky Ulitsa, 125047 Moscow Russia. **LC** Z165; .K59.

RU/0131-4122
**KNIZHNAIA TORGOVLIA. REFERATIVNAIA INFORMATSIIA.** **Added/Corp** Gosudarstvennyi Komitet Soveta Ministrov SSSR po Delam Izdatelstv, Poligrafii i Knizhnoi Torgovli. Gosudarstvennyi Komitet SSSR po Delam Izdatelstv, Poligrafii i Knizhnoi Torgovli. Vsesoiuznaia Knizhnaia Palata. Tsentralnoe Biuro Nauchno-Tekhnicheskoi Informatsii i Tekhniko-Ekonomicheskikh Issledovanii po Poligraficheskoi Promyshlennosti, Izdatelskomu Delu, Knigovedeniiu i Knizhnoi Torgovle. Nauchno-Informatsionnyi Tsentr po Izdatelskomu Delu, Poligraficheskoi Promyshlennosti i Knizhnoi Torgovle. Vol. 1 (1973)-. Russian. bm. 0.15rub single issue. Izdatelstvo Kniga, 50 Gorky Ulitsa, 125047 Moscow Russia. **LC** Z278; .K55.

KO
**KYOBO MUNGO.** Periodical. Korean. bm. Kyobo Mungo, 1-1 1-ka Chong-ro Korea. **LC** Z1003.5.K8; K96.

US/1053-363X
**LAMBDA RISING NEWS.** [Lambda Rising news]. **Added/Corp** Lambda Rising, Inc. (1984)-. Periodical. English. Four times a year. Free. Lambda Rising Inc, 1625 Connecticut Avenue Northwest, Washington DC 20009. **Tel** (202)462-7924, FAX (202)462-7257. **DD** 305.
**Ind/Abst** Expand. Acad. Index (1992-).

CN/0229-4370
**LARGE PRINT BOOKS / GEORGIAN BAY REGIONAL LIBRARY SYSTEM.** [Large print books - Georgian Bay Reg. Libr. Syst.]. **Main/Corp** Georgian Bay Regional Library System. English. Free. Georgian Bay Regional Library System, 30 Morrow Road, Barrie Ontario L4N 3V8 Canada. **DD** 018/.163. ctrl circ.

US
**LAW BOOKS IN PRINT / EDITED AND COMPILED BY J. MYRON JACOBSTEIN AND MEIRA G. PIMSLEUR.** See Law.

US/0023-9240
**LAW BOOKS PUBLISHED.** See Law.

GW
**LESELAND.** Periodical. German. an. Borsenverein der Deutschen Buchhandler, Gerichtsweg 26, Postfach 146, 7010 Leipzig Germany. **LC** Z321.7; .L47. **DD** 380.1/450705/09431.

IT
**LIBER : LIBRI PER BAMBINI E RAGAZZI.** Libreria Ragazzi, Serv Abbon, Bia Unione 3, 20122 Milan Italy.

US/0894-8631
**LIBRARIES & CULTURE.** [Libr. cult.]. **VFOAT** Libraries and Culture; L and C; L & C. Vol. 23, No. 1 (Winter 1988)-. Periodical. English. qt. $44.00 (institutions), $26.00 (individuals) US; add $6.00 postage other. University of Texas Press, PO Box 7819, Austin TX 78713. **Tel** (512)471-4531, FAX (512)320-0668, telex 776453 UTEXPRES AUS. **ED** Don G. Davis Jr. **LC** Z671; .J67. **DD** 027. **[CCC]. Bk Rev. Ad Acc. Pr Rev. Circ:** 733 (ctrl). available on microfilm and microfiche from University Microfilms International (UMI). Documents available from The Genuine Article. ***Continues*** *Journal of Library History (Tallahassee, Fla. : 1974), 0275-3650.*
**Desc:** Explores the significance of collections of recorded knowledge. Their creation, organization, preservation and utilization-in the context of cultural and social history, unlimited as to time and place.
**Ind/Abst** Acad. Search (July 1993-); Am. Hist. Life (1966-); Am. Bibliogr. Slavic East Europ. Stud. (1987-); Book Rev. Index (1988-); Child. Lit. Abstr. (19??-); Curr. Contents Soc. Behav. Sci.; INFO-SOUTH Abstr.; Inf. Instruc. Technol. (1988-); Inf. Sci. Abstr.; Libr. Inf. Sci.

Abstr. (1988-); Libr. Lit. (1988-); Mag. Search; MLA Int. Bibl. Books Artic. Mod. Lang. Lit. (1988-); Res. Alert [Full Cov.]; Soc. Sci. Cit. Index (1988-) [Full Cov.].

SZ/0024-2152
**LIBRARIUM.** [Librarium]. **Added/Corp** Schweizerische Bibliophilen-Gesellschaft. Vol. 1 (Apr. 1958)-. Periodical. German (French, Italian and English). Three times a year. 150.00F. Swiss Society of Bibliophiles, Hoffnungsstr 3, CH 8038 Zurich Switzerland. **Tel** 01/242 63 49. **(Subscription address:** A Zwingli, Steinwiesstrasse 76, CH-8032 Zurich, Switzerland.**) ED** Werner Zimmermann. **LC** Z990; .L46. Index available. **Ad Acc.** ***Supersedes*** *Stultifera Navis.*
**Ind/Abst** MLA Int. Bibl. Books Artic. Mod. Lang. Lit.

SP
**LIBRERIA.** ***Suspended.*** **Added/Corp** Gremio Sindical de Libreros de Barcelona. (19??)-Suspended. Spanish. ir. 20 single issue. Mallorca 274 1 Planta, Barcelona Spain. **LC** Z416; .L53.

IT
**LIBRI NUOVI E USATI.** No. 1 (Feb. 1991)-. Periodical. Italian. qt. L30000. Libri Nuovi e Usati, Via Lepido 203 24, 40132 Bologna Italy. **Tel** 011 39 51 401285. **LC** IN PROCESS.

IT
**LIBRINOVITA.** Federico Ceratti Editore, C Postale 1, Via XXV Aprile 11, 20060 Vignate Milan Italy. **Tel** 011 39 2 9560530.

CK/0121-1242
**LIBRO EN AMERICA LATINA Y EL CARIBE, EL.** **Added/Corp** Regional Center for Book Promotion in Latin America and the Caribbean. **VFOAT** Libro. No. 54-55 (July/Dec. 1987)-. Periodical. Spanish. Four times a year. $26.00. Centro Regional para el Fomento del Libro en America, CLL 70 N 9 52, Apdo Aereo 57438, Bogota Columbia. **Tel** 011 57 1 2554574, 011 57 1 2495141, FAX 011 57 1 2554614, telex CERLACO 44637. **ED** Luis Horacio Lopez. **LC** Z490; .C455a. **DD** 381/.45002/098. Index available. **Ad Acc. Circ:** 2,000 (ctrl). ***Continues*** *Cerlalc Noticias Sobre el Libro.*

CK
**LIBROS.** ***Ceased.*** **Added/Corp** Camara Colombiana de la Industria Editorial. (19??)-(19??). Periodical. Spanish. bm. Camara Columbiana de la Industria Editorial, Calle 15 Num 9-30, Oficina 206 Apartado Aereo 8998, Bogota Colombia. **LC** Z523.7; .L52.

VE
**LIBROS AL DIA.** Vol. 1 No. 1 (Aug. 15 1975)-. Periodical. Spanish. bw. Lialdi Edificio la Linea, Officina 153 A, Caracas Venezuela. **LC** F2308; .L52.

MX
**LIBROS EN ESPANOL ... TITULOS.** **VFOAT** Titulos. Spanish. **LC** Z2685; .L56. **DD** 056/.1. ***Continues in part*** *Publicaciones Editadas en Espanol.*

US/0741-0107
**LICENSING BOOK, THE.** [Licens. book]. **VFOAT** Licensing. Vol. 1, No. 1 (Oct. 1983)-. Periodical. English. mo. $36.00 (1 year), $60.00 (2 year), $72.00 (3 year) US and Canada; $250.00 (1 year) other. Adventure Publishing Group Inc, 264 West 40th Street, New York NY 10018. **Tel** (212)575-4510, FAX (212)575-4521, telex 177368 IEBUT. **DD** 338. **Ad Acc. Circ:** 21,000 (ctrl).
**Desc:** Information on various aspects of the licensing industry.

CN/1188-7494
**LITERARY REVIEW OF CANADA, THE.** **See** Literature.

CN/0714-9948
**LIVRE D'ICI (MENSUEL).** (LIVRE D'ICI.). [Livre ici]. **Added/Corp** Societe de Promotion du Livre. Vol. 8, No. 1 (Nov. 1982)-. Trade Publication. French. mo (except July/Aug.). 30.00Can$ Canada; 38.00Can$ other. Periodica Inc, PO Box 444, Outremont Quebec H2V 4R6 Canada. **Tel** (514)274-5468, FAX (514)274-0201. **ED** Jacques Theriault. **DD** 028.1/09714. **Circ:** 7,000.
**Desc:** A trade magazine of book industry in Canada, and primarily in Quebec; for publishers, booksellers, librarians, printers, etc.

BE/0024-533X
**LIVRE ET L'ESTAMPE, LE.** **Added/Corp** Societe des Bibliophiles et Iconophiles de Belgique. (Dec 1954)-. Periodical. French. sa. 1200F (Belgium); 1750F (other). Societe Royale des Bibliophiles et Iconophiles Belgium, 4 et Boulevard de L'Empereur, 1000 Brussels Belgium. **Tel** 11 32 2 5195311. **ED** A Grisay. **LC** Z990; .L5. cum. index. **Ad Acc. Circ:** 300 (ctrl).
**Desc:** History of books (old and contemporary) and prints.
**Ind/Abst** BHA : Biblio. Hist. Art.

FR
**LIVRES DISPONIBLES, LES.** **VFOAT** French Books in Print. (1977). French. an. 910.00Can$ Montreal; 890.00Can$ Canada. Cercle de la Librairie, 35 rue Gregoire de Tours, F-75279 Paris Cedex 06 France. **Tel** 011 33 1 43291000, FAX 011 33 1 43296895, telex LIFRAN 270 838. **LC** Z2161; .L8. **DD** 015/.44. **NLM** Z 2161 L788. ***Formed by the union of*** *Repertoire des Livres de Langue Francaise Disponibles, 0080-1003* ***and*** *Catalogue de l'Edition Francaise.*
**Desc:** Exhaustive repertory listing the 263,000 books published in the French language. (263,000 entries, 25,000 new titles, 201, 648 amendments of entries in 1987 edition. Schedule of publishers and distributors, schedule of collections.

CN/0710-5231
**LIVROS EM PORTUGUES.** [Livros Port.]. **VFOAT** Portuguese Books on Deposit in the Public Libraries of Metropolitan Toronto. 1st Ed. (1981)-. English (Portuguese). be. Metropolitan Toronto Library Board, 789 Yonge Street, Toronto Ontario M4W 2G8 Canada. **Tel** (416)393-7134, telex 06-22232. **DD** 011/.269.

UK/0957-9656
**LOGOS.** Vol. 1, No. 1 (1990)-. Periodical. English. qt. £62.00 (institution), £40.00 (individual) UK; $70.00 (individual), $105.00 (institution) US. Whurr Publishers Ltd, 19B Compton Terrace, London N1 2UN England. **Tel** 011 44 71 359 5979, FAX 011 44 71 226 5290. **(Subscription address:** Turpin Distribution Services Limited, Blackhorse Road, Letchworth, Hertfordshire SG6 1HN, United Kingdom.**) ED** Gordon Graham. **LC** Z284; .L64. **DD** 070.5/025. **CODEN** LGOSEL. Index available. **Bk Rev.**
**Desc:** Serves the international book community. Aims to deal in depth with issues which unite, divide, excite and concern the world of books.

US/0890-7722
**MAGILL BOOK REVIEW.** [Magill book rev.]. (1987)-. Periodical. English. an (monthly installments). Salem Press/Magill Books, 150 South Main Street, Woodridge NJ 07095. **ED** Frank McGill. **LC** Z1035.A1; M29. **DD** 028.1.
**Ind/Abst** Acad. Abstr. (Jan. 1987-); Mag. Artic. Summar. Elite (Jan. 1987-) [Full Txt.]; Mag. Artic. Summar. Select (Jan. 1987-) [Full Txt.]; Mag. Artic. Summar. CD-ROM (Jan. 1987-); Mid. Search (?-?); Vocat. Search.

US/0198-9960
**MANHATTAN BOOK HOUND.** (Apr. 1980)-. Periodical. English. Twelve times a year. $15.00. Butler Communications, PO Box 5347, New York NY 10150.

NE/0920-0401
**MANUSCRIPTS OF THE MIDDLE EAST.** **VFOAT** MME. Vol. 1 (1986)-. English. an. Fl150.00. Ter Lugt Press, Donkersteeg 19, 2312 Ha Leiden Netherlands. **Tel** 011 31 71 120916. **LC** Z6620.M6; M36. **DD** 091/.0956.
**Ind/Abst** Art Archaeol. Tech. Abstr.

II
**MARATHI PRAKASANA VARSHIKA ANI PRAKASANA DAYARI.** **VFOAT** Prakasana-Dayari. Marathi. an. Rs35.00. Aniruddha Sahitya, 1493 C Sadashiv, Pune 411030 India. **Tel** 441004. **ED** Gajanan Kshirsagar. **LC** Z454; .M37. **Ad Acc. Circ:** 3,500.
**Desc:** Covers list of books printed during the year, lists of publishers, booksellers, periodicals, colleges, artists, etc.

SZ
**MEDBOOKS.** Periodical. English. sa. **(Subscription address:** Karger Libri AG, Petersgraben 31, CH-4009 Basel 11 Switzerland; telephone: 011 41 61 3061500 or FAX: 011 41 61 3061234**)**

US
**MEI-KUO CHU PAN CHIH CHUNG-KUO YEN CHIU LUN CHU HSUAN CHAI.** **Added/Corp** Chinese Information and Culture Center (New York, N.Y.). **VFOAT** Digest of Books & Articles on U.S. China Studies. (Feb. 11, 1991)-. Periodical. Chinese (English). sm. **LC** Z3106; .M4. ***Continues*** *Mei-Kuo Chung-Kuo Yen Chiu Lun Chu Hsuan Chai.*

US
**MEMBERSHIP DIRECTORY / GUILD OF BOOK WORKERS.** **Main/Corp** Guild of Book Workers. **VFOAT** Guild of Book Workers Membership List. (1986)-. Directory. English. $40.00 US; $47.50 Canada; $60.00 other (national membership); $50.00 (national membership (incls) one chapter membership). Guild of Book Workers, 521 Fifth Avenue, New York NY 10175. **Tel** (212)757-6454. ***Continues*** *Membership list.*

GW
**MERKBLATTER - KOMMISSION FUR EINBANDFRAGEN VEREINS DEUTSCHER BIBLIOTHEKARE.** **Main/Corp** Verein Deutscher Bibliothekare. Kommission fur Einbandfragen. German. Kommission fur Eingandfragen, Fehrbelliner Platz 3, W-1000 Berlin 3 Germany. **LC** Z267; .V42A. ***Supersedes*** *Verein Deutscher Bibliothekare. Kommission fur Einbandfragen. Einband Buchpflege.*

US/0026-4377
**MILWAUKEE READER.** **Main/Corp** Milwaukee. Public Library. (1942)-. Newsletter. English. mo. $5.00. Milwaukee Public Library, 814 West Wisconsin Avenue, Milwaukee WI 53233. **Tel** (414)278-3032. **ED** Lorelei Starck. **Bk Rev. Circ:** 4,500 (ctrl).
**Desc:** Covers books, events, and community affairs.

IT
**MINIATURA / A CURA DELLA SOCIETA DI STORIA DELLA MINIATURA.** **Added/Corp** Societa di Storia Della Miniatura. (1988)-. Periodical. Italian (summaries and/or abstracts in English). Twice a year. L180000. Fratelli Alinari IDEA SPA, Largo Fratelli Alinari 15, 50123 Florence Italy. **Tel** 011 39 55 210202, 011 39 55 218950. **LC** ND2900; .M64.
**Ind/Abst** BHA : Biblio. Hist. Art.

US/0894-5489
**MINIATURE BOOK SOCIETY NEWSLETTER, THE.** [Miniat. Book Soc. newsl.]. **Added/Corp** Miniature Book Society. (1986)-. Periodical. English. qt. $25.00 US; $40.00 other. Miniature Book Society, PO Box 127, Sudbury MA 01776. **Tel** (617)527-7560, (617)924-9110. **DD** 099.

XR
**MISCELANEA ODDELENI RUKOPISU A VZACNYCH TISKU / STATNI KNIHOVNA CESKE SOCIALISTICKE REPUBLIKY, NOSITELKA RADU REPUBLIKY.** **Added/Corp** Statni Knihovna CSR. Oddeleni Rukopisu a Vzacnych Tisku. **VFOAT** Miscellanea Oddeleni Rukopisu a Vzacnych Tisku; Miscellanea. (1984)-. Czech (Czech; summaries and/or abstracts in English and Russian). ir. Statni Knihovna CSR, Liliova 5, Prague Czech Republic. **LC** Z1029; .M57.
**Desc:** Includes information on rare books and manuscripts.

US
**MOBILE IDEAS.** **Added/Corp** Library Administrators Conference of Northern Illinois. Bookmobile Librarians. (1980)-. English. Wynne Weiss, Des Plaines Public Library, 841 Graceland Avenue, Des Plaines IL 60016.

GW
**MOHR-KURIER.** German. Three times a year. JCB Mohr / Paul Siebeck, Postfach 2040, D 72010 Tuebingen Germany. **Tel** 011 49 7071 9230, FAX 011 49 7071 51104, telex 7/262872 mohr d.

AT/0159-7191
**MOROCCO BOUND.** (MOROCCO BOUND. QUARTERLY JOURNAL OF THE GUILD OF CRAFT BOOKBINDERS.). (1980)-. Periodical. English. Four times a year (Feb., May, Aug., Nov.). 28.00Aus$. Guild of Craft Bookbinders, PO Box 1110, Rozelle NSW 2039 Australia. **Tel** 011 61 2 4983522. cum. index (1st ten years).
**Desc:** Imparts of information on binding, restoration, and associated book topics for hobbyists.

US/0739-5272
**MOTHEROOT JOURNAL.** ***Suspended.*** [Motheroot j.]. Vol. 1 No. 1 (Spring 1979)-(199?). Periodical. English. qt. $5.00. Motheroot Publications, PO Box 8306, Pittsburgh PA 15218. **Tel** (412)241-0628. **LC** WMLC 90/0409. **Bk Rev. Ad Acc.**
**Ind/Abst** Altern. Press Index (-199?).

CN/0710-5207
**NEDERLANDSE BOEKEN.** **VFOAT** Dutch Books on Deposit in the Public Libraries of Metropolitan Toronto. 1st Ed. (1981)-. English (Dutch). be. Metropolitan Toronto Library Board, 789 Yonge Street, Toronto Ontario M4W 2G8 Canada. **Tel** (416)393-7134, telex 06-22232. **DD** 011/.23931.

US
**NEW BOOK ANNOUNCEMENTS. ANNUAL BOOK CATALOG.** **Main/Corp** AMACOM. Catalog. English. an. Amacom, 135 West 50th Street, New York NY 10020. **Tel** (212)903-8075. ***Supersedes*** *AMACOM Resources for Professional Management.*

UK/0261-5363
**NEW BOOKBINDER, THE.** [New bookbind.]. **Added/Corp** Designer Bookbinders. Vol. 1 (1981)-. Periodical. English. an. $75.00. Designer Bookbinders, Wardens Cottage, Leintwardine, Shrops SY7 OLL England. **Tel** 011 44 81 5473443, FAX 011 44 81 5473488. **ED** G.C. Nicholson. Index available. **Bk Rev,** (Qty: 3-5). **Ad Acc. Pr Rev. Circ:** 700. available on microfiche. ***Continues*** *Designer Bookbinders Review.*
**Desc:** Modern designer bookbindings exhibitions, binding techniques and design. Profiles of contemporary bookbinders.
**Ind/Abst** Art Archaeol. Tech. Abstr.; Libr. Inf. Sci. Abstr.; Print. Abstr.

US/0734-8142
**NEW BOOKS IN THE COMMUNICATIONS LIBRARY.** **See** Communication.

●US/1064-7511
**NEW BOOKTALKER, THE.** **VFOAT** New Book Talker; Booktalker; Book Talker. Vol. 1 (Fall 1992)-. English. sa. $17.00. Libraries Unlimited Inc., PO Box 6633, Department 920, Englewood CO 80155. **Tel** (800)237-6124. **ED** Joni Richards Bodart. **LC** Z716.3; .N36. **DD** 028. ***Continues*** *Booktalker.*

**Desc:** Covers 150 to 200 fiction and nonfiction titles for all ages. Informative articles written by professionals to encourage the joy of reading.

NZ/1170-9103
**NEW ZEALAND BOOKS.** [N.Z. books]. (1991)-. Periodical. English. Five times a year (Feb., May, July, Sept., Nov.). 36.00NZ$ New Zealand; 45.00NZ$ Australia; 50.00NZ$ other (except US). Peppercorn Press, PO Box 6341, Wellington 2 New Zealand. **Tel** 4-499 1569, FAX 4-499 1424. **ED** Colin James (phone:4-3847030). **DD** 028.1099305. **Bk Rev**. **Ad Acc**, **Adv Mgr:** Jane Gayers.
**Desc:** Indepth reviews of New Zealand books.

US/0569-2229
**NEWS-LETTER OF THE AMERICAN ANTIQUARIAN SOCIETY. Main/Corp** American Antiquarian Society. No. 1 (Jan. 1968)-. Newsletter. English. Twice a year. Free with subscription to the Proceedings. American Antiquarian Society, 185 Salisbury Street, Worcester MA 01609. **Tel** (508)752-5813, (508)755-5221. **ED** Lynnette P. Sodha. **LC** E172; .A335. **DD** 973/.06/273. **Circ:** 1,649 (ctrl). available on microfilm from University Microfilms International (UMI).
**Desc:** Presents news and information about the activities of the society's members and staff, as well as news of collections and acquisitions of the society.

CN/0822-9538
**NEWSLETTER (CANADIAN BOOKBINDERS AND BOOK ARTISTS GUILD).** (NEWSLETTER / THE CANADIAN BOOKBINDERS AND BOOK ARTISTS GUILD.). **Added/Corp** Canadian Bookbinders and Book Artists Guild. Vol. 1, No. 1 (1983)-. Newsletter. English. Four times a year. 55.00Can$ institutions; 35.00Can$ indivduals Canada; $35.00 individuals other (comes with membership). Canadian Bookbinders and Book Artists Guild, 35 McCaul Street, Suite 220, Toronto Ontario M5T 1V7 Canada. **Tel** (416)851-1554, (416)581-1071. **ED** Richard Miller. **DD** 686.3/006/071. Index available. **Bk Rev**. **Ad Acc. Circ:** 540 (ctrl).
**Desc:** Technical, philosophical and critical articles on the book arts as well as listing exhibition, workshops, lecture series, and more of interest to book artists, collectors, librarians, etc.

US
**NEWSLETTER (UNITED STATES BOARD ON BOOKS FOR YOUNG PEOPLE).** (NEWSLETTER / THE UNITED STATES BOARD ON BOOKS FOR YOUNG PEOPLE, INC., THE UNITED STATES SECTION OF THE INTERNATIONAL BOARD ON BOOKS FOR YOUNG PEOPLE (IBBY).). **Added/Corp** United States Board on Books for Young People. **VFOAT** USBBY Newsletter. Vol. 9, No. 2 (Fall 1984)-. Newsletter. English. sa. $25.00 (members), $75.00 (institutional members). US Board on Books for Young People, 800 Barksdale Road, Newark DE 19714. **Tel** (302)731-1600, FAX (302)731-1057. **ED** Arlene M. Pillar (editor's address: 67 Forester Street, Long Beach, New York 11561). ctrl circ. ***Continues*** *Newsletter (Friends of IBBY), 0888-5079.*

NR
**NIGERIAN BOOKS IN PRINT.** 1967-. English. ir. Nigerian Book Suppliers Ltd, PO Box 3870, Lagos Nigeria. **LC** Z965; .N38 subser; Z3597. **DD** 027.5669 S; 015.669.

CN/0710-5304
**NIHONGO-NO-TOSHO.** [Nihongo-no-tosho]. **VFOAT** Japanese Books on Deposit in the Public Libraries of Metropolitan Toronto. 1st. Ed. (1981)-. English (Japanese). be. Metropolitan Toronto Library Board, 789 Yonge Street, Toronto Ontario M4W 2G8 Canada. **Tel** (416)393-7134, telex 06-22232. **DD** 011/.2956.

JA
**NISSHOREN ZENKOKU SHOTEN MEIBO. Main/Corp** Nihon Shoten Kumiai Rengokai. **VFOAT** Zenkoku Shoten Meibo. (1973)-. Periodical. Japanese. Nihon Shoten Shougyou Kumiai Rengokai, 2 Kanda Surguadai 1- Chome Chiyoda-ku, Tokyo Japan. **LC** Z463.5; .N537a.

US/0886-5256
**NORTHWEST REVIEW OF BOOKS, THE.** [Northwest rev. books]. Vol. 1, No. 1 (June 1985)-. Periodical. English. qt. $10.00. Northwest Review of Books, PO Box 45370, Seattle WA 98145. **DD** 028.

FR/0335-752X
**NOUVELLES DU LIVRE ANCIEN. Added/Corp** Centre National du Livre Ancien (France) Bibliotheque Nationale (France). Service du Livre Ancien. Institut de Recherche et d'Histoire des Textes (France). Section de l'Humanisme. (19??)-. French. Four times a year. Free on Request. Service du Livre Ancien Bibliotheque Nationale, 58 rue de Richelieu, 75084 Paris Cedex 02 France. **Tel** 011 33 1 47236104. **LC** Z4; .N68. **DD** 002/.05.

US
**OFFICIAL PRICE GUIDE, PAPERBACKS, THE. VFOAT** Paperbacks. 1st Ed. (1991)-. English. $12.95. House of Collectibles, 201 East 50th Street, New York NY 10022. **LC** Z1033.P3; O34. **DD** 070.5/73.

US/0747-5047
**OFFICIAL PRICE GUIDE TO OLD BOOKS & AUTOGRAPHS, THE.** **See** Hobbies.

GR
**PANELLENIA EKTHESE VIVLIOU : KATALOGOS. Main/Conf** Panellenia Ekthese Vivliou. **VFOAT** Katalogos Ekdoseon. Greek, Modern. Panellenia Homospondia Ekdoton Vivliopolon, Arachobes 61, Athens Greece. **LC** Z333.7; .P36A.

US
**PAPER COLLECTORS' MARKETPLACE : PCM. VFOAT** PCM. Vol. 3, No. 8 (Aug. 1985)-. Periodical. English. mo. $17.95 (one year), $32.95 (two year), $45.95 (three year); add 13.00 postage per year to other. Watson Graphic Designs, PO Box 127, Scandinavia WI 54977. **Tel** (715)467-2379. **LC** PN4877; .M34. **DD** 002/.075/05. available on microfilm from The State Historical Society of Wisconsin. ***Continues*** *Magazine Collectors' Marketplace, 0741-4927.*

CN/0822-5818
**PAPERBACKS BY MAIL.** [Paperb. mail]. **Main/Corp** Chinook Regional Library. **Added/Corp** Chinook Regional Library. (1976)-. English. sa. Chinook Regional Library, 1240 Chaplin Street West, Swift Current Saskatchewan S9H 0G8 Canada. **Tel** (306)773-3186. **DD** 017/.532. **Circ:** 175.
**Desc:** A duration collection intended for library patrons who cannot easily visit a library.

US
**PASS IN REVIEW.** Vol. 1, No. 1 (May 1, 1981)-. English. mo. $5.00 US; $12.00 (surface mail), $18.00 (airmail) other. Merriam Press, 218 Beech Street, Bennington VT 05201. **ED** Ray Merriam. **Bk Rev**.
**Desc:** Newsletter to inform readers of the latest military history books and publications.

US/0553-6774
**PERMANENCE/DURABILITY OF THE BOOK.** [Perm.-durab. book]. **VFOAT** Publication. No. 1-. Monographic series. English. Price varies per volume. W J Barrow Research Laboratory Building, Box 7311, Richmond VA 23221. **LC** Z701; .P4. **DD** 025/.84.

●US/1064-4741
**PLANT'S REVIEW OF BOOKS. VFOAT** Review of Books. (1992)-. Periodical. English. qt. Free. Plant's Review of Books, PO Box 14081, Portland OR 97214-0081. **Tel** (503)274-6345.

CN/0710-5290
**POLSKIE KSIAZKI (TORONTO).** (POLSKIE KSIAZKI). **Added/Corp** Metropolitan Toronto Library Board. Metropolitan Toronto Library Board. Regional Multilanguage Services. **VFOAT** Polish Books on Deposit in the Public Libraries of Metropolitan Toronto. 1st Ed. (1981)-. English (Polish). be. Metropolitan Toronto Library Board, 789 Yonge Street, Toronto Ontario M4W 2G8 Canada. **Tel** (416)393-7134, telex 06-22232. **DD** 011/.291851.

UK
**PRIVATE PRESS BOOKS. Added/Corp** Private Libraries Association. (1959)-. English. an. £40.00. Private Libraries Association, Ravelston South View Road, Pinner Middlesex HA5 3YD England. **(Subscription address:** Private Libraries Association, British Library, Great Russell Street, London WC1B 3DG England.**) ED** Philip Kerrigan. **DD** 015. cum. index. **Ad Acc. Circ:** 800.
**Desc:** List of books and pamphlets printed by private presses in Britain, USA, Canada, Australia and the Western World.

SP
**PROLOGO (MADRID, SPAIN).** (PROLOGO.). **Added/Corp** Centro de Exportacion de Libros Espanoles. Sociedad Estatal para la Ejecucion de Programas del Quinto Centenario (Spain). No. 1 (Feb. 1989)-. Periodical. Spanish. bm. Prolongo Revista del Lector, Bailen 39, Madrid 28005 Spain. **Tel** 011 34 1 2663713. **LC** Z1035.7; .P76. **DD** 028.1/0946.

PL
**PRZEGLED KSIEGARSKI I WYDAWNICZY. Added/Corp** Dom Ksiezki, Warsaw. Zjednoczenie Ksiegarstwa. (19??)-. Periodical. Polish. Twelve times a year. **(Subscription address:** ARS Polona, PO Box 1001, 00068 Warsaw Poland.**) LC** Z365; .P68. ***Continues*** *Praca Ksiegarska.*

US/0000-0019
**PUBLISHERS WEEKLY.** [Publ. wkly.]. **Added/Corp** R.R. Bowker Company. Publishers' Board of Trade (U.S.) Book Trade Association of Philadelphia. Am. Book Trade Association. American Book Trade Union. Vol. 3 (Jan. 1873)-. Periodical. English. wk (51 issues). $139.00 US; $187.00 Canada; $270.00 other. Cahners Publishing Company, 249 West 17th Street, New York NY 10011. **Tel** (212)645-0067, FAX (212)242-6987. **(Subscription address:** Publishers Weekly, PO Box 6457, Torrance CA 90504-0457.**) ED** John Baker. **LC** Z1219; .P98. **DD** 070. **[CCC]**. Index available. cum. index. **Bk Rev**. **Ad Acc. Circ:** 37,000. available on microfilm and microfiche from University Microfilms International (UMI); available on CD-ROM (Books in Print with Reviews) from R.R. Bowker; available on an online database (files 647,648/Full-Text) from DIALOG. Documents available from UMI Article Clearinghouse, Magazine Collection. ***Continues*** *Publishers' and Stationers' Weekly Trade Circular.*
**Desc:** International news magazine of the book publishing industry. Covers trade news, book design and manufacture, bookselling and merchandising, plus interviews with influential authors and publishing principles. Includes reviews of over 7,000 new books each year plus regular columns on rights, people, paperback and hardcover bestsellers and controversial issues.
**Ind/Abst** ABI/INFORM Glob. Ed.; ABI Inform Ondisc (Feb. 1975-March 1977); Abstr. Graphic Arts Tech. Found. (1984); Acad. Abstr. Full Text Elite (Jan. 1989-); Acad. Abstr. (Jan. 1989-); Acad. Ind. [Computer File] (1984-); Acad. Search (Jan. 1989-); Am. Bibliogr. Slavic East Europ. Stud.; Book Rev. Index; Bus. Index (1985-); Bus. Period. Index; Child. Lit. Abstr. (19??-); Curr. Lit. Fam. Plan.; Expand. Acad. Index (1984-); Garden Lit. (1992-); Gen. BusinessFile (1985-); Gen. Period. Index (1985-); Graph. Arts Bull. Inst. Pap. Sci. Technol. (Jan. 1989-Mar. 1989, May 1989-July 1989, Sept. 1989-Nov. 1989); Index Period. Artic. Relat. Law; INFO-SOUTH Abstr.; Inf. Instruc. Technol.; Int. Aerosp. Abstr.; Law Office Inf. Serv.; Libr. Inf. Sci. Abstr.; Libr. Lit.; Mag. Artic. Summar. Elite (Jan. 1989-); Mag. Artic. Summar. Select (Jan. 1989-); Mag. Artic. Summar. CD-ROM (Jan. 1989-); Mag. Index Plus (1989-); Mag. Index. Sel. (1986-); Mag. Search; Middle East Abstr. Index; Newsp. Period. Abstr. (1986-); Print. Abstr.; Read. Guide Abstr. Select Ed.; Read. Guide Period. Lit.; Sci. Fict. Fantasy Book Rev. Index; Stat. Ref. Index; Mag. Index (1977-); Trade Ind. ASAP [Full Txt.]; Trade Ind. Index [Full Txt.]; Vocat. Search (Jan. 1989-); Wilson Bus. Abstr.

NE/0014-9527
**QUAERENDO.** [Quaerendo]. Vol. 1, No. 1 (Jan. 1971)-. Periodical. English (French and German). Four times a year. Fl130.00 (institutions) Netherlands; $74.50 (institutions) other. E. J. Brill, Postbus 9000, 2300 PA Leiden Netherlands. **Tel** 011 31 71 312624, FAX 011 31 71 317532, telex 39296 BRILL NL. **ED** A. R. A. Crouset van Uchelen. **[CCC]**. Index available (Free). **Bk Rev**. **Ad Acc.** ctrl circ.
**Desc:** Articles, notes and news in the science of manuscripts and books. It is divided into the following rubrics: manuscripts; early printing; 16th-century printing; 17th-century humanism; book illustration; bibliophily and bookbinding; the history of libraries; and news.
**Ind/Abst** Am. Hist. Life (1989-); Annu. Bibliogr. Engl. Lang. Lit.; BHA : Biblio. Hist. Art.

II
**QUARTERLY - NATIONAL BOOK CENTRE BANGLADESH. Main/Corp** Jatiya Granthakendra Bamladesa. Vol. 1 (Winter 1974)-. Periodical. English. qt. National Book Centre, 67-A Purana Paltan, Dacca India. **LC** Z1003.5.B36; N37a. **DD** 028/.9/095492.

US/0006-7202
**QUARTERLY NEWS-LETTER - BOOK CLUB OF CALIFORNIA. Main/Corp** Book Club of California. **VFOAT** Quarterly News-Letter of the Book Club of California. Vol. 1 (May 1933)-. Periodical. English. Four times a year (Mar., June, Sept., Dec.). $55.00 (regular membership), $75.00 (sustaining memebership), $150.00 (patron) Comes with Book Club of California membership. Book Club of California, 312 Sutter Street, Room 510, San Francisco CA 94108. **Tel** (415)781-7532, FAX (415)781-7537. **ED** Harlan Kessel. **LC** Z1008; .B74. **DD** 028. Index available. cum. index. **Bk Rev.** (Qty: 3-4). **Ad Acc**, **Adv Mgr Tel** (415)781-7532. **Circ:** 1,000 (ctrl).
**Ind/Abst** MLA Int. Bibl. Books Artic. Mod. Lang. Lit.; Predicasts F&S Index, U. S. Annu. Ed.

US/0739-070X
**QUEBEC BOOKS.** [Quebec books]. **VFOAT** QB; Q.B. Vol. 1, No. 1 (Fall 1983)-. Periodical. English (French). sa. $6.00 US; $7.00 other. Information Center on Canada, 130 Green Acres Drive, Burlington VT 05401.

CN/0033-6491
**QUILL & QUIRE.** [Quill quire]. **VFOAT** Forthcoming Books. (1935)-. Periodical. English. mo. 48.15Can$ Canada; 75.00Can$ (includes postage) other. Quill & Quire, 70 The Esplanade, 4th Floor, Toronto Ontario M5E 1R2 Canada. **Tel** (416)360-0044, (416)946-0406. **(Subscription address:** Indas Customer Service, 35 Riviera Drive, Unit 17, Markham Ontario L3R 8N4 Canada**) LC** Z487; .Q8. **DD** 655.505. **[CCC]**. Index available. **Bk Rev**. **Ad Acc. Circ:** 7,000. ***Absorbed*** *Books for Young People (Toronto. Ont), 0835-8885.*
**Desc:** Magazine about books and the book business, featuring news, reviews of Canadian books, interviews with authors, profiles of up-and-coming writers, and

in-depth reports on all aspects of the publishing business. **Ind/Abst** AGRICOLA; Book Rev. Digest; Book Rev. Index; Can. Index; Can. Period. Index; Libr. Inf. Sci. Abstr.

CN/0824-7919
**QUILL & QUIRE. GENERAL INDEX.** [Quill quire, Gen. index]. 1973-. Periodical. English. an. Free to subscribers of the microfilm edition of Quill & Quire. McLaren Micropublishing, PO Box 972 Station F, Toronto Ontario M4Y 2N9 Canada. **DD** 070.5/0971. ***Continues*** *Quill and Quire Index.*

UK
**RARE BOOKS NEWSLETTER. Added/Corp** Library Association. Rare Books Group. (Nov. 1989)-. Newsletter. English. Three times a year. £11.00 UK and Europe; £15.00 other. Library Association/Rare Books Group, Birmingham Central Library, Arts, Language, and Literature, Birmingham BC 3HQ England. **Tel** 011 021 235 4227. **ED** Richard Ovenden. **Bk Rev. Ad Acc. Circ:** 1,300. ***Continues*** *Newsletter - Library Association, Rare Books Group, 0307-5826.*

US
**RARE BOOKS : TRENDS, COLLECTIONS, SOURCES.** ***Ceased.*** **See** Hobbies.

US/0743-1481
**RBMS NEWSLETTER.** [RBMS newsl.]. **Added/Corp** Association of College and Research Libraries. Rare Books and Manuscripts Section. **VFOAT** R.B.M.S. Newsletter. **VAT** Rare Books and Manuscripts Section Newsletter. No. 1 (April 1984)-. Periodical. English. sa. $20.00. American Library Association, 50 East Huron Street, Chicago IL 60611. **Tel** (312)944-6780, (800)545-2433, FAX (312)944-2641. **(Subscription address:** American Library Association, Subscription Department, 434 West Downer, Aurora IL 60506-9936.**)**

CN/0827-4940
**READER (VANCOUVER).** (THE READER.). [Reader]. Vol. 1 No. 1 (Dec. 1981)-. Periodical. English. qt (Jan., Apr., July, Oct., plus special Christmas issue). 10.00Can$; 15.00Can$. Duthie Books Ltd, 1701 West Third Avenue, Vancouver British Columbia, V67 1K7 Canada. **Tel** (604)732-7631, FAX (604)732-3765. **ED** Lisa Broadfoot & Keri Korteling. **DD** 028.1.
**Desc:** Publication deals with books.

FR/0257-2222
**REGISTRE DE L'ISDS (ED. SUR MICROFICHE).** **See** Publishing.

CN/0715-8130
**REPERTOIRE (UNIVERSITE DU QUEBEC A MONTREAL).** (REPERTOIRE : LIVRES ET PERIODIQUES DES PROFESSEURS.). [Repert., Livres period. profr.]. **Added/Corp** Universite du Quebec a Montreal. (1983)-. French. an. University Quebec at Montreal - Service des Publications, PO Box 8888 Succursale Centre-Ville, Montreal Quebec H3C 3P8 Canada. **Tel** (514)987-7747, FAX (514)987-3251. **DD** 013/.379/09714281. ***Continues*** *Repertoire des Productions, 0822-4722.*

US/0892-6212
**REVIEW OF TEXAS BOOKS.** [Rev. Tex. books]. Vol. 1, No. 1 (Spring 1986)-. English. qt (Feb., May, Aug., Nov.). $10.00. Review of Texas Books, PO Box 10021, Beaumont TX 77710. **Tel** (409)880-8118, FAX (409)880-2309. **DD** 028. **Bk Rev**, (Qty: 160 per year). **Pr Rev. Circ:** 200.
**Desc:** Each issue contains approximately 25 reviews of current books either published in Texas, by Texan authors published out of state, or on Texas subjects.

SP
**REVISTA DE LIBRERIA ANTIQUARIA.** **See** Library and Information Sciences.

IT
**RIVISTA DEI LIBRI, LA.** Vol. 1, No. 1 (April 1991)-. Periodical. Italian. mo. L60000 Italy; L100000 other. FSM, Abbon/C So Novara 99, 10154 Turin Italy. **Tel** 011 39 11 26171.

CN/0822-5443
**SALON DU LIVRE DE MONTREAL.** (PROGRAMME DES ACTIVITES.). [Salon livre Montr.]. **Main/Corp** Salon du Livre de Montreal. **VAT** Salon du Livre, Montreal. 21/26 Nov. 1978-. French (English, German, Spanish and Italian). an. Free. Salon du Livre de Montreal, 911 rue Jean-Talon Est, Bureau 207, Montreal Quebec H2R 1V5 Canada. **Tel** (514)277-2250. **DD** 002/.074/0114281. **Circ:** 15,000 (ctrl).

II/0036-4835
**SARVODAYA.** Began with July(?) 1952. Periodical. English. ir. Hindustan Book Agency, 17 UB Jawahar Nagar, Delhi 7 India. ***Continues*** *Khadi World.*

AT
**SCHOLARLY BOOKS IN AUSTRALIA.** ***Ceased.*** (19??)-(19??). English. Association of Australian University Presses, University of Queensland, Box 42 Post Office, St Lucia Queensland 4067 Victoria Australia. **LC** Z1033.U64; S33. **DD** 016.0705/94/0994.

AU
**SCHONSTEN BUCHER OSTERREICHS, DIE. Added/Corp** Verband der Osterreichischen Buch-, Kunst-, Musikalien-, Zeitungs- und Zeitschriftenhandler. (1953)-. Periodical. German. an. **LC** Z1035; .S33.

●UK/0963-0171
**SHEPPARD'S BOOK DEALERS IN EUROPE. VFOAT** Book Dealers in Europe. (1992)-. English. be. $48.00 (UK); $51.00 (US & Canada); $53.00 (other). Richard Joseph Publishers Ltd, Unit 2 Monks Walk, Farnham, Surrey GU9 8HT England. **Tel** 11 44 252 734347, FAX 11 44 252 734307. **Ad Acc. *Continues*** *Sheppard's European Book Dealers.*
**Desc:** Lists of Antiquarian & secondhand books dealers in the European countries.

UK/0269-1469
**SHEPPARD'S BOOK DEALERS IN NORTH AMERICA. VFOAT** Book Dealers in North America. 10th Ed. (1986/87)-. English. be. $48.00 (UK); $51.00 (US & Canada); $53.00 (other). Richard Joseph Publishers Ltd, Unit 2 Monks Walk, Farnham, Surrey GU9 8HT England. **Tel** 11 44 252 734347, FAX 11 44 252 734307. **(Subscription address:** Sheppard's Book Dealers in North America, 1 Church Road, Shedfield, Hampshire, S03 2HW England.**) LC** Z475; .B63. **DD** 381/.45002025/7. **Ad Acc. Circ:** 2,000. ***Continues*** *Book Dealers in North America, 0068-0109.*
**Desc:** Standard guide to the antiquarian book trade in North America lists all known dealers in antiquarian and secondhand books throughout the United States and Canada. Entries are grouped geographically and each shows name, address, name of proprietor, telephone number, year established, type of premises occupied, size of stock, specialties, etc.

UK/0950-0715
**SHEPPARD'S BOOK DEALERS IN THE BRITISH ISLES. VFOAT** Book Dealers in the British Isles. 12th Ed. (1987)-. English. an. $48.00 (UK); $51.00 (US & Canada); $53.00 (other). Richard Joseph Publishers Ltd, Unit 2 Monks Walk, Farnham, Surrey GU9 8HT England. **Tel** 11 44 252 734347, FAX 11 44 252 734307. **LC** Z327; .D57. **DD** 070.5/025/41. **NLM** Z 327; D598. Index available. **Ad Acc. Circ:** 5,000. ***Continues*** *Directory of Dealers in Secondhand and Antiquarian Books in the British Isles, 0070-5411.*
**Desc:** A directory of dealers in secondhand and antiquarian books in the British Isles. Twelfth edition.

SI/0080-9659
**SINGAPORE BOOK WORLD.** [Singap. book world]. **Added/Corp** National Book Development Council of Singapore. **VFOAT** Dunia Buku Singapura; Buku Dunia Singapura. (Apr. 1970)-. English (Chinese, English and Malay). an. 49.00Sing$. Chopmen Publishers Pty Ltd., 37 Jalan Peminpin, Singapore 2057 Republic of Singapore. **Tel** 011 65 3441495, FAX 011 65 3440180. **LC** Z464.S55; S57. **DD** 338.4/70705/095957. cum. index.
**Ind/Abst** Libr. Inf. Sci. Abstr.

SI/0129-4431
**SINGAPORE BOOKS IN PRINT.** [Singap. books print]. **Added/Corp** National Book Development Council of Singapore. (1978)-. English. ir. Chopmen Publishers Pty Ltd., 37 Jalan Peminpin, Singapore 2057 Republic of Singapore. **Tel** 011 65 3441495, FAX 011 65 3440180. **LC** Z3248.S5; S53. **DD** 015/.595/2.

US/8756-7202
**SMALL PRESS BOOK REVIEW, THE.** ***Suspended.*** [Small press book rev.]. Vol. 1, No. 1 (July/August 1985)-(1993). Periodical. English. qt. $28.00. Greenfield Press, PO Box 176, Southport CT 06490. **Tel** (203)268-4878. **ED** Henry Berry. **LC** Z1215; .S6. **DD** 015.73/034. Index available. **Bk Rev. Ad Acc. Circ:** 3,000 (ctrl).
**Desc:** Reviews of books, periodicals, audiocassettes and videocassettes from independent publishers.
**Ind/Abst** Book Rev. Index.

US/0148-9720
**SMALL PRESS RECORD OF BOOKS IN PRINT. VFOAT** Small Press Record of Books. (1975)-. English. an. $43.95. Dustbooks, PO Box 100, Paradise CA 95969. **Tel** (916)877-6110. **ED** Len Fulton. **LC** Z1033.L73; S52. **DD** 070.5/93. **Ad Acc. *Continues*** *Small Press Record of Books, 0361-364X.*
**Desc:** A listing of 20,000 books published by small, independent presses worldwide.

IT
**SOLATHIA.** ***Title Change.*** **VFOAT** Informatore Librario. Vol. 16 No. 1/2 (Jan.-Feb. 1986)-No. 5 (May 1992). Periodical. Italian. mo. Informatore Librario Srl, Via Trionfale 8406, 00135 Rome Italy. ***Continues*** *Informatore Librario (Rome, Italy : 1981).* ***Continued by*** *Nonsololibri.*

KO
**SOPYONG MUNHWA. Added/Corp** Hanguk Kanhaengmul Yulli Wiwonhoe. Vol. 1 (1991)-. Periodical. Korean. Hanguk Kanhaengmul Yulli Wiwonhoe, 257-3 Kongdok-Dong Mapo-Ku, Seoul 121-020 Korea. **LC** Z1035.8.K6; S67.

US/0742-8936
**SOUTH DAKOTA AUTHORS' CATALOG.** 1981-. Catalog. English. an. $5.00. 909 East 34th Street, Sioux Falls SD 57105. **Tel** (605)361-6942. **ED** Janet Leih. **Bk Rev. Circ:** 500.
**Desc:** Catalog of current books by South Dakota writers.

US/0895-254X
**SPECIALTY BOOKSELLERS DIRECTORY.** **See** Publishing.

CN/0225-9044
**SPIRALE (MONTREAL).** **See** The Arts-Art.

GW
**STICHWORT- UND TITEL-REGISTER. VFOAT** Stichwort- und Titel Register. (1987/88)-. German. an. Verlag Hase & Koehler, Postfach 2269, D-55012 Mainz Germany. **Tel** 011 49 6131 232334. ***Continues in part*** *Barsortiment Lagerkatalog.*

US/0000-0159
**SUBJECT GUIDE TO BOOKS IN PRINT.** **See** Literature-Abstracting, Bibliographies and Statistics.

CN/0710-5215
**SUOMENKIELISIA KIRJOJA. VFOAT** Finnish Books on Deposit in the Public Libraries of Metropolitan Toronto. 1st Ed. (1981)-. English (Finnish). be. Metropolitan Toronto Library Board, 789 Yonge Street, Toronto Ontario M4W 2G8 Canada. **Tel** (416)393-7134, telex 06-22232. **DD** 011/.294541.

CN/0821-1590
**SUPPLEMENT ONE, HEALTH SCIENCES BOOKS & JOURNALS.** [Suppl. one health sci. books j.]. Sept. 1982-. English. be. Ontario Medical Association, 525 University Avenue, Suite 300, Toronto Ontario M5G 2K7, Canada. **Tel** (416)599-2580. **DD** 016.61. ***Formed by the union of*** *Supplement One, Medical Books & Journals, 0821-1566* ***and*** *Supplement Two, Health Sciences Books & Journals, 0821-1574.*

SW/0039-6451
**SVENSK BOKHANDEL. Added/Corp** Svenska Bokforlaggareforeningen. Svenska Bokhandlareforeningen. (Jan. 4, 1952)-. Periodical. Swedish. wk. **LC** Z407; .S84. ***Formed by the union of*** *Bokhandlaren* ***and*** *Svensk Bokhandelstidning.*
**Ind/Abst** Child. Lit. Abstr. (19??-).

US/0193-5526
**SWANN GALLERIES, INC.** ([CATALOGUE] - SWANN GALLERIES, INC.). **Main/Corp** Swann Galleries, Inc. (19??)-. English. Forty times a year. $300.00 US, Canada and Mexico; $350.00 other. Swann Galleries Inc., 104 East 25th Street, New York NY 10010. **Tel** (212)254-4710. **LC** Z999; .S97. **Circ:** 1,000 (ctrl).
**Desc:** Book auction catalogues, including prints, maps, autographs and manuscripts, and photographica.

UK/0265-8119
**SWEDISH BOOK REVIEW. SUPPLEMENT.** 1983-. English. an. St. David's University College, Lampeter Dyfed Swedish Unit, 5A48 7ED Wales England. **Tel** 011 44 570422351. **LC** PT9368; .S92. **DD** 839.7/09.

US/1041-1453
**TAA REPORT.** (TAA REPORT / TEXTBOOK AUTHORS ASSOCIATION.). [TAA rep.]. **Added/Corp** Textbook Authors Association. **VAT** Textbook Authors Association Report. (198?)-. Periodical. English. Four times a year (Jan., Apr., July, Oct.). $30.00. Text and Academic Authors Association, PO Box 535, Orange Springs FL 32182. **Tel** (904)546-5419, FAX (904)546-5419. **DD** 371. **Bk Rev**, (Qty: 2). **Ad Acc. Circ:** 1,000 (ctrl).

US/0039-9183
**TALKING BOOK TOPICS.** **See** Physically Impaired.

CN/0225-5723
**TALKING BOOKS.** [Talking books]. 1st- Ed.; 1980-. Periodical. English. be. Free. Southwestern Regional Library System, 660 Ouellette Avenue/Suite 216, Windsor Ontario N9A 1L1 Canada. **DD** 018/.138. ctrl circ.

CN/0700-3277
**TALKING BOOKS AVAILABLE IN THE PUBLIC LIBRARIES OF METROPOLITAN TORONTO. Added/Corp** Metropolitan Toronto Library Board. 1st Ed. (1976)-. Periodical. English. $40.00 (catalog); $35.00 (supplement). Metropolitan Toronto Library Board, 789 Yonge Street, Toronto Ontario M4W 2G8 Canada. **Tel** (416)393-7134, telex 06-22232. **DD** 011. ***Supersedes*** *Talking Books in the Public Library Systems of Metropolitan Toronto, 0380-2973.*

CN/0229-4028
**TALKING BOOKS CATALOGUE SUPPLEMENT.** [Talking books cat. suppl.]. **Main/Corp** Northwestern Regional Library System (Ont.).

(197?)-. English. Northwestern Regional Library System, 910 Victoria Avenue, Thunder Bay Ontario P7C 1B4 Canada. **DD** 018/.138.

CN/0842-5116
**TALKING BOOKS (THUNDER BAY).**
(TALKING BOOKS.). [Talk. books]. **Main/Corp** Ontario Library Service, Nipigon. (1987)-. English. Talking Books Catalogue, Northwestern Regional Library System, 910 Victoria Avenue, Thunder Bay Ontario P7C 1B4 Canada. **DD** 018/.138. **Continues** *Talking Books Catalogue., 0711-7434.*

GW
**TASCHENBUCH-KATALOG.** VFOAT
Taschenbuch Katalog. German. DM135.00. Koch Neff Oetinger & Company, Schockenriedstrasse 37, W-7000 Stuttgart 80 Germany. **Tel** 7860-2215. **LC** Z2225; .T37. **DD** 015.43. **Ad Acc. Circ:** 3,000.
**Desc:** Pocket edition books listed by author, series and number, most important word, key word, and title index.

US/0739-3202
**TEXAS BOOKS IN REVIEW.** [Tex. books rev.]. **Added/Corp** Tarleton State University. North Texas State University. Center for Texas Studies. Vol. 1, (1977)-. English. Four times a year (Summer, Fall, Winter). $10.00 one year; $18.00 two years; $25.00 three years. Center for Texas Studies, PO Box 13018, North Texas Station, Denton TX 76203-3018. **Tel** (817)565-2124, FAX (817)369-8770. **ED** Jane L. Tanner. **LC** F381; .T325. **DD** 976.4. **Bk Rev,** (Qty: 125). **Ad Acc. Circ:** 500 (ctrl).
**Desc:** Publishes reviews of books by and about Texans and Texas. In addition, each issue contains articles from different regions around the state.
**Ind/Abst** Am. Humanit. Index; Annu. Bibliogr. Engl. Lang. Lit.

US/0733-8228
**TEXTBOOK NEWS.** **Ceased.** See Education.

IT
**TITOLO.** Italian. qt. L20000 Italy; L30000 other. Grafiche Benucci Srl, Via Volta, 06087 Pte S Giovanni PG Italy. **Tel** 011 39 75 39441. **Continues** *Artinumbria.*

UK
**TLS, TIMES LITERARY SUPPLEMENT MICROFORM.** [TLS. Times lit. suppl.]. No. 3488 (Jan. 2, 1969)-. Periodical. English. Times Newspapers Ltd / England, POB 7, 200 Gray's Inn Road, London WC1X 8EZ England. **Continues** *Times Literary Supplement.*

JA
**TOSHO.** (Nov. 1949)-. Periodical. Japanese. mo. $50.50. **(Subscription address:** Japan Publications Trading Company, Ltd., PO Box 5030, Tokyo International, Tokyo 100-31 Japan.**)**

US/1044-7644
**TRACKING THE UPCOMING BESTSELLERS.** **Ceased.** [Track. upcom. bestsell.]. May/June (1989)-Ceased with Jan (1993). Periodical. English. bm. Impossible Dreams Publications 85702. **DD** 011.

US/0731-5589
**TRENDS UPDATE (NEW YORK, N.Y.).**
(TRENDS UPDATE.). [Trends update]. **Added/Corp** Book Industry Study Group. Vol. 1, No. 1 (May 1982)-. Periodical. English. Four times a year. $125.00 (members); $450.00 (non-members) Comes with Book Industry Study Group membership. Book Industry Study Group, 160 5th Avenue, New York NY 10010. **Tel** (212)929-1393, FAX (212)989-7542. **LC** Z477; .T73. **Circ:** 250. **Continues in part** *Book Industry Study Group. BISG Bulletin, 0276-4806.*
**Desc:** Enhances and expands upon the statistics provided in the Trends annual, explains the forecasting techniques used in preparing the data and highlights areas of importance.

FR/0294-0035
**TROIS MOIS DE NOUVEAUTES.** [Trois mois nouv.]. (Jan./March 1982)-. Periodical. French. sa. Editions Professionnelles Livr, BP 180, 75326 Paris Cedex 06 France. **Bk Rev. Formed by the union of** *Trois Mois de Nouveautes (Edition Destinee a l'Etranger), 0245-7229* **and** *Trois Mois de Nouveautes (Edition Avec Prix Cession de Base), 0245-7237.*
**Desc:** All the references of publishing's books in print in French and French speaking for a year.

FR/0294-1090
**UN AN DE NOUVEAUTES.** [Un an nouv.]. (1981)-. French. an. 336.45F. Cercle de la Librairie, 35 rue Gregoire de Tours, F-75279 Paris Cedex 06 France. **Tel** 011 33 1 43291000, FAX 011 33 1 43296895, telex LIFRAN 270 838. Index available (price of index-430.00F). cum. index. **Formed by the union of** *An de Nouveautes (Edition Avec Prix Cession de Base), 0223-5218* **and** *An de Nouveautes (Edition Destinee a l'Etranger), 0223-5226.*
**Desc:** Listing of most titles published during the year in the French language.

US/0191-4146
**UNIVERSITY PUBLISHING.** **Ceased.** 1984. Periodical. English. qt. University of California Press, 2120 Berkeley Way, Berkeley CA 94720. **Tel** (510)642-4191, (510)642-3907, FAX (510)642-9917. **ED** William McClung, Leonard Michaels, and Christine Taylor. **LC** Z1033.U64; U54. **DD** 070.5/94. **[CCC]. Bk Rev. Ad Acc. Circ:** 1,500.
**Desc:** Independent, international, quarterly review of University Press books.
**Ind/Abst** Annu. Bibliogr. Engl. Lang. Lit. (19??-19??).

GW
**VERZEICHNIS LIEFERBARER BUCHER. ISBN-REGISTER.** VFOAT German Books in Print - ISBN Register. (1979)-. German (English; summaries and/or abstracts in English and German). ir. K.G. Saur Verlag KG, A Reed Reference Publishing Company, Part of Reed International PLC, Ortlerstrasse 8, D 81373 Munich Germany. **Tel** 011 49 89 769020, FAX 011 49 89 76902150, telex 5212067-SAUR-D. **(Subscription address:** Reed Reference Publishing Company / New Jersey, 131 Chanlaon Road, PO Box 31, New Providence NJ 07974.**)**

US/0738-9973
**WALDENBOOKS BESTSELLERS.**
**Ceased.** (WALDENBOOKS BESTSELLERS, FOR THE WEEK ENDING.). Ceased (Feb. 1989). English. wk. Waldenbooks, PO Box 10218, Stamford CT 06904.

US
**WASHINGTON POST BOOK WORLD, THE.** VFOAT Book World. Began with Vol. 1 (Sept. 10, 1967)-. Periodical. English. wk. $13.00 US; $15.60 other. Washington Post, 1150 15th Street NW, Washington DC 20071. **Tel** (202)334-6000. **ED** Brigitte Weeks. **Bk Rev. Ad Acc. Formed by the union of** *Book Week* **and** *Books Today.*
**Ind/Abst** Sci. Fict. Fantasy Book Rev. Index.

UK
**WHITAKER'S BOOKS NOW OP. MICROFORM.** 1988-. Periodical. English. an. J. Whitaker & Sons Ltd, 12 Dyott Street, London WC1A 1DF England. **Tel** 011 44 71 8368911, FAX 011 44 71 836 2909. **Continues** *Books ... Now OP - On Microfiche, 0264-097X.*

UK/0043-4868
**WHITAKER'S BOOKS OF THE MONTH & BOOKS TO COME. Ceased.** VFOAT Whitaker's Books of the Month and Books to Come. Jan. (1970)-Ceased with issue for Sept. (1992). Periodical. English. mo. J. Whitaker & Sons Ltd, 12 Dyott Street, London WC1A 1DF England. **Tel** 011 44 71 8368911, FAX 011 44 71 836 2909. **LC** Z2005; .W56. **DD** 015/.42.
**Desc:** Complete listing of new English language books added to Whitaker's database plus, forthcoming books for the next two months under author title and keyword.

UK/0265-7775
**WHITAKER'S ISBN LISTING.** VFOAT Whitaker's International Standard Book Number Listing. 1982-. Periodical. sa. £172.00 UK; £185.00 other. J. Whitaker & Sons Ltd, 12 Dyott Street, London WC1A 1DF England. **Tel** 011 44 71 8368911, FAX 011 44 71 836 2909. **Continues** *Standard Book Number Listing, 0141-6693.*

US
**WHITAKER'S NEW AND FORTHCOMING BOOKS. [MICROFORM].** (19??)-. Periodical. English. wk. £80.00. J. Whitaker & Sons Ltd, 12 Dyott Street, London WC1A 1DF England. **Tel** 011 44 71 8368911, FAX 011 44 71 836 2909.

GW
**WHO'S WHO AT THE FRANKFURT BOOK FAIR.** (1970)-. Periodical. English (German). an. $40.00. K.G. Saur Verlag KG, A Reed Reference Publishing Company, Part of Reed International PLC, Ortlerstrasse 8, D 81373 Munich Germany. **Tel** 011 49 89 769020, FAX 011 49 89 76902150, telex 5212067-SAUR-D. **LC** WMLC L 82/289.

US/1063-0686
**WILEY LIBRARIANS' NEWSLETTER.** [Wiley libr. newsl.]. **Added/Corp** John Wiley & Sons. (Nov./Dec. 1991)-. Newsletter. English. qt. Free. John Wiley & Sons, Inc., 605 Third Avenue, New York NY 10158-0012. **Tel** (212)850-6000, (212)850-6645, FAX (212)850-6088, telex 12-7063. **(Subscription address:** John Wiley & Sons / England, Baffins Lane, Chichester, West Sussex PO19 1UD England.**) DD** 015. **CODEN** WLINEU. **Continues** *Librarians' Newsletter, 0194-0112.*
**Desc:** Advance title information for professional, technical, trade and young adult books.

GW/0341-2253
**WOLFENBUTTELER NOTIZEN ZUR BUCHGESCHICHTE.** Vol. 1- May 1976-. Periodical. German (English and French). sa. DM54.00. Dr. Ernst Hauswedell & Co. Verlag, Rosenbergstrasse 113, D 70193 Stuttgart Germany. **Tel** 011 49 711 638265. **(Subscription address:** Otto Harrassowitz Verlag,

Postfach 2929, Taunusstr 14, D-6200 Wiesbaden 1 West Germany**) LC** Z119; .W64. cum. index. **Bk Rev. Ad Acc. Circ:** 450.

KO
**WOLGAN TOKSO.** VFOAT Tokso. Periodical. Korean. W5,000. Wolgan Tokso, 73 Soron-dong, Chongno-ku, Seoul South Korea. **LC** Z1003.5.K8; W64.

US/0192-9666
**WORTHWHILE PRICE GUIDE, THE.** V. 1- 1979-. Periodical. English. an. $27.95. Worthwhile Books, PO Box 2143, Riverside CA 92516. **ED** L Hill and S Sykora. **LC** Z1000.5; .W67. **DD** 018/.4/0973.

# REAL ESTATE

US
**36 CITIES : REAL ESTATE FORECAST AND REVIEW.** (1987)-. English. an. Gavilon Publishing & Information Services, 109 Grant Street/Suite 300, Denver CO 80203.
**Desc:** Gives profiles and forecasts of 36 top U.S. cities.

US/0746-2751
**ACCREDITED RESIDENT MANAGER NEWS / INSTITUTE OF REAL ESTATE MANAGEMENT OF THE NATIONAL ASSOCIATION OF REALTORS.** Title Change. See Business-General Management.

CN/0701-0516
**ACTUALITE IMMOBILIERE.** [Actual. immobil.]. **Added/Corp** Universite du Quebec a Montreal. Vol. 1 (Oct. 1976)-. Periodical. French. qt. 32.00Can$. University Quebec at Montreal - Service des Publications, PO Box 8888 Succursale Centre-Ville, Montreal Quebec H3C 3P8 Canada. **Tel** (514)987-7747, FAX (514)987-3251. **ED** Marcel Lizee. **DD** 333.3/3/09714. **Bk Rev. Ad Acc. Circ:** 4,000 (ctrl).
**Desc:** Studies in real estate applied to Montreal, Quebec, and Canada.
**Ind/Abst** Point Repere (1983-).

US
**AD VALOREM PROPERTY TAX LEVEY REPORT. Added/Corp** Michigan. State Tax Commission. **VFOAT** State Equalized Valuations & Average Tax Rate Data, City Tax Levies, Village Tax Levies, Township Tax levies; State Equalized Valuations and Average Tax Rate Data, City Tax Levies, Village Tax Levies, Township Tax Levies. (1984)-. Periodical. **Continues** *State Equalized Valuations & Average Tax Rate Data, City Tax Levies, Village Tax Levies, Township Tax Levies, E.*

US/0198-9448
**ADVANCED REAL ESTATE LAW COURSE.** See Law.

CN/0701-7502
**AGRICULTURAL REAL ESTATE VALUES IN ALBERTA.** [Agric. real estate values Alta.]. **Main/Corp** Alberta. Alberta Agriculture. Resource Economics Branch. **Added/Corp** Alberta. Alberta Agriculture. Resource Economics Branch. Alberta. Alberta Agriculture. Production and Resource Economics Branch. Alberta. Alberta Agriculture. Production Economics Branch. **VFOAT** Agriculture Real Estate Values in Alberta. (1976)-. English. **LC** HD319.A4; A29b. **DD** 333.3/35/097123. **Continues** *Rural Real Estate Values in Alberta, 0383-3585.*

GW/0001-1673
**AIZ. ALLGEMEINE IMMOBILIEN-ZEITUNG.** VFOAT Allgemeine Immobilien-Zeitung (1960). (1960)-. Periodical. German. mo. R D M Verlags GmbH, Moenckebergstr 27, W-2000 Hamburg 1 Germany. **UDC** 332.

US/0277-3252
**ALI-ABA COURSE OF STUDY. ABA SECTION OF TAXATION, ANNUAL OF TAXATION, ANNUAL ADVANCED STUDY SESSIONS, ADVANCED TAX PLANNING FOR REAL ESTATE TRANSACTIONS: MATERIALS.** See Law.

US/0270-9708
**ALI-ABA COURSE OF STUDY. FOREIGN INVESTMENT IN U.S. REAL ESTATE : MATERIALS.** VAT American Law Institute-American Bar Association Course of Study. Foreign Investment in United States Real Estate. Periodical. English. an. American Law Institute, 4025 Chestnut Street, Philadelphia PA 19104-3099. **Tel** (215)243-1661, (800)253-6397, FAX (215)243-1664. **LC** KF573; .A923. **DD** 346.7304/3.

US/0191-2003
**ALI-ABA COURSE OF STUDY : MODERN REAL ESTATE TRANSACTIONS : MATERIALS.** See Law.

US/0190-9347
**ALI-ABA COURSE OF STUDY. REAL ESTATE CONDOMINIUMS AND PUDS : MATERIALS.** See Law.

US/0730-4722
**ALI-ABA COURSE OF STUDY. REAL ESTATE SYNDICATIONS. MATERIALS.** See Law.

US/1055-2472
**ALI-ABA REAL ESTATE COURSE MATERIALS JOURNAL.** **Added/Corp** American Law Institue. America Bar Association. **VAT** American Law Institue, America Bar Association Real Estate Course Materials Journal. (1991)-. Periodical. English. bm. $30.00. American Law Institute, 4025 Chestnut Street, Philadelphia PA 19104-3099. **Tel** (215)243-1661, (800)253-6397, FAX (215)243-1664.

CN/0703-9743
**ALL ABOUT HOMES.** Apr. 15, 1977-. Periodical. English. wk. 0.25Can$ per issue. All About Homes, 1262 Don Mills Road, Don Mills Ontario M3B 2W7. **DD** 333.3/37/09713541.

US/0892-0850
**ANDREWSREPORT (INDIANAPOLIS, IND.).** ***Ceased.*** (ANDREWSREPORT.). [Andrewsreport]. **VFOAT** Andrews Report. Vol. 1, No. 1 (Jan. 1987)-(19??). Periodical. English. mo. Report Communications, 9595 Whitley Drive, PO Box 80209, Indianapolis IN 46280. **Tel** (800)344-5058, (317)844-9024, FAX (317)848-6953. **ED** William R Wilburn. **DD** 338. **[CCC]**. Index available. **Bk Rev**. **Circ:** 1,000.
**Desc:** Newsletter for the owners, developers, managers and marketers of small shopping centers.

CN/0828-3117
**ANNUAL REPORT / BRITISH COLUMBIA PLACE LTD.** [Annu. rep. - B.C. Place Ltd.]. **Main/Corp** British Columbia Place Ltd. English. an. University of British Columbia 2075 Wesbrook Place, Vancouver British Columbia V6T 1W5 Canada. **LC** HD319.B8; B76A. **DD** 338.7/6133338/0971.

US/0092-413X
**ANNUAL REPORT - NEW MEXICO. REAL ESTATE COMMISSION.** (ANNUAL REPORT.). **Main/Corp** New Mexico. Real Estate Commission. English. an. New Mexico Real Estate Commission, Room 1031, 505 Marquette NW, Albuquerque NM 87101. **LC** HD266.N6; N47A. **DD** 353.9/789/008243.

CN/0709-258X
**ANNUAL REPORT OF THE LAND VALUE APPRAISAL COMMISSION.** (ANNUAL REPORT - LAND VALUE APPRAISAL COMMISSION.). **Main/Corp** Manitoba. Land Value Appraisal Commission. (1966)-. English. an. Lanark, Leeds and Grenville Information BAnk, Box 172, Smiths Falls Ontario K7A 4T1. **LC** HD1387; .M363a. **DD** 354/.7127/00724213.

AT
**ANNUAL REPORT OF THE REAL ESTATE AND BUSINESS AGENTS SUPERVISORY BOARD FOR THE PERIOD 1ST JULY ... TO 30TH JUNE ... (WESTERN AUSTRALIA).** **Main/Corp** Western Australia. Real Estate and Business Agents Supervisory Board. English. an. **LC** HD1039.W47; W436A. **DD** 354.9410082/43.

AT
**ANNUAL REPORT / SETTLEMENT AGENTS SUPERVISORY BOARD.** **Main/Corp** Western Australia. Settlement Agents Supervisory Board. (July 1981)-. English. an. Settlement Agents Supervisory Board, Perth WA Australia. **LC** HD1039.W47; W437a. **DD** 354.9410082/43.

CN/0842-4632
**ANNUAL REPORT / THE MANITOBA FARM LANDS OWNERSHIP BOARD.** See Agriculture.

US/8756-1387
**APARTMENT & CONDOMINIUM NEWS.** [Apartm. condomin. news]. **VFOAT** Apartment and Condominium News. Periodical. English. bm. $20.00. Relocation Consultants, Inc. of Chicago, 579 West North Avenue, Suite 302, Elmhurst IL 60126. **DD** 333.

US/0744-9143
**APARTMENT MANAGEMENT NEWSLETTER.** **VFOAT** Apartment Newsletter. (19??)-. Periodical. English. Twelve times a year. $95.00. Apartment Management Publishing Company, Inc., 122 East 42nd Street, Suite 1700, New York NY 10168. **Tel** (212)966-8957. **ED** Harold Mann. **Bk Rev**. **Ad Acc**. **Circ:** 5,000.
**Desc:** Practical information and news for better cost-saving apartment management, renting and marketing, finance, tenant relations, maintenance and legal matters.

US/0003-7060
**APPRAISAL DIGEST.** ***Suspended.*** [Appraisal dig.]. **VFOAT** Appraisal Digest of the New York State Society of Real Estate Appraisers of the New York State Association of Realtors, Inc. Vol. 1 (1950)-(?). Periodical. English. qt. $5.00. New York State Society of Real Estate Appraisers, 107 Washington Avenue, PO Box 122, Albany NY 12260.

US/0003-7087
**APPRAISAL JOURNAL, THE.** [Appraisal j.]. **Added/Corp** American Institute of Real Estate Appraisers. Appraisal Institute (U.S.). Vol. 7, No. 2, (1939)-. Periodical. English. Four times a year (Jan., Apr., July, Oct.). Free (members & candidates of appraisal institute); $35..00 (non-members). Appraisal Institute, 875 North Michigan Avenue, Suite 2400, Chicago IL 60601-7601. **Tel** (312)335-4100, FAX (312)335-4400. **LC** HD251; .A7. **DD** 333.33205. **CODEN** APPJA5. Index available. cum. index. **Bk Rev**, (Qty: 12-15/yr). **Circ:** 38,000 (ctrl). available on microfilm and microfiche from University Microfilms International (UMI); available in print. Documents available from UMI Article Clearinghouse. ***Continues*** *Journal of the American Institute of Real Estate Appraisers; Real Estate Appraiser.*
**Desc:** Professional articles on real estate appraisal or closely related subjects.
**Ind/Abst** ABI/INFORM Glob. Ed.; ABI Inform Ondisc (Oct. 1971-); Acad. Search (Jan. 1993-); Account. Tax Datab. (Oct. 1971-); Account. Art.; AGRICOLA; Bus. ASAP (1992-) [Full Txt.]; Bus. Index (1985-); Bus. Period. Index; Bus. Source (Jan. 1993-); Fed. Tax Artic.; Gen. BusinessFile (1985-); Gen. Period. Index (1985-); INFO-SOUTH Abstr.; Mag. Search; Manage. Contents; PAIS Int. Print (1991-); Trade Ind. ASAP [Full Txt.]; Trade Ind. Index [Full Txt.]; UMI ABI/Inform--Bus. Period. Ondisc (Jan. 1988-) [Full Txt.]; Vocat. Search (Jan. 1993-); Wilson Bus. Abstr.

US/1041-1585
**APPRAISAL REVIEW & MORTGAGE UNDERWRITING JOURNAL.** [Appraisal rev. mort. underwrit. j.]. **Added/Corp** National Association of Review Appraisers & Mortgage Underwriters (U.S.). **VFOAT** Appraisal Review and Mortgage Underwriting Journal. Vol. 8, No. 1 (Summer 1985)-. Periodical. English. sa. $45.00. National Association of Review Appraisers, 8383 East Evans Road, Scottsdale AZ 85260. **Tel** (602)998-3000. **ED** Joe Iacuzzo. **LC** HD1387; .A67. **DD** 333.33/2/05. **Ad Acc, Adv Mgr:** Editor. ctrl circ. ***Continues*** *Appraisal Review Journal, 0195-4407.*
**Desc:** For the review of the appraisal/mortgage underwriting business.

US/1054-5999
**APPRAISER NEWS.** (APPRAISER NEWS /APPRAISAL INSTITUTE.). [Apprais. news]. **Added/Corp** Appraisal Institute (U.S.). Vol. 1, No. 1, (Jan. 15, 1991)-. Periodical. English. Twelve times a year. Free ( members & candidates of appraisal institute); $20.00 (non-members). Appraisal Institute, 875 North Michigan Avenue, Suite 2400, Chicago IL 60601-7601. **Tel** (312)335-4100, FAX (312)335-4400. **LC** HD251; .A66. ***Formed by the union of*** *Appraiser, 0003-7095* ***and*** *Briefs (Society of Real Estate Appraisers), 0899-8779.*

US/8755-4348
**APPRAISERS' INFORMATION EXCHANGE, THE.** (THE APPRAISERS' INFORMATION EXCHANGE / INTERNATIONAL SOCIETY OF APPRAISERS.). [Appraisers inf. exch.]. Periodical. English. bm. International Society of Appraisers, PO Box 726, Hoffman Estates IL 60195. **Tel** (708)882-0706. **ED** Maurice E Fry. **DD** 332. **Bk Rev**. **Ad Acc**. **Circ:** 2,500 (ctrl).
**Desc:** Newsletter about appraisers, appraising of appraisals pertaining to personal property of all types for all reasons.

US/1048-6534
**AREA DEVELOPMENT SITES & FACILITY PLANNING.** [Area dev. sites facil. plan.]. **VFOAT** Area Development Sites and Facility Planning; Area Development. Periodical. English. mo. Halcyon Business Publications, 400 Post Avenue, Westbury NY 11590. **Tel** (516)829-8990, FAX (516)829-8230. **LC** HD58; .A8. **DD** 658.2/1/05. available on microfilm from University Microfilms International (UMI). ***Continues*** *Area Development, 0004-0908.*

US/1064-1092
**AREEA REPORT, THE.** [AREEA rep.]. **Added/Corp** Appraisal and Real Estate Economics Associates, Inc. **VFOAT** AREEA Report for South Florida. **VAT** Appraisal and Real Estate Economics Associates Report. (19??)-. Periodical. English. Ten times a year (every 5 to 6 weeks). $250.00. Appraisal & Real Estate Economic, 9400 South Dadeland Boulevard, Sutie PH 1, Miami FL 33156. **Tel** (305)661-1571. **ED** David M. Diabray (phone: (305)670-0001 ext. 258). **DD** 333. **Pr Rev.** ctrl circ.

US/0199-9206
**ARIZONA REALTOR DIGEST.** (ARIZONA REALTOR DIGEST / ARIZONA ASSOCIATION OF REALTORS.). Vol. 1, No. 1 (Mar./Apr. 1979)-. Periodical. English. bm. $6.00 US and Canada. Arizona Realtors Subsidiary Corporation, 4414 North 19th Avenue/Suite R, Phoenix AZ 85015. **Tel** (602)248-7787, FAX (602)277-8423. **ED** Sue Scholz. **LC** HD266.A7; A76. **DD** 333.33/09791. **Ad Acc**. **Circ:** 21,000 (ctrl).
**Desc:** Information and articles about the Realtor Organization and the industry for members of the Arizona Association of Realtors and its local boards.

US/0731-0277
**ASSESSMENT DIGEST.** ***Title Change.*** **See** Public Administration-Public Finance and Taxation.

CN/0225-9761
**AT HOME IN CANADA'S CAPITAL.** [home Can. cap.]. **VAT** At Home (Ottawa). V. 1- Sept. 1979-. Periodical. English. mo. $8.00. At Home in Canada's Capital, Suite 2, 430 Maclaren Street, Ottawa K2P 0M8. **DD** 643/.12/0971384. ctrl circ.

US
**AUDIT REPORT, DEPARTMENT OF INSURANCE, TENNESSEE REAL ESTATE COMMISSION.** **Main/Corp** Tennessee. Division of State Audit. **Added/Corp** Tennessee. Real Estate Commission. (19??)-. English. an. Free on request. Tennessee Division of the State Auditor, 505 Deadrick Street, JK Polk State Office, Nashville TN 37243. **Tel** (615)741-2501. **LC** HD266.T2; T45a. **DD** 353.9/768/008243.

●US/1071-5142
**AUSTIN REAL ESTATE FINANCE SOURCEBOOK.** (1994)-. English. Real Estate Finance Sourcebooks, 14340 Memorial Drive, Suite 118, Houston TX 77079.

US/0749-5714
**BAHAMAS DATELINE.** **See** Business-Investments.

US/0005-5409
**BANKER & TRADESMAN.** (BANKER & TRADESMAN : MASSACHUSETTS' REAL ESTATE, BANKING, AND COMMERCIAL WEEKLY.). **VFOAT** Banker and Tradesman. Vol. 24, No. 1 (Feb. 5, 1896)-. Periodical. English. wk (Wed.). $176.00. Warren Publishing Corporation, 210 South Street, Boston MA 02111. **Tel** (617)426-4495, FAX (617)423-1335. **ED** Nena Groskin. **Ad Acc, Adv Mgr:** Jeffery Keller. **Circ:** 8,000. available on microfilm from University Microfilms International (UMI). ***Continues*** *Banker and Tradesman and Massachusetts Law Reporter.*
**Desc:** Publishes news articles pertaining to real estate and banking in Massachusetts. Also abstracts of official public records such as deed transfers and mortgage filings, tax liens, and bankruptcies.

US/0891-5539
**BAYSTATE REALTOR.** [Baystate realt.]. Vol. 62, No. 9 (Sept. 1986)-. Periodical. English. mo (except July and Nov.). $30.00. Massachusetts Association of Realtors, 256 Second Avenue, PO Box 9036, Waltham MA 02254-9036. **Tel** (617)890-4919. **ED** Chris LaFontaine. **DD** 333. **Ad Acc, Adv Mgr:** Bonnie Michaud, **Tel** (508)887-9371. **Circ:** 20,000. ***Continues*** *Baystate Realtor Hi-Lites, 0746-3146.*
**Desc:** Designed to provide association and industry news, including market reports, educational opportunities, articles on new trends, and stories on government and regulatory issues affecting the real estate industry.

US/0893-9519
**BERNARD ZICK'S REAL ESTATE FINANCING & MORTGAGE REPORT.** **See** Business-Banking and Finance.

US/0738-2170
**BOMA EXPERIENCE EXCHANGE REPORT.** **Added/Corp** Building Owners and Managers Association International. **VFOAT** B.O.M.A. Experience Exchange Report; BOMA Report; BOMA Experience Report for Downtown & Suburban Office Buildings; Experience Exchange Report; Experience Exchange Report. **VAT** Building Owners and Managers Association Experience Exchange Report. (1982)-. English. an (July). $145.00 (members), $277.00 (non-members) US; $296.00 (non-members) Canada; $$289.00 (non-members) others. Building Owners and Managers Association, 1201 New York Avenue Northwest, Suite 300, Washington DC 20005. **Tel** (202)408-2662, FAX (202)371-0181. **ED** Sandra Beard and Ellen Ku. **LC** TX980; .N33. **DD** 333.33/8. **Circ:** 11,000 (ctrl). ***Continues*** *Downtown and Suburban Office Building Experience Exchange Report, 0196-982X.*

**Desc:** The most complete income and expense analysis for over 4,000 office buildings in North America, by city, size, height and age.

US/0193-3221
**BUSINESS OPPORTUNITIES JOURNAL.** **See** Business-Investments.

US/8755-3732
**CAAS NEWS.** (CAAS NEWS : COMPUTER ASSISTED APPRAISAL SECTION NEWS.). [CAAS news]. **Added/Corp** International Association of Assessing Officers. Computer Assisted Appraisal Section. **VFOAT** C.A.A.S. News; Computer Assisted Appraisal Section News. (Summer 1984)-. Periodical. English. Four times a year. $40.00 Comes with International Association of Assessing Officers Computer Assisted Apprasial Section membership. International Association of Assessing Officers, 130 East Randolph Street, Suite 850, Chicago IL 60601. **Tel** (312)819-6100. **DD** 336. **Circ:** 1,000 (ctrl). ***Continues*** *EDP.*

US/1042-8631
**CAIN AND SCOTT APARTMENT INVESTMENT STUDY, THE.** [Cain Scott apartm. investm. study]. (1989)-. Periodical. English. qt. $250.00. Cain and Scott Inc, 220 West Mercer 407, Seattle WA 98119. **Tel** (206)285-7100. **DD** 333. ***Continues*** *Cain and Scott Apartment Market Study, 0882-4185.*

US/0896-6435
**CAIN AND SCOTT COMMERCIAL INVESTMENT STUDY, THE.** [Cain Scott commer. investm. study]. Vol. 1, No. 1, (1987). English. $150.00. Cain and Scott Inc, 220 West Mercer 407, Seattle WA 98119. **Tel** (206)285-7100. **DD** 332.

US/1043-3678
**CAIN AND SCOTT MARKET SUMMARY, THE.** ***Title Change.*** (THE CAIN AND SCOTT MARKET SUMMARY.). [Cain Scott mark. summ.]. **Added/Corp** Cain and Scott, Inc. **VFOAT** Market Summary. Vol. 12, No. 1, Winter/Spring (1989)-(1992). Periodical. English. sa (published Summer and Fall). Cain and Scott Inc, 220 West Mercer 407, Seattle WA 98119. **Tel** (206)285-7100. **DD** 332. ***Continues*** *Cain and Scott Apartment Letter, 0882-4177.* ***Continued by*** *Apartment Letter, 1067-1498.*

US/1058-8205
**CALIFORNIA LAND USE LAW & POLICY REPORTER.** **See** Law.

US/0008-1450
**CALIFORNIA REAL ESTATE (1975).** (CALIFORNIA REAL ESTATE.). **Added/Corp** California Association of Realtors. Vol. 56, (Dec. 1975)-. Periodical. English. mo (Jan./Feb. & July/Aug. iss. combined). $12.00 (one year), $22.00 (two year) US; $44.00 (one year), $82.00 (two year) other. California Association of Realtors, 525 South Virgil Avenue, Los Angeles CA 90020. **Tel** (213)739-8320. **ED** Anne Framroze. Index available. cum. index. **Ad Acc, Adv Mgr:** Cindi Richardson, **Tel** (212)739-8321. **Circ:** 105,000. ***Continues*** *California Real Estate Magazine, 0732-2194.*
**Desc:** Information that serves to improve the business approach, professionalism and day-to-day procedures of real estate agents with generic and how-to articles.
**Ind/Abst** Calif. Period. Index (19??-).

US/1053-4164
**CALIFORNIA REAL ESTATE TRENDS. FORECAST FOR HOUSING AND THE ECONOMY.** [Calif. real estate trends, Forecast hous. econ.]. **Added/Corp** California Association of Realtors. **VFOAT** Trends, California Real Estate. Forecast for Housing and the economy; Forecast for Housing and the Economy. (19??)-. English. mo. $54.00 Cal. Association of Realtors affiliates; $38.00 C.A.R. members; $70.00 other. California Association of Realtors, 525 South Virgil Avenue, Los Angeles CA 90020. **Tel** (213)739-8320. **DD** 333.

US/1052-2921
**CALIFORNIA REAL PROPERTY JOURNAL.** **See** Law.

US/0748-2396
**CAMP RESORT LAW REPORT.** **See** Law.

US/1052-1208
**CANADA REGISTER.** (Nov. 1990)-. English. $95.00. Mead Ventures Inc, PO Box 44952, Phoenix AZ 85064. **Tel** (602)234-0044, FAX (602)234-0076. Index available.
**Desc:** A unique directory describing more than 100 Canadian real estate-related companies with activities in the United States. Listings of the names, addresses, and phone and fax numbers of more than 200 Canadian real estate executives.

CN/0827-2697
**CANADIAN APPRAISER, THE.** [Can. appraiser]. **Added/Corp** Appraisal Institute of Canada. **VFOAT** Evaluateur Canadien. Vol. 28, Book 2 (May 1984)-. Periodical. English (French; summaries and/or abstracts in French). Four times a year (Mar., June, Sept., Dec.). 20.00Can$ (one year); 35.00Can$ (two years). Appraisal Institute of Canada, 1111 Portage Avenue, Winnipeg Manitoba R3G 0S8 Canada. **Tel** (204)783-2224, FAX (204)783-5575. **ED** Tanya Dube. **DD** 333.33/2/0971. Index available. **Bk Rev. Ad Acc. Circ:** 6,600 (ctrl). available on microfiche from University Microfilms International (UMI). Documents available from UMI Article Clearinghouse. ***Continues*** *A I M, Appraisal Institute Magazine, 0383-6649.*
**Desc:** Provides a record of individual opinions concerning appraisal theory and practice as well as additional related subjects.
**Ind/Abst** ABI/INFORM Glob. Ed.; ABI Inform Ondisc (Aug. 1980-).

CN/0709-0757
**CANADIAN PROFESSIONAL REAL ESTATE DIRECTORY FOR THE PROVINCE OF BRITISH COLUMBIA.** (1979)-. Directory. English. **DD** 333.3/3/025711.

CN/0823-8197
**CANADIAN REAL ESTATE (DON MILLS. 1983).** ***Title Change.*** (CANADIAN REAL ESTATE.). [Can. real estate]. **Added/Corp** Canadian Real Estate Association. **VFOAT** L'Immobilier Canadien; Immobilier Canadien. **VAT** Immobilier Canadien (1983). (1983)-Sept. (1992). Periodical. English (French). qt. Canadian Real Estate Association, 320 Queen Street, Suite 2100, Ottawa Ontario K1R 5A3 Canada. **Tel** (613)234-3372. **DD** 333.33/0971. ***Continues*** *Panorama (Don Mills, Ont.), 0713-3847.* ***Continued by*** *Canadian Realtor News, 1193-8021.*

●CN/1193-8021
**CANADIAN REALTOR NEWS.** (THE CANADIAN REALTOR NEWS / LE REALTOR CANADIEN.). [Can. realtor news]. **Added/Corp** Canadian Real Estate Association. **VFOAT** Realtor Canadien; Realtor Canadien. (Oct. 1992)-. Periodical. English (French). Twelve times a year. 40.00Can$. Canadian Real Estate Association, 320 Queen Street, Suite 2100, Ottawa Ontario K1R 5A3 Canada. **Tel** (613)234-3372. **DD** 333.33/0971/05. ***Continues*** *Canadian Real Estate (1983)., 0823-8197.*

CN/0381-7687
**CANADIAN REALTY NEWS (EDITION FRANCAISE).** (CANADIAN REALTY NEWS.). V. 1-May 1974-. Periodical. French. ir. Tankoos Yarmon Ltd, 8 Est rue King, Toronto Ontario M5C 1B5 Canada. **DD** 333/.00971.

US/0742-5678
**CAROLINA REAL ESTATE JOURNAL.** ***Ceased.*** (198?)-Vol. 8, No. 4 (Apr. 1993). Periodical. English. sm. Shaw Publishing Inc, 128 S Tryon Street, Suite 2200, Charlotte NC 28202. **Tel** (704)375-7404, (407)231-7788.

US
**CENTERS; UPSCALE SPECIALTY, URBAN MIXED-USE AND FESTIVAL.** English. an. $195.00 (prepaid); $205.00 (if invoiced). Jomurpa Publishing Corporation, PO Box 1708, 7 South Myrtle Avenue, Spring Valley NY 10977. **Tel** (914)426-0040, FAX (914)426-0802. **ED** Murray Shor. **Ad Acc.**
**Desc:** Directory of niche market of shopping centers. Included are upscale specialty centers, urban mixed-use and festival. Data provided on location, tenants, developer information and other pertinent information for each listing.

US/0890-4154
**CHANGING HOMES.** ***Ceased.*** [Chang. homes]. Vol. 1, No. 1 (Summer 1986)-(1988). Periodical. English. qt. 70 East Sunrise Highway, Suite 409, Valley Stream NY 11581.

UK/0264-049X
**CHARTERED SURVEYOR WEEKLY.** [Chart. surv. wkly.]. **Added/Corp** Royal Institution of Chartered Surveyors. Vol. 1, No. 1 (Oct. 28, 1982)-. Periodical. English. wk. £42.00 UK; $105.00 US. RICS Journals Ltd, PO Box 87, 1 Pemberton Row, London EC4P 4HL England. **Tel** 01-353-2300, FAX 01-583-2253, telex 25212 BUILDA G. **ED** C Branson. **LC** TA501; .R6252. **DD** 333/.00941. Index available. cum. index. **Bk Rev. Ad Acc. Circ:** 48,104 (ctrl). available in microform. ***Continues*** *Chartered Surveyor, 0009-1936.*
**Desc:** A magazine for Britain's real estate industry. It covers building, agriculture, as well as commercial real estate.
**Ind/Abst** Archit. Period. Index (1982-); Ecol. Abstr. (?-?); Infomat Int. Bus.; Int. Civil Eng. Abstr.; Leis. Recreat. Tour. Abstr.

US/0743-5630
**CIT REAL ESTATE REPORT.** **VFOAT** C.I.T. Real Estate Report; Real Estate Report. Vol. 1, No. 1 (May 1984)-. Periodical. English. mo.

US
**CITRUS DEED REPORT.** English. mo. $650.00. Florida New Business Report, 7402 North 56th Street, Suite 895, Tampa FL 33680. **Tel** (813)988-8148, FAX (813)988-8422. **ED** Ken Guthery. **Circ:** n.
**Desc:** A compilation of all real estate sales giving granter, grantee, address, legal description, O R book, page, selling price and mortgage amount.

AT
**CITYSCOPE - BRISBANE EDITION.** English. Three times a year (Jan., May, Sept.). 825.00Aus$. Cityscope Publications, PO Box 807, Manly New South Wales 2095 Australia. **Tel** 011 61 2 957 4811, FAX 011 61 2 922 2247.

AT
**CITYSCOPE - CANBERRA.** English. Three times a year (Jan., May, Sept.). 795.00Aus$. Cityscope Publications, PO Box 807, Manly New South Wales 2095 Australia. **Tel** 011 61 2 957 4811, FAX 011 61 2 922 2247.

AT
**CITYSCOPE - GOLD COAST EDITION.** English. Three times a year (Mar., July, Nov.). 790.00Aus$. Cityscope Publications, PO Box 807, Manly New South Wales 2095 Australia. **Tel** 011 61 2 957 4811, FAX 011 61 2 922 2247.

AT
**CITYSCOPE - SPRING HILL EDITION.** English. Three times a year (Feb., June, Oct.). 710.00Aus$. Cityscope Publications, PO Box 807, Manly New South Wales 2095 Australia. **Tel** 011 61 2 957 4811, FAX 011 61 2 922 2247.

US/1047-6083
**CLAYTON-FILLMORE REPORT, THE.** (THE CLAYTON-FILLMORE REPORT : PERSPECTIVES ON ECONOMICS AND REAL ESTATE.). [Clayton-Fillmore rep.]. **VFOAT** Clayton Fillmore Report. (1990)-. Periodical. English. mo. $175.00 US; $205.00 other. Clayton-Fillmore Limited, 2849 West 23rd Avenue, Denver CO 80211. **Tel** (303)433-5323, FAX (303)861-2610. **ED** Howard Treibutz. **DD** 333. Index available. **Bk Rev,** (Qty: 12/yr). **Circ:** 1,000. ***Continues*** *Robert Fuller Real Estate Market Report.*
**Desc:** Special report for real estate investors, lenders and developers.

US/0748-2019
**COASTAL BEND APARTMENT & RENTAL GUIDE.** **VFOAT** Coastal Bend Apartment and Rental Guide; Apartment & Rental Guide. (Feb 1984)-. Periodical. English. mo. Free. Coastal Bend Apartment & Rental Guide, PO Box 72925, Corpus Christi TX 78472. **DD** 643.

●US/1060-4383
**COLORADO REAL ESTATE JOURNAL.** (1992)-. Periodical. English. Twenty-six times a year. $50.00. Colorado Real Estate Journal, 1630 Welton Street, Suite 300, Denver CO 80202. **Tel** (303)623-1148.

US/0887-4778
**COMMERCIAL INVESTMENT REAL ESTATE JOURNAL.** [Commer. investm. real estate j.]. **Added/Corp** Realtors National Marketing Institute. Commercial-Investment Real Estate Council. Vol. 5, No. 1 (Winter 1986)-. Periodical. English. qt. $32.00 US & Canada; $38.00 other. Commercial Investment Real Estate Council, 430 North Michigan Avenue, Suite 600, Chicago IL 60611. **Tel** (312)321-4470. **LC** HD1361; .C65. **DD** 332.63/24/05. Documents available from UMI Article Clearinghouse. ***Continues*** *Commercial Investment Journal, 0744-6446.*
**Ind/Abst** ABI/INFORM Glob. Ed.; ABI Inform Ondisc (Winter 1985).

US/0736-0517
**COMMERCIAL LEASE LAW INSIDER.** **See** Law.

US/0898-5634
**COMMERCIAL LEASING LAW & STRATEGY.** **See** Law.

US/1043-1675
**COMMERCIAL PROPERTY NEWS.** [Commer. prop. news]. Vol. 3, No. 7 (April 1, 1989)-. Periodical. English. sm. $70.00 US; $176.00 Canada & Mexico; $240.00 other. Miller Freeman Inc., 600 Harrison Street, San Francisco CA 94107. **Tel** (415)905-2337, FAX (415)905-2240, telex 278273. **(Subscription address:** Sunbelt Fulfillment Services, PO Box 41530, Nashville TN 37204.) **LC** WMLC 93/1023; HD1393.25; .C66. **DD** 333. ***Continues*** *Real Estate Times (New York, N.Y.), 0893-1968.*

US/0882-7664
**COMMERCIAL REAL ESTATE BROKERS DIRECTORY, THE.** [Commer. real estate brok. dir.]. 1985-. Directory. English. an. $77.00. Whole World Publishing Inc, 400 Lake Cook Road/Suite 207, Deerfield IL 60015. **Tel** (312)945-8050. **LC** HD166; .C65. **DD** 333.33/025/73.

US/0192-3897
**COMMERCIAL REAL ESTATE LEASES.** [Commer. real estate leases]. **Added/Corp** Practising Law Institute. (19??)-. English. an. $77.00. Practising Law Institute, 810 Seventh Avenue, New York NY

10019-5818. **Tel** (212)765-5700, FAX (212)581-4670 general correspondence, (212)265-4742 orders and billing inquiries. **LC** KF593.C6; C65. **DD** 346/.73/04346. Index available. cum. index.

●US/1062-5879
**COMMERCIAL REAL ESTATE PROPERTY DIRECTORY.** (1992)-. Directory. English. mo. $300.00. Kathleen Moore, 5560 Wilmin Way, Jacksonville FL 32207.

US/0010-3098
**COMMERCIAL RECORD (SOUTH WINDSOR, CT.), THE.** (THE COMMERCIAL RECORD.). (1882)-. Periodical. English. wk. $208.00. Commercial Record, PO Box 902, South Windsor CT 06074-0902. **Tel** (203) 644-3489, FAX (203) 644-7363. **ED** Nena Groskind. **Bk Rev**. **Ad Acc**. **Circ:** 4,000 (ctrl).
**Desc:** Information from real estate deeds: sales price, seller, buyer, mortgage, address, liens, attachments, bankruptcies, new corps and building permits.

US/1066-0933
**COMPARATIVE STATISTICS OF INDUSTRIAL AND OFFICE REAL ESTATE MARKETS.** [Comp. stat. ind. off. real estate mark.]. **Added/Corp** Society of Industrial and Office Realtors. Landauer (Firm). (1991)-. English. an. $45.00 (SIOR members), $60.00 (nonmembers). Society of Industrial and Office Realtors, 777 14th Street Northwest, Suite 400, Washington DC 20005-3271. **Tel** (202)373-1150, FAX (202)373-3142. **ED** Linda Nasvaderani and Hugh Kelly (Editor's Address: Landaver Assoc., 335 Madison Avenue, New York, NY 10017). **DD** 333. ***Continues*** *Guide to Industrial and Office Real Estate Markets, 1048-2784.*

US/8750-1236
**CONDO SALES REPORT.** **Added/Corp** Yale Robbins, Inc. (1983)-. English. Twelve times a year. $487.13 New York residents; $450.00 others. Yale Robbins Inc., 31 East 28th Street, 3rd Floor, New York NY 10157. **Tel** (212)683-5700, FAX (212)545-0764. Index available. **Ad Acc**. **Pr Rev**.
**Desc:** Reviews condo sales transactions with a careful analysis of each sale, including prices, square footages, dates, dollars per square foot and per room, and actual floor plans.

CN/0849-6714
**CONDOMINIUM (TORONTO. 1989).** (CONDOMINIUM.). [Condominium]. **VFOAT** Condominium Magazine. (July/Aug. 1989)-. Periodical. English. mo. 65.00Can$. Shelter Publications Ltd, 366 Adelaide Street West, Suite 501, Toronto Ontario M5V 1R9 Canada. **Tel** (416)585-2552. **DD** 333.33. ***Continues*** *Condominium Magazine, 0826-502X.*

US
**CONNECTICUT REAL ESTATE LAW JOURNAL, THE.** **See** Law.

CN/0703-119X
**CONTACT (DON MILLS).** (CONTACT.). [Contact]. **Added/Corp** Real Estate Institute of Canada. (1977)-. Periodical. English (summaries and/or abstracts in French). qt. 30.00Can$ (add GST). Real Estate Institute of Canada, 2200 Lakeshore Boulevard West/Suite 305, Toronto Ontario M8V 1A4 Canada. **Tel** (416)253-0803, FAX (416)253-0884. **ED** Susan Arnold. **DD** 333.3/3/06271. **Bk Rev**, (Qty: 2-4). **Ad Acc**, **Adv Mgr:** Christine Paetkau. **Pr Rev**. **Circ:** 5000 (ctrl). ***Absorbed*** *Resource (Don Mills, Ont.), 0828-9522;* ***Supersedes in part*** *Real Estate Instiute of Canada. Journal, 0703-6914.*
**Desc:** Published for real estate professionals Seeks to increase the knowledge, skill and competency of those engaged in real estate and advance the interest of its members by maximizing public respect and confidence.

CN/0712-9564
**CORPIQ VOUS INFORME.** [CORPIQ vous inf.]. **VAT** Corporation des Proprietaires Immobiliers du Quebec Vous Informe. V. 1, No. 1, (Dec. 1980)-. Periodical. French. bm. CORPIQ, 1750 rue de Vitre, Quebec Quebec G1J 1Z6 Canada. **DD** 333.33/09714.

US/1042-9115
**CORPORATE REAL ESTATE EXECUTIVE.** [Corp. real estate exec.]. **Added/Corp** NACORE International. (198?)-. Periodical. English. mo. $65.00 (one year). International Association Corporation Real Estate Executive, 440 Columbia Drive, Suite 100, West Palm Beach FL 33409. **Tel** (407) 683-8111, FAX (407) 697-4853. **DD** 333.

US/1048-7948
**CORRIDOR REAL ESTATE JOURNAL, THE.** [Corridor real estate j.]. Vol. 1, No. 1 (May 19, 1989)-. Periodical. English. wk. $84.00 (one year), $152.00 (two year). Journal Two Publishing Inc, PO Box 1008-236, Route 8, Moorestown NJ 08057. **ED** Heidi Daniel. **LC** CURRENT ISSUES ONLY. **DD** 333. **Ad Acc**. **Circ:** 9,000 (ctrl). ***Continues*** *Washington Real Estate News (Washington, D.C.).*

**Desc:** Trade newspaper covering all aspects of commercial real estate in Maryland, Virginia and Washington D.C.

US/0194-7222
**CREATIVE REAL ESTATE MAGAZINE.** **VFOAT** Creative Real Estate. (197?)-. Periodical. English. mo. $72.00 one year, $85.00 two year, $99.00 three year. Creative Real Estate Magazine, Drawer L Rancho, Santa Fe CA 92067. **Tel** (619)756-1441. **ED** A. D. Kessler and J. S. McNary. Index available. cum. index. **Bk Rev**. **Ad Acc**. **Circ:** 40,000. ***Absorbed*** *The Real Estate News Observer TRENO.*
**Desc:** National reference journal for creative real estate investors and professionals with how-to formulas by recognized experts, includes national and international directory of exchange groups and an educational calendar.

US/0732-751X
**CREATIVE TAX PLANNING FOR REAL ESTATE TRANSACTIONS.** (CREATIVE TAX PLANNING FOR REAL ESTATE TRANSACTIONS : ALI-ABA COURSE OF STUDY, MATERIALS.). **Added/Corp** American Law Institute-American Bar Association Committee on Continuing Professional Education. **VFOAT** ALI-ABA Course of Study, Materials. (19??)-. English. an. $150.00. American Law Institute, 4025 Chestnut Street, Philadelphia PA 19104-3099. **Tel** (215)243-1661, (800)253-6397, FAX (215)243-1664. **LC** KF6540.Z9; C73. **DD** 343.7305/46; 347.303546.

US/0888-9147
**CRITTENDEN INCOME PROPERTY DEALS.** ***Title Change.*** [Crittenden income prop. deals]. **Added/Corp** Crittenden Publishing (Novato, Calif.). **VFOAT** Income Property Deals. (198?)-(19??). Periodical. English. wk. Crittenden Research Inc., PO Box 1150, Novato CA 94948. **Tel** (415)382-2400, FAX (415)382-2476. **DD** 333. ***Continues*** *Crittenden Bulletin Income Property Deals, 0740-5340.* ***Continued by*** *Crittenden Income Property Rates.*

US/0888-9139
**CRITTENDEN REAL ESTATE BUYERS.** [Crittenden real estate buy.]. **Added/Corp** Crittenden Publishing (Novato, Calif.). **VFOAT** Real Estate Buyers. (1984)-. Periodical. English. ir (49 issues per year). $387.00. Crittenden Research Inc., PO Box 1150, Novato CA 94948. **Tel** (415)382-2400, FAX (415)382-2476. **DD** 333.

US/0736-0339
**CRITTENDEN REPORT REAL ESTATE FINANCING.** (CRITTENDEN REPORT.). [Crittenden rep. real estate financ.]. **Added/Corp** Crittenden Publishing (Novato, Calif.). **VFOAT** Crittenden Report Real Estate Financing. (19??)-. Periodical. English. ir (49 issues per year). $387.00 North America; $472.00 other (includes Crittenden Mortgage Report). Crittenden Research Inc., PO Box 1150, Novato CA 94948. **Tel** (415)382-2400, FAX (415)382-2476. **DD** 333. ***Absorbed*** *Crittenden Hard-To-Finance Deals.*

US/1055-1700
**CYCLE PROJECTIONS.** **See** Business-Banking and Finance.

US/0279-4195
**DAILY COMMERCE.** **See** Business-Commerce.

●US/1071-5134
**DALLAS/FORT WORTH REAL ESTATE FINANCE SOURCEBOOK.** **VFOAT** Dallas Fort Worth Real Estate Finance Sourcebook. (1994)-. English. Real Estate Finance Sourcebooks, 14340 Memorial Drive, Suite 118, Houston TX 77079.

US/1055-0771
**DEALMAKERS (BELLE MEAD, N.J.), THE.** (THE DEALMAKERS.). [Dealmakers]. Vol. 1, No. 1 (Jan. 18, 1991)-. Periodical. English. Forty-eight times a year. $197.00 (one year), $310.00 (two year). Dealmakers, PO Box 2630, Mercerville NJ 08690. **Tel** (609)587-6200, FAX (609)587-3511. **ED** Ann O'Neal. **DD** 333. **Bk Rev**. **Ad Acc**. **Circ:** 6,000. available on CD-ROM and an online database. ***Continues*** *Retail Leasing Reporter, 1049-8265.*
**Desc:** Covers retailing and real estate. Lists properties for sale, expanding retailers, and new developments.

FR/0291-1191
**DEMEURES & CHATEAUX.** **See** Architecture.

FR/1145-2099
**DEVELOPPEURS LEVALLOIS-PERRET.** (DEVELOPPEURS.). **VFOAT** Developpeurs (Gennevilliers). (1989)-. Periodical. French. Ten times a year. 783.55F France; 800.00F other. Chaptal International Svc Abon, 30 rue Alemendre, 32238 Gennevilliers CDX France. **Tel** 011 33 1 47480055. **UDC** 72. Index available. **Ad Acc**.
**Desc:** Commercial real estate particularly in France; also in Europe , North America, and Asia.

US/0739-6368
**DIGEST OF STATE LAND SALES REGULATIONS, THE.** [Dig. state land sales regul.]. **Added/Corp** Land Development Institute. American Land Development Association. **VFOAT** State Digest. (19??)-. Periodical. English. Four times a year. $235.00 state supremem courts, universities, and their libraries; $265.00 other. Land Development Institute Ltd, 1401 16th Street Northwest, Washington DC 20036. **Tel** (202)232-2144, FAX (202)232-4757. Index available. **Circ:** 400 (ctrl).
**Desc:** State-by-state summary of laws and administrative policy affecting real estate, land development, campgrounds, timesharing, advertising, and related laws.

FR
**DIRECTORY - INTERNATIONAL REAL ESTATE FEDERATION.** **Main/Corp** International Real Estate Federation. Directory. English (French, German and Spanish). an. Editions Hervas, 123 Avenue Philippe Auguste, F 75011 Paris France. **Tel** 011 33 1 43791095. **LC** HD1361; .I5414. **DD** 333.33/025. ***Continues*** *FIABCI International Directory.*

US/0730-7357
**DIRECTORY, LICENSED REAL ESTATE BROKERS AND SALES ASSOCIATES.** **VFOAT** Directory of Oklahoma Licensed Real Estate Brokers and Sales Association. Directory. English. Oklahoma Real Estate Commission, Suite 100/4040 North Lincoln Boulevard, Oklahoma City OK 73105. **LC** HD266.O5; A33. **DD** 333.33/025/766.

CN/0316-9839
**DIRECTORY OF DESIGNATED MEMBERS - APPRAISAL INSTITUTE OF CANADA.** **Main/Corp** Appraisal Institute of Canada. **VFOAT** Liste de Membres Designes; Annuaire des Membres Autorises; Annuaire des Membres Titulaires. 1972-. Directory. English (French). an. Free. Institut Canadien Des Evaluateurs, Bureau 502, 177, Av., Lombard Winnipeg Manitoba R3B 0W6 Canada. **DD** 333.3/32/06271. ***Supersedes*** *Institut Canadien des Evaluateurs. Directory, 0316-9820.*

US/0361-4980
**DIRECTORY OF LICENSED REAL ESTATE APPRAISERS.** Directory. English. Nebraska Real Estate Commission, 600 South 11th Street, Suite 200, Lincoln NE 68508. **LC** HD266.N2; D57. **DD** 333.3/32/025782.

US/0732-5983
**DIRECTORY OF MAJOR MALLS.** **See** Business-Retail.

US/1061-1673
**DIRECTORY OF MEMBERS - APPRAISAL INSTITUTE (U.S.).** (DIRECTORY OF MEMBERS / APPRAISAL INSTITUTE.). [Dir. memb. - Apprais. Inst. (U.S.)]. **Main/Corp** Appraisal Institute (U.S.). (1991)-. Directory. English. an (Feb.). Free. Appraisal Institute, 875 North Michigan Avenue, Suite 2400, Chicago IL 60601-7601. **Tel** (312)335-4100, FAX (312)335-4400. **LC** HD251; .A455. **DD** 333. ***Formed by the union of*** *Society of Real Estate Appraisers. Directory of Designated Members (1990), 1050-5229* ***and*** *American Institute of Real Estate Appraisers. Directory of Members, 0569-5821.*

US/0569-5821
**DIRECTORY OF MEMBERS / THE INSTITUTE.** ***Title Change.*** **Main/Corp** American Institute of Real Estate Appraisers. (19??)-(19??). Directory. English. an. American Institute of Real Estate Appraisers, 430 North Michigan Avenue, Chicago IL 60611-4088. **Tel** (312)329-8559, FAX (312)329-8354. **LC** HD251; .A455. ***Merged with*** *Society of Real Estate Appraisers. Directory of Designated Members (1990), 1050-5229* ***to form*** *Appraisal Institute (U.S.). Directory of Members, 1061-1673.*
**Desc:** Lists current members (MAI's and RM's) of the Appraisal Institute.

US/0731-8553
**DIRECTORY OF MEMBERS / THE NATIONAL ASSOCIATION OF REAL ESTATE INVESTMENT TRUSTS, INC.** **Main/Corp** National Association of Real Estate Investment Trusts. **VFOAT** Membership Directory. (1981)-. Directory. English. an (Jan.). $195.00 (nonmembers), $35.00 (members). National Association of Real Estate Boards, 1129 20th Street Northwest, Suite 705, Washington DC 20036. **Tel** (202)785-8717. **LC** HG5095; .N245b. **DD** 332.6/3247/02573. ***Continues*** *National Association of Real Estate Investment Trusts, 0097-8191.*

US
**DIRECTORY OF PROFESSIONAL RELOCATION AND REAL ESTATE SERVICES.** **Added/Corp** Relocation Information Service. **VFOAT** National Relocation and Real Estate ... Directory of Professional Relocation and Real Estate Services. (1991)-. Directory. English. an. $95.00 US.

Relocation Information Service Inc., PO Box 445, Norwalk CT 06852. **Tel** (203)227-3800. **Ad Acc.** ***Continues*** *Directory of Professional Relocation Services, 1056-9731.*

US/0093-9439
**DIRECTORY OF REAL ESTATE AND BUSINESS CHANCE BROKERS AND SALESMEN.** Directory. English. PO Box 44095 Capitol Station, Baton Rouge LA 70804. **LC** HD266.L8; A33. **DD** 333.3/3. ***Continues*** *Roster of Real Estate and Business Chance Brokers and Salesmen.*

US/0161-3154
**DIRECTORY, PROFESSIONAL REAL ESTATE MANAGEMENT WHO'S WHO.** Directory. English. Institute of Real Estate Management, 430 North Michigan Avenue, Chicago IL 60611. **Tel** (312)661-1930, FAX (312)661-0217, telex 025-3742. **LC** HD251; .D57. **DD** 658/.91/33333.

US/0731-9525
**DIRECTORY - SOUTH DAKOTA REAL ESTATE BOARD.** (DIRECTORY / COMPILED BY SOUTH DAKOTA REAL ESTATE BOARD.). **Added/Corp** South Dakota Real Estate Board. (1981)-. English. an. $3.00. South Dakota Real Estate Board, PO Box 490, Pierre SD 57501. **LC** HD266.S8; D57a. **DD** 333.33/025/783. ***Continues*** *Directory (South Dakota Real Estate Commission).*

US/0892-4198
**DISTRESSED REAL ESTATE LAW ALERT.** ***Ceased.*** **See** Law-Banking Law.

US/0738-6931
**DISTRICT OF COLUMBIA REAL ESTATE REPORTER.** **VFOAT** Real Estate Reporter. (19??)-. Periodical. English. Twelve times a year. $280.90 Washington DC; $265.00 other. Land Development Institute Ltd, 1401 16th Street Northwest, Washington DC 20036. **Tel** (202)232-2144, FAX (202)232-4757. **ED** Stuart Marshall Bloch, William B. Ingersoll and Lisa Marsh. Index available. **Circ:** 250 (ctrl).
**Desc:** Reports on the latest land use, historic preservation, zoning, licensing and permits, rental housing and administrative and court decisions in the District of Columbia.

US/0070-704X
**DOLLARS & CENTS OF SHOPPING CENTERS, THE.** [Dollars cents shopp. cent.]. **Added/Corp** Urban Land Institute. **VFOAT** Dollars and Cents of Shopping Centers. (1961)-. Trade Publication. English. te. $206.95 members, $256.95 non-members. Urban Land Institute, 625 Indiana Ave Northwest, Washington DC 20004. **Tel** (202)624-7000, (800)321-5011. **ED** Michael Beyard. **LC** HF5430.3; .U7. **DD** 658.1/55. available in reprints from University Microfilms International (UMI).
**Desc:** Contains the most comprehensive data available on shopping centers in the US and Canada. In addition to the in-depth financial figures from 950 shopping centers, the book contains statistics on type and age of center, geographic location, and kinds of tenants.

US
**E-R-C DIRECTORY OF EMPLOYEE RELOCATION REAL ESTATE SERVICES.** **Added/Corp** Employee Relocation Council. **VFOAT** ERC Directory of Employee Relocation Real Estate Services. 9th Ed. (1983)-. English. an (published in March). $35.00. Employee Relocation Council, 1720 North Street Northwest, Washington DC 20036. **Tel** (202)857-0905, FAX (202)467-4012. ***Continues*** *Employee Relocation Council. ERC Directory.*
**Desc:** Identifies companies and individuals that provide real estate appraising and real estate brokerage services for transferring employees and corporations.

US/1053-0339
**EAST ASIAN INVESTMENT IN U.S. AND CANADIAN REAL ESTATE DIRECTORY.** [East Asian investm. U. S. Can. real estate dir.]. (Dec. 1990)-. Directory. English. $195.00. Mead Ventures Inc, PO Box 44952, Phoenix AZ 85064. **Tel** (602)234-0044, FAX (602)234-0076. **DD** 333. Index available.
**Desc:** Contains listings of more than 750 real estate investment- related offices including more than 80 in North America, with contact names, addresses, and phone and fax numbers.

US/0898-4050
**EMERGING TRENDS IN REAL ESTATE.** [Emerg. trends real estate]. **Added/Corp** Real Estate Research Corporation. First National Bank of Chicago. Balcor/American Express Inc. (198?)-. English. an. $25.00. Equitable Real Estate, 787 7th Avenue, New York NY 10019. **LC** HD251; .E47. **DD** 333.33/0973.

●US/1066-954X
**ENVIRONMENT & DEVELOPMENT / APA, AMERICAN PLANNING ASSOCIATION.** **See** Environmental Issues.

US/1049-8877
**ENVIRONMENTAL WATCH (CHICAGO, ILL.).** ***Ceased.*** (ENVIRONMENTAL WATCH : A PUBLICATION OF THE RESEARCH DEPARTMENT OF THE AMERICAN INSTITUTE OF REAL ESTATE APPRAISERS.). [Environ. watch]. **Added/Corp** American Institute of Real Estate Appraisers. American Institute of Real Estate Appraisers. Research Dept. (1988)-Vol. 7 No. 4 (19??). Periodical. English. Four times a year (Mar., June, Sept., Dec.). Appraisal Institute, 875 North Michigan Avenue, Suite 2400, Chicago IL 60601-7601. **Tel** (312)335-4100, FAX (312)335-4400. **DD** 333.

UK/0014-1240
**ESTATES GAZETTE.** [Estates gaz.]. (1858)-. Periodical. English. wk. ***Continues*** *Property Market Review and Auction Chronicle* ***and*** *Estates Journal.*
**Ind/Abst** Aust. Leg. Mon. Dig.; Infomat Int. Bus.

UK/0014-1259
**ESTATES TIMES.** [Estates times]. (1968)-. English. wk. £82.00 UK and Northern Ireland; $160.00 other. Morgan Grampian, 40 Beresford Street Woolwich, London SE18 6BQ England. **Tel** 011 44 81 855 7777, FAX 011 44 81 855 5548, telex 896238. **DD** 333.33.
**Ind/Abst** Infomat Int. Bus.

KE
**EURO AFRICA'S REVIEW OF THE NAIROBI PROPERTY MARKET.** **Main/Corp** Euro Africa International Ltd. **Added/Corp** Euro Africa International Ltd. Euro Africa Property Review. **VFOAT** Euro Africa Property Review. (1979/80)-. Periodical. English. an. **LC** HD983.Z9; N343a. **DD** 333.33/09676/25.

US/1049-8508
**EUROPEAN INVESTMENT IN U.S. AND CANADIAN REAL ESTATE DIRECTORY.** [Eur. investm. U. S. Can. real estate dir.]. **Added/Corp** Mead Ventures, Inc. **VAT** European Investment in United States and Canadian Real Estate Directory. (1990)-. Directory. English. $195.00. Mead Ventures Inc, PO Box 44952, Phoenix AZ 85064. **Tel** (602)234-0044, FAX (602)234-0076. **LC** HD251; .E95. **DD** 333.33/025/73. ***Continues*** *European Investment in U.S. Real Estate Directory, 1043-2582.*
**Desc:** This unique directory includes over 400 European and Europe-related firms -- investors, developers, lenders, brokers -- that are involved in the American real estate industry. Listings include company names, addresses, and more.

US/0161-5882
**EXISTING HOME SALES.** ***Title Change.*** **Main/Corp** National Association of Realtors. Dept. of Economics and Research. (1976)-(19??). English. an. National Association of Realtors, 430 North Michigan Avenue, Chicago IL 60611. **Tel** (312)329-8494, (800)874-6500. **LC** HD255; .N32. **DD** 333.33/8. ***Continues*** *Existing Home Sales Series, Annual Report.* ***Continued by*** *Home Sales Yearbook.*

US/0191-2208
**EXPENSE ANALYSIS, CONDOMINIUMS, COOPERATIVES, & PLANNED UNIT DEVELOPMENTS.** **Added/Corp** Institute of Real Estate Management. **VFOAT** Expense Analysis. Condominiums, Cooperatives, and Planned Unit Developments; Expense Analysis. Condominiums, Cooperatives, and PUDs; Expense Analysis. Condominium, Co-Ops & PUD's; Condominiums, Cooperatives, & Planned Unit Developments; Condominiums, Cooperatives, and PUDs; Condominium, Co-Ops & PUD's; Condominium, Coops, and PUDs; Income/Expense Analysis. Condominiums, Cooperatives & PUDs. **VAT** Expense Analysis, Condominiums, Cooperatives, and Planned Unit Developments. (1978)-. English. an. $157.95. Institute of Real Estate Management, 430 North Michigan Avenue, Chicago IL 60611. **Tel** (312)661-1930, FAX (312)661-0217, telex 025-3742. **ED** Kenneth Anderson. **LC** HD7287.67.U5; E96. **DD** 658.1/5933. **Circ:** 5,500. ***Continues in part*** *Income-Expense Analysis. Apartments, Condominiums & Cooperatives, 0161-5262.*
**Desc:** Survey of homeowners association operating costs, including administration, maintenance, contract services, amenities and replacement research.
**Ind/Abst** Stat. Ref. Index.

●US
**FAIRFAX DIRECTORY SERVICE.** (1992)-. Directory. English. Four times a year (Jan., Apr., July, Oct.). $675.00 (includes 1 directory and 3 quarterly supplements). Rufus S. Lusk and Son Inc., 1110 Bonifant Street, Silver Spring MD 20910-3374. **Tel** (301)588-6700.

US/0738-9434
**FAIRFAX NEWSLETTER, THE.** (19??)-. Newsletter. English. wk (except Aug., last week in Dec., and last week in Jan.). $150.00 Fairfax County Public Libraries; $240.00 other. Dulles International Airport, Box 17162, Washington DC 20041. **Tel** (703)860-2666.

US
**FEDERAL INCOME TAXATION OF REAL ESTATE. SUPPLEMENTS.** (19??)-. English. Twice a year. $110.00 US; $143.00 other. Warren Gorham & Lamont Inc., Park Square Building, 31 St. James Avenue, Boston MA 02116-4112. **Tel** (617)423-2020, (800)950-1207, FAX (617)423-2026.

●US
**FEDERAL SUPPLY CATALOG. SECTION VII, CLASSIFICATION OF PROPERTY WITH ALPHABETICAL INDEX OF EXPENDABLE ITEMS.** **Main/Corp** United States. Dept. of Veterans Affairs. Office of Acquisition and Materiel Management. **VFOAT** Classification of Property With Alphabetical Index of Expendable items; Alphabetical Index and Expendability Class Classification of Property. Mar. (1992)-. Catalog. English. be. ***Formed by the union of*** *Federal Supply Catalog. Section VII, Classification of Property* ***and*** *Federal Supply Catalog. Section IV, Alphabetical Index of Expendable Items.*

FR
**FIABCI INTERNATIONAL DIRECTORY.** **Main/Corp** International Real Estate Federation. Directory. English (French, German and Spanish). Federation Internationale des Professions Inmobilieres, Clayton Promotion, 99 rue de Fichelieu, 75002 Paris France. **LC** HD1361; .I5414. **DD** 333.3/3/025.

FR
**FIABCI PANORAMA.** French. an. FIABCI Paris, 68 rue des Archives, Paris (3E) France. **LC** HD1361; .F5.

FR
**FIABCI REPORTER.** **Main/Corp** International Real Estate Federation. (19??)-. Periodical. English (French, German and Spanish). FIABCI Paris, 68 rue des Archives, Paris (3E) France. **LC** HD251; .I64. **DD** 333.3/3/05. ***Continues*** *International Real Estate Federation. FIABCI.*

●US/1066-7350
**FINANCE, INSURANCE & REAL ESTATE USA.** **See** Business-Banking and Finance.

US/0196-514X
**FINANCIAL FREEDOM REPORT.** ***Title Change.*** **See** Business-Investments.

US/0272-8230
**FIRST TUESDAY.** (1979)-. Periodical. English. mo. $119.00. First Tuesday, PO Box 20068, Riverside CA 92516. **Tel** (714)781-7300. **ED** Simon Sykes. **LC** HD251; .F57. **DD** 33.33/0973. **Circ:** 95,087.
**Desc:** A journal for the real estate industry.

US/0899-9147
**FLEET'S GUIDE.** [Fleet's guide]. (July-Dec. 1988)-. Periodical. English. Four times a year. $385.00. Fleet Press Inc, 3337 Duke Street, Alexandria VA 22314. **Tel** (703)370-3246, (703)336-3246. **LC** HG2040.5.U5; A1367. **DD** 332.3/2/02573.
**Desc:** Approximately 200 active commercial real estate lenders nationwide.

US/1053-3060
**FLORIDA LAND OWNER.** [Fla. land own.]. **Added/Corp** Florida Association of Land Owners. **VFOAT** FALO Florida Land Owner. Periodical. English. mo. C F Cline Publishes, 321 Tamilami Trail, Punta Gorda FL 33950. **Tel** (813)637-6566. **DD** 333. ***Continues*** *Florida Land Owner Magazine, 1047-1413.*

US/1047-1413
**FLORIDA LAND OWNER MAGAZINE.** ***Title Change.*** [Fla. land owner mag.]. **VFOAT** Florida Land Owner. (1989)-?. Periodical. English. mo. C F Cline Publishes, 321 Tamilami Trail, Punta Gorda FL 33950. **Tel** (813)637-6566. **(Subscription address:** PO Box 512241, Punta Gorda, FL 33951-2241**)** **ED** George Collins. **DD** 333. Index available. **Ad Acc. Circ:** 25,000 (ctrl). ***Continued by*** *Florida Land Owner, 1053-3060.*
**Desc:** News and information on the the growth in Charlotte County, Florida.

US/0897-9383
**FLORIDA REAL ESTATE.** [Fla. real estate]. (1987)-. Periodical. English. Four times a year. $22.00. J J Publication, 3381 Ocean Drive, Vero Beach FL 32963. **Tel** (407)231-7788. **ED** Don Sider. **DD** 333. **Circ:** 100,000 (ctrl).
**Desc:** Targets individuals, especially in the Northeast and Midwest who are looking to purchase a second home in Florida.

US/0887-3208
**FLORIDA REAL ESTATE & DEVELOPMENT UPDATE.** [Fla. real estate devel. update]. **Added/Corp** Data Directions, Inc. **VFOAT** Florida Real Estate and Development Update. Vol. 1, No. 1 (1985)-. Periodical. English. Twenty-four times a year. $100.00. Data Directions Inc., PO Box 1052, Port Washington NY 11050. **Tel** (516)876-2108, (516)333-7730. **ED** Hank Boerner and Harry Prior. **DD** 332. cum. index. **Circ:** 3,000.
**Desc:** Covers land use, real property, development, construction, and related topics in State of Florida for senior management, entrepreneur, and financial audiences.

US/0735-9071
**FLORIDA REAL ESTATE BROKER & THE LAW, THE.** **VFOAT** Florida Real Estate Broker and the Law. Periodical. English. $24.00. C.E. Hartle Associates, PO Box 23091, Jacksonville FL 32223. **LC** KFF126.A59; F55. **DD** 333.33/09759.

US
**FLORIDA REAL ESTATE COMMISSION HANDBOOK / STATE OF FLORIDA.** **Main/Corp** Florida Real Estate Commission. **VFOAT** F.R.E.C. Handbook; FREC Handbook. (19??)-. English. an. $4.50. Florida Division of Real Estate, PO Box 1900, Orlando FL 32802. **Tel** (407)423-6071. **LC** KFF282.R4; A296. **DD** 346.75904/37; 347.5906437. **Circ:** 50,000. ***Continues*** *Florida. Board of Real Estate. Board of Real Estate Handbook, 0734-8363.*

US/0744-6152
**FLORIDA REAL ESTATE COMMISSION NEWS & REPORTS.** (FLORIDA REAL ESTATE COMMISSION NEWS & REPORT / DEPARTMENT OF PROFESSIONAL REGULATION.). **Added/Corp** Florida Real Estate Commission. (19??)-. Periodical. English. qt. Free on request. Florida Real Estate Commission, PO Box 1900, Orlando FL 32802. **Tel** (407)423-6071. ***Continues*** *Florida Board of Real Estate News & Report, 0199-4565.*

US/0892-0524
**FLORIDA REAL ESTATE JOURNAL.** [Fla. real estate j.]. (1986)-. Periodical. English. wk. Florida Real Estate Journal, PO Box 1270, Sanford FL 32772-1270. **DD** 333.

US/0199-5839
**FLORIDA REALTOR.** [Fla. realtor]. **Added/Corp** Florida Association of Realtors. (19??)-. Periodical. English. Eleven times a year. $15.90. Florida Association of Realtors, PO Box 725025, Orlando FL 32872. **Tel** (407)438-1400, FAX (407)438-1411. **ED** Pam Littlefield, 7025 Augusta National Drive, Orlando, FL 32822 USA; Telephone: (407)438-1400 Ext. 2315. Index available in last issue of volume--attached. cum. index. **Ad Acc, Adv Mgr:** Tracy Lawton, **Tel** (407)438-1400 Ext. 2322. **Circ:** 65,000 (ctrl). ***Continues*** *Florida Realty Journal.*
**Desc:** A combination of practical information and trend analysis for real estate professionals.

US/1042-6817
**FORUM.** [Forum]. 1988-. Periodical. English. qt. Free. Arizona Real Estate Center, College of Business, Arizona State University, Tempe AZ 85287-4406. **Tel** (602)965-5440, FAX (602)965-5458. **ED** Jay Q Butler and Nan Beams. **DD** 333. **Circ:** 2,500 (ctrl).
**Desc:** Current articles on issues pertinent to the real estate industry in Arizona and elsewhere.

JA
**FUDOSAN KANKEI HOREI SHU.** **Main/Corp** Japan. **Added/Corp** Jutaku Shimpo Sha. (19??)-. Periodical. Japanese. ¥2600. Jutaku Shimpo Sha, c/o Tokyo Toranomon Building, 10 Shiba Toranomon Minato-ku, Tokyo 105 Japan. **LC** LAW.

JA
**FUDOSAN SHINROPPO.** **Main/Corp** Japan. **Added/Corp** Shukan Jutaku Shimbun Sha. Shukan Jutaku Shimbun Sha. Shikaku Shiken Shido Senta. (19??)-. Periodical. Japanese. ¥2600. Shukan Jutaku Shimbun Sha, 9-4 Shinjuku 1, Shinjuku-ku 160, Tokyo Japan. **LC** LAW.

US
**GAO'S ... BIENNIAL REPORT ON THE TRANSFER OF EXCESS AND SURPLUS FEDERAL PERSONAL PROPERTY TO NONFEDERAL ORGANIZATIONS.** **See** Public Administration.

US/0069-9047
**GENERAL SERIES - CENTER FOR REAL ESTATE AND URBAN ECONOMIC STUDIES, SCHOOL OF BUSINESS ADMINISTRATION, UNIVERSITY OF CONNECTICUT.** (GENERAL SERIES - CENTER FOR REAL ESTATE AND URBAN ECONOMIC STUDIES.). **Main/Corp** University of Connecticut. Center for Real Estate and Urban Economic Studies. Began with No. 1 in 1968. Monographic series. English. ir. Price varies per volume. Center for Real Estate and Urban Economic Studies, U-41RE/Room 426, University of Connecticut, 368 Fairfield Road, Storrs CT 06268. **Tel** (203)486-3227. **LC** HD251; .C745. **DD** 333.3/3.

US/1040-4805
**GEORGIA REAL ESTATE LAW LETTER.** **See** Law.

CN/0229-0723
**GOLD POST.** [Gold post]. Vol. 1, Issue 1 (1978)-. Periodical. English. mo. Free. Goldpost Publications for Century 21 Members, Suite 204, 1992 Yonge Street, Toronto Ontario. **DD** 333.33/0971.

US
**GOLF PROPERTY.** (Winter 1991)-. English. bm. $18.00 US; $32.00 other. Golf Property, PO Box 809, Hendersonville NC 28793. **Tel** (800)248-6994. **Ad Acc. Circ:** 130,000.
**Desc:** International golf real estate and resorts portfolio.

US/1059-6607
**GOULD'S PRIVATE SECURITY REPORTER : SERVING THE HOSPITALITY AND REAL ESTATE INDUSTRIES.** [Gould's priv. secur. report.]. **VFOAT** Private Security Reporter. Vol. 1, No. 1 (Dec. 1991)-. Periodical. English. mo. $149.00. Gould Publications, 199/300 State Street, Binghamton NY 13901. **Tel** (607)724-3000, FAX (607)723-4285. **DD** 344.

US
**GOWER FEDERAL SERVICES PLAN.** (19??)-. English. ir. $1,025.00. Rocky Mountain Mineral Law Foundation, Porter Administration Building, 7039 East 18th Avenue, Denver CO 80220. **Tel** (303)321-8100, FAX (303)321-7657. Index available (Bound in Dec. issue). cum. index (available with subscription only). **Circ:** 55. available on an online database; available on microfiche.

US/1056-5604
**GSI REPORT ON REAL ESTATE AND FACILITY MANAGEMENT AUTOMATION.** ***Title Change.*** [GSI rep. real estate facil. manage. autom.]. **Added/Corp** Graphic Systems, Inc. **VFOAT** GSI Report. Vol. 1, No. 1 (May 1991)-(199?). Periodical. English. mo. Graphic Systems, 1815 Massachussetts Avenue, Suite 308, Cambridge MA 02140. **DD** 004. ***Continued by*** *FM Technology Report, 1067-6244.*

US/0895-5360
**GUFFEY'S JOURNAL.** **VFOAT** Guffey's Tulsa Real Estate Journal. Vol. 1, No. 1 (August 19, 1987)-. Periodical. English. sm. $15.00. Guffey's Tulsa Real Estate Journal, 409 Mayo Building, 420 South Main Street, Tulsa OK 74103. **Tel** (918)587-4734. ***Continues*** *Guffey's Executive Journal, 0744-6977.*

US
**GUIDE TO CONSTRUCTION ACTIVITY IN MANHATTAN.** English. an. $495.00. Yale Robbins Inc., 31 East 28th Street, 3rd Floor, New York NY 10157. **Tel** (212)683-5700, FAX (212)545-0764. **ED** Yale Robbins. Index available. cum. index. **Pr Rev.**
**Desc:** Locates sites of new apartment and office construction giving gross building area, square footage, name of developer and architect with phone numbers, and accompanying maps.

US
**HARRIS COUNTY REAL ESTATE REPORT.** (19??)-. Periodical. English. mo. $703.63 Texas (includes tax), $650.00 other. Revac Publications, 11777 Katy Freeway, Suite 500, Houston TX 77079. **Tel** (713)496-2388. **ED** Marcia Forrest. Index available. **Ad Acc. Circ:** 500 (ctrl). available on an online database.

US/0745-7073
**HAWAII INVESTOR.** [Hawaii investor]. **VFOAT** Hawaii Inve$tor. (198?)-. Periodical. English. mo. $15.00 (1 year), $24.00 (2 year), $36.00 (3 year) Hawaii; $21.00 (1 year), $36.00 (2 year), $54.00 (3 year) US; $27.00 (1 year), $48.00 (2 year), $72.00 (3 year) other. Honolulu Publishing Company Ltd, 36 Merchant Street, Honolulu HI 96813. **Tel** (800)272-5245, (808)524-7400. **ED** Bill Wood. **Ad Acc, Adv Mgr:** Mary Winpenny, **Tel** (808)524-7400. **Circ:** 10,000 (ctrl). available on an online database (file 635/Full-Text) from DIALOG. Documents available from UMI Article Clearinghouse. ***Continues*** *Hawaii Real Estate Investor, 0273-5806.*
**Desc:** Articles regarding various businesses throughout the state of Hawaii, including government effects upon them.
**Ind/Abst** Bus. Dateline (April 1991-) [Full Txt.].

CN/0848-8541
**HEMSON TORONTO LAND USE REPORT.** **See** Public Administration.

US
**HERNANADO DEED REPORT.** English. mo. $650.00. Florida New Business Report, 7402 North 56th Street, Suite 895, Tampa FL 33680. **Tel** (813)988-8148, FAX (813)988-8422. **ED** Ken Guthery.
**Desc:** A compilation of all real estate sales giving granter, grantee, address, legal description, O R book and page, selling price, mortgage amount.

US/0733-1304
**HGS INTERNATIONAL'S REAS LETTER.** **VFOAT** H.G.S. International's R.E.A.S. Letter; International's REAS Letter; International's R.E.A.S. Letter. **VAT** Henry G. Sobeck International's Real Estate Agent's Survival Letter. Vol. 1, No. 1 (May 1983)-. Periodical. English. mo. $147.00. Sobeck International, 516 Jackson Avenue, Westwood NJ 07675.

US/1063-0511
**HOME SALES.** ***Title Change.*** (HOME SALES : EXISTING AND NEW SINGLE-FAMILY, APARTMENT CONDOS AND CO-OPS / NATIONAL ASSOCIATION OF REALTORS.). [Home sales]. **Added/Corp** National Association of Realtors. (Feb. 1987)-(1993). English. mo. National Association of Realtors / Washington, 777 14th Street Northwest, Washington DC 20005. **Tel** (202)383-1137. **LC** HD251; .H63. **DD** 333.33/83/0973021. ***Continues*** *Existing Home Sales, Monthly Report.* ***Absorbed by*** *Real Estate Outlook Market Trends and Insights.*
**Ind/Abst** Stat. Ref. Index.

US
**HOME SALES REPORT.** English. mo. $75.00 (non-members), $50.00 (members of the National Association of Realtors). National Association of Realtors / Washington, 777 14th Street Northwest, Washington DC 20005. **Tel** (202)383-1137.

US
**HOME SALES YEARBOOK.** **Added/Corp** National Association of Realtors. (19??)-. English. National Association of Realtors, 430 North Michigan Avenue, Chicago IL 60611. **Tel** (312)329-8494, (800)874-6500. **LC** HD1390.5; .H65. ***Continues*** *National Association of Realtors. Dept. of Economics and Research.; Existing Home Sales, 0161-5882.*

US/0894-0258
**HOMEBUYER'S GUIDE. DALLAS/FT. WORTH.** **VFOAT** Homebuyer's Guide. Dallas, Fort Worth; Dallas, Ft. Worth Homebuyer's Guide; Dallas, Forth Worth Homebuyer's Guide; Dallas/Ft. Worth Homebuyer's Guide. Vol. 16, No. 4 (July/Aug. 1987)-. Periodical. English. bm. $12.00. Living Partners Ltd, 5501 LBJ Freeway/Suite 300, Dallas TX 75240. ***Continues*** *Living (Dallas/Fort Worth Edition), 0741-5494.*

US/1046-1655
**HONG KONG REGISTER.** [Hong Kong regist.]. (1990)-. English. an. $195.00. Mead Ventures Inc, PO Box 44952, Phoenix AZ 85064. **Tel** (602)234-0044, FAX (602)234-0076. **LC** HD941; .H68. **DD** 333.33/025/5125.
**Desc:** Locate nearly 700 companies and 800 executives who invest in North American real estate. Introductory chapters analyze current Hong Kong investment trends and economic conditions.

US/1200-2062
**HOUSE PRICE TRENDS.** (199?)-. English. an. Toronto Real Estate Board, 1400 Don Mills Road, J Samaroo, Don Mills Ontario, M3B 3N1 Canada. **Tel** (905)443-8128. ***Continues*** *House Price Trends and Residential Construction Costs in the Toronto Real Estate Board Market Area and in Canada, 0705-9515.*

CN/0705-9515
**HOUSE PRICE TRENDS AND RESIDENTIAL CONSTRUCTION COSTS IN THE TORONTO REAL ESTATE BOARD MARKET AREA AND IN CANADA.** ***Title Change.*** [House price trends resid. constr. costs Tor. Real Estate Board mark. area Can.]. **Added/Corp** Toronto Real Estate Board. Research Dept. (1978)-(199?). English. an. Toronto Real Estate Board, 1400 Don Mills Road, J Samaroo, Don Mills Ontario, M3B 3N1 Canada. **Tel** (905)443-8128. **DD** 338.4/3/690809713541. ***Continues*** *House Price Trends and Residential Construction Costs in Metropolitan Toronto and Canada, 0319-7522.* ***Continued by*** *House Price Trends, 1200-2062.*

UK/0263-3639
**HOUSE PRICES.** [House Prices]. **VFOAT** House Prices in the ... Quarter. (1981)-. Periodical. English. qt. Free. Nationwide Building Society, Nationwide House (LG/C), Pipers Way, Swindon L, SN38 1NW England. **Tel** 011 44 0793 456374, FAX 011 44 0793 455903. **ED** Barry Bissett. **DD** 333.33. cum. index. **Bk Rev. Ad Acc. Circ:** 30,000 (ctrl). ***Continues*** *Housing trends, 0262-8821.*

US
**HOUSTON AREA APARTMENT OWNERSHIP GUIDE.** (19??)-. Periodical. English. Four times a year (March, June, Sept., Dec.). $995.00. O'Conner and Associates, 2100 West 18th, Suite 102, Houston TX 77008. **Tel** (713)862-7545, FAX (713)862-1949. **ED** Pat O'Connor. Index available (bound in each issue). **Circ:** 100 (ctrl).
**Desc:** Guide available for the Houston apartment market. Research for this report includes researching Harris County deed records, calling the owners, calling the management companies, calling the projects, reviewing County Appraisal District (HCAD) records and driving by the projects.

●US/1065-853X
**HOUSTON REAL ESTATE FINANCE SOURCEBOOK.** (1993)-. English. Real Estate Finance Sourcebooks, 14340 Memorial Drive, Suite 118, Houston TX 77079.

US/1045-8638
**HOUSTON REAL ESTATE TRENDS.** (Mar. 1987)-. Periodical. English. mo. $92.00. O'Conner and Associates, 2100 West 18th, Suite 102, Houston TX 77008. **Tel** (713)862-7545, FAX (713)862-1949. **ED** Pat O'Connor. **Circ:** 1,200 (ctrl). ***Continues*** *Houston Apartment Trends.*
**Desc:** Includes significant sales of commercial real estate in Harris County, including apartments, office buildings, retail centers, industrial buildings and vacant land; sales and foreclosure data as well as building and demolition permits; rental and occupancy studies for residential, apartment, office retail and industrial markets are reviewed and compared. Third party lenders are listed by name, phone number, type of property and amount of loan.

GW/0934-5693
**IMMOBILIEN-BERATER.** (19??)-. German. bm. DM200.00. Verlag Norman Rentrop, Theodor Heuss Strasse 4, D-53177 Bonn Germany. **Tel** 011 49 228 82050, FAX 011 49 228 364411, telex 17228309 TTX D. **ED** Norman Rentrop. Index available. **Bk Rev.**
**Desc:** Loose-leaf publication concerning real estate.

US
**INCOME/EXPENSE ANALYSIS. OFFICE BUILDINGS, DOWNTOWN AND SUBURBAN.** **Added/Corp** Institute of Real Estate Management. Institute of Real Estate Management. Experience Exchange Committee. **VFOAT** Office Buildings, Downtown and Suburban; Income/Expense Analysis. Office Buildings; Office Buildings. (1982)-. English. an. $157.95. Institute of Real Estate Management, 430 North Michigan Avenue, Chicago IL 60611. **Tel** (312)661-1930, FAX (312)661-0217, telex 025-3742. **Circ:** 8,000. ***Continues*** *Income/Expense Analysis. Suburban Office Buildings, 0146-9630.*
**Desc:** Statistical analysis of income and expense items for office buildings.

CK
**INFORME SOBRE ESTADO JURIDICO DE LAS SOLICITUDES VIGENTES DE LICENCIAS, PERMISOS, APORTES, ANTIGUOS PERMISOS DE ESMERALDAS Y RECONOCIMIENTO DE PROPIEDAD PRIVADA, PRESENTADAS ANTE EL MINISTERIO Y LAS GOBERNACIONES.** No. 1 (Oct. 1984)-. Spanish. qt. Ministerio de Minas y Energia, Ave el Dorado-Can-A A, 80319 Oficina No 417, Bogota de Colombia.

US
**INNSIDE ISSUES.** (19??)-. Periodical. English. an (July). $182.50. Hotel and Motel Brokers of America, 10220 North Executive Hills Boulevard, Kansas City MO 64153. **Tel** 800 821-5191. **ED** Patrick Ford (editor's address: 500 market Street, Suite 13, Portsmouth, NH 03801; (603)821-8740. **Ad Acc. Circ:** 2,000.

US/1065-2310
**INSIDER FORECLOSURE GUIDE.** ***Title Change.*** [Insid. foreclos. guide]. (1992)-(1992). Periodical. English. mo. Insider Foreclosure Guide, 6272 South Dixie Highway, Miami FL 33143. **DD** 333. ***Continues*** *Institutional Real Estate Monitor. Florida Ed.* ***Continued by*** *Insider Real Estate Guide, 1068-1264.*

●US/1068-1264
**INSIDER REAL ESTATE GUIDE, THE.** [Insid. real estate guide]. (1992)-. Periodical. English. mo. Insider Foreclosure Guide, 6272 South Dixie Highway, Miami FL 33143. **DD** 333. ***Continues*** *Insider Foreclosure Guide, 1065-2310.*

US/1044-1662
**INSTITUTIONAL REAL ESTATE LETTER, THE.** [Inst. real estate lett.]. Vol. 1, No. 1 (Jan. 1989)-. Periodical. English. Twelve times a year. $795.00 one year. Institute Real Estate letter, 2211 Olympic Boulevard, Walnut Creek CA 94595. **Tel** (510)933-4040. **ED** Karen Stearns, (phone: (713)242-1998). **LC** HD 1361; .I58. **DD** 333. **Ad Acc, Adv Mgr:** Mike Mollo, **Tel** (510)933-4040. **Circ:** 3,500 (ctrl).

US/0149-2039
**INTERNATIONAL DIRECTORY OF MEMBERS.** [Int. dir. memb.]. Directory. English. St Louis Homes for Living Headquarters International, 2632 Woodson Road, St Louis MO 63114. **LC** HD251; .I62. **DD** 333.3/3.

US/8755-6138
**INTERNATIONAL REAL ESTATE JOURNAL.** [Int. real estate j.]. **Added/Corp** International Institute of Valuers. International Real Estate Institute. Vol. 1, No. 1 (1982)-. Periodical. English. Four times a year. $48.00 (one year), $90.00 (two year). International Real Estate Institute, 8383 East Evans Road, Scottsdale AZ 85260. **Tel** (602)998-8267, telex 165092. **ED** Robert C. Johnson. **LC** HD1361; .I55. **DD** 333.33/05. **Bk Rev. Ad Acc, Adv Mgr:** Troy E. Johnson. **Circ:** 10,000. ***Continues*** *International Property Report.*
**Desc:** Journal specializes in international real estate concerning investment, development, finance and real estate on a general basis.

US/0882-1879
**ISLAND PROPERTIES REPORT.** **Added/Corp** Gene Cowell & Associates. (198?)-. Periodical. English. Twelve times a year. $44.00 one year; $79.00 two years. Island Properties Report, 4061 Bonita Beach Road, Suite 201, Bonita Springs FL 33932. **Tel** (813)495-1604, FAX (813)495-1738. **ED** Joan Kelly-Plate. **DD** 332. cum. index. **Circ:** 11,000.
**Desc:** Newsletter for potential retirees/investors seeking business or residential properties in the Caribbean and Central America. Reviews current economic, political climate, real estate purchase procedures, taxes, ect..

US/0882-1887
**ISLAND PROPERTIES REPORT. QUARTERLY REPORT.** Periodical. English. mo. $39.00 US; $49.00 other. Gene Cowell & Associates, Box 58, Woodstock VT 05091. **Tel** (802)457-3734. **ED** Deborah Stearno Sullivan. **DD** 332. Index available. **Bk Rev. Circ:** 8,500.
**Desc:** Reports on Caribbean for real estate buyers and covers economy, politics, tax and incentive programs, quality of life on each island, plus property listings (unpaid).

NE
**JAARVERSLAG.** **Main/Corp** Netherlands. Centrale Landinrichtingscommissie. **Added/Corp** Netherlands. Landinrichtingsdienst. Dutch. Landinrichtingsdienst, Rijkskantorengebouw Westraven Griffioenlaan 2, Utrecht Netherlands. **LC** HD1335.N4; N47a. ***Continues*** *Jaarverslag - Landinrichtingsdienst.*

US/1047-7233
**JAPANESE INVESTMENT IN U.S. AND CANADIAN REAL ESTATE DIRECTORY.** [Jpn. investm. U. S. Can. real estate dir.]. **VFOAT** Japanese Investment in US and Canadian Real Estate Directory. **VAT** Japanese Investment in United States and Canadian Real Estate Directory. (1990)-. Directory. English. an. $195.00. Mead Ventures Inc, PO Box 44952, Phoenix AZ 85064. **Tel** (602)234-0044, FAX (602)234-0076. **ED** Dawn N Erdos. **LC** HD251; .J37. **DD** 332.63/24/02552. ***Continues*** *Japanese Investment in U.S. Real Estate Directory, 1027-2447.*
**Desc:** Lists information on investors, lenders, accountants, and others involved in Japanese real estate investment in the U.S. and Canada.

US/0898-9761
**JAPANESE INVESTMENT IN U.S. REAL ESTATE REVIEW. WESTERN REGION.** ***Ceased.*** [Jpn. investm. U. S. real estate rev., West. reg.]. **VFOAT** Western Region. **VAT** Japanese Investment in United States Real Estate Review. Western Region. Vol. 1, No. 1 (May, 1988)-?. Periodical. English. mo. Mead Ventures Inc, PO Box 44952, Phoenix AZ 85064. **Tel** (602)234-0044, FAX (602)234-0076. **ED** Christopher Mead, Gail Maiorana. **LC** HD266.A17; J37. **DD** 332.63/24/02552. ctrl circ. available on diskette; available on an online database (files 16,636.Full-Text) from DIALOG.
**Desc:** Provides information on the latest Japanese investment and on related matters.

US/0887-1922
**JOHN T. REED'S REAL ESTATE INVESTOR'S MONTHLY.** [John T. Reed's real estate investor's mon.]. **VFOAT** Real Estate Investor's Monthly. Vol. 1, No. 1 (Feb. 1986)-. Periodical. English. Twelve times a year. $125.00. Reed Publishing Company / Concord, CA, PO Box 27311, Concord CA 94527. **Tel** (800)635-5425, (415)820-6292. **DD** 332. Index available.

UK/0958-868X
**JOURNAL OF PROPERTY FINANCE.** **VFOAT** Property Finance. Vol. 1, No. 1 (Summer 1990)-. Periodical. English. qt. $379.00. MCB University Press, 60 62 Toller Lane, Bradford West Yorkshire BD8 9BX England. **Tel** 011 44 274 499821, FAX 011 44 274 547143, telex 51317 MCBUNI G. **(Subscription address:** MCB University Press / US and Canada Subscriptions, PO Box 10812, Birmingham AL 35201-0812.**)**

US/0022-3905
**JOURNAL OF PROPERTY MANAGEMENT.** [J. prop. manage.]. **Added/Corp** Institute of Real Estate Management. Vol. 6, No. 4 (June 1941)-. Periodical. English. bm (6 issues). $38.95 US. Institute of Real Estate Management, 430 North Michigan Avenue, Chicago IL 60611. **Tel** (312)661-1930, FAX (312)661-0217, telex 025-3742. **[CCC].** Index available (bound in Jan. issue). ***Continues*** *Journal of Certified Property Managers.*
**Ind/Abst** Acad. Search (July 1993-).

UK/0959-9916
**JOURNAL OF PROPERTY RESEARCH.** **Added/Corp** Land Development Studies Education Trust (Great Britain). Vol. 8, No. 1 (Spring 1991)-. Periodical. English. Three times a year (Jan., May, Sep.). $225.00 US and Canada; £130.00 European Community; £145.00 other. E & FN Spon Ltd, 2 6 Boundary Row, London SE1 8HN England. **Tel** 011 44 71 865 0066. **(Subscription address:** Chapman & Hall, Subscription Department, International Thomson Publishing Services, Cheriton House, North Way, Andover, Hants SP10 5BE, UK**) ED** Bryan MacGregor, David Hartzell, Mike Miles. **LC** HD251; .L36. **DD** 333.33/0941/05. **Bk Rev. Ad Acc. Pr Rev. Circ:** 300. ***Continues*** *Land Development Studies, 0264-0821.*
**Desc:** All aspects of real estate investment and developments. Publishes theoretical and empirical papers, case studies and critical literature surveys, concentrating on property investment portfolios and land development.

UK/0960-2712
**JOURNAL OF PROPERTY VALUATION & INVESTMENT.** **VFOAT** Journal of Property Valuation and Investment; Property Valuation & Investment; A.Property valuation and investment. Vol. 9, No. 1 (Autumn 1990)-. Academic Scholarly Publication. English. qt. $399.00. MCB University Press, 60 62 Toller Lane, Bradford West Yorkshire BD8 9BX England. **Tel** 011 44 274 499821, FAX 011 44 274 547143, telex 51317 MCBUNI G. **(Subscription address:** MCB University Press / US and Canada Subscriptions, PO Box 10812, Birmingham AL 35201-0812.**) ED** Nick French. **LC** IN PROCESS. Index available. **Bk Rev.** ***Continues*** *Journal of Valuation.*
**Desc:** Aims to provide an international forum for the interchange and ideas relating to property valuation and investment.

SI
**JOURNAL OF REAL ESTATE & CONSTRUCTION.** Vol. 1, No. 1 (Aug. 1990)-. Periodical. English. Three times a year (Mar., Sept., Dec.). $50.00. Singapore University Press Pte Ltd, Yusof Ishak House, National University of Singapore, 10 Kent Ridge Crescent, Singapore 0511 Republic of Singapore. **Tel** 011 65 7761148, FAX 011 65 7740652. **ED** George Ofori (editor's address: National University of Singapore 10 Kent Ridge Crescent, Singapore 0511 Singapore). **Circ:** 200 (ctrl).
**Desc:** Referred academic papers on a broad spectrum of real estate and construction issues.

US/0895-5638
**JOURNAL OF REAL ESTATE FINANCE AND ECONOMICS, THE.** [J. real estate financ. econ.]. Vol. 1 No. 1 (Apr. 1988)-. Periodical. English. bm. $564.00. Kluwer Academic Publishers / Massachusetts, PO Box 358, Accord Station, Hingham MA 02018. **Tel** (617)871-6600. **ED** James B Kau, C F Sirmans, and Edwin S Mills. **LC** HG2040; .J66. **DD** 332.7/2/05. **CODEN** JREEEI. **[CCC]. Bk Rev. Ad Acc. Acid Free.** available on microfilm and microfiche from University Microfilms International (UMI).
**Desc:** The subject areas in which the papers published in the journal include urban economics, housing, regional science and public policy.
**Ind/Abst** Econ. Lit. Index (199?-); J. Econ. Lit.; Soc. Sci. Cit. Index [Full Cov.].

US/0927-7544
**JOURNAL OF REAL ESTATE LITERATURE.** **See** Literature.

US/0896-5803
**JOURNAL OF REAL ESTATE RESEARCH, THE.** [J. real estate res.]. **Added/Corp** American Real Estate Society. Vol. 1, No. 1 (Fall 1986)-. Periodical. English. Three times a year. $70.00. University of North Dakota, Grand Forks ND 58202. **Tel** (701)777-2941. **(Subscription address:** University of North Dakota Department of Finance, Theron Nelson, Grand Forks, ND 58202**) ED** G. Donald Jud. **DD** 332. **Circ:** 1,300 (ctrl).
**Desc:** Micro-oriented issues in real estate.
**Ind/Abst** Avery Index Archit. Period. Suppl. Colum. Univ. (Fall 1987); Econ. Lit. Index; Int. Bibliogr. Sociol.; J. Plan. Lit.; Sage Urban Stud. Abstr.

US/0093-5107
**JOURNAL OF REAL ESTATE TAXATION.** **See** Public Administration-Public Finance and Taxation.

US/1055-4211
**JOURNAL OF RTC REAL ESTATE.** ***Ceased.*** [J. RTC real estate]. **VFOAT** RTC Real Estate. **VAT** Journal of Resolution Trust Corporation Real Estate. Vol. 1, No. 1 (May/June 1991)-(May/June 1992). Periodical. English. bm. Warren Gorham & Lamont Inc., Park Square Building, 31 St. James Avenue, Boston MA 02116-4112. **Tel** (617)423-2020, (800)950-1207, FAX (617)423-2026. **DD** 333.

●US/1067-8433
**JOURNAL OF THE AMERICAN REAL ESTATE AND URBAN ECONOMICS ASSOCIATION.** [J. Am. Real Estate Urban Econ. Assoc.]. **Added/Corp** American Real Estate and Urban Economics Association. **VFOAT** Real Estate Economics. Vol. 20, No. 1 (Spring 1992)-. Periodical. English. Four times a year (Mar., June, Sept., Dec.). $50.00 (individuals), $25.00 (students), $70.00 (libraries),

# Real Estate

$350.00 (institutional membership), $1,000.00 (institutional sponsorship). The American Real Estate and Urban Economics Association - AREUEA, Tenth Street & Fee Lane, Indiana University/School of Business, Room 428, Bloomington IN 47405. **Tel** (812)855-7794, FAX (812)855-8679. **ED** John Glascock. **LC** HD251; .A493a. **DD** 333. *Continues* AREUEA Journal, 0270-0484. **Ind/Abst** Acad. Search (Jan. 1994-).

US/0738-6494
**JUST COMPENSATION.** See Law.

US/0279-9960
**KANSAS REALTOR.** (KANSAS REALTOR : OFFICIAL PUBLICATION OF THE KANSAS ASSOCIATION OF REALTORS.). **Added/Corp** Kansas Association of Realtors. (198?)-. Periodical. English. Twelve times a year. $5.00. Kansas Association Realtors, 3644 Southwest Burlingame, Topeka KS 66611. **Tel** (913)267-3610. *Continues* Jayhawk Realtor.

JA
**KOKUDO RIYO HAKUSHO / KOKUDOCHO HEN.** Japanese. Okurasho Insatukyoku, 2-4, Toranomon 2 chome, Minatoku, Tokyo 105 Japan. **LC** HD911.A1; K63.

JA
**KYUSHU KEIZAI HAKUSHO.** **Main/Corp** Kyushu Keizai Chosa Kyokai. (19??)-. Japanese. an. Kyushu Keizai Chosa Kyokai, 9-48 Daimyomachi 1 Chuo-ku, Fukuoka 810 Japan. **LC** HD919.K9; K9a.

MY/0126-6160
**LAND DEVELOPMENT DIGEST.** V. 1-. Periodical. English. sa. $7.50 airmail, $4.00 surface mail. Felda Institute of Land Development, PO Sungkai, Perak Malaysia. **LC** HD890.6.A1; L36. **DD** 333.73/15/09595.

US/0891-7337
**LAND INVESTMENT NEWS.** See Business-Investments.

AT/0313-6353
**LAND RIGHTS NEWS.** (19??)-. English. Four times a year. 25.00Aus$ Australia; 30.00Aus$ others. Land Rights News, PO Box 42921, Casuarina NT 0811 Australia. **Tel** 011 61 89 205118.

US/0739-6376
**LAND TRENDS (NEW YORK, N.Y.).** (LAND TRENDS.). [Land trends]. **Added/Corp** Land Development Institute. Vol. 1, No. 1 (July 1974)-. Periodical. English. Twelve times a year. $345.00 university libraries, state supreme courts and their libraries, $395.00 other. Land Development Institute Ltd, 1401 16th Street Northwest, Washington DC 20036. **Tel** (202)232-4724, FAX (202)232-4757. **ED** Stuart Marshall Bloch, William B. Ingersoll, and Lisa Flyer Marsh. **LC** KF5698.3.A15; .L36. **DD** 346.7304/3; 347.30643. Index available. cum. index. **Circ**: 250 (ctrl).
 **Desc:** Newsletter and reference update services on the state and federal regulation of land development, including court decisions.

US/0023-768X
**LAND USE DIGEST.** **Added/Corp** Urban Land Institute. Vol. 1 (Nov. 1968)-. Periodical. English. mo. $15.00 (subscription). Urban Land Institute, 625 Indiana Ave Northwest, Washington DC 20004. **Tel** (202)624-7000, (800)321-5011.

US/0094-7598
**LAND USE LAW & ZONING DIGEST.** See Law.

US/0145-8620
**LAND USE PLANNING IN NEBRASKA.** [Land use plan. Neb.]. English. University of Nebraska / College of Architecture, Lincoln NE 68508. **LC** HD211.N2; L34. **DD** 333.7/09782.

NE/0166-5839
**LANDEIGENAAR.** [Landeigenaar]. (1955)-. Periodical. Dutch. mo (with July-Aug. issue combined). F92.45. Vuga Uitgeverij B.V., Postbus 16400, Zeestraat 65, 2500 BK Gravenhage Netherlands. **Tel** 011 31 70 3614011, FAX 011 31 70 3632338. **(Subscription address:** Infolio BV, Postbus 16500, 2500 BM Den Haag Netherlands.) **UDC** 347.23. Index available. **Ad Acc**. **Circ**: 3,861.
 **Desc:** Covers land utilization and ownership of land for policymakers, workers, or decision makers who have to deal with real estate.

US/1050-3196
**LANDLORD-TENANT RELATIONS REPORT.** See Housing and Urban Development.

US/1060-8826
**LANDWATCH (REDLANDS, CALIF.).** (LANDWATCH : LOCAL LAND USE AND REAL PROPERTY BULLETIN.). [LandWatch]. **VFOAT** Land Watch. (Oct./Dec. 1991)-. Bulletin. English. qt. $125.00. Pacific Horizon Co., 104 East State Street, Suite A, Redlands CA 92373. **DD** 333.

IO
**LAPORAN PASARAN HARTA.** *Title Change*. **VFOAT** Property Market Report. 1978-. English (Malay). **LC** HD890.6.Z63; M34A. **DD** 333.33/2/09595. *Superseded by* Property Market Report.

MY
**LAPURAN TAHUN DAN KIRA-KIRA - MALAYSIA INDUSTRIAL ESTATES SENDIRIAN BERHAD.** See Economics.

US/0741-5486
**LIVING (HOUSTON, ED.).** (LIVING.). **VFOAT** Houston Living. (1983)-. Periodical. English. Six times a year. Free. Lash Publications Inc., 6700 West Loop South 100, Bellaire TX 77401. **Tel** (713)777-4636. **ED** Francine Carbajal. Index available. **Bk Rev**. **Ad Acc**. **Circ**: 80,000 (ctrl). *Continues* Houston Living, 0192-9143.

US/0741-3440
**LIVING (SOUTH FLORIDA ED.).** (LIVING.). Vol. 3, No. 3 (June/July 1983)-. Periodical. English. bm. South Texas Housing Guide Limited, 4242 Medical OR 2175, San Antonio TX 78229. **Tel** (214)239-2399. **LC** HD266.F6. **DD** 333.33/09759. *Continues* South Florida Living, 0279-8506.

US
**LOG HOME LIVING ANNUAL BUYER'S GUIDE.** See Building and Construction-Carpentry and Woodwork.

US/0146-3438
**LOWER BUCKS COUNTY REAL ESTATE DIRECTORY.** Directory. English. Philadelphia Real Estate Directories Inc, 1010 Arch Street, Philadelphia PA 19107. **LC** HD266.P4; L68. **DD** 333.3/3.

US/0099-1686
**LUSK'S ANNE ARUNDEL COUNTY REAL ESTATE DIRECTORY, PROPERTY TRANSFERS.** Directory. English. Rufus S Lusk & Son Inc, 1110 Bonifant St., Attn: J B Hardt, Silver Springs MD 20910. **Tel** (301)588-6700. **LC** HD266.M3; L86. **DD** 333.3/3.

US/0099-104X
**LUSK'S BALTIMORE COUNTY REAL ESTATE DIRECTORY, PROPERTY TRANSFERS.** Directory. English. Rufus S Lusk & Son Inc, 1110 Bonifant St., Attn: J B Hardt, Silver Springs MD 20910. **Tel** (301)588-6700. **LC** HD266.M3; L87. **DD** 333.3/3/02575271.

US/0360-0874
**LUSK'S CARROLL COUNTY REAL ESTATE DIRECTORY.** Directory. English. Rufus S Lusk & Son Inc, 1110 Bonifant St., Attn: J B Hardt, Silver Springs MD 20910. **Tel** (301)588-6700. **LC** HD266.M3; L88. **DD** 333.3/3.

US/0196-4119
**LUSK'S DISTRICT OF COLUMBIA REAL ESTATE DIRECTORY SERVICE.** **VFOAT** District of Columbia Real Estate Directory Service. Directory. English. an. **LC** HD268.W3; L84. **DD** 333.3/37/025753. *Supersedes* Lusk's District of Columbia Assessment Directory Service.

US/0363-0668
**LUSK'S EAST SUFFOLK COUNTY REAL ESTATE DIRECTORY.** (19??)-. English. Rufus S Lusk & Son Inc, 1110 Bonifant St., Attn: J B Hardt, Silver Springs MD 20910. **Tel** (301)588-6700. **LC** HD266.N72; S94. **DD** 333.3/3.

US/0197-0305
**LUSK'S FAIRFAX COUNTY, VIRGINIA REAL ESTATE DIRECTORY SERVICE.** *Title Change*. **VFOAT** Fairfax County, Virginia Real Estate Directory Service. (19??)-(1992). Directory. English. Rufus S. Lusk and Son Inc., 1110 Bonifant Street, Silver Spring MD 20910-3374. **Tel** (301)588-6700. **ED** Rufus S. Lusk III. **LC** HD266.V82; F25. **DD** 333.305875529. *Continued by* Fairfax Directory Service.
 **Desc:** We publish real estate information for the Washington metropolitan areas, Baltimore and surrounding counties.

US/0557-4447
**LUSK'S MONTGOMERY COUNTY, MARYLAND, ASSESSMENT DIRECTORY.** **VFOAT** Montgomery County, Maryland, Assessment Directory. Directory. English. $400.00. Rufus S Lusk & Son Inc, 1110 Bonifant St., Attn: J B Hardt, Silver Springs MD 20910. **Tel** (301)588-6700. **ED** Rufus S Lusk III. **LC** HJ9253.M65; L85. **DD** 336.2/2/02575284.
 **Desc:** We publish real estate information for the Washington metropolitan areas, Baltimore and surrounding counties.

US/0745-8878
**LUSK'S NORTHERN VIRGINIA REAL ESTATE GUIDE.** **VFOAT** Northern Virginia Real Estate Guide. English. wk. $230.00. Rufus S. Lusk and Son Inc., 1110 Bonifant Street, Silver Spring MD 20910-3374. **Tel** (301)588-6700.

US/0094-8713
**LUSK'S PRINCE WILLIAM COUNTY REAL ESTATE DIRECTORY SERVICE.** Directory. English. ir. $400.00. Rufus S. Lusk and Son Inc., 1110 Bonifant Street, Silver Spring MD 20910-3374. **Tel** (301)588-6700. **ED** Rufus S Lusk III. **LC** HD266.V82; P735. **DD** 333.3/3/025755273. **Ad Acc**.
 **Desc:** We publish real estate information for the Washington metro area, Baltimore and surrounding counties, New York, Richmond and New Orleans.

US/0886-2737
**MANHATTAN OFFICE BUILDINGS. DOWNTOWN.** [Manhattan off. build., Downt.]. **VFOAT** Downtown; Manhattan Office Building/Downtown. (198?)-. English. an (May). $119.00. Yale Robbins Inc, 31 East 28th Street, 3rd Floor, New York NY 10157. **Tel** (212)683-5700, FAX (212)545-0764. **LC** HD1393.55; .M355. **DD** 333.33/87/0257471. **Ad Acc**. ctrl circ.
 **Desc:** A six volume set detailing major office buildings in midtown, midtown south, downtown and Westchester. Lists major tenants, rentable floor areas, GBA, plot size, ownership, rental agents, location maps, etc.

US/0886-3725
**MANHATTAN OFFICE BUILDINGS. MIDTOWN.** [Manhattan off. build., Midtown]. **VFOAT** Midtown; Manhattan Office Buildings/Midtown. (198?)-. English. an (Aug.). $119.00. Yale Robbins Inc, 31 East 28th Street, 3rd Floor, New York NY 10157. **Tel** (212)683-5700, FAX (212)545-0764. **LC** HD1393.55; .M36. **DD** 333.33/8. Index available. **Ad Acc**. **Pr Rev**. ctrl circ.
 **Desc:** A six volume set detailing major office buildings in midtown, midtown south, downtown and Westchester. Lists major tenants, rentable floor areas, GBA, plot size, ownership, rental agents, location maps, etc.

US/1046-8943
**MANHATTAN OFFICE BUILDINGS. MIDTOWN SOUTH.** [Manhattan off. build., Midtown south]. **VFOAT** Office Buildings; Midtown South; Manhattan Office Buildings Midtown South. (198?)-. English. an (Mar.). $119.00. Yale Robbins Inc., 31 East 28th Street, 3rd Floor, New York NY 10157. **Tel** (212)683-5700, FAX (212)545-0764. **LC** HD1393.55; .M363. **DD** 333.33/87/0257471.

US
**MARKET HISTORY REPORTS.** **Added/Corp** Ernst & Young. **VFOAT** National Real Estate Index Market History Reports. (19??)-. English. an. $295.00. Liquidity Fund, 2200 Powell Street, Suite 700, Emeryville CA 94608. **Tel** (415)652-8738, (800)992-7257, FAX (415)652-9701. **LC** HD251; .M37.
 **Desc:** Reports semiannual property price, rent and cap rate data since 1985 in 22 largest markets.

US
**MARKETSCORE.** English. qt. $195.00. Liquidity Fund, 2200 Powell Street, Suite 700, Emeryville CA 94608. **Tel** (415)652-8738, (800)992-7257, FAX (415)652-9701.
 **Desc:** Forecasts performance using a proprietary model based on key real estate, economic and demographic variables in five property sectors and 53 local markets.

JA
**MEIJI DAIGAKU KEIJI HAKUBUTSUKAN SHIRYO.** **Main/Corp** Meiji Daigaku. Keiji Hakubutsukan. (1977)-. Japanese. Meiji Daigaku, 1 Kanda Surugadai 1 Chiyoda-ku, Tokyo Japan. **LC** HD1295.J3; M44a.

US/0192-9909
**MEMBERSHIP/COMMITTEE DIRECTORY - BUILDING OWNERS AND MANAGERS ASSOCIATION INTERNATIONAL.** **Main/Corp** Building Owners and Managers Association International. Directory. English. an. Building Owners and Managers Association, 1201 New York Avenue Northwest, Suite 300, Washington DC 20005. **Tel** (202)408-2662, FAX (202)371-0181. **LC** TX955; .B793A. **DD** 643/.06/21.

US/0148-9348
**MEMBERSHIP DIRECTORY - APPRAISERS ASSOCIATION OF AMERICA, INC.** **Main/Corp** Appraisers Association of America. (19??)-. Directory. English. be (once every two years). $3.00. Appraisers Association of America, 60 East 42nd Street, New York NY 10017. **Tel** (212)867-9775. **LC** HF5681.V3; A66a. **DD** 333.3/32.

US/0737-4267
**MEMBERSHIP DIRECTORY - INTERNATIONAL ASSOCIATION OF ASSESSING OFFICERS. PERSONAL PROPERTY SECTION.** See Public Administration-Public Finance and Taxation.

US/0893-0775
**METRO CHICAGO REAL ESTATE.** **VFOAT** Real Estate. Vol. 74, No. 4 (Feb. 1987)-. Periodical. English. bw. $30.00. Law Bulletin Publishing Co., 415 North State Street, Chicago IL 60610. **Tel** (312)644-7800. ***Continues*** *Real Estate Magazine (Chicago, Ill.), 0746-164X.*

US/0893-2719
**MIDWEST REAL ESTATE NEWS.** [Midwest real estate news]. (Sept. 1985)-. Periodical. English. mo. $38.00 (one year), $60.00 (two year). Argus Business, 6151 Powers Ferry Road, Atlanta GA 30339. **Tel** (404)995-2500, (800)233-3359. **(Subscription address:** Hallmark Data System, PO Box 1147, Skokie, IL 60076 (708-647-6933)) **ED** Editor: 1985- Hal Schwartz. **DD** 333. **[CCC]. Circ:** 21,500. available on microfilm and microfiche from University Microfilms International (UMI); available on an online database (file 648/Full-Text) from DIALOG.
**Desc:** Covers commercial and industrial real estate activity in 10 Midwestern states: Illinois, Indiana, Iowa, Kansas, Michigan, Minnesota, Missouri, Nebraska, Ohio, and Wisconsin.
**Ind/Abst** Trade Ind. Index.

US/1054-9684
**MINNEAPOLIS AREA REALTOR.**
**Added/Corp** Minneapolis Area Association of Realtors (Minneapolis, Minn.). Periodical. English. mo. Great Minneapolis Board of Realtor, 5750 Lincoln Drive, Minneapolis MN 55436. ***Continues*** *Minneapolis Realtor, 0745-3906.*

US/0745-3906
**MINNEAPOLIS REALTOR.** ***Title Change.*** Periodical. English. mo. Great Minneapolis Board of Realtor, 5750 Lincoln Drive, Minneapolis MN 55436. **ED** Lee Coucette. **Circ:** 5,700 (ctrl). ***Continued by*** *Minneapolis Area Realtor, 1054-9684.*
**Desc:** Published for Greater Minneapolis Area Board of REALTORS.

US/0360-8077
**MINNESOTA REAL ESTATE DIRECTORY.** Directory. English. Metro Square Building, 5th Floor, St Paul MN 55101. **LC** HD266.M6; M48. **DD** 333.3/3.

US/0893-2255
**MINNESOTA REAL ESTATE JOURNAL.** [Minn. real estate j.]. **VFOAT** Real Estate Journal; MREJ. Vol. 1, No. 1 (Jan. 1985)-. Periodical. English. bw. $65.00 (one year), $95.00 (two years), $115.00 (three years). Minnesota Real Estate Journal, 8900 Wentworth Avenue S, Bloomington MN 55420. **Tel** (612)885-0815, FAX (612)885-0818. **ED** John Share. **DD** 333. **Ad Acc, Adv Mgr:** Mike Kramer. available on microfilm.
**Desc:** Covers information on the commercial real estate industry for the state of Minnesota, primarily for the Minneapolis/St. Paul area.

US/0278-7628
**MINNESOTA REAL ESTATE LAW JOURNAL.** See Law.

US/0195-1963
**MINNESOTA REALTOR.** V. 1- Aug. 1979-. Periodical. English. mo. Minnesota Association of Realtors, 5750 Lincoln Drive, Edina MN 55436. ***Supersedes*** *Minnesota Realtor, 0195-1963.*

US/0195-8194
**MOBILITY (WASHINGTON).** See Business.

US/8756-9124
**MONEY & REAL ESTATE.** **VFOAT** Money and Real Estate. (1985)-. Periodical. English. mo. $120.00 charter, $180.00 regular. Executive Enterprises, 22 West 21st Street, New York NY 10010-6990. **Tel** (800)332-8804, FAX (212)645-8689.

US
**MONTGOMERY COUNTY REAL ESTATE REPORT.** English. $324.75. Revac Publications, 11777 Katy Freeway, Suite 500, Houston TX 77079. **Tel** (713)496-2388.

CN/0839-6361
**MONTHLY MLS STATISTICAL SURVEY.** [Mon. MLS stat. surv.]. **Added/Corp** Canadian Real Estate Association. Research & Publications Dept. Canadian Real Estate Association. Communications Dept. **VFOAT** Monthly Multiple Listing Service Statistical Survey; Preliminary MLS Statistical Survey. **VAT** Releve Mensuel des Statistiques SIA. (1982)-. Statistical Publication. English. mo. 60.00Can$. Canadian Real Estate Association, 320 Queen Street, Suite 2100, Ottawa Ontario K1R 5A3 Canada. **Tel** (613)234-3372. **DD** 333.33/0971/021. ***Continues*** *Monthly MLS Statistical Summary, 0839-6353.*

CN/0712-9769
**MORGUARD REPORT.** (MORGUARD REPORT / MORGUARD.). [Morguard rep.]. Periodical. English. qt. Free. Morguard Group Ltd, 6 Crescent Road, Toronto Ontario M4W 3K9 Canada. **DD** 332.63/24/0971.

US/0047-813X
**MORTGAGE AND REAL ESTATE EXECUTIVES REPORT, THE.** (MORTGAGE AND REAL ESTATE EXECUTIVES REPORT.). (19??)-. Periodical. English. sm (24 issues). $160.00 US and Canada; 223.20 other. Warren Gorham & Lamont Inc., Park Square Building, 31 St. James Avenue, Boston MA 02116-4112. **Tel** (617)423-2020, (800)950-1207, FAX (617)423-2026. **ED** Alvin L. Arnold. **[CCC].**
**Desc:** Report service for real estate professionals. Provides a constant source of ideas and new updates.
**Ind/Abst** Trade Ind. Index.

US/0545-0659
**MORTGAGE AND REAL ESTATE INVESTMENT GUIDE.** (MORTGAGE AND REAL ESTATE INVESTMENT GUIDE / BY MALCOLM C. SHERMAN.). [Mort. real estate investm. guide]. (1952)-. English. Twice a year (May, Nov.). $132.50 Massachusetts; $125.00 others. Mrs. Malcolm Sherman, Box 703, Marshfield MA 02050. **Tel** (617)834-8702. **ED** Malcolm C. Sherman and Alan C. Sherman. **DD** 332.

CN/0713-8369
**MOVING TO & AROUND ALBERTA.** [Mov. Alta.]. **VAT** Moving To and Around Alberta. Vol. 9, No. 6 (Feb. 5, 1982)-. English. an. $6.95. Moving Publications Ltd., 44 Upjohn Road, Suite 100, Don Mills Ontario M3B 2W1 Canada. **Tel** (416)441-1168, FAX (416)441-1641. **ED** Lorraine Hunter. **DD** 917.123/044. **Ad Acc.** Full Page (B&W) $6540.00. Half Page (B&W) $3940.00 (island). Full Page (Color) $7995.00. Half Page (Color) $4845.00 (island). ***Continues*** *Moving to Alberta, 0702-9195.*
**Desc:** Relocation magazine packed with information for people moving across town, or to a new city. Answers questions on housing, education, health care and shopping.

CN/0843-9214
**MOVING TO & AROUND HAMILTON, C.T.T., BRANTFORD, BURLINGTON & NIAGARA.** [Mov. around Hamilt. C.T.T. Brantford Burlingt. Niagara]. **VFOAT** Moving to and Around Hamilton, C.T.T., Brantford, Burlington and Niagara. Vol. 17, No. 7 (Sept. 1990/1991)-. English. Twice a year. $6.95. Moving Publications Ltd., 44 Upjohn Road, Suite 100, Don Mills Ontario M3B 2W1 Canada. **Tel** (416)441-1168, FAX (416)441-1641. **ED** Lorraine Hunter. **DD** 917.13/2.
**Desc:** Relocation magazine packed with information for people moving across town, or to a new city. Answers questions about housing, education, health care, and shopping.

CN/0713-8385
**MOVING TO & AROUND SASKATCHEWAN.** [Mov. Sask.]. **VAT** Moving To and Around Saskatchewan. Vol. 9, No. 5 (Jan. 29 1982/1983)-. English. Twice a year. $6.95. Moving Publications Ltd., 44 Upjohn Road, Suite 100, Don Mills Ontario M3B 2W1 Canada. **Tel** (416)441-1168, FAX (416)441-1641. **ED** Lorraine Hunter. **DD** 917.124/044. **Ad Acc.** Full Page (B&W) $6130.00. Half Page (B&W) $3670.00 (island). Full Page (Color) $7620.00. Half Page (Color) $4720.00 (island). ***Continues*** *Moving to Saskatchewan, 0225-5383.*
**Desc:** Relocation magazine packed with information for people moving across town, or to a new city. Answers questions on housing, education, health care, and shopping.

CN/0713-8377
**MOVING TO & AROUND TORONTO & AREA.** [Mov. Tor. area]. **VAT** Moving To and Around Toronto and Area. Vol. 9, No. 3 (Jan. 15, 1982)-. English. an. $6.95. Moving Publications Ltd., 44 Upjohn Road, Suite 100, Don Mills Ontario M3B 2W1 Canada. **Tel** (416)441-1168, FAX (416)441-1641. **ED** Lorraine Hunter. **DD** 917.13/54044. **Ad Acc.** Full Page (B&W) $6680.00. Half Page (B&W) $4040.00 (island). Full Page (Color) $8270.00. Half Page (Color) $4985.00 (island). ***Continues*** *Moving to Toronto & Area, 0226-7829.*
**Desc:** Relocation magazine packed with information for people moving across town, or to a new city. Answers questions on housing, education, health care, and shopping.

CN/0713-8407
**MOVING TO & AROUND VANCOUVER & B.C.** [Mov. Vanc. B.C.]. **VAT** Moving To and Around Vancouver and British Columbia. Vol. 9, No. 3 (Jan. 15, 1982)-. English. an. $6.95. Moving Publications Ltd., 44 Upjohn Road, Suite 100, Don Mills Ontario M3B 2W1 Canada. **Tel** (416)441-1168, FAX (416)441-1641. **ED** Lorraine Hunter. **DD** 917.11/33044. **Ad Acc.** Full Page (B&W) $6540.00. Half Page (B&W) $3940.00 (island). Full Page (Color) $7995.00. Half Page (Color) $4845.00 (island). ***Continues*** *Moving to Vancouver & B.C., 0226-7276.*
**Desc:** Relocation magazine packed with information for people moving across town, or to a new city. Answers questions on housing, education, health care, and shopping.

CN/0715-7053
**MOVING TO & AROUND WINNIPEG & MANITOBA.** [Mov. around Winn. Manit.]. **VAT** Moving to and Around Winnipeg and Manitoba. Vol. 10, No. 4 (Feb. 4, 1983/1984)-. English. Twice a year. $6.95. Moving Publications Ltd., 44 Upjohn Road, Suite 100, Don Mills Ontario M3B 2W1 Canada. **Tel** (416)441-1168, FAX (416)441-1641. **ED** Lorraine Hunter. **DD** 917.127/4. **Ad Acc.** Full Page (B&W) $6130.00. Half Page (B&W) $3670.00 (island). Full Page (Color) $7620.00. Half Page (Color) $4720.00 (island). ***Continues*** *Moving to Winnipeg, 0702-9209.*
**Desc:** Relocation magazine packed with information for people moving across town, or to a new city. Answers questions on housing, education, health care, and shopping.

CN/0702-9225
**MOVING TO MONTREAL.** **VFOAT** Emmenager a Montreal. (1975)-. English (French). Twice a year. $6.95. Moving Publications Ltd., 44 Upjohn Road, Suite 100, Don Mills Ontario M3B 2W1 Canada. **Tel** (416)441-1168, FAX (416)441-1641. **ED** Lorraine Hunter. **DD** 971.4/28/005.
**Desc:** Relocation magazine packed with information for people moving across town, or to a new city. Answers questions about housing, education, health care, and shopping.

CN/0226-7837
**MOVING TO OTTAWA/HULL (1978).** (MOVING TO OTTAWA/HULL.). [Moving Ottawa/Hull]. **VFOAT** Emmenager a Ottawa/Hull. **VAT** Emmanager a Ottawa/Hull (1978). (1978)-. English (French). an. $6.95. Moving Publications Ltd., 44 Upjohn Road, Suite 100, Don Mills Ontario M3B 2W1 Canada. **Tel** (416)441-1168, FAX (416)441-1641. **ED** Lorraine Hunter. **DD** 917.13/84. **Ad Acc.** Full Page (B&W) $6130.00. Half Page (B&W) $3670.00 (island). Full Page (Color) $7620.00. Half Page (Color) $4720.00 (island). ***Continues*** *Emmenager a Ottawa/Hull, 0226-7837.*
**Desc:** Relocation magazine packed with information for people moving across town, or to a new city. Answers questions about housing, education, health care, and shopping.

CN/0828-4601
**MOVING TO THE SAN FRANCISCO BAY AREA AND GREATER SACRAMENTO.** [Mov. San Francisco Bay Area Gt. Sacram.]. Vol. 11, No. 12 (1985)-. English. an. $6.95. Moving Publications Ltd., 44 Upjohn Road, Suite 100, Don Mills Ontario M3B 2W1 Canada. **Tel** (416)441-1168, FAX (416)441-1641. **ED** Lorraine Hunter. **DD** 917.94/60453/05. ***Continues*** *Moving to San Francisco and the Bay Area, 0714-7295.*
**Desc:** Relocation magazine packed with information for people moving across town, or to a new city. Answers questions about housing, education, health care, and shopping.

AT/0727-0062
**N.S.W. REALTY AUCTIONEER.** (1973)-. Periodical. English. mo. 215.00Aus$. Ian Huntley Publishers Pty Limited, PO Box 99, Cremorne NSW, 2090 Australia. **Tel** 11 61 2 9535788.

US/0745-0893
**N.Y. HABITAT.** **VFOAT** NY Habitat; New York Habitat. Vol. 1, No. 1 (May 1982)-. Periodical. English. Eight times a year. $34.95. New York Habitat, 928 Broadway, New York NY 10010. **Tel** (212)505-2030. **ED** Carol J. Ott. cum. index. **Bk Rev. Ad Acc. Circ:** 10,000 (ctrl). ***Absorbed*** *Loft Living.*
**Desc:** A business magazine for co-op and condo boards of directors, owners and would-be owners. Covering aspects of ownership-management, value sales, group leadership.

US/1053-7902
**NATIONAL DIRECTORY OF REAL ESTATE ATTORNEYS, THE.** See Law.

US/0739-5647
**NATIONAL MONTHLY CONDOMINIUM EXECUTIVE REPORT.** (NATIONAL MONTHLY CONDOMINIUM EXECUTIVE REPORT : A JOHN GORNALL COMMUNICATIONS PUBLICATION.). **VFOAT** Condominium Executive Report. (19??)-. Periodical. English. mo. $136.00 US; $150.00 Canada. Gornall Communications, PO Box 911, Millsboro DE 19966. **Tel** (302)945-9313, FAX (302)945-8636. **ED** John M. Gornall. **Bk Rev. Circ:** 1,000.
**Desc:** Monthly newsletter of updates on real estate and housing development. Includes articles, on sales, management problems, dealing with and giving bad news to customers, and upcoming events on conferences.

US
**NATIONAL REAL ESTATE INDEX.**
**Added/Corp** Liquidity Fund (Firm). **VFOAT** Index Quarterly Report. (Summer 1986)-. Periodical. English. qt. $895.00. Liquidity Fund, 2200 Powell Street, Suite 700, Emeryville CA 94608. **Tel** (415)652-8738, (800)992-7257, FAX (415)652-9701. **ED** Dan O'Conner.

**LC** HD255; .N37. **Circ:** 3,500 (ctrl).
**Desc:** Indexes all National Real Estate Index publications, plus Index Special Reports.

US
**NATIONAL REAL ESTATE INDEX. MARKET MONITOR.** **Added/Corp** Liquidity Fund (Firm) Standard and Poor's Corporation. **VFOAT** Market Monitor. Ist Quarter (1989)-. Periodical. English. qt. $295.00. Liquidity Fund, 2200 Powell Street, Suite 700, Emeryville CA 94608. **Tel** (415)652-8738, (800)992-7257, FAX (415)652-9701. **ED** Dan O'Conner. **Ad Acc, Adv Mgr:** Ami Loventhal. **Circ:** 5,000. ***Continues*** *National Real Estate Index. Research Bulletin.*
**Desc:** Primary source of prices, rents, and cap rates for the CBD office, warehouse, retail, and apartment sectors in 51 markets. Compares current quarter with prior quarter and one year before. Reports Class A suburban office and Class B apartments as well.

US/0027-9994
**NATIONAL REAL ESTATE INVESTOR.** **See** Business-Investments.

US/0731-8693
**NATIONAL REAL ESTATE INVESTOR. DIRECTORY ISSUE.** [Natl. real estate invest. Dir. issue]. **VFOAT** National Real Estate Investor Directory; NREI Directory. (197?)-. Directory. English. an. $75.95. Argus Business, 6151 Powers Ferry Road, Atlanta GA 30339. **Tel** (404)995-2500, (800)233-3359. **ED** Paula S Stephens and Barbara Katinsky. **Ad Acc. Circ:** 31,000 (ctrl). ***Continues*** *National Real-Estate Investor Directory, 0547-8383.*
**Desc:** Over 7,000 individual and company listings in 19 real estate classifications. Plus a real estate executive salary survey.

CN/1181-9359
**NATIONAL REAL PROPERTY LAW REVIEW.** [Natl. real prop. law rev.]. **VFOAT** National Property Review. Vol. 3, No. 9 (Sept. 1990)-. Periodical. English. mo. 150.00Can$. Butterworth & Company Ltd. / Canada, 75 Clegg Road, Markham Ontario L6G 1A1 Canada. **Tel** (905)479-2665, (800)668-6481. **ED** Paul Perell. **DD** 346.7104/3. ***Continues*** *National Property Review, 0836-057X.*
**Desc:** Provides ongoing commentary on recent decisions, new developments, and established practices.
**Ind/Abst** Index Can. Leg. Period. Lit. (1992-).

●US/1075-1084
**NATIONAL REFERRAL ROSTER.** (1994)-. English. an (Feb.). $75.00 real estate firms; $30.00 other. Stamats Communications Inc., 427 Sixth Avenue Southeast, Cedar Rapids IA 52406. **Tel** (319)364-6167, FAX (319)365-5421. **ED** Candy Holub. **Ad Acc, Adv Mgr:** Mark Neujahr, **Tel** same as publisher. **Circ:** 18,000. ***Continues*** *National Roster of Realtors, 0090-1741.*
**Desc:** Contains the most complete list of US residential real estate firms and is designed to serve the estimated $1.8 billion national referral market.

●US/1062-6352
**NATIONAL REGISTER OF COMMERCIAL REAL ESTATE, THE.** **VFOAT** Commercial Property Exchange. (1992)-. Periodical. English. qt. Sigma Communications, 300 First Stamford Place, 6th Floor West, Stamford CT 06902.

US
**NATIONAL RELOCATION AND REAL ESTATE MAGAZINE.** (19??)-. English. bm (plus one special issue). $41.65. Relocation Information Service Inc., PO Box 445, Norwalk CT 06852. **Tel** (203)227-3800. **Ad Acc.**

US/0090-1741
**NATIONAL ROSTER OF REALTORS.** ***Title Change.*** **Added/Corp** National Association of Real Estate Boards. (19??)-(1993). English. an. Stamats Communications Inc., 427 Sixth Avenue Southeast, Cedar Rapids IA 52406. **Tel** (319)364-6167, FAX (319)365-5421. **ED** Evelyn Oldridge. **LC** HD253; .N34. **DD** 333.3/3. **Ad Acc. Circ:** 10,000. ***Continued by*** *National Referral Roster, 1075-1084.*
**Desc:** Lists the names and addresses alphabetically by board and state of every realtor. Also information on the National Association of Realtors.

US/8750-6580
**NATION'S BUILDING NEWS.** **See** Building and Construction.

US
**NCREIF REAL ESTATE PERFORMANCE REPORT, THE.** **Added/Corp** National Council of Real Estate Investment Fiduciaries. Frank Russell Company. **VFOAT** National Council of Real Estate Investment Fiduciaries Real Estate Performance Report; Performance Report. (1987)-. Periodical. English. qt. $1000.00 (one year). NCREIF, PO Box 1616, Tacoma WA 98401. **Tel** (206) 572-9500, FAX (206) 591-3495, telex 327431. **LC** HD1382.5; .N374. ***Continues*** *NCREIF Report.*

●US/1060-5789
**NELSON'S DIRECTORY OF INSTITUTIONAL REAL ESTATE.** [Nelson's dir. inst. real estate]. **VFOAT** Directory of Institutional Real Estate; Institutional Real Estate. 1st Annual Ed. (1992)-. Directory. English. an. $295.00. Nelson Publications, One Gateway Plaza, PO Box 591, Port Chester NY 10573. **Tel** (914)937-8400, (800)333-6357, FAX (914)937-8908. **ED** Marcia Boysen. **LC** HD251; .N38. **DD** 333.33/029/473. Index available (bound in each issue). **Ad Acc, Adv Mgr:** Peter McCuen, **Tel** (914)937-8400. **Circ:** 2,000+. ***Continues*** *Nelson's Directory of Real Estate Consultants, 1058-854X.*
**Desc:** Contains detailed profiles (including key executives) of firms providing real estate investment management services as well as specialized real estate services such as asset management, appraisals, lease negotiations, property management and consulting.

US/1058-854X
**NELSON'S DIRECTORY OF REAL ESTATE INVESTMENTS.** ***Title Change.*** **VFOAT** Directory of Real Estate Investments. (1992)-(1992). Directory. English. an. Nelson Publications, One Gateway Plaza, PO Box 591, Port Chester NY 10573. **Tel** (914)937-8400, (800)333-6357, FAX (914)937-8908. ***Continued by*** *Nelson's Directory of Institutional Real Estate, 1060-5789.*

US/0028-4890
**NEW ENGLAND REAL ESTATE JOURNAL.** [N. Engl. real estate j.]. (19??)-. Periodical. English. wk. $96.00 (one year), $172.00 (two year). New England Real Estate, PO Box 55, Accord MA 02018. **Tel** (617)878-4540. **ED** Roland Hopkins. **DD** 332. **Ad Acc, Adv Mgr Tel** (617)878-4540. **Circ:** 30,000 (ctrl).
**Desc:** Commercial, industrial andor investment real estate.

US/1042-9689
**NEW ENGLAND REAL ESTATE NEWS.** ***Title Change.*** [New Engl. real estate news]. Vol. 1, No. 1 (March 1989)-(1992). Periodical. English. mo. Argus Business, 6151 Powers Ferry Road, Atlanta GA 30339. **Tel** (404)995-2500, (800)233-3359. **DD** 333. **[CCC].** available on microfilm and microfiche from University Microfilms International (UMI); available on an online database (file 648/Full-Text) from DIALOG. ***Merged into*** *Northeast - New England Real Estate News.*
**Ind/Abst** Trade Ind. Index.

US/0890-4723
**NEW HOMES.** **VFOAT** New homes Magazine; Southern California New Homes; A.New homes magazine and map guide to new home communities; A.New homes magazine & map guide to new home communities. Vol. 7, No. 1 (Feb./Mar. 1974)-. Periodical. English. Six times a year. $30.00. New Homes Magazine, 3151 Air Way Avenue, Building D1, Costa Mesa CA 92626. **Tel** (800)247-6996, (714)751-5813, FAX (714)755-5500. **ED** Jim Turnbull. **Ad Acc, Adv Mgr:** Dan Ciavri. ctrl circ. ***Continues*** *Southern California New Homes.*

US/0192-4893
**NEW HOMES MAGAZINE.** (1973)-. Periodical. English. **ED** Kele Dooley.

US/0028-5919
**NEW JERSEY REALTOR.** **Added/Corp** New Jersey Association of Realtors. (19??)-. Periodical. English. Ten times a year. $10.00. New Jersey Association of Realtors, 295 Pierson Avenue, Box 2098, Edison NJ 08818. **Tel** (201)494-4723. **ED** Donna Jean Schratwieser. **Bk Rev. Ad Acc. Circ:** 46,000 (ctrl).
**Desc:** Trends of the New Jersey Association of Realtors; including legal questions and guidelines, real estate issues and member inquiries.

UK/0264-8121
**NEW LAW FOR SURVEYORS.** [New law surv.]. **VFOAT** New Law for General Practice Surveyors. (1984)-. Periodical. English. sa. $40.00 European Union; $44.00 other. E & FN Spon Ltd, 2 6 Boundary Row, London SE1 8HN England. **Tel** 011 44 71 865 0066. **ED** Vera McEwan. **Bk Rev. Ad Acc.**
**Desc:** Provides general practice surveyors with selected summaries of legal developments relevant to their day-to-day concerns. Provides notes on recently decided cases and gives details of recent statutes and statutory instruments.

US/0951-547X
**NEW MEXICO REAL ESTATE LAW REPORTER.** **See** Law.

US/1057-2104
**NEW YORK REAL ESTATE JOURNAL.** [N. Y. real estate j.]. (198?)-. Periodical. English. sm (24 issues). $48.00. New York Real Estate Journal, PO Box 55, Accord MA 02018. **Tel** (800)654-4993. **ED** Linda Christman. **DD** 333. **Bk Rev,** (Qty: 3). **Ad Acc. Circ:** 7,000 (ctrl).

US/0894-4903
**NEW YORK REAL ESTATE LAW REPORTER.** [N. Y. real estate law report.]. **Added/Corp** Leader Publications, Inc. Benjamin N. Cardozo School of Law. Real Estate Law Society. **VFOAT** Real Estate Law Reporter. Vol. 1, No. 1 (Nov. 1986)-. Periodical. English. mo. $185.00. Leader Publications, 345 Park Avenue South, New York NY 10010. **Tel** (800)888-8300 ext. 6170, (212)545-6170, FAX (212)696-1848. **ED** Stewart Sterk (editor's phone: (212)790-0230). **LC** KFN5140.A59; N49. **DD** 346.74704/3; 347.470643.
**Desc:** Reports on recent New York state real estate cases.

US/0883-1726
**NEWSLETTER - COMMON SHORES.** (NEWSLETTER / COMMON SHORES INC.). [Newsl. - Common Shores]. Newsletter. English. qt. Common Shores Inc, 45 Dixon Avenue, Amityville NY 11701. **DD** 333.

US/0270-255X
**NMM WEEKLY.** **Main/Corp** National Mall Monitor. **VAT** National Mall Monitor Weekly. Periodical. English. wk. $195.00. National Mall Monitor, Arbor Office Center, 1321 US 19 South/Suite 500, Clearwater FL 33516. **Tel** (813)796-8870, telex (813)791-3763.

US/1047-8833
**NORTHEAST REAL ESTATE NEWS.** ***Title Change.*** [Northeast real estate news]. (1990)-(1992). Periodical. English. bm. Argus Business, 6151 Powers Ferry Road, Atlanta GA 30339. **Tel** (404)995-2500, (800)233-3359. **ED** Fora Hatras. **DD** 332. **[CCC]. Circ:** 19,000. available on microfilm and microfiche from University Microfilms International (UMI). ***Merged into*** *Northeast - New England Real Estate News.*
**Desc:** Covers commercial and industrial real estate activity in New York, New Jersey, Pennsylvania and Delaware.

CN
**NOVA SCOTIA REAL PROPERTY PRACTICE MANUAL.** **See** Law.

●CN/1189-5993
**OFFICE LEASING DIRECTORY.** [Off. leas. dir.]. **Added/Corp** BOMA Manitoba. **VFOAT** BOMA Manitoba Office Leasing Directory. (1992)-. Directory. English. Free to members of BOMA Manitoba. Naylor Communications Ltd, 100 Sutherland Avenue, Winnipeg Manitoba R2W 3C7 Canada. **Tel** (204)947-0222, FAX (604)985-7399. **DD** 333.33. ***Continues*** *Official and Industrial Leasing Directory (Winnipeg, Man.)., 1185-4219.*

US/1057-9486
**OFFICIAL PROPERTY MANAGEMENT DIRECTORY (METROPOLITAN WASHINGTON), THE.** (THE OFFICIAL PROPERTY MANAGEMENT DIRECTORY.). [Off. prop. manage. dir.]. **VFOAT** Metropolitan Washington Official Property Management Directory. 2nd ed. (Spring 1991)-. Directory. English. sa. $119.00. Adler Group Inc., 8601 Georgia Avenue, Silver Spring MD 20910. **Tel** (609)988-0092, FAX (609)988-0093. **LC** HD1394; .P75. **DD** 333. ***Continues*** *Property Management Directory, 1049-2712.*

US/0745-5046
**OKLAHOMA REALTOR.** **Added/Corp** Oklahoma Association of Realtors. (19??)-. Periodical. English. bm. $3.00 (members), $4.00 (non-members). Oklahoma Realtor, 9807 North Broadway, Oklahoma City OK 73114. **Tel** (4050848-9944, FAX (405)848-9947. **ED** Trey Richardson and Laura Wells. **Bk Rev. Ad Acc. Circ:** 7,000 (ctrl).
**Desc:** Real Estate Industry and membership news.

US/0147-1929
**OPERATIONS MANUAL OF THE NATIONAL ASSOCIATION OF REALTORS.** **Main/Corp** National Association of Realtors. English. $4.00. 430 North Michigan Avenue, Chicago IL 60611. **LC** HD251; .N339316. **DD** 333.3/3.

IT
**OSSERVATORIO SUL MERCATO IMMOBILIARE.** (19??)-. Periodical. Italian. Three times a year. L600000. Nomisma, Strada Maggiore 44, 40125 Bologna, Italy. **Tel** 011 39 51 239422. cum. index. **Bk Rev. Ad Acc.**
**Desc:** Analysis on the urban real estate market.

●US/1059-6526
**PENNSYLVANIA COMMERCIAL REAL ESTATE.** (1992)-. Periodical. English. mo. Pennsylvania Publishing Company, PO Box 170, Coalport PA 16627.

●US/1059-6534
**PENNSYLVANIA REAL ESTATE.** (1992)-. English. mo. Pennsylvania Publishing Company, PO Box 170, Coalport PA 16627.

US/0190-5449
**PHOTO ROSTER.** **Main/Corp** Society of Industrial Realtors. English. be. Society of Industrial and Office Realtors, 777 14th Street Northwest, Suite 400,

# Real Estate

Washington DC 20005-3271. **Tel** (202)373-1150, FAX (202)373-3142. **LC** HD251; .S62A. **DD** 333.3/3/02573. ctrl circ.

**US/0746-746X**
**PINELLAS COUNTY REVIEW.** See Business-Banking and Finance.

**US/8756-0372**
**PRACTICAL REAL ESTATE LAWYER, THE.** See Law.

**US/0882-715X**
**PRESERVATION LAW REPORTER.** See Law.

**US**
**PREVIEWS GUIDE TO THE WORLD'S FINE REAL ESTATE. Ceased. Main/Corp** Previews Incorporated. **VFOAT** Previews' International Real Estate Guide; Guide to the World's Fine Real Estate. Ceased (1988/89). English. an. Previews Inc, 400 Northridge/Suite 1100, Atlanta GA 30350. **Tel** (800)243-4006, telex 4750075. **ED** Helene Nichols and Betty Moore. **LC** HD1361; .P73A. **DD** 333.33/05. **Ad Acc. Circ:** 20,000.
**Desc:** Guide showing the world's finest real estate for sale around the world.

**US**
**PRIME REAL ESTATE.** English. bm. $18.95 US; (add $12.00) other. Prime Publishing Company, 4141 State Street, No E14, Santa Barbara CA 93110. **Tel** (805)967-3663. **ED** Jennifer Downes. **Ad Acc. Circ:** 40,000 (ctrl).
**Desc:** Lifestyle environment, community real estate, residential oriented.

**US/0271-0897**
**PRIVATE REAL ESTATE LIMITED PARTNERSHIPS.** [Priv. real estate ltd. partnersh.]. 1977-. Periodical. English. an. Practising Law Institute, 810 Seventh Avenue, New York NY 10019-5818. **Tel** (212)765-5700, FAX (212)581-4670 general correspondence, (212)265-4742 orders and billing inquiries. **LC** KF1079; .P75. **DD** 346/7304/37.

**US/0164-0372**
**PROBATE AND PROPERTY (CHICAGO, ILL. : 1987).** See Law-Estate Planning.

**US/0891-2599**
**PROFESSIONAL APARTMENT MANAGEMENT.** [Prof. apartm. manage.]. (Oct. 1986)-. Periodical. English. mo. $168.00. Brownstone Publishers, 149 Fifth Avenue, 16th Floor, New York NY 10010. **Tel** (212)473-8200, (800)643-8095, FAX (212)995-9205. **ED** Glenn Demby. **DD** 333. Index available.
**Desc:** Newsletter for property managers, leasing agents and owners that strives to help them run their apartment buildings.

**US/0749-8012**
**PROFESSIONAL REAL ESTATE REPORTS.** [Prof. real estate rep.]. Vol. 1, No. 1 (Sept. 1984)-. Periodical. English. bm. $235.00. Tribune Media Services, 435 North Michigan Avenue, Chicago IL 60611. **Tel** (800)637-4082, FAX (312)222-2581. **DD** 333.

●**US/1067-4764**
**PROFESSIONAL REPORT : A PUBLICATION OF THE SOCIETY OF INDUSTRIAL AND OFFICE REALTORS.** [Prof. rep. - Soc. Ind. Off. Realt.]. **Added/Corp** Society of Industrial and Office Realtors. (1992)-. Periodical. English. ir (6 issues per year). $35.00 members; $45.00 others. Society of Industrial and Office Realtors, 777 14th Street Northwest, Suite 400, Washington DC 20005-3271. **Tel** (202)373-1150, FAX (202)373-3142. **DD** 333. **Continues** Professional Report of Industrial and Office Real Estate, 1060-9636.

**US/0742-5074**
**PROFILE OF REAL ESTATE FIRMS.** (PROFILE OF REAL ESTATE FIRMS / PREPARED BY THE ECONOMICS AND RESEARCH DIVISION, NATIONAL ASSOCIATION OF REALTORS.). **Added/Corp** National Association of Realtors. Economics & Research Division. (19??)-. English. te. $18.00. National Association of Realtors Economics and Research Division, 777 14th Street Northwest, Washington DC 20005. **Tel** (202)383-1059. **LC** HD278; .P75. **DD** 338.7/61333330973. **Circ:** 2,000.
**Desc:** Presents findings on the organizational, operational and structural characteristics of real estate firms. The objective is to provide a current profile of real estate firms and develop information on trends in the industry.

**US/0033-1287**
**PROPERTIES.** Periodical. English. mo. $10.00. Properties Magazine, 4900 Euclid Avenue, Cleveland OH 44103. **Tel** (216)431-7666. **ED** Gene E Bluhm. **Circ:** 2,500.
**Desc:** Publishes distinctive, new income property real estate developments.

**UK/0955-8658**
**PROPERTY FINANCE.** See Business-Banking and Finance.

**AT**
**PROPERTY INVESTOR.** See Business-Investments.

**UK/0263-7472**
**PROPERTY MANAGEMENT. (LONDON).** [Prop. manage.Lond.]. Periodical. English. qt. $249.00. MCB University Press, 60 62 Toller Lane, Bradford West Yorkshire BD8 9BX England. **Tel** 011 44 274 499821, FAX 011 44 274 547143, telex 51317 MCBUNI G. **(Subscription address:** MCB University Press / US and Canada Subscriptions, PO Box 10812, Birmingham AL 35201-0812.**) DD** 344.10643. Index available. cum. index. **Bk Rev. Ad Acc. Pr Rev. Acid Free. Circ:** 2,000.
**Desc:** Each issue contains up to 8 refereed papers, a legal update and a market comment. Publication is specifically aimed at property managers, surveyors, solicitors and property academics.

**US/1054-3848**
**PROPERTY MANAGEMENT MONTHLY.** [Prop. manage. mon.]. **VFOAT** Property Management. Vol. 1, No. 1 (Feb. 1991)-. Periodical. English. mo. $12.00. Adler Group Inc., 8601 Georgia Avenue, Silver Spring MD 20910. **Tel** (609)988-0092, FAX (609)988-0093. **LC** HD1394; .P765. **DD** 647/.92/05. **Continues** Apartment & Office Management News, 1049-2372.

**MY**
**PROPERTY MARKET REPORT ... / MINISTRY OF FINANCE MALAYSIA, KUALA LUMPUR.** Began with Vol. for 1979. English. an. $16.00. **LC** HD890.6.Z63; P76. **DD** 333.33/2/09595. **Separated from** Laporan Pasaran Harta.

**MY**
**PROPERTY OUTLOOK.** Vol. 1, No. 1 (Sept. 1983)-. Periodical. English. $3.00 each issue. Multiple Listing Systems, SDN BHD 943 Japan 19/13, Petaling Jaya Selangor Malaysia. **LC** HD890.6.A1; P76. **DD** 333.33/2/095951.

**HK**
**PROPERTY REVIEW. Main/Corp** Hong Kong. Rating and Valuation Dept. (19??)-. English. **LC** HD943.2; H65a. **DD** 333.33/0951/25.

**UK/0966-8225**
**PROPERTY REVIEW OXFORD.** [Prop. rev. Oxf.]. (1992)-. Periodical. English. mo. £150.00 UK; £165.00 other. Eclipse Publications Ltd, 18 20 Highbury Place, London N5 1QP England. **Tel** 011 44 71 354 5858.

**US/0731-0285**
**PROPERTY TAX JOURNAL. Title Change.** See Public Administration-Public Finance and Taxation.

**IS/0302-6248**
**QRQ.** (KARKA.). **VFOAT** Karka. V. 1- September 1971-. Hebrew. 8. Tsevi Shapira, Street 11, PO Box 11380, Tel Aviv Israel. **Tel** (0)246828. **ED** Alexander Poznanski. **LC** HD951.P3; A15. **Bk Rev. Circ:** 750.
**Desc:** Land use research land policy in Israel, land appraisal and land prices planning.

**US/1052-5521**
**QUARTERLY BYTE, THE.** (THE QUARTERLY BYTE : A PUBLICATION OF THE AMERICAN INSTITUTE OF REAL ESTATE APPRAISERS.). [Q. byte]. **Added/Corp** American Institute of Real Estate Appraisers. **VFOAT** QB. Vol. 6, No. 1 (1st Quarter 1990)-. Periodical. English. Four times a year (Feb., May, Aug., Nov.). $30.00 one year; $55.00 two years. Appraisal Institute, 875 North Michigan Avenue, Suite 2400, Chicago IL 60601-7601. **Tel** (312)335-4100, FAX (312)335-4400. **DD** 333. **Continues** Appraisal Institute Quarterly Byte, 0884-7649.

**CN/0839-640X**
**QUARTERLY MLS STATISTICAL SURVEY.** [Q. MLS stat. surv.]. **Added/Corp** Canadian Real Estate Association. Communications Dept. **VFOAT** Preliminary MLS Statistical Survey; Quarterly Multiple Listing Service Statistical Survey; Releve des Statistiques SIA. 3rd Quarter (1986)-. Statistical Publication. English. qt. 40.00Can$. Canadian Real Estate Association, 320 Queen Street, Suite 2100, Ottawa Ontario K1R 5A3 Canada. **Tel** (613)234-3372. **DD** 333.33/0971/021. **Continues** MLS Statistical Survey (Quarterly), 0839-6396.

**AT**
**QUEENSLAND PROPERTY REPORT.** English. Nine times a year (published every six weeks). 68.00Aus$ Australia; 84.00Aus$ other. Queensland Property Report, Box 6660 Gold Coast Mail Center, Queensland 4217 Australia. **Tel** 011 61 75 972144, FAX 011 61 75 972819. **ED** Frank Mahoney. **Bk Rev. Ad Acc, Adv Mgr:** R. Weiler. **Circ:** 14,400 (ctrl).

**UK**
**QUEST: MANHATTAN PROPERTIES & COUNTRY ESTATES.** English. Ten times a year. Quest Magazines Inc, 152 East 79th Street, New York NY 10021. **Tel** (212)288-6060, FAX (212)288-4536. **ED** Heather Cohane and Alexander Cohane. **Bk Rev. Ad Acc. Circ:** 100,000 (ctrl). available on diskette.

**US/0147-9059**
**RAM DIGEST, THE.** See Housing and Urban Development.

**IT**
**RASSEGNA DELLE LOCAZIONI E DEL CONDOMINIO.** (19??)-. Italian. L90000 Italy; L110000 Other. Cedam Spa, Via Jappelli 5 6, 35121 Padua Italy. **Tel** 011 39 49 65667.

**UK**
**RATING APPEALS.** See Law.

**CN/0712-5976**
**RE/MAX INTER.** Vol. 1, No. 1 (Oct. 1982)-. Periodical. French. Re/Mas Quebec, 1200 Ouest, Boul. St-Martin, Laval, Quebec H7S 2E4 Canada. **DD** 333.33/06/0714.

**US/0897-0262**
**REAL ESTATE ACCOUNTING & TAXATION. Ceased.** [Real estate account. tax.]. **Added/Corp** Warren, Gorham & Lamont, inc. **VFOAT** Real Estate Accounting and Taxation. Vol. 1, No. 1 (Spring 1986)-(1993). Periodical. English. qt. Warren Gorham & Lamont Inc., Park Square Building, 31 St. James Avenue, Boston MA 02116-4112. **Tel** (617)423-2020, (800)950-1207, FAX (617)423-2026. **ED** Benedetto Bongiorno. **LC** K18; .E13. **DD** 343.7305/4; 347.30354. **[CCC].** available on microfilm and microfiche from University Microfilms International (UMI). Documents available from UMI Article Clearinghouse.
**Desc:** A professional journal that provides all the industry- specific knowledge needed to successfully evaluate, manage and profit from your real estate activities.
**Ind/Abst** ABI/INFORM Glob. Ed.; ABI Inform Ondisc (Fall 1987-); Account. Tax Datab. (Fall 1987-); Gen. BusinessFile (1992-).

**US**
**REAL ESTATE AGENCY LAW QUARTERLY.** English. mo (12 issues per year). $157.00. Real Estate Agency Law, PO Box 3422, Arlington VA 22203. **Tel** (703)920-2210.

**US/0882-9144**
**REAL ESTATE ANALYSIS AND PLANNING SERVICE.** [Real estate anal. plann. serv.]. English. DRI McGraw Hill, 24 Hartwell Avenue, Lexington MA 02173. **Tel** (617)863-5100. **LC** HD251; .R16. **DD** 333.33/0973.

**US**
**REAL ESTATE ANALYST, THE. Main/Corp** Wenzlick (Roy) and Company. Periodical. English. **LC** HD251. **DD** 333.33. available on microfilm from University Microfilms International (UMI).
**Desc:** Composed of continuously paged bulletins, digests, etc., having individual titles, e.g., Agricultural bulletin, Appraisal bulletin, Executive digest, etc.

**US/0147-9946**
**REAL ESTATE AND CONSTRUCTION REPORT. Main/Corp** Real Estate Research Council of Southern California. (1977)-. Periodical. English. qt. Real Estate Res Counc Col of Bus, 3801 W Temple Avenue, Pomona CA 91768. **Tel** (909)869-2410. **LC** HD266.C22; L63. **DD** 333.33/09794. **Continues** Residential Research Report, 0147-9636.

**US/0732-0701**
**REAL ESTATE AND PUBLIC UTILITY PROPERTY TAXES.** (REAL ESTATE AND PUBLIC UTILITY PROPERTY TAXES. GROSS TAXES LEVIED, TAXES CHARGED, AND VALUE OF PROPERTY, BY CLASS OF PROPERTY AND CITY, CALENDAR YEAR ... / OHIO DEPARTMENT OF TAXATION.). 1976-. English. Department of Taxation / Ohio, Research and Statistics Section, PO Box 530, Columbus OH 43216. **LC** HJ4255; .A37. **DD** 336.22/09771. **Continues** Property Taxes, Real Estate and Public Utility.

**US/0270-7683**
**REAL ESTATE & THE LAW. VAT** Real Estate and the Law. V. 1- Sept. 1979-. Periodical. English. mo. $29.00. Philip Clarke Baten Reports, PO Box 2171, Washington DC 20013. **LC** KF2042.R4; A497. **DD** 346.7304/3/05.

**US/0095-3032**
**REAL ESTATE ASSESSMENT/SALES RATIO STUDY. Main/Corp** Minnesota. Dept. of Revenue. English. Department of Revenue / Minnesota, 10 River Park Plaza, St Paul MN 55146. **LC** HJ4231; .A3A. **DD** 336.2/2/09776.

US/0276-4792
**REAL ESTATE BOARD REPORT, THE.** Vol. 1, No. 1 (Apr. 1981)-. Periodical. English. mo. $72.00. Newsletter Management Corporation, 10076 Boca Entrada Boulevard, Boca Raton FL 33431. **Tel** (407)241-1800.

US/0734-7839
**REAL ESTATE BULLETIN (SACRAMENTO, CALIF.).** (REAL ESTATE BULLETIN : OFFICIAL PUBLICATION OF THE CALIFORNIA DIVISION OF REAL ESTATE.). **Added/Corp** California. State Real Estate Division. California. Dept. of Real Estate. (19??)-. Periodical. English. qt. $3.00 (three year). Department of Real Estate / California, PO Box 187000, Sacramento CA 95818. **Tel** (916)739-3684.

US/0744-642X
**REAL ESTATE BUSINESS.** [Real estate bus.]. **Added/Corp** Realtors National Marketing Institute. Vol. 1, No. 1 (May/June 1982)-. Periodical. English. qt. $18.00 members; $20.00 nonmembers. Realtors National Marketing Institute, 430 North Michigan Avenue, Chicago IL 60611. **Tel** (312)670-3780. **LC** HD1361; .R42. **DD** 333.33/05.

US/0893-3332
**REAL ESTATE CENTER JOURNAL.** ***Title Change.*** [Real estate cent. j.]. **Added/Corp** Texas Real Estate Research Center. Texas A & M University. Real Estate Center. Vol. 1, No. 1 (1987)-(1993). Periodical. English. qt. Texas A & M University / Real Estate, Texas Real Estate Research Center, College Station TX 77843. **ED** David S Jones. **LC** WMLC L 83/317; HD268.T4; R42. **DD** 333. **Circ:** 65,000 (ctrl). ***Continues*** *Tierra Grande, 0164-5781.* ***Continued by*** *Tierra Grande (College Station, Tex. : 1993), 1070-0234.*
**Desc:** Reports on latest real estate research results, emphasizing Texas. Audience is primarily licensed real estate brokers.

US/0148-2718
**REAL ESTATE CLOSINGS. Main/Corp** Practising Law Institute. 4th (1973)-. Periodical. English. Practising Law Institute, 810 Seventh Avenue, New York NY 10019-5818. **Tel** (212)765-5700, FAX (212)581-4670 general correspondence, (212)265-4742 orders and billing inquiries. **LC** KF665; .N48. **DD** 346/.73/0437. ***Continues*** *Real Estate Closing Workshop, 0148-2645.*

US/0742-5600
**REAL ESTATE COMPUTER REVIEW.** [Real estate comput. rev.]. Vol. 1, No. 1 (Jan. 1984)-. Periodical. English. mo. $97.00. Real Estate Computer Review, 1564 Fitzgerald Drive, Pinole CA 94564.

US
**REAL ESTATE COORDINATOR. SUPPLEMENT.** English. bw. $579.00. Research Institute of America, 117 East Stevens Avenue, Valhalla NY 10595. **Tel** (800)431-9025. **ED** James E Cheeks.
**Desc:** Expert advice on how to evaluate a real estate deal, how to support the transaction, and how to execute it.

CN/0319-1087
**REAL ESTATE DEVELOPMENT ANNUAL, THE.** VFOAT REDA Directory. (1974)-. English. an. 31.00Can$ Canada; 37.00Can$ other. Crailer Communications, 113 Davenport Road, Toronto Ontario M5R 1H8 Canada. **Tel** (416)966-9944. **LC** HD311.A1; C36. **DD** 338.4/7/6900971. ***Supersedes*** *The Canadian Real Estate Annual, 0068-9564.*

CN/1187-6468
**REAL ESTATE DEVELOPMENT (OTTAWA).** (AMENAGEMENT EN IMMOBILIER.). [Real estate dev.]. **Added/Corp** Canada. Industrie, Sciences et Technologie Canada. **VFOAT** Real Estate Development. (1990/1991)-. French (English). Ottawa: Industrie, Sciences et Technologie, Ottawa, Canada. **DD** 333.33.

US/0882-8733
**REAL ESTATE DIGEST, THE.** [Real estate dig.]. Periodical. English. mo. $48.00. The Real Estate Digest, PO Box 26555, Birmingham AL 35226. **Tel** (205)991-8988. **ED** Richard E Dewberry. **DD** 332. Index available. **Bk Rev. Ad Acc. Circ:** 10,000 (ctrl).
**Desc:** How-to-do-it guide for real estate investing, creative financing techniques, and up-to-date strategies. Plus guest authors famous in the real estate field.

US/0098-8936
**REAL ESTATE DIRECTORY OF MANHATTAN.** (19??)-. English. an. Real Estate Data Inc, 475 Fifth Avenue, Suite 1901, New York NY 10017. **Tel** (212)532-2705. **LC** HD268.N5; R3. **DD** 333.3/3. ***Continues*** *Real Estate Directory of the Borough of Manhattan.*

US
**REAL ESTATE EDUCATION AND RESEARCH SPECIAL ACCOUNT / DEPARTMENT OF COMMERCE, DIVISION OF REAL ESTATE.** English. an. Ohio Department of Commerce, 77 South High Street, 23rd Floor, Columbus OH 43266. **Tel** (614)466-3636, FAX (614)644-8292. **LC** HD1381.5.U5; R4. **DD** 353.97710082/6533333.

US/1046-9966
**REAL ESTATE/ENVIRONMENTAL LIABILITY NEWS.** (REAL ESTATE/ENVIRONMENTAL LIABILITY NEWS : THE BIWEEKLY REPORT ON LITIGATION, REGULATION, AND INDUSTRY PRACTICE.). [Real estate/environ. liabil. news]. **VFOAT** Real Estate Environmental Liability News. Vol. 1, No. 1 (Nov. 9, 1989)-. Periodical. English. sm. $547.00 US, Canada and Mexico; $569.00 other. Buraff Publications Inc., 714 Church Street, Alexandria VA 22314. **Tel** (800)333-1291, (703)739-8500. **LC** KF1298.A15; R43. **DD** 346.7303/2; 347.30632. **[CCC].**

US/0748-318X
**REAL ESTATE FINANCE.** [Real estate finance]. Vol. 1, No. 1 (Spring 1984)-. Periodical. English. qt. $98.00 US; $127.40 other. Institutional Investor Inc., 488 Madison Avenue, New York NY 10022. **Tel** (212)303-3234, (212)303-3233, FAX (212)303-3353. **ED** Barbara Grizincic. **LC** HD1361; .R423. **DD** 332.7/2/05. **Ad Acc, Adv Mgr:** Frank Eaton, **Tel** (617)457-0600. **Circ:** 3,500. available on an online database (files 15,485/Full-Text) from DIALOG. Documents available from UMI Article Clearinghouse. ***Absorbed*** *Journal of Real Estate Development, 0887-5812* ***and*** *Real Estate Leasing Report.*
**Desc:** A professional journal covering the financing of commercial real estate. Each issue includes case studies of actual real estate projects and articles that analyze new financing techniques as well as traditional financing methods.
**Ind/Abst** ABI/INFORM Glob. Ed.; ABI Inform Ondisc (Fall 1988-); Account. Tax Datab. (Fall 1988-) [Full Txt.]; Avery Index Archit. Period. Suppl. Colum. Univ. (Winter 1990-); UMI ABI/Inform--Bus. Period. Ondisc (Fall 1988-) [Full Txt.].

US/0898-0209
**REAL ESTATE FINANCE JOURNAL, THE.** [Real estate finance j.]. **Added/Corp** Warren, Gorham & Lamont, Inc. Vol. 1, No. 1 (1985)-. Periodical. English. qt. $130.98 US and Canada; $206.45 other. Warren Gorham & Lamont Inc., Park Square Building, 31 St. James Avenue, Boston MA 02116-4112. **Tel** (617)423-2020, (800)950-1207, FAX (617)423-2026. **ED** William Zucker. **LC** HD1361; .R4235. **DD** 332.7/2/05. **[CCC].** available on microfilm and microfiche from University Microfilms International (UMI). Documents available from UMI Article Clearinghouse.
**Desc:** Covers financing aspects of major real estate trends, problems and new developments. Geared toward entrepreneurs, lenders, and independent minded investors.
**Ind/Abst** ABI/INFORM Glob. Ed.; ABI Inform Ondisc (Summer 1985-); Account. Tax Datab. (Summer 1985-); Gen. BusinessFile (1992-).

US/0742-0021
**REAL ESTATE FINANCE TODAY.** (REAL ESTATE FINANCE TODAY / MORTGAGE BANKERS ASSOCIATION OF AMERICA.). [Real estate financ. today]. **Added/Corp** Mortgage Bankers Association of America. Vol. 1, No. 1 (March 1984)-. Periodical. English. sm. $85.00 (one year), $217.00 (three year). Mortgage Bankers Association of America, Department 0021, Washington DC 20073-0021. **Tel** (202)861-6992. **LC** PAR. **DD** 333. **[CCC].**

US/0735-0678
**REAL ESTATE FINANCING REPORT.** Vol. 1, No. 1 (Sept. 1982)-. Periodical. English. mo. $36.00. Owl Publishing Company, 10440 Culver Boulevard, PO Box 167, Culver City CA 90230.

US/0891-9852
**REAL ESTATE FINANCING UPDATE.** ***Ceased.*** [Real estate financ. update]. Vol. 1, No. 1 (Sept. 1984)-(Spring 1993). Periodical. English. mo. Warren Gorham & Lamont Inc., Park Square Building, 31 St. James Avenue, Boston MA 02116-4112. **Tel** (617)423-2020, (800)950-1207, FAX (617)423-2026. **[CCC].**

US/0034-0707
**REAL ESTATE FORUM.** [Real estate forum]. **VFOAT** Forum. (1946)-. Periodical. English. mo. $65.00. Real Estate Forum, 111 8th Avenue, Suite 1511, New York NY 10011-5201. **Tel** (212)929-6900. **ED** Michael Desiato. **DD** 333. **Ad Acc, Adv Mgr:** J. Schein, **Tel** same as publisher. **Circ:** 34,000.
**Desc:** Provides the most comprehensive national coverage of real estate industry news, trends and opinions.
**Ind/Abst** Avery Index Archit. Period. Suppl. Colum. Univ. (May, Dec. 1989, 1990-).

US/0034-0715
**REAL ESTATE INSIDER.** [Real estate insid.]. **VFOAT** Real Estate Insider Newsletter. (19??)-. Newsletter. English. bw. $225.00 (one year), $420.00 (two year), $610.00 (three year) US, Canada and Mexico; $250.00 (one year), $470.00 (two year), $685.00 (three year) other. Walker Communications Inc., 1541 Morris Avenue, Bronx NY 10457. **Tel** (800)524-3785, (212)583-8060, FAX (212)583-8258, . **ED** Suzie Mitchell. **DD** 338. **[CCC]. Circ:** 1,000.
**Desc:** Newsletter for owners, managers and brokers of real estate firms.

US
**REAL ESTATE INVESTING LETTER.** Vol. 2, No. 5 (May 1977)-. Periodical. English. mo (12 issues). $96.00 (one year), $179.00 (two year). Management Resources Inc, 861 LaFayette Road, Suite 5, Hampton NH 03842. **Tel** (603)929-1600. **Bk Rev**, (Qty: 6). ***Continues*** *Real Estate Investor Letter.*

US/0146-0595
**REAL ESTATE ISSUES.** [Real estate issues]. **Added/Corp** American Society of Real Estate Counselors. Vol. 1 (Fall 1976)-. English. Three times a year (Apr., Aug., Dec.). $21.00 (one year), $33.00 (two years), $42.00 (three years) students and faculty; $29.00 (one year), $40.00 (two years), $49.00 (three years) others. American Society of Real Estate Counselors, 430 North Michigan Avenue, Chicago IL 60611. **Tel** (312)329-8427, FAX (312)329-8881, telex 0253742. **ED** Linda Magad; (phone: (312)329-8431). **LC** HD251; .R2. **DD** 333.3/3. cum. index. **Ad Acc. Pr Rev. Circ:** 1,400. available on microfilm and microfiche from University Microfilms International (UMI); available on an online database (file 15/Full-Text) from DIALOG. Documents available from UMI Article Clearinghouse.
**Desc:** The journal contains articles that focus on theoretical and empirical approaches to timely problems and topics in the field of real estate.
**Ind/Abst** ABI/INFORM Glob. Ed.; ABI Inform Ondisc (Spring 1983-); Avery Index Archit. Period. Suppl. Colum. Univ. (Fall-Winter 1989); J. Plan. Lit.; UMI ABI/Inform--Bus. Period. Ondisc (Spring 1988-) [Full Txt.].

AT
**REAL ESTATE JOURNAL.** (19??)-. English. bm (6 issues). 36.00Aus$. Real Estate Institute of New South Wales, PO Box A624 / Sydney, South NSW 2000 Australia. **Tel** 011 61 2 2642343, FAX 011 61 2 2679190. **ED** Danielle Watts. **Bk Rev. Ad Acc, Adv Mgr:** Gordon Durnford, **Tel** 011 61 2 9572033. **Circ:** 4,500 (ctrl).

CN/0832-0780
**REAL ESTATE JOURNAL, THE.** [Real estate j.]. (1985)-. Periodical. English. ir. Toronto Real Estate Board, 1400 Don Mills Road, J Samaroo, Don Mills Ontario, M3B 3N1 Canada. **Tel** (905)443-8128. **DD** 333.33/09713/541. ***Continues*** *Realtor, 0704-6707.*

US/0548-7366
**REAL ESTATE LAW AND PRACTICE COURSE HANDBOOK SERIES.** **See** Law.

US/0034-0758
**REAL ESTATE LAW BRIEF CASE.** (19??)-. Periodical. English. Twelve times a year. $10.00 (one year), $14.00 (two year). Legal Research Institute, PO Box 26, San Antonio TX 78291.

US/0048-6868
**REAL ESTATE LAW JOURNAL.** **See** Law.

US/0162-752X
**REAL ESTATE LAW REPORT.** **See** Law.

US/0748-3163
**REAL ESTATE LEASING REPORT.** ***Title Change.*** [Real estate leas. rep.]. Vol. 1, No. 1 (April 1984)-(19??). Periodical. English. mo. Federal Research Press, 210 Lincoln Street, Boston MA 02111. **ED** Barbara Grizincic. **DD** 333. ***Merged into*** *Real Estate Finance, 0748-318X.*

US
**REAL ESTATE LICENSE LAW AND RULES AND REGULATIONS.** **See** Law.

US/0273-6667
**REAL ESTATE NEWS (BALTIMORE).** (REAL ESTATE NEWS.). **Added/Corp** Greater Baltimore Board of Realtors. (19??)-. Periodical. English. mo.
**Ind/Abst** Trade Ind. Index.

CN/0225-2783
**REAL ESTATE NEWS (TORONTO).** (REAL ESTATE NEWS.). [Real estate news]. Vol. 1 (Oct. 5, 1979)-. Periodical. English. wk. Free. Toronto Real Estate Board, 1400 Don Mills Road, J Samaroo, Don Mills Ontario, M3B 3N1 Canada. **Tel** (905)443-8128. **DD** 333.3/3/09713541. ***Supersedes*** *Toronto Real Estate, 0225-2775.*

US/0749-8640
**REAL ESTATE NEWSLINE.** (REAL ESTATE NEWSLINE / AN INFORMATION SERVICE OF KENNETH LEVENTHAL & COMPANY.). [Real estate newsline]. Vol. 1, No. 1 (Nov. 1984)-. Periodical. English. mo. Free. Kenneth Leventhal & Company, 2049 Century Park East/Suite 1700, Los Angeles CA 90067. **Tel** (310)277-0880. **ED** James Carberry. **DD** 333. **Circ:** 10,000 (ctrl).
**Desc:** Real estate news and analysis.

US/1054-0458
**REAL ESTATE NEWSLINE (KNOXVILLE, TENN.).** (REAL ESTATE NEWSLINE.). **VFOAT** Newsline. Vol. 1, Issue 1 (1991)-. Periodical. English. mo. Free. Steven M Albin, 8905 Kingston Pike, Suite 12448, Knoxville TN 37923.

US
**REAL ESTATE OUTLOOK MARKET TRENDS AND INSIGHTS.** English. mo. $95.00 members, National Association of Realtors; $135.00 nonmembers. National Association of Realtors / Washington, 777 14th Street Northwest, Washington DC 20005. **Tel** (202)383-1137. ctrl circ. ***Continues*** *Home Sales.*

US/0744-4516
**REAL ESTATE PROFESSIONAL, THE.** [Real estate prof.]. Vol. 5, No. 1 (Jan./Feb. 1982)-. Periodical. English. bm. 72.00Aus$. Real Estate Institute of Australia, PO Box 234, Curtin Act 2605 Australia. **Tel** 61-62-824277, 062-824277, FAX 06-285-2444. **DD** 333. ***Continues*** *Real Estate Agent.*

US
**REAL ESTATE PROFILES.** (19??)-. English. $2200.00. Evaluation Associates Inc., 200 Connecticut Avenue, Norwalk CT 06854. **Tel** (203)855-2200, FAX (203)855-2301. **ED** Dawn Nelson. ctrl circ.
**Desc:** Contains information on funds that invest in properties and other facts of interest to those involved with real estate.

US/0034-0774
**REAL ESTATE RECORD AND BUILDER'S GUIDE (1941).** ***Title Change.*** (REAL ESTATE RECORD AND BUILDER'S GUIDE.). **VFOAT** Record and Guide. (1941)-(19??). Periodical. English. wk. Real Estate Data Inc, 475 Fifth Avenue, Suite 1901, New York NY 10017. **Tel** (212)532-2705. **ED** Venice Kelly. **DD** 332. **Ad Acc. Circ:** 1,200. ***Continues*** *Real Estate Record.* ***Continued by*** *Redi Realty Report, 1051-0737.*
**Desc:** Lists real estate information on properties that have sold in Manhattan. Includes owner's name, address and phone number as well as financial data.

US
**REAL ESTATE REPORT (REAL ESTATE RESEARCH CORPORATION).** (REAL ESTATE REPORT.). **Added/Corp** Real Estate Research Corporation. (19??)-. Periodical. English. bm. $195.00. Real Estate Research Corporation, 2 North Lasalle Street, Suite 400, Chicago IL 60602. **Tel** (312)346-5885.

US/0079-9890
**REAL ESTATE REPORT (STORR, CONN.).** (REAL ESTATE REPORT.). [Real estate rep.]. English. ir. Real Estate Report, 1208 Main Street, Georgetown TX 78626. **LC** HD251; .R283.

US/0034-0790
**REAL ESTATE REVIEW (BOSTON, MASS.).** (REAL ESTATE REVIEW.). [Real estate rev.]. **Added/Corp** New York University. Real Estate Institute. Vol. 1, No. 1 (Spring 1971)-. Periodical. English. qt. $104.48 US and Canada; $173.30 other. Warren Gorham & Lamont Inc., Park Square Building, 31 St. James Avenue, Boston MA 02116-4112. **Tel** (617)423-2020, (800)950-1207, FAX (617)423-2026. **ED** Alvin L. Arnold. **LC** HD251; .R286. **DD** 333.33/0973. **[CCC]. Pr Rev.** available on microfilm and microfiche from University Microfilms International (UMI). Documents available from The Genuine Article, UMI Article Clearinghouse. ***Absorbed*** *Condominium World.*
**Desc:** Provides advice from the leaders of the real estate field.
**Ind/Abst** ABI/INFORM Glob. Ed.; ABI Inform Ondisc (Summer 1972-); ABI/INFORM Ondisc: Expr. Ed.; Acad. Search (Jan. 1994-); Bus. Index (1985-); Bus. Period. Index; Bus. Source (Jan. 1993-); Curr. Contents Soc. Behav. Sci.; Gen. BusinessFile (1985-); Gen. Period. Index (1985-); INFO-SOUTH Abstr.; J. Plan. Lit.; Mag. Search; Res. Alert [Full Cov.]; Soc. Sci. Cit. Index [Full Cov.]; Trade Ind. Index; Vocat. Search (Jan. 1993-); Wilson Bus. Abstr.

US/0737-3600
**REAL ESTATE REVIEW'S WHO'S WHO IN REAL ESTATE.** **See** Biographies.

US/8755-8262
**REAL ESTATE SALES/CLOSINGS LAW BULLETIN.** [Real estate sales/closings law bull.]. **VFOAT** Real Estate Sales Closings Law Bulletin; SCB; S.C.B. Began with issue for Oct. 1984?. Bulletin. English. mo. $36.50. Entre Deux Mers Ltd, 7 S River Lane E, Duxbury MA 02332. **DD** 346.

US/1052-4622
**REAL ESTATE SECURITIES & CAPITAL MARKETS.** ***Suspended.*** [Real estate secur. cap. mark.]. **VFOAT** Real Estate Securities and Capital Markets. (February 1985)-Suspended. Periodical. English. mo. $185.00. Leader Publications, 345 Park Avenue South, New York NY 10010. **Tel** (800)888-8300 ext. 6170, (212)545-6170, FAX (212)696-1848. **ED** Don Augustine and Richard J. Behrens. **DD** 332. ***Continues*** *Real Estate Syndicator, 8756-8411.*

US/0275-1127
**REAL ESTATE SECURITIES LETTER.** (REAL ESTATE SECURITIES LETTER AN INFORMATION SERVICE OF QUESTOR ASSOCIATES.). **Added/Corp** Questor Associates. (1981)-. English. mo. $150.00. Questor Associates, 115 Sansome Street, San Francisco CA 94104. ***Continues*** *Real Estate Syndication Reporter Newsletter, 0197-1107.*

US/8750-510X
**REAL ESTATE SYNDICATION ALERT.** ***Ceased.*** [Real estate synd. alert]. Vol. 1, No. 1 (Jan. 1984)-Ceased (1989). Periodical. English. mo. Warren Gorham & Lamont Inc., Park Square Building, 31 St. James Avenue, Boston MA 02116-4112. **Tel** (617)423-2020, (800)950-1207, FAX (617)423-2026.
**Desc:** Provides all the information needed to succeed in real estate group investments, from structuring to managing to selling. Examines how syndicators are restructuring their operations and managing their assets.

US/1048-7492
**REAL ESTATE SYNDICATIONS.** [Real estate synd.]. English. an. Practising Law Institute, 810 Seventh Avenue, New York NY 10019-5818. **Tel** (212)765-5700, FAX (212)581-4670 general correspondence, (212)265-4742 orders and billing inquiries. **LC** KF1079.Z9; R4195. **DD** 346.7304/3; 347.30643.

US/8756-8411
**REAL ESTATE SYNDICATOR, THE.** ***Title Change.*** [Real estate synd.]. (1985)-Vol. 6, No. 4 (1991). Periodical. English. mo. Leader Publications, 345 Park Avenue South, New York NY 10010. **Tel** (800)888-8300 ext. 6170, (212)545-6170, FAX (212)696-1848. **DD** 332. ***Continued by*** *Real Estate Securities & Capital Markets, 1052-4622.*

US/8756-3835
**REAL ESTATE TAX DIGEST (ALBANY, N.Y.), THE.** (THE REAL ESTATE TAX DIGEST / BY MARVIN B. STARR.). [Real estate tax dig.]. (19??)-. Periodical. English. Twelve times a year. $260.00. Matthew Bender & Company Inc., 1275 Broadway, Albany NY 12204. **Tel** (800)833-9844, (518)487-3000. **LC** KF6535.A15; R43. **DD** 343.7305/4/05; 347.3035405.

US/0162-7538
**REAL ESTATE TAX IDEAS.** (Apr. 1972)-. Periodical. English. mo. $126.25 US; $180.95 other. Warren Gorham & Lamont Inc., Park Square Building, 31 St. James Avenue, Boston MA 02116-4112. **Tel** (617)423-2020, (800)950-1207, FAX (617)423-2026. **ED** Gerald J. Robinson and Lewis R. Kaster. **[CCC].**
**Desc:** Provides analysis of the current marketplace and regulatory agencies and alerts new opportunities. It shows how to make use of the existing tax structure and achieve the most profitable tax treatment possible.

US/0034-0804
**REAL ESTATE TODAY.** [Real estate today]. **Added/Corp** National Institute of Real Estate Brokers (U.S.) Realtors National Marketing Institute. National Association of Realtors. Vol. 1 (1968)-. Periodical. English. mo (ten issues per year). $25.00. National Association of Realtors, 430 North Michigan Avenue, Chicago IL 60611. **Tel** (312)329-8494, (800)874-6500. **ED** Dali R Hoover. **LC** HD251; .R293. **DD** 333.3/3/05. Index available. cum. index. **Bk Rev. Ad Acc. Pr Rev. Circ:** 800,000 (ctrl). available on microfilm and microfiche from University Microfilms International (UMI); available on an online database (files 647,648/Full-Text) from DIALOG. Documents available from UMI Article Clearinghouse. ***Absorbed*** *Realtors Review.*
**Desc:** Official magazine of the National Association of Realtors. Contains ideas, opinions and practical applications that aid in elevating professionalism and earning power of realtors.
**Ind/Abst** Acad. Search (July 1993-); Bus. ASAP (1990-) [Full Txt.]; Bus. Index (1985-); Bus. Period. Index; Bus. Source (Jan. 1993-); Gen. BusinessFile (1985-); Gen. Period. Index (1985-); INFO-SOUTH Abstr.; Mag. ASAP Plus [Full Txt.]; Mag. Index Plus (1989-); Mag. Search; Newsp. Period. Abstr. (1989-); Mag. Index (1977-); Trade Ind. ASAP [Full Txt.]; Trade Ind. Index (1981-) [Full Txt.]; Vocat. Search (Jan. 1993-); Wilson Bus. Abstr.

CN/0085-5405
**REAL ESTATE TRENDS IN METROPOLITAN VANCOUVER.** **Added/Corp** Real Estate Board of Greater Vancouver. Statistical and Survey Committee. British Columbia. Bureau of Economics and Statistics. 5th Ed. (1964)-. Periodical. English. an. 37.20Can$. Real Estate Board of Greater Vancouver, 1101 West Broadway, Vancouver British Columbia V6H 1G2 Canada. **Tel** (604)736-4551, FAX (604)734-1778. **ED** Ray A. Nelson. **LC** HD319.B8; V3. **DD** 333.3/0971133. **Circ:** 500. ***Continues*** *Real Estate and Business Trends in Metropolitan Vancouver and British Columbia, 0318-6083.*
**Desc:** Benchmark values and statistics of real estate in the lower mainland of British Columbia.

US/0092-3672
**REAL ESTATE VENTURE ANALYSIS.** English. Practising Law Institute, 810 Seventh Avenue, New York NY 10019-5818. **Tel** (212)765-5700, FAX (212)581-4670 general correspondence, (212)265-4742 orders and billing inquiries. **LC** HD1375; .R4. **DD** 333.3/3.

●US/1063-4290
**REAL ESTATE WORKOUTS & ASSET MANAGEMENT.** (1992)-. Periodical. English. mo. $154.25 US & Canada; $208.60 other. Warren Gorham & Lamont Inc., Park Square Building, 31 St. James Avenue, Boston MA 02116-4112. **Tel** (617)423-2020, (800)950-1207, FAX (617)423-2026. **ED** Howard Zuckerman. **[CCC].** available in Loose-leaf.

US
**REAL ESTATE WORKOUTS AND BANKRUPTCIES.** **See** Business-Banking and Finance.

NZ
**REAL ETATE MARKET IN NEW ZEALAND, THE.** **Main/Corp** New Zealand. Valuation Dept. (1975)-. English. sa. 11.00NZ$. Valuation New Zealand, PO Box 5098, Wellington New Zealand. **Tel** 738-555, FAX 738-552. **LC** HD1387; .N38 subser; HD11205. **DD** 333.33/09931 S; 333.33/5/09931. **Circ:** 50. ***Continues*** *New Zealand. Valuation Dept. Rural Real Estate Market in New Zealand.*
**Desc:** Shows provisional national real estate sales statistics in New Zealand.

●CN/1187-7200
**REAL PROPERTY ASSESSMENT. YEAR ONE.** [Real prop. assess., Year one]. **Added/Corp** University of British Columbia. Real Estate Division. International Association of Assessing Officers. **VFOAT** Certificate Programme in Real Property Assessment. (1991/92)-. English. $80.00. University of British Columbia / Real Estate, Real Estate Division, 202-2053 Main Mall, Vancouver BC V6T 1Z2. **DD** 333.33/2.

US/0198-893X
**REAL PROPERTY (GARDENA).** **See** Law.

US/0147-135X
**REAL PROPERTY LAW SECTION NEWSLETTER.** **Main/Corp** New York State Bar Association. Real Property Law Section. (1973)-. English. qt. $25.00. New York State Bar Association, One Elk Street, Albany NY 12207. **Tel** (518)463-3200. **ED** Board. **LC** KFN5140.A15; N48. **DD** 346/.747/04305. **Bk Rev. Ad Acc. Circ:** 5,000 (ctrl).
**Desc:** Newsletter of real property law section. Section notes and current issues are discussed.

US
**REAL PROPERTY SECTION NEWS.** **See** Law.

US/1071-1805
**REAL TRENDS.** [Real trends]. (May 1987)-. Periodical. English. Twelve times a year. $120.00 (one year), $200.00 (two years). Real Trends, PO Box 796364, Dallas TX 75397-6341. **Tel** (214)250-1483, FAX (214)931-8545. **ED** Laurie Moore and Steve Murray. **DD** 333.

US/1053-8917
**REALSCAN. BROWARD COUNTY.** (REALSCAN. BROWARD COUNTY [COMPUTER FILE] : REAL ESTATE INFORMATION MANAGEMENT SYSTEMS.). [RealScan, Broward Cty.]. **VFOAT** Broward County. (July 1987)-. Periodical. English. mo. $145.00 (average price). LaserScan Systems, Inc., 5310 NW 33 Avenue, Suite 115, Ft Lauderdale FL 33309. **DD** 333.
**Desc:** System requirements: compatible CD-ROM, RealScan System I, II, or III software program.

US/1053-8925
**REALSCAN. DADE COUNTY.** (REALSCAN. DADE COUNTY [COMPUTER FILE] : REAL ESTATE INFORMATION MANAGEMENT SYSTEMS.). [RealScan, Dade Cty.]. **VFOAT** Dade County. (Aug. 1988)-. Periodical. English. mo. $145.00 (average price). LaserScan Systems, Inc., 5310 NW 33 Avenue, Suite 115, Ft Lauderdale FL 33309. **DD** 333.

US/1056-8344
**REALSCAN. PALM BEACH COUNTY [COMPUTER FILE] : REAL ESTATE MARKET INFORMATION SYSTEMS.** [RealScan, Palm Beach Cty.]. **VFOAT** Palm Beach County. (Mar 1991)-. Periodical. English. mo. $120.00 (average price). LaserScan Systems, Inc., 5310 NW 33 Avenue, Suite 115, Ft Lauderdale FL 33309. **DD** 333.
**Desc:** System requirements: RealScan System I, II, or III software program; compatible CD-ROM.

US/0886-8794
**REALTOR (LANSING, MICH.).** ***Title Change.*** (REALTOR.). **VFOAT** Michigan Realtor. (1985)-?. Periodical. English. mo. Michigan Association of Realtors,

PO Box 40725, Lansing MI 48901. ***Continues** Michigan Realtor, 8750-670X.* ***Continued by** Michigan Realtor (Lansing, Mich. : 1990), 1053-4598.*

US/0279-6309
**REALTOR NEWS.** [Realtor news]. **Added/Corp** National Association of Realtors. (1980)-. Periodical. English. Twenty-six times a year. $12.00. National Association of Realtors, 430 North Michigan Avenue, Chicago IL 60611. **Tel** (312)329-8494, (800)874-6500. **ED** Bill Adkinson. **DD** 338. **Bk Rev. Ad Acc. Circ:** 118,500 (ctrl). available on an online database (file 648/Full-Text) from DIALOG.
**Desc:** Official newspaper of the National Association of Realtors; reports and analyzes legislative and political news for the real estate industry and examines significant economic and political trends.

IT
**REALTY.** Italian (English, French, German and Spanish). be. L50000 Italy; L80000 other. FC Editore Srl, Via Vivaio 24, 21022 Milan Italy. **Tel** (39-2)76 009 001, FAX (39-2)78 13 46. **ED** Fabrizio Capsoni. **Ad Acc. Circ:** 30,000.
**Desc:** Deals with luxury real estate.

US/0481-9004
**REALTY.** (19??)-. Periodical. English. bw. $20.00 (one year); $32.50 (two year); $40.00 (three year). Realty, 80-34 Jamaica Avenue, Woodhaven NY 11421. **Tel** (212)296-2233. **ED** Lester A Sobel. **Bk Rev. Ad Acc.**
**Desc:** Important news of real estate, finance, regulation, management, sales, leases, mortgages, trends, personnel.

US/0034-1045
**REALTY AND BUILDING. VFOAT** Realty & Building. Vol. 115, No. 19 (May 11, 1946)-. Periodical. English. wk. $35.00 (one year), $55.00 (two years). Realty and Building Inc, 311 West Superior, Suite 316, Chicago IL 60610. **Tel** (312)944-1204, FAX (312)944-1824. **ED** John Cutler. **LC** HG1; .E3. **DD** 333.33/09773/11. **Ad Acc. Circ:** 4,000 (ctrl). ***Continues** Economist (Chicago, Ill.).*
**Desc:** News articles of property sales and construction and organizational activities mostly local. We have a national section. Regular features, names of buyers and sellers of real estate, building permits, wrecking permits, and weekly construction reports.

US/0090-399X
**REALTY BLUEBOOK.** [Realty blueb.]. (19??)-. English. an (Nov.). $31.00. Professional Publishing Corporation, 122 Paul Drive, San Rafael CA 94903. **Tel** (415)472-1964. **ED** Robert W. De Heer. **LC** HD253; .R4. **DD** 333.3/3.
**Desc:** Contains new tax laws, tables, financing, checklists, and clauses.

US
**REALTY PARTNERSHIP IN DEFAULT, THE. Added/Corp** Practising Law Institute. (1991)-. English. Practising Law Institute, 810 Seventh Avenue, New York NY 10019-5818. **Tel** (212)765-5700, FAX (212)581-4670 general correspondence, (212)265-4742 orders and billing inquiries. **LC** KF1535.R43; R414. **DD** 346. ***Continues** Real Estate Partnership in Default, 1058-0093.*

US/0270-7721
**REALTY. RELOCATION. REVIEW. Added/Corp** Hertz Relocation Services. (19??)-. Periodical. English. mo. $75.00. Realty Relocation Review, Saugatuck POB 114, Connecticut Office Building, Westport CT 06880. **Tel** (203)226-7801.

US
**REALTY STOCK REVIEW. Added/Corp** Audit Investments, Inc. **VFOAT** Audit's Realty Stock Review. (1981)-. Periodical. English. sm (except 1 issue in Aug.). $325.00. Charter Financial Publishing, 179 Avenue at the Commons, Shrewsbury NJ 07702. **Tel** (908)389-8700, FAX (908)389-8701. **ED** Barry Vinocur. **Ad Acc, Adv Mgr:** A. Goldfinger, **Tel** (908)389-8700 Ext.122. **Circ:** 3,500. ***Continues** Realty Trust Review.*
**Desc:** Covers issues about real estate investments trusts.

US/1051-0737
**REDI REALTY REPORT.** ***Title Change.*** [REDI realty rep.]. Vol. 243, No. 17 April 28 (1990)-(199?). Periodical. English. Fifty-two times a year. Real Estate Data Inc, 475 Fifth Avenue, Suite 1901, New York NY 10017. **Tel** (212)532-2705. **DD** 333. ***Continues** Real Estate Record and Builder's Guide, 0034-0774.* ***Continued by** TRW REDI Realty Report, 1075-3664.*

US/0279-5965
**REGARDIE'S.** ***Ceased.*** [Regardie's]. **VFOAT** Regardie's of Washington. Vol. 1, No. 3 (Jan./Feb. 1981)-Ceased December (1992). Periodical. English. mo. Regardie's Magazine, 1010 Wisconsin Avenue NW, Washington DC 20007. **LC** HC108.W3; R43. **DD** 330.9753/005. Documents available from UMI Article Clearinghouse. ***Continues** Regardie's Business & Real Estate Washington, 0274-984X.*
**Ind/Abst** Bus. Dateline; Bus. Index (1985-1990); Gen. BusinessFile (1985-1990); Gen. Period. Index (1985-); Mag. ASAP Plus [Full Txt.]; Mag. Index Plus (1989-); Mag. Search; Newsp. Period. Abstr. (1988-); Mag. Index.

●US
**REIT HANDBOOK : COMPLETE GUIDE TO THE REAL ESTATE INVESTMENT TRUST INDUSTRY. Added/Corp** National Association of Real Estate Investment Trusts. **VFOAT** Real Estate Investment Trust Handbook. (1993)-. Periodical. English. National Association of Real Estate Investment Trusts, 1129 20th Street Northwest, Suite 705, Washington DC 20036. **Tel** (202)785-8717. **LC** HG5095; .R47. ***Continues** REIT Sourcebook.*

US
**REIT HANDBOOK OF MEMBER TRUSTS. See** Business-Investments.

US
**REIT SOURCEBOOK.** ***Title Change.*** **Added/Corp** National Association of Real Estate Investment Trusts. **VAT** Real Estate Investment Trust Sourcebook. (1991)-(1992). English. National Association of Real Estate Investment Trusts, 1129 20th Street Northwest, Suite 705, Washington DC 20036. **Tel** (202)785-8717. **LC** HG5095; .R47. ***Continues** REIT Facts, 1051-1644.* ***Continued by** REIT Handbook.*

US
**RELIA+IBLE.** (RELIA+IBLE : REAL ESTATE LITERATURE INDEX & ABSTRACTS, INTERNATIONAL BOOKSHELF FOR LAND ECONOMISTS.). **VFOAT** RELIA + IBLE; RELIA and IBLE; RELIAIBLE; RELIABLE; Real Estate Literature Index & Abstracts, International Bookshelf; Land Economists; Real Estate Literature Index and Abstracts, International; International Bookshelf for Land Economists. (19??)-. English. sm. $195.00. Real Estate Infosources, 2500 Van Ness Avenue/Suite 11, San Francisco CA 94109-1658.

US
**RELOCATION FACT BOOK.** (19??)-. English. an. $100.00. Runzheimer International / Wisconsin, Runzheimer Park, Rochester WI 53167. **Tel** (414)767-2200, FAX (414)767-2254, (800)558-1702.

UK/0967-0424
**RELOCATION HANDBOOK.** (THE RELOCATION HANDBOOK.). [Relocat. handb.]. (1992)-. English. an. £120.00 (institutions), £94.00 (individuals) UK; £120.00 (institutions), £100.00 (individuals) other. Mark Allen Publishing Limited, Robjohns Farm, Vicarage Road, Finchingfield CM7 4LJ England. **Tel** 11 44 371 810433. **DD** 338.70941.

US
**RELOCATION / REALTY UPDATE. See** Business-Personnel Management.

US/0275-7613
**RELOCATION REPORT, THE. Added/Corp** Kinsale Corporation. (19??)-. Periodical. English. bm. $89.00. Federal News Services Inc., PO Box 13460, Silver Spring MD 20911. **Tel** (301)608-9322, FAX (301)608-9057. **ED** Ken Groh. **[CCC]. Bk Rev. Circ:** 2,000 (ctrl).
**Desc:** Newsletter concerning the employee relocation industry.

UK/0263-7499
**RENT REVIEW & LEASE RENEWAL.** [Rent rev. lease renew.]. **VFOAT** Rent Review and Lease Renewal. (19??)-. Periodical. English. qt. $249.00. MCB University Press, 60 62 Toller Lane, Bradford West Yorkshire BD8 9BX England. **Tel** 011 44 274 499821, FAX 011 44 274 547143, telex 51317 MCBUNI G. **(Subscription address:** MCB University Press / US and Canada Subscriptions, PO Box 10812, Birmingham AL 35201-0812.**) DD** 344.2064344. ***Continues** Rent Review., 0260-907X.*

US
**REPAIR & REMODEL QUARTERLY, THE. See** Building and Construction.

CN/0834-9908
**REPERTOIRE DES BIENS A STATUT PARTICULIER.** [Repert. biens statut part.]. **Main/Corp** Conseil Scolaire de l'Ile de Montreal. French. an. $10.00. Conseil Scolaire de l'Ile de Montreal, 500 Est Boul Cremazie, Montreal Quebec H2P 1E7 Canada. **Tel** (514)384-1830, telex 05-825-871. **ED** Albert Cote. **DD** 371.6/25. Index available (in the repertory). **Circ:** 200 (ctrl).
**Desc:** List and description of closed schools and other real estate properties owned by the eight school boards of the island of Montreal.

US
**REPORT OF THE STATE COMMISSION ON EMINENT DOMAIN AND REAL PROPERTY TAX ASSESSMENT REVIEW. Main/Corp** New York (State). State Commission on Eminent Domain and Real Property Tax Assessment Review. (1974)-. English. an. State Commission on Eminent Domain, 844 State Office Building, 333 East Washington Street, Syracuse NY 13202. ***Continues** New York (State). State Commission on Eminent Domain. Report of the State Commission on Eminent Domain.*

US/0731-7999
**RESEARCH IN REAL ESTATE : A RESEARCH ANNUAL.** [Res. real estate]. Vol. 1 (1982)-. Monographic series. English. an. $73.25. JAI Press Inc., 55 Old Post Road, Suite 2, PO Box 1678, Greenwich CT 06836-1678. **Tel** (203)661-7602, FAX (203)661-0792. **ED** C.F. Sirmans. **LC** HD251; .R4. **DD** 333.33/0973.

US/1042-0517
**RESIDENTIAL FLORIDA REAL ESTATE.** [Resid. Fla. real estate]. **VFOAT** Florida Residential Real Estate; Residential Florida. Winter 1989-. Periodical. English. sa. Resort Publications Inc, 1010 Wisconsin Avenue NW/Suite 600, Washington DC 20007. **DD** 333.

●US/1059-3047
**RESOURCE BOOK, REAL ESTATE. LOS ANGELES COUNTY.** [ReSour. book real estate, Los Angel. Cty.]. **VFOAT** Resource Book; Los Angeles County; Real Estate ReSource Book. (1992)-. English. $29.95. EIP Inc, 2350 West Sepulveda Blvd., Suite B, Torrance CA 90501.

●US/1060-3948
**RESOURCE BOOK, REAL ESTATE. ORANGE, RIVERSIDE & SAN BERNARDINO COUNTIES. VFOAT** ReSource Book. (1992)-. Periodical. English. $29.95. EIP Inc, 2350 West Sepulveda Blvd., Suite B, Torrance CA 90501.

CN/0828-9522
**RESOURCE (DON MILLS, ONT.).** ***Title Change.*** (RESOURCE.). **Added/Corp** Real Estate Institute of Canada. May 1985- Vol. 8, No. 3 (July 1992). Periodical. English (French). qt (March, June, Sep., Dec.). Real Estate Institute of Canada, 2200 Lakeshore Boulevard West/Suite 305, Toronto Ontario M8V 1A4 Canada. **Tel** (416)253-0803, FAX (416)253-0884. **ED** Barbara Sosin. **DD** 333.33/0971. Index available. cum. index. **Bk Rev. Ad Acc. Circ:** 4,000 (ctrl). ***Continues** Education Quarterly, 0703-1173.* ***Absorbed by** Contact, 0703-119X.*
**Desc:** Explores in depth contemporary developments and research in the business of real estate.

US/0199-3534
**RESSI REVIEW.** (THE RESSI REVIEW.). **Main/Corp** Real Estate Securities and Syndication Institute. **VFOAT** Real Estate Securities and Syndication Institute Review. (197?)-. Periodical. English. mo (except June/July and Nov./Dec. combined). Real Estate Securities & Syndication Institute, 430 North Michigan Avenue, Chicago IL 60611. **Tel** (312)670-6760. **ED** Lisa B. Johnson. **Bk Rev. Circ:** 3,000 (ctrl).
**Desc:** Provides RESSI's membership with reporting on current regulatory and legislative issues affecting the real estate securities industry as well as institute affairs.

US/0887-0470
**RETAIL TENANT DIRECTORY. See** Business-Retail.

FR/0048-7953
**REVUE DE L'HABITAT FRANCAIS.** (1961)-. Periodical. French. mo (except Aug.). 130.26F. Revue de l'Habitat Francais, 274 Blvd St. Germain, 75007 Paris France. **Tel** 011 33 1 47058762. **UDC** 333.3.

FR/0242-5629
**REVUE DES LOYERS ET DES FERMAGES, DE LA PROPRIETE COMMERCIALE, DES FONDS DE COMMERCE, DE LA CONSTRUCTION ET DE LA COPROPRIETE IMMOBILIERES.** [Rev. loyers fermages propr. commer. fonds commer. constr. copropr. immobil.]. (1957)-. Periodical. French. Ten times a year. 410.00F France; 435.00F other. Societe d'Edition de la Revue des Loyers et Fermages, 8 rue Ventadour, 75001 Paris France. **UDC** 347.453.

US/0035-5275
**RIGHT OF WAY.** [Right way]. **Added/Corp** American Right of Way Association. (1954)-. Periodical. English. bm. Comes with the International Right of Way Association membership. International Right of Way Association, 13650 Gramercy Place, Gardena CA 90249-2465. **Tel** (310)538-0233. **ED** Mike Powell. **LC** LAW. **DD** 333. **Bk Rev. Ad Acc. Circ:** 9,000 (ctrl). ***Supersedes** American Right of Way Association. News.*
**Desc:** Land acquisition for public use, engineering, appraisal, acquisition, real property law, and property management.
**Ind/Abst** Energy Inf. Abstr.

US
**ROBERT FULLER REAL ESTATE REPORT.** English. $175.00 US; $200.00 other. Gavilon Publishing, 1009 Grant Street/Suite 300, Denver

# Real Estate

CO 80203. **Tel** (303)832-9100. **ED** Howard Treibitz. **Desc:** Special report for real estate investors, lenders and developers. Provides authoritative information regarding subjects covered.

US/8756-7784
**ROBERT G. ALLEN'S REAL ESTATE ADVISOR.** [Robert G. Allen's real estate advis.]. Periodical. English. mo. $126.00. The Allen Group, PO Box 300, Provo UT 84603. **DD** 332. **Continues** Nothing Down Advisor.

US
**RODDY REPORT. BOULDER COUNTY.** English. $535.84 (includes 8.25% sales tax) Texas; $495.00 other. Dresco Inc., 4851 Keller Springs Road, Suite 100, Dallas TX 75248. **Tel** (214)248-9186, FAX (214)407-1040. **Ad Acc**, **Adv Mgr:** G Roddy.

US/0889-1842
**RODDY REPORT. DALLAS COUNTY, THE.** **Added/Corp** Dresco, Inc. (19??)-. Periodical. English. mo. $297.69 (includes 8.25% sales tax) Texas; $275.00 other. Dresco Inc., 4851 Keller Springs Road, Suite 100, Dallas TX 75248. **Tel** (214)248-9186, FAX (214)407-1040. **Ad Acc**, **Adv Mgr:** G Roddy.

US
**RODDY REPORT. TARRANT COUNTY, THE.** (1983)-. Periodical. English. mo. $644.09 (includes 8.25% sales tax) Texas; $595.00 other. Dresco Inc., 4851 Keller Springs Road, Suite 100, Dallas TX 75248. **Tel** (214)248-9186, FAX (214)407-1040. **Ad Acc**, **Adv Mgr:** G Roddy.

US/0194-3723
**RON JANOFF'S GUIDE TO COMMERCIAL REAL ESTATE.** **VFOAT** Guide to Commercial Real Estate. 1st- 1977-. English. $50.00. Ronald C Janoff, 549 N 6th Avenue, Tucson AZ 85705. **LC** HD7287.6.U5; J35. **DD** 333.3/37.

US/0098-0315
**ROSTER OF LICENSED REAL ESTATE BROKERS AND SALESMEN BY COMPANY.** English. Delaware Real Estate Commission, Department of Administrative Services, Division of Business and Occupational Regulations, State House Annex, Dover DE 19901. **LC** HD266.D3; A3. **DD** 658.89/3333/3. **Continues** Roster of Real Estate Brokers and Salesmen.

US
**ROSTER OF REAL ESTATE LICENSEES (IOWA).** **Main/Corp** Iowa Real Estate Commission. **VFOAT** Roster of Licensed Real Estate Brokers and Salespersons. Began with 1977 issue. Periodical. an. English. Iowa Real Estate Commission / Des Moines, Executive Hills, 1223 East Court Avenue, Des Moines IA 50319. **LC** HD266.I8; I67C. **DD** 333.33/025/777. **Continues** Roster of Licensed Real Estate Brokers and Sales Persons. **Desc:** SUMMARY: Rosters of licensed real estate brokers and salespersons in Iowa, licensed real estate apprentice salesperson, and licensed non-resident brokers and salespersons.

US/1049-7013
**RTC PROPERTY DISPOSITION REPORT.** [RTC prop. dispos. rep.]. **VAT** Resolution Trust Corporation Property Disposition Report. (1989)-. Periodical. English. mo. $290.00 (one year), $522.00 (two year) US, Canada and Mexico; $338.00 (one year), $618.00 (two year). DataTrends Publications, 895 Harrison Street SE, Suite B, Leesburg VA 22075. **Tel** (703)779-0574, (800)766-8130, FAX (703)779-2267. **DD** 333. available on an online database (file 636/Full-Text) from DIALOG.

US
**RTC REPORT.** (19??)-. English. wk (50 issues). $475.00. Land Development Institute Ltd, 1401 16th Street Northwest, Washington DC 20036. **Tel** (202)232-2144, FAX (202)232-4757.

US/0731-9150
**RUNZHEIMER REPORTS ON RELOCATION.** **Added/Corp** Runzheimer and Company. **VFOAT** Reports on Relocation; Runzheimer Reports. Vol. 1, No. 1 (March 1982)-. Periodical. English. Twelve times a year. $354.00. Runzheimer International / Wisconsin, Runzheimer Park, Rochester WI 53167. **Tel** (414)767-2200, FAX (414)767-2254, (800)558-1702. **ED** Kenneth Groh. **[CCC].** Index available. cum. index. **Desc:** Covers all aspects of corporate employee transfer programs.

US/0886-8611
**RURAL DEVELOPMENT NEWS.** [Rural dev. news]. **Added/Corp** North Central Regional Center for Rural Development. (19??)-. Periodical. English. ir. North Central Regional Center for Rural Development, 216 East Hall, Iowa State University, Ames IA 50011. **Tel** (515)294-8321. **DD** 333. Documents available from Documents on Demand.
**Ind/Abst** AGRICOLA [Full Cov.]; Environ. Abstr.

NZ/0549-0111
**RURAL REAL ESTATE MARKET IN NEW ZEALAND (WELLINGTON, N.Z. : 1981).** (RURAL REAL ESTATE MARKET IN NEW ZEALAND.). English. sa. 65.00NZ$ New Zealand. Valuation New Zealand, PO Box 5098, Wellington New Zealand. **Tel** 738-555, FAX 738-552. **LC** HD1120; .5. **DD** 333.33/5. **Circ:** 350.
**Desc:** Bulletins showing real estate sales and price indices by districts in New Zealand with some historical series.

US/1063-5513
**SAN DIEGO COMMERCE.** **See** Business-Commerce.

US
**SCAN.** English. qt. $25.00 members; $50.00 other. Florida Association of Realtors, PO Box 725025, Orlando FL 32872. **Tel** (407)438-1400, FAX (407)438-1411. **ED** Tara Thompson.
**Ind/Abst** Geogr. Abstr. Phys. Geogr.; Int. Dev. Abstr.

US/0272-3484
**SERVICE CORPORATION DIRECTORY.** **See** Business-Banking and Finance.

US/0049-0393
**SHOPPING CENTER WORLD.** Vol. 1 (Feb. 1972)-. Periodical. English. mo. $60.00. Argus Business, 6151 Powers Ferry Road, Atlanta GA 30339. **Tel** (404)995-2500, (800)233-3359. **[CCC].** available on microfilm and microfiche from University Microfilms International (UMI).

US/1041-3073
**SITE SELECTION & INDUSTRIAL DEVELOPMENT.** **Title Change.** [Site sel. ind. dev.]. **VFOAT** Site Selection and Industrial Development; Site Selection. Vol. 33, No. 5 (Oct. 1988)-(19??). Periodical. English. bm. Conway Data Inc., 40 Technology Park Suite 200, Norcross GA 30092. **Tel** (404)446-6996, (800)554-5686, FAX (404)263-8825. **ED** Jack Lyne, Tim Venable, Deborah Fusi. **LC** HD58; .I48. **DD** 338/.0973/05. Index available. **Bk Rev**. **Ad Acc**. **Circ:** 31,600 (ctrl). available on microfilm and microfiche from University Microfilms International (UMI). **Continues** Industrial Development and Site Selection Handbook. **Merged into** Site Selection.
**Desc:** Information for the corporate real estate profession.
**Ind/Abst** Acad. Search (Jan. 1993-); Bus. Per. Index; Bus. Source (Jan. 1993-); INFO-SOUTH Abstr.; Mag. Search; PAIS Int. Print; Vocat. Search (Jan. 1993-); Wilson Bus. Abstr.

DK/0105-1164
**SKATTER OG AFGIFTER.** **See** Public Administration-Public Finance and Taxation.

US/0892-7847
**SKYLINES (WASHINGTON, D.C.).** (SKYLINES.). [Skylines]. **Added/Corp** Building Owners and Managers Association International. (May 1986)-. Periodical. English. Ten times a year (July/Aug. and Nov./Dec. issues combined). $65.00 (members); $95.00 (non-members). Building Owners and Managers Association, 1201 New York Avenue Northwest, Suite 300, Washington DC 20005. **Tel** (202)408-2662, FAX (202)371-0181. **LC** HD1393.55; .S59. **DD** 658. Index available (Free). **Continues** BOMA International Skylines, 0279-2044.

US/8755-6065
**SOFTWHERE. REAL ESTATE.** [Softwhere. Real estate]. **VFOAT** Software. Real Estate; Real Estate; Real Estate Softwhere. Jan. 1984-. English. $21.90. Moore Data Management Services, Minneapolis MN 55416. **Tel** (612)588-7205. **LC** HD1380; .S65. **DD** 333.33/028/5425.

US/0733-4605
**SOUND ADVICE.** (SOUND ADVICE : THE ENGLISH & CARDIFF REAL ESTATE & INVESTMENT ADVISORY LETTER.). [Sound advice]. Periodical. English. qt. $78.00. Sound Advice, 2120 Omega Road, San Ramon CA 94583. **Tel** (510)838-8100. **ED** John Wesley English. **Bk Rev**. **Circ:** 1,000. **Continues** English & Cardiff Real Estate Advisory Letter.
**Desc:** Advisory letter containing original and in-depth research in all sectors of real estate. Clearly-written articles on tax matters and laws affecting investors.

US/0192-1630
**SOUTHEAST REAL ESTATE NEWS.** (19??)-. Periodical. English. Twelve times a year. $38.00. Argus Business, 6151 Powers Ferry Road, Atlanta GA 30339. **Tel** (404)995-2500, (800)233-3359. **(Subscription address:** Sunbelt Subfulfillment Services, PO Box 41369, Nashville, TN 37204; telephone: (615)377-3322, (800)888-5139) **ED** Coles McKagen. **[CCC].** **Circ:** 16,013. available on microfilm and microfiche from University Microfilms International (UMI); available on an online database (file 648/Full-Text) from DIALOG.
**Ind/Abst** Trade Ind. Index.

US/0192-9194
**SOUTHWEST REAL ESTATE NEWS.** (19??)-. Periodical. English. Six times a year. $38.00 (one year), $60.00 (two years). Argus Business, 6151 Powers Ferry Road, Atlanta GA 30339. **Tel** (404)995-2500, (800)233-3359. **[CCC].** available on microfilm and microfiche from University Microfilms International (UMI); available on an online database (file 648/Full-Text) from DIALOG. **Absorbed** Texas Real Estate News.
**Ind/Abst** Trade Ind. Index.

SP
**SPANISH REAL ESTATE MAGAZINE.** qt. $45.00. Nuevas Ed Inmobiliarias Sa, Gran Via 67, 28013 Madrid Spain. **Tel** 247 6115 6943.

●US/1063-9098
**SPAULDING & SLYE REPORT. GREATER BOSTON, THE.** (THE SPAULDING & SLYE REPORT. GREATER BOSTON : A QUARTERLY REVIEW OF COMMERCIAL REAL ESTATE TRENDS IN THE OFFICE, R&D, AND INDUSTRIAL MARKETS.). [Spaulding Slye rep., Gt. Boston]. **Added/Corp** Spaulding & Slye. **VFOAT** Spaulding and Slye Report. Greater Boston; Greater Boston. (July 1992)-. English. qt (Jan., Apr., July, Oct.). $200.00. Spaulding & Slye Research, 125 High Street, Boston MA 02110-2701. **Tel** (617)523-8000, FAX (617)523-8001. **ED** Louisa Kussin. **LC** HD1393.25; .S63. **DD** 333. **Circ:** 3,000 (ctrl). **Continues** Spaulding & Slye Report. Greater Boston Market (Boston, Mass. : 1992), 1063-908X.

●US/1063-9101
**SPAULDING & SLYE REPORT. WASHINGTON, D.C, THE.** (THE SPAULDING & SLYE REPORT. WASHINGTON, D.C. : A QUARTERLY REVIEW OF COMMERCIAL REAL ESTATE TRENDS IN THE OFFICE MARKET.). [Spaulding Slye rep., Wash. D.C.]. **Added/Corp** Spaulding & Slye. **VFOAT** Spaulding and Slye Report. Washington, D.C.; Washington, D.C. (July 1992)-. English. qt. **DD** 333. **Continues** Spaulding & Slye Report. Washington, D.C. Market.

SW
**STOCKHOLM FASTIGHETS KALENDER.** Periodical. Swedish. Stockholms Fastighetskalender, Fach 104, 22 Stockholm Sweden. **LC** HD770.S75; S75.

US
**STRUCTURING COMMERCIAL REAL ESTATE WORKOUTS : ALTERNATIVES TO FORECLOSURE.** (19??)-. English. an. $103.08. Prentice-Hall Law and Business, 270 Sylvan Avenue, Englewood Cliffs NJ 07632. **Tel** (800)223-0231, (201)894-8538, FAX (201)894-8666.

US
**SUMMARY OF REAL ESTATE ASSESSMENT/SALES RATIO STUDY / COMPILED BY STATE OF IOWA, DEPARTMENT OF REVENUE.** **Added/Corp** Iowa. Dept. of Revenue. (19??)-. English. Free. Department of Revenue / Iowa, Hoover State Office Building, Des Moines IA 50319. **LC** HD266.I8; S86. **DD** 333.33/2/09777.

US/0145-4595
**SUMMARY REPORT ON REAL PROPERTY OWNED BY THE UNITED STATES THROUGHOUT THE WORLD AS OF ... .** Began with 1975. English. an. **LC** JK1613; .A245. **DD** 333.1/0973. **Continues** Inventory Report on Real Property Owned by the United States Throughout the World.

US/0745-354X
**SUN BELT BUILDINGS JOURNAL.** **Title Change.** Periodical. English. mo. Rockwell, 3501 N 16th Street, Phoenix AZ 85016. **Tel** (602)264-3500. **ED** Karl Tunberg. **Circ:** 13,700. **Continues** Sun Belt Real Estate Press. **Continued by** Sun Belt Real Estate Press, 0279-0904.

US
**SURVEY OF ACCOUNTING AND REPORTING PRACTICES OF REAL ESTATE DEVELOPERS, A.** **Main/Corp** Price, Waterhouse and Company. **VFOAT** Real Estate Developers. English. an. Price Waterhouse & Company, 1177 Avenue of the Americas, New York NY 10020. **Tel** (212)596-7000.

HK
**SURVEY OF BUILDING, CONSTRUCTION, AND REAL ESTATE SECTORS.** **See** Building and Construction.

US/1044-470X
**TAIWAN REGISTER.** (1989)-. English. an. $195.00. Mead Ventures Inc, PO Box 44952, Phoenix AZ 85064. **Tel** (602)234-0044, FAX (602)234-0076. **LC** HD936; .T36. **DD** 332.63/24/02551249.

## Real Estate

**Desc:** 100 Taiwanese companies which invest in, or lend on, US property are profiled. Entries review company activities, future projects, and capital turnover.

US/8755-0628
**TAX MANAGEMENT REAL ESTATE JOURNAL.** See Law.

UK
**TAX ON PROPERTY.** (19??)-. English. £298.15. Croner Publ Ltd, Croner House, London Road, Kingston upon Thames, Surrey KT2 6SR England. **Tel** 011 44 81 5473333, FAX 081 547-2637.

US/1059-5090
**TENNESSEE REAL ESTATE LAW LETTER.** See Law.

US/0267-8896
**TEXAS REAL ESTATE LAW REPORTER.** See Law.

US
**TIMESHARING LAW REPORTER (WASHINGTON, D.C. : 1987).** See Law.

JA
**TOCHI HAKUSHO / KOKUDOCHO HEN.**
**Added/Corp** Japan. Kokudocho. (1990)-. Japanese. Okurasho Insatukyoku, 2-4, Toranomon 2 chome, Minatoku, Tokyoto 105 Japan. **LC** IN PROCESS.

US/8750-5088
**TRI-STATE REAL ESTATE JOURNAL (CHERRY HILL, N.J.).** (TRI-STATE REAL ESTATE JOURNAL.). **VFOAT** Tri State Real Estate Journal. Vol. 1, No. 1 (Apr. 13, 1984)-. Periodical. English. wk. $84.00. Adler Group Inc., 8601 Georgia Avenue, Silver Spring MD 20910. **Tel** (609)988-0092, FAX (609)988-0093.

●US/1075-3664
**TRW REDI REALTY REPORT.** [TRW REDI realty rep.]. **VFOAT** REDI Realty Report. (1993)-. Periodical. English. Fifty-two times a year. Real Estate Data Inc, 475 Fifth Avenue, Suite 1901, New York NY 10017. **Tel** (212)532-2705. **DD** 333. **Continues** REDI Realty Report, 1051-0737.

US/1061-4184
**TURNAROUNDS & WORKOUTS. SURVEY.** [Turnarounds workouts, Surv.]. **Added/Corp** Beard Group, Inc. **VFOAT** Turnarounds and Workouts. Survey; Survey; Real Estate Workouts Survey; Real Estate Workouts. (1991)-. Periodical. English. mo. $195.00. Beard Group, PO Box 9867, Washington DC 20016. **Tel** (301)951-6400. **DD** 333.

US/8755-1608
**U.S. REAL ESTATE REGISTER.** [U.S. real estate regist.]. **VFOAT** US Real Estate Register. Vol. 17 (1984/1985)-. English. an. $46.00. Barry Inc, PO Box 551, Wilmington MA 01887. **Tel** (617)658-0441. **LC** HD1394; .I45. **DD** 332.63/24/02573; 333. **Ad Acc**. **Continues** Industrial/Commercial Real Estate Managers' Directory, 0737-1950.

US/0894-6108
**ULI MARKET PROFILES.** [ULI mark. profiles]. **VFOAT** Market Profiles. **VAT** Urban Land Institute Market Profiles. 1986-. English. an. $236.00 (nonmembers), $192.00 (members). Urban Land Institute, 625 Indiana Ave Northwest, Washington DC 20004. **Tel** (202)624-7000, (800)321-5011. **LC** HD251; .U45. **DD** 333.3/8/0973. **Circ:** 2,500. **Continues in part** Development Review and Outlook, 0740-1574.
**Desc:** Annual profiles of US real estate development markets.

NZ
**URBAN REAL ESTATE MARKET IN NEW ZEALAND.** **Main/Corp** New Zealand. Valuation Dept. English. sa. 45.00NZ$ New Zealand. Valuation New Zealand, PO Box 5098, Wellington New Zealand. **Tel** 738-555, FAX 738-552. **LC** HD1387; .N38 subser; HD1120.5. **DD** 333.3/3 S 333.3/37/09931. **Circ:** 350.
**Desc:** Bulletins showing real estate sales and price indices by districts in New Zealand with some historical series.

US/0042-238X
**VALUATION (AMERICAN SOCIETY OF APPRAISERS).** See Business-Banking and Finance.

CE
**VALUATION JOURNAL, THE.** V. 1 (Oct. 1974)-. English. Valuation Department, 748 Maradana 10, Colombo Ceylon Sri Lanka. **LC** HD1393; .V34. **DD** 333.3/32/095493.

AT/0815-3132
**VICTORIAN REAL ESTATE JOURNAL.** [Vic. real estate j.]. (1984)-. Periodical. English. qt. Free to qualified subscribers; 20.00Aus$ other. Real Estate Institute of Victoria Ltd., 335 Camberwell Road, PO Box 443, Camberwell Victoria 3124 Australia. **Tel** 011 61 03 8829188, FAX 011 61 03 8828112. **ED** Graham Stanley. **DD** 333.3309945. **Ad Acc, Adv Mgr:** G. Kyrros. **Circ:** 2,700. **Continues** Real Estate and Stock Journal, 0034-0669.

US
**VIRGINIA LAND USE DIGEST.** English. Four times a year. $25.00 (one year); $45.00 (two years). Cenva Publishing Company, PO Box 2315, Lynchburg VA 24501. **Tel** (804)896-6128, FAX (804)847-5678. **ED** William W. Hibbert. Index available (Winter issues in Jan.). cum. index. **Ad Acc**. **Circ:** 400 (ctrl).
**Desc:** Articles about land use issues in Virginia.

CN/0821-2120
**WARNOCK HERSEY APPRAISAL COMPANY.** (WARNOCK HERSEY APPRAISAL COMPANY : BULLETIN.). [Warnock Hersey Appraisal Company]. Bulletin. English. Warnock Hersey Appraisal Company, 128 Elmslie Street, Lasalle Quebec H8R 1V8 Canada. **DD** 333.33/2/05. **Continues** Warnock Hersey Appraisal Company. Bulletin, 0821-2112.

US
**WASHINGTON PROPERTY LAW REPORTER.** See Law.

US/0277-8475
**WG & L REAL ESTATE OUTLOOK.** **Ceased.** [WGL real estate outlook]. **VFOAT** Real Estate Outlook. **VAT** Warren, Gorham and Lamont Real Estate Outlook. Began publication in 1979-Ceased (1990). Periodical. English. qt. Warren Gorham & Lamont Inc., Park Square Building, 31 St. James Avenue, Boston MA 02116-4112. **Tel** (617)423-2020, (800)950-1207, FAX (617)423-2026.

US/0279-2583
**WISCONSIN REALTOR, THE.** **Title Change.** Vol. 1, No. 1 (June 1981)-. Periodical. English. sa. Wisconsin Realtors Association, 4801 Hayes Road, Madison WI 53704. **Tel** (608)241-2047. **ED** William E Malkasian. **Ad Acc**. **Circ:** 10,500 (ctrl). **Superseded by** Wisconsin Realtor Update, 0886-0777.
**Desc:** Reference manual and directory of members.

US/8756-0259
**YANKEE HOMES.** **Ceased.** (Jan. 1985)-(Dec. 1989). Periodical. English. mo (except Jan. and Feb.). Yankee Publishing Inc., Main Street, Dublin NH 03444. **Tel** (603)563-8111, (800)736-1100. **ED** Georgia Orcutt. **Bk Rev**. **Ad Acc**. **Circ:** 15,000.
**Desc:** Features New England real estate for sale, from seaside to mountaintop, in styles from Federal to contemporary, including homes, inns, farms, and cabins.

JA
**ZENKOKU SHIGAICHI KAKAKU SHISU.**
**Main/Corp** Nihon Fudosan Kenkyujo. **VFOAT** Zenkoku Mokuzo Kenchikuhi Shisu. Japanese (English). sa. ¥310. Nihon Fudosan Kenkyujo, c/o Kangin Fujiya Building, 3-2 Toranomon 1-chome Minto-ku, Tokyo Japan. **Tel** (03)503-5335, FAX (03)597-8063. **LC** HD918; .N53A. Index available. cum. index. **Circ:** 7,700.
**Desc:** Urban land price indexes in Japan compiled by the Japan Real Estate Institute.

## ABSTRACTING, BIBLIOGRAPHIES AND STATISTICS

CN/0381-0917
**INDICATOR (NANAIMO).** (THE INDICATOR.). **Main/Corp** Vancouver Island Real Estate Board. 1976-. English. an. $15.00. Vancouver Island Real Estate Board, PO Box 592, Nanaimo British Columbia V9R 5L5 Canada. **Tel** (604)390-4212, FAX (604)390-3911. **ED** D Gardner. **DD** 333.3/3/0971134. **Bk Rev**. **Ad Acc**. **Circ:** 1,500 (ctrl).
**Desc:** A statistical review of market activities in real estate, also a review of demographics and commercial development.

US/0098-0056
**STATISTICAL REPORT OF PROPERTY ASSESSMENT AND TAXATION.** **Main/Corp** Kansas. Division of Property Valuation. Statistical Publication. English. an. Division of Property Valuation, State Capitol Building, Topeka KS 66606. **LC** HJ4217; .A25. **DD** 333.3/32/09781. **Continues** Statistical Report of General Property Assessment and Taxation.

## RECREATION, LEISURE

FR/0247-6886
**4X4 MAGAZINE.** **VFOAT** Quatre Fois Quatre Magazine. (1981)-. Periodical. French. mo. 4 X 4 Magazine, 122 Avenue des Champs Elysees, 75008 Paris France. **UDC** 796.7.

US/0279-8689
**ACTION NOW (SAN JUAN CAPISTRANO, CALIF.).** **Ceased.** (ACTION NOW.). Vol. 7, No. 9 (Apr. 1981)-Ceased Feb. 1992. Periodical. English. mo. Surfer Publications Inc., PO Box 1028, Dana Point CA 92629. **Tel** (714)496-5922, (800)289-0636, FAX (714)496-7849. **LC** GV561; .S55. **DD** 796/.05. **Continues** Skateboarder's Action Now, 0274-7170.
**Ind/Abst** Mag. Index (April 1981-?).

UK/0957-8870
**AMENITY MANAGEMENT.** [Amenity manag.]. (1989)-. Periodical. English. mo (12 issues). £20.00 UK; £40.00 Eire & Europe; £50.00 America, Middle East, Africa & India; £60.00 Australia, New Zealand & Japan; £40.00 other. Haymarket Publishing Ltd., 12 14 Ansdell Street, London W8 5TR England. **Tel** 011 44 483 733800, FAX 011 44 483 776573. **(Subscription address:** Haymarket Publishing Ltd, PO Box 219, Subscriptions Department, Woking Surrey GU21 1ZW, United Kingdom.) **DD** 333.70941.

GW/0171-7243
**AMUSEMENT-INDUSTRIE.** [Amus.-Ind.]. (1971)-. Periodical. German. Four times a year. DM40.00. Junfermannische Verlagsbuchhand, Imadstrasse 40 Postfach 18 40, W 4790 Paderborn F R Germany. **Tel** 011 49 521 34034. **UDC** 379.8.
**Ind/Abst** Leis. Recreat. Tour. Abstr.

US
**AMUSEMENT PARK GUIDEBOOK.** 1987-. English. an. $11.50. Reed Publishing Company / Pennsylvania, c/o James W Reed, 38 Meadow View Drive, Leola PA 17540-1624. **Tel** (717)656-0125. **ED** James W Reed. **Bk Rev**. **Circ:** 5,000.
**Desc:** Description, rating, location, season and hours, admission charges, complete list of rides and shows for every amusement park with 8 or more adult rides in the U.S. and Canada.

US
**ANNUAL IN THERAPEUTIC RECREATION.** See Physical Therapy.

AT
**ANNUAL REPORT - COMMUNITY RECREATION COUNCIL OF WESTERN AUSTRALIA.** **Main/Corp** Community Recreation Council of Western Australia. (19??)-. English. **LC** GV146.W4; C65a. **DD** 350/.85.

AT
**ANNUAL REPORT OF THE DEPARTMENT FOR YOUTH, SPORT, AND RECREATION / GOVERNMENT OF WESTERN AUSTRALIA.** **Main/Corp** Western Australia. Dept. for Youth, Sport, and Recreation. (1979)-. English. **LC** GV146.W4; W48a. **DD** 790/.09941. **Absorbed** Youth, Community Recreation, and National Fitness Council (W.A.). Report of the Youth, Community Recreation, and National Fitness Council.

AT
**ANNUAL REPORT OF THE DEPARTMENT OF SPORT AND RECREATION FOR THE YEAR ENDED.** (19??)-. Government Publication. English. an. Department of Sport and Recreation, Marland House, 570 Bourke Street, Melbourne Victoria 3000 Australia. **Circ:** 700. **Continues** Report for the Department of Sport and Recreation for the Year Ended.

US
**ANNUAL REPORT - STATE PARK AND RECREATION COMMISSION.** **Main/Corp** New Mexico. State Park and Recreation Commission. (19??)-. English. an. State Capitol, Santa Fe NM 87503. **LC** GV191.42.N6; N47a. **DD** 333.7/8/09789.

US
**ATLANTA LAKE LIFE.** English. Four times a year (plus yearly guide book). $9.95 North America. Allison Andrews Ed & Publisher, 3169 Holcomb Bridge Road, Suite 205, Norcross GA 30071. **Tel** (404)446-3925. **ED** Allison Andrews. **Ad Acc**. **Circ:** 52,700.
**Desc:** Leisure, lifestyle magazine focusing on Georgia's lakes.

AT/0311-8223
**AUSTRALIAN PARKS AND RECREATION.** See Public Administration-Parks and Recreation.

AT
**AUSTRALIAN SKIING.** (19??)-. Consumer Publication. English. mo. 18.81Aus$ (one year), 33.93Aus$ (two year). Mason Stewart Publishing, PO Box 746, Darlinghurst NSW 2010 Australia. **Tel** 011 61 2 331 5006. **ED** Matt Johnson. **Bk Rev**, (Qty: 3). **Ad Acc, Adv Mgr:** Stephen Kay. **Circ:** 13,000. **Continues** Australian Skiing Surry Hills, 0818-9307.
**Desc:** Equipment buyers' guides, test, instruction, travel and resort infomation.

GW/0935-0454
**AZUR-CAMPING-MAGAZIN.** [Azur-Camp.-Mag.]. (1987)-. Periodical. German. Twice a year. Free. Azur Freizeit GmbH, Rohracker Strasse 272, W-7000 Stuttgart 61 Germany. **Tel** 0711 42 70 23, FAX 0711 49 711 427030. **UDC** 379.85. **Ad Acc. Circ:** 70,000.

US/8756-4661
**BALLOON (IRVINE, CALIF.).** **See** Physically Impaired.

US/0887-6061
**BALLOON LIFE.** **See** Recreation, Leisure-Sports.

HU/0865-9222
**BALNEOLOGIA, GYOGYFURDOUGY, GYOGYIDEGENFORGALOM.** [Balneol. Gyogyfurdou. Gyogyidforg.]. (1990)-. Periodical. Hungarian. qt. **UDC** 615.8. ***Continues** Balneologia, Rehabilitacio, Gyogyfurdougy, 0230-0494.*
**Ind/Abst** Leis. Recreat. Tour. Abstr.

US/0735-4711
**BAND & FESTIVAL GUIDE.** **See** Music.

US
**BIENNIAL REPORT OF THE NORTH CAROLINA RECREATION COMMISSION.** **Main/Corp** North Carolina. Recreation Commission. Periodical. English. be. North Carolina Recreation Commission, Raleigh NC 27603. **LC** GV54.N8; A3. **DD** 790.61756.

US/0503-9967
**BIENNIAL REPORT OF THE VERMONT RECREATION BOARD.** **Main/Corp** Vermont. Recreation Board. **VFOAT** Recreation in Vermont; Biennial Report of the State Recreation Board. Periodical. English. be. Vermont Recreation Board, Montpelier VT 05602. **LC** GV54.V5; A32. **DD** 790; 790.9743.

CN/0826-0508
**BODY POLITIC XTRA.** **See** Homosexuality.

BE/0771-8020
**BONNE SOIREE.** **VFOAT** BS. Bonne Soiree. (1922)-. Periodical. French. wk. 300.00F France; 506.00F other. Editions Mondiales, 9 11 13 Rue du Col Pierre Avia, 75754 Paris Cedex 15 France. **Tel** 011 33 1 46622162. **(Subscription address:** Bonne Soiree, BP 52, F 77932 Perthes France.**)** **UDC** 007.

UK
**BRITISH ROWING ALMANACK AND ARA YEAR BOOK.** **Main/Corp** Amateur Rowing Association (Great Britain). **VFOAT** ARA Year Book; A.R.A. Year Book; British Rowing Almanack. English. an. £9.00 UK; £10.00 other. Amateur Rowing Association, 6 Lower Mall/Hammersmith, London W6 9DJ England. **Tel** 011 44 81 748 3632, FAX 011 44 81 741 4658. **ED** Keith Osbane. **LC** GV791; .A46A. **DD** 797.1/23/0941. Index available. **Ad Acc. Circ:** 2,500.
**Desc:** Subject matter of contemporary and historical interest.

US/0279-8158
**BULLETIN / AMERICAN SUNBATHING ASSOCIATION, THE.** **Added/Corp** American Sunbathing Association. (19??)-. Periodical. English. Eleven times a year. $28.00. American Sunbathing Association, 1703 North Main Street Suite E, Kissimmee FL 34744. **Tel** (407)933-2064, FAX (407)933-7577. **Bk Rev. Ad Acc. Circ:** 30,000 (ctrl).
**Desc:** Newspaper of nudist news and club events.

CN/1187-0818
**BULLETIN - CANADIAN INTRAMURAL RECREATION ASSOCIATION.** (BULLETIN.). [Bull. - Can. Intramural Recreat. Assoc.]. **Added/Corp** Canadian Intramural Recreation Association. **VFOAT** CIRA Bulletin; Bulletin de l'ACLI. **VAT** Bulletin - Association Canadienne de Loisirs Intramuros. Vol. 15, No. 5 (June/July 1990)-. Bulletin. English (French). bm. Free to members. Canadian Intramural Recreation Association, 1600 James Naismith Drive, Gloucester Ontario K1B 5N4 Canada. **Tel** (613)748-5639. **DD** 793. ***Continues** CIRA Bulletin (Canadian Intramural Recreation Association), 0847-0189.*
**Ind/Abst** SPORT Discus.

US/0362-6180
**BUYERS' GUIDE FOR THE MASS ENTERTAINMENT INDUSTRY.** ***Title Change.*** Consumer Publication. English. an. Amusement Business, PO Box 24970, Nashville TN 37202. **Tel** (615)321-4250, FAX (615)327-1575. **LC** GV1851.A3; B88. **DD** 381/.45/790068. ***Continued by** Mass Entertainment Buyers Guide, 0748-1675.*

US/0273-6896
**CAHPERD JOURNAL TIMES.** **See** Public Health and Safety.

FR
**CALENDRIER MURAL.** French. an. $10.00. Sogedil, 146 rue du FG Poissonniere, 75010 Paris France.

US
**CALIFORNIA RECREATION ACTION PROGRAM REPORT.** **Main/Corp** California. Dept. of Parks and Recreation. 1981-82-. English. an. California Department of Parks & Recreation, PO Box 9422896, Sacramento CA 94296. **Tel** (916)445-9663. **LC** GV54.C2; C33A. **DD** 333.78/3/09794.

CN/1181-8689
**CAMP DITES-VOUS?.** (CAMP DITES-VOUS? : BULLETIN DU REGROUPEMENT DES ANIMATRICES ET ANIMATEURS DE CENTRES DE VACANCES DU QUEBEC.). [Camp dites-vous]. **Added/Corp** Regroupement des Animatrices et Animateurs de Centres de Vacances du Quebec. (Fall/Winter 1990)-. Bulletin. French. qt. Free for members. Regroupement des Animatrices et Animateurs de Centres de Vacances du Quebec, 4ME Etage, 985 Notre Dame, Joliette, Quebec J6E 3K1 Canada. **DD** 796.54/2/060714.

US/0896-5706
**CAMPING AND RV MAGAZINE.** [Camping RV mag.]. **VFOAT** Camping and RV; Camping & RV Magazine. **VAT** Camping and Recreational Vehicle Magazine; Camping & Recreational Vehicle Magazine. (Nov. 1985)-. Periodical. English. mo. D$17.95 one year; $32.50 two year; $46.50 three year. Jim Radtke, PO Box 458, Washburn WI 54891. **Tel** (715)373-5556, FAX (715)373-5003. **ED** Debora Radtke. **DD** 796. **Bk Rev.** (Qty: 30-40). **Ad Acc. Circ:** 13,500 (ctrl). ***Continues** Camping & RV Trader.*
**Desc:** Feature articles, new product, and technical information on RV and Camping lifestyle.

CN/0711-6470
**CANADIAN POOL & PATIO CONSUMERS HANDBOOK.** [Can. pool patio consum. handb.]. Vol. 8, No. 1 (Spring 1981)-. English. an. $2.00 per issue. Canadian Pool and Patio Consumers Handbook, c/o Southam Business Publishers, 1450 Don Mills Road, Don Mills Ontario M3B 2X7 Canada. **DD** 643/.55. ***Continues** Canadian Pool & Patio, 0317-2791.*

CN/0823-0145
**CANSPA COMMUNICATOR.** [CANSPA commun.]. **VAT** Canadian Swimming Pool Association Communicator. Vol. 3, No. 3 (June 1982)-. Periodical. English. Free to members. Canadian Swimming Pool Association, Suite 503/6303 Airport Road, Mississauga Ontario L4V 1R8 Canada. **DD** 690/.574/06071. ctrl circ. ***Continues** National Newsletter (Canadian Swimming Pool Association), 0229-2866.*

US/0090-2985
**CARNIVAL & CIRCUS BOOKING GUIDE.** ***Ceased.*** (1972)-?. English. an. Amusement Business, PO Box 24970, Nashville TN 37202. **Tel** (615)321-4250, FAX (615)327-1575. **LC** GV1851.A3; C37. **DD** 658/.91/7910680973.

US
**CASINO PLAYER.** (Apr. 1991)-. Consumer Publication. English. mo (12 issues per year). $24.00. Las Vegas Casino Journal, 3100 West Sahara Avenue, Suite 207, Las Vegas NV 89102. **Tel** (705)253-6230, (800)394-2467, FAX (702)253-6804. **(Subscription address:** Casino Player, 2524 Arctic Avenue, Atlantic City NJ 08401.**)** **LC** GV1301; .C36. ***Continues** Player (Atlantic City, N.J.).*
**Desc:** Targets the gaming enthusiast. Each issue focuses on a popular segment of this growing industry. Includes features on gaming around the world, columns by professional gamblers, interviews with famous entertainers, updates on the newest gaming technology and advice that helps the average gambler play to win.

CN/0705-3991
**CATALYST (VANCOUVER).** (CATALYST.). **Added/Corp** Recreation Society of British Columbia. (April 1977)-. Periodical. English. bm. Free. Recreation Society of British Columbia, 1200 Hornby Street, Vancouver British Columbia V6Z 1W2 Canada. **DD** 790/.06/2711. ctrl circ. ***Supersedes** Recreation Society of British Columbia. Newsletter.*

DK/0106-7303
**CENTRING SLAGELSE.** (CENTRING.). [CentringSlagelse]. (1980)-. Periodical. Danish. Forlaget Bavnebanke, Gerlav Idraethojskole, 4200 Slagelse Denmark. **Tel** 4553584065, FAX 4553584382. **DD** 796.
**Ind/Abst** Leis. Recreat. Tour. Abstr.

US/0162-4652
**CHURCH RECREATION MAGAZINE.** ***Ceased.*** **Added/Corp** Southern Baptist Convention. Sunday School Board. Vol. 1, (Oct./Dec. 1970)-(Jan. 1995). Periodical. English. Four times a year (Jan., Apr., July, Oct.). Southern Baptist Convention, 901 Commerce, Suite 750, Nashville TN 37203. **Tel** (615)244-2355, FAX (615)742-8919. **ED** Joe Williamson. **LC** BV1620; .C43. **DD** 259. **Bk Rev. Ad Acc.** ctrl circ. available on microfilm and microfiche from University Microfilms International (UMI). ***Supersedes** Church Recreation, 0529-7028.*
**Desc:** Reaching people for Christ through recreation. Exciting reading for church leaders and for families and individuals. Includes step-by-step how-to articles.
**Ind/Abst** South. Baptist Period. Index.

US/0889-5996
**CIRCUS REPORT, THE.** [Circus rep.]. (19??)-. Periodical. English. wk (publ Mon.). $35.00 US; $45.00 Canada; $50.00 other. The Circus Report, 525 Oak Street, El Cerrito CA 94530. **Tel** (510)525-3332. **ED** Don Marcks. **DD** 791. **Bk Rev. Ad Acc. Circ:** 2,100 (ctrl).
**Desc:** Circus information, news, routes, data on show people, reviews of shows, books, etc.

CN
**CITY PARENT.** (19??)-. English. Twelve times a year. 20.56Can$ Canada; 36.00Can$ others. City Parent, 467 Speers Road, Oakville Ontario L6K 3S4 Canada. **Tel** (905)815-0017. ***Continues** Kids Toronto.*

UK
**CLASSIC RACER.** (19??)-. English. bm. £19.50. Bob Berry Publishing Services, Deene House C Market Square Corby, Northants NN17 1PB England. **Tel** 011 44 536 203003. **(Subscription address:** World-Wide Subscription Services, Unit 4, Gibbs Reed Farm Pashley Road, Ticehurst TN5 7HE England.**)**

UK/0955-3045
**CLIMBER AND HILL WALKER.** [Climb. hill walker]. **VFOAT** Climber (1988). (198?)-. Periodical. English. mo. £55.00 UK; £75.00 other. George Outram & Co Ltd, 195 Albion Street, Glasgow G1 1QP Scotland. **Tel** 011 44 355246444, FAX 011 44 355263013. **(Subscription address:** Caledonian Magazines Ltd, Plaza Tower Plaza, East Kilbride, Glasgow G74 1LW Scotland**)** **DD** 796-522. ***Continues** Climber (1986), 0953-1319.*

US/0898-4603
**COLORADO SKI INDUSTRY CHARACTERISTICS AND FINANCIAL ANALYSIS.** **See** Recreation, Leisure-Sports.

●US/1063-763X
**COLUMBIA GORGE VISITOR & RECREATION GUIDE (1992).** (COLUMBIA GORGE VISITOR & RECREATION GUIDE.). **VFOAT** Columbia Gorge Visitor and Recreation Guide; Columbia Gorge. Vol. 3 (1992)-. Periodical. English. an. $2.50 (per copy). Gorge Publishing, PO Box 918, Hood River OR 97031. **Tel** (503)386-7440, FAX (503)386-7480. **ED** Carol York. **Ad Acc, Adv Mgr:** Marie Cordell. **Circ:** 60,000. ***Continues** Columbia Gorge Magazine, 1063-7621.*
**Desc:** Visitor and recreation guide to the Columbia River Gorge. Includes information on historic sites, comprehensive calendar of events, lodging, dining and shopping, along with maps and color photography.

●US/1062-4503
**COMICS VALUES ANNUAL.** (COMICS VALUES ANNUAL: THE COMIC BOOK PRICE GUIDE.). [Comics values annu.]. (1992)-. English. $15.95. Wallace-Homestead Book Company / Pennsylvania, 201 King of Prussia Road, Radnor PA 19089.

●US/1062-9653
**CONDO VACATIONING.** [Condo vacat.]. Vol. 1, No. 1 (Spring 1992)-. Periodical. English. qt. $24.95. Condo Vacations, 855 Hanover Street, Suite 110, Manchester NH 03104. **DD** 333.

CN/0838-2395
**COTTAGE LIFE.** [Cottage life]. Vol. 1, No. 1 (June/July 1988)-. Periodical. English. Six times a year. 17.50Can$ Canada; 23.50Can$ US; 27.50Can$ other. Cottage Life, 111 Queen Street East, Suite 408, Toronto Ontario M5C 1S2 Canada. **Tel** (416)360-6880, FAX (416)360-6814. **(Subscription address:** Cottage Life, 35 Riviera Drive, Unit 17, Markham Ontario L3R 8N4 Canada**)** **DD** 643/.2. available on microfilm and microfiche from Micromedia Limited.
**Ind/Abst** Can. Index.

CN/0229-5229
**COUNTRY VACATIONS IN ALBERTA.** [Ctry. vacat. Alta.]. Periodical. English. Alberta Agriculture / Market Analysis, 9718 107th Street, Edmonton Alberta T5K 2C8 Canada. **Tel** (403)427-2121, FAX (403)435-4725. **DD** 796.5/6/097123. ***Continues in part** Alberta Country Vacations, 0229-5199.*

US
**COUNTY AND MUNICIPAL RECREATION AND PARK SERVICES STUDY (MARYLAND).** **Main/Corp** Maryland. Office of Recreation and Leisure Services. Fiscal Year 1982-. English. an. Department of Natural Resources / Maryland, Tawes State Office Building, 580 Taylor Avenue, Baltimore MD 21401. **Tel** (410)974-3015. **LC** GV54.M3; M34A. **DD** 353.97520085/8. ***Continues** Maryland. Dept. of Natural Resources. Assistance and Information. County and Municipal Recreation and Park Services Study.*

US
**COURIER (WASHINGTON, D.C.).** ***Ceased.*** (COURIER : THE NATIONAL PARK SERVICE NEWSLETTER.). **VFOAT** National Park Service

# Recreation, Leisure

Newsletter. (1977)-(19??). Newsletter. English. mo. National Park Service, Room 5103/1100 L Street NW, Washington DC 20240. **LC** SB482.A1; C6. **Continues** Newsletter (United States. National Park Service).

UK
**CRICKETERS' WHO'S WHO, THE.** **VFOAT** Cricketers' Who is Who; Who's Who. (19??)-. English. an. Queen Anne Press, Maxwell House, 74 Worship Street, London EC2A 2EN England. **LC** GV915.A1; C75. **DD** 796.35/8/0922; B.

US/1064-2579
**CUE MAGAZINE.** (CUE MAGAZINE : NORTHERN CALIFORNIA FILM, VIDEO, TELEVISION PRODUCTION.). [Cue mag.]. (19??)-. Periodical. English. mo. $24.00. Cue Magazine, 1430 Benito Avenue, Burlingame CA 94010. **Tel** (415)348-8004, FAX (415)348-7781. **ED** Pat Henry and Karen Pathmell (editor's address: PO Box 2027 Burlingame CA 94011-2027). **DD** 791. **Ad Acc.** ctrl circ.

UK/0140-6000
**DARTS WORLD.** See Recreation, Leisure-Sports.

US/0194-178X
**DIRECTORY OF NIGHTCLUBS, HOTELS, THEATRES, LOUNGES & DISCOTHEQUES.** See Theater.

US
**DISCOVERY YMCA.** **Added/Corp** YMCA of the USA. Vol. 1, No. 1 (Oct. 1982)-. Periodical. English. qt. $8.00. YMCA of the USA, 101 North Wacker Drive, Chicago IL 60606. **Tel** (312)269-0505, FAX (312)977-9063. **ED** Anthony Ripley. **LC** BV1040; .D57. **Ad Acc.** **Circ:** 75,000 (ctrl).
**Desc:** Includes features, photo essays, and news stories spotlighting YMCA programs across the country.

US/0095-7178
**DISNEY NEWS.** **Title Change.** **Added/Corp** Disney (Walt) Productions. Disneyland Division. Vol. 1 (Winter 1965/66)-(Spring 1994). Periodical. English. qt. Disney Magazine, PO Box 4489, Anaheim CA 92803. **Tel** (714)520-2533. **ED** Anne OKey. **LC** GV1853.D5; D57. **DD** 791./068/79496. **Ad Acc, Adv Mgr:** K. Helgason. **Circ:** 300,000 (ctrl). **Continued by** Disney Magazine.
**Desc:** Behind the scenes Disney information.

US/0363-4825
**DIVERSION (TITUSVILLE).** (DIVERSION.). [Diversion]. Vol. 1 (Apr./May 1973)-. Periodical. English. ir. Diversion Magazine, 60 East 42nd Street, Room 2424, New York NY 10165. **ED** Tom Passavant. **LC** G149; .D57. **DD** 910/.5. **Bk Rev.** **Ad Acc.** **Circ:** 160,085 (ctrl).
**Desc:** A leisure magazine edited by physicians. It includes articles of interest to the doctor as a traveler, gourmet, investor, gardener, photographer and sportsman. The editorial tone reflects its readers lifestyles and their personal interests. Articles are prepared by authorities in their respective fields.

US/1042-1343
**DIVING WORLD (VAN NUYS, CALIF.).** See Recreation, Leisure-Sports.

UK/0264-9691
**DOCKLANDS NEWS.** See Business.

CN/0821-5758
**DOCTOR'S REVIEW.** [Dr. rev.]. Vol. 1, No. 1 (Jan./Feb 1983)-. English. mo. 45.00Can$. Parkhurst Publishing, 400 McGill 3rd Floor, Montreal Quebec H2Y 2G1 Canada. **Tel** (514)397-8833, (514)397-9393. **ED** David Elkins and Madeleine Partous. **DD** 790/.05. **Ad Acc. Circ:** 34,000 (ctrl).
**Desc:** Leisure time journal specifically focused on the interests of Canadian physicians; topics include travel, sports, art, food and wine.

FR
**DOCUMENTATION TOURISTIQUE.** See Travel and Tourism.

HU/0139-0252
**DUNAKANYAR.** [Dunakanyar]. (1978)-. Hungarian. ir. **Continues** Dunakanyar Tajekoztato, 0200-1985. **Ind/Abst** Leis. Recreat. Tour. Abstr.

US
**EC CLASSICS.** 1985-. Periodical. English. Three times a year. Russ Cochran Publishers Ltd, 202 Aid Avenue, Box 469, West Plains MO 65775. **Tel** (417)256-2224. **ED** Russ Cochran. **Circ:** 10,000.

CN/1185-1635
**ECHANGER POUR MIEUX FAIRE.** [Echanger mieux faire]. **Added/Corp** Federation Quebecoise du Loisir en Institution. No 1 (Dec. 1990)-. Periodical. French. qt. Federation Quebecoise du Loisir en Institution, 525 Boulevard Hamel, Quebec, Quebec G1M 2S8 Canada. **DD** 790.1.

●US/1070-9231
**ECONOMIC ANALYSIS OF UNITED STATES SKI AREAS.** See Recreation, Leisure-Sports.

US/0746-2999
**ELECTRONIC ENTERTAINMENT.** [Electron. entertain.]. Vol. 2, No. 9 (Sept. 1983)-. Periodical. English. mo. $24.00. Infotainment World Inc., 951 Mariners Island Boulevard, San Mateo CA 94404. **Tel** (415)349-4300. (**Subscription address:** Neodata / Colorado, PO Box 2606, Boulder Boulder CO 80322.) **Continues** Arcade (Long Beach, Calif.), 0736-0304.

US/0744-3676
**EMPLOYEE SERVICES MANAGEMENT.** See Business-Personnel Management.

US/0883-1890
**ENTERTAINMENT MAGAZINE, THE.** Periodical. English. mo. $6.00. Southwest Alternatives Institute, Inc., 738 North 5th Avenue, PO Box 3355, Tucson AZ 85722. **Bk Rev.** **Ad Acc.** **Circ:** 20,000 (ctrl).
**Desc:** City-wide entertainment for all ages. Distribution in schools, colleges, convenience stores and hundreds of businesses.

FR
**EQUIPE DE LUNDI.** French. Fifty-two times a year. $151.50. International Subscriptions Inc., 30 Montgomery Street 7th Floor, Jersey City NJ 07302. **Tel** (800)544-6748, (201)451-9420, FAX (201)451-5745.

FR/0078-9585
**ETUDES ET MEMOIRES.** See Travel and Tourism.

●US/1066-6346
**EVENTS USA.** [Events USA]. **VAT** Events United States of America. (Oct./Nov. 1992)-. Periodical. English. bm. $15.00. Events USA, 386 Park Avenue South 301, New York NY 10016. **Tel** (212)684-2222. (**Subscription address:** Subscriptions Service Department P O Box 3000 Denville, NJ 07834 (201)627-2427) **DD** 973.
**Ind/Abst** Access (1992-July 1993).

US/1059-5929
**FAIRS AND FESTIVALS, NORTHEAST AND SOUTHEAST.** **Title Change.** (FAIRS AND FESTIVALS NORTHEAST AND SOUTHEAST/ ARTS EXTENSION SERVICE, DIVISION OF CONTINUING EDUCATION, UNIVERSITY OF MASSACHUSETTS AT AMHERST.). [Fairs festiv. Northeast Southeast].
**Added/Corp** University of Massachusetts at Amherst. Arts Extension Service. (1992)-(1992). English. University of Massachuttes, Arts Extension Service, Division of Continuing Education, 604 Goodell, Amherst MA 01003. **DD** 394. **Formed by the union of** Fairs and Festivals in the Southeast, 1051-9513 and Fairs and Festivals in the Northeast, 1051-9505. **Continued by** Fairs and Festivals (Amherst, Mass.), 1067-1846.

US/0740-3690
**FEDERAL PARKS & RECREATION.** [Fed. parks recreat.]. **VFOAT** Federal Parks and Recreation. Vol. 1, No. 1 (June 16, 1983)-. Periodical. English. Twenty-four times a year. $167.00. Resources Publishing Company, 1010 Vermont Avenue Northwest, Suite 708, Washington DC 20005. **Tel** (202)638-7529, FAX (202)393-2075. **ED** James B. Coffin.

US/0736-8364
**FEDERAL RECREATION FEE REPORT.** **Title Change.** (FEDERAL RECREATION FEE REPORT : INCLUDING FEDERAL AND STATE AND PRIVATE SECTOR RECREATION VISITATION AND FEE DATA : A REPORT TO CONGRESS BY THE U.S. DEPARTMENT OF THE INTERIOR, NATIONAL PARK SERVICE.). **Main/Corp** United States. National Park Service. (1981)-(19??). English. an. US Department of the Interior / US Geological Survey, Virginia, National Technical Information Service, 5285 Port Royal Road, Springfield VA 22161. **Tel** (800)553-6847, (703)487-4812. **LC** GV191.4; .U547a. **DD** 333.78/0973. **Continues** United States. Heritage Conservation and Recreation Service. Federal Recreation Fee Program, 0192-5369. **Continued by** United States. National Park Service. Federal Recreation Fee Report to Congress.

US
**FEDERAL RECREATION FEE REPORT TO CONGRESS : INCLUDING FEDERAL RECREATION VISITATION AND FEE DATA WITH STATE PARK INFORMATION SUPPLEMENT.** **Main/Corp** United States. National Park Service. (19??)-. English. **LC** GV191.4; .U547a. **DD** 333.78/0973. **Continues** United States. National Park Service. Federal Recreation Fee Report, 0736-8364.
**Desc:** Government information concerning national parks and reserves.

●CN/1196-4790
**FESTIVALS & ATTRACTIONS.** (FESTIVALS & ATTRACTIONS : REVUE DE LA SOCIETE DES FETES ET FESTIVALS DU QUEBEC ET DE LA SOCIETE DES ATTRACTIONS TOURISTIQUES DU QUEBEC.). [Festiv. attract.]. **Added/Corp** Societe des Fetes et Festivals du Quebec. Societe des Attractions Touristiques du Quebec. Vol. 18, No. 1 (1993)-. Periodical. French. qt. Societe Fetes et Festivals du Quebec, 4545 Ave P Couber, CP1000 Succursale M, Montreal Quebec H1V 3R2 Canada. **Tel** (514)252-3037, (800)361-7688, FAX (514)521-1067. **DD** 790/.09714/05.
**Continues** Fetes & Festivals., 0836-6926.

CN/0836-6926
**FETES ET FESTIVALS.** **Title Change.** [Fetes festiv.]. **Added/Corp** Societe des Festivals Populaires du Quebec. **VAT** Fetes et Festivals. Vol. 12, No. 3 (Autumn 1987)-(Vol. 17, No. 4 (Autumn 1992). Periodical. French. qt. Societe Fetes et Festivals du Quebec, 4545 Ave P Couber, CP1000 Succursale M, Montreal Quebec H1V 3R2 Canada. **Tel** (514)252-3037, (800)361-7688, FAX (514)521-1067. **DD** 394.2/5/060714. **Continues** Tam ti Delam., 0705-3428; **Absorbed** Fetes Populaires au Quebec, Bottin. **Continued by** Festivals & Attractions, 1196-4790.

●CN/1189-3303
**FITNESS, PHYSICAL HEALTH AND RECREATION EDUCATION (WESTERN U.S. ED.).** See Health and Personal Fitness.

US
**FLOATING.** No. 1 (Nov. 1974)-. Periodical. English. qt. Free. Flotation Tank Association, Box 1396, Grass Valley CA 95945. **Tel** (916)432-3794, FAX (916)265-4321. **ED** Lee Perry. **Bk Rev.** **Ad Acc.** **Circ:** 500.
**Desc:** Contains information on all aspects of floating.

US/0430-7739
**FLORIDA J.O.H.P.E.R.** See Public Health and Safety.

BE/0770-321X
**FOOT MAGAZINE.** [Foot mag.]. (1982)-. Periodical. French. mo. 850.00F Belgium; 1500.00F US and Canada; 1150.00F other. Hayex Sprl, Rue Fin 4, 1080 Brussels Belgium. **Tel** 011 32 2 4240064. **UDC** 769.332.

SW/0283-7560
**FRIA TIDER.** [Fria tider]. (1986)-. Periodical. Swedish. bm. Fria Tider, Karlbregsvagen 86A, 3tr. 113 35, Stockholm Sweden. **UDC** 364.65-053.6. **Continues** Fritidsgarden, 0016-1500; **Absorbed** Samspel for Fritid, 0349-7518.
**Ind/Abst** Leis. Recreat. Tour. Abstr.

CN/0229-2319
**FRIDAY (TORONTO).** (FRIDAY.). [Friday]. Vol. 1, No. 12 (Aug. 21, 1980)-. Periodical. English. Free. Friday Magazine, 130 Merton Street/Suite 306, Toronto Ontario M4S 1A4 Canada. **DD** 790/.09713/541. **Continues** Friday in and About Toronto, 0229-2300.

NE/0165-313X
**FRIESLAND POST.** [Friesland Post]. (1974)-. Periodical. Dutch. mo. Fl54.25. Friesland Post, Postbus 619, 9200 AP Drachten, Netherlands. **Tel** 011 31 5120 84488. **UDC** (492.71).

FR/0016-1446
**FRIPOUNET PARIS.** **Title Change.** (FRIPOUNET.). (1969)-(1994). Periodical. French. wk. Fleurus Presse International, 21 rue Faubourg St Antoine, 75550 Paris Cedex 11 France. **Tel** 011 33 1 40026300. **UDC** 087.5. **Continues** Fripounet et Marisette, 0992-7891. **Absorbed by** Infos Junior.

CN/0046-6042
**GO (EDMONTON).** (GO.). Began publication in 1965. English. Free. Go Publishing Ltd, 13366-140th, Edmonton Alberta Canada. **DD** 790/.097123/3.

●US/1063-7656
**GORGE GUIDE.** [Gorge guide]. Vol. 10 (1992)-. Periodical. English. an. $3.95. Gorge Publishing, PO Box 918, Hood River OR 97031. **Tel** (503)386-7440, FAX (503)386-7480. **LC** WMLC 91/5909. **DD** 797. **Continues** Northwest Sailboard's Gorge Guide, 1063-7648.
**Desc:** The original and complete guide to windsurfing in the Columbia River Gorge.

US
**GRANT$ FOR RECREATION, SPORTS, & ATHLETICS.** See Philanthropy.

US/0072-8705
**GUIDE TO SUMMER CAMPS AND SUMMER SCHOOLS, THE.** **VFOAT** Sargent Guide to Summer Camps and Summer Schools. 13th ed. (1962-1963)-. English. be. $23.60 Massachusetts; $22.55 other. Porter Sargent Publishers Inc., 11 Beacon Street, Suite 1400, Boston MA 02108. **Tel** (617)523-1670. **LC** GV193; .G8. Index available. **Bk Rev.** **Ad Acc.** **Continues** Sargent Guide to Summer Camps and Summer Schools.
**Desc:** Information on location and enrollment, director's winter address, fees, length of camping period, and other pertinent facts.

US/0896-6001
**GUN SHOW CALENDAR.** [Gun show cal.]. **VFOAT** Gun Show Calendar Quarterly. (Jan. 1988)-. Periodical. English. qt. $12.95 US; $20.50 Canada & Mexico; $16.50 other. Krause Publications, 700 East State Street, Iola WI 54990-0001. **Tel** (715)445-2214,

FAX (715)445-4087, telex 55 6461. **DD** 799. **Circ:** 5,728. ***Continues*** *Dave Reecer's Gun and Knife Show Calendar.*
**Desc:** Listing of gun shows happening nationwide, up to a year in advance. Shows throughout the US and Canada are listed chronologically, in alphabetical order by state. Information presented also includes show hours, location, admission fee, and dealer set-up times and cost.

US/0895-433X
**HANG GLIDING. See** Recreation, Leisure-Sports.

CN/0225-7009
**HAPPENINGS IN KAMLOOPS.** [Happen. Kamloops]. **VFOAT** Happenings. V. 1- March 1979-. Periodical. English. mo. Free. Suncastle Holdings, Happenings in Kamloops, PO Box 869 Station Main, Kamloops British Columbia V2C 5M8 Canada. **DD** 790/.09711/4.

US/0893-6447
**HARLEY WOMEN.** [Harley women]. (198?)-. Periodical. English. bm. $14.00 (one year), $25.00 (two years). Asphalt Angels Publications, PO Box 374, Streamwood IL 60107. **ED** Linda Jo Giovannoni (editor's phone: (708)888-2645). **DD** 796. **Bk Rev**, (Qty: 0-2). **Ad Acc**, **Adv Mgr:** Bonnie, **Tel** (602)451-9655. **Circ:** 15,000.
**Desc:** First magazine to recognize women motorcyclists; covers profiles on women riders.

CN/0827-2484
**HOME ENTERTAINMENT GUIDE (FM GUIDE ED.).** ***Title Change.*** (HOME ENTERTAINMENT GUIDE.). [Home entertain. guide]. Vol. 13, No. 5 (May 1983)-. Periodical. English. mo. FM Guide, 1659 Bayview Avenue, Toronto Ontario M4G 3C1 Canada. **DD** 790/.05. ***Continues*** *FM Guide, 0316-2400.* ***Continued by*** *Andrew Marshall's Audio Ideas Guide, 0833-9198.*

US/0736-6736
**HONEYMOON HIDEAWAYS. See** Travel and Tourism.

US/0199-2708
**HUMMER, THE. Added/Corp** Association of Wisconsin Snowmobile Clubs. (19??)-. Periodical. English. ir. The Hummer, PO Box 6236, Madison WI 53716.

UK
**IBRM. See** Hotels/Motels.

FR/1240-4454
**INFOS JUNIOR PARIS.** (INFOS JUNIOR.). (1992)-. Periodical. French. wk. 313.42F France; 476.00F other. Fleurus Presse International, 21 rue Faubourg St Antoine, 75550 Paris Cedex 11 France. **Tel** 011 33 1 40026300. **UDC** 087.5(44). ***Absorbed*** *Fripounet, 0016-1446.*

US/1061-480X
**INSIDE INDIANA.** [Inside Indiana]. (1991)-. Periodical. English. wk. $29.95. Inside Indiana, PO Box 1231, Bloomington IN 47402-1231. **ED** Rick Notter. **DD** 796.
**Desc:** Complete sports coverage of the Indiana Hoosiers. Primarily focus is on Indiana University Basketball and Football. 32 page tabloid-style newspaper with some advertising.

US/1052-1607
**INSIDE TRACK (HAMMONTON, N.J.).** (INSIDE TRACK.). (1987)-. Periodical. English. Twelve times a year. $20.00 US & Canada; $30.00 other. Inside Track, PO Box 7956, Newark DE 19714-7956. **Tel** (302)322-9453, FAX (302)322-1828. **ED** Mark Wiatt. **DD** 791. **Bk Rev**, (Qty: 8). **Ad Acc**, **Adv Mgr:** Gary Slade, **Tel** (817)640-8316. **Circ:** 3,000.

US/1059-8227
**INSIDE U.S.A. VOLLEYBALL. See** Recreation, Leisure-Sports.

CN/0831-9103
**INTERCOMM - INTERPRETATION CANADA. ONTARIO SECTION. See** Public Administration-Parks and Recreation.

●UK/1352-2809
**INTERNATIONAL JOURNAL OF LEISURE.** (1994)-. Periodical. English. Four times a year. £67.00 Europe; £70.00 Other (Institutions). Churchill Livingstone, 1-3 Baxter's Place, Leith Walk, Edinburgh EH1 3AF Scotland. **Tel** 011 44 31 556 2424, FAX 011 44 31 558 1278, telex 727511. **(Subscription address:** Maruzen Company Ltd., PO Box 5050, Import & Export Department, Tokyo 100 31 Japan.**)**

●UK
**INTERNATIONAL PLAY JOURNAL.** (1993)-. English. Three times a year. $135.00 US and Canada; £79.00 Europe; £85.00 other. Chapman & Hall, 2-6 Boundary Row, London SE1 8HN England. **Tel** 011 44 71 865 0066, FAX 011 44 71 522 9623, telex 290164 Chapmag. **(Subscription address:** Chapman & Hall, Cheriton House, North Way, Andover, Hampshire, SP10 5BE England.**) ED** Bob Hughes.
**Desc:** Covers all aspects of play. Aims to develop the subject of play from the perspectives of practice, provision, politics, science, art, culture, and philosophy and will be a vehicle for exploring, experimenting and developing all facets of play in an attempt to improve the level and quality of knowledge, awareness and practice to practitioners and academics alike.

UK/0951-1555
**INTERNATIONAL POPULAR BRIDGE MONTHLY.** [Int. pop. bridge mon.]. (1980)-. Periodical. English. Twelve times a year. £27.00 UK; £30.00 other. Probray Press Ltd, 455 Alfreton Road, Nottingham NG7 5LS England. **Tel** 011 44 602 422615, FAX 011 44 889 565939. **ED** Tony Sowder, (phone: (0602)422615). **DD** 795.414. **Bk Rev. Ad Acc. Circ:** 3,000. ***Continues*** *Popular Bridge Monthly.*
**Desc:** Bridge reports, competitions, bridge stories, system developments and ideas.

CN/0843-9117
**JOURNAL OF APPLIED RECREATION RESEARCH.** (JOURNAL OF APPLIED RECREATION RESEARCH / ONTARIO RESEARCH COUNCIL ON LEISURE.). [J. appl. recreat. res.]. **Added/Corp** Ontario Research Council on Leisure. **VFOAT** JARR. Vol. 15, No. 1 (1989)-. Periodical. English. qt. 50.00Can$ Canada; $50.00 other. Wilfrid Laurier University Press, 75 University Avenue West, Waterloo Ontario N2L 3C5 Canada. **Tel** (519)884-1970, FAX (519)725-1399. **DD** 790/.05. **Bk Rev. *Continues*** *Recreation Research Review, 0702-9284.*
**Ind/Abst** SPORT Discus.

●US/1050-7051
**JOURNAL OF HOSPITALITY & LEISURE MARKETING.** [J. hosp. leis. mark.]. **VFOAT** Journal of Hospitality and Leisure Marketing; JHLM. Vol. 1, No. 1 (1992)-. Periodical. English. qt. $60.00 US; $84.00 other. The Haworth Press Inc, 10 Alice Street, Binghamton NY 13904-1580. **Tel** (607)722-5857, (800)3-HAWORTH, FAX (607)722-1424. **ED** Francis A. Buttle (editor's address: Department of Hotel, Restaurant and Travel Administration, University of Massachusetts and Ahmerst, Flint Laboratory, Amherst, MA 01003). **LC** TX911.3.M3; J68. **DD** 381/.45647/05. **CODEN** JHLME7. **Bk Rev. Ad Acc. Pr Rev. Acid Free.** available on microfiche. Documents available from Haworth Document Delivery Service.
**Desc:** Examines marketing issues in the hospitality and leisure industries. Aims to improve our understanding of relationships between hospitality/leisure organizations and their customers and to improve the management of those relationships.
**Ind/Abst** Contents Pages Educ.; Contents Pages Manage.; Hum. Resour. Abstr. (?-?); SPORT Discus.

CN/0711-222X
**JOURNAL OF LEISURABILITY (1980). See** Physically Impaired.

US/0022-2216
**JOURNAL OF LEISURE RESEARCH.** [J. leis. res.]. **Added/Corp** National Recreation and Park Association. Vol. 1 (Winter 1969)-. Periodical. English. qt. $25.00 (members), $40.00 (nonmembers), $60.00 (insitutions). National Recreation and Park Association, 2775 South Quincy Street, Suite 300, Arlington VA 22206. **Tel** (703)820-4940, (703)578-5564, FAX (703)671-6772. **LC** GV1; .J6. **DD** 790/.05. **CODEN** JLERA. **Pr Rev.** available on microfilm and microfiche from University Microfilms International (UMI). Documents available from The Genuine Article, UMI Article Clearinghouse, Documents on Demand.
**Ind/Abst** Acad. Abstr. Full Text Elite (Jan. 1992-); Acad. Abstr. (Jan. 1992-); Acad. Search (Jan. 1992-); AGRICOLA [Select. Cov.]; Appl. Soc. Sci. Index Abstr.; Curr. Contents Soc. Behav. Sci.; Curr. Geogr. Publ. (199?-); Curr. Index J. Educ.; Energy Inf. Abstr.; Environ. Abstr.; Expand. Acad. Index (1989-); For. Abstr.; Geogr. Abstr. Human Geogr. (?-?); Health Source (Jan. 1992-); INFO-SOUTH Abstr.; Int. Bibliogr. Sociol.; Leis. Recreat. Tour. Abstr.; Mag. Search; Newsp. Period. Abstr. (1991-); Phys. Educ. Index; Psychol. Abstr. (1981-); PsycINFO; PsycLit; Res. Alert [Full Cov.]; Rural Dev. Abstr.; Soc. Plann. Policy Dev. Abstr.; Soc. Sci. Source (Jan. 1992-); Soc. Sci. Cit. Index [Full Cov.]; Soc. Sci. Index; Soc. Sci. Index Fulltext (1988-) [Full Txt.]; Sociol. Abstr. (?-?); SPORT Discus; SportSearch; Urban Aff. Abstr.; World Agric. Econ.

SZ
**KIDOU. *Ceased.*** (19??)-(April 1994). English. mo. Periodica Inc, PO Box 444, Outremont Quebec H2V 4R6 Canada. **Tel** (514)274-5468, FAX (514)274-0201.

CN/0826-9696
**KIDS TORONTO. *Title Change.*** [Kids Tor.]. (June 1984)-(19??). Periodical. English. Twelve times a year. City Parent, 467 Speers Road, Oakville Ontario L6K 3S4 Canada. **Tel** (905)815-0017. **ED** Leslie Garret. **DD** 790.1/922/09713541. **Bk Rev. Ad Acc. Circ:** 60,000 (ctrl). ***Continued by*** *City Parent.*
**Desc:** A magazine for parents with children under the age of 12. It focuses on entertainment and events for the parents and child in and around Toronto. Includes features on school, tutoring, day camps, birthdays and summer fun.

US/0192-3439
**KITELINES.** [Kitelines]. **Added/Corp** American Kitefliers Association. **VFOAT** Kite Lines. Vol. 1 (Spring 1977)-. Periodical. English. qt. $14.00 US; $18.00 other. Kite Lines, PO Box 466, 8807 Liberty Road, Randallstown MD 21133. **Tel** (410)922-1212, FAX (410)922-4262. **ED** Valerie Govig. **LC** TL759.A1; K575. **DD** 629.133/32/05. **Bk Rev**, (Qty: 12-16). **Ad Acc. Circ:** 13,000. available on microfiche. ***Supersedes*** *Kite Tales, 0192-3420.*
**Desc:** International kite news, features, techniques, reviews of kites and books, personality profiles, and in-depth feature articles.
**Ind/Abst** Index Inf. (1979-).

SZ
**KODI.** French. mo. Periodica Inc, PO Box 444, Outremont Quebec H2V 4R6 Canada. **Tel** (514)274-5468, FAX (514)274-0201.

CN/1184-6224
**KOOTENAY WEEKLY EXPRESS, THE.** [Kootenay wkly. express]. Vol. 2, Issue 12 (Oct. 3rd, 1990)-. Periodical. English. wk. Kootenay Weekly Express, Box 922, Nelson, British Columbia V1L 6A5 Canada. **DD** 790/.09711/6205. ***Continues*** *What's on Magazine (Nelson, B.C.), 1184-6232.*

SP/0047-3863
**LABORES DEL HOGAR.** [Labor hogar]. (1928)-. Periodical. Spanish. ir. 2400ptas. HYMSA, Muntaner 40-42, 08011 Barcelona, Spain. **Tel** 011 34 3 4546431. **UDC** 646.

US/1070-8103
**LAKE MARTIN LIVING MAGAZINE.** [Lake Martin living mag.]. **VFOAT** LML; Lake Martin Living. (19??)-. Periodical. English. mo. $15.00 (one year), $24.00 (two year). Lake Martin Living, 375 Windy Wood, Alexander City AL 35010. **Tel** (205)329-2460. **ED** Jim Bain, Jr. **DD** 976. **Ad Acc**, **Adv Mgr:** Debbie Bain. **Circ:** 8,500, 34,000 (estimated readership) (ctrl).
**Desc:** Published for the residents and visitors of Lake Martin and its surrounding communities. Dedicated to the conservation and preservation of the lake, the magazine lists community news, recipes, poetry, a calendar of events and much more.

CN/0713-7761
**LEADER (GLOUCESTER). *Ceased.*** (THE LEADER.). **Added/Corp** Gloucester (Ont.). **VFOAT** Leader. Vol. 1, No. 1 (Sept. 1981)-(199?). Periodical. English (French). bm. Leader, PO Box 8333, Ottawa Ontario K1G 3V5 Canada. **DD** 071/.1383.

CN/0711-5377
**LEADER (OTTAWA. 1976).** (THE LEADER.). [Leader]. **VFOAT** Canadian Leader. **VAT** Canadian Leader (1976). Vol. 7, No. 1 (Aug./Sept. 1976)-. Periodical. English. mo (Jun/July & Aug/Sept issues combined). 10.00Can$ (Canada); 15.00Can$ (other). Canyouth Publications, PO Box 5112 Station F, Ottawa Ontario K2C 3H4 Canada. **Tel** (613)224-5131, FAX (613)224-3571. **ED** Allen Macartney. **DD** 369.43/.0971. Index available. **Bk Rev. Ad Acc. Circ:** 45,000. ***Continues*** *Canadian Leader, 0036-9462.*
**Desc:** A program and activity resource recommended to adult members of the Boy Scouts of Canada.

●US/1053-4814
**LEISURE AND FAMILY FUN: LAFF.** **VFOAT** LAFF; LAFF Magazine. (1992)-. Periodical. English. qt. $9.00. D Phelicia Smith, 1969 Lown Farm Trail, Lithonia GA 30058.

JA/0915-1729
**LEISURE & RECREATION.** [Leis. recreat.]. **VFOAT** Jiyu Jikan Kenkyu; Research Quarterly of Freetime. (1988)-. Periodical. Japanese. qt. **DD** 790.
**Ind/Abst** Leis. Recreat. Tour. Abstr.

CN/0704-643X
**LEISURE FORUM.** V. 4- Jan./Feb. 1977-. Periodical. English. ir. Free to members, 0.50Can$ others. Leisure Forum, 2799 Roblin Boulevard, Winnipeg Manitoba R3R 0B8 Canada. **DD** 790/06/27127. ***Continues*** *Manitoba Parks and Recreation Association. Newsletter, 0704-6448.*

US
**LEISURE INDUSTRY REPORT.** Vol. 8, (Jan. 1988)-. Periodical. English. Ten times a year. $65.00 (one year), $110.00 (two year), $150.00 (three year). Leisure Industry / Recreation News, PO Box 43563, Washington DC 20010. **Tel** (202)232-7107, FAX (202)462-6021. **ED** Marj Jensen. **Bk Rev. Ad Acc.** ctrl circ. ***Continues*** *Leisure Industry Digest.*
**Desc:** Summaries of discretionary spending on movies, concerts, gaming, and spectator sports.

US
**LEISURE INFORMATION QUARTERLY / NEW YORK UNIVERSITY, SCHOOL OF EDUCATION, HEALTH, NURSING AND ARTS PROFESSIONS, DEPT. OF RECREATION, LEISURE STUDIES, PHYSICAL EDUCATION & SPORT.** **Added/Corp** New York University. Dept. of Recreation, Leisure Studies, Physical Education & Sport. Vol. 10, No.

1 (Summer 1983)-. Periodical. English. qt. $27.00 (institutions), $16.00 (individuals). New York University / Education, Health, Nursing and Arts Profession, 635 East Bldg., Washington Square, New York NY 10003. **Bk Rev. Circ:** 300. ***Continues*** *Leisure Information Newsletter.*
**Desc:** Topical issues in the study of leisure including information articles dealing with leisure counseling and leisure education, resource listings conferences new publications.
**Ind/Abst** Leis. Recreat. Tour. Abstr.; SPORT Discus; SportSearch (May 1987-).

UK/0266-9102
**LEISURE MANAGEMENT.** [Leis. manage.]. Vol. 1, No. 1 (June/July 1981)-. Periodical. English. Twelve times a year. £36.00 UK; £45.00 other Europe; $65.00 other (combined with Leisure Opportunities). Dicestar Ltd., 40 Bancroft, 1st Floor Suite 40, Hitchin Herts SG5 1LA England. **Tel** 011 44 462 431385, FAX 011 44 462 433909. **ED** Liz Teary.
**Desc:** Covering developments in the leisure industry.
**Ind/Abst** Leis. Recreat. Tour. Abstr.; Museum Abstr.

UK/0267-3754
**LEISURE MANAGER : THE JOURNAL OF THE INSTITUTE OF LEISURE & AMENITY MANAGEMENT, THE.** **Added/Corp** Institute of Leisure & Amenity Management (Great Britain). Vol. 3, No. 1 (Jan. 1985)-. Periodical. English. mo. £25.00 UK; £35.00 other. ILAM Services Ltd, Ilam House, Lower Basildon, Reading, Berkshire, RG8 9NE England. **Tel** 011 4 491 874222. ***Continues*** *ILAM.*
**Desc:** Covers specific management topics, product and equipment news for those engaged in this rapidly expanding industry.
**Ind/Abst** Leis. Recreat. Tour. Abstr.; SPORT Discus.

UK/0952-8210
**LEISURE OPPORTUNITIES.** (1987)-. Periodical. English. mo. comes with Leisure Management. Dicestar Ltd., 40 Bancroft, 1st Floor Suite 40, Hitchin Herts SG5 1LA England. **Tel** 011 44 462 431385, FAX 011 44 462 433909.
**Desc:** Features cover news, forecasts, reviews, market research reports, and product and personality profiles.
**Ind/Abst** Leis. Recreat. Tour. Abstr.; Museum Abstr.

AT/1036-0573
**LEISURE OPTIONS.** [Leis. options]. **VFOAT** Australian Journal of Leisure and Recreation. (1991)-. Periodical. English. qt. 20.00Aus$. Leisure Options, PO Box 611, Townsville QLD 4810 Australia. **Tel** 011 61 77 21010. **DD** 790.099405.
**Ind/Abst** SPORT Discus.

UK/0261-1392
**LEISURE, RECREATION, AND TOURISM ABSTRACTS.** **See** Recreation, Leisure-Abstracting, Bibliographies and Statistics.

US/0149-0400
**LEISURE SCIENCES.** **See** Social Sciences.

UK/0261-4367
**LEISURE STUDIES.** (LEISURE STUDIES : THE JOURNAL OF THE LEISURE STUDIES ASSOCIATION.). [Leis. stud.]. **Added/Corp** Leisure Studies Association (Great Britain). Vol. 1, No. 1 (Jan. 1982)-. Periodical. English. Four times a year. $145.00 US and Canada; £83.00 Europe; £95.00 other. E & FN Spon Ltd, 2 6 Boundary Row, London SE1 8HN England. **Tel** 011 44 71 865 0066. **(Subscription address:** Chapman & Hall, Cheriton House, North Way, Andover, Hampshire, SP10 5BE England.**) ED** Jonathon Long. **[CCC].** Index available. **Bk Rev. Ad Acc. Pr Rev. Circ:** 600. available on microfilm and microfiche from University Microfilms International (UMI).
**Desc:** Publishes papers on leisure behaviour from a wide range of disciplinary bases including sociology, psychology, planning and economics as well as leisure professionals.
**Ind/Abst** Geogr. Abstr. Human Geogr.; Leis. Recreat. Tour. Abstr.; Multicult. Educ. Abstr.; Phys. Educ. Index (1991-); Psychol. Abstr. (1982-); PsycINFO; PsycLit; Soc. Plann. Policy Dev. Abstr.; Sociol. Educ. Abstr.; SPORT Discus; SportSearch.

US
**LEISURE TODAY, SELECTED READINGS.** Vol. 1 (1975)-. English. ir. Price varies. American Alliance for Health, Physical Education, Recreation, and Dance / AAHPERD, 1900 Association Drive, Reston VA 22091. **Tel** (703)476-3493, (800)321-0789.

CN/1184-146X
**LEISURE WORLD.** **See** Travel and Tourism.

CN/0712-5747
**LEISUREWAYS.** [Leisureways]. **Added/Corp** Canadian Motorist Publishing Company. **VFOAT** Leisure Ways. Vol. 1 (Feb. 1982)-. Periodical. English. bm (Feb., Apr., Jun., Aug., Oct., Dec.). 6.00Can$. Canada Wide Magazine, 1707/ 2 Carlton Street, Toronto Ontario M5B 1J3 Canada. **Tel** (416)595-5007, FAX (416)924-6308. **ED** Robin Roberts. **DD** 790/.05. **Ad Acc, Adv Mgr:** J. Tarbat. **Circ:** 600,000. ***Continues*** *Canadian Motorist, 0008-4530.*
**Desc:** Contains information on travel, auto, photography, and cooking.

AT
**LIVE TO RIDE.** (19??)-. Periodical. English. mo. 59.00Aus$ Australia; 94.00Aus$ New Zealand & Papua New Guinea; 118.00Aus$ US & Canada; 125.00Aus$ Europe & Africa; 100.00Aus$ Singapore, Malaysia, Indonesia; 109.00Aus$ Hong Kong, China, Japan, India. Federal Publishing Co Pty Ltd, PO Box 199, 180 Bourke Road, Alexandria New South Wales, 2015 Australia. **Tel** 011 61 2 693 6666, FAX 011 61 2 693 9935. **(Subscription address:** Federal Publishing Co. Pty Ltd., PO Box 199, Alexandria NSW 2015 Australia.)

IT
**LO SPETTACOLO IN ITALIA.** **Added/Corp** Societa Italiana degli Autori ed Editori. (1936)-. Italian. an. Soieta Italiana degli Autori ed Editori, Viale della Letteratura 30, 00144, Rome, Italy. **Tel** 06-59901, FAX 06-5923351, telex 611423. **LC** GV85; .S6. **DD** 790.945.

CN/0705-3436
**LOISIR ET SOCIETE.** (LOISIR ET SOCIETE. SOCIETY AND LEISURE.). [Loisir soc.]. **Added/Corp** International Sociological Association. Research Group on Leisure. **VFOAT** Loisir & Societe. Vol. 1 (April 1978)-. Periodical. English (French; summaries and/or abstracts in Multiple languages). Twice a year. 35.51Can$ (institutions) Canada; 43.00Can$ (institutions) other. Les Presses de L'Universite de Quebec, 2875 Boulevard Laurier, St. Foy Quebec G1V 2M3 Canada. **Tel** (418)657-4390 Ext. 2860. **ED** Gilles Pronovost and Max d'Amours. **LC** GV14.45; .L63. **DD** 301.5/7/05. cum. index. **Bk Rev. Circ:** 1,000. ***Continues*** *Society and Leisure, 0037-9670.*
**Desc:** Multidisciplinary journal on leisure studies with thematic issues.
**Ind/Abst** Leis. Recreat. Tour. Abstr.; Point Repere (1983-); Soc. Plann. Policy Dev. Abstr.; Sociol. Abstr.; SPORT Discus; SportSearch; Stud. Women Abstr.

CN/0701-1342
**LOISIR. INFORMATION.** (LOISIR INFORMATION. LEISURE NEWSLETTER.). **Added/Corp** Association Internationale de Sociologie. Groupe de Recherche sur le Loisir. **VFOAT** Leisure Newsletter. (1976)-. Newsletter. French (English). Three times a year. Research Comm Sociology Leisure, Univ Utrecht Fact Soc Sciences, 3508 TC Utrecht Netherlands. **DD** 790/.05. ***Continues*** *Leisure Newsletter, 0701-1334.*

CN/0711-3293
**LOISIR LONGUEUIL.** [Loisir Longueuil]. Summer- 81. Periodical. French. Bureau d'Information, Direction du Loisir, CP 5000 Longueuil Quebec J4K 4Y7 Canada. **DD** 790/.09714/37.

BE
**LOISIRAMA.** Ministere de l'Education Natl, Galerie Ravenstein 4 27, B-1000 Bruxelles Belgium.

●US/1062-8223
**LONG ISLAND EXPRESS QUARTERLY.** [Long isl. express q.]. Vol. 5, No. 2 (Spring 1992)-. Periodical. English. qt. $12.00. National Heritage Press, PO Box 20489, Ferndale MI 48220. **DD** 795. ***Continues*** *Long Island Monthly Express.*

US/0744-7590
**LONG ISLAND'S NIGHTLIFE MAGAZINE.** ***Title Change.*** [Long Isl. nightlife mag.]. **VFOAT** Long Island's Nightlife. Periodical. English. mo. Long Island Update, 990 Motor Parkway, Central Islip NY 11722. **Tel** (516)435-8890. **ED** Bill Ervilino. **DD** 790. **Bk Rev. Ad Acc. Circ:** 22,500. ***Continued by*** *Long Island's Nightlife, 1054-0016.*
**Desc:** Exciting things to see and do in New York.

CN/0715-2361
**LOOK AT LEISURE, A.** [Look leis.]. **Added/Corp** Alberta. Recreation Development Division. No. 1 (1981)-. Periodical. English. ir. Free. Alberta Tourism Parks & Recreations, 10405 Jasper Avenue, Suite 901, Edmonton Alberta T5J 3N4 Canada. **Tel** (403)427-2968. **DD** 790.1/097123.
**Ind/Abst** Leis. Recreat. Tour. Abstr.

●US/1063-1372
**LOST TREASURE'S TREASURE CACHE.** **VFOAT** Treasure Cache. (1992)-. English. an. $7.95. Lost Treasure Inc, PO Box 1589, Grove OK 74344. **Tel** (918)496-8169. **ED** Grace Michael. **Circ:** 40 (per year).
**Desc:** Information on treasure hunting and cache stories.

SZ/0254-1246
**MAGGLINGEN.** [Magglingen]. (1944)-. Periodical. German. mo. **UDC** 362.83.
**Ind/Abst** Leis. Recreat. Tour. Abstr.

FR/0761-9529
**MARIONNETTES PARIS.** [Marionnettes Paris]. (1984)-. Periodical. French. qt. 161.61F France; 180.00F other. Unima France, 5 Cite Voltaire, F-75011 Paris France. **Tel** 011 33 1 43737447. **UDC** 791.5. ***Continues*** *UNIMA France, 0503-2032.*

CN/0838-5513
**MASCOUCHOIS.** [Mascouchois]. **Added/Corp** Mascouche (Quebec). Vol. 1, No 1 (March 1988)-. Periodical. French. qt. Gratuit pour les residents. Ville de Mascouche, 3034 rue Sainte-Marie, Mascouche Quebec J0N 1C0 Canada. **DD** 352.0714/416. ***Continues*** *Chez Vous., 0715-920X.*

BE
**MEDIA BOX.** ***Ceased.*** (19??)-(1993). French. bm. Edimedia ASBL, rue de la Constitution 22, 1030 Brussels Belgium. **Tel** 011 32 2 2180031. **Bk Rev. Ad Acc. Circ:** 1,000.

US
**METROPARKS EMERALD NECKLACE.** **See** Recreation, Leisure-Outdoor Life.

CN/0708-9627
**MILIEU DE VIE.** **Added/Corp** Federation Quebecoise des Centres Communautaires de Loisirs. Vol. 1 (June 1977)-. Periodical. French. Four times a year. 5.00Can$. Federation Quebecoise des Centres Communautaires, 2301 1 ERE Avenue, Montreal Quebec G1L 3M9 Canada. **Tel** (418)647-4536. **DD** 790/.06/2714.

UK
**MINTEL LEISURE INTELLIGENCE.** English. qt. £745.00. Mintel International Group Ltd., 18-19 Long Lane, London EC1A 9HE England. **Tel** 011 44 71 606 4533. **ED** Fenella McCarthy. Index available. **Pr Rev.** ctrl circ.
**Desc:** Journal of market research into the leisure sector. Each issue contains market reports with consumer research and topline market statistics.
**Ind/Abst** Leis. Recreat. Tour. Abstr.

CN/0316-8530
**MONTREAL CE MOIS-CI.** ***Ceased.*** Vol. 1 (Oct. 11/Nov. 14, 1974)-Ceased (April/May 1987). Periodical. French. mo. Mondo Media, 1844 William Street, Montreal Quebec H3J 1R7 Canada. **Tel** (514)937-5771. **ED** Andre Ducharme. **DD** 790/.09714/281. **Bk Rev. Ad Acc. Circ:** 90,000 (ctrl).
**Desc:** Lifestyle magazine focussing on Montreal. Comprehensive events plus restaurant listings.

US
**MOTOR HOMES, CAMPERS, VAN CONVERSIONS, SURFER VANS.** **See** Transportation.

US/0744-074X
**MOTORHOME.** **See** Transportation.

FR/1169-8152
**NATATION (PARIS).** (NATATION.). **VFOAT** Natation Infos. (1922)-. Periodical. French. ir (27 issues). 260.00F France; 440.00F other. Federation Francaise Natation, 148 Av Gambetta, 75020 Paris France. **Tel** 011 33 1 40311770, FAX 011 33 1 40311990, telex 215429. **ED** Catherine Poirot. **UDC** 797.2(44). **Ad Acc, Adv Mgr:** B. Rayaune, **Tel** same as editor. **Circ:** 4,000 (ctrl).
**Desc:** Swimming publication.

US
**NATIONAL CONFERENCE TASK FORCE ON RECREATION USE AND RESOURCE MANAGEMENT / EDISON ELECTRIC INSTITUTE.** **Main/Corp** Edison Electric Institute. Task Force on Recreation Use and Resource Management. National Conference. 3rd (1980)-. English. Edison Electric Institute, 701 Pennsylvania Avenue Northwest, Washington DC 20004. **Tel** (202)508-5607, (202)508-5610, FAX (202)508-5030. ***Continues*** *National Conference on Recreation and Resource Management.*

US/0083-2316
**NATIONAL PARK SERVICE SOURCE BOOK SERIES.** **Main/Corp** United States. National Park Service. **Added/Corp** United States. National Park Service. No. 1 (1941)-. Monographic series. English. ir. Price varies per volume. Superintendent of Documents, US Government Printing Office, Washington DC 20402. **Tel** (202)275-3328, FAX (202)786-2377. **LC** E160; .U629. **DD** 917.3.

US/0028-1964
**NEBRASKALAND.** [Nebraskaland]. **Added/Corp** Nebraska Game, Forestation, and Parks Commission. Nebraska Game and Parks Commission. **VFOAT** Nebraska Land; Nebraskaland Magazine; News Edition Nebraskaland. Vol. 42, No. 5 (June 1964)-. Periodical. English. Ten times a year. $14.00 (one year), $27.00 (two year). Nebraska Game and Parks Commission, 2200 North 33rd Street, Box 30370, Lincoln NE 68503. **Tel** (402)471-0641. **ED** Lowell A. Johnson. Index available. **Bk Rev. Ad Acc. Circ:** 65,000 (ctrl). ***Continues*** *Outdoor Nebraskaland, 0091-6404.*
**Desc:** Covers conservation and recreation (hunting and fishing), plus historical stories about Nebraska.

CN/0713-7745
**NEWFOUNDLAND AND LABRADOR : CAMPGROUND GUIDE.** **Added/Corp** Newfoundland. Tourist Services Division. **VFOAT** Newfoundland and Labrador : Accommodation Guide.

# Recreation, Leisure

(197?)-. English. an. Department of Environmental and Lands, PO Box 8700, St John's Newfoundland A1B 4J6 Canada. **Tel** (709)576-6205. **DD** 647/.94718. **Continues** *Where to Stay in Newfoundland, 0700-2920.*

US/0887-140X
**NEWSLETTER - THE ASSOCIATION FOR THE ANTHROPOLOGICAL STUDY OF PLAY.** [Newsl. - Assoc. Anthropol. Study Play]. **Main/Corp** Association for the Anthropological Study of Play. Vol. 1; 1974-. Newsletter. English. qt. $7.50 (students and retirees), $15.00 (professionals), $20.00 (institutions). LBRL, Childrens Research Center, University of Illinois Champaign IL 61820. **DD** 790. **Ind/Abst** SPORT Discus; SportSearch (May 1987-).

CN/0384-5842
**NIGHTOUT. See** Music.

US
**NIRSA JOURNAL. See** Recreation, Leisure-Sports.

US/0164-4254
**NORTH CAROLINA RECREATIONAL AND PARK REVIEW. Added/Corp** North Carolina Recreation and Park Society. (19??)-. Periodical. English. Four times a year (Feb., May, Aug., Nov.). $6.00 (individuals), $12.00 (institutions), $35.00 Comes with North Carolina Recreation & Park Society membership. North Carolina Recreation and Park Society, 883 Washington Street, Raleigh NC 27605. **Tel** (919)832-5868, FAX (919)832-5868. **ED** Karla Henderson, (editor's address: University of North Carolina-Chapel Hill, LSRA Curriculum, Evergreen House, Chapel Hill, NC 27599, phone: (919)962-1222). Index available. cum. index. **Ad Acc, Adv Mgr:** Mike Waters, **Tel** (919)832-5868. **Circ:** 2,000 (ctrl).

US
**NORTHWESTERN CAMPING & TRAILERING; INCLUDING LOCATION MAPS. VFOAT** Camping & Trailering. English. an. American Automobile Association, 1000 AAA Drive, Heathrow FL 32746. **Tel** (407)444-7000. **LC** GV191.4; .N68. **DD** 917.8/04/3.

US/0736-1394
**NOTIFICATIONS / HCRS INFORMATION EXCHANGE. See** Environmental Issues-Conservation and Natural Resources.

CN/0712-1326
**NOW (TORONTO. 1981).** (NOW : TORONTO'S WEEKLY NEWS AND ENTERTAINMENT VOICE.). [Now]. Vol. 1 No. 1 (Sept. 10, 1981)-. Periodical. English. wk (Published on Thursday). 42.06Can$ Canada; 103.00Can$ other. Now, 150 Danforth Avenue, Toronto Ontario M4K 1N1 Canada. **Tel** (416)461-0871, FAX (416)461-2886. **ED** Michael Hollett. **DD** 790/.09713/541. **Bk Rev,** (Qty: 52). **Ad Acc, Adv Mgr:** Bill Malcolm, **Tel** (416)461-0871. **Circ:** 100,000 (ctrl). available on microfiche.
**Desc:** Young adult, news and entertainment weekly with an emphasis on the downtown scene.

US/0744-9976
**NSPI NEWSLETTER.** (NSPI NEWSLETTER / NATIONAL SPA AND POOL INSTITUTE.). **Added/Corp** National Spa and Pool Institute (U.S.). **VFOAT** N.S.P.I. Newsletter. **VAT** National Spa and Pool Institute Newsletter. (19??)-. Periodical. English. sm. Comes with National Spa and Pool Institute membership. National Spa and Pool Institute, 2111 Eisenhower Avenue, Alexandria VA 22314-4698. **Tel** (202)331-8844.

GW
**OFF DUTY.** (19??)-. German. Free on request. Rios Group, Ischersheimer Landstr 69, W 6000 Frankfurt 1 Germany.

CN/0711-7760
**OFFICIAL BULLETIN / RECREATION ASSOCIATION OF NOVA SCOTIA. Added/Corp** Recreation Association of Nova Scotia. No. 1 (1977)-. Bulletin. English. Free to members. Recreation Association of Nova Scotia, PO Box 3010, South Halifax Nova Scotia B3J 3G6 Canada. **Tel** (902)425-5450, FAX (902)425-5606. **DD** 790/.09716. **Continues** *Official Bulletin of-- R.A.N.S., 0711-7752.*

US/1056-8263
**OFFSHORE WORLDWIDE.** [Offshore worldw.]. Vol. 1 (1991)-. Periodical. English. mo. $40.00 US; $58.00 Canada. Offshore Worldwide Inc, 2000 South Dixie Highway, Suite 206-C, Miami FL 33133. **Tel** (305)858-0970. **ED** J. D. Berg. **LC** WMLC 91/734. **DD** 797. cum. index.
**Desc:** International offshore powerboat racing.

US
**OHIO STATEWIDE COMPREHENSIVE OUTDOOR RECREATION PLAN. ACTION PROGRAM.** 1979/80-. English. an. Department of Natural Resources / Ohio, Fountain Square, Columbus OH 43224. **Tel** (614)265-6590. **ED** William E Daehler Jr. **LC** GV191.42.O3; O45. **DD** 790/.09771. **Circ:** 2,000 (ctrl).
**Desc:** Policy document for outdoor recreation development for the state of Ohio.

CN/0382-8220
**ON S'PARLE.** No. 1- June 10 1972-. Periodical. French. Communication Inter-Media, Sherbrooke Local 120, 180 Acadie, Sherbrooke Quebec J1H 2T3 Canada. **DD** 791.45/06/271466.

CN
**ONTARIO RECREATION FACILITIES ASSOCIATION.** English. Six times a year. 30.00Can$. Ontario Recreation Facilities Association, Inc., 1220 Shipard Avenue E / Suite 210, North York Ontario M2K 2X1 Canada. **Tel** 416 495-4200, FAX 416 495 4329. **Continues** *Ontario Arenas Association.*

US
**OUTDOOR RECREATION IN ILLINOIS ... ACTION PROGRAM.** 1980-1981-. English. an. **LC** GV191.42.I3; O88. **DD** 790/.09773. **Continues** *Outdoor Recreation in Illinois, Action Plan.*

AT/0156-0832
**OVERLANDER.** [Overlander]. (1976)-. Periodical. English. mo. 52.00Aus$ Australia; 93.00Aus$ New Zealand & Papua New Guinea; 117.00Aus$ US & Canada; 124.00Aus$ Europe & Africa; 99.00Aus$ Singapore, Malaysia, Indonesia; 108.00Aus$ other. Federal Publishing Co Pty Ltd, PO Box 199, 180 Bourke Road, Alexandria New South Wales, 2015 Australia. **Tel** 011 61 2 693 6666, FAX 011 61 2 693 9935. (Subscription address: Federal Publishing Co. Pty Ltd., PO Box 199, Alexandria NSW 2015 Australia.) **DD** 796.70994.

US/1059-6313
**PAINT CHECK.** [Paint check]. **VFOAT** Paintcheck. (May 1989)-. Periodical. English. mo. $24.00. C B Publications Inc, Box 347, Ossinig NY 10562. **Tel** (914)923-3543. **ED** Len Canter and Julie Davis. **DD** 796. **Bk Rev. Ad Acc. Circ:** 15,000 (ctrl).
**Desc:** Keeps you updated on the new upcoming sport called paintball. Over 100,000 people are now playing.

UK/0962-0184
**PEAK PERFORMANCE.** [Peak perform.]. (1990)-. Periodical. English. mo. Stonehart Leisure Magazines, Unit 1 Hainault Road, Little Heath Romford RM6 5NP England. **Tel** 011-44-81-597-7335, FAX 011-44-81-599-5965. **DD** 796.42.
**Ind/Abst** SPORT Discus.

US/0279-0033
**PENNSYLVANIA JOURNAL OF HEALTH, PHYSICAL EDUCATION, RECREATION, DANCE. See** Education-Teaching and Curriculum.

US/0894-9417
**PETERSON'S SUMMER OPPORTUNITIES FOR KIDS AND TEENAGERS.** [Peterson's summer oppor. kids teenagers]. **Added/Corp** Peterson's Guides, Inc. **VFOAT** Summer Opportunities for Kids and Teenagers. 6th Ed. (1989)-. English. an. $21.95. Peterson's Guides, 202 Carnegie Center, Department 2342, Princeton NJ 08543. **Tel** (800)338-3282, FAX (609)452-0966. **DD** 790. **Continues** *Summer Opportunities for Kids and Teenagers, 0739-9006.*
**Desc:** Covers over 300 types of activities, including academic programs, sports, foreign travel, arts, music, theater/dance, wilderness trips, and career exploration.

FR
**PLAGES.** (19??)-. French. Four times a year. 1500.00F. Roberto Gutierrez, 1762 R du Vieux, Pont de Sevres, 92100 Boulogne France. **Tel** 46 08 35 56. **ED** Roberto Gutierrez. **Circ:** 1,000.
**Desc:** Magazine made by artists for artists containing various works of art.
**Ind/Abst** BHA : Biblio. Hist. Art.

US
**POOL & SPA NEWS DIRECTORY ISSUE.** (19??)-. Trade Publication. English. an. $24.50. Leisure Publishing Company, 3923 West 6th Street, Los Angeles CA 90020. **Tel** (213)385-3926, FAX (213)383-1152. **ED** Eve Freeman. **LC** HD9993.S953; U56. **DD** 381/.4569089. **Bk Rev. Ad Acc. Circ:** 12,000. **Continues** *Pool News Directory, 0194-1380.*
**Desc:** Pool and spa magazine going to pool and spa trade.

FR
**POURQUOI. Ceased.** (19??)-Issue 277 (Nov. 1992). French. Ten times a year. Edilig, 3 rue Recamier, 75341 Paris Cedex 07 France. **Tel** 011 33 1 43589693.

FR/0399-3698
**PREMIERE PARIS.** (PREMIERE.). (1976)-. Periodical. French. mo. 217.43F France; 322.00F other. Edimonde Loisirs, 90 rue de Flandre, 75947 Paris Cedex 19 France. **Tel** 011 33 1 44894489. **UDC** 791.43.

CN/0229-2572
**PROGRAMME SOUVENIR. FESTIVAL DU VOYAGEUR, ST. BONIFACE, MANITOBA.** (PROGRAMME SOUVENIR / FESTIVAL DU VOYAGEUR.). **Main/Corp** Festival du Voyageur (St-Boniface, Man.). **VFOAT** Souvenir Program. Feb. 16/23, 1975-. Periodical. an. Free. Festival du Voyageur, 768 Tache Avenue, Saint Boniface Manitoba R2H 2C4 Canada. **Tel** (204)237-7692. **DD** 791/.624/0971274. Index available. **Ad Acc. Circ:** 25,000 (ctrl). **Continues** *Festival du Voyageur (St. Boniface, Man.). Official Program, 0229-2564.*

US
**PUBLICATION - STATE OF CALIFORNIA RECREATION COMMISSION. Main/Corp** California. Recreation Commission. **VFOAT** Recreation in California; Publication of the State of California Recreation Commission. No. 1 (1948!)-. Monographic series. English. Price varies per volume. **DD** 790.61794.

NE/0165-4179
**RECREATIE EN TOERISME. See** Travel and Tourism.

US
**RECREATION AND OUTDOOR LIFE DIRECTORY. Ceased.** 1st Ed.-?. Directory. English. ir. Gale Research Inc., 835 Penobscot Building, Detroit MI 48226. **Tel** (800)877-GALE, (313)961-2242, FAX (313)961-6083, telex TWX 810-221-7086. **ED** Steven R Wasserman.
**Desc:** Part I covers general sources such as organizations, federal and state agencies, etc. Part II covers details on outdoor recreational facilities provided by state and federal governments.

US
**RECREATION AND PARK YEARBOOK.** Periodical. English. ir. National Recreation and Park Association, 2775 South Quincy Street, Suite 300, Arlington VA 22206. **Tel** (703)820-4940, (703)578-5564, FAX (703)671-6772. **LC** GV185; .R4. **Continues** *Yearbook - Playground and Recreation Association of America.*

CN/0830-1913
**RECREATION BRITISH COLUMBIA (1985).** (RECREATION BRITISH COLUMBIA.). [Recreat. B.C.]. **Added/Corp** British Columbia Recreation and Park Association. **VFOAT** Recreation BC. (July/Aug. 1985)-. Periodical. English. Four times a year (Jan., Apr., July, Oct.). 26.00Can$ (one year). British Columbia Recreation and Parks Association, 10551 Shellbridge Way, Suite 30, Richmond British Columbia V6X 2W9 Canada. **Tel** (604)273-8055, FAX (604)273-8059. **DD** 790/.09711. **Ad Acc. Circ:** 1,300 (ctrl). **Continues** *Recreation Reporter, 0380-2647.*

CN/0031-2231
**RECREATION CANADA.** (RECREATION CANADA.). [Recreat. Can.]. **Added/Corp** Canadian Parks/Recreation Association. No. 27/5 (Sept. 1969)-. Periodical. English (summaries and/or abstracts in French). Five times a year. 45.00Can$ Canada; 50.00Can$ other. Canadian Parks/Recreation Association, 1600 James Naismith Drive, Gloucester Ontario K1B 5N4 Canada. **Tel** (613)748-5651, FAX (613)748-5706. **ED** Denny Neider. **Ad Acc. Circ:** 3,500 (ctrl). **Continues** *P & R, 0380-2558.*
**Desc:** Articles and opinion essential to the education and professional development of anyone involved or interested in the provision of parks, recreation and leisure services.
**Ind/Abst** AQUAREF; Leis. Recreat. Tour. Abstr.; SportSearch.

CN/0031-2231
**RECREATION CANADA (FRENCH EDITION).** (RECREATION CANADA.). [Recreat. Can.]. **Added/Corp** Canadian Parks/Recreation Association. No. 27/5 (Sept. 1969)-. Periodical. French (English; summaries and/or abstracts in English). Five times a year. 45.00Can$ Canada; 50.00Can$ other. Canadian Parks Recreation Association / National Office-Siege Social ACL/P, 1600 James Naismith Drive, Gloucester Ontario K1B 5N4 Canada. **Tel** (613)748-5651, FAX (613)748-5706. **ED** S. Beckman. Index available. **Ad Acc. Pr Rev. Circ:** 2,500 (ctrl). **Continues** *P & R, 0380-2558.*
**Ind/Abst** AQUAREF; Can. Index (?-?); SPORT Discus.

AT
**RECREATION EXCHANGE.** (19??)-. Newsletter. English. qt. 40.00Aus$ Australia; 45.00Aus$ other. Institute of Recreation WA, PO Box 179, Wembley WA, 6014 Australia. **Tel** 011 61 9 345 8562, FAX 011 61 9 345 8693. **ED** Zoe Jack, Susan Quay. **Bk Rev,** (Qty: 4). **Ad Acc. Circ:** 800 (ctrl).
**Desc:** Official publication of the Institute of Recreation of WA and the Ministry of Sport and Recreation. Provides information about IOR membership, the recreation industry and coming events aimed at bettering the people who work in the industry.

## Recreation, Leisure

**US/0890-2194**
**RECREATION EXECUTIVE REPORT.**
(RECREATION EXECUTIVE REPORT / LEISURE INFORMATION SERVICE.). [Recreat. exec. rep.]. **Added/Corp** Leisure Information Service. Vol. 13, (Jan. 16, 1984)-. Periodical. English. Ten times a year. $65.00 one year; $110.00 two years; $150.00 three years. Leisure Industry / Recreation News, PO Box 43563, Washington DC 20010. **Tel** (202)232-7107, FAX (202)462-6021. **ED** Marj Jensen. **DD** 790. **Bk Rev**, (Qty: 5). **Ad Acc.** ctrl circ. *Formed by the union of Leisure Business, 0739-0890 and Fund Development & Revenue Sources Report, 0739-0866.*
**Desc:** Reports on outdoor recreation, parks and sports.

**UK/0961-2580**
**RECREATION MELTON MOWBRAY.**
(RECREATION.). [Recreation Melton Mowbray]. (1990)-. Periodical. English. mo (with Jan./Feb., July/Aug., and Nov./Dec. combined). £30.00 UK; £35.00 other. Institute of Baths & Recreation Management, Giffard House, 36-38 Sherrard Street, Leicestershire LE13 1XJ England. **Tel** 011 44 664 65531, FAX 0664 501155. **DD** 790.069. *Continues Baths Service and Recreation Management (1989), 0961-2572.*

**CN/0824-7323**
**RECREATION PRACTITIONERS BULLETIN.** (RECREATION PRACTITIONERS BULLETIN / NEWFOUNDLAND LABRADOR PARKS/RECREATION ASSOC.). [Recreat. pract. bull.]. Feb. 1983-. Bulletin. English. qt. Free to members. N/LP/RA Torbay Recreation Centre, c/o Confederation Building, St John's Newfoundland A1C 5T7 Canada. **DD** 790./06/909718.

**US/1046-316X**
**RECREATION RESOURCES.** [Recreat. resour.]. Vol. 9 No. 70 (Sept. 1989)-. Periodical. English. Nine times a year. $24.00 US; $27.00 Canada; $50.00 other. Adams / Recreation Publishing, 527 Marquette Avenue, Suite 1300, Minneapolis MN 55402. **Tel** (800)923-2326, (612)342-2121, FAX (612)342-2480. **ED** Galenn Nordstrom. **LC** GV181.5; .R435. **DD** 790. **Ad Acc.** *Continues Recreation, Sports & Leisure, 0277-707X.*
**Desc:** Directed at the professional interests of managers of fitness and leisure facilities. Designed to inform, instruct, and communicate information on products and services of value in achieving their recreational and facility development and maintenance goals.

**CN/0833-9791**
**RECREATIONAL VEHICLE LIFE (1984).**
*Ceased.* (RECREATIONAL VEHICLE LIFE.). [Recreat. veh. life]. **VFOAT** Snowmobile Canada. (1984)-(199?). Periodical. English. sa. Recreational Vehicle Life, Suite 2211/3414 Park Avenue, Montreal Quebec H2X 2H5 Canada. **DD** 796.94/0971. *Continues Snowmobile Canada, 0705-3789.*

**NE/0166-2651**
**REKREAKSIE.** [Rekreaksie]. (1970)-. Periodical. Dutch. Twelve times a year. Fl70.00. Recron Tav Mevr J Huiskamp, Zypendaalsweg 91, 6814 CG Arnhem Netherlands. **Tel** 011 085 59111. **UDC** 379.81.
*Continues Orkava.*
**Ind/Abst** Leis. Recreat. Tour. Abstr.

**JA**
**REKURIESHON KENKYU. VFOAT** Journal of Leisure and Recreation Studies. V. 1, No. 1, (Nov. 1971)-. Japanese (summaries and/or abstracts in English). an. Nihon Rekurieshon Gakkai, c/o Kishimoto Kinen Taiikukan, 1-1 Jinnan 1 Shibuya-ku, Tokyo-to 150 Japan. **LC** PAR.

**US/0090-4015**
**REPORT - N.H. STATE PLANNING PROJECT.** (REPORT.). **Main/Corp** New Hampshire. State Planning Project. **VFOAT** Land, Water, Recreation. No. 1- 1964-. English. New Hampshire State Planning Project, Concord NH 03301. **LC** GV54.N4; A2. **DD** 309.2/5/09742.

**NZ**
**REVIEW OF THE NEW ZEALAND COUNCIL FOR RECREATION AND SPORT. Main/Corp** New Zealand. State Services Commission. English. an. State Services Commission, Private Bag, Wellington New Zealand. **LC** GV149; .N49A. **DD** 796./06/0931.

**US/1064-1785**
**RICHMOND SURROUNDINGS.** [Richmond surround.]. (Spring 1986)-. Periodical. English. mo. $14.95 US; $17.95 Canada; $16.95 Pan-American nations; $18.95 other. Target Communications Incorporated, 7814 Carousel Lane, Suite 110, Richmond VA 23294. **Tel** (804)346-4130, FAX (804)965-0083. **ED** Frances Helms. **DD** 051. **Ad Acc, Adv Mgr:** R. Malkman. **Circ:** 25,000-40,000. *Continues Surroundings (Richmond, Va.).*
**Desc:** City and lifestyle magazine for metro Richmond.

**JA/0386-7137**
**RIDERS CLUB TOKYO. 1978.** [Riders club Tokyo. 1978.]. (1978)-. Periodical. Japanese. Twelve times a year. $200.50. **(Subscription address:** Japan Publications Trading Company, Ltd., PO Box 5030, Tokyo International, Tokyo 100-31 Japan.) **DD** 796.7.
*Continues Riders Club (Tokyo. 1975), 0386-703X.*

**US/0191-7617**
**ROLLER SKATING BUSINESS.** Periodical. English. mo. Roller Skating Rink Operators Association, PO Box 81846, Lincoln NE 68501. **Tel** (402)489-8811. **ED** Nance Kirk. **LC** GV859.4; .R64. **DD** 796.2/1068/2. Index available. **Ad Acc. Circ:** 1,100 (ctrl).
**Desc:** Management, marketing, maintenance, and news features for skating center operators. Available only to members of the Roller Skating Rink Operators Association.

**US/1041-9772**
**RV WEST MAGAZINE.** [RV west mag.]. **VFOAT** RV West. **VAT** Recreational Vehicle West Magazine. Vol. 1 No. 1 (Nov. 1988)-. Periodical. English. Twelve times a year. $12.00 US; $18.00 Canada. Outdoor Publications Inc, 4133 Mohr Avenue, Suite 1, Pleasanton CA 94566. **Tel** (415)426-3200. **DD** 917. *Continues Western RV Traveler, 0888-8477.*

**US**
**RV WORLD.** Vol. 1 (June 1973)-. Periodical. English. bm. $7.50. Hi-Torque Publications, PO Box 9502, Mission Hills CA 91395. **Tel** (805)295-1910. **LC** SK600; .R18. **DD** 796.54/05.

**CN/0229-7698**
**SAGAMIE.** [Sagamie]. V. 1, No. 1 (Summer 1980)-. Periodical. French. qt. Free. La Maison De L'Arche, 85 Jean-Allard, Jonquiere, Quebec, G7X 3E8. **DD** 790/.09714/16.

**US/0029-3431**
**SALMON TROUT STEELHEADER.** (1967)-. Periodical. English. bm (Feb., April, June, Aug., Oct., Dec.). $14.95 US, $19.95 others (one year); $24.95 US, $34.95 others (two years). $21.95 US, $31.95 others (1 year); $39.95 US, $59.95 others (two years) combined with Flyfishing. Frank Amato Publications, PO Box 82112, Portland OR 97282. **Tel** (503)653-8108, (800)541-9498. **ED** Nick Amato, PO Box 82112, Portland, OR 97282 (phone# (503)653-8108). **Ad Acc, Adv Mgr:** Sherry Gullings, **Tel** (503)653-8108. **Circ:** 30,000.
**Desc:** All information on where to fish for salmon, trout and steelhead in the USA.

●**CN/1187-4562**
**SANFORD EVANS GOLD BOOK, OFFICIAL SNOWMOBILE DATA AND USED PRICES. See** Transportation.

**FR/0182-4708**
**SAVOIR MARIN, LE.** (1978)-. Monographic series. French. ir. Price varies per volume. Sodis, 128 Ave Marechal Lattre Tassig, 77400 Lagny France. **Tel** 011 33 1 64305557. **UDC** 790.

**GW/0036-102X**
**SB. SPORTSTATTENBAU UND BADERANLAGEN. See** Building and Construction.

**US**
**SCHOLE : A JOURNAL OF LEISURE STUDIES AND RECREATION EDUCATION. Added/Corp** Society of Park and Recreation Educators. Vol. 4 (Aug. 1989)-. English. an. $16.00 (members), $20.00 (nonmembers). National Recreation and Park Association, 2775 South Quincy Street, Suite 300, Arlington VA 22206. **Tel** (703)820-4940, (703)578-5564, FAX (703)671-6772. **LC** GV14.5; .S34. **DD** 790/.0135/0711. *Continues SPRE Annual on Education.*
**Ind/Abst** SPORT Discus.

**CN/0318-9279**
**SEEKER (SARNIA).** (SEEKER.). V. 1- May 15, 1975-. English. wk. $5.00. Seeker Publishing Company, PO Box 82, Sarnia Ontario N7T 7H8 Canada. **DD** 790/.09713/27. *Supersedes Pleasure Seeker, 0318-9287.*

**IT**
**SETTIMANA ENIGMISTICA.** (19??)-. Italian. wk. L75000 Italy; L150000 other. Bresi Spa, Piazza 5, Giornate 10, 20129 Milan Italy. **Tel** 011 39 2 55190591.

●**US/1060-376X**
**SIOUXLAND EVENTS. Added/Corp** Sioux City Public Library (Sioux City, Iowa). **VFOAT** Events. Vol. 1, No 1 (Jan. 1992)-. Periodical. English. mo. Free. Sioux City Public Library, 529 Pierce Street, Sioux City IA 51101. **Tel** (712)255-8829. *Continues What Where When.*

**US/1076-9110**
**SLAP.** (19??)-. English. mo (12 issues). $16.50 US; $25.00 Canada; $30.00 other. High Speed Productions Inc, PO Box 884570, San Francisco CA 94188. **Tel** (415)822-3083. **ED** Lance Dawes.
**Desc:** Focuses on skateboarding.

**CN/0833-2010**
**SNOWMAN NEWS. See** Recreation, Leisure-Sports.

**US**
**SNOWMOBILE TRADE-IN GUIDE BLUE BOOK. Added/Corp** Intertec Publishing Corporation. Technical Publications Division. **VFOAT** Blue Book; Official Snowmobile Trade-In Guide. (19??)-. Periodical. English. an. $16.70. Intertec Publishing Corporation, 9800 Metcalf, Overland Park KS 66212. **Tel** (913)341-1300. **(Subscription address:** Intertec Publishing Corporation, PO Box 2901, Overland Park KS 66282.) **LC** HD9714.A1; S66. **DD** 629.2/2042.

●**US**
**SNOWWEST SNOWMOBILE WEST MAGAZINE.** (1993)-. English. Five times a year. $15.95 (one year), $26.95 (two year), $34.95 (three year) US; $27.95 Canada; $30.95 others. Harris Publishing Inc, 520 Park Avenue, Idaho Falls ID 83402. **Tel** (208)524-7000, FAX (208)522-5241.

**CN/0712-3205**
**SOCIAL ACTIVITIES FOR ADULTS.** [Soc. act. adults]. **VFOAT** Social Activities for Adults in Metropolitan Toronto. Periodical. English. be. $3.00 each volume. Community Information Centre of Metropolitan Toronto, 590 Jarvis Street, Toronto Ontario M4Y 2J4 Canada. **Tel** (416)392-4575, FAX (416)392-4404. **DD** 367/.025/713541.

**CN/0827-9772**
**SOUS-TERRE. See** Earth Sciences-Geophysics.

**US/0279-2249**
**SOUTH COAST SPORTFISHING.** *Title Change.* **VFOAT** South Coast Sport Fishing. (198u)-(19??). Periodical. English. mo. South Coast Sportfishing, PO Box 26047, Santa Ana CA 92799-6047. **Tel** (714)540-2144. **ED** Kenneth J Kukuda. **Ad Acc.** *Merged into California Angler.*
**Desc:** The number one saltwater fishing magazine covering Southern California and Baja.

**US/1063-9640**
**SOUTHERN RE-ENACTING VETERAN, THE.** *Title Change.* [South. re-enacting veteran]. Vol. 1, No. 1 (Nov. 1992)-(1993). Periodical. English. bm. National Lineage Publishing, Inc., PO Box 3181, Merrifield VA 22116. **LC** WMLC 93/2401. **DD** 973. *Continued by Southern Heritage Magazine, 1069-5125.*

**US/0747-0185**
**SPECIAL RECREATION DIGEST.**
*Suspended.* [Spec. recreat. dig.]. Vol. 1, No. 1 (Jan.-Mar. 1984)-Suspended Vol. 6, No. 4. Periodical. English. qt. $39.95. Special Recreation Digest, 362 Koser Avenue, Iowa City IA 52246. **Tel** (319)337-7578. **ED** John A Nesbitt. **LC** GV183.5; .S68. **DD** 790.1/96/0973. Index available. cum. index. **Bk Rev. Ad Acc. Circ:** 700 (ctrl).
**Desc:** Recreation for people with vision, hearing, mental, physical and social problems. Current information on recreation programs, services, grants, equipment, supplies, publications, etc. provided by 1,250 national and US organizations.

**AU**
**SPIEL SPORT FREIZEIT MODE.** mo. Osterreichische Wirtschaftsverlag, Nikolsdorfergasse 7-11, A-1501 Vienna Austria. **Tel** 011 43 222 555585, FAX 0222/55 55 85/215, telex 1-11669.

**US**
**SPORT AMERICANA BASKETBALL CARD PRICE GUIDE AND ALPHABETICAL CHECKLIST, THE. VFOAT** Basketball Card Price Guide and Alphabetical Checklist. (1991)-. English. Edgewater Book Co, PO Box 40238, Cleveland OH 44140. **Tel** (216)835-3108. **LC** GV885.15; .S68. **DD** 769/.49796323/0973.

**CN/0838-4061**
**SPORT & LEISURE.** *Ceased.* [Sport leis.]. **VFOAT** Sport and Leisure. Vol. 1, No. 1 Spring (1989)-?. Periodical. English. Three times a year. University of Waterloo Press Dana Porter Library, Waterloo Ontario N2L 3G1 Canada. **Tel** (519)885-1211 ext. 3369, FAX 519 747 4606. **DD** 306/.48. *Continues Sociology of Leisure and Sport Abstracts, 0167-580X.*

**UK**
**SPORT AND LEISURE.** *Title Change.* **See** Recreation, Leisure-Sports.

**US/0898-4301**
**SPORT PARACHUTIST'S SAFETY JOURNAL.** [Sport parachutist's saf. j.]. **VFOAT** SPSJ. Vol. 1, No. 1; May/June 1988-. Periodical. English. bm. $7.00 US; $11.00 other. Sports Parachutists, 2671 W 20th Street, Yuma AZ 85364. **ED** Jan Meyer. **DD** 797.

●**US/1061-5512**
**SPORTS CARD PRICE GUIDE MONTHLY. See** Recreation, Leisure-Sports.

# Recreation, Leisure

UK
**SPORTS COUNCIL STUDY.** See Recreation, Leisure-Sports.

CN/0319-5082
**SUMMER IN CANADA.** See Economics-Labor.

CN
**SUPERTRAX.** (19??)-. English (French). Twice a year (Sept. & Oct.). 12.95Can$. Supertrax Publishing Inc, Box 20219, 856 Upper James Street, Hamilton Ontario L9C 7M8 Canada. **Tel** (416)549-1370. **ED** D. Kent Lester (phone: (905)575-1621). **Ad Acc, Adv Mgr:** T. Kehoe. **Pr Rev. Circ:** 160,000 (ctrl).
**Desc:** Covers snowmobile products. Industry, and organizational guide.

RU
**SVOBODNOE VREMIA I ORGANIZATSIIA DOSUGA V SOTSIALISTICHESKOM OBSHCHESTVE NA SOVREMENNOM ETAPE.** **Added/Corp** Gosudarstvennaia Biblioteka SSSR Imeni V.I. Lenina. Nauchno-Isslyedovatelskii Otdel Bibliografovedeniia i Nauchno-Vspomogatelnoi Bibliografii. (19??)-. Russian. ir.

US
**SWIMMING POOL AGE & SPA MERCHANDISER, DATA & REFERENCE ANNUAL.** **VFOAT** Swimming Pool Age and Spa Merchandiser, Data & Reference Annual; Data and Reference Annual. **VAT** Swimming Pool Age and Swimming Pool Age Merchandiser, Data and Reference Annual. 49th Ed. (Spring 1982)-. English. an. Swimming Pool Age & Spa Merchandiser, 3000 NE 30 Place, Fort Lauderdale FL 33306. **Continues** Swimming Pool Weekly and Swimming Pool Age, Data & Reference Annual, 0082-0466.

US/0899-1022
**SWIMMING POOL/SPA AGE.** [Swim. pool/spa age]. **VFOAT** Swimming Pool Spa Age. Vol. 62, No. 5; April 1988-. Periodical. English. mo. $39.00. Argus Business, 6151 Powers Ferry Road, Atlanta GA 30339. **Tel** (404)995-2500, (800)233-3359. **LC** GV837.A1; S9. **DD** 338. **[CCC].** available on microfilm and microfiche from University Microfilms International (UMI). **Continues** Swimming Pool Age & Spa Merchandiser, 0279-134X.

IT
**T-SPORT.** See Architecture.

IT
**TECHNICS AND LEISURES.** qt. L80000 Italy; 160000 other. Sinopia Ed, Via G. Murat 84, 20159 Milan Italy. **Tel** 011 39 2 688-3641, FAX 011 39 2 668-02971.

CN/0229-4052
**TEMPS FORT.** (TEMPS FORT : BULLETIN D'INFORMATION DU CRL RIVE SUD.). [Temps fort]. No. 1 (March 1977)-. Bulletin. French. mo. Free. Temps Fort, 780 rue St-Jean, Longueuil Quebec J4H 2Y7 Canada. **DD** 790/.09714/3. ctrl circ. **Continues** Bulletin d'Information (Conseil Regional des Loisirs de la Rive Sud), 0229-4036.

HU/0209-6811
**TESTNEVELES ES SPORTTUDOMANY.** (1980)-. Periodical. Hungarian. qt. **UDC** 796. **CODEN** 798.
**Ind/Abst** Leis. Recreat. Tour. Abstr.

US/0040-5914
**THERAPEUTIC RECREATION JOURNAL.** See Physically Impaired.

MX
**TIEMPO LIBRE / PUBLICACION SEMANAL DE UNO MAS UNO.** (19??)-. Periodical. Spanish (English). wk. 20.00ptas. Tiempo Libre, Edificio No 5 bis, Nochebuena Mixcoac, 03720 Mexico DF Mexico. **Tel** 5 611-28-84. **ED** Angeles Aguilar Zinser. Index available (bound in each issue). **Ad Acc, Adv Mgr:** Javier Flores. Acid Free. **Circ:** 90,000.
**Desc:** How to spend your free time in Mexico city. A weekly guide of what to do any day at any time in Mexico city.
**Ind/Abst** Leis. Recreat. Tour. Abstr.

CN/0827-4207
**TORONTO TONIGHT.** Ceased. [Tor. tonight]. Vol. 1, No. 1 (Dec. 1983)-(199?). Periodical. English. sm. Toronto Tonight Productions, 531 St Lawrence Avenue West, Toronto Ontario M6A 1A3 Canada. **DD** 790/.09713/541.

CN/0826-5224
**TOUR DE SUTTON, LE.** [Tour Sutton]. Vol. 1, No. 1 (Sept. 1983)-. Periodical. English (French). qt. Free. Bureau du Tourisme et des Congres de Sutton, PO Box 810, Sutton Quebec J0E 2K0 Canada. **ED** Betsy Johnston and Denis Boulangen. **DD** 790/.09714/64. **Ad Acc, Circ:** 7,000 (ctrl).
**Desc:** Covers local tourism, developments, nature, astronomy, architecture, and current events and history.

US/0194-4894
**TOURIST ATTRACTIONS & PARKS.** [Tour. attract. parks]. **VAT** Tourist Attractions and Parks. Periodical. English. Seven times a year. $25.00 (one year), $36.00 (two year);US. Tourist Attractions & Parks, 7000 Terminal Square, Suite 210, Upper Darby PA 19082. **Tel** (215)734-2420, FAX (215)734-2423. **ED** Sandy Meschbcow. **Bk Rev. Ad Acc. Circ:** 20,000 (ctrl).
**Desc:** Largest circulated publication for the amusement and leisure facility market.

CN/0822-5524
**TOUT A LOISIR.** (TOUT A LOISIR / CONSEIL REGIONAL DES LOISIRS, SAGUENAY-LAC-SAINT-JEAN, CHIBOUGAMAU-CHAPAIS.). [Tout loisir]. Periodical. French. mo. Free. Conseil Regional des Loisirs Saguenay-Lac-Saint-Jean, 414 rue Collard, Alma Quebec G8B 1N2 Canada. **DD** 790/.09714/16.

US/0892-3922
**TRAIL RIDER MAGAZINE.** [Trail rider mag.]. **VFOAT** Trail Rider. (198?)-. Periodical. English. mo. $18.00. Windemede Publications, PO Box 129, Medford NJ 08055. **Tel** (609)953-7805. **ED** Paul Clipper. **DD** 796. **Ad Acc. Circ:** 2,500. **Continues** Trail Rider, 0890-9393.
**Desc:** Written for the East Coast off-road motorcycle enthusiast. Contents include competition reports, mechanical how-tos, product evaluations and riding features.

US/0041-0780
**TRAILER LIFE.** [Trailer life]. (19??)-. Periodical. English. mo. $22.00. TL Enterprises, 29901 Agoura Road, Agoura CA 91301. **Tel** (800)234-3450, (805)389-0300. **(Subscription address:** Neodata / Colorado, PO Box 2606, Boulder Boulder CO 80322.**)** **ED** Bill Estes. **LC** TX1100; .T7. **Ad Acc. Circ:** 314,000. available on microfilm and microfiche from University Microfilms International (UMI). Documents available from UMI Article Clearinghouse.
**Desc:** Represents the RV lifestyle, featuring various articles from RV maintenance to travel and cooking tips. Dedicated to the motor home, travel trailer and truck camper.
**Ind/Abst** Consum. Index Prod. Eval. Inf. Source; Mag. Artic. Summar. Elite (Jan. 1984-June 1989); Mag. Artic. Summar. Select (Jan. 1984-June 1989); Mag. Artic. Summar. CD-ROM (Jan. 1984-June 1989); Mag. Index Plus (1989-); Mag. Search; Newsp. Period. Abstr. (1989-); Pop. Mag. Rev. (1984-); Mag. Index (1977-);(1959-).

US/1041-5203
**TRAVEL LEISURE & ENTERTAINMENT NEWS MEDIA.** See Travel and Tourism.

US/1054-8246
**TREASURE FACTS.** (TREASURE FACTS : HOW-TO GUIDE FOR TREASURE HUNTERS.). [Treas. facts]. Vol. 1, Issue 1 (Apr./May 1991)-. Periodical. English. bm. $15.95. Treasure Facts, PO Box 1589, Grove OK 74344. **LC** WMLC 91/975. **DD** 622.

XO
**TRENER.** Czech. mo. $44.00. Slovak Physical Training Organization, Vajnorska Cesta 100-A, 832 58 Bratislava, Slovakia. **(Subscription address:** Slovart GTG Ltd., Krupinska 4, 852 99 Bratislava Slovakia.**)**

FR
**TRIOLO.** French. Fleurus Presse International, 21 rue Faubourg St Antoine, 75550 Paris Cedex 11 France. **Tel** 011 33 1 40026300.

CH
**TSAO KEN JEN.** First published in Oct. 1982. Periodical. Chinese. mo. NT$500.00. Tsao Ken Jen Tsa Chih She, PO Box 551766, Taipei Taiwan. **LC** AP95.C4; T66.

NE
**UITVOERINGSORGANEN BUURT- EN KLUBHUISWERK.** **Main/Corp** Netherlands. Centraal Bureau voor de Statistiek. 1976-. Dutch. Fl10.75. Centraal Bureau voor de Statistiek, AFD ALG Zaken, Postbus 959, 2270 AZ Voorburg Netherlands. **Tel** 011 31 70 3373800, FAX 011 31 038 7429, telex 32692 CBS NL. **LC** HN46.N4; N35A.

HU/0865-9435
**UJ ERDEKES UJSAG.** [Uj erdek. ujs.]. (1990)-. Periodical. Hungarian. bm. **(Subscription address:** Kultura, PO Box 149, H 1389 Budapest 62 Hungary**)** **UDC** 070. **Continues** Erdekes Ujsag (Budapest. 1988), 0239-0051.

US/0740-1930
**UNDERSEA JOURNAL, THE.** Periodical. English. qt. $15.00 US / $20.00 other. Professional Association of Diving Instructors, 1243 East Warner Avenue, Santa Ana CA 92705.
**Ind/Abst** SportSearch (May 1987-).

●US/1049-6351
**VACATION HOME REPORT.** (1992)-. Periodical. English. bm. $12.00. Rundown/Standish Publishing, POB 335, Ardmore PA 19003. **Tel** (215)664-3322, FAX (215)664-3322.

US
**VARIA BELADIRI.** 923-. Periodical. Indonesian. mo. Rp350. Pt Badan Penerbit & Percetakan Vaira, Jl Abdulrachman Saleh No 28, Jakarta Pusat Indonesia. **LC** GV111; .V28. **Continues** Varia.

US/0277-5204
**VISIONS IN LEISURE AND BUSINESS.** [Vis. leis. bus.]. **Added/Corp** Appalachian Associates. Vol. 1 (Spring 1982)-. Periodical. English. qt. $25.00 individuals, $45.00 institutions. Appalachian Associates, 615 Pasteur Avenue, Bowling Green OH 43402. **Tel** (419)352-9111. **ED** David L. Groves. **LC** GV188.3.U6; V57. **DD** 338.4/7790/01350973. available on microfiche.
**Desc:** An international journal of personal services, programming and administration. It addresses the interface between the leisure and business communities.
**Ind/Abst** Leis. Recreat. Tour. Abstr. (19??-).

NE/0167-966X
**VRIJETIJD EN SAMENLEVING.** [Vrijetijd samenlev.]. (1982)-. Periodical. Dutch. qt. Stichting Recreatie, Postbus 80547, 2508 GM Den Haag Netherlands. **Tel** 070-500111. **UDC** 379.8.
**Ind/Abst** Leis. Recreat. Tour. Abstr. (19??-).

●US/1072-558X
**WILD STEELHEAD AND ATLANTIC SALMON.** (19??)-. English. qt. $39.95 US; $49.95 Canada; $59.95 other. Wild Steelhead & Atlantic Salmon, PO Box 3666, Seattle WA 98124. **Tel** (206)483-4818.

CN/0825-4044
**WINTER RECREATION DIRECTORY.** [Winter recreat. dir.]. 1982/83-. Directory. English. an. Free upon request. Tourism Saskatchewan, 1919 Saskatchewan Drive, Regina Saskatchewan S4P 3V7 Canada. **Tel** (306)787-2473, (800)667-7191. **ED** Bob Ellis. **DD** 796.9/025/7124. **Circ:** 20,000 (ctrl). **Formed by the union of** Winter Events, 0715-724X **and** Welcome to Winter, 0825-4036.
**Desc:** Contains information on where to ski, snowmobile, ice fish or participate in other sports and special winter events in the province of Saskatchewan.

NE
**WINTERSPORT.** (Oct. 1977)-. Periodical. Dutch. mo. BV Dienst en Centrum Tourisme DCT, POB 278, 3400 AG Ijsselstein Netherlands. **LC** GV841; .W58.

US/0163-4313
**WOODALL'S FLORIDA & SOUTHERN STATES RETIREMENT AND RESORT COMMUNITIES.** **VFOAT** Florida & Southern States Retirement and Resort Communities. **VAT** Woodall's Florida and Southern States Retirement and Resort Communities. English. an. $3.95, $5.95 includes additional editorial material. Woodall Publishing Company, 28167 North Keith Drive, Lake Forest IL 60015. **Tel** (708)362-6700. **LC** HQ1063; .W64. **DD** 301.43/5.

US/0145-577X
**WOODALL'S RETIREMENT AND RESORT COMMUNITIES. EASTERN EDITION.** (WOODALL'S RETIREMENT AND RESORT COMMUNITIES.). [Woodall's retire. resort communities, East. ed.]. **VFOAT** Woodall's Eastern Edition Retirement & Communities Directory; Retirement and Resort Communities. English. $2.95. Woodall Publishing Company, 28167 North Keith Drive, Lake Forest IL 60015. **Tel** (708)362-6700. **LC** HQ1063; .W65. **DD** 301.43/5.

US/0146-4892
**WOODALL'S RETIREMENT AND RESORT COMMUNITIES. NATIONAL EDITION.** (WOODALL'S RETIREMENT AND RESORT COMMUNITIES.). **VFOAT** Woodall's National Edition Retirement & Resort Communities Directory; Retirement and Resort Communities. English. $5.95. Woodall Publishing Company, 28167 North Keith Drive, Lake Forest IL 60015. **Tel** (708)362-6700. **LC** HQ1063; .W66. **DD** 301.5/4.

US/0191-4960
**WORCESTER MAGAZINE (WORCESTER).** (WORCESTER MAGAZINE.). (1976)-. Periodical. English. Fifty-two times a year. $26.00. Worcester Magazine, 172 Shrewsbury Street, Worcester MA 10614. **Tel** (508)755-8004. **ED** Jay Whearley. **Bk Rev. Ad Acc. Circ:** 50,000 (ctrl). available on microfilm from University Microfilms International (UMI).
**Desc:** Local art and entertainment guide, alternative newsweekly.

US
**WORLD LEISURE & RECREATION.** **Added/Corp** World Leisure and Recreation Association. **VAT** World Leisure and Recreation. Vol. 26, No. 5 (Dec. 1984)-. Periodical. English. qt (4 issues). $60.00 (includes 2 issues of WLRA Newsletter) US; Also comes with World Leisure and Recreation Association membership. World Leisure & Recreation Association, PO Box 309, Sharbot Lake K0H 2P0 Canada. **Tel** (613)279-3172, FAX (613)279-3372. **ED** Tina Kelly. **LC** GV1; .W67. **Bk Rev.**

**Ad Acc. Circ:** 1,000. ***Continues*** *WLRA Journal.*
**Ind/Abst** Am. Bibliogr. Slavic East Europ. Stud.; Leis. Recreat. Tour. Abstr.; SPORT Discus; SportSearch (May 1987-).

IT/1120-2424
**YACHT PREMIERE ENGLISH ED.** [Yacht prem.Engl. ed.]. (1990)-. Periodical. English (Italian, German and Spanish). bm. L56000 Italy; $55.00 US. Edizioni Internazionali SRL, P Le Brescia 6, 20149 Milan Italy. **Tel** 39 2 48012905, FAX 39 2 48012925. **ED** Dott. Cinzia Boschiero. **UDC** 797.1. **Ad Acc, Adv Mgr:** Paola Pellegrino, **Tel** 39 2 48012417. **Pr Rev. Circ:** 75,000.
**Desc:** International magazine of yachting life.

SZ
**YMCA WORLD.** (19??)-. Periodical. English. qt. 25.00F. World Alliance of Young Men's Christian Associations, 37 Quai Wilson, CH-1201 Geneva, Switzerland. **Tel** 011 41 22 7323100, FAX 011 41 22 7384015. **ED** Bart Shaba.

## ABSTRACTING, BIBLIOGRAPHIES AND STATISTICS

CN/0821-0683
**ALBERTA PROVINCIAL PARKS USER STATISTICS.** [Alts. prov. parks user stat.]. **VFOAT** User Statistics, Alberta Provincial Parks. English. an. Limited free distribution. Alberta Recreation and Parks, 10405 Jasper Avenue, Edmonton Alberta T5J 3N4 Canada. **LC** GV191.46.A43; A46. **DD** 333.7/83/097123.

US/0361-8048
**ANNUAL - ASSOCIATION OF TRACK AND FIELD STATISTICIANS.** ***Ceased.*** **Main/Corp** Association of Track and Field Statisticians. (19??)-?. English. an. Tafnews Press, Box 296, Los Altos CA 94022. **LC** GV1060.67; .A85a. **DD** 796.4/2/0212.

●US/1066-3746
**BIBLIOGRAPHIES AND INDEXES ON SPORTS HISTORY.** (1993)-. Periodical. English. Greenwood Press Inc., PO Box 5007, Westport CT 06881-5007. **Tel** (203)226-3571, FAX (203)222-1502.

US
**CURRENT BASEBALL PUBLICATIONS.** (19??)-. Newsletter. English. qt. $8.00 US; $10.00 Canada; $12.00 other. Society for American Baseball Research, PO Box 93183, Cleveland OH 44101. **Tel** (216)575-0500.
**Desc:** Bibliography/newsletter listing newly published books, magazines, and newsletters on baseball.

US
**HUNTER CASUALTY REPORT / ARKANSAS GAME AND FISH COMMISSION.** **Main/Corp** Arkansas Game and Fish Commission. (19??)-. English. an. Free. Arkansas Game and Fish Commission, Game & Fish Building, No 2 Natural Resources Drive, Little Rock AR 72205. **Tel** (501)223-6300, (800)364-4163, FAX (501)223-6447. **ED** H. Dykes Reber. **LC** SK53; .A74a. **DD** 363.1/4. **Circ:** 2,000 (ctrl).
**Desc:** Covers information, analysis, and statistics concerning all hunting accidents within the state of Arkansas for the fiscal year.

UK
**LEISURE AND RECREATION STATISTICS ESTIMATES.** English. an. £7.50. Chartered Institute of Public Finance and Accountancy, 2 3 Robert Street, London WC2N 6BH England. **Tel** 011 44 1 895 8823. **LC** GV76.E5; L44. **DD** 990/.01/35/0942.

UK/0261-1392
**LEISURE, RECREATION, AND TOURISM ABSTRACTS.** **Added/Corp** Commonwealth Agricultural Bureaux. World Leisure and Recreation Association. Vol. 6, No. 1 (March 1981)-. Abstracting/Indexing Service. English. qt. $251.00 US. CAB International Centre, Wallingford, Oxon OX10 8DE United Kingdom. **Tel** 44 491 832111, FAX 44 491 833508, telex 847964 (COMAGG G). **ED** Margaret A. Leighfield. **LC** GV191.6; .R86. **DD** 333.78. **Ad Acc. Circ:** 400. ***Continues*** *Rural Recreation and Tourism Abstracts, 0308-0137.*
**Desc:** Brings together information on the many aspects of leisure for those interested in research and strategic development of leisure, recreation, sport, tourism and hospitality activities, facilities, products and services.

US/0162-542X
**OFFICIAL BASEBALL REGISTER.** ***Title Change.*** (1973)-(199?). English. an (Mar.). Sporting News, c/o Sharon Moore, 1212 North Lindbergh Boulevard, PO Box 56, St Louis MO 63166. **Tel** (314)997-7111, (800)825-8508. ***Supersedes*** *Baseball Register.* ***Continued by*** *Sporting News Official Baseball Register.*
**Desc:** Statistical information on the major league players and active managers.

US
**OFFICIAL NATIONAL COLLEGIATE ATHLETIC ASSOCIATION BASKETBALL STATISTICIANS' MANUAL, THE.** **Main/Corp** National Collegiate Athletic Association. **VFOAT** Basketball Statisticians' Manual. English. an. National Collegiate Athletic Association / NCAA, PO Box 7347, Overland Park KS 66207. **Tel** (913)339-1900, FAX (913)339-0030. **LC** GV885.45; .O35. **DD** 796.323/63/02022. **UDC** 796.323.093(73).

US/0362-7837
**RECREATION STATISTICS.** (RECREATION STATISTICS / DEPARTMENT OF THE ARMY, CORPS OF ENGINEERS, CIVIL WORKS DIRECTORATE.). English. Image Southwest, 517 Main Street, Texarkana TX 75501. **Tel** (903)793-5528, FAX (903)794-0080. **LC** GV191.4; .U53A. **DD** 333.78/0973.

●US
**SPORTING NEWS OFFICIAL BASEBALL REGISTER, THE.** **VFOAT** Official Baseball Register. (1992)-. Periodical. English. an. $12.95. Sporting News, c/o Sharon Moore, 1212 North Lindbergh Boulevard, PO Box 56, St Louis MO 63166. **Tel** (314)997-7111, (800)825-8508. **LC** GV862; .S69. ***Continues*** *Official Baseball Register.*
**Desc:** Statistical information on the major league players and active managers.

US/0882-553X
**SPORTSEARCH.** (SPORTSEARCH.). [SportSearch]. **Added/Corp** Coaching Association of Canada. Sport Information Resource Centre. **VFOAT** Sport Search. Vol. 1, No. 1 (Sept. 1985)-. Abstracting/Indexing Service. English. mo. 295.00Can$ (institutions and libraries), 170.00Can$ (individuals) Canada; 298.00Can$ (institutions), 173.00Can$ (individuals) US; 314.00Can$ (institutions), 189.00Can$ (individuals) other. Sport Information Resource Centre, 1600 promenade James Naismith Drive, Gloucester Ontario K1B 5N4 Canada. **Tel** (613)748-5658, FAX (613)748-5701, telex 053-3660 Sportrec Ott. **LC** GV561; .S745. **DD** 016.796/05. **Ad Acc.** available on CD-ROM (Sport Discus) from SilverPlatter (US).
**Desc:** Current awareness tool that monitors over 960 sport and physical education periodicals published in English or French. Relevant articles from non-sport journals are also included.

## GAMES AND AMUSEMENTS

CN/0227-261X
**2000, AN.** (L'AN 2000 : LE PREMIER MAGAZINE INTERPLANETAIRE.). [An 2000]. **VAT** An Deux Mille. Vol. 1, No. 1 (1980)-. Periodical. French. bw. $1.25 per no. Distributions Eclair, 8320 Place de Lorraine, Anjou Quebec H1J 1E6 Canada. **DD** 741.5/9714.

US/0899-2843
**ACTION COMICS.** (19??)-. Periodical. English. mo (12 issues). $18.00 US; $24.30 Canada; $30.00 other. DC Comics, 1325 Avenue of the Americas, Floor 27, New York NY 10019. **Tel** (212)636-5443. **(Subscription address:** DC Comics, PO Box 0528, Baldwin NY 11510.**)** **DD** 741. ***Continues*** *Action Comics Weekly.*

US/0899-2843
**ACTION COMICS WEEKLY.** ***Title Change.*** [Action comics wkly.]. No. 601 (1988)-(19??). Periodical. English. wk. $18.00 US; $24.30 Canada; $30.00 other. DC Comics, 1325 Avenue of the Americas, Floor 27, New York NY 10019. **Tel** (212)636-5443. **DD** 741. ***Continues*** *Action Comics.* ***Changed back to*** *Action Comics.*

US/0893-9489
**ACTION PURSUIT GAMES.** [Action purs. games]. Vol. 1, No. 1 (Fall 1987)-. Periodical. English. mo. $24.50. CFW Enterprises Inc., 4201 West Van Owen Place, Burbank CA 91505. **Tel** (818)845-2656. **(Subscription address:** Kable Publishers Aide, 308 East Hitt Street, Subscription Department, Mt. Morris IL 61054-1473.**)** **DD** 793.

US/0362-5923
**ACTIVITY PROGRAMMERS SOURCEBOOK.** **See** Education.

US/0893-4428
**ADVENTURES OF SUPERMAN, THE.** [Adventures Superman]. No. 424 (Jan. 1987)-. Periodical. English. mo. $18.00 US; $24.30 Canada; $30.00 other. DC Comics, 1325 Avenue of the Americas, Floor 27, New York NY 10019. **Tel** (212)636-5443. **(Subscription address:** DC Comics Subscriptions, PO Box 0528, Baldwin, NY 11510**)** **DD** 741. ***Continues*** *Superman, 0272-4243.*

US/0737-1381
**AFTERMATH.** Issue 1, (1983)-. Periodical. English. Gulf Coast Comics, PO Box 310, Winnie TX 77665. **Tel** (409)296-2867. **ED** Charles Thurber. **Bk Rev. Ad Acc. Circ:** 10,000 (ctrl).
**Desc:** Science fiction action adventure comic about US military operations and a struggling civilian populace after a nuclear war in the year 2025.

US/1044-6745
**ALF.** ***Ceased.*** [ALF]. No. 1 (March 1988)-(Feb. 1992). Periodical. English. mo. Marvel Entertainment Group Inc., 387 Park Avenue South, New York NY 10016. **Tel** (212)576-8595, FAX (212) 576-9289. **DD** 741.

US/0894-3397
**ALIEN LEGION, THE.** [Alien legion]. No. 1 (April 1984)-. Periodical. English. bm. Marvel Entertainment Group Inc., 387 Park Avenue South, New York NY 10016. **Tel** (212)576-8595, FAX (212) 576-9289.

US/8750-0558
**ALPHA FLIGHT.** **Added/Corp** Marvel Comics Group. Vol. 1, No. 1 (Aug. 1983)-. Periodical. English. Twelve times a year. $21.00. Marvel Entertainment Group Inc., 387 Park Avenue South, New York NY 10016. **Tel** (212)576-8595, FAX (212) 576-9289. **ED** J. Shooter. **Ad Acc. Circ:** 240,000.

US/0274-5232
**AMAZING SPIDER-MAN, THE.** **Added/Corp** Marvel Comics Group. Non-Pareil Publishing Corp. **VFOAT** Spider-Man. **VAT** Amazing Spider Man. No. 1 (Mar. 1963)-. Periodical. English. mo. $15.00 (US); $23.00 (Canada); $27.00 (other). Marvel Entertainment Group Inc., 387 Park Avenue South, New York NY 10016. **Tel** (212)576-8595, FAX (212) 576-9289. **ED** Jim Shooter. **DD** 741. **Ad Acc. Circ:** 350,000.
**Desc:** Comic book adventures of Spider-Man.

●US/1066-8292
**AMERICAN CHESS JOURNAL (CAMBRIDGE, MASS.).** (AMERICAN CHESS JOURNAL.). [Am. chess j.]. No. 1 (1992)-. Periodical. English. Three times a year. $30.00 US; $36.00 Canada & Mexico; $42.00 others. American Chess Journal, PO Box 2967, Harvard Square Station, Cambridge MA 02238. **Tel** (617)876-5759. **DD** 794.
**Desc:** A work of chess writing, graphics, and analysis in book format.

US/0148-0243
**AMERICAN GO JOURNAL, THE.** [Am. Go j.]. **Main/Corp** American Go Association. Began in 1949. Periodical. English (Japanese). qt. $25.00 North America; $30.00 other. American Go Association, PO Box 397 Old Chelsea Station, New York NY 10113. **Tel** (212)397-1945, FAX (212)477-2812. **ED** Roy J Laird. **LC** GV1459; .A44A. **DD** 794/.05. **Bk Rev. Ad Acc. Circ:** 1,200 (ctrl).
**Desc:** A magazine of information about the game of Go-4000 year old intellectual board game claiming 50,000,000 players in the orient and growing thousands in the U.S. and Europe. Articles on tactics, history, game analysis, theory, philosophy, club information, and news. The national magazine of the American Go Association.

US/1058-1669
**AMUSE USA.** (1991)-. Periodical. English. qt. $35.00. 9 Muses Publications, Inc., Box 365, Pacific Palisades CA 90272.

US/0003-2344
**AMUSEMENT BUSINESS.** [Amus. bus.]. Vol. 73 (Jan. 9, 1961)-. Periodical. English. wk. $99.00 US; $115.00 Canada; $125.00 other (surface mail). Billboard Publications Inc., 1515 Broadway Billboard, New York NY 10036. **Tel** (212)764-7300, FAX (305)755-7048, telex WU TWX 710-581-6279. **(Subscription address:** Amusement Business, PO Box 5022, Brentwood, TN 37024**)** **ED** Tom Powell, Karen Oertley, Tom Sullivan. **LC** GV1851.A3; A55. **DD** 338.7/61/79006805. Index available. cum. index. **Ad Acc. Circ:** 13,111. available on microfilm and microfiche from University Microfilms International (UMI); available on an online database (files 16,570,648/Full-Text) from DIALOG. ***Continues*** *Funspot;* ***Continues in part*** *Billboard (Cincinnati, Ohio : 1894).*
**Desc:** Covers the spectrum of the international sports and mass entertainment industry - primarily live large numbers of people. Provides news on events, revenue, attendance, talent, promotions, financial and business operations, sponsorships, and endorsements. Edited for owners and managers of arenas, stadiums, auditoriums, etc. Also covers services allied to these industries.
**Ind/Abst** Bus. ASAP (1990-) [Full Txt.]; Bus. Index (1985-); Gen. BusinessFile (1985-); Gen. Period. Index (1985-); Mag. Search; Trade Ind. ASAP [Full Txt.]; Trade Ind. Index (1981-) [Full Txt.].

US/1044-8268
**AMUSEMENT INDUSTRY BUYERS GUIDE.** [Amus. ind. buy. guide]. 1987-. Consumer Publication. English. an (October). $28.00 US and Canada; $38.00 other. Amusement Business, PO Box 24970, Nashville TN 37202. **Tel** (615)321-4250, FAX (615)327-1575. **LC** GV1851.A3; A557. **DD** 380.1/456887/02573. **Circ:** 8,550. ***Continues*** *Amusement Rides & Games Buyers' Guide, 0149-8010.*
**Desc:** Contains comprehensive listing of manufacturers, importers and suppliers of all types of games, rides and merchandise. Listing of ride suppliers and manufacturers and distributors are cross referenced. Also lists companies providing services and supplies to the amusement industry.

CN/0709-2415
**AMUSEMENT JEUNESSE.** First issue in May 1978?. Periodical. French. Three times a year. $1.00 Canada, $1.25 others. Deuel & Associates, 7208 Jefferson Street NE, Albuquerque NM 87109. **Tel** (505)345-8732. **DD** 793.7/3/05.

US/0271-7999
**AMUSEMENT PARK JOURNAL.** ***Ceased.*** (19??)-(1987). Periodical. English. qt. Amusement Business, PO Box 24970, Nashville TN 37202. **Tel** (615)321-4250, FAX (615)327-1575. **ED** Charles J Jacques Jr. **LC** GV1851.A3; A556. **DD** 791/.06/805. Index available. **Bk Rev. Ad Acc. Circ:** 13,000.
**Desc:** A speciality publication on amusement parks and amusement rides-past and present.

US
**ANDERSON PLANNER, THE.** English. Twelve times a year. $28.00. Rosewood Pulbishers, Star Route Box 145, Sarona WI 54870. **Tel** (715)635-8538.
**Desc:** An activities planning guide, including crafts and games, for people who work with the elderly.

US
**ANECDOTA SCOWAH.** **Added/Corp** Roxburghe Club of San Francisco. Grabhorne Press, San Francisco. (19??)-. English.

US
**ANNUAL U.S. OPEN CHESS CHAMPIONSHIP.** English. **LC** GV1313; .S66; GV1313; .C59. **DD** 794.1 S; 794.1/57.

●US/1062-502X
**APHELION (SANTA ANA, CALIF.).** (APHELION : A JOURNAL OF MAGIC HISTORY AND BIBLIOGRAPHY.). [Aphelion]. Vol. 1, No.1 Mar. (1992)-. Bibliography. English. bm. $36.00. Thomas Sawyer, 12502 Red Hill Avenue, Santa Ana CA 92705. **DD** 793.

US
**APOCALYPSE.** (Spring 1975)-. Periodical. English. Twelve times a year. $53.00. Apocalypse, 62 Jane Street, c/o Harry Lorayne, New York NY 10014. **Tel** (212)989-5694, FAX (212)989-2646. **ED** Harry Lorayne. Index available. cum. index. **Ad Acc.**
**Desc:** Focuses on close-up magic as entertainment.

CN/0846-3409
**APPRENTI SORCIER (GATINEAU).** (APPRENTI SORCIER.). [Apprenti sorcier]. **Added/Corp** Guilde des Problemistes du Nouveau Monde. No 1 (June 1991)-. Periodical. French. Three times a year. 2.00Can$ per issue. Guilde des Problemistes du Mouveau Monde, 34 Plateau du Reservoir, Gatineau Quebec J8V 1G2 Canada. **DD** 794.1.

CN/0706-7399
**APPRENTICE (OTTAWA).** (THE APPRENTICE.). No. 1 (May 1978)-. Periodical. English. qt. $5.50 (six issues) Canada and US. D. Berman, 7381 Bank Street, The Theatre, Ottawa Ontario K1S 3V4 Canada. **Tel** (613)237-6268. **ED** Daid Berman. **DD** 796.1. **Bk Rev. Ad Acc. Pr Rev. Circ:** 1,000 (ctrl).

US/0199-5596
**APPROVED CROSSWORD PUZZLES.** ***Title Change.*** (19??)-(199?). Periodical. English. Twelve times a year. Penny Press Inc., 6 Prowitt Street, Norwalk CT 06855. **Tel** (203)866-6688. ***Continued by*** *Approved Variety Puzzles Plus Crosswords, 1076-9021.*

US/1076-9021
**APPROVED VARIETY PUZZLES PLUS CROSSROADS.** **VFOAT** Variety Puzzles. (199?)-. Periodical. English. bm. $15.47. Penny Press Inc., 6 Prowitt Street, Norwalk CT 06855. **Tel** (203)866-6688. ***Continues*** *Approved Crossword Puzzles, 0199-5596.*

US/0746-8660
**ARCHIE AT RIVERDALE HIGH.** No. 1 (Aug. 1972)-. Periodical. English. an. $0.75 one copy, $1.00 two copies. Archie Comic Publications, 325 Fayette Avenue, Mamaroneck NY 10543. **Tel** (914)381-5155. **ED** Victor Gorelick and Richard H Goldwater. **Ad Acc.** ctrl circ.
**Desc:** Comic stories and games.

US/8750-0620
**ARCHIE COMICS DIGEST MAGAZINE.** ***Title Change.*** [Archie comics dig. mag.]. (19??)-(19??). Periodical. English. bm. Archie Comic Publications, 325 Fayette Avenue, Mamaroneck NY 10543. **Tel** (914)381-5155. ***Continued by*** *Archie Digest Magazine, 1059-1877.*

US/0735-6455
**ARCHIE (NEW YORK, N.Y.).** (ARCHIE.). [Archie]. (19??)-. Periodical. English. Eight times a year. $11.87. Archie Comic Publications, 325 Fayette Avenue, Mamaroneck NY 10543. **Tel** (914)381-5155. **ED** Victor Gorelick and Richard H. Goldwater. **DD** 741. **Ad Acc.** ctrl circ. ***Continues*** *Archie Comics.*

CN
**ARCHIE (ST. LAMBERT).** (ARCHIE.). French. ir. 60.00Can$. Les Editions Heritage Inc., 300 Avenue Arran, St. Lambert Quebec J4R 1K5 Canada. **Tel** (514)875-0327, (514)672-6710. **(Subscription address:** Informatique Rive Sud Inc., 25 Taschereau Bur 201, Greenfield Park, Quebec J4V 2G8 Canada.**)**

US/1069-0999
**ARCHIE'S PAL JUGHEAD COMICS.** [Archie's pal Jughead comics]. (1993)-. Periodical. English. mo. Archie Comic Publications, 325 Fayette Avenue, Mamaroneck NY 10543. **Tel** (914)381-5155. **DD** 741. ***Continues*** *Jughead, 0022-5991.*

US/0745-7774
**ARCHIE'S PALS 'N GALS.** ***Ceased.*** **VFOAT** Archie's Pals and Gals. Periodical. English. bm. Archie Comic Publications, 325 Fayette Avenue, Mamaroneck NY 10543. **Tel** (914)381-5155. **ED** Victor Gorelick and Richard H Goldwater. **Ad Acc.** ctrl circ.
**Desc:** Comic stories and games.

US/1048-9118
**AT-THE-PARK (CHICAGO, ILL.).** (AT-THE-PARK : A JOURNAL FOR THE AMUSEMENT PARK INDUSTRY.). [At-the-park]. **VFOAT** At the Park. Premiere Issue (Jan./Feb. 1990)-. Periodical. English. bm (6 issues). $24.95 (surface mail), $34.95 (first class). At the Park, PO Box 597783, Chicago IL 60659. **Tel** (312)465-4880, FAX (312)465-4880. **ED** Allen Ambrosini. **DD** 791. **Bk Rev. Ad Acc. Circ:** 4,000.
**Desc:** About and for the amusement park and attractions industry. Places, attractions, and people in the industry are profiled.

US/1043-9064
**ATARIAN VIDEO GAME MAGAZINE.** [Atarian video game mag.]. **VFOAT** Atarian. Vol. 1, No. 1 (May/June 1989)-. Periodical. English. bm. $12.00 US; $17.00 Canada. Atarian, 7 Hilltop Road, Mendham NJ 07945. **DD** 794.

AT
**AUSTRALIAN GAMESTAR.** (19??)-. Periodical. English. mo. 45.00Aus$ Australia; 82.60Aus$ New Zealand; 96.00Aus$ other. Australian Consolidated Press Ltd, GPO Box 5252, Sydney New South Wales 2001 Australia. **Tel** 011 61 2 2600000.

AT
**AUSTRALIAN MAD MAGAZINE.** English. Eight times a year. $24.00. Horwitz Grahame Pty Ltd, 506 Miller Street, Cammeray New South Wales, 2062 Australia. **Tel** 011 61 2 9296144, FAX 011 61 2 9571814.

US/0888-1081
**AVALON HILL GENERAL.** **VFOAT** General, Avalon Hill. Vol. 1 (1964)-. Periodical. English. Six times a year (Jan., Mar., May, July, Sept., Nov.). $18.00 (one year); $29.00 (two years). Avalon Hill Game Company, 4517 Harford Road, Baltimore MD 21214. **Tel** (410)254-9200, FAX (410)254-0991. **ED** Don Hawthorne. **DD** 794. **Bk Rev**, (Qty: 6). **Circ:** 25,000.
**Desc:** The authoritative voice in the studies & tactics of historical games.

US/0274-5240
**AVENGERS, THE.** [Avengers]. **Added/Corp** Marvel Comics Group. **VFOAT** Mighty Avengers. No. 1 (Sept. 1963)-. Periodical. English. mo. $15.00 (12 issues). Marvel Entertainment Group Inc., 387 Park Avenue South, New York NY 10016. **Tel** (212)576-8595, FAX (212) 576-9289. **ED** Jim Shooter. **DD** 741. **Ad Acc. Circ:** 245,000.
**Desc:** The adventures of one of the world's foremost teams of superhuman crimefighters banded together to battle menaces too big for anyone else to handle.

US/1044-8195
**AVENGERS WEST COAST.** **Added/Corp** Marvel Comics Group. (198?)-. Periodical. English. Twelve times a year. $18.00. Marvel Entertainment Group Inc., 387 Park Avenue South, New York NY 10016. **Tel** (212)576-8595, FAX (212) 576-9289. **DD** 741. ***Continues*** *West Coast Avengers, 0887-9737.*

●US/1060-474X
**B.B. DUCKWOOD'S WORD SEARCH IN RUSSIAN.** [B.B. Duckwood's word search Russ.]. **VFOAT** Word Search in Russian; Word Search; B.B. Duckwood's Word Search; B.B. Duckwood's Word Search Po-Russkii. (Winter 1991/1992)-. English. $7.95 (single issue). Tangent Graphics, 9609 49th Avenue, College Park MD 20740-1617. **DD** 793.

CN/0707-9672
**BALOUNE.** No. 1- Feb. 1977-. Periodical. French. mo. $1.00 per no. Editions Baloune Enrg, #161 East Ontario, Montreal Quebec H2X 1H5 Canada. **DD** 741.5/9714.

US/0005-4968
**BANDWAGON (COLUMBUS, OHIO : 1957).** (BANDWAGON.). [Bandwagon]. **Added/Corp** Circus Historical Society. Vol. 1 (1957)-. Periodical. English. bm (Jan., Mar., May, July, Sept., Nov.). $19.00 US; $24.00 other. Circus Historical Society, 2515 Dorset Road, Columbus OH 43221. **Tel** (614)294-5361, FAX (614)294-1633. **ED** Fred D. Pfening Jr. **Bk Rev. Ad Acc. Circ:** 1,500 (ctrl).
**Desc:** Bandwagon, the journal of the Circus Historical Society, records in print the written and illustrated history of the circus in America.

US/1055-940X
**BARBIE FASHION.** [Barbie fash.]. Vol. 1, No. 1 (Jan. 1991)-. English. ir. $15.00 (12 issues). Marvel Entertainment Group Inc., 387 Park Avenue South, New York NY 10016. **Tel** (212)576-8595, FAX (212) 576-9289. **DD** 741.

US/1055-601X
**BARBIE (NEW YORK, N.Y. 1990).** (BARBIE.). [Barbie]. No. 1 (Jan. 1991)-. Monographic series. English. mo. $15.00 (12 issues). Marvel Entertainment Group Inc., 387 Park Avenue South, New York NY 10016. **Tel** (212)576-8595, FAX (212) 576-9289. **DD** 741.

PL/0866-9902
**BAZAR KATOWICE.** (BAZAR.). [Bazar Katow.]. (1989)-. Periodical. Polish. qt. z3.00 Europe. **(Subscription address:** ARS Polona, PO Box 1001, 00068 Warsaw Poland.**)** **UDC** 793.7.

US/1054-3422
**BEST OF TV GUIDE CROSSWORDS, THE.** (1991)-. Periodical. English. bm. $10.95. Murdoch Magazines, 200 Madison Avenue, 8th Floor, New York NY 10016. **Tel** (212)447-4700, (212)447-4732. **DD** 793.

US/0006-0267
**BETTY AND ME.** ***Title Change.*** [Betty me]. **VFOAT** Betty & Me. No. 1 (Aug. 1965)-(19??). Periodical. English. bm. Betty & Me, c/o Archie Enterprises Inc, 325 Fayette Avenue, Mamaroneck NY 10543. **Tel** (914)381-5155, telex (ITT) 949-9036. **ED** Victor Gorelick and Richard H Goldwater. **DD** 741. **Ad Acc.** ctrl circ. ***Continued by*** *Betty, 1064-9395.*
**Desc:** Comic stories and games.

US/0895-4194
**BETTY AND VERONICA.** [Betty Veronica]. **VFOAT** Betty & Veronica. No. 1 (June 1987)-. Periodical. English. Twelve times a year. $16.00. Archie Comic Publications, 325 Fayette Avenue, Mamaroneck NY 10543. **Tel** (914)381-5155. **DD** 741. ***Continues*** *Archie's Girls Betty and Veronica, 0735-6463.*

US/0886-134X
**BETTY AND VERONICA COMICS DIGEST MAGAZINE.** ***Title Change.*** **VFOAT** Betty and Veronica; Betty & Veronica Comics Digest Magazine. No. 5 (198?)-(19??). Periodical. English. bm. Archie Comic Publications, 325 Fayette Avenue, Mamaroneck NY 10543. **Tel** (914)381-5155. **ED** Victor Gorelick, Richard H Goldwater. **Ad Acc.** ctrl circ. ***Continues*** *Betty and Veronica Digest Magazine.* ***Continued by*** *Betty and Veronica Digest Magazine, 1059-1915.*
**Desc:** Comic stories and games.

●US/1064-9395
**BETTY (MAMARONECK, N.Y.).** (BETTY.). [Betty]. No. 1 (Sept. 1992)-. Periodical. English. Eight times a year. $10.00. Archie Comic Publications, 325 Fayette Avenue, Mamaroneck NY 10543. **Tel** (914)381-5155. **DD** 741. ***Continues*** *Betty and Me, 0006-0267.*

US/0740-3321
**BIG CROSSWORDS.** **VFOAT** Big Cross Words. (1983)-. English. bm (Feb., Apr., June, Aug., Oct., Dec.). $8.00 (one year), $15.25 (two year). Harle Publications, PO Box 207, Ft. Washington PA 19034. **Tel** (215)643-6385.

US/1061-2351
**BILL & TED'S EXCELLENT COMIC BOOK.** [Bill Ted's excell. comic book]. **VFOAT** Bill and Ted's Excellent Comic Book. No. 1 (Dec. 1991)-. Periodical. English. mo. $12.00. Marvel Entertainment Group Inc., 387 Park Avenue South, New York NY 10016. **Tel** (212)576-8595, FAX (212) 576-9289. **DD** 741.

●US
**BILLIARD INDUSTRY SOURCE BOOK, THE.** (1992/1993 Ed.)-. English. Que House, PO Box 2009, Manteca CA 95336. **LC** IN PROCESS.

US/0164-761X
**BILLIARDS DIGEST.** Vol. 1 (Sept./Oct. 1978)-. Periodical. English. bm. $15.00 US; $31.00 Canada & Mexico; $37.00 other. Billiards Digest, 200 South Michigan, Suite 1430, Chicago IL 60604. **Tel** (312)341-1110. **ED** Michael E. Panozzo. **Bk Rev. Ad Acc. Circ:** 9,000.
**Desc:** Focuses on the billiard industry and the professional tour.

US/1053-3087
**BLITZ CHESS.** [Blitz chess]. **Added/Corp** World Blitz Chess Association. Vol. 1, No. 1 (May-June, 1988)-. Periodical. English. qt. $12.00 US; $13.00 Canada and Mexico; $16.00 other. World Blitz Chess Association, 8 Parnassus Road, Berkeley CA 94708. **Tel** (510)549-1169. **ED** Walter and Raquel Browne. **DD** 794.

**Ad Acc. Circ:** 3,000.
**Desc:** The voice of the WBCA which promotes Blitz Chess worldwide.

US/0194-3111
**BLUE RIBBON FILL-IT-INS.** **VFOAT** Fill-It-Ins. Periodical. English. mo. $12.00. Official Publications Inc., PO Box 937, Fort Washington PA 19034. **Tel** (215)628-0924. **Ad Acc.**

US/0194-312X
**BLUE RIBBON WORD-FINDS.** **VFOAT** Word-Finds. **VAT** Blue Ribbon Word Finds. (19??)-. Periodical. English. mo. $12.30. Official Publications Inc., PO Box 937, Fort Washington PA 19034. **Tel** (215)628-0924. **Bk Rev. Ad Acc.**

US/0006-8446
**BOWLING PROPRIETOR.** [Bowl. propr.]. Periodical. English. mo. $30.00. Bowling Proprietors' Association of America, 615 Six Flags Drive, Arlington TX 76011. **Tel** (817)649-5105, FAX (817)633-2940. **(Subscription address:** PO Box 5802, Arlington, TX 76005**) ED** Steve Welch. **DD** 794. **Circ:** 5,000. available on microfilm from University Microfilms International (UMI).
**Desc:** Provides information to help bowling centers operate more efficiently and profitably.
**Ind/Abst** SportSearch (May 1987-).

UK
**BRIDGE, THE.** (1946)-. Periodical. English. mo. £35.00. Pergamon Bridge, Railway Roadsutton Coldfield, West Midlands B73 6AZ England. **Tel** 011 44 21 354 2536. **(Subscription address:** US/ 395 Saw Mill River Road, Elmsford, NY 10523; Can/ 150 Consumers Road/Suite 104, Willowdale Ontario M2J 1P9; Aus-NZ/ POB 544, Potts Point NSW 2011**) ED** Alan Hiron. **Bk Rev. Ad Acc. Circ:** 7,000.
**Desc:** For over 50 years the leading journal on bridge. Sells to over 85 countries. News, stories, letters, theory, bookshop, all regularly featured.

NE
**BRIDGE.** (19??)-. Dutch. ir (11 issues). Nederlandse Bridge Bond, Emmapark 9 2595 ES, The Hague Netherlands.

US/1043-6383
**BRIDGE TODAY!.** [Bridge today]. (1988)-. Periodical. English. Six times a year. $21.00 US; $29.00 other. Granovetter Books, 3838 Catalina Street, Los Alamitos CA 90720. **Tel** (518)899-6670, (800)872-2081, FAX (518)899-7254. **ED** Pamela Granovetter and Matthew Granovetter. **DD** 795. Index available. **Bk Rev. Ad Acc. Circ:** 6,000.

US/0006-9876
**BRIDGE WORLD, THE.** Began publication (1929)-. Periodical. English. mo. $38.00 (one year), $71.00 (two years). Bridge World, 39 West 94th Street, New York NY 10025. **Tel** (212)866-5860. **ED** Ed Gar Kaplan and Jeff Rubens. **Bk Rev. Ad Acc. Circ:** 95,000.
**Desc:** Covers bridge for serious players and fans.

FR
**BRIDGEUR.** **See** Recreation, Leisure-Sports.

CN/0383-8498
**BRISEBOIS ET COMPAGNIE.** (1977)-. Periodical. French. ir. 50.00Can$. Les Editions Heritage Inc., 300 Avenue Arran, St. Lambert Quebec J4R 1K5 Canada. **Tel** (514)875-0327, (514)672-6710. **DD** 741.5/9714.

UK/0007-0440
**BRITISH CHESS MAGAZINE, THE.** [Br. chess mag.]. Vol. 1 (1881)-. Periodical. English. Twelve times a year. £24.00 UK; £26.00 Europe; £29.00 others. British Chess Magazine Ltd., The Chess Shop, 69 Masbro Road, Kensington W14 OLS London. **Tel** 011 44 71 6032877, FAX 011 44 71 3711477. **ED** B. Cafferty. **LC** GV1313; .B7. **DD** 794. Index available. **Bk Rev. Ad Acc. Circ:** 4,000.
**Desc:** Chess news, games, and puzzles from the whole world.

CN/0317-0187
**BROKEN CUE NEWS, THE.** Began with Jan. 1974 issue. Periodical. English. bm. $3.00. Editor Broken Cue News, 16 Kenora Street, Ottawa Ontario K1Y 3K8 Canada. **DD** 794.7/2/05.

●US/1068-6800
**BUCK NAKED CRIME FIGHTER.** (1993)-. Periodical. English. bm. $14.00 (four issues). Heroic Publishing Inc, 6433 California Avenue, Long Beach CA 90895.

US/1071-3131
**BULLETIN - AMERICAN CONTRACT BRIDGE LEAGUE (1993), THE.** (THE BULLETIN.). [Bull. - Am. Contract Bridge Leag.]. **Added/Corp** American Contract Bridge League. (19??)-. Periodical. English. mo. American Contract Bridge League, 2990 Airways Boulevard, Memphis TN 38116. **Tel** (901)332-5586. **DD** 795. ***Continues*** *Contract Bridge Bulletin, 0010-7840.*

CN/0381-0003
**BULLETIN - SOCIETE DES JEUX DU QUEBEC.** (LE BULLETIN - SOCIETE DES JEUX DU QUEBEC.). **Main/Corp** Societe des Jeux du Quebec. (1976)-. Bulletin. French. bm. Free to clients of the Society. Societe des Jeux de Quebec Inc, Quebec H2E 2Z7 Canada. **DD** 796.06/2714.

CN/0707-9524
**CANADIAN BRIDGE DIGEST (1977).** (CANADIAN BRIDGE DIGEST.). **Added/Corp** Canadian Bridge Federation. Vol. 7, No. 3 (Sept. 1977)-. Periodical. English. Free to members. Canadian Bridge Federation, 2692 Bendale Place, North Vancouver British Columbia V7H 1G9 Canada. **DD** 795.4/15/06271. ***Continues*** *Bridge Digest, 0317-9281.*

CN
**CANADIAN CHESS CHAT.** **Added/Corp** Canadian Chess Federation. Vol. 4, No. 6 (1950)-. Periodical. English. Six times a year. 16.00Can$. Glenquaich Press Ltd., PO Box 553, Postal Station Q, Toronto Ontario M4T 2M5 Canada. **Tel** (416)616-0684. **ED** Frank J. Szarka. **Circ:** 5,000. ***Continues*** *Maritime Chess Chat.*
**Desc:** International chess, and chess problems.

CN/0383-0462
**CAPTAIN CANUCK.** No. 1- July 1975-. Periodical. English. $3.00. Comely Comix, 1854 Portage Avenue, Winnipeg Manitoba R3J 0G9. **DD** 741.5/9/71.

CN/0317-6134
**CAPTAIN GEORGE'S YELLOW JOURNAL.** V. 1- April 4, 1975-. English. Vast Whizzbang Organization, 594 Markham Street, Toronto Ontario M6G 2L8 Canada. **DD** 741.5.

US/1049-1473
**CAPTAIN N, THE GAME MASTER.** [Capt. N. game master]. **VFOAT** Captain N; Game Master. (1990)-. Periodical. English. mo. $1.95 (single issue). Voyager Communications Inc, 1560 Broadway/Suite 500, New York NY 10036. **DD** 741.

US/1060-8745
**CAPTAIN PLANET AND THE PLANETEERS.** [Capt. Planet Planeteers]. Vol. 1, No. 1 (Oct. 1991)-. Periodical. English. mo. $12.00 US; $17.00 Canada. Marvel Entertainment Group Inc., 387 Park Avenue South, New York NY 10016. **Tel** (212)576-8595, FAX (212) 576-9289. **DD** 741.

US/0889-9797
**CASINO CHRONICLE.** **See** Hotels/Motels.

US/8755-6103
**CASINO DIGEST.** [Casino dig.]. Vol. 101 (Nov. 1984)-. Periodical. English. mo. $36.00 US; $46.00 other. Landmark Publications, 1901-G Ashwood Ct., Suite 123, Greensboro NC 27408. **DD** 338.

US
**CASINO EXPLORER.** English. mo. $22.95 (one year), $39.95 (two year). Casino Explorer, PO Box 1498, Ridgland MS 39158. **Tel** (601)853-1989, FAX (601)856-0926. **ED** John McCommon. Index available. cum. index. **Bk Rev. Ad Acc. Circ:** 60,000.

US/1040-9920
**CASINOS : THE INTERNATIONAL CASINO GUIDE.** English. an. $16.95 US; $26.95 other. Bain Dror International Travel Inc, PO Box 7708, Flushing NY 11352. **Tel** (718)445-2471, FAX (718)939-8647, telex 6719473 BDIT UW. **ED** Eli Dror and Joseph H Bain. **LC** HV6711; .C37. **DD** 795/.025. Index available. cum. index. **Bk Rev. Ad Acc. Circ:** 50,000 (ctrl).
**Desc:** A reference guide to the world's casinos. Designed for individuals or travel agents that wish to include casino gaming as part of their holiday.

FR/0243-1327
**CASSUS BELLI.** **See** Recreation, Leisure-Sports.

CN/0712-7774
**CEREBUS.** [Cerebus]. **VAT** Cerebus the Aardvark (1979). No. 11 (Aug. 1979)-. Periodical. English. mo. $1.50 per no. Cerebus, PO Box 1674 Station C, Kitchener Ontario N2G 4R2 Canada. **Tel** FAX (519)576-0955. **DD** 741.5/971. **Pr Rev.** ctrl circ. ***Continues*** *Cerebus the Aardvark, 0229-0103.*

XR/0009-0743
**CESKOSLOVENSKY SACH.** ***Ceased.*** **Added/Corp** Ceskoslovensky Svaz Telesne Vychovy. (1906)-(1992). Periodical. Czech. Twelve times a year. **(Subscription address:** Artia Pegas Press Ltd., Palac Metro Narodni Trida 25, 11210 Prague 1 Czech Republic.**)** ***Continues*** *Sach.*

US/0894-5535
**CHALLENGE (BLOOMINGTON, ILL.).** (CHALLENGE.). [Challenge]. **Added/Corp** Game Designers' Workshop (Firm). Began with No. 25 (1986)-. Periodical. English. bm. $15.00. Game Designers Workshop, PO Box 1646, Bloomington IL 61701. **Tel** (309)452-3032, FAX (309)454-3127. **ED** Loren K. Wiseman and Timothy B. Brown. **LC** GV1469.T75; J68. **DD** 794.8/2. **Ad Acc. Circ:** 10,000. ***Continues*** *Journal of the Travellers' Aid Society, 0193-3124.*
**Desc:** Publishes additional material for a number of near future boardgames and role-playing games.

US/0892-4341
**CHAMPIONS.** [Champions]. Vol. 1, No. 1 (1986)-. Periodical. English. mo. $18.00. Heroic Publishing Inc, 6433 California Avenue, Long Beach CA 90895. **DD** 741.

UK/0009-3319
**CHESS.** Vol. 1, No. 1 (1935)-. Periodical. English. mo. £25.95 UK; £33.95 Europe; $55.00 US; £33.95 (surface mail), £49.95 (airmail) other. Chess & Bridge Ltd., 369 Euston Road, London NW1 3AR England. **Tel** 011 44 71 3882404, FAX 011 44 71 3882407. **ED** Jimmy Adams. Index available. cum. index. **Bk Rev. Ad Acc. Circ:** 12,000. ***Absorbed*** *Canadian Chessner; Social Chess Quarterly.*
**Desc:** Covers chess tournament news, prize competitions, articles and analysis by leading chess players, beginners and teaching features, etc.

UK
**CHESS COLLECTOR.** (1988)-. English. Twice a year. Chess Collector International, 35 Shepherds Hill, London N6 5QJ England. **Tel** FAX 071-831-9188. **ED** Michael Mark. **Bk Rev**, (Qty: 2-4). **Ad Acc, Adv Mgr:** Gareth Williams, **Tel** 071 262 6410.
**Desc:** Articles and other information on chess history, chess sets and books about the the different aspects of chess collecting.

US/0009-3327
**CHESS CORRESPONDENT, THE.** **Added/Corp** Correspondence Chess League of America. (19??)-. Periodical. English. Ten times a year (Mar./Apr. & July/Aug. issue combined). $13.00 (institutions); $8.00 (individuals). Correspondence Chess League of America, PO Box 3481, Barringtone IL 60011. **ED** Jerry Honn. **LC** GV1313; .C48. **DD** 794.105. Index available. **Bk Rev. Ad Acc. Circ:** 1,500.
**Desc:** Chess games, articles and columns by America's leading correspondence players.

US/0009-3335
**CHESS DIGEST MAGAZINE.** **VFOAT** Chess Digest. V. 1- Jan. 1968-. Periodical. English. ir. $13.50. Chess Digest Magazine, PO Box 21225, Dallas TX 75211. **LC** GV1313; .C483. **DD** 794.1/05.

US/0147-2569
**CHESS HORIZONS.** (19??)-. Periodical. English. bm. $6.00 (libraries & prison), $12.00 (others) US; $12.00 (libraries & prison), $18.00 (others) other. Massachusetts Chess Association, 64 Asbury Stret, Lexington MA 02173-6521. **Tel** (617)973-7345. **ED** Joseph W Sparks (editor's address: 40 Boston Street, Somerville MA 02143; editor's phone: (617)623-5619). **Bk Rev**, (Qty: 10). **Ad Acc, Adv Mgr:** same as editor. **Circ:** 1,800.
**Desc:** New England and international chess news and feature articles by top US and foreign players. Tournament reports and annotated games.

US/1044-8888
**CHESS IN INDIANA.** [Chess Ind.]. Vol. 1, No. 1 (Dec. 1988)-. Periodical. English. qt. $8.00. Indiana State Chess Association, 214 South 4th Street, Elkhart IN 46516. **Tel** (219)293-2241. **ED** Roger E Blaine. **DD** 794. **Bk Rev. Ad Acc. Circ:** 250. ***Continues*** *Hoosier Chess Journal.*
**Desc:** Chess clubs, tournaments, and champions in Indiana.

US/0197-260X
**CHESS LIFE (1980).** (CHESS LIFE.). [Chess life]. **Added/Corp** United States Chess Federation. **VFOAT** Chess Life & Review. Vol. 35 (Jan. 1980)-. Periodical. English. mo (12 issues). $33.00 US, $38.00 Canada and Mexico; $48.00 other. US Chess Federation, 186 Route 9 West, New Windsor NY 12553. **Tel** (914)562-8350. **ED** Larry Parr. **LC** GV1313; .C487. **DD** 794.1/05. Index available. **Bk Rev. Ad Acc. Circ:** 55,000. available on microfilm and microfiche from University Microfilms International (UMI). ***Continues*** *Chess Life & Review, 0009-3351.*
**Desc:** Contains instruction, games, puzzles, personality profiles, history, reviews, and news, both U.S. and international, for members of U.S. Chess Federation.

●UK/0964-6221
**CHESS (OXFORD).** (CHESS MONTHLY.). [Chess]. **VFOAT** Chess. Vol. 56, No. 10 (Jan. 1992)-. Periodical. English. mo. $52.95. Chess & Bridge Ltd., 369 Euston Road, London NW1 3AR England. **Tel** 011 44 71 3882404, FAX 011 44 71 3882407. Index available (published in April). ***Continues*** *Maxwell Macmillan Chess Monthly.*

US/0009-3971
**CHILD LIFE (INDIANAPOLIS, IND. 1922).** **See** Children and Youth Interests.

●UK
**CHILDREN'S ENVIRONMENTS.** **See** Education-Early Childhood and Primary Education.

Recreation, Leisure —Games and Amusements

US/0886-4284
**CHILDREN'S FUN PUZZLES (1985).** (CHILDREN'S FUN PUZZLES.). [Child. fun puzzles]. Vol. 25, No. 1 (Jan. 1986)-. Periodical. English. bm. $5.00 (US); $6.50 (other). Official Publications Inc, PO Box 750, Fort Washington PA 19034. **Tel** (215)643-6385. **DD** 793. ***Continues*** *Official's Fun Puzzles, 8755-9293.*

CN/0705-3819
**CHILDRENS' MYSTERY WORD.** V. 1- Dec. 1977-. Periodical. English. ir. $1.00 per no. Mystery Word Publications, 5 Highburn Crescent, Blackburn Hamlet Ontario K1B 3H7 Canada. **DD** 793.7/3/05.

US/0194-3146
**CIRCLE-A-WORD PUZZLES. VAT** Circle a Word Puzzles. (19??)-. Periodical. English. Twelve times a year. $12.50 (one year); $22.00 (two years). Editorial Services Inc., PO Box 687, Old Lyme CT 06371.

●AG
**CIRCO CRIOLLO : PUBLICACION DE LA ESCUELA DE CIRCO CRIOLLO DE BUENOS AIRES. See** The Arts-Performing Arts.

US/0199-5588
**CLASSIC CROSSWORD PUZZLES.** (19??)-. Periodical. English. mo. $15.97 (one year), $29.97 (two year). Penny Press Inc., 6 Prowitt Street, Norwalk CT 06855. **Tel** (203)866-6688.

●US/1078-389X
**COMBO (EVANSTON, ILL.).** (COMBO.). (1994)-. Periodical. English. mo. $39.95 US; $60.00 other. Century Publishing Company, 990 Grove Street, Evanston IL 60201-4370. **Tel** (708)491-6440, (800)321-3333, FAX (708)491-0459. **(Subscription address:** Kable Publishers Aide, 308 East Hitt Street, Subscription Department, Mt. Morris IL 61054-1473.**)** ***Absorbed*** *Comic Book Collector* ***and*** *Card Collectors Price Guide.*

US/1063-7982
**COMIC BOOK COLLECTOR. *Title Change.*** [Comic book collect.]. Vol. 1, No. 1 (Jan. 1993)-(Dec. 1994). Periodical. English. mo. Century Publishing Company, 990 Grove Street, Evanston IL 60201-4370. **Tel** (708)491-6440, (800)321-3333, FAX (708)491-0459. **(Subscription address:** Kable Publishers Aide, 308 East Hitt Street, Subscription Department, Mt. Morris IL 61054-1473.**) DD** 741. ***Merged into*** *Combo, 1078-389X.*

US
**COMIC PRESS NEWS.** English. mo. $15.00 US; $30.00 Canada; $35.00 other. Comic Press News, PO Box 434, North San Juan CA 95960. **Tel** (916)292-0117. **ED** James Israel. **Ad Acc. Circ:** 35,000 (ctrl).
**Desc:** Current editorial / political cartoons by nationally syndicated cartoonists; also local cartoons and other features.

US/1055-9639
**COMIC RELIEF.** [Comic relief]. **VFOAT** Comic Relief Magazine. Vol. 1, No. 1 (May 1989)-. Periodical. English. Fifteen times a year. $24.75 US; $35.00 other. Page One Publishers Bookworks, PO Box 6606, Eureka CA 95502. **Tel** (707)443-2820. **LC** PN6700; .C665. **DD** 741.

US/0745-4570
**COMICS BUYER'S GUIDE, THE.** No. 482 (Feb. 11, 1983)-. Periodical. English. wk. $34.95 US; $94.25 other. Krause Publications, 700 East State Street, Iola WI 54990-0001. **Tel** (715)445-2214, FAX (715)445-4087, telex 55 6461. **ED** Maggie Thompson. **Circ:** 19,070. ***Continues*** *Buyer's Guide for Comic Fandom.*
**Desc:** Contains news about comics and the people who write, draw and publish them from the past and present. Includes a marketplace for collectible and new comic books, columns, and a comics convention calendar.

US/1053-8704
**COMICS BUYER'S GUIDE PRICE GUIDE.** [Comics buyer's guide price guide]. **VFOAT** CBG Price Guide; Price Guide. (1990)-. Periodical. English. qt. $14.95 US; $22.25 other. Krause Publications, 700 East State Street, Iola WI 54990-0001. **Tel** (715)445-2214, FAX (715)445-4087, telex 55 6461. **LC** IN PROCESS. **DD** 741.

US/0199-7459
**COMICS FEATURE.** Vol. 1 (March 1980)-. Periodical. English. mo. New Media Publishing Company, 8399 Topanga Canyon Boulevard/210, Canoga Park CA 91304. **Tel** (818)340-4170.

US/1055-7164
**COMICS MANIFESTO, THE.** (1991)-. Periodical. English. qt. $6.00. Rogers Cadenhead, 1510-B McCormick, Denton TX 76205.

US/1053-0398
**COMICS SCENE.** [Comics scene]. (Aug. 1987)-. Periodical. English. Nine times a year. $29.99 US; $38.99 other. Starlog Press Inc., 475 Park Avenue South, New York NY 10016. **Tel** (212)689-2830, FAX (212)889-7933. **(Subscription address:** Kable Publishers Aide, 308 East Hitt Street, Subscription Department, Mt. Morris IL 61054-1473.**) LC** WMLC L 83/292. **DD** 741. ***Continues*** *Starlog Presents Comics Scene, 0732-5622.*

UK
**COMMODORE FORCE. *Ceased.* See** Computers-Computer Sales, Service and Supply.

IT
**COMPUTER & VIDEOGIOCHI.** (19??)-. Italian. mo (11 issues). L44000 Italy; L88000 other. Gruppo Editoriale Jackson Spa, Via Gorki 69, 20092 Cinisello Balsamo Italy. **Tel** 011 39 2 66034401. **ED** Fabio Rossi. Index available. **Ad Acc. Circ:** 40,000 (ctrl).
**Desc:** Magazine dedicated to videogames.

US/0748-4461
**COMPUTER GAMES. See** Computers-Computer Games.

US/0273-0782
**CONAN THE BARBARIAN. *Ceased.*** **Added/Corp** Marvel Comics Group. No. 1 (Oct. 1970)-Ceased with No. 275, Dec. (1993). Periodical. English. mo. Marvel Entertainment Group Inc., 387 Park Avenue South, New York NY 10016. **Tel** (212)576-8595, FAX (212) 576-9289. **ED** Jim Shooter. **Ad Acc. Circ:** 165,000.
**Desc:** The steel-thewed Cimmerian swashbuckles through sorcerors, mad kings, pirates and giant spiders on his quest for the Topaz Throne of Aquilonia.

US/0746-8237
**CONAN THE KING. *Ceased.*** (Jan. 1984)-?. Periodical. English. bm. Marvel Entertainment Group Inc., 387 Park Avenue South, New York NY 10016. **Tel** (212)576-8595, FAX (212) 576-9289. **ED** J Shooter. **Ad Acc. Circ:** 106,000. ***Continues*** *King Conan, 0279-0076.*

US/0195-9735
**CONTEST HOTLINE.** (19??)-. Periodical. English. Eleven times a year. $11.00 (U.S.), $13.50 (Canada). Contest Hotline, PO Box 4013, Burbank CA 91503-4013. **Tel** (714)970-0790.

US/0010-7840
**CONTRACT BRIDGE BULLETIN, THE. *Title Change.* Added/Corp** American Contract Bridge League. (19??)-(1993). Periodical. English. mo. American Contract Bridge League, 2990 Airways Boulevard, Memphis TN 38116. **Tel** (901)332-5586. ***Continues*** *American Contract Bridge League. Bulletin.* ***Continued by*** *Bulletin (American Contract Bridge League : 1993), 1071-3131.*

CN/0229-9852
**COOPERATIVE GAMES NEWSLETTER.** (COOPERATIVE GAMES NEWSLETTER / JEUX COOPERATIFS NEWSLETTER.). [Coop. games newsl.]. **Added/Corp** University of Ottawa. Community Affairs Service. **VFOAT** Jeux Cooperatifs Newsletter; Jeux Cooperatifs; Cooperative Games Bulletin; Bulletin de Jeux Cooperatifs. **VAT** Bulletin Jeux Cooperatifs; Jeux Cooperatifs. Bulletin. Vol. 1, No. 1 (May 1979)-. Newsletter. English (French). qt. $2.00. Cooperative Games Newsletter, 12 Bedale Drive, Ottawa Ontario K2H 5M1 Canada. **DD** 613.7/1/019.

UK
**CORRESPONDENCE CHESS. Added/Corp** British Correspondence Chess Association. Vol. 1 (1954)-. Periodical. English. qt. £6.60. British Correspondence Chess Association, Whitestones Maddox Lane, Leatherhead Surrey KT23 3BS England. **Tel** 011 44 372 454795. **ED** N.J. Blake. **Bk Rev. Ad Acc. Circ:** 800. ***Continues*** *B.C.C.A. Magazine.*
**Desc:** Correspondence chess games and related material.

US/1062-8371
**COURIER (BROCKTON, MASS.), THE.** (THE COURIER : AMERICA'S FOREMOST MINIATURE WARGAMING MAGAZINE.). [Courier]. Vol. 1, No. 1 (June-July 1979)-. Periodical. English. Four times a year. $15.00. Courier Publishing Co Inc, PO Box 1878, Brockton MA 02403. **Tel** (508)587-3176. **ED** Richard L. Bryant. **LC** U310; .C68. **DD** 793.9/2/05. **Bk Rev**, (Qty: 20+). **Ad Acc, Adv Mgr:** Tom Desmond. **Circ:** 15,000. ***Continues*** *Courier.*
**Desc:** Covers historical miniature wargaming.

●US/1065-2922
**CROSSWORD CHALLENGE.** [Crossword chall.]. (June 1992)-. Periodical. English. mo. $19.95. Pace Publications Inc., 1020 North Broadway, Suite 111, Milwaukee WI 53202. **Tel** (414)272-9977, FAX (414)297-9973. **DD** 793.

US/0194-3154
**CROSSWORD TREAT.** (19??)-. Periodical. English. mo. $12.30. Official Publications Inc, PO Box 750, Fort Washington PA 19034. **Tel** (215)643-6385. **Ad Acc.**
**Desc:** Crossword puzzles for crossword fans.

US/0194-3162
**CROSSWORD VARIETIES.** (19??)-. Periodical. English. bm (6 issues). $12.00 (one year), $17.50 (two years). Official Publications Inc., PO Box 937, Fort Washington PA 19034. **Tel** (215)628-0924. **Ad Acc.**
**Desc:** From easy to expert, these crosswords and word games appeal to every puzzle appetite.

US/0743-7005
**CROSSWORDS GALORE.** Began in 1984. Periodical. English. bm. $6.98. American Astrology, 475 Park Avenue South, New York NY 10016. **DD** 793.

US/1058-4781
**CROSSWORDS TO RELAX WITH.** [Crosswords relax]. **VFOAT** Crosswords to Relax With. Vol. 6, No. 5 (May 1991)-. Periodical. English. bm. Three PM Inc., 60 Goldstein Road, PO Box 1800, Prince Frederick MD 20678. **DD** 793. ***Continues*** *Crosswords, Crosswords, Crosswords to Relax With, 0892-0052.*

US/0732-5495
**CRYPTOGRAPHY MAGAZINE. See** Hobbies.

US/1048-972X
**DAILY CLOG, THE.** [Dly. clog]. (1984)-. Periodical. English. Twelve times a year. $8.00. Daily Clog, 95 East Wayne Avenue, #312, Silver Spring MD 20901-4245. **Tel** (301)495-0082. **ED** Julie Mangin. **DD** 793. **Bk Rev.** ctrl circ.

US/0279-8271
**DAREDEVIL.** (DAREDEVIL / MARVEL COMICS GROUP.). **Added/Corp** Marvel Comics Group. **VFOAT** Here Comes--Daredevil : The Man Without Fear. No. 1 (April 1964)-. Periodical. English. ir. $18.00. Marvel Entertainment Group Inc., 387 Park Avenue South, New York NY 10016. **Tel** (212)576-8595, FAX (212) 576-9289. **ED** Jim Shooter. **Ad Acc.**
**Desc:** Daredevil is blind. His sight has been replaced with an internal radar sense, his other senses have been heightened to an extreme degree, and this helps in his war against organized crime.

US/1056-3830
**DARKHAWK (NEW YORK, N.Y.).** (DARKHAWK.). [Darkhawk]. (Mar. 1991)-. Periodical. English. ir. $18.00. Marvel Entertainment Group Inc., 387 Park Avenue South, New York NY 10016. **Tel** (212)576-8595, FAX (212) 576-9289. **DD** 741.

US/1052-5548
**DAVID ANTHONY KRAFTS COMICS INTERVIEW.** [David Anthony Kraft's Comics interview]. **VFOAT** Comics Interview. (Jan. 1983)-. Periodical. English. mo. $36.00 (US); $51.00 (Canada). Fictioneer Books, 1 Screamer Mountain, Box 1241, Clayton GA 30525. **Tel** (404) 782-3318, FAX (706) 782-6625. **LC** IN PROCESS. **DD** 741.
**Desc:** Brings you interviews with the pros, by the pros and gives you an inside ear to what the comics industry is saying. It's a magazine for the creators and inside-the-industry sorts to just talk about comics.

AT/0311-0435
**DAVID LORD'S WORLD OF CRICKET. VFOAT** World of Cricket. Vol. 1 (1973)-. Periodical. English. mo. $1.00. David Lord Publishing Pty Ltd, Suite 5 & 6/340 Victoria Avenue, Chatswood New South Wales 2067 Australia. **LC** GV911; .D35. **DD** 796.358/05.

US/0747-590X
**DELL CHAMPION CROSSWORD PUZZLES. VFOAT** Champion Crossword Puzzles; Crossword Puzzles. (198?)-. Periodical. English. bm. $9.97 US; $12.97 other. Dell Publishing Company Inc., 1540 Broadway, 9th Floor, New York NY 10036-4021. **Tel** (212)782-8532, FAX (212)782-8338. **(Subscription address:** CDS Agency Hard Copy, PO Box 4966, Des Moines IA 50340.**)**

US/0747-5888
**DELL CHAMPION VARIETY PUZZLES. VFOAT** Champion Variety Puzzles; Variety Puzzles. (198?)-. Periodical. English. bm. $9.97 US; $12.97 other. Dell Publishing Company Inc., 1540 Broadway, 9th Floor, New York NY 10036-4021. **Tel** (212)782-8532, FAX (212)782-8338. **(Subscription address:** CDS Agency Hard Copy, PO Box 4966, Des Moines IA 50340.**)**

US/0274-6301
**DELL CROSSWORD PUZZLES. VFOAT** Crossword Puzzles. (19??)-. Periodical. English. mo. $15.97. Dell Publishing Company Inc., 1540 Broadway, 9th Floor, New York NY 10036-4021. **Tel** (212)782-8532, FAX (212)782-8338. **(Subscription address:** CDS Agency Hard Copy, PO Box 4966, Des Moines IA 50340.**) Ad Acc.**

US/0747-5896
**DELL CROSSWORD SPECIAL. VFOAT** Crossword Special. (19??)-. Periodical. English. bm (6 issues). $9.97 US; $12.97 other. Dell Publishing Company Inc., 1540 Broadway, 9th Floor, New York NY 10036-4021. **Tel** (212)782-8532, FAX (212)782-8338. **(Subscription address:** CDS Agency Hard Copy, PO Box 4966, Des Moines IA 50340.**)** ***Continues*** *Dell Crossword Annual.*

US/0747-5934
**DELL CROSSWORDS AND VARIETY PUZZLES.** [Dell crosswords var. puzzles]. **VFOAT** Crosswords and Variety Puzzles. (198?)-. Periodical.

English. bm. $7.97 US; $10.97 other. Dell Publishing Company Inc., 1540 Broadway, 9th Floor, New York NY 10036-4021. **Tel** (212)782-8532 FAX (212)782-8338. **(Subscription address:** CDS Agency Hard Copy, PO Box 4966, Des Moines IA 50340.**)** **DD** 793.

US/1059-3985
**DELL EASY FAST 'N' FUN CROSSWORDS.** [Dell easy fast fun crosswords]. **VFOAT** Dell Easy Fast and Fun Crosswords; Easy Fast 'n' Fun; Easy Fast 'n' Fun Crosswords. (Dec. 1991)-. Periodical. English. mo. $6.97 US; $9.97 other. Dell Publishing Company Inc., 1540 Broadway, 9th Floor, New York NY 10036-4021. **Tel** (212)732-8532, FAX (212)782-8338. **(Subscription address:** CDS Agency Hard Copy, PO Box 4966, Des Moines IA 50340.**)** **DD** 793.

US/1058-3343
**DELL LOGIC PUZZLES.** [Dell logic puzzles]. (198?)-. Periodical. English. bm. $12.97 US and US possessions; $15.97 other. Dell Publishing Company Inc., 1540 Broadway, 9th Floor, New York NY 10036-4021. **Tel** (212)782-8532, FAX (212)782-8338. **(Subscription address:** CDS Agency Hard Copy, PO Box 4966, Des Moines IA 50340.**)** **DD** 793.

US/1070-4078
**DELL MATH PUZZLES AND LOGIC PROBLEMS.** [Dell math puzzles logic probl.]. **VFOAT** Math Puzzles and Logic Problems. No. 1 (1989)-. English. $17.94 US; $20.94 other. Dell Publishing Company Inc., 1540 Broadway, 9th Floor, New York NY 10036-4021. **Tel** (212)782-8532, FAX (212)782-8338. **(Subscription address:** CDS Agency Hard Copy, PO Box 4966, Des Moines IA 50340.**)** **DD** 793.

US/0274-6239
**DELL OFFICIAL CROSSWORD PUZZLES.** [Dell off. crossword puzzles]. **VFOAT** Official Crossword Puzzles; Official (19??)-. English. Twelve times a year. $14.97 US and US possessions; $17.97 other. Dell Publishing Company Inc., 1540 Broadway, 9th Floor, New York NY 10036-4021. **Tel** (212)782-8532, FAX (212)782-8338. **(Subscription address:** CDS Agency Hard Copy, PO Box 4966, Des Moines IA 50340.**)** **DD** 793.

US/0747-5926
**DELL OFFICIAL WORD SEARCH PUZZLES.** **VFOAT** Official Word Search Puzzles; Official Word Search. (198?)-. Periodical. English. Eight times a year. $6.97 US; $9.97 Canada. Dell Publishing Company Inc., 1540 Broadway, 9th Floor, New York NY 10036-4021. **Tel** (212)782-8532, FAX (212)782-8338.

US/0274-6220
**DELL PENCIL PUZZLES & WORD GAMES.** **VFOAT** Pencil Puzzles & Word Games. **VAT** Dell Pencil Puzzles and Word Games. (19??)-. Periodical. English. mo. $15.97 US and Possessions; $18.97 other. Dell Publishing Company Inc., 1540 Broadway, 9th Floor, New York NY 10036-4021. **Tel** (212)782-8532, FAX (212)782-8338.

US/0274-6425
**DELL POCKET CROSSWORD PUZZLES.** **VFOAT** Pocket Crossword Puzzles. (19??)-. English. mo. $12.97. Dell Publishing Company Inc., 1540 Broadway, 9th Floor, New York NY 10036-4021. **Tel** (212)782-8532, FAX (212)782-8338. **(Subscription address:** CDS Agency Hard Copy, PO Box 4966, Des Moines IA 50340.**)**

US/0274-6190
**DELL WORD SEARCH PUZZLES.** **VFOAT** Word Search Puzzles. (19??)-. Periodical. English. Twelve times a year. $9.97 US; $12.97 Canada. Dell Publishing Company Inc., 1540 Broadway, 9th Floor, New York NY 10036-4021. **Tel** (212)782-8532, FAX (212)782-8338. **(Subscription address:** CDS Agency Hard Copy, PO Box 4966, Des Moines IA 50340.**)**

PL/0860-4436
**DETEKTYW.** [Detektyw]. (1987)-. Polish. mo. $27.00. **(Subscription address:** ARS Polona, PO Box 1001, 00068 Warsaw Poland.**)** **UDC** 884-91.

GW/0012-0669
**DEUTSCHE SCHACHZEITUNG / ORGAN FUR DAS GESAMMTE SCHACHLEBEN.** V. 27, No. 1 (Jan. 1872)-. Periodical. German. mo. Walter de Gruyter Inc., PO Box 303421, D 10728 Berlin Germany. **Tel** 011 49 30 260050, FAX 011 49 30 26005251. **(Subscription address:** US and Canada/ 200 Saw Mill River Road, Hawthorne, NY 10532**)** **LC** GV1313; .D5. ***Continues*** *Schachzeitung;* ***Absorbed*** *Deutsche Schachrundshau; Caissa.*

US/1059-5457
**DIGITAL GAMES REVIEW.** (DIGITAL GAMES REVIEW [COMPUTER FILE].). [Dig. games rev.]. (1990)-. English. mo. Free. Intuitive Systems, PO Box 4012, Menlo Park CA 94026. **DD** 794.
**Desc:** Mode of access: Email on Internet.

●XR
**DIKOBRAZ.** **Added/Corp** Eurostudio (Firm). (1993)-. Periodical. Czech. wk. **(Subscription address:** Artia Pegas Press Ltd., Palac Metro Narodni Trida 25, 11210 Prague 1 Czech Republic.**)** ***Continues*** *Novy Dikobraz.*

US/0093-8823
**DIRECT LEVIES ON GAMING IN NEVADA.** **See** Public Administration-Public Finance and Taxation.

US
**DIRECTORY OF NORTH AMERICAN FAIRS AND EXPOSITIONS.** Vol. 2, No. 1 (Spring 1977)-. Directory. English. an (Jan.). $45.00. Amusement Business, PO Box 24970, Nashville TN 37202. **Tel** (615)321-4250, FAX (615)327-1575. **ED** Leslie Shaver. **Ad Acc. Circ:** 1,000.
**Desc:** A comprehensive directory of every fair and exposition in the US and Canada which run three or more days. Contains data on managers, demographics, size of grounds and budgets, plus chronological cross reference of fairs.

US
**DIRECTORY OF NORTH AMERICAN FAIRS, FESTIVALS, AND EXPOSITIONS.** **VFOAT** North American Fairs, Festivals, and Expositions; Fairs, Festivals, and Expositions. 1986-. Directory. English. an (January). $45.00 US and Canada; $55.00 other. Amusement Business, PO Box 24970, Nashville TN 37202. **Tel** (615)321-4250, FAX (615)327-1575. **LC** T391; .D57. **Circ:** 1,500. ***Continues*** *Directory of North American Fairs & Expositions, 0361-4255.*
**Desc:** Comprehensive directory of over 6,000 fairs, festivals and expositions in the US and Canada which run three days or more. Contains data on managers, demographics, size of grounds and budgets plus chronological cross reference of event dates.

US
**DOOM PATROL, THE.** No. 1 (Oct. 1987)-. Periodical. English. mo. $23.40 US; $29.35 Canada; $35.40 other. DC Comics, 1325 Avenue of the Americas, Floor 27, New York NY 10019. **Tel** (212)636-5443. **(Subscription address:** DC Comics Subscriptions, PO Box 0528, Baldwin, NY 11510**)**

US/0279-6848
**DRAGON (LAKE GENEVA, WIS.).** ***Title Change.*** (DRAGON.). Vol. 1, No. 1 (June 1976)-(19??). Periodical. English. mo. Dragon Publishing, Division of TSR Hobbies Inc, PO Box 110, Lake Geneva WI 53147. **Tel** (414)248-3625. **ED** Roger E Moore. Index available. **Bk Rev. Ad Acc. Circ:** 85,000 (ctrl). ***Continued by*** *Dragon Magazine, 1062-2101.*
**Desc:** Articles on role-playing games, especially the Advanced Dungeons and Dragons game. Some fiction, and reviews of games and books.

US/1062-2098
**DRAGON MAGAZINE.** [Dragon mag.]. (19??)-. Periodical. English. mo. $30.00 (one year), $60.00 (two year), $90.00 (three year) US; $36.00 (one year), $72.00 (two year), $108.00 (three year), Canada; $50.00 (one year), $100.00 (three year) other. TSR Inc., PO Box 5695, Boston MA 02206. **Tel** (414)248-3625, FAX (414)248-0389. **DD** 051. Index available (free). ***Continues*** *Dragon (Lake Geneva, Wis.), 0279-6848.*

US/8750-3271
**DREADSTAR.** **Added/Corp** Marvel Comics Group. **VFOAT** Dread Star. (198?)-. Periodical. English. bm. $8.00 US; $10.00 Canada. Marvel Entertainment Group Inc., 387 Park Avenue South, New York NY 10016. **Tel** (212)576-8595, FAX (212) 576-9289.

US/0890-7102
**DUNGEON (LAKE GENEVA, WISC.).** (DUNGEON.). Issue No. 1 (1986)-. Periodical. English. bm. $18.00 (one year), $36.00 (two year), $54.00 (three year) US; $23.00 (one year), $46.00 (two year), $69.00 (three year), Canada; $35.00 (one year), $70.00 (two year) other. TSR Inc., PO Box 5695, Boston MA 02206. **Tel** (414)248-3625, FAX (414)248-0389. **ED** Roger E. Moore. **DD** 741. **Circ:** 8,500.
**Desc:** Each issue contains 3-5 short adventures designed for the "Dungeons and Dragons" and "Advanced Dungeons and Dragons" games.

US/1062-323X
**EASY & FUN WORD SEEK PUZZLES.** [Easy fun word seek puzzles]. **VFOAT** Penny Press Easy & Fun Word Seek Puzzles; Penny Press Means Puzzle Pleasure. (1991)-. Periodical. English. bm. $5.88 US; $7.88 Canada. Penny Press Inc., 6 Prowitt Street, Norwalk CT 06855. **Tel** (203)866-6688. **DD** 793.

CN/0825-0049
**ECHEC +.** [Echec +]. **VAT** Echec Plus. No. 34 (March/April 1984)-. Periodical. French. Six times a year. 34.00Can$ Canada; 37.00Can$ US; 39.00Can$ other. Quebec Chess Federation, PO Box 640, Station C, Montreal Quebec H2L 4L5 Canada. **Tel** (514)252-3034, FAX (514)251-8038. **DD** 794.1/05. Index available. **Bk Rev. Ad Acc, Adv Mgr:** Robert Finta, **Tel** same as publisher. **Circ:** 2,500. ***Continues*** *Petit Roque, 0227-8340.*
**Desc:** International and national tournament news, games, analysis, problems, and contests. Authoritative articles, and columns on middle, end games and chess computers.

RU
**EKSPRESS-SHAKHMATY : NAUCHNO-METODICHESKII ZHURNAL.** **Added/Corp** Shakhmatnaia Federatsiia SSSR. TSentralnyi Shakhmatnyi Klub SSSR. Assotsiatsiia Razvitiia Shakhmat. **VAT** Ekspress Shakhmaty. (1991)-. Periodical. Russian. sm. Fizkultura i Sport, Luzhneskaia Nab 8, 119270 Moscow Russia. **LC** GV1313; .S46. ***Continues*** *Shakhmatnyi Biulleten.*

●US/1063-8326
**ELECTRONIC GAMES.** (1992)-. Periodical. English. mo. $23.95. Sendai Publications, 1920 Highland Avenue, Suite 222, Lombard IL 60148. **Tel** (708)916-7222.

US/1058-918X
**ELECTRONIC GAMING MONTHLY.** [Electron. gaming mon.]. **VFOAT** Electronic Gaming; EGM. (1988)-. Periodical. English. mo. $23.95 US; $34.95 Canada. Sendai Publications, 1920 Highland Avenue, Suite 222, Lombard IL 60148. **Tel** (708)916-7222. **LC** WMLC 91/3434. **DD** 794.

US/1060-4677
**ELECTRONIC GAMING RETAIL NEWS.** [Electr. gaming retail news]. (June 1991)-. Periodical. English. mo. Sendai Publications, 1920 Highland Avenue, Suite 222, Lombard IL 60148. **Tel** (708)916-7222. **DD** 794.

US/0887-9745
**ELFQUEST.** [Elfquest]. **VFOAT** Elf Quest. Vol. 1 (Aug. 1985)-. Periodical. English. mo. $9.00 US; $11.00 Canada. Marvel Entertainment Group Inc., 387 Park Avenue South, New York NY 10016. **Tel** (212)576-8595, FAX (212) 576-9289.

US/1062-2950
**ENGLAND'S FINEST LOGIC PROBLEMS.** [Engl. finest log. probl.]. **VFOAT** Finest Logic Problems. No. 1 (July 1991)-. Periodical. English. Six times a year. $11.47. Penny Press Inc., 6 Prowitt Street, Norwalk CT 06855. **Tel** (203)866-6688. **DD** 793.

US/0279-246X
**EPIC ILLUSTRATED.** Vol. 1, No. 1 (Spring 1980)-. Periodical. English. bm. Marvel Entertainment Group Inc., 387 Park Avenue South, New York NY 10016. **Tel** (212)576-8595, FAX (212) 576-9289.

FR/0014-2794
**EUROPE ECHECS.** [Eur. Echecs]. (1959)-. Periodical. French. Eleven times a year (Except August). 305.00F France; 335.00F other. DIFFEC, 4 Rue Xavier Marmier, 25000 Besancon Cedex France. **Tel** 011 33 81 510126. **UDC** 794.1.

UK/0966-0259
**EUROSLOT OLDHAM.** (EUROSLOT). [EuroslotOldham]. (1990)-. Periodical. English (summaries and/or abstracts in French, German, Italian and Spanish). mo (12 issues). £68.00 UK; $135.00 Europe; $180 US and Canada; $210.00 Far East; $180.00 Middle East. Worlds Fair Ltd, PO Box 57 / Daltry Street, Oldham OL1 4BB England. **Tel** 011 44 61 624-3687, FAX 011 44 61 665-1260, 011 44 61 628-6921, telex 667352. **ED** Phil Klegg. **DD** 338.476887. **Bk Rev,** (Qty: 12/yr). **Ad Acc, Adv Mgr:** J. Lancaster. **Circ:** 13,500 (ctrl). available on microfiche.
**Desc:** International coin-operated games journal.

US/0745-7766
**EVERYTHING'S ARCHIE.** ***Ceased.*** [Everything's Archie]. **VFOAT** Everything is Archie. No. 1 (May 1969)-?. Periodical. English. bm. Archie Comic Publications, 325 Fayette Avenue, Mamaroneck NY 10543. **Tel** (914)381-5155. **ED** Victor Gorelick and Richard H Goldwater. **DD** 741. ctrl circ.
**Desc:** Contains comic stories games.

US/0888-0743
**EWOKS.** [Ewoks]. 1 (May 1985)-. Periodical. English. bm. $12.00 US; $14.00 other. Marvel Entertainment Group Inc., 387 Park Avenue South, New York NY 10016. **Tel** (212)576-8595, FAX (212) 576-9289. **ED** T De Falco and S Jacobson. **Ad Acc. Circ:** 80,000.

US/1045-1366
**EXCALIBUR.** [Excalibur]. (1989)-. Periodical. English. mo. Marvel Entertainment Group Inc., 387 Park Avenue South, New York NY 10016. **Tel** (212)576-8595, FAX (212) 576-9289. **DD** 741.

US/0889-0714
**FAIR TIMES.** ***Title Change.*** [Fair times]. **Added/Corp** Independent Dealers Association of America. (198?)-(19??). Periodical. English. mo. 21st Century Marketing, 930 Fox Pavilion, Jenkintown PA 19046. **Tel** (215)887-5700, FAX (215)887-7536. **ED** Marshall Davis. **DD** 338. **Ad Acc, Adv Mgr:** Jack McAndrew, **Tel** (215)887-5700. **Circ:** 72,000. ***Continued by*** *Special Events News, 1066-1417.*

**Desc:** Editorial focuses on information to the special events industry and fair, flea market and festival vendors and concessionaires.

US/1054-2167
**FAIRES & FESTIVALS.** ***Ceased.*** [Faires festiv.]. **Added/Corp** California Print Media Services. **VFOAT** Fairs & Festivals; Faires and Festivals; Faires n' Festivals. (July/Sept. 1990)-(1992). English. California Print Media Services, 10487 Folsom Boulevard, Suite E, Rancho Cordova CA 95670. **Tel** (916)722-5003. **DD** 791.

●US/1064-542X
**FAMILY ENTERTAINMENT CENTER.** (FAMILY ENTERTAINMENT CENTER : A PUBLICATION OF THE IAAPA.). [Fam. entertain. cent.]. **Added/Corp** International Association of Amusement Parks and Attractions. Vol. 1, No. 1 (Summer 1992)-. Periodical. English. qt. $20.00. International Association of Amusement Parks and Attractions, 1448 Duke Street, Alexandria VA 22314. **Tel** (703)836-4800, FAX (703)824-8365, telex 853485. **DD** 791. ***Continues*** *Minature Golf Magazine.*

US/0274-5291
**FANTASTIC FOUR.** **Added/Corp** Marvel Comics Group. No. 1 (Nov. 1961)-. Periodical. English. ir. $18.00. Marvel Entertainment Group Inc., 387 Park Avenue South, New York NY 10016. **Tel** (212)576-8595, FAX (212) 576-9289. **ED** Jim Shooter. **Ad Acc. Circ:** 253,000.
**Desc:** Super-heroic team defending the world against various perils. Team's made up of four members: mister fantastic, invisible woman, human torch, and she-hulk or the thing.

US
**FAT FREDDY'S COMICS & STORIES.** **VFOAT** Fat Freddy's Comics and Stories. (198?)-. Periodical. English. Rip Off Press Inc, PO Box 4686, Auburn CA 95604. **Tel** (916)885-8183, FAX (916)885-8219.

US/0195-0142
**FAVORITE CROSSWORD PUZZLES.** (19??)-. English. mo. $18.00. Quinn Publishing Company, PO Box 988, Department 2, Ft Washington PA 19034. **Tel** (215)628-0924.

US/0194-3170
**FEATURED FILL-IT-INS.** **VAT** Featured Fill It Ins. Periodical. English. mo. $12.00 one year, $22.00 two years. Official Publications Inc., PO Box 937, Fort Washington PA 19034. **Tel** (215)628-0924. **Ad Acc.**
**Desc:** Fun and easy crossword-style puzzles. The answers are given.

●US/1064-6302
**FEMME FATALE.** (1992)-. Periodical. English. qt. $8.00 US; $10.00 Canada. A & B Comics, 135 Lawrence Street, Brooklyn NY 11201.

US/0147-0051
**FIRE & MOVEMENT.** [Fire mov.]. **VAT** Fire and Movement. No. 1 (May 1976)-. Periodical. English. Seven times a year. $25.00 US; $32.00. Fire & Movement, PO Box 3104, Quartz Hill CA 93586. **Tel** (805)943-6832. **DD** 793. **Bk Rev**, (Qty: 2-4). **Ad Acc**, **Adv Mgr:** James Cason.
**Desc:** For review of historical simulations.

UK
**FIRST DROP / COASTER NEWS.** English. bm. $25.00. Coaster House, 16 Charles Street, Hillingdon, Middlesex UB10 0S4 England. **Tel** 44 81 8484073, FAX 44 81 5693478. **ED** Andrew Hine and Justin Garvanovic. **Bk Rev**, (Qty: unlimited). **Ad Acc**, **Adv Mgr:** A. Hine. **Circ:** 600 (ctrl).
**Desc:** Information news and features on amusement parks and roller coasters.

US/0826-256X
**FLAMING CARROT COMICS.** **VFOAT** Flaming Carrot. Vol. 1, No. 1 (May 1984)-. Periodical. English. bm. $12.00. Flaming Carrot Comics, PO Box 1674 Station C, Kitchener Ontario N2G 4RC Canada. **DD** 741.5/971.

US
**FLORIDA PAINTBALL PRESS.** **See** Recreation, Leisure-Sports.

CC
**FU-CHUN-CHIANG HUA PAO : FCJ.** **VFOAT** Fuchunjianghuabao. Periodical. Chinese. RMBY0.32. Science Press, 16 Donghuangchenggen North Street, Beijing 100707, People's Republic of China. **Tel** 011 86 1 4019821, 011 86 1 4010642, FAX 011 86 1 4012180, 011 86 1 4019810, telex 210147. **LC** PN6700; .F8. **DD** 741.5/951.

US/1059-3209
**FUN E LAFFS.** [Fun e laffs]. Series 9, Vol. 1 (1991)-. Periodical. English. bm. $24.00. Camille Publications, PO Box 30067, Arlington TX 76010. **DD** 741.

US/1059-6135
**FUN ZONE, THE.** ***Ceased.*** [Fun zone]. **VFOAT** Fun Zone Magazine. Vol. 1, No. 1 (Jan./Feb. 1992)-Ceased December (1992). Periodical. English. mo. Highlights for Children, PO Box 18275, 2300 West 5th Avenue, Columbus OH 43218-0275. **Tel** (614)486-0631, (800)255-9517. **DD** 051. ***Continues*** *Hidden Pictures Magazine, 1042-0622.*

PK
**FUNLINE.** Vol. 1, No. 1 (1991)-. English. mo. **LC** WMLC 91/1312.

US/0071-9943
**FUNNYWORLD.** [Funnyworld]. No. 1, (Oct. 1966)-. English. ir. $1.50. Funny World, PO Box 1633, New York NY 10001. **LC** PN6725; .F86. **DD** 741.5/973. available on microfilm and microfiche from University Microfilms International (UMI).
**Ind/Abst** Film Lit. Index (1977-1981).

US/0147-5606
**FUNPARKS DIRECTORY.** Directory. English. an (February). $48.00 US and Canada; $58.00 other. Amusement Business, PO Box 24970, Nashville TN 37202. **Tel** (615)321-4250, FAX (615)327-1575. **ED** Leslie Shaver and Rusty Terry. **LC** GV1851; .F85. **DD** 790/.068/02573. **Ad Acc. Circ:** 6,140 (ctrl).
**Desc:** Lists over 2,000 amusement and theme parks, kiddielands, water parks, tourist attractions, museums, zoos, and state and national parks.

US/0892-3752
**FUNWORLD.** (FUNWORLD / INTERNATIONAL ASSOCIATION OF AMUSEMENT PARKS AND ATTRACTIONS.). [Funworld]. **Added/Corp** International Association of Amusement Parks and Attractions. **VFOAT** Fun World. (19??)-. Periodical. English. mo (11 issues). $22.00 (members), $40.00 (nonmembers). International Association of Amusement Parks and Attractions, 1448 Duke Street, Alexandria VA 22314. **Tel** (703)836-4800, FAX (703)824-8365, telex 853485. **ED** Rick Henderson, Bill Phillips. Index available. cum. index. **Ad Acc. Circ:** 7,900 (ctrl).
**Desc:** Primary purpose is to keep amusement park executives abreast of the state of the industry. Status reports detail industry related subjects that may impact on park profitability.

US/0746-7397
**G.I. JOE.** ***Ceased.*** **VFOAT** GI Joe; G. I. Joe. (198?)-(Dec. 1994). Periodical. English. Twelve times a year. Marvel Entertainment Group Inc., 387 Park Avenue South, New York NY 10016. **Tel** (212)576-8595, FAX (212) 576-9289. **(Subscription address:** Marvel Direct Marketing Corporation, PO Box 1979, Danbury CT 06813.**)** **ED** J. Shooter. **Ad Acc. Circ:** 442,000.
**Desc:** An adventure for boys. Articles on sports heroes, action stories, real-life stories, poster, games, and activities.

US/0092-069X
**GAMBLERS WORLD.** Vol. 1 (Dec./Jan. 1974)-. Periodical. English. $15.00 (11 issues). Gamma III Ltd, 1414 Avenue Americas/2nd Floor, New York NY 10019. **LC** GV1301; .G3. **DD** 795/.01.

US/8755-0989
**GAME NEWS.** [Game news]. No. 1 (March 1985)-. Periodical. English. mo. $20.00. Game News, 700 Orange Street, Wilmington DE 19801. **DD** 794.

US/1041-0376
**GAME PLAYER'S NINTENDO BUYER'S GUIDE.** ***Title Change.*** [Game play. Nintendo buy. guide]. **VFOAT** Game Player's Nintendo Strategy Guide. (1988)-?. Periodical. English. bm. Signal Research Inc / North Carolina, PO Box 29364, 300 Westgate Drive, Greensboro NC 27407. **Tel** (919)299-9902, (201)703-9500, FAX (919)854-0963. **DD** 794. ***Continues*** *Game Player's Guide to Nintendo, 0899-9643.* ***Continued by*** *Game Player's Strategy Guide to Nintendo Games, 1054-884X.*

US/1059-2172
**GAME PLAYERS NINTENDO GUIDE.** ***Title Change.*** [Game Play. Nintendo guide]. Vol. 4, No. 12 (Dec. 1991)-(1993). Periodical. English. mo. Game Player's Nintendo Guide, PO Box 54163, Boulder CO 80322-4163. **LC** GV1469.3; .G39. **DD** 794.8/15365. ***Continues*** *Game Player's Strategy Guide to Nintendo Games, 1054-884X.* ***Merged with*** *Game Players Sega Guide, 1065-3376* ***to form*** *Game Players Nintendo-Sega, 1068-1809.*

US/1068-1809
**GAME PLAYERS NINTENDO-SEGA.** ***Title Change.*** [Game play. Nintendo-Sega]. **VFOAT** Game Players Nintendo Sega; Game Players. (June 1993)-(1993). Periodical. English. mo. GP Publications, 1350 Old Bayshore, Burlingame CA 94010. **Tel** (415)696-1688. **LC** GV1469.15; .G35. **DD** 794.8. ***Formed by the union of*** *Game Players Nintendo Guide, 1059-2172* ***and*** *Game Players Sega Guide, 1065-3376.* ***Continued by*** *Game Players Sega-Nintendo, 1074-2425.*

US/1046-0918
**GAME PLAYER'S PC BUYER'S GUIDE.** [Game play. PC buy. guide]. **VFOAT** PC Buyer's Guide. **VAT** Game Player's Personal Computer Buyer's Guide. Vol. 1, No. 1- (1989)-. Periodical. English. bm. $18.95 US; $30.95 Canada. Signal Research Inc / North Carolina, PO Box 29364, 300 Westgate Drive, Greensboro NC 27407. **Tel** (919)299-9902, (201)703-9500, FAX (919)854-0963. **LC** GV1469.15; .G36. **DD** 794.8/05.

US/1059-2180
**GAME PLAYERS PC ENTERTAINMENT.** ***Title Change.*** [Game Play. PC entertain.]. **VFOAT** Game Players Personal Computer Entertainment. **VAT** Game Players Personal Computer Entertainment. Vol. 5, No. 1 (Jan./Feb. 1992)-(19??). Periodical. English. Six times a year. GP Publications, 1350 Old Bayshore, Burlingame CA 94010. **Tel** (415)696-1688. **(Subscription address:** Neodata / Colorado, PO Box 2606, Boulder Boulder CO 80322.**)** **LC** GV1469.2; .G35. **DD** 794.8. ***Continues*** *Game Player's PC Strategy Guide, 1056-6414.* ***Continued by*** *PC Gamer.*

US/1065-3376
**GAME PLAYERS SEGA GUIDE.** ***Title Change.*** [Game play. Sega guide]. Vol. 3, No. 4 (Aug./Sept. 1992)-(1993). Periodical. English. bm. GP Publications, 1350 Old Bayshore, Burlingame CA 94010. **Tel** (415)696-1688. **LC** WMLC L 83/9156. **DD** 794. ***Continues*** *Game Player's Sega Genesis Strategy Guide, 1052-763X.* ***Merged with*** *Game Players Nintendo Guide, 1059-2172* ***to form*** *Game Players Nintendo-Sega, 1068-1809.*

●US/1074-2425
**GAME PLAYERS SEGA NINTENDO.** (1993)-. English. mo. $24.95. GP Publications, 1350 Old Bayshore, Burlingame CA 94010. **Tel** (415)696-1688. ***Continues*** *Game Players Nintendo Sega.*

US/1042-8658
**GAMEPRO (BELMONT, CALIF.).** (GAMEPRO.). [Gamepro]. **VFOAT** Gamepro Magazine. Premiere Issue (1989)-. Periodical. English. Twelve times a year. $24.95. Infotainment World Inc., 951 Mariners Island Boulevard, San Mateo CA 94404. **Tel** (415)349-4300. **(Subscription address:** Neodata / Colorado, PO Box 2606, Boulder Boulder CO 80322.**)** **ED** Leanne McDermotte. **DD** 794. **Ad Acc. Circ:** 300,000.
**Desc:** Features game reviews, interviews with players and developers, puzzles, strategies and tips, and more.

US/1049-3948
**GAMEROOM (NEW ALBANY, IND.).** (GAMEROOM.). [Gameroom]. **VFOAT** Gameroom Magazine. (19??)-. Periodical. English. Twelve times a year. $24.00 US; $28.00 Canada; $42.00 other. Gameroom Magazine, 1014 Mt. Tabor Road, New Albany IN 47150. **Tel** (812)945-7971, 945-6966, FAX (812)945-7971, 945-6966. **ED** Dave Cooper. **DD** 794. **Ad Acc.** ***Continues*** *Gameroom Magazine, 1043-8181.*

●US/1061-611X
**GAMER'S CONNECTION, THE.** [Gamer's connect.]. **VFOAT** TGC. (1992)-. Periodical. English. mo. $15.00. M.T.A. Graphics, PO Box 278331, Sacramento CA 95827. **DD** 794.

US/0199-9788
**GAMES (BASIC ED.).** (GAMES.). [Games]. **Added/Corp** Playboy Enterprises. (19??)-. Periodical. English. bm. $17.97. B and P Publishing Company Incorporated, 575 Boylston Street, Boston MA 02116. **Tel** (617)536-5536. **(Subscription address:** Kable Publishers Aide, 308 East Hitt Street, Subscription Department, Mt. Morris IL 61054-1473.**)** **LC** GV1199; .G35. **DD** 794/.05. ***Absorbed*** *Games (Deluxe ed.), 0896-3924* ***and*** *Games (Special Ed.), 0896-3916.*
**Ind/Abst** Mag. Artic. Summar. Select.

UK/0955-4424
**GAMES INTERNATIONAL.** (GAMES INTERNATIONAL : THE JOURNAL OF FUN AND GAMES.). [Games int.]. **VFOAT** G.I. No. 13 (Feb./March 1990)-. Periodical. English. mo. Games International, Lamerton House, 23A High Street, London W5 5DF England. **Tel** 011 44 579 6485. **DD** 796.

US/0897-196X
**GAMES JUNIOR.** ***Ceased.*** [Games jr.]. Vol. 1, No. 1 (1988)-?. Periodical. English. bm. Games Junior, 810 Seventh Avenue, New York NY 10019. **Tel** (212)246-4640. **ED** Wayne Schmittberger. **DD** 793. **Ad Acc. Circ:** 250,000.
**Desc:** Designed more to be played than read, and is aimed at 6-12 year olds and their parents. The aim is recreation rather than education, although it will stress that solving puzzles and other challenging games can often help improve skills in language and math, as well overall mental agility.

US
**GAMING REVENUE REPORT QUARTERLY.** **See** Public Administration-Public Finance and Taxation.

CN/0831-2591
**GARGOUILLE MAGAZINE.** ***Ceased.*** [Gargouille mag.]. **VFOAT** Gargouille. (1983)-(199?). Periodical. French. ir. Gargouille Magazine, PO Box 461 Jan Talon, Montreal Quebec H1S 2Z4 Canada. **Tel** (514)722-6861. **ED** Tristan Demers. **DD** J741.5/9714/05.

## Recreation, Leisure —Games and Amusements

CN/0828-4733
**GENERAL STAFF JOURNAL, THE.** [Gen Staff j.]. Aug. 1982-. Periodical. English. Association Miniere Du Canada, 20, Rue Toronto, Toronto Ontario M5C 2C2. **DD** 793/.9.

US/0016-6855
**GENII.** [Genii]. **Added/Corp** Pacific Coast Association of Magicians. (1936)-. Periodical. English. Twelve times a year. $30.00 (one year), $55.00 (two years). William Larson and Corporation, PO Box 36068, Los Angeles CA 90036. **Tel** (213)935-2848, FAX (213)933-4820. **ED** William Larsen Jr. **Bk Rev**. **Ad Acc**. **Circ**: 10,000. *Absorbed Conjurors' Magazine.*
**Desc:** The world leading independent magazine of magic published continuously since 1936. It is aimed at the professional and amateur magician and contains original tricks and effects, news, feature articles, reviews and advertising from all over the magic world.

●US/1065-8785
**GHOST RIDER & BLAZE : SPIRITS OF VENGEANCE.** [Ghost rider Blaze]. **VFOAT** Ghost Rider and Blaze. Vol. 1 No. 1 (Aug. 1992)-. Periodical. English. mo. Marvel Entertainment Group Inc., 387 Park Avenue South, New York NY 10016. **Tel** (212)576-8595, FAX (212) 576-9289. **DD** 741.

US
**GI JOE.** English. Twelve times a year. $18.00. Marvel Entertainment Group Inc., 387 Park Avenue South, New York NY 10016. **Tel** (212)576-8595, FAX (212) 576-9289.

JA/0286-0376
**GO WORLD.** [Go world]. No. 1 (May-June 1977)-. English. qt. $12.00. ISHI Press, CPO Box 2126, Tokyo Japan. **(Subscription address:** ISHI Press International, 1400 North Shoreline Boulevard, A-7, Mountain View CA 94043) **ED** John Power. **LC** GV1459; .G6. **DD** 794.2. **Bk Rev**. **Ad Acc**. ctrl circ.
**Desc:** Quarterly magazine on the Japanese game of GO news, tournament games and instructional articles.

US/8756-3908
**GOREN BRIDGE LETTER.** [Goren bridge lett.]. **Added/Corp** Goren International. Vol. 1, No. 1 (May 1984)-. Periodical. English. mo. $27.95. Tribune Media Services, 435 North Michigan Avenue, Chicago IL 60611. **Tel** (800)637-4082, FAX (312)222-2581. **DD** 795.

CN/0225-381X
**GRATIS (SCARBOROUGH, ONT.).** (GRATIS.). [Gratis]. 1st Issue (Mar. 1979)-. English. qt. $1.25. Gratis Publications, 36 Ivy Green Crescent, Scarborough Ontario M1G 2X Canada. **DD** 741./5/05.

US/1052-102X
**GUARDIANS OF THE GALAXY.** [Guard. galaxy]. Vol. 1 (June 1990)-. Periodical. English. Twelve times a year. $18.00. Marvel Entertainment Group Inc., 387 Park Avenue South, New York NY 10016. **Tel** (212)576-8595, FAX (212) 576-9289. **DD** 741.

US/0145-8159
**GUIDE TO AMUSEMENT RIDES.** English. Amusement Business, PO Box 24970, Nashville TN 37202. **Tel** (615)321-4250, FAX (615)327-1575. **LC** HD9999.A68; G84. **DD** 338.4/7/68.

US
**GUIDE TO SIMULATIONS/GAMES FOR EDUCATION AND TRAINING, THE.** See Education.

US/1060-6688
**HARPOON (BUFFALO, N.Y.).** **Title Change.** (HARPOON.). [Harpoon]. (1991)-(1992). Periodical. English. bw. American Media of New York, Inc., 1685 Elmwod Avenue, Suite 208, Buffalo NY 14207. **LC** E839.5; .H37. **Continued by** *American Harpoon*, 1064-7139.

US/0888-0751
**HEATHCLIFF.** Ceased. [Heathcliff]. Vol. 1 (April 1985)-Ceased (Nov. 1990). Periodical. English. bm. Marvel Entertainment Group Inc., 387 Park Avenue South, New York NY 10016. **Tel** (212)576-8595, FAX (212) 576-9289.

US/1054-8149
**HERALD TRIBUNE CROSSWORD PUZZLES ONLY.** **VFOAT** Crossword Puzzles Only; Herald Tribune. (19??)-. Periodical. English. Twelve times a year. $22.00. Kappa Publishers Group, 7002 West Butler Pike, Ambler PA 19002. **Tel** (215)643-5800. **Continues** *New York Herald Tribune Crossword Puzzles Only*, 0886-9936.

US/1054-8165
**HERALD TRIBUNE CROSSWORDS & OTHER WORD GAMES.** **VFOAT** Herald Tribune Crosswords and Other Word Games; Crosswords & Other Word Games; Crosswords and Other Word Games; Herald Tribune Crosswords. Periodical. English. bm. $8.97 US; $11.97 Canada. New York Herald Tribune, 575 Eighth Avenue, New York NY 10018. **Tel** (212)268-7270, FAX (212)268-7218. **Continues** *New York Herald Tribune Crossword & Other Word Games*, 8750-2240.

IT
**HUMOR GRAPHIC.** **Added/Corp** Museo Internazionale dell'Umorismo di Milano. (1960)-. Periodical. Italian. qt. Museo Internazionale dell'Umorismo, Via Arzaya 28, 20146 Milan Italy. **ED** Luciano Consigli. **LC** NC1528.H85; H85. **DD** 741.5/945.

US/0274-5275
**INCREDIBLE HULK, THE.** **Added/Corp** Marvel Comics Group. No. 102 (Apr. 1968)-. Periodical. English. ir. $18.00. Marvel Entertainment Group Inc., 387 Park Avenue South, New York NY 10016. **Tel** (212)576-8595, FAX (212) 576-9289. **ED** Jim Shooter. **Ad Acc**. **Circ**: 125,000. **Continues in part** *Tales to Astonish* (1959).
**Desc:** A mild-mannered scientist becomes a huge, raging monster when angered.

●US/1062-7405
**INSIDE COMICS (GLASSBORO, N.J.).** (INSIDE COMICS.). (1992)-. Periodical. English. mo. $36.00 (US), $46.00 (Can.). Double Barrel Productions, PO Box 67, Sewell NJ 08080.

US/1061-7183
**INTERACTION (COARSEGOLD, CALIF.).** (INTERACTION.). [InterAction]. **VFOAT** InterAction Magazine; Inter Action. (1991)-. Periodical. English. Four times a year. Free. Sierra On-Line, Inc., PO Box 485, Coarsegold CA 93614. **Tel** (800)743-7725. **DD** 794. **Continues** *Sierra/Dynamix Newsmagazine.*

US/0742-700X
**INTERNATIONAL PLAYERS CHESS NEWS, THE.** (THE INTERNATIONAL PLAYERS CHESS NEWS : OFFICIAL PUBLICATION OF THE COMMITTEE ON PUBLICATIONS OF F.I.D.). [Int. play. chess news]. **VFOAT** PCN; P.C.N. Began in 1983?. Periodical. English. wk. $68.00 US, $72.72 Canada and Mexico. Players Chess Association, Circulatio Department, PO Box 5721, Pasadena CA 91107. **DD** 794. **Continues** *Players Chess News*, 0744-4222.

US
**IRONMAN.** (19??)-. English. ir. $18.00. Marvel Entertainment Group Inc., 387 Park Avenue South, New York NY 10016. **Tel** (212)576-8595, FAX (212) 576-9289. **(Subscription address:** Marvel Direct Marketing Corporation, PO Box 1979, Danbury CT 06813.)

US/1054-2620
**IT'S A FANZINE.** [It's fanzine]. **VFOAT** IAF. (1989)-. Periodical. English. qt. $5.50. It's a Fanzine, 6223 Forest Avenue, Des Moines IA 50311. **DD** 741.

CN/0703-1785
**JACKPOT.** **VAT** Jackpot Magazine (Toronto): V. 1-June/July 1977-. Periodical. English. ir. $5.00. Jackpot Magazine, 41 Roehampton Avenue, Toronto Ontario M4P 1P9 Canada. **DD** 795/.0971.

CN/0227-4450
**JACQUES.** [Jacques]. Dec. 1979-. Periodical. English. $1.25 per no. Jacques, PO Box 8008, Ottawa Ontario K1G 3H6 Canada. **DD** 741.5/9713.

SP
**JAQUE.** (19??)-. Periodical. Spanish. Twenty-four times a year. Jaque, C General Pardinas, 48, 3o A, 28001 Madrid Spain. **Tel** 011 34 1 3090379, FAX 011 34 1 3092655. **Bk Rev**.

US/0888-532X
**JIM HENSON'S MUPPET BABIES.** Ceased. [Jim Henson's Muppet babies]. **Added/Corp** Marvel Comics Group. **VFOAT** Muppet Babies. Vol. 1 (May 1985)-?. Periodical. English. bm. Marvel Entertainment Group Inc., 387 Park Avenue South, New York NY 10016. **Tel** (212)576-8595, FAX (212) 576-9289.

US/0192-9917
**JOURNAL OF MAGIC HISTORY, THE.** [J. magic hist.]. V. 1- Mar. 1979-. Periodical. English. Three times a year. $11.00. The Journal of Magic History, PO Box 7149, Toledo OH 43615. **LC** GV1541; .J64. **DD** 793.8/05.
**Ind/Abst** Am. Hist. Life (1979-).

UK/0305-2133
**JOURNAL OF THE PLAYING-CARD SOCIETY.** [J. Play.-card Soc.]. (1972)-. Periodical. English. qt. £3.00 plus postage. The International Playing-Card Society, 188 Sheen Lane, East Sheen, London SW14 8LF England. **(Subscription address:** Adrienne Gurr, Shortacre, Peasmarsh, RYE, East Sussex TN31 6SX England) **Bk Rev**. **Ad Acc**. **Circ**: 500.
**Desc:** Journal of the International Playing-Card Society. Promotes the study and collection of playing-cards, society news, details of new and older packs, reviews of periodicals, books, exhibitions and catalogues.

●US/1063-729X
**JOURNEYS (BLOOMINGTON, ILL.).** (JOURNEYS : JOURNAL OF MULTIDIMENSIONAL ROLEPLAYING). [Journeys]. Issue no. (Sept. 1992)-. Periodical. English. mo. $20.00. Game Designers' Workshop, PO Box 1646, Bloomington IL 61702-1646. **DD** 793.

US
**JOYSTICK : HOW TO WIN AT VIDEO GAMES.** Ceased. **VFOAT** Joy Stik. Vol. 1, No. 1 (1982)-Vol. 2, No. 4 (1983). Periodical. English. bm. Publications International Ltd., 7373 North Cicero Avenue, Lincolnwood IL 60646. **Tel** (708)676-3470.

US/0022-5991
**JUGHEAD (MAMARONECK, ILL.).** **Title Change.** (JUGHEAD.). No. 127 (Dec. 1965)-(199?). Periodical. English. bm. Archie Comic Publications, 325 Fayette Avenue, Mamaroneck NY 10543. **Tel** (914)381-5155. **ED** Victor Gorelick and Richard H. Goldwater. **Ad Acc**. ctrl circ. **Continues** *Archie's Pal Jughead*. **Continued by** *Archie's Pal Jughead Comics*, 1069-0999.
**Desc:** Comic stories and games.

US/8750-0639
**JUGHEAD WITH ARCHIE.** **Title Change.** **VFOAT** Jughead with Archie Comics Digest Magazine. (1974)-(19??). Periodical. English. bm. Archie Comic Publications, 325 Fayette Avenue, Mamaroneck NY 10543. **Tel** (914)381-5155. **ED** Victor Gorelick and Richard H Goldwater. cum. index. **Ad Acc**. ctrl circ. **Continued by** *Jughead with Archie Digest Magazine*, 1059-1885.
**Desc:** Contains comic stories and games.

US/0896-3282
**JUSTICE LEAGUE INTERNATIONAL.** [Justice Leag. Int.]. **Added/Corp** DC Comics, Inc. (198?)-. Periodical. English. mo. $18.00 US; $24.30 Canada; $30.00 other. DC Comics, 1325 Avenue of the Americas, Floor 27, New York NY 10019. **Tel** (212)636-5443. **DD** 741. **Continues** *Justice League of America*.

US/0886-4748
**KATY KEENE.** Ceased. Periodical. English. bm. Archie Comic Publications, 325 Fayette Avenue, Mamaroneck NY 10543. **Tel** (914)381-5155. **ED** Victor Gorelick and Richard H Goldwater. **Ad Acc**. ctrl circ. **Continues** *Katy Keene Special*, 0886-1358.
**Desc:** Comic stories and games.

CN/0700-9054
**KEBEK KOMIK.** V. 1- June 1976-. Periodical. French. ir. 0.50Can$ per no. Editions La Feuille De Chou, CP 1845, Succursale Place, D'Armes Montreal Quebec H2Y 3L9 Canada. **DD** 741.5/9/714.

JA
**KIDO.** **Added/Corp** Nihon Kiin. (1976)-. Periodical. Japanese. mo. ¥480. Japan Go Association, 7-2 Gobancho, Chiyoda-ku Tokyo 102 Japan. **Tel** 03 2632464, FAX 03 2637875. **LC** GV1459; .K5.

US
**KIDS' PUZZLE EXPRESS.** See Children and Youth Interests.

CN/0711-7094
**KILLSHOT.** [Killshot]. (1980)-. Periodical. English. Five times a year. $16.95 US; $26.95 Canada; $41.95 South America; $56.95 Europe; $66.95 other. Ontario Handball Association, c/o Group Sport Office, 160 Vanderhoof Avenue, Toronto Ontario M4G 4B8. **ED** Marvin Quertermous. **DD** 796.31/09713. **Bk Rev**. **Ad Acc**. **Circ**: 15,000 (ctrl).

UK
**KIPPING CHESS CLUB MAGAZINE, THE.** 1945/46-. English. an. **Continues** *Kipping Chess Club Yearbook*.

US/8756-5404
**KREATIVE KIDS KOPY FUNLETTERS.** [Kreat. kids kopy funlett.]. **VFOAT** Creative Kids Copy Funletters. Vol. 1, No. 1 (Dec. 1984)-. Periodical. English. mo. $8.00. Kreative Kids Kopy Funletters, PO Box 6361, Arlington VA 22206-0361. **DD** 793.

PL/0137-7663
**KRZYZOWKA.** [Krzyzowka]. (1957)-. Periodical. Polish. mo. $18.00. **(Subscription address:** ARS Polona, PO Box 1001, 00068 Warsaw Poland.) **UDC** 793.7.
**Desc:** Features crosswords and other puzzles.

●US
**LAS VEGAS CASINO JOURNAL.** **VFOAT** Casino Journal; Nevada Casino Journal. Vol. 4, No. 1 (Feb. 1992)-. Periodical. English. mo (12 issues). $36.00. Las Vegas Casino Journal, 3100 West Sahara Avenue, Suite 207, Las Vegas NV 89102. **Tel** (705)253-6230, (800)394-2467, FAX (702)253-6804. **Continues** *Nevada Casino Journal*.

US/8750-0612
**LAUGH COMICS DIGEST MAGAZINE.** **Title Change.** [Laugh comics dig. mag.]. **VFOAT** Laugh. (19??)-(19??). Periodical. English. bm. Close-Up Inc, 325 Fayette Avenue, Mamaroneck NY 10543. **Tel** (914)381-5155, telex (ITT) 949-9036. **ED** Victor Gorelick

and Richard H Goldwater. **DD** 741. **Ad Acc.** ***Continued by*** *Laugh Digest Magazine, 1059-1907.*
**Desc:** Comic stories and games.

US/0023-8945
**LAUGH (MAMARONECK, N.Y.).** ***Ceased.*** (LAUGH.). No. 1 (June 1987)-(199?). Periodical. English. bm. Archie Comic Publications, 325 Fayette Avenue, Mamaroneck NY 10543. **Tel** (914)381-5155. **DD** 741. ***Continues*** *Laugh, 0023-8945.*

US/0731-1788
**LAUGHING MATTERS.** **Added/Corp** Humor Project. Vol. 1, No. 1 (1981)-. Periodical. English. Four times a year. $16.00 US and Canada; $18.30 other. The Humor Project, 110 Spring Street, Saratoga Springs NY 12866. **Tel** (518)587-8770, FAX (518)587-8771. **ED** Joel Goodman. **Circ:** 5,000.
**Desc:** Focuses on the positive power of humor, humorous ideas, practical tips on how to develop and apply humor personally and on-the-job to get more smileage out of life.

US
**LEGION OF SUPER-HEROES.** **VFOAT** Legion of Super Heroes. (1989)-. Periodical. English. mo. $23.40 US; $29.35 Canada; $35.40 other. DC Comics, 1325 Avenue of the Americas, Floor 27, New York NY 10019. **Tel** (212)636-5443. ***Continues*** *Tales of the Legion of Super-Heroes, 0883-7074.*

US/0024-3248
**LIFE WITH ARCHIE.** ***Ceased.*** [Life Archie]. No. 1 (Sept. 1958)-?. Periodical. English. bm. Archie Comic Publications, 325 Fayette Avenue, Mamaroneck NY 10543. **Tel** (914)381-5155. **ED** Victor Gorelick and Richard H Goldwater. **Ad Acc.** ctrl circ.
**Desc:** Comic stories and games.

US/0024-4023
**LINKING RING, THE.** Vol. 1 (1923)-. Periodical. English. mo. International Brotherhood of Magicians, c/o Howard Bamman, 42 Fiddlers Green Drive, Huntington NY 11743. **LC** GV1541; .L5. cum. index.

US/0024-5801
**LOG (ANNAPOLIS), THE.** (THE LOG.). **Added/Corp** United States. Naval Academy, Annapolis. Brigade of Midshipmen. LOG staff. **VFOAT** Lodski. (19??)-. Periodical. English. mo. $28.00. United States Naval Academy / The Log, c/o Captain R. C. Adams, Officer Representative, Annapolis MD 21402. **Tel** (301)267-2492. **Ad Acc. Circ:** 5,500.
**Desc:** Humor magazine for midshipmen. Includes humor, satire and entertainment. Most valuable advertising for career, starting assistance firms, e.g. banks, insurances, car dealers and credit cards.

US/8756-7369
**LONE STAR HUMOR DIGEST, THE.** (1985)-. Periodical. English. ir. $6.00 per issue. Lone Star Publications of Humor, PO Box 29000, Suite 103, San Antonio TX 78229. **ED** Lauren Barnett. **Bk Rev.** ***Continues*** *Lone Star (Houston, Tex. : 1983), 0735-1623.*
**Desc:** A humor 'book-by-subscription' for the comedy connoisseur and general reader. Each issue contains jokes, cartoons, essays, reviews, letters and stories.

CN/0828-7503
**LOTTERY & GAMING REVIEW.** Vol. 5, No. 1 (March 1984)-. Periodical. English. ir. $19.95. Rubin-Thomas, PO Box 7700, London Ontario N5Y 5A3 England. **DD** 795. ***Continues*** *Lottery News & Contest Review, 0828-749X.*

US/0277-5565
**LOTTERY PLAYER'S MAGAZINE.** [Lottery play. mag.]. Vol. 1, No. 1 (Aug. 1981)-. Periodical. English. Eleven times a year (July/Aug. issues combined). $24.00. Lottery Players, PO Box 5013, Cherry Hill NJ 08034. **Tel** (609)778-8900, (800)367-9681, FAX (609)273-6350. **ED** Samuel W. Valenza Jr. **DD** 795. **Ad Acc. Circ:** 180,000 (ctrl). ***Absorbed*** *National Lottery List.*
**Desc:** Winning numbers, news and features relating to state and foreign lotteries including Western and Eastern recreational gaming information.

US/0024-9319
**MAD (NEW YORK, N.Y.).** (MAD.). (Nov. 1958)-. Periodical. English. Eight times a year. $15.50 US; $18.22 Canada; $19.50 other. EC Publishing Inc, 485 Madison Avenue, New York NY 10022. **Tel** (212)752-7685. **ED** John Ficirra and Nick Meglin. **Circ:** 1,000,000. ***Continues*** *New Mad.*

PL/0867-0404
**MAGAZYN KRYMINALNY 997.** (1990)-. Periodical. Polish. Twenty-four times a year. $36.00. **(Subscription address:** ARS Polona, PO Box 1001, 00068 Warsaw Poland.**)** **UDC** 351.74.
**Desc:** Presents detective stories.

US/0736-704X
**MAGIC DIRECTORY, THE.** [Magic dir.]. Directory. English. an. Monson Productions, PO Box 5324, Madison WI 53705. **LC** GV1541; .M28135. **DD** 793.8/028.

US/1062-2845
**MAGIC (LAKEWOOD, CALIF.).** (MAGIC : AN INDEPENDENT MAGAZINE FOR MAGICIANS.). [Magic]. Vol. 1, No. 1 (Sept. 1991)-. Periodical. English. mo. $30.00. Stan Allen & Associates, 4067 Hardwick, Suite 322, Lakewood CA 90712. **DD** 793.

US/0097-5176
**MAGIC MAGAZINE (NEW YORK).** (THE MAGIC MAGAZINE.). Periodical. English. mo. $10.00. Magic Industries, 20 East 46th Street, New York NY 10017. **LC** GV1541; .M2814. **DD** 793.8.

CN/0829-3848
**MANIE DES JEUX, LA.** [Manie jeux.]. No. 1 (1984)-. Periodical. French. Six times a year. 21.50Can$. Super Magazine Inc, 8050 Boul Metropolitan Est, Montreal Quebec H1K 1A1 Canada. **DD** 793.73/05.

●US
**MANN-MALLIN FANTASY BASEBALL GUIDE, THE.** **See** Recreation, Leisure-Sports.

US/8750-4367
**MARVEL AGE.** ***Ceased.*** (1983)-(19??). Periodical. English. ir. Marvel Entertainment Group Inc., 387 Park Avenue South, New York NY 10016. **Tel** (212)576-8595, FAX (212) 576-9289. **(Subscription address:** Marvel Direct Marketing Corporation, PO Box 1979, Danbury CT 06813.**)** **Ad Acc. Circ:** 90,000.

US/1044-7180
**MARVEL COMICS PRESENTS.** [Marvel Comics presents]. (1989)-. Periodical. English. Twenty-six times a year. $18.00. Marvel Entertainment Group Inc., 387 Park Avenue South, New York NY 10016. **Tel** (212)576-8595, FAX (212) 576-9289. **DD** 741.

US/0746-7664
**MARVEL FANFARE (NEW YORK, N.Y.).** (MARVEL FANFARE / MARVEL COMICS GROUP.). [Marvel fanfare]. **Added/Corp** Marvel Comics Group. (198?)-. Periodical. English. Six times a year. $27.00. Marvel Entertainment Group Inc., 387 Park Avenue South, New York NY 10016. **Tel** (212)576-8595, FAX (212) 576-9289. **(Subscription address:** Marvel Direct Marketing Corporation, PO Box 1979, Danbury CT 06813.**)** **ED** J. Shooter. **DD** 741. **Ad Acc. Circ:** 73,500.

US
**MARVEL TALES (CHICAGO, ILL.).** (MARVEL TALES.). Vol. 1, No. 6 (Dec. 1939)-. Periodical. English. Twelve times a year. $15.00. Marvel Entertainment Group Inc., 387 Park Avenue South, New York NY 10016. **Tel** (212)576-8595, FAX (212) 576-9289. ***Continues*** *Marvel Science Stories.*

US/0748-1675
**MASS ENTERTAINMENT BUYERS GUIDE.** ***Title Change.*** (MASS ENTERTAINMENT BUYERS GUIDE / AMUSEMENTS BUSINESS PRESENTS.). [Mass entertain. buy. guide]. **VFOAT** Buyers Guide for the Mass Entertainment Industry. Consumer Publication. English. Amusement Business, PO Box 24970, Nashville TN 37202. **Tel** (615)321-4250, FAX (615)327-1575. **LC** GV1851.A3; B88. **DD** 338.7/61791/06802573. ***Continues*** *Buyers' Guide for the Mass Entertainment Industry, 0362-6180.* ***Continued by*** *Entertainment Facility Buyers Guide.*

US/0274-533X
**MIGHTY THOR, THE.** **Added/Corp** Marvel Comics Group. **VFOAT** Thor. No. 126 (Mar. 1966)-. Periodical. English. Twelve times a year. $15.00. Marvel Entertainment Group Inc., 387 Park Avenue South, New York NY 10016. **Tel** (212)576-8595, FAX (212) 576-9289. **DD** 741. ***Continues*** *Journey into Mystery.*

CN/0711-3307
**MINI-JEUX, LES.** [Mini-jeux]. No. 1-. Periodical. French. Three times a year. $2.50 per no. Les Mini-Jeux, CP 71, Succursale R, Montreal Quebec H2S 3K8. **DD** 793.73/05.

CN/0714-489X
**MINI RECREATION.** [Mini recreat.]. No. 1 (1981)-. Periodical. French. ir. $2.50 per no. Messageries Dynamiques Inc, 775 Boulevard Lebeau, Saint-Laurent Quebec H4N 1S5 Canada. **Tel** (800)463-4645, (514)332-0680. **DD** 793.73.

CN/0827-3812
**MISTER X.** Vol. 1, No. 1 (June 1984)-. Periodical. English. bm. Vortex Comics, 9th Floor/96 Spadina Avenue, Toronto Ontario M5V 2J6 Canada. **DD** 741.5/971.

US/0899-8116
**MONKEYSHINES ON YOU!.** (MONKEYSHINES ON YOU! : THE ORIGINAL MONKEYSHINES JOKE BOOK.). **Added/Corp** NC Learning Institute for Fitness & Education. **VFOAT** Original Monkeyshines Joke Book; Monkey Shines on You. (1988)-. English. an. $5.95. North Carolina Learning Institute for Fitness & Education, PO Box 10245, Greensboro NC 27404. **Tel** (919)292-6999. **DD** 810.

CN/0831-5213
**MONTREAL MAGAZINE.** [Montr. mag.]. Vol. 1 (Jan. 15/Feb. 28, 1986)-. Periodical. English. Ten times a year. 18.00Can$. Montreal Magazine, 4984 Place de la Savane, Montreal Quebec H4P 2MP Canada. **Tel** (514)933-2555, FAX (514)933-7327. **ED** Jim Cormier. **DD** 790/.0714/281. **Ad Acc. Circ:** 60,000. ***Continues*** *Montreal Calendar Magazine, 0315-0534.*
**Ind/Abst** Can. Index (?-?).

CN/0228-569X
**MOT A TROUVER MYSTERIEUX.** [Mot trouver mysterieux]. **VAT** Mot Mysterieux Eclair. Vol. 1, No. 2-. Periodical. French. bm. $6.00. Mot a Trouver Mysterieux Bert-Hold Inc, CP 1050 Succursale Anjou, Montreal Quebec H1K 4H2 Canada. **DD** 793.73/05. ***Continues*** *Mot Mystere, 0228-5681.*

CN/0228-5681
**MOT MYSTERE.** ***Title Change.*** [Mot mystere]. **VAT** Mot Mystere Eclair. Vol. 1, No 1. Periodical. French. Distributions Eclair, 8320 Place de Lorraine, Anjou Quebec H1J 1E6 Canada. **DD** 793.73/05. ***Continued by*** *Mot A Trouver Mysterieux, 0228-569X.*

CN/0228-6475
**MOTS A TROUVER POPULAIRES.** [Mots trouver pop.]. Vol. 1, No 1- . -. Periodical. French. qt. $4.00. Distribution Eclair, 8320 Place de Lorraine, Montreal Quebec H1J 1E6 Canada. **DD** 793.73/05.

CN/0823-7123
**MOTS A TROUVER RG.** [Mots trouver RG]. No 1 (1980)-. Periodical. French. qt. 11.00Can$ (two year) Canada; $14.00 (two year) US. Supermagazine, 8050 Metropolitan Boulevard East, Montreal Quebec H1K 1A1 Canada. **Tel** (514)353-7660. **ED** Guy Chabot. **DD** 793.73/05. **Ad Acc. Circ:** 12,000 (ctrl).
**Desc:** Crossword book.

CN/0826-4740
**MOTS CACHES J'AIME, LES.** [Mots caches aime]. 1-. Periodical. French. qt. 11.00Can$ (two year) Canada; 14.00Can$ (two year) US. Supermagazine, 8050 Metropolitan Boulevard East, Montreal Quebec H1K 1A1 Canada. **Tel** (514)353-7660. **ED** Daniele Moisan-Dubois. **DD** 793.73. **Ad Acc. Circ:** 12,000 (ctrl).

CN/0822-4145
**MOTS CACHES SUPERMAGAZINE.** [Mots caches supermag.]. Vol. 1, No 1-. Periodical. French. bm. 11.00Can$ (two year) Canada; $14.00 (two year) US. Supermagazine, 8050 Metropolitan Boulevard East, Montreal Quebec H1K 1A1 Canada. **Tel** (514)353-7660. **ED** 3534935350. **DD** 793.73. **Ad Acc. Circ:** 12,000 (ctrl).
**Desc:** Crosswords book.

CN/0384-8191
**MOTS CROISES ECLAIR (EDITION SEMESTRIELLE).** (MOTS CROISES ECLAIR.). V. 1- Jan. 1977-. Periodical. French. mo. $1.50 each number. Distributions Eclair, 8320 Place de Lorraine, Anjou Quebec H1J 1E6 Canada. **DD** 793.73/2/05.

CN/0822-8728
**MOTS CROISES FRANCAIS ANGLAIS.** [Mots croises fr. angl.]. V. 1, No. 1, (Fall '83)-. Periodical. English (French). qt. $1.50 each number. Mots Croises Francais Anglais, c/o Roland Dolce, 580 71th Street East, Charlesbourge Quebec G1H 1M1 Canada. **DD** 793.73/2/05.

CN/0712-5631
**MOTS CROISES POUR TOUT L'MONDE.** **VFOAT** Mots Croises Pour Tout le Monde. Vol. 1, No 1 (1980)-. Periodical. French. mo. Supermagazine, 8050 Metropolitan Boulevard East, Montreal Quebec H1K 1A1 Canada. **Tel** (514)353-7660. **DD** 793.73/2/05.

CN/0319-7115
**MOTS CROISES T V HEBDO.** **VFOAT** T V Hebdo. No 1 1974-. Periodical. French. $1.25 each number. Publications Eclair, 9393 Aveneu Edison, Montreal Quebec H1J 1T5 Canada. **DD** 793.73/2/05.

CN/0228-6483
**MOTS ENTRE-CROISES POPULAIRES.** [Mots entre-croises pop.]. Vol. 1, No 1- . -. Periodical. French. qt. $1.00 each number. Distributions Eclair, 8320 Place de Lorraine, Anjou Quebec H1J 1E6 Canada. **DD** 793.73/05.

UK
**MYRA.** (19??)-. Periodical. English.

CN
**NATIONAL NEWSLETTER.** Newsletter. English. Hang Gliding Association of Canada, c/o Aero Club of Canada, 209-485 Bank Street, Ottawa Ontario K2P 1Z2 Canada. **Tel** (604)533-4456.

US/0192-6837
**NATIONAL OBSERVER BOOK OF CROSSWORDS, THE.** (19??)-. Periodical. English. mo. $21.00. Hachette Magazines Inc., 1633 Broadway, New York NY 10019. **Tel** (212)767-6000. **(Subscription address:** Neodata / Colorado, PO Box

Recreation, Leisure —Games and Amusements

2606, Boulder Boulder CO 80322.) available on microfilm and microfiche from University Microfilms International (UMI).

US/0745-2276
**NATIONAL SHUFFLER.** Periodical. English. mo. $5.00. California Association of Residential Care Homes, 1600 Sacramento Inn Way Suite 110, Sacramento CA 95815-3458.

US/1047-529X
**NEVADA CASINO JOURNAL.** ***Title Change.*** [Nev. casino j.]. (1989-1992). Periodical. English. mo. Nevada Casino Journal, 953 East Sahara B-28/Suite 202, Las Vegas NV 89104. **DD** 795. ***Continued by*** *Las Vegas Casino Journal.*

US
**NEVADA GAMING ABSTRACT / STATE GAMING CONTROL BOARD.** **See** Public Administration.

CN/0382-7313
**NEW COMIC WORLD, THE.** No. 1- 1976-. Periodical. English. Vast Whizzbang Organization, 594 Markham Street, Toronto Ontario M6G 2L8 Canada. **DD** 741.5/971. **UDC** 741.5.

NE/0168-7697
**NEW IN CHESS YEARBOOK.** **VFOAT** New in Chess; New in Chess Jahrbuch; N C Yearbook. Vol. 1 (1984)-. Periodical. English (Multiple languages). Eight times a year. $70.00 one year; $133.00 two years. New in Chess, PO Box 2423, Bridgeport CT 06608. **Tel** (203)367-1555. **ED** Jan Tiararnn. **LC** GV1449.5; .N49. **DD** 794.1/22. cum. index. **Bk Rev.** **Ad Acc.** ctrl circ.
**Desc:** International tournaments and news on the players.

US
**NEW JERSEY TRACK.** **See** Health and Personal Fitness.

US/1053-7325
**NEW WARRIORS, THE.** [New warriors]. (1990)-. Periodical. English. ir. $18.00. Marvel Entertainment Group Inc., 387 Park Avenue South, New York NY 10016. **Tel** (212)576-8595, FAX (212) 576-9289. **DD** 741.

US/0886-9936
**NEW YORK HERALD TIMES CROSSWORD PUZZLES ONLY.** ***Title Change.*** **VFOAT** Crossword Puzzles Only. Periodical. English. bm (three special issues). New York Herald Tribune, 575 Eighth Avenue, New York NY 10018. **Tel** (212)268-7270, FAX (212)268-7218. **(Subscription address:** PO Box 187, Brewster NY 10509-0187**) ED** Ronni Berger. **UDC** 793.7. **Bk Rev.** **Ad Acc.** **Circ:** 300,000. ***Continues*** *New York Herald Tribune Crossword Puzzles. Pocket Size, 0195-2641.* ***Continued by*** *Herald Tribune Crossword Puzzles Only, 1054-8149.*
**Desc:** Crossword puzzles including special "Beat the Clock", on how to solve and construct puzzles.

US/0892-0168
**NEW YORK HERALD TRIBUNE LARGE PRINT CROSSWORDS.** ***Title Change.*** **VFOAT** Large Print Crosswords. (Mar. 1987)-?. Periodical. English. bm. New York Herald Tribune, 575 Eighth Avenue, New York NY 10018. **Tel** (212)268-7270, FAX (212)268-7218. **(Subscription address:** PO Box 187, Brewster, NY 10509-0187**) ED** Ashley Griffin. **UDC** 793.7. **Bk Rev.** **Ad Acc.** **Circ:** 100,000. ***Continued by*** *Herald Tribune Large Print Crosswords, 1054-8157.*
**Desc:** Puzzles and related pastimes, including features on celebrities who enjoy puzzles, reviews of games and books about them. Also, tips on how to solve and construct puzzles.

US/0364-3700
**NEW YORK TIMES CROSSWORD PUZZLES, THE.** **VFOAT** Crossword Puzzles. V. 1- 1976-. English. Quadrangle/New York Times Book Company, Times Square, New York NY 10036. **LC** GV1507.C7; N685. **DD** 793.7/32. **UDC** 793.7.

US/0149-9394
**NEWS RELEASE FROM THE CHESS PRESS SYNDICATE.** **Main/Corp** Chess Press Syndicate. V. 1- (Issue 1- ); Oct. 20, 1977-. Periodical. English. KV Press, PO Box 2204, Chapel Hill NC 27514. **UDC** 794.1.

US/1060-3514
**NFL SUPERPRO.** **VFOAT** NFL Super Pro; SuperPro. (Oct. 1991)-. English. mo. $12.00 US; $17.00 Canada. Marvel Entertainment Group Inc., 387 Park Avenue South, New York NY 10016. **Tel** (212)576-8595, FAX (212) 576-9289. **DD** 741.

US/1056-3660
**NIGHTMARES ON ELM STREET.** [Nightmares on Elm Str.]. (Sept. 1991)-. Periodical. English. mo. $3.00 (single issue). Innovation Publishing, 3622 Jacob Street, Wheeling WV 26003. **DD** 741.

AT
**NINTENDO.** (19??)-. Periodical. English. mo. 54.45Aus$ Australia; 60.00Aus$ New Zealand & Papua New Guinea; 105.00Aus$ US & Canada; 112.00Aus$ Europe & Africa; 90.00Aus$ Singapore, Malaysia, Indonesia; 100.00Aus$ Hong Kong, China, Japan, India. Federal Publishing Co Pty Ltd, PO Box 199, 180 Bourke Road, Alexandria New South Wales, 2015 Australia. **Tel** 011 61 2 693 6666, FAX 011 61 2 693 9935. **(Subscription address:** Federal Publishing Co. Pty Ltd., PO Box 199, Alexandria NSW 2015 Australia.**)**

US/1041-9551
**NINTENDO POWER.** **Added/Corp** Nintendo of America. (June 1988)-. Periodical. English. mo. $18.00 (one year), $33.00 (two year), $45.00 (three year). Nintendo of America Inc., 4820 150th Avenue Northeast, Redmond WA 98052. **Tel** (800)255-3700, (206)861-2865, FAX (206)882-3585. **(Subscription address:** Nintendo of America Inc., PO Box 97043, Redmond, WA 98073**) ED** Gail Tilden, Pam Sather. **DD** 794. **Circ:** 2,000,000 (ctrl).

US/0146-6941
**NORTHWEST CHESS.** **Added/Corp** Washington Chess Federation. **VFOAT** Northwest Chess Magazine. No. 1 (Nov. 1947)-. Periodical. English. mo. $16.00 US; $20.00 other. Northwest Chess, PO Box 84746, Seattle WA 98124. **Tel** (206)935-8440, (206)882-1746. **ED** Ralph Dubisch. **Bk Rev.** **Ad Acc.** **Circ:** 600 (ctrl).

CS
**NOVY DIKOBRAZ.** ***Title Change.*** **Added/Corp** Studio Dobre Nalady. Vol. 1 No. 1 (1990)-(1993). Periodical. Czech. wk. **(Subscription address:** Artia Pegas Press Ltd., Palac Metro Narodni Trida 25, 11210 Prague 1 Czech Republic.**) LC** AP115; .D5. ***Continues*** *Dikobraz, 0012-284X.* ***Continued by*** *Dikobraz (Prague, Czech Republic : 1993).*

US/1047-7462
**NTH MAN.** (NTH MAN : THE ULTIMATE NINJA.). [Nth man]. **VFOAT** NTH Man, The Ultimate Ninja. (1989)-. Periodical. English. mo. $12.00 US; $14.00 Canada. Marvel Comics, 387 Park Avenue South/9th Floor, New York NY 10016. **Tel** (212)576-9259. **DD** 741.

US/0891-8872
**OFFICIAL OVERSTREET COMIC BOOK PRICE GUIDE, THE.** (THE OFFICIAL OVERSTREET COMIC BOOK PRICE GUIDE / BY ROBERT M. OVERSTREET.). [Off. Overstreet comic book price guide]. **VFOAT** Comic Book Price Guide; Overstreet Comic Book Price Guide. 17th Ed. (1987/1988)-. English. an. $17.90 (includes shipping/handling). Random House Inc., 400 Hahn Road, Westminster MD 21157. **Tel** (800)726-0600, (800)733-3000, FAX (800)659-2436. **LC** Z1000; .O94. **DD** 741.5/0973/075. ***Continues*** *Comic Book Price Guide, 0730-2916.*

US/0278-9884
**OFFICIAL PENCIL PUZZLES & WORD GAMES.** (OFFICIAL PENICL PUZZLES & WORD GAMES / DELL.). **VFOAT** Dell Official Pencil Puzzles & Word Games; Official Pencil Puzzles and Word Games. No. 1 (Dec. 1981)-. Periodical. English. bm. $7.97 US; $10.97 Cananda. Dell Publishing Company Inc., 1540 Broadway, 9th Floor, New York NY 10036-4021. **Tel** (212)782-8532, FAX (212)782-8338. **LC** Discard.

US/0885-6583
**OHIO CHESS BULLETIN.** [Ohio chess bull.]. **Added/Corp** Ohio Chess Association. Vol. 9, No. 4 (Aug. 1954)-. Bulletin. English. Six times a year (Jan., Mar., May, July, Sept., Nov.). $10.00. Ohio Chess Association, 7722 Lucerne Drive, #N35 J Pechac, Middleburg Heights OH 44130. **Tel** (614)587-6682. **ED** Andrew Rea, (editor's address: 1750 Patrick Place T20, Library, PA 15129). **DD** 794. Index available (Volume F). **Circ:** 500. ***Continues*** *Ohio Chess Association Bulletin.*
**Desc:** News of tournaments and other chess games events in Ohio.

●US/1062-2594
**OMNIFORCE (BROOKLYN, NEW YORK, N.Y.).** (OMNIFORCE.). **VFOAT** Keepers of the Central Flame. (1992)-. English. qt. $7.00. A & B Comics, 135 Lawrence Street, Brooklyn NY 11201.

CN/0712-2195
**ONTARIO CHESS NEWS.** [Ont. chess news]. Issue 1 (May 1981)-. Periodical. English. Three times a year. Free to OCA members, $1.00 each number. Ontario Chess News, c/o Erik Malmsten, #1715 620 James Street, Toronto Ontario M4Y 2R8 Canada. **DD** 794.1/05. **UDC** 794.1.

US/0048-2099
**ORBEN'S COMEDY FILLERS.** **VFOAT** Comedy Fillers. Periodical. English. mo. Comedy Center, 300 Water Street, Wilmington DE 19801. **Tel** (302)656-2209. **ED** R Orben. **UDC** 741.5.

US/0896-9337
**ORIGINAL NINJA, THE.** ***Ceased.*** [Orig. ninja]. **VFOAT** Ninja. (19??)-(19??). Periodical. English. mo. Condor Books Inc, 351 West 54th Street, New York NY 10019.

KO
**PADUK.** Periodical. Korean. mo. W24,000. Hanguk Kiwon, 13-4 Kwanchol-dong Chongno-ku, Seoul Korea. **LC** GV1459; .P27.

KO
**PADUK YONGAM.** '85-. Korean. an. W5,000. Hanguk Kiwon, 13-4 Kwanchol-dong Chongno-ku, Seoul Korea. **LC** GV1459.35.K6; P33.

US/1043-4771
**PAINTBALL (BURBANK, LOS ANGELES COUNTY, CALIF.).** ***Ceased.*** (PAINTBALL.). [Paintball]. **VFOAT** Paintball Magazine. (Winter 1988)-(Fall 1992). Periodical. English. mo. CFW Enterprises Inc., 4201 West Van Owen Place, Burbank CA 91505. **Tel** (818)845-2656. **ED** Jessica Sparks. **DD** 799. **Circ:** 65,000.
**Desc:** Focus is on games, rules and equipment.

CN/0822-5672
**PASSANT, EN.** [En passant]. **Added/Corp** Chess Federation of Canada. No. 62 (9/10 1983)-. Periodical. English (French; summaries and/or abstracts in French). Six times a year (Feb., Apr., June, Aug. Oct., Dec.). 14.02Can$. En Passant, 2212 Gladwin Crescent E 1 B, Ottawa Ontario K1B 5N1 Canada. **Tel** (613)733-2844. **(Subscription address:** Box 7339, Ottawa Ontario K1L 8E4 Canada**) ED** Stephen Ball and Jacques Dube. **DD** 794.1/06/071. Index available. **Ad Acc.** **Circ:** 3,600. ***Continues*** *Chess Canada, 0225-7351.*
**Desc:** Chess in Canada, chess news, instructional articles, annotated and unannotated games. National rankings and tournament announcements.

●US/1351-3540
**PC GAMER.** (1993)-. English. Twelve times a year. $47.95. GP Publications, 1350 Old Bayshore, Burlingame CA 94010. **Tel** (415)696-1688. **(Subscription address:** Neodata / Colorado, PO Box 2606, Boulder Boulder CO 80322.**)** ***Continues*** *Game Players.*

US/1042-2943
**PC GAMES (PETERBOROUGH, N.H.).** ***Title Change.*** (PC GAMES.). [PC games]. **VFOAT** PCGames; PCGames Magazine. **VAT** Personal Computer Games. (1989)-(19??). Periodical. English. Eight times a year. IDG Communications / New Hampshire, 86 Elm Street, Peterborough NH 03458. **Tel** (603)924-9471, (800)343-0728. **DD** 794. **[CCC].** ***Continues*** *PC Resource's PC Games, 1042-1351.* ***Continued by*** *Electronic Entertainment.*

CN/0700-9127
**PENNY PRESS, THE.** ***Title Change.*** June 15, 1976-. Periodical. English (French). The Penny Press, PO Box 4346, Station E Ottawa K1S 5B3. **DD** 917/.13/84005. **UDC** 917.1. ***Continued by*** *Revue, 0826-0656.*

US/0031-5060
**PEP (MAMARONECK, N.Y.).** (PEP.). [Pep]. Periodical. English. an. $0.75 one issue, $1.00 two issues. Pep, c/o Archie Enterprises Inc, 325 Fayette Avenue, Mamaroneck NY 10543. **Tel** (914)381-5155, telex ITT 494-9036. **ED** Victor Gorelick and Richard H Goldwater. **UDC** 741.5. **Ad Acc.** ctrl circ.
**Desc:** Comic stories and games.

CN/0709-3497
**PETIT INTELLECTUEL, LE.** [Petit intellect.]. V. 1- Oct. 1979-. Periodical. French. bw. 0.75Can$. Editions Le Compagnon, CP 143, Succursale A, Hull Quebec J8Y 6M8. **DD** 793.73/05. **UDC** 793.7.

FR/0300-3639
**PHENIX.** No. 1 (Oct. 1966)-. Periodical. French. Three times a year. 200.00F France; 260.00F other. Denis Blondel, 22 Allee des Bouleaux, La Queve en Brie 94510 France. **Tel** 011 33 1 45931396. **ED** Denis Blondel and Jean-Marc Loustau. **Bk Rev.** **Ad Acc.** **Circ:** 300 (ctrl).

CN/1186-2289
**PLAISIR DES JEUX (MONTREAL).** (LE PLAISIR DES JEUX.). [Plaisir jeux]. No 1 (1990)-. Periodical. French. bm. 2.50Can$ per issue. Plaisir des Jeux, 8050 Est Boulevard Metropolitain, Montreal, Quebec H1K 1A1 Canada. **DD** 793.7.

●US/1062-6956
**PLAY (GAINESVILLE, FLA.).** (PLAY MAGAZINE). [Play]. **VFOAT** Play Magazine. Vol. 1, No. 1 (Winter 1992/1993)-. Periodical. English. Four times a year. $12.00 US; $16.00 Canada & Mexico; $24.00 others. Meg Inc., 3620 Northwest 43rd Street, Suite D, Gainesville FL 32606. **Tel** (904)375-3705. **DD** 791.

US/1048-8243
**PLAY METER MAGAZINE.** [Play meter mag.]. **VFOAT** Play Meter. (19??)-. Periodical. English. mo. $50.00. Skybird Publishing Co., Inc., PO Box 24170, New Orleans LA 70184. **Tel** (504)488-7003. **DD** 338. Index

# Recreation, Leisure —Games and Amusements

available. **Ad Acc. Circ:** 5,000. available with charts; available with illustrations. **Continues** Play Meter, 0162-1343.

US/1047-5303
**PLAYER (ATLANTIC CITY, N.J.), THE.** **Title Change.** (THE PLAYER : AMERICA'S GAMING GUIDE.). [Player]. (1988)-(199?). Periodical. English. mo. Las Vegas Casino Journal, 3100 West Sahara Avenue, Suite 207, Las Vegas NV 89102. **Tel** (705)253-6230, (800)394-2467, FAX (702)253-6804. **DD** 795. **Continued by** Casino Player.

UK/0966-4033
**PLAYING-CARD WORLD.** [Play. card world]. (1981)-. Periodical. English. qt. £2.00 plus postage. The International Playing-Card Society, 188 Sheen Lane, East Sheen, London SW14 8LF England. **(Subscription address:** Adrienne Gurr, Shortacre, Peasmarsh, RYE, East Sussex TN31 6SX England) **Bk Rev. Ad Acc. Circ:** 500. **Continues** Newsletter of the International Playing-Card Society.
**Desc:** Newsletter of the International Playing-Card Society. Promotes the study and collection of playing-cards, society news, details of new and older packs, reviews of periodicals, books, exhibitions and catalogues.

US/1053-7236
**POOL PLAYER'S NATIONAL POCKET BILLIARDS DIRECTORY, THE.** [Pool play. natl. pocket billiards dir.]. (1991)-. Directory. English. Lawco Ltd., PO Box 2009, Manteca CA 95336. **LC** GV891.A1; P66. **DD** 794.7/3.

US/0194-6749
**POPULAR CROSSWORDS (NEW YORK, N.Y.).** (POPULAR CROSSWORDS.). (19??)-. English. mo. $17.88. Hachette Magazines Inc., 1633 Broadway, New York NY 10019. **Tel** (212)767-6000. **(Subscription address:** Neodata / Colorado, PO Box 2606, Boulder Boulder CO 80322.)

US/0162-3060
**POST SCRIPTS (INDIANAPOLIS). Ceased.** (POST SCRIPTS.). (19??)-Vol. 20, No. 4 (April 1993). Periodical. English. mo. Curtis Publishing Company / Bonnie Kanter, 1000 Waterway Boulevard, Indianapolis IN 46202. **Tel** (317)633-2061. **ED** James Thom. **Circ:** 1,500.
**Desc:** Wit, wisdom, and amusing anecdotes from cover to cover.

CN/0383-1833
**PRISME (MONTREAL).** (PRISME.). **VFOAT** Revue Prisme. No. 1 (March 1976)-. Periodical. French. ir. $1.00 each number. Editions Phase, CP 454 Succursale Place d'Armes, Montreal Quebec H2Y 3H3 Canada. **DD** 741.5/9/714.

UK
**PROBLEM OBSERVER.** (19??)-. English. bm (6 issues). £4.00. JF Ling, 41 Tiverton Road, Loughborough LE11 2RU England. **Tel** 011 44 0509 266372. **ED** John F. Ling. **Bk Rev. Circ:** 75 (ctrl).
**Desc:** Original chess problems and and their solutions. Articles on chess problems, reviews of chess books and magazines.

SP/0032-9223
**PROBLEMAS BARCELONA.** [Problemas Barc.]. **VFOAT** Boletin de la Sociedad Espanola de Problemistas de Ajedrez. (194?)-. Periodical. Spanish. Four times a year. 2000ptas. Sociedad Espanola de Problemistas de Ajedrez, Avenida Prin Ast 35 4 2, Barcelona 08012 Spain. **Tel** 011 34 1 3552159. **UDC** 794.1. **Pr Rev. Circ:** 1,000.
**Desc:** Information on problems in the game of chess.

UK/0032-9398
**PROBLEMIST, THE. Added/Corp** British Chess Problem Society. **VFOAT** Proceedings of the British Chess Problem Society. Vol. 1 (1928)-. Periodical. English. Six times a year (Jan., Mar., May, July, Sept., Nov.). £18.00 one year, surface mail; £16.00 Europe, £18.50 other, airmail. British Chess Problem Society, 123 Cockerell Close Wimborne, Dorset BH21 1XR England. **Tel** 011 44 81 202 889810. **ED** Paul Valois. Index available. cum. index. **Bk Rev**, (Qty: varies); **Circ:** 600.
**Desc:** Articles, lectures reports, national and international meeting reports, tours announcements, awards, society and members news are included on the game of Chess.

PL
**PROBLEMISTA.** Polish. qt. $15.00. Eugeniusz Iwanow, 42-2000 Czestochowa, Kilinskiego 57M 53 Poland. **ED** E Iwanow. **Pr Rev.**
**Desc:** Information on chess composition.

US/0899-7888
**PSI FORCE.** [PSI force]. English. mo. Marvel Entertainment Group Inc., 387 Park Avenue South, New York NY 10016. **Tel** (212)576-8595, FAX (212) 576-9289. **DD** 741.

US/0196-2558
**PUBLIC GAMING NEWSLETTER. Ceased.** (19??)-(19??). Newsletter. English. sm. Public Gaming Research Institute, 15825 Shady Grove Road, Suite 130, Rockville MD 20850. **Tel** (301)330-7600. **UDC** 794.

US/1040-5372
**PUNISHER (NEW YORK, N.Y. 1987), THE.** (THE PUNISHER.). [Punisher]. Vol. 1 (July 1987)-. Periodical. English. ir (Published every six weeks). $18.00. Marvel Entertainment Group Inc., 387 Park Avenue South, New York NY 10016. **Tel** (212)576-8595, FAX (212) 576-9289. **DD** 741.

US/1044-4610
**PUNISHER WAR JOURNAL, THE.** [Punisher war j.]. No. 1 (Nov. 1988)-. Periodical. English. Twelve times a year. $21.00. Marvel Entertainment Group Inc., 387 Park Avenue South, New York NY 10016. **Tel** (212)576-8595, FAX (212) 576-9289. **DD** 741.

UK
**PUPPET MASTER, THE.** (19??)-. Periodical. English. qt. British Puppet and Model Theatre Guild, 18 Maple Road, Yeading Hayes Middlesex England.

●US/1062-1164
**PUZZLER (MINNETONKA, MINN.), THE.** (THE PUZZLER.). [Puzzler]. (1992)-. Periodical. English. mo. $24.95. CY Decosse, Inc., 5900 Green Oak Drive, Minnetonka MN 55343. **DD** 793.

US/0480-676X
**QUALITY CROSSWORD PUZZLES.** (19??)-. Periodical. English. mo. $18.00. Quinn Publishing Company, PO Box 988, Department 2, Ft Washington PA 19034. **Tel** (215)628-0924.

US/1056-3679
**QUANTUM LEAP.** [Quantum leap]. Vol. 1, No. 1 (Sept. 1991)-. Periodical. English. mo. $2.50 (U.S., single issue), 2.95 (Can., single issue). Innovation Publishing, 3622 Jacob Street, Wheeling WV 26003. **DD** 741.

US/0195-4709
**QUARTERLY REPORT - STATE GAMING CONTROL BOARD. Title Change.** See Public Administration.

CN/0381-6443
**QUEBEC AU BOUT DES DOIGTS.** V. 1- May 1975-. Periodical. Multiple languages (English and French). mo. Publicites Cascades, 1155 Ste-Foy Road, Quebec G1S 2M8 Canada. **DD** 790/.09714/471. **UDC** 791(714).

US/1042-9174
**RACING GREYHOUNDS.** [Racing greyhounds]. Vol. 1, No. 1 (July 1988)-. Periodical. English. mo. $46.00 US; $61.00 Canada; $76.00 other. Pico Publishing, 5906 10th Avenue, Kenosha WI 53140. **Tel** (414)652-3278, FAX (414)652-2906. **ED** Gordon Waite. **DD** 798. Index available. **Ad Acc. Pr Rev. Circ:** 2,000 (ctrl).
**Desc:** Each issue features articles on different aspects of greyhound handicapping, pari-mutuel wagering, and greyhound wagering strategies written by the nation's leading handicappers and industry experts. Information on the greyhound tracks' schedules are published regularly.

PL/0239-8796
**REBUS.** [Rebus]. (1983)-. Periodical. Polish. mo. $18.00. **(Subscription address:** ARS Polona, PO Box 1001, 00068 Warsaw Poland.) **UDC** 793.7.

CN/0847-432X
**RECREATION QUEBEC.** (RECREATION QUEBEC : REVUE DE LA FEDERATION QUEBECOISE DES JEUX RECREATIFS.). [Recreat. Que.]. **Added/Corp** Federation Quebecoise des Jeux Recreatifs. (Jan./Feb. 1990)-. Periodical. French. bm. Gratuit pour les membres. Federation Quebecoise des Jeux Recreatifs, 1415 Est rue Jarry, Montreal Quebec H2E 2Z7 Canada. **DD** 794/.06/0714. **Continues** Informa' Jeux, 0705-3835.

CN/0711-3455
**REVUE JEUNESSE.** [Rev. jeun.]. No. 1-. Periodical. French. Three times a year. $2.50 per number. Les Editions Publication, CP 123, Succursale R, Montreal Quebec H2S 3K6. **DD** 793.73/05. **UDC** 793.7.

CN/0828-5012
**REVUE QUEBECOISE DE BRIDGE, LA.** [Rev. que. bridge]. Vol. 1, No 1 (Oct. 1984)-. Periodical. French. qt. $1.00 per no. Federation Quebecoise de Bridge, 1415 East rue Jarry, Montreal Quebec H2E 2Z7 Canada. **DD** 795.41/5/05. **UDC** 794.41.

PL/0137-8295
**REWIA ROZRYWKI.** [Rewia Rozryki]. (1972)-. Periodical. Polish. bm. $12.00. **(Subscription address:** ARS Polona, PO Box 1001, 00068 Warsaw Poland.) **UDC** 793.7.

US/0194-3189
**RING-A-WORD PUZZLES. VAT** Ring a Word Puzzles. Periodical. English. mo $9.00. Editorial Services Inc., PO Box 687, Old Lyme CT 06371. **UDC** 793.7.

CN/0821-5782
**RINGETTE REVIEW.** (RINGETTE REVIEW : RINGETTE CANADA'S NATIONAL NEWSLETTER.). [Ringette rev.]. **VFOAT** Revue Ringuette. Vol. 1 No. 1 (Apr. 1979)-. Newsletter. English (French). ir. Free. Ringette Canada, PO Box 2162, Stettler Alberta T0C 2L0 Canada. **DD** 796.9/6. **UDC** 796.96. ctrl circ.
**Ind/Abst** SPORT Discus.

US
**RIP OFF COMIX.** No. 1 (1977)-. English. qt. $13.00 US; $16.60 other. Rip Off Comix, PO Box 4686, Auburn CA 95604. **Tel** (800)634-0668, (916)885-8183 IN CALIFORNIA, FAX (916)-885-8219. **ED** Kathe Todd. **UDC** 741.5. **Circ:** 5,000.
**Desc:** Presents new comics from the cream of American and European cartoonists for the mature audience.

CN/0227-5953
**ROBERT CAMPBELL'S SOUP TO NUTS.** [Robert Campbell's soup nuts]. **VFOAT** Soup to Nuts. No. 1-. Periodical. English. mo. $1.00 for 4 mo. Soup to Nuts, c/o R Campbell, 63 Lanyard Road, Weston Ontario M9M 1Y8 Canada. **DD** 793./9.05. **UDC** 793.7. **Continues** Cheader's Digest, 0703-8186.

US/1058-8248
**ROGER RABBIT'S TOONTOWN.** [Roger Rabbit's Toontown]. **VFOAT** Welcome To- Roger Rabbit's Toontown. No. 1 (Aug. 1991)-. Periodical. English. mo. $18.00. Roger Rabbit's Toontown, PO Box 2079, Prescott AZ 86302. **DD** 741.

US/0896-7261
**ROLLERCOASTER! MAGAZINE.** **Added/Corp** American Coaster Enthusiasts (Organization). **VFOAT** Roller Coaster Magazine; Rollercoaster; Roller Coaster; Rollercoaster! Magazine (Coaster World). (19??)-. Periodical. English. Four times a year (Jan., Apr., July, Oct.). $50.00 US / $60.00 Canada & Mexico, $80.00 others (individuals); $65.00 US, $75.00 Canada & Mexico, $95.00 others (institutions) Comes with American Coaster Enthusiasts membership. American Coaster Enthusiasts, PO Box 8226, Chicago IL 60680. **Tel** (410)385-1222, FAX (410)385-1222. **DD** 791. Index available. cum. index (Dec. in 1994). **Bk Rev. Ad Acc. Pr Rev. Circ:** 4,000 (ctrl). **Continues** Coaster World.
**Desc:** Pictures and text describing rollercoasters of the past and present, with technical features and interviews.

●US
**ROTISSERIE LEAGUE FOOTBALL.** (1992)-. English. Bantam Books Inc, 666 Fifth Avenue, New York NY 10019. **Tel** (212)340-7500. **LC** GV1202.F34; R68. **DD** 793.93.

PL/0137-8252
**ROZRYWKA.** [Rozrywka]. (1957)-. Periodical. Polish. Twenty-six times a year. $32.00. **(Subscription address:** ARS Polona, PO Box 1001, 00068 Warsaw Poland.) **UDC** 793.7.

CI
**SAHOVSKI GLASNIK. Added/Corp** Sahovski Savez Hrvatske. (19??)-. Periodical. Slovak (Slovenian and Macedonian). Twelve times a year. $20.00. Sahovska Nalzada, Zrinjski TRG 3, PO Box 759, Zagreb Croatia. **Tel** 041-273-692. **ED** Drazen Marovic. **LC** GV1313; .S27. Index available. cum. index. **Bk Rev. Ad Acc. Circ:** 5,500 (ctrl).
**Desc:** Chess-review bringing great number of important commented games of international tournaments theoretical news, results and scores and photos.

CI/0351-1375
**SAHOVSKI INFORMATOR.** [Sah. inf.]. **Added/Corp** Savezni Centar za Unapreivanje Saha (Yugoslavia) Centar za Unapreivanje Saha (Sahovski Savez Srbije). **VFOAT** Shakhmatnyi Informator; Chess Informant. (1966)-. Periodical. English (Multiple languages). ir. $18.00. Sahovski Informator, Francuska 31, 11001 Belgrade Yugoslavia. **Tel** 011 38 11 626583. **(Subscription address:** Mladost Export Import, PO Box 1028, Ilica 30, 41000 Zagreb Croatia.) **LC** GV1313; .S28.

HU/0237-2525
**SAKKELET.** [Sakkelet]. (1985)-. Periodical. Hungarian. Twelve times a year. $38.00. **(Subscription address:** Kultura, PO Box 149, H 1389 Budapest 62 Hungary (phone: 011 36 1 359370)). **UDC** 794.1. **Continues** Magyar Sakkelet, 0464-4689.

PL/0867-4310
**SAM NA SAM.** [Sam Sam]. (1990)-. Periodical. Polish. mo $33.00. **(Subscription address:** ARS Polona, PO Box 1001, 00068 Warsaw Poland.) **UDC** 793.7. **Continues** Sam na Sam z Soba, 0239-5185.

US
**SANDMAN, THE.** (19??)-. English. Twelve times a year. $23.40 US; $29.35 Canada; $35.40 other. DC Comics, 1325 Avenue of the Americas, Floor 27, New York NY 10019. **Tel** (212)636-5443.

Recreation, Leisure —Games and Amusements

US/1054-7789
**SCANDAL SHEET.** [Scandal sheet]. Vol. 1, No. 1 (1991)-. Periodical. English. qt. $2.50 (single issue). Arriba Comics, 7210 Jordan Avenue, Suite A56, Canoga Park CA 91303. **DD** 741. ***Continues*** *Scandal Sheet, 1054-7789.*

NE
**SCHAAK JAARBOEK.** Dutch. Spectrum / Netherlands, Uttgeverij Het Spectrum, Utrecht Netherlands. **LC** GV1313; .S328. **DD** 794.1/5. **UDC** 794.1(058).

GW/0048-9328
**SCHACH.** [Schach]. (1947)-. Periodical. German. Twelve times a year. DM72.00 Germany; DM84.00 other. Sport & Gesundheit Verlag GmbH, Lindenstrasse 76, D 10969 Berlin Germany. **Tel** 011 49 30 25913028. **(Subscription address:** DSB ABO Betreuung GmbH, Heiner Fleischmann Strasse 2, D 74168 Neckarsulm Germany.)

GW
**SCHACH GERMANY.** German. mo. DM72.00 Germany; DM84.00 other. Sport & Gesundheit Verlag GmbH, Lindenstrasse 76, D 10969 Berlin Germany. **Tel** 011 49 30 25913028. **(Subscription address:** DSB ABO Beteruung GmbH, Frau Weilmann D 74168 Neckarsulm, Germany)

US/1040-7707
**SCHOOL MATES.** (SCHOOL MATES : THE U.S. CHESS FEDERATION'S MAGAZINE FOR YOUNG CHESSPLAYERS.). [Sch. mates]. **Added/Corp** United States Chess Federation. **VFOAT** Schoolmates. (198?)-. Periodical. English. bm (6 issues). $7.50 (age 20 and over), $7.00 (age 19 and under) North America; $17.50 (age 20 and over), $17.00 (age 19 and under) other. US Chess Federation, 186 Route 9 West, New Windsor NY 12553. **Tel** (914)562-8350. **ED** Jennie Simon, Michele Spione and Bob Nasiff. **DD** 794. **Circ:** 5,000.
**Desc:** Chess magazine for children and beginning players.

NE
**SCORE.** Dutch. qt. Fl25.00. Cinemuzika, PO Box 406, 8200 AK Lelystad Netherlands.
**Ind/Abst** Film Lit. Index (19??-).

US/1059-8359
**SEEK-A-WORD.** [Seek-a-word]. **VFOAT** Seek a Word. (19??)-. English. Seventeen times a year. $18.40. Stavrolex Publications, Inc., PO Box 1207, Fort Washington PA 19034. **Tel** (215)628-0964. **DD** 793.
**Desc:** A game to solve these 72 large-print word find puzzles..

US/0887-5952
**SERGIO ARAGONES GROO THE WANDERER (NEW YORK, N.Y.).** (SERGIO ARAGONES GROO THE WANDERER.). **VFOAT** Groo the Wanderer. 1 (Mar. 1985)-. Periodical. English. mo. $12.00 US; $14.00 other. Marvel Entertainment Group Inc., 387 Park Avenue South, New York NY 10016. **Tel** (212)576-8595, FAX (212) 576-9289. **ED** J Shooter. **Ad Acc. Circ:** 132,000. ***Continues*** *Sergio Aragones Groo the Wanderer (San Diego, Calif.), 0887-5952.*

RU/0132-0947
**SHAKHMATY V SSSR.** ***Title Change.*** **Added/Corp** Russia (1917- R.S.F.S.R.). Vyshii Sovet Fizicheskoi Kultury. Russia (1923- U.S.S.R). Komitet po Fizicheskoi Kulture i Sportu. Shakhmatnaia Federatsiia SSSR. (1931)-(19??). Periodical. Russian. mo. **(Subscription address:** Victor Kamkin, 4956 Boiling Brook Parkway, Rockville MD 20852.) **LC** GV1313; .S48. ***Continues*** *Shakmatnyi Listok.* ***Continued by*** *Shakhmatnyi Vestnik.*

US
**SHE HULK.** English. ir. $18.00. Marvel Entertainment Group Inc., 387 Park Avenue South, New York NY 10016. **Tel** (212)576-8595, FAX (212) 576-9289.

US/0897-9111
**SILVER SURFER.** [Silver Surfer]. Vol. 1 (July 1987)-. English. ir. $18.00. Marvel Entertainment Group Inc., 387 Park Avenue South, New York NY 10016. **Tel** (212)576-8595, FAX (212) 576-9289. **DD** 741.

US/0196-7231
**SIMON AND SCHUSTER CROSSWORD PUZZLE BOOK.** **Main/Corp** Simon and Schuster, Inc. **VAT** Simon and Schuster Cross Word Puzzle Book. English. $3.95. Simon & Schuster, 1230 Avenue of the Americas, New York NY 10020. **Tel** (212)698-7000. **LC** GV1507.C7; S47A. **DD** 793.73/05. **UDC** 793.7.

US/1058-3475
**SLEEPWALKER (NEW YORK, N.Y.).** (SLEEPWALKER.). [Sleepwalker]. **VFOAT** Sleep Walker. No. 1 (June 1991)-. English. ir. $18.00. Marvel Entertainment Group Inc., 387 Park Avenue South, New York NY 10016. **Tel** (212)576-8595, FAX (212) 576-9289. **DD** 741.

CN/0715-5522
**SNAFU (LOW).** (SNAFU.). [Snafu]. Periodical. English. ir. $8.00, 10 no. R.J. Brown, RR 1 Low, Quebec J0X 2C0 Canada. **DD** 794.2. **UDC** 794.2.

US/1049-0159
**SOAP OPERA WORD-FIND.** [Soap opera word-find]. **VFOAT** Soap Opera Word Find. (19??)-. Periodical. English. bm. $6.25. Official Publications Inc., PO Box 937, Fort Washington PA 19034. **Tel** (215)628-0924. **DD** 793. ***Continues*** *Soap Opera Word-Find Hidden Word Puzzles, 0194-3197.*

US/0194-3197
**SOAP OPERA WORD-FIND HIDDEN WORD PUZZLES.** ***Title Change.*** [Soap opera word-find hidden word puzzles]. **VAT** Soap Opera Word Find Hidden Word Puzzles. Periodical. English. bm. Official Publications Inc., PO Box 937, Fort Washington PA 19034. **Tel** (215)628-0924. **DD** 793. **UDC** 793.7. **Ad Acc.** ***Continued by*** *Soap Opera Word-Find, 1049-0159.*

US/1056-3938
**SOLAR, MAN OF THE ATOM.** [Solar man atom]. **VFOAT** Solar. No. 1 (Sept. 1991)-. Periodical. English. mo. $21.00 US; $27.00 Canada. Voyage Communications, 65 Commerce Road, Stamford CT 06902-4546. **DD** 741.

US/0147-3441
**SPARTAN, THE.** Periodical. English. qt. $9.00. Spartan International, Inc., Box 1017, Bellflower CA 90706. **LC** U310; .S67. **DD** 793/.9.

US/0898-1833
**SPECTACULAR SPIDER-MAN.** (198?)-. Periodical. English. Twelve times a year. $18.00. Marvel Entertainment Group Inc., 387 Park Avenue South, New York NY 10016. **Tel** (212)576-8595, FAX (212) 576-9289. ***Continues*** *Peter Parker, The Spectacular Spider-Man, 0273-6632.*

US/1055-4874
**SPRING FEVER.** [Spring fever]. **VFOAT** Walt Disney's Spring Fever. (1990)-. Periodical. English. $2.95 (US single issue) $3.95 (Canada single issue). Walt Disney Publishing Inc., 500 South Buena Vista Street, Burbank CA 91521. **Tel** (818)567-5661. **DD** 741.

FR/0980-5338
**ST MAGAZINE.** (STANDARD ATARI.). **VFOAT** Sept Trente-Deux Bits Magazine; 7 32 Magazine. (1985)-. Periodical. French. Ten times a year. 250.00F France; 310.00F Europe; 350.00F other. Pressimage, 19 rue Hegesippe Moreau, 75018 Paris, France. **Tel** 011 33 1 45223860, 011 33 1 43870139. **UDC** 681.3.

US/1061-1037
**STRAT FAN.** (STRAT FAN : SF.). [Strat fan]. **VFOAT** SF. (1991)-. Periodical. English. mo. $32.00. Strat Fan, PO Box 302, Springfield PA 19064. **DD** 794.

US/0164-3975
**STREET MACHINE (CANOGA PARK, LOS ANGELES, CALIF.).** (STREET MACHINE.). [Str. mach.]. Vol. 1 No. 1 (June 1987)-. Periodical. English. bm. $11.50 US; $15.50 other. Street Machine, 10968 Via Frontera, San Diego CA 92127. **DD** 796. ***Continues*** *Street Machine (Canoga Park, Los Angeles, Calif. : 1979), 0164-3975.*

US/0897-5760
**STRIKEFORCE MORITURI.** ***Ceased.*** Vol. 1 (Dec. 1986)-?. Periodical. English. mo. Marvel Entertainment Group Inc., 387 Park Avenue South, New York NY 10016. **Tel** (212)576-8595, FAX (212) 576-9289. **DD** 741.

US/1060-4685
**SUPER GAMING.** (SUPER GAMING : VIDEO GAME PREVIEWS.). [Super gaming]. Began in 1991. Periodical. English. qt. $9.95 (U.S.), $19.95 (foreign). Sendai Publications, 1920 Highland Avenue, Suite 222, Lombard IL 60148. **Tel** (708)916-7222. **DD** 794.

US/0732-5657
**SUPER MAZE CRAZE PUZZLE PICTURES.** **VFOAT** Super Maze Craze; Maze Craze. (19??)-. Periodical. English. bm. Can Am Media Inc., 151 Hempstead Turnpike, West Hempstead NY 11552.

US/1040-144X
**SUPER SCIENCE (BLUE ED.).** (SUPER SCIENCE.). **Added/Corp** Scholastic Inc. **VFOAT** Superscience Blue; Superscience. (1989)-. Periodical. English. ir (8 issues per year). $27.00. Scholastic Inc., 2931 East McCarty Street, PO Box 3710, Jefferson City MO 65102-9957. **Tel** (314)636-5271, (800)631-1586. available on microfilm and microfiche from University Microfilms International (UMI).
**Ind/Abst** Child. Mag. Guide; Gen. Sci. Source (Jul. 1993-); Mag. Search; Mid. Search (Jul. 1993-); Prim. Search (Jul. 1993-).

US/1040-1431
**SUPER SCIENCE (RED ED.).** (SUPER SCIENCE.). **Added/Corp** Scholastic Inc. **VFOAT** Superscience Red. (1989)-. Periodical. English. ir (8 issues per year). $27.00. Scholastic Inc., 2931 East McCarty Street, PO Box 3710, Jefferson City MO 65102-9957. **Tel** (314)636-5271, (800)631-1586. **(Subscription address:** Scholastic Inc., PO Box 3710, Jefferson City, MO 65102) available on microfilm and microfiche from University Microfilms International (UMI).
**Ind/Abst** Child. Mag. Guide; Gen. Sci. Source (Jul. 1993-); Mag. Search; Mid. Search (Jul. 1993-); Prim. Search (Jul. 1993-).

US/0894-6469
**SUPERB CROSSWORDS.** [Superb crosswords]. (198?)-. Periodical. English. mo. $12.30 US; $15.30 Canada. Official Publications Inc, PO Box 750, Fort Washington PA 19034. **Tel** (215)643-6385.

US/0194-3227
**SUPERB FILL-IT-INS.** **VFOAT** Fill-It-Ins. **VAT** Superb Fill It Ins. (19??)-. Periodical. English. Twelve times a year. $9.60 US; $12.80 others. Official Publications Inc., PO Box 937, Fort Washington PA 19034. **Tel** (215)628-0924. **Ad Acc.**
**Desc:** Loads of puzzles for easy solving. All the answers are supplied.

US/0194-3235
**SUPERB WORD-FIND PUZZLES.** **VFOAT** Word-Find Puzzles. **VAT** Superb Word Find Puzzles. (19??)-. Periodical. English. Twelve times a year. $12.00 one year, $22.00 two years. Official Publications Inc., PO Box 937, Fort Washington PA 19034. **Tel** (215)628-0924. **Ad Acc.**
**Desc:** An ever-popular magazine filled with hidden-word puzzles on your favorite subjects, plus special word-twists, angle-finds, and number puzzles.

US/0199-218X
**SUPERB WORD-TWISTS.** **VFOAT** Superb Word Twists. **VAT** Superb Word Twists. (19??)-. Periodical. English. mo. $12.30. Official Publications Inc., PO Box 937, Fort Washington PA 19034. **Tel** (215)628-0924. **Ad Acc.**
**Desc:** Games involving hidden words with a twist.

US/0887-1035
**SUPERSTAR WRESTLER.** (1986)-. Periodical. English. ir (nine times a year). $19.98. Comics World Corporation, 475 Park Avenue South, New York NY 10016. **Tel** (212)689-2830. **(Subscription address:** Kable Publishers Aide, 308 East Hitt Street, Mt. Morris, IL 61054) **ED** George Napolitano and Richard Gilbert. **DD** 796. **Ad Acc. Circ:** 134,000.
**Desc:** Information on famous wrestlers and special wrestling events.

US
**SWAMP THING.** **VFOAT** Saga of the Swamp Thing. Vol. 31 (Dec. 1984)-. Periodical. English. mo. $23.40. DC Comics, 1325 Avenue of the Americas, Floor 27, New York NY 10019. **Tel** (212)636-5443. ***Continues*** *Saga of the Swamp Thing.*

●PL/1230-2309
**SZACHISTA WARSZAWA.** (SZACHISTA.). [Szachista Warsz.]. (1991)-. Periodical. Polish. mo. Price on Request. **(Subscription address:** ARS Polona, PO Box 1001, 00068 Warsaw Poland.) **UDC** 794.1.

PL
**SZACHY.** **Added/Corp** Polski Zwiazek Szachowy. (1946)-. Periodical. Polish. Twelve times a year. **(Subscription address:** ARS Polona, PO Box 1001, 00068 Warsaw Poland.) Index available. **Bk Rev. Ad Acc. Circ:** 14,000 (ctrl).
**Desc:** Chess news, information, theory, history, interviews, chess composition, correspondence chess, statistics annotated games, description of the players, etc.

CN/0703-8178
**T V B.** Began with Jan. 1977 issue (No. 4). Periodical. English. ir. $1.00. Games by Mail, 48 Elsfield Road, Toronto Ontario M8Y 3R5 Canada. **DD** 793. ***Continues*** *Vulgar Bloatman, 0705-7024.*

US/0887-7114
**TALES OF THE TEEN TITANS.** ***Ceased.*** **VFOAT** Teen Titans. 41 (Apr. 84)-?. Periodical. English. mo. DC Comics, 1325 Avenue of the Americas, Floor 27, New York NY 10019. **Tel** (212)636-5443. **UDC** 741.5. ***Continues*** *New Teen Titans, 0887-7122.*

US
**TAVERN SPORTS INTERNATIONAL.** English. bm. $13.00 North America. National Bowlers Journal Inc, 101 East Erie Street, Suite 850, Chicago IL 60611. **Tel** (312)266-9499, FAX (312)266-7215. **ED** Jocelyn Hathaway and Louise Collins. Index available. **Ad Acc. Circ:** 25,000 (ctrl).
**Desc:** Focusing on the phenomenon of coin-op sports.

US/1049-0183
**TEENAGE MUTANT NINJA TURTLES MAGAZINE.** ***Ceased.*** [Teenage Mutant Ninja Turt. mag.]. (1990)-(Summer 1993). Periodical. English. qt. Welsh Publishing Group Inc., 300 Madison Avenue, New York NY 10017. **Tel** (212)687-0680, FAX (212)986-5849. **DD** 741.

●US/1065-1764
**TERROR, INC.** [Terror Inc.]. Vol. 1, No. 1 (July 1992)-. English. mo. Marvel Entertainment Group Inc., 387 Park Avenue South, New York NY 10016. **Tel** (212)576-8595, FAX (212) 576-9289. **DD** 741.

US/0274-5372
**THE UNCANNY X-MEN.** [Uncanny X-men]. **VFOAT** Uncanny X Men; X-Men. **VAT** Uncanny X Men. No. 114 (Oct. 1978)-. English. Twelve times a year. $18.00. Marvel Entertainment Group Inc., 387 Park Avenue South, New York NY 10016. **Tel** (212)576-8595, FAX (212) 576-9289. **ED** Jim Shooter. **DD** 741. **Ad Acc. Circ:** 480,000. ***Continues*** *X-Men.*
**Desc:** A group of young mutant outcasts from all over the world band together at Professor Xavier's school for gifted youngsters and use their varied superpowers to protect humanity from itself.

CN/0827-4703
**THOSE ANNOYING POST BROS.** ***Ceased.*** **VFOAT** Post Bros. No. 1 (Jan. 1985)-(199?). Periodical. English. bm. Vortex Comics, 9th Floor/96 Spadina Avenue, Toronto Ontario M5V 2J6 Canada. **DD** 741.5/971. **UDC** 741.5.

US/1050-7760
**TINY TOON ADVENTURES MAGAZINE.** ***Ceased.*** [Tiny toon advent. mag.]. **VFOAT** Tiny Toon Adventures; Warner Bros. Presents Tiny Toon Adventures; TV's Newest Stars! Tiny Toon Adventures Magazine. No. 1 (Oct. 1990)-No. 7 (Spring 1992). Periodical. English. qt. DC Comics, 1325 Avenue of the Americas, Floor 27, New York NY 10019. **Tel** (212)636-5443. **DD** 741.

UK
**TOUGH PUZZLES.** English. ir. £22.00 UK; £22.50 others. British European Association Publishers Limited, Glenthorne House, Hammersmith Grove, London W6 0LG England. **Tel** 011 44 81 846-992, FAX 011 44 81 919001, 011 44 81 741 7762.

UK/0276-7090
**TOURNAMENT CHESS.** [Tournament chess]. Vol. 1 (1982)-. Periodical. English. bm. $150.00 Japan; $125.00 other. TUI Enterprises, 35 Ceres Road England, Plumstead London SE18 England. **Tel** 0865 64881. **ED** Nigel Davies. **LC** GV1455; .T68. **DD** 794.1/57. **[CCC]. Ad Acc. Circ:** 1,000.
**Desc:** Provides coverage of the modern grandmaster tournaments, plus a major openings survey.

●US/1064-4261
**TOXIC CRUSADERS.** [Toxic crusad.]. (May 1992)-. Periodical. English. mo. Marvel Entertainment Group Inc., 387 Park Avenue South, New York NY 10016. **Tel** (212)576-8595, FAX (212) 576-9289. **DD** 741.

CN/0381-9930
**TOYS & GAMES. See** Gifts, Toys.

UK/0041-0187
**TOYS AND PLAYTHINGS.** [Toys & playthings]. (1957)-. Periodical. English. bm. £45.00 UK; £55.00 Europe; £75.00 (airmail) other. Lema Publishing Company, Unit 1 Queen Mary's Avenue, Waterford W01 7JR England. **Tel** 011 44 603 250909. **ED** Georgina Godwin. **DD** _a380.1456887. **Ad Acc, Adv Mgr:** John Baulch. **Circ:** 4,500 (ctrl).

●US/1063-8334
**TURBOFORCE (LOMBARD, ILL.).** (TURBOFORCE.). [Turboforce]. **VFOAT** Turbo Force. Vol. 1 (June 1992)-. Periodical. English. qt. $9.95. Turboforce, PO Box 7597, Red Oak IA 51591-0311. **DD** 794.

US/0734-5585
**TV CROSSWORDS.** [TV crosswords]. **VFOAT** Television Crosswords; T.V. Crosswords. (Feb. 1983)-. Periodical. English. Seventeen times a year. $25.33. Hachette Magazines Inc., 1633 Broadway, New York NY 10019. **Tel** (212)767-6000. **(Subscription address:** Neodata / Colorado, PO Box 2606, Boulder Boulder CO 80322.**) DD** 793. **Ad Acc. *Continues*** *Best of TV Guide Crosswords, 0195-2153.*

US/0884-4992
**TV GAME SHOW MAGAZINE.** ***Ceased.*** [TV game show mag.]. **VFOAT** TV Game Show. **VAT** Television Game Show Magazine. Aug. 1986-?. Periodical. English. mo. Video Age International, 216 East 75th Street 1W, New York NY 10021. **Tel** (212)288-3933. **DD** 795.

US
**VALOR.** (195?)-. Periodical. Spanish (translations available in English). mo. $18.00 US; $24.30 Canada; $30.00 other. DC Comics, 1325 Avenue of the Americas, Floor 27, New York NY 10019. **Tel** (212)636-5443. **(Subscription address:** DC Comics Subscriptions, PO Box 0528, Baldwin, NY 11510)

US/0194-3278
**VARIETY CROSSPATCHES.** (19??)-. Periodical. English. bm (6 issues). $6.25 one year, $12.00 two year. Official Publications Inc., PO Box 937, Fort Washington PA 19034. **Tel** (215)628-0924. **Ad Acc.**
**Desc:** Digest size for challenging, absorbing entertainment on the go.

US/0194-3286
**VARIETY WORD-FIND PUZZLES. VAT** Variety Word Find Puzzles. Periodical. English. mo. $12.00 one year, $22.00 two year. Official Publications Inc., PO Box 937, Fort Washington PA 19034. **Tel** (215)628-0924. **UDC** 793.7. **Ad Acc.**
**Desc:** Search forwards, backwards, up, and down and diagonally for the cleverly concealed words. The number one selling hidden-word puzzle magazine in the world.

US/1059-2938
**VIDEO GAMES & COMPUTER ENTERTAINMENT.** ***Title Change.*** **See** Computers-Computer Games.

US
**VIDEO GAMES : THE ULTIMATE GAMING MAGAZINE.** (19??)-. Periodical. English. mo. $19.95. LFP Inc., 9171 Wilshire Boulevard/Suite 300, Beverly Hills CA 90210. **Tel** (310)858-7100, FAX (310)274-7985. **(Subscription address:** Kable Publishers Aide, 308 East Hitt Street, Subscription Department, Mt. Morris IL 61054-1473.**) *Continues*** *Video Games & Computer Entertainment.*

CN/0711-7914
**VIDEOMANIA.** ***Title Change.*** [Videomania]. **VFOAT** Video. Vol. 1, No. 1 (1980)-?. Periodical. English. mo. Videomania, 1314 Britannia Road East, Mississauga Ontario L4W 1C8 Canada. **ED** Salah Bachir. **DD** 778.59/9/05. **Bk Rev. Ad Acc. Circ:** 38,000. ***Continued by*** *Premiere (Mississauga, Ont.)., 0831-9782.*
**Desc:** Canadian video magazine, with feature articles about video, personalities and film greats, movie reviews, test reports on the latest video equipment, hardware tips, video new release listings, video news and new product reports.
**Ind/Abst** Can. Index (?-?).

US/0889-1990
**VOLLEYBALL MONTHLY. See** Recreation, Leisure-Sports.

CN/0823-7034
**VORTEX (TORONTO).** (VORTEX.). [Vortex]. Vol. 1 No. 1 (Nov. 1982)-. Periodical. English. bm. $1.95 each number. Vortex Magazine, 93A Bloor Street West, Toronto Ontario M5S 1Y2 Canada. **DD** 741.5/971. **UDC** 741.5.

CN/0712-757X
**VOTRE BOTTIN DE CROSSE. See** Recreation, Leisure-Sports.

US/0894-5268
**WALT DISNEY UNCLE SCROOGE.** [Walt Disney's Uncle Scrooge]. **Added/Corp** Walt Disney Company. **VFOAT** Uncle Scrooge; Uncle $croogе; Walt Disney's Uncle $crooge. (19??)-. Periodical. English. bm. $18.00 (two years). Walt Disney Publishing Inc., 500 South Buena Vista Street, Burbank CA 91521. **Tel** (818)567-5661. **(Subscription address:** Gladstone Publishing Ltd., PO Box 2079 D, Prescott AZ 86302.**)**

US/0894-5284
**WALT DISNEY'S COMICS AND STORIES.** [Walt Disney's comics stories]. **Added/Corp** Walt Disney Company. **VFOAT** Comics and Stories; Walt Disney's Comics & Stories. No. 1 (Oct. 1940)-. Periodical. English. bm (6 issues). $18.00. Walt Disney Publishing Inc., 500 South Buena Vista Street, Burbank CA 91521. **Tel** (818)567-5661. **(Subscription address:** Gladstone Publishing Ltd., PO Box 2079 D, Prescott AZ 86302.**) DD** 741. ***Continues*** *Mickey Mouse Magazine.*

US/1041-3170
**WALT DISNEY'S DONALD DUCK ADVENTURES.** [Walt Disney's Donald Duck adventures]. **VFOAT** Donald Duck Adventures. No. 1 (Nov. 1987)-. Periodical. English. bm. $18.00. Walt Disney Publishing Inc., 500 South Buena Vista Street, Burbank CA 91521. **Tel** (818)567-5661. **(Subscription address:** Gladstone Publishing Ltd., PO Box 2079 D, Prescott AZ 86302.**) DD** 741.

US/1055-4882
**WALT DISNEY'S HOLIDAY PARADE.** [Walt Disney's holiday parade]. **VFOAT** Holiday Parade. (1990)-. Periodical. English. $2.95 (US single issue) $3.95 (Canada single issue). Walt Disney Publishing Inc., 500 South Buena Vista Street, Burbank CA 91521. **Tel** (818)567-5661. **DD** 741.

US/1041-1615
**WALT DISNEY'S MICKEY & DONALD.** [Walt Disney's Mickey Donald]. **VFOAT** Walt Disney's Mickey and Donald; Mickey and Donald; Mickey & Donald. No. 1 (March 1988)-. Periodical. English. mo. $7.60 US; $9.60 other. Walt Disney Publishing Inc., 500 South Buena Vista Street, Burbank CA 91521. **Tel** (818)567-5661. **DD** 741.

US/1057-817X
**WALT DISNEY'S SUMMER FUN.** [Walt Disney's summer fun]. **VFOAT** Summer Fun. (1991)-. Periodical. English. $2.95 (single issue). Walt Disney Publishing Inc., 500 South Buena Vista Street, Burbank CA 91521. **Tel** (818)567-5661. **DD** 741.

US/0887-9702
**WEB OF SPIDER-MAN. Added/Corp** Marvel Comics Group. (April 1985)-. Periodical. English. Twelve times a year. $18.00. Marvel Entertainment Group Inc., 387 Park Avenue South, New York NY 10016. **Tel** (212)576-8595, FAX (212) 576-9289. **(Subscription address:** Marvel Direct Marketing Corporation, PO Box 1979, Danbury CT 06813.**) ED** J. Shooter. **Ad Acc. Circ:** 283,000.

●US/1060-779X
**WEEKLY PUZZLER, THE.** [Wkly. puzzler]. (1992)-. English. wk. $100.80. CY Decosse, Inc., 5900 Green Oak Drive, Minnetonka MN 55343. **DD** 793.

CN/1182-1981
**WHERE CALGARY.** [Where Calg.]. Vol. 9, No. 12 (May 1990)-. Periodical. English. mo. 20.00Can$ Canada; 25.00Can$ other. Key West Publishers, Suite 250, 125-9th Avenue SE, Calgary, Alberta T2G 0P6 Canada. **Tel** (403)266-9085, FAX (403)290-0573. **ED** Jennifer MacLeod. **DD** 790/.097123/38. **Ad Acc. Circ:** 25,000 (ctrl). ***Continues*** *Key to Calgary., 0711-4400.*

US/0043-499X
**WHITE TOPS, THE.** [White tops]. **Added/Corp** Circus Fans Association of America. (193?)-. Periodical. English. bm (Jan., Mar., May, Jul., Sep., Nov.). $24.00. Circus Fans Association of America, PO Box 59710, Potomac MD 20859. **Tel** (805)435-2951, (301)762-8272, FAX (805)435-3784. **ED** James G Saunders. **Bk Rev. Ad Acc. Circ:** 2,600 (ctrl). ***Continues*** *Chatter from Around the White Tops.*
**Desc:** Past and present history of the circus. News items regarding the local Tent and Top activities of the members and legislation as it relates to circus animals.

US/0897-9391
**WHITE WOLF MAGAZINE.** [White wolf mag.]. **VFOAT** White Wolf. (August 1986)-. Periodical. English. Twelve times a year. $24.00. White Wolf Publishing, 4598 B Stonegate Boulevard, Stone Mountain GA 30083. **Tel** (404)832-9994. **ED** Steward Wieck. **DD** 794. **Bk Rev. Ad Acc. Circ:** 10,000.
**Desc:** Provides supplemental material for players of role-playing games and prints reviews of new game and book products.

US/1047-854X
**WIN MAGAZINE (VAN NUYS, CALIF.).** (WIN MAGAZINE.). [Win mag.]. **Added/Corp** Gambling Times Incorporated. **VFOAT** Win. (Feb. 1990)-. Periodical. English. Twelve times a year. $44.00. Win Magazine, 16760 Stagg Street, Suite 213, Van Nuys CA 91406-1642. **Tel** (818)781-9355 or (818)760-8983. **LC** GV1301; .G34. **DD** 795.01/05. ***Continues*** *Gambling Times, 0149-0214.*
**Desc:** Covers how to win, where to play and what's happening in sports, racing and lotteries and at legal gambling casinos worldwide. Includes best bets and discount travel information.

CN/0700-4990
**WINNING.** (Jan. 1977)-. Periodical. English. bm. $8.00. Winning, PO Box 412 Station F, Toronto Ontario M4Y 2L8 Canada. **DD** 795/.01. ***Supersedes*** *Gambling Quarterly, 0316-6163.*

US/0744-2467
**WINNING (TULSA, OKLA.).** (WINNING.). (19??)-. Periodical. English. mo. $24.00 (one year), $42.00 (two year). Natcom Inc, 5300 City Plex Tower, 2448 East 81st Street, Tulsa OK 74137-4207. **Tel** (918)491-6100, FAX (918)491-9410. **ED** Thayne Smith. **Bk Rev. Ad Acc. Circ:** 250,000.
**Desc:** Tips on winning contests, sweepstakes, and lotteries, including monthly listings of current sweepstakes and lotteries.

US/1044-453X
**WOLVERINE.** [Wolverine]. No. 1 (Nov. 1988)-. Periodical. English. mo. Marvel Entertainment Group Inc., 387 Park Avenue South, New York NY 10016. **Tel** (212)576-8595, FAX (212) 576-9289. **DD** 741.

US/0732-054X
**WOMAN'S DAY CROSSWORDS.** Periodical. English. mo. $.99 per issue. Diamandis Communications Inc, 1499 Monrovia Avenue, New Port Beach CA 92663. **Tel** (714)720-5300. **UDC** 793.7. ***Continues*** *Woman's Day Puzzles, 0276-8216.*

US/1060-7595
**WONDER MAN.** [Wonder Man]. Vol. 1, No. 1 (Sept. 1991)-. Periodical. English. mo. Marvel Entertainment Group Inc., 387 Park Avenue South, New York NY 10016. **Tel** (212)576-8595, FAX (212) 576-9289. **DD** 741. ***Continues*** *Wonder Man, 1060-7595.*

US
**WONDER WOMAN.** No. 1 (Feb. 1987)-. Periodical. English. mo. $18.00 US; $24.30 Canada;

$30.00 other. DC Comics, 1325 Avenue of the Americas, Floor 27, New York NY 10019. **Tel** (212)636-5443. **(Subscription address:** DC Comics Supscriptions, PO Box 0528, Baldwin, NY 11510**)**

●US/1065-2930
**WORD SEARCH CHALLENGE.** [Word search chall.]. (1992)-. Periodical. English. mo. $19.95. Pace Publications Inc., 1020 North Broadway, Suite 111, Milwaukee WI 53202. **Tel** (414)272-9977, FAX (414)297-9973. **DD** 793.

US/1048-6852
**WORD WIZE.** (WORD WIZE : WORD CIRCLE PUZZLES.). Vol. 1, Issue 1 (Feb. 1990)-. English. bm (6 issues). $21.00. Hochman Associates, 950 Third Avenue, 16th Floor, New York NY 10022. **Tel** (212)371-4932. **(Subscription address:** CDS Agency Hard Copy, PO Box 4966, Des Moines IA 50340.**)** ***Continues*** *Word Sleuth, 0894-5578.*
**Desc:** Puzzle book that strives to stimulate, entertain and challenge puzzle solvers.

UK
**WORLD'S FAIR, THE.** (1904)-. Periodical. English. wk. £61.00 UK; £108.00 other. Worlds Fair Ltd, PO Box 57 / Daltry Street, Oldham OL1 4BB England. **Tel** 011 44 61 624-3687, FAX 011 44 61 665-1260, 011 44 61 628-6921, telex 667352. **ED** Phill Clegg. cum. index. **Bk Rev. Ad Acc, Adv Mgr:** B. Gunn. **Circ:** 30,000 (ctrl). available on microfilm.
**Desc:** News, etc., on amusement, theme and leisure parks, fairgrounds, coin-operated amusement machines and market trading.

US/0894-6604
**X-FACTOR.** [X factor]. **Added/Corp** Marvel Comics Group. **VFOAT** X Factor. Vol. 1 (Feb. 1986)-. Periodical. English. Twelve times a year. $18.00. Marvel Entertainment Group Inc., 387 Park Avenue South, New York NY 10016. **Tel** (212)576-8595, FAX (212) 576-9289. **DD** 741.

US/1057-6800
**X-FORCE (NEW YORK, N.Y.).** (X-FORCE.). [X-force]. **VFOAT** X Force. Vol. 1, No. 1 (Aug. 1991)-. Periodical. English. ir. $18.00. Marvel Entertainment Group Inc., 387 Park Avenue South, New York NY 10016. **Tel** (212)576-8595, FAX (212) 576-9289. **DD** 741.

US/1049-7382
**X-MEN CLASSIC.** [X-men class.]. **VFOAT** X Men Classic. No. 46 (Apr. 1990)-. Periodical. English. Twelve times a year. $18.00. Marvel Entertainment Group Inc., 387 Park Avenue South, New York NY 10016. **Tel** (212)576-8595, FAX (212) 576-9289. **DD** 741. ***Continues*** *Classic X-Men, 0897-5779.*

US/1057-6819
**X-MEN (NEW YORK, N.Y.).** (X-MEN.). [X-men]. **VFOAT** X Men. (Oct. 1991)-. Periodical. English. Twelve times a year. $15.00. Marvel Entertainment Group Inc., 387 Park Avenue South, New York NY 10016. **Tel** (212)576-8595, FAX (212) 576-9289. **DD** 741.

US/0897-7704
**YO YO TIMES. See** Children and Youth Interests.

CN/0229-0383
**YUKON KOMIX.** Vol. 1, No. 1 (1978)-. Periodical. English. John Lodder, PO Box 87, Dawson Yukon Territory Y0B 1G0 Canada. **DD** 741.5/971.

US/0732-5649
**ZANY WORD SEARCH & FIND PUZZLES. VFOAT** Zany Word Search and Find Puzzles; Zany Word; Zany Word Search & Find. (19??)-. Periodical. English. ir. Can Am Media Inc., 151 Hempstead Turnpike, West Hempstead NY 11552.

UK/0954-867X
**ZZAP! 64.** ***Title Change.*** **See** Computers-Computer Sales, Service and Supply.

## OUTDOOR LIFE

US/0514-9738
**A.M.C. MAINE MOUNTAIN GUIDE, THE. Main/Corp** Appalachian Mountain Club. **VFOAT** Maine Mountain Guide. **VAT** Appalachian Mountain Club Maine Mountain Guide. 1st Ed.; 1961-. Periodical. English. ir. Appalachian Mountain Club, 5 Joy Street, Boston MA 02108. **Tel** (617)523-0636, FAX (617)523-0722. **LC** F17.3; .A6. **DD** 917.41/0443. **UDC** 796.52(036)(741). ***Absorbed*** *A.M.C. Katahdin Guide.*

UK
**AA CAMPING AND CARAVANNING IN BRITAIN. VFOAT** Camping and Caravanning in Britain. 1979-. English. an.

UK
**AA GUIDE TO CAMPING AND CARAVANNING. See** Travel and Tourism-Abstracting, Bibliographies and Statistics.

US/0065-082X
**ACCIDENTS IN NORTH AMERICAN MOUNTAINEERING. Added/Corp** American Alpine Club. Safety Committee. Alpine Club of Canada. Safety Committee. (1968)-. English. an. $7.50. American Alpine Club, 710 10th Street, Golden CO 80401. **Tel** (303)384-0110. **LC** GV199.8; .A28. **DD** 363.1/4. ***Continues*** *Accidents in American Mountaineering.*

US/0001-8236
**ADIRONDAC.** [Adirondac]. **Added/Corp** Adirondack Mountain Club. (1945)-. Periodical. English. Six times a year (Jan., Mar., May, July, Sept., Nov.). $12.00 one year; $20.00 other. Adirondack Mountain Club Inc, RR 3 Box 3055, Lake George NY 12845-9523. **Tel** (518)668-4447, FAX (518)668-3746. **ED** Neal S. Burdick. **LC** F127.A2; A17. **DD** 796.5. Index available. **Bk Rev**, (Qty: 12). **Ad Acc. Circ:** 12,000. Documents available from Documents on Demand. ***Continues*** *Adirondack Mountain Club. Bulletin of the Adirondack Mountain Club.*
**Desc:** Focuses on the history, hiking, backpacking, skiing, snowshoeing, ecology and other current issues.
**Ind/Abst** Environ. Abstr.

US/1056-2370
**ADIRONDACK MOUNTAIN CLUB : [NEWSLETTER], THE.** [Adiron. Mt. Club]. **Added/Corp** Adirondack Mountain Club. **VFOAT** Adirondack Mountain Club Newsletter; ADK Newsletter. Vol. 1, No. 1 (June 1991)-. Periodical. English. qt. Adirondack Mountain Club Inc, RR 3 Box 3055, Lake George NY 12845-9523. **Tel** (518)668-4447, FAX (518)668-3746. **DD** 917.

●US
**ADVENTURE WEST.** (Summer/Fall 1992)-. Periodical. English. Six times a year. $11.97 (six issues); $19.97 (twelve issues). Ski West Publications, PO Box 3210, Incline Village NV 89450. **Tel** (702)832-3700, FAX (702)832-3775. **ED** Katrina V. Hackley. **LC** GV191.42.W47; A38. **Ad Acc, Adv Mgr:** Rick Yess, **Tel** (702)832-3700. **Circ:** 190,000.
**Desc:** The America's guide to discovering the West.

US/1058-9805
**AFRICAN WILDLIFE UPDATE. VFOAT** African Wildlife. (Mar. 1991)-. Periodical. English. Six times a year (Jan., Mar., May, July, Sept. Nov.). $15.00. African Wildlife News Service, PO Box 546, Olympia WA 98507-0546. **Tel** (206)459-8862. **ED** Stephen R. Mishkin. **DD** 333. Index available. cum. index (Late in 1994). **Bk Rev**, (Qty: 6). **Circ:** 5,000.

US/0279-6783
**ALABAMA GAME & FISH. VAT** Alabama Game and Fish. (19??)-. Periodical. English. mo. $14.95 (one year), $27.95 (two year), $39.95 (three year). Game & Fish Publications Inc., PO Box 741, Marietta GA 30061. **Tel** (404)953-9222. **ED** David Morris. **Circ:** 19,808.

US/0894-8356
**ALABAMA WILDLIFE.** [Ala. wildl.]. **Added/Corp** Alabama Wildlife Federation. **VFOAT** Alabama Wild Life. (198?)-. Periodical. English. qt. $25.00. Alabama Wildlife Federation, PO Box 1109, Montgomery AL 36102. **Tel** (205)832-9453. **ED** Dan Dumont. **DD** 639. **Ad Acc. Circ:** 6,000 (ctrl). ***Continues*** *Alabama Out-of-Doors, 0889-2814.*

US/0002-4562
**ALASKA (ANCHORAGE, ALASKA).** (ALASKA.). [Alaska]. **VFOAT** Alaska Magazine. Vol. 35, No. 10 (Oct. 1969)-. Periodical. English. Ten times a year. $24.00 (1 year), $42.00 (2 year). Yankee Publishing Inc., Main Street, Dublin NH 03444. **Tel** (603)563-8111, (800)736-1100. **(Subscription address:** CDS / SIFD Agency Control, 1901 Bell Avenue, Des Moines IA 50315.**) ED** Grant Simms. **LC** SK1; .A35. **DD** 799/.09798. **Bk Rev. Ad Acc. Circ:** 260,000. Documents available from UMI Article Clearinghouse. ***Continues*** *Alaska Sportsman.*
**Desc:** Captures the vitality and excitement of Alaskan life; news, stories and color photography. Special hunting, fishing and travel issues each year.
**Ind/Abst** Acad. Abstr. Full Text Elite (May 1984-); Acad. Abstr. (May 1984-); Acad. Search (May 1984-); Access (1975-); Gen. Period. Index (1985-); GeoRef; Mag. Artic. Summar. Elite (May 1984-); Mag. Artic. Summar. Select (May 1984-); Mag. Artic. Summar. CD-ROM (May 1984-); Mag. Index Plus (1989-); Mag. Search; Newsp. Period. Abstr. (1988-); Mag. Index (1977-)(1969-).

US/0095-5760
**ALASKA HUNTING GUIDE.** English. an. $3.95. Alaska Northwest Publishing Company, 130 Second Avenue South, Edmonds WA 98020-3588. **Tel** (206)774-4111, (800)533-7381. **LC** SK49; .A473. **DD** 799.2/09798. **UDC** 799.2(036)(798); 639.1(036)(798).

US/1052-2727
**ALASKA'S WILDLIFE.** ***Ceased.*** [Alsk. wildl.]. **Added/Corp** Alaska. Dept. of Fish and Game. Vol. 22, No. 4 (July/Aug. 1990)-(1993). Periodical. English. bm. Alaska Department of Fish and Game, PO Box 3-2000, Juneau AK 99802. **Tel** (907)465-4100, (907)465-4286. **LC** SK367; .A44. **DD** 639. **Pr Rev. Circ:** 10,000 (ctrl). ***Continues*** *Alaska Fish & Game, 0747-038X.*
**Desc:** Features articles and photographs describing wildlife resource management in the state.

CN/1184-2687
**ALBERTA GAME WARDEN, THE.** [Alta. game ward.]. **Added/Corp** Alberta Fish and Wildlife Officers' Association. Vol. 2, No. 1 (Winter Ed. 1990)-. Periodical. English. qt. $10.00 Canada; $15.00 other. Alberta Game Warden, Box 64, Oten Alberta TOJ 2JO Canada. **Tel** (403)664-3614. **DD** 639.9/097123/05. ***Continues*** *The Alberta Game Warden Conservation Magazine., 0848-0443.*

CN/1185-2836
**ALBERTA GUIDE TO SPORTFISHING.** [Alta. guide sportfish.]. **Added/Corp** Alberta. Fish and Wildlife Division. (1991)-. English. **DD** 799.1/1/097123. ***Continues*** *Guide to Sportfishing., 1182-2600.*

CN/0835-5851
**ALCES. See** Environmental Issues-Conservation and Natural Resources.

CN/0381-8233
**ALMANACH DE KUYPER DE CHASSE ET PECHE, L'.** (1972)-. French. an. John de Kupyer & Fils Ltd, 950 Chemin de l'Adacport, Montreal Quebec H3C 3W5 Canada. **DD** 799/.9714. ***Supersedes*** *Petit Almanach du Chasseur et du Pecheur, 0555-991X.*

SZ
**ALPES (QUARTERLY).** (LES ALPES : REVUE DU CLUB ALPIN SUISSE.). **VFOAT** Alpi; Alpen. Began in 1957. Periodical. French (German, Italian and Romanian). qt. 40.00F. Hallerstrasse 79, Postfach 2728, CH 3001 Berne Switzerland. **LC** DQ820; .A68. **DD** 914.94/7/005. **UDC** 796.52(494).

UK/0065-6569
**ALPINE JOURNAL, THE.** [Alp. j.]. **Added/Corp** Alpine Club (London, England). Vol. 1 (March 1863)-. English. an (Sept.). £21.50. Cordee, 3A de Montfort Street, Leicester LE1 7HD England. **Tel** 011 44 533 543579. **LC** DQ821; .E1. **DD** 949.4/7005. cum. index. **Bk Rev. Ad Acc. Circ:** 3,500.
**Desc:** Is unique in mountain literature. Published as a record of mountain adventure and scientific observation and follows peaks, passes and glaciers.
**Ind/Abst** GeoRef; SportSearch.

FR/0759-2167
**ALPIRANDO. See** Recreation, Leisure-Sports.

●US/1067-5604
**AMC OUTDOORS.** (AMC OUTDOORS : THE MAGAZINE OF THE APPALACHIAN MOUNTAIN CLUB.). [AMC outdoors]. **Added/Corp** Appalachian Mountain Club. **VAT** Appalachian Mountain Club Outdoors. Vol. 59, No. 1 (Jan./Feb. 1993)-. Periodical. English. mo (10 issues). $15.00. Appalachian Mountain Club, 5 Joy Street, Boston MA 02108. **Tel** (617)523-0636, FAX (617)523-0722. **LC** G505; .A56. **DD** 796. ***Continues*** *Appalachia. Bulletin Issue, 1052-5319.*

US/0065-6925
**AMERICAN ALPINE JOURNAL, THE.** [Am. alp. j.]. **Added/Corp** American Alpine Club. Vol. 1 (1929)-. English. an (June). $25.00. American Alpine Club, 710 10th Street, Golden CO 80401. **Tel** (303)384-0110. **LC** GV199.8; .A4. Index available. available on microfilm and microfiche from University Microfilms International (UMI).
**Ind/Abst** GeoRef; Int. Aerosp. Abstr.; SportSearch.

US/0002-8452
**AMERICAN FIELD.** (1881)-. Periodical. English. Twenty-six times a year. $30.00 (one year); $55.00 (two years); $80.00 (three years). American Field, 542 South Dearborn, Chicago IL 60605. **Tel** (312)663-9797. **ED** William F. Brown Sr. **LC** SK1; .A5. **Bk Rev. Ad Acc. Circ:** 13,000. ***Continues*** *Chicago Field.*
**Desc:** Sporting dog and hunting magazine, field trials and bird dog competition.

US/0279-9472
**AMERICAN HIKER.** (AMERICAN HIKER : THE OFFICIAL PUBLICATION OF THE AMERICAN HIKING SOCIETY AND INTERNATIONAL BACKPACKERS ASSOCIATION.). **Added/Corp** American Hiking Society. Vol. 1, No. 1 (Mar., 1981)-. Periodical. English. Four times a year. $25.00. The American Hiking Society, PO Box 20160, Washington DC 20041. **Tel** (703)385-3252, FAX (703)754-9008. **ED** Wayne Curtis. **Ad Acc. Circ:** 2,000. ***Continues*** *American Hiking Society American Hiking Society News, 0164-5722.*

US/0092-1068
**AMERICAN HUNTER, THE. Added/Corp** National Rifle Association of America. Vol. 1 (Oct. 1973)-. Periodical. English. Ten times a year. $15.00 US; $20.00 Canada; $25.00 other. National Rifle Association of America, 11250 Waples Mill Road, Fairfax VA 22030-9100. **Tel** (703)267-1560, (703)267-1583, (800)231-4672, FAX (703)267-3994. **ED** Thomas Fulgham. **LC** SK1; .A517. **DD** 799.2/05. **Circ:** 1,403,337. available on microfilm and microfiche from University

Microfilms International (UMI). Documents available from UMI Article Clearinghouse.
**Ind/Abst** Newsp. Period. Abstr. (1988-).

US/0003-083X
**AMERICAN RIFLEMAN. See** Recreation, Leisure-Sports.

US/0162-153X
**AMERICAN SHOTGUNNER, THE. See** Recreation, Leisure-Sports.

GW
**AMERICANA (BRAUNSCHWEIG, GERMANY).** (AMERICANA : ZEITSCHRIFT FUER INDIANISTIK-CORRAL BRAUNSCHWEIG.). **Added/Corp** Westerners. Corral Braunschweig. (1918)-. Periodical. German. Four times a year (Jan., Apr., July, Oct.). DM25.00 Germany; DM34.00 others. Americana Zeitschrift, Schuetzenstrasse 15, M Grieger, D 38100 Braunschweig Germany. **Tel** 011 49531 43146.

US/0163-268X
**ANDERSON'S CAMPGROUND DIRECTORY. VFOAT** Campground Directory. Directory. English. $4.95. Anderson's Campground Directory, Rural Route 1 Box 58, Boyce VA 22620. **Tel** (703)837-2555. **ED** M Flues. **LC** GV191.42.M52; F57. **DD** 647/.9475. **UDC** 379.83(036)(73); 796.54(73). **Bk Rev. Ad Acc. Circ:** 18,000 (ctrl). ***Continues*** *Campground Directory, Mid Atlantic, 0098-5236.*
**Desc:** A guide to camping in the Mid-Atlantic and Southeast. Each annual issue includes information on private, state and federal campgrounds including rates.

CN/0828-7341
**ANGLER & HUNTER (PETERBOROUGH, ONT.).** ***Ceased.*** (ANGLER & HUNTER.). [Angler hunt.]. **VAT** Angler & Hunter in Ontario (1982); Angler and Hunter (Peterborough, 1982). Vol. 7, No. 1 (Sept. 1982)-Ceased 6/92 with Vol. 16, No. 8. Periodical. English. ir. Ontario Outdoor Publishing Ltd, Box 1541, Peterborough Ontario K9J 7H7 Canada. **DD** 799/.09713. **UDC** 639.1/.2(713); 799.1/.2(713). ***Continues*** *Angler and Hunter Featuring Wildlife in Ontario, 0709-0110.*

CN/0226-5877
**ANNUAIRE - ASSOCIATION DES CAMPS DU QUEBEC.** (ANNUAIRE - QUEBEC CAMPING ASSOCIATION.). [Annu. - Assoc. camps Que.]. **Main/Corp** Quebec Camping Association. **VFOAT** Directory. **VAT** Directory - Association des Camps du Quebec. 1981-. English (French). an. $1.00 per vol. Annuaire, c/o Quebec Camping Association, 1415 Jarry Street East, Montreal Quebec H2E 2L7 Canada. **DD** 796.54/2/025714. **UDC** 796.54(058)(714); 379.83(058)(714). ***Continues*** *Quebec Camping Association. Directory, 0226-5877.*

US
**ANNUAL FINANCIAL REPORT - SOUTH DAKOTA DEPARTMENT OF WILDLIFE, PARKS AND FORESTRY. Main/Corp** South Dakota. Dept. of Wildlife, Parks and Forestry. English. an. South Dakota Department of Wildlife, Parks, and Forestry, Sigurd Anderson Building, 445 E Capitol, Pierre SD 57501. **LC** SK447; .S68A. **DD** 353.97830072/31. **UDC** 502.4(783). ***Continues*** *Annual Financial Report - South Dakota Department of Game, Fish and Parks, 0146-8987.*

US
**ANNUAL PERFORMANCE REPORT OF SURVEY-INVENTORY ACTIVITIES / ALASKA DEPARTMENT OF FISH AND GAME, DIVISION OF WILDLIFE CONSERVATION. See** Environmental Issues-Conservation and Natural Resources.

US/0362-6962
**ANNUAL REPORT OF SURVEY-INVENTORY ACTIVITIES.** ***Title Change.*** **Main/Corp** Alaska. Division of Game. (19??)-(19??). English. an. Alaska Department of Fish and Game, PO Box 3-2000, Juneau AK 99802. **Tel** (907)465-4100, (907)465-4286. **LC** SK367; .A65b. **DD** 353.9/798/00823305. ***Continued by*** *Annual Performance Report of Survey-Inventory Activities.*

US/0003-6587
**APPALACHIA (BOSTON).** (APPALACHIA.). [Appalach.]. Vol. 1, No. 1 (June 1876)-. Periodical. English. sa. $10.00. Appalachian Mountain Club, 5 Joy Street, Boston MA 02108. **Tel** (617)523-0636, FAX (617)523-0722. **ED** Sandy Stott. **LC** G505; .A55. **DD** 796. Index available. cum. index. **Bk Rev. Ad Acc. Circ:** 10,000 (ctrl).
**Desc:** Oldest journal of mountaineering and conservation.
**Ind/Abst** AGRICOLA [Full Cov.]; Am. Hist. Life (1986-1988); GeoRef.

US/1052-5319
**APPALACHIA. BULLETIN ISSUE.** ***Title Change.*** [Appalach., Bull. issue]. **Added/Corp** Appalachian Mountain Club. **VFOAT** Bulletin Issue. Vol. 40, No. 8 (Aug.-Sept./74)-(1992). Bulletin. English. mo. Appalachian Mountain Club, 5 Joy Street, Boston MA 02108. **Tel** (617)523-0636, FAX (617)523-0722. **LC** G505; .A56. **DD** 796. ***Continues*** *Appalachia Bulletin.* ***Continued by*** *AMC Outdoors, 1067-5604.*

US/0003-6641
**APPALACHIAN TRAILWAY NEWS.** [Appalach. trailw. news]. **Added/Corp** Appalachian Trail Conference. Vol. 1 (Jan. 1939)-. Periodical. English. Five times a year. $15.00 US; $22.50 Canada & Mexico; $32.50 other. Appalachian Trail Conference, PO Box 807, Harpers Ferry WV 25425. **Tel** (304)535-6331, FAX (304)535-2667. **ED** Judith Jenner. **LC** F106; .A623. **DD** 917.4. Index available. **Bk Rev. Circ:** 24,500 (ctrl).
**Desc:** News and features about the Appalachian Trail; general coverage regarding environmental and conservation topics.
**Ind/Abst** GeoRef.

US/0190-3322
**APPALACHIAN VOICE, THE. See** Environmental Issues-Conservation and Natural Resources.

US/1069-0298
**ARIZONA GREAT OUTDOORS.** [Ariz. great outdoors]. (1989)-. Periodical. English. Four times a year (Mar., June, Sept., Dec.). $6.00. Arizona Great Outdoors, Box 6243, Scottsdale AZ 85261. **Tel** (602)945-6746. **ED** Janet L. Jacobson (editor's address: 7432 East Diamond, Scottsdale, AZ 85257). **DD** 796. **Ad Acc. Circ:** 27,000.
**Desc:** Covers outdoor recreation and conservation in Arizona. Primarily focus on hiking and camping, calendar of events, and directories of outdoors groups and government agencies.

US/0882-5572
**ARIZONA WILDLIFE VIEWS. See** Environmental Issues-Conservation and Natural Resources.

US/0744-4184
**ARKANSAS SPORTSMAN.** (198?)-. Periodical. English. mo. $14.95 (one year), $27.95 (two year), $39.95 (three year). Game & Fish Publications Inc., PO Box 741, Marietta GA 30061. **Tel** (404)953-9222.

●US/1063-0953
**ARKANSAS WILDLIFE. See** Environmental Issues-Conservation and Natural Resources.

●US/1059-5708
**ASSAULT RIFLES. See** Military and Defense.

AT/0159-6322
**AUSTRALIAN GEM & TREASURE HUNTER.** [Aust. gem treas. hunt.]. **VAT** Australian Gem and Treasure Hunter. No. 43-. Periodical. English. mo. $16.23. Gemcraft, 291-295 Wattletree Road, East Malvern Victoria 3145 Australia. **Tel** 03-5091181. **ED** Gladys Rangott. **UDC** 553.8(94). **Bk Rev. Ad Acc. Circ:** 12,000. ***Continues*** *Australian Gems & Crafts Magazine.*
**Desc:** Family outdoor activities of prospecting, mining, detecting, gold prospecting, treasure hunting, gemstones and minerals, camping, etc.
**Ind/Abst** GeoRef.

US/0277-867X
**BACKPACKER.** [Backpacker]. **VFOAT** Backpacker Including Wilderness Camping; Backpacker Including Wilderness Camping and Backpacker Footnotes. Vol. 1, No. 1 (Spring 1973)-. Periodical. English. Nine times a year. $27.00 US; $31.78 Canada; $46.00. Rodale Press Inc., 400 South 10th Street, Emmaus PA 18098. **Tel** (215)967-5171, (800)666-2503. **LC** GV199.6; .B3. **DD** 796.5. available on microfiche from University Microfilms International (UMI); available on an online database (file 647/Full-Text) from DIALOG. Documents available from UMI Article Clearinghouse, Magazine Collection. ***Absorbed*** *Wilderness Camping, 0043-5430; Backpacker Footnotes, 0271-6534.*
**Desc:** Contains expedition planners, maps and illustrations.
**Ind/Abst** Acad. Abstr. Full Text Elite (Jan. 1984-); Acad. Abstr. (Jan. 1984-); Acad. Ind. [Computer File] (1984-); Consum. Index Prod. Eval. Inf. Source; Expand. Acad. Index (1980, 1984-1988); Gen. Period. Index (1985-); Health Source (Jan. 1984-); Mag. Artic. Summar. Elite (Jan. 1984-); Mag. Artic. Summar. Select (Jan. 1984-); Mag. Artic. Summar. CD-ROM (Jan. 1984-); Mag. Index Plus (1989-); Mag. Search; Newsp. Period. Abstr. (1988-); Phys. Educ. Index; Read. Guide Period. Lit.; SPORT Discus; SportSearch (1980-); Mag. Index (1980-); Vocat. Search (Jan. 1984-).

US/0005-3775
**BADGER SPORTSMAN.** (19??)-. Periodical. English. Twelve times a year. $9.00 (one year); $16.00 (two years); $22.00 (three years). Vercauteren Publishing, 19 East Main Street, Chilton WI 53014. **Tel** (414)849-4651. **ED** Mike Maricqurrdt. **Bk Rev. Ad Acc. Circ:** 26,200.
**Desc:** A fishing, hunting and camping guide to Wisconsin and the midwest.

●US
**BASS & WALLEYE BOATS. VFOAT** Bass and Walleye Boats. (1994)-. Periodical. English. Five times a year. $20.97 (2 year). Poole Publications Inc, 20700 Belshaw Avenue, Carson CA 90746. **Tel** (310)537-6322, FAX (310)537-8735. **(Subscription address:** Kable Publishers Aide, 308 East Hitt Street, Subscription Department, Mt. Morris IL 61054-1473.**)**

CN/0045-2998
**BC MOUNTAINEER, THE.** Vol. 1 (March 1923)-. English. be. $6.00. British Columbia Mountaineering Club, PO Box 2674, Vancouver British Columbia V6B 3W8 Canada. **Bk Rev. Ad Acc. Circ:** 400.

CN/0045-3013
**BC OUTDOORS.** (B C OUTDOORS.). [BC outdoors]. Vol. 23, No. 4 (July/Aug. 1967)-. Periodical. English. Eight times a year. 23.95Can$ Canada; 31.95Can$ other. Special Interest Publications / Canada, 1132 Hamilton Street/Suite 202, Vancouver BC V6B 2S2 Canada. **Tel** (604)687-1581, FAX (604)687-1925. **ED** George Will. **Bk Rev. Ad Acc. Circ:** 35,000. available on an online database. ***Continues*** *British Columbia Digest, 0382-5639.*
**Desc:** Outdoor recreation in British Columbia - fishing, camping, hunting, hiking, cross-country skiing, backroad travel, wildlife conservation, outdoor equipment, and book reviews.
**Ind/Abst** AQUAREF; Can. Index; Can. Period. Index.

GW/0340-1294
**BERGWELT.** [Bergwelt]. Jan. 1974-. German. 36.00. Berverlag R Rother, Landshuter Allee 49, 8 Munchen 19 Germany. **LC** DQ820; .B46. **UDC** 796.52. ***Continues*** *Winter, Bergkamerad, 0005-8939.*

US/0507-0503
**BIENNIAL REPORT - VIRGINIA COMMISSION OF OUTDOOR RECREATION. Main/Corp** Virginia. Commission of Outdoor Recreation. (1968)-. Periodical. English. be. Virginia Commission of Outdoor Recreation, Recreation Services Section, James Monroe Building, 101 North 14th Street, Richmond VA 23219. **LC** GV191.42.V8; V57c. **DD** 301.5/7.

●US/1059-5767
**BIG GAME HUNTING.** (1992)-. Periodical. English. $4.95. Petersen Publishing Company, 6420 Wilshire Bouldevard, Los Angeles CA 90048. **Tel** (213)782-2485.

US/0894-7856
**BOW & ARROW HUNTING.** [Bow arrow hunt.]. **VFOAT** Bow and Arrow Hunting. Vol. 22, No. 5 (Jan./Feb. 1985)-. Periodical. English. Seven times a year. $18.00 (US); $22.00 (others). Gallant Charger Publishing Inc., Box HH, 34249 Camino Capistrano, Capistrano Beach CA 92624. **Tel** (714)493-2101, FAX (714)240-8680. **LC** GV1183; .B6. **DD** 799.2/028/5. ***Continues*** *Bow and Arrow, 0006-8403.*

US/0273-7434
**BOWHUNTER (FORT WAYNE).** (BOWHUNTER.). (19??)-. Periodical. English. bm. $24.00. Cowles Magazines, PO Box 8200, Harrisburg PA 17105. **Tel** (717)657-9555, (800)435-9610. **LC** WMLC L 83/6983. available on microfilm from University Microfilms International (UMI).

US/1043-5492
**BOWHUNTING WORLD.** [Bowhunt. world]. Vol. 38, No. 3 (June 1989)-. Periodical. English. ir. $20.00 US; $26.00 Canada. Ehlert Publishing Group, 601 Lakeshore Parkway, Suite 600, Minnetonka MN 55305. **Tel** (612)476-2200. **DD** 799. available on microfilm and microfiche from University Microfilms International (UMI). ***Continues*** *Archery World (Boyertown, PA.), 0003-827X.*
**Desc:** The magazine of all-season bowhunter action.
**Ind/Abst** Phys. Educ. Index.

UK
**BRITISH WILDLIFE.** (1989)-. English. Six times a year (Feb., Apr., June, Aug., Oct., Dec.). £21.95 UK; £22.50 Europe; £28.50 other. British Wildlife Publishing, Lower Barn/Rooks Farm, Basingstoke RG27 9BG England. **Tel** 011 44 256 760663. **ED** Andrew Branson. Index available. **Bk Rev. Ad Acc, Adv Mgr:** A.Branson, **Tel** 0256 760663. **Circ:** 4,750 (ctrl).
**Desc:** Covers all aspects of the wildlife including conservation news and environmental issues.
**Ind/Abst** Curr. Aware. Biol. Sci., CABS; Ecol. Abstr.

CN/0383-9249
**BRUCE TRAIL NEWS.** (THE BRUCE TRAIL NEWS.). **Added/Corp** Bruce Trail Association. (196?)-. Periodical. English. Three times a year. Free to members, $30.00 other (US and Canada). Bruce Trail Association, PO Box 857, Hamilton Ontario L8N 3N9 Canada. **Tel** (416)529-6821. **DD** 796.5/1/05.
**Desc:** Information on hiking and outdoor excursions.

US/0895-481X
**BUCKMASTERS WHITETAIL MAGAZINE. Added/Corp** Buckmasters (Organization). Vol. 1, No. 1 (July/August 1987)-. Periodical. English. ir (monthly Sept. through Dec., bi-monthly Jan./Feb. and July/Aug/). $20.00 (membership). Buckmasters Inc, PO Box 235006, Montgomery AL 36197. **Tel** (205)269-3337. **DD** 799.

CN/0709-2172
**BULLETIN A L'USAGE DES TRAPPEURS.** See Recreation, Leisure-Sports.

CN/1186-2785
**BULLETIN DU PROGRAMME D'EDUCATION SCOLAIRE SUR LES PECHES.** [Bull, Programme educ. sc. pech.]. **Main/Corp** Ontario. Programme d'Education Scolaire sur les Peches. **Added/Corp** Ontario. Ministere des Richesses Naturelles. (1991)-. Bulletin. French. **DD** 333.95.

CN/0706-4667
**C. O. E. Q. JOURNAL, THE.** See Education.

CN/0821-235X
**CALEDON COMMENT.** (CALEDON COMMENT : THE MAGAZINE OF THE CALEDON HILLS BRUCE TRAIL CLUB.). [Caledon comment]. Periodical. English. qt. Free to members. Caledon Hills Bruce Trail Club, PO Box 302, Waterloo Ontario N2Y 4A4 Canada. **DD** 796.5/1/060713535. **UDC** 796.51(713).

US/0164-8748
**CALIFORNIA EXPLORER.** See Travel and Tourism.

US/1056-0122
**CALIFORNIA GAME & FISH.** [Calif. game fish]. **VFOAT** California Game and Fish. (19??)-. Periodical. English. mo. $14.95 (one year), $27.95 (two year), $39.95 (three year). Game & Fish Publications Inc., PO Box 741, Marietta GA 30061. **Tel** (404)953-9222. **DD** 799.

US
**CAMPBOOK. EASTERN CANADA.** **VFOAT** Eastern Canada Campbook. Began with 1980. English. an. American Automobile Association, 1000 AAA Drive, Heathrow FL 32746. **Tel** (407)444-7000. **LC** GV191.46.M4; A46A. **DD** 647/.9471. **UDC** 379.839(71); 796.54(71). ***Continues*** *Eastern Canada Camping.*

US/0734-2705
**CAMPBOOK. MIDEASTERN.** **Added/Corp** American Automobile Association. **VFOAT** Camp Book. Mideastern; Mideastern. (1980)-. English. American Automobile Association, 1000 AAA Drive, Heathrow FL 32746. **Tel** (407)444-7000. **LC** GV191.42.A84; A5a. **DD** 647/.9474. ***Continues*** *Mideastern Camping, 0147-7285.*

US/0732-2585
**CAMPBOOK. NORTH CENTRAL.** [CampB., North Cent.]. **VFOAT** Camp Book. North Central; North Central. English. an. American Automobile Association, 1000 AAA Drive, Heathrow FL 32746. **Tel** (407)444-7000. **LC** GV198.65.N67; A45A. **DD** 647/.9477. **UDC** 379.83(77); 796.54(77). ***Continues*** *North Central Camping, 0147-8613.*

US/0732-7315
**CAMPBOOK. NORTHEASTERN.** [CampB., Northeast.]. **VFOAT** Camp Book. Northeastern; Northeastern. English. an. American Automobile Association, 1000 AAA Drive, Heathrow FL 32746. **Tel** (407)444-7000. **LC** GV191.42.N74; N67. **DD** 917.4. **UDC** 379.83(74); 796.54(74). ***Continues*** *Northeastern Camping, 0196-6456.*

US/0732-2577
**CAMPBOOK. NORTHWESTERN.** [CampB., Northwest.]. **VFOAT** Camp Book. Northwestern; Northwestern. English. an. American Automobile Association, 1000 AAA Drive, Heathrow FL 32746. **Tel** (407)444-7000. **LC** GV191.35; .N67. **DD** 647/.9779. **UDC** 379.83(79); 796.54(79). ***Continues*** *Northwestern Camping, 0095-4411.*

US/0731-535X
**CAMPBOOK. SOUTH CENTRAL.** [CampB., South Cent.]. **VFOAT** Camp Book. Began with 1980 ed. English. an. American Automobile Association, 1000 AAA Drive, Heathrow FL 32746. **Tel** (407)444-7000. **LC** GV198.65.S68; A43A. **DD** 647/.94767. **UDC** 379.83(76); 796.54(76). ***Continues*** *South Central Camping, 0364-7161.*

US/0731-5112
**CAMPBOOK. SOUTHEASTERN.** [CampB., Southeast.]. **VFOAT** Camp Book. Southeastern; Southeastern. Began with 1980 Ed. English. an. American Automobile Association, 1000 AAA Drive, Heathrow FL 32746. **Tel** (407)444-7000. **LC** GV191.42.S83; S66. **DD** 647.94/75. **UDC** 379.83(75); 796.54(75). ***Continues*** *Southeastern Camping, 0162-9166.*

US/0731-8103
**CAMPBOOK. SOUTHWESTERN.** [CampB., Southwest.]. **VFOAT** Camp Book. Southwestern; Southwestern. Began with 1980 Ed. English. an. American Automobile Association, 1000 AAA Drive, Heathrow FL 32746. **Tel** (407)444-7000. **LC** GV191.42.A165; S68. **DD** 647/9479. **UDC** 379.83(79); 796.54(79). ***Continues*** *Southwestern Camping, 0094-2855.*

US/0732-5347
**CAMPBOOK. WESTERN CANADA AND ALASKA.** [CampB., West. Can. Alsk.]. **VFOAT** Camp Book. Western Canada and Alaska; Western Canada and California. Began in 1980. English. an. American Automobile Association, 1000 AAA Drive, Heathrow FL 32746. **Tel** (407)444-7000. **LC** GV198.67.C2; W47. **DD** 647/.9471. **UDC** 379.83(71); 796.54(71). ***Continues*** *Western Canada. Alaska Camping.*

US/0094-0054
**CAMPER'S GUIDE TO AREA CAMPGROUNDS.** English. be. $3.95. M.B. Pearsall, Box 305, Hillsdale IL 61257. **LC** GV191.42.M53; C34. **DD** 917.7/04/3. **UDC** 379.83(036)(73).

US/0896-5706
**CAMPING AND RV MAGAZINE.** See Recreation, Leisure.

US/0361-5812
**CAMPING AND TRAILERING GUIDE.** **VFOAT** Camping Guide. Periodical. English. mo. $6.45. Woodall Publishing Company, 28167 North Keith Drive, Lake Forest IL 60015. **Tel** (708)362-6700. **LC** GV191.68; .C34. **DD** 796.54/0973. **UDC** 379.83(036)(73).

CN/0384-9856
**CAMPING CANADA.** Vol. 1 (1972)-. Periodical. English. ir. 16.00Can$ (Canada); 35.00Can$ (other). CRV Publications, 2585 Skymark Ave, Suite 306, Mississauga Ontario L4W 4L5 Canada. **Tel** (416)624-8218, FAX (416)624-6764. **ED** Norman Rosen. **DD** 917.1/04/644. Index available (Free). **Bk Rev.** **Ad Acc.** **Circ:** 56,000 (ctrl).

FR
**CAMPING, CARAVANING FRANCE.** **VFOAT** Camping, Caravaning. French (German, Dutch and English). Michelin Guides and Maps, PO Box 3305, Spartanburg SC 29304. **Tel** (803)599-0850. **LC** GV191.48.F8; C34. **DD** 914.40483/7. **UDC** 379.83(44); 796.54(44). ***Continues*** *Camping, Caravanning en France.*

CN/1187-1334
**CAMPING, CARAVANING (MONTREAL).** (CAMPING, CARAVANING.). [Camping caravan.]. **Added/Corp** Conseil de Developpement du Camping au Quebec. (1991)-. French (English). Conseil du Developpment du Camping au Quebec, 4545 av Pierre-de-Courbetin, CP 1000 Succursale M, Montreal, Quebec H1V 3R2. **DD** 647.94714/09. ***Formed by the union of*** *Guide Camping Quebec., 0849-0082* ***and*** *Hebergement, Camping, 1187-7987 Camping Accommodation, 1187-7979 Hebergement, Camping.*

CN/0822-6474
**CAMPING CLUES.** [Camping clues]. Periodical. English. Town Talk Publications, 89 Oriole Parkway, Toronto Ontario M5P 2G7 Canada. **DD** 796.54/2. **UDC** 379.83(71); 796.54(71). ***Continues*** *Town Talk About Toronto Presents Camping Clues, 0822-6466.*

GW
**CAMPING-FUHRER. BAND I: SUDEUROPA.** **Added/Corp** ADAC. (19??)-. German. an. Free. ADAC Verlag, Postfach 70 00 86, 8 Munchen 70 Germany. **Tel** (089)76762315. **ED** Horst Nitschke. **LC** GV198.67.E855; C34. Index available. **Ad Acc.** **Circ:** 280,000 (ctrl).
**Desc:** Guide to European camping-sites, based on accurate inspection and research. Insertions: multicoloured map; special brochure with listings of camping sites ordered into fields of interest.

GW
**CAMPING FUHRER BAND II : DEUTSCHLAND, MITTEL- UND NORD-EUROPA.** **VFOAT** Campingfuhrer Band II: Deutschland, Mittel- und Nordeuropa. **VAT** Camping Fuhrer Bank Zwei: Deutschland, Mittel- und Nord-Europa. German. an. Free. Postfach 70 00 86, 8 Munich 70 Germany. **Tel** (089)76762315, telex 26. **ED** Horst Nitschke. **LC** GV191.48.E8; C34. **UDC** 379.83(4); 796.54(4). **Ad Acc.** **Circ:** 90,226 (ctrl).
**Desc:** Guide to European camping-sites, based on accurate inspection and research.

US/8755-9773
**CAMPING HOTLINE.** **Added/Corp** National Campers & Hikers Association. (198?)-. Periodical. English. mo. Free (members), $15.00 (nonmembers). HAP Enterprises Inc, 500 Hyacinth Place, Highland Park IL 60035. **LC** GV191.4; .W66. **DD** 796.54/0973. ***Continues*** *Woodall's Camping Hotline, 0277-0075.*

US/0740-4131
**CAMPING MAGAZINE, THE.** [Camping mag.]. **Added/Corp** Camp Directors Association (U.S.) American Camping Association. Vol. 1 (Jan. 1930)-. Periodical. English. Six times a year (Jan., Mar., May, July, Sept., Nov.). $23.95 US; $30.00 Alaska, Hawaii, Canada, Mexico, & Puerto Rico; $36.50 others; $30.50 US, $39.00 Alaska, Hawaii, Canada, Mexico, & Puerto Rico, $48.00 others, (one years) Comes with a guide. American Camping Association, 5000 State Road 67 North, Martinsville IN 46151-7902. **Tel** (317)342-8456, (800)428-2267, FAX (317)342-2065. **ED** Nancy LaMarca Gordon. **LC** SK601.A1; C36. **DD** 796. Index available. **Bk Rev.** **Ad Acc.** **Circ:** 8,000. available on microfilm and microfiche from University Microfilms International (UMI); available on CD-ROM. Documents available from UMI Article Clearinghouse, Magazine Collection. ***Continues*** *Camping (Cambridge, Mass.).*
**Desc:** For professionals working with youth and adult camps and outdoor programming. Geared toward camp and conference center owners/directors/staff and educators. Includes practical articles and applicable academic research on camp management, staffing and programming, camper development, environmental and legislative issues.
**Ind/Abst** Curr. Index J. Educ.; Gen. Period. Index (1985-); Mag. Index Plus (1989-); Newsp. Period. Abstr. (1988-); Phys. Educ. Index; Read. Guide Period. Lit.; SPORT Discus; SportSearch; Mag. Index (1978-);(1959-).

BL
**CAMPING QUATRO RODAS.** (1980)-. Portuguese. $131.00. Editora Abril SA, Rua do Curtume 769 Lapa, 05066 900 Sao Paulo SP Brazil. **Tel** 011 55 11 8239222, 011 55 11 2623322, FAX 011 55 11 8643796. **LC** GV191.48.B6; C35. **DD** 647/.9481. **UDC** 379.83(81); 796.54(81).

US/0746-1259
**CAMPNEWS (PHILADELPHIA, PA.).** (CAMPNEWS : OFFICIAL PUBLICATION OF THE PATRIOTIC ORDER SONS OF AMERICA.). **Added/Corp** Patriotic Order Sons of America. **VFOAT** Camp News. (1???)-. Periodical. English. bm. Patriotic Order Sons of America, 115 Rochelle Avenue, Philadelphia PA 19128.

CN/0068-8207
**CANADIAN ALPINE JOURNAL, THE.** **Added/Corp** Alpine Club of Canada. **VFOAT** Journal Alpin Canadien. Vol. 1 (1907)-. Periodical. English (French). an. 26.95Can$ Canada; 27.95Can$ other. Alpine Club of Canada, PO Box 1026, Banff Alberta T0L 0C0 Canada. **Tel** (403)678-3200. **ED** Geoff Powter. **LC** F1090; .C2. **DD** 796.5/22/0971. **CODEN** CNAJA6. Index available. cum. index. **Bk Rev.** **Circ:** 3,000 (ctrl).
**Desc:** Covers mountaineering and expeditions.
**Ind/Abst** GeoRef; SportSearch.

CN
**CANADIAN ANGLER.** See Fish and Fisheries.

CN/0846-3182
**CANADIAN BOWHUNTING.** [Can. bowhunt.]. **VFOAT** Bowhunting. (1991)-. Periodical. English. sa. $13.95. Canadian Outdoor Publications, 140 Avenue F North, Saskatoon Sask S7L 1V8 Canada. **Tel** (306)665-6302, FAX (306)244-8859. **DD** 799.2. ***Continues*** *The ... Canadian Bowhunting Annual., 0846-3174.*

CN/0316-280X
**CANADIAN CAMPER, THE.** **Added/Corp** Canadian Family Camping Federation. Vol. 3, Issue 4 (July 1970)-. Periodical. English. Four times a year. 9.00Can$. Canadian Family Camping Federation, Box 397, Rexdale Ontario Canada. **ED** Carol Nagel and Gerald Nagel (editor's address: RR9 Dunnville, Ontario N1A 2W8 Canada; editor's phone: (905)774-4030). **Ad Acc.** **Circ:** 350. ***Continues*** *C.F.C.F. News for the Canadian Camper, 0045-4729.*
**Desc:** Information of interest to camping families.

CN/0833-0948
**CANADIAN CAVER, THE.** [Can. caver]. **Added/Corp** McMaster University. Dept. of Geology. (1969)-. Periodical. English (French; summaries and/or abstracts in French). sa. 12.00Can$. The Canadian Caver, PO Box 22324 Bankers Hall, Calgary Alberta T2P 4J1 Canada. **Tel** (403)276-1545. **ED** Ian McKenzie, Chas Yonge and Tich Morris. **DD** 796.5/25/0971. Index available. cum. index. **Bk Rev.** **Ad Acc.** **Pr Rev.** **Circ:** 200 (ctrl).
**Desc:** A blend of sports and science; accounts of explorations and geomorphological investigations of caves in Canada and abroad. Includes surveys (plan and profile), maps and photos.

CN/0846-3042
**CANADIAN HUNTING & SHOOTING MAGAZINE, THE.** [Can. hunt. shoot. mag.]. **VFOAT** Hunting & Shooting. **VAT** Canadian Hunting and Shooting Magazine. Vol. 1, Issue 1 (Fall 1990)-. Periodical. English. Eight times a year. 19.95Can$ (one year) Canada; 28.32Can$ (one year) other. Canadian Outdoor Publications, 140 Avenue F North, Saskatoon Sask S7L 1V8 Canada. **Tel** (306)665-6302, FAX (306)244-8859. **ED** R. A. Johnson. **DD** 799.2.

UK/0141-2302
**CANAL & RIVERBOAT.** (1978)-. Consumer Publication. English. mo. £21.00. A E Morgan Publications Ltd, Stanley House, 9 West Street, Epsom Surrey KT18 7RL England. **Tel** 011 44 3727 41411, FAX 0372 744493, telex 291561 VIA SOS G. **ED** C.J. Beadsmoore. **Bk Rev.** **Ad Acc.** **Circ:** 15,000.

US/0194-8954
**CASCADES EAST.** Vol. 1 (May 1976)-. Periodical. English. Four times a year (Mar., June, Sept., Dec.). $12.00 (one year) US; $16.00 (one year) others. Sun Publishing Company / Oregon, PO Box 5784, 716 Northeast 4th Street, Bend OR 97708. **Tel** (503)382-0127, FAX (503)382-7057. **ED** Geoff Hill. **Bk Rev**. **Ad Acc**. **Circ:** 10,000.
**Desc:** For all ages interested in outdoor recreation in Central Oregon. Covers fishing, hunting, sight-seeing, hiking, bicycling, mountain climbing, backpacking, rockhounding, skiing, snowmobiling, etc.

CN/0706-8166
**CAVING INTERNATIONAL.** [Caving int.]. **VFOAT** Caving International Magazine. No. 1-. Periodical. English. qt. 3.00Can$. Caving International, PO Bag 4014 Station C, Calgary Alberta T2T 5M9 Canada. **DD** 796.5/25/05. **UDC** 796.55.
**Ind/Abst** GeoRef.

●CN/1185-247X
**CHASSE AU QUEBEC, PRINCIPALES REGLES, LA.** [Chasse Que. princ. regles]. **Added/Corp** Quebec (Province). Ministere du Loisir, de la Chasse et de la Peche. (1992)-. French. Ministere du Loisir de la Chasse et de la Peche, 150 Est Boulevard St. Cyrille, Quebec Quebec G1R 4Y1 Canada. **Tel** (418)643-5526. **DD** 799.2. ***Continues in part*** *La Chasse et le Piegeage au Quebec, Principales Regles., 0838-4134.*

UK
**CINEMANTICS.** No. 1- Jan. 1970-. Periodical. English. qt. 117 Hartfield Road, London SW19 England.

UK/0955-3045
**CLIMBER AND HILL WALKER.** **See** Recreation, Leisure.

US/0045-7159
**CLIMBING (ASPEN, COLO.).** (CLIMBING.). (1970)-. Periodical. English. bm. $24.00 (one year), $42.00 (two year) US; $34.00 (one year), $62.00 (two year) Canada; $39.00 (one year), $72.00 (two year) other. Elk Mountain Press, Box 339, 502 Main Street, Carbondale CO 81623. **Tel** (303)963-9449, FAX (303)963-9442. **ED** Michael Kennedy. **LC** GV199.4; .C58. **DD** 796.5/223/0973. **Bk Rev**. **Ad Acc**. **Circ:** 36,000.
**Desc:** Covers technicalities of rock, snow and ice climbing and Alpine mountaineering throughout North America and the world. Profusely illustrated in four colors, with news, reviews, commentary and equipment reviews.
**Ind/Abst** SportSearch (May 1987-).

US/0734-7251
**COLEMAN GUIDE TO CAMPING & THE GREAT OUTDOORS.** [Coleman guide camping gt. outdoors]. **VFOAT** Coleman Guide to Camping and the Great Outdoors; Guide to Camping & the Great Outdoors; Guide to Camping and the Great Outdoors; Coleman Camping. Periodical. English. $2.50 US; $2.95 other. Aqua Field Publications Inc, 66 West Gilbert Street, Shrewsbury NJ 07702. **Tel** (201)842-8300. **LC** GV191.68; .C64A. **DD** 796.54/05. **UDC** 379.83(73); 796.54(73). ***Continues*** *Coleman Outdoor Annual, 0195-3958.*

US/0891-3145
**COLORADO OUTDOOR JOURNAL.** ***Ceased.*** [Colo. outdoor j.]. Vol. 1, No. 1 (1986)-Vol. 2, No. 3 (1987). Periodical. English. qt. Colorado Outdoor Journal, 2418 Greenway Circle, Canon City CO 81212. **DD** 799. **UDC** 379.83/.85(788); 799.1/.2(788).

US/0010-1699
**COLORADO OUTDOORS.** **See** Environmental Issues-Conservation and Natural Resources.

US/0276-8992
**COLORADO WILDLIFE RESEARCH REVIEW.** ***Title Change.*** [Colo. wildl. res. rev.]. **Added/Corp** Colorado. Wildlife Research Section. (1977-1979)-(19??). English. Research Center Library, Division of Wildlife, 317 West Prospect, Fort Collins CO 80526. **LC** SK375; .A325. **DD** 596.09788/05. ***Continues*** *Colorado Game Research Review.* ***Merged with*** *Colorado Fisheries Research Review, 0588-4462* ***to form*** *Research Review (Colorado. Division of Wildlife), 1055-4238.*

US/1047-1669
**COMPETITION ANGLER.** [Compet. angler]. (1989)-. Periodical. English. mo. $15.00. Competition Angler, 2160 Renwick Drive, Poland OH 44514. **Tel** (216)757-8171, FAX (216)533-3865. **ED** Jack Wollitz. **DD** 799. **Bk Rev**. **Ad Acc**. **Circ:** 1,000 (ctrl).
**Desc:** Targeted at tournament-style bass fishermen, primarily in Ohio. Offers in-depth coverage of Ohio bass tournaments, schedules and related bass fishing news. Publishes news and results from the national bass tournament trail, and monthly columns by well-known professional fishermen on topics ranging from fitness and nutrition to sponsorships, tips and tactics.

●US/1059-5783
**COMPLETE GUIDE TO 9MM.** (1992)-. English. $3.95. Petersen Publishing Company, 6420 Wilshire Bouldevard, Los Angeles CA 90048. **Tel** (213)782-2485.

US/0092-5764
**CONNECTICUT WALK BOOK.** 1st- Ed.; 1937-. English. te. $15.00. Connecticut Forest and Park Association, Middlefield, 16 Meriden Road, Rockfall CT 06481-2961. **Tel** (203)346-2372, FAX (203)347-7463. **ED** Linda Rapp. **LC** SD1; .C62 subser; F92.3. **DD** 333.7/8/09746; 917.46/04/4. **UDC** 796.51(746); 379.852(746).
**Desc:** Scenery, wildlife, and outdoor recreation in Connecticut.

US/0092-8216
**CORD SPORTFACTS HUNTING.** (CORD SPORTFACTS: HUNTING.). **VFOAT** Hunting. (19??)-. English. an (Oct.). $2.25. Cord Communications Corporation, 130 West 42nd Street, New York NY 10036. **Tel** (212)840-0660. **LC** SK1; .C67. **DD** 799.2/05.

CN/0712-4570
**COURANT (MONTREAL).** (LE COURANT : BULLETIN DE LA FEDERATION QUEBECOISE DU CANOT-CAMPING.). [Courant]. **Added/Corp** Federation Quebecoise du Canot-Camping. (June/July 1982)-. Bulletin. French. qt (Jan., Apr., July, Oct.). 40.00Can$ Canada; 50.00Can$ other. Federation Quebecoise du Canot-Camping, 4545 Pierre de Coubertin, C P 1000 Succursale M, Montreal Quebec H1V 3R2 Canada. **Tel** (514)252-3001. **DD** 797.1/22/060714. **Bk Rev**. **Ad Acc**. **Circ:** 2,000 (ctrl). ***Continues*** *Contre-Courant (Federation Quebecoise du Canot-Camping), 0229-8813.*
**Desc:** Recreational canoeing and canoe camping activities in Quebec province.
**Ind/Abst** SportSearch (May 1987-).

CN/0701-3558
**CRAG AND CANYON.** Vol. 1, (Dec. 8, 1900)-. English. Fifty-two times a year. 53.13Can$ Canada; 88.13Can$ others. Banff Crag & Canyon, PO Box 129, Banff Alberta Canada. **Tel** (403)762-2453, FAX (403)762-5274. **ED** Stewart Muir. **Bk Rev**. **Ad Acc**. **Circ:** 4,500 (ctrl).

US/0362-7160
**DAISY SHOOTING ANNUAL.** English. an. $1.75. Aqua Field Publications Inc, 66 West Gilbert Street, Shrewsbury NJ 07702. **Tel** (201)842-8300. **LC** GV1151; .D34. **DD** 799/.05. **UDC** 799.2(058).

US/0194-5769
**DAKOTA COUNTRY.** Vol. 1, (April 1979)-. Periodical. English. Twelve times a year. $14.95 (one year); $25.00 (two years); $35.00 (three years). Karen Ziegler, PO Box 2714, Bismarck ND 58502. **Tel** (701)255-3031. **ED** William Mitzel. **Ad Acc**, **Adv Mgr:** Sylvia Shockman. **Circ:** 10,000 paid (ctrl).
**Desc:** Outdoor magazine that focuses on hunting and fishing in North and South Dakota.

US/1041-1968
**DAKOTA OUTDOORS.** [Dak. outdoors]. (Oct. 1988)-. Periodical. English. Twelve times a year. $10.00 one year; $18.00 two years; $25.00 three years. Kevin Hipple Dakota Outdoors, PO Box 669, Pierre SD 57501. **Tel** (605)224-7301, FAX (605)224-9210. **ED** Kevin Hipple. **DD** 799. **Bk Rev**, (Qty: 12). **Ad Acc**, **Adv Mgr:** Terry Hipple. **Circ:** 7,000 (ctrl). ***Continues*** *Kevin Woster's Dakota Outdoors, 0891-902X.*

US/1055-0364
**DECOY MAGAZINE.** **See** Hobbies.

US/0164-7318
**DEER AND DEER HUNTING.** [Deer deer hunt.]. **VFOAT** Deer & Deer Hunting. (19??)-. Periodical. English. Eight times a year. $17.95 US; $25.95 other. Krause Publications, 700 East State Street, Iola WI 54990-0001. **Tel** (715)445-2214, FAX (715)445-4087, telex 55 6461. **DD** 799. **Bk Rev**. **Ad Acc**.
**Desc:** Focuses on all phases of deer activity. Information for white-tailed deer hunters.

US/0362-1952
**DEER SPORTSMAN.** Periodical. English. bm. $6.00. Deer Sportsman of America, PO Box 142, Marlinton WV 24954. **LC** SK301; .D393. **DD** 799.2/77/357. **UDC** 799.2:639.111.

US
**DEL-MAR-VA HEARTLAND.** **See** Agriculture.

US
**DESERT LIFE.** ***Ceased.*** (19??)-(19??). Periodical. English. mo. Our Land, PO Box 1244, Barstow CA 92312. **Tel** (619)241-9131 Bill Delaney. Index available. **Bk Rev**, (Qty: 5). **Ad Acc**. **Circ:** 19,300 (ctrl).

CN/0316-1226
**DIRECTORY OF ACCREDITED CAMPS.** **VFOAT** Annuaire des Camps Membres Accredites. 1973-. Directory. Multiple languages (English and French). an. Free. Quebec Camping Association, 952 Cherrier Street, Montreal Quebec H2L 1H7 Canada. **DD** 796.54/22/025714. **UDC** 379.83(036)(714). ***Supersedes*** *Directory of Accredited Camps.*

US/1058-5761
**DISCOVERING AND EXPLORING NEW JERSEY'S FISHING STREAMS.** ***Title Change.*** [Discov. explor. N. J. fish. streams]. 1st Ed. (1991)-(199?). English. New Jersey Sportsmen's Guides, PO Box 100, Somerdale NJ 08083. **LC** WMLC 91/3834. **DD** 799. ***Continued by*** *Discovering and Exploring New Jersey's Fishing Streams and the Delaware River, 1071-6432.*

US
**EASTERN CAMPING & TRAILERING AREAS IN EASTERN UNITED STATES AND CANADA.** English. an. American Automobile Association, 1000 AAA Drive, Heathrow FL 32746. **Tel** (407)444-7000. **LC** GV191.35; .A53A. **DD** 647/.947. ***Continues*** *Eastern Campground Directory: Areas in the Eastern United States and Canada.*

US/0363-2091
**EASTERN CANADA CAMPING.** **Main/Corp** American Automobile Association. English. an. American Automobile Association, 1000 AAA Drive, Heathrow FL 32746. **Tel** (407)444-7000. **LC** GV191.46.M4; A46A. **DD** 917.1.

CN/0827-8911
**EASTERN WOODS & WATERS.** [East. woods waters]. **VFOAT** Woods & Waters. **VAT** Eastern Woods and Waters. Vol. 1, No. 1 (Spring 1985)-. Periodical. English. bm. 16.95Can$ Canada; 23.00Can$ US; 30.00Can$ other. James Publications Ltd, PO Box 428, Dartmouth Nova Scotia B2Y 3Y5 Canada. **Tel** (902)468-2682, FAX (902)468-3996. **ED** Jim Gourlay. **DD** 799/.09715.
**Desc:** Dedicated to the concepts of a clean environment, responsible wildlife management, true sportsmanship and the recognition of outdoor pursuits as an important and integral element of the Canadian way of life. Published for the outdoor community of Atlantic Canada, the editorial line-up features articles on hunting, fishing, new products, trapping, environmental concerns and wildlife management.

GW
**EUROPA CAMPING + CARAVANING.** **VFOAT** Europa-Camping. **VAT** Europa Camping und Caravaning. (19??)-. Periodical. English (French and German). an. DM19.80. Drei Brunnen Verlag, Friedhofstrasse 11, D 70191 Stuttgart Germany.

CN/0714-816X
**EXPLORE (CALGARY).** (EXPLORE.). [Explore]. No. 4 (Jan. 1982)-. Periodical. English. Six times a year (Feb., Apr., June, Aug., Oct., Dec.). 22.47Can$ (one year), 39.10Can$ (two year) Canada; 26.00Can$ (one year), 45.25Can$ (two year) US; 31.00Can$ (one year), 56.55Can$ (two year) other. Thompson and Gordon Publ. Limited, 301 14th Street Northwest, Suite 470, Calgary Alberta T2N 2A1 Canada. **Tel** (403)270-8890, FAX (403)270-7922. **ED** Marion Harrison, (phone: (403)270-8911). **DD** 917.123/043/05. **Ad Acc**. **Circ:** 25,000. ***Continues*** *Explore Alberta! Magazine, 0706-8174;* ***Absorbed*** *Whiskey Jack Magazine, 0226-7462.*
**Desc:** For people who enjoy "self-propelled" outdoor recreational activities such as hiking, cycling, paddling and skiing. Topics include adventure travel destinations in all parts of Canada, equipment evaluations, new products for outdoors people, environmental and management issues, outdoor photography, first aid and survival. Two yearly special issues devoted to adventure travel.
**Ind/Abst** Can. Index; Can. Period. Index.

IT
**FAO TRAINING SERIES.** **Added/Corp** Food and Agriculture Organization of the United Nations. (1980)-. Monographic series. English. ir. Price varies per volume. Food and Agriculture Organization (FAO) / Italy, GIPC166 via Terme di Caracalla, 00100 Rome Italy. **Tel** 011 39 6 522 52925, FAX 011 39 6 522 55784. **(Subscription address:** UNIPUB, 4611 F Assembly Drive, Lanham MD 20706.**)**
**Ind/Abst** Aquat. Sci. Fish. Abstr. (Computer File); For. Prod. Abstr. (1991-); Hortic. Abstr.; Postharvest News Inf.

SZ/0014-9756
**FELD WALD WASSER. SCHWEIZERISCHE JAGDZEITUNG.** [Feld Wald Wasser, Schweiz. Jagdztg.]. Began in 1973. Periodical. German. mo. 64.00F. Meier & Cie Ag Schaffhausen, Offset Buchdruck, 8200 Schaffhausen Switzerland. **Tel** 053/881 11. **ED** Jakob W Reiff. **LC** SK219; .F44. **DD** 799.29494. **Bk Rev**. **Ad Acc**. **Circ:** 8,000.
**Desc:** Hunting, dogs, fishing, book reviews, nature, news from the advertiser, hunting club news, and reports on hunting.
**Ind/Abst** AGRICOLA; Key Word Index Wildl. Res.

UK
**FIELD, THE.** **VFOAT** Field, The Farm, The Garden; Field, The Country Gentlemen's Newspaper. (19??)-. English. Twelve times a year. £93.60 (one year), £165.75 (two years), £234.00 (three years) US & Canada (surface mail); £154.04 US & Canada (airmail); £35.00 UK, £48.00 others. IPC Magazines Ltd., Perrymount Road, Haywards Heath, West Sussex RH16 3DH England. **Tel** 011 44 444 440421. **LC** GV1; F4. **DD** 799/.0941.

US/0163-5042
**FIELD & STREAM DEER HUNTING ANNUAL.** **VAT** Field and Stream Deer Hunting Annual. English. an. $1.50. Diamandis Communications Inc, 1499 Monrovia Avenue, New Port Beach CA 92663. **Tel** (714)720-5300. **LC** SK301; .F53. **DD** 799.2/7/7357.

US/8755-8572
**FIELD & STREAM (FAR WEST ED.).** (FIELD & STREAM.). [Field stream]. **VFOAT** Field and Stream. (19??)-. Periodical. English. mo. $15.94 (one year), $32.00 (two year), $48.00 (three year). Times Mirror Magazines, Two Park Avenue, New York NY 10016. **Tel** (212)779-5000. **(Subscription address:** Neodata / Colorado, PO Box 2606, Boulder Boulder CO 80322.**)** **DD** 799. Documents available from Magazine Collection. ***Continues in part*** *Field & Stream, 0015-0673;* ***Absorbed*** *Living Outdoors.*
**Desc:** Provides in-depth articles on fishing and hunting, conservation news, and tips on perfecting skills - from flycasting to stalking big game. Provides regional fishing reports, and also contains updates on new equipment and appeal.
**Ind/Abst** Gen. Period. Index (1985-); Mag. Index Plus (1989-); Mag. Index. Sel. (1986-); TOM Gen. Index (1985-) [Full Txt.].

US
**FIELD & STREAM GUIDE TO CAMPING ON WHEELS.** **VFOAT** Guide to Camping on Wheels; Camping on Wheels; Field & Stream Camping on Wheels. 1973-. English. an. $1.25. Diamandis Communications Inc, 1499 Monrovia Avenue, New Port Beach CA 92663. **Tel** (714)720-5300. **LC** TL298; .P49. **DD** 338.4/7/629226. ***Continues*** *Field & Stream Camping on Wheels.*

US/0361-3011
**FIELD & STREAM HUNTING ANNUAL.** **VFOAT** Hunting Annual. **VAT** Field and Stream Hunting Annual. English. an. $1.25. Diamandis Communications Inc, 1499 Monrovia Avenue, New Port Beach CA 92663. **Tel** (714)720-5300. **LC** SK1; .F46. **DD** 799.2/05.

US/8755-8599
**FIELD & STREAM (MIDWEST ED.).** (FIELD & STREAM.). [Field stream]. **VFOAT** Field and Stream. Vol. 89, No. 1 (May 1984)-. Periodical. English. mo. $15.94 (one year), $32.00 (two year), $48.00 (three year). Times Mirror Magazines, Two Park Avenue, New York NY 10016. **Tel** (212)779-5000. **(Subscription address:** Neodata / Colorado, PO Box 2606, Boulder Boulder CO 80322.**)** **DD** 799. ***Continues in part*** *Field & Stream, 0015-0673;* ***Absorbed*** *Living Outdoors.*
**Desc:** Provides in-depth articles on fishing and hunting, conservation news, and tips on perfecting skills - from flycasting to stalking big game. Provides regional fishing reports, and also contains updates on new equipment and appeal.

US/8755-8580
**FIELD & STREAM (NORTHEAST ED.).** (FIELD & STREAM.). [Field stream]. **VFOAT** Field and Stream. (19??)-. Periodical. English. mo. $15.94. Times Mirror Magazines, Two Park Avenue, New York NY 10016. **Tel** (212)779-5000. **(Subscription address:** Neodata / Colorado, PO Box 2606, Boulder Boulder CO 80322.**)** **LC** SK1; .F44. **DD** 799/.05. ***Continues in part*** *Field & Stream, 0015-0673;* ***Absorbed*** *Living Outdoors.*
**Desc:** Provides in-depth articles on fishing and hunting, conservation news, and tips on perfecting skills - from flycasting to stalking big game. Provides regional fishing reports. and also contains updates on new equipment and appeal.
**Ind/Abst** Acad. Search (Jan. 1984-); Mag. Artic. Summar. Elite (Jan. 1984-); Mag. Artic. Summar. Select; Mag. Artic. Summar. CD-ROM (Jan. 1984-); Mag. Index Sel. Microfiche (1990-) [Full Txt.]; Mag. Search; Prim. Search (Jan. 1984-); Read. Guide Abstr. Select Ed.; Vocat. Search (Jan. 1984-).

US/8755-8602
**FIELD & STREAM (SOUTH ED.).** (FIELD & STREAM.). [Field stream]. **VFOAT** Field and Stream. Vol. 89, No. 1 (May 1984)-. Periodical. English. mo. $15.94 (one year), $32.00 (two year), $48.00 (three year). Times Mirror Magazines, Two Park Avenue, New York NY 10016. **Tel** (212)779-5000. **(Subscription address:** Neodata / Colorado, PO Box 2606, Boulder Boulder CO 80322.**)** **DD** 799. Documents available from UMI Article Clearinghouse. ***Continues in part*** *Field & Stream, 0015-0673;* ***Absorbed*** *Living Outdoors.*
**Desc:** Provides in-depth articles on fishing and hunting, conservation news, and tips on perfecting skills - from flycasting to stalking big game. Provides regional fishing reports, and also contains updates on new equipment and appeal.
**Ind/Abst** Acad. Abstr. Full Text Elite (Jan. 1984-); Acad. Abstr. (Jan. 1984-); Mag. Express (1988-) [Full Txt.]; Mid. Search (Jan. 1984-); Newsp. Period. Abstr. (1988-); Resource/One Ondisc.

US/0091-0651
**FIELD & STREAM SPORTSMAN.** **VFOAT** Sportsman. English. $1.25. Diamandis Communications Inc, 1499 Monrovia Avenue, New Port Beach CA 92663. **Tel** (714)720-5300. **LC** SK1; .T36. **DD** 799.

US/8755-8610
**FIELD & STREAM (WEST ED.).** (FIELD & STREAM.). [Field stream]. **VFOAT** Field and Stream. (19??)-. Periodical. English. mo. $15.94 (one year), $32.00 (two year), $48.00 (three year). Times Mirror Magazines, Two Park Avenue, New York NY 10016. **Tel** (212)779-5000. **(Subscription address:** Neodata / Colorado, PO Box 2606, Boulder Boulder CO 80322.**)** **DD** 799. ***Continues in part*** *Field & Stream, 0015-0673;* ***Absorbed*** *Living Outdoors.*
**Desc:** Provides in-depth articles on fishing and hunting, conservation news, and tips on perfecting skills - from flycasting to stalking big game. Provides regional fishing reports, and also contains updates on new equipment and appeal.
**Ind/Abst** Mag. Index (1977-).

UK
**FIELD (LONDON, ENGLAND : 1853).** (THE FIELD.). **VFOAT** Field Illustrated; Field, The Farm, The Garden. No. 1 (Jan. 1, 1853)-. Periodical. English. wk. £20.00 (one year), £39.00 (two year) UK; £30.00 (one year), £59.00 (two year) Ireland; £33.00 (one year), £65.00 (two year) surface mail; £60.00 (one year), £119.00 (two year) airmail - other. The Harmsworth Press Ltd, Watling Street, Bletchley, Buckinghamshire England. **Tel** (0442)876661, FAX (0442)877279. **LC** GV1; .F4. **DD** 072/.1. ***Absorbed*** *Land and Water.*

US
**FINS AND FEATHERS.** ***Title Change.*** **VFOAT** Delaware/Maryland Fins and Feathers. Vol. 4, No. 8 (Sept. 1986)-(19??). Periodical. English. mo. Fins and Feathers, 318 West Franklin Avenue, Minneapolis MN 55040-9989. ***Formed by the union of*** *Fins and Feathers (Delaware Edition), 0741-7055* ***and*** *Fins and Feathers (Maryland Edition), 0741-708X.* ***Continued by*** *Fins and Feathers (Mount Morris, Ill.), 1053-6965.*

GW/0342-5703
**FISCHER UND TEICHWIRT.** (1972)-. Periodical. German. mo. DM43.50 Germany; DM59.00 other. Fischer und Teichwirt, Koenigstorgraben 11, D 90402 Nuernberg Germany. **Tel** 011 49 911 223910, FAX 011 49 911 241453. **UDC** 639.211.
**Ind/Abst** Aquat. Sci. Fish. Abstr. (Computer File).

US
**FISH AND GAME CODE.** **Main/Corp** California. **Added/Corp** California. Fish and Game Commission. (19??)-. Periodical. English. be (includes supplements). California Department of Fish and Game, 1416 9th Street, Sacramento CA 95814. **Tel** (916)653-7664.

US/1041-4762
**FISH & GAME HIGHLIGHTS.** [Fish game highl.]. **Added/Corp** New Hampshire. Fish and Game Dept. **VFOAT** Fish and Game Highlights. (1988)-. Periodical. English. mo. $8.00. New Hampshire Fish and Game Department, 2 Hazen Drive, Concord NH 03301. **Tel** (603)271-3512. **DD** 639.

US/0160-4740
**FISH AND WILDLIFE REFERENCE SERVICE NEWSLETTER.** **Added/Corp** Fish and Wildlife Reference Service (U.S.) Denver Public Library. Informatics General Corporation. Sterling Software (Firm) Maxima Corporation. No. 28 (Sept. 1974)-. Newsletter. English. qt. Free on request. Fish and Wildlife Reference Service, 5430 Grosvenor Lane, Bethesda MD 20814. **Tel** (800)582-3421. ***Continues*** *Newsletter, Library Reference Service, Federal Aid in Fish and Wildlife Restoration, 0190-4353.*

US/1059-5295
**FISHERMAN (FLORIDA ED.), THE.** **See** Fish and Fisheries.

US/0886-3008
**FISHING & HUNTING JOURNAL.** [Fish. hunt. j.]. **VFOAT** Fishing and Hunting Journal. Vol. 1, No. 1 (Apr. 1986)-. Periodical. English. Twelve times a year. $29.95 US; $49.95 other. Fishing & Hunting Journal, 1869 Craig Park Court, St Louis MO 63146.
**Ind/Abst** Ozark Period. Index.

US/0015-301X
**FISHING & HUNTING NEWS (WESTERN WASHINGTON ED.).** (FISHING & HUNTING NEWS.). [Fish. hunt. news]. **VFOAT** A.Fishing and hunting news. (19??)-. Periodical. English. wk. $39.95 (one year), $69.95 (two year). Fishing & Hunting News, c/o Kim Rancans, PO Box 19000, Seattle WA 98109. **Tel** (206)624-3845. **ED** Vence Malernee. **DD** 799. **Ad Acc. Circ:** 150,000.

US
**FISHING GUIDEBOOK.** **See** Fish and Fisheries.

US/1063-1577
**FISHING HOLES.** [Fish. holes]. Vol. 18, No. 2 (Dec. 1991)-. Periodical. English. mo. $14.95. Fishing Holes Magazine, 27247 Northeast Union Hill Road, Redmond WA 98053. **LC** SH559; .W35. **DD** 799. ***Continues*** *Washington Fishing Holes, 0194-7729.*

US/0164-0941
**FISHING IN MARYLAND.** **See** Fish and Fisheries.

US
**FISHING IN NEW JERSEY.** ***Ceased.*** **See** Fish and Fisheries.

●US/1060-5444
**FISHING TRIP MAGAZINE.** (1992)-. Periodical. English. mo. Pennsylvania Publishing Company, PO Box 170, Coalport PA 16627.

AT/0158-572X
**FISHING WORLD SYDNEY.** [Fish. world Syd.]. **VFOAT** Australian Angler's Fishing World. (1977)-. Periodical. English. mo. 54.00Aus$ Australia; 145.00Aus$ other. Yaffa Publishing Group Pty Ltd., GPO Box 606, Sydney NSW 2001 Australia. **Tel** 011 61 2 2812333, FAX 011 61 2 2812750. **DD** 799.105. ***Continues*** *Australian Angler.*

US/0889-3322
**FLORIDA GAME & FISH (MARIETTA, GA.).** (FLORIDA GAME & FISH.). **VFOAT** Florida Game and Fish; Florida Game & Fish Magazine; Florida Game and Fish Magazine. (198?)-. Periodical. English. mo. $14.95 (one year), $27.95 (two year), $39.95 (three year). Game & Fish Publications Inc., PO Box 741, Marietta GA 30061. **Tel** (404)953-9222.

US/0015-4369
**FLORIDA WILDLIFE.** **See** Environmental Issues-Conservation and Natural Resources.

US/1051-046X
**FLY FISHING DIRECTORY, THE.** [Fly fish. dir.]. (1991)-. Directory. English. an. $10.00. Anglers Information Services, 2389 Camino Pintores, Sante Fe NM 87505. **LC** WMLC L 83/7260. **DD** 799.

US/1056-2273
**FOLDING KAYAKER.** **See** Recreation, Leisure-Sports.

GW
**FORSCHUNGSBERICHT / DEUTSCHE SPORTHOCHSCHULE KOLN.** **Main/Corp** Deutsche Sporthochschule Koln. German. **LC** GV368.D49; D48A. **DD** 796/.071/143.

US/0884-9137
**FRED TROST'S OUTDOORS DIGEST.** ***Title Change.*** [Fred Trost's outdoor dig.]. **VFOAT** Outdoor Digest. Vol. 4 No. 2 (March/April 1985)-(1992). Periodical. English. bm. Michigan Outdoors Inc, PO Box 1000, Bath MI 48808. **DD** 799. ***Continues*** *Club Digest, 8750-1996.* ***Continued by*** *Fred Trost's Practical Sportsman, 1067-5914.*

US/0016-2620
**FULL CRY (SEDALIA).** (FULL CRY.). (19??)-. Periodical. English. mo. $16.00 (one year); $30.00 (two year). Gault Publications Inc, PO Box 10, Boody IL 62514. **Tel** (217)865-2332, FAX (217)865-2334. **ED** Seth R. Gault. **Bk Rev**, (Qty: 3-4). **Ad Acc. Circ:** 24,000.
**Desc:** For trail and treehound enthusiasts: raccoon, lion and bear hunters. Includes club news, breed association and state news, stories, articles and training material for the entire family.

US/0016-2922
**FUR-FISH-GAME.** **VAT** Fur Fish Game. (1905)-. Periodical. English. mo (12 issues). $15.95. A R Harding Publishing Company, 2878 East Main Street, Columbus OH 43209. **Tel** (614)231-9585. **ED** Mitch Cox. **Ad Acc. Circ:** 145,000.
**Desc:** Contains articles on fishing, camping, dogs, guns, ammunition and hunting in the US. Includes articles on trapping fur bearing animals, sale of pelts and prices, outdoor questions and answers and conservation.

US
**GAME JOURNAL : THE BEST OF HUNTING AND FISHING.** **VFOAT** Game Journal. Vol. 1 (Jan./Feb. 1992)-. English. bm. $24.95 (one year), $43.95 (two year). Game Journal Inc, PO Box 1208, Williamsport PA 17703. **Tel** (800)225-7949, (717)321-5070. **ED** David A Wonderlich. **Ad Acc.** ***Continues*** *Game Country.*
**Desc:** Contains columns dedicated solely to the world of big game hunting.

US/0733-0340
**GARDEN IDEAS & OUTDOOR LIVING.** **See** Gardening and Horticulture.

US/0895-3295
**GEORGIA OUTDOOR NEWS.** (GEORGIA OUTDOOR NEWS : GON.). [Ga. outdoor news]. **VFOAT** GON. (1987)-. Periodical. English. bw. $11.95 (one year); $22.95 (two year). Georgia Outdoor News, 1625 Williams Drive, Suite 208, Marietta GA 30066. **Tel** (404) 425-0990. **DD** 796.

US/0199-6517
**GEORGIA SPORTSMAN.** Vol. 1 (1976)-. Periodical. English. mo. $14.95 (one year), $27.95 (two year), $39.95 (three year). Game & Fish Publications Inc., PO Box 741, Marietta GA 30061. **Tel** (404)953-9222. **ED** David E Morris. **Circ:** 54,608.

# Recreation, Leisure —Outdoor Life

SA
**GETAWAY.** English. mo. R40.00 South Africa; R73.00 other. Ramsay Son & Parker Pty Ltd., PO Box 180, Howard Place, Pinelands 7450 South Africa. **Tel** 011 27 21 531 1391, FAX 011 27 21 531 3333, telex 526933. **ED** David Steele. **Ad Acc. Circ:** 42,000.
 **Desc:** Carries articles on outdoor places of interest, game parks, nature conservation, photography, trailing and caravaning.

US/0273-6691
**GRAY'S SPORTING JOURNAL.** [Gray's sport. j.]. Vol. 1 (Winter 1976)-. Periodical. English. Six times a year. $35.95 (one year), $58.00 (two years). Gray's Sporting Journal, PO Box 1207, Augusta GA 30903. **Tel** (706)722-6060, FAX (706)724-3873. **ED** David C. Foster. **LC** GV191.2; .G73. **DD** 796.5/05. **Bk Rev. Ad Acc, Adv Mgr:** Lea Cockerherm, **Tel** (800)458-4010. **Circ:** 30,000.
 **Desc:** Each issue is written for the advanced angler and shooter. Includes outdoor photography and literature.

US/0734-8517
**GREAT LAKES CAMPBOOK.** VFOAT Great Lakes Camp Book. 1982 Ed.-. English. an. $3.00. American Automobile Association, 1000 AAA Drive, Heathrow FL 32746. **Tel** (407)444-7000. **LC** GV198.65.G7; A45A. **DD** 647/.9477. **Continues** Great Lakes Camping, 0363-5171.

UK/0140-7570
**GREAT OUTDOORS.** [Great outdoors]. (1978)-. English. mo. £25.00 UK; £30.00 other. George Outram & Co Ltd, 195 Albion Street, Glasgow G1 1QP Scotland. **Tel** 011 44 355246444, FAX 011 44 355263013. **DD** 796.
 **Ind/Abst** SportSearch (May 1987-).

SA
**GREAT OUTDOORS.** English. mo. R42.50 South Africa; R120.50 other. Great Outdoors, PO Box 33873, 2042 Jeppestown South Africa. **Tel** 011 27 11 3379138, FAX 011 27 11 3378061. **ED** Jill Dunstone. **Bk Rev. Ad Acc. Circ:** 20,000.
 **Desc:** Covers general outdoor activity, including camping, fishing, hunting, travel, and conservation.

US/1055-6532
**GREAT PLAINS GAME & FISH.** [Great Plains game fish]. VFOAT Great Plains Game and Fish; Great Plains Game & Fish Magazine. Vol. 1, No. 1 (Jan. 1991)-. Periodical. English. mo. $14.95 (one year), $27.95 (two year), $39.95 (three year). Game & Fish Publications Inc., PO Box 741, Marietta GA 30061. **Tel** (404)953-9222. **DD** 799. **Continues** Kansas Game & Fish, 0897-9200.

CN/0712-1822
**GREENSCAPE.** See Gardening and Horticulture.

US/0017-4297
**GRIT AND STEEL.** (1899)-. Periodical. English. mo. $16.00 (one year), $30.00 (two year), $45.00 (three year). Grit and Steel, Box 280, Gaffney SC 29342. **Tel** (803)489-2324, FAX (803)489-2324. **ED** Beverly Early. **Bk Rev,** (Qty: n). **Ad Acc. Circ:** 5,000.
 **Desc:** Published in the interest of those devoted to game fowl.

CN/0847-4834
**GUIDE PLEIN AIR DU QUEBEC.** [Guide plein-air que.]. (1989)-. French. an (Apr. or May). 9.95Can$ Canada; 12.95US$ US and Mexico; 13.95Can$ other. Traffic Communication, 3575 Boulevard St. Laurent, Suite 509, Montreal Quebec H2X 2T7 Canada. **Tel** (514)288-7730. **DD** 796.5/025/714.

US/1046-5774
**GUIDE TO ACCREDITED CAMPS.** See Children and Youth Interests.

US/0279-5086
**GUN DOG.** [Gun dog]. Vol. 1, No. 1 (Sept./Oct. 1981)-. Periodical. English. bm (6 issues). $23.97 (one year), $37.97 (two year), $49.97 (three year). Stover Publishing Company Inc., PO Box 35098, 1901 Bell Avenue, Suite 2, Des Moines IA 50315. **Tel** (515)243-2472, FAX (515)243-0233. **ED** Bob Wilbanks. **Bk Rev. Ad Acc, Adv Mgr:** Mary Stearns, **Tel** same as publisher. **Circ:** 68,000.
 **Desc:** For upland bird and waterfowl hunters and their favorite hunting companion. Breed features, hunting stories, gun dog training, veterinary advice, humor, nostalgia and much more. For the serious sportsman and hunting dog enthusiast.

US/0894-8119
**GUN LIST.** [Gun list]. (198?)-. Periodical. bw. $24.95 US; $83.50 other. Krause Publications, 700 East State Street, Iola WI 54990-0001. **Tel** (715)445-2214, FAX (715)445-4087, telex 55 6461. **DD** 799. **Circ:** 65,353.
 **Desc:** Marketplace for buying and selling collectible firearms. More than 50,000 guns for sale each issue. Guns are categorized alphabetically by make.

US/0896-6001
**GUN SHOW CALENDAR.** See Recreation, Leisure.

US/0362-4749
**GUN WORLD HUNTING GUIDE.** See Recreation, Leisure-Sports.

US/1044-6257
**GUNS MAGAZINE.** See Recreation, Leisure-Sports.

US/0731-1885
**GUTMANN PUMA/EXPLORER KNIFE ANNUAL.** Title Change. [Gutmann puma/explor. knife annu.]. VFOAT Puma/Explorer Knife. VAT Gutmann Puma Explorer Knife Annual. (198?)-(19??). Periodical. English. an. Aqua Field Publications Inc, 66 West Gilbert Street, Shrewsbury NJ 07702. **Tel** (201)842-8300. **LC** TS380; .G88. **DD** 621.9/32/05. **Continues** Gutmann Knife Annual, 0271-762X. **Continued by** Explorer Knife Journal, 1067-3202.

CN/0846-3654
**HALIBURTON FISHING GUIDE.** See Fish and Fisheries.

●US/1060-068X
**HANDGUNNING.** See Recreation, Leisure-Sports.

CN/1183-6288
**HIKE CANADA.** [Hike Can.]. Added/Corp National Trail Association of Canada. No. 1 (June 1991)-. Periodical. English. bm. $3.00 per year. National Trail Association of Canada, Box 3098, Station B, Calgary Alberta T2M 4L6. **DD** 796.5/1/0971.

SA
**HIKING AFRICA.** English. mo. R20.00. Hiking Africa, PO Box 33873, 2042 Jeppestown South Africa. **Tel** 011 27 11 3379138, FAX 011 27 11 3378061. **ED** Jill Dunstone. **Circ:** 8,000. **Continues** SA Hiker.
 **Desc:** Covers hiking trails within southern Africa.

US/0094-0291
**HIKING (HIGHLAND PARK).** (HIKING.). V. 1- Spring 1974-. Periodical. English. $2.00. Woodall Publishing Company, 28167 North Keith Drive, Lake Forest IL 60015. **Tel** (708)362-6700. **LC** GV199; .H54. **DD** 796.5/05.

II
**HIMALAYAN JOURNAL, THE.** Added/Corp Himalayan Club. Vol. 1 (Apr. 1929)-. Periodical. an. Rs369.75. The Himalayan Club, PO Box 1905, Bombay 400 001 India. **Tel** 011 22 2021029 or, 2021198. **(Subscription address:** Oxford University Press / India, PO Box 31, Bombay 400 039 India.) **ED** Hansh Kapadia. **LC** DS485.H6; H55. **DD** 915.42. **Bk Rev. Ad Acc. Circ:** 1,500. (ctrl).
 **Desc:** Journal on climbing in Himalaya, Karakoram and China.

US/0018-4780
**HOOSIER OUTDOORS.** (19??)-. Periodical. English. bm (Jan., Mar., May, Sept., Nov.). $7.88 (one year), $21.00 (two year) Indiana, $7.50 (one year), $20.00 (two year) other. High Point Communications, PO Box 447, Cloverdale IN 46120. **Tel** (317)795-6312. **ED** Thomas J. Glancy. **LC** SK75; .H65. **DD** 917.72/04/4. Index available. **Bk Rev. Ad Acc. Circ:** 35,000.
 **Desc:** Magazine covers outdoor sports and is geared towards Indiana residents. Also contains articles on the conservation of natural resources.

CH
**HU WAI SHENG HUO.** VFOAT Outdoor Life. Began with July 5, 1976 issue. Periodical. Chinese. mo. $39.00. Hu Wai Sheng Huo Tsa Chi She, 12 Yen Ping S Road, Taipei Taiwan. **LC** GV191.2; .H8. **DD** 796.5/05.

US
**HUNT.** English. bm. $19.97. Timberline-B Inc, Hunt Magazine, 58069, Renton WA 98058. **Tel** (206)226-4534, FAX (206)255-0320. **ED** William Boylon. **Bk Rev. Ad Acc. Circ:** 110,000. (ctrl).

US
**HUNTER CASUALTY REPORT / ARKANSAS GAME AND FISH COMMISSION.** See Recreation, Leisure-Abstracting, Bibliographies and Statistics.

CN/0846-104X
**HUNTER EDUCATION NEWS (PETERBOROUGH).** (HUNTER EDUCATION NEWS : THE INSTRUCTORS' PUBLICATION OF THE ONTARIO FEDERATION OF ANGLERS AND HUNTERS). [Hunt. educ. news]. Added/Corp Ontario Federation of Anglers & Hunters. (May 1990)-. Periodical. English. qt. Includes free distribution. Ontario Federation of Anglers & Hunters, PO Box 2800, Peterborough, Ontario K9J 8L5 Canada. **DD** 799.29713/05.

US
**HUNTERS FRONTIER TIMES.** English. mo. $14.95 (1 year), $26.00 (2 year) US; $19.95 (one year), $36.00 (two year) other; add 7% GST in Canada. Western Publications / Oklahoma, PO Box 2107, Stillwater OK 74076. **Tel** (405)743-3370, (800)749-3369, FAX (405)743-3374.

●US/1059-3837
**HUNTING HORIZONS.** [Hunt. horiz.]. (1992)-. Periodical. English. qt. $34.00 US; $42.00 other. Wolfe Publishing Company, 6471 Airpark Drive, Prescott AZ 86301. **Tel** (602)445-7810. **LC** SK274; .H86. **DD** 799.2/028. **Ad Acc, Adv Mgr:** Jana Kosco.
 **Desc:** Designed to reach the upscale hunter and shooter. Celebrates the lifestyle of the sophisticated sportsman. Also covers fine art, destinations, and product evaluations.

US
**HUNTING REGULATIONS.** Added/Corp United States. Fish and Wildlife Service. United States. Bureau of Sport Fisheries and Wildlife. No. 88 (1972)-. Monographic series. English. Price varies per volume. Office of Biological Services, Fish & Wildlife Service, Department of the Interior, Washington DC 20240. **Continues** Regulatory Announcement.

US/8750-6629
**HUNTING RETRIEVER.** (HUNTING RETRIEVER : THE NEWSLETTER OF THE HUNTING RETRIEVER CLUB, INC.). [Hunt. retriev.]. Added/Corp Hunting Retriever Club. (1984)-. Periodical. English. Six times a year. $15.00. Hunting Retriever Club, 100 East Kilgore Road, Kalamazoo MI 49001. **Tel** (616)343-9020. **DD** 799.

●US/1060-5452
**HUNTING TRIP MAGAZINE.** (1992)-. Periodical. English. mo. Pennsylvania Publishing Company, PO Box 170, Coalport PA 16627.

US/8755-2469
**IDAHO WILDLIFE.** Added/Corp Idaho. Dept. of Fish and Game. Vol. 1, No. 1 (Jan./Feb. 1978)-. Periodical. English. bm $12.95 (1 year), $24.95 (2 year) US; $15.95 (1 year), $30.95 (2 year) other. Idaho Department of Fish and Game, PO Box 25, Boise ID 83707. **Tel** (208)334-3748, FAX (208)334-2114. **ED** Diane Ronayne. **LC** SK387; .I33. **DD** 639.9/05. Index available. cum. index. **Circ:** 11,000 (ctrl). **Continues** Idaho Wildlife Review, 0019-1248.
 **Ind/Abst** Fish Rev.; Wildl. Rev.

US/0276-9905
**IN-FISHERMAN, THE.** See Fish and Fisheries.

US/1048-4892
**IN-FISHERMAN ANGLING ADVENTURES TRAVEL GUIDE.** [In-Fisherman angling adventures travel guide]. VFOAT In-Fisherman Angling Adventures; In Fisherman Angling Adventures Travel Guide; Angling Adventures Travel Guide; Angling Adventures. Vol. 3 (Jan. 1989)-. Periodical. English. qt. In-Fisherman Communications Network, Box 999, 651 Edgewood Drive, Brainerd MN 56401-0999. **LC** WMLC L 83/6984. **DD** 799. **Continues** Angling Adventures, 1044-6826.

II
**INDIAN MOUNTAINEER.** Added/Corp Indian Mountaineering Foundation. (May 1978)-. Periodical. English. an. $20.00. Indian Mountaineering Foundation, 18-Q Block Behind South Block Central Sect, New Delhi 110055 India. **(Subscription address:** Prints India, 11 Darya Ganj, New Delhi, 110002 India, (Phone: 011 91 11 3268645)) **LC** GV199.44.I532; H554. **DD** 796.5/22/0954.

US/0897-8980
**INDIANA GAME & FISH.** [Indiana game fish]. VFOAT Indiana Game and Fish; Indiana Game & Fish Magazine. (19??)-. Periodical. English. mo. $14.95 (one year), $27.95 (two year), $39.95 (three year). Game & Fish Publications Inc., PO Box 741, Marietta GA 30061. **Tel** (404)953-9222. **DD** 799.

US/0892-1180
**INSIDER GUN NEWS, THE.** [Insid. gun news]. Vol. 1, No. 1 (Jan. 1987)-. Periodical. English. Twelve times a year. Gunpress Publishing Company, PO Box 3257, Alexandria VA 22302. **DD** 799.

US/0747-007X
**INSIGHTS (WASHINGTON, D.C.).** See Recreation, Leisure-Sports.

US/0091-6986
**INTERNATIONAL DIVER INDEX. WORLD INDIVEX EDITION.** See Recreation, Leisure-Sports.

US/0092-1769
**INTERNATIONAL SKI TRAILS.** See Recreation, Leisure-Sports.

US/0897-9197
**IOWA GAME & FISH.** [Iowa game fish]. VFOAT Iowa Game and Fish; Iowa Game & Fish Magazine.

## Recreation, Leisure —Outdoor Life

(198?)-. Periodical. English. mo. $14.95 (one year), $27.95 (two year), $39.95 (three year). Game & Fish Publications Inc., PO Box 741, Marietta GA 30061. **Tel** (404)953-9222. **DD** 799.

CN/0712-6336
**IROQUOIAN, THE.** [Iroquoian]. **Main/Corp** Iroquoia Bruce Trail Club. Periodical. English. qt. Iroquoia Bruce Trail Club, PO Box 183, Hamilton Ontario L8N 3A2 Canada. **DD** 796.5/1/06071352.

CN/1185-7145
**ISLAND FISH FINDER MAGAZINE.** [Isl. fish finder mag.]. Vol. 1, No. 1 (May 1991)-. Periodical. English. ir. $2.25 per no. Rosebrugh Holdings Inc, 6404 Metral Drive, Suite 3, Navaimo BC V9T 2L8. **DD** 799.1.

US/0361-4999
**ITHACAGUN HUNTING & SHOOTING ANNUAL.** See Recreation, Leisure-Sports.

BE
**JACHT EN NATUURBEHEER.** Periodical. Dutch. Koninklijke Sint-Hubertusclub van Belgie, Jan Jacobsplein 1, 1000 Brussels Belgium. **LC** SK205; .J3.

●US/1062-5224
**JOE FELLEGY'S MILLE LACS FISHING DIGEST.** (MILLE LACS FISHING DIGEST.). [Joe Fellegy's Mille Lacs Fish. Dig.]. **Added/Corp** Fellegy, Joe 1944-. **VFOAT** Mille Lacs Fishing Digest. (1992)-. Periodical. English. qt. $1.25. Millie Lacs Press, RT. 1, Box 149 A, Aitkin MN 56431. **DD** 799.

UK
**JOURNAL OF ADVENTURE EDUCATION AND OUTDOOR LEADERSHIP : THE JOURNAL OF THE NATIONAL ASSOCIATION FOR OUTDOOR EDUCATION, THE ASSOCIATION OF HEADS OF OUTDOOR EDUCATION CENTRES, [AND] THE OUTDOOR EDUCATION ASSOCIATION OF IRELAND, THE.** **Added/Corp** National Association for Outdoor Education (Great Britain) Association of Heads of Outdoor Education Centres (Great Britain) Outdoor Education Association of Ireland. **VFOAT** JAEOL. Vol. 8, No. 1 (Spring 1991)-. English. qt. **Continues** Adventure Education and Outdoor Leadership.
 **Ind/Abst** Br. Educ. Index.

US/0021-9649
**JOURNAL OF CHRISTIAN CAMPING.** **Added/Corp** Christian Camping International. **VFOAT** CCI Journal of Christian Camping. (1969)-. Periodical. English. bm $24.95 US; $26.95 (members) other; $31.95 (nonmembers) other. Christian Camping International, PO Box 62189, Colorado Springs CO 80962. **Tel** (719)260-9400.
 **Ind/Abst** Christ. Period. Index (19??-).

US/0022-3336
**JOURNAL OF OUTDOOR EDUCATION.** See Education.

US/0097-6253
**JOURNAL OF THE NORTH AMERICAN FALCONERS' ASSOCIATION, THE.** **Main/Corp** North American Falconers' Association. Began with Vol. for 1962. English. an. North American Falconers' Association, Route 3, Box 301, Durango CO 81301. **LC** SK321; .N67A. **DD** 799.2/32/0973.

CN/1189-5152
**KANAWA MAGAZINE FOR RECREATIONAL PADDLING IN CANADA.** [Kanawa mag. recreat. paddling Can.]. **Added/Corp** Canadian Recreational Canoeing Association. **VFOAT** Kanawa Magazine. (1990)-. Periodical. English (summaries and/or abstracts in French). Four times a year. $15.00. Canadian Recreational Canoeing Association, 1029 Hyde Park Road Box 500, Hyde Park Ontario N0M 1Z0 Canada. **Tel** (519)473-2109, (519)641-1261, FAX (519)473-6560. **ED** Joseph Agnew. **DD** 796.1/22/097105. **Bk Rev**, (Qty: 6-8). **Ad Acc. Pr Rev. Circ:** 10,500. **Continues** Kanawa (Magazine : 1975)., 1189-5144.

●US/1059-9177
**KENTUCKY AFIELD.** **Added/Corp** Kentucky. Dept. of Fish and Wildlife Resources. (1992)-. Periodical. English. Six times a year. $5.00 (one year), $9.00 (two years). Kentucky Department of Fish & Wildlife Resources, 1 Game Farm Road, Frankfort KY 40601. **Tel** (502)564-4336, FAX (502)564-6508. **LC** SK1; .K45. **DD** 799. **Bk Rev**, (Qty: 5). **Circ:** 40,000. **Continues** Kentucky Happy Hunting Ground, 0023-0235.
 **Desc:** Presents a myriad of articles on outdoor / wildlife-related issues, conservation of wildlife resources, Kentucky Department of Fish and Wildlife Resources programs and activities.

US/0889-3802
**KENTUCKY GAME & FISH.** [Ky. game fish]. **VFOAT** Kentucky Game and Fish; Kentucky Game & Fish Magazine. (1986)-. Periodical. English. mo. $14.95 (one year), $27.95 (two year), $39.95 (three year). Game & Fish Publications Inc., PO Box 741, Marietta GA 30061. **Tel** (404)953-9222.

US/0023-0235
**KENTUCKY HAPPY HUNTING GROUND.** **Title Change.** [Ky. happy hunt. ground]. **Added/Corp** Kentucky. Division of Game and Fish. Kentucky. Dept. of Fish and Wildlife Resources. League of Kentucky Sportsmen. **VFOAT** Happy Hunting Ground; HHG. Vol 1 (Dec. 1945)-(199?). Periodical. English. bm. Kentucky Department of Fish & Wildlife Resources, 1 Game Farm Road, Frankfort KY 40601. **Tel** (502)564-4336, FAX (502)564-6508. **ED** John Wilson. **LC** SK1; .K45. **DD** 799. **Bk Rev. Circ:** 35,000 (ctrl). **Continued by** Kentucky Afield, 1059-9177.
 **Desc:** Official publication of Kentucky Department of Fish and Wildlife Resources; devoted to wildlife conservation, outdoor sports, wise and ethical use of natural resources.
 **Ind/Abst** Fish Rev.; Wildl. Rev.

CN/0706-3180
**LIVRET DES REGLEMENTS DE LA FEDERATION CANADIENNE DES ARCHERS (1974).** See Recreation, Leisure-Sports.

US/0744-3692
**LOUISIANA GAME & FISH.** **VFOAT** Louisiana Game and Fish. (1981)-. Periodical. English. mo. $14.95 (one year), $27.95 (two year), $39.95 (three year). Game & Fish Publications Inc., PO Box 741, Marietta GA 30061. **Tel** (404)953-9222.

US/0738-8098
**LOUISIANA OUT-OF-DOORS.** (LOUISIANA OUT-OF-DOORS: OFFICIAL PUBLICATION OF THE LOUISIANA WILDLIFE FEDERATION.). **Added/Corp** Louisiana Wildlife Federation. **VFOAT** Louisiana Out Of Doors. (19??)-. Periodical. English. Ten times a year (two combination issues per year/ combined months vary). $6.00 (one year), $11.00 (two years), $15.00 (three years). Louisiana Wildlife Federation, PO Box 65239 Audubon Station, Baton Rouge LA 70896-5239. **Tel** (504)344-6707. **ED** Randy P Lanctot (editor's address: 337 South Acadion Thruway, Boton Rouge LA 70806). **Bk Rev**, (Qty: Varies). **Ad Acc. Circ:** 5,500 (ctrl).
 **Desc:** Contains state, local and national news, features and information concerning the environment and natural resource conservation issues.

PL/0137-1266
**LOWIEC POLSKI.** [Low. Pol.]. (1899)-. Periodical. Polish. mo. Price on Request. (Subscription address: ARS Polona, PO Box 1001, 00068 Warsaw Poland.) UDC 639.1.

US/0360-005X
**MAINE FISH AND WILDLIFE.** See Fish and Fisheries.

CN/0823-8588
**MANITOBA CAMPING DIRECTORY.** [Manit. camping dir.]. Directory. English. an. Free. Manitoba Camping Association, 1495 St Matthews Avenue, Winnipeg Manitoba R3G 3L3 Canada. **Tel** (204)985-4166, FAX (204)985-4028. **DD** 796.54/2/0257127.

US/0025-4924
**MASSACHUSETTS WILDLIFE.** See Environmental Issues-Conservation and Natural Resources.

US
**METROPARKS EMERALD NECKLACE.** **Added/Corp** Cleveland Metroparks System. Vol. 24, No. 6 (May 1975)-. Periodical. English. Twelve times a year. Free Cuyahoga County; $10.00 others. Cleveland Metroparks System, 4101 Fulton Parkway, Cleveland OH 44144. **Tel** (216)351-6300, FAX (216)351-2584. **ED** Brenda Lightner. **Bk Rev**, (Qty: 4). **Circ:** 40,000 (ctrl). **Continues** Emerald Necklace.
 **Desc:** Articles on resources of the park system, both natural and recreational. Listing of scheduled activities and programs.

US/0885-0674
**MEXICAN SPORTFISHING NEWS.** [Mex. sportfish. news]. Periodical. English. qt. $12.00 US; $16.00 other. International Sport Fishing Publications, 11000 Metro Parkway/Suite 4, Captiva Island FL 33912. **DD** 799.

US/1057-2856
**MICHIGAN HUNTING & FISHING.** [Mich. hunt. fish.]. **VFOAT** Michigan Hunting and Fishing; Michigan Hunt & Fishing. Vol. 1, No. 1 (Fall 1991)-. Periodical. English. Eight times a year. $15.97 (one year), $29.97 (two year). Northwoods Publications, PO Box 90, Lemoyne PA 17043. **Tel** (717)761-1400, FAX (717)761-4579. **DD** 799. **Continues** Michigan Fisherman, 0274-4783.

US/0539-8908
**MICHIGAN SPORTSMAN (OSHKOSH WIS.).** (MICHIGAN SPORTSMAN). **VFOAT** Michigan Sportsman Magazine. (197?)-. Periodical. English. mo. $14.95 (one year), $27.95 (two year), $39.95 (three year). Game & Fish Publications Inc., PO Box 741, Marietta GA 30061. **Tel** (404)953-9222. **ED** Ken Dunwoody. **LC** SK91; .M47. **DD** 799.29774. **Ad Acc.**
 **Desc:** Covers fishing, hunting and other outdoor participation activities in Michigan.

US/1055-6540
**MID-ATLANTIC GAME & FISH.** [Mid-Atl. game fish]. **VFOAT** Mid Atlantic Game and Fish; Mid-Atlantic Game and Fish; Mid Atlantic Game & Fish; Mid Atlantic Game & Fish Magazine. Vol. 1991, No. 1 (Jan. 1991)-. Periodical. English. mo. $14.95 (one year), $27.95 (two year), $39.95 (three year). Game & Fish Publications Inc., PO Box 741, Marietta GA 30061. **Tel** (404)953-9222. **LC** WMLC 93/1040. **DD** 799. **Continues** Maryland-Delaware Game & Fish, 0897-9022.

CN/1185-2143
**MID-CANADA OUTDOORS.** [Mid-Can. outdoors]. Vol. 2, No. 2 (Winter/Spring 1991)-. Periodical. English. Four Scware Pub. Ltd., 253-375 York Avenue, Winnipeg Manitoba R3C 3J3 Canada. **DD** 799. **Continues** The Manitoba Outdoorsman., 0849-4983.

US/0894-7767
**MID-SOUTH HUNTING & FISHING NEWS.** [Mid-South hunt. fish. news]. **VFOAT** Mid-South Hunting and Fishing News; Hunting and Fishing News; Mid South Hunting & Fishing News; Hunting & Fishing News. (198?)-. Periodical. English. bw. $17.95. S S & J Publications Inc, 3251 Poplar Ave #100, Memphis TN 38111. **Tel** (901)458-7899, FAX (901)458-7951. **ED** L. Peter Schutt. **DD** 799. **Ad Acc. Circ:** 12,000.

US/0747-3648
**MIDWEST OUTDOORS.** **VFOAT** Mid West Outdoors. (19??)-. Periodical. English. mo. $11.95. MidWest Outdoors, 111 Shore Drive, Hinsdale IL 60521. **Tel** (708)887-7722, FAX (708)887-1958.

US/0026-5608
**MINNESOTA OUT-OF-DOORS.** **Added/Corp** Minnesota Conservation Federation. Vol. 1, No. 1 (Apr. 1954)-. Periodical. English. bm. $10.00. Minnesota Conservation Federation, 1036 Cleveland Avenue South, Suite B, St Paul MN 55116-1887. **Tel** (612)690-3077, FAX (612)690-3077. **ED** Melissa Schmidt. **Ad Acc, Adv Mgr:** Dan Hinton. **Circ:** 5,000 (ctrl).
 **Desc:** Official publication of the Minnesota Conservation Federation. Features news and educational articles on current conservation issues and outdoor recreation.

US/0274-8622
**MINNESOTA SPORTSMAN.** [Minn. sportsman]. Vol. 1 (July/Aug 1977)-. Periodical. English. mo. $14.95 (one year), $27.95 (two year), $39.95 (three year). Game & Fish Publications Inc., PO Box 741, Marietta GA 30061. **Tel** (404)953-9222. **ED** Ken Dunwoody. **LC** WMLC L 83/6909. **Ad Acc.**
 **Desc:** Covers fishing, hunting and other outdoor participation activities in Minnesota.

US/0428-6472
**MINUTES OF THE FLORIDA OUTDOOR RECREATIONAL DEVELOPMENT COUNCIL, FLORIDA OUTDOOR RECREATIONAL PLANNING COMMITTEE.** **Main/Corp** Florida Outdoor Recreational Development Council. **Added/Corp** Florida Outdoor Recreation Planning Committee. (1964)-. Periodical. English. Florida Outdoor Recreational Planning Committee, Tallahassee FL 32304. **LC** GV54.F6; A2. **DD** 790.

US/0744-4192
**MISSISSIPPI GAME & FISH (MARIETTA, GA.).** (MISSISSIPPI GAME & FISH). **VFOAT** Mississippi Game and Fish. (198?)-. Periodical. English. mo. $14.95 (one year), $27.95 (two year), $39.95 (three year). Game & Fish Publications Inc., PO Box 741, Marietta GA 30061. **Tel** (404)953-9222. **LC** WMLC 93/898.

US/1041-9306
**MISSISSIPPI OUTDOORS (1987).** (MISSISSIPPI OUTDOORS.). [Miss. outdoors]. **Added/Corp** Mississippi. Dept. of Wildlife Conservation. Vol. 50, No. 6 (Nov./Dec. 1987)-. Periodical. English. bm (6 issues). $6.00. Mississippi Department of Wildlife Conservation, POB 451, Jackson MS 39205. **Tel** (601)362-9212. **LC** SH11.M7; A32. **DD** 799/.09762. **Continues** MS Outdoors.

## Recreation, Leisure —Outdoor Life

US/1044-0062
**MISSISSIPPI WILDLIFE.** [Miss. wildl.].
**Added/Corp** Mississippi Wildlife Federation. Vol. 1, No. 1 (Apr./May 1989)-. Periodical. English. Six times a year. $25.00. Mississippi Wildlife Federation, 520 North President Street, Jackson MS 39201. **Tel** (601)353-6922. **ED** Elizabeth Rooks. **DD** 639. **Ad Acc. Circ:** 15,000 (ctrl) *Continues Mississippi Out-Of-Doors, 0279-9146.*

US/0889-3799
**MISSOURI GAME & FISH.** [Mo. game fish]. **VFOAT** Missouri Game and Fish; Missouri Game & Fish Magazine. (1986)-. Periodical. English. mo. $14.95 (one year), $27.95 (two year), $39.95 (three year). Game & Fish Publications Inc., PO Box 741, Marietta GA 30061. **Tel** (404)953-9222.

AU
**MITTEILUNGEN (OSTERREICHISCHER ALPENVEREIN (1950)-.** (MITTEILUNGEN / OEAV OSTERREICHISCHER ALPENVEREIN.). **Added/Corp** Osterreichischer Alpenverein (1950)-. (19??)-. Periodical. German. bm. University of Innsbruck, Faculty of Theology, Innsbruck Austria. **Tel** 05222 5078501, FAX 05222 579799. **LC** JQ821; .G733. **DD** 796.5/22/05. *Continues Mitteilungen (Osterreichischer Alpenverein (1950)-. Akademische Sektion).*

AT/0026-7732
**MODERN FISHING.** See Recreation, Leisure-Sports.

FR/0047-7923
**MONTAGNE ET ALPINISME, LA.** **Added/Corp** Club Alpin Francais. Groupe de Haute Montagne. (Oct. 1955)-. Periodical. French. qt. 130.00F France; 165.00F other. Club Alpin Francais, 24 Avenue de Laumiere, 75019 Paris France. **Tel** 011 33 1 47423846. **ED** Annie Bertholet. Index available. **Bk Rev. Ad Acc. Circ:** 45,000 (ctrl). *Supersedes Montagne.*
**Desc:** National magazine of the Association "Club Alpine Francais" dealing with mountain climbing, trekking, and so on.
**Ind/Abst** SportSearch (May 1987-).

FR/0184-2595
**MONTAGNES MAGAZINE GRENOBLE.** (1978)-. Periodical. French. mo (11 issues). 296.00F France; 366.00F other. Montagnes Magazine, BP 53, 77932 Perthes Cedex France. **Tel** 011 33 1 64380125. **UDC** 790. **CODEN** 799.

US/0027-0016
**MONTANA OUTDOORS.** **Added/Corp** Montana. Dept. of Fish and Game. Montana Fish and Game Commission. Vol. 1 (Nov./Dec. 1970)-. Periodical. English. bm. $7.00 US; $10.00 Canada; $22.00 other. Montana Outdoors, 930 Custer Avenue West, Helena MT 59620. **Tel** (406)444-2474. **ED** David J. Books. Index available. **Bk Rev. Circ:** 40,000 (ctrl) *Formed by the union of Montana Outdoors, 0027-0016 and Montana Wildlife (Helena, Mont. : 1950).*
**Desc:** Covers natural resource conservation, wildlife management, outdoor recreation, fishing, and hunting.
**Ind/Abst** Fish Rev.; Wildl. Rev.

US
**MOTORCAMPING HANDBOOK.** English. $1.50. Grolier Book Club, Old Sherman Turnpike, Danbury CT 66816. **LC** SK600; .M68. **DD** 796.54/05.

UK/0959-3160
**MOUNTAIN EAR.** (THE MOUNTAIN EAR.). [Mt. ear]. (198?)-. Periodical. English. Ten times a year. £100.00 UK; £110.00 other. Mark Allen Publishing Limited, Robjohns Farm, Vicarage Road, Finchingfield CM7 4LJ England. **Tel** 11 44 371 810433. **DD** 796.522.

CN
**MOUNTAINEER. ROCKY MOUNTAIN HOUSE.** English. Fifty-two times a year. 21.00Can$ Canada (within 65 km Rocky Mountain House); 40.00Can$ others in Canada; 80.00Can$ others. The Mountaineer Publishing Co. Ltd., 4814 49 Street, Rocky Mountain House ALTA, T0M1T1 Canada. **Tel** (403)845-3334.

US/0027-2620
**MOUNTAINEER (SEATTLE, WASH.).** (MOUNTAINEER.). [Mountaineer]. **Added/Corp** Mountaineers (Society). Vol. 1, No. 1 (Mar. 1907)-. Periodical. English. mo. $15.00 US; $27.00 Canada; $40.00 other. Mountaineer, 300 3rd Avenue West, Seattle WA 98119. **ED** Brad Stracener. **LC** F886; .M92. **DD** 917.95/0943/0060797. **Bk Rev.** (Qty: 3-4). **Ad Acc. Pr Rev. Circ:** 14,000 (ctrl).
**Desc:** Serves The Mountaineers members with each of their activities' monthly trips schedules. Also contains feature articles and news of general readership interest.
**Ind/Abst** GeoRef.

CN/0712-3817
**MOUSQUETON, LE.** [Mousqueton]. **Added/Corp** Federation Quebecoise de la Montagne. (1971)-. Periodical. French. Ten times a year. $6.00. Federation Quebecoise de la Montagne, 1415 East rue Jarry, Montreal Quebec H2E 2Z7 Canada. **Tel** (514)252-3004. **DD** 796.5/22/05.
**Ind/Abst** SportSearch (May 1987-).

US
**MUSKIE : THE OFFICIAL PUBLICATION OF MUSKIES, INC.** Periodical. English. mo. Muskies Inc International Office, 1708 University Avenue, St. Paul MN 55104. **LC** SH691.M8; M87. **DD** 799.1/753. *Continues Newsletter (Muskies, Inc.).*

US/1041-6366
**MUSKY HUNTER MAGAZINE.** [Musky hunt. mag.]. **VFOAT** Musky Hunter. Vol. 1, No. 1 (Feb./March 1989)-. Periodical. English. Six times a year (Feb., Apr., June, Aug., Oct., Dec.). $18.00 (one year); $35.00 (two years). Outlook Publishing Inc, PO Box 881, Minocqua WI 54548. **Tel** (715)356-6301, FAX (715)358-2807. **ED** Joe Bucher. **DD** 799. **Bk Rev.** (Qty: 30). **Ad Acc, Adv Mgr:** B. Krammer, **Tel** (800)23-Musky. **Circ:** 22,000.
**Desc:** Dedicated specifically to the sport of fishing for muskies, with articles on tackle selection and modification, techniques and lakes.

CN/0828-1327
**NASTAWGAN.** See Boats and Boating.

US/0736-6450
**NATIONAL SURVEY OF FISHING, HUNTING, AND WILDLIFE-ASSOCIATED RECREATION.** 1980-. Government Publication. English. ir. Free. Department of the Interior, 1849 C Street Northwest, Washington DC 20240. **Tel** (202)343-3171, FAX (202)208-5048. **LC** SK41; .U54A. **DD** 333.95/413/0973. available on diskette (and data tape). *Continues National Survey of Hunting, Fishing, and Wildlife-Associated Recreation, 0191-6947.*
**Desc:** Contains statistics on US residents' participation in fishing, hunting and other wildlife related recreation, and their expenditures for those activities.

US
**NATIONAL SURVEY OF FISHING, HUNTING, AND WILDLIFE-ASSOCIATED RECREATION. ALASKA.** Government Publication. English. ir. US Department of Interior, Division of Federal Aid, Washington DC 70240. **LC** SK49; .N38. **DD** 333.95/413/09798021.

US/0742-7174
**NATIONAL SURVEY OF FISHING, HUNTING, AND WILDLIFE-ASSOCIATED RECREATION. ARKANSAS.** [Natl. surv. fish., hunt., wildl.-assoc. recreat., Ark.]. Government Publication. English. ir. US Department of Interior, Division of Federal Aid, Washington DC 70240. **LC** SK53; .N38. **DD** 333.95/4/09767.

US/0742-7166
**NATIONAL SURVEY OF FISHING, HUNTING, AND WILDLIFE-ASSOCIATED RECREATION. CONNECTICUT.** [Natl. surv. fish., hunt., wildl.-assoc. recreat., Conn.]. Government Publication. English. ir. US Department of Interior, Division of Federal Aid, Washington DC 70240. **LC** SK59; .N38. **DD** 333.95/4/09746.

US
**NATIONAL SURVEY OF FISHING, HUNTING, AND WILDLIFE-ASSOCIATED RECREATION. IDAHO.** Government Publication. English. ir. US Department of Interior, Division of Federal Aid, Washington DC 70240. **LC** SK69; .N38. **DD** 799/.09796/021.

US/0742-7158
**NATIONAL SURVEY OF FISHING, HUNTING, AND WILDLIFE-ASSOCIATED RECREATION. ILLINOIS.** [Natl. surv. fish., hunt., wildl.-assoc. recreat., Ill.]. **Added/Corp** U.S. Fish and Wildlife Service. United States. Bureau of the Census. (19??)-. Government Publication. English. ir. US Department of Interior, Division of Federal Aid, Washington DC 70240. **LC** SK71; .N38. **DD** 333.95/4/09773.

US/0742-714X
**NATIONAL SURVEY OF FISHING, HUNTING, AND WILDLIFE-ASSOCIATED RECREATION. LOUISIANA.** [Natl. surv. fish., hunt., wildl.-assoc. recreat., La.]. Government Publication. English. ir. US Department of Interior, Division of Federal Aid, Washington DC 70240. **LC** SK83; .N38. **DD** 333.95/4/09763.

US
**NATIONAL SURVEY OF FISHING, HUNTING, AND WILDLIFE-ASSOCIATED RECREATION. MICHIGAN.** Government Publication. English. ir. US Department of Interior, Division of Federal Aid, Washington DC 70240. available on microfiche (Vols. for (1980-) distributed to depository libraries).

US/0742-7190
**NATIONAL SURVEY OF FISHING, HUNTING, AND WILDLIFE-ASSOCIATED RECREATION. NEW YORK.** [Natl. surv. fish., hunt., wildl.-assoc. recreat., N.Y.]. Government Publication. English. ir. US Department of Interior, Division of Federal Aid, Washington DC 70240. **LC** SK111; .N35. **DD** 333.95/4/09747.

●US/1058-8221
**NATIONAL VOLUNTEERS IN PARKS DIRECTORY (U.S. ED.).** (NATIONAL VOLUNTEERS IN PARKS DIRECTORY.). [Natl. volunt. parks dir.]. **VFOAT** Volunteers in Parks Directory. (1992)-. Directory. English. $4.95 (U.S.), $5.95 (Can.). Solutions / Tennessee, 652 Spruce Drive, Erwin TN 37650. **DD** 796.

US/1044-4971
**NATIONAL WILDLIFE FEDERATION SCIENTIFIC AND TECHNICAL SERIES.** [Natl. Wildl. Fed. sci. tech. ser.]. **Added/Corp** Institute for Wildlife Research (Washington, D.C.) National Wildlife Foundation. (19??)-. Monographic series. English. ir. Price varies per volume. National Wildlife Federation / Virginia, 8925 Leesburg Pike, Vienna VA 22184. **Tel** (703)790-4000, (800)822-9919, FAX (703)442-7332. **DD** 639. **CODEN** STSFEY. Documents available from BIOSIS Document Express.
**Ind/Abst** Biol. Abstr. (1989-); Fish Rev.; Wildl. Rev.

US/0897-8999
**NEBRASKA GAME & FISH.** [Nebr. game fish]. **VFOAT** Nebraska Game and Fish; Nebraska Game & Fish Magazine. (19??)-. Periodical. English. mo. $14.95 (one year), $27.95 (two year), $39.95 (three year). Game & Fish Publications Inc., PO Box 741, Marietta GA 30061. **Tel** (404)953-9222. **DD** 799.

US/1059-7484
**NEW ALASKA OUTDOORS, THE.** [New Alsk. outdoors]. Vol. 1, No. 1 (July 1991)-. Periodical. English. mo. Alaska Outdoors Development Corporation, 400 D Street, Suite 200, Anchorage AK 99501. **DD** 796. *Continues Alaska Outdoors, 0274-8282.*

US/0897-8972
**NEW ENGLAND GAME & FISH.** [N. Engl. game fish]. **VFOAT** New England Game and Fish; New England Game & Fish Magazine. (1988)-. Periodical. English. mo. $14.95 (one year), $27.95 (two year), $39.95 (three year). Game & Fish Publications Inc., PO Box 741, Marietta GA 30061. **Tel** (404)953-9222. **DD** 799.

US/0028-5889
**NEW JERSEY OUTDOORS.** See Environmental Issues-Conservation and Natural Resources.

US/0197-4874
**NEW WILDERNESS LETTER.** *Ceased.* [New wilderness lett.]. Vol. 1 (Jan. 1977)-Vol. 13 (?). Periodical. English. sa. New Wilderness Foundation, 325 Spring Street/Room 208, New York NY 10013. **Tel** (212)807-7944.

US/0897-9189
**NEW YORK GAME & FISH.** [N. Y. game fish]. **VFOAT** New York Game and Fish; New York Game & Fish Magazine. Vol. 1987, No. 1 (Feb. 1987)-. Periodical. English. mo. $14.95 (one year), $27.95 (two year), $39.95 (three year). Game & Fish Publications Inc., PO Box 741, Marietta GA 30061. **Tel** (404)953-9222. **DD** 799. *Continues New York in the Field, 0893-1445.*

●US
**NEW YORK OUTDOORS.** (1992)-. Periodical. English. mo. Allsport Publishing Corporation, 51 Atlantic Avenue, Floral Park NY 11001. **Tel** (516)352-9700, FAX (516)437-6841. **LC** WMLC 91/5523.

NZ/0028-8802
**NEW ZEALAND WILDLIFE.** **Added/Corp** New Zealand Deerstalkers' Association. (1962)-. Periodical. English. Four times a year. 20.00NZ$. New Zealand Wildlife, PO Box 6514, Wellington New Zealand. **Tel** 04 896 773. **ED** Smelby Grant. **[CCC].** Each issue contains an index to its own contents (no volume index)--loose. **Bk Rev. Ad Acc. Circ:** 10,000.
**Desc:** Hunting, shooting, wildlife, game management and outdoor recreation articles, stories and information.
**Ind/Abst** Key Word Index Wildl. Res.

CN/0225-7335
**NEWSLETTER - BLUE MOUNTAINS BRUCE TRAIL CLUB.** [Newsl. - Blue Mt. Bruce Trail Club]. **Main/Corp** Blue Mountains Bruce Trail Club.

**VAT** News Letter - Blue Mountains Bruce Trail Club; Bulletin - Blue Mountains Bruce Trail Club. Spring 1979-. Newsletter. English. ir. Blue Mountains Bruce Trail Club, PO Box 306, Barrie Ontario L4M 4T5 Canada. **DD** 796.5/1/06071317. ***Continues*** *BMBTC Newsletter, 0708-0867.*

US/0588-5035
**NEWSLETTER - COLORADO RIVER ASSOCIATION. Main/Corp** Colorado River Association. Newsletter. English. mo. 417 South Hill Street, Los Angeles CA 90013.

CN/0706-7429
**NIAGARA BRUCE TRAIL CLUB. *Title Change.*** [Niagara Bruce Trail Club]. **Main/Corp** Niagara Bruce Trail Club. (197?)-Winter (1991/92). Periodical. English. Three times a year. Niagara Bruce Trail Club, PO Box 1, St Catharines Ontario L2R 6R4 Canada. **ED** Martha Deeker. **DD** 796.5/1/05. **Bk Rev. Ad Acc. Circ:** 550 (ctrl). ***Continued by*** *Niagara Bruce Trail Club Grapevine, 1189-6310.*
**Desc:** Includes a hike schedule of weekly activities with the name and telephone number of the leader and the meeting place for the start of each hike. As well there are descriptions of past hikes and letters of interest to club members.

HU/0549-494X
**NIMROD : A MAGYAR VADASZOK ORSZAGOS SZOEVETSEGENEK LAPJA. Added/Corp** Magyar Vadaszok Orszagos Szoevetsege. Vol. 1, No. 4 (April 1969)-. Hungarian. mo. $44.00. **(Subscription address:** Kultura, PO Box 149, H 1389 Budapest 62 Hungary.**)** **LC** SK223.H9; N55.
**Ind/Abst** Index Am. Period. Verse.

●IT/1121-6379
**NO LIMITS WORLD.** (1992)-. Italian. mo. L60000. Cooperativa Giornalisti del Estremo RL, Via Corridoni 11, 20122 Milan Italy. **Tel** 02-76005205, FAX 02-7600717. **ED** Francesco Lacono. **Circ:** 100,000.
**Desc:** Covers adventurous sports such as rock climbing, deep-sea fishing, piloting, and skiing.

US/0194-4320
**NORTH AMERICAN HUNTER.** (NORTH AMERICAN HUNTER : OFFICIAL PUBLICATION OF THE NORTH AMERICAN HUNTING CLUB.). [North Am. hunt.]. **Added/Corp** North American Hunting Club. (Winter 1979)-. Periodical. English. Six times a year (Jan., Mar., May, July, Sept., Nov.). $18.00 includes membership. North American Hunting Club, 12301 Whitewater Drive, Minnetonka MN 55343. **Tel** (612)936-9404, FAX (612)936-9755. **ED** Mark LaBarbera and Bill Miller. **LC** SK40; .N68. **DD** 799.297. **Bk Rev. Ad Acc. Circ:** 200,000.
**Desc:** The technical, how-to, and pleasurable aspects of hunting. Distribution and information to members of the North American Hunting Club.

US
**NORTH AMERICAN HUNTING DIRECTORY.** (19??)-. Directory. English. ir (approx. every 5 years). $79.95. North American Hunting Club, 12301 Whitewater Drive, Minnetonka MN 55343. **Tel** (612)936-9404, FAX (612)936-9755.
**Desc:** Directory of member information in two volumes.

US/0746-6250
**NORTH AMERICAN WHITETAIL.** (198?)-. Periodical. English. Eight times a year. $14.95 (one year), $27.95 (two year), $39.95 (three year). Game & Fish Publications Inc., PO Box 741, Marietta GA 30061. **Tel** (404)953-9222.

US/0897-8816
**NORTH CAROLINA GAME & FISH.** [N. C. game fish]. **VFOAT** North Carolina Game and Fish; North Carolina Game & Fish Magazine. (198?)-. Periodical. English. mo. $14.95 (one year), $27.95 (two year), $39.95 (three year). Game & Fish Publications Inc., PO Box 741, Marietta GA 30061. **Tel** (404)953-9222. **ED** Jeff Samsel. **DD** 799. ***Continues in part*** *Carolina Game & Fish, 0744-4176.*

US/0029-2761
**NORTH DAKOTA OUTDOORS.** [N.D. outdoors]. **Added/Corp** North Dakota. State Game and Fish Dept. Junior Game Wardens' League (N.D.). **VFOAT** ND Outdoors. Vol. 1 (July 1938)-. Periodical. English. Ten times a year (April/May, September/October are special issues). $7.00. North Dakota Game & Fish Department, 100 North Bismarck Expressway, Bismarck ND 58501. **Tel** (701)221-6300, FAX (701)221-6352. **ED** Harold Umber. **LC** SK351; .N878. **DD** 799.05. **Bk Rev. Circ:** 23,000 (ctrl). ***Supersedes*** *North Dakota Outdoors, 0029-2761.*
**Desc:** A state game and fish department publication.
**Ind/Abst** Wildl. Rev.

US/0199-8463
**NORTH EAST OUT DOORS. VFOAT** Northeast Outdoors. (1966)-. Periodical. English. mo. $8.00 (one year), $11.00 (two year), $13.00 (three year). Northeast Outdoors, PO Box 2180, Waterbury CT 06722. **Tel** (203)755-0158. **ED** Debbie Nealley. **Bk Rev. Ad Acc. Circ:** 27,500 (ctrl).
**Desc:** Covers camping and recreational vehicle travel in the Northeastern United States.

US/0029-2958
**NORTH WOODS CALL, THE.** Vol. 1 (Nov. 11, 1953)-. Periodical. English. Twenty-three times a year. $20.00. North Woods Call, Route 1, 00509 Turkey Run, Charlevoix MI 49720. **Tel** (616)547-9797. **ED** Glenn Sheppard. **Bk Rev. Ad Acc. Circ:** 2,000 (ctrl).
**Desc:** Regional conservation and outdoor recreation journal.

US/1071-2615
**NYLON HIGHWAY. See** Earth Sciences-Geophysics.

AU
**OESTERREICHS WEIDWERK : ILLUSTRIERTE MONATSHEFTE FUER JAGD, FISCHEREI UND NATURSCHUTZ MIT DEN OFFIZIELLEN NACHRICHTEN OESTERREICHISCHER LANDESJAGDVERBAENDE. Added/Corp** Oesterreichischer Landesjagdverband. (19??)-. German. Oesterreichischer Jagd- und Fischerei-Verlag, Vienna Austria. **LC** WMLC L 83/8737.
**Ind/Abst** Helminthol. Abstr. (1991-).

US/0889-2407
**OHIO FISHERMAN.** [Ohio fisherman]. (19??)-. Periodical. English. mo. Ohio Fisherman, PO Box 06355, Columbus OH 43206. **Tel** (614)241-2313. **DD** 799.

US/0897-9170
**OHIO GAME & FISH.** [Ohio game fish]. **VFOAT** Ohio Game and Fish; Ohio Game & Fish Magazine. (198?)-. Periodical. English. mo. $14.95. Game & Fish Publications Inc., PO Box 741, Marietta GA 30061. **Tel** (404)953-9222. **ED** Steve Carpenteri. **DD** 799.

CN/0707-3178
**ONTARIO OUT OF DOORS.** [Ont. out doors]. Vol. 9, Issue 11 (Dec. 1977)-. Periodical. English. Ten times a year. 21.50Can$ Canada; 29.50Can$ other. MacLean Hunter Publ. Limited / Toronto, 777 Bay Street, 8th Floor Agency Control, Toronto Ontario M5W 1A7 Canada. **Tel** (416)596-5000, (800)268-6811, FAX (416)596-5526. **(Subscription address:** Indas, 35 Riviera Drive, Building 17, Markham Ontario L3R 8N4 Canada.**)** **ED** Burt Myers. **DD** 799/.09713. **Bk Rev. Ad Acc. Circ:** 60,000. available on microfilm and microfiche from University Microfilms International (UMI). ***Continues*** *Ontario Fisherman & Hunter Out of Doors, 0319-6941.*
**Desc:** Covers fishing and hunting in Ontario.
**Ind/Abst** Can. Index.

CN/0827-2352
**ONTARIO OUTDOOR GUIDE & CALENDAR.** [Ont. outdoor guide cal.]. **VFOAT** Ontario Outdoor Guide. No. 1 (Spring '84)-. Periodical. English. ir. Ontario Outdoor Guide, 296 Glen Road, Toronto Ontario M4W 2X3 Canada. **DD** 799/.09713.

CN/0823-6453
**ONTARIO OUTDOORSMAN.** (1980)-. Periodical. English. ir. $10.00. Ontario Outdoorsman, PO Box 7054, Ancaster Ontario L9G 3L1. **DD** 799/.09713.

NE/0168-3845
**OP PAD (DEN HAAG). See** Travel and Tourism.

CN/1183-4889
**OPTION GRAND AIR.** [Option grand air]. Vol. 1, No 1 (April 1991)-. Periodical. French. mo. 1.50Can$ per issue. Option Grand Air, 7356 St. Hubert, Montreal Quebec H2R 2N3 Canada. **DD** 799.

CN/0826-3019
**ORC REPORT.** (THE ORC REPORT.). [ORC rep.]. **Added/Corp** Outdoor Recreation Council of British Columbia. No. 1 (Oct. 1983)-. Bulletin. English. Four times a year. 10.00Can$. Outdoor Recreation Council of British Columbia, 334-1367 West Broadway, Vancouver British Columbia V6Z 4A9 Canada. **Tel** (604)737-3058, FAX (607)737-3666. **DD** 796.5/09711. **Ad Acc. Circ:** 1,000.
**Desc:** Dedicated to promoting outdoor recreation in the province of British Columbia.

US/0362-8264
**OREGON WILDLIFE COMMISSION FINANCIAL STATEMENT. Main/Corp** Oregon. Wildlife Commission. English. Oregon Department of Fish & Wildlife, PO Box 59, 2501 Southwest 1st Street, Portland OR 97201. **Tel** (503)229-5400. **LC** SK439; .O78B. **DD** 353.9/795/008232.

US/0883-6809
**OUT OF DOORS (PIERRE, S.D.).** (OUT OF DOORS : OFFICIAL PUBLICATION OF THE SOUTH DAKOTA WILDLIFE FEDERATION.). **Added/Corp** South Dakota Wildlife Federation. **VFOAT** South Dakota Wildlife Federation Out of Doors. (19??)-. Periodical. English. mo (12 issues). $5.00. Out of Doors, 812 North Monroe, Pierre SD 57501.
**Desc:** Hunting, fishing, and environmental concerns to outdoorsmen.

UK
**OUTDOOR.** (19??)-. Periodical. English. Twelve times a year. £45.00 (institutions), £30.00 (individuals) UK; £50.00 (institutions), £40.00 (individuals) other. Mark Allen Publishing Ltd., Croxped Mews, 288 Croxped Road, London SE24 9DA England. **Tel** 011 44 1 671 7521.

CN/0827-2964
**OUTDOOR ALBERTA.** [Outdoor Alta.]. Summer 1984-. Periodical. English. ir. $5.00. Outdoor Alberta, 12514-124 Street, Edmonton Alberta T5L 0N5 Canada. **DD** 799/.097123.

CN/0228-0604
**OUTDOOR ATLANTIC.** [Outdoor Atl.]. V. 1-Oct./Nov. 1979-. Periodical. English. ir. 5.00Can$. Fundy Group Publications, PO Box 128, Yarmouth Nova Scotia B5A 4B1 Canada. **Tel** (902)453-2330, FAX (902)455-7162. **DD** 639/.09715.

US/0030-7025
**OUTDOOR CALIFORNIA.** [Outdoor Calif.]. **Added/Corp** California. Dept. of Fish and Game. Vol. 1 (July 1930)-. Periodical. English. bm. $6.50. California Department of Fish and Game, 1416 9th Street, Sacramento CA 95814. **Tel** (916)653-7664. **(Subscription address:** PO Box 15087, Sacramento, CA 95851-0087**)** **ED** Dave Dick. **LC** SH11; .C272. **Circ:** 50,000.
**Desc:** Covers California wildlife, fish and plants.
**Ind/Abst** Calif. Period. Index (19??-); Calif. Period. Microfi. (19??-); Fish Rev.; Wildl. Rev.

CN/0315-0542
**OUTDOOR CANADA.** [Outdoor Can.]. Vol. 1 (Dec. 1972)-. Periodical. English. Nine times a year. 21.00Can$ Canada, 29.00Can$ other. Outdoor Canada Magazine Ltd., 703 Evans Avenue, Ontario M9C 5E9 Canada. **Tel** (905)695-0311. **(Subscription address:** Indas, 35 Riviera Drive, Building 17, Markham Ontario L3R 8N4 Canada.**)** **ED** Teddi Brown. **Ad Acc. Circ:** 143,000. available on microfiche (from Toronto : Micromedia).
**Desc:** Shows you how to get the most out of your outdoor adventures with how-to's, interviews and tips from the pros. Brings the people, the places and the action of the outdoors to your door. Covers fishing, boating, hiking, canoeing, camping and wildlife.
**Ind/Abst** AQUAREF; Can. Index; Can. Period. Index.

US
**OUTDOOR COMMUNICATOR : THE OFFICIAL JOURNAL OF THE NEW YORK STATE OUTDOOR EDUCATION ASSOCIATION, THE. *Title Change.*** **Added/Corp** New York State Outdoor Education Association. (1980)-(19??). Periodical. English. sa. NYSOEA, PO Box 71, Raquette Lake NY 13436. ***Continues*** *Communicator (New York State Outdoor Education Association).* ***Merged with*** *Outdoor Path* ***to form*** *Pathways to Outdoor Communication.*
**Ind/Abst** Curr. Index J. Educ.

CN/0700-9909
**OUTDOOR CREST (1975).** (OUTDOOR CREST.). Began publication in 1975?. Periodical. English. ir (approximately 9 times a year). Free. The Outdoor Crest, 17 Mill Street, Willowdale Ontario M2P 1B3 Canada. **Tel** (416)487-4477. **ED** Peter Edwards. **DD** 799/.06/2713541. **Ad Acc. Circ:** 800 (ctrl). ***Supersedes*** *Outdoor Crest Newsletter, 0700-9895.*

CN/1186-8023
**OUTDOOR EDGE.** (THE OUTDOOR EDGE.). [Outdoor edge]. Vol. 1, Issue 1 (Apr./May 1991)-. Periodical. English. bm. Hunting Guide Publications, 6922-104 Street, Edmonton Alberta T6H 2L7 Canada. **DD** 799/.09712. ***Continues*** *Wildlife Crusader., 0043-5457.*

US/0048-2420
**OUTDOOR GUIDE.** No. 1- 1970-. Periodical. English. mo. Outdoor Guide, 2718 Montana Avenue, Billings MT 59101.

US/0279-8700
**OUTDOOR HIGHLIGHTS. *Title Change.*** **Added/Corp** Illinois. Dept. of Conservation. Information/Education Division. Vol. 3, No. 4 (Feb. 24, 1975)-(19??). Periodical. English. sm. Illinois Department of Conservation, 524 South Second Street, Springfield IL 62706. **Tel** (217)782-7454. **ED** Gary C. Thomas. Index available. **Bk Rev. Circ:** 45,000. ***Continues*** *Illinois. Dept. of Conservation. Information/Education Division. News - Illinois Dept. of Conservation.* ***Continued by*** *Outdoor Illinois.*
**Desc:** Covers outdoor recreation and natural resources.

●US/1072-7175
**OUTDOOR ILLINOIS (SPRINGFIELD, ILL.).** (OUTDOOR ILLINOIS.). (1993)-. Periodical. English. mo. $10.00 (one year), $19.00 (two year). Illinois Department of Conservation, 524 South Second Street, Springfield IL 62706. **Tel** (217)782-7454. ***Continues*** *Outdoord Highlights, 0279-8700.*

US/0030-7068
**OUTDOOR INDIANA. See** Public Administration-Parks and Recreation.

US/0890-7196
**OUTDOOR JOURNAL. *Ceased.*** [Outdoor j.]. (1963)-(19??). Periodical. English. mo. Outdoor Journal, PO Box 8, Hubbard OH 44425. **ED** Jerry Blinzley. **DD** 796. Index available. **Bk Rev. Ad Acc. Circ:** 24,000 (ctrl).
**Desc:** Contains information about hunting, fishing, camping, trapping, boating, Canadian news and bow hunting.

US/0734-2918
**OUTDOOR LIFE DEER HUNTER'S YEARBOOK.** [Outdoor life deer hunt. yearb.]. **VFOAT** Outdoor Life Deerhunter's Yearbook; Deerhunter's Yearbook; Deer Hunter's Yearbook. (1983)-. English. an. $16.95. Stackpole Magazines, 500 Vaughn Street, Harrisburg PA 17110. **Tel** (717)234-5041, (800)732-3669, FAX (717)234-1359. **LC** SK301; .O94. **DD** 639/.117357.

US/0030-7076
**OUTDOOR LIFE (NEW YORK, N.Y.).** (OUTDOOR LIFE.). [Outdoor life]. Vol. 1 (1897)-. Periodical. English. mo. $15.94 (one year), $27.97 (two year), $38.97 (three year). Times Mirror Magazines, Two Park Avenue, New York NY 10016. **Tel** (212)779-5000. **(Subscription address:** Neodata / Colorado, PO Box 2606, Boulder Boulder CO 80322.**) ED** Clare Conley. **LC** SK1; .O7. **DD** 796. **Ad Acc.** available on microfilm and microfiche from University Microfilms International (UMI); available on an online database (file 647/Full-Text) from DIALOG. Documents available from UMI Article Clearinghouse, Magazine Collection. ***Absorbed*** *Outdoor Recreation; Fisherman.*
**Desc:** Provides in-depth regional coverage for fishermen, hunters, and outdoorsmen. Filled with tips on tracking and hunting waterfowl, deer and big game. Also contains tips for reeling in fresh and saltwater fish.
**Ind/Abst** Abr. Read. Guide Period. Lit.; Acad. Abstr. Full Text Elite (Jan. 1984-); Acad. Abstr. (Jan. 1984-); Consum. Index Prod. Eval. Inf. Source; Gen. Period. Index (1985-); Health Source (Jan. 1984-); Mag. Artic. Summar. Elite (Jan. 1984-); Mag. Artic. Summar. Select (Jan. 1984-); Mag. Artic. Summar. CD-ROM (Jan. 1984-); Mag. Express (1988-) [Full Txt.]; Mag. Index Plus (1989-); Mag. Index Sel. Microfiche (1990-) [Full Txt.]; Mag. Index. Sel. (1986-); Mag. Search; Mid. Search (Jan. 1984-); Newsp. Period. Abstr. (1988-); Prim. Search (Jan. 1984-); Read. Guide Abstr. Select Ed.; Read. Guide Period. Lit.; Resource/One Ondisc; Mag. Index (1977-); TOM Gen. Index (1985-) [Full Txt.]; Vocat. Search (Jan. 1984-).

US/0030-7106
**OUTDOOR OKLAHOMA.** [Outdoor Okla.]. **Added/Corp** Oklahoma. Dept. of Wildlife Conservation. Vol. 21, No. 8 (Sept. 1965)-. Periodical. English. Six times a year (Jan., Mar., May, July, Sept., Nov.). $8.00 (one year); $14.00 (two years); $20.00 (three years). Department of Wildlife Conservation, 1801 North Lincoln, PO Box 53465, Oklahoma City OK 73125. **Tel** (405)521-3851, FAX (405)521-6535. Index available (Bound in 6th issue. ($8.00)). **Bk Rev**, (Qty: 6). **Ad Acc. Pr Rev. Circ:** 21,000 (ctrl). Documents available from Documents on Demand. ***Continues*** *Oklahoma Wildlife, 0199-9524.*
**Desc:** Hunting, fishing and conservation information.
**Ind/Abst** Environ. Abstr.; Wildl. Rev.

US/0739-0602
**OUTDOOR PRESS, THE.** (19??)-. Periodical. English. wk (except first & last weeks of the year). $30.00 (one year), $45.00 (two year) US; $48.00 (one year), $81.00 (two year) other. Outdoor Press, N 2012 Ruby Street, Spokane WA 99207. **Tel** (509) 328-9392.

US/0148-401X
**OUTDOOR RECREATION IN GEORGIA.** V. 1- 1977-. English. an. $4.95. Terminus Media Inc, 1819 Peachtree Road, Atlanta GA 30309. **LC** GV191.42.G4; O94. **DD** 647/.94758.

US/0892-8355
**OUTDOOR SPORTS & RECREATION.** [Outdoor sports recreat.]. **Added/Corp** Sports & Recreation, Inc. (Alexandria, Minn.). Sports Publications, Inc. (Minneapolis, Minn.). **VFOAT** OS&R; OS & R; Outdoor Sports and Recreation; Sports & Recreation; Sports and Recreation. Vol. 43, No. 2 (Mar./Apr. 1986)-. Periodical. English. Six times a year. $9.95. Sports Publications / Outdoor Sports and Recreation, PO Box 5023, Hopkins MN 55343-1023. **Tel** (612)944-1230. **ED** Nicki Harper. **DD** 799. **Bk Rev. Ad Acc. *Continues*** *Sports & Recreation.*
**Desc:** Fishing and hunting reports on Minnesota and Wisconsin. Informative articles on outdoor recreation.

US/0272-9342
**OUTDOOR SPORTSMAN (POINT PLEASANT).** (OUTDOOR SPORTSMAN.). (19??)-. English. $2.25 single issue US, $2.75 single issue Canada. Aqua Field Publications Inc, 66 West Gilbert Street, Shrewsbury NJ 07702. **Tel** (201)842-8300. **LC** SK1; .O816. **DD** 799/.05.

US/1048-8871
**OUTDOOR WOMAN.** [Outdoor woman]. Vol. 1, No. 1 (Jan. 1990)-. Periodical. English. mo. $30.00 US; $35.00 Canada. Gentian Mountain Inc, PO Box 834, Nyack NY 10960. **DD** 796.

UK/0962-1016
**OUTDOORS ILLUSTRATED. *Ceased.*** [Outdoors illus.]. (1991)-(Feb. 1994). Periodical. English. Ten times a year. Outdoors Illustrated Inc, PO Box 845, Bath Avon, BA1 3TW England. **Tel** 011 44 225 443194, FAX 011 44 225 443195. **ED** Fabian Russell-Cobb. **Bk Rev**, (Qty: 10). **Ad Acc.**

US/0199-3666
**OUTDOORS TODAY.** (19??)-. Periodical. English. wk. $15.00. Outdoors Today, PO Box 6852, St Louis MO 63144.

US
**OUTDOORS WEST. Added/Corp** Federation of Western Outdoor Clubs. (1977)-. Periodical. English. Twice a year (June & Dec.). $10.00. Federation of Western Outdoor Clubs, 512 Boylston East, Suite 106, Seattle WA 98102. **Tel** (206)322-3041. **ED** Hazel Wolf. **Bk Rev. Circ:** 1,000 (ctrl). ***Continues*** *Western Outdoors Annual, 0091-7524.*
**Desc:** Conservation issues in eight Western states and British Columbia.

US/0278-1433
**OUTSIDE (1980).** (OUTSIDE.). [Outside]. (Feb./March 1980)-. Periodical. English. Twelve times a year. $18.00 (one year), $32.00 (two year), $42.00 (three year). Outside, 400 Market Street, Santa Fe NM 87501. **Tel** (505)989-7100. **(Subscription address:** Neodata / Colorado, PO Box 2606, Boulder Boulder CO 80322.**) ED** Mark Bryant. **LC** GV191.2; .M373. **DD** 796.5/0973. **Bk Rev. Ad Acc. Circ:** 400,000 (ctrl). available on microfilm and microfiche from University Microfilms International (UMI). Documents available from UMI Article Clearinghouse. ***Continues*** *Mariah Outside, 0194-4371.*
**Desc:** The active outdoor lifestyle magazine dedicated to inspiring people to enjoy fuller, more rewarding lives through editorial coverage of sports, travel events, people, politics, art and literature of the world outside.
**Ind/Abst** Acad. Search (Aug. 1984-June 1989); Access (1980-); INFO-SOUTH Abstr.; Mag. Artic. Summar. Elite (Aug. 1984-June 1989); Mag. Artic. Summar. Select (Aug. 1984-June 1989); Mag. Artic. Summar. CD-ROM (Aug. 1984-June 1989); Mag. Search; Newsp. Period. Abstr. (1992-); Pop. Period. Index; SPORT Discus; SportSearch (May 1987-).

US/0749-4459
**OUTWARD BOUND.** [Outw. bound]. 1985-. Periodical. English. an. $3.95. Telepictures Publications Inc, 300 Madison Avenue/8th Floor, New York NY 10017. **LC** GV191.2; .O95. **DD** 613.6/9.

US/1077-3703
**OVER THE EDGE. *Ceased.*** [Over edge]. Vol. 1, No. 1 (July 1994)-(1994). Periodical. English. bm (6 issues). LFP Inc., 9171 Wilshire Boulevard/Suite 300, Beverly Hills CA 90210. **Tel** (310)858-7100, FAX (310)274-7985. **LC** GV191.2 IN PROCESS. **DD** 796.

AT/0818-0210
**PADDLE POWER. *Suspended.*** [Paddle power]. (1985)-(19??). Periodical. English. bm. Paddle Power, PO Box 305, Gordon NSW 2072 Australia. **Tel** 011 61 02 498 8900, FAX 011 61 02 498 8695. **DD** 797.1220994. **Ad Acc.**
**Desc:** Magazine for canoe, kayak, wave and surf ski enthusiasts.

US/1058-5710
**PADDLER (FALLBROOK, CALIF.).** (PADDLER.). Vol. 11, No. 3 (July 1991)-. Periodical. English. bm (6 issues). $15.00 (one year), $25.00 (two year), $34.00 (three year) US; $27.00 (one year), $49.00 (two year), $70.00 (three year) other. Paddling Group, 4061 Oceanside Boulevard, Oceanside CA 92056. **Tel** (619)630-2293. **DD** 797. ***Continues*** *River Runner (Vista, Calif.), 0886-9197;* ***Absorbed*** *Canoesport Journal.*

UK/0031-224X
**PARKS & SPORTS GROUNDS. See** Travel and Tourism.

CN/1191-4335
**PARLONS PLEIN AIR, CHASSE, PECHE. *Title Change.*** [Parlons plein air chasse peche]. **VFOAT** Chasse, Peche; Parlons Plein Air, Chasse et Peche. Vol. 1, No 1 (Jan. 1992)-(1994). Periodical. French. mo. Quebecor Ventes Media, 2E Etage, 801 Est Rue Sherbrooke, Montreal Quebec H2L 4X9 Canada. **DD** 799/.09714/05. ***Continued by*** *Sports Nature, 1199-8458.*

CN/0227-2881
**PATHFINDER (CALGARY).** (THE PATHFINDER.). Winter 1980-. Periodical. English. qt. Free to members. Pathfinder Great Divide Trail Association, PO Box 5322 Station A, Calgary Alberta T2H 1X6 Canada. **DD** 917.11/005. ***Supersedes*** *Great Divide Trail Association Newsletter, 0227-2873.*

●US/1057-8331
**PENNSYLVANIA FISHERMAN.** (1992)-. Periodical. English. mo.

US/0897-8808
**PENNSYLVANIA GAME & FISH.** [Pa. game fish]. **VFOAT** Pennsylvania Game and Fish; Pennsylvania Game & Fish Magazine. (198?)-. Periodical. English. mo. $14.95 (one year), $27.95 (two year), $39.95 (three year). Game & Fish Publications Inc., PO Box 741, Marietta GA 30061. **Tel** (404)953-9222. **DD** 799. ***Continues*** *Pennsylvania Outdoors, 0745-225X.*

US/0031-451X
**PENNSYLVANIA GAME NEWS. Added/Corp** Pennsylvania Game Commission. Pennsylvania. Board of Game Commissioners. Vol. 1 (Apr. 1930)-. Periodical. English. mo (12 issues). $9.00 Pennsylvania (one year); $25.50 others (three years). Pennsylvania Game Commission, 2001 Elmerton Avenue, Harrisburg PA 17110-9797. **Tel** (717)787-3745, FAX (717)772-0542. **ED** Robert C. Mitchell. **LC** SK351; .P3. Index available (Bound in Dec. iss. ($1.00)). **Bk Rev**, (Qty: 15). **Circ:** 140,000 (ctrl). available on microfilm and microfiche from University Microfilms International (UMI).
**Desc:** Primary interest is hunting in Pennsylvania.
**Ind/Abst** Biol. Dig.

US/0274-6336
**PENNSYLVANIA SPORTSMAN, THE. Added/Corp** Pennsylvania Federation of Sportsman's Clubs. (198?)-. Periodical. English. Eight times a year (Feb., Mar., Apr., June, Aug., Sept., Nov., Dec.). $15.97 (one year), $29.97 (two year). Northwoods Publications, PO Box 90, Lemoyne PA 17043. **Tel** (717)761-1400, FAX (717)761-4579. ***Continues*** *Pennsylvania's Outdoor People, 0199-9494.*

●US/1059-1753
**PETERSEN'S ... ANNUAL TURKEY HUNTING. VFOAT** Petersen's Turkey Hunting Annual; Petersen's Turkey Hunting; Turkey Hunting. (1992)-. English. $4.95. Petersen Publishing Company, 6420 Wilshire Bouldevard, Los Angeles CA 90048. **Tel** (213)782-2485.

US/1049-9768
**PETERSEN'S BOWHUNTING.** [Petersen's bowhunt.]. **VFOAT** Bowhunting. (198?)-. Periodical. English. Eight times a year. $15.95 US; $22.42 Canada; $21.95 other. Petersen Publishing Company, 6420 Wilshire Bouldevard, Los Angeles CA 90048. **Tel** (213)782-2485. **(Subscription address:** Neodata / Colorado, PO Box 2606, Boulder Boulder CO 80322.**) DD** 799. available on microfilm and microfiche from University Microfilms International (UMI).

US/0095-5124
**PETERSEN'S HUNTING ANNUAL. *Title Change.* VFOAT** Hunting Annual. (1975)-(19??). English. an. Petersen Publishing Company, 6420 Wilshire Bouldevard, Los Angeles CA 90048. **Tel** (213)782-2485. **LC** SK1; .P43. **DD** 799.2/05. ***Continued by*** *Petersen's Annual Hunting, 1059-1737.*

US/0098-8154
**POTOMAC APPALACHIAN (MAY 1972).** (POTOMAC APPALACHIAN.). **Main/Corp** Potomac Appalachian Trail Club. **Added/Corp** Potomac Appalachian Trail Club. Potomac Appalachian (May 1972). Vol. 1 May (1972)-. English. mo. $6.00. Potomac Appalachian Trail Club, 118 Park Street Southeast, Vienna VA 22180. **Bk Rev. Circ:** 3,200. ***Supersedes*** *Bulletin of the Potomac Appalachian Trail Club, Washington, D.C.;* ***Formed by the union of*** *Potomac Appalachian Trail Club Bulletin* ***and*** *Forecast.*
**Desc:** Review of recent events and descriptions of upcoming activities regarding outdoor life, trails, and mountaineering.

US/1058-2274
**PRACTICAL SURVIVAL.** [Pract. surviv.]. Vol. 1, No. 1 (Aug./Sept. 1991)-. Periodical. English. bm (6 issues). $18.00. Mountain Star International Inc., 1750 30th Street, Suite 498, Boulder CO 80301. **Tel** (303)449-4128. **LC** GF86; .P73. **DD** 613.6/9.

US/0048-5144
**PRECISION SHOOTING.** [Precis. shoot.]. **Added/Corp** Precision Shooting, Inc. (19??)-. Periodical. English. mo. $29.00 (one year) US; $36.00 (one year surface), $52.00 (one year air) other. Precision Shooting Inc, 5735 Sherwood Forest Drive, Akron OH 44319. **Tel** (203)643-1157. **ED** David Brennan (phone: (203)645-8776). **DD** 799. Index available. cum. index. **Ad Acc.**
**Ind/Abst** SportSearch (May 1987-).

## Recreation, Leisure — Outdoor Life

**US**
**PROCEEDINGS OF THE NATIONAL CONFERENCE ON OUTDOOR RECREATION RESEARCH.** Main/Conf National Conference on Outdoor Recreation Research, Ann Arbor. **Added/Corp** University of Michigan. School of Natural Resources. United States. Bureau of Outdoor Recreation. (1963)-. Proceedings. English.

US/0198-9154
**PSE OUTDOOR ADVENTURES BOWHUNTING ANNUAL.** VFOAT PSE Bowhunting; Outdoor Adventures Bowhunting Annual; Bowhunting Annual. English. an. $1.95. Aqua Field Publications Inc, 66 West Gilbert Street, Shrewsbury NJ 07702. **Tel** (201)842-8300. **LC** SK36; .P18. **DD** 799.2/028/5.

CN/0381-1123
**QUEBEC NATURE.** V. 1- Dec. 1976-. Periodical. French. mo. $1.25 each number. Editaouais Ltee, C.P. 1066, Succursale B, 111,, Rue Carillon, Hull, Quebec J8X 2P8. **DD** 796.5/09714.

CN/0710-5789
**RAPPEL (MONTREAL).** (LE RAPPEL : JOURNAL DU CLUB DE CANOT-CAMPING LES PAGAYEURS INC.). [Rappel]. Periodical. French. ir. Free to members. Les Pagayeurs, CP 579 Succursale Desjardins, Montreal Quebec H5B 1B7 Canada. **DD** 797.1/22/060714.

US/0364-7153
**RECORDS OF EXOTICS.** See Recreation, Leisure-Sports.

**US**
**RECREATION AND OUTDOOR LIFE DIRECTORY.** Ceased. See Recreation, Leisure.

NE/0166-2651
**REKREAKSIE.** See Recreation, Leisure.

**SA**
**REPORT OF THE NATIONAL HIKING WAY BOARD.** Main/Corp National Hiking Way Board (South Africa). **Added/Corp** National Hiking Way Board (South Africa). Verslag van die Nasionale Voetslaanpadraad. **VFOAT** Verslag van die Nasionale Voetslaanpadraad. (19??)-. Afrikaans (English). R2.15. The Government Printer, Bosman Street, Private Bag X85, Pretoria 0001 South Africa. **Tel** 012-323-9731, FAX 012-323-0009. **LC** GV199.44.S6; N37a.

US/1055-4238
**RESEARCH REVIEW - COLORADO. DIVISION OF WILDLIFE.** (RESEARCH REVIEW : TERRESTRIAL AND AQUATIC WILDLIFE RESEARCH OF THE COLORADO DIVISION OF WILDLIFE.). [Res. rev. - Colo., Div. Wildl.]. **Added/Corp** Colorado. Division of Wildlife. Review No. 1 (June 1991)-. English. $1.50. Colorado Division of Wildlife, 6060 Broadway, Denver CO 80216. **DD** 639. **Formed by the union of** Colorado Fisheries Research Review, 0588-4462 **and** Colorado Wildlife Research Review, 0276-8992.

CN/0711-2572
**RESEAU PLEIN-AIR.** [Reseau plein-air]. **VFOAT** Bulletin de la Societe Quebecoise du Plein-Air. April 81-. Periodical. French. ir. Free to members, $5.00 others. Societe Quebecoise du Plein-Air, 1415 Est rue Jarry, Montreal Quebec H2E 2Z7 Canada. **DD** 796.5/09714. **Continues** P.A. (Societe Quebecoise du Plein-Air), 0711-2580.

**FR**
**REVUE NATIONALE DE LA CHASSE.** French. mo. 190.00F France; 250.00F other. Gerpresse, 8 10 rue Pierre Brossolette, 92300 Levallois Perr France. **Tel** 011 33 1 40874085.

CN/0709-7085
**RIDEAU TRAIL NEWSLETTER, THE.** Main/Corp Rideau Trial Association. Began with Summer 1971 issue. Newsletter. English. qt. Free to members. Rideau Trail Association, Box 15, Kingston Ontario K7L 4V6 Canada. **DD** 796.5/1/0627137.

US/0885-5722
**ROCK & ICE.** [Rock ice]. **VFOAT** Rock and Ice. (1984)-. Periodical. English. bm. $24.00 US; $34.00 Canada; $36.50 other. Eldorado Publishing Inc, PO Box 3595, Boulder CO 80308. **Tel** (303)499-0165, FAX (303)499-4131. **ED** George Bracksieck. **DD** 796. **Bk Rev** (Qty: 1 each issue). **Ad Acc. Adv Mgr:** Wendy Levison. **Pr Rev. Circ:** 45,000 (ctrl).
**Desc:** Offers coverage of the entire mountain scene, from rock and ice climbing to alpine ascents in the Himalaya. Also covers other outdoor adventures, such as ballooning, trekking and mountaineering.

US/1056-0114
**ROCKY MOUNTAIN GAME & FISH.** [Rocky Mt. game fish]. **VFOAT** Rocky Mountain Game and Fish. (19??)-. Periodical. English. mo. $14.95 (one year), $27.95 (two year), $39.95 (three year). Game & Fish Publications Inc., PO Box 741, Marietta GA 30061. **Tel** (404)953-9222. **DD** 799.

US/0278-0194
**ROCKY MOUNTAIN MAGAZINE ... WINTER GUIDE, THE.** [Rocky Mt. mag. winter guide]. **VFOAT** Winter Guide. Winter 1981/82-. English. an. $2.95. Rocky Mountain Country Limited Partnership, 1741 High Street, Denver CO 80218.

US/0893-746X
**ROCKY MOUNTAIN SPORTSMAN (COLORADO SPRINGS, COLO.).** Ceased. (ROCKY MOUNTAIN SPORTSMAN.). [Rocky Mt. sportsman]. Vol. 1, No. 1 (July/Aug. 1986)-Ceased ?. Periodical. English. bm. Rocky Mountain Sportsman, 226 East Monument, Colorado Springs CO 80903. **DD** 799.

US/0197-1883
**ROYAL RED BALL OUTDOOR SPORTSMAN.** (19??)-. Periodical. English. an. $1.95 per copy. Aqua Field Publications Inc, 66 West Gilbert Street, Shrewsbury NJ 07702. **Tel** (201)842-8300. **LC** SK1; .R68. **DD** 799/.05.

US/0199-5316
**SAFARI (TUCSON, ARIZ.).** See Recreation, Leisure-Sports.

FI/0355-0656
**SAMMANFATTNING AV ARTIKLARNA.** See Recreation, Leisure-Sports.

CN/1185-4839
**SASKATCHEWAN GAME MANAGEMENT.** (SASKATCHEWAN GAME MANAGEMENT / SASKATCHEWAN PARKS AND RENEWABLE RESOURCES, WILDLIFE BRANCH, POPULATION MANAGEMENT SECTION.). [Sask. game manage.]. **Added/Corp** Saskatchewan. Wildlife Branch. Population Management Section. (1984/1985)-. English. **LC** SK152.S26; S24a. **DD** 354.71240082/36; 333.95/411/097124021. **Continues** Saskatchewan Game Harvest Management, 0826-2136.
**Desc:** Information on hunting and wildlife management.

US/0195-7538
**SCI RECORD BOOK OF TROPHY ANIMALS, THE.** [SCI rec. book trophy anim.]. **Added/Corp** Safari Club International. **VFOAT** S.C.I. Record Book of Trophy Animals; Records Book of Trophy Animals. (1978)-. English (French, German and Spanish). an. $35.00 (field edition), $125.00 (hardbound edition). Safari Club International, 4800 West Gates Pass Road, Tucson AZ 85745. **Tel** (602)620-1220, FAX (602)622-1205, telex 880149. **ED** C. J. McElney, William Quimby, Jack Schwabland. **LC** SK277; .S39. **DD** 799.2/6. **Bk Rev**.
**Desc:** A 720 page edition devoted entirely to the continent and wildlife of Africa. Profusely illustrated.

**US**
**SCORP DIGEST.** (SCORP DIGEST / HCRS, U.S. DEPARTMENT OF THE INTERIOR, HERITAGE CONSERVATION AND RECREATION SERVICE.). **Added/Corp** United States. Heritage Conservation and Recreation Service. **VAT** Statewide Comprehensive Outdoor Recreation Planning Digest. Vol. 1, No. 1 (July 1980)-. English. Heritage Conservation and Recreation Service, US Department of the Interior, 550 G Street NW, Washington DC 20243.

CN/0383-0853
**SCOUT-JEUNESSE.** No. 1- Feb. 1976-. Periodical. French. ir. $5.00. les Amis du Signe de Piste, 16 Place du Fort, Repentigny Quebec J6A 3H7 Canada. **DD** 769.5/05. ctrl circ.

**AT**
**SCOUT MAGAZINE.** English. mo (11 issues). 25.00Aus$ Australia; 36.00Aus$ other. Scout Association of Australia, PO Box 190, Carlton South 3053 Australia. **Tel** 03 3492500, FAX 03 3492499.

**NE**
**SCOUTING MAGAZINE.** Dutch. ir. Scouting Nederland, Larikslaan 5, 6500 AH Nijmegen Netherlands. **Tel** 31 033 960911. **Continues** Scouting.

CN/0711-7957
**SENTIER CHASSE-PECHE.** [Sentier chasse-peche]. **VFOAT** Chasse-peche. Vol. 11, No. 4 (Feb. 1982)-. Periodical. French. Eleven times a year. 37.76Can$ Canada; 55.00Can$ other. Groupe Polygone Editeur Inc., 11450 Boul Albert Hudon, Montreal Quebec H1G 3J9 Canada. **Tel** (514)327-4464. **ED** Jeannot Ruel. **DD** 799/.09714. **Bk Rev. Ad Acc. Circ:** 75,000 (ctrl). **Formed by the union of** Quebec Chasse et Peche, 0315-260X **and** Sentier, 0228-3107.
**Desc:** French magazine for anglers, hunters, trappers, outdoorsmen.
**Ind/Abst** AQUAREF; Point Repere (1983-).

●US/1053-0304
**SHOOTER'S GUIDE (CALIFORNIA ED.).** (SHOOTER'S GUIDE.). (1992)-. English. $5.95. Pro-Ref Publications, 904 Silver Spur Road, #683, Rolling Hills Estates CA 90274.

**US/1069-6822**
**SHOOTING SPORTS USA.** See Recreation, Leisure-Sports.

US/1050-5717
**SHOOTING SPORTSMAN (WILLIAMSPORT, PA.).** (SHOOTING SPORTSMAN : THE MAGAZINE OF WINGSHOOTING & FINE GUNS.). [Shoot. sportsman]. Vol. 1, Issue 1 (Dec. 1987/Jan. 1988)-. Periodical. English. bm. $29.95 (one year), $54.95 (two year) US; $44.95 (one year), $84.95 (two year) other. Down East Enterprise Inc., PO Box 1357, Camden ME 04843. **Tel** (207)594-9544, FAX (207)594-5144. **(Subscription address:** CDS / SIFD Agency Control, 1901 Bell Avenue, Des Moines IA 50315.) **ED** Ralph P. Stuart. **LC** SK313; .S48a. **DD** 799.2/4/05. **Bk Rev**. **Ad Acc, Adv Mgr:** Bill Anderson. **Circ:** 12,000.
**Desc:** Covers the traditions of the sport, the birds, the hunting dogs, and the destinations. Honors the craftsmanship in shotguns, with stories about gunsmiths, engravers, and stock makers.

US/0038-8084
**SHOOTING TIMES.** See Recreation, Leisure-Sports.

**AU**
**SICHERHEIT IM BERGLAND.** Periodical. German. an. Kuratorium, Prinz-Eugen-Strasse 12, 1040 Vienna Austria. **LC** GV200.18; .S52. **DD** 363.1/4. **Continues** Fur die Sicherheit Im Bergland.

US/1069-2177
**SIGNPOST FOR NORTHWEST TRAILS (1988).** (SIGNPOST FOR NORTHWEST TRAILS.). [Signpost Northwest trails]. **Added/Corp** Washington Trails Association. **VFOAT** Signpost. Vol. 23, No. 1 (Jan. 1988)-. Periodical. English. Twelve times a year. $25.00. Washington Trails Association, 1305 4th Avenue, Suite 512, Seattle WA 98101. **Tel** (206)625-1367. **ED** Dan A. Nelson. **LC** GV199.42.N69; S55. **DD** 796. **Continues** Signpost (Seattle, Wash.), 0896-7989.
**Desc:** This is the information and news on the Pacific Northwest hikings.

US/0745-8517
**SKEETER, THE.** See Recreation, Leisure-Sports.

US/0091-1461
**SKI RACING REDBOOK.** See Recreation, Leisure-Sports.

**UK**
**SKIER'S HOLIDAY GUIDE.** See Recreation, Leisure-Sports.

US/0037-7473
**SNOWY EGRET.** See Natural History.

US/0889-7891
**SOUTH AMERICAN EXPLORER.** [South Am. explor.]. **Added/Corp** South American Explorers Club. Vol. 1, No. 1 (Oct. 1977)-. Periodical. English. Four times a year. $15.00. South American Explorers Club, 126 Indian Creek Road, Ithaca NY 14850. **Tel** (607)277-0488. **ED** Don Montague and Linda Rojas. **LC** F2224; .S68. **DD** 918/.043. Index available. cum. index. **Bk Rev**, (Qty: 15). **Ad Acc. Circ:** 9,200.
**Desc:** Features articles on South America related to exotic and unusual travel, ecology, the Andes, Amazon mountaineering, hiking, history and field sciences such as botany, anthropology, archaeology, geology, etc.

US/0897-9154
**SOUTH CAROLINA GAME & FISH.** [S. C. game fish]. **VFOAT** South Carolina Game and Fish; South Carolina Game & Fish Magazine. (19??)-. Periodical. English. mo. $14.95 (one year); $27.95 (two year); $39.95 (three year). Game & Fish Publications Inc., PO Box 741, Marietta GA 30061. **Tel** (404)953-9222. **ED** Jeff Samsel. **DD** 799. **Continues in part** Carolina Game & Fish, 0744-4176.

US/0279-2249
**SOUTH COAST SPORTFISHING.** Title Change. See Recreation, Leisure.

US/0199-3372
**SOUTHERN OUTDOORS (MONTGOMERY).** (SOUTHERN OUTDOORS.). [South. outdoors]. (19??)-. Periodical. English. Nine times a year. $18.00. Southern Outdoors, PO Box 17915, Montgomery AL 36141. **Tel** (205)272-9530, FAX (205)279-7148. **ED** Larry Teague. **LC** SK1; .S58. **DD** 799. Index available. **Ad Acc. Circ:** 252,000 (ctrl).
**Desc:** Edited and written for southern sportsmen. Features articles on fishing, hunting, and boating in the South.

US/0093-1977
**SOUTHWESTERN CAMPING & TRAILERING.** **VFOAT** Camping & Trailering: Southwestern. **VAT** Southwestern Camping and Trailering. English. an. American Automobile Association, 1000 AAA Drive, Heathrow FL 32746. **Tel** (407)444-7000. **LC** SK601.4.S68; S6. **DD** 917.8/04/3.

## Recreation, Leisure — Outdoor Life

US/0734-5895
**SPELEONEWS.** [Speleonews]. **Added/Corp** National Speleological Society. Nashville Grotto. National Speleological Society. Chattanooga Grotto. (19??)-. Periodical. English. Six times a year. $12.00. Nashville Grotto, PO Box 23114, Nashville TN 37201. **Tel** (615)356-2244.
 **Desc:** Notes and history on the exploration of caves and grottoes.
 **Ind/Abst** GeoRef.

US/1061-2424
**SPORTING CLAYS.** (SPORTING CLAYS : THE SHOTGUN HUNTER'S MAGAZINE : OFFICIAL PUBLICATION OF NSCA, NATIONAL SPORTING CLAYS ASSOCIATION.). [Sport. clays]. **Added/Corp** National Sporting Clays Association. (Sept.-Oct. 1989)-. Periodical. English. Nine times a year. $29.95. Patch Publishing, 5211 South Washington Avenue, Titusville FL 32780. **Tel** (407)268-5010, FAX (407)267-7216. **LC** WMLC 91/2308. **DD** 799. **Ad Acc.**
 **Desc:** Reports on one of the newest shooting activities with instructional columns, equipment reviews and range listings. Each issue features top tournament coverage as well as news, conservation and wildlife issues. Special sections on gear, clothing and accessories are also included.

US/0193-8401
**SPORTING GOODS MARKET IN ..., THE.** English. an. $165.00 non members, $132.00 members. National Sporting Goods Association, 1699 Wall Street, Mt Prospect IL 60056-5780. **Tel** (708)439-4000, FAX (708)439-0111. **LC** HD9992.U5; S657. **DD** 381/.456887/0973. Index available. available on microfiche.
 **Desc:** Contains information on consumer purchases of sports equipment, footwear and clothing.
 **Ind/Abst** Stat. Ref. Index.

US/0160-1830
**SPORTS AFIELD DEER.** **VFOAT** Deer. Periodical. English. an. $2.50. The Hearst Corporation, 250 West 55th Street, New York NY 10019. **Tel** (212)649-4014. **ED** Mike Schwanz. **LC** SK301; .S73. **DD** 799.2/77357. **Ad Acc.** **Circ:** 300,000.
 **Desc:** How-to stories about deer hunting.

US/0190-1249
**SPORTS AFIELD OUTDOOR ALMANAC, THE.** English. The Hearst Corporation, 250 West 55th Street, New York NY 10019. **Tel** (212)649-4014. **LC** SK1; .S714. **DD** 799/.05. **Continues** Sports Afield Almanac, 0092-7082.

FR/0990-0845
**SUBAQUA MARSEILLE.** See Recreation, Leisure-Sports.

US
**SUMMARY OF FEDERAL HUNTING REGULATIONS, ATLANTIC FLYWAY.** **VFOAT** Atlantic Flyway. Government Publication. English. an. Department of the Interior Fish and Wildlife Service, C Street Between Eighteenth and Nineteenth Streets Northwest, Washington DC 20240. **Tel** (202)343-3171.

US
**SUMMARY OF FEDERAL HUNTING REGULATIONS, CENTRAL FLYWAY.** **VFOAT** Central Flyway. Government Publication. English. an. Department of the Interior Fish and Wildlife Service, C Street Between Eighteenth and Nineteenth Streets Northwest, Washington DC 20240. **Tel** (202)343-3171.

US
**SUMMARY OF FEDERAL HUNTING REGULATIONS, MISSISSIPPI FLYWAY.** **VFOAT** Mississippi Flyway. Government Publication. English. an. Department of the Interior Fish and Wildlife Service, C Street Between Eighteenth and Nineteenth Streets Northwest, Washington DC 20240. **Tel** (202)343-3171.

US
**SUMMARY OF FEDERAL HUNTING REGULATIONS, PACIFIC FLYWAY.** **VFOAT** Pacific Flyway. Government Publication. English. an. Department of the Interior Fish and Wildlife Service, C Street Between Eighteenth and Nineteenth Streets Northwest, Washington DC 20240. **Tel** (202)343-3171.

CN/0226-482X
**SUMMARY OF THE HUNTING REGULATIONS (TORONTO).** (SUMMARY OF THE HUNTING REGULATIONS.). [Summ. hunt. regul.]. **Main/Corp** Ontario. Ministry of Natural Resources. 1978-. Periodical. English. an. Ministry of Natural Resources / Ontario, Whitney Block, Parliament Buildings, Toronto Ontario M7A 1W3 Canada. **DD** 346.71304/6954.
 **Continues** Hunting, 0226-188X.

CN/0846-7145
**SUMMER VISITATION AND OUTDOOR RECREATION STATISTICAL REPORT.** [Summer visit. outdoor recreat. stat. rep.]. **Added/Corp** Saskatchewan. Saskatchewan Parks, Recreation and Culture. Policy and Statistics Unit. (1989)-. Statistical Publication. English. **DD** 354.71240086/3/021. **Continues** Visitation and Outdoor Recreation Statistical Report., 0837-6298.

US/0039-5056
**SUMMIT (BIG BEAR LAKE).** (SUMMIT.). [Summit]. 1955. Periodical. English. bm. $15.00. Summit Magazine, PO Box 1889, Big Bear Lake CA 92315. **Tel** (909)866-3682. **ED** Jene Crenshaw and H Kilness. **LC** G505; .S94. **DD** 796. **Bk Rev.** **Ad Acc.** **Circ:** 7,500 (ctrl). available on microfilm and microfiche from University Microfilms International (UMI). **Continues** Summit Magazine.
 **Desc:** Up-to-date information on all phases of mountaineering expeditions, rock climbing, ski mountaineering, climbing and backpacking. Includes medical notes.
 **Ind/Abst** SportSearch (May 1987-).

GW/0342-7560
**SURF.** [Surf]. (1977)-. Periodical. German. mo. DM69.50. Delius Klasing & Co GmbH, Siekerwall 21, D 33602 Bielefeld Germany. **Tel** 011 49 521 559291, telex 9 32 934 DEKLA. **UDC** 797.17.

SW/0039-6583
**SVENSK JAKT.** **Added/Corp** Svenska Jagareforbundet. (18??)-. Periodical. Swedish. Eleven times a year. Svenska Jagareforbundets Tidskrift, Box 1, S-163 21 Spanga Sweden. **Tel** 011 46 8 7953300.

●US/1068-5812
**TACKLE TESTER.** See Hobbies.

US/0190-2792
**TECHNICAL ASSISTANCE BULLETIN (ANN ARBOR).** (TECHNICAL ASSISTANCE BULLETIN.). No. 1-. Bulletin. English. Price varies per volume. US Bureau of Outdoor Recreation, Lake Central Region, 3853 Research Park Drive, Ann Arbor MI 48104. **LC** GV191.42.M52; T42. **DD** 301.5/7/0977.

US/0077-8389
**TECHNICAL CIRCULAR - NEW HAMPSHIRE FISH AND GAME DEPARTMENT.** **Main/Corp** New Hampshire. Fish and Game Department. No. 1- 1937-. Monographic series. English. Price varies per volume. New Hampshire Fish and Game Department, 2 Hazen Drive, Concord NH 03301. **Tel** (603)271-3512. **DD** 799.

FR
**TECHNIQUE CHAUSSURE.** French. mo (June & July and Aug. & Sept. issues combined). 375.00F France; 480.00F other. SOPROGE SA, 7 Ter Cour des Petites Ecuries, 75010 Paris France. **Tel** 011 33 1 42471205, FAX 011 33 1 47703394.

US/0161-3871
**TENNESSEE SPORTSMAN.** Vol. 1 (Aug. 1980)-. Periodical. English. mo. $14.95 (one year), $27.95 (two year), $39.95 (three year). Game & Fish Publications Inc., PO Box 741, Marietta GA 30061. **Tel** (404)953-9222. **ED** David Morris. **Circ:** 15,059. **Supersedes** Tennessee Sportsman, 0161-3871.

US/0049-3481
**TETON.** **Suspended.** (1969)-(19??). Periodical. English. an. $3.00. Teton Magazine, Box 1903-10 West Broadway, Jackson WY 83001. **Tel** (307)733-9220. **ED** Gene Downer. **Bk Rev.** **Ad Acc.** **Circ:** 15,000.
 **Desc:** Concerns nature, wildlife, individual outdoor activities, and pioneer history.

US/0887-4174
**TEXAS FISH & GAME.** [Tex. fish game]. **VFOAT** Texas Fish and Game. (198?)-. Periodical. English. mo. $15.00. Texas Fish and Game, 7600 West Tidwell, Suite 708, Houston TX 77040. **Tel** (713)690-3474. **ED** Marvin Spivey. **DD** 799.

US/0748-9854
**TEXAS HUNTER'S DIRECTORY.** [Tex. hunt. dir.]. **Added/Corp** Outdoor Worlds of Texas (Firm). (19??)-. English. an. $4.45 (per copy). Outdoor Worlds of Texas Inc., 1647 South Alameda, Corpus Christi TX 78404. **Tel** (512)882-2953.

US/0163-4771
**TEXAS RIVERS AND RAPIDS.** (1972)-. English. $5.95. B.M. Nolen, PO Box 60, Pipe Creek TX 78063. **LC** GV776.T4; T49. **DD** 917.64.

US/0279-8875
**TEXAS SPORTSMAN.** (19??)-. Periodical. English. mo. $14.95 (one year), $27.95 (two year), $39.95 (three year). Game & Fish Publications Inc., PO Box 741, Marietta GA 30061. **Tel** (404)953-9222. **ED** Hugh Kinard. **Continues** Texas Sportsman Magazine.

CN/0380-6197
**THUNDER BAY CAMPING GUIDE.** 1972-. English. Guide Publishing & Print, PO Box 510, Ignace Ontario P0T 1T0. **DD** 917.13/12/044.

CN/0318-8477
**THUNDER COUNTRY OUTDOORS.** V. 2, No. 1- Oct. 1974-. Periodical. English. mo. Thunder Country Promotions, Box 1242 Station F, 1184 Roland Avenue, Thunder Bay Ontario P7C 4X9 Canada. **DD** 796.9/3/0971312. **Continues** Thunder Country Skier, 0318-8469.

US/1040-2098
**TODAY'S AQUARIST (DEVON, CONN.).** (TODAY'S AQUARIST.). [Today's aquar.]. Vol. 1, No. 1 (Sept. 1988)-. Periodical. English. bm. $22.50 US; $28.00 Canada and Mexico; $35.00 other. Pisces Publishing Group, 417 Bridgeport Avenue, Devon CT 06460. **Tel** (203)877-4427, FAX (203)877-1927. **ED** Don Johnson, (203)877-1927. **DD** 639. **Bk Rev.** (Qty: Varies). **Circ:** 1,000+. available on an online database from Compuserve. **Continues** Today's Aquarist, 1040-2098.
 **Desc:** World's leading publication for public aquarium personnel. Covers exhibits, conservation, breeding, maintenance of aquatic animals.

US/0041-0756
**TRAIL AND TIMBERLINE.** **Added/Corp** Colorado Mountain Club. No. 1 (Apr. 1918)-. Periodical. English. Eleven times a year (monthly with July/Aug. combined). $8.00 members, $10.00 other, US; $13.00 other. Colorado Mountain Club, 710 10th Street #200, Golden CO 80401. **Tel** (303)279-3080, (303)279-5643, FAX (303)279-5643. **ED** Marilyn Peterson. **LC** F782.R6; T77. Index available. cum. index. **Bk Rev.** (Qty: 12-15). **Ad Acc,** **Adv Mgr Tel** (303)279-3080. **Circ:** 9,000. **Supersedes** Trail and Timberline.
 **Desc:** Our members share their interests, concerns, and experiences in the mountains of Colorado and of the world.

US/0090-2241
**TRAIL CAMPING.** V. 1- Jan. 1973-. Periodical. English. mo. $9.00. Cramax Publications Inc, PO Box 310, Canoga Park CA 91305. **LC** SK600; .T73. **DD** 796.5/05.

US/0099-0191
**TRAILER LIFE'S RV CAMPGROUND & SERVICES DIRECTORY.** **VFOAT** RV Campground & Services Directory. **VAT** Trailer Life's Recreational Vehicle Campground and Services Directory. 9th- 1975-. Directory. English. an. $5.95. TL Enterprises, 29901 Agoura Road, Agoura CA 91301. **Tel** (800)234-3450, (805)389-0300. **LC** GV198.56; .T72. **DD** 647/.947. **Continues** Trailer Life's Recreational Vehicle Campground and Services Guide.

US/0194-5394
**TRAILS-A-WAY. OHIO EDITION.** (TRAILS-A-WAY.). (19??)-. Periodical. English. Eight times a year. $5.00 (one year), $8.00 (two year). Taw Publishing Company, 9731 Riverside Drive, Greenville MI 48838.

CN/1184-7417
**TRAPPER (NORTH BATTLEFORD. 1990).** (THE TRAPPER.). [Trapper]. Vol. 4, No. 6 (1990)-. Periodical. English. qt. Free to Trapper Association members; 15.00Can$ other. McIntosh Publications Co Ltd, Box 430, North Battleford 291 2Y5 Canada. **Tel** (306)445-7477, FAX (306)445-1977. **DD** 639. **Formed by the union of** The Trapper. Alberta-Manitoba-Saskatchewan., 1182-6894; The Trapper. British Columbia-Yukon., 1182-6908 **and** The Trapper. Newfoundland/Labrador, Nova Scotia, New Brunswick., 1182-6983.

CN/0836-7248
**TRAPPEUR QUEBECOIS, LE.** **Ceased.** [Trapp. que.]. **Added/Corp** Association Provinciale des Trappeurs Independants. (1976)-(19??). Periodical. French. qt. 1370 Bagot Ville de la Baie, Quebec Quebec G7B 2R2 Canada. **DD** 639/.1/09714.

US
**TRAPPING SEASONS AND REGULATIONS / STATE OF WASHINGTON, DEPARTMENT OF GAME.** **Main/Corp** Washington (State). Dept. of Game. (19??)-. English. Washington Game Department, 600 North Capitol Way, Olympia WA 98504. **LC** KFW453.A39; W37. **DD** 346.79704/6954; 347.970646954. **Circ:** 10,000.

UK
**TROUT FISHERMAN.** English. mo. £18.00 UK; £22.00 other. EMAP National Publications Ltd, Farndon Road, Market Harborough, Leicestershire, LE16 9NR England. **Tel** 011 44 733 555161. (**Subscription address:** Alan Wells International, Memberline House, Farndon Road, Leicestershire LE169NR England)

US/1067-4942
**TURKEY & TURKEY HUNTING.** [Turk. turk. hunt.]. **VFOAT** Turkey and Turkey Hunting. (Spring 1991)-. Periodical. English. Six times a year. $11.95 US; $17.95 other. Krause Publications, 700 East State Street, Iola WI 54990-0001. **Tel** (715)445-2214, FAX (715)445-4087, telex 55 6461. **LC** WMLC 91/1203. **DD** 799. **Absorbed** Turkey Hunter, 0896-1786.

US/1064-6094
**TURKEY CALL.** [Turk. call]. **Added/Corp** National Wild Turkey Federation (U.S.). (19??)-. Periodical. English. bm. $10.00 (library subscription only); $20.00 (membership to National Wild Turkey Federation). National Wild Turkey Federation, PO Box 530, Edgefield SC 29824. **Tel** (803)637-3106, FAX (803)637-0034. **ED** Gene Smith. **LC** SK325.T8; T87. **DD** 799.2/48619.

US/0896-1786
**TURKEY HUNTER, THE.** ***Title Change.*** [Turk. hunt.]. **VFOAT** Turkey. (198?)-(1992). Periodical. English. Eight times a year. Krause Publications, 700 East State Street, Iola WI 54990-0001. **Tel** (715)445-2214, FAX (715)445-4087, telex 55 6461. **LC** SK325.T8; T875. **DD** 799.2/48619. ***Continues*** *Turkey (Sutton, Neb.), 8750-0205.* ***Split into*** *Turkey & Turkey Hunting, 1067-4942.*
**Desc:** The sport's savviest writers pack each issue with assorted tom-taking know-how to help you bag this classic American bird. It features shooting tips for both firearm and archery hunters, forecasts of upcoming seasons, new product comparisons, updates on state legislative developments, and book reviews to help avid turkey hunters stock their libraries with confidence. Also features a solid marketplace for the best in turkey calls, ammunition, clothing, boots, videos, and other essential hunting and outdoor supplies.

GW
**UNSERE JAGD.** **Added/Corp** Germany (East). Oberste Jagdbehorde. (19??)-. Periodical. German. Twelve times a year. DM41.16 Germany; DM59.50 others. BLV Verlagsgesellschaft MBH, Lothstrasse 29, D80797 Munich Germany. **Tel** 011 49 89 12705214. **LC** SK201; .U54.
**Ind/Abst** Key Word Index Wildl. Res.

US/0883-6841
**USA OUTDOORS.** [U.S.A. outdoors]. (198?)-. Periodical. English. bm. USA Outdoors, PO Box 796908, Dallas TX 75379-6908. **Tel** (214)380-2656, FAX (214)380-2621. **ED** John H. Brett, Jr. **DD** 796. **Bk Rev**. **Ad Acc**. **Circ:** 22,000 (ctrl). ***Continues*** *Military Outdoors, 0194-6846.*
**Desc:** Results, news, views, and information on fishing tournaments.

US/0741-9708
**UTAH BIG GAME RANGE TREND STUDIES.** **See** Recreation, Leisure-Sports.

US
**UTAH COUGAR HARVEST.** **See** Recreation, Leisure-Sports.

US/0897-7283
**UTAH FISHING.** [Utah fish.]. **VFOAT** Utah Fishing Magazine. (1987)- Vol.25 (Jan. 1993)-. Periodical. English. Twenty-four times a year. $16.95. Utah Fishing, PO Box 728, Centerville UT 84014. **Tel** (801)451-0857. **ED** Sam Webb, 205 N 400 West, Salt Lake City, UT 84103 (801)521-8223. **DD** 799. **Bk Rev**. **Ad Acc, Adv Mgr:** James Archie, **Tel** (801)521-8223. **Circ:** 10,000.
**Desc:** The cat fishing continues strong at Utah Lake and is picking up at Willard Bay and on the Bear River.

CN/0524-5613
**VARSITY OUTDOOR CLUB JOURNAL, THE.** **Main/Corp** University of British Columbia. Varsity Outdoor Club. V. 1- 1958-. Periodical. English. an. 10.00Can$. The Varsity Outdoor Club Journal, Box 98, University of British Columbia, Vancouver British Columbia V6T 1W5 Canada. **ED** Ken Legg. **DD** 378.1/9/84796522. **Ad Acc**. **Circ:** 150.

US/0897-8794
**VIRGINIA GAME & FISH.** [Va. game fish]. **VFOAT** Virginia Game and Fish; Virginia Game & Fish Magazine. (198?)-. Periodical. English. mo. $14.95 (one year), $27.95 (two year), $39.95 (three year). Game & Fish Publications Inc., PO Box 741, Marietta GA 30061. **Tel** (404)953-9222. **DD** 799. ***Continues in part*** *Virginia-West Virginia Game & Fish, 0889-3314.*

US
**VIRGINIA OUTDOORS PLAN. EXECUTIVE SUMMARY, THE.** **Main/Corp** Virginia. Commission of Outdoor Recreation. **VFOAT** Executive Summary, the Virginia Outdoors Plan. English. Commission of Outdoor Recreation, 101 North 8th Street, Richmond VA 23219. **LC** GV191.42.V8; V57B. **DD** 790/.09755.

US/0194-6927
**VOICE OF THE TRAPPER.** ***Title Change.*** [Voice trapp.]. (1959)-?. Periodical. English. qt. National Trappers Association, PO Box 3667, Bloomington IL 61702. **Tel** (309)829-2422, FAX (309)829-7615. **ED** Tom Krause. **DD** 639. **Ad Acc**. **Circ:** 17,000 (ctrl). ***Continued by*** *American Trapper, 1050-4036.*
**Desc:** To educate and promote trapping.

US/0744-1266
**WALLEYE.** (WALLEYE / AMERICAN WALLEYE ASSOCIATION.). **Added/Corp** American Walleye Association. **VFOAT** Walleye Magazine. (198?)-. Periodical. English. Six times a year. $12.50. Walleye Magazine, PO Box 40210, Cleveland OH 44140. **Tel** (216)333-9494. **LC** Discard. **Bk Rev**. **Ad Acc**. **Circ:** 40,000. ***Continues*** *American Walleye Association. A.W.A. Monthly, 0274-5062.*
**Desc:** Tells readers how, when, and where to catch walleye and sauger across North America. It also contains recipes, vacation spots, and information on conservation and legislative issues.

US/1068-2112
**WALLEYE IN-SIDER.** **See** Fish and Fisheries.

●PL/0867-4663
**WEDKARSTWO I TY.** [Wedkar. Ty]. (1991)-. Periodical. Polish. mo. Price on Request. **(Subscription address:** ARS Polona, PO Box 1001, 00068 Warsaw Poland.**)** **UDC** 799.1.

US/0743-460X
**WEEKLY BULLET, THE.** **See** Recreation, Leisure-Sports.

US/0897-9162
**WEST VIRGINIA GAME & FISH.** [W. V. game fish]. **VFOAT** West Virginia Game and Fish; West Virginia Game & Fish Magazine. (198?)-. Periodical. English. mo. $14.95 (one year), $27.95 (two year), $39.95 (three year). Game & Fish Publications Inc., PO Box 741, Marietta GA 30061. **Tel** (404)953-9222. **LC** WMLC 93/874. **DD** 799. ***Continues in part*** *Virginia-West Virginia Game & Fish, 0889-3314.*

US/0890-0876
**WESTERN & EASTERN TREASURES.** [West. east. treasures]. **VFOAT** Western and Eastern Treasures. (197?)-. Periodical. English. Twelve times a year. $21.95 one year; $37.95 two year. Peoples Publishing Company, 5440 Ericson Way, PO Box 1095, Arcata CA 95521. **Tel** (707)822-8442, FAX (707)822-0973. **ED** Rosemary Anderson, PO Box 1598, Mercer Island, WA 98040 (phone: (206)230-9224). **LC** G521; .W47. **DD** 622/.1905. Index available. **Bk Rev**, (Qty: 30-50). **Ad Acc, Adv Mgr:** S. Anderson, **Tel** (206)230-9224. **Circ:** 30,000. ***Continues*** *Western Treasures.*
**Desc:** Written for metal detecting enthusiasts.

US/0194-4398
**WESTERN BACKCOUNTRY MAGAZINE.** **VFOAT** Western Backcountry. Periodical. English. mo. Western Backcountry, Inc., PO Box Q, Quincy CA 95971. ***Continues*** *Wild Country, 0164-601X.*

US/0274-7219
**WESTERN BOWHUNTER.** (19??)-. Periodical. English. Twelve times a year. $12.00 (one year); $20.00 (two years). Western Bowhunter, PO Box 511, Squaw Valley CA 93646. **Tel** (209)332-2535. ***Continues*** *Pacific Coast Bowhunter.*

US/0146-6585
**WESTERN CANADA : ALASKA CAMPING.** **VFOAT** Alaska Camping. English. an. American Automobile Association, 1000 AAA Drive, Heathrow FL 32746. **Tel** (407)444-7000. **LC** GV198.67.C2; W47. **DD** 647/.9471.

US/0049-7479
**WESTERN OUTDOOR NEWS.** [West. outdoor news]. (19??)-. Periodical. English. wk. $34.95. Western Outdoors Publications, 3197-E Airport Loop Drive, Costa Mesa CA 92626. **Tel** (714)546-4370, FAX (714)662-3486. **(Subscription address:** Hutchins and Associates, 1865 East Valley Parkway, Suite 206, Escondido CA 92072.**)** **ED** Pat McDonell. **DD** 799. **Ad Acc**. **Circ:** 72,000.
**Desc:** Coverage of fishing and hunting in California.

US/0043-4000
**WESTERN OUTDOORS.** [West. outdoors]. (1953)-. Periodical. English. ir (nine issues per year). $11.95 US; $21.95 other. Western Outdoors Publications, 3197-E Airport Loop Drive, Costa Mesa CA 92626. **Tel** (714)546-4370, FAX (714)662-3486. **ED** Jack Brown. **LC** SK1; .W39. **DD** 799/.05. Index available. **Bk Rev**. **Ad Acc**. **Circ:** 143,128.
**Desc:** Editorial coverage on where to go in the West for recreational activities, with emphasis on new places for fishing, hunting, camping and pleasure boating.
**Ind/Abst** Calif. Period. Index (19??-); Calif. Period. Microfi. (19??-).

US/0194-0384
**WHEELERS RV RESORT & CAMPGROUND GUIDE.** **VFOAT** RV Resort & Campground Guide. **VAT** Wheelers Recreational Vehicle Resort and Campground Guide. (1979)-. English (French and Spanish). an (current year edition publ Dec. prior year). $12.95, $19.41. Print Media Services Ltd, 1310 Jarvis Avenue, Elk Grove Village IL 60007. **Tel** (800)323-8899, (708)981-0100, FAX (708)981-0106. **ED** Gerri Bossiere. **LC** GV198.56; .W47. **DD** 647/.947. Index available. **Ad Acc, Adv Mgr:** Kevin Dempsey. **Circ:** 200,000. ***Continues*** *Wheelers Recreational Vehicle Resort and Campground Guide. North American Edition, 0362-9759.*
**Desc:** Guide to campgrounds and RV resorts in North America and a toll-free reservation directory for its US advertisers. Plus travel articles and information.

US/0090-600X
**WHEELER'S TRAILER RESORT AND CAMPGROUND GUIDE. SUN BELT EDITION.** (WHEELERS TRAILER RESORT AND CAMPGROUND GUIDE.). English. an. $2.95. Aventour Marketing Ltd., 1150 Northwest Highway, Park Ridge IL 60068. **LC** SK601.3; .W482. **DD** 796.54/0257.

AT/1030-469X
**WILD PRAHRAN.** [Wild Prahran]. (1987)-. Periodical. English. Four times a year. 69.00Aus$ Australia; 89.00Aus$ others. Wild Publications Pty Ltd., PO Box 415, Prahran VIC 3181 Australia. **Tel** 011 61 3 8268482. **DD** 796.50994. ***Continues*** *Australian Wild, 0726-2809.*
**Ind/Abst** SPORT Discus.

CN/0705-3150
**WILDERNESS ARTS AND RECREATION (1977).** (WILDERNESS ARTS AND RECREATION.). V. 2, No. 3-. Periodical. English. bm. 1.00Can$ each number. Big Bear Wilderness Services, Box 2640, Edson Alberta T0E 0P0 Canada. **DD** 796.5/097123. ***Continues*** *Alberta Wilderness Arts and Recreation, 0381-6303.*

US
**WILDERNESS MEDICINE LETTER : THE OFFICIAL NEWSLETTER OF THE WILDERNESS MEDICAL SOCIETY.** **See** Medical Science and Technology.

●US/1056-3318
**WILDERNESS SERIES.** 1992-. Monographic series. English. $30.00 (libraries and institutions), $38.00 (individuals), $45.00 (single copies). Ohio Valley Publishing Company, 452 West Haller Street, Lima OH 45801. **ED** Michael Michand. Index available (Bound in first issue). cum. index. **Acid Free.** ctrl circ.
**Desc:** A complete handbook for campers, hikers, those who love the out of doors. How-to magazine for comfort while living in the wilderness, camping or cooking in the out of doors.

CN/0828-9654
**WILDERNESS TRAILS 'N' TALES.** [Wilderness trails tales]. Vol. 1, Issue 1 (April 1983)-. Periodical. English. mo. 12.00Can$. Wilderness Trails 'N' Tales, PO Box 4321 Station A, Fredericton New Brunswick E3B 5G4 Canada. **DD** 799/.09715.

US/0886-0637
**WILDFOWL (ADEL, IOWA).** (WILDFOWL.). [Wildfowl]. Vol. 1, No. 1 (Aug./Sept. 1985)-. Periodical. English. bm (6 issues). $23.97 (one year), $37.97 (two year), $49.97 (three year). Stover Publishing Company Inc., PO Box 35098, 1901 Bell Avenue, Suite 4, Des Moines IA 50315. **Tel** (515)243-2472, FAX (515)243-0233. **ED** Bob Wilbanks. **Ad Acc, Adv Mgr:** Mary Stearns, **Tel** same as publisher.

US/0886-3458
**WILDLIFE HARVEST.** [Wildl. harvest]. **Added/Corp** North American Game Breeders and Shooting Preserve Operators Association, Inc. North American Gamebird Association. **VFOAT** Wildlife Harvest Magazine. Vol. 1 (1970)-. Periodical. English. mo. $25.00. John M. Mullin / Publ Editor, North American Gamebird Association, Goose Lake IA 52750. **Tel** (319)242-3046. **ED** John M. Mullin and Peggy Mullin Boehman. **DD** 799. **Ad Acc**. **Circ:** 2,453.

US/0892-1849
**WING & SHOT.** [Wing shot]. **VFOAT** Wing and Shot; Wing & Shot Magazine. (1986)-. Periodical. English. bm (6 issues). $23.97 (one year), $37.97 (two year), $49.97 (three year). Stover Publishing Company Inc., PO Box 35098, 1901 Bell Avenue, Suite 4, Des Moines IA 50315. **Tel** (515)243-2472, FAX (515)243-0233. **ED** Bob Wilbanks. **Bk Rev**. **Ad Acc, Adv Mgr:** Mary Stearns, **Tel** same as publisher.
**Desc:** A periodical for upland bird hunters.

US
**WISCONSIN DEER AND BEAR HARVEST SUMMARY.** **Main/Corp** Wisconsin. Dept. of Natural Resources. 1968-. English. an. Wisconsin Deer and Bear Harvest Summary, PO Box 7921, Madison WI 53707. **DD** 799.2/77/357. ***Continues*** *Deer Hunt.*

US/0893-5769
**WISCONSIN OUTDOOR JOURNAL.** [Wis. outdoor j.]. Vol. 1, No. 1 (Aug./Sept. 1987)-. Periodical. English. Eight times a year. $14.95 US; $23.95 other. Krause Publications, 700 East State Street, Iola WI 54990-0001. **Tel** (715)445-2214, FAX (715)445-4087, telex 55 6461. **DD** 799.

US
**WISCONSIN OUTDOORS AND CONSERVATION NEWS.** ***Title Change.*** **Main/Corp** Wisconsin. Dept. of Natural Resources. Feb. 19-20, 1977-. Periodical. English. wk. Wisconsin Outdoors and Conservation News, PO Box 7921, Madison WI 53707. **ED** Jeff L Welsch. **Circ:** 1,000 (ctrl). ***Formed by the union of*** *Wisconsin Outdoors.* ***Absorbed by*** *News Release - Department of Natural Resources.*

US/0361-9451
**WISCONSIN SPORTSMAN.** [Wis. sportsman]. **VFOAT** Wisconsin Sportsman Magazine. (19??)-. Periodical. English. mo. $14.95 (one year), $27.95 (two year), $39.95 (three year). Game & Fish Publications Inc., PO Box 741, Marietta GA 30061. **Tel** (404)953-9222. **ED** Ken Dunwoody. **LC** SK143; .W55. **DD** 977.5/005. **Ad Acc.**
**Desc:** Covers fishing, hunting and other outdoor participation activities in Wisconsin.

US/1041-1291
**WISCONSIN WOODS & WATER.** [Wis. woods waters]. **VFOAT** Wisconsin Woods and Waters; Woods and Waters; Woods & Waters. (198?)-. Periodical. English. bm (6 issues). $14.95 (one year), $27.95 (two year), $39.95 (three year). Laken Enterprises, PO Box 983, Fond du Lac WI 54936. **Tel** (414)921-1890. **ED** Barbara Laken. **DD** 799. **Ad Acc. Circ:** 40,000. ***Continues*** *Woods "N" Waters Magazine, 0279-0807.*
**Desc:** Deals with fishing, hunting and camping in Wisconsin.

US/1042-6426
**WOLF! (CLIFTON HEIGHTS, PA.).** (WOLF!.). [Wolf]. (1983)-. Periodical. English. Four times a year (Feb., May, Aug., Nov.). $18.50 US; $25.00 Canada & Mexico; $33.50 others. Wolf, PO Box 29, Lafayette IN 47902. **Tel** (317)567-2265, FAX (317)567-2084. **ED** Brian F. Bailey. **DD** 639.
**Desc:** This magazine continues its tradition of objective reporting of both local and global issues concerning the current status of wolves in the wild, government recovery programs, legislation affecting the wolves and other current news.
**Ind/Abst** Fish Rev. (Jan. 1989-July 1992); Wildl. Rev. (Jan. 1989-July 1992).

KO
**WOLGAN NAKKSI. VFOAT** Nakksi. 1st Vol. ('84/5)-. Periodical. Korean. mo. W36,000. Choson Ilbosa, 61 Taepyong-no 1-ka, Chung-ku, Seoul South Korea. **LC** SH667.K8; W64.

US/0030-7157
**WONDERFUL WEST VIRGINIA. See** Environmental Issues-Conservation and Natural Resources.

US/0091-2018
**WOODALL'S BETTER CAMPING. VFOAT** Better Camping. Periodical. English. mo. $6.00. Woodall Publishing Company, 28167 North Keith Drive, Lake Forest IL 60015. **Tel** (708)362-6700. **LC** SK600; .W66. **DD** 796.54/05.

US/0162-7406
**WOODALL'S CAMPGROUND DIRECTORY. EASTERN EDITION.** (WOODALL'S CAMPGROUND DIRECTORY.). **VFOAT** Campground Directory. 5th- Ed.; 1977-. Directory. English. an. $12.95. Woodall Publishing Company, 28167 North Keith Drive, Lake Forest IL 60015. **Tel** (708)362-6700. **ED** Linda Profaizer. **DD** 647/.9473. **Bk Rev. Ad Acc. Circ:** 450,000 (ctrl).
**Desc:** Directory contains complete listings of campgrounds in the United States; public and private campgrounds, inspection rated.

US/0146-1362
**WOODALL'S CAMPGROUND DIRECTORY. NORTH AMERICAN EDITION.** (WOODALL'S CAMPGROUND DIRECTORY.). **VFOAT** Campground Directory. 11th Ed. (1977)-. Directory. English. an. $12.95. Woodall Publishing Company, 28167 North Keith Drive, Lake Forest IL 60015. **Tel** (708)362-6700. **LC** GV198.56; .W66. **DD** 647/.9473. **Bk Rev. Ad Acc. *Continues*** *Woodall's Trailering Parks & Campgrounds. North American Ed.*
**Desc:** Includes full color US map, interesting travel section, a description of each state containing information about climate, time zone, and most popular attractions, etc.

US/0162-7414
**WOODALL'S CAMPGROUND DIRECTORY. WESTERN EDITION.** (WOODALL'S CAMPGROUND DIRECTORY.). **VFOAT** Campground Directory. 6th Ed. (1977)-. Directory. English. an. $8.95. Woodall Publishing Company, 28167 North Keith Drive, Lake Forest IL 60015. **Tel** (708)362-6700. **DD** 647/.9473.

US/0090-5151
**WOODALL'S FLORIDA CAMPGROUND DIRECTORY. VFOAT** Florida Campground Directory. 1st- 1973-. Directory. English. an. $3.95. Woodall Publishing Company, 28167 North Keith Drive, Lake Forest IL 60015. **Tel** (708)362-6700. **LC** SK601.5.F6; W66. **DD** 917.59/04/6. **UDC** 379.838(036)(759).

US/0163-5328
**WOODALL'S MISSOURI/ARKANSAS CAMPGROUND DIRECTORY. VFOAT** Missouri/Arkansas Campground Directory. Directory. English. an. $8.95. Woodall Publishing Company, 28167 North Keith Drive, Lake Forest IL 60015. **Tel** (708)362-6700. **UDC** 379.838(036)(767+778). **Bk Rev. Ad Acc.**
**Desc:** Contains expanded listings for all campgrounds listed in each state or group of states.

US/0742-3969
**WOODALL'S ... TENT CAMPING GUIDE. EASTERN EDITION. VFOAT** Woodall's Tent Camping Guide. Eastern Region. 1988-. English. an. Woodall Publishing Company, 28167 North Keith Drive, Lake Forest IL 60015. **Tel** (708)362-6700. **LC** PAR. ***Continues*** *Woodall's The Tenting Directory. Eastern Region, 0742-3969.*

US/0742-3977
**WOODALL'S THE TENTING DIRECTORY. CENTRAL REGION. Added/Corp** Woodall Publishing Company. **VFOAT** Tenting Directory. Central Region; Central Tenting Directory; Woodall's ... Tenting Directory. Central Edition; Woodall's ... Tenting Directory. Central Region. 1st Ed. (1984)-. Directory. English. an. $7.80 US; $7.95 Canada. Woodall Publishing Company, 28167 North Keith Drive, Lake Forest IL 60015. **Tel** (708)362-6700. **LC** GV191.42.M525; W66. **DD** 647/.9477.
**Desc:** Lists campgrounds in the Midwestern states and the Canadian provinces of Ontario and Manitoba.

US
**WOODALL'S TRAILERING PARKS AND CAMPGROUNDS DIRECTORY. VFOAT** Trailering Parks and Campgrounds Directory. Directory. English. Woodall Publishing Company, 28167 North Keith Drive, Lake Forest IL 60015. **Tel** (708)362-6700. **LC** GV191.35; .W66. **DD** 647/.9473. **UDC** 379.838(036)(73).

US/0095-9243
**WOODALL'S TRAILERING PARKS & CAMPGROUNDS. WESTERN EDITION.** (WOODALL'S TRAILERING PARKS & CAMPGROUNDS.). **VFOAT** Trailering Parks & Campgrounds. English. an. $2.95. Woodall Publishing Company, 28167 North Keith Drive, Lake Forest IL 60015. **Tel** (708)362-6700. **LC** GV191.35; .W65. **DD** 917.8/04/3. **UDC** 379.838(036)(73).

US/0194-8253
**WOODS 'N' WATER. VAT** Woods and Water. (19??)-. Periodical. English. Twelve times a year. $7.00 Florida & Georgia; $8.00 other. Woods 'N' Water, 702 North Calhoun Street, Perry FL 32347. **Tel** (904)584-3824. **ED** Patricia O. Pillow. **Bk Rev. Ad Acc. Circ:** 9,000.
**Desc:** Hunting and fishing news articles in Florida's Big Bend Area.

US/0276-4865
**WORLDWIDE HUNTING ANNUAL.** (WORLDWIDE HUNTING ANNUAL : OFFICIAL PUBLICATION OF SAFARI CLUB INTERNATIONAL.). [Worldw. hunt. annu.]. **VFOAT** Safari Worldwide Hunting Annual. 1981-. Periodical. English. an. $5.50. Safari Magazine, 4800 West Gates Pass Road, Tucson AZ 85745. **LC** SK1; .W69. **DD** 799.2/6/05. **UDC** 799.2.

## SPORTS

●US/1066-6834
**.22 RIMFIRE.** (1993)-. English. $3.95. Petersen Publishing Company, 6420 Wilshire Bouldevard, Los Angeles CA 90048. **Tel** (213)782-2485.

US/0884-7126
**3 & 4 WHEEL ACTION.** [3 & 4 wheel action]. **VFOAT** 3&4 Wheel Action; Three and Four Wheel Action. (1984)-. Periodical. English. mo. $18.98 (one year), $36.95 (two year). Hi-Torque Publications, PO Box 9502, Mission Hills CA 91395. **Tel** (805)295-1910. **DD** 796.

CN/0229-3684
**4 FOR 20.** (4 FOR 20 / ONTARIO ASSOCIATION OF ARCHERS.). ["4 20"]. **VFOAT** Four for Twenty. June 1980-. Periodical. English. bm. Ontario Association of Archers, Willowdale Ontario M2K 2X1 Canada. **DD** 799.3/2/060713. **UDC** 799.322(713). ***Continues*** *Ontario Association of Archers : Newsletter, 0229-3676;* ***Formed by the union of*** *J.D.P. Newsletter, 0828-6337.*

IT
**18 KARATI. VFOAT** Diciotto Karati. **VAT** Eighteen Karati. (19??)-. Periodical. Italian (English). Six times a year. $129.00. Overseas Publishing Representatives, 47 West 34th Street, New York NY 10001. **Tel** (212)564-3954.

CN/0826-2314
**A.H.M.H. INC. : ASSOCIATION DU HOCKEY MINEUR DE HULL INC.** [A.H.M.H. inc. Assoc. hockey mineur Hull inc.]. **VAT** Association du Hockey Mineur de Hull Inc. Vol. 1, No 1 (Dec. 1983)-. Periodical. French. ir. Association du Hockey Mineur de Hull, C P 1970 Succursale B, Hull Quebec J8K 3X5 Canada. **DD** 796.96/26. **UDC** 796.966(714).

US/0001-1754
**A.L.B.A. BOWLS. Main/Corp** American Lawn Bowls Association. **VAT** American Lawn Bowls Association Bowls. Vol. 3, 13th Issue (Jan. 1965)-. Periodical. English. qt. $3.00. American Lawn Bowls, 445 Surfview Drive, Pacific Palisades CA 90272. **LC** GV909; .A53a. **DD** 796.31. Index available. **Ad Acc. Circ:** 6,000. ***Continues*** *A.L.B.A. Bowls, 0001-1754.*

US/1071-1414
**AAAD BULLETIN, THE.** (THE AAAD BULLETIN : OFFICIAL PUBLICATION OF THE AMERICAN ATHLETIC ASSOCIATION OF THE DEAF.). [AAAD bull.]. **VAT** American Athletic Association of the Deaf bulletin. (1948)-. Bulletin. English. Four times a year. $4.00. American Athletic Association of the Deaf, 3607 Washington Blvd., Suite 4, Ogden UT 84403. **Tel** (801)393-7916 TDD. **ED** Shirley H Platt (editor's phone: (801)393-8710). **DD** 796. **Ad Acc.**

US/0193-7960
**ACC BASKETBALL. VAT** Atlantic Coast Conference Basketball. Vol. 1, (1979)-. English. Capitol Sports Network Publications, Capitol Broadcasting Company, 2619 Boulevard, Raleigh NC 27601. **LC** GV885.72.A85; A14. **DD** 796.32/363/0975.

US/0733-0448
**ACC BASKETBALL HANDBOOK. VFOAT** A.C.C. Basketball Handbook. **VAT** Atlantic Coast Conference Basketball Handbook. (19??)-. Periodical. English. an. $6.00. University Microfilms International, 300 North Zeeb Road, Ann Arbor MI 48106-1346. **Tel** (313)761-4700, (800)521-0600 Exts. 2490, 2491, FAX (313)973-1540. **ED** Ivan Mothershead. **Ad Acc. Circ:** 100,000.
**Desc:** Covers all aspects of ACC basketball.

US/0733-043X
**ACE (NEW YORK, N.Y.).** (ACE.). [Ace]. Periodical. English. bm. $17.50 US; $20.00 Canada. Burlesque Publishing Inc, 300 West 43rd Street, New York NY 10036.

XO
**ACTA - BRATISLAVA. UNIVERZITA. FAKULTA TELESNEJ VYCHOVY A SPORTU. Main/Corp** Bratislava. Univerzita. Fakulta Telesnej Vychovy a Sportu. Periodical. English (Slovak). an. Free. Fakulta Telesnej Vychovy a Sportu, nabr arm gen Svobodu 9, 814 69 Bratislava Slovakia. **Tel** +42 7 31 16 24. **UDC** 796. Index available. ctrl circ.
**Desc:** Scientific research works of pedagogues of the Faculty of Physical Education of Commenius University.

CN/0849-0759
**ACTION - CANADIAN ASSOCIATION FOR THE ADVANCEMENT OF WOMEN IN SPORT AND PHYSICAL ACTIVITY.** (ACTION.). [Action - Can. Assoc. Adv. Women Sport Phys. Act.]. **Added/Corp** Canadian Association for the Advancement of Women and Sport and Physical Activity. **VAT** Action - Association Canadienne pour l'Avancement des Femmes, du Sport et de l'Activite Physique. (1989)-. Periodical. English (French). tq. Free to members. Canadian Association Women and the Advancement of Sport, 1600 Prom James Naismith Drive, Gloucester Ontario K1B 5N4 Canada. **Tel** (613)748-5793. **DD** 796/.0194. ***Continues*** *The Starting Line., 0849-0740.*

FR/0292-5370
**ACTION GUNS.** [Action guns]. (1981)-. Periodical. French. Twelve times a year. 284.04F France; 390.00F other. Editions de Acacias, 122 Champs Elysees, 75008 Paris Cedex France. **Tel** 011 33 1 43592771. **UDC** 799. ***Continues*** *Action Digest, 0249-4639.*

US/1072-9291
**ACTION SPORTS RETAILER (1993). See** Business-Retail.

US/1068-2619
**ACTION SPORTS (SOUTH LAGUNA, CALIF.).** ***Title Change.*** (ACTION SPORTS.). [Action sports]. (199?)-(199?). Periodical. English. mo. Miller Freeman Inc., 600 Harrison Street, San Francisco CA 94107. **Tel** (415)905-2337, FAX (415)905-2240, telex 278273. ***Continues*** *Action Sports Retailer, 0199-4972.* ***Continued by*** *Action Sports Retailer, 1072-9291.*

AT/1031-282X
**ACTIVE (BELCONNEN).** (ACTIVE.). [Act.Belconnen]. **Added/Corp** Australian Sports Commission. Women's Sports Promotion Unit. (1988)-. Periodical. English. qt. Free. Australian Sports Commission, PO Box 176, Belconnen Australian Capital Territory, 2616 Australia. **Tel** 011 61 62 521594, FAX 011 61 62 521681, telex AA 62400. **ED** Sue Baker-Finch, Anne Marie Mioche and Michelle O'Rourke. **DD** 796.01940994. **Bk Rev. Circ:** 25,000 (ctrl).
**Desc:** Includes information about women in sports; the athletes, coaches, administrators and the related issues.
**Ind/Abst** SPORT Discus.

US/0149-4082
**ADDVANTAGE.** Periodical. English. bm. $18.00. Two Commerce Park Square/Suite 100, 23200 Chargrin Boulevard, Cleveland OH 44122. **Tel** (216)464-8546. **ED**

Recreation, Leisure —Sports

Bernice Adams. **LC** GV991; .A26. **DD** 796.34/2/0973. **UDC** 796.342(73). **Bk Rev**. **Ad Acc**. **Circ:** 5,000 (ctrl).
**Desc:** Tennis magazine for teaching professionals.
**Ind/Abst** SPORT Discus; SportSearch (May 1987-).

US/1048-3756
## AETHLON (SAN DIEGO, CALIF.).
(AETHLON.). [Aethlon]. **Added/Corp** Sport Literature Association. (Spring 1988)-. Periodical. English. sa. $35.00 US; $40.00 other. Eastern Tennessee State University / Department of English, PO Box 70270, Johnson City TN 37614-0270. **Tel** (615)929-4339, 929-6675, FAX (615)461-7193. **ED** Don Johnson. **LC** PN56.S73; A73. **DD** 810.8/355. Index available. cum. index. **Bk Rev**. **Ad Acc, Adv Mgr:** J. Duncan, **Tel** (615)929-4339. **Circ:** 600. ***Continues*** *Arete (San Diego, Calif.), 0894-0827.*
**Ind/Abst** Phys. Educ. Index; SPORT Discus.

US/0164-2863
## AIR GUN.
V. 1- Nov. 1978-. Periodical. English. qt. $10.00 US; $13.00 other. Quaker Point Professional Center, 1100 Quaker Road, Macedon NY 14502. **LC** TS537.5; .A38. **DD** 799.3. **UDC** 799.315.

TS
## AL-RIYADAH WA-AL-SHABAB. VFOAT
Alriada wa Ashabab. Periodical. Arabic. $200.00. Muassasat Al-Bayan, Lil-Sihafah Wa-Al-Tibaah, Wa-Al-Nashr Dubayy S B 2710, Dubayy Trucial States United Arab Emirates. **Tel** 444400. **ED** Hasher Maktoum. **LC** GV561.R57. **UDC** 796/799. **Bk Rev**. **Ad Acc**. **Circ:** 40,000 (ctrl).
**Desc:** Concerned with Arabic and international sports and youths. Includes interviews with stars of different Olympic sports, publishes weekly Arabic sports activities plus outstanding international ones.

QA
## AL-SAQR. VFOAT
Alsaqer. Periodical. Arabic. Al-Quwat Al-Musallahah Al-Qatariyah Al-Dawahah, PO Box 4925, Al-Dawahah Qatar. **LC** GV561; .S26.

US
## ALABAMA JUNIOR & COMMUNITY COLLEGE CONFERENCE BASEBALL NEWS BUREAU.
(19??)-. English. wk (During baseball season). $20.00. Alabama Junior & Community College Conference, 401 Adams Avenue, Montgomery AL 36130-2130. **Tel** (205)242-2890.

US
## ALABAMA JUNIOR & COMMUNITY COLLEGE CONFERENCE WOMEN'S BASKETBALL NEWS BUREAU.
(19??)-. English. $20.00. Alabama Junior & Community College Conference, 401 Adams Avenue, Montgomery AL 36130-2130. **Tel** (205)242-2890.

CN/0848-838X
## ALBERTA & BRITISH COLUMBIA GOLF GUIDE.
***Title Change.*** [Alta. B.C. golf guide]. **VFOAT** Annual Golf Course Directory Golf Guide; Alberta and British Columbia Golf Guide. **VAT** Alberta and British Columbia Golf Guide. Vol. 6, No. 1 (1989)-?. English. an. Sylvester Publications Ltd, Postal Bag 5022, Red Deer Alberta T4N 6A1 Canada. **DD** 796.352/06/87123. ***Formed by the union of*** *Alberta Golf Guide, 0832-8803* ***and*** *British Columbia Golf Guide, 0848-8398.* ***Continued by*** *Golf Guide, Annual Golf Course Directory, British Columbia, Alberta, Saskatchewan, 1184-6291.*

US/1047-546X
## ALL-AROUND, THE.
[All-around]. (19??)-. Periodical. English. mo. $15.00. The All-Around, 6121 East Milton, Cave Creek AZ 85331-9992. **Tel** (602)585-0785, (602)780-0891, FAX (602)585-0785. **ED** Jim Shephard. **DD** 791. ***Continues*** *Arizona All-Around.*
**Desc:** Covers the Southwest's rodeo, roping, and barrel-racing news.

US/0733-9356
## ALPINE SKIING COMPETITION GUIDE. EASTERN/CENTRAL EDITION.
(ALPINE SKIING COMPETITION GUIDE / UNITED STATES SKI ASSOCIATION. COMPETITION DIVISION.). [Alp. ski. compet. guide, East./Cent. ed.]. 1983-. English. an. United States Ski Association, US Alpine Office, 1750 East Boulder Street, Colorado Springs CO 80909. **Tel** (303)578-4600, telex 51051000530 USSA SKI. **UDC** 796.926.093(036)(73). ***Formed by the union of*** *Alpine Skiing Competition Guide, 0733-6659* ***and*** *Alpine Skiing Competition Guide, 0733-6667.*

US/0278-2960
## ALPINE SKIING COMPETITION GUIDE. ROCKY MOUNTAIN EDITION.
(ALPINE SKIING COMPETITION GUIDE.). [Alp. ski. compet. guide, Rocky Mt. ed.]. 1982-. English. an. $6.75. United States Ski Association, US Alpine Office, 1750 East Boulder Street, Colorado Springs CO 80909. **Tel** (303)578-4600, telex 51051000530 USSA SKI. **LC** WMLC L 83/26. **UDC** 796.926.093(036)(78).

US/0733-9348
## ALPINE SKIING COMPETITION GUIDE. WESTERN/ROCKY EDITION.
(ALPINE SKIING COMPETITION GUIDE.). [Alp. ski. compet. guide, West./Rocky Mt. ed.]. 1983-. English. an. $8.75. United States Ski Association, US Alpine Office, 1750 East Boulder Street, Colorado Springs CO 80909. **Tel** (303)578-4600, telex 51051000530 USSA SKI. **ED** Bruce Crane and S D Valentine-Ramey. **UDC** 796.926.093(036)(78). Index available. **Bk Rev**. **Ad Acc**. **Circ:** 15,000. ***Formed by the union of*** *Alpine Skiing Competition Guide, 0733-6675* ***and*** *Alpine Skiing Competition Guide, 0278-2960.*
**Desc:** A comprehensive guide to amateur alpine ski racing in the United States.

FR/0759-2167
## ALPIRANDO.
[AlpiRando]. (1984)-. Periodical. French. Twelve times a year. 274.24F France; 320.00F other. Societe Francaise d'Edition Presse, 48 50 Boulevard Senard, 92210 St Cloud France. **Tel** 011 33 1 47112000. **UDC** 796.5. ***Continues*** *Alpinisme et Randonnee (Paris. 1978), 0154-1757.*

US/1067-4535
## ALSA SWIMMERS' GUIDE.
[ALSA swim. guide]. **Added/Corp** American Lap Swimmers Association. **VFOAT** Swimmers' Guide. **VAT** American Lap Swimmers Association Swimmers' Guide. (1993). English. an. $14.95. American Lap Swimmers Association, Inc., PO Box 014220, Flagler Station, Miami FL 33101-4220. **Tel** (305)672-2900, FAX (305)531-0804. **DD** 797.
**Desc:** Includes information on 1,166 lap swimming facilities in 755 cities and towns in all 50 states and the District of Columbia. It has 55 maps to help swimmers locate pools in unfamiliar territory. Provides names and addresses, telephone numbers, admissions fees, pool sizes, water temperature. lane setups, schedules, disabled access data and locker and towel availability.

US/0002-6816
## AMATEUR BASEBALL NEWS.
**Added/Corp** American Amateur Baseball Congress. (19??)-. Periodical. English. ir (8 issues). $5.00. American Amateur Baseball Congress, 215 East Green, Box 467, Marshall MI 49068. **Tel** (616)781-2002.

CN/0824-4049
## AMATEUR SPORT NEWS.
[Amat. sport news]. Periodical. English. sa. Free. Amateur Sport News, 701-10240-124 Street, Edmonton Alberta T5N 3W6 Canada. **DD** 796/.097123. **UDC** 796.077(712).

CN/0824-4014
## AMATEUR SPORT NEWS (BRITISH COLUMBIA ED.).
(AMATEUR SPORT NEWS.). [Amat. sport news]. Periodical. English. sa. Free. Amateur Sport News, 701-10240-124 Street, Edmonton Alberta T5N 3W6 Canada. **DD** 796/.09711. **UDC** 796.077(711).

CN/0824-4065
## AMATEUR SPORT NEWS (CENTRAL ALBERTA ED.).
(AMATEUR SPORT NEWS.). [Amat. sport news]. Periodical. English. sa. Free. Amateur Sport News, 701-10240-124 Street, Edmonton Alberta T5N 3W6 Canada. **DD** 796/.097123/3. **UDC** 769.077(712).

CN/0824-4057
## AMATEUR SPORT NEWS (EDMONTON ED.).
(AMATEUR SPORT NEWS.). [Amat. sport news]. Periodical. English. sa. Free. Amateur Sport News, 701-10240-124 Street, Edmonton Alberta T5N 3W6 Canada. **DD** 796/.097123/3. **UDC** 796.077(712).

CN/0824-4006
## AMATEUR SPORT NEWS (NORTHERN BRITISH COLUMBIA ED.).
(AMATEUR SPORT NEWS.). [Amat. sport news]. Periodical. English. sa. Free. Amateur Sport News, 701-10240-124 Street, Edmonton Alberta T5N 3W6 Canada. **DD** 796/.09711. **UDC** 796.077(711).

CN/0824-4030
## AMATEUR SPORT NEWS (NORTHERN SASKATCHEWAN ED.).
(AMATEUR SPORT NEWS.). [Amat. sport news]. Periodical. English. sa. Free. Amateur Sport News, 701-10240-124 Street, Edmonton Alberta T5N 3W6 Canada. **DD** 796/.097124. **UDC** 796.077(712).

CN/0822-8280
## AMATEUR SPORT NEWS (SOUTHERN ALBERTA ED.).
(AMATEUR SPORT NEWS.). [Amat. sport news]. Periodical. English. sa. Free. Amateur Sport News, 701-10240-124 Street, Edmonton Alberta T5N 3W6 Canada. **DD** 796/.097123. **UDC** 796.077(712).

CN/0824-3999
## AMATEUR SPORT NEWS (SOUTHERN BRITISH COLUMBIA ED.).
(AMATEUR SPORT NEWS.). [Amat. sport news]. Periodical. English. sa. Free. Amateur Sport News, 701-10240-124 Street, Edmonton Alberta T5N 3W6 Canada. **DD** 796/.09711. **UDC** 796.077(711).

CN/0824-4022
## AMATEUR SPORT NEWS (SOUTHERN SASKATCHEWAN ED.).
(AMATEUR SPORT NEWS.). [Amat. sport news]. Periodical. English. sa. Free. Amateur Sport News, 701-10240-124 Street, Edmonton Alberta T5N 3W6 Canada. **DD** 796/.097124. **UDC** 796.077(712).

US/0569-1796
## AMATEUR WRESTLING NEWS.
[Amateur wrestl. news]. **Added/Corp** National Wrestling Coaches Association (U.S.). National Collegiate Athletic Association of Wrestling Coaches and Officials (U.S.). Vol. 3 (1957)-. Periodical. English. Twelve times a year. $28.00 (one year), $53.00 (two years), $77.00 (three years). Amateur Wrestling News, PO Box 54679, Oklahoma City OK 73154. **Tel** (405)524-8551, FAX (405)524-8193. **ED** Ron Good. **DD** 796. **Bk Rev**. **Ad Acc, Adv Mgr:** Johanna, **Tel** (405)524-8551. **Circ:** 9,000 (ctrl). ***Continues*** *Wrestling News and Reports.*
**Desc:** Covers all phases of amateur wrestling (Olympic to high school to college).
**Ind/Abst** SPORT Discus; SportSearch (May 1987-).

US
## AMERICAN ATHLETICS ANNUAL.
**Added/Corp** Athletics Congress (U.S.). (1980)-. English. an (Apr.). $15.00. TAC USA / Book Order Department, PO Box 120, Indianapolis IN 46206. **Tel** (317)297-2900.

US/0002-807X
## AMERICAN COONER.
(19??)-. Periodical. English. Twelve times a year. $15.00. American Cooner, PO Box 211, Sesser IL 62884. **Tel** (618)625-2711. **ED** George O. Slankard. **Ad Acc**. **Circ:** 30,000. ***Absorbed*** *Mountain Music.*
**Desc:** Coon hound events, supplies and stories.

US/0738-9795
## AMERICAN COWBOY.
**Added/Corp** Professional Rodeo Cowboys Association (U.S.). **VFOAT** American Cowboy Magazine; American Cowboy Magazine (Hoof and Horn). (19??)-. Periodical. English. bm. $16.95. Web Publications Inc., 650 Westdale Drive, PO Box 12830, Wichita KS 67277. **Tel** (316)946-0600. **LC** GV1834.5; .A47. **DD** 791.8. ***Continues*** *American Cowboy Magazine, 0199-4220.*

US/0002-8436
## AMERICAN FENCING.
**Added/Corp** Amateur Fencers League of America. Vol. 1 (Nov. 1949)-. Periodical. English. Four times a year. $12.00 US; $18.00 other. United States Fencing Association, 1750 East Boulder Street, Colorado Springs CO 80909. **Tel** (719)578-4511. **ED** Albert Axelrod. **LC** U860; .A48. **DD** 796.8605. **Bk Rev**. **Ad Acc**. **Circ:** 8,000 (ctrl). available on microfilm and microfiche from University Microfilms International (UMI). ***Supersedes*** *Amateur Fencers League of America. A.F.L.A. Secretary's Newsletter; Riposte.*
**Desc:** Promotion of the sport of fencing and activities of USFA membership.
**Ind/Abst** SPORT Discus; SportSearch (May 1987-).

US/0145-4250
## AMERICAN HANDGUNNER, THE.
[Am. handgunner]. **VFOAT** American Handgunner ... Annual. Vol. 1 (Sept./Oct. 1976)-. Periodical. English. bm. $16.95 (one year), $31.75 (two year), $44.87 (three year). Publishers Development Corporation, 591 Camino de La Reina, Suite 200, San Diego CA 92108. **Tel** (619)297-5350, FAX (619)297-5353, telex 695-478. **ED** Jerry Rakusan. **LC** TS537; .A53. **DD** 799.2/02833/05. cum. index. **Bk Rev**. **Ad Acc**. **Circ:** 155,054.
**Desc:** Publication devoted exclusively to the sport of handgunning.

US
## AMERICAN HIGH SCHOOL ATHLETE / COMPILED BY ATHLETIC PUBLISHING GROUP, INC.
**Added/Corp** Athletic Publishing Group. (19??)-. English. qt. Athletic Publishing Group Inc, PO Box 248, Andover MA 01810. **LC** GV697.A1; A47. **DD** 796/.092/2; B.

US/8756-3789
## AMERICAN HOCKEY MAGAZINE.
[Am. hockey mag.]. **Added/Corp** Amateur Hockey Association of the United States. (198?)-. Periodical. English. Ten times a year. $13.00. American Hockey Magazine, 4965 North 30th Street, Colorado Springs CO 80919. **Tel** (719)599-5500. **ED** Darryl Seibel. **LC** GV848.4.U6; U54. **DD** 796.96/2/0973. **Bk Rev**. **Ad Acc, Adv Mgr:** Jensen, **Tel** (612)522-1200. **Circ:** 30,000 (ctrl). ***Continues*** *American Hockey & Arena.*
**Desc:** Covers the news of the association, events, tournament schedules and game schedules.
**Ind/Abst** SportSearch (May 1987-).

US/1045-3598
## AMERICAN KITE.
[Am. kite]. Vol. 1, No. 1 (Summer 1988)-. Periodical. English. qt. $14.00 (1 year), $25.00 (2 year) US; $24.00 (1 year), $45.00 (2 year) other. American Kite, PO Box 699, Cedar Ridge CA 95924. **Tel** (916)273-3855. **DD** 796. **Bk Rev**. **Ad Acc**.

US/0736-0444
**AMERICAN LEAGUE REDBOOK.** **Added/Corp** American League of Professional Baseball Clubs. **VFOAT** Official American League Red Book. (19??)-. Periodical. English. an. $11.95. Sporting News, c/o Sharon Moore, 1212 North Lindbergh Boulevard, PO Box 56, St Louis MO 63166. **Tel** (314)997-7111, (800)825-8508. **(Subscription address:** Contemporary Books, Two Prudential Plaza, Suite 1200, Chicago IL 60601.**) LC** GV875.A15; A47a. **DD** 796.357/64/0973. ***Continues*** *Rookie and Record Book.*

US/0199-6770
**AMERICAN MARKSMAN, THE.** ***Title Change.*** Periodical. English. mo. National Rifle Association of America, 11250 Waples Mill Road, Fairfax VA 22030-9100. **Tel** (703)267-1560, (703)267-1583, (800)231-4672, FAX (703)267-3994. **ED** John Zent. **Circ:** 5,000. ***Continued by*** *NRA Tournament News.*

US/0732-8176
**AMERICAN POOL PLAYER.** [Am. pool play.]. Vol. 1, No. 1, (July 1982)-. Periodical. English. mo. $18.00 US; $20.00 Canada and Mexico; $22.00 other. PO Box 277, Lincolndale NY 10540.

●US/1069-1693
**AMERICAN RACING CLASSICS.** [Am. racing classics]. Vol. 1, No. 1 (Jan. 1992)-. Periodical. English. qt. $32.95. Griggs Publishing Company Inc., PO Box 500, Concord NC 28026. **Tel** (704)786-7132, (800)883-7323, FAX (704)788-4420. **DD** 796.

US/0003-083X
**AMERICAN RIFLEMAN.** [Am. riflem.]. **Added/Corp** National Rifle Association of America. (1923)-. Periodical. English. Ten times a year. $15.00 US; $20.00 Canada; $25.00 other. National Rifle Association of America, 11250 Waples Mill Road, Fairfax VA 22030-9100. **Tel** (703)267-1560, (703)267-1583, (800)231-4672, FAX (703)267-3994. **ED** Bill Parkerson. **LC** SK1; .A52. **DD** 799.205. **Circ:** 1,360,319. available on microfilm and microfiche from University Microfilms International (UMI). Documents available from UMI Article Clearinghouse. ***Continues*** *Arms and the Man, 0271-6917.*
**Ind/Abst** Acad. Abstr. Full Text Elite (July 1984-June 1989); Acad. Abstr. (July 1984-June 1989); Acad. Search (July 1984-June 1989); Art Archaeol. Tech. Abstr.; Consum. Index Prod. Eval. Inf. Source; Gen. Period. Index (1985-); INFO-SOUTH Abstr.; Mag. Artic. Summar. Elite (July 1984-June 1989); Mag. Artic. Summar. Select (July 1984-June 1989); Mag. Artic. Summar. CD-ROM (July 1984-June 1989); Mag. Index Plus (1989-); Mag. Search; Newsp. Period. Abstr. (1988-); Mag. Index (1977-)(1959-).

US/0888-1154
**AMERICAN ROWING.** (AMERICAN ROWING / THE UNITED STATES ROWING ASSOCIATION.). **Added/Corp** United States Rowing Association. Vol. 18, No. 1 (Feb./Mar. 1986)-. Periodical. English. Six times a year. $30.00. US Rowing Association, 201 South Capitol Avenue, Suite 400, Indianapolis IN 46225-1054. **Tel** (317)237-5656, FAX (317)237-5646. **ED** Maureen Merhoff and Trudy Bunge. **LC** GV790.6; .A47. **DD** 797.1/23/0973. **Ad Acc. Circ:** 26,000 (ctrl). ***Continues*** *Rowing U.S.A., 0744-4788.*
**Ind/Abst** Phys. Educ. Index; SPORT Discus; SportSearch.

US/0162-153X
**AMERICAN SHOTGUNNER, THE.** (19??)-. Periodical. English. Twelve times a year. The American Shotgunner, PO Box 3351, Reno NV 89505. **Tel** (702)826-3825. **ED** Robert Thruston and Kerry Watkins. **LC** WMLC L 83/19. **Bk Rev. Ad Acc. Circ:** 134,000.
**Desc:** The connoisseur's hunting, fishing, outdoor recreation and travel magazine. Columns on shooting sports, exotic hunting and fishing trips, wildlife art and gun investments.

US/0744-1363
**AMERICAN SKATING WORLD.** (19??)-. Periodical. English. mo. $22.95. Group Publications Ltd. Inc., 1816 Brownsville Road, Pittsburgh PA 15210. **Tel** (800)245-6280, (412)885-7600, FAX (412)885-7617. **ED** Bob Mack & H. Kermit Jackson. Index available. cum. index. **Bk Rev**, (Qty: 8). **Ad Acc**, **Adv Mgr:** P. Weber. **Circ:** 15,000.
**Desc:** Contains information on eligible and professional skating. Includes news and views on competitions, shows, profiles, music and choreography, both domestic and international. Also covers speedskating, in-line and related activities.

US
**AMERICAN SKI COACH.** English. Five times a year. $35.00. US Ski Coaches Association, PO Box 100, Park City UT 84060.
**Ind/Abst** Phys. Educ. Index (1990-); SPORT Discus.

US/1055-0615
**AMERICAN SKIER.** [Am. skier]. **Added/Corp** American Ski Association. Vol. 15, Issue 3 (Jan. 1991)-. Periodical. English. qt. American Ski Association, 155 South Madison Street, Denver CO 80209. **Tel** (303)399-9924. **DD** 796. ***Continues*** *Skiers Advocate, 0195-1300.*

US/0747-6000
**AMERICAN SWIMMING : A PUBLICATION OF THE AMERICAN SWIMMING COACHES ASSOCIATION.** **Added/Corp** American Swimming Coasches Association. **VFOAT** American Swimming Magazine. (1991)-. Periodical. English. bm. American Swimming Coaches Association, 301 SE 20th Street, Fort Lauderdale FL 33316. **Tel** (305)462-6267, (800)356-2722. **LC** WMLC 91/2900. ***Continues*** *American Swimming Coaches Association Magazine, 0747-6000.*

US/0747-5853
**AMERICAN SWIMMING COACHES ASSOCIATION WORLD CLINIC YEARBOOK.** ***Title Change.*** [Am. Swim. Coaches Assoc. World Clinic yearb.]. **Added/Corp** American Swimming Coaches Association. American Swimming Coaches Association. ASCA Clinic Talks (1969-1973). **VFOAT** World Clinic Yearbook; World Clinic Year Book. (1974)-(19??). English. an. ASCA, 1 Hall of Fame Drive, Fort Lauderdale FL 33316. **Tel** (305)462-6267. **ED** John Leonard. **Ad Acc. Circ:** 1,500. ***Continued by*** *World Clinic Yearbook.*
**Desc:** Serials of international swim coaches talks.

US/1045-7186
**AMERICAN VOLLEYBALL.** [Am. volleyb.]. Periodical. English. bm. $15.00 US and Canada; $20.00 other. American Volleyball Coaches Association, 1227 Lake Plaza Drive, Suite B, Colorado Springs CO 80906. **Tel** (719)576-7777, FAX (719)576-7778. **LC** GV1015.55; .A47. **DD** 796.325/0973.

US/0300-7626
**AMERICAN WHITEWATER.** [Am. whitewater]. **Added/Corp** American Whitewater Affiliation. **VFOAT** Whitewater. (19??)-. Periodical. English. Six times a year (Jan., Mar., May, July, Sept., Nov.). $20.00. American Whitewater Affiliation, PO Box 85, Phoenicia NY 12464. **Tel** (914)688-5569, FAX (914)688-5569. **ED** Bob Gedekoh, (phone: (412)384-7275. **Bk Rev. Ad Acc. Circ:** 5000.
**Desc:** Conservation, safety and adventure on the Whitewater River.
**Ind/Abst** SPORT Discus; SportSearch (May 1987-).

FR
**ANNEE DU TENNIS, L'.** Began with Vol. for 1979. French. an. **LC** GV991; .A66. **DD** 796.342/05.

FR
**ANNEE PLANCHE A VOILE, L'.** 1980-81-. French. an. **LC** GV811.63.W56; A55. **DD** 797.1/72/05.

CN/0228-7005
**ANNUAIRE DU SPORT UNIVERSITAIRE QUEBECOIS ET CALENDRIERS DES ACTIVITES.** (ANNUAIRE DU SPORT UNIVERSITAIRE QUEBECOIS ET CALENDRIERS DES ACTIVITIES ... / ASSOCIATION SPORTIVE UNIVERSITAIRE DU QUEBEC.). **Main/Corp** Association Sportive Universitaire du Quebec. **VFOAT** Directory of University Sports in Quebec and Schedules of Activities ... . **VAT** Annuaire - Association Sportive Universitaire du Quebec; Directory - Quebec University Athletic Association; Quebec University Athletic Association. Directory of University Sports in Quebec and Schedules of Activities. French (English). an. ASUQ, 4545 Avenue Pierre-de-Coubertin, CP 1000 Succursale M, Montreal Quebec H1V 3R2 Canada. **DD** 796/.025/714. **UDC** 796/799(059)(714).

FR
**ANNUAIRE (FRANCE. MINISTERE DE LA JEUNESSE, DES SPORTS ET DES LOISIRS. DIVISION DES ETUDES ET DE LA STATISTIQUE).** ***Title Change.*** (ANNUAIRE / DIRECTION DE L'ADMINISTRATION, DIVISION DES ETUDES ET DE LA STATISTIQUE.). **Added/Corp** France. Ministere de la Jeunesse, des Sports et des Loisirs. Division des Etudes et de la Statistique. France. Ministere de la Jeunesse, des Sports et des Loisirs. Lettre d'Information du Ministere de la Jeunesse, des Sports et des Loisirs. **VFOAT** Regards sur les Statistiques Jeunesse et Sports. (19??)-(19??). French. an. 118 Avenue du President-Kennedy, 75775 Paris Cedex 16 France. **LC** GV79; .S8. **DD** 790/.0944. ***Continues*** *Statistiques Jeunesse, Sports et Loisirs.* ***Continued by*** *Statistiques Temps Libre, Jeunesse et Sports.*

US/0361-8048
**ANNUAL - ASSOCIATION OF TRACK AND FIELD STATISTICIANS.** ***Ceased.*** **See** Recreation, Leisure-Abstracting, Bibliographies and Statistics.

CN/1180-4491
**ANNUAL GUIDE TO SYNCHRONIZED SWIMMING.** (ANNUAL GUIDE TO SYNCHRONIZED SWIMMING / SYNCHRO CANADA.). [Annu. guide synchron. swim.]. **Main/Corp** Canadian Amateur Synchronized Swimming Association. **VFOAT** Guide Annuel a la Nage Synchronisee. (1990)-. English (French). Limited free distribution. Canadian Amateur Synchronized Swimming Association, 333 River Road, Ottawa Ontario K1L 8H9 Canada. **DD** 797.2/1.

UK
**ANNUAL HANDBOOK.** **Main/Corp** Badminton Association of England. (19??)-. English. an. £2.50. National Badminton Center, Bradwell Road, Milton Keynes MK89LA England. **Tel** 011 44 908 568822. **LC** GV1007; .B26a. **DD** 796.34/5/0942.

CN/0229-0618
**ANNUAL - KAJAKS TRACK AND FIELD CLUB.** **Main/Corp** Kajaks Track and Field Club. 1979-. English. an. Free. Kajaks Track and Field Club, 11540 Seabrook, Richmond British Columbia V7A 3H3 Canada. **DD** 796.4/2/0971133. **UDC** 796.42(058). ctrl circ. ***Continues*** *Richmond Track and Field Club. Annual, 0708-2150.*

US
**ANNUAL OFFICIAL VOLLEYBALL REFERENCE GUIDE OF THE UNITED STATES VOLLEYBALL ASSOCIATION, THE.** **Added/Corp** United States Volleyball Association. **VFOAT** Volleyball Official Guide; Official Volleyball Guide; United States Volleyball Association Official Guide. No. 60 (1980)-. English. an (Sept.). $8.85. Nashbar, 4111 Simon Road, Youngstown OH 44512. **Tel** (800)937-7453. **LC** GV1017.V6; O4. **Ad Acc. Circ:** 25,000. ***Continues*** *Annual Official Volleyball Rules and Reference Guide of the United States Volleyball Association, 0083-3592.*

US/0884-1276
**ANNUAL REPORT / LOS ANGELES OLYMPIC ORGANIZING COMMITTEE.** [Annu. rep. - Los Angel. Olymp. Organ. Comm.]. **Main/Corp** Los Angeles Olympic Organizing Committee. (1979)-. English. an. Los Angeles Olympic Organizing Committee, 10100 Santa Monica Boulevard/6th Floor, Los Angeles CA 90067. **LC** GV721.4.U6; L67a. **DD** 796.4/8.

US
**ANNUAL REPORT OF THE CALIFORNIA HORSE RACING BOARD FOR THE PERIOD JULY 1 ... TO JUNE 30 ... .** **See** Horses and Horsemanship.

AT
**ANNUAL REPORT OF THE DEPARTMENT OF SPORT AND RECREATION FOR THE YEAR ENDED.** **See** Recreation, Leisure.

US/0077-3794
**ANNUAL REPORTS OF THE NATIONAL COLLEGIATE ATHLETIC ASSOCIATION.** **Main/Corp** National Collegiate Athletic Association. **VFOAT** Annual Reports, NCAA. 1965/66-. English. an. $12.00. National Collegiate Athletic Association / NCAA, PO Box 7347, Overland Park KS 66207. **Tel** (913)339-1900, FAX (913)339-0030. **LC** GV563; .N25292. **DD** 796/.06/273. **UDC** 796.077(73). **Bk Rev. Ad Acc.** ctrl circ. ***Continues in part*** *The ... Yearbook / The National Collegiate Athletic Association.*
**Desc:** Reports of various NCAA committees, minutes of council, President's Commission, and executive committee meetings, complete financial report.

SP
**ANO AUTOMOVIL, EL.** Spanish. 1,600. Edisport S L, Isaac Peral 12, Madrid 15 Spain. **LC** GV1029; .A57. **DD** 796.7/2.

SP
**ANO DE LOMATO, EL.** **See** Motorcycles.

SP
**ANUARIO DE LA NIEVE.** Spanish. an. 700ptas. Trazo Editorial SL, Camino de los Molinos 155, Apartado Correos 611, 50015 Zaragoza Spain. **Tel** 976 517586, FAX 976 517464. **ED** Maria Jose Garcia - Arguelles. Index available. cum. index. **Ad Acc. Circ:** 24,000 (ctrl).
**Desc:** Publication is dedicated to the world of the snow and mountain sports, equipment, and novelties.

US/0742-910X
**AQUA-FIELD SPORTSMAN.** **See** Manufacturing.

AT/1032-6189
**AQUALINK.** [Aqualink]. (1988)-. Periodical. English. qt. Market Link Publishing, Unit B-3 23-25 Windsor Road, Northmead NSW 2152, Australia. **Tel** 11 61 02 630 25541. **DD** 790.069. ***Continues*** *Aquarec, 0819-2413.*
**Ind/Abst** SPORT Discus.

US/1058-7039
**AQUATICS INTERNATIONAL.** [Aquat. int.]. (1991)-. Periodical. English. bm (July/Aug. issue is Buyers' Guide). $39.00. Argus Business, 6151 Powers Ferry Road, Atlanta GA 30339. **Tel** (404)995-2500, (800)233-3359. **ED** Terri Simmons. **LC** WMLC 91/3439. **DD** 338. Index available. **Bk Rev. Ad Acc. Circ:** 30,000

# Recreation, Leisure —Sports

(ctrl). available on microfilm and microfiche from University Microfilms International (UMI). *Continues Aquatics (Atlanta, Ga.), 1042-9697.*

US/0274-5704
**ARC (ARLINGTON, TEX. : MAY 20, 1980).** (ARC.). May 20, 1980-. Periodical. English. mo. ARC, The Softball Magazine of Texas, c/o Conner, PO Box 1774, Buna TX 77612. **UDC** 796.357.4(764).

US/0003-8237
**ARCHER (CAMAS VALLEY, OR.), THE.** (THE ARCHER.). V. 1- Autumn 1951-. Periodical. English. qt. Camas Press, 2284 Rogers Lane NW, Salem OR 97304. **Tel** (503)445-2327. **LC** AP2; .A5966. **DD** 811/.008. **UDC** 799.322.2.

AT/1037-6720
**ARCHERY ACTION WITH OUTDOOR CONNECTIONS.** (ARCHERY ACTION.). (1987)-. Periodical. English. Six times a year (Jan., Mar., May, July, Sept., Nov.). 20.00Aus$ Australia; 40.00Aus$ other. Archery Action, PO Box 227, Aspley Queensland 4034 Australia. **Tel** 011 61 7 2644910, **FAX** 011 61 7 2644963. **ED** Susan Green. **Bk Rev**, (Qty: varies). **Ad Acc**, **Adv Mgr:** Jo Whitmore, **Tel** 07 2644910. **Circ:** 11,000 (ctrl).
  *Desc:* Target fraternity with the magazine and look forwards to the reports of archery.
  **Ind/Abst** SPORT Discus.

CN/0704-0822
**ARGO NEWS.** V. 1- Feb. 1977-. Periodical. English. 0.50Can$ per no. Argonaut Inc., Unit 52, 655 Dixon Road, Rexdale Ontario M9W 1J4 Canada. **DD** 796.33/5/06. **UDC** 796.33.

US/0888-840X
**ARIZONA HUNTER & ANGLER.** [Ariz. hunt. angler]. **VFOAT** Arizona Hunter and Angler; AZ Hunter & Angler. (1984)-. Periodical. English. mo. $19.17 Arizona; $18.00 other. Arizona Hunter and Angler, PO Box 859, Mesa AZ 85211. **Tel** (602)890-2547. **ED** Harry Morgan. **DD** 799. **Bk Rev**, (Qty: 6-12). **Ad Acc**, **Adv Mgr:** Tom Stiles. ctrl circ.

US/0744-4184
**ARKANSAS SPORTSMAN.** See Recreation, Leisure-Outdoor Life.

US/0747-6000
**ASCA NEWSLETTER (FORT LAUDERDALE, FLA.).** (ASCA NEWSLETTER / THE AMERICAN SWIMMING COACHES ASSOCIATION.). **Added/Corp** American Swimming Coaches Association. **VFOAT** A.S.C.A. Newsletter. (198?)-. Newsletter. English. bm. $45.00 US; $55.00 other. American Swimming Coaches Association, 301 SE 20th Street, Fort Lauderdale FL 33316. **Tel** (305)462-6267, (800)356-2722. **ED** John Leonard. **Bk Rev**. **Ad Acc**. **Circ:** 3,000 (ctrl).
  *Desc:* Information for swimming coaches.
  **Ind/Abst** SPORT Discus.

US/0892-6166
**ATHLETE, THE.** **Added/Corp** Kentucky High School Athletic Association. **VFOAT** Kentucky High School Athlete. Vol. 48, No. 2 (Sept. 1985)-. Periodical. English. bm. $10.00. Kentucky High School Athletic Association, 2280 Executive Drive, Lexington KY 40505. **Tel** (606)299-5472, **FAX** (606)293-5999. **ED** Tom Mills. **Circ:** 3,700 (ctrl). *Continues Kentucky High School Athlete.*

US/0004-6639
**ATHLETES IN ACTION.** Vol. 1, Spring 1967-. Periodical. English. qt. Athletes in Action, 4790 Irvine Boulevard 105-325, Irvine CA 92720. **Tel** (714)669-1720. **UDC** 796.42. **Circ:** 25,000.

US/0044-9873
**ATHLETIC ADMINISTRATION.** See Education-Physical Education and Training.

US/0747-315X
**ATHLETIC BUSINESS.** See Business.

US
**ATHLETIC DIRECTORY.** (19??)-. Directory. English. Six times a year. $25.00. Scholastic Resources Unlimited, 20622 Ottawa Road, Apple Valley CA 92308. **Tel** (619)247-4717. **ED** Dick Sauers. Index available. cum. index. **Circ:** 5,000.
  *Desc:* Newsletter dealing with issues of sports behavior and sports ethics.

US
**ATHLETIC MANAGEMENT.** Vol. 3, No. 5 (Sept. 1991)-. Periodical. English. Six times a year. $14.00 US; $18.00 Canada. College Athletic Management, PO Box 4806, Ithaca NY 14852-4806. **Tel** (607)272-0265, **FAX** (607)272-0701. **ED** Eleanor Frankel (editor's address: 438 West State Street, Ithaca, NY 14850 USA). **LC** GV347; .C6. **Ad Acc**, **Adv Mgr:** Bill Kaprelian, **Tel** (708)568-9289. ctrl circ. *Formed by the union of Athletic Director (Wayzata, Minn.), 1048-339X and College Athletic Management, 1041-5432.*

*Desc:* How-to articles for high school and college athletic departments. Also product/service information on maintaining and running athletic departments in the most efficient manner.
  **Ind/Abst** Phys. Educ. Index (1990-).

UK
**ATHLETICS.** English. an. **LC** GV1060.5; .A83. **DD** 796.4/2.
  **Ind/Abst** Can. Index.

UK/0267-0267
**ATHLETICS COACH.** **Added/Corp** British Amateur Athletic Board. (19??)-. Periodical. English. Four times a year (Mar., June, Sept., Dec.). £15.00 UK; £17.00 (surface mail) others; £20.50 US; £21.50 (airmail) others. British Amateur Athletic Board, 56 Rolls Aveuen, Penpedairheol, Mid Glamorgan CF8 8HQ England. **Tel** 011 44 443 832186, **FAX** 011 44 443 822291, telex 334253. **ED** Malcolm Arnold. **Bk Rev**. **Ad Acc**. **Circ:** 1,000.
  *Desc:* Up-to-dates articles and interest to all aspects and branches of "Track & Field". Photo's sequences of currently successful athletes.
  **Ind/Abst** Phys. Educ. Index; SPORT Discus; SportSearch (May 1987-).

US/0888-4870
**ATHLETICS EMPLOYMENT WEEKLY.**
  See Occupations and Careers.

UK/0269-1302
**ATHLETICS TODAY.** *Ceased.* [Athl. today]. (1985)-(19??). Periodical. English. wk. Athletics Today, Limited 2-6 High Street, Kingston-upon-Thames, Surrey KT1 1Ey England. **Tel** 081 679 1899, **FAX** 081 547 2271, telex 265451. **ED** Randall Northam. **DD** 796.405. **Ad Acc**. *Continues Athletes World, 0260-499X.*
  *Desc:* Britain's athletic magazine.

CN/0229-4966
**ATHLETICS (TORONTO. 1981).** (ATHLETICS.). [Athletics]. **VFOAT** Athletics Magazine. No. 27 (Mar./Apr. 1981)-. Periodical. English. Nine times a year. 18.50Can$ Canada; 22.50Can$ US; 33.00Can$ other. Athletics, 1220 Sheppard Avenue East, Willowdale Ontario M2K 2X1 Canada. **Tel** (416)495-4056, **FAX** (416)495-4052, telex 06-986157. **ED** Greg Lockhart. **DD** 796.4/2/09713. **Bk Rev**. **Ad Acc**. **Circ:** 18,000. available on microfilm and microfiche from Micromedia Limited. *Continues Ontario Athletics, 0229-0014.*
  *Desc:* Covers track and field and road racing in Canada, including major competitions across the world and Canada. Along with all results, it publishes profiles, ranking lists and other interesting information.
  **Ind/Abst** Can. Period. Index (19??-); SPORT Discus; SportSearch (May 1987-).

UK/0004-6671
**ATHLETICS WEEKLY.** [Athl. Wkly.]. (1945)-. Periodical. English. Fifty-two times a year. £46.00 UK; £69.00 others. EMAP National Publications Ltd, Farndon Road, Market Harborough, Leicestershire, LE16 9NR England. **Tel** 011 44 733 555161. (Subscription address: Alan Wells International, Memberline House, Farndon Road, Leicestershire LE16 9NR England.)
  **Ind/Abst** SPORT Discus.

CN/0822-9953
**ATHLETISME ET COURSE SUR ROUTE.** *Ceased.* (ATHLETISME ET COURSE SUR ROUTE : REVUE OFFICIELLE DE LA FEDERATION D'ATHLETISME DU QUEBEC.). (1976)-?. French. mo. Federation d'Athletisme du Quebec, 1415 Est rue Jarry, Montreal Quebec H2E 2Z7 Canada. **DD** 796.4/2/09714. **UDC** 796.42(714). *Continues Athletisme, 0381-6214.*
  **Ind/Abst** SportSearch (May 1987-).

US/0734-2888
**ATHLON'S PRO FOOTBALL.** [Athlon's pro footb.]. **VFOAT** Pro Football. Vol. 1 (1982)-. Periodical. English. an. $6.95. Athlon Publications, 220 25th Avenue North, Nashville TN 37203. **Tel** (615)627-1747. **LC** GV937; .A85. **DD** 796.332/64/0973. **Ad Acc**.

US/1060-362X
**ATLANTIC COAST COLLEGIATE SPORTS MAGAZINE.** [Atl. coast coll. sports mag.]. (1991)-. Periodical. English. ir. $45.00. Collegiate Sportsmagazines, Inc., 3274 Longleaf Road, Tallahassee FL 32310. **DD** 796.

US
**ATLANTIC COASTAL KAYAKER.** English. Ten times a year (published monthly except Jan., and Feb.). $20.00. Cycle Sport Publishing, 29 Burley Street, Wenham MA 01984. **Tel** (508)774-0906. **ED** Tamsin Venn (508)356-2057 PO Box 520 Ipswich, MA 01938. **Bk Rev**, (Qty: varies). **Ad Acc**, **Adv Mgr:** Bob Hicks, **Tel** (508)356-2057. **Circ:** 2,000.
  *Desc:* Publication concerned with the sport of kayaking.

IT/0392-2251
**ATLETICA LEGGERA.** *Ceased.* See Health and Personal Fitness.

IT
**ATLETICA : RIVISTA MENSILE DELLA FIDAL.** (19??)-. Italian. mo. L30000 Italy; L115000 other. Fidal, Via Della Camilluccia 703, 00135 Rome Italy. **Tel** 011 39 6 326831. **Bk Rev**. **Ad Acc**. **Circ:** 30,000 (ctrl).
  *Desc:* Contains chronicle and results on athletics and events worldwide.

IT
**ATLETICASTUDI.** **Added/Corp** Federazione Italiana di Atletica Leggera. Centro Studi & Ricerche. (19??)-. Periodical. Italian. bm. L100000 Italy; L150000 Europe; L200000 other. Fidal, Via Della Camilluccia 703, 00135 Rome Italy. **Tel** 011 39 6 326831. **LC** GV1060.5; .A847. **DD** 796.4/205.

XR
**ATLETIKA : VYDAVA CESKOSLOVENSKY SVAZ TELESNE VYCHOVY.** **Added/Corp** Ceskoslovensky Svaz Telesne Vychovy. (1948)-. Periodical. Czech. mo. Olympia, Klimentska 1, 115 88 Prague 1, Czech Republic. (Subscription address: Artia Pegas Press Ltd., Palac Metro Narodni Trida 25, 11210 Prague 1 Czech Republic.)

DK/0905-3883
**ATLETIK'EN.** [Atletik'en]. **VFOAT** Atletikken. (1989)-. Periodical. Danish. Sixteen times a year. kr170.00. Dansk Athletik Forbund, Brondby Station 20, DK 2600 Glostrup Denmark. **ED** Niels Larsen, Lunden 5, 5540 Wlerslen, Denmark, 05 351135. **DD** 769.409 489. **Circ:** 3,000. *Continues Action (Brndby), 0903-5680.*

IT/1120-3633
**ATTIVITA FISICA & SPORT.** [Attiv. fis. sport]. **VFOAT** Attivita Fisica e Sport. (1990)-. Periodical. Multiple languages. qt. L20000 Italy; L26000 other Europe; L30000 Western Hemisphere & Asis; L32000 Africa; L37000 other. ESI Stampa Medica Spa, Casella Postale 42, 20097 San Donato Milan Italy. **Tel** 011 39 2 527-4241. **UDC** 61 :796.

US/0892-3183
**ATV SPORTS.** *Ceased.* **VAT** All Terrain Vehicle Sports. Vol. 8, No. 3 (March 1987)-Vol. 10 (1989). Periodical. English. mo. Wright Publishing Company Inc, Box 2260, Costa Mesa CA 92628. **Tel** (714)533-4083. **Bk Rev**. **Ad Acc**. **Circ:** 65,241. *Continues 3Wheeling, 0196-5549.*
  *Desc:* Edited for all terrain vehicle and off-road enthusiasts. Features include new models, technical articles, how-to-do-it's, and competition coverages.

CN/0710-2038
**AUDIBLE (TORONTO).** (AUDIBLE / ONTARIO AMATEUR FOOTBALL ASSOCIATION.). [Audible]. **Added/Corp** Ontario Amateur Football Association. Ontario Sports Administrative Centre. (1975)-. Periodical. English. Four times a year. 8.00Can$. Ontario Amateur Football Association, 1220 Sheppard Avenue East, Willowdale Ontario M2K 2X1 Canada. **Tel** (416)495-4290, **FAX** (416)495-4310, telex 06-986157 OSAC Tor. **ED** Edward Slabikowski. **DD** 796.33/5/09713. cum. index. **Bk Rev**. **Ad Acc**. **Circ:** 2,000 (ctrl).
  *Desc:* Football-related articles on techniques, systems, safety, training, and officiating with emphasis on the amateur coach and volunteer.
  **Ind/Abst** SPORT Discus; SportSearch (May 1987-).

AT/1035-4573
**AUSSIE SPORTS ACTION.** [Aussie sports action]. **Added/Corp** Australian Sports Commission. **VFOAT** Aussie Sport Action. (1990)-. Periodical. qt. Free. Australian Sports Commission, PO Box 176, Belconnen Australian Capital Territory, 2616 Australia. **Tel** 011 61 62 521594, **FAX** 011 61 62 521681, telex AA 62400. **DD** 796.0994. *Formed by the union of Aussie Sports News, 0817-9875 and Aussie Sports Club News, 1032-8300.*
  **Ind/Abst** Leis. Recreat. Tour. Abstr.; SPORT Discus.

AT/0819-3363
**AUSTRALASIAN CYCLING AND TRIATHLON NEWS.** [Australas. cycl. triathlon news]. (1985)-. Periodical. English. mo. **DD** 796.60994. *Formed by the union of Australasian Cycling, 0819-3347 and Triathlon News.*
  **Ind/Abst** SPORT Discus.

AT/0810-5928
**AUSTRALASIAN SPORTING SHOOTER.** [Australas. sport. shoot.]. (1982)-. Periodical. English. Twelve times a year. 48.00Aus$ Australia; 135.00Aus$ other. Yaffa Publishing Group Pty Ltd., GPO Box 606, Sydney NSW 2001 Australia. **Tel** 011 61 2 2812333, **FAX** 011 61 2 2812750. **DD** 799.2130994. *Continues Sporting Shooter, 0038-8076.*
  **Ind/Abst** SPORT Discus.

# Recreation, Leisure —Sports

AT
**AUSTRALIAN ALPINE NEWS.** English. Seven times a year (monthly April through Sept., plus special issue in Dec.). 14.00Aus$. Australian Alpine News, PO Box 252, Richmond VIC 3121 Australia. **Tel** 011 61 3 4293888, FAX 011 61 3 4287607.
**Desc:** Australia's national skiing newspaper.

AT/0811-2541
**AUSTRALIAN BASKETBALLER.** [Aust. basketb.]. **Added/Corp** Australian Basketball Federation. (1983)-. Periodical. English. mo. 40.00Aus$ Australia. Sports Fusion Pty Ltd, PO Box 374, 18-22 Thomson Street, South Melbourne Victoria 3205 Australia. **Tel** 011 61 03 690 8155. **DD** 796.323.
**Ind/Abst** SPORT Discus.

AT/0004-895X
**AUSTRALIAN CRICKET. Ceased.** (1968)-(Oct. 1993). Periodical. English. mo. Mason Stewart Publishing, PO Box 746, Darlinghurst NSW 2010 Australia. **Tel** 011 61 2 331 5006.
**Ind/Abst** SPORT Discus.

AT/0817-6604
**AUSTRALIAN CROQUET GAZETTE.** [Aust. croquet gaz.]. **Added/Corp** Australian Croquet Council. (1951)-. Periodical. English. qt. 11.00Aus$ Australia; 15.00Aus$ other. Australian Croquet Association, PO Box 296, Rosny Park, TAS 7018 Australia. **Tel** 011 61 2 444788. **DD** 796.35406.
**Ind/Abst** SPORT Discus.

AT
**AUSTRALIAN GLIDING YEAR BOOK.** **Added/Corp** Gliding Federation of Australia. (1969)-. English. an. 28.20Aus$ Australia; 40.50Aus$ other. Gliding Federation of Australia, GPO Box 1650, Adelaide 5001 South Australia. **Tel** 08 410 4711, FAX 08 410 4711. **ED** Noel Matthews. **LC** GV750; .A92. **DD** 797.5/5/0994. **Bk Rev. Ad Acc. Circ:** 4,500.
**Desc:** Covers the sport of gliding world-wide, but primarily focuses on Australian activities. Official journal of the Gliding Federation of Australia.

AT/1034-3938
**AUSTRALIAN GOLF DIGEST ... HANDBOOK.** [Aust. golf dig. handb.]. **VFOAT** Golf Handbook. (1989)-. English. mo. 58.00Aus$ Australia; 93.00Aus$ New Zealand and Papau New Guinea; 117.00Aus$ US and Canada; 124.00Aus$ Europe and Africa; 108.00Aus$ other. Federal Publishing Co Pty Ltd, PO Box 199, 180 Bourke Road, Alexandria New South Wales, 2015 Australia. **Tel** 011 61 2 693 6666, FAX 011 61 2 693 9935. **(Subscription address:** Federal Publishing Co. Pty Ltd., PO Box 199, Alexandria NSW 2015 Australia.) **DD** 796.3520994.
**Ind/Abst** SPORT Discus.

AT
**AUSTRALIAN GYMNAST.** English. Four times a year. 20.00Aus$ Australia; 30.00Aus$ other. Australian Gymnastic Federation, 416 St. Kilda Road, Melbourne Victoria 3004 Australia. **Tel** 011 61 3 5513833, FAX 011 61 3 5513119, telex 134972. **ED** Peggy Brolone (editor's phone: 011 61 3 8666011). Index available. **Ad Acc. Circ:** 3,000.
**Ind/Abst** SPORT Discus.

AT
**AUSTRALIAN OLYMPIAN.** (19??)-. English. qt. Free on request. Australian Olympic Committee, Level 13, 207 Kent Street, Sydney 2000 Australia. **Tel** 011 61 2 9312075, FAX 011 61 2 9312098. **ED** Robyn Price. **Pr Rev. Circ:** 5,000 (ctrl).
**Desc:** Magazine for Olympians and others interested in news of the Australian Olympic Committee, Olympic sports, athletes and the Olympic movement in Australia.
**Ind/Abst** SPORT Discus.

AT/0818-6510
**AUSTRALIAN ORIENTEER JAMISON.** [Aust. orienteer Jamison]. (1979)-. Periodical. English. Six times a year. 34.00Aus$ US, Canada and Israel; 28.00Aus$ New Zealand and Papau New Guinea; 29.00Aus$ Indonesia, Malaysia and Singapore; 32.00Aus$ Japan, Hong Kong, and the Philippines; 37.00Aus$ Europe (airmail); 25.00Aus$ (surface mail) Australia; 28.00Aus$ (surface mail) other. Australian Orienteer, PO Box 263, Jamison Ctr ACT 2614 Australia. **Tel** 011 61 6 2513885. **DD** 796.42605.
**Ind/Abst** SPORT Discus.

AT/0727-3126
**AUSTRALIAN ROWING.** (197?)-. Periodical. English. qt. 10.00Aus$ Australia; 18.00Aus$ New Zealand; 24.00Aus$ other. Australian Rowing Council Inc., 118 Church Street, Suite 10, Hawthorn VIC Australia. **Tel** 011 61 3 8181965.

AT
**AUSTRALIAN RUGBY NEWS. Ceased.** (19??)-(Dec. 1993). English. mo. Australian Rugby News, PO Box 134, West Ryde NSW 2114 Australia. **Tel** 011 61 2 8073118.
**Ind/Abst** SPORT Discus.

AT
**AUSTRALIAN RUNNER.** English. bm. 38.00Aus$ Australia; 71.00Aus$ Asia and Oceania; 75.00Aus$ other. Australian Runner, PO Box 396, South Yarra VIC 3141 Australia. **Tel** 011 61 3 8199225.
**Ind/Abst** SPORT Discus.

AT/0005-0245
**AUSTRALIAN SHOOTERS JOURNAL.** (1968)-. Periodical. English. mo. 40.00Aus$ Australia; 50.00Aus$ other. Sporting Shooters Association, PO Box 2366, Kent Town SA 5071 Australia. **Tel** 011 61 8 3382446.
**Ind/Abst** SPORT Discus.

AT/0818-9307
**AUSTRALIAN SKIING SURRY HILLS.** **Title Change.** [Aust. skiing Surry Hills]. (1986)-(19??). Periodical. English. mo. Mason Stewart Publishing, PO Box 746, Darlinghurst NSW 2010 Australia. **Tel** 011 61 2 331 5006. **DD** 796.930994. **Continues** Fall-Line (South Melbourne), 0818-9315. **Continued by** Australian Skiing.
**Ind/Abst** SPORT Discus.

AT/0727-6850
**AUSTRALIAN SOCCER WEEKLY.** [Aust. soccer wkly.]. (1980)-. Periodical. English. wk. 160.00Aus$. Australian Soccer Weekly, 1 9 Glebe Point Road, Glebe New South Wales, 2037 Australia. **Tel** 11 61 2 660 2033, FAX 011 61 2 692 0649, telex 22141. **DD** 796.3340994.

AT/0817-2048
**AUSTRALIAN SOCIETY FOR SPORTS HISTORY BULLETIN.** [Aust. Soc. Sports Hist. bull.]. **Added/Corp** Australian Society for Sports History. (1985)-. Periodical. English. tq. 25.00Aus$ (membership). Australian Society Sports History, PO Box 968, Fischer Catholic University, North Sydney 2060 Australia. **Tel** 011 61 8 2752195. **ED** Richard Cashman. **DD** 796.0994.
**Desc:** Strives to promote, stimulate and encourage discussion, study, research and publication of information on sporting traditions with special reference to Australia.
**Ind/Abst** SPORT Discus.

AT/0157-6542
**AUSTRALIAN SPORTS DIRECTORY.** [Aust. sports dir.]. (1979)-. English. an. 15.00Aus$ (one year). Australian Sports Commission, PO Box 176, Belconnen Australian Capital Territory, 2616 Australia. **Tel** 011 61 62 521594, FAX 011 61 62 521681, telex AA 62400. **DD** 796.0994. **Continues** Australian Sports Calendar, 0156-3580.

AT
**AUSTRALIAN SURFING WORLD.** (19??)-. English. qt. 40.00Aus$ Australia; 70.00Aus$ other. Australian Surfing World, PO Box 128, Mona Vale NSW 2103 Australia. **Tel** 011 61 2 9972657, FAX 011 61 2 9978944.

AT/0814-3668
**AUSTRALIAN TABLE TENNIS.** [Aust. table tennis]. **Added/Corp** Australian Table Tennis Association. (1983)-. English. Four times a year (Mar., June, Sept., Dec.). 16.00Aus$ Australia; 20.00Aus$ New Zealand & Pacific; 26.00Aus$ others. Australian Table Tennis Association, Private Bag 1994, South Melbourne VIC 3205 Australia. **Tel** 011 61 3 8208507, FAX 011 61 3 8208510. **ED** Ron Carlton. **DD** 796.3460994. **Bk Rev. Ad Acc. Circ:** 3,000 (ctrl). **Continues** Table Tennis Newsletter, 0814-365X.
**Desc:** News and information about table tennis and other related topics in Australia.

AT/1036-3491
**AUSTRALIA'S SURFING LIFE.** (198?)-. Periodical. English. mo. 19.30Aus$(6 issues), 35.50Aus$ (12 issues), 51.35Aus$ (18 issues), 35.40Aus$ (6 issues) New Zealand; 44.00Aus$ (6 issues) other. Morrison Media Services, PO Box 823, Burleigh Heads Queensland 4220 Australia. **Tel** 075 561 388, FAX 075 561 527.

AT/1033-6001
**AUSTRALIA'S SURFING LIFE ANNUAL.** [Aust. surf. life annu.]. (1989)-. English. an. 19.30Aus$(6 issues), 35.50Aus$ (12 issues), 51.35Aus$ (18 issues) Australia; 35.40Aus$ (6 issues) New Zealand; 44.00Aus$ (6 issues) other. Morrison Media Services, PO Box 823, Burleigh Heads Queensland 4220 Australia. **Tel** 075 561 388, FAX 075 561 527. **DD** 797.320994.

CN/0822-1006
**AUTO MODIFIEE, L'.** [Auto modif.]. Vol. 1, No 1 (1982)-. Periodical. French. mo. L'Auto Modifiee, CP 848, Rawdon Quebec J0K 1S0 Canada. **Tel** (514)834-5359. **ED** Luc Richard. **DD** 629.2/28/09714. **Ad Acc. Circ:** 8,000.
**Desc:** Covers motorsport racing of all kinds, with track and club listing information, flashbacks, schedules, past major event reports and what's new and plenty of photographs.

GW/0005-0806
**AUTO, MOTOR UND SPORT.** See Transportation-Automobiles.

US
**AUTO MUNDO DEPORTIVO.** Periodical. Spanish. Twelve times a year. $84.00. Ruiz Spanish Language Magazines, PO Box 2389, El Paso TX 79952. **Tel** (915)544-6282.

●US/1059-8367
**AUTO RACEPAGES.** (AUTO RACEPAGES: THE ULTIMATE RACING SOURCEBOOK.). [Auto racepages]. **VFOAT** Auto Race Pages; Race Pages. Inaugural Issue (1992)-. English. $19.95. Youngson Publisihing Company, PO Box 8127, La Jolla CA 90238-8127. **DD** 796.

US/0090-8029
**AUTO RACING DIGEST.** Vol. 1 (July 1973)-. Periodical. English. bm (6 issues). $22.00 US; $30.00 other. Century Publishing Company, 990 Grove Street, Evanston IL 60201-4370. **Tel** (708)491-6440, (800)321-3333, FAX (708)491-0459. **ED** Michael Herbert. **LC** GV1029; .A779. **DD** 796.7/2/0973. **Bk Rev. Ad Acc. Circ:** 75,000. available on microfilm from University Microfilms International (UMI).
**Desc:** Covers all forms of auto racing, including Stock, Indy and Formula One.

US/0743-7129
**AUTO RACING MEMORIES & MEMORABILIA.** **VFOAT** Auto Racing Memories and Memorabilia. Periodical. English. bm. $19.00. ARM Publishing & Promotion Inc, 75 S E 4th Avenue, Delray Beach FL 33444. **UDC** 796.71.

US/8756-9353
**AUTO RACING/USA (DALLAS, TEX.).** (AUTO RACING, USA.). [Auto racing/USA]. **VFOAT** Autoracing/USA. 1983-. English. a. $39.95. Motorbooks International Publishers & Wholesalers, PO Box 2, 729 Prospect Avenue, Osceola WI 54020. **LC** GV1033; .A95. **DD** 796.7/2/0973. **UDC** 796.71(73).

US/0164-369X
**AUTO RACING USA (FRANKLIN LAKES, N.J.).** (AUTO RACING USA). [Auto racing USA]. **VAT** Auto Racing United States of America. Vol. 1 (1978)-. Periodical. English. mo. $8.95 US; $9.95 Canada. Auto Racing USA, PO Box 72, 916 Franklin Avenue, Franklin Lakes NJ 07417. **UDC** 796.71(73).

CN/0714-7104
**AUTO SPORT.** [Auto sport]. Vol. 8, Issue 3 (May 1982)-. Periodical. English. mo. $10.95. Wheelspin News, 3045 Universe Drive, Mississauga Ontario L4X 2E2. **DD** 796.7/2. **UDC** 796.71. **Continues** Auto Sport Canada, 0317-3798.

CN/1191-3401
**AUTO SPORT (MONTREAL. 1992).** **Title Change.** (L'AUTOSPORT.). [Auto sport]. No. 69 (Febr. 1992)-No. 73 (June 1992). Periodical. French. mo. Editions de la Competion Inc., 3600 Avenue du Parc, Montreal Quebec H2X 3R2 Canada. **DD** 796.7/2/0971405. **Continues** Le Journal de l'Auto Sport., 0832-8900. **Continued by** Auto Sports Moteur, 1193-509X.

●CN/1193-509X
**AUTO SPORTS MOTEUR, L'.** [Auto sports mot.]. **VFOAT** Sports-Moteur. No. 74 (July 1992)-. Periodical. French. mo. 1.70Can$ per issue. Editions de la Competion Inc., 3600 Avenue du Parc, Montreal Quebec H2X 3R2 Canada. **DD** 796.7. **Continues** L'Autosport., 1191-3401.

IT/0005-1349
**AUTOMOBILE.** [Automobile]. (1945)-. Periodical. Italian. mo (11 issues per year). L10000 Italy; L30000 other. Editrice dell'Automobile, V le Regina Margherita 290, 00198 Rome Italy. **Tel** 011 39 6 440-2061. **UDC** 388.

UK/0269-946X
**AUTOSPORT (TEDDINGTON).** See Transportation-Automobiles.

FR/0005-2094
**AVIASPORT.** (1954)-. French. Twelve times a year. 38.00F. Soc Edn Period Aviation Gen, 59 Avenue Artistide Briand, 93190 Livry Gargan France. **Tel** 011 33 1 43021064, FAX 011 33 1 43018311. **ED** Dominique Meglioli. Index available. cum. index. **Ad Acc, Adv Mgr:** Gebard Pabot. **Circ:** 15,000.
**Desc:** News and information on sports and business in aviation waters field.

FR/1154-9041
**AVIRON (FRANCE).** (19??)-. French. bm (6 issues). 160.00F France; 225.00F other. Federation Francaise des Socs d'Aviron, 7 Rue La Fayette, 75009 Paris France. **Tel** 011 33 1 48744377, FAX 011 33 1 49959331. **UDC** 797.1(44).
**Ind/Abst** SPORT Discus.

IT
**AZIMUT.** (19??)-. Italian. bm. Edaco, Via Lombardia 27, 20131 Milan Italy. **Tel** 011 39 2 2666460.

CN/0226-7691
**B. C. ARCHER, THE.** [B.C. archer]. **VAT** British Columbia Archer. Periodical. English. mo. $15.00 membership. British Columbia Archery Association, 1905-37th Avenue, Vernon BC V1T 2W9 Canada. **DD** 799.3/2/060711. **UDC** 799.322.2(711).

CN/0315-999X
**B. C. SPORTS ANNUAL.** (1974)-. Periodical. English. an. Optimist Club of Vancouver, 164-11th Avenue East, Vancouver British Columbia V5T 2C2 Canada. **DD** 796/.09711. ***Supersedes*** *Sports Annual, 0316-0092.*

US/0005-3775
**BADGER SPORTSMAN.** **See** Recreation, Leisure-Outdoor Life.

CN/0710-0051
**BADMINTON CHALLENGE.** (THE BADMINTON CHALLENGE : BRITISH COLUMBIA BADMINTON ASSOCIATION NEWSPAPER.). [Badminton chall.]. Periodical. English. qt. Free. British Columbia Badminton Association, 6326 Collingwood Street, Vancouver British Columbia V6N 1T6 Canada. **DD** 796.34/5/09711. **UDC** 796.344(711).

US/0747-9069
**BADMINTON MAGAZINE, THE.** ***Ceased.*** [Badminton mag.]. (1983)-Vol. 4, No. 3 (Sept. 1989). Periodical. English. Five times a year. Badminton Magazine, PO Box 3796, Manhattan Beach CA 90266. **Tel** (310)546-3652. **(Subscription address:** 5873 E Paradise Lane, Scottsdale AZ 85254**) ED** W Guy Chadwick. **DD** 796. **UDC** 796.344. **Ad Acc. Circ:** 2,500 (ctrl).
**Desc:** Scholastic and tournament badminton scene in the USA, A new olympic sport.

CN/0229-3862
**BADMINTON NEW-NOUVEAU BRUNSWICK : NEWSLETTER.** Sept. 1979-. Newsletter. English (French). ir. Free. Badminton New-Nouveau Brunswick, 5 Neck Road, Rothesay New Brunswick E0G 2W0 Canada. **DD** 796.34/5/09715. **UDC** 796.344(715). ctrl circ. ***Continues*** *Badminton New Brunswick, 0229-3854.*

UK
**BADMINTON NOW.** (1990)-. Periodical. English. Six times a year. £10.50 UK; £13.50 Europe; £18.50 other. Badminton Now / National Badminton Centre, Bradwell Road, Loughton Lodge, Milton Keynes MK8 9LA England. **Tel** 011 44 908 568822, FAX 011 44 908 566922. **ED** William Kings & Sue Ashton. **Bk Rev. Ad Acc, Adv Mgr:** Joanne James, **Tel** 011 44 61 486 6159. **Circ:** 5,500 (ctrl).
**Desc:** The magazine devoted exclusively to the sport - Badminton.
**Ind/Abst** SPORT Discus.

CN/0822-6784
**BADMINTON REVIEW (ST. ALBERT).** (BADMINTON REVIEW.). [Badminton rev.]. **Added/Corp** Alberta Badminton Association. Vol. 1 (1982)-. Periodical. English. mo. Comes with membership. Alberta Badminton Association, 11759 Groat Road, Edmonton Alta. T5M 3K6. **Tel** (403)453-8536. **DD** 796.34/5/097123. ***Continues*** *Alberta Badminton Review, 0714-3893.*
**Ind/Abst** SportSearch (May 1987-).

AT/0813-006X
**BADMINTON SIDELINES.** (19??)-. English.
**Ind/Abst** SPORT Discus.

CN/0841-6036
**BADMINTON TODAY.** [Badminton today]. **Added/Corp** Ontario Badminton Association. Vol. 9, No. 1 (1987)-. Periodical. English. Six times a year. 15.00Can$. Ontario Badminton Association, 1220 Sheppard Avenue East, Toronto Ontario M2K 2X1 Canada. **Tel** (416)495-4080. **DD** 796.34/5/09713. ***Continues*** *Ontario Badminton., 0709-8308.*

US/0045-1312
**BADMINTON U S A.** [Badminton U. S. A.]. Vol. 27, No. 1 (Nov. 1967)-. Periodical. English. bm. $10.00 US; $20.00 other. United States Badminton Association, 1750 East Boulder Street, Colorado Springs CO 80909. **Tel** (800)798-8459. **ED** Richard Kimball and Warren K Everson. **LC** GV1007.6.U6; B33. **DD** 796.34/5/0973. **Ad Acc.** ctrl circ. available on microfilm and microfiche from University Microfilms International (UMI). ***Continues*** *Bird Chatter.*
**Desc:** Tournament results, tournament listings, national and local stories, and action pictures.
**Ind/Abst** SPORT Discus.

CN/0228-0698
**BADMINTONIEN.** (LE BADMINTONIEN.). [Badmintonien]. **Added/Corp** Federation de Badmonton du Quebec. (May 1979)-. Periodical. French. bm. Free to members. Federation Quebecoise Badminton, 4545 Avenue Pierre de Coubertin, Montreal Quebec H1V 3S4 Canada. **Tel** (514)252-3066. **DD** 796.34/5/05.

US/0887-6061
**BALLOON LIFE.** [Balloon life]. Vol. 1, No. 1 (Feb. 1986)-. Periodical. English. Twelve times a year. $30.00 (one year), $54.00 (two years). Balloon Life Magazine Inc., 2145 Dale Avenue, Sacramento CA 95815. **Tel** (916)922-9648, FAX (916)922-4730. **ED** Tom Hamilton. **LC** WMLC L 83/6806. **DD** 797. **Bk Rev**, (Qty: 12). **Ad Acc, Adv Mgr:** Tom Hamilton. **Circ:** 4,000.
**Desc:** The magazine dedicated to the sport of ballooning. Each issue is packed with stories, pictures, and graphics to bring the reader the pulse of ballooning. Exciting features help to satisfy your curiosity and indulge your wanderlust. An indispensable tool for today's balloon enthusiast.

US/0199-2406
**BALLS AND STRIKES.** ***Title Change.*** **Added/Corp** Amateur Softball Association of America. (19??)-(19??). Periodical. English. mo (March through Oct.). Amateur Softball Association of America, 2801 Northeast 50th Route 4, Box 385, Oklahoma City OK 73111. **Tel** (405)424-5266. **ED** Bill Plummer III. **Ad Acc. Circ:** 260,000 per month. ***Continued by*** *USA Softball Magazine.*
**Desc:** News, columns and listings of tournaments about softball and the amateur softball association.

US/0195-0975
**'BAMA.** Vol. 1 (June 1979)-. Periodical. English. Ten times a year (Aug. to May). $35.00 US & Canada; $45.00 other. College Sports Publishing Inc, PO Box 6104, Tuscaloosa AL 35486. **Tel** (205)345-5074. **ED** Kirk McNair. **Bk Rev. Ad Acc. Circ:** 15,000 (ctrl).
**Desc:** Official full-color magazine of the University of Alabama athletics, emphasizing football and men's basketball but including all men's and women's sports.

JA
**BAREI BORU MAGAJIN.** **VFOAT** Volleyball Magazine. (19??)-. Periodical. Japanese. mo. $168.00. **(Subscription address:** Maruzen Company Ltd., PO Box 5050, Import & Export Department, Tokyo 100 31 Japan.**)**

US/0745-5372
**BASEBALL AMERICA.** [Baseb. Am.]. (198?)-. Periodical. English. Twenty-six times a year. $38.95 one year; $67.95 two years. Baseball America, PO Box 2089, Circulation Department, Durham NC 27702-9998. **Tel** (919)682-9635, FAX (919)682-2880. **LC** GV863.A1; A43. **DD** 796.357/0973. **Bk Rev**, (Qty: 20). **Ad Acc, Adv Mgr:** Kris Grubbs, **Tel** (800)845-2776. **Circ:** 65,000. ***Continues*** *All-America Baseball News, 0228-6033.*
**Desc:** Major league columnists for each division, player features, pre-season previews and spring training coverage - rookie previews, off-season organizational reports, and complete 40-man rosters. It gives complete pitching and batting statistics for each team from Triple A through the rookie leagues, in-depth reports from each league, listings of all transactions in each league and organization.

US/0199-0128
**BASEBALL BULLETIN.** ***Ceased.*** (19??)-(19??). Bulletin. English. bm. Donald Publications Inc, PO Box 413, Troy MI 48099. **Tel** (313)879-1676. **ED** Larry Donald and Michael Sheridan. **Bk Rev. Ad Acc. Circ:** 20,000 (ctrl).
**Desc:** Tabloid newspaper, nostalgia and in-depth columns by nationally known writers.

US/0896-7563
**BASEBALL CARD PRICE GUIDE MONTHLY.** ***Title Change.*** **See** Hobbies.

US/1058-0433
**BASEBALL CARD UPDATE.** **See** Hobbies.

US/8750-5851
**BASEBALL CARDS.** ***Title Change.*** **See** Hobbies.

US/0270-4218
**BASEBALL CASE BOOK.** **Added/Corp** National Federation of State High School Associations. (19??)-. English. an. National Federation of State High School Associations, 11724 Northwest Plaza Circle, PO Box 20626, Kansas City MO 64195-0626. **Tel** (816)464-5400, FAX (816)464-5571. **LC** GV877; .B26. **DD** 796.357/02/022.

US/0005-609X
**BASEBALL DIGEST.** Vol. 1, (Aug. 1942)-. Periodical. English. mo. $22.00 US; $30.00 other. Century Publishing Company, 990 Grove Street, Evanston IL 60201-4370. **Tel** (708)491-6440, (800)321-3333, FAX (708)491-0459. **(Subscription address:** Kable Publishers Aide, 308 East Hitt Street, Subscriptions Department, Mt. Morris, IL 61054**) ED** Jack Kuenster. **LC** GV862; .B36. **DD** 796.35705. **Bk Rev. Ad Acc. Circ:** 300,000. available on microfilm and microfiche from University Microfilms International (UMI).
**Desc:** Baseball's only monthly magazine.
**Ind/Abst** Mag. Artic. Summar. Elite (Jan. 1994-); Mag. Artic. Summar. CD-ROM (Jan. 1994-).

US
**BASEBALL GUIDE.** **VFOAT** Sporting News Baseball Guide. (1990)-. English. Sporting News, c/o Sharon Moore, 1212 North Lindbergh Boulevard, PO Box 56, St Louis MO 63166. **Tel** (314)997-7111, (800)825-8508. **LC** GV877; .B324. **DD** 796.357/0973. ***Continues*** *Official Baseball Guide, 0078-3838.*

US/0199-946X
**BASEBALL HOBBY NEWS.** ***Ceased.*** **See** Hobbies.

US/1057-235X
**BASEBALL MAGAZINE (BELLEVILLE, ILL.).** (BASEBALL MAGAZINE.). [Baseb. mag.]. (1991)-. Periodical. English. mo. Baseball Magazine, PO Box 1436, Belleville IL 62223-1436. **DD** 796. ***Continues*** *Baseball Magazine, St. Louis Style.*

CN/0821-4123
**BASEBALL (MONTREAL).** (BASEBALL.). [Baseball]. Periodical. English (French). ir. $2.25 per no. Montreal Baseball Club, PO Box 500 Station M, Montreal Quebec H1V 3P2 Canada. **Tel** (514)253-3434. **ED** Rene Guimond. **DD** 796.357/64/09714281. **Ad Acc. Circ:** 350,000.
**Desc:** Baseball editorial content with photography. Articles on players, teams, players' families, Hall of Fame stars and special interest stories. Goal of articles is to get the fans to know the team and its players.

US/1066-2448
**BASEBALL QUARTERLY REVIEWS.** Vol. 1, No. 1 (1986)-. English. qt. $28.00 US; $30.00 Canada and Mexico; $32.00 other. Krabbenhoft, PO Box 9343, Schenectady NY 12309. **Tel** (518)399-7890. **ED** Herman Krabbenhoft. **LC** WMLC L 83/4337. **Circ:** 200.
**Desc:** Provides authoritative reports and comprehensive summaries of in-depth research on topics of historical interest and statistical significance.

US/0734-6891
**BASEBALL RESEARCH JOURNAL.** [Baseb. res. j.]. **Added/Corp** Society for American Baseball Research. (1972)-. English. an. Free to members, $6.00 nonmembers. Society for American Baseball Research, PO Box 93183, Cleveland OH 44101. **Tel** (216)575-0500. **ED** Jim Kaplan. **LC** GV862; .B435. **DD** 796.357/05. Index available. cum. index. **Bk Rev. Ad Acc. Circ:** 8,000 (ctrl).
**Ind/Abst** Am. Hist. Life (1985-); Phys. Educ. Index; SPORT Discus; SportSearch.

US/0270-1537
**BASEBALL RULE BOOK. NATIONAL FEDERATION EDITION.** ***Title Change.*** (BASEBALL RULE BOOK.). **Added/Corp** National Federation of State High School Associations. (19??)-(19??). English. an. National Federation of State High School Associations, 11724 Northwest Plaza Circle, PO Box 20626, Kansas City MO 64195-0626. **Tel** (816)464-5400, FAX (816)464-5571. **ED** Bradley A Rumble. **LC** GV877; .B335. **DD** 796.357/02/022. **Ad Acc. Circ:** 55,000. ***Continues*** *Baseball Rules.* ***Continued by*** *High School Baseball Rules.*
**Desc:** The official rules of high school baseball.

US
**BASEBALL'S FORGOTTEN HEROES.** **See** Biographies.

CN/0229-3471
**BASELINE, THE.** [Baseline]. **Added/Corp** B.C.A.B.A. Vol. 1, No. 1 (Feb. 1980)-. Periodical. English. qt. Free to members, $5.00 membership. B.C.A.B.A., 1200 Hornby Street, Vancouver British Columbia V6Z 2E2 Canada. **DD** 796.32/3/060711.

FR/0755-7337
**BASKET-BALL.** [Basket-ball]. (1933)-. Periodical. French. mo (11 issues). 230.00F France; 270.00F other. Basket Ball, 14 rue Froment, 75011 Paris France. **Tel** 011 33 1 43382000. **UDC** 796.323.

US/0094-9175
**BASKETBALL BULLETIN, THE.** **Added/Corp** National Association of Basketball Coaches of the United States. (19??)-. Bulletin. English. Fifteen times a year. $50.00. Sports Publishing, 6000 Camp Bowie Boulevard, Suite 197, Forth Worth TX 76116. **Tel** (817)737-0925. **LC** GV882; .B36. **DD** 796.32/363/0973.

US/0525-4663
**BASKETBALL CASE BOOK.** **Added/Corp** National Federation of State High School Associations. (19??)-. English. an. National Federation of State High School Associations, 11724 Northwest Plaza Circle, PO Box 20626, Kansas City MO 64195-0626. **Tel** (816)464-5400, FAX (816)464-5571. **LC** GV885.45; .B37. **DD** 796.32/362.

US/0098-5988
**BASKETBALL DIGEST.** Vol. 1, (Nov. 1973)-. Periodical. English. Eight times a year. $22.00 US; $30.00 other. Century Publishing Company, 990 Grove Street, Evanston IL 60201-4370. **Tel** (708)491-6440, (800)321-3333, FAX (708)491-0459. **(Subscription address:** Kable Publishers Aide, 308 East Hitt Street, Subscriptions Department, Mt. Morris, IL 61054**) ED**

Michael Herbert. **LC** GV885.5; .B36. **DD** 796.32/3/05. **Bk Rev. Ad Acc. Circ:** 130,000. available on microfilm and microfiche from University Microfilms International (UMI). **Desc:** Coverage of the National Basketball Association. **Ind/Abst** Mag. Artic. Summar. Elite (Jan. 1994-); Mag. Artic. Summar. CD-ROM (Jan. 1994-).

US/0160-5747
**BASKETBALL FORECAST.** English. $1.25 single issue. Lexington Library, 355 Lexington Avenue, New York NY 10017. **LC** GV885.6; B37. **DD** 796.32/3/0973.

UK
**BASKETBALL NEWS.** English. mo. £26.00 UK; £32.00 Europe; £37.00 other. Clearmark Productions Limited, PO Box 74, Loughborough LE12 5ET England. **Tel** 011 44 509 880208. ***Continues*** *Basketball Monthly.* **Desc:** Covers basketball in the UK and abroad.

US/0270-4226
**BASKETBALL OFFICIALS MANUAL.** **Added/Corp** National Federation of State High School Associations. National Collegiate Athletic Association. (19??)-. English. an. National Federation of State High School Associations, 11724 Northwest Plaza Circle, PO Box 20626, Kansas City MO 64195-0626. **Tel** (816)464-5400, FAX (816)464-5571. **LC** GV885.2; .B37. **DD** 796.32/3/02022.

US/0737-5212
**BASKETBALL RULES SIMPLIFIED AND ILLUSTRATED ... FOR OFFICIALS, COACHES, PLAYERS, SPECTATORS.** **Main/Corp** National Federation of State High School Associations. **VFOAT** Official High School Basketball Rules Simplified and Illustrated. English. an. $2.25. National Federation of State High School Associations, 11724 Northwest Plaza Circle, PO Box 20626, Kansas City MO 64195-0626. **Tel** (816)464-5400, FAX (816)464-5571. **LC** GV885.45; .N39B. **DD** 796.32/3/02022.

US/0744-2866
**BASKETBALL TIMES.** (19??)-. Periodical. English. Twelve times a year. $32.00. Basketball Times, PO Box 370, Rochester MI 48063. **Tel** (313)879-1676. **ED** Larry W. Donald. **Bk Rev. Ad Acc. Circ:** 37,000. ***Continues*** *College and Pro Basketball Times, 0164-3096.* **Desc:** Tabloid newspaper covers junior college, college, and professional teams.

US/0005-6170
**BASKETBALL WEEKLY.** (19??)-. Periodical. English. Twenty times a year (weekly in season). $39.95 US; $44.95 Canada; $69.95 other. Football News/Basketball Weekly, 17820 East Warren Avenue, Detroit MI 48224. **Tel** (313)881-9555, (800)521-8808, FAX (313)881-2027. **ED** P Stanton. **Ad Acc, Adv Mgr:** K Ballew, **Tel** (313)881-9554. **Circ:** 60,000 (ctrl). **Desc:** Complete coverage of college, prep, and pro basketball; weekly ratings of top teams, college and pro; outstanding predictions of all major games.

CN/0822-9759
**BC ATHLETICS RECORD.** [BC athl. rec.]. **Added/Corp** BC Athletic/Track & Field Association. **VAT** British Columbia Athletics Record. (Mar./Apr. 1983)-. Periodical. English. Six times a year. 12.00Can$. BC Amateur Athletics Association, 1132 Hamilton Street, Vancouver British Columbia V6B 2S2 Canada. **Tel** (604)688-6266. **DD** 796.4/2/09711. **Circ:** 4,000. ***Continues*** *BC Track Record, 0711-0006.*

US/1072-1061
**BDS (CULVER CITY, CALIF.).** (BDS.). [BDS]. (199?)-. Periodical. English. mo. Miramar Publishing Company, 6133 Bristol Parkway, PO Box 3640, Culver City CA 90231. **Tel** (800)543-4116, (310)337-9717. **DD** 380. ***Continues*** *Bicycle Dealer Showcase, 0361-381X.*

US/0886-0599
**BECKETT BASEBALL CARD MONTHLY.** **See** Hobbies.

US/1055-8179
**BECKETT BASKETBALL MAGAZINE.** **See** Hobbies.

US/1055-2294
**BECKETT FOOTBALL CARD MONTHLY.** [Beckett footb. card mon.]. **VFOAT** Beckett Football. Issue #10 (Jan. 1991)-. Periodical. English. mo. $19.95 US; $29.86 Canada; $31.95 other. Beckett Publications, 15850 Dallas Parkway, Dallas TX 75248. **Tel** (214)991-6657, FAX (214)991-8930. **(Subscription address:** PO Box 1915, Marion, OH 43305, Telephone: (614)383-5772**) LC** WMLC L 83/8682. **DD** 796. ***Continues*** *Beckett Football Card Magazine, 1053-1521.*

US/1058-5958
**BECKETT HOCKEY MONTHLY.** [Beckett hockey mon.]. **VFOAT** Hockey Monthly; Beckett Hockey. Vol. 2, No. 1 (Jan. 1991)-. Periodical. English. mo. $19.95 US; $29.86 Canada; $31.95 other. Beckett Publications, 15850 Dallas Parkway, Dallas TX 75248. **Tel** (214)991-6657, FAX (214)991-8930. **(Subscription address:** PO Box 1915, Marion, OH 43305, Telephone: (614)383-5772**) LC** WMLC 91/512. **DD** 796. ***Continues*** *Beckett Hockey Magazine, 1058-8434.*

CN/0820-9863
**BECOIS-VOLANT.** Periodical. French. ir. 15.00Can$. Association de Vol Libre du Quebec, C P 332, Saint-Laurent Quebec H4L 4V6 Canada. **ED** Jean Letourneau. **DD** 797.5/5. **Ad Acc. Circ:** 300. **Desc:** Hang-gliding activity in Quebec Province training club meets, competitions and safety records.

US/0275-3626
**BEHIND THE WHISTLE.** (19??)-. Periodical. English. Six times a year. $8.50. Behind the Whistle, PO Box 67952, Los Angeles CA 90067-0952. **LC** GV943.9.R43; B43. **DD** 796.334/3/05.

BM
**BERMUDIAN, THE.** (1930)-. Periodical. English. mo. $32.00 (Bermuda); $38.00 (other). Bermudian Publishing Company, PO Box Hm 283, Hamilton 5 Bermuda. **Tel** (809)295-7104, FAX (809)295-8616. **ED** Kevin Stevenson. **Ad Acc, Adv Mgr:** Ms. Daveby, **Tel** (809)295-7104. **Circ:** 10,000. **Desc:** Personalities, sports, and social news.

US/1056-8034
**BEST AMERICAN SPORTS WRITING, THE.** **See** Journalism.

US/0097-9767
**BEST OF GOAL, THE.** 1973/74-. English. $2.95. Spartan Publishing Inc., Box 2001, New Canaan CT. **LC** GV846; .B47. **DD** 796.9/62/05.

CN/0712-2446
**BEYOND SIGHT.** [Beyond sight]. **Added/Corp** Canadian Blind Sports Association. **VFOAT** Actualite. (1981)-. Periodical. English (French). qt. 5.00Can$ Canada; $5.00 US. Canadian Blind Sports Association, 1600 James Naismith, Gloucester Ontario K1B 5N4 Canada. **Tel** (613)748-5609, telex 053-3660. **ED** Janet Lommen. **DD** 796/.01/9605. **Ad Acc. Circ:** 2,000 English, 500 French (ctrl). ***Formed by the union of*** *Au-dela du Regard, 0844-0433;* ***Absorbed*** *Actualite (Association Canadienne des Sports pour Avaeugles), 0824-0892.* ***Continued in part by*** *Actualite (Association Canadienne des Sports pour Aveugles : 1985), 0828-2048.* **Desc:** Informs our membership of the development of organized sport and recreation programs for the blind.

US/0161-7710
**BFLO. VAT** Buffalo. V. 4- Winter 1978-. Periodical. English. bm. $3.00. 983 Jefferson Avenue, Buffalo NY 14204. ***Continues*** *Buffalo Fan.*

●US/1065-1802
**BICYCLE TRAVELER, THE.** (1992)-. Periodical. English. mo. $65.00. PKD Publishing Co., 540 Frontage Road, Suite 3140, Northfield IL 60093.

US/1056-845X
**BIG BLUE REVIEW.** [Big Blue rev.]. (1991)-. Periodical. English. sm. $30.00. Weston Communications, 85 Old Ridge Road, Stamford CT 06903. **DD** 796.

US/0361-588X
**BIG EIGHT, THE.** [Big eight]. English. an. $3.50. Football Enterprises, PO Box 20688, Oklahoma City OK 73120. **Tel** (405)364-1050. **LC** GV958.5.B53; B5. **DD** 796.33/263/0973.

US
**BIG TEN CONFERENCE RECORDS BOOK.** **Added/Corp** Big Ten Conference (U.S.). Communications Dept. **VFOAT** Big 10 Records. 43rd. Ed. (1991)-. English. $8.00. **LC** GV741; .B592. ***Continues*** *Big Ten Records Book (Schaumburg, Ill. : 1989).*

US/0197-8128
**BIG TEN FOOTBALL ALMANAC.** V. 1- 1978-. English. an. $4.95. Alpine Book Company, 527 Madison Avenue, New York NY 10022. **LC** GV985.5.I55; B53. **DD** 796.332/63/0977.

US/0889-5988
**BIGGER, FASTER, STRONGER JOURNAL.** **Added/Corp** Bigger, Faster, Stronger (Organization). **VFOAT** Bigger, Faster, Stronger; BFS Journal. (19??)-. Periodical. English. Four times a year (Mar., June, Sept., Dec.). $14.95 (one year), $27.95 (two year), $39.95 (three year). Bigger Faster Stronger Journal, 805 West 2400 South, Salt Lake City UT 84119. **Tel** (800)628-9737, FAX (801)975-7159. **ED** Greg Shepard. **DD** 796. **Circ:** 25,000. **Desc:** This publication is designed for junior and senior high schools and colleges and athletes in general, as well as coaches. It contains motivational and training information for coaches and athletes in all sports.

●US/1064-492X
**BIKE (MIDDLETOWN, R.I.), THE.** (BIKE.). (1992)-. Periodical. English. bm. $26.00. NGU Publishing, Inc., Suite 1A, 747 Aquidneck Avenue, Middletown RI 02840.

US/0277-3066
**BLACK BELT (BURBANK, CALIF.).** (BLACK BELT.). [Black belt]. Vol. 1 (1962)-. Periodical. English. mo. $45.95 (one year), $91.90 (two year). Rainbow Publications Inc., PO Box 16298, North Hollywood CA 91615. **Tel** (818)760-8983, (800)257-4066, FAX (818)985-1213. **ED** Jim Coleman. **DD** 796. **Ad Acc.** ***Continues*** *Black Belt Magazine.* **Desc:** Covers all aspects of material arts. **Ind/Abst** Phys. Educ. Index; SPORT Discus; SportSearch.

US/0744-6179
**BLADE MAGAZINE, THE.** ***Title Change.*** **See** Hobbies.

●US/1067-750X
**BLUE BOOK OF COLLEGE ATHLETICS FOR SENIOR, JUNIOR & COMMUNITY COLLEGES, THE.** [Blue book coll. athl. sr. jr. community coll.]. **VFOAT** Blue book of College Athletics; Blue Book of Senior, Junior & Community College Athletics. (1992)-. English. an. $29.95. Athletic Publishing Company, PO Box 931, Montgomery AL 36102. **Tel** (205)263-4436, FAX (205)263-4437. **LC** GV351; .B58. **DD** 796/.071/173. ***Continues*** *Blue Book of Sr. College, University, and Junior & Community College Athletics.*

US
**BOB CARR'S INSIDE SPORTING GOODS.** **See** Business-Retail.

US/1047-2223
**BODY BOARDING.** [Body board.]. **VFOAT** Body Boarding Magazine. (198?)-. Periodical. English. Four times a year. $9.95. Western Empire Publishing, PO Box 3010, San Clemente CA 92672. **Tel** (714)492-7873. **(Subscription address:** Hudson & Associates, PO Box 469005, Escondido CA 92672.**) LC** GV840.S8; B6. **DD** 797.3. ***Continues*** *Surfing Magazine's Body Boarding, 0896-7318.* **Desc:** A surfing publication.

CN/1191-0100
**BODYCHECK (NEPEAN).** (BODYCHECK.). [Bodycheck]. **Added/Corp** Senateurs d'Ottawa (Equipe de Hockey). No. 1 (1991)-. Periodical. French (English). ir. Club de Hockey les Senateurs D'Ottawa, Bureau 200, 301 Promenade Moodie, Nepean Ontario K2H 9C4 Canada. **DD** 796.962.

US/1064-6507
**BOICE LYDELL'S SPORT KARATE INTERNATIONAL.** [Boice Lydell's sport karate int.]. **VFOAT** Sport Karate International; Sport Karate; SKI. (19??)-. Periodical. English. Six times a year. $17.50. Smash, 341 East Fairmont Avenue, Lakewood NY 14750. **Tel** (716)763-1111, FAX (716)763-5555. **ED** Boice Lydell. **DD** 796. **Ad Acc.** ***Continues*** *Sport Karate Magazine.*

BL
**BOLETIM INFORMATIVO - CONSELHO NACIONAL DE DESPORTOS.** **Main/Corp** Brazil. Conselho Nacional de Desportos. Bulletin. Portuguese. Rua da Imprensa 16-11 Andar, Rio de Janeiro Brazil. **LC** GV597.B73A.

CN/0710-3905
**BONNYVILLE NOUVELLE.** [Bonnyville nouv.]. (1935)-. Newspaper. English. Fifty-one times per year. 20.56Can$ Canada (residents within 40 km radius of Bonnyville), 55.06Can$ Canada (outside 40 km radius of Bonnyville); 124.56Can$ other. Bonnyville Nouvelle Ltd., PO Box 8174, Bonnyville ALTA T9N 2J5 Canada. **ED** Janet Olsen (editor's phone: (403)826-3876). **DD** 071.123. **Bk Rev. Ad Acc, Adv Mgr:** Rene VanBrabant, **Tel** (403)826-3876. **Circ:** 6,000.

CN/0821-0098
**BOOK OF RECORDS, NATIONALS - SOFTBALL CANADA.** (BOOK OF RECORDS, NATIONALS.). **Main/Corp** Canadian Amateur Softball Association. **VFOAT** Livre de Records, Nationaux. Sept. 1980-. English (French). an. Canadian Amateur Softball Association, National Sport and Recreation Centre, 355 River Road, Vanier Ontario K1L 8C1 Canada. **Tel** (613)748-5668. **DD** 796.357/8. ***Continues*** *Canadian Amateur Softball Association. Book of Records, 0821-008X.*

US/0739-4667
**BOOK ON STARTING PITCHERS.** (1983)-. English. an. $20.00. Research Analysis Publications, PO Box 49213, Los Angeles CA 90049. **ED** Ron Lewis. **Circ:** 3,500.

US/0361-6398
**BOSTON BRUINS OFFICIAL YEARBOOK.** English. an. $2.50. RA Production Inc, PO Box 9100, Boston MA 02114. **LC** GV848.B6; B68. **DD** 796.9/62/0922 B.

US/0361-6894
**BOSTON CELTICS.** English. an. $2.50. Shamrock Publishing Company, PO Box 9100, Boston MA 02114. **LC** GV885.52.B67; B68. **DD** 796.32/364/0974461.

Recreation, Leisure —Sports

●US/1065-7134
**BOTTOM TIME.** [Bottom time]. (1992)-. Periodical. English. mo. $38.00. Bottom Time, 78-365 Highway 111, Suite 361, La Quinta CA 92253-1981. **DD** 797.

CN/0827-2638
**BOWBENDER MAGAZINE.** [Bowbender mag.]. **VFOAT** Bowbender. Vol. 1 (Aug. 1984)-. Periodical. English. qt. 9.00Can$ Canada; $14.00 other. Bowbender Magazine, PO Box 912 Canada. **Tel** (403)337-3023, FAX (403)337-3460. **ED** Kathleen Windsor. **DD** 799.3/2/097123. **Bk Rev**. **Ad Acc**. **Circ:** 33,000.
**Desc:** Intended to provide information and enjoyment for the archery enthusiast. Regardless of the type of bow, shafting, shooting style or pursuit, if your launching of arrows employs healthy and responsible attitudes, then we salute you.

US/0164-9183
**BOWLERS JOURNAL.** **Added/Corp** Billiard & Bowling Institute of America. Vol. 65, No. 9 (Sept. 1978)-. Periodical. English. Twelve times a year. $20.00 US; $36.00 Canada and Mexico; $42.00 other. National Bowlers Journal, Inc., 200 South Michigan Suite 1430, Chicago IL 60604. **Tel** (312)341-1110. **LC** WMLC L 83/6462. ***Continues*** *National Bowlers Journal & Billiard Review.*
**Ind/Abst** Phys. Educ. Index; SPORT Discus; SportSearch.

US/8750-3603
**BOWLING DIGEST.** Vol. 1, No. 1 (Mar./Apr. 1983)-. Periodical. English. bm (6 issues). $22.00 US; $30.00 other. Century Publishing Company, 990 Grove Street, Evanston IL 60201-4370. **Tel** (708)491-6440, (800)321-3333, FAX (708)491-0459. **(Subscription address:** Kable Publishers Aide, 308 East Hitt Street, Subscriptions Department, Mt. Morris, IL 61054**)** **ED** Michael Herbert. **LC** WMLC L 83/129. **Bk Rev**. **Ad Acc**. **Circ:** 110,000. available in microform.
**Desc:** Covers professional and amateur bowling.
**Ind/Abst** SPORT Discus.

US/1050-5121
**BOWLING MAGAZINE (1988).** (BOWLING MAGAZINE.). [Bowl. mag.]. **Added/Corp** American Bowling Congress. **VFOAT** Bowling. Vol. 55, No. 1 (Aug./Sept. 1988)-. Periodical. English. Six times a year. $10.95 North America; $13.95 other. American Bowling Congress, 5301 South 76th Street, Greendale WI 53129. **Tel** (414)421-6400, FAX (414)421-1194. **ED** Bill Vint. **LC** GV901; .B75. **DD** 794.6/0973. **Ad Acc**, **Adv Mgr:** John Dill, **Tel** (612)856-2465. ***Continues*** *Bowling (Milwaukee, Wis. : 1970), 0162-0274.*
**Desc:** Newsworthy, educational, informative, and entertaining items about the sport of bowling.
**Ind/Abst** SPORT Discus.

US
**BOX Y LUCHA.** (19??)-. Periodical. Spanish. Twenty-four times a year. $15.60. EDIMEX, PO Box 2145, San Ysidro CA 92073. **Tel** (310)626-1205. **(Subscription address:** Order Assistance Department, PO Box 1943, Birmingham AL 35201.**)**
**Desc:** Covers articles on sports, boxing, and wrestling.

US/0006-8500
**BOXING ILLUSTRATED.** [Box. illus.]. (1959)-. Periodical. English. mo. $30.00. National Sports Publishing Corporation, 25 West 43rd, Suite 1403, New York NY 10036. **Tel** (212)730-1374. **(Subscription address:** Subco, PO Box 10233, Eugene OR 97404.**)** **DD** 796. ***Continues*** *Boxing Illustrated Ringside News, 0524-1774.*

UK/0956-098X
**BOXING MONTHLY.** [Box. mon.]. (1989)-. Consumer Publication. English. mo. £26.00 UK; £58.00 Australia, Japan, New Zealand & Philippines; £37.00 Europe; £48.00 other. Plan It Publishing, 24 Notting Hill Gate, London W11 3JE England. **Tel** 011 44 71 229 9944, FAX 011 44 71 727 5442. **ED** Glyn Leach. **DD** 796.83. **Bk Rev**, (Qty: 15). **Ad Acc**, **Adv Mgr:** Jo Eady. **Circ:** 35,000.

UK/0006-8519
**BOXING NEWS.** (1940)-. Periodical. English. wk. £50.00 UK except Eire; £60.00 Europe; £65.00 America; £55.00 other. Boxing News Limited, 30 34 Langham Street, London WIN 5LB England. **Tel** 011 44 71 4365199.

US/1056-5353
**BOXING REGISTRY'S RATINGS GUIDE.** [Box. regist. rat. guide]. Vol. 1, No. 1 (Winter 1991)-. Periodical. English. qt. Boxing Registry, PO Box 6336, Rosemead CA 91770. **LC** GV1131; .B69. **DD** 796.8/3.

US/0274-7979
**BOXING TODAY.** [Box. today]. (19??)-. Periodical. English. mo. Boxing Today, 155 West 29th Street, New York NY 10001. **Tel** (203)735-3381.

US/1054-8106
**BOXING TODAY (NEW YORK, N.Y. 1991).** (BOXING TODAY.). **VFOAT** Boxing. (1991)-. Periodical. English. qt. $30.00 US; $36.00 Canada. Spectator Sports, 519 8th Avenue, New York NY 10018.

UK/0959-8944
**BOXING WEEKLY.** [Box. wkly.]. (1989)-. Periodical. English. wk. $120.00. Plan It Publishing, 24 Notting Hill Gate, London W11 3JE England. **Tel** 011 44 71 229 9944, FAX 011 44 71 727 5442.

US/0744-8295
**BREAKOUT.** ***Ceased.*** **VFOAT** Break Out. Periodical. English. bm. Breakout Magazine, POB 820, Carlsbad CA 92008. **Tel** (619)434-3322. **ED** George Salvador and Chris Ahrens. **LC** WMLC L 83/254. **DD** 797.
**Desc:** Focuses on the California surfing lifestyle. Concentrating on Californian surfers as individuals and as a force in the world competition.

GW/0932-8823
**BRENNPUNKTE DER SPORTWISSENSCHAFT / HERAUSGEGEBEN VON DER DEUTSCHEN SPORTHOCHSCHULE KOLN.** **Added/Corp** Deutsche Sporthochschule Koln. **VFOAT** BSW. (19??)-. Periodical. German. sa (May & Nov.). DM5050.00. Academia Verlag Richarz GmbH, Postfach 1163, D 53734 St. Augustin Germany. **Tel** 011 49 2241 333349. **LC** GV428; .B74. **DD** 613.7/1.

FR
**BRIDGEUR.** French. mo. Editions de Presse Specialisee, 28 rue de Richelieu, 75001 Paris France. **Tel** 011 33 1 42 96 25 50.

UK/0007-0289
**BRITISH ARCHER, THE.** (June/July 1949)-. Periodical. English. Six times a year. £8.20 UK; £10.80 other. BA Publishing Company Ltd., 4345 Milford Road, Reading RG1 8LG England. **Tel** (0734) 55444. **ED** John Histead. **Bk Rev**. **Ad Acc**.
**Desc:** A magazine for target and field archers.
**Ind/Abst** SPORT Discus; SportSearch (May 1987-).

CN/0711-3862
**BRITISH COLUMBIA SPORT SALMON FISHING NEWS.** ***Title Change.*** **See** Fish and Fisheries.

CN/0228-3263
**BRITISH COLUMBIA SPORTS HALL OF FAME AND MUSEUM.** [B.C. Sports Hall Fame Mus.]. **VFOAT** Sports Hall of Fame and Museum. 1977-. English. an. British Columbia Sports Hall of Fame and Museum, Exhibition Park, Vancouver British Columbia V5K 4A9 Canada. **DD** 796/.074/011133. ***Continues*** *British Columbia Sports Hall of Fame, 0318-3645.*

US/0278-9973
**BROWNS NEWS/ILLUSTRATED.** **Added/Corp** Cleveland Browns (Football Team). **VFOAT** Browns News Illustrated. **VAT** Browns News Illustrated. (198?)-. Periodical. English. ir (weekly, Aug.-Jan., monthly, Feb.-July). $29.95. Cleveland Browns Publishing Co., Inc., 2 Berea Commons/Suite 200, Berea OH 44017. **Tel** (216)826-4640. **ED** Frank Derry. **Ad Acc**. **Circ:** 20,000.
**Desc:** Delivers the inside story on the players, coaches, front office, and the entire NFL. Takes you behind the scenes delivering statistics, standings, scouting reports, key matchups, postgame reports, weekly game previews, photographs from cover-to-cover, and a poster-size centerspread of your favorite player.

US/0883-6833
**BUCKEYE SPORTS BULLETIN.** (198?)-. Periodical. English. Thirty times a year. $40.00. Buckeye Sports Bulletin, 1350 West 5th Avenue 25, Columbus OH 43212. **Tel** (614)486-2202.

JA
**BUDO.** **Added/Corp** Nihon Budokan. **VFOAT** Budo. (19??)-. Periodical. Japanese. mo. Nihon Budokan, 2-3 Kitanomaru Koen, Chiyoda-ku, Tokyo 102 Japan. **LC** GV1112; .B8.

●US/1065-2140
**BUFFALO SPORTS NEWS, THE.** [Buffalo sports news]. Vol. 1, No. 1 (July 21, 1992)-. Periodical. English. ir. The Buffalo Sports News, 1085 14th Street, Suite 1257, Boulder CO 80302. **DD** 796.

CN/0382-4713
**BULLETIN 78.** (BULLETIN 78. (COMMONWEALTH GAMES).). **Main/Conf** Commonwealth Games, 11th, Edmonton, Alta., 1978. V. 1- Dec. 1976-. Bulletin. English. mo. Free. Commonwealth Games Canada, PO Box 1978, Edmonton Alta T5J 5J5 Canada. **DD** 796.4/09171/241. **UDC** 796.4.

CN/0709-2172
**BULLETIN A L'USAGE DES TRAPPEURS.** No. 2-. Bulletin. French. Price varies per volume. Direction de la Peche Sportive et de la Chasse, Ministere des Ressources Naturelles, CP 6000, Fredericton New Brunswick E3B 5H1 Canada. **UDC** 799.1/.2(715).

CN/0826-1326
**BULLETIN DE NOUVELLES / FEDERATION QUEBECOISE DES SPORTS AERIENS, SECTEUR PARACHUTISME.** [Bull. nouv. - Fed. que. sports aer., Sect. parachutisme]. **Main/Corp** Federation Quebecoise des Sports Aeriens. Secteur Parachutisme. Vol. 3, No. 1 (March 31 1983)-. Bulletin. French. Federation Quebecoise des Sports Aeriens, 1415 Est rue Jarry, Montreal Quebec H2E 2Z7 Canada. **Tel** (514)252-3055. **DD** 797.5/6/09714. **UDC** 797.561(714). ***Continues*** *Federation Quebecoise des Sports Aeriens. Commission Sectorielle de Parachutisme. Bulletin de Nouvelles, 0822-5249.*

CN/0822-854X
**BULLETIN DE NOUVELLES / FEDERATION QUEBECOISE DES SPORTS AERIENS, SECTEUR VOL LIBRE.** [Bull. nouv. - Fed. que. sports aer., Sect. vol libre]. **Main/Corp** Federation Quebecoise des Sports Aeriens. Secteur Vol Libre. Vol. 3, No 1 (19 April 1983)-. Bulletin. French. Federation Quebecoise des Sports Aeriens, 1415 Est rue Jarry, Montreal Quebec H2E 2Z7 Canada. **Tel** (514)252-3055. **DD** 797.5/5. **UDC** 797.55(714). ***Continues*** *Federation Quebecoise des Sports Aeriens. Commission Sectorielle de Vol Libre. Bulletin de Nouvelles, 0822-532X.*

BE/1012-0491
**BULLETIN D'INFORMATION SPORTIVE BRUXELLES.** **VFOAT** Sports Information Bulletin. (1985)-. Periodical. French (English, French, Dutch, Spanish and Portuguese). qt. 1000.00F Belgium & Luxembourg; 1500.00F other. Clearing House Belgium, Espace du 27 Septembre, Boulevard Leopold II nr 44, 1080 Brussels Belgium. **Tel** 011 32 2 4132893, FAX 011 32 2 4132890. **ED** Albert Remons. **UDC** 796. **Pr Rev**.
**Desc:** Sports policy information.
**Ind/Abst** SPORT Discus.

SZ/0428-1659
**BULLETIN / FEDERATION INTERNATIONALE DE GYMNASTIQUE.** **Main/Corp** Federation Internationale de Gymnastique. **VFOAT** Bulletin d'Information de la FIG; Bulletin de la FIG. (19??)-. Bulletin. French (English). qt. 30.00F. Federation Internationale Gymnastique, Rue de Oeuches 10, 2740 Moutier 1 Switzerland. **Tel** 011 41 32 936666, FAX 11 41 32 936671, telex 934961 FIG CH. **LC** UNC. **Ad Acc**. ctrl circ.
**Ind/Abst** SPORT Discus.

CN/0700-8090
**BULLETIN - I C S S.** **Main/Corp** International Committee for Sociology of Sport. Bulletin. English. sa. $15.00. School of Physical Education, McMaster University, c/o Peter Donnelly, 1280 Main Street West, Hamilton Ontario 48S 4K1 Canada. **DD** 796. **UDC** 316:796. ctrl circ.

CN/0824-0906
**BULLETIN SKI NAUTIQUE.** [Bull. ski naut.]. **VFOAT** Ski Nautique. **VAT** Ski Nautique (Montreal). Vol. 1, No 1 (May 1983)-. Bulletin. French. bm. 10.00Can$. Federation Quebecoise de Ski Nautique, 4545 Pierre de Coubertin, CP 1000 Succursale M, Montreal Quebec H1V 3R2 Canada. **Tel** (514)252-3092. **ED** Pierre Laforest. **DD** 797.3/5/05. **UDC** 797.176. **Ad Acc**. **Circ:** 2,000 (ctrl).
**Desc:** Instruction calendar of activities, equipment, physical conditioning, safety, and interviews.

AU
**BULLETIN UNION INTERNATIONALE DE PENTATHLON MODERNE ET BIATHLON.** Bulletin. English (German, Czech, French and Spanish). ir. Union Internationale de Pentathlon Moderne et Biathlon (UIPMB), Prinz Eugen St 12 Dr Vld Cerny, A-1040 Vienna Austria.

US/0885-0771
**BULL'S-EYE NEWS.** [Bull's-eye news]. **VFOAT** Bull's Eye News. (19??)-. Periodical. English. Twelve times a year. $24.00. Bulls Eye News, 281 East Broadway, Westerville OH 43081. **Tel** (614)899-1338, FAX (614)899-6696. **ED** Michelle Huskey. **LC** WMLC L 83/2598. **DD** 794. **Ad Acc**, **Adv Mgr:** Jay Tomlinson. **Circ:** 5,000.
**Desc:** Is an national publication directed towards dart players of all levels from the grass roots shooter to the tournament pro. Readers are interested in all aspects of the game, from how to improve their skills to keeping informed on the latest in product advancement.

US
**BUSINESS DIRECTORY / NATIONAL FOOTBALL LEAGUE RETIRED PLAYERS ASSOCIATION.** **Main/Corp** National Football League Retired Players Association (U.S.). **VFOAT** NFLRPA Business Directory. Sept. 1984-. Directory. English. National Football League Retired Player Association, 1300 Connecticut Avenue NW, Washington DC 20036. **LC** GV955.5.N36; N37A. **DD** 796.332/092/2. **UDC** 796.333.7-057.75(73).

US/0191-1902
**BYLAWS, RULES, AND SPECIFICATIONS - WOMEN'S INTERNATIONAL BOWLING CONGRESS.** **Main/Corp** Women's International Bowling Congress. English. an (July). Free. Women's International Bowling Congress, 5301 South 76th Street, Greendale WI 53129. **Tel** (414)421-9000, FAX (414)421-4420. **LC** GV901.W6; A417. **DD** 794.6. **UDC** 796.28:063-055.2. **Ad Acc.** ctrl circ.
**Desc:** Contains rules governing sanctioned league and tournament competition for the game of American bowling. Also WIBC Bylaws and bylaws governing affiliated local and state associations.

CN/0381-9906
**C. A. S. C. RACE REGULATIONS.** [C.A.S.C. race regul.]. **Main/Corp** Canadian Automobile Sport Clubs. **VFOAT** Race Regulations. **VAT** Canadian Automobile Sport Clubs Race Regulations. (1975)-. English. Canadian Automobile Sport Clubs, Suite 203, 5385 Yonge Street, Willowdale Ontario M2N 5R7. **DD** 796.7/2/0971. ***Continues in part*** *Canadian Automobile Sport Clubs. Race & Solo Regulations, 0381-9892.*

CN/0382-4055
**C C A RODEO NEWS.** **Main/Corp** Canadian Cowboys Association. Periodical. English. sm. $7.74. CCA Rodeo News, Box 276, North Battleford Saskatchewan S9A 2Y3 Canada. **Tel** (306)445-3233. **DD** 791.8. **UDC** 791.8. ***Continues*** *C A C A Rodeo News, 0382-4268.*

US/0279-6945
**CAA MAGAZINE.** (CAA MAGAZINE : OFFICIAL PUBLICATION OF THE CHICAGO ATHLETIC ASSOCIATION.). **VAT** Chicago Athletic Association Magazine. Periodical. English. an. Chicago Athletic Association, 12 South Michigan Avenue, Chicago IL 60603. **UDC** 796.42(773). ***Continues*** *Cherry Circle, 0009-3238.*

US
**CABLESPORTS NEWSLETTER.** ***Title Change.*** **See** Communication-Broadcasting.

FR
**CAHIERS DU PISTOLIER ET DU CARABINIER.** (19??)-. French. mo (10 issues). 295.00F France; 360.00F other. Editions Tir Armes Total, Boinville Legaillard, 78660 Ablis France. **Tel** 33 30 59 00 80.

US/0008-0918
**CALIFORNIA BOWLING NEWS.** (1940)-. Periodical. English. Fifty-two times a year. $12.00. California Bowling News, 2606 West Burbank Boulevard, Burbank CA 91505. **Tel** (818)845-4458, (213)849-4664. **ED** Ken Lowman. **Bk Rev.** **Ad Acc.** **Circ:** 15,000 (ctrl).
**Desc:** Nation's leading bowling newspaper, published continuously since 1940. Covers local, regional, national and world bowling news, with columns and editorials.

US
**CALIFORNIA CITY SPORTS MAGAZINE.** (1990)-. Periodical. English. Six times a year. $25.00. Competitor Inc., 214 South Cedros, Solana Beach CA 92075. **Tel** (619)793-2711.

US
**CALIFORNIA DIVING NEWS.** English. mo. $17.00. Saint Brendan Corporation, PO Box 11231, Torrance CA 90510. **Tel** (213)538-8856.

CN/0383-1191
**CANADA GUNSPORT.** Began with V. 1, No. 5, Feb. 1976 issue. Periodical. English. G.N. Dentay, Box 201, Willowdale Ontario M2N 5S8 Canada. **DD** 683/.4/00971. **UDC** 799.3(71). ***Continues*** *Journal of Military, Police and Sporting Arms, 0383-1205.*

CN/0045-4222
**CANADA SKI.** Vol. 1 (Nov. 1968)-. Periodical. English. qt. $2.00. Fred Roberts, Box 180, Pointe Claire Quebec H9R 4N9 Canada. **LC** GV854.8. **UDC** 796.92(71).

CN/0823-6674
**CANADIAN AMPUTEE SPORTS ASSOCIATION.** (CANADIAN AMPUTEE SPORTS ASSOCIATION : NEWSLETTER.). **Added/Corp** Canadian Amputee Sports Association. **VFOAT** Association Canadienne des Sports pour Ampute : Journal. Vol. 1, Issue 1 (1980)-. Newsletter. English. qt. Free. Canadian Amputee Sports Association, 428 Lake Bonavista Drive SE, Calgary Alberta T2J 0M1 Canada. **DD** 796/.01/96. ctrl circ.

CN/0316-8131
**CANADIAN AND PROVINCIAL GOLF RECORDS.** 1972-. Periodical. English. an. Royal Canadian Golf Association, Golf House, R.R. #2, Oakville Ontario L6J 4Z3. **DD** 796.352/7/0971. **UDC** 796.352.2.092(71). ***Supersedes*** *National Tournament Records, 0316-8212.*

CN/0712-5135
**CANADIAN AQUATICS.** [Can. aquat.]. Vol. 1, No. 1 (July 1982)-. Periodical. English. ir. Free to aquatic clubs and organizations, $18.00 Canada; $21.00 other. Canadian Aquatics, Subscription Department, Canadian Aquatics Publications Boulevard, Willowdale Ontario M2J 1S3 Canada. **DD** 797.2/0971. **UDC** 797.2(71).

CN/0228-9504
**CANADIAN CRICKETER, THE.** **Added/Corp** Canadian Cricket Association. Sports Federation of Canada. National Sport and Recreation Centre. Vol. 1, No. 1 (March 1972)-. Periodical. English. an. 5.00Can$. Canadian Cricket Association, 41 Ivybridge Drive, Brampton Ontario L6V 2X1 Canada. **DD** 796.35/8/0971.
**Ind/Abst** SportSearch (May 1987-).

CN/0045-4648
**CANADIAN CURLING NEWS.** [Can. curling news]. **Added/Corp** Canadian Curling Association. (Oct. 4, 1957)-. Periodical. English. mo. 14.02Can$ Canada; $22.00 US; 28.00Can$ other. Canadian Curling News, PO Box 245, Markdale Ontario NOC 1HO Canada. **Tel** (800)661-2418. **ED** Doug Maxwell. **DD** 796.9/6. **Ad Acc.** **Circ:** 10,000 (ctrl).

CN/0319-2997
**CANADIAN EQUINE SPORTS.** Oct. 1974-. Periodical. English (French). mo. $9.00. Canadien Equine Sports, 1117 St Catherine Street West, Montreal Quebec H3B 1H9 Canada. **DD** 798/.2/05. **UDC** 798.2(71). ***Supersedes*** *Equine Sports, 0319-2989.*

CN/0703-7074
**CANADIAN HORSESHOE PITCHERS YEAR BOOK.** No. 1- 1977-. English. an. $3.50 per no. E H Murray, Canadian Horseshoe Pitchers Year Book, Delmas Saskatchewan S0M 0P0 Canada. **DD** 796.2/4/05. **UDC** 796.24(71).

CN/0712-9815
**CANADIAN JOURNAL OF HISTORY OF SPORT.** [Can. j. hist. sport]. **VFOAT** Revue Canadienne de l'Histoire des Sports. Vol. 12, No. 1 (May 1981)-. Periodical. English (French). sa. 12.00Can$. Faculty of Human Kinetics, c/o Dr Metcalfe, University of Windsor, Windsor Ontario N9B 3P4 Canada. **Tel** (519)254-9955, FAX (519)253-4232, . **ED** Alan Metcalfe. **DD** 796/.09. **[CCC].** Index available. **Bk Rev.** **Pr Rev.** **Circ:** 500. ***Continues*** *Canadian Journal of History of Sport and Physical Education, 0008-4115.*
**Desc:** Sport history, in particular North American. Some articles are on international topics.
**Ind/Abst** Am. Hist. Life (1973-)(1981-); Leis. Recreat. Tour. Abstr.; Phys. Educ. Index; Spec. Educ. Needs Abstr.; SPORT Discus; SportSearch.

CN/0709-0269
**CANADIAN MARATHON ANNUAL.** 1979-. English. an. E Thomas, Canadian Marathon Annual, 22 Findlay Avenue, Ottawa Ontario K1S 2T9 Canada. **DD** 796.4/26/0971. **UDC** 796.422.16(058)(71).

CN/1183-4269
**CANADIAN OFFICIAL, THE.** [Can. off.]. Vol. 1, No 1 (Fall 1991)-. Periodical. English. qt. $3.75 (single issue). Canadian Official, PO Box 23069, 1315 Pembina Highway, Winnipeg Manitoba R3T 2B6 Canada. **DD** 796.

CN/1185-9792
**CANADIAN RULE BOOK FOR TACKLE FOOTBALL.** [Can. rule book tack. footb.]. **Main/Corp** Canadian Amateur Football Association. **Added/Corp** Canadian Interuniversity Athletic Union. (1991)-. English. Football Canada, 1600 James Naismith Drive, Gloucester Ontario K1B 5N4 Canada. **DD** 796.335/02022. ***Continues*** *Rule Book for Tackle Football., 1184-0331.*

CN/0823-874X
**CANADIAN SPORTS AWARDS, ATHLETE OF THE MONTH.** [Can. sports awards athl. month]. 1980-. English. an. Free. Sports Federation of Canada, 333 River Road, Vanier Ontario K1L 8B9 Canada. **Tel** (613)748-5670, FAX 613-748-5706. **DD** 796/.092/2. **UDC** 796.092(71).

CN/0831-229X
**CANADIAN WRESTLER (1985).** (CANADIAN WRESTLER.). [Can. wrestl.]. **Added/Corp** Canadian Amateur Wrestling Association. **VFOAT** Lutteur Canadien. **VAT** Wrestler (Vanier. 1985). Vol. 9, No. 2 (Fall 1985)-. Periodical. English (French). qt. 16.00Can$. Canadian Amateur Wrestling, 1600 James Naismith Drive, Gloucester Ontario K1B 5N4 Canada. **Tel** (613)748-5686, FAX (613)748-5756. **ED** Greg Mathieu. **DD** 796.8/12/0971. **Ad Acc.** **Circ:** 4,000. ***Continues*** *Canadian Wrestler Newsletter, 0829-3767.*
**Desc:** Concerning amateur wrestling in Canada. Includes news information, event updates and results.
**Ind/Abst** SPORT Discus.

US
**CANOE AND KAYAK RACING NEWS.** ***Ceased.*** **See** Boats and Boating.

IT
**CANOTTAGGIO.** (19??)-. Italian. Ten times a year. $35.00. Federazione Ital Canottaggio, Viale Tiziano 70, 00196 Rome Italy. **Tel** 011 39 6 3233770.

CN/0227-5880
**CANPARA (1976).** (CANPARA.). [Canpara]. **Added/Corp** Canadian Sport Parachuting Association. **VFOAT** Parachutiste Canadien; Canadian Parachutist. Vol. 10, No. 4 (Aug. 1976)-. Periodical. English (French). bm (6 issues). 35.00Can$ Canada; 45.00Can$ other. Canadian Sport Parachuting Association, 4185 Dunning Road, Navan Ontario K4B 1J1 Canada. **Tel** (613)835-3731. **ED** P.J. Perdue (editor's telephone/fax: (604)854-1426). **DD** 797.5/6/0971. **Ad Acc,** **Adv Mgr:** same as editor. **Pr Rev.** **Circ:** 5,000 (ctrl). ***Continues*** *Canadian Parachutist, 0319-3896.*
**Desc:** Sport parachuting and other aviation sports.
**Ind/Abst** SportSearch (May 1987-).

US/1041-5742
**CAPITAL SPORTS FOCUS.** [Cap. sports focus]. (Feb. 8, 1989)-. Periodical. English. Twelve times a year. Capital Sports Focus, 4733 Bethesda Avenue Suite 300, Bethesda MD 20814. **Tel** (301)657-1580. **ED** Dave Ungrady. **DD** 796. **Bk Rev.** **Ad Acc.** **Circ:** 100,000 (ctrl).
**Desc:** Features coverage of local sports teams as well as boating, running, cycling, walking and other sports.

US/0094-5889
**CAPTAIN'S MATE.** Periodical. English. mo. $9.00. 833 Dover Drive, Suite 3, Newport Beach CA 92660. **LC** GV771; .C36. **DD** 797.1/05. **UDC** 797.1.

US/1056-912X
**CARDEALS (WASHINGTON, D.C.).** (CARDEALS.). [Cardeals]. **Added/Corp** Center for the Study of Services (Washington, D.C.). **VFOAT** Car Deals. (1991)-. Periodical. English. bw. $4.50 (single issue). Center for Study of Services, 733 15th Street Northwest, Suite 820, Washington DC 20005. **Tel** (202)347-9612, (202)347-7283. **DD** 629.

US/8755-7703
**CART NEWS MEDIA GUIDE.** [CART news media guide]. **Added/Corp** Championship Auto Racing Teams (Organization). **VFOAT** C.A.R.T. News Media Guide; News Media Guide. **VAT** Championship Auto Racing Teams News Media Guide. (19??)-. English. an. $18.25. Championship Auto Racing Team, 390 Enterprise Court, Bloomfield Hills MI 48302. **Tel** (313)334-8500. **LC** GV1033; .C36. **DD** 796.7/2/0973.

FR/0243-1327
**CASSUS BELLI.** [Cassus belli]. (1980)-. Periodical. French. bm. 36.00F. Excelsior Publications, 1 rue du Colonel Pierre Avia, 75503 Paris Cedex 15 France. **Tel** 011 33 1 46484848, FAX 011 33 1 46484793. **UDC** 794.

US
**CCHA MEDIA GUIDE.** (19??)-. English. an (Oct.). $10.00. Central Collegiate Hockey Association, 1000 South State Street, Ann Arbor MI 48109. **Tel** (313)764-2590, FAX (313)764-0131.
**Desc:** 88 pages of pictures and information on all member schools including outlook, roster, schedule, previous year statistics, league history and award winners.

US
**CCHA NEWS RELEASE.** (19??)-. Periodical. English. wk (during hockey season). $40.00. Central Collegiate Hockey Association, 1000 South State Street, Ann Arbor MI 48109. **Tel** (313)764-2590, FAX (313)764-0131.
**Desc:** Updated standings, past weekend scores, list of upcoming games, statistics, game boxscores and notes on each school.

US/0747-6817
**CENTER FOR SPORTS SPONSORSHIP'S SPONSOR QUEST, THE.** **VFOAT** Sponsor Quest. Began in 1984. Periodical. English. mo. $30.00. Center for Sports Sponsorship, 34 Washington Road, Princeton Junction NJ 08550.

CN/0712-1334
**CENTRE THIRD.** (CENTRE THIRD : THE ONTARIO AMATEUR NETBALL ASSOCIATION'S NEWSLETTER.). [Cent. third]. **Added/Corp** Ontario Amateur Netball Association. (1980)-. Newsletter. English. ir. Free. Centre Third, Ontario Amateur Netball Association, 160 Vanderhoof Avenue, Toronto Ontario M4G 4B8 Canada. **DD** 796.32. ctrl circ.
**Ind/Abst** SportSearch (May 1987-).

CN/0822-5621
**CHAMPIONS DU SPORT AMATEUR, LES.** **VFOAT** Champions. **VAT** Champions (Montreal-Nord). V. 1, No 1 (Summer 83)-. French. mo. $1.75 per no. Les Champions du Sport Amateur, Montreal-Nord Quebec H1H 1V5 Canada. **DD** 796/.09714/27. **UDC** 796.092(714).

US/0893-8091
**CHEER NEWS TODAY.** [Cheer news today]. (Spring 1987)-. Periodical. English. qt (Apr., June, Oct.,

Dec.). $5.50 (one year), $9.99 (two year), $13.99 (three year). Cheer News Today, PO Box 3742, Minneapolis MN 55403. **Tel** (612)525-8653. **ED** Tamara Lindley. **DD** 796. **Bk Rev**. **Ad Acc**. **Circ:** 30,000 (ctrl).
**Desc:** Edited for high school and college coaches, administrators, athletic directors and cheerleaders. Issues regularly include coverage of national high school and college championships, as well as practical information on appearance, fund raising and school leadership.

KO
**CHEYUGIN.** First issue Sept. 1984. Periodical. Korean. mo. W2,800. Supochu Nyushu Sa, 25-27 Sangdo-dong Tongjak-ku, Seoul Korea. **LC** GV561; .C49.

US/0882-7346
**CHICAGO ATHLETIC ASSOCIATION ANNUAL.** **Main/Corp** Chicago Athletic Association. **VFOAT** Annual. English. an. Chicago Athletic Association, 12 South Michigan Avenue, Chicago IL 60603. **LC** GV584.5.C4; C48A. **DD** 796/.06/077311. **UDC** 796.42(058)(773).

US/1056-4284
**CHICAGO BEAR REPORT.** [Chic. Bear rep.]. **VFOAT** Bear Report. (199?)-. Periodical. English. Twenty-seven times a year. $29.95. Royle Publishing Company Inc., 112 Market Street, Sun Prairie WI 53590. **Tel** (608)837-5161. **DD** 796. ***Continues*** *Bear Report, 1048-6526.*

US/0009-3513
**CHICAGO BOWLER.** ***Title Change.*** Periodical. English. wk. **UDC** 796.28(773). ***Continued by*** *Chicago Bowler, Inc., 11056-3547.*

US/1056-3547
**CHICAGO BOWLER, INC, THE.** (THE CHICAGO BOWLER, INC. : WORLD'S GREATEST BOWLING WEEKLY.). **Added/Corp** Chicago Metropolitan Bowling Association. Illinois Bowling Association. **VFOAT** Chicago Bowler. (19??)-. Periodical. English. wk. $10.00. Chicago Bowler Inc., 350 West 22nd Street, Suite 109, Lombard IL 60148. **Tel** (708)629-7665. **ED** Terri Weglarz. **Ad Acc**, **Adv Mgr:** Mariann Weglarz. **Circ:** 3000 (ctrl). ***Continues*** *Chicago Bowler, 0009-3513.*

CC
**CHINA SPORTS.** **VFOAT** Chung-Kuo Ti Yu. (1980)-. Periodical. English. mo. $54.00 institution, $39.00 individual. **(Subscription address:** China Books & Periodicals Inc., 2929 24th Street, San Francisco CA 94110.**)** **LC** GV651; .C53. **DD** 796/.0951. ***Continues*** *China's Sports, 0577-8948.*
**Desc:** Keeps sports fans around the world informed on achievements in Chinese sports. Discusses the techniques and methods of training, reports on China's participation in international athletic competitions, and introduces subjects of topical interest.
**Ind/Abst** SPORT Discus; SportSearch (May 1987-).

CN/1191-4009
**CHRYSLER CUP CANADIAN HOCKEY LEAGUE EAST-WEST ALL-STAR CHALLENGE OFFICIAL GUIDE.** ***Title Change.*** [Chrysler Cup Can. Hockey Leag. East-West all-star chall. off. guide]. **Added/Corp** Canadian Hockey League. (1992)-(1992). English. Canadian Hockey League, Jim Price, 305 Milner Avenue, Suite 208, Scarborough Ontario M1B 3V4 Canada. **DD** 796.962/06/071. ***Continued by*** *Defi Coupe Chrysler de la Ligue Canadienne de Hockey, 1202-0583.*

CH
**CHUNG-HUA MIN KUO TI YU HSIEH CHIN HUI CHI KAN.** **Main/Corp** Chung-Hua Min Kuo Ti Yu Hsieh Chin Hui. **VFOAT** Republic of China Amateur Athletic Federation Quarterly. (Sept. 1973)-. Periodical. Chinese (Chinese). **LC** GV663.T3; C48A. **UDC** 796.077(529).

JA
**CHUO KEIBA NENKAN.** **See** Horses and Horsemanship.

●CN/1191-3851
**CIEL BLEU (SAINT-EDOUARD).** (CIEL BLEU.). [Ciel bleu]. (Spring 1992)-. Periodical. French. qt. Limited free distribution. L'Equipe de Redaction, Ciel Bleu, 3221 Rang Ruisseau Plat, Saint-Edouard Quebec J0K 2H0 Canada. **DD** 797.5/6/0971405.

US/0746-1127
**CINCINNATI BENGALS REPORT, THE.** **VFOAT** Bengals Report. Periodical. English. ir. $24.95. Sports News Inc, 2501 West Peterson Avenue, Chicago IL 60659. ***Continues*** *Cincinnati Bengals Weekly, 0745-2004.*

US/1052-9624
**CIRCLE TRACK.** [Circ. track]. **VFOAT** Petersen's Circle Track. Vol. 9, No. 3 (March 1990)-. Periodical. English. mo. $23.95 US; $36.33 Canada; $34.95 other. Petersen Publishing Company, 6420 Wilshire Bouldevard, Los Angeles CA 90048. **Tel** (213)782-2485. **(Subscription address:** Neodata / Colorado, PO Box 2606, Boulder Boulder CO 80322.**)** **LC** TL236; .P44. **DD** 629.228. available on microfilm from University Microfilms International (UMI). ***Continues*** *Petersen's Circle Track, 0734-5437.*

CN/0846-3492
**CITADELS NEWS.** ***Ceased.*** [Citadels news]. **Added/Corp** Halifax Citadels (Hockey Team). Vol. 1, Issue 1 (Oct. 1991)-(1992). Periodical. English. mo. Effective Communications and Marketing Ltd., PO Box 31085, Halifax Nova Scotia B3K 5T9 Canada. **DD** 796.962.

CN/0713-052X
**CLASS / CANADIAN LADIES ASSOCIATION OF SHOOTING SPORTS.** **Added/Corp** Sport Canada. Vol. 1, No. 1 (Spring 1980)-. Periodical. English. wk. Free to members. M Spinney Class, 1514-1050 Markham Road, Scarborough Ontario M1H 2Y7 Canada. **DD** 799.3/1/0971.

US/0045-7159
**CLIMBING (ASPEN, COLO.).** **See** Recreation, Leisure-Outdoor Life.

CN/0228-4839
**CLUB DES AMIS DE GILLES VILLENEUVE INC.** (LE CLUB DES AMIS DE GILLES VILLENEUVE INC. : BULLETIN.). [Club amis Gilles Villeneuve inc.]. **Main/Corp** Club des Amis de Gilles Villeneuve. V. 1, No. 1, (April 1979)-. Bulletin. French. bm. Free. Club Des Amis De Gillles Villeneuve, C.P. 1365, Place D'Armes, Montreal Quebec H2Y 3K5. **DD** 796.7/2/05. **UDC** 796.77(714). ctrl circ.

US/0160-6166
**CLUB LIVING.** (1978)-. Periodical. English. Ten times a year. Club Living Inc, 16 Copper Beech Circle, White Plains NY 10605-4702. **ED** Diana Davis Lyons. **Ad Acc**. **Circ:** 51,000 (ctrl).

NE
**COACHEN.** Dutch. ir. NFWS, Herenstraat 35, 3512 KB Utrecht Netherlands. **Tel** 011 31 030 316207.

US/0009-9880
**COACHING CLINIC, THE.** (1963)-. Periodical. English. Ten times a year. $35.00 US; $45.00 Canda; $50.00 other. Princeton Educational Publishers, PO Box 280, Plainsboro NJ 08536. **Tel** (908)297-6920. **LC** GV711; .C6. ***Continues*** *Women's Coaching Clinic, 0146-1143; Coaching Clinics Basketball Coach.*
**Ind/Abst** Phys. Educ. Index (1978-19??); SPORT Discus; SportSearch.

US/1053-1904
**COACHING CLINIC'S BASKETBALL COACH.** ***Title Change.*** [Coach. clin. basketb. coach]. **VFOAT** Basketball Coach. Vol. 22, No. 1 (Sept. 1990)-. Periodical. English. mo. Princeton Educational Publishers, PO Box 280, Plainsboro NJ 08536. **Tel** (908)297-6920. **DD** 372. ***Continues*** *Basketball Clinic, 0146-5007.* ***Merged into*** *Coaching Clinic, 0009-9880.*

AT/0814-7752
**COACHING DIRECTOR.** [Coach. dir.]. **Added/Corp** Australian Coaching Council. (1984)-. Periodical. English. qt. 12.00Aus$ Australia; 20.00Aus$ other. Australian Coaching Council, PO Box 176, Belconnen ACT 2616 Australia. **Tel** 011 61 6 2521550, FAX 011 61 6 2521200, telex 62400. **ED** Andrew Dee. **DD** 796.0770994. **Pr Rev**. **Circ:** 1,000.
**Desc:** Contains articles on all facets of coaching, developing courses, new from Australia and overseas, book reviews and so on.
**Ind/Abst** SPORT Discus.

US/0146-1265
**COACHING : MEN'S ATHLETICS.** V. 1- Jan./Feb. 1977-. Periodical. English. bm. $10.00. Drebus, 3720 Pau/Ko/Tuk Lane, Oshkosh WI 54901. **LC** GV711; .C62. **DD** 796/.077. **UDC** 796.42.071.4.

US/0894-4237
**COACHING VOLLEYBALL.** (COACHING VOLLEYBALL : OFFICIAL JOURNAL OF THE AVCA.). [Coach. volleyb.]. **Added/Corp** American Volleyball Coaches' Association. **VFOAT** CV. (1987)-. Periodical. English. Six times a year. $40.00 (institution), $20.00 (individual) US; $50.00 (institution), $40.00 (individual) other. American Volleyball Coaches Association, 1227 Lake Plaza Drive, Suite B, Colorado Springs CO 80906. **Tel** (719)576-7777, FAX (719)576-7778. **ED** Kinda S. Asher. **DD** 796. Index available. cum. index. **Bk Rev**, (Qty: 2-3). **Ad Acc**, **Adv Mgr:** Kevin Kaneshiro. **Circ:** 3,000.
**Desc:** Addresses the concerns of coaches at all levels and provides up-to-date information on the latest techniques, tactics, and issues; current sports medicine and sport science research; and new resources, equipment, and facilities.
**Ind/Abst** Phys. Educ. Index (1989-); SPORT Discus.

US/0894-4245
**COACHING WOMEN'S BASKETBALL.** (COACHING WOMEN'S BASKETBALL : OFFICIAL JOURNAL OF THE WBCA.). [Coach. women's basketb.]. **Added/Corp** Women's Basketball Coaches' Association. **VFOAT** CWB. (1987)-. Periodical. English. bm (6 issues). $30.00 (institutions), $20.00 (individuals). WBCA, 4646B Lawrenceville Highway, Lilburn GA 30247. **Tel** (404)279-8027. **ED** Scott Wikgren. **DD** 796. **Bk Rev**. **Ad Acc**. **Circ:** 545.
**Desc:** The only professional journal geared specifically to women's basketball coaches. It contains game winning techniques and tactics; mental training programs; research in the sports medicine and sport science fields; and interviews with today's leading coaches.
**Ind/Abst** Phys. Educ. Index (1989-); SPORT Discus.

US/0897-750X
**COASTAL CRUISING.** [Coast. cruis.]. Vol. 4, No. 1 (Feb./Mar. 1988)-. Periodical. English. bm. $19.75 US; $37.75 other. Nautilus Publishing Inc, 108 Middle Lane, Beaufort NC 28516-2157. **Tel** (919)728-6050, FAX (919)728-2233. **ED** Ted Jones. **DD** 797. ***Continues*** *Carolina Cruising, 0893-3723.*

US
**COFFIN CORNER: OFFICIAL NEWSLETTER/MAGAZINE OF P.F.R.A, THE.** **Added/Corp** Professional Football Researchers Association (U.S.). (19??)-. Periodical. English. Six times a year. $25.00. Professional Football Research Association, 12870 Route 30, North Huntingdon PA 15642. **Tel** (412)863-6345.
**Ind/Abst** SPORT Discus.

US/0279-1153
**COLLEGE AND JUNIOR TENNIS.** [Coll. jr. tennis]. (19??)-. Periodical. English. bm (6 issues). $18.00 (1 year), $33.00 (2 year), $45.00 (3 year) US; $24.00 (1 year), $45.00 (2 year), $63.00 (3 year) other. Junior Tennis, 100 Harbor Road, Port Washington NY 11050. **Tel** (516)883-6601. **ED** Wendy Peterson. **Bk Rev**. **Ad Acc**. **Circ:** 5,000 (ctrl). ***Continues*** *College & Jr. Tennis, 0164-5668.*
**Desc:** The only publication in the world that's specifically aimed at the college and junior tennis players. We cover all match results, biographies and any other related info-worldwide.

US/0092-881X
**COLLEGE FOOTBALL MODERN RECORD BOOK.** **Main/Corp** National Collegiate Sports Services. (19??)-. English. $2.00. National Collegiate Sports Services, 420 Lexington Avenue, New York NY 10017. **LC** GV956.8; .N37a. **DD** 796.33/263/0973.

US/1059-4825
**COLLEGE FOOTBALL TODAY.** [Coll. footb. today]. Fall (1991)-. Periodical. English. $2.95 (U.S., single issue), $3.50 (Canada, single issue). Spectator Sports, 519 8th Avenue, New York NY 10018. **DD** 796.

US/1061-6357
**COLLEGE HOCKEY.** ***Title Change.*** [Coll. hockey]. **VFOAT** College Hockey Magazine. (19??)-(19??). Periodical. English. ir (Approx. every 2 weeks during hockey season, Oct.-Apr.). Eastern College Sports, 37 Trask Road, Peabody MA 01960. **Tel** (508)531-4311. **ED** Ed Granger. **LC** WMLC 91/2962. **DD** 796. **Bk Rev**. **Ad Acc**. **Circ:** 10,000. ***Continues*** *Eastern College Hockey Magazine, 0897-4713.* ***Continued by*** *US College Hockey Magazine.*
**Desc:** Complete coverage of all divisions of ice hockey played in the Northeastern United States.

●US/1065-8270
**COLLEGE SPORTS (RUTHERFORD, N.J.).** (COLLEGE SPORTS.). [Coll. sports]. (Winter 1992)-. Periodical. English. mo. $14.97. College Sports Publishing Ltd, 51 Craigwood Road, Suite 300, Plainfield NJ 07080. **Tel** (908)753-6600. **(Subscription address:** College Sports, PO Box 1982, Danbury CT 06813.**)** **DD** 796.

US/0530-9751
**COLLEGIATE BASEBALL.** **Added/Corp** American Association of College Baseball Coaches. United States Baseball Federation. (1957)-. Periodical. English. Fourteen times a year (semi-monthly Jan-June, monthly Sept., Oct.). $18.00. Collegiate Baseball Newspapers, PO Box 50566, Tucson AZ 85703. **Tel** (602)623-4530, FAX (602)624-5501. **ED** Louis Pavlovich. **Bk Rev**, (Qty: 5-10). **Ad Acc**, **Adv Mgr:** Diane Pavlovich. **Circ:** 7,500. available on microfilm from University Microfilms International (UMI). ***Continues*** *Collegiate Baseball Digest.*
**Desc:** Covers technical and factual information on amateur baseball, conduct polls on leaders among schools and compiles statistics.

US/0748-9668
**COLLEGIATE SPORTS REPORT.** (COLLEGIATE SPORTS REPORT : AN OFFICIAL PUBLICATION OF THE INTERNATIONAL UNIVERSITY PRESS.). Vol. 1, No. 1 (Sept. 1973)-. Periodical. English. qt. $200.00. The International University Press, 1301 South Noland Road, Independence MO 64055. **Tel** (816)461-3633. **ED** John Wayne Johnston. **UDC** 796(73). ctrl circ.
**Desc:** Major sports developments related to international higher education.

## Recreation, Leisure —Sports

US/0898-4603
**COLORADO SKI INDUSTRY CHARACTERISTICS AND FINANCIAL ANALYSIS.** [Colo. ski ind. charact. financ. anal.]. **Added/Corp** University of Colorado, Boulder. Business Research Division. **VFOAT** Colorado Ski Industry. (19??)-. English. an. $30.00. Business Research Division, Campus Box 420, University of Colorado at Boulder, Boulder CO 80309-0420. **Tel** (303)492-8227, FAX (303)492-3620. **LC** GV854.5.C6; C65. **DD** 338.4/779693/09788.

US/8755-8653
**COLORADO SPORTS MONTHLY.** (19??)-. Periodical. English. mo. Colorado Sports Monthly, PO Box 3519, Evergreen CO 80439-3423. **Tel** (303)670-3700. **ED** Robert Erdmann. **Circ:** 35,000.

US/0364-071X
**COLT AMERICAN HANDGUNNING ANNUAL.** **VFOAT** Colt Handgunning. 1976-. English. an. $1.75 single issue. Aqua Field Publications Inc, 66 West Gilbert Street, Shrewsbury NJ 07702. **Tel** (201)842-8300. **LC** TS537. **DD** 799.2/0233/05. **UDC** 799.311(058)(73).

UK
**COMMERCIAL DIVER AND UNDERWATER CONTRACTOR.** English. qt. £31.80 UK; £43.60, $67.50 other. Argus Press Group, Queensway House, 2 Queensway Redhill, Surrey RH1 1QS England. **Tel** 011 44 737 768611, 011 44 737 761685, FAX 011 44 737 760510, telex 948669 TOPJNL G.

SZ
**COMMUNICATION - INTERNATIONAL SKATING UNION.** **Main/Corp** International Skating Union. (19??)-. Multiple languages (English, French and German). 40.00F. International Skating Union, Postfach 7270, Davos-Platz Switzerland. **Tel** 083 37577, FAX 083 36671, telex 853123 ISU CH. **ED** Beat Hasler. **LC** GV849; .I59a. **DD** 769.9/1/0601. **Bk Rev. Circ:** 1,700 (ctrl).
**Desc:** Includes 54 new melodies and titles that have been carefully chosen and tested in the presence of international trainers and dance couples with a view to character, rhythm and sound.
**Ind/Abst** SPORT Discus; SportSearch (May 1987-).

CN/0226-8701
**COMMUNIQUE - SYNCHRO SWIM CANADA.** [Commun. - Synchro Swim Can.]. **Main/Corp** Canadian Amateur Synchronized Swimming Association. No. 1- Jan. 1979-. Periodical. English (French). Five times a year. Free to members. Canadian Amateur Synchronized, 1600 James Naismith Drive, Gloucester Ontario K1B 5N4 Canada. **Tel** (613)748-5674, FAX (613)748-5724, telex 053-3660. **ED** Barbara Theman. **DD** 797.2/1/06071. **UDC** 797.217.2(71). **Ad Acc. Circ:** 2,700 (ctrl).
**Desc:** A newsletter for members of Synchro Canada. Provides reports on events and people in the sport as well as upcoming items of interest.

UK/0263-6697
**COMPASS SPORT/THE ORIENTEER.** [Compass sport/orienteer]. (1982)-. Periodical. English. Eight times a year. £15.50 UK; £17.00 other. Compass Sport, 37 Sandycombe Road, Twickenham TW1 2LR United Kingdom. **Tel** 011 44 81 8929429. **(Subscription address:** Compass Sport, 25 The Hermitage Eliot Hill, London SE13 7EH United Kingdom.) **DD** 796.505. **Formed by the union of** Compass Sport and Orienteer, 0306-0705.
**Ind/Abst** SPORT Discus.

US
**COMPETITION RULES FOR ATHLETICS / ATHLETICS CONGRESS USA.** **VFOAT** Competition Rules. English. sa. $8.00. TAC/USA Book, PO Box 120, Indianapolis IN 46206. **Tel** (317)297-2900. **ED** Heliodoro R Rico. **LC** GV1060.67; .C65. **UDC** 796.42.063(73).
**Desc:** Includes rules of competition for track and field, long distance running and race walking-senior, junior, youth athletics and masters. Also includes adaptations to rules of competition for individuals with disabilities.

SA/1015-8014
**COMPLEAT GOLFER.** [Compleat golf.]. (1989)-. Periodical. English. Eleven times a year (Except Feb.). R59.80 South Africa; R78.00 North America. Compleat Golfer Pty Ltd., PO Box 55231, 2116 Northlands South Africa. **Tel** 011 27 11 8837820, FAX 011 27 11 8835872. **ED** Dennis Bruyns (phone: (011) 8837820). **UDC** 796.352. cum. index. **Bk Rev. Ad Acc. Adv Mgr:** Dale Hayes, **Tel** 011 8837820. **Circ:** 30,000 (ctrl).
**Desc:** This golf magazine gives instruction and information journal for golfers. It also the official journal of South Africa PGA.

US/0885-9183
**COMPLETE BASEBALL RECORD BOOK, THE.** (1986)-. Periodical. English. an. $16.95. Sporting News, c/o Sharon Moore, 1212 North Lindbergh Boulevard, PO Box 56, St Louis MO 63166. **Tel** (314)997-7111, (800)825-8508. **(Subscription address:** Contemporary Books, Two Prudential Plaza, Suite 1200, Chicago IL 60601.) **LC** GV877; .C66. **DD** 796.357/0973. **Formed by the union of** Official Baseball Dope Book, 0162-5411; Official Baseball Record Book (Saint Louis, MO. : 1982), 0162-5438 and Official World Series Records, 0078-3900.
**Desc:** Contains major league baseball records.

US/1058-3823
**COMPLETE BOOK OF AUTOPISTOLS : BUYER'S GUIDE.** [Complete book autopistols buy. guide]. **VFOAT** A.Complete book of autopistols. Vol. 1, No. 1 (1991)-. Periodical. English. sa. $4.95 US; $5.95 Canada. Harris Publications, 1115 Broadway/8th Floor, New York NY 10010. **Tel** (212)807-7100. **LC** TS537; .C617. **DD** 683.4/32.

●US/1072-8457
**COMPLETE GUIDE TO .38/.357.** **Added/Corp** Petersen Publishing Company. **VFOAT** Complete Guide to .38 .357. (1994)-. English. $3.95. Petersen Publishing Company, 6420 Wilshire Bouldevard, Los Angeles CA 90048. **Tel** (213)782-2485.

●US/1059-5716
**COMPLETE GUIDE TO 45'S.** (1992)-. English. $3.95. Petersen Publishing Company, 6420 Wilshire Bouldevard, Los Angeles CA 90048. **Tel** (213)782-2485.

US/0149-0168
**COMPLETE HANDBOOK OF COLLEGE FOOTBALL, THE.** (1977)-. English. ir. $2.25 single issue. The New American Library, PO Box 999, Bergenfield NJ 07621. **LC** GV951; .C63. **DD** 796.33/263/0973.

US
**COMPLETE HANDBOOK OF PRO BASKETBALL, THE.** English. New American Library, 120 Woodbine Street, Bergenfield NJ 07621. **Tel** (201)387-0600. **LC** GV885.55; .C64. **DD** 796.32/364/0973. **UDC** 796.323.071(73).

US/0361-2988
**COMPLETE HANDBOOK OF PRO FOOTBALL, THE.** (1975)-. English. an. New American Library, 120 Woodbine Street, Bergenfield NJ 07621. **Tel** (201)387-0600. **LC** GV955; .C64. **DD** 796.33/264/0973.

US/0363-6046
**COMPLETE HANDBOOK OF SOCCER, THE.** 1976-. English. an. $1.95. New American Library, 120 Woodbine Street, Bergenfield NJ 07621. **Tel** (201)387-0600. **LC** GV944.U5; C64. **DD** 796.33/4/0973.

US/0749-9248
**COMPLETE HANDBOOK OF THE OLYMPIC GAMES, THE.** [Complet. handb. Olymp. games]. English. ir. $4.50. New American Library, 120 Woodbine Street, Bergenfield NJ 07621. **Tel** (201)387-0600. **LC** GV721.5; .C615. **DD** 796.4/8/05.

US
**COMPLETE HANDBOOK OF THE OLYMPIC WINTER GAMES, THE.** English. ir. $3.50. New American Library, 120 Woodbine Street, Bergenfield NJ 07621. **Tel** (201)387-0600. **LC** GV841.5; .C66. **DD** 796.9/8/05.

US/1052-7133
**COMPLETE HOCKEY BOOK.** [Complete hockey book]. **VFOAT** Hockey Book; Sporting News Complete Hockey Book. (1991)-. Periodical. English. an. $17.95. Sporting News, c/o Sharon Moore, 1212 North Lindbergh Boulevard, PO Box 56, St Louis MO 63166. **Tel** (314)997-7111, (800)825-8508. **(Subscription address:** Contemporary Books, Two Prudential Plaza, Suite 1200, Chicago IL 60601.) **LC** GV847.5; .C66. **DD** 796.962/0973. **Formed by the union of** Hockey Guide, 0278-4955 and Hockey Register, 0090-2292.
**Desc:** Statistics and facts from the National Hockey League to college play, including award winners, rosters, schedules, and career statistics.

US/1071-8958
**COMPLETE SUPER BOWL BOOK, THE.** [Complete super bowl book]. **VFOAT** Sporting News Complete Super Bowl Book. (1991)-. Periodical. English. an. $12.95. Sporting News, c/o Sharon Moore, 1212 North Lindbergh Boulevard, PO Box 56, St Louis MO 63166. **Tel** (314)997-7111, (800)825-8508. **(Subscription address:** Contemporary Books, Two Prudential Plaza, Suite 1200, Chicago IL 60601.) **LC** GV956.2.S8; S89. **DD** 796.332/648. **Continues** Super Bowl Book, 0275-4487.

US/1057-6908
**CONDITIONING FOR CYCLING.** Ceased. [Cond. cycl.]. **Added/Corp** National Strength & Conditioning Association (U.S.). Vol. 1, No. 1 (Summer 1991)-(19??). Periodical. English. qt. National Strength Conditioning Association, PO Box 81410, Lincoln NE 68501. **Tel** (402)472-3000, FAX (402)476-6976. **LC** WMLC 91/1439. **DD** 796.
**Ind/Abst** SPORT Discus.

CN/0229-5156
**CONGRESS ... PROCEEDINGS - FEDERATION DES SPORTS DU CANADA.** (CONGRESS... : PROCEEDINGS.). [Congr. ... proc. - Fed. sports Can.]. **Main/Corp** Federation des Sports du Canada. Congres. **VFOAT** Congres : Compte Rendus. Proceedings. French. an. Federation des Sports du Canada, 333 Chemin River, Vanier Ontario K1L 8B9 Canada. **DD** 796/.06/071.

FR
**CONNAISSANCE DE LA CHASSE.** Periodical. French. 114.00F. Editions Lariviere Naryse Menn, 15 17 Quai de l Oise Sec. Abonn., 75166 Paris Cedex 19 France. **Tel** 011 33 1 40342207, FAX 33 1 40358441, telex 211678. **LC** SK1; .C66. **DD** 799.2/05.

CN/0834-3055
**CONSTITUTION, BY-LAWS, REGULATIONS, HISTORY / CANADIAN AMATEUR HOCKEY ASSOCIATION.** [Const. by-laws regul. hist. - Can. Amat. Hockey Assoc.]. **Main/Corp** Canadian Amateur Hockey Association. (1985/86)-. English. an. Canadian Amateur Hockey Association, 1600 Promenade James Naismith, Gloucester Ontario K1B 5N4 Canada. **Tel** (613)748-5617. **DD** 796.96/2/06. **Formed by the union of** C.A.H.A. Regulations, 0831-0904 and Constitution, By-Laws, History - Canadian Amateur Hockey Association, 0317-9540.

US
**CONVERSE BASKETBALL YEARBOOK.** English. an. Converse Rubber Company, 55 Fordham Road, Wilmington MA 01887. **Tel** (617)657-5500. **LC** GV885.

US/0591-0374
**CORD SPORTFACTS HOCKEY GUIDE.** (19??)-. English. Cord Communications Corporation, 130 West 42nd Street, New York NY 10036. **Tel** (212)840-0660. **LC** GV846; .C65. **DD** 796.9/62/05.

US/0092-8216
**CORD SPORTFACTS HUNTING.** See Recreation, Leisure-Outdoor Life.

US/0197-7105
**CORD SPORTFACTS PRO FOOTBALL GUIDE.** **Added/Corp** Cord Communications Corporation. **VFOAT** Pro Football Guide. (19??)-. English. Cord Communications Corporation, 130 West 42nd Street, New York NY 10036. **Tel** (212)840-0660. **LC** GV955.5.N35; C67. **DD** 796.332/64/0973.

CN/0227-6909
**COUP D'OEIL SUR L'HALTEROPHILIE.** [Coup oeil halterophilie]. Periodical. French. Four times a year. $16.00 US. Federation d'Halterophilie du Quebec, 4545 Ave Pierre de Coubertin, CP 1000 Succursale M, Montreal Quebec H1V 3R2 Canada. **Tel** (514)252-3046, telex 05829647 SECADMIBEC. **DD** 796.4/1/09714. **Bk Rev. Ad Acc.**
**Desc:** Political aspects of federation.
**Ind/Abst** Point Repere (19??-19??); SPORT Discus; SportSearch.

FR
**COURSES ET ELEVAGE.** Periodical. French (English). bm. $80.00 US. Union Natl Interprofessionnell Cheval, 51 rue Dumont d'Urville, 75116 Paris France. **Tel** (4)500 03 10, telex 612-292 EQUUS. **Bk Rev. Ad Acc. Circ:** 8,500.
**Desc:** Racing and breeding of bloodhorses for flat, jump and trot.

US/0956-5620
**CRICKET LIFE INTERNATIONAL.** Periodical. English. mo. $49.00. South Publications Ltd, 230 Park Avenue, The Helmsley/Suite 932, New York NY 10169. **Tel** (212)682-8714, FAX (212)697-8280, telex 710-581-3722 TRIMED NYK. **ED** Shahed Sadullah. **Circ:** 50,000.
**Desc:** The only professional magazine to provide full and balanced coverage of the world game, from domestic competitions in cricket planning countries to the Middle East and outposts of the game like the U.S., Canada, Africa, and the Far East.

AT
**CRICKETER.** Ceased. (19??)-(April 1994). English. ir. David Syme & Co. Ltd., PO Box 257C, Melbourne VIC 3001 Australia. **Tel** 011 61 3 6012005. **(Subscription address:** Syme Magazines, GPO 55A, Melbourne VIC 3001 Australia)
**Ind/Abst** SPORT Discus.

UK/0266-7398
**CRICKETER INTERNATIONAL.** [Cricket. int.]. (1974)-. Periodical. English. mo. £27.00 UK, Channel Islands, BFPO; £34.40 other. Cricketer Ltd, Beech Hanger, Ashurst Tunbridge, Wells Kent TN3 9ST, England. **Tel** 011 44 892 740256. **DD** 796.358. **Continues** Cricketer, 0011-1260.
**Ind/Abst** SPORT Discus.

UK/0266-7401
**CRICKETER QUARTERLY FACTS AND FIGURES.** [Cricket q. facts fig.]. **VFOAT** Cricketer Quarterly; Cricketer International Quarterly Facts and Figures. (1974)-. Periodical. English. qt. £11.70 UK; £11.80 other. Cricketer Ltd, Beech Hanger, Ashurst Tunbridge, Wells Kent TN3 9ST, England. **Tel** 011 44 892 740256. **DD** 790.1.

US/0746-083X
**CROSS COUNTRY JOURNAL.** (1983)-. Periodical. English. bm. $23.00 (one year), $41.00 (two year), $56.00 (three years) US; $29.00 (one year), $47.00 (two years), $62.00 (three year) other (includes postage). Sunrise Valley Press, PO Box 1004, Austin TX 55912. **Tel** (800)828-1231, (507)433-6562.

US/0278-9213
**CROSS COUNTRY SKIER.** [Cross ctry. skier]. Vol. 1, No. 1 (Oct. 1981)-. Periodical. English. Five times a year. $14.97 (one year), $23.97 (two year). Collins Chase Publishers, 1823 Freemont Avenue South, Minneapolis MN 55403. **Tel** (612)377-0312. **(Subscription address:** Kable Publishers Aide, 308 East Hitt Street, Mt. Morris, IL 61054**) ED** James C. McCullagh. **LC** GV854.4; .C74. **DD** 796.93/0973. **Ad Acc. Circ:** 45,000. available on microfilm from University Microfilms International (UMI). ***Continues** Nordic Skiing, 0164-6974.*
**Desc:** America's leading nordic magazine for skiers of all levels. The latest on products and equipment, and information on training technique, touring and cross country vacations.
**Ind/Abst** SPORT Discus; SportSearch (May 1987-).

US/0273-9135
**CROSSFACE, THE.** ***Title Change.*** Periodical. English. ir. Stoughton Newspapers Inc, 301 W Main Street, PO Box 577, Stoughton WI 53589. **Tel** (608)873-6671. **ED** Russel Hellickson and Nancy Hellickson. **Ad Acc. Circ:** 2,500. ***Continued by** Wisconsin Crossface.*
**Desc:** All styles and levels of wrestling are covered with emphasis on Wisconsin.

US/1061-6519
**CROSSWORDS (WALNUT CREEK, CALIF.).** **See** Motorcycles.

US
**CSSS DIGEST : CENTER FOR THE STUDY OF SPORT IN SOCIETY.** **Added/Corp** Northeastern University Center for the Study of Sport in Society. Vol. 1, No. 1 (Oct. 1988)-. English. Three times a year. $10.00. CSSS, Northeastern University, 271 Huntington Avenue, CP 161, Boston MA 02115. **Tel** (617)373-4025, FAX (617)552-3199. **ED** Tina Leduc. ctrl circ.
**Desc:** Review of recent events in the world of sports which pertain to contemporary social issues.
**Ind/Abst** SPORT Discus.

CN/0828-9034
**CURLING CANADA.** [Curl. Can.]. 1983/84-. English. an. $2.00 (each volume). National All-Sport Promotions, 1623 Yonge Street, Toronto Ontario M4T 2A1 Canada. **DD** 796.9/6. ***Continues** Curling Canada Magazine, 0828-9026.*
**Ind/Abst** SportSearch (May 1987-).

US
**CURRENT BASEBALL PUBLICATIONS.** **See** Recreation, Leisure-Abstracting, Bibliographies and Statistics.

UK
**CYCLE INDUSTRY.** **See** Economics-Industry and Production.

US/1049-8990
**CYCLING SCIENCE.** **See** Bicycles and Bicycling.

UK/0143-0238
**CYCLING WORLD.** [Cycling world]. (1979)-. Periodical. English. Eleven times a year (Dec./Jan. issues combined). £20.00 UK; £30.00 others. Stone Leisure Limited, Andrew House, 2A Granville Road, Sidcup Kent DA14 4BN England. **Tel** 011 44 81 3026150, FAX 011 44 81 3002315. **Bk Rev**, (Qty: 4). **Ad Acc**, **Adv Mgr Tel** 011 41 332 874731. ctrl circ.

US/0160-2543
**CYNEGETICUS.** Vol. 1 (Jan. 1977)-. Academic Scholarly Publication. English. qt. $6.00. Cynegeticus, Box 315, Helena MT 59624. **Tel** (406)227-8766. **ED** Douglas C. Stange. **Bk Rev**.
**Desc:** A bibliographical resource and scholarly vehicle devoted to an interdisciplinary approach to the discussion and exploration of hunting.

PL/0867-3993
**CZARNY PAS.** [Czarny Pas]. (1989)-. Polish. mo. Price on Request. **(Subscription address:** ARS Polona, PO Box 1001, 00068 Warsaw Poland.**) UDC** 796.8.

US/0011-4707
**D.A.C. NEWS.** **Main/Corp** Detroit Athletic Club. **Added/Corp** Detroit Athletic Club. **VAT** Detroit Athletic Club News. (19??)-. Periodical. English. Nine times a year. Detroit Athletic Club, 241 Madison Avenue, Detroit MI 48226. **Tel** (313)963-5993. **ED** John H. Worthington. **Ad Acc. Circ:** 4,000 (ctrl).
**Desc:** A glossy, four-color magazine, ranging 48-84 pages, containing national and local advertising. Contents directed to mostly male membership with club social activities, sports, travel, health, and dining.

US/0745-0370
**DALLAS COWBOYS OFFICIAL WEEKLY.** **VFOAT** Dallas Cowboys Weekly; Dallas Cowboys. (198?)-. Periodical. English. Thirty-two times a year (weekly during football season; 6 monthly issues off-season). $29.95 (one year), $51.00 (two year), $72.00 (three year). Dallas Cowboys, Cowboys Center, One Cowboys Parkway, Irving TX 75063. **Tel** (214)556-9900. **ED** Steve Perkins. **Ad Acc. Circ:** 83,075 (ctrl). ***Continues** Official Dallas Cowboys Weekly.*
**Desc:** Complete coverage of all cowboy's games, individual player stories, past and present, and a section on the Dallas Cowboy cheerleaders.

UK/0140-6000
**DARTS WORLD.** [Darts world]. (19??)-. Periodical. English. mo. £30.00 (one year), £72.00 (two year). Darts World, 9 Kelsley Park Road, Beckenham Kent BR3 2LH England. **Tel** 011 44 81 650 6580, FAX 011 44 81 681 6492. **ED** A. J. Wood. **Bk Rev**. **Ad Acc. Circ:** 28,000.
**Desc:** International magazine covering all aspects of the sport of darts.
**Ind/Abst** SportSearch (May 1987-).

AT/0817-1440
**DATASPORT.** [Datasport]. **Added/Corp** Australia. Dept. of Sport, Recreation and Tourism. (1986)-. Periodical. English. qt. Free on request. Australian Sports Commission, PO Box 176, Belconnen Australian Capital Territory, 2616 Australia. **Tel** 011 61 62 521594, FAX 011 61 62 521681, telex AA 62400. **DD** 790.06894.
**Ind/Abst** SPORT Discus.

US/0147-1295
**DAVE CAMPBELL'S ARKANSAS FOOTBALL.** **VFOAT** Arkansas Football. (19??)-. Periodical. English. Twenty times a year. $15.00. Host Communications Inc., 1300 West Mockingbird Lane, Suite 444, Dallas TX 75247. **Tel** (214)631-1160.

US/0147-1287
**DAVE CAMPBELL'S TEXAS FOOTBALL.** [Dave Campbell's Tex. footb.]. **VFOAT** Texas Football. (1960)-. Periodical. English. an. $17.50. Host Communications Inc., 1300 West Mockingbird Lane, Suite 444, Dallas TX 75247. **Tel** (214)631-1160. **ED** Dave Campbell. **DD** 796. **Ad Acc. Circ:** 100,000.
**Desc:** Coverage of football in the SWC.

US/1051-1849
**DAVE HEEREN'S BASKETBALL ABSTRACT.** [Dave Heeren's basketb. abstr.]. **VFOAT** Basketball Abstract. (1990/91)-. English. an. $12.95. Prentice-Hall General Reference and Travel, 200 Old Tappan Road, Old Tappan NJ 07675. **Tel** (800)922-0579. **ED** Dave Heeren. **DD** 796. ***Continues** Basketball Abstract, 1053-1645.*
**Desc:** Features up-to-the-minute ratings of professional and college players, teams, and coaches. Supplies stats based on Heeren's revolutionary and highly regarded Tendex rating system, used by many NBA teams for scouting and salary negotiations. It is the only book that publishes ratings of college players and coaches.

US/1059-3063
**DEAF SPORTS REVIEW.** [Deaf sports rev.]. **Added/Corp** American Athletic Association of the Deaf. **VFOAT** Sports Review; American Athletic Association of the Deaf / Deaf Sports Review; AAAD Deaf Sports Review. Vol. 1, No. 1 (July 1991)-. Periodical. English. qt. $12.00. American Athletic Association of the Deaf, 3607 Washington Blvd., Suite 4, Ogden UT 84403. **Tel** (801)393-7916 TDD. **ED** Shirley H. Platt (editor's phone: (801)393-8710). **LC** WMLC 91/5151. **DD** 796. **Ad Acc.**

US/0732-457X
**DELLBOOK OF SUPERWINNERS, THE.** [DellBook superwinners]. **Added/Corp** Dell Publishing Company. **VFOAT** Superwinners. (19??)-. English. an. Dell Publishing Company Inc., 1540 Broadway, 9th Floor, New York NY 10036-4021. **Tel** (212)782-8532, FAX (212)782-8338. **LC** GV1201.6; .D44. **DD** 001.4/4/0973.

CU
**DEPORTE, EL.** Periodical. Spanish (summaries and/or abstracts in English and French). mo. $0.30 single issue. Empresa de Medios de Propaganda Deportiva Inder, Apartado Postal No 5104, La Habana Cuba. **LC** GV592.C9; D46. **DD** 796/.097291.

US/0199-5928
**DERBY (NORMAN, OKLA.).** ***Ceased.*** **See** Horses and Horsemanship.

CN/0711-3331
**DESK-REFERENCE DIRECTORY.** (DESK-REFERENCE DIRECTORY = GUIDE DE L'ACHETEUR.). [Desk-ref. dir.]. **VFOAT** Guide de l'Acheteur. **VAT** Guide de l'Acheteur (Toronto); Guide de l'Acheteur (Collingwood). (1979)-. Directory. English (French). Jim Rennie's Sports Letter, Box 1000, Collingwood Ontario L9Y 4L4 Canada. **Tel** (705)445-7161, FAX (705)445-8650. **ED** Jim Rennie and Sheila Johnston. **DD** 338.4/7796/02571.

CN/0229-7906
**DESPORTO (TORONTO, ONT.).** (DESPORTO : REVISTA LUSO-CANADIANA DE DESPORTO : PORTUGUESE CANADIAN SPORTS MAGAZINE.). [Desporto]. Vol. 1, No. 1 (July 1977)-. Periodical. Portuguese. wk. Portuguese Business Promotions, Toronto Ontario M6K 2B2 Canada. **DD** 796/.08969071.

GW/0323-8628
**DEUTSCHES SPORTECHO AUSGABE A.** [Dtsch. Sportecho, A]. Newspaper. German. da. DM142.80. Sportverlag, Neustaedtische Kirchstr 15, D 10117 Berlin Germany. **UDC** 79.

GW/0232-4814
**DEUTSCHES SPORTECHO AUSGABE B.** [Dtsch. Sportecho, B]. Newspaper. German. da. DM142.80. Sportverlag, Neustaedtische Kirchstr 15, D 10117 Berlin Germany. **UDC** 79.

US/1054-2213
**DICK VITALE'S BASKETBALL.** [Dick Vitale's basketb.]. **VFOAT** Basketball. English. an. $4.95. Preview Publishing, PO Box 19200, Seattle WA 98119. **Tel** (206)282-2322. **LC** WMLC L 83/9178. **DD** 796.

US
**DIRECTORY / AMATEUR ATHLETIC UNION OF THE UNITED STATES.** **Main/Corp** Amateur Athletic Union of the United States. (19??)-. Directory. English. an. $10.00. Amateur Athletic Union / AAU, 3400 West 86th Street, PO Box 68207, Indianapolis IN 46268. **Tel** (317)872-2900, FAX (317)875-0548. ctrl circ.
**Desc:** A membership directory.

UK
**DIRECTORY & CALENDAR / IAAF.** **Main/Corp** International Amateur Athletic Federation. **VFOAT** Directory and Calendar. (19??)-. Directory. English. an. £7.00 UK; $14.00 North America. International Amateur Athletic Federation, 3 Hans Crescent Knightsbridge, London SW1X OLN England. **Tel** 011 44 71 5818771, FAX 011 44 71 5845907, telex 9419338. **ED** Ms Jo Dick. **LC** GV563; .I74414. **DD** 796/.06/025. Index available. ctrl circ. ***Continues** I.A.A.F. Directory.*
**Desc:** Contains names and addresses of IAAF member federations as well as extensive details of world track and field meets.

CN/0706-697X
**DIRECTORY - CANADIAN INTERUNIVERSITY ATHLETIC UNION.** **Main/Corp** Canadian Interuniversity Athletic Union. **VFOAT** Repertoire - Union Sportive Interuniversitaire Canadienne; Annuaire. 1978/79-. Directory. English (French). an. Free to members. Canadian Interuniversity Athletic Union, 333 River Road Canada. **DD** 796/.025/71.

US/0273-5172
**DIRECTORY - FORUM COMMITTEE ON THE ENTERTAINMENT AND SPORTS INDUSTRIES.** **See** Law.

SZ
**DIRECTORY OF ADDRESSES - FEDERATION INTERNATIONALE DE FOOTBALL ASSOCIATION.** **Main/Corp** Football Association International Federation. Directory. English. 8.00F. Fifa-House, Hitziwet 11, CH-8032 Zurich Switzerland. **LC** GV943.55.F65; F66A. **DD** 796.33/2/0601.

US/0270-3815
**DIRECTORY OF NEW ENGLAND SKI TOURING CENTERS, A.** [Dir. N. Engl. ski tour. cent.]. (1979)-. English. an. Puckerbrush Press, PO Box 28, East Longmeadow MA 01028. **LC** GV854.5.N35; D57. **DD** 796.93/025/74.
**Desc:** Information on cross-country skiing & ski resorts .

UK
**DIRECTORY OF SCOTTISH SPORTS.** Directory. English. **LC** GV605.2; .D57. **DD** 796/.06/025411.

US
**DIRECTORY OF WOMEN IN SPORTS BUSINESS, THE.** (1991)-. Directory. English. Women's Sports Guide, PO Box 1417, Princeton NJ 08524.

CN/0713-6781
**DIRECTORY / ONTARIO AMATEUR FOOTBALL ASSOCIATION.** [Dir. - Ont. Amat. Footb. Assoc.]. **Main/Corp** Ontario Amateur Football Association. Directory. English. an. $10.00. Ontario Amateur Football Association, 1220 Sheppard Avenue East, Willowdale Ontario M2K 2X1 Canada. **Tel** (416)495-4290, FAX (416)495-4310, telex 06-986157

OSAC TOR. **ED** Jennifer Bennett. **DD** 796.33/5/060713. **Ad Acc.** ctrl circ.
**Desc:** Listing of amateur football board of directors, regional executives, member flag, tackle and touch leagues, associate and high school members, provincial association contacts and related football contacts.

CN/0229-3161
**DIRECTORY - SPORTS FEDERATION OF CANADA.** (DIRECTORY.). [Dir. - Sports Fed. Can.]. **Main/Corp** Sports Federation of Canada. **Added/Corp** National Sport and Recreation Centre. **VFOAT** Repertoire Sports; Sports Directory. **VAT** Directory - Sports Federation of Canada; Directory - Federation des Sports du Canada; Repertoire Sports - Federation des Sports du Canada; Recreation Directory - Sports Federation of Canada. (1970)-. Directory. English (French). an. 15.00Can$. Sports Federation of Canada, 333 River Road, Vanier Ontario K1L 8B9 Canada. **Tel** (613)748-5670, FAX 613-748-5706. **ED** Margaret J. Barber. **DD** 796/.025/71. **Ad Acc.**
**Desc:** The only who's who and where of Canadian amateur sports. Abstracts on some associations and support services included. Media listings and professional sport included as well.

US/1060-4804
**DIRT WHEELS.** [Dirt wheels]. **VFOAT** Dirt Wheels Magazine. (19??)-. Periodical. English. mo. $18.98 (one year), $35.95 (two year). Hi-Torque Publications, PO Box 9502, Mission Hills CA 91395. **Tel** (805)295-1910. **DD** 796. ***Continues*** *Dirt Wheels Magazine, 0745-0192.*

US/0745-0192
**DIRT WHEELS MAGAZINE.** ***Title Change.*** [Dirt wheels mag.]. **VFOAT** Dirt Wheels. (19??)-(19??). Periodical. English. mo. Hi-Torque Publications Inc, 10600 Sepulveda Boulevard, PO Box 9502, Mission Hills CA 91345-9502. **Tel** (818)365-6831, FAX (818)361-4512. **ED** Dennis Cox. **DD** 796. **Ad Acc. Circ:** 110,000. ***Continued by*** *Dirt Wheels, 1060-4804.*
**Desc:** Directed to three- and four-wheel ATV enthusiasts; includes race coverage, technical articles, testing and riding tips.

US/1067-098X
**DISABLED OUTDOORS MAGAZINE.** **See** Physically Impaired.

US/1055-4785
**DISC GOLF JOURNAL.** (1991)-. Periodical. English. bm. $20.00. The Disc Connection, 1801 Richardson Drive, Number 6, Urbana IL 61801.

US/0747-9956
**DISC SPORTS.** ***Ceased.*** **VFOAT** International Disc Sports Magazine. (Oct. 1983)-?. Periodical. English. bm. Sports Ink Magazines Inc, 2 South Park Place, PO Box 159, Fair Haven VT 05743-1223. **Tel** (802)265-3533, FAX (802)265-4746. **ED** Robert Gray. **Bk Rev. Ad Acc. Circ:** 15,000 (ctrl).
**Desc:** The international magazine for flying games.

US/1061-3323
**DIVE TRAINING.** [Dive train.]. Vol. 1, No. 1 (Nov. 1991)-. Periodical. English. mo. Dive Training Ltd., 405 Main Street, Parkville MO 64152-3737. **LC** WMLC 91/2861. **DD** 797.

UK
**DIVER.** **Added/Corp** British Sub-Aqua Club. (19??)-. Periodical. English. mo. £30.00 (1 year), £55.00 (2 year). Eaton Publications, 55 High Street Teddington, Middlesex TW11 8HA England. **Tel** 011 44 81 943-4288, FAX 011 44 81 943-4312. **ED** Bernard Eaton. **LC** GV840.S78; T75. **DD** 797.2/3. **Bk Rev. Ad Acc. Circ:** 39,376 (ctrl). ***Continues*** *Triton;* ***Absorbed*** *Underwater World (March 1982).*
**Desc:** Diving and underwater exploration and discovery.
**Ind/Abst** SPORT Discus; SportSearch (May 1987-).

CN/0700-3994
**DIVER DOWN.** Fall 1975-. Periodical. English. qt. Free. New Brunswick Underwater Council, PO Box 382, Chatham NB E1N 3A7 Canada. **DD** 797.2/3/062715. ctrl circ.

CN/0706-5132
**DIVER MAGAZINE.** [Diver mag.]. **VFOAT** Diver; Diver. Vol. 4, No. 6 (August 1978)-. Periodical. English. Nine times a year. 23.50Can$ Canada; 26.75Can$ other. Seagraphic Publications Ltd., 295-10991 Shellbridge Way, Richmond British Columbia V6X 3C6 Canada. **Tel** (604)273-4333, FAX (604)273-0813. **ED** Stephanie Bold. **DD** 797.2/3/05. Index available. **Bk Rev. Ad Acc, Adv Mgr Tel** (604)273-4333. **Circ:** 20,000 (ctrl). ***Continues*** *Diver and Underwater Adventure, 0704-5220;* ***Absorbed*** *Diver Travel Annual, 0820-9952.*
**Desc:** Sport diving in North America and abroad with emphasis on destinations, photography, marine life equipment, education and safety and shipwreck adventures, highlighting the histories of the wrecks.

US/0273-8589
**DIVER (PORTLAND CONN.), THE.** (THE DIVER.). [Diver]. Vol. 1 (Nov./Dec. 1980)-. Periodical. English. bm. $15.00 (1 year), $28.00 (2 year) US; $20.00 (1 year) other. Taylor Publishing / Portland, PO Box 313, Portland CT 06480. **Tel** (203)342-4730, FAX (203)342-1977. **ED** Bob Taylor. **DD** 797. **Bk Rev**, (Qty: 2). **Ad Acc. Circ:** 3,000.
**Desc:** Everything to do with platform and springboard diving: results, profiles, etc.

US/8755-5573
**DIVER'S ALMANAC.** (DIVER'S ALMANAC : SCUBA DIVING ON THE WEST COAST.). **VFOAT** Scuba Diving on the West Coast. 1st Ed. (1984)-. English. $11.95. Adventure Series Productions, Diver's Almanac, PO Box 1119, Jacksonville OR 97530. **LC** GV840.S78; D55. **DD** 797.2/3. **UDC** 797.215.

CN/0846-0477
**DIVERS FREE PRESS.** [Divers free press]. Vol. 0, No. 1 (Summer 1990)-. Periodical. English. qt. Free to members of diving clubs. Atlantic Diver, PO Box 8216, St. John's, Newfoundland A1B 3N4 Canada. **DD** 797.2/3/0971.

●US/1062-1210
**DIVING & SNORKELING QUARTERLY.** **VFOAT** Diving and Snorkeling Quarterly; Aqua Field Diving and Snorkeling; Aqua-Field Diving & Snorkeling. (Spring 1992)-. English. qt. Aqua Field Publications Inc, 66 West Gilbert Street, Shrewsbury NJ 07702. **Tel** (201)842-8300. **LC** WMLC 91/3833. **DD** 797.

●US/1063-0767
**DIVING (BLOOMSBURG, PA.).** (DIVING.). (1992)-. Periodical. English. bm. $15.00. Underwater USA, 3185 Lackawanna Avenue, Bloomsburg PA 17815. **Tel** (717)784-6081, (800)422-1164 PENNSYLVANIA, FAX (717)784-9226.

US/1042-1343
**DIVING WORLD (VAN NUYS, CALIF.).** (DIVING WORLD.). [Diving world]. Vol. 1 No. 1 (1988)-. Periodical. English. mo. $14.00. Diving World, 7628 Densmore Avenue, Van Nuys CA 91406. **Tel** (818)782-7328, FAX (818)782-7450. **ED** Barbara Feiner, Marie Nordberg. **DD** 797. **Ad Acc. Circ:** 11,000 (ctrl).
**Desc:** Editorial consists of how-to and retail-related articles written by experienced divers, diving industry professionals, and retail experts / consultants.

UK/0264-9691
**DOCKLANDS NEWS.** **See** Business.

US/0279-4144
**DOG SPORTS.** **See** Pets.

FR
**DOJO ARTS MARTIAUX.** ***Ceased.*** (19??)-(Aug. 1993). French. Eleven times a year. Siam Abonnement, 54 rue Rene Boulanger, 75010 Paris France. **Tel** 011 33 1 42457474.

US/0744-3226
**DOLPHIN DIGEST.** **See** Newspapers.

SP
**DON BALON.** (19??)-. Periodical. Spanish. wk. 26260ptas Spain; 15600ptas US; 32760ptas Europe. Editorial Don Balon, Av Diagonal 435 10 2A, E 08036 Barcelona, Spain. **Tel** 011 34 3 2092000.

US/1050-2262
**DOUBLE-GUN JOURNAL, THE.** [Double-gun j.]. **VFOAT** Double Gun Journal; D.G.J.; DGJ. Vol. 1, Issue 1 (Winter 1989)-. Periodical. English. qt (Mar., June, Sept., Dec.). $28.00 US; $38.00 Canada; $40.00 other. Double-Gun Journal Inc., Route 1 Box 319, East Jordan MI 49727. **Tel** (616)536-7439, (800)447-1658, FAX (616)536-7450. **ED** Daniel & Joanna Cote. **DD** 799. Index available. cum. index. **Bk Rev**, (Qty: 4-8). **Ad Acc. Circ:** 10,000.
**Desc:** Dedicated to double guns (double barreled shotguns and rifles) and to what is done with them.

US/0747-4148
**DRAG RACING WORLD / AMERICAN HOT ROD ASSOCIATION, AHRA.** [Drag racing world]. **VFOAT** Drag World. Began in 1984. Periodical. English. bw. $25.00. Drag Racing World, 12425 US Highway 19S, Clearwater FL 33546. **DD** 796. **UDC** 796.71(73).

US/0277-4771
**DRAG RULES.** **Main/Corp** National Hot Rod Association. English. an. $3.00. National Hot Rod Association, 2035 Financial Way, Glendora CA 91740. **Tel** (818)914-4761. **ED** Graham Light. **LC** GV1029.3; .N32A. **DD** 796.7/2. **UDC** 796.71.063. **Ad Acc. Circ:** 75,000.
**Desc:** A technical book giving competitors the information necessary for them to race at sanctional races.

●US/1062-9394
**DRIVER (MIAMI, FLA.).** (DRIVER.). (1992)-. Periodical. English. Four times a year. $85.00 US; $127.00 Canada; $105.00 other. Fitness Information Technology, Inc., PO Box 4425, University Avenue, Morgantown WV 26504. **Tel** (304)599-3482, (800)477-4348, FAX (304)599-3482. **ED** Dr. Dallas Branch, Jr. **Bk Rev**, (Qty: 8). **Ad Acc, Adv Mgr:** Mary Rizzotti, **Tel** (304)599-3482. **Pr Rev. Acid Free. Circ:** 1,000.
**Desc:** Highlights feature articles on sport marketing written by the nation's leading experts in the private sector and in academia. Also contains book/video reviews, conference schedules, sport marketing success stories, profiles of influential people and more.

CN
**DRUG FILE UPDATE.** English. sa. 54.00Can$. Sport Information Resource Centre, 1600 promenade James Naismith Drive, Gloucester Ontario K1B 5N4 Canada. **Tel** (613)748-5658, FAX (613)748-5701, telex 053-3660 Sportrec Ott.
**Desc:** A current awareness index to publications on drugs and doping in sports.

●CN/1188-0260
**DRUGS IN SPORTS.** **See** Drug Abuse and Alcoholism.

US/0012-7132
**DUNE BUGGIES AND HOT VWS.** **See** Transportation-Automobiles.

US/8750-1732
**DUSTY TIMES.** [Dusty times]. (198?)-. Periodical. English. mo. $15.00. Dusty Times, 5331 Derry Avenue/Suite O, Agoura CA 91301. **DD** 796. ***Absorbed*** *Off Road Action News, 0161-7974.*

GW
**DWJ, DEUTSCHES WAFFEN-JOURNAL.** **VFOAT** Deutsches Waffen-Journal. (19??)-. Periodical. German. mo. DM93.00. Journal-Verlag Schwend GmbH, PO Box 10 03 40, D 74523 Schwabisch Hall Germany. **Tel** 011 49 791 404 515, FAX 011 49 791 404 505. **ED** Michael Schwend, Klaus Schinmeyer, Gerhard Wirnsberger. **LC** TS532; .D18. **Bk Rev**, (Qty: 80-100). **Ad Acc, Adv Mgr:** Norbert Rieger. Full Page (Color) DM4028.00. Half Page (Color) DM2014.00. **Acid Free. Circ:** 72,000 (ctrl).
**Desc:** Specialized weapons magazine for hunters, shooters and collectors.

CN/1185-8788
**DYNAMO (VANCOUVER).** (THE DYNAMO.). [Dynamo]. (Mar. 1991)-. Periodical. English. Free to members. Membership $25.00 per year. Vancouver Bicycle Club, 206-7028 17th Avenue, Burnaby, BC V3n 1K5. **DD** 796.6.

PL/0137-6187
**DZIENNIK URZEDOWY GOWNEGO KOMITETU KULTURY FIZYCZNEJ I SPORTU.** **See** Health and Personal Fitness.

US/0162-5144
**EAGLE (UNITED STATES FIELD HOCKEY ASSOCIATION, INC.), THE.** ***Suspended.*** (THE EAGLE.). **Added/Corp** United States Field Hockey Association. Periodical. English. bm (eight no. a year). $8.00 US; $12.00 other. USFHA National Office, 4415 Buffalo Road North, Chili NY 14514. **LC** GV1017.H7; E18. **DD** 796.35/5.05.

US/0195-0223
**EASTERN BASKETBALL.** (1976)-. Periodical. English. Eleven times a year. $32.00. Eastern Basketball, PO Box 370, Rochester MI 48308. **Tel** (313)879-1676, FAX (313)879-1977. **ED** Larry Donald. **Bk Rev. Ad Acc. Circ:** 10,000 (ctrl).
**Desc:** College and high school basketball (including recruiting) from Maine to North Carolina.

US/0896-8233
**EASTERN COLLEGE FOOTBALL MAGAZINE.** ***Title Change.*** [East. coll. footb. mag.]. **VFOAT** Eastern College Football. Periodical. English. Twelve times a year. Eastern College Sports, 37 Trask Road, Peabody MA 01960. **Tel** (508)531-4311. **DD** 796. **UDC** 796.333(74). ***Continued by*** *College Football Magazine, 1053-895X.*
**Desc:** Complete coverage of all teams - all divisions - of football in Northeast US, Ivy League, Colonial League, and Yankee Conference, Division 1A Independent, Division II, and III.

CN/0228-2348
**EASTERN ZONE NEWSLETTER - ONTARIO ASSOCIATION OF ARCHERS.** [East. Zone newsl. - Ont. Assoc. Archers]. **Main/Corp** Ontario Association of Archers. Eastern Zone. V. 1- Oct. 1979-. Newsletter. English. Ontario Association of Archers Eastern Zone, R Sunstrum, RR 1 1K0 Canada. **DD** 799.3/2/060713. **UDC** 799.322.2(713).

●US/1070-9231
**ECONOMIC ANALYSIS OF UNITED STATES SKI AREAS.** (ECONOMIC ANALYSIS OF UNITED STATES SKI AREAS / PREPARED BY UNITED SKI INDUSTRIES ASSOCIATION IN CONJUNCTION WITH KPMG PEAT MARWICK.). [Econ. anal. U.S ski areas]. **Added/Corp** United States Ski Association. KPMG Peat Marwick. (1991/92)-. English. **LC** GV854.8.N58; G63. **DD** 338.4/779693/0973. ***Continues*** *Economic Analysis of North American Ski*

*Areas, 0147-4243.*
**Desc:** Recreational surveys on winter sports facilities, skis and skiing.

US/0891-7329
**EDELSTEIN PRO FOOTBALL LETTER, THE.** [Edelstein pro footb. lett.]. (198?)-. Periodical. English. Thirty-six times a year. $54.00 one-half year; $89.00 one year; $159.00 two years; $235.00 three years. Fred Edelstein, Benjamin Fox Pavilion, Suite 432, Jenkintown PA 19046. **Tel** (800)523-1312 (215)576-8112, FAX (215)576-5830. **ED** Fred Edelstein. **DD** 796. **Circ:** 1,000.
**Desc:** A newsletter that covers the business side of professional football. It is aimed at pro football owners, general managers and agents.

CN/0229-7450
**ELITE SPORTIVE QUEBECOISE, L'.** 1980-. French. an. $6.95 per no. Societe des Sports du Quebec, 1415 Est rue Jarry, Montreal Quebec H2E 2Z7 Canada. **DD** 796/.06/0714. **UDC** 796(714).

US/1044-9574
**EMPLOYMENT OPPORTUNITIES (ATHLETICS).** [Employ. oppor. athl.]. (1989)-. Periodical. English. Twenty-six times a year. $40.00. Employment Opportunities Athletics, 1210 Auburn Way North, Suite P-147, Auburn WA 98002. **Tel** (206)735-3048. **DD** 796.
**Desc:** Comprehensive listing of coaching, P.E. and recreation opportunities in the states of California, Washington, Oregon, Alaska and Hawaii.

US/0732-1880
**ENTERTAINMENT AND SPORTS LAWYER : PUBLICATION OF THE FORUM COMMITTEE ON THE ENTERTAINMENT AND SPORTS INDUSTRIES, THE.** **See** Law.

CN/0828-4954
**ENTRAINEUR, L'.** ***Ceased.*** [Entraineur]. **VAT** Revue de l'Entraineur (1984). (Jan./Mar. 1984)-Ceased (Jan. 1987). Periodical. French. qt. Entraineur, c/o Societe des Sports du Quebec, 1415 Est rue Jarry, Montreal Quebec H2E 2Z7 Canada. **DD** 796/.07/705. **UDC** 796.071.4(714). ***Continues*** *Revue de l'Entraineur, 0705-5625.*

CN/0228-071X
**ENTREFILET.** [Entrefilet]. **Added/Corp** Federation de Badminton du Quebec. (Sept. 1978)-. Periodical. French. qt. 7.48Can$. Federation Quebecoise Badminton, 4545 Avenue Pierre de Coubertin, Montreal Quebec H1V 3S4 Canada. **Tel** (514)252-3066. **DD** 796.34/5/05.
**Ind/Abst** SPORT Discus; SportSearch (May 1987-).

CN/0823-1834
**ENVOI (MONTREAL).** (L'ENVOI : REVUE OFFICIELLE DE LA FEDERATION DE HOCKEY SUR GAZON DU QUEBEC.). [Envoi]. **Added/Corp** Federation de Hockey sur Gazon du Quebec. Vol. 1, No. 1 (June 1983)-. Periodical. French. Three times a year (Mar., July, Sept.). 5.00Can$. Quebec Field Hockey Federation, PO Box 1000, Succ M, Montreal Quebec H1V 3R2 Canada. **ED** Joceline Dion. **DD** 796.35/5/05. **Bk Rev. Ad Acc.** ctrl circ.
**Desc:** Covers international and Canadian competitions, the certification program and other official functions, as well as hockey training programs and a calendar of events.

FR/0245-8969
**EPS. EDUCATION PHYSIQUE ET SPORT.** **VFOAT** Revue EPS; Education Physique et Sport. (1976)-. Periodical. French. bm. 205.68F (France); 260.00F (other). Etablissements de Joinville, 11 Av de Tremblay, F-75012 Paris France. **Tel** 011 33 1 48083087. **UDC** 796:373.3.
**Ind/Abst** Point Repere (1989-); SPORT Discus.

US/0737-3449
**EPSCC NEWSLETTER.** (EPSCC NEWSLETTER / EASTERN PENNSYLVANIA SPORTS COLLECTORS CLUB, EPSCC.). **Added/Corp** Eastern Pennsylvania Sports Collectors Club. **VFOAT** E.P.S.C.C. Newsletter. **VAT** Eastern Pennsylvania Sports Collectors Club Newsletter. (19??)-. Newsletter. English. qt. $3.50 or Free to members. Eastern Pennsylvania Sports Collectors Inc, PO Box 37, Maple Glen PA 19002.

FR/0153-1069
**EQUIPE. PARIS, L'.** (L'EQUIPE.). [Equipe Paris]. (1946)-. Periodical. French. da (312 issues). 1547.50F France; 2732.00F other. L'Equipe, 4 rue Rouget de l Isle, 92137 Issy Moulineaux France. **Tel** 011 33 1 40932020. **UDC** 790 + 793/799.
**Ind/Abst** SPORT Discus.

FR/0153-4661
**ESCRIME.** **Added/Corp** International Fencing Federation. Federation Francaise d'Escrime. (19??)-. Periodical. French. bm. 165.00F (France); 220.00F (other). Federation Francaise d Escrime, 14 rue Moncey, 75009 Paris, France. **Tel** 11 33 1 44532750. **LC** GV1143; .E72. **DD** 796.8/6. ***Continues*** *Escrime Francaise.*
**Ind/Abst** SportSearch (May 1987-).

US
**ESQUIRE SPORTSMAN.** (Fall 1992)-. English. qt. $3.95 (per issue). Esquire Sportsman, 250 West 55th Street, New York NY 10019. **ED** Terry McDonnell.
**Desc:** Provides features on outdoor sports. The "Global Sporting" section offers a list of sports vacations the world over.
**Ind/Abst** Access (1993-).

CN/0823-793X
**ESQUIVE (MONTREAL, QUEBEC).** (L'ESQUIVE.). [Esquive]. Vol. 1, No. 1 (10 June 1981)-. Periodical. French. Federation Quebecoise de Boxe Amateur, 1415 Est rue Jarry, Montreal Quebec H2E 2Z7 Canada. **DD** 796.8/3/09714. ctrl circ.

GW
**EUROPAPOKAL.** (19??)-. German. Copress-Verlag, Schellingstrasse 39, 8 Munchen 40 Germany. **LC** GV943.52; .E95. **DD** 796.33/464/094.

UK
**EUROPEAN CUPS.** English (French, German, Italian and Spanish). Kenneth Mason Publications Ltd Street, Emsworth Hants PO10 7DQ England. **Tel** 0243 377977, FAX 0243 379136.
**Desc:** Covers who won which cup, where, and when.

UK
**EUROPEAN FOOTBALL BOOK, THE.** No. 1 (1968/69)-. English. an. £1.00. European Football Book, 178-202 Great Portland Street, London W1 England. **LC** GV942; .E87. **DD** 796.33/4/094.

US/1067-3202
**EXPLORER KNIFE JOURNAL.** [Explor. knife j.]. **VFOAT** Knife Journal; Explorer Knives; Gutmann Knives. (19??)-. Periodical. English. $2.50. **LC** TS380; .G88. **DD** 621.9/32/05. ***Continues*** *Gutmann Puma/Explorer Knife Annual, 0731-1885.*
**Desc:** Journal aimed at those who have an interest in the area of collectable and all-purpose knives.

●US/1072-0510
**EXTRA INNINGS.** **See** Education-Physical Education and Training.

CN/0712-5585
**F.I.B.A. RULES CASEBOOK.** [F.I.B.A. rules casebook]. **Main/Corp** International Amateur Basketball Federation. **VFOAT** FIBA Basketball Rules Casebook; Official Rule Interpretations; Federation Internationale de Basketball Amateur Rules Casebook. **VAT** Federation Internationale de Basketball Amateur Rules Casebook. English (French). ir (one issue every 4 years). 5.00Can$ Canada; $4.00 US. F I B A Rules Casebook, c/o Basketball Canada, 333 River Road, Vanier Ontario K1L 8B9 Canada. **Tel** (613)748-5607, telex 053-3660. **ED** Allen G Rae. **DD** 796.32/3/02022. Index available. **Bk Rev. Ad Acc. Circ:** 10,000 (ctrl).
**Desc:** Play situations giving rule interpretations for Federation Internationale de Basketball Amateur Rules Casebook.

CN/1184-6208
**FACT BOOK - SASKATCHEWAN ROUGHRIDERS, FOOTBALL TEAM.** (FACT BOOK / SASKATCHEWAN ROUGHRIDERS.). [Fact book - Sask. Roughriders Footb. team]. **Main/Corp** Saskatchewan Roughriders (Football Team). **VFOAT** Saskatchewan Roughriders Fact Book. (1990)-. English. Saskatchewan Roughriders, PO box 1277, Regina, Saskatchewan S4P 3B8 Canada. **DD** 796.335/64. ***Continues*** *Saskatchewan Roughriders (Football Team) Yearbook., 0846-7137.*

US/1046-9125
**FANTASY BASEBALL.** [Fantasy baseb.]. (Mar. 1991)-. Periodical. English. qt. $9.95 US; $16.95 other. Krause Publications, 700 East State Street, Iola WI 54990-0001. **Tel** (715)445-2214, FAX (715)445-4087, telex 55 6461. **ED** Kit Kiefer. **DD** 796. **Circ:** 150,000.
**Desc:** League players receive information on picks for drafting players, including complete statistics from the previous year for all baseball players. Every major league ballplayer is ranked. Contains batting averages, pitching ratios, player interviews, and new product reviews.

US/0898-9672
**FANTASY FOOTBALL.** English. an. $4.95. Sportspage Publications, 8433 Southside Boulevard/Suite 1803, Jacksonville FL 32256.

US
**FCCAA STATISTICAL REPORTING SERVICE / MEN'S BASEBALL.** (19??)-. Statistical Publication. English. Thirteen times a year (published during baseball season). $50.00. Miami-Dade South, c/o James Carrig, 11011 Southwest 104th Street, Miami FL 33176. **Tel** (305)237-2309, FAX (305)347-2606. **ED** James Carrig. ctrl circ.

SZ/0014-9756
**FELD WALD WASSER. SCHWEIZERISCHE JAGDZEITUNG.** **See** Recreation, Leisure-Outdoor Life.

UK
**FENCING.** ***Ceased.*** Vol. 10, No. 2 (May 1975)-Ceased (Jan. 1979). English. qt. Roy Goodall, 20 Dent's Grove Lower Kingswood, Tadworth Surrey KT20 7DX England. ***Continues*** *Fencing Master.*
**Ind/Abst** SPORT Discus.

UK/0959-888X
**FIBA BASKETBALL MONTHLY.** **Main/Corp** International Amateur Basketball Federation. **VFOAT** FIBA Basketball. (1990)-. English. mo. £46.00 UK; £50.00 other. Lawrence Publishing UK Ltd., Unicorn House 3 Plough Yard, London EC2A 3LP England. **Tel** 011 44 71 3753773.
**Desc:** Official publication of F I B A . Includes all regional basketball results, articles on coaching, refereeing, medical breakthroughs, reports on events, features from players, coaches and managers.

US/0275-5394
**FIELD HOCKEY RULES. NATIONAL FEDERATION ED.** (FIELD HOCKEY RULES.). **Main/Corp** National Federation of State High School Associations. **VFOAT** Field Hockey Rule Book. (19??)-. English. an. National Federation of State High School Associations, 11724 Northwest Plaza Circle, PO Box 20626, Kansas City MO 64195-0626. **Tel** (816)464-5400, FAX (816)464-5571. **ED** Susan True. **LC** GV1017.H7; N37a. **DD** 796.35/5. **Ad Acc. Circ:** 1,300.
**Desc:** Rules governing high school competition in field hockey.

SZ
**FIFA MAGAZINE : A PUBLICATION OF THE FEDERATION INTERNATIONALE DE FOOTBALL ASSOCIATION.** **Added/Corp** Federation Internationale de Football Association. **VAT** Federation Internationale de Football Association Magazine. 1st Ed. (1983)-. Periodical. English. qt. Federation Internationale de Football Association, PO Box 85, 8030 Zurich 30 Switzerland. **LC** IN PROCESS. ***Separated from*** *Federation Internationale de Football Association. FIFA News.*
**Ind/Abst** SPORT Discus.

SZ
**FIFA NEWS.** **Main/Corp** Federation Internationale de Football Association. **Added/Corp** Federation Internationale de Football Association. News. **VAT** Federation Internationale de Football Association News. (19??)-. Periodical. English (French, German and Spanish). Fifteen times a year. Combined with FIFA Magazine: 70.00F North & Central America, Middle East, and all African countries except North Africa; 50.00F Europe, North Africa, and Near East; 80.00F other. Federation Internationale de Football Association, PO Box 85, 8030 Zurich 30 Switzerland. **LC** GV942; .F6514. **DD** 796.33/4/0621. **Circ:** 6,000 (ctrl). ***Continued in part by*** *FIFA Magazine.*
**Desc:** Presents the official results of football games, and international and official communications within the International Football Association.

US/8756-2340
**FIGHT BEAT.** [Fight beat]. **VFOAT** Fight. Periodical. English. bm. $27.50 US; $30.00 other. Fight Beat, 155 Avenue of the Americas, New York NY 10013. **DD** 796.

●AU
**FIL MAGAZIN.** (1994)-. Periodical. German (English). ir (3-4 times per year). 50.00F. FIL / International Luge Federation, Olympiastrasse 168-a, A 8786 Rottenmann Austria. **Tel** 011 43 3614 2266, FAX 011 43 3614 3381. **ED** Herbert Wurzer (editor's address: Meinonggasse 7, A 8010 Graz Austria; telephone/FAX: 316 381257. **Photos.**
**Desc:** Official publication of the International Luge Federation.

FR
**FINAL REPORT / INTERGOVERNMENTAL COMMITTEE FOR PHYSICAL EDUCATION AND SPORT.** **Main/Corp** Intergovernmental Committee for Physical Education and Sport. (1979)-. English. ir. UNESCO / France, 31 rue Francois Bonvin, 75732 Paris Cedex 15 France. **Tel** 011 33 1 45684564, 011 33 1 45684565, FAX 011 33 1 42733007, telex 204461 Paris. **LC** GV563; .I74313. **DD** 613.7/05. ***Continues*** *Interim Intergovernmental Committee for Physical Education and Sport. General Report.*

GW/0015-2838
**FISCH UND FANG.** (1960)-. Periodical. German. mo. DM86.40 (includes postage), $58.00 (includes postage) US; 84.00F (includes postage) Switzerland. Paul Parey (Berlin), Seelbuschring 9-17, 1000 Berlin 42 Germany. **Tel** 030-70784-00. **[CCC]. Bk Rev. Ad Acc. Pr Rev.**
**Desc:** A special interest journal on sports fishing.

Recreation, Leisure —Sports

US/1040-0117
**FISHERMAN (NEW JERSEY, DELAWARE BAY ED.), THE.** (THE FISHERMAN.). [Fisherman]. (19??)-. Periodical. English. Fifty times a year (Except for two weeks in Dec.). $23.00. New Jersey Fisherman, 1622 Beaver Dam Road, Point Pleasant NJ 08742. **Tel** (908)295-8600. **ED** Don Eisenhuth. **DD** 799. **Bk Rev**. **Ad Acc**, **Adv Mgr:** Cullen Monahan. **Circ:** 35,000 (ctrl). ***Continues** New Jersey Fisherman.*

●US/1068-5952
**FITNESS AND SPORTS REVIEW INTERNATIONAL.** **See** Education-Physical Education and Training.

RU
**FIZKULTURA I SPORT.** **Added/Corp** Vysshii Sovet Fizicheskoi Kultury R.S.F.S.R. Vsesoiznyi Sovet Fizicheskoi Kultury (Soviet Union) Soviet Union. Vsesoiuznyi Komitet po Delam Fizicheskoi Kultury i Sporta. Soviet Union. Komitet po Delam Fizicheskoi Kultury i Sporta. Soviet Union. Ministerstvo Zdravookhraneniia. Soviet Union. Komitet po Fizicheskoi Kulture i Sportu. Soiuz Sportivnykh Obshchestv i Organizatsii SSSR. **VFOAT** FIS. (1928)-. Periodical. Russian. mo. $69.95. **(Subscription address:** East View Publications Inc., 3020 Harbor Lane North, Suite 110, Minneapolis MN 55447.**)** ***Formed by the union of** Izvestiia Fizicheskoi Kultury **and** Krasnyi Sport (Moscow, R.S.F.S.R. : 1924).*

CN/1182-9265
**FLASH (BANFF).** (THE FLASH! / NATIONAL SPORT CLIMBING COMMITTEE, ALPINE CLUB OF CANADA/FEDERATION QUEBECOISE DE LA MONTAGNE.). [Flash]. **Added/Corp** Alpine Club of Canada. National Sport Climbing Committee. Vol. 1, No. 1 (Spring 1990)-. Periodical. English. qt. Free to individuals registered with the Sport climbing registry. National Sport Climbing Committee, c/o Alpine Club of Canada, PO Box 1026, Banff, Alberta T0L 0C0 Canada. **DD** 796.5/223.

US/1044-9000
**FLORIDA COACHING DIRECTORY.** (FLORIDA COACHING DIRECTORY : AN OFFICIAL PUBLICATION OF THE NATIONAL INTERSCHOLASTIC ATHLETIC ADMINISTRATORS ASSOCIATION AND THE FLORIDA INTERSCHOLASTIC ATHLETIC ADMINISTRATORS ASSOCIATION.). [Fla. coach. dir.]. **Added/Corp** National Interscholastic Athletic Administrators Association. Florida Interscholastic Athletic Administrators Association. National Federation Interscholastic Coaches Association. **VFOAT** Florida Coaches Directory of High Schools and Colleges. (1989)-. English. an (Sept.). $9.95. Clell Wade Coaches Directory, PO Box 177, Cassville MO 65625. **Tel** (417)847-2783. **DD** 796. ***Continues** Florida Coaches Directory of High Schools and Colleges.*

US
**FLORIDA PAINTBALL PRESS.** English. mo. $9.00. Florida Paintball Press, PO Box 12341, St. Petersburg FL 33733. **Tel** (813)321-7926, (813)971-8805. **ED** Kenneth R. Gilder. **Ad Acc**. ***Continues** West Florida Paintball Press, 1071-1929.*

US/0897-2621
**FLORIDA SCUBA NEWS.** (1984)-. Periodical. English. mo. $12.95. Wet Set Publications, 1324 Placid Place, Jacksonville FL 32205. **Tel** (904)384-7336.

US/0015-3885
**FLORIDA SPORTSMAN (MIAMI).** (FLORIDA SPORTSMAN.). Vol. 1 (1969)-. English. mo. $16.95 (one year), $27.95 (two year), $36.95 (three year) US; $24.95 (one year), $43.95 (two year), $60.95 (three year) other. Wickstrom Publishers Inc, 5901 SW 74th Street/Suite 310, Miami FL 33143. **Tel** (305)661-4222. **ED** Vic Dunaway. **Ad Acc**. **Circ:** 90,498.
**Desc:** Covers fishing, boating and other outdoors activities in Florida.

CN/0317-2481
**FLYPAPER (CALGARY).** (THE FLYPAPER.). [Flypaper]. V. 1- ; March 1974-. English. qt. Free to members. Alberta Hang Gliding Association, PO Box 2011 Station M, Calgary Alberta T2P 2M2 Canada. **Tel** (403)286-7599. **DD** 797.5/5/0627123. **Bk Rev**. **Ad Acc**. ***Absorbed** National Newsletter (Hang Gliding Association of Canada), 0847-9399.*
**Desc:** Newsletter on hang gliding.
**Ind/Abst** SportSearch (May 1987-).

US/1069-7004
**FOCUS ON. SPORTS, SCIENCE AND MEDICINE.** (FOCUS ON. SPORTS, SCIENCE AND MEDICINE [COMPUTER FILE].). **Added/Corp** Institute for Scientific Information. **VFOAT** Sports, Science and Medicine. (1993)-. Periodical. English. mo. $217.00. Institute for Scientific Information, 3501 Market Street, Philadelphia PA 19104. **Tel** (215)386-0100, (800)523-1850, FAX (215)386-6362, telex 84-5305. **(Subscription address:** Institute for Scientific Information, PO Box 71416, Chicago IL 60694.**)**

US/1056-2273
**FOLDING KAYAKER.** [Fold. kayak.]. Vol. 1, No. 1 (May 1991)-. Periodical. English. Six times a year. $28.00 US; $35.50 other. Folding Kayaker, Inc., PO Box 0754, Planetarium Station, New York NY 10024-0539. **Tel** (212)724-5069. **ED** Ralph Diaz. **DD** 797. Index available (published separately). cum. index. **Bk Rev**, (Qty: 3). **Circ:** 500.
**Desc:** Newsletter that offers unique tips and insights on using and enjoying folding kayaks. Latest news on manufacturers and product changes. Technical advice to readers for modifying foldtables. Kayak and ancillary product reviews. Specialized techniques on paddling, sailing, other activities. Safety tips. Features on equipment selected for major expeditions.

US/1051-1997
**FOOTBALL, BASKETBALL & HOCKEY COLLECTOR.** ***Ceased.*** **See** Hobbies.

US/0163-6200
**FOOTBALL CASE BOOK.** **Added/Corp** National Federation of State High School Associations. (19??)-. English. an. National Federation of State High School Associations, 11724 Northwest Plaza Circle, PO Box 20626, Kansas City MO 64195-0626. **Tel** (816)464-5400, FAX (816)464-5571. **LC** GV955; .F62. **DD** 796.33/2/02022.

US/0015-6760
**FOOTBALL DIGEST.** Vol. 1, (Sept. 1971)-. Periodical. English. Ten times a year. $22.00 US; $30.00 other. Century Publishing Company, 990 Grove Street, Evanston IL 60201-4370. **Tel** (708)491-6440, (800)321-3333, FAX (708)491-0459. **(Subscription address:** Kable Publishers Aide, 308 East Hitt Street, Subscriptions Department, Mt. Morris, IL 61054**)** **ED** Michael Herbert. **Bk Rev**. **Ad Acc**. **Circ:** 200,000. available on microfilm and microfiche from University Microfilms International (UMI).
**Desc:** Covers NFL football.
**Ind/Abst** Mag. Artic. Summar. Elite (Jan. 1994-); Mag. Artic. Summar. CD-ROM (Jan. 1994-).

US
**FOOTBALL HANDBOOK.** **Main/Corp** National Federation of State High School Associations. (19??)-. English. be. National Federation of State High School Associations, 11724 Northwest Plaza Circle, PO Box 20626, Kansas City MO 64195-0626. **Tel** (816)464-5400, FAX (816)464-5571. **LC** GV937; .N27a. **DD** 796.33205.

US
**FOOTBALL HANDBOOK.** **Added/Corp** National Research Bureau, Inc. (19??)-. English. an. $1.70. National Research Bureau Inc. / Iowa, 200 North Fourth, PO Box 1, Burlington IA 52601. **Tel** (319)752-5415, FAX (319)752-3421. **LC** GV937; .F65. **DD** 796.332/0973.

CN/0317-2163
**FOOTBALL JOURNAL.** **VFOAT** CAFA Journal. V. 1- Aug./Sept. 1974-. English. bm. $3.00 U.S. Canadian Amateur Football Association, 333 River Road, Vanier Ontario K1L 8B9 Canada. **DD** 796.33/5/05.

UK
**FOOTBALL KICK.** English. mo. £19.00. Mid Angle Ltd, PO Box 18, Thornham Magna, NR Eye Suffolk England.

UK/0266-481X
**FOOTBALL MONTHLY (1980).** [Footb. mon. 1980]. (1980)-. Periodical. English. mo. £24.80 Europe. World Wide Subscription Services, Unit 4, Gibbs Reed Farm, East Sussex TN5 7HE England. **Tel** (0580)200657, FAX (0580)200616. **DD** 796.334. ***Continues** Football Magazine (London), 0307-8108.*

US/0161-9020
**FOOTBALL NEWS (DETROIT).** (FOOTBALL NEWS.). (19??)-. Periodical. English. Twenty times a year (weekly in season). $39.95 US; $44.95 Canada; $69.95 other. Football News/Basketball Weekly, 17820 East Warren Avenue, Detroit MI 48224. **Tel** (313)881-9555, (800)521-8808, FAX (313)881-2027. **ED** P Stanton. **Ad Acc**, **Adv Mgr:** K Ballew, **Tel** (313)881-9554. **Circ:** 120,000 (ctrl).
**Desc:** Complete coverage of college and pro football; weekly ratings of top teams, college and pro; outstanding predictions of all major games.

US/0163-6219
**FOOTBALL OFFICIALS MANUAL.** **Added/Corp** National Federation of State High School Associations. (19??)-. English. an. National Federation of State High School Associations, 11724 Northwest Plaza Circle, PO Box 20626, Kansas City MO 64195-0626. **Tel** (816)464-5400, FAX (816)464-5571. **LC** GV954.35; .F66. **DD** 796.33/2/0202.

US/8755-9048
**FOOTNOTES (RESTON, VA.).** (FOOTNOTES / ROAD RUNNERS CLUB OF AMERICA.). [Footnotes]. **VFOAT** Foot Notes. Periodical. English. qt. $1.00 single issue. Road Runners Club of America, 629 South Washington Street, Alexandria VA 22314. **Tel** (703)836-0558, FAX (703)836-4430. **ED** Steve Clapp. **DD** 796. **Bk Rev**. **Ad Acc**. **Circ:** 115,000.
**Desc:** A journal for members of the Road Runners Club of America, which promotes long distance running as a sport and as healthy exercise.

US/0300-8509
**FORE (NORTH HOLLYWOOD, CALIF.).** (FORE.). **Added/Corp** Southern California Golf Association. (1968)-. Periodical. English. bm. Southern California Golf Association, 3740 Cahuenga Boulevard, North Hollywood CA 91604. **ED** Robert Thomas. **Circ:** 110,000.

CN/0846-4618
**FQSE EN ACTION, LA.** [FQSE action]. **Added/Corp** Federation Quebecoise du Sport Etudiant. **VAT** Federation Quebecoise du Sport Etudiant en Action. Vol. 2, No. 4 (March 1989)-. Periodical. French. bm. Limited free distribution. Federation du Sport Scolaire du Quebec, 1415 Est rue Jarry, Montreal Quebec H2E 2Z7 Canada. **DD** 796/.09714. ***Continues** Acti Presse, 0836-2998.*

FR
**FRANCE FOOTBALL.** (1945)-. Periodical. French. Twenty-six times a year. 288.75F France; 410.00F others. L'Equipe, 4 rue Rouget de l Isle, 92137 Issy Moulineaux France. **Tel** 011 33 1 40932020. **(Subscription address:** Service Abbonements, 1 rue de Lille, 75007 Paris France.**)** **LC** GV944.F8; F7. **DD** 796.334/0944.

FR/0984-421X
**FRANCE TENNIS DE TABLE MAGAZINE.** (1987)-. Periodical. French. bm. **UDC** 796.3.
**Ind/Abst** SPORT Discus.

●US/1067-5914
**FRED TROST'S PRACTICAL SPORTSMAN.** [Fred Trost's pract. sportsman]. **VFOAT** Practical Sportsman. Vol. 1, No. 1 (Dec./Jan. 1992)-. Periodical. English. Six times a year. $20.00 (institutions), $12.00 (individuals) Comes with Practical Sportsman membership. Practical Sportsman, 14099 Webster Road, PO Box 1001, Bath MI 48808. **Tel** (517)641-6701. **DD** 799. ***Continues** Fred Trost's Outdoors Digest, 0884-9137.*

CN/0827-2557
**FREE FLIGHT (OTTAWA ONT.).** (FREE FLIGHT.). [Free flight]. **Added/Corp** Soaring Association of Canada. **VFOAT** Vol Libre. (196?)-. Periodical. English (French; summaries and/or abstracts in French). Six times a year (Jan., Mar., May, July, Sept., Nov.). $22.00 Canada; $28.00 other. Soaring Association of Canada, 1355 Banks Street, Suite 306, Ottawa Ontario K1H 8K7 Canada. **Tel** (613)739-1063, FAX (613)739-1826. **ED** T. Burton. **DD** 797.5/5/05. **Bk Rev**. **Ad Acc**. **Circ:** 1,500.
**Desc:** For the enjoyment of soaring enthusiasts.
**Ind/Abst** SPORT Discus.

AT/0727-615X
**FREESAIL.** [Freesail]. (1981)-. Consumer Publication. English. Five times a year. 38.61Aus$ Australia; 63.00Aus$ other. Mason Stewart Publishing, PO Box 746, Darlinghurst NSW 2010 Australia. **Tel** 011 61 2 331 5006. **ED** Mike McGrath. **DD** 797.17205. **Ad Acc**, **Adv Mgr:** Stephen Kay. **Circ:** 15,500.
**Desc:** For local enthusiasts of boardsailing; reviews of equipment, hints and tips, with accompanying photographs.
**Ind/Abst** SPORT Discus.

US/0193-0443
**FRIENDLY FAIRWAYS OF MICHIGAN.** English. an. $5.70. Friendly Fairways of America, Po Box 237-A, Royal Oak MI 48068. **LC** GV962; .F73. **DD** 796.352/068/025774.

US/1054-1950
**FROM THE GYM TO THE JURY.** **See** Law.

AT/0157-5295
**FUN RUNNER.** ***Title Change.*** [Fun runner]. (1979)-(19??). Periodical. English. mo. Triathlon Sports, PO Box 2590, Taren Point 2229 Australia. **Tel** 011 61 2 5241455, FAX 011 61 2 5241454. **DD** _a796.426. ***Continued by** New Fun Runner.*
**Ind/Abst** SPORT Discus.

GW
**FUSSBALL MAGAZIN.** **VFOAT** Fussballmagazin. (19??)-. German. Olympia Verlag GmbH, Badstrasse 4-6, Abholfach, D 90402 Nuernberg 1 Germany. **Tel** 011 49 911 2162230.

GW/0016-3228
**FUSSBALL TRAINER.** German. DM60.60. Achalm Verlag, Postfach 1642, 72706 Reutlingen 1 Germany. **Tel** 011 49 7121 272.

US/1059-3853
**GADGETS FOR DIVERS.** [Gadgets divers]. **VFOAT** GFD. Vol. 1, No. 1 (Dec. 22, 1991)-. Periodical. English. mo. $59.95. Gadgets for Divers, PO Box 319, Madison AL 35758. **DD** 688.

Recreation, Leisure —Sports

IE
**GAELIC SPORT.** Vol. 1, No. 1 (1958)-. English. qt. Gaelic Sport, 139A Lower Drumcondra Road, Dublin 9 Ireland.
**Ind/Abst** SportSearch (May 1987-).

US/8755-1470
**GAMEDAY.** (GAMEDAY : AN OFFICIAL PRO PUBLICATION OF THE NFL.). [GameDay]. **VFOAT** Game Day. Periodical. English. mo. National Football League Properties Inc, 410 Park Avenue, New York NY 10022. **LC** GV937; .G36. **DD** 796.332/64/0973.

US/1055-9256
**GAMEPLAN COLLEGE FOOTBALL ... ANNUAL PREVIEW.** [GamePlan coll. footb. annu. preview]. **VFOAT** Game Plan College Football Annual Preview; College Football; GamePlan College Football; GamePlan College Football Magazine. (19??)-. English. an (July). $7.95. Sports Associates Inc., PO Box 3169, Syracuse NY 13220. **Tel** (315)458-1287. **LC** WMLC 91/5153. **DD** 796.

US/0161-7834
**GATER RACING PHOTO NEWS.** Periodical. English. Thirty-seven times a year. $25.00 US; $48.00 North America; $100.00 other. Gater Racing Photo News, PO Box 2187, Syracuse NY 13220. **Tel** (315)457-0175, FAX (315)457-0346. **ED** Norman W Patrick and Joseph J Patrick. **Circ:** 85,000.
**Desc:** Oval track auto racing.

US/0744-0995
**GATOR BAIT.** (19??)-. Periodical. English. ir (Weekly Aug. through Apr.; Monthly May through July). $47.00. Gator Bait, PO Box 14022, Gainesville FL 32604. **Tel** (904)372-1215, FAX (904)371-9420. **ED** Marty Cohen. **Ad Acc, Adv Mgr:** Dwight Johnson, **Tel** (813)351-5469. **Circ:** 22,000.
**Desc:** A sports tabloid covering all aspects of University of Florida athletic competition with a heavy emphasis on football and recruiting.

●CN/1194-5303
**GEO PLEIN-AIR.** [Geo plein-air]. **VFOAT** Magazine Geo Plein-Air. Vol. 4, No. 3/4 (Oct./Dec. 1992)-. Periodical. French. bm (Feb., Apr., June, Aug., Oct., Dec.). 22.50Can$. Magazine Expedition Plein Air, 4058 rue Parthenais, Montreal Que H2K 3T9 Canada. **Tel** (514)528-7103, FAX (514)982-6065. **DD** 796.5/05. **Bk Rev**, (Qty: 20). **Ad Acc, Adv Mgr:** Dalpe, **Tel** (514)228-7559. **Circ:** 25,000 (ctrl). ***Continues*** *Plein Air (Montreal, Quebec)., 0843-8552.*

US/0279-0238
**GIANTS NEWSWEEKLY, THE.** Vol. 1, No. 1 (Apr. 13, 1981)-. Periodical. English. ir (monthly January through July; weekly August through December). $29.95 (one year), $53.95 (two year). Giants Newsweekly, PO Box 816, 43 West Front Street, Suite 9, Red Bank NJ 07701. **Tel** (201)747-1085. **ED** Rick Maddock. **Ad Acc, Adv Mgr:** Dave Klein. **Circ:** 48,000 (ctrl).
**Desc:** Complete coverage of New York Giants football.

IT
**GINNASTA.** Il Ginnasta, Redazione Viale Tiziano 70, 00196 Rome Italy.

US/0882-5920
**GIRLS' AND WOMEN'S TAEKWONDO NEWSLETTER, THE.** [Girls' Women's taekwondo newsl.]. Newsletter. English (Korean, Chinese, French and Spanish). Three times a year. $25.00. The Girls' and Women's Taekwondo Newsletter, 14125 Berryville Road, Germantown MD 20874. **Tel** (301)869-5518. **ED** Karen Lunquist. **DD** 796. ctrl circ.

US/0361-5839
**GIRLS BASKETBALL RULES BOOK. NATIONAL FEDERATION EDITION.** (GIRLS BASKETBALL RULES BOOK.). **Main/Corp** National Federation of State High School Associations. English. $0.85. National Federation of State High School Associations, 11724 Northwest Plaza Circle, PO Box 20626, Kansas City MO 64195-0626. **Tel** (816)464-5400, FAX (816)464-5571. **LC** GV886; .N385A. **DD** 796.32/38.

US/0197-162X
**GIRLS GYMNASTICS JUDGING MANUAL. NATIONAL FEDERATION EDITION.** (GIRLS GYMNASTICS JUDGING MANUAL.). [Girls gymnast. judg. man., Natl. Fed. ed.]. **Main/Corp** National Federation of State High School Associations. English. National Federation of State High School Associations, 11724 Northwest Plaza Circle, PO Box 20626, Kansas City MO 64195-0626. **Tel** (816)464-5400, FAX (816)464-5571. **LC** GV464; .N37A. **DD** 796.4/1.

US
**GLADIATOR SPORTS MAGAZINE.** English. qt. $14.00. Flo Anthony, 142 West 72nd Street #2A, New York NY 10023. **Tel** (212)769-8423, FAX (212)594-9712. **ED** Vinette Pryce. Index available. **Bk Rev. Ad Acc.**
**Desc:** Black sports magazine.

US
**GLOBOSPORTS. See** Communication-Broadcasting.

CN/0704-0385
**GO FOR SPORTS.** V. 1- Fall 1977-. Periodical. English. Monday Publications Ltd, 1609 Blanshard Street, Victoria BC Canada V8W 2J5. **Tel** (604)382-6188, FAX (604)381-2662. **DD** 796/.09711/34.

IT
**GOAL FLASH.** (19??)-. Italian. mo. L55000.00. Forte Editore, Via Asiago 114, 20128 Milan Italy. **Tel** 011 39 2 2594241, FAX 011 39 2 2591493.

US/0273-5601
**GOAL (NEW YORK, N.Y.).** ***Ceased.*** (GOAL : THE NATIONAL HOCKEY LEAGUE MAGAZINE.). [Goal]. **Added/Corp** National Hockey League. (19??)-(Summer 1992). Periodical. English. ir (7 issues a year). National Hockey League Enterprises, 1633 Broadway, 40th Floor, New York NY 10019. **Tel** (212)767-4600. **Ad Acc, Adv Mgr:** Neil Butwin, **Tel** (212)308-6666.
**Ind/Abst** SPORT Discus.

CN/0708-5427
**GOALGETTER.** Vol. 1, (Feb. 28, 1979)-. Periodical. English. bw. **DD** 796.33/4/09711.

US/0092-6914
**GOLF & CLUB YEARBOOK.** (19??)-. English. an. $1.00. Werner Book Corporation, 606 Wilshire Boulevard, Santa Monica CA 90401. **LC** GV961; .G55024.

AT/0818-5077
**GOLF AUSTRALIA.** [Golf Aust.]. (1987)-. Periodical. English. mo. 49.95Aus$ (1 year), 89.00Aus$ (2 year) Australia; 56.00Aus$ (1 year), 102.00Aus$ (2 year) (surface mail), $70.00 (1 year), $135.00 (2 year) (air mail) other. Horwitz Grahame Pty Ltd, 506 Miller Street, Cammeray New South Wales, 2062 Australia. **Tel** 011 61 2 9296144, FAX 011 61 2 9571814. **DD** 796.3520994.
**Ind/Abst** SPORT Discus.

US/0148-3706
**GOLF BUSINESS (1976).** (GOLF BUSINESS.). Periodical. English. mo. $18.00, Free (qualified management personnel at golf facilities). Golf Business, 9800 Detroit Avenue, Cleveland OH 44102. **LC** GV961; .G55028. **DD** 796.352/05. available on microfilm from University Microfilms International (UMI). ***Continues*** *Golfdom, 0017-1905.*

US/0192-3048
**GOLF COURSE MANAGEMENT.** [Golf course manage.]. Vol. 47 (Jan. 1979)-. Periodical. English. mo. $30.00 (1 year), $55.00 (2 years), $80.00 (3 years). Golf Course Superintendents Association of America, 1421 Research Park Drive, Lawrence KS 66049. **Tel** (913)841-2240, FAX (913)832-4433. **ED** Clay Loyd (913)832-4490. **LC** GV975; .G6. **DD** 796.352/06/8. **CODEN** GCMAEA. Index available. cum. index. **Ad Acc. Circ:** 20,000. ***Continues*** *Golf Superintendent, 0017-1840.*
**Desc:** Golf course management.
**Ind/Abst** SPORT Discus; SportSearch (May 1987-).

US/0017-176X
**GOLF DIGEST.** [Golf dig.]. Vol. 1 (Spring 1950)-. Periodical. English. mo. $27.94 (one year), $41.94 (two year), $55.88 (three year). Golf Digest- Tennis Inc., 5520 Park Avenue, Trumbull CT 06611. **Tel** (203)373-7256, FAX (203)371-2102. **(Subscription address:** CDS Agency Hard Copy, PO Box 4966, Des Moines IA 50340.) **ED** Jerry Tarde. **LC** GV961; .G5505. **DD** 796. **Ad Acc, Adv Mgr:** Peter Gross, **Tel** (212)789-3030. **Circ:** 1,220,204. available on microfilm and microfiche from University Microfilms International (UMI). Documents available from UMI Article Clearinghouse. ***Continues*** *Arrowhead Golf Digest.*
**Desc:** Covers the world of golf, with instructional tips, coverage of PGA and international events, and features on the game's top players and instructors.
**Ind/Abst** Consum. Index Prod. Eval. Inf. Source; Mag. Artic. Summar. Elite (July 1993-); Mag. Artic. Summar. CD-ROM (July 1993-); Mag. Search; Newsp. Period. Abstr. (1988-); Phys. Educ. Index; Resource/One Ondisc (1988-); SPORT Discus; SportSearch (1984-).

US/0742-4485
**GOLF DIGEST ALMANAC, THE.** (1984)-. English. ir. Macmillan Publishing Company, 866 3rd Avenue, New York NY 10022. **Tel** (212)702-2000, (800)257-5755. **LC** GV981; .G63. **DD** 796.352/0973.

US/0275-5734
**GOLF DIRECTORY.** (GOLF ... DIRECTORY.). [Golf dir.]. (19??)-. Directory. English. ir. $2.95. Ziff-Davis, One Park Avenue, 5th Floor, New York NY 10016. **Tel** (212)503-3500, (609)786-8230. **LC** GV961; .G5506. **DD** 796.352/05.

US/0898-4719
**GOLF FOR WOMEN : GFW.** [Golf women]. **VFOAT** GFW. Vol. 1, No. 1 (July/Aug. 1988)-. Periodical. English. bm (6 issues). $16.97. Meredith Corporation, Locust at 17th, Des Moines IA 50309. **Tel** (515)284-3000. **(Subscription address:** Neodata / Colorado, PO Box 2606, Boulder Boulder CO 80322.) **ED** Glen Zediker. **DD** 796. **Ad Acc, Adv Mgr:** Vicki Richards, **Tel** (212)551-7177. **Circ:** 300,000.
**Desc:** Magazine for women golfers that features articles on instruction, equipment, vacation ideas, tournament listings and results.

CN/1184-6291
**GOLF GUIDE, ANNUAL GOLF COURSE DIRECTORY, BRITISH COLUMBIA, ALBERTA, SASKATCHEWAN.** ***Title Change.*** [Golf guide annu. golf course dir. B.C. Alta. Sask.]. **VFOAT** Annual Golf Course Directory, British Columbia, Alberta, Saskatchewan; Golf Guide, British Columbia, Alberta, Saskatchewan; Golf Guide. Vol. 7, No. 1 (1990)-(199?). Directory. English. Sylvester Publications Ltd, Postal Bag 5022, Red Deer Alberta T4N 6A1 Canada. **DD** 796.352/068712. ***Continues*** *Alberta & British Columbia Golf Guide., 0848-838X.* ***Continued by*** *Golf Guide (Edmonton, Alta.), 1199-3057.*

US/0099-1783
**GOLF GUIDE (SANTA MONICA).** (GOLF GUIDE.). Periodical. English. mo. $9.00. Werner Book Corporation, 606 Wilshire Boulevard, Santa Monica CA 90401. **LC** GV961; .G615. **DD** 796.352/05. ***Continues*** *Golfguide and Golf & Club.*

US/0160-6808
**GOLF ILLUSTRATED (COVINA, CALIF.).** ***Ceased.*** (GOLF ILLUSTRATED.). [Golf illus.]. Vol. 1, No. 1 (Winter 1985)-(19??). Periodical. English. mo. Golf Illustrated, 381 Park Avenue South, New York NY 10016. **ED** Mike Corcoran. **LC** GV961; .G612. **DD** 796. **Ad Acc. Circ:** 350,000. available on microfilm from University Microfilms International (UMI). ***Continues*** *Golf Illustrated, 0160-6808.*

US/0160-6824
**GOLF INDUSTRY.** ***Ceased.*** Vol. 1 (Oct. 1975)-(April 1992). English. Nine times a year. Sterling Northeast, 1156 Avenue of the Americas, New York NY 10036. **Tel** (212) 921-3784, telex (212) 921-3777. **ED** Michael J Keighley. **LC** HD9993.G65; U54. **DD** 338.4/7/688763520973. **Circ:** 19,057.
**Ind/Abst** SPORT Discus; SportSearch (May 1987-).

●CN/1189-4830
**GOLF INTERNATIONAL.** [Golf int.]. **VFOAT** Golf. (1992)-. Periodical. French. mo. 2.95Can$ per issue. Golf International, 283 20E Avenue Nord, Saint-Antoine-des-Laurentides Quebec J7Z 2W6 Canada. **DD** 796.352.

US/0017-1794
**GOLF JOURNAL.** (GOLF JOURNAL : THE OFFICIAL PUBLICATION OF THE UNITED STATES GOLF ASSOCIATION.). **Added/Corp** United States Golf Association. (19??)-. Periodical. English. Eight times a year. $35.00 Comes with United States Golf Association Adult membership. US Golf Association, Golf House, PO Box 708, Far Hills NJ 07931. **Tel** (908)234-2300. **ED** Robert T. Sommers. **LC** GV961; .G613. **DD** 796.352/0973. **Bk Rev. Circ:** 140,000 (ctrl). available on microfilm from University Microfilms International (UMI). ***Continues*** *USGA Golf Journal.*
**Desc:** Focuses its attention on the history, humor, latest developments, agronomy, equipment, rules, and technical issues of golf.
**Ind/Abst** SPORT Discus; SportSearch (May 1987-).

GW/0933-7415
**GOLF-MAGAZIN HAMBURG. 1987.** [Golf-Mag.Hambg., 1987]. (1987)-. Periodical. German. mo. DM96.00 Germany; DM99.00 other. Jahr Verlag GmbH & Co, Jessenstrasse 1, 22767 Hamburg Germany. **Tel** 011 49 40 389060. **UDC** 796.352.2. ***Continues*** *Golf (Hamburg), 0017-1735.*

US/1056-5493
**GOLF MAGAZINE (1991).** (GOLF MAGAZINE.). [Golf mag.]. **VFOAT** Golf. Vol. 33, No. 6 (June 1991)-. Periodical. English. mo. $19.94 (one year), $29.94 (two year), $39.98 (three year). Times Mirror Magazines, Two Park Avenue, New York NY 10016. **Tel** (212)779-5000. **(Subscription address:** Neodata / Colorado, PO Box 2606, Boulder Boulder CO 80322.) **LC** GV961; .G623. **DD** 796.352/05. Documents available from Magazine Collection. ***Continues*** *Golf (New York, N.Y. : 1986), 1056-5485.*
**Desc:** Provides regular how-to instruction features, tournament coverage and extensive articles on travel and lifestyle.
**Ind/Abst** Acad. Abstr. Full Text Elite (Jan. 1992-) [Full Txt.]; Acad. Abstr. (Jan. 1992-); Gen. Period. Index; Health Source (Jan. 1992-); Mag. Artic. Summar. Elite (Jan. 1992-) [Full Txt.]; Mag. Index Plus (1989-); Read. Guide Abstr. Select Ed.; Read. Guide Period. Lit. (1991-).

UK/0017-1816
**GOLF MONTHLY.** [Golf mon.]. (1911)-. Periodical. English. mo. $90.00. IPC Magazines Ltd., Perrymount Road, Haywards Heath, West Sussex RH16 3DH England. **Tel** 011 44 444 440421. **DD** 796.352.

US
**GOLF NEWS MAGAZINE.** English. Limited free distribution; $17.00 (12 issues), $32.00 (24 issues),

$44.00 (36 issues) for mailing costs. GOLF NEWS Magazine, PO Box 1040, Rancho Mirage CA 92270. **Tel** (619)324-8333, FAX (619)324-8011. **ED** Dan Poppers. **Bk Rev**. **Ad Acc**. ctrl circ.
**Ind/Abst** SPORT Discus.

US/1072-1274
**GOLF PRO.** [Golf pro]. (1993)-. Periodical. English. bm (6 issues). $30.00. Fairchild Publications Inc, 7 West 34th Street, 4th Floor, New York NY 10001. **Tel** (212)630-4230. **DD** 796. **Ad Acc. Circ:** 12,000 (ctrl). available on an online database. ***Continues*** *Golf Pro Merchandiser, 1067-3415.*
**Ind/Abst** F&S Index Plus Text, Int.; Mark. Advert. Ref. Serv.; PROMT.

US/0745-7502
**GOLF REPORTER, THE.** Periodical. English. wk. $29.00. The Golf Reporter, PO Box 370, Cornelius NC 28031-0370. **Tel** (704)892-7272, FAX (704)892-4832. **ED** Richard Sinn. **Bk Rev**. **Ad Acc. Circ:** 15,000. ***Continues*** *Carolinas Golf Reporter, 0199-3461.*
**Desc:** Coverage of golf events in, and players from, the Carolina and Georgia; includes a calendar of events.

US/1051-7758
**GOLF TIPS.** [Golf tips]. (1989)-. Periodical. English. bm. $11.97 (1 year), $19.97 (2 year) US; $16.97 (1 year), $29.97 (2 year) other. Werner Publishing Corporation, 12121 Wilshire Boulevard, Suite 1220, Los Angeles CA 90025. **Tel** (213)820-1500. **LC** WMLC 93/923. **DD** 796.
**Desc:** Instructions to make better golfers, covers all aspects of the game.

US/0191-717X
**GOLF TRAVELER, THE.** (GOLF TRAVELER : OFFICIAL PUBLICATION OF GOLF CARD INTERNATIONAL.). **Added/Corp** Golf Card International. (197?)-. Periodical. English. bm (6 issues). $12.00. Golf Card International Inc, 1137 East 2100 South, Salt Lake City UT 84106. **Tel** (801)453-4260. **ED** Bill Roland and Annette Holyoak. **LC** GV975; .G665. **DD** 796.352/06/873. **Ad Acc. Circ:** 70,000 (ctrl).
**Desc:** For the 92,000 members of "The Golf Card." Serves as a directory of affiliated golf courses including editorial support.

●CN/1189-4849
**GOLF VACATIONS (BURLINGTON).** (GOLF VACATIONS : A DIRECTORY OF HOLIDAY GOLF DESTINATIONS.). [Golf vacat.]. **VFOAT** Golf Connections. (1992/1993)-. Directory. English. $9.95 per volume. Golf Connections, Unit 2, 3455 Harvester Road, Burlington Ontario L7N 3P2 Canada. **DD** 796.352.

UK/0017-1883
**GOLF WORLD.** Vol. 1 (1962)-. Periodical. English. mo. £35.20 UK; £90.00 other. Tower Publishing, Tower House, Sovereign Park, Market Harborough, Leicester LE16 9EF England. **Tel** 011 44 858 468888. **DD** 796.352. **Ad Acc. Circ:** 80,000 (ctrl).
**Desc:** Strives to bring instruction and worldwide coverage of the golf scene.
**Ind/Abst** SportSearch (May 1987-).

US/0017-1891
**GOLF WORLD.** [Golf world]. Vol. 1, (1947)-. Periodical. English. Forty-Four times a year. $43.94 (one year); $65.91 (two year); $87.88 (three year). Golf Digest-Tennis Inc., 5520 Park Avenue, Trumbull CT 06611. **Tel** (203)373-7256, FAX (203)371-2102. **(Subscription address:** CDS Agency Hard Copy, PO Box 4966, Des Moines IA 50340.**) ED** Richard Taylor. **LC** GV961; .G63. **DD** 796.35205. **Bk Rev**. **Ad Acc**, **Adv Mgr:** Robert Carney, **Tel** (212)789-3009. **Circ:** 130,000.
**Desc:** News magazine of golf, with analysis of PGA and LPGA action and collegiate, senior and amateur coverage. Contains travel features and regular instructional series.

US/0360-0858
**GOLFGUIDE ANNUAL.** English. an. $1.50. Werner Book Corporation, 606 Wilshire Boulevard, Santa Monica CA 90401. **LC** GV961; .G55023. **DD** 796.352/05. ***Continues*** *Golf & Club Annual.*

US/0017-1824
**GOLFSHOP OPERATIONS. See** Business-Marketing.

US/0890-3514
**GOLFWEEK.** [Golfweek]. **VFOAT** Golf Week. (198?)-. Periodical. English. wk. $56.97 (one year), 89.97 (two year), $113.94 (three year). Golfweek Ltd, PO Box 1458, Winter Haven FL 33882-1458. **Tel** (813)294-5511. **ED** Charles Stine. **LC** WMLC 93/76. **DD** 796. **Bk Rev**. **Ad Acc. Circ:** 35,000 (ctrl). ***Continues*** *Florida Golfweek, 0745-7464.*
**Desc:** America's golf newspaper focusing on the Southeast.

HK/0376-6535
**GONG FU.** (KUNG FU.). [Gong fu]. **VFOAT** Kung Fu Magazine. Periodical. Chinese (Chinese). ir. $2.00 single issue. **LC** GV1112; .K86.

CN/0822-5222
**GRAND PRIX LABATT DU CANADA. REGLEMENTS. See** Transportation-Automobiles.

CN/0701-0745
**GRAND SLAM (OTTAWA).** (GRAND SLAM.). **Added/Corp** Softball Canada. Nov. (1972)-(1988). Periodical. English (French; summaries and/or abstracts in French). bm. $4.00. Canadian Amateur Softball Association, National Sport and Recreation Centre, 355 River Road, Vanier Ontario K1L 8C1 Canada. **Tel** (613)748-5668. **ED** Terry Manns. **DD** 796.357/8. **Bk Rev**. **Ad Acc. Circ:** 10,000 (ctrl).
**Desc:** News and views about softball in Canada. Technical information for umpires and coaches.
**Ind/Abst** SportSearch (May 1987-).

●US/1056-5116
**GREAT AMERICAN BASEBALL STAT BOOK.** (1992)-. English. $12.95. Harper Collins Publishers, Keystone Industrial Park, Scranton PA 18512. **Tel** (800)242-7737, (800)233-4727, FAX (800)822-4090.

CN/0823-6380
**GREEN.** (THE GREEN : THE OFFICIAL VOICE OF CANADIAN LAWN BOWLING COUNCIL.). [Green]. Issue No. 1 (Apr. 1972)-. Periodical. English (French). ir (four times a year, during the Summer). Free to association members Canada; 10.00Can$ US; 12.00Can$ other. Lawn Bowls Canada, 333 River Road/A-3, Ottawa Ontario K1L 8H9 Canada. **Tel** (613)748-5643, FAX (613)748-5706. **DD** 796.31. **Bk Rev**. **Ad Acc. Circ:** 15,000 (ctrl).
**Desc:** Information and news on the sport of lawn bowls in Canada and abroad.

CN/0380-3333
**GREENMASTER.** (THE GREENMASTER.). [Greenmaster]. **Added/Corp** Canadian Golf Superintendents Association. Ontario Golf Superintendents Association. **VFOAT** Green Master. Vol. 2 No. 3 (Feb. 1966)-. Periodical. English (French). bm (Jan., Mar., May, July, Sept., Nov.). 35.00Can$ Canada; $35.00 US. Canadian Golf Superintendents Association, 5580 Expplorer Drive, Suite 509 Mississauga, Ontario L4W 4Y1 Canda. **Tel** 800-387-1056, (905)602-8873, FAX (416)249-8467. **ED** Jane Vale. **DD** 796.352/068/05. Index available. **Bk Rev**. **Ad Acc. Circ:** 2,850 (ctrl). ***Continues*** *Ontario Golf Course Superintendents Association. News Bulletin, 0380-3341.*
**Desc:** Publishes technical and practical articles about golf course and fine turf management.
**Ind/Abst** SPORT Discus; SportSearch (May 1987-).

US/1071-1902
**GRIDIRON COACH.** [Gridiron coach]. (1991)-. Periodical. English. Eight times a year. $18.95. Klemmer - Halley and Associates Inc., 707 Wellman Avenue, North Chelmsford MA 01863. **Tel** (508)251-8278, FAX (508)251-9849. **ED** Mark Leaeriaos. **DD** 796. cum. index. **Bk Rev**, (Qty: 1). **Ad Acc. Circ:** 10,000.

UK/0017-4696
**GROUNDSMAN. See** Gardening and Horticulture.

CN/0820-0645
**GUIDE MEDIA - CONCORDES.** ***Title Change.*** (GUIDE MEDIA.). [Guide Media - Concordes]. **Main/Corp** Concordes (Football team). **VFOAT** Fact Book; Annuaire des Concordes; Concordes Directory. (1982)-(1984). English (French). Montreal Alouette Football Club, PO Box Station M, Montreal Quebec H1V 3L6 Canada. **DD** 796.33/56. ***Continues*** *Alouettes., 0318-9759.* ***Continued by*** *Fact Book, 0820-0645.*

US/1054-4178
**GUINNESS BOOK OF SPORTS RECORDS, THE.** [Guinness book sports rec.]. (1991)-. English. an. $21.95. Facts on File Publications, 460 Park Avenue South, New York NY 10016. **Tel** (212)683-2244, (800)322-8755, FAX (212)683-3633, telex 238 552 FACTS UR. **LC** GV741; .G843. **DD** 796/.021. Index available. available with charts. ***Continues*** *Guinness Sports Record Book (New York, N.Y. : 1985), 1054-4542.*
**Desc:** Offers little-known facts and odd feats for more than seventy sports, and incorporates in-depth coverage of the whole sporting spectrum.

US
**GUN.** English. an. $69.00. Orion Research Corporation, 14555 North Scottsdale Road, Suite 330, Scottsdale AZ 85260. **Tel** (800)844-0759, (602)951-1114, FAX (602)951-1117.
**Desc:** Gives information on used prices for 7,586 products

●US/1061-6918
**GUN TRADER.** [Gun trader]. Vol. 1, No. 1 (Apr. 1992)-. Periodical. English. mo. $12.00. Literati, Inc., PO Box 32, Patchougue NY 11772. **DD** 683.

US/0017-5641
**GUN WORLD.** [Gun world]. Vol. 1 (1960)-. Periodical. English. Thirteen times a year. $25.00 (US), $33.00 (others). Gallant Charger Publishing Inc., Box HH, 34249 Camino Capistrano, Capistrano Beach CA 92624. **Tel** (714)493-2101, FAX (714)240-8680. **ED** Jack Lewis. **DD** 799. **Bk Rev**. **Ad Acc. Circ:** 136,000. available on microfilm and microfiche from University Microfilms International (UMI).
**Desc:** Edited for shooters and hunters, with features on firearms, and tests and evaluation of new equipment. Contents aimed at the firearms enthusiast.

US/0362-2495
**GUN WORLD ANNUAL. VFOAT** GWA. English. an. $1.50. Gallant Charger Publishing Inc., Box HH, 34249 Camino Capistrano, Capistrano Beach CA 92624. **Tel** (714)493-2101, FAX (714)240-8680. **LC** TS532; .G78. **DD** 683/.4/005.

US/0362-4749
**GUN WORLD HUNTING GUIDE.** Began with issue for 1973. English. an. $1.50. Gallant Charger Publishing Inc., Box HH, 34249 Camino Capistrano, Capistrano Beach CA 92624. **Tel** (714)493-2101, FAX (714)240-8680. **LC** SK1; .G83. **DD** 799.2/13/05.

CN
**GUNRUNNER.** English. mo. 23.00Can$ Canada; 45.00Can$ other. Gunrunner, Box 565, Lethbridge Alberta, T1J 3Z4 Canada. **Tel** (403)327-3030, FAX (403)328-3006. **ED** Anna Burla. **Ad Acc. Circ:** 12,000 (ctrl).
**Desc:** Information on firearms trade.

US/0017-5684
**GUNS & AMMO.** [Guns ammo]. **VAT** Guns and Ammo. Vol. 1, (Summer 1958)-. Periodical. English. mo. $21.94 US; $32.04 Canada; $30.94 other. Petersen Publishing Company, 6420 Wilshire Bouldevard, Los Angeles CA 90048. **Tel** (213)782-2485. **(Subscription address:** Neodata / Colorado, PO Box 2606, Boulder Boulder CO 80322.**) ED** Jay Hard. **LC** TS535; .G83. **Circ:** 478,462. available on microfilm and microfiche from University Microfilms International (UMI); available on an online database (file 647/Full-Text) from DIALOG.
**Ind/Abst** Gen. Period. Index (Jan. 1985-Dec. 1985); Mag. Index (1977-Dec. 1985).

US/0883-9468
**GUNS & AMMO ACTION SERIES.** [Guns ammo action ser.]. **VFOAT** Guns and Ammo Action Series. No. 1-. Monographic series. English. bm. Price varies per volume. Petersen Publishing Company, 6420 Wilshire Bouldevard, Los Angeles CA 90048. **Tel** (213)782-2485. **LC** SK274; .G79. **DD** 799.2/028/33.

AT/0157-1729
**GUNS AUSTRALIA.** [Guns Aust.]. (1978)-. Periodical. English. Six times a year. 24.00Aus$ Australia; 70.00Aus$ other. Yaffa Publishing Group Pty Ltd., GPO Box 606, Sydney NSW 2001 Australia. **Tel** 011 61 2 2812333, FAX 011 61 2 2812750. **DD** 683.40994.

US/1044-6257
**GUNS MAGAZINE.** [Guns mag.]. **VFOAT** Guns. (198?)-. Periodical. English. mo. $19.95 (one year), $34.95 (two year), $46.95 (three year). Publishers Development Corporation, 591 Camino de La Reina, Suite 200, San Diego CA 92108. **Tel** (619)297-5350, FAX (619)297-5353, telex 695-478. **LC** TS519; .G82. **DD** 683.4. ***Continues*** *Guns, 0017-5676.*

UK
**GUNS REVIEW. Added/Corp** British Sporting Rifle Club. (19??)-. Periodical. English. mo. £18.00 UK, £21.00 other. Teesdale Publishing Company, Ltd., PO Box 35, Standard House, Bonhill Street, London EC2A 4DA England. **Tel** 011 44 71 6284741, FAX 011 44 71 6388497, telex 888602. **ED** Colin Greenwood. **LC** TS532; .G87. **DD** 683/.4/005. Index available. **Bk Rev**. **Ad Acc. Circ:** 20,000.
**Desc:** Covers all aspects of guns and shooting, with a wide variety of shooting subjects for enthusiasts and collectors.
**Ind/Abst** Acoust. Abstr.

US/0731-1885
**GUTMANN PUMA/EXPLORER KNIFE ANNUAL.** ***Title Change.*** **See** Recreation, Leisure-Outdoor Life.

FR
**GYMNASTE.** French. Fed Francaise de Gymnastique, 7 Ter Cour des Petites Ecuries, 75010 Paris France.
**Ind/Abst** SPORT Discus.

NO
**GYMNASTIKK OG TURN.** (1948)-. Periodical. Norwegian. ir. $10.00. Norges Gymnastikk-OG, Hauger Skolovei 1, 1351 Rud Norway. **ED** Rolf Rustad.

FR
**HANDBALL.** French. Federation Francaise de Handball, 62 rue Gabriel Peri, 94250 Gentilly France.

GW/0178-2983
**HANDBALL-MAGAZIN.** [Handball-Mag.]. (1984)-. Periodical. German. mo. DM67.20 Germany; DM74.40 other. Philippka Verlag, Postfach 6540, D-48034 Muenster Germany. **Tel** 011 49 251 230-0522. **UDC** 796.322. ***Continues*** *Handball, 0138-1296.*

US/0046-6778
**HANDBALL (SKOKIE, ILL.).** (HANDBALL.). **Added/Corp** United States Handball Association. (June 1971)-. Periodical. English. bm. $25.00 (one year), $70.00 (three year); add 15.00 postage per year to other. US Handball Association, 2333 North Tuscon Ave., Tucson AZ 85716. **Tel** (602)795-0434. available on microfilm and microfiche from University Microfilms International (UMI). ***Continues*** *Ace, 0515-2488.*
**Ind/Abst** Phys. Educ. Index (1978-); SPORT Discus.

CN/0849-097X
**HANDBOOK - ALBERTA BADMINTON ASSOCIATION.** (HANDBOOK.). [Handb. - Alta. Badminton Assoc.]. **Main/Corp** Alberta Badminton Association. (1990)-. English. Free to members. Alberta Badminton Association, 11759 Groat Road, Edmonton Alta. T5M 3K6. **Tel** (403)453-8536. **DD** 796.34/5/0607123. ***Continues*** *Badminton Rule Book, 0826-5208.*

CN/0225-0314
**HANDBOOK AND DIRECTORY - CANADIAN FIELD HOCKEY ASSOCIATION.** [Handb. dir. - Can. Field Hockey Assoc.]. **Main/Corp** Canadian Field Hockey Association. Began publication in 1972?. Directory. English. an. Free to members. Canadian Field Hockey Council, 333 River Road, Vanier Ontario K1L 8B9 Canada. **Tel** (613)748-5634, telex 053-3660. **DD** 796.35/5/02571. ctrl circ.
**Desc:** Listing of national and provincial executives, standing committees. Plus the constitution and bylaws of the association.

CN/0225-0306
**HANDBOOK AND DIRECTORY - CANADIAN WOMEN'S FIELD HOCKEY ASSOCIATION.** [Handb. dir. - Can Field Hockey Assoc.]. **Main/Corp** Canadian Women's Field Hockey Association. Began publication in 1972?. Directory. English. an. Free to members. Canadian Field Hockey Council, 333 River Road, Vanier Ontario K1L 8B9 Canada. **Tel** (613)748-5634, telex 053-3660. **DD** 796.35/5/02571. ctrl circ.
**Desc:** Listing of current national and provincial executives, standing committees plus constitution and bylaws of the associations.

CN/0229-5806
**HANDBOOK - CANADIAN BADMINTON ASSOCIATION.** (HANDBOOK / CANADIAN BADMINTON ASSOCIATION, CANADIAN BADMINTON COACHES ASSOCIATION, CANADIAN BADMINTON UMPIRES ASSOCIATION.). [Hand. - Can. Badminton Assoc.]. **Main/Corp** Canadian Badminton Association. **VAT** Handbook - Canadian Badminton Coaches Association; Handbook - Canadian Badminton Umpires Association. English (French). an. $5.00. Canadian Badminton Association, 1600 James Naismith Drive, Gloucester Ontario K1N 5B4 Canada. **Tel** (613)748-5605, FAX (613)746-5695, telex 053-3660. **DD** 796.34/5/0971.

US
**HANDBOOK - NEW YORK STATE PUBLIC HIGH SCHOOL ATHLETIC ASSOCIATION.** **Main/Corp** New York State Public High School Athletic Association. English. be. $3.00. New York State Public High School Athletic Association Inc, 88 Delaware Avenue, Delmar NY 12054-1536. **Tel** (518)439-8872. **ED** A B Doyle. **Circ:** 18,000 (ctrl).
**Desc:** A ready source of reference and information on the philosophy, policies and rules of the association.

UK/0306-8218
**HANDBOOK - RUGBY FOOTBALL UNION.** [Handb. - Rugby Footb. Union]. **Main/Corp** Rugby Football Union. Began in 1894?. English. an. £/50. **LC** GV945.4; .R83B. **DD** 796.33/3/0621.

UK/0260-8693
**HANDGUNNER.** [Handgunner]. (1980)-. Periodical. English. Six times a year. £13.00 UK; £15.00 Europe; £17.00 other. Handgunner Ltd, Seychelles Regent Road, Essex Brightlingsea CO7 0NN England. **Tel** 011 44 206 305204. **ED** R.A.I. Monday. **DD** 683.4305. **Bk Rev**, (Qty: 6). **Ad Acc**, **Adv Mgr:** A.Smith. **Circ:** 17,000.
**Desc:** All aspects of classic and modern firearms; design, use, technology, law, administration, military, police, sport, competition, trade, manufacture, politics.

●US/1060-068X
**HANDGUNNING.** **VFOAT** Handgunning. Vol. 6, No. 1 (Jan.-Feb. 1992)-. Periodical. English. Six times a year. $19.98 US; $27.98 other. PJS Publications Inc., News Plaza, PO Box 1790, Peoria IL 61656. **Tel** (309)682-6626, FAX (309)682-7394. **(Subscription address:** CDS Agency Hard Copy, PO Box 4966, Des Moines IA 50340.**)** **LC** TS537; .S46. **DD** 683.4/005. ***Continues*** *Shooting Times Handgun Quarterly, 1042-6108.*

US/1054-4135
**HANDGUNS FOR SPORT & DEFENSE.** ***Title Change.*** [Handguns sport defense]. **VFOAT** Handguns; Handguns for Sport and Defense; Petersen's Handguns for Sport and Defense; Petersen's Handguns for Sport & Defense; Petersen's Handguns. Vol. 5, No. 1 (Jan. 1991)-(199?). Periodical. English. mo. Petersen Publishing Company, 6420 Wilshire Bouldevard, Los Angeles CA 90048. **Tel** (213)782-2485. **DD** 683. ***Continues*** *Petersen's Handguns, 1040-1865.* ***Continued by*** *Handguns (Los Angeles, Calif.), 1068-2635.*
**Desc:** Specializes in the thorough testing and evaluation of a wide variety of handguns. Topics of special interest include self-defense, law enforcement, handgun hunting, handgun history, competitions, and handloading. Also featured are in-depth evaluations of new guns, ammunition, handgun safety, and much more.

US/1068-2635
**HANDGUNS (LOS ANGELES, CALIF.).** (HANDGUNS.). [Handguns]. (199?)-. Periodical. English. mo. $23.94 US; $34.18 Canada; $32.94 other. Petersen Publishing Company, 6420 Wilshire Bouldevard, Los Angeles CA 90048. **Tel** (213)782-2485. **(Subscription address:** Neodata / Colorado, PO Box 2606, Boulder Boulder CO 80322.**)** **LC** WMLC 93/933. **DD** 683. ***Continues*** *Handguns for Sport & Defense, 1054-4135.*

US/0017-7393
**HANDLOADER.** [Handloader]. **VFOAT** Handloader Magazine. (19??)-. Periodical. English. bm. $19.00 (1 year), $35.00 (2 year), $50.00 (3 year) US; $25.00 (1 year), $47.00 (2 year), $68.00 (3 year) other. Wolfe Publishing Company, 6471 Airpark Drive, Prescott AZ 86301. **Tel** (602)445-7810. **ED** Tom Gresham. **LC** WMLC 93/926. Index available. cum. index. **Bk Rev**. **Ad Acc**. **Circ:** 35,000 (ctrl).
**Desc:** Directed to those who reload centerfire ammunition, shotshells and who cast or swage bullets.

US
**HANDLOADER BULLETIN MAKING ANNUAL.** ***Ceased.*** (19??)-(1992 ed.). Bulletin. English. an. Wolfe Publishing Company, 6471 Airpark Drive, Prescott AZ 86301. **Tel** (602)445-7810.

US/0895-433X
**HANG GLIDING.** [Hang glid.]. **Added/Corp** United States Hang Gliding Association. (19??)-. Periodical. English. mo. $35.00 US; $40.00 Canada & Mexico; $50.00 other. US Hang Glider Association Inc., PO Box 8300, Colorado Springs CO 80933. **Tel** (719)632-8300, FAX (719)632-6417. **ED** Gil Dodgen. **DD** 797. **Bk Rev**. **Ad Acc**, **Adv Mgr:** Jeff Elgart, **Tel** (719)632-8300. **Circ:** 9,110 (ctrl).
**Desc:** Magazine is published for hang gliding sport enthusiasts to create further interest in the sport, by means of open communication and to advance hang gliding methods and safety.
**Ind/Abst** SPORT Discus; SportSearch (May 1987-).

US
**HANK STRAM'S PRO FOOTBALL SCOUTING REPORT.** **VFOAT** Pro Football Scouting Report. (1991)-. English. Bonus Books, Inc., 160 East Illinois Street, Chicago IL 60611. **LC** GV953.4; .H36. **DD** 796.332/64/0973.

US/1045-0017
**HAWAII, WASHINGTON, ALASKA, OREGON COACHING DIRECTORY : AN OFFICIAL PUBLICATION OF THE NATIONAL INTERSCHOLASTIC ATHLETIC ADMINISTRATORS ASSOCIATION, THE ALASKA INTERSCHOLASTIC ATHLETIC ADMINISTRATORS ASSOCIATION, AND THE WASHINGTON SECONDARY SCHOOL ATHLETIC ADMINISTRATORS ASSOCIATION.** [Hawaii Wash. Alsk. Or. coach. dir.]. **VFOAT** Washington, Oregon, Alaska, Hawaii Coaches Directory of High Schools and Colleges. (1988/89)-. Directory. English. an. $7.95. Clell Wade Coaches Directory, PO Box 177, Cassville MO 65625. **Tel** (417)847-2783. **LC** GV711; .H28. **DD** 796/.025. ***Continues*** *Washington, Oregon, Alaska, Hawaii Coaches Directory of High Schools and Colleges.*

US/1060-8672
**HAWG (MT. MORRIS, N.Y.).** (HAWG : THE AMERICAN MOTORCYCLE SPORTS MAGAZINE.). [Hawg]. **VFOAT** Hawg Magazine. Vol. 1, Issue 1 (1991)-. Periodical. English. qt. Free. McBride Associates, Ltd., 12 Spring Street, Mt. Morris NY 14510. **DD** 796.

US
**HIGH SCHOOL BASEBALL RULES.** **Main/Corp** National Federation of State High School Associations. **VFOAT** Baseball Rules. (199?)-. English. **LC** GV877; .B335. **DD** 796.357/02/022. ***Continues*** *Baseball Rule Book.*
**Desc:** Official rules governing high school baseball in the United States.

●US/1069-6393
**HIGH SCHOOL GIRLS GYMNASTICS RULES AND MANUAL.** [High sch. girls gymnast. rules man.]. **Main/Corp** National Federation of State High School Associations. **VFOAT** Girls Gymnastics Rules and Manual. (1992)-. English. an. $3.00. National Federation of State High School Associations, 11724 Northwest Plaza Circle, PO Box 20626, Kansas City MO 64195-0626. **Tel** (816)464-5400, FAX (816)464-5571. **LC** GV464; .N37b. **DD** 796.4/1/088042. ***Continues*** *National Federation of State High School Associations. Official High School Girls Gymnastics Rules and Manual, 0739-9804.*

US
**HIGH SCHOOL SOFTBALL RULES.** **Main/Corp** National Federation of State High School Associations. **VFOAT** Softball Rules; High School Softball Rules for Boys and Girls Competition. (19??)-. English. an. National Federation of State High School Associations, 11724 Northwest Plaza Circle, PO Box 20626, Kansas City MO 64195-0626. **Tel** (816)464-5400, FAX (816)464-5571. **LC** GV881.2; .N37a. ***Continues*** *National Federation of State High School Associations. Official High School Softball Rules.*

●US/1075-1920
**HIGH SCHOOL SOFTBALL UMPIRES MANUAL.** [High sch. softb. ump. man.]. **Main/Corp** National Federation of State High School Associations. **VFOAT** Softball Umpires Manual. (1994/1995)-. English. be. National Federation of State High School Associations, 11724 Northwest Plaza Circle, PO Box 20626, Kansas City MO 64195-0626. **Tel** (816)464-5400, FAX (816)464-5571. **LC** IN PROCESS. **DD** 796. ***Continues in part*** *National Federation of State High School Associations. Official High School Softball Case Book and Umpires Manual.*

US
**HIGH SCHOOL SPORTS.** English. bm. $1.50. National Federation of State High School Associations, 11724 Northwest Plaza Circle, PO Box 20626, Kansas City MO 64195-0626. **Tel** (816)464-5400, FAX (816)464-5571. ctrl circ.

US
**HIGH SCHOOL SWIMMING, DIVING, AND WATER POLO RULES.** **Main/Corp** National Federation of State High School Associations. **VFOAT** Swimming, Diving, and Water Polo Rules. (1990/1991)-. English. National Federation of State High School Associations, 11724 Northwest Plaza Circle, PO Box 20626, Kansas City MO 64195-0626. **Tel** (816)464-5400, FAX (816)464-5571. **LC** GV837; .N323a. **DD** 797.2007120973. ***Continues*** *National Federation of State High School Associations. Official High School Swimming and Diving, Water Polo Rules.*

US/1054-3600
**HIGH SCHOOL WRESTLING RULES.** [High sch. wrestl. rules]. **Main/Corp** National Federation of State High School Associations. **VFOAT** Wrestling Rules; High School Rules. Wrestling. (1990/91)-. English. National Federation of State High School Associations, 11724 Northwest Plaza Circle, PO Box 20626, Kansas City MO 64195-0626. **Tel** (816)464-5400, FAX (816)464-5571. **LC** GV1195; .W72. **DD** 796.8/12/0712. ***Continues*** *Official High School Wrestling Rules, 0735-8946.*

US/0094-0291
**HIKING (HIGHLAND PARK).** **See** Recreation, Leisure-Outdoor Life.

JA
**HISTORY OF PHYSICAL EDUCATION AND SPORT: RESEARCH AND STUDIES.** ***Ceased.*** **See** Education-Physical Education and Training.

CN/0826-5313
**HOCKEY AMATEUR.** [Hockey amat.]. **Main/Corp** Canadian Amateur Hockey Association. English. an. Free. Hockey Amateur, 8928 Boulevard St-Michel, Montreal Quebec H1Z 3G4 Canada. **DD** 796.96/2/02022.

●US/1064-6892
**HOCKEY, ART OF THE STATE.** **VFOAT** Hockey Magazine. Vol. 5, No. 1 (Oct. 1992)-. Periodical. English. mo. **LC** GV848.4.U6; M6. **DD** 796.962/09776/05. ***Continues*** *Minnesota Hockey, 1050-740X.*

CN/0841-6982
**HOCKEY AUJOURD'HUI.** (HOCKEY AUJOURD'HUI / CAHA.). [Hockey aujourd'hui]. **Added/Corp** Association Canadienne de Hockey Amateur. (1977/1978)-. French. Free to minor hockey players in Canada; 2.00Can$ other. Canadian Amateur Hockey Association, 1600 Promenade James Naismith, Gloucester Ontario K1B 5N4 Canada. **Tel** (613)748-5617. **DD** 796.96/26.
**Ind/Abst** SPORT Discus.

US/1064-6892
**HOCKEY (BLOOMINGTON, MINN.).** (HOCKEY.). (1992)-. Periodical. English. bm. Hockey Publications, 1022 West 80th Street, Bloomington MN 55420-1009. ***Continues*** *Minnesota Hockey, 1050-740X.*

## Recreation, Leisure —Sports

**AT**
**HOCKEY CIRCLE.** English. Four times a year. 25.00Aus$ Australia; 27.50Aus$ New Zealand and Papua New Guinea; 37.50Aus$ US, Canada and Israel. Hockey Circle, PO Box 127, Glen Iris 3146 Australia. **Tel** 011 61 3 8857235. **ED** Richard Blaze. **Ad Acc.** ctrl circ.

CN/0835-8044
**HOCKEY COACHING JOURNAL.** [Hockey coach. j.]. Vol. 1, Issue 1 (Dec. 1987)-. Periodical. English. ir. 24.00Can$ Canada; 34.00Can$ other. Hockey Coaching Journal, 20 Sir Pellias Perr, Markham Ontario L3P 2Z8 Canada. **Tel** (416)472-4582. **DD** 796.96/2/077. **Ind/Abst** SPORT Discus.

US/0046-7693
**HOCKEY DIGEST (EVANSTON, ILL.).** (HOCKEY DIGEST.). [Hockey dig.]. Vol. 1, (Nov. 1972)-. Periodical. English. Eight times a year. $22.00 US; $30.00 other. Century Publishing Company, 990 Grove Street, Evanston IL 60201-4370. **Tel** (708)491-6440, (800)331-3333, FAX (708)491-0459. **(Subscription address:** Kable Publishers Aide, 308 East Hitt Street, Subscriptions Department, Mt. Morris, IL 61054) **ED** Michael Herbert. **LC** GV846; .H57. **DD** 796.9/62/05. **Bk Rev. Ad Acc. Circ:** 135,000. available on microfilm and microfiche from University Microfilms International (UMI). **Desc:** Covers the National Hockey League. **Ind/Abst** Mag. Artic. Summar. Elite (Jan. 1994-); Mag. Artic. Summar. CD-ROM (Jan. 1994-); SPORT Discus; SportSearch (May 1987-).

UK/0950-9550
**HOCKEY DIGEST (HARROW).** [Hockey dig. Harrow]. (1975)-. Periodical. English. Ten times a year. £21.50 UK; £20.00 other. Hockey Digest, 426 Long Drive, Unit E6 Aladdin, Middlesex UB6 8UH England. **Tel** 011 44 81 575 3121, FAX 011 44 81 575 1320. **ED** P.J. Luck. **Ad Acc. Circ:** 5,000 (ctrl). **Continues** Indoor Hockey News. **Desc:** Hockey news, results, league tables, tournaments, etc. mainly in Britain.

UK/0018-3008
**HOCKEY FIELD.** Vol. 43, No. 1 (Sept. 17, 1955)-. Periodical. English. mo $14.00 surface mail, $24.00 airmail. Miss Gertrude Hooper, 369 Atlantic Avenue, Cohasset MA 02025. **ED** J Whitehead. **Continues** Women's Hockey Field. **Ind/Abst** SPORT Discus; SportSearch (May 1987-).

CN/0704-7983
**HOCKEY (MONTREAL).** (HOCKEY.). V. 1- Dec. 1977-. Periodical. French. ir. $10.00. Publications Belseg, Hockey Inc, Bureau 2202/1115 Ouest rue Sherbrooke, Montreal Quebec H3A 1H3 Canada. **DD** 796.9/62/05.

CN/0018-3016
**HOCKEY NEWS, THE.** [Hockey news]. (Oct. 1, 1947)-. Periodical. English. Forty-two times a year. $49.95 (one year); $94.85 (two year); $137.85 (three year). Transcontinental Publications, 85 Scarsdale Road, Suite 100, Don Mills, Ontario M3B 2R2 Canada. **Tel** (800)268-7793. **ED** Michael Lawton and Bob McKenzie. cum. index. **Bk Rev. Ad Acc. Circ:** 112,000. available on microfilm and microfiche from University Microfilms International (UMI). **Desc:** Covers all levels of the game of hockey from minors, colleges, amateurs, European and international teams to the NHL. Behind-the-scenes happenings are included giving comprehensive, in-depth reportage of the sport. A team of columnists, reporters and statisticians keeps readers up-to-date on all the trades, opinions, promotions, controversies, wins, losses, goals, assists, points, and penalty minutes. **Ind/Abst** Can. Index; Can. Period. Index (19??-).

CN/0845-2563
**HOCKEY NEWS ... YEARBOOK, THE.** [Hockey news yearb.]. (19??)-. English. an. 9.95Can$. Transcontinental Publications, 85 Scarsdale Road, Suite 100, Don Mills, Ontario M3B 2R2 Canada. **Tel** (800)268-7793. **DD** 796.96/26.

US/0361-5847
**HOCKEY (NORWALK).** (HOCKEY.). V. 1- Nov. 1975-. Periodical. English. bm. $6.00. Golf Digest, Inc., 297 Westport Avenue, Norwalk CT 06856. **LC** GV846; .H56. **DD** 796.9/62/05.

CN/0821-4700
**HOCKEY ONTARIO MAGAZINE.** [Hockey Ont. mag.]. **Added/Corp** Hockey Ontario. **VFOAT** Hockey Ontario. Vol. 3, No. 6 (Sept./Oct. 1984)-. Periodical. English. ir. $4.50. Hockey Ontario Development Committee, 1220 Sheppard Avenue East, Willowdale Ontario M2K 2X1 Canada. **DD** 796.96/2/05. **Continues** Hockey Scope.

CN/0712-8428
**HOCKEY PROFESSIONNEL.** [Hockey prof.]. French. an. $6.95 Per Volume. Hockey Professionnel, c/o Presses Boucherville Polymédias, 175 le Montagne, Boucherville Quebec J4B 6G4 Canada. **DD** 796.96/2/06. **Continues** Hockey L N H, 0704-7894.

●CN/0836-5148
**HOCKEY SCOUTING REPORT.** (HOCKEY SCOUTING REPORT / FRANK BROWN; SHERRY ROSS.). [Hockey scout. rep.]. (1991/1992)-. English. $14.95 per vol. Douglas & McIntyre, 1615 Venables Street, Vancouver BC V5L 2H1. **DD** 796.962/64. **Continues** Hockey Scouting Report., 0836-5148.

US/0073-2869
**HOCKEY STARS OF ... .** [Hockey stars]. English. $0.95. Pyramid Books, 919 Third Avenue, New York NY 10022. **LC** GV846.5.A1; F49. **DD** 796.9/62/0922.

CN/0833-0859
**HOCKEY TODAY.** [Hockey today]. **Added/Corp** Canadian Amateur Hockey Association. (1978)-. English. an. $2.00 (each volume). Canadian Amateur Hockey Association, 1600 Promenade James Naismith, Gloucester Ontario K1B 5N4 Canada. **Tel** (613)748-5617. **DD** 796.96/26. **Ind/Abst** SPORT Discus; SportSearch (May 1987-).

US/1059-4795
**HOCKEY TODAY (NEW YORK, N.Y.).** (HOCKEY TODAY.). (1991)-. Periodical. English. qt. $2.95 (single issue). Dojo Publishing, 300 West 43rd Street, New York NY 10036.

CN/0317-9257
**HOCKEY'S HERITAGE.** *Suspended.* 1969-Suspended 1982. Periodical. English. be. Hockey Hall of Fame, Canadian National Exhibition Grounds, Toronto Ontario M6K 3C3 Canada. **Tel** (416)595-1345. **DD** 796.9/62/0922. **Continues** Hockey Hall of Fame Book, 0317-9265.

RU/0302-7260
**HOKKEJ (MOSKVA).** (KHOKKEI; KALENDAR-SPRAVOCHNIK.). [Hokkej]. (19??)-. Russian. wk. $89.95. Fizkultura i Sport, Luzhneskaia Nab 8, 119270 Moscow Russia. **(Subscription address:** East View Publications Inc., 3020 Harbor Lane North, Suite 110, Minneapolis MN 55447.) **LC** GV848.4.R8K48.

FR/0018-4411
**HOMMES VOLANTS PARIS, LES.** (LES HOMMES VOLANTS.). (1964)-. Periodical. French. mo. 146.91F France, 250.00F other. Les Hommes Volants, 28 Rue de Navarin, f 75009 Paris France. **Tel** 011 33 1 45260275, FAX 011 33 1 40160951, telex 642717. **ED** Gardes Rene. **UDC** 797.5. Index available. cum. index. **Circ:** 20,000 (ctrl). **Continues** Para Presse Aviation (Paris), 1144-3626. **Ind/Abst** SPORT Discus.

US/0895-4046
**HONEY HOLE.** [Honey hole]. **Added/Corp** Texas Black Bass Unlimited (Organization). (198?)-. Periodical. English. Nine times a year. $18.00 US; $35.82 Canada; $32.94 Mexico; $39.42 other. Honey Hole Magazine Inc., PO Box 9027, Forth Worth TX 76147. **Tel** (817)738-5596. **DD** 799. **Bk Rev. (Qty: 1). Ad Acc. Adv Mgr:** Roger Romines, **Tel** (817)738-5596. **Circ:** 20,000.

US/0749-5285
**HOOP/NBA TODAY.** (HOOP.). [Hoop]. Vol. 11, Issue 1 (Nov. 1984)-. Periodical. English. Eight times a year. $20.95 (US); $24.95 (Canada); $39.95 (other). Professional Sports Publ, PO Box Hoop, Lowell MA 01852. **Tel** (508)452-6310, FAX (212)949-6109. **LC** GV885.515.N37; H66. **DD** 796.32/364/0973.

US
**HOOSIER SCENE.** V. 12, No. 5- Sept. 27, 1976-. Periodical. English. Indiana University Varsity, Club Assembly Hall, Bloomington IN 47401. **Continues** Indiana Football News.

UK
**HORSE AND HOUND HUNTER CHASERS AND POINT-TO-POINTERS.** *See* Horses and Horsemanship.

CN/0380-2779
**HORSE RACING MAGAZINE.** *See* Horses and Horsemanship.

US
**HORSESHOE PITCHER'S NEWS DIGEST, THE.** **Added/Corp** National Horseshoe Pitcher's Association. (19??)-. Periodical. English. mo. $12.00. National Horseshoe Pitchers Association of America, PO Box 278, Munroe Falls OH 44262. **Tel** (216)688-6522. **ED** F. Ellis Cobb. **Ad Acc. Circ:** 3,000.

US/0018-6031
**HOT ROD.** *See* Transportation-Automobiles.

US
**HOT ROD BIKES.** (19??)-. Periodical. English. bm (6 issues). $13.95 US; $24.56 Canada; $23.95 other. Petersen Publishing Company, 6420 Wilshire Boulevard, Los Angeles CA 90048. **Tel** (213)782-2485. **(Subscription address:** Neodata / Colorado, PO Box 2606, Boulder Boulder CO 80322.)

US/1057-0179
**HOT STOVE BASEBALL.** [Hot stove baseb.]. Vol. 1 (Winter 1991)-. Periodical. English. sa. Vanguard Sports Publications, PO Box 667, Chapel Hill NC 27514. **DD** 796.

US/0737-6227
**HUNTER SAFETY INSTRUCTOR.** *Title Change.* (HUNTER SAFETY INSTRUCTOR : THE OFFICIAL PUBLICATION OF THE NORTH AMERICAN ASSOCIATION OF HUNTER SAFETY COORDINATORS.). [Hunt. saf. instr.]. **Added/Corp** North American Association of Hunter Safety Coordinators. Vol. 2, No. 3 (June/July 1983)-(199?). Periodical. English. mo. Outdoor Empire Publishing Company, 511 Eastlake Avenue, Box 19000, Seattle WA 98109. **Tel** (206)624-3845. **Continues** Hunter Safety News (Seattle, Wash.). **Continued by** Hunter Education Instructor, 1066-3460.

US/0018-7860
**HUNTER'S HORN, THE.** (19??)-. Periodical. English. Twelve times a year. $14.00. Hunters Horn, 114 120 Franklin Avenue, Sesser IL 62884. **Tel** (618)625-2711. **ED** George O. Slankard. **Ad Acc. Circ:** 10,000. **Desc:** Fox hunting events and supplies plus fox hunting stories.

US/0276-8895
**HUNTING (NEW YORK, N.Y.).** (HUNTING.). **VFOAT** Sports Afield Hunting. Periodical. English. an. $2.50 (per issue). Sports Afield, 250 West 55th Street, New York NY 10019. **Tel** (212)649-4014. **ED** Mike Schwanz. **LC** SK7; .S6. **DD** 799.2/05. **UDC** 639.7; 799.2. **Ad Acc. Circ:** 300,000. **Continues** Sports Afield Hunting Annual. **Desc:** How-to articles about big-game hunting and birdshooting.

CN/0715-495X
**HUSKY FEVER.** [Husky fever]. Vol. 1, No. 1 (1978)-. Periodical. English. mo. $10.50. Husky Fever, PO Box 2212, Yellowknife Northwest Territories X0E 1H0 Canada. **DD** 798/.8.

UK
**I.A.A.F. DIRECTORY / I.A.A.F.** *Title Change.* **Main/Corp** International Amateur Athletic Federation. **VFOAT** IAAF Directory; Repertoire FIAA; Repertoire F.I.A.A. Directory. English. an. International Amateur Athletic Federation, 3 Hans Crescent Knightsbridge, London SW1X OLN England. **Tel** 011 44 71 5818771, FAX 011 44 71 5845907, telex 9419338. **ED** Joanne Dick. **LC** GV563; .I74414. **DD** 796./06/01. **Circ:** 4,000-5,000. **Continued by** Directory & Calendar (International Amateur Athletic Federation).

US/8755-2469
**IDAHO WILDLIFE.** *See* Recreation, Leisure-Outdoor Life.

US/0892-9130
**ILLINOIS INTERSCHOLASTIC, THE.** *Ceased.* (1940)-(19??). Periodical. English. ir (8 issues yearly). Illinois High School Association, 2715 McGraw Drive, Box 2715, Bloomington IL 61702. **Tel** (309)663-6377. **UDC** 796.422. **Continues** Illinois High School Athlete.

US
**ILLINOIS PREP TOP TIMES. CROSS COUNTRY EDITION.** English. Ten times a year (Aug.-Nov.). $20.00. Illinois Prep Top Times, 669 North Eagle Street, Naperville IL 60563. **Tel** (708)717-1744, FAX (708)717-9522.

US
**ILLINOIS PREP TOP TIMES. TRACK FIELD EDITION.** English. Sixteen times a year. $30.00. Illinois Prep Top Times, 669 North Eagle Street, Naperville IL 60563. **Tel** (708)717-1744, FAX (708)717-9522.

US/0747-4911
**ILLINOIS RUNNER.** (Oct. 1983)-. Periodical. English. mo (10 issues). $10.00. Illinois Runner, PO Box 53, Fairbury IL 61739-0053. **ED** Rich Elliott. **Circ:** 15,000. **Desc:** Coverage of amateur athletics with particular emphasis on running and tri-athletics.

US/0091-3901
**ILLUSTRATED DIGEST OF BASEBALL.** English. $1.50. Stadia Sports Publications, 180 Madison Avenue, New York NY 10016. **LC** GV877; .I53. **DD** 796.357/64/0973. **UDC** 796.333.071(73).

IT
**IMPIANTI ATTREZZATURE SPORTIVE E RICREATIVE.** Rima SRL, Via Barzini 20, 20125 Milan Italy.

US/1043-6839
**IMPRESSIONS (DALLAS, TEX.).** *See* Clothing Industry and Fashion.

US/0744-5172
**IN THE CREASE.** *Ceased.* (19??)-(19??). Periodical. English. ir. in the Crease/The Lacrosse, PO Box 281, Riderwood MD 21139. **Tel** (301)433-0743.

US/1041-2859
**INDEX TO THE SPORTING NEWS.** [Index Sport. news]. (1990)-. English. te. $40.00 (Vol. 1). John Gordon Burke Publisher Inc., PO Box 1492, Evanston IL

Recreation, Leisure —Sports

60204. **Tel** (708)866-8625, FAX (708)866-8625. **ED** Ned Kehde. **LC** GV583; .I73. **DD** 796/.0973. Index available. cum. index. available on an online database.
**Desc:** Subject index to The Sporting News.

US/0278-5900
**INDEX (TULSA, OKLA.), THE.** (THE INDEX.). Vol. 1, No. 1 (Jan. 1977-Dec. 1980)-. English. sa. $8.50. Lynn A. Freiheit, PO Box 33093, Tulsa OK 74135. **LC** GV1061; .I53. **DD** 796.4/26.

●US
**INDIANA BASKETBALL HISTORY : A PUBLICATION OF THE INDIANA BASKETBALL HALL OF FAME.**
**Added/Corp** Indiana Basketball Hall of Fame. Vol. 1, No. 1 (Fall 1992)-. Periodical. English. qt. $10.00. Indiana Basketball Hall of Fame, 1 Hall of Fame Court, New Castle IN 47362. **LC** GV885.72.I6; I518. ***Absorbed*** *News (Indiana Basketball Hall of Fame).*

US
**INDIANA GRAPPLER.** (19??)-. English. Seven times a year. $20.00. The American Grappler, PO Box 5205, Bloomington IN 47407. **ED** Rick Chitwood (phone: (812)339-6989). **Ad Acc, Adv Mgr:** Dianne Chitwood. **Circ:** 1,200. Documents available from the publisher.
**Desc:** This is state wrestling magazine. Covers high school, college, freestyle, Greco-Roman, national and amateur wrestling.

US/1055-3355
**INDIANAPOLIS 500 YEARBOOK, THE.**
**See** Transportation-Automobiles.

US/1071-1759
**INDY CAR RACING MAGAZINE.** [Indy car racing mag.]. **VFOAT** Indycar Racing Magazine; Indy Car Racing. (19??)-. Periodical. English. Twelve times a year. $29.00 US; $44.00 Canada; $49.00 other. Indy Car Racing Publications, 617 South 94th Street, Milwaukee WI 53214. **Tel** (414)774-6211, FAX (414)774-6740. **ED** Ned Wicker, (414)774-6291. **DD** 796. **Bk Rev**, (Qty: 10). **Ad Acc, Adv Mgr:** Kevin Kelly. **Circ:** 40,000. ***Continues*** *Indy Car Racing, 0747-0894.*
**Desc:** Covers completely all aspects of Indy car racing.

US/1059-3179
**INDY REVIEW.** [Indy rev.]. **Added/Corp** Indianapolis Motor Speedway Corp. Indy 500 Publications. Vol. 1 (1991)-. Periodical. English. $24.95. Indy Review, Indianapolis Motor Speedway Corp., 4790 West 16th Street, Indianapolis IN 46240. **LC** WMLC 91/3314. **DD** 796.

CN/0710-1414
**INFO BASKET.** [Info basket]. No. 1 (Oct. 1970)-V. 6, No 3 (Feb. 1976). Periodical. French (English). Federation de Basketball du Quebec, 1415 Est rue Jarry, Montreal Quebec H2E 2Z7 Canada. **DD** 796.32/3/060714. **UDC** 796.325(714).

CN/0823-6305
**INFO-VOLLEY.** (INFO-VOLLEY / A.R.V.N.Q.). [Info-volley]. No. 1 (1st Oct. 1980)-. Periodical. French. mo. Association Regionale de Volleyball de Quebec, Bureau 225/1990 Ouest Boulevard Charest, Sainte-Foy Quebec G1N 4K8 Canada. **DD** 796.32/5/06071447. **UDC** 379.8(714). ***Continues*** *Bulletin de Nouvelles (Association Regionale de Volleyball de Quebec), 0710-734X.*

US/0279-9863
**INFOAAU.** **See** Health and Personal Fitness.

US/1046-4980
**INFORMATION PLEASE SPORTS ALMANAC, THE.** [Inf. please sports alm.]. **VFOAT** Sports Almanac. (1990)-. English. an. $10.95. Houghton Mifflin Company, Wayside Road, Burlington MA 01803. **Tel** (800)225-3362, (617)272-1500. **LC** GV741; .I58. **DD** 796/.05.

CN/0711-1126
**INSIDE EDGE.** (INSIDE EDGE : THE OFFICIAL PUBLICATION OF THE WESTERN ONTARIO SECTION, C.F.S.A.). [Inside edge]. Periodical. English. ir. $3.50. Canadian Figure Skating Association, Western Ontario Section, Box 1074, Hagersville Ontario N0A 1H0 Canada. **DD** 796.91/09713. **UDC** 796.97.

CN/0835-9806
**INSIDE HOCKEY (DON MILLS, ONT.).**
***Ceased.*** (INSIDE HOCKEY.). [Inside hockey]. **VAT** Hockey News. Inside Hockey. Vol. 1, No. 1 (Nov./Dec. 1987)-Vol. 7, No. 1 (Aug. 1993). Periodical. English. Seven times a year. Inside Hockey, 85 Scarsdale Road/Suite 100, Don Mills Ontario M3B 2R2 Canada. **Tel** (800)268-7793. **ED** Michael Lawton and Bob McKenzie. **DD** 796.96/26. ctrl circ.
**Desc:** Features coverage of the stars of the professional hockey league, player profiles, posters, photographs, interviews etc. A look at the players at home and at the arena. Also contains trivia, crosswords and word games, cartoons and humor directed at stars in the National Hockey League.

US
**INSIDE KARATE.** English. mo. $18.00. CFW Enterprises Inc., 4201 West Van Owen Place, Burbank CA 91505. **Tel** (818)845-2656. **(Subscription address:** Kable Publishers Aide, 308 East Hitt Street, Subscriptions Department, Mt. Morris, IL 61054**)** ***Continues*** *Kick Illustrated.*
**Ind/Abst** SPORT Discus.

US/0199-8501
**INSIDE KUNG-FU.** **See** Health and Personal Fitness.

AT/1037-1648
**INSIDE SPORT CAMMERAY.** (INSIDE SPORT.). [Inside sport Cammeray]. (1991)-. Periodical. English. bm. 54.00Aus$ Australia; 65.00Aus$ (surface mail), 83.00Aus$ (air mail) other. Horwitz Grahame Pty Ltd, 506 Miller Street, Cammeray New South Wales, 2062 Australia. **Tel** 011 61 2 9296144, FAX 011 61 2 9571814. **DD** 796.0994.
**Ind/Abst** SPORT Discus.

US/0195-3478
**INSIDE SPORTS.** [Inside sports]. Vol. 1, (Oct. 1979)-. Periodical. English. mo. $22.00 US; $34.00 other. Century Publishing Company, 990 Grove Street, Evanston IL 60201-4370. **Tel** (708)491-6440, (800)321-3333, FAX (708)491-0459. **(Subscription address:** Kable Publishers Aide, 308 East Hitt Street, Subscriptions Department, Mt. Morris, IL 61054**) ED** Michael Herbert. **LC** GV561; .I58. **DD** 796.05. **Bk Rev**. **Ad Acc. Circ:** 600,000. available on microfilm and microfiche from University Microfilms International (UMI).
**Desc:** In-depth look at sports today; colorful, exciting, up-close and personal.
**Ind/Abst** Access (1981-); SportSearch.

●US/1065-4682
**INSIDE TAE KWON DO.** **VFOAT** Tae Kwon Do. (1992)-. Periodical. English. bm. D. F. W. Enterprises, 4201 Vanowen Place, Burbank CA 91505-1139.

US/1042-3664
**INSIDE TEXAS RUNNING.** [Inside Tex. run.]. (198?)-. Periodical. English. Twelve times a year. $12.50. Inside Running & Fitness, 9514 Bristlebrook Drive, Houston TX 77083. **Tel** (713)498-3208. **(Subscription address:** PO Box 720757, Houston, TX 77272**) DD** 796. **Ad Acc. Circ:** 10,000. ***Continues*** *Inside Running, 0194-6552.*
**Desc:** Road racing in Texas. Also triathlons, cycling and cross training.

US/0279-2273
**INSIDE THE AUBURN TIGERS (AUBURN, ALA.).** (INSIDE THE AUBURN TIGERS.). **Added/Corp** Auburn University. Athletic Dept. Vol. 1, No. 1 (Aug. 1981)-. Periodical. English. Ten times a year (Aug.-May). $30.00 US & Canada; $45.00 other. College Sports Publishing Inc, PO Box 6104, Tuscaloosa AL 35486. **Tel** (205)345-5074. **ED** Mark Murphy. **Bk Rev**. **Ad Acc. Circ:** 12,000 (ctrl).
**Desc:** Official full-color magazine of Auburn University athletics emphasizing football and men's basketball. Also includes all men's and women's sports.

US
**INSIDE THE BLUE CHIPS : EXCLUSIVE NATIONAL COLLEGIATE RECRUITERS' REPORT.** (19??)-. Periodical. English. bm. $24.00. Blue Chip Communications Ltd, PO Box 1775, Norman OK 73070. **Tel** (405)364-1050. **LC** Discard.

US/1059-8227
**INSIDE U.S.A. VOLLEYBALL.** [Inside U. S. A. volleyb.]. **Added/Corp** United States Volleyball Association. **VFOAT** Inside USA Volleyball. **VAT** Inside United States of America Volleyball. Vol. 19 No. 1 (Spring 1991)-. Periodical. English. Four times a year (Mar., June, Sept., Dec.). $10.00. US Volleyball Association, 3595 East Fountain Boulevard, Colorado Springs CO 80910. **Tel** (800)637-8300. **LC** WMLC 91/1436. **DD** 796. ***Continues*** *Volleyball USA.*

US/0738-7040
**INSIDE WOMEN'S TENNIS.** (INSIDE WOMEN'S TENNIS : OFFICIAL PUBLICATION OF THE WOMEN'S TENNIS ASSOCIATION.). [Inside women's tennis]. **Added/Corp** Women's Tennis Association (U.S.). (197?)-. Periodical. English. mo (10 issues). $48.00. Womens Tennis Association, 133 First Street Northeast, St Petersburg FL 33701. **Tel** (813)895-5000, FAX (813)894-1982. **ED** Douglas Clery. **Ad Acc. Circ:** 2,500.
**Desc:** A monthly look at the Kraft Tour. Results, inside gossip, player features, and rankings.
**Ind/Abst** SPORT Discus.

US/1047-9562
**INSIDE WRESTLING.** [Inside wrestl.]. (19??)-. Periodical. English. Thirteen times a year. $19.00. London Publishing Company, PO Box 910, Fort Washington PA 19034. **Tel** (215)643-6385, FAX (215)540-0146. **DD** 796. **Ad Acc.**

US/0731-8162
**INSIDERS BASEBALL FACT-BOOK.**
**VFOAT** Insiders Baseball Fact Book. English. an. $8.00 single issue. Research Analysis Publications, PO Box 49213, Los Angeles CA 90049. **ED** Ron Lewis. **LC** GV877; .I57. **DD** 796.357/0973. **UDC** 796.357.2(73). **Circ:** 2,000.

US/0731-8146
**INSIDERS BASEBALL FACT-BOOK EXTRA.** **VFOAT** Insiders Baseball Fact Book Extra; Insiders Baseball Fact-Book. 1st Ed. (1982)-. English. an. $7.00. Research Analysis Publications, PO Box 49213, Los Angeles CA 90049. **LC** GV877; .I573. **DD** 796.357/0973. **UDC** 796.357.2(73).

US/0747-007X
**INSIGHTS (WASHINGTON, D.C.).**
(INSIGHTS : NRA NEWS FOR YOUNG SHOOTERS.). [InSights]. **Added/Corp** National Rifle Association of America. **VFOAT** In Sights. Vol. 2, Issue 1 (Jan./Feb. 1982)-. Periodical. English. Twelve times a year. $7.50. National Rifle Association of America, 11250 Waples Mill Road, Fairfax VA 22030-9100. **Tel** (703)267-1560, (703)267-1583, (800)231-4672, FAX (703)267-3994. **ED** John Robbins and Brenda Dalessandro. **DD** 799. **Ad Acc. Circ:** 35,000 (ctrl). ***Continues*** *NRA Junior News.*
**Desc:** InSights uses educational stories that promote the shooting sports as well as firearm safety. Directed to audience of 10 to 20 year-olds.
**Ind/Abst** Bowne Dig. Corp. Sec. Lawyers.

HU/0139-4932
**INTERNATIONAL BASKETBALL.** [Int. basketb.]. (1978)-. Periodical. Multiple languages. mo. $12.00 (one year), $23.00 (two year). International Basketball, PO Box 229, H-1425 Budapest Hungary. **Tel** 011 36 1 634430. **UDC** 796.3.
**Ind/Abst** SportSearch (May 1987-).

NE/0378-4037
**INTERNATIONAL BULLETIN OF SPORTS INFORMATION.** **Added/Corp** International Association for Sports Information. (1977)-. English. ir (2-4 issues per volume). $30.00 (latest volume). Clearing House Belgium, Espace du 27 Septembre, Boulevard Leopold II nr 44, 1080 Brussels Belgium. **Tel** 011 32 2 4132893, FAX 011 32 2 4132890.
**Desc:** News, abstracts and documentation related to sport, sport sciences and physical education.
**Ind/Abst** SPORT Discus.

US/0091-6986
**INTERNATIONAL DIVER INDEX. WORLD INDIVEX EDITION.**
(INTERNATIONAL DIVER INDEX.). Multiple languages (English, French, German and Spanish). sa. $3.95. Stuart Publishing House, 18025 Sky Park Circle/Suite F, Irvine CA 92714. **LC** GV840.S78; I55. **DD** 797.2/3/025. **UDC** 797.26.

●US/1070-9568
**INTERNATIONAL FIGURE SKATING.**
(1994)-. Periodical. English. mo. $25.00. Paragraph Communications, 55 Ideal Road, Worcester MA 01604.

US/0272-1775
**INTERNATIONAL GOLF DIRECTORY, THE.** [Int. golf dir.]. (19??)-. Directory. English. sa. $25.00. Ingledue Travel Publishing, 444 Burchett Street, Glendale CA 91203. **LC** GV962; .I57. **DD** 796.352/06/8025.

US/0891-6616
**INTERNATIONAL GYMNAST (1986).**
(INTERNATIONAL GYMNAST.). [Int. gymnast]. (Dec. 1986)-. Periodical. English. mo (10 issues). $24.00 US; $27.00 Canada and Mexico; $29.00 other. International Gymnast, 225 Brooks Street, PO Box 2450, Oceanside CA 92051. **Tel** (619)722-0030. **ED** Dwight Normile. **DD** 796. Index available (free). cum. index. **Bk Rev**. **Ad Acc, Adv Mgr:** Peter Koch, **Tel** (310)836-2642. **Circ:** 25,000. available on microfilm and microfiche from University Microfilms International (UMI). Documents available from UMI Article Clearinghouse. ***Continues*** *International Gymnast Magazine (Santa Monica, Calif. : 1982), 0890-2437.*
**Desc:** Features worldwide reports of gymnastics competitions with interviews, posters and profiles. Includes hints for coaches and gymnasts.
**Ind/Abst** Acad. Search (July 1993-); INFO-SOUTH Abstr.; Mag. Search; Newsp. Period. Abstr. (1988-); Phys. Educ. Index; SPORT Discus; SportSearch.

US/0740-2082
**INTERNATIONAL JOURNAL OF SPORT BIOMECHANICS.** ***Title Change.*** **See** Biology-Biophysics.

US/1050-1606
**INTERNATIONAL JOURNAL OF SPORT NUTRITION.** **See** Nutrition and Dietetics.

IT/0047-0767
**INTERNATIONAL JOURNAL OF SPORT PSYCHOLOGY.** (INTERNATIONAL JOURNAL OF SPORT PSYCHOLOGY : OFFICIAL JOURNAL OF THE

INTERNATIONAL SOCIETY OF SPORTS PSYCHOLOGY.). [Int. j. sport psychol.]. **Added/Corp** International Society of Sports Psychology. Vol. 1 (1970)-. Periodical. Italian (English, French and Italian; summaries and/or abstracts in German and Spanish). qt. L80000 (Italy); $100.00 (other). Edizioni Luigi Pozzi Srl, Via Panama 68, 00198 Rome Italy. **Tel** (06)8553548, FAX (06)8554105. **ED** Ferruccio Antonelli. **LC** GV706.4; .I58. **DD** 796/.05. **NLM** W1 IN791D. **CODEN** ISPYAN. **Bk Rev. Ad Acc. Pr Rev. Circ:** 1,500. Documents available from The Genuine Article.
**Ind/Abst** Curr. Contents Soc. Behav. Sci.; Leis. Recreat. Tour. Abstr.; Phys. Educ. Index; Psychol. Abstr. (1970-); PsycINFO; PsycLit; Res. Alert [Full Cov.]; Soc. Sci. Cit. Index [Full Cov.]; SPORT Discus; SportSearch.

UK/0952-3367
**INTERNATIONAL JOURNAL OF THE HISTORY OF SPORT, THE.** Vol. 4, No. 1 (May 1987)-. Periodical. English. Three times a year. $165.00. Frank Cass & Company Ltd, Newbury House, 890-900 Eastern Avenue, Newbury Park, Ilford, Essex IG2 7HH United Kingdom. **Tel** 011 44 81 599 8866, FAX 011 44 81 599 0984, telex 897719. **ED** J.A. Mangan, Richard Holt, William J. Baker and Arnd Kruger. **LC** GV571; .I6. **DD** 796/.09. **UDC** 796/799(09). **Ad Acc, Adv Mgr:** Anne Kidson. available on microfilm and microfiche from University Microfilms International (UMI). ***Continues*** *British Journal of Sports History, 0264-9373.*
**Desc:** Aims to stimulate, promote and co-ordinate interest in the history of sport, recreation and leisure. This international journal provides a forum for contemplation of issues of concern to those historians, social scientists and other academics who increasingly reflect on the historical role of sport in society throughout the world.
**Ind/Abst** Br. Humanit. Index; Leis. Recreat. Tour. Abstr.; Phys. Educ. Index; SPORT Discus.

US/0739-5396
**INTERNATIONAL OLYMPIC LIFTER.** (INTERNATIONAL OLYMPIC LIFTER : IOL.). **VFOAT** IOL; I.O.L. (19??)-. Periodical. English. mo. $25.00 US; $28.00 Canada and Mexico; $36.00 other. International Olympic Lifter, PO Box 65855, Los Angeles CA 90065. **Tel** (213)257-8762. **ED** Bob Hise. Index available. cum. index. **Bk Rev**, (Qty: 4-6). **Ad Acc, Adv Mgr:** Sandra Hise. **Circ:** 2,000.
**Desc:** Each issue contains training articles, information on nutrition, a doctor's column, biographies of lifters, results from AWA and USWF meets, up to date international results, statistical data and analyses, and more.
**Ind/Abst** SportSearch (May 1987-).

GW/0074-7769
**INTERNATIONAL REVIEW FOR THE SOCIOLOGY OF SPORT. Added/Corp** International Committee for Sociology of Sport. Vol. 19, No. 1 (1984)-. Periodical. English (summaries and/or abstracts in German, French and Russian). qt. DM148.00. R Oldenbourg Verlag, Postfach 801360, D 81613 Munich Germany. **Tel** 011 49 89 450190, FAX 011 49 89 45019305. **ED** Klaus Heinemann. **LC** GV706; .I54. **DD** 306/.483. **[CCC]. Bk Rev. Ad Acc. *Continues*** *International Review of Sport Sociology, 0074-7769.*
**Desc:** Contains stimulating material for readers far beyond just those interested in the sociology of sport; for scholars and students of sociology, anthropology and sport.
**Ind/Abst** Leis. Recreat. Tour. Abstr.; Middle East Abstr. Index; Phys. Educ. Index; Soc. Plann. Policy Dev. Abstr.; Sociol. Abstr. (1966-) [Full Cov.]; SPORT Discus; SportSearch.

US/0092-1769
**INTERNATIONAL SKI TRAILS.** English. an. $3.95. International Ski Trails, Subscription Department, 3700 Wilshire Boulevard/Suite 538, Los Angeles CA 90010. **LC** GV854.A1; I55. **DD** 796.9/3. **UDC** 796.92.

HU
**INTERNATIONAL SPORTS MAGAZINE.** ir (double issues twice per year). $25.00. AIPS Secretariat, Hold UTCA 1, 1054 Budapest Hungary. **Tel** 011 36 1 1112689, FAX 011 36 1 1533807. **ED** Tamas Gyarfas. **Ad Acc. Circ:** 8,000.

HU
**INTERNATIONAL SWIMMING AND WATER POLO, DIVING & SYNCHRONIZED SWIMMING.** (1985)-. Multiple languages (English). Four times a year. International Swimming & Water Polo, Gyarmat Utca 52, 1145 Budapest Hungary. **Tel** 011 36 1 1633239 OR 1634430.

US/1063-0333
**INTERNATIONAL TENNIS.** [Int. tennis]. **Added/Corp** Association of Tennis Professionals. ATP Tour. Vol. 16, No. 1 (Jan. 14, 1991)-. Periodical. English. Twelve times a year. $36.00 (one year) US; $65.00 (one year) Canada and Mexico; $84.00 (one year) others. ATP Tour, 200 ATP Tour Boulevard, Ponte Vedra Beach FL 32082. **Tel** (904)285-8000, FAX (904)285-5966. **ED** Ellen Alfano. **DD** 796. **Ad Acc, Adv Mgr:** Erika Green. **Circ:** 3,500 (ctrl). ***Continues*** *International Tennis Weekly, 0199-0853.*
**Desc:** This contains news and information of the men's professional tennis. It features player and news items.
**Ind/Abst** SPORT Discus.

US/0199-0853
**INTERNATIONAL TENNIS WEEKLY. *Title Change.*** [Int. tennis wkly.]. **Added/Corp** Association of Tennis Professionals. ATP Tour. (197?)-(199?). Periodical. English. wk. International Tennis Weekly, 200 Tournament Players Road, Ponte Vedra FL 32082. **Tel** (904)285-8000, FAX (904)285-5966, telex 6829028. **ED** Michael Curet. **DD** 796. **Ad Acc. Circ:** 3,300. ***Continued by*** *International Tennis, 1063-0333.*
**Desc:** News features, tournament reports, player profiles, rankings.

GW/0942-721X
**INTERNATIONAL VOLLEY TECH.** [Int. volley tech]. **VFOAT** International Volleytech. (1990)-. Periodical. Multiple languages. qt. DM24.00 Germany; DM28.00 other. Philippka Verlag, Postfach 6540, D-48034 Muenster Germany. **Tel** 011 49 251 230-0522. **UDC** 796.325. ***Continues*** *Volley Tech, 0938-443X.*

US
**INTERNATIONAL VOLLEYBALL REVIEW.** Vol. 1 (1940)-. Periodical. English (French; summaries and/or abstracts in French, English and German; translations available in English, French and German). qt.

SZ/1017-5547
**INTERNATIONALES WAFFEN-MAGAZIN. See** Military and Defense.

US/0097-871X
**INTERSCHOLASTIC ATHLETIC ADMINISTRATION. Added/Corp** National Federation of State High School Associations. Vol. 1 (Winter 1974)-. Periodical. English. qt. $12.00 (one year), $33.00 (three year) US; $15.00 (one year), $42.00 (three year) other. National Federation of State High School Associations, 11724 Northwest Plaza Circle, PO Box 20626, Kansas City MO 64195-0626. **Tel** (816)464-5400, FAX (816)464-5571. **ED** Richard G Fawcett. Index available. cum. index. **Bk Rev**, (Qty: 4). **Ad Acc, Adv Mgr:** Brad Rumble, **Tel** (816)464-5400. **Pr Rev. Circ:** 6,200.
**Desc:** Contains articles on a wide spectrum of topics which are beneficial to the school athletic or activities director.
**Ind/Abst** Phys. Educ. Index (1978-); SPORT Discus.

NE
**INVENTARISATIE SPORTACCOMMODATIES. Main/Corp** Netherlands. Centraal Bureau Voor de Statistiek. Dutch. an. Fl14.50. Centraal Bureau voor de Statistiek, AFD ALG Zaken, Postbus 959, 2270 AZ Voorburg Netherlands. **Tel** 011 31 70 3373800, FAX 011 31 038 7429, telex 32692 CBS NL. **LC** GV433.N4; N47A.

GW
**IPPON : DEUTSCHER JUDO VERBAND.** (19??)-. German. mo. DM27.90. Deutscher Judo Verband, Redaktion Ippon Segewaldweg 40, D 12557 Berlin Germany. **Tel** 011 49 711 210770, telex 051 678. ***Continues*** *Judo.*

IE/0332-2947
**IRISH RUNNER.** [Ir. runn.]. **VFOAT** Irish Runner Magazine. (1981)-. Periodical. English. Eight times a year. $55.00. Athletic Promotions Ltd., 109 Old Country Road, Crumlin Dublin 12 Ireland. **Tel** 011 353 1 506824. **DD** 796.426.

US/0740-6266
**ISLANDWIDE RUNNER. *Ceased.* VFOAT** Islandwide Running Magazine. (198?)-(1992). Periodical. English. mo. Islandwide Runner, 36 Rollstone Avenue, W Sayville NY 11796. **Tel** (516)842-7034. **ED** Ralph Epifanio. **Bk Rev. Ad Acc. Circ:** 1,500 (ctrl).
**Desc:** Regional running magazine (Long Island and Metropolitan New York) covering calendar and results of road racing, also human interest stories.

US/0361-4999
**ITHACAGUN HUNTING & SHOOTING ANNUAL. VFOAT** Ithacagun Annual. Vol. 1 (1976)-. English. an. Aqua Field Publications Inc, 66 West Gilbert Street, Shrewsbury NJ 07702. **Tel** (201)842-8300. **LC** SK1; .I74. **DD** 799/.05.

US/0274-886X
**IT'S SPORTS.** Periodical. English. mo. $15.00. Fox and Fink, 14782 W Village Drive/Suite 392, Tampa FL 33624. **Tel** (813)932-4441.

US/0047-2956
**J U C O REVIEW. Main/Corp** National Junior College Athletic Association. (1991)-. Periodical. English. Six times a year (September-May). $20.00. National Junior Collegiate Athletic Association, PO Box 7305, Colorado Springs CO 80933. **Tel** (719)590-9788, FAX (719)590-7324. **ED** George E. Killian. **Ad Acc. Circ:** 3,650. available on microfilm from University Microfilms International (UMI).
**Desc:** Articles on a variety of topics covering the major sport areas by the nation's outstanding junior college coaches and administrators. Specific information on the current program of the National Junior College Athletic Association.
**Ind/Abst** Phys. Educ. Index (1978-); SPORT Discus.

US/8750-8680
**JACKPOT & RODEO NEWS. VFOAT** Jackpot and Rodeo News; California Jackpot and Rodeo News. Periodical. English. mo. $12.00. Jackpot and Rodeo News, 2901 Redwood Road, Ceres CA 95307. **UDC** 791.8.

GW
**JAHRBUCH DER TURNKUNST.** 72.- Yearly volume; 1977/78-. Periodical. German. an. DM17.00. Bernecker-Verlag, Unter Dem Schoneberg, 3508 Melsungen, Germany. **Tel** 069/678010, telex 411513 DTUBU. **LC** GV204.G4; J3. **DD** 613.7/0943. **Ad Acc. Circ:** 15,000. ***Continues*** *Amtliches Jahrbuch des Deutschen Turner-Bundes.*
**Desc:** Addresses of German Gymnastics Association members. Includes statistical data, competition reports and results.

JA/0286-9322
**JAPANESE JOURNAL OF SPORTS SCIENCES.** [Jpn. j. sports sci.]. (1982)-. Periodical. Multiple languages. mo. $219.50. **(Subscription address:** Japan Publications Trading Company, Ltd., PO Box 5030, Tokyo International, Tokyo 100-31 Japan.**) DD** 796.

SZ
**JEUNESSE ET SPORT.** French (German and Italian). mo. 29.00F Switzerland; 33.00F other. Jeunesse et Sport, Service PTT des Abonnements et Journaux, 3029 Berne Switzerland. **Tel** 011 41 32 225644.

CN/0712-2632
**JIM RENNIE'S SPORTS LETTER.** [Jim Rennie's sports lett.]. **VFOAT** Sports Letter; Jim Rennie's Previewing ... Merchandise. (1977)-. Periodical. English. wk. 210.00Can$. Jim Rennie Publications Sports Letter, PO Box 1000, Collingwood Ontario L9Y 4L4 Canada. **Tel** (705)445-7161, FAX (705)445-8650. **ED** Jim Rennie. **DD** 338.4/768876/0971. **Bk Rev. Ad Acc. Circ:** 1,400.
**Desc:** Reports on developments in the Canadian sporting goods and ski trades.
**Ind/Abst** SPORT Discus; SportSearch (May 1987-).

US/0882-7877
**JOHN HORAN'S SPORTS INK. *Title Change.* VFOAT** Sports Ink. Periodical. English. ir. John Horan's Sports Ink, PO Box 1263, Morrisville PA 19067. **Tel** (215)493-2720. **ED** John Horan. **LC** HD9992.A1; J64. **DD** 688.7/068. Index available. cum. index. **Circ:** 750. ***Continued by*** *Sporting Goods Management News.*
**Desc:** Business news and analysis of sports industry.

CN/0826-5887
**JOURNAL - CANADIAN OLDTIMERS' HOCKEY ASSOCIATION.** (JOURNAL.). **VFOAT** Canadian Oldtimers' Hockey Association Journal. **VAT** COHA Journal. Vol. 1, No. 1 (Oct. 1981)-. Periodical. English (French). Six times a year. Free to members. COHA, 1600 James Naismith Drive, Gloucester Ontario K1B 5N4 Canada. **Tel** (613)748-5646, FAX 748-5706. **ED** Pat Curran. **DD** 796.96/26. **UDC** 796.966(71). **Ad Acc. Circ:** 22,000 (ctrl).
**Desc:** Complete coverage of oldtimers hockey in Canada, U.S., and parts of Europe. Special section for National Hockey Alumni Association.

US/1041-3200
**JOURNAL OF APPLIED SPORT PSYCHOLOGY. See** Psychology.

GW/1010-8262
**JOURNAL OF COMPARATIVE PHYSICAL EDUCATION AND SPORT / ISCPES, INTERNATIONAL SOCIETY ON COMPARATIVE PHYSICAL EDUCATION AND SPORT. See** Education-Physical Education and Training.

US/1072-0316
**JOURNAL OF LEGAL ASPECTS OF SPORT. See** Law.

US
**JOURNAL OF MARTIAL ARTS.** (19??)-. English. qt. $75.00 (institutions), $50.00 (individuals). Via Media Publishing Company, 821 West 24th Street, Erie PA 16502. **Tel** (814)455-9517, FAX (814)838-7811. **ED** Michael DeMarco.
**Desc:** Provides an intellectual approach to martial arts. Topics include martial arts traditions, and the physical effects of martial arts and injuries.

II
**JOURNAL OF PHYSICAL EDUCATION AND SPORT SCIENCES : A BI-ANNUAL PUBLICATION OF SPORTS AUTHORITY OF INDIA. See** Education-Physical Education and Training.

US/0895-2779
**JOURNAL OF SPORT & EXERCISE PSYCHOLOGY.** [J. sport exerc. psychol.]. **VFOAT** Sport & Exercise Psychology Journal of Sport and Exercise Psychology; Sport and Exercise Psychology. Vol. 10, No. 1 (March 1988)-. Periodical. English. qt (Mar., June, Sept., Dec.). $36.00 (individual), $88.00 (institution) US; $40.00 (individual), $92.00 (institution) other. Human Kinetics Publishers Inc, 1607 North Market Street, PO Box 5076, Champaign IL 61825-5076. **Tel** (217)351-5076, FAX (217)351-2674. **ED** Thelma Horn. **LC** GV706.4; .J68. **DD** 796/.01. **NLM** W1; JO902R. **[CCC].** Index available (Included in Dec. issue). **Pr Rev.** Documents available from The Genuine Article, BIOSIS Document Express, UMI Article Clearinghouse. ***Continues** Journal of Sport Psychology, 0163-433X.*
**Desc:** Designed to stimulate and communication research and theory in all areas of sport and exercise psychology.
**Ind/Abst** Acad. Search (July 1993-); Biol. Abstr. (1988-); Curr. Contents Soc. Behav. Sci.; Educ. Index (1988-); Ergon. Abstr.; Expand. Acad. Index (1992-); Gen. Sci. Source (Jul. 1993-); Health Source (Jul. 1993-); INFO-SOUTH Abstr.; Mag. Search; Newsp. Period. Abstr. (1992-); Psychol. Abstr. (1988-); PsycINFO (1990-); PsycLit; Res. Alert [Full Cov.]; Soc. Sci. Cit. Index [Full Cov.]; SPORT Discus.

US/0193-7235
**JOURNAL OF SPORT AND SOCIAL ISSUES.** **See** Sociology.

US/0162-7341
**JOURNAL OF SPORT BEHAVIOR.** [J. sport behav.]. **Added/Corp** United States Sports Academy. (1978)-. Periodical. English (summaries and/or abstracts in French). qt (Mar., June, Sept., Dec.). $20.00. University of South Alabama / HPELS, Department of HPELS, Room 1011, Mobile AL 36688. **Tel** (205)460-7131. **ED** Dr. W. F. Gilley. **LC** GV561; .J68. **DD** 796/.05. Index available (4th issue). **Bk Rev**, (Qty: 2 per year). **Circ:** 450 (ctrl). Documents available from UMI Article Clearinghouse.
**Desc:** Publishes original, empirical investigations and theoretical papers dealing with studies of social behavior in the areas of games and sport.
**Ind/Abst** Expand. Acad. Index (1992-); Leis. Recreat. Tour. Abstr.; Newsp. Period. Abstr. (1992-); Phys. Educ. Index; Psychol. Abstr. (1980-); PsycINFO; PsycLit; SPORT Discus; SportSearch.

US/0094-1700
**JOURNAL OF SPORT HISTORY.** [J. sport hist.]. **Added/Corp** North American Society for Sport History. Vol. 1 (Spring 1974)-. Periodical. English. Three times a year. $40.00 (regular individual), $20.00 (student or retired individual), $45.00 (foreign individual), $55.00 (sustaining individual), $450.00 (LIFE membership); $50.00 (regular institution), $55.00 (foreign institution)-all countries except US and Canada. North American Society for Sport History, Penn State University, 101 White Building, University Park PA 16802. **Tel** (814)865-2416, (814)238-1288. **ED** Steven Riess. **LC** GV571; .J68. **DD** 796/.09. **Bk Rev.** **Ad Acc.** **Pr Rev.** **Circ:** 1,000 (ctrl). Documents available from The Genuine Article.
**Desc:** Covers the critical issues and themes of sport history through the publication of interpretive essays and historical research which advance the understanding of sport and its impact on society.
**Ind/Abst** Am. Hist. Life (1974-); Am. Bibliogr. Slavic East Europ. Stud.; Arts Humanit. Citation Index [Select. Cov.]; Curr. Contents Soc. Behav. Sci.; Phys. Educ. Index; Res. Alert [Full Cov.]; Soc. Sci. Cit. Index [Full Cov.]; SPORT Discus; SportSearch.

US/0888-4773
**JOURNAL OF SPORT MANAGEMENT.** [J. sport manage.]. **Added/Corp** North American Society for Sport Management. **VFOAT** JSM. Vol. 1, No. 1 (Jan. 1987)-. Periodical. English. Three times a year (January, May, September). $30.00 (individual), $64.00 (institution) US; $35.00 (individual), $69.00 (institution) other. Human Kinetics Publishers Inc, 1607 North Market Street, PO Box 5076, Champaign IL 61825-5076. **Tel** (217)351-5076, FAX (217)351-2674. **ED** Joy DeSensi & Trevoe Slack. **DD** 790. **[CCC].** Index available (Included in Sept. issue). **Bk Rev.** **Ad Acc.** **Circ:** 425.
**Desc:** Contains articles focusing on the theory and application of management to sport, exercise, dance and play. Articles cover various setting - professional sport, intercollegiate and interscholastic sport, health/sport clubs, sport arenas and community recreational sports.
**Ind/Abst** Leis. Recreat. Tour. Abstr.; Phys. Educ. Index; Soc. Sci. Cit. Index [Select. Cov.]; SPORT Discus.

UK/0264-0414
**JOURNAL OF SPORTS SCIENCES.** [J. sports sci.]. **Added/Corp** Society of Sports Sciences (Great Britain) British Association of Sports Sciences. International Society for Advancement of Kinanthropometry. Vol. 1, No. 1 (Spring 1983)-. Periodical. English. bm. $385.00 US and Canada; £225.00 Europe; £250.00 other. E & FN Spon Ltd, 2 6 Boundary Row, London SE1 8HN England. **Tel** 011 44 71 865 0066. **(Subscription address:** Chapman & Hall, Cheriton House, North Way, Andover, Hampshire, SP10 5BE England.**)** **ED** Thomas Reilly, Roger Bartlett, John Annett, Ron Maughan and Lew Hardy. **LC** GV561; .J684. **DD** 796/.05. **NLM** W1; JO903P. **CODEN** JSSCEL. **[CCC].** Index available. **Bk Rev.** **Ad Acc.** **Pr Rev.** **Circ:** 600. available on microfilm and microfiche from University Microfilms International (UMI). Documents available from BIOSIS Document Express, Ask*IEEE.
**Desc:** Publishes articles of a high standard on various aspects of the sports sciences covering a number of disciplinary bases including anatomy, biochemistry, biomechanics, psychology, sociology, as well as ergonomics, kinanthropometry and other interdisciplinary perspectives.
**Ind/Abst** Biol. Abstr. (1987-); Curr. Aware. Biol. Sci., CABS; EMBASE; Ergon. Abstr. (?-?); Index Med. (Vol. 3, No. 1, 1985-);; INSPEC; Phys. Educ. Index; SPORT Discus.

IT/1120-3137
**JOURNAL OF SPORTS TRAUMATOLOGY AND RELATED RESEARCH.** [J. sports traumatol. relat. res.]. (1990)-. Periodical. English. Four times a year. $80.00. Editrice Kurtis Srl, Via Luigi Zoja 30, 20153 Milan Italy. **Tel** 011 39 2 48202740, FAX 011 39 2 48201219. **UDC** 616.71. ***Continues** Italian Journal of Sports Traumatology, 0391-4089.*
**Ind/Abst** EMBASE; Phys. Educ. Index; SPORT Discus.

●US/1064-8011
**JOURNAL OF STRENGTH AND CONDITIONING RESEARCH.** **VFOAT** Journal of Applied Sport Science Review. (1993)-. Periodical. English. qt (Feb., May, Aug., Nov.). $32.00 (individual), $64.00 (institution) US; $36.00 (individual), $68.00 (institution) other. Human Kinetics Publishers Inc, 1607 North Market Street, PO Box 5076, Champaign IL 61825-5076. **Tel** (217)351-5076, FAX (217)351-2674. **ED** William J. Kraemer. **NLM** W1; JO904TE. **[CCC].** Index available (Included in Nov. issue). **Bk Rev.** ***Continues** Journal of Applied Sport Science Research.*
**Desc:** Presents current sport science research along with advice on how to apply the findings.
**Ind/Abst** Acad. Search (July 1993-); Mag. Search; Soc. Sci. Cit. Index [Select. Cov.]; SPORT Discus.

US/0747-5993
**JOURNAL OF SWIMMING RESEARCH, THE.** [J. swim. res.]. **Added/Corp** American Swimming Coaches Association. USS Sports Medicine Committee. Vol. 1 No. 1 (Fall 1984)-. Periodical. English. an. $35.00 US; $45.00 Canada and Mexico; $55.00 other. American Swimming Coaches Association, 301 SE 20th Street, Fort Lauderdale FL 33316. **Tel** (305)462-6267, (800)356-2722. **ED** Mary Sutton. **DD** 797. Index available. **Ad Acc.** ctrl circ.
**Desc:** Scientific journal devoted to research in competitive swimming.
**Ind/Abst** Phys. Educ. Index; SPORT Discus; SportSearch (May 1987-).

US/0736-7724
**JOURNAL OF THE AMERICAN SPORTING BOOK COLLECTOR, THE.** **See** Hobbies.

US/0097-6253
**JOURNAL OF THE NORTH AMERICAN FALCONERS' ASSOCIATION, THE.** **See** Recreation, Leisure-Outdoor Life.

US/0094-8705
**JOURNAL OF THE PHILOSOPHY OF SPORT.** [J. philos. sport]. **Added/Corp** Philosophic Society for the Study of Sport. Vol. 1 (1974)-. English. an. $19.00 (individual), $30.00 (institution) US; $21.00 (individual), $32.00 (institution) other. Human Kinetics Publishers Inc, 1607 North Market Street, PO Box 5076, Champaign IL 61825-5076. **Tel** (217)351-5076, FAX (217)351-2674. **ED** Klaus V. Meier. **LC** GV706; .J68. **DD** 796/.01. **[CCC].** **Bk Rev.** **Pr Rev.** **Circ:** 300. Documents available from The Genuine Article.
**Desc:** Contains articles and discussions, synthesis statements, and critical reviews dealing with the philosophy of sport.
**Ind/Abst** Acad. Search (July 1993-); Curr. Contents Soc. Behav. Sci.; INFO-SOUTH Abstr.; Mag. Search; Philos. Index; Phys. Educ. Index; Res. Alert [Full Cov.]; Soc. Sci. Cit. Index [Full Cov.]; SPORT Discus; SportSearch.

UK/0560-6152
**JOURNAL OF THE SOCIETY OF ARCHER-ANTIQUARIES.** **Main/Corp** Society of Archer-Antiquaries. **VFOAT** Journal - Society of Archer-Antiquaries. Vol. 1 (1958)-. Academic Scholarly Publication. English. an. £7.00. Society of Archer Antiquaries, 61 Lambert Road, Bridlington, N Humberside YO16 5Rd England. **ED** E. McEwen (editor's address: 10 Richmond Way, Wanstead London E11 3QT). **LC** GV1183; .S6. **DD** 799.3/2/05. Index available. **Bk Rev.** **Circ:** 550 (ctrl).
**Ind/Abst** SPORT Discus.

UK/0561-6832
**JOURNAL OF THE SPORTS TURF RESEARCH INSTITUTE, THE.** **Main/Corp** The Sports Turf Research Institute, Bingley, Yorkshire. Vol. 1 (Nov. 1929)-. English. an. £25.00 UK; £39.00 other. Sports Turf Research Institute, Bingley, West Yorkshire BD16 1AU England. **Tel** 011 44 274 565131, FAX 011 44 274 561891. cum. index.
**Ind/Abst** AGRICOLA [Select. Cov.]; Hortic. Abstr.; Irr. Drain. Abstr.; Ornamental Hort. (19??-19??); Plant Breed. Abstr.; Rev. Plant Pathol.; Soils Fert.; SPORT Discus; SportSearch (May 1987-).

CN/0849-1623
**JOURNAL QUEBEC QUILLES, LE.** [J. Que. quilles]. **VFOAT** Quebec Quilles. (Jan. 1990)-. Periodical. French. ir. Le Journal Quebec Quilles, CP 66, Succursale St-Michel, Montreal, Quebec H2A 3L2 Canada. **DD** 794.6/09714/05. ***Continues** Quebec Quilles., 0840-4593.*

UK/0022-5819
**JUDO.** ***Suspended.*** Vol. 1 (Oct. 1956)-. Periodical. English. bm. $19.01. Judo Ltd, Candem House, 717 Manchester Old Road, Rhodes Mdltn, Manchester M24 4JF England. **Tel** 061 653 1499. **ED** John Drogan. **LC** GV475.J9. **UDC** 796.853.23(410). **Bk Rev.** **Ad Acc.** **Circ:** 5,000 (ctrl).
**Desc:** Contains reports which include British international competitions, profiles, technical articles, training schedules, and reviews.

FR
**JUDO (FRANCE).** (JUDO.). French. bm. 150.00F France; 180.00F other. FFJDA, 43 rue des Plantes, 75014 Paris France. **Tel** 011 33 1 45428090.
**Ind/Abst** SPORT Discus.

US/1066-6257
**JUDO JOURNAL.** [Judo j.]. (1978)-. Periodical. English. bm (6 issues). $18.00. Judo Journal Publications, PO Box 18485, Irvine CA 92713. **Tel** (714)645-1674, FAX (714)722-9331. **DD** 796.

US/1019-4835
**JUGGLERS' WORLD.** [Jugglers' world]. (19??)-. Periodical. English. qt. $30.00 (membership International Jugglers Association) US; $35.00 (membership International Jugglers Association) other. International Jugglers Association, PO Box 218, Montague MA 01351. **Tel** (413)367-2401. **ED** Bill Giduz. **UDC** 791.83(05).
**Desc:** Communications with members of the International Jugglers Association and forum for exchange of information and ideas on juggling.

US/0273-9100
**JUNIOR BOWLER.** V. 1- Nov. 1964-. Periodical. English. mo. American Junior Bowling Congress Inc, 1572 E Capitol Drive, Milwaukee WI 53211. **LC** GB901; .J8. **DD** 794.6/05. **UDC** 796.28. ***Supersedes** Prep Pin Patter.*

CN/0826-4279
**JUNIOR HOCKEY ACTION.** [Jr. hockey action]. Vol. 1, No. 1 (Sept. 1982)-. Periodical. English. $22.00 for 20 issues, Canada. Junior Hockey Action, PO Box 3311, Langley British Columbia V3A 4R6 Canada. **DD** 796.96/26. **UDC** 796.66(71).

●US/1074-0554
**JUNIOR TENNIS.** (1993)-. Periodical. English. Five times a year. $14.95 (one year), $24.95 (two year). Junior Tennis / Seattle, PO Box 9921, Seattle WA 98109. **Tel** (206)284-4574, FAX (206)285-4366. **Ad Acc.**

US/0894-4431
**KANSAS SPORTS.** [Kans. sports]. **VFOAT** Kansas Sports Magazine. (19??)-. Periodical. English. Six times a year. $16.00. Kansas Sports/ Statewide High, PO Box 35, Abilene KS 67410. **Tel** (913)263-7403. **DD** 796.

UK
**KARATE AND ORIENTAL ARTS.** (1966)-. Periodical. English. bm (6 issues). $12.00. Paul H. Crompton Ltd, 638 Fulham Road, London SW6 England. **Tel** 01-736-2551. **ED** Paul Crompton. **LC** GV476; .K3. **DD** 796.8/153/05. **Bk Rev.** **Ad Acc.** **Circ:** 15,500. ***Continues** Karate Magazine & Oriental Arts.*
**Desc:** Topics include martial arts of the East and West, health and strength, survival systems, and modern self defence systems, Zen Buddhism, etc.

FR/1243-3853
**KARATE, BUSHIDO.** (1988)-. Periodical. French. Eleven times a year. 269.34F France; 323.21F other. Editions du Monde, 2 Bis rue Mercoeur, 75011 Paris, France. **Tel** 011 33 1 43676424. **UDC** 796.8. ***Formed by the union of** Bushido (Paris), 0760-0097 **and** Karate (Paris), 0335-2552.*

CN/0383-6517
**KARATE KEBEC.** Vol. 1 (Oct. 1975)-. Periodical. French. $12.00. Karate Kebec, C P 10 Succursale Beaubien, Montreal Quebec H2G 3C8 Canada. **DD** 796.8/153/05.

US/0888-031X
**KARATE, KUNG-FU ILLUSTRATED.** [Karate kung-fu illus.]. **VFOAT** Karate, Kung Fu Illustrated; Karate/Kung Fu Illustrated; Karate/Kung-Fu Illustrated. Vol. 17, No. 5 (May 1986)-. Periodical.

## Recreation, Leisure —Sports

English. bm (publishes 3 months in advance of cover date). $17.70 (one year), $35.40 (two year). Rainbow Publications Inc., PO Box 16298, North Hollywood CA 91615. **Tel** (818)760-8983, (800)257-4066, FAX (818)985-1213. **ED** Marion Castinado. **LC** GV1114.3; .K36. **DD** 796.8/153/05. **Bk Rev. Ad Acc. Continues** Karate Illustrated, 0022-9016.
**Ind/Abst** SPORT Discus.

US/1062-3558
**KARATE PROFILES MADE IN AMERICA.** [Karate profiles made Am.]. (July 1991)-. Periodical. English. Twelve times a year. $21.00. Karate Profiles Made in America, PO Box 1187, West Chester OH 45071. **Tel** (513)874-8678. **DD** 796.

US/0279-8816
**KART-TECH.** [Kart-tech]. **VFOAT** Kart Tech; Karttech. Vol. 1, No. 1 (Apr. 1981)-. Periodical. English. mo $23.95. Kart-Tech Magazine, 31 H Street, Suite 2, Bakersfield CA 93304. **Tel** (919)428-4068. **DD** 796.

US/0096-3216
**KARTER NEWS.** (19??)-. Periodical. English. Twelve times a year. $18.00 US/ $20.00 Canada; $25.00 other. International Kart Federation, 4650 Arrow Highway, Suite B-4, Montclair CA 91763. **Tel** (714)625-5497. **ED** Jan Gaspar. **LC** GV1029.5; .K32. **DD** 796.7/6. **Bk Rev. Ad Acc. Circ:** 5,000.
**Desc:** Karting events, photos of karts at karting events, race reports, technical and rule update, minutes of board meetings and other karting related information.

UK/0022-913X
**KARTING.** (19??)-. Periodical. English. mo. £37.00 US; £23.00 UK. Lodgemark Press, Bank House, Sidcup, Chislehurst, Kent BR7 5RD England. **Tel** 011 44 81 4676533, FAX 011 44 81 4687999. **ED** M.C. Burgess. **Bk Rev, (Qty: 1). Ad Acc. Circ:** 12,000 (ctrl).
**Desc:** Contains information on kart racing.

SZ
**KATAPULT.** mo. 60.00F Switzerland; 86.00F Europe; 104.00F other. Jean Frey Druck, Postfach 299, CH-8021 Zurich, Switzerland. **Tel** 011 41 1 2078919.

IR
**KAYHAN-I VARZISHI.** Periodical. Persian. wk. 150.00IR, 80.00 IR (single issues) Iran; $63.00 Persian Gulf region; $156.00 North America and Africa; $111.00 Europe; $131.00 Far East; $177.00 Oceania. Khiyaban-I Firdawsi, Kuchah-I Atabak, Muassasah-I Kayhan, Daftar-I Kayhan-I Farhang I, Tehran Iran. **Tel** 302313, telex 212467. **LC** GV657; .K38. **Ad Acc. Circ:** 220,000 (ctrl).

US/0882-8180
**KICK (NEW YORK, N.Y. 1983).** (KICK.). [Kick]. Began in 1983. Periodical. English. bm. $18.00 US; $28.00 other. Kick Enterprises, Inc., 509 Madison Avenue, Suite 2700, New York NY 10022. **DD** 796. **UDC** 796.332(7).

GW
**KICKER SPORTMAGAZIN.** (19??)-. Periodical. German. sw (Published on Mon. & Thurs.). $240.00. Olympia Verlag GmbH, Badstrasse 4-6, Abholfach, D 90402 Nuernberg D Germany. **Tel** 011 49 911 2162230. **LC** GV611; .K47.

US/1054-7002
**KIDSPORTS (ARLINGTON, VA.). Ceased.**
See Children and Youth Interests.

US/1069-2614
**KILLSHOT (PADUCAH, KY.).** (KILLSHOT.). [Killshot]. **Added/Corp** Quertemous and Quertemous. Vol. 1, No. 1 (Aug. 1991)-. Periodical. English. Five times a year. $16.95 US; $26.95 Canada; $41.95 South America; $56.95 Europe; $66.95 other. Quertemous & Quertemous, Inc., PO Box 8036, Paducah KY 42002. **Tel** (502)441-7723. **ED** Marvin Quertemous. **DD** 796. **Ad Acc, Adv Mgr Tel** same as publisher.
**Desc:** Information about racquetball.

CN/0709-8456
**KIRON, LE.** [Kiron]. Periodical. French. bm. Free. Club De Coureurs De Fonde De Quebec, CP 183, St. Sauveur, Quebec G1K 6W3 Canada. **DD** 796.4/26/060714. **UDC** 796.4(714). ctrl circ. **Continues** Bulletin des Centaures.

●US/1068-7645
**KUNG FU MASTERS. VFOAT** Kung-Fu Masters; Kung Fu. Vol. 1, No. 1 (June 1993)-. Periodical. English. mo. $3.00 (single issue). CFW Enterprises Inc., 4201 West Van Owen Place, Burbank CA 91505. **Tel** (818)845-2656. **(Subscription address:** Box 404 Mt. Morris, IL 61054) **ED** Dave Cater. **DD** 796. **Ad Acc.**

HK
**KUNG FU MI AO. VFOAT** Secrets of Kung Fu. First published Sept. 1974-. Periodical. Chinese (Chinese). $28.50. Lung Publisher Inc, PO Box 20606, Causeway Bay Post Office, Hsiang-Kang Hong Kong. **LC** GV1112; .K87. **UDC** 796.855.

US/0194-7893
**LACROSSE (BALTIMORE, MD.). Title Change.** (LACROSSE.). [Lacrosse]. **Added/Corp** Lacrosse Foundation. Vol. 1, No. 1 (Mar. 1979)-(19??)-. Periodical. English. bm. Lacrosse Foundation Inc, 113 West University Parkway, Baltimore MD 21210. **Tel** (301)235-6882, FAX (301)366-6735. **ED** Jamie Hunt. **LC** GV989; .L33. **DD** 796.34/7/0973. **Ad Acc, Adv Mgr:** Network Publications, **Tel** (410)235-0500. **Circ:** 10,000. **Continued by** Lacrosse Magazine, 1069-5893.
**Desc:** Features men's and women's lacrosse at all age levels. Serves as a directory for lacrosse information.

UK/0023-7086
**LACROSSE (LONDON, ENG.). Title Change.** (LACROSSE.). **Added/Corp** All England Ladies Lacrosse Association. All England Women's Lacrosse Association. (1948?)-(19??). Periodical. English. mo. All England Women's Lacrosse Association, 4 Western Court, Bromley Street, Digbeth Birmingham B9 England. **Tel** 011-44-21-7734422. **ED** J Harper and R Davies. **Continued by** Lacrosse Talk.
**Ind/Abst** SportSearch (May 1987-).

US/1069-5893
**LACROSSE MAGAZINE.** [Lacrosse mag.]. **Added/Corp** Lacrosse Foundation. (19??)-. Periodical. English. Seven times a year. $50.00 Australia and Japan; $35.00 other. Lacrosse Foundation Inc, 113 West University Parkway, Baltimore MD 21210. **Tel** (301)235-6882, FAX (301)366-6735. **DD** 796. **Continues** Lacrosse, 0194-7893.
**Ind/Abst** SPORT Discus.

●UK
**LACROSSE TALK.** (1993)-. English. Eight times a year. £20.00. All England Womens Lacrosse, 4 Western Court, Bromley Street, Digbeth Birmingham, B9 England. **Tel** 11 44 21 7734422.

US/0092-8909
**LADY GOLFER (SCOTTSDALE).** (THE LADY GOLFER.). Periodical. English. ir. $7.00. Seidal Publications, Box 1118, Scottsdale AZ 85252. **LC** GV966; .L33. **DD** 796.352/024042. **UDC** 796.352-055.2.

CC
**LAN CHIU / CHUNG-KUO LAN CHIU HSIEH HUI CHU PAN. Added/Corp** Chung-kuo Lan Chiu Hsieh Hui. (19??)-. Periodical. Chinese. bm. RMBY0.28. Lan Chiu, Post Office, Beijing, People's Republic of China. **LC** GV885.8.C6; L36. **DD** 796.32/3/0951.

UK
**LAWN TENNIS ALMANACK, THE. Added/Corp** Dunlop Sports Company Limited. **VFOAT** Dunlop Lawn Tennis Almanak. (19??)-. English. an. **LC** GV991; .L355. **DD** 796.34.

SZ
**LAWS OF THE GAME AND UNIVERSAL GUIDE FOR REFEREES. See** Law.

UK
**LAWS OF THE GAME OF RUGBY FOOTBALL WITH INSTRUCTIONS AND NOTES FOR GUIDANCE OF REFEREES. Main/Corp** Rugby Football Union. English. £60.00. **LC** GV945.4; .R83A. **DD** 796.33/3/02022.

US/1067-4748
**LEGENDS SPORTS MEMORABILIA.** [Legends sports memorab.]. (19??)-. Periodical. English. Six times a year (Jan., Mar., May, July, Sept., Nov.). $27.00 US; $43.50 other. Legends Sports Memorabilia, 9950 Campo Road, Suite 202, Spring Valley CA 91977. **Tel** (800)835-2835 (619)460-9219, FAX (619)460-4919. **DD** 769.

GW/0323-4134
**LEICHTATHLET BERLIN, DDR. 1953. Title Change.** [LeichtathletBerl. DDR, 1953]. (1953)-(1992). Periodical. German. wk. Deutscher Judo Verband, Redaktion Ippon Segewaldweg 40, D 12557 Berlin Germany. **Tel** 011 49 711 210770, telex 051 678. **UDC** 796.4. **Continues** Leichtathletik (Berlin, DDR. 1952), 0323-7346. **Continued by** Leichtathletik.

GW
**LEICHTATHLETIK. VFOAT** Track and Field. (19??)-. Periodical. German. wk. DM283.40. Deutscher Sportverlag K Stoof, Eintrachstr 110, D 50668 Cologne Germany. **Tel** 011 49 221 1648247. **LC** WMLC L 83/3794. **Continues** Der Leichtathlet.

US/0733-9674
**LET'S CHEER. Added/Corp** North American Association for Drill Teams. **VAT** Let Us Cheer. (19??)-. Periodical. English. Five times a year. $13.50 US; $27.00 others. Miss Drillteam USA Pageant, 1212 Ynez Avenue, Redondo Beach CA 90277. **Tel** (310)540-3364. **ED** Kay Crawford. **Ad Acc. Circ:** 3,000 (ctrl).
**Desc:** A national pep arts magazine for drill teams, flags, cheerleaders, baton, songleaders, pom-pom and dance teams. Excellent for instructors and students. Edited by the worlds greatest authorities.

●CN/1188-5416
**LET'S GO RACIN'.** (LET'S GO RACIN'/ BY JOAN ROUE.). [Let's go racin']. (1992)-. English. $9.00 per volume. Jr. Motorsports, PO Box 41035, Dartmouth Nova Scotia B2Y 4P7 Canada. **DD** 796.7.

US/0889-4795
**LET'S PLAY HOCKEY.** [Let's play hockey]. **VFOAT** Hockey. (19??)-. Periodical. English. Twenty-six times a year (Weekly from Nov. thru Apr. and once in Aug. and Oct.). $26.00 US; $60.00 Canada. Lets Play Inc., 2721 East 42nd Street, Minneapolis MN 55406. **Tel** (612)729-0023, FAX (612)729-0023. **ED** Arnold Hamel. **DD** 796. **Bk Rev, (Qty: 2). Ad Acc. Adv Mgr:** Doug Johnson. **Circ:** 20,000 (ctrl).
**Desc:** Focuses on all levels of ice hockey in the United States and Canada. Special columns deal with playing, training, and coaching. Complete team rankings and a tournament calendar are featured in each issue.

FI/0358-7010
**LIIKUNTA JA TIEDE.** [Liik. tiede]. (1981)-. Periodical. Finnish. bm. **UDC** 796. **Continues** Stadion, 0561-7731.
**Ind/Abst** SPORT Discus.

US
**LINKS MAGAZINE.** (199?)-. English. Six times a year. $12.00. Southern Links, PO Box 7628, Hilton Head Island SC 29938. **Tel** (803)842-6200, FAX (803)842-6233. **Continues** Southern Links, 1043-6375.

CN/0821-4603
**LIVRE DE REGLEMENTS ADMINISTRATIFS / FEDERATION QUEBECOISE DE HOCKEY SUR GLACE INC.** [Livre reglem. adm. - Fed. que. hockey glace]. **Main/Corp** Federation Quebecoise de Hockey sur Glace. Seasons 1982/1983 - 1983/1984-. French. an. Federation Quebecoise de Hockey sur Glace, 1415 Est rue Jarry, Montreal Quebec H2E 2Z7 Canada. **DD** 796.96/2/02022. **UDC** 796.66.063(714). **Continues** Federation Quebecoise de Hockey sur Glace. Livre de Reglements, 0710-4758.

FR
**LIVRE D'OR DE LA MOTO, LE. See** Motorcycles.

CN/0225-7203
**LIVRE OFFICIEL DES RECORDS - LIGUE CANADIENNE DE FOOTBALL.** [Livre off. rec. - Ligue can. footb.]. **Main/Corp** Ligue Canadienne de Football. First issue in 1978?. French. an. Ligue Canadienne de Football, Bureau 1800/11 Ouest rue King, Toronto Ontario M5H 1A3 Canada. **DD** 796.33/56. **UDC** 796.333.092(71).

CN/0706-3180
**LIVRET DES REGLEMENTS DE LA FEDERATION CANADIENNE DES ARCHERS (1974).** (LIVRET DES REGLEMENTS DE LA FEDERATION CANADIENNE DES ARCHERS.). **Main/Corp** Federation Canadienne des Archers. First issue in 1975?. French (English). an. $10.00 Canada; $15.00 other. Federation Canadienne des Archers, National Office, 1600 James Naismith Drive, Gloucester Ontario K1B 5N4 Canada. **Tel** (613)748-5604, FAX (613)748-5706, telex 053 3660. **DD** 799.3/2/0971. **UDC** 799.322.2.063(71).

CN/0713-553X
**LOISIRS-PRESSE.** [Loisirs-presse]. No. 1 (Jan. 15, 1982)-. Periodical. French. fw. Free. Loisirs-Presse, 1414 East rue Jarry, Montreal Quebec H2E 2Z7 Canada. **DD** 790./09714. **UDC** 379.8(714).

US/8750-9016
**LOUISIANA SPORTSMAN. VFOAT** South Louisiana Sportsman. (198?)-. Periodical. English. Eleven times a year ((Dec. and Jan. issue combined)). $14.00 US; $20.00 other. Louisiana Sportsman Magazine / Louisiana, PO Box 1199, Boutte LA 70039. **Tel** (504)758-7217, FAX (504)758-7000. **ED** Ann Taylor. **Ad Acc, Adv Mgr:** L. Behan. **Continues** South Louisiana Sportsman, 0744-3560.

IT
**LUDOTECA.** (19??)-. Italian. bm (6 issues). L80000 (institutions), L40000 (individuals). Ludoteca, Cigi Via del Proconsolo 26, 50122 Florence Italy. **Tel** 011 39 55 214069, 011 39 55 284621.

CN/0821-1329
**MAGAZINE CONTRE-JOUR.** [Mag. contre-jour]. **VFOAT** Contre-Jour. Vol. 1, No 1 (1982)-. Periodical. French. 3.50Can$. Contre-Jour, CP 477, Succursale Limoilou, Quebec, Quebec G1L 4W3. **DD** 796.7/2/05.

CN/0713-4290
**MAGAZINE DES ARTS MARTIAUX DU QUEBEC, LE.** Vol. 1 No. 1 (May/June 1982)-. Periodical. French. mo. $12.00. Le Magazine des Arts Martiaux du Quebec, 4337 rue Papineau, Montreal Quebec H2H 1T3 Canada. **DD** 796.8/15/05. **UDC** 796.85(714).

SZ/0254-1246
**MAGGLINGEN.** See Recreation, Leisure.

US/1054-6723
**MAGIC MAGAZINE (ORLANDO, FLA.).** (MAGIC MAGAZINE.). (1990)-. Periodical. English. mo (Oct.-June plus additional in April). $14.95. Orlando Sentinel / Public Services, P.O.Box 1100, Orlando FL 32802. **Tel** (800)788-1225, (407)420-5236, FAX (407)420-5759. **ED** Bruce Carden. **DD** 796. **Ad Acc. Circ:** 15,000 (ctrl).

HU/0238-0412
**MAGYAR OLIMPIAI AKADEMIA EVKONYVE, A.** (1986)-. Hungarian. an. Magyar Olimpiai Akademia, Alkotas U 44, Budapest 1123 Hungary. **LC** GV721.4.H9; M34.

US/0195-2870
**MAINE SNOWMOBILER.** Periodical. English. mo (eight issues per year). $2.80. Maine Snowmobiler, Box 77, Augusta ME 04330. **ED** Michael B Gregory. Index available. **Ad Acc. Circ:** 11,000 (ctrl).

US/0199-0365
**MAINE SPORTSMAN, THE.** [Me. sportsman]. (19??)-. Periodical. English. Twelve times a year. $20.00 (one year); $35.00 (two years). Maine Sportsman, PO Box 507, Yarmouth ME 04096. **Tel** (207)846-9501. **ED** Harry P. Vanderweide. **Bk Rev. Ad Acc. Circ:** 30,000 (ctrl).
**Desc:** Seasonal activities: hunting, fishing, canoeing, archery, dogs, by the columnists. Some activities also covered regionally by other columnists.

US
**MAJOR LEAGUE BASEBALL OFFICIAL ... PREVIEW.** **VFOAT** MLB Official ... Preview. (1990)-. English. an. Diamandis Communications Inc, 1499 Monrovia Avenue, New Port Beach CA 92663. **Tel** (714)720-5300. **ED** Barry Shapiro. **LC** GV863.A1; M34. **DD** 796.357/64/0973.
**Desc:** Each regional issue will feature a local star on its batting and statistical averages.

SA
**MAN MAGNUM.** **VFOAT** Man/Magnum; Magnum; Man. (19??)-. Periodical. English. mo. R75.00 South Africa; R89.00 other. South Africa Man Pty Ltd., PO Box 35204, Northway 4065 South Africa. **Tel** 11 27 31 526551, FAX 11 27 31 5628389. **LC** WMLC L 83/125.
**Desc:** The shooter's magazine.

CN/0383-7777
**MAN UNDERWATER.** 1967. Periodical. English. bm. $13.82. Manitoba Underwater Council, PO Box 711, Winnipeg Manitoba R3C 2K3 Canada. **ED** Joan Eggett. **DD** 797.2/3/0627127. **UDC** 797.215(714). **Ad Acc. Circ:** 300 (ctrl). ***Continues** Manitoba Underwater Council. Newsletter, 0383-7742.*
**Desc:** Scuba diving publication containing information on safety, education, activities and information of interest to the Manitoba Diver.

BL
**MANCHETE ESPORTIVA.** Periodical. Portuguese. Cr$20.00 per issue. Bloch, rua do Resenda 100, Rio de Janeiro Brazil. **LC** GV561; .M24. **DD** 796/.05.

CN/0823-8448
**MANITOBA CURLING REVIEW.** Periodical. English. mo. $8.00. Manitoba Curling Review, PO Box 182, Rosenfeld Manitoba R0G 1X0 Canada. **DD** 796.9/6. **UDC** 796.96(714).

CN/0225-9273
**MANITOBA HIGH SCHOOLS ATHLETIC DIRECTORY.** [Man. high sch. athl. dir.]. 1978/79-. Directory. English. be. Maitoba High Schools Athletic Association, 1301 Ellice Avenue, Winnipeg Manitoba R3G 0G1. **DD** 796/.025/7127. **UDC** 796.42(036)(714). ***Continues** Contact Personnel in Sport Recreation & Schools, 0225-9265.*

●US/1072-3595
**MANN FANTASY BASEBALL GUIDE, THE.** [Mann fantasy baseb. guide]. (1994)-. Periodical. English. $10.00. Harper Collins Publishers, Keystone Industrial Park, Scranton PA 18512. **Tel** (800)242-7737, (800)233-4727, FAX (800)822-4090. **LC** WMLC 91/5125. **DD** 796. ***Continues** Mann-Mallin Fantasy Baseball Guide, 1056-5108.*

●US
**MANN-MALLIN FANTASY BASEBALL GUIDE, THE.** **VFOAT** Mann Mallin Fantasy Baseball Guide. (1992)-. English. Harper Collins Publishers, Keystone Industrial Park, Scranton PA 18512. **Tel** (800)242-7737, (800)233-4727, FAX (800)822-4090. **DD** 793.93.

US/1056-5108
**MANN-MALLIN FANTASY BASEBALL GUIDE, THE.** ***Title Change.*** [Mann-Mallin fantasy baseb. guide]. **VFOAT** Mann Mallin Fantasy Baseball Guide. (1992)-(199?). English. Harper Collins Publishers, Keystone Industrial Park, Scranton PA 18512. **Tel** (800)242-7737, (800)233-4727, FAX (800)822-4090. **LC** WMLC 91/5125. **DD** 796. ***Continued by** Mann Fastasy Baseball Guide, 1072-3595.*

CN/0227-5996
**MANUEL - ASSOCIATION CANADIENNE DE BADMINTON.** (MANUEL / ASSOCIATION CANADIENNE DE BADMINTON, ASSOCIATION CANADIENNE D'ENTRAINEURS DE BADMINTON, ASSOCIATION CANADIENNE DES ARBITRES DE BADMINTON.). [Man. - Assoc. can. badminton]. **Main/Corp** Association Canadienne de Badminton. French (English). an. $5.00. Association Canadienne de Badminton, 1600 James Naismith Drive, Gloucester Ontario K1N 5B4 Canada. **Tel** (613)748-5605, FAX (613)746-5695, telex 053-3660. **DD** 796.34/5/06071. **UDC** 796.344(035.3)(71). ctrl circ.

IT
**MAPPI DEI FORNITORI DI IMPIANTI SPORTIVI RICREATIVI.** Italian. ir. Free. Sinopia Ed, Via G. Murat 84, 20159 Milan Italy. **Tel** 011 39 2 688-3641, FAX 011 39 2 668-02971.

US/0360-9928
**MARATHON HANDBOOK.** English. an. $1.95. World Publications, Box 366, Mountainview CA 94040. **LC** GV1065; .M36. **DD** 796.4/26. **UDC** 796.422.16(035.3).

CN/1187-4775
**MARCHE (MONTREAL).** (MARCHE.). [Marche]. **Added/Corp** Federation Quebecoise de la Marche. Vol. 3, No 1 (Fall 1991)-. Periodical. French. qt. $2.95 per issue. Federation Quebecoise de la Marche, 4545 de Coubertin, Montreal Quebec H1V 3R2 Canada. **Tel** (514)252-3157. **DD** 796.5. ***Continues** La Revue Marche., 0843-7769.*

AT
**MARKSMAN.** English. Six times a year. 15.00Aus$. New South Wales Rifle Association, PO Box 386, Maroubra NSW 2036 Australia. **Tel** 011 61 2 6614532, FAX 011 61 2 616042.

US/1057-6029
**MARQUETTE SPORTS LAW JOURNAL.** See Law.

US/0898-4786
**MARTIAL ARTS TRAINING.** [Martial arts train.]. **VFOAT** MA Training; MA; M.A. Training. Vol. 15, No. 2 (Summer 1988)-. Periodical. English. bm (publishes 3 months in advance of cover date). $17.70 (one year), $35.40 (two year). Rainbow Publications Inc., PO Box 16298, North Hollywood CA 91615. **Tel** (818)760-8983, (800)257-4066, FAX (818)985-1213. **LC** GV1102.7.T7; M37. **DD** 796.8/05. ***Continues** MA Weapons, 0893-2514.*

CN/1185-2127
**MASTERATHLETE NEWS.** [MasterAthl. news]. **Added/Corp** Canadian MasterAthlete Federation. Vol. 1, No. 1 (June 1990)-. Periodical. English. mo. $22.00. Canadian Masterathlete Federation, Unit 310, 200 Silver Star Boulevard, Scarborough, Ontario H1V 4H5 Canada. **DD** 796. ***Continues** Masterathlete Letter., 0835-6815.*

US/0191-8117
**MASTERS (AUGUSTA).** (MASTERS.). 1978-. English. an. Augusta National Golf Club, Augusta GA 30901. **LC** GV970; .M37. **DD** 796.352/7. **UDC** 796.352.

US/0743-6580
**MEDALIST FLASHBACK NOTEBOOK.** Began with 1976 volume. English. an. Macgregor Sports Ed, 7001 Orchard Lake Road K #420C, West Bloomfield MI 48322-3608. **LC** GV885.3; .M35. **DD** 796.32/3/077.

●CN/1191-3991
**MEDIA INFORMATION FOR THE ... IIHF WORLD JUNIOR HOCKEY CHAMPIONSHIPS / PREPARED BY THE CANADIAN HOCKEY LEAGUE.** [Media inf. IIHF World jr. hockey championships]. **Added/Corp** Canadian Hockey League. **VFOAT** IIHF World Junior Hockey Championships; International Ice Hockey Federation World Junior Hockey Championships. **VAT** Media Information for the International Ice Hockey Federation World Junior Hockey Championships. (1992)-. English. Canadian Hockey League, Jim Price, 305 Milner Avenue, Suite 208, Scarborough Ontario M1B 3V4 Canada. **DD** 796.962/06/071. ***Continues** Media Information for the ... World Junior Hockey Championships., 1191-3983.*

US/0025-9969
**MERCURY (LOS ANGELES, CALIF.).** (MERCURY.). **Added/Corp** Los Angeles Athletic Club. Riviera Country Club. Riviera Tennis Club. California Yacht Club. (19??)-. Periodical. English. Los Angeles Athletic Club, 431 West 7th Street, Los Angeles CA 90014. **Tel** (310)625-2211. **ED** Dan Bayless. **Circ:** 9,700.

SZ/1011-405X
**MESSAGE OLYMPIQUE.** **Added/Corp** International Olympic Committee. **VFOAT** Olympic Message. No. 1 (May 1982)-. Multiple languages (English and French; table of contents in English and French; translations available in Spanish). tq. Free upon request. International Olympic Committee / Comite International Olympique, Chateau de Vidy, CH-1007 Lausanne Switzerland. **Tel** 011 41 21 621-6111, FAX 011 41 21 621-6216, telex 45-4024ACIOCH. **ED** Raymond Gafner. **LC** GV721.5; .M3999. **DD** 796.98.
**Desc:** Information on Olympics.
**Ind/Abst** Leis. Recreat. Tour. Abstr.; Phys. Educ. Index (1985-); SPORT Discus; SportSearch (May 1987-).

US
**MESSING ABOUT IN BOATS.** English. sm (published on the 1st and 15th of each month). $20.00. Cycle Sport Publishing, 29 Burley Street, Wenham MA 01984. **Tel** (508)774-0906. **ED** Bob Hicks. **Bk Rev**, (Qty: varies). **Ad Acc. Circ:** 4,000.
**Desc:** Articles relating to the enjoyment of small boating.

US/1042-7678
**MET GOLFER, THE.** [Met golf.]. Periodical. English. Sports Marketing Group Inc, 1 Selleck Street/Suite 550, Norwalk CT 06855-1120. **DD** 796.

US
**METRO SPORTS MAGAZINE.** (19??)-. Periodical. English. mo. $18.00 (one year), $25.00 (two year). Metro Sports Magazine, 695 Washington Street, New York NY 10014. **Tel** (212)627-7040. **ED** Miles Jaffe. **Bk Rev**, (Qty: 10). **Ad Acc.** ctrl circ. ***Continues** City Sports Monthly.*

US/0273-6683
**MIAA NEWSLETTER, THE.** **Main/Corp** Massachusetts Interscholastic Athletic Association. **VAT** Massachusetts Interscholastic Athletic Association Newsletter. Newsletter. English. mo. Massachusetts Interscholastic Athletic Association, 75 Central Street, PO Box 269, Ashland MA 01721.

US
**MICHIGAN GOLFER.** (19??)-. English. Six times a year (Feb., May., June, July, Aug., Sept.). $9.00 (one year); $16.00 (two years). Great Lakes Sports Publishing Inc., 7990 West Grand River, Suite C, Brighton MI 48116. **Tel** (313)227-4200. **ED** Terry Moore. **Bk Rev**, (Qty: 1). **Ad Acc, Adv Mgr Tel** (312)227-4200. **Circ:** 16,000.
**Desc:** Regional golf magazine with course, new products reviews, calendar of events and golf news coverage of regional tournaments and outings.

US/1071-2313
**MICHIGAN GOLFER.** [Mich. golf.]. (198?)-. Periodical. English. ir (Feb., May, June, July, Aug., Sept.). $10.00 (one year), $18.00 (two year). Great Lakes Sports Publishing Inc., 7990 West Grand River, Suite C, Brighton MI 48116. **Tel** (313)227-4200. **ED** Jerry Moore. **DD** 796. **Bk Rev. Ad Acc. Circ:** 17,000.

US/0279-1773
**MICHIGAN RUNNER, THE.** (19??)-. Periodical. English. Nine times a year (Jan./Feb., Mar./Apr. and Nov./Dec. issues combined). $13.50. Great Lakes Sports Publishing Inc., 7990 West Grand River, Suite C, Brighton MI 48116. **Tel** (313)227-4200. **ED** Dave Foley. **Bk Rev. Ad Acc. Circ:** 10,000.
**Desc:** Running news update, calendar of state wide events, medical and health reviews and race coverage.

US/0199-2465
**MID AMERICAN AUTO RACING NEWS.** **VFOAT** Mid-American Auto Racing News. (19??)-. Periodical. English. ir (weklky Apr. through Oct., monthly Nov. through Mar.). $18.00 (one year), $30.00 (two year). Mid-American Auto Racing News, PO Box 178, Swanton OH 43558. **Tel** (419)866-0771, FAX (419)866-4569. **ED** Nancy and Phil Cole.

US/1042-3516
**MID SPORTS.** [Mid sports]. (1988)-. Periodical. English. bm. $25.00 (1 year), $45.00 (2 year). Joe Bournonville, PO Box 207, Pittsburg KS 66762. **Tel** (316)231-5740, (316)231-5883, FAX (316)232-3521. **DD** 796.
**Desc:** Designed to provide ideas for the people who develop, administer, and coach middle school activity programs, to provide a forum for professionals who develop and reevaluate goals and objectives, and to promote the positive effect that age-appropriate activities have on middle school students.

US/0889-5279
**MIDGETS & MINI-SPRINTS RACING NEWS.** ***Title Change.*** **VFOAT** Midgets and Mini-Sprints Racing News. Periodical. English. bm. J.L. Quinn and Associates, PO Box 8389, Fresno CA 93727. **Tel** (307)266-3838, (800)443-9250, FAX 1-307-472-5106. **ED** Marlon Atkins. **DD** 796. **UDC** 796.71(73). **Bk Rev. Ad Acc. Circ:** 6,000. ***Continued by** J.L. Quinn's Midgets & Motorsports Illustrated, 1050-0243.*
**Desc:** Concerns racing results and coverage of various midget and mini-sprint kart races across the United States.

US/0047-732X
**MIDWEST RACING NEWS.** **VFOAT** MRN. (19??)-. Periodical. English. Thirty times a year. $15.00 (one year), $27.00 (two year). Midwest Racing News Inc, 6646 West Fairview Avenue, Milwaukee WI 53213. **Tel**

(414)778-4700. **ED** Phil Hall and James K. Engel. **Bk Rev. Ad Acc. Circ:** 9,000.
**Desc:** Results, stories, features and upcoming events of general interest to the auto racing enthusiast.

US/0893-3367
**MIDWEST VOLLEYBALL MAGAZINE.** ***Ceased.*** [Midwest volleyb. mag.]. (1984)-?. Periodical. English. bm. Midwest Volleyball Magazine, PO Box 41116, Chicago IL 60641. **Tel** (312)777-0319. **DD** 796.

●US/1061-7140
**MILES TO GO.** (MILES TO GO: A DISTANCE RIDING MAGAZINE.). [Miles go]. Vol. 1, Issue 1 (May 1992)-. Periodical. English. bm. $18.00. Carol Clark, PO Box 364, Jupiter FL 33468-0364. **DD** 798.

US/1052-0961
**MINITRUCKIN' (ANAHEIM, CALIF.).** (MINITRUCKIN'.). **VFOAT** Mini Truckin'. (198?)-. Periodical. English. Nine times a year. $17.95 (one year), $29.95 (two years). McMullen Publishing Inc, 2145 West La Palma Avenue, PO Box 70015, Anaheim CA 92801-1785. **Tel** (714)572-2255, FAX (714)572-1864. **LC** WMLC 93/3942. **DD** 388.

US/1050-740X
**MINNESOTA HOCKEY.** ***Title Change.*** [Minn. hockey]. **VFOAT** Minnesota Hockey Magazine. (198?)-(1992). Periodical. English. mo. Minnesota Hockey Magazine, 1000 W 80th Street, Bloomington MN 55420. **Tel** (612)884-4490, FAX (612)881-2172. **ED** Bruce Brothers. **LC** GV848.4.U6; M6. **DD** 796.962/09776/05. ***Continues*** *Hockey (Bloomington, Minn.), 1064-6892.* ***Continued by*** *Hockey, Art of the State, 1064-6892.*
**Desc:** In depth coverage of youth programs, training, college hockey, celebrities, North Stars, tournaments, juniors, and coaching.

US/1058-6288
**MISSOURI JOURNAL OF HEALTH, PHYSICAL EDUCATION, RECREATION AND DANCE.** **See** Education-Physical Education and Training.

AT
**MODERN ATHLETE AND COACH.** **Added/Corp** Australian Track & Field Coaches Association. Vol. 1 (1963)-. Periodical. English. qt. 22.00Aus$ Australia; 25.00Aus$ (surface mail) other. Track & Field Coaches Association / Australia, 1 Fox Avenue, Athelstone South Australia 5076 Australia. **Tel** 011 61 8 3374510. **ED** Jess Jarver. **Bk Rev. Ad Acc, Adv Mgr:** same as editor. **Circ:** 2600.
**Ind/Abst** Phys. Educ. Index; SPORT Discus; SportSearch (May 1987-).

AT/0026-7732
**MODERN FISHING.** (19??)-. Periodical. English. mo. 53.00Aus$ Australia; 88.00Aus$ New Zealand & Papua New Guinea; 112.00Aus$ US & Canada; 119.00Aus$ Europe & Africa; 94.00Aus$ Singapore, Malaysia, Indonesia; 103.00Aus$ other. Federal Publishing Co Pty Ltd, PO Box 199, 180 Bourke Road, Alexandria New South Wales, 2015 Australia. **Tel** 011 61 2 693 6666, FAX 011 61 2 693 9935. **(Subscription address:** Federal Publishing Co. Pty Ltd., PO Box 199, Alexandria NSW 2015 Australia.**)**

CN/1183-4846
**MONDE DU LOISIR ET DES SPORTS AU QUEBEC.** ***Title Change.*** (REPERTOIRE DESCRIPTIF.LE MONDE DU LOISIR ET DES SPORTS AU QUEBEC.). [Monde loisir sports Que.]. **Added/Corp** Alliance Champlain. **VFOAT** Monde du Loisir et des Sports au Quebec. (1992)-(1992). French. be. Quebec Dans Le Monde, CP 8503, Sainte-Foy Quebec G1V 4N5 Canada. **Tel** (418)659-5540, FAX (418)659-4143. **DD** 790/.025/714. ***Continued by*** *Repertoire Descriptif. Loisir et Sport au Quebec, 1192-3326.*

FR
**MONDE DU RUGBY, LE.** 1973/74-. French. 25. Stock, 14 rue de l'Ancienne-Comedie, Paris 6E France. **LC** GV945.5; .D86. **DD** 796.33/3/05. **UDC** 796.333.

IT
**MONDO DEL NUOTO.** (19??)-. Italian. Ten times a year. L60000 Italy; L70000 other. Societa Editrice Aquarius, Via Albere 19, 37138 Verona Italy. **Tel** 011 39 45 577399.

US/1056-3393
**MOTHER ROAD JOURNAL, THE.** [Mother road j.]. No. 1 (July 1991)-. Periodical. English. qt. $10.00 US; $12.00 Canada. Mother Road Publishing, Robert L Moore, PO Box 27232, Lakewood CO 80227. **DD** 796.

CN/0836-7264
**MOTONEIGE QUEBEC.** [Motoneige Qu,e.]. (1975)-. Periodical. French. ir. 10.00Can$. Editions Motoneige / Quebec, 60 rue Villeneuve, Vaudreuil Quebec, J7V 8B9 Canada. **Tel** (514)252-3163, FAX (514)251-8038, telex 005 62358. **DD** 796.94/09714. **Ad Acc. Circ:** 65,000. ***Continues*** *Magazine Motoneige., 0381-7326.*

NE
**MOTOR.** **See** Motorcycles.

UK
**MOTOR-CYCLE SPORT.** English. Teesdale Publishing Company, Ltd., PO Box 35, Standard House, Bonhill Street, London EC2A 4DA England. **Tel** 011 44 71 6284741, FAX 011 44 71 6388497, telex 888602.

US/0090-2144
**MOTOR RACING YEAR, THE.** 1971-. English. W W Norton & Company Inc, 500 Fifth Avenue, New York NY 10110. **Tel** (800)233-4830. **LC** GV1029; .P754. **DD** 796.7/2/05. **UDC** 796.7.

UK/0027-2019
**MOTOR SPORT.** Vol. 1 (May 1924)-. English. mo. $42.00 US; $49.00 Canada & Mexico. Teesdale Publishing Company, Ltd., PO Box 35, Standard House, Bonhill Street, London EC2A 4DA England. **Tel** 011 44 71 6284741, FAX 011 44 71 6388497, telex 888602. **(Subscription address:** Eric Waiter Associates, PO Box 188, Berkely Heights NJ 07922.**)**

US/0091-8822
**MOTOR SPORT YEARBOOK.** English. $4.95. Collier Books, 866 Third Avenue, New York NY 10022. **LC** GV1029; .M69. **DD** 796.7/2/05. **UDC** 796.7(058).

UK
**MOTOR SPORTS CAR ROAD TESTS, THE.** **VFOAT** Sports Car Road Tests. English. **LC** WMLC L 83/8118.

US/0027-2094
**MOTOR TREND.** **See** Transportation-Automobiles.

US/0883-7228
**MOTORCYCLE DRAG RACING.** **See** Motorcycles.

US/0164-9256
**MOTORCYCLIST'S POST, THE.** **See** Transportation.

UK/0027-2264
**MOTORING NEWS LONDON.** (MOTORING NEWS.). [Mot. news Lond.]. (1955)-. Newspaper. English. wk. £45.00 UK; £55.00 other. Teesdale Publishing Company, Ltd., PO Box 35, Standard House, Bonhill Street, London EC2A 4DA England. **Tel** 011 44 71 6284741, FAX 011 44 71 6388497, telex 888602. **ED** Mark Skews and David Treymane. Index available. cum. index. **Ad Acc.** ctrl circ.
**Desc:** Motor racing reports and interviews, and road tests for new cars.

US
**MOTORSPORTS MARKETING NEWS.** **See** Business-Advertising and Public Relations.

US/1063-0422
**MOTORSPORTS WEEKLY.** [Motorsports wkly.]. **VFOAT** Motor Sports Weekly. (1991)-. Periodical. English. wk. Motorsports Weekly, PO Box 1540, Perry GA 31069. **DD** 796.

US/0897-5213
**MOUNTAIN BIKE.** [Mt. bike]. **VFOAT** Mountain Bike Magazine. Vol. 6, No. 1 (Feb. 1990)-. Periodical. English. Eleven times a year. $19.97 US; $35.97 others. Rodale Press Inc., 400 South 10th Street, Emmaus PA 18098. **Tel** (215)967-5171, (800)666-2503. **(Subscription address:** CDS Agency Hard Copy, PO Box 4966, Des Moines, IA 50340**) LC** WMLC 91/279. **DD** 796. ***Continues*** *Mountain Bike, 0897-5213.*

US/0895-8467
**MOUNTAIN BIKE ACTION.** [Mt. bike action]. **VFOAT** Mountain Bike. Vol. 1, No. 1 (Oct. 1986)-. Periodical. English. Twelve times a year. $19.98 (one year), $36.95 (two year). Hi-Torque Publications, PO Box 9502, Mission Hills CA 91395. **Tel** (805)295-1910.

US/0160-726X
**MOUNTAIN GAZETTE.** Began in Sept. 1972. Periodical. English. mo. $8.00. Mountain Gazette, 2025 York Street, Denver CO 80205. **UDC** 796.92. ***Supersedes*** *Skier's Gazette.*

IT
**MOVIMENTO.** **See** Psychology.

US/0749-4122
**MULTIHULLS.** [Multihulls]. **VFOAT** Multihulls Magazine. (1975)-. Periodical. English. bm (6 issues). $21.00 US; $27.00 other. Chiodi Advertising & Publishing Inc, 421 Hancock Street, North Quincy MA 02171. **Tel** (617)328-8181, FAX (617)471-0118. **ED** Charles Chiodi. **DD** 797. Index available. cum. index. **Bk Rev. Ad Acc. Circ:** 30,000.
**Desc:** Complete coverage of all size multihulls, design, racing, boat tests, cruising information and safety information.

US/0895-9668
**MUSHING (ESTER, ALASKA).** (MUSHING.). [Mushing]. Vol. 1, No. 1 (Feb./Mar. 1988)-. Periodical. English. bm. $21.00 (1 year), $36.00 (2 year) US; $30.00 (1 year), $54.00 (2 year) Canada; $41.00 (1 year), $76.00 (2 year) other. Mushing, PO Box 149, Ester AK 99725. **Tel** (907)479-0454, FAX (907)479-0454. **ED** Todd Hoener and Diane Herrman. **DD** 796. Index available (Published in March). **Bk Rev**, (Qty: 4). **Ad Acc, Adv Mgr:** Roy Earnest. **Circ:** 5,000. available on microfiche.
**Desc:** Contains articles on the adventures, technology, history, politics and appeal of dog mushing. Aimed at both beginners and experts, there are updates on health, safety, food, training, techniques, equipment and events. There are also interviews of people who have influenced mushing, as well as articles on the history and traditions of the sport.

●US/1062-9513
**MUSSELMAN'S ORIGINAL PRO BASKETBALL SCOUTING HANDBOOK.** [Musselman's orig. pro basketb. scout. handb.]. **VFOAT** Original Pro Basketball Scouting Handbook; Pro Basketball Scouting Handbook; Musselman's Original. (1992)-. Periodical. English. sa. $19.99. Goose Productions, 1230 Shirestone Lane, Dallas TX 75244. **DD** 796.

US/0894-5179
**MUSTANG (LOS ANGELES, CALIF.).** ***Title Change.*** **See** Transportation-Automobiles.

US
**MUZZLE BLASTS.** Periodical. English. mo. $19.75. National Muzzle Loading Rifle Association, PO Box 67, Friendship IN 47021. **Tel** (812)667-5131. **ED** Sharon Cunningham. **Bk Rev. Circ:** 27,000.
**Desc:** History and educational material on muzzle loading firearms.

US/0274-5720
**MUZZLELOADER, THE.** **VFOAT** Muzzle Loader. Vol. 1, (April 1974)-. Periodical. English. Six times a year (Jan., Mar., May, July, Sept., Nov.). $16.00 (one year); $28.00 (two years). Rebel Publishing Company Inc, Route 5 Box 347-M, Texarkana TX 75501. **Tel** (903)832-4726, FAX (903)831-3177. **ED** William Scurlock. **LC** TS536.6.M8; M885. **DD** 683.4/22. Index available (Bound in Nov./Dec. issues). cum. index. **Bk Rev**, (Qty: 18). **Ad Acc, Adv Mgr Tel** (903)832-4347. **Circ:** 20,500.
**Desc:** This magazine is for the black powder shooters, hunters and re-enactors.

CN/0829-6146
**MVP.** (MVP : CANADA'S NATIONAL SPORTS MAGAZINE.). [MVP]. **VFOAT** MVP Magazine. Dec. 1984-. Periodical. English. ir. MVP Magazine, 304-3 Church Street, Toronto Ontario M5E 1M2 Canada. **DD** 796/.0971.
**Ind/Abst** SportSearch (May 1987-).

CN/0711-3986
**N.S.U.C. UNDERWATER NEWS.** [N.S.U.C. underw. news]. **VAT** Nova Scotia Underwater Council News. Issue 3 (1979)-. Periodical. English. Free to members. Nova Scotia Underwater Council, Nova Scotia Canada. **DD** 797.2/3/060716. **UDC** 797.215(716). ***Continues*** *NSUC Newsletter, 0711-3994.*

US
**NAGWS SOFTBALL GUIDE.** **Main/Corp** National Association for Girls & Women in Sport. **Added/Corp** American Alliance for Health, Physical Education, Recreation, and Dance. (1987)-. English. ir. $6.25 members; $6.95 non-members. American Alliance for Health, Physical Education, Recreation, and Dance / AAHPERD, 1900 Association Drive, Reston VA 22091. **Tel** (703)476-3493, (800)321-0789. **Circ:** 8,000. ***Continues*** *NAGWS Guide: Softball, 0363-2504.*

US
**NAGWS VOLLEYBALL GUIDE.** **Main/Corp** National Association for Girls & Women in Sport. **VFOAT** Volleyball Guide. **VAT** National Association for Girls & Women in Sport Volleyball Guide. (1987)-. English. an. $7.45. American Alliance for Health, Physical Education, Recreation, and Dance / AAHPERD, 1900 Association Drive, Reston VA 22091. **Tel** (703)476-3493, (800)321-0789. **LC** GV1017.V6; N32a. **DD** 796.325. ***Continues*** *National Association for Girls & Women in Sport. NAGWS Guide. Volleyball, 0145-1987.*

US/0740-5995
**NAIA NEWS.** [NAIA news]. **Main/Corp** National Association of Intercollegiate Athletics. **VFOAT** NAIA News and Coach. **VAT** National Association of Intercollegiate Athletics News. Vol. 1 (1950)-. Periodical. English. mo (11 issues). $25.00. National Association of Intercollegiate Athletics, 6120 South Yale Avenue, Suite 1450, Tulsa OK 74136. **Tel** (918)494-8828. **ED** Mary Beth Brutton. **Ad Acc. Circ:** 7,500. available on microfilm and microfiche from University Microfilms International (UMI).
**Ind/Abst** SPORT Discus; SportSearch (May 1987-).

US/1059-745X
**NARA PYLON : OFFICIAL PUBLICATION OF THE NATIONAL AIR RACING ASSOCIATION.** [NARA pylon]. **Added/Corp** National Air Racing Association. **VAT** National Air Racing Association Pylon. Vol. 1, No. 1 (Sept./Oct. 1991)-. Periodical. English. bm. $35.00. National Air Racing Association, 1090 Lawrence Drive, Suite 107, Newbury Park CA 91320. **DD** 797.

PL/0860-9519
**NARTY KRAKOW.** (NARTY.). [Narty Krak.]. (1989)-. Periodical. Polish. mo. Price on Request. **(Subscription address:** ARS Polona, PO Box 1001, 00068 Warsaw Poland.**)** **UDC** 796.92.

CN/0705-7423
**NATIONAL 5-PIN BOWLERS NEWS.** **VFOAT** Bowlers News. **VAT** National Five-Pin Bowlers News; Bowlers' News (1978). V. 3, No. 2- Jan. 1978-. Periodical. English. mo. National 5-Pin Bowlers News, Suite 215, 2487 Kaladar Avenue, Ottawa K1V 9A9. **DD** 796.358/22/05. ***Continues*** *Canadian 5-Pin Bowlers News, 0381-1530.*

US/0005-2116
**NATIONAL AERONAUTICS.** **See** Aeronautics, Astronautics.

US
**NATIONAL AQUATICS JOURNAL.** English. qt. $75.00 US; $85.00 other. Council of National Aquatic Cooperation, PO Box 351743, Toledo OH 43635. **Tel** (419)867-3326.
**Ind/Abst** SPORT Discus.

US
**NATIONAL AQUATICS JOURNAL.** English. qt. $65.00. Council of National Aquatic Cooperation, PO Box 351743, Toledo OH 43635. **Tel** (419)867-3326.
**Ind/Abst** SPORT Discus.

US
**NATIONAL ASSOCIATION FOR GIRLS & WOMEN IN SPORT.** **Main/Corp** National Association for Girls & Women in Sport. **VFOAT** Tennis Guide. (1986)-. Periodical. English. an. American Alliance for Health, Physical Education, Recreation, and Dance / AAHPERD, 1900 Association Drive, Reston VA 22091. **Tel** (703)476-3493, (800)321-0789. ***Continues*** *NAGWS Guide: Tennis, 0272-863X.*

US/0278-1867
**NATIONAL BASEBALL HALL OF FAME AND MUSEUM YEARBOOK.** **Main/Corp** National Baseball Hall of Fame and Museum. English. an. $3.00. National Baseball Hall of Fame, Box 590 Main Street, Cooperstown NY 13326. **LC** GV863.A1; N37A. **DD** 796.357/64/074014774.

US/0747-3265
**NATIONAL BILLIARD NEWS, THE.** **VFOAT** Billiard News. (19??)-. Periodical. English. mo. $21.00. PUHK Publishing Company, PO Box 807, 104 West Main, Northville MI 48167. **Tel** (313)348-0053.

US/0190-4329
**NATIONAL COLLEGIATE CHAMPIONSHIPS (1978).** (NATIONAL COLLEGIATE CHAMPIONSHIPS.). **Main/Corp** National Collegiate Athletic Association. **VFOAT** History and Records of the NCAA Men's and Women's Championships; History and Records; History and Records of National Collegiate Championships and National College Division Championships. (1977/78)-. Periodical. English. an. $9.95. National Collegiate Athletic Association / NCAA, PO Box 7347, Overland Park KS 66207. **Tel** (913)339-1900, FAX (913)339-0030. **LC** GV741; .N37a. **DD** 796/.06/273. ***Continues*** *National Collegiate Championships Records Book, 0148-9798.*
**Desc:** Detailed summary of the championships of the previous year for both men and women, plus history and records of championships conducted since 1883.

US
**NATIONAL COLLEGIATE FENCING CHAMPIONSHIPS HANDBOOK.** **VFOAT** National Collegiate Championships Handbook: Fencing; Fencing. Periodical. English. an. National Collegiate Athletic Association / NCAA, PO Box 7347, Overland Park KS 66207. **Tel** (913)339-1900, FAX (913)339-0030.
**Desc:** Contains policies and procedures governing the administration and conduct of the National Collegiate Fencing Championships.

US
**NATIONAL DIRECTORY OF BASEBALL CAMPS.** ***Ceased.*** (19??)-(1992). Directory. English. Clell Wade Coaches Directory, PO Box 177, Cassville MO 65625. **Tel** (417)847-2783.

US
**NATIONAL DIRECTORY OF BASKETBALL CAMPS.** ***Ceased.*** (19??)-(1992). Directory. English. Clell Wade Coaches Directory, PO Box 177, Cassville MO 65625. **Tel** (417)847-2783.

US/0739-1226
**NATIONAL DIRECTORY OF COLLEGE ATHLETICS (WOMEN'S EDITION), THE.** (THE NATIONAL DIRECTORY OF COLLEGE ATHLETICS.). [Natl. dir. coll. athl.]. (1976/77)-. Directory. English. an. $17.45. Collegiate Directories, Inc., Box 4546640, Cleveland OH 44145. **Tel** (216)835-1172, FAX (216)835-8835. **ED** Kevin Cleary. **LC** GV439; .N35. **DD** 796/.071/173025. **Ad Acc. Circ:** 18,000. ***Continues*** *National Directory of Women's Athletics, 0092-5489.*
**Desc:** Pertinent information about athletic departments of 2,100 senior and junior colleges in US and Canada, such as addresses, enrollment, athletic personnel, coaches, phone numbers, etc.

US
**NATIONAL DIRECTORY OF FOOTBALL & SOCCER CAMPS.** ***Ceased.*** (19??)-(1992). Directory. English. Clell Wade Coaches Directory, PO Box 177, Cassville MO 65625. **Tel** (417)847-2783.

US
**NATIONAL DIRECTORY OF HIGH SCHOOL COACHES, THE.** **VFOAT** High School Coaches. (1963)-. Directory. English. an. $49.95. Athletic Publishing Company, PO Box 931, Montgomery AL 36102. **Tel** (205)263-4436, FAX (205)263-4437. **ED** John Allen Dees. **LC** GV697.A1; D5. **DD** 796/.07/702573. Index available. **Ad Acc. Circ:** 10,000 (ctrl). ***Continues*** *Directory of High School Coaches.*
**Desc:** Nationwide listing of high schools, coaches addresses, sport the coach teaches and telephone numbers.

US/0466-2199
**NATIONAL DRAGSTER.** **Added/Corp** National Hot Rod Association. (1960)-. Periodical. English. wk (except 4 weeks from Dec. 15-Jan. 15). $34.00 (nonmembers), $52.00 (members) US; $90.00 (members) Canada; $93.00 (members) other. National Dragster, 2035 Financial Way, Glendora CA 91740. **Tel** (818)914-4761. **ED** John Raffa. **Bk Rev. Ad Acc. Circ:** 60,000 (ctrl).
**Desc:** Reaches automotive enthusiasts interested in the sport of drag racing. Devoted to coverage of NHRA racing events, includes technical articles, new product data, current performance standards, and race previews. Special features include interviews, and official rule changes.

US/0737-5204
**NATIONAL FEDERATION HANDBOOK.** [Natl. Fed. handb.]. **Main/Corp** National Federation of State High School Associations. **VFOAT** National Federation of State High School Associations Handbook; Handbook. (19??)-. English. ir. must order direct. National Federation of State High School Associations, 11724 Northwest Plaza Circle, PO Box 20626, Kansas City MO 64195-0626. **Tel** (816)464-5400, FAX (816)464-5571. **LC** GV710; .N34a. **DD** 371.8/9. ***Continues*** *National Federation of State High School Associations. Official Handbook, 0146-8626.*

US
**NATIONAL FEDERATION NEWS.** English. Ten times a year. $10.00. National Federation of State High School Associations, 11724 Northwest Plaza Circle, PO Box 20626, Kansas City MO 64195-0626. **Tel** (816)464-5400, FAX (816)464-5571.
**Desc:** Timely articles of national significance as well as all major athletic rule changes, questions and answers for various sports while in session, plus a section containing music and speech information.
**Ind/Abst** SPORT Discus.

US/0192-978X
**NATIONAL HIGH SCHOOL SPORTS RECORD BOOK.** **Main/Corp** National Federation of State High School Associations. (1979)-. Periodical. English. an. National Federation of State High School Associations, 11724 Northwest Plaza Circle, PO Box 20626, Kansas City MO 64195-0626. **Tel** (816)464-5400, FAX (816)464-5571. **LC** GV346; .N37a. **DD** 796.

US/0896-6400
**NATIONAL LEAGUE GREEN BOOK.** [Natl. Leag. green book]. **Main/Corp** National League of Professional Baseball Clubs. **Added/Corp** National League of Professional Baseball Clubs. **VFOAT** Green Book. (19??)-. Periodical. English. an. $11.95. Sporting News, c/o Sharon Moore, 1212 North Lindbergh Boulevard, PO Box 56, St Louis MO 63166. **Tel** (314)997-7111, (800)825-8508. **(Subscription address:** Contemporary Books, Two Prudential Plaza, Suite 1200, Chicago IL 60601.**)** **LC** GV875.A3; N38; GV875.A3; N37. **DD** 796.357/64/0973.
**Desc:** Information on baseball's National League.

US/0734-6905
**NATIONAL PASTIME, THE.** [Natl. pastime]. **Added/Corp** Society for American Baseball Research. **VFOAT** T.N.P.; TNP. Vol. 1, No. 1 (Fall 1982)-. Periodical. English. an. Membership: $35.00 US; $45.00 Canada and Mexico; $50.00 other. Society for American Baseball Research, PO Box 93183, Cleveland OH 44101. **Tel** (216)575-0500. **ED** John Thorn. **LC** GV863.A1; N39. **DD** 796.357/0973. Index available. cum. index. **Bk Rev. Ad Acc. Circ:** 8,000.
**Desc:** Publication on baseball.
**Ind/Abst** SPORT Discus; SportSearch (May 1987-).

CN
**NATIONAL RUGBY POST.** Newspaper. English. bm (published Feb., Apr., June, Aug., Oct., Dec.). 20.00Can$ Canada; 30.00Can$ US; 39.00Can$ other. Natioal Rugby Post, 13228 76 Street, Edmonton T5C 1B6, Alberta, Canada. **Tel** (403)476-0268, FAX (403)473-1066. **Ad Acc, Adv Mgr:** D. Graham. **Circ:** 6,000.
**Desc:** Newspaper covering the sport of rugby in Canada.

US/0098-5945
**NATIONAL SKI AREA NEWS.** ***Title Change.*** [Natl. ski area news]. **Main/Corp** National Ski Areas Association. Vol. 1 (Spring 1973)-(19??). Periodical. English. qt. 61 South Main Street, West Hartford CT 06107. **LC** GV854.4; .N37a. **DD** 796.9/3/0973. ***Continued by*** *NSAA News, 1042-6256.*

US/0028-0208
**NATIONAL SPEED SPORT NEWS.** (1934)-. Periodical. English. wk (fifty issues per year). $30.00 US; $65.00 Canada & Mexico; $75.00 Pan Am; $100.00 other. National Speed Sport News, Box 608/79 Chestnut Street, Ridgewood NJ 07451. **Tel** (201)445-3117, FAX (201)445-7677. **ED** Corinne Economaki (201)445-3117. **Bk Rev. Ad Acc. Circ:** 75,000 (ctrl). available on microfilm from The Library of Congress Photoduplication Service.
**Desc:** News information weekly race results from motorsports events throughout the world.

●US/1071-555X
**NATURAL BODYBUILDING AND FITNESS.** [Nat. bodybuild. fit.]. **VFOAT** Natural Physique. (1993)-. Periodical. English. qt (4 issues). $10.90. Chelo Publishing Inc, 350 5th Avenue, Suite 8216, New York NY 10118. **Tel** (212)947-4322, FAX (212)563-4774. **ED** Steve Dawns, (editor's phone: (212)947-4322). **DD** 796. **Ad Acc, Adv Mgr Tel** (212)947-4322. ctrl circ. ***Continues*** *Natural Physique, 1044-6583.*

US/1044-6583
**NATURAL PHYSIQUE.** ***Title Change.*** [Nat. phys.]. Vol. 1, No. 1 (Oct. 1988)-(Aug. 1993). Periodical. English. Four times a year (Feb., May, Aug., Nov.). Chelo Publishing Inc, 350 5th Avenue, Suite 8216, New York NY 10118. **Tel** (212)947-4322, FAX (212)563-4774. **ED** Steve Dawns, (editor's phone: (212)947-4322). **DD** 796. **Ad Acc, Adv Mgr:** Bruce Soffer, **Tel** (212)947-4322. ctrl circ. ***Continued by*** *Natural Bodybuilding and Fitness, 1071-555X.*

US/0739-3067
**NBA REGISTER.** [NBA regist.]. **VFOAT** Sporting News Official N.B.A. Register; N.B.A. Register; Sporting News Official NBA Register. **VAT** National Basketball Association Register. 1982/83 Ed.-. English. an. $9.95. Sporting News, c/o Sharon Moore, 1212 North Lindbergh Boulevard, PO Box 56, St Louis MO 63166. **Tel** (314)997-7111, (800)825-8508. **LC** GV885.515.N37; O34. **DD** 796.32/3/0922; B. **Circ:** 12,000. ***Continues*** *Official National Basketball Association Register, 0894-315X.*
**Desc:** Full collegiate and professional records for every active player. Includes photos of each player.

US/0736-5209
**NCAA BASEBALL RULES.** **Main/Corp** National Collegiate Athletic Association. **VFOAT** N.C.A.A. Baseball Rules. **VAT** National Collegiate Athletic Association Baseball Rules. (1983)-. Periodical. English. an. $3.00. National Collegiate Athletic Association, PO Box 7347, Overland PArk KS 66207. **Tel** (913)339-1900. **LC** GV877; .N29a. **DD** 796.357/0973. ***Continues in part*** *National Collegiate Athletic Association. NCAA Baseball.*
**Desc:** Baseball rules.

US/0276-1017
**NCAA BASKETBALL.** ***Title Change.*** [NCAA basketb.]. **Added/Corp** National Collegiate Athletic Association. **VAT** National Collegiate Athletic Association Basketball. (1980)-(19??). English. an. National Collegiate Athletic Association / NCAA, PO Box 7347, Overland Park KS 66207. **Tel** (913)339-1900, FAX (913)339-0030. **LC** GV885.45; .N42. **DD** 796.32/363/0973. **Bk Rev. Ad Acc.** ctrl circ. ***Continues*** *Official National Collegiate Athletic Association Basketball Guide;* ***Absorbed*** *Basketball Records, 0733-8376.* ***Continued by*** *Official ... NCAA Basketball, 1063-1089.*
**Desc:** Contains individual and team records, statistical leaders, all-America teams, game-by-game results from the preceding year and schedules for the upcoming season.

US/0162-1467
**NCAA DIRECTORY.** **Main/Corp** National Collegiate Athletic Association. **Added/Corp** National Collegiate Athletic Association. Directory. National Collegiate Athletic Association. NCAA Membership Directory. **VFOAT** NCAA Membership Directory. **VAT** National Collegiate Athletic Association Directory. (1977)-. Directory. English. an. $6.00. National Collegiate Athletic Association / NCAA, PO Box 7347, Overland Park KS 66207. **Tel** (913)339-1900, FAX (913)339-0030. **LC** GV347; .N34a. **DD** 796/.07/1102573.
**Desc:** Contains roster of members by district and by division as well as listing of NCAA committees and structure.

US/0736-5160
**NCAA FOOTBALL RULES AND INTERPRETATIONS.** **Main/Corp** National Collegiate Athletic Association. **VFOAT** N.C.A.A. Football Rules and Interpretations; Football Rules and

Interpretations. **VAT** National Collegiate Athletic Association Football Rules and Interpretations. (1979)-. Periodical. English. an. $3.00. National Collegiate Athletic Association / NCAA, PO Box 7347, Overland Park KS 66207. **Tel** (913)339-1900, FAX (913)339-0030. **LC** GV956.8; .N36a. **DD** 796.332/63/02022. **Bk Rev. Ad Acc.** ctrl circ. ***Continues*** *Official National Collegiate Athletic Association Football Rules & Interpretations which Supplements the NCAA Official Football Rules, 0094-5226.*
**Desc:** Football rules and interpretations.

US/1053-0886
**NCAA MANUAL.** [NCAA man.]. **Main/Corp** National Collegiate Athletic Association. **VAT** National Collegiate Athletic Association Manual. English. an. $11.00. National Collegiate Athletic Association / NCAA, PO Box 7347, Overland Park KS 66207. **Tel** (913)339-1900, FAX (913)339-0030. **LC** GV563; .N25296. **DD** 338.4/6796/071173. ***Continues*** *Manual of the National Collegiate Athletic Association, 0077-3816.*

US/1042-3877
**NCAA MEN'S AND WOMEN'S BASKETBALL RULES AND INTERPRETATIONS.** [NCAA men's women's basketb. rules interpret.]. **Main/Corp** National Collegiate Athletic Association. **VFOAT** Men's and Women's Basketball Rules and Interpretations; NCAA Basketball, Men's and Women's Rules and Interpretations. **VAT** National Collegiate Athletic Association Men's and Women's Basketball Rules and Interpretations. 1988-. English. an. $3.00 (add $3.00 first class mail). National Collegiate Athletic Association, PO Box 7347, Overland PArk KS 66207. **Tel** (913)339-1900. **ED** Michelle A. Pond and Edward Steitz. **LC** GV885.45; .N37D. **DD** 796. Index available. cum. index. **Ad Acc. Circ:** 30,000. ***Formed by the union of*** *NCAA Men's Basketball Rules and Interpretations, 0736-5187* ***and*** *NCAA Women's Basketball Rules, 0882-6293.*
**Desc:** Basketball (collegiate) rules of play.

US/0882-3170
**NCAA MEN'S AND WOMEN'S CROSS COUNTRY AND TRACK AND FIELD RULES.** ***Title Change.*** [NCAA men's women's cross ctry. track field rules]. **Main/Corp** National Collegiate Athletic Association. **VFOAT** N.C.A.A. Men's and Women's Cross Country and Track and Field Rules; Men's and Women's Cross Country and Track and Field Rules. **VAT** National Collegiate Athletic Association Men's and Women's Cross Country and Track and Field Rules. (1984)-(1992). English. an. National Collegiate Athletic Association / NCAA, PO Box 7347, Overland Park KS 66207. **Tel** (913)339-1900, FAX (913)339-0030. **LC** GV1060.6; .N36a. ***Continues*** *National Collegiate Athletic Association. NCAA Men's and Women's Track and Field Rules, 0736-7783.* ***Continued by*** *National Collegiate Athletic Association. NCAA Men's and Women's Track and Field and Cross Country Rules.*
**Desc:** Men's and women's cross country and track and field rules.

US/0736-5144
**NCAA MEN'S AND WOMEN'S RIFLE RULES.** **Added/Corp** National Collegiate Athletic Association. **VFOAT** Men's and Women's Rifle Rules; N.C.A.A. Men's and Women's Rifle Rules; A.NCAA rifle; A.NCAA rifle men's and women's rules. **VAT** National Collegiate Athletic Association Rifle Rules. (1984)-. English. an (Oct.). $4.00. National Collegiate Athletic Association / NCAA, PO Box 7347, Overland Park KS 66207. **Tel** (913)339-1900, FAX (913)339-0030. **LC** WMLC L 83/136. ***Continues*** *NCAA Rifle Rules.*

US/0741-9279
**NCAA MEN'S AND WOMEN'S SKIING RULES.** (NCAA MEN'S AND WOMEN'S SKIING RULES / NATIONAL COLLEGIATE ATHLETIC ASSOCIATION.). **Main/Corp** National Collegiate Athletic Association. **VFOAT** N.C.A.A. Men's and Women's Skiing Rules; Men's and Women's Skiing Rules; NCAA Skiing, Men's and Women's Rules; NCAA Skiing. (1984)-. Periodical. English. an. $4.00. National Collegiate Athletic Association, PO Box 7347, Overland PArk KS 66207. **Tel** (913)339-1900. **LC** GV854.A1; N26. **DD** 796.93. ***Continues*** *NCAA Men's Skiing Rules, 0736-5136.*
**Desc:** Men's and women's skiing rules.

US/0735-0368
**NCAA MEN'S AND WOMEN'S SOCCER RULES.** **Main/Corp** National Collegiate Athletic Association. **VFOAT** Men's and Women's Soccer Rules. **VAT** National Collegiate Athletic Association Men's and Women's Soccer Rules. (1989)-. English. an (June). $3.00. National Collegiate Athletic Association / NCAA, PO Box 7347, Overland Park KS 66207. **Tel** (913)339-1900, FAX (913)339-0030. **LC** GV943.4; .N365a. **DD** 796.334/02/022. ***Continues*** *National Collegiate Athletic Association. NCAA Men's Soccer Rules.*

US/0736-5128
**NCAA MEN'S AND WOMEN'S SWIMMING AND DIVING RULES.** **Added/Corp** National Collegiate Athletic Association. **VFOAT** Men's and Women's Swimming and Diving Rules; N.C.A.A. Men's and Women's Swimming and Diving Rules. (198?)-. English. an. $3.00. National Collegiate Athletic Association / NCAA, PO Box 7347, Overland Park KS 66207. **Tel** (913)339-1900, FAX (913)339-0030. **LC** WMLC L 83/119.
**Desc:** Men's and women's swimming and diving rules.

●US
**NCAA MEN'S AND WOMEN'S TRACK AND FIELD AND CROSS COUNTRY RULES.** **Main/Corp** National Collegiate Athletic Association. **VFOAT** NCAA Track and Field, Cross Country Men's and Women's Rules; NCAA Track & Field/Cross Country Men's and Women's Rules. (1992)-. English. an (Dec.). $3.00. National Collegiate Athletic Association / NCAA, PO Box 7347, Overland Park KS 66207. **Tel** (913)339-1900, FAX (913)339-0030. **LC** GV1060.6; .N36a. ***Continues*** *National Collegiate Athletic Association. NCAA Men's and Women's Cross Country and Track and Field Rules, 0882-3170.*

US/0735-9195
**NCAA MEN'S ICE HOCKEY RULES AND INTERPRETATIONS.** **Main/Corp** National Collegiate Athletic Association. **VFOAT** N.C.A.A. Men's Ice Hockey Rules and Interpretations; Men's Ice Hockey Rules and Interpretations; NCAA Ice Hockey Men's Rules and Interpretations. (1983)-. English. an (published in September). $3.00. National Collegiate Athletic Association, PO Box 7347, Overland PArk KS 66207. **Tel** (913)339-1900. **LC** GV847; .O33. **DD** 796.96/2/0711. ***Continues*** *NCAA Ice Hockey, 0734-5011.*
**Desc:** Men's ice hockey rules and interpretations.

US/0742-4361
**NCAA MEN'S LACROSSE RULES.** **Main/Corp** National Collegiate Athletic Association. **VFOAT** N.C.A.A. Men's Lacrosse Rules; Men's Lacrosse Rules. 1984-. English. an. $3.00. National Collegiate Athletic Association, PO Box 7347, Overland PArk KS 66207. **Tel** (913)339-1900. **LC** GV989; .N37A. **DD** 796.34/7. ***Continues*** *NCAA Lacrosse Rules, 0736-7775.*
**Desc:** Rules and interpretations governing NCAA lacrosse competition.

US/0734-0508
**NCAA MEN'S WATER POLO RULES.** [NCAA men's water polo rules]. **Main/Corp** National Collegiate Athletic Association. **VFOAT** N.C.A.A. Men's Water Polo Rules. (1982)-. English. an. $3.00. National Collegiate Athletic Association / NCAA, PO Box 7347, Overland Park KS 66207. **Tel** (913)339-1900, FAX (913)339-0030. **LC** GV839; .N37a. **DD** 797.2/5. **Bk Rev. Ad Acc.** ctrl circ. ***Continues*** *NCAA Water Polo Rules, 0271-860X.*
**Desc:** Men's water polo rules.

US/0027-6170
**NCAA NEWS, THE.** (NCAA NEWS.). **Main/Corp** National Collegiate Athletic Association. **Added/Corp** National Collegiate Athletic Association. News. **VAT** National Collegiate Athletic Association News. (19??)-. Periodical. English. Forty-six times a year. $24.00. National Collegiate Athletic Association / NCAA, PO Box 7347, Overland Park KS 66207. **Tel** (913)339-1900, FAX (913)339-0030. **ED** Thomas A. Wilson. **Bk Rev. Ad Acc.** ctrl circ.
**Desc:** Covers the business of college athletics throughout the year.
**Ind/Abst** SPORT Discus.

US/0272-8095
**NCAA SWIMMING; ANNUAL GUIDE.** [NCAA swim.]. **Main/Corp** National Collegiate Athletic Association. **VAT** National Collegiate Athletic Association Swimming. 56th- 1980-. English. an. National Collegiate Athletic Association / NCAA, PO Box 7347, Overland Park KS 66207. **Tel** (913)339-1900, FAX (913)339-0030. **LC** GV837.A1; O3. **DD** 797.2/1. ***Continues*** *Official National Collegiate Athletic Association Swimming Guide.*

US/1042-3869
**NCCA ILLUSTRATED MEN'S AND WOMEN'S BASKETBALL RULES.** [NCAA illus. men's women's basketb. rules]. **Main/Corp** National Collegiate Athletic Association. **VFOAT** Illustrated Men's and Women's Basketball Rules; NCAA Illustrated Basketball, Men's and Women's Rules. **VAT** National Collegiate Athletic Association Illustrated Men's and Women's Basketball Rules. (1988)-. English. an. $3.00. National Collegiate Athletic Association, PO Box 7347, Overland PArk KS 66207. **Tel** (913)339-1900. **LC** GV885.45; .N37a. **DD** 796.323/02/022. **Ad Acc. Circ:** 10,000. ***Continues*** *NCAA Illustrated Men's Basketball Rules, 0736-5179.*
**Desc:** Produces rules of play in 12 different sports, with each book containing diagrams of playing areas, official signals, and official interpretations and rulings.

FR/0247-1906
**NEIGE, LA.** (1979)-. Periodical. French. qt. 90.00F France; 130.00F other Europe; 190.00F other. Publications Jean Suard, BP 4, 74320 Sevrier France. **Tel** 50465173. **UDC** 796.9.

UK/0959-1117
**NETBALL MAGAZINE.** (1933)-. Periodical. English. qt. £11.00 Europe; £13.00 airmail zone 1; £14.00 airmail zone 2. All England Netball Association, Netball House, 9 Paynes Park, Hitchin Hert SG5 1EH England. **Tel** 011 44 462 442344. **ED** Geoff Harrold. **Bk Rev**, (Qty: 3). **Ad Acc. Circ:** 6,000 (ctrl).
**Desc:** Keeps member clubs and schools in touch with events and competitions at the national and international level. Provides information for coaches, umpires, and players, with articles on sports injuries, rules forum, coaching hints, and team selection.
**Ind/Abst** SPORT Discus.

US/1055-9604
**NEVADA GOLF AND TENNIS.** [Nev. golf tennis]. (1991)-. Periodical. English. $13.50. Nevada Magazine, Capitol Complex, Carson City NV 89710. **Tel** (702)687-5416, FAX (702)687-6159. **DD** 796. ***Continues*** *Nevada Golf, 1048-0714.*

US/1041-4800
**NEW ENGLAND RUNNER.** [N. Engl. runn.]. (198?)-. Periodical. English. Eight times a year. $18.95 US; $23.95 Canada; $28.95 other. New England Sports Publications, PO Box 252, Boston MA 02113. **Tel** (617)891-1844. **ED** John McGrath and Tom Derderian. **DD** 796. Index available ($2.50). **Bk Rev. Ad Acc. Pr Rev. Circ:** 15,000 (ctrl). ***Continues*** *Boston Running News, 8750-8621.*
**Desc:** Covers running, triathlon, track and field, and recreational sports and fitness throughout the six state New England region.

AT
**NEW FUN RUNNER.** (19??)-. English. Six times a year. 43.00Aus$ Australia; 87.00Aus$ New Zealand & PNG; 97.00Aus$ Fiji, Indonesia & Malaysia; 107.00Aus$ India & Japan; 122.00Aus$ US & Israel; $132.00 UK & Europe. Triathlon Sports, PO Box 2590, Taren Point 2229 Australia. **Tel** 011 61 2 5241455, FAX 011 61 2 5241454. ***Continues*** *Funrunner.*

US/0195-1599
**NEW GUN WEEK, THE.** **VFOAT** Gun Week. Vol. 14 Issue 665 (Aug. 10, 1979)-. Periodical. English. Fifty times a year (weekly except Memorial Day week and Christmas week). $32.00 (one year), $56.00 (two year) US; 40.00 (one year), $72.00 (two year) other. Second Amendment Foundation, PO Box 488, Station C, Buffalo NY 14209. **Tel** (716)885-6408, FAX (716)884-4471. **ED** Joseph P Tartaro. **Bk Rev**, (Qty: 15-20 per year). **Ad Acc, Adv Mgr:** Peggy Tartaro, **Tel** (716)885-6408. **Circ:** 23,000. ***Continues*** *Gun Week, 0017-5633.*
**Desc:** The only newspaper serving gunowners, hunters and collectors as well as the firearms industry and gun issue activists and influentials tabloid format.

US/0897-0319
**NEW HAMPSHIRE SPIRIT.** [N. H. spirit]. **VFOAT** Spirit; New Hampshire Spirit Magazine. Vol. 1, No. 1 (Winter 1987)-. Periodical. English. qt. $12.00. Flair Publishing & Marketing Corporation, PO Box 440, Tamworth NH 03886. **DD** 796.

UK/0961-933X
**NEW STUDIES IN ATHLETICS.** [New stud. athl.]. (1986)-. Periodical. English. qt. $25.00 certified coaches and members of recognized coaches association; $30.00 other. International Amateur Athletic Federation, 3 Hans Crescent Knightsbridge, London SW1X OLN England. **Tel** 011 44 71 5818771, FAX 011 44 71 5845907, telex 9419338. **ED** Bill Glad, Helmar Hommel, Bjorn Wangemann. **Bk Rev**, (Qty: 4). **Circ:** 2,600 (ctrl).
**Desc:** IAAF magazine for coaches, technical research, development information, and bibliographic documentation.

●US/1060-5908
**NEW WAVE WRESTLING.** [New wave wrestl.]. (1992)-. Periodical. English. mo. $19.50. Michael O'Hara, PO Box 651, Gracie Station, New York NY 10028-0006. **DD** 796.

US/0887-5863
**NEW YORK METS INSIDE PITCH.** (NEW YORK METS INSIDE PITCH : THE OFFICIAL NEWSPAPER OF THE NEW YORK METS.). (198?)-. Periodical. English. mo. $21.95. Coman Publishing Company, PO Box 2331, Durham NC 27702. **Tel** (919) 688-0218. **ED** Steve Almasey. **Ad Acc, Adv Mgr:** Jan Cheves. **Circ:** 11,000 (ctrl). ***Continues*** *Mets Inside Pitch, 0746-0651.*
**Desc:** Sports newspaper covering New York Mets professional baseball team; articles and photos on current and former teams and players.

US/0161-7338
**NEW YORK RUNNING NEWS.** **Added/Corp** New York Road Runners Club. No. 75 (Spring 1978)-. Periodical. English. bm. $20.00. New York Road Runners Club, PO Box 881, FDR Station, New York NY 10150. **Tel** (212)860-4455, FAX (212)860-9754. **ED** Raleigh Mayer and Michele White. **Bk Rev. Ad Acc. Circ:** 35,000 (ctrl). ***Continues*** *New York Road Runners Club Newsletter, 0160-9726.*
**Desc:** Contains articles and calendar of events for the New York area Road Runners Club.

US/0740-2384
**NEW YORK SPORTS.** Vol. 1 No. 1 (May/June 1983)-. Periodical. English. mo. $15.00. M J C Publishers, 1770 Deer Park Avenue, Deer Park NY 11729. **Tel** (516)242-7722. **Ad Acc.**

NZ/0113-9606
**NEW ZEALAND FISHERMAN.** [N.Z. fisherman]. **VFOAT** Fisherman. (1988)-. Periodical. English. mo. 110.00NZ$. Vantage Publishing Ltd, Private Bag 9, Parnell, Aukland, New Zealand. **Tel** 011 64 9 7149244, FAX (09)3096 361. **ED** William E. Kirk. **DD** 799.109931. **Bk Rev. Ad Acc. Pr Rev. Circ:** 25,000.
**Desc:** Sportfishing magazine in tabloid form for all recreational anglers. Fresh and salt water fishing.

NZ/1171-3771
**NEW ZEALAND SPORTSWOMAN.** [N.Z. sportswom.]. **VFOAT** Sportswoman; New Zealand Sports Woman. (1992)-. Periodical. English. mo. **DD** 796.0194099305.
**Ind/Abst** SPORT Discus.

CN
**NEWFOUNDLAND SPORTSMAN.** English. qt. 15.00Can$. Newfoundland Sportsman, PO Box 13754, St Johns NFLD, A1B 4G5 Canada. **Tel** (709) 368-7670, (709) 368-4662, FAX (709) 368-7676.

CN/0823-7948
**NEWSLETTER (CANADIAN MODERN PENTATHLON ASSOCIATION).** (NEWSLETTER / THE CANADIAN MODERN PENTATHLON ASSOCIATION.). **VFOAT** Bulletin. **VAT** Bulletin - Association Canadienne du Pentathlon Moderne. Newsletter. English. bm. Canadian Modern Pentathlon Association, 1893 Stonehenge Crescent, Gloucester Ontario K1B 4N7 Canada. **DD** 796.

CN/0826-2969
**NEWSLETTER - FIGURE SKATING COACHES OF CANADA.** (NEWSLETTER.). **Main/Corp** Figure Skating Coaches of Canada. **VFOAT** Figure Skating Coaches of Canada Newsletter. (1983)-. Periodical. English. ir (3 or 4 per year). Figure Skating Coaches Canada, PO Box 93, Agincourt Ontario M1S 3B4 Canada. **Tel** (905)479-9497. **DD** 796.91/07/071. ***Continues*** *Circle, 0227-2091.*

CN/0383-7742
**NEWSLETTER - MANITOBA UNDERWATER COUNCIL.** ***Title Change.*** **Main/Corp** Manitoba Underwater Council. Sept. 1964-. Newsletter. English. mo. Manitoba Underwater Council, PO Box 711, Winnipeg Manitoba R3C 2K3 Canada. **ED** Joan Eggett. **DD** 797.2/3/0627127. **Ad Acc. Circ:** 500 (ctrl). ***Continued by*** *Man Underwater, 0383-7777.*

US
**NEWSLETTER - NORTH AMERICAN SOCIETY FOR SPORT HISTORY.** **Main/Corp** North American Society for Sport History. **Added/Corp** Sports Literature Association. Vol. 1, (1973)-. Periodical. English. Free to subscribers of The Journal of Sport History. North American Society for Sport History, Penn State University, 101 White Building, University Park PA 16802. **Tel** (814)865-2416, (814)238-1288.

US/0364-8079
**NEWSLETTER (PRESIDENT'S COUNCIL ON PHYSICAL FITNESS AND SPORTS (U.S.)).** See Health and Personal Fitness.

US/0364-8273
**NFL FOOTBALL FORECAST.** **VFOAT** Football Forecast. **VAT** National Football League Football Forecast. (19??)-. English. $1.25. Lexington Library, 355 Lexington Avenue, New York NY 10017. **LC** GV955.5.N35; N13. **DD** 796.33/264/0973.

GW/0934-8913
**NIKEPHOROS : ZEITSCHRIFT FUER SPORT & KULTUR IM ALTERTUM.** **VFOAT** Nike. Vol. 1 (1988)-. German (English and French). an. Georg Olms Verlag AG Weidmann, Hagentorwall 6 7, D 31134 Hildesheim Germany. **Tel** 011 49 5121 15010, telex 927454 OLMS D. **LC** GV573; .N55. **DD** 796/.09. **[CCC].**

US
**NIRSA JOURNAL.** **Added/Corp** National Intramural-Recreational Sports Association (U.S.). **VFOAT** N.I.R.S.A Journal. **VAT** National Intramural-Recreational Sports Association journal. Vol. 6, No. 1 (Oct. 1981)-. Periodical. English. Three times a year (Fall, Winter, Spring). $35.00 US; $40.00 other. National Intramural Recreational Sports Association, 850 Southwest 15th Street, Corvallis OR 97333. **Tel** (503)737-2088, FAX (503)737-2026. **LC** GV710; .N54. **DD** 371.8/9. **Ad Acc. Circ:** 2,500 (ctrl). ***Continues*** *NIRSA, Journal of the National Intramural-Recreational Sports Association.*
**Ind/Abst** Phys. Educ. Index; SPORT Discus; SportSearch (May 1987-).

II/0970-7557
**NIS SCIENTIFIC JOURNAL.** [NIS Sci. J.]. **VFOAT** Netaji Subhas National Institute of Sports Scientific Journal. (1987)-. Periodical. English. Four times a year (Jan., Apr., July, Oct.). $20.00. Sports Authority of India, Netaji Subhas National Institute of Sports, Patiala 174001 India. **Tel** 011 91 70336. **(Subscription address:** Prints India, 11 Darya Ganj, New Delhi 110002 India.**)** **UDC** 796. ***Continues*** *SNIPES Journal, 0253-6706.*
**Ind/Abst** SPORT Discus.

●IT/1121-6379
**NO LIMITS WORLD.** See Recreation, Leisure-Outdoor Life.

US/0163-5905
**NORDIC.** [Nordic]. English. an. $5.00. Nordic Skiing, PO Box 106, West Brattleboro VT 05301. **LC** GV855.5.E67; N67. **DD** 688.7/693.

US/0277-7452
**NORDIC SKIING COMPETITION GUIDE.** (NORDIC SKIING COMPETITION GUIDE / USSA.). **Added/Corp** United States Ski Association. **VFOAT** Skiing Competition Guide. (1981)-. English. an. $6.00. Human Kinetics Publishers Inc, 1607 North Market Street, PO Box 5076, Champaign IL 61825-5076. **Tel** (217)351-5076, FAX (217)351-2674. **LC** GV855.4; .N67. **DD** 796.93.
**Desc:** Covers cross-country ski racing and ski jumping.

US/0749-601X
**NORDIC WEST.** (198?)-. Periodical. English. Twice a year. $5.00. Nordic West, PO Box 7077, Bend OR 97708. **Tel** (503)382-8908. **ED** Richard Coon (editor's address: 20357 Shahala Ct. Bend OR 97702; editor's phone: (503)389-6156). **Ad Acc. Circ:** 42,000.
**Desc:** Information on cross-country skiing and snowshoeing.

US/0197-8349
**NORM EVANS' SEAHAWK REPORT.** **VFOAT** Seahawk Report. Periodical. English. ir. $15.75. Evans, 18831 Pacific Highway S 225, Seattle WA 98188.

FR
**NORMANDIE.** **Added/Corp** Pneu Michelin (Firm). (19??)-. French (English). $8.95. Michelin Guides and Maps, PO Box 3305, Spartanburg SC 29304. **Tel** (803)599-0850. **LC** GV1025.F7; N6.
**Desc:** Covers farming and dairy production.

NO/0029-1994
**NORSK IDRETT.** [Nor. idrett]. (1940)-. Periodical. Norwegian. Eight times a year. Free on request. Norges Idrettsforbund, Hauger Skolevei 1, 1351 Rud Norway. **Tel** 011 47 2 874600. **ED** Tor K. Karlsen. **DD** 796. **[CCC]. Ad Acc. Circ:** 5,000. ***Continues*** *Landsidrett, 0803-138X; Start, 0800-1588.*
**Desc:** Covering general questions within the area of sports.

CN/0829-3856
**NORTHERN CURLING REVIEW.** ***Title Change.*** [North. curl. rev.]. Vol. 21, No. 1 (Oct. 1984)-(1992). Periodical. English. mo. Northern Curling Review, 1063 Kingsway Avenue, Edmonton Alberta T5G 2Z6 Canada. **DD** 796.7/6. ***Continues*** *Curling Review, 0011-3115.* ***Continued by*** *Curling Review (Northern Ed.), 1193-879X.*

US/0737-5530
**NORTHWEST PLAYER.** **Added/Corp** Northwest Sports Foundation (U.S.). Vol. 1, No. 1 (Dec. 1979)-. Periodical. English. Twelve times a year. $4.00. Northwest Sports Foundation, 946 North 83rd Street, Seattle WA 98103. **Tel** (206)524-0741.

US/0883-7945
**NORTHWEST RUNNER.** (NORTHWEST RUNNER : A CLUB NORTHWEST PUBLICATION.). **Added/Corp** Club Northwest (Seattle, Wash.). Vol. 13, No. 3 (Apr. 1985)-. Periodical. English. Twelve times a year. $18.97 (one year), $33.97 (two year),$46.97 (three year). Northwest Runner, 1231 Northeast 94th Street, Seattle WA 98115. **Tel** (206)526-9000. **ED** Jim Whiting. **Ad Acc. Circ:** 7,000. ***Continues*** *Nor'Wester (Seattle, Wash.), 8750-6076.*
**Desc:** Schedule of running events, event results, articles of local interest to runners in Washington State.

US/1063-8164
**NORTHWEST SAILBOARD.** [Northwest sailboard]. (19??)-. Periodical. English. Six times a year. $9.97 US; $16.00 Canada; $39.00 other. Gorge Publishing, PO Box 918, Hood River OR 97031. **Tel** (503)386-7440, FAX (503)386-7480. **ED** Carol S. York. **DD** 797. **Bk Rev. Ad Acc, Adv Mgr:** Marie Cordell. **Circ:** 25,000.
**Desc:** Informative consumer windsurfing magazine, focusing on the Northwest.

US/0164-3134
**NORTHWESTERN SPORTSMAN.** (19??)-. Periodical. English. mo. Northwestern Publishing Company Inc, PO Box 1208, Big Timber MT 59011. **Tel** (406)932-3646.

US
**NRA TOURNAMENT NEWS.** ***Title Change.*** (19??)-(198?). English. Twelve times a year. National Rifle Association of America, 11250 Waples Mill Road, Fairfax VA 22030-9100. **Tel** (703)267-1560, (703)267-1583, (800)231-4672, FAX (703)267-3994. ***Continues*** *American Marksman.* ***Continued by*** *Shooting Sports USA, 1069-6822.*
**Desc:** Regular features include critiques on newly-marketed firearms and accessories, researched historical studies, and firearms displays.

US/1042-6256
**NSAA NEWS.** [NSAA news]. **VAT** National Ski Areas Association News. Periodical. English. bm. National Ski Areas Association, 20 Maple Street, PO Box 288, Springfield MA 01101. **LC** GV854.4; .N37A. **DD** 796.93/0973. ***Continues*** *National Ski Area News.*
**Ind/Abst** SportSearch (May 1987-).

US
**NSGA BUYING GUIDE.** **Main/Corp** National Sporting Goods Association. (1974/75)-. Consumer Publication. English. an. $95.00. National Sporting Goods Association, 1699 Wall Street, Mt Prospect IL 60056-5780. **Tel** (708)439-4000, FAX (708)439-0111. **ED** K. Lindgren.

US/1045-2087
**NSGA RETAIL FOCUS.** [NSGA retail focus]. **Added/Corp** National Sporting Goods Association. **VFOAT** Retail Focus. **VAT** National Sporting Goods Association Retail Focus. Vol. 42, No. 1 (Jan. 1989)-. Periodical. English. mo (11 issues). $50.00. National Sporting Goods Association, 1699 Wall Street, Mt Prospect IL 60056-5780. **Tel** (708)439-4000, FAX (708)439-0111. **LC** GV743; .S4. **DD** 381/.45796/0973. ***Continues*** *NSGA Sports Retailer, 0884-6278.*
**Ind/Abst** SPORT Discus.

●US
**OCEAN SEA DIVERS WORLDWIDE DIVING DIRECTORY.** 1st Ed. (1992/1993)-. Directory. English. Ocean Sea Publishers, PO Box 890267, Houston TX 77289-0267. **LC** GV840.S78; O26. **DD** 797.2/3/025.

US/0899-2622
**OCEAN SPORTS INTERNATIONAL.** ***Title Change.*** [Ocean sports int.]. **VFOAT** Ocean Sports. (19??)-(19??). Periodical. English. qt. PO Box 1388, Soquel CA 95073. **Tel** (408)459-0425. **ED** Susan Watrous. **DD** 797. **Ad Acc.** ***Continued by*** *Ocean Sports International's Dive Travel.*

FR
**OCEANS.** No. 1 (Jan. 1970)-. Periodical. French (summaries and/or abstracts in English, German, Italian and Spanish). ir. 178.00F. Oceans / France, 2 rue Saint Simon, 75007 Paris France. **Tel** 011 33 1 42221682. **ED** Yves Baix. **LC** GV840.S78; O27. **Ad Acc. Circ:** 30,000 (ctrl).
**Desc:** Covers Diving.
**Ind/Abst** Aquat. Sci. Fish. Abstr. (Computer File); Biol. Agric. Index; Gen. Sci. Index; Ocean. Abstr.

US/0090-4414
**OFFICIAL A.A.U. BASKETBALL HANDBOOK.** **Main/Corp** Amateur Athletic Union of the United States. (19??)-. English. $5.00. Amateur Athletic Union / AAU, 3400 West 86th Street, PO Box 68207, Indianapolis IN 46268. **Tel** (317)872-2900, FAX (317)875-0548. **LC** GV882; .A45. **DD** 796.32/3/05.

US
**OFFICIAL AAU CODE AND DIRECTORY.** **Main/Corp** Amateur Athletic Union of the United States. **VFOAT** AAU Code and Directory. **VAT** Official Amateur Athletic Union of the United States Code and Directory. (1981)-. Directory. English. an. AAU House, POB 68207, Indianapolis IN 46268. **LC** GV563; .A448. **DD** 796/.0973. ***Formed by the union of*** *AAU Directory* ***and*** *Official Handbook of the AAU Code, 0091-3405.*

US
**OFFICIAL AAU SYNCHRONIZED SWIMMING HANDBOOK.** **Main/Corp** Amateur Athletic Union of the United States. **VFOAT** Synchronized Swimming Rules. English. be. $10.00. United States Synchronized Swimming, 201 S Capitol Avenue/Suite 510, Indianapolis IN 46225. **Tel** (317)237-5705. **LC** GV837; .A45C. **DD** 797.2/1/0202. **UDC** 797.217.2(035.3).

US/0198-7941
**OFFICIAL AAU TAE KWON DO RULES.** [Off. AAU Tae Kwon Do rules]. **Main/Corp** Amateur Athletic Union of the United States. **VFOAT** Taekwondo; Tae Kwon Do Rules. **VAT** Official Amateur Athletic Union Tae Kwon Do Rules. 1977/80-. English. Amateur Athletic Union / AAU, 3400 West 86th Street, PO Box 68207, Indianapolis IN 46268. **Tel** (317)872-2900, FAX (317)875-0548. **LC** GV1114.3; .A42B. **DD** 796.8/153. **UDC** 796.853.27.063.

US/0361-347X
**OFFICIAL AAU TRACK AND FIELD HANDBOOK.** **Main/Corp** Amateur Athletic Union of the United States. **Added/Corp** Amateur Athletic Union of

the United States. AAU Official Handbook, Track & Field. **VFOAT** AAU Official Handbook, Track & Field. **VAT** Official Amateur Athletic Union Track and Field Handbook. (19??)-. English. an. $5.00. Amateur Athletic Union / AAU, 3400 West 86th Street, PO Box 68207, Indianapolis IN 46268. **Tel** (317)872-2900, FAX (317)875-0548. **LC** GV1060.67; .A4a. **DD** 796.4/02/02. ***Continues*** *Amateur Athletic Union of the United States. A.A.U. Official Track and Field Handbook.*

US/0361-2899
**OFFICIAL AAU TRAMPOLINE AND TUMBLING HANDBOOK.** **Main/Corp** Amateur Athletic Union of the United States. **VFOAT** AUU Official Handbook: Trampoline & Tumbling. **VAT** Official Amateur Athletic Union of the United States Trampoline and Tumbling Handbook. English. an. $5.00. Trampoline & Tumbling, 3400 West 86th Street, Indianapolis IN 46268. **LC** GV555; .A52A. **DD** 796.4/7. **UDC** 796.418.7(035.3).

US/0078-3838
**OFFICIAL BASEBALL GUIDE.** **VFOAT** Baseball Guide.; Baseball Official Guide. (1940)-. Periodical. English. an. $12.95. Total Environment Centre, 18 Argyle Street, Sydney New South Wales, 2000 Australia. **Tel** 11 61 2 22478476. **(Subscription address:** Contemporary Books, Two Prudential Plaza, Suite 1200, Chicago IL 60601.**)** **ED** J. G. T. Spink and others; C. C. Spink and others. **LC** GV877; .B32. ***Supersedes*** *Spaldings Official Baseball Guide.; Reach Official American League Base Ball guide.*
**Desc:** Review of last year's professional baseball season.

US/0162-542X
**OFFICIAL BASEBALL REGISTER.** ***Title Change.*** **See** Recreation, Leisure-Abstracting, Bibliographies and Statistics.

US/0078-3846
**OFFICIAL BASEBALL RULES.** (19??)-. Periodical. English. an. $3.95. Sporting News, c/o Sharon Moore, 1212 North Lindbergh Boulevard, PO Box 56, St Louis MO 63166. **Tel** (314)997-7111, (800)825-8508. **(Subscription address:** Contemporary Books, Two Prudential Plaza, Suite 1200, Chicago IL 60601.**)**
**Desc:** Official baseball playing rules.

CN/0473-8853
**OFFICIAL BASKETBALL RULES FOR MEN AND WOMEN.** [Off. basketb. rules men women]. **Main/Corp** International Amateur Basketball Federation. **VFOAT** Official Basketball Rules. English. ir (every 4 years). 5.00Can$ Canada; $4.00 US. Official Basketball Rules, c/o Basketball Canada, 10th Floor 333 River Road, Vanier Ontario K1L 8H9 Canada. **Tel** (613)748-5607, telex 053-3660. **ED** Allen G Rae. **DD** 796.32/3/02022. **UDC** 796.323.063. Index available. **Circ:** 20,000 (ctrl).
**Desc:** Rules of basketball (international).

US
**OFFICIAL CODE/DIRECTORY / AMATEUR ATHLETIC UNION OF THE UNITED STATES, INC.** **Main/Corp** Amateur Athletic Union of the United States. **VFOAT** Official Code Directory; Official Code and Directory. (1991)-. English. AAU House, POB 68207, Indianapolis IN 46268. **LC** GV563; .A448. ***Formed by the union of*** *Directory* ***and*** *Official Code.*

US
**OFFICIAL DIVING RULES AND REGULATIONS OF UNITED STATES DIVING, INC.** **VFOAT** United States Diving Rules and Regulations. 1982-. English. an. United States Diving Inc, 901 West New York Street, Indianapolis IN 46202. **UDC** 797.26.063(73). ***Continues*** *Official Diving Rules ... of United States Diving, Inc.*

US/0362-3270
**OFFICIAL FIELD HOCKEY RULES FOR SCHOOL GIRLS.** **Main/Corp** United States Field Hockey Association. English. US Field Hockey Association, 25 Front Street, Marblehead MA 01945. **LC** GV1017.H7; U52A. **DD** 796.35/5. **UDC** 796.355.063(73).

CN/0828-6647
**OFFICIAL GUIDE & RECORD BOOK / THE NATIONAL HOCKEY LEAGUE.** [Off. guide rec. book - Natl. Hockey Leag.]. **Main/Corp** National Hockey League. (1984/85)-. English. an. $13.95 per vol. National Hockey League, 1155 Metcalf Suite 960, Montreal Quebec H3B 2W2 Canada. **Tel** (514)871-9220. **LC** GV847.8.N3; N36A. **DD** 796.96/2/06. **UDC** 796.966.09(71). ***Formed by the union of*** *National Hockey League. Official Guide, 0826-5038* ***and*** *National Hockey League. Official Record Book, 0826-0214.*

UK
**OFFICIAL HANDBOOK / INTERNATIONAL AMATEUR ATHLETIC FEDERATION.** **Main/Corp** International Amateur Athletic Federation. **VFOAT** IAAF Handbook; I.A.A.F. Handbook. (19??)-. English. an. £5.00. International Amateur Athletic Federation, 3 Hans Crescent Knightsbridge, London SW1X OLN England. **Tel** 011 44 71 5818771, FAX 011 44 71 5845907, telex 9419338. **LC** GV1060.5; .I57a. **DD** 796.4/2/0202.

US/0091-3405
**OFFICIAL HANDBOOK OF THE AAU CODE.** ***Title Change.*** **Main/Corp** Amateur Athletic Union of the United States. **VFOAT** AAU Code. (19??)-(19??). English. Amateur Athletic Union / AAU, 3400 West 86th Street, PO Box 68207, Indianapolis IN 46268. **Tel** (317)872-2900, FAX (317)875-0548. **LC** GV563; .A454. **DD** 796/.0973. **Bk Rev.** **Ad Acc.** ctrl circ. ***Merged with*** *Amateur Athletic Union of the United States. AAU Directory* ***to form*** *Amateur Athletic Union of the United States. Official AAU Code and Directory.*
**Desc:** Code of the Amateur Athletic Union and listing of all personnel and functions within the Union.

US/0736-7821
**OFFICIAL HIGH SCHOOL BASEBALL RULES.** ***Title Change.*** (OFFICIAL HIGH SCHOOL BASEBALL RULES / NATIONAL FEDERATION OF STATE HIGH SCHOOL ASSOCIATIONS.). **Main/Corp** National Federation of State High School Associations. (19??)-(19??). English. National Federation of State High School Associations, 11724 Northwest Plaza Circle, PO Box 20626, Kansas City MO 64195-0626. **Tel** (816)464-5400, FAX (816)464-5571. **LC** GV877; .N3a. **DD** 796.357/02/022. ***Continued by*** *Official High School Baseball Case Book.*

US/0740-9532
**OFFICIAL HIGH SCHOOL BOYS GYMNASTICS RULES.** (OFFICIAL HIGH SCHOOL BOYS GYMNASTICS RULES / NATIONAL FEDERATION OF STATE HIGH SCHOOL ASSOCIATIONS.). **Main/Corp** National Federation of State High School Associations. **VFOAT** Boys Gymnastics Rules. (1982/1983)-. English. an. $7.00. National Federation of State High School Associations, 11724 Northwest Plaza Circle, PO Box 20626, Kansas City MO 64195-0626. **Tel** (816)464-5400, FAX (816)464-5571. **ED** Susan True. **LC** GV461; .N33a. **DD** 796.4/1. **Ad Acc.** **Circ:** 400. ***Continues*** *National Federation of State High School Associations. Boys Gymnastics Rule Book, 0277-8386.*
**Desc:** Rules governing high school competition in boys gymnastics.

US/0747-9808
**OFFICIAL HIGH SCHOOL FOOTBALL RULES.** [Off. high sch. footb. rules]. **Main/Corp** National Federation of State High School Associations. **VFOAT** Official Football Rules. 1983-. English. an. National Federation of State High School Associations, 11724 Northwest Plaza Circle, PO Box 20626, Kansas City MO 64195-0626. **Tel** (816)464-5400, FAX (816)464-5571. **LC** GV956.8; .N38B. **DD** 796.332/02022. **UDC** 796.333.063(73).

US/0735-651X
**OFFICIAL HIGH SCHOOL ICE HOCKEY RULES.** **Main/Corp** National Federation of State High School Associations. (1983)-. English. an. National Federation of State High School Associations, 11724 Northwest Plaza Circle, PO Box 20626, Kansas City MO 64195-0626. **Tel** (816)464-5400, FAX (816)464-5571. **LC** GV847.5; .N37a. **DD** 796.96/2/02022. ***Continues*** *National Federation of State High School Associations. Ice Hockey Rule Book, 0732-8117.*

US
**OFFICIAL HIGH SCHOOL SPIRIT RULES BOOK.** **Main/Corp** National Federation of State High School Associations. **VFOAT** Spirit Rules Book. (1991)-. English. National Federation of State High School Associations, 11724 Northwest Plaza Circle, PO Box 20626, Kansas City MO 64195-0626. **Tel** (816)464-5400, FAX (816)464-5571. **LC** LB3635; .N38a. **DD** 791.6/4. ***Continues*** *Official High School Cheerleading, Pom Pon & Drill Team Guide.*

US
**OFFICIAL LOS ANGELES LAKERS YEARBOOK, THE.** **VFOAT** Los Angeles Lakers Yearbook. (1991)-. English. Taylor Publishing Company, 1550 West Mockingbird Land, Dallas TX 75221.

●US/1061-9178
**OFFICIAL MAJOR LEAGUE BASEBALL ROOKIE LEAGUE MAGAZINE FOR KIDS.** **VFOAT** Rookie League Magazine. (1992)-. Periodical. English. sa. $1.95), (single issue).

US/1054-4038
**OFFICIAL MAJOR LEAGUE BASEBALL STAT BOOK, THE.** (THE OFFICIAL MAJOR LEAGUE BASEBALL ... STAT BOOK / COMPILED BY MAJOR LEAGUE BASEBALL PROPERTIES, INC. AND THE EDITORS OF THE BASEBALL ENCYCLOPEDIA.). [Off. major leag. baseb. stat book]. **Added/Corp** Major League Baseball Properties, Inc. (1991)-. English. an. $14.95. Macmillan Publishing Company, 100 Front Street, Box 500, Riverside NJ 08075-7500. **Tel** (800)257-5755, (609)461-6500, FAX (609)461-7070. **LC** GV877; .O46. **DD** 796.357/0973.

US/0891-4648
**OFFICIAL NASCAR YEARBOOK AND PRESS GUIDE, THE.** (THE OFFICIAL NASCAR ... YEARBOOK AND PRESS GUIDE.). [Off. NASCAR yearb. press guide]. **Added/Corp** NASCAR (Association). **VFOAT** Official NASCAR Yearbook and Press Guide. **VAT** Official National Association for Stock Car Auto Racing Yearbook and Press Guide. (1986)-. English. an. $6.00. University Microfilms International, 300 North Zeeb Road, Ann Arbor MI 48106-1346. **Tel** (313)761-4700, (800)521-0600 Exts. 2490, 2491, FAX (313)973-1540. **ED** Ivan Mothershead. **LC** GV1029.9.S74; O37. **DD** 796.7/2/0973. **Ad Acc.** **Circ:** 60,000. ***Formed by the union of*** *NASCAR Winston Cup Grand National Yearbook; Official NASCAR Winston Cup Record Book and Press Guide* ***and*** *NASCAR Winston Cup Series Media Guide.*

US/0163-2817
**OFFICIAL NATIONAL COLLEGIATE ATHLETIC ASSOCIATION BASKETBALL RULES & INTERPRETATIONS, THE.** ***Title Change.*** **Main/Corp** National Collegiate Athletic Association. **VFOAT** NCAA Official Basketball Rules & Interpretations; Basketball Rules & Interpretations. **VAT** The Official National Collegiate Athletic Association Basketball Rules and Interpretations. English. an. National Collegiate Athletic Association / NCAA, PO Box 7347, Overland Park KS 66207. **Tel** (913)339-1900, FAX (913)339-0030. **LC** GV885.45; .N37C. **DD** 796.32/3/02022. **UDC** 796.323.063(73). ***Continued by*** *NCAA Basketball Rules and Interpretations.*

US
**OFFICIAL NATIONAL COLLEGIATE ATHLETIC ASSOCIATION BASKETBALL STATISTICIANS' MANUAL, THE.** **See** Recreation, Leisure-Abstracting, Bibliographies and Statistics.

US
**OFFICIAL NATIONAL COLLEGIATE ATHLETIC ASSOCIATION FOOTBALL STATISTICIANS' MANUAL, THE.** **Added/Corp** National Collegiate Athletic Association. **VFOAT** Football Statisticians' Manual; Official ... Football Statisticians' Manual; NCAA Football Statisticians' Manual; Official ... Football Statistics Rules. (19??)-. English. $2.75. National Collegiate Athletic Association / NCAA, PO Box 7347, Overland Park KS 66207. **Tel** (913)339-1900, FAX (913)339-0030. **LC** GV956.8; .O35. **DD** 796.332/0973.
**Desc:** Official statistics rules, including special interpretations and approved rulings.

US/0270-8280
**OFFICIAL NATIONAL FEDERATION BASKETBALL RULE BOOK.** ***Title Change.*** **Main/Corp** National Federation of State High School Associations. **VFOAT** Basketball Rule Book. English. National Federation of State High School Associations, 11724 Northwest Plaza Circle, PO Box 20626, Kansas City MO 64195-0626. **Tel** (816)464-5400, FAX (816)464-5571. **LC** GV885.45; .N39A. **DD** 796.32/3/02022. **UDC** 796.323.063(73). ***Continued by*** *National Federation Basketball Rule Book (National Federation of State High School Association).*

US/0091-0821
**OFFICIAL NATIONAL FOOTBALL LEAGUE GUIDE.** (OFFICIAL GUIDE.). **Main/Corp** National Football League. **VFOAT** National Football League Guide. 1972-. English. an. New American Library, 120 Woodbine Street, Bergenfield NJ 07621. **Tel** (201)387-0600. **LC** GV955.5.N35; N28A. **DD** 796.33/264/0973. **UDC** 796.333(036)(73).

US/0883-4199
**OFFICIAL ... NATIONAL FOOTBALL LEAGUE RECORD & FACT BOOK.** **Main/Corp** National Football League. **Added/Corp** National Football League. Public Relations Dept. **VFOAT** Official ... National Football League Record and Fact Book; Record and Fact Book; Record & Fact Book; National Football League Record & Fact Book. (1984)-. English. an. $14.95. Workman Publishing Company, 708 Broadway, New York NY 10003. **Tel** (800)722-7202, (212)254-5900, FAX 212-254-8098, telex 291233. **LC** GV955; .N334b. **DD** 796.332/64/0973. ***Formed by the union of*** *National Football League. Official Record Manual* ***and*** *National Football League ... Media Information Book, 0743-7080.*

US
**OFFICIAL NBA GUIDE.** ***Title Change.*** **Added/Corp** National Basketball Association. **VFOAT** Official National Basketball Association Guide; Sporting News Official NBA Guide. (1981/82)-(1992). English. an. Sporting News, c/o Sharon Moore, 1212 North Lindbergh Boulevard, PO Box 56, St Louis MO 63166. **Tel** (314)997-7111, (800)825-8508. **LC** GV885; .N26. **DD** 796.32/3/0973. ***Continues*** *National Basketball Association Official Guide, 0078-3862.* ***Continued by*** *Sporting News NBA Guide.*

●US/1063-1089
**OFFICIAL ... NCAA BASKETBALL.** [Off. NCAA basketb.]. **Added/Corp** National Collegiate Athletic Association. (1992)-. English. National Collegiate Athletic Association / NCAA, PO Box 7347, Overland Park KS 66207. **Tel** (913)339-1900, FAX (913)339-0030. **LC** GV885.45; .N42. **DD** 796. ***Continues*** *NCAA Basketball, 0276-1017.*

US
**OFFICIAL ... NCAA FOOTBALL / NATIONAL COLLEGIATE ATHLETIC ASSOCIATION.** **Main/Corp** National Collegiate Athletic Association. **VFOAT** Official ... National Collegiate Athletic Association Football; NCAA Football. (1991)-. English. National Collegiate Athletic Association / NCAA, PO Box 7347, Overland Park KS 66207. **Tel** (913)339-1900, FAX (913)339-0030. **LC** GV937; .N37. ***Continues*** *NCAA Football.*

US/1042-8798
**OFFICIAL PGA TOUR BOOK.** [Off. PGA tour book]. **Main/Corp** Professionel Golfers' Association of America. **VFOAT** PGA Tour; Tour Book; Official ... PGA Tour Media Guide; PGA Tour Book. **VAT** Official Professional Golfers' Association Tour Book. English. an. Qmpac, 4366B, Rue St. Hubert, Montreal Quebec H2J 2W8. **DD** 796. ***Continues*** *Official PGA Tour Media Guide, 0193-9653.*

CN/0316-151X
**OFFICIAL PLAYING RULES FOR THE CANADIAN FOOTBALL LEAGUE, THE.** **Main/Corp** Canadian Football League. **VFOAT** Official Playing Rules for Canadian Football. 1974-. Periodical. English. an. Free. Canadian Football League, 1200 Bay Street/12th Floor, Toronto Ontario M5R 2A5 Canada. **Tel** (416)928-1200. **DD** 796.33/5/02022. ***Supersedes*** *Official Playing Rules for the Canadian Football League and the Canadian Amateur Football Association, 0316-1501.*

US/1062-7227
**OFFICIAL PRICE GUIDE TO HOCKEY AND BASKETBALL CARDS.** ***Title Change.*** **See** Hobbies.

US
**OFFICIAL PRICE GUIDE TO HOCKEY CARDS.** **See** Hobbies.

US/0748-1160
**OFFICIAL PRICE GUIDE TO SPORTS COLLECTIBLES, THE.** (THE OFFICIAL PRICE GUIDE TO SPORTS COLLECTIBLES / BY THE HOUSE OF COLLECTIBLES, INC.). **Added/Corp** House of Collectibles. **VFOAT** Sports Collectibles; Sports. 1st Ed. (1984)-. English. an. Price varies. Random House Inc., 400 Hahn Road, Westminster MD 21157. **Tel** (800)726-0600, (800)733-3000, FAX (800)659-2436. **LC** GV568.5; .O36. **DD** 796/.0973.

US
**OFFICIAL READ-EASY BASKETBALL RULES OF THE NATIONAL COLLEGIATE ATHLETIC ASSOCIATION.** **VAT** Official Read Easy Basketball Rules of the National Collegiate Athletic Association. English. an. National Collegiate Athletic Association / NCAA, PO Box 7347, Overland Park KS 66207. **Tel** (913)339-1900, FAX (913)339-0030.

US
**OFFICIAL REGULATIONS AND PLAYING RULES. LITTLE LEAGUE, SENIOR LEAGUE, BIG LEAGUE SOFTBALL.** **Main/Corp** Little League Baseball, Inc. (19??)-. English. an. Little League Baseball Inc, PO Box 3485, Williamsport PA 17701. **LC** GV881.2; .L57a. **DD** 796.357/62.

US/0091-3413
**OFFICIAL RULES FOR COMPETITIVE SWIMMING.** **Main/Corp** Amateur Athletic Union of the United States. **VFOAT** AAU Official Rules Swimming. English. an. $6.00. United States Swimming, 1750 East Boulder Street, Colorado Springs CO 80909. **Tel** (719)578-4578, FAX (719)578-4669. **ED** William A Lippman Jr and Carol Zaleski. **LC** GV837; .A45A. **DD** 797.2/1. **Ad Acc. Circ:** 22,000 (ctrl).
**Desc:** Complete rules and regulations for competitive swimming in the United States. Also includes current records.

US/0196-7827
**OFFICIAL RULES FOR PROFESSIONAL FOOTBALL.** **Main/Corp** National Football League. English. National Football League Properties Inc, 410 Park Avenue, New York NY 10022. **LC** GV955; .N334A. **DD** 796.332/64/0973.

CN/0711-0537
**OFFICIAL RULES / RINGETTE CANADA.** [Offic. rules - Ringette Can.]. **Main/Corp** Ringette Canada. 1980/1981-. English (French). sa. $3.00. Ringette Canada, PO Box 2162, Stettler Alberta T0C 2L0 Canada. **ED** W Clark and D MacQuarrie. **DD** 796.9/6. **Ad Acc. Circ:** 10,000. ***Continues*** *Ontario Ringette Association. Official Rules, 0316-7615.*
**Desc:** Outlines the rules for Ringette, a winter team game played on ice (with skates). Invented mainly for females. The rules emphasize team play and no body contact.

US
**OFFICIAL UNITED STATES TENNIS ASSOCIATION TENNIS YEARBOOK.** ***Title Change.*** **Main/Corp** United States Tennis Association. **VFOAT** Tennis Yearbook; Official USTA Tennis Yearbook. (1989)-(1992). English. an. HO Zimman Inc, Seaport Landing #152, The Lynnway, Lynn MA 01902. **Tel** (617)598-9230. **ED** Miles Dumont. **LC** GV991; .U54. ***Continues*** *United States Tennis Association. Official United States Tennis Association Yearbook and Tennis Guide with the Official Rules, 0196-5425.* ***Continued by*** *USTA Tennis Yearbook.*

US/0196-5425
**OFFICIAL UNITED STATES TENNIS ASSOCIATION YEARBOOK AND TENNIS GUIDE WITH THE OFFICIAL RULES, THE.** ***Title Change.*** **Main/Corp** United States Tennis Association. **VFOAT** Tennis Yearbook. (197?)-. English. an ((published in May)). HO Zimman Inc, Seaport Landing #152, The Lynnway, Lynn MA 01902. **Tel** (617)598-9230. **ED** Miles Dumont. **Bk Rev. Ad Acc. Circ:** 50,000 (ctrl). ***Continues*** *Official United States Lawn Tennis Association Yearbook and Tennis Guide with the Official Rules.* ***Continued by*** *United States Tennis Association. Official United States Tennis Association Tennis Yearbook.*
**Desc:** Up-to-date information on tournaments, committees, rankings, members, records, tournament regulations, and the official rules of tennis and cases and decisions.

US/0145-7977
**OFFICIAL UNITED STATES TENNIS TOURNAMENT DIRECTORY.** [Off. U. S. tennis tournament dir.]. **Added/Corp** United States Tennis Survey. **VFOAT** Official U.S. Tennis Tournament Directory; U.S. Tennis Tournament Directory. **VAT** United States Tennis Tournament Directory. Supplement. (Feb. 28, 1977-Mar. 1, 1978)-. Directory. English. sa. **LC** GV999; .O44. **DD** 796.34/2/0973.

US
**OFFICIAL ... UNITED STATES VOLLEYBALL RULES.** **Main/Corp** United States Volleyball Association. **VFOAT** United States Volleyball Rules. English. an. US Volleyball Association, 3595 East Fountain Boulevard, Colorado Springs CO 80910. **Tel** (800)637-8300. **LC** GV1015.39; .U56A. ***Continues*** *Official Rules of the United States Volleyball Association.*

US/0742-4299
**OFFICIAL USFL GUIDE AND REGISTER.** **VFOAT** Official U.S.F.L. Guide and Register; USFL Guide and Register; U.S.F.L. Guide and Register; Sporting News Official USFL Guide and Register; Sporting News Official U.S.F.L. Guide and Register. **VAT** Official United States Football League Guide and Register. 1984 Ed.-. English. an. $9.95. Sporting News, c/o Sharon Moore, 1212 North Lindbergh Boulevard, PO Box 56, St Louis MO 63166. **Tel** (314)997-7111, (800)825-8508. **LC** GV955.5.U8; O35. **DD** 796.332/64/0973.

US
**OFFICIAL VOLLEYBALL RULES FOR GIRLS AND WOMEN.** **Main/Corp** National Association for Girls & Women in Sport. **VFOAT** Volleyball Rules for Girls and Women. English. National Association for Girls and Women in Sports, 1900 Association Drive, Business Office, Reston VA 22091.

US
**OFFICIAL WATER POLO RULES.** (1980)-. English. an. $8.00 US and Canada; $16.00 other. US Water Polo Incorporated, 201 South Capitol Avenue, Suite 520, Indianapolis IN 46225. **Tel** (317)237-5599, FAX (317)237-5590. **ED** Eileen Sexton. **Ad Acc. Circ:** 1,500 (ctrl). ***Continues*** *Official AAU Water Polo Rules.*
**Desc:** Contains rules of US Water Polo; also corporate rules.

CN/1185-135X
**OFSAA BULLETIN.** [OFSAA bull.]. **Added/Corp** Ontario Federation of School Athletic Associations. **VAT** Ontario Federation of School Athletic Associations Bulletin. (Sept. 1977)-. Bulletin. English. qt. 15.00Can$. Ontario Federal School Athletic Associations, 11 Victoria Street, Unit 218, Berrie ONT L4N 6T3 Canada. **Tel** (416)494-0022. **DD** 796/.09713.

US/0743-6874
**OHIO GOLFER MAGAZINE.** **VFOAT** Ohio Golfer. Vol. 1, No. 1 (May/June 1984)-. Periodical. English. Six times a year. $14.95 (one year), $24.95 (two years). Ohio Golfer Magazine, PO Box 509, renoldsburgs OH 43068. **Tel** (614)759-7744.

US/1064-0908
**OHIO HIGH SCHOOL ATHLETE, THE.** **Added/Corp** Ohio High School Athletic Association. Vol. 1 (1941)-. Periodical. English. qt. $12.00. Ohio High School Athletic Association, 4080 Roselea Place, Columbus OH 43214. **Tel** (614)267-2502.

US
**OHIO RACEWALKER.** English. Twelve times a year. $10.00 US; $12.00 others. Ohio Racewalker, 3184 Summit Street, Columbus OH 43202. **Tel** (614)424-7004. **ED** Jack Mortland. **Circ:** 650.
**Desc:** News and information on racewalking.

US/0279-9634
**OHIO RUNNER, THE.** (19??)-. Periodical. English. Six times a year. $14.00 (one year), $26.00 (two years) US and Canada; $18.00 (one year), $28.00 (two years) other. Ohio Runner, 1001 Eastwind Drive, Suite 304, Westerville OH 43081. **Tel** (614)882-3441. **ED** Linda K Gambaiani. **Bk Rev. Ad Acc, Adv Mgr:** same as editor. **Circ:** 2,000.
**Desc:** For the long-distance runner and related sports enthusiast in Ohio and neighboring states.

●US/1061-8368
**OHIO SPORTS ALMANAC.** (1992)-. English. $10.00. Orange Frazer Press, PO Box 214, 37 1/2 West Main Street, Wilmington OH 45177. **LC** GV584.03; 038. **DD** 796/.09771.

RU
**OLIMPIISKAIA PANORAMA : [ORGAN OLIMPIISKOGO KOMITETA SSSR].** **Added/Corp** Olimpiiskii Komitet SSSR. No. 1 (Autumn/Winter 1981)-. Periodical. Russian (French, German, Spanish and Russian). qt. $12.50 US. Fizkultura i Sport, Luzhneskaia Nab 8, 119270 Moscow Russia. **LC** GV721.4.S65; O44. **DD** 796.4/8/0947.
**Desc:** Magazine on major sports events in the Russia and other countries, covering preparations for the Olympic Games and introducing star Russia athletes.

US/0094-9787
**OLYMPIAN (NEW YORK, N.Y.), THE.** (THE OLYMPIAN.). [Olympian]. **Added/Corp** United States Olympic Committee. Vol. 1 (July/Aug. 1974)-. Periodical. English. Ten times a year. $19.96 Comes with United States Olympic Society membership. US Olympic Committee, 1750 East Boulder Street, Colorado Springs CO 80909. **Tel** (303)632-5551. **ED** Bob Condron. **LC** GV721.5; .O38. **DD** 796.4/8/05. **Ad Acc. Circ:** 60,000 (ctrl).
**Desc:** The official publication of the United States Olympic Committee, devoted to amateur sports and the Olympic movement in the United States.
**Ind/Abst** SPORT Discus; SportSearch (May 1987-).

US/0030-2163
**OLYMPIAN (SAN FRANCISCO).** (OLYMPIAN.). Periodical. English. mo. $10.00. Olympic Club, 524 Post Street, San Francisco CA 94102. **LC** GV563; .O6. **DD** 796/.05.

SZ
**OLYMPIC ENCYCLOPEDIA.** **Added/Corp** International Olympic Committee. (19??)-. Periodical. English. qt. 35.00F. International Olympic Committee / Comite International Olympique, Chateau de Vidy, CH-1007 Lausanne Switzerland. **Tel** 011 41 21 621-6111, FAX 011 41 21 621-6216, telex 45-4024ACIOCH. **LC** GV721.5; .O39.
**Ind/Abst** SPORT Discus.

RU
**OLYMPIC PANORAMA.** ***Suspended.*** (19??)-. Periodical. English (French, German, Spanish and Russian). qt. $15.00. **(Subscription address:** Victor Kamkin, 4956 Boiling Brook Parkway, Rockville MD 20852.**) LC** GV721.5; .O4227. **DD** 796.4/8/05.
**Desc:** Covers major events in sport life in the Russia and other countries, acquaints the reader with the activity and intitiatives of the National Olympic Committee of the Russia and introduces Russia and foreign Olympic athletes known in many countries, throughout the world.

SZ/0377-192X
**OLYMPIC REVIEW.** **Added/Corp** International Olympic Committee. No. 28 (Jan. 1970)-. Periodical. English (French and Spanish). Ten times a year (eight regular and two double issues per year). $42.46 US. Comite International Olympique, Chateau de Vidy, CH 1007 Lausanne Switzerland. **Tel** 011 41 21 6216111. **ED** Raymond Gafner and Denis Echard. **LC** GV721.5; .O423. **DD** 796.4/8/05. Index available. **Bk Rev. Ad Acc. Circ:** 7,000. ***Continues*** *International Olympic Committee. Newsletter.*
**Desc:** Official organ of the International Olympic Committee, distributed to the highest international and national sports authorities and to the international press.
**Ind/Abst** Leis. Recreat. Tour. Abstr.; Phys. Educ. Index; SPORT Discus; SportSearch.

GW/0471-5640
**OLYMPISCHES FEUER.** [Olymp. Feuer]. **VFOAT** OF. Olympisches Feuer. (1951)-. Periodical. German. bm (6 issues). DM30.00. Deutsche Olympische Gesellschaft, 12 Haus II, D 60528 Frankfurt Germany. **Tel** 011 49 69 747094 95. **UDC** 796.

CN/0316-6384
**OLYMPRESS 1976.** V. 2, No. 3- May 1974-. Periodical. Multiple languages (French and English). mo. Olympic Games, PO Box 1976, Montreal Quebec H3C 3A6. **DD** 796.4/8. ***Formed by the union of*** *Olympress 1976* ***and*** *Olympresse 1976.*

CN/0824-6629
**ON COURT.** [On Court]. July 1983-. Periodical. English. Free. ON Court, Suite 501, 1200 Sheppard Avenue East, Willowdale Ontario M2K 2S5 Canada. **DD** 796.34/0971. ctrl circ.

CN/0229-088X
**ON THE RUN.** (ON THE RUN / NATIONAL CAPITAL RUNNERS' ASSOCIATION.). [On run]. **VFOAT** En Courant. Periodical. English. mo. Free to members. National Capital Runners Association, 22 Findlay Avenue Canada. **DD** 796.4/26/0971383.

US/1054-836X
**ON TRACK (HARLINGEN, TEX.).** (ON TRACK : ENJOYING TEXAS GREYHOUND RACING.). Vol. 1, No. 1 (April 1991)-. Periodical. English. mo. $19.00 US; $28.00 Canada. On Track Magazine Company, PO Box 1408, Harlingen TX 78551. **DD** 798.

US/0279-2737
**ON TRACK (SANTA ANA, CALIF.).** (ON TRACK.). [On track]. Vol. 1, No. 1 (April 16, 1981)-. Periodical. English. ir (every other Thurs.). $33.97 (one year), $64.00 (two year). Paul Oxman Publishing Company, 17165 New Hope Street, Unit M, Fountain Valley CA 92708. **Tel** (800)228-0787, (714)966-1131, FAX (714)556-9776. **(Subscription address:** OT Publishing Inc., Subscription Department, Box 8509, Fountain Valley CA 92728.**) ED** Tim Tuttle (phone: (702)897-8100). **DD** 796. Index available. **Bk Rev**, (Qty: 12). **Ad Acc**, **Adv Mgr:** David Amette, **Tel** same as publisher. **Circ:** 29,000.

CN/0822-6806
**ONTARIO AMATEUR WRESTLING ASSOCIATION RESULTS BOOK.** (RESULTS BOOK /ONTARIO AMATEUR WRESTLING ASSOCIATION.). [Ont. Amat. Wrestl. Assoc. results book]. **Main/Corp** Ontario Amateur Wrestling Association. 1981/1982-. English. an. 5.00Can$. Ontario Amateur Wrestling Association, 1220 Sheppard Avenue East, Willowdale Ontario M2K 2X1 Canada. **Tel** (416)495-4165, FAX (416)495-4310. **ED** Ingrid Leslie and Tim MaGarrey. **DD** 796.8/12/09713. **Bk Rev**. **Ad Acc**. **Circ:** 3,000 (ctrl). ***Continues*** *Ontario Olympic Wrestling Federation. Results Book, 0820-6082.*
**Desc:** Results of Canadian amateur wrestlers in international, national, provincial and local competitions.

CN/1183-4072
**ONTARIO CRICKET "PITCH".** (THE ONTARIO CRICKET "PITCH".). [Ont. cricket "pitch"]. **Added/Corp** Ontario Cricket Association. (1978)-. Periodical. English. Three times a year (Mar., July, Nov.). 15.00Can$. Ontario Cricket Association Inc, 1220 Sheppard Avenue East, Willowdale Ontario, M2K 2X1 Canada. **Tel** (905)495-4280, FAX (905)495-3406. **ED** Randy Borde. **DD** 796.358/09713. **Ad Acc**. **Circ:** 10,000 (ctrl).

CN/0228-9075
**ONTARIO FENCER.** (ONTARIO FENCER : MAGAZINE.). **Added/Corp** Ontario Fencing Association. (1958)-. Periodical. English. ir. 5.00Can$. Ontario Fencing Association, 75 Leacrest Road/8, Toronto Ontario M4G 1E7 Canada. **DD** 796.8/6/09713.

CN/0710-2801
**ONTARIO GOLF NEWS.** [Ont. golf news]. **VFOAT** Golf News. **VAT** Golf News (Thornhill). Vol. 1, No. 1 (May 1981)-. Periodical. English. ir. $6.00. Ontario Golf News, PO Box 5400, Thornhill Ontario L3T 4S5 Canada. **DD** 796.352/09713.

CN/0834-2105
**ONTARIO JUDO NEWSLETTER.** ***Title Change.*** [Ont. Judo newsl.]. **Added/Corp** Judo Ontario. (1986)-(1992). Newsletter. English. bm. Judo Ontario, 1220 Sheppard Avenue East, Willowdale Ontario M2K 2N1 Canada. **DD** 796.8/152/09713. ***Continues*** *Ontario Judoka, 0823-9134.* ***Continued by*** *Judo Ontario Newsletter, 1193-7149.*

CN/0383-7009
**ONTARIO SNOWMOBILER.** Vol. 1 (Sept. 1972)-. Periodical. English. Five times a year (Sept., Oct., Nov., Dec., Jan.). 17.00Can$ Canada; 22.00Can$ other. Ontario Snowmobiler, RR #3 Center Road, Mt. Albert, Ontario L0G 1M0 Canada. **Tel** (416)473-7009, FAX (416)473-5217. **ED** Mark and Kent Lester. **Ad Acc**, **Adv Mgr:** J Hildebrandt, **Tel** (705)484-1511. **Circ:** 60,000.

CN/0225-5782
**ONTARIO SPORTSCENE. Added/Corp** Ontario Sports Administrative Centre. Vol. 1 (Nov. 1979)-. Periodical. English. bm (6 issues). Ontario Sports Administrative Centre Inc., 1220 Sheppard Avenue East, Willowdale Ontario M2K 2X1 Canada. **DD** 796/.09713. ctrl circ.
**Ind/Abst** SportSearch (May 1987-).

CN/0226-5702
**ONTARIO WATER SKIER, THE.** [Ont. water skier]. **Added/Corp** Canadian Water Ski Association. Ontario Region. Ontario Water Ski Association. Sport Ontario. Ontario Sports Administrative Centre. Vol. 1 (Feb. 1974)-. Periodical. English. qt. Comes with membership to Ontario Water Ski Association. Ontario Sports Administrative Centre Inc., 1220 Sheppard Avenue East, Willowdale Ontario M2K 2X1 Canada. **ED** Walter Sokolowski. **DD** 797.1/73/05. Index available. **Bk Rev**. **Ad Acc**. **Circ:** 1,500 (ctrl).
**Desc:** Articles and information relating to water skiing as a sport and recreation.
**Ind/Abst** SportSearch (May 1987-).

CN/0226-1561
**ONTARIO WRESTLER.** [Ont. wrestler]. **Added/Corp** Ontario Amateur Wrestling Federation. Ontario Olympic Wrestling Federation. Wrestling Ontario. **VFOAT** Newsletter. Vol. 1 (Sept. 1979)-. Periodical. English. Four times a year. 20.00Can$ (supporter), 35.00Can$ (associate) Comes with Ontario Amateur Wrestling Association membership. Ontario Amateur Wrestling Association, 1220 Sheppard Avenue East, Willowdale Ontario M2K 2X1 Canada. **Tel** (905)495-4165. **DD** 796.8/12/09713.
**Ind/Abst** SportSearch (May 1987-).

US/0279-0254
**OPEN WHEEL.** [Open wheel]. **VFOAT** Stock Car Racing Magazine's Open Wheel; Stock Car Racing Open Wheel; Open Wheel Magazine. Vol. 1, No. 1 (1981)-. Periodical. English. mo. $21.95. General Media Publishing Company, 1965 Broadway, New York NY 10023. **Tel** (212)496-6100. **(Subscription address:** CDS Agency Hard Copy, PO Box 4966, Des Moines IA 50340.**) ED** Dick Berggren. **LC** GV1029.9.S74; O63. **DD** 796.7/20/5. **Bk Rev**. **Ad Acc**. **Circ:** 55,000.
**Desc:** Dedicated to behind the scenes coverage of events and personalities along with in-depth technical articles and brilliant color photography.

CN/0227-6658
**ORIENTEERING CANADA.** [Orienteer. Can.]. **Added/Corp** Canadian Orienteering Federation. (1973)-. Periodical. English. Four times a year. 12.00Can$. Canadian Orienteering Federation, 333 River Road, Ottawa Ontario K1L 8H9 Canada. **Tel** (613)748-5649. **DD** 796.4/2.
**Ind/Abst** SPORT Discus; SportSearch (May 1987-).

US/0886-1080
**ORIENTEERING NORTH AMERICA.** [Orienteer. North Am.]. (19??)-. Periodical. English. Ten times a year (Mar./Apr. and Sept./Oct. issues combined). $23.50. SM & L Berman Publishing Company, 23 Fayette Street, Cambridge MA 02139. **Tel** (617)868-7416. **ED** Sara Mae Berman. **LC** GV200.4; .O75. **DD** 796.5/097. Index available. **Bk Rev**, (Qty: 2-3). **Ad Acc**. **Circ:** 1,800.
**Desc:** Covers all aspects of orienteering including training, organization, course planning, equipment, and technique. Coverage mostly about United States and Canada but contains some international news.

SW/1015-4965
**ORIENTEERING WORLD.** English. Four times a year. Kr125.00 Sweden; Kr155.00 other. Intl Orienteeering Federation, Secretary General, PO Box 76, S-191 21 Sollentuna Sweden. **ED** Peter Gehrmann (editors address: 39, D-4815 Schloss Holte, Germany. **Ad Acc**. ***Continues*** *IOF Report; IOF Bulletin.*
**Desc:** Information about orienteering events around the world, international discussion about orienteering matters, news of all major international events; world championships, etc..

SW/1015-4965
**ORIENTEERING WORLD : ORIENTIERUNGSLAUF AUS ALLER WELT. Added/Corp** International Orienteering Federation. (1989)-. Periodical. English. Six times a year. Kr125.00. International Orienteering Federation, Secretary General, PO Box 76, S 191 21 Sollentuna Sweden. **ED** Lennart Levin. **LC** WMLC 93/1460. ***Continues*** *IOF Bulletin.*

TU
**ORTA DERECELI OKULLAR OKUL ICI SPOR FAALIYETLERI. VFOAT** Sports Activities in Secondary Schools. English (Turkish). **LC** HA1911; .A3 subser; GV346.

US/0747-0991
**OSCEOLA (TALLAHASSEE, FLA.), THE.** (THE OSCEOLA: AN INDEPENDENT WEEKLY NEWSPAPER FEATURING FLORIDA STATE UNIVERSITY SPORTS.). (198?)-. Periodical. English. Thirty-four times a year. $45.00. Florida State University / The Osceola, 402 Dunwoody Street, Tallahassee FL 32304. **Tel** (800)733-3781.

CN/0846-1074
**OTTAWA CITIZEN SKI GUIDE, THE.** [Ott. citiz. ski guide]. **VFOAT** Ski Guide. Winter (1991)-. English. Ottawa Citizen, 1101 Baxter Road, Ottawa Ontario K2C 3M4 Canada. **Tel** (613)829-9100. **DD** 796.93.

US/0892-8355
**OUTDOOR SPORTS & RECREATION.** **See** Recreation, Leisure-Outdoor Life.

CN/0229-3463
**PACER (WINNIPEG, MAN.).** (PACER.). [Pacer]. Periodical. English. bm. Free. International Correspondence Schools, Scranton PA 18515. **DD** 796/.097127. **UDC** 796.42 (712). ctrl circ.
**Ind/Abst** SportSearch (May 1987-).

CN/0319-2113
**PACIFIC MOTORSPORT.** V. 1- July 1975-. Periodical. English. mo. $5.00. North 60 Publications, PO Box 77, Chemainus BC V0R 1K0 Canada. **DD** 796.7/2/90795. **UDC** 796.7.

US/1059-4493
**PACK & PADDLE.** [Pack paddle]. **VFOAT** Pack and Paddle. Vol. 1, No. 1 (Dec. 1991)-. Periodical. English. Twelve times a year. $15.00 one year; $28.00 two year. Pack & Paddle, PO Box 1063, Port Orchard WA 98366. **Tel** (206)871-1862, FAX 206876-2139. **ED** Ann Marshall. **DD** 796. Index available. cum. index. **Bk Rev**, (Qty: 12-20). **Ad Acc**. **Circ:** 1,500 (ctrl).
**Desc:** An informed, black-white magazine for hikes, paddles, climbers, and snow tourers; A lot of enthusiastic reader input; Covers backcountry areas everywhere but focuses on Pacific Northwest; photographs and maps. Free sample to libraries on request.

US/1058-5710
**PADDLER (FALLBROOK, CALIF.). See** Recreation, Leisure-Outdoor Life.

US/1043-4771
**PAINTBALL (BURBANK, LOS ANGELES COUNTY, CALIF.).** ***Ceased.*** **See** Recreation, Leisure-Games and Amusements.

PK
**PAKISTAN BOOK OF CRICKET.** 1976-. English. an. Rs10.00. Q Ahmed, 3rd Floor/Spencers Building, II Chundrigar Road, GPO Box 3721, Karachi Pakistan. **LC** GV928.P3; P34. **DD** 796.358/0954/9. **UDC** 796.358 (549.1).

US/8756-5811
**PALAESTRA (MACOMB, ILL.). See** Physically Impaired.

IT/0390-3133
**PALLAVOLO.** [Pallavolo]. (1973)-. Periodical. Italian. mo. L48000 Italy; L90000 Europe; L120000 other. Ecofin Spa, V Garibaldi 55, 43100 Parma Italy. **Tel** 011 39 521 279729. **UDC** 796.

US/0886-4527
**PAR EXCELLANCE MAGAZINE.** [Par excell. mag.]. (198?)-. Periodical. English. Five times a year (Mar.,Apr., June, Aug., Nov.). $12.00 Canada; $16.00 other. Par Excellance Magazine, 10401 West Lincoln Avenue, West Allis WI 53227. **Tel** (414)327-7707, FAX (414)545-1729. **ED** Neal Kotlarek. **DD** 796. **Bk Rev**, (Qty: 10-12). **Ad Acc**. **Circ:** 20,000.
**Desc:** Stories and articles on golf along with reviews of golf courses.

US
**PARACHUTE PAGES.** English. mo. $24.95 (one year). Skydiving Book Service, 1725 North Lexington Avenue, Deland FL 32724. **Tel** (904)736-4793, FAX (904)736-9786. **ED** Ann Marie Forkey. ctrl circ.
**Desc:** International directory of the parachute industry. Includes manufactures, dealers, parachute drop zones, riggers, associations and periodicals.

US/0031-1588
**PARACHUTIST (WASHINGTON).** (PARACHUTIST.). [Parachutist]. **Added/Corp** United States Parachute Association. Parachute Club of America. (Sept. 1957)-. Periodical. English. Twelve times a year. $21.50. United States Parachute Association, 1440 Duke Street, Alexandria VA 22314. **Tel** (703)836-3495, FAX (703)836-2843. **LC** GV770; .P36. **Ad Acc**. **Circ:** 20,000.
**Ind/Abst** SPORT Discus; SportSearch (May 1987-).

CN/0228-9938
**PARAVOICE.** (PARAVOICE : THE NEWSLETTER FOR PARACHUTISTS.). [Paravoice]. Newsletter. English. bm. $5.00. Sport Parachuting Clubs of Ontario, 160 Vanderhoof Avenue Canada. **DD** 797.5/6/09713. **UDC** 797.561 (713).
**Ind/Abst** SPORT Discus; SportSearch (May 1987-).

CN/0820-070X
**PASSE-SPORTS.** (PASSE-SPORTS / SPORT SCOLAIRE RICHELIEU.). [Passe-sports]. Vol. 3, No. 1 (Nov. 1980)-. Periodical. French. qt. Free. Passe-Sports, c/o Commission Scolaire Regionale, Honore-Mercier, 69 Boulevard St Joseph, Saint-Jean-Sur-Richelieu Quebec J3B 1V8 Canada. **DD** 796/.09714/51. **UDC** 372.879.6 (714). ctrl circ. ***Continues*** *Mini-Franc Jeu Regional, 0226-7675.*

US
**PEAK RUNNING PERFORMANCE.** English. bm. $29.00 US; $34.00 other. Peak Running

Performance, PO Box 128036, Nashville TN 37212. **(Subscription address:** Fulco 30 Broad Street, Denville NJ 07834) **ED** Guy Avery. Index available. cum. index. **Bk Rev**, (Qty: 2). **Ad Acc. Pr Rev. Circ:** 12,000.
**Desc:** Training and racing strategies for runners and coaches.

CN/0703-9107
**PECHEUR ET CHASSEUR QUEBECOIS.** V. 1, No. 5- Sept. 1976-. Periodical. French. ir. $1.00 per no. Pecheur Et Chasseur Quebecois, 3580, Rue Masson, Montreal Quebec H1X 1S2. **DD** 799/.09714. **UDC** 799.1/.2 (714). ***Continues*** *Pecheur Quebecois, 0384-1073.*

●US/1060-5460
**PENNSYLVANIA GOLFER MAGAZINE.** (1992)-. Periodical. English. mo. Pennsylvania Publishing Company, PO Box 170, Coalport PA 16627.

US/0734-0230
**PENNSYLVANIA HIGH SCHOOL ATHLETIC YEARBOOK.** Vol. 1 (1978-79)-. English. an. $19.95. Sportron Publications, 3162 Glenwood Park Avenue, Erie PA 16508. **LC** GV346; .P46. **DD** 796/.07/12748. **UDC** 796.42 (748).

US/0274-6336
**PENNSYLVANIA SPORTSMAN, THE. See** Recreation, Leisure-Outdoor Life.

CN/0832-8196
**PERFORMANCE (VANIER).** (PERFORMANCE.). [Performance]. **Added/Corp** Canadian Weightlifting Federation. No. 1 (Aug. 1986)-. Periodical. English (French). ir. Free. Canadian Weightlifting Federation, 333 River Road, Ottawa Ontario K1L 8H9 Canada. **Tel** (613)749-7237, FAX (613)748-5706, telex 053-3660. **ED** Claude Ranger. **DD** 796.4/1. **Bk Rev. Ad Acc.**

US/0162-3214
**PETERSEN'S 4 WHEEL & OFF-ROAD. VFOAT** 4 Wheel & Off-Road. **VAT** Petersen's Four Wheel and Off Road. (1978)-. Periodical. English. mo. $19.94 US; $30.97 Canada; $28.94 other. Petersen Publishing Company, 6420 Wilshire Bouldevard, Los Angeles CA 90048. **Tel** (213)782-2485. **(Subscription address:** Neodata / Colorado, PO Box 2606, Boulder Boulder CO 80322.) **ED** Michael Coates. **LC** TL235.6; .P47. **DD** 629.22. **Ad Acc. Circ:** 300,900. available on microfilm from University Microfilms International (UMI).
**Desc:** Each issue features detailed how-to's on bolt-ons and build-ups, in-depth road tests, and buyers' guides to off-road products. Readers also get exciting race and special event coverage, articles on readers' vehicles, and more.

●US/1059-5805
**PETERSEN'S ... COLLEGE BASKETBALL.** [Petersen's coll. basketb.]. **VFOAT** College Basketball. (1992)-. English. Peterson Publishing Company, 6725 Sunset Boulevard, Los Angeles CA 90028. **LC** GV885.4; .P48. **DD** 796.323/63/0973.

US/0276-2129
**PETERSEN'S ... COLLEGE FOOTBALL.** ***Title Change.*** [Petersen's coll. footb.]. **VFOAT** College Football. (1980)-(19??). English. an. Petersen Publishing Company, 6420 Wilshire Bouldevard Los Angeles CA 90048. **Tel** (213)782-2485. **LC** GV937; .P47. **DD** 796.332/63/05. ***Continued by*** *Petersen's Preview ... College Football, 1059-2571.*

US/1041-4703
**PETERSEN'S FISHING.** ***Ceased.*** [Petersen's fish.]. **VFOAT** Fishing. Vol. 1, Issue 1 (April/May 1987)-(April 1991). Periodical. English. bm. Petersen Publishing Company, 6420 Wilshire Bouldevard, Los Angeles CA 90048. **Tel** (213)782-2485. **ED** Bob Robb. **LC** WMLC L 83/6366. **DD** 799. Index available. cum. index. **Ad Acc. Circ:** 150,000. available on microfilm and microfiche from University Microfilms International (UMI).
**Desc:** Complete sportfishing journal covering all aspects of fresh water, salt water, lake reservoir, river and stream angling.

●US/1073-4716
**PETERSEN'S GOLFING.** [Petersen's golf.]. Vol.1, No. 1 (Mar. 1994)-. Periodical. English. mo. $19.94 US; $30.97 Canada; $29.94 other. Petersen Publishing Company, 6420 Wilshire Bouldevard, Los Angeles CA 90048. **Tel** (213)782-2485. **(Subscription address:** Neodata / Colorado, PO Box 2606, Boulder Boulder CO 80322.) **DD** 796.

US/0146-4671
**PETERSEN'S HUNTING. VFOAT** Hunting. Vol. 1 (Nov. 1973)-. Periodical. English. mo. $19.94 US; $29.90 Canada; $27.94 other. Petersen Publishing Company, 6420 Wilshire Bouldevard, Los Angeles CA 90048. **Tel** (213)782-2485. **(Subscription address:** Neodata / Colorado, PO Box 2606, Boulder Boulder CO 80322.) **ED** Craig Boddington. **LC** SK1; P428. **DD** 799.2/05. **Ad Acc. Circ:** 301,183. available on microfilm and microfiche from University Microfilms International (UMI).
**Desc:** Devoted exclusively to the sport of recreational hunting. Every issue includes articles on big and small game, waterfowl and upland game, and hunting in a wide variety of locales. Monthly departments focus on hunting vehicles, gun dogs, knives, clothing, bowhunting, firearms and much more.

US/0095-5124
**PETERSEN'S HUNTING ANNUAL.** ***Title Change.*** **See** Recreation, Leisure-Outdoor Life.

US/1059-2571
**PETERSEN'S PREVIEW ... COLLEGE FOOTBALL.** [Petersen's preview coll. footb.]. **VFOAT** College Football; Petersen's College Football. (1991)-. English. $3.95. Petersen Publishing Company, 6420 Wilshire Bouldevard, Los Angeles CA 90048. **Tel** (213)782-2485. **DD** 796. ***Continues*** *Petersen's College Football, 0276-2129.*

US/1059-1680
**PETERSEN'S PREVIEW ... PRO FOOTBALL. VFOAT** Pro Football; Petersen's Pro Football. 1988-. English. an. $2.95. Petersen Publishing Company, 6420 Wilshire Bouldevard, Los Angeles CA 90048. **Tel** (213)782-2485. **LC** GV955.5.N35; P46. ***Continues*** *Petersen's ... Annual Pro Football, 0731-0161.*

US/0148-3153
**PETERSEN'S PRO BASEBALL.** Periodical. English. an. $1.95 single issue. Petersen Publishing Company, 6420 Wilshire Bouldevard, Los Angeles CA 90048. **Tel** (213)782-2485. **LC** GV875.A1; P47. **DD** 796.357/64/0973. **UDC** 796.357.071 (058)(73).

US/1045-120X
**PETERSEN'S ROD & CUSTOM.** ***Title Change.*** **See** Transportation-Automobiles.

US/1044-1204
**PGA MAGAZINE (1989).** (PGA MAGAZINE : THE OFFICIAL PUBLICATION OF THE PGA OF AMERICA.). [PGA mag.]. **Added/Corp** Professional Golf Association of America. **VFOAT** PGA. **VAT** Professional Golf Association Magazine. Vol. 70, No. 6 (June 1989)-. Periodical. English. mo. $19.95. Professional Golfers Association of America, PO Box 109601, Palm Beach Garden FL 33410. **DD** 796. ***Continues*** *PGA (Troy, Mich.), 1042-6310.*

CN/0843-2635
**PHYSICAL EDUCATION DIGEST.** [Phys. educ. dig.]. Vol. 5, No. 1 (Sept. 1988)-. Periodical. English. mo. $24.00 (one year), $42.00 (two year), $72.00 (three year). Physical Education Digest, PO Box 1385 Station B, Sudbury Ontario P3E 5K4 Canada. **Tel** (705)675-7055, FAX (705)675-5539. **DD** 796/.07. ***Continues*** *Coaching Digest., 0829-8076.*

PL/0137-4710
**PIKA NOZNA.** [Pika Nozna]. (1956)-. Periodical. Polish. wk. $78.00. **(Subscription address:** ARS Polona, PO Box 1001, 00068 Warsaw Poland.) **UDC** 796.333.

CC
**PING PANG SHIH CHIEH. Added/Corp** Chung-Kuo Ping Pang Chiu Hsieh Hui. **VFOAT** Pingpang Shijie. (1982)-. Chinese. sa (2 issues). $2.00. Jen Min Ti Yu Chu Pan She, Beijing, People's Republic of China. **Tel** 757161. **ED** Cen Yuefang and Ma Guanghong. **LC** GV1004.9; .P56. **DD** 796.34/6/05. **Bk Rev. Ad Acc, Adv Mgr:** Mr. Su Pixian, **Tel** 7031505. Full Page (B&W) £3000.00. Half Page (B&W)£1500.00. Full Page (Color) £7000.00 (back cover), £6000.00 (inside back cover), £5000.00 (center spread). Half Page (Color) £3500.00 (back cover), £3000.00 (inside back cover), £2500.00 (center spread). **Circ:** 20,000.
**Desc:** Reports on major competitions at home and abroad; commentaries; results of competitions; trend of world table tennis developments; new tactics and techniques; training of young players; etc.

IT/0390-3230
**PISCINE OGGI.** [Piscine oggi]. (1973)-. Periodical. Italian. qt. L42000 Italy; L75000 Europe; L130000 other. Editrice Il Campo, Via G Amendola 11, 40121 Bologna Italy. **Tel** 011 39 51 255544. **UDC** 725.

US
**PISTONS INSIDER : OFFICIAL MAGAZINE OF THE DETROIT PISTONS. Added/Corp** Detroit Pistons (Basketball team). Vol. 1, Issue 1 (May 1990)-. Periodical. English. Twelve times a year. $18.95. Detroit Pistons Basketball Co, 2 Championship Drive, Auburn Hill MI 48326. **Tel** (313)377-0100 or (313)222-2419. **LC** WMLC L 83/8865.

BL
**PLACAR.** No. 1 (20 Mar. 1970)-. Periodical. Portuguese. Editora Abril SA, Rua do Curtume 769 Lapa, 05066 900 Sao Paulo SP Brazil. **Tel** 011 55 11 8239222, 011 55 11 2623322, FAX 011 55 11 8643796.

FR/0242-6986
**PLANCHE MAGAZINE.** (1981)-. Periodical. French. mo. **UDC** 797.1. ***Continues*** *Force 6., 0246-8603.*
**Ind/Abst** SPORT Discus.

US/0361-3976
**PLAYING RULES.** [Play. rules]. **Main/Corp** Women's International Bowling Congress. English. Women's International Bowling Congress, 5301 South 76th Street, Greendale WI 53129. **Tel** (414)421-9000, FAX (414)421-4420. **LC** GV905; .W65A. **DD** 794.6. **UDC** 796.28-055.2 (73).

CN/0228-3530
**PLONGEE.** (LA PLONGEE.). [Plongee]. **Added/Corp** Federation Quebecoise des Activites Subaquatiques. Vol. 5, No 2 (March/April 1978)-. Periodical. French (English). bm. 25.00Can$ Canada; $25.00 US; $30.00 other. Les Editions Quebecoise des Activities Subaquatiques, 4545 Pierre de Coubertin, CP 1000 Succursale M, Montreal Quebec H1V 3R2 Canada. **Tel** (514)252-3009, FAX (514)252-3162, telex 05-829647. **ED** Tristan Leonard (editor's address: 6, rud Saint-Francois, Mercier, Quebec J6R 2L1 Canada; phone (514)691-8433, fax (511)692-8630. **DD** 797.2/3/05. **Bk Rev**, (Qty: 20). **Ad Acc. Circ:** 6,000. ***Continues*** *Plongee Sous-Marine, 0704-7096.*
**Desc:** Scuba diving magazine with editorial, equipment, photography, technics, news, story, instruction, and leading article.
**Ind/Abst** SportSearch (May 1987-).

US/0148-8007
**POCKET BOOK OF PRO FOOTBALL, THE.** English. $1.95 single issue. Pocket Books, 1230 Avenue of the Americas, New York NY 10020. **ED** H M Furlow. **LC** GV955; .P6. **DD** 796.332/64/0973. **UDC** 796.333.071 (73).

CN/0821-2023
**POCKET PRO GOLF MAGAZINE.** [Pocket pro golf mag.]. **VFOAT** Pocket Pro Golf Magazine & Course Guide; Pocket Pro. 1982 Ed.-. English. an. Free to golfers. Longhurst Golf Enterprises, Suite 202/2 St Clair Avenue East, Toronto Ontario M4T 2T5 Canada. **DD** 796.352/3/0971. **UDC** 796.352.071 (71). ***Continues*** *Pro Pocket Guide Golf Magazine, 0711-4079.*

US/0273-3420
**POINT SPREAD PLAYBOOK.** [Point spread playb.]. **VAT** Point Spread Play Book. 1979-. English. an. Point Spread Playbook, 1314 Watling Road, Arlington Heights IL 60004. **LC** GV955; .O36. **DD** 796.332/64/0212. **UDC** 796.333 (73).

US/0146-4574
**POLO (GAITHERSBURG, MD.).** (POLO.). **Added/Corp** United States Polo Association. Vol. 2, No. 6 (Oct./Nov. 1976)-. Periodical. English. ir (ten issues a year). $30.00 (one year), $45.00 (two year). Fleet Street Corporation, 656 Quince Orchard Road, Gaithersburg MD 20878. **Tel** (301)977-3900. **ED** Ami Shinitzky. **LC** GV1010; .P64. **DD** 796.35/3/05. **Ad Acc. Circ:** 5,000. ***Continues*** *Polonews, 0146-4612.*
**Desc:** Covers the sport of polo.
**Ind/Abst** SPORT Discus; SportSearch (May 1987-).

CN/0226-5443
**POLOISTE, LE.** [Poloiste]. Mar. 1979-. Periodical. French. qt. Federation de Water Polo du Quebec, 1415 Est rue Jarry, Montreal Quebec H2E 2Z7 Canada. **DD** 797.2/5. **UDC** 797.25. ***Continues*** *Federation de Water Polo du Quebec. Bulletin, 0226-5435.*

US/1049-2852
**POOL & BILLIARD MAGAZINE. VFOAT** Pool and Billiard Magazine. (19??)-. Periodical. English. mo. $29.95 US; $39.95 Canada and Mexico; $68.95 other. Pool & Billiard Magazine, 1701 Bloomingdale Road, Glendale Heights IL 60139. **Tel** (708)260-8500, FAX (708)260-8566. **ED** Shari J. Stauch. **DD** 794. **Bk Rev**, (Qty: 6). **Ad Acc, Adv Mgr:** Mark Haddad. **Circ:** 14,000.
**Desc:** Deals with billiard sports.

US/0195-0037
**POOP SHEET, THE.** (197?)-. Periodical. English. Twenty-one times a year. $35.00 (one year), $66.00 (two year). Sports Letter Inc, 31 Rogerson Street, Chapel Hill NC 27514. **Tel** (919)967-7789. **ED** Dennis Wuycik. **Bk Rev. Ad Acc.**

US/0092-5969
**POPULAR SPORTS FACE-OFF.** (Jan. 1973)-. Periodical. English. sa. $0.75 per copy. Popular Library Columbia Broad, 355 Lexington Avenue, New York NY 10017. **LC** GV846; .F3. **DD** 796.9/62/0973. ***Continues*** *Face-Off.*

US/0195-9476
**POPULAR SPORTS. SOCCER ILLUSTRATED. VFOAT** Soccer Illustrated. 1979-. English. an. CBS Publications, 1515 Broadway, New York NY 10036. **Tel** (212)503-5064. **LC** GV942; .P66. **DD** 796.334/05. **UDC** 796.332. ***Continues*** *Popular Sports. Soccer, 0195-9441.*

SZ
**POSEIDON.** No. 1- 1964-. Periodical. German. mo. Deutscher Judo Verband, Redaktion Ippon Segewaldweg 40, D 12557 Berlin Germany. **Tel** 011 49 711 210770, telex 051 678. **LC** GV840.S78; P66.

UK
**POST FOOTBALL GUIDE.** English. T Bailey Forman Ltd, Forman Street, PO Box 99, Nottingham NG1 4AB England. **LC** GV944.G7; P67. **DD** 796.33/4/0942. **UDC** 796.333 (036).

GW/0343-4168
**POST UND SPORT.** [Post Sport]. (1952)-. Periodical. German. Twelve times a year. DM24.60 (plus postage). Josef Keller GmbH & Co. Verlags KG, Postfach 1455, D 82317 Starnberg Germany. **Tel** 011 49 (08151)771-0, FAX 011 49 (08151)771-152, telex 566438. **UDC** 796.

CN/0824-4170
**POUR LA SUITE DES JEUX.** (POUR LA SUITE DES JEUX : BULLETIN D'INFORMATION DE LA FONDATION DES JEUX DU QUEBEC.). [Pour suite Jeux]. **Added/Corp** Fondation des Jeux du Quebec. Vol. 1, No. 1, (April 1983)-. Periodical. English (French). Free. Fondation des Jeux du Quebec, 1415 Jarry West, Montreal Quebec H2E 2Z7 Canada. **DD** 796.4/06/0714. ctrl circ.

US/0145-4471
**POWDER.** (19??)-. Periodical. English. Seven times a year (published Sept.-Mar.). $12.95. Surfer Publications Inc., PO Box 1028, Dana Point CA 92629. **Tel** (714)496-5922, (800)289-0636, FAX (714)496-7849. **(Subscription address:** Neodata / Colorado, PO Box 2606, Boulder Boulder CO 80322.**) ED** Pat Cochran. **LC** GV854.A1; P68. **DD** 796.9/3/05. **Circ:** 100,000.
**Ind/Abst** SPORT Discus; SportSearch (May 1987-).

AT/0818-1128
**POWDERHOUND SKI MAGAZINE'S NEW ZEALAND SKI GUIDE.** (1977)-. English. qt. 19.80Aus$. Powderhound, PO Box 44, Avalon 2107, Australia. **Tel** 11 61 2 9187203.

US/0032-6089
**POWERBOAT (VAN NUYS, CALIF.).** See Boats and Boating.

US/0199-8536
**POWERLIFTING USA.** [Powerlift. U. S. A.]. **VAT** Powerlifting United States of America. (197?)-. Periodical. English. Twelve times a year. $26.95 US; $36.00 other. Powerlifting USA, PO Box 467, Camirillo CA 93010. **Tel** (805)482-2378. **ED** Mike Lambert. **Bk Rev**. **Ad Acc**. **Circ:** 16,750.
**Desc:** Covers the sport of powerlifting, with contest results, training techniques and athlete profiles.
**Ind/Abst** SPORT Discus; SportSearch (May 1987-).

US/0199-0705
**PREDICAMENT, THE.** (19??)-. Periodical. English. Nine times a year. $15.00 US; $25.00 other. Predicament, PO Box 545, Emmetsburg IA 50536. **Tel** (712)852-2288. **ED** Ron Seaman. **Bk Rev**. **Ad Acc**. **Circ:** 2,000 (ctrl).
**Desc:** Wrestling newspaper covering high school wrestling with some college and JR wrestling.

US
**PREP POWER POLL.** English. Seven times a year. $20.00. The American Grappler, PO Box 5205, Bloomington IN 47407. **ED** Rick Chitwood (phone: (812)333-4210). **Ad Acc**. **Circ:** 450.
**Desc:** This is a wrestling poll of the top 16 high school wrestlers, printed during each high school wrestling season.

CN/0318-9325
**PRESTO.** Began in 1974?. Multiple languages (French and English). wk. Organizing Committee of the 1976 Olympic Games, PO Box 1976, Montreal Quebec. **DD** 796.4/8. **UDC** 796.032 (714).

US/0360-2125
**PRO BASKETBALL.** English. $1.50. Simon & Schuster Reference Division, One Gulf & Western Plaza, New York NY 10023. **LC** GV882; .P7. **DD** 796.32/364/0973. **UDC** 796.323.071 (73).

US/0732-1902
**PRO FOOTBALL GUIDE.** [Pro footb. guide]. **VFOAT** Sporting News Pro Football Guide. (1982)-. Periodical. English. an. $12.95. Sporting News, c/o Sharon Moore, 1212 North Lindbergh Boulevard, PO Box 56, St Louis MO 63166. **Tel** (314)997-7111, (800)825-8508. **(Subscription address:** Contemporary Books, Two Prudential Plaza, Suite 1200, Chicago IL 60601.**) LC** GV937; .P68. **DD** 796.332/64/0973. **Circ:** 15,000. ***Continues*** *Sporting News' National Football Guide, 0081-3788.*
**Desc:** Complete review of the previous season - every game and every team. Includes club rosters, college draft picks, individual records.

US/1054-0156
**PRO FOOTBALL ILLUSTRATED.** [Pro footb. illus.]. (1965)-. English. an. $2.95. Pro Football Illustrated, 355 Lexington Avenue, New York NY 10017. **DD** 796.

US/1059-4833
**PRO FOOTBALL TODAY.** [Pro footb. today]. Vol. 1, No. 1 (1991)-. Periodical. English. $2.95 (U.S., single issue), $3.50 (Canada, single issue). Spectator Sports, 519 8th Avenue, New York NY 10018. **DD** 796.

US/0032-9053
**PRO FOOTBALL WEEKLY.** (19??)-. Periodical. English. ir (28 issues a year). $54.00. Football World Incorporated, 666 Dundee Road, Suite 1101, Northbrook IL 60062. **Tel** (708)272-1237. **ED** Hub Arkush. **Ad Acc**, **Adv Mgr:** Bob Sherman.
**Desc:** Devoted to professional football.

US/1043-7576
**PRO WRESTLING ILLUSTRATED.** [Pro wrestl. illus.]. (198?)-. Periodical. English. Thirteen times a year. $30.00. London Publishing Company, PO Box 910, Fort Washington PA 19034. **Tel** (215)643-6385, FAX (215)540-0146. **DD** 796. **Ad Acc**.

US/0072-4947
**PROCEEDINGS. Added/Corp** Golf Course Superintendents Association of America. **VFOAT** Conference Proceedings. (19??)-. Periodical. English. an. $30.00. Golf Course Superintendents Association of America, 1421 Research Park Drive, Lawrence KS 66049. **Tel** (913)841-2240, FAX (913)832-4433. **LC** WMLC L 83/2484.

US/0276-7929
**PROCEEDINGS OF THE ... ANNUAL CONFERENCE SOUTHEASTERN ASSOCIATION OF FISH AND WILDLIFE AGENCIES.** [Proc. annu. conf. Southeast. Assoc. Fish Wildl. Agencies]. **Main/Corp** Southeastern Association of Fish and Wildlife Agencies. 30th (Oct. 24-27, 1976)-. English. an. $2.50 (per copy). Southeastern Association of Fish Wildlife Agencies, 7221 Covey Trace, Tallahassee FL 32308. **LC** SK1; .S57. **DD** 333.95/6/0975. ***Continues*** *Southeastern Association of Game and Fish Commissioners. Proceedings.*
**Ind/Abst** Curr. Ref. Fish Res.; Fish Rev.; Key Word Index Wildl. Res.; Life Sci. Collect.; Wildl. Rev.

US/0077-3808
**PROCEEDINGS OF THE ANNUAL CONVENTION OF THE NATIONAL COLLEGIATE ATHLETIC ASSOCIATION (1967).** (PROCEEDINGS OF THE ANNUAL CONVENTION.). **Main/Corp** National Collegiate Athletic Association. **VFOAT** Convention Proceedings; NCAA Convention Proceedings; National Collegiate Athletic Association Convention Proceedings. (1967)-. Proceedings. English. an (Jan.). $12.00. National Collegiate Athletic Association / NCAA, PO Box 7347, Overland Park KS 66207. **Tel** (913)339-1900, FAX (913)339-0030. ***Continues in part*** *National Collegiate Athletic Association. Yearbook.*
**Desc:** Transcripts of all general sessions at the NCAA Convention, summaries of round tables and a roster of delegates and visitors.

UK
**PROCEEDINGS OF THE ... INTERNATIONAL MATADOR CONFERENCE.** Proceedings. Collier McMillan Ltd, Dictionaries Development Division, 12A Golden Square, London W1R 3AF England.

US/0094-4459
**PROCEEDINGS OF THE SPECIAL CONVENTION OF THE NATIONAL COLLEGIATE ATHLETIC ASSOCIATION.** (PROCEEDINGS OF THE SPECIAL CONVENTION.). **Main/Corp** National Collegiate Athletic Association. 1st (Aug. 1973)-. Proceedings. English. ir. $4.00. National Collegiate Athletic Association / NCAA, PO Box 7347, Overland Park KS 66207. **Tel** (913)339-1900, FAX (913)339-0030. **LC** GV563; .N25298. **DD** 796/.06/273. **UDC** 796.42(063)(73). **Bk Rev**. **Ad Acc**. ctrl circ.
**Desc:** The proceedings of the special conventions.

CN/0709-7069
**PROCEEDINGS - SPORT B. C., ANNUAL GENERAL MEETING.** [Proc. - Sport B.C., Annu. Gen. Meet.]. **Main/Corp** Sport B.C. General Meeting. 1978-. Proceedings. English. an. Sport B C, 1200 Hornby Street, Vancouver British Columbia V6Z 2E2 Canada. **DD** 796/.06/0711. **UDC** 796(063)(71). ***Continues*** *B.C. Sports Federation. General Meeting. Proceedings, 0709-7050.*

US/0098-0706
**PROFESSIONAL KARATE.** V. 1- Summer 1973-. English. ir. $4.50. Universal Publications of America, 1880 Century Park East/Suite 325, Oklahoma City CA 90067. **LC** GV476; .P76. **DD** 796.8/153/05. **UDC** 796.853.26.071.

US/8750-9369
**PROFESSIONAL SKATER, THE.** (THE PROFESSIONAL SKATER : A NEWSLETTER OF THE PROFESSIONAL SKATERS GUILD OF AMERICA.). [Prof. skat.]. **VFOAT** PS Magazine; Professional Skaters Magazine. **VAT** Professional Skaters Magazine. (1985)-. Periodical. English. bm. $19.95. Professional Skaters Guild of America, PO Box 5904, Rochester MN 55903. **Tel** (507)281-5122, FAX (507)281-5441. **ED** Carole Shulman. **DD** 796. Index available. cum. index. **Bk Rev**. **Ad Acc**. **Circ:** 1,200 (ctrl). ***Continues*** *Newsletter (Professional Skaters Guild of America), 0273-5571.*
**Desc:** A newsletter of the Professional Skaters Guild of America. The publication brings technical advice, rule changes, trends, and articles of human interest.

US/1065-1314
**PROFESSIONAL SKIER, THE.** [Prof. skier]. **Added/Corp** Professional Ski Instructors of America. United States Ski Coaches Association. (19??)-. Periodical. English. Three times a year (Jan., Sept., Nov.). $20.00 US; $30.00 other. Professional Ski Instructors of America, 133 South Van Gordon Street #101, Lakewood CO 80288. **Tel** (303)987-9390, FAX (303)988-3005. **DD** 796.
**Ind/Abst** Phys. Educ. Index (1990-); SPORT Discus.

US/0095-151X
**PROFILE (LOS ANGELES, CALIF. 1974).** (PROFILE.). [Profile]. **Added/Corp** National Football League. (1974)-. English. $1.95. Dell Publishing / California, 10880 Wilshire Boulevard, Los Angeles CA 90024. **LC** GV955.5.N35; P75. **DD** 796.33/264/0973.
**Ind/Abst** ARTbibliogr. Mod.

CN/0828-5705
**PROGRAMME DES ACTIVITES CULTURELLES ET SPORTIVES.** ***Title Change.*** (CULTURAL AND SPORTS ACTIVITIES PROGRAM.). [Programme act. cult. sport.]. **Main/Corp** Saint-Laurent (Ile-de-Montreal, Quebec). **Added/Corp** Saint-Laurent (Ile-de-Montreal, Quebec). Centre des Loisirs. Sports and Cultural Dept. **VFOAT** Programme des Activites Culturelles et Sportives. Fall/Winter/Spring (1983/84)-(198?). Periodical. English (French). sa. Centre des Loisirs de Saint-Laurent, Sports and Cultural Department, 1870 Decelles Street, Saint Laurent Quebec H4M 1A8 Canada. **DD** 790/.09714/28. ***Continues*** *Saint-Laurent (Ile-de-Montreal, Quebec). Programme des Activites Culturelles et Sportives., 0828-5705.* ***Continued by*** *Leisure and Culture, 1193-3577.*

US/0095-3946
**PROLOG (LOS ANGELES).** (PROLOG.). **Added/Corp** National Football League. (19??)-. English. an. Dell Publishing / California, 10880 Wilshire Boulevard, Los Angeles CA 90024. **LC** GV955.5.N35; O16. **DD** 796.33/264/0973. ***Continues*** *Oates, Bob. Prolog.*

US/0194-6218
**PROPELLER (EAST DETROIT).** (PROPELLER.). **Added/Corp** American Power Boat Association. (19??)-. Periodical. English. mo. $25.00. American Power Boat Association, 17640 East Nine Mile Road, PO Box 377, Detroit MI 48021. **Tel** (313)773-9700, FAX (313)773-6490. **ED** Renee J. Mahn. **Bk Rev**. **Ad Acc**. **Circ:** 9,000.
**Desc:** Update on American Power Boat Association racing news and technical information. Annual photo issue in November.

US/0161-5815
**PRORODEO SPORTS NEWS.** [Prorodeo sports news]. **Added/Corp** Professional Rodeo Cowboys Association (U.S.). **VFOAT** Pro Rodeo Sports News. Vol. 26, No. 11 (Apr. 19, 1978)-. Periodical. English. bw. $24.00 US; $31.00 other. Professional Rodeo Cowboy Association, 101 Pro Rodeo Drive, Colorado Springs CO 80919. **Tel** (719)593-8840, FAX (719)593-8235. **ED** Tim Bergsten. **DD** 791. **Ad Acc**. **Circ:** 28,000. ***Continues*** *Rodeo Sports News.*
**Desc:** Official voice of pro rodeo, with inside information on the world's top rodeo cowboys, a calendar of upcoming pro contests in the United States and Canada, and information on equipment.
**Ind/Abst** SportSearch (May 1987-).

CN/0822-5141
**PROSPECTUS - CONCORDES.** (PROSPECTUS.). [Prospectus - Concordes]. **Main/Corp** Concordes (Equipe de Football). 1983-. French (English). an. Free to the Media. Concordes De Montreal, CP 100, Succursale M, Montreal Quebec H1V 3L6 Canada. **DD** 796.33/56. **UDC** 796.33. ctrl circ.

PL/0137-9267
**PRZEGLAD SPORTOWY.** [Prz. Sport.]. (1921)-. Newspaper. Polish. da. $130.00. **(Subscription address:** ARS Polona, PO Box 1001, 00068 Warsaw Poland.**) UDC** 796.

US/0198-9154
**PSE OUTDOOR ADVENTURES BOWHUNTING ANNUAL.** See Recreation, Leisure-Outdoor Life.

US/1063-1518
**PUCK STOPS HERE!, THE.** (THE PUCK STOPS HERE!: DIE HARD BRUINS FAN MAGAZINE.). [Puck stops here]. (1992)-. Periodical. English. mo. The Puck Stops Here, 386 Riverway, Boston MA 02115. **DD** 796.

US/1050-2173
**QIGONG (SAN FRANCISCO, CALIF.).** (MARTIAL ARTS OF CHINA PRESENTS CH I KUNG.).

[Qigong]. **VFOAT** Chi Kung; Quigong Magazine. Issue 1 (Spring 1991)-. Periodical. English. qt. $19.80. China Direct Publishing, Inc., PO Box 31578, San Francisco CA 94131. **LC** WMLC 91/678. **DD** 613.

CN/0228-6351
**QUEBEC SOCCER.** [Que. soccer]. **VFOAT** Quebec Soccer Magazine. Periodical. French (English). ir. $10.00. Les Promotions Socbec Inc, 3270 Est rue Belanger, Montreal Quebec H2X 1A1 Canada. **DD** 796.334/09714. **UDC** 796.332(714).

US/1062-757X
**R/C MODEL BOATS & RACING.** ***Title Change.*** [R/C model boats racing]. **VFOAT** R/C Model Boats and Racing; Boats & Racing; Boats and Racing. **VAT** Radio Controlled Model Boats & Racing. Vol. 15, No. 4 (June 1992)-. Periodical. English. mo. Challenge Publications Inc., 7950 Deering Avenue, Canoga Park CA 91304. **Tel** (818)887-0550. **DD** 623. ***Formed by the union of*** *Scale Ship Modeler, 0194-780X* ***and*** *R/C Race Boats, 1057-0322.* ***Continued by*** *Scale Ship Modeler (Canoga Park, Calif.), 1066-0275.*

UK
**RACEFORM UP-TO-DATE FORM BOOK.** **See** Horses and Horsemanship.

CN/0380-7762
**RACER (TORONTO).** (THE RACER.). [Racer]. **Added/Corp** Canadian Amateur Speed Skating Association. Vol. 1 Nov. (1965)-. Periodical. English (French). Four times a year (Feb. June, Sept., Dec.). 15.00Can$. Canadian Amateur Speed Skating, 33 River Road, Vanier ONT K1L 8B9 Canada. **Tel** (613)748-5669. **ED** Brenda Gallagher (editor's address: 1600 James Naismith Drive, #804, Gloucester, Ontario K1J8N9, phone: (613)748-5669). **DD** 796.91/062. **Ad Acc, Adv Mgr:** Brenda Gallagher, **Tel** (613)748-5669. **Circ:** 3,500 (ctrl).
**Desc:** Articles and news on speed skating.

●US/1066-6060
**RACER (TUSTIN, CALIF.).** (RACER.). [Racer]. (1992)-. English. mo. $30.00 (1 year), $55.97 (2 year) US; $35.00 (1 year), $63.00 (2 year) other. Racer Communications Incorporated, 1371 East Warner Avenue Suite E, Tustin CA 92680. **Tel** (714)259-8240. **ED** John Zimmermann. **LC** WMLC 91/4937. **DD** 796. **Ad Acc, Adv Mgr:** Donna Chamberlain. **Circ:** 38,500.
**Desc:** Features coverage of American auto racing.

CN/0834-311X
**RACER WEST, THE.** [Racer west]. Vol. 3, No. 1 (Jan./Feb./March 1987)-. Periodical. English. qt. $2.95 per issue. The Racer Magazine, PC Box 1848, Lake Oswego OR 97034. **DD** 796.4/26. **UDC** 796.42. ***Continues*** *Racer (Vancouver, B.C.), 0826-7111.*
**Desc:** A magazine and guide for runners, triathletes and cross-country skiers in northern California, Oregon, Washington, and British Columbia.

AT
**RACETRACK.** (19??)-. Periodical. English. mo. 64.00Aus$ Australia; 123.00Aus$ US & Canada; 130.00Aus$ Europe & Africa; 105.00Aus$ Singapore & Malaysia; 99.00Aus$ New Zealand & Papua New Guinea; 114.00Aus$ Hong Kong, China, Japan, India. Federal Publishing Co Pty Ltd, PO Box 199, 180 Bourke Road, Alexandria New South Wales, 2015 Australia. **Tel** 011 61 2 693 6666, FAX 011 61 2 693 9935. **(Subscription address:** Federal Publishing Co. Pty Ltd., PO Box 199, Alexandria NSW 2015 Australia.**)**

US/1042-9174
**RACING GREYHOUNDS.** **See** Recreation, Leisure-Games and Amusements.

UK/0033-7390
**RACING PIGEON, THE.** Vol. 1 (1898)-. Periodical. English. wk. £34.00 UK; £44.00 other. Racing Pigeon Publishing Company Ltd, Unit 13 21 Wren Street, London WC1X 0HF England. **Tel** 011 44 71 8335959. **ED** Cae Osman. **Bk Rev. Ad Acc. Circ:** 33,000 (ctrl).
**Desc:** Care of, keeping, training, and showing racing pigeons.

US/0146-8383
**RACING PIGEON BULLETIN.** (1946)-. Bulletin. English. wk (50 issues). $30.00 US; $39.00 other. American Racing Pigeon News, 34 East Franklin Street, Bellebrook OH 45305. **Tel** (513 848-4972, FAX (513)848-3012. **ED** Wayne A. Rinke. **Bk Rev. Ad Acc. Circ:** 6,000. ***Absorbed*** *Western Racing Pigeon Bulletin, 0195-3249.* ***Superseded in part by*** *Western Racing Pigeon Bulletin, 0195-3249.*
**Desc:** Serving the social and informational needs of the sport of pigeon racing.

UK/0033-7404
**RACING PIGEON PICTORIAL.** V. 1- (No. 1- ); Jan. 1970-. Periodical. English. mo. £15.20 UK; £17.20 US. Racing Pigeon Publishing Company Ltd, Unit 13 21 Wren Street, London WC1X 0HF England. **Tel** 011 44 71 8335959. **ED** Cae Osman. **UDC** 798.9:656.596. **Bk Rev. Ad Acc. Circ:** 12,000.
**Desc:** Care of, keeping, training and showing racing pigeons.

US/0883-8429
**RACQUET (NEW YORK, N.Y. : 1985).** (RACQUET.). [Racquet]. (Spring 1985)-. Periodical. English. qt. $10.00 US; $13.00 Canada. PO Box 3000, Boulder CO 80303. **DD** 796. ***Continues*** *Racquet Quarterly, 0273-9194.*

CN/0229-7396
**RACQUETBALL CANADA (1981).** (RACQUETBALL CANADA.). Winter 1981-. Periodical. English. qt. $5.00. Harvid Publications, Suite 430, 5180 Queen Mary Road, Montreal Quebec H3W 3E7 Canada. **DD** 796.34. **UDC** 796.346(71). ***Continues*** *Racquetball Canada Bulletin, 0226-0069.*

CN/0381-9493
**RALLY REGULATIONS (WILLOWDALE).** (RALLY REGULATIONS.). **Main/Corp** Canadian Automobile Sport Clubs. 1974/75-. English. Canadian Automobile Sport Clubs, Suite 203, 5385 Yonge Street, Willowdale Ontario M2N 5R7. **DD** 796.7/2/0971. **UDC** 796.71.063(71).

US/0363-7697
**RALLYE.** V. 1- Oct. 1975-. Periodical. English. mo. $10.00. Spectrum IV Corporation, 2880 LBJ Freeway/Suite 243, Dallas TX 75234. **LC** GV1029.2; .R34. **DD** 796.7/2. **UDC** 796.71.09..54(73).

CN/0822-529X
**RALLYE : REGLEMENTS.** [Rallye. Reglem.]. **Main/Corp** Federation Auto-Quebec. French. an. $1.00 each number. Federation Auto-Quebec, 1415 Est rue Jarry, Montreal Quebec H2E 2Z7 Canada. **DD** 796.7/2/09714. **UDC** 796.71.063(714).

AT
**RAMBLING ON.** (19??)-. English. Four times a year. 32.00Aus$ Australia; 55.00Aus$ other. Ramblers Parachute Centre, 15 Wynnua Road, Norman Park QLD 4170 Australia. **Tel** 011 61 7 3996400, FAX 011 61 7 8992863. **ED** Dave McEvoy. **Ad Acc. Circ:** 800 (ctrl).
**Desc:** Skydiving magazine including photos, reviews of competitions, upcoming events, trivia, skydiving stories and more.

●US/1074-6242
**READ-EASY BASKETBALL RULES.** [Read-easy basketb. rules]. **Main/Corp** National Collegiate Athletic Association. **VFOAT** Read Easy Basketball Rules; NCAA Read-Easy Basketball Rules. (1994)-. English. ir. National Collegiate Athletic Association / NCAA, PO Box 7347, Overland Park KS 66207. **Tel** (913)339-1900, FAX (913)339-0030. **LC** GV885.45; .O37. **DD** 796.32/3/02022. ***Continues*** *National Collegiate Athletic Association. Read-Easy Men's and Women's Basketball Rules, 1070-079X.*

US
**READ-EASY FOOTBALL RULES.** **Main/Corp** National Collegiate Athletic Association. **VFOAT** NCAA Read-Easy Football Rules. 21st Annual Ed. (1990)-. English. $1.50. National Collegiate Athletic Association / NCAA, PO Box 7347, Overland Park KS 66207. **Tel** (913)339-1900, FAX (913)339-0030. **LC** GV956.8; .N36c. ***Continues*** *National Collegiate Athletic Association. Official Read-Easy Football Rules.*

US/1070-079X
**READ-EASY MEN'S AND WOMEN'S BASKETBALL RULES.** ***Title Change.*** [Read-easy men's women's basketb. rules]. **Main/Corp** National Collegiate Athletic Association. **VFOAT** Read Easy Men's and Women's Basketball Rules; National Collegiate Athletic Association Men's and Women's Read Easy Basketball rules; Men's and Women's Basketball Rules; NCAA Men's and Women's Read-Easy Basketball Rules. 21st Annual Ed. (1991)-(1993). English. (Aug.). National Collegiate Athletic Association / NCAA, PO Box 7347, Overland Park KS 66207. **Tel** (913)339-1900, FAX (913)339-0030. **LC** GV885.45; .O37. **DD** 796.32/3/02022. ***Continues*** *Official Read-Easy Men's Basketball Rules, 0736-5195.* ***Continued by*** *National Collegiate Athletic Association. Read-Easy Basketball Rules, 1074-6242.*

●CN/1191-3975
**RECORD BOOK / CANADIAN HOCKEY LEAGUE.** [Rec. book - Can. Hockey Leag.]. **Main/Corp** Canadian Hockey League. (1991/1992)-. English. Canadian Hockey League, Jim Price, 305 Milner Avenue, Suite 208, Scarborough Ontario M1B 3V4 Canada. **DD** 796.962/06/071.

US/0364-7153
**RECORDS OF EXOTICS.** V. 1- 1976-. English. T B Temple, Box 181, Mountain Home TX 78058. **LC** SK277; .R42. **DD** 799.2/6/0973. **UDC** 799.2(73).

US/0363-8766
**RECORDS OF SELECTED PLAYERS.** **Main/Corp** United States Tennis Association. English. HO Zimman Inc, Seaport Landing #152, The Lynnway, Lynn MA 01902. **Tel** (617)598-9230. **LC** GV991; .U53A. **DD** 796.34/2/0212. **UDC** 796.342.092.

US
**RECREATIONAL SPORTS DIRECTORY.** (1985)-. Directory. English. an. $27.90. National Intramural Recreational Sports Association, 850 Southwest 15th Street, Corvallis OR 97333. **Tel** (503)737-2088, FAX (503)737-2026. **ED** Will Holsberry. **Ad Acc. Circ:** 1,500. ***Continues*** *NIRSA Directory (National Intramural Recretional Sports Association).*
**Desc:** Lists over 2,500 recreational sports programs and over 7,500 professionals in college/universities and US military installations.

US/1057-9540
**REDS REPORT.** [Reds rep.]. Vol. 1, No. 1 (Feb. 1988)-. Periodical. English. mo. $21.95. Coman Publishing Company, PO Box 2331, Durham NC 27702. **Tel** (919) 688-0218. **DD** 796. **Ad Acc, Adv Mgr:** Jan Cheves. **Circ:** 6,000 (ctrl).

US/0733-1436
**REFEREE (FRANKSVILLE, WIS.).** (REFEREE.). Vol. 1 (1976)-. Periodical. English. mo. $29.95 (one year); $51.95 (two years); $69.95 (three years). Referee Enterprises Inc, PO Box 161, Franksville WI 53126. **Tel** (414)632-8855, FAX (414)632-5460. **ED** Barry Mano, Tom Hammill, Scott Ehret, and Jeff Wilson. **DD** 796. **Bk Rev. Ad Acc. Circ:** 55,000.
**Desc:** Rule interpretations and viewpoints, miscellaneous sports, health and feature stories.
**Ind/Abst** Phys. Educ. Index; SPORT Discus; SportSearch.

UK
**REGATTA.** (19??)-. English. Ten times a year (Dec./Jan. & Aug./Sept. issues combined). £23.00 UK; £26.00 Europe; £32.00 other. Amateur Rowing Association, 6 Lower Mall/Hammersmith, London W6 9DJ England. **Tel** 011 44 81 748 3632, FAX 011 44 81 741 4658. **ED** Christopher Dodd. **Bk Rev. Ad Acc, Adv Mgr:** A. Todd. **Pr Rev. Circ:** 14,000 (ctrl).
**Desc:** Articles, features, letters, calendars, reviews, events and other related articles pertaining to rowing and sailing.

CN/0316-1536
**REGLEMENT OFFICIEL DE JEU POUR LA LIGUE CANADIENNE DE FOOTBALL.** **Main/Corp** Ligue Canadienne de Football. **VFOAT** Reglement Officiel de Jeu du Football Canadien. (1974)-. Periodical. French. an. Free. Ligue Canadienne de Football, Bureau 1800/11 Ouest rue King, Toronto Ontario M5H 1A3 Canada. **DD** 796.33/5/02022. ***Supersedes*** *Reglement Officiel du Jeu pour la Ligue Canadienne de Football et l'Association Canadienne de Football Amateur, 0316-1528.*

CN/0710-4391
**REGLEMENTS OFFICIELS / ASSOCIATION CANADIENNE D'ATHLETISME.** [Reglem. off. - Assoc. can. athl.]. **Main/Corp** Association Canadienne d'Athletisme. **VFOAT** Statuts et Reglements. **VAT** Statuts et Reglements - Association Canadienne d'Athletisme. French. te. Reglements Officeils Association Canadienne d'Athletisme, 355 Chemin River Canada. **DD** 796.4/2/06071. **UDC** 796.42.063(71). ***Continues*** *Association Canadienne d'Athletisme. Manuel Oficiel, Statuts et Reglements, 0381-9701.*

CN/1187-1865
**REGLES DU JEU CANADIENNES POUR LE FOOTBALL AVEC PLAQUE.** [Regles jeu can. footb. plaque]. **Main/Corp** Association Canadienne de Football Amateur. (1990/1991)-. French. Association Canadienne de Football Amateur, 333 Chemin River, Vanier Ontario K1L 8H9 Canada. **DD** 796.335. ***Continues*** *Regles du Jeu Pour Plaquage de Football., 1187-1857.*

SZ
**REGULATIONS / INTERNATIONAL SKATING UNION.** **Main/Corp** International Skating Union. English. be. International Skating Union, Postfach 7270, Davos-Platz Switzerland. **Tel** 083 37577, FAX 083 36671, telex 853123 ISU CH. **LC** GV850.2; .I57A. **DD** 796.91. **UDC** 796.91.063. Index available. **Bk Rev. Circ:** 2,700.

GW/0720-5104
**REITEN UND FAHREN.** ***Ceased.*** (19??)-Vol. 13, No. 6 (1992). German. Six times a year. Blackwell Wissenschafts-Verlag, Kurfuerstendamm 57, D 10707 Berlin Germany. **Tel** 011 49 30 32790623, 011 49 30 32790624, FAX 011 49 30 327 90610. **[CCC]. Bk Rev. Ad Acc.**

BL
**RELATORIO - CONSELHO NACIONAL DE DESPORTOS.** **Main/Corp** Brazil. Conselho Nacional de Desportos. (19??)-. Portuguese. **LC** GV597; .B73b.

CN/0318-2843
**RENDEZ-VOUS 76 MONTREAL.** 1- Aug. 1973-. English (French). Free. Organizing Committee of the 1976 Olympic Games, PO Box 1976, Montreal Quebec. **DD** 796.4/8. **UDC** 796.032(714). ctrl circ.

CN/0828-4725
**RENDEZVOUS & LONGRIFLES.** [Rendezvous longrifles]. **VAT** Rendezvous and

## Recreation, Leisure —Sports

Longrifles. (1981)-. Periodical. English. ir. $10.00 Canada; $12.00 US; $15.00 other. Rendezvous & Longrifles, 1465 Paddington Court, Burlington Ontario L7M 1W7 Canada. **DD** 683.4/2/05.

CM
### REPERTOIRE D'ADRESSES - CONSEIL SUPERIEUR DU SPORT EN AFRIQUE.
**Main/Corp** Supreme Council for Sport in Africa. **VFOAT** Address Directory - Supreme Council for Sport in Africa. English (French). Conseil Superieur du Sport en Afrique, PO Box 1363, Yaounde Cameroon. **LC** GV665; .S9A. **DD** 796/.025/68. **UDC** 696/699(058)(6).

ER
### REPORT - INTERNATIONAL CONGRESS ON PHYSICAL EDUCATION AND SPORTS FOR GIRLS AND WOMEN.
**Main/Corp** International Congress on Physical Education and Sports for Girls and Women. **VFOAT** Expanding Horizons in Physical Education. Periodical. English (German and French). **LC** GV205; .I577. **UDC** 696-055.2(063).

US
### REPORT OF THE ... RACING SEASON / MAINE STATE HARNESS RACING COMMISSION.
**Main/Corp** Maine State Harness Racing Commission. English. an. **LC** SF335.U6; M2. **DD** 338.4/779846/09741. **UDC** 798.4(047)(741). **Continues** Annual Report of the Harness Racing Commission to the Governor of Maine.

GR/0538-8910
### REPORT OF THE ... SUMMER SESSION OF THE INTERNATIONAL OLYMPIC ACADEMY. See Education-Physical Education and Training.

US/0145-8191
### REPORT OF THE VIRGINIA ATHLETIC COMMISSION TO THE GOVERNOR OF VIRGINIA.
**Main/Corp** Virginia. Athletic Commission. English. Fulfillment, PO box 1231, Sisters OR 97759. **LC** GV584.V8; V57A. **DD** 796.4/06/1755. **UDC** 796.42(047)(755).

US/0091-942X
### REPORT - OFFICE OF ATHLETIC COMMISSIONER (LINCOLN). (REPORT.).
**Main/Corp** Nebraska. Office of Athletic Commissioner. English. an. Office of the Athletic Commissioner, Lincoln NE 68508. **LC** GV1116.U5; N43A. **DD** 353.9/782/00858. **UDC** 796.42(047)(782).

US/0276-7627
### REPRESENTING PROFESSIONAL ATHLETES AND TEAMS. See Law.

BL/0101-3289
### REVISTA BRASILEIRA DE CIENCIAS DO ESPORTE. [Rev. Bras. Cienc. Esporte]. (1979)-. Periodical. Portuguese. **UDC** 796/799.
**Ind/Abst** SPORT Discus.

SZ/1018-1008
### REVISTA OLIMPICA. [Rev. olimp.]. (19??)-.
Periodical. Spanish. Ten times a year (Published monthly with 2 double issues). 60.00F. Comite International Olympique, Chateau de Vidy, CH 1007 Lausanne Switzerland. **Tel** 011 41 21 6216111. **UDC** 79.

CN/1187-4627
### REVUE CURLING QUEBEC, LA. [Rev. Curl. Que.] **Added/Corp** Curling Quebec. Vol. 6, No 1 (Oct.1991)-. Periodical. French. Three times a year. Free for members. Curling Quebec, CP1000, Succursale M, Montreal Quebec H1V 3R2 Canada. **DD** 796.9. **Continues** Curling Quebec., 0833-1782.

FR
### REVUE DE L'AEFA. French. Five times a year. 180.00F France; 210.00F other. Amicale des Entraineurs, 10 rue du Faubourg Poissonnier, 75010 Paris France. **Tel** 011 33 1 47263075.
**Ind/Abst** SPORT Discus.

SZ/0251-3498
### REVUE OLYMPIQUE. [Rev. olymp.]. (19??)-.
Periodical. French. Ten times a year (Published monthly with 2 double issues). 60.00F. Comite International Olympique, Chateau de Vidy, CH 1007 Lausanne Switzerland. **Tel** 011 41 21 6216111. **UDC** 79. **Continues** Lettre d'Informations - Comite International Olympique, 1018-3760.
**Ind/Abst** SPORT Discus.

US/0162-3583
### RIFLE. **VFOAT** Rifle Magazine. (19??)-. Periodical. English. bm. $19.00 (1 year), $35.00 (2 year), $50.00 (3 year) US; $25.00 (1 year), $47.00 (2 year), $68.00 (3 year) other. Wolfe Publishing Company, 6471 Airpark Drive, Prescott AZ 86301. **Tel** (602)445-7810. **ED** Tom Greham. **LC** SK274; .R54. **DD** 683.4/22. Index available. cum. index. **Bk Rev**. **Ad Acc**. **Circ:** 25,000 (ctrl).
**Desc:** Designed for hunters, competitors, collectors and handloaders interested in technically-oriented information about centerfire, rimfire, muzzleloading and air rifles.

●US/1059-5759
### RIFLE & SHOTGUN ANNUAL. **VFOAT** Rifle and Shotgun Annual. 1992-. Periodical. English. $3.95. Petersen Publishing Company, 6420 Wilshire Bouldevard, Los Angeles CA 90048. **Tel** (213)782-2485.

UK
### RIFLEMAN. (19??)-. English. Three times a year. £7.00 UK; £10.00 Europe; £12.00 other. National Small-Bore Rifle Association, Lord Roberts House, Bisley Camp, Brkwd Working GU240NP England. **Tel** 011 44 483 476969, FAX 011 44 486 76392, telex 859969 NSRAG. **Ad Acc**. **Circ:** 7,500.
**Desc:** Journal of NSRA, which is the governing body in the UK for smallbore and airweapon shooting.
**Ind/Abst** SPORT Discus.

US/0035-5410
### RING (NEW YORK), THE. (THE RING.). Vol. 1, (Feb. 15, 1922)-. Periodical. English. Thirteen times a year. $30.00. London Publishing Company, PO Box 910, Fort Washington PA 19034. **Tel** (215)643-6385, FAX (215)540-0146. **ED** N.S. Fleischer. **LC** GV1115; .R5. available on microfilm and microfiche from University Microfilms International (UMI).
**Desc:** Covers the sport of boxing.
**Ind/Abst** SportSearch (May 1987-).

GW
### RINGKAMPF. German. mo. DM10.80. Deutscher Ringerverband, Dr. Manasse Strasse 47, D 15370 Petershagen Germany.

IT/0392-9221
### RIVISTA DEL CLUB ALPINO ITALIANO.
**Added/Corp** Club Alpino Italiano. Vol. 98, No. 1/2 (Jan./Febr. 1979)-. Periodical. Italian. bm. L50000.00 Italy; L80000.00 other (includes Lo Scarpone). Club Alpino Italiano, V Pimentel Fonseca 7, 20121 Milan Italy. **Tel** 011 39 2 26141378. **Continues** Rivista Mensile (Club Alpino Italiano : 1946), 0009-9511.

CN/0702-7885
### ROAD & MOTOR SPORT. Began publication in 1965. Periodical. English. mo. 0.25Can$ per no. Road and Motor Sprot Magazine, PO Box 264, Burnaby 1, BC. **DD** 796.7/2/09711. **UDC** 796.7.

US/0739-3784
### ROAD RACE MANAGEMENT. **VFOAT** Road Race Management Newsletter. (19??)-. Periodical. English. mo. $89.00. Road Race Management Inc, 2101 Wilson Blvd, Suite 437, Arlington VA 22201. **Tel** (703)276-0093, FAX (703)979-4960. **ED** Philip B Stewart. **Circ:** 600.
**Desc:** Information and news for organizers of road racing events. Covers organization, medical, legal, and financial issues. Also includes tips for racing directors.
**Ind/Abst** SPORT Discus; SportSearch (May 1987-).

US
### ROAD RACE MANAGEMENT ... GUIDE TO ELITE ATHLETES AND PRIZE MONEY RACES. **Added/Corp** Road Race Management, Inc. **VFOAT** Guide to Elite Athletes and Prize Money Races; Road Race Management Guide. (19??)-. Periodical. English. $48.95 US and Canada, $54.50 other. Road Race Management Inc, 2101 Wilson Blvd, Suite 437, Arlington VA 22201. **Tel** (703)276-0093, FAX (703)979-4960. **LC** GV1061.2; .R63. **DD** 796.4/26.

US
### ROCHESTER GOLF WEEK & SPORTS LEDGER. English. wk. $17.50 US; $25.00 other. George Morgenstern, 2535 Brighton-Henrietta Town Line Road, Rochester NY 14623-2711. **Tel** (716)427-2468. **ED** George Morgenstern. **Bk Rev**. **Ad Acc**. **Circ:** 2,500 (ctrl).
**Desc:** Technical material on all phases of the golf industry.

●US/1060-9563
### RODALE'S SCUBA DIVING. [Rodale's scuba diving]. **VFOAT** Scuba Diving. (June 1992)-. Periodical. English. bm. $14.97. Rodale Press Inc., 400 South 10th Street, Emmaus PA 18098. **Tel** (215)967-5171, (800)666-2503. **DD** 797.

US/0149-6425
### RODEO NEWS. **Added/Corp** International Rodeo Association. (19??)-. Periodical. English. Eleven times a year (Dec/Jan. issues combined). $20.00 one year; $35.00 two years; $47.00 three years. Rodeo News, PO Box 587, Pauls Valley OK 73075, FAX (405)238-3725. **ED** John Cravens (editor's address: 721 North Cedar, Pauls Valley OK 73075, phone: (405)238-3310). **Bk Acc**, **Ad Acc**, **Adv Mgr:** Tom Vietzke.
**Desc:** The total rodeo industry magazine and the voice of the International Pro Rodeo Association.

US
### RODEO TIMES /NATIONAL HIGH SCHOOL RODEO ASSOCIATION. Vol. 1, No. 1 (Sept. 1980)-. English. mo (July/Aug. combined issue). $15.00 US; $18.00 other. National High School Rodeo Association, 11178 North Huron, Suite 7, Denver CO 80234. **Tel** (303)452-0820, FAX (303)452-0912. **ED** Kent L. Sturman. **LC** Discard. **Ad Acc**. ctrl circ.

UK
### ROTHMANS FOOTBALL YEARBOOK. **VFOAT** Football Yearbook. English. £1.20. **LC** GV942; .R68. **DD** 796.33/4/0942. **UDC** 796.332.

US/1043-2345
### ROW (PETALUMA, CALIF.). (ROW.). [Row]. **VFOAT** Row Magazine. Vol. 1, No. 1 (Premier 1989)-. Periodical. English. bm. $24.95. Row Magazine, 4390 Bodega Avenue, Petaluma CA 94952. **Tel** (707)762-6297. **ED** Greg Sabourin. **DD** 797. **Ad Acc**. **Circ:** 35,000.
**Desc:** Covers local, national and international news. Regular columns will feature people, races, rowing events, equipment, medicine, technique.

NE/0926-7638
### RSG. RICHTING SPORT-GERICHT. See Education-Teaching and Curriculum.

FR
### RUGBY. English. Ten times a year. 20.00F France; 58.00F other. Federation Francaise de Rugby, 7 Cite d'Antin, 75009 Paris France.

UK
### RUGBY FOOTBALL LEAGUE OFFICIAL GUIDE. (19??)-. English. an. £9.00. Rugby Football League, 180 Chapeltown Road, Leeds 7 England. **Tel** 011 44 532 624637, FAX 011 44 532 623386.

AT/0035-9742
### RUGBY LEAGUE WEEK. [Rugby leag. week]. **Added/Corp** Australian Consolidated Press. (1970)-. Periodical. English. Thirty-seven times a year. 118.40Aus$ Australia; 128.10Aus$ New Zealand; 210.00Aus$ other. Australian Consolidated Press Ltd, GPO Box 5252, Sydney New South Wales 2001 Australia. **Tel** 011 61 2 2600000. **DD** 796.3330994.
**Ind/Abst** SPORT Discus.

US/0162-1297
### RUGBY (NEW YORK). (RUGBY.). [Rugby]. (1975)-. Periodical. English. mo (except Jan.). $29.00. The Rugby Press Ltd., 2350 Broadway/Suite 220, New York NY 10024. **Tel** (212)787-1160, FAX (212)595-0934. **ED** Ed Hagerty. **DD** 796. **UDC** 796.333. **Bk Rev**. **Ad Acc**. **Circ:** 11,000.
**Desc:** In-depth coverage of US and international rugby plus updates on changes and developments in the game.
**Ind/Abst** SPORT Discus; SportSearch (May 1987-).

UK/0035-9777
### RUGBY WORLD. **Title Change**. Vol. 1 (Oct. 1960)-?. Periodical. English. mo. Reed Business Publishing / West Sussex, England, Perrymount Road, Haywards Heath, West Sussex RH16 3DH England. **Tel** 011 44 81 6523500. **UDC** 796.333. **Continued by** Rugby World & Post.
**Ind/Abst** SportSearch (May 1987-).

UK
### RUGBY WORLD & POST. (Aug. 1985)-. Periodical. English. mo. Rugby Publishing, PO Box 142, Reading RG4 9DX England. **Formed by the union of** Rugby Post; Rugby World, 0035-9777 and Rugby Wales.
**Ind/Abst** SPORT Discus; SportSearch (May 1987-).

CN/0834-2946
### RULE BOOK / CANADIAN VOLLEYBALL ASSOCIATION. [Rule book - Can. Volleyb. Assoc.]. **Main/Corp** Canadian Volleyball Association. **VFOAT** Volleyball Rule Book. (1986/87)-. English. an. Canadian Volleyball Association, 1600 James Naismith Drive, Gloucester Ontario K1B 5N4 Canada. **Tel** 613 748 5681. **DD** 796.32/5. **Continues** Rule Book and Annual / Canadian Volleyball Association, 0831-8794.

US/0278-615X
### RULE BOOK - MIDWEST 4 WHEEL DRIVE ASSOCIATION. (RULE BOOK / MIDWEST 4 WHEEL DRIVE ASSOCIATION.). **Main/Corp** Midwest 4 Wheel Drive Association. **VFOAT** Off-Road Racing Rules and Regulations. **VAT** Rule Book - Midwest Four Wheel Drive Association. (1981)-. English. $2.00. **LC** GV1029.3; .M5a. **DD** 796.7/2.

CN/0710-4383
### RULES AND BY-LAWS / CANADIAN TRACK AND FIELD ASSOCIATION.
**Main/Corp** Canadian Track and Field Association. English. te. Rules and By-Laws, Canadian Track and Field Association, 355 River Road, Vanier Ontario K1L 8C1 Canada. **DD** 796.4/2/06071. **UDC** 796.42.063(71). **Continues** Official C T F A Rules and Bylaws, 0381-9698.

UK
**RULES AND STANDING ORDERS OF THE INTERNATIONAL TENNIS FEDERATION.** **Main/Corp** International Tennis Federation. English. £1.50. International Tennis Federation, Barons Court, West Kensington London W1R 9EG England. **LC** GV991; .I5715. **DD** 796.342/02/022. **UDC** 796.342.063.

CN/0226-773X
**RULES BOOK OF THE FEDERATION OF CANADIAN ARCHERS.** [Rules book Fed. Can. Archers]. **Main/Corp** Federation of Canadian Archers. 1978-. English (French). an. $10.00 Canada; $15.00 other. Federation of Canadian Archers, 1600 James Naismith Drive, Gloucester Ont K1B 5N4 Canada. **Tel** (613)748-5604. **DD** 799.3/2/0971. **UDC** 799.322.063(71). **Circ:** 1,200. ***Continues*** *Rules Booklet of the Federation of Canadian Archers, 0318-4250.*
**Desc:** Shooting rules of archery.

US/0272-3468
**RULES FOR INBOARD, INBOARD ENDURANCE, UNLIMITED RACING.** **See** Boats and Boating.

US/0272-3514
**RULES FOR OUTBOARD PERFORMANCE, CRAFT AND DRAG RACING.** **See** Boats and Boating.

US/0272-3476
**RULES FOR STOCK OUTBOARD, PRO OUTBOARD, MODIFIED OUTBOARD.** **See** Boats and Boating.

US
**RULES OF GOLF AS APPROVED BY THE UNITED STATES GOLF ASSOCIATION AND THE ROYAL AND ANCIENT GOLF CLUB OF ST. ANDREWS, SCOTLAND, THE.** **Added/Corp** United States Golf Association. (19??)-. English. an. $25.00 Comes with United States Golf Association membership. United States Golf Association, Golf House, PO Box 708, Far Hills NJ 07931. **Tel** (201)234-2300. **LC** WMLC L 83/960. **Circ:** 800,000 (ctrl).

●US
**RULES OF GOLF FOR ... AND THE RULES FOR AMATEUR STATUS.** **Main/Corp** United States Golf Association. **VFOAT** Rules of Amateur Status. (1992)-. English. United States Golf Association, Golf House, PO Box 708, Far Hills NJ 07931. **Tel** (201)234-2300. **LC** GV971; .U5c. **DD** 796.352/02/022.

CN/0708-5125
**RULES OF STANDARDBRED RACING.** **See** Horses and Horsemanship.

UK
**RULES OF TENNIS.** **Main/Corp** International Tennis Federation. English. £0.40. International Tennis Federation, Barons Court, West Kensington London W1R 9EG England. **LC** GV1001; .I57A. **DD** 796.342/02/022. **UDC** 796.342.063.

CN/0707-8919
**RULES OF THOROUGHBRED RACING.** **See** Horses and Horsemanship.

US/0272-0353
**RUNNER YEARBOOK, THE.** [Runner yearb.]. 1980-. English. $1.95. New Times Communications Corporation, One Park Avenue, New York NY 10016. **LC** GV1061; .R832. **DD** 796.4/26. **UDC** 796.422(058).

US/0199-6983
**RUNNER'S GAZETTE.** (19??)-. Periodical. English. Twelve times a year. $12.00. Runner's Gazette, 566 Fairfield Road, Lewisburg PA 17837-8830. **Tel** (717)524-9713. **ED** Freddi Carlip. **Bk Rev. Ad Acc. Circ:** 10,000.
**Desc:** Race coverage of running and triathlons, sportsmedicine features, training techniques, book reviews, and calendar listing of upcoming outdoor events.

US/0897-1706
**RUNNER'S WORLD (1987).** (RUNNER'S WORLD.). [Runn. world]. **VFOAT** Runner's World. Vol. 22, No. 6 (June 1987)-. Periodical. English. Twelve times a year. $24.00 US; $50.00 other. Rodale Press Inc., 400 South 10th Street, Emmaus PA 18098. **Tel** (215)967-5171, (800)666-2503. **ED** Chuck McCullagh. **LC** GV1061; .R8336. **DD** 796.42/05. **Ad Acc. Circ:** 420,000. available on microfilm and microfiche from University Microfilms International (UMI). Documents available from UMI Article Clearinghouse. ***Continues*** *Rodale's Runner's World, 0892-3744.*
**Desc:** A running magazine containing profiles on running personalities, coverage of major races, medical and training advice, diet and nutritional information.
**Ind/Abst** Abr. Read. Guide Period. Lit.; Acad. Abstr. Full Text Elite (Jan. 1984-) [Full Txt.]; Acad. Abstr. (Jan. 1984-); Acad. Ind. [Computer File] (1984-1988); Acad. Search (Jan. 1984-); Expand. Acad. Index (1984-1988); Health Index (1989-); Health Period. Database [Full Txt.]; Health Ref. Cent. (Jan. 1989-) [Full Txt.] [Full Cov.]; Health Source (Jan. 1984-) [Full Txt.]; INFO-SOUTH Abstr.; Mag. Artic. Summar. Elite (Jan. 1984-) [Full Txt.]; Mag. Artic. Summar. Select (Jan. 1984-) [Full Txt.]; Mag. Artic. Summar. CD-ROM (Jan. 1984-); Mag. ASAP Plus [Full Txt.]; Mag. ASAP Sel. [Full Txt.]; Mag. Index Plus (1989-); Mag. Index. Sel. (1986-); Mag. Search; Newsp. Period. Abstr. (1988-); Phys. Educ. Index; Read. Guide Abstr. Select Ed.; Read. Guide Period. Lit. (June 1987-); Resource/One Ondisc (1988-); SPORT Discus; SportSearch; Mag. Index (June 1987-); Vocat. Search (Jan. 1984-) [Full Txt.].

UK
**RUNNING.** English. mo. £25.40 UK; £29.20 Europe; £55.00 other. Stonehart Leisure Magazines, Unit 1 Hainault Road, Little Heath Romford RM6 5NP England. **Tel** 011-44-81-597-7335, FAX 011-44-81-599-5965. **ED** Nick Troop. **Bk Rev. Ad Acc. Circ:** 50,731.
**Desc:** Features for the recreational and serious runner. Athletic news and competition reports, interviews with top runners, how to run faster, recover from injury, and where to race.
**Ind/Abst** SPORT Discus.

US/0898-5162
**RUNNING & FITNEWS.** **See** Health and Personal Fitness.

US/0892-5038
**RUNNING JOURNAL.** [Runn. j.]. **Added/Corp** Carolina Runner, Inc. Vol. 3, No. 6 (Jan./Feb. 1987)-. Periodical. English. Twelve times a year. $22.00 one year; $39.00 two year. Running Journal, PO Box 157, Greenville TN 37744. **Tel** (615)638-4177, FAX (615)638-3328. **ED** Mary Lou Day. **DD** 796. **Ad Acc, Adv Mgr:** M.L. Day, **Tel** same as publisher. **Circ:** 11,000. ***Continues*** *Carolina Runner, 0883-1629;* ***Absorbed*** *Racing South Magazine, 8750-507X* ***and*** *Running in Georgia.*
**Desc:** Contains a comprehensive race calendar of events and results of races in the Southeast. Features columns by coaches and runners on running, walking, and fitness. Also has coverage of racewalking, multi-sport events, ultra-running, wheelchair racing and the Grand Prix Circuit.

US/0887-7033
**RUNNING RESEARCH NEWS.** [Runn. res. news]. (198?)-. Periodical. English. Six times a year (Jan., Mar., May, July, Sept., Nov.). $17.00 (one year); $31.00 (two years); $45.00 (three years). Running Research News, PO Box 27041, Lansing MI 48909. **Tel** (517)393-3150. **ED** Owen Anderson. **DD** 617. Index available ($10.00). cum. index. **Bk Rev. Circ:** 3,500 (ctrl).
**Desc:** Summarizes important new scientific research concerning training for endurance athletics-running, cycling, swimming, etc. Also provides candid evaluations of commercial products sold to athletes.

US/0147-2968
**RUNNING TIMES.** [Run. Times]. No. 1 (Jan. 1977)-. Periodical. English. mo. $25.00 (one year), $46.00 (two year), $64.00 (three year). Fitness Publishing, 98 North Washington Street, Boston MA 02114. **Tel** (617)367-2350. **(Subscription address:** PO Box 511, Mt. Morris, IL 61054; Tel: 1-800-877-5402**) ED** Ed Ayres. **LC** GV1061; .R84. **DD** 796.4/26. **Bk Rev. Ad Acc. Circ:** 41,000.
**Desc:** Offers runners training advice, nutrition and sports medicine tips and a calendar of upcoming events. Features present general-interest and sophisticated information on running, health and fitness, cross training, and worldwide coverage of running events and personalities; also latest information on new products and apparel.
**Ind/Abst** SportSearch (May 1987-).

●US/1067-5094
**RUNNING WILD.** [Run. wild]. **VFOAT** RW. (199?)-. Periodical. English. bm. $18.00 US. Running Wild, 494 North Avenue, Weston MA 02193. **Tel** (617)899-9896, FAX (617)899-9896. **DD** 796.
**Desc:** The trailrunner's magazine providing information on the outdoors, the environment, and running.

US/0746-1585
**SACRAMENTO SPORTS.** **VFOAT** Sports Magazine; Sacramento Sports Magazine. Periodical. English. mo. $8.95. Anpac Publishing Inc, 2414 16th Street, Sacramento CA 95818. **UDC** 796/799(794). ***Continues*** *Sacramento Sports News & Calendar Magazine, 0745-1156.*

US/0199-5316
**SAFARI (TUCSON, ARIZ.).** (SAFARI.). [Safari]. **Added/Corp** Safari Club International. **VFOAT** Safari Magazine. (19??)-. Periodical. English. Six times a year (Jan., Mar., May, July, Sept., Nov.). $30.00. Safari Club International, 4800 West Gates Pass Road, Tucson AZ 85745. **Tel** (602)620-1220, FAX (602)622-1205, telex 880149. **ED** William R. Quimby. **LC** SK1; .S23. **DD** 799.2/6/05. **Bk Rev**, (Qty: 25). **Ad Acc, Adv Mgr:** Eric Hubbell, **Tel** (602)620-1220. **Pr Rev. Circ:** 18,000 (ctrl).
**Desc:** Journal of big game hunting. Dedicated to wildlife and habitat conservation, endangered species, and protection of hunters.

US/0886-9626
**SAIL BOARDER INTERNATIONAL.** ***Ceased.*** **VFOAT** Sail Boarder Magazine. (1983)-(1986). Periodical. English. bm. Surfer Publications Inc., PO Box 1028, Dana Point CA 92629. **Tel** (714)496-5922, (800)289-0636, FAX (714)496-7849. **DD** 797. ***Continues*** *Sail Boarder, 0744-1886.*
**Ind/Abst** SportSearch (May 1987-).

AT/0817-2773
**SAILBOARD EXTRA.** [Sailboard extra]. (1985)-. English. mo. 18.00Aus$ Australia; 60.00Aus$ other. Publicity Press Pty Ltd, 252 Bay Street, Port Melbourne 3207 Australia. **Tel** 011 61 03 6466788. **DD** 797.1240994.
**Ind/Abst** SPORT Discus.

US/1063-8180
**SAILBOARD RETAILER.** [Sailboard retail.]. **Added/Corp** American Windsurfing Industries Association. National Sailboard Retailers & Instructors. (19??)-. Trade Publication. English. Eight times a year. $20.00 (1 year), $40.00 (2 year) US; $28.00 Canada and Mexico; $38.00 other. Gorge Publishing, PO Box 918, Hood River OR 97031. **Tel** (503)386-7440, FAX (503)386-7480. **ED** Carol York. **DD** 338. **Bk Rev. Ad Acc, Adv Mgr:** Marie Cordell. **Circ:** 3,500.
**Desc:** The only trade magazine for the windsurfing industry. Includes business tips and industry and product news.

JA
**SAKKA MAGAJIN.** (19??)-. Periodical. Japanese. wk. $378.00. **(Subscription address:** Maruzen Company Ltd., PO Box 5050, Import & Export Department, Tokyo 100 31 Japan.)

US/0036-3618
**SALT WATER SPORTSMAN.** [Salt water sportsman]. (19??)-. Periodical. English. mo. $24.95 (one year), $38.95 (two year), $49.95 (three year). Times Mirror Magazines, Two Park Avenue, New York NY 10016. **Tel** (212)779-5000. **(Subscription address:** CDS / SIFD Agency Control, 1901 Bell Avenue, Des Moines IA 50315.**) ED** C. M. Cunningham, Barry Gibson. **Ad Acc. Circ:** 122,095. available on microfilm and microfiche from University Microfilms International (UMI).
**Desc:** Aimed at the serious saltwater sport fisherman interested in improving his skills. Keeps you abreast of trends in tackle and technique, and in proper management of marine finfish resources.
**Ind/Abst** Consum. Index Prod. Eval. Inf. Source.

FI/0355-0656
**SAMMANFATTNING AV ARTIKLARNA.** (SUOMEN RIISTA.). [Suom. riista]. **Added/Corp** Suomen Riistanhoito-Saatio. (1946)-. Finnish (summaries and/or abstracts in English). ir. $4.00. Academic Bookstore Akateeminen, Postilokero 23, FIN-00371 Helsinki Finland. **Tel** 011 358 0 12141. **(Subscription address:** Bookstore Tiedekirja, Kirkkokatu 14, SF 00170 Helsinki Finland.**) LC** SK1; .S88.
**Ind/Abst** Key Word Index Wildl. Res.; Life Sci. Collect.

US/0193-7332
**SAN DIEGO SPORTS DIGEST.** (197?)-. Periodical. English. Twelve times a year. $9.00 (one year); $15.00 (two years). San Diego Sports Digest, 3681 Fifth Avenue, San Diego CA 92103. **Tel** (714)295-1120.

FR
**SANTE ET SPORTS.** (19??)-. French. ir (6 issues). 130.00F. Sante et Sports, 123 rue Saint Maur, 75011 Paris, France. **Tel** 43 57 90 03.

US/0899-9066
**SCARLET & GRAY ILLUSTRATED.** **VFOAT** Scarlet and Gray Illustrated. (1987)-. Periodical. English. ir (32 issues per year). $53.00. Sports Communications Inc / Ohio, 6025 Frantz Road, Dublin OH 43017. **Tel** (614)766-9801.

GW
**SCHACH MAGAZIN 64 SCHACH ECHO.** German. mo. Eilers & Schuenemann Verlag, Postfach 106067, D 2800 Bremen Germany. **Tel** 011 49 421 3690347, FAX 011 49 421 3690339, telex 841 244397. ***Formed by the union of*** *Schach Echo, 0036-5831* ***and*** *Schach Magazin 64.*

CN/0842-0947
**SCHEDULE & RULE BOOK - NATIONAL HOCKEY LEAGUE.** (SCHEDULE & RULE BOOK.). [Sched. rule book - Natl. Hockey Leag.]. **Main/Corp** National Hockey League. **VFOAT** Official Schedule; Official Rule Book; Schedule and Rule Book. **VAT** Schedule and Rule Book - National Hockey League. (198?)-. English. an. 3.50Can$. National Hockey League, 1155 Metcalf Suite 960, Montreal Quebec H3B 2W2 Canada. **Tel** (514)871-9220. **DD** 796.9/62/05. ***Continues*** *Official Rule Book of the National Hockey League, 0316-831X.*

US/0160-1253
**SCHIESSPORTSCHULE DIALOGUES.** 1-. Periodical. English. $6.00. Reliable Productions Inc, PO Box 865, Mesa AZ 85201. **LC** GV1151; .S33. **DD** 799.2/05. **UDC** 799.3.

US/0036-6382
**SCHOLASTIC COACH.** ***Title Change.*** [Scholast. coach]. **Added/Corp** Sportsmanship Brotherhood (New York, N.Y.). **VFOAT** Coach. (Sept. 1931)-(1994). Periodical. English. Ten times a year (monthly Aug.-May). Scholastic Inc., 2931 East McCarty Street, PO Box 3710, Jefferson City MO 65102-9957. **Tel** (314)636-5271, (800)631-1586. **ED** Herman L. Masin. **LC** GV561; .S3. **DD** 796. **Bk Rev. Ad Acc. Circ:** 37,000 (ctrl). available on microfilm and microfiche from University Microfilms International (UMI). Documents available from UMI Article Clearinghouse. ***Absorbed*** *Athletic Journal, 0004-6655* ***and*** *Coach & Athlete, 0009-9872.* ***Continued by*** *Scholastic Coach and Athletic Director, 1077-5625.*
**Desc:** Professional journal for high school, college, and recreational athletic directors and coaches. Features technical articles, editorials, and other helpful materials for target audience.
**Ind/Abst** Acad. Ind. [Computer File] (1987-); Biogr. Index; Educ. Index; Expand. Acad. Index (1987-); Mag. Search; Newsp. Period. Abstr. (1989-); Phys. Educ. Index; SPORT Discus; SportSearch.

●US/1077-5625
**SCHOLASTIC COACH AND ATHLETIC DIRECTOR.** [Scholast. coach athl. dir.]. **VFOAT** Scholastic Coach. Vol. 64, No. 1 (Aug. 1994)-. Periodical. English. Ten times a year. $23.95. Scholastic Inc., 2931 East McCarty Street, PO Box 3710, Jefferson City MO 65102-9957. **Tel** (314)636-5271, (800)631-1586. **(Subscription address:** Neodata / Colorado, PO Box 2606, Boulder Boulder CO 80322.**)** **DD** 796. **Bk Rev. Ad Acc. Circ:** 37,000 (ctrl). ***Continues*** *Scholastic Coach, 0036-6382.*
**Desc:** Professional journal for high school, college, and recreational athletic directors and coaches. Features technical articles, editorials, and other helpful materials for target audience.
**Ind/Abst** Acad. Ind. [Computer File]; Biogr. Index; Educ. Index; Expand. Acad. Index; Mag. Search; Newsp. Period. Abstr.; Phys. Educ. Index; SPORT Discus; SportSearch.

GW
**SCHWALBE.** (SCHWALBE / DEUTSCHE VEREINIGUNG FUER PROBLEMSCHACH.). (19??)-. Periodical. German. bm (Feb., Apr., June, Aug., Oct., Dec.). DM40.00. Achim Schoneberg, Paul Hindemith Str. 58, D-37574 Einbeck Germany. **Tel** 011 49 5561 4727. Index available (free).

SZ/0253-4878
**SCHWEIZER WAFFEN-MAGAZIN.** ***Title Change.*** **See** Military and Defense.

US/0195-7538
**SCI RECORD BOOK OF TROPHY ANIMALS, THE.** **See** Recreation, Leisure-Outdoor Life.

IT
**SCIARE.** (19??)-. Italian. Eleven times a year. L60000 Italy; L80000 Europe; L105000 other. DMK Ed, Via Boscovich 14, 20124 Milan Italy. **Tel** 011 39 2 66984827.

SW/1012-0602
**SCIENTIFIC JOURNAL OF ORIENTEERING.** [Sci. j. orienteer.]. (1985)-. Periodical. English. sa. Kr70.00. International Orienteering Federation, Secretary General, PO Box 76, S 191 21 Sollentuna Sweden. **ED** Dr. Roland Seiler Biberweg 6, D-5000 Koln 40, Germany. **UDC** 796.422.
**Ind/Abst** SPORT Discus.

CN/0711-3226
**SCORE (TORONTO).** (SCORE : CANADA'S GOLF MAGAZINE.). [Score]. No. 1 (Apr./May 1981)-. Periodical. English. Five times a year (May, June/July, Aug./Sept., and Oct.). $11.68 (one year), $23.36 (two year), $35.05 (three year). Control Media Communication, 287 Macpherson Avenue, Toronto ONT M4V 1A4 Canada. **Tel** (416)928-2909, FAX (416)966-1181. **ED** Bob Weeks. **DD** 796.352/0971. **Bk Rev**, (Qty: 2-4). **Ad Acc, Adv Mgr:** Peter Simpson. **Circ:** 140,000 (ctrl). Documents available.

US/1055-8608
**SCOREBOARD (OWINGS MILLS, MD. NORTHWEST ED.).** (SCOREBOARD : THE SPORTS AND RECREATION WEEKLY.). [Scoreboard]. **VFOAT** Scoreboard Northwest; Scoreboard NW. Vol. 1, No. 1 (Mar. 29, 1991)-. Periodical. English. wk. $40.00. Scoreboard Northwest, PO Box 303, Owings Mills MD 21117. **DD** 796.

US/0743-1309
**SCOUTING REPORT, THE.** (THE SCOUTING REPORT : AN IN-DEPTH ANALYSIS OF THE STRENGTHS AND WEAKNESSES OF EVERY ACTIVE MAJOR LEAGUE BASEBALL PLAYER.). 1st Ed. (1983)-. English. an. $16.00. Harper Collins Publishers, Keystone Industrial Park, Scranton PA 18512. **Tel** (800)242-7737, (800)233-4727, FAX (800)822-4090. **LC** GV877; .S392. **DD** 796.357/092/2.
**Desc:** An assessment of the strengths and weaknesses of all major league baseball players.

AT/0729-5529
**SCUBA DIVER.** [Scuba diver]. (1981)-. Periodical. English. bm (6 issues). 28.50Aus$ Australia; 82.00Aus$ other. Yaffa Publishing Group Pty Ltd., GPO Box 606, Sydney NSW 2001 Australia. **Tel** 011 61 2 2812333, FAX 011 61 2 2812750. **DD** 797.23.
**Ind/Abst** SPORT Discus.

US/0739-568X
**SCUBA TIMES.** [Scuba times]. (1980)-. Periodical. English. Six times a year. $15.00 (one year), $26.00 (two year), $37.00 (three year). Scuba Times, PO Box 40702, Nashville TN 37204. **Tel** (800)950-7282.
**Desc:** Comprehensive equipment reviews, travel articles, advanced diving and environmental topics.

IT
**SCUOLA DELLO SPORT : RIVISTA DI CULTURA SPORTIVA.** (19??)-. Italian. qt. L16000.00. Coni, SDS/V Campi Sportivi 48, 00197 Rome Italy. **Tel** 011 39 6 36851.

IT
**SCUOLA DELLO SPORT RIVISTA DI CULTURA SPORTIVA.** Italian. qt. L16000.00. Coni, SDS/V Campi Sportivi 48, 00197 Rome Italy. **Tel** 011 39 6 36851.
**Ind/Abst** SPORT Discus.

US/0883-6817
**SCWDC.** (SCWDC / SKI CLUB OF WASHINGTON, D.C.). **Added/Corp** Ski Club of Washington, D.C. **VAT** Ski Club of Washington, D.C. (19??)-. Periodical. English. mo. Ski Club of Washington DC (SCWDC), 5309 Lee Highway, Arlington VA 22207.

US/0829-3279
**SEA KAYAKER.** **See** Boats and Boating.

US/0746-8601
**SEA (LOS ANGELES, CALIF.).** **See** Boats and Boating.

US/0885-9078
**SEC REPORT.** **VAT** Southeastern Conference Report. Periodical. English. ir. Sec Report Inc, PO Box 59238, Birmingham AL 35259. **Tel** (205)871-8398. **UDC** 796.32/.33(75). **Bk Rev. Ad Acc. Circ:** 20,000 (ctrl). ***Continues*** *Southsports, 8750-667X.*
**Desc:** Complete coverage of all Southeastern conference sports (football, basketball, features, recruiting and commentaries).

CN/0822-7853
**SECURITAIRE.** (LE SECURITAIRE / REGIE DE LA SECURITE DANS LES SPORTS.). [Securitaire]. **Added/Corp** Quebec (Province). Regie de la Securite dans les Sports. Service des Communications et de la Recherche. Vol. 1, No. 1 (Dec. 1983)-. Periodical. French. Four times a year. Free on request. Regie de la Securite dans les Sports du Quebec, 100 rue Laviolette, Bureau 114, Trois Rivieres Quebec G9A 5S9 Canada. **Tel** (819)376-6371, (800)567-7902. **DD** 796/.06/9. **Circ:** 12,000 (ctrl).
**Ind/Abst** SPORT Discus.

CN/0226-8728
**SELECTION DE PRESSE / CLUB MULTI-SPORTS INTERNATIONAL DE MONTREAL.** [Sel. presse - Club multi-sports int. Montr.]. **VFOAT** Selection de Presse (Quotidiens et Hebdomadaires). May 1979/June 1980-. French. an. Club Multi-Sports International de Montreal, CP 1976 Succursale St Michel, Montreal Quebec H2A 2M3 Canada. **DD** 796/.09714. **UDC** 796/799(714).

CU
**SEMANARIO DEPORTIVO LPV.** **VAT** Semanario Deportivo Listos Para Vencer. Spanish. $0.15 single issue. Inder, Apartado 5104, La Habana Cuba. **LC** GV592.C9; S45.

CN/0380-3082
**SERVO LOISIR.** ***Title Change.*** V. 1- Jan. 1972-. Periodical. French. bm. Conseil Regional Des Loisirs De Quebec, Bureau 300, 917 Rue Mgr Grandin, Ste-Foy Quebec G1V 3X8. **DD** 790/.09714/47. **UDC** 379.8(714). ***Continued by*** *Informo Loisir, 0380-3090.*

US/1059-4310
**SETON HALL JOURNAL OF SPORT LAW.** **See** Law.

US/0085-6592
**SFI BULLETIN.** **Added/Corp** Sport Fishing Institute. **VFOAT** Sport Fishing Institute Bulletin; S.F.I. Bulletin. **VAT** Sport Fishing Institute Bulletin. No. 101 (April 1960)-. Bulletin. English. Ten times a year (Jan./Feb. & Nov./Dec. issues combined). Free. Sport Fishing Institute, 1010 Massachusetts Avenue Northwest, Suite 320, Washington DC 20001. **Tel** (202)898-0770. **ED** Gilbert Radonski. **LC** IN PROCESS. **Bk Rev. Circ:** 15,000. Documents available from Documents on Demand. ***Continues*** *Bulletin - Sport Fishing Institute, 0097-0492.*
**Ind/Abst** Environ. Abstr.

YE
**SHABAB WA-AL-RIYADAH (MAJLIS AL-ALA LIL-SHABAB WA-LA-RIYADAH (YEMEN). ALAQAT WA-AL-ILAM).** (AL-SHABAB WA-AL-RIYADAH / TUSDIRUHA AL-ALAQAT WA-AL-ILAM BI-AL-MAJLIS AL-ALA LIL-SHABAB WA-AL-RIYADAH.). **VFOAT** Majallat Al-Shabab Wa-Al-Riyadah. Periodical. Arabic. Shari Al-Matar, Sana Yemen. **LC** GV663.Y46; S52.

TI
**SHABAB WA-AL-RIYADAH (TUNIS, TUNISIA).** (AL-SHABAB WA-AL-RIYADAH.). Periodical. Arabic. qt. $2.00 Single Issue. Jamiat Al-Duwal, Al-Arabiyah 37 Nahj Khayr Al-Din Basha, 1002 Tunis Tunisia. **LC** GV664; .S52.

MR
**SHABAB WADI AL-DHAHAB.** **VFOAT** Jeunesse Oued Eddahab. Periodical. Arabic (French). 5.00 Single Issue. 3 Zanqat Al-Duktur Jiyur, RAQM 30, Al-Dar Al-Bayda Morocco. **LC** HQ799.M8; S5.

US/0745-1245
**SHARING THE VICTORY.** (SHARING THE VICTORY : PUBLICATION OF THE FELLOWSHIP OF CHRISTIAN ATHLETES.). **Added/Corp** Fellowship of Christian Athletes. Vol. 1, No. 1 (Sept./Oct. 1982)-. Periodical. English. Nine times a year. $18.00 US and Canada; $36.00 other. Fellowship of Christian Athletes, 8701 Leeds Road, Kansas City MO 64129. **Tel** (816)921-0909, (800)289-0909. **ED** John Dodderidge. **Bk Rev. Ad Acc, Adv Mgr:** John Dodderidge, **Tel** (816)921-0909. **Circ:** 55,000. ***Formed by the union of*** *Christian Athlete, 0744-0227* ***and*** *Widening Circle.*
**Desc:** Presents to athletes and coaches, and all whom they influence, the challenge and adventure of receiving Jesus Christ as Saviour and Lord.

US/0080-9365
**SHOOTER'S BIBLE, THE.** [Shoot. bible]. No. 44 (1953)-. English. an. $21.95 US; $30.95 other. Stoeger Publishing Company, 55 Ruta Court, South Hackensack NJ 07606. **Tel** (201)440-2700, telex 134511. **ED** William S. Jarrett. **DD** 799. Index available. **Bk Rev.** ***Continues*** *Stoeger's Catalog and Handbook.*
**Desc:** Complete listing along with specifications and retail prices of all currently manufactured firearms.

US/0037-4148
**SHOOTING INDUSTRY, THE.** [Shoot. ind.]. (19??)-. Periodical. English. mo. $25.00 (one year), $45.00 (two year), $60.00 (three year). Publishers Development Corporation, 591 Camino de La Reina, Suite 200, San Diego CA 92108. **Tel** (619)297-5350, FAX (619)297-5353, telex 695-478. **ED** Jerome Rakusan and John Mack. Index available. **Bk Rev. Ad Acc. Circ:** 23,000 (ctrl). available on microfilm from University Microfilms International (UMI); available on an online database (file 648/Full-Text) from DIALOG.
**Desc:** A business publication for federal firearms license holders actively involved in the sale of firearms and related equipment.
**Ind/Abst** Bus. ASAP (1990-) [Full Txt.]; Bus. Index (1985-); Gen. BusinessFile (1985-); Trade Ind. ASAP [Full Txt.]; Trade Ind. Index (1981-) [Full Txt.].

US/0887-9397
**SHOOTING SPORTS RETAILER.** **See** Business-Retail.

US/1069-6822
**SHOOTING SPORTS USA.** [Shoot. sports USA]. **Added/Corp** National Rifle Association of America. (198?)-. Periodical. English. Twelve times a year. $15.00. National Rifle Association of America, 11250 Waples Mill Road, Fairfax VA 22030-9100. **Tel** (703)267-1560, (703)267-1583, (800)231-4672, FAX (703)267-3994. **DD** 799. ***Continues*** *NRA Tournament News.*

US/0038-8084
**SHOOTING TIMES.** [Shoot. times]. (March 1960)-. Periodical. English. Twelve times a year. $21.98 US; $29.98 other. PJS Publications Inc., News Plaza, PO Box 1790, Peoria IL 61656. **Tel** (309)682-6626, FAX (309)682-7394. **(Subscription address:** CDS Agency Hard Copy, PO Box 4966, Des Moines IA 50340.**)** **LC** GV1151; .S5. **Ad Acc, Adv Mgr:** Ken Ramage.
**Desc:** Information on firearms, ammunition, accessories, outerwear, and hunting and camping gear.
**Ind/Abst** Consum. Index Prod. Eval. Inf. Source.

US/0049-0415
**SHOTGUN NEWS.** (19??)-. Periodical. English. ir (3 times per month). $20.00 US; $100.00 other. Shotgun News, PO Box 669, Hastings NE 68901. **Tel** (402)463-4589, FAX (402)463-3893.

US/0744-3773
**SHOTGUN SPORTS.** [Shotgun sports]. Vol. 4, No. 1 (Feb. 1982)-. Periodical. English. mo (10 issues per year). $26.00. Shotgun Sports Magazine, PO Box 6810, Auburn CA 95604. **Tel** (916)889-2220. **DD** 799. ***Continues*** *Shootin' Trap, 0194-665X.*

CN/0712-5801
**SHUTTLE.** (THE SHUTTLE : NEWSLETTER OF THE SASKATCHEWAN BADMINTON ASSOCIATION.). [Shuttle]. **Added/Corp** Saskatchewan Badminton Association. (Feb. 1982)-. Newsletter. English. ir. Free to Members. Saskatchewan Badminton Association, 2205 Victoria Avenue, Regina Saskatchewan S4P 0S4 Canada. **DD** 796.34/5/097124. ***Continues*** *Saskatchewan Badminton Association. Newsletter, 0227-6704.*

AU
**SICHERHEIT IM BERGLAND. See** Recreation, Leisure-Outdoor Life.

US
**SIDELINE VIEW.** English. ir. $5.00. Institute for Athletic Medicine, 9750 Rockford Road, Plymouth MN 55441. **Tel** (612)371-6697.
**Ind/Abst** SPORT Discus.

US
**SIDELINES.** ***Ceased.*** (19??)-(Oct. 1990). English. SportsMedia Inc, 701 South 37th Street, Suite 9, Birmingham AL 35222. **Tel** (205)324-0460, FAX (205)324-4947. **ED** Ben Cook and Lyn Scarbrough. **Ad Acc. Circ:** 21,046.
**Desc:** In depth coverage of personalities, events and issues relating to deep south sports.

US/0037-6132
**SKATING. Added/Corp** United States Figure Skating Association. Vol. 1 (Dec. 1923)-. Periodical. English. mo (except Aug. and Sept.). $25.00. US Figure Skating Association, 20 First Street, Colorado Springs CO 80906. **Tel** (719)635-5200. **ED** Jay Miller. **LC** GV849.A1; S5. **Ad Acc, Adv Mgr:** Luann Duda, **Tel** (719)635-5200. **Circ:** 38,000 (ctrl).
**Desc:** Includes coverage of all major US figure-skating competitions and coverage from international correspondents of foreign and world championships, along with interviews, profiles and regular features of interest to figure skaters, including sports medicine, choreography, club management and music.
**Ind/Abst** SPORT Discus; SportSearch (May 1987-).

US/0037-6140
**SKEET SHOOTING REVIEW. Added/Corp** National Skeet Shooting Association. (1947)-. Periodical. English. mo. $15.00. National Skeet Shooting Association, PO Box 680007, San Antonio TX 78268. **Tel** (210)688-3371. **LC** GV1181; .N298. **DD** 799.3/13/05. **Ad Acc, Adv Mgr:** Susie Fluckiger, **Tel** (800)US-SKEET.
**Desc:** Official publication of the National Skeet Shooting Association.
**Ind/Abst** SPORT Discus; SportSearch (May 1987-).

US/0745-8517
**SKEETER, THE.** [Skeeter]. Periodical. English. bm. The Skeeter, PO Box 11789, Fresno CA 93775-1789. **DD** 799. **UDC** 799.312.54.

US/0037-6175
**SKI AREA MANAGEMENT.** [Ski area manage.]. **Added/Corp** National Ski Areas Association. (19??)-. Periodical. English. Six times a year. $26.00. Beardsley Publishing Corporation, PO Box 644, Woodbury CT 06798. **Tel** (203)263-0888. **ED** David Rowan. **LC** GV854.A1; S48. **DD** 796.93/068. **Ad Acc. Circ:** 4,000 (ctrl).
**Desc:** Edited for the North American Ski Resort Industry. Published bimonthly, it covers technical engineering data lifts, snowmaking, oversnow vehicles; also market and research data; plus material on the many component disciplines involved, such as the rental shop, the ski school, the touring operation etc.
**Ind/Abst** Leis. Recreat. Tour. Abstr.; SPORT Discus; SportSearch (May 1987-).

US/0037-6191
**SKI BUSINESS.** ***Title Change.*** [Ski bus.]. (19??)-(19??). Trade Publication. English. Six times a year. NYT Sports Leisure Magazine, 5520 Park Avenue, Trumball CT 06611. **Tel** (203)373-7249. **ED** Glenn Heitsmith. **DD** 338. **Ad Acc. Circ:** 14,871. ***Continued by*** *Snow Country Business.*
**Desc:** Business-to-business publication aimed at ski retailers.
**Ind/Abst** SportSearch (May 1987-).

CN/0702-701X
**SKI CANADA.** [Ski Can.]. **VFOAT** Sun Sports. Vol. 5, No. 1 (Oct. 1976)-. Periodical. English. Seven times a year. 16.45Can$ Canada; 26.45Can$ other. Solstice Publishing Inc., 19 Albany Avenue, Toronto Ontario M5R 3C2 Canada. **Tel** (416)368-0607. **(Subscription address:** Indas, 35 Riviera Drive, Building 17, Markham Ontario L3R 8N4 Canada.**) ED** Clive Hobson. **DD** 796.9/3/05. **Ad Acc. Circ:** 51,000. ***Continues*** *Ski Canada Journal, 0316-2648.*
**Desc:** Covers alpine skiing in Canada and abroad. Features ski travel and resort reviews, reports on racing, new gear and equipment, ski fashion, ski trips and more.
**Ind/Abst** Can. Index; Can. Period. Index (19??-); SPORT Discus.

CN/0229-1940
**SKI INDUSTRY BULLETIN.** [Ski ind. bull.]. **VFOAT** Bulletin de l'Industrie du Ski. Bulletin. English (French). ir. Free. National Ski Industries Association, 306A Youville Sq., Montreal Quebec H2Y 2B6. **DD** 338.4/779693/0971. **UDC** 338.46:796.92. ctrl circ.

US/0197-3479
**SKI INDUSTRY LETTER, THE.** (19??)-. Periodical. English. Fifty-two times a year. $296.00. Ski Letter Inc., 115 Lilly Pond Lane, Katonah NY 10536. **Tel** (914)232-5094, FAX (914)232-4499. **ED** Greg Berry (editor's address: 1550 Sherman, Suite 102, Denver, CO 80203, phone: (303)863-7865). **Bk Rev**, (Qty: 5-10). available on an online database; available via fax.
**Desc:** News and information about skiing business.

CN/0714-8267
**SKI NAUTIQUE NEWS.** [Ski naut. news]. **Added/Corp** Canadian Water Ski Association. (Feb. 1982)-. Periodical. English. Three times a year. Free on request. Canada Water Ski Association, 1600 James Naismitt Drive, Gloucester Ontario K1B 5N4, Canada. **Tel** (613)748-5683, FAX (613)748-5867, telex 053-3660. **ED** Margaret McGregor and Dan Wolfenden. **DD** 797.1/73/0971. Index available. **Bk Rev. Ad Acc. Circ:** 3,000 (ctrl). ***Continues*** *Ski Canada Nautique, 0315-3665.*
**Desc:** Promotional and educational content on water skiing activities.

US/0037-6159
**SKI (NEW YORK, N.Y.).** (SKI.). [Ski]. **VFOAT** Ski Magazine. (Nov. 1, 1948)-. Periodical. English. Eight times a year. $11.94 (one year), $22.97 (two year), $32.97 (three year). Times Mirror Magazines, Two Park Avenue, New York NY 10016. **Tel** (212)779-5000. **(Subscription address:** Neodata / Colorado, PO Box 2606, Boulder Boulder CO 80322.**) LC** GV854; .A1S57. **DD** 796.93/05. **Ad Acc.** available on microfilm and microfiche from University Microfilms International (UMI). Documents available from UMI Article Clearinghouse. ***Absorbed*** *Ski Life;* ***Formed by the union of*** *Ski News (National Ski Association of America); Western Skiing; Ski Sheet* ***and*** *Ski Illustrated.*
**Desc:** The how-to magazine of skiing for all skiers.
**Ind/Abst** Acad. Abstr. Full Text Elite (Oct. 1984-June 1989); Acad. Abstr. (Oct. 1984-June 1989); Acad. Search (Oct. 1984-June 1989); Consum. Index Prod. Eval. Inf. Source; INFO-SOUTH Abstr.; Mag. Artic. Summar. Elite (July 1994-); Mag. Artic. Summar. Select (Jan. 1984-June 1989); Mag. Artic. Summar. CD-ROM (Oct. 1984-June 1989); Mag. Search; Newsp. Period. Abstr. (1988-); Phys. Educ. Index; SPORT Discus.

US/0890-6076
**SKI PATROL MAGAZINE. See** Public Health and Safety.

CN/0703-2056
**SKI QUEBEC (SAINT-LAURENT).** (SKI QUEBEC.). (1974)-. Periodical. French. Six times a year. Gouvernement du Quebec, 600 St Amable 4E Etage, Quebec Quebec G1R 4Z1 Canada. **DD** 796.9/3/05.

US/0037-6213
**SKI RACING.** (1968)-. Periodical. English. Twenty times a year. $19.95 US; $30.00 Canada; $80.00 others. Ski Racing International, PO Box 1125, Waitsfield VT 05673. **Tel** (802)496-7700, FAX (802)496-7704. **ED** Tim Etchells. **Bk Rev**, (Qty: 1-5). **Ad Acc, Adv Mgr:** Phil Knaub. **Circ:** 25,000.
**Desc:** Provides comprehensive race information, race techniques and conditioning secrets, and up-to-date coverage of World Cup, pro, collegiate, Jr. and club competition.
**Ind/Abst** SportSearch (May 1987-).

US/0091-1461
**SKI RACING REDBOOK.** English. an. $1.00. Paper House, Inc., 1801 York Street, Denver CO 80206. **LC** GV854.9.R3; S57. **DD** 796.9/3. **UDC** 796.92.

US/0195-5640
**SKI RUN.** Periodical. English. bm. Free. Ski Run, 115 Mission Street, San Francisco CA 94112. **UDC** 796.92.

US/1058-3246
**SKI TECH.** [Ski tech]. (1986)-. Periodical. English. mo. $16.00. Ski Tech, Box 9042, Braintree MA 02184. **DD** 796.
**Ind/Abst** SPORT Discus.

CN/0710-0523
**SKI TRAILS (VANCOUVER, B.C. : CA. 1978).** (SKI TRAILS.). [Ski trails]. Periodical. English. mo. $.50 each number. Raipub Enterprises, 726 Richards, Vancouver British Columbia V6B 3L2 Canada. **DD** 796.93/09711. **UDC** 796.92(711). ***Continues*** *Ski Trails West, 0381-8675.*

US/0161-1054
**SKI X-C. VFOAT** Ski XC. **VAT** Ski Cross-Country. (1978/79)-. English. sa. $3.95. Rodale Press Inc., 400 South 10th Street, Emmaus PA 18098. **Tel** (215)967-5171, (800)666-2503. **LC** GV855; .S55. **DD** 796.93. **UDC** 796.92.

US/0195-1300
**SKIERS ADVOCATE.** ***Title Change.*** [Skiers advocate]. Periodical. English. Five times a year. American Ski Association, 155 South Madison Street, Denver CO 80209. **Tel** (303)399-9924. **ED** Carolyn A Martin. **DD** 796. **UDC** 796.92. **Circ:** 194,388. ***Continued by*** *American Skier, 1055-0615.*

UK
**SKIER'S HOLIDAY GUIDE.** English. £1.20. Ski Specialists, 4 Douro Place, London W8 5PH England. **LC** GV854.8.E9; S5. **DD** 796.9/3/0254. **UDC** 796.92(036).

●US
**SKIING FOR WOMEN.** (1994)-. English. an. Times Mirror Magazines, Two Park Avenue, New York NY 10016. **Tel** (212)779-5000. **LC** GV854.34; .S52. **DD** 796.93/05.

US/0037-6264
**SKIING (NEW YORK, N.Y.).** (SKIING.). [Skiing]. Vol. 11, No. 1 (Oct. 1958)-. Periodical. English. Seven times a year. $11.94 (one year), $22.97 (two year), $32.97 (three year). Times Mirror Magazines, Two Park Avenue, New York NY 10016. **Tel** (212)779-5000. **(Subscription address:** Neodata / Colorado, PO Box 2606, Boulder Boulder CO 80322.**) ED** Bill Grout. **LC** GV854.A1; S63. **DD** 796.93/05. **Ad Acc.** available on microfilm and microfiche from University Microfilms International (UMI); available on an online database (files 149,647/Full-Text) from DIALOG. Documents available from UMI Article Clearinghouse, Magazine Collection. ***Continues*** *National Skiing.*
**Desc:** Brings you in-depth profiles on ski resorts. Contains tips on purchasing equipment, the latest in ski fashions and accessories, and fast ways to get in shape for the season. Also contains advice on improving your techniques on the slopes.
**Ind/Abst** Acad. Abstr. Full Text Elite (Jan. 1984-) [Full Txt.]; Acad. Abstr. (Jan. 1984-); Acad. Ind. [Computer File] (1984-); Acad. Search (Jan. 1984-); Consum. Index Prod. Eval. Inf. Source; Expand. Acad. Index (1984-); Gen. Period. Index (1985-); Health Source (Jan. 1984-); INFO-SOUTH Abstr.; Mag. Artic. Summar. Elite (Jan. 1984-) [Full Txt.]; Mag. Artic. Summar. Select (Jan. 1984-); Mag. Artic. Summar. CD-ROM (Jan. 1984-); Mag. Express (1988-) [Full Txt.]; Mag. Index Plus (1989-); Mag. Index. Sel. (1986-); Mag. Search; Newsp. Period. Abstr. (1988-); Read. Guide Abstr. Select Ed.; Read. Guide Period. Lit.; Resource/One Ondisc; SPORT Discus; Mag. Index (1977-); TOM Gen. Index (1985-); Vocat. Search (Jan. 1984-).

US/0037-6299
**SKIING TRADE NEWS.** ***Title Change.*** [Ski. trade news]. **VFOAT** STN, Skiing Trade News; STN. Vol. 1 (Sept. 1964)-. Periodical. English. bm. Diamandis Communications Inc, 1499 Monrovia Avenue, New Port Beach CA 92663. **Tel** (714)720-5300. **LC** GV854.A1; S67. **DD** 796.9/3/05. available on microfilm from University Microfilms International (UMI); available on an online database (file 648/Full-Text) from DIALOG. ***Supersedes*** *Wintersports.* ***Continued by*** *STN, 1061-4524.*
**Ind/Abst** Acad. Search (Jan. 1994-); Bus. Index (1985-1989); Gen. BusinessFile (1985-1989); Gen. Period. Index (1989-1992); Mag. Search.

US/0037-6345
**SKIN DIVER.** [Skin diver]. **VFOAT** Skin Diver Magazine. Vol. 1 (Dec. 1951)-. Periodical. English. mo. $21.94 US; $36.32 canada; $34.94 other. Petersen Publishing Company, 6420 Wilshire Bouldevard, Los Angeles CA 90048. **Tel** (213)782-2485. **(Subscription address:** Neodata / Colorado, PO Box 2606, Boulder Boulder CO 80322.**) ED** Bill Gleason. **LC** SH458; .S5. Index available. **Bk Rev. Ad Acc. Circ:** 211,724 (ctrl). available on microfilm and microfiche from University Microfilms International (UMI); available on an online database (file 647/Full-Text) from DIALOG. Documents available from UMI Article Clearinghouse.
**Desc:** Magazine for skin and scuba diving. It showcases the most spectacular dive spots, and offers helpful advice on scuba techniques, wreck exploration, and travel. Every issue also includes underwater photography, safety and medicine features, and worldwide coverage of dive resorts and live-aboards.
**Ind/Abst** Acad. Search (July 1993-); Calif. Period. Index (19??-); Consum. Index Prod. Eval. Inf. Source; Gen. Period. Index (1985-); Health Source (Jul. 1993-); INFO-SOUTH Abstr.; Mag. Index Plus (1989-); Mag. Search; Newsp. Period. Abstr. (1988-); SportSearch; Mag. Index (1977-)(1959-).

US/1050-7078
**SKYBOX (CINCINNATI, OHIO).** (SKYBOX : INSIDE THE SPORTS BUSINESS.). [Skybox]. **VFOAT** Sky Box. Vol. 1, No. 1 (1990)-. Periodical. English. Four times a year (Jan., March, July, Oct.). $19.95 (one year), $34.95 (two year), $45.95 (three year) US; $28.95 (one year), $52.95 (two year), $72.95 (three year) Canada. Dorsey Publishing, 1328 Elam Avenue, Cincinnati OH 45225. **Tel** (513)541-0269, FAX (513)541-0057. **DD** 338.

US/0192-7361
**SKYDIVING.** [Skydiving]. Vol. 1, (1979)-. Periodical. English. Twelve times a year. $22.00 US; $32.00 others. Skydiving Book Service, 1725 North Lexington Avenue, Deland FL 32724. **Tel** (904)736-4793, FAX (904)736-9786. **DD** 797. Index available. cum. index ($5.00). **Bk Rev. Ad Acc. Circ:** 8,700 (ctrl).
**Desc:** Both national and international news magazine

that covers the techniques, equipment, places, events and people of parachuting.
**Ind/Abst** SPORT Discus.

AT/0313-363X
**SKYSAILOR.** [Skysailor]. (1975)-. Periodical. English. ir. **DD** _a797.550994. ***Continues*** *Journal of T.A.S.S.A., 0311-5186.*
**Ind/Abst** SPORT Discus.

●US/1072-625X
**SLAM (NEW YORK, N.Y.).** (SLAM.). [Slam]. (1994)-. Periodical. English. bm. $14.97. Harris Publications, 1115 Broadway/8th Floor, New York NY 10010. **Tel** (212)807-7100. **DD** 796.

US/0149-3620
**SLO PITCH.** V. 1- Mar./Apr. 1978-. Periodical. English. ir. SLO Pitch Magazine, 7120 Hayvenhurst Avenue, Suite 214, Van Nuys CA 91406. **UDC** 796.357.4.

AT
**SMALLBORE AUSTRALIA.** English. bm. 6.00Aus$. Australian Smallbore Rifle Association, Box C13, Clarence Street, Sydney NSW 2000 Australia. **Tel** 02 492489.
**Ind/Abst** SPORT Discus.

US/1046-0403
**SNOW BOARDER.** [Snow board.]. **VFOAT** Snowboarder Magazine; Snowboarder. Vol. 1, No. 1 (Winter 1988)-. Periodical. English. Seven times a year. $13.95 US. Surfer Publications Inc., PO Box 1028, Dana Point CA 92629. **Tel** (714)496-5922, (800)289-0636, FAX (714)496-7849. **DD** 796.
**Desc:** Provides features and photos for snowboarding enthusiasts. Each issues provides technique and equipment tips and equipment reviews, as well as profiles of ski areas that allow snowboarding.

US/0896-758X
**SNOW COUNTRY.** [Snow ctry.]. (March 1988)-. Periodical. English. Eight times a year. $13.97. Golf Digest- Tennis Inc., 5520 Park Avenue, Trumbull CT 06611. **Tel** (203)373-7256, FAX (203)371-2102. **(Subscription address:** CDS Agency Hard Copy, PO Box 4966, Des Moines IA 50340.**)** **ED** John Fry. **LC** GV191.4; .S66. **DD** 796.5/0973. Index available. **Ad Acc, Adv Mgr:** Tom Brown, **Tel** (212)789-3090. **Circ:** 225,000 (ctrl).
**Desc:** Tells readers locations for skiing, mountain climbing, golf, tennis, backpacking, whitewater rafting, biking, hang gliding, etc.

US
**SNOW COUNTRY BUSINESS.** (19??)-. Periodical. English. Six times a year. $30.00. NYT Sports Leisure Magazine, 5520 Park Avenue, Trumball CT 06611. **Tel** (203)373-7249. ***Continues*** *Ski Business, 0037-6191.*

CN/0711-6454
**SNOW-GOER.** (SNOW-GOER : THE MAGAZINE OF CANADIAN SNOWMOBILING.). [Snow-goer]. Vol. 1, No. 1 (Winter 1981)-. Periodical. English. Four times a year. $5.99. Camar Publications Ltd., 130 Spy Court, Markham Ontario L3R 5H6 Canada. **Tel** (416)475-8440, FAX (416)475-9246. **DD** 796.94/0971.

US/0191-8095
**SNOW GOER.** (19??)-. Periodical. English. mo. $10.97. Ehlert Publishing Group, 601 Lakeshore Parkway, Suite 600, Minnetonka MN 55305. **Tel** (612)476-2200.
**Desc:** Magazine geared to in-season snowmobilers.

US/1056-4209
**SNOW GOER (WAYZATA, MINN.).** (SNOW GOER.). **VFOAT** Snowgoer. 1st Ed. (Dec. 1990)-. Periodical. English. Four times a year. $10.97. Ehlert Publishing Group, 601 Lakeshore Parkway, Suite 600, Minnetonka MN 55305. **Tel** (612)476-2200. **(Subscription address:** Kable Publishers Aide, 308 East Hitt Street, Subscription Department, Mt. Morris IL 61054-1473.**)** **LC** WMLC 93/3381. **DD** 796.

CN/0833-2010
**SNOWMAN NEWS.** [Snoman news]. Vol. 1, No. 1; Oct. 1985-. Periodical. English. mo. Free to members. Snowmobilers of Manitoba, PO Box 1577, Winnipeg Manitoba R3C 2Z4 Canada. **DD** 796.94/097127. ***Continues*** *Snoman, 0712-256X.*

US
**SNOWMOBILE & ATV SPORTS.** English. Formula Publications Ltd, 447 Speers Road, Suite 4, Oakville ONT L6K 3S7 Canada. **Tel** (905)842-6591, FAX (905)842-6843.

CN/0700-3315
**SNOWMOBILE ANNUAL.** 1974/75-. English. an. Formula Publications Ltd, 447 Speers Road, Suite 4, Oakville ONT L6K 3S7 Canada. **Tel** (905)842-6591, FAX (905)842-6843. **DD** 796.9. **UDC** 796.97(058). **Ad Acc.** ctrl circ. ***Supersedes*** *Snowmobile, 0700-3307.*

US/0274-8363
**SNOWMOBILE (MILWAUKEE).** (SNOWMOBILE.). Vol. 1 (Aug./Sept. 1980)-. Periodical. English. qt. $11.00. Ehlert Publishing Group, 601 Lakeshore Parkway, Suite 600, Minnetonka MN 55305. **Tel** (612)476-2200. **(Subscription address:** Kable Publishers Aide, 308 East Hitt Street, Subscription Department, Mt. Morris IL 61054-1473.**)** ***Formed by the union of*** *Snotrack, 0049-0822* ***and*** *Midwest Snowmobiler, 0195-1203.*
**Desc:** Primarly for the snowmobile-owning households.

US/0163-4070
**SOCCER AMERICA.** Vol. 2, No. 10 (Mar. 7, 1972)-. Periodical. English. Fifty times a year. $46.94 (US); $65.00 (other). Soccer America Weekly, PO Box 23704, Oakland CA 94623-0704. **Tel** (510)528-5000, FAX (510)528-5177. **ED** Lynn Berling-Manuel. **Bk Rev. Ad Acc. Circ:** 18,000. available on microfilm and microfiche from University Microfilms International (UMI). ***Supersedes*** *Soccer West.*
**Desc:** Edited for the soccer enthusiast; covers MISL, outdoor pro, college, amateur and international games. Includes stories, features, statistics, playing and coaching tips and much more.
**Ind/Abst** SportSearch (May 1987-).

CN/0227-1834
**SOCCER CANADA.** [Soccer Can.]. **Added/Corp** Canadian Soccer Association. **VAT** Soccer (Toronto). (Apr. 1980)-. Periodical. English. Eight times a year. 20.00Can$ Canada; 30.00Can$ other. Canadian Soccer Association, 1600 James Naismith Drive, Gloucester Ontario K1B 5N4 Canada. **Tel** (613)747-2900. **DD** 796.334/0971. ***Continues*** *Canadian Soccer News, 0319-4469.*

US/0149-2365
**SOCCER DIGEST (EVANSTON).** (SOCCER DIGEST.). (1978)-. Periodical. English. bm (6 issues). $22.00 US; $30.00 other. Century Publishing Company, 990 Grove Street, Evanston IL 60201-4370. **Tel** (708)491-6440, (800)321-3333, FAX (708)491-0459. **(Subscription address:** Kable Publishers Aide, 308 East Hitt Street, Subscriptions Department, Mt. Morris, IL 61054**)** **ED** Michael Herbert. **LC** GV942; .S552. **DD** 796.334/05. **Bk Rev. Ad Acc. Circ:** 60,000. available on microfilm and microfiche from University Microfilms International (UMI).
**Desc:** Covers indoor, outdoor and world cup soccer.

CN/0710-2577
**SOCCER ILLUSTRATED (TORONTO).** (SOCCER ILLUSTRATED.). [Soccer illus.]. Vol. 1, No. 9 (Nov. 1980)-. Periodical. English. mo. $30.18. Soccer Illustrated, 69 Belgrave Avenue, Toronto Ontario M5M 3S9 Canada. **DD** 796.334/0971. **UDC** 796.332(71). ***Continues*** *Soccer in Canada, 0710-2585.*

US/1053-4199
**SOCCER INTERNATIONAL.** [Soccer intern.]. (1990)-. Periodical. English. Twelve times a year. $19.94 (one year); $36.94 (two years); $52.94 (three years). Soccer International, PO Box 1060, Newton PA 18940. **ED** Grahaule Jones. **DD** 796. **Ad Acc, Adv Mgr:** P. Herbison. **Circ:** 40,000.
**Desc:** Dedicated to covering soccer around the world. Stunning photography, revealing graphics and incisive comment capture the color of the world's greatest game.

US/0560-3617
**SOCCER JOURNAL. Added/Corp** National Soccer Coaches Association of America. (19??)-. Periodical. English. bm (Jan., Mar., May, July, Sept., Nov.). $50.00 US and Canada; $70.00 Europe; $80.00 other. National Soccer Coaches Association of America, West Gym SUNY Binghamton, Binghamton NY 13901. **Tel** (607)777-2133, (607)248-0213, FAX (607)777-4597. **ED** Tim Schum. **Bk Rev. Ad Acc, Adv Mgr:** Lee & Associates, **Tel** (800)364-0426. **Circ:** 10,000 (ctrl).
**Desc:** Information about and for soccer coaches. Contains technical pieces on soccer coaching plus information also on activities of the NSCAA.
**Ind/Abst** Phys. Educ. Index; SPORT Discus; SportSearch (May 1987-).

●US/1060-9911
**SOCCER JR.** **See** Children and Youth Interests.

●US/1070-9754
**SOCCER MAGAZINE (TITUSVILLE, FLA.).** (SOCCER MAGAZINE.). (1993)-. Periodical. English. Nine times a year. $17.95. Patch Publishing, 5211 South Washington Avenue, Titusville FL 32780. **Tel** (407)268-5010, FAX (407)267-7216. **Ad Acc.**
**Desc:** Each issue features full color coverage of the top tournaments, international news, youth and women's development, amateur and professional leagues, plus instructional columns on coaching, nutrition and training tips and special sections on World Cup.

US/0744-964X
**SOCCER MATCH.** [Soccer match]. (19??)-. Periodical. English (Spanish). sm. Soccer Match, 302 South Brand Boulevard/Suite 1, Glendale CA 91204. **Tel** (818)242-9959. **Ad Acc.** ctrl circ.
**Desc:** Covers youth and pro-level soccer.

US/0731-9541
**SOCCER RULE BOOK.** ***Title Change.*** [Soccer rule book]. **Main/Corp** National Federation of State High School Associations. (1979/1980)-(1993). English. an. National Federation of State High School Associations, 11724 Northwest Plaza Circle, PO Box 20626, Kansas City MO 64195-0626. **Tel** (816)464-5400, FAX (816)464-5571. **LC** GV943.4; .N37a. **DD** 796.334/02/022. ***Continues*** *National Federation of State High School Associations. Soccer Rules, 0163-4763.* ***Continued by*** *National Federation of State High School Associations. Soccer Rules (1993/1994), 1072-0170.*

●US/1072-0170
**SOCCER RULES.** [Soccer rules]. **Main/Corp** National Federation of State High School Associations. (1993/1994)-. English. National Federation of State High School Associations, 11724 Northwest Plaza Circle, PO Box 20626, Kansas City MO 64195-0626. **Tel** (816)464-5400, FAX (816)464-5571. **LC** GV943.4; .N37a. **DD** 796.334/02/022. ***Continues*** *National Federation of State High School Associations. Soccer Rule Book, 0731-9541.*

US/0882-9632
**SOCCER TEXAS.** Vol. 1, No. 1 (Mar. 1985)-. Periodical. English. mo. $3.00. Texas Sports Marketing, 13650 Rolling Hill, Dallas TX 75240. **UDC** 796.332(764).

US/0098-8707
**SOCCER WORLD. VFOAT** Soccer World Magazine. Began in 1974. Periodical. English. mo. $7.50. Runner's World Magazine Company, 1400 Stierlin Road, Mountain View CA 94042. **LC** GV942; .S57. **DD** 796.334/05. **UDC** 796.332. available on microfilm and microfiche from University Microfilms International (UMI).

US/0741-1235
**SOCIOLOGY OF SPORT JOURNAL.** [Sociol. sport j.]. Vol. 1, No. 1 (1984)-. Periodical. English. qt (mar., June, Sept., Dec.). $36.00 (individual), $80.00 (institution) US; $40.00 (individual), $84.00 (institution) other. Human Kinetics Publishers Inc, 1607 North Market Street, PO Box 5076, Champaign IL 61825-5076. **Tel** (217)351-5076, FAX (217)351-2674. **ED** Cynthia A. Hasbrook. **DD** 306. Index available (Included in Dec. issue). **Bk Rev. Ad Acc. Circ:** 490. Documents available from The Genuine Article.
**Desc:** Focuses on the relationship between sport, society, and social institutions from the perspectives of social psychology, sociology, and anthropology. Its purpose is to communicate research, critical thought, and theory development toward understanding sport related behavior or social organization.
**Ind/Abst** Arts Humanit. Citation Index [Select. Cov.]; Curr. Contents Soc. Behav. Sci.; Leis. Recreat. Tour. Abstr.; Phys. Educ. Index; Res. Alert [Full Cov.]; Soc. Plann. Policy Dev. Abstr.; Soc. Sci. Cit. Index [Full Cov.]; Sociol. Abstr. (1984-) [Full Cov.]; SPORT Discus; SportSearch (May 1987-).

AT
**SOUTH AUSTRALIAN ANGLER.** (19??)-. English. Six times a year. 20.00Aus$ (institutions), 23.50Aus$ (individuals). South Australian Angler, 8 Lysander Crescent / N Haven, South Australia 5018 Australia. **Tel** 08 341-8938, 08 381 5384, FAX 08 248-5180. **ED** Shane Mensforth and Greg Irving. Index available. cum. index. **Ad Acc, Adv Mgr:** S. Mensforth. **Circ:** 4,500.
**Desc:** Covers fishing and boating.

US/0194-8911
**SOUTH FLORIDA SPORTSCENE MAGAZINE. VFOAT** SportScene Magazine. **VAT** South Florida Sport Scene Magazine. Vol. 1 (June 1979)-. Periodical. English. mo. RPM Publishing, PO Box 7916, La Verne CA 91750.

US
**SOUTHEAST DRAGSTER : AN NHRA PUBLICATION. Added/Corp** National Hot Rod Association. Southeast Division. (198?)-. Periodical. English. mo. National Dragster, 2035 Financial Way, Glendora CA 91740. **Tel** (818)914-4761. **LC** WMLC L 83/7488. **Ad Acc, Adv Mgr:** Scott Lowden.
**Desc:** For those interested in the sport of drag racing in the southeast region. Devoted mainly to photo and journalistic coverage of NHRA sanctioned racing events at tracks in Southern states. Other coverage includes racer and other industry-related personality interviews and new product news.

US/0146-8251
**SOUTHERN GOLF.** (197?)-. Periodical. English. bm. $9.00 (one year), $20.00 (three year) US; $20.00 (one year), $40.00 (three year) other. Brantwood Publications Inc, 3023 Eastland Boulevard/Suite 103, Clearwater FL 34621. **Tel** (813)796-3877, FAX (813)791-4126. **LC** GV975; .S65. **DD** 338.4/7/7963520975. ***Continues*** *Southern Golf Course Operations for the Bermudagrass Belt, 0145-4196;* ***Absorbed*** *Southern Landscape & Turf, 8755-2256.*

US/1043-6375
**SOUTHERN LINKS (HILTON HEAD ISLAND, S.C.).** ***Title Change.*** (SOUTHERN LINKS.). (1988)-(199?). Periodical. English. bm. Southern Links, PO Box 7628, Hilton Head Island SC 29938. **Tel** (803)842-6200, FAX (803)842-6233. **ED** Mark Brown. **DD** 796. **Ad Acc, Adv Mgr Tel** (203)977-8600. **Circ:** 170,000. ***Continued by*** *Links Magazine.*

# Recreation, Leisure —Sports

US/0049-1616
**SOUTHERN MOTORACING.** See Transportation-Automobiles.

US/0199-3372
**SOUTHERN OUTDOORS (MONTGOMERY).** See Recreation, Leisure-Outdoor Life.

●US/1065-4763
**SPALDING BOOK OF RULES AND ... SPORTS ALMANAC.** (1992)-. English. $14.95. Masters Press, 2647 Waterfront Parkway East, Suite 300, Indianapolis IN 46214.

IT
**SPAZIO SPORT.** Coni Spazio Sport, Via Leopoldo Franchetti 2, 00194 Rome Italy. **Tel** 011 39 6 36857418.

US/0747-5403
**SPEEDWAY SCENE.** [Speedw. scene]. (19??)-. Periodical. English. wk. $35.00. Speedway Scene, Box 300, North Easton MA 02356-0300. **Tel** (508)238-7016, FAX (508)230-2381. **ED** Val Le Sieur. **DD** 796. **Bk Rev**. **Ad Acc**. **Circ**: 46,000.
**Desc**: The most comprehensive auto racing coverage, including Winston Cup, World of Outlaws, ASA and other top racing organizations.

US/8755-741X
**SPITBALL.** See Literature.

US/0898-8951
**SPLASH (ANAHEIM, CALIF.).** (SPLASH.). (1987)-. Periodical. English. Twelve times a year. $19.95 (one year), $36.95 (two years). McMullen Publishing Inc, 2145 West La Palma Avenue, PO Box 70015, Anaheim CA 92801-1785. **Tel** (714)572-2255, FAX (714)572-1864. **DD** 797.
**Ind/Abst** Annu. Bibliogr. Engl. Lang. Lit.; Geogr. Abstr. Phys. Geogr.; Int. Dev. Abstr.; Rural Dev. Abstr.; Soils Fert.; World Agric. Econ.

US
**SPLASH / WORLD WATERPARK ASSOCIATION.** **Added/Corp** World Waterpark Association. **VFOAT** News Splash. (May-June 1985)-. Periodical. English. ir (9 issues). $45.00. World Waterpark Association, PO Box 14826, Lenexa KS 66214. **Tel** (913)362-9440, FAX (913)599-0520. **Continues** News Splash.
**Desc**: Covers aquatic sports and sports facilities.

TU
**SPOR FAALIYETLERI VE TESISLERI.** **VFOAT** Sports Activities and Facilities. (1982)-. English (Turkish). **LC** HA1911; .A3 subser; GV661.

TU
**SPOR KULUPLERI.** See Societies and Clubs.

AU
**SPORT.** German (German). **LC** GV607; .S58.

BE
**SPORT.** (19??)-. Newsletter. Dutch. bm. Free on request. Bloso, Kolonienstraat 31, B-1000 Brussels, Belgium. **Tel** 02 510 34 11, FAX 02 510 35 05. **Circ**: 1,000.

UK
**SPORT.** (19??)-. Periodical. English. bm (6 issues). £20.00 UK & EIRE; £35.00 other. The Sports Council, 16 Upper Wolburn Place, London WC1H 0QP England. **Tel** 011 44 71 388-1277, FAX 011 44 71 383-5740, telex 27830 SPORTC G. **(Subscription address**: Sports Council, PO Box 99, Sudbury Suffolk CO10 6SN UK; Phone: 011 44 787 880011**) Continues** Sport & Leisure.

FR
**SPORT A L'UNIVERSITE.** (19??)-. French. ir. 100.00F. Paris Universite Club, 31 Avenue Georges Bernanos, 75231 Paris Cedex 05 France.

CN/0824-7900
**SPORT ADMINISTRATOR, THE.** [Sport adm.]. Vol. 1, No. 1; Sept./Oct. 1984-. Periodical. English. ir. $8.95. Sport Administrator, PO Box 15974, Station F, Ottawa Ontario K2C 3S8 Canada. **DD** 796/.06/9.
**Ind/Abst** SportSearch (May 1987-).

US/0161-5351
**SPORT AEROBATICS.** **Added/Corp** International Aerobatic Club. (19??)-. Periodical. English. Twelve times a year. $35.00. Experimental Aircraft Association Inc., PO Box 3086, Oshkosh WI 54903-3086. **Tel** (414)426-4800, FAX (414)426-4828. **LC** TL711.S8; S66. **DD** 797.5/4/05.

CN/0700-9046
**SPORT ALBERTA NEWS.** Vol. 1 (June 7, 1974)-. Periodical. English. bw. $6.00. Sport Alberta News, PO Box 3950 Station B, Calgary Alberta T2M 4M5 Canada. **DD** 796/.097123.

US/0190-1389
**SPORT AMERICANA BASEBALL CARD PRICE GUIDE, THE.** See Hobbies.

US/0738-1212
**SPORT AMERICANA BASEBALL MEMORABILIA AND AUTOGRAPH PRICE GUIDE, THE.** **VFOAT** Baseball Memorabilia and Autograph Price Guide; Sport Americana Baseball Memorabilia & Autograph Price Guide. No. 1-. English. $8.95. Den's Collectors Den, PO Box 606, Laurel MD 20810. **LC** GV875.2; .S657. **DD** 769/.49796357/0973.

US
**SPORT AMERICANA HOCKEY CARD PRICE GUIDE, THE.** See Hobbies.

UK
**SPORT AND LEISURE.** **Title Change**. Vol. 21, No. 2 (April/May 1980)-(19??). Periodical. English. bm. The Sports Council, 16 Upper Wolburn Place, London WC1H 0QP England. **Tel** 011 44 71 388-1277, FAX 011 44 71 383-5740, telex 27830 SPORTC G. **ED** Louise Fyfe. **UDC** 79. **Continues** Sport & Recreation. **Continued by** Sport.
**Ind/Abst** Leis. Recreat. Tour. Abstr.; Phys. Educ. Index; SPORT Discus; SportSearch (May 1987-).

●UK
**SPORT AND SPORT 2.** (1994)-. Newsletter. English. bm. £20.00. The Sports Council, 16 Upper Wolburn Place, London WC1H 0QP England. **Tel** 011 44 71 388-1277, FAX 011 44 71 383-5740, telex 27830 SPORTC G. **ED** Louise Fyfe. **Bk Rev**. **Circ**: 8,000.

GW
**SPORT AUTO.** (1969)-. Periodical. German. Twelve times a year. DM91.89 France; DM92.70 Luxembourg & Spain; DM93.60 Greece & Italy; DM95.40 Belgium & Netherlands; DM96.30 Portugal & Ireland; DM112.20 Denmark; DM90.00 others. Vereinigte Motor Verlag GmbH, Motor Presse, POB 106036, D 70049 Stuttgart Germany. **Tel** 011 49 711 1821506, 011 49 711 1821545. **(Subscription address**: Deutscher Pressevertrieb Buch, POB 101602 Hansa GMBH, D 20010 Hamburg Germany.**) LC** GV1029; .S718. **DD** 796.7/2/05.

FR/0151-6353
**SPORT AUTO, VIRAGE AUTO, CHAMPION.** See Transportation-Automobiles.

US/0038-7835
**SPORT AVIATION.** [Sport aviat.]. **Added/Corp** Experimental Aircraft Association. (1961)-. Periodical. English. Twelve times a year. $20.00 (schools & libraries); $35.00 (others) Comes with Experimental Aircraft Association Membership. Experimental Aircraft Association Inc., PO Box 3086, Oshkosh WI 54903-3086. **Tel** (414)426-4800, FAX (414)426-4828. **ED** Jack Cox. Index available. cum. index. **Bk Rev**. **Ad Acc**. **Circ**: 133,000 (ctrl). **Continues** Sport Aviation and the Experimenter.
**Desc**: Coverage of the international aviation community from the ground up. Includes the people and airplanes that have made sport aviation an exciting experience.
**Ind/Abst** Index Inf.

GW/0344-6492
**SPORT-, BADER-, FREIZEIT-BAUTEN.** See Building and Construction.

FR/0398-8341
**SPORT BOWLING.** (1963)-. Periodical. French. mo. **UDC** 790.
**Ind/Abst** SPORT Discus.

BE
**SPORT : COMMUNAUTE FRANCAISE DE BELGIQUE.** (19??)-. French. qt. 350.00F Belgium; 450.00F other. Communnaute Francaise de Belgique, Boulevard Leopold II 44, 1080 Brussels Belgium. **Tel** 011 32 2 4132311.

FR/0397-4707
**SPORT ET PLEIN AIR.** (1953)-. Periodical. French. Ten times a year. 122.00F France; 240.00F other. Sport et Plein Air, 14 rue de Scandicci, 93508 Pantin Cedex France. **Tel** 011 33 1 49422319. **UDC** 7.

FR/1152-9563
**SPORT ET VIE DIJON.** (SPORT ET VIE.). (1990)-. Periodical. French. bm. 170.00F (1 year), 315.00F (2 year) France; 215.00F (1 year), 405.00F (2 year) other. Editions Faton, BP90, 21803 Quetigny Cedex France. **Tel** 011 33 80 469393, FAX 011 33 80 469350. **UDC** 796.

US/8750-8117
**SPORT FLYER.** [Sport flyer]. 4th year, No. 10 (Jan. 1985)-. Periodical. English. mo. $9.00. Sport Flyer, PO Box 98786, Tacoma WA 98499. **Tel** (206)588-1743. **ED** Bruce Williams. **DD** 797. **UDC** 797.5. **Bk Rev**. **Ad Acc**. **Circ**: 25,000 (ctrl). **Continues** Ultralight Flyer, 0279-0181.
**Desc**: For enthusiasts of sport-recreational flying, including ballooning, ultralights, homebuilt, kites, etc. News articles report on new products, safety tips, competitions and people.

NE
**SPORT GERICHT.** **Title Change**. (19??)-(19??). Sport Gericht, Scheltuslaan 53 Netherlands. **Merged with** Richting **to form** RSG.

SZ
**SPORT / HERAUSGEGEBEN VOM SCHWEIZERISCHEN LANDESVERBAND FUER SPORT.** **Added/Corp** Schweizerischer Landesverband fur Sport. (1990)-. German (French). **LC** GV637; .S68. **DD** 796/.09494. **Continues** Sport ... Von A-Z.

GW
**SPORT INTERN.** English. sm. DM300.00 (1 year), DM450.00 (2 year). Extra Press, Karl Heinz Huba, Postfach 710420, D-81424 Munich F. R. Germany. **Tel** 011 49 89 796177, FAX 011 49 89 7900626.

BE
**SPORT INTERNATIONAL.** qt. 400.00F. CISM Magazine, Avenue Jacques Jordaens 26, B-1050 Brussels Belgium. **Tel** 011 32 2 647 68 52.
**Ind/Abst** SportSearch (May 1987-).

IT
**SPORT ITALIA.** Sisal Sport Italia, Via Giolitti 6, 10123 Turin Italy.

PL/0137-9305
**SPORT KATOWICE.** (SPORT.). [Sport Katow.]. (1945)-. Newspaper. Polish. ir (260 issues). $130.00. **(Subscription address**: ARS Polona, PO Box 1001, 00068 Warsaw Poland.**) UDC** 796.

AU
**SPORT MAGAZIN.** German. ir. $30.00 single issue. Wirtschafts Trend Zeitschrifte Verlagsges MBH, Marc Aurel Strasse 10, A-1010 Vienna Austria. **Continues** Ski Welt.

CN/1195-7956
**SPORT MAGAZINE.** (19??)-. French. Ten times a year. 19.95Can$ Canada; 32.74Can$ other. Publications Transcontinental Inc, 1100 Rene-Levesque, 24Fl Boulevard West, Montreal Quebec H3B 4X9 Canada. **Tel** (514)392-9000, FAX (514)392-4724.

●US/1061-6934
**SPORT MARKETING QUARTERLY.** [Sport mark. q.]. **VFOAT** SMQ. (1992)-. Periodical. English. qt. $39.00 individual, $85.00 institutions, $27.00 students US; $43.00 individual (surface mail), $59.00 individual (air mail), $89.00 institution (surface mail), $105.00 institution (air mail), $31.00 student (surface mail), $47.00 student (airmail) other. Fitness Information Technology, Inc., PO Box 4425, University Avenue, Morgantown WV 26504. **Tel** (304)599-3482, (800)477-4348, FAX (304)599-3482. **ED** Dallas Branch Jr. **LC** GV716; .S6355. **DD** 796/.06/91. **Bk Rev**, (Qty: 4). **Ad Acc**, **Adv Mgr**: Eric Noble. **Pr Rev**. **Circ**: 1,000.
**Desc**: Serves as a unique forum for the exchange of information among academicians and sport marketing practitioners. Highlights sports marketing success stories, research, books/video, sport marketing programs, upcoming events/conferences, and profiles influential leaders in the rapidly growing sport marketing field.
**Ind/Abst** SPORT Discus.

US
**SPORT MEDIA BUYERS GUIDE.** (19??)-. Consumer Publication. English. an. International Sport Summit, 200 West 60th Street, Suite 310, New York NY 10023-8510. **Tel** (212)502-5306, telex RCA 261239. **ED** Monica Hellerman. Index available. **Ad Acc**. **Circ**: 7,000 (ctrl).
**Desc**: Information for sport media buyers.

US/0038-7797
**SPORT (NEW YORK).** (SPORT.). [Sport]. Vol. 1 (Sept. 1946)-. Periodical. English. mo. $19.94 US; $27.76 Canada; $27.94 other. Petersen Publishing Company, 6420 Wilshire Bouldevard, Los Angeles CA 90048. **Tel** (213)782-2485. **(Subscription address**: Neodata / Colorado, PO Box 2606, Boulder Boulder CO 80322.**) ED** Neil Cohen. **LC** GV561; .S66. **DD** 796.05. **Bk Rev**. **Ad Acc**. **Circ**: 930,000. available on microfilm and microfiche from University Microfilms International (UMI). Documents available from UMI Article Clearinghouse, Magazine Collection.
**Desc**: Articles and photography on baseball, football, basketball and hockey. All the action from the front row and from behind the scenes.
**Ind/Abst** Acad. Abstr. Full Text Elite (Feb. 1989-); Acad. Abstr. (Feb. 1989-); Acad. Ind. [Computer File] (1984-); Acad. Search (Feb. 1989-); Expand. Acad. Index (1984-); Gen. Period. Index (1985-); INFO-SOUTH Abstr.; Infobank (Jan. 1969-); Mag. Artic. Summar. Elite (Jan. 1989-); Mag. Artic. Summar. Select (Jan. 1989-); Mag. Artic. Summar. CD-ROM (1989-); Mag. Index Plus (1989-); Mag. Index Sel. Microfiche (1990-) [Full Txt.]; Mag. Index. Sel. (1989-); Mag. Search; Mag. Search (Jan. 1989-); Newsp. Period. Abstr. (1988-); Read. Guide Abstr. Select Ed.; Read. Guide Period. Lit.; SportSearch; Mag. Index (1977-); TOM Gen. Index (1985-) [Full Txt.].

CN/0708-6113
**SPORT ONTARIO DIRECTORY OF SPORTS, RECREATION AND PHYSICAL EDUCATION.** (DIRECTORY OF SPORTS, RECREATION AND PHYSICAL EDUCATION.). 1977/78-. Directory. English. an. Sport Ontario, 559 Jarvis Street, Toronto Ontario M4Y 2J1. **DD** 796/.025/713. **UDC** 79(036)(713).

CN/0707-1906
**SPORT ONTARIO NEWS. Main/Corp** Sport Ontario. Vol. 1 (June 1972)-. Periodical. English. bm. Free. **DD** 796/.09713. **UDC** 796/799(713).

UK
**SPORT PARACHUTIST. Added/Corp** British Parachute Association. (19??)-. Periodical. English. Six times a year. £30.00 (surface mail), £35.00 (airmail). British Parachute Association, 5 Wharf Way, Glen Parva, Leicester, LE2 9TF England. **Tel** 011 44 533 785271, FAX 011 44 533 477662. **LC** GV770; .S66.
**Ind/Abst** SPORT Discus; SportSearch (May 1987-).

NE
**SPORT PARTNER.** English. mo (10 issues). Fl89.00. Inter Events Holland BV, Winthontlaan 200, 3526 KV Utrecht Netherlands. **Tel** 011 31 30 891073.

US
**SPORT PLACE INTERNATIONAL : AN INTERNATIONAL MAGAZINE OF SPORTS GEOGRAPHY.** ***Title Change.*** (198?)-(19??). Periodical. English. Three times a year. Black Oak Press, 2624 Black Oak Drive, Stillwater OK 74074. **Tel** (405)744-6250. ***Continues*** *Sport Place.* ***Continued by*** *Sport Place (1990).*
**Ind/Abst** SPORT Discus.

CN/0227-7417
**SPORT PRESTIGE.** [Sport prestige]. 1st Year, No. 1 (1 Nov. 1979)-. Periodical. French. wk. Free. Sport Prestige, 251 St. Geeorges, St. Jerome Quebec J7Z 5A1. **DD** 796/.09714/24.

US/0888-4781
**SPORT PSYCHOLOGIST, THE. See** Psychology.

US/1044-3118
**SPORT PSYCHOLOGY TRAINING BULLETIN.** [Sport psychol. train. bull.]. (Sept./Oct. 1989)-. Bulletin. English. Six times a year (Jan., Mar., May, July, Sept., Nov.). $18.00. Sport Pshchology Training Bulletin, PO Box 187, Carrboro NC 27510. **Tel** (919)942-4020, FAX (804)258-5201. **ED** Dr. Charles J. Hardy Ph.D. and Dr. R. Kelly Crace, Ph.D. **DD** 796. **Bk Rev**, (Qty: varies). ctrl circ.
**Desc:** To provide athletes, coaches, and parents with information on the mental aspects of sports performance.

CN/0700-8791
**SPORT QUEBEC.** ***Title Change.*** Oct. 1970-. Periodical. French. Service des Communications de la Confederation des Sports du Quebec, 1415 East rue Jarry, Montreal Quebec H2E 2Z7 Canada. **DD** 796/.09714/005. **UDC** 796/799(714). ***Continued by*** *Sport Illustre.*

AT
**SPORT REPORT.** (19??)-. English. qt. 12.00Aus$ Australia; 20.00Aus$ other. Sport Report, PO Box 342, Curtin ACT 2605 Australia. **Tel** 011 61 62 851887. **ED** Melanie Collins. **Bk Rev**, (Qty: 4). **Ad Acc.** Full Page (B&W) 550.00Aus$. Half Page (B&W) 350.00Aus$. Full Page (Color) 850.00Aus$. **Circ:** 5,000.
**Desc:** Official publication of the Confederation of Australian Sport, an independent industry grouping of 125 national sporting organizations representing 6.5 million sports participants.
**Ind/Abst** SPORT Discus.

●US/1065-7649
**SPORT RIDER.** [Sport rider]. Issue 1 (Apr. 1993)-. Periodical. English. bm (6 issues). $13.95 US; $20.28 Canada; $18.95 other. Petersen Publishing Company, 6420 Wilshire Bouldevard, Los Angeles CA 90048. **Tel** (213)782-2485. **(Subscription address:** Neodata / Colorado, PO Box 2606, Boulder Boulder CO 80322.**) LC** WMLC 93/1583. **DD** 796.
**Desc:** Only magazine to showcase the exciting world of high-performance street sport bikes. Each issue features track tests and comparisons of the hottest bikes around along with wild, full-color action shots. Offers tips and techniques for getting the most performance without compromising safety.

US/0270-1812
**SPORT SCENE. Added/Corp** North Carolina Youth Sport Institute. North American Youth Sport Institute. Vol. 1, No. 1 (Dec. 1979)-. Periodical. English. qt (Feb., May, Aug., Nov.). $24.00 (institution), $16.00 (individual) North America; $25.00 other. Sport Scene, 4985 Oak Garden Drive, Kernersville NC 27284. **Tel** (919)784-4926. **ED** Jack Hutslar. Index available. **Bk Rev. Ad Acc. Circ:** 15,000 (ctrl).
**Desc:** For parents, coaches, teachers, community leaders and others interested in sports, recreation, education, fitness, and health. Focus is on kids, their programs and how adults can work with them in a positive, safe manner.

●US/1056-6724
**SPORT SCIENCE REVIEW (CHAMPAIGN, ILL.).** (SPORT SCIENCE REVIEW.). [Sport sci. rev.]. **Added/Corp** International Council of Sport Science and Physical Education. Vol. 1, No. 1 (1992)-. Periodical. English. sa (Jan. & July). $26.00 (individual), $52.00 (institution) US; $29.00 (individual), $55.00 (institution) other. Human Kinetics Publishers Inc, 1607 North Market Street, PO Box 5076, Champaign IL 61825-5076. **Tel** (217)351-5076, FAX (217)351-2674. **LC** GV557; .S67. **DD** 613.7/1/05; 613.7/1/05; 612. **NLM** W1; SP488R. **[CCC].** ***Continues*** *Sport Science Review, 0256-4327.*
**Desc:** Reviews the new achievements in the various areas of sport sciences.
**Ind/Abst** Phys. Educ. Index; Soc. Sci. Cit. Index [Select. Cov.]; SPORT Discus.

US/0162-2242
**SPORT STYLE. See** Clothing Industry and Fashion.

CN/0831-6317
**SPORT THESAURUS.** (SPORT THESAURUS / COMPILED BY THE SPORT INFORMATION RESOURCE CENTRE.). [Sport thesaurus]. **Added/Corp** Coaching Association of Canada. Sport Information Resource Centre. **VFOAT** SIRC Thesaurus. **VAT** Sport Information Resource Centre Thesaurus. (1981)-. English. ir. $95.00 US; $115.00 other. Sport Information Resource Centre, 1600 promenade James Naismith Drive, Gloucester Ontario K1B 5N4 Canada. **Tel** (613)748-5658, FAX (613)748-5701, telex 053-3660 Sportrec Ott. **ED** Richard W. Stark, Marion Fourner and Jean-Michel Johnson. **DD** 025.4/9796.

PL/0239-4405
**SPORT WYCZYNOWY.** [Sport Wyczyn.]. (1966)-. Periodical. Multiple languages. mo. Price on Request. **(Subscription address:** ARS Polona, PO Box 1001, 00068 Warsaw Poland.**) UDC** 796. ***Continues*** *Materiay Szkoleniowe - Polski Komitet Olimpijski, 1230-0144.*

RU/0234-8004
**SPORT ZA RUBEZHOM.** ***Ceased.*** (19??)-(19??). Russian. ir. **(Subscription address:** Victor Kamkin, 4956 Boiling Brook Parkway, Rockville MD 20852.**)**

US/1060-8419
**SPORTBIKE (NEW YORK, N.Y.).** (SPORTBIKE / BY THE EDITORS OF CYCLE MAGAZINE.). [Sportbike]. (1991)-. English. Cycle Magazine, PO Box 56406, Boulder CO 80322-6406. **LC** WMLC 91/1294. **DD** 629.

US/1047-210X
**SPORTBOSTON (PHILADELPHIA, PA.).** (SPORTBOSTON.). [SportBoston]. **VFOAT** Sport Boston. Vol. 1, No. 1 (1989)-. Periodical. English. Six times a year. $19.95. SportBoston, PO Box 692, Holmes PA 19043-9963. **DD** 796.

US/0899-3815
**SPORTCARE & FITNESS.** ***Ceased.*** [SportCare fit.]. **VFOAT** Sport Care & Fitness; Sportcare and Fitness; Sport Care and Fitness. 1988-?. Periodical. English. bm. Sportcare Inc, 2400 West 4th Street, Wilmington DE 19385. **Tel** (302)984-2600. **ED** Linda Jones. **DD** 613. **Ad Acc. Circ:** 35,000 (ctrl).
**Desc:** Addresses the needs of those involved with the athlete, presented in an easy-to-read, colorful format. Coaches, athletic trainers, sport physical therapists, nutritionists, psychologists, facility directors, and instructors can all benefit from the comprehensive special reports, innovative features, and regular columns on sports medicine.

GW/0170-2890
**SPORTDOKUMENTATION : LITERATUR DER SPORTWISSENSCHAFT.** ***Ceased.*** **Added/Corp** Bundesinstitut fuer Sportwissenschaft. **VFOAT** Sport Dokumentation. (19??)-(1994). German. Four times a year. Verlag Karl Hofmann, Postfach 1360, D-73603 Schorndorf Germany. **Tel** 011 49 7181 4020. **[CCC].**

US
**SPORTING CLASSICS.** [Sport. class.]. Vol. 1, No. 1 (19??)-. English. Six times a year. $23.95. Sporting Classics, PO Box 1017, Highway 521 South, Camden SC 29020. **Tel** (803)425-1003. **ED** John Culler. **Bk Rev. Ad Acc. Circ:** 80,000 (ctrl).
**Desc:** Rapidly becoming America's highest quality hunting and fishing magazine.
**Ind/Abst** Am. Hist. Life (1984-).

US/0146-0889
**SPORTING GOODS BUSINESS. See** Business.

US/0038-8017
**SPORTING GOODS DEALER, THE.** Vol. 1 (Oct. 1899)-. Trade Publication. English. mo. $100.00 US; $140.00 other. Sporting Goods Dealer, 1212 North Lindbergh Boulevard, St Louis MO 63132. **Tel** (314)997-7111, (800)825-8508, FAX (314)993-7726. **LC** GV743; .S7.
**Desc:** Trade magazine for sporting goods dealers, manufacturers and educated consumers. Areas of focus includes footwear, licensed products, activewear, outdoor and team sporting goods.

US/1060-2550
**SPORTING GOODS INTELLIGENCE. See** Business-Marketing.

FR/1143-2462
**SPORTING GOODS INTELLIGENCE (BRY-SUR-MARNE).** (SPORTING GOODS INTELLIGENCE.). (1990)-. Periodical. Multiple languages. Thirty-six times a year (3 times per month). $375.00. EDM Publications, 9 rue du Pre-aux-Merles, F-94360 Bry-sur-Marne France. **Tel** 011 33 1 49838242, FAX 011 33 1 49838224. **UDC** 338.

US/0193-8401
**SPORTING GOODS MARKET IN ..., THE. See** Recreation, Leisure-Outdoor Life.

US/0363-1478
**SPORTING GOODS REGISTER, THE.** (19??)-. English. ir. $50.00 US, $80.00 others (latest volume). Sporting News, c/o Sharon Moore, 1212 North Lindbergh Boulevard, PO Box 56, St Louis MO 63166. **Tel** (314)997-7111, (800)825-8508. **(Subscription address:** Contemporary Books, Two Prudential Plaza, Suite 1200, Chicago IL 60601.**) LC** HD9992 .U5; S66. **DD** 380.1/45/6887602573.

CN/0827-5726
**SPORTING GOODS REVIEW.** [Sport. goods rev.]. Vol. 1; Jan./Feb. 1985-. Periodical. English. mo. 20.00Can$ Canada; 30.00Can$ other. Sporting Goods Review, Box 3061, Winnipeg Manitoba R3C 4E5 Canada. **DD** 688.7/6/0971.
**Ind/Abst** SportSearch (May 1987-).

CN/0826-5992
**SPORTING LIFE (WESTMOUNT, QUEBEC).** (SPORTING LIFE.). [Sport. life]. Vol. 1, No. 1 (Feb./March 1984)-. Periodical. English. bm. $2.50 each number. Sporting Life, 4827-A St Catherine Street West, Westmount Quebec H3Z 1S9 Canada. **DD** 796/.0971. **UDC** 796/799(71).

US/0038-805X
**SPORTING NEWS, THE.** [Sport. news]. (1886)-. Periodical. English. Sixty times a year. $60.00. Times Mirror Magazines, Two Park Avenue, New York NY 10016. **Tel** (212)779-5000. **(Subscription address:** CDS / SIFD Agency Control, 1901 Bell Avenue, Des Moines IA 50315.**) LC** GV561; .S74. **DD** 796. **Ad Acc. Circ:** 725,000. available on microfilm and microfiche from University Microfilms International (UMI). Documents available from UMI Article Clearinghouse.
**Desc:** Weekly analysis and previews on football, baseball, basketball and hockey.
**Ind/Abst** Access (1975-1987); Gen. Period. Index (1985-); Mag. Index Plus (1989-); Mag. Index. Sel. (1986-); Newsp. Period. Abstr. (1988-); SPORT Discus; Mag. Index (1977-).

US
**SPORTING NEWS BASEBALL GUIDE AND REGISTER. CD-ROM.** English. $129.00. Quanta Press, Inc., 1313 Fifth Street Southeast, Suite 208C, Minneapolis MN 55414. **Tel** (612)379-3956, FAX (612)623-4570.
**Desc:** Guide to the statistics, personalities, and games of Major League Baseball. Gives you a multimedia database on America's favorite pastime. Available in DOS and MAC formats.

US/0275-0732
**SPORTING NEWS ... BASEBALL YEARBOOK, THE.** [Sport. news baseb. yearb.]. **VFOAT** Baseball Yearbook. (1981)-. Periodical. English. an. $6.50. Sporting News, c/o Sharon Moore, 1212 North Lindbergh Boulevard, PO Box 56, St Louis MO 63166. **Tel** (314)997-7111, (800)825-8508. **(Subscription address:** Sporting News, PO Box 11229, Des Moines IA 50340.**) LC** GV863.A1; S75. **DD** 796.357/0973. **Bk Rev. Ad Acc. Circ:** 300,000 (ctrl).

US/0895-0598
**SPORTING NEWS COLLEGE BASKETBALL, THE. VFOAT** College Basketball; College Basketball Yearbook; Sporting News College Basketball Yearbook. (1988)-. Periodical. English. an. $6.50. Sporting News, c/o Sharon Moore, 1212 North Lindbergh Boulevard, PO Box 56, St Louis MO 63166. **Tel** (314)997-7111, (800)825-8508. **(Subscription address:** Contemporary Books, Two Prudential Plaza, Suite 1200, Chicago IL 60601.**) LC** WMLC L 83/6459. **DD** 796. ***Continues in part*** *Sporting News College and Pro ... Basketball Yearbook.*

US/0733-2823
**SPORTING NEWS ... COLLEGE FOOTBALL YEARBOOK, THE. VFOAT** College Football Yearbook; College Football Year Book. (1982)-. Periodical. English. an. $6.50. Sporting News, c/o

Sharon Moore, 1212 North Lindbergh Boulevard, PO Box 56, St Louis MO 63166. **Tel** (314)997-7111, (800)825-8508. **LC** WMLC L 83/138.

US/1052-7591
**SPORTING NEWS ... FANTASY BASEBALL OWNER'S MANUAL, THE.** [Sport. news fantasy baseb. own. man.]. **VFOAT** Fantasy Baseball Owner's Manual. (1991)-. English. $4.95 (single issue). Sporting News, c/o Sharon Moore, 1212 North Lindbergh Boulevard, PO Box 56, St Louis MO 63166. **Tel** (314)997-7111, (800)825-8508. **DD** 796.

US/1051-6018
**SPORTING NEWS HOCKEY, THE.** [Sport. news hockey]. **VFOAT** Hockey; Hockey Yearbook; Hockey Year Book; Sporting News ... Hockey Year Book; Sporting News ... Hockey Yearbook. (1991)-. English. an. $6.50. Sporting News, c/o Sharon Moore, 1212 North Lindbergh Boulevard, PO Box 56, St Louis MO 63166. **Tel** (314)997-7111, (800)825-8508. **(Subscription address:** Sporting News, PO Box 11229, Des Moines IA 50340.**) LC** GV848.4.U6; S67. **DD** 796/.962/0973.

US/1062-2071
**SPORTING NEWS INSIDER REPORT, THE.** ***Ceased.*** [Sport. news insid. rep.]. **VFOAT** Insider Report. Vol. 1, No. 1 (Mar. 16, 1992)-(1993). Periodical. English. wk. The Sporting News Insider Report, PO Box 10753, Des Moines IA 50340. **Tel** (515)246-6924. **DD** 796.

●US
**SPORTING NEWS NBA GUIDE, THE.** **Added/Corp** National Basketball Association. **VFOAT** Sporting News National Basketball Association Guide; NBA Guide; Official NBA Guide; Sporting News Official NBA Guide. (1992/93)-. Periodical. English. an. $12.95. Sporting News, c/o Sharon Moore, 1212 North Lindbergh Boulevard, PO Box 56, St Louis MO 63166. **Tel** (314)997-7111, (800)825-8508. **LC** GV885; .N26; GV885; .N26. **DD** 796.323/64/0973. ***Continues*** *Official NBA Guide.*
**Desc:** News guide for followers of NBA basketball.

●US
**SPORTING NEWS OFFICIAL BASEBALL REGISTER, THE.** **See** Recreation, Leisure-Abstracting, Bibliographies and Statistics.

US/0895-0601
**SPORTING NEWS ... PRO BASKETBALL YEARBOOK, THE.** **VFOAT** Pro Basketball Yearbook. (1987/1988)-. Periodical. English. an. $6.50. Sporting News, c/o Sharon Moore, 1212 North Lindbergh Boulevard, PO Box 56, St Louis MO 63166. **Tel** (314)997-7111, (800)825-8508. **(Subscription address:** Sporting News, PO Box 11229, Des Moines IA 50340.**) LC** GV885.7; .S66. **DD** 796.32/3/0973. ***Continues in part*** *Sporting News College and Pro ... Basketball Yearbook.*

US
**SPORTING NEWS PRO FOOTBALL REGISTER, THE.** **VFOAT** Football Register; Pro Football Register; Sporting News Football Register. (1991)-. Periodical. English. an. $12.95. Sporting News, c/o Sharon Moore, 1212 North Lindbergh Boulevard, PO Box 56, St Louis MO 63166. **Tel** (314)997-7111, (800)825-8508. **(Subscription address:** Contemporary Books, Two Prudential Plaza, Suite 1200, Chicago IL 60601.**) LC** GV955; .F64. **DD** 796.332/0973. ***Continues*** *Football Register, 0071-7258.*

US/0276-2307
**SPORTING NEWS ... PRO FOOTBALL YEARBOOK, THE.** [Sport. news pro footb. yearb.]. **VFOAT** Pro Football Yearbook. (1981)-. Periodical. English. an. $6.50. Sporting News, c/o Sharon Moore, 1212 North Lindbergh Boulevard, PO Box 56, St Louis MO 63166. **Tel** (314)997-7111, (800)825-8508. **LC** GV937; .S73. **DD** 796.332/64/0973.

US/1046-7017
**SPORTING NEWS ROTISSERIE & FANTASY BASEBALL LEAGUE GUIDE, THE.** ***Ceased.*** [Sport. news Rotisserie fantasy baseb. leag. guide]. **VFOAT** Sporting News Rotisserie and Fantasy Baseball League Guide; Rotisserie and Fantasy Baseball League Guide; Rotisserie & Fantasy Baseball League Guide. (1990)-Ceased in (1990). English. an. Sporting News, c/o Sharon Moore, 1212 North Lindbergh Boulevard, PO Box 56, St Louis MO 63166. **Tel** (314)997-7111, (800)825-8508. **LC** GV1202.F33; S67. **DD** 793.93.

US/0275-4487
**SPORTING NEWS SUPER BOWL BOOK, THE.** ***Title Change.*** (SUPER BOWL BOOK.). [Sport. news super bowl book]. **VFOAT** Sporting News Super Bowl Book. (1981)-(19??). Periodical. English. an. Sporting News, c/o Sharon Moore, 1212 North Lindbergh Boulevard, PO Box 56, St Louis MO 63166. **Tel** (314)997-7111, (800)825-8508. **ED** Bob McCoy. **LC** GV956.2.S8; S89. **DD** 796.332/7. **Circ:** 10,000. ***Continued by*** *Complete Super Bowl Book, 1071-8958.*
**Desc:** Recap of past Super Bowl Games records, rosters of players. Covers football championship games since 1933.

CN/0824-9849
**SPORTING SCENE (SCARBOROUGH, ONT.).** (SPORTING SCENE.). [Sport. scene]. Vol. 21, (July 1982)-. Periodical. English. mo. Free. Martens Graphic Promotions, 70 Romulus Drive, Scarborough Ontario M1K 4C2. **DD** 796/.09713/541. **UDC** 796/799(713). ***Continues*** *Scarborough Sporting Scene, 0824-9830.*

CN/1180-5080
**SPORTING TIMES (VERNON).** (THE SPORTING TIMES.). [Sport. times]. Vol. 1, No. 1 (June 15, 1990)-. Periodical. English. mo. $15.00. Adams Enterprises, Suite 3, 3105-30th Avenue, Vernon, British Columbia V1T 2C4 Canada. **DD** 796/.09711/505.

AT/0813-2577
**SPORTING TRADITIONS.** **VFOAT** Journal of the Australian Society for Sports History. (1984)-. English.
**Ind/Abst** APAIS, Aust. Public Aff. Inf. Ser. (1986-); Leis. Recreat. Tour. Abstr.; SPORT Discus.

NE
**SPORTMASSAGE.** mo (10 issues). Ned Genootschap V Sportmassage, Keizersgracht 23A, 5611 GC Eindhoven Netherlands. **Tel** 011 31 040-449614.

SI
**SPORTS.** **Added/Corp** Singapore Sports Council. Vol. 1, (Oct. 1972)-. Periodical. English. Ten times a year (May/June & Nov/Dec. issues combined). 4.00Sing$ Singapore; 15.00Sing$ Brunei; 17.00Sing$ Malaysia; 21.00Sing$ other. Singapore Sports Council, National Stadium, Kallang Singapore 1439. **Tel** 011 65 3457111, 011 65 3409660, FAX 011 65 3452541, 011 65 4409205, telex RS 35467 NASTAD. **ED** Nora Yap. **Bk Rev**, (Qty: 3). **Ad Acc**, **Adv Mgr:** Sharon Lau, **Tel** 011 65 3409663. ctrl circ.

US
**SPORTS ADDRESS BIBLE.** (19??)-. English. an. $21.95. Ed Kobak Global Sports Productions, 1223 Broadway, Suite 102, Santa Monica CA 90404. **Tel** (310)454-9480, FAX (310)454-6590. **ED** Edward Kobak Jr. ***Continues*** *Comprehensive Directory of Sports Addresses.*

US/1064-573X
**SPORTS ADVANTAGE.** ***Ceased.*** [Sports advant.]. **Added/Corp** Standard Rate & Data Service. Vol. 1, No. 1 (1991)-(Fall 1993). Periodical. English. sa. Standard Rate & Data Service, 3004 Glenview Road, Wilmette IL 60091. **Tel** (708)441-2263, FAX (708)441-2400. **(Subscription address:** Neodata / Colorado, PO Box 2606, Boulder Boulder CO 80322.**) LC** GV716; .S645. **DD** 338.4/7796.
**Desc:** Source for sports marketing opportunities; current sports media rates and data; national, international, and regional sports marketing information.

US/0038-8149
**SPORTS AFIELD (1940).** (SPORTS AFIELD.). [Sports afield]. Vol. 103, No. 3 (March 1940)-. Periodical. English. mo. $13.97. The Hearst Corporation, 250 West 55th Street, New York NY 10019. **Tel** (212)649-4014. **(Subscription address:** CDS Agency Hard Copy, PO Box 4966, Des Moines IA 50340.**)** available on microfilm and microfiche from University Microfilms International (UMI). Documents available from UMI Article Clearinghouse. ***Continues*** *Sports Afield and Trails of the Northwoods.*
**Ind/Abst** Access (1975-); Gen. Period. Index (1985-); Mag. Index Plus (1989-); Newsp. Period. Abstr. (1988-); Mag. Index (1977-).

US/0160-1830
**SPORTS AFIELD DEER.** **See** Recreation, Leisure-Outdoor Life.

US/0733-0669
**SPORTS AND THE COURTS.** **See** Law.

US/0273-2572
**SPORTS (BOCA RATON).** (SPORTS.). [Sports]. Vol. 1, Article 1-. English. ir (approximately 20 articles each year). Social Issues Resources Series Inc, PO Box 2348, Boca Raton FL 33427. **Tel** (800)327-0513, (407)994-0079. **ED** Eleanor C Goldstein. **LC** GV583; .S6848. **DD** 796/.0973. **UDC** 796/799(73).
**Desc:** Interdisciplinary resource material consisting of reprinted articles from popular and professional journals, newspapers, magazines and government documents.

US/1042-9662
**SPORTS CAR INTERNATIONAL.** **See** Transportation-Automobiles.

●US/1061-5512
**SPORTS CARD PRICE GUIDE MONTHLY.** [Sports card price guide mon.]. **VFOAT** Sports Collectors Digest Sports Card Price Guide Monthly; Sports Card Price Guide; Price Guide Monthly. No. 49 (Apr. 1992)-. Periodical. English. mo. $18.95 US; $24.95 other. Krause Publications, 700 East State Street, Iola WI 54990-0001. **Tel** (715)445-2214, FAX (715)445-4087, telex 55 6461. **LC** GV568.5; .S64. **DD** 769/.49796/0973. ***Continues*** *Baseball Card Price Guide Monthly, 0896-7563.*

CN/0225-1876
**SPORTS CLUB MAGAZINE.** [Sports club mag.]. V. 2, No 6. (Jan./Feb. 1979)-. Periodical. French. ir. $1.50 per no. Publisysteme Inc, 9851 Parkway Boulevard, Ville St Laurent Quebec H1J 1P3 Canada. **DD** 796/.05. **UDC** 796/799. ***Continues*** *Sports Plus, 0703-1904.*

AT
**SPORTS COACH.** **Added/Corp** Western Australia. Dept. for Youth, Sport, and Recreation. Western Australia. Dept. for Sport and Recreation. Australian Sports Commission. Vol. 1, No. 1 (1976)-. Periodical. English. qt. 15.00Aus$ Australia; 20.00Aus$ (surface mail), 30.00Aus$ (air mail) other. Australian Coaching Council, PO Box 176, Belconnen ACT 2616 Australia. **Tel** 011 61 6 2521550, FAX 011 61 6 2521200, telex 62400.
**Ind/Abst** Phys. Educ. Index (1983-); SPORT Discus.

CN/0820-6457
**SPORTS (COACHING ASSOCIATION OF CANADA : 1980).** ***Title Change.*** **See** Education-Physical Education and Training.

US/0278-2693
**SPORTS COLLECTORS DIGEST.** [Sports collect. dig.]. (19??)-. Periodical. English. wk. $49.95 US; $75.75 other. Krause Publications, 700 East State Street, Iola WI 54990-0001. **Tel** (715)445-2214, FAX (715)445-4087, telex 55 6461. **ED** Steve Ellingboe. **DD** 796. **Circ:** 47,076.
**Desc:** Information baseball cards and sports collectibles. Weekly news updates on the hobby and a weekly updated price guide to more than 30,000 cards Baseball card show calendar in each issue.

US
**SPORTS COLLECTORS DIGEST FOOTBALL, BASKETBALL & HOCKEY PRICE GUIDE / BY THE STAFF OF SPORTS COLLECTORS DIGEST.** **See** Hobbies.

UK
**SPORTS COUNCIL STUDY.** **Added/Corp** Sports Council (Great Britain). **VFOAT** Studies; Study. (19??)-. Monographic series. English. **LC** GV605; .S74. **DD** 796/.0941.
**Ind/Abst** Leis. Recreat. Tour. Abstr.

CN/0380-5751
**SPORTS DIRECTORY.** 1st- Ed.; 1973-. Directory. English. an. Northwestern Ontario Sports Council, 189 Arthur Street, Thunder Bay P, Ontario P7B 1A2. **DD** 796/.025/7131. **UDC** 796/799(036)(713).

UK
**SPORTS DOCUMENTATION MONTHLY BULLETIN.** **Added/Corp** University of Birmingham. Sports Documentation Centre. (1971)-. Bulletin. English. mo. £40.00 (individuals), £51.00 (institutions) UK; £53.00 other. University of Birmingham / England, Edgbaston, Center for Byzantine Ottoman, Greek Street, Birmingham B15 2TT England. **Tel** 011 44 21 414 5733, FAX 011 44 21 414 5726. Index available. cum. index. **Circ:** 350 (ctrl).
**Desc:** Sport, biomechanics, psychology, physiology, sociology, recreation, physical education, sports medicine, and sports injuries.
**Ind/Abst** Ergon. Abstr.

●UK/1351-0029
**SPORTS, EXERCISE AND INJURY.** **See** Medical Science and Technology-Sports Medicine.

●US/1059-0862
**SPORTS FAN'S CONNECTION.** [Sports fan's connect.]. **Added/Corp** Gale Research Inc. 1st ed. (1992)-. English. be. Gale Research Inc., 835 Penobscot Building, Detroit MI 48226. **Tel** (800)877-GALE, (313)961-2242, FAX (313)961-6083, telex TWX 810-221-7086. **LC** GV583; .S6853. **DD** 796/.02573.

US/0895-0350
**SPORTS HERITAGE.** [Sports herit.]. Vol. 1, No. 1 (Jan./Feb. 1987)-. Periodical. English. bm. Commonwealth Communications Service, PO Box 15760, Harrisburg PA 17105.

US/0733-8740
**SPORTS HIGH.** Vol. 1, No. 1 (Sept. 198?)-. Periodical. English. mo. $20.00 US; $27.00 other. Oxley International Corporation, PO Box 2836, Farmington Hills MI 48018.

US/0038-822X
**SPORTS ILLUSTRATED.** [Sports illus.]. Vol. 1 (Aug. 16, 1954)-. Periodical. English. wk. $80.46. Time Inc. / New York, Time & Life Building, Rockefeller Center, New York NY 10020. **(Subscription address:** Time Customer Service, PO Box 60050, Tampa FL 33609.**) LC** GV561; .S733. **DD** 796/.05. **Ad Acc**. available on microfilm and microfiche from University Microfilms International (UMI); available on an online database (files

647,648,746/Full-Text) from DIALOG. Documents available from UMI Article Clearinghouse.
**Desc:** Covers football, basketball, baseball, hockey, and more.
**Ind/Abst** Abr. Read. Guide Period. Lit.; Acad. Abstr. Full Text Elite (Jan. 1984-) [Full Txt.]; Acad. Abstr. (Jan. 1984-); Acad. Ind. [Computer File] (1977-); Acad. Search (Jan. 1984-); Biogr. Index; Book Rev. Index; Can. Index (?-?); Can. Period. Index (19??-); Expand. Acad. Index (1977-); Gen. Period. Index (1985-); Health Ref. Cent. (1987-) [Select. Cov.]; Index Period. Artic. Relat. Law; INFO-SOUTH Abstr.; Infobank (Jan. 1969-); Mag. Artic. Summar. Elite (Jan. 1984-) [Full Txt.]; Mag. Artic. Summar. Select (Jan. 1984-) [Full Txt.]; Mag. Artic. Summar. CD-ROM (Jan. 1984-); Mag. ASAP Plus [Full Txt.]; Mag. ASAP Sel. [Full Txt.]; Mag. Express (1986-) [Full Txt.]; Mag. Index Plus (1989-); Mag. Index Sel. Microfiche (1986-1991) [Full Txt.]; Mag. Index Sel. (1986-); Mag. Search; Mid. Search (Jan. 1984-) [Full Txt.]; Newsp. Period. Abstr. (1986-); NEXIS (1981-); Prim. Search (Jan. 1984-); Read. Guide Abstr. Select Ed.; Read. Guide Period. Lit.; Resource/One Ondisc; SPORT Discus; SportSearch; Mag. Index (1977-); TOM Gen. Index (1985-) [Full Txt.]; Vocat. Search (Jan. 1984-) [Full Txt.].

US/1042-394X
**SPORTS ILLUSTRATED FOR KIDS.** See Children and Youth Interests.

●US/1056-7887
**SPORTS ILLUSTRATED ... SPORTS ALMANAC, THE.** [Sports illus. sports alm.]. **VFOAT** Sports Almanac. (1992)-. English. Little Brown and Company / New York, 666 5th Avenue, 9th Floor, New York NY 10103. **LC** GV741; .S768; GV741; .S73. **DD** 796/021.

RM
**SPORTS IN ROMANIA : MAGAZINE OF THE ROMANIAN OLYMPIC COMMITTEE.** **Added/Corp** Romanian Olympic Committee. (1957)-. Periodical. English (French). Four times a year. $15.00. Romanian Olympic Committee, 16 Vasile Conta Street, Bucharest Romania. **LC** GV645; .S67. **DD** 796/.09498.

GW/0584-9209
**SPORTS IN THE GDR.** ***Ceased.*** **VAT** Sports in the German Democratic Republic. Ceased with Dec. (1985). Periodical. English. qt. Deutscher Judo Verband, Redaktion Ippon Segewaldweg 40, D 12557 Berlin Germany. **Tel** 011 49 711 210770, telex 051 678. **LC** GV612.6; .S63. **UDC** 796(430.20.

US/0742-2024
**SPORTS INDUSTRY NEWS.** [Sports ind. news]. (198?)-. Periodical. English. Fifty times a year. $197.00 US & Canada & Mexico Universities; $244.00 US & Canada & Mexico; $262.00 other. Gamepoint Publications, PO Box 946, Camden ME 04840. **Tel** (207)236-8346. **ED** Ray Swan.

NZ
**SPORTS INSTRUCTION SERIES.** **Added/Corp** New Zealand. Physical Education Branch. New Zealand. Dept. of Education. Curriculum Development Unit. New Zealand. Curriculum Development Division. New Zealand Rugby Football Union. (19??)-. Monographic series. English. **LC** GV561; .N485. **DD** 796/.0993.

UK
**SPORTS LAW AND FINANCE.** (19??)-. Periodical. English. bm. $198.00. IBC Publishing, 57-61 Mortimer St., London W1N 7TD England. **Tel** 011 44 71 637 4383, FAX 011 44 71 636 6314. **ED** Stephen Townley.

US/0195-8623
**SPORTS LAW REPORTER.** See Law.

US/0195-8100
**SPORTS LITERATURE INDEX.** [Sports lit. index]. 1978-. English. an. Marathon Press, Box 8140, Albany NY 12203. **LC** GV561; .S737. **DD** 796/.016. **UDC** 796/799(048.3).

CN/0826-5305
**SPORTS-LOISIRS (MONTREAL).** (SPORTS-LOISIRS.). [Sports-loisirs]. Vol. 1, No. 1 (Summer 1984)-. Periodical. French. Free. Sports-Loisirs, c/o Publ Antisquebec 8928 rue St-Michel Canada. **DD** 796/.09714. **UDC** 796/799(714).

US/1055-8020
**SPORTS MARKET PLACE.** [Sports mark. place]. **VFOAT** Sports Marketplace. (1984)-. Directory. English. an. $199.00 (single book), $259.00 (extended service), $279.00 (double book). Sportsguide Inc., PO Box 1417, Princeton NJ 08542. **Tel** (609)921-8599, FAX (609)921-8599. **(Subscription address:** Sports Careers, PO Box 10129, Phoenix AZ 85064.**)** **ED** Richard A. Lipsey. **LC** HD9992.U5; S667. **DD** 380.1/456887/02573. Index available (bound in Jan. issue). ***Continues*** *Sportsguide Master Reference, 0277-0296.*
**Desc:** A 1,100 page reference directory of sports organizations, teams, publications, TV/radio programmers, sports marketing firms, equipment footwear suppliers, and market statistics reports.

US/0898-6541
**SPORTS MARKETING NEWS.** ***Ceased.*** [Sports market. news]. Vol. 1, No. 1 Oct.(1986)-?. Periodical. English. bw. Technical Marketing Corporation, PO Box 453, Winchester MA 01890. **DD** 796.

GW
**SPORTS. MIT SPORT ILLUSTRIERTE.** German. mo. DM90.00. Gruner und Jahr Ag & Co, Abonnenten Service, D 20080 Hamburg Germany. **Tel** 011 49 40 37030. **(Subscription address:** Deutscher Pressevertrieb Buch, PO Box 101602 Hansa GmbH, D 20010 Hamburg Germany**)**

●US/1062-8215
**SPORTS-N-REVIEW.** (SPORTS-N-REVIEW / SPORTS ANALYSIS INC.). **VFOAT** Sports n Review. (1992)-. Periodical. English. qt. $9.95. Sports Analysis, Inc., PO Box 56503, Harwood Heights IL 60656-0503.

US/0161-6706
**SPORTS 'N SPOKES.** **Added/Corp** Crase, Nancy. Vol. 1 (May/June 1975)-. Periodical. English. bm. $12.00 (one year), $22.00 (two year), $32.00 (three year). Paralyzed Veterans of America Publications, 2111 East Highland, Suite 180 B, Phoenix AZ 85016. **Tel** (602)246-9426, FAX (602)224-0507. **ED** Cliff and Nancy Crase. **LC** GV709.3; .S69. **DD** 796/.06/0880810973. Index available. cum. index. **Bk Rev**. **Ad Acc**. **Adv Mgr Tel** (602)246-9426. **Circ:** 9,500.
**Desc:** Covers wheelchair sports and recreation. Competitive sports coverage, recreational opportunities, how-to tips, calendar, and new product news.
**Ind/Abst** Phys. Educ. Index; SPORT Discus; SportSearch (May 1987-).

UK
**SPORTS NUTRITION.** See Nutrition and Dietetics.

US/0883-1580
**SPORTS PERIODICALS INDEX, THE.** ***Ceased.*** [Sports period. index]. Vol. 1, No. 1, Jan. (1985)-?. English. mo. National Information Systems Inc, 2750 South State, Ann Arbor MI 48104-6738. **LC** GV561; .S743. **DD** 796/.05. **UDC** 796(048.3).

US
**SPORTS PROFILES.** English. Six times a year (Jan., Mar., May, July, Sept., Nov.). $10.00. Sports Profiles, 4711 Golf Road, Suite 715, Skokie IL 60076. **Tel** (312)673-0592. **ED** Paula Blaine. **Ad Acc. Circ:** 50,000, 100.000 readership.
**Desc:** News and information on sports.

US/0732-0043
**SPORTS QUARTERLY PRESENTS INSIDE HOCKEY.** **VFOAT** Inside Hockey. Periodical. English. an. $2.25 each issue. Lopez Publications Inc., 152 Madison Avenue, Suite 905 & 906, New York NY 10016. **Tel** (212)689-3933. **UDC** 796.96.

US/1073-1326
**SPORTS REVIEW WRESTLING (AMBLER, PA.).** (SPORTS REVIEW WRESTLING.). [Sports rev. wrestl.]. **VFOAT** Wrestling. (1993)-. Periodical. English. bm. $25.50. London Publishing Company, PO Box 910, Fort Washington PA 19034. **Tel** (215)643-6385, FAX (215)540-0146. **DD** 796. **Ad Acc.**

UK/0490-5474
**SPORTS TURF BULLETIN.** [Sports turf bull.]. (1951)-. Bulletin. English. Four times a year. Free to members; £7.00 other. Sports Turf Research Institute, Bingley, West Yorkshire BD16 1AU England. **Tel** 011 44 274 565131, FAX 011 44 274 561891. **ED** R.D.C. Evans. Index available. cum. index. **Bk Rev**, (Qty: varies). **Acid Free. Circ:** 5,500 (ctrl). Documents available from BLDSC. ***Continues*** *Notes from the St. Ives Research Station.*
**Ind/Abst** SPORT Discus.

US
**SPORTS WEEKLY NEWSLETTER/BASKETBALL.** English. Sixteen times a year (During basketball season). $50.00. Sports Weekly Newsletter, PO Box 60008, North Charleston SC 29419. **Tel** (803)797-6173.

US
**SPORTS WEEKLY NEWSLETTER/ FOOTBALL/ THE LITTLE GREEN SHEET.** English. Twenty-two times a year (During football season only). $60.00. Sports Weekly Newsletter, PO Box 60008, North Charleston SC 29419. **Tel** (803)797-6173.

US/0272-7579
**SPORTSCAPE.** V. 1- Winter 1981-. Periodical. English. qt. Free. Sportscape Inc, 400 Commonwealth Avenue, Boston MA 02215. **Tel** (617)277-3823.

US/0882-553X
**SPORTSEARCH.** See Recreation, Leisure-Abstracting, Bibliographies and Statistics.

AT/1033-8977
**SPORTSNETWORK.** [Sportsnetw.]. **Added/Corp** Australian Society of Sport Administrators. (1986)-. Periodical. English. qt. **DD** 796.05.
**Ind/Abst** SPORT Discus.

GW
**SPORTSTATTEN IN NORDRHEIN-WESTFALEN / HERAUSGEBER LANDESAMT FUR DATENVERARBEITUNG UND STATISTIK NORDRHEIN-WESTFALEN.** German. DM18.00. Landesamt fuer Datenverarbeitung und Statistik Nordrhein-Westfalen, Postfach 101105, 40002 Duesseldorf Germany. **Tel** (0211)944901, FAX (0211)442006, telex 8586654 LDST D. **LC** HA1320.N6; A32 subser; GV433.G43 G43N67. **DD** 690/.58043/094356.

US/0733-8708
**SPORTSTYLE (CONSUMER EDITION).** (SPORTSTYLE.). [Sportstyle]. **VFOAT** Sport Style. Vol. 1, No. 1 (Apr. 1983)-. Periodical. English. Six times a year. $35.00. Fairchild Publications Inc, 7 West 34th Street, 4th Floor, New York NY 10001. **Tel** (212)630-4230. **ED** Mark Sullivan. **LC** WMLC L 83/124. **[CCC].**
**Ind/Abst** F&S Index Plus Text, Int. [Full Txt.] [Select. Cov.]; Mark. Advert. Ref. Serv. [Full Txt.]; PROMT [Full Txt.].

US/0099-0388
**SPORTSWOMAN, THE.** V. 1- Spring 1973-. Periodical. English. bm. $4.50. Jensen-Fane Publishing, PO Box 2611, Culver City CA 90230. **LC** GV709; .S677. **DD** 796/.019/4. **UDC** 796-055.2. available on microfilm and microfiche from University Microfilms International (UMI).

GW/0342-2402
**SPORTUNTERRICHT.** See Education-Physical Education and Training.

HU
**SPORTVEZETO.** **Added/Corp** Hungary. Magyar Testnevelesi es Sportszovetseg. (19??)-. Academic Scholarly Publication. Hungarian. Twelve times a year. $20.00. Akademiai Kiado, Publishing House of the Hungarian Academy of Sciences, Prielle Kornelia u. 19-35, H-1117 Budapest Hungary. **Tel** 011 36 1 1811991, FAX 011 36 1 1811991, telex 22-6228 AKNYO H. **(Subscription address:** Kultura, Hungarian Foreign Trading Company, PO Box 149, H-1389 Budapest 62 Hungary**)** **LC** GV648.H8; S66.

GW
**SPORTWISSENSCHAFT.** (1971)-. Periodical. Multiple languages (English, French and German; summaries and/or abstracts in French). qt. DM83.20. Verlag Karl Hofmann, Postfach 1360, D-73603 Schorndorf Germany. **Tel** 011 49 7181 4020. **LC** GV201; .S66. **Bk Rev. Ad Acc.** ctrl circ.
**Desc:** Deals with theoretical discussions and research results in the theory of sport, intended to form a basis for the development of sport and to advance the cooperation between physical education and other sciences.
**Ind/Abst** Leis. Recreat. Tour. Abstr.; SportSearch (May 1987-).

GW
**SPORTWISSENSCHAFT UND SPORTPRAXIS.** (1970)-. Monographic series. German. ir (4-8 books per year). Price varies per volume. Verlag Ingrid Czwalina, Reesenbuettler Redder 75, D-22926 Ahrensburg Germany. **Tel** 011 49 4102 59190. **(Subscription address:** Feldhaus Verlag GmbH, Postfach 730240, D-22122 Hamburg Germany.**)** **ED** Clemens Czwalina. **LC** GV565; .S36. ***Continues*** *Schriftenreihe fur Sportwissenschaft und Sportpraxis.*
**Desc:** Books on sport science and practice.

US/0740-0802
**SPOTLIGHT ON YOUTH SPORTS.** (SPOTLIGHT ON YOUTH SPORTS : A PUBLICATION OF THE INSTITUTE FOR THE STUDY OF YOUTH SPORTS.). [Spotlight youth sports]. **Added/Corp** Institute for the Study of Youth Sports (Michigan). **VFOAT** Spotlight. (19??)-. Periodical. English. Four times a year (Mar., June, Sept., Dec.). Free, Michigan; $3.00 other. Michigan State University / Youth Sports Institute, East Lansing MI 48824. **Tel** (517)353-6689, FAX (517)353-2944. **ED** Vern Seefeldt. **Circ:** 1,000 (ctrl).
**Desc:** For educators, parents, coaches, and administrators of youth sports.

US/0745-4368
**SPURS & FEATHERS.** **VFOAT** Spurs and Feathers. **VAT** Spurs and feathers. (19??)-. Periodical. English. Thirty-eight times a year (Weekly during school year). $31.00. Gamecock Associates, PO Box 8055, Columbia SC 29202. **Tel** (803)256-1789, FAX (803)256-1789. **ED** Dexter D Hudson. **Ad Acc.** ctrl circ.
**Desc:** Special interest sports newspaper that covers the University of South Carolina.

CN/0821-025X
**SQUASH LIFE.** (SQUASH LIFE / SQUASH ONTARIO.). [Squash life]. **Added/Corp** Squash Ontario. Vol. 5, No. 3 (Sept./Oct. 1981)-. Periodical. English. Five

times a year. 20.00Can$. Squash Ontario, 1220 Sheppard Avenue East, Willowdale Ontario M2K 2X1 Canada. **Tel** (905)495-4140. **DD** 796.34/3/09713. ***Continues*** *'Let Point', 0821-0241.*
**Ind/Abst** SPORT Discus; SportSearch (May 1987-).

US/0164-7148
**SQUASH NEWS (HOPE VALLEY, R.I.).** (SQUASH NEWS.). [Squash news]. Vol. 1 (Apr. 1978)-. Periodical. English. Ten times a year (July/August issue combined). $20.00 (one year); $35.00 (two years). Squash News, 186 Arcadia Road, Hope Valley RI 02832. **Tel** (401)539-2381, FAX (401)539-2490. **ED** Hazel White Jones. **DD** 796. **Bk Rev**, (Qty: 4-6). **Ad Acc**, **Adv Mgr:** Tom Jones. **Circ:** 10,000.
**Desc:** A publication on the game of squash. Features tournament results from professional to novice level, instruction columns, and articles on prominent players.

UK
**SQUASH PLAYER INTERNATIONAL.** English. Ten times a year (April/May and July/August issues combined). £29.95 UK; £31.15 Europe; £35.15 other. Stonehart Leisure Magazines, Unit 1 Hainault Road, Little Heath Romford RM6 5NP England. **Tel** 011-44-81-597-7335, FAX 011-44-81-599-5965. **ED** Robin Clark.
**Desc:** The magazine for the serious squash players.
**Ind/Abst** SPORT Discus.

CN/0229-2351
**SQUASH REVIEW.** (SQUASH REVIEW : NATIONAL CAPITAL SQUASH RACQUETS ASSOCIATION NEWSLETTER.). [Squash rev.]. Vol. 1, No. 1 (Nov. 12, 1976)-. Newsletter. English. Free. National Capital Squash Racquets Association, Box 8943, Ottawa K1G 3J2 Canada. **DD** 796.34/3/0971383. **UDC** 796.346.

GW/0172-4029
**STADION (COLOGNE, GERMANY).** (STADION.). [Stadion]. **VFOAT** Arena. (1975)-. Periodical. German (English and French). Twice a year. DM96.00. Academia Verlag Richarz GmbH, Postfach 1163, D 53734 St. Augustin Germany. **Tel** 011 49 2241 333349. **ED** M. Laemmer (phone: (02241) 4982383). **LC** GV561; .S77. **DD** 796/.09. Index available. **Bk Rev**. **Ad Acc**. **Circ:** 400 (ctrl). ***Continues*** *Arena.*
**Desc:** This periodical aims on one hand to make the results of various kinds of basic historical and philological research available to sports historians, and on the other hand to stimulate the interest of social historians and historians of culture in questions connected with the history of sport so that international co-operation and exchange of information between those working in these fields can be increased.
**Ind/Abst** Am. Hist. Life (1975-); BHA : Biblio. Hist. Art; SPORT Discus.

GW/0233-2736
**START BERLIN, DDR. 1986.** (START.). [Start Berl. DDR, 1986]. (1986)-. Periodical. German. mo. $30.00. Sportverlag, Neustaedtische Kirchstr 15, D 10117 Berlin Germany. **UDC** 79.

US/0362-4579
**STATE LAWS GOVERNING BOXING AND WRESTLING IN CALIFORNIA, WITH RULES AND REGULATIONS.** **See** Law.

FR
**STATISTIQUES TEMPS LIBRE, JEUNESSE ET SPORTS.** **Added/Corp** France. Ministere du Temps, de la Jeunesse et de Sports. Direction de l'Administration. Bureau des Etudes et de la Statistique. (19??)-. French. 118 Avenue du President-Kennedy, 75775 Paris Cedex 16 France. **LC** GV79; .S8. **DD** 790.1/92. ***Continues*** *France. Ministere de la Jeunesse, des Sports et des Loisirs. Division des Etudes et de la Statistique. Annuaire.*

US/1061-4524
**STN (NEW YORK, N.Y.).** (STN.). [STN]. **VFOAT** STN, Skiing Trade News. (199?)-. Periodical. English. bm (6 issues). $25.00. Times Mirror Magazines, Two Park Avenue, New York NY 10016. **Tel** (212)779-5000. **DD** 796. available on an online database (file 648/Full-Text) from DIALOG. ***Continues*** *Ski Trade News, 0037-6299.*
**Desc:** Provides objective information on extensive product testing of ski apparel and equipment. Also, up-to-the-minute information on new products.
**Ind/Abst** Bus. Index (1992-); Gen. BusinessFile (1992-); Gen. Period. Index (1992-); Trade Ind. ASAP [Full Txt.]; Trade Ind. Index [Full Txt.]; Vocat. Search (July 1993-).

US/0731-2008
**STOCK CAR CLASSIFICATION GUIDE.** **See** Transportation-Automobiles.

US/0734-7340
**STOCK CAR RACING.** **VFOAT** Stock Car Racing Magazine. (19??)-. Periodical. English. mo. $18.95. General Media Publishing Company, 1965 Broadway, New York NY 10023. **Tel** (212)496-6100. **(Subscription address:** CDS Agency Hard Copy, PO Box 4966, Des Moines IA 50340.**)** **ED** Dick Berggren. **LC** GV1029.9.S74; S76. **DD** 796.7/2/0973. **Bk Rev**. **Ad Acc**. **Circ:** 81,000.
**Desc:** America's oval track racer's "Bible". It strives to reach virtually every participant in closed wheel oval track racing.

US/1064-1629
**STRATTON MAGAZINE.** [Stratton mag.]. **Added/Corp** Stratton Corporation. Vol. 8, No. 8 (Fall 1980)-. Periodical. English. qt (Feb., June, Sept., Dec.). $8.00 US; $12.00 other. Stratton Magazine, PO Box 85, Dorset VT 05251. **Tel** (802)867-0242, FAX (802)867-0102. **ED** Marsha Norman. **DD** 917. **Bk Rev**. **Ad Acc**, **Adv Mgr:** Lee Romand. **Circ:** 20,000 (ctrl). ***Continues*** *Stratton Mountain News.*
**Desc:** Lifestyle publication dealing with regional topics of interest, sports, skiing, arts, nature, and Vermont history.

US
**STREET & SMITH'S PRO BASKETBALL.** **VFOAT** Pro Basketball; Street and Smith's Pro Basketball. (1988)-. English. an. $6.00 US; $8.50 other. Street and Smiths, 304 East 45th Street, New York NY 10017. **Tel** (212)880-8698. **LC** GV885.7; .S85. **DD** 796.323/64/0973. ***Continues*** *Street & Smith's Basketball.*

US/1053-2641
**STREET & SMITH'S PRO FOOTBALL.** [Street Smith's pro footb.]. **VFOAT** Street and Smith's Pro Football; Pro Football. 25th Year (1987)-. Periodical. English. an. $6.00 US; $8.50 other. Street and Smiths, 304 East 45th Street, New York NY 10017. **Tel** (212)880-8698. **LC** GV937; .S85. **DD** 796. available on microfilm from University Microfilms International (UMI). ***Continues*** *Street and Smith's Official Yearbook: Pro Football, 0092-3214.*

US/0192-1967
**STREET MACHINES & BRACKET RACING.** **See** Transportation-Automobiles.

US/0277-5735
**STREET RODDER.** (19??)-. Periodical. English. Twelve times a year. $23.95 (one year), $37.95 (two years). McMullen Publishing Inc, 2145 West La Palma Avenue, PO Box 70015, Anaheim CA 92801-1785. **Tel** (714)572-2255, FAX (714)572-1864. **ED** Geoff Carter.

US/1059-793X
**STUDENT SPORTS (CAL-HI SPORTS ED.).** (STUDENT SPORTS.). [Stud. sports]. (1991)-. Periodical. English. mo. $29.00. Cal-Hi Sports, 777 Convention Way, Suite 100, Anaheim CA 92802. **Tel** (714)740-4717. **DD** 796. ***Continues*** *Cal-Hi Sports, 1054-5905.*

FR/0990-0845
**SUBAQUA MARSEILLE.** (SUBAQUA.). (1988)-. Periodical. French. bm (6 issues). 160.00F France; 250.00F other. Federation Francaise d'Etudes et de Sports Sous Marins, 24 Quai de Rive Neuve, 13007 Marseille France. **Tel** 011 33 91 339931. **UDC** 797.2. ***Continues*** *Etudes et Sports Sous-Marins (1973), 0425-5054.*

●CN/1192-523X
**SUKCES W AMERYCE.** [Sukces Am.]. (1992)-. Periodical. English. mo. $1.80 (single issue). Sukces y Ameryce, 2559 Lakeshore Boulevard, Suite 40, Toronto, Ontario M8V 1E5 Canada. **DD** 796. ***Continues*** *Na Wirazu., 1188-8377.*

FI
**SUOMEN SHAKKI.** **Added/Corp** Suomen Keskusshakkiliitto. Suomen Shakkiliitto. Tyoevaeen Shakkiliitto. Suomen Tehtaevaeniekat. (1943)-. Periodical. Finnish. Twelve times a year. Fmk200.00 Finland; Fmk230.00 others. Suomen Shakki, PL 61 SF 04401, Jarvenpaa Finland. **Tel** 011 358 0 2919319, FAX 011 358 0 2918336. **Bk Rev**. **Ad Acc**. **Circ:** 2,100.
**Desc:** Information on national and international games, theory, etc.

US/0733-1630
**SUPER BOWL FACT BOOK.** ***Title Change.*** [Super bowl fact book]. **VFOAT** Sporting News Super Bowl Fact Book. (1982)-(19??). English. an. Sporting News, c/o Sharon Moore, 1212 North Lindbergh Boulevard, PO Box 56, St Louis MO 63166. **Tel** (314)997-7111, (800)825-8508. **LC** GV956.2.S8; S9. **DD** 796.332/7. ***Continued by*** *Super Bowl Book.*

US/0039-5692
**SUPER STOCK & DRAG ILLUSTRATED.** **VFOAT** Super Stock; Super Stock & Dl. **VAT** Super Stock and Drag Illustrated. (19??)-. Periodical. English. mo. $19.95. General Media Publishing Company, 1965 Broadway, New York NY 10023. **Tel** (212)496-6100. **(Subscription address:** CDS Agency Hard Copy, PO Box 4966, Des Moines IA 50340.**)** **ED** Steve Collison. **Bk Rev**. **Ad Acc**. **Circ:** 56,000.
**Desc:** Dedicated to the drag racing enthusiast, with articles and color photos on latest events and in-depth technical features.

US
**SUPERPREP. AMERICA'S RECRUITING MAGAZINE.** English. Three times a year (Jan., Mar., Aug.). $59.00 (one year); $110.00 (two years); $165.00 (three years). JCW Publishing, PO Box 487, Laguna Beach CA 92652. **Tel** (714)494-7866, FAX (714)497-3173. **ED** Allen Wallace. **Ad Acc**. ctrl circ.
**Desc:** Information on evaluation, descriptions and college enrollment of high school football propects in the US.

KO
**SUPOCHU REJO.** **VFOAT** Sports, Leisure. 1st Vol. (1984/4)-. Periodical. Korean (Korean). mo. Hanguk Ilbosa, 14 Chunghak-dong Chongno-ku, Seoul Korea. **LC** AP95.K6; S86. **UDC** 796/799(519.5).

KO
**SUPOCHU SAJIN YONGAM.** **Added/Corp** Hanguk Ilbosa. (1983)-. Korean. W30,000. Hanguk Ilbosa, 14 Chunghak-dong Chongno-ku, Seoul Korea. **LC** GV663.K6; S86.

US/0270-2630
**SURF REPORT, THE.** Vol. 1 (July 1980)-. Periodical. English. mo. $35.00 US; $42.00. Surfer Publications Inc., PO Box 1028, Dana Point CA 92629. **Tel** (714)496-5922, (800)289-0636, FAX (714)496-7849. **(Subscription address:** Neodata / Colorado, PO Box 2606, Boulder Boulder CO 80322.**)** **ED** Rus Calisch. **Circ:** 1,000.
**Desc:** Summary and forecast of worldwide surf conditions.

AT
**SURF SKI QUARTERLY.** English. qt (Mar., June, Sep., Dec.). Surf Ski Quarterly Pty Ltd., PO Box 854, Brookvale 2100 Australia. **Tel** 011 61 2 9050162.
**Ind/Abst** SPORT Discus.

US/0276-6582
**SURFBOARD.** [Surfboard]. 1980-. English (French and Spanish). $12.95. Transmedia, PO Box 9024, La Jolla CA 92038-9024. **ED** Stephen Shaw. **LC** GV840.S8; S76. **DD** 797.1/72/05. **UDC** 797.178. ***Continues*** *Surfboard Builder's Yearbook.*
**Desc:** Contains complete instructions, detailed with photos and illustrations for designing, shaping, laminating, air brushing, finishing and repairing surfboards, as well as sailboards. Includes product data on materials and supplies and a chapter on how to surf.

US/0039-6036
**SURFER.** **VFOAT** Surfer Monthly. (1960)-. Periodical. English. mo (12 issues). $19.95. Surfer Publications Inc., PO Box 1028, Dana Point CA 92629. **Tel** (714)496-5922, (800)289-0636, FAX (714)496-7849. **(Subscription address:** Neodata / Colorado, PO Box 2606, Boulder Boulder CO 80322.**)** **ED** Matt Warshaw. **LC** GV840.S8; S78. **DD** 797.1/72/05. **Bk Rev**. **Ad Acc**. **Circ:** 120,000.
**Ind/Abst** Gen. Period. Index (Jan. 1985-Dec. 1985); SportSearch; Mag. Index (1978-Dec. 1985)(1977-).

●US/1062-3892
**SURFER'S JOURNAL, THE.** [Surfer's j.]. (Jan. 1992)-. Periodical. English. Four times a year. $35.00 US; $55.00 other. Surfers Journal, 1050 Calle Cordillera Unit 106, San Clemente CA 92672. **Tel** (714)361-0331. **ED** Steve Pezman. **DD** 797. **Ad Acc**.
**Desc:** Edited for the older mature surfing enthusiast (age 25 and up).

US/0194-9314
**SURFING (SAN CLEMENTE, CALIF.).** (SURFING.). **VFOAT** Surfing Magazine. (1964)-. Periodical. English. mo. $19.95 US; $42.00 Canada; $43.00 other. Western Empire Publishing, PO Box 3010, San Clemente CA 92672. **Tel** (714)492-7873. **ED** David Gilovich. **LC** WMLC L 83/514. **DD** 797. **Circ:** 88,000 (ctrl).
**Desc:** Edited for the serious participant as well as the beach lifestyle audience. Color photos, interviews with top pros, contest results and beach lifestyle fashion complete the editorial scope.
**Ind/Abst** Calif. Period. Index (19??-); SportSearch (May 1987-).

SW
**SVENSK JAKTKALENDER.** Began with vol. for 1972/73. Swedish. Forlagahuset Norden, Box 305, 201 23 1 Malmo Switzerland. **LC** SK210; .S88. **UDC** 799.2(485).

●PL/0867-6410
**SWIAT KARATE.** [Swiat Karate]. (1991)-. Periodical. Polish. mo. Price on Request. **(Subscription address:** ARS Polona, PO Box 1001, 00068 Warsaw Poland.**)** **UDC** 796.8.

CN/0319-0560
**SWIM.** Vol. 1 (Feb. 1974)-. Periodical. English. Ten times a year. 30.00Can$ Canada; 65.00Can$ others. Swim Canada, 356 Sumach Street, Toronto Ontario M4X 1VA Canada. **Tel** (416)963-5599. **ED** N. J. Thierry. **DD** 797.2/1/0971.
**Ind/Abst** SPORT Discus; SportSearch (May 1987-).

US/8755-2027
**SWIM (ARLINGTON, VA.).** (SWIM.). [Swim]. **VFOAT** Swim Magazine. Vol. 1, No. 1 (Oct./Nov. 1984)-. Periodical. English. bm (6 issues). $16.95 (one year), $32.50 (two year), $46.95 (three year). Sports Publications Inc., PO Box 91870, Pasadena CA 91109. **Tel** (818)304-7755. **ED** Kim A. Hansen. **DD** 797. **Bk Rev**. **Ad Acc**. **Circ:** 8,000 (ctrl). available on microfilm.

## Recreation, Leisure —Sports

Desc: Dedicated to adult fitness and competitive swimmers; a must for adult swimmers everywhere. Ind/Abst SPORT Discus.

US/0163-2884
**SWIMMING AND DIVING RULES.** Main/Corp National Federation of State High School Associations. VFOAT Swimming and Diving Rules and Case Book. English. an. $1.75. National Federation of State High School Associations, 11724 Northwest Plaza Circle, PO Box 20626, Kansas City MO 64195-0626. Tel (816)464-5400, FAX (816)464-5571. LC GV837; .N32A. DD 797.2. UDC 797.2.063. Continues Swimming and Diving Case Book, 0145-3831.

UK
**SWIMMING POOL NEWS.** English. bm (6 issues). £34.00 UK; £39.00 other. MGS Publishing Ltd., 172 London Road, Guildford Surr GU1 1XR England. Tel 011 44 483 306304.

UK/0306-0403
**SWIMMING TEACHER.** [Swim. teach.]. (1952)-. Periodical. English. mo. Free to members. Swimming Teachers Association, Anchor House, Birch Street, Walsall WMid WS2 8H2 England. Bk Rev, (Qty: occassionally). Ad Acc. Acid Free. ctrl circ. Continues Northern Messenger.

US/0039-7415
**SWIMMING TECHNIQUE.** (SWIMMING TECHNIQUE : OFFICIAL PUBLICATION OF THE AMERICAN SWIMMING COACHES ASSOCIATION.). Added/Corp American Swimming Coaches Association. Vol. 1 (April 1964)-. Periodical. English. qt (Feb., May, Aug., Nov.). $13.95 (one year); $26.95 (two year); $38.95 (three year). Sports Publications Inc., PO Box 91870, Pasadena CA 91109. Tel (818)304-7755. ED Mark Muckenfuss. LC WMLC L 83/3578. Bk Rev. Ad Acc. Circ: 8,000 (ctrl). available on microfilm and microfiche from University Microfilms International (UMI).
 Desc: Features instructional, 'how to' material on swimming for both participants and those engaged in aquatic sports.
 Ind/Abst Phys. Educ. Index; SPORT Discus; SportSearch (May 1987-).

UK
**SWIMMING TIMES.** (1923)-. Periodical. English. Twelve times a year. £16.75 UK; £21.50 other. Swimming Times Ltd, Harold Fern House, Derby Square, Loughborough LE11 0AL England. Tel 011 44 509 234433. ED Richard H. Brown. Ad Acc. Circ: 15,236.
 Desc: Official journal of the Amateur Swimming Association and the Institute of Swimming Teachers and Coaches.
 Ind/Abst SPORT Discus; SportSearch (May 1987-).

US
**SWIMMING WORLD.** (1960)-. Periodical. English. mo. Swimming World Publications, 116 West Hazel Street, Inglewood CA 90045. Tel (310)674-2120. UDC 797.2. Continues Swimming World (New Haven).

US/0039-7431
**SWIMMING WORLD AND JUNIOR SWIMMER (1965).** (SWIMMING WORLD AND JUNIOR SWIMMER.). Added/Corp National Interscholastic Swimming Coaches Association. American Swimming Coaches Association. College Swimming Coaches Association of America. United States Swimming. Vol. 6, No. 9 (Sept. 1965)-. Periodical. English. mo. $21.50 (one year), $39.95 (two year), $57.95 (three). Sports Publications Inc., PO Box 91870, Pasadena CA 91109. Tel (818)304-7755. ED Bob Ingram. LC GV837; .S94. DD 797.2/1/05. Bk Rev Ad Acc. Circ: 31,000 (ctrl). available on microfilm and microfiche from University Microfilms International (UMI). Continues Swimming World (North Hollywood, Los Angeles, Calif.)
 Desc: The national magazine for competitive aquatics, swimming, diving and water polo at all levels, including the Olympics. Articles on coaching, nutrition and training.
 Ind/Abst Acad. Abstr. (Jan. 1994)-; Mag. Artic. Summar. Elite (Jan. 1994-); Mag. Artic. Summar. CD-ROM (Jan. 1994-); Phys. Educ. Index; SPORT Discus; SportSearch (May 1987-).

US/0746-5726
**SYNCHRO.** Title Change. [Synchro]. Vol. 17, No. 3 (June 1979)-(199?). Periodical. English. bm. Dawn P Bean, 11902 Red Hill Avenue, Santa Ana CA 92705. DD 797. Continues Synchro-Info. Continued by Synchro Swimming USA, 1069-2290.
 Ind/Abst SPORT Discus; SportSearch (May 1987-).

FI
**SYYSRIISTATIEDUSTELU.** Finnish. an. Riista Ja Kalatalouden Tutkimuslaitos, Kalantutkimusosasto PL 193, 00131 Helsinki Finland. LC SK543.F5; S96.

PL
**SZACHY.** See Recreation, Leisure-Games and Amusements.

IT
**T-SPORT.** Italian. L90000 Italy; L180000 other. Sinopia Ed, Via G. Murat 84, 20159 Milan Italy. Tel 011 39 2 688-3641, FAX 011 39 2 668-02971.

IT
**T-SPORT : INSERTI TECNICI CALCIO.** (19??)-. Italian. ir. Sinopia Ed, Via G. Murat 84, 20159 Milan Italy. Tel 011 39 2 688-3641, FAX 011 39 2 668-02971.

IT
**T-SPORT : INSERTI TECNICI GESTIONE E MANUTENZIONE.** Italian. ir. Sinopia Ed, Via G. Murat 84, 20159 Milan Italy. Tel 011 39 2 688-3641, FAX 011 39 2 668-02971.

IT
**T-SPORT : INSERTI TECNICI GLI SPORT TENNIS ATLETICA GOLF.** (19??)-. Italian. ir. L18000. European Magazines Guides Srl, Via Murat 84, 20159 Milan Italy. Tel 011 39 2 6682261.

IT
**T-SPORT : INSERTI TECNICI PALAZZETTI PALESTRE SALE SPORTIVE.** (19??)-. Italian. ir. L18000. European Magazines Guides Srl, Via Murat 84, 20159 Milan Italy. Tel 011 39 2 6682261.

IT
**T-SPORT : RACCOLTA SCHEDE TECNICHE.** Italian. ir. Sinopia Ed, Via G. Murat 84, 20159 Milan Italy. Tel 011 39 2 688-3641, FAX 011 39 2 668-02971.

CN/0828-4539
**TABLE TENNIS TECHNICAL.** [Table tennis tech.]. VFOAT Technique Tennis de Table; TTT-Tennis Technical; TTT-Technique Tennis de Table. Periodical. English (French). ir. Free. Canadian Table Tennis Association, 333 River Road, Vanier Ontario K1L 8B9 Canada. DD 796.34/6/06071. UDC 796.386(71). ctrl circ.

US
**TAC/USA OFFICIAL RULES FOR ATHLETICS.** Added/Corp Athletics Congress (U.S.). VFOAT T.A.C. U.S.A. Official Rules for Athletics; TAC USA Official Rules for Athletics; Official Rules for Athletics. VAT The Athletics Congress of the USA Official Rules for Athletics. (19??)-. Periodical. English. ir. $6.00 US; $8.00 Canada; $10.00 other. TAC USA / Book Order Department, PO Box 120, Indianapolis IN 46206. Tel (317)297-2900.

US/0141-028X
**TAE KWON DO TIMES.** [Tae kwon do times]. VFOAT Tae-Kwon-Do-Times. (198?)-. Periodical. English. Eight times a year. $16.00 (one year), $27.00 (two year). Tri-Mount Publications, 1423 18th Street, Bettendorf IA 52722. Tel (319)359-7200. ED Rod Speidel and Carol Hart. DD 796. Ad Acc, Adv Mgr: C Hart.
 Desc: Martial arts, fitness and health.

JA/0286-6951
**TAIIKU KENKYUJO KIYO.** See Education-Physical Education and Training.

US/0899-6849
**TALKIN' TWINS BASEBALL.** Periodical. English. bw. $8.00 US; $12.00 other. Que Publishing Company, 8009 Irving Avenue North, Brooklyn Park MN 55444.

US/1059-6364
**TAPER & SHAVE.** [Taper shave]. VFOAT Taper and Shave. (1990)-. Periodical. English. Eighteen times a year. $49.00. Taper & Shave, PO Box 192022, San Francisco CA 94119. Tel (415)777-4567, FAX (415)777-4567. ED Stuatr Corliss. DD 796. Ad Acc.
 Desc: Results of top college, high school swimming meets (dual, conference, state, & national). Recruiting updates & occasional features for serious coaches, swimmers and hard core fans.

UK/0143-8751
**TARGET GUN.** (19??)-. English. mo. £23.00 UK; £30.00 other. Peterson Publications Ltd, Accts Dept, High House, Vigo, Bromsgrove Worcs B601LL England. Tel 011 44 905 795564, FAX 0905-795905. Bk Rev. Ad Acc. Circ: 25,000.

GW
**TAUCHEN.** Periodical. German. 51.60. Jahr-Verlag, Schlossstrasse 6, 2000 Hamburg 70 Germany. LC GV840.S78; T38. DD 797.2/3 UDC 797.26. Formed by the union of Delphin and Taucher.

US
**TEAM AND TRAIL.** English. mo. $24.00 US; $29.00 Canada; $30.00 other, (surface mail) $45.00 (air mail). Box 128, Center Harbour NH 03226-0128. Tel (603)253-6265, FAX (603)253-9513. ED Cynthia J Molburg. Bk Rev. Ad Acc.
 Desc: Focuses on sled dog sports and related subjects.

US
**TEAM MARKETING REPORT.** Vol. 1, Issue 1 (Oct. 1988)-. Periodical. English. Twelve times a year. $169.00 (one year). Team Marketing Report, 660 West Grand Street, Suite 100E, Chicago IL 60610. Tel (312)829-7060. ED Alan Friedman. cum. index. Bk Rev. Ad Acc.

CN/0705-7504
**TECHNICAL MANUAL - CANADIAN SOCCER ASSOCIATION.** Main/Corp Canadian Soccer Association. V. 1- Nov. 1977-. Periodical. English. qt. $5.00 Canada; $6.00 US and Caribbean; $7.00 other. Canadian Soccer Association, 1600 James Naismith Drive, Gloucester Ontario K1B 5N4 Canada. Tel (613)747-2900. DD 796.33/4/077. UDC 796.332(035.3)(71). Supersedes Coach, 0701-001X.

US/0748-5999
**TECHNIQUE (INDIANAPOLIS, IND.).** (TECHNIQUE : THE OFFICIAL TECHNICAL PUBLICATION OF THE UNITED STATES GYMNASTICS FEDERATION.). [Technique]. Added/Corp United States Gymnastics Federation. (19??)-. Periodical. English. Twelve times a year. $25.00. US Gymnastics Federation, 201 South Capitol, Suite 300, Indianapolis IN 46225-1054. Tel (317)237-5050, telex 27-2385 USGYM-IND. ED Mike Jaeki, Luan Peszek and Steve Whitlock. LC GV461; .T4. DD 796.4/1/0973. Continues USGF Technical Journal.
 Desc: Contains technical articles related to the coaching and judging of gymnastics.

IT
**TECNICA DEL NUOTO, LA.** Societa Editrice Aquarius, Via Albere 19, 37138 Verona Italy. Tel 011 39 45 577399.

XV
**TELESNA VZGOJA, SPORT IN SPORTNA REKREACIJA.** See Education-Physical Education and Training.

PL/0137-933X
**TEMPO KRAKOW.** (TEMPO.). [Tempo Krak.]. (1959)-. Periodical. Polish. tw $104.00. (Subscription address: ARS Polona, PO Box 1001, 00068 Warsaw Poland.) UDC 796. Continues Gos Sportowca, 0431-9834.

CN/0228-6629
**TEMPS LIBRE (LAUZON).** (TEMPS LIBRE : BULLETIN DE LA SOCIETE QUEBECOISE D'HISTOIRE DU LOISIR.). [Temps libre]. Vol. 4, No. 1 (May 1980)-. Bulletin. French. Free to members, $10.00 others. Temps Libre / Canada, 36 Chemin du Vieux Fort, Lauzon Quebec G6V 2C5 Canada. DD 796/.09714. UDC 379.8(09)(714). Continues Universite Laval. Groupe de Recherche sur l'Histoire de l'Activite Physique. GRHAP, 0705-1573.

PL/0867-1486
**TENIS STOOWY.** [Tenis Stoowy]. (1989)-. Periodical. Polish. bm (6 issues). Price on Request. (Subscription address: ARS Polona, PO Box 1001, 00068 Warsaw Poland.) UDC 796.38.

AT
**TENNIS.** English. mo. 40.00Aus$ Australia; 45.00Aus$ other. Nicholson Media Group, 1 457 Malvern Road, South Varra VIC 3141 Australia. Tel 011 61 3 8268446.

US/0749-6478
**TENNIS BUYER'S GUIDE (NORWALK, CONN.).** (TENNIS BUYER'S GUIDE.). [Tennis buy. guide]. (Apr. 1984)-. Periodical. English. Six times a year. Free (members), $36.00 (nonmembers) US & Canada; $90.00 (nonmembers) other. Golf Digest - Tennis Inc., 5520 Park Avenue, Trumbull CT 06611. Tel (203)373-7256, FAX (203)371-2102. DD 688.

FR
**TENNIS DE FRANCE.** French. mo. 263.75F France; 288.75 other. Tennis de France, 36 rue de Picpus, F-75012 Paris France. Tel 011 33 1 43425800.

US/1057-6851
**TENNIS ILLUSTRATED.** Suspended. English. mo. Family Media Inc, 3 Park Avenue, New York NY 10016.
 Ind/Abst Mag. Index.

US/0191-5851
**TENNIS INDUSTRY.** [Tennis ind.]. Vol. 1 (Sept. 1972)-. Periodical. English. Six times a year. $22.00 (one year), $40.00 (two year), $55.00 (three year). Sterling Northeast, 1156 Avenue of the Americas, New York NY 10036. Tel (212) 921-3784, telex (212) 921-3777. ED Jeff Williams. DD 796. Ad Acc. Circ: 26,841 (ctrl).
 Ind/Abst SPORT Discus; SportSearch (May 1987-).

IT/0393-0890
**TENNIS ITALIANO, IL.** [Tennis ital.]. (1929)-. Periodical. Italian. mo. L77000.00 Italy; L115000.00. Edisport Editoriale, V Gradisca 11, 20151 Milan Italy. Tel 011 39 2 380851. UDC 796.342.

US/0279-9979
**TENNIS LIFE.** Periodical. English. bm. Tennis Life Magazine, 700 Horton Drive, Silver Spring MD 20902. Tel (301)593-3222. UDC 796.342.

Recreation, Leisure —Sports

UK/0262-9224
**TENNIS LONDON. 1981.** ***Ceased.*** [Tennis Lond. 1981]. (1981)-(1992). Periodical. English. mo. Tennis Magazine, 85 Castle Lane W, Bournemouth, Dorset BH9 3LH England. **Tel** 0 1 44 202 517555, FAX 0202 536439. **ED** Charles Elder. **DD** 796.34205. **Bk Rev. Ad Acc. Circ:** 15,000 (ctrl). ***Continues*** *Top Tennis, 0143-2184.*
**Desc:** Lawn tennis in the UK and on coaching, players, and equipment. Also court tennis coverage of tournaments and coaching techniques.

FR
**TENNIS MAGAZINE.** French. mo. 276.00F France; 377.00F other. Edimonde Loisirs, 90 rue de Flandre, 75947 Paris Cedex 19 France. **Tel** 011 33 1 44894489.
**Ind/Abst** SPORT Discus.

AT
**TENNIS MAGAZINE. AUSTRALIA.** English. Twelve times a year. 40.00Aus$ Australia; 45.00Aus$ others. Nicholson Media Group, 1 457 Malvern Road, South Varra VIC 3141 Australia. **Tel** 011 61 3 8268446. **ED** S. Petrovski. **Bk Rev. Ad Acc, Adv Mgr:** Cameron. **Circ:** 28,000.
**Desc:** News and information of the national & international tennis games.

US/0040-3423
**TENNIS (NORWALK, CONN.).** (TENNIS.). [Tennis]. **Added/Corp** United States Professional Tennis Association. Vol. 1 (May 1965)-. Periodical. English. mo. $23.94. Golf Digest- Tennis Inc., 5520 Park Avenue, Trumbull CT 06611. **Tel** (203)373-7256, FAX (203)371-2102. **(Subscription address:** CDS Agency Hard Copy, PO Box 4966, Des Moines IA 50340.) **LC** GV991; .T42. **DD** 796.34/2/05. **Ad Acc.** available on microfilm and microfiche from University Microfilms International (UMI). Documents available from UMI Article Clearinghouse.
**Desc:** Magazine of membership of the United States Tennis Association.
**Ind/Abst** Acad. Abstr. Full Text Elite (Jan. 1984-June 1989); Acad. Abstr. (Jan. 1984-June 1989); Acad. Search (Feb. 1984-June 1989); Consum. Index Prod. Eval. Inf. Source; Gen. Period. Index (1985-); INFO-SOUTH Abstr.; Mag. Artic. Summar. Elite (Jan. 1984-June 1989); Mag. Artic. Summar. Select (Jan. 1984-June 1989); Mag. Artic. Summar. CD-ROM (Jan. 1984-June 1989); Mag. Index Plus (1989-); Mag. Search; Newsp. Period. Abstr. (1988-); Phys. Educ. Index (1984-); Read. Guide Period. Lit.; SPORT Discus; SportSearch; Mag. Index.

US/0745-1547
**TENNIS TALK & SPORTS REVIEW.** **VFOAT** Tennis Talk and Sports Review. (198?)-. Periodical. English. Twelve times a year. Tennis Talk & Sports Review, 21016 Ventura Boulevard, Woodland Hills CA 91364. ***Continues*** *Tennis Talk & Racquetball Report.*

US/0194-9098
**TENNIS WEEK.** [Tennis week]. (19??)-. Periodical. English. Twenty times a year. $40.00 US; $50.00 Canada; $125.00 other. Tennis News Inc., 124 East 40th Street, New York NY 10016. **Tel** (212 808-4750, FAX (212)983-6302. **ED** Nina Talbot. **LC** WMLC L 83/7972. **DD** 796. **Bk Rev. Ad Acc, Adv Mgr:** Roberta Faig. **Circ:** 86,000.
**Desc:** Edited for the avid tennis player. In addition to articles on tennis politics and personalities, it covers tournament results, player rankings and earnings, as well as new product development, business summaries and industry analyses.

UK/0040-3474
**TENNIS WORLD.** Vol. 1 (Apr. 1969)-. Periodical. English. mo. £19.50 UK; £27.50 other (surface mail), £57.00 (airmail). Dennis Fairey Publishing Ltd, Presswatch LTD, Spendlove Center/Enstone Road, Oxford OX7 3PQ England. **Tel** 011/44/608/811446. **ED** Henry Wancke. **UDC** 796.342. **Bk Rev. Ad Acc. Circ:** 15,500.
**Desc:** British and international tennis magazine containing previews, results, instruction, competitions; richly illustrated with full color and black and white photographs.
**Ind/Abst** SPORT Discus; SportSearch (May 1987-).

US
**TENNISPRO.** English. bm. Free North America; $30.00 other. US Professional Tennis Registry Foundation, Box 6754, Hilton Head Island SC 29938. **Tel** (803)686-8733, FAX (803)785-7032. **ED** Steve Milano. **Bk Rev. Ad Acc.** ctrl circ.

US
**TEXAS BASKETBALL MAGAZINE.** 1988-. English. an. $4.50 North America; $6.50 other. Texas Basketball Magazine, 12815 Memorial Drive, Houston TX 77024-4809. **Tel** (713)468-1658. **ED** Robert P Springer. Index available. **Bk Rev. Ad Acc. Circ:** 25,000 (ctrl).
**Desc:** High school basketball magazine that covers over 2,000 schools; top 100 players; top coaches in the state and 300 photos.

US/0040-4241
**TEXAS COACH.** **Added/Corp** Texas High School Coaches Association. (1958)-. Periodical. English. Nine times a year (Jan., Feb., Mar., April, May, Aug., Sept., Oct., Nov.). $13.00 US; $15.00 other (1 year) $25.00 US; $27.00 other (2 year). Texas High School Coaches Association, PO Box 14627, 5300 North IH 35, Austin TX 78761. **Tel** (512)454-6709. **ED** Eddie Joseph. **Bk Rev. Ad Acc, Adv Mgr:** E Wolski, **Tel** (512)454-6709. **Circ:** 11,500 (ctrl).
**Desc:** Articles of interest to coaches of sports; football, basketball, baseball, track, and soccer. Articles also include sports for females.
**Ind/Abst** Phys. Educ. Index; SPORT Discus; SportSearch.

US/0199-3062
**TEXAS GOLF.** (197?)-. Periodical. English. mo. $15.00 Texas; $20.00 other. Texas Golf, 4316 Main Street, Dallas TX 75226.

US/0889-0692
**THRASHER (SAN FRANCISCO, CALIF.).** (THRASHER.). [Thrasher]. **VFOAT** Thrasher Magazine. (198?)-. Periodical. English. mo. $18.50 US; $26.00 Canada; $35.00 other. High Speed Productions Inc, PO Box 884570, San Francisco CA 94188. **Tel** (415)822-3083. **DD** 796. ***Continues*** *Thrasher Skateboard Magazine, 0742-4922.*
**Desc:** Geared toward active youth into skateboarding, music and related pursuits. Features interviews, color action photos, comics, contest coverage, news and product reviews.

CN/0821-7114
**THUMPER (ST. ALBERT, ALTA.).** (THUMPER / ALBERTA VOLLEYBALL ASSOCIATION.). [Thumper]. Jan. 1981-. Periodical. English. ir. Alberta Volleyball Assocaition, 13 Mission Avenue, St. Albert Alta. T8N 1H6. **DD** 796.32/5/0607123. **UDC** 796.325(712). ***Continues*** *Newsletter (Alberta Volleyball Association), 0821-7122.*

CC
**TI TSAO.** **VFOAT** Ticao Mulu. Periodical. Chinese. qt. RMBY0.28. Science Press, 16 Donghuangchenggen North Street, Beijing 100707, People's Republic of China. **Tel** 011 86 1 4019821, 011 86 1 4010642, FAX 011 86 1 4012180, 011 86 1 4019810, telex 210147. **LC** GV461; .T475. **DD** 796.4/1/05. **UDC** 796.4.

CC
**TI YU KO HSUEH.** **Added/Corp** Chung-kuo ti yu ko Hsueh Hsueh Hui. **VFOAT** Sports Science. (19??)-. Periodical. Chinese. qt. RMBY0.65. Science Press, 16 Donghuangchenggen North Street, Beijing 100707, People's Republic of China. **Tel** 011 86 1 4019821, 011 86 1 4010642, FAX 011 86 1 4012180, 011 86 1 4019810, telex 210147. **LC** GV561; .T5. **DD** 796/.05.
**Ind/Abst** SPORT Discus.

CC
**TIEN CHING.** **VFOAT** Tian Jing. Periodical. Chinese. bm. RMBY0.28. Science Press, 16 Donghuangchenggen North Street, Beijing 100707, People's Republic of China. **Tel** 011 86 1 4019821, 011 86 1 4010642, FAX 011 86 1 4012180, 011 86 1 4019810, telex 210147. **LC** GV1060.5; .T53. **DD** 796.4/2/05. **UDC** 796.4.

CN/0710-1643
**TIGER-CAT FACT BOOK / TIGER-CATS FOOTBALL.** [Tiger-Cat fact book]. **Main/Corp** Hamilton Tiger-Cat Football Club. **VFOAT** Fact Book. English. an. $2.00 each number. Hamilton Tiger-Cat Football Club, PO Box 170, Hamilton Ontario L8N 3A Canada. **DD** 796.33/56/0922. **UDC** 796.333(713).

US/0744-7604
**TIGER RAG.** (THE TIGER RAG.). Vol. 1 (Sept. 1, 1978)-. Periodical. English. wk. $48.00 US; $70.00 other. Bayou Bengal Publishing Company, PO Box 2305, Hammond LA 70893. **Tel** (504)345-7458. **ED** Steve Myers. **Ad Acc. Circ:** 12,000.
**Desc:** Sports publication covering Louisiana State University and the southeastern conference.

US/8756-8497
**TIME OUT (KANNAPOLIS, N.C.).** (TIME OUT.). **VFOAT** Timeout. (1984)-. Periodical. English. mo. $30.00. Time Out, PO Box 548, Spencer NC 28159. **Tel** (704)522-0092, FAX (704)522-0092. **ED** Jim Baker. **Ad Acc. Circ:** 1,000.
**Desc:** Features basketball drills, plays and strategies for coaches and players at all levels.

GW/0138-1547
**TISCHTENNIS.** German. mo. 19.80F Switzerland; 24.50F other. Deutscher Judo Verband, Redaktion Ippon Segewaldweg 40, D 12557 Berlin Germany. **Tel** 011 49 711 210770, telex 051 678.

FR/0248-2339
**TOBOGGAN TOULOUSE.** **VFOAT** Toboggan Magazine (Toulouse). (1980)-. Periodical. French. mo. 305.58F France; 377.00F other Europe; 447.00F other. Milan Presse/Serv Abonnement, 300 Rue Leon Joulin, 31101 Toulouse Cedex France. **Tel** 011 33 1 61766464, FAX 011 33 1 61766400. **UDC** 087.5.

UK/0268-4977
**TODAY'S RUNNER.** [Today's runn.]. (1985)-. Periodical. English. Twelve times a year. £17.50 UK; £27.00 others. EMAP National Publications Ltd, Farndon Road, Market Harborough, Leicestershire, LE16 9NR England. **Tel** 011 44 733 555161.

CN/1181-6341
**TODAYS SKATER.** [Today's skat.]. **VFOAT** Skater. (198?)-. English. an. $3.19. National All Sport Promotions, 30 St. Clair Avenue West, Suite 805, Toronto Ont M4V 3A1 Canada. **Tel** (416)926-7595. **DD** 796.91/2/05.

US/8750-6726
**TOLEDO SPORTSMAN, THE.** **VFOAT** Sportsman. (19??)-. Periodical. English. mo. $7.25. Grissom Publications, PO Box 288, Carthage TX 75633. **Tel** (214)693-7678. **ED** Loyd C. Grissom. **Bk Rev. Ad Acc. Circ:** 10,000.
**Desc:** Fishing and hunting magazine-newspaper.

US/1047-1871
**TOPPS MAGAZINE.** ***Ceased.*** [Topps mag.]. (1990)-(Fall 1993). Periodical. English. Four times a year. Topps Company, 254 36th Street, Brooklyn NY 11232. **Tel** (718)768-8900. **ED** Bob Woods. **DD** 796.
**Desc:** Comprised of articles on popular baseball players, as well as other sports players. The magazine will focus on the players, with interest in card collecting secondary.

CN/0227-6526
**TORONTO ARGONAUTS FACT BOOK.** (FACT BOOK / ARGONAUT FOOTBALL CLUB.). [Tor. Argonauts fact book]. **Main/Corp** Toronto Argonaut Football Club. **VFOAT** Toronto Argonauts Fact Book and Media Guide. (19??)-. English. an. Free. Toronto Argonaut Football Club Exhibition Stadium, Exhibition Place, Toronto Ontario M6K 3C3 Canada. **DD** 796.33/56. ctrl circ.

●US/1065-1977
**TOTAL TRIATHLON ALMANAC, THE.** (1992)-. English. $16.95. Trimarket, PO Box 60871, Palo Alto CA 94306.

US/0090-4228
**TOUCHDOWN (PHOENIX, ARIZ.).** (TOUCHDOWN.). [Touchdown]. Vol. 1 (Nov. 1972)-. Periodical. English. ir. $2.75. Touchdown Publishing Inc, 450 Sansome Street, c/o M Bushing, San Francisco CA 94111. **Tel** (415)398-1919. **LC** GV955.5.N35; T68. **DD** 796.33/264/0973.

US/0146-1796
**TOUR BOOK, THE.** (THE TOUR BOOK - TOURNAMENT PLAYERS DIVISION, PROFESSIONAL GOLFERS' ASSOCIATION OF AMERICA.). **Main/Corp** Professional Golfers' Association of America. Tournament Players Division. English. an. Professional Golfers' Association of America, Tournament Players Division, 5101 River Road, Washington DC 20016. **LC** GV964.A1; P72A. **DD** 796.352/092/2. **UDC** 796.352.071(73).

KE
**TRACK.** English. 15.00 each issue. International Professional Hunters Association, Eastern Hemisphere Office, Hilton Hotel, PO Box 40528, Nairobi Kenya. **LC** SK1; .T75. **DD** 799.2/05. **UDC** 799.2(676.2).

US/1042-878X
**TRACK AND FIELD AND CROSS COUNTRY RULE BOOK.** [Track field cross ctry. rule book]. **Main/Corp** National Federation of State High School Associations. **VFOAT** Official High School Track and Field and Cross Country Rules. (1988)-. English. an. $6.75. National Federation of State High School Associations, 11724 Northwest Plaza Circle, PO Box 20626, Kansas City MO 64195-0626. **Tel** (816)464-5400, FAX (816)464-5571. **LC** GV1060.67; .N37a. **DD** 796.42. ***Continues*** *Track and Field Rule Book.*

US/0041-0284
**TRACK & FIELD NEWS.** [Track field news]. **VAT** Track and Field News. (Feb. 1948)-. Periodical. English. mo. $33.00 US; $41.00 other (surface mail). Track & Field News, 2570 El Camino Real, Suite 606, Mountain View CA 94040. **Tel** (415)948-8188. **ED** Bert Nelson. **Bk Rev. Ad Acc. Circ:** 35,000 (ctrl). available on microfilm and microfiche from University Microfilms International (UMI).
**Desc:** Magazine devoted exclusively to coverage of track and field in the United States and worldwide.
**Ind/Abst** SPORT Discus; SportSearch (May 1987-).

US/0041-0292
**TRACK & FIELD QUARTERLY REVIEW.** (TRACK & FIELD QUARTERLY REVIEW / THE UNITED STATES TRACK COACHES ASSOCIATION.). [Track field q. rev.]. **Added/Corp** United States Track Coaches Association. **VFOAT** Track and Field Quarterly Review. (1968)-. Periodical. English. Four times a year (Mar., June, Sept., Dec,). $20.00 US; $30.00 other. Track & Field Coaches Association USA, 1705 Evanston Street, Kalamazoo MI 49008. **Tel** (616)349-1008. **ED** George G. Dales. **LC** GV1060.6; .T7. **DD** 796.4/2/0973. Index available (published in Dec. issue). **Bk Rev**, (Qty: 3-4). **Ad Acc, Adv Mgr:** George Dales, **Tel** same as publisher. **Circ:** 1,500. available on microfilm and microfiche from University Microfilms International (UMI). ***Continues*** *Quarterly Review (United States Track*

*Coaches Association).*
**Desc:** Technical educational journal for track and field coaches and athletes.
**Ind/Abst** Phys. Educ. Index; SPORT Discus; SportSearch.

US/0041-0306
**TRACK NEWSLETTER.** (1955)-. Newsletter. English. Twenty-six times a year. $38.50 US, Canada and Mexico; $57.00 other. Track & Field News, 2570 El Camino Real, Suite 606, Mountain View CA 94040. **Tel** (415)948-8188. **ED** Garry Hill. **Circ:** 500 (ctrl). ***Absorbed*** *Trackstats.*
**Desc:** Devoted to the US/worldwide track and field, and in-depth statistics of all track and field results.

US/0742-3918
**TRACK TECHNIQUE.** [Track tech.]. No. 1 (Sept. 1960)-. Periodical. English. Four times a year (published within the seasons). $15.00 US; $16.00 other. Track & Field News, 2570 El Camino Real, Suite 606, Mountain View CA 94040. **Tel** (415)948-8188. **LC** GV561; .T74. **DD** 796. available on microfilm and microfiche from University Microfilms International (UMI).
**Desc:** Official publication of the Athletics Congress/USA.
**Ind/Abst** Phys. Educ. Index.

AT
**TRACKS.** (19??)-. Consumer Publication. English. mo. 77.40Aus$ Australia; 138.00Aus$ other. Mason Stewart Publishing, PO Box 746, Darlinghurst NSW 2010 Australia. **Tel** 011 61 2 331 5006. **ED** Gary Dunne. **Ad Acc, Adv Mgr:** Stephen Kay. **Circ:** 30,000.
**Desc:** Reports on the professional surfing circuit, latest news in surfboard design, environmental issues, surfing techniques, profiles on surfing stars and information on travel, health and fitness.
**Ind/Abst** SPORT Discus.

US/0888-5443
**TRADITIONAL ARCHERY.** [Tradit. archery]. (198?)-. Periodical. English. Four times a year. Traditional Archery, Route 3 Box 258, North Platte NE 69103. **DD** 799. ***Continues*** *Traditional Archery Digest, 0745-5666.*

US
**TRADITIONAL BOWHUNTER.** English. qt. $16.00 (US); $40.00 (Canada); $43.00 (other). Traditional Bowhunter, PO Box 15583, Department MM, Boise ID 83715.

US/0745-2365
**TRADITIONAL TAEKWON-DO.** ***Ceased.*** **VFOAT** Taekwondo. Periodical. English. qt. Traditional Taekwondo, 6202 South Sheridan, Tulsa OK 74136. **Tel** (918)494-9691. **ED** D W Kang. **UDC** 796.85. **Bk Rev. Ad Acc. Circ:** 70,000.
**Desc:** Martial arts magazine for all ages around the world. We accept articles from our readers and cover every aspect of the martial arts world.

US/0274-8274
**TRAIL BLAZER (PASO ROBLES). See** Horses and Horsemanship.

US/0748-7401
**TRANSWORLD SKATEBOARDING.** **Added/Corp** United Skate Front (Firm). **VFOAT** Trans World Skateboarding; Transworld Skateboarding Magazine. (198?)-. Periodical. English. mo. $19.95. Transworld Publications, 353 Airport Road, Oceanside CA 92054. **Tel** (619)722-7777. **(Subscription address:** Skateboarding, PO Box 469006, Escondido CA 92046.) ***Continues*** *Transworld Skateboarding Magazine.*

US/1046-4611
**TRANSWORLD SNOWBOARDING. VFOAT** Transworld Snow Boarding; Trans World Snow Boarding; Transworld Snowboarding Magazine. (198?)-. Periodical. English. Eight times a year. $19.95 (one year), $34.95 (two year). Transworld Publications, 353 Airport Road, Oceanside CA 92054. **Tel** (619)722-7777. **(Subscription address:** Transworld Snowboarding, PO Box 469019, Escondido CA 92046.) **DD** 796.

US/0041-1760
**TRAP & FIELD. Added/Corp** Amateur Trapshooting Association (U.S.). **VAT** Trap and Field. (19??)-. Periodical. English. mo. $20.00. Trap & Field Magazine, 1000 Waterway Boulevard, Indianapolis IN 46202. **Tel** (317)633-2080, FAX (317)634-1791. **ED** Bonnie Nash. **Bk Rev. Ad Acc. Circ:** 14,500.
**Desc:** Official publication of the Amateur Trapshooting Association, governing body of the clay target sport in North America, the largest association in the world regulating clay target firing.
**Ind/Abst** SPORT Discus; SportSearch (May 1987-).

US/0898-3410
**TRIATHLETE (ALLENTOWN, PA.).** (TRIATHLETE.). **VFOAT** Tri-athlete; Triathlete Magazine. (June 1986)-. Periodical. English. Eleven times a year (Jan./Feb. issues combined). $23.95 US; $39.95 Canada; $43.95 Mexico; $50.00 others. Winning Magazine, 744 Roble Road, Suite 190, Allentown PA 18103. **Tel** (215)266-6893. **LC** GV1060.7; .T75. **DD** 796. ***Continues*** *Triathlon, 0745-5917.*
**Ind/Abst** SPORT Discus; SportSearch (May 1987-).

AT
**TRIATHLON SPORTS.** English. Ten times a year. 45.00Aus$ Australia; 127.00Aus$ US, and Canada; 92.00Aus$ New Zealand, and Papau New Guinea; 102.00Aus$ South Pacific; 112.00Aus$ Asia, Japan, Hong Kong, and Thailand; 137.00Aus$ Europe, UK and South Africa. Triathlon Sports, PO Box 2590, Taren Point 2229 Australia. **Tel** 011 61 2 5241455, FAX 011 61 2 5241454. **ED** Paul Oliver. **Bk Rev. Ad Acc, Adv Mgr:** A. Mitchell.
**Desc:** Multi-sport and endurance magazine including swim/bike/run and all multi-sport events.
**Ind/Abst** SPORT Discus.

GW/0931-3850
**TRIATHLON UND SPORTWISSENSCHAFT.** Monographic series. German. Price varies per volume. Verlag Ingrid Czwalina, Reesenbuettler Redder 75, D-22926 Ahrensburg Germany. **Tel** 011 49 4102 59190. **NLM** W1; TR448.

US/0883-2951
**TROPHY BIG GAME INVESTIGATIONS AND HUNTING SEASON RECOMMENDATIONS / STATE OF NEVADA, DEPARTMENT OF WILDLIFE, DIVISION OF GAME. Main/Corp** Nevada. Division of Game. 1980-. English. an. Nevada Department of Wildlife, 1100 Valley Road, PO Box 10678, Reno NV 89520. **LC** SK421; .N49A. **DD** 639.9/79. **UDC** 639.111(793). ***Continues*** *Nevada. Division of Game. Big Game Investigations and Hunting Season Recommendations, 0160-1547.*

CC
**TSU CHIU SHIH CHIEH / CHUNG-KUO TSU CHIU HSIEH HUI CHU PAN. Added/Corp** Chung-kuo Tsu Chiu Hsieh Hui. (19??)-. Periodical. Chinese. bm. RMBY0.28. Tsu Chiu Shih Chieh, Post Office, Beijing, People's Republic of China. **LC** GV942; .T78.

HU
**TUDOMANYOS KOZLEMENYEK. See** Education-Physical Education and Training.

US/1041-4258
**TUFF STUFF. See** Hobbies.

US/0041-4158
**TURF AND SPORT DIGEST.** Periodical. English. bm. $12.00. Turf & Sport Digest, 118 W Pennsylvania Avenue, Baltimore MD 21204-5001. **Tel** (301)337-0300. **ED** Dave Betz. **UDC** 798.42. **Bk Rev. Ad Acc. Circ:** 30,000 (ctrl).
**Desc:** A favorite of thoroughbred racing fans. Features articles on everything that's happening in the exciting world of thoroughbred racing. Handicapping hints, racing statistics, jockey, horses, and trainer profiles.

AT/0819-8632
**TURF CRAFT AUST.** [Turf craft Aust.]. (1987)-. Periodical. English. bm. 39.00Aus$ Australia; 66.50Aus$ New Zealand; 71.50Aus$ Fiji, Indonesia and Malaysia; 76.50Aus$ Hong Kong, India and Japan; 84.00Aus$ North America; 89.00Aus$ other. Turf Craft Australia, 9 George Street, PO Box 133, Sandringham VIC 3191 Australia. **Tel** 011 61 3 5988642. **DD** 635.964205.
**Ind/Abst** SPORT Discus.

GW
**U.I.T. JOURNAL. Added/Corp** International Shooting Union. **VFOAT** UIT Journal; International Shooting Sport. (1981)-. Periodical. English (French, German and Spanish). bm. DM44.00 Europe; DM50.00 other. UIT International Schuetzenunion, Bavariaring 21, D 80336 Munich Germany. **Tel** 011 49 89 531012, FAX 011 49 89 5309481, telex 52 16792 UITD. **ED** Wolfgang Schreiber. **LC** GV1151; .I54. **DD** 799.3/05. **Bk Rev. Ad Acc. Circ:** 4,200 (ctrl). ***Continues*** *International Shooting Sport.*
**Desc:** Current reports on competitors in shooting sports. Regular documentations in the fields of medicine and psychology and the effects in the world of sports, as well as the presentation of the technical developments with regards to shooting equipment.
**Ind/Abst** SPORT Discus.

●US/1076-0008
**U.S. COLLEGE HOCKEY MAGAZINE.** (1994)-. English. Twelve times a year. $27.00. Eastern College Sports, 37 Trask Road, Peabody MA 01960. **Tel** (508)531-4311. ***Continues*** *College Hockey Magazine, 1061-6357.*

US/0363-7050
**U.S.H.L. YEARBOOK. Main/Corp** United States Hockey League. **VAT** United States Hockey League Yearbook. 1975/76-. English. an. $1.00. PO Box 1093, Green Bay WI 54305. **LC** GV847.8.U53; U53A. **DD** 796.9/62/0973. **UDC** 796.9(058)(73).

US/1044-0801
**U.S. ROLLER SKATING.** [U. S. roll. skat.]. **Added/Corp** United States Amateur Confederation of Roller Skating. **VFOAT** Roller Skating. **VAT** United States Roller Skating. Vol. 1, Issue 1 (Jan. 1989)-. Periodical. English. mo (11 issues). $10.00. USAC RS / US Amateur Confederation of Roller Skating, 4730 South Street, Lincoln NE 68506. **Tel** (402)483-7551. **DD** 796.
**Ind/Abst** SPORT Discus.

●US
**ULTIMATE FANTASY FOOTBALL LEAGUE ... GUIDE AND HANDBOOK, THE.** (1992)-. English. Prometheus Books, 59 John Glenn Drive, Amherst NY 14228-2197. **LC** GV1202.F34; U47. **DD** 793.93.

●US/1063-9349
**ULTRA CYCLING.** (ULTRA CYCLING : THE VOICE OF UMCA AND RAAM.). [Ultra cycl.]. **Added/Corp** Ultra Marathon Cycling Association. Race Across America. **VFOAT** Ultracycling. Vol. 1, No. 1 (1992)-. Periodical. English. qt. $30.00 (membership). UMCA, Ultra Marathon Cycling Association, 2761 North Marengo Avenue, Altadena CA 91001. **DD** 796.

US/0744-3609
**ULTRARUNNING.** Vol. 1, No. 1 (May 1981)-. Periodical. English. mo. $25.00 (one year), $45.00 (two year). Ultrarunning, PO Box 481, Sunderland MA 01375. **Tel** (413)665-7573. **LC** GV1065.2; .U43. **DD** 796.4/26.
**Ind/Abst** SPORT Discus.

US
**UMI'S SOUTHEASTERN BASKETBALL HANDBOOK. VFOAT** Southeastern Basketball Handbook. (1987/88)-. Periodical. English. an. $7.00. University Microfilms International, 300 North Zeeb Road, Ann Arbor MI 48106-1346. **Tel** (313)761-4700, (800)521-0600 Exts. 2490, 2491, FAX (313)973-1540. **ED** Ivan Mothershead. **LC** GV885.72.S85; U47. **DD** 796.32/362/0975. **Ad Acc. Circ:** 150,000.

US/0192-0871
**UNDERCURRENT (NEW YORK).** (UNDERCURRENT: THE PRIVATE, EXCLUSIVE GUIDE FOR SERIOUS DIVERS.). [Undercurrent]. (19??)-. Periodical. English. mo (11 issues per year). $39.00. Insighful Newsletters Inc., 175 Great Neck Road, Suite 307, Great Neck NY 11021. **Tel** (516)466-7816. **ED** Ben Davidson. **LC** GV840.S78; U353. **DD** 797.2/3/05. **[CCC]. Bk Rev,** (Qty: 2). **Circ:** 13,600.
**Desc:** A newsletter for the sport diver, featuring resort and equipment reviews safety tips and ways to have more fun under water.

US/0740-1930
**UNDERSEA JOURNAL, THE. See** Recreation, Leisure.

US/0749-1794
**UNDERWATER USA.** [Underw. USA]. **VFOAT** Underwater U.S.A. (198?)-. Periodical. English. Twelve times a year. $15.95. Underwater USA, 3185 Lackawanna Avenue, Bloomsburg PA 17815. **Tel** (717)784-6081, (800)422-1164 PENNSYLVANIA, FAX (717)784-9226. **ED** Tim Pelton and Carl Boyer. Index available. **Ad Acc. Circ:** 40,000.
**Desc:** Publication for scuba diving enthusiasts. Covers topics such as dive spot reviews. Marine science and dive medicine legislation affecting the sport.
**Ind/Abst** Biol. Dig.

US/0742-7808
**UNITED STATES SWIMMING RULES AND REGULATIONS.** (UNITED STATES SWIMMING RULES AND REGULATIONS : OFFICIAL PUBLICATION OF UNITED STATES SWIMMING.). [U.S. Swim. rules regul.]. **Added/Corp** United States Swimming (Organization). **VFOAT** Rules and Regulations. (19??)-. English. an (Jan.). $6.00. United States Swimming, 1750 East Boulder Street, Colorado Springs CO 80909. **Tel** (719)578-4578, FAX (719)578-4669. **ED** William a Lippman, Arvydas Barzdukas, Bernard Favaro and Dudley Smith. **LC** WMLC L 83/117. **Ad Acc. Circ:** 25,000 (ctrl).
**Desc:** Technical rules for competitive swimming by-laws of US Swimming, Inc.

US/0364-8214
**UNITED STATES TENNIS CLUB REGISTRY.** 1st- Ed.; 1976-. English. Tennis Club Registry, Inc., PO Box 4231, Irvine CA 92716. **LC** GV991; .U55. **DD** 796.34/2/0973. **UDC** 796.342(73).

US/0738-9949
**US ARCHER, THE.** (THE US ARCHER : OFFICIAL PUBLICATION OF THE NATIONAL ARCHERY ASSOCIATION.). [US archer]. **Added/Corp** National Archery Association of the United States. Professional Archers Association. National Field Archery Association. Pro Division. International Field Archery Association. **VAT** United States Archer. (198?)-. Periodical. English. bm. $17.50 (1 year), $27.50 (2 year), $37.50 (3 year). US Archer, 7315 North San Anna Drive, Tucson AZ 85704-1943. **Tel** (602)742-5846, FAX (602)742-0027. **ED** R. Arlyne Rhode. **LC** GV1187; .U8. **DD** 799.3/2/0973. **Ad Acc. Circ:** 10,000.
**Desc:** Worldwide coverage of recreational archery from Olympic style to 3-D. The official publication of the National Archery Association and the Professional Archers Association.

US/0883-0347
**US SWIMMING NEWS.** ***Ceased.*** [U. S. swim. news]. **VAT** United States Swimming News. (1944)-(July 1993). Periodical. English. mo. US Swimming News, 1750 East Boulder Street, Colorado Springs CO 80909. **Tel** (719)578-4578, FAX (719)578-4669, telex 258878. **ED** Jeff Dimond. **DD** 797. **UDC** 797.21(73). **Circ:** 3,000 (ctrl).
**Desc:** The newsletter of United States swimming; national governing body for competitive swimming carries items for the record about swimming.
**Ind/Abst** SPORT Discus.

US/0748-6006
**USA GYMNASTICS.** [U. S. A. gymnast.]. **Added/Corp** United States Gymnastics Federation. **VFOAT** U.S.A. Gymnastics. Vol. 13, No. 1 (Jan./Feb. 1984)-. Periodical. English. Six times a year. $15.00. US Gymnastics Federation, 201 South Capitol, Suite 300, Indianapolis IN 46225-1054. **Tel** (317)237-5050, telex 27-2385 USGYM-IND. **ED** Luan Reszek. **DD** 796. **Ad Acc.** ctrl circ. ***Continues*** *USGF Gymnastics.*
**Desc:** Features about gymnastics in America from U.S. teams and events to grassroots.

US
**USA KARATE FEDERATION RULES & REGULATIONS.** (19??)-. English. ir. Pat Hickey, 1544 Ritchie, Stow OH 44224. **Tel** (216)753-3114. ***Continues*** *Official AAU Karate Rules, 0148-737X.*

US/0883-6841
**USA OUTDOORS.** **See** Recreation, Leisure-Outdoor Life.

●US/1057-9532
**USA TODAY BASEBALL WEEKLY.** [USA today baseb. wkly.]. **VFOAT** Baseball Weekly; U.S.A. Today Baseball Weekly. Vol. 1, No. 1 (Apr. 11, 1991)-. Periodical. English. Forty-Four times a year. $34.00. Gannett International, 535 Madison Avenue, New York NY 10022. **Tel** (212)715-5426, (800)872-0001, FAX (212)207-8982. **(Subscription address:** Subscription Processing, PO Box 4179, Silver Springs, MD 20914, telephone: (301)622-7474**)** **DD** 796. available on microfilm and microfiche from University Microfilms International (UMI).
**Desc:** The most complete guide to baseball, features: indepth, team-by-team reports; offseason scouting; spring training updates; expanded box scores; computerized player rankings; the latest injury reports and more.

●US
**USA TODAY BASEBALL WEEKLY ALMANAC.** **VFOAT** Baseball Weekly Almanac. (1992)-. English. Hyperion, 114 Fifth Avenue, New York NY 10011. **LC** GV863.A1; U84. **DD** 796.357/0973/05.

US
**USA VOLLEYBALL REVIEW.** **Added/Corp** United States Volleyball Association. United States Volleyball Association. Volleyball Review. (1???)-. Periodical. English. ir. US Volleyball Association, 3595 East Fountain Boulevard, Colorado Springs CO 80910. **Tel** (800)637-8300.

US/0882-5009
**USDF CALENDAR OF COMPETITIONS.** **See** Horses and Horsemanship.

US/0041-5502
**USGA GREEN SECTION RECORD.** [USGA Green Sect. rec.]. **Main/Corp** United States Golf Association. Green Section. **VAT** United States Golf Association Green Section Record. (1963)-. Periodical. English. bm. $15.00. US Golf Association, Golf House, PO Box 708, Far Hills NJ 07931. **Tel** (908)234-2300. **ED** James T. Snow. **LC** GV975; .U54a. **DD** 711/.558. **Circ:** 16000. ***Supersedes in part*** *USGA Journal and Turf Management.*
**Desc:** The magazine discusses issues in turfgrass science and research, with an emphasis on its effects on the golf industry.
**Ind/Abst** AGRICOLA (19??-) [Select. Cov.]; SPORT Discus (19??-); SportSearch (May 1987-).

US
**USTA COLLEGE TENNIS GUIDE / USTA EDUCATION AND RESEARCH CENTER.** **Added/Corp** United States Tennis Association. USTA Education and Research Center. USTA Center for Education and Recreational Tennis. **VFOAT** U.S.T.A. College Tennis Guide; College Tennis Guide. **VAT** United States Tennis Association College Tennis Guide. (1979)-. English. be. $10.00. US Tennis Association, 707 Alexander Road, Princeton NJ 08540. **Tel** (609)452-2580. **ED** Anne B. Humes. **LC** GV991.5; .U77. **DD** 796.342/07/1173. **Circ:** 6,000.
**Desc:** For the college-bound tennis player, a comprehensive index to intercollegiate tennis teams and scholarships for both men and women. Nearly 1,500 colleges and universities listed alphabetically by state.

US
**USYSA NETWORK.** (19??)-. English. qt. Free to members of USYSA; $6.00 other. United State Youth Soccer Association / USYSA, 2050 NOrth Plano Road, Suite 100, Richardson TX 75082. **Tel** (918)582-6397, (800)476-2237. **ED** Jon de Stefano. **Bk Rev**, (Qty: 4). **Ad Acc. Circ:** 96,000.

US/0741-9708
**UTAH BIG GAME RANGE TREND STUDIES.** 1981-. English. an. Department of Natural Resources / Utah, 1636 West North Temple, Suite 316, Salt Lake City UT 84116. **Tel** (801)538-7200, FAX (801)538-7315. **LC** SK453; .A25 subser. **DD** 639.9/797357. **UDC** 639.111(792). ***Continues*** *Utah. Division of Wildlife Resources. Big Game Range Inventory, 0145-8337.*

US
**UTAH COUGAR HARVEST.** **Main/Corp** Utah. Division of Wildlife Resources. **VFOAT** Utah Cougar Harvest Book. English. an. Department of Natural Resources / Utah, 1636 West North Temple, Suite 316, Salt Lake City UT 84116. **Tel** (801)538-7200, FAX (801)538-7315. **LC** SK453; .A25 subser. **DD** 799.2/77/4428. **UDC** 639.16(77).

IO/0506-4155
**VARIA.** ***Title Change.*** Vol. 1- No. 1-. Periodical. Indonesian (Indonesian). wk. **LC** GV1111; .V28. **DD** 796.8/15. **UDC** 796.8. ***Continued by*** *Varia Beladiri.*

US/0161-1798
**VELO-NEWS.** **See** Bicycles and Bicycling.

●US/1058-8442
**VERMONT GOLF JOURNAL & DIRECTORY.** **VFOAT** Vermont Golf Journal and Directory. (1992)-. Directory. English. $4.95 (U.S.), $6.95 (single issue), $6.50 (Can.). Divot Communications Corp., 431 Pine Street, Burlington VT 05401.

AT
**VICTORIAN NETBALLER.** English. Five times a year (Feb., Mar., June, Aug., Oct.). 20.00Aus$; Free to readers of affiliated associations. Netball Victoria, PO Box 60, North Melbourne 3051 Australia. **Tel** 011 61 3 329 7766, FAX 011 61 9 329 8175. **ED** Ms. Leigh Mawby. **Bk Rev**. **Ad Acc, Adv Mgr:** same as editor. ctrl circ.
**Ind/Abst** SPORT Discus.

US/0887-1426
**VICTORY LANE.** [Vic. lane]. Vol. 1, No. 1 (April 1986)-. Periodical. English. Twelve times a year. $39.95 one year; $62.50 two years. Victory Lane Magazine, 2460 Park Boulevard, Suite 4, Palo Alto CA 94306. **Tel** (415)321-1411, FAX (415)321-4426. **ED** Tom Gano. **DD** 796. **Bk Rev**, (Qty: 10). **Ad Acc, Adv Mgr:** R. Lichty, **Tel** (415)321-4605. **Circ:** 10,000.
**Desc:** The news magazine of vintage auto racing and it featuring articles such as, race sports, technology reports, inside columns, schedules, and classified ads.

CN/0844-1804
**VIE EN PLEIN AIR.** **See** Transportation-Automobiles.

US/1046-7823
**VIKING UPDATE.** ***Title Change.*** [Viking update]. (198?)-(19??). Periodical. English. bw. Viking Update, 6250 Excelsior Boulevard/Suite 102, Minneapolis MN 55416. **DD** 796. ***Continues*** *Tommy Kramer's Viking Update, 0890-9407.* ***Continued by*** *Bob Lurtsema's Viking Update, 1060-5509.*

SZ
**VISIER.** Periodical. German. mo. Deutscher Judo Verband, Redaktion Ippon Segewaldweg 40, D 12557 Berlin Germany. **Tel** 011 49 711 210770, telex 051 678. **LC** GV1151; .V57.

NE/0923-2486
**VOETBAL INTERNATIONAL SPECIAL.** [Voetb. spec.]. **VFOAT** Voetbal Special. (1989)-. Periodical. Dutch. wk. Fl131.80 Belgium and Netherlands; Fl238.40 other. Weekbladpers, Postbus 1050, 1000 BB Amsterdam, Netherlands. **Tel** 011 31 20 5518711. **UDC** 796.332. ***Continues*** *Voetbal-Magazine, 0921-6847.*

US/0892-7421
**VOICE OF THE HAWKEYES, THE.** (198?)-. Periodical. English. ir (Published weekly Sept.-Mar., and monthly Apr., May, and Aug.). $37.95. Sports Tabloid Corporation, PO Box 8576, Cedar Rapids IA 52408. **Tel** (319)390-3715.

CN/0826-4511
**VOILE LIBRE (MONTREAL, QUEBEC).** ***Ceased.*** (VOILE LIBRE.). [Voile libre]. Vol. 1, No. 1 (1982)-(Spring 1988). Periodical. French. qt. Voile Libre, CP 306, Succursale Bourassa, Montreal Quebec H2C 3G8. **DD** 797.1/72/05. **UDC** 797.14.
**Ind/Abst** SPORT Discus; SportSearch (May 1987-).

FR
**VOLLEY BALL.** French (English). bm. 80.00F France; 90.00F other. Fedn Francaise de Volleyball, 43 Bis rue d'Hautpoul, 75019 Paris France. **Tel** 011 33 1 42002234.

GW/0323-5211
**VOLLEYBALL.** (1956)-. Periodical. German. mo. 21.40F Switzerland; 26.20F other. Deutscher Judo Verband, Redaktion Ippon Segewaldweg 40, D 12557 Berlin Germany. **Tel** 011 49 711 210770, telex 051 678. **UDC** 796.3.

UK
**VOLLEYBALL.** (19??)-. Periodical. English. Six times a year. £8.40 UK; £12.40. English Volleyball Association, 27 South Road, West Bridgeford, Nottingham NG2 1AQ England. **Tel** 0602 816324.

US/0749-1832
**VOLLEYBALL CASE BOOK AND OFFICIALS MANUAL.** **Main/Corp** National Federation Volleyball Rules Committee. **VFOAT** Official High School Volleyball Case Book and Officials Manual. English. National Federation of State High School Associations, 11724 Northwest Plaza Circle, PO Box 20626, Kansas City MO 64195-0626. **Tel** (816)464-5400, FAX (816)464-5571. **LC** GV1015.39; .N37A. **DD** 796.32/5/0202. **UDC** 796.325.

CN/0842-2958
**VOLLEYBALL COACHES JOURNAL.** [Volleyb. coach. j.]. (1988/89)-. English. an. $25.00 per issue. Volleyball Coaches Journal, 1110 Emerald Way, Saskatoon Saskatchewan S7J 4J9 Canada. **DD** 796.32/5/07.

US/0274-6662
**VOLLEYBALL MAGAZINE.** (1976)-. Periodical. English. qt. $17.95 US; $30.00 Canada; $31.00 other. Western Empire Publishing, PO Box 3010, San Clemente CA 92672. **Tel** (714)492-7873. **LC** GV1015; .V64. **DD** 796.32/505.
**Ind/Abst** SPORT Discus (19??-).

US/0889-1990
**VOLLEYBALL MONTHLY.** [Volleyb. mon.]. (19??)-. Periodical. English. Twelve times a year. $19.95 US; $29.95 Canada & Mexico; $32.00 other. Straight Down Inc., PO Box 3137, San Luis Obispo CA 93403. **Tel** (805)541-2294, FAX (805)541-2438. **DD** 796.
**Desc:** Numerous training tip articles from the world's number one player, Karch Kiraly, and coverage of Olympic, professional and college volleyball. Dynamic color photos. Numerous volleyball posters enclosed in many issues.
**Ind/Abst** SPORT Discus; SportSearch (May 1987-).

IT/1012-1730
**VOLLEYBALL ROME.** [Volleyball Rome]. (1984)-. Periodical. Multiple languages. bm. **UDC** 796.32.
**Ind/Abst** SPORT Discus.

US/0882-1372
**VOLLEYBALL RULE BOOK.** **Main/Corp** National Federation of State High School Associations. **VFOAT** Official High School Volleyball Rules for Boys and Girls Competition. (1979/80)-. English. an. $6.75. National Federation of State High School Associations, 11724 Northwest Plaza Circle, PO Box 20626, Kansas City MO 64195-0626. **Tel** (816)464-5400, FAX (816)464-5571. **ED** Susan True. **LC** GV1017.V6; N33a. **DD** 796.32/5. **Ad Acc. Circ:** 11,000. ***Continues*** *Volleyball Rules, 0363-2156.*
**Desc:** Rules covering high school competition in volleyball.

GW
**VOLLEYBALL TRAINING.** German. mo. DM67.80. Philippka Verlag, Postfach 6540, D-48034 Muenster Germany. **Tel** 011 49 251 230-0522.

UK/0955-8047
**VOLLEYBALL WORLD.** [Volleyb. world]. (1988)-. Periodical. English. bm. £8.40 UK; £12.40 other. English Volleyball Association, 27 South Road, West Bridgeford, Nottingham NG2 7AQ England. **Tel** 0602 816324, FAX 0602 455429, telex 378604. **DD** 796.325.

SZ
**VOLLEYWORLD.** English. bm. 60.00F (one year), 110.00F (two year). Fivb Subscription Dept, 12 Avenue de la Gare, 1001 Lausanne Switzerland. **Tel** 011 41 21 208932.

CN/0712-757X
**VOTRE BOTTIN DE CROSSE.** [Votre bottin crosse]. **Main/Corp** Federation de Crosse du Quebec. French. an. Free. Federation De Crosse Du Quebec, 1415 Est, Rue Jarry, Montreal Quebec H2E 2Z7 Canada. **DD** 796.34/7/060714. **UDC** 796.34(714).

US/0888-3491
**WALKER'S WORLD NEWSLETTER.** (WALKER'S WORLD NEWSLETTER : PREVENTION WALKING CLUB.). [Walker's world newsl.]. Vol. 1, No. 1 (Summer 1986)-. Newsletter. English. bm. $9.97. Rodale Press Inc., 400 South 10th Street, Emmaus PA 18098. **Tel** (215)967-5171, (800)666-2503. **DD** 796.

US/0043-0501
**WASHINGTON COACH, THE.** **Added/Corp** Washington State Coaches Association. (19??)-. Periodical. English. qt (Mar., June, Oct., Dec.). free (member coaches and Washington State High School libraries); $4.00 other. Washington State Coaches Association, 18468 8th Avenue Northeast, Poulsbo WA 98370. **Tel** (206)779-2986 or, 779-8863.
**Ind/Abst** SportSearch (May 1987-).

US/0049-7002
**WATER SKIER (WINTER HAVEN), THE.** (THE WATER SKIER.). [Water skier]. **Added/Corp** American Water Ski Association. (1951)-. Periodical. English. Seven times a year. $8.00 US and Canada; $12.00 (surface mail) other; available to libraries and schools only. American Water Ski Association, 799 Overlook Drive, Winter Haven FL 33884. **Tel** (813)324-4341, FAX (813)325-8259. **ED** John Baker. **LC** GV840.S5; W29. **DD** 797.1/73/0973; 797.13. **Bk Rev. Ad Acc. Circ:** 24,000 (ctrl). available on microfiche.
**Desc:** Information about the sport of water skiing, both recreational and organized competition. Includes instruction, equipment, personalities, events.
**Ind/Abst** Gen. Period. Index (Jan. 1985-Dec. 1985); SPORT Discus; SportSearch (May 1987-); Mag. Index (1977-dEC. 1985)(1977-).

NE
**WATERKAMPIOEN, DE. Added/Corp** A.N.W.B. Toeristenbond voor Nederland. Afdeeling Watertoerisme. Koninklijke Verbonden Nederlandsche Watersport Vereenigingen. Nederlandsche Bond van Kano-Vereenigingen. Nederlandse Kano Bond. Koninklijke Nederlandse Toeristen Bond ANWB. Afdeeling Watertoerisme. Koninklijke Nederlandse Toeristen Bond ANWB. Koninklijk Nederlands Watersport Verbond. Vol. 1 (Jan. 7 1927)-. Periodical. Dutch. bm. ANWB, PB 93557, 2509 AN Den Haag The Netherlands. **Tel** 011 31 70 3146726. **LC** GV771; .W35. **DD** 797.05.

CN/1183-6377
**WATERLINE (WINDSOR).** (WATERLINE.). [Waterline]. (June/July 1991)-. Periodical. English. $2.50 per issue. Waterline Publications Ltd., 1524 Mathew Brady Boulevard, Windsor Ontario N8S 3K6 Canada. **DD** 797.

US/0883-7813
**WATERSKI (WINTER PARK, FLA.).** (WATERSKI.). [WaterSki]. **VFOAT** Water Ski; Waterski Magazine; Water Ski Magazine. Vol. 7, No. 1 (Apr. 1985)-. Periodical. English. Ten times a year. $18.97. World Publications, Inc., PO Box 2456, 809 South Orlando Ave., Winter Park FL 32790. **Tel** (407)628-4802, (800)394-6006. **ED** Terry T. Temple. **DD** 797. **Ad Acc. Circ:** 103,000. ***Formed by the union of** World Waterskiing Magazine, 0194-6633* ***and** Spray's Water Ski, 8750-5509.*
**Desc:** Deals with helpful how-to's, in-depth features on boats, equipment and tournaments, plus colorful pro-circuit and personality coverage and stunning fast-action photography.

US
**WATERSPORTS BUSINESS.** Vol. 1, No. 1 (Feb. 1989)-. English. mo. $3.00 per issue. Two South Park Place, Fair Haven VT 05743. **Tel** (802)265-4746. **ED** Robert Gray.
**Desc:** Offers a voice for retailers, suppliers and manufacturers of active water sports products to help them reach their current and potential subscribers. Currently available with "Sailboard News."

●US/1078-2958
**WB (GREENDALE, WIS.).** (WB : FOR THE WOMAN WHO BOWLS.). [WB]. (Fall 1994)-. Periodical. English. qt. Woman Bowler, 5301 South 76th Street, Greendale WI 53129. **Tel** (414)421-9000, FAX (414)421-3013. **DD** 794. ***Continues** Woman Bowler, 0043-7255.*

US/1062-4368
**WBF BODYBUILDING LIFESTYLES : THE OFFICIAL PUBLICATION OF THE WORLD BODYBUILDING FEDERATION.** **See** Health and Personal Fitness.

US/1062-3752
**WCW COLLECTORS EDITIONS.** ***Ceased.*** **VAT** World Championship Wrestling Collectors Editions. (1992)-(19??). Periodical. English. mo. London Publishing Company, PO Box 910, Fort Washington PA 19034. **Tel** (215)643-6385, FAX (215)540-0146.

IT
**WEEKEND.** Year 1- June 1973-. Periodical. Italian (Italian). mo. $56.00. Bolaffi Mondadori, Via Cavour 17, 10123 Turin Italy. **LC** GV1; .W43.
**Ind/Abst** Index Philip. Period.

US/0743-460X
**WEEKLY BULLET, THE. Added/Corp** Second Amendment Foundation. (19??)-. Periodical. English. wk (50 / year). $32.00 (US); $40.00 (other). Second Amendment Foundation, PO Box 488, Station C, Buffalo NY 14209. **Tel** (716)885-6408, FAX (716)884-4471. **ED** Joseph P Tartaro. **Circ:** 20,000.
**Desc:** Reporting on firearms & hunting subjects with news focus on legislation, regulations, court decisions, summaries from general news, plus feature articles, book reviews, and commentaries.

US/0895-5387
**WEST MICHIGAN BOWLER.** [West Mich. bowler]. **VFOAT** Bowler. (198?)-. Periodical. English. ir. $7.50. Sports News, 2045 Lake Michigan Drive, Grand Rapids MI 49504. **Tel** (616)453-3351. **DD** 794. ***Continues** Sports News, 0194-7923.*

US/0746-7060
**WESTERN BOWLER.** Periodical. English. mo. Western Bowler, 941 Bench Boulevard, Billings MT 59105. **UDC** 796.2.

US/1052-3219
**WESTERN LINKS (HILTON HEAD ISLAND, S.C.).** (WESTERN LINKS.). (Sept./Oct. 1990)-. Periodical. English. bm. Southern Links, PO Box 7628, Hilton Head Island SC 29938. **Tel** (803)842-6200, FAX (803)842-6233. **ED** Mark Brown. **DD** 796. ctrl circ.
**Desc:** Editorial includes in-depth travel pieces on golf locations in 13 Western states, interviews with golf legends and leaders and coverage of emerging trends and controversial issues.

US/0510-2626
**WESTERN RACING NEWS.** **See** Transportation-Automobiles.

CN/1184-2679
**WESTERN SKIER.** [West. skier]. **VFOAT** Western Canada Outdoors Skier; Western Skier Directory. Vol. 17, No. 1 (Oct. 1990)-. Periodical. English. Four times a year (Jan., Feb., Nov., Dec.). 10.00Can$ Canada; 16.00Can$ others. McIntosh Publications Co Ltd, Box 430, North Battleford 291 2Y5 Canada. **Tel** (306)445-7477, FAX (306)445-1977. **ED** Becky McIntosh McDonald. **DD** 796.93/097124. **Bk Rev**, (Qty: varies). **Ad Acc. Circ:** 30,000 (ctrl). ***Continues** Saskatchewan Skier, 0849-6927.*

CN/0709-1532
**WESTERN SPORTSMAN.** Vol. 11 (Spring 1979)-. Periodical. English. bm (Feb, Apr, Jun, Aug, Oct, Dec). 15.95Can$ (one year), 27.00Can$ (two year), 36.00Can$ (three year) Canada; 22.95Can$ (one year), 41.00Can$ (two year), 57.00Can$ (three year) other. Nimrod Publishers Ltd., Western Sportsman, PO Box 737, Regina Saskatchewan, S4P 3A8 Canada. **Tel** (306)352-2773, FAX (306)565-2440. **ED** Brian Bowman. **DD** 799.2/97123. **Ad Acc. Circ:** 24,000 (ctrl). ***Continues** Fish and Game Sportsman, 0015-2897.*
**Desc:** Covers fishing and hunting in Western Canada.

US/0279-9707
**WHAT'S BREWING?.** ***Ceased.*** **Added/Corp** Milwaukke Brewers. (19??)-(19??). Periodical. English. ir (9 times a year). Whats Brewing, PO Box 14155, Milwaukee WI 53214. **Tel** (414)933-4114. **ED** Mario Ziino. **Ad Acc.**
**Desc:** Contains a color-action centerfold and features articles on players and coaches of the Brewers.

CN/0227-0862
**WHISTLE (VANCOUVER).** (THE WHISTLE.). [Whistle]. **Added/Corp** British Columbia Youth Soccer Association. British Columbia Juvenile Soccer Association. (1977)-. Periodical. English. bm. Free to members. British Columbia Youth Soccer Association, 1200 Hornby Street, Vancouver British Columbia V6Z 1W2 Canada. **DD** 796.334/09711. ctrl circ.

US/0163-9684
**WHITE BOOK OF SKI AREAS. U.S. AND CANADA, THE.** (THE WHITE BOOK OF SKI AREAS.). [White book ski areas]. **VAT** White Book of Ski Areas. United States and Canada. 3rd Edition (1978)-. English. an. $18.00. Inter Ski Services, PO Box 9595, Washington DC 20016. **Tel** (202)342-0886, FAX (202)338-1940. **ED** Robert G. Enzel. **LC** GV854.4; .W47. **DD** 796.9/3/02573. cum. index. **Bk Rev. Circ:** 10,000-20,000 (ctrl). ***Continues** White Book of U.S. Ski Areas, 0145-6075.*
**Desc:** Provides information on all of ski areas in the US and Canada and various services. Rates and photos are also included.

CN/0229-611X
**WHO'S WHO DIRECTORY OF SPORTS, RECREATION AND PHYSICAL EDUCATION.** (ANNUAIRE DES SPORTS, DES LOISIRS, ET DE L'EDUCATION PHYSIQUE.). [Who's who dir. sports recreat. phys. educ.]. **Added/Corp** Sport New Brunswick. **VFOAT** Directory of Sports, Recreation and Physical Education; Who's Who : Directory of Sports, Recreation and Physical Education; Who's Who Directory of Sport, Recreation and Physical Education. (1983)-. English (French). an. Sport New Brunswick, 65 Brunswick Street, Fredericton New Brunswick E3B 1G5 Canada. **DD** 796/.025/715. ***Continues** Who's Who Directory of Sports, Recreation and Physical Education, 0229-611X.*

US/1044-9906
**WHO'S WHO IN ATHLETICS IN AMERICAN COLLEGES AND UNIVERSITIES.** [Who's who athl. Am. coll. univ.]. (1990)-. English. be. $75.00. Athletic Press of America, 8268 Streamwood Drive, Baltimore MD 21208. **Tel** (410)922-8115, FAX (410)922-4903. **ED** Dr. Gladson. **LC** GV697.A1; W523. **DD** 796.071/173. Index available (bound in June issue). **Pr Rev.**

US
**WHO'S WHO IN GOLF COURSE MANAGEMENT : DIRECTORY & SOURCE BOOK. Main/Corp** Golf Course Superintendents Association of America. **VFOAT** Directory & Source Book; Directory and Source Book; GCSAA Directory and Source Book; Membership Directory and Source Book; GCSAA Directory & Source Book. Directory. English. an. Golf Course Superintendents Association of America, 1421 Research Park Drive, Lawrence KS 66049. **Tel** (913)841-2240, FAX (913)832-4433. **LC** GV975; .G63A. **DD** 796.352/06/802573. ***Continues** Membership Directory / Golf Course Superintendents Association of America, 0436-1474.*

US/1040-7464
**WHO'S WHO OF AMERICAN HIGH SCHOOL BASKETBALL COACHES.** [Who's who Am. high sch. basketb. coach.]. 1st Ed. (1988/89)-. English. be. $25.00. Gunther Publishing Company, 10207 Heather Hill, Houston TX 77086. **LC** GV884.A1; W48. **DD** 796.323/092/2.

PL/0137-8112
**WIADOMOSCI SPORTOWE.** [Wiad. Sport.]. **VFOAT** WS Wiadomosci Sportowe. (1967)-. Periodical. Polish. mo. $15.00. **(Subscription address:** ARS Polona, PO Box 1001, 00068 Warsaw Poland.**) UDC** 796.

GW
**WILD UND HUND.** Vol. 11 (1885)-. Periodical. German. Twenty-six times a year. DM176.00 (includes postage) Germany; $117.50 (includes postage) US; 171.00F (includes postage) Switzerland. Paul Parey (Berlin), Seelbuschring 9-17, 1000 Berlin 42 Germany. **Tel** 030-70784-00. **ED** H. Reetz. **Bk Rev. Ad Acc. Circ:** 2,500.
**Desc:** Popular magazine for hunters and wildlife lovers.
**Ind/Abst** Key Word Index Wildl. Res.

US/1057-0799
**WIND SURFING.** (WINDSURFING.). [Wind surfing]. **VFOAT** Wind Surfing; Windsurfing Magazine. Vol. 10, No. 1 (March 1991)-. Periodical. English. Eight times a year. $18.97. World Publications, Inc., PO Box 2456, 809 South Orlando Ave., Winter Park FL 32790. **Tel** (407)628-4802, (800)394-6006. **(Subscription address:** Windsurfing, PO Box 8500, Winter Park FL 32790.**) LC** GV811.63.W56; W537. **DD** 797.3/3/05. ***Continues** Windrider, 0279-4659.*

US/0279-4659
**WINDRIDER.** ***Title Change.*** [Windrider]. **VFOAT** Windrider Magazine. **VAT** Wind Rider. Vol. 1, Iss. 1 (Fall 1981)-(199?). Periodical. English. ir (eight issues per year). Windrider, PO Box 183, Mt Morris IL 61054. **Tel** (305)628-4802. **ED** Terry L Snow. **LC** GV811.63.W56; W537. **DD** 797.3/3/05. **Ad Acc. Circ:** 60,000. ***Continued by** Wind Surfing, 1057-0799.*
**Desc:** The No. 1 windsurfing magazine. Step-by-step instruction, equipment and product reviews, regatta coverage and stunning photography.
**Ind/Abst** SPORT Discus; SportSearch (May 1987-).

CN/0826-5003
**WINDSPORT.** [Windsport]. **VFOAT** Windsport Canada. **VAT** Windsport Canada (1983). Vol. 2, Issue No. 2 (April 1983)-. Periodical. English. Four times a year. 20.06Can$ Canada; 30.06Can$ others. Windsport Magazine, 2255 B Queen Street East, Suite 3266, Toronto Ontario M4E 1G3 Canada. **Tel** (416)698-0138, telex 06-986766. **ED** Steve Jarrett. **DD** 797.1/72/0971. **Bk Rev. Ad Acc. Circ:** 15,000. ***Continues** Windsport Canada, 0714-8852.*
**Desc:** Presents articles on all aspects of this new sport "windsurfing". Writers cover everything from how to get started to advanced high-speed windsurfing. Plus, it provides extensive analysis of sailboards and accessories as well as coverage of the best places to windsurf in Canada.
**Ind/Abst** Can. Period. Index (19??-19??); SPORT Discus.

US/1063-8172
**WINDSURFING CALIFORNIA.** [Windsurf. Calif.]. (19??)-. Periodical. English. bm. $9.97 US; $16.00 Canada and Mexico; $38.00 other. Gorge Publishing, PO Box 918, Hood River OR 97031. **Tel** (503)386-7440, FAX (503)386-7480. **ED** Carol York. **DD** 797. **Bk Rev. Ad Acc, Adv Mgr:** Marie Cordell. **Circ:** 25,000.
**Desc:** Regional windsurfing magazine providing positive and informative editorial for consumers.

US
**WINNING EDGE, THE.** 1st Ed. (1990/91)-. English. $14.95. Octameron Associates, PO Box 2748, Alexandria VA 22301. **Tel** (703)836-5480.

US/0893-6439
**WINNING HOOPS.** [Winning hoops]. (Sept. 1986)-. Periodical. English. Six times a year. $34.95. Cornerstone Enterprises, PO Box 604023, Bay Terrace NY 11360. **Tel** (516)227-1402, (718)428-1957. **ED** Paul M. Eckstein. **DD** 796. Index available. cum. index. **Circ:** 200.

Recreation, Leisure —Sports

**Desc:** Advice, strategy, plays for scholastic basketball coaches (high school, junior high school, and boys/girls clubs) written by college basketball coaches.

US/1048-6119
**WINSTON CUP ILLUSTRATED.** [Winst. Cup Illus.]. **Added/Corp** NASCAR (Association). **VFOAT** WCI. Vol. 8, No. 6 (Nov. 1989)-. Periodical. English. Six times a year. $40.00 (one year), $70.00 (two year) US; $60.00 Canada and Mexico; $100.00 other. Griggs Publishing Company Inc., PO Box 500, Concord NC 28026. **Tel** (704)786-7132, (800)883-7323, FAX (704)788-4420. **ED** Steve Waid, PO Box 500 Concord, NC 28026 (phone: (704)786-7132). **DD** 796. **Ad Acc**, **Adv Mgr:** Zeta Smith, **Tel** (704)-786-7131. **Circ:** 18,000 (ctrl). ***Continues** Grand National Illustrated, 0744-4869.*
**Desc:** The Winston Cup Race Series is featured in this publication. Photos and interviews of the sports' personalities.

US/1053-461X
**WINSTON CUP SCENE.** Periodical. English. ir (weekly mid-February through mid-November). $40.00 (one year), $75.00 (two years) US; $95.00 Canada/Mexico; $150.00 other. Griggs Publ Company Inc, PO Box 500, Concord NC 28026. **Tel** (704)786-7132, FAX (704)788-4420. **ED** Steve Waid. **Ad Acc**, **Adv Mgr:** Zeta Smith, **Tel** (704)786-7131. **Circ:** 82,000 (ctrl). ***Continues** Grand National Scene, 0274-4910.*
**Desc:** Weekly recap of the NASCAR Winston Cup Series racing circuit.

CN/1188-8377
**WIRAZU, NA.** ***Title Change.*** [Na Wirazu]. **Added/Corp** Polski Klub Sportowy w Kanadzie. **VAT** Sharp Turn. (1992)-(199?). Periodical. English. mo. Polski Klub Sportowy w Kanadzie, Suite 40, 2559 Lakeshore Boulevard, Toronto Ontario M8V 1E5 Canada. **DD** 796. ***Continued by** Sukces w Ameryce, 1192-523X.*

US/1042-6620
**WISCONSIN GOLF.** [Wis. golf]. **Added/Corp** Golf Foundation of Wisconsin. Professional Golfers' Association of America. Wisconsin Section. (Oct. 1988)-. Periodical. English. Seven times a year. $12.95 (one year); $23.95 (two year); $32.05 (three year). Wisconsin Golf, PO Box 14439, Madison WI 53714. **Tel** (608) 244-2600, FAX (608) 244-2603. **ED** John Hughes. **DD** 796. **Bk Rev**, (Qty: 6 /yr). **Ad Acc**.

US/0882-9640
**WISCONSIN SILENT SPORTS.** Periodical. English. mo. $14.00 (1 year), $25.00 (2 year), $36.00 (3 year). Waupaca County Publishing Company, PO Box 152/717 10th Street, Waupaca WI 54981. **Tel** (715)258-5546, FAX (715)258-8162. **DD** 796. **UDC** 796(775). **Bk Rev**. **Ad Acc**. **Circ:** 10,000.
**Desc:** Directed toward bicyclists, cross county skiers, runners, triathletes, canoeists, kayakers, hikers, backpackers, and participants in related activities.

UK
**WISDEN'S CRICKETERS ALMANAC.** (19??)-. English. an. £22.50 (hardback), £20.00 (softback). Gollancz Victor Ltd, Villiers House, 41/47 Strand, London WC2N 5JE United Kingdom. **Tel** 011 44 71 839 4900, FAX 011 44 839 1804. **ED** Matthew Engel. **Bk Rev**. **Ad Acc**, **Adv Mgr:** Colin Ackehurst.
**Desc:** Coverage and examination of contemporary cricket in England and overseas, including all score cards and records.

KO
**WOLGAN SSIRUM.** **VFOAT** Ssirum. Periodical. Korean. mo. W10,000. Taehan Ssirum Hyophoe, 19 Mugyo-dong Chung-ku, Seoul 100 Korea. **LC** GV1198.81.K6; W64.

US/1048-9940
**WOLVERINE (ANN ARBOR, MICH.), THE.** (THE WOLVERINE : COVERING UNIVERSITY OF MICHIGAN SPORTS.). [Wolverine]. (1989)-. Periodical. English. Twenty-five times a year. $35.95. Wolverine, PO Box 1304, Ann Arbor MI 48106. **Tel** (800)421-7751. **DD** 796.
**Desc:** Covers sports at the University of Michigan.

US/0043-7255
**WOMAN BOWLER, THE.** ***Title Change.*** **Added/Corp** Women's International Bowling Congress. (1936)-(1994). Periodical. English. qt. Woman Bowler, 5301 South 76th Street, Greendale WI 53129. **Tel** (414)421-9000, FAX (414)421-3013. **ED** Jeffrey R. Nowak. **LC** GV901; .W57. **DD** 794.6; 796.31*. **Ad Acc**, **Adv Mgr:** Leslie Smith, **Tel** (414)421-9000. **Circ:** 120,000. ***Continued by** WB (Greendale, Wis.), 1078-2958.*
**Desc:** Features articles of interest to bowling. Coverage of bowling and WIBC events and programs on local, national and international level.
**Ind/Abst** SPORT Discus.

US/1054-8580
**WOMAN DIVER.** [Woman diver]. Vol. 1, No. 1 (Winter 1991)-. Periodical. English. qt. $30.00. Woman Diver, Inc., 6631 Wakefield Drive, Suite 820 Alexandria VA 22307. **DD** 797.

US/0146-1133
**WOMEN'S COACHING CLINIC.** ***Title Change.*** [Women's coach. clin.]. Vol. 1, No. 1 (Sept. 1977)-(?). Periodical. English. mo (except July and Aug.). Princeton Educational Publishers, PO Box 280, Plainsboro NJ 08536. **Tel** (908)297-6920. **ED** Annette R van Deusen. **LC** GV709.14; .W65. **DD** 796/.01/94. **UDC** 796/799.07.072-055.2. **Bk Rev**. **Circ:** 2,500. ***Continued by** The Coaching Clinic, 0009-9880.*
**Desc:** Each issue conveys the best thinking, the newest strategies devised by some of the most successful coaches of women's sports today.
**Ind/Abst** Phys. Educ. Index; SPORT Discus; SportSearch.

US/0899-5508
**WOMEN'S FASTPITCH WORLD.** Vol. 1, No. 1 (Feb. 1988)-. Periodical. English. Twelve times a year. $39.99 (U.S.). Windmill Publishing LTD, PO Box 326, St Charles IL 60174. **Tel** (312)377-7369. **ED** Julie Olsen (editor's phone: (314)625-8803). **DD** 796. **Ad Acc**.

US/8750-653X
**WOMEN'S SPORTS AND FITNESS.** [Women's sports fitness]. **Added/Corp** Women's Sports Foundation. **VFOAT** Women's Sports. Vol. 6, No. 5 (May 1984)-. Periodical. English. ir (8 issues). $19.97. Sports & Fitness Publishing Group, 2025 Pearl Street, Boulder CO 80302. **Tel** (303)440-5111. **(Subscription address:** Kable Publishers Aide, 308 East Hitt Street, Mt Morris, IL 61054**)** **ED** Martha Nelson. **LC** GV709; .W587. **DD** 796/.01/94. **[CCC]**. **Ad Acc**. **Circ:** 250,000. available on microfilm and microfiche from University Microfilms International (UMI); available on an online database (file 149,647/Full-Text) from DIALOG. Documents available from UMI Article Clearinghouse. ***Continues** Women's Sports, 0163-7428.*
**Desc:** Covers sports medicine, aerobics, cycling, swimming, rowing, gymnastics, running, rope jumping and other sports, with related health topics such as nutrition, from the woman's point of view.
**Ind/Abst** Abr. Read. Guide Period. Lit.; Acad. Abstr. Full Text Elite (May 1984-); Acad. Abstr. (May 1984-); Acad. Ind. [Computer File] (1985-); Acad. Search (May 1984-); Consum. Health Nutr. Index (?-?); Expand. Acad. Index (1985-); Gen. Period. Index (1985-); Health Index (1989-); Health Period. Database [Full Txt.]; Health Ref. Cent. (Jan. 1989-) [Full Txt.] [Full Cov.]; Health Source (Mar. 1985-); INFO-SOUTH Abstr.; Mag. Artic. Summar. Elite (March 1985-); Mag. Artic. Summar. Select (March 1985-); Mag. Artic. Summar. CD-ROM (May 1984-); Mag. ASAP Plus [Full Txt.]; Mag. ASAP Sel. [Full Txt.]; Mag. Index Plus (1989-); Mag. Index. Sel. (1986-); Mag. Search; Mid. Search (Mar. 1985-); Newsp. Period. Abstr. (1988-); Phys. Educ. Index; Read. Guide Abstr. Select Ed.; Read. Guide Period. Lit.; Resource/One Ondisc (1988-); SPORT Discus; SportSearch; Mag. Index (May 1984-); TOM Gen. Index (1992-) [Full Txt.]; Vocat. Search (May 1984-).

●US/1061-1568
**WOMEN'S SPORTS EXPERIENCE, THE.** (THE WOMEN'S SPORTS EXPERIENCE: A NEWSLETTER FROM THE WOMEN'S SPORTS FOUNDATION.). [Women's sports exp.]. **Added/Corp** Women's Sports Foundation. (1992)-. Newsletter. English. qt. $25.00 (membership). Women's Sports Foundation, 342 Madison Avenue, Suite 728, New York NY 10173. **DD** 796. ***Continues** Headway (New York, N.Y.), 1044-7377.*

US/0095-7240
**WORLD ALMANAC GUIDE TO PRO HOCKEY, THE.** English. $1.95. Bantam Books Inc, 666 Fifth Avenue, New York NY 10019. **Tel** (212)340-7500. **LC** GV847.5; .W67. **DD** 796.9/62/097. **UDC** 796.355(036).

GW
**WORLD AMATEUR BOXING MAGAZINE.** German. Three times a year. $15.00. World Amateur Boxing Magazine Editor's Office, P.O.Box 0141, 10321 Berlin/GERMANY. **Tel** (049.30)423 5932, (049.30)423 6766, FAX (049.30)423 5943. **Bk Rev**.

UK/0255-4429
**WORLD BADMINTON.** [World badminton]. (1972)-. Periodical. English. Four times a year (Mar., June, Sept., Dec.). £8.00. International Badminton Federation, 4 Manor Park, Mackenzie Highway, Cheltenham Glos England. **Tel** 011 44 242 34904, FAX 011 44 242 221030, telex 43495. **UDC** 796.34.
**Ind/Abst** SPORT Discus.

US/1040-5216
**WORLD BASEBALL MAGAZINE.** (WORLD BASEBALL MAGAZINE / IBA.). [World baseb. mag.]. **Added/Corp** International Baseball Association. **VFOAT** World Baseball; IBA World Baseball. **VAT** International Baseball Association World Baseball. (19??)-. Periodical. English (Spanish). qt. $10.00. International Baseball Association, Pan Am Plaza, 201 South Capitol Avenue/Suite 490, Indianapolis IN 46225. **DD** 796.

UK/0966-9884
**WORLD BOWLS.** [World bowls]. (1954)-. Periodical. English. mo.
**Ind/Abst** SPORT Discus.

US/1051-9033
**WORLD BOXING.** [World box.]. (19??)-. Periodical. English. Fourteen times a year. $24.60 (comes with Boxing). London Publishing Company, PO Box 910, Fort Washington PA 19034. **Tel** (215)643-6385, FAX (215)540-0146. **DD** 796.

US/1057-1396
**WORLD CHAMPIONSHIP WRESTLING MAGAZINE : WCW.** ***Ceased.*** [World championship wrestl. mag.]. **VFOAT** WCW Magazine. Vol. 1, No. 1 (Nov. 1991)-(19??). Periodical. English. mo. London Publishing Company, PO Box 910, Fort Washington PA 19034. **Tel** (215)643-6385, FAX (215)540-0146. **DD** 796.

US/0747-5853
**WORLD CLINIC YEARBOOK / AMERICAN SWIMMING COACHES ASSOCIATION.** **Added/Corp** American Swimming Coaches Association. World Clinic. American Swimming Coaches Association. **VFOAT** American Swimming Coaches Association World Clinic Yearbook. (19??)-. Periodical. English. an. $29.95 US; $34.95 (includes postage) other. American Swimming Coaches Association, 301 SE 20th Street, Fort Lauderdale FL 33316. **Tel** (305)462-6267, (800)356-2722. **LC** GV837.65; .W67. **DD** 797.2/1/0973. ***Continues** American Swimming Coaches Association World Clinic Yearbook, 0747-5853.*

PK
**WORLD CRICKET ANNUAL.** 1979-80-. English. an. A/12 Gaushala Building, Moolji Street, Kharadar Karachi 2 Pakistan.

SZ/0255-884X
**WORLD HANDBALL MAGAZINE.** [World handball mag.]. (1984)-. Periodical. Multiple languages. sa. 40.00F. Internationale Handball Federation, Postfach 312, CH 4020 Basel, Switzerland. **Tel** 11 41 61 2721344.

UK/0964-0681
**WORLD HOCKEY.** [World Hockey]. (1969)-. English. Four times a year (Jan., Apr., Aug., Oct.). £7.00 UK; £10.00 Europe & Eire; £18.50 other. Harrow Press, 426 Long Drive, Unite E6 Aladdinw, Greenford MID UB6 8UH England. **Tel** 011 44 81 575-3121, FAX 011 44 81 5751320. **ED** Chris Moore. **Ad Acc**. **Circ:** 3,000 (ctrl).
**Desc:** Hockey results and news around the world.

SZ
**WORLD OF GYMNASTICS.** Four times a year. 30.00F Europe; 45.00F other. Federation Internationale Gymnastique, Rue de Oeuches 10, 2740 Moutier 1 Switzerland. **Tel** 011 41 32 936666, FAX 11 41 32 936671, telex 934961 FIG CH. **ED** Andre F. Gueisbuhler. **Ad Acc**.
**Desc:** Provides features, news, and interviews from the world of gymnastics.

UK
**WORLD SOCCER.** (1960)-. Periodical. English. mo. $55.00. IPC Magazines Ltd., Perrymount Road, Haywards Heath, West Sussex RH16 3DH England. **Tel** 011 44 444 440421. **ED** Philip Rising. **LC** GV942; .W67. **DD** 796.33/4/05. cum. index. **Bk Rev**. **Ad Acc**. **Circ:** 25,000.
**Desc:** The largest circulated international soccer magazine in English, in the world, with sales and subscribers in 97 countries. Sent to all FIFA member organizations and the world's top soccer clubs.
**Ind/Abst** SPORT Discus; SportSearch (May 1987-).

CN/0711-3919
**WORLD SOCCER NEWS.** [World soccer news]. Vol. 1, No. 1 (Oct. 7, 1981)-. Periodical. English. wk. $1.00 each issue. World Soccer News, Suite 205, 4250 Westo Road, Weston Ontario M9L 1W9 Canada. **DD** 796.334/05. **UDC** 796.332; 799.2:599.742.7(77).

HU/0230-3035
**WORLD WEIGHTLIFTING.** **See** Health and Personal Fitness.

US/0093-2477
**WORLD-WIDE GOLF DIRECTORY.** 1973-. Directory. English. an. $9.75. World Sprots Publishers, 1511 K Street NW, Suite 1036, Washington DC 20005. **LC** GV975; .W65. **DD** 796.352/06/025. **UDC** 796.352(058).

US/1056-3946
**WORLD WRESTLING FEDERATION BATTLEMANIA.** [World Wrestling Fed. battlemania]. **Added/Corp** World Wrestling Federation. **VFOAT** Battlemania. No. 1 (Aug. 1991)-. Periodical. English. mo. $30.00 US; $39.00 Canada. Voyager Communications, 65 Commerce Road, Stamford CT 06902-4546. **DD** 741.

US/1052-0899
**WRESTLER (ROCKVILLE CENTRE, N.Y.), THE.** (THE WRESTLER.). [Wrestler]. (1968)-. Periodical. English. Thirteen times a year. $19.00. London Publishing Company, PO Box 910, Fort

Washington PA 19034. **Tel** (215)643-6385, FAX (215)540-0146. **ED** Stu Saks. **DD** 796. **Ad Acc**, **Adv Mgr Tel** (800)678-9321. **Circ:** 147,000.

US/0885-8551
**WRESTLING ALL STARS, HEROES & VILLAINS.** **VFOAT** Wrestling All Stars, Heroes and Villains; Wrestling All Stars. No. 1 (Dec. 1985)-. Periodical. English. Eight times a year. Comics World Corporation, 475 Park Avenue South, New York NY 10016. **Tel** (212)689-2830. ***Continues*** *Wrestling All Stars, 0742-518X.*

US/1059-0706
**WRESTLING EYE.** ***Ceased.*** [Wrestl. eye]. **VFOAT** Wrestling Eye Magazine. (Nov. 1985)-(19??). Periodical. English. mo. Jems Inc., 55 6th Avenue, Suite 309, New York NY 10013. **Tel** (212)925-3115, (212)925-3377. **LC** WMLC 91/2864. **DD** 796.

US/1059-0714
**WRESTLING FURY.** ***Ceased.*** [Wrestl. fury]. (1986)-(19??). Periodical. English. bm. Jems Inc., 55 6th Avenue, Suite 309, New York NY 10013. **Tel** (212)925-3115, (212)925-3377. **DD** 796.

US/8755-3767
**WRESTLING MASTERS.** [Wrestl. masters]. **Added/Corp** Professional Freestyle Wrestling Association. (Jan. 1983)-. Periodical. English. Eight times a year. $20.95. Sports Masters Publishing Co., PO Box 618, Lakewood NJ 08701-9988. **Tel** (201)363-7576. **LC** GV1195; .W718. **DD** 796.8/12/0973.

US/1042-5284
**WRESTLING SUPERSTARS.** (19??)-. Periodical. English. qt. $35.40. London Publishing Company, PO Box 910, Fort Washington PA 19034. **Tel** (215)643-6385, FAX (215)540-0146. **DD** 796. **Ad Acc.**

US/0199-6258
**WRESTLING USA (LAHABRA).** (WRESTLING USA.). [Wrestl. U. S. A.]. **VFOAT** Wrestling U.S.A. **VAT** Wrestling United States of America. Vol. 15, No. 6 (Feb. 1, 1980)-. Periodical. English. mo. $27.00 US; $37.00 other. Wrestling USA, 109 Apple House Lane, Missoula MT 59802. **Tel** (406)549-4448. **ED** Lanny Bryant. **DD** 796. Index available. **Ad Acc. Circ:** 13,000 (ctrl). available on microfiche. ***Continues*** *Scholastic Wrestling News.*
**Desc:** The nation's school boy magazine devoted exclusively to wrestling. A publication for the coach, athlete and wrestling fan.
**Ind/Abst** SPORT Discus; SportSearch (May 1987-).

US/0891-0707
**WRESTLING (VERNON CENTER, MINN.).** (WRESTLING.). [Wrestling]. **VFOAT** Wrestling Magazine; Wrestling News. (198?)-. Periodical. English. qt. $16.00 (one year), $26.00 (two year), $36.00 (three year) US; $20.00 (one year), $34.00 (two year), $48.00 (three year) other. Norman Kietzer, Route 1 Box 103, Vernon Center MN 56090. **Tel** (507)549-3677. **DD** 796. ***Formed by the union of*** *Major League Wrestling* ***and*** *Ring's Wrestling, 0745-8843 Wrestling Writers Association of America Hall of Fame Wrestling Revue, 0043-9487.*
**Desc:** Covers the sport of professional wrestling.

US/0278-9612
**WRESTLING'S MAIN EVENT.** **VFOAT** Main Event. Vol. 1, No. 1 (June 1982)-. Periodical. English. Six times a year (Feb., Apr., June, Aug., Oct., Dec.). $22.50 (two year). Pumpkin Press Inc, Empire State Building, 350 5th Avenue, New York NY 10118. **Tel** (212)947-4322, FAX (212)563-4774. **ED** Sandra Krebs. **Ad Acc. Circ:** 108,000 (ctrl).
**Desc:** We profile the most popular wrestlers of the day through first person interviews and in-depth authoritative articles. There are many full page, full color photos suitable for framing.

KO
**WTF TAEKWONDO.** **Added/Corp** World Taekwondo Federation. (19??)-. Periodical. English. Four times a year. $30.00. World Taekwondo Federation, 635 Yuksam Dong, Kangnam ku, Seoul Korea. **Tel** 566 2505 Korea Chong Ho Bae. **LC** WMLC L 83/6591.
**Ind/Abst** SPORT Discus.

US/8756-7792
**WWF MAGAZINE.** (WWF MAGAZINE / OFFICIAL PUBLICATION OF THE WORLD WRESTLING FEDERATION.). [WWF mag.]. **Added/Corp** World Wrestling Federation. **VFOAT** Official World Wrestling Federation Magazine. **VAT** World Wrestling Federation Magazine. (198?)-. Periodical. English. mo. $20.00 (one year), $35.00 (two year). WWF Magazine, PO Box 420174, Palm Coast FL 32142. **Tel** (203)353-2855, FAX (203)353-2821. **(Subscription address:** Palm Coast Data, PO Box 420235, Agency Department, Palm Coast FL 32142.**)** **LC** WMLC L 83/3731. **DD** 796. **Ad Acc**, **Adv Mgr Tel** (212)593-2228. ***Continues*** *Official World Wrestling Federation's Magazine, 0747-4016.*

US/0744-0006
**YANKEES MAGAZINE.** (YANKEES MAGAZINE : THE OFFICIAL NEWSPAPER OF THE NEW YORK YANKEES.). **Added/Corp** New York Yankees (Baseball team). (19??)-. Periodical. English. mo. $14.97. Yankees Magazine, Yankee Stadium, Bronx NY 10451. **Tel** (718)293-4300.
**Desc:** Official publication of the New York Yankees.

CN/0316-2559
**YEAR BOOK - CANADIAN RACING PIGEON UNION.** **Main/Corp** Canadian Racing Pigeon Union. (1???)-. Periodical. English. an. Free to members. Canadian Racing Pigeon Union, 246 Blakie Road, Unit 107, London Ontario N6L 1G4 Canada. **Tel** (519)652-5704. **DD** 798/.8. **Ad Acc. Circ:** 1,800.

US/0146-2458
**YEARBOOK - ENSIGN CLASS ASSOCIATION.** [Yearb. - Ensign Cl. Assoc.]. **Main/Corp** Ensign Class Association. (19??)-. English. an. $3.50. Ensign Class Association, 96 Washington Street, Newport RI 02840. **LC** GV810.5; .E5718. **DD** 797.1/24/06273.

US/0160-5771
**YOUNG WRESTLER, THE.** V. 1- Sept./Oct. 1974-. English. qt. $3.00. PO Box 60387, Oklahoma City OK 73106. **LC** GV1198.12; .Y68. **DD** 796.8/12/0973. **UDC** 796.81(73).

US/0894-4377
**YOUTH SPORTS.** [Youth sports]. (Sept. 1987)-. Periodical. English. Thirteen times a year. $19.50. Youth Sports, 141 North Orlando Avenue, Cocoa Beach FL 32931. **DD** 796.

GW/0044-2887
**ZEITSCHRIFT FUER JAGDWISSENSCHAFT.** [Z. Jagdwiss.]. Vol. 1 (1955)-. Academic Scholarly Publication. German (summaries and/or abstracts in English and French). qt. DM298.00. Blackwell Wissenschafts-Verlag, Kurfuerstendamm 57, D 10707 Berlin Germany. **Tel** 011 49 30 32790623, 011 49 30 32790624, FAX 011 49 30 327 90610. **ED** E. Veckermann. **CODEN** ZEJAAA. **[CCC].** Index available. cum. index. **Bk Rev. Ad Acc. Pr Rev. Circ:** 2,500. Documents available from The Genuine Article, BIOSIS Document Express.
**Desc:** Reports on wildlife diseases, game management, hunting, hunting laws and history.
**Ind/Abst** Agrofor. Abstr. (1991-); Anim. Breed. Abstr.; Biol. Abstr.; Curr. Contents, Agric. Biol. Environ. Sci.; EMBASE; For. Abstr.; Grasslands For. Abstr.; Helminthol. Abstr. (1991-); Index Vet.; Key Word Index Wildl. Res.; Leis. Recreat. Tour. Abstr.; Nutr. Abstr. Rev., Ser. B, Live Feeds and Feed.; Life Sci. Collect.; Pig News Inf.; Poult. Abstr.; Protozoolog. Abstr.; Res. Alert [Select. Cov.]; Rev. Med. Vet. Entomol.; Vet. Bull.; Wildl. Rev.

# RELIGION AND THEOLOGY

CN/0820-8778
**4E JOUR.** [4e jour]. **VAT** Quatrieme Jour. Periodical. French. ir. $3.00. Mouvement Cursillo D'Ottawa, 256 Avenue King Edward, Ottawa Ont. K1N 7N1. **DD** 269/.6.

US/1048-4124
**21ST CENTURY CHRISTIAN MAGAZINE.** **Added/Corp** 20th Century Christian Foundation. **VFOAT** Twenty-First Century Christian Magazine. Vol. 52, No. 4 (Jan. 1990)-. Periodical. English. Twelve times a year. $10.95 (one year), $17.95 (two years), $23.95 (three years) 21st Century Christian; $16.95 (one year), $28.95 (two years), $38.95 (three years), Power Today 21st Century Christian. 20th Century Christian Foundation, 2809 Granny White Pike, PO Box 40526, Nashville TN 37204. **Tel** (800)331-5991. ***Continues*** *20th Century Christian, 0162-6418.*

US/0360-3725
**A.M.E. CHURCH REVIEW, THE.** [A.M.E. church rev.]. **Added/Corp** African Methodist Episcopal Church. Vol. 1 (July 1884)-. Periodical. English. Four times a year (Mar., June, Sept., Dec.). $10.00. AME Church Review, 500 Eight Avenue South, Nashville TN 37203-4119. **Tel** (615)256-7020, FAX (615)256-7020. **ED** Paulette Coleman. **Bk Rev**, (Qty: 4-6). **Pr Rev. Circ:** 4,000. available on microfilm and microfiche from University Microfilms International (UMI).

US/0145-2789
**AAR STUDIES IN RELIGION.** [AAR stud. relig.]. **Main/Corp** American Academy of Religion. **Added/Corp** American Academy of Religion. **VFOAT** Studies in Religion. **VAT** American Academy of Religion Studies in Religion. (1970)-. Monographic series. English. ir. Price varies per volume. Scholars Press / Georgia, PO Box 15399, Atlanta GA 30333-0399. **Tel** (404)636-4757, (404)727-2320, FAX (404)727-2348. **ED** James Wiggins. **LC** UNC. **DD** 290. **Bk Rev. Ad Acc.** ctrl circ.
**Desc:** Monographs representing historical, methodological, critical, and constructive aspects of scholarship in the field of religion.

US
**ABBEY LETTER.** **Added/Corp** St. Gregory's Abbey, Three Rivers, Mich. No. 81 (June 1969)-. Periodical. English. Four times a year. Free on request. St Gregory's Abbey, 56500 Abbey Road, Three Rivers MI 49093. **Tel** (616)244-5893. **ED** Jude Bell. **Circ:** 30,000. ***Continues*** *Benedicite.*
**Desc:** Short articles on topics relating to the monastic life and Christian spiritual life, usually written by the monks of St. Gregory's. Also news of the abbey and photographs.

US/1047-5486
**ABINGDON PREACHER'S ANNUAL.** ***Title Change.*** (1991)-(1994). English. an. Abingdon Press, PO Box 801, Nashville TN 37202. **Tel** (615)749-6451, (800)251-3320. **DD** 252. ***Continues*** *Minster's Annual.* ***Continued by*** *Abingdon Preaching Annual, 1075-2250.*

US/0164-1816
**ABSTRACTS / AMERICAN ACADEMY OF RELIGION.** **Main/Corp** American Academy of Religion. **VFOAT** AAR/SBL Abstracts. (19??)-. English. an. $20.00. Scholars Press / Georgia, PO Box 15399, Atlanta GA 30333-0399. **Tel** (404)636-4757, (404)727-2320, FAX (404)727-2348. **LC** BL48; .A49a. **DD** 200/.5. ***Absorbed*** *Society of Biblical Literature. Abstracts.*

US/0733-2599
**ABSTRACTS OF RESEARCH IN PASTORAL CARE AND COUNSELING.** **See** Religion and Theology-Abstracting, Bibliographies and Statistics.

US/1071-376X
**ACADEMY ACCENTS.** (ACADEMY ACCENTS : THE NEWSLETTER OF THE ACADEMY OF PREACHERS.). [Acad. accents]. **Added/Corp** Academy of Preachers. Lutheran Theological Seminary at Philadelphia. Vol. 1, No. 1 (Fall 1984)-. Newsletter. English. qt. $8.00. Lutheran Theological Seminary / Philadelphia, PA, 7301 Germantown Road, Academy of Preachers, Philadelphia PA 19119. **Tel** (215)248-4616. **ED** Robert G. Hughes. **DD** 284. Index available. cum. index. **Bk Rev**, (Qty: 4). **Circ:** 1,200 (ctrl).

US/0162-1955
**ACCENT.** Vol. 1 (1970)-. Periodical. English. mo. $11.00 US; $13.50 other. Woman's Missionary Union, PO Box 830010, Birmingham AL 35283. **Tel** (205)991-8100, (205)991-4933. **ED** Jan Turrentine. **Circ:** 106,000 (ctrl).
**Desc:** The Woman's Missionary Union magazine for AcTeens and AcTeens leaders. Seeks to lead AcTeens and their leaders not only to feel a part of the Acteens organization but also to feel a part of the total Woman's Missionary Union organization through missions support and involvement.
**Ind/Abst** South. Baptist Period. Index.

US/0276-2358
**ACCENT ON WORSHIP.** ***Suspended.*** (ACCENT ON WORSHIP : A PUBLICATION OF THE LITURGICAL CONFERENCE.). **Added/Corp** Liturgical Conference, Inc. Vol. 1, No. 1 (1981)-(?). Periodical. English. Free to members. The Liturgical Conference, 8750 Georgia Avenue, Suite 123, Silver Spring MD 20910. **Tel** (301)495-0885. **ED** Rachel Reeder. **LC** Discard. **Bk Rev. Circ:** 4,500 (ctrl). ***Continues*** *Accent on Liturgy, 0272-7951.*
**Desc:** A benefit of membership in the Liturgical Conference, it provides two-to-three articles of interest to pastoral liturgists on music, art, preaching, etc., as well as book reviews.

US/0277-9102
**ACCENT/REVIEWS.** [Accent/rev.]. **VFOAT** Accent. **VAT** Accent Reviews. 1-. Periodical. English. qt. Free US; $10.00 other. Accent/Reviews, PO Box 4463, Washington DC 20017. **Tel** (202)543-1075. **ED** William E Hartgen Jr. **Bk Rev. Ad Acc. Circ:** 14,000.
**Desc:** Reviews and resources for local church ministry cross-cultural and cross-confessional.

UK/0305-9286
**ACT DIGEST.** [ACT dig.]. **VFOAT** Association of Christian Teachers Digest. (1974)-. Periodical. English. Three times a year (Jan., May, Sept.). £6.00. Association of Christian Teachers, 94A London Road, St. Albans, Herts Al1 1NX England. **Tel** 011 44 727 40298.

US/0001-5083
**ACT (WHITING).** (ACT: A QUARTERLY NEWSPAPER OF CHRISTIAN FAMILY MOVEMENT.). **Added/Corp** Christian Family Movement. Christian Family Movement. Coordinating Committee. (1946)-. Newsletter. English. mo (except combined Nov./Dec. and July/Aug.). $8.00 US; $10.00 other. Christian Family Movement, PO Box 272, Ames IA 50010. **Tel** (515)232-7432. **ED** Laurie Przyhysz (phone: (412)795-7156). **Bk Rev. Circ:** 2,800. ***Continues*** *Agape.*
**Desc:** Information on Christian family movement. Ideas and resources of interest to families and family life ministers.

NE/0065-1672
**ACTA THEOLOGICA DANICA.** Vol. 1 (1958)-. Monographic series. Latin. ir. Price varies per volume. E. J. Brill, Postbus 9000, 2300 PA Leiden Netherlands. **Tel** 011 31 71 312624, FAX 011 31 71 317532, telex 39296

BRILL NL. **ED** Edward Nielsen. **Bk Rev. Ad Acc. Circ:** 1,000.
**Desc:** A series of theological dissertations, dealing with the Bible, religion, philosophy, and church history or dogmatic issues.

UK
**ACTION.** No. 1 (July 1, 1966)-. Periodical. English. World Association for Christian Communication, 357 Kennington Lane, London SE11 5QY England. **Tel** 011 44 71 582 9139. **ED** Ann Shakespeare. **Bk Rev. Circ:** 2,000 (ctrl). ***Supersedes*** *National European.*
**Desc:** Communication and church trends. Information on journalism, radio, video projects in third world countries and news of books on communication.

US/0363-731X
**ACTION (CENTRAL ILLINOIS CONFERENCE EDITION).** (ACTION.). **Added/Corp** United Methodist Church (U.S.). Illinois Area Commission. Vol. 1 (1962)-. Newspaper. English. bm. $0.40. Illinois Area Commission on United Methodist Communication, Springfield IL 62701.

US
**ACTION INFORMATION.** ***Title Change.*** **Added/Corp** Alban Institute. **VFOAT** Alban Institute Action Information. Vol. 1 (1975)-(19??). Periodical. English. bm. Alban Institute, 4550 Montgomery Avenue, Suite 433 N, Bethesda MD 20814. **Tel** (301)718-4407. **ED** Celia Allison Hahn. Index available. cum. index. **Bk Rev. Circ:** 7,000 (ctrl). ***Continued by*** *Congregations Alban Journal.*
**Desc:** Practical aid to ministers and lay leaders to help dynamics of congregational life.

CN/0227-2040
**ACTION (LIMOILOU).** (L'ACTION.). [Action]. V. 1, No. 8- Dec. 1979-. Periodical. French. $1.00 per no. without supplement, $2.50 per no. with supplement. Centre Unev l'Action, CP 97, Limoilou Quebec G1N 2N9 Canada. **DD** 261.8/3/09714. ***Continues*** *Action Sociale Catholique, 0707-8005.*

FR/0184-6345
**ACTION MISSIONNAIRE PARIS.** (1978)-. Periodical. French. qt. 60.00F France; 80.00F other. France Mission, 22 Ave de Saint Mande, 75012 Paris France. **Tel** 33 1 43420521. **ED** Gilbert Presle. **UDC** 283. **Circ:** 5,000 (ctrl).
**Desc:** An update on church planning activities in France, and exposition on biblical topics.

US/8750-1333
**ACTION (REDONDO BEACH, CALIF.).** (ACTION / WORLD BIBLE SCHOOL.). [Action]. Periodical. English. mo. Action / Redondo Beach, CA, PO Box 488, Redondo Beach CA 90277-0488.

CN/0315-6036
**ACTION (TORONTO. 1970).** ***Title Change.*** (ACTION.). Mar. 1970-. Periodical. English. qt. Overseas Missions Department of the Pentecostal Assemblies of Canada, 10 Overlea Boulevard, Toronto Ontario M4H 1A5 Canada. **Tel** (416)425-1010, FAX (416)425-8308. **ED** George W Grosshans. **Circ:** 30,000 (ctrl). ***Superseded in part by*** *Know, 0381-5617; Dominion Outreach, 0419-6414;* ***Continued by*** *Missionary Outlook, 0315-6044.*

KO
**ACTIVITY REPORT - KOREA THEOLOGICAL STUDY INSTITUTE.** **Main/Corp** Hanguk Sinhak Yonguso. **VFOAT** Report of the Activities. 1973/75-. English. Korea Theological Study Institute, Room 201/Hyangrin Building 164-11 2-ka Ulchi-ro 2-ga Chung-gu, Seoul Korea. **LC** BR1320; .H3613. **DD** 230/.05.

US
**ACTS AND FACTS.** **Added/Corp** Institute for Creation Research. (197?)-. Periodical. English. mo. Free on request. Institute of Creation Research, 10946 Woodside Avenue North, Santee CA 92071. **Tel** (619)448-0900. **ED** Henry M. Morris. ctrl circ. ***Continues*** *Institute for Creation Research. ICR Acts & Facts.*

CN/1183-4153
**ACTS IN ACTION.** (ACTS IN ACTION / ASSOCIATED CANADIAN THEOLOGICAL SCHOOLS INSTITUTE FOR CHURCH GROWTH AND GLOBAL MISSIONS.). [ACTS action]. **Added/Corp** Associated Canadian Theological Schools Institute for Church Growth and Global Missions. **VAT** Associated Canadian Theological Schools in Action. Vol. 1, No. 1 (Winter 1991)-. Periodical. English. Three times a year. Limited free distribution. Associated Canadian Theological Schools Institute for Church Growth and Global Missions, 7600 Glover Road, Langley British Columbia V3A 6H4 Canada. **DD** 254.

SP/0211-4143
**ACTUALIDAD BIBLIOGRAFICA DE FILOSOFIA Y TEOLOGIA.** **See** Philosophy.

CN/0823-552X
**ACTUALITE DIOCESAINE.** (ACTUALITE DIOCESAINE : JOURNAL DE L'EGLISE DE SAINT-JEAN-LONGUEUIL.). [Actual. dioc.]. **Added/Corp** Eglise Catholique. Diocese de Saint-Jean-Longueuil. Vol. 14, No 9 (Fall 1983)-. Periodical. French. mo. $7.00. Diocese de Saint-Jean-Longueuil, 740 bd. Ste-Foy, Longueuil PQ J4K 4X8 Canada. **Tel** (514)679-1100, FAX (514)679-1102. **DD** 282/.71437. **Bk Rev. Ad Acc. Circ:** 8,000 (ctrl). ***Continues*** *Au Rythme de Notre Eglise, 0383-0152.*
**Desc:** News from Christian communities of the diocese plus editorial content stating the policies and position of the church on a variety of subjects.

FR/0757-3529
**ACTUALITE RELIGIEUSE DANS LE MONDE (1983).** (L'ACTUALITE RELIGIEUSE DANS LE MONDE.). [Actual. relig. monde]. **VFOAT** Actualite Religieuse. No. 1 (May 1983)-. Periodical. French. mo (11 issues per year). 360.00F. Malesherbes Publications, 163 Boulevard Malesherbes, 75859 Paris France. **Tel** 011 33 1 48884600, FAX 011 33 1 48884601. Index available. **Bk Rev. Ad Acc. Circ:** 20,000 (ctrl). ***Continues*** *ICI, Informations Catholiques Internationales.*
**Desc:** Published for all believers from all faiths, who want to be informed, to analyse and understand international issues with the vital religious light.
**Ind/Abst** PAIS Int. Print; Point Repere (1983-).

AT/1031-8453
**AD 2000.** [AD 2000]. **VFOAT** AD Two Thousand. (1988)-. Periodical. English. Eleven times a year (Dec./Jan. issue combined). 30.00Aus$ Australia; 35.00Aus$ others. Australian Family Association, 582 Queensberry Street, N Melbourne VIC 3051 Australia. **Tel** 011 61 3 3265757, FAX 011 61 3 3282877. **ED** B. A. Santamaria. **DD** 200.5. Index available. cum. index. **Bk Rev**, (Qty: 35). **Circ:** 8,000 (ctrl).
**Desc:** This journal of religious opinion is dealing with mainstream Churches with a bias towards traditional and Orthodox positions.

IT
**ADISTA : AGENZIA D'INFORMAZIONE STAMPA.** **See** Political Science.

US/0300-7022
**ADRIS NEWSLETTER.** ***Suspended.*** **VAT** Association for the Development of Religious Information Systems Newsletter. Vol. 1, No. 1 (Summer 1971)-(?). Newsletter. English. qt. $10.00. ADRIS Newsletter, 3601 Lindell Boulevard, St Louis MO 63108. **Tel** (314)658-2588. **ED** R F Smith. Index available. **Bk Rev**, (Qty: 175 per year). **Circ:** 500.
**Desc:** Bibliographical and informational control and understanding, both retrospective and current in the area of religion and cognate fields.

US/0898-9729
**ADULT FAITH RESOURCES NETWORKER.** (ADULT FAITH RESOURCES NETWORKER / AFR.). [Adult Faith Resour. netw.]. **Added/Corp** Adult Faith Resources. **VFOAT** Networker. Vol. 1, Issue 1 (Feb. 1988)-. Periodical. English. bm (6 issues). $15.00. Adult Faith Resources, 9709 Rich Road, Bloomington MN 55437. **Tel** (612)835-1579. **ED** Cathryn Benntson-Hantsmen. **DD** 291. **Bk Rev**, (Qty: (6-10)). **Circ:** 800 (ctrl).
**Desc:** Written for practitioners in the field of adult religious development and education. It interprets both research and scholarship into practical application articles for clergy, religious educators, counselors, etc..

US/0732-3573
**ADULT LIFE AND WORK LESSON ANNUAL.** [Adult life work lesson annu.]. English. an. Editor Sunday School Board, 127 Ninth Avenue North, Nashville TN 37234. **LC** BX6225; .L5. **DD** 230/.61. ***Continues*** *Life and Work Lesson Annual.*

●US/1059-3225
**ADULT STUDENT GUIDE.** **Added/Corp** Assemblies of God. General Council. (1992)-. Periodical. English. qt. $5.40. Gospel Publishing House, 1445 Boonville Avenue, Springfield MO 65802. **Tel** (417)862-2781, FAX (417)866-1146. ***Continues*** *Adult Student, 0190-4000.*

●US/1059-3233
**ADULT TEACHER GUIDE.** **Added/Corp** Assemblies of God. General Council. (1992)-. Periodical. English. qt. $9.60. Gospel Publishing House, 1445 Boonville Avenue, Springfield MO 65802. **Tel** (417)862-2781, FAX (417)866-1146. ***Continues*** *Adult Teacher, 0567-9702.*

US/1059-7905
**ADVENTIST THEOLOGICAL SOCIETY MONOGRAPHS.** **Added/Corp** Adventist Theological Society. **VFOAT** Adventist Theological Society Publications. (1991)-. Monographic series. English. $11.95. Adventist Theological Society, 9984 Red Bud Trail, Berrien Springs MI 49103.

US/0001-8783
**ADVENTURE (NASHVILLE).** (ADVENTURE.). **Added/Corp** Southern Baptist Convention. Sunday School Board. (19??)-. Periodical. English. Twelve times a year. $16.10. Southern Baptist Convention, 901 Commerce, Suite 750, Nashville TN 37203. **Tel** (615)244-2355, FAX (615)742-8919. **(Subscription address:** Sunday School Board, Customer Service, 127 9th Avenue North, Nashville TN 37234.**)**

US
**AEIC JOURNAL.** **VFOAT** Journal of the Association of Evangelical Institutional Chaplains. **VAT** Association of Evangelical Institutional Chaplains Journal. No. 1 (July 1976)-. Periodical. English. sa. AEIC, 2912 Chamberlayne Avenue, Richmond VA 23222.

II
**AETEI JOURNAL.** English. Twice a year (Jan., & July). $10.00 (one year); $18.00 (two years); $25.00 (three years). AETEI Journal, PO Box 9522, Bangalore 560095 India. **Tel** 011 91 080 531154, FAX 011 91 080 533387. **ED** Dr. Ken R. Gnanakan and Dr. S. Sumithra, (editor's address: 54 Migi Colony, 5th Block, Koramangala, Bangalore 560 095 India, phone: (91)080 531154). **Bk Rev**, (Qty: 12-15). **Ad Acc. Circ:** 2,000 (ctrl).
**Desc:** Articles and news of the Association of Evangelical Theological Education in India.

●US/1063-0937
**AETHERIUS SOCIETY NEWSLETTER, THE.** **Added/Corp** Aetherius Society. Vol. 1, Issue 1 (Feb. 1992)-. Newsletter. English. qt. The Aetherius Society, 6202 Afton Place, Hollywood CA 90028-8298. **DD** 299. ***Continues*** *Aetherius Society Newsletter (Hollywood, Calif. : 1962).*

KE/0250-4650
**AFER.** [Afer]. **Added/Corp** AMECEA Pastoral Institute (Gaba) Pastoral Institute of Eastern Africa. **VFOAT** AFER, African Ecclesial Review; AFER, African Ecclesiastical Review; African Ecclesial Review; African Ecclesiastical Review. Vol. 7 (Jan. 1965)-. Periodical. English. bm. $50.25 Europe and Asia; $36.25 Africa; $55.25 other. AMECEA Pastoral Institute (Gaba), PO Box 4002, Eldoret Kenya Africa. **Tel** 011 254 321 33286, 011 254 321 32244. **ED** Boniface K Zabajungu. **LC** BX1675.A1; A15. **DD** 276. Index available. cum. index. **Bk Rev. Circ:** 2,500. ***Continues*** *African Ecclesiastical Review, 0001-1134.*
**Desc:** Offers and invites discussion, reflection, information, and documentation, regarding making the Christian message relevant for Africa today.
**Ind/Abst** Bibliogr. Mission.; Canon Law Abstr.; Index Book Rev. Relig.; New Testam. Abstr.; Relig. Index One Period. (1980-); Abr. Cathol. Period. Lit. Index; Cathol. Period. Lit. Index.

US/0001-9674
**AFFIRMATION (RICHMOND, VA.).** (AFFIRMATION / UNION THEOLOGICAL SEMINARY IN VIRGINIA.). [Affirmation]. **Added/Corp** Union Theological Seminary in Virginia. Vol. 1, No. 1 (Spring 1988)-. Periodical. English. Four times a year (Seasonally). Union Theological Seminary, 3401 Brook Road, Richmond VA 23227. **Tel** (804)355-0671 Ext. 296, FAX (804)355-3919. **DD** 230. ***Continues*** *Affirmation, 0001-9674.*
**Ind/Abst** Index Book Rev. Relig.; Relig. Index One Period.

US/0162-8038
**AFFIRMATIONS.** **Added/Corp** Boston Theological Institute. Women's Theological Coalition. Vol. 1 (Jan. 1974)-. Periodical. English. ir. Affirmations, Boston Theological Institute, 11 Garden Street, Cambridge MA 02138. **Tel** (617)492-5622. **ED** Chris Vanin Bishop. **Bk Rev. Ad Acc.** ctrl circ. ***Supersedes*** *Sisterhood.*

UK/0267-842X
**AFKAR INQUIRY.** ***Suspended.*** **VFOAT** Afkar/Inquiry; Inquiry. Vol. 1, No. 4 (Sept. 1984)-Suspended May 1988 with Vol. 5. Periodical. English. mo. £30.00. Tropvale Ltd, 55 Banner Street, London EC1Y 8PX England. **Tel** 01-2534726, telex 262028. **ED** M I Asaria. **Bk Rev. Ad Acc. Circ:** 30,000. ***Continues*** *Afkar.*
**Desc:** Current affairs from an Islamic perspective.

CN/0824-3166
**AFRICA INLAND MISSION, CANADA.** (AFRICA INLAND MISSION (CANADA) : [LETTER].). [Afr. Inland Mission Can.]. **Added/Corp** Africa Inland Mission (Canada). (1965)-. Periodical. English. bm. Free. Africa Inland Mission (Canada), Scarborough Ontario M1R 1P8 Canada. **DD** 266/.0096.

KE
**AFRICA JOURNAL OF EVANGELICAL THEOLOGY.** **Added/Corp** Scott Theological College. ACTEA (Organization). Consortium of Theological Colleges. **VFOAT** AJET. Vol. 9, No. 1 (1990)-. Periodical. English. sa (June and Dec.). $10.00 (one year) $25.00 (three year) Africa; $12.00 (one year) $30.00 (three year) Europe; $15.00 (one year), $37.50 (three year) other. Scott Theological College, Box 49, Machakos Kenya. **Tel** 011 254 21086. **LC** BR11642.A35; A47. **DD** 230/.046. ***Continues*** *East Africa Journal of Evangelical Theology, 1018-8975.*
**Ind/Abst** Christ. Period. Index (19??-); Index Book Rev. Relig.; Relig. Index One Period.

CN/0706-8581
**AFRICA (LEVIS).** (AFRICA.). May/June 1967-. Periodical. French. bm. $2.00. Soeurs Blanches,

Missionnaires De Notre-Dame D'Afrique, 34, Rue Fraser, Levis Quebec G6V 3R7 Canada. **DD** 266/.2/6. ***Continues*** *Soeurs Blanches, 0706-8573.*

TZ/0253-9322
**AFRICA THEOLOGICAL JOURNAL.** [Afr. theol. j.]. **Added/Corp** Lutheran Theological College (Makumira, Tanzania) Lutheran World Federation. No. 1 (1968)-. English. Three times a year. $25.00 Africa; $30.00 Europe; $35.00 others. ALICE / Tanzania, PO Box 314, ELCT Building, Arusha Tanzania. **Tel** 011 255 2318, telex 42054. **ED** Naaman Laiser and Mutembe Gaetan. **LC** BR1; .A32. **DD** 230/.096. Index available. cum. index. **Bk Rev. Ad Acc. Circ:** 1,500. available on microfilm and microfiche from University Microfilms International (UMI).
**Desc:** A forum for African Theologians who are anxious to develop theology in the Africa context.
**Ind/Abst** Bibliogr. Mission.; Index Book Rev. Relig.; Missionalia; New Testam. Abstr.; Relig. Index One Period. (1978-); Relig. Theol. Abstr.

NR/0001-9968
**AFRICAN CHALLENGE.** (1951)-. Periodical. English. All Africa Conference of Churches, PO Box 20301, Nairobi Kenya.
**Ind/Abst** Hum. Rights Intern. Rep.

KE/1013-171X
**AFRICAN CHRISTIAN STUDIES.** [Afr. christ. stud.]. **VFOAT** CHIEA Journal : African Christian Studies. (1985)-. Periodical. English. Four times a year (Mar., June, Sept., Dec.). $50.00 Europe & Middle East; $40.00 Africa; $60.00 other. CHIEA Publications, PO Box 62157, Nairobi Kenya. **Tel** 011/254/11/891601, telex 25050.

KE
**AFRICAN CHRISTIAN STUDIES: THE JOURNAL OF THE FACULTY OF THEOLOGY OF THE CATHOLIC HIGHER INSTITUTE OF EASTERN AFRICA, NAIROBI.** **Added/Corp** Catholic Higher Institute of Eastern Africa. Faculty of Theology. **VFOAT** CHIEA African Christian Studies; C.H.I.E.A. African Christian Studies. Vol. 1, No. 1 (Aug. 1985)-. Periodical. English. qttq (March, June, Sep., Dec.). $120.00 (Africa except Kenya); $150.00 (Europe & Middle East); $180.00 (other). CHIEA Publications, PO Box 62157, Nairobi Kenya. **Tel** 011/254/11/891601, telex 25050. **ED** Leonard Mamwera. **LC** BR1359; .A373. **DD** 276/.005. **Bk Rev.**

US/0885-9795
**AGAIN MAGAZINE.** [Again]. **Added/Corp** Evangelical Orthodox Church. Vol. 1, No. 1 (Jan./March 1978)-. Periodical. English. Four times a year (Mar., June, Sept., Dec.). $12.00 (one year), $30.00 (three year). Conciliar Press, PO Box 76, Ben Lomond CA 95005. **Tel** (408)338-3644, FAX (408)336-8882. **ED** Raymond L. Zell, (phone: (408)336-5118). **DD** 281. **Circ:** 4,500.
**Desc:** Eastern Orthodox Christian thought, in a contemporary format.

BE
**AGAPE MAGAZINE.** (19??)-. Multiple languages (French and Dutch). Six times a year. 471.70F. Agape A S B L, rue de Bertrimont 50, 7000 Mons Belgium. **Tel** 011 32 65 318384. **Bk Rev. Ad Acc.**
**Desc:** News, studies, and reports communicating to the Christian world.

FR/0294-1155
**AGE D'OR, L'.** Vol. 1, (Winter 1983)-. Periodical. French. BP 47, 45390 Puiseaux France. **LC** BL624; .A35. **DD** 291/.05.

IT/0002-094X
**AGGIORNAMENTI SOCIALI.** [Aggiorn. soc.]. (Jan. 1950)-. Italian. Ten times a year. L35000 (Italy); L50000 other. San Fedele Edizioni Srl, Piazza S Fedele 4, 20121 Milan MI Italy. **Tel** 011 39 2 86352212. Index available. cum. index. **Ad Acc. Circ:** 13,000.
**Ind/Abst** Bibliogr. Mission.; Int. Polit. Sci. Abstr.

US/0748-6677
**AGLOW.** ***Ceased.*** [Aglow]. No. 1 (Nov. 1969)-Ceased ?. Periodical. English. bm. Women's Aglow Fellowship International, PO Box 1548, Lynnwood WA 98046-1557. **Tel** (206)775-6282, FAX (206)778-9615. **ED** G Weising. **DD** 248. **Ad Acc. Circ:** 27,000.
**Desc:** A magazine for charismatic Christian women. Uses inspirational and teaching articles, 1500 words.
**Ind/Abst** Christ. Period. Index (1976-19??).

CN/1183-2118
**AHA!!!--THE PREACHER'S RESEARCH ASSISTANT.** [Aha preach. res. assist.]. **VFOAT** Preacher's Research Assistant. Vol. 1, No. 1 (Sept. 1, 1991)-. Periodical. English. Five times a year. 52.97Can$. Practice of Ministry in Canada, PO Box 700, Winfield British Columbia V0H 2C0 Canada. **Tel** (604)766-2778. **DD** 251.

US/0884-6316
**AIM INTERNATIONAL.** [AIM int.]. **Added/Corp** Africa Inland Mission International. Africa Inland Mission. **VAT** Africa Inland Mission International. Vol. 67 No. 1 (Winter 1983)-. Periodical. English. qt. Free on request. Africa Inland Mission International, PO Box 178, Pearl River NY 10965. **Tel** (914)735-4014. **DD** 266. available on microfilm from University Microfilms International (UMI). ***Continues*** *Inland Africa, 0020-1464.*

US/0745-6786
**ALABAMA ECHOES.** **VFOAT** Echoes. Began in 1943?. Periodical. English. bm. Church of God Publishing House, PO Box 2250, Cleveland TN 37320. **Tel** (615)476-4512.

US
**ALASKA MISSION OUTREACH.** **VFOAT** Outreach. Vol., No. 1 (Fall 1979)-. Periodical. English. qt. 1134 South 8th Street, Minneapolis MN 55404. ***Continues*** *Norsk Ungdom.*

UK/0951-2667
**ALCUIN/GROW LITURGICAL STUDY.** [Alcuin/GROW liturg. study]. **VFOAT** Alcuin/Group for Renewal of Worship Liturgical Study. (1987)-. Monographic series. English. ir. £16.00 UK; £17.00 US & Canada. Dispatch Printery, 420 Howertown Road, Catasauqua PA 18032. **Circ:** 650.

CN/0711-2769
**ALDERSGATE NEWS.** [Aldersgate news]. **Main/Corp** Aldersgate College. Vol. 25, No. 2 (Dec. 1980)-. Periodical. English. qt. Aldersgate College, Box 460, Moose Jaw Saskatchewan S6H 4P1 Canada. **Tel** (306)693-7773. **ED** David Jahn. **DD** 207/7124/4. **Circ:** 4,000 (ctrl). ***Continues*** *Aldersgate College Newsletter, 0705-1395.*
**Desc:** This is an alumni newsletter. Publishes articles about alumni and current news of Aldersgate College.

CN/0383-896X
**ALERTE (STE-PETRONILLE. 1976).** (ALERTE.). Vol. 1, No. 6 (Jan. 1976)-. Periodical. French. mo. $5.00 Canada; $8.00 other. Publications Alerte, 25, Av. Royale, Ste-Petronille Quebec G0A 4C0. **DD** 248/.05. ***Continues*** *Alerte au Quebec, 0319-6984.*

US/0891-8767
**ALIVE NOW!.** [Alive now!]. (1971)-. Periodical. English. bm. $8.95 (one year), $14.95 (two years), $19.95 (three years). Upper Room, 1908 Grand Avenue, PO Box 189, Nashville TN 37202. **Tel** (800)925-6847, FAX (615)340-7275. **ED** Mary Ruth Coffman, Beth A Richardson. **DD** 242. **Circ:** 70,000.
**Desc:** Meditative material in a thematic style.

US/0733-1231
**ALL ABOUT ISSUES.** ***Title Change.*** **Added/Corp** American Life Lobby. **VFOAT** About Issues; A.L.L. About Issues. **VAT** ALL About Issues for God, for Life, for the Family, for the Nation; American Life Lobby About Issues. (1979)-(19??). Periodical. English. mo. American Life League, PO Box 1350, Stafford VA 22555. **Tel** (703)659-4171, FAX (703)659-2586. ***Continued by*** *Celebrate Life.*
**Ind/Abst** Curr. Lit. Fam. Plan. (19??-199?).

UK/0002-5623
**ALL THE WORLD. [A QUARTERLY REVIEW OF THE WORLD-WIDE WORK OF THE SALVATION ARMY].** **See** Sociology-Social Services and Welfare.

US/1040-6794
**ALLIANCE LIFE.** [Alliance life]. **Added/Corp** Christian and Missionary Alliance. Vol. 122, No. 10 (May 13, 1987)-. Periodical. English. Twenty-two times a year. $9.50 US; $16.00 Canada; $13.00 other. Alliance Life, PO Box 35000, Colorado Springs CO 80935-3500. **Tel** (719)599-5999. **ED** Maurice Irvin, (editor's address: 8595 Explorer Avenue, Colorado Springs, CO 80935-3500). **DD** 266. Index available (Published separately). cum. index. **Bk Rev**, (Qty: 2). **Ad Acc, Adv Mgr:** Doug Wicks. **Circ:** 55,000 (ctrl). available on microfilm and microfiche from University Microfilms International (UMI); available on audiocassette from Clearer Vision Ministries, Inc. ***Continues*** *Alliance Witness, 0745-3256.*
**Desc:** This is a Christian literature publication.
**Ind/Abst** Christ. Period. Index; Guide Soc. Sci. Relig.

US/0270-9678
**ALLIANCE WORLD (CAMP HILL, PA.), THE.** (THE ALLIANCE WORLD.). **Added/Corp** Christian and Missionary Alliance. (19??)-. Periodical. English. qt. $25.00. Christian Publications Inc., 3825 Hartzdale Drive, Camp Hill PA 17011. **Tel** (717)761-7044.

●US/1052-2670
**ALMANAC OF THE CHRISTIAN WORLD, THE.** [Alm. Christ. world]. (1992)-. English. $16.95. Tyndale House Publishers, Box 220, 203 East Farnham Lane, Wheaton IL 60189. **LC** BR1; .A345. **DD** 209/.04/05.

CN/0228-5320
**ALPEC : ANIMATION ET LITURGIE PAR L'EXPRESSION ET LA COMMUNICATION.** [ALPEC. Anim. liturg. expr. commun.]. **Added/Corp** Centre Alpec. **VFOAT** ALPEC : Animation et Liturgie par l'Expression et la Communication; Animation et Liturgie par l'Expression et la Communication. Vol. 1, No. 1 (Nov. 1980)-. Periodical. French. Three times a year. Free to members. ALPEC, CP 10.000, Ste Foy Quebec G1V 4C6 Canada. **DD** 264/.02/005.

IT/1120-0685
**ALTRA EUROPA / CENTRO RUSSIA CRISTIANA, L'.** ***Title Change.*** **Added/Corp** Centro Studi Russia Cristiana. Vol. 10, No. 1 (Jan./Feb. 1985)-(19??). Periodical. Italian. bm. Centro Russia Cristiana, Via Ponzio 44, 20133 Milan Italy. **Tel** 011 39 2 2663432, FAX 011 39 2 2365011. ***Continues*** *Rivista del Centro Studi Russia Cristiana, 0391-2795.* ***Continued by*** *La Nuova Europa.*
**Ind/Abst** Bibliogr. Mission.

IO/0215-255X
**AMANAH (JAKARTA, INDONESIA).** (AMANAH.). No. 1 (July 1986)-. Periodical. Indonesian. bw. Jl Kramat VI No 14A, Jakarta Indonesia. **LC** BP63.I5; A687.

US/1055-7008
**AMANECER (ENGLISH ED.).** ***Ceased.*** (AMANECER.). [Amanecer]. **Added/Corp** Centro Ecumenico Antonio Valdivieso. No. 1 (Jan. 1988)-(19??). Periodical. English. bm. New York Circus Publications, Box 681, Audubon Station, New York NY 10032. **Tel** (212)928-7600, FAX (212)928-2757. **ED** Rigoberto Avila. **DD** 282. Index available. cum. index. **Circ:** 3,000 (ctrl).
**Desc:** Offers the English speaking world the first systematically prepared and distributed information and reflection from the Christian experience in Nicaragua.

US/0882-2123
**AMBASSADOR REPORT.** Periodical. English. qt. $20.00. Ambassador Report, PO Box 60068, Pasadena CA 91116. **Tel** (818)798-0072. **ED** John Trechak. **DD** 289. Index available. **Bk Rev. Circ:** 3,000.
**Desc:** Exposes on Armstrongism, Ambassador College and cults in general.

US/0277-1071
**AMERICAN ACADEMY OF RELIGION ACADEMY SERIES.** (AMERICAN ACADEMY OF RELIGION ACADEMY SERIES / AAR.). [Am. Acad. Rel. acad. ser.]. **Added/Corp** American Academy of Religion. **VFOAT** AAR Academy Series; A.A.R. Academy Series; Academy Series. No. 37 (1981)-. Monographic series. English. ir. Price varies per volume. Syracuse University - Hall of Languages, 501 Hall of Languages, Syracuse NY 13244. **Tel** (315)443-1870. **(Subscription address:** Scholars Press Customer Service, PO Box 6996, Professional Book District, Alpharetta, GA 30239, telephone: (800)437-6692 or (404)442-8633**) ED** Susan Thistlethwaite. ***Continues*** *Dissertation Series - American Academy of Religion, 0145-272X.*
**Desc:** Books representing outstanding doctoral research in the field of religion.

US/1055-873X
**AMERICAN ASSOCIATION OF CHRISTIAN COUNSELORS MEMBERSHIP REGISTRY.** (AMERICAN ASSOCIATION OF CHRISTIAN COUNSELORS MEMBERSHIP REGISTRY / THE AMERICAN ASSOCIATION OF CHRISTIAN COUNSELORS.). [Am. Assoc. Christ. Couns. membersh. regist.]. **Main/Corp** American Association of Christian Counselors. **VFOAT** AACC Membership Registry; AACC Membership Registry. (1990/1991)-. English. an. American Association of Christian Counselors, PO Box 739, Forest VA 24551. **Tel** 800 526-8673. **LC** BV4012.2; .A48a. **DD** 253.5/025/73.

US/0516-9623
**AMERICAN ATHEIST, THE.** ***Suspended.*** **Added/Corp** American Atheists. (19??)-(19??). Periodical. English. mo. $12.50 (one year), $20.00 (two years) libraries US; $25.00 (one year), $40.00 (two years) other US; $22.50 (one year), $30.00 (two years) libraries other; $35.00 (one year), $50.00 (two years) other. American Atheist Press, PO Box 140195, Austin TX 78714-0195. **Tel** (512)458-1244, FAX (512)467-9525. **(Subscription address:** 7215 Cameron Road, Austin, TX 78752-2973**) ED** R Murray-O'Hair. **LC** BL2747.3; .A64. **DD** 211/.8/05. **Bk Rev. Ad Acc. Circ:** 30,000 (ctrl).
**Desc:** Covers topics of interest to Atheists, ranging from the latest antics of the New Right to the latest deeds of Atheist activists.
**Ind/Abst** Altern. Press Index (199?-); Index Period. Artic. Relat. Law.

US/1056-7380
**AMERICAN GOSPEL MAGAZINE.** ***Suspended.*** **See** Music.

US
**AMERICAN HOLINESS JOURNAL.** (1944)-. Periodical. English. Ten times a year (except July and August). West Publishing Company / Pennsylvania, RD 1 Box 54A, Avonmore PA 15618-9618. **Tel** (412)726-8828. **ED** A. J. West. **Ad Acc.**
**Desc:** Religious, conservative, holiness.

●US/1065-8068
**AMERICAN INDIAN RELIGIONS.** (AMERICAN INDIAN RELIGIONS : AN INTERDISCIPLINARY JOURNAL.). [Am. Indian relig.].

**Added/Corp** Center for Academic Publication (Stanford, Calif.). Vol. 1, No. 1 (Winter 1994)-. Periodical. English. qt. $50.00 (institutions); $30.00 (individuals). Center for Academic Publication, 160 North Fairview Avenue, Santa Barbara CA 93117. **Tel** (805)683-1676, FAX (805)683-4876. **LC** E98.R3; A47. **DD** 299/.7/05.

US/0002-905X
**AMERICAN JEWISH ARCHIVES.** **See** Ethnic Interests.

US/0003-1402
**AMERICAN THEOSOPHIST, THE.**
**Added/Corp** Theosophical Society in America. (19??)-?. Periodical. English. Eleven times a year. $12.50. Theosophical Society of America, Box 270, Wheaton IL 60187. **Tel** (312)668-1571. **ED** William Metzger. **Bk Rev. Circ:** 5,200. ***Continued in part by*** *Quest (Wheaton, Ill.), 1040-533X.*
**Desc:** Dedicated to forming a nucleus of human brotherhood; encouraging study of comparative religion, philosophy and science; and investigating unexplained laws of nature.

US/0740-0446
**AMERICAN UNIVERSITY STUDIES. SERIES VII, THEOLOGY AND RELIGION.**
**VFOAT** Theology and Religion; American University Studies. Series Seven, Theology and Religion; American University Studies. Series 7, Theology and Religion. Monographic series. English. ir. Price varies per volume. Peter Lang Publishing, 62 West 45th Street, 4th Floor, New York NY 10036. **Tel** (212)764-1471, (800)770-5264, telex 6973364 PLNY.

IT
**AMICI DEL BURUNDI.** **Added/Corp** Scuola Beato Angelico. Volontari Internazionali. (19??)-. Periodical. Italian. Via S Gimignano 19 Milan 20146 Italy. **LC** BV3625.B8; A45.

DR
**AMIGO DEL HOGAR.** Spanish. Twelve times a year. $15.00. Amigo Del Hogar, Apartado Postal 1104, Santo Domingo Dominican Republic.

CN/0318-5729
**AMIGO (MONTREAL).** (AMIGO.). **Added/Corp** Service Mond-ami. Vol. 1 (Sept./Oct. 1973)-. Periodical. French. Five times a year. 6.00Can$. Service Mond-Ami, 4055 Avenue Du Mont Royal Est., Montreal Quebec HIX 1Y5 Canada. **Tel** (514)251-2664, FAX (514)251-7449. **ED** Therese Roy. **Bk Rev. Ad Acc. Circ:** 25,000.
**Desc:** Includes Christian values, missionary projects, crosswords, crafts, Biblical reflections and prayers, school year events and history.

CN/0823-6178
**AMIS DE JESUS, LES.** [Amis Jesus]. No. 1, (Dec. 1980)-. Periodical. French. Free. Association des Amis de Jesus, C P 5185, Beauport Quebec G1E 6B5 Canada. **DD** 248.8/2/05. ctrl circ.

●US/1059-7255
**AMS STUDIES IN RELIGIOUS TRADITION.** **VFOAT** Studies in Religious Tradition. (1992)-. Monographic series. English. Price varies per volume. AMS Press Inc., 56 East 13th Street, New York NY 10003. **Tel** (212)777-4700, FAX (212)995-5413, telex 710 581 2302.

●US/1065-6812
**ANABAPTIST TIMES, THE.** [Anabapt. times]. Vol. 1, No. 1 (July 1992)-. Periodical. English. Six times a year (Feb., Apr., June, Aug., Oct., Dec.). $8.00. Anabaptist Times, 7300 Holdrege, Lincoln NE 68505. **Tel** (402)467-1526. **ED** Steve Ratzlaff. **DD** 284. **Circ:** 50.

GW
**ANALECTA ANSELMIANA. UNTERSUCHUNG UBER PERSON U. WERK ANSELMUS VON CANTERBURY.** (1969)-. Multiple languages (English, French, German and Italian). ir. Minerva GmbH, Morgensternstrasse 37, W6000 Frankfurt Germany.

BE/0003-2468
**ANALECTA BOLLANDIANA.** [Analecta bollandiana]. **Added/Corp** Bollandists. Vol.1 (1882)-. Periodical. Latin (English, Italian, German and French). sa (two double issues). 3250F. Societe des Bollandistes, 24 Boulevard Saint-Michel, B-1040 Bruxelles Belgium. **Tel** 011 32 2 7393338, FAX 011 32 2 7393338. **LC** BX4655; .A3. Index available (bound in Dec. issue). cum. index. **Bk Rev**, (Qty: 60). **Circ:** 500. available on microfilm from University Microfilms International (UMI).
**Desc:** Critical history about lives of saints from the ancient and Middle Ages.
**Ind/Abst** BHA : Biblio. Hist. Art; MLA Int. Bibl. Books Artic. Mod. Lang. Lit.

AU/0253-1593
**ANALECTA CARTUSIANA.** [Analecta cartus.]. **Added/Corp** Universitat Salzburg. Institut fuer Englische Sprache und Literatur. Universitat Salzburg. Institut fuer Anglistik und Amerikanistik. (1970)-. Monographic series. Multiple languages (English and German). ir. Price varies per volume. Institute Anglistic & Amerikanistik, A-5020 Salzburg, Akademiestrasse Austria. **ED** James Hogg. **Ad Acc. Circ:** 200.
**Desc:** History and spirituality of the Carthusian Order.
**Ind/Abst** Annu. Bibliogr. Engl. Lang. Lit.; MLA Int. Bibl. Books Artic. Mod. Lang. Lit.

IT/0003-2476
**ANALECTA CISTERCIENSIA.** (1945)-. Multiple languages (English, French, German and Latin). sa. L90000.00. Edizioni Cisterciensi, Piazza Tempio di Diana 14, 1-00153 Rome Italy. **Tel** 011 39 6 5755110, FAX 011 39 6 5741827. cum. index.
**Desc:** History and spirituality.

IT/0066-1376
**ANALECTA GREGORIANA.** **Added/Corp** Rome (city). Pontifica Universita Gregoriana. Issue 1 (1930)-. Monographic series. Italian (English, Spanish, French and German). ir. Price varies per volume. Edit Pontif Instituto Biblio, Piazza Della Pilotta 35, 00187 Rome Italy. **Tel** 011 39 6 6781567, FAX 011 39 66985378. **ED** M. A. Anton. **Bk Rev. Ad Acc.**

SP/0304-4300
**ANALECTA SACRA TARRACONENSIA.** (ANALECTA SACRA TARRACONENSIA; REVISTA DE CIENCIAS HISTORICO-ECLESIASTICAS.). [An. sacra Tarraconensia]. **Added/Corp** Fundacion Balmesiana. Vol. 1 (1925)-. Periodical. Spanish (Catalan, French and English). ir. 40ptas. Libreria Balmes, Calle Duran y Bas 11, Barcelona 08002 Spain. **Tel** 317 9443. **ED** P. Francesc de P. Sola S. J. **LC** BX806.C3; A6. **DD** 205. Index available. cum. index. **Circ:** 1,000.
**Ind/Abst** Am. Hist. Life (1959-); BHA : Biblio. Hist. Art; MLA Int. Bibl. Books Artic. Mod. Lang. Lit.

SP/0210-0460
**ANALES VALENTINOS.** **Added/Corp** Facultad de Teologia San Vicente Ferrer. Vol. 1 (1975)-. Periodical. Spanish. sa. **LC** BX805; .A66. **DD** 230/.2/05. ***Supersedes*** *Moncada, Spain. Seminario Metropolitano de Valencia. Anales del Seminario de Valencia.*
**Ind/Abst** Bibliogr. Mission.; BHA : Biblio. Hist. Art.

US/0732-4340
**ANCHOR (LOMITA, CALIF.).** (ANCHOR : NEWSLETTER OF THE AMERICAN MINISTERIAL ASSOCIATION.). Vol. 1, Issue 1 (Mar. 1982)-. Newsletter. English. qt. $10.00 nonmembers, free to members. American Ministerial Association, 25920 Narbonne Avenue No 16, Lomita CA 90717.

US/0066-1597
**ANCIENT CHRISTIAN WRITERS : THE WORKS OF THE FATHERS IN TRANSLATION.** No. 1 (1946)-. Monographic series. English. ir. Price varies per volume. Paulist Press, 997 McArthur Boulevard, Mahwah NJ 07430. **Tel** (201)825-7300, FAX (201)825-8345. **LC** BR60; .A35. **DD** 281.1082.

US/0279-7216
**ANCLA (EL PASO, TEX.).** (ANCLA.). **Added/Corp** Southern Baptist Convention. Sunday School Board. (19??)-. Periodical. Spanish. qt. $5.50. Southern Baptist Convention, 901 Commerce, Suite 750, Nashville TN 37203. **Tel** (615)244-2355, FAX (615)742-8919. **(Subscription address:** Sunday School Board, Customer Service, 127 9th Avenue North, Nashville TN 37234.**)** **LC** Discard.

US
**ANDOVER NEWTON REVIEW.** (1990)-. English. an. Free. Andover Newton Theological School, Newton Centre MA 02159.
**Ind/Abst** Index Book Rev. Relig.; Relig. Index One Period.

US/0003-2980
**ANDREWS UNIVERSITY SEMINARY STUDIES.** [Andrews Univ. Semin. stud.]. **Main/Corp** Andrews University. Seventh-Day Adventist Theological Seminary. Vol. 1 (1963)-. Periodical. English (German and French). Three times a year (Spring, Summer, and Fall). $18.00 (individual), $24.00 (institutiton) US; $21.00 (individual), $27.00 (institution) other. Andrews University, Seminary Studies, Berrien Springs MI 49104. **Tel** (616)471-6023, (616)471-7771, FAX (616)473-4472. **ED** Nancy J. Vyhmeister. Index available (Bound in 3rd issue in the Fall). **Bk Rev**, (Qty: 40). **Circ:** 1,000.
**Desc:** Founded in 1963 by renowned archaeologist and biblical scholar Siegfried Horn, AUSS is the journal of the Seventh-day Adventist Theological Seminary. It provides articles and book reviews in biblical archaeology, biblical studies, Christian ethics, church and ancient history, textual critism, theology, etc., plus book notices and selected A.U. dissertation abstracts.
**Ind/Abst** Index Book Rev. Relig.; Int. Zeitschriftenschau Bibelwissenschaft Grenzgeb.; Middle East Abstr. Index; New Testam. Abstr.; Old Testam. Abstr.; Relig. Index One Period. (1965-); Relig. Theol. Abstr.; Seventh-Day Adventist Period. Index (1971-).

IT/0003-3081
**ANGELICUM.** **See** Philosophy.

CN/0710-0612
**ANGELOS (HALIFAX).** (ANGELOS.). [Angelos]. **Main/Corp** Atlantic School of Theology. **VFOAT** Angelos : A Bulletin of Atlantic School of Theology. Vol. 1, No. 1 (Summer 1981)-. Periodical. English. sm. $5.00. Angelos, c/o Atlantic School of Theology, 640 Francklyn Street, Halifax Nova Scotia B3H 3B5 Canada. **Tel** (902)423-6801. **DD** 207/.71622. **Bk Rev. Circ:** 2,400.

CN/1193-9737
**ANGLICAN CHURCH DIRECTORY / THE ANGLICAN CHURCH OF CANADA.** [Angl. Church dir.]. **Main/Corp** Anglican Church of Canada. **Added/Corp** Anglican Church of Canada. General Synod. Anglican Book Centre. (1993)-. Directory. English. Anglican Book Centre, 600 Jarvis Street, Toronto Ontario M4Y 2J6 Canada. **Tel** (416)924-9192. **DD** 283/.71/025. ***Continues*** *Anglican Year Book, 0317-8765.*

CN/0847-978X
**ANGLICAN JOURNAL.** [Angl. j.]. **Added/Corp** Anglican Church of Canada. **VFOAT** Journal Episcopal. Vol. 115, No. 1 Jan. (1989). Periodical. English (summaries and/or abstracts in French). Ten times a year (Except July/Aug.). 7.00Can$ Canada; 14.00Can$ other. Anglican Journal, 600 Jarvis Street, Toronto Ontario M4Y 2J6 Canada. **Tel** (416)924-9192, FAX (416)924-4452. **ED** Carolyn Purden. **DD** 283/.71. cum. index. **Bk Rev. Ad Acc, Adv Mgr:** B. Trotter, **Tel** (416)924-9192. **Circ:** 270,000. available on an online database from Canadian Business and Public Affairs Database. ***Continues*** *Canadian Churchman, 0008-3216.*
**Desc:** This is a national magazine for the Anglican Church of Canada.
**Ind/Abst** Can. Index; Can. Period. Index.

US
**ANGLICAN OPINION.** **Added/Corp** Episcopal Committee on Religion and Freedom. Vol. 1, No. 1 (June 1986)-. Periodical. English. qt. $25.00. Institute on Religion & Democracy, 1331 H Street Northwest, Suite 900, Washington DC 20005. **Tel** (202)393-3200, FAX (202)638-4948.

US/0003-3286
**ANGLICAN THEOLOGICAL REVIEW.** [Angl. theol. rev.]. Vol. 1 (May 1918)-. Periodical. English. Four times a year (Feb., May, Aug., Nov.). $23.00 (individual), $30.00 (institution). Anglican Theological Review, 600 Haven Street, Evanston IL 60201. **Tel** (708)864-6024, FAX (708)328-9624. **ED** Reverend James E. Griffiss (editor's address: PO Box 1794, Racine, WI 53401, phone: (414)637-4289). **LC** BR1; .A5. cum. index. **Bk Rev. Ad Acc, Adv Mgr:** J. Winter, **Tel** (708)864-6024. **Pr Rev. Circ:** 1,600. available on microfilm from University Microfilms International (UMI).
**Desc:** General theological journal which seeks to promote discussion of basic contemporary issues to increase understanding of the role of the church in a society.
**Ind/Abst** Acad. Search (July 1993-); Am. Hist. Life (1955-1979); Index Book Rev. Relig.; INFO-SOUTH Abstr.; Int. Bibliogr. Zeitschriftenliteratur Allen Gebieten Wissens; Mag. Search; New Testam. Abstr.; Old Testam. Abstr.; Relig. Index One Period. (1949-); Relig. Theol. Abstr.

US/0097-4951
**ANGLICAN THEOLOGICAL REVIEW. SUPPLEMENTARY SERIES.** [Angl. theol. rev., Suppl. ser.]. Began with No. 1 (July 1973). Periodical. English. qt. $20.00. Anglican Theological Review, 600 Haven Street, Evanston IL 60201. **Tel** (708)864-6024, FAX (708)328-9624. **ED** Richard E Wentz; telephone: (602)965-4689. **LC** BX5001; .A649. **DD** 230/.3/05. **Pr Rev.**
**Desc:** A journal devoted to intellectual pursuit of religious issues; dialogue on theological and historical issues; unofficial organ of the theological faculties of the Episcopal Church.

CN/0317-8765
**ANGLICAN YEAR BOOK.** ***Title Change.*** [Angl. yearb.]. **Added/Corp** Anglican Church of Canada. General Synod. (1965)-(19??). Periodical. English. an. Anglican Book Centre, 600 Jarvis Street, Toronto Ontario M4Y 2J6 Canada. **Tel** (416)924-9192. **DD** 283/.71. **Ad Acc. Circ:** 1,200. ***Supersedes*** *Anglican Church of Canada. General Synod. Yearbook of the Anglican Church of Canada, 0517-774X.* ***Continued by*** *Anglican Church of Canada. Year Book, 1193-9737.*

IT/0394-8226
**ANNALES THEOLOGICI.** [Ann. theol.]. (1987)-. Periodical. Multiple languages. Twice a year (July & Dec.). L35000. Annales Theologici, via San Girolamo Carita 64, 00186 Rome Italy. **Tel** 011 39 6 6861592, FAX 011 39 6 6897021. **UDC** 2. Index available. **Bk Rev**, (Qty: 45). **Ad Acc, Adv Mgr:** Anbrogio Piras, **Tel** 68802208. **Circ:** 650 (ctrl).
**Desc:** News and information of theological studies.
**Ind/Abst** Relig. Theol. Abstr. (199?-).

CN/0318-434X
**ANNALS OF SAINT ANNE DE BEAUPRE (1974).** (THE ANNALS OF SAINT ANNE DE BEAUPRE.). **Added/Corp** Redemptorists. Vol. 88, No. 1 (Jan. 1974)-. English. mo (except combined July/Aug.). 9.25Can$ (1 year), 17.25Can$ (2 year), 25.00Can$ (3 year) Quebec; 8.50Can$ (1 year), 16.00Can$ (2 year), 23.00Can$ (3 year) other Canada; $8.00 (1 year), $15.00 (2 year), $22.00 (3 year) US; 16.00Can$ (1 year),

28.00Can$ (2 year) surface mail, 25.00Can$ (1 year) air mail, other. The Annals of Sainte Anne de Beaupre, PO Box 1000, Quebec G0A 3C0 Canada. **Tel** (418)827-4538, FAX (418)827-4530. **ED** Rock Achard. **DD** 248/.05. Index available. **Circ:** 50,000. ***Continues*** *The Annals of Good Saint Anne de Beaupre, 0318-4331.*
**Desc:** Specifically speaks of Saint Anne and other Church's concerns. Various events at our shrine also family education, comments from our readers, etc.

FR/0570-1953
**ANNEE CANONIQUE, L'. See** Law.

CN/0319-7166
**ANNEE SAINTE AVEC PAUL VI.** 1- Feb. 1974-. Periodical. French. bm. 60.00Can$ per no. Cahiers d'Animation Spirituelle, c/o Bureau Regional des Freres de l'Instruction Chretienne, 1293 Est Boulevard St-Joseph, Montreal Quebec H2J 1L9 Canada. **DD** 242/.05.

CN/0826-5119
**ANNUAIRE / FRERES PRECHEURS, PROVINCE SAINT-DOMINIQUE DU CANADA.** [Annu. - Freres precheurs, Prov. St-Dominique Can.]. **Main/Corp** Dominicains. Province Canadienne de Saint-Dominique. **VFOAT** Province Saint-Dominique du Canada. Annuaire Officiel des Dominicains de la Province Canadienne de Saint-Dominique. **VAT** Province Saint-Dominique du Canada (1984). 1984-. French. an. Les Dominicains Administration Provinciale, 5353 Av Notre-Dame de Grace, Montreal Quebec H4A 1L2 Canada. **DD** 255/.2/002571. ***Continues*** *Annuaire de la Province Saint-Dominique du Canada, 0713-4576.*

II
**ANNUAL BIBLIOGRAPHY OF CHRISTIANITY IN INDIA. VFOAT** Bibliography of Christianity in India. No. 1 (1981)-. Bibliography. English. an. Rs25.00 India; $5.00 US. Heras Institute of Indian History and Culture, St Xavier's College, Bombay 400 001 India. **Tel** 011 91 22 262 0661. **ED** B Anderson and J Correia-Afonso. **LC** Z7778.I4; A56; BR1155. **DD** 016.2. Index available. **Circ:** 350.
**Desc:** An instrument of study and research on Christianity in its various denominations in India. Sections: generalia, philosophy and theology, social action, art, literature and history.

US/0730-1561
**ANNUAL CONFERENCE / NATIONAL ASSOCIATION OF CHURCH BUSINESS ADMINISTRATORS. Main/Conf** National Association of Church Business Administrators. English. an. National Association of Church Business Administration, PO Box 7181, Kansas City MO 64113. **Tel** (817)784-1732. **LC** BV652.A1; N33A. **DD** 254/.005. ***Continues*** *Proceedings of the ... Annual Conference of the National Association of Church Business Administrators, 0730-1553.*

US/0732-4928
**ANNUAL OF THE SOCIETY OF CHRISTIAN ETHICS, THE.** [Annu. Soc. Christ. ethics]. **Main/Corp** Society of Christian Ethics (U.S.). (1981)-. Academic Scholarly Publication. English. an (Nov.). $14.39 US; $15.30 others. Society of Christian Ethics, Georgetown University Press, Intercultural Center, Washington DC 20057. **Tel** (202)687-5889, FAX (202)687-5712. **ED** Diane Yeager. **LC** BJ1188.5; .S65a. **DD** 241/.05. Index available. cum. index. **Ad Acc. Pr Rev. Circ:** 920. available on microfilm. ***Continues*** *Society of Christian Ethics (U.S.). Meeting. Selected Papers from the ... Annual Meeting, 0278-4645.*
**Desc:** Collects scholarly papers chosen for presentation at the yearly professional meeting of the SCE. Addresses University professors in religion, philosophy, the social sciences, professional people in law, medicine and politics, the clergy and others working in Christian educational and social action programs.

RH
**ANNUAL REPORT - MINDOLO ECUMENICAL FOUNDATION. Main/Corp** Mindolo Ecumenical Foundation. English. sa. K40.00 Africa; $45.00 North America. Mindolo Ecumenical Foundation, PO Box 21493, Kitwe Zambia Africa, C. Africa. **Tel** 02-211488, telex ZA 52050. **ED** Isaac Phiri. **LC** BR1446.6; .M55A. **DD** 262/.001. **Ad Acc.**
**Desc:** Contains feature articles and stories.

US/0145-0824
**ANNUAL REPORT - UNITED CHURCH BOARD FOR WORLD MINISTRIES.** **Main/Corp** United Church Board for World Ministries. 151st (1961)-. English. an. United Church Board for World Ministries, 475 Riverside Drive, New York NY 10027. **Tel** (212)870-2183. **ED** Sandra J Rooney. **LC** BV2360; .A3. **DD** 262/.001. ***Continues*** *American Board of Commissioners for Foreign Missions. Annual Report, 0362-7632;* ***Absorbed*** *United Church Treasurer's Report; United Church Board for World Ministries. Directory and Calendar of Prayer.* ***Continued in part by*** *United Church Board for World Ministries. Financial Report.*
**Desc:** Reviews the work of the United Church Board for World Ministries, the overseas arm of the United Church of Christ.

US/1056-4578
**ANNUAL REVIEW OF WOMEN IN WORLD RELIGIONS, THE.** [Annu. rev. women world relig.]. **VFOAT** Women in World Religions. Vol. 1 (1991)-. Periodical. English. an. $39.50 hardcover; $12.95 paperback. State University of New York Press, State University Plaza, Albany NY 12246. **Tel** (518)472-5000, FAX (518)472-5038. **ED** William D. Eastman. **LC** BL458; .A56. **DD** 291/.082. **Ad Acc. Circ:** 300.
**Desc:** Exploring the study of women and religion; traditional religions and new religious movements.

US/1056-1994
**ANSWERS FOR LIFE'S QUESTIONS.** [Answ. life's quest.]. **Added/Corp** Southern Baptist Convention. Sunday School Board. (1991)-. Periodical. English. qt. $3.90. Southern Baptist Convention, 901 Commerce, Suite 750, Nashville TN 37203. **Tel** (615)244-2355, FAX (615)742-8919. **(Subscription address:** Sunday School Board - Customer Service, 127 Ninth Avenue North, Nashville, TN 37234 USA; telephone: (800)458-2772**) DD** 248.

IT/0003-6064
**ANTONIANUM.** (ANTONIANUM; PERIODICUM TRIMESTRE.). [Antonianum]. **Added/Corp** Pontificio Ateneo Antoniano (Rome, Italy). Vol. 1 (1926)-. Periodical. English (German, Italian, Latin and Spanish). qt (4 issues). $65.00 US. Editore Antonianum, Via Merulana 124, 00185 Rome Italy. **Tel** 011 39 6 70373462. **ED** Marco Nobile. Index available (bound in last issue). cum. index. **Bk Rev. Circ:** 1,000 (ctrl).
**Desc:** Antonianum service in faith and in Christian science.
**Ind/Abst** Am. Hist. Life (1955-1958, 1970-); Bibliogr. Mission.; BHA : Biblio. Hist. Art; MLA Int. Bibl. Books Artic. Mod. Lang. Lit.; New Testam. Abstr.; Old Testam. Abstr.; Relig. Theol. Abstr.

UK
**ANVIL (NOTTINGHAM, NOTTINGHAMSHIRE).** (ANVIL.). Vol. 1, No. 1 (1984)-. Periodical. English. Three times a year (Mar., July, Nov.). £14.50 UK; £16.50 other. Anvil Trust, 58 Yokecliffe Drive, Wirksworth, Derbysmire DE4 4EX England. **Tel** 011 44 629 822896, FAX 011 44 629 822896. **ED** Michael C. Sansom. Index available. **Bk Rev. Ad Acc. Circ:** 900.
**Ind/Abst** Missionalia.

GW/0721-1937
**ANZEIGER FUER DIE SEELSORGE.** (1981)-. Periodical. German. mo. DM32.40. Verlag Herder Freiburg, Postfach 79080, Frieburg, Germany. **Tel** (0761)27-17-0, FAX (0761)27 17-520, telex 761489. **ED** K. Sclemmer. **UDC** 242:282.
**Desc:** Periodical concerning the work of pastors in the Catholic church in German speaking areas.

US
**APACHE LUTHERAN.** (19??)-. Periodical. English. Twelve times a year. $5.00. Apache Lutheran, Box 18, Bylas AZ 85530. **Tel** (602)475-2213. **ED** Willis Hadler.

CN/0828-4695
**APPELES A LA LIBERTE (LEGARDEUR, QUEBEC).** (APPELES A LA LIBERTE.). [Appeles lib.]. Jan. 84-. Periodical. French. qt. Free. R Theberge, CP 81, Legardeur Quebec J5Z 2N4 Canada. **DD** 269/.2/05.

CN/0827-1690
**APPROCHES (MONTREAL, QUEBEC).** (APPROCHES.). [Approch.]. No. 1 (March 86)-. Periodical. French. qt. 2.00Can$ per no. Revue Approches, CP 613 Succ Cote des Neiges, Montreal Quebec H3C 3J7 Canada. **DD** 230/.05.

US/0279-9804
**APUNTES (DALLAS, TEX.).** (APUNTES.). [Apuntes]. **Added/Corp** Perkins School of Theology. Mexican American Program. Vol. 1, No. 1 (Spring 1981)-. Periodical. Spanish (English). qt. $10.00. Apuntes, Perkins School of Theology, PO Box 750133, Dallas TX 75275. **Tel** (214)768-2265. **ED** Justo L. Gonzalez. **Bk Rev.**
**Desc:** Theology from a Hispanic perspective; theological issues relevant to Hispanics.
**Ind/Abst** Index Book Rev. Relig.; Relig. Index One Period. (1981-).

CR
**APUNTES PASTORALES.** Spanish (French). bm. $9.90. Desarrollo Cristiano, APDO. 204-2150 Morvia, San Jose, Costa Rica. **Tel** 011 54 21 791 3506. Index available. **Ad Acc, Adv Mgr:** Randall M. Wittig, **Tel** 853919. **Circ:** 20,000.
**Desc:** Journal for leaders with articles in theology, practice councelling, news etc.

CE
**AQUINAS JOURNAL. See** Social Sciences.

US/0145-7519
**ARALDO DELLA SCIENZA CRISTIANA, L'. Added/Corp** Christian Science Publishing Society. **VFOAT** The Herald of Christian Science. Vol. 9 (Jan./March 1959)-. Periodical. Italian (English and Italian). qt. $29.00. Christian Science Publishing Society, One Norway Street, Boston MA 02115. **Tel** (617)450-2678, (617)450-2504. **LC** BX6901; .H552. ***Continues in part*** *Herald of Christian Science. Spanish-Portuguese-Italian Edition.*

US/0145-7489
**ARAUTO DA CIECIA CRISTA, O. Added/Corp** Christian Science Publishing Society. **VFOAT** The Herald of Christian Science. (19??)-. Periodical. Portuguese (English and Portuguese). mo. $29.00. Christian Science Publishing Society, One Norway Street, Boston MA 02115. **Tel** (617)450-2678, (617)450-2504. **LC** BX6901; .A72.

NE
**ARBEITEN ZUR GESCHICHTE DES ANTIKEN JUDENTUMS UND DES URCHRISTENTUMS.** (1961)-. Monographic series. German. ir. Price varies per volume. E. J. Brill, Postbus 9000, 2300 PA Leiden Netherlands. **Tel** 011 31 71 312624, FAX 011 31 71 317532, telex 39296 BRILL NL.

GW
**ARBEITEN ZUR GESCHICHTE DES PIETISMUS. Added/Corp** Historische Kommission zur Erforschung des Pietismus. Vol. 1 (1967)-. Monographic series. German. ir. Price varies per volume. Vandenhoeck & Ruprecht, Robert Bosch Breite 6, D-37079 Goettingen Germany. **Tel** 011 49 551 695911, FAX 011 49 551 695917, telex 965226 VAN d. **Ad Acc.**

GW/0518-2107
**ARBEITEN ZUR KIRCHENGESCHICHTE HAMBURGS.** Vol. 1 (1958)-. Monographic series. German. ir. Price varies per volume. Friedrich Wittig Verlag, In der Masch 6, D-22453 Hamburg Germany. **Tel** 011 49 40 5535019.

GW
**ARBEITEN ZUR KIRCHLICHEN ZEITGESCHICHTE. REIHE B: DARSTELLUNGEN. Added/Corp** Evangelische Arbeitsgemeinschaft fuer Kirchliche Zeitgeschichte. Vol. 1 (1975)-. Monographic series. German. ir. Price varies per volume. Vandenhoeck & Ruprecht, Robert Bosch Breite 6, D-37079 Goettingen Germany. **Tel** 011 49 551 695911, FAX 011 49 551 695917, telex 965226 VAN d. **ED** Georg Kretschmer and Klans Scholder. **Ad Acc.**

UK/0570-6378
**ARCHETYPAL IMAGES IN GREEK RELIGION.** Vol. 1 (1959)-. Monographic series. English. ir. Price varies per volume. Princeton University Press, 41 William Street, Princeton NJ 08540. **Tel** (609)258-4900.

GW/0066-6432
**ARCHI FUER MITTELRHEINISCHE KIRCHENGESCHICHTE. Added/Corp** Gesellschaft fuer Mittelrheinische Kirchengeschichte. Vol. 1 (1949)-. German (French, German and Latin). an. DM50.00. Gesellschaft fuer Mittelrheinische Kirchen, Jesuitenstr 13B, D 54290 Trier Germany. **ED** F. Jurgensmeier. **LC** BR857.R5; A73. **DD** 274.3/005. cum. index. **Circ:** 1,900 (ctrl).
**Ind/Abst** Bibliogr. Carto.; BHA : Biblio. Hist. Art.

GW/0066-6386
**ARCHIV FUER LITURGIEWISSENSCHAFT.** [Arch. liturgiewiss.]. **Added/Corp** Abt-Herwegen-Institut fur Liturgische und Monastische Forschung. Vol. 1 (1950)-. German. Three times a year. DM230.00. Kunstverlag ARS Liturgica, ABT Herwegen Institut, W-5471 Maria Laach Germany. **Tel** 011 49 2652 59360, FAX 011 49 2652 386. **LC** BX1970.A1; A7. **DD** 264/.02/005. cum. index. ***Continues*** *Jahrbuch fur Liturgiewissenschaft.*
**Ind/Abst** BHA : Biblio. Hist. Art; Index Book Rev. Relig.; New Testam. Abstr.; Relig. Index One Period.

GW/0341-8375
**ARCHIV FUER REFORMATIONSGESCHICHTE. BEIHEFT, LITERATURBERICHT. See** History(General)-History of Europe.

GW
**ARCHIV FUER RELIGIONSPSYCHOLOGIE. Added/Corp** Internationale Gesellschaft fuer Religionspsychologie. Vol. 7 (1962)-. Monographic series. German (English and French). ir. price varies per volume. Vandenhoeck & Ruprecht, Robert Bosch Breite 6, D-37079 Goettingen Germany. **Tel** 011 49 551 695911, FAX 011 49 551 695917, telex 965226 VAN d. ***Continues*** *Archiv fur Religionspsychologie und Seelenfuhrung.*

FR/0335-5985
**ARCHIVES DE SCIENCES SOCIALES DES RELIGIONS.** [Arch. sci. soc. relig.]. **Added/Corp** Institut de Sciences Sociales des Religions. Vol. 18 No. 35 (Jan./June 1973)-. French (summaries and/or abstracts in English). Four times a year. 440.00F France; 530.00F other. Editions du CNRS, 22 rue Saint Armand, F 75015 Paris France. **Tel** 011 33 1 45075050. **(Subscription address:** Centrale des Revues, 11 rue Gossin, 92543 Montrouge Cedex France.**)** **LC** BL60; .A7. **DD** 301.5/8/05. **Bk Rev**. Documents available from The Genuine Article. ***Continues*** *Archives de Sociologie des Religions, 0003-9659.*
**Desc:** Methodology, epistemology and status of scientific approaches to religions, classics of the sociology of religions and new religious movements.
**Ind/Abst** Am. Hist. Life (1979-); Arts Humanit. Citation Index (19??-19??) [Full Cov.]; Bibliogr. Mission.; Curr. Contents Arts Humanit.; Index Book Rev. Relig.; Int. Bibliogr. Sociol.; Int. Polit. Sci. Abstr.; Linguist. Lang. Behav. Abstr.; Relig. Index One Period. (1973-); Relig. Theol. Abstr.; Res. Alert; Romant. Move.; Soc. Plann. Policy Dev. Abstr.; Soc. Sci. Cit. Index [Select. Cov.]; Sociol. Abstr.

IT/0066-6785
**ARCHIVUM HISTORIAE PONTIFICIAE.** **Added/Corp** Pontificia Universita Gregoriana. Facolta di Storia Ecclesiastica. (1963)-. Multiple languages (English, French, German, Italian, Latin and Spanish). an (Dec.). L110000 Italy; $100.00 other. Editrice Pontificio Istituto Biblico, Piazza della Pilotta 35, 00187 Rome Italy. **Tel** 011 39 6 6781567, FAX 011 39 6 6780588. **ED** Paulius Rabikauskas. **LC** BR1.Al; .A73. Index available. **Circ:** 650.
**Ind/Abst** Am. Hist. Life (1981-); Bibliogr. Mission.; BHA : Biblio. Hist. Art.

CN/0518-3839
**ARCTIC NEWS.** (THE ARCTIC NEWS.). **Added/Corp** Anglican Church of Canada. Diocese of the Arctic. (1959)-. Periodical. English. Twice a year (Spring and Fall). Diocese of the Arctic, 1055 Avenue Road, Toronto Ontario M5N 2C8 Canada. **Circ:** 4,000 (ctrl).
**Desc:** This magazine informs supporters of the work of the Anglican Church in the Arctic of events, work and personnel of the Diocese of the Arctic.

HK
**AREOPAGUS : A LIVING ENCOUNTER WITH TODAY'S RELIGIOUS WORLD.** **Added/Corp** Dialog Center (Arhus, Denmark). (Fall 1987)-. Periodical. English (Chinese). qt. $16.00 Hong Kong; $24.00 other. Tao Fong Shan Christian Center, PO Box 33 Shatin, New Territories, Hong Kong Hong Kong. **Tel** 852 6911904, FAX 852 6940354. **ED** John G LeMond. **Bk Rev**, (Qty: 5-10). **Circ:** 1,000. available on microfiche from University Microfilms International (UMI). ***Continues*** *Update (Arhus, Denmark), 0108-7029.*
**Desc:** Seeks to engage readers in a living encounter with today's religious world. Respecting the integrity of religious communities, provides a forum for dialog between the good news of Jesus Christ and people of faith in major world religions and new religious movements.
**Ind/Abst** Bibliogr. Mission.; Index Book Rev. Relig.; Relig. Index One Period.

PL/0518-5289
**ARGUMENTY (WARSAW, POLAND).** (ARGUMENTY.). **Added/Corp** Stowarzyszenie Ateistow i Wolnomyslicieli. Towarzystwo Krzewienia Kultury Swieckiej. No. 1 (1957)-. Periodical. Polish. Fifty-two times a year. **(Subscription address:** ARS Polona, PO Box 1001, 00068 Warsaw Poland.**)** **LC** BL2700; .A78.

US/1044-0186
**ARIZONA BAPTIST BEACON (ARIZONA SOUTHERN BAPTIST CONVENTION).** (ARIZONA BAPTIST BEACON.). **Added/Corp** Arizona Southern Baptist Convention. **VFOAT** Baptist Beacon. (1989)-. Periodical. English. bw. $7.00. Baptist Beacon, 4520 North Central Avenue, Phoenix AZ 85012. **Tel** (602)264-9421. **ED** Elizabeth Young. **Ad Acc. Circ:** 10,200. ***Continues*** *Baptist Beacon (Phoenix, Ariz.), 0745-4139.*
**Desc:** News journal published mainly for Arizona Southern Baptists. Includes news, features, and photos.

IT/0004-3400
**ARTE CRISTIANA.** **See** The Arts-Art.

US
**ARTS / THE ARTS IN RELIGIOUS & THEOLOGICAL STUDIES.** **See** The Arts.

CN/0227-499X
**AS THE SPIRIT MOVES.** Periodical. English. mo. Free. D. Varcoe, 60 McNaughton Avenue, Regina Sask S5M 4M3 Canada. **DD** 269/.4/0971.

US
**ASBURY THEOLOGICAL JOURNAL, THE.** **Added/Corp** Asbury Theological Seminary. Vol. 41, No. 1 (Spring 1986)-. Academic Scholarly Publication. English. Twice a year (Apr., & Oct.). $5.00 (one year), $8.00 (two years), $11.00 (three years). The Asbury Theological Journal, Asbury Theological Seminary, 204 North Lexington Avenue, Wilmore KY 40390. **Tel** (606)858-3581, FAX (606)858-3581. **ED** Scott Burson (phone: (606)858-2310). **Bk Rev**, (Qty: 10). **Circ:** 1,200. available on microfilm. ***Continues*** *The Asbury Seminarian.*
**Desc:** Provides a scholarly forum for discussion of issues relevant to Christian thought and faith, and to the nature and mission of the Church. It addresses concerns and ideas across the curriculum which interface with Christian thought and life and ministry.
**Ind/Abst** Christ. Period. Index (19??-); Index Book Rev. Relig.; Relig. Index One Period.; Relig. Theol. Abstr.

US
**ASBURY THEOLOGICAL SEMINARY HERALD, THE.** **Added/Corp** Asbury Theological Seminary (Wilmore, Ky.). **VFOAT** Herald. (1???)-. Periodical. English. bm. The Asbury Theological Journal, Asbury Theological Seminary, 204 North Lexington Avenue, Wilmore KY 40390. **Tel** (606)858-3581, FAX (606)858-3581.

CN/0315-8179
**ASCENT (KOOTENAY BAY).** (ASCENT.). **Added/Corp** Yasodhara Ashram Society. Vol. 1 (Sept. 1969)-. Periodical. English. tq. 8.00Can$. Yasodhara Ashram Society, Box 9, Kootenay Bay British Columbia V0B 1X0 Canada. **Tel** (604)227-9224. **ED** Linda Pelton. **DD** 181/.48/05. Index available. **Bk Rev. Circ:** 1,500 (ctrl).
**Desc:** Published twice a year, and carries a major article by Swami Radha. Book reviews and contributions from friends and associates.

US/1044-6494
**ASHLAND THEOLOGICAL JOURNAL.** [Ashl. theol. j.]. **Added/Corp** Ashland Theological Seminary. Vol. 14, No. 1 (Fall 1981)-. Periodical. English. an (Sept.). $6.00. Ashland Theological Seminary, 910 Center, Ashland OH 44805. **Tel** (419)289-4142, FAX (419)289-5969. **ED** David W. Baker, (phone: (419)289-5177). **DD** 230. **Bk Rev**, (Qty: 35). **Pr Rev. Circ:** 2,000. ***Continues*** *Ashland Theological Bulletin, 0888-2185.*
**Desc:** An analysis of theological thought and review from an evangelical perspective.
**Ind/Abst** Index Book Rev. Relig.; New Testam. Abstr.; Relig. Index One Period.; Relig. Theol. Abstr. (199?-).

SI/0218-0812
**ASIA JOURNAL OF THEOLOGY.** **Added/Corp** Association for Theological Education in South East Asia. North East Asia Association of Theological Schools. Serampore College. Board of Theological Education. Vol. 1, No. 1 (April 1987)-. Periodical. English. sa. $12.00 (institutions), $9.00 (individuals) Asia and Third World countries; $23.00 (institutions), $19.00 (individuals) other. Association for Theological Education in Southeast Asia, 324 Onan Road, Republic of Singapore 1542 Singapore. **Tel** 011 65 3447316. **ED** Choo-Lak Yeow. **LC** BR1.A1; A85. **DD** 230/.095/05. Index available. cum. index. **Bk Rev**. available on microfilm. ***Continues*** *East Asia Journal of Theology, 0217-3859.*
**Desc:** A popularization of contextual theological literature.
**Ind/Abst** Bibliogr. Mission.; Index Book Rev. Relig.; Int. Bibliogr. Sociol.; New Testam. Abstr.; Relig. Index One Period.; Relig. Theol. Abstr.

CH
**ASIA THEOLOGICAL NEWS.** ***Ceased.*** **Added/Corp** Asia Theological Association. Vol. 1 (June 1975)-(Dec. 1992). Periodical. English. qt. Asia Theological Association / Taiwan, PO Box 1477, Taichung 400 Taiwan. **ED** Bong Rin Ro. **Bk Rev. Ad Acc. Circ:** 2,000 (ctrl).
**Desc:** Intended to upgrade the quality of evangelical Christian education in Asia and to build up church leaders.

US/0741-0336
**ASIAN AMERICAN JOURNEY, THE.** **VFOAT** TAJ. (19??)-. Periodical. English. bm. $4.00 general issues, $5.00 general and religious issues. Agape Fellowship, 801 Northeast Edgeware Road, Los Angeles CA 90026-5127.

US/1070-3969
**ASIAN AMERICAN NEWS (HOUSTON, TEX.).** **See** Ethnic Interests.

KO
**ASIAN MISSIONS ADVANCE: BULLETIN OF THE ASIAN MISSIONS ASSOCIATION.** **Added/Corp** Asia Missions Association (Korea) Tongso Songyo Yongu Kaebarwon (Korea). No. 1 (Jan. 1978)-. Bulletin. English. Six times a year. $12.00. Asia Missions Association, 110-1 Wolmoon Paltan, Hwasung Kyunggi 445-910, Korea. **Tel** 011 82 2 33921301. **LC** BV3151; .A84. **DD** 266/.0095.

US/0896-4394
**ASSEMBLIES OF GOD HERITAGE.** [Assem. God herit.]. **Added/Corp** Assemblies of God Archives. Assemblies of God Heritage Society. **VFOAT** Heritage; A/G Heritage. Vol. 1, No. 1 (Fall 1981)-. Periodical. English. Four times a year. $10.00 (one year); $100.00 (lifetime) Comes with Assemblies of God Heritage Society membership. Assemblies of God Archives, 1445 Boonville Avenue, Springfield MO 65802-1894. **Tel** (417)862-2781, (417)862-1447, FAX (417)862-8558. **ED** Wayne E. Warner (phone: (417)862-2781 Ext. 4401). **LC** BX8765.5.A1; A87. **DD** 289.9/4/05. Index available. cum. index. **Bk Rev**, (Qty: 10). **Ad Acc. Circ:** 3,000. available on microfilm from TREN - Theological Research Exchange Network; available on CD-ROM from H W Wilson; available on an online database from WILSONLINE; DIALOG; and BRS.
**Desc:** Assemblies of God, Pentecostal movement history, and photographs.
**Ind/Abst** Index Book Rev. Relig.; Relig. Index One Period.

US/0162-2234
**ASSEMBLIES OF GOD HOME MISSIONS.** **Main/Corp** Assemblies of God. General Council. **Added/Corp** Assemblies of God. Division of Home Missions. **VFOAT** Home Missions. (1978)-. Periodical. English. bm. Gospel Publishing House, 1445 Boonville Avenue, Springfield MO 65802. **Tel** (417)862-2781, FAX (417)866-1146.

CN/0820-7836
**ASSOCIATION DE MESSES DES MISSIONNAIRES DES SAINTS-APOTRES, L'.** [Assoc. messes Mission. St.-Apotres]. No. 1-. Periodical. French. ir. Free. Fondation Pere Eusebe Menard, 65 Ouest rue de Castelnau, Montreal Quebec H2R 2W3 Canada. **DD** 264/.02036. ***Absorbed*** *Missionnaires des Saints-Apotres (Bulletin), 0820-7828.*

US/0190-4280
**AT EASE.** Periodical. English. bm. Free. Assemblies of God Archives, 1445 Boonville Avenue, Springfield MO 65802-1894. **Tel** (417)862-2781, (417)862-1447, FAX (417)862-8558. **ED** Lemuel D McElyea and Traci L Countryman. **Bk Rev. Circ:** 25,000.
**Desc:** A publication for military personnel.

II
**ATA JOURNAL. ASIA THEOLOGICAL ASSOCIATION. INDIA.** English (Multiple languages). Twice a year (Jan., & July). $100.00 (members) Comes with Asia Theological Association membership & ATA News. Asia Theological Association / India, PO Box 3432, Bangalore 560 095 S India. **Tel** 91 080 531154, FAX 91 080 533387. **ED** Dr. Ken R. Gnanakan and Dr. S. Sumithra, (editor's address: 54 Migi Colony, 5th Block, Koramangala, Bangalore 560 095 India, phone: (91)080 531154). **Bk Rev**, (Qty: 8). **Circ:** 700 (ctrl).

II
**ATA NEWS.** English. Four times a year. $100.00 (members) Comes with Asia Theological Association membership. Asia Theological Association / India, PO Box 3432, Bangalore 560 095 S India. **Tel** 91 080 531154, FAX 91 080 533387. **ED** Dr. Ken R. Gnanakan and Dr. S. Sumithra, (editor's address: 54 Migi Colony, 5th Block, Koramangala, Bangalore 560 095 India, phone: (91)080 531154). **Bk Rev**, (Qty: 8). **Circ:** 700 (ctrl).

II
**ATAMA-SAIMSA.** **VFOAT** Atam-Science. (19??)-. Periodical. Panjabi (Panjabi). mo. 12.00. Raghabira Singha Bira, 82-A Ashutosh Mukherji Road, Calcutta 25 India. **LC** BL2017; .A85.

VC
**ATEISMO E DIALOGO.** **Added/Corp** Catholic Church. Secretarius pro Non Credentibus. **VFOAT** Atheism and Dialogue; Atheisme et Dialogue; Ateismo y Dialogo. Began with Vol. 1 (1966)-. Periodical. Multiple languages (French, English and Spanish). qt (Mar., Jun., Sep., Dec.). $30.00. Atheism and Faith/ Pontifical, CNCL Dialogue W/ Non Believers, 00120 Vatican City Rome Italy. **Tel** 011 39 6 6987104, telex 2013 CULT VAT VA. **ED** Cardinal Paul Poupard. Index available. **Bk Rev. Circ:** 1,000.
**Desc:** Informs and reflects on the various forms of atheism, the factors which occasion it, dialogue with non-believers and other responses to this modern challenge.

RU
**ATEIZM I RELIGIIA, VOPROSY I OTVETY.** (1985)-. Russian. Izdatelstvo Polit Lit-ry, A-47 Miussadaia Pl7, Moscow Russia. **LC** PAR.

US
**ATLA MONOGRAPH SERIES.** **See** Library and Information Sciences.

US
**ATLANTIC UNION GLEANER, THE.** **Main/Corp** Seventh-Day Adventists. Atlantic Union Conference. English. bm. $6.00. PO Box 1189, South Lancaster MA 01561.
**Ind/Abst** Seventh-Day Adventist Period. Index (19??-).

II
**ATMA VISVASA.** (Jan, 23, 1982)-. Periodical. Hindi (Hindi). ir. Rs1.50. Jawaharlal Nehru University Campus, New Mehrauli Road, New Delhi 110067 India. **LC** BL1280.9; .A85.

BD
**AU COEUR DE L'AFRIQUE.** Vol. 9 (Jan. 1969)-. Periodical. French. bm. $16.50 US, Canada, Asia, Oceania; $9.00 Burundi; $15.00 Europe; $13.50 other. Conference des Ordinaires du, BP 1390, Bujumbura Burundi. **Tel** 011 257 2223263, FAX 011 257 22 232 70. **LC** BX1682.R8; T54. **DD** 282/.6757. Index available. cum. index. **Ad Acc. Circ:** 1,000 (ctrl). ***Continues*** *Theologie et Pastorale au Rwanda et au Burundi.*
**Ind/Abst** Bibliogr. Mission.

UK/0004-7481
**AUDENSHAW PAPERS. Added/Corp** Audenshaw Foundation. (1967)-. Periodical. English. Six times a year. Westminster College / Audenshaw Papers, Hinksey Centre, Oxford OX2 9AT England. **Tel** 865 247644. ***Continues*** *Christian Comment, 0144-9184.*

US/0044-9997
**AUDITOR, THE.** Periodical. English. mo. Free. Church of Scientology of California, 1413 North Berendo Street, Los Angeles CA 90027-0972. **Tel** (310)660-5553.

SZ/0004-7880
**AUFTRAG (BASEL. 1967).** (AUFTRAG.). V. 1, No. 1 (Feb./March 1967)-. Periodical. German. Six times a year. 15.00F. Auftrag Administration, Missionsstr 21, 4003 Basel 3 Switzerland. **Tel** (061)253725, 963315, FAX (061)2688 268, telex 963315. **ED** Armin Nettler and Anne-Marie Prevost. **Circ:** 47,000 (ctrl). ***Formed by the union of*** *Dienst und Zeugnis; Auftrag (Basel, Switzerland : 1956); Pionier; Ostasien* ***and*** *Bruder Uberall.*
**Desc:** Religion and theology related to 3rd world countries, religion and development aid.

US/0888-2274
**AUGUSTINIAN HERITAGE.** ***Title Change.*** **Added/Corp** Augustinians. Province of Saint Thomas of Villanova. Vol. 32, No. 1 (1986)- Vol. 39, No. 2 (19??). Periodical. English. sa. Augustinian Heritage, PO Box 476, Villanova PA 19085. **Tel** (215)527-3330. **ED** John E Rotelle. **LC** BX2901; .T32. **DD** 255/.4. **Circ:** 500. ***Continues*** *Tagastan, 0749-6451.*
**Desc:** Articles which treat of Saint Augustine of Hippo, his writings, legacy, and spirituality. Also the history of the Augustinian family.

US/1057-9338
**AUGUSTINIAN JOURNEY.** [Augustin. journey]. Vol. 1, No. 1 (1991)-. Periodical. English. mo. $15.00. Assumption Communications, 101 Barry Road, Worcester MA 01609. **Tel** (508)756-2893. **DD** 242.

IT/0004-8011
**AUGUSTINIANUM. See** Philosophy.

SP/0004-802X
**AUGUSTINUS.** [Augustinus]. **Added/Corp** Augustinian Recollects. (Jan./March 1956)-. Periodical. Spanish (English, French and German). Four times a year. $47.50. Augustinus, General Davila 5 Bajo D, 28003 Madrid Spain. **Tel** 011 34 1 5342070. **ED** Jose Oroz Reta. **LC** WMLC L 83/7408. Index available. **Bk Rev. Pr Rev. Circ:** 700 (ctrl).
**Desc:** Studies on life, doctrine, thought, spirituality, and influence of St Augustine, his relation with other authors, and history of his time.
**Ind/Abst** MLA Int. Bibl. Books Artic. Mod. Lang. Lit.; Philos. Index.

CN/0383-2554
**AUJOURD'HUI CREDO. Added/Corp** Eglise Unie du Canada. Vol. 21, No. 8-9 (Aug./Sept. 1974)-. Periodical. French. Ten times a year (monthly with Jan./Feb. and July/Aug. issues combined). 18.00Can$ Canada; 25.00Can$ other. Aujourd'Hui Credo, 132 Victoria Greenfield Park, Quebec J4V 1L8 Canada. **Tel** (514)466-7733, FAX (514)671-4354. **ED** Daniel Fines. **Bk Rev. Ad Acc, Adv Mgr:** G. Gautier. **Circ:** 1,000 (ctrl). ***Continues*** *Credo, 0383-2546.*
**Desc:** Contains a French protestant perspective on the religious life in Canada and throughout the world, on the cultural, social, economic and political issues in Canada, ecumenical news from all over the world, biblical and theological thinkings on the christian life in our society today.

CN/0228-9148
**AURORE. TRAITE, L'.** No. 1-. Periodical. French. L'Aurore Publishing Company Ltd, 1174 rue Duvernay, St Bruno Quebec J3V 2T2 Canada. **Tel** (514)766-3403. **DD** 284/.09714.

AT/1033-2626
**AUSTRALASIAN RELIGION INDEX.** **Added/Corp** Australian and New Zealand Theological Library Association. Charles Sturt University. Centre for Information Studies. **VFOAT** ARI.; A.R.I. Vol. 1, No. 1 (June 1989)-. English. sa. 50.00Aus$ ANZTLA members; 65.00Aus$ other. Charles Sturt University CRSR, PO Box 588, Wagga Wagga NSW 2650 Australia. **Tel** 011 61 69 222763, FAX 011 61 69 222764. **LC** Z7753; .A87. **DD** 016.2/005.

AT/0004-8852
**AUSTRALIAN CHRISTIAN.** (1898)-. Periodical. English. Twenty-two times a year. 25.00Aus$ Australia; 42.00Aus$ others. Australian Christian, Box 101 Essendon, N Victor VIC 3041 Australia. **Tel** 011 61 3 3791219, FAX 011 61 3 3790015. **ED** Chris Ambrosia. Index available. **Bk Rev**, (Qty: 70-100). **Ad Acc, Adv Mgr:** C. Ambrosia. **Circ:** 3,850.
**Desc:** News and opinions of the Churches and the Christians of Australia.

AT/0812-4353
**AUSTRALIAN EVANGEL.** (1943)-. Periodical. English. Ten times a year. 23.00Aus$ Australia; 43.00Aus$ other. Australian Evangel, PO Box 336, Mitcham Victoria 336 Australia. **Tel** 011 61 8 3365005, FAX 011 61 9 3365502. **ED** Dr. W. Robert McQuillan, (phone: 03 8 4811). **Bk Rev. Ad Acc. Pr Rev. Circ:** 7,000.
**Desc:** Denominational Magazine, informative, inspirational, nons items, testimonies, and doctrines

AT
**AUSTRALIAN FRIEND (SYDNEY, N.S.W.).** (THE AUSTRALIAN FRIEND : THE ORGAN OF THE SOCIETY OF FRIENDS (QUAKERS) IN AUSTRALIA.). (19??)-. Periodical. English. Five times a year (Mar., May, July, Sept., Nov.). Free to (members), 12.50Aus$ (non members) Australia; 18.50Aus$ other. Australia Yearly Meeting Religious, Society of Friends, Box 259, Greenacres SA 5086 Australia. **Tel** 11 61 08 2613142. **ED** Charles & Elizabeth Stevenson. **Bk Rev. Circ:** 1,100. ***Continues*** *Friend of Australia and New Zealand.*
**Desc:** Articles of general interest of the society and friends.

AT/1030-617X
**AUSTRALIAN JOURNAL OF LITURGY.** [Aust. j. liturgy]. **Added/Corp** Australian Academy of Liturgy. (1987)-. Periodical. English. Twice a year (May & Oct.). 15.00Aus$. Australian Academy of Liturgy, GPO Box 282, Brisbane 4001 Australia. **Tel** 011 61 7 7224 3332, FAX 011 61 7 221 1706. **ED** R. W. Hartley (phone: 011 61 3 379 3404). **DD** 264.005. Index available. **Bk Rev. Ad Acc. Circ:** 250.
**Desc:** Liturgy and worship with particular reference to Australia.

AT/1031-2943
**AUSTRALIAN RELIGION STUDIES REVIEW.** [Aust. Relig. Stud. Rev.]. **Added/Corp** Australian Association for the Study of Religions. (1988)-. Periodical. English. Twice a year (April and September). 40.00Aus$. Australian Association of Study of Religion (AASR), 6 Balfour Street, Wollestone Craft 2065 Australia. **Tel** (02)438 2837, FAX 011 61 7 3715896. **ED** Tricia Blombery. **DD** 200.7. **Bk Rev**, (Qty: 15). **Ad Acc. Circ:** 350.
**Desc:** Short, academic and descriptive articles on religion and religious studies. Reports of conferences and network news of religious studies in Australia.

●US/1059-1001
**AUTOCEPHALOUS ORTHODOX CHURCHES, THE.** (1992)-. Monographic series. English. Price varies per volume. Borgo Press, PO Box 2845, San Bernardino CA 92406. **Tel** (714)884-5813, (714)885-1161. Index available.
**Desc:** Histories, indexes, chronologies, directories, and guides to the independent Eastern churches, prepared by well-known scholars and churchmen, with bibliographies, chronologies, and indexes.

CN/0228-4146
**AUTRE PAROLE, L'.** [Autre parole]. No. 1 (Sept. 1976)-. Periodical. French. qt. 8.00Can$ Canada; $7.00 US; 10.00Can$ other. Monique Dumais, Department des Sciences Religieuses, Universite du Quebec, 300 Av des Ursulines, Rimouski Quebec G5L 3A1 Canada. **Tel** (418)724-1552. **(Subscription address:** CP 393, Succ C, Montreal Quebec H2L 4K3 Canada) **ED** L'autre Parole. **DD** 261.8/344/09714. **Bk Rev. Circ:** 400.

FR
**AUTRES TEMPS. Added/Corp** Mouvement du Christianisme Social (France). (Spring 1984)-. Periodical. French. qt (4 issues). 220.00F France; 250.00F other. Movement Francais du Christianisme Social, 32 Rue Olivier Noyer, 75014 Paris France. **Tel** 011 33 1 45439111. **ED** Pierre Olivier Monteil. **LC** BT738; .A89. **DD** 261.8/05. **Bk Rev**, (Qty: 4). ctrl circ. ***Formed by the union of*** *Itineris* ***and*** *Parole + Societe.*

US/0890-5541
**AVALOKA.** ***Ceased.*** [Avaloka]. Vol. 1 (Winter 1986)-(199?). Periodical. English. an. Avaloka, PO Box 21085, Topeka KS 66621. **Tel** (913)267-9518. **ED** Arthur Versluis. **DD** 200. **Bk Rev**, (Qty: 10). **Ad Acc. Pr Rev. Circ:** 500 (ctrl).

US/0005-237X
**AWAKE (BROOKLYN).** (AWAKE.). [Awake]. 1919. Periodical. English. sm. Watch Tower Bible and Tract Society / Canadian Branch, PO Box 4100, Georgetown Ontario L7G 4Y4 Canada. **Tel** (718)625-3600. **ED** W L Barry. **Circ:** 8,900,000. ***Continues*** *Consolation.*
**Desc:** Articles focus on God's purpose to make earth a paradise, while dealing with nature, science, health, lands, peoples, religion, and world affairs.

UK/0017-8271
**AWARE.** (19??)-. English. Six times a year. £17.95 UK; £19.50 other. Paternoster Press, A division of Send the Light Ltd., PO Box 300, Kingstown Broadway, Cumbria CA3 0QS England. **Tel** 011 44 228 512512, FAX 011 44 228 514949. **ED** John Allan. available on microfilm from University Microfilms International (UMI). ***Continues*** *Harvester, 0017-8271.*

US/0162-6833
**AWARE.** Periodical. English. qt. $7.50 US; add $1.75 postage other. Woman's Missionary Union, PO Box 830010, Birmingham AL 35283. **Tel** (205)991-8100, (205)991-4933. **ED** Barbara Massey. **Circ:** 39,000 (ctrl).
**Desc:** The magazine for Girls in Action leaders. Girls in Action is a Woman's Missionary Union organization for girls, ages six through eleven or grades one through six.
**Ind/Abst** South. Baptist Period. Index.

US/0145-7934
**B.T.I. NEWSLETTER. Main/Corp** Boston Theological Institute. **VAT** Boston Theological Institute Newsletter. V. 1- Oct. 1968-. Newsletter. English. wk. $10.00. Boston Theological Institute, 11 Garden Street, Cambridge MA 02138. **Tel** (617)492-5622. ctrl circ.

●US/1059-3292
**BABY & TODDLER TEACHER GUIDE.** **Added/Corp** Assemblies of God. General Council. **VFOAT** Baby and Toddler Teacher Guide. (1992)-. Periodical. English. qt. $3.75 (each quarter). Gospel Publishing House, 1445 Boonville Avenue, Springfield MO 65802. **Tel** (417)862-2781, FAX (417)866-1146. **ED** Dawn N Hartman. **Circ:** 2000. ***Continues*** *Complete Morning of Baby & Toddler Programs, 0273-5040.*
**Desc:** Teacher's manual containing weekly bible lessons for babies and toddlers. Includes instructions for starting and operating a baby/toddler classroom.

US/0005-3643
**BACK TO GODHEAD. See** Philosophy.

SZ
**BACKGROUND INFORMATION / COMMISSION OF THE CHURCHES ON INTERNATIONAL AFFAIRS, WORLD COUNCIL OF CHURCHES. See** Political Science-International Relations.

US
**BADGER BAPTIST.** (19??)-. English. Six times a year (Jan., Mar., May, July, Sept., Nov.). $3.00. Badger Baptist, 520 JoAnn Court, Sun Prairie WI 53590. **Tel** (607)837-4800. **ED** Leon and Dorothy Leeds. **Circ:** 1,600 (ctrl).
**Desc:** News and information on the churches.

IT
**BAILAMME.** Vol. 1, No. 1 (April 1987)-. Periodical. Italian. sa. Editoriale del Drago, Via Pascoli 60, 20133 Milan Italy.

II/0253-9365
**BANGALORE THEOLOGICAL FORUM.** [Banglore theol. forum]. **Added/Corp** United Theological College, Bangalore. Department of Research and Post-Graduate Studies. Vol. 1 (Jan. 1967)-. Periodical. English. qt. $10.00. United Theological College, 17 Millers Road, Bangalore 560046 Karnataka India. **Tel** 55844. **(Subscription address:** Prints India, 11 Darya Ganj, New Delhi 110002 India.) available on microfilm from University Microfilms International (UMI).
**Ind/Abst** Bibliogr. Mission.; Index Book Rev. Relig.; Missionalia; New Testam. Abstr.; Relig. Index One Period. (1980-); Relig. Theol. Abstr.

US/0005-5557
**BANNER (GRAND RAPIDS), THE.** (THE BANNER.). **Added/Corp** Christian Reformed Church. Vol. 1 (1907)-. Periodical. English. wk. $35.00 US; $46.00 Canada; $80.00 other. CRC Publications, 2850 Kalamazoo Avenue Southeast, Grand Rapids MI 49560. **Tel** (616)246-0799, (800)333-8300, FAX (616)246-0834. **ED** John Suk. Index available (separate). cum. index (by calendar year). **Ad Acc. Circ:** 48,000. available on microfilm and microfiche from University Microfilms International (UMI). ***Continues*** *Banner of Truth, 0731-6089.*
**Desc:** It seeks to inspire, to inform, to educate, and to challenge the denomination.
**Ind/Abst** Guide Soc. Sci. Relig.

US/0408-4748
**BANNER OF TRUTH, THE. Added/Corp** Banner of Truth Trust. No. 1 (Sept. 1955)-. Periodical. English. Eleven times a year (Aug./Sep. issue combined). $20.00 (one year), $38.00 (two years) US and Canada; £10.50 (one year), £19.50 (two years) England northern Ireland Scotland & Wales; £12.50 (one year), £22.50 (two years) other. Banner of Truth-Pennsylvania, PO Box 621, Carlisle PA 17013. **Tel** (717)249-5747, FAX (717)249-0604. **(Subscription address:** for all except US and Canada: 3 Murrayfield Road, Edinburgh EH12 6EL Scotland) **ED** Maurice Roberts. Index available. cum. index. **Bk Rev. Circ:** 5,000 (ctrl). available on microfilm

from University Microfilms International (UMI).
**Desc:** A periodical with articles dealing with doctrinal and practical issues related to Christian life. Also book reviews and items of correspondence.

US
**BAPTIST BIBLICAL HERITAGE.** English. Four times a year. $8.00. Pilgrim Publishing, PO Box 66, Pasadena TX 77501. **Tel** (713)477-4261, (713)477-2329, FAX (713)477-7561. **ED** Bob L. Ross. **Circ:** 1,000 (ctrl).
**Desc:** Historic Baptist views on the Bible with emphasis on the King James Version controversy.

US/0005-5700
**BAPTIST HERALD, THE.** [Baptist her.]. **Added/Corp** North American Baptist Conference. (1923)-. Periodical. English. mo (except combined Jan./Feb. and July/Aug.). $8.00 (1 year), $15.00 (2 year) US; $18.50 (1 year), $36.00 (2 year) Canada; $24.00 (1 year), 45.00 (2 year) other. North American Baptists Inc, 1 South 255 Summit Avenue, Oakbrook Terrace IL 60181. **Tel** (312)495-2000. **ED** Barbara J. Binder. Index available. **Ad Acc. Circ:** 8,000. available on microfilm from University Microfilms International (UMI).

US/1059-5104
**BAPTIST HERITAGE JOURNAL, THE.** (1991)-. Periodical. English. qt. $15.00 US; $18.00 other. Baptist Heritage Press, PO Box 112, Wilmington OH 45177.

US/0005-5727
**BAPTIST LEADER (PHILADELPHIA).** (BAPTIST LEADER.). [Baptist lead.]. **Added/Corp** American Baptist Churches in the U.S.A. Board of Educational Ministries. (1939)-. Periodical. English. Four times a year. $8.00. American Baptist Board of Education & Publishers, Po Box 851, Valley Forge PA 19482. **Tel** (800)458-3766, (610)768-2101, FAX (610)768-2107. **ED** Linda Isham (phone: (610)768-2153). Index available. cum. index (annual index only (Winter)). **Bk Rev**, (Qty: 4). **Ad Acc, Adv Mgr:** M. Brown, **Tel** (610)768-2151. **Circ:** 4,300. ***Formed by the union of*** *Adult Leader; Young People's Leader; Children's Leader;* ***Absorbed*** *Judson Journal.*
**Desc:** Practical "how-to-do" or thought provoking articles for lay leaders, pastors and Christian education staff persons who are concerned and responsible for supporting the teaching ministry and leader development in local churches.

CN/1192-4241
**BAPTIST REVIEW OF THEOLOGY, THE.** [Baptist rev. theol.]. **Added/Corp** Central Baptist Seminary (Toronto, Ont.). **VFOAT** Revue Baptiste de Theologie. Vol. 1, No. 1 (Autumn 1991)-. Periodical. English (summaries and/or abstracts in French). sa. 20.00Can$ Canada; 22.00Can$ other. Heritage Theological Seminary Baptist College, 30 Grand Avenue, London ONT N6C 1K8 Canada. **ED** Michael A.G. Haykin. **DD** 230/.6/05. Index available. cum. index. **Bk Rev**, (Qty: 40). **Pr Rev. Circ:** 200.

US/1072-7787
**BAPTISTS TODAY.** [Baptists today]. Vol. 9, No. 15 (Aug. 9, 1991)-. Periodical. English. Twelve times a year. $20.00. Baptists Today, 222 East Lake Drive, Decatur GA 30030. **Tel** (404)377-6822. **ED** Jack Harwell. **DD** 286. **Bk Rev**, (Qty: 12). **Ad Acc, Adv Mgr:** Karen Cheponis, **Tel** (414)377-6822. **Circ:** 15,000. ***Continues*** *SBC Today, 0890-0272.*

CN/0228-9873
**BARATAINKNAK A MAGYAR JEZSUITAK.** English (Hungarian). an. Free. Hungarian Jesuit Fathers, 282 Spadina Avenue, Toronto Ontario M5T 2E5 Canada. **DD** 255/.53/005. ctrl circ.

US/1063-1437
**BARNA REPORT, THE.** [Barna rep.]. (1991)-. Monographic series. English. $16.99. Regal Books, PO Box 3875, Ventura CA 93003. **Tel** (800) 235-3415. **LC** BR526; .B33. **DD** 277.3/0829/021.

SZ
**BASLER UND BERNER STUDIEN ZUR HISTORISCHEN UND SYSTEMATISCHEN THEOLOGIE.** V. 23-. Monographic series. German. ir. Price varies per volume. Verlag Peter Lang AG, Jupiterstrasse 15, CH-3000 Bern 15 Switzerland. **Tel** 011 41 31 9411122, FAX 011 41 31 321131. **Circ:** 350. ***Continues*** *Basler Studien zur Historischen und Systematischen Theologie.*
**Desc:** Monographs on swiss studies of historical and systematical theology, ecumenical studies, social aspects of religion.

US/1053-8631
**BASTA! (CHICAGO, ILL.).** ***Ceased.*** (BASTA : NEWSLETTER OF THE CHICAGO RELIGIOUS TASK FORCE ON CENTRAL AMERICA.). [Basta!]. **Added/Corp** Chicago Religious Task Force on Central America. (Feb. 1983)-(December 1992). Newsletter. English. ir. Chicago Religious Task Force, 59 East Van Buren 1400, Chicago IL 60605. **DD** 261.
**Ind/Abst** Hum. Rights Intern. Rep. (?-?).

CN/0382-6384
**BEACON (TORONTO. 1970).** (BEACON.). **Added/Corp** Basilian Order of Saint Josaphat. Vol. (5 Mar. 1970)-. Periodical. English. bm (Jan., Mar., May, July, Sept., Nov.). 12.00Can$. Basilian Press, 265 Bering Avenue, Toronto, Ontario M8Z 3A5 Canada. **Tel** (905)234-1212. **ED** Roman Kravec. **Bk Rev. Ad Acc. Circ:** 1,500. ***Continues*** *Life Beacon.*
**Desc:** Digest of Ukrainian press, news of Ukrainian and Roman Catholic Church, articles of spiritual value and preservation of Ukrainian cultural heritage.

US
**BEADS OF TRUTH. Added/Corp** 3HO Foundation. (19??)-. Periodical. English. Twice a year (Mar. & Sept.). $10.00. 3 HO Foundation, 1620 Preuss Road, Los Angeles CA 90035. **Tel** (310)273-9422.

US/0275-6587
**BEAR & COMPANY. VFOAT** Bear and Company. Began in 1981. Periodical. English. mo. $15.00 US; $17.00 other. Bear & Company Inc, Drawer 2860, Santa Fe NM 87504.

US/0190-3950
**BEGINNER TEACHER.** ***Title Change.*** (19??)-(1992). Periodical. English. qt. Gospel Publishing House, 1445 Boonville Avenue, Springfield MO 65802. **Tel** (417)862-2781, FAX (417)866-1146. **ED** Dawn N Hartman. ***Continued by*** *Beginner Teacher Guide, 1059-325X.*
**Desc:** A teacher publication for 4 and 5 year olds. Contains weekly Bible-based lessons which include an opening session, worship activities, story time (Bible and life application), learning center suggestions, Bible verse, and how to use the supplemental handwork and teaching helps. Also includes teacher training articles, supplemental craft projects and music.

US/1059-325X
**BEGINNER TEACHER GUIDE.** ***Title Change.*** **Added/Corp** Assemblies of God. General Council. Vol. 52, No. 1 (Sept./Oct./Nov. 1992)-(199?). Periodical. English. qt. Gospel Publishing House, 1445 Boonville Avenue, Springfield MO 65802. **Tel** (417)862-2781, FAX (417)866-1146. ***Continues*** *Beginner Teacher, 0190-3950.* ***Continued by*** *Kindergarten Teacher Guide, 1072-1444.*

GW/0175-7652
**BEITRAEGE AUS DER EV. MILITARSEELSORGE. VFOAT** Beitraege Aus der Evangelischen Militarseelsorge. (1987)-. Periodical. German. qt. Ev Kirchenamt fur die Bundeswehr, Godesberger Allee 107A, 5300 Bonn 2 Germany. **LC** BV4457; .B44. **DD** 259/.088355. ***Continues*** *Beitrage Aus der Ev. Militarseelsorge.*

GW/0067-5172
**BEITRAEGE ZUE OKUMENISCHEN THEOLOGIE.** V. 1-. Monographic series. German. Price varies per volume. Ferdinand Schoeningh Verlag, Postfach 2540, D 33055 Paderborn Germany. **Tel** 011 49 5251 127665.

GW
**BEITRAEGE ZUR EVANGELISCHEN THEOLOGIE.** Vol. 1 (1940)-. Monographic series. German. ir. Price varies per volume. Chr Kaiser Verlag GmbH, Lilienstrabe 70, W-8000 Munchen 80 Germany. **LC** BX4801; .B4.

GW
**BEITRAEGE ZUR GESCHICHTE DER PHILOSOPHIE UND THEOLOGIE DES MITTELALTERS. SUPPLEMENTBAND.** **See** Philosophy.

GW/0067-5024
**BEITRAEGE ZUR GESCHICHTE DER PHILOSOPHIE UND THEOLOGIE DES MITTELALTERS. TEXTE UND UNTERSUCHUNGEN.** **See** Philosophy.

GW/0067-5024
**BEITRAGE ZUR GESCHICHTE DER PHILOSOPHIE UND THEOLOGIE DES MITTELALTERS.** **See** Linguistics.

GW
**BEITRAGE ZUR HISTORISCHEN THEOLOGIE.** (1929)-. Monographic series. German. ir. Price varies per volume. JCB Mohr / Paul Siebeck, Postfach 2040, D 72010 Tuebingen Germany. **Tel** 011 49 7071 9230, FAX 011 49 7071 51104, telex 7/262872 mohr d. **ED** Lilian G. Katz.

GW
**BEITRAGE ZUR WISENSSOZIOLOGIE, BEITRAGE ZUR RELIGIONS-SOZIOLOGIE.** **See** Sociology.

IT/0392-0356
**BENEDICTINA.** [Benedictina]. Vol. 1 (Jan./June 1947)-. Periodical. Italian (English and French). Twice a year (June & Dec.). L55000 (Italy); L65000 (other). Benedictina, Via Ostiense 186, 00146 Rome Italy. **Tel** 011 39 6 5410341, 011 39 6 5410342 or 43, FAX 011 39 6 5403381. **ED** Abbazia Paola. Index available. cum. index. **Bk Rev. Circ:** 1,000 (ctrl).
**Desc:** Concerned with studies and research on monasticism and related topics.
**Ind/Abst** Bibliogr. Mission.; BHA : Biblio. Hist. Art; New Testam. Abstr.

GW/0522-9014
**BENSHEIMER HEFTE.** (BENSHEIMER HEFTE / HERAUSGEGEBEN VOM EVANGELISCHEN BUND.). **Added/Corp** Evangelischer Bund. Issue 1-19 (1961)-. Monographic series. German. ir. Price varies per volume. Vandenhoeck & Ruprecht, Robert Bosch Breite 6, D-37079 Goettingen Germany. **Tel** 011 49 551 695911, FAX 011 49 551 695917, telex 965226 VAN d. **ED** Er Bund. **LC** BR45; .B44. **Ad Acc.** ***Continues*** *Aus der Arbeit des Evangelischen Bundes, 0421-8264.*

GW/0724-6137
**BERLINER THEOLOGISCHE ZEITSCHRIFT : THEOLOGIA VIATORUM NEUE FOLGE : HALBJAHRESSCHRIFT FUER THEOLOGIE IN DER KIRCHE. Added/Corp** Kirchliche Hochschule Berlin. (1984)-. Periodical. German. Twice a year. DM50.60. Wichern Verlag GmbH, Bachstrasse 1-2, D 10555 Berlin Germany. **Tel** 011 49 30 3915075. Index available. **Bk Rev. Ad Acc. Circ:** 1,000 (ctrl). ***Continues*** *Theologia Viatorum (Berlin, Germany).*
**Ind/Abst** New Testam. Abstr.

US/0737-4682
**BETHESDA MESSENGER. Added/Corp** Bethesda Lutheran Home. (19??)-. Periodical. English. Four times a year. Free. Bethesda Lutheran Home, 700 Hoffmann Drive, Watertown WI 53094. **Tel** (414)261-3050.

US/0887-6053
**BIBELOT (DAYTON, OHIO).** ***Suspended.*** (BIBELOT.). [Bibelot]. **Added/Corp** United Theological Seminary (Dayton, Ohio). Vol. 1, No. 1 (Nov. 1985)-Vol. 5 No. 3-6. Periodical. English. qt. United Theological Seminary, 1810 Harvard Boulevard, Dayton OH 45406. **Tel** (513)278-5817. **DD** 287.

US
**BIBLE AND SPADE.** Vol. 6 No. 2 (Spring 1993)-. English. Four times a year (Jan., Apr., July, Oct.). $20.00 (associates), $35.00 (supporting), $50.00 (sustaining) Comes with Associates Biblical Research membership. Associates for Biblical Research, PO Box 125, Ephrata PA 17522. **Tel** (717)733-3585, FAX (717)733-3585. **ED** David Livingston. Index available. cum. index. ctrl circ. ***Continues*** *Archaeology and Biblical Research.*
**Desc:** Designed to strengthen faith in and increase knowledge of the Bible. It also seeks to encourage non-believers to investigate the Bible and the gospel. It carries both articles and news items which help confirm and illuminate the Scripture.

US
**BIBLE JOURNEYS FOR CHRISTIANS.** English. wk. $35.00 North America; $50.00 other. ALT Publishing Company, PO Box 400, Green Bay WI 54305. **Tel** (414)432-1413. **ED** James L Alt. **Circ:** 800 (ctrl).
**Desc:** Homily service for Catholic priests and deacons.

UK/0006-0763
**BIBLE LANDS.** **See** Religion and Theology-Bible.

US/0006-081X
**BIBLE STANDARD AND HERALD OF CHRIST'S KINGDOM, THE.** [Bible stand. her. Christ's kingd.]. **Added/Corp** Laymen's Home Missionary Movement (U.S.). **VFOAT** Bible Standard. (19??)-. Periodical. English. mo. Free on request to libraries and educational institutions; $1.00 other. Laymen's Home Missionary Movement, PO Box 67, Chester Springs PA 19425. **Tel** (215)827-7665. **ED** Bernard W. Hedman. **DD** 248. **Circ:** 6,000.
**Desc:** Interdenominational mission dealing especially with the end of the Christian era and ushering in the coming Kingdom of Christ and the church.

US/0749-9280
**BIBLICAL BULLETIN.** **See** Religion and Theology-Bible.

US/0740-7998
**BIBLICAL EVANGELIST, THE.** [Bibl. Evang.]. 1 (1966)-. Periodical. English. mo. free on request. Biblical Evangelism, PO Drawer 940, Ingleside TX 78362. **Tel** (512)776-2867. **ED** Robert L. Sumner. **Bk Rev. Ad Acc. Circ:** 27,300 (ctrl).
**Desc:** Promoting Biblical Christianity through Bible studies, sermons, music, trends in religion, family life, and evangelism from a fundamentalist point of view.

US/0195-1351
**BIBLICAL ILLUSTRATOR. Added/Corp** Southern Baptist Convention. Sunday School Board. **VFOAT** Illustrator. (Fall 1979)-. Periodical. English. Four times a year. $12.00. Southern Baptist Convention, 901 Commerce, Suite 750, Nashville TN 37203. **Tel** (615)244-2355, FAX (615)742-8919. **(Subscription**

**address:** Sunday School Board - Customer Service, 127 Ninth Avenue North, Nashville, TN 37234 USA; telephone: (800)458-2772) **ED** Michael J. Mitchell. **LC** BX6225; .B55. **DD** 220/.05. **Bk Rev. Ad Acc. Circ:** 82,000 (ctrl). ***Continues*** *Sunday School Lesson Illustrator, 0162-4407.*
**Desc:** Biblical background articles for illuminating lessons in the three adult Sunday School curricula of the Baptist Sunday School Board of the Southern Baptist Convention.
**Ind/Abst** South. Baptist Period. Index.

IS/0792-4739
**BIBLICAL POLEMICS.** [Biblic. polemics]. (1988)-. Academic Scholarly Publication. English. mo. $35.00. Jerusalem Institute of Biblical Polemics, PO Box 13099, Jerusalem 91130 Israel. **Tel** 972-2-414299, FAX 972-2-414522. **ED** Shmuel Golding. **UDC** 296. Index available. **Bk Rev. Circ:** 1,000.
**Desc:** Contains rational answers refuting Christian fundamentalism, repudiating bibliotary and religious intolerance, education, against anti-semitism. Viable alternatives to dogmas and creeds.

US/1043-5522
**BIBLICAL PREACHING JOURNAL.** [Biblic. preach. j.]. **Added/Corp** Biblical Preaching Institute. (1988)-. Periodical. English. Four times a year (Jan., Apr., July, Oct.). $29.00 (one year); $56.00 (two years); $81.00 (three years). Biblical Preaching Institute, PO Box 503, Versailles KY 40383-0503. **Tel** (606)873-0308, FAX (606)873-0308. **ED** Gary W. Kidwell, (editor's address: 321 4th Court East, Carmel, IN 46033-1991, phone: (317)571-8776). **DD** 251. **Circ:** 3,000.
**Desc:** Contains samples of sermon and exegesis for each Sunday, following the revised common lectionary.

US/1047-6946
**BIBLICAL REFLECTIONS ON MODERN MEDICINE.** [Biblic. reflect. mod. med.]. Vol. 1, No. 1 (Jan. 1990)-. Periodical. English. bm. $17.00. Covenant Enterprises, PO Box 14488, Augusta GA 30919. **Tel** (404)736-0161. **DD** 248.

US/0146-1079
**BIBLICAL THEOLOGY BULLETIN.** **See** Religion and Theology-Bible.

SW
**BIBLICUM.** (1972)-. Periodical. Swedish. qt. Kr75.00 Sweden; $15.00 US. Biblicum-Tidskrift for Biblisk Tro Och Forskning, c/o Hedegard, Jakob Ulfssonsvag 7B, S-150 30 Mariefred Sweden. **Tel** 018-10 69 25. **ED** Lars Engquist, Ingemar Furberg, Carl Petterson. **Bk Rev.**
**Desc:** Theological journal and a monograph series in Scandinavian and foreign languages; also book reviews.

IT/0392-2588
**BIBLIOGRAFIA IDG. B, DIRITTO CANONICO ED ECCLESIASTICO.** [Bibliogr. IDG, B, Diritto canonico ecclesiastico]. **Added/Corp** Istituto per la Documentazione Giuridica. **VFOAT** Diritto Canonico Ed Ecclesiastico. (1979)-. Italian. an. L4,500. Giuffre Editore SPA, Via Busto Arsizio 40, 20151 Milan Italy. **Tel** 011 398 2 38089200. **LC** LAW. **DD** 016.2629.

AG
**BIBLIOGRAFIA TEOLOGICA COMENTADA DEL ARIA IBEROAMERICANA.** **Added/Corp** Instituto Superior Evangelico de Estudios Teologicos. Vol. 1/2, (1974)-. Spanish. an (Dec.). $93.00. Instituto Superior Evangelico, Camacua 282, 1406 Buenos Aires Argentina. **Tel** 011 54 1 6325030, 011 54 1 6325039. **ED** Eduardo Bierzychudek. **Circ:** 550.
**Desc:** Bibliography of books and articles of periodical publications from the Latin American and Iberian area about religion, theology and human sciences.
**Ind/Abst** Bibliogr. Mission.

VC/0394-9869
**BIBLIOGRAPHIA MISSIONARIA / PONTIFICAL MISSIONARY LIBRARY OF THE CONGREGATION FOR THE EVANGELIZATION OF PEOPLES.** **See** Religion and Theology-Abstracting, Bibliographies and Statistics.

GW/0523-2252
**BIBLIOGRAPHIA PATRISTICA.** **VFOAT** Internationale Patristische Bibliographie. Vol. 1 (1956)-. Monographic series. Latin (German, English and French). be. Walter De Gruyter Inc, 200 Saw Mill River Road, Hawthorne NY 10532. **Tel** (914)747-0110. **ED** W. Schneemelcher. **LC** Z7791; .B5.

US/0065-8847
**BIBLIOGRAPHIC SERIES.** **See** Religion and Theology-Abstracting, Bibliographies and Statistics.

GW/0067-706X
**BIBLIOGRAPHIE ZUR SYMBOLIK, IKONOGRAPHIE UND MYTHOLOGIE.** Vol. 1 (1968)-. German (English, German, French and Italian). an. DM48.00. Verlag Valentin Koerner GmbH, Postfach 304, D-76482 Baden Baden Germany. **Tel** 011 49 7221 22423. **ED** Werner Bies and Hermann Jung. **LC** Z7836; .B5; BL311. Index available (Published every ten years). **Bk Rev. Circ:** 1,000.
**Desc:** Yearbook with abstracts of new books and articles on symbolics, iconography and mythology.
**Ind/Abst** BHA : Biblio. Hist. Art.

GW/0939-0154
**BIBLIOGRAPHIE ZUR SYMBOLIK, IKONOGRAPHIE UND MYTHOLOGIE. ERGANZUNGSBAND.** (1982)-. German. Verlag Valentin Koerner GmbH, Postfach 304, D-76482 Baden Baden Germany. **Tel** 011 49 7221 22423. **LC** IN PROCESS.
**Ind/Abst** BHA : Biblio. Hist. Art.

US/0742-6836
**BIBLIOGRAPHIES AND INDEXES IN RELIGIOUS STUDIES.** [Bibliogr. indexes relig. stud.]. No. 1 (1984)-. Monographic series. English. ir. Price varies per volume. Greenwood Press Inc., PO Box 5007, Westport CT 06881-5007. **Tel** (203)226-3571, FAX (203)222-1502. **LC** UNC. **DD** 016.

US
**BIBLIOGRAPHY IN CHRISTIAN EDUCATION FOR SEMINARY AND COLLEGE LIBRARIES. ADDENDA ... .** 1966-. Bibliography. English. an. ***Continues*** *Suggested Bibliography in Christian Education for Presbyterian College Libraries.*

BE
**BIBLIOTHECA EPHEMERIDUM THEOLOGICARUM LOVANIENSIUM.** **Main/Corp** Louvain. Universite Catholique. (19??)-. Monographic series. Latin. Three times a year. Price varies per volume. Editions Peeters SA, Bondgenotenlaan 153, BP 41, B-3000 Leuven Belgium. **Tel** 32 16 235170, FAX 32 16 228500, telex 65987 PUL B. **Ad Acc.** ctrl circ.

IT
**BIBLIOTHECA FRANCISCANA SCHOLASTICA MEDII AEVI.** 1- 1903-). Periodical. ir. International College of St Bonaventure, 00046 Grottaferrata Rome Italy. **Tel** (06)945.82.48. **ED** Jacques Guy Bougerol. **Circ:** 900 (ctrl).
**Desc:** Edition of unpublished texts of Franciscan medieval masters; theological or philosophical.

SW
**BIBLIOTHECA HISTORICO-ECCLESIASTICA LUNDENSIS.** Vol. 1 (1972)-. Monographic series. Swedish. Price varies per volume. Lund University Press, Box 141, S-22100 Lund Sweden. **Tel** 011 46 46 312000, FAX 011 46 46 305338, telex 33345 EDUCATE S.

US/0006-1921
**BIBLIOTHECA SACRA (1864).** (THE BIBLIOTHECA SACRA.). [Bibl. sacra]. **Added/Corp** Xenia Theological Seminary. Pittsburgh-Xenia Theological Seminary. Evangelical Theological College (Dallas, Tex.) Dallas Theological Seminary and Graduate School of Theology. Dallas Theological Seminary. **VFOAT** Bibliotheca Sacra and Theological Eclectic. Vol. 21, No. 81 (Jan. 1864)-. Periodical. English. qt (Jan., April, July, Oct.). $18.00 (one year), $30.00 (two year) US; $23.00 (one year), $36.00 (two year) other. Dallas Theological Seminary, 3909 Swiss Avenue, Dallas TX 75204. **Tel** (800)992-0998. **ED** Roy B. Zuck. **LC** BR1; .B8. **DD** 205. **CODEN** BSTQAA. Index available. cum. index. **Bk Rev. Circ:** 10,000 (ctrl). available on microfilm and microfiche from University Microfilms International (UMI). ***Absorbed*** *Theological Eclectic; Christian Faith and Life;* ***Formed by the union of*** *Bibliotheca Sacra and Biblical Repository* ***and*** *Christian Review.*
**Desc:** Seeks to provide continuing Biblical and theological instruction to Biblical scholars, alumni, pastors, teachers, and serious Bible students.
**Ind/Abst** Christ. Period. Index (19??-); Curr. Thoughts Trends; GeoRef; Index Book Rev. Relig.; New Testam. Abstr.; Old Testam. Abstr.; Relig. Index One Period. (1963-); Relig. Theol. Abstr.

SW
**BIBLIOTHECA THEOLOGIAE PRACTICAE.** 1- 1957-. Monographic series. Latin. ir. Price varies per volume. Liber International, S-205 10 Malmo Sweden. **Tel** 46-40-70650.

NE
**BIJDRAGEN TIJDSCHRIFT VOOR FILOSOFIE EN THEOLOGIE.** **See** Philosophy.

CN/0006-4327
**BLACKBOARD BULLETIN.** Vol. 1 (1957)-. Bulletin. English. mo (except June and July). $6.00. Pathway Publishers, Route 4, Aylmer Ontario N5H 2R3 Canada. **Bk Rev**, (Qty: 10). **Circ:** 15,500.

GW/0341-9479
**BLATTER FUER WURTTEMBERGISCHE KIRCHENGESCHICHTE.** [Bl. wurttemb. Kirchengesch.]. **Added/Corp** Verein fur Wurttembergische Kirchengeschichte. (1886)-. Periodical. German. an. DM70.00. Verein Fuer Wuerttembergische Kirchengeschichte, Gaensheidestr. 4, Postfach 101342, 7000 Stuttgart 10, Germany. **Tel** FAX 0711-2149236. **ED** Martin Brecht, Hermann Ehmer. Index available. cum. index. **Bk Rev. Circ:** 1,250.
**Ind/Abst** Am. Hist. Life (1970-).

XV/0006-5722
**BOGOSLOVNI VESTNIK.** Began in 1920. Periodical. Serbo-Croatian (Roman) (summaries and/or abstracts in Latin and German). ir. Teoloska Fakulteta v Ljubljana, Institut za Zgodovino Cerkve, Ljubljana Slovenia. **Tel** 061/312-593. **LC** BR9.S5.

CK
**BOLETIN / CEHILA.** **Added/Corp** Comision de Estudios de Historia de la Iglesia en Latinoamerica. Secretaria Ejecutiva. No. 6 (1975)-. Periodical. Spanish (Portuguese and English). Three times a year. $15.00 Spain; $20.00 other. Secretaria Ejecutiva, Apartado 20439, Bogota Colombia. **Tel** 011 55 11 284 6299, FAX 011 55 11 284 6220. **ED** Jose Oscar Beozzo. **LC** BR600; .B64. **DD** 278.005. Index available. cum. index. **Bk Rev. Circ:** 1,500. available on audiocassette; available on diskette. ***Continues*** *Boletin Informativo (Comision de Estudios de Historia de la Iglesia en Latinoamerica).*
**Desc:** Church history of Latin America, Caribean and the US Spanish population, from a ecumenical point of view.

MX
**BOLETIN / COMITE CRISTIANO DE SOLIDARIDAD MONSENOR ROMERO.** **Added/Corp** Comite Cristiano de Solidaridad Monsenor Romero (Mexico City, Mexico). (19??)-. Periodical. Spanish.
**Ind/Abst** Hum. Rights Intern. Rep.

SP
**BOLETIN DE LA PROVINCIA DE SAN JOSE DE LA ORDEN DE AGUSTINOS RECOLETOS.** **Main/Corp** Recollets (Augustinian). Provincia de San Jose. Spanish. Colegio San Augustin, Alberite 104-122, Logrono Spain. **LC** BX2944.S25; R4A.

IT/0037-8739
**BOLLETTINO DELLA SOCIETA DI STUDI VALDESI.** [Boll. Soc. studi valdesi]. **Main/Corp** Societa di Studi Valdesi. 54th Yr. No. 64 (Sept. 1935)-. Periodical. Italian (French and English). sm. $40.00. Via Roberto d'Azeglio 2, 10066 Torre Pellice Italy. **Tel** (0121)932179. **Bk Rev. Ad Acc. Circ:** 850 (ctrl). ***Continues*** *Bollettino Della Societa di Storia Valdese.*
**Desc:** History of the Waldensians and of the Protestantism in Italy.
**Ind/Abst** Am. Hist. Life; Index Book Rev. Relig.; Relig. Index One Period. (1980-).

IT
**BOLLETTINO DELL'ARCHIVIO PER LA STORIA DEL MOVIMENTO SOCIALE CATTOLICO IN ITALIA.** **Added/Corp** Archivio per la Storia del Movimento Sociale Cattolico in Italia. (1966)-. Periodical. Italian. Three times a year. $84.00. Vita e Pensiero, Pubblic University, Largo Gemelli 1, 20123 Milan Italy. **Tel** 011 39 2 72342310, 011 39 2 72342370. **LC** HN39.I8; B64. **DD** 261.8/3/0945. cum. index.
**Ind/Abst** Am. Hist. Life (1981-).

BE/0774-5230
**BONNE NOUVELLE.** [Bonne nouv.]. (1978)-. Monographic series. French. bm. Price varies per volume. Bonne Nouvelle, rue de l'Armistice 37, B-1080 Brussels Belgium. **Tel** 011 32 2 4103011. **UDC** 226. ***Continues*** *Magnificat (Bruxelles), 0774-5222.*
**Ind/Abst** Bibliogr. Mission.

US/1043-352X
**BOOK NEWSLETTER (MINNEAPOLIS, MINN.).** **See** Literary and Political Reviews.

US/0890-0841
**BOOKS & RELIGION.** ***Ceased.*** [Books relig.]. **Added/Corp** Duke University. Divinity School. Trinity Church (New York, N.Y.). **VFOAT** Books and Religion; B&R. Vol. 13, No. 1 (Jan./Feb. 1985)-Vol. 19, No. 1 (1992). Periodical. English. qt. Trinity Episcopal Church, 74 Trinity Place, New York NY 10006-2088. **Tel** (212)602-0880. **ED** Christopher Walters-Burgee. **LC** BL1; .N48. **DD** 200. Index available. **Bk Rev. Ad Acc. Circ:** 15,000. available on microfilm and microfiche from University Microfilms International (UMI). ***Continues*** *Review of Books and Religion (Forward Movement Publications), 0732-5800.*
**Desc:** A review offering panoramic coverage of religious books and all other aspects of the interplay of religion and culture.
**Ind/Abst** Book Rev. Digest; Book Rev. Index; Index Book Rev. Relig.; Relig. Index One Period.

US/0006-7563
**BOOKSTORE JOURNAL.** **See** Business.

CN/0824-555X
**BORN-AGAIN CHRISTIAN DIRECTORY-CATALOG, THE.** [Born-again Christ. dir.-cat.]. No. 1-. Catalog. English. an. $4.00. Born-Again Christian Directory-Catalog, PO Box 317 Station A, Ottawa Ontario K1N 9Z9 Canada. **DD** 248/.05.

US
**BOSTON UNIVERSITY STUDIES IN PHILOSOPHY AND RELIGION. See** Philosophy.

US
**BOTH SIDES NOW.** English. ir. $10.00. Both Sides Now, 10547 State Hwy 110 North, Tyler TX 75704-9537. **Tel** (903)592-4263. **ED** Elihu Edelson. **Bk Rev. Ad Acc. Circ:** 200.
**Desc:** An alternative journal of spiritual and political synthesis with emphasis on New Age spirituality.

CN/0822-8949
**BOTTIN / UNION CANADIENNE DES RELIGIEUSES CONTEMPLATIVES.** ***Ceased.*** [Bottin - Union can. relig. contempl.]. **Main/Corp** Union Canadienne des Religieuses Contemplatives. **VFOAT** Directory. (1975)-(19??). French. be. Union Canadienne des Religieuses Contemplatives, CP 479, Berthierville Quebec J0K 1A0 Canada. **DD** 255/.901/02571.

CN
**BOZJA BESEDA. Added/Corp** Slovenski Misijonarji (Lazaristi). **VFOAT** Word of God. (19??)-. Periodical. Slovenian. mo (10 issues). $15.00 US and Canada; $20.00 other. Bozja Beseda / The Word of God, 739 Browns Line, Toronto Ontario M8W 3V7 Canada. **Tel** (416)255-2721. **LC** WMLC L 83/587. Index available. **Ad Acc. Circ:** 1,650.

US/0006-8918
**BRAILLE STAR THEOSOPHIST, THE. See** Physically Impaired.

US
**BRAZIL GOSPEL NEWS.** (19??)-. Periodical. English. qt. Free on request. Brazil Gospel Fellowship Mission, 121 North Glenwood, Springfield IL 62702. **Tel** (217)523-7176.

BL
**BRAZILIAN BIBLE QUARTERLY.** (19??)-. qt. $25.00. Padre Caetano Minette de Tillesse, Revista Biblica Brasileira, Caixa Postal 1577, Fortaleza Ceara 60001 Brazil. Index available. **Bk Rev**, (Qty: 200). **Ad Acc**. Full Page (B&W) $100.00. Half Page (B&W) $50.00. **Circ:** 1,000 (ctrl).
**Desc:** A scholarly periodical of theological analysis, dealing with the Bible and related subjects (exegesis, Judaism, Ancient Middle East, etc.) through original articles and literature reviews.

CN/0821-168X
**BREAD OF LIFE (ANCASTER).** (THE BREAD OF LIFE.). [Bread life]. **Added/Corp** Catholic Charismatic Services Committee of Ontario. Vol. 1, No. 1 (Nov. 1977)-. Periodical. English. bm. By donation only. Bread of Life, 370 Main Street E Suite B1, Hamilton ONT L8N 1J6 Canada. **Tel** (416)529-4496, FAX (416)529-5373. **ED** Peter B Coughlin. **DD** 269/4/05. **Circ:** 5,400.
**Desc:** Designed to encourage spiritual growth in areas of renewal in the Catholic Church today.

US/1062-2837
**BREAK POINT WITH CHARLES COLSON.** [Break point Charles Colson]. **Added/Corp** Prison Fellowship Ministries. **VFOAT** Break Point. Vol. 1, No. 1 (March 1991)-. Periodical. English. mo. $5.00 per month for 100 copies. Break Point with Charles Colson, Subscription Services, PO Box 1916, Marion OH 43305. **DD** 248.

US/1048-2881
**BREAKAWAY (POMONA, CALIF.). See** Family and Marriage.

US
**BRETHREN IN CHRIST CHURCH / GENERAL CONFERENCE MINUTES.** English. be. $6.50. Evangel Press, PO Box 189, Napanee IN 46550. **Tel** (416)871-7769.

US/0006-9663
**BRETHREN LIFE AND THOUGHT.** [Brethr. life thought]. **Added/Corp** Church of the Brethren. Bethany Theological Seminary, Oak Brook, Ill. Brethren Journal Association. Vol. 1 (Autumn 1955)-. Periodical. English. Four times a year (Jan., Apr., July, Oct.). $15.00 (individual); $25.00 (institution). Brethren Press Association, Butterfield & Meyers Roads, Oak Brook IL 60521. **Tel** (312)620-2200. **ED** Christina Bucher. **LC** BX7801; .B74. **DD** 289. **Bk Rev. Circ:** 850 (ctrl). available on microfilm and microfiche from University Microfilms International (UMI).
**Desc:** Religious and theological issues are relating to the"Peace" churches. History, current events, and other articles are also included.
**Ind/Abst** Index Book Rev. Relig.; Relig. Index One Period. (1956-); Relig. Theol. Abstr.

US/0161-5238
**BRETHREN MISSIONARY HERALD.** (1940)-. Periodical. English. mo (12 issues per year). $13.50 (one year), $25.00 (two year). Brethren Missionary Herald, Box 544, Winona Lake IN 46590. **Tel** (219)267-7158. **ED** Charles W Turner. **Ad Acc, Adv Mgr:** Charles Turner, **Tel** (219)267-7158. **Circ:** 2,600 (ctrl).
**Desc:** Denominational interest for national fellowship of Brethren Churches.

HK/1018-8983
**BRIDGE (HONG KONG).** (BRIDGE : CHURCH LIFE IN CHINA TODAY.). [Bridge]. **Added/Corp** Tao Fong Shan Ecumenical Centre (Sha Tin, Hong Kong) Christian Study Centre on Chinese Religion and Culture. No. 1 (Sept. 1983)-. Periodical. English (Chinese). bm. $12.00 (sea mail), $15.00 (air mail) Asia; $15.00 (sea mail), $18.00 (air mail) other. Christian Study Centre on China Religion and Culture, Sixth Floor Kiu Kin Mansion, 566 Nathan Road, Kowloon Hong Kong. **Tel** 011 852 3 7703310, FAX 011 852 3 7826869. **ED** Deng Zhaoming. **Bk Rev. Ad Acc. Circ:** 3,000.
**Ind/Abst** Index Book Rev. Relig. (1986-); Relig. Index One Period.

CN/1184-6542
**BRIDGING THE GAP (CALGARY).** (BRIDGING THE GAP / GENESIS INTERNATIONAL RESEARCH ASSOCIATION AND PUBLISHERS.). [Bridg. gap]. **Added/Corp** Genesis International Research Association and Publishers. Vol. 1, No. 2 (Summer 1990)-. Periodical. English. qt. Free to members. Genesis International Research Association and Publishers, PO Box 30202, Chinook Postal Outlet, Calgary, Alberta T2H 2V9 Canada. **DD** 231.7/65/05. ***Continues*** *Newsletter (Genesis International Research Association and Publishers)., 1184-6550.*

CN/0821-5839
**BRIERCREST ECHO.** [Briercrest echo]. Vol. 41, No. 2 (Sept. 1982)-. Periodical. English. qt. Free. Briercrest Bible College, 510 College Drive, Caronport Saskatchewan S0H 0S0 Canada. **Tel** (306)756-3200, FAX (306)756-3366. **(Subscription address:** US/ Briercrest Bible College, Box 401, Plentywood, MT 59254-0401**) ED** Klaus H Tonn. **DD** 207/.71244. **Circ:** 24,000 (ctrl). ***Continues*** *Echo (Caronport, Sask.), 0824-9288.*
**Desc:** A thematic topical approach to current issues within the evangelical Christian world. Primarily deals with biblical and theological topics.

US/0740-4107
**BRIGHAM YOUNG UNIVERSITY ... FIRESIDE AND DEVOTIONAL SPEECHES. Added/Corp** Brigham Young University. (198?)-. Periodical. English. an (publish after each school year). $8.95. Brigham Young University Publishers, BYU 210, University Press Building, Provo UT 84602. **Tel** (801)378-4137. **ED** Karen Seely. **Circ:** 4,000. ***Continues*** *Speeches of the Year.*
**Desc:** Written copies of Devotional and Fireside speeches given at Brigham Young University.

US/0007-0106
**BRIGHAM YOUNG UNIVERSITY STUDIES (1984).** (BRIGHAM YOUNG UNIVERSITY STUDIES.). **VFOAT** BYU Studies. Vol. 24, No. 1 (Winter 1984)-. Academic Scholarly Publication. English. Four times a year (Mar., June, Sept., Dec.). $15.00 (one year); $28.50 (two years). Brigham Young University Press / 2246 Smith Family Living Center, Provo UT 84602. **Tel** (801)378-4647. **ED** John W. Welch, (editor's address: 551 JRBC, Provo, UT 84602, (801)378-6691). Index available (index bound in issue 31, price $6.00). cum. index. **Bk Rev. Circ:** 2,500. available on microfilm and microfiche from University Microfilms International (UMI). Documents available from The Genuine Article. ***Continues*** *BYU Studies, 0278-1980.*
**Desc:** Scholarly perspectives on LDS topics.
**Ind/Abst** Am. Hist. Life (1974-); Arts Humanit. Citation Index [Full Cov.]; Ceram. Abstr.; Curr. Contents Arts Humanit.; Curr. Contents Soc. Behav. Sci.; Index Book Rev. Relig.; MLA Int. Bibl. Books Artic. Mod. Lang. Lit.; Relig. Index One Period.; Res. Alert [Full Cov.]; Romant. Move.; Soc. Sci. Cit. Index [Select. Cov.].

US/1056-778X
**BRIGHT (MIDDLETOWN, CALIF.), THE.** (THE BRIGHT : CELEBRATIONS OF THE DIVINE WORLD TEACHER DA AVABHASA (THE "BRIGHT").). [Bright]. **Added/Corp** Free Daist Communion. (1991)-. Periodical. English. bm. $12.00. The Bright, PO Box 3680, Clearlake CA 95422. **DD** 291.

US
**BRINGING RELIGION HOME.** (19??)-. English. mo. $12.00. Claretian Publications, 205 West Monroe Street, Chicago IL 60606. **Tel** (312)236-7782, (800)328-6515.

US/1048-2873
**BRIO (POMONA, CALIF.). See** Family and Marriage.

UK/0141-6200
**BRITISH JOURNAL OF RELIGIOUS EDUCATION.** Vol. 1 (Autumn 1978)-. Periodical. English. Three times a year. £24.00. Christian Education Movement, Royal Buildings, Victoria Street, Derby DE1 1GW England. **Tel** 011 44 332 296655, FAX 011 44 332 43253. **ED** John Hull (editor's address: PO Box 363, The University of Birmingham, Birmingham B15 2TT England; editor's telephone number: 021-414-4836). Index available. **Bk Rev. Ad Acc. Circ:** 2,600. available on microfilm and microfiche from University Microfilms International (UMI). ***Supersedes*** *Learning for Living; The British Journal of Religion in Education.*
**Desc:** Professional academic journal for religious education in county schools including curriculum, theory and practice.
**Ind/Abst** Br. Educ. Index; Index Book Rev. Relig.; Relig. Index One Period.

UK
**BRITISH JOURNAL OF THEOLOGICAL EDUCATION.** English. Three times a year (Fall, Summer & Winter (Volume changes each Fall)). £7.50 UK; £9.50 US and Canada; £10.00 other. British Journal ofTheological Education, 16 Towers Avenue Jesmond, Newcastle U T NE2 3QE England. **Tel** 011 44 91 2810714 or 2321939.

US/0007-2494
**BROWN GOLD.** (19??)-. Periodical. English. Twelve times a year. $7.00 one year; $18.00 two years. New Tribes Mission, Sanford FL 32771. **Tel** (407)323-3430, FAX (407)330-1580.

US
**BTI UNION LIST OF SERIALS. MICROFORM. VFOAT** Union List of Serials. (19??)-. English. Boston Theological Institute, 11 Garden Street, Cambridge MA 02138. **Tel** (617)492-5622.

US/0897-8115
**BUILDING TIMES MAGAZINE.** [Build. times mag.]. **VFOAT** Building Times. Vol. 1, No. 1 (Jan./Feb. 1988)-. Periodical. English. bm. Edification Ministries, 109 White Oak Lane/Suite 521, Old Bridge NJ 08857-1945. **DD** 248. ***Continues*** *Edification (Shrewsbury, N.J.), 0894-0428.*

FR/1142-2300
**BULLETIN - AIDE AUX CROYANTS DE L'URSS.** (BULLETIN.). **Added/Corp** Edition Chretienne des Etudiants Russes (Paris). **VFOAT** Bulletin - Aide aux Croyants de l'Union des Republiques Socialistes Sovietiques. (198?)-. Periodical. French. **UDC** 267 (4).
**Ind/Abst** Hum. Rights Intern. Rep.

CN/0316-8743
**BULLETIN - CANADIAN RELIGIOUS CONFERENCE.** [Bull. - Can. Relig. Conf.]. **Main/Corp** Canadian Religious Conference. V. 1- Jan. 1955-. Bulletin. English. CRC Bulletin, 324 Laurier Avenue East, Ottawa Ontario K1N 6P6 Canada. **DD** 255/.006/271.

US/0163-6561
**BULLETIN - CENTER FOR THE STUDY OF WORLD RELIGIONS, HARVARD UNIVERSITY. Main/Corp** Harvard University. Center for the Study of World Religions. (Oct. 1974)-. Bulletin. English. qt. Free. Center for the Study of World Religions, 42 Francis Avenue, Cambridge MA 02138.
**Ind/Abst** Index Book Rev. Relig.; Relig. Index One Period.

CN/0316-8751
**BULLETIN - CONFERENCE RELIGIEUSE CANADIENNE.** [Bull. - Conf. relig. can.]. **Main/Corp** Conference Religieuse Canadienne. **VFOAT** Bulletin CRC. V. 1- Jan. 1955-. Bulletin. French (English). Four times a year. Bulletin CRC, 324 Est Avenue Laurier, Ottawa Ontario K1N 6P6 Canada. **Tel** (613)236-0824. **ED** Rita Montreuil. **DD** 255/.006/271.

US
**BULLETIN / COUNCIL OF SOCIETIES FOR THE STUDY OF RELIGION. Added/Corp** Council of Societies for the Study of Religion. Vol. 17, No. 1 (Feb. 1988)-. Bulletin. English. qt. $24.00 (institutions), $30.00 (foreign institutions). Council Society for Study of Religion, Valparaiso University, Valparaiso IN 46383. **Tel** (219)464-5340. **(Subscription address:** CSSR Bulletin, Valparaiso University, Valparaiso, IN 46383, (219)464-5515**) ED** Richard Busse, 1706 N. Calumet Avenue, Valparaiso, IN, 46383, (219)464-7278. **Ad Acc.** ***Continues in part*** *Religious Studies News, 0885-0372.*
**Ind/Abst** Index Book Rev. Relig. (1988-); Relig. Index One Period.

FR/0153-3851
**BULLETIN DE LA CATHEDRALE DE STRASBOURG. See** Architecture.

US/0007-4314
**BULLETIN DE L'A.I.M.** **Main/Corp** AIDE a l'Implantation Monastique. **VFOAT** A.I.M. Bulletin. 1969. Bulletin. English. sa. $10.00 North America; $12.00 other. Inter-Monastic Aid, St Scholastica Priory, PO Box 606 MA 01366-0606. **Tel** (508)724-3213. **ED** Dom Paul Gordan. **Bk Rev. Circ:** 750.
**Desc:** Invaluable historical witness and documentation of monastic life in the Mission World and the beginning efforts of dialogue between Christian and Non-Christian monks and nuns.

CN/0382-9472
**BULLETIN DE L'ENTRAIDE MISSIONNAIRE.** **Main/Corp** Entraide Missionnaire, Inc. (1954)-. Bulletin. French. Four times a year. 15.00Can$ Canada; 20.00Can$ other. Bulletin de l'Entraidemissionnaire, 15 Ouest de Castelnau, Montreal Quebec H3L 2J2 Canada. **Tel** (514)270-6089, FAX (514)270-6156. Index available. **Bk Rev. Circ:** 600.
**Desc:** Topics include missionary work, politics, health, etc. Also book reviews.

CN
**BULLETIN DE LIAISON.** (19??)-. French. Four times a year. 25.00$Can. Conference de la Pastorale Scolaire, 11 rue Pauline, Coteau-Station, Quebec, J0P 1E0 Canada. **Tel** (514)267-2906.

US
**BULLETIN DE SAINT-SULPICE.** Bulletin. English (French and Spanish). an. $15.00. Bulletin de Saint-Sulpice, 5408 Roland Ave., Baltimore MD 21210. **Tel** (410)323-5070, FAX (410)433-6524.

CG/0253-9969
**BULLETIN DE THEOLOGIE AFRICAINE.** (BULLETIN DE THEOLOGIE AFRICAINE / BULLETIN OF AFRICAN THEOLOGY.). [Bull. theol. afr.]. **Added/Corp** Ecumenical Association of African Theologians. **VFOAT** Bulletin of African Theology. Vol. 1, No. 1 (Jan./June 1979)-. Periodical. French (English). Twice a year. Kapongo Kazadi / Bulletin de Theologie Africaine, PO Box 479, Kinshasa 23 Zaire. **LC** BR1.A1; B84.
**Ind/Abst** Index Book Rev. Relig.; Relig. Index One Period. (1980-).

BE/0007-442X
**BULLETIN DE THEOLOGIE ANCIENNE ET MEDIEVALE.** **Added/Corp** Abbaye du Mont Cesar. Vol. 1 (Jan. 1929)-. Bulletin. French (English and German). an. 943.40F Belgium; 1056.60F other. Editions Peeters SA, Bondgenotenlaan 153, BP 41, B-3000 Leuven Belgium. **Tel** 32 16 235170, FAX 32 16 228500, telex 65987 PUL B. **LC** Z7753; .B95.
**Ind/Abst** Bibliogr. Mission.; Abr. Cathol. Period. Lit. Index; Cathol. Period. Lit. Index.

US/0744-768X
**BULLETIN DIGEST.** (198?)-. Periodical. English. mo. Bulletin Digest, HC69, Box 29A, Anselma NE 68813. **Tel** (308)749-2349.

FR
**BULLETIN D'INFORMATION ET DE LIAISON DE L'ASSOCIATION INTERNATIONALE D'ETUDES PATRISTIQUES.** **Main/Corp** Association Internationale d'Etudes Patristiques. No. 1 (1968)-. English (French and German). an. AIEP, 14 rue Saint Louis, F57158 Montigny Metz France. **Tel** 011 33 1 87638906. **LC** WMLC L 83/652.

US/8755-450X
**BULLETIN FROM THE HILL.** (BULLETIN FROM THE HILL / COLGATE-ROCHESTER DIVINITY SCHOOL, BEXLEY HALL, CROZER THEOLOGICAL SEMINARY.). **Added/Corp** Colgate-Rochester Divinity School, Bexley Hall, Crozer Theological Seminary. Vol. 54, No. 1 (Dec. 1981)-. Bulletin. English. Three times a year. Free. Colgate Rochester Divinity School, 1100 South Goodman Street, Rochester NY 14620. **Tel** (716)271-1320. **LC** BV4070.C66; A15. **DD** 207/.74789. ***Continues*** *Colgate-Rochester Divinity School, Bexley Hall, Crozer Theological Seminary. Bulletin - Colgate-Rochester Divinity School, Bexley Hall, Crozer Theological Seminary.*

UK/0018-828X
**BULLETIN - HYMN SOCIETY OF GREAT BRITAIN AND IRELAND.** **See** Music.

US/0739-0459
**BULLETIN / INSTITUTE FOR ANTIQUITY AND CHRISTIANITY.** [Bull. Inst. Antiq. Christ.]. **Main/Corp** Institute for Antiquity and Christianity (Claremont, Calif.). **VFOAT** Bulletin of the Institute for Antiquity and Christianity. No. 1, (Nov. 1970)-. Bulletin. English. Four times a year (Mar., June, Sept., Dec.). $25.00. Institute Antiquity and Christianity, Claremont Graduate School, Claremont CA 91711. **Tel** (714)621-8066, FAX (714)621-8390. **ED** Jon M. Asgeirsson. **Bk Rev**, (Qty: varies). **Ad Acc. Circ:** 1,000 (ctrl). available on an online database from University Microfilms International (UMI).

US/1073-5976
**BULLETIN / INSTITUTE FOR THEOLOGICAL ENCOUNTER WITH SCIENCE AND TECHNOLOGY.** **VFOAT** ITEST Bulletin. (19??)-. English. Four times a year. Free to members; $35.00 membership. Institute for Theological Encounter with Science and Technology, 221 North Grand Boulevard, St. Louis MO 63103. **Tel** (314)658-2703. **Bk Rev. Circ:** 1,000. ***Continues*** *ITEST Bulletin.*

CN/1186-8937
**BULLETIN MARIE DE L'INCARNATION.** [Bull. Marie Incarnation]. **Added/Corp** Centre Marie-de-l'Incarnation. No. 1 (Jan. 1991)-. Bulletin. French. qt. Limited free distribution. Centre Marie-de-L'Incarnation, 10 Rue Donnacona, Quebec Quebec G1R 4T1 Canada. **DD** 271/.974.

US/0540-8644
**BULLETIN - MORAVIAN THEOLOGICAL SEMINARY, THE.** **Main/Corp** Moravian Theological Seminary. (19??)-. Bulletin. English. ir. $3.00 (per issue). Moravian Theological Seminary, 1200 Main Street, Bethlehem PA 18018. **Tel** (215)861-1516.
**Desc:** Includes the Weber memorial lectures.
**Ind/Abst** Relig. Index One Period.

JA/0386-720X
**BULLETIN - NANZAN INSTITUTE FOR RELIGION AND CULTURE.** **Main/Corp** Nanzan Institute for Religion and Culture. (1???)-. Bulletin. English. an. Free. Nanzan Institute for Religion and Culture, 18 Yamazato-cho Showa-ku, 466 Nagoya Japan. **Tel** (052)832-3111, FAX (052)833-6157. **ED** Jan Van Bragt. **Circ:** 1,000.
**Desc:** An organ of communication with actual and potential collaborators. Presents a description of the main activities of the Nanzan Institute and ordinarily one feature article on the everyday Japanese religious scene.
**Ind/Abst** Bibliogr. Mission.

UK
**BULLETIN OF DR. WILLIAMS'S LIBRARY.** **Main/Corp** Dr. Williams's Library. (195?)-. English. an (Jan.). £4.00. Dr. Williams Trust, 14 Gordon Square, London WC1H 0AG England. **Tel** 011 44 71 3873727. **LC** Z921.L87; B84. **Circ:** 2,000. ***Continues*** *Bulletin and Classified List of Accessions to the Library.*
**Desc:** Contains recent accessions.

II/0254-9182
**BULLETIN OF THE CHRISTIAN INSTITUTE OF SIKH STUDIES.** [Bull. Christ. Inst. Sikh Stud.]. **Added/Corp** Christian Institute of Sikh Studies. (1972)-. Bulletin. English. sa. $25.00. Christian Institute of Sikh Studies, Baring Union Christian College, Batala-143505, Punjab India. **(Subscription address:** Prints India, 11 Darya Ganj, New Delhi 110002 India.**)**
**Ind/Abst** Bibliogr. Mission.; Index Book Rev. Relig.; Relig. Index One Period.

US/0010-5821
**BULLETIN OF THE CONGREGATIONAL LIBRARY.** **See** Library and Information Sciences.

US
**BULLETIN OF THE EVANGELICAL PHILOSOPHICAL SOCIETY.** **See** Philosophy.

US/1052-8202
**BULLETIN OF THE GENERAL THEOLOGICAL CENTER OF MAINE.** [Bull. - Gen. Theol. Cent. Me.]. **Main/Corp** General Theological Center of Maine. **VFOAT** Bulletin. Vol. 83, No. 3/4 (Sept./Dec. 1988)-. Bulletin. English. Four times a year (Mar., June, Sept., Dec.). $15.00. Bangor Theological Seminary, 159 State Street, Portland ME 04101. **Tel** (207)874-2214. **ED** Clifton Davis, (phone: (207)942-6781). **DD** 200. **Bk Rev**, (Qty: 75). **Circ:** 1,200. available on an online database from Internet. ***Continues*** *Bulletin of the General Theological Library, 0361-0837.*

UK/0048-9778
**BULLETIN OF THE SCOTTISH INSTITUTE OF MISSIONARY STUDIES, THE.** **Main/Corp** Scottish Institute of Missionary Studies. No. 1, June (1967)-. Bulletin. English. ir. $4.10. Scott Institute of Missionary Studies, University of Aberdeen, Religious Studies, Aberdeen AB9 2UB Scotland. available on microfilm and microfiche from University Microfilms International (UMI).

UK/0081-1297
**BULLETIN OF THE SOCIETY FOR AFRICAN CHURCH HISTORY, THE.** ***Suspended.*** **Main/Corp** Society for African Church History. **VFOAT** Bulletin de la Societe d'Histoire de l'Eglise en Afrique. Vol. 1 (April 1963)-Suspended. Bulletin. English (summaries and/or abstracts in French). an. Society for African Church History, University of Aberdeen, Kings College, Aberdeen Scotland.

CN/0823-7883
**BULLETIN OZANAM / SOCIETE DE SAINT-VINCENT DE PAUL, HULL ET GATINEAU.** [Bull. Ozanam]. March 1983-. Bulletin. French. bm. Free. Societe de Saint-Vincent de Paul Hull et Gatineau, 102 rue Eddy, Hull Quebec J8X 2W4 Canada. **DD** 267/.242714221/05. ctrl circ.

SP/0521-8195
**BURGENSE.** [Burgense]. **Added/Corp** Facultad de Teologia del Norte de Espana. Seminario Metropolitano (Burgos, Spain). (1960)-. Periodical. Spanish. Twice a year (Jan., & July). 21ptas Spain; 28ptas. Facultad de Teologia Burgosedit, Aldecoa Martinez de Compo 7, 09003 Burgos Spain. **Tel** 011 34 947 267000. **ED** Don Nicolas Lopez Martpinez. **LC** BR7; .B86. **Bk Rev.**
**Ind/Abst** Bibliogr. Mission.; New Testam. Abstr.; Old Testam. Abstr.

US/1071-0523
**BUSH-MEETING DUTCH, THE.** (THE BUSH-MEETING DUTCH : A QUARTERLY NEWSLETTER OF LOCAL HISTORY AND GENEALOGY OF THE FORMER EVANGELICAL UNITED BRETHREN CHURCH, ITS PREDECESSORS, AND SISTER CHURCHES.). [Bush-meet. Dutch]. **VFOAT** Bush Meeting Dutch. Vol. 1, No. 1 (Jan. 1984)-. Periodical. English. qt. $4.00. The Bush-Meeting Dutch, c/o D H Koss, 114 Dundee Avenue, Barrington IL 60010. **Tel** (312)381-6672. **ED** David H. Koss. **DD** 929. **Bk Rev. Circ:** 50.

CN/0701-2837
**BUZZ (THUNDER BAY).** (BUZZ.). Began with Nov. 2, 1976 issue. Periodical. English. mo. 9.95Can$. Buzz Christian Ministries, 37 Elm Road, New Malden Surrey KT3 3HB England. **Tel** (01)942-9761. **ED** Steve Goddard. **DD** 027.4/713/1. **Bk Rev. Ad Acc. Circ:** 23,616. ***Supersedes*** *Northwestern Regional Library System (Ontario). Newsletter, 0701-2829.*
**Desc:** News and current affairs regarding: significance for contemporary Christian arts, media reviews, features, etc.

GW/0935-0373
**C-MAGAZIN.** [C-Mag.]. (1987)-. Periodical. German. qt. DM24.00 Germany; DM30.00 other (regular). Gemeinschaft Immanuel Ravensburg, Rudolfstrasse 16, Postfach 1271, W-7980 Ravensburg Germany. **Tel** 49 751 17035, FAX 49 751 23899. **ED** Rainer Straub. **UDC** 070.482. **Bk Rev. Ad Acc. Pr Rev. Circ:** 4,000.
**Desc:** Encourages Christians to live their faith in daily life.

US
**CA NEWSERVICE.** **VFOAT** CA News Service; Newservice. **VAT** Churches Alive Newservice. Periodical. English. qt. Free. Churches Alive!, PO Box 3800, San Bernardino CA 92413. **Tel** (214)886-5361. **ED** Ronald A Wormser Sr and Ron Wormser Jr. **Circ:** 15,000.
**Desc:** Ideas and insights for church leaders to grow their ministry following Jesus Christ's concepts and model.

BL
**CADERNOS ABESC.** **Main/Corp** Associacao Brasileira de Escolas Superiores Catolicas. **VAT** Cadernos Associacao Brasileira de Escolas Superiores Catolicas. Yearly V. 1-. Portuguese. Av Dom Jose Gaspar 500/30.000. **LC** LC505.B7; A87A.

●CN/1188-6749
**CAHIER DE L'ENVOLEE LUMIERE.** (LE CAHIER DE L'ENVOLEE LUMIERE.). [Cah. envol. lumiere]. **VFOAT** Envolee Lumiere. (Spring 1992)-. Periodical. French. qt. Le Cahier de l'Envolee Lumiere, 89, Ch du Fleuve, Coteau-du-Lac Quebec J0P 1B0 Canada. **DD** 232.

CN/0381-7652
**CAHIERS D'ANIMATION MISSIONNAIRE.** V. 1, No. 1, (Aug./Sept. 1973)-. Periodical. French. qt. $5.00. Women's Commission, 230 North Washington Avenue, Lansing MI 48933. **DD** 266/.2/05. ***Continues*** *Messages, 0381-7628.*
**Ind/Abst** Bibliogr. Mission.

SZ/0250-6971
**CAHIERS DE LA REVUE DE THEOLOGIE ET DE PHILOSOPHIE.** [Cah. rev. theol. philos.]. (1977)-. Monographic series. French. ir. Price varies per volume. Librairie Droz SA, 11 rue Massot BP 389, CH 1211 Geneva 12 Switzerland. **Tel** 011 41 22 3466666, FAX 011 41 22 472391. **Circ:** 600.
**Ind/Abst** Index Book Rev. Relig.; Relig. Index One Period.

FR
**CAHIERS DE L'APF.** **Main/Corp** Association des Pasteurs de France. No. 1- May 1974-. Periodical. French. 10.00. Association des Pasteurs de France, 47 rue de Clichy, Paris 75011 France. ***Supersedes*** *Confiance.*

CN/0705-8942
**CAHIERS DE SPIRITUALITE IGNATIENNE.** [Cah. spiritual. ignatienne]. **Added/Corp** Centre de Spiritualite Ignatienne. Vol. 1 (Jan./March 1977)-. Periodical. French. Four times a year

(Jan., May, Aug., Nov.). 30.00Can$ Canada; 40.00Can$ other. Centre de Spiritualite Ignatie, 2370 Rue Nicolas Pinel, Ste Foy Quebec G1V 4L6 Canada. **Tel** (418)653-6353, FAX (418)653-1208. **ED** Jean Avy Saint Arnaud. **DD** 248/.05. cum. index. **Bk Rev. Circ:** 800.
**Desc:** Spirituality of Ignatius de Loyola in his spiritual exercises.

CG/0008-0047
**CAHIERS DES RELIGIONS AFRICAINES.** [Cah. relig. afr.]. **Added/Corp** Universite Lovanium de Kinshasa. Centre d'Etudes des Religions Aricaines. Universite Natonale du Zaire, Campus de Kinshasa. Centre d'Eudes des Religions Africaines. Faculte de Theologie Catholique de Kinshasa. Centre d'Etudes de Religions Africaines. Vol. 1, (Jan./July 1967)-. Periodical. French (English). Twice a year (Jan., Apr.). $70.00. Cen D Etudes des Relig Afric, PO Box 712, Kinshasa Limete Zaire. **Tel** 011 243 78476. **LC** BL2400; .C3. **DD** 229/.6/05. Index available. **Bk Rev. Ad Acc. Circ:** 1,000 (ctrl).
**Desc:** Publishes articles on African traditional religions, sociology of religion, cultural anthropology, mythologies, lore, religious literature and art.
**Ind/Abst** Anthropol. Index; Bibliogr. Mission.; Index Book Rev. Relig.

FR/0008-0063
**CAHIERS D'ETUDES CATHARES.** **Added/Corp** Societe du Souvenir et des Etudes Cathares. Vol. 1 (1949)-. Periodical. French. Four times a year. 200.00F France; 250.00F other. Societe du Souvenir et des Etudes Cathares, Chateau de Ferrieres, 81260 Ferrieres France. **Tel** 011 33 63 740353. cum. index. **Bk Rev.**

FR
**CAHIERS DU TEMOIGNAGE CHRETIEN.** **VFOAT** Temoignage Chretien. (Nov. 1941)-. Periodical. French. Fifty-two times a year. 910.00F (US, Canada and Mideast); 770.00F (EEC countries); 820.00F (Morocco, Algeria and other European countries); 1000.00F (Latin America and Asia); 710.00F (Tunisia); 1100.00F (Oceania); 800.00F (French speaking Africa, Mayotte, St Pierre and Miquelon); 1000.00F (French Polynesia). ETC, BP 63, F-77932 Perthes France. **Tel** 011 33 1 64380155, FAX 011 33 1 64310053, telex 290562.
**Ind/Abst** Int. Labour Doc.

FR/0222-9714
**CAHIERS EVANGILE.** [Cah. evang.]. (Aug. 1972)-. Periodical. French. Four times a year. 107.74F France; 155.00F other. Serv Biblique Evangile et Vie, 8 rue Jean Bart, 75006 Paris France. **Tel** 011 33 1 43263832. ***Supersedes** Evangile, 0423-8559.*
**Ind/Abst** Old Testam. Abstr.; Point Repere (1983-).

FR/0987-2213
**CAHIERS POUR CROIRE AUJOURD'HUI.** (1987)-. Periodical. French. ir. 279.00F France; 400.00F other. Assas Editions, 14 rue d'Assas, 75006 Paris France. **Tel** 011 33 1 44394848, FAX 011 33 1 40490192. **UDC** 261. ***Formed by the union of** Croire Aujourd'Hui (Paris. 1971), 0223-4734 **and** Cahiers de l'Actualite Religieuse et Sociale, 0007-9669.*

US/0739-9189
**CALC REPORT.** (CALC REPORT / CLERGY AND LAITY CONCERNED.). **Added/Corp** Clergy and Laity Concerned (U.S.). **VFOAT** C.A.L.C. Report; CALC Report, TWC Bulletin; TWC Bulletin. **VAT** Clergy and Laity Concerned Report. (197?)-. Periodical. English. Six times a year. $30.00. Clergy & Laity Concerned, 340 Mead Road, Decatur GA 30030. **Tel** (404)377-1983. **ED** Leslie Withers.
**Desc:** Clergy and Laity Concerned is a nation-wide, multiracial network of people of different races, religions, ages, ethnic and economic backgrounds. Brings moral, ethical and religious values to bear on issues of human rights, racial and gender justice, militarism and economic justice at home and abroad.
**Ind/Abst** Hum. Rights Intern. Rep.

CN/0701-0729
**CALEDONIA TIMES.** **Added/Corp** Anglican Church of Canada. Diocese of Caledonia. Vol. 9 (Jan. 1968)-. Newspaper. English. Fifty-two times a year (Tues.). 78.13Can$. Brabant Newspapers Ltd., 333 Alvin Avenue, Stoney Creek Ontario L83 2M6 Canada. **Tel** (905)523-5800. **DD** 283/.711/32. ***Continues** Caledonia Diocesan Times, 0383-6509.*

CN/0228-9229
**CALGARY EVANGELICAL DIRECTORY.** [Calgary evang. dir.]. (1975)-. Directory. English. an. $2.00 per issue. Christian News Inc., 8734 61st Avenue, Edmonton Alta T6E 5P6 Canada. **Tel** (403)468-6408. **DD** 280/.025/71233.

CN/0319-3829
**CALGARY Y F C FOCUS.** ***Title Change.*** **Main/Corp** Calgary Youth for Christ. Sept./Oct. 1970-. Periodical. English. ir. Calgary Youth for Christ, PO Box 6151, Station D, Calagry Alta. T2P 2C8. **DD** 269. ***Superseded by** Focus on Calgary Youth for Christ, 0319-3837.*

US/0008-1795
**CALVIN THEOLOGICAL JOURNAL.** [Calvin theol. j.]. **Added/Corp** Calvin Theological Seminary. Vol. 1 (April 1966)-. Periodical. English. sa. $15.00 (one year), $24.00 (two year), $30.00 (three year). Calvin Theological Seminary, 3233 Burton Street Southeast, Grand Rapids MI 49506. **Tel** (616)957-6044, FAX (616)957-8621. **ED** John Bolt. **LC** BR1; .C14. **DD** 200./5. Index available. cum. index. **Bk Rev. Circ:** 2,700. available on microfilm and microfiche from University Microfilms International (UMI).
**Ind/Abst** Christ. Period. Index; Index Book Rev. Relig.; Int. Zeitschriftenschau Bibelwissenschaft Grenzgeb.; New Testam. Abstr.; Old Testam. Abstr.; Relig. Index One Period. (1966-); Relig. Theol. Abstr.

UK/0961-7272
**CALVINISM TODAY.** ***Title Change.*** [Calvin. today]. (1991)-(1994). Periodical. English. qt. Calvinism Today, PO Box 1, New Yorkshire Y021 111P England. **Tel** 11 44 947 810854, FAX 11 44 742 750822. ***Continued by** Christianity and Society.*

CN/0008-2988
**CANADIAN BAPTIST, THE.** [Can. Baptist]. **Added/Corp** Baptist Convention of Ontario and Quebec. Baptist Union of Western Canada. Vol. 7 (1860)-. Periodical. English. Ten times a year. 16.82Can$ (1 year), 28.04Can$ (2 year) US; 18.00Can$ (1 year), 30.00Can$ (2 year) other. Canadian Baptist, 195 The West Mall, Suite 414, Etobicake, Ontario M9C 5K1 Canada. **Tel** (416)821-3533, FAX (416)922-4369. **ED** Larry Matthews. Index available. **Bk Rev**, (Qty: 2). **Ad Acc, Adv Mgr:** Don Besler. **Pr Rev. Circ:** 15,000. available on microfiche from Micromedia Limited. ***Continues** Christian Messenger; **Absorbed** Western Baptist.*
**Desc:** A platform for discussion regarding Canadian Baptist beliefs.
**Ind/Abst** Can. Index; Can. Period. Index (19??-).

CN/0828-6930
**CANADIAN CHALLENGE.** (CANADIAN CHALLENGE / CAMPUS CRUSADE FOR CHRIST OF CANADA.). [Can. chall.]. Vol. 1, No. 1 (Spring 1984)-. Periodical. English. qt. Campus Crusade for Christ of Canada, PO Box 368, Abbotsford BC V2S 4N9 Canada. **DD** 267/.61. ***Continues** Canadian Report (Abbotsford, B.C.), 0821-6339.*

CN/0008-3410
**CANADIAN DISCIPLE.** [Can. disciple]. **Added/Corp** Disciples of Christ (Canada). (193?)-. Periodical. English. Four times a year (Mar., June, Sept., Dec.). 8.50Can$ Canada; 11.90Can$ other. Canadian Disciple, PO Box 64, Guelph Ont N1H 6J6 Canada. **Tel** (519)823-5190, FAX (519)823-5190. **ED** Stanley L. Litke (phone: (403)256-3280). **Bk Rev**, (Qty: varies). **Circ:** 600 (ctrl).
**Desc:** This is the official publication of the Christian Church (disciples of Christ) in Canada. Editor chooses subjects of religious and social action plus church news.

CN/0227-8782
**CANADIAN ECUMENICAL NEWS.** [Can. ecum. news]. **Added/Corp** Canadian Ecumenical Action. **VFOAT** B.C. Ecumenical News. Vol. 5, No. 1 (Feb. 1980)-. Periodical. English. Five times a year. 5.00Can$. Canadian Ecumenical News, 385 Boundary Road, Vancouver British Columbia V5T 4S1 Canada. **Tel** (604)291-1865. **DD** 262/.0011. ***Continues** Ecumenical News, 0227-8243.*

CN/0382-7658
**CANADIAN FRIEND, THE.** **Added/Corp** Society of Friends (Canada). (1903)-. Periodical. English. bm. 18.00Can$ Canada; 23.00Can$ other. Canadian Friend, Argenta Friends Press, Argenta British Columbia V0G 1B0, Canada. **Tel** (604)366-4314. **ED** Dorothy Parshall. **Circ:** 1,000.
**Desc:** Lively exchange of Quaker (Religious Society of Friends) news and thought.
**Ind/Abst** Peace Res. Abstr. J. (1961-1969, 1975-1976).

CN/0316-2907
**CANADIAN GIDEON.** (THE CANADIAN GIDEON.). [Can. Gideon]. **Added/Corp** Gideons International in Canada. Vol. 12 (Feb. 1955)-. Periodical. Multiple languages (English and French). Six times a year. 8.50Can$ Canada; $6.30 US. Gideons International in Canada, 501 Imperial Road North, Guelph Ontario N1H 7A2 Canada. **Tel** (519)823-1140. **ED** Henry Braun and Mark Fowke. **Circ:** 4,200 (ctrl). ***Continues** Torch and Trumpet, 0316-2915.*
**Desc:** An in-house publication for the encouragement, motivation and education of association members.

CN/0045-544X
**CANADIAN THEOSOPHIST, THE.** **Added/Corp** Theosophical Society in Canada. (Mar. 1920)-. Periodical. English. Six times a year. 9.00Can$. Theosophical Society in Canada, R R No. 3 Burk's Falls, Ontario POA 1CO Canada. **Tel** (705)382-6012. **ED** S. Treloar. Index available in last issue of volume--attached. **Bk Rev. Circ:** 500.
**Desc:** Covers theosophy, comparative religion, philosophy, science, etc.

CN/0527-9860
**CANADIAN UNITARIAN, THE.** V. 1- Summer 1957-. Periodical. English. ir (five issues per year). 0.15Can$ per issue. Canadian Unitarian Council, 175 St Clair Avenue West, Toronto Ontario M4V 1P7 Canada. **Tel** (416)921-4506. **ED** Brian Kiely. **Circ:** 5,000.
**Desc:** National newsletter of Canadian Unitarians and Universalists.

BL
**CANCHIM : RESUMOS INFORMATIVOS.** **See** Religion and Theology-Catholicism.

UK/0008-5650
**CANON LAW ABSTRACTS.** **See** Religion and Theology-Abstracting, Bibliographies and Statistics.

US/0008-5898
**CAPITAL VOICE.** Periodical. English. mo. $3.00. National Bible Knowledge Association, 200 Laurel Street, Culpeper VA 22701.

US/0739-3113
**CARE CASSETTES.** (CARE CASSETTES [SOUND RECORDING].). **Added/Corp** College of Chaplains. (19??)-. Periodical. English. mo. $62.40. College of Chaplains, 1701 East Woodfield Road, Suite 311, Schaumburg IL 60173. **Tel** (708)240-1014. Index available (Free).

TR
**CARIBBEAN CONTACT.** ***Ceased.*** **Added/Corp** Caribbean Conference of Churches. **VFOAT** Contact. (19??)-(19??). Periodical. English (French and Spanish). mo. Caribbean Contact Ltd, PO Box 616, Bridgetown Barbados West Indies. **Tel** (809)427-2681. **ED** Chamberlain M Hope. **LC** F2155; .C3635. **DD** 972.9/005. **Bk Rev. Ad Acc.** ctrl circ.
**Desc:** Analyses of social, political economical and cultural happenings in the Caribbean and abroad.
**Ind/Abst** Hum. Rights Intern. Rep.

JM/0253-066X
**CARIBBEAN JOURNAL OF RELIGIOUS STUDIES.** [Caribb. j. relig. stud.]. **Added/Corp** United Theological College of the West Indies. Vol. 1 (Sept. 1975)-. Periodical. English (French, Spanish and Dutch). sa. 65.00Jam$ Jamaica; $10.00 US. United Theological College West Indies, PO Box 136, Golding Avenue, Kingston 7 Jamaica. **Tel** (809)927-2868. **(Subscription address:** The Press - University of West Indies, 1A Aqueduct Flats, Mona Campus, Kingston 7 Jamaica.**) ED** Dr. Howard Gregory. **LC** BR1; .C158. **DD** 200/.5. Index available. **Circ:** 500.
**Desc:** Research on religious issues done especially by Caribbean scholars and persons involved in pastoral work in the region or in other Third World situations.
**Ind/Abst** Index Book Rev. Relig.; Relig. Index One Period. (1975-).

US
**CARING : THE BENEVOLENCES STORY.** Vol. 1 (1960)-. English (Spanish). Nine times a year. Free. Assemblies of God Archives, 1445 Boonville Avenue, Springfield MO 65802-1894. **Tel** (417)862-2781, (417)862-1447, FAX (417)862-8558. **ED** Owen Wilkie. **Circ:** 50,000 (ctrl).
**Desc:** Articles deal exclusively with the National Benevolences Department of The Assemblies of God.

US
**CARMELITE DIGEST.** **Added/Corp** Discalced Carmelites. California-Arizona Province. Vol. 1, No. 1 (Winter 1986)-. English. qt (Jan., Apr., July, Oct.). $15.00 (one year), $28.00 (two year), $41.00 (three year). Carmelite Digest, PO Box 3180, San Jose CA 95156. **Tel** (408)251-1361. **(Subscription address:** Resource Publishers Inc, 160 E Virgina Street, Suite 290, San Jose CA 95112.**) DD** 282.

US/0008-672X
**CAROLINA CHRISTIAN.** (19??)-. Periodical. English. mo. $8.00 (one year), $15.00 (two year), $22.00 (three year). Carolina Christian Publications, Route 2 Box 137, Conover NC 28613. **ED** Johnny R. Melton (editor's address: 3305 12th Avenue Place Southeast, Conover, NC 28613-9609). **Bk Rev**, (Qty: 15-20). **Ad Acc, Adv Mgr Tel** (704)465-6739. **Circ:** 2,000. ***Continues** Carolina Messenger of Truth.*

CN/0824-2062
**CATALYST / CITIZENS FOR PUBLIC JUSTICE.** **See** Political Science.

US/1040-659X
**CATECHUMENATE (CHICAGO, ILL.).** (CATECHUMENATE.). [Catechumenate]. Vol. 9, No. 3 (Jan. 1987)-. Periodical. English. bm (6 issues). $20.00 US; $25.00 other. Liturgy Training Publications, 1800 North Hermitage Avenue, Chicago IL 60622. **Tel** (312)486-8970, (800)933-1800, FAX (800)933-7094. **ED** Victoria Tufano. **DD** 282. ***Continues** Chicago Catechumenate.*

US/0008-7874
**CATHEDRAL AGE.** **See** Architecture.

GY
**CATHOLIC STANDARD.** (19??)-. Periodical. English. wk. **LC** BX1476.A1; C37. **DD** 282/.881. **Ind/Abst** Hum. Rights Intern. Rep.

SI/0129-9891
**CCA NEWS / CHRISTIAN CONFERENCE OF ASIA.** **Added/Corp** Christian Conference of Asia. **VFOAT** Christian Conference of Asia CCA News; News. **VAT** Christian Conference of Asia News. (19??)-. Periodical. English. mo. HK$55.00 Hong Kong; $14.00 (air mail) Asia; $10.00 (surface mail), $21.00 (air mail) other. Christian Conference of Asia / Hong Kong, 96 District 2 Pak Tim Village, Mei Tim Road, Shatin Hong Kong. **Tel** 011 852 6911068, FAX 011 852 6924378, telex 37618. **ED** Godfrey Raymond Karat. Index available. **Bk Rev.** **Ind/Abst** Hum. Rights Intern. Rep.

SZ
**CCPD ACTIVITY REPORT.** **Main/Corp** World Council of Churches. Commission on the Churches' Participation in Development. English. Commission on the Churches' Participation in Development, World Council of Churches, 150 Route de Ferney, 1211 Geneva 20 Switzerland. **LC** BR115.U6; W67A. **DD** 261.8.
**Desc:** Puts emphasis on study, reflection and education, on enpowerment of the poor and the oppressed, and on communication.

US
**CD WORLDLIBRARY : THE INTERACTIVE BIBLICAL LIBRARY. CD-ROM.** English. sa. $595.00. CDWord Library Inc, PO Box 803133, Dallas TX 75380-3133. **Tel** (214)770-2414, FAX (214)770-2345. ***Continues*** *CDWord.*
**Desc:** Merges two technologies in an single Biblical studies CD-ROM package: hypertext and interactive concording. The technology permits anyone to explore Biblical texts and reference tools without having intimate knowledge of the original languages nor the paths normally traced by the Biblical scholar.

AT
**CELEBRATE.** 1970-. Periodical. English. bm. 10.95Aus$. Dove Communications, 60-64 Railway Road, Box 316, Blackburn Victoria 3130 Australia. **Tel** (03)877-1333, FAX (03)894-1352. **ED** Madeleine Wright. **Circ:** 5,041 (ctrl).
**Desc:** Junior secondary level religious education magazine: comments, stories, reflections, activities, liturgy-oriented and doctrine-based.

US
**CELEBRATE LIFE.** (19??)-. English. Six times a year. Free to libraries; $12.95 others. American Life League, PO Box 1350, Stafford VA 22555. **Tel** (703)659-4171, FAX (703)659-2586. ***Continues*** *ALL About Issues, 0733-1231.*

CN/0843-2538
**CELEBRATE! (OTTAWA).** (CELEBRATE!). [Celebrate!]. **Added/Corp** Novalis (Firm). Vol. 27, No. 1 (Jan./Feb. 1988)-. Periodical. English. bm. $24.00 (one year), $46.00 (three year). Novalis, PO Box 990, Outremont Quebec H2V 4S7 Canada. **Tel** (514)948-1222. **ED** Jerome Herauf. **DD** 264/.02/005. **Circ:** 2,443. ***Continues*** *Homiletic Service, 0381-7466.*

US/0889-0765
**CENTER FOCUS.** (CENTER FOCUS : NEWS FROM THE CENTER OF CONCERN.). [Cent. focus]. **Added/Corp** Center of Concern (Washington, D.C.). (197?)-. Periodical. English. bm (6 issues). Free. Center of Concern, 3700 13th Street NW, Washington DC 20017. **Tel** (202)635-2757. **DD** 261.
**Ind/Abst** Hum. Rights Intern. Rep.

NE
**CENTRAALWEEKBLAD.** Centraal Weekblad, Antwoordnummer 119, 8900VC Leeuwarden Netherlands.

CN/0821-4107
**CENTRAL THEMES.** (CENTRAL THEMES : A QUARTERLY BULLETIN OF CENTRAL PENTECOSTAL COLLEGE.). [Cent. themes]. **Main/Corp** Central Pentecostal College. Bulletin. English. qt. Central Pentecostal College, 1303 Jackson Avenue, Saskatoon Saskatchewan S7H 2M9 Canada. **Tel** 374-6655. **ED** J Harry Faught. **DD** 207/.71242. **Ad Acc. Circ:** 1,500.
**Desc:** Alumni news and current events of Central Pentecostal Colleges. News and needs expressed to friends of the college.

CN/1184-9827
**CFCM REPORT.** [CFCM rep.]. **Added/Corp** Canadian Fellowship of Churches and Ministers. **VFOAT** Canadian Fellowship of Churches and Ministers Report. No. 1 (1991)-. Periodical. English. Canadian Fellowship of Churches and Ministers, 2202 Speers Avenue, Saskatoon Sask. S7L 5X7 Canada. **DD** 269. ***Continues*** *Canada Arise., 0843-0942.*

HK
**CGST JOURNAL.** Chinese (English). sa. $17.00 Hong Kong and Asia; $25.00 other. China Graduate School of Theology, 5 Devon Road, Kowloon Tong Hong Kong. **Tel** 011 852 3374106, FAX 011 852 3385934. **ED** Wilson Chow and Esther Ng. Index available. cum. index. **Bk Rev. Pr Rev. Circ:** 1,000.
**Desc:** Each issue comprises three sections: articles, book reviews and theological news. Articles deal with biblical exegesis, theological topics, historical and contemporary issues from a Christian perspective and Christianity among the Chinese.

US/1062-1849
**CHALLENGE (WASHINGTON, D.C. 1989).** (CHALLENGE.). [Challenge]. **Added/Corp** Ecumenical Program on Central America and the Caribbean. Center for Educational Design and Communication. Vol. 1, No. 1 (Aug. 1989)-. Periodical. English. bm. $50.00 institutions; $30.00 individuals. Challenge / Israel, PO Box 32107, Jerusalem 91320 Israel. **Tel** 011 972 2 255382, FAX 011 972 2 251614. **DD** 230. **Bk Rev**, (Qty: 12). **Circ:** 2,000.
**Desc:** For the international community concerned with a solution to the Palestinian-Israeli conflict.

US/0744-4079
**CHANNELS (NEWBURY PARK, CALIF.).** (CHANNELS.). Periodical. English. qt. Channels It Is Written, PO Box O, Thousand Oaks CA 91360. **Tel** (805)373-7733, telex 65-9245. **ED** Steven R Mosley. **Circ:** 60,000 (ctrl).
**Desc:** Publishes news related to the It Is Written Ministry. Includes descriptions of upcoming programs and articles of general interest on the Christian life.

US/0895-7916
**CHAPLAINCY TODAY.** [Chaplain. today]. **Added/Corp** College of Chaplains. Vol. 1, No. 1 (March/April 1986)-. Periodical. English. bm. $20.00 (one year), $37.00 (two year). College of Chaplains, 1701 East Woodfield Road, Suite 311, Schaumburg IL 60173. **Tel** (708)240-1014. **DD** 253. **Ad Acc.**

US/0895-156X
**CHARISMA AND CHRISTIAN LIFE.** [Charism. Christ. life]. **VFOAT** Charisma & Christian Life; Charisma. Vol. 12, No. 11 (June 1987)-. Periodical. English (Spanish). Twelve times a year. $16.97 (one year); $26.97 9two years); $36.97 (three years). Strang Communications Company, 600 Rinehart Road, Lake Mary FL 32746. **Tel** (407)333-0600, FAX (407)333-9753. **(Subscription address:** Kable Publishers Aide, 308 East Hitt Street, Subscription Department, Mt. Morris IL 61054-1473.**)** **ED** Lee Grady. **LC** BV4485; .C36. **DD** 270.8/2/05. **Bk Rev. Ad Acc, Adv Mgr:** Bob Minotti, **Tel** (407)333-0600. **Circ:** 200,000. available in microform from Xerox; available on microfilm and microfiche from University Microfilms International (UMI). ***Formed by the union of*** *Charisma, 0279-0424* ***and*** *Christian Life, 0009-5427.*
**Desc:** The magazine for dynamic Christian living in today's world.
**Ind/Abst** Christ. Period. Index (1987-).

AT
**CHECKPOINT.** **Added/Corp** War Control Planners. (1972)-. English. Five times a year. 10.00Aus$ Australia; 20.00Aus$ other. Church Missionary Society of Australia, 93 Bathurst Street, Sydney New South Wales 2000 Australia. **Tel** 011 41 61 2 2846777, FAX 011 41 61 2 2673626. **ED** Diana McIntosh. **Circ:** 7,500 (ctrl).
**Desc:** Content mainly on Christian mission, both overseas and in North Australia. Articles, news items, and pictures.

US/0739-5124
**CHICAGO THEOLOGICAL SEMINARY REGISTER, THE.** **Main/Corp** Chicago Theological Seminary. Vol. 1 (Mar. 1908)-. Periodical. English. Three times a year (Fall, Winter, and Spring). $4.00. The Register / Illinois, 5757 South University Avenue, Chicago IL 60637. **Tel** (312)752-5757 ext.264. **ED** Perry LeFevre. **LC** BV4070; .C413. **DD** 207.773. **Bk Rev. Circ:** 4,000.
**Desc:** Includes annual report, alumni news, news issue and catalogue.
**Ind/Abst** Index Book Rev. Relig.; Relig. Index One Period.; Relig. Theol. Abstr.

US/1054-1144
**CHILDREN'S MINISTRY.** [Child. minist.]. Vol. 1, No. 1 (Mar./Apr. 1991)-. Periodical. English. bm (Jan., Mar., May, July, Sept., Nov.). $24.95. Group Publishing, PO Box 481, c/o Shelia Augustine, Loveland CO 80539. **Tel** (303)669-3836, FAX (303)669-3269. **ED** Rick Lawrence. **DD** 649. **Bk Rev**, (Qty: 20-30). **Ad Acc, Adv Mgr:** Larry Boryour, **Tel** (303)669-3836. **Circ:** 34,000.
**Desc:** For adults who work in churches with children from birth to 6th grade. Contains crafts, games, resources, articles, bible adventures etc.

CN/0828-1602
**CHINA AND OURSELVES.** (CHINA AND OURSELVES : NEWSLETTER OF THE CANADA CHINA PROGRAMME.). [China ourselves]. **Added/Corp** Canada China Program. **VFOAT** Hui Tan Chung-Kuo. No. 1 (May 1976)-. Newsletter. English (Chinese and French). Four times a year (Seasonally). 10.00Can$ Canada; 12.00Can$ other. Canada China Program, 129 St Clair Avenue East, Toronto Ontario M4V 1N5 Canada. **Tel** (416)921-1923, FAX (416)921-3843. **ED** Cynthia K. McLean. **DD** 275.1/082. **Bk Rev. Pr Rev. Circ:** 250 (ctrl).
**Desc:** This newsletter reports events involving Canada and China, and promotes understanding of China informed by Christian faith.
**Ind/Abst** Hum. Rights Intern. Rep.

US/0009-4412
**CHINA NOTES.** ***Ceased.*** **Added/Corp** National Council of the Churches of Christ in the United States of America. Division of Overseas Ministries. East Asia Office. National Council of the Churches of Christ in the United States of America. Division of Foreign Missions. China Committee. National Council of the Churches of Christ in the United States of America. Division of Overseas Ministries. China Committee. National Council of the Churches of Christ in the United States of America. Division of Overseas Ministries. East Asia Dept. Vol. 1 (Sept. 1962)-Vol. 30 (1992). Periodical. English. qt. China Notes, Room 616/475 Riverside Drive, New York NY 10027. **Tel** (212)870-2372. **ED** Franklin J Woo. **LC** WMLC L 83/1494. **Bk Rev. Circ:** 1,000. ***Continues*** *National Council of the Churches of Christ in the United States of America. Division of Foreign Missions. Far Eastern Office. China Bulletin of the Far Eastern Office, 0529-3146.*
**Desc:** Current developments and relationships of Chinese christian churches inside and outside of the Chinese society, religion and culture.

UK/0956-4314
**CHINA STUDY JOURNAL.** (1986)-. English. Three times a year. £10.00 (individuals), £15.00 (institutions) UK; £15.00 (individuals), £20.00 (institutions) other. China Study Project, 35-41 Lower Marsh, Inter-Church, London SE1 7RL England. **Tel** 011 44 1 620-4444. **ED** Edmond Tang. **Bk Rev. Circ:** 300. ***Continues*** *China Study Project Journal.*
**Desc:** Scholarly articles on religion in China and documentation of China publications on the subject and some political and social items.

HK/1011-2979
**CHINESE AROUND THE WORLD.** [Chinese around world]. (1979)-. Periodical. English. mo. Free. Chinese Coordination Center of World Evangelism, PO Box 98435, Tsimshatsui Hong Kong. **Tel** 011 852 3 910411.

US/1056-358X
**CHINESE OUR MISSIONS WORLD.** **Added/Corp** Southern Baptist Convention. Woman's Missionary Union. **VFOAT** Chuan Tao Tien Ti. (1991)-. Periodical. English (Chinese and English). mo. Woman's Missionary Union, PO Box 830010, Birmingham AL 35283. **Tel** (205)991-8100, (205)991-4933.

US/0896-7660
**CHINESE THEOLOGICAL REVIEW.** [Chin. theol. rev.]. **Added/Corp** Tung Nan Ya Shen Hsueh Chiao Yu Chi Chin Hui. (1985)-. Periodical. English (translations available in Chinese). an. $10.00 (one year), $18.00 (two year), $25.00 (three year). Foundation for Theological Education, 86 East 12th Street, Holland MI 49423. **Tel** (616)399-9585, FAX (616)392-7717. **ED** Janice Wickeri. **DD** 230. **Bk Rev.**
**Ind/Abst** Index Book Rev. Relig.; Relig. Index One Period.; Relig. Theol. Abstr. (199?-).

HK/0009-4668
**CHING FENG (ENGLISH EDITION).** (CHING FENG.). [Ching feng]. **Added/Corp** Christian Study Centre on Chinese Religion and Culture. Vol. 1 (Winter 1964)-. Periodical. English (Chinese). qt. $24.00 (sea mail); $28.00 (air mail). Christian Study Centre on China Religion and Culture, Sixth Floor Kiu Kin Mansion, 566 Nathan Road, Kowloon Hong Kong. **Tel** 011 852 3 7703310, FAX 011 852 3 7826869. **ED** Peter K.H. Lee. **LC** WMLC L 83/3796. **DD** 291. Index available. **Bk Rev. Ad Acc. Circ:** 1,000 (ctrl). available on microfilm and microfiche from University Microfilms International (UMI); available on CD-ROM. ***Continues*** *Quarterly Notes on Christianity and Chinese Religion.*
**Desc:** Devoted to the contextualization of Christian thought in China and also in the Asian setting and deals with the encounter of Christianity with Chinese religions and culture.
**Ind/Abst** Bibliogr. Mission.; Index Book Rev. Relig.; Int. Bibliogr. Sociol.; Missionalia; Relig. Index One Period. (1978-); Relig. Theol. Abstr. (19??-).

GW/0170-5148
**CHRIST IN DER GEGENWART.** [Christ Ggw.]. (1967)-. Periodical. German. wk. DM91.00. Verlag Herder Freiburg, Postfach 79080, Frieburg, Germany. **Tel** (0761)27-17-0, FAX (0761)27 17-520, telex 761489. **ED** M. Plate, K. Janssen, J. Roser. ***Continues*** *Der Christliche Sonntag, 0170-513X.*

FR/0750-2087
**CHRIST SEUL.** **Added/Corp** Eglises Evangeliques Mennonites de France. (June 1907)-. Periodical. French. ir (Aug./Sept. combined). $50.00. Christ Seul, 3 Route de Grand-Charmont, 25200 Montbeliard France. **Tel** 011 33 81 945914. ***Continues*** *Bulletin de la Conference des Eglises Evangeliques Mennonites de France.*

IT/0011-1465
**CHRIST TO THE WORLD.** [Christ world]. Vol. 1 (1955)-. Periodical. English (French). bm. L35000 (Europe); $30.00 (other). Christ to the World, Via di

Propaganda 1-C, Rome 00187 Italy. **Tel** 06 6793226. **ED** Basil Mary Arthadeva. Index available. **Bk Rev. Circ:** 5,000.
**Desc:** Directives of the Pope on the appropriate experiences of mission and parish, and work problems of current doctrinal errors.
**Ind/Abst** Abr. Cathol. Period. Lit. Index; Cathol. Period. Lit. Index.

US/0746-8253
**CHRISTADELPHIAN ADVOCATE, THE.** Periodical. English. mo. $7.50 US; $8.00 Canada. Christadelphian Advocate Publishing Committee, 2506 Huntington Road, Charlottesville VA 22901.

GE/0009-5192
**CHRISTENLEHRE, DIE.** Vol. 1, No. 1 (April 1948)-. Periodical. German. Twelve times a year. DM84.00 Germany; DM98.00 other. Evangel Verlagsanstalt Gmbh, Postfach 1467, D 04025 Leipzig Germany. **Tel** 011 49 341 7114122, FAX 49 341 295383.

UK
**CHRISTIAN.** (1989)-. Periodical. English. bm. £17.00 US and Canada. Morgan & Scott Publications, 3 Beggarwood Lane, Basingstoke Hants RG23 7LP England. **LC** BV4485; .C435. **DD** 205. ***Continues*** *Christian.*

US/8756-9930
**CHRISTIAN ACTIVIST, THE.** ***Ceased.*** (THE CHRISTIAN ACTIVIST : A SCHAEFFER V PRODUCTIONS NEWSLETTER.). [Christ. act.]. Vol. 1, No. 1 (Spring 1984)-?. Newsletter. English. qt. Schaeffer V Productions, PO Box 33283, Los Gatos CA 95031-3383. **DD** 261.

US/0883-4210
**CHRISTIAN ACTIVITIES CALENDAR (MIDDLE ATLANTIC ED.).** (CHRISTIAN ACTIVITIES CALENDAR.). **VFOAT** Calendar. (19??)-. Periodical. English. Six times a year. $14.95 (two years). Christian Activities Calendar, PO Box 730, Ojai CA 93023. **Tel** (805)646-4382. **Bk Rev. Ad Acc. Circ:** 20,000 (ctrl).

●US/1062-970X
**CHRISTIAN ADVOCATE (AUSTIN, TEX.).** (CHRISTIAN ADVOCATE.). [Christ. advocate]. **Added/Corp** Faith Communication Ministries. Vol. 1, No. 1 (May 1992)-. Periodical. English. mo. $10.00. Faith Communication Ministries, Inc., PO Box 309, Del Valle TX 78617. **DD** 248.

US/1064-1602
**CHRISTIAN ANTHROPOLOGY.** **See** Anthropology.

UK/0264-598X
**CHRISTIAN ARENA.** [Christ. arena]. (1983)-. Periodical. English. qt. £6.00. U C C F Subscriptions Dept, 38 De Montfort Street, Leicester LE1 7GP England. **Tel** 011 44 533 551700. **DD** 205. ***Continues*** *Christian Graduate, 0045-6802.*

US/0009-5265
**CHRISTIAN BEACON.** ***Suspended.*** [Christ. beac.]. Vol. 1 (Feb. 13, 1936)-Suspended (Feb. 1990). Periodical. English. wk. $12.00. Christian Beacon, 756 Haddon Avenue, Collingswood NJ 08108. **Tel** (609)858-0700. **ED** C McIntire.

US/1058-8558
**CHRISTIAN BEGINNINGS.** [Christ. begin.]. Vol. 1, No. 1 (Oct. 1990)-. Periodical. English. Five times a year. $19.95 US; $22.00 other. Our Sunday Visitor Inc., 200 Noll Plaza, Box 920, Huntington IN 46750. **Tel** (219)356-8400, (800)348-2440, FAX (219)356-8472. **ED** Beth McNamara. **DD** 268. **Bk Rev. Circ:** 2,500.
**Desc:** A periodical of original articles, ideas, and stories from religious educators throughout the country. Also includes articles to help fine-tune teaching skills as well as articles to improve teaching effectiveness.

NE/1380-3603
**CHRISTIAN BIOETHICS.** (199?)-. Periodical. English. Three times a year. Fl250.00 (institution). Swets & Zeitlinger BV, Heereweg 347B PO Box 825, 2160 SZ Lisse Holland. **Tel** 011 31 2521 35111, FAX 02521-15888, telex 41325. **(Subscription address:** Swets & Zeitlinger BV, P.O. Box 825, 2160 SZ LISSE, Holland**)**

UK/0306-7467
**CHRISTIAN BRETHREN REVIEW : THE JOURNAL OF THE CHRISTIAN BRETHREN RESEARCH FELLOWSHIP.** **Added/Corp** Christian Brethren Research Fellowship. **VFOAT** Christian Brethren Review Journal. Nos. 31, 32 (Feb. 1982)-. Periodical. English. Twice a year. £18.00 UK; £15.00 other. Paternoster Press, A division of Send the Light Ltd., PO Box 300, Kingstown Broadway, Cumbria CA3 0QS England. **Tel** 011 44 228 512512, FAX 011 44 228 514949. **LC** BX8799; .C47. **DD** 289.9. **Circ:** 1,000. available on CD-ROM. ***Continues*** *Journal of the Christian Brethren Research Fellowship.*
**Desc:** Analysis of current trends and movements; aims to develop church ministries in context of forward-looking "Plymouth" Brethren thought and action.
**Ind/Abst** Index Book Rev. Relig.; Relig. Index One Period.; Relig. Theol. Abstr. (199?-).

AT/0312-9519
**CHRISTIAN BROTHERS STUDIES.** **See** Education.

US/0009-5281
**CHRISTIAN CENTURY (1902), THE.** (THE CHRISTIAN CENTURY.). [Christ. century]. **Added/Corp** Christian Century Company. Disciples Publication Society. Christian Century Press. Christian Century Foundation. Vol. 19, No. 1 (Jan. 2, 1902)-. Periodical. English. Forty times a year. $35.00. Christian Century Foundation, 407 South Dearborn Street, Suite 1405, Chicago IL 60605. **Tel** (312)427-2714, (312)427-5380, FAX (312)427-1302. **ED** James M Wall, David Heim, Gretchen Ziegenhals, Victoria Rebeck, Martin E Marty, Dean Peerman, Mark R Halton. **LC** BR1; .C45. **DD** 261. Index available. **Bk Rev. Ad Acc. Circ:** 38,000. available on microfilm and microfiche from University Microfilms International (UMI). Documents available from UMI Article Clearinghouse, Magazine Collection. ***Continues*** *Christian Century of the Disciples of Christ;* ***Absorbed*** *Christian Work (New York, N.Y. : 1914); Baptist; World Tomorrow, 0364-8583; New Christian.*
**Desc:** An ecumenical journal of opinion and news with a broad approach to topics of religion, culture and world affairs.
**Ind/Abst** Acad. Abstr. Full Text Elite (Jan. 1989-); Acad. Abstr. (Jan. 1989-); Acad. Ind. [Computer File] (1984-); Acad. Search (Jan. 1989-); Am. Hist. Life (1954-1956); Annu. Bibliogr. Engl. Lang. Lit.; Book Rev. Digest; Book Rev. Index; Curr. Thoughts Trends; Expand. Acad. Index (1984-); Film Lit. Index; Gen. Period. Index (1985-); Guide Soc. Sci. Relig.; Humanit. Source (Jan. 1989-); Index Am. Period. Verse; Index Book Rev. Relig.; INFO-SOUTH Abstr.; Mag. Artic. Summar. Elite (Jan. 1989-); Mag. Artic. Summar. Select (Jan. 1989-); Mag. Artic. Summar. CD-ROM (Jan. 1989-); Mag. Express (1986-) [Full Txt.]; Mag. Index Plus (1989-); Mag. Index Sel. Microfiche (1989-) [Full Txt.]; Mag. Index. Sel. (1986-); Mag. Search; Med. Rev. Dig.; Middle East Abstr. Index; Newsp. Period. Abstr. (1986-); Peace Res. Abstr. J. (1969-1983); Read. Guide Abstr. Select Ed.; Read. Guide Period. Lit.; Relig. Index One Period. (1972-); Relig. Theol. Abstr.; Resource/One Ondisc; Mag. Index (1977-); TOM Gen. Index (1985-) [Full Txt.].

CN/0009-5303
**CHRISTIAN COMMUNICATIONS.** [Christ. commun.]. V. 1- Dec. 1962-. Periodical. English. qt. $2.00. St Paul University, 223 Main Street, Ottawa Ontario K1S 1C4 Canada. **Tel** (613)236-1393 ext. 2294, FAX (613)236-5278. available on microfilm from University Microfilms International (UMI).

US/1043-1225
**CHRISTIAN COMMUNICATOR, THE.** [Christ. commun.]. Jan. (1989)-. Periodical. English. mo. $19.95 (one year), $37.95 (two years), $49.95 (three years). Joy Publishing, PO Box 827, San Juan Capistrano CA 92693. **Tel** (714)493-8161, FAX (714)493-6552. **DD** 808. ***Continues*** *Inspirational Writer, 0899-1790.*
**Desc:** This publication contains the tools to help you strengthen your writing skills.

UK
**CHRISTIAN COMMUNITY : A JOURNAL FOR THE NEW AGE OF CHRISTIANITY PUBLISHED BY THE CHRISTIAN COMMUNITY IN GREAT BRITAIN, THE.** No. 1 (Jan./Feb. 1970)-. Periodical. English.

US/0145-3297
**CHRISTIAN COMMUNITY (COLUMBUS), THE.** (THE CHRISTIAN COMMUNITY.). [Christ. community]. **Added/Corp** Council of Community Churches. International Council of Community Churches. Vol. 1 (1949)-. Periodical. English. Eight times a year. $14.00. International Council of Community Churches, 7808 College Dr./Suite #2SE, Palos Heights IL 60463-1027. **Tel** (312)798-2264. **ED** J Ralph Shotwell. **DD** 250. **Bk Rev. Ad Acc.**
**Desc:** News and views of postdenominational Christianity and ecumenism.

UK
**CHRISTIAN COMMUNITY : THE MAGAZINE OF THE NATIONAL CENTRE FOR CHRISTIAN COMMUNITIES AND NETWORKS.** (19??)-. English. Three times a year (Mar., July., Nov.). £10.00 UK; £11.00 other. NACCAN, 1046 Bristol Road, Selly Oak, Birmingham B29 6LJ England. **Tel** 011 44 21 472 8079. **ED** Roger Sawtell (editor's address: The Neighbours, 140/148 Ardington Road, Northampton NN15LT, phone: 0604 33918). **Bk Rev. Circ:** 700 (ctrl).
**Desc:** Articles from Christian groups, communities, and networks in the UK and overseas.

US/1063-7672
**CHRISTIAN COMPUTING MAGAZINE.** **See** Computers.

US/0892-9300
**CHRISTIAN CONQUEST.** [Christ. conqu.]. Vol. 1, No. 1 (Jan./Feb. 1987)-. Periodical. English (Spanish). bm. $15.00 (contribution). Charles Simpson Ministries, PO Box Z, Mobile AL 36616. **Tel** (205)633-7900. **ED** Charles Simpson. ctrl circ. ***Continues*** *New Wine, 0194-438X.*
**Desc:** Designed to equip people for action and to help them be conquerors in every area of their lives.

●US/1076-9668
**CHRISTIAN COUNSELING TODAY.** [Christ. couns. today]. **Added/Corp** American Association of Christian Counselors. Vol. 1, No. 1 (Jan. 1993)-. Periodical. English. Four times a year (Jan., Apr., July, Oct.). $35.00. American Association Christian Counselors, 2421 West Pratt, Suite 1398, Chicago IL 60645. **DD** 253. **Bk Rev** (Qty: 12). **Ad Acc, Adv Mgr:** Dawn Emeigh, **Tel** (804)384-0564. **Circ:** 15,000. ***Continues*** *Christian Journal of Psychology and Counseling, 1051-9866.*
**Desc:** News and information on Christian counseling.

US/0195-265X
**CHRISTIAN CRUSADE.** (19??)-. Periodical. English. mo. $5.00 (US & Canada); $7.80 (other). Christian Crusade, PO Box 977, Tulsa OK 74102. **Tel** (918)665-2345. **ED** Billy James Hargis. **Circ:** 38,000. available on microfilm from University Microfilms International (UMI).

TH
**CHRISTIAN DIRECTORY.** **VFOAT** Christian Thailand Directory. Directory. English. 15.00. Suthep Chaviwan, PO Box 1405, Bangkok Thailand. **LC** BR1195; .C45. **DD** 275.93/025.

US/1045-4977
**CHRISTIAN EARLY CHILDHOOD CONNECTION : METHODS AND MATERIALS FOR THE PRE-SCHOOL YEARS.** **See** Education.

US/8756-1751
**CHRISTIAN EDUCATION DIGEST.** [Christ. educ. dig.]. Vol. 1, No. 1 (Fall 1984)-. Periodical. English. Four times a year (Jan., Apr., July. Oct.). Free. Baptist Publishing House, 1319 Magnolia Street, Texarkana TX 75501-4493. **Tel** (214)793-6531. **ED** James L. Silvey. **DD** 207. **Bk Rev. Circ:** 11,000.
**Desc:** Articles related to Christian education at the administrative and classroom levels.

US/0740-1876
**CHRISTIAN EDUCATION INFORMER, THE.** **VFOAT** Informer. Periodical. English. qt. $5.00. National Baptist Convention USA, 330 Charlotte Avenue, Nashville TN 37201. ***Continues*** *Leadership in Action.*

US/0739-8913
**CHRISTIAN EDUCATION JOURNAL.** [Christ. educ. j.]. **Added/Corp** Scripture Press Ministries (U.S.) National Association of Professors of Christian Education (U.S.). Vol. 3, No. 2 (Jan. 1983)-. Periodical. English. Three times a year. $10.00 US; $12.00 other. Scripture Press Ministries, PO Box 650, Glen Ellyn IL 60138. **Tel** (708)260-6440 Ext. 2640, FAX (708)668-3806. **ED** Ronald R. Ramsey. **LC** BV1460; .C485. **DD** 207. Index available (included in Spring issue). cum. index. **Bk Rev**, (Qty: 3 per year). **Pr Rev. Circ:** 2,500. available on microfilm and microfiche from University Microfilms International (UMI); available in microform. ***Continues*** *Journal of Christian Education.*
**Desc:** Designed to promote growth and advancement in the field of Christian education.
**Ind/Abst** Index Book Rev. Relig.; Relig. Index One Period.; Relig. Theol. Abstr.

US/0884-5506
**CHRISTIAN EDUCATION TODAY.** ***Ceased.*** [Christ. educ. today]. Vol. 37, No. 4 (Fall 1985)-(1992). Periodical. English. qt. Accent Publications, 12100 West 6th Avenue, Box 15337, Denver CO 80215. **Tel** (303)988-5300. **ED** James E Burkett Jr and Kenneth O Gangel. **DD** 268. ***Continues*** *Success (Denver, Colo.).*

US/0091-2867
**CHRISTIAN EDUCATOR.** V. 1- May 1973-. Periodical. English. qt. $7.50. Christian Warriors for Christian Education (CWCE), Drawer C, Cape Canaveral FL 32920. **LC** BV1460; .C49. **DD** 207/.73.

US
**CHRISTIAN EDUCATORS JOURNAL.** (19??)-. Periodical. English. qt (Feb., Apr., Oct., Dec.). $7.50 (one year), $15.00 (two year), $21.00 (three year). Christian Educators Journal, 1828 Mayfair Drive Northeast, Grand Rapids MI 49503-3835. **Tel** (616)245-1305, (616)451-3274. **ED** Lorna Van Gilst. cum. index. **Bk Rev. Ad Acc, Adv Mgr:** P. Boogaart. **Circ:** 4,100.
**Desc:** The general purpose is to foster the continuing improvement of educational theory and practice in Christian schools.
**Ind/Abst** Christ. Period. Index; Guide Soc. Sci. Relig.

US
**CHRISTIAN ENDEAVOR LEADER'S MONTHLY, INTERMEDIATE NUMBER.** Periodical. English.

US
**CHRISTIAN ENDEAVOR LEADER'S MONTHLY, JUNIOR NUMBER.** Periodical. English.

US/0009-5338
**CHRISTIAN ENDEAVOR WORLD, THE.** **Added/Corp** International Society of Christian Endeavor. United Society of Christian Endeavor. Vol. 1 (1897)-. Periodical. English. Four times a year. Free to non-profit organizations; $30.00 others. Christian Endeavor International, 3575 Valley Road, Liberty Corner NJ 07938. **Tel** (908)604-9440. **ED** F. E. Clark, A. R. Well, Phyllis I. Rike and David G. Jackson. **LC** BV1420; .C4. ctrl circ. available in microform. ***Continues*** *Golden Rule (1886).*
**Desc:** Report and promote activities of christian endeavor groups in the United States and throughout the world.

IE
**CHRISTIAN EXAMINER AND CHURCH OF IRELAND MAGAZINE, THE.** **VFOAT** Church of Ireland Magazine. (1825)-. Periodical. English. mo. available on microfilm from University Microfilms International (UMI).

US/0279-5310
**CHRISTIAN FAMILY (BLOWNTVILLE, TEX.).** (CHRISTIAN FAMILY.). [Christ. fam.]. **Added/Corp** Life of America Foundation (Dallas, Tex.). (197?)-. Periodical. English. mo. $13.95. Christian Family Publishing Ministry, PO Box 4514, Brownsville TX 78523. **DD** 248.

UK
**CHRISTIAN FAMILY NEW MALDEN.** ***Title Change.*** [Christ. fam. New Malden]. (1986)-(1993). English. Twelve times a year. ***Continues*** *Family (London. 1980), 0144-7696.* ***Continued by*** *Parentwise.*

US/0009-5354
**CHRISTIAN HERALD.** **See** Biographies.

US/0009-5354
**CHRISTIAN HERALD (CHAPPAQUA).** ***Ceased.*** (CHRISTIAN HERALD.). [Christ. her.]. (1901)-(19??). Periodical. English. bm. **LC** BR1; .C63. **DD** 205. ***Continues*** *Christian Herald and Signs of our Times;* ***Absorbed*** *World Outlook, 0190-4345; American Messenger.*
**Ind/Abst** Gen. Period. Index (1985-); Mag. Index (1977-).

UK
**CHRISTIAN HISTORY.** (19??)-. Periodical. English. Four times a year. £15.80 UK; £16.90 other. Paternoster Press, A division of Send the Light Ltd., PO Box 300, Kingstown Broadway, Cumbria CA3 0QS England. **Tel** 011 44 228 512512, FAX 011 44 228 514949.

US/0891-9666
**CHRISTIAN HISTORY (WORCESTER, PA.).** (CHRISTIAN HISTORY.). [Christ. hist.]. **Added/Corp** Christian History Institute. **VFOAT** Christian History Magazine. Vol. 1, No. 1 (1982)-. Academic Scholarly Publication. English. qt. $19.95. Christianity Today Inc., 465 Gundersen Drive, Carol Stream IL 60188. **Tel** (708)260-6200. **(Subscription address:** CDS / SIFD Agency Control, 1901 Bell Avenue, Des Moines IA 50315.**)** **ED** Kevin Miller. **LC** BR140; .C48. **DD** 270/.05. **Circ:** 8,000 (ctrl). available on CD-ROM; available on microfilm and microfiche from University Microfilms International (UMI).
**Desc:** A scholarly readable magazine focusing on issues and significant individuals or topics in Church History to promote greater awareness of our spiritual heritage. Designed for lay people, and scholars or students of Christian history.
**Ind/Abst** Acad. Abstr. Full Text Elite (Jan. 1994-) [Full Txt.]; Acad. Abstr. (Jan. 1994-); Acad. Search (Jan. 1994-); Am. Hist. Life (1985-); Christ. Period. Index (19??-); Mag. Artic. Summar. Elite (Jan. 1994-) [Full Txt.].

●US/1065-8386
**CHRISTIAN HOME JOURNAL, THE.** [Christ. home j.]. No. 1 (Sept./Oct. 1992)-. Periodical. English. bm. $24.00. Flight Development Corporation, 2111 Highland Hills, Sugar Land TX 77478. **DD** 248.

CN/0229-0219
**CHRISTIAN INFO COMMUNIGRAM.** Vol. 1, No. 1 (Jan./Feb. 1981)-. English. $2.00. Christian News Inc., 8734 61st Avenue, Edmonton Alta T6E 5P6 Canada. **Tel** (403)468-6408. **DD** 277.123/3082.

CN
**CHRISTIAN INFO DIRECTORY.** [Chris. info dir.]. **Added/Corp** Christian INFO. (1985)-. Directory. English. an. 10.00Can$. Christian News Inc., 8734 61st Avenue, Edmonton Alta T6E 5P6 Canada. **Tel** (403)468-6408. **DD** 280/.025/71233. **Ad Acc. Circ:** 200. ***Continues*** *Calgary Evangelical Directory, 0228-9229.*

CN/0315-6532
**CHRISTIAN INQUIRER (NATIONAL EDITION).** ***Title Change.*** (CHRISTIAN INQUIRER.). **VFOAT** Inquirer. National Ed. May 1972-. Periodical. English. mo. International Christian Communications, PO Box 339, Ridgeway Ontario L0S 1N0. **DD** 269/.2/05. ***Supersedes*** *Enquirer. National Ed., 0315-6516.* ***Merged with*** *Christian Inquirer. Toronto Ed., 0315-6559* ***to form*** *Christian Inquirer. Canadian Ed., 0383-8773.*

CN/0315-6559
**CHRISTIAN INQUIRER (TORONTO EDITION).** ***Title Change.*** (CHRISTIAN INQUIRER.). **VFOAT** Inquirer. May 1972-. Periodical. English. mo. Christian Inquirer / Canada, PO Box 339, Canada. **DD** 269/.2/05. ***Supersedes*** *Enquirer. Toronto Ed., 0315-6540.* ***Merged with*** *Christian Inquirer. National Ed., 0315-6532* ***to form*** *Christian Inquirer. Canadian Ed., 0383-8773.*

US/1040-8622
**CHRISTIAN IRELAND TODAY.** [Christ. Irel. today]. Periodical. English. mo. Christian Ireland Ministries Inc, PO Box 11057, Albany NY 12211. **Tel** (518)329-3003, FAX (518)329-3003. **ED** Francis G McCloskey and Gary Moorehead. **DD** 274. **Circ:** 475 (ctrl).
**Desc:** Promotes reconciliation in Northern Ireland.

US/1056-3644
**CHRISTIAN JOURNAL (FORT WORTH, TEX.).** (CHRISTIAN JOURNAL.). Vol. 5, No. 1 (April 12, 1963)-. Periodical. English. mo. $6.00 US; $8.00 other. Christian Journal, PO Box 7385, Ft. Worth TX 76111. **Tel** (817)838-2644, FAX (817)595-2737. **ED** J.E. Snelson Jr. **Bk Rev**, (Qty: 6-10). **Ad Acc. Circ:** 9-10,000 (ctrl). ***Continues*** *Fort Worth Christian Journal.*

US/0412-3131
**CHRISTIAN LIBRARIAN (CEDARVILLE, OHIO), THE.** **See** Library and Information Sciences.

US/0739-6422
**CHRISTIAN LIFE COMMUNITIES HARVEST.** [Christ. life communities harvest]. **Added/Corp** National Federation of Christian Life Communities (U.S.). **VFOAT** Harvest. (19??)-. Periodical. English. qt. $15.00. National Federation of Christian Life Communities, 3601 Lindell Blvd, St Louis MO 63108. **Tel** (314)533-3185. **ED** Fred C. Leone (Editor's address: 201 E. Wayne Ave., Silver Spring MD, 20901; Editor's telephone:(301)495-2969). **DD** 248. **[CCC]**. **Bk Rev**, (Qty: 20-25). **Circ:** 800. ***Continues*** *Christian Life Communicator, 0194-6137.*

US/0162-9255
**CHRISTIAN LIVING (ELGIN).** (CHRISTIAN LIVING.). English. qt. $4.25. David C Cook Publishing Company, 850 North Grove Avenue, Elgin IL 60120.

US
**CHRISTIAN MEDICAL & DENTAL SOCIETY JOURNAL.** **See** Medical Science and Technology.

GH/0009-5478
**CHRISTIAN MESSENGER.** 1960-. Periodical. English (Twi and Ga). mo. $5.25 US. Christian Messenger, Post Office Box 3075, Accra Ghana West Africa. **Tel** 662415. **ED** G B K Owusu. Index available. **Bk Rev**. **Ad Acc. Circ:** 40,000. available on microfilm from University Microfilms International (UMI).
**Desc:** Patronized by Christians from different denominations.

US/0033-4138
**CHRISTIAN MINISTRY, THE.** [Christ. ministr.]. **Added/Corp** Christian Century Foundation. Vol. 1 (Nov. 1969)-. Periodical. English. bm. $14.00. Christian Century Foundation, 407 South Dearborn Street, Suite 1405, Chicago IL 60605. **Tel** (312)427-2714, (312)427-5380, FAX (312)427-1302. **ED** James M Wall. **LC** BV4000; .C47. **DD** 250/.5. Index available. **Bk Rev**. **Ad Acc. Circ:** 13,000. available on microfilm and microfiche from University Microfilms International (UMI). ***Supersedes*** *Pulpit, 0362-4617.*
**Desc:** A periodical for practicing parish clergy, focusing on theory and ministry presentation.
**Ind/Abst** Curr. Thoughts Trends; Guide Soc. Sci. Relig.; Index Book Rev. Relig.; Relig. Index One Period. (1979-).

US/8750-7765
**CHRISTIAN MISSION.** [Christ. mission]. **Added/Corp** Christian Aid Mission. (197?)-. Periodical. English. qt. Free on request. Christian Aid Mission, 3045 Ivy Road, Charlottesville VA 22903. **Tel** (804)977-5650. **ED** John Lindner. **DD** 266. **Circ:** 15,000 (ctrl).
**Desc:** Presents the work of indigenous mission groups.

US/0744-4052
**CHRISTIAN MISSIONS IN MANY LANDS.** **VFOAT** Missions. Periodical. English. mo. Christian Missions in Many Lands Inc, PO Box 13, Spring Lake NJ 07762. **DD** 266/.005. ***Absorbed*** *Christian Missions in Many Lands. Canadian Ed., 0316-2990.*

US/0009-5494
**CHRISTIAN MONTHLY.** **Added/Corp** Apostolic Lutheran Church of America. (1943)-. Periodical. English (Russian). Twelve times a year. $12.00 US; $15.00 Canada; $30.00 others. Apostolic Lutheran Book Concern, PO Box 537, Brush Prairie WA 98606. **Tel** (206)687-7088. **ED** Alvar Helmes, (editor's address: 27307 Northeast 85th Court, Battle Ground, WA 98604, phone: (206)687-7088). **Circ:** 2,000 (ctrl).
**Desc:** A publications of religious news from the church federation. Articles and notices of meetings are sent in by various members and pastors.

US/0899-7292
**CHRISTIAN NEW AGE QUARTERLY.** [Christ. new age q.]. **Added/Corp** Bethsheva's Concern. **VFOAT** Christian New Age Quarterly. Vol. 1, No. 1 (Jan./March 1989)-. Periodical. English. qt. $12.50 North America; $18.50 other. Bethsheva's Concern, PO Box 276, Clifton NJ 07011-0276. **ED** Catherine Groves. **DD** 205. **Bk Rev**. **Ad Acc**. **Pr Rev**.
**Desc:** Purpose is to stimulate substantive dialogue between Christians and new agers. Articles and columns explore the areas both of unity and distinction between Christianity and the new age.

IS/0009-5532
**CHRISTIAN NEWS FROM ISRAEL.** (CHRISTIAN NEWS FROM ISRAEL / ISSUED BY THE DEPARTMENT FOR CHRISTIAN COMMUNITIES, MINISTRY FOR RELIGIOUS AFFAIRS.). [Christ. news Isr.]. **Added/Corp** Israel. Misrad ha-Datot. Israel. Mahlakah le-Edot Notsriyot. **VFOAT** Nouvelles Chretiennes d'Israel. (1949)-. Periodical. English (French). qt. $4.00. Christian News from Israel, 30 Jaffa Street, PO Box 1167, Jerusalem Israel. **LC** BR1110; .C45. cum. index. available on microfilm and microfiche from University Microfilms International (UMI).
**Ind/Abst** New Testam. Abstr.; Old Testam. Abstr.

US/0009-5516
**CHRISTIAN NEWS (NEW HAVEN, MO.).** (CHRISTIAN NEWS.). [Christ. news]. Vol. 1 (Jan. 1968)-. Periodical. English. Forty-eight times a year. $20.00 US; $24.00 other. Lutheran News, 3277 Boeuf Lutheran Road, New Haven MO 63068-9568. **Tel** (314)237-3110, FAX (314)237-3858. **ED** Herman Otten. Index available (Bound in 48th issue, in December). **Bk Rev**, (Qty: 250). **Pr Rev. Circ:** 14,000. ***Continues*** *Lutheran News.*
**Desc:** Religious news: conservative, independent and biblical dealing with the issues of the day.

US/0899-2584
**CHRISTIAN OBSERVER (MANASSAS, VA.).** (CHRISTIAN OBSERVER.). Vol. 165, No. 1 (Nov. 27, 1987)-. Periodical. English. wk. $27.00 US; $47.00 (includes postage) other. Christian Observer, 9400 Fairview Avenue, Manassas VA 22110. **Tel** (703)361-2300, FAX (703)368-4817. **ED** Dr. Edwin P. Elliott Jr. **DD** 285. cum. index. **Bk Rev**. **Ad Acc. Circ:** 2,000. available on microfilm and microfiche from University Microfilms International (UMI). ***Continues*** *Journey.*

UK/0009-5559
**CHRISTIAN ORDER.** (1960)-. Periodical. English. mo. $20.00. Christian Order, c/o Rev Paul Crane, 53 Penerley Road, Catford LND SE6 2LH England. **Tel** 011 44 71 6972265. **LC** BT738.

CN/0701-0451
**CHRISTIAN OUTREACH.** Periodical. English. mo. $3.50. Dellcraft Publishing Company, 111 Broadway East, Vancouver BC V5T 1W1. **DD** 205.

US/0069-3871
**CHRISTIAN PERIODICAL INDEX.** **See** Religion and Theology-Abstracting, Bibliographies and Statistics.

US/1064-9239
**CHRISTIAN READER, THE.** [Christ. read.]. Vol. 1, No. 1 (Oct.-Nov. 1963)-. Periodical. English. bm (6 issues). $17.50. Christianity Today Inc., 465 Gundersen Drive, Carol Stream IL 60188. **Tel** (708)260-6200. **(Subscription address:** CDS / SIFD Agency Control, 1901 Bell Avenue, Des Moines IA 50315.**)** **DD** 051.
**Ind/Abst** Guide Soc. Sci. Relig.

CN/0820-7593
**CHRISTIAN RENEWAL.** [Christ. renew.]. **Added/Corp** Abraham Kuyper Christian Citizen Foundation. Vol. 1, No. 1 (Oct. 11, 1982)-. Periodical. English. Twenty times a year (Except July/Aug.). $40.00. Abraham Kuyper Christian Foundation, PO Box 770, Lewiston NY 14092. **Tel** (716)284-7784, FAX (905)562-7828. **ED** J. Hultink and John Van Dyk, (editor's address: Box 777, Jordan Station, Ontario L0R 1S0 Canada, phone: 562-5719). **DD** 248/.05. Index available. **Bk Rev**, (Qty: 25-40). **Ad Acc**, **Adv Mgr Tel** (905)562-5719. **Circ:** 4,300.
**Desc:** Church news and comment on events taking place in reformed presbyterian communities. Information on social and political issues.

US
**CHRISTIAN RESEARCH JOURNAL.** English (Russian, Portuguese and Spanish). Four times a year. $16.00 (one year); $29.00 (two years); 30.00Can$

Canada. Christian Research Institute, PO Box 500, San Juan Capistra CA 92693. **Tel** (714)855-9926. **ED** Elliot Miller. **Bk Rev**, (Qty: 8-12). **Ad Acc**, **Adv Mgr:** Melanie Cogdill, **Tel** (714)899-4428.

CN/0846-3905
**CHRISTIAN RESOURCE DIRECTORY.** (CHRISTIAN RESOURCE DIRECTORY / CHRISTIAN INFO.). [Christ. resour. dir.]. **Added/Corp** Christian Info (Vancouver-Lower Mainland) Society. **VFOAT** Christian Info Christian Resource Directory; Christian Info Resource Directory. (1991)-. Directory. English. be. $12.00 per volume. Christian Info (Vancouver-Lower Mainland) Society, Box 58307, Station L, Vancouver British Columbia V6P 6K2 Canada. **DD** 280/.025/711.

US/0017-2251
**CHRISTIAN SCHOLAR'S REVIEW.** [Christ. sch. rev.]. Vol. 1 (Fall 1970)-. Periodical. English. qt. $17.00 (one year), $31.50 (two year), $45.00 (three year) institutions; $14.00 (one year), $26.50 (two year), $36.00 (three year) individuals. Calvin College, 3201 Burton Street, Grand Rapids MI 49546. **LC** BR1; .C6372. **DD** 230/.05. **Bk Rev**. **Ad Acc**. **Circ:** 4,200. available on microfilm and microfiche from University Microfilms International (UMI). ***Continues*** *Gordon Review, 0436-1644.*
**Ind/Abst** Abstr. Engl. Stud.; Am. Hist. Life (1970-); Annu. Bibliogr. Engl. Lang. Lit.; Christ. Period. Index (19??-); Guide Soc. Sci. Relig.; Index Book Rev. Relig. (1970-); Middle East Abstr. Index; MLA Int. Bibl. Books Artic. Mod. Lang. Lit.; Old Testam. Abstr.; Relig. Index One Period. (1970-); Relig. Theol. Abstr.; Romant. Move.

US/0009-5613
**CHRISTIAN SCIENCE JOURNAL, THE.** **Added/Corp** First Church of Christ, Scientist (Boston, Mass.). (Apr. 14, 1883)-. Periodical. English. mo. $39.00. Christian Science Publishing Society, One Norway Street, Boston MA 02115. **Tel** (617)450-2678, (617)450-2504. **LC** BX6901; .C5.

US/0578-0144
**CHRISTIAN SCIENCE MONITOR (INDEXES).** (CHRISTIAN SCIENCE MONITOR INDEX.). Vol. 1 (Jan. 1960)-. Periodical. English. ir. $175.00. University Microfilms International, 300 North Zeeb Road, Ann Arbor MI 48106-1346. **Tel** (313)761-4700, (800)521-0600 Exts. 2490, 2491, FAX (313)973-1540. **DD** 016; 070. cum. index. available on microfilm from University Microfilms International (UMI).
**Desc:** Comprehensive subject index; includes access by personal and corporate name headings, with informative abstracts.
**Ind/Abst** BioBusiness.

US/0009-5621
**CHRISTIAN SCIENCE QUARTERLY.** (18??)-. Periodical. English. qt. $19.50. Christian Science Publishing Society, One Norway Street, Boston MA 02115. **Tel** (617)450-2678, (617)450-2504.

US
**CHRISTIAN SCIENCE SENTINEL.** **Added/Corp** Christian Science Publishing Society. Vol. 1, No. 22 (Jan. 26, 1899)-. English. wk (52 issues). $54.00. Christian Science Publishing Society, One Norway Street, Boston MA 02115. **Tel** (617)450-2678, (617)450-2504. **LC** BX6901; .C6. Index available in last issue of volume--attached. ***Continues*** *Christian Science Weekly.*

US/0191-4294
**CHRISTIAN SINGLE.** **Added/Corp** Southern Baptist Convention. Sunday School Board. (April 1979)-. Periodical. English. Twelve times a year. $15.50. Southern Baptist Convention, 901 Commerce, Suite 750, Nashville TN 37203. **Tel** (615)244-2355, FAX (615)742-8919. **(Subscription address:** Sunday School Board - Customer Service, 127 Ninth Avenue North, Nashville, TN 37234; telephone: (800)458-2772) **LC** BV4596.S5; C47. **DD** 248.4/8613204.
**Ind/Abst** South. Baptist Period. Index.

US/0897-0459
**CHRISTIAN SOCIAL ACTION (WASHINGTON, D.C.).** (CHRISTIAN SOCIAL ACTION.). [Christ. soc. action]. Vol. 1. No. 1 (Jan. 1988)-. Periodical. English (Spanish). mo (July-August are combined). $13.50. Christian Social Action, 100 Maryland Avenue NE, Washington DC 20002. **Tel** (202)488-5632, FAX (202)488-5619. **ED** Lee Ranck and Stephen Brockwell. **LC** HN37.M4; C43. **DD** 361.7/5/096805. Index available. **Bk Rev**. **Ad Acc**. **Circ:** 3,500 (ctrl). available on microfilm and microfiche from University Microfilms International (UMI). ***Continues*** *Engage/Social Action, 0164-5528.*
**Desc:** Analysis social issues from the perspective of the Christian faith.
**Ind/Abst** Index Book Rev. Relig.; Relig. Index One Period. (1988-); Relig. Theol. Abstr.

US/0009-5656
**CHRISTIAN STANDARD.** Vol. 1 (Apr. 7, 1866)-. Periodical. English. wk. $17.00 US; $19.50 Canada and Mexico; $21.50 other. Standard Publishers Company, 8121 Hamilton Avenue, Cincinnati OH 45231. **Tel** (800)543-1353, FAX (513)931-0904. **ED** Sam E Stone. Index available. **Bk Rev**. **Circ:** 75,000. available on microfilm and microfiche from University Microfilms International (UMI).
**Desc:** Journal of essays, news, and inspirational material. Devoted to the restoration of New Testament Christianity.
**Ind/Abst** Christ. Period. Index (19??-); Guide Soc. Sci. Relig.

US/0009-5664
**CHRISTIAN STATESMAN.** **Added/Corp** National Reform Association (Founded 1863). Vol. 1, (1867)-. Periodical. English. bm. $15.00 (new subscriptions), $12.50 (renew). National Reform Association, PO Box 97086, Pittsburgh PA 15229. **Tel** (412)661-2943. **ED** Gerald L Bowyer. **LC** HN51; .C6. **DD** 261.8/05. **Bk Rev**, (Qty: (6-8)). **Ad Acc**. **Circ:** 2,000 (ctrl). available on microfilm from University Microfilms International (UMI); and University Microfilms International (UMI). ***Continues*** *Journey.*
**Desc:** The application of reformational, Biblical Christianity to society, culture, and political science.

US/1050-4125
**CHRISTIAN STUDIES (AUSTIN, TEX.).** (CHRISTIAN STUDIES.). [Christ. stud.]. **Added/Corp** Institute for Christian Studies. No. 10 (Fall 1989)-. Periodical. English. sa. Free. Institute for Christian Studies, 1909 University Avenue, Austin TX 78705. **Tel** (512)476-2772. **DD** 207. ***Continues*** *Faculty Bulletin of the Institute for Christian Studies.*
**Ind/Abst** Index Book Rev. Relig.; Relig. Index One Period.

US/0529-472X
**CHRISTIAN THEOLOGICAL SEMINARY BULLETIN.** (BULLETIN - CHRISTIAN THEOLOGICAL SEMINARY.). **Main/Corp** Christian Theological Seminary. V. 1- June 1959-. Bulletin. English. Four times a year. Christian Theological Seminary, 1000 West 42nd Street, Box 88267, Indianapolis IN 46208. **Tel** (317)924-1331, FAX (317)923-1961 *2. **ED** R Coalson. **Circ:** 16,000 (ctrl).

CN/0843-7602
**CHRISTIAN VISION.** **See** Literature.

CN/0835-412X
**CHRISTIAN WEEK.** [Christ. week]. Vol. 1, No. 1 (Apr. 7, 1987)-. Periodical. English. Twenty-four times a year (Alternate Tuesdays, except July, & Aug.). 24.61Can$ (one year), 42.80Can$ (two year) Canada; 35.00Can$ (one year), 70.00Can$ (two year) other. Christian Week, PO Box 725, Winnipeg Manitoba R3C 2K3 Canada. **Tel** (204)943-1147, FAX (204)947-5632. **ED** Harold Jantz and Doug Koop. **DD** 277.1/005. **Bk Rev**. **Ad Acc**, **Adv Mgr:** Bryan Rempel. **Circ:** 11,000.
**Desc:** A Canadian Christian newspaper aimed at providing news and comment on Christianity in Canada.

US/0009-5702
**CHRISTIAN WOMAN.** [Christ. woman]. (1933)-. Periodical. English. bm. $16.98 (one year), $28.98 (two year). Gospel Advocate, 1006 Elm Hill Pike, Nashville TN 37210. **Tel** (615)254-8781, (800)251-8446. **DD** 248.

CN/0846-4243
**CHRISTIAN WORLD REPORT, THE.** [Christ. world rep.]. Vol. 1, No. 1 (Feb. 1989)-. Periodical. English. mo (11 issues). $24.95. Christian World Report, PO Box 1440, Niagara Falls NY 14302. **Tel** (800)776-7432, (905)684-7700, FAX (905)684-7946. **ED** Patti Lalonde. **DD** 973.92/05. **Ad Acc**, **Adv Mgr:** T. Gray. **Circ:** 21,000. ***Absorbed*** *Omega-Letter, 0834-146X.*

US/0736-7600
**CHRISTIAN WRITER'S SERVICE GUIDE.** [Christ. writ. serv. guide]. **VFOAT** Service Guide. 1983-. Periodical. English. an. Christian Horizons Unlimited, PO Box 5650, Lakeland FL 33803.

FR/0009-5729
**CHRISTIANISME AU VINGTIEME SIECLE, LE.** **VFOAT** Christianisme au XXe Siecle. (1872)-. Periodical. French. wk. 560.00F France; 710.00F other. Le Christianisme Au XXe Siecle, 27 rue de Rome, 75008 Paris France. **Tel** 33 1 46347323, FAX 33 1 40469399. **Bk Rev**. **Ad Acc**. **Circ:** 5,000 (ctrl).

US/0278-8187
**CHRISTIANITY & CIVILIZATION.** ***Ceased.*** [Christ. civiliz.]. **Added/Corp** Geneva Divinity School. **VFOAT** Christianity and Civilization. No. 1 (Spring 1982)-Series complete. Periodical. English. sa. Geneva Ministries, PO Box 572, Brentwood TN 37024.

US/0009-5745
**CHRISTIANITY AND CRISIS.** ***Ceased.*** [Christ. crisis]. **VFOAT** C & C; C&C. Vol. 1 (Feb. 10, 1941)-(1993). Periodical. English. bw (twice monthly, Feb., March, April, May, Sept., Oct., Nov.). Christianity and Crisis, 537 West 121st Street, New York NY 10027. **Tel** (212)662-5907. **(Subscription address:** C&C Subscription Department, 202 Twin Oaks Drive, Suite 105, Syracuse, New York 13206**)** **ED** Leon Howell. **LC** BR1; .C6417. **DD** 205. Index available. **Bk Rev**. **Ad Acc**. **Circ:** 15,000. available on microfilm and microfiche from University Microfilms International (UMI). Documents available from UMI Article Clearinghouse.
**Desc:** Distinguished ecumenical journal of opinion on contemporary issues.
**Ind/Abst** Am. Hist. Life (1954-1959); Curr. Thoughts Trends; Expand. Acad. Index (1989-); Hum. Rights Intern. Rep.; Humanit. Index; Humanit. Source (Jul. 1993-); Index Book Rev. Relig. (1954-1959, 19??-); INFO-SOUTH Abstr.; Linguist. Lang. Behav. Abstr.; Mag. Search; Middle East Abstr. Index (1954-1959); Newsp. Period. Abstr. (1989-); PAIS Int. Print (1991-?); Peace Res. Abstr. J. (1976-1983); Relig. Index One Period. (1949-1972, 19??-); Relig. Theol. Abstr.; Soc. Plann. Policy Dev. Abstr.; Sociol. Abstr.

US/0148-3331
**CHRISTIANITY & LITERATURE.** **See** Literature.

US/0009-5753
**CHRISTIANITY TODAY (WASHINGTON).** (CHRISTIANITY TODAY.). [Christ. today]. Vol. 1, (Oct. 15, 1956)-. Periodical. English. Fourteen times a year. $24.95. Christianity Today Inc., 465 Gundersen Drive, Carol Stream IL 60188. **Tel** (708)260-6200. **(Subscription address:** CDS / SIFD Agency Control, 1901 Bell Avenue, Des Moines IA 50315.**)** **ED** George Brushaber, David Neff, Lyn Cryderman. **LC** BR1; .C6418. **DD** 230.05. Index available. **Bk Rev**. **Ad Acc**. **Circ:** 170,000. available on microfilm and microfiche from University Microfilms International (UMI). Documents available from UMI Article Clearinghouse, Magazine Collection.
**Desc:** A transdenominational (conservative) protestant magazine. Offers readers a balanced fare.
**Ind/Abst** Acad. Abstr. Full Text Elite (Jan. 1984-) [Full Txt.]; Acad. Abstr. (Jan. 1984-); Acad. Ind. [Computer File] (1984-); Acad. Search (Jan. 1984-); Book Rev. Digest; Book Rev. Index; Christ. Period. Index; Curr. Thoughts Trends; Expand. Acad. Index (1984-); Gen. Period. Index (1985-); Guide Soc. Sci. Relig.; Humanit. Source (Jan. 1988-); Index Book Rev. Relig.; INFO-SOUTH Abstr.; Inf. Instruc. Technol.; Mag. Artic. Summar. Elite (Jan. 1984-) [Full Txt.]; Mag. Artic. Summar. Select (Jan. 1984-); Mag. Artic. Summar. CD-ROM (Jan. 1984-); Mag. Index Plus (1989-); Mag. Index. Sel. (1986-); Mag. Search; Middle East Abstr. Index; New Testam. Abstr.; Newsp. Period. Abstr. (1986-); Peace Res. Abstr. J. (1956-); Read. Guide Abstr. Select Ed.; Read. Guide Period. Lit.; Relig. Index One Period. (1956-); Relig. Theol. Abstr.; Mag. Index (1977-); Vocat. Search (Jan. 1984-).

CN/0317-0772
**CHRISTIANS AGAINST TERRORISM.** **Added/Corp** Christians Against Terrorism (Organization). (March 1974)-. Periodical. English. Christians Against Terrorism, PO Box 332, Rexdale Ontario M9W 5L3 Canada. **DD** 261.8/7.

US/1073-2209
**CHRISTIAN'S EXPOSITOR.** (CHRISTIAN EXPOSITOR.). [Christ. expo.]. **VFOAT** Christian's Expositor. (198?)-. Periodical. English. qt. $15.00. Christian Expositor, PO Box 1390, Buffalo MO 65622. **Tel** (417)345-8302. **ED** Smith H. Bibens. **DD** 205. Index available. **Bk Rev**, (Qty: 10). **Circ:** 1,000.

CN/0225-5367
**CHRISTIANS, JEWS TODAY.** (CHRISTIANS, JEWS TODAY. CHRETIENS, JIFS AJOURD'HI.). **Added/Corp** Centre MI-CA-EL Notre Dame de Sion. League for Human Rights of B'nai B'rith. **VFOAT** Chretiens, Juifs Aujourd'Hui. **VAT** Chretiens, Juifs Aujourd'Hui (Edition Anglaise). Vol. 6, No. 2 (Oct. 1979)-. Periodical. English. ir. League for Human Rights, 15 Hove Street, Downsview ONT M3H 4Y8 Canada. **Tel** (905)633-6224. **DD** 296.3/872. ***Continues*** *Christians and Jews Today; Canadian Newsletter., 0319-3349.*

●US/1064-9751
**CHRISTO, EN.** (EN CHRISTO : A PUBLICATION OF INSTITUTES OF [I.E. FOR] CHRISTIAN SPIRITUALITY.). [En Christo]. **Added/Corp** Institutes for Christian Spirituality. Vol. 5, No. 1 (Spring 1992)-. Periodical. English. qt. $12.00 US; $17.00 Canada. **DD** 248. ***Continues*** *En Christo Book Reviews, 1040-3019.*

US/8755-6901
**CHRISTOPHER NEWS NOTES.** **Added/Corp** Christophers (Firm). **VFOAT** News Notes. (1946)-. Periodical. English (Spanish). Ten times a year (monthly except Apr. & Oct.). Free. The Christophers, 12 East 48th Street, New York NY 10017. **Tel** (212)759-4050, FAX (212)838-5073. **ED** Stephanie Raha. **DD** 271. **Circ:** 500,000.

MX
**CHRISTUS (MEXICO CITY, MEXICO.** (CHRISTUS.). Periodical. Spanish. mo. $35.30. R P Xavier Garibay SJ, Auguste Redin No 355, Mexico 19 DF Mexico. **LC** BR7; .C48. **DD** 230/.2.
**Ind/Abst** Abr. Cathol. Period. Lit. Index; Cathol. Period. Lit. Index.

UK/0529-5025
**CHRYSOSTOM : QUARTERLY BULLETIN OF THE SOCIETY OF ST JOHN CHRYSOSTOM.** **Added/Corp** Society of St John Chrysostom. No. 1 (Spring 1960)-No. 32 (Winter 1967-68); Vol. 2, No. 1 (Spring 1968)-. Periodical. English. sa. £5.00. Society of St John Chrysostom,

Marian House, Holden Avenue, London N12 8HY England. available on microfilm and microfiche from University Microfilms International (UMI).

KO
**CHUGAN KIDOKKYO.** Periodical. Korean. wk. W4,800. Chugan Kidokkyosa, 319-7 Sinsa-dong, Kangnam-ku, Seoul South Korea. **LC** BR1320; .C545.

KO
**CHUIL HAKKYO KYOSA UI POT. VFOAT** The Sunday School Teacher; Sunday School Teacher; Kyosa Ui Pot. Periodical. Korean. mo. W7.700. Hanguk Kidokkyo Kyoyuk, Yonguwon 35-14 Tongja-dong, Yongsan-ku Seoul Korea. **LC** BV1500; .C49.

US/0412-4553
**CHURCH ADMINISTRATION. Added/Corp** Southern Baptist Convention. Sunday School Board. Vol. 1 (Oct. 1959)-. Periodical. English. mo. $21.60 (one year), $51.58 (two year), $77.06 (three year). Southern Baptist Convention, 901 Commerce, Suite 750, Nashville TN 37203. **Tel** (615)244-2355, FAX (615)742-8919. **(Subscription address:** Sunday School Board, Customer Service, 127 9th Avenue North, Nashville TN 37234.**)** available on microfilm and microfiche from University Microfilms International (UMI).
**Ind/Abst** Christ. Period. Index (19??-); South. Baptist Period. Index.

US/0009-630X
**CHURCH ADVOCATE (FINDLAY, OHIO), THE.** (THE CHURCH ADVOCATE. CHURCHES OF GOD, GENERAL CONFERENCE.). [Church advocate]. **Added/Corp** Churches of God, General Conference. (1???)-. Periodical. English. mo. $10.00 one year; $19.00 two year. Churches of God Publications, PO Box 926, Findlay OH 45840. **Tel** (419)424-1961, FAX (419)424-3433. **ED** Linda M. Draper. Index available (Bound in May issue). **Bk Rev. Circ:** 7,800.
**Desc:** A denominational publication intended to encourage and inform people to live as the Church.

SZ
**CHURCH ALERT.** Periodical. English. $5.00. Ecumenical Centre, 150 Route de Ferney, PO Box 66, 1211 Geneva 20 Switzerland.

US/0037-7805
**CHURCH AND SOCIETY (NEW YORK).** (CHURCH AND SOCIETY.). [Church soc.]. **Added/Corp** United Presbyterian Church in the U.S.A. Program Agency. Presbyterian Church in the U.S. Division of Corporate and Social Mission. Presbyterian Church (U.S.A.). Social Justice and Peacemaking Unit. **VFOAT** Church & Society. Vol. 60, No. 3, (Jan./Feb. 1970)-. Periodical. English. bm. $12.00. Presbyterian Church (USA), 100 Witherspoon St, Room 5628, Louisville KY 40202. **Tel** (502)569-5637, FAX (502)569-8073. **(Subscription address:** Church and Society Magazine, 100 Witherspoon Street, Room 3044, Louisville KY 40202-1396.**) ED** Kathy Lancaster. **DD** 285. **Bk Rev. Circ:** 5,000. ***Continues*** *Social Progress.*
**Desc:** Forum for the church on subjects of social concerns for Christians: reflective comment, models and resources for individuals and groups.
**Ind/Abst** Index Book Rev. Relig.; Middle East Abstr. Index; Relig. Index One Period. (1970-).

US/0009-6334
**CHURCH AND STATE. See** Political Science.

US/0009-6342
**CHURCH & SYNAGOGUE LIBRARIES. See** Library and Information Sciences.

CN/1183-2339
**CHURCH BUSINESS.** [Church bus.]. Vol. 1, Issue 1 (Nov./Dec. 1991)-. Periodical. English. bm. $15.00 Canada; $30.00 US. Momentum Magazine, 4040 Creditview Road, Unit 11, PO Box 6900, Mississauga Ontario L5C 3Y8 Canada. **DD** 254.

US/0884-7193
**CHURCH BYTES.** [Church bytes]. (1983)-. Periodical. English. bm. $14.95. Church Bytes Inc., 562 Brightleaf Square #9, 905 West Main Street, Durham NC 27701. **Tel** (919)490-8927. **ED** Neil Houk. **DD** 253. Index available. cum. index. **Ad Acc. Circ:** 1,000.
**Desc:** Related to church computing, computers and theology-Bible-church management, software reviews, and news. Written for pastors, church staff, teachers, and church secretaries.

US/0164-5625
**CHURCH EDUCATOR.** [Church educ.]. **Added/Corp** Educational Ministries, Inc. (1976)-. Periodical. English. mo. $28.00 (one year); $48.00 (two year). Educational Ministries, 165 Plaza Drive, Prescott AZ 86303. **Tel** (602)771-8601, 800 221-0910, FAX (602)771-8621. **ED** Linda Davidson. **DD** 268. **Circ:** 5,500.
**Desc:** A magazine filled with practical "how-to" tips for Christian educators. Written for ministers, youth advisors, CE directors, church school teachers, church libraries, and CE committees.

KO
**CHURCH GROWTH.** (19??)-. English. qt (4 issues). $8.00. Church Growth International, Yoido PO Box 7, Seoul Korea 150-600. **Tel** 011 82 2 7839920, FAX 011 82 2 7841990, telex K28200. **ED** Peggy Kannaday. **Circ:** 12,615 (ctrl).
**Desc:** For Christian leaders and lay people to equip the saints for the work of the ministry.

UK/0268-7658
**CHURCH GROWTH DIGEST.** [Church growth dig.]. (1979)-. Periodical. English. Four times a year (Jan., Apr., July, Oct.). £8.00 UK; £10.00 (surface mail), £12.00 (air mail) other. British Church Growth Association, The Park, Moggerhanger, Bedford MK44 3RW England. **Tel** 011 767-61001, FAX 011 767-61001. **ED** Monica Hill. **DD** 274.10828. **Bk Rev**, (Qty: 40). **Circ:** 1,000.
**Desc:** Articles on leadership, church government, strategy, information on courses and conferences, evangelism, planning and goal-setting.

US
**CHURCH GROWTH JOURNAL.** (19??)-. English. $12.50. North American Society for Church Growth, 1202 East Austin, Bolivar MO 65613. **Tel** (417)326-3870, FAX (417)326-3212. **ED** Dr. John N. Vaughan. **Circ:** 200.

US
**CHURCH GROWTH TODAY.** English. Six times a year (Jan., Mar., May, July, Sept., Nov.). $15.00. Church Growth Today, 1202 East Austin, Bolivar MO 65613. **Tel** (417)326-3870. **ED** Dr. John N. Vaughan, (phone: (417)326-3212). Index available. cum. index.

US/0009-6393
**CHURCH HERALD, THE. Added/Corp** Reformed Church in America. Vol. 1 (Jan. 7, 1944)-. Periodical. English. mo (11 issues). $15.00. The Church Herald, 4500 60th Street Southeast, Grand Rapids MI 49512. **Tel** (616)698-7071, FAX (616)698-6606. **ED** Jeff Japinga. Index available. **Ad Acc, Adv Mgr:** S.Smith. **Circ:** 108,000 (ctrl). available on microfilm and microfiche from University Microfilms International (UMI). ***Supersedes*** *Intelligence-Leader.*
**Desc:** Narrator and interpreter of the life and ministry of the RCA. Purpose is to inform and inspire its readership with news of people, churches, missions, and with ideas and reflections on corporate and personal Christian journeys.
**Ind/Abst** Guide Soc. Sci. Relig.

AT/0156-224X
**CHURCH HERITAGE.** [Church herit.]. (1978)-. Periodical. English. Twice a year (Mar. and Sept.). 16.00Aus$ Australia; 22.00Aus$ other. Eskdale, PO Box 2395, North Parramatta NSW 2151 Australia. **Tel** 011 61 2 6833147. **ED** Dr. M. D. Prentis. **DD** 287.9305. **Bk Rev**, (Qty: 6-8). ***Continues*** *Journal and Proceedings of the Australasian Methodist Historical Society.*

US/0009-6407
**CHURCH HISTORY.** [Church hist.]. **Added/Corp** American Society of Church History. Vol. 1 (Mar. 1932)-. Periodical. English. qt (4 issues). $30.00. American Society of Church History, PO Box 8517, Red Bank NJ 07701. **LC** BR140; .A45. **DD** 270.05. Index available (bound in Dec. issue). cum. index. **Bk Rev. Ad Acc. Circ:** 2,950. available on microfilm and microfiche from University Microfilms International (UMI). Documents available from The Genuine Article, UMI Article Clearinghouse.
**Desc:** Seeks to advance and deepen historical knowledge of Christianity in all periods and places.
**Ind/Abst** Acad. Search (July 1993-); Am. Hist. Life (1954-); Am. Bibliogr. Slavic East Europ. Stud.; Annu. Bibliogr. Engl. Lang. Lit.; Arts Humanit. Citation Index [Full Cov.]; BHA : Biblio. Hist. Art; Book Rev. Index; Christ. Period. Index (19??-); Curr. Contents Arts Humanit.; Expand. Acad. Index (1989-); Hist. Source (July 1993-); Humanit. Index; Humanit. Source (Jul. 1993-); Index Book Rev. Relig. (1954-); INFO-SOUTH Abstr.; Linguist. Lang. Behav. Abstr.; Mag. Search; Newsp. Period. Abstr. (1991-); Old Testam. Abstr.; Relig. Index One Period. (1949-); Relig. Theol. Abstr.; Res. Alert [Full Cov.]; Romant. Move.; Soc. Plann. Policy Dev. Abstr.; Soc. Sci. Cit. Index [Select. Cov.]; Soc. Work Abstr. (?-?); Sociol. Abstr.; West. Hist. Q.; Women Stud. Abstr.

US
**CHURCH LAW & TAX REPORT. See** Law.

US/0009-6431
**CHURCH MANAGEMENT. Added/Corp** National Association of Church Business Administrators. **VFOAT** Clergy Journal. Vol. 1 (Oct. 1924)-. Periodical. English. Ten times a year. $54.00 (libraries), $27.00 (other). Logos Art Productions, PO Box 240, South St. Paul MN 55075. **Tel** (800)328-0200, (612)451-9945, FAX (612)457-4617. **LC** BV652.A1; C4. **DD** 254. **Bk Rev**, (Qty: 50 per year). **Ad Acc. Circ:** 20,000. available on microfilm from University Microfilms International (UMI). ***Absorbed*** *Record of Christian Work, 0364-4855.*
**Desc:** Sermons and "how to" in church management.

US/0888-0255
**CHURCH MINISTRIES WORKER. *Ceased.*** [Church minist. work.]. **VFOAT** Worker. Periodical. English. bm. General Conference of SDA, 12051 Old Columbia Pike, Silver Springs MD 20904. **DD** 286. ***Continues*** *Worker, Journal of Sabbath School Action, 0163-8815.*

UK/0268-7518
**CHURCH MONUMENTS.** (CHURCH MONUMENTS : JOURNAL OF THE CHURCH MONUMENTS SOCIETY.). [Church monum.]. **Added/Corp** Church Monuments Society. Vol. 1, Pt. 1 (1985)-. Periodical. English. an. £15.00. Church Monument Society, c/o Royal Armouries HM Tower, London EC3N 4AB England. **Tel** 011 44 71 9370155. **ED** R. Knowles. **LC** N7943; .C55. **DD** 730/.941/05. **Circ:** 500. ***Continues in part*** *Bulletin (International Society for the Study of Church Monuments), 0143-4128.*
**Desc:** Covers church monuments of any period or location.
**Ind/Abst** Archit. Period. Index; BHA : Biblio. Hist. Art.

UK/0307-6334
**CHURCH MUSIC QUARTERLY. See** Music.

US/1071-9903
**CHURCH MUSIC REPORT : TCMR, THE. See** Music.

US/0009-6466
**CHURCH MUSICIAN, THE. See** Music.

US/0883-5667
**CHURCH (NEW YORK, N.Y.).** (CHURCH.). [Church]. **Added/Corp** National Pastoral Life Center (U.S.). Vol. 1, No. 1 (Spring 1985)-. Periodical. English. qt. $56.00 (institution); $50.00 (individual) Comes with membership to National Pastoral Life. National Pastoral Life Center, 299 Elizabeth Street, New York NY 10012. **Tel** (212)431-7825, FAX (212)274-9786. **ED** Karen Sue Smith. **DD** 253. Index available (In December). cum. index. **Bk Rev. Ad Acc. Circ:** 8,500. available on microfilm from University Microfilms International (UMI).
**Desc:** Designed to provide information, insight, and interpretation for pastoral ministers. It combines serious longer essays on theology, scripture, history, spirituality, and sociology with shorter, concrete articles on parish matters.
**Ind/Abst** New Testam. Abstr.; Abr. Cathol. Period. Lit. Index; Cathol. Period. Lit. Index.

UK/0009-6482
**CHURCH OBSERVER. Added/Corp** Church Union. Seven Years Association. (Jan. 1948)-. Periodical. English. Three times a year. The Church Union, Faith House, 7 Tufton Street, Westminister SWIP 3QN England. **Tel** (01)222-6952, FAX (01)976-7180. **ED** Martin Flatman. **Bk Rev. Ad Acc. Circ:** 5,500 (ctrl). available on microfilm from University Microfilms International (UMI). ***Formed by the union of*** *Church Union Gazette* ***and*** *Platform.*
**Desc:** A Catholic Renewal journal.

UK/0069-3987
**CHURCH OF ENGLAND YEAR BOOK, THE. Main/Corp** Church of England. General Synod. 88th (1971/72)-. English. an. Church House Publishing, Church House Westminster, Great Smith Street, London SW1P 3NZ England. **Tel** (01)222 9011. **ED** Jo Linzey. **Ad Acc. Circ:** 3,000. ***Continues*** *Church of England Year Book.*
**Desc:** Official yearbook of the Church of England containing detailed information on dioceses throughout the Anglican communion, with an extensive who's who and list of organisations.

US/0009-6504
**CHURCH OF GOD MISSIONS. Added/Corp** Missions Education. (19??)-. Periodical. English. mo (11 issues). $7.00. Missions Education, PO Box 2337, Anderson IN 46018. **Tel** (317)649-7597. **ED** Dondeena Caldwell. **Bk Rev. Circ:** 8,500 (ctrl).
**Desc:** Missions education materials include stories and reports from missionaries and national workers in seventy-eight countries. Also considered are social issues, such as peace, hunger, and poverty.

IE
**CHURCH OF IRELAND GAZETTE, THE.** (19??)-. Periodical. English. Fifty-two times a year. 16.50p Ireland: 22.50p others. Church of Ireland Press, 48 Bachelors Walk, Lisburn BT28 1XN North Ireland.

US/0273-5059
**CHURCH PROGRAMS FOR MIDDLERS & JUNIORS. *Title Change.* VAT** Church Programs for Middlers and Juniors. (1981-1992). Periodical. English. qt. Gospel Publishing House, 1445 Boonville Avenue, Springfield MO 65802. **Tel** (417)862-2781, FAX (417)866-1146. ***Continued by*** *Middler & Junior Children's Church Teacher Guide, 1059-3411.*

US/0273-5113
**CHURCH PROGRAMS FOR PRIMARIES. *Title Change.*** Vol. 7, No. 1 (Fall 1981)-(19??). Periodical. English. qt. Gospel Publishing House, 1445 Boonville Avenue, Springfield MO 65802. **Tel** (417)862-2781, FAX (417)866-1146. ***Continues*** *Children's Church, 0190-4221.* ***Continued by*** *Primary Children's Church Teacher Guide, 1059-3403.*

US/0162-4652
**CHURCH RECREATION MAGAZINE. *Ceased.* See** Recreation, Leisure.

US
**CHURCH RESOURCE DIRECTORY.** **Added/Corp** Christian Literature Crusade. (19??)-. Directory. English. an. Free. Keener Marketing Inc, 124 East Main Avenue, Dayton TN 37321. **Tel** (617)775-3300. **ED** Marvin Keenec and Mareta Keenec. **LC** TS2301.C5; C48. **DD** 202/.9/473. Index available. **Bk Rev. Ad Acc. Circ:** 150,000 (ctrl).
**Desc:** A valuable resource tool for church leaders with approximately 800 suppliers of church services listed with their updated addresses.

AT/0009-6563
**CHURCH SCENE (MELBOURNE, AUSTRALIA).** (CHURCH SCENE.). (198?)-. Periodical. English. wk (48 issues per year). 49.50Aus$ Australia; 95.50Aus$ other. Church Press Ltd, PO Box 358, Carnegie Victoria, 3163 Australia. **Tel** 011 61 3 5635311.

US/0738-6885
**CHURCH SECRETARY'S SWAP SHOP, THE.** ***Ceased.*** **VFOAT** Swap Shop. (19??)-(19??). Periodical. English. mo (except July and August). Betty Atchinson, Publisher & Editor, 12 Meadow View Road, Wilbraham MA 01095. **Tel** (413)596-3282. **ED** Betty Atchinson. **Bk Rev.**
**Desc:** A sharing, caring publication exclusively for church secretaries, which qualifies as 'continuing education,' therefore, a high percentage of churches pay for their secretaries' subscriptions.

US/0164-6451
**CHURCH TEACHERS.** ***Ceased.*** **Added/Corp** Association of Church Teachers. National Teacher Education Project. (1973)-(Dec. 1993). Periodical. English. ir. Harper San Francisco, PO Box 2357, San Francisco CA 94126. **Tel** (800)842-4307, (415)372-6002. **ED** Locke E Bowman Jr. **Bk Rev. Circ:** 10,000 (ctrl).
**Desc:** An innovative magazine prepared for persons who teach in churches.
**Ind/Abst** Christ. Period. Index (19??-).

US
**CHURCH TIMES, THE.** (1863)-. Periodical. English. wk. £31.00 UK & Eire, £38.00 other, surface mail; £43.00 UK & Eire, £48.00 other airmail. G. J. Palmer & Sons limited, 16 Blyburgate, Beccles Suffolk NR34 9TB England. **Tel** 011 44 502 711171. **LC** Microfilm 03107BX; BX 5011. **Bk Rev. Ad Acc.** available on microfiche from University Microfilms International (UMI).

US/0009-6598
**CHURCH WOMAN, THE.** (THE CHURCH WOMAN. INCORPS LEAD TIME.). **Added/Corp** National Council of Federated Church Women. National Council of Church Women. Council of Women for Home Missions. Foreign Missions Conference of North America. Committee on Women's Work. United Council of Church Women. **VFOAT** CW; Churchwoman. (19??)-. Periodical. English. Six times a year. $10.00 one year; $24.00 three years. Church Women United, 475 Riverside Drive, Room 812, New York NY 10015. **Tel** (212)870-3048, FAX (212)870-2338. **LC** BV4415; .C55. **DD** 259.

US/1063-9187
**CHURCH WORSHIP.** [Church worsh.]. (19??)-. Periodical. English. mo. $24.00 (two year), $40.00 (two year). Educational Ministries, 165 Plaza Drive, Prescott AZ 86303. **Tel** (602)771-8601, 800 221-0910, FAX (602)771-8621. **ED** Linda Davidson. **DD** 205. **Circ:** 1,200.

US/1043-9609
**CHURCHES SPEAK, THE.** ***Ceased.*** [Churches speak]. **VFOAT** Churches Speak On. (1989)-Vol. 8. Monographic series. English. qt. Gale Research Inc., 835 Penobscot Building, Detroit MI 48226. **Tel** (800)877-GALE, (313)961-2242, FAX (313)961-6083, telex TWX 810-221-7086. **ED** J Gordon Melton.
**Desc:** Provides the full text of official church statements regarding issues of current interest. It presents the positions of various religious groups on homosexuality, women's ordination, euthanasia, and sex and the family life. Each title begins with an introductory essay that provides an overview of the topic itself and traces its recent historical manifestations. This essay also summarizes, compares, and contrasts the opinions found in the individual statements. Then, official statements on the issue from Roman Catholic, Protestant, Eastern Orthodox, Jewish, and other religious organizations are given. A brief annotation providing background information on the issuing organization and on the statement itself are also included.

UK/0009-661X
**CHURCHMAN (LONDON. 1879).** (CHURCHMAN.). [Churchman]. **Added/Corp** Church Society. Vol. 1 (Oct. 1879)-Vol. 14 (Sept. 1886); New Series Vol. 1 (Oct. 1886)-Vol. 19 (Dec. 1905); Vol. 20 (New Series Vol. 1) (Jan. 1906)-. Periodical. English. qt. £17.00 (UK students in full-time training), £20.00 other. Church Society, Dean Wace House, 16 Rosslyn Road, Watford, Herts WD1 7EY England. **Tel** 44 923 235111. **ED** Gerald Bray. **LC** BX5011; .C5. **[CCC]**. Index available (bound in Dec. issue). **Bk Rev. Ad Acc, Adv Mgr:** M J W Barker. **Circ:** 700. available on microfilm and microfiche from University Microfilms International (UMI).
**Desc:** Anglican theological journal written from a conservative evangelical standpoint. Deals in-depth with issues facing the church of England and the Anglican communion.
**Ind/Abst** Christ. Period. Index (19??-); Index Book Rev. Relig.; New Testam. Abstr.; Old Testam. Abstr.; Relig. Index One Period. (1963-).

SP/0045-6896
**CIERVO, EL.** No. 1 (1952)-. Periodical. Spanish. Ten times a year (monthly with June/July and Aug./Sep. issues combined). 6000ptas Spain; 8000ptas other. El Ciervo SA, Calvet 56 Entresuelo 3, 08021 Barcelona Spain. **Tel** 34 3 2005145, FAX 34 3 2011015. **ED** Lorenzo Gomis Sanahuja. **LC** AP60; .C54. Index available. **Bk Rev. Ad Acc. Circ:** 5,000 (ctrl).
**Desc:** Covers the presence of free Christians in the cultural Laic world.

UK
**CIIR ANNUAL REVIEW.** **Main/Corp** Catholic Institute for International Relations. (198?)-. English. an. Free on request. Catholic Institute for International Relations, 190A New N Road, Unit 3, Canonb Yd, London N1 7BJ United Kingdom. **Tel** 011 44 71 3540883, FAX 011 44 71 3590017, telex 21118 CIIR G. **LC** HN37.C3; C298a. **DD** 261.8/3. ***Continues*** *Catholic Institute for International Relations. Annual Review.*

US/1057-8102
**CIRCUIT RIDER (COLORADO SPRINGS, COLO.), THE.** ***Title Change.*** (THE CIRCUIT RIDER / FELLOWSHIP OF CHRISTIAN COWBOYS.). [Circuit rider]. **Added/Corp** Fellowship of Christian Cowboys. Vol. 1, No. 1 (July 1991)-(1993). Periodical. English. mo. Circuit Rider, PO Box 3010, Colorado Springs CO 80934-3010. **DD** 248. ***Continued by*** *Line Rider (Colorado Springs, Colo.), 1074-3049.*

US/0009-7527
**CITHARA.** [Cithara]. **Added/Corp** St. Bonaventure University. Vol. 1, No. 1 (Nov. 1961)-. Periodical. English. sa. $6.00. St. Bonaventure University Department of English, PO Box BC, St Bonaventure NY 14778. **Tel** (716)375-2405. **LC** AS36; .S2. **DD** 205. **Ad Acc.** available on microfilm and microfiche from University Microfilms International (UMI). Documents available from The Genuine Article.
**Ind/Abst** Abstr. Engl. Stud.; Am. Hist. Life (1963-); Annu. Bibliogr. Engl. Lang. Lit.; Arts Humanit. Citation Index [Full Cov.]; Curr. Contents Arts Humanit.; MLA Int. Bibl. Books Artic. Mod. Lang. Lit.; Res. Alert [Full Cov.]; Soc. Sci. Cit. Index [Select. Cov.]; Abr. Cathol. Period. Lit. Index; Cathol. Period. Lit. Index.

IT/0009-7632
**CITTA DI VITA.** [Citta vita]. Vol. 1 (1946)-. Periodical. Italian. Six times a year. L40000 Italy; L60000 other. Citta di Vita, Piazza Santa Croce 16, 50122 Firenze Italy. **Tel** 011 39 55 242783. **ED** Massimiliano Giuseppe Rosito. **Bk Rev. Ad Acc. Circ:** 2,000 (ctrl).
**Desc:** An up-to-date and lively teaching of the revealed thought which attempts to experiment with the deep vitality of the theology as to the problems which distress the spirit of the modern world.
**Ind/Abst** MLA Int. Bibl. Books Artic. Mod. Lang. Lit.

UK
**CITY CRIES.** **Added/Corp** Evangelical Coalition for Urban Mission (Great Britain). **VFOAT** Journal of E.C.U.M. No. 1 (Spring 1983)-. Periodical. English. Three times a year. £15.00. Evangelical Coalition for Urban Mission, 85A Allerton Road, Liverpool L18 2DA England. ***Continues*** *Christians in Industrial Areas.*

SP/0009-7756
**CIUDAD DE DIOS, LA.** [Ciudad Dios]. Vol. 152 (1936)-. Periodical. Spanish (summaries and/or abstracts in English and French). Three times a year (Apr., Sept., Dec.). $52.00. Ediciones Escurialenses, Real Monasterio, 28200 Madrid Spain. **Tel** 011 34 1 8905011, FAX 011 34 1 8905421. Index available. cum. index. **Bk Rev. Ad Acc, Adv Mgr:** Saturnino Alvarez. **Pr Rev. Circ:** 650. ***Continues*** *Ciudad de Dios; Religion y Cultura.*
**Desc:** This publication includes four regular sections, articles, unpublished texts, notes, and bibliography. It stands out in the field of ecclesiastical by reason of its Augustine inspiration.
**Ind/Abst** Am. Hist. Life (1956-1965); Bibliogr. Mission.; BHA : Biblio. Hist. Art; MLA Int. Bibl. Books Artic. Mod. Lang. Lit.; New Testam. Abstr.

II
**CIVANANA PUJA MALAR.** Periodical. Tamil (Tamil). an. Rs5.00. S Venkatesa, Sarma 5 Telipost Colony Kurukkut Street, Melmampalam Madras 600033 India. **LC** BL1280.5; .C57.

BE
**CLAIRLIEU : TIJDSCHRIFT GEWIJD ANN DE GESCHIEDENIS DER KRUISHEREN.** **See** History(General)-History of Europe.

US/0896-8071
**CLARION CALL (SAN FRANCISCO, CALIF.), THE.** (THE CLARION CALL.). [Clar. call]. **VFOAT** Clarion Call Magazine. Vol. 1, No. 1 (Winter 1988)-. Periodical. English. qt. $11.80 US; $14.67 Canada. Clarion Call Magazine, PO Box 146392, San Francisco CA 94114-6392. **DD** 294.
**Ind/Abst** Except. Hum. Exp.

US/1054-3147
**CLASSIC CYCLE REVIEW.** [Class. cycle rev.]. Vol. 1, No. 1 (Mar. 1991)-. Periodical. English. bm (6 issues). $24.00. DT Howards Classic Cycle Review, 641 645 Seneca Street, Harrisburg PA 17110. **Tel** (717)233-5569. **DD** 629.

US
**CLASSICS OF WESTERN SPIRITUALITY.** (1978)-. Monographic series. English. ir. Price varies per volume. Paulist Press, 997 McArthur Boulevard, Mahwah NJ 07430. **Tel** (201)825-7300, FAX (201)825-8345.

●US/1061-527X
**CLERGY FOCUS.** **Added/Corp** National Association of Pastoral Musicians (U.S.). (1992)-. Periodical. English. qt. $10.00. National Association of Pastoral Musicians, 225 Sheridan Street Northwest, Washington DC 20011. **Tel** (202)723-5800, FAX (202)723-2262.

US
**CLERGY JOURNAL.** V. 45, No. 9- June 1969-. Periodical. English. mo. $10.00. Logos Art Productions, PO Box 240, South St. Paul MN 55075. **Tel** (800)328-0200, (612)451-9945, FAX (612)457-4617. available on microfilm from University Microfilms International (UMI). ***Continues*** *Church Management, 0009-6431.*
**Ind/Abst** Curr. Thoughts Trends.

US/0893-3596
**CLERGY MALPRACTICE ALERT.** ***Suspended.*** **See** Law.

SA
**CLERICAL DIRECTORY / CHURCH OF THE PROVINCE OF SOUTHERN AFRICA.** **Main/Corp** Church of the Province of Southern Africa. Directory. English. CPSA, PO Box 1032, Pretoria 0001 South Africa. **Tel** 012-3226580. **LC** BX5700.6.A1; C48a. **DD** 283/.68/025. ***Continues*** *Year Book and Clerical Directory.*

CN/0823-9614
**CLINS D'OEIL DE DIEU.** [Clins oeil Dieu]. Periodical. French. ir. Free. Guides du Canada Guides Catholiques du Canada Secteur Francaise, 3827 rue St-Hubert, Montreal Quebec H2L 4A4 Canada. **DD** 248.4/82.

US/1071-4073
**CLUBHOUSE (BERRIEN SPRINGS, MICH.).** (CLUBHOUSE.). [Clubhouse]. (19??)-. Periodical. English. bm. $5.00. Clubhouse, Box 15, Berrien Springs MI 49103. **Tel** (616)471-9009, FAX (616)471-4661. **ED** Krista Phillips. **DD** 268. **Circ:** 5,000. ***Continues*** *Good Deeder.*

UK
**CMS NEWS-LETTER.** **Main/Corp** Church Missionary Society. (19??)-. Periodical. English. Seven times a year. £12.00. Church Missionary Society, 157 Waterloo Road, London SE1 8UU England. **Tel** 011 44 71 9288681, telex 8950907 ANGCOM G. **ED** Pauline Bower. **Circ:** 5,000 (ctrl).

US/0735-8628
**COCK-A-DOODLE WAKE UP WORLD.** **Added/Corp** Rhema Christian Center (Washington, D.C.). (198?)-. Periodical. English. mo. $15.00. Rhema Christian Center, 4915 Sargent Road NE, Washington DC 20017.

CK
**COLECCION TEMAS.** **Main/Corp** Centro Arquidiocesano de Pastoral, Lima. 1- 1970-. Periodical. Spanish. Apt Aereo 4817, Bogota Colombia.

US/0164-1522
**COLLABORATION (HIGH FALLS).** **See** Philosophy.

AT/0588-3237
**COLLOQUIUM.** (COLLOQUIUM; THE AUSTRALIAN AND NEW ZEALAND THEOLOGICAL REVIEW.). [Colloquium]. Vol. 2, No. 2 (May 1967)-. Periodical. English. sa. 25.00Aus$ individual; 35.00Aus$ institutions;. Australian and New Zealand Society for Theological Studies, PO Box 63, Everton Park 4053, Australia. **Tel** 11 61 7 3541761. **ED** Brian J Jackson. Index available. cum. index. **Bk Rev. Ad Acc. Pr Rev. Circ:** 400. ***Continues*** *New Zealand Theological Review.*
**Desc:** An established forum for exchange among scholars, particularly from Australia and New Zealand, on a wide range of theological areas: Bible, doctrine, ethics, liturgy, study of religions, church history and related areas.
**Ind/Abst** Annu. Bibliogr. Engl. Lang. Lit.; APAIS, Aust. Public Aff. Inf. Ser. (1973-); Index Book Rev. Relig.; New Testam. Abstr.; Relig. Index One Period. (1979-); Relig. Theol. Abstr.

US/0095-4438
**COLUMBAN MISSION.** **Added/Corp** St. Columban's Foreign Mission Society. (1918)-. Periodical. English. Ten times a year (May/June and July/Aug. issues combined). $10.00. Columban Missions, Columban Fathers Street, St Columbans NE 68056. **Tel** (402)291-1920, FAX (402)291-8693. **ED** Rev. Richard Steinhilber. **LC** BV3410; .F3. **DD** 266/.2/05. **Bk Rev**. **Circ:** 150,000 (ctrl). ***Continues*** *Columban Fathers Missions.*
**Desc:** Intended to educate, inform and inspire its readers about the missionary work of the Catholic Church; specifically about the work of the Columban Fathers.
**Ind/Abst** Bibliogr. Mission.

US/0279-3652
**COMBONI MISSIONS.** [Comboni missions]. (19??)-. Periodical. English. qt. $6.00. Comboni Mission Center, 8108 Beechmont Avenue, Cincinnati OH 45230. **Tel** (513)474-4997. **ED** Joseph Bragotti, Jose Marques, Patricia Meder. **Circ:** 22,000 (ctrl). ***Continues*** *Verona Missions, 0164-4211.*
**Desc:** Mission work of Comboni missionaries and their contribution to Third World development.
**Ind/Abst** Bibliogr. Mission.

US/0010-2474
**COMMAND (DENVER, COLO.).** **See** Military and Defense.

US/1063-7575
**COMMENTS FROM THE FRIENDS.** [Comments friends]. Vol. 1, No. 1 (Jan. 1982)-. Periodical. English. Four times a year (Mar., June, Sept., Dec.). $9.00. Comments from the Friends, PO Box 840, Stoughton MA 02072. **ED** David A. Reed (phone: (508)584-3838). **DD** 289. **Bk Rev**, (Qty: 4). **Circ:** 2,000 (ctrl).
**Desc:** Written for the Jehovah's Witness and persons concerned about JW relatives, friends, and neighbors.

US/0010-3179
**COMMISSION, THE.** **Added/Corp** Southern Baptist Convention. Foreign Mission Board. (1938)-. Periodical. English. Nine times a year. $8.75 US; $14.75 other. Southern Baptist Convention / Virginia, Foreign Mission Board, PO Box 6767, Richmond VA 23230. **Tel** (804)353-0151. ***Supersedes*** *Home and Foreign Fields.*
**Ind/Abst** South. Baptist Period. Index.

US/0885-8500
**COMMON BOUNDARY, THE.** **See** Psychology.

UK/0010-325X
**COMMON GROUND.** **Added/Corp** Council of Christians and Jews. Vol. 1-30A, No. 3, (Nov./Dec. 1946)-(Autumn 1976); (1978)-. Periodical. English. qt. £25.00. Council of Christians and Jews, 1 Dennington Park Road, West End Lane, London NW6 1AX England. **Tel** 011 44 1 794 8178, FAX 011 44 1 431 3500. **ED** Marcus Braybrooke. **Bk Rev**. **Ad Acc**. **Circ:** 4,000 (ctrl). available on microfilm from University Microfilms International (UMI). ***Supersedes*** *Christians and Jews.*
**Desc:** Features articles and reviews on Christianity and Judaism and relations between these two religions.

CN/0010-3454
**COMMUNAUTE CHRETIENNE.** ***Title Change.*** [Communaute chretienne]. **Added/Corp** Institut Dominicain de Pastorale, Montreal, Quebec. (1962-1992). Periodical. French. Eight times a year. 2715 Chemin de la Cote, Ste Catherine Montreal Quebec H3T 1B6 Canada. **Tel** (514)739-9797. **ED** Jean-Paul LeFebure. Index available. **Bk Rev**. **Circ:** 1,300 (ctrl). ***Continued by*** *Presence (Institut Dominicain de Pastorale (Montreal, Quebec)), 1188-5580.*
**Desc:** Pastoral theology.
**Ind/Abst** Point Repere (1983-).

BE
**COMMUNAUTES ET LITURGIES.** ***Ceased.*** Vol. 57 (1975)-?. Periodical. French. bm. Communautes et Liturgies, 1 Allee de Clerlande, B-1340 Ottignies Belgium. **Tel** 32 10 417461. **DD** 282. ***Continues*** *Paroisse et Liturgie, 0031-2347.*
**Desc:** One of the oldest liturgical review articles about celebration, prayers. liturgists and theologians. Special liturgy for the church holidays, including a bibliography.
**Ind/Abst** Old Testam. Abstr.

CN/0706-3644
**COMMUNICANTES.** (COMMUNICANTES : LE BULLETIN DU PRIEURE.). [Communicantes]. Vol. 2, No. 1 (March 1978)-. Bulletin. French. ir. Fraternite Saint-Pie X Canada, CP 1190, Shawinigan-Sud Quebec G9P 4E8 Canada. **DD** 269/.609714465. ***Continues*** *Bulletin du Prieure, 0706-3636.*

US/0279-1196
**COMMUNICARE.** ***Ceased.*** Vol. 56, No. 1 (1981)-?. Periodical. English. bm. Christian Communications Inc, PO Box 1601, Wichita KS 67201. **ED** Hart Armstrong. **Circ:** 10,000. available on microfilm from Xerox. ***Continues*** *Defender Magazine.*
**Desc:** Covers religion, theology and Bible prophecy.
**Ind/Abst** Commun. Abstr.

CN/0384-661X
**COMMUNICATE (KAMLOOPS).** (COMMUNICATE.). **Added/Corp** Evangelistic Enterprises Society. (1???)-. English. Five times a year. 7.00Can$. Evangelistic Enterprises, PO Box 600, Beaverlodge Alberta T0H 0C0 Canada. **Tel** (403)345-2818. ***Continues*** *Bible Evangelism.*

II/0970-0382
**COMMUNICATIO SOCIALIS YEARBOOK.** [Commun. social. yearb.]. 1981-1982-. English. an. Rs45.00 India; $12.00 US. Rev Clarence Srambical, Satprakashan Sanchar Kendra, Bhanwarkua Chowraha, Khandwa Road, Indore 452001 India. **Tel** 67131. **ED** Tomy Luiz. **LC** BV652.95; .C648. **DD** 260. **UDC** 22/28. **Bk Rev**. **Ad Acc**. **Circ:** 1,000.
**Desc:** Journal of Christian communication in the Third World, containing articles, reports, documentation, chronicle, innovation, personality and review. It provides and sustains a scientific basis for all questions connected with Christian communications.
**Ind/Abst** Bibliogr. Mission.; Missionalia.

●US/1061-4133
**COMMUNICATOR (NASHVILLE, TENN., 1992), THE.** (THE COMMUNICATOR.). [The Communicator]. **Added/Corp** African Methodist Episcopal Church. Sunday School Union. Vol. 1, No. 1 (Spring Issue 1992)-. Periodical. English. bm. $18.00 (U.S.), $24.00 (Can.). AMEC Sunday School Union/Legacy Publishing, 500-8th Avenue South, Nashville TN 37203-4181. **DD** 051.

UK
**COMMUNIO.** (1972)-. English. £19.00 (individuals), £25.00 (institutions) UK; £21.00 (individuals), £27.00 (institutions) other. T & T Clark Ltd., 59 George Street, Edinburgh EH2 2LQ Scotland. **Tel** 011 44 31 2254703, FAX 011 44 31 2204260.

SP/0010-3705
**COMMUNIO (SEVILLA).** (COMMUNIO; COMMENTARII INTERNATIONALES DE ECCLESIA ET THEOLOGIA.). [Communio]. Vol. 1 (1968)-. Periodical. Spanish (English, French and German). Three times a year. $40.00. Studium Generale O P, Apartado 820, E 41080 Seville Spain.
**Ind/Abst** New Testam. Abstr.; Old Testam. Abstr.

US/0094-2065
**COMMUNIO (SPOKANE, WASH.).** (COMMUNIO.). [Communio]. **VFOAT** International Catholic Review. Vol. 1, No. 1 (Spring 1974)-. Periodical. English. qt (Apr., July, Oct., Dec.). $33.00 (institutions), $23.00 (individuals) US; $29.00 other. Communio, PO Box 4468, Washington DC 20017. **Tel** (202)526-0251, FAX (202)526-0251. **ED** David L. Schindler. **LC** BX801; .C63. **DD** 282/.05. Index available (bound in fourth issue). cum. index. **Bk Rev**, (Qty: 1-2). **Ad Acc**, **Adv Mgr:** David Spesia. **Circ:** 2,700 (ctrl). available on microfilm from University Microfilms International (UMI).
**Desc:** Theological and cultural reflections from a Catholic perspective by noted theologians, philosophers, historians and other scholars.
**Ind/Abst** Bibliogr. Mission.; Index Book Rev. Relig.; New Testam. Abstr.; Old Testam. Abstr.; Relig. Index One Period. (1979-); Relig. Theol. Abstr. (199?-); Abr. Cathol. Period. Lit. Index; Cathol. Period. Lit. Index.

FR/0224-0254
**COMMUNION ET DIACONIE WATTRELOS.** (1979)-. Periodical. French. qt. 22.00Can$. Communion et Diaconie, 24 Avenue Aristide Briand, F 59150 Wattrelos France. **(Subscription address:** Periodica Inc., PO Box 444, 1155 Ducharme, Outrement Quebec H2V 4R6 Canada.**)** **ED** Lemettre Bernard. **UDC** 282. **Bk Rev**.

US/1043-0695
**COMMUNIQUE (COLUMBUS, OHIO).** (COMMUNIQUE.). [Commun.]. **Added/Corp** Business Professionals of America. Periodical. English. Eleven times a year. $3.00 (1-10 copies), $1.50 (10 or more). Synod of the Covenant, 6172 Busch Blvd, Office of Communications, Columbus OH 43229. **Tel** (614)436-3310. **ED** Doris Campbell. **DD** 371. **Ad Acc**. **Circ:** 10,000. ***Continues*** *OEA Communique, 0889-4817.*
**Desc:** THE COMMUNIQUE interprets the life and work of the synod of the Covenant (Presbyterian Church (USA) for the constituents in Michigan/Ohio and others outside the boundaries. It is a vehicle to inform church members about the mission of the church.

UK
**COMMUNITY BROADSHEET, THE.** 1940-. Periodical. English. ir.

US/0886-1293
**COMPANY (CHICAGO, ILL.).** (COMPANY.). [Company]. **Added/Corp** Jesuit Conference. Vol. 1, No. 1 (Sept. 1983)-. Periodical. English. qt. Free. Company, 3441 North Ashland Avenue, Chicago IL 60657. **ED** E. J. Mattimoe. **DD** 255.
**Desc:** Magazine of the American Jesuits.

AT/1036-9686
**COMPASS KENSINGTON.** (COMPASS.). [Compass Kensington]. **VFOAT** Compass Theology Review. (1990)-. Periodical. English. qt. 20.00Aus$ Australia; 24.80Aus$ Asia & Oceania; 25.60Aus$ other. Chevalier Press, PO Box 13, Kensington New South Wales 2033 Australia. **Tel** 011 61 2 6627894. **DD** 230.05.

AT
**COMPASS THEOLOGY REVIEW.** ***Title Change.*** **Added/Corp** Missionaries of the Sacred Heart. Australian Province. **VFOAT** Compass. Vol. 7, (June 1973)-(19??). Periodical. English. qt. Chevalier Press, PO Box 13, Kensington New South Wales 2033 Australia. **Tel** 011 61 2 6627894. ***Continues*** *Compass.* ***Continued by*** *Compass.*

CN/0715-8777
**COMPASS (TORONTO).** (COMPASS : A JESUIT JOURNAL.). [Compass]. **Added/Corp** Jesuits. Upper Canada Province. Vol. 1, No. 1 (1983)-. Periodical. English. bm. 25.00 Can$ institutions; 19.00 Can$ (one year), 34.00 Can$ (two years) individuals, Canada; 22.50 Can$ individuals other. Compass / Toronto, 10 St Mary Street/Suite 300, Toronto Ontario M4Y 1P9 Canada. **Tel** (416)921-1864, FAX (416)921-0653. **DD** 248.4/82/005. ctrl circ.
**Desc:** Forum of lively debate on contemporary, social and religious questions; ecumenical in spirit, it provides a moral and ethical perspective on such issues as Canada-US relations, international development and economic policy, along with informed and critical examination of the role of the Church in society.

IT
**CONCILIUM.** (19??)-. Italian. bm (6 issues). L65000 Italy; L80000 other. Editrice Queriniana, Casella Postale 403, 25100 Brescia Italy. **Tel** 39 30 294653.

UK/0010-5236
**CONCILIUM (ENGLISH LANGUAGE EDITION).** (CONCILIUM.). [Concilium]. **VFOAT** New Concilium. (1965)-. Monographic series. English. Six times a year (Feb., Apr., June, Aug., Oct., Dec.). $60.00 (individual); $75.00 (institution); $15.00 (single issue). Orbis Books, PO Box 308, Pinesbridge Road, Maryknoll NY 10545-0308. **Tel** (800)258-5838, (924)941-7590. **LC** UNC.
**Ind/Abst** Canon Law Abstr.; New Testam. Abstr.

SP/0210-1041
**CONCILIUM (MADRID).** (CONCILIUM : REVISTA INTERNACIONAL DE TEOLOGIA.). [Concilium]. No. 1 (1965)-. Monographic series. Spanish. Six times a year (Feb., Apr., June, Aug., Oct., Dec.). £71.00 Europe; £75.00 other. Editorial Verbo Divino, AVDA de Pamplona 41, 31200 Estella Navarra Spain. **Tel** 011 34 48 550449, FAX 011 34 48 554506. Index Available Received separately--bound from publisher. cum. index.
**Ind/Abst** Am. Hist. Life (1970-).

US/0162-7929
**CONCORDIA COMMENTATOR.** **See** Publishing-Books and Bookmaking.

US/0145-7233
**CONCORDIA JOURNAL.** [Concordia j.]. **Added/Corp** Concordia Seminary (Saint Louis, Mo.). (1975)-. Academic Scholarly Publication. English. qt (Jan., Apr., July, Oct.). $10.00 (US); $11.00 (Canada); $14.00 (other). Concordia Seminary, 801 de Mun Avenue, St Louis MO 63105. **Tel** (314)721-5934. **ED** Quentin F. Wesselschmidt (phone: (314)721-5934 ext. 475). **LC** BX8001; .C54. **DD** 230/.4/173. Index available. **Bk Rev**. **Circ:** 9,400. available on CD-ROM; available on microfilm and microfiche from University Microfilms International (UMI). ***Supersedes*** *CTM, 0090-9823.*
**Desc:** Publishes scholarly and practical articles dealing with exegetical, historical, practical, and systematic theology. It also contains editorials, homiletical helps, and book reviews.
**Ind/Abst** Christ. Period. Index (19??-); Index Book Rev. Relig.; Int. Zeitschriftenschau Bibelwissenschaft Grenzgeb.; New Testam. Abstr.; Old Testam. Abstr.; Relig. Index One Period. (1975-); Relig. Theol. Abstr.

US/0038-8610
**CONCORDIA THEOLOGICAL QUARTERLY.** [Concordia theol. q.]. **Added/Corp** Lutheran Church--Missouri Synod. Concordia Theological Seminary. **VFOAT** CTQ. Vol. 41, (Jan. 1977)-. Periodical. English. qt (Jan., Apr., July, Oct.). $10.00 US; $15.00 Canada; $20.00 other. Concordia Theological Seminary, 6600 North Clinton, Ft Wayne IN 46825. **Tel** (219)481-2100, FAX (219)481-2121. **ED** Dr. Heino Kadai (phone: (219)481-2131). **LC** NOT IN LC. **DD** 284. **Bk Rev**, (Qty: varies). **Ad Acc**. **Circ:** 9,000 (ctrl). available on microfilm and microfiche from University Microfilms International (UMI). ***Continues*** *Springfielder, 0884-2825.*
**Desc:** Articles on theology, also homiletical studies designed to aid the busy parish pastor.
**Ind/Abst** Index Book Rev. Relig.; New Testam. Abstr.; Old Testam. Abstr.; Relig. Index One Period. (1977-); Relig. Theol. Abstr.

CN/1180-0682
**CONFRATERNITAS (TORONTO).** (CONFRATERNITAS : THE NEWSLETTER OF THE SOCIETY FOR CONFRATERNITY STUDIES.). [Confraternitas]. **Added/Corp** Society for Confraternity Studies. **VFOAT** Newsletter of the Society for

Confraternity Studies. Vol. 1, No. 1 (Spring 1990)-. Periodical. English. sa. 12.00Can$. Society for Confraternity Studies, Victoria College, University of Toronto, Toronto, Ontario M5S 1K7 Canada. **Tel** (416)585-4486, FAX (416)585-4591. **ED** William R. Bowen and Konrad Eisenbichler. **DD** 248/.06.

IT
**CONFRONTI.** (19??)-. Italian. mo. L65000 Italy; L95000 others. Societa Coop Com Nuovi Tempi, Via Firenze 38, 00184 Rome Italy. **Tel** 011 39 6 4820503, FAX 011 39 6 4827901. Index available. **Bk Rev. Ad Acc. Circ:** 5,000.
**Desc:** Comparisons and meetings between Protestantism, Catholicism, Judaism and Islam on the events involving daily life. Covers ecology and ethics.

US/0010-5856
**CONGREGATIONALIST (BELOIT), THE.** (THE CONGREGATIONALIST.). **Added/Corp** National Association of Congregational Christian Churches (U.S.). Vol. 1-6, (Feb. 1958)-(Dec. 1964); Vol. 125 (Jan. 1965)-. Periodical. English. Six times a year. $10.00. National Association Christian Churches, PO Box 1620, Oak Creek WI 53154. **Tel** (414)764-1620. **ED** Mary Woolsey. **LC** BX7101; .C77. **DD** 285/.8/05. **Bk Rev. Ad Acc. Circ:** 5,000 (ctrl). available on microfilm from University Microfilms International (UMI). ***Supersedes*** *Free Churches.*
**Desc:** Denominational publication of literary items and current event coverage.

US
**CONGREGATIONS ALBAN JOURNAL.** (19??)-. English. Six times a year. $30.00. Alban Institute, 4550 Montgomery Avenue, Suite 433 N, Bethesda MD 20814. **Tel** (301)718-4407.

CN/0821-1752
**CONGRES - ENTRAIDE MISSIONNAIRE.** (CONGRES.). [Congr. - Entraide mission.]. **Main/Corp** Entraide Missionnaire, Inc. Congres. **Added/Corp** Entraide Missionnaire, Inc. (1982)-. French. an. Entraide Missionnaire, 2295 rue Chambly, Montreal Quebec H1W 3J6 Canada. **DD** 261.8/05. ***Continues*** *Entraide Missionnaire, Inc. Congres. Dossier du Congres, 0821-1744.*

FR
**CONNAISSANCEG DES PERES DE L'EGGLISE.** Editions Nouvelle Cite, 131 rue Castagnary, F 75015 Paris France. **Bk Rev. Ad Acc.**

CN/0829-044X
**CONRAD GREBEL REVIEW, THE.** [Conrad Grebel rev.]. **Added/Corp** Conrad Grebel College. Vol. 1, No. 1 (Winter 1983)-. Periodical. English. Three times a year. 21.00Can$ (1 year), 36.00Can$ (2 year), 50.00 Can$ (3 year). Conrad Grebel College, Kathleen Boutet, Waterloo Ontario N2L 3G6 Canada. **Tel** (519)885-0220, FAX (519)885-0014. **ED** Rodney Sawatsky. **DD** 289.7/05. **Bk Rev. Circ:** 400 (ctrl).
**Desc:** Interdisciplinary journal of Christian inquiry exploring contemporary issues in light of Christian faith. Includes book reviews of interest to academics and professionals.
**Ind/Abst** Index Book Rev. Relig.; Relig. Index One Period.; Relig. Theol. Abstr.

UK
**CONSCIENCE AND LIBERTY : INTERNATIONAL JOURNAL OF RELIGIOUS FREEDOM.** (1989)-. English. sa.
**Ind/Abst** Index Book Rev. Relig.; Relig. Index One Period.

SZ
**CONSCIENCE ET LIBERTE.** No. 1-3, 1948-50; New Series, No. 1- 1971-. Periodical. French (German, Italian, Portuguese, Spanish and Serbo-Croatian (Roman)). sa. 22.00F Switzerland; 60.00F France; 24.00F other. Association Internationale pour la Defense del la Liberte Religieuse, Schlosshaldenstrasse 17, 3006 Berne Switzerland. **Tel** 031/44 62 62, telex 845-912950. **ED** Gianfranco Rossi. Index available. **Bk Rev.**
**Desc:** Attempts to stress the importance of religious liberty, to inform about respect or violations of this freedom, and to emphasize the legal, social and political implications thereof.

US/0884-7010
**CONSECRATED LIFE (ENGLISH ED.).** (CONSECRATED LIFE.). **Added/Corp** Institute on Religious Life. Catholic Church. Congregatio pro Religiosis et Institutis Saecularibus. **VFOAT** Informationes. Vol. 1 (1975)-. Periodical. English (Italian; translations available in Multiple languages). sa. $15.00. Institute on Religious Life, PO Box 41007, Chicago IL 60641. **Tel** (312)267-1195. **ED** James Downey, (editor's address: 44 Frank Lloyd Wright Drive, PO Box 555, Ann Arbor, MI 48106; editor's phone: (313)930-7470). **DD** 261. **Circ:** 2,300 (ctrl).
**Desc:** Various talks the Holy Father gives to different religious orders, and talks on religious life in general.
**Ind/Abst** Abr. Cathol. Period. Lit. Index; Cathol. Period. Lit. Index.

CN/0317-1493
**CONSENSUS (WINNIPEG).** (CONSENSUS.). [Consensus]. **Added/Corp** Lutheran Council in Canada. Division of Theological Studies. Waterloo Lutheran Seminary. Lutheran Theological Seminary (Saskatoon, Sask.). Vol. 1 (Jan. 1975)-. Periodical. English. Twice a year (Spring & Fall). $13.50 one year; $25.00 two year. Consensus Canada, Waterloo Lutheran Seminary, 75 University Avenue W, Waterloo Ontario N2L 3C5 Canada. **Tel** (519)884-1970 ext 2258 or ext 2512, FAX (519)725-2434. **ED** Eduard Riegert. **DD** 230/.4/171. **Bk Rev**, (Qty: 40). **Pr Rev. Circ:** 350.
**Ind/Abst** Index Book Rev. Relig. (1979-); Relig. Index One Period. (1979-).

CN/0826-7499
**CONSOLATA MISSIONARIES. Added/Corp** Consolata Missionaries of Canada. (1981)-. Periodical. English. bm (6 issues). 3.00Can$. Consolata Missionaries Canada, 2671 Islington Avenue, Toronto Ontario M9V 2X6 Canada. **Tel** (416)749-8907. **ED** Francesco Cialini. **DD** 266/.2/05. ***Continues*** *Consolata, 0226-8957.*

UK/0573-777X
**CONTACT. Added/Corp** Scottish Pastoral Association. Clinical Theology Association. Institute of Religion and Medicine. Association for Pastoral Care and Counseling. (Oct. 1960)-. Periodical. English. Three times a year. £6.00 UK; £7.50 other. Isobel Bennie, 62 Anson Avenue, Flakirk FK1 5JE Scotland. **Tel** 44 324 21388. **ED** Dr. Stephen Cattison. cum. index. **Bk Rev. Ad Acc. Circ:** 2500. available on microfilm from University Microfilms International (UMI).
**Desc:** To allow a dialogue to take place between the "pastoral" disciplines; to expose areas of agreement and disagreement, and to clarify rather than synthesize.

FR/0045-8325
**CONTACTS; REVUE FRANCAISE DE L'ORTHODOXIE. Added/Corp** Eglise Orthodoxe de France. **VFOAT** Revue Francaise de l'Orthodoxie. Vol. 1 (1949)-. Periodical. French. qt. $53.00. Revue Orthodoxe "Contacts", 37 rue des Cornouillers, 46090 Pradines, CCP Paris 74 95 15 W France. **Tel** 33 1 45358098. **ED** S Balzon and Revault d'Allonnes. **Bk Rev. Circ:** 1,000.
**Desc:** Orthodox theology and spirituality.

US/0162-1971
**CONTEMPO (BIRMINGHAM, ALA.).** (CONTEMPO.). [Contempo]. **Added/Corp** Southern Baptist Convention. Woman's Missionary Union. Baptist Young Women. (19??)-. Periodical. English. mo. $12.95. Woman's Missionary Union, PO Box 830010, Birmingham AL 35283. **Tel** (205)991-8100, (205)991-4933. **ED** Ele Clay. **DD** 266. **Circ:** 61,000 (ctrl).
**Desc:** A magazine for Baptist Young Women, ages 18-34, one of Woman's Missionary Union's five organizations.
**Ind/Abst** South. Baptist Period. Index.

US/1049-3379
**CONTEMPORARY CHRISTIAN MUSIC (1986).** **See** Music.

US/0190-0986
**CONTEMPORARY RELIGIOUS MOVEMENTS.** (19??)-. Monographic series. English. ir. Price varies per volume. John Wiley & Sons, Inc., 605 Third Avenue, New York NY 10158-0012. **Tel** (212)850-6000, (212)850-6645, FAX (212)850-6088, telex 12-7063. **(Subscription address:** John Wiley & Sons / England, Baffins Lane, Chichester, West Sussex PO19 1UD England.**)**

FI/0782-7342
**CONTENTA RELIGIONUM.** [Contenta relig.]. (1985)-. Multiple languages. ir. Kluwer Academic Publishers, Postbus 322, 3300 AH Dordrecht, The Netherlands. **Tel** 011 (31) 78 524400, FAX 011 31 78 183273, telex 20083.

US/0361-8854
**CONTEXT (CHICAGO. 1969).** (CONTEXT; A COMMENTARY ON THE INTERACTION OF RELIGION AND CULTURE.). Vol. 1 (Oct. 15, 1969)-. Periodical. English. sm (combined Aug./Sept.). $24.95. Claretian Publications, 205 West Monroe Street, Chicago IL 60606. **Tel** (312)236-7782, (800)328-6515. **ED** Martin E. Marty. **Circ:** 5,790. available on microfilm from University Microfilms International (UMI).
**Desc:** Martin E. Marty's commentary on the interaction of religion and culture.

CN/0226-8949
**CONTINENTAL REFLECTIONS.** [Cont. reflect.]. Vol. 1, No. 1 (May 1980)-. Periodical. English. bm. Free. Continental Reflections, PO Box 98, Thompson Manitoba R8N 1M9 Canada. **Tel** (204)778-4491. **ED** Bill Martens. **DD** 226/.009719. **Circ:** 1,700.

US/1070-9495
**CONTRA MUNDUM.** (CONTRA MUNDUM : A REFORMED CULTURAL REVIEW.). [Contra mundum]. No. 1 (Fall 1991)-. Periodical. English. qt. $18.50 US; $19.30 Canada and Mexico; $20.50 other. Contra Mundum, PO Box 32652, Fridley MN 55432. **Tel** (612)378-0359. **DD** 285. **Bk Rev**, (Qty: 35). **Ad Acc. Circ:** 250.
**Desc:** Information on the Reformed Church.

US/0196-7053
**CONTRIBUTIONS TO THE STUDY OF RELIGION.** [Contrib. study relig.]. (1981)-. Monographic series. English. ir. Price varies per volume. Greenwood Press Inc., PO Box 5007, Westport CT 06881-5007. **Tel** (203)226-3571, FAX (203)222-1502. **ED** Henry W. Bowden. **Bk Rev. Ad Acc.**

CN/0826-0621
**CONVENING CIRCULAR AND SYNOD JOURNAL FOR THE ... SESSION OF SYNOD. Main/Corp** Anglican Church of Canada. Diocese of Ottawa. Synod. **VFOAT** Meeting of the Synod. 95th (May 26/27/28, 1983)-. English. an. Free. Anglican Church of Canada / Ottawa, Diocese of Ottawa, 71 Bronson Avenue, Ottawa Ontario K1R 6O6 Canada. **DD** 283/.713/84. ***Continues*** *Journal of Proceedings of the Incorporated Synod of the Diocese of Ottawa, 0317-3003.*

CN/0229-1134
**COPTOLOGIA.** (COPTOLOGIA : STUDIA COPTICA ORTHODOXA : A RESEARCH PUBLICATION IN COPTIC ORTHODOX STUDIES.). [Coptologia]. **Added/Corp** St. Mark's Coptic Canadian Cultural Centre. Society for Coptic and Ancient Egyptian Studies. **VFOAT** Gyptologia. Vol. 1 (1981)-. Periodical. English. an (Sept.). 10.00Can$ Canada; 11.50Can$ US; 12.50Can$ other. Coptologia Publications, PO Box 235 / Don Mills Postal Station, Don Mills Ontario M3C 2S2 Canada. **Tel** (416)391-1774. **ED** Fayek M. Ishak. **LC** BX130; .C67. **DD** 281/.7/05. **Bk Rev. Circ:** 350 (ctrl).
**Desc:** Journal of Coptic thought and orthodox spirituality.

US/0360-649X
**COPTS, THE. Added/Corp** American Coptic Association. **VFOAT** Aqbat. (Jan./Feb. 1974)-. Periodical. Arabic (English). Four times a year. $10.00. American Coptic Association, PO Box 9119, Jersey City NJ 07304. **Tel** (201)451-0972, (201)333-7057. **LC** DT72.C7; C66.
**Ind/Abst** Hum. Rights Intern. Rep.

CN/0318-4374
**COQUILLE, LA.** V. 1- 1972-. French. qt. La Coquille, 61 Promenade Riverside, Saint-Lambert Quebec Canada. **DD** 267/.18/2.

US/0275-2743
**CORNERSTONE (CHICAGO, ILL.).** (CORNERSTONE.). **Added/Corp** Jesus People USA. (19??)-. Periodical. English. bm (varies). $15.00 (12 issues). Cornerstone Communications, 920 West Wilson, Chicago IL 60640. **Tel** (312)561-2450, FAX (312)989-2076. **ED** Dawn Herrin (phone: (312)989-2080). **Bk Rev. Ad Acc. Pr Rev. Circ:** 40,000.
**Desc:** Full length articles on social problems, christian ethics, cults, poetry, and current news events. A oriented magazine for the contemporary evangelical Christians.

US/0883-6108
**CORNERSTONE (SAN ANTONIO, TEX.), THE.** (THE CORNERSTONE.). [Cornerstone]. Began with June 1985?. Periodical. English. mo. $24.00. Cornerstone Publishing Company, PO Box 37226, San Antonio TX 78218-6727. **DD** 277.

BE
**CORPUS CHRISTIANORUM. CLAVIS PATRUM GRAECORUM.** ***Ceased.*** **VFOAT** Clavis Patrum Graecorum. Vol. 1 (19??)-Vol. 5 (19??). Periodical. Latin. ir. Brepols Publishers, Steenweg OP Tielen 68, B-2300 Turnhout Belgium. **Tel** 011 32 14 402500.
**Desc:** The series contains the works of Christian Latin literature of the 1st to the 12th Century and of the Greek Post-Nicene fathers.

BE
**CORPUS CHRISTIANORUM. CONTINUATIO MEDIAEVALIS. VFOAT** Continuatio Mediaevalis. (1971)-. Monographic series. Latin. ir. Price varies per volume. Brepols Publishers, Steenweg OP Tielen 68, B-2300 Turnhout Belgium. **Tel** 011 32 14 402500. **ED** Abbey Steenbrugge. **DD** 270.
**Desc:** Patristic texts of the 8th to the 14th century.

BE
**CORPUS CHRISTIANORUM. INITIA.** (1971)-. Latin. ir. Brepols Publishers, Steenweg OP Tielen 68, B-2300 Turnhout Belgium. **Tel** 011 32 14 402500.
**Desc:** Incipits of the two Latin series of the Corpus Christianorum.

BE
**CORPUS CHRISTIANORUM. SERIES APOCRYPHORUM. Added/Corp** Association pour l'Etude de la Litterature Apocryphe Chretienne. **VFOAT** Series Apocryphorum. (1983)-. Monographic series. French (French). an. Price varies per volume. Brepols Publishers, Steenweg OP Tielen 68, B-2300 Turnhout Belgium. **Tel** 011 32 14 402500.

BE
**CORPUS CHRISTIANORUM: SERIES GRAECA.** (1977)-. Monographic series. Greek, Modern (Latin; summaries and/or abstracts in French). ir. Price varies per volume. Brepols Publishers, Steenweg OP Tielen 68, B-2300 Turnhout Belgium. **Tel** 011 32 14 402500.
**Desc:** Greek patrology with principally Post-Nicene fathers.

BE
**CORPUS CHRISTIANORUM. SERIES LATINA.** Vol. 1 (1953)-. Monographic series. Latin (French). ir. Price varies per volume. Brepols Publishers, Steenweg OP Tielen 68, B-2300 Turnhout Belgium. **Tel** 011 32 14 402500. **LC** BR60; .C49.

FR
**CORPUS SCRIPTORUM CHRISTIANORUM ORIENTALIUM.** **Added/Corp** Louvain. Universite Catholique. Catholic University of America. (19??)-. Monographic series. Latin (Arabic, Armenian, Ethiopic, Coptic, Syriac, Greek, Modern, Latin and French, English). ir. Price varies per volume. Editions Peeters SA, Bondgenotenlaan 153, BP 41, B-3000 Leuven Belgium. **Tel** 32 16 235170, FAX 32 16 228500, telex 65987 PUL B. Index available. ctrl circ.
**Desc:** Scientific text editions and studies on Early Oriental Churches.

AU
**CORPUS SCRIPTORUM ECCLESIASTICORUM LATINORUM.** **Added/Corp** Kaiserl. Akademie der Wissenschaften in Wien. Akademie der Wissenschaften in Wien. Osterreichische Akademie der Wissenschaften. Vol. 1 (1866)-. Monographic series. Latin. ir. Price varies per volume. Holder Pichler Tempsky, Frankgasse 4, Postfach 127, 1096 Vienna Austria. **Tel** 011 43 1 4389930. **LC** BR60; .C6.

US/1052-3790
**COVENANT DISCIPLESHIP QUARTERLY.** [Covenant disciplesh. q.]. **Added/Corp** United Methodist Church (U.S.) Center for Congregational Life. United Methodist Church (U.S.). Office of Covenant Discipleship and Christian Foundation. Vol. 1, No. 1 (Oct. 1985)-. Periodical. English (Spanish). Four times a year (Jan., Apr., July, Oct.). $10.00. Covenant Discipleship General, Board Discipleship, PO Box 840, Nashville TN 37202. **Tel** (615)340-7010, FAX (615)340-7565. **ED** Ellen Bourne. **DD** 248. **Bk Rev**, (Qty: 1). **Ad Acc. Circ:** 1,000 (ctrl).
**Desc:** Covers covenant discipleship members and their efforts to look beyond their church congregations and neighborhood and discover the world of proverty, homelesssness, drug addition, rundown housing development, unemployment, illiteracy, broken families, and the uninsured sick.

US/0361-0934
**COVENANT QUARTERLY, THE.** [Covenant q.]. Vol. 1 (1941)-. Periodical. English. qt. $12.00 US; $24.00 other. Covenant Publications, 3200 West Foster Avenue, Chicago IL 60625. **Tel** (312)478-4676. **ED** Wayne Weld (phone: (312)478-2696). **Bk Rev**. **Ad Acc. Circ:** 1,800 (ctrl).
**Desc:** The theological journal of the Evangelical Covenant Church, aimed at ministers, missionaries, and interested laypeople.
**Ind/Abst** Index Book Rev. Relig.; Relig. Index One Period. (1976-); Relig. Theol. Abstr.

US/0749-4319
**COVENANTER WITNESS.** **Added/Corp** Reformed Presbyterian Church of North America. Vol. 1 (July 11, 1928)-. Periodical. English. Eleven times a year (July/Aug. issues combined). $20.00. Covenanter Witness, 7418 Penn Avenue, Pittsburgh PA 15208-2531. **Tel** (412)241-0436. **ED** Drew Gordon and Lynne Gordon. **LC** BX8990.A1; C6. **DD** 285. Index available ($1.95 separately). cum. index. **Bk Rev**. **Ad Acc, Adv Mgr:** Steve, **Tel** (412)241-0436. **Circ:** 2,000 (ctrl).
***Supersedes*** *Christian Nation;* ***Absorbed*** *Olive Trees.*

XR
**CPC INFORMATION.** **Main/Corp** Christian Peace Conference. **VAT** Christian Peace Conference Information. No. 68 (Dec. 1970)-. Periodical. English. mo. Free on request. Christian Peace Conference, Jungmanova 9, Information Department, Prague 1 Czech Republic. ***Continues*** *Christian Peace Conference. Information Bulletin of the Christian Peace Conference, 0578-0136.*

AT/0819-1530
**CREATION EX NIHILO.** [Creat. ex nihilo]. (1985)-. Periodical. English. Four times a year (Mar., June, Sept., Dec.). $22.00 (one year), $42.00 (two year), $60.00 (three year). Creation Science Foundation Ltd, PO Box 6302, Acacia Ridge QLD 4110 Australia. **Tel** 011 61 7 273 7650, FAX 011 61 7 273 7672. **ED** Robert Doolan. **DD** 231.76505. **Circ:** 35,000. ***Continues*** *Ex Nihilo, 0726-6782.*
**Desc:** Presents scientific and biblical evidence for creation and related subjects.

AT/1036-2916
**CREATION EX NIHILO TECHNICAL JOURNAL.** [Creat. ex nihilo tech. j.]. (1991)-. Periodical. English. sa. $25.00 (one year), $48.00 (two year), $69.00 (three year). Creation Science Foundation Ltd, PO Box 6302, Acacia Ridge QLD 4110 Australia. **Tel** 011 61 7 273 7650, FAX 011 61 7 273 7672. **ED** A. Snelling. **DD** 231.765. **Circ:** 2,000. ***Continues*** *Ex Nihilo Technical Journal, 0814-6764.*

CN/0229-253X
**CREATION SCIENCE DIALOGUE.** **See** Science and Technology.

US/1053-9891
**CREATION SPIRITUALITY.** [Creat. spiritual.]. **Added/Corp** Friends of Creation Spirituality. Vol. 7, No. 1 (Jan./Feb. 1991)-. Periodical. English. qt (Jan., Apr., July, Oct.). $24.00 (one year), $45.00 (two year). Friends of Creation Spirituality Inc, PO Box 19216, Oakland CA 94619. **Tel** (510)482-4984, FAX (510)482-0387. **ED** John R. Mabry. **LC** BL624; .C73. **DD** 291/.05. **Bk Rev**, (Qty: 20). **Ad Acc. Circ:** 13,000. ***Continues*** *Creation (Oakland, Calif.), 8756-3088.*
**Desc:** Magazine of spirituality applied to the personal social and ecological issues of our day.

US/1062-4708
**CREATIVE TRANSFORMATION.** [Creat. transform.]. **Added/Corp** Claremont Center for Process Studies. Process and Faith. Vol. 1, No. 1 (Summer 1991)-. Periodical. English. Four times a year. $40.00 (membership), $20.00 (library). Process & Faith Program, School of Theology, 1325 North College Avenue, Claremont CA 91711. **Tel** (909)626-3521 Ext. 288. **ED** John Quiring; (909)621-5330. **DD** 210. **Bk Rev**, (Qty: 8). **Pr Rev. Circ:** 350.

NO
**CREDO.** (19??)-. Periodical. Norwegian. Eighteen times a year. Kr98.00 US & Canada; Kr65.00 other. Credo Forlag AS, Holbergs Plass 4, Oslo 1 Norway. **ED** Jens-Petter Johnsen and Haakon Soedal. cum. index. **Bk Rev**. **Ad Acc. Circ:** 4,000 (ctrl).
**Desc:** A student magazine with theological, scientific and other actual items for Christians. Covers family problems and problems between faith and study.

AG
**CREER.** No. 1 (April/May 1975)-. Periodical. Spanish. mo. Editorial el Pais Saicf e Defensa, 570 Buenos Aires Argentina.

MX
**CRIE : CENTRO REGIONAL DE INFORMACIONES ECUMENICAS, A.C.** **Added/Corp** Centro Regional de Informaciones Ecumenicas (Mexico City, Mexico). **VFOAT** Centro Regional de Informaciones Ecumenicas. (1976)-. Periodical. Spanish. Twenty-seven times a year. $35.00 North America & Europe; $30.00 other. Centro Reg Info Ecumenicas, Yosemite 45, Colonia Napoles, 03810 Mexico DF Mexico. **Tel** 011 52 5369321.
**Ind/Abst** Hum. Rights Intern. Rep.

IT/0393-3598
**CRISTIANESIMO NELLA STORIA.** [Cristianes. stor.]. **Added/Corp** Istituto per le Scienze Religiose di Bologna. Universita di Bologna. Vol. 1, Issue 1 (April 1980)-. Periodical. Italian (English, French, German and Spanish; summaries and/or abstracts in English). Three times a year. L59000 Italy; L71000 other. Centro Editoriale Dehoniano, Via Nosadella 6, Casella Postale 568, 40123 Bologna Italy. **Tel** 011 39 51 306811. **ED** Giuseppe Alberigo. **LC** BR140; .C74. **DD** 270/.05. Index available. **Bk Rev**. **Ad Acc. Circ:** 1,200 (ctrl).
**Desc:** The journal publishes critical essays on the history of Christianity from the Judaic origins to the present age, and research articles of the Istituto Scienze Religiose.
**Ind/Abst** Am. Hist. Life (1984-); Bibliogr. Mission.; Canon Law Abstr.; Index Book Rev. Relig.; New Testam. Abstr.; Old Testam. Abstr.; Relig. Theol. Abstr.

AG/0326-5633
**CRISTIANISMO Y SOCIEDAD (BUENOS AIRES).** (CRISTIANISMO Y SOCIEDAD.). [Crist. soc.]. **Added/Corp** Junta Latino Americana de Iglesia y Sociedad. Movimiento Latino Americano de Iglesia y Sociedad. Vol. 1, No. 1 (Jan./April 1963)-. Periodical. Spanish. qt. $11.00 Mexico; $22.00 other. Accion Social Ecumenica Latino Americana, Casilla 15067, Guayaquil Ecuador. **Tel** 011 593 4 237385. **LC** BR115.W6; C7. **DD** 261. ***Supersedes*** *Iglesia y Sociedad en America Latina.*
**Ind/Abst** HAPI Hisp. Am. Period. Index; Index Book Rev. Relig.; Relig. Index One Period. (1981-); Relig. Theol. Abstr.

US/0892-5712
**CRISWELL THEOLOGICAL REVIEW.** (CRISWELL THEOLOGICAL REVIEW : CTR.). [Criswell theol. rev.]. **Added/Corp** Criswell College. **VFOAT** CTR. Vol. 1, No. 1 (Fall 1986)-. Periodical. English. sa (May & Oct.). $15.00 (one year), $27.00 (two years), $39.00 (three years). Criswell College, 4010 Gaston Ave, Dallas TX 75246. **Tel** (214)821-5433. **ED** George L Klein. **DD** 230. **Bk Rev**. **Ad Acc, Adv Mgr:** Klein, **Tel** (214)821-5433. **Circ:** 1,250 (ctrl).
**Desc:** Theological journal includes articles and book reviews.
**Ind/Abst** Index Book Rev. Relig.; Relig. Index One Period. (1986-1988, 19??-).

US/0590-0980
**CRITERION (CHICAGO).** (CRITERION.). [Criterion]. **Added/Corp** University of Chicago. Divinity School. Vol. 1 (1962)-. Periodical. English. Three times a year (Feb., May, Nov.). Free to alumni and donors; $9.00 other. The Divinity School, University of Chicago, Chicago IL 60637. **Tel** (312)702-8222, FAX (312)702-6048. **ED** Elena Vassallo. **LC** BR1; .C6965. **Circ:** 5,000. ***Supersedes*** *Divinity School News.*
**Desc:** Religious studies and scholarship for a popular audience, and news from the University of Chicago Divinity School.
**Ind/Abst** Index Book Rev. Relig.; Relig. Index One Period. (1963-); Relig. Theol. Abstr. (1963-).

VE
**CRITERIOS HOY.** **Added/Corp** Organizacion Democrata Cristiana de America. No. 1 (1991)-. Periodical. Spanish.

US/0890-3654
**CRITICAL MASS (BERKELEY, CA).** ***Ceased.*** (CRITICAL MASS.). [Crit. mass]. Vol. 1, No. 1 (1986)-?. Periodical. English. qt. Starr King School, 2241 Leconte, Berkeley CA 94709. **DD** 288.

CN/0712-2292
**CROITRE.** [Croitre]. Vol. 1 No. 1-. Periodical. French. ir. Free. Oasis Maison Rivat, Cap-Rouge Quebec G0A 1K0 Canada. **DD** 248/.05.

DM
**CROIX, LA.** **VFOAT** Croix du Dahomey. Periodical. French. 1000. BP 105, Cotonou Dahomey. **LC** BX1682.D34; C76.

UK/0260-6313
**CROSS CURRENT.** **See** Education.

US/0011-1953
**CROSS CURRENTS.** [Cross curr.]. **Added/Corp** Association for Religion & Intellectual Life. Associates for Religion and Intellectual Life (U.S.). Vol. 1 (Fall 1950)-. Periodical. English. qt (4 issues). $25.00 (individuals), $32.50 (libraries). Cross Currents, College of New Rochelle, New Rochelle NY 10805. **Tel** (914)654-5425, FAX (914)654-5554. **(Subscription address:** Cambey & West Cross Currents, PO Box 147, Pearl River NY 10965.**)** **ED** William Birmingham, Joseph Cunneen and Nancy Malone, O.S.U. **LC** BR1; .C6978. **DD** 205. Index available (bound in 4th issue). **Bk Rev**, (Qty: 35). **Ad Acc, Adv Mgr:** Ronnie Carpini. **Circ:** 4,000. available on microfilm and microfiche from University Microfilms International (UMI); available on CD-ROM. Documents available from UMI Article Clearinghouse. ***Absorbed*** *Religion & Intellectual Life, 0741-0549.*
**Desc:** A review to explore the implications of Christianity for our times. It is international, ecumenical and interdisciplinary.
**Ind/Abst** Acad. Search (July 1993-); Am. Bibliogr. Slavic East Europ. Stud.; Annu. Bibliogr. Engl. Lang. Lit.; Guide Soc. Sci. Relig.; Humanit. Index; Humanit. Source (Jul. 1993-); Index Book Rev. Relig.; INFO-SOUTH Abstr.; Mag. Search; MLA Int. Bibl. Books Artic. Mod. Lang. Lit.; Newsp. Period. Abstr. (1990-); Old Testam. Abstr.; Relig. Index One Period.; Relig. Theol. Abstr.; Abr. Cathol. Period. Lit. Index; Cathol. Period. Lit. Index.

US/1064-4490
**CROSS POINT.** [Cross point]. **Added/Corp** Community of Jesus (Orleans, Mass.). Vol. 1, No. 1 (Fall 1988)-. Periodical. English. Four times a year (Feb., May, Aug., Nov.). $12.95. Community of Jesus, PO Box 1094, Orleans MA 02653. **Tel** (508)255-1094. **ED** Hal M. Helins. **DD** 248. **Bk Rev**, (Qty: 10-12). **Ad Acc, Adv Mgr:** Paraclete Press, **Tel** (508)255-4685. **Circ:** 4,100.

●US/1065-6863
**CROSSROADS (SUNNYVALE, CALIF.).** (CROSSROADS.). [Crossroads]. (1992)-. Periodical. English. qt. $25.00. Coalition on Revival, 789 El Camino Real, Sunnyvale CA 94087. **DD** 269.

UK/0011-2100
**CRUCIBLE.** **Added/Corp** Church of England. National Assembly. Board for Social Responsibility. (1963)-. Periodical. English. qt. £8.00 UK; £9.00 Europe; £10.00 other. General Synod Board of Education, 118 Duxford Road, E Wolstencroft, Cambridge CB2 4NA United Kingdom. **Tel** 011 44 71 223 832331. **ED** Ian Kenway. **LC** HN30; .C75. **DD** 261. Index available. **Bk Rev**. **Ad Acc. Circ:** 2,000 (ctrl). available on microfiche; available in microform. ***Supersedes*** *Moral Welfare.*
**Desc:** Christian comment on current issues, international affairs, faith and morals, social problems and politics.
**Ind/Abst** Appl. Soc. Sci. Index Abstr.

US/8756-1247
**CRUCIBLE (MERCEDES, TEX.), THE.** (THE CRUCIBLE.). [Crucible]. (19??)-. Periodical. English. qt. $10.00. De Young Press, Box 7252, Spencer IA 51301-7252. **DD** 211.

CN/0011-2186
**CRUX.** [Crux]. Vol. 15, No. 2 (June 1979)-. Periodical. English. qt. $14.00. Crux, 5800 University Boulevard,

Vancouver British Columbia V6T 2E4 Canada. **Tel** (800)663-8664, (604)224-3245, FAX (604)224-3097. **[CCC]. Circ:** 2,000. ***Continues*** *Crux, 0011-2186.*
**Ind/Abst** Index Book Rev. Relig.; New Testam. Abstr.; Old Testam. Abstr.; Relig. Index One Period.; Relig. Theol. Abstr.

US/0591-2296
**CRUX OF THE NEWS.** Vol. 1 (Aug. 18, 1980)-. Periodical. English. wk. $79.50 (one year) (surface mail), $97.00 (air mail) US; $99.00 (one year) (air mail) Canada and Mexico; $128.00 (air mail) other. Clarity Publishing Inc., 3 Enterprise Drive, Albany NY 12204. **Tel** (518)465-4591, FAX (518)465-4333. **ED** Richard A. Dowd and Patricia A. Crewell. **Bk Rev. Ad Acc. Pr Rev. Circ:** 4,500. ***Supersedes*** *Crux of the News, 0591-2296.*
**Desc:** Management newsletter for church professionals covering all news of interest.

US
**CSSR BULLETIN.** Bulletin. English. qt. $24.00 US; $30.00 other. Council of Societies for the Study of Religion, Valparaiso University, Valparaiso IN 46383. **Tel** (219)464-5515. **ED** Rick Busse. **Ad Acc. Circ:** 6,000 (ctrl).
**Desc:** An inter-societal newsletter designed to carry news to its members as well as information to members of other societies.

US
**CSSR DIRECTORY OF DEPARTMENTS OF RELIGIOUS STUDIES IN NORTH AMERICA.** Directory. English. ir. Council of Societies for the Study of Religion, Valparaiso University, Valparaiso IN 46383. **Tel** (219)464-5515. **ED** Watson E Mills. Index available. **Ad Acc.**
**Desc:** In-depth information from participating departments of religion/religious studies regarding admissions requirements, description of department, faculty listing, financial information, etc.

SI
**CTC BULLETIN : OCCASIONAL BULLETIN OF THE COMMISSION ON THEOLOGICAL CONCERNS, CHRISTIAN CONFERENCE OF ASIA.** **Added/Corp** Christian Conference of Asia. Commission on Theological Concerns. Vol. 1, No. 2 (Nov. 1979)-. Periodical. English. Three times a year. $4.00 Asia; $8.00 other. Christian Conference of Asia / Hong Kong, 96 District 2 Pak Tim Village, Mei Tim Road, Shatin Hong Kong. **Tel** 011 852 6911068, FAX 011 852 6924378, telex 37618. **ED** Salvador T. Martinez. **Bk Rev. Circ:** 700 (ctrl). ***Continues*** *Hayyim.*

AG
**CUADERNOS DE TEOLOGIA.** **Added/Corp** Instituto Superior Evangelico de Estudios Teologicos. Vol. 1 (1970)-. Periodical. Spanish. sa. $6.00 Brazil, Uruguay & Paraguay; $8.00 Chile, Bolivia & Peru; $14.00 The Americas; $16.00 Europe; $20.00 other. Instituto Superior Evangelico, Camacua 282, 1406 Buenos Aires Argentina. **Tel** 011 54 1 6325030, 011 54 1 6325039. **Bk Rev.** ***Formed by the union of*** *Ekklesia* ***and*** *Cuadernos Teologicos.*
**Desc:** Organ of the protestant institute for higher theological studies with articles related to ecclesiastical and historical subjects.

BL
**CULTURA E FE.** **Added/Corp** Instituto de Desenvolvimento Cultural (Porto Alegre, Brazil). Vol. 1 No. 1 (April/June 1978)-. Periodical. Portuguese. qt. $40.00. Institute Desenvolvimento Cultural, Caixa Postal 702, 90001 Porto Alegre RS, Brazil. **Tel** 011 55 51 2240496. **LC** BR115.C8; C83. **DD** 261/.05. Index available. **Bk Rev. Ad Acc. Circ:** 2,500 (ctrl).
**Desc:** Covers Christianity and culture.

US/0097-952X
**CULTURAL INFORMATION SERVICE.** Periodical. English. mo. $37.00 (1 year), $72.00 (2 year) regular membership; $49.00 (1 year), $95.00 (2 year), $140.00 (3 year) full membership. Cultural Information Service, PO Box 786 Madison Square Station, New York NY 10159. **Tel** (212)691-5240. **ED** Frederic A Brussat. **LC** BR115.C8; C84. **DD** 261.8/3. Index available. **Bk Rev. Circ:** 4,000 (ctrl).
**Desc:** Reviews and previews of literature, television, videos, films, popular music. TV and film viewers' guides, posters and bookmarks.

US/0011-2968
**CUMBERLAND FLAG, THE.** **Added/Corp** Second Cumberland Presbyterian Church. Board of Public and Christian Education. (19??)-. Periodical. English. mo. $6.00. Second Cumberland Presbyterian Church, 226 Church Street Northwest, Huntsville AL 35801. **Tel** (205)536-7481. **ED** Robert S. Wood. **Bk Rev. Ad Acc. Circ:** 750 (ctrl).

US/0590-3386
**CUMBERLAND SEMINARIAN, THE.** [Cumberl. semin.]. Vol 1 (Fall 1953)-. Periodical. English. Three times a year. free. 168 East Parkway South, Memphis TN 38104.
**Ind/Abst** Index Book Rev. Relig.; Relig. Index One Period. (1979-).

SZ
**CURRENT DIALOGUE.** **Added/Corp** World Council of Churches. Sub-Unit for Dialogue with People of Living Faiths and Ideologies. No. 1 (Winter 1980/81)-. Periodical. English (French and German). ir. Free on request. Newsletter DFI, 150 Route de Ferney, 1211 Geneva 20 Switzerland. **LC** WMLC 93/3394. ***Continues*** *Church and the Jewish People.*
**Ind/Abst** Bibliogr. Mission.

US
**CURRENT LC SUBJECT HEADINGS IN THE FIELD OF RELIGION / PUBLISHED BY THE BIBLIOGRAPHIC SYSTEMS COMMITTEE OF THE AMERICAN THEOLOGICAL LIBRARY ASSOCIATION.** ***Ceased.*** **Added/Corp** American Theological Library Association. Bibliographic Systems Committee. American Theological Library Association. Pattern Subdivisions for Christian Denominations. **VFOAT** Library of Congress subject Headings in the Field of Religion. **VAT** Current Library of Congress Subject Headings in the Field of Religion. Vol. 1, No. 1 (Sept. 1983)-Vol. 8 (19??). Periodical. English. Four times a year. American Theological Library Association, 820 Church Street, 3rd Floor, Evanston IL 60201. **Tel** (708)869-7788, FAX (708)869-8513. **ED** Alice Runis. **Circ:** 130.

US/1054-8688
**CURRENT THOUGHTS AND TRENDS.** **See** Religion and Theology-Abstracting, Bibliographies and Statistics.

US/0098-2113
**CURRENTS IN THEOLOGY AND MISSION.** [Curr. theol. mission]. **Added/Corp** Christ Seminary-Seminex. Evangelical Lutherans in Mission. Concordia Seminary-in-Exile. Vol. 1 (Aug. 1974)-. Periodical. English. Six times a year (Feb., Apr., Jun., Aug., Oct., Dec.). $13.50 (one year), $25.00 (two years), $36.00 (three years). Currents in Theology and Mission, 1100 East 55th Street, Chicago IL 60615. **Tel** (312)753-0763. **ED** Ralph W Klein. Index available. **Bk Rev. Ad Acc. Circ:** 4,000. available in microform from University Microfilms International (UMI). ***Continues*** *Preaching Helps, 0098-2156.*
**Desc:** Essays and reviews aimed at pastors and laypersons dealing with questions of belief and ministry, now includes sermon studies based on the three year lectionary.
**Ind/Abst** Index Book Rev. Relig.; Missionalia; New Testam. Abstr.; Old Testam. Abstr.; Relig. Index One Period. (1974-); Relig. Theol. Abstr.

US/0092-7147
**DAILY BREAD.** (19??)-. English. mo. £21.60. Royal National Institute for the Blind, PO Box 173, Peterborough PE2 6WS England. **Tel** 011 44 733 730777. **LC** BV4810; .D23. **DD** 242/.2.
**Desc:** Daily commentary on portions of scripture selected by The Scripture Union. The scripture passages themselves are not included.

US/0190-5457
**DAILY GUIDEPOSTS.** Began with 1977 Vol. English. an. $4.95. Guideposts, 39 Seminary Hill Road, Carmel NY 10512. **Tel** (914)225-3681, (800)431-2344. **LC** BV4810; .D254. **DD** 242/.1/05.

CN/0227-096X
**DAILY PRAYER REMINDER.** (DAILY PRAYER REMINDER / INTERNATIONAL INTERCESSORS.). [Dly. prayer remind.]. **VAT** International Intercessors Daily Prayer Reminder. Periodical. English. mo. Free to members. International Intercessors, Box 2500, Streetsville Ontario L5M 2H2 Canada. **ED** Bernard Camper. **DD** 248.3/2. **Circ:** 3,000.

US/0011-5525
**DAILY WORD.** **Added/Corp** Unity School of Christianity, Kansas City, Mo. (19??)-. Periodical. English (Spanish, Dutch, French, German, Afrikaans, Indonesian and Portuguese). mo. $5.00, $7.00 (large type-English only). Unity School of Christianity, Unity Village MO 64065. **Tel** 251-3571524-3550, FAX (816)251-3550. **ED** Colleen Zuck. **Circ:** 2,380,700. available in large print. ***Continues*** *Unity Daily Word.*
**Desc:** A monthly non-denominational magazine of daily Christian devotions and inspirational articles and poetry; convenient pocket size with full-color photography.

DK
**DANMARKS KIRKER.** **Main/Corp** Nationalmuseet (Denmark). Vol. 1 (1973)-. Periodical. Danish. Gec Gad Forlag, Vimmelskaftet 32, 1161 Copenhagen K Denmark. **Tel** 011 45 3 3150558.

DK/0105-3191
**DANSK TEOLOGISK TIDSSKRIFT.** [Dan. teol. tidsskr.]. Vol. 1 (1938)-. Periodical. Danish. qt. kr326.00. Forlaget Anis, Frederiksberg Alle 10A, DK 1820 Frederiksberg Denmark. **Tel** 011 45 31249250. cum. index. **Bk Rev.** ctrl circ.
**Ind/Abst** Index Book Rev. Relig.; New Testam. Abstr.; Old Testam. Abstr.; Relig. Index One Period. (1964-); Relig. Theol. Abstr.

II/0011-6734
**DARSHANA INTERNATIONAL.** **See** Philosophy.

US
**DATELINE NAMIBIA.** **Added/Corp** Lutheran Church in America. Division for Mission in North America. American Lutheran Church (1961- ). Division for World Mission and Inter-Church Cooperation. American Lutheran Church (1961- ). Office of Church in Society. No. 1 (1981)-. Periodical. English. Dateline : Namibia, 231 Madison Avenue, New York NY 10016.
**Ind/Abst** Hum. Rights Intern. Rep.

US/0739-1749
**DAUGHTERS OF SARAH.** **Added/Corp** People's Christian Coalition. Daughters of Sarah (Organization). Vol. 1, No. 1 (Nov. 1974)-. Periodical. English. Four times a year. $18.00 (one year), $35.00 (two year), $50.00 (three year). Daughters of Sarah, 2121 Sheridan Road, Evanston IL 60201. **Tel** (708)866-3882. **ED** Lareta Halteman Finger. **LC** BV4527; .D36. **DD** 208/.2. Index available. cum. index. **Bk Rev. Ad Acc. Circ:** 6,700. available on microfilm and microfiche from University Microfilms International (UMI).
**Desc:** A Christian feminist forum. Articles on theology, Bible, social justice issues, women's history, personal issues, spirituality, marriage, children, health, and the church.
**Ind/Abst** Index Book Rev. Relig.; Relig. Index One Period.

CN/0703-6485
**DAVANTAGE.** V. 1- April 1967-. Periodical. French. mo. $5.00. Conseil Central De Quebec, Societe St. Vincent De Paul, 777 Des Glacis, Quebec G13 3R1. **DD** 267/.24/2714471.

II
**DAYANANDA SANDESA.** Periodical. Hindi (Sanskrit). mo. Rs1500. Arsha Sahitya Pracara Trasta, 2-F Kamla Nagar, Dilhi 110 007 India. **Tel** 233112, 238360, 2922612. **(Subscription address:** Arsh Sahitya Prachar Trust, 455 Khari Baoli, Delhi 110 006 India) **LC** BL1250; .D38. Index available. cum. index. **Bk Rev. Circ:** 2,000.

US/8750-7749
**DEACON DIGEST.** Vol. 1, No. 1 (Nov. 1984)-. Periodical. English. Six times a year (Jan., Mar., May, July, Sept., Nov.). $18.00 (one year); $32.00 (two years). ALT Publishing Company, PO Box 400, Green Bay WI 54305. **Tel** (414)432-1413. **ED** James Alt. **Ad Acc. Circ:** 4,000 (ctrl). ***Continues*** *Diaconal Quarterly.*
**Desc:** Educational journal primarily for the Catholic Deacons.

NE/0929-0761
**DEAD SEA DISCOVERIES.** (199?)-. English. Three times a year. Fl160.00 Netherlands; $91.50 other. E. J. Brill, Postbus 9000, 2300 PA Leiden Netherlands. **Tel** 011 31 71 312624, FAX 011 31 71 317532, telex 39296 BRILL NL. **ED** Lawrence Schiffman, George Brooke, James Vanderkam.
**Desc:** Dedicated to the study of the Dead Sea Scrolls and associated literature. Primarily devoted to the discussion of the significance of the Qumran finds for the study of Palestinian Judaism and the history and ideas of early Christianity.

CN/0820-9057
**DECISION (CANADIAN ED.).** (DECISION.). [Decision]. **Added/Corp** Billy Graham Evangelistic Association of Canada. (1960)-. Periodical. English. Eleven times a year. 8.00Can$. Billy Graham Evangelistic Association of Canada, Box 841, Winnipeg Manitoba R3C 2R3 Canada. **Tel** (204)943-0529. **ED** Roger C Palms. **DD** 269/.2/05. Index available. cum. index. **Bk Rev. Ad Acc. Circ:** 2,000,000 (ctrl).
**Desc:** To present the good news of salvation in Jesus Christ and to encourage, teach and strengthen Christians.

FR/0751-6274
**DECISION (EDITION FRANCAISE).** (DECISION.). [Decision]. Began in 1963. Periodical. English (French, German and Spanish). bm. $5.00F. Decision Magazine, 1300 Harmon Place, Minneapolis MN 55403. **Tel** (612)338-0500. **ED** Roger C Palms. Index available. cum. index. **Circ:** 2,000,000 (ctrl).
**Desc:** To present the gospel of Jesus Christ and to encourage, teach and strengthen Christians.

US/0011-7307
**DECISION (NORTH AMERICA ED.).** (DECISION.). [Decision]. **Added/Corp** Billy Graham Evangelistic Association. Vol. 1 (Nov. 1960)-. Periodical. English (French, German and Spanish). Eleven times a year (monthly except July and August). $7.00 (surface mail), $22.00 (airmail). Billy Graham Evangelistic Association, Box 779, Minneapolis MN 55440. **Tel** (612)338-0500, FAX (612)338-6362, telex 290259. **ED** Roger C Palms. **LC** BV3750; .D4. **DD** 269/.2/05. Index available. cum. index. **Circ:** 2,000,000 (ctrl). available in braille; available on microfilm and microfiche from University Microfilms International (UMI).
**Desc:** A message by Billy Graham, personal testimonies, inspirational poems, reports from around the world, articles on the spiritual life, and a Bible study.
**Ind/Abst** Christ. Period. Index; Curr. Thoughts Trends.

UK
**DEO.** See Music.

US/0011-9229
**DESERT CALL / SPIRITUAL LIFE INSTITUTE.** *Title Change.* **Added/Corp** Spiritual Life Institute. (19??)-(19??). Periodical. English. qt. Spiritual Life Institute, PO Box 219, Crestone CO 81131. **Tel** (719)256-4778, FAX (719)256-4719. **ED** Tessa Bielecki and David Denny. **Bk Rev. Circ:** 2,300. ***Continued by** Forefront.*
**Desc:** Fosters contemplation as the way to lead an integrated, God-centered life.

CN/0225-9796
**DESTINY.** [Destiny]. V. 1- May 1979-. Periodical. English. mo. $7.95 Canada; $8.95 other. Paradise Publishers Company, Destiny Magazine, Suite 606/3 Church Avenue, Toronto Ontario M5E 1M2 Canada. **DD** 248/.05.

US/1070-7875
**DIAKONEO (NEW ORLEANS, LA.).** (DIAKONEO.). [Diakoneo]. **Added/Corp** North American Association for the Diaconate. National Center for the Diaconate (Episcopal Church). Vol. 1, No. 1 (Fall 1978)-. Periodical. English. Five times a year (Jan., Mar., May, Sept., Nov.). $25.00. North American Association Diaconate, PO Box 750156, New Orleans LA 70175-0156. **Tel** (504)895-0058. **ED** Ormonde Platter. **DD** 283. **Bk Rev**, (Qty: 3-4). **Circ:** 1,500.
**Desc:** Newsletter for deacons and diaconal ministry in North America (Anglican and Lutheran).

GW/0341-9592
**DIAKONIA (MAINZ, GERMANY : 1972).** (DIAKONIA.). [Diakonia]. (1972)-. Periodical. German. Six times a year (Jan., Mar., May, July, Sept., Nov.). DM92.40. Matthias Grunewald Verlag Gmbh, Postfach 3080, D 55020 Mainz Germany. **Tel** 011 49 6131 839055. **ED** H. Erharter. **LC** BX1913; .D46. Index available. cum. index. **Bk Rev. Ad Acc. Circ:** 1,050 (ctrl). ***Continues** Daikonia. Der Seelsorger.*
**Desc:** Theological journal for liturgical practice; offers many suggestions through reports, models and examples.
**Ind/Abst** New Testam. Abstr.

CN/0382-7933
**DIAKONIA MAS TES BASILEIAS (KANADE EKDOSIS).** (E DIAKONIA MAS TES BASILEIAS.). V. 19, No. 7- July 1976-. Periodical. Greek, Modern. mo. Watch Tower Bible and Tract Society / Canadian Branch, PO Box 4100, Georgetown Ontario L7G 4Y4 Canada. **Tel** (718)625-3600. **DD** 289.9. ***Continues** E Yperesia Mas Tes Basileias, 0382-7925.*

CN/0316-6864
**DIAKONIA TES BASILEIAS.** V. 17, No. 6- June 1974-. Periodical. Greek, Modern. mo. Free. Watch Tower Bible and Tract Society / Canadian Branch, PO Box 4100, Georgetown Ontario L7G 4Y4 Canada. **Tel** (718)625-3600. **DD** 289.9.

GW/0341-826X
**DIAKONIE.** **Added/Corp** Evangelische Kirche in Deutschland. Diakonische Werk. **VFOAT** Diakonie; Impulse, Erfahrungen, Theorien; Diakonie; Theorien, Erfahrungen, Impulse. (Jan./Feb. 1975)-. Periodical. German. bm (6 issues). DM48.00. Kaiser Verlag Zeitschriften, Quell Verlag Furtbachstr 12A, D 70178 Stuttgart Germany. **Tel** 011 49 711 6010057, FAX 011 49 711 6010076. Index available. ***Supersedes** Innere Mission.*

GW/0174-5506
**DIAKRISIS.** (198?)-. Periodical. German. Four times a year (Mar., June, Sep., Dec.). DM15.00. Diakrisis, Stiffurtstr 5, 72074 Tubingen Germany. **Tel** 49 7071 26104, FAX 49 7071 293314. **UDC** 284. cum. index. **Bk Rev**, (Qty: 8). **Circ:** 2,500.

US/0012-2033
**DIALOG (ST. PAUL).** (DIALOG.). [Dialog]. Vol. 1 (Winter 1962)-. Periodical. English. qt (Jan., Apr., July, Oct.). $21.00 (one year), $37.00 (two year), US and Canada; $22.00 (one year), $39.00 (two year), other. Dialog / US, 2375 Como Avenue, St Paul MN 55108. **Tel** (612)641-3482. **ED** Ted Peters. **LC** BR1; .D5. **DD** 230/.05. **Bk Rev**, (Qty: 16). **Ad Acc, Adv Mgr:** Ruth Taylor, **Tel** (207)799-4387. available on microfilm and microfiche from University Microfilms International (UMI).
**Desc:** A journal of theology, primarily Lutheran.
**Ind/Abst** Index Book Rev. Relig.; New Testam. Abstr.; Old Testam. Abstr.; Relig. Index One Period. (1962-); Relig. Theol. Abstr.

CL
**DIALOGANDO : BOLETIN INFORMATIVO DE LA VICARIA DE PASTORAL OBRERA DE SANTIAGO-CHILE.** **Added/Corp** Catholic Church. Archdiocese of Santiago (Chile). Vicaria de Pastoral Obrera. (19??)-. Periodical. Spanish. mo. Vicaria de Pastoral Obrera, Av. Libertador B O'Higgins, 3155 20 Piso Santiago chile. **LC** HD6338.2.C5; D5.
**Ind/Abst** Hum. Rights Intern. Rep.

SP/0210-2870
**DIALOGO ECUMENICO.** **Added/Corp** Centro de Estudios Orientales y Ecumenicos Juan XXIII. Centro Ecumenico Juan XXIII. Instituto Ecumenico Juan XXIII. (1966)-. Periodical. Spanish. ir. $44.00. Universidad Pontificia de Salamanca, Apartado de Correos 541, 37080 Salamanca Spain. **Tel** 011 34 23 215140. **ED** Adolfo Gonzalez Montes. **Bk Rev. Ad Acc. Circ:** 500.
**Desc:** A theological journal which focuses on the fundamental issues of ecumenical thinking in the Roman Catholic Church, Eastern Christian Churches and Protestantism.

US/0891-5881
**DIALOGUE & ALLIANCE.** (DIALOGUE & ALLIANCE : JOURNAL OF THE INTERNATIONAL RELIGIOUS FOUNDATION, INC.). [Dialogue alliance]. **Added/Corp** International Religious Foundation. **VFOAT** Dialogue and Alliance. Vol. 1, No. 1 (Spring 1987)-. Periodical. English. sa. $15.00 (institutions) US, Canada, and Mexico; $20.00 (institutions) other; $10.00 (individuals, US only). Dialogue & Alliance, c/o International Religious Foundation, 4 West 43rd Street, New York NY 10036. **Tel** (212)869-6023, FAX (212)869-6424, telex 4991393. **ED** Thomas Walsh. **LC** BL1; .D48. **DD** 291/.05. Index available. cum. index. **Bk Rev**, (Qty: 30). **Ad Acc. Circ:** 2000 (ctrl). available on microfilm.
**Desc:** Covers world peace through interreligious dialogue.
**Ind/Abst** Bibliogr. Mission.; Guide Soc. Sci. Relig.; Relig. Index One Period.; Relig. Theol. Abstr. (199?-).

CN/1184-6283
**DIALOGUE - ANGLICAN CHURCH OF CANADA. DIOCESE OF ONTARIO.** (DIALOGUE.). [Dialogue - Angl. Church Can., Dioc. Ont.]. **Added/Corp** Anglican Church of Canada. Diocese of Ontario. Anglican Church of Canada. Diocese of Ontario. Board of Parish Services. Vol. 33, No. 1, Jan. (1991)-. Periodical. English. Ten times a year. $4.00 per year. Synod of the Diocese of Ontario, Parish Services Board, 90 Johnson Street, Kingston Ontario K7L 1X7 Canada. **Tel** (613)544-4774, FAX (613)547-3745. **ED** Helene Hannah. **DD** 283.7137. **Bk Rev**, (Qty: varies). **Ad Acc, Adv Mgr Tel** (613)544-4774. **Acid Free. Circ:** 7,000 (ctrl). ***Continues** The Ontario Churchman., 0030-2848.*
**Desc:** The official media publication of the Diocese of Ontario (Anglican), provides news, opinion, features concerning interests of the Anglican parishes in Eastern Ontario. It carries news of current happenings in the parishes and publicity for them.

US
**DIALOGUE : JOURNAL OF ADDIS ABABA UNIVERSITY MAIN CAMPUS TEACHERS ASSOCIATION.** See Education-Higher Education.

PO/0253-1674
**DIDASKALIA (LISBOA).** (DIDASKALIA.). [Didaskalia]. **Added/Corp** Faculdade de Teologia de Lisboa. Vol. 1 (1971)-. English (French, German, Latin, Spanish and English). sa. 3000$00 Portugal; $40.00 North America; $35.00 Europe, Itacau and Portuguese's African languages countries. Didaskalia, Universidade Catolica Portuguesa, Palma de Cima, 1600 Lisbon Portugal. **Tel** 726 55 50/65094 UNICAPP. **LC** BR7; .D53. Index available. **Bk Rev. Circ:** 1,000 (ctrl).
**Ind/Abst** New Testam. Abstr.; Old Testam. Abstr.; Relig. Theol. Abstr. (199?-).

CN/0847-1266
**DIDASKALIA (OTTERBURNE).** (DIDASKALIA : THE JOURNAL OF THE WINNIPEG THEOLOGICAL SEMINARY.). [Didaskalia]. **Added/Corp** Winnipeg Theological Seminary. **VFOAT** Didaskalia. Vol. 1, No. 1 Nov. (1989)-. Periodical. English. Twice a year (April and October). $11.00 US; $12.50 Canada; $16.00 other. Providence Theological Seminary, Otterburne, Manitoba R0A 1G0 Canada. **ED** David Smith, (204)433-7488. **DD** 230/.044/05. **Bk Rev.**
**Ind/Abst** Index Book Rev. Relig.; Relig. Index One Period.

FR
**DIMANCHE EN PAROISSE.** French. mo (except Aug.). 95.00F. Soceval, 12 rue Edmond Valentin, 75007 Paris France. **Tel** 011 33 1 47054331.

CN/0317-2198
**DIMANCHE ET FETE.** No. 1- Jan. 1975-. French. ir. $3.00. Dimanche et Fete, 2715 Chemin de la Cote Ste-Catherine, Montreal Quebec H3T 1B6 Canada. **DD** 264/.02/005.

US/0162-6825
**DIMENSION.** Periodical. English. qt. $9.00 US (add $2.75 for postage) other. Woman's Missionary Union, PO Box 830010, Birmingham AL 35283. **Tel** (205)991-8100, (205)991-4933. **ED** Gina Howard. **Circ:** 45,700 (ctrl).
**Desc:** Administrative magazine for planning WMU in a church.
**Ind/Abst** South. Baptist Period. Index.

US/1047-6318
**DIRECCION (KANSAS CITY, MO.).** *Title Change.* (DIRECCION.). [Direccion]. **Added/Corp** Church of the Nazarene. Publications Services. Periodical. Spanish. mo. Casa Nazarena de Publicaciones, 6401 The Paseo, Kansas City MO 64131. **Tel** (816)333-7000. **DD** 230. ***Continues** Heraldo de Santidad, 0746-4509.* ***Continued by** Herldo de Santidad, 1060-2135.*

US/0384-8515
**DIRECTION (WINNIPEG).** (DIRECTION.). [Direction]. **Added/Corp** Mennonite Brethren Schools. Vol. 1, (Jan. 1972)-. Periodical. English. Twice a year (Spring and Fall). $9.00 US; $10.00 other. Mennonite Brethren Biblical Direction, 4824 East Butler, Fresno CA 93727-5097. **Tel** (209)453-2041, FAX (209)453-2007. **ED** Elmer Martens. Index available. cum. index. **Bk Rev**, (Qty: 12-15). **Circ:** 500 (ctrl). ***Formed by the union of** Voice, 0384-8507 **and** Journal of Church & Society.*
**Desc:** Seeks to serve its constituency by addressing biblical, theological and church-related issues. Church and conference leaders, pastors, educators, and informed church members are the intended audience.
**Ind/Abst** Index Book Rev. Relig.; Manage. Market. Abstr.; New Testam. Abstr.; Relig. Index One Period.

US
**DIRECTIONS (BROOKLINE, MASS.).** (DIRECTIONS / HELLENIC COLLEGE AND HOLY CROSS GREEK ORTHODOX SCHOOL OF THEOLOGY.). Began publication in 1977. Periodical. English. wk. Hellenic College, 50 Goddard Avenue, Brookline MA 02146.

US/0885-4335
**DIRECTIONS IN FAITH.** Vol. 1, No. 1 (Fall 1986)-. Periodical. English. qt. $14.75. Methodist Publishing House / US, PO Box 801, Nashville TN 37202.

US/0362-1472
**DIRECTORY.** **Main/Corp** Association of Theological Schools in the United States and Canada. **VFOAT** ATS Directory. (1975)-. Directory. English. sa. $27.75 US; $28.45 other. Association of Theological Schools, 10 Summit Park Drive, Pittsburgh PA 15275. **Tel** (412)788-6505, FAX (412)788-6510. **Circ:** 4,000. ***Continues** AATS Directory of Theological Schools.*
**Desc:** Lists graduate schools of theology in the US and Canada which are members of the Association. Members may be accredited, candidates, or affiliates.

CN/0705-3118
**DIRECTORY - CANADIAN RELIGIOUS CONFERENCE.** **Main/Corp** Canadian Religious Conference. **VFOAT** Bottin - Conference Religieuse Canadienne. Began with 1970 issue. Directory. English (French). an. $2.50. Canadian Religious Conference, 324 Laurier Avenue East, Ottawa Ontario K1N 6P6 Canada. **Tel** (613)236-0824. **DD** 255/.0025/71. ctrl circ.

US/0070-5209
**DIRECTORY OF CAMPUS MINISTRY.** [Dir. campus minist.]. Directory. English. United States Catholic Conference, 1312 Massachusetts Avenue NW, Washington DC 20005. **LC** BV4376; .D57. **DD** 253/.025/73.

US
**DIRECTORY OF GRADUATE STUDIES.** Directory. English. $4.00 US; $7.50 other. Council of Societies for the Study of Religion, Valparaiso University, Valparaiso IN 46383. **Tel** (219)464-5515. **ED** Watson E Mills.
**Desc:** A compilation of departmental information for institutions who are members of the Council on Graduate Studies in Religion. Information includes program description, faculty listings, research facilities, admission information, etc.

US/0731-0331
**DIRECTORY OF RELIGION BROADCASTING (1982/83), THE.** (THE DIRECTORY OF RELIGIOUS BROADCASTING.). [Dir. relig. broadcast.]. **Added/Corp** National Religious Broadcasters (U.S.). (1983)-. English. an (Jan.). $69.95. National Religious Broadcasters, 7839 Ashton Avenue, Manassas VA 22110. **Tel** (703)330-7000, FAX (703)330-7100. **ED** Mark Ward Sr., Ron J. Kopczick. **LC** BV655; .D57. **DD** 384.54/53/02573. **Ad Acc, Adv Mgr:** Dick Reynolds, **Tel** (704)393-0602. **Circ:** 2,500. ***Continues** Annual Directory of Religious Broadcasting, 0160-029X.*
**Desc:** Listing of religious broadcasters and related services. Radio, TV stations, program producers, suppliers of equipment, consultants, representatives, and agencies. Reference source for the religious broadcasting industry containing 4400-plus listings covering radio and television stations. Program producers, manufacturers, etc. plus statistics and historical information.

CN/1187-7227
**DIRECTORY OF SPIRITUALIST ORGANIZATIONS IN CANADA.** [Dir. spiritual. organ. Can.]. (Nov. 1991)-. Directory. English. Walter J Meyer Zu Erpen, PO Box 8697, Victoria British Columbia V8W 3S3 Canada. **DD** 291.2/025/71.

US/0066-8710
**DIRECTORY / THE ASSOCIATED CHURCH PRESS.** [Dir. - Assoc. Church Press]. **Main/Corp** Associated Church Press. **VFOAT** Associated Church Press Directory. (19??)-. Newspaper. English. an. $7.00 (academics); $21.00 (others). The Associated Church Press, PO Box 162, Ada MI 49301. **ED** Donald F. Hetzler and Mary Best. **LC** Z7753; .A7; BR1. **DD** 291/.05. **Ad Acc. Circ:** 600.

US/0416-0274
**DISCERNER.** [Discerner]. (1947). Periodical. English. mo. $3.00 US; $4.44 Canada; $4.92 other. Religion Analysis Service Inc, 2708 East Lake Street, Minneapolis MN 55406. **Tel** (612)722-4463. **ED** Dr. A. Bevier. **DD** 273. **Bk Rev. Circ:** 4,000 (ctrl).
**Desc:** Information concerning cults and non-Christian religions.

US/0888-1111
**DISCIPLES THEOLOGICAL DIGEST, THE.** Vol. 1, No. 1 (1986)-. Periodical. English. ir. $12.00 (one year), $20.00 (two year) US; $15.00 (one year), $26.00 (two year) other. Division of Higher Education, 11780 Borman Drive, Suite 100, St Louis MO 63146. **Tel** (314)991-3000. **ED** John M Imber. **DD** 286. **Circ:** 700 (ctrl).
**Desc:** Abstracts of current disciples of Christ, related books and journal articles.
**Ind/Abst** Relig. Theol. Abstr.

US/0273-5865
**DISCIPLESHIP JOURNAL.** [Disciplesh. j.]. **Added/Corp** Navigators (Religious Organization). Vol. 1, No. 1 (Jan./Feb. 1981)-. Periodical. English. bm. $18.97 (one year), $29.97 (two year), $39.97 (three year). Navpress, PO Box 35004, Colorado Springs CO 80935. **Tel** (719)548-9222, FAX (719)593-7128. **(Subscription address:** Neodata, PO Box 2606, Boulder, CO 80322**)** **ED** Susan Maycinik; (719)531-3529. **LC** BV4485; .D58. **DD** 248.4. Index available. cum. index. **Bk Rev. Ad Acc, Adv Mgr:** Dave Wilson, **Tel** (719)531-3579. **Circ:** 100,000.
**Desc:** Designed to help Christians develop a deeper relationship with God and to provide practical help in understanding the Scriptures and applying them to daily life and ministry.
**Ind/Abst** Christ. Period. Index (19??-); Curr. Thoughts Trends.

US/1047-9449
**DISCIPLESHIP TRAINING.** [Disciplesh. train.]. **Added/Corp** Southern Baptist Convention. Sunday School Board. (Jan. 1990)-. Periodical. English. mo. $11.00. Southern Baptist Convention, 901 Commerce, Suite 750, Nashville TN 37203. **Tel** (615)244-2355, FAX (615)742-8919. **(Subscription address:** Sunday School Board - Customer Service, 127 Ninth Avenue North, Nashville, TN 37234 USA; telephone: (800)458-2772**)** **DD** 268. available on microfilm and microfiche from University Microfilms International (UMI). ***Continues** Church Training, 0162-4601.*
**Ind/Abst** South. Baptist Period. Index (1990-).

US/0732-9881
**DISCIPLIANA (1960).** (DISCIPLIANA.). [Discipliana]. **Added/Corp** Disciples of Christ. Historical Society. Vol. 20, No. 1 (Mar. 1960)-. Periodical. English. qt. $15.00 US; $20.00 other (comes with membership). Disciples of Christ Historical Society, 1101 19th Avenue South, Nashville TN 37212. **Tel** (615)327-1444, FAX (615)327-1445. **ED** D. Newell Williams. **LC** BX7301; .H3. **DD** 286.6/05. **Bk Rev. Ad Acc, Adv Mgr:** J.Seale. **Circ:** 4,800. ***Continues** Harbinger and Discipliana.*
**Desc:** The holdings of this society relate to the religious movement which began in 19th Century American and is known as the Campbell-Stone movement and embraces three distinct church bodies.

US/1052-3804
**DISCIPULOS RESPONSABLES.** [Discipulos responsab.]. **Added/Corp** United Methodist Church (U.S.). Office of Covenant Discipleship and Christian Foundation. (1987)-. Periodical. Spanish (English). Four times a year (Jan., Apr., July, Oct.). $10.00. Covenant Discipleship General, Board Discipleship, PO Box 840, Nashville TN 37202. **Tel** (615)340-7010, FAX (615)340-7565. **ED** Marigene Chamberlain. **DD** 248. **Bk Rev**, (Qty: 1). **Circ:** 750 (ctrl).

NE/0419-4233
**DISSERTATIONES AD HISTORIAM RELIGIONUM PERTINENTES.** (1967)-. Monographic series. English. ir. Price varies per volume. E. J. Brill, Postbus 9000, 2300 PA Leiden Netherlands. **Tel** 011 31 71 312624, FAX 011 31 71 317532, telex 39296 BRILL NL. **ED** C. J. Blecker. **DD** 200.

VC/0012-4222
**DIVINITAS.** [Divinitas]. **Added/Corp** Pontificia Accademia Teologica Romana. Pontificia Universita Lateranense. Facolta di Teologia. Pontificio Ateneo Lateranense. Facolta di Teologia. Vol. 1, (April 1957)-. Periodical. English (French, German, Italian, Latin and Spanish). Three times a year. $35.00. Pontificia Accademia Teologica, Romana Palazzo Cananici, 00120 Vatican City. **Tel** 011 39 6 7852630. **LC** BR1.A1; D5.
**Ind/Abst** Bibliogr. Mission.; New Testam. Abstr.; Relig. Theol. Abstr.

IT/0012-4257
**DIVUS THOMAS; COMMENTARIUM DE PHILOSOPHIA ET THEOLOGIA.** **Added/Corp** Collegio Alberoni. Vol. 1-6,(1880)-. Periodical. Italian (English). Three times a year. L40000 Italy; L80000 other. Studio Domenicano, Via Osservanza 72, 40136 Bologna Italy. **Tel** 011 39 51 582034.
**Ind/Abst** Bibliogr. Mission.; MLA Int. Bibl. Books Artic. Mod. Lang. Lit.

IE/0012-446X
**DOCTRINE AND LIFE.** [Doctrine life]. (Feb/Mar 1951)-. Periodical. English. Ten times a year. $33.21. Dominican Publications, 42 Parnell Square, Dublin 1 Ireland. **Tel** 11 353 1 8731355, FAX 731760, telex 725201. Index available. cum. index. **Bk Rev. Ad Acc. Circ:** 5,000. available on microfilm from Xerox; available on microfilm and microfiche from University Microfilms International (UMI).
**Ind/Abst** New Testam. Abstr.; Old Testam. Abstr.; Abr. Cathol. Period. Lit. Index; Cathol. Period. Lit. Index.

FR
**DOCUMENTS EXPERIENCES.** French. qt. 84.00F France; $22.00 North America; 105.00F other. Documents Experiences, Coat Y Louarn, 29270 Carhaix France. **Tel** 011 33 1 98930864, FAX 011 33 1 98991460. **ED** Yvon Charles. Index available. cum. index. **Pr Rev. Circ:** 20,000.
**Desc:** A protestant, evangelical publication dealing with one subject at a time, through different articles. Themes concerning faith, the religious world, society and events are treated in a biblical perspective.

●US/1062-3426
**DONKEY TALK.** (DONKEY TALK: A CHRISTIAN CHILDREN'S MAGAZINE.). Vol. 1, No. 1 (Apr. 1992)-. Periodical. English. bm. $30.00. Christian Family Publishing Ministry, PO Box 4514, Brownsville TX 78523. **DD** 248.

CN/0318-0123
**DONUM DEI (ENGLISH ED.).** (DONUM DEI; A PUBLICATION OF THE CANADIAN RELIGIOUS CONFERENCE.). [Donum Dei]. **VFOAT** Donum Dei Series. 1- 1959-. Periodical. English. Canadian Religious Conference, 324 Laurier Avenue East, Ottawa Ontario K1N 6P6 Canada. **Tel** (613)236-0824. **ED** Albert Landry.

NE
**DOOPSGEZIND JAARBOEKJE.** 1902-. Dutch. an. Algemene Doopsgezinde Societei, Singel 450, 1017 AV Amsterdam Netherlands. **Tel** 011 31 020 6230914.

US/1044-7512
**DOOR (EL CAJON, CALIF.).** (THE DOOR.). [Door]. No. 104 (March/April 1989)-. Periodical. English. Six times a year. $22.95 US; $29.95 other. Youth Specialties Inc., 1224 Greenfield Drive, El Cajon CA 92021. **Tel** (619)440-2333. **ED** Mike Yaconelli (editor's phone: (916)842-2701). **DD** 808. **Circ:** 20,000. ***Continues** Wittenburg Door, 0199-8285.*
**Desc:** Dedicated to church reform and renewal. Contains editorials, features and interviews in humorous satire.
**Ind/Abst** Christ. Period. Index (19??-).

FR/0761-7267
**DOSSIERS DE LA BIBLE, LES.** **VFOAT** Bible. (Jan./Feb. 1984)-. Periodical. English. qt. 110.00F (EEC countries); 130.00F (other). Editions du CERF, BP 65, 77932 Perthes Cedex France. **Tel** 011 33 1 44181212. ***Continues** Bible et Son Message.*
**Ind/Abst** Point Repere (1984-).

US/0748-4682
**DOXOLOGY.** (DOXOLOGY : JOURNAL OF THE ORDER OF ST. LUKE IN THE UNITED METHODIST CHURCH.). [Doxology]. **Added/Corp** Order of St. Luke. Vol. 1 (1984)-. English. an. Only available with Sacramental Life. Order of St. Luke, PO Box 22279, Akron OH 44302. **Tel** (607)962-3512. **DD** 242.

US/8750-4901
**DR. C.S. LOVETT'S MARANATHA FAMILY MINI-MAGAZINE.** **Added/Corp** Personal Christianity Chapel (Baldwin Park, Calif.). **VFOAT** Dr. C. S. Lovett's Maranatha Family Mini-Magazine; Maranatha Family Mini-Magazine; Marantha Family. **VAT** Doctor C.S. Lovett's Maranatha Family Mini-Magazine. (198?)-. Periodical. English. Six times a year. Free. Personal Christianity, PO Box 549, Baldwin Park CA 91706. **Tel** (818)338-7333. ***Continues** Personal Christianity, 0745-1288.*

CN/0701-0214
**DRAUDZES VESTIS.** Began publication in Jan. 1953. Periodical. Latvian. qt. 20.00Can$. E Lange, 364 Pleasant Park Road, Ottawa Ontario K1H 5M8 Canada. **Tel** (613)733-3906. **ED** Edgars Lange. **DD** 284/.1/71384. **Bk Rev. Ad Acc. Circ:** 180.
**Desc:** Church news and Latvian community life in Canada, the USA and other countries.

CN/0843-445X
**DREAMS & VISIONS.** **See** Literature.

US/0012-6152
**DREW GATEWAY, THE.** ***Ceased.*** [Drew gatew.]. **Added/Corp** Drew University. Theological School. Drew Theological Seminary. Vol. 1, (1930)-Vol. 61, No. 2 (Jan. 1993). Periodical. English. Three times a year. Drew University Theological School, Madison NJ 07940. **Tel** (201)408-3279. **ED** Janet F. Fishburn. **LC** BX8201; .D73. **DD** 287/.673. cum. index. **Bk Rev. Ad Acc. Circ:** 600 (ctrl). available on microfilm and microfiche from University Microfilms International (UMI).
**Desc:** Theological and ethical issues related to the practice of ministry.
**Ind/Abst** Index Book Rev. Relig.; Relig. Index One Period. (1959-); Relig. Theol. Abstr.

CM
**DRUM CALL, THE.** **Added/Corp** Presbyterian Church in the U.S.A. West Africa Mission. United Presbyterian Church in the U.S.A. West Africa Mission. (Jan. 1922)-. Periodical. English. ir. United Presbyterian Church in Africa, Box 32, Ebolowa Cameroun West Africa.

VM
**DUC ME HANG CUU GIUP.** Periodical. Vietnamese. mo. 360$00. Ao Hien Toan, 38 Ky Dong, Saigon South Vietnam. **LC** BX806.V5; D83.

US/1044-0178
**DYNAMIC PREACHING.** [Dyn. preach.]. (198?)-. Periodical. English. Twelve times a year. $29.00 US, $36.50 Canada, (one year); $49.00 (two years). Seven Worlds Corporation, PO Box 11565, Knoxville TN 37939. **Tel** (615)584-7350. **ED** C. King Duncan. **DD** 252. **Circ:** 8,200. available in reprints; available on diskette.
**Desc:** Adult sermons and childrens sermons for each Sunday of each month.

US
**EARNEST CHRISTIAN.** (19??)-. Periodical. English. mo. $5.00. Earnest Christian, Rural Route 1, Box 87, Cooperstown PA 16317. **Tel** (814)789-3855. **ED** William Sarber.

CN/1183-630X
**EARTHKEEPING ONTARIO.** **See** Agriculture.

KE/1018-8975
**EAST AFRICA JOURNAL OF EVANGELICAL THEOLOGY.** ***Title Change.*** [East Afr. j. evang. theol.]. **Added/Corp** Scott Theological College. Vol. 1, (1982)-(19??). Periodical. English. sa. EAJET, Box 49, Machakos Kenya. ***Continued by** Africa Journal of Evangelical Theology.*
**Ind/Abst** Index Book Rev. Relig. (1983-); Relig. Index One Period.

US/0012-8406
**EAST ASIA MILLIONS (ROBESONIA).** (EAST ASIA'S MILLIONS.). **Added/Corp** Overseas Missionary Fellowship. China Inland Mission. **VFOAT** Millions. Vol. 69, No. 5 (May 1961)-. Periodical. English (Chinese, Korean, German and Dutch). Four times a year (Feb., May, Aug., Nov.). $4.00 one year; $10.00 three year. OMF International, 10 West Dry Creek Circle, Littleton CO 80120-4413. **Tel** (303)730-4160, FAX (303)730-4165. **ED** Rev. E. David Dougherty. **LC** BV3410.C56; A3. **DD** 266/.0095/05. Index available. cum. index. **Circ:** 28,000 (ctrl). available on microfilm from University Microfilms International (UMI). ***Continues** Millions (Philadelphia, Pa.), 0740-400X.*
**Desc:** Focuses on the work OMF is doing in East Asia to share Christ.

PH/0116-0257
**EAST ASIAN PASTORAL REVIEW.** [East Asian pastor. rev.]. **Added/Corp** East Asian Pastoral Institute. Vol. 16, No. 4 (1979)-. Periodical. English. Four times a year (Jan., Apr., July, Oct.). $12.00 one year; $23.40 two years; $34.55 three years. East Asian Pastoral Institute, PO Box 221, 1101 UP Campus, Quezon City 1101 Philippines. **Tel** 63 2 924 1561, FAX 63 2 924 4359. **ED** Rev. Fr. Geoffrey J. King, S. J. Index available (Bound in 4th iss.). cum. index. **Bk Rev. Circ:** 1,200 (ctrl). ***Formed by the union of** Teaching All Nations **and** Good Tidings.*
**Desc:** This review hopes to contribute, in a thought provoking manner, to the maturing process of Christian thought in Asia and the Pacific and to the growth and inculturation of our churches.
**Ind/Abst** Bibliogr. Mission.; Index Philip. Period.; Missionalia; Abr. Cathol. Period. Lit. Index; Cathol. Period. Lit. Index.

US/0898-9346
**EASTERN CHALLENGE.** [East. chall.]. **Added/Corp** International Missions, Inc. (19??)-. Periodical. English. qt. Free. International Missions Inc, 621 Centre Avenue, Box 14866, Reading PA 19612-4866. **Tel** (215)375-0300. **DD** 266. **Circ:** 22,000 (ctrl).
**Desc:** Reporting on the overseas ministries of international missions.

IT/1010-3872
**ECCLESIA ORANS.** [Eccl. orans]. **Added/Corp** Pontificio Ateneo S. Anselmo. Pontificio Istituto Liturgico. Vol. 1 (1984)-. Periodical. English (French, German, Italian, Portuguese and Spanish). Three times a year. $43.00. Pontificio Ateneo S Anselmo, Via di Porta Lavernale 19, 00153 Rome Italy. **Tel** 11 39 6 5743569. **(Subscription address:** Ecclesia Orans, Pontificio Istituto Liturgico, Piazza Cavalieri di Malta 5, 00153, Roma Italia) **ED** Adrien Nocent. Index available. cum. index. **Bk Rev. Pr Rev. Circ:** 1,000 (ctrl).
**Desc:** Periodical of scientific liturgical studies under the auspices of the faculty of sacred liturgy of the pontifical university of Sant'Angelmo, Rome.

FR
**ECHANGES.** No 239 (Janv. 1990)-. Periodical. French. **LC** BX802; .E24. **DD** 282/.05. ***Continues*** *Echanges Mensuel, 0249-9312.*
**Desc:** Journal of theology.

SZ
**ECHOES.** (19??)-. English. Twice a year. Free on request. World Council of Churches, PO Box 2100, CH 1211 Geneva 2 Switzerland. **Tel** 011 41 22 7906076, FAX 011 41 22 7910361, telex 23 423 OIK CH. ***Absorbed*** *PCR Information.*

●CN/1193-0748
**ECHOES (MEDICINE HAT).** (ECHOES.). [Echoes]. Vol. 63, No. 1 (Jan./Feb. 1992)-. Periodical. English. ir. $10.00 per year. Evangelical United Brethren Church, Northwest Canada Conference, 2801-13th Avenue South East, Medicine Hat Alberta T1A 3R1 Canada. **DD** 289.9. ***Continues*** *Northwest Canada Echoes., 0384-5486.*

US/0890-8117
**ECLECTIC THEOSOPHIST, THE.** [Eclect. theosoph.]. No. 1 (Mar. 5, 1971)-. Periodical. English. Four times a year (Jan., Apr., July, Oct.). $7.00 US; $10.00 other. Point Loma Production, PO Box 6507, San Diego CA 92166. **Tel** (619)222-9609 or 222-3291. **ED** W. E. Small, Kenneth Small and John Cooper. **DD** 299. Index available. cum. index. **Bk Rev. Circ:** 800.

SP
**ECO DE AFRICA Y DE OTROS CONTINENTES.** **Added/Corp** Instituto de San Pedro Claver. (19??)-. Periodical. Spanish. bm. 1500ptas. Instituto de San Pedro Claver, Travesia del Cano 10, Aravaca, Madrid 23 Spain. **Tel** 011 34 1 3572250. **LC** BV2130; .E36. **DD** 266/.26. ***Continues*** *Eco de Africa.*
**Ind/Abst** Bibliogr. Mission.

US/0882-3707
**ECOS CRISTOFOROS.** [Ecos cristoforos]. Periodical. English (Spanish). bm. Free. The Christophers, 12 East 48th Street, New York NY 10017. **Tel** (212)759-4050, FAX (212)838-5073. **ED** Joseph R Thomas. **DD** 271. **Circ:** 80,000.
**Desc:** An easy to read leaflet that promotes sound values, contemporary topics of interest to the community such as aids, marriage, youth.

UK/0263-662X
**ECUM BULLETIN.** ***Suspended.*** **Added/Corp** Evangelical Coalition for Urban Mission (Great Britain). **VFOAT** Evangelical Coalition for Urban Mission Bulletin; Coalition News. (19??)-Suspended. Bulletin. English. Three times a year. £10.00. Evangelical Coalition for Urban Mission, 85A Allerton Road, Liverpool L18 2DA England.

US/0361-2236
**ECUMENICAL DIRECTORY OF RETREAT AND CONFERENCE CENTERS.** 1st Ed. (1974)-. Directory. English. an. $15.00. Jarrow Press Inc, 552 de Haro Street, San Francisco CA 94107. **LC** BV1652; .E38. **DD** 269/.6/02573.

SZ/0013-0796
**ECUMENICAL REVIEW, THE.** [Ecum. rev.]. **Added/Corp** World Council of Churches. Vol. 1 (Autumn 1948)-. Periodical. English. qt. $32.50. World Council of Churches, PO Box 2100, CH 1211 Geneva 2 Switzerland. **Tel** 011 41 22 7906076, FAX 011 41 22 7910361, telex 23 423 OIK CH. **ED** Emilio Castro. **LC** BX1; .E33. **DD** 280. Index available. **Bk Rev. Ad Acc. Circ:** 3,500. available on microfilm and microfiche from University Microfilms International (UMI). Documents available from The Genuine Article, UMI Article Clearinghouse. ***Absorbed*** *Christendom, 0190-4043.*
**Desc:** Journal of the World Council of Churches in which the major current theological, ethical and other issues relating to the work of the WCC in particular and the Ecumenical movement as a whole are discussed and debated. Each issue devoted to a specific theme.
**Ind/Abst** Acad. Search (July 1993-); Arts Humanit. Citation Index [Full Cov.]; Bibliogr. Mission.; Book Rev. Index; Curr. Contents Eng. Tech. Appl. Sci.; Expand. Acad. Index (1989-); Humanit. Index; Humanit. Source (Jul. 1993-); Index Book Rev. Relig.; INFO-SOUTH Abstr.; Mag. Search; Middle East Abstr. Index; New Testam. Abstr.; Newsp. Period. Abstr. (1991-); Old Testam. Abstr.; Relig. Index One Period. (1948/1949-); Relig. Theol. Abstr.; Res. Alert [Full Cov.]; Soc. Sci. Cit. Index [Select. Cov.].

US/0360-9073
**ECUMENICAL TRENDS.** **Added/Corp** Graymoor Ecumenical Institute. National Council of the Churches of Christ in the United States of America. Commission on Faith and Order. Vol. 1 (April 1972)-. Periodical. English. Eleven times a year. $10.00 (one year), $18.00 (two year), $25.00 (three year). Graymoor Ecumenical Institute, Graymoor, Garrison NY 10524. **Tel** (914)424-3671. available on microfilm and microfiche from University Microfilms International (UMI).
**Desc:** Ecumenical publication which presents news reports, documentation, book reviews, resources, key events, and analyses.
**Ind/Abst** Index Book Rev. Relig.; Relig. Index One Period.; Abr. Cathol. Period. Lit. Index; Cathol. Period. Lit. Index.

CN/0383-431X
**ECUMENISM.** [Ecumenism]. **Added/Corp** Canadian Centre for Ecumenism. No. 64 (Jan. 1982)-. Periodical. English. qt. 15.00Can$ (one year), 27.00Can$ (two years) Canada; $17.50 (one year), $32.50 (two years) US. Canadian Center for Ecumenism, 2065 West Sherbrook Street, Montreal Que H3H 1G6 Canada. **Tel** (514)937-9176. **ED** Thomas Ryan. **DD** 262/.0011. Index available (bound in March issue). **Bk Rev. Pr Rev. Circ:** 2,500. available on microfilm from University Microfilms International (UMI). ***Continues*** *Oecumenisme (English Ed.), 0383-431X.*
**Desc:** Serves Christian unity and interfaith understanding through dialogue, study, documentation, and news of ecumenical significance in Canada and internationally.

SA
**ECUNEWS : ECUMENICAL NEWS SERVICE OF THE SOUTH AFRICAN COUNCIL OF CHURCHES.** **Added/Corp** South African Council of Churches. **VFOAT** Ecunews Bulletin. (19??)-. Periodical. English. mo.
**Ind/Abst** Hum. Rights Intern. Rep.

RH
**EDICESA NEWS / ECUMENICAL DOCUMENTATION AND INFORMATION CENTRE FOR EASTERN AND SOUTHERN AFRICA.** **Added/Corp** Ecumenical Documentation and Information Centre for Eastern and Southern Africa. **VAT** Ecumenical Documentation and Information Centre for Eastern and Southern Africa News. (1988)-. Periodical. English. bm. EDICESA, PO Box H94, Hatfield, Harare,, Zimbabwe. **LC** BR1446; .E34. **DD** 276.76/082/05.
**Ind/Abst** Hum. Rights Intern. Rep.

SP
**EDIFICACION CRISTIANA.** Spanish. Five times a year. 2500ptas. Edificacion Cristiana, Trafalgar No 32-2 A, Madrid 28010 Spain. **Tel** 011 34 1 4488968. **ED** Amable Moralis, Pablo Le More, and Antonio Ruiz. Index available. **Bk Rev. Pr Rev. Circ:** 1,160.
**Desc:** Articles for women, young people and several pages of international and national news. Including book reviews and poetry mainly for the evangelical churches.

UK/1354-991X
**EDINBURGH REVIEW OF THEOLOGY AND RELIGION.** (19??)-. English. Twice a year. £30.00 UK & Europe; $50.00 North America; £33.00 other. Edinburgh University Press, 22 George Square, Edinburgh EH8 9LF Scotland. **Tel** 011 44 31 650 6207, FAX 011 44 31 662 0053.

CN
**EDITIONS SR.** **VFOAT** EDSR; Editions in the Study of Religion. Monographic series. English. Price varies per volume. Humanities Press, 165 1st Avenue, Atlantic Highlands NJ 07716. **Tel** (908)872-1441, (800)221-3845, FAX (908)872-0717, telex 752233. Index available.
**Desc:** Studies on religious and church history, missionary policies, etc.

PE
**EDUCACION (LIMA, PERU).** (EDUCACION / COMISION EVANGELICA LATINO AMERICANO DE EDUCACION CRISTIANA.). **Added/Corp** Comision Evangelica Latinoamericana de Educacion Cristiana. (19??)-. Periodical. Spanish. qt. Ave General Gazon 2267, Lima 11 Peru. **LC** BV1460; .E35. **DD** 207/.08.

SZ/0013-144X
**EDUCATION NEWSLETTER.** **Added/Corp** World Council of Churches. Office of Education. Programme Unit III. Vol. 1 (1972)-. Newsletter. English. Three times a year. Free on request. World Council of Churches, PO Box 2100, CH 1211 Geneva 2 Switzerland. **Tel** 011 41 22 7906076, FAX 011 41 22 7910361, telex 23 423 OIK CH. ***Supersedes*** *World Christian Education.*

UK/0951-1105
**EFAC BULLETIN.** [EFAC bull.]. **VFOAT** Evangelical Fellowship in the Anglican Community Bulletin. (19??)-. Periodical. English. sa. $4.80 (one year), $9.60 (two year). Wordmakers, 35 H M Road, St. Thomas Town, Bangalore 560084 India. **(Subscription address:** Riverbank, c/o Mrs. J. Dann, Treas., Reybridge Lacock Chippenham, Wiltshire SN15 2PS England.) **ED** David Evans. **DD** 270.82. ctrl circ.
**Desc:** The bulletin of the evangelical fellowship in the Anglican Community, founded in 1961 in order to foster fellowship between Anglican evangelicals throughout the world.

CN/0317-851X
**EGLISE, EN.** **Added/Corp** Eglise Catholique. Diocese de Chicoutimi. Vol. 1, (Jan. 1974)-. Periodical. French. Seven times a year. 12.00Can$. Office des Communications Sociales / Chicoutimi, 602 rue Racine Est CP 278, Chicoutimi Quebec G7H 5C3 Canada. **Tel** (418)543-0783. **Circ:** 1,200.
**Desc:** Presents the diocese of Chicoutimi's life and reflection to orient pastors and pastoral agents.

CN/0013-2322
**EGLISE CANADIENNE, L'.** Vol. 1 (Jan. 1968)-. Periodical. French. Eleven times a year (June/July issues combined). 30.00Can$ Canada; 42.00Can$ US; 65.00Can$ others. L'Eglise Canadienne, 6255 rue Hutchison, Bureau 103, Montreal Quebec H2V 4C7 Canada. **Tel** (514)278-3020, (800)668-2547. **ED** Rolande Parrot. **Bk Rev. Ad Acc. Circ:** 6,500 (ctrl).
**Desc:** Documents, studies and information about the life of Roman Catholic Church in Canada.
**Ind/Abst** Point Repere.

CN/0013-2349
**EGLISE ET THEOLOGIE.** [Eglise theol.]. **Added/Corp** Universite Saint-Paul, Ottawa, Ont. Faculte de Theologie. Vol. 1 (Jan. 1970)-. Periodical. French (English). Three times a year. 37.00Can$. St Paul University, 223 Main Street, Ottawa Ontario K1S 1C4 Canada. **Tel** (613)236-1393 ext. 2294, FAX (613)236-5278. **ED** Leo Laberge. Index available. **Bk Rev. Circ:** 500 (ctrl). available on microfilm and microfiche from University Microfilms International (UMI).
**Desc:** Doctrinal and practical theology, Bible, history of ideas: Christianity and church history/problems of culture.
**Ind/Abst** Bibliogr. Mission.; Canon Law Abstr.; Index Book Rev. Relig.; New Testam. Abstr.; Old Testam. Abstr.; Relig. Index One Period. (1970-); Relig. Theol. Abstr.

US/0018-3229
**EL HOGAR CRISTIANO.** Periodical. Spanish. qt. $6.00. Southern Baptist Convention, 901 Commerce, Suite 750, Nashville TN 37203. **Tel** (615)244-2355, FAX (615)742-8919. **(Subscription address:** Sunday School Board - Customer Service, 127 Ninth Avenue North, Nashville, TN 37234 USA; telephone: (800)458-2772**)**

US/0360-6120
**ELDER CHURCHMAN, THE.** V. 1- June 1969-. Periodical. English. Three times a year. Rev Max A Kapp, Box 1392, Vineyard Haven MA 02568.

GW/0724-4452
**ELEMENTA THEOLOGIAE.** No. 1 (1984)-. Monographic series. German. Price varies per volume. Verlag Peter Lang GmbH, Eschborner Landstrasse 42-50, D 60489 Frankfurt Germany. **Tel** 011 49 69 7807050.

IT
**ELENCHUS OF BIBLICA.** **Added/Corp** Pontificio Istituto Biblico. (1985)-. English (English). ir. L180000 Italy; $165.00 US. Editrice Pontificio Istituto Biblico, Piazza della Pilotta 35, 00187 Rome Italy. **Tel** 011 39 6 6781567, FAX 011 39 6 6780588. **ED** Robert North. **LC** Z7770; .E63; BS1171.2. **DD** 016.22. **Ad Acc. Circ:** 1,000 (ctrl). ***Continues*** *Elenchus Bibliographicus Biblicus of Biblica.*
**Desc:** Covers all areas of investigation which involve the scientific study of the Bible.

US/0889-8936
**EMERGING TRENDS.** (EMERGING TRENDS / PRRC.). [Emerg. trends]. **Added/Corp** Princeton Religion Research Center. **VFOAT** PRRC Emerging Trends. Vol. 1, No. 1 (Jan. 1979)-. Periodical. English. Ten times a year. $40.00 US, Canada & Puerto Rico; $50.00. Princeton Religion Research Centre, PO Box 389, Princeton NJ 08542. **Tel** (609)921-8112. **LC** BL2525; .E45. **DD** 291/.0973/05. cum. index. **Circ:** 1,500. available on microfilm and microfiche from University Microfilms International (UMI).
**Desc:** Provides answers to current levels of involvement in Bible study groups, religious education classes, the charismatic movement, evangelism, and the public's views on prayer in public schools and the moral majority.
**Ind/Abst** Stat. Ref. Index.

US/0013-6719
**EMMANUEL (NEW YORK, N.Y.).** (EMMANUEL.). [Emmanuel]. **Added/Corp** Priests' Eucharistic League. Congregation of the Blessed Sacrament. Apostolic Union of Secular Priests. Priests' Communion League. **VFOAT** Emmanuel Magazine. Vol. 1 (Jan. 1895)-. Periodical. English. mo. $19.95 (1 year), $32.95 (2 year) US; $24.95 (1 year), $42.95 (2 year) other. Emmanuel Magazine, 5384 Wilson Mills Road, Cleveland OH 44143. **Tel** (216)449-2103, FAX (216)449-3862. **ED** Rev. Anthony Schueller. **DD** 282. Index available (Bound in Nov. issue). **Bk Rev. Ad Acc. Circ:** 6,000.
**Desc:** Purpose is to meet the spiritual needs of those

engaged in church ministry. The focus of our spirituality is Eucharistic.
**Ind/Abst** New Testam. Abstr.; Abr. Cathol. Period. Lit. Index; Cathol. Period. Lit. Index.

US/1043-5816
**EMORY STUDIES IN EARLY CHRISTIANITY.** [Emory stud. early Christ.]. (1991)-. Monographic series. English. ir. Price varies per volume. Peter Lang Publishing, 62 West 45th Street, 4th Floor, New York NY 10036. **Tel** (212)764-1471, (800)770-5264, telex 6973364 PLNY. **DD** 200.

US/1053-9743
**EMPHASIS (LIMA, OHIO).** (EMPHASIS.). [Emphasis]. (197?)-. Periodical. English. mo. $27.50. CSS Publishing Company, 628 South Main Street, Lima OH 45804. **Tel** (419)227-1818. **DD** 251.

US/0013-7081
**ENCOUNTER (INDIANAPOLIS).** (ENCOUNTER.). [Encounter]. **Added/Corp** Christian Theological Seminary (Indianapolis, Ind.) Butler University. School of Religion. Vol. 17 (Winter 1956)-. Periodical. English. qt. $18.00 (one year), $32.00 (two year), $48.00 (three year). Christian Theological Seminary, 1000 West 42nd Street, Box 88267, Indianapolis IN 46208. **Tel** (317)924-1331, FAX (317)923-1961 *2. **ED** Clark M Williamson. **LC** BR1; .S5. **DD** 205. **UDC** 205. Index available (bound in fourth issue). **Bk Rev**, (Qty: Approx 10 in each issue). **Circ:** 600 (ctrl). available on microfilm (indexed in Religion Index One) from University Microfilms International (UMI). ***Continues*** *Shane Quarterly, 0362-4609.*
**Desc:** Creative discussion among Christians of various communions throughout the world: among theologians and other scholars, among believers in Christ and people of other faiths.
**Ind/Abst** Am. Hist. Life; Arts Humanit. Citation Index (19??-19??) [Full Cov.]; Index Book Rev. Relig.; Index Relig. Period. Lit.; Int. Zeitschriftenschau Bibelwissenschaft Grenzgeb.; Middle East Abstr. Index; New Testam. Abstr.; Old Testam. Abstr.; Relig. Index One Period. (1956-); Relig. Theol. Abstr.; Writ. Am. Hist.

CN/0842-8409
**ENSEMBLE.** [Ensemble]. Vol. 10, No. 4 (Sept. 1988)-. Periodical. French. ir. Ensemble, CP 602/Succ B, Montreal Quebec H3B 3K3 Canada. **Tel** (514)878-3035. **DD** 253.7/09714. **Bk Rev. Ad Acc.** ***Continues*** *Vigneron, 0225-1183.*

CN/1184-0447
**ENTRE-NOUS - CANADIAN COUNCIL OF CHURCHES.** (ENTRE-NOUS : NEWSLETTER OF THE CANADIAN COUNCIL OF CHURCHES.). [Entre-nous - Can. Counc. Churches]. **Added/Corp** Canadian Council of Churches. Vol. 1, No. 1 (June 1990)-. Newsletter. English (French). Three times a year (Mar., July, and Nov.). free. Canadian Council of Churches, 40 St Clair Avenue East, Suite 201, Toronto, Ontario M4T 1M9 Canada. **Tel** (416)921-4152, FAX (416)921-7478. **ED** Jim Hodgson, (Editor) and Helene Leclerc, (Assistant Editor). **DD** 262/.001/10971. **Circ:** 2,000. ***Continues*** *News Bulletin (Canadian Council of Churches)., 0835-8427.*

CN
**ENTRETIENS D'ORAISON.** **VFOAT** Oraison. V. 1- Sept./Oct. 1974-. Periodical. French. bm. Free. Entretiens d'Oraison, 4120 Avenue de Vendome, Montreal Quebec H4A 3N1 Canada. **DD** 248/.3/05.

US/0013-9408
**ENVOY (PITTSBURGH).** ***Title Change.*** (ENVOY.). [Envoy]. **Added/Corp** Institute of Man. Center of Religion and Personality. Institute of Man. Center for the Study of Spirituality. (1964)-(19??)-. Periodical. English. bm. Institute of Formative Spirituality, 906 Rockwell Hall, Duquesne University, Pittsburgh PA 15282. **Tel** (412)396-6026. **ED** Adrian van Kaam. **Circ:** 2,000. available on microfilm and microfiche from University Microfilms International (UMI). ***Continued by*** *Inspiration, 1065-8092.*
**Desc:** A journal of reflective reading bringing the word of God into one's everyday life through inspirational articles, poetry and spiritual reading of scripture and the masters.
**Ind/Abst** Abr. Cathol. Period. Lit. Index; Cathol. Period. Lit. Index.

US/8750-7064
**EP NEWS SERVICE.** (EP NEWS SERVICE : OFFICIAL WEEKLY NEWS SERVICE OF THE EVANGELICAL PRESS ASSOCIATION.). [EP news serv.]. **Added/Corp** Evangelical Press Association. **VFOAT** News Service. **VAT** Evangelical Press News Service. (19??)-. Periodical. English. Fifty-one times per year. $104.00 (libraries or radio stations), $176.00 (publishers of newspapers or magazines), $68.00 (others) US; $180.00 other. EP News Service, 1619 Portland Avenue South, Minneapolis MN 55404. **Tel** (612)339-9579, FAX (612)339-6973. **ED** Doug Trouten. Index available (published separately). cum. index. **Circ:** 350 (ctrl). available on an online database.
**Desc:** The official weekly news service of the Evangelical Press Association.

IT/0013-9505
**EPHEMERIDES LITURGICAE.** Vol. 1 (Jan. 1887)-. Periodical. Italian (English, German, Italian and Latin). bm. L35000 (Italy), L45000 (Europe), $48.60 (other). Centro Liturgico Vincenziano, Via Pompeo Magno 21, 00192 Rome Italy. **Tel** (0039-6)3216114, or 6628, FAX (0039-6)3221078. **LC** WMLC 93/1574. Index available in last issue of volume--attached.
**Ind/Abst** Bibliogr. Mission.; Canon Law Abstr.; New Testam. Abstr.; Abr. Cathol. Period. Lit. Index; Cathol. Period. Lit. Index.

SP/0425-1466
**EPHEMERIDES MARIOLOGICAE.** [Ephemer. Mariol.]. Vol. 1 (Jan./Mar. 1951)-. Periodical. Spanish (French, English, German, Italian and Latin). qt. 3100ptas Spain; $32.00 other. Publicaciones Claretianas, Buen Suceso 22, 28008 Madrid Spain. **Tel** 011 34 1 2486601. **ED** P Domiciano Fernandez. **LC** BT595; .E6. Index available. cum. index (until 1975). **Bk Rev. Pr Rev. Circ:** 800 (ctrl).
**Desc:** It offers systematical studies, researchers, actual questions on mariological thoelogie and spirituality, notices about the Marian Congresses, documents of the ecclesiastical magistery and bibliography.
**Ind/Abst** Bibliogr. Mission.; New Testam. Abstr.

BE/0013-9513
**EPHEMERIDES THEOLOGICAE LOVANIENSES.** [Ephemer. theol. Lovan.]. **Added/Corp** Universite Catholique de Louvain (1835-1969) Universite Catholique de Louvain--Katholieke Universiteit te Leuven. Vol. 1 (Jan. 1924)-. Periodical. French (English and German). qt. 2000F. Editions Peeters SA, Bondgenotenlaan 153, BP 41, B-3000 Leuven Belgium. **Tel** 32 16 235170, FAX 32 16 228500, telex 65987 PUL B. **ED** E. Brito, L. de Fleurquin, A. de Halleux, J. Etienne, A. Haquin, J. Lust, F. Neirynck, B. Willaert, and R. Willockx. **LC** BR1.A1; E55. Index available. cum. index. **Bk Rev.** ctrl circ.
**Desc:** Articles on theology, biblical exegesis, the church fathers, church history and canon law; authored by the professors of theology and canon law of the Catholic University of Louvain. Contains yearly bibliography.
**Ind/Abst** Bibliogr. Mission.; Index Book Rev. Relig.; New Testam. Abstr.; Old Testam. Abstr.; Relig. Index One Period.; Relig. Theol. Abstr.; Abr. Cathol. Period. Lit. Index; Cathol. Period. Lit. Index.

US
**EPIPHANY.** (19??)-. English. Four times a year. $22.50 US; $28.50 other. Epiphany Journal, PO Box 2250, South Portland ME 04116. **Tel** (207)767-1889. **ED** Michael Crowley. **Bk Rev**, (Qty: 15). **Ad Acc. Circ:** 1,000. available on microfilm from University Microfilms International (UMI); available on an online database from BRS.

US/0195-0681
**EPISCOPAL NEWS, THE.** (THE EPISCOPAL NEWS : THE CHURCH IN THE DIOCESE OF LOS ANGELES.). [Episcop. news]. **Main/Corp** Episcopal Church. Diocese of Los Angeles. (19??)-. Periodical. English (Spanish). Ten times a year. $10.00. Diocese of Los Angeles, PO Box 2164, Los Angeles CA 90054. **Tel** (213)482-2040, FAX (213)482-5304. **ED** Ruth Nicastro and Bob Williams. **DD** 283. **Bk Rev. Ad Acc. Circ:** 35,000 (ctrl).
**Desc:** News of the Diocese of Los Angeles, the Episcopal Church in the USA, the worldwide Anglican Communion, and the larger Christian Church, for diocesan members.

US/0149-3043
**EPOCHE (LOS ANGELES).** (EPOCHE.). **Added/Corp** University of California, Los Angeles. Dept. of History. Vol. 4, No. 2 (Fall 1976)-. Periodical. English (English). an. $7.00 (institutions), $5.00 (individuals). Epoche, UCLA Department of History, Los Angeles CA 90024. **Tel** (310)825-3780. **LC** BL41; .E65. **DD** 291/.05. ***Continues*** *History of Religions Newsletter, 0360-6147.*
**Ind/Abst** Index Book Rev. Relig.; Relig. Index One Period.

SZ
**EPS, ECUMENICAL PRESS SERVICE.** **Added/Corp** World Council of Churches. World Alliance of YMCAs. World Young Women's Christian Association. World Student Christian Federation. United Bible Societies. World Council of Christian Education and Sunday School Association. No. 46 (Dec. 1962)-. Periodical. English (French). wk. 69.00F Switzerland; $37.50 US; £24.90 UK. Ecumenical Press Service, World Council of Churches Publications, BP 66, CH-1211 Geneve 20 Switzerland. **Tel** 022/91 61 11, telex 23 423 OIK CH. **ED** Ken Mubu. Index available. **Circ:** 2,300. ***Continues*** *Ecumenical Press Service.*
**Desc:** This press service, approx. 30 mailings a year (news bulletins and documentation) - is published in English and French. The first issue of each month of the French Edition (SOEPI), Mensuel, is especially designed for local congregations.

IS
**ERETZ MAGAZINE.** See Archaeology.

SP/0210-3133
**ESCRITOS DEL VEDAT.** [Escr. Vedat]. V. 1- 1971-. Periodical. Spanish. an. $17.00 US. Seccion PP Dominicos, Facultad Teologia San Vicente, Torrente Valencia Spain. **Tel** (96)3517750. **ED** Martin Gelabert. **LC** BR45; .E86. **Ad Acc.** ctrl circ.
**Desc:** Scientific research in history, the Bible, theology, morality, canon law and philosophy.
**Ind/Abst** Bibliogr. Mission.; New Testam. Abstr.

FR/0014-0775
**ESPRIT ET VIE.** [Esprit vie]. **VFOAT** Esprit et vie Doctrine. (Jan. 1969)-. Periodical. French. wk. 125F. L Ami du Clerge, BP 4, 52200 Langres France. ***Continues*** *Ami du Clerge.*
**Ind/Abst** New Testam. Abstr.

SP
**ESTUDIO AGUSTINIANO.** Spanish. Three times a year. $11.00. Estudio Agustiniano, Paseo de Filipinos 7, Valladolid Spain. **Tel** 983 30 68 00. **UDC** 23.
**Ind/Abst** Canon Law Abstr.

SP
**ESTUDIOS MARIANOS.** **Added/Corp** Sociedad Mariologica Espanola. (1942)-. Spanish. an. $30.00. Editorial de Espiritualidad, Sociedad Mariologica Espanola, Triana 9 28016 Madrid 16 Spain. **Tel** 011 34 1 3504922. **LC** BT596; .E8.

SP/0210-0363
**ESTUDIOS TRINITARIOS.** [Estud. trinitarios]. (1963)-. Periodical. Spanish. Three times a year. $55.00. Ediciones Sec Trinitario, Filiberto Villalobos 82, Salamanca Spain. **Tel** 011 34 923 235602. **UDC** 23. Index available. cum. index. ctrl circ.
**Desc:** Articles on religion and theology.

BL
**ESTUDOS BIBLICOS.** No. 1 (1983)-. Monographic series. Portuguese. Four times a year. $30.00. Editora Vozes Ltda, R Frei Luis, 100 CP 90023, 25689 Petropolis RJ Brazil. **Tel** 11 55 242 435112.

BL/0101-3130
**ESTUDOS TEOLOGICOS.** (ESTUDOS TEOLOGICOS : ORGAO DA FACULDADE DE TEOLOGIA.). [Estud. teol.]. **Added/Corp** Igreja Evangelica de Confissao Luterana no Brasil. Faculdade de Teologia. (1961)-. Periodical. Portuguese (German). tq (Apr., July, Oct.). $15.00. Estudos Teologicos, EST CP 14, 93001 Sao Leopoldo RS Brazil. **Tel** 011 55 512 213433, , FAX 011 55 61 2257244. **ED** Nelio Schneider. Index available. **Circ:** 550. ***Continues*** *Estudos Teologicos - Studien und Berichte.*
**Desc:** Contains articles from the practical, biblical and historical-systematic areas with special emphasis on the challenges of the Latin American reality for the pastoral ministry.
**Ind/Abst** Index Book Rev. Relig.; Old Testam. Abstr.; Relig. Index One Period.

PL
**ETNOS (LUBLIN, POLAND).** (ETHOS.). No. 1 (1988)-. Periodical. Polish (English). qt. Z20.00. Instytyt Jana Pawa II, Al Racawickie 14, 20-950 Lublin Poland. **LC** BJ1188.5; .E83. Index available. cum. index. **Bk Rev. Ad Acc.** ctrl circ.

NE/0531-1950
**ETUDES PRELIMINAIRES AUX RELIGIONS ORIENTALES DANS L'EMPIRE ROMAIN.** Vol. 1 (1961)-. Monographic series. French. ir. Price varies per volume. E. J. Brill, Postbus 9000, 2300 PA Leiden Netherlands. **Tel** 011 31 71 312624, FAX 011 31 71 317532, telex 39296 BRILL NL. **ED** M.J. Vermaseren.

FR/0014-2239
**ETUDES THEOLOGIQUES ET RELIGIEUSES.** [Etud. theol. relig.]. **Added/Corp** Faculte de Theologie Protestante (Montpellier, France). Institut Protestant de Theologie Faculte de Theologie Pprotestante (Montpellier, France). Vol. 1, Mar. (1926)-. Periodical. French. qt. 156.71F France; 180.00F other. Etudes Theologiques et Religieuses, 13 rue Louis Perrier, 34000 Montpellier France. **ED** Andre Gounelle. Index available. cum. index. **Bk Rev. Ad Acc. Circ:** 2,500 (ctrl). available on microfilm and microfiche from University Microfilms International (UMI). Documents available from The Genuine Article.
**Desc:** Studies on religion, Bible, church history, theology and philosophy of religion.
**Ind/Abst** Arts Humanit. Citation Index [Full Cov.]; Curr. Contents Arts Humanit.; Index Book Rev. Relig.; Int. Zeitschriftenschau Bibelwissenschaft Grenzgeb.; New Testam. Abstr.; Old Testam. Abstr.; Relig. Index One Period. (1963-); Res. Alert [Full Cov.]; Romant. Move. (1963-); Soc. Sci. Cit. Index [Select. Cov.].

IT
**EUNTES DOCETE.** Vol. 1- 1948-. Periodical. Italian (English, French, Latin and Spanish). Three times a year. L35000. Urbaniana University Press, Vatican City, 00120 Rome Italy. **Tel** 06 6868640. Index available in last issue of volume--attached. cum. index. **Bk Rev. Ad Acc. Circ:** 1,000 (ctrl).
**Desc:** Missionary, law, missionology, and psychology.
**Ind/Abst** Bibliogr. Mission.; New Testam. Abstr.

GW/0531-2450
**EUROPAISCHE SAGEN.** V. 1- 1961-. Monographic series. German. Price varies per volume. Erich Schmidt Verlag GmbH, Postfach 304240, D 10724 Berlin Germany. **Tel** 011 49 30 25008525. **ED** Will-Erich Peuckert.
**Desc:** European myths.

UK/0960-2720
**EUROPEAN JOURNAL OF THEOLOGY.** (19??)-. English (French and German). Twice a year. £19.90 UK; £20.80 other. Paternoster Press, A division of Send the Light Ltd., PO Box 300, Kingstown Broadway, Cumbria CA3 0QS England. **Tel** 011 44 228 512512, FAX 011 44 228 514949.
**Desc:** Founded and edited with the aid of scholars and church leaders from many countries, this journal offers ministers, students and theologians a new European focus for their theology.

UK/0265-4547
**EVANGEL : QUARTERLY REVIEW OF BIBLICAL, PRACTICAL AND CONTEMPORARY THEOLOGY.** (19??)-. English. Three times a year (March, June and October). £13.50 UK; £14.20 other. Paternoster Press, A division of Send the Light Ltd., PO Box 300, Kingstown Broadway, Cumbria CA3 0QS England. **Tel** 011 44 228 512512, FAX 011 44 228 514949. **Circ:** 1,300.
**Desc:** An interdenominational publication for ministers and other church leaders and thinking Christians.

US/0162-1890
**EVANGEL (WINONA LAKE).** (EVANGEL.). Periodical. English. wk. $4.475. Light & Life Press, PO Box 535002, Indianapolis IN 46253-5002. **Tel** (219)267-7656. **ED** Raymond G Feldman. **Circ:** 35,000 (ctrl). available on microfilm and microfiche from University Microfilms International (UMI).
**Desc:** This publication is a Sunday School take home.
**Ind/Abst** Guide Soc. Sci. Relig.

US/0014-3332
**EVANGELICAL BEACON, THE. Added/Corp** Evangelical Free Church of America. (19??)-. Periodical. English. Seventeen times a year. $12.00 US; $14.00 others. Evangelical Beacon, 901 East 78th Street, Minneapolis MN 55420. **Tel** (612)854-1300. **ED** George M. Keck. **LC** BX7548.A1; E92. **DD** 289.9. Index available. **Bk Rev. Ad Acc. Circ:** 37,500. ***Continues*** *Evangelical Beacon and Evangelist.*
**Desc:** Devoted to inspirational articles, general religious news, denominational news and information.
**Ind/Abst** Curr. Thoughts Trends.

US/0014-3340
**EVANGELICAL FRIEND. *Ceased.* Added/Corp** Evangelical Friends Alliance (U.S.). Vol. 1, (Sept. 1967)-Vol. 27, No. 6. Periodical. English. Six times a year (Jan., Mar., May, July, Sept., Nov.). Evangelical Friend, 600-3rd Street, PO Box 232, Newburg OR 97132. **Tel** (503)538-7345, FAX (503)538-7033, . **ED** Dan McCracken. **Bk Rev. Ad Acc. Circ:** 12,000 (ctrl). ***Formed by the union of*** *Evangelical Friend; Southwest Friend; Rocky Mountain Friend; Northwest Friend* ***and*** *Missionary Voice of Evangelical Friends.*
**Desc:** General denominational magazine covering a variety of themes and of friends denomination (Quaker).

US/0741-1758
**EVANGELICAL JOURNAL.** [Evang. j.]. **Added/Corp** Evangelical School of Theology (Myerstown, Pa.). Vol. 1, No. 1, Spring (1983)-. Academic Scholarly Publication. English. sa. $8.00 US; $9.00 Other. Evangelical School of Theology, 121 South College Street, Myerstown PA 17067. **Tel** (717)866-5775. **ED** William S Sailer. **Bk Rev**, (Qty: 15-20/yr). **Circ:** 600.
**Desc:** Purposes is to provide a forum for scholarly theological expression consistent with the Wesleyan-Arminian tradition of Evangelical Protestantism.
**Ind/Abst** Index Book Rev. Relig.; Relig. Index One Period.; Relig. Theol. Abstr.

UK/0421-8094
**EVANGELICAL MAGAZINE OF WALES.** (THE EVANGELICAL MAGAZINE OF WALES.). [Evang. mag. Wales]. (1955)-. Periodical. English. Six times a year. £9.60. Evangelical Movement of Wales, Bryntirion Bridgend Mid, Glamorgan CF31 4DX Wales. **Tel** 011 44 1 656 655886, FAX 011 44 1 656 656095.

US/0014-3359
**EVANGELICAL MISSIONS QUARTERLY. Added/Corp** Evangelical Missions Information Service. Vol. 1 (Fall 1964)-. Periodical. English. qt (Jan., Apr., July, Oct.). $31.95 (one year) $59.90 (two year), $80.85 (three year). Evangelical Missions Information Service, PO Box 794, Wheaton IL 60189. **Tel** (703)653-2158, FAX (708)653-0520. **ED** Jim Reapsome. **LC** BV2350; .E83. **DD** 266/.005. Index available (Bound in volume every two year, $17.95 price.). **Bk Rev**, (Qty: 32). **Ad Acc, Adv Mgr:** Jan Warren. **Circ:** 7,300. available on microfilm and microfiche from University Microfilms International (UMI).
**Desc:** Written for missionaries, teachers, students and clergymen, emphasizing on evangelical missionary life, thought, and practice.
**Ind/Abst** Bibliogr. Mission.; Christ. Period. Index; Index Book Rev. Relig.; Relig. Index One Period.; Relig. Theol. Abstr. (19??-).

US/1065-4852
**EVANGELICAL MORMON OUTREACH QUARTERLY, THE.** [Evang. Mormon outreach q.]. **Added/Corp** IBC Outreach Ministries. (Sept. 1990)-. Periodical. English. qt. $2.00 (each copy). IBC Outreach Ministries, 5211 Backlick Road, Springfield VA 22151. **Tel** (703)941-4124, FAX (703)941-3896. **ED** Bob Tozler. **DD** 289. **Circ:** 10,000.
**Desc:** Strives to inform, alert, and motivate Christians with news about Mormon activities, insight on Mormon teachings, and ideas for witnessing to members of The Church of Jesus Christ of Latter-Day Saints.

UK/0014-3367
**EVANGELICAL QUARTERLY.** (THE EVANGELICAL QUARTERLY.). [Evang. q.]. (1929)-. Periodical. English. qt (January, April, July and October). £19.80 UK; £20.90 other. Paternoster Press, A division of Send the Light Ltd., PO Box 300, Kingstown Broadway, Cumbria CA3 0QS England. **Tel** 011 44 228 512512, FAX 011 44 228 514949. **ED** I. Howard Marshall. **LC** BR1; .E86. **DD** 230/.05. **[CCC]. Bk Rev. Ad Acc.** available on microfilm and microfiche from University Microfilms International (UMI).
**Desc:** Committed to the historic Christian faith, it promotes a theology based on scripture, yet it is sensitive to practical contemporary issues.
**Ind/Abst** Christ. Period. Index (19??-); Index Islam. Lit.; Index Book Rev. Relig.; Missionalia; New Testam. Abstr.; Old Testam. Abstr.; Relig. Index One Period. (1949-); Relig. Theol. Abstr.

II/0144-8153
**EVANGELICAL REVIEW OF THEOLOGY.** [Evang. rev. theol.]. **Added/Corp** World Evangelical Fellowship. Theological Commission. Vol. 1 (Oct. 1977)-. Periodical. English. Four times a year. £19.80 UK; £20.90 other. Paternoster Press, A division of Send the Light Ltd., PO Box 300, Kingstown Broadway, Cumbria CA3 0QS England. **Tel** 011 44 228 512512, FAX 011 44 228 514949. **ED** Sunand Sumithra. **[CCC]. Bk Rev. Ad Acc.** available on microfilm and microfiche from University Microfilms International (UMI).
**Desc:** Offers the thinking Christian articles and reviews from international publications, covering the spectrum of evangelical thought.
**Ind/Abst** Christ. Period. Index (19??-); Index Book Rev. Relig.; Missionalia; Relig. Index One Period.; Relig. Theol. Abstr.

US/0890-703X
**EVANGELICAL STUDIES BULLETIN.** [Evang. stud. bull.]. **Added/Corp** Institute for the Study of American Evangelicals (Wheaton, Ill.). Vol. 1, No. 1 (Jan. 1984)-. Bulletin. English. sa. $7.50. Evangelical Studies Bulletin, ISAE Wheaton College, c/o L Eskridge, Wheaton IL 60187. **Tel** (708)752-5437, FAX (708)752-5916. **ED** Edith Blumhofer and Larry Eskridge. **DD** 285. **Bk Rev**, (Qty: 2-3). **Ad Acc. Circ:** 2,300 (ctrl).
**Desc:** Reviews on American evangelicalism and its relations to American culture, and provides news on upcoming conferences, projects, and sources of financial support for academics. Each issue carries lists of important dissertations, articles, and books relevant to the study of American evangelicalism.

US/0731-0463
**EVANGELICAL SUNDAY SCHOOL TEACHER'S GUIDE, THE.** [Evang. Sunday sch. teach. guide]. 1982-83-. English. an. $5.95. Fleming H Revell Company, 184 Central Avenue, Old Tappan NJ 07675.

US/0745-0486
**EVANGELICAL VISITOR. Added/Corp** Brethren in Christ Church. Vol. 1 (1888)-. Periodical. English. mo. $10.25 US; $12.25 other. Evangel Press, PO Box 189, Napanee IN 46550. **Tel** (416)871-7769.

GW/0177-8706
**EVANGELIKALE MISSIOLOGIE.** [Evang. Missiol.]. **VFOAT** EM. Evangelikale Missiologie. (1985)-. Periodical. German. Four times a year (Jan., April, July, and Oct.). DM17.00. Arbeitskreis Evangelikale Missiologie, Hindenburstrasse 36, D-70825 Korntal, Germany. **Tel** 011 49 711 83987131, FAX 011 49 711 8380545. **UDC** 266. **Bk Rev**, (Qty: 20). **Circ:** 1,300 (ctrl).

GW/0014-3413
**EVANGELISCHE ERZIEHER, DER.** (1949)-. Periodical. German. bm (Feb., Apr., June, Aug., Oct., Dec.). DM62.18. Moritz Diesterweg, Postfach 630180, D-60351 Frankfurt Germany. **Tel** 11 49 69 420810, FAX 11 49 69 42081100. **ED** Karl Dienst. **[CCC]. Bk Rev. Ad Acc.**
**Desc:** One of the leading journals for religious instruction which links theory and practice. Of interest to teachers of religious subjects at all school levels.

GW
**EVANGELISCHE INFORMATION : NACHRICHTENSPIEGEL DES EVANGELISCHEN PRESSEDIENSTES.** Began in Jan. 1977. Periodical. German. wk. Evangelisher Press, Friedrichster 34, W-6000 Frankfurt 4 Germany. ***Continues*** *Nachrichtenspiegel des Evangelischen Pressedienstes.*

GW/0300-4236
**EVANGELISCHE KOMMENTARE.** [Evang. Komment.]. Vol. 1 (Jan. 1968)-. Periodical. German. Twelve times a year. DM132.00 Germany; DM144.60 other. Kreuz-Verlag Zeitschriften GmbH, Postfach 800669, Breitwiesenstr 30, D 70506 Stuttgart Germany. **Tel** 011 49 711 7880318, FAX 011 49 711 7880310. **ED** G. Brandt, H. Hamm-Brucher, E. Jungel, J. Moltmann, J. Rau, W. Trillhaas, R. Weeber and R. V. Weizsacker. **[CCC].** Index available. **Bk Rev. Ad Acc. Circ:** 10,000. ***Formed by the union of*** *Evangelische Welt; Kirche in der Zeit* ***and*** *Evangelischer Literaturbeobachter;* ***Absorbed*** *Ubergange (Berlin, Germany).*
**Desc:** Magazine with analysis, reports, notes, commentaries, interviews, and documentations to the contemporary history in church and society.
**Ind/Abst** Energy Res. Abstr. (Sept. 1980-).

GW/0014-3502
**EVANGELISCHE THEOLOGIE.** [Evang. Theol.]. Vol. 1, (Apr. 1934)-. Periodical. German. bm. DM68.50 Germany; DM74.00 other. Kaiser Verlag Zeitschriften, Quell Verlag Furtbachstr 12A, D 70178 Stuttgart Germany. **Tel** 011 49 711 6010057, FAX 011 49 711 6010076. **ED** Gunter Altner, Frank Crusemann, Helmut Gollwitzer, Ferdinand Hahn, Diether Koch, Ulrich Luz, Joachim Mehlhausen, Jurgen Moltmann, Gerhard Sauter, Werner H Schmidt, Wolfgang Schrage, Jurgen Seim, Theo Sundermeier, Lukas Vischer, Michael Welker and Elisabeth Moltmann-Wendel. **LC** BR4; .E88. **[CCC].** Index available. cum. index. **Bk Rev. Ad Acc. Circ:** 3,000. available on microfilm and microfiche from University Microfilms International (UMI). ***Formed by the union of*** *Blatter zur Kirchlichen Lage* ***and*** *Zwischen den Zeiten.*
**Desc:** Evangelical theology.
**Ind/Abst** Energy Res. Abstr. (Nov. 1981-); Index Book Rev. Relig.; New Testam. Abstr.; Old Testam. Abstr.; Relig. Index One Period. (1971-); Relig. Theol. Abstr.

GW
**EVANGELISCHES GEMEINDEBLATT FUER WUERTTEMBERG / [IM AUFTRAG VON LANDESBISCHOF D. WURM HERAUSGEGEBEN VON DER EVANG. GESELLSCHAFT IN STUTTGART].** **Added/Corp** Evangelische Gesellschaft in Stuttgart. (Oct. 1, 1905)-. Periodical. German. Fifty-two times a year. DM80.40. Evangelische Gemeindepresse GmbH, Postfach 101353, D 70012 Stuttgart 1 Germany. **Tel** 011 49 711-601000.

US/0890-667X
**EVANGELISM (MEQUON, WIS.).** (EVANGELISM.). [Evangelism]. Vol. 1, No. 1 (Fall 1986)-. Periodical. English. Four times a year (Feb., May, Aug., Nov.). $16.00 (institutions), $12.00 (individuals). Concordia University Wisconsin Evang, 12800 North Lakeshore Drive, Mequon WI 53097. **Tel** (414)243-5700, FAX (414)243-4409, (414)243-4351. **ED** Joel D. Heck (phone: (414)243-4207). **DD** 253. Index available (12th iss.). **Bk Rev**, (Qty: 4). **Ad Acc. Circ:** 1,000.
**Desc:** Practical and theological articles related to the Great Commission for an interdenominational readership.

CN/0821-0985
**EVANGELIST (HAMILTON).** (EVANGELIST MICROFORM.). [Evangelist]. **VAT** Evangelist (Toronto). Vol. 1, No. 1 (Jan. 1848)-. Periodical. English. Preston Microfilming Services, 2215 Queen Street East, Toronto Ontario M4E 1E8 Canada. **Tel** (416)699-7154. **DD** 287/.471.

GW
**EVANGELIUM / GOSPEL / EUAGGELION. *Ceased.* Added/Corp** German Lutheran Hour (Organization). **VFOAT** Gospel; Euaggelion. (1974)-No. 5 (Dec. 1992)-. Periodical. German (English). bm. Die Lutherische Stunde, PO Box 1162, W 2724 Sottrum F R Germany. **Tel** 011 49 4264 9103. **ED** Hans Lutz Poetsch. Index available. **Bk Rev. Ad Acc. Circ:** 3,000 (ctrl). ***Continues*** *Verkungdigung.*
**Desc:** Offers theological contributions of Lutheran scholars throughout the world; the accent is laid on practical implications.

GW/0934-0769
**EVANGELIUM UND WISSENSCHAFT.** [Evang. Wiss.]. (1980)-. Periodical. German. sa. DM6.00. Karl Heim Gesellschaft EV, Unter Den Eichen 13, D 35041 Marburg Germany. **Tel** 011 49 6421 83129. **UDC** 226 :001. Index available. cum. index. **Bk Rev**, (Qty:

10-20). **Circ:** 650.
**Desc:** Contributions, reports and reviews related to the field of science and Christian thought.

US/0891-3846
**EVANGELIZING TODAY'S CHILD.** **Added/Corp** Child Evangelism Fellowship. Vol. 1, No. 1, May/June (1974)-. Periodical. English. bm. $17.95 (one year), $32.95 (two year) US; $21.95 (one year), $40.95 (two year) other. Evangelizing Today's Child, PO Box 348, Warrenton MO 63383. **Tel** (314)456-4321, FAX (314)456-2078. **(Subscription address:** Canada/ PO Box 165, Winnipeg Manitoba R3C 2G9**) ED** Elsie Lippy. **Bk Rev**, (Qty: 20/yr). **Ad Acc**, **Adv Mgr:** AA Baker, **Tel** (803)370-3717. **Circ:** 25,000. ***Continues*** *Child Evangelism.*
**Desc:** Articles on teaching the Bible to children (4-12) in church, club and home, plus full-color lesson, puzzle and read-aloud story, lesson and verse reviews, bulletin and board designs, object lessons, handcrafts, attendance booster and Christian growth activities.
**Ind/Abst** Christ. Period. Index.

US/0423-8699
**EVERLASTING NATION, THE.** V. 1- Jan. 1952-. Periodical. English. bm. $2.00. International Board of Jewish Missions, PO Box 3307, Chattanooga TN 37404.

US/0883-0053
**EX AUDITU.** ***Title Change.*** Vol. 1 (1985)-Vol. 6 (1990). English. an. Pickwick Publications, 4137 Timberlane Drive, Allison Park PA 15101-2932. **Tel** (412)487-2159, FAX (412)487-8862. **ED** Robert E Guelich. **LC** BS543; .E92. **DD** 220.6/05. **Ad Acc.** ctrl circ. ***Continued by*** *Ex Auditu : An International Journal of Theological Interpretation of Scripture.*
**Ind/Abst** Relig. Index One Period.; Relig. Theol. Abstr.

US
**EX AUDITU : AN INTERNATIONAL JOURNAL OF THEOLOGICAL INTERPRETATION OF SCRIPTURE.** English. an. $20.00 (institutions), $12.00 (individuals) Canada; $25.00 (institutions), $15.00 (individuals) other. Pickwick Publications, 4137 Timberlane Drive, Allison Park PA 15101-2932. **Tel** (412)487-2159, FAX (412)487-8862. **ED** Klyne R Snodgrass. **Ad Acc. Pr Rev. Circ:** 240 (ctrl). ***Continues*** *Ex Auditu : An Annual of the Frederick Neumann Symposium on Theological Interpretation Scripture.*
**Desc:** Theological interpretation of scripture from the perspective of various disciplines.
**Ind/Abst** Index Book Rev. Relig.; Relig. Index One Period.

AT/0814-6764
**EX NIHILO TECHNICAL JOURNAL.** ***Title Change.*** **Added/Corp** Creation Science Foundation. Vol. 1 (1984)-(19??). English. an. Creation Science Foundation Ltd, PO Box 6302, Acacia Ridge QLD 4110 Australia. **Tel** 011 61 7 273 7650, FAX 011 61 7 273 7672. ***Continued by*** *Creation Ex Nihilo Technical Journal, 1036-2916.*

US/1046-3798
**EXALTATION.** [Exaltation]. Vol. 1, No. 1 (Oct./Dec. 1990)-. Periodical. English. qt. $7.50. Southern Baptist Convention, 901 Commerce, Suite 750, Nashville TN 37203. **Tel** (615)244-2355, FAX (615)742-8919. **(Subscription address:** Sunday School Board - Customer Service, 127 Ninth Avenue North, Nashville, TN 37234 USA; telephone: (800)458-2772**) DD** 783. ***Continues*** *Choral Praise, 0362-0409.*

NE/0166-2740
**EXCHANGE.** **Added/Corp** Interuniversitair Instituut voor Missiologie en Oecumenica (Netherlands). Afdeling Missiologie. No. 1 (Apr. 1972)-. Periodical. English (Dutch and French). Three times a year. Fl45.00. Department of Missiology Iimo, Rapenburg 61, NL 2311 GJ Leiden Netherlands. **Tel** 011 31 71 144248, FAX 011 31 72 273118. **ED** L. Lagerwerf. **Bk Rev**, (Qty: 20). **Ad Acc. Pr Rev. Circ:** 700 (ctrl).
**Desc:** Theological discussion on current missiological and ecumenical topics.
**Ind/Abst** Index Book Rev. Relig.; Missionalia; Relig. Index One Period.

US/0362-0867
**EXPLOR (EVANSTON, ILL.).** (EXPLOR.). [Explor]. **Added/Corp** Garrett-Evangelical Theological Seminary. Vol. 1 (Spring 1975)-. Periodical. English. Three times a year. Garrett Evangelical Theological Seminary, c/o Kenneth I Clawson, 2121 Sheridan Road, Evanston IL 60201. **LC** BR1; .E94. **DD** 230. available on microfilm and microfiche from University Microfilms International (UMI).
**Ind/Abst** Index Book Rev. Relig.; Old Testam. Abstr.; Relig. Index One Period. (1976-).

US/0889-8693
**EXPLORATIONS (DAYTON, OHIO).** (EXPLORATIONS : JOURNAL FOR ADVENTUROUS THOUGHT.). [Explorations]. Vol. 1, No. 1 (Sept. 1982)-. Periodical. English. qt. $12.00 (one year), $22.00 (two year). College Press, PO Box 922, Dayton OH 45409. **Tel** (513)293-2687. **ED** William F. Frost (phone: (513)229-4320). **DD** 230. **Bk Rev**, (Qty: 29). **Ad Acc.**

US
**EXPONENT II.** **VFOAT** Exponent 2; Exponent Two. Vol. 1, No. 1 (July 1974)-. Periodical. English. ir. $15.00. Exponent II, PO Box 128, Arlington MA 02174. **Tel** (617)868-3464. **ED** Sue Paxman. **Bk Rev**, (Qty: 4). **Pr Rev. Circ:** 2,000 (ctrl).

US/0014-5238
**EXPOSITOR BIBLICO. MAESTROS DE ADOLESCENTES-JOVENES-ADULTOS, EL.** (EL EXPOSITOR BIBLICO.). Spanish. qt. $5.75. Southern Baptist Convention, 901 Commerce, Suite 750, Nashville TN 37203. **Tel** (615)244-2355, FAX (615)742-8919. **(Subscription address:** Sunday School Board - Customer Service, 127 Ninth Avenue North, Nashville, TN 37234 USA; telephone: (800)458-2772**)**

CN/0824-474X
**EXPRESSION (WINNIPEG, DEUTSCHE AUSG.).** (EXPRESSION / MENNONITE BRETHREN COMMUNICATIONS.). [Expression]. Periodical. German. qt. Free. Mennonite Brethren Communications, PO Box 2 Station F, Winnipeg Manitoba R2L 2A5 Canada. **Tel** (204)667-9576. **ED** Gerhard Friesen. **DD** 289.7/06/07127. **Circ:** 1,600 (ctrl).
**Desc:** Describes the current activities of Mennonite Brethren Communications in religious radio and television broadcasting.

CN/0824-4731
**EXPRESSION (WINNIPEG. ENGLISH ED.).** (EXPRESSION / MENNONITE BRETHREN COMMUNICATIONS.). [Expression]. Vol. 1, No. 1 (June 1983)-. Periodical. English. bm. Free. Mennonite Brethren Communications, PO Box 2 Station F, Winnipeg Manitoba R2L 2A5 Canada. **Tel** (204)667-9576. **DD** 289.7/06/07127. ctrl circ.

US/0361-6061
**FACE TO FACE (NEW YORK).** ***Suspended.*** (FACE TO FACE; AN INTERRELIGIOUS BULLETIN.). **Added/Corp** B'nai B'rith. Anti-Defamation League. (Fall 1975)-(19??). Bulletin. English. Three times a year. Antidefamation League BNAI, Brith 823 United Nations Plaza, New York NY 10017. **Tel** (212)490-2525.

US/8756-2146
**FACULTY DIALOGUE.** [Fac. dial.]. **Added/Corp** Institute for Christian Leadership. No. 1 (Fall 1984)-. Periodical. English. Three times a year. $15.00 (1 year), $28.00 (2 year), $39.00 (3 year) institutions; $11.00 (1 year), $19.50 (2 year), $27.00 (3 year) individuals. Institute for Christian Leadership, 12753 SW 68th Avenue, Suite 299, Tigard OR 97223. **Tel** (503)598-7889. **ED** Ted Ward and Martin W Bush. **LC** LC383; .F33. **DD** 377/.8/097305. **Ad Acc. Circ:** 11,000 (ctrl).
**Desc:** Examines issues related to strength and success of church related colleges and universities, particularly in the area of fulfilling mission and goals.
**Ind/Abst** Christ. Period. Index (19??-).

US/0734-1539
**FACULTY STUDIES - CARSON-NEWMAN COLLEGE.** (FACULTY STUDIES.). [Fac. stud. - Carson-Newman Coll.]. Began in 1965?. Periodical. English. an. Carson-Newman College, Box 1898, Jefferson City TN 37760. **ED** Robert M Shurden (editor's address: Carson Newman, PO Box 1899, Jefferson City TN 37760). **LC** BX6201; .F3. **DD** 286/.132/05. **Circ:** 400 (ctrl).
**Desc:** Journal published by Carson Newman College including articles from faculty members on subjects related to their discipline.

FR/0760-6443
**FAIM DEVELOPPEMENT MAGAZINE PARIS.** [Faim dev. mag.Paris]. (1983)-. Periodical. French. Nine times a year (monthly except July, Aug., Sep.). 93.00F France; 123.00F other. Com Catholique Contre Faim Dev, 4 rue Jean Lantier, 75001 Paris France. **Tel** 33 615160, telex CCFD 213918. **UDC** 266.5. ctrl circ. ***Continues*** *CCFD Info (Paris), 0339-0489.*

UK
**FAITH AND FREEDOM.** Vol. 1 (Oct. 1947)-. English. Three times a year. University of Winnipeg, Winnipeg Manitoba R3B 2E9 Canada.
**Ind/Abst** Index Book Rev. Relig.; Relig. Index One Period.; Relig. Theol. Abstr. (199?-).

UK/0014-701X
**FAITH AND FREEDOM OXFORD.** [Faith freedom Oxf.]. **VFOAT** Faith and Freedom (Leeds). (1947)-. Periodical. English. Twice a year (Apr. and Nov.). $20.00 (US & Canada); £10.00 (all others). Manchester College, Mansfield Road, % P B Godfrey, Oxford OX1 3TD, England. **Tel** 11 44 81 393-9122, FAX 11 44 81 393-9122. **(Subscription address:** US and Canada: Faith and Freedom Agency, Meadville/Lombard Theological School, 5701 Woodlawn Avenue, Chicago, Illinois 60637**) ED** Pete B. Godfrey. **DD** 200. **Bk Rev. Ad Acc. Circ:** 600. available on microfilm and microfiche from University Microfilms International (UMI); available on an online database from DIALOG.
**Desc:** Articles on liberal & progressive religious, social, and philosophical topics.

US/0740-0659
**FAITH AND MISSION.** **Added/Corp** Southeastern Baptist Theological Seminary. Vol. 1, No. 1 (Fall 1983)-. Periodical. English. sa. $9.00. Faith and Mission, PO Box 1889, Southeastern Seminary, Wake Forest NC 27587. **Tel** (919)556-3101. **ED** Fred Grissom and T Furman Hewitt. **Bk Rev. Circ:** 2,000. available on microfilm and microfiche from University Microfilms International (UMI).
**Ind/Abst** Index Book Rev. Relig.; Missionalia; Relig. Index One Period.; Relig. Theol. Abstr.; South. Baptist Period. Index.

US/0739-7046
**FAITH AND PHILOSOPHY : JOURNAL OF THE SOCIETY OF CHRISTIAN PHILOSOPHERS.** **See** Philosophy.

US/0098-5449
**FAITH & REASON.** [Faith reason]. **VFOAT** Faith and Reason. **VAT** Faith and Reason. Vol. 1 (Spring 1975)-. Periodical. English. Four times a year (Mar., June, Sept., Dec.). $20.00. Christendom Press, 2101 Shenandoah Shores Road, Front Royal VA 22630. **Tel** (703)636-2900, FAX (703)636-1655. **ED** Rev. James McLucas, (phone: (703)636-2900). **LC** BR1; .F26. **DD** 230/.05. **Bk Rev**, (Qty: 2). **Circ:** 1,000.
**Desc:** An academic journal with articles by Catholic scholars in fields such as theology, philosophy, politics, literature, history and philosophy of science.
**Ind/Abst** Abr. Cathol. Period. Lit. Index; Cathol. Period. Lit. Index.

US/1051-8762
**FAITH & RENEWAL.** ***Ceased.*** (FAITH & RENEWAL : FOR CHRISTIAN LEADERS.). [Faith renew.]. **Added/Corp** Alliance for Faith & Renewal. **VFOAT** Faith and Renewal. Vol. 15, No. 1 (July/Aug. 1990)-(Dec. 1994). Periodical. English. bm. Alliance for Faith and Renewal, PO Box 8229, Ann Arbor MI 48107. **Tel** (313)761-8505. **DD** 262. ***Continues*** *Pastoral Renewal, 0744-8279.*
**Ind/Abst** Curr. Thoughts Trends.

UK
**FAITH (PORTSLADE BY SEA, E. SUSSEX).** (FAITH.). Periodical. English. bm.

CN/0706-7003
**FAITH TODAY (TORONTO).** (FAITH TODAY.). V. 1- Feb. 1978-. Periodical. English. bm. 16.50Can$ Canada; $19.50 US; $22.50 other. FT Communications, PO Box 186 Station U, Toronto Ontario M8Z 5P1 Canada. **Tel** (416)479-5885, FAX (416)479-4742. **ED** Brian C Stiller and Audrey Dorsch. **DD** 269/.2/0971. **Bk Rev. Ad Acc. Circ:** 18,000.
**Desc:** Canada's evangelical news/feature magazine providing news of interest to and/or about the church community and discussing current issues from a Christian perspective.

CN/0832-1191
**FAITH TODAY (WILLOWDALE).** (FAITH TODAY.). [Faith today]. **Added/Corp** Evangelical Fellowship of Canada. (Mar./Apr. 1986)-. Periodical. English. bm (Jan., Mar., May, July, Sept., Nov.). 16.50Can$ Canada; 19.50Can$ US and Mexico; 22.50Can$ other. Evangelical Fellowship Office, Box 88000, Station B, Willowdale, Ontario, M2K 2R6 Canada. **Tel** (416)479-5885, FAX (416)479-4742. **ED** Audrey Dorsch. **DD** 269/.2/05. **Bk Rev. Ad Acc. *Continues*** *Faith Alive., 0822-5087.*
**Ind/Abst** Christ. Period. Index (19??-).

US/0360-9057
**FAITHFUL WORD, THE.** **Added/Corp** Lutheran Churches of the Reformation. (1961)-. Periodical. English. qt. $6.00. One Accord, 3000 Van Horn Drive, Hood River OR 97031. **Tel** FAX (503)386-6488.

US/0277-4518
**FAMILY MINISTRIES.** (FAMILY MINISTRIES : ASSEMBLIES OF GOD NEWSLETTER.). **VFOAT** Family Ministries Newsletter. Newsletter. English. qt. Gospel Publishing House, 1445 Boonville Avenue, Springfield MO 65802. **Tel** (417)862-2781, FAX (417)866-1146.

CN/0713-0163
**FATIMA CRUSADER.** (THE FATIMA CRUSADER / THE NATIONAL PILGRIM VIRGIN OF CANADA.). [Fatima crusad.]. Issue No. 1 (Summer 1978)-. Periodical. English. qt. Free. The National Pilgrim Virgin of Canada, PO Box 602, Fort Erie Ontario L2A 5X3 Canada. **Tel** (416)871-7607, FAX (416)871-5274. **ED** Coralie Graham. **DD** 232.91/7. **Circ:** 500,000.
**Desc:** Promoting the message of our Lady of Fatima.

US
**FELLOWSCRIP.** Assemblies of God Archives, 1445 Boonville Avenue, Springfield MO 65802-1894. **Tel** (417)862-2781, (417)862-1447, FAX (417)862-8558.

US/0014-9837
**FELLOWSHIP IN PRAYER.** [Fellowsh. pray.]. (1950)-. Periodical. English. bm. $16.00. Fellowship in Prayer, 291 Witherspoon Street, Princeton NJ 08542. **DD** 242.

# Religion and Theology

CN/0316-7909
**FELLOWSHIP OF BELIEVERS BULLETIN.** (BULLETIN - FELLOWSHIP OF BELIEVERS.). **Main/Corp** Fellowship of Believers. Vol. 3, No. 4 (July/Aug. 1971)-. Bulletin. English. bm. Fellowship of Believers, PO Box 537, Gladstone Manitoba R0J 0T0 Canada. **DD** 269/.2/05. **Continues** Anointed Life, 0316-7895.

US/8750-3530
**FESTIVAL QUARTERLY.** [Festiv. q.] Vol 1, No. 1 (Spring 1974)-. Periodical. English. Four times a year (Mar., June, Sept., Dec.). $14.00 (one year), $27.00 (two years), $40.00 (three years). Festival Quarterly, 3513 Old Philadelphia Pike, Intercourse PA 17534. **Tel** (717)768-7171. **ED** Phyllis Pellman Good and David Graybill. **DD** 289. **Bk Rev. Ad Acc. Circ:** 4,000. **Desc:** Exploring the art, faith and culture of mennonite people.

FR/0015-0371
**FETES ET SAISONS.** [Fetes saisons]. Periodical. French. mo. Editions du CERF, BP 65, 77932 Perthes Cedex France. **Tel** 011 33 1 44181212.
**Ind/Abst** Point Repere (1983-).

BE
**FEU NOUVEAU.** French. mo. 55.00Can$, 70.00Can$ (airmail). Periodica Inc, PO Box 444, Outremont Quebec H2V 4R6 Canada. **Tel** (514)274-5468, **FAX** (514)274-0201.

CN/0824-1546
**FEUILLET SPIRITUEL DE L'OEUVRE DU PELERINAGE DES MALADES.** (LE FEUILLET SPIRITUEL DE L'OEUVRE DU PELERINAGE DES MALADES / ORATOIRE SAINT-JOSEPH.). Vol. 1, No. 1 (Mar. 1980)-. Periodical. French. bm. $1.00. l'Oeuvre du Pelerinage des Malades de l'Oratoire Saint-Joseph, 3800 Ch Reine-Marie, Montreal Quebec H3V 1H6 Canada. **DD** 232.9/32/05.

US/0730-0271
**FIDELITY (MARSHFIELD, WIS.).** (FIDELITY.). **Added/Corp** Wanderer Forum Foundation. Ultramontane Associates, Inc. Vol. 1, No. 1 (Dec 1989)-. Periodical. English. mo (with July and Aug. combined). $19.00 individuals; $23.00 institutions. Fidelity, 206 Marquette Avenue, South Bend IN 46617. **Tel** (219)289-9786. **ED** E. Michael Jones. **LC** BX801; .F53. **DD** 282/.05.
**Desc:** Features, commentaries, and reviews on current issues.

US/0884-5379
**FIDES ET HISTORIA.** (FIDES ET HISTORIA : OFFICIAL PUBLICATION OF THE CONFERENCE ON FAITH AND HISTORY.). [Fides hist.]. **Added/Corp** Conference on Faith and History. Vol. 1 (Fall 1968)-. Periodical. English. Three times a year. $15.00 (one year), $40.00 (three year). Conference on Faith & History, Department of History, Indiana State University, Terre Haute IN 47809. **Tel** (812)237-2707. **LC** BR1; .F5. **DD** 261. available on microfilm and microfiche from University Microfilms International (UMI).
**Ind/Abst** Am. Hist. Life (1970-); Christ. Period. Index (19??-); Index Book Rev. Relig. (1970-); Old Testam. Abstr.; Relig. Index One Period. (1979-); Relig. Theol. Abstr.

CN/0836-6918
**FILET (MONTREAL, QUEBEC).** (LE FILET.). [Filet]. Vol. 1, No. 1 (May 1987)-. Periodical. French. qt. Sameta, 3719 Est Boul Gouin, Montreal Quebec H1H 5L8 Canada. **Tel** (514)322-0560. **DD** 255/.79. **Continues** Sameta, 0705-0518.

US
**FINANCIAL STATEMENTS AND SCHEDULES : (WITH ACCOUNTANTS' REPORT THEREON) / UNITED CHURCH BOARD FOR WORLD MINISTRIES.** **Main/Corp** United Church Board for World Ministries. (Dec. 31, 1979)-. English. an. United Church Board for World Ministries, 475 Riverside Drive, New York NY 10027. **Tel** (212)870-2183. **Continues** Financial Report for the Year - United Church Board for World Ministries.

NE/0168-5481
**FINANCIELE GEGEVENS KERKGENOOTSCHAPPEN / CENTRAAL BUREAU VOOR DE STATISTIEK, HOOFDAFDELING FINANCIELE STATISTIEKEN.** VFOAT Financial Data of Religious Denominations. Dutch (summaries and/or abstracts in English). Fl7.15. Centraal Bureau voor de Statistiek, AFD ALG Zaken, Postbus 959, 2270 AZ Voorburg Netherlands. **Tel** 011 31 70 3373800, **FAX** 011 31 038 7429, telex 32692 CBS NL. **LC** BR903; .F56. **DD** 338.4/328/09342.

GW/1050-7507
**FIRST DAYS RECORD : A JOURNAL OF LIBERAL RELIGIOUS RESPONSES, THE.** [First days rec.]. (1984)-. Periodical. English. mo. $30.00. First Days Record, 420 Willa Road, Newark DE 19711. **Tel** (302)368-5980. **ED** Roberta Emmons. **DD** 288. Index available. cum. index. **Circ:** 600.
**Desc:** Ordered distribution of materials written on the first day of each month by contributing Unitarian Universalist Ministers.

US/1047-5141
**FIRST THINGS (NEW YORK, N.Y.).** (FIRST THINGS : A MONTHLY JOURNAL OF RELIGION AND PUBLIC LIFE.). [First things]. **Added/Corp** Institute on Religion and Public Life. No. 1 (Mar. 1990)-. Periodical. English. mo (except combined June/July and Aug./Sept.). $29.00. Institute on Religion and Public Life, 156 5th Avenue, Suite 400, New York NY 10010. **Tel** (212)627-2288. **(Subscription address:** First Things Subscriber Services FT, PO Box 3000, Denville, NJ 07834) **DD** 291. Index available. **Bk Rev. Ad Acc, Adv Mgr:** Richard Vaughan, **Tel** (815)398-8569. **Circ:** 20,000.
**Ind/Abst** Curr. Thoughts Trends; Index Book Rev. Relig.; Relig. Index One Period.

US/1064-136X
**FIVE STONES, THE. See** Religion and Theology-Protestantism.

US
**FLAME (SEATTLE, WASH.). See** Women's Interests.

US/0274-6522
**FLASHLIGHT (PASADENA, CALIF.).** (FLASHLIGHT.). [Flashlight]. **VFOAT** VOCA Flashlight. Periodical. English. bm. VOCA, PO Box 15-M, Pasadena CA 91102. **DD** 266.

US
**FLOODTIDE.** **Added/Corp** Christian Literature Crusade. Vol. 1 (Mar. 1948)-. Periodical. English. qt. Free on request. Christian Literature Crusade, PO Box 1449, Fort Washington PA 19034. **Tel** (215) 542-1242, **FAX** (215) 542-7580. **ED** Leona Hepburn. **Bk Rev. Ad Acc. Circ:** 2,000.
**Desc:** News and ideas in Christian literature distribution.

US
**FLYER (EVANSTON, ILL.). See** Women's Interests.

UK/0950-9720
**FOCUS ON CHRISTIAN-MUSLIM RELATIONS. Ceased. Added/Corp** Islamic Foundation (Great Britain). (19??)-(1993). Periodical. English. mo. Islamic Foundation Publishing Unit, Unit 9/Old Dunlop Factory, 62 Evington Valley Road, Leicester LE5 5LJ England. **Tel** 011 44 533 734860, **FAX** 011 44 533 244946, telex 341539 ISLAMF G.

US
**FOCUS ON MISSIONS; OCCASIONAL NEWS SUPPLEMENT FOR MISSIONARIES.** **Added/Corp** Fellowship of Missions. (1970)-. Periodical. English. Five times a year. Free on request. Fellowship of Missions, PO Box 136, Middleton DE 19709. **Tel** (302)378-1525. **ED** Bernice Inman. **Bk Rev. Circ:** 25,000 (ctrl).
**Desc:** A conservative fundamental news supplement for missionaries.

US/0894-3346
**FOCUS ON THE FAMILY (ARCADIA, CALIF. 1982). See** Family and Marriage.

CN/0319-3837
**FOCUS ON YOUTH FOR CHRIST CALGARY.** (FOCUS / YOUTH FOR CHRIST/CALGARY.). [Focus Youth Christ Calg.]. **Added/Corp** Youth for Christ/Calgary. (1980)-. Periodical. English. qt. Calgary Youth for Christ, PO Box 6151, Station D, Calagry Alta. T2P 2C8. **DD** 267/.61/0971233. **Continues** Focus on Youth for Christ Calgary, 0319-3837.

FR/0015-5357
**FOI ET LA VIE, LA.** (FOI ET VIE.). [Foi vie]. (1898)-. Periodical. French. Five times a year (January, April, July, September, and December). 200.00F France; 220.00F other. Foi et Vie, 139 Boulevard Montparnasse, Paris 75006 France. **Tel** 11 33 1 43221599. **ED** Olivier Millet, 130 Avenue de Versailles, 75016 Paris France. Index available in last issue of volume--attached. **Bk Rev,** (Qty: 5). **Circ:** 1,200 (ctrl)
**Desc:** Covers Jewish studies, spiritual life, commemoration of the revocation of the Edit de Nantes, Bible studies on Paul, creation of the world, etc.
**Ind/Abst** Index Book Rev. Relig.; New Testam. Abstr.; Relig. Index One Period. (1963-); Relig. Theol. Abstr.; Romant. Move.

BE/0430-8522
**FOI ET LE TEMPS.** Vol. 1. (Jan./Feb. 1968); New Series, Vol. 1 (Jan./Feb. 1971)-. Periodical. French. Six times a year. 900F Belgium; 1060F other. La Foi et le Temps, 28 rue des Jesuites, 7500 Tournai Belgium. **Tel** 011 32 69 221429. **Formed by the union of** Revue Ecclesiastique de Liege **and** Revue Diocesaine de Namur.

US
**FOREFRONT CO.** (19??)-. English. Four times a year (Feb., May, Aug, Nov.). $16.00 (one year); $30.00 (two years). Spiritual Life Institute, PO Box 219, Crestone CO 81131. **Tel** (719)256-4778, **FAX** (719)256-4719. **ED** Reverend David Denny. **Bk Rev,** (Qty: 4-6). **Circ:** 2,700 (ctrl). **Continues** Desert Call, 0011-9229.
**Desc:** Seeks to restore contemplation to the forefront of culture and celebrates Christ at the forefront of history. It takes truth of the desert---where the deepest encounters with God takes place--to the cities. Articles apply the principles of the spiritual life to everyday life and evaluate contemporary trends in light of the world's wisdom traditions. While Catholic in origin, ecumenical spirit embraces the deepest values of the great religious traditions.

GW
**FORSCHUNG ZUR BIBEL.** Vol. 1 (1972)-. Monographic series. German. ir. Price varies per volume. Echter Wuerzburg, Postfach 5560, Julius Promenade 64, D 97070 Wuerzburg Germany. **Tel** 011/49/931/3091153, **FAX** 011/49/931/16735.

GW/0532-2154
**FORSCHUNGEN ZUR KIRCHEN- UND DOGMENGESCHICHTE.** Vol. 1 (1952)-. German. Vandenhoeck & Ruprecht, Robert Bosch Breite 6, D-37079 Goettingen Germany. **Tel** 011 49 551 695911, **FAX** 011 49 551 695917, telex 965226 VAN d.

GW/0429-162X
**FORSCHUNGEN ZUR SYSTEMATISCHEN UND OEKUMENISCHEN THEOLOGIE.** Vol. 1 (1962)-. Monographic series. German. ir. Price varies per volume. Vandenhoeck & Ruprecht, Robert Bosch Breite 6, D-37079 Goettingen Germany. **Tel** 011 49 551 695911, **FAX** 011 49 551 695917, telex 965226 VAN d. **Ad Acc. Continues** Forschungen zur Systematischen Theologie und Religionsphilosophie.

US
**FORUM.** **Added/Corp** North American Forum on the Catechumenate. (1984)-. Periodical. English. qt. Free. North American Forum on the Catechumenate, 5510 Columbia Pike, Suite 310, Arlington VA 22204. **Tel** (703)671-0330. **ED** Lorie Catsos. **LC** BX1968; .F67. **DD** 268/.82/05. **Bk Rev,** (Qty: 4). **Circ:** 4,000.

US/0015-9182
**FOURSQUARE WORLD ADVANCE.** VFOAT Advance. Periodical. English. bm. International Church of the Foursquare Gospel, 1910 W Sunset Boulevard/Suite 200, Los Angeles CA 90026-3282. **Tel** (310)484-2400. **ED** Ron Williams. **Bk Rev. Circ:** 85,000.

US
**FOURTH R, THE.** (1981)-. Periodical. English. Six times a year. $18.00. Polebridge Press, 19678 8th Street East, Sonoma CA 95476. **Tel** (707)996-9228, **FAX** (707)996-5022. **ED** Culver H. Nelson. **Circ:** 1,500. **Continues** Westar Magazine.
**Desc:** Advocates biblical and religious literacy. Addresses a broad range of questions about religion, past and present.

CN/0711-2211
**FRAGMENTS (SCARBOROUGH, ONT.).** (FRAGMENTS.). Mar. 1977)-. Periodical. English. Toronto Pastoral Centre for Liturgy, 2661 Kingston Road, Scarborough Ontario M1M 1M3 Canada. **DD** 264/.02. **Continues** Untitled Publication (Toronto Pastoral Center for Liturgy), 0711-2203.

FR/1157-3775
**FRANCIS BULLETIN SIGNALETIQUE. 527, HISTOIRE ET SCIENCES DES RELIGIONS.** **Added/Corp** Institut de l'Information Scientifique et Technique (France). Sciences Humaines et Sociales. VFOAT Histoire et Sciences des Religions; History and Sciences of Religion. Vol. 45, No. 1 (1991)-. Bulletin. French. qt (4 issues). 585.00F France; 615.00F other. CNRS / Institut d'Information Scientifique et Technique, (Centre National de la Recherche Scientifique), 15 Quai Anatole France, Paris 75700 France. **Tel** 011 33 1 47531515, telex 299 356 F. **(Subscription address:** Institut d'Information Scientifique et Technique Diffusion, 2 Allee du Parc de Brabois, 54514 Vandoeuvre Nancy France.) **LC** Z7751; .B85. Index available (free). available on CD-ROM. **Continues** Bulletin Signaletique. 527, Histoire et Sciences des Religions, 0180-9296.

UK/0532-579X
**FRANCISCAN, THE.** Vol. 4, No. 3 (Summer 1962)-V. 30, No. 3 (Sept. 1988)-. Periodical. English. Three times a year. **Continues** Franciscan News.

UK
**FRANCISCAN ESSAYS.** English. **LC** BX3601; .B7. **DD** 271.306242; 271.304.

CK/0120-1468
**FRANCISCANUM. See** Philosophy.

CN/0821-3488
**FRANCOIS AUJOURD'HUI.** No. 1 (Sept. 1982)-. Periodical. French. bm. $5.00. Fraternite Provinciale de l'Ordre Franciscain Seculier, 836 rue d'Aiguillon, Quebec Quebec G1R 1M9 Canada. **DD** 271/.3. **Circ:** 2,000.

UK/0016-0326
**FREE CHURCH CHRONICLE. Added/Corp** Free Church Federal Council. National Council of the Evangelical Free Churches. (Jan. 1899)-. Periodical. English. qt. Free Church Federal Council, 27 Tavistock Square, London WC1H 9HH England. **Tel** 01 387 8413. **ED** David Staple. **Bk Rev. Ad Acc. Circ:** 2,000 (ctrl).

US/0272-0701
**FREE INQUIRY (BUFFALO). See** Philosophy.

US/1059-6372
**FREEDOM WRITER (GREAT BARRINGTON, MASS.).** (FREEDOM WRITER.). [Freedom writ.]. **Added/Corp** Simon, Porteous & Associates, Inc. Institute for First Amendment Studies. Vol. 2, No. 3 (Mar. 1985)-. Periodical. English. bm. Free to members; $25.00 membership. Institute of First Amendment Studies, PO Box 589, Great Barrington MA 01230. **Tel** (413)274-3786, FAX (413)274-0245. **ED** Skipp Porteous. **DD** 322. **Ad Acc, Adv Mgr:** 6. **Circ:** 18,000. available on microfilm. ***Continues*** *Control Q.*

US/0882-8512
**FREETHOUGHT TODAY.** [Freethought today]. **Added/Corp** Freedom From Religion Foundation (Madison, Wis.). **VFOAT** Free Thought Today. (Jan. 1984)-. Periodical. English. mo (Jan./Feb and Jun./Jul. issues are combined). $15.00 US; $20.00 Canada and Mexico; $30.00 other; Add $7.50 for Canada postage, add $15.00 for other postage. Freedom from Religion Foundation, PO Box 750, Madison WI 53701. **Tel** (608)256-5800. **ED** Annie Laurie Gaylor. **DD** 211. **Bk Rev. Ad Acc. Circ:** 3,500 (ctrl).
**Desc:** The only freethought newspaper in the US. Hard-hitting critique of religion, Bible, advancement of freethought, state/church separation. For atheists, agnostics, humanists, and freethinkers.

GW/0344-1385
**FREIBURGER RUNDBRIEF.** [Freibg. Rd.br.]. **Added/Corp** Arbeitskreis fuer Christlich-Juedische Begegnung (Germany) Deutscher Caritasverband. Catholic Church. Deutsche Bischofskonferenz. (Feb. 1954)-. Periodical. German. Four times a year. DM40.00. Frieberger Rundbrief, Postfach 5766, D 79025 Freiburg Germany. **Tel** 011 49 761 386790. ***Continues*** *Rundbrief zur Foerderung der Freundschaft Zwischen dem Alten und dem Neuen Gottesvolk im Geiste der Beiden Testamente.*
**Ind/Abst** Old Testam. Abstr.

GW
**FREIBURGER THEOLOGISCHE STUDIEN. Added/Corp** Freiburg i. B. Universitaet. Vol. 1 (1910)-. Monographic series. German. ir. Price varies per volume. Verlag Herder Freiburg, Postfach 79080, Frieburg, Germany. **Tel** (0761)27-17-0, FAX (0761)27 17-520, telex 761489. **(Subscription address:** Verlag Herder Freiburg / KNO, PF 800620 Koch, Neff & Oetinger, D 70506 Stuttgart Germany.**) ED** Gerbert Brunner. **Circ:** 500.
**Desc:** Covers Catholic theology, dogmatic theology and development of doctrine. Includes history of dogmas, history of theology, theology and philosophy, Biblical theology and history of moral theology.

SZ/0016-0725
**FREIBURGER ZEITSCHRIFT FUER PHILOSOPHIE UND THEOLOGIE. See** Philosophy.

US/0009-4102
**FRIEND (SALT LAKE CITY), THE.** (FRIEND.). **Added/Corp** Church of Jesus Christ of Latter-Day Saints. Corporation of the First Presidency. (19??)-. Periodical. English. mo (11 issues). $8.00. LDS Church Magazines, 50 East Temple, 24th Floor, Salt Lake City UT 84150. **Tel** (801)531-2947. **ED** Vivian Paulsen. Index available. **Bk Rev. Circ:** 200,000. ***Supersedes*** *Children's Friend.*

US/0016-1322
**FRIENDS JOURNAL.** [Friends j.]. Vol. 1, (July 2, 1955)-. Periodical. English. Twelve times a year. $21.00 US & Canada & Mexico; $27.00 other. Friends Journal, 1501 Cherry Street, Philadelphia PA 19102. **Tel** (215)241-7277, FAX (215)568-1377. **ED** Vinton Deming (phone: (215)241-7280). **LC** BX7601; .F66. **DD** 289.605. Index available (Mar. iss.). **Bk Rev. Ad Acc, Adv Mgr:** Caitlyn Frost, **Tel** (215)241-7277. **Circ:** 10,000. available on microfilm and microfiche from University Microfilms International (UMI). ***Formed by the union of*** *Friend, 0362-8957* ***and*** *Friends Intelligencer, 0362-8965.*
**Desc:** Covers the spectrum of Quaker interests through meditative pieces and action stories, history and current issue analysis, poetry and art, book reviews, reports, reader's forum, etc.
**Ind/Abst** Peace Res. Abstr. J. (1964-1987).

UK/0016-1357
**FRIENDS' QUARTERLY, THE.** Vol. 1 (1947)-. Periodical. English. qt. $17.50. Headley Brothers Ltd., The Invicta Press, Queens Road, Ashford Kent TN24 8HH England. **Tel** 011 44 233 623131. **ED** Stephen Allott. **Circ:** 1,000. ***Continues*** *Friends' Quarterly Examiner, 0144-9168.*
**Ind/Abst** Peace Res. Abstr. J. (1964-1967).

UK/0016-1365
**FRIENDS WORLD NEWS : NEWS BULLETIN OF THE FRIENDS WORLD COMMITTEE FOR CONSULTATION.** No. 3 (July 1940)-. Bulletin. English. sa. $2.00. Friends World Committee, Section of the Americas, 1506 Race Street, Philadelphia PA 19102. **Tel** (215)241-7250. **ED** Val Ferguson and Thomas Taylor. ctrl circ. ***Continues*** *News Bulletin (Friends World Committee for Consultation).*
**Desc:** Newsletter for members and interested others, world-wide, Religious Society of Friends (Quakers).

GW/0340-6091
**FROHE BOTSCHAFT GOTTINGEN.** [Frohe Botsch. Gott.]. (1895)-. Periodical. German. Four times a year. DM31.00. Vandenhoeck & Ruprecht, Robert Bosch Breite 6, D-37079 Goettingen Germany. **Tel** 011 49 551 695911, FAX 011 49 551 695917, telex 965226 VAN d. **UDC** 252.

UK/0951-7677
**FRONTIER. See** Political Science-Socialism, Communism, Anarchism, Utopianism.

GW
**FULDAER HOCHSCHULSCHRIFTEN / HERAUSGEGEBEN VON DER THEOLOGISCHEN FAKULTAT FULDA.** (1987)-. Monographic series. German. an. Price varies per volume. EOS Verlag, Erzabtei St Ottilien, D 86941 St Ottilien Germany. **Tel** 011 49 8193 71261, FAX 011 49 8193 6844. **Bk Rev. Ad Acc. Circ:** 300. ***Continues*** *Fuldaer Theologische Schriften.*

US/0042-8264
**FULL GOSPEL BUSINESS MEN'S VOICE. Added/Corp** Full Gospel Business Men's Fellowship International. **VFOAT** Voice. (1953)-. Periodical. English. mo. $7.95. Full Gospel Businessmens Voice, PO Box 5050, Costa Mesa CA 92628. **Tel** (714)754-1400, FAX (715)557-9916. **ED** Jerry Jensen. **Circ:** 500,000.
**Desc:** Features Christian business men's testimonials.

CN/0712-8320
**FUTURE IS TODAY, THE.** [Future today]. Vol. 1, No. 1 (Apr./May/June 1982)-. Periodical. English. qt. $7.50. Future is Today, 566 21st Avenue, Hanover Ontario N4N 3H4 Canada. **DD** 248.4/05.

CN/0823-1869
**GATHERING.** [Gathering]. **Added/Corp** United Church of Canada. Working Unit on Worship and Liturgy. Advent/Christmas (1983)-. Periodical. English. Three times a year (Jan., Apr., Oct.). 12.00Can$ Canada; 17.00Can$ other. Canec Publishing & Supple House, 85 St Clair Avenue East, 5th Floor, Toronto ONT M4T 1M8 Canad. **Tel** (416)925-5931, FAX (416)925-3394. **ED** Fred Graham. **DD** 264/.0792/005. Index available. cum. index. **Bk Rev**, (Qty: 3). **Circ:** 3,200. ***Continues*** *Getting it all Together (United Church of Canada. Committee on Liturgy), 0713-3669.*
**Desc:** Seasonal liturgical resources, primarily for the Sunday gathering, including lectionary-related homiletical ideas, prayers and new hymns. Includes articles and book reviews.

CN/0226-0441
**GAY CHRISTIAN WITNESS. See** Homosexuality.

SZ/0016-5867
**GEGENWART.** Vol. 1- ; April 1939-. Periodical. German. bm. 48.00F Switzerland; 55.00F other. Administration Gegenwart, Frau C Graf, Obere Bahnhofstrasse 22A, CH-3700 Spiez Switzerland. **Tel** 033/54 79 94. **ED** Kurt Brotbeck. **LC** BP595. **Bk Rev. Ad Acc.**
**Desc:** Articles on social philosophy, pedagogics, religion, intellectual life, and the encounter of technology. Also reports on courses and conventions, new books and chronological up-dates.
**Ind/Abst** Am. Hist. Life (1955-1956).

GW/0016-5921
**GEIST UND LEBEN (WURZBURG). See** Literature.

US/0745-3019
**GEM (FINDLAY, OHIO), THE.** (THE GEM.). Periodical. English. mo. Churches of God Publications, PO Box 926, Findlay OH 45840. **Tel** (419)424-1961, FAX (419)424-3433.

US/0893-6617
**GENESIS (MITCHELLVILLE, MD.).** ***Ceased.*** (GENESIS.). [Genesis]. Vol. 1, No. 1 (July 1987)-(1993). Periodical. English. Four times a year. Berea Publications, PO Box 100, Powhatan PA 23139. **Tel** (804)598-7557. **DD** 261.

NE/0016-8610
**GEREFORMEERD THEOLOGISCH TIJDSCHRIFT.** [Geref. theol. tijdschr.]. **Added/Corp** Gereformeerde Kerken in Nederland. (May 1912)-. Periodical. Dutch. qt. F70.00. J H Kok, Postbus 130, 8260 AC Kampen Netherlands. **Tel** 011 31 520292555, FAX 011 31 520227331. Index available. **Bk Rev. Circ:** 5,000. ***Continues*** *Gereformeerd Tijdschrift.*
**Desc:** Theological articles.
**Ind/Abst** New Testam. Abstr.; Old Testam. Abstr.; Relig. Theol. Abstr.

GW/0934-0785
**GLAUBE UND DENKEN : JAHRBUCH DER KARL-HEIM-GESELLSCHAFT.** Vol. 1 (1988)-. Periodical. German. an. Brendow Verlag, Postfach 1280, W-4130 Moers 1 Germany. **LC** BR4; .G58. **DD** 230/.05.

GW/0179-3551
**GLAUBE UND LERNEN.** Vol. 1, No. 1, (May 1986)-. Periodical. German. Twice a year. DM46.00. Vandenhoeck & Ruprecht, Robert Bosch Breite 6, D-37079 Goettingen Germany. **Tel** 011 49 551 695911, FAX 011 49 551 695917, telex 965226 VAN d.
**Ind/Abst** Relig. Theol. Abstr. (199?-).

US/0897-9723
**GLEANER (KOKOMO, IND.).** (GLEANER : PUBLICATION OF THE EVANGELICAL BAPTIST MISSIONS.). **Added/Corp** Evangelical Baptist Missions. (Winter 1988)-. Periodical. English. qt (Feb., May, Aug., Nov.). Free. Evangelical Baptist Missions, PO Box 2225, Kokomo IN 46904. **Tel** (317)453-4488, FAX (317)455-0889. **ED** Carol Barnes. ***Continues*** *Evangelical Baptist (Kokomo, Ind.), 0279-9227.*
**Desc:** Contains information relating to missionary activity through Evangelical Baptist Missions. Missionaries are presently serving in 18 countries.

US/0746-5874
**GLEANER (PORTLAND, OR.).** (GLEANER / NORTH PACIFIC UNION CONFERENCE.). **Added/Corp** North Pacific Union Conference of the Seventh-Day Adventists. (19??)-. Periodical. English. sm. $6.50. North Pacific Union Gleaner, PO Box 16677, Portland OR 97216-8677.
**Ind/Abst** Seventh-Day Adventist Period. Index.

US/0160-2373
**GLEANINGS (CAMBRIDGE).** (GLEANINGS.). [Gleanings]. V. 1- Winter 1973-. Periodical. English. Three times a year. $9.50. New Skete Monastery, Cambridge NY 12816. **Tel** (518)677-3928.
**Ind/Abst** Am. Hist. Life.

US/0731-1125
**GLOBAL CHURCH GROWTH.** [Glob. church growth]. **Added/Corp** Church Growth Center. (1982)-. Periodical. English. Four times a year (Mar., June, Sept., Dec.). $19.50 one year; $36.50 two year. Church Growth Center, 1230 US Highway Six, PO Box 145, Corunna IN 46730. **Tel** (219)281-2452, FAX (219)281-2167. **ED** Kent R. Hunter. **LC** WMLC L 83/510. **DD** 291. **Bk Rev**, (Qty: 12). **Ad Acc, Adv Mgr:** Shelly Hinkley. **Circ:** 1,000. ***Continues*** *Global Church Growth Bulletin, 0273-7183.*
**Desc:** A worldwide missiological magazine dedicated exclusively to the Great Commission. Based on the idea that the main thrust of Scripture is the evangelization of the world.
**Ind/Abst** Bibliogr. Mission.; Christ. Period. Index (19??-).

US/0894-6159
**GNOSIS (SAN FRANCISCO, CALIF.).** (GNOSIS.). [Gnosis]. **Added/Corp** Lumen Foundation. **VFOAT** Gnosis Magazine. No. 1 (Fall/Winter 1985)-. Periodical. English. Four times a year (Jan., Apr., July, Oct.). $20.00 (individual); $25.00 (institution). Lumen Foundation, PO Box 14217, San Francisco CA 94114. **Tel** (415)255-0400, FAX (415)255-6329. **ED** Richard Smoley. **DD** 299. Index available (Publishes separately 1-17, ($6.00)). cum. index. **Bk Rev**, (Qty: 50-60). **Ad Acc, Adv Mgr:** Jeff Chiutouras, **Tel** (415)255-0400. **Circ:** 16,000.
**Desc:** Readable and non-sectarian discussions of the spiritual paths within and outside the Judeo/Christian/Islamic traditions, from the perspectives of comparative religions. Jungian psychology and more.

US/0896-2413
**GOD'S SPECIAL PEOPLE.** [God's spec. people]. **Added/Corp** Grays Harbor Baptist Church (Grays Harbor City, Wash.). (198?)-. Periodical. English. qt. $8.00. God's Special People, PO Box 729, Ocean Shores WA 98569. **Tel** (206)289-2540. **ED** Dan Lindsey. **DD** 362. **Bk Rev. Ad Acc. Circ:** 450.
**Desc:** Conservative Christian magazine concerning disabilities.

US/1054-1837
**GOD'S WORLD TODAY. See** Children and Youth Interests.

UK/0954-562X
**GOOD NEWS EXETER.** (GOOD NEWS.). [Good news Exeter]. (1988)-. Periodical. English. Six times a year. £49.75 UK; £55.00 other. Paternoster Press, A division of Send the Light Ltd., PO Box 300, Kingstown Broadway, Cumbria CA3 0QS England. **Tel** 011 44 228 512512, FAX 011 44 228 514949.

CN/0229-091X
**GOOD NEWS FROM NARAMATA CENTRE.** [Good news Naramata Cent.]. **Added/Corp** Naramata Centre. **VFOAT** Good News. (1973)-. Periodical. English. qt. Free. Naramate Centre, PO Box 68, Naramata British Columbia V0H 1N0 Canada. **Tel** (604)496-5751. **DD** 267/.1. **Circ:** 12,000 (ctrl).
**Desc:** Description of the programs offered at the Naramata Centre for Continuing Education, including course fees and costs for accommodations and meals.

CN/0713-3677
**GOOD-NEWS-LETTER.** (GOOD-NEWS-LETTER : DIALOGUE ON EVANGELISM IN THE UNITED CHURCH OF CANADA.). [Good-news-lett.]. **Added/Corp** United Church of Canada. Division of Mission in Canada. Vol. 1, No. 1 (Jan. 1980)-. Periodical. English. ir. Free. United Church of Canada, 85 Saint Clair Avenue East Room 711, Toronto Ontario M45 1M8 Canada. **Tel** (416)925-5931. **ED** Gordon Bruce Turner. **DD** 269/.0971. **Bk Rev. Circ:** 6,000 (ctrl).
**Desc:** Commentary, critique, and resources in the field of evangelization; continuing education events in evangelism highlighted for North America and program directions of National Working Unit highlighted.

US/1047-2320
**GOOD NEWS (NEW BERLIN, WIS.).** (GOOD NEWS.). [Good news]. (19??)-. Periodical. English. mo. $59.00. Liturgical Publications Inc, 2875 South James Drive, New Berlin WI 53151. **Tel** (414)785-1188, (800)876-4574. **ED** Rev. Joseph Nolan, (editor's address: 8 Wesley St, Newton, MA 02158). **DD** 251. **Circ:** 2,700.
**Desc:** An Ecumenical homily resource providing the clergy with ideas for preaching the lectionary. It contains both long and short homily models, two commentaries, a newsletter and prayers to make the entire package an effective resource for worship. Follows the Catholic Lectionary.

US/0093-5026
**GOOD NEWS OF TOMORROW'S WORLD.** (THE GOOD NEWS OF TOMORROW'S WORLD.). **Added/Corp** Pasadena, Calif. Ambassador College. Graduate School of Theology. Pasadena, Calif. Ambassador College. School of Theology. **VFOAT** Tomorrow's World. Vol. 1 June (1969)-. Periodical. English (French, Spanish, German and Dutch). bm. Free. The Good News of Tommorows World, 300 West Green, Pasadena CA 91123. **Tel** (818)304-6077. **ED** Dexter H Faulkner. **LC** BR1; .G63. **DD** 248/.48/99. **Circ:** 1,000,000 (ctrl).
**Desc:** Covers biblical instruction, family topics and practical christian living published for members and supporters of the Worldwide Church of God and others who request it.

PL/0137-7604
**GOSC NIEDZIELNY.** [Gosc Niedz.]. (1923)-. Periodical. Polish. wk. $52.00. **(Subscription address:** ARS Polona, PO Box 1001, 00068 Warsaw Poland.**) UDC** 2.

US/0195-1297
**GOSPEL ADVOCATE (NASHVILLE).** (GOSPEL ADVOCATE.). (1855)-. Periodical. English. sm. $16.98 (one year), $28.98 (two year). Gospel Advocate, 1006 Elm Hill Pike, Nashville TN 37210. **Tel** 800 251-8446, (615)254-8781. **DD** 243.

US/0744-2203
**GOSPEL EVANGEL, THE.** Periodical. English. mo. Gospel Evangel, 117 River Vista Drive, Goshen IN 46526. **Tel** (219)293-4923.

US/0746-0880
**GOSPEL HERALD AND THE SUNDAY SCHOOL TIMES.** Vol. 1, No. 1 (Spring Quarter 1983)-. Periodical. English. qt. $5.00 US; $5.75 other. Gospel Worker Society, Union Gospel Press Division, 2000 Brookpark Road, Cleveland OH 44109. ***Continues*** *Sunday School Times and Gospel Herald.*

CN/0829-4666
**GOSPEL HERALD BEAMSVILLE.** [Gospel Her. Beamsv.]. Periodical. English. mo. 10.28Can$ Canada; 16.36Can$ other. Gospel Herald / Canada, 4904 King Street, Beamsbille, Ontario, L04 1B6 Canada. **Tel** (905)563-7503, FAX (905)563-7503. **ED** Wayne Turner. **DD** 220. Index available. cum. index. **Bk Rev**, (Qty: 30-40). **Ad Acc**, **Adv Mgr:** E.C. Perry. **Circ:** 1450.

US/0273-7167
**GOSPEL HERALD (JELLICO), THE.** (THE GOSPEL HERALD.). Periodical. English. mo. The Gospel Herald, PO Box 157, Jellico TN 37762. available on microfilm from University Microfilms International (UMI).

US/0744-5814
**GOSPEL MESSAGE, THE.** [Gospel message]. **Added/Corp** Gospel Missionary Union. (April 1892)-. Periodical. English. qt. Gospel Message, Gospel Missionary Union, Smithville MO 64089. **LC** BV2350; .G73. **DD** 266.005.

US/0199-2953
**GOSPEL MISSION OF SOUTH AMERICA.** Periodical. English. bm. Gospel Mission of South America, 1401 Southwest 21st Avenue, Ft Lauderdale FL 33312.

UK/0017-2367
**GOSPEL STANDARD.** [Gospel stand.]. (?835)-. Periodical. English. Twelve times a year. £9.36 UK; £11.40 others. Gospel Standard Publications, 12 G Roundwood Lane, Harpenden Herts AL53DD England. **Tel** 011 44 582 765448, FAX 011 44 582 469148. **ED** Mr. B. A. Ramsbottom (phone: 0582 26042). **Circ:** 2,500 (ctrl).

UK
**GOSPEL STANDARD, OR, FEEBLE CHRISTIAN'S SUPPORT, THE. VFOAT** Feeble Christian's Support; Gospel Standard. No. 1 (Aug. 1835)-. English.

US/0017-2375
**GOSPEL TIDINGS (AUSTIN, TEX.).** (GOSPEL TIDINGS.). (19??)-. Periodical. English. mo. $7.20. Gospel Tidings, 7533 East Easter Way, Englewood CO 80112. **Tel** (303)694-3560.

CN/0828-1769
**GOSPEL WITNESS (TORONTO. 196?).** (THE GOSPEL WITNESS.). [Gospel witn.]. (196?)-. Periodical. English. Eighteen times a year. 10.00Can$ one year; 18.00Can$ two years; 25.00Can$ three years. Gospel Witness, 130 Gerrard Street East, Toronto Ontario M5A 3T4 Canada. **Tel** (416)925 3261. **ED** Rev. W. P. Bauman. cum. index. **Bk Rev. Circ:** 1,800 (ctrl). ***Continues*** *Gospel Witness and Protestant Advocate, 0702-570X.*
**Desc:** Contains information on sermons, articles, current religious interest, missionary news, and book reviews.

GW/0343-8732
**GOTTESDIENST.** [Gottesdienst]. **VFOAT** Gottesdienst (Freiburg). (1967)-. Periodical. German. Twenty-four times a year. DM55.20. Verlag Herder Freiburg, Postfach 79080, Frieburg, Germany. **Tel** (0761)27-17-0, FAX (0761)27 17-520, telex 761489. **ED** B. Fischer, A. Heinz, E. Nagel. **UDC** 264.
**Desc:** Information and sharing of knowledge of the Liturgical Institutes of Germany, Austria and Switzerland.

GW/0017-2499
**GOTTESDIENST UND KIRCHENMUSIK.** **See** Music.

GW/0340-6083
**GOTTINGER PREDIGTMEDITATIONEN.** [Gott. Predigtmedit.]. (1946)-. Periodical. German. qt. DM92.00. Vandenhoeck & Ruprecht, Robert Bosch Breite 6, D-37079 Goettingen Germany. **Tel** 011 49 551 695911, FAX 011 49 551 695917, telex 965226 VAN d. **UDC** 252.

GW
**GOTTINGER THEOLOGISCHE ARBEITEN.** Vol. 1-. Monographic series. German. ir. Price varies per volume. Vandenhoeck & Ruprecht, Robert Bosch Breite 6, D-37079 Goettingen Germany. **Tel** 011 49 551 695911, FAX 011 49 551 695917, telex 965226 VAN d. **ED** George Strecker.
**Desc:** This is a series of monographs.

US/0198-666X
**GRACE THEOLOGICAL JOURNAL.** ***Ceased.*** [Grace theol. j.]. **Added/Corp** Grace Theological Seminary. Vol. 1, No. 1 (Spring 1980)-(1993). Periodical. English. sa. Grace Theological Seminary, 200 Seminary Drive, Winona Lake IN 46590. **Tel** (219)372-5117, FAX (219)372-5265. **ED** John J Davis. Index available. cum. index. **Bk Rev. Circ:** 1,500. available on microfilm and microfiche from University Microfilms International (UMI). ***Continues*** *Grace Journal; A Publication of Grace Theological Seminary.*
**Desc:** Deals with many areas of Christian scholarship, including Bible, theology, biblical languages and backgrounds, Church history, hermeneutics, philosophy, and Christian ministry.
**Ind/Abst** Christ. Period. Index (19??-); Index Book Rev. Relig.; New Testam. Abstr.; Old Testam. Abstr.; Relig. Index One Period. (1980-); Relig. Theol. Abstr.

CN/0828-4083
**GRAIL (WATERLOO).** (GRAIL.). [Grail]. **Added/Corp** University of St. Jerome's College. Vol. 1, Issue 1 (March 1985)-. Periodical. English. qt. 14.00Can$(individuals), 22.00Can$ (institutions). University of St Jerome's College, Waterloo Ontario N2L 3G3 Canada. **Tel** (519)884-8110. **ED** Michael W Higgins. **DD** 261/.05. **Bk Rev. Circ:** 2,000.
**Desc:** Multi-disciplinary journal inspired by Vatican II's investigations of the human condition in light of modern scholarship and its encouragement of ecumenical understanding. Has set out to promote dialogue, debate and understanding, both among scholars and generally-educated readers.
**Ind/Abst** Index Book Rev. Relig.; Relig. Index One Period.

US
**GRANT$ FOR RELIGION, RELIGIOUS WELFARE, & RELIGIOUS EDUCATION.** **See** Philanthropy.

US/0017-3894
**GREEK ORTHODOX THEOLOGICAL REVIEW, THE.** [Greek Orthodox theol. rev.]. **Added/Corp** Greek Archdiocese Holy Cross Orthodox Theological School. Holy Cross Greek Orthodox School of Theology (Hellenic College). Vol. 1 (Aug. 1954)-. Periodical. English. Four times a year. $22.00 US; $27.00 other. Holy Cross Greek Orthodox Press, 50 Goddard Avenue, Brookline MA 02146. **Tel** (617)232-4544. **ED** Rev. Dr. N. Michael Vaporis and Mr. Constantine Moralis. **LC** BX200; .G7. **DD** 230/.19. **Bk Rev**, (Qty: 50/year). **Circ:** 1,000 (ctrl). available on microfilm from University Microfilms International (UMI); available on microfiche from Xerox.
**Desc:** Contains theological abstracts from reviewed texts spanning the globe of beliefs with a strong Orthodox Christian axis.
**Ind/Abst** Am. Hist. Life (1955-1981); Am. Bibliogr. Slavic East Europ. Stud.; Index Book Rev. Relig.; New Testam. Abstr.; Old Testam. Abstr.; Relig. Index One Period. (1954-); Relig. Theol. Abstr.

IT/0017-4114
**GREGORIANUM.** [Gregorianum]. **Added/Corp** Pontificia Universita Gregoriana. Vol. 1 (1920)-. Periodical. English (French, German, Italian, Latin and Spanish). qt. L80000 Italy; $75.00 US. Editrice Pontificio Istituto Biblico, Piazza della Pilotta 35, 00187 Rome Italy. **Tel** 011 39 6 6781567, FAX 011 39 6 6780588. **ED** Jacques Dupuis. **LC** BX800.A1; G7. cum. index.
**Desc:** A scientific review of theology and philosophy with occasional discussions of problems in church history, Canon law, and social sciences.
**Ind/Abst** Bibliogr. Mission.; Canon Law Abstr.; Index Book Rev. Relig.; New Testam. Abstr.; Old Testam. Abstr.; Philos. Index; Relig. Index One Period.; Relig. Theol. Abstr.; Abr. Cathol. Period. Lit. Index; Cathol. Period. Lit. Index.

GR/1011-3010
**GREGORIOS HO PALAMAS.** [Gregor. Palamas]. Periodical. Greek, Modern. bm. Hiera Metropolis Thessalonikes. **Tel** 031 261 216, FAX 031 227 677. **LC** BX610; .G73. **Bk Rev. Circ:** 1,200 (ctrl).
**Ind/Abst** MLA Int. Bibl. Books Artic. Mod. Lang. Lit.

US/0163-8971
**GROUP (LOVELAND, COLO.).** **See** Children and Youth Interests.

US
**GROWTH REPORT.** **Added/Corp** Institute for American Church Growth. Vol. 1, No. 1 (1983)-. Periodical. English. Church Growth, 2670 So Myrtle Avenue/Suite 201, Monrovia CA 91016. ***Continues in part*** *Church Growth, America.*
**Ind/Abst** Curr. Thoughts Trends.

DK/0107-4164
**GRUNDTVIG STUDIER.** [Grundtvig stud.]. **Added/Corp** Grundtvig-Selskabet. **VFOAT** Grundtvig-Studier. (1948)-. Academic Scholarly Publication. Danish (summaries and/or abstracts in English). an. kr150.00. Gruntvig-Selskabet, c/o Danske Boghandleres Anstalt,, Siljangade 6,, 2300 Copenhagen Denmark. **Tel** 011 45 33 137670. **Bk Rev. Circ:** 800. ***Continues*** *Grundtvig-Studier.*
**Ind/Abst** MLA Int. Bibl. Books Artic. Mod. Lang. Lit.

US/0273-5504
**GUARDIAN OF TRUTH.** **Added/Corp** Cogdill Foundation. Guardian of Truth Foundation. Vol. 25, No. 1 (Jan. 1, 1981)-. Periodical. English. sm (published 1st and 3rd Thursday of each month). $18.00. Guardian of Truth Foundation, PO Box 9670, Bowling Green KY 42101. **Tel** (502)781-2223. **ED** Mike Willis (editor's address: 6567 King's Court, Danville, IN 46122; (317)745-4708. Index available (bound in 1st issue). cum. index. **Ad Acc. Circ:** 6,000. ***Formed by the union of*** *Gospel Guardian, 0161-9888* ***and*** *Truth Magazine.*

US
**GUIDE TO JEWISH USA.** (1987)-. Periodical. English. $11.95. Israelowitz Publishing, Box 228, Brooklyn NY 11229. **Tel** (718)951-7072, FAX (718)951-7072. **ED** Oscar Israelowitz.

US/0891-1452
**GUIDELINES FOR TODAY.** [Guidel. today]. (1966)-. Periodical. English. Six times a year (Jan., Mar., May, July, Sept., Nov.). $11.75 US; $23.25 other. Guidelines for Today, PO Box 575, Harrisonburg VA 22801. **Tel** (814)288-1388. **ED** Maurice W. Landis. **DD** 289. **Bk Rev. Circ:** 3,500.
**Desc:** Independent publication supported by donations.

US/0017-5331
**GUIDEPOSTS (CARMEL).** (GUIDEPOSTS.). Vol. 1 (1946)-. Periodical. English. mo. $9.97 (one year),

$16.97 (two year), $22.97 (three year). Guideposts, 39 Seminary Hill Road, Carmel NY 10512. **Tel** (914)225-3681, (800)431-2344. **LC** BV4800; .G8. available in large print; available in braille.
**Desc:** Features dramatic first person, true-life narratives designed to show how people from all walks of life have overcome their difficulties through faith and positive attitudes.

PK
**GUL-I KHANDAN.** Urdu (Urdu). Rs4.00. Kashmiri Bazar 8, Malik Sirajuddin and Sons Publishers, Lahor Pakistan. **Tel** (042)52169, telex 44942 CLOTH PK. **ED** Ayaz Ahmed Malik. **LC** AP95.U7; G853. **Circ:** 2,000.
**Desc:** Covers information about religion.

CN/0823-261X
**HALTE JEUNESSE ET FOI (1982).** (HALTE JEUNESSE ET FOI : BULLETIN D'INFORMATION DU CENTRE JEUNESSE ET FOI.). [Halte jeun. foi]. **VFOAT** Bulletin d'Information du Centre Jeunesse et Foi. Sept. 1982-. Bulletin. French. Free. Societe Amour Des Jeunes CP 2532, Quebec, Quebec G1K 7R3 Canada. **DD** 259/.5/0971447. ***Continues*** *Societe Amour des Jeunes et Centre Jeunesse et Foi : Bulletin, 0820-6139.*

NZ/0304-1603
**HANDBOOK, ANNUAL CONFERENCE - ASSOCIATED CHURCHES OF CHRIST IN NEW ZEALAND.** (HANDBOOK : ANNUAL CONFERENCE.). **Main/Corp** Associated Churches of Christ in New Zealand. English. an. 5.00NZ$. Associated Churches of Christ in New Zealand, Department of Administration, PO Box 30516, Lower Hut New Zealand. **Tel** (054)89873. **LC** BR1480; .A87A. **DD** 286/.6331.

GW
**HANDBUCH DER DOGMENGESCHICHTE.** (19??)-. Monographic series. German. ir. Price varies per volume. Verlag Herder Freiburg, Postfach 79080, Frieburg, Germany. **Tel** (0761)27-17-0, FAX (0761)27 17-520, telex 761489.

US/0017-8047
**HARVARD DIVINITY BULLETIN. Main/Corp** Harvard Divinity School. Vol. 24-30, (1959-1967); New Series Vol. 1-3, (1967-1969); Third Series Vol. 1 (1970)-. Bulletin. English. qt. Free. Harvard Divinity School, 45 Francis Avenue, Cambridge MA 02138. **Tel** (617)495-5786, FAX (617)495-9489. **ED** Andrew Rasanen. **LC** BV4070; .H423. **Bk Rev. Ad Acc. Circ:** 24,000 (ctrl). ***Continues*** *Harvard Divinity School School Bulletin, 0362-5117.*
**Desc:** Covers religion, theology, values and ethics.
**Ind/Abst** Index Book Rev. Relig.; Relig. Index One Period. (1959-).

US/0017-8160
**HARVARD THEOLOGICAL REVIEW, THE.** [Harv. theol. rev.]. **Added/Corp** Harvard Divinity School. **VFOAT** HTR. Vol. 1 (Jan. 1908)-. Periodical. English. qt. $45.00 (institutions), $25.00 (individuals). Harvard Divinity School, 45 Francis Avenue, Cambridge MA 02138. **Tel** (617)495-5786, FAX (617)495-9489. **ED** Helmut Koester. **LC** BR1; .H4. **DD** 205. Index available. cum. index. **Ad Acc. Pr Rev. Circ:** 2,000. Documents available from The Genuine Article, UMI Article Clearinghouse.
**Desc:** Investigations, discussions and essays in the various areas of religious studies that contribute to enlargement of knowledge and scholarship.
**Ind/Abst** Abstr. Engl. Stud.; Acad. Search (July 1993-); Am. Hist. Life (1975-); Annu. Bibliogr. Engl. Lang. Lit.; Arts Humanit. Citation Index [Full Cov.]; BHA : Biblio. Hist. Art; Curr. Contents Arts Humanit.; Expand. Acad. Index (1989-); Humanit. Index; Humanit. Source (Jul. 1993-); Index Book Rev. Relig.; INFO-SOUTH Abstr.; Mag. Search; Middle East Abstr. Index; MLA Int. Bibl. Books Artic. Mod. Lang. Lit.; New Testam. Abstr.; Newsp. Period. Abstr. (1990-); Old Testam. Abstr.; Relig. Index One Period. (1949-); Relig. Theol. Abstr.; Res. Alert [Full Cov.]; Soc. Sci. Cit. Index [Select. Cov.].

US/0073-0726
**HARVARD THEOLOGICAL STUDIES.** (1916)-. Monographic series. English. ir. Price varies per volume. Augsburg Fortress, 426 South 5th Street, Box 1209, Minneapolis MN 55440. **Tel** 800 328-4648 or, (612)330-3300. **LC** UNC.

CN/0848-9386
**HARVEST FIELD MINISTRIES : NEWSLETTER.** [Harv. Field Minist.]. **Added/Corp** Harvest Field Ministries. Vol. 14, No. 5 (Sept. 1989)-. Newsletter. English. qt. Limited free distribution. Harvest Field, PO Box 1145, South Porcupine Ontario P0N 1H0 Canada. **DD** 266/.022/0971. ***Continues*** *Harvest Field, 0702-7117.*

JA
**HAYAMA MISSIONARY SEMINAR ANNUAL REPORT.** English. an. $9.50 Japan; $11.00 other. Tokyo Mission Research Institute, 1-30-1 Megurita, Robert Lee, Higashimurayama Tokyo Japan. **Tel** 011 81 3 423929890, FAX 011 81 3 423977558. **ED** Robert Lee. **Circ:** 1,000 (ctrl). ***Continues*** *Hayama Handbook.*

UK
**HEALING HAND, THE.** Vol. 23-32, No. 1, (May 1966)-(Summer/Autumn 1975); (Winter 1975)-. Periodical. English. Three times a year. £3.00. Edinburgh Medical Missionary Society, 7 Washington Lane, Edinburgh EH11 2HA Scotland. **Tel** 011 31 313 3828, FAX 011 31 313 4662. **ED** F.M. Aitken. **Bk Rev**, (Qty: 2-3). **Circ:** 2,000 (ctrl). ***Continues*** *Edinburgh Medical Missionary. Quarterly Paper.*
**Desc:** Christian medical work including reports from the society hospital in Nazareth, Israel.

US/1047-1014
**HEARTBEAT.** [Heartbeat]. (1988)-. Periodical. English. Free. Luis Palau Evangelistic Association, Box 1173, Portland OR 97207. **Tel** (503)643-0777, FAX (503)643-6851, telex 350076. **ED** Mike Umlandt. **DD** 269. ctrl circ.
**Desc:** News concerning the Luis Palau Evangelistic Association.

AU/0017-9620
**HEILIGER DIENST.** [Hl. Dienst]. Periodical. German. qt. S250.00. Institutum Liturgicum, Verlag St. Peter, Postfach 113, A 5010 Salzeburg Austria. **Tel** 011 43 662 844576-84, FAX 011 43 662 844576. **UDC** 200. Index available. cum. index. **Bk Rev. Ad Acc, Adv Mgr:** P. Winfried. **Circ:** 800 (ctrl).
**Desc:** Specialist publication concerned with themes of liturgy and worship.

GR
**HELLENIKE THEOLOGIKE VIVLIOGRAPHIA.** Began with 1977 Volume. Greek, Modern. an. Ioannou Gennadiou 14, Athens 140 Greece. **LC** Z7842.A3; H44; BX320.2.

US/0745-029X
**HELPING HAND (JANESVILLE, WIS.), THE.** (THE HELPING HAND.). **Added/Corp** Seventh Day Baptist. Board of Christian Education. Vol. 9 (Winter Quarter 1977/1978)-. English. qt. $4.50. American Sabbath Tract Society, 3120 Kennedy Road, PO Box 1678, Janesville WI 53547. **Tel** (608)752-5055. **ED** Linda Harris. **Circ:** 2,300 (ctrl). ***Continues*** *Helping Hand in Bible-School Work.*

US/0895-7622
**HENCEFORTH.** [Henceforth]. **Added/Corp** Berkshire Christian College (Lenox, Mass.). Vol. 1, No. 1 (Fall 1972)-. Periodical. English. Twice a year (Apr., Oct.). $8.00 (1 year); $13.00 (2 years). Henceforth, c/o Robert Mayer, PO Box 23152, Charlotte NC 28212. **Tel** (704)545-6161, FAX (704)573-0712. **ED** Freeman Barton, Gordon-Canwell Theological Seminary, 130 Essex St., South Hamilton, MA 01982. **DD** 230. **Bk Rev**, (Qty: 5-10). **Circ:** 300.
**Desc:** A journal by the faculty of Berkshire Christian College particularly for Advent Christian ministers.
**Ind/Abst** Relig. Theol. Abstr.

UK/0144-0241
**HENRY BRADSHAW SOCIETY (SERIES).** (HENRY BRADSHAW SOCIETY.). (1891)-. Monographic series. English. Price varies per volume. Henry Bradshaw Society, 19 Thorpe Road, Banbury OX17 2JW United Kingdom.

US/0146-7174
**HERALD OF CHRISTIAN SCIENCE, THE. Added/Corp** Christian Science Publishing Society. (19??)-. Periodical. English. qt. $29.00. Christian Science Publishing Society, One Norway Street, Boston MA 02115. **Tel** (617)450-2678, (617)450-2504.

US/1061-6659
**HERALD OF CHRISTIAN SCIENCE (AUDIO CASSETTE ED.), THE. *Title Change.*** (THE HERALD OF CHRISTIAN SCIENCE [SOUND RECORDING].). [Herald Christ. Sci.]. Vol. 1, No. 1 (Mar. 1992)-(1992). Periodical. English. mo. Christian Science Publishing Society, One Norway Street, Boston MA 02115. **Tel** (617)450-2678, (617)450-2504. **DD** 289. ***Continues*** *Herald of Christian Science (Audio Cassette Ed. : 1988).* ***Continued by*** *Christian Science Sentinel (Radio Ed.), 1065-1241.*

US
**HERALD OF HIS COMING.** (1941)-. Periodical. English. Twelve times a year. Free on request. Herald of His Coming, PO Box 886, Newton KS 67114. **Tel** (316)283-7747. **ED** Lois J Stucky. **Circ:** 120,000.
**Desc:** Helps for christian living prayer revival.

US/0439-0148
**HERALDO DE LA CIENCIA CRISTIANA, EL. Added/Corp** Christian Science Publishing Society. **VFOAT** The Herald of Christian Science. Vol. 9 (Jan./March 1959)-. Periodical. Spanish (English and Spanish). mo. $29.00. Christian Science Publishing Society, One Norway Street, Boston MA 02115. **Tel** (617)450-2678, (617)450-2504. **LC** BX6901; .H5523. ***Continues in part*** *Herald of Christian Science. Spanish-Portuguese-Italian Edition.*

●US/1060-2135
**HERALDO DE SANTIDAD (1992), EL.** (EL HERALDO DE SANTIDAD.). **Added/Corp** Church of the Nazarene. Vol. 46, No. 991 (Enero 1992)-. Periodical. English. mo. $5.00. Casa Nazarena de Publicaciones, 6401 The Paseo, Kansas City MO 64131. **Tel** (816)333-7000. **ED** Jose Pacheco. **DD** 230. **Circ:** 6,000. ***Continues*** *Direccion (Kansas City, Mo.), 1047-6318.*

US/0145-7470
**HERAUT DE LA SCIENCE CHRETIENNE, LE. Added/Corp** Christian Science Publishing Society. **VFOAT** Herald of Christian Science. (19??)-. Periodical. French (English and French). mo. $29.00. Christian Science Publishing Society, One Norway Street, Boston MA 02115. **Tel** (617)450-2678, (617)450-2504. **LC** BX6901; .H48. **DD** 289.505.

US/0145-756X
**HERAUT VAN DE CHRISTELIJKE WETENSCHAP, DE. Added/Corp** Christian Science Publishing Society. **VFOAT** The Herald of Christian Science. (19??)-. Periodical. Dutch (English). qt. $29.00. Christian Science Publishing Society, One Norway Street, Boston MA 02115. **Tel** (617)450-2678, (617)450-2504. **LC** BX6901; .H47. **DD** 289.505.

GE/0437-3014
**HERBERGEN DER CHRISTENHEIT; JAHRBUCH FUER DEUTSCHE KIRCHENGESCHICHTE. See** Architecture.

CN/0711-4737
**HERITAGE BOOK, THE.** [Herit. book]. 1st Ed. (1977)-. English. an. $4.50 per volume. Collier Macmillan Canada, 1125B Leslie Street, Don Mills Ont. M3C 2K2. **LC** BV4810; .M34. **DD** 242/.2.

GW/0930-6897
**HERMENEIA. See** The Arts-Art.

US/0145-7578
**HEROLD DER CHRISTLICHEN WISSENSCHAFT, DER. Added/Corp** Christian Science Publishing Society. **VFOAT** The Herald of Christian Science. Vol. 1 (April 1903)-. Periodical. German (English and German). mo. $29.00. Christian Science Publishing Society, One Norway Street, Boston MA 02115. **Tel** (617)450-2678, (617)450-2504. **LC** BX6901; .H5. **DD** 289.5/05.

US/0300-8851
**HEROLD DER WAHRHEIT.** (1912)-. Periodical. Multiple languages (English and German). mo. Herold der Wahr Heit, Kalona IA 52247.

NE
**HERVORMD UTRECHT. *Title Change.*** (19??)-(199?). Dutch. sm. Hervormde Gemeente, Postbus 299, 3500 AG Utrecht Netherlands. **Tel** 011 31 20 316460. ***Continued by*** *Kerk in de Stad.*

SA
**HERVORMDE TEOLOGIESE STUDIES. Added/Corp** University of Pretoria. Navorsings- en Publikasiekomitee. South Africa. Dept. of National Education. **VFOAT** HTS. (1943)-. Periodical. Afrikaans (English and German; summaries and/or abstracts in English). qt. R35.00. PO Box 5777, Pretoria 0001 South Africa. **Tel** (012) 322 8885. **ED** A G Van Aarde. **LC** BR9.A34; H47. cum. index. **Bk Rev. Ad Acc. Circ:** 900 (ctrl).
**Desc:** Publishes scientific articles on current theological issues, and reviews on major publications obtained.
**Ind/Abst** Index Book Rev. Relig.; Relig. Index One Period.; Relig. Theol. Abstr.

SA
**HERVORMER, DIE.** Began with Vol. for 1909/10. Periodical. Afrikaans. mo. R18.50. Nederduitse Hervormde Kerk Van Suid-Afrika, Posbus 5777, Pretoria 0001 South Africa. **Tel** (012)322-8885. **ED** Dr Wyk. Index available. **Bk Rev. Ad Acc. Circ:** 27,500 (ctrl). available on diskette.
**Desc:** Official magazine of The Nederduitsch Hervormde Kerk van Suid-AfriKa.

●US/1059-3365
**HI-TEEN STUDENT GUIDE. Added/Corp** Assemblies of God. General Council. **VFOAT** Hi, Teen Student Guide. (1992)-. Periodical. English. qt. $5.20. Gospel Publishing House, 1445 Boonville Avenue, Springfield MO 65802. **Tel** (417)862-2781, FAX (417)866-1146. ***Continues*** *Hi-Teen Student, 0190-3810.*

●US/1059-3357
**HI-TEEN TEACHER GUIDE. Added/Corp** Assemblies of God. General Council. **VFOAT** Hi, Teen Teacher Guide. (1992)-. Periodical. English. qt. $9.20. Gospel Publishing House, 1445 Boonville Avenue, Springfield MO 65802. **Tel** (417)862-2781, FAX (417)866-1146. ***Continues*** *Hi-Teen Teacher, 0190-3829.*

US/0018-120X
**HICALL. *Title Change.* VAT** Hi Call. (19??)-(199?). Periodical. English. qt. Gospel Publishing House, 1445 Boonville Avenue, Springfield MO 65802. **Tel** (417)862-2781, FAX (417)866-1146. **ED** Gary Legget.

***Continued by*** *Teen Life, 1076-9897.*
**Desc:** Paper designed to help build Christian character for teens.

CN/0825-4850
**HIGHLIGHT QUEBEC.** [Highlight Que.]. Vol. 4, No. 1 (Feb. 1984)-. Periodical. English. qt. 12.00Can$ Canada; 15.00Can$ other. Highlight Quebec, PO Box 602 Station B, Montreal Quebec H3B 3K3 Canada. **Tel** (514)878-3035, FAX (514)878-8048. **ED** Sandra H. Smith. **DD** 289.9. **Bk Rev. Ad Acc, Adv Mgr:** Carole Tapin. **Circ:** 1,200. ***Continues*** *Highlight (Lachine, Quebec), 0823-8146.*
**Desc:** Information about Christian activities in Quebec, and to encourage an interest in foreign missions.

UK/0018-1927
**HINDUISM.** Jan. 1965?-. Periodical. English. qt. Bharat Sevashram Sangha, 17 Stanlake Villas, London W12 England.

CN/0229-7175
**HIS DOMINION (REGINA).** (HIS DOMINION.). [His dom.]. **Added/Corp** Canadian Church Growth Centre. Vol. 4, No. 1 (1977)-. Periodical. English. qt. 7.00Can$ Canada; $7.00 other. Canadian Theological Seminary, 4400 Fourth Avenue, Regina Saskatchewan S4T 0H8 Canada. **Tel** (306)545-1515. **ED** W. David Buschant, Peter H. Davids, Martin P. Sanders and T. V. Thomas. **DD** 262/.001. Index available. cum. index. **Bk Rev. Circ:** 2,700 (ctrl). ***Continues*** *Church Growth Canada, 0315-8152.*
**Desc:** A journal of special interest to ministerial personnel and Christian leaders pertaining to the thought and practice of Christianity in North America and around the world.

CN/0440-8934
**HISTOIRE RELIGIEUSE DU CANADA.** (19??)-. Monographic series. French. ir. Price varies per volume. Editions Fides / Canada, 5710 Ave Decelles, Montreal Quebec H3S 2O5 Canada.

SW/0439-2132
**HISTORIA RELIGIONUM.** Monographic series. Multiple languages. Price varies per volume. Almqvist & Wiksell International, PO Box 4627, S-11691 Stockholm Sweden. **Tel** 011-46-8-6408800.

CN/0848-1563
**HISTORICAL PAPERS / CANADIAN SOCIETY OF CHURCH HISTORY.** [Hist. pap. - Can. Soc. Church Hist.]. **Added/Corp** Canadian Society of Church History. June 2/3 (1988)-. English. an. 20.00Can$. Canadian Society of Church History, 75 Queen's Park Crescent E, Toronto Ontario M5S 1K7 Canada. **Tel** (416)585-4542. **DD** 277.1. **Circ:** 100. ***Continues*** *Canadian Society of Church History. Meeting. Proceedings of the Canadian Society of Church History., 0842-1056.*

CN/1193-1981
**HISTORICAL STUDIES OTTAWA. 1990.** **See** History(General).

US/0018-2710
**HISTORY OF RELIGIONS.** [Hist. relig.]. Vol. 1 (Summer 1961)-. Periodical. English. qt (Aug., Nov., Feb., May). $70.00 institution; $32.00 individual; $22.00 UC Divinity School Alumni and students. University of Chicago Press / Journals Division, PO Box 37005, 5720 South Woodlawn, Chicago IL 60637. **Tel** (312)753-3347, FAX (312)753-0811. **(Subscription telephone:** (312)753-8083) **ED** Frank E. Reynolds, Wendy Doniger and Gary L. Ebersole. **LC** BL1; .H5. **DD** 220/.9. **[CCC]. Bk Rev. Ad Acc. Acid Free.** available on microfilm and microfiche from University Microfilms International (UMI). Documents available from The Genuine Article, UMI Article Clearinghouse.
**Desc:** Devoted to the study of religious phenomena from prehistory to modern times, both within particular traditions and across cultural boundaries.
**Ind/Abst** Acad. Search (July 1993-); Am. Hist. Life (1961-); Anthropol. Lit.; Arts Humanit. Citation Index [Full Cov.]; Curr. Contents Arts Humanit.; Expand. Acad. Index (1989-); Guide Soc. Sci. Relig.; Hist. Source (July 1993-); Humanit. Index; Humanit. Source (Jul. 1993-); Index Islam. Lit.; Index Book Rev. Relig.; INFO-SOUTH Abstr.; Mag. Search; Middle East Abstr. Index; New Testam. Abstr.; Newsp. Period. Abstr. (1990-); Old Testam. Abstr.; Relig. Index One Period. (1961-); Relig. Theol. Abstr.; Res. Alert [Full Cov.]; Romant. Move.; Soc. Sci. Cit. Index [Select. Cov.].

US/1054-545X
**HISTORY OF WOMEN RELIGIOUS NEWS AND NOTES.** [Hist. women relig. news notes]. **VFOAT** HWR Newsletter; History of Women Religious. Vol. 1, No. 1 (Feb. 1988)-. Periodical. English. Three times a year (Feb., June, Oct.). $5.00 (one year); $10.00 (two years); $15.00 (three years). Conference on History of Women Religious, 12001 Chalon Road, Los Angeles CA 90049. **Tel** (213)471-9500, FAX (213)476-9296. **ED** Karen Kennelly. **DD** 270. **Bk Rev**, (Qty: varies). **Circ:** 600.

XR
**HLAS PRAVOSLAVI : ORGAN PRAVOSLAVNE CIRKVE V CESKOSLOVENSKU.** **Added/Corp** Pravoslavna Cirkev v Ceskoslovensku. (19??)-. Periodical. Czech. ir. **(Subscription address:** Artia Pegas Press Ltd., Palac Metro Narodni Trida 25, 11210 Prague 1 Czech Republic.**)**

NE/0168-8693
**HN MAGAZINE.** **VFOAT** HN. Vol. 39, No. 13 (April 2, 1983)-. Periodical. Dutch. wk. Boekencentrum B V, PO Box 29, 2700 EE Zoetemeer Netherlands. **Tel** 011 31 079 615481. ***Continues*** *Hervormd Nederland;* ***Formed by the union of*** *Voorlopig, 0166-3380.*

US/1040-8584
**HOLINESS DIGEST.** [Holin. dig.]. **Added/Corp** Christian Holiness Association. Vol. 1, No. 1 (fall 1987)-. Periodical. English. sa. $25.00. Christian Holiness Association, Post Office Box 100, Wilmore KY 40390. **Tel** (606)858-4091, FAX (606)858-4096. **DD** 289.

CN/0381-5129
**HOLOS SPASYTELIA.** **VFOAT** Redeemer's Voice. Periodical. English (Ukrainian). mo. Holos Spaystela, Box 220, 165 Catherine Street, Yorktown Saskatchewan S3N 0B9 Canada. **LC** BX4711.74; .H62.

US
**HOLY CROSS.** V. 1-. Periodical. English. qt. Order of the Holy Cross, West Park NY 12493. ***Supersedes in part*** *Holy Cross, 0018-3725.*

US
**HOLY LAND.** **Added/Corp** Franciscans. Commissariat of the Holy Land (Washington, D.C.). Franciscans. Custody of the Holy Land. Vol. 1 No. 1 (Spring 1981)-. Periodical. English (Italian, Spanish and Arabic). qt (Mar., June, Sept., Dec.). $10.00. Holy Land, PO Box 186, Jerusalem 91001 Israel. **Tel** 011 972 2 286594. **ED** Peter Vasko. Index available. **Bk Rev. Ad Acc. Circ:** 2,500 (ctrl). ***Continues*** *Holy Land Review.*
**Desc:** An illustrated quarterly on the Holy places; a Catholic voice on the troubled Middle East; an armchair visit to the land of Jesus. Back issues treated peace proposals, Saints, Eastern churches, Mt. Tabor, pilgrims, Cyprus, Bethlehem, Holy Grail, The Land, Capharnaum, ect.

US
**HOME MISSIONS IMPACT / THE WESLEYAN CHURCH.** Periodical. English. qt. Free for constituency. Wesleyan Publishing House, PO Box 50434, Indianapolis IN 46250-0434. **Tel** (317)842-0444, (317)576-0444, FAX (317)842-9188. **ED** Thomas E Phillippe. **Circ:** 50,000.

CN/0823-8464
**HOME MISSIONS (TORONTO).** (HOME MISSIONS.). [Home missions]. Sept. 1982-. Periodical. English. qt. $2.00 per year. Catholic Church Extension Society of Canada, 67 Bond Street, Toronto Ontario M5B 1X5 Canada. **DD** 266/.271/05.

US/0738-0534
**HOMILETIC.** [Homiletic]. **Added/Corp** Religious Speech Communication Association. Academy of Homiletics (U.S.) American Academy of Homiletics. College of Preachers. Vol. 1, (1976)-. Periodical. English. sa. $9.00 US; $10.00 other (institutions); $7.00 US; $8.00 other (individuals). Lutheran Theological Seminary / Gettysburg, PA, Bulletin 61, NW Confederate Avenue, Gettysburg PA 17325. **Tel** (717)334-6286. **(Subscription address:** 61 W Confederate Avenue, Gettysburg, PA 17325**)** **ED** Richard L Thulin. **DD** 251. **Bk Rev**, (Qty: 50-75/yr). **Ad Acc. Circ:** 1,200.
**Desc:** A review of publications in religious communication.

US/1040-6255
**HOMILETICS (NORTH CANTON, OHIO).** (HOMILETICS.). [Homiletics]. **Added/Corp** Communication Resources and Development Company. Vol. 1, No.1 (Jan./March 1989). Periodical. English. qt. $37.95 (one year), $70.90 (two year), $98.80 (three year). Communication Resources Inc, 4150 Belden Village Street NW, Suite 400, North Canton OH 44718. **Tel** (216)493-7880, FAX (216)493-7897. **ED** Sandord C Mitchell, C P Mitchell, and Robert W Fisher. **DD** 251. Index available. cum. index. **Bk Rev.** ctrl circ.
**Desc:** Christian sermon resource based on the new common lectionary.

CN/1184-2652
**HOMILY HINTS.** [Homily hints]. Issue 498, (Aug. 26, 1990)-. Periodical. English. wk. 52.00Can$ (1 year), 125.00Can$ (3 year). Capsulized Communications Ltd, Box 968, Vernon British Columbia V1T 6N2 Canada. **Tel** (604)545-8632, FAX (613)458-7286. **ED** R.G. Fitzpatrick. **DD** 251/.02/05. **Ad Acc. Circ:** 3000. ***Continues*** *Homily Hints for Contemporary Preaching., 0227-0676.*
**Desc:** Freshly written sermon outlines for every Sunday.

US/0732-1872
**HOMILY SERVICE.** [Homily serv.]. **Added/Corp** Liturgical Conference, Inc. (1968)-. Periodical. English. Twelve times a year. $55.00 (one year); $98.00 (two years). Liturgical Conference / Maryland, 8750 Georgia Avenue, Suite 123, Silver Spring MD 20910. **Tel** (301)495-0885. **ED** Rachel Reeder. **DD** 252. **Circ:** 4,200 (ctrl).
**Desc:** The publication offers aids to preachers of the various Christian churches: scriptural exegesis, "ideas and illustrations", homily models, etc.

FR
**HOMMES ET EGLISE; ANNUAIRE DU QUEBEC.** **VFOAT** Annuaire du Cerdic. No. 1 (1970)-. Monographic series. French. an. Price varies per volume. CERDIC Universite des Sciences Humaines de Strasbourg, Palais Universitaire, 2 rue Goethe, 67000 Strasbourg France. **ED** Jean Schlick and Marie Zimmermann.

US/1042-8461
**HORIZON (CHICAGO, ILL.).** (HORIZON : JOURNAL OF THE NATIONAL RELIGIOUS VOCATION CONFERENCE.). [Horizon]. **Added/Corp** National Religious Vocation Conference (U.S.). Vol. 14, No. 2 (Winter 1989)-. Periodical. English. Four times a year (Published within the seasons & volume change in the Fall). $17.00 one year; $30.00 two year. National Religious Vocation Conference, 1603 South Michigan Avenue, Suite 400, Chicago IL 60616. **Tel** (312)663-5454, FAX (312)663-5030. **ED** Patricia Knopp Sndden. **LC** WMLC 93/1382. **DD** 248. Index available. cum. index. **Circ:** 2,000 (ctrl). ***Continues*** *Call to Growth/Ministry, 0883-6280.*
**Desc:** Exploration of questions of information gathering confidentiality, liability, and related matters.

CN/0712-6077
**HORIZONS (OAKVILLE).** (HORIZONS.). [Horizons]. Jan. 1981-. Periodical. English. bm. Horizons / Salvation Army Editorial Department, 455 North Service Road East, Oakville Ontario L6H 1A5 Canada. **ED** Major Ira Barrow. **DD** 267/.15/05. **Bk Rev.** ctrl circ. ***Continues*** *Officer Bulletin.*

US/0360-9669
**HORIZONS (VILLANOVA).** (HORIZONS.). [Horizons]. **Added/Corp** College Theology Society. Vol. 1 (Fall 1974)-. Periodical. English. sa (Spring & Fall). 36.00Can$ Canada; $36.00 other. Wilfrid Laurier University Press, 75 University Avenue West, Waterloo Ontario N2L 3C5 Canada. **Tel** (519)884-1970, FAX (519)725-1399. **ED** Walter E. Conn. **LC** BR1; .H83. **DD** 230/.2/05. Index available. **Bk Rev. Ad Acc. Pr Rev. Circ:** 1,425 (ctrl). available on microfilm and microfiche from University Microfilms International (UMI). Documents available from The Genuine Article.
**Desc:** Explores developments in Catholic theology, total Christian tradition, human religious experience, and the concerns of creative teaching from the college and university environment.
**Ind/Abst** Arts Humanit. Citation Index [Full Cov.]; Index Book Rev. Relig.; INIS Atomindex [Micro.]; Middle East Abstr. Index; New Testam. Abstr.; Old Testam. Abstr.; Relig. Index One Period. (1974-); Relig. Theol. Abstr. (199?-); Res. Alert [Full Cov.]; Soc. Sci. Cit. Index [Select. Cov.]; Abr. Cathol. Period. Lit. Index; Cathol. Period. Lit. Index.

US/8756-3029
**HORUS (SILVER SPRINGS, MD.).** (HORUS.). [Horus]. Vol. 1, No. 1 (Winter 1985)-. Periodical. English. Three times a year. $15.00. Institute for the Study of Collective Behavior and Memory, PO Box 9026, Silver Spring MD 20906. **DD** 291.

US
**HOSANNA (PHOENIX, ARIZ.).** (HOSANNA.). [Hosanna]. **Added/Corp** North American Liturgy Resources. Loyola Pastoral Institute (New York, N.Y.). Vol. 1, No. 1 (1982)-. Periodical. English. qt. **DD** 242. ***Continues*** *Hosanna, 0276-3729.*
**Desc:** Deals with liturgics.

US/0276-3729
**HOSANNA (PHOENIX, ARIZ.).** ***Title Change.*** (HOSANNA.). [Hosanna]. **Added/Corp** North American Liturgy Resources. (197?)-(19??). Periodical. English. North American Liturgy Review, 10802 North 23rd Avenue, Phoenix AZ 85029-4968. **DD** 242. ***Continued by*** *Hosanna (Phoenix Ariz. : 1982), 0276-3729.*

CI
**HRVATSKA KRSCANSKA BIBLIOGRAFIJA.** **See** Religion and Theology-Abstracting, Bibliographies and Statistics.

US/0018-6910
**HRVATSKI KATOLICKI GLASNIK.** **VFOAT** Croatian Catholic Messenger. Periodical. Serbo-Croatian (Roman). mo. $20.00. Croatian Franciscan Fathers, 4851 Drexel Boulevard, Chicago IL 60615. **ED** Diomzije Lasic. **Circ:** 2,000.
**Desc:** Religion and mythology.

US/0197-3096
**HUMAN DEVELOPMENT (NEW YORK).** **See** Psychology.

US/0897-8786
**HUMAN QUEST.** **VFOAT** Churchman's Human Quest. Vol. 203, No. 6 (Nov./Dec. 1989)-. Periodical.

English. Eighteen times a year (Monthly Oct.-March; bimonthly April-Sept.). $10.00 (1 year), $17.00 (2 year) US; $13.00 (1 year), $23.00 (2 year)other. The Churchman, 1074 23rd Avenue North, St Petersburg FL 33704. **Tel** (813)894-0097. **LC** BX5800; C7. **DD** 270.8/05. available on microfilm and microfiche from University Microfilms International (UMI). ***Continues*** *Churchman's Human Quest, 0897-8786.*

GW
**HWAHAE.** **VFOAT** Versohnung. Periodical. German (Korean). Korean Christen-Verband IM Ausland, Gunthersburgallee 96, W-6000 Frankfurt AM Main Germany. **LC** BR1320; .H93.

US/0018-8271
**HYMN, THE.** **See** Music.

DK/0106-4940
**HYMNOLOGISKE MEDDELELSER.** **See** Music.

KO
**HYONDAE MOKHOE.** Periodical. Korean. mo. 19.000. Chu, Hyondae Mokhoe, PO Box 144, Youido Ucheguk Seoul 150 Korea. **LC** BV4000; .H9.

US/0422-4108
**I.E. (CHICAGO).** (I.E.). **VAT** Id Est. V. 1- 1964-. Periodical. English. bm. The Ecumenical Institute, 3444 West Congress Parkway, Chicago IL 60624.

SZ
**ICMC TODAY / INTERNATIONAL CATHOLIC MIGRATION COMMISSION.** **Added/Corp** International Catholic Migration Commission. **VAT** International Catholic Migration Commission Today. Vol. 1, No. 1 (Feb. 1991)-. Periodical. English. qt. Coordinator of Communications, ICMC, 37-39 Rue de Vermont, Case Oistale 96, CH-1211 Geneva 20 Switzerland. **LC** BX2347.8.R44; I27. **DD** 261.8/368/05. ***Continues*** *ICMC Newsletter.*

US
**ICUIS METRO-MINISTRY NEWS : THE INTERDENOMINATIONAL NEWSLETTER OF THE INSTITUTE ON THE CHURCH IN URBAN INDUSTRIAL SOCIETY.** **VFOAT** Metro-Ministry News. Vol. 1, No. 1 (Fall 1985)-. Newsletter. English. Four times a year. $8.00. Institute on the Church in Urban Industrial Society, 5700 South Woodlawn Avenue, Chicago IL 60637. **ED** Clinton E Stockwell and Tom Wakely. **Bk Rev**. **Circ:** 6,000.
**Desc:** A vehicle for exchanging information across denominational lines about urban ministry programs, events, strategies and resources.

GW
**IDEA SPEKTRUM.** German. wk. DM163.20. Informationsdienst Ev Allianz, Moritz Hensoldt Str 22, PF 1820, W 6330 Wetzlar 1 Germany. **Tel** 011 49 6441 90140. **ED** Helmut Mathies. Index available. **Bk Rev**. **Ad Acc. Circ:** 2,000 (ctrl).
**Desc:** News and opinion from the Christian world with an emphasis on Protestantism and Central Europe.

IT
**IDOC INTERNAZIONALE.** **Added/Corp** IDOC (Center). (1970)-. Periodical. English (Italian and Spanish). Four times a year. $30.00. IDOC Internazionale, Via S Maria dell Anima 30, 00186 Rome Italy. **Tel** 011 39 6 6868332. **Circ:** 1,500. available on microfilm and microfiche from University Microfilms International (UMI). ***Absorbed*** *International IDOC Bulletin, 0250-7633.*
**Desc:** Review publishing documents and articles coming from groups or individuals involved in social, political, and religious renewal and change throughout the third world.

US/1065-1675
**IFCO NEWS.** [IFCO news]. **Main/Corp** Interreligious Foundation for Community Organization (U.S.). **VFOAT** Interreligious Foundation for Community Organization News. (19??)-. Periodical. English. qt. $20.00 (institutions), $15.00 (individuals). Interreligious Foundation, 402 West 145th Street, New York NY 10031. **Tel** (212)926-5757. **ED** Gail Walker. **DD** 291. Index available. cum. index. **Bk Rev**. **Ad Acc. Circ:** 10,000 (ctrl).
**Desc:** Highlights the work of IFCO and issues related to social justice.

UK/1010-8734
**IFES REVIEW.** [IFES rev.]. **VFOAT** International Fellowship of Evangelical Students Review. (1976)-. Periodical. English (Spanish). Twice a year. £10.00 UK; $18.00 other. International Fellowship of Evangelical Students, 55 Palmerston Road, Wealdstone Harrow, Middlesex HA3 7RR United Kingdom. **Tel** 081-863 8688, FAX 081-863 8229. **ED** Sue Brown. **UDC** 25. Index available. cum. index. **Bk Rev. Circ:** 750 (ctrl).
**Desc:** Training articles and resources for those involved in Christian ministry among students.

US/0019-1795
**ILIFF REVIEW, THE.** ***Ceased.*** [Iliff rev.]. Vol. 1 (1944)-Vol. 45 No. 3 (1988). Periodical. English. Three times a year. The Iliff School of Theology, 2233 South University, Denver CO 80210. **Tel** (303)744-1287. **ED** Charles S Milligan. **LC** BR1; .I37. **DD** 205. **Bk Rev. Circ:** 500 (ctrl). available on microfilm from ATLA.
**Desc:** Religious studies including standard academic areas in the field.
**Ind/Abst** Index Book Rev. Relig. (?-?); MLA Int. Bibl. Books Artic. Mod. Lang. Lit. (?-?); Old Testam. Abstr. (?-?); Relig. Index One Period. (1974-).

SI/0129-704X
**IMAGE.** **Added/Corp** Asian Christian Art Association. (Oct. 1979)-. Periodical. English. Four times a year (Mar., June, Sept., Dec.). $30.00 (institutions), $20.00 (individuals) Comes with Asian Christian Art Association membership. Asian Christian Art Association, Kansai Seminar House, 23 Takenouchi-cho, Kyoto 606 Japan. **Tel** 075 711 2115, FAX 075 701 5256. **ED** Alison O'Grady, (editor's address: 264 Titirangi Road, PO Box 15-774, Auckland 7 New Zealand, Fax: (64-9-817-3574). **Circ:** 600.
**Desc:** It contains news of interest to the Asian Art world, articles on theology and art, and well-produced color and black and white reproductions of contemporary art.

US/0194-0422
**IMPACT (CLAREMONT).** (IMPACT.). [Impact]. **Added/Corp** Disciples Seminary Foundation. No. 1 (1978)-. Periodical. English. sa (June and Nov.). $7.50 (one year), $13.00 (two year), $18.00 (three year). Disciples Seminary Foundation, PO Box 1177, Claremont CA 91711. **Tel** (909)624-0712. **ED** Donald D Reisinger and Mary Anne Parrott. **LC** BX7301; .I47. **DD** 286/.679. Index available. cum. index. **Circ:** 300.
**Desc:** Publishes works by Disciples of Christ or presentations to that constituency, primarily on the Pacific Slope.
**Ind/Abst** Index Book Rev. Relig.; Relig. Index One Period. (1978-).

CN/0384-7543
**IMPACT (MONTREAL).** (IMP A C T.). **Main/Corp** Provincial Association of Catholic Teachers of Quebec. **Added/Corp** Provincial Association of Catholic Teachers of Quebec. Negotiating Assembly. Vol. 1 (Dec. 1975)-. Periodical. English. ir. Provincial Association of Catholic Teachers of Quebec, 5767 Monkland Avenue, Montreal Quebec H4A 1E8 Canada. **DD** 377/.8/209714.

SI/0129-2862
**IMPACT SINGAPORE.** [Impact Singap.]. (1976)-. Periodical. English. bm (6 issues). $22.00. Impact Christian Communication, 12B East Coast Road, Singapore 1543 Singapore. **Tel** 011 65 3450444. **ED** Andrew Boh. **DD** 205. **Bk Rev**, (Qty: 6). **Ad Acc. Circ:** 6,000 (ctrl).

CN/0823-8812
**IMSS NEWSLETTER.** (IMSS NEWSLETTER / INTER MENNONITE STUDENT SERVICES.). [IMSS newsl.]. **VAT** Inter Mennonite Student Services Newsletter. Vol. 1, No. 1 (Nov. 1982)-. Newsletter. English. Three times a year. Free to Young Ontario Mennonites. IMSS Newsletter, University Community Centre/Room 4, University of Western Ontario, London Ontario N6A 3K7 Canada. **DD** 259/.24/09713.

NE
**IN DE WAAGSCHAAL.** Vol. 1, No. 1 (Oct. 6, 1945)- Vol. 25, No. 26 (Sept. 26, 1970). Periodical. Dutch. bw. Fl17.00. Mevr Geuze, Oranje Nassauplein, 3708 BL Zeist, Netherlnds. **Tel** 011 31 3404 13993. ***Continues*** *Woord en Geest.*

SA/1018-6441
**IN DIE SKRIFLIG.** [In skriflig]. (1966)-. Periodical. Afrikaans (English and Dutch). Four times a year (Mar., June, Sept., Dec.). R30.00. Bureau for Scholarly Journals, Private Bag X6001, Potchefstroom 2520 South Africa. **Tel** 011 27 148 991769, FAX 011 27 148 991562, telex 346019. **ED** Professor J. H. Van Wyk and Mariana Venter. **UDC** 24. Index available in last issue of volume--attached. cum. index. **Bk Rev**, (Qty: 25). **Pr Rev. Circ:** 430.
**Desc:** Articles promoting reformational theology are published. All domains of theology are accepted.

KO
**IN GOD'S IMAGE.** (19??)-. English. Four times a year. $15.00 Europe & North America; $10.00 Australia, Hong Kong, Japan, Taiwan, Korea, New Zealand; $5.00 Asian countries. Asian Womens Resource Centre, PO Box 16 Chungchongno, Seoul 120 650 Korea. **Tel** 011 82 2 3636147.
**Desc:** Presents Asian feminist theology.

US
**IN SEASON.** English. mo. $36.00. Cathedral Directories, 1401 West Girard Avenue, Madison Heights MI 48071. **Tel** (313)545-1415, (800)544-6903, FAX (313)544-1611. **ED** Dean Lueking (editor's address: 7300 West Division Street, River Forest, IL 60305).

US/1064-0649
**IN THE MARKETPLACE.** (IN THE MARKETPLACE : EQUIPPING BUSINESS PEOPLE FOR WORKPLACE WITNESS AND SPIRITUAL LEADERSHIP IN THE MARKETPLACE.). [In marketpl.]. **Added/Corp** Marketplace Ministries, Inc. (1987)-. Periodical. English. Six times a year (Jan., Mar., May, July, Sept., Nov.). Free. Marketplace Ministries, PO Box 27813, San Diego CA 92198. **Tel** (619)673-8544, FAX (619)673-3977. **ED** Judy Hanawalt. **DD** 261. **Ad Acc, Adv Mgr:** Roy Taylor. **Circ:** 4,000.
**Desc:** Newsletter designed to equip the reader for confident workplace witness and spiritual leadership in the marketplace.

AT/0442-3844
**IN UNITY.** **Added/Corp** Australian Council of Churches. (1953)-. Periodical. English. sa (May and Dec.). Australian Council of Churches, PO Box C199, Clarence Street, Sydney 2000 Australia. **Tel** (02)2992215. **ED** Joan Dugdale. **Bk Rev. Circ:** 6,500 (ctrl).
**Desc:** Covers work of Australian and world councils of churches, ecumenical and inter-faith dialogue within Australia and world-wide, theology, aid, development, and education.

US/0274-5569
**INCREASE.** **Added/Corp** Bible Christian Union. (19??)-. Periodical. English. Four times a year. Free on request. Bible Christian Union, PO Box 410, Hatfield PA 19440-0410. **Tel** (215)361-0500. **ED** George W. Murray. **Circ:** 15,000 (ctrl).
**Desc:** Covers topics of missionary interest, particularly the work of missionaries with the Bible Christian Union.

US/0887-1574
**INDEX TO BOOK REVIEWS IN RELIGION.** **See** Religion and Theology-Abstracting, Bibliographies and Statistics.

II/0019-4530
**INDIAN CHURCH HISTORY REVIEW.** [Indian church hist. rev.]. **Added/Corp** Church History Association of India. Vol. 1 (June 1967)-. Periodical. English. sa (June and Dec.). $15.00. Church History Association of India, Business Manager/Dharmaram College, Bangalore 560 029 India. **Tel** 845 2270, 845 2653, FAX 91 080 8452653. **(Subscription address:** Prints India, 11 Darya Ganj, New Delhi, 110002 India, (Phone: 011 91 11 3268645)) **ED** J. Rosario Narchison. **LC** BR1150; .I5. **DD** 275.4. **Bk Rev. Ad Acc.** ctrl circ. ***Supersedes*** *Church History Association of India. Bulletin of the Church History Association of India.*
**Desc:** Ideas and essays on the origin, growth and present features of the church in India.
**Ind/Abst** Bibliogr. Mission.; Index Book Rev. Relig.; Relig. Index One Period. (1973-); Relig. Theol. Abstr.

II/0019-5685
**INDIAN JOURNAL OF THEOLOGY, THE.** ***Ceased.*** [Indian j. theol.]. (1952)-(19??). Periodical. English. qt. Bishops College, 224 Lower Circular Road, Calcutta 700017 India. **LC** BR1. ***Continues in part*** *Society for Biblical Studies. Bulletin.*
**Ind/Abst** Bibliogr. Mission.; Index Book Rev. Relig.; Missionalia; New Testam. Abstr.; Relig. Index One Period. (1952-19??); Relig. Theol. Abstr.

II
**INDIAN MISSIOLOGICAL REVIEW : IMR / SACRED HEART THEOLOGICAL COLLEGE.** **Added/Corp** Sacred Heart Theological College (Shillong, India). **VFOAT** IMR; I.M.R. Vol. 1, No. 1 (Jan. 1979)-. Periodical. English. qt. $20.00. Satprakashan Sanchar Kendra, Bhanwarkua Chow Indore 452 001, Madhya Pradesh India. **(Subscription address:** Prints India, 11 Darya Ganj, New Delhi 110002 India.) **ED** Father Joseph Futhenpurackal. **LC** BV2000; .I53. **DD** 266/.00954/05.

II/0253-620X
**INDIAN THEOLOGICAL STUDIES.** [Indian theol. stud.]. **Added/Corp** St. Peter's Pontifical Institute of Theology. Vol. 14, No. 1 (Mar. 1977)-. Periodical. English (Multiple languages). Four times a year (Mar., June, Sept., Dec.). $15.00. Indian Theologica Studies, St. Peters Seminary, Bangalore 560 055 India. **Tel** 011 91 812 341407 or 349621. **(Subscription address:** Prints India, 11 Darya Ganj, New Delhi, 110002 India, (Phone: 011 91 11 3268645)) **ED** Fr. L. Legrand. **LC** BR1; .I53. **DD** 230/.254. Index available (Bound in Dec. iss.). cum. index. **Bk Rev**, (Qty: 1,000). **Ad Acc. Circ:** 1,000 (ctrl). ***Continues*** *Indian Ecclesiastical Studies.*
**Desc:** Provides a forum for theological research either conducted in India or relevant to India.
**Ind/Abst** Bibliogr. Mission.; Missionalia; New Testam. Abstr.; Old Testam. Abstr.

US
**INDIANA BAPTIST.** Newspaper. English. Forty-eight times a year (Tues.). $8.00. Indiana Baptist, PO Box 24189, Indianapolis IN 46224. **Tel** (317)241-9317. **ED** Gary Ledbetter. **Circ:** 5,500 (ctrl).
**Desc:** State paper for the state convention of Baptists in Indiana.

CN/0833-9228
**INFORMATEUR CATHOLIQUE (1985).** (L'INFORMATEUR CATHOLIQUE.). [Inf. cathol.]. Vol. 4, No. 24 (Dec. 14, 1985). Periodical. French. sm. 35.00Can$ (Quebec); 32.00Can$ (other provinces); 41.00Can$ (other countries). Spirimedia Inc., CP 330, Chertsey Quebec J0K 3K0 Canada. **DD** 261.8/3/09714. **Bk Rev. Ad Acc. Circ:** 10,000. ***Continues*** *Informateur*

*(Montreal, Quebec), 0824-4111.*
**Desc:** Provides objective religious information on events pertinent to the faith and of social interest.

PL
**INFORMATION BULLETIN - CHRISTIAN SOCIAL ASSOCIATION.** ***Ceased.*** **Main/Corp** Christian Social Association. **VFOAT** CHSS Information Bulletin. Ceased (Jan. 1990). Bulletin. English. mo. **(Subscription address:** ARS Polona, PO Box 1001, 00068 Warsaw Poland.**)**

IT
**INFORMATION SERVICE.** **Main/Corp** Catholic Church Secretariatus Ad Christianorum Unitatem Fovendam. No. 1 (1967)-. Periodical. English (French). qt. L40,000 Italy; $30.00 (surface mail), $40.00 (air mail) other. Pontifical Council For Promoting Christian Unity, Via Del Erba 1, 00120 Vatin City, Italy. **Tel** (6)698 4085, FAX (6)698 5365. **ED** John A Radano. **Circ:** 3,500.
**Ind/Abst** Bibliogr. Mission.

CN/0227-5406
**INFORMER (CALGARY).** (THE INFORMER.). [Informer]. **VFOAT** Christian Informer. June 1979-. Periodical. English. qt. Free. Christian Info, 223-10 Street NW, Calgary Alta. T2N 1V5. **DD** 267/.1.

CN/0836-866X
**INITIATIVES (TORONTO).** **See** Education-Teaching and Curriculum.

US/1049-9709
**INNER WOMAN.** **See** Women's Interests.

UK/0020-1723
**INQUIRER, THE.** No. 4789- April 14, 1934-. Periodical. English. bw. £12.50 UK; $32.00 other. Inquirer Publishing Company Inc, 1-6 Essex Street, London WC2R 3HY England. **Tel** (0710240-2384. **ED** Keith Gilley. **Bk Rev.** **Ad Acc.** **Circ:** 2,500. ***Continues*** *Inquirer and Christian Life;* ***Absorbed*** *General Assembly Bulletin.*
**Desc:** Religious journal.

IT/1121-1555
**INSEGNARE RELIGIONE.** (1988)-. Periodical. Italian. Nine times a year. L21500 (Italy); L35000 (other). Editrice Elle di Ci, Corso Francia 214, 10090 Rivoli Turin Italy. **Tel** 39 11 9591091, FAX (011)9574048. **UDC** 37.

NR/0794-7968
**INSIGHT LAGOS. 1987.** [InsightLagos, 1987]. (1987)-. Periodical. English. mo. $24.00. OAL Research Publications Ltd, Cleanjohn House, 90 Ladipo Street, PO Box 9802, Lagos Nigeria. **Tel** (01)520342, 523420, 962119, telex 27358. **ED** O A Lawal. **DD** 269.4. **Bk Rev.** **Ad Acc.** **Circ:** 25,000.
**Desc:** A magazine for spiritual development.

US/1056-0548
**INSIGHTS : A JOURNAL OF THE FACULTY OF AUSTIN SEMINARY.** [Insights]. **Added/Corp** Austin Presbyterian Theological Seminary. Vol. 106, No. 1 (Fall 1990)-. Periodical. English. sa. $1.00 US; $5.00 other. Austin Presbyterian Theological Seminary, 100 East 27th Street, Austin TX 78705. **Tel** (512)472-6736, FAX (512)479-0738. **DD** 285. Index available. cum. index. **Circ:** 7500 (ctrl). available on microfilm from University Microfilms International (UMI). ***Continues in part*** *Austin Seminary Bulletin, 0191-8613.*
**Desc:** A planned selection of essays focusing on a central theme, of importance to the church or its ministry.
**Ind/Abst** Index Book Rev. Relig.; Relig. Index One Period.

US/1056-1978
**INSIGHTS FOR LIFE.** [Insights life]. **Added/Corp** Southern Baptist Convention. Sunday School Board. (1991)-. Periodical. English. qt. $10.60. Southern Baptist Convention, 901 Commerce, Suite 750, Nashville TN 37203. **Tel** (615)244-2355, FAX (615)742-8919. **(Subscription address:** Sunday School Board - Customer Service, 127 Ninth Avenue North, Nashville, TN 37234 USA; telephone: (800)458-2772**)** **DD** 248.

US/8756-3347
**INSIGHTS INTO CHRISTIAN EDUCATION.** ***Ceased.*** [Insights Christ. educ.]. **VFOAT** Insights. Periodical. English. qt. Parish Ministries Resource, 619 North 6th Avenue, Maywood IL 60153. **ED** Thomas Couser. **DD** 268. **Bk Rev.** **Ad Acc.** **Circ:** 400 (ctrl).
**Desc:** An independent journal serving religious educators.

US/0164-7709
**INSIGHTS (SPRINGFIELD, OHIO).** (INSIGHTS FOR PREACHERS.). (1973)-. Periodical. English. Four times a year (Jan., Apr., July, Oct.). $22.00 one year; $40.00 two years. King Publications, 5697 Applebutter Hill Road, Cooperburg PA 18036. **Tel** (215)967-3901. **ED** Rev. Richard H. Stough. **Pr Rev.** **Circ:** 500.
**Desc:** Provides a sermon for every Sunday of the church year for many special occasions and events. Scripture-based materials are prepared by a team of experienced clergy from several denominations.

US/1065-8092
**INSPIRATION (PITTSBURGH, PA.).** ***Ceased.*** (INSPIRATION.). **Added/Corp** Duquesne University. Institute of Formative Spirituality. (1993)-(Dec. 1994). Periodical. English. Four times a year. Institute of Formative Spirituality, 906 Rockwell Hall, Duquesne University, Pittsburgh PA 15282. **Tel** (412)396-6026. **ED** Helen Douglas. **DD** 248. **Bk Rev**, (Qty: 3). **Circ:** 3,000. available on microfilm and microfiche from University Microfilms International (UMI).
**Desc:** Contains upward in openness to the Holy and helps to return to the richness of our ordinary lives with renewed vigor.

US
**INSTITUTE FOR CHRISTIAN ECONOMICS.** **See** Economics.

BE
**INSTRUMENTA LEXICOLOGICA LATINA. SERIES A, ENUMERATIO FORMARUM, CONCORDANTIA FORMARUM, INDEX FORMARUM A TERGO ORDINATARUM.** **Added/Corp** CETEDOC. **VFOAT** Corpus Christianorum. Instrumenta Lexicologica Latina; Instrumenta Lexicologica Latina. Series A, Formae. No. 1 (1982)-. Monographic series. Latin. Ten times a year. Price varies per volume. Brepols Publishers, Steenweg OP Tielen 68, B-2300 Turnhout Belgium. **Tel** 011 32 14 402500. available on microfiche.

BE
**INSTRUMENTA LEXICOLOGICA LATINA. SERIES B, ENUMERATIO LEMATUM, CONCORDANTIA LEMMATUM ET FORMARUM, INDEX FORMARUM ET LEMMATUM, INDEX LEMMATUM A TERGO ORDINATORUM, TABULA FREQUENTIARUM.** **See** Classical Studies.

NE/0534-4255
**INSTRUMENTA PATRISTICA.** (1959)-. Monographic series. Multiple languages. ir. Price varies per volume. Martinus Nijhoff Publishers, Subsidiary of Kluwer Academic Publishers, Koraalrood 50, 2718 SC Zoetermeer Netherlands. **Tel** 011 31 79 684400.
**Desc:** History and theology of early and modern Christianity.

US/0161-1380
**INTEGRAL YOGA.** **See** Philosophy.

CN/0849-133X
**INTENTION MISSIONNAIRE.** [Intent. mission.]. **Added/Corp** Oeuvres Pontificales Missionnaires. Service d'Animation Missionnaire. (1990)-. Periodical. French. Service D'Animation Missionnaire Des Oeuvres Pontificales, CP 220 Limoilou, Quebec G1L4V7 Canada. **DD** 282/.05. ***Continues*** *Intentions de l'Eglise, 0845-4604.*

CN/0828-797X
**INTERCULTURE.** [Interculture]. (1984)-. Periodical. English (French and English). qt. 30.00Can$ (one year), 55.00Can$ (two year), 80.00Can$ (three year) institutions, 17.00Can$ (one year), 32.00Can$ (two year), 47.00Can$ (three year) individuals Canada; $35.00 (one year), $65.00 (two year), $95.00 (three year) institutions, $22.00 (one year), $42.00 (two year), $62.00 (three year) individuals other. Centre Interculturel Monchanin, 4917 St Urban Street, Montreal Quebec H2T 2W1 Canada. **Tel** (514)288-7229. **ED** Jacques Langlais and Robert Vachon. **DD** 291/.05. Index available. cum. index. **Bk Rev.** **Circ:** 1,000 (ctrl). available on microfilm (35mm) from Microfilms Publications. ***Continues in part*** *Interculture (Montreal, Quebec), 0712-1571.*
**Desc:** To inform on contemporary cultures as living realities; to promote research and encounter in full intercultural reciprocity; to explore and raise intercultural questions and issues.
**Ind/Abst** Index Book Rev. Relig.; Relig. Index One Period.; Relig. Theol. Abstr.

CN/0712-1571
**INTERCULTURE (MONTREAL. ED. FRANCAISE).** (INTERCULTURE.). [Interculture]. **Added/Corp** Centre interculturel Monchanin. Vol. 17, No. 4 (Oct./Dec. 1984)-. Periodical. French (English). Twice a year. $23.00 (individual); $37.00 (institution). Monchanin Cross-Cultural Centre, 4917 rue Urbain Street, Montreal Quebec H2T 2W1 Canada. **Tel** (514)288-7229. **ED** Jacques Langlais and Robert Vachon. **DD** 291/.05. Index available. cum. index. **Bk Rev.** **Circ:** 1,000 (ctrl). ***Continues in part*** *Interculture (Montreal, Quebec), 0712-1571.*
**Desc:** Seeking a cross-cultural response to the deep contemporary crisis of civilizations and to the recent human condition of cultural pluralism.
**Ind/Abst** Index Book Rev. Relig.; Point Repere (1991-); Relig. Index One Period.

US/0362-4668
**INTERDEPENDENCE.** 1969-. Periodical. English. Unitarian Church of Evanston, 1130 Ridge Avenue, Evanston IL 60201.

US/0273-6187
**INTERMOUNTAIN CATHOLIC.** (19??)-. Periodical. English. Forty-Five times a year (Weekly on Friday except during the summer, paper is every other week;). $13.50. Intermountain Catholic, Box 2489, Salt Lake City UT 84110. **Tel** (801)328-8641 Ext. 23, 24, or 35. **ED** Barbara S. Lee. **Bk Rev.** **Ad Acc**, **Adv Mgr:** Ann. **Circ:** 13,500. ***Continues*** *Intermountain Catholic Register, 0199-2910.*
**Desc:** News to do with the Catholic Church.

US/0272-6122
**INTERNATIONAL BULLETIN OF MISSIONARY RESEARCH.** [Int. bull. mission. res.]. **Added/Corp** Overseas Ministries Study Center. **VFOAT** International Bulletin. Vol. 5, No. 1 (Jan. 1981)-. Periodical. English. qt. $18.00. Overseas Ministries Study Center, 490 Prospect Street, New Haven CT 06511. **Tel** (203)624-6672. **(Subscription address:** Subscriptions Service Department, PO Box 3000, Denville NJ 07834.**)** **LC** BV2350; .O3. **DD** 266/.005. **Bk Rev.** **Ad Acc.** **Circ:** 9,000. available on microfilm and microfiche from University Microfilms International (UMI). Documents available from UMI Article Clearinghouse. ***Continues*** *Occasional Bulletin of Missionary Research, 0364-2178.*
**Desc:** Christian missionary magazine about the church throughout the world.
**Ind/Abst** Acad. Search (July 1993-); Bibliogr. Mission.; Christ. Period. Index; Expand. Acad. Index (1989-); Guide Soc. Sci. Relig.; Humanit. Index; Humanit. Source (Jul. 1993-); Index Book Rev. Relig.; INFO-SOUTH Abstr.; Missionalia; Newsp. Period. Abstr. (1991-); Relig. Index One Period. (1981-); Relig. Theol. Abstr.

US/0890-4081
**INTERNATIONAL CHRISTIAN DIGEST : ICD.** ***Ceased.*** [Int. Christ. dig.]. **VFOAT** ICD. Vol. 1, No. 1 (1987)-Vol. 3, No. 8 ( ). Periodical. English. mo. United Methodist Publishing House, PO Box 801, 201 8th Avenue South, Nashville TN 37202. **Tel** (615)749-6732, (615)749-6615, FAX (615)749-6578, (615)749-6579. **DD** 205.
**Ind/Abst** Guide Soc. Sci. Relig.

US
**INTERNATIONAL FELLOWSHIP NEWSLETTER, THE.** Newsletter. English. qt. $2.00. The International University Press, 1301 South Noland Road, Independence MO 64055. **Tel** (816)461-3633. **ED** John Wayne Johnston. **Bk Rev.** **Circ:** 2,500 (ctrl).

NE/0020-7047
**INTERNATIONAL JOURNAL FOR PHILOSOPHY OF RELIGION.** [Int. j. philos. relig.]. Vol. 1 (Spring 1970)-. Periodical. English. bm. $372.00. Kluwer Academic Publishers, Postbus 322, 3300 AH Dordrecht, The Netherlands. **Tel** 011 31 78 524400, FAX 011 31 78 183273, telex 20083. **ED** Eugene Thomas Long and Frank R Harrison III. **LC** BL51; .I65. **DD** 200/.1. **CODEN** IJPREB. **[CCC].** **Pr Rev.** available on microfilm and microfiche from University Microfilms International (UMI). Documents available from The Genuine Article, UMI Article Clearinghouse.
**Desc:** Provides a medium for the exposition, development and criticism of important philosophical insights and theories relevant to religion in any of its varied forms. Also provides a forum for critical, constructive, and interpretive consideration of religion from an objective philosophical point of view. Articles, symposia, discussions, reviews, notes, and news in this journal are intended to serve the interests of a wide range of thoughtful readers, especially teachers and students of philosophy, philosophical theology and religious thought.
**Ind/Abst** Acad. Search (July 1993-); Arts Humanit. Citation Index [Full Cov.]; Curr. Contents Arts Humanit.; Expand. Acad. Index (1989-); Humanit. Index; Humanit. Source (Jul. 1993-); Index Book Rev. Relig.; INFO-SOUTH Abstr.; Middle East Abstr. Index; Newsp. Period. Abstr. (1991-); Philos. Index; Relig. Index One Period. (1975-); Relig. Theol. Abstr.; Res. Alert [Full Cov.].

US/1050-8619
**INTERNATIONAL JOURNAL FOR THE PSYCHOLOGY OF RELIGION, THE.** [Int. j. psychol. relig.]. Vol. 1, No. 1 (1991)-. Periodical. English. qt. $145.00 US & Canada; $170.00 other. Lawrence Erlbaum Associates, 365 Broadway, Suite 102, Hillsdale NJ 07642. **Tel** (201)666-4110, (800)926-6579, FAX (201)666-2394. **LC** BL53.A1; I53. **DD** 291.01/9. **CODEN** IPRLEB.
**Ind/Abst** Index Book Rev. Relig.; Relig. Index One Period.; Soc. Plann. Policy Dev. Abstr.; Abr. Cathol. Period. Lit. Index; Cathol. Period. Lit. Index.

US/0743-2429
**INTERNATIONAL JOURNAL OF FRONTIER MISSIONS.** [Int. j. front. missions]. **Added/Corp** International Student Leaders Coalition for Frontier Missions. Vol. 1, No. 1 (1984)-. Periodical. English. qt (Jan., April, July, Oct.). $15.00 (one year), $28.00 (two year), $40.00 (three year). International Student Leaders Coalition for Frontier Missions, 7665 Wenda Way, El Paso TX 79915. **Tel** (915)779-5655, FAX (915)778-6440. **ED** Hans M. Weerstra. **DD** 266. **Bk Rev**, (Qty: 2-3 per year). **Ad Acc.** **Circ:** 500 (ctrl).

**Desc:** A professional journal of evangelical persuasion, focusing on missionary endeavor in societies presently without Christian churches.

UK/0951-5429
**INTERNATIONAL JOURNAL OF THEOLOGY AND PHILOSOPHY IN AFRICA : TPA, THE.** **VFOAT** TPA. Vol. 1, No. 1 (Jan. 1989)-. Periodical. English. qt. OS Journals, Center Research & Publs, 27 Pattison Road, London NW2 2HL England. **LC** BT30.A4; I57. **DD** 230/.096. **[CCC].**

CN
**INTERNATIONAL LAZARITE.** V. 1 (Jan./Mar. 1975)-. Periodical. English. qt. $25.00. Puller, Rt 3 Box 357, Moneta VA 24121-9424. **LC** CR5037; .I58. **DD** 255/.8.

US/0074-6770
**INTERNATIONAL LESSON ANNUAL, THE.** (1956)-. Monographic series. English. an. Price varies per volume. Abingdon Press, PO Box 801, Nashville TN 37202. **Tel** (615)749-6451, (800)251-3320. **ED** Horace R. Weaver. **LC** BV1560; .I64. **DD** 268.61. Index available in last issue of volume--attached.
**Desc:** An interdenominational resource for teachers of Sunday school and church school. Contains step-by-step lesson plans for every Sunday.

SZ/0020-8582
**INTERNATIONAL REVIEW OF MISSIONS.** [Int. rev. mission]. **Added/Corp** World Council of Churches. Commission on World Mission and Evangelism. World Missionary Conference, Edinburgh, 1910. Continuation Committee. International Missionary Council. **VFOAT** International Review of Mission; IRM. Vol. 1, No. 1 (Jan. 1912)-. Periodical. English. Four times a year (Jan., Apr., July, Oct.). $32.50. World Council of Churches, PO Box 2100, CH 1211 Geneva 2 Switzerland. **Tel** 011 41 22 7906076, FAX 011 41 22 7910361, telex 23 423 OIK CH. **ED** Christopher Duraisingh. **LC** BV2351; .I6. Index Available, published separately, free-automatically sent. cum. index. available on microfilm and microfiche from University Microfilms International (UMI). Documents available from UMI Article Clearinghouse.
**Desc:** A journal of mission and evangelism in six continents.
**Ind/Abst** Acad. Search (July 1993-); Am. Hist. Life (1964-1970); Anthropol. Index; Humanit. Index (1964-1970); Humanit. Source (Jul. 1993-); Index Book Rev. Relig. (1964-1970); INFO-SOUTH Abstr.; Int. Bibliogr. Sociol.; Newsp. Period. Abstr. (1991-); Relig. Index One Period.

SZ/0020-9252
**INTERNATIONALE KIRCHLICHE ZEITSCHRIFT.** [Int. kirchl. Z.]. **VFOAT** Revue Internationale Ecclesiastique; International Church Review. Vol. 1, (1911)-. Periodical. German (English and French). Four times a year (Mar., June, Sept., Dec.). 64.00F Switzerland; $48.75 other. Staempfli & Cie SA, Postfach 8326, CH-3001 Bern Switzerland. **Tel** 011 41 31 3006666, telex 031 911 515 EDMZ CH. **ED** Hans Alfred Frei. **[CCC].** Index available. cum. index. **Bk Rev. Circ:** 580 (ctrl). ***Supersedes*** *Revue Internationale de Theologie.*
**Desc:** Old Catholicism and regular chronicle of the eastern orthodox churches both historical and systematical issues.
**Ind/Abst** New Testam. Abstr.; Old Testam. Abstr.

US/0020-9643
**INTERPRETATION (RICHMOND).** (INTERPRETATION.). [Interpret.]. **Added/Corp** Union Theological Seminary in Virginia. Vol. 1 (Jan. 1947)-. Periodical. English. qt. $22.00 (one year), $41.00 (two year), $56.00 (three year) institutions; $15.50 (one year), $29.00 (two year), $41.00 (three year) individuals, US; $17.00 (one year), $31.50 (two year), $46.00 (three year) individuals, other; $42.32 (one year), $81.64 (two year), $116.96 (three year) institutions, airmail; $37.32 (one year), $72.14 (two year), $106.96 (three year) individuals, airmail; cumulative index free. Union Theological Seminary, 3401 Brook Road, Richmond VA 23227. **Tel** (804)355-0671 Ext. 296, FAX (804)355-3919. **ED** Paul J Achtemeier. **LC** BR1; .I57. **DD** 205. Index available. cum. index. **Bk Rev. Ad Acc. Circ:** 11,000 (ctrl). available on microfilm and microfiche from University Microfilms International (UMI). Documents available from The Genuine Article, UMI Article Clearinghouse. ***Supersedes*** *Union Seminary Review, 0362-904X.*
**Desc:** Articles and essays of "biblical and theological interpretation in the community of faith" for scholars, clergy, and laity of all denominational backgrounds.
**Ind/Abst** Acad. Abstr. (Jan. 1993-); Acad. Ind. [Computer File] (1992-); Acad. Search (Jan. 1993-); Arts Humanit. Citation Index [Full Cov.]; Book Rev. Index; Christ. Period. Index; Expand. Acad. Index (1989-); Guide Soc. Sci. Relig.; Humanit. Index; Index Book Rev. Relig.; Int. Zeitschriftenschau Bibelwissenschaft Grenzgeb.; Middle East Abstr. Index; New Testam. Abstr.; Newsp. Period. Abstr. (1990-); Old Testam. Abstr.; Relig. Index One Period. (1949-); Relig. Theol. Abstr.; Res. Alert [Full Cov.]; Soc. Sci. Cit. Index [Select. Cov.]; U.S. Polit. Sci. Doc.

CN/0712-9904
**INVESTORS' BULLETIN (MILTON).** (INVESTORS' BULLETIN.). [Investors' bull.]. **VAT** Investors' Bulletin (Cambridge); Investors' Bulletin (Willowdale); Investors Bulletin of the Ken Campbell Evangelistic Association. Jan. 1973-. Bulletin. English. Campbell-Reese Evangelistic Team, PO Box 100, Milton Ontario L9T 2Y3 Canada. **DD** 269/.2/06071.

US/0893-6331
**INVITATION. BIBLE STUDIES FOR AGES 3-4. TEACHER.** **Added/Corp** United Methodist Church (U.S.). Board of Discipleship. Curriculum Resources Committee. **VFOAT** Bible Studies for Ages 3-4. Teacher. Vol. 1, No. 1 (Fall 1988)-. Periodical. English. qt. Graded Press, 201 Eighth Avenue South, Box 801, Nashville TN 37202. **Tel** (615)749-6417. ***Continues*** *Children's Bible Study. Ages 3-4. Teacher, 0276-346X.*

US/0893-6366
**INVITATION. BIBLE STUDIES FOR AGES 5-6 (LEAFLETS).** **Added/Corp** United Methodist Church (U.S.). Board of Discipleship. Division of Church School Publications. **VFOAT** Bible Studies for Ages 5-6. Vol. 1, No. 1 (Fall 1988)-. Periodical. English. qt. $11.00 US; $12.00 Canada and Mexico. Graded Press, 201 Eighth Avenue South, Box 801, Nashville TN 37202. **Tel** (615)749-6417. ***Continues*** *Church & Home Leaflets. Ages 4-6, 0276-3435.*

US/0893-6382
**INVITATION. BIBLE STUDIES FOR AGES 5-6. TEACHER.** **Added/Corp** United Methodist Church (U.S.). Board of Discipleship. Division of Church School Publications. **VFOAT** Bible Studies for Ages 5-6. Teacher. Vol. 1, No. 1 (Fall 1988)-. Periodical. English. qt. $17.50 US, $18.50 Canada and Mexico. Graded Press, 201 Eighth Avenue South, Box 801, Nashville TN 37202. **Tel** (615)749-6417. ***Continues*** *Children's Bible study. Ages 4-6. Teacher, 0276-3451.*

US/0893-6390
**INVITATION. BIBLE STUDIES FOR ELEMENTARY A (LEAFLETS).** **Added/Corp** United Methodist Church (U.S.). Board of Discipleship. Division of Church School Publications. **VFOAT** Bible Studies for Elementary A. Vol. 1, No. 1 (Fall 1988)-. Periodical. English. qt. $11.00 US; $12.00 Canada and Mexico. Graded Press, 201 Eighth Avenue South, Box 801, Nashville TN 37202. **Tel** (615)749-6417. ***Continues*** *Church & Home Leaflets. Elementary A, 0278-3533.*

US/0893-679X
**INVITATION. BIBLE STUDIES FOR ELEMENTARY C (LEAFLETS).** **Added/Corp** United Methodist Church (U.S.). Board of Discipleship. Division of Church School Publications. **VFOAT** Bible Studies for Elementary C. Vol. 1, No. 1 (Fall 1988)-. Periodical. English. qt. $11.00 US; $12.00 Canada and Mexico. Graded Press, 201 Eighth Avenue South, Box 801, Nashville TN 37202. **Tel** (615)749-6417. ***Continues*** *Elementary C. Church & Home Leaflets, 0882-794X.*

US/0021-0250
**INWARD LIGHT.** No. 1- Fall 1937-. Periodical. English. ir. $10.00 US; $12.00 Canada and Mexico. Inward Light, 749 Polo Road, Bryn Mawr PA 19010. **Tel** (215)525-6031. **ED** Charles Perry and Eleanor Perry. **DD** 205. **Bk Rev. Circ:** 500.
**Desc:** An organ of expression and intercommunication relating inner life to problems of our time.

BE/0021-0978
**IRENIKON.** [Irenikon]. Vol. 1 (April 1926)-. Periodical. French (English). qt. 190.00F France; $40.00 US; $46.00 Canada. Monastere Benediction, B-5395, Chevetogne Belgium. **Tel** (083)21 17 63. **ED** Don Emmanuel Lanne, Don Maxime Gimenez. **LC** BX1; .I7. Index available. cum. index. **Bk Rev. Circ:** 7,250.
**Desc:** Ecumenism, theology and history of eastern and western churches, economical church news.
**Ind/Abst** Bibliogr. Mission.; Index Book Rev. Relig.; New Testam. Abstr.; Relig. Index One Period. (1963-).

IE/0021-1400
**IRISH THEOLOGICAL QUARTERLY.** [Irish theol. q.]. **Added/Corp** St. Patrick's College (Maynooth, Ireland). Faculty of Theology. Vol. 1 (Jan. 1906)-. Periodical. English. qt (Jan., Apr., July, Oct.). 16.12p UK; 18.20p other. St Patricks College / Theology, Maynooth Ireland. Index available. cum. index. available on microfilm and microfiche from University Microfilms International (UMI).
**Desc:** Covers theological issues.
**Ind/Abst** Bibliogr. Mission.; Canon Law Abstr.; New Testam. Abstr.; Old Testam. Abstr.; Relig. Theol. Abstr.; Abr. Cathol. Period. Lit. Index; Cathol. Period. Lit. Index.

US/8756-3142
**IRON MOUNTAIN.** [Iron mt.]. Summer 1984-. Periodical. English. sa. $9.00. Iron Mountain Journal, 8060 Niwot Road 31, Longmont CO 80501-8693. **DD** 291.

US/0886-6910
**ISKCON REVIEW.** [ISKCON rev.]. Vol. 1, No. 1 (Spring 1985)-. Periodical. English. sa. Free. Bhaktivedanta Institute of Religion and Culture, c/o Subhananda, 41 West Allens Lane, Philadelphia PA 19119. **DD** 294.

US/0748-2280
**ISKCON WORLD REVIEW, THE.** [ISKCON world rev.]. **VFOAT** I.S.K.C.O.N. World Review. Periodical. English. mo. $8.00 (bulk mail), $15.00 (first class mail) US; $16.00 (airmail) other. The Iskcon World Review, PO Box 1487, Culver City CA 90232. **Tel** (310)839-0903. **ED** Uddhava Dasa, Mukunda Goswami, Nandini Dasi. **DD** 294. **Bk Rev. Ad Acc. Circ:** 5,000.
**Desc:** The newspaper of the Hare Krishna Movement, containing news on its worldwide network of temples, cultural centers, vegetarian restaurants, and farming communities.

CN/0021-1761
**ISKRA (GRAND FORKS).** (ISKRA.). **Added/Corp** Union of Spiritual Communities of Christ. No. 28 (Mar. 4 1945)-. Periodical. Multiple languages (English and Russian). Twenty-five times a year. 30.00Can$ Canada; 50.00Can$ others. Iskra Publications, Box 760, Grand Folks British Columbia, V0H 1HO Canada. **Tel** (604)442-8252. **ED** D. E. (Jim) Popoff. **Circ:** 1,000. ***Continues*** *Sten-Gazeta Soiuza Dukhovnikh Obshchin Khrista.*
**Desc:** Publication of Union of Spiritual Communities of Christ, main body in Canada of Doukhobors, centuries old sect espousing nonviolence, world brotherhood, East-West friendship.

UK/0021-1842
**ISLAMIC QUARTERLY, THE.** [Islam. q.]. **Added/Corp** Islamic Cultural Centre (London, England). Vol. 1 (Apr. 1954)-. Periodical. English. qt. £20.00 UK and Europe; £25.00 other. Islamic Culture Center, 146 Park Road, London NW8 7RG England. **Tel** 01 724 3363. **ED** Bashir Ebrahim-Khan. **LC** DS198; .I8. **DD** 956.005. **Bk Rev. Circ:** 2,000 (ctrl). available on microfilm from University Microfilms International (UMI).
**Ind/Abst** Am. Hist. Life (1973-); Index Islam. Lit.; Index Book Rev. Relig.; Int. Bibliogr. Sociol.; Middle East Abstr. Index; Relig. Index One Period.

IT
**ISLAMOCHRISTIANA. ISLAMIYAT MASIHIYAT.** **Added/Corp** Pontificio Istituto di Studi Arabi. **VFOAT** Islamiyat Masimiyat. Vol. 1, (1975)-. Periodical. French (English and Arabic). an (Feb.). L41000.00. Pontificio Istituto di Studi Arabi, Viale di Trastevere 89, 00153 Rome Italy. **Tel** 011 39 6 5882676. **LC** BP172; .I84. **DD** 261.2/7. **Bk Rev. Ad Acc. Circ:** 600.
**Desc:** Christian-Muslim dialogue in history and today comparative theologies and mystics bibliography about these topics.
**Ind/Abst** Bibliogr. Mission.; Index Islam. Lit.

US/8755-402X
**ISRAEL MY GLORY.** (ISRAEL MY GLORY, ISAIAH 46:13.). [Israel my glory]. **Added/Corp** Friends of Israel Gospel Ministry. Friends of Israel Missionary and Relief Society. (Dec. 1942)-. Periodical. English. bm (Feb., Apr., June, Aug., Oct., Dec.). $10.95 (one year), $18.95 (two year), $25.95 (three year) US; $12.95 (one year), $2.95 (two year), $31.95 (three year), Canada; $23.95 (two year minimum), $33.95 (3 year) other. Friends of Israel Gospel Ministry, PO Box 908, Bell Mawr NJ 08099. **ED** Elwood McQuaid. **DD** 266. **Circ:** 220,000 (ctrl).
**Desc:** Official publication of the Friends of Israel Gospel Ministry committed to evangelism, education and edification.

FR/0021-2423
**ISTINA.** [Istina]. **Added/Corp** Centre d'etudes Istina (Boulogne-Billancourt, France). Vol.1 (Jan./Mar. 1954)-. Periodical. French. qt. 325.00F. Centre d'Etudes Istina, 45 rue de la Glaciere, 75013 Paris France. **Tel** 011 33 1 45353704. **ED** RP Dupuy. **LC** BX1781; .I8. Index available. **Ad Acc. Pr Rev. Circ:** 800. available on microfilm and microfiche from University Microfilms International (UMI). ***Continues*** *Russie et Chretiente.*
**Desc:** Ecumenical journal; theological dialogue between Christian churches, Jewish Christian dialogue, religious liberty and human rights in East-European countries.
**Ind/Abst** Bibliogr. Mission.; Index Book Rev. Relig.; Int. Polit. Sci. Abstr.; New Testam. Abstr.; Relig. Index One Period. (1954-).

BL
**ISTO E SENHOR.** ***Title Change.*** No. 982 (July 11, 1988)-No. 1173 (Mar. 25, 1992). Periodical. Portuguese. wk. Editora Tres, Rua William Speers, No 1000, 10 Andar, CEP 05065 Sao Paulo Brazil. **LC** AP66; .I845. **DD** 056/.9. ***Formed by the union of*** *Istoe* ***and*** *Senhor (Sao Paulo, Brazil).* ***Continued by*** *Istoe.*

US/0278-9809
**IT'S GOD'S WORLD.** (19??)-. English. ir. $12.95. God's World Publications, Box 2330, Asheville NC 28802. **Tel** (704)253-8063, (800)951-5437.

SP/0021-325X
**IUS CANONICUM.** **See** Law.

IT
**IUS ECCLESIAE : RIVISTA INTERNAZIONALE DI DIRITTO CANONICO.** See Law.

GW/0072-4238
**JAHRBUCH DER GESELLSCHAFT FUER NIEDERSACHSISCHE KIRCHENGESCHICHTE.** **Main/Corp** Gesellschaft fur Niedersachsische Kirchengeschichte. **Added/Corp** Gesellschaft fur Niedersachsische Kirchengeschichte. Zeitschrift. (1896)-. German. an. **LC** BR857.S3; G4.
**Ind/Abst** BHA : Biblio. Hist. Art.

GW/0075-2541
**JAHRBUCH FUER ANTIKE UND CHRISTENTUM.** [Jahrb. Antike Christ.]. **Added/Corp** Rheinisch-Westfalische Akademie der Wissenschaften. Universitat Bonn. Franz Joseph Dolger-Institut. Vol. 1 (1958)-. German (French and English). an. DM98.00 (cloth bound), DM88.00 (paper bound). Aschendorffsche Verlagsbuchhandlung, Postfach 1124, D-48135 Muenster Germany. **Tel** 011 49 251 690132, telex 08-92 830 WN MS D. **ED** Ernst Dassmann, Klaus Thraede, and Josef Engemann. **LC** BR128.A2; J3. **Bk Rev.** ***Supersedes*** *Antike und Christentum.*
**Desc:** The studies of antiquity and christianity.
**Ind/Abst** Art Archaeol. Tech. Abstr.; BHA : Biblio. Hist. Art; Br. Archaeol. Bibliogr. (-?); New Testam. Abstr.

GW/0448-1488
**JAHRBUCH FUER ANTIKE UND CHRISTENTUM. ERGANZUNGSBAND.** **Added/Corp** Universitat Bonn. Franz Joseph Dolger Institut. Rheinisch-Westfalische Akademie der Wissenschaften. (1964)-. Monographic series. German. Aschendorffsche Verlagsbuchhan, Postfach 1124, D 48135 Muenster Germany. **Tel** 011 49 251 690132.
**Ind/Abst** BHA : Biblio. Hist. Art.

GW
**JAHRBUCH FUER BIBLISCHE THEOLOGIE : JBTH.** **VFOAT** JBTh. No. 1 (1986)-. Monographic series. German. ir. Price varies per volume. Neukirchener Verlag des Erziehungsvereins, Andreas Braem Strasse 18-20, D-47506 Neukirchen Vlu Germany. **Tel** 011 49 2845 392227. **LC** BS543.A1; J33. **DD** 220.6.

GW/0075-2681
**JAHRBUCH FUER LITURGIK UND HYMNOLOGIE.** See Music.

JA/0021-4353
**JAPAN CHRISTIAN ACTIVITY NEWS.** ***Suspended.*** **Added/Corp** National Christian Council of Japan. National Christian Council of Japan. Commission on Public Relations. **VFOAT** JCAN. (1952)-(19??). Periodical. English. mo. ¥3000 Japan; $25.00 US. National Christian Council of Japan, 2 13 18 Nishi Waseda, Room 24, Shinji-ku Tokyo 160 Japan. **Tel** 011 81 3 32030372, telex J27890 CCRAI. **ED** Aiko Y. Carter. **Bk Rev. Circ:** 500.
**Desc:** A newsletter of the National Christian Council in Japan, with news of ecumenical activities in Japan.

●JA/0918-516X
**JAPAN CHRISTIAN REVIEW, THE.** **Added/Corp** Christian Literature Society of Japan. Vol. 58 (1992)-. Periodical. English. an. $24.00. Japan Christian Review, Kyo Bun Kwan, 4 5 1 Ginzachuo Ku, Tokyo 104, Japan. **Tel** 011 81 1 35615549. **LC** BV3440; .J25. ***Continues*** *Japan Christian Quarterly.*

JA/0021-440X
**JAPAN HARVEST.** **Added/Corp** Japan Evangelical Missionary Association. Evangelical Missionary Association of Japan. (195?)-. Periodical. English. qt. $25.00. Japan Evangelical Missionary Association, OCC Building, 2 1 Kanda Surugaddai, Chiyoda-Ku Tokyo 101 Japan. **Tel** 011 81 3 32951949, FAX 011 81 3 32951949. **ED** Katie Sisco. Index available. **Bk Rev. Ad Acc. Circ:** 1,100 (ctrl).
**Desc:** The magazine for today's Japan missionary with special news of what's happening across Japan and around the world.

JA
**JAPAN MISSION JOURNAL.** (19??)-. Bulletin. English. qt. $35.00. Oriens Institute for Religious Research, 2-28-5 Matsubara Setagaya-ku, Tokyo 156 Japan. **Tel** 011 81 3 33257601, telex 011 81 3 3255322. ***Continues*** *Japan Missionary Bulletin.*

JA/0021-4531
**JAPAN MISSIONARY BULLETIN, THE.** ***Title Change.*** **Added/Corp** Katorikku Chuo Kyogikai. Fukyo Iinkai (Japan) Oriensu Shukyo Kenkyujo. **VFOAT** Fukyo. Vol. 13 (Jan./Feb. 1959)-(19??). Bulletin. English (Japanese). qt. Oriens Institute for Religious Research, 2-28-5 Matsubara Setagaya-ku, Tokyo 156 Japan. **Tel** 011 81 3 33257601, telex 011 81 3 3255322. **ED** M. Christiaens. **Bk Rev. Ad Acc. Circ:** 600. ***Continues*** *Missionary Bulletin.* ***Continued by*** *Japan Mission Journal.*
**Ind/Abst** Bibliogr. Mission.; Missionalia.

JA/0304-1042
**JAPANESE JOURNAL OF RELIGIOUS STUDIES.** **Added/Corp** Kokusai Shukyo Kenkyujo (Japan). (Mar. 1974)-. Periodical. English. Three times a year. $35.00 (Institutions); $25.00 (Individuals). Nanzan University, 18 Yamazato-cho, Showa-ku Nagoya 466 Japan. **Tel** 011 81 52 8323111, FAX 011 81 52 8336157. **ED** Paul L. Swanson. **LC** BL2202; .J35. **DD** 200/.5. Index available. cum. index. **Bk Rev**, (Qty: 12-16). **Pr Rev. Circ:** 300. available on microfilm and microfiche from University Microfilms International (UMI). ***Supersedes*** *Contemporary Religions in Japan.*
**Desc:** Presents studies in Japanese religious traditions.
**Ind/Abst** Index Book Rev. Relig.; Int. Bibliogr. Sociol.; Relig. Index One Period.; Relig. Theol. Abstr.

JA/0448-8954
**JAPANESE RELIGIONS.** [Jpn. relig.]. **Added/Corp** Nihon Kiristokyo Kyogikai. Shukyo Kenkyujo. Shoshukyo Kenkyu Senta (Japan). (1959)-. Periodical. English (Japanese). Twice a year. $30.00. NCC Center, Study Japanese Religions, Karasuma, Shimotachiuri Kyoto 602 Japan. **Tel** 11 81 75 4321945, FAX 11 81 75 4321945. **ED** Yuki Hideo. **LC** BL2202; .J37. **DD** 291/.0952. **Bk Rev**, (Qty: 3-5). **Ad Acc. Circ:** 600. available on microfilm. ***Continues*** *Quarterly Notes (Shoshukyo Kenkyu Senta (Japan)).*
**Desc:** Studies of Japanese religions and the encounter between Christianity and Eastern religions.
**Ind/Abst** Index Book Rev. Relig.; Int. Bibliogr. Sociol.; Missionalia; Relig. Index One Period. (1959-); Relig. Theol. Abstr. (1959-).

UK
**JARROW LECTURES.** Monographic series. English. an. Price varies per volume. St Pauls Church Jarrow, Team Vicar, 28 Kitchener Terrace, Jarrow T&W NE32 5PU England.

II/0970-1125
**JEEVADHARA (ENGLISH ED.).** (JEEVADHARA; A JOURNAL OF CHRISTIAN INTERPRETATION.). [Jeevadhara]. Vol. 1, No. 1 (Jan./Feb. 1971)-. Periodical. English (Malayalam). Six times a year (Jan., Mar., May, July, Sept., Nov.). $18.00. Theology Center, Kottayam 686 041, Kerala India. **Tel** 091 481 597430. **(Subscription address:** Prints India, 11 Darya Ganj, New Delhi 110002 India.**)** **ED** Joseph Constantine Manalel. Index available. **Bk Rev. Ad Acc. Pr Rev. Circ:** 2000.
**Desc:** A interest in every human problem. Whole area of theology is divided into six areas: anthropology, scriptures, doctrinal theology, ecclesiology, ecumenism and practical theology.
**Ind/Abst** Bibliogr. Mission.; New Testam. Abstr.; Old Testam. Abstr.

CN/0383-2635
**JESUS, MARIE ET NOTRE TEMPS.** [Jesus Marie notre temps]. **VFOAT** Notre Temps. V. 4, No. 2- Jan. 1974-. Periodical. French. mo. Jesus Marie et Notre Temps, 5055 Saint Dominique, Montreal Quebec H2T 1V1 Canada. **Tel** (514)271-7731. **DD** 232.91/05. ***Continues*** *Jesus Marie et Notre Temps, 0383-2627;* ***Absorbed*** *Annoncer Jesus-Christ, 0705-1018.*

FR/1154-7138
**JESUS PARIS. 1973.** (JESUS LES CAHIERS DU LIBRE AVENIR.). (1973)-. Periodical. French. Four times a year (Mar., June, Sept., Dec.). 120.00F France; 130.00F other. Jesus Michel Pinchon, Presbytere Gouville, 27240 Damville France. **Tel** 011 33 32 298316. **ED** Georges Levesque. **UDC** 232. Index available. cum. index. **Bk Rev**, (Qty: 4). **Ad Acc, Adv Mgr:** M. Ponchon. **Circ:** 2,500 (ctrl).

CN/0822-5559
**JEUNESSE FRANCOIS D'ASSISE.** (JEUNESSE FRANCOIS D'ASSISE : BULLETIN.). [Jeun. Francois Assise]. **Added/Corp** Jeunesse Francois d'Assise. **VAT** Bulletin - Jeunesse Francois d'Assiee. (1983)-. Bulletin. French. bm. Free. Jeunesse Francois d'Assise, C P 5185, Beauport Quebec G1E 6B5 Canada. **DD** 248.8/3/05.

CN/0828-9662
**JIM TAYLOR'S CURRENTS.** (CURRENTS.). [Jim Taylor's currents]. Vol. 1, No. 1 (Sept. 1984)-. Periodical. English. Five times a year. $10.00 Canada, US; $14.00 other. Wood Lake Books Inc., PO Box 700, Winfield British Columbia V0H 2C0 Canada. **Tel** (604)766-2778. **ED** Jim Taylor. **DD** 248.4/05. **Bk Rev. Ad Acc. Circ:** 350.

CN
**JOHN MILTON MAGAZINE.** Periodical. English. John Milton Society for the Blind, Room 455, 475 Riverside Drive, New York NY 10115. available in large print; available in braille.
**Desc:** A digest of informative and devotional reading materials selected from more than 50 religious periodicals.

CN/0703-2757
**JOSEMARIA ESCRIVA DE BALAGUER (EDITION FRANCAISE).** (JOSEMARIA ESCRIVA DE BALAGUER : FONDATEUR DE L'OPUS DEI : BULLETIN D'INFORMATION.). [Josemaria Escriva de Balaguer]. No. 1, (Dec. 1976)-. Bulletin. French (English, Portuguese, German, Dutch, Polish, Spanish and Italian). ir. Free. Vice-Postulation de l'Opus dei au Canada, 5643 rue Plantagenet, Montreal Quebec H3T 1S3 Canada. **Tel** (514)731-5500. **DD** 271/.095. **Circ:** 75,000 (ctrl).
**Desc:** Informs on the life, spirit, and apostolic initiatives of the Servant of God Monsignor Josemaria Escriva de Balaguer, founder of Opus Dei.

CN/0703-9093
**JOSEMARIA ESCRIVA DE BALAGUER (ENGLISH EDITION).** (JOSEMARIA ESCRIVA DE BALAGUER; BULLETIN.). No. 1 (Jan. 1977)-. Bulletin. English (French, Portuguese, German, Dutch, Polish, Spanish and Italian). ir. Free. Vice-Postulation de l'Opus dei au Canada, 5643 rue Plantagenet, Montreal Quebec H3T 1S3 Canada. **Tel** (514)731-5500. **DD** 255.094. **Circ:** 75,000 (ctrl).
**Desc:** Informs on the life, spirit, and apostolic initiatives of the Servant of God Monsignor Josemaria Escriva de Balaguer, founder of Opus Dei.

US/0021-7603
**JOSEPHITE HARVEST, THE.** **Added/Corp** Josephite Fathers. (196?)-. Periodical. English. Four times a year. $2.00. St Joseph's Society, 1130 North Calvert Street, Baltimore MD 21202. **Tel** (410)727-3386. ***Continues*** *Colored Harvest.*

US/0021-8235
**JOURNAL FOR ANTHROPOSOPHY.** **Added/Corp** Anthroposophical Society of America. (Spring 1965)-. Periodical. English. Twice a year (May & Nov.). $12.00. Journal of Anthroposophy, 3700 South Ranch Road 12, Drippings Springs TX 78620. **ED** Christy Barnes and Arthur Zajone. **LC** BP595.A1; J67. **DD** 212/.53. **Bk Rev. Ad Acc. Circ:** 1,800. ***Supersedes*** *Anthropological Society of America. Newsletter.*
**Desc:** New, practical impulses in science, art, education and medicine arising from the insights of the spiritual science by Rudolf Steiner.

US/0889-5848
**JOURNAL FOR CHRISTIAN STUDIES, A.** [J. Christ. stud.]. **Added/Corp** Lincoln Christian Seminary (Ill.) Chi-Lambda Fellowship (Lincoln, Ill.). Vol. 1, No. 1 (Oct. 1981)-. Periodical. English. an. $12.00. Chi Lambda Fellowship, 100 Campus View Drive, Lincoln IL 62656. **Tel** (217)732-3168. **(Subscription address:** Chi Lambda of Fellowship, PO Box 178, 866 Lincoln Christian Seminary, Lincoln IL 62656.**)** **ED** Dennis Duret. **DD** 205. **Bk Rev**, (Qty: 2/yr).

US/1057-266X
**JOURNAL FOR PREACHERS.** [J. preach.]. Vol. 1, No. 1 (1977)-. Periodical. English. qt. $10.00 US; $15.00 other. Journal for Preachers, PO Box 520, Decatur GA 30030. **Tel** (404)378-8821. **ED** T. Erskine Clarke. **DD** 251.
**Ind/Abst** Index Book Rev. Relig.; Relig. Index One Period. (1983-).

US/0021-8294
**JOURNAL FOR THE SCIENTIFIC STUDY OF RELIGION.** [J. sci. study relig.]. **Added/Corp** Society for the Scientific Study of Religion. Vol. 1 (Oct. 1961)-. Periodical. English. qt (4 issues). $45.00. Society for the Scientific Study of Religion, 1365 Stone Hall, Purdue University, West Lafayette IN 47907-1365. **Tel** (317)494-6286, FAX (317)496-1476. **ED** David G. Bromley (editor's address: 539 Cabel Hall, University of Virginia, Charlottesville, VA 22903). **LC** BL1; .J6. **CODEN** JSSRBT. **Bk Rev. Ad Acc, Adv Mgr:** Harve Horowitz, **Tel** (410)997-0763. **Pr Rev. Circ:** 3,000. available on microfilm and microfiche from University Microfilms International (UMI). Documents available from The Genuine Article, UMI Article Clearinghouse.
**Desc:** Theoretical, methodological and empirical studies and reviews of current books on religious institutions and experiences.
**Ind/Abst** Abstr. Res. Pastor. Care Couns. (1974-); Acad. Search (July 1993-); Am. Hist. Life (1974-); Am. Bibliogr. Slavic East Europ. Stud.; Arts Humanit. Citation Index [Full Cov.]; Bibliogr. Mission.; Crim. Justice Abstr. (-199?); Curr. Contents Arts Humanit.; Except. Hum. Exp.; Expand. Acad. Index (1989-); Guide Soc. Sci. Relig.; High. Educ. Abstr. (1975-); Humanit. Index; Humanit. Source (Jul. 1993-); Index Islam. Lit.; Index Book Rev. Relig.; INFO-SOUTH Abstr.; Int. Bibliogr. Sociol.; Mag. Search; Middle East Abstr. Index; MLA Int. Bibl. Books Artic. Mod. Lang. Lit.; Newsp. Period. Abstr. (1991-); Old Testam. Abstr.; Peace Res. Abstr. J. (1973, 1985, 1987); Psychol. Abstr. (1961-); PsycINFO; PsycLit; Ref. Sources; Relig. Index One Period. (1961-); Relig. Theol. Abstr.; Res. Alert [Full Cov.]; Soc. Plann. Policy Dev. Abstr.; Soc. Sci. Cit. Index [Select. Cov.]; Soc. Welf. Soc. Plan./Policy Soc. Dev.; Sociol. Abstr. [Full Cov.].

SA/1011-7601
**JOURNAL FOR THE STUDY OF RELIGION.** **Added/Corp** Association for the Study of Religion (Southern Africa). **VFOAT** JSR. Vol. 1, No. 1 (Mar. 1988)-. Periodical. English. Twice a year (March, Sep.). R20.00 Africa; $35.00 US & Canada; $45.00 other. Journal for the Study of Religion, Department of Religious Studies, University of Natal, PO Box 375, Pietermaritzburg, 3200 South Africa. **Tel** 011 27 331 955571. **ED** M. H. Prozesky and P. S. Maxwell. Index

available (Bound in 4th iss. (Free)). **Bk Rev**. **Ad Acc**. **Pr Rev**. ***Continues*** *Religion in Southern Africa, 0258-3224.*
**Desc:** Covers the study of religion, science of religion, history of religions, philosophy of religion, and comparative religion.
**Ind/Abst** Index Book Rev. Relig.; Relig. Index One Period.

UK/0951-8207
**JOURNAL FOR THE STUDY OF THE PSEUDEPIGRAPHA.** **VFOAT** Journal for the Study of the Pseudepigrapha and Related Literature. Issue 1 (1987)-. Periodical. English. Three times a year. Sheffield Academic Press Ltd, 343 Fulwood Road, Sheffield S10 3BP England. **Tel** 011 44 742 670044, 011 44 742 668431, FAX 011 44 742 660291. **(Subscription address:** US/ PO Box 620000, Orlando, FL 32891-8340; UK/ Foots Cray High Street, Sidcup, Kent DA14 5HP England; Aus-NZ/ Locked Bag 16, Marrickville NSW 2204 Australia; telephone: US/ (800)543-9534, FAX: (407)363-9661; UK/ 081-300-3322, FAX: 081-309-0807**)**
**Ind/Abst** Index Book Rev. Relig.; Relig. Index One Period.; Relig. Theol. Abstr.

US/1058-3084
**JOURNAL FROM THE RADICAL REFORMATION, A.** (A JOURNAL FROM THE RADICAL REFORMATION: A TESTIMONY TO BIBLICAL UNITARIANISM.). [J. radic. reform.]. **Added/Corp** Church of God General Conference. **VFOAT** Radical Reformation. Vol. 1, No. 1 (Fall 1991)-. Periodical. English. Four times a year (Seasonally). $20.00. Atlanta Bible College, PO Box 1000, Morrow GA 30260. **Tel** (404)362-0052. **ED** Kent Ross, Kent Ross and Mark Mattison. **LC** BX6181; .J68. **DD** 286.7/3. Index available. cum. index. **Bk Rev**, (Qty: 8-12). **Pr Rev. Circ:** 350 (ctrl).
**Desc:** Examines historical and theological issues related to the anti-Trinitarian branch of the Radical Reformation, especially in 17th-Century Poland. This journal represents contemporary Biblical unitarianism with a strong emphasis on eschatology.
**Ind/Abst** New Testam. Abstr.; Relig. Theol. Abstr.

CN/1186-6020
**JOURNAL JEUNESSE TIMOTHEE.** [J. jeun. Timothee]. (1990)-. Periodical. French. mo. Journal Jeunesse Timothee, CP 2521, Sherbrooke, Quebec J1J 3Y4 Canada. **DD** 248.8.

CN/0838-0430
**JOURNAL OF BAHA'I STUDIES.** (THE JOURNAL OF BAHAI STUDIES / LA REVUE DES ETUDES BAHAIES.). [J. Baha'i stud.]. **Added/Corp** Association for Bahai Studies. **VFOAT** Revue des Etudes Bahaies. **VAT** Revista de Estudios Baha'is. Vol. 1, No. 1 (1989)-. Periodical. English (French and Spanish; summaries and/or abstracts in English, French and Spanish). qt. 30.00Can$ institution. Association for Bahai Studies, 34 Copernicus Street, Ottawa, Ontario K1N 7K4 Canada. **Tel** (613)233-1903. **ED** Christine Zerbinis. **LC** BP300; .J68. **DD** 297/.93/05. **Bk Rev**. **Pr Rev. Circ:** 1,800.
**Desc:** Publishes current studies on the meanings of the texts that comprise the writings of the Bahai Faith and examines their application to contemporary life and thought.

●US/1063-2166
**JOURNAL OF BIBLICAL COUNSELING, THE.** [J. biblic. couns.]. **Added/Corp** Christian Counseling & Educational Foundation. (1993)-. Periodical. English. Three times a year (Fall, Winter, Spring). $18.00 (individuals), $24.00 (institutions), US; $23.00 (individuals), $29.00 (institutions), other. Christian Counseling & Education Foundation, 1803 East Willow Grove Avenue, Glenside PA 19038. **Tel** (215)884-7676, FAX (215)884-9435. **ED** David A.C. Powlison. **DD** 253. **Bk Rev**, (Qty: 6-10). **Circ:** 1,700. ***Continues*** *Journal of Pastoral Practice, 0196-9072.*
**Desc:** Contains articles on counseling, preaching and book reviews, all written from and vantage point that is distinctly biblical.
**Ind/Abst** Curr. Thoughts Trends.

US/1050-3404
**JOURNAL OF BIBLICAL ETHICS IN MEDICINE.** **See** Ethics.

US/0021-9231
**JOURNAL OF BIBLICAL LITERATURE.** **See** Religion and Theology-Bible.

SA/1015-2296
**JOURNAL OF BLACK THEOLOGY IN SOUTH AFRICA.** [J. black theol. S. Afr.]. (1988)-. Periodical. English. sa (2 issues). $14.00 Africa; R23.00 South Africa; $24.00 other (institutions). Journal of Black Theology, PO Box 392, UNISA, Pretoria 0001 South Africa. **Tel** 011 27 12 4294302, 011 27 12 4294571, FAX 011 27 12 3730369. **(Subscription address:** Journal of Black Theology, c/o the editor, PO Box 287, Atteridgeville 0008 South Africa.**)** **ED** Takatso A. Mofokeng.
**Desc:** A forum for the exchange of theological ideas and a contribution to the development of black theology in South Africa and elsewhere.

●US/1065-9366
**JOURNAL OF BOOK OF MORMON STUDIES, THE.** **Added/Corp** Foundation for Ancient Research and Mormon Studies. (1992)-. Periodical. English. sa. $7.95 (single issue). Foundation for Ancient Research and Mormon Studies, PO Box 7131, University Station, Provo UT 84602. **Tel** (801)378-3295.

US/0737-769X
**JOURNAL OF CHINESE RELIGIONS.** [J. Chin. relig.]. **Added/Corp** Society for the Study of Chinese Religions (U.S.). No. 10 (Fall 1982)-. Periodical. English. an. $25.00. Society for the Study of Chinese Religions, Bard College, Annadale on Hudson NY 12504. **Tel** (914)758-1539. **(Subscription address:** University of Pittsburgh / Department of Religious Studies, Pittsburgh PA 15260.**)** **ED** Julian F. Pas. **LC** BL1802; .S65a. **DD** 299/.51/05. **Bk Rev**. **Circ:** 350. ***Continues*** *Bulletin (Society for the Study of Chinese Religions (U.S.)), 0271-3446.*
**Desc:** Strives to provide information on current research in the area of Chinese religions, and to share ideas and materials for courses in different aspects of Chinese religious experiences.

US/0146-0366
**JOURNAL OF CHRISTIAN COUNSELING.** **Added/Corp** Institute of Christian Counseling. Vol. 1 (Winter 1977)-. Periodical. English. qt. $12.00. PO Box 548, Mt Pleasant MI 48858. **Tel** (517)773-2674. **LC** BV4012; .J67. **DD** 253.5/05.

AT/0021-9657
**JOURNAL OF CHRISTIAN EDUCATION.** [J. Christ. educ.]. **Added/Corp** Australian Teacher's Christian Fellowship. (1957)-. Periodical. English. Three times a year. 40.00Aus$ (institution); 30.00Aus$ (individual). Australian Teachers Christian Fellowship, 16 Mill Hill Road, Bondi Junction 2022, Australia. **Tel** 011 61 2 3691688. **ED** Neil Holm. Index available. cum. index. **Bk Rev**. **Circ:** 900. available on microfilm from University Microfilms International (UMI).
**Desc:** Considers implications of Christianity on all aspects of education. Articles from several countries examine, philosophically, the Christian views on education.
**Ind/Abst** Aust. Educ. Index (1977-); Christ. Period. Index (19??-); Index Book Rev. Relig.; Relig. Index One Period. (1973-); Relig. Theol. Abstr.

US/0738-2944
**JOURNAL OF CHRISTIAN HEALING, THE.** [J. christ. heal.]. **Added/Corp** Institute for Christian Healing (Narberth, Pa.) Association of Christian Therapists (Rochester, N.Y.). (1979)-. Periodical. English. Four times a year. $24.00. Journal of Christian Healing, 103 Dudley Avenue, Narberth PA 19072. **Tel** (215)667-0460. **ED** Douglas W. Schoeninger. **LC** BT732; .J68. **DD** 150.19/0882. Index available. cum. index. **Bk Rev**. **Ad Acc**. **Circ:** 1,450.
**Desc:** Interdisciplinary journal advancing the knowledge and practice of healing through Jesus Christ by the power of the Holy Spirit of all dimensions of the person - physical, emotional, relational and spiritual.

US/0741-6075
**JOURNAL OF CHRISTIAN JURISPRUDENCE.** ***Suspended.*** **See** Law.

US/0743-2550
**JOURNAL OF CHRISTIAN NURSING.** **See** Medical Science and Technology-Nursing.

US/0360-1420
**JOURNAL OF CHRISTIAN RECONSTRUCTION, THE.** **Added/Corp** Chalcedon Foundation. Vol. 1 (Summer 1974)-. Periodical. English. ir. Price varies. Chalcedon, PO Box 158, Vallecito CA 95251. **Tel** (209)736-4365. **ED** Garry J. Moes (editor's address: Box 2066, Murphys CA 95247; phone: (209)728-3510). **LC** BR1; .J62. **DD** 230/.05. **Bk Rev**. **Ad Acc**. **Circ:** 1,500 (ctrl). available on microfilm and microfiche from University Microfilms International (UMI).
**Desc:** A compendium of original monographs and reviews applying Christian principles of analyses to contemporary and historical situations, persons, and trends.
**Ind/Abst** Christ. Period. Index.

US/0021-969X
**JOURNAL OF CHURCH AND STATE.** **See** Political Science.

US/0894-2838
**JOURNAL OF COMMUNICATION AND RELIGION, THE.** [J. commun. relig.]. **Added/Corp** Religious Speech Communication Association. Vol. 10, No. 1 (March 1987)-. Periodical. English. Twice a year (Mar. & Sept.). $10.00 US; $12.00 other. Religious Speech Communication Association, c/o Dr Roxane Lulofs - RSCA Executive Secratary, Department of English and Communication, Azusa Pcific University, 901 East Alosta Avenue, Azusa CA 91702. **Tel** (818)815-6000, FAX (818)969-7180. **ED** Ronald Arnett. **DD** 251. Index available. **Bk Rev**. **Circ:** 275. ***Continues*** *Religious Communication Today.*
**Desc:** Solicits manuscripts on any aspect of religious speech communication no matter what the persuasion. Any recognized research approach is acceptable.
**Ind/Abst** Index Book Rev. Relig.; Relig. Index One Period.; Relig. Theol. Abstr. (199?-).

US/0041-7211
**JOURNAL OF CURRENT SOCIAL ISSUES.** [J. curr. soc. issues]. V. 9, No. 5- Spring 1971-. Periodical. English. qt. $3.00. United Church of Christ / New York, 287 Park Avenue South, New York NY 10010. **LC** BX9884.A1; U48A. **DD** 261.8/3/05. available on microfilm and microfiche from University Microfilms International (UMI). ***Continues*** *Journal - United Church of Christ, Division of Higher Education.*
**Ind/Abst** Am. Hist. Life (1968-1971).

II/0253-7222
**JOURNAL OF DHARMA.** [J. Dharma]. **Added/Corp** Dharmaram College. Centre for the Study of World Religions. Dharma Research Association. Vol. 1 (July 1975)-. Periodical. English. Four times a year. $28.00 (one year), $78.00 (three years). Journal of Dharma, Dharmaram College, Bangalore 560-029 India. **Tel** 805 536866, 805 536867, FAX 805 536046. **(Subscription address:** Prints India, 11 Darya Ganj, New Delhi 110002 India.**)** **ED** Dr. Thomas Manninezhath. **LC** BL1; .J62. **DD** 291/.05. Index available in last issue of volume--attached. **Bk Rev**, (Qty: 50/year). **Pr Rev. Circ:** 1,200. available on microfilm and microfiche from University Microfilms International (UMI). Documents available from The Genuine Article.
**Desc:** Published by an international team of scholars coming from and specializing in various religious, cultural and philosophical traditions.
**Ind/Abst** Arts Humanit. Citation Index [Full Cov.]; Bibliogr. Mission. (1980-); Curr. Contents Arts Humanit.; Index Book Rev. Relig.; Missionalia; Philos. Index; Relig. Index One Period. (1980-); Relig. Theol. Abstr.; Res. Alert [Full Cov.]; Soc. Sci. Cit. Index [Select. Cov.].

●US/1067-6341
**JOURNAL OF EARLY CHRISTIAN STUDIES.** [J. early Christ. stud.]. **Added/Corp** North American Patristic Society. Vol. 1, No. 1 (Spring 1993)-. Periodical. English. qt. $56.00 US; $61.90 Canada and Mexico; $62.90 other. Johns Hopkins University Press, 2715 North Charles Street, Baltimore MD 21218-4319. **Tel** (410)516-6987, FAX (410)516-6968. **LC** BR66; .J68. **DD** 270.1/05. ***Continues*** *Second Century (Abilene, Tex.), 0276-7899.*
**Ind/Abst** Arts Humanit. Citation Index [Full Cov.]; New Testam. Abstr.; Relig. Index One Period.; Soc. Sci. Cit. Index [Select. Cov.].

UK/0022-0469
**JOURNAL OF ECCLESIASTICAL HISTORY, THE.** [J. eccles. hist.]. Vol. 1 (April 1950)-. Academic Scholarly Publication. English. qt. $169.00 US, Canada & Mexico; £93.00 other. Cambridge University Press, The Edinburgh Building, Shaftesbury Road, Cambridge CB2 2RU United Kingdom. **Tel** 011 44 223 312393, FAX 011 44 223 325959. **(Subscription address:** Cambridge University Press / North America, 110 Midland Avenue, Port Chester NY 10573.**)** **ED** Brendan Bradshaw and Martin Brett. **LC** BR140; .J6. **DD** 270.05. Index Available, published separately, free-automatically sent. **Bk Rev**. available on microfilm and microfiche from University Microfilms International (UMI). Documents available from The Genuine Article, UMI Article Clearinghouse.
**Desc:** Publishes material on all aspects of the history of the Christian Church. Deals with the Church both as an institution and in its relations with other religions and society at large. Each volume includes about twenty articles and roughly two hundred reviews, and short notices of recently published books relevant to the interests of the journal's readers.
**Ind/Abst** Acad. Search (Jan. 1994-); Am. Hist. Life (1954-); Arts Humanit. Citation Index [Full Cov.]; BHA : Biblio. Hist. Art; Br. Archaeol. Bibliogr.; Br. Humanit. Index; Curr. Contents Arts Humanit.; Expand. Acad. Index (1989-); Guide Soc. Sci. Relig.; Hist. Source (July 1993-); Humanit. Index; Humanit. Source (Jul. 1993-); Index Book Rev. Relig.; INFO-SOUTH Abstr.; Mag. Search; New Testam. Abstr.; Newsp. Period. Abstr. (1991-); Relig. Index One Period. (1950-); Relig. Theol. Abstr.; Res. Alert [Full Cov.]; Romant. Move.; Soc. Sci. Cit. Index [Select. Cov.].

US/0022-0558
**JOURNAL OF ECUMENICAL STUDIES.** [J. ecum. stud.]. **Added/Corp** Council on the Study of Religion. Vol. 1 (Winter 1964)-. Periodical. English. qt. $30.00 (one year), $55.00 (two year), $75.00 (three year). Journal of Ecumenical Studies, Temple University (022-38), Philadelphia PA 19122. **Tel** (215)204-7714, FAX (215)204-4569. **ED** Leonard Swidler. **LC** BX1; .J6. **DD** 262/.001. Index available in last issue of volume--attached. **Bk Rev**, (Qty: 200). **Ad Acc**, **Adv Mgr:** Nancy Krody. **Pr Rev. Circ:** 1,800 (ctrl). available in microform from Hein and Company. Documents available from The Genuine Article, UMI Article Clearinghouse. ***Absorbed*** *College Theology Notes.*
**Desc:** Articles, reviews and abstracts related to interreligious, interideological dialogue, worldwide.
**Ind/Abst** Acad. Ind. [Computer File] (1992-); Acad. Search (July 1992-); Am. Hist. Life (1970-); Am. Bibliogr.

Slavic East Europ. Stud.; Arts Humanit. Citation Index [Full Cov.]; Bibliogr. Mission.; Curr. Contents Arts Humanit.; Expand. Acad. Index (1989-); Guide Soc. Sci. Relig.; Humanit. Index; Humanit. Source (Jul. 1993-); Index Book Rev. Relig.; INFO-SOUTH Abstr.; Int. Zeitschriftenschau Bibelwissenschaft Grenzgeb.; Mag. Search; Middle East Abstr. Index; Missionalia; New Testam. Abstr.; Newsp. Period. Abstr. (1991-); Old Testam. Abstr.; Relig. Index One Period. (1964-); Relig. Theol. Abstr.; Res. Alert [Full Cov.]; Soc. Sci. Cit. Index [Select. Cov.]; Abr. Cathol. Period. Lit. Index; Cathol. Period. Lit. Index.

NE/0922-2936
**JOURNAL OF EMPIRICAL THEOLOGY : JET.** **VFOAT** JET; J E T. Vol. 1 (1988)-. English. sa. J H Kok Pharos Publishing House, Postbus 130, 8260 AC Kampen Netherlands. **Tel** 31 520292555.
**Ind/Abst** Index Book Rev. Relig.; Relig. Index One Period.

US/8755-4178
**JOURNAL OF FEMINIST STUDIES IN RELIGION.** [J. fem. stud. relig.]. **VFOAT** JFSR. Vol. 1, No. 1 (Spring 1985)-. Periodical. English. sa. $15.60. T & T Clark Ltd., 59 George Street, Edinburgh EH2 2LQ Scotland. **Tel** 011 44 31 2254703, FAX 011 44 31 2204260. **(Subscription address:** Scholars Press, PO Box 15399, Atlanta, GA 30333**) ED** J. Plaskow and E. S. Fiorenza. **LC** HQ1393; .J68. **DD** 261.8/3442. **Bk Rev. Ad Acc. Circ:** 1,000. available on microfilm and microfiche from University Microfilms International (UMI). Documents available from The Genuine Article, UMI Article Clearinghouse.
**Desc:** Feminist research in religion. Encourages discussion and dialogue among men and women of differing feminist perspectives on studies in religion.
**Ind/Abst** Acad. Search (Jan. 1993-); Arts Humanit. Citation Index [Full Cov.]; Curr. Contents Arts Humanit.; Expand. Acad. Index (1989-); Guide Soc. Sci. Relig.; Humanit. Index; Humanit. Source (Jul. 1993-); Index Book Rev. Relig.; INFO-SOUTH Abstr.; Mag. Search; New Testam. Abstr.; Newsp. Period. Abstr. (1991-); Relig. Index One Period.; Relig. Theol. Abstr.; Res. Alert [Full Cov.]; Soc. Sci. Cit. Index [Select. Cov.]; Women Stud. Abstr.

US/0885-4726
**JOURNAL OF HEALTH CARE CHAPLAINCY.** [J. health care chaplain.]. **VFOAT** Health Care Chaplaincy; JHCC. Vol. 1, No. 1 (Fall/Winter 1987)-. Periodical. English. sa (Published during the academic year). $85.00 US; $119.00 other. The Haworth Press Inc, 10 Alice Street, Binghamton NY 13904-1580. **Tel** (607)722-5857, (800)3-HAWORTH, FAX (607)722-1424. **ED** Laurel Burton (editor's address: 1210 North Woodrine Avenue, Oak Park, IL 60302). **LC** BV4335; .J63. **DD** 259/.4/05. **NLM** W1; JO67BGI. **Bk Rev. Ad Acc. Pr Rev. Acid Free. Circ:** 269. available on microfilm and microfiche from University Microfilms International (UMI). Documents available from Haworth Document Delivery Service.
**Desc:** Devoted to promoting both foundational and applied interdisciplinary research related to chaplaincy as practiced in community hospitals, medical centers, nursing homes, and other health care institutions. Publishes work from both the academic and professional communities that pertains to pastoral care issues.
**Ind/Abst** Health Plan. Adminis.; Hospit. Health Admin. Index (1987-).

US
**JOURNAL OF HISPANIC LATINO THEOLOGY.** Periodical. English. qt. $20.00 (one year), $39.00 (two year) US; $24.00 (one year), $47.00 (two year) other. Liturgical Press, St. Johns Abbey, Collegeville MN 56321. **Tel** (612)363-2213, (800)858-5450, FAX (612)363-3299, (800)445-5899.

US/0890-0132
**JOURNAL OF INTERDISCIPLINARY STUDIES.** [J. interdiscip. stud.]. **Added/Corp** Institute for Interdisciplinary Research (Santa Monica, Calif.) International Christian Studies Association. Vol. 1, No. 1/2 (1989)-. Academic Scholarly Publication. English (German and French). an. $25.00 (institutions), $15.00 (individuals). Institute for Interdisciplinary Res, 2828 Third Street/Suite 11, Santa Monica CA 90405. **Tel** (310)396-0517. **ED** Oskar Gruenwald. **LC** BD255; .J68. **DD** 001/.05. **CODEN** JISTE2. Index available. cum. index. **Bk Rev**, (Qty: 10-12 per year). **Ad Acc. Pr Rev. Circ:** 1,200.
**Desc:** Offers a scholarly forum for recovering the lost unity of Renaissance learning while affirming transcendental values and faith. Its themes and insights are cumulative, exploring the principles of liberty, methodological pluralism, complementarity and dialogue.
**Ind/Abst** Index Book Rev. Relig.; Relig. Index One Period.; Soc. Plann. Policy Dev. Abstr.; Abr. Cathol. Period. Lit. Index; Cathol. Period. Lit. Index.

US/0748-0814
**JOURNAL OF LAW AND RELIGION, THE.** **See** Law.

CN/0824-5053
**JOURNAL OF MENNONITE STUDIES.** [J. Mennon. stud.]. **Added/Corp** University of Winnipeg. Chair in Mennonite Studies. Canadian Mennonite Bible College. Manitoba Mennonite Historical Society. Mennonite Literary Society. Vol. 1, (1983)-. English (German). an (Aug.). 10.00Can$. University of Winnipeg / Mennonite Study, 515 Portage Avenue, Winnipeg Manitoba R3B 2E9 Canada. **Tel** (204)786-9895. **ED** Harry Loewen. **LC** BX8101; .J68. **DD** 289.7/71. **Bk Rev. Ad Acc. Pr Rev. Circ:** 400.
**Desc:** Canadian interdisciplinary journal dealing with mennonite issues.
**Ind/Abst** Am. Hist. Life (1988-).

●US/1053-8755
**JOURNAL OF MINISTRY IN ADDICTION & RECOVERY.** **See** Drug Abuse and Alcoholism.

US/0094-7342
**JOURNAL OF MORMON HISTORY.** V. 1-1974-. English. sa. $10.00, $7.50 (students). Mormon History Association, PO Box 7010 University Station, Provo UT 84602. **Tel** (801)378-4048. **ED** Lowell Durham. **LC** BX8601; .J62. **DD** 289.3/09. **UDC** 289.3. cum. index. **Circ:** 1,000 (ctrl). available on an online database from DIALOG.
**Desc:** Articles on LDS, RLDS, and other Mormon group tradition-past, present and future. Promotes fellowship and communication among all those interested in the Mormon past.
**Ind/Abst** Am. Hist. Life (1986-).

US/0022-3409
**JOURNAL OF PASTORAL CARE, THE.** [J. pastor. care]. **Added/Corp** Association for Clinical Pastoral Education. Institute of Pastoral Care. Council for Clinical Training. American Association of Pastoral Counselors. Vol. 1 (Sept. 1947)-. Periodical. English. qt. $20.00 US; $22.00 other. Kutztown Publishing Company, PO Box 346, Kutztown PA 19530. **Tel** (215)683-7341. **ED** Orlo Strunk. **LC** BV4000; .J6. **DD** 250.5. **NLM** W1 JO828. **CODEN** JPACA8. Index available. **Bk Rev**, (Qty: 25). **Ad Acc. Pr Rev. Circ** 13,000. available on microfilm and microfiche from University Microfilms International (UMI). ***Absorbed*** *Journal of Clinical Pastoral Work.*
**Ind/Abst** Abstr. Res. Pastor. Care Couns. (19??-); Appl. Soc. Sci. Index Abstr.; Curr. Thoughts Trends; Health Plan. Adminis.; Hospit. Health Admin. Index; Index Book Rev. Relig.; Middle East Abstr. Index; Psychol. Abstr. (1947-); PsycINFO (?-?); PsycLit; Relig. Index One Period. (1949-); Relig. Theol. Abstr.; Soc. Work Abstr. (?-?).

US/0449-508X
**JOURNAL OF PASTORAL COUNSELING, THE.** [J. pastoral couns.]. **Added/Corp** Iona College. Graduate Division of Pastoral Counseling. Academy of Pastoral Counselors. Vol. 1 (1966)-. Periodical. English. an. $25.00 (individuals), $40.00 (institutions). Iona College, 715 North Avenue, New Rochelle NY 10801. **Tel** (914)633-2000. **ED** Samuel M. Natale. **DD** 253. **Bk Rev. Ad Acc. Circ:** 1,000. available on microfilm and microfiche from University Microfilms International (UMI). ***Continues*** *Iona Journal of Pastoral Counseling.*
**Desc:** Counseling and religious values.
**Ind/Abst** Abstr. Res. Pastor. Care Couns.; Index Book Rev. Relig.; Relig. Index One Period. (1970-); Relig. Theol. Abstr.

US/1064-9867
**JOURNAL OF PASTORAL THEOLOGY.** [J. pastor. theol.]. **Added/Corp** Society for Pastoral Theology. Vol. 1 (1991)-. Periodical. English. an (June). $15.00. Society of Pastoral Theology, Anderson School of Theology, Anderson IN 46012. **Tel** (317)649-9071, (317)641-4528. **ED** Christie Cozad Neuger (editor's address: United Theological Seminary, 3000 5th Street Northwest, New Brighten, MN 55112 phone: (612)633-4311); Larry Graham (editor's address: Iliff School of Theology, 2201 South University Boulevard, Denver, CO 80210, phone: (303)744-1287). **LC** BV4000; .J6. **DD** 253/.05. **Bk Rev. Ad Acc, Adv Mgr:** Glenn Asquith, **Tel** (215)861-1521. **Pr Rev. Circ:** 450.
**Desc:** To maintain a view of pastoral theology as a constructive theology growing out of the exercise of caring relationships, with attention both to present lived experience and to knowledge derived from the past.

SW/0283-8486
**JOURNAL OF PREHISTORIC RELIGION.** **VFOAT** JPR. Vol. 1 (1987)-. Periodical. English (French and German). ir (usually once a year). $15.00. Journal of Prehistoric Religion, William Gibsons Vaeg 11, S-43376 Partille Sweden. **Tel** 31-956600. **ED** Paul Astrom and Jon van Leuven. **Bk Rev. Ad Acc. Circ:** 3,000 (ctrl).
**Desc:** Interests include: methodology, comparative studies, regional surveys, excavations and interpretation of relevant evidence such as shrines, tombs, iconography and inscriptions, cult practices, ritual customs, theological beliefs, social and cultural effects and continuity of religion in space and time.
**Ind/Abst** Anthropol. Lit.

US/0733-4273
**JOURNAL OF PSYCHOLOGY AND CHRISTIANITY.** [J. psychol. Christ.]. **Added/Corp** Christian Association for Psychological Studies. **VFOAT** J.P.C.; JPC. Vol. 1, No. 1 (1982)-. Periodical. English. Four times a year. $50.00 libraries; $55.00 (individuals) others; $70.00 US & Canada. Christian Association for Psychological Studies, PO Box 310400, New Braunfels TX 78131. **Tel** (210)629-2277. **ED** Peter C. Hill and Robert R. King. **LC** BR110; .J64. **DD** 150.19/0882. **NLM** W1; JO8588. Index available. cum. index. **Bk Rev. Ad Acc. Pr Rev. Circ:** 2,100 (ctrl). available on microfilm and microfiche from University Microfilms International (UMI). ***Continues*** *Christian Association for Psychological Studies. Bulletin, 0147-7978.*
**Desc:** Addresses the interface of religion and social sciences and the cutting edge issues of all related subjects.
**Ind/Abst** Abstr. Res. Pastor. Care Couns. (19??-); Guide Soc. Sci. Relig.; Index Book Rev. Relig.; Psychol. Abstr. (1982-); PsycINFO; PsycLit; Relig. Index One Period.; Relig. Theol. Abstr.

US/0091-6471
**JOURNAL OF PSYCHOLOGY AND THEOLOGY.** **See** Psychology.

US/0022-4189
**JOURNAL OF RELIGION, THE.** [J. relig.]. **Added/Corp** University of Chicago. Divinity School. University of Chicago. Federated Theological Faculty. Vol. 1, No. 1 (Jan. 1921)-. Periodical. English. qt (4 issues). $53.00 institution, $25.00 indiviual, $19.00 UC Divinity School alumni and student; $61.71 institutions, $31.75 individual, $25.33 UC Divinity School Alumni and students, Canada; $58.00 institutions, $30.00 individual, $24.00 UC Divinity School Alumni and students. University of Chicago Press / Journals Division, PO Box 37005, 5720 South Woodlawn, Chicago IL 60637. **Tel** (312)753-3347, FAX (312)753-0811. **(Subscription telephone:** (312)753-8083**) ED** Don S. Browning, Franklin I. Gamwell and Bernard McGinn. **LC** BR1; .J65. **[CCC]. Acid Free.** available on microfilm and microfiche from University Microfilms International (UMI); available on microfiche from Johnson Associates. Documents available from The Genuine Article, UMI Article Clearinghouse. ***Formed by the union of*** *Biblical World, 0190-3578* ***and*** *American Journal of Theology.*
**Desc:** Promotes critical and systematic inquiry into the meaning and import of religion. Not limited by ideological orientation, it embraces all areas of theology as well as other types of religious studies.
**Ind/Abst** Acad. Abstr. Full Text Elite (July 1990-); Acad. Abstr. (July 1990-); Acad. Ind. [Computer File] (1987-); Acad. Search (July 1990-); Am. Hist. Life (1955-1974); Annu. Bibliogr. Engl. Lang. Lit.; Arts Humanit. Citation Index [Full Cov.]; Book Rev. Digest; Book Rev. Index; Expand. Acad. Index (1987-); Guide Soc. Sci. Relig.; Humanit. Index; Humanit. Source (Jul. 1990-); Index Book Rev. Relig.; INFO-SOUTH Abstr.; Mag. Search; Middle East Abstr. Index; New Testam. Abstr.; Newsp. Period. Abstr. (1991-); Old Testam. Abstr.; Relig. Index One Period. (1949-); Relig. Theol. Abstr.; Res. Alert [Full Cov.]; Romant. Move.; Soc. Sci. Cit. Index [Select. Cov.].

US/0022-4197
**JOURNAL OF RELIGION AND HEALTH.** [J. relig. health]. **Added/Corp** Institutes of Religion and Health (New York, N.Y.) Academy of Religion and Mental Health. **VFOAT** Religion & Health. Vol. 1 (Oct. 1961)-. Academic Scholarly Publication. English. qt. $215.00 US; $250.00 other. Human Sciences Press, PO Box 735, 233 Spring Street, New York NY 10013. **Tel** (212)620-8000, FAX (212)807-1047, telex 23421139. **(Subscription address:** Eurospan Ltd., Journals and Serials Division, 3 Henrietta Street, Covent Garden, London WC2E 8LU England.**) ED** Harry Meserve. **LC** RC321; .J85. **DD** 616.8/9/005. **NLM** W1 JO868. **CODEN** JRHEAT. **[CCC].** cum. index. **Pr Rev.** available on microfilm and microfiche from University Microfilms International (UMI). Documents available from The Genuine Article.
**Desc:** A thoughtful journal which critically explores the most contemporary modes of religious thought with particular emphasis on its relevance to current medical and psychological research. Using an eclectic approach to the study of human values, health and emotional welfare, this journal provides a scholarly forum for the discussion of topical themes on both a theoretical and practical level.
**Ind/Abst** Abstr. Res. Pastor. Care Couns. (19??-); Arts Humanit. Citation Index [Full Cov.]; Cumul. Index Nurs. Allied Health Lit.; Curr. Contents Arts Humanit.; Curr. Contents Soc. Behav. Sci.; Guide Soc. Sci. Relig.; Index Book Rev. Relig.; Index Jew. Period. (199?-); Middle East Abstr. Index; Psychol. Abstr. (1964-); PsycINFO (1961-); PsycLit; Relig. Index One Period. (1961-); Relig. Theol. Abstr.; Res. Alert [Full Cov.]; Soc. Sci. Cit. Index [Full Cov.].

US/0731-2148
**JOURNAL OF RELIGION AND PSYCHICAL RESEARCH, THE.** [J. relig. psych. res.]. **Added/Corp** Academy of Religion and Psychical Research. Vol. 4, No. 1 (Jan. 1982)-. Academic Scholarly Publication. English. Four times a year (Jan., Apr., July, Oct.). $20.00 (one year); $35.00 (two years), $45.00 (three years). Academy of Religion and Psychical Research, PO Box 614, Bloomfield CT 06002. **Tel** (203)242-4593. **ED** Claire G. Walker, (editor's address: 14001 Thunderbird Drive, 4K, Seal Beach, CA 90740, phone: (310)493-0355). **LC** BL65.P3; J68. **DD** 291.1/75. Index available (bound in Oct. issue). **Bk Rev**, (Qty: 20-30). **Circ:** 300. ***Continues*** *Academy of Religion and Psychical Research. Journal of the Academy of Religion*

*and Psychical Research, 0272-7188.*
**Desc:** A scholarly journal dealing with the area in which religion and psychical research interface.
**Ind/Abst** Except. Hum. Exp.; Index Book Rev. Relig. (1981-); Relig. Index One Period. (1981-).

US/0275-1402
## JOURNAL OF RELIGION AND THE APPLIED BEHAVIORAL SCIENCES.
(JOURNAL OF RELIGION AND THE APPLIED BEHAVIORAL SCIENCES : A PUBLICATION OF ASSOCIATION FOR CREATIVE CHANGE WITHIN RELIGIOUS AND OTHER SOCIAL SYSTEMS.). [J. relig. appl. behav. sci.]. **Added/Corp** Association for Creative Change Within Religious and Other Social Systems (U.S.). Vol. 1, No. 2 (Fall 1979)-. Periodical. English. tq. Free to members, $15.00 nonmembers. Association for Creative Change, 1340 Welch Road, Franklin NC 28734. **Tel** FAX (803)654-8416. **ED** Judith Guttman. **LC** BL1; .J628. **DD** 291.6/5/019. **Bk Rev. Circ:** 600. available with charts. ***Continues*** *Journal of Religion & the Applied Behavioral Sciences.*

NE/0022-4200
## JOURNAL OF RELIGION IN AFRICA.
[J. relig. Afr.]. **VFOAT** Religion en Afrique. Vol 1 (1967)-. Periodical. English (French). qt (4 issues). Fl195.00 (institutions) Netherlands; $111.50 (institutions) other. E. J. Brill, Postbus 9000, 2300 PA Leiden Netherlands. **Tel** 011 31 71 312624, FAX 011 31 71 317532, telex 39296 BRILL NL. **ED** Adrian Hastings. **LC** BL2400; .J68. **[CCC]. Bk Rev. Ad Acc. Circ:** 320 (ctrl). ***Absorbed*** *African Religious Research, 0044-6602.*
**Desc:** Devoted to the study of the forms and history of religion within the African continent and in sub-Saharan Africa in particular. The issues include articles and book reviews.
**Ind/Abst** Abstr. Anthropol.; Am. Hist. Life (1973-); Bibliogr. Mission.; Index Book Rev. Relig.; Int. Bibliogr. Sociol.; Missionalia; Relig. Index One Period. (1971-); Relig. Theol. Abstr.

●US/1059-9258
## JOURNAL OF RELIGION IN DISABILITY & REHABILITATION.
**VFOAT** Journal of Religion in Disability and Rehabilitation. (March 1993)-. English. qt (4 issues). $60.00 US; $84.00 other. The Haworth Press Inc, 10 Alice Street, Binghamton NY 13904-1580. **Tel** (607)722-5857, (800)3-HAWORTH, FAX (607)722-1424. **NLM** W1; JO868E. **Bk Rev. Acid Free.** Documents available from Haworth Document Delivery Service.
**Desc:** Brings religious professionals, along with those in other helping disciplines, greater knowledge and kinship so that they might join alongside each other in helping persons who experience disability.
**Ind/Abst** Abstr. Anthropol. (1993-); Abstr. Res. Pastor. Care Couns. (1993-); Appl. Soc. Sci. Index Abstr. (1993-); Cumul. Index Nurs. Allied Health Lit. (1993-); Hum. Resour. Abstr. (1993-); Sage Fam. Stud. Abstr. (1993-).

●US/1045-5876
## JOURNAL OF RELIGION IN PSYCHOTHERAPY.
**See** Medical Science and Technology-Psychiatry.

●US/1047-7845
## JOURNAL OF RELIGIOUS & THEOLOGICAL INFORMATION.
**See** Library and Information Sciences.

US/1050-2289
## JOURNAL OF RELIGIOUS GERONTOLOGY.
**See** Medical Science and Technology-Geriatrics.

AT/0022-4227
## JOURNAL OF RELIGIOUS HISTORY, THE.
[J. relig. hist.]. **Added/Corp** Association for the Journal of Religious History. Vol. 1 (June 1960)-. Academic Scholarly Publication. English. Twice a year (June & Dec.). $95.00 North America; £61.50 other. Basil Blackwell Publishers Ltd, 108 Cowley Road, Oxford 0X4 1JF England. **Tel** 011 44 865 791100, FAX 011 44 865 791347, telex 837022 OXBOOK G. **(Subscription address:** Blackwell Publishers / UK, Marston Book Services, PO Box 87, Oxford OX2 0DT England.**) ED** Bruce E. Mansfield. **LC** BR140; .J65. **[CCC].** Index available. **Bk Rev. Ad Acc. Circ:** 600. available on microfilm and microfiche from University Microfilms International (UMI). Documents available from The Genuine Article.
**Desc:** Articles and reviews on all fields of religious history (ancient, medieval, or modern) and on bearing of religion on general history.
**Ind/Abst** Am. Hist. Life (1960-); APAIS, Aust. Public Aff. Inf. Ser. (1963-); Arts Humanit. Citation Index [Full Cov.]; Br. Archaeol. Bibliogr.; Curr. Contents Arts Humanit.; Index Book Rev. Relig. (1960-); Middle East Abstr. Index (1960-); Relig. Index One Period. (1960-); Relig. Theol. Abstr. (1963-); Res. Alert [Full Cov.]; Romant. Move. (1960-); Soc. Sci. Cit. Index [Select. Cov.].

II/0047-2735
## JOURNAL OF RELIGIOUS STUDIES.
**Added/Corp** Punjabi University. Dept. of Religious Studies. Vol. 1 (Sept. 1969)-. Periodical. English. sa. $15.00. Punjabi University Registrar, Production and Sales Officer, Patiala 147002 India. **Tel** 73262. **(Subscription address:** Prints India, 11 Darya Ganj, New Delhi, 110002 India, (Phone: 011 91 11 3268645)**) ED** Wazir Singh. **LC** BL1; .J63. **DD** 200/.5. **Bk Rev. Circ:** 1,000 (ctrl).
**Desc:** Devoted to the study and understanding of the religious nature of mankind on historical, comparative and philosophical lines.

US/0193-3604
## JOURNAL OF RELIGIOUS STUDIES (CLEVELAND, OHIO).
(JOURNAL OF RELIGIOUS STUDIES.). [J. relig. stud.]. **Added/Corp** Ohio Academy of Religion. (Spring 1979)-. Periodical. English. sa. $6.00. Cleveland State University / Religious Studies, Department of Religious Studies, Cleveland OH 44115. **Tel** (216)687-2000. **ED** Derwood C. Smith. **Circ:** 175. ***Continues*** *Ohio Journal of Religious Studies, 0094-5668.*
**Ind/Abst** Index Book Rev. Relig.; New Testam. Abstr.; Relig. Index One Period.

US/0022-4235
## JOURNAL OF RELIGIOUS THOUGHT, THE.
[J. relig. thought]. **Added/Corp** Howard University. School of Religion. Vol. 1 (Autumn 1943)-. Periodical. English. sa. $14.00 (institutions), $12.00 (individuals). Howard University School of Divinity, 1400 Shephard Street Northeast, Washington DC 20017. **Tel** (202)806-0500. **ED** Cain H. Felder. **LC** BR1; .J67. **DD** 205. **Bk Rev. Ad Acc. Circ:** 800 (ctrl). available on microfilm and microfiche from University Microfilms International (UMI). Documents available from UMI Article Clearinghouse.
**Desc:** Focuses on issues in religion and ministry relating to Afro-American, Caribbean and African people through feature articles, pastor's corner segment and book reviews/notes.
**Ind/Abst** Am. Hist. Life (1983-); Expand. Acad. Index (1992-); Index Book Rev. Relig.; Middle East Abstr. Index; New Testam. Abstr.; Newsp. Period. Abstr. (1992-); Relig. Index One Period. (1949-); Relig. Theol. Abstr.

●US/1065-6219
## JOURNAL OF RESEARCH ON CHRISTIAN EDUCATION.
(JOURNAL OF RESEARCH ON CHRISTIAN EDUCATION : JRCE.). [J. res. christ. educ.]. **Added/Corp** Andrews University. School of Education. **VFOAT** JRCE. Vol. 1, No. 1 (Autumn 1992)-. Periodical. English. Twice a year (Fall and Spring). $35.00 (instituitons); $27.00 (individuals). Andrews University Press, Information Services Building, Suite 211, Berrien Springs MI 49104-1800. **Tel** (616)471-6080, FAX (616)471-6224. **ED** Paul S. Brantley, (editor's address: Department of Teaching and Learning, Bell Hall, Andrews University, Berrien Springs, MI 49104, phone: (616)471-3416). **LC** BV1460; .J685. **DD** 268/.05. **Bk Rev**, (Qty: 6). **Ad Acc, Adv Mgr:** Debi Robertson, **Tel** (616)471-6080. **Pr Rev. Circ:** 1,000.
**Desc:** Emphasis on Christian education or Christian schooling at all levels. News on articles by leading scholars; discussion on controversial trends and methodologies.

US/0890-1112
## JOURNAL OF RITUAL STUDIES.
**Added/Corp** University of Pittsburgh. Dept. of Religious Studies. Vol. 1 No. 1 (Winter 1987)-. Academic Scholarly Publication. English. Twice a year (Mar. & Aug.). $25.00 (individuals), $45.00 (institutions). University of Pittsburgh / Religion, 2604 Cathedral Learning Religion, Pittsburgh PA 15206. **Tel** (412)624-5990. **ED** Ronald L. Grimes, Fred W. Clothey, Madeline Duntley and Bennetta Jules-Rosette. **Bk Rev. Ad Acc.** ctrl circ. available on microfilm and microfiche from University Microfilms International (UMI).
**Desc:** An interdisciplinary forum for the scholarly study of ritual in its various forms.
**Ind/Abst** Ethnoarts Index; Index Book Rev. Relig.; MLA Int. Bibl. Books Artic. Mod. Lang. Lit.; Relig. Index One Period.; Relig. Theol. Abstr.

II/0379-8194
## JOURNAL OF SIKH STUDIES.
[J. Sikh stud.]. **Added/Corp** Guru Nanak Dev University. Dept. of Guru Nanak Studies. Guru Nanak University. Dept. of Guru Nanak Studies. (Feb. 1974)-. Periodical. English (Panjabi). Twice a year (Feb., Aug.). Rs100.00. Guru Nanak Development University, Department of Sociology, Amritsar India. **Tel** 65278. **(Subscription address:** Registrar Guru Nanak, Development University Press, Publication Department, Amritsar 143005 India.**) ED** Madanjit Kaur. **LC** BL2017; .J67. **DD** 294.6. Index available. **Bk Rev. Ad Acc. Circ:** 750 (ctrl).
**Desc:** The journal contains original articles by eminent writers on subjects concerning Sikh history, religion and philosophy.

US
## JOURNAL OF SPIRITUAL FORMATION.
***Ceased.*** **Added/Corp** Duquesne University. Institute of Formative Spirituality. Vol. 15, No. 1 (Feb. 1994)-(Dec. 1994). Periodical. English. tq. Institute of Formative Spirituality, 906 Rockwell Hall, Duquesne University, Pittsburgh PA 15282. **Tel** (412)396-6026. **LC** BX2350.2; .S74. ***Continues*** *Studies in Formative Spirituality, 0193-2748.*

US/0891-0235
## JOURNAL OF STEWARDSHIP.
[J. steward.]. **Added/Corp** National Council of the Churches of Christ in the United States of America. Commission on Stewardship. Vol. 28 (1975)-. Periodical. English. an (January). $5.00. Ecumenical Center for Stewardship Studies, 1100 West 42nd Street, Suite 225, Indianapolis IN 46208. **Tel** (317)926-3525, FAX (317)926-3521. **DD** 253. ***Continues*** *Stewardship.*

US/0160-7774
## JOURNAL OF SUPERVISION AND TRAINING IN MINISTRY.
[J. superv. train. minist.]. **Added/Corp** Association for Clinical Pastoral Education. North Central Region. American Association of Pastoral Counselors. Central Region. Vol. 1 (Winter 1978)-. English. an (Dec.). $20.00. Journal of Supervision and Training in Ministry, 1549 Clairmont Road, Suite 103, Decatur GA 30033. **Tel** (404)320-1472. **ED** Roger Fallot. **LC** BV4012; .J69. **DD** 207/.73. **Bk Rev**, (Qty: 10). **Pr Rev. Circ:** 1,000 (ctrl).
**Desc:** Only publication devoted exclusively to consideration of practice-based aspects of education for religious leadership, both theoretical and applied aspects.
**Ind/Abst** Abstr. Res. Pastor. Care Couns.; Index Book Rev. Relig.; Relig. Index One Period. (1978-).

US/0894-9034
## JOURNAL OF THE ACADEMY FOR EVANGELISM IN THEOLOGICAL EDUCATION.
[J. Acad. Evang. Theol. Educ.]. **Added/Corp** Academy for Evangelism in Theological Education. Vol. 1 (1986)-. English. an (Oct.). $10.00. ACAD Evangelism, 6009 Northwest Expressway, Oklahoma City OK 73132. **LC** BV3750; .J68. **DD** 269/.2/05.
**Ind/Abst** Relig. Theol. Abstr. (199?-).

US/0002-7189
## JOURNAL OF THE AMERICAN ACADEMY OF RELIGION.
**Main/Corp** American Academy of Religion. **Added/Corp** National Association of Biblical Instructors. Vol. 1 (1933)-. Academic Scholarly Publication. English. qt. $60.00. Scholars Press / Georgia, PO Box 15399, Atlanta GA 30333-0399. **Tel** (404)636-4757, (404)727-2320, FAX (404)727-2348. **LC** BV1460; .N23. cum. index. **Bk Rev. Ad Acc. Circ:** 5,750. available on microfilm and microfiche from University Microfilms International (UMI). Documents available from The Genuine Article, UMI Article Clearinghouse. ***Supersedes*** *Christian Education.*
**Desc:** Includes scholarly articles on the full range of world religious traditions together with studies of the methodologies by which they are explored. Each issue contains major articles of general interest and importance and a lengthy book section.
**Ind/Abst** Acad. Ind. [Computer File] (1992-); Acad. Search (July 1993-); Am. Hist. Life (1963-); Arts Humanit. Citation Index [Full Cov.]; Book Rev. Digest; Book Rev. Index; Curr. Contents Arts Humanit.; Expand. Acad. Index (1989-); Humanit. Index; Humanit. Source (Jul. 1993-); Index Book Rev. Relig.; Mag. Search; Middle East Abstr. Index; MLA Int. Bibl. Books Artic. Mod. Lang. Lit.; New Testam. Abstr.; Newsp. Period. Abstr. (1990-); Relig. Theol. Abstr.; Res. Alert [Full Cov.]; Soc. Sci. Cit. Index [Select. Cov.].

CN/0008-3208
## JOURNAL OF THE CANADIAN CHURCH HISTORICAL SOCIETY.
[J. Can. Church Hist. Soc.]. **Main/Corp** Canadian Church Historical Society. **Added/Corp** Canadian Church Historical Society. Vol. 1, No. 1 (Sept. 1950)-. Periodical. English. sa (Apr. and Oct.). 20.00Can$ Canada; $20.00 other. Canadian Church Historical Society, 600 Jarvis Street, Toronto Ont M4Y 2J6 Canada. **Tel** (416)924-9192, FAX (416)968-7983. **ED** Ian C. Storey (editor's address:Traill College, Trent University, Peterborough ONT K9J 7B8). **LC** BR570; .C34a. **DD** 283/.71. **Bk Rev.** available on microfilm from Micromedia Limited; available on microfilm and microfiche from University Microfilms International (UMI).
**Ind/Abst** Am. Hist. Life (1973-); Index Book Rev. Relig. (1973-); Relig. Index One Period. (1973-).

II
## JOURNAL OF THE CHRISTIAN MEDICAL ASSOCIATION OF INDIA.
**See** Medical Science and Technology.

UK
## JOURNAL OF THE CHRISTIAN MEDICAL FELLOWSHIP.
English. qt. £5.00 per year UK; £7.50 other. Christian Medical Fellowship, 157 Waterloo Road, London SE1 8XN England. **Tel** 011 44 71 928-4694, FAX (04)44 71 620 2453. **ED** Andrew Brown and Rebecca Torry. Index available. **Bk Rev. Pr Rev. Circ:** 6,000 (ctrl).
**Desc:** The purpose is to promote discussion of the interests and problems of Christians within the medical profession. Authors have reasonable freedom of expression as long as articles are consonant with Christian faith as recorded in the bible. Views expressed are not official views of CMF.

US/0360-8808
**JOURNAL OF THE EVANGELICAL THEOLOGICAL SOCIETY.** [J. Evang. Theol. Soc.]. **Main/Corp** Evangelical Theological Society. Vol. 12 (Winter 1969)-. Periodical. English. qt. $20.00. Evangelical Theological Society, 112 Russell Woods, Lynchburg VA 24502. **Tel** (804)237-1486. **LC** BR21; .E92. **DD** 205. **Circ:** 2,700. available on microfilm and microfiche from University Microfilms International (UMI). ***Continues*** *Bulletin of the Evangelical Theological Society, 0361-5138.*
**Ind/Abst** Christ. Period. Index; Index Book Rev. Relig.; New Testam. Abstr.; Old Testam. Abstr.; Relig. Index One Period. (1969-); Relig. Theol. Abstr.

US/0092-6558
**JOURNAL OF THE INTERDENOMINATIONAL THEOLOGICAL CENTER, THE.** [J. Interdenominatl. Theol. Cent.]. **Main/Corp** Interdenominational Theological Center, Atlanta. Vol. 1 (Fall 1973)-. Periodical. English. sa. $8.00. Journal of Interdenominational Theological Center, 671 Beckwith Street SW, Atlanta GA 30314. **Tel** (404)527-7726. **ED** John C Diamond. **LC** BR1; .I54a. **DD** 230/.05. **Bk Rev. Circ:** 1,000. available on microfilm from University Microfilms International (UMI).
**Desc:** A theological interpretation to social, ethical, economical, and religious issues from the perspective of worldwide scholars.
**Ind/Abst** Index Book Rev. Relig.; New Testam. Abstr.; Relig. Index One Period. (1973-); Relig. Theol. Abstr.

II/0970-0609
**JOURNAL OF THE K.R. CAMA ORIENTAL INSTITUTE.** (JOURNAL.). [J. K.R. Cama Orient. Inst.]. **Main/Corp** K.R. Cama Oriental Institute. No. 1 (1922)-. English. an. $20.00. **(Subscription address:** Prints India, 11 Darya Ganj, New Delhi 110002 India.) **LC** PK6001; .C3. **DD** 491.06254. **UDC** 954.

US/1051-0605
**JOURNAL OF THE NEW ENGLAND LUTHERAN HISTORICAL SOCIETY.** [J. N. Engl. Lutheran Hist. Soc.]. **Added/Corp** New England Lutheran Historical Society. Vol. 1 (Spring 1983)-. Periodical. English. an (published Spring). $25.00 (institutions), $10.00 (individuals). Journal of the New England Lutheran Historical Society, 40 Pitkin Street, Manchester CT 06040. **Tel** (203)649-5311. **ED** Rev. K.E. Williams. **LC** BX8042.N48; J68. **DD** 284.1/74/05. **Circ:** 500 (ctrl).
**Desc:** Annual publication featuring articles on the history of Lutheran churches or personalities in New England.

UK/0022-5185
**JOURNAL OF THEOLOGICAL STUDIES.** [J. theol. stud.]. (1899)-. Periodical. English. sa. £77.00 UK and Europe; $150.00 other. Oxford University Press, Walton Street, Oxford OX2 6DP England. **Tel** 011 44 865 56767, FAX 011 44 865 267773, telex 837330 OXPRES G. **(Subscription address:** Oxford University Press / USA, Journals Marketing Department, Oxford University Press, 2001 Evans Road, Cary NC 27513.) **ED** Morna Hooker and Maurice Wiles. **LC** BR1; .J8. **DD** 230.05. **[CCC].** Index available. **Bk Rev. Ad Acc. Circ:** 1,200. available on microfilm and microfiche from University Microfilms International (UMI). Documents available from The Genuine Article, UMI Article Clearinghouse.
**Desc:** Academic study of Christian theology: Old and New Testaments, church history, and philosophy of religion and ethics. Reviews of English and other theological works.
**Ind/Abst** Acad. Search (July 1993-); Arts Humanit. Citation Index [Full Cov.]; BHA : Biblio. Hist. Art; Br. Humanit. Index; Curr. Contents Arts Humanit.; Expand. Acad. Index (1989-); Humanit. Index; Humanit. Source (Jul. 1993-); Index Book Rev. Relig.; INFO-SOUTH Abstr.; Mag. Search; MLA Int. Bibl. Books Artic. Mod. Lang. Lit.; New Testam. Abstr.; Newsp. Period. Abstr. (1991-); Old Testam. Abstr.; Relig. Index One Period. (1949-); Relig. Theol. Abstr.; Res. Alert [Full Cov.]; Soc. Sci. Cit. Index [Select. Cov.].

US/0361-1906
**JOURNAL OF THEOLOGY.** **Added/Corp** Church of the Lutheran Confession. (196?)-. Periodical. English. Four times a year. $5.00 (one year), $9.00 (two year). Church of the Lutheran Confession, Immanuel Lutheran College, 501 Grover Road, Eau Claire WI 54701-7199. **Tel** (715)836-6621. **(Subscription address:** Journal of Theology, 2750 North Oxford Street, Roseville MN 55113.) **ED** John Lau. Index available. cum. index. **Bk Rev**, (Qty: 12 per year). **Pr Rev. Circ:** 300.
**Desc:** Professional journal of confessional Lutheran theology for pastors and teachers.

SA/0047-2867
**JOURNAL OF THEOLOGY FOR SOUTHERN AFRICA.** [J. theol. South. Afr.]. No. 1 (Dec. 1972)-. Periodical. English. Four times a year (Mar., June, Sept., Dec.). R25.00 (individual), R30.00 (institution) South Africa; R40.00 (individual), $60.00 (institution) others. University Cape Town, Department of Religious Studies, Rondebosch 7700 South Africa. **Tel** 011 27 21 650-3453. **ED** John W. de Gruchy. **LC** BR1; .J82. **DD** 230/.0968. Index available. **Bk Rev. Ad Acc. Circ:** 1,000. available on microfilm and microfiche from University Microfilms International (UMI). ***Formed by the union of*** ***Credo and*** *Ministry.*
**Desc:** Exists to encourage theological reflection and dialogue especially within the southern African context. A contribution to theological thought from within, and a means to keep southern Africa informed about theological developments elsewhere.
**Ind/Abst** Bibliogr. Mission.; Index Book Rev. Relig.; New Testam. Abstr.; Old Testam. Abstr.; Relig. Index One Period. (1977-); Relig. Theol. Abstr.

US
**JOURNAL OF THEOLOGY (UNITED THEOLOGICAL SEMINARY).** English. an.
**Ind/Abst** Index Book Rev. Relig.; Relig. Index One Period.

US/8756-4785
**JOURNAL OF THETA ALPHA KAPPA.** [J. Theta Alpha Kappa]. **Added/Corp** Theta Alpha Kappa. **VFOAT** JTAK. (197?)-. Periodical. English. Twice a year (Apr. & Nov.). $15.00. Theta Alpha Kappa / New Jersey, Caldwell College of Religious Studies, Caldwell NJ 07006. **Tel** (201)228-4424 ext. 250. **ED** Anthong J. Tambasco, (editor's address: Theology Department, Georgetown University, Washington, DC 20057, phone: (202)687-6234). **DD** 200. Index available. cum. index (Thru Vol. 15). **Bk Rev. Pr Rev. Circ:** 1,000.
**Desc:** Academic studies, essays, art, poetry, and reviews in religious and theology. Focus primarily from both faculty and students members of "Theta Alpha Kappa".

●US/1062-1237
**JOURNAL OF VAISNAVA STUDIES, THE.** [J. Vaisnava stud.]. **VFOAT** JVS. Vol. 1, No. 1 (Fall 1992)-. Periodical. English. Four times a year. $35.00. Folk Books Journal Vaisnava Studies, PO Box 400716, Brooklyn NY 11240. **Tel** (718)522-2335. **ED** Steven Rosen. **LC** BL1284.5; .J68. **DD** 305. **Bk Rev**, (Qty: 12). **Ad Acc, Adv Mgr:** Barbara Berasl, **Tel** (718)522-2335. **Pr Rev. Circ:** 500 per issue (ctrl).
**Desc:** This publication allows scholars to publish academic papers concerning the religion, philosophy, history and culture of all forms of Vaisnavism.

US/1046-543X
**JOURNAL OF VITAL CHRISTIANITY, A.** ***Title Change.*** [J. vital Christ.]. **Added/Corp** Church of God (Anderson, Ind.). **VFOAT** Vital Christianity. (198?)-(199?). Periodical. English. mo. Warner Press Inc, PO Box 2499, Anderson IN 46018. **Tel** (317)644-7721. **DD** 289. ***Continues*** *Vital Christianity, 0042-7381.* ***Continued by*** *Vital Christianity (Anderson, Ind. : 1994), 1077-6982.*

US/0888-5621
**JOURNAL OF WOMEN AND RELIGION.** [J. women relig.]. **Added/Corp** Graduate Theological Union. Center for Women and Religion. Vol.1 No.1 (Spring 1981)-. Periodical. English. an. $50.00. Center for Women and Religion, 2400 Ridge Road, Berkeley CA 94709. **Tel** (510)649-2490. **LC** BL458; .J68. **DD** 291.2/082. Index available. cum. index. **Bk Rev. Circ:** 3,000. Documents available from UMI Article Clearinghouse. ***Continues*** *Newsletter / Graduate Theological Union. Center for Women and Religion.*
**Ind/Abst** Expand. Acad. Index (1992-); Index Book Rev. Relig.; Newsp. Period. Abstr. (1989-); Relig. Index One Period.

US/1064-1084
**JOURNAL OF WOMEN'S MINISTRIES.** [J. women's minist.]. **Added/Corp** Episcopal Church. Council for Women's Ministries. No. 1 (Winter 1984)-. Periodical. English. ir (3-4 times per year). Free on request. Domestic and Foreign Missionary Society, Episcopal Church, 815 2nd Avenue, New York NY 10017. **Tel** (212)867-8400. **ED** Marcy Darin. **DD** 280. **Bk Rev. Circ:** 10,000.

US/0887-8854
**JOURNEY (LYNCHBURG, VA.).** ***Title Change.*** (JOURNEY.). **Added/Corp** Grace Orthodox Presbyterian Church (Lynchburg, Va.). **VFOAT** Journey Magazine. Vol. 1, No. 1 (Jan./Feb. 1986)-(19??). Periodical. English. bm. Journey, 1021 Federal Street, Lynchburg VA 24504. **Tel** (804)845-8572. **ED** R E Knodel Jr. **Bk Rev. Ad Acc. Circ:** 2,000 (ctrl). ***Continued by*** *Christian Statesman; Christian Observer.*
**Desc:** Historically confessional and reformed protestant.

US/1055-1409
**JR. HIGH MINISTRY.** [Jr. high minist.]. Vol. 6, No. 2 (Jan./Feb. 1991)-. Periodical. English. Five times a year (Feb., Apr., Aug., Oct., Dec.). $19.95 one year; $36.00 two years. Group Publishing, PO Box 481, c/o Shelia Augustine, Loveland CO 80539. **Tel** (303)669-3836, FAX (303)669-3269. **ED** Rick Lawrence. **DD** 268. **Bk Rev**, (Qty: 10-20). **Ad Acc, Adv Mgr:** Larry Boryour, **Tel** (303)669-3836. **Circ:** 25,000. ***Continues*** *Group's Jr. High Ministry, 0884-0504.*
**Desc:** For leaders of Christian youth from 6th to 9th grade. Contains articles, games, ready-to-go meeting, and resource reviews.

US/0736-9662
**JUBILEE INTERNATIONAL.** **VFOAT** Jubilee. Spring 1981; Vol. 1, No. 1, (Jan./March 1983)-. Periodical. English (French and Spanish). qt. Free. Prison Fellowship International, PO Box 17500, Washington DC 20041-0500. **ED** Martha Anderson. **Circ:** 5,500 (ctrl).
**Desc:** Newsletter of prison fellowship international to motivate, encourage and inform ministry volunteers, staff, donors as well as prisoners and their families worldwide.

GW/0022-6319
**JUNGE KIRCHE; EINE ZEITSCHRIFT EUROPAISCHER CHRISTEN.** **Added/Corp** Marburger Christen fuer den Sozialismus. Vol. 1 (21 June 1933)-. Periodical. German. mo. DM66.00 Germany; DM75.00 other. Vertrieb Junge Kirche, Mathildenstrasse 86, D 28203 Bremen Germany. **Tel** 011 49 421 71648. **ED** D. Casalis, H. Gollwitzer, K. Lubbert, F.W. Marquardt, D. Solle, M. Veit. **LC** BX8001; .J8. Index available. **Bk Rev. Ad Acc. Circ:** 7,200. ***Absorbed*** *Akid; Zeitschrift fur Theorie und Praxis in Gesellschaft und Kirche.*
**Desc:** Topics include theology, ecumenism, Third World, environment, peace movements and nonviolence.

US/0748-6928
**JUNIOR (HAGERSTOWN, MD.).** (JUNIOR : SABBATH SCHOOL LESSON QUARTERLY OF SEVENTH-DAY ADVENTISTS.). **VFOAT** Junior Sabbath School Lessons. Vol. 51, No. 1 (Jan.-Mar. 1985)-. Periodical. English. Four times a year. $16.64. Review and Herald Publishing Association, 55 West Oak Ridge Drive, Hagerstown MD 21740. **Tel** (301)791-7000 ext. 2534, FAX (301)790-9734. **Circ:** 33,000. ***Continues*** *Junior Bible Explorer, 0163-8777.*
**Desc:** Sabbath school lesson material for the Junior Department.

US/0277-917X
**JUNIOR STUDENT.** ***Title Change.*** **Added/Corp** Assemblies of God. General Council. (1982-1992). English. qt. Gospel Publishing House, 1445 Boonville Avenue, Springfield MO 65802. **Tel** (417)862-2781, FAX (417)866-1146. ***Continues*** *Junior. Grades 5, 6 Student, 0273-5121.* ***Continued by*** *Junior Student Guide, 1059-3373.*

●US/1059-3373
**JUNIOR STUDENT GUIDE.** **Added/Corp** Assemblies of God. General Council. (1992)-. Periodical. English. qt. $5.20. Gospel Publishing House, 1445 Boonville Avenue, Springfield MO 65802. **Tel** (417)862-2781, FAX (417)866-1146. ***Continues*** *Junior Student, 0277-917X.*

●US/1059-3322
**JUNIOR TEACHER GUIDE.** **Added/Corp** Assemblies of God. General Council. (1992)-. Periodical. English. qt. $9.20. Gospel Publishing House, 1445 Boonville Avenue, Springfield MO 65802. **Tel** (417)862-2781, FAX (417)866-1146. ***Continues*** *Junior Teacher, 0277-9161.*

US/0022-6718
**JUNIOR TRAILS.** Periodical. English. qt. Gospel Publishing House, 1445 Boonville Avenue, Springfield MO 65802. **Tel** (417)862-2781, FAX (417)866-1146.

JM
**JUSTICE.** No. 1- May 1971-. Periodical. English. Social Action Centre, 8 Oliver Road, Kingston 8 Jamaica West Indies. **LC** HN39.J28; J87. **DD** 261.8/3/097292.

KO
**KAEHYOK SINANG.** **VFOAT** Reformed Faith. (19??)-. Periodical. Korean. qt. The Korea Society for Reformed Faith and Action, 3-47 3 Ga Chungjungro Sudaemungu Seoul Korea. **Tel** (02)312-6758. **ED** Pyeng Seh Oh. **LC** BV4485; .K33. Index available. **Bk Rev. Ad Acc. Circ:** 3,000.

AU/0022-7757
**KAIROS; ZEITSCHRIFT FUER RELIGIONSWISSENSCHAFT UND THEOLOGIE.** (Jahrg. 1 1959)-. Periodical. German. an. Otto Mueller Verlag, Ernest Thun Strasse 11, Postfach 167, A-5020 Salzburg Austria. **Tel** 011 43 662 881974, or 881975. **ED** Kurt Schubert. **LC** BL1; .K3. **Bk Rev. Ad Acc. Circ:** 600.
**Desc:** History of religion; includes Judaistic, Islamic and Biblical research.
**Ind/Abst** Index Book Rev. Relig.; New Testam. Abstr.; Relig. Index One Period. (1959-).

PL/0209-1291
**KATECHETA.** [Katecheta]. (1957)-. Periodical. Polish. bm. Price on Request. **(Subscription address:** ARS Polona, PO Box 1001, 00068 Warsaw Poland.) **UDC** 268.

SW
**KATOLSK ARSSKRIFT.** Swedish. an. Kr40.00. Katolska Teologforeningen, Hogbergsgatan 67, 116 20 Stockholm Sweden. **LC** BR50; .K36.

US
**KEEP THE FAITH.** English. qt. $25.00. Center Ministry Laity, 210 Herrick Road, Newton Centre MA 02159. **Tel** 964-1100. **ED** Susan Rosen. **Bk Rev. Circ:**

675. ***Continues*** *Centering.*
**Desc:** Gives information on what is happening at our center, The Center for the Ministry of the Laity, and it presents articles, sermons and book reviews on doing ministry in the world.

NE/0450-1489
**KERK EN THEOLOGIE.** (1950)-. Periodical. Dutch. qt. Boekencentrum B V, PO Box 29, 2700 EE Zoetemeer Netherlands. **Tel** 011 31 079 615481. Index available. **Bk Rev**. **Ad Acc**. ***Continues*** *Onder Eigen Vaandel.*

NE
**KERKELIJK JAARBOEKJE DER GEREFORMEERDE GEMEENTEN.** **Main/Corp** Gereformeerde Gemeenten in Nederland en Noord-Amerika. **VFOAT** Kerkelijk Jaarboekje. Dutch. **LC** WMLC L 83/7991.

NE/0169-8451
**KERKHISTORISCHE BIJDRAGEN.** [Kerkhist. bijdr.]. (1970)-. Monographic series. Multiple languages. ir. Price varies per volume. E. J. Brill, Postbus 9000, 2300 PA Leiden Netherlands. **Tel** 011 31 71 312624, FAX 011 31 71 317532, telex 39296 BRILL NL. **UDC** 27.

BE
**KERNOS.** **Added/Corp** Kentro Meletes tes Archaias Hellenikes Threskeias. (1988)-. French (English, German, Greek and Modern, Italian). an (May). 1500.00F Belgium and Greece; 1700.00F other. Kernos - University of Liege, 32 Place du XX Aout, B-4000 Liege Belgium. **Tel** 011 32 2 41665568. **ED** Andre Motte. **LC** BL700; .K47. **DD** 292.08/05. Index available. cum. index. **Bk Rev**. ctrl circ.
**Desc:** Information on the aspects of Greek religion.

US/0888-3513
**KERUX.** [Kerux]. **VFOAT** Journal of Biblical Theological Preaching. Vol. 1, No. 1 (May 1986)-. Periodical. English. Three times a year (May, Sept., Dec.). $15.00. Kerux Publishing Company, 1131 Whispering Highlands Drive, Escondido CA 92027. **Tel** (619)741-8276. **ED** James T. Dennison Jr. **DD** 220. **Bk Rev**.
**Ind/Abst** Relig. Theol. Abstr.

CN/0023-0693
**KERYGMA (OTTAWA).** ***Title Change.*** (KERYGMA.). [Kerygma]. **Added/Corp** Conseil Oblat des Missions Indiennes et Esquimaudes. Universite Saint-Paul (Ottawa, Ont.). Centre Canadien de Recherches en Anthropologie. Universite Saint-Paul (Ottawa, Ont.) Institut des Sciences Missionnaires. Universite Saint-Paul (Ottawa, Ont.) Institut de Missiologie. Universite Saint-Paul (Ottawa, Ont.). Institut des Sciences de la Mission. Vol. 1 (1967)-(1993). Periodical. French (English). sa. Institute of Mission Studies, St Paul University, 233 Main Street, Ottawa Ontario K1S 1C4 Canada. **Tel** (613)236-1393, FAX (613)236-5278. **ED** Achiel Peelman. **DD** 266/.2/05. **Bk Rev**. **Ad Acc**. **Circ:** 220 (ctrl). ***Continued by*** *Mission (Ottawa, Ont.), 1198-0400.*
**Desc:** Communication medium between missionaries and researchers for discussion on contemporary issues: inculturation traditional religions and Christianity faith-cultures social challenges.
**Ind/Abst** Bibliogr. Mission.; Missionalia.

GW/0023-0707
**KERYGMA UND DOGMA.** [Kerygma & Dogma]. Vol. 1 (Jan. 1955)-. Periodical. German. qt. DM79.00. Vandenhoeck & Ruprecht, Robert Bosch Breite 6, D-37079 Goettingen Germany. **Tel** 011 49 551 695911, FAX 011 49 551 695917, telex 965226 VAN d. **LC** BR4; .K47. **[CCC]**. available on microfilm from University Microfilms International (UMI).
**Ind/Abst** Index Book Rev. Relig.; New Testam. Abstr.; Old Testam. Abstr.; Relig. Index One Period. (1955-); Relig. Theol. Abstr.

GW/0453-7726
**KERYGMA UND DOGMA. BEIHEFT.** **VFOAT** Beiheft Zu Kerygma und Dogma. 1-. Monographic series. German. ir. Price varies per volume. Vandenhoeck & Ruprecht, Robert Bosch Breite 6, D-37079 Goettingen Germany. **Tel** 011 49 551 695911, FAX 011 49 551 695917, telex 965226 VAN d. **Bk Rev**. ctrl circ.

US/0023-0839
**KEY TO CHRISTIAN EDUCATION.** **VFOAT** Key. Vol. 1 (Oct./Dec. 1962)-. Periodical. English. qt. $6.50 US; $9.00 Mexico; 9.99Can$ Canada; $11.00 other. Standard Publishers Company, 8121 Hamilton Avenue, Cincinnati OH 45231. **Tel** (800)543-1353, FAX (513)931-0904. **ED** Barbara Bolton and Lowellette Lauderdale. **LC** BV1500; .K46. **Circ:** 65,000 (ctrl).
**Desc:** Articles offering encouragement and ideas for the Christian educator, primarily Sunday school teachers.
**Ind/Abst** Christ. Period. Index (19??-).

KO
**KIDO (SEOUL, KOREA).** (KIDO.). **VFOAT** The Prayer; Prayer. Periodical. Korean. mo. W7.000. Wolgan Kidosa, 37-1 1-ka Wonhyoro Yongsan-ku, Seoul 140 Korea. **LC** BV4485; .K53.

KO
**KIDOKKYO SASANG.** Periodical. Korean. W5,000. Taehan Kidokkyo Sohoe, 84-8 2-ka Chongno, Seoul South Korea. **LC** BR9.K6; K52.

US/0745-8258
**KINDERGARTEN TEACHER.** ***Title Change.*** **Added/Corp** American Baptist Churches in the U.S.A. Board of Educational Ministries. (19??)-(19??). Periodical. English. qt. Nazarene Publishing House, PO Box 419527, Kansas City MO 64141. **Tel** (816)931-1900. ***Continued by*** *Early Childhood Level D.*

●US/1072-1444
**KINDERGARTEN TEACHER GUIDE.** [Kindergart. teach. guide]. **Added/Corp** Assemblies of God. General Council. Vol. 1, No. 1 (Sept.-Oct.-Nov. 1994)-. Periodical. English. qt. $2.65 (single issue). Gospel Publishing House, 1445 Boonville Avenue, Springfield MO 65802. **Tel** (417)862-2781, FAX (417)866-1146. **DD** 289. ***Continues*** *Beginner Teacher Guide, 1059-325X.*

US
**KINDRED SPIRIT.** **Added/Corp** Dallas Theological Seminary. Vol. 1 (Winter 1977)-. Periodical. English. Three times a year (Jan., May, Sept.). Free. Dallas Theological Seminary, 3909 Swiss Avenue, Dallas TX 75204. **Tel** (800)992-0998. **Bk Rev**, (Qty: 3). ctrl circ.

UK/0143-5922
**KING'S THEOLOGICAL REVIEW.** ***Ceased.*** (19??-(199?). Periodical. English. sa. King's Theological Review, Kings College University of London, Strand London WC2R 2LS England. **Tel** 011 44 71 836 5454. ***Absorbed*** *Kingsman.*
**Ind/Abst** Index Book Rev. Relig.; New Testam. Abstr.; Relig. Index One Period.; Relig. Theol. Abstr.

GW/0453-929x
**KIRCHE UND KONFESSION.** **Added/Corp** Evangelischer Bund. Konfessionskundliches Institut. Vol. 1 (1962)-. Monographic series. German. ir. Price varies per volume. Vandenhoeck & Ruprecht, Robert Bosch Breite 6, D-37079 Goettingen Germany. **Tel** 011 49 551 695911, FAX 011 49 551 695917, telex 965226 VAN d. **Ad Acc**.

AU
**KIRCHE UND RECHT.** (1???)-. Monographic series. German. ir. Price varies per volume. Institut fuer Kirchenrecht, Freyungasse 6, A-1010 Vienna Austria.

GW/0932-9951
**KIRCHLICHE ZEITGESCHICHTE.** **VFOAT** KZG. **VAT** KZG. Vol. 1, No. 1 (May 1988)-. Periodical. German (English; summaries and/or abstracts in English). Twice a year (May & Nov.). DM96.00. Vandenhoeck & Ruprecht, Robert Bosch Breite 6, D-37079 Goettingen Germany. **Tel** 011 49 551 695911, FAX 011 49 551 695917, telex 965226 VAN d. **LC** BR140; .K56. **DD** 270/.05.
**Ind/Abst** Am. Hist. Life (1988-).

GW
**KIRCHLICHES AMTSBLATT DER EVANGELISCHEN KIRCHE IM RHEINLAND.** **Main/Corp** Evangelische Kirche Im Rheinland. Periodical. German. 7.50 quarterly. Verlag Landeskirchenamt, Hand-Bockler-Strasse 7, 4000 Dusseldorf Germany. **LC** BX7567.A1; E93A.

US/0145-8019
**KIRISUTOKYO KAGAKU SAKIGAKE.** **VFOAT** Herald of Christian Science. Japanese Edition. (19??)-. Periodical. Multiple languages ( and English). qt. $29.00. Christian Science Publishing Society, One Norway Street, Boston MA 02115. **Tel** (617)450-2678, (617)450-2504.

NO/0023-186X
**KIRKE OG KULTUR.** [Kirke kult.]. **VFOAT** For Kirke og Kultur. Vol. 1 (1919)-. Periodical. Norwegian. bm. Kr420.00, $76.00. Scandinavian University Press, PO Box 2959 Toeyen, N 0608 Oslo 6 Norway. **Tel** 011 47 2 2575400, FAX 011 47 2 2575353, telex 71896 UROR N. **(Subscription address:** Scandinavian University Press, 200 Meacham Ave., Elmont NY 11003.**)** **ED** Inge Loenning. **LC** AP45; .K57. **Bk Rev**. **Ad Acc**. **Circ:** 3,000 (ctrl). ***Continues*** *For Kirke og Kultur.*
**Desc:** Forum for essays and debate on ethics in society, religion, and culture.
**Ind/Abst** Annu. Bibliogr. Engl. Lang. Lit.; MLA Int. Bibl. Books Artic. Mod. Lang. Lit.

GR
**KLERONOMIA : PERIODIKON DEMODIEUMA TOU PATRIARCHIKOU HIDRYMATOS PATERIKON MELETON.** **Added/Corp** Patriarchikon Hidryma Paterikon Meleton. Vol. 1 (Jan. 1969)-. Periodical. Greek, Modern (English, German, Italian and French). Twice a year (June & Dec.). $36.00. Patriarchikon Hidryma Paterikon Meleton, 64 Eptapyrigiou St Moni Vlattadon, 546 34 Thessalonike Greece. **Tel** 011 30 31 202 301, 011 30 31 202 300. **ED** P. K. Christou, V. N. Fanourgakis, and E. K. Litsas. **LC** BR66; .K57. **Bk Rev**. **Ad Acc**.
**Ind/Abst** BHA : Biblio. Hist. Art.

US/1047-1057
**KOINONIA (PRINCETON, N.J.).** (KOINONIA : PRINCETON THEOLOGICAL SEMINARY GRADUATE FORUM.). [Koinonia]. **Added/Corp** Princeton Theological Seminary. **VFOAT** Koinonia Journal. Vol. 1 (Spring 1989)-. Periodical. English. Twice a year (Spring and Fall). $24.00 (institutions), $18.00 (individuals). Koinonia Journal, Princeton Theological Seminary, CN 821, Princeton NJ 08542. **Tel** (609)497-7788, FAX (609)921-8300. **ED** Gregory L. Glover, (editor's phone: (609)243-9634). **LC** BR1; .K65. **DD** 230/.05. Index available. **Bk Rev**, (Qty: 20-30). **Ad Acc**. **Circ:** 350 (ctrl).
**Desc:** Provides a scholarly forum for interdisciplinary discussion and for exploring new and emerging areas and issues among graduate students in the study of religion.

JA
**KOKUGAKUIN DAIGAKU NIHON BUNKA KENKYUJO HO.** **Main/Corp** Kokugakuin Daigaku. Nihon Bunka KenkyÂujo. (Feb. 1964)-. Periodical. Japanese. Kokugakuin Daigaku, 10-28 Higashi 4-chome, Shiuya-ku, Tokyo Japan. **Tel** (03)409-0111. **LC** DS820.8; .K637a. **Bk Rev**.

GW
**KOMMENTAR ZUM ALTEN TESTAMENT.** ***Ceased.*** (19??)-(Spring 1994). German. Guetersloher Verlagshaus, Postfach 450, D 33311 Guetersloh Germany. **Tel** 011 49 5241 74050. **(Subscription address:** VVA Bertelsmann Dist. GmbH, Postfach 7777, D 33310 Guetersloh Germany**)**

US/0197-7776
**KOREAN CHURCH DIRECTORY OVERSEAS.** [Korean church dir. overs.]. **VFOAT** Hoeoe Hanin Kyohoe (Kidokkyo Kigwan) Chusorok. Directory. English (Japanese). Clarendon Presbyterian Church, 1305 North Jackson Street, Arlington VA 22201. **LC** BX4800.5; .K67.

NE
**KOSMOS + OEKUMENE.** **VFOAT** Kosmos en Oekumene. 6E Volume Number 1-. Periodical. Dutch. mo. $30.00. St Willibrord Vereniging, Walpoort 10, S-Hertogenbosch Netherlands. **Tel** (073)136471. Index available. cum. index. **Bk Rev**. **Ad Acc**. **Circ:** 1,300. ***Continues*** *Kosmos + Oecumene.*
**Desc:** Covers issues about the ecumenical movement.

US/0145-7551
**KRISTEN VIDENSKABS HEROLD.** **Added/Corp** Christian Science Publishing Society. **VFOAT** Herald of Christian Science. (19??)-. Periodical. Danish (English). qt. $29.00. Christian Science Publishing Society, One Norway Street, Boston MA 02115. **Tel** (617)450-2678, (617)450-2504. ***Continues*** *Christian Science Herold.*

RU
**KULTURA I RELIGIIA.** ***Ceased.*** (1992)-(1992). Periodical. Russian. mo. Izdatelstvo Znanie, Novaya Pl., 3-4,, 101835 Moscow Russia. **LC** BL9.R8; N68. ***Continues*** *Novoe v Zhizni, Nauke. Kultura i Religiia.*

JA
**KYODAN NEWS LETTER.** **Added/Corp** Nihon Kirisuto Kyodan. No. 1 (Jan. 20, 1966)-. Newsletter. English. bm (6 issues). $12.00. United Church of Christ in Japan, 2 3 18 31 Nishiwaseda Shinjuku, Tokyo 169 Japan. **Tel** 011 81 3 3202 0546.
**Ind/Abst** Hum. Rights Intern. Rep.

KO
**KYOHOE WA YOKSA.** **VFOAT** Church and History. V. 1- (Sept. 1975)-. Periodical. Korean (Korean). Hanguk Kyohoesa Yonguso, 367-27 Hapchong-dong Mapo-ku, Seoul Korea. **LC** BX1670.5; .K894.

SW/0085-2619
**KYRKOHISTORISK AARSSKRIFT.** [Kyrkohist. -Aarsskr.]. **Added/Corp** Svenska Kyrkohistoriska Foereningen. Kyrkohistoriska Foereningen (Sweden). (1900)-. English (Swedish; summaries and/or abstracts in English, French and German). an. kr175.00. Uppsala Universitet, Teologiska Institutionen, Box 1604 S-751 46 Sweden. **Tel** FAX 011 46 18 12 68 75. **ED** Harry Lenhammar. **LC** BR140; .K9. cum. index. **Bk Rev**. **Ad Acc**. **Circ:** 1,000.
**Ind/Abst** Am. Hist. Life (1962-).

PL/0208-7723
**LAD WARSZAWA.** (LAD.). (1981)-. Periodical. Polish. wk. $52.00. **(Subscription address:** ARS Polona, PO Box 1001, 00068 Warsaw Poland.**)** **UDC** 3.

PE/0360-3350
**LADOC.** **Added/Corp** United States Catholic Conference. **VAT** Latin America Documentation. No. 1, (June 1970)-. Periodical. English. Six times a year (Jan., Mar., May, July, Sept., Nov.). $10.00 Peru; $20.00 Latin America; $25.00 others. Ladoc Latin America Documentation, Apartado 18 0964, Lima 18 Peru. **Tel** 011 51 14 475210, FAX 011 51 14 454681. **ED** Maeve O'Driscoll C.P. **LC** BX1425.A1; L18. **DD** 282/.8. Index available. **Circ:** 1000. available on microfilm from University Microfilms International (UMI).
**Desc:** Documents from the Latin American churches.
**Ind/Abst** Bibliogr. Mission.; Hum. Rights Intern. Rep.; Abr. Cathol. Period. Lit. Index; Cathol. Period. Lit. Index.

VC/1010-7215
**LATERANUM.** [Lateranum]. **Added/Corp** Pontificia Universita Lateranense. Facolta di Teologia. (1919)-. Monographic series. Italian (English and German). sa. L65000 Italy; L90000 others. Pontificia Universita Lateranense, Piazza S Giovanni Laterano 4, 00120 Citta del Vaticano. **Tel** 011 39 6 69886401, FAX 011 39 6 69886103. **LC** BX800.A1; L37. Index available. **Bk Rev.** **Ind/Abst** Bibliogr. Mission.; Old Testam. Abstr.

US
**LATIN AMERICA EVANGELIST.** **Added/Corp** Latin America Mission. Vol. 1 (1921)-. Periodical. English. qt (Jan., Apr., July and Oct.). Free. Latin America Mission, PO Box 52-7900, Miami FL 33152-7900. **Tel** (305)884-8400. **ED** John Maust. **Bk Rev. Circ:** 32,000.
**Desc:** To give readers factual reporting, thoughtful analysis, human interest and spiritual uplift; and to reflect the real situation in the Latin world.

US
**LATVIJAS EV.-LUT. BAZNICAS GADA GRAMATA UN KALENDARS.** **Main/Corp** Latvijas Evan. **VFOAT** Baznicas Gada Gramata. 1973-. Latvian. an. 425 Elm Street, Glenview IL 60025. ***Continues*** *Latvijas Ev.-Lut. Baznicas Kalendars.*

CN/0023-9054
**LAVAL THEOLOGIQUE ET PHILOSOPHIQUE.** [Laval theol. philos.]. **Added/Corp** Universite Laval. Faculte de Theologie. Universite Laval. Faculte de Philosophie. **VFOAT** Laval Theologique Philosophique. **VAT** Laval Theologique Philosophique. Vol. 1 (1944)-. Periodical. French (English). Three times a year. 20.00Can$ Canada; $15.00 US. Presses de l'Universite Laval, CP 2447 Avenue de la Medicine, Saint Foy Quebec G1K 7P4 Canada. **Tel** (418)656-5106, (418)656-2590. **ED** Yvan Pelletier. **LC** BX802; .L3. **DD** 282.05. Index available in last issue of volume--attached. cum. index. **Bk Rev. Ad Acc. Circ:** 600. available on microfilm from Micromedia Limited; available on microfilm and microfiche from University Microfilms International (UMI).
**Desc:** A Quebec journal to promote research and discussion in all fields of theological and philosophical thinking.
**Ind/Abst** Index Book Rev. Relig.; New Testam. Abstr.; Old Testam. Abstr.; Philos. Index; Point Repere (1983-); Relig. Theol. Abstr.; Abr. Cathol. Period. Lit. Index; Cathol. Period. Lit. Index.

CN/0023-9054
**LAVAL THEOLOGIQUE ET PHILOSOPHIQUE.** [Laval theol. philos.]. **Added/Corp** Universite Laval. Faculte de Theologie. Universite Laval. Faculte de Philosophie. **VFOAT** Laval Theologique Philosophique. Vol. 1 (1944/1945)-. Periodical. French (English). Three times a year. 32.00Can$ (institutions), 25.00Can$ (individuals). Presses de l'Universite Laval, CP 2447 Avenue de la Medicine, Saint Foy Quebec G1K 7P4 Canada. **Tel** (418)656-5106, (418)656-2590. **(Subscription address:** Periodica Inc., PO Box 444, 1155 Ducharme, Outrement Quebec H2V 4R6 Canada.**)** **ED** Lionel Ponton. Documents available from The Genuine Article.
**Ind/Abst** Arts Humanit. Citation Index [Full Cov.]; Curr. Contents Arts Humanit.; New Testam. Abstr. (1983-); Old Testam. Abstr.; Philos. Index; Res. Alert [Full Cov.]; Soc. Sci. Cit. Index [Select. Cov.]; Abr. Cathol. Period. Lit. Index; Cathol. Period. Lit. Index.

US/1055-2626
**LEADER (ANDERSON, IND.).** (LEADER : A RESOURCE FOR CHRISTIAN LEADERSHIP.). **Added/Corp** Church of God (Anderson, Ind.). Board of Christian Education. (19??)-. Periodical. English. Six times a year (Jan., Mar., May, July, Sept., Nov.). $7.00 (one year); $12.00 (two years). Board of Christian Education Church of God, Box 2458, Anderson IN 46018. **Tel** (317)642-0257. **ED** Joseph L. Cookston. **DD** 268. Index available. cum. index. **Bk Rev**, (Qty: 7). **Circ:** 4,000. ***Continues*** *Christian Leadership, 1041-4460.*
**Desc:** Primary commitment is to leadership development and educational ministries of congregations.

US/0895-1403
**LEADER IN THE CHURCH SCHOOL TODAY.** [Lead. church sch. today]. **Added/Corp** United Methodist Church (U.S.) Board of Discipleship Curriculum Resources Committee. Vol. 1, No. 1 (Summer 1988)-. Periodical. English. qt. $14.00 (one year), $22.00 (two year). United Methodist Publishing House, PO Box 801, 201 8th Avenue South, Nashville TN 37202. **Tel** (615)749-6732, (615)749-6615, FAX (615)749-6578, (615)749-6579. **DD** 268. ***Continues*** *Church School Today, 0276-8569.*

US/0199-7661
**LEADERSHIP (CAROL STREAM).** (LEADERSHIP : A PUBLICATION OF CHRISTIANITY TODAY, INC.). [Leadership]. **Added/Corp** Christianity Today, Inc. Vol. 1, No. 1 (Winter 1980)-. Periodical. English. qt. $22.00. Christianity Today Inc., 465 Gundersen Drive, Carol Stream IL 60188. **Tel** (708)260-6200. **(Subscription address:** CDS / SIFD Agency Control, 1901 Bell Avenue, Des Moines IA 50315.**)** **ED** Marshall Shelley. **LC** BV4000; .L38. **DD** 253/.05. Index available. cum. index. **Bk Rev. Ad Acc. Circ:** 80,000. available on microfilm and microfiche from University Microfilms International (UMI).
**Desc:** Published by Christianity Today to provide local church leaders with practical, biblical guidelines for their everyday work. Our editorial premise is that the readers have had ample exposure to theory. Now they need down-to-earth, proven concepts that other churches are benefiting from.
**Ind/Abst** Curr. Thoughts Trends; Index Book Rev. Relig.; Relig. Index One Period.

GW
**LEBENDIGE SEELSORGE.** (1???)-. Periodical. German. Six times a year. DM49.00. Echter Wuerzburg, Postfach 5560, Julius Promenade 64, D 97070 Wuerzburg Germany. **Tel** 011/49/931/3091153, FAX 011/49/931/16735. **Bk Rev. Ad Acc. Circ:** 6,300.
**Desc:** Articles on ministerial work and pastoral duties.

US/1050-5393
**LECCIONES CHRISTIANAS PARA JOVENES. ALUMNO.** [Lecciones Christ. jovenes. Alumno]. No 1 (Sept/Aug 1991)-. Periodical. Spanish. $2.95 (single issue). Graded Press, 201 Eighth Avenue South, Box 801, Nashville TN 37202. **Tel** (615)749-6417. **DD** 268.

US/0149-8363
**LECCIONES CRISTIANAS.** Periodical. Spanish. qt. $4.75, $9.75 (teacher book). Graded Press, 201 Eighth Avenue South, Box 801, Nashville TN 37202. **Tel** (615)749-6417.

US/1050-5385
**LECCIONES CRISTIANAS PARA JOVENES. LIBRO DEL MAESTRO.** [Lecciones Crist. jovenes.]. **Added/Corp** United Methodist Church (U.S.) Board of Discipleship. Curriculum Resources Committee. United Presbyterian Church in the U.S.A. **VFOAT** Christian Lessons for Youth. (Sept/Aug 1991)-. Periodical. Spanish. $1.95 (single issue). Graded Press, 201 Eighth Avenue South, Box 801, Nashville TN 37202. **Tel** (615)749-6417. **DD** 268.

US/8750-4448
**LECCIONES DE LA ESCUELA SABATICA.** **VFOAT** Sabbath School Lessons. Periodical. Spanish. qt. $4.50. Lecciones de la Escuela Sabatica, PO Box 7000, Boise ID 83707. **DD** 268.
**Desc:** A Bible study for those interested in Bible study.

US/0746-763X
**LECTERN RESOURCE.** Vol. 1, No. 1 (Jan./Feb./Mar. 1984)-. Periodical. English. qt. $36.00 (libraries), $18.00 (other). Logos Art Productions, PO Box 240, South St. Paul MN 55075. **Tel** (800)328-0200, (612)451-9945, FAX (612)457-4617. **Circ:** 1,500.
**Desc:** Aid for planning worship, scriptural resource material, word for children intercession and includes international focus.

US/1043-2310
**LECTIONARY HOMILETICS.** [Lection. homilet.]. (1989)-. Periodical. English. mo. $65.00. Lectionary Homilectics, PO Box 2012, 6006 Moss Creek Court, Midlothian VA 23112. **Tel** (804)744-8631. **DD** 251.

CN/0225-5391
**LEGAL SHOCK.** **See** Law.

US/0891-3927
**LET THE PEOPLE WORSHIP.** [Let people worsh.]. **Added/Corp** Schuyler Creative Arts Institute. Vol. 1, Issue 1 (Spring 1985)-. Periodical. English. Four times a year (Feb., June, Sept., Dec.). $20.00 (individuals); $50.00 (institutions). Schuyler Creative Arts Institute, 2757 Melendy Drive, PO Box 790, San Carlos CA 94070. **Tel** (415)595-2443. **ED** Pamela Payne Allen. **DD** 254. ctrl circ.

US
**LETTER FROM TAIZE.** **Added/Corp** Communaute de Taize. No. 1 (May 1970)-. Periodical. English (German, Italian, Spanish and Dutch). bm. $9.00. Letter From Taize, 2150 Almaden Road, San Jose CA 95123. **LC** BV4408.A1; L46.

UK
**LETTERS AND NOTICES.** Began with V. 1 in June 1862. Periodical. English. ir. $20.00. Jesuit Information Office, 114 Mount Street, London W1Y 6AH England. **Tel** (01)49-7596. **ED** Hugh Kay. **Bk Rev. Circ:** 2,300.
**Desc:** A review of Christian thought and world affairs i.e. China in Deng's last years, God in the nuclear age, arms control: a new perspective and detente by way of Germany.

FR
**LETTRE DES AMIS : BULLETIN DES QUAKERS EN FRANCE.** No. 1 (April/May/June 1984)-. Bulletin. French. qt. Societe Religieuses des Amis, 114 Rud de Vaugirard, 75006 Paris France. ***Continues*** *Vie Quaker.*

US/0024-1628
**LEXINGTON THEOLOGICAL QUARTERLY.** [Lexingt. theol. q.]. **Added/Corp** Lexington Theological Seminary. Vol. 1 (Jan. 1966)-. Academic Scholarly Publication. English. qt. Lexington Theological Seminary, 631 South Limestone, Lexington KY 40508. **Tel** (606)252-0361. **ED** William R. Barr. **LC** BR1; .L38. Index available. cum. index. **Bk Rev. Circ:** 2,500 (ctrl). available on microfilm and microfiche from University Microfilms International (UMI). ***Supersedes*** *College of the Bible Quarterly, 0160-8770.*
**Desc:** For ministers and professors of religion. Includes scholarly articles on Bible, theology, church history, ethics, sermons and sermon preparation, Christian unity, and pastoral care.
**Ind/Abst** Index Book Rev. Relig.; New Testam. Abstr.; Old Testam. Abstr.; Relig. Index One Period. (1966-); Relig. Theol. Abstr.

US
**LIBERAL RELIGIOUS EDUCATION.** (19??)-. Periodical. English. sa. $20.00 US, Canada & Mexico; $23.00 other. Unitarian Universalist Association, 25 Beacon Street, Boston MA 02108. **Tel** (617)742-2100. **(Subscription address:** Liberal Religious Education, 22 Ardley Road, Winchester, MA 01890**)** **ED** M. Elizabeth Anastos.
**Desc:** Mission is to inform the philosophy and practice of religious education through regular publication which critically reflects on ideas and events important to religious education.

CN/0227-2687
**LIBERATION (MILTON).** (LIBERATION.). [Liberation]. No. 1- Jan. 1979-. Periodical. English. Renaissance International, PO Box 100, Milton Ontario L9T 2Y3 Canada. **DD** 269/.2/0971.

CN/0829-0954
**LIBERATION (MILTON. 1984).** (LIBERATION.). [Liberation]. **Added/Corp** Ken Campbell Evangelistic Association. Vol. 13, No. 2/3 (Oct./Nov. 1984)-. Periodical. English. qt. Free to contributors of the Association. Ken Campbell Evangelistic Association Inc, PO Box 100, Milton Ontario L9T 2Y3 Canada. **Tel** (416)878-8461. **ED** Ken Campbell. **DD** 269/.2/0971. **Bk Rev. Ad Acc. Circ:** 40,000. ***Continues*** *Encounter., 0315-0097.*
**Desc:** An independent quarterly speaking to, and for, the evangelistic Christian.

US
**LIBRARY OF RELIGIOUS PHILOSOPHY.** **See** Philosophy.

SW/0284-0200
**LIFE & PEACE REVIEW.** **VFOAT** Life and Peace Review. (1987)-. Periodical. English. Four times a year. Kr22.00 US & Canada; Kr25.00 others. Life & Peace Institute, Box 297, S-75105 Uppsala Sweden. **Tel** 011 46 18 169500, FAX 011 46 18 693059. **ED** Tom Dorris (phone: (46)18 16 9500). **UDC** 241. **Bk Rev. Ad Acc.** ctrl circ.
**Desc:** This magazine covers peace and justice issues, with an emphasis on church involvement.

US
**LIFE PURPOSE JOURNALS.** Periodical. English. Four times a year. $15.00. IBLP Publications Office, PO Box 1, Oak Brook IL 60522. **Tel** (708)323-9800.

●US/1063-794X
**LIFELINES FOR YOUTH TEACHER.** [Lifelines youth teach.]. Vol. 1, No. 1 (June, July, Aug. 1992)-. Periodical. English. qt. $11.70. Herald and Banner Press, 7415 Metcalf, Overland Park KS 66204. **DD** 268. ***Continues*** *Junior High, Senior Youth Teacher.*

US/0190-6569
**LIGHT 'N' HEAVY.** **Added/Corp** Assemblies of God. General Council. Assemblies of God. Youth Dept. **VAT** Light and Heavy. Vol. 52, No. 3 (Spring 1979)-. Periodical. English. qt. $5.00. Gospel Publishing House, 1445 Boonville Avenue, Springfield MO 65802. **Tel** (417)862-2781, FAX (417)866-1146. ***Continues*** *Youth Alive, 0009-5826.*
**Desc:** Stories on personalities or youth-oriented issues. Also humor page, and question/ answer column.

US
**LIGHT (NASHVILLE, TENN.).** (LIGHT.). Periodical. English. qt. $5.00. Christian Life Commission, PO Box 25266, Nashville TN 37202. **ED** Louis A Moore. Index available. cum. index. **Bk Rev. Circ:** 75,000 (ctrl).
**Desc:** Commentary on social, ethical, public policies as per theology of Southern Baptist Convention.
**Ind/Abst** Seventh-Day Adventist Period. Index (1971-); South. Baptist Period. Index.

US/1040-7448
**LIGHT OF CONSCIOUSNESS.** [Light conscious.]. **VFOAT** Chit-Jyoti. Vol. 1, No. 1 (Sept./Oct. 1988)-. Periodical. English. Three times a year. Truth Consciousness Inc, Gold Hill Salina Star Route, Boulder CO 80302. **Tel** (303)447-1637. **ED** Bob Conrow. **LC** BP605.T78; T78. **DD** 299/.93. **Bk Rev. Ad Acc. Circ:** 650 (ctrl). ***Continues*** *Truth Consciousness Journal, 0191-5207.*

**Desc:** Devoted to the realization of the true self within; a vehicle for Swami Amar Jyoti's message of spiritual awakening. Professes a universal outlook of religion.

II/0970-2571
**LIGHT OF LIFE.** (1957)-. Periodical. English. Eleven times a year. $15.00. Light of Life, 21 YMCA Road, Bombay 400 008 India. **ED** P. Abraham (editor's phone: 022 307 6941). **UDC** 22. **Bk Rev**, (Qty: 11). **Ad Acc**. Full Page (B&W) Rs600.00. Half Page (B&W) Rs350.00. **Circ:** 5,000.
**Desc:** Oriented to the Christian family and endeavours to inspire, instruct, inform and influence Christians to become better followers of Jesus Christ.

PL/0342-0884
**LINGUISTICA BIBLICA.** [Linguist. Biblica]. **Added/Corp** Arbeitskreis Theologie und Linguistik. (Nov. 1970)-. Periodical. German. sa. $15.01. Linguistica Biblica Bonn, Postfach 130150, D 53061 Bonn Germany. **Tel** 011 49 2225 7645. **LC** BL65.L2; L53. **DD** 201/.4. Documents available from The Genuine Article.
**Ind/Abst** Arts Humanit. Citation Index (19??-19??) [Full Cov.]; Curr. Contents Arts Humanit.; Linguist. Lang. Behav. Abstr. (1972-) [Full Cov.]; MLA Int. Bibl. Books Artic. Mod. Lang. Lit.; New Testam. Abstr.; Old Testam. Abstr.; Relig. Theol. Abstr.; Res. Alert [Full Cov.]; Soc. Plann. Policy Dev. Abstr.

CN/0845-4507
**LISTE DES RELIGIEUX ET CATALOGUE DES MAISONS ET OEUVRES / CONGREGATION DE SAINTE-CROIX, SOCIETE DES PERES, LA PROVINCE CANADIENNE.** [Liste relig. cat. maisons oeuvres - Congregat. St.-Croix Soc. Peres Prov. can.]. **Main/Corp** Peres de Sainte-Croix. Province Canadienne. (1988/1989)-. French. an. Province Canadienne des Peres de Sainte-Croix, 4961 rue Coronet, Montreal Quebec H3V 1C9 Canada. **DD** 255/.79. ***Continues*** *Peres de Sainte-Croix. Province Canadienne. Liste des Religieux, des Residences et des Oeuvres., 0820-0629.*

US/0024-4414
**LISTENING (RIVER FOREST).** (LISTENING.). [Listening]. **Added/Corp** Aquinas Institute of Philosophy and Theology. Vol. 1 (Winter 1966)-. Periodical. English. Three times a year (Feb., May, Oct.). $10.00 (individuals), $13.00 (institutions) US; $12.00 (individuals), $15.00 (institutions) other. Listening, Journal of Religion and Culture, Lewis University, Box 1108 Rt 53, Romeoville IL 60441-2298. **Tel** (815)838-0500 Ext 342. **ED** Victor S LaMotte. **LC** AP2; .L5515. cum. index. **Bk Rev**. **Ad Acc**. **Circ:** 1,000 (ctrl). available on microfilm and microfiche from University Microfilms International (UMI).
**Desc:** Interested in ideas, persons, in dialogue and in explorations, it is interested in anything that is cogent. A journal of religion and culture.
**Ind/Abst** Old Testam. Abstr.; Philos. Index; Abr. Cathol. Period. Lit. Index; Cathol. Period. Lit. Index.

US/0732-1929
**LITERATURE AND BELIEF.** **See** Literature.

UK/0269-1205
**LITERATURE & THEOLOGY.** **See** Literature.

US/0460-1297
**LITTLE LAMP, THE.** Periodical. English. qt. $15.00 (one year), $42.00 (three year). Blue Mountain Center of Meditation, Box 477, Petaluma CA 94953. **Tel** (707)878-2369. **ED** Christine Easwaran. **LC** BL624; .L57. **DD** 294.5/44/05. Index available. **Circ:** 2,000. ***Continues*** *Newsletter (Blue Mountain Center of Meditation).*
**Desc:** A journal for leading the spiritual life in the home and the community.

US
**LITURGICAL CONFERENCE.** ***Ceased.*** -Ceased May 1984. Monographic series. English. mo. Liturgical Newsletter, Box 3554, Albuquerque NM 87110. **Tel** (505)883-0469.

●US/1059-7786
**LITURGICAL MINISTRY.** [Liturg. minist.]. **Added/Corp** Maria Stein Center. Institute for Liturgical Ministry. (Winter 1992)-. Periodical. English. qt. $20.00. Institute for Liturgical Ministry, 2365 St. John's Road, PO Box 128, Maria Stein OH 45860. **Tel** (419)925-4538. **ED** Joyce Ann Zimmerman. **DD** 264. **Bk Rev**. **Circ:** 350.
**Desc:** Thematic periodical addressing topics concerning worship/liturgy in both scholarly and pastoral contexts.

FR
**LITURGIE.** French. Four times a year (Mar., June, Sept., Dec.). 140.00F. Liturgie, Abbaye la Joie Notre Dame, 56800 Campeneac France.

CN
**LITURGIE FOI ET CULTURE.** Four times a year. 14.00Can$ Canada; 27.00Can$ other. Publications Service of the Canadian Conference of Catholic Bishops, 90 Parent Avenue, Ottawa Ontario K1N 7B1 Canada. **Tel** (613)236-9461, FAX (613)236-8117.

GW/0076-0048
**LITURGIEWISSENSCHAFTLICHE QUELLEN UND FORSCHUNGEN.** **Added/Corp** Maria Laach (Benedictine Monastery). Vol. 32 (1957)-. Monographic series. German. ir. Price varies per volume. Aschendorffsche Verlagsbuchhandlung, Postfach 1124, D-48135 Muenster Germany. **Tel** 011 49 251 690132, telex 08-92 830 WN MS D. **LC** BV170; .L5513. ***Continues*** *Liturgiegeschichtliche Quellen und Forschungen.*
**Desc:** Research and documentation on doctrinal theology, from the beginnings of Christianity through the middle ages and the reformation.

GW/0024-5100
**LITURGISCHES JAHRBUCH.** **Added/Corp** Liturgisches Institut Trier. (1951)-. Periodical. German. qt. DM70.00. Aschendorffsche Verlagsbuchhandlung, Postfach 1124, D-48135 Muenster Germany. **Tel** 011 49 251 690132, telex 08-92 830 WN MS D. **[CCC]**. Index available. cum. index. **Bk Rev**. **Ad Acc**. **Circ:** 1,400.
**Desc:** Discussions of current questions of the worship service, attempts to analyze today's worship based on anthropological, historical and theological foundations, background information on liturgy and reform.
**Ind/Abst** BHA : Biblio. Hist. Art; Index Book Rev. Relig.; Relig. Index One Period.; Relig. Theol. Abstr.

US
**LITURGY DOCUMENTARY SERIES.** 1-. Monographic series. English. Price varies per volume. Office of Publishing Services, United States Catholic Conference, 1312 Massachusetts Avenue NW, Washington DC 20005.

US/0458-063X
**LITURGY (WASHINGTON).** (LITURGY.). [Liturgy]. **Added/Corp** Liturgical Conference, Inc. (1980)-. Periodical. English. qt. Free to members of the Liturgical Conference. Liturgical Conference / Maryland, 8750 Georgia Avenue, Suite 123, Silver Spring MD 20910. **Tel** (301)495-0885. **ED** Rachel Reeder. **LC** BV169; .L58. **DD** 264/.005. **Circ:** 4,500 (ctrl). available on microfilm from University Microfilms International (UMI). ***Continues*** *Liturgy (Washington, D.C. : 1956), 0458-063X.*
**Desc:** Addresses the subject of worship that is ecumenical, imaginative and free; sacramental celebrations; liturgical ministries. Explores themes in relation to worship, music, and the arts, social justice and the Bible in the assembly.
**Ind/Abst** Relig. Theol. Abstr.; Abr. Cathol. Period. Lit. Index; Cathol. Period. Lit. Index.

US/0024-5240
**LIVING CHURCH (1942), THE.** (THE LIVING CHURCH.). **VFOAT** Living Church and the Layman's Magazine. Vol. 104 (Jan. 7, 1942)-. Periodical. English. wk. $39.50 (one year), $70.72 (two year). The Living Church, 816 East Juneau, Milwaukee WI 53202. **Tel** (414)276-5420. **ED** H. Boone Porter. **Bk Rev**. **Ad Acc**. **Circ:** 10,000. ***Continues*** *Living Church and the Layman's Magazine, 0161-8482.*
**Desc:** Publishes current news of Episcopal church. Containing articles, special reports, letters from readers and clergy changes.

US/0193-5968
**LIVING CITY (NEW YORK).** (LIVING CITY.). [Living city]. **Added/Corp** Focolare Movement. Focolare Movement. Women's Branch. **VFOAT** LivingCity. (19??)-. Periodical. English. Eleven times a year. Living City / NY, PO Box 126, Jamaica NY 11415. **Tel** (718)896-0334. **ED** Sharry Silvi. **LC** BX809.F6; L58. **DD** 270.8/2. **Circ:** 7,000 (ctrl).
**Desc:** Articles focusing on the spirituality of the Focolare movement, a spirituality of unity; articles on ecumenism and current events regarding the Catholic Church, family life, youth and human development.

US/0890-5568
**LIVING PRAYER.** [Living pray.]. Vol. 19, No. 3 (Sept./Oct. 1986)-. Periodical. English. bm (6 issues). $17.00 (1 year), $32.00 (2 year) US; $22.00 (1 year), $44.00 (2 year) other. Living Prayer Inc, Beckley Hill, Rural Route 2 Box 4784, Barre VT 05641. **Tel** (802)476-8362. **ED** Mary Roman. **DD** 248. **Bk Rev**. **Circ:** 6,500 (ctrl). available on microfilm and microfiche from University Microfilms International (UMI). ***Continues*** *Contemplative Review, 0193-8452.*
**Desc:** Contains articles, book meditations to promote understanding of the Christian tradition of meditation, mysticism and contemplation, and to practice contemporary prayer.
**Ind/Abst** Abr. Cathol. Period. Lit. Index; Cathol. Period. Lit. Index.

●US/1059-2733
**LIVING PULPIT, THE.** [Living pulpit]. Vol. 1, No. 1 (Jan.-Mar. 1992)-. Periodical. English. qt. $39.00 US; $41.00 Canada; $45.00 other (membership). Living Pulpit, Inc., PO Box 3000, Denville NJ 07834. **Tel** (914)758-5219, FAX (212)549-6113. **ED** Ginger Grab. **DD** 251. **Bk Rev**, (Qty: 20). ctrl circ.
**Desc:** Resource for sermon preparation. Each issue focuses on a specific theme. Subject matter includes biblical research, theological interpretation, relevant material from science, literature, philosophy, politics. Provides provocative ideas, useful information.

US/0883-7236
**LIVING THE WORD. LEVEL 8, GRADES TEN-TWELVE STUDENT'S RESOURCE.** (LIVING THE WORD. LEVEL 8, GRADES TEN-TWELVE.). **VFOAT** Living the Word. Level Eight, Grades Ten-Twelve; Living the Word. Level 8, Older Youth. Periodical. English. qt. United Church Press, 475 Riverside Drive 10th Floor, New York NY 10115. **Tel** (800)537-3394, (212)870-2100. **DD** 268.

CN/0703-6752
**LIVING WITH CHRIST. COMPLETE EDITION.** (LIVING WITH CHRIST.). Vol. 1 (Apr./May 1977)-. Periodical. English. Twelve times a year. Novalis, PO Box 990, Outremont Quebec H2V 4S7 Canada. **Tel** (514)948-1222. **ED** Jerome Herauf. **DD** 264/.023. **Circ:** 96,100. ***Continues in part*** *Living with Christ, 0383-2481.*
**Desc:** Prayers and texts for daily masses.

CN/0703-6760
**LIVING WITH CHRIST. SUNDAY EDITION.** (LIVING WITH CHRIST.). Vol. 42, No. 4 (Apr./May 1977)-. Periodical. English. Twelve times a year. 13.85Can$. Novalis, PO Box 990, Outremont Quebec H2V 4S7 Canada. **Tel** (514)948-1222. **ED** Jerome Herauf. **DD** 264/.023. **Circ:** 217,350. ***Continues in part*** *Living with Christ, 0383-2481.*
**Desc:** Liturgical texts for Sunday masses.

CN/0714-7880
**LOAVES & FISHES (TORONTO, ONT.).** (LOAVES & FISHES.). **VAT** Loaves and Fishes. Vol. 1 (Fall 1978)-. Periodical. English. sa. $10.00. Canec Publishing and Supply House, 85 St Clair Avenue East, Toronto Ontario M4T 1M8 Canada. **DD** 268/.432.

●US/1064-0398
**LOGIA (FORT WAYNE, INDIANA).** (LOGIA : A JOURNAL OF LUTHERAN THEOLOGY.). [Logia]. **Added/Corp** Luther Academy (Fort Wayne, Ind.). (Reformation/Oct. 1992)-. Periodical. English. Four times a year. $18.00 US; $25.00 Canada and Mexico; $35.00 (airmail), $25.00 (surface mail) other. The Luther Academy, 2829 Fox Chase Run, Fort Wayne IN 46825-3985. **(Subscription address:** Logia, 800 South Military, Dearborn, MI 48124**)** **DD** 284. **Bk Rev**, (Qty: 20). **Ad Acc**, **Adv Mgr:** Rodney E Zwonitzer. **Circ:** 1,500.
**Desc:** A journal of Lutheran theology, Logia publishes articles on exegetical, historical, systematic, and liturgical theology that promotes the orthodox theology of the Evangelical Lutheran Church.

US/0194-3820
**LOGOS JOURNAL.** **Added/Corp** Logos International Fellowship. (197?)-. Periodical. English. Six times a year. Logos Journal, 201 Church Street, Plainfield NJ 07061. **LC** BR1644; .L63. **DD** 269. ***Supersedes*** *Herald of Faith-Harvest Time Magazine.*

CN/0828-184X
**LONERGAN STUDIES NEWSLETTER.** [Lonergan stud. newsl.]. **Added/Corp** Lonergan Research Institute. Vol. 1, No. 1 (Jan. 1980)-. Newsletter. English. qt. $5.00. Lonergan Research Institute, 10 St. Mary Street, Suite 500, Toronto ONT M4Y 1P9 Canada. **Tel** (416)922-8374. **ED** F. E. Crowe. **DD** 016.230/092/4. **Bk Rev**. **Circ:** 250.
**Desc:** International quarterly presenting and reviewing scholarship related to the methodology proposed by Bernard Lonergan for contemporary philosophy and theology.

US/0148-2009
**LONERGAN WORKSHOP.** ***Suspended.*** (LONERGAN WORKSHOP: [COLLECTED ESSAYS].). **Main/Corp** Lonergan Workshop. Vol. 1 (1978)-Vol. 8. Periodical. English. sa. $18.00. Scholars Press / Georgia, PO Box 15399, Atlanta GA 30333-0399. **Tel** (404)636-4757, (404)727-2320, FAX (404)727-2348. **ED** Fred Lawrence. **LC** BX4705.L7133; L66. **DD** 230/.05. **Circ:** 200.
**Desc:** Features symposia on the work of such authors as Hans-Georg Gadamer and Eric Voegelin, and includes new essays by these authors.

US
**LOOKOUT, THE.** Periodical. English. wk. $15.00. Standard Publishing Company / Ohio, 8121 Hamilton Avenue, Cincinnati OH 45231. **Tel** (513)931-4050, (800)543-1353. **ED** Mark A Taylor. **LC** BX7312.A1; L6. **DD** 268.43305. **Bk Rev**. **Circ:** 145,000.
**Desc:** Helps build Sunday schools, individual Christian commitment, and Christian family life. Deals with contemporary issues in light of Biblical teaching.

US/0024-6425
**LOOKOUT (NEW YORK), THE.** **See** Sociology-Social Services and Welfare.

MX
**LOS CUATRO VIENTOS, DE.** **VFOAT** Cuatro Vientos. Vol. 1, No. 1 (May/July 1990)-. Periodical. Spanish. bm.

BE/0024-6964
**LOUVAIN STUDIES.** [Louv. stud.]. **Added/Corp** Katholieke Universiteit te Leuven (1970- ). Faculteit der Godgeleerdheid. American College (Louvain, Belgium). Vol. 1, No. 1 (Fall 1966)-. Periodical. English. qt. $30.00 (one year), $55.00 (two year), $80.00 (three year). Louvain Studies, Faculty of Theology, KU Leuven, St Michielsstraat 6, 3000 Leuven Belgium. **Tel** 011 32 16 283894, FAX 011 32 16 283858. **ED** John A. Dick. **LC** BX801; .L6. Index available. **Bk Rev. Circ:** 1,500 (ctrl). available on microfilm and microfiche from University Microfilms International (UMI).
**Desc:** Presents current scholarship in Roman Catholic theology.
**Ind/Abst** Bibliogr. Mission.; Canon Law Abstr.; Index Book Rev. Relig.; New Testam. Abstr.; Old Testam. Abstr.; Relig. Theol. Abstr.; Abr. Cathol. Period. Lit. Index; Cathol. Period. Lit. Index.

AT/1030-4428
**LUCAS.** [Lucas]. (1987)-. Periodical. English. Twice a year (June, Dec.). 32.00Aus$. Evangelical History Association, Centre Study Australia Christ, PO Box 1505, Marquarie CTR 2113 Australia. **Tel** 61 2 5192131. **ED** Geoff Treloar (phone: 02 887 3698). **DD** 253.7. Index available. cum. index. **Bk Rev. Ad Acc. Pr Rev. Circ:** 200 (ctrl).
**Desc:** Review journal of the Evangelical History Association, publishing christian and church history.

US/8756-8012
**LUCRURI NOI SI VECHI.** Began in 1984. Periodical. Romanian (English). mo. $25.00. Motz Publications, 9304 Annapolis Court, Fairfax VA 22032. **Tel** (703)323-0708. **(Subscription address:** PO Box 2426, Fairfax, VA 22031) **ED** Dorin Motz. **DD** 947. **Bk Rev. Ad Acc. Circ:** 3,000 (ctrl).
**Desc:** Non-denominational Christian publication with many additional subjects geared for preservation of Romanian language. Also many articles on English language.

BE/0024-7324
**LUMEN VITAE.** [Lumen vitae]. **Added/Corp** International Centre for Studies in Religious Education. (1946)-. French. Four times a year (Mar., June, Sept., Dec.). 1090F Belgium; 1380F Europe; 1410F others. Lumen Vitae, 184 186 rue Washington, B-1050 Bruxelles Belgium. **Tel** 011 32 2 3441882, FAX 011 32 2 3465745. **ED** P. Mourlon Beernaert. Index available. cum. index. **Bk Rev. Ad Acc. Circ:** 1,500. available on microfilm from University Microfilms International (UMI).
**Desc:** Religious education, faith formation, and pastoral theology.
**Ind/Abst** Bibliogr. Mission.; Educ. Index; New Testam. Abstr.; Relig. Theol. Abstr.; Abr. Cathol. Period. Lit. Index; Cathol. Period. Lit. Index.

FR/0024-7359
**LUMIERE ET VIE.** [Lumiere vie]. **Added/Corp** College Theologique Dominicain de Saint-Alban-Leysse (Savoie). No. 1 (Dec. 1951)-. Periodical. French. Five times a year. 220.00F France; 250.00F (surface mail), 300.00F (air mail) other. Lumiere et Vie, 2 Place Gailleton, 69002 Lyon France. **Tel** 011 33 78 426683. cum. index. **Bk Rev. Ad Acc. Circ:** 3,000.
**Desc:** Journal dealing with theological structure and reflection.
**Ind/Abst** Bibliogr. Mission.; Index Book Rev. Relig.; New Testam. Abstr.; Old Testam. Abstr.; Romant. Move.; Abr. Cathol. Period. Lit. Index; Cathol. Period. Lit. Index.

CN/1183-935X
**LUMINANCE (MONTREAL).** (LUMINANCE : LA REVUE DU NOUVEL AGE AU QUEBEC.). [Luminance]. (Spring 1991)-. Periodical. French. qt. 15.84Can$. Ariane Publishers and Distributors, 5427 Avenue du Parc, Montreal Quebec H2V 4G9 Canada. **Tel** (514)273-6467. **DD** 299.

●SW/1102-769X
**LUND STUDIES IN ETHICS AND THEOLOGY.** See Ethics.

PO/0076-1508
**LUSITANIA SACRA.** See History(General).

US/0894-0304
**LUTHERAN COMMENTATOR.** [Lutheran comment.]. **Added/Corp** Lutherans for Political and Religious Freedom. Vol. 1, No. 1 (Summer 1987)-. Periodical. English. qt (Jan., Apr., July, Oct.). $12.00 (one year), $22.00 (two year), $30.00 (three year) US; $19.00 (one year), $36.00 (two year), $51.00 (three year) other. Lutheran Commentator, PO Box 1093, Minnetonka MN 55345. **Tel** (612)938-6771. **DD** 261.

US/0024-7464
**LUTHERAN LAYMAN, THE.** **Added/Corp** International Lutheran Laymen's League. (19??)-. Periodical. English. Ten times a year. $5.00. Lutheran Layman, 2185 Hampton Avenue, St Louis MO 63139. **Tel** (314)647-4900. **ED** Gerald Perschbacher. **Bk Rev**, (Qty: varies). **Circ:** 90,000 (ctrl). available on audiocassette.
**Desc:** Official publication of the Lutheran layman's league. Gives information about the League's media ministries and stories about laymen serving Christ in the Church and the League.

US/0024-7499
**LUTHERAN QUARTERLY (GETTYSBURG. 1949).** (LUTHERAN QUARTERLY.). [Lutheran q.]. Vol. 1, No. 1 (Spring 1987)-. Periodical. English. Four times a year. $27.00 (one year); $48.00 (two years). Lutheran Quarterly, 2715 South Ray Street, Spokane WA 99223. **Tel** (509)535-3333. **DD** 284. available on microfilm and microfiche from University Microfilms International (UMI). ***Continues** Lutheran Quarterly (Gettysburg, Pa. : 1949), 0024-7499.*
**Ind/Abst** Am. Hist. Life (1963-1977, 1987-); Index Book Rev. Relig.; Relig. Index One Period.

GW/0024-7618
**LUTHERISCHE MONATSHEFTE.** Vol. 1 (Jan. 1962)-. Periodical. German. Twelve times a year. DM66.00 Germany; DM73.20 other. Lutherisches Verlagshaus GmbH, Knochenhauer 38/40, W 3000 Hannover 1 F R Germany. **Tel** 0511/1241-733, FAX 011 49 511 1649595. **LC** BX8001; .L96. **DD** 261/.05. **Circ:** 6,400 (ctrl). ***Formed by the union of** Evangelisch-Lutherische Kirchenzeitung; Informationsblatt fur die Gemeinden in Den Niederdeutschen Lutherischen Landeskirchen **and** Lutherische Nachrichten.*
**Desc:** Information and opinion on church, religion, culture and politics.

GW
**LUTHERISCHE THEOLOGIE UND KIRCHE.** **Added/Corp** Lutherische Theologische Hochschule, Oberursel. (Feb. 1977)-. Periodical. German. Four times a year. DM25.00. Lutherische Theologie und Kirche, Altkoenigstrasse 150, D 61440 Oberursel Germany. **Tel** 011 41 6171 24340. Index available. **Bk Rev. Circ:** 700 (ctrl). ***Continues** Lutherischer Rundblick.*
**Desc:** Essays concerning Lutheran theology, including doctrinal and practical theology.

GW/0342-0914
**LUTHERJAHRBUCH.** [Lutherjahrbuch]. **Added/Corp** Luthergesellschaft. **VFOAT** Luther-Jahrbuch. Vol. 1 (1919)-. German. ir. Price varies per volume. Vandenhoeck & Ruprecht, Robert Bosch Breite 6, D-37079 Goettingen Germany. **Tel** 011 49 551 695911, FAX 011 49 551 695917, telex 965226 VAN d. **ED** Helmar Junghans. **Bk Rev. Ad Acc. Circ:** 390.
**Ind/Abst** Am. Hist. Life (1985-); MLA Int. Bibl. Books Artic. Mod. Lang. Lit.

IT
**LUX BIBLICA : RIVISTA TEOLOGICA SEMESTRALE EDITA A CURA DI IBEI E VERITAS EDIZIONI.** (19??)-. Italian. sa. L20000 Italy; L25000 other. Istituto Biblico Evangelico Italiano, Via des Casale Corvio 50, 00132 Rome Italy. **Tel** 011 39 6 20762293.

GW/0174-1756
**LWF DOCUMENTATION.** [LWF doc.]. **Main/Corp** Lutheran World Federation. **VAT** Lutheran World Federation Documentation. No. 1 (Sept. 1978)-. Periodical. English. ir. DM22.00. Lutheran World Federation, 150 Route de Ferney, CP 2100, Geneva 20 Switzerland. **Tel** 011 41 22 7916111. **LC** BX8001; .L82a. **DD** 284.1/0601. **Circ:** 3,000. ***Supersedes in part** Lutheran World.*
**Ind/Abst** Index Book Rev. Relig.; Relig. Index One Period. (1978).

●US/1066-5749
**LWML QUARTERLY ECHO.** (LWML QUARTERLY ECHO / NEBRASKA DISTRICT SOUTH.). **Added/Corp** Lutheran Women's Missionary League. Nebraska District South. **VFOAT** Quarterly Echo; Lutheran Women's Missionary League Quarterly Echo. Vol. 18, No. 3 (Fall 1992)-. Periodical. English. qt. LWML Quarterly Echo, 537 E Memorial Drive, Grand Island NE 68801. ***Continues** Lutheran Women's Missionary League Quarterly Echo, 8750-5207.*

CN/0315-9655
**M I C MISSION NEWS.** **Main/Corp** Missionary Sisters of the Immaculate Conception. V. 1- Jan./Feb. 1974-. Periodical. English. bm. Missionary Sisters of the Immaculate Conception, PO Box 157 Laval Branch PO, Laval Quebec H7N 424 Canada. **DD** 266/.2. ***Supersedes** Precursor, 0315-9663.*

BL
**MACAE ESPIRITA.** **Added/Corp** Uniao Espirita Macaense. Departamento Social. (19??)-. Periodical. Portuguese. ir. Uniao Espirita Macaense Departamento Social, Caixa Postal 74, Macae RJ Brazil.

US/8756-4564
**MAGAZINE FOR CHRISTIAN YOUTH, THE.** [Mag. Christ. youth]. **Added/Corp** United Methodist Church (U.S.). Board of Discipleship. Curriculum Resources Committee. **VFOAT** Youth. (Sept. 1985)-. Periodical. English. mo. $18.00 (1 year), $30.00 (2 year) US; $20.00 (1 year), $32.00 (2 year) other. Graded Press, 201 Eighth Avenue South, Box 801, Nashville TN 37202. **Tel** (615)749-6417. **ED** Christopher B. Hughes. **DD** 051. **Bk Rev. Circ:** 50,000.
**Desc:** Purpose is to help teens develop Christian identity and live the Christian faith in their contemporary culture.

US
**MANANAM PUBLICATION SERIES.** The Stock Show, 2100 North Highway 360/#1205, Grand Prairie TX 75050-1015. **Tel** (915)762-2352.

II
**MANASABHARATI : SRI RAMACARITAMANASA CATUSSATABDI SAMAROHA SAMITI, MADHYAPRADESA, BHOPALA KI MASIKA MUKHAPATRIKA.** See Literature.

CN/0225-7068
**MANDATE (TORONTO. 1979).** (MANDATE.). [Mandate]. **Added/Corp** United Church of Canada. Vol. 10, No. 7 (Oct. 1979)-. Periodical. English. Six times a year. $6.50. United Church of Canada, 85 Saint Clair Avenue East Room 711, Toronto Ontario M45 1M8 Canada. **Tel** (416)925-5931. **ED** Rebekah Chevalier. **DD** 266/.792/05. **Ad Acc. Circ:** 32,000 (ctrl). ***Continues** Mandate Newsletter, 0383-1493.*

●US
**MANY PATHS.** English. Twelve times a year. $25.00. CRES, PO Box 4165, Overland Park KS 66204. **Tel** (913)649-5114. **ED** Vern Barnet. **Bk Rev**, (Qty: varies). **Circ:** 500 (ctrl).
**Desc:** Interfaith news and articles of interest to Kansas City.

US
**MAPS NEWS.** English. qt. free. Assemblies of God Archives, 1445 Boonville Avenue, Springfield MO 65802-1894. **Tel** (417)862-2781, (417)862-1447, FAX (417)862-8558. **ED** Helen Braxton. **Pr Rev.**
**Desc:** Contains testimonies and stories of short-term personnel and teams assignments. Also, Gives listing of openings for construction teams.

NE/0921-3848
**MARA (KAMPEN).** (MARA.). [Mara Kampen]. (1987)-. Periodical. Dutch. Three times a year. F40.00. J H Kok, Postbus 130, 8260 AC Kampen Netherlands. **Tel** 011 31 520292555, FAX 011 31 520227331. **UDC** 239.

CN/0318-9147
**MARANATHA (ST-HYACINTHE).** (LE SEIGNEUR VIENT.). **VFOAT** Marantha. V. 1- Feb. 1972-. Periodical. French. qt. 15.00Can$ per no. Maranatha, CP 603 St-Hyacinth, Quebec J2S 7C2. **DD** 248/.2/05.

GW/0542-657X
**MARBURGER THEOLOGISCHE STUDIEN.** Began publication in 1963. Monographic series. German. ir. Price varies per volume. N G Elwert Verlag, Postfach 1128, Reitgasse 7+9, W-3550 Marburg Germany. **Tel** 06421 25023, FAX 06421 15487.

US/0461-0636
**MARCH OF FAITH.** [March faith]. Periodical. English. qt. Wings of Healing Inc, 110 South Garfield Avenue, Montebello CA 90604. **DD** 269.

IT
**MARIANUM; EPHEMERIDES MARIOLOGIAE.** **Added/Corp** Pontificia Facultas Theologica "Marianum" Ordinis Fratrum Servorum S. Mariae. Collegium Internationale S. Alexii Falconieri de Urbe. Facultas Theologicae. Vol. 1, (1939)-. Periodical. Latin (French, Italian, English, Spanish and German). Twice a year. L60000 Italy; L70000 other. Edizioni Marianum, Viale Trenta Aprile 6, 00153 Rome Italy. **Tel** 011 39 6 5814441. Index available in last issue of volume--attached. cum. index.
**Ind/Abst** Bibliogr. Mission.; MLA Int. Bibl. Books Artic. Mod. Lang. Lit.; New Testam. Abstr.

CN/1187-5402
**MARIE-CLEMENT STAUB, A.A., SKETCHES OF HIS LIFE AND WORK.** [Marie-Clement Staub A.A. sketches life work]. **Added/Corp** Soeurs de Sainte-Jeanne d'Arc. Secretariat-Father Marie-Clement. Soeurs de Sainte-Jeanne d'Arc. No. 1 (Autumn 1991)-. Periodical. English. sa. Free. Soeurs de Sainte-Jeanne D'Arc, Secretariat-Father Marie-Clement, 1505 de L'Assomption, Sillery Quebec G1S 4T3 Canada. **DD** 271. ***Continues** Echo of the Cause of Father Marie-Clement., 1187-5399.*

US
**MARK-UP / WASHINGTON OFFICE, NATIONAL COUNCIL OF CHURCHES.** Began in 1970?. Periodical. English. mo. $12.50. Washington Office, National Council of Churches, 110 Maryland Avenue NE, Washington DC 20002. **Tel** (202)544-2350. **ED** Mary Anderson Cooper. **Circ:** 850 (ctrl).
**Desc:** Mark-up reports regularly on public policy issues of concern to the churches, especially related to the NCC's peace with justice agenda.

US/0897-5469
**MARRIAGE PARTNERSHIP.** [Marriage partnersh.]. **Added/Corp** Christianity Today, Inc. **VFOAT** Partnership. Vol. 4, No. 5 (Sept./Oct. 1987)-. Periodical. English. qt (4 issues). $19.95 (one year), $29.90 (two year). Christianity Today Inc., 465 Gundersen Drive, Carol Stream IL 60188. **Tel** (708)260-6200. **(Subscription address:** CDS / SIFD Agency Control, 1901 Bell Avenue, Des Moines IA 50315.**) ED** Ron Lee. **DD** 253. **Bk Rev. Ad Acc. Circ:** 65,000. available on microfilm and microfiche from University Microfilms International (UMI). ***Continues*** *Partnership (Carol Stream, Ill.), 0747-9190.*
**Desc:** Celebrates marriage, with candor, humor and a Christian perspective. Every issue brings meaningful articles, thoughtful interviews, practical ideas, and spiritual insights to make marriages vital and strong.
**Ind/Abst** Christ. Period. Index; Curr. Thoughts Trends.

•US/1052-181X
**MARTIN LUTHER KING, JR. MEMORIAL STUDIES IN RELIGION, CULTURE, AND SOCIAL DEVELOPMENT.** **See** Sociology.

FR/0181-057X
**MASSES OUVRIERES.** **See** Economics-Labor.

US/0362-0808
**MASTER SERMON SERIES.** ***Ceased.*** (MSS, MASTER SERMON SERIES.). **VFOAT** Master Sermon Series. Vol. 1 (1970)-(Aug. 1992). Periodical. English. mo. Cathedral Directories, 1401 West Girard Avenue, Madison Heights MI 48071. **Tel** (313)545-1415, (800)544-6903, FAX (313)544-1611. **ED** Carl Howie. **Bk Rev. Ad Acc. Circ:** 2,000 (ctrl).
**Desc:** Sermons and prayers to aid the minister in preparing weekly sermons.

US/1066-3959
**MASTER'S SEMINARY JOURNAL, THE.** [Master's semin. j.]. (1990)-. Periodical. English. sa. $10.00. Master's Seminary Journal, 13248 Roscoe Boulevard, Sun Valley CA 91352. **Tel** (818)909-5619. **DD** 207.
**Ind/Abst** Christ. Period. Index (199?-); Index Book Rev. Relig.; Relig. Index One Period.; Relig. Theol. Abstr. (199?-).

UK
**MATRIMONIAL DECISIONS OF GREAT BRITAIN AND IRELAND FOR ... .** **Added/Corp** Canon Law Society of Great Britain and Ireland. Vol. 16 (1980)-. English. an. £21.00; £30.00 (membership). Canon Law Society of Great Britain and Ireland, Cathedral House, Ingrave Road, Brentwood ESX CM15 8AT England. **Tel** 011 44 277 214821. ***Continues*** *Matrimonial Decisions for England and Wales for ... .*

US/0025-6021
**MATURE YEARS.** **Added/Corp** United Methodist Church (U.S.). Board of Education. Division of Curriculum Resources. Vol. 1 (Sept./Nov. 1968)-. Periodical. English. qt. $12.00 (one year), $20.00 (two year). United Methodist Publishing House, PO Box 801, 201 8th Avenue South, Nashville TN 37202. **Tel** (615)749-6732, (615)749-6615, FAX (615)749-6578, (615)749-6579. **ED** Donn C. Downall. **LC** BV4580.A1; M32. **DD** 248/.85. available on microfilm from University Microfilms International (UMI). ***Supersedes*** *Mature Years.*

UK/0025-7597
**MC : THE MODERN CHURCHMAN.** New Ser., V. 25, No. 1 (1982)-. Periodical. English. qt. $10.73. Modern Churchpeoples Union, Chirburyviskerage, Powys SY15 6BN England. **Tel** 011 44 93 872218. **ED** A O Dyson. Index available. **Bk Rev. Ad Acc. Circ:** 1,200 (ctrl). available on microfilm. ***Continues*** *Modern Churchman, 0026-7597.*
**Desc:** Informed Christian thinking and a questioning approach to issues of theology and the ethical, pastoral, spiritual and socio-political aspects of contemporary life.
**Ind/Abst** New Testam. Abstr.; Relig. Theol. Abstr.

CN/0831-6074
**MCCAUSLAND'S ORDER OF DIVINE SERVICE.** [McCausland's order divine serv.]. **Main/Corp** Anglican Church of Canada. (1984/85)-. English. an. Anglican Book Centre, 600 Jarvis Street, Toronto Ontario M4Y 2J6 Canada. **Tel** (416)924-9192. **DD** 264/.031. ***Continues*** *Order of Divine Service, 0319-2679.*

CN/0849-0899
**MCMASTER JOURNAL OF THEOLOGY.** ***Ceased.*** [McMaster j. theol.]. **Added/Corp** McMaster Divinity College. Vol. 1, No. 1 (Spring 1990)-Vol. 3, No. 2, (1993). Periodical. English. sa. McMaster Divinity College, Hamilton Ontario L8S 4K1 Canada. **Tel** (416)525-9140. **DD** 230/.05. ***Continues*** *Theodolite., 0225-7270.*

GW
**MD, MATERIALDIENST DES KONFESSIONSKUNDLICHEN INSTITUTS.** **Main/Corp** Evangelischer Bund. Konfessionskundliches Institut. (1970)-. Periodical. German. bm. DM25.00. Eifelstrasse 35, Postfach 1255, D 64602 Bensheim Germany. **Tel** 06251 38000, FAX 06251 2045. Index available. cum. index. **Acid Free.** ***Continues*** *Materialdienst des Konfessionskundlichen Instituts.*
**Desc:** Publication covering religion and theology.
**Ind/Abst** Archit. Period. Index.

US/0094-5633
**MEASURING MORMONISM.** V. 1- Apr. 1974-. English. an. Association for the Study of Religion, 3646 East 3580 South, Salt Lake City UT 84109. **LC** BX8601; .M34. **DD** 289.3/3.

UK
**MEDIA DEVELOPMENT.** **See** Communication.

US/1057-0608
**MEDIEVAL PHILOSOPHY & THEOLOGY.** **See** Philosophy.

UK/0140-1211
**MEDIEVAL SERMON STUDIES NEWSLETTER.** **Added/Corp** University of Warwick. English Department. **VFOAT** MSS Newsletter. No. 1 (Summer 1977)-. Newsletter. English. sa (Mar. and Oct.). Comes with International Medieval Sermon Studies Society membership. Medieval Sermon Studies, University of Leeds, School of History, Leeds LS2 9JT England. **Tel** 011 44 532 333614. **(Subscription address:** International Medieval Sermon Studies, 670 West End Avenue, Apartment 10B, New York NY 10025.**)**
**Desc:** Contains information on medieval sermons.
**Ind/Abst** Annu. Bibliogr. Engl. Lang. Lit.

PP
**MELANESIAN JOURNAL OF THEOLOGY : JOURNAL OF THE MELANESIAN ASSOCIATION OF THEOLOGICAL SCHOOLS.** Vol. 1, No. 1 (Apr. 1985)-. Periodical. English. sa. $7.00 (surface mail), $10.00 (airmail). Martin Luther Seminary, Rev Kasek Kautil, PO Box 80, Lae Morobe Province, Paupua New Guinea. **Tel** 425180. **ED** Christopher Garland (editor's address: Newton Theological College, PO Box 162, Popondetta Papua New Guinea). Index available. **Bk Rev. Ad Acc.** ctrl circ.
**Ind/Abst** Bibliogr. Mission.; Index Book Rev. Relig.; Relig. Index One Period.; Relig. Theol. Abstr.

FR/0025-8911
**MELANGES DE SCIENCE RELIGIEUSE.** [Mel. sci. relig.]. **Added/Corp** Lille. Facultes Catholiques. Vol. 1 (1944)-. Periodical. French. Four times a year (Mar., June, Sept., Dec.). 150.00F France; 180.00F others. Melanges de Science Religieuse, 60 Boulevard Vauban, BP 109, 59016 Lille Cedex France. **Tel** 011 33 50 308827. **LC** BR3; .M4. **DD** 230/.05. **Bk Rev. Ad Acc. Circ:** 500.
**Desc:** Theology, philosophy, religious history, institutions and law history, anthropology, sociology, pedagogics, literature and art history.
**Ind/Abst** Index Book Rev. Relig.; MLA Int. Bibl. Books Artic. Mod. Lang. Lit.; New Testam. Abstr.; Old Testam. Abstr.; Relig. Index One Period. (1973-); Relig. Theol. Abstr.; Abr. Cathol. Period. Lit. Index; Cathol. Period. Lit. Index.

MM/1012-9588
**MELITA THEOLOGICA.** (MELITA THEOLOGICA : THE REVIEW OF THE ROYAL UNIVERSITY STUDENTS' THEOLOGICAL ASSOCIATION, MALTA.). [Melita theol.]. **Added/Corp** Royal University Students' Theological Association, Malta. University Students' Theological Association, Malta. Theological Students' Association (Malta) University of Malta. Faculty of Theology. (1947)-. Periodical. English (French and Italian). Twice a year (June & Nov.). Price varies. Theology Students Association, Faculty of Theology, University of Malta, Msida Malta. **Tel** 675497/8. **ED** Anthony Abela and Hector Scerri. **LC** BX804; .M4. **DD** 282/.05. cum. index. **Bk Rev. Ad Acc. Circ:** 600.
**Ind/Abst** New Testam. Abstr.; Old Testam. Abstr.; Relig. Theol. Abstr.

IT
**MEMORIE DOMENICANE (PISTOIA : 1970).** **See** History(General)-History of Europe.

US/0885-7776
**MEMOS (SPRINGFIELD, MO.).** (MEMOS.). [Memos]. Vol. 31, No. 2 (Spring 1986)-. Periodical. English. qt. $4.50. Gospel Publishing House, 1445 Boonville Avenue, Springfield MO 65802. **Tel** (417)862-2781, FAX (417)866-1146. **ED** Linda Upton and Aleda Swartzendruber. **DD** 289. **Bk Rev. Circ:** 15,000. ***Continues*** *Missionettes Memos, 0190-4418.*
**Desc:** General leadership magazine for Women's Ministries, Missionettes, leaders, including Rainbows, Daisies, Prims, Stars and Y's sponsors.

US
**MEMPHIS THEOLOGICAL SEMINARY JOURNAL.** English. Three times a year.
**Ind/Abst** Index Book Rev. Relig.; Relig. Index One Period.

GW
**MENNONITISCHES GEMEINDEBLATT, BRUCKE.** **Added/Corp** Vereinigung der Deutschen Mennonitengemeinden. **VFOAT** Brucke; Brucke, Mennonitisches Gemeindeblatt. Vol. 1, No. 1 (Jan. 1986)-. Periodical. German. mo. DM40.00. Peter J. Foth, Mennonitenstrasse 20, D 22769 Hamburg Germany. **Tel** 011 49 40 857112. ***Formed by the union of*** *Mennonitische Blatter* ***and*** *Gemeinde Unterwegs.*

CL/0025-956X
**MENSAJE (SANTIAGO, CHILE).** (MENSAJE.). Vol. 1, No. 1 (Oct. 1951)-. Periodical. Spanish. mo. Revista Mensaje, Casilla 10445, Almir Barosso 24, Santiago Chile. **Tel** 011 56 2 6960653. **LC** HN39.L3; M46. Index available in last issue of volume--attached. cum. index. **Bk Rev. Ad Acc.** available on microfilm.
**Ind/Abst** HAPI Hisp. Am. Period. Index; Hum. Rights Intern. Rep.

MX
**MENSAJERO DEL CORAZON DE JESUS, EL.** **Added/Corp** Apostleship of Prayer. (1???)-. Periodical. Spanish. mo. Apartado 2181, Mexico 1 DF Mexico.

US/0894-4857
**MERTON ANNUAL, THE.** [Merton ann.]. Vol. 1 (1988)-. English. an. $42.50. AMS Press Inc., 56 East 13th Street, New York NY 10003. **Tel** (212)777-4700, FAX (212)995-5413, telex 710 581 2302. **ED** Robert E Daggy, Patrick Hart, Dewey W and Victor A Kramer. **LC** BX4705.M542; M38. **DD** 271/.125/024. Index available. **Pr Rev.**
**Desc:** Studies in Thomas Merton, religion, culture, literature, and social concerns.
**Ind/Abst** MLA Int. Bibl. Books Artic. Mod. Lang. Lit.

US/0271-5732
**MESSAGE (CHERRY HILL), THE.** (THE MESSAGE.). [Message]. **Added/Corp** Association of Baptists for World Evangelism. Association of Baptists for Evangelism in the Orient. (1934)-. Periodical. English. Four times a year. Free upon request. Association of Baptists in World Evangelism, PO Box 500, Cherry Hill NJ 08034. **Tel** (609)424-4606. **ED** Ruth Trott. **LC** BV2520.A1; M4. Index available (published separately). cum. index. **Circ:** 90,000.
**Desc:** Attempt is to bridge the gap between the missionary and the local church. Published quarterly, field news, prayer concerns and reports are shared.

US
**MESSAGE OF THE CROSS.** (19??)-. Periodical. English (Spanish and Portuguese). Four times a year. Free. Bethany Fellowship, 6820 Auto Club Road, Minneapolis MN 55438-2898. **Tel** (617)944-2121, FAX (617)829-2753. **ED** David P. Renich, Nancy L. Renich, and Cathy Brokke. **Circ:** 5,000.
**Desc:** Inspirational, cross-cultural reports on international mission activities, and personnel profiles.

FR
**MESSAGER EVANGELIQUE, LE.** Feb. 22, 1970-. Periodical. French (German). 30.00. Messager Evangelique, 19 rue des Francs-Bourgeois, Strasbourg France. ***Continues*** *Messager Evangelique de l'Eglise de la Confession d'Augsburg d'Alsace et de Lorraine.*

US
**MESSENGER, THE.** English. bm (Jan., Mar., May, July, Sept., and Nov.). $6.00. Western Baptist College, 5000 Deer Park Drive Southeast, Salem OR 97301. **Tel** FAX (503)585-4316. **ED** David Miller & Clark Greer.
**Desc:** Serves all Regular Baptist churches of the western states keeping individuals informed of upcoming events, provide a forum for individual churches, introduce new personnel, assist missionaries and to make camps and agencies more visible.

CN/0381-5293
**MESSENGER (KITCHENER).** (THE MESSENGER.). V. 186, No. 7/8- July/Aug. 1966-. Periodical. English. mo. Swedenborgian Church, Box 2642, Station B, Kitchener Ontario N2H 6N2 Canada. **DD** 289.4/05. ***Continues*** *New Church Messenger, 0028-4424.*

US/0892-6662
**MESSENGER OF TRUTH (MOUNDRIDGE, KAN.).** (MESSENGER OF TRUTH.). **Added/Corp** Mennonite Church. (19??)-. Periodical. English. bw. $11.00. Messenger of Truth, PO Box 230, Moundridge KS 67107. **Tel** (316)345-2532. **ED** Gladwin Koehn. **DD** 289. **Circ:** 7,750.

CN/0701-3299
**MESSENGER (STEINBACK).** (THE MESSENGER.). V. 1- Jan. 11, 1963-. Periodical. English. bw. Evangelical Mennonite Conference, Box 1268, Steinbach Manitoba Canada.

•UK
**MESSIANIC JEW (AND HEBREW CHRISTIAN) / INTERNATIONAL MESSIANIC JEWISH (HEBREW CHRISTIAN) ALLIANCE, THE.** **Added/Corp** International Messianic Jewish (Hebrew Christian)

Alliance. Vol. 64, No. 4 (Dec. 1991/Feb. 1992)-. Periodical. English. Four times a year (Jan., Apr., July, Oct.). $4.00. Hebrew Christian Alliance, PO Box 524, North Pembroke MA 02358. **LC** BV2619; .H35. ***Continues** Hebrew Christian, 0017-9477.*

CN
**METHOD & THEORY IN THE STUDY OF RELIGION. Added/Corp** University of Toronto. Centre for Religious Studies. North American Association for the Study of Religion. **VFOAT** Method and Theory in the Study of Religion. Vol. 1, No. 1 (Spring 1989)-. Periodical. English. Four times a year. $101.00. Walter de Gruyter Inc. / Hawthorne, 200 Saw Mill River Road, Hawthorne NY 10532. **Tel** (914)747-0110, GERMANY: 011/49/30/260050, FAX (914)747-1326, telex 646677.

US/0736-7392
**METHOD (LOS ANGELES, CALIF.). See** Philosophy.

CN/0227-0978
**MICHAEL FIGHTING.** [Michael fight.]. **Added/Corp** Pilgrims of Saint Michael. (197?)-. English. Pilgrims of Saint Michael, Rougement Quebec Canada. **DD** 261.8/05.

US/0026-2072
**MICHIGAN CHRISTIAN ADVOCATE. Added/Corp** United Methodist Church (United States). Detroit Conference. United Methodist Church (United States). West Michigan Conference. **VFOAT** Advocate. (1875)-. Periodical. English. ir. $11.00 one year; $20.00 two years; $30.00 three years. Michigan Christian Advocate, 316 Springbrook Avenue, Adrian MI 49221. **Tel** (517)265-2075. **ED** Edward L. Duncan. **Bk Rev. Ad Acc. Circ:** 21,000 (ctrl).
**Desc:** Weekly news for Michigan United Methodist Church.

US/1048-2709
**MICHIGAN THEOLOGICAL JOURNAL.** (MICHIGAN THEOLOGICAL JOURNAL : MTJ.). [Mich. theol. j.]. **Added/Corp** Michigan Theological Society. **VFOAT** MTJ. Vol. 1, No. 1 (Spring 1990)-. Periodical. English. an. $18.00 (one year), $32.00 (two year). Michigan Theological Society, 429 Orchard, Hazel Park MI 48030. **Tel** (810)542-0011. **ED** Dr. John A. Jelinek. **LC** WMLC L 83/7258. **DD** 200. cum. index. **Bk Rev**, (Qty: 10).

US/0734-9882
**MID-AMERICA THEOLOGICAL JOURNAL.** [Mid-Am. Theol. j.]. **Added/Corp** Mid-America Baptist Theological Seminary. (19??)-. Periodical. English. an (June). $5.50 one year; $11.00 two year. Mid America Baptist Theological Seminary, PO Box 3624, Memphis TN 38173-0624. **Tel** (901)726-9171. **ED** R. David Skinner. **LC** BR1; .M43. **DD** 230/.6132/05. Index available (Bound in Vol. 10 No. 2 issue). cum. index. **Bk Rev. Ad Acc. Circ:** 180 (ctrl).
**Desc:** Studies on biblical and theological themes from both a practical and technical perspective.
**Ind/Abst** Guide Soc. Sci. Relig.

US/0544-0653
**MID-STREAM (INDIANAPOLIS).** (MID-STREAM.). [Mid-stream]. **Added/Corp** Council on Christian Unity (U.S.). Vol. 1 (Nov. 1961)-. Periodical. English. qt. $30.00 institutions, $23.00 individuals. Council on Christian Unity, 222 South Downey Avenue, PO Box 1986, Indianapolis IN 46206. **Tel** (317)353-1499, FAX (317)359-7546. **ED** Paul A Crow Jr. **LC** BX1; .M5. **DD** 262/.001. Index available. **Bk Rev. Circ:** 1,300 (ctrl). available on microfilm and microfiche from University Microfilms International (UMI). ***Absorbed in part** Digest of the Proceedings of the Meeting of the Consultation on Church Union, 0589-4867.*
**Desc:** A journal bringing together articles, documentation and book reviews on the direction and history of the ecumenical movement in the United States and internationally.
**Ind/Abst** Abstr. Engl. Stud.; Index Book Rev. Relig.; Missionalia; Relig. Index One Period. (1976-); Relig. Theol. Abstr.

●US/1059-3411
**MIDDLER & JUNIOR CHILDREN'S CHURCH TEACHER GUIDE. Added/Corp** Assemblies of God. General Council. **VFOAT** Middler and Junior Children's Church Teacher Guide. (1992)-. Periodical. English. qt. $13.20. Gospel Publishing House, 1445 Boonville Avenue, Springfield MO 65802. **Tel** (417)862-2781, FAX (417)866-1146. ***Continues** Church Programs for Middlers & Juniors, 0273-5059.*

●US/1059-3314
**MIDDLER STUDENT GUIDE. Added/Corp** Assemblies of God. General Council. (1992)-. Periodical. English. qt. $5.20. Gospel Publishing House, 1445 Boonville Avenue, Springfield MO 65802. **Tel** (417)862-2781, FAX (417)866-1146. ***Continues** Middler Student, 0277-9145.*

●US/1059-3306
**MIDDLER TEACHER GUIDE. Added/Corp** Assemblies of God. General Council. (1992)-. Periodical. English. qt. $9.20. Gospel Publishing House, 1445 Boonville Avenue, Springfield MO 65802. **Tel** (417)862-2781, FAX (417)866-1146. ***Continues** Middler Teacher, 0277-9153.*

US/0026-3958
**MILITARY CHAPLAIN, THE. See** Military and Defense.

IE/0332-1428
**MILLTOWN STUDIES.** [Millt. stud.]. **Added/Corp** Milltown Institute of Theology and Philosophy. (1978)-. Periodical. English. Twice a year (May, Oct.). $16.30. Milltown Institute of Theology and Philosophy, Milltown Park, Dublin 6 Ireland. **Tel** 011 353 1 2697257. **ED** Gervase Corcoran. **LC** BR1; .M45. **DD** 230/.2/05. Index available. **Bk Rev. Circ:** 300.
**Desc:** Theological and philosophical reviews.
**Ind/Abst** New Testam. Abstr.; Old Testam. Abstr.

US/0026-4474
**MINDSZENTY REPORT, THE.** [Mindszenty rep.]. **Added/Corp** Cardinal Mindszenty Foundation. (19??)-. Periodical. English. Twelve times a year. $14.00 US; $17.00 other. Cardinal Mindszenty Foundation, PO Box 11321, St. Louis MO 63105. **Tel** (314)991-2939, FAX (314)991-2047. **Bk Rev.** available on microfilm and microfiche from University Microfilms International (UMI).
**Desc:** Education for faith, freedom, and family against militant atheism.

SZ/0255-8777
**MINISTERIAL FORMATION.** (MINISTERIAL FORMATION / PROGRAMME ON THEOLOGICAL EDUCATION, WORLD COUNCIL OF CHURCHES.). [Minist. form.]. **Added/Corp** World Council of Churches. Programme on Theological Education. (1978)-. Periodical. English. Four times a year (Jan., Apr., July, Oct.). $10.00. World Council of Churches, PO Box 2100, CH 1211 Geneva 2 Switzerland. **Tel** 011 41 22 7906076, FAX 011 41 22 7910361, telex 23 423 OIK CH. available on microfilm from University Microfilms International (UMI).
**Ind/Abst** Index Book Rev. Relig.; Missionalia; Relig. Index One Period.

US/0891-5725
**MINISTRIES TODAY.** [Minist. today]. Vol. 4, No. 5 (Sept./Oct. 1986)-. Periodical. English. bm. $19.95 (one year); $29.95 (two years). Strang Communications Company, 600 Rinehart Road, Lake Mary FL 32746. **Tel** (407)333-0600, FAX (407)333-9753. **(Subscription address:** Kable Publishers Aide, 308 East Hitt Street, Subscription Department, Mt. Morris IL 61054-1473.**) ED** Stephen Strang. **LC** BV4000; .M538. **DD** 253/.05. **Bk Rev. Ad Acc, Adv Mgr:** Bob Minotti, **Tel** (407)333-0600. **Circ:** 25,000. available on microfilm and microfiche from University Microfilms International (UMI). ***Continues** Ministries (Winter Park, Fla.), 0739-3997; **Absorbed** Buckingham Report.*
**Desc:** Magazine about renewal in leadership.
**Ind/Abst** Curr. Thoughts Trends; Guide Soc. Sci. Relig.

US/1069-1766
**MINISTRY CURRENTS. *Ceased.*** [Minist. curr.]. **Added/Corp** Barna Research Group. Vol. 1, No. 1 (April 1991)-(April 1994). Periodical. English. qt. Barna Research Group, PO Box 4152, Glendale CA 91222. **Tel** (818)241-9684. **ED** George Barna (editor's address: 647 West Broadway, Glendale, CA 91204; Phone: (818)241-9300). **DD** 254. **Bk Rev**, (Qty: 32). **Circ:** 2,000 (ctrl).

US
**MINISTRY IN ACTION NEWSLETTER.** Newsletter. Assemblies of God Archives, 1445 Boonville Avenue, Springfield MO 65802-1894. **Tel** (417)862-2781, (417)862-1447, FAX (417)862-8558.

US/0026-5314
**MINISTRY (WASHINGTON, D.C.).** (MINISTRY.). **Added/Corp** Ministerial Association of Seventh-Day Adventists. (1928)-. Periodical. English. Twelve times a year. $22.00. Review and Herald Publishing Association, 55 West Oak Ridge Drive, Hagerstown MD 21740. **Tel** (301)791-7000 ext. 2534, FAX (301)790-9734. **LC** BX6101; .M52. **DD** 253/.05. **Bk Rev. Ad Acc. Circ:** 240,000. available on microfilm and microfiche from University Microfilms International (UMI).
**Desc:** Ministerial journal for Seventh-Day Adventist pastors and clergy of other faiths.
**Ind/Abst** Curr. Thoughts Trends; Seventh-Day Adventist Period. Index (1971-).

SZ
**MINUTES OF THE ... MEETING / CENTRAL COMMITTEE OF THE WORLD COUNCIL OF CHURCHES. Main/Corp** World Council of Churches. Central Committee. Began with 27th (1974). English (French, German and Spanish). an. World Council of Churches, PO Box 2100, CH 1211 Geneva 2 Switzerland. **Tel** 011 41 22 7906076, FAX 011 41 22 7910361, telex 23 423 OIK CH. **LC** BX6.W773; C4. **DD** 270.8/2. **Circ:** 2,000. ***Continues** World Council of Churches. Central Committee. Minutes and Reports of the Meeting.*
**Desc:** Minutes of the Central Committee Meetings and Assemblies of the World Council of Churches.

JA
**MINZOKU SHUKYO KENKYU.** V. 1, No. 1 (Fall 1980)-. Periodical. Japanese. qt. ¥2800. Minzoku Shukyo Kenkyujo, c/o Imperiaru Ochanomizu 810, 11-2 Kanda Ogawamachi, Chiyoda-ku 101, Tokyo Japan. **LC** BL9.J3; M55.

US/1061-3927
**MIRACLES MAGAZINE.** [Miracles mag.]. No. 1 Autumn (1991)-. Periodical. English. qt. $25.00. Heartways Press, PO Box 8118, Brattleboro VT 05304. **DD** 299.
**Desc:** A publication for students of "A Course in Miracles" as well as for the general new age/self-help audience. Features articles by top authors in the miracles community. Also contains beautiful photographs, plus poetry and book reviews.

US/0738-7237
**MIRROR, THE.** English. bm. $20.00 available as part of society membership. Lancaster Mennonite Historical Society, 2215 Mill Stream Road, Lancaster PA 17602-1499. **Tel** (717)393-9745. **ED** Carolyn C Wenger. **Circ:** 8,500.
**Desc:** News of Lancaster Mennonite Historical Society, library and archival and museums accessions, seminars, field trips, lectures, family reunions, and updates on membership.

SP
**MISA DOMINICAL CASTILIAN.** (19??)-. Periodical. Spanish. sm (23 issues). $62.00. Centre de Pastoral Liturgica, Rivadeneyra 6 7, 08002 Barcelona Spain. **Tel** 011 34 3 3022235. **UDC** 25. **Bk Rev. Circ:** 10,000 (ctrl).

SP
**MISA DOMINICAL CATALONIAN.** Catalan (Spanish). Two issues per month. $39.00 Spain; £67.00 US; $49.00 other. Centre de Pastoral Liturgica, Rivadeneyra 6 7, 08002 Barcelona Spain. **Tel** 011 34 3 3022235. **UDC** 25. **Bk Rev.** ctrl circ.

SP/0210-9522
**MISCELANEA COMILLAS.** [Misc. Comillas]. **Main/Corp** Universidad Pontificia de Comillas. (1945)-. Periodical. Spanish. Twice a year (Apr., Nov.). $32.50. Univ Pontificia Comillas, Department Teologia Y Humanidades, 28049 Madrid Spain. **Tel** 011 34 1 7343950, FAX 011 34 1 7344570. **LC** BX880; .U54a. **DD** 230/.2. cum. index. **Circ:** 400. ***Continues** Miscelanea de Colaboracion Cientifica de los Antiguos Alumnos de la Universidad Pontificia de Comillas.*
**Ind/Abst** Am. Hist. Life (1956-1969); Bibliogr. Mission.; BHA : Biblio. Hist. Art; Index Book Rev. Relig.; New Testam. Abstr.; Relig. Index One Period.

IT
**MISCELLANEA HISTORIAE PONTIFICIAE. Main/Corp** Rome (City). Pontificia Universita Gregoriana. Facolta di Storia Ecclesiastica. Vol. 1 (1939)-. Monographic series. Multiple languages (Italian, German, French and English). ir. Price varies per volume. Universita Gregoriana Editrice, 00187 Rome Italy. **Tel** (06)6781567. **ED** Vincenzo Monachino.

IS
**MISHKAN. Added/Corp** United Christian Council in Israel. Issue No. 1 (Summer 1984)-. Periodical. English. sa. £9.00; $15.00 (airmail) US. United Christian Council in Israel, PO Box 116, Jerusalem 91000, Israel. **Tel** 972-2-286553, FAX 972-2-284561.
**Desc:** Covers Hebrew Christianity, Jewish-Christian relations, Biblical theology and Jewish mission.

AG
**MISION (BUENOS AIRES, ARGENTINA).** (MISION.). Vol. 1, No. 1 (March/June 1982)-. Periodical. Spanish. Four times a year. $8.00 Latin America; $20.00 others. Mision Rene Padilla, Jose Marmol, 1734 - 1602 Florida, Buenos Aires Argentina. **(Subscription address:** Orientacion Cristiana / US, PO Box 522241, Miami FL 33152.**) ED** C. Rene Padilla. Index available. cum. index. **Bk Rev. Ad Acc. Circ:** 3,000 (ctrl).
**Desc:** Offers articles to inspire and educate pastors and lay leaders in the Latin American church; also provides an opportunity for national writers to present articles.
**Ind/Abst** Bibliogr. Mission.; Missionalia.

SP
**MISIONES EXTRANJERAS.** Periodical. Spanish. $8.00. **LC** BV2130; .M35.
**Ind/Abst** Bibliogr. Mission.

US/1068-3151
**MISSIO APOSTOLICA : JOURNAL OF THE LUTHERAN SOCIETY FOR MISSIOLOGY. Added/Corp** Lutheran Society for Missiology. (1993)-. Periodical. English. sa. $15.00 US; $16.50 other. Missio Apostolica, 801 Demun Avenue W-207, St. Louis MO 63105. **Tel** (314)721-5934, FAX (314)721-5902. **ED** Won Yong Ji.

US/0091-8296
**MISSIOLOGY.** [Missiology]. **Added/Corp** American Society of Missiology. Vol. 1 (Jan. 1973)-. Periodical. English. Four times a year (Jan., April, July, Oct.). $18.00 (individuals), $25.00 (institutions) surface mail; $32.40

(individuals), $39.40 (institutions) airmail. American Society of Missiology, 616 Walnut Avenue, Scottdale PA 15683. **Tel** (412)887-8500, FAX (412)887-3111. **ED** Darrell Whiteman (editor's address: Asbury Theological Seminary, Wilmore, KY 40390-1199; phone: (606)858-2215). **LC** BV2000; .M55. **DD** 266/.007. Index available. cum. index. **Bk Rev**. **Ad Acc**, **Adv Mgr:** Steve Shenk, **Tel** (703)433-7477. **Circ:** 2,500 (ctrl). available on microfilm and microfiche from University Microfilms International (UMI). ***Supersedes*** *Practical Anthropology, 0032-633X.*
**Desc:** Official journal of the American Society of Missiology.
**Ind/Abst** Anthropol. Index; Bibliogr. Mission.; Christ. Period. Index; Index Book Rev. Relig.; Relig. Index One Period. (1973-); Relig. Theol. Abstr.

DK
**MISSION.** **Added/Corp** Dansk Missionsrad. Vol. 3, No. 81 (1970)-. Periodical. Norwegian. qt. kr150.00 Denmark; $50.00 North America. Dansk Missionsrad, Skt Lukas Vej 13, DK 2900 Hellerup Denmark. **Tel** 31612777, FAX 39401954. Index available. **Bk Rev**. Documents available from FAXON Xpress. ***Continues*** *Nordisk Missions-Tidskrift.*
**Desc:** Brings Danish, as well as international, mission thinking and practice to the readers' attention.

US/0889-9436
**MISSION FRONTIERS.** (MISSION FRONTIERS : THE BULLETIN OF THE UNITED STATES CENTER FOR WORLD MISSION.). [Mission front.]. **Added/Corp** U.S. Center for World Mission. Vol. 1 No. 1 (Jan. 1979)-. Bulletin. English. bm. $4.00. US Center for World Mission, 1605 East Elizabeth Street, Pasadena CA 91104. **Tel** (818)797-1111, (818)398-2317. **ED** Ralph D Winter, John Holzmann. **DD** 266. **Bk Rev**. **Circ:** 70,000 (ctrl).
**Desc:** Focuses on the activities of the US Center for World Mission with a basic purpose of reaching the unreached people groups with the gospel.

US/0095-2036
**MISSION HAND BOOK.** **Main/Corp** United States Catholic Mission Council. English. 1325 Massachusetts Avenue NW, Room 500, Washington DC 20005. **LC** BV2190; .U54A. **DD** 266/.2/05.

US/1050-771X
**MISSION HANDBOOK. USA/CANADA PROTESTANT MINISTRIES OVERSEAS.** [Mission handb., U. S. A./Can. Protestant minist. overseas]. **Added/Corp** Missions Advanced Research and Communication Center. **VFOAT** USA/Canada Protestant Ministries Overseas; USA Canada Protestant Ministries Overseas. 14th Ed. (1989)-. Periodical. English. ir (every 3 years). $39.95. Marc Publications, 121 East Huntington Drive, Monrovia CA 91016. **Tel** (818)303-8811, (800)777-7752, FAX (818)301-7786. **LC** BV2050; .D55. **DD** 266/.02373. ***Continues*** *Mission Handbook: North American Protestant Ministries Overseas, 0093-8130.*

US
**MISSION INTERCOM.** ***Ceased.*** **Added/Corp** United States Catholic Mission Council. (19??)-(March 1992). Periodical. English. ir (10 times per year). US Catholic Mission Council, 1233 Lawrence Street NE, Washington DC 20017. **Tel** (202)785-9450. **ED** Anne Pope. **Circ:** 843.
**Desc:** Newsletter containing items of mission interest gleaned from a broad spectrum of publications.
**Ind/Abst** Bibliogr. Mission.

●CN/1198-0400
**MISSION: JOURNAL OF MISSION STUDIES.** (1994)-. Periodical. French. Institute of Mission Studies, St Paul University, 233 Main Street, Ottawa Ontario K1S 1C4 Canada. **Tel** (613)236-1393, FAX (613)236-5278. **Bk Rev**. **Ad Acc**. **Circ:** 220 (ctrl).
**Desc:** Communication medium between missionaries and researchers for discussion on contemporary issues: inculturation traditional religions and Christianity faith-cultures social challenges.
**Ind/Abst** Bibliogr. Mission.; Missionalia.

CN/0822-837X
**MISSION (ST-LAMBERT, QUEBEC), EN.** (EN MISSION.). [En mission]. **Added/Corp** Amis du Pere Jean-Marie Labonte. Vol. 1 No. 1 (Mar. 1984)-. Periodical. French. mo. $15.00. Amis du Pere Jean-Marie Labonte, CP 241, St-Lambert Quebec J4P 3N8 Canada. **DD** 266/.272945.

NE/0168-9789
**MISSION STUDIES.** (MISSION STUDIES : JOURNAL OF THE INTERNATIONAL ASSOCIATION FOR MISSION STUDIES.). [Mission stud.]. **Added/Corp** International Association for Mission Studies. (1984)-. Academic Scholarly Publication. English. sa. $20.00. International Association for Mission Studies, Normannenweg 17 21, D 20537 Hamburg Germany. **Tel** 011 49 40 254560, FAX 011 49 40 252987. **ED** Horst Rzepkowski and Joachim Wietzke. **LC** BV2000; .M57. **Bk Rev**. **Circ:** 1,000. ***Continues*** *IAMS News Letter.*
**Desc:** A forum for the scholarly study of theological, historical, and practical questions related to mission. The journal is multi-denominational and multi-cultural.
**Ind/Abst** Bibliogr. Mission.; Index Book Rev. Relig.; Relig. Index One Period.; Relig. Theol. Abstr.

SA/0256-9507
**MISSIONALIA.** **See** Religion and Theology-Abstracting, Bibliographies and Statistics.

US/0273-6780
**MISSIONARY EVANGEL.** **Added/Corp** Mennonite Church. Pacific Coast Conference. (19??)-. Periodical. English. qt. Missionary Evangel, Route 1 Box 404, Salem OR 97305.

US/0161-7133
**MISSIONARY MONTHLY.** (1896)-. Periodical. English. Nine times a year. $14.00 (1 year), $25.00 (2 year), $35.00 (3 year) US; $16.00 (1 year), $28.00 (2 year), $39.00 (3 year) Canada & Mexico; $17.00 (1 year), $30.00 (2 year), $41.00 (3 year) other. Missionary Monthly, c/o I.D.E.A. Ministeries, 4595 Broadmoor Avenue, S.E., Suite 237, Grand Rapids MI 49512-5337. **Tel** (616)698-8393, FAX (616)698-3080. **ED** DR Dick L. Van Halsema, (616)698-8393. **Ad Acc**. **Circ:** 4,000 (ctrl). ***Continues*** *Missionary Monthly Reformed Review.*
**Desc:** Devoted to the worldwide evangelistic and missionary outreach of Christian reformed and reformed churches of North America.

US/0026-6051
**MISSIONARY NEWS SERVICE.** ***Ceased.*** [Mission. news serv.]. **VFOAT** MNS. Vol. 9, No. 12 (June 15, 1962)-Ceased Vol. 34, No. 24, Dec.1987. Periodical. English. sm. Evangelical Missions Information Service, PO Box 794, Wheaton IL 60189. **Tel** (703)653-2158, FAX (708)653-0520. **ED** James Reapsome. **DD** 266. **Circ:** 1,600 (ctrl). ***Continues*** *EFMA Missionary News Service.*
**Desc:** Reports of missionary activity around the world.

US
**MISSIONARY SEER.** (19??)-. English. Six times a year. $12.00. Missionary Seer, 475 Riverside Drive, Suite 1935, New York NY 10115. **Tel** (212)870-2952, FAX (212)870-2055. **ED** K. Graffenreidt. Index available. **Ad Acc**, **Adv Mgr:** Seth Moulton. **Circ:** 4,500 (ctrl).
**Desc:** Official organ of the Home and Overseas Missions, African Methodist Episcopal Zion Church.

US/1043-0725
**MISSIONARY TIDINGS (WINONA LAKE, IND.).** (THE MISSIONARY TIDINGS.). [Mission. tidings]. **Added/Corp** Free Methodist Church of North America. General Woman's Missionary Society. General Women's Missionary Fellowship International. (1897)-. Periodical. English. Six times a year (Jan., Mar., May, July, Sept., Nov.). $10.00 (one year); $19.00 (two years); $27.00 (three years). Free Methodist World Missions, PO Box 535002, Indianapolis IN 46253. **Tel** (517)750-3163, FAX (517)750-1863. **ED** Daniel V. Runyon. **DD** 266. Index available (included in Nov./Dec. issue). **Bk Rev**, (Qty: 50). **Circ:** 9,000 (ctrl). available on audiocassette.

US
**MISSIONGRAMS / BEREAN MISSION.** **Added/Corp** Berean Mission. (19??)-. Periodical. English. ir. Free. Berean Mission Inc., 3536 Russell Boulevard, St. Louis MO 63104. **Tel** (314)773-0110. ctrl circ.

CN/0838-7052
**MISSIONNAIRES ENSEMBLE.** [Mission. ensemble]. **Added/Corp** Capucins. (1988)-. Periodical. French. qt. Distribution gratuite restreinte. Centre Missionnaire Ste-Therese, 4387 Av Esplanade, Montreal Quebec H2W 1T3 Canada. **DD** 266/.271/05. ***Continues*** *Capucins Canadiens., 0821-6355.*

CN/0229-0928
**MISSIONS DES ILES.** (MISSIONS DES ILES / MISSIONS MARISTES.). [Missions des iles]. Periodical. French. qt. $2.00. Missions des Iles, Missions Maristes, 2315 Chemin St-Louis Canada. **DD** 266/.29.

CN/0026-6116
**MISSIONS ETRANGERES.** **Added/Corp** Pretres des Missions-Etrangeres du Quebec. (1955)-. Periodical. French. Six times a year. 5.00Can$ US & Canada; 10.00Can$ other. Societe des Missions Etrangeres, 160 Place Juge Desnoyers, Ville de Laval Quebec H7G 1A5 Canada. **Tel** (514)667-4190, FAX (514)667-4194. **ED** Jean Greffard. **DD** 266/.2/05. **Circ:** 35,000 (ctrl). ***Continues*** *Missions-Etrangeres du Quebec, 0706-845X.*
**Desc:** Presentation of the content of the issue to the readers.

US/1051-3345
**MISSIONS TODAY (MEMPHIS, TENN.).** (MISSIONS TODAY.). **Added/Corp** Southern Baptist Convention. Brotherhood Commission. (1990)-. Periodical. English. Twelve times a year. $11.28 Annual; $2.82 quarterly. Baptist Brotherhood Commission, 1548 Popular Avenue, Memphis TN 38104. **Tel** (901)272-2461. **ED** Jim Burton. **Circ:** 25,000. ***Continues*** *World Mission Journal.*
**Desc:** Missions education for men in Southern Baptist churches.
**Ind/Abst** South. Baptist Period. Index (1990-).

GW/0076-9428
**MISSIONSWISSENSCHAFTLICHE FORSCHUNGEN.** Vol. 1- 1962-. Monographic series. German. ir. Price varies per volume. Guetersloher Verlagshaus, Postfach 450, D 33311 Guetersloh Germany. **Tel** 011 49 5241 74050. Index available. **Circ:** 400.
**Desc:** Published by the West German Society of Mission Studies on Christian Missionaries in the past and in the world today.

US/0746-827X
**MISSOURI NEWS.** Periodical. English. qt. Church of God Publishing House, PO Box 2250, Cleveland TN 37320. **Tel** (615)476-4512.

GW/0026-6779
**MITARBEIT, DIE.** ***Ceased.*** [Mitarbeit]. Vol. 1 (Apr. 1952)-Ceased 1986. Periodical. German. ir. Verlag Otto Schwartz & Company, Annastrasse 7, D 37075 Goettingen Germany. **Tel** 011 49 551 31051, 011 49 551 31052, FAX 011 49 551 372812. **LC** H5; .M55. **DD** 261/.05. ***Formed by the union of*** *Arbeiterbrief* ***and*** *Evangelische Sozialakademie Friedewald. Mitteilungen.*

UK
**MODERN BELIEVING.** (19??)-. English. Four times a year. £9.25 UK; £10.95 others. Modern Churchpeoples Union, Chirburyviskerage, Powys SY15 6BN England. **Tel** 011 44 93 872218. ***Continues*** *Modern Churchman.*

UK/0026-7597
**MODERN CHURCHMAN, THE.** ***Title Change.*** [Mod. churchm.]. **Added/Corp** Modern Churchmen's Union. Vol. 1-46, (Apr. 1911-Dec. 1956); New Series, Vol. 1 (July 1957)-(19??). Periodical. English. qt. Modern Churchpeoples Union, Chirburyviskerage, Powys SY15 6BN England. **Tel** 011 44 93 872218. **ED** Professor A. O. Dyson. **LC** BX5011; .M6. **DD** 283/.3. Index available. cum. index. **Bk Rev**. **Circ:** 1,100. available on microfilm and microfiche from University Microfilms International (UMI). ***Continued by*** *Modern Believing.*
**Desc:** A journal with a questioning approach to the ethical, pastoral theological aspects of contemporary living, bringing together theory and practice, knowledge and faith.
**Ind/Abst** Index Book Rev. Relig.; Middle East Abstr. Index; New Testam. Abstr.; Relig. Index One Period. (1949-).

US/0363-504X
**MODERN LITURGY.** [Mod. liturg.]. Vol. 3, No. 6 (Aug./Sept. 1976)-. Periodical. English. Ten times a year. $40.00. Resource Publications, 160 East Virginia Street, Suite 290, San Jose CA 95112. **Tel** (408)286-8505. **ED** Ken Guentert. **LC** BV169; .F64. **DD** 264/.005. Index available. **Bk Rev**. **Ad Acc**. **Circ:** 16,000 (ctrl). available on microfilm and microfiche from University Microfilms International (UMI). ***Continues*** *Folk Mass and Modern Liturgy Magazine, 0094-775X.*
**Desc:** The creative idea journal for Parish worship leaders and religious educators.
**Ind/Abst** Index Book Rev. Relig.; Music Artic. Guide (?-?); Music Index (-19??); Abr. Cathol. Period. Lit. Index; Cathol. Period. Lit. Index.

II/0304-1727
**MODERN RATIONALIST, THE.** Periodical. English. K Veeramani, 2 Rundalls Road 7, Madras India. **LC** BL2700; .M56. **DD** 149/.7/05.

UK/0266-7177
**MODERN THEOLOGY.** [Mod. theol.]. Vol. 1, No. 1 (Oct. 1984)-. Academic Scholarly Publication. English. Four times a year. £94.50 UK and Europe; $170.50 North America; £114.00 other. Basil Blackwell Publishers Ltd, 108 Cowley Road, Oxford 0X4 1JF England. **Tel** 011 44 865 791100, FAX 011 44 865 791347, telex 837022 OXBOOK G. **(Subscription address:** Blackwell Publishers / UK, Marston Book Services, PO Box 87, Oxford OX2 0DT England.**) [CCC]**. available on microfilm and microfiche from University Microfilms International (UMI). Documents available from UMI Article Clearinghouse.
**Ind/Abst** Acad. Search (July 1993-); Br. Humanit. Index; Expand. Acad. Index (1989-); Humanit. Index; Humanit. Source (Jul. 1993-); Index Book Rev. Relig.; INFO-SOUTH Abstr.; Mag. Search; Newsp. Period. Abstr. (1991-); Philos. Index; Relig. Index One Period.; Relig. Theol. Abstr.

US/0026-914X
**MOMENTUM (WASHINGTON).** (MOMENTUM.). [Momentum]. **Added/Corp** National Catholic Educational Association. (Feb. 1970)-. Periodical. English. Four times a year. $20.00. National Catholic Education Association, 1077 30th Street NW, Suite 3100, Washington DC 20007-3852. **Tel** (202)337-6232. **ED** Patricia Feistritzer. **LC** LC461; .N4316. **DD** 377/.8/205. Index available. cum. index. **Bk Rev**. **Ad Acc**. **Circ:** 20,000. available on microfilm and microfiche from University Microfilms International (UMI). ***Supersedes*** *National Catholic Educational Association. NCEA Bulletin.*
**Desc:** Emphasizes research, innovative programs for Catholic education and "how-to" pieces for the classroom teacher.
**Ind/Abst** Curr. Contents Educ.; Curr. Index J. Educ.; Educ. Index; Except. Child Educ. Resour. (19??-19??); Public Aff. Inf. Serv. Bull.; Abr. Cathol. Period. Lit. Index; Cathol. Period. Lit. Index.

# Religion and Theology

CN/0316-0785
**MON FRERE ET MOI.** 1- June 1968-. Periodical. French. qt. Centre de l'Association Missionaire de Marie Imaculee, C P 721, Winnipeg Manitoba R3C 2K3 Canada.

GW
**MONATSHEFTE FUER EVANGELISCHE KIRCHENGESCHICHTE DES RHEINLANDES. Added/Corp** Presseverband der Evangelischen Kirche im Rheinland. Verein fuer Rheinische Kirchengeschichte. (1952)-. Monographic series. German. ir. Price varies per volume. Dr. Rudolf Habelt GmbH, Postfach 150104, D 53040 Bonn Germany. **Tel** 011 49 228 232015. **ED** H. Faulenbach, D. Meyer, and W. Schmidt. **LC** BX8022.R5; M66. **Supersedes** Monatshefte fuer Rheinische Kirchengeschichte.

UK
**MONOGRAPH SERIES / SOCIETY FOR NEW TESTAMENT STUDIES. Added/Corp** Society for New Testament Studies. (19??)-. Monographic series. English. ir. Price varies per volume. Cambridge University Press, The Edinburgh Building, Shaftesbury Road, Cambridge CB2 2RU United Kingdom. **Tel** 011 44 223 312393, FAX 011 44 223 325959. **(Subscription address:** Cambridge University Press / North America, 110 Midland Avenue, Port Chester NY 10573.**)**
**Desc:** Series presenting works on the study of the New Testament. Contains volumes on the theology of St. Paul and more.

US
**MONOGRAPH SERIES / SOCIETY FOR THE SCIENTIFIC STUDY OF RELIGION. Main/Corp** Society for the Scientific Study of Religion. **Added/Corp** Society for the Scientific Study of Religion. No. 1 (1978)-. Monographic series. English. ir. Price varies per volume. Society for the Scientific Religion, University of Connecticut, Box U 68-A, Storrs CT 06268. **Tel** (203)486-4424.

NE
**MONOGRAPHS OF THE PESHITTA INSTITUTE, LEIDEN. Added/Corp** Rijksuniversiteit te Leiden. Peshitta-Instituut. (19??)-. Monographic series. English. Price varies per volume. E. J. Brill, Postbus 9000, 2300 PA Leiden Netherlands. **Tel** 011 31 71 312624, FAX 011 31 71 317532, telex 39296 BRILL NL.

FR/1014-9759
**MONTH AT UNESCO, THE. Added/Corp** International Catholic Center for U.N.E.S.C.O. International Catholic Coordinating Center for UNESCO. (19??)-. Periodical. English (French, Spanish and German). qt. 200.00F France; 220.00F other. SEPIC, 9 rue Cler, 75007 Paris France. **Tel** 11 33 1 47051759, FAX 11 33 1 45569092. **LC** AS4.U83; M56. **Bk Rev. Circ:** 5,000.
**Desc:** Information for the Christian world about UNESCO activities and publications.

UK/0027-0172
**MONTH (LONDON. 1882), THE.** (THE MONTH.). [Month]. Vol. 44-186 (No. 211-976) (Jan. 1882-Dec. 1948); New Series, Vol. 1-42, Jan. 1949-Dec.1969; 2nd New Ser., V. 1 (Jan. 1970). Periodical. English. mo. £15.00 UK; £37.00 other. The Month, 114 Mount Street, London W1Y 6AH England. **Tel** 11 41 71 491 7596, FAX 11 41 71 495 1673, telex 22234 J. **ED** John McDade. Index available. cum. index. **Bk Rev. Ad Acc. Pr Rev. Circ:** 3,000. available on microfilm and microfiche from University Microfilms International (UMI). **Continues** Month and Catholic Review; **Absorbed** Dublin Review; **Absorbed in part** Herder Correspondence.
**Desc:** Review of Christian comment and world affairs.
**Ind/Abst** Br. Humanit. Index; Middle East Abstr. Index; New Testam. Abstr.; Abr. Cathol. Period. Lit. Index; Cathol. Period. Lit. Index.

SZ/0540-8059
**MONTHLY LETTER ABOUT EVANGELISM. LETTRE MENSUELLE SUR L'EVANGELISATION, A. Added/Corp** World Council of Churches. Commission on World Mission and Evangelism. World Council of Churches. Division of Studies. Department of Evangelism. World Council of Churches. Division of World Mission and Evangelism. **VFOAT** Monatlicher Informationsbrief uber Evangelisation; Lettre Mensuelle sur l'Evangelisation. (Jan. 1956)-. Periodical. English (German and French). Ten times a year. Free. World Council of Churches, PO Box 2100, CH 1211 Geneva 2 Switzerland. **Tel** 011 41 22 7907906, FAX 011 41 22 7910361, telex 23 423 OIK CH. **ED** Raymong Fung. **Circ:** 8,000.
**Desc:** An ecumenical reflection on communicating the Christian faith.

US
**MONTHLY NEWSLETTER - AMERICAN ASSOCIATION OF THEOLOGICAL SCHOOLS. Main/Corp** American Association of Theological Schools. Vol. 1 (Sept. 1970)-. Newsletter. English. mo. Association of Theological Schools, 10 Summit Park Drive, Pittsburgh PA 15275. **Tel** (412)788-6505, FAX (412)788-6510. ctrl circ. **Continues** Highlights.

SP
**MONUMENTA HISPANIAE SACRA. SERIE LITURGICA / CONSEJO SUPERIOR DE INVESTIGACIONES CIENTIFICAS. Added/Corp** Escuela de Estudios Medievales. Seccion de Barcelona. Consejo Superior de Investigaciones Cientificas (Spain). **VFOAT** Serie Liturgica. Vol. 1 (1946)-. Spanish (Latin). ir. Consejo Superior Investigacion Cientificas (CSIC), Vitruvio 8, 28006 Madrid Spain. **Tel** 011 34 1 5612833, FAX 011 34 1 4113077, telex 42182.

IT
**MONUMENTA ORDINIS FRATRUM PRAEDICATORUM HISTORICA.** V. 1-. Monographic series. Latin. ir. Price varies per volume. Instituto Storico Domenicano, Convento S Sabina Avenito Roma.
**Desc:** History of the Dominican Order.

GW/0254-9948
**MONUMENTA SERICA. See** History(General).

US/1052-2271
**MOODY (CHICAGO, ILL.).** (MOODY.). [Moody]. **Added/Corp** Moody Bible Institute. Vol. 91, No. 1 (Sept. 1990)-. Periodical. English. Eleven times a year. $23.95. Moody Bible Institute, 820 North La Salle Boulevard, Chicago IL 60610. **Tel** (312)329-2164. **(Subscription address:** Neodata / Colorado, PO Box 2606, Boulder Boulder CO 80322.**) LC** BR1; .M6. **DD** 205. available on microfilm and microfiche from University Microfilms International (UMI). **Continues** Moody Monthly, 0027-0806.
**Ind/Abst** Christ. Period. Index (19??-); Curr. Thoughts Trends.

US/1041-0961
**MORAVIAN (1989), THE.** (THE MORAVIAN.). **Added/Corp** Moravian Church in America. Vol. 20, No. 1 (Jan./Feb. 1989)-. Periodical. English. mo (except combined Jan.-Feb. and July-Aug.). $9.00 US; $11.00 other. The Moravian, PO Box 1245, Bethlehem PA 18016. **Tel** (215)867-0594, FAX (215)866-9223. **ED** Hermann I. Weinlick. Index available (Bound in Dec. issue). **Bk Rev (Qty:** 6-8). **Ad Acc. Circ:** 25,000 (ctrl). **Continues** North American Moravian, 0027-1012.
**Desc:** A church journal publishing articles of general church interest, and going to each home of members in the US and Canada as privilege of membership.

US/0745-5968
**MORNING GLORY. Added/Corp** Hauge Lutheran Innermission Federation. Periodical. English. sm. $8.00. Morning Glory, c/o Mrs D Erickson, 2016 Elton Hills Drive, Rochester MN 55901.

US
**MOTHER'S MAGAZINE AND FAMILY CIRCLE (MICROFORM), THE. See** Education.

UK/0307-5958
**MOUNT CARMEL.** (MOUNT CARMEL JOURNAL.). [Mt. Carmel]. (1952)-. Periodical. English. qt (Within the seasons of the year). $14.00. Mount Carmel Journal, Carmelite Priory Chilswell, Boars Hill OXF OX1 5HB England. **Tel** 011 44 865 735133 or, 730183, FAX 011 44 865 326478. **ED** Father John Magowan. **Bk Rev. Ad Acc. Circ:** 1,000 (ctrl).

US/0164-7253
**MOUNTAIN MOVERS. Added/Corp** Assemblies of God. Division of Foreign Missions. Vol. 21 (Jan. 1979)-. Periodical. English. mo. $5.00. Gospel Publishing House, 1445 Boonville Avenue, Springfield MO 65802. **Tel** (417)862-2781, FAX (417)866-1146. **ED** Joyce Wells Booze. **Circ:** 185,000. **Continues** Good News Crusades, 0017-2162.

US
**MULTI-BIBLE IBM. CD-ROM.** English. $130.00 (one disc); $255.00 (network unlimited users). Innotech Inc, 2001 Sheppard Avenue East 118, North York, Ontario M2J 4Z7 Canada. **Tel** (416)492-3838.
**Desc:** Contains a collection of six Bible databases. Includes the New International, New Revised Standard, Revised Standard, King James (Authorized), and New King James Versions. The Bibles are displayed in parallel for each verse so that the wording of the versions can be compared instantly. Indexing includes every word in all versions, common phases, plus subject index entries based on the Naves Topical Concordance.

LE
**MUNTADA (BEIRUT, LEBANON).** (AL-MUNTADA / MAKTAB AL-ILAM WA-AL-TAWTHIQ.). Periodical. Arabic. £L50.00. Mudir Tahrir Al-Muntada Majlis Kanais Al-Sharq Al-Awsat, SB 5376, Beirut Lebanon. **LC** BR1070; .M83.

PK
**MUSHIR (RAWALPINDI, PAKISTAN).** (AL-MUSHIR.). **Added/Corp** Christian Study Centre (Rawalpindi, Pakistan). **VFOAT** Counselor. (Jan. 1959)-. Periodical. English (Urdu). Four times a year (Mar., June, Sept., Dec.). $17.00. Christian Study Centre, 126-B Murree Road, Rawalpindi Cantt Pakistan. **Tel** 567412. **ED** Charles Amjad-Ali. **LC** BR1.A1; M87. Index available. **Bk Rev, (Qty:** varies). **Circ:** 750.
**Desc:** The study of local culture, and to study the faith of Muslims and Christians, their relationships of both past and present.
**Ind/Abst** Bibliogr. Mission.; Missionalia.

US/0027-4372
**MUSIC LEADER, THE. See** Music.

US/0203-5936
**MUSLIMS OF THE SOVIET EAST.** English (French, Arabic, Faroese and Uzbek). qt. $10.00. **(Subscription address:** Victor Kamkin, 4956 Boiling Brook Parkway, Rockville MD 20852.**) LC** BP65.S58; M87. **DD** 297/.0958/4.
**Desc:** Illustrated journal of the Muslim Religious Board of Central Asia and Kazakhstan; publishes articles on the life of Muslims, printing theological matter and answering readers' questions.
**Ind/Abst** Index Islam. Lit.

US
**MUSU ZINIOS.** 1- Saus. 2, 1972-. Periodical. Lithuanian. mo. $8.00. Tevai Jezuitai Cikagoje, 2345 West 56th Street, Chicago IL 60636. **Tel** (312)737-8400. **ED** Anthony Saulaitis. **LC** BX806.L5; M85. **Bk Rev. Ad Acc. Circ:** 1,400.
**Desc:** Information about activities of Lithuanian ethnic groups in the Lithuanian Cultural Center and of Lithuanian Jesuit Fathers.

CN/0316-8913
**MY BROTHER AND I. Added/Corp** Missionary Association of Mary Immaculate. Vol. 1, (Oct. 1968)-. Periodical. English. Missionary Association of Mary Immaculate Oblate Missionary Center, PO Box 721, Winnipeg Manitoba R3C 2K3 Canada. **DD** 266/.2.

US/0027-5387
**MY DEVOTIONS.** (19??)-. Periodical. English. Twelve times a year. $6.50. Concordia Publishing House, 3558 South Jefferson Avenue, St Louis MO 63118. **Tel** (314)268-1000, (800)325-3381, FAX (314)268-1329. **ED** Don Hoeferkamp. **Circ:** 62,000.
**Desc:** Daily devotions for young Christians ages 8-12. Consists of Bible reading, inspirational reading and a prayer.

FR
**MYTHES, CROYANCES ET RELIGIONS DANS LE MONDE ANGLO-SAXON. Added/Corp** Faculte des Lettres et Sciences Humaines d'Avignon. Section d'Anglais. No. 1 (1983)-. Periodical. English (French). an. 60.00F. Universite d'Avignon Section d'Anglais, Faculte des Letters et des Sciences Humaines, Rue Violette, 84000 Avignon France. **ED** Maurice Abieteboul and Jacques Chouleur. **LC** BL3; .M96. **DD** 291/.0917/52105.
**Ind/Abst** MLA Int. Bibl. Books Artic. Mod. Lang. Lit.

US/0199-3038
**NAE WASHINGTON INSIGHT (NEWSLETTER ED.).** (NAE WASHINGTON INSIGHT.). [NAE Wash. insight]. **Added/Corp** National Association of Evangelicals. **VFOAT** Washington Insight; Insight. **VAT** National Association of Evangelicals Washington Insight. (March 1979)-. Periodical. English. mo. $15.00 US; $21.00 other. National Association of Evangelicals, PO Box 28, Wheaton IL 60189. **Tel** (708)665-0500. **ED** Robert Dugan. **Bk Rev. Circ:** 165,000 (ctrl).
**Desc:** Informs evangelical Christians about important issues and bills in Washington; also encourages evangelicals to be concerned about political activities.

NE
**NAG HAMMADI STUDIES.** Vol. 1 (1971)-. Monographic series. Multiple languages (English and French). ir. Price varies per volume. E. J. Brill, Postbus 9000, 2300 PA Leiden Netherlands. **Tel** 011 31 71 312624, FAX 011 31 71 317532, telex 39296 BRILL NL.

CN/0821-5995
**NAPJAINK (WEST-HILL).** (NAPJAINK.). [Napjaink]. **VFOAT** Our Days. **VAT** Our Days (West-Hill). Nov. 1974-. Periodical. Hungarian. bm. 0.25Can$. Magyar Church of Canada, Missionary Service, PO Box 67, West Hill Ontario M1E 4R4. **DD** 289.9.

CN/0824-3522
**NASE ZAJEDNISTVO. VFOAT** Our Croatian Community. No. 1 (1981)-. Periodical. Serbo-Croatian

(Roman). qt. 1.00Can$. Nase Zajednistvo, PO Box 664, Streetsville Ontario L5M 2C2 Canada. **DD** 282/.08991823071.

US
**NATIONAL AND INTERNATIONAL RELIGION REPORT.** (19??)-. English. bw. $49.00. Media Management, PO Box 21433, Roanoke VA 24018. **Tel** (703)989-1330, FAX (703)989-5890. **ED** Cheryl Hoffman & Mark Henry, Tel. (703)989-7500. **Circ:** 8,000.

CN/0084-8425
**NATIONAL BULLETIN OF LITURGY.** **Added/Corp** Canadian Conference of Catholic Bishops. Canadian Catholic Conference. Vol. 20, (Jan. 1987)-. Bulletin. English. qt (Mar, June, Sept, Dec). 10.00Can$ Canada; $12.00 US; $25.00 other. Publications Service of the Canadian Conference of Catholic Bishops, 90 Parent Avenue, Ottawa Ontario K1N 7B1 Canada. **Tel** (613)236-9461, FAX (613)236-8117. **ED** Patrick Byrne. Index available. cum. index. **Bk Rev. Circ:** 7,000. available on microfilm from University Microfilms International (UMI). ***Continues*** *Canadian Catholic Conference. National Commission on Liturgy. Bulletin of the National Commission on Liturgy., 0700-7442.*
**Desc:** Canada's own liturgical journal treating all aspects of liturgical questions; written for those who are involved in liturgy.
**Ind/Abst** Abr. Cathol. Period. Lit. Index; Cathol. Period. Lit. Index.

US/0279-8913
**NATIONAL CHRISTIAN REPORTER, THE.** **Added/Corp** United Methodist Communications Council. Newspaper Division. **VFOAT** Reporter. (198?)-. Periodical. English. wk. $20.00. United Methodist Church / Dallas, PO Box 660275, Dallas TX 75266. **Tel** (214)630-6495, FAX (214)630-0079. **ED** Spurgeon M Dunnam III. **Bk Rev**. **Ad Acc. Circ:** 25,000.
**Desc:** News and comment primarily on mainstream protestantism.

●US/1070-3314
**NATIONAL DIRECTORY OF CHURCHES, SYNAGOGUES, AND OTHER HOUSES OF WORSHIP.** **Added/Corp** Gale Research Inc. (1993)-. Directory. English. te. $300.00. Gale Research Inc., 835 Penobscot Building, Detroit MI 48226. **Tel** (800)877-GALE, (313)961-2242, FAX (313)961-6083, telex TWX 810-221-7086. **ED** John Krol. available on magnetic tape; available on diskette.
**Desc:** Offers information on 350,000 churches and other centers of worship in the United States.

US/0199-0284
**NATIONAL JESUIT NEWS.** [Natl. Jesuit news]. **Added/Corp** Jesuits. American Jesuit Assistancy. **VFOAT** NJ. (19??)-. Periodical. English. mo. National Jesuit News, St Joseph's University, 5600 City Avenue, Philadelphia PA 19131. **DD** 255.

AT/0158-6270
**NATIONAL OUTLOOK SYDNEY.** **See** Sociology.

UK/0309-4308
**NATIONAL REVIEW FOR LITURGY.** [Natl. rev. liturg.]. **VFOAT** Liturgy. (1976)-. Periodical. English. bm. £10.00 UK and Europe; £10.00 (surface mail), £14.00 (air mail) other. Bishops' Conference of England and Wales, 39 Eccleston Square, Liturgy Office, London SW1V 1PL England. **Tel** 011 44 71 821 0553, FAX 011 44 71 630 5166.

US/0882-1275
**NATIONAL SPIRITUALIST (INDIANAPOLIS, IND.), THE.** (THE NATIONAL SPIRITUALIST.). **Added/Corp** National Spiritualist Association of Churches. Began with: Vol. 56, No. 598 (Aug./Sept. 1974). Periodical. English. mo. $12.00 US; $18.00 other (includes postage). National Spiritualist Association of the Church, 2020 West Turney, c/o Rev. P. Fortmiller, Phoenix AZ 85014. **Tel** (602)274-3161. **LC** BF1001; .N3. **DD** 299/.93. ***Continues*** *Summit of Spiritual Understanding.*

SP/0470-3790
**NATURALEZA Y GRACIA.** Vol. 1 (1954)-. Periodical. Spanish. Three times a year. $21.00. Administration/Spain, Apartado 87, 37080 Salamanca Spain. **Tel** 214653. **ED** Manuel Gonzalez Garcia. Index available (last issue of the year). **Bk Rev. Circ:** 300.
**Desc:** Ecclesiastic sciences, particularly theology, philosophy and Franciscanism.

RU/0130-7045
**NAUKA I RELIGIJA.** (NAUKA I RELIGIIA.). [Nauka relig.]. **Added/Corp** Vsesoiuznoe Obshchestvo Po Rasprostraneniiu Politicheskikh i Nauchnykh Znanii. Vsesoiuznoe Obshchestvo "Znanie.". (Sept. 1959)-. Periodical. Russian. mo. $79.95. Izdatelstvo Znanie, Novaya Pl., 3-4,, 101835 Moscow Russia. **(Subscription address:** East View Publications Inc., 3020 Harbor Lane North, Suite 110, Minneapolis MN 55447.**) LC** BL2700; .N35. available on microfilm from University Microfilms International (UMI).
**Ind/Abst** Int. Aerosp. Abstr.; Curr. Dig. Post Sov. Press.

SA/0378-9888
**NED. GEREF. TEOLOGIESE TYDSKRIF.** [Ned. geref. teol. tydskr.]. **Added/Corp** Nederduitse Gereformeerde Kerk. **VAT** Nederduitse Gereformeerde Teologiese Tydskrif. Vol. 1 (Dec. 1959)-. Periodical. Afrikaans (English). qt. R72.00 South Africa & Namibia; R77.00 other. Nederduitse Gereformeerde Kerk Uitgewers, Postbus 4539, Cape Town 8000 South Africa. **Tel** 011 27 21 215540, telex 52-6922. **ED** E. Brown. **LC** BR9.A34; N4. Index available. **Bk Rev**, (Qty: 30). **Circ:** 1,800 (ctrl). ***Continues*** *Gereformeerde Vaandel.*
**Desc:** Articles on theological issues.
**Ind/Abst** New Testam. Abstr.; Old Testam. Abstr.

NE/0028-2030
**NEDERLANDS ARCHIEF VOOR KERKGESCHIEDENIS.** Vol. 1-7 (1884-99); New Ser., Vol. 1, (1900)-. Periodical. Dutch. sa (2 issues bi-annually). Fl103.00 Netherlands; $59.00 other. E. J. Brill, Postbus 9000, 2300 PA Leiden Netherlands. **Tel** 011 31 71 312624, FAX 011 31 71 317532, telex 39296 BRILL NL. **ED** J. Trapman and E. G. E. van der Wall. **LC** BR900; .N4. **[CCC]. Circ:** 256.
**Desc:** Primarily devoted to church and dogmatic history and is open to any contributions in these fields as well as in other specialised related field.
**Ind/Abst** Am. Hist. Life (1954-); BHA : Biblio. Hist. Art.

NE/0028-212X
**NEDERLANDS THEOLOGISCH TIJDSCHRIFT.** [Ned. theol. tijdschr.]. **Added/Corp** Rijksuniversiteit te Leiden. Rijksuniversiteit te Groningen. Rijksuniversiteit te Utrecht. Universiteit van Amsterdam. (1946)-. Periodical. Dutch. qt. Fl54.75. Boekencentrum B V, PO Box 29, 2700 EE Zoetemeer Netherlands. **Tel** 011 31 079 615481. Index available. **Bk Rev. Ad Acc.** ***Supersedes*** *Nieuwe Theologische Studien.*
**Ind/Abst** Index Book Rev. Relig.; New Testam. Abstr.; Relig. Index One Period. (1962-); Relig. Theol. Abstr.

SA/0254-8356
**NEOTESTAMENTICA.** [Neotestamentica]. (19??)-. Periodical. English. Twice a year (May & Oct.). $25.00. NTSSA Dept New Testament, University of Orange, Free State P 339, Bloemfontein 9300 South Africa. **Tel** 011 27 51 4012789. **[CCC].** available on microfilm from University Microfilms International (UMI).
**Ind/Abst** Relig. Theol. Abstr. (199?-).

US/0270-4900
**NET RESULTS.** **Added/Corp** Christian Church (Disciples of Christ). National Evangelistic Association. Vol. 1 (Aug. 1980)-. Periodical. English. mo. $29.95 (one year), $54.95 (two years) US; $38.00 (one year), $69.00 (two years) other. Net Results, 5001 Avenue North, Lubbock TX 79412. **Tel** (806)762-8094, FAX (806)762-8873. **ED** Herb Miller. Index available. **Bk Rev**, (Qty: 30). **Ad Acc, Adv Mgr:** J. Latimer. **Circ:** 11,000.

US/1061-9615
**NETWORK CONNECTION.** **Added/Corp** Network (Washington, D.C.). Vol. 18, No. 2 (Mar./Apr. 1990)-. Periodical. English. bm. $30.00. Network Connection, 806 Rhode Island Avenue NE, Washington DC 20018. **Tel** (202) 526-4070, FAX (202) 832-4635. ***Continues*** *Network (Washington, D.C. : 1980), 0199-5723.*

GW
**NEUE ORDNUNG, DIE.** **Added/Corp** Institut fur Gesellschaftswissenschaften Walberberg. Vol. 37, No. 1 (Feb. 1983)-. Periodical. German (English). bm. DM49.00 (7 year subscription) Germany; DM34.30 US. IFG Verlagsgesellschaft MBH, Simrockstrasse 19, W-5300 Bonn 1 Germany. **Tel** (0228)216852. **ED** Heinrich Basilius Streithofen. Index available. **Bk Rev. Ad Acc. Circ:** 2,400. ***Continues*** *Neue Ordnung in Kirche, Staat, Gesellschaft, Kultur.*
**Desc:** Contains essays on church, public, social and cultural problems.

SZ/0028-3495
**NEUE ZEITSCHRIFT FUER MISSIONSWISSENSCHAFT. NOUVELLE REVUE DE SCIENCE MISSIONAIRE.** **Added/Corp** Verein zur Forderung der Missionswissenschaft. Schoneck, Switzerland. Bruder-Klausen-Seminar. **VFOAT** Nouvelle Revue de Science Missionaire. Vol. 1 (1945)-. Periodical. English (French, German and Italian). qt (Feb., May, Aug., Nov.). 36.00F Switzerland; 40.40F Europe; 42.60F other. Neue Zeitschrift fur Missionswissenschaft, PO Box 62, CH 6405 Immensee Switzerland. **Tel** 011 41 81 51 81. **ED** F Folmli. **LC** BV2130; .N47. Index available. cum. index. **Bk Rev. Ad Acc. Circ:** 800. ***Supersedes*** *Missionswissenschaft und Religionswissenschaft.*
**Desc:** International review which covers all branches of missionology.
**Ind/Abst** Bibliogr. Mission.

GW/0028-3517
**NEUE ZEITSCHRIFT FUER SYSTEMATISCHE THEOLOGIE UND RELIGIONSPHILOSOPHIE.** [Neue Z. syst. Theol. Religionsphilos.]. (1963)-. Periodical. German. Three times a year. $119.25. Walter de Gruyter Inc., PO Box 303421, D 10728 Berlin Germany. **Tel** 011 49 30 260050, FAX 011 49 30 26005251. **[CCC].** Documents available from The Genuine Article. ***Continues*** *Neue Zeitschrift fuer Systematische Theologie.*
**Ind/Abst** Arts Humanit. Citation Index [Full Cov.]; Curr. Contents Arts Humanit.; Index Book Rev. Relig.; Relig. Index One Period. (1959-); Relig. Theol. Abstr.; Res. Alert [Full Cov.].

GW/0720-3772
**NEUERWERBUNGEN THEOLOGIE UND ALLGEMEINE RELIGIONSWISSENSCHAFT.** **Main/Corp** Universitat Tubingen. Universitatsbibliothek. Theologische Abteilung. No. 1 (1981)-. Periodical. German (English, French, Italian and Spanish). mo. DM33.00. Universitaetsbibliothek Tuebin Gen Theologische, ABT Postfach 2620, D 72016 Tubingen 1 Germany. **Tel** 011 49 7071 296499. ***Continues*** *Mitteilungen und Neueuwerbungen.*

RU
**NEUES LEBEN.** (1945)-. Periodical. German. mo. $77.00 airmail. **(Subscription address:** Victor Kamkin, 4956 Boiling Brook Parkway, Rockville MD 20852.**) LC** AP205; .N45. **DD** 053.

US/0279-4535
**NEVADA BAPTIST, THE.** **Added/Corp** Nevada Baptist Convention. (19??)-. Periodical. English. Twelve times a year. $4.00. Nevada Baptist, 406 California Avenue, Reno NV 89509. **Tel** (702)786-0406. **ED** Michael B. McCullough. **Ad Acc. Circ:** 4,200.
**Desc:** Features news of Southern Baptists in Nevada and the Southern Baptist Convention.

US/1048-8545
**NEW ATHENAEUM (LEWISTON, N.Y.).** (NEW ATHENAEUM : A SCHOLARLY JOURNAL SPECIALIZING IN SCHLEIERMACHER RESEARCH AND NINETEENTH CENTURY STUDIES/). [New athen.]. **VFOAT** Neues Athenaeum. Vol. 1 (1989)-. Periodical. English (German). ir. $34.95 (US) postage included; $37.95 (other) postage included. Delaware Nurses Association, 2634 Capitol Trail, Suite C, Newark DE 19711. **Tel** (302)368-2333, FAX (302)366-1775. **LC** B3090; .N49. **DD** 230/.044/092.

UK/0028-4289
**NEW BLACKFRIARS.** [New Blackfriars]. Vol. 46 (No. 532-Oct. 1964)-. Periodical. English. mo (except combined July/Aug.). $40.00. New Blackfriars, Blackfriars, Oxford 0X1 3LY England. **Tel** 011 44 865 278401. **ED** John Orme Mills. Index available. **Bk Rev. Ad Acc. Circ:** 1,500. available on microfilm and microfiche from University Microfilms International (UMI). ***Formed by the union of*** *Blackfriars* ***and*** *Life of the Spirit.*
**Desc:** A critical review surveying the field of theology, philosophy, sociology and the arts from the standpoint of Christian principles in the modern world.
**Ind/Abst** Br. Humanit. Index; Index Book Rev. Relig.; Middle East Abstr. Index; New Testam. Abstr.; Old Testam. Abstr.; Abr. Cathol. Period. Lit. Index; Cathol. Period. Lit. Index.

US/0360-0181
**NEW CONVERSATIONS.** **Added/Corp** United Church Board for Homeland Ministries. Vol. 1 (Spring/Summer 1975)-. Periodical. English. Three times a year. $10.00 (one year), $19.00 (two year). United Church Board of Homeland Ministries, 700 Prospect Avenue East, Cleveland OH 44115. **Tel** (212)870-3470. **ED** Nanette Roberts. **Pr Rev. Circ:** 1,500.
**Desc:** Explores mission issues facing churches in the United States, with special attention to the United Church of Christ.

US/0028-453X
**NEW DAY (PHILADELPHIA).** ***Suspended.*** (THE NEW DAY.). (1937)-(19??). Periodical. English. bw. $7.50. New Day Publishing Company, 1600 West Oxford Street, Philadelphia PA 19121. **Tel** 03-9940. **ED** Eugene Amman. **LC** BX7350.A1; N4. **DD** 289.9. **Ad Acc.** available on microfilm.
**Desc:** Publish works - works of Father and Mother Divine, and general news items included.

US
**NEW DIMENSIONS IN GIVING.** **See** Philanthropy.

US/1059-5902
**NEW DIRECTION (LOS ANGELES, CALIF.).** (NEW DIRECTION.). [New dir.]. No. 1 (1991)-. Periodical. English. bm (6 issues). $25.00 (1 year), $45.00 (2 year), $65.00 (3 year) North America; $35.00 (1 year), $65.00 (2 year), $95.00 (3 year) other. New Direction, 6529 Selma Avenue, Suite 440, Los Angeles CA 90028. **DD** 261.

US/1050-4214
**NEW ENGLAND CHRISTIAN.** ***Ceased.*** [New Engl. Christ.]. (1990)-(May 1991). Periodical. English. mo. Evangelistic Assn New England, 279 Cambridge Street, Burlington MA 01803. **DD** 280. ***Continues*** *New England Church Life, 0891-7094.*

US/0277-3082
**NEW ERA (BARRYTOWN, N.Y.).** ***Ceased.*** (NEW ERA : A NEWSLETTER OF THE NEW ECUMENICAL RESEARCH ASSOCIATION.). [New era]. Vol. 1, No. 1 (March/April 1981)-?. Newsletter. English. bm. International Religious Foundation Inc, 10 Dock Road, Barrytown NY 12507.

US/0164-5285
**NEW ERA (SALT LAKE CITY), THE.** (THE NEW ERA.). [New era]. **Added/Corp** Church of Jesus Christ of Latter-Day Saints. (19??)-. Periodical. English. mo (11 issues). $7.00. Church of Jesus Christ Latter Day Saints, 50 East North Temple, Salt Lake City UT 84150. **Tel** (801)531-2947. **ED** Brian K. Kelly. **DD** 289. **Circ:** 185,000.

US/0748-6804
**NEW FOUNDATION PAPERS.** [New found. pap.]. **Added/Corp** George Fox Fund. No. 1 (July 1980)-. Periodical. English. Four times a year (Jan., Apr., July, Oct.). $7.00. George Fox Fund Inc., PO Box 1101, Wingate NC 28174-1101. **Tel** (704)283-8248. **ED** J. H. McCandless. **Bk Rev. Circ:** 400 (ctrl).
**Desc:** Promoting the everlasting gospel preached by George Fox and the early Quakers.

US/0363-6976
**NEW HORIZONS (COLUMBIA).** (NEW HORIZONS.). V. 1- Mar. 1956-. Periodical. English. qt. Missouri School of Religion, Ninth and Lowry, Columbia MO 65201.

US/0883-0215
**NEW MENORAH.** (NEW MENORAH : THE B'NAI OR JOURNAL OF JEWISH RENEWAL.). **Added/Corp** B'nai Or Religious Fellowship (Philadelphia, Pa. (1985)-. Periodical. English. Four times a year. $22.00 (one year), $49.00 (two years) US; $28.00 Canada; $34.00 other. B'Nai or Journal of Jewish Renewal, 6723 Emlen Street, Philadelphia PA 19119. **Tel** (215)849-5385, (215)849-0821. **ED** Arthur Waskow (editor's address: 7318 Germantown Ave. Philadelphia PA 19119; editor's phone: (214)247-9700). **DD** 296. **Bk Rev. Ad Acc, Adv Mgr:** M Katz, **Tel** (215)247-9700. **Circ:** 4,000. ***Continues*** *Menorah (Washington, D.C.).*
**Desc:** Theory and practice of the movement for Jewish renewal; new liturgies and feminist, Torah-rooted politics, etc.

US/0895-7460
**NEW MERCERSBURG REVIEW, THE.** (THE NEW MERCERSBURG REVIEW : JOURNAL OF THE MERCERSBURG SOCIETY.). [New Mercersbg. rev.]. **Added/Corp** Mercersburg Society. No. 1 (Aug. 1985)-. Periodical. English. Twice a year (Apr. & Oct.). $10.00. New Mercersburg Review, 762 Tamarack Trail, Reading PA 19607. **Tel** (215)777-0679. **ED** R. Howard Paine. **DD** 230. **Bk Rev**, (Qty: 2). **Circ:** 120.
**Desc:** This journal contains papers by its members.

US/0149-4244
**NEW OXFORD REVIEW.** [New Oxford rev.]. **Added/Corp** American Church Union. Vol. 44, No. 2 (Feb. 1977)-. Periodical. English. Ten times a year (Except combined Jan./Feb. and July/Aug.). $19.00 (one year); $35.00 (two years); $48.00 (three years). New Oxford Review Inc., 1069 Kains Avenue, Berkeley CA 94706. **Tel** (510)526-5374, FAX (510)526-3492. **ED** Dale Vree. **LC** BR1; .N66. **Bk Rev. Ad Acc. Circ:** 13,300. available on microfilm and microfiche from University Microfilms International (UMI). ***Continues*** *American Church News.*
**Desc:** An Christian journal of ideas, edited by Lay Roman Catholics; interested in doctrinal orthodoxy, morality, evangelism, social justice, peace and family life.
**Ind/Abst** Index Book Rev. Relig.; Abr. Cathol. Period. Lit. Index; Cathol. Period. Lit. Index.

CN/0704-5883
**NEW RELIGIONS NEWSLETTER.** V. 1- Apr. 1977-. Newsletter. English. mo. $10.00. Herbert Richardson, Box 164, Toronto M5S IJ4 Canada.

US/1040-0974
**NEW RELIGIOUS MOVEMENTS.** [New relig. mov. ser.]. (1988)-. Monographic series. English. ir. Price varies per volume. Borgo Press, PO Box 2845, San Bernardino CA 92406. **Tel** (714)884-5813, (714)885-1161. **ED** Peter B Clarke. **DD** 291. Index available. **Circ:** 300. ***Continues*** *New Religious Movements Series.*
**Desc:** Clear, objective histories of the new religions which have sprung forth in the twentieth century, with each movement's origins, beliefs, practices, aims, and appeal, plus illustrations, notes, bibliographies, and indexes.

UK
**NEW STUDIES IN THEOLOGY.** (1980)-. English. an. $15.00. Gerald Duckworth and Company Ltd, Old Piano Fctry, 43 Glou Cresc, London NW1 England. **LC** BR1; .N67. **DD** 230/.05.

US/0896-4297
**NEW THEOLOGY REVIEW.** [New theol. rev.]. Vol. 1, No. 1 (Feb. 1988)-. Periodical. English. qt. $24.00 (one year), $47.00 (two year) US; $27.00 (one year), $53.00 (two year) other. Liturgical Press, St. Johns Abbey, Collegeville MN 56321. **Tel** (612)363-2213, (800)858-5450, FAX (612)363-3299, (800)445-5899. **LC** WMLC 93/1809. **DD** 282.
**Ind/Abst** Relig. Theol. Abstr.

US/0146-7832
**NEW THOUGHT (SCOTTSDALE, ARIZ.).** (NEW THOUGHT.). [New thought]. **Added/Corp** International New Thought Alliance. **VFOAT** New Thought Bulletin; New Thought Quarterly. (1950)-. Periodical. English. qt. $10.00. International New Thought Alliance, 5003 E. Broadway Road, Mesa AZ 85206. **Tel** (602)830-2461. **ED** Blaine C. Mays. **DD** 131. **Bk Rev. Ad Acc. Circ:** 5,000. available with illustrations. ***Continues*** *New Thought Bulletin, 0146-8170.*
**Desc:** Dedicated to the spiritual enlightenment of the individual and of the world.

US/1043-2221
**NEW WOMEN/NEW CHURCH.** [New women new church]. **Added/Corp** Women's Ordination Conference. Rochester Regional Task Force on Women in the Church (N.Y.). **VFOAT** New Women New Church. Vol. 1, No. 1 (Jan./March 1978)-. Periodical. English. bm. $35.00. Women's Ordination Conference, PO Box 2693, Fairfax VA 22031. **Tel** (703)352-1006. **DD** 253. ***Absorbed*** *Women's Ordination Conference. WOC Newsletter.*
**Desc:** For members of Women's Ordination conference working for women priests in Roman Catholic Church.

CN/0227-5422
**NEW WYCLIF SOCIETY NEWSLETTER, THE.** [New Wyclif Soc. newsl.]. No. 1 (Fall 1979)-. Newsletter. English. sa. $3.00 Canada; $2.50 US. New Wyclif Society, Department of English, University of Ottawa, Ottawa Ontario K1N 6N5 Canada. **DD** 270.5/092/4.

US/0893-9063
**NEW YORK BAPTIST, THE.** (NEW YORK BAPTIST : MONTHLY JOURNAL OF THE SOUTHERN BAPTIST CHURCHES IN THE NEW YORK STATE, NORTHERN NEW JERSEY AND SOUTHWESTERN CONNECTICUT AREA: PUBLISHED ... BY THE BAPTIST CONVENTION OF NEW YORK, COOPERATING WITH THE SOUTHERN BAPTIST CONVENTION.). **Added/Corp** Baptist Convention of New York. Southern Baptist Convention. (196?)-. Periodical. English. mo. $3.00. New York Baptist, 6538 Collamer Road, East Syracuse NY 13057. **Tel** (315)433-1001. **ED** Rev. Quentin Lockwood Jr.

CN/0549-0898
**NEWFOUNDLAND CHURCHMAN.** **Added/Corp** Anglican Church of Canada. Diocese of Newfoundland. Vol. 1 (Jan. 1959)-. Periodical. English. Ten times a year. 5.00Can$ Labrador & Newfoundland; 7.50Can$ others. Newfoundland Churchman, 19 Kings Bridge Road, St Johns Newfoundland A1C 3K4 Canada. **Tel** (709)726-6697. ***Supersedes*** *Diocesan Magazine.*

CN/0710-5770
**NEWS-GRAM - CHRISTIAN BUSINESS MEN OF CANADA.** (NEWS-GRAM.). [News-gram - Christ. Bus. Men Can.]. Vol. 1, No. 1 (Jan. 1974)-. Periodical. English. qt. Free. Christian Business Men's Committee of Canada, 501-177 Lombard Avenue, Winnipeg Manitoba R3B 0W5 Canada. **Tel** (204)942-2148. **ED** Marvin Wall. **DD** 267/.23/0971. **Bk Rev. Circ:** 900 (ctrl).

UK/0263-2306
**NEWS OF HYMNODY.** (Jan. 1982)-. Periodical. English. qt. $4.40 US and Canada; £2.20 other. Grove Books, Bramcote, Nottingham NG9 3DS England. **Tel** 011 44 0602 430786, FAX 011 44 0602 220134.

UK
**NEWS OF LITURGY.** Issue No. 1 (Jan. 1975)-. Periodical. English. mo. $12.00. Grove Books, Bramcote, Nottingham NG9 3DS England. **Tel** 011 44 0602 430786, FAX 011 44 0602 220134. **ED** C O Buchanan. **Bk Rev. Circ:** 1,500.

UK/0958-2770
**NEWSBRIEF - UNITED SOCIETY FOR THE PROPAGATION OF THE GOSPEL.** (1990)-. English. qt. £4.00. United Society for the Propagation of the Gospel, 15 Tufton Street, London SW1 England.
**Desc:** News and views from the world church.

CN/1193-8722
**NEWSLETTER - ALBERTA TEACHERS' ASSOCIATION. RELIGIOUS AND MORAL EDUCATION COUNCIL.** (NEWSLETTER.). [Newsl. - Alta. Teach. Assoc., Relig. Moral Educ. Counc.]. **Added/Corp** Alberta Teachers' Association. Religious and Moral Education Council. Vol. 16, No. 3 (July 1990)-. Newsletter. English. qt. Free to members of the Religious and Moral Education Council. Religious and Moral Education Council, % Alberta Teachers' Association, 11010-142nd Street, Edmonton, Alberta, T5N 2R1 Canada. **DD** 291/.071/27123. ***Continues*** *Alberta Teachers' Association. Religious Studies and Moral Education Council. Newsletter - Religious Studies and Moral Education Council, Alberta Teachers' Association., 0701-1237.*

US/0736-2595
**NEWSLETTER - AMERICAN ASSOCIATION OF BIBLE COLLEGES.** (NEWSLETTER.). **Added/Corp** American Association of Bible Colleges. (19??)-. Newsletter. English. Three times a year. $6.00 (one year), $10.00 (two years) non-members; Free to members. American Association of Bible Colleges, PO Box 1523, Fayetteville AR 72702. **Tel** (501)521-8164, FAX (501)521-9202. **ED** Randall E. Bell and J. Mondragon. **LC** BV4019; .A5. **Circ:** 1,200. available on CD-ROM from TREN; available on microfiche from TREN. ***Continues*** *AABC Newsletter, 0094-260X.*
**Desc:** Contains articles pertaining to Christian higher education, including employment opportunities, highlights of news from AABC colleges, AABC criteria changes and proposed changes.

US/1065-383X
**NEWSLETTER / AMERICAN ASSOCIATION OF PASTORAL COUNSELORS.** [Newsl. - Am. Assoc. Pastor. Couns.]. **Added/Corp** American Association of Pastoral Counselors. (19??)-. Periodical. English. Four times a year (Apr., July, Sept., Dec.). $15.00. American Association Pastoral Counselors, 9504A Lee Highway, Fairfax VA 22031. **Tel** (703)385-6967, FAX (703)352-7725. **ED** Barbara L. Gyomory. **DD** 253. **Ad Acc. Circ:** 3,200 (ctrl).

US/0003-1399
**NEWSLETTER - AMERICAN THEOLOGICAL LIBRARY ASSOCIATION.** **See** Library and Information Sciences.

CN/0823-9606
**NEWSLETTER - BILL PRANKARD EVANGELISTIC ASSOCIATION.** (NEWSLETTER.). [Newsl. - Bill Prankard Evang. Assoc.]. May 1983-. Newsletter. English. ir. Free. Bill Prankard Evangelistic Association, PO Box 5555 Station F, Ottawa Ontario K3C 3M1 Canada. **DD** 269/.2/06071.

US/0362-563X
**NEWSLETTER - CENTER FOR REFORMATION RESEARCH.** **Main/Corp** Center for Reformation Research. (1974)-. Newsletter. English. qt. Free on Request. Center for Reformation Research, 6477 San Bonita Avenue, St Louis MO 63105. **Tel** (314)727-6655. available on microfilm from University Microfilms International (UMI). ***Continues*** *Newsletter - Foundation for Reformation Research, 0360-9707.*

US
**NEWSLETTER (ENABLEMENT INFORMATION SERVICE (BOSTON, MASS.)).** ***Ceased.*** (NEWSLETTER / ENABLEMENT INFORMATION SERVICE.). (19??)-Vol. 22, No. 5 (Sept. 1993). Newsletter. English. Eleven times a year. Enablement Inc, 14 Beacon Street/Room 715, Boston MA 02108. **Tel** (617)742-1460. **ED** James L Lowery Jr. Index available. **Bk Rev. Circ:** 600.
**Desc:** Tested new alternatives in clergy ministry development. Special sections on tentmakers, clergy associations and the clergy career spectrum.

US/0732-9253
**NEWSLETTER FROM C.A.R.E.E.'S CHRISTIAN-MARXIST ENCOUNTER TASK GROUP.** [Newsl. C.A.R.E.E.'s Christ.-Marx. Encounter Task Group]. **VFOAT** Newsletter from CAREE's Christian-Marxist Encounter Task Group. **VAT** Newsletter from Christians Associated for Relationships with Eastern Europe's Christian Marxist Encounter Task Group. Newsletter. English. Three times a year. $3.00. Dr Nicholas Piediscalzi, Department of Religion, Wright State University, Dayton OH 45435.

●US/1068-302X
**NEWSLETTER FROM DICK B. ON THE SPIRITUAL ROOTS OF ALCOHOLICS ANONYMOUS, A.** [Newsl. Dick B. spirit. roots Alcohol. Anon.]. **VFOAT** Spiritual Roots of Alcoholics Anonymous. Vol. 1, No. 1 (Nov. 1992)-. Newsletter. English. bm. Free. Good Book Publishing Co., Box 276, Corte Madera CA 94976-0276. **Tel** (415)924-8902. **ED** Richard G. Burns. **DD** 362. Index available. **Bk Rev. Circ:** 500 (ctrl). available in Loose-leaf.
**Desc:** Features research news concerning the spiritual roots of Alcoholics Anonymous.

US/0364-667X
**NEWSLETTER - MASSACHUSETTS BAY DISTRICT, UNITARIAN UNIVERSALIST CHURCHES.** **Main/Corp** Unitarian Universalist Association. Massachusetts Bay District. **VFOAT** Mass Bay District Newsletter. Vol. 1, (Jan. 15, 1976)-.

Newsletter. English. Massachusetts Bay District, Unitarian Universalist Churches, 110 Arlington Street, Boston MA 02116.

US/0740-6460
**NEWSLETTER - MISSIONS ADVANCED RESEARCH AND COMMUNICATIONS CENTER.** (NEWSLETTER / MISSIONS ADVANCED RESEARCH & COMMUNICATION CENTER.). **Main/Corp** Missions Advanced Research and Communication Center. **VFOAT** MARC Newsletter; A.M.A.R.C. Newsletter. (19??)-. Newsletter. English. Four times a year. Free. Marc Publications, 121 East Huntington Drive, Monrovia CA 91016. **Tel** (818)303-8811, (800)777-7752, FAX (818)301-7786.

US/0885-6966
**NEWSLETTER NEWSLETTER, THE.** **See** Journalism.

US/0889-6178
**NEWSLETTER OF THE AFRO-AMERICAN RELIGIOUS HISTORY GROUP OF THE AMERICAN ACADEMY OF RELIGION.** **See** History(General)-History of North, South, and Central America.

US/0360-618X
**NEWSLETTER OF THE CENTER FOR PROCESS STUDIES.** **Main/Corp** Center for Process Studies. Vol. 1 (Spring 1975)-. Newsletter. English. Three times a year (Feb., June, Nov.). $5.00. Center for Process Studies, 1325 North College Avenue, Claremont CA 91711. **Tel** (909)626-3521 Ext. 224. **ED** Laurel Huff. **Bk Rev**. **Circ:** 750.
**Desc:** News of conferences, publications, and personalities that involved in the process studies.

CN/0225-5758
**NEWSLETTER - PRAIRIE RELIGIOUS LIBRARY ASSOCIATION.** (NEWSLETTER.). [Newsl. - Prairie Relig. Libr. Assoc.]. Vol. 1, No. 1 (Mar. 1980)-. Newsletter. English. Free to members, membership $15.00. PRLA Newsletter, c/o Campion College Library, University of Regina, Regina Saskatchewan S4S 0A2 Canada. **DD** 027.6/7/060712.

US/0362-4676
**NEWSLETTER - WOMEN'S CAUCUS-RELIGIOUS STUDIES.** **Main/Corp** Women's Caucus-Religious Studies (Organization). V. 1- Fall 1972-. Newsletter. English. qt. $5.00. Loyola University of the South, Box 58, New Orleans LA 70118. **Tel** (504)861-5558.

CN/0822-2061
**NEWSLETTER - WOMEN'S INTER-CHURCH COUNCIL OF CANADA.** (NEWSLETTER.). [Newsl. - Women's Inter-Church Counc. Can.]. **Main/Corp** Women's Inter-Church Council of Canada. Newsletter. English. ir. Free. WICC, 77 Charles Street West, Toronto Ontario M5S 1K5 Canada. **DD** 261.8/344/05. ***Continues*** *Women's Inter-Church Council of Canada. Hi There, 0826-3078.*

UK/0048-0304
**NEWSPEACE.** **Added/Corp** Fellowship of Reconciliation. (May 1971)-. Periodical. English. bm. £6.00 UK; £10.00 others. Fellowship of Reconciliation, 40 46 Harleyford Road, London SE11 5AY England. **Tel** 011 44 71 5289054, FAX 011 44 71 5829180. **ED** Benn Rees. **Bk Rev**, (Qty: 12). **Ad Acc**, **Adv Mgr:** Ben Rees, **Tel** 051 724 1989. **Circ:** 700/1,500. ***Continues*** *Reconciliation (New Malden, Surrey).*

US/0738-3886
**NFPC NEWS NOTES / NATIONAL FEDERATION OF PRIESTS' COUNCILS.** ***Title Change.*** **Added/Corp** National Federation of Priests' Councils. **VFOAT** News Notes; N.F.P.C. News Notes. (Sept. 1979)-(1993). Periodical. English. mo. National Federation of Priests Council, 1337 West Ohio Street, Chicago IL 60622. **Tel** (312)226-3334, FAX (312)829-8915. ***Continued by*** *Touchstone IL.*

US
**NICM ASSOCIATES NEWSLETTER.** **VFOAT** Associates Newsletter; Newsletter. **VAT** National Institute for Campus Ministries Associates Newsletter. Vol. 1, No. 1 (Aug. 1977)-. Newsletter. English. sa. National Institute for Campus Ministries, Annabel Taylor Hall, Cornell University, Ithaca NY 14853. ***Continues*** *National Newsletter (National Institute for Campus Ministries).*

NR/0029-005X
**NIGERIAN CHRISTIAN, THE.** Vol. 1 (1967)-. Periodical. English. mo. $33.00. Daystar Press, PO Box 1261, Literature Department, Ibadan Nigeria. **Tel** 234 302 412670. **ED** Adeola Idowu Esther. **LC** BR1463.N5; N53. **Bk Rev**. **Ad Acc**. **Circ:** 1,500.
**Desc:** Views of Christians on issues of contemporary national interests, Christian/Muslim dialogues and Bible based studies. Ecumenical news and home and family life issues. Christian Council of Nigeria.

NR
**NIGERIAN JOURNAL OF THEOLOGY, THE.** **Added/Corp** Catholic Theological Association of Nigeria. Vol. 1, No. 1 (Dec. 1985)-. Periodical. English. an. $30.00. Nigerian Journal of Theology, Seat Wisdom Seminary, Box 2124, Owerri IMO State of Nigeria. **Tel** 011 234 83 232479. **ED** T. Okere. **LC** WMLC 93/1983; BR1.; N53. **Bk Rev**.

IT/0029-0173
**NIGRIZIA.** [Nigrizia]. **Added/Corp** Comboni Missionaries. (1882)-. Periodical. Italian. Twelve times a year. L30000 Italy; L70000 Africa; L75000 US and Asia; L50000 Europe; L85000 other. Collegio Missioni Africane, Ufficio Abbon/Vicolo Pozzo 1, 37129 Verona Italy. **Tel** 39 45 8003534, FAX 39 45 8031455. **LC** BV3500; .A43. Index available. **Bk Rev**, (Qty: 50). **Pr Rev. Circ:** 35,000.
**Desc:** Studies of problems of the third world countries.
**Ind/Abst** Bibliogr. Mission.; MLA Int. Bibl. Books Artic. Mod. Lang. Lit.

JA
**NIHON NO SHINGAKU / NIHON KIRISUTOKYO GAKKAI HEN.** **Added/Corp** Nihon KirisutokyÂo Gakkai. **VFOAT** Theological Study in Japan; Theological Studies in Japan. (1962)-. Periodical. Japanese (English). an. $56.00. Nihon Kiristokyo Gakkai, c/o Kyobunkan, 4-5-1 Ginza Chuo-ku, Tokyo 104 Japan. **Tel** 03(561)8446. **(Subscription address:** Japan Publications Trading Company, Ltd., PO Box 5030, Tokyo International, Tokyo 100-31 Japan.) **ED** Hiroshi Shigeru. **LC** BR9.J3; N53. **Bk Rev**. **Circ:** 1,000 (ctrl).

CN/0703-4512
**NOR SEROUNT.** 1955-. Periodical. Armenian. mo. Holy Trinity Armenian Church, 14 Woodlawn Avenue West, Toronto Ontario M4V 1G7 Canada. **Tel** (416)924-6514.

NO/0029-2176
**NORSK TEOLOGISK TIDSSKRIFT.** [Nor. teol. tidsskr.]. **VFOAT** Norsk Theologisk Tidsskrift. Vol. 1 (1900)-. Periodical. Norwegian. qt. Kr365.00, $64.00. Scandinavian University Press, PO Box 2959 Toeyen, N 0608 Oslo 6 Norway. **Tel** 011 47 2 2575400, FAX 011 47 2 2575353, telex 71896 UROR N. **(Subscription address:** Scandinavian University Press, 200 Meacham Ave., Elmont NY 11003.) **ED** Svein Aage Christoffersen. Index available. cum. index. **Bk Rev**. **Ad Acc**. **Circ:** 700.
**Desc:** Theological research.
**Ind/Abst** Am. Hist. Life (1959-1990); Index Book Rev. Relig.; Int. Bibliogr. Rezen. Wissen. Lit.; Int. Bibliogr. Zeitschriftenliteratur Allen Gebieten Wissens; New Testam. Abstr.; Old Testam. Abstr.; Relig. Index One Period. (1967-); Relig. Theol. Abstr.

NO/0029-2214
**NORSK TIDSSKRIFT FOR MISJON.** **Added/Corp** Egede-instituttet. Vol. 1, (1947)-. Periodical. Norwegian. qt (Mar., June, Sept., Dec.). Kr300.00 Scandinavia; Kr350.00 other. Egede Instituttet, Gydas Vei 4, N 0363 Oslo Norway. **Tel** 011 47 22 606817. **ED** Notto R. Thelle. Index available. cum. index (1947-1976). **Bk Rev**. **Ad Acc**. **Circ:** 800. ***Continues*** *Norsk Misjonstidsskrift.*
**Desc:** Contains mission and missionary questions.
**Ind/Abst** Bibliogr. Mission.; Missionalia.

II
**NORTH INDIA CHURCHMAN, THE.** **Added/Corp** Church of North India. Vol. 1 (Feb. 1971)-. Periodical. English. mo. $20.00 (air mail), $15.00 (sea mail). North India Churchman, 938 Hendricks, Port Townsend WA 98368. **Tel** (206)385-5412. ***Continues*** *United Church Review.*

US/0744-0278
**NORTH STAR BAPTIST.** **Added/Corp** Minnesota Baptist Convention. Minnesota Baptist Association of Independent Churches. Vol. 1, No. 2, (1916)-. Periodical. English. Four times a year (Jan. Apr., July, Oct.). $4.00. Minnesota Baptist Association, 5000 Golden Valley Road, Minneapolis MN 55422. **Tel** (612)588-2755. **ED** Dr. Richard Paige. **Bk Rev**, (Qty: 40). **Circ:** 1,100 (ctrl). ***Continues*** *Minnesota Baptist.*
**Desc:** Spiritual challenge and message news for fundamental Christians, and reports from the churches of our fellowship along with missionary reports.

CN/0820-7526
**NOTRE PAIN QUOTIDIEN (CAP-DE-LA-MADELEINE, QUEBEC).** (NOTRE PAIN QUOTIDIEN.). [Notre pain quotid.]. 1982-. Periodical. French. qt. Free. Notre Pain Quotidien, c/o Publications Chretiennes, 230 Lupien, Cap-de-la-Madeleine Quebec G8T 6W4 Canada. **Tel** (819)378-4023. **DD** 242/.2/05. **Circ:** 16,500 (ctrl).
**Desc:** A devotional booklet primarily for French speaking persons world-wide for all Christians and other interested persons.

CN/0384-0530
**NOTRE SEMAINE COMMUNAUTAIRE.** V. 2, No. 2- Dec. 6/12, 1970-. Periodical. French. wk. $5.00. Notre Semaine Communautaire, 5750 Boulevard Rosemont, Montreal Quebec H1T 2H2 Canada. **DD** 248/.05. ***Continues*** *Vie Paroissiale, 0384-0522.*

FR/0297-7486
**NOUVEAUX CAHIERS MARIALS.** (1986)-. Periodical. French. qt. 130.00F France; 160.00F other. Nouveaux Cahiers Marials, 27 rue Juliette Recamier, 69006 Lyon France. **Tel** 011 33 78 241821. **UDC** 25.

CN/0823-6240
**NOUVEL ESSOR MARCELLE MALLET.** [Nouv. Essor Marcelle Mallet]. Vol. 1, No 1 (Jan. 1981) -. Periodical. French. ir (Jan., Mar., May, and Aug.). Essor Marcelle Mallet, 2655 rue le Pelletier, Beauport Quebec G1C 3X7 Canada. **Tel** 628-8860. **ED** Sister Viviane Deschenes. **DD** 271/.91. **Circ:** 6,000.
**Desc:** Reconstruction of the life of the founder of the Sisters of Charity of Quebec from 1805 to 1871.

BE/0029-4845
**NOUVELLE REVUE THEOLOGIQUE.** [Nouv. rev. theol.]. **Added/Corp** Centre de Documentation et de Recherche Religieuses de la Compagnie de Jesus a Louvain. College Philosophique et Theologique Saint-Albert de la Compagnie de Jesus. Vol. 1 (1869)-. Periodical. French. bm. $47.00 Central & South America; $70.00 other. Casterman S A, 28 rue des Soeurs Noires, 7500 Tournai Belgium. **Tel** (326)922-4141, telex 57328. **ED** S A Casterman. **LC** BX802; .N6. **DD** 282.05. cum. index. **Bk Rev**. **Ad Acc**. **Circ:** 4,000. ***Supersedes*** *Revue Theologique.*
**Desc:** Concerned with theological subjects in a broad meaning, at a high but not strictly specialized level.
**Ind/Abst** Bibliogr. Mission.; Canon Law Abstr.; New Testam. Abstr.; Old Testam. Abstr.; Relig. Theol. Abstr.; Abr. Cathol. Period. Lit. Index; Cathol. Period. Lit. Index.

CN/0707-7211
**NOUVELLES ET DOCUMENTS - LA PROVINCE CANADIENNE DES PERES DE SAINTE-CROIX.** **Main/Corp** Peres de Sainte-Croix. Province Canadienne. No 1- Oct. 1977-. Periodical. French. Archives Provinciale des Peres de Sainte-Croix, 4994 Cote-des-Neiges, Montreal Quebec H3V 1A4 Canada. **DD** 271/.79.

SZ/0029-5027
**NOVA ET VETERA (FRIBOURG).** (NOVA ET VETERA.). [Nova vetera]. (1926)-. Periodical. French. qt. 50.00F. Editions Universitaires, Boulevard de Perolles 42, CH-1700 Fribourg Switzerland. **Tel** 011 41 37 246812, FAX 011 41 37 249147. **LC** AP24; .N6. Index available. **Bk Rev**. **Ad Acc**. **Circ:** 650 (ctrl).
**Desc:** The journal presents an instrument of research and a reflection to the light of the gospel.
**Ind/Abst** New Testam. Abstr.

RU/0134-2932
**NOVAIA OTECHESTVENNAIA I INOSTRANNAIA LITERATURA PO OBSHCHESTVENNYM NAUKAM. RELIGIOVEDENIE / ROSSIISKAIA AKADEMIIA NAUK, INSTITUT NAUCHNOI INFORMATSII PO OBSHCHESTVENNYM NAUKAM.** ***Title Change.*** **Added/Corp** Institut Nauchnoi Informatsii po Obshchestvennym Naukam (Rossiiskaia Akademiia Nauk). (1992)-(1992). Periodical. Russian. mo. Inion An SSSR, Ulitsa Krasikova D 28/45, Moscow Russia. **Tel** 128.89.71. **(Subscription address:** East View Publications Inc., 3020 Harbor Lane North, Suite 110, Minneapolis MN 55447.) **LC** Z7755; .N6. ***Continues*** *Novaia Sovetskaia i Inostrannaia Literatura po Obshchestvennym Naukam. Problemy Ateizma i Religii.* ***Continued by*** *Novaia Literatura po Sotsialnym i Gumanitarnym Naukam. Religiovedenie.*
**Desc:** Information on religion and atheism.

CN/1186-2017
**NOVI SKRIZALI.** (NOVI SKRYZHALI.). [Novi skrizali]. **Added/Corp** Sobornyi Khram Ridnoi Viry. Rada Initsiiatoriv. Sobornyi Khram Sviatai Ukrainsko Viry. Dukhavne Vohnyshche Ridnoi Viry. (1971)-. Periodical. Ukrainian (summaries and/or abstracts in English). qt. Novi Skryzhali, PO Box 11 Station F, Winnipeg Manitoba R2L 2A5 Canada. **LC** BL980.C2; N68. **DD** 299.

US
**NUESTRA PARROQUIA.** (19??)-. Spanish. mo. $12.00. Claretian Publications, 205 West Monroe Street, Chicago IL 60606. **Tel** (312)236-7782, (800)328-6515.

NE/0029-5973
**NUMEN (INTERNATIONAL ASSOCIATION FOR THE HISTORY OF RELIGIONS).** (NUMEN.). [Numen]. **Added/Corp** International Association for the History of Religions. **VFOAT** International Review for the History of Religions. Vol. 1 (Jan. 1954)-. Periodical. English (French, German and Italian). Three times a year. Fl140.00 (institutions) Netherlands; $80.00 (institutions) other. E. J. Brill, Postbus 9000, 2300 PA Leiden Netherlands. **Tel** 011 31 71 312624, FAX 011 31 71 317532, telex 39296 BRILL NL. **ED** H. G. Kippenberg and E. T. Lawson. **LC** BL1; .N8. **[CCC]**. **Bk Rev**. **Ad Acc**. **Circ:** 296 (ctrl). Documents available from The Genuine Article.
**Desc:** Ensures a regular interchange of the results of investigations carried out in the field of history of religions.
**Ind/Abst** Anthropol. Index; Arts Humanit. Citation Index

[Full Cov.]; Index Book Rev. Relig.; Int. Bibliogr. Sociol.; Middle East Abstr. Index; MLA Int. Bibl. Books Artic. Mod. Lang. Lit.; New Testam. Abstr.; Relig. Index One Period. (1954-); Relig. Theol. Abstr.; Res. Alert [Full Cov.].

IT
**NUOVA EUROPA, LA.** (19??)-. Periodical. Italian. Six times a year (Jan., Mar., May, July, Sept., Nov.). L40000 Italy; L60000 others. Centro Russia Cristiana, Via Ponzio 44, 20133 Milan Italy. **Tel** 011 39 2 2663432, FAX 011 39 2 2365011. **Bk Rev**, (Qty: 30). **Ad Acc. Circ:** 10,000 (ctrl). ***Continues*** *Altra Europe, 1120-0685.*

IT/0394-8846
**NUOVO AREOPAGO, IL.** [Nuovo areopago]. (1982)-. Periodical. Italian. qt. CSEO Edizioni, CAS Postale 232, 47100 Forli Italy. **Tel** 011 39 543 24266. **UDC** 008.

US/1059-3241
**NURSERY TEACHER GUIDE (SPRINGFIELD, MO.).** ***Title Change.*** (NURSERY TEACHER GUIDE.). **Added/Corp** Assemblies of God. General Council. Vol. 39, No. 1 (Sept./Oct./Nov. 1992)-(199?). Periodical. English. qt. Gospel Publishing House, 1445 Boonville Avenue, Springfield MO 65802. **Tel** (417)862-2781, FAX (417)866-1146. ***Continues*** *Twos and Threes Teacher, 0744-7620.* ***Continued by*** *Preschool Teacher Guide, 1072-1460.*

CN/0821-2686
**OBRA (MONTREAL).** (LA OBRA : THE WORK OF THE MISSIONARIES OF THE HOLY APOSTLES.). [Obra]. **VFOAT** Work of the Missionaries of the Holy Apostle; Obra. Vol. 1, No. 1 (Easter 1981)-. Periodical. French (English). Three times a year. Free. La Obra, c/o Fondation Pere Eusebe Menard, 65 Castelneau Street West, Montreal Quebec H2R 2W3 Canada. **Tel** (514)274-7645. **ED** Jean-Pierre Bonhomme, Yvon Allard, and Robert Cormier. **DD** 266/.28. **Circ:** 35,000.
**Desc:** News from the missionaries of Holy Apostles working in Latin America.

CN/0824-653X
**OBSERVATEUR ORTHODOXE, L'.** [Obs. orthodoxe]. No. 1 (June 1983)-. Periodical. French. qt. L'Eglise Orthodoxe Russe Hors Frontieres, 8011 Av Champagneur, Montreal Quebec H3N 2K4 Canada. **DD** 281.9/05.

CR
**OCCASIONAL ESSAYS.** **Main/Corp** Latin American Evangelical Center for Pastoral Studies. **Added/Corp** CELEP. Centre Evangelico Latinoamerican de Estudes Pastorales. Vol. 4 (Jan. 1977)-. Periodical. English. sa. $7.00. Centro Evangelico Latinoamerica, Apartado Postal 1307, 1000 San Jose Costa Rica. **Tel** 22-50-38. **ED** William Cook and James C Dekker. **Bk Rev. Circ:** 1,000 (ctrl). ***Supersedes in part*** *Occasional Essays.*
**Desc:** Latin American missiology and pastoral theology.

UK
**OCCASIONAL PAPERS.** (19??)-. Periodical. English. ir. £2.00. Selly Oak Colleges, Bristol Road South, Birmingham B29 6LQ England. **Tel** 011 44 21 4724231, FAX 011 44 21 4728852, telex 334349 SELLYO G. **Circ:** 500 (ctrl).
**Desc:** Contains a piece of scholarly work including, lectures, reports, and an analysis of an issue which is related to one of the educational programs or research concerns of the Federation of Selly Oak Colleges.

US/0731-5465
**OCCASIONAL PAPERS ON RELIGION IN EASTERN EUROPE.** ***Title Change.*** (OCCASIONAL PAPERS ON RELIGION IN EASTERN EUROPE / CHRISTIANS ASSOCIATED FOR RELATIONSHIPS WITH EASTERN EUROPE.). [Occs. pap. relig. East. Eur.]. **Added/Corp** Christians Associated for Relationships with Eastern Europe (U.S.). **VFOAT** O.P.R.E.E.; OPREE. Vol. 1 No. 1 (1981)-(1992). Periodical. English. bm. Caree/Dr Paul Mojzes, Rosemont College, Rosemont PA 19010. **Tel** (215)527-0200, FAX (215)525-2930. **ED** Paul Mojzes. **LC** BR738.6; .O25. **DD** 274.7/082/05. Index available. **Bk Rev. Ad Acc. Circ:** 600. available on microfilm. ***Continued by*** *Religion in Eastern Europe, 1069-4781.*
**Desc:** Church-state relations and religious developments in socialist Eastern Europe (includes USSR). Includes both regional and country by country academic studies.
**Ind/Abst** Am. Bibliogr. Slavic East Europ. Stud.; Relig. Index One Period.

US/0273-0960
**OCCASIONAL PAPERS - UNITED METHODIST BOARD OF HIGHER EDUCATION AND MINISTRY.** **See** Education-Higher Education.

SA
**OCCASIONAL RESEARCH PAPERS - DEPARTMENT OF RELIGIOUS STUDIES AND PHILOSOPHY, MAKERERE UNIVERSITY.** **Main/Corp** Makerere University. Dept. of Religious Studies and Philosophy. V. 8- Dec. 1972-. English. R40.-. Makerere University / Department of Religious Studies, PO Box 7062, Kampala Uganda. **LC** BL2400; .O24. **DD** 200/.96. ***Continues*** *Occasional Papers in African Traditional Religion and Philosophy.*

VE
**ODCA INFORMA.** **Added/Corp** Organizacion Democrata Cristiana de America. **VFOAT** Organizacion Democrata Cristiana de America Informa. No. 1 (Feb. 1991)-. Periodical. Spanish. ***Continues*** *Informe ODCA.*

MW
**ODINI.** Vol. 35, No. 1 (6th-19th Jan. 1984)-. Periodical. Nyanja (Nyanja). bw. K.7.50. Likuni Press, PO Box 133, Lilongwe Malawi. ***Continues*** *African.*

CN/0383-4301
**OECUMENISME (EDITION FRANCAISE).** (OECUMENISME.). [Oecumenisme]. **VFOAT** Ecumenism. No. 1 (Feb. 1966)-. Periodical. French (English). qt. 12.00Can$ Canada; 15.00Can$ other. Centre d'Oecumenisme, 2065 Ouest rue Sherbrooke, Montreal Quebec H3H 1G6 Canada. **Tel** (514)937-9176. **Circ:** 1,000. ***Supersedes in part*** *Oecumenisme en Marche, 0383-428X.*
**Desc:** Serves grassroots ecumenism, featuring a dossier of in-depth articles by members of various churches and religions coordinated around a central theme; includes ecumenical news items, bibliographies, resources and book surveys.
**Ind/Abst** Index Book Rev. Relig.; Relig. Index One Period.

NR/1115-232X
**OGBOMOSO JOURNAL OF THEOLOGY.** [Ogbomoso j. theol.]. **Added/Corp** Nigerian Baptist Theological Seminary. (Jan. 1986)-. Periodical. English. an (Dec.). $5.00. Nigerian Baptist Theological Seminary, Box 30, Ogbomoso, Oyo State, Nigeria. **Tel** 038 710 011.
**Ind/Abst** Index Book Rev. Relig.; Relig. Index One Period.; South. Baptist Period. Index (1987-).

US/0030-0845
**OHIO CHRISTIAN NEWS.** (OHIO CHRISTIAN NEWS / OHIO COUNCIL OF CHURCHES.). **Added/Corp** Ohio Council of Churches. (19??)-. Periodical. English. mo. Ohio Council of Churches, 89 East Wilson Bridge Road, Columbus OH 43085.

US/0889-745X
**OKLAHOMA BAPTIST CHRONICLE, THE.** [Okla. Baptist chron.]. **Added/Corp** Baptist General Convention of Oklahoma. Historical Commission. Oklahoma Baptist Historical Society. Vol. 1 (Spring 1958)-. Periodical. English. Twice a year (Spring and Fall). $2.00. Oklahoma Baptist Chronicle, 2231 Gershwin Drive, Durant OK 74701. **Tel** (405)236-434144. **DD** 286. **Circ:** 400.
**Desc:** General information on the Baptists General Convention of Oklahoma, and the Historical Commission.

GW/0029-8654
**OKUMENISCHE RUNDSCHAU.** Vol. 1 (Jan. 1952)-. Periodical. German. Four times a year. DM48.00. Verlag Otto Lembeck, Leerbachstrasse 42, D 60322 Frankfurt 1 Germany. **Tel** 011 49 69 5970988. **ED** Gunther Gassmann, Gerhard Grohs and Ako Haarbeck. cum. index. **Bk Rev. Ad Acc.** available on microfilm from Microfilm Service & Sales.
**Ind/Abst** Index Book Rev. Relig.; Relig. Index One Period.

GW
**OKUMENISCHER TASCHENBUCHKOMMENTAR ZUM NEUEN TESTAMENT.** (19??)-. Monographic series. German. ir. Price varies per volume. VVA Bertelsmann Dist GmbH, Postfach 7600, D 33310 Gutersloh Germany. **Tel** 011 49 5241 803294.

US/0274-9459
**OMS OUTREACH.** [OMS outreach]. **Main/Corp** OMS International. **VFOAT** Outreach. **VAT** Oriental Missionary Society Outreach. Vol. 72, No. 4 (April 1973)-. Periodical. English. qt (Jan., Apr., July, Oct.). $10.00 (surface mail), $15.00 (air mail). OMS International Inc, PO Box A, Greenwood IN 46142-6599. **Tel** (317)881-6751, FAX (317)888-5275. **ED** Eleanor L. Burr. **DD** 266. **Circ:** 60,000. ***Continues*** *Missionary Standard, 0738-4521.*
**Desc:** The journal is a missionary outreach to 14 Third World countries.

●US/1061-0952
**ON COURSE (SPRINGFIELD, MO.).** (ON COURSE.). **Added/Corp** Assemblies of God. Dept. of Education. Assemblies of God. Dept. of Youth. Vol. 1, No. 1 (Apr. 1992)-. Periodical. English. qt. Free. Assemblies of God Archives, 1445 Boonville Avenue, Springfield MO 65802-1894. **Tel** (417)862-2781, (417)862-1447, FAX (417)862-8558.

US/0738-758X
**ON GUARD (CLEVELAND, TENN.).** (ON GUARD; PENTECOSTAL SERVICEMEN'S MAGAZINE.). [On guard]. Periodical. English. qt. $6.00. On Guard, 900 Walker Street, PO Box 3330, Cleveland TN 37311. **Tel** (615)478-1131. **ED** Robert D Crick and John E Taylor. **Bk Rev. Ad Acc. Circ:** 13,000.
**Desc:** Christian pentecostal servicemen's magazine.

US
**ONE ACCORD.** Periodical. English. mo. $8.00 US; $15.00 Canada; $24.00 other. One Accord, 3000 Van Horn Drive, Hood River OR 97031. **Tel** FAX (503)386-6488.

UK/0030-252X
**ONE IN CHRIST.** [One Christ]. Vol 1 (1965)-. Periodical. English. qt. £21.00 UK; $22.00 US. One in Christ, Turvey Abbey Turvey, Bedfordshire MK43 8DE England. **Tel** 011 44 234 881432, FAX 011 44 234 881538. **ED** Paschal Anne Hardiment. **LC** BX1781; .O5. **DD** 282/.05. Index available. **Bk Rev. Circ:** 1,000. available on microfilm and microfiche from University Microfilms International (UMI). ***Continues*** *Eastern Churches Quarterly;* ***Absorbed*** *Ecumenical Notes.*
**Desc:** Christian unity and documentation ecumenical initiatives. Theology, history spirituality relating to ecumenism.
**Ind/Abst** Bibliogr. Mission.; Index Book Rev. Relig.; New Testam. Abstr.; Old Testam. Abstr.; Relig. Index One Period. (1980-); Abr. Cathol. Period. Lit. Index; Cathol. Period. Lit. Index.

SZ/0303-125X
**ONE WORLD (GENEVA).** (ONE WORLD.). [One world]. **Added/Corp** World Council of Churches. Dept. of Communication. No. 1 (Nov. 1974)-. Periodical. English. Ten times a year. $29.90. World Council of Churches, PO Box 2100, CH 1211 Geneva 2 Switzerland. **Tel** 011 41 22 7906076, FAX 011 41 22 7910361, telex 23 423 OIK CH. **ED** Marlin Van Elderen. **LC** BR1; .O53. **DD** 262/.001. **Bk Rev. Ad Acc. Circ:** 7,500. available on microfilm and microfiche from University Microfilms International (UMI). ***Formed by the union of*** *This Month* ***and*** *Justice and Service.*
**Desc:** News and feature articles for a general church audience on the activities of the World Council of Churches and its member churches worldwide; illustrated.
**Ind/Abst** Index Book Rev. Relig.; Peace Res. Abstr. J. (1964-1970); Relig. Index One Period. (1974-); Relig. Theol. Abstr.

BE/0774-2827
**ONS GEESTEILJK ERF.** [Ons geest. erf]. **Added/Corp** Ruusbroec-Vereniging. Universitaire Faculteiten St.-Ignatius. Ruusbroecgenootschap (Antwerp, Belgium). Centrum voor Spiritualiteit. (19??)-. Periodical. Dutch (English, French, German and Latin). qt. 1450F Belgium; 1900F other. Ruusbroecgenootschap, Prinsstraat 13, 2000 Antwerpen Belgium. **Tel** (03)220 43 67. **ED** F Hendrickx. **LC** BX806.D8; O54. Index available. cum. index. **Bk Rev. Circ:** 400 (ctrl).
**Desc:** Historical study of the spirituality of the Low Countries before 1800.
**Ind/Abst** MLA Int. Bibl. Books Artic. Mod. Lang. Lit.

●CN/1192-5515
**ONTARIO MENNONITE HISTORY.** (ONTARIO MENNONITE HISTORY : THE NEWSLETER OF THE MENNONITE HISTORICAL SOCIETY OF ONTARIO.). [Ont. Mennon. hist.]. **Added/Corp** Mennonite Historical Society of Ontario. Vol. 11, No. 1 (Mar. 1993)-. Periodical. English. sa. Free to members. Mennonite Historical Society of Ontario, Conrad Grebel College, Waterloo Ontario N2L 3G6 Canada. **Tel** (519)885-0220. **DD** 289.7/713/09. ***Continues*** *Mennogesprach., 0824-5673.*

CN/0229-4540
**ONTARIO NEWS BULLETIN / WCTU.** [Ont. news bull. - WCTU]. **VFOAT** Ontario WCTU News Bulletin Ontario Woman's Christian Temperance News Bulletin. **VAT** Ontario News Bulletin - Woman's Christian Temperance Union. Bulletin. English. ir. Free. Ontario Woman's Christian Temperance Union News Bulletin, Spencerville Ontario K0E 1X0 Canada. **DD** 178/.06/0713. ctrl circ.

US/8756-5234
**OPEN DOORS (SANTA ANA, CALIF.).** (OPEN DOORS.). [Open doors]. **VFOAT** Open Doors with Brother Andrew. (197?)-. Periodical. English. bm (Jan., Mar., May, July, Sept., Nov.). $5.00. Brother Andrew Ministries, PO Box 2020, Orange CA 92669. **Tel** (714)751-4080. **ED** Chris Woehr. **DD** 320. **Bk Rev. Circ:** 1,600 (ctrl).
**Desc:** International news service covering news of persecuted Christians around the world.

US/0888-8833
**OPEN HANDS.** **See** Homosexuality.

US/0162-4296
**OPEN WINDOWS.** **Added/Corp** Southern Baptist Convention. Sunday School Board. (19??)-. Periodical. English. Four times a year. $5.20. Southern Baptist Convention, 901 Commerce, Suite 750, Nashville TN 37203. **Tel** (615)244-2355, FAX (615)742-8919. **(Subscription address:** Sunday School Board - Customer Service, 127 Ninth Avenue North, Nashville, TN 37234 USA; telephone: (800)458-2772) **LC** BV4800; .O6. **DD** 242.05.

IT/1121-1563
**ORA DI RELIGIONE, L'.** (1988)-. Periodical. Italian. Nine times a year. L21000 (Italy); L35000 (other). Editrice Elle di Ci, Corso Francia 214, 10090 Rivoli Turin Italy. **Tel** 39 11 9591091, FAX (011)9574048. **UDC** 37.

SP
**ORACION DE LAS HORAS.** Spanish. mo. $29.00 Spain; $48.00 US; $39.00 other. Centre de Pastoral Liturgica, Rivadeneyra 6 7, 08002 Barcelona Spain. **Tel** 011 34 3 3022235. **UDC** 24. **Bk Rev. Ad Acc. Circ:** 2,500 (ctrl).

CN/0384-1871
**ORATORY, THE.** ***Ceased.*** **Added/Corp** Congregation of Holy Cross. Saint Joseph's Oratory. (1???)-(1???). Periodical. English (French). bm. St Joseph Oratory, 3800 Chemin Reine-Marie, Montreal Quebec H3B 1H6 Canada. **Tel** (514)733-8211. **ED** Therese Baron. **Circ:** 10,000 (ctrl).
**Desc:** Official reviews of the Saint Joseph Oratory, Montreal, Canada.

US/0361-5472
**ORB (HARVARD), THE.** (THE ORB.). V. 1-1972/73-. Periodical. English. qt. First Unitarian Church of Harvard, PO Box 217, Harvard MA 01451.

SZ
**ORBIS BIBLICUS ET ORIENTALIS.** **Added/Corp** Fribourg (City). Universite. Biblische Institut. (1973)-. Monographic series. German. ir. Price varies per volume. Vandenhoeck & Ruprecht, Robert Bosch Breite 6, D-37079 Goettingen Germany. **Tel** 011 49 551 695911, FAX 011 49 551 695917, telex 965226 VAN d. **ED** Othmar Keel and Bernard Tremel. **Ad Acc.**

CN/0226-9996
**ORDRE HOSPITALIER.** (L'ORDRE HOSPITALIER : BULLETIN D'INFORMATION.). [Ordre hosp.]. **Main/Corp** Ordre Hospitalier de St-Jean de Dieu. Vol. 1, No. 1 (March 1978)-. Bulletin. French. Three times a year. Free. Comite Central Ordre Hospitalier de St-Jean de Dieu, 555 Ouest Boul Bouin, Montreal Quebec H3L 1K5 Canada. **DD** 271/.49.

CN/0472-0490
**ORIENT (MONTREAL).** (ORIENT.). **Added/Corp** Congregation of Holy Cross. (May/June 1953)-. Periodical. French. Six times a year. 2.00Can$. Orient, 4901 rue Piedmont, Montreal Quebec H3V 1E3 Canada. **Tel** (514)731-6231, FAX (514)731-7820. **ED** Marcel Descheneaux. **Circ:** 10,500.
**Desc:** Reflections on the presence of Christians in the world.

IT
**ORIENTE CRISTIANO.** Italian. qt. L15000 Italy; L25000 other. Oriente Cristiano, Piazza Bellini 3, 90133 Palermo Italy.

AG/0325-8823
**ORIENTE-OCCIDENTE / INSTITUTO LATINOAMERICANO DE INVESTIGACIONES COMPARADAS SOBRE ORIENTE Y OCCIDENTE (ILICOD), UNIVERSIDAD DEL SALVADOR Y CONICET.** **Added/Corp** Universidad del Salvador. Instituto Latinoamericano de Investigaciones Comparadas Sobre Oriente y Occidente. Universidad del Salvador. Consejo Nacional de Investigaciones Cientificas y Tecnicas (Argentina). **VFOAT** Oriente Occidente. Vol. 1 No. 1 (Jan. 1980)-. Periodical. Spanish. sa. Universidad del Salvador, Rodriguez Pena 640, 2 Piso, 1020 Buenos Aires Argentina. **Tel** 40-6645. **LC** BL7; .O74. **DD** 105.
**Ind/Abst** Bibliogr. Mission.

SZ/0030-5502
**ORIENTIERUNG (ZURICH).** (ORIENTIERUNG; KATHOLISCHE BLATTER FUER WELTANSCHAULICHE INFORMATION.). [Orientierung]. **Added/Corp** Institut fuer Weltanschauliche Fragen. Apologetisches Institut des Schweizerischen Katholischen Volkvereins. (Jahrg. 19??)-. Periodical. German. bm. Apologetisches Inst, Scheideggstr 45, CH 8002 Zurich Switzerland. ***Continues** Apologetische Blatter.*

UK/0953-2773
**ORIGINS BIBLICAL CREATION SOCIETY.** [Origins Bibl. Creat. Soc.]. (1987)-. Periodical. English. Twice a year. £5.30 (surface mail); £7.80 (airmail). Biblical Creation Society, PO Box 22, Rugby CV22 7SY England. **Tel** 011 44 788 810633, 011 44 788 107881. **DD** 222.11005. **Circ:** 900 (ctrl). ***Continues** Biblical Creation, 0260-9460.*

NR/0030-5596
**ORITA.** [Orita]. **Added/Corp** University of Ibadan. Dept. of Religious Studies. Vol. 1 (June 1967)-. Periodical. English. sa (June and Dec.). $16.00. University of Ibadan / Department of Religious Studies, Ibadan Nigeria West Africa. **Tel** 011 09234 22 400550. **ED** J. Kenny. **LC** BL80.2; .O74. cum. index. **Bk Rev. Ad Acc. Circ:** 400 (ctrl).
**Desc:** Promotes the study and understanding of "the phenomenon and the social implications of religion in general and religion in Africa in particular".
**Ind/Abst** Bibliogr. Mission.; Int. Bibliogr. Sociol.; Middle East Abstr. Index.

US
**ORTHODOX MONITOR, THE.** No. 1 (Nov.-Dec. 1978)-. Periodical. English.
**Ind/Abst** Hum. Rights Intern. Rep.

US/0731-2547
**ORTHODOX OBSERVER.** (ORTHODOX OBSERVER. / ORTHODOXOS PARATERETES.). [Orthodox obs.]. **Added/Corp** Greek Orthodox Archdiocese of North and South America. **VFOAT** Orthodoxos Parateretes. Vol. 37 No. 619 (Oct. 20, 1971)-. Periodical. English (Greek, Modern). Eleven times a year. $5.50 US; $25.00 Canada; $35.00 others. Greek Orthodox Archdio N & S AM, 8 East 79th Street, New York NY 10021. **Tel** (212)628-2590. **ED** P. J. Gazouleas. **DD** 281. **Bk Rev. Ad Acc. Circ:** 125,000 (ctrl). ***Continues in part** Orthodox Observer, 0731-2547.*
**Desc:** We publish the activities of our more than 500 communities.

US/0737-738X
**ORTHODOX THOUGHT AND LIFE : A JOURNAL DEVOTED TO POPULAR ORTHODOX ENLIGHTENMENT AND EASTERN CHRISTIAN SPIRITUALITY.** (1984)-. English. Three times a year. R R #1 Box 353-A, Kingston NY 12401.
**Ind/Abst** Index Book Rev. Relig.; Relig. Index One Period.

US/0742-4019
**ORTHODOX TRADITION.** (ORTHODOX TRADITION / CENTER FOR TRADITIONALIST ORTHODOX STUDIES.). **Added/Corp** Center for Traditionalist Orthodox Studies (St. Gregory Palmas Monastery). Vol. 1, No. 1 (1984)-. Periodical. English (Greek, Modern). qttq. $10.00 US, $13.00 Canada, $25.00 others. St Gregory Palamas Monastery, PO Box 398, Etna CA 96027. **Tel** (916)467-3228, FAX (916)467-3996. **ED** Rt. Rev. Dr. Auxentios. **Bk Rev. Circ:** 1,800.
**Desc:** A traditional (old calendarist) Greek orthodox theological periodical.

AU/0029-9820
**OSTERREICHISCHES ARCHIV FUER KIRCHENRECHT.** [Osterr. Arch. Kirchenr.]. **Added/Corp** Osterreichische Gesellschaft fuer Kirchenrecht. Vol. 1 (1950)-. Periodical. German. qt. DM89.00 Volume 41. Verband der Wissenschaftlichen Gesellschaften Osterreichs, Lindengasse 37, A-1070 Vienna Austria. **Tel** 011 43 1 932166, 011 43 1 934756, telex 847/134981.
**Desc:** Covers Ecclesiastical and Canon law.
**Ind/Abst** Am. Hist. Life (1955-1986).

US
**OTHER SIDE OF THE BOAT.** English. qt. Free. Canadian Council of Churches, 40 St Clair Avenue East, Suite 201, Toronto, Ontario M4T 1M9 Canada. **Tel** (416)921-4152, FAX (416)921-7478. **ED** Jim Hodgson. **Pr Rev. Circ:** 500 (ctrl).
**Desc:** An ecumenical youth publication.

US/0145-7675
**OTHER SIDE (SAVANNAH), THE.** (THE OTHER SIDE.). [Other side]. (1965)-. Periodical. English. bm. $34.97 (1 year), $64.97 (2 year), $94.97 (3 year). The Other Side, 300 West Apsley Street, Philadelphia PA 19144. **Tel** (215)849-2178. **(Subscription address:** The Other Side, PO Box 2007, Hagerstown MD 21742.**) ED** Mark Olson, (703)372-6504. **DD** 261. Index available. **Bk Rev. Ad Acc. Pr Rev. Circ:** 13,000. available on microfilm and microfiche from University Microfilms International (UMI).
**Desc:** Contains provocative opinions, biblical analyses, and personal experiences which provide help and encouragement for Christians who care about peace and justice.
**Ind/Abst** Christ. Period. Index (19??-); Index Book Rev. Relig.; Relig. Index One Period. (1978-); Relig. Theol. Abstr.

CN/0030-6843
**OUR FAMILY (BATTLEFORD).** (OUR FAMILY.). **Added/Corp** Oblates of Mary Immaculate of St. Mary's Province of Canada. (Jan. 1949)-. Periodical. English. mo. 15.97Can$ (Canada); 21.97Can$ (other). Our Family, PO Box 249, Battleford Saskatchewan, S0M 0E0 Canada. **Tel** (306)937-7771, FAX (306) 937-7644. **ED** Albert Lalonde. **Ad Acc. Circ:** 14,100 (ctrl).
**Desc:** Articles that challenge, inform, and inspire our readers and that help them apply the gospel to everyday life situations.

CN/0823-2547
**OUR KINGDOM MINISTRY. FOR CANADA.** [Our kingd. minist. Can.]. Vol. 25, No. 1 (Jan. 1982)-. Periodical. English. mo. Watch Tower Bible and Tract Society / Canadian Branch, PO Box 4100, Georgetown Ontario L7G 4Y4 Canada. **Tel** (718)625-3600. **DD** 289.9/2/05. ***Continues** Our Kingdom Service, 0382-4837.*

US/0030-6886
**OUR LADY'S DIGEST.** ***Ceased.*** ( )-Vol. 45, No. 4 ( ). Periodical. English. qt. Our Ladys Digest, Box 777, Twin Lakes WI 53181. **Tel** (414)877-3886. **ED** Stanley Matuszewski. **LC** BT595; .O8. **DD** 232.931. **Bk Rev. Circ:** 50,000.
**Desc:** A national Catholic publication on Mary, Mother of Christ, from Catholic books and magazines and articles by an eminent staff of associate and contributing editors.

US/0887-977X
**OUTLOOK (LINCOLN, NEB.).** (OUTLOOK / MID-AMERICA UNION CONFERENCE OF SEVENTH-DAY ADVENTISTS.). [Outlook]. **Added/Corp** Mid-America Union Conference of Seventh-Day Adventists. (198?)-. Periodical. English. mo. $8.00. Mid-America Union Conference of Seventh-Day Adventists, PO Box 6127, Lincoln NE 68506. **DD** 286. ***Continues** Mid-America Adventist Outlook, 0274-922X.*
**Ind/Abst** Seventh-Day Adventist Period. Index (19??-).

●UK/0969-1049
**OUTLOOK NEW CHURCH. GENERAL CONFERENCE.** [OutlookNew Church, Gen. Conf.]. **VFOAT** Outlook (General Conference of the New Church). (1992)-. Periodical. English. qt. Free. Swedenborg Movement, Oaklands New Church Centre, Winleigh Road, Birmingham B20 2HN England. **Tel** 0959-534220. **ED** G. Roland Smith. **Bk Rev. Circ:** 2,500 (ctrl). ***Continues** Swedenborg Movement Newsletter.*

CN/1181-9286
**OUVROIR (SAINTE-MARIE-DE-BEAUCE).** (L'OUVROIR.). [Ouvroir]. **Added/Corp** Ouvroir Missionnaire Ste-Marie. Vol. 1, No 1 (Autumn 1990)-. Periodical. French. Limited free distribution. Ouvrier Missionnaire Ste-Marie, Inc, 538 Rue Notre-Dame Nord, Ste-Marie-de-Beauce, Quebec G6E 2K9 Canada. **DD** 266/.2/06071471.

FR/0758-802X
**P.J.R. PRAXIS JURIDIQUE ET RELIGION.** (PRAXIS JURIDIQUE ET RELIGION : PJR.). [P.J.R. Prax. jurid. relig.]. **Added/Corp** Cerdic. **VFOAT** PJR. Vol. 1 (1984)-. Periodical. French (summaries and/or abstracts in English and Spanish). sa. 250.00F. CERDIC Publications, 2 rue Goethe, Palais Universitaire, F-67000 Strasbourg France. **Tel** 88 25 97 09. **Ad Acc.**
**Desc:** Covers law and religion.
**Ind/Abst** Bibliogr. Mission.; Index Book Rev. Relig.; Relig. Index One Period.

US/1048-4523
**PACE (HUNTINGTON, IND.).** (PACE; PROFESSIONAL APPROACHES FOR CHRISTIAN EDUCATORS.). [PACE]. **VFOAT** Professional Approaches for Christian Educators. (1970)-. Periodical. English. Eight times a year. $95.00. Brown-Roa, PO Box 539, Dubuque IA 52004. **Tel** (800)922-7696. **ED** Mary Perkins Ryan. **DD** 268. Index available. cum. index. **Circ:** 1,800 (ctrl).
**Desc:** Current ideas are explored in approaches, directions, issues, teaching and community subscribers may reproduce all articles.

FJ/0552-7414
**PACIFIC JOURNAL OF THEOLOGY, THE.** **Added/Corp** Pacific Conference of Churches. Continutation Committee. (Dec. 1961)-. Periodical. English. qt. $9.00 Pacific; $13.00 Fiji; $15.00 other. Pacific Journal of Theology, PO Box 2426 Government Bldgs., Suva, Fiji Islands. **Tel** (011 679)303924, FAX (011 679)303205. **ED** Linda Johnson-Hill.

US/0360-1897
**PACIFIC THEOLOGICAL REVIEW.** ***Suspended.*** **Added/Corp** San Francisco Theological Seminary. Vol. 6, No. 2 (1974)-Suspended with Vol. 26 (1993). Periodical. English. Twice a year. San Francisco Theological Seminary, 2 Kensington Road, San Anselmo CA 94960. **Tel** (415)258-6500. **ED** Robert B. Coote. **Bk Rev. Ad Acc. Circ:** 6,400 (ctrl). ***Continues** Action, Reaction, 0001-7485.*
**Desc:** Articles on Biblical studies, theology, pastoral ministry, and church history.

US/0744-6381
**PACIFIC UNION RECORDER.** (PACIFIC UNION RECORDER : OFFICIAL BIWEEKLY OF THE PACIFIC UNION CONFERENCE OF SEVENTH-DAY ADVENTISTS.). **Added/Corp** Pacific Union Conference of Seventh-day Adventists. (1???)-. Periodical. English. bw. Pacific Union Conference of Seventh-Day Adventists, Circulation Department, Box 5005, Thousand Oaks CA 91359.
**Ind/Abst** Seventh-Day Adventist Period. Index (19??-).

AT
**PACIFICA : AUSTRALIAN THEOLOGICAL STUDIES.** **Added/Corp** Pacifica Theological Studies Association. Vol. 1, No. 1 (Feb. 1988)-. Periodical. English. Three times a year (Feb., June, Oct.). 40.00Aus$ (1 year), 76.00Aus$ (2 year) surface mail institutions; 35.00Aus$ (1 year), 66.00Aus$ (2 year) surface mail individuals; 56.00Aus$ airmail institutions US, UK, Africa & Europe; 50.00Aus$

airmail institutions Asia, India, New Zealand & Pacific. Pacifica, PO Box 271, Brunswick East Victoria 3057 Australia. **Tel** (03)347-6366. Index available. **Bk Rev. Ad Acc. Pr Rev. Circ:** 600 (ctrl).
**Desc:** Scholarly journal covering all areas of theology, with particular emphasis on the work of theologians of Pacific region.
**Ind/Abst** Index Book Rev. Relig.; Relig. Index One Period.

US/0030-9222
**PADRES' TRAIL. Added/Corp** Franciscans. Province of St. John the Baptist. (19??)-. Periodical. English. Four times a year (Mar., June, Sept., Dec.). $2.00. Franciscan Mission Center, PO Box 645, St Michaels AZ 86511-0645. **Tel** (602)871-4171. **ED** Father Martan Rademaker. **Circ:** 12,000 (ctrl).
**Desc:** This newsletter lets you know some of the things going on in the missions and getting you acquainted with some of the people that is in the mission.

PE
**PAGINAS (CENTRO DE ESTUDIOS Y PUBLICACIONES).** (PAGINAS.). **Added/Corp** Centro de Estudios y Publicaciones. (19??)-. Periodical. Spanish. bm. $65.00 US and Canada; $60.00 Latin America; $70.00 other. Centro de Estudios y Publicaciones, Apartado 11 0107, Lima 11 Peru. **Tel** 011 51 14 336453, FAX 011 51 14 331078. **ED** Cecilia Tovar. **LC** HN30; .P33. **DD** 261.8/3/098. Index available. cum. index. **Bk Rev. Ad Acc, Adv Mgr:** Eduardo Urdanivia. **Circ:** 2,500 (ctrl).
**Desc:** Theological, cultural and philosophical articles of academic nature.

SP
**PALABRA.** Spanish. mo. 3.200ptas Spain; 5.125ptas other. Ediciones Palabra SA, PO Castellana 210-2B, 28046 Madrid Spain. **Tel** 250 83 11, FAX 259 02 30. **Bk Rev. Ad Acc. Circ:** 13,000 (ctrl).

CN/0705-0879
**PALAN, LE.** V. 1- June 1976-. Periodical. French. qt. Free to members. J.G. Gilles Charron, 181 6E Avenue, Boisbriand Quebec J7G 1Y5. **DD** 248/.05.

IT
**PALESTRA DEL CLERO. Added/Corp** Istituto Padano di Arti Grafiche. (1921)-. Periodical. Italian. Twelve times a year. L70000 Italy; L120000 others. Palestra del Clero, Viale Indutrie 1, 45100 Rovigo Italia Italy. **Tel** 011 39 425 28164.
**Ind/Abst** Bibliogr. Mission.; New Testam. Abstr.

US/0274-9009
**PAN Z WAMI.** Polish. ir (6 times per year). $4.50 US; $6.00 Canada. Polish-American Liturgical Center, The Orchard Lake Schools, PO Box 5042, Orchard Lake MI 48033. **Tel** (313)683-0409. **ED** Eugene Edyk. **DD** 264. **Circ:** 58,000 (ctrl).
**Desc:** Polish missalette and prayer book for Roman Catholic church services.

CN/0226-3564
**PAPERS OF THE CANADIAN SOCIETY OF CHURCH HISTORY.** [Pap. Can. Soc. Church Hist.]. **Main/Corp** Canadian Society of Church History. (1975)-. English. an. 20.00Can$. Canadian Society of Church History, 75 Queen's Park Crescent E, Toronto Ontario M5S 1K7 Canada. **Tel** (416)585-4542. **DD** 277.1. **Circ:** 130. ***Continues*** *Canadian Society of Church History. Papers, 0226-3564.*

GW
**PAPYROLOGISCHE TEXTE UND ABHANDLUNGEN.** Vol. 1 (1968)-. Monographic series. German. ir. Price varies per volume. Dr. Rudolf Habelt GmbH, Postfach 150104, D 53040 Bonn Germany. **Tel** 011 49 228 232015. **ED** D. Hagedorn, R. Kassel, L. Koenen and R. Merkelbach.

SZ
**PAPYRUS BODMER. See** Literature.

US/0744-2017
**PARABLES, ETC. VAT** Parables, et Cetera. (198?)-. Periodical. English. mo. $29.95. Saratoga Press, Box 8 311 Elizabeth Avenue, Suite B, Platteville CO 80651. **Tel** (303)785-2990. Index available.

AT/0362-1596
**PARABOLA (MT. KISCO). See** Folklore.

US
**PARENTAL GUIDANCE. See** Family and Marriage.

●UK
**PARENTWISE.** (April 1993)-. Periodical. English. mo. £20.90 UK. Elm House Christian Community Ltd, 37 Elm Road, New Malden, Surrey KT3 3NB England. **Tel** 011 44 81 9429761, FAX 011 44 81 9492313. **ED** Clive Price. **Bk Rev. Ad Acc. Circ:** 10,000. available with illustrations. ***Continues*** *Christian Family, 0269-4689.*
**Desc:** Christian perspectives on marriage, children and home life.

US/0279-7828
**PARISH COMMUNICATION.** Vol. 1, No. 1 (Mar. 1981)-. Periodical. English. qt. $23.00. Growth Associates / New Hampshire, PO Box 142, New Hampton NH 03256. **Tel** (800)637-9144, (508)779-6142. **ED** Patty R. Coleman. **Bk Rev. Circ:** 1,000 (ctrl).
**Desc:** Aids for church bulletins, art, essays, quotes and information on communication for church leaders.

US
**PARISH PAPER, THE.** (1971)-. Periodical. English. Twelve times a year. Yokefellow Institute, 530 North Brainard Street, Naperville IL 60540. **Tel** (312)355-0817. **ED** Lyle E. Lehaller.

US/0738-7962
**PARISH TEACHER. Added/Corp** American Lutheran Church (1961-). Augsburg Publishing House, Minneapolis, Minn. Vol. 1 (Sept. 1977)-. Periodical. English. mo (10 issues). Augsburg Fortress Publishers, 426 South Fifth Street, Box 1209, Minneapolis MN 55440. **Tel** (800)328-4648, (612)330-3300. **ED** Rebecca Grothe. Index available. **Circ:** 50,000 (ctrl). ***Supersedes*** *Learning with: Everyone in the Congregation.*
**Desc:** An informative periodical for Sunday church school teachers.

LE
**PAROLE DE L'ORIENT.** V. 1-. Periodical. French (English). sa. University St Esprit Kaslik, BP 446, Jounieh Lebanon. **Tel** 01 215700. **LC** BR3; .P35. **DD** 201.1. ***Formed by the union of*** *Orient Syrien* ***and*** *Melto.*

FR/0294-0531
**PARTIE PRENANTE. See** Education.

CR/1016-9857
**PASOS SAN JOSE.** (1985)-. Periodical. Spanish. Six times a year. $12.00 Latin America; $18.00 other. Editorial Dei, Apartado 390-2070 Sabanilla, San Jose Costa Rica. **Tel** 506 530229, FAX 506 531541, telex 3472. **UDC** 25(728)(8). **Ad Acc. Circ:** 1,500.

TR
**PASTORAL BULLETIN, THE.** (1984)-. Bulletin. English. Five times a year. $12.00. Archdiocesan Pastoral Centre, 2 Carmody Road, St. Augustine, Trinidad. **(Subscription address:** The Press - University of the West Indies, 1A Aqueduct Flats, Mona Campus, Kingston 7, Jamaica**)**
**Desc:** Records articles, projects, poems and short stories expressing a theology of the Caribbean.

US/0031-2762
**PASTORAL LIFE. Added/Corp** Society of St. Paul. Vol. 1 (Nov./Dec. 1952)-. Periodical. English. Eleven times a year (July/Aug issues combined). $17.00 US; $21.00 other. Pastoral Life, PO Box 595, Canfield OH 44406-0595. **Tel** (216)533-5503, FAX (216)533-1076. **ED** Anthony L. Chenevey. Index available (Bound in December issue). **Bk Rev**, (Qty: 40-50). **Ad Acc, Adv Mgr:** D' Ann J. Montpet, **Tel** (216)799-1306. **Circ:** 3,400 (ctrl). available on microfilm and microfiche from University Microfilms International (UMI).
**Desc:** Pastoral life: ministers to priests, sisters, brothers, deacons, and anyone interested in or involved with today's ministry.
**Ind/Abst** Abstr. Res. Pastor. Care Couns.

CL
**PASTORAL POPULAR.** (19??)-. Monographic series. Spanish. ir (5 issues). $25.00 Latin America; $35.00 other. Centro Ecumenico Diego De Medellin, Casilla 390 V, Santiago, Chile. **Tel** 011 56 2 341804, 344653.

US/0031-2789
**PASTORAL PSYCHOLOGY. See** Psychology.

CN/0713-3383
**PASTORAL SCIENCES.** [Pastor. sci.]. **Added/Corp** Saint Paul University (Ottawa, Ont.). Institute of Pastoral Studies. **VFOAT** Sciences Pastorales. Vol. 1 (1982)-. English (French). an. 17.25Can$ (institutions), 14.25Can$ (individuals) Canada; 19.45Can$ (institutions), 16.45Can$ (individuals) other. Saint Paul University, 223 Main Street, Ottawa Ontario K1S 1C4 Canada. **Tel** (613)236-1393 ext. 2294, FAX (613)782-3005. **ED** Maureen Slattery. **DD** 253/.05. **Bk Rev**, (Qty: 15). **Ad Acc, Adv Mgr:** Jacques Gauthier. **Pr Rev. Circ:** 500.
**Desc:** Forum for dialogue among researchers, trainers and practitioners in the area of pastoral studies. Aims to contribute to the integration of theology and the human sciences in an ecumenical framework.
**Ind/Abst** Abstr. Res. Pastor. Care Couns.

HK
**PASTORAL SHARING.** Chinese. bm. Free. Chinese Coordination Center of World Evangelism, PO Box 98435, Tsimshatsui Hong Kong. **Tel** 011 852 3 910411.

CN/0227-1095
**PASTORALE SCOLAIRE (QUEBEC).** (LA PASTORALE SCOLAIRE.). [Pastor. sc.]. V. 15, No. 2- Nov./Dec. 1979-. Periodical. French. ir. Conference de la Pastorale Scolaire, 1073 Ouest Boulevard Saint-Cyrille, Quebec Quebec G1S 4R5 Canada. **DD** 259/.23/060714. ***Continues*** *Conference de la Pastorale Scolaire. Bulletin de Liaison, 0227-1087.*

GW/0031-2827
**PASTORALTHEOLOGIE.** Vol. 70, No. 1 (Jan. 1981)-. Periodical. German. mo. DM94.00 (regular), DM70.00 (students); DM125.00 (regular), DM78.00 (students) for combined subscription with GPM. Vandenhoeck & Ruprecht, Robert Bosch Breite 6, D-37079 Goettingen Germany. **Tel** 011 49 551 695911, FAX 011 49 551 695917, telex 965226 VAN d. **LC** BV4000; .M6. **DD** 253/.05. ***Continues*** *Wissenschaft und Praxis in Kirche und Gesellschaft.*

CN/0226-5001
**PASTOR'S BULLETIN.** [Pastor's bull.]. V. 1- Feb. 1980-. Bulletin. English. Canadian Home Bible League, PO Box 524 Station A, Weston Ontario M9N 3N3 Canada. **DD** 266.

US/0882-3545
**PASTOR'S STORY FILE, THE.** [Pastor's story file]. (198?)-. Periodical. English. mo. $29.95. Saratoga Press, Box 8 311 Elizabeth Avenue, Suite B, Platteville CO 80651. **Tel** (303)785-2990. **DD** 252.

●US/1061-978X
**PASTOR'S TAX & MONEY. VFOAT** Pastor's Tax and Money; Tax & Money; Tax and Money. (Mar. 1992)-. Periodical. English. qt. Pastor's Tax and Money, PO Box 50188, Indianapolis IN 46250. **ED** DAniel D. Busby. **DD** 254. **Circ:** 6,000 (ctrl).
**Desc:** Tax and finance for ministers.

II
**PATHWAY TO GOD. Added/Corp** Academy of Comparative Philosophy and Religion (India). (19??)-. Periodical. English. qt. $20.00. Academy of Comparative Philosophy & Religion, Gurudeo Mandir, Post Hindwadi, Belgaum Pin 590 011 India. **Tel** 22231. **(Subscription address:** Prints India, 11 Darya Ganj, New Delhi, 110002 India, (Phone: 011 91 11 3268645)**) ED** B R Modak. **LC** BL1; .P3. **DD** 291/.05. **Bk Rev. Ad Acc. Circ:** 2,000 (ctrl).

US/1040-1822
**PATHWAYS FOR YOUNG ADULTS. STUDENT.** Periodical. English. qt. Gospel Publishing House, 1445 Boonville Avenue, Springfield MO 65802. **Tel** (417)862-2781, FAX (417)866-1146.

US/1040-1830
**PATHWAYS FOR YOUNG ADULTS. TEACHER.** Periodical. English. qt. Gospel Publishing House, 1445 Boonville Avenue, Springfield MO 65802. **Tel** (417)862-2781, FAX (417)866-1146.

SP
**PATMOS.** (19??)-. Monographic series. Spanish. ir. Price varies per volume. Ediciones Rialp SA, Batalla Salado 34 Escalera B1A, 28045 Madrid Spain. **Tel** 011 34 1 5390103. **UDC** 24.

US/0737-738X
**PATRISTIC AND BYZANTINE REVIEW, THE.** (THE PATRISTIC AND BYZANTINE REVIEW / THE AMERICAN INSTITUTE FOR PATRISTIC AND BYZANTINE STUDIES.). [Patrist. Byz. rev.]. **Added/Corp** American Institute for Patristic and Byzantine Studies. **VFOAT** PBR. Vol. 1, No. 1 (1982)-. Periodical. English (Greek, Modern and French, Italian). Three times a year. $55.00. American Institute Patristic Byzantine Studies, Rural Route 1 Box 353-A, Minuet Lane, Kingston NY 12401. **Tel** (914)336-8797. **ED** Constantine Tsirpanlis. **DD** 270. Index available. cum. index. **Bk Rev. Ad Acc. Circ:** 2,000.
**Ind/Abst** Index Book Rev. Relig.; Relig. Index One Period.; Relig. Theol. Abstr.

US/0360-652X
**PATRISTICS.** ***Title Change.*** **Added/Corp** North American Patristic Society. Vol. 1 (April 1972)-(19??). Periodical. English. Twice a year. North American Patristics Society, Frederick W. Norris Emmanuel, School of Religion, Johnson City TN 37601. **Tel** (615)926-1186. **ED** Frederick W. Norris. **Bk Rev. Circ:** 350. ***Merged into*** *Journal of Early Christian Studies.*
**Desc:** Review of early Christianity, 1st-7th centuries. Conference news and international coverage are also included.

GW/0553-4003
**PATRISTISCHE TEXTE UND STUDIEN.** (1964)-. Monographic series. German. ir. Price varies per volume. Walter de Gruyter Inc. / Hawthorne, 200 Saw Mill River Road, Hawthorne NY 10532. **Tel** (914)747-0110, GERMANY: 011/49/30/260050, FAX (914)747-1326, telex 646677.

US/0897-9545
**PAX CHRISTI USA.** [Pax Christi U. S. A.]. **Added/Corp** Pax Christi USA. (19??)-. Periodical. English. qt. comes with Pax Christi USA Membership. Pax Christi USA, 348 East 10th Street, Erie PA 16503. **Tel** (814)453-4955. **DD** 261.

CN/0031-3335
**PAX REGIS. Added/Corp** Westminster Abbey, Mission, B.C. Seminary of Christ the King. (1???)-. English. Twice a year. 3.00Can$. Pax Regis, Westminster Abbey, Mission City British Columbia, V2V 4J2 Canada. **Tel** (604)826-8975.

US/0191-4162
**PCA MESSENGER, THE.** ***Ceased.*** **Main/Corp** Presbyterian Church in America. **Added/Corp** Presbyterian Church in America. Committee for Christian Education and Publications. **VAT** Presbyterian Church in America Messenger. Vol. 1, No. 1 (July 1, 1977)-(Dec. 1994). Periodical. English. Eleven times a year (July/August issue combined). Presbyterian Church in America, 1852 Century Place, Suite 101, Atlanta GA 30345. **Tel** (404)320-3388, FAX (404)329-1280. **ED** Robert G Sweet. **Bk Rev**, (Qty: 11 or more). **Ad Acc**, **Adv Mgr:** Bill Savage. **Circ:** 10,000. ***Continues*** *Continuing--.*

UK
**PEACE AND TRUTH. Added/Corp** Sovereign Grace Union. (19??)-. Periodical. English. qt (Mar., June, Sept., Dec.). £7.00 US; £8.00 others. Sovereign Grace Union, 5 Rosier Crescent Swanwick, Derbys DE55 1RS England. **Tel** 011 44 773 608431. Index available. cum. index. **Ad Acc. Circ:** 800.

FR/0764-4663
**PELERIN MAGAZINE.** (1984)-. Periodical. French. wk. 149.00F. Bayard Presse, Svc Client, 3 rue Bayard/Dept 2, 75393 Paris Cedex 08 France. **Tel** 011 33 1 44356060, 011 33 1 44356262. **(Subscription address:** Novalis, PO Box 990, Outremont H2V 4S7 Canada.**) UDC** 087.2.000.28.
**Desc:** World news and general interest articles from a Christian perspective.

IO
**PENINJAU.** V. 1- 1974-. Periodical. Indonesian. 900. Lembaga Penelitan dan Studi-Dewan, Gereja-Gereja, Jalan Salemba Raya 10, Jakarta Indonesia. **LC** BR1220; .P45.

US/0279-7038
**PENTECOSTAL MINISTER, THE.** ***Ceased.*** (THE PENTECOSTAL MINISTER / A CHURCH OF GOD PUBLICATION.). Vol. 1, No. 1 (Spring 1981)-(Fall 1989). Periodical. English. qt. Pathway Press, 1080 Montgomery Avenue, Cleveland TN 37311. **Tel** (615)472-3361. **ED** Clyne W Buxton. **Bk Rev. Circ:** 3,000.
**Desc:** A journal for ministers designed to provide resources, insights, interaction, inspiration, helps, and motivation for effective personal ministry.

CN/0031-4927
**PENTECOSTAL TESTIMONY, THE.**
**Added/Corp** Pentecostal Assemblies of Canada. (1928)-. English. Twelve times a year. 17.00Can$ Canada; 24.00Can$ others. Pentecostal ASSB Canada, 6745 Century Avenue, Mississauga L5N 6P7 Canada. **Tel** (905)542-7400. **ED** Robert J. Skinner. **Bk Rev**, (Qty: 3/year). **Ad Acc**, **Adv Mgr:** D. Niles. **Circ:** 30,000 (ctrl).
**Desc:** Denominational, inspirational articles, news of our fellowship locally and worldwide, some theological articles, letters to the editor, book reviews, some missions and social concerns articles.
**Ind/Abst** Guide Soc. Sci. Relig.

US/1050-8597
**PEOPLE OF DESTINY.** [People destiny]. Vol. 5, No. 1 (Jan./Feb. 1987)-. Periodical. English. bm. People of Destiny International, 7881-B Beechcraft Avenue, Gaithersburg MD 20879. **DD** 289. ***Continues*** *People of Destiny Magazine, 8750-8346.*

US
**PERE MARQUETTE LECTURE IN THEOLOGY, THE. Added/Corp** Marquette University. Theology Dept. (1989)-. Monographic series. English. Marquette University Press, Marquette University, Milwaukee WI 53233. **Tel** (414)288-1564. ***Continues*** *Pere Marquette Theology Lecture.*

IT
**PERIODICA DE RE CANONICA.**
**Added/Corp** Pontificia Universita Gregoriana. Vol. 80, No. 1 (1991)-. Periodical. Latin. qt. L80000 Italy; $75.00 US. Editrice Pontificio Istituto Biblico, Piazza della Pilotta 35, 00187 Rome Italy. **Tel** 011 39 6 6781567, FAX 011 39 6 6780588. ***Continues*** *Periodica de re Morali, Canonica, Liturgica, 0031-529X.*

US/0730-2142
**PERKINS JOURNAL.** [Perkins j.]. Vol. 26 No. 1 (Fall 1972)-. Periodical. English. Four times a year. Free. Perkins School of Theology, Southern Methodist University, Dallas TX 75275. **ED** Roger Loyd. **LC** BR1; .D28. **DD** 230/076/05. **Bk Rev.** available on microfilm and microfiche from University Microfilms International (UMI). ***Continues*** *Perkins School of Theology Journal.*
**Ind/Abst** Index Book Rev. Relig.; New Testam. Abstr.; Old Testam. Abstr.; Relig. Index One Period. (1973-).

BL/0102-4469
**PERSPECTIVA TEOLOGICA. Added/Corp** Faculdade de Teologia Cristo Rei. Jesuits. Faculdade de Teologia (Belo Horizonte, Brazil) Jesuits. Centro de Estudos Superiores (Belo Horizonte, Brazil). (1969)-. Periodical. Portuguese. Three times a year (Apr., Aug., Dec.). $25.00. Perspectiva Teologica, Caixa Postal 5047, 31611 Belo Horizonte, MG Brazil. **Tel** 11 55 31 4410233. **ED** Danilo Momdani and Carlos Palacio (phone: (031)441-0233). **LC** BR7; .M45. **DD** 230/.2/05. Index available (3rd & Dec. iss.). **Bk Rev**, (Qty: 4-5). **Ad Acc. Circ:** 1,500 (ctrl).
**Ind/Abst** Bibliogr. Mission.; New Testam. Abstr.; Old Testam. Abstr.; Abr. Cathol. Period. Lit. Index; Cathol. Period. Lit. Index.

CN/0384-8922
**PERSPECTIVE (TORONTO. 1967).** (PERSPECTIVE.). [Perspective]. **Added/Corp** Association for the Advancement of Christian Scholarship. Association for Reformed Scientific Studies. Institute for Christian Studies. **VFOAT** Perspective Newsletter. Vol. 1 (Dec. 1967)-. Newsletter. English. Four times a year. 20.00Can$. Institute for Christian Studies / Toronto, 229 College Street, Toronto ONT M5T 1R4 Canada. **Tel** (416)979-2331, FAX (416)979-2332. **ED** Robert VanderVennen. **Circ:** 4,200 (ctrl).
**Desc:** House organ of the Institute for Christian Studies, giving information about its activities and programs and publications.

US
**PERSPECTIVES : A JOURNAL OF REFORMED THOUGHT. Added/Corp** Reformed Church in America. Vol. 1, No. 1 (Jan. 1986)-. Periodical. English. Ten times a year (Except July & Aug.). $21.00 US; $26.00 Canada; $35.00 other. Reformed Church Press, PO Box 470, Ada MI 49301. **Tel** (616)392-8555. **ED** James W. Van Hoeven. Index available. **Bk Rev**, (Qty: 30/yr). **Ad Acc. Circ:** 3,300. available on microfilm from University Microfilms International (UMI).
**Desc:** The purpose is to express the reformed faith theologically. To engage issues that reformed Christians meet in personal, ecclesiastical, and societal life, and to contribute to the mission of the church of Jesus Christ.

US/0888-5281
**PERSPECTIVES (GRAND RAPIDS, MICH.).** (PERSPECTIVES.). [Perspectives]. **Added/Corp** Reformed Church in America. Vol. 1, No. 1 (Jan. 1986)-. Periodical. English. mo (10 issues). $18.00 US; $21.00 other. Reformed Church Press, PO Box 470, Ada MI 49301. **Tel** (616)392-8555.**DD** 285. available on microfilm and microfiche from University Microfilms International (UMI). ***Absorbed*** *Reformed Journal, 0486-252X.*
**Ind/Abst** Christ. Period. Index (19??-); Index Book Rev. Relig.; Relig. Index One Period.

US/0093-531X
**PERSPECTIVES IN RELIGIOUS STUDIES.** [Perspect. relig. stud.]. **Added/Corp** Association of Baptist Professors of Religion. Vol. 1 (Spring 1974)-. Periodical. English. Four times a year. $18.00 (individuals), $25.00 (institutions), US; $40.00 other. NABPR, Mercer University, Macon GA 31207. **Tel** (912)752-2880. **ED** Rollin S. Armour, Sr. (phone: (912)752-2759). **Bk Rev. Ad Acc. Circ:** 700. available on microfilm and microfiche from University Microfilms International (UMI).
**Desc:** Promotes communication and cooperation providing opportunities for consideration of literature, movements, and ideas developing in the field of religion. Also, provides aid to the sharing of curricular concepts, teaching methods, and new approaches to study.
**Ind/Abst** Index Book Rev. Relig.; New Testam. Abstr.; Old Testam. Abstr.; Relig. Index One Period. (1974-); Relig. Theol. Abstr.

US/0892-2675
**PERSPECTIVES ON SCIENCE AND CHRISTIAN FAITH.** (PERSPECTIVES ON SCIENCE AND CHRISTIAN FAITH : JOURNAL OF THE AMERICAN SCIENTIFIC AFFILIATION.). [Perspect. sci. Christ. faith]. **Added/Corp** American Scientific Affiliation. Vol. 39, No. 1 (March 1987)-. Periodical. English. qt (Mar., June, Sept., Dec.). $35.00 (one year), $68.00 (two years), $101.00 (three years). American Scientific Affiliation, PO Box 668, Ipswich MA 01938. **Tel** (508)356-5656. **ED** J. W. Haas. **LC** BL240.2; .A55. **DD** 261.5/5/05. **[CCC].** Index available (available every 3 years). **Bk Rev. Ad Acc. Pr Rev. Circ:** 3,600. available on magnetic tape, an online database, and CD-ROM; available on microfilm and microfiche from University Microfilms International (UMI). ***Continues*** *American Scientific Affiliation. Journal of the American Scientific Affiliation, 0003-0988.*
**Desc:** Papers of academic caliber which address issues pertaining both to science and the Christian faith. Both the 'hard' sciences and the 'soft' sciences are represented. Provides a forum for material dealing with the interaction of science and Christian faith in a matter consistent with scientific and theological integrity.
**Ind/Abst** Christ. Period. Index; Guide Soc. Sci. Relig.; Index Book Rev. Relig.; Relig. Index One Period.; Relig. Theol. Abstr.; Soc. Work Abstr. [Select. Cov.].

FR/0555-9952
**PEUPLES DU MONDE.** (May 1967)-. Periodical. French. Ten times a year. 245.00F France; 295.00F other. Peuples du Monde, 8 rue Francois Villon, 75015 Paris France. **Tel** 11 33 1 45311300, FAX 11 33 1 48288657. **ED** Marc Lardret. **LC** BV2130; .P48. **DD** 266/.2. Index available. cum. index. **Bk Rev. Ad Acc. Circ:** 35,000 (ctrl).
**Desc:** Covers Christian life in the third world.
**Ind/Abst** Bibliogr. Mission.; Point Repere (1980-1981).

US/0149-4376
**PHILOSOPHY OF RELIGION AND THEOLOGY : PROCEEDINGS. Main/Corp** American Academy of Religion. Philosophy of Religion and Theology Section. Proceedings. English. Scholars Press / Georgia, PO Box 15399, Atlanta GA 30333-0399. **Tel** (404)636-4757, (404)727-2320, FAX (404)727-2348. **LC** BL51; .A54A. **DD** 200/.1.

US/0890-2461
**PHILOSOPHY, THEOLOGY. See** Philosophy.

AT/0819-4920
**PHRONEMA. See** College and School Publications.

US
**PHYSICIAN. See** Medical Science and Technology-Physicians and Medical Personnel.

CN/0846-5320
**PIONEER CHRISTIAN MONTHLY.** [Pioneer Christ. mon.]. **Added/Corp** Reformed Church in America. Reformed Church in Canada. Vol. 14 (Jan. 1963)-. Periodical. English (Dutch). mo. $13.00 per year. Reformed Churches in Canada, 201 Paradise Road North, Hamilton Ontario L8S 3T3 Canada. **Tel** (416)527-0998. **DD** 285.7/32/05. ***Continues*** *Pioneer., 0480-5321.*

US/0893-5254
**PIONEER (MEMPHIS, TENN.).** (PIONEER.). Vol. 1, No. 1 (Oct. 1987)-. Periodical. English. mo. Baptist Brotherhood Commission, 1548 Popular Avenue, Memphis TN 38104. **Tel** (901)272-2461. ***Continues*** *Pioneer Probe, 8750-4065.*
**Ind/Abst** South. Baptist Period. Index.

US/0032-0420
**PLAIN TRUTH (PASADENA, CALIF.), THE.** (THE PLAIN TRUTH.). [Plain truth]. (Feb. 1934)-. Periodical. English (French, German, Spanish, Dutch, Italian and Norwegian). mo (10 issues). Free. Worldwide Church of God, 300 West Green Street, Pasadena CA 91123. **Tel** (818)304-6077, FAX (818)792-5106. **ED** Joseph W. Tkach. **DD** 205. **Bk Rev. Circ:** 7,800,000. available on microfilm from University Microfilms International (UMI). ***Absorbed*** *Good News, 0432-0816.*
**Desc:** Explains world events and social developments in light of Bible prophecy. Offers practical solutions for everyday problems. It encourages growth and stability of family.
**Ind/Abst** Middle East Abstr. Index.

CN/0319-4078
**PLEIN MONDE, EN. VFOAT** Cette Nouvelle Ecole du Quebec: le Peuple N'en Veut Pas; Pourquoi?. First issue in 1967?. Periodical. French. qt. $3.00. Des Auxiliaires Franciscaines, 1215 Boul. Masson, Les Saules, Quebec G1P 1J4. **DD** 205.

●US/1069-2479
**PLENTY GOOD ROOM.** [Plenty good room]. Vol. 1, No. 1 (May/June 1993)-. Periodical. English. bm (6 issues). $20.00 (one year), $30.00 (two year), $40.00 (three year). Liturgy Training Publications, 1800 North Hermitage Avenue, Chicago IL 60622. **Tel** (312)486-8970, (800)933-1800, FAX (800)933-7094. **ED** David Lysik. **DD** 305.

US/0740-9125
**PLOUGH, THE.** (THE PLOUGH : PUBLICATION OF THE BRUDERHOF COMMUNITIES.). [Plough]. **Added/Corp** Hutterian Society of Brothers (Rifton, N.Y.). No. 1 (Nov. 1983)-. Periodical. English (German). ir (Publishes three to four times per year). Free. The Plough Publishing House, R D 2 Box 446, Farmington PA 15437. **Tel** (914)658-3141, FAX (914)658-6685. **ED** Art Wiser and Derek Wardle. Index available. cum. index. **Bk Rev. Circ:** 15,000. ***Continues*** *Plough (1953), 0740-9125.*
**Desc:** Dedicated to all who work for a personal transformation in Christ and radical turn from the materialism, militarism, racism, and impurity of this world, looking toward the coming of God's Kingdom here on earth.

US/1059-2881
**PLUMB LINE (ONEONTA, ALA.), THE.** (THE PLUMB LINE.). Vol. 1, No. 1 (Sept. 19, 1991)-. Periodical. English. wk. $19.98 (6 months). The Plumb Line, 319 First Avenue East, Oneonta AL 35121-1406. **DD** 243.

US/0747-217X
**PLUS (PAWLING, N.Y.).** (PLUS. THE MAGAZINE OF POSITIVE THINKING). **Added/Corp** Foundation for Christian Living (Pawling, N.Y.). (19??)-. Periodical. English. mo (Published monthly except Jan. and Aug.). $10.00. Peale Center for Christian Living, 66 East Main Street, Pawling NY 12564-1409. **Tel** (914)855-5000, FAX (914)855-1036. **ED** Ric Cox. **Circ:** 640,000 (ctrl). ***Continues*** *Creative Help for Daily Living.*

CN/0825-0391
**PMC. PRACTICE OF MINISTRY IN CANADA.** (PMC : THE PRACTICE OF MINISTRY IN CANADA.). [PMC, Pract. minist. Can.]. **Added/Corp** Co-ordinating Committee on Theological Education in Canada. Ecumenical Foundation of Canada. **VFOAT** Practice of Ministry in Canada. Vol. 1, No. 1 (Mar. 1984)-. Periodical. English. Four times a year. 25.00Can$. Wood Lake Books Inc., PO Box 700, Winfield British Columbia V0H 2C0 Canada. **Tel** (604)766-2778. **ED** James Taylor and Mike Schwartzentraber. **DD** 253/.05. **Bk Rev**, (Qty: 14-16). **Ad Acc. Circ:** 2,200.

US/0734-4570
**PNCC STUDIES.** [PNCC stud.]. **VFOAT** P.N.C.C. Studies. **VAT** Polish National Catholic Church Studies. 1980-. Periodical. English (Polish). an. $8.00. Polish National Catholic Church, Commission of History and Archives, 1004 Pittston Avenue, Scranton PA 18505. **Tel** (717)343-0100. **ED** Joe Wieczerzak. **LC** BX4795.P64; P53. **DD** 284/.8. **Bk Rev. Ad Acc. Circ:** 300.
**Desc:** Articles, reviews, and translations which are relevant to the study of the Polish National Catholic Church and the "independent" religious movements among the Polish and other ethnic groups in the United States.

US/0278-565X
**POCKETS.** **See** Children and Youth Interests.

PP/0253-2913
**POINT SERIES.** **Added/Corp** Melanesian Institute for Pastoral & Socio-Economic Service. **VFOAT** Point. (1982)-. Periodical. English. an. k14.00 US and Europe; k10.00 Australia and New Zealand; k8.00 Pacific and Asia. Melanesian Institute, PO Box 571, Goroka EHP, Papua New Guinea. **Tel** 675 72 1777, FAX 675 72 1214. **ED** Mr. Alphonse Aime. Index available. cum. index. **Bk Rev. Ad Acc.** ctrl circ. ***Continues** Point (Goroka, Papua New Guinea), 1012-0300.*
**Desc:** Devoted to special topics, relevant to the developing countries in Melanesia such as, theology, missiology, anthropology, sociology, economics, politics, law and order, ecology and the arts.
**Ind/Abst** Index Book Rev. Relig.; Relig. Index One Period.

FR
**POINT THEOLOGIQUE, LE.** **Added/Corp** Institut Catholique de Paris. Vol. 1 (1971)-. Monographic series. French. ir. Price varies per volume. Beauchesne Editeur, 72 rue des Saints Peres, 75007 Paris France. **Tel** 011 33 1 45488028. **Bk Rev. Ad Acc.**
**Desc:** Publishes practical theology of today, accomplishments in research groups, theological schools, or Christian communities.

FR
**POLITICA HERMETICA.** No. 1 (1987)-. Periodical. French. an. 113.74F France; 120.00F other. Editions l'Age d'Homme / France, 5 rue Ferou, 75006 Paris France. **Tel** 011 33 1 46341851, FAX 011 33 1 40517102.
**Desc:** Connections between religion and political problems.

PL/0303-2272
**POLSKA BIBLIOGRAFIA NAUK KOSCIELNYCH.** Polish. Dzia Administracyjno-Gospodarczy, Akademii Teologii Katolickiej, Dewajtis 3, 01-653 Warszawa UL Poland. **LC** Z7757.P6; P64.

US/0741-1588
**POOR KONRAD.** [Poor Konrad]. No. 1 (Dec. 1982)-. Periodical. English. sm. $6.00. Carmarthen Oak Press, PO Box 4770, Berkeley CA 94704. ***Continues** Second Coming (Berkeley, Calif.), 0741-1596.*

CN/0383-7653
**PRAIRIE HARVESTER.** (THE PRAIRIE HARVESTER.). **Added/Corp** Prairie Bible Institute. Vol. 1 (Winter 1982)-. Periodical. English. qt. Free upon request. Prairie Bible Institute, Box 400, Three Hills Alberta, T0M 2A0 Canada. **Tel** (403)443-5511. **ED** Phil Calloway. **DD** 207/.7123/3. **Circ:** 30,000 (ctrl). ***Continues** Prairie Harvesters., 0383-7653.*
**Desc:** News and information for friends of Prairie Bible Institute.

SA/1010-8017
**PRAKTIESE TEOLOGIE IN S.A.** [Prakt. teol. in S.A.]. **VFOAT** Praktiese Teologie in Suid-Afrika. (1986)-. Periodical. Afrikaans. sa.
**Ind/Abst** Index Book Rev. Relig.; Relig. Index One Period.

NE
**PRAKTISCHE THEOLOGIE.** Vol. 1, (1974)-. Periodical. Dutch. Five times a year. F71.50. Waanders Uitgevers, Postbus 1129, 8001 BC Zwolle Netherlands. **Tel** 011 31 38 658628, FAX 038-655989. **ED** F. Wolswijh. Index available. **Bk Rev. Ad Acc. Circ:** 2,500. ***Formed by the union of** Ministerium; Theologie en Pastoraat **and** Tijdschrift voor Pastorale Psychologie.*
**Desc:** Periodical for practical theology.

US/0032-7018
**PRAVOSLAVNAIA RUS.** **Added/Corp** Jordanville, N.Y. Holy Trinity Monastery. Bratstvo Prepodnogo Iova Pochaevskogo. **VFOAT** Orthodox Russia. (19??)-. Periodical. Russian. sm. $28.00. Holy Trinity Monastery, PO Box 36, Jordanville NY 13361. **Tel** (315)858-0940. **Bk Rev. Circ:** 1,700.

US
**PRAY TOGETHER INSTRUCTIONS FOR LECTORS AND COMMENTATORS.** Periodical. English. Twelve times a year. $22.50 US; $33.50 Canada; $47.50 other. Sunday Missal Service, 1012 Vermont Street, Quincy IL 62301. **Tel** (217)222-4030, FAX (217)222-6808. **Circ:** 3,500. ***Continues** Catholic.*

US/0274-600X
**PRAYERS FOR WORSHIP.** [Pray. worsh.]. (19??)-. Periodical. English. qt. $25.00. Liturgical Publications Inc, 2875 South James Drive, New Berlin WI 53151. **Tel** (414)785-1188, (800)876-4574. **ED** Rev. Leroy Koopman, (editor's address: 1750 Plateau Dr, Wyoming, MI 49509). **DD** 251. **Circ:** 1,600.
**Desc:** Creative prayers for community and individual worship. It is ecumenial in scope and follows the Common Lectionary.

US/0162-3982
**PREACHER'S MAGAZINE, THE.** (Jan. 1926)-. Periodical. English. qt (Mar., June, Sep., Dec.). $7.50. Nazarene Publishing House, PO Box 419527, Kansas City MO 64141. **Tel** (816)931-1900. **ED** Wesley Tracy. **Bk Rev. Circ:** 20,000 (ctrl).
**Desc:** Practical helps for clergy to assist them in ministry and in their own personal growth.
**Ind/Abst** Guide Soc. Sci. Relig.

US/0744-8562
**PREACHER'S PERIODICAL, THE.** ***Title Change.*** Periodical. English. mo. Preachers Periodical, 109 Indian Trail, Searcy AR 72143. **Tel** (501)268-7588. **DD** 251. ***Continued by** Truth for Today.*
**Desc:** Designed to encourage the preacher in his great work of gospel preaching by giving sermon ideas, full-length manuscript sermons, and illustrations for his study.

US/0882-7036
**PREACHING (JACKSONVILLE, FLA.).** (PREACHING.). [Preaching]. Vol. 1, No. 1 (July/Aug. 1985)-. Periodical. English. Six times a year (Jan., Mar., May, July, Sept., Nov.). $24.95 (one year); $44.95 (two years); $64.95 (three year). Preaching Resources Inc, PO Box 7728, Louisville KY 40257. **Tel** (502)899-3119. **ED** Michael Duduit. **DD** 251. **[CCC].** Index available. cum. index. **Bk Rev. Ad Acc. Circ:** 7,000 (ctrl).
**Desc:** An interdenominational, evangelical publication offering information and inspiration in the area of preaching through articles, sermons, features and homiletical helps.
**Ind/Abst** Index Book Rev. Relig.; Relig. Index One Period.

US
**PRECEPTOR.** (19??)-. Periodical. English. mo. $10.00. Preceptor Co, PO Box 187, Beaumont TX 77704. **Tel** (409)866-3598. **ED** Danny Brown.

AG
**PREGON DE LA TFP.** **Added/Corp** Sociedad Argentina de Defensa de la Tradicion, Familia y Propiedad. **VFOAT** Pregon de la T.F.P. (19??)-. Periodical. Spanish. bm. $30.00 US. Sociedad Argentina de Defensa de la Tradicion, Familia y Propiedad Avda, Figueroa Alcorta, 1425 Buenos Aires 3260 Argentina. **Tel** 802-6295, FAX 54-1-11-2021. **ED** Cosme Beccar Varela, Raul de Corpal. **LC** AP63; .P726. **DD** 056/.1. **Bk Rev**, (Qty: 6). **Circ:** 3,500.
**Desc:** Analysis of the current national and international scene as reflected in the principles of social doctrine of the Roman Catholic Church.

CN/0827-9713
**PRESBYTERIAN HISTORY.** **Added/Corp** Presbyterian Church in Canada. Committee on History. Historical Society of the Presbyterian Church in Canada. Vol.1, No. 1 (Mar. 1957)-. Periodical. English. sa. 5.00Can$. Presbyterian History, 200 Whitney Street, Flin Flon MANI, 481 019 Canada. **Tel** (204)687-6440. **ED** Peter Bush. **DD** 285/.271/05. **Bk Rev. Circ:** 1,000.

●US/1059-339X
**PRESCHOOL CHILDREN'S CHURCH TEACHER GUIDE.** **Added/Corp** Assemblies of God. General Council. (1992)-. Periodical. English. qt. $13.20. Gospel Publishing House, 1445 Boonville Avenue, Springfield MO 65802. **Tel** (417)862-2781, FAX (417)866-1146. ***Continues** Church Programs for Preschoolers, 0736-4288.*

●US/1072-1460
**PRESCHOOL TEACHER GUIDE.** [Presch. teach. guide]. **Added/Corp** Assemblies of God. General Council. Vol. 54, No. 1 (Sept.-Oct.-Nov. 1994)-. Periodical. English. qt. $2.65 (single issue). Gospel Publishing House, 1445 Boonville Avenue, Springfield MO 65802. **Tel** (417)862-2781, FAX (417)866-1146. **DD** 289. ***Continues** Nursery Teacher Guide (Springfield, Mo.), 1059-3241.*

US/1048-5260
**PRESCHOOLERS AT CHURCH AND HOME.** (1990)-. Periodical. English. qt. $7.75. Southern Baptist Convention, 901 Commerce, Suite 750, Nashville TN 37203. **Tel** (615)244-2355, FAX (615)742-8919. **(Subscription address:** Sunday School Board - Customer Service, 127 Ninth Avenue North, Nashville, TN 37234 USA; telephone: (800)458-2772**)**

●CN/1188-5580
**PRESENCE (MONTREAL. 1992).** (PRESENCE.). [Presence]. **Added/Corp** Institut Dominicain de Pastorale (Montreal, Quebec). Vol. 1, No 1 (April 1992)-. Periodical. French. Eight times a year. 30.00Can$ Canada; 55.00Can$ other. Institut Dominicain de Pastorale, a/s Presence, 2715 ch. Cote-Sainte-Catherine, Montreal Quebec H3T 1B6 Canada. **Tel** (514)739-9797, FAX (514)739-1664. **ED** Louis Lesage. **DD** 248. **Bk Rev**, (Qty: 8). **Ad Acc. Circ:** 2,000 (ctrl). ***Continues** Communaute Chretienne., 0010-3454.*

VE
**PRESENCIA ECUMENICA : BOLETIN INFORMATIVO DE ACCION ECUMENICA.** **Added/Corp** Accion Ecumenica (Organization). (Sept. 1985)-. Periodical. Spanish. qt. $16.00 (Americas except Venezuela); $20.00 (other). Accion Ecumenica, Apartado 6314 Carmelitas, Caracus 1010A Venezuela.
**Ind/Abst** Hum. Rights Intern. Rep.

US/0032-7700
**PRESENT TRUTH AND HERALD OF CHRIST'S EPIPHANY, THE.** (19??)-. Periodical. English (Danish, French and Polish). bm (6 issues). $2.00. Laymen's Home Missionary Movement, PO Box 67, Chester Springs PA 19425. **Tel** (215)827-7665. **ED** Bernard W. Hedman. **Circ:** 1,000.
**Desc:** Undenominational mission dealing especially with the Christian era and ushering in the coming Kingdom of Christ and the church. Deals with advanced subjects.

US/0745-192X
**PRESENT TRUTH OF THE APOKALYPSIS, THE.** English. bm. Laodician Home Missionary Movement, 18386 Otsego Drive, Fort Myers FL 33908.

SP
**PRESUPUESTO - IGLESIA EVANGELICA ESPANOLA.** **Main/Corp** Iglesia Evangelica Espanola. Multiple languages (English and French). Iglesia Evangelica Espanola, Raimundo Lulio 2, Madrid Spain. **LC** BX7990.I45; I34A.

CN/0383-8307
**PRETRE ET PASTEUR.** **Added/Corp** Congregation du Tres Saint-Sacrement. Vol. 74, (Jan. 1971)-. Periodical. French. Eleven times a year. 25.00Can$ Canada; 42.00Can$ others. Pretre et Pasteur, 4450 St. Hubert, Montreal Quebec H2J 2W9 Canada. **Tel** (514)525-6210. **Bk Rev. Ad Acc. Circ:** 2,200 (ctrl). ***Continues** Revue Eucharistique du Clerge, 0383-8293.*
**Desc:** A review concerned with up-to-date pastoral theology and liturgical renewal.

FR
**PRIER.** (19??)-. French. ir (10 issues). 49.00Can$. Malesherbes Publications, 163 Boulevard Malesherbes, 75859 Paris France. **Tel** 011 33 1 48884600, FAX 011 33 1 48884601.

US/0161-0090
**PRIESTHOOD AND BROTHERHOOD.** (PRIESTHOOD AND BROTHERHOOD : DIRECTORY OF VOCATIONS FOR MEN.). **VFOAT** Directory of Vocations for Men. Directory. English. 545 Island Road, Ramsey NJ 07446. **LC** BX2505; .P74. **DD** 255/.0025/73.

●US/1059-3403
**PRIMARY CHILDREN'S CHURCH TEACHER GUIDE.** **Added/Corp** Assemblies of God. General Council. **VFOAT** Primary Children's Church. Vol. 18, No. 1 (Sept./Nov. 1992)-. Periodical. English. qt. $13.20. Gospel Publishing House, 1445 Boonville Avenue, Springfield MO 65802. **Tel** (417)862-2781, FAX (417)866-1146. ***Continues** Church Programs for Primaries, 0273-5113.*

US/0032-8413
**PRINCETON SEMINARY BULLETIN, THE.** [Princeton Semin. bull.]. **Main/Corp** Princeton Theological Seminary. Vol. 1-68 No. 3 (May 1907)-(Winter 1976)-. Bulletin. English. Three times a year. Free to alumni. Princeton Theological Seminary, Princeton NJ 08542. **Tel** (609)497-7974. **ED** Daniel L Migliore. **LC** BV4070; .P712. **DD** 230/.05. **Bk Rev. Circ:** 10,000 (ctrl). available on microfilm and microfiche from University Microfilms International (UMI).
**Desc:** No. 1 of each vol. is the academic catalog of the Siminary, 1907-76.

**Ind/Abst** Index Book Rev. Relig.; New Testam. Abstr.; Old Testam. Abstr.; Relig. Index One Period. (1948/1949-).

CN/0383-8277
**PRIONS EN EGLISE (EDITION DOMINICALE).** (PRIONS EN EGLISE.). **Added/Corp** Novalis (Firme) Universite d'Ottawa. Centre Catholique. Universite Saint-Paul, Ottawa, Ont. Centre Catholique. Vol. 29, No. 5A (Jan. 1965)-. French. wk. 7.36Can$. Novalis, PO Box 990, Outremont Quebec H2V 4S7 Canada. **Tel** (514)948-1222. **ED** Pierre Dufresne. **Circ:** 472,483. ***Continues*** *Prie Avec l'Eglise, 0383-8269.*
**Desc:** Liturgical texts for Sunday masses.

US/0898-753X
**PRISCILLA PAPERS.** [Priscilla pap.]. **Added/Corp** Christians for Biblical Equality. (1986)-. Periodical. English. Four times a year (Seasonally). $20.00. Christians Biblical Equality, PO Box 7155, St. Paul MN 55107-0155. **Tel** (612)224-2416, FAX (612)224-3504. **ED** Gretchen Gaebelein Hall. **DD** 261. Index available (bound in vol. 7 #4). cum. index. **Bk Rev**, (Qty: varies). **Circ:** 1,800 (ctrl).
**Desc:** Deals with the issues of women's equality with men in the church for the most part, although issues of race, ethnic, economic classes, and age are also important. Many of the articles are written by scholars in these areas. There are some articles related to news of the organization.

US/0887-5049
**PRISM (SAINT PAUL, MINN.).** (PRISM.). [Prism]. (Fall 1985)-. Periodical. English. sa (Jul. and Dec.). $10.00 (one year), $16.00 (two year) US. Prism Publishers, 3000 5th Street Northwest, New Brighton MN 55112. **Tel** (612)633-4311 ext. 138, FAX (612)633-4315. **ED** Clyde Steckel and Elizabeth Nordbeck (Editor's address: Andrew Newton Theological School, Newton Centre, MA 02159: phone: (617)964-1100). **DD** 289. **Circ:** 2,500.
**Desc:** A journal for the whole church with theological reflections from a diversity of viewpoints on issues of faith, missions and ministry.

NO/0032-8447
**PRISMET. Added/Corp** Institute for Christian Education. (1950)-. Periodical. Norwegian. Six times a year. Kr315.00, $58.00. Scandinavian University Press, PO Box 2959 Toeyen, N 0608 Oslo 6 Norway. **Tel** 011 47 2 2575400, FAX 011 47 2 2575353, telex 71896 UROR N. **(Subscription address:** Scandinavian University Press, 200 Meacham Ave., Elmont NY 11003.**) ED** Sverre Mogstad, Per Karstensen and Ragnhild Veiteberg (editor (editor's address: Institutt For Kristen Oppseding, Box 2623 St Hanshaugen, 0131 Oslo 3 Norway). Index available. **Bk Rev. Ad Acc. Circ:** 2,500 (ctrl).
**Desc:** Educational science, pedagogics for religious-Christian education. Contains research, teaching and schoolwork/churchwork. For teachers, students and churchworkers.

XR
**PRITEL LIDU : CASOPIS SLEZSKE CIRKVE EVANGELICKE. Added/Corp** Slezska Cirkev Evangelicka Augsburgskeho Vyznania. **VFOAT** Przyjaciel Ludu : Pismo Slaskiego Kosciola Ewangelickiego A.W. (19??)-. Periodical. Czech (Polish). ir. $24.20. **(Subscription address:** Artia Pegas Press Ltd., Palac Metro Narodni Trida 25, 11210 Prague 1 Czech Republic.**) Bk Rev. Ad Acc. Circ:** 2,250 (ctrl).
**Desc:** Theological articles, information of the church life.

●US/1063-8512
**PRO ECCLESIA (NORTHFIELD, MINN.).** (PRO ECCLESIA.). [Pro eccles.]. **Added/Corp** American Lutheran Publicity Bureau. Center for Catholic and Evangelical Theology. (1992)-. Periodical. English. Four times a year (Jan., Mar., June, Sept.). $25.00 (individuals), $30.00 (institutions) US; $28.00 (individual), $33.00 (institutions) Canada; $30.00 (individuals), $35.00 (institutions) other. Center for Catholic and Evangelical Theology, 5642 Endwood Trail, Northfield MN 55057. **(Subscription address:** American Lutheran Publicity Bureau, PO Box 327, Delhi, NY 13753, phone: (607)746-7511**) ED** Carl Braaten and Robert Jenson. **DD** 260. **Bk Rev. Ad Acc.**
**Desc:** Seeks to give contemporary expression to the one apostolic faith and its traditions, working for and manifesting the church's unity by research, theological construction, and the free exchange of opinion.

US/0276-4830
**PRO REGE. See** Education-Higher Education.

US
**PROBE (CHICAGO, ILL.).** (PROBE.). Vol. 1, No. 1 (Sept. 1970)-. Periodical. English. ir. $445.00 corporations; $95.00 individuals. Probe Inc., RT 1 Box 88A, Nanjemoy MD 20662. **Tel** (800)477-7623. **ED** Edward Keenan. **Circ:** 2000.
**Desc:** A national publication of theological reflection, social analysis and steps for feminist women of faith in justice ministry.
**Ind/Abst** South. Baptist Period. Index.

US/0069-5750
**PROCEEDINGS. Main/Corp** College Theology Society. (1967)-. Proceedings. English. an. $21.50 (paper), $52.00 (cloth). Loyola University / College Theology Society, 6525 North Sheridan Avenue, Chicago IL 60626. **Tel** (312)508-2357. **ED** Michael Barnes. **Circ:** 1,000. ***Continues*** *Society of Catholic College Teachers of Sacred Doctrine. Proceedings.*
**Ind/Abst** Abr. Cathol. Period. Lit. Index; Cathol. Period. Lit. Index.

US/0069-1267
**PROCEEDINGS OF THE ANNUAL CONVENTION. Main/Corp** Catholic Theological Society of America. (1946)-. Proceedings. English. an. $18.00 US and Canada; $20.00 other. Catholic Theological Society of America, LaSalle University, Box 125, Philadelphia PA 19141. **Tel** (215)951-1335. **LC** BX810; .C285. **DD** 282.06273. **Circ:** 2,000. available on microfilm and microfiche from University Microfilms International (UMI).
**Desc:** Includes major papers and seminar and workshop reports from annual meetings.
**Ind/Abst** New Testam. Abstr.; Cathol. Period. Lit. Index.

US/0092-072X
**PROCEEDINGS OF THE ANNUAL CONVENTION - CHRISTIAN ASSOCIATION FOR PSYCHOLOGICAL STUDIES.** (PROCEEDINGS OF THE ANUUAL CONVENTION.). [Proc. annu. conv. - Christ. Assoc. Psychol. Stud.]. **Main/Corp** Christian Association for Psychological Studies. Proceedings. English. an. $3.00. 6850 Division Avenue South, Grand Rapids MI 49508. **LC** BL53.A1; C43A. **DD** 201/.1. **CODEN** PACSDU. available on microfilm from University Microfilms International (UMI).

US/0887-4913
**PROCEEDINGS OF THE CENTER FOR JEWISH-CHRISTIAN LEARNING.** [Proc. Cent. Jew.-Christ. Learn.]. **Main/Corp** Center for Jewish-Christian Learning. **Added/Corp** College of St. Thomas (Saint Paul, Minn.). (1986)-. Proceedings. English. an (May). Free. Center Jewish Christian Learning, Saint Thomas ML#5010, 2115 Summit, St Paul MN 55105. **Tel** (612)647-5740. **ED** Sr. M. Christine Athans, BVM. **DD** 291. **Bk Rev**, (Qty: 1-2). **Circ:** 6,000 (ctrl).

AT
**PROCEEDINGS OF THE ... GENERAL SYNOD, OFFICIAL REPORT / ANGLICAN CHURCH OF AUSTRALIA. Main/Corp** Anglican Church of Australia. General Synod. 6th (1981)-. Corporate Report. English. an. General Synod Office, St Andrews House, Sydney Square New South Wales 2000 Australia. **LC** BX5703; .C45a. **DD** 283/.94. **Circ:** 600 (ctrl). ***Continues*** *Church of England in Australia. General Synod. Proceedings of the General Synod, Official Report.*

CN/0227-4337
**PROCEEDINGS OF THE ... TRIENNIAL ASSEMBLY ( ... MEETING) OF THE CANADIAN COUNCIL OF CHURCHES, THE.** [Proc. trienn. assem. Can. Counc. Churches]. **Main/Corp** Canadian Council of Churches. Assembly. 4th Triennial Assembly (1979) = 20th meeting (1979)-. Proceedings. English. te. Canadian Council of Churches, 40 St Clair Avenue East, Suite 201, Toronto, Ontario M4T 1M9 Canada. **Tel** (416)921-4152, FAX (416)921-7478. **DD** 277.1. **Circ:** 400. ***Continues*** *Canadian Council of Churches. Assembly. Record of Proceedings, 0701-4309.*

UK/0043-2873
**PROCEEDINGS OF THE WESLEY HISTORICAL SOCIETY.** [Proc. Wesley Hist. Soc.]. **Main/Corp** Wesley Historical Society. Vol. 1, Pt. 1, (1897)-. Proceedings. English. Three times a year (Feb., May and October). £8.00 (individuals), £10.00 (institutions) UK; £10.00 (individuals), £12.00 (institutions) other. Wesley Historical Society, 1A School Lane, c/o V. E. Vickers, Emswrth Hants PO10 7ED England. **ED** E. A. Rose. Index available (Free). **Bk Rev**, (Qty: varies). **Ad Acc, Adv Mgr:** same as Editor. **Circ:** 1,000 (ctrl).
**Desc:** Denominational history.
**Ind/Abst** Am. Hist. Life (1955-).

US/0162-4326
**PROCLAIM (NASHVILLE).** (PROCLAIM.). **Added/Corp** Southern Baptist Convention. Sunday School Board. (19??)-. Periodical. English. Four times a year. $13.30. Southern Baptist Convention, 901 Commerce, Suite 750, Nashville TN 37203. **Tel** (615)244-2355, FAX (615)742-8919. **(Subscription address:** Sunday School Board - Customer Service, 127 Ninth Avenue North, Nashville, TN 37234 USA; telephone: (800)458-2772**) ED** James Hightower. **Bk Rev. Ad Acc. Circ:** 18,000 (ctrl).
**Desc:** A preaching journal for the Southern Baptist Convention.
**Ind/Abst** South. Baptist Period. Index.

US
**PROGRESSIVE WORLD.** Began with issue for Mar. 1947. Periodical. English. mo. United Secularists of America, 1301 E Venture Boulevard 36, Oxnard CA 93030. **LC** BL2700; .P85.

CN/0705-0917
**PROVIDENCE DES PAUVRES, MERE GAMELIN, LA. Added/Corp** Centre Emilie-Gamelin. Vol. 1 (Feb. 1978)-. Periodical. French (English). qt. Free. Centre Emilie-Gemelin, 5655 rue de Salaberry, Montreal Quebec H4J 2J5 Canada. **Tel** (514)331-4810. **ED** Therese Frigon. **DD** 255/.979. **Circ:** 2,000.

CN/0705-0925
**PROVIDENCE OF THE POOR, MOTHER EMILIE GAMELIN. Added/Corp** Emilie Gamelin Centre. Vol. 1 (Feb. 1978)-. Periodical. English (French). sa. Free. Emilie Gemelin Centre, 5655 de Salaberry Street, Montreal Quebec H4J 2J5 Canada. **Tel** (514)331-4810. **ED** Therese Frigon. **DD** 255/.979. **Circ:** 400.
**Desc:** Articles on Mother Emilie Gamelin.

SP/0478-6378
**PROYECCION (GRANADA).** (PROYECCION.). [Proyeccion]. **Added/Corp** Facultad de Teologia S.I. Facultad de Teologia (Granada, Spain). **VFOAT** Proyeccion Teologia y Mundo Actual; Proyeccion Teologica. Vol. 1, No. 1, (May 1954)-. Periodical. Spanish. qt. $32.00. Facultad de Teologica, Apartado 2002, 18080 Granada Spain. **LC** BX805; .P73.
**Ind/Abst** Old Testam. Abstr.

US/0030-8250
**PRS JOURNAL. See** Philosophy.

PO
**PRZEGLAD POWSZECHNY.** (1884)-. Periodical. Polish. mo. Price on Request. **(Subscription address:** ARS Polona, PO Box 1001, 00068 Warsaw Poland.**)**

PL
**PRZEGLAD RELIGIOZNAWCZY. Added/Corp** Polskie Towarzystwo Religioznawcze. (19??)-. Periodical. Polish. qt. $54.00. **(Subscription address:** ARS Polona, PO Box 1001, 00068 Warsaw Poland.**) LC** BL9.P6; E8. ***Continues*** *Euhemer.*

US/0160-838X
**PULPIT DIGEST (1978).** (PULPIT DIGEST.). [Pulpit dig.]. (Jan./Feb. 1978)-. Periodical. English. bm. $49.90 libraries, schools & universities; $24.95 other. Logos Art Productions, PO Box 240, South St. Paul MN 55075. **Tel** (800)328-0200, (612)451-9945, FAX (612)457-4617. **LC** BV4200; .P83. **DD** 251/.005. Index available. **Bk Rev. Ad Acc. Circ:** 5,000. ***Continues*** *New Pulpit Digest, 0145-7969.*
**Desc:** An ecumenical preaching journal presenting sermons and feature material by contemporary preachers for enhancing the preacher's creativity in the pulpit ministry and for devotional purposes.

US/0195-1548
**PULPIT RESOURCE.** (19??)-. Periodical. English. qt. $71.90 (libraries), $35.95 (other). Logos Art Productions, PO Box 240, South St. Paul MN 55075. **Tel** (800)328-0200, (612)451-9945, FAX (612)457-4617. **ED** Glendon E. Harris. **DD** 251. Index available. cum. index. **Circ:** 9,000 (ctrl).
**Desc:** Homiletical aid designed to provide sermon approaches and illustrative material.

US/0747-8631
**PULSE (1984).** ***Title Change.*** (PULSE / EVANGELICAL MISSIONS INFORMATION SERVICE.). **Added/Corp** Evangelical Missions Information Service. Vol. 19 (Jan. 1984)-(19??). Periodical. English. sm. Evangelical Missions Information Service, PO Box 794, Wheaton IL 60189. **Tel** (703)653-2158, FAX (708)653-0520. **ED** James Reapsome. **DD** 266. Index available. **Circ:** 2,500. available on microfilm from University Microfilms International (UMI). ***Formed by the union of*** *Europe Pulse, 0739-0521* ***and*** *Latin American Pulse, 0739-0513 Asia Pulse, 0739-0548 Africa Pulse, 0739-0556 Chinese World Pulse, 0739-053X Muslim World Pulse, 0739-0505.* ***Continued by*** *World Pulse, 1063-7931.*
**Desc:** Reports of world news in the context of world missions.

US/0895-9498
**PUNTOS CARDINALES.** [Puntos cardinales]. Vol. 1, No. 1; 1987-. Periodical. Spanish. qt. $10.00. Nazarene Publishing House, PO Box 419527, Kansas City MO 64141. **Tel** (816)931-1900. **ED** Sylvette Rivera. **DD** 266. **Circ:** 4,000.
**Desc:** Review of the missionary education concerning the work of the Nazarene Church in 89 worldwide areas.

US/1055-839X
**PYM NEWS: A PUBLICATION OF THE RELIGIOUS SOCIETY OF FRIENDS.** **Main/Corp** Society of Friends. Philadelphia Yearly Meeting. **VAT** Philadelphia Yearly Meeting news. (19?)-. Periodical. English. bm. Religious Society of Friends, 1515 Cherry Street, Philadelphia PA 19102. **Continues** *Philadelphia Yearly Meeting News, 0429-7326*.

CN/0828-5780
**Q.T.C. TODAY.** (Q.T.C. TODAY : NEWS OF THE QUEEN'S THEOLOGICAL COLLEGE.). [Q.T.C. today]. **VAT** Queen's Theological College Today. No. 1-. Periodical. English. Free. Queen's Theological College, Kingston Ontario K7L 3N6 Canada. **DD** 207/.71372. ctrl circ.

IT
**QUADERNI DELLA FONDAZIONE S. CARLO.** **VFOAT** Quaderni della Fondzaione San Carlo. Periodical. Italian. qt. Mucchi Editore, PB 64 Centro, 41100 Modena Italy.

IT
**QUADERNI DELL'ARCHIVIO DIOCESANO DI MOLFETTA-RUVO-GIOVINAZZO TERLIZZI.** **VFOAT** Serie Quaderni dell'Archivio Diocesano di. Monographic series. Italian. Price varies per volume. **Continues** *Quaderni dell'Archivio Diocesano di*.

IT
**QUADERNI DI DIRITTO E POLITICA ECCLESIASTICA.** **Added/Corp** Universita di Parma. Istituto di Diritto Pubblico. Vol. 1 (1984)-. Periodical. Italian. Three times a year. L125000.00 Italy; L150000.00 (surface mail), L170000.00 (airmail) other. Societa Editrice il Mulino, Strada Maggiore 37, 40125 Bologna Italy. **Tel** 011 39 51 256011, FAX 011 39 51 256034. **LC** KKH2690.A13; Q83.

GW/0481-1216
**QUAESTIONES DISPUTATAE.** Vol. 1 (1958)-. Monographic series. German. ir. Price varies per volume. Verlag Herder Freiburg, Postfach 79080, Frieburg, Germany. **Tel** (0761)27-17-0, FAX (0761)27 17-520, telex 761489.

US/0033-5053
**QUAKER HISTORY.** [Quaker hist.]. **Added/Corp** Friends Historical Association. (1962)-. Academic Scholarly Publication. English. sa. $15.00. Friends Historical Association, Membership Office, Haverford College Library, Haverford PA 19041. **Tel** (215)896-1161. **ED** Charles L. Cherry. **DD** 289. Index available. cum. index. **Bk Rev**, (Qty: 10). **Pr Rev. Circ:** 800 (ctrl). **Continues** *Bulletin of Friends Historical Association, 0361-1957*.
 **Desc:** Contains scholarly articles, book reviews, and brief notices regarding history and activities of Quakers, mostly in the U.S.
 **Ind/Abst** Am. Hist. Life (1962-); Annu. Bibliogr. Engl. Lang. Lit.; Index Book Rev. Relig.; Relig. Index One Period. (1966-); West. Hist. Q.

US/0033-5061
**QUAKER LIFE.** (1960)-. Periodical. English. Ten times a year (Monthly with Jan./Feb. and July/Aug. issues combined). $17.00 (one year), $42.00 (three year) US; $25.00 (one year), $55.00 (three year) other. Friends United Meeting, 101 Quaker Hill Drive, Richmond IN 47374-1980. **Tel** (317)962-7573, FAX (317)966-1293. **ED** John Maures. **LC** BX7601; .Q33. **DD** 289.6/05. Index available. cum. index. **Bk Rev**, (Qty: 20). **Ad Acc, Adv Mgr:** Carol Beals. **Pr Rev. Circ:** 9,000. **Formed by the union of** *American Friend, 0364-5878* **and** *Quaker Action*.
 **Desc:** Denominational magazine for Friends United Meeting (Society of Friends/Quaker) with inspirational articles and news for a largely Quaker readership.

GW
**QUAKER : MONATSHEFTE DER DEUTSCHEN FREUNDE, DER.** Began in 1932. Periodical. German. mo. DM40.00. Relig Ges Freunde/Gertrud Benz Pars Germany, Germany. **ED** Klaus Rosenbrauf. **Bk Rev. Circ:** 600 (ctrl). **Continues** *Monatshefte der Deutschen Freunde*.

UK/0033-507X
**QUAKER MONTHLY.** [Quaker mon.]. **Added/Corp** Friends Home Service Committee. Friends Service Council. Quaker Home Service. Vol. 43, No. 4 (Apr. 1964)-. Periodical. English. mo. £9.90 UK; £12.00 other. Quaker Home Service, Friends House, Euston Road, London NW1 2BJ England. **Tel** 011 44 71 3873601. **ED** Carol Gardiner. **LC** IN PROCESS. **Bk Rev. Circ:** 3,500. **Continues** *Wayfarer, 0144-915X*.
 **Desc:** Articles, reviews, photos and poetry by members of the Religious Society of Friends on all aspects of Quaker life and service.

FR/0292-5451
**QUAND DIEU PARLE AUX HOMMES.** [Quand Dieu parle hommes]. (1979)-. Monographic series. French. ir. Price varies per volume. Editions du CERF, BP 65, 77932 Perthes Cedex France. **Tel** 011 33 1 44181212. **UDC** 221.

US/0736-0142
**QUARTERLY / CHRISTIAN LEGAL SOCIETY.** See Law.

II
**QUARTERLY JOURNAL OF THE MYTHIC SOCIETY (BANGALORE), THE.** **Main/Corp** Mythic Society, Bangalore, India. Vol. 1 (Oct. 1909)-. Periodical. English. qt. $10.00. Hindustan Book Agency, 17 UB Jawahar Nagar, Delhi 7 India. **(Subscription address:** Prints India, 11 Darya Ganj, New Delhi, 110002 India, (Phone: 011 91 11 3268645)) **LC** DS401; .M8.

US/1062-6565
**QUARTERLY NEWSLETTER - WOMEN'S THEOLOGICAL CENTER (BOSTON, MASS.).** (QUARTERLY NEWSLETTER / WOMEN'S THEOLOGICAL CENTER.). [Q. newsl. - Women's Theol. Cent. (Boston Mass.)]. **Added/Corp** Women's Theological Center (Boston, Mass.). **VFOAT** WTC Newsletter. Vol. 9, No. 1 (Mar. 1991)-. Newsletter. English. qt $35.00. Women's Theological Center, PO Box 1200, Boston MA 02117. **Tel** (617)277-1330. **DD** 291. **Continues** *Women's Theological Center : An Occasional Newsletter, 0892-6263*.

US
**QUEEN OF PEACE WILDERNESS GAZETTE.** (19??)-. English. Six times a year. Yellowstone Information Services, 7 View Road, Elkview VW 25071. **Tel** (304)965-5548. **ED** Roger C Thibault and Thomas Sayre. **Bk Rev. Pr Rev. Circ:** 1,000 (ctrl). available on diskette.
 **Desc:** Covers the apparitians of the Blessed Virgin Mary in Mejugorje, Yugoslavia and other places around the world.

GW
**QUELLEN UND FORSCHUNGEN ZUR REFORMATIONSGESCHICHTE.** Vol. 1 (1911)-. Monographic series. German. ir. Price varies per volume. Guetersloher Verlagshaus Gerd Mohn, Postfach 1343, Koenigstr 23, W4830 Guetersloh Germany. **LC** BR300.

BE
**QUESTIONS LITURGIQUES.** **Added/Corp** Katholieke Universiteit te Leuven. Liturgisch Instituut. Vol. 51-. Periodical. French (English). qt. 700F Belgium; $27.00 North America; 900F other. Abbaye du Mont Cesar, Mechelse Straat 202, B 3000 Louvain Belgium. **Tel** 011 32 16 224174. ((index available in last issue of volume)). **Continues** *Questions Liturgiques et Paroissiales*.
 **Desc:** The study of the liturgy; historically and theologically.

US
**QUIET REVOLUTION (JACKSON, MISS.).** (A QUIET REVOLUTION : MINISTRY OF VOICE OF CALVARY MINISTRIES). **Added/Corp** Voice of Calvary Ministries (U.S.). (19??)-. Periodical. English. Four times a year. Voice of Calvary Ministries, PO Box 10562, Jackson MS 39209. **Tel** (601)353-1635.

UK
**R. E. TODAY.** (R. E.: RELIGIOUS EDUCATION TODAY.). **VFOAT** Religious Education Today. (19??)-. Academic Scholarly Publication. English. Three times a year. £6.00 (single issues); £15.50 (one year). Christian Education Movement, Royal Buildings, Victoria Street, Derby DE1 1GW England. **Tel** 011 44 332 296655, FAX 011 44 332 43253. **ED** Dr. Stephen Orchard. **Bk Rev. Ad Acc, Adv Mgr:** Mr. Cyril Lowden, **Tel** 0628 890700. **Ind/Abst** Child. Lit. Abstr. (19??-).

GW/0033-8532
**RADIUS (STUTTGART, GERMANY).** **Ceased.** (RADIUS). (Dec. 1955)-Ceased (Nov. 1990). Periodical. German. qt. Radius Verlag, Kniebisstrasse 29, W-7000 Stuttgart 1 Germany. **Tel** 711-28391. **Bk Rev. Ad Acc. Circ:** 9,000.
 **Desc:** Monographic issues on literature and religion.

US/0275-0147
**RADIX (BERKELEY, CALIF.).** (RADIX.). [Radix]. Vol. 8 (July/Aug. 1976)-. Periodical. English. Four times a year. $12.00. Radix Magazine Inc., Box 4307, Berkeley CA 94704. **Tel** (510)548-5329. **ED** Sharon Gallagher. **Bk Rev. Ad Acc. Circ:** 5,000 (ctrl). available on microfilm. **Continues** *Right On*.
 **Desc:** Interviews with people who influence the church and the society. Features, reviews, and editorials when dealing with the interface of faith and culture.
 **Ind/Abst** Philip. Sci. Technol. Abstr.

US/0748-7312
**RAINBOW HERALD, THE.** Vol. 1, No. 1 (Oct.-Dec. 1983)-. Periodical. English. qt. $7.00. Rainbow's End Company, PO Box 173, Baden PA 15005.

CN/0228-7870
**RAISON (MONTREAL).** (LA RAISON : BULLETIN RATIONALISTE DE LIBRE CRITIQUE.). [Raison]. Vol. 1, No. 1 (March/April 1979)-. Bulletin. French. La Raison, CP 628 Succursale Desjardins, Montreal Quebec H5B 1B7 Canada. **DD** 211.4/05.

IT/0033-9644
**RASSEGNA DI TEOLOGIA.** [Rass. teol.]. (1960)-. Periodical. Italian. Six times a year (Feb., Apr., June, Aug., Oct., Dec.). L64000 Italy; L130000 other. Editrice A V E, Via Aurelia 481, 00165 Rome Italy. **Tel** 011 39 6 6633041, FAX 011 39 6 6620207.
 **Ind/Abst** Bibliogr. Mission.; New Testam. Abstr.

US/1061-656X
**RCDA (NEW YORK, N.Y.).** (RCDA.). [RCDA]. **Added/Corp** Research Center for Religion and Human Rights in Closed Societies. **VAT** Religion in Communist Dominated Areas. Vol. 30, No. 1 (1991)-. Periodical. English. qt. $28.00. Research Center for Religion and Human Rights in Closed Societies, 475 Riverside Drive, Suite 448, New York NY 10115. **Tel** (212)870-2481. **ED** Olga S Hruby. **LC** BR738.6; .R425. **DD** 200/.947. **Bk Rev. Continues** *Religion in Communist Dominated Areas, 0034-3978*.

US/0034-3978
**RCDA. RELIGION IN COMMUNIST DOMINATED AREAS.** See Political Science-Socialism, Communism, Anarchism, Utopianism.

UK/0266-7738
**RE TODAY.** [RE today]. **VFOAT** Religious Education Today. (1984)-. Periodical. English. Three times a year. £15.50. Christian Education Movement, Royal Buildings, Victoria Street, Derby DE1 1GW England. **Tel** 011 44 332 296655, FAX 011 44 332 43253. **Ad Acc. Circ:** 11,000.

US
**REACHOUT.** (19??)-. English. Four times a year. $10.00 US; $18.00 other. Horizons International, PO Box 18478, Boulder CO 80308. **Tel** (303)442-3333. **ED** George Houssney. **Circ:** 12,000.
 **Desc:** Information about Islamic countries, Muslim teachings and practices as compared with Christianity.

US
**READINGS IN MORAL THEOLOGY.** No. 1 (1979)-. Monographic series. English. ir. Price varies per volume. Paulist Press, 997 McArthur Boulevard, Mahwah NJ 07430. **Tel** (201)825-7300, FAX (201)825-8345. **LC** UNC.

SZ/0254-301X
**REALITES DE LA FOI. DIGEST.** [Real. foi, Dig.]. (1980)-. Periodical. French. qt. 30.00F. Realites de la Foi, Case Postale 93, CH 1816 Chailly Switzerland. **Tel** 11 41 21 9646501, FAX 11 41 21 9647383. **UDC** 2.

NZ/0034-107X
**REAPER; NEW ZEALAND'S EVANGELICAL MONTHLY.** (1970)-. Periodical. English. bm. 22.00NZ$ New Zealand; 26.00NZ$ other. Bible College of New Zealand, 221 Lincoln Road, Henderson Auckland 8 New Zealand. **Tel** +69 9 837 0675, FAX 69-9-837-4209. **ED** S J Sands. **Bk Rev. Ad Acc. Circ:** 5,000.
 **Desc:** Official publication of Bible College of New Zealand. Evangelical and protestant topical and devotional articles. Also, news of the Bible College and graduates.

US
**REC NEWS EXCHANGE.** (19??)-. English. mo. $7.00. Reformed Ecumenical Council, 2017 Eastern Avenue Southeast, Suite 201, Grand Rapids MI 49507. **Tel** (616)241-4424, FAX (616)241-4424. **Continues** *R.E.S. News Exchange, 0033-6904*.

FR/0484-0887
**RECHERCHES AUGUSTINIENNES.** [Rech. augustin.]. (1958)-. French (Italian, English and German). ir. Price varies. Brepols Publishers, Steenweg OP Tielen 68, B-2300 Turnhout Belgium. **Tel** 011 32 14 402500. **LC** BR65.A62; R43.
 **Desc:** History, philosophy and theology.
 **Ind/Abst** BHA : Biblio. Hist. Art; MLA Int. Bibl. Books Artic. Mod. Lang. Lit.

FR/0034-1258
**RECHERCHES DE SCIENCE RELIGIEUSE.** [Rech. sci. relig.]. **VFOAT** RSR. Vol. 1 (1910)-. Periodical. French (summaries and/or abstracts in English). qt (4 issues). 255.00F France. Recherches Science Religieuse, 15 rue Monsieur, 75007 Paris, France. **Tel** 11 33 1 40616400. **ED** Joseph Moingt. Index available (bound in last issue). cum. index. **Bk Rev. Ad Acc.** available on microfilm.
 **Desc:** Covers religious sciences, theology, philosophy of religion, and world religions.
 **Ind/Abst** Bibliogr. Mission.; Index Book Rev. Relig.; MLA Int. Bibl. Books Artic. Mod. Lang. Lit.; New Testam. Abstr.; Old Testam. Abstr.; Relig. Index One Period. (1969-).

BE/0034-1266
**RECHERCHES DE THEOLOGIE ANCIENNE ET MEDIEVALE.** [Rech. theol. anc. mediev.]. **Added/Corp** Abbaye du Mont Cesar. Vol. 1 (1929)-. Periodical. French (English and German). an. 1200.00F. Abbaye du Mont Cesar, Mechelse Straat 202, B 3000 Louvain Belgium. **Tel** 011 32 16 224174. **LC** BX800.A1; R4.
**Ind/Abst** Bibliogr. Mission.; MLA Int. Bibl. Books Artic. Mod. Lang. Lit.; New Testam. Abstr.; Relig. Theol. Abstr.; Abr. Cathol. Period. Lit. Index; Cathol. Period. Lit. Index.

FR/1156-833X
**RECHERCHES, HANDICAPS ET VIE CHRETIENNE.** See Sociology-Social Services and Welfare.

UK/0034-1479
**RECONCILIATION QUARTERLY (NEW MALDEN, SURREY).** (RECONCILIATION QUARTERLY : RQ.). **Added/Corp** Fellowship of Reconciliation. **VFOAT** RQ. No. 1 (Oct. 1967)- No. 10 I.E. 13 (Dec. 1970). Academic Scholarly Publication. English. Four times a year (Mar., June, Sept., Dec.). £6.00 UK; £10.00 others. Fellowship of Reconciliation, 40 46 Harleyford Road, London SE11 5AY England. **Tel** 011 44 71 5289054, FAX 011 44 71 5829180. **ED** Ben Rees. **Bk Rev**, (Qty: 12). **Ad Acc, Adv Mgr:** Ben Rees, **Tel** 051 724 1989. **Circ:** 700/1,500. available on microfilm from University Microfilms International (UMI). ***Continues in part*** *Reconciliation (London, England : 1947).*

AT/0819-5633
**RECORD WARBURTON.** [RecordWarburton]. **Added/Corp** Seventh-Day Adventist Church. South Pacific Division. (1987)-. Periodical. English. wk. **DD** 286.732099. ***Continues*** *South Pacific Record and Adventist World Survey, 0818-7258.*
**Ind/Abst** Seventh-Day Adventist Period. Index.

NE/0922-4238
**REFLECTION.** Vol. 1, No. 1 (Feb. 1988)-. English (Dutch). qt (Mar., May, Sept., Nov.). $54.00. International Reformed Review of Missiology, PO Box 2232, 9704 GC Groningen Netherlands. Index available. **Pr Rev.**

US/0362-0611
**REFLECTION (NEW HAVEN).** (REFLECTION.). [Reflect.]. V. 63- 1965/66-. Periodical. English. Three times a year. Yale Divinity School, 409 Prospect Street, New Haven CT 06510. **Tel** (203)436-2498. **ED** Harry B Adams. **DD** 205. **Bk Rev. Circ:** 7,000. available on microfilm from University Microfilms International (UMI). ***Continues*** *Yale Divinity News, 0364-8613.*
**Desc:** Articles of interest to clergy and other religious professionals. Deals with a broad range of topics.
**Ind/Abst** Relig. Index One Period.

US/1055-1581
**REFLECTIONS ON REALITY.** [Reflect. real.]. **Added/Corp** Church at Bozeman. Vol. 1, No. 1 (May 1991)-. Periodical. English. mo. $25.00. The Church at Bozeman, PO Box 7290, Bozeman MT 59771. **DD** 243.

US
**REFLECTIONS ... : THE WANDERER REVIEW OF LITERATURE, CULTURE, THE ARTS.** **VFOAT** Wanderer Review of Literature, Culture, the Arts. (198?)-. Periodical. English. qt. Wanderer Printing Co., 201 Ohio Street, St. Paul MN 55107. **Tel** (612)224-5733.

US
**REFORMATION AND REVIVAL.** English. qt. $16.00 (one year), $30.00 (two year). Reformation and Revival, PO Box 88216, Carol Stream IL 60188. **Tel** (708)653-4165.
**Ind/Abst** Christ. Period. Index (19??-).

●US/1071-7277
**REFORMATION & REVIVAL JOURNAL.** (REFORMATION & REVIVAL.). [Reform. revival]. **Added/Corp** Reformation and Revival Ministries, Inc. **VFOAT** Reformation and Revival; Reformation and Revival Journal; Reformation & Revival Journal. Vol. 1, No. 1 (Winter 1992)-. Periodical. English. Four times a year (Feb., May, Aug., Nov.). $16.00 (one year); $30.00 (two years). Reformation and Revival, PO Box 88216, Carol Stream IL 60188. **Tel** (708)653-4165. **ED** John H. Armstrong. **DD** 269. **Bk Rev. Circ:** 850 (ctrl).
**Desc:** This journal is published with the desire to foster reformation and to promote prayer for, and interest in, revival and spiritual awakening.

UK/0034-3048
**REFORMATION TODAY.** **Added/Corp** Cuckfield Baptist Church. (Jan. 1970)-. Periodical. English. Six times a year (Jan., Mar., May, July, Sept., Nov.). £10.00 (one year), £18.50 (two years); £15.00 (one year), £27.00 (two years) without index. Reformation Today, 75 Woodhill Road, Leeds LS16 7BZ England. **ED** Errol Hulse (phone: 011 3 2612513). Index available. cum. index. **Bk Rev. Circ:** 2,000. ***Supersedes*** *Christians Pathway.*
**Desc:** Publishes relevant doctrinal, expository articles as well as historical and biographical material, all written by contemporary authors. Provides information and news from churches around the world, inspiring vision prayer and unity. Seeks to promote reformation and prayer for global revival and spiritual awakening. The doctrinal basis is the 1689 Confession.

US/0362-0476
**REFORMED LITURGY AND MUSIC.** (REFORMED LITURGY & MUSIC.). [Reform. liturg. music]. **Added/Corp** Joint Office of Worship (U.S.) Presbyterian Association of Musicians (U.S.). **VFOAT** Reformed Liturgy and Music. (Winter 1981)-. Periodical. English. Four times a year. $15.00. Reformed Liturgy & Music, Unit on Theology and Worship, 100 Witherspoon Street, Louisville KY 40202-1396. **Tel** (502)569-5289, FAX (502)569-5018. **ED** Peter C. Bower. **LC** BX9185; .R43. **DD** 264/.051. Index available (bound in issue). cum. index. **Bk Rev. Circ:** 4,000 (ctrl). available on microfilm and microfiche from University Microfilms International (UMI). ***Continues*** *Reformed Liturgy and Music, 0362-0476.*
**Desc:** Historical, theological and practical articles - journal is thematic - contains book reviews, news columns of what is happening in worship - music, lectionary aids, viewpoints.
**Ind/Abst** Index Book Rev. Relig.; Music Artic. Guide; Relig. Index One Period. (1981-); Relig. Theol. Abstr.

CN/0714-8208
**REFORMED PERSPECTIVE.** [Reform. perspect.]. **VAT** Perspective (Winnipeg. 1982). Vol. 1, No. 1 (Jan. 1982)-. Periodical. English. mo (except July and Aug.). 29.00Can$ Canada; 34.50Can$ other. Reformed Perspective, 1 Beghin Avenue, Winnipeg Manitoba R2J 3X5 Canada. **Tel** (204)663-9000, FAX (204)663-9202. **DD** 248.4/05. Index available (bound in Nov. issue). **Bk Rev. Ad Acc. Circ:** 2,200 (ctrl).
**Desc:** A social-political magazine for the family from a Biblical perspective.

US/0034-3064
**REFORMED REVIEW (HOLLAND, MICH.).** (THE REFORMED REVIEW; A JOURNAL OF THE SEMINARIES OF THE REFORMED CHURCH IN AMERICA.). [Reform. rev.]. **Added/Corp** Western Theological Seminary of the Reformed Church in America, Holland, Mich. (1955)-. Periodical. English. Three times a year (Mar., May, Oct.). $15.00 US and Canada; $18.00 other. Western Theological Seminary, 86 East 12th Street, Holland MI 49423. **Tel** (616)392-8555, FAX (616)392-7717. **ED** James I. Cook. **Bk Rev**, (Qty: 50). **Ad Acc, Adv Mgr:** Norman Donkersloot. **Circ:** 2,800. available on microfilm and microfiche from University Microfilms International (UMI). ***Continues*** *Western Seminary Bulletin, 0361-5480.*
**Desc:** A journal aimed at christian clergy and laity - Containing 3-4 articles on a theme plus book reviews.
**Ind/Abst** Index Book Rev. Relig.; Int. Bibliogr. Zeitschriftenliteratur Allen Gebieten Wissens; Missionalia; New Testam. Abstr.; Relig. Index One Period. (1962-); Relig. Theol. Abstr.

AT/0034-3072
**REFORMED THEOLOGICAL REVIEW, THE.** [Reform. theol. rev.]. Vol. 1 (1941)-. Periodical. English. Three times a year (March, July, November). 12.00Aus$ Australia, New Zealand, Asia; $15.00 other. Reformed Theological Review, PO Box 635, Doncaster Victoria, 3108 Australia. **Tel** 61 3 2111846. **ED** A M Harman, D G Peterson. Index available. **Bk Rev. Circ:** 650 (ctrl).
**Desc:** Biblical and theological articles and book reviews.
**Ind/Abst** Index Book Rev. Relig.; Int. Zeitschriftenschau Bibelwissenschaft Grenzgeb.; New Testam. Abstr.; Relig. Index One Period. (1949-); Relig. Theol. Abstr.

SZ/0034-3056
**REFORMED WORLD.** [Reform. world]. **Added/Corp** World Alliance of Reformed Churches (Presbyterian and Congregational). Vol. 31 No. 5 (Mar. 1971)-. Periodical. English. qt. $9.00 (one year), $17.00 (two years), $25.00 (three years). World Alliance of Reformed Churches, PO Box 2100-150, route de Ferney, 1211 Geneva 2 Switzerland. **Tel** (022)7916236, FAX (022)7916505, telex 415 730 OIK CH (WARC). **ED** Edmond Perret. **LC** BX8901; .R3. Index available. **Bk Rev. Circ:** 17,000. available on microfilm and microfiche from University Microfilms International (UMI). ***Formed by the union of*** *Bulletin of the Department of Theology of the World Alliance of Reformed Churches* ***and*** *Reformed and Presbyterian World.*
**Desc:** Theological articles with special reference to reformed and ecumenical concerns and practical theology. News of members of the World Alliance of Reformed Churches.
**Ind/Abst** Index Book Rev. Relig.; Relig. Index One Period. (1971-); Relig. Theol. Abstr.

US/0890-8583
**REFORMED WORSHIP.** [Reform. worsh.]. **Added/Corp** Christian Reformed Church. No. 1 (Fall 1986)-. Periodical. English. Four times a year (Mar., June, Sept., Dec.). $22.00 US; $29.80 Canada; $30.00 other. CRC Publications, 2850 Kalamazoo Avenue Southeast, Grand Rapids MI 49560. **Tel** (616)246-0799, (800)333-8300, FAX (616)246-0834. **ED** Emily Brink. **DD** 286. Index available. cum. index.
**Ind/Abst** Index Book Rev. Relig.; Relig. Index One Period.

US/0887-8331
**REGISTRY OF WOMEN IN RELIGIOUS STUDIES, A.** ***Suspended.*** [Regist. women relig. stud.]. **Added/Corp** Doctoral Placement Service for Women in Religious Studies (U.S.) Women's Caucus-Religious Studies (Organization). (1972)-(19??). English. be. Youngstown State University, 1069 Edgewood Dr, c/o R. McClain, Chillicothe OH 44601. **Tel** (614)775-7494. **DD** 200/.7/1173. ctrl circ.

GW
**REGULAE BENEDICTI STUDIA.** **Added/Corp** Regula Benedicti Institute. Vol. 1 (1972)-. French (German, Italian and English). ir. EOS Verlag, Erzabtei St Ottilien, D 86941 St Ottilien Germany. **Tel** 011 49 8193 71261, FAX 011 49 8193 6844. **Ad Acc.** ctrl circ.
**Desc:** Essays about Benedicti events.

BL/0100-8587
**RELIGIAO E SOCIEDADE.** ***Suspended.*** **Added/Corp** Universidade Estadual de Campinas. Centro de Estudos de Religiao. Instituto de Estudos da Religiao (Rio de Janeiro, Brazil). No. 1 (May 1977)-Suspended. Periodical. Portuguese (summaries and/or abstracts in English). Three times a year. Editora de Humanismo Ciencia e Technologia, rue Conde de Sarzedas 38, Sao Paulo Brazil. **LC** HN39.L3; R44. **DD** 261.8/3/098.

RU
**RELIGII MIRA.** **Added/Corp** Institut Vostokovedeniia (Akademiia Nauk SSSR). (1982)-. Periodical. Russian. an. 1.60rub. Glav Red Vostochnoi, Lit-Ry Izd-Va Nauka Moscow K-31, Ulitsa Zhdanova 12/1 Russia. **LC** BL9.R8; R44.

CN/1180-0135
**RELIGIOLOGIQUES (MONTREAL).** (RELIGIOLOGIQUES.). [Religiologiques]. **Added/Corp** Universite du Quebec a Montreal. Departement des Sciences Religieuses. No. 1 (1990)-. Periodical. French. sa. Departement des Sciences Religieuses, Universite du Quebec a Montreal, CP 8888, Succursale H, Montreal Quebec H3C 3P8 Canada. **DD** 200/.5.

US/1052-1151
**RELIGION AND AMERICAN CULTURE.** (RELIGION AND AMERICAN CULTURE : R & AC.). [Relig. Am. cult.]. **Added/Corp** Indiana University-Purdue University at Indianapolis. Center for the Study of Religion and American Culture. **VFOAT** R & AC; R and AC. Vol. 1, No. 1 (Winter 1991)-. Periodical. English. sa. $30.00. Indiana University Press, 601 North Morton Street, Bloomington IN 47404. **Tel** (812)855-3830, (800)842-6796. **LC** BL65.C8; R42. **DD** 291/.0973/05.
**Ind/Abst** Am. Hist. Life (1991-).

US
**RELIGION & DEMOCRACY.** **Added/Corp** Institute on Religion and Democracy. **VFOAT** Religion and Democracy. (197?)-. Periodical. English. ir. $25.00. Institute on Religion & Democracy, 1331 H Street Northwest, Suite 900, Washington DC 20005. **Tel** (202)393-3200, FAX (202)638-4948.

US/0730-2363
**RELIGION AND LIFE LETTERS.** Periodical. English. bw. $25.00 US; $35.80 other. Spiritual Studies Center, PO Box 1104, Rockville MD 20850. **Tel** (301)963-9243. **ED** Elisabeth Nachtwey. available on an online database.

US/0888-3769
**RELIGION & LITERATURE.** [Relig. lit.]. **Added/Corp** University of Notre Dame. Dept. of English. **VFOAT** Religion and Literature; R & R & L; R and L; R. & L. Vol. 16 (Winter 1984)-. Periodical. English. Three times a year. $20.00 (one year), $34.00 (two year) individual; $25.00 (one year), $45.00 (two year), $65.00 (three year) institution, US; $29.00 (one year), $52.00 (two year), $75.00 (three year) institutions, other. University of Notre Dame Department of English, Notre Dame IN 46556. **Tel** (219)631-5725. **ED** Thomas Werge and James Dougherty. **LC** PN49; .R39. **DD** 809/.005. Index available. cum. index. **Bk Rev. Ad Acc. Circ:** 500 (ctrl). available on microfilm and microfiche from University Microfilms International (UMI). Documents available from The Genuine Article. ***Continues*** *Notre Dame English Journal, 0029-4500.*
**Desc:** A forum for an on-going discussion of the relations between the religious impulses and the literary forms of any era, place or language.
**Ind/Abst** Abstr. Engl. Stud.; Am. Humanit. Index; Annu. Bibliogr. Engl. Lang. Lit.; Arts Humanit. Citation Index [Full Cov.]; Curr. Contents Arts Humanit.; Index Book Rev. Relig.; Lit. Crit. Regist.; MLA Int. Bibl. Books Artic. Mod. Lang. Lit.; Relig. Theol. Abstr.; Res. Alert [Full Cov.]; Romant. Move.; Abr. Cathol. Period. Lit. Index; Cathol. Period. Lit. Index.

US/1056-7224
**RELIGION & PUBLIC EDUCATION.** See Education.

NE/0080-0848
**RELIGION AND REASON.** 1- 1971-. Monographic series. Multiple languages (English and French). ir. Price varies per volume. Walter de Gruyter

Inc. / Hawthorne, 200 Saw Mill River Road, Hawthorne NY 10532. **Tel** (914)747-0110, GERMANY: 011/49/30/260050, FAX (914)747-1326, telex 646677. **(Subscription address:** Germany/ PO Box 110240, 1 Berlin 11)

II/0034-3951
**RELIGION AND SOCIETY (BANGALORE, INDIA).** (RELIGION AND SOCIETY.). [Relig. soc.]. **Added/Corp** Christian Institute for the Study of Religion and Society, Bangalore. Vol. 4, No. 3 (Dec. 1957)-. Periodical. English. qt. $30.00 US and Canada; $20.00 other. CISRS Publications Trust, 73 Millers Road, PO Box 4600, Bangalore 560046 India. **Tel** 011 91 080 332981, FAX 011 91 080 330335. **(Subscription address:** Prints India, 11 Darya Ganj, New Delhi 110002 India.) **ED** J. Victor Koilpillai. Index available. **Bk Rev. Circ:** 1,000. available on microfilm and microfiche from University Microfilms International (UMI). ***Continues*** *Bulletin of the Christian Institute for the Study of Society.*
**Desc:** Christian journal of research and study of social and religious issues; especially from perspective of oppressed sections of society to promote social justice.
**Ind/Abst** Bibliogr. Mission.; Index Islam. Lit.; Index Book Rev. Relig.; Relig. Index One Period. (1973-).

II/0578-0039
**RELIGION AND SOCIETY REPORT.** (REPORT - CHRISTIAN INSTITUTE FOR THE STUDY OF RELIGION AND SOCIETY.). **Main/Corp** Christian Institute for the Study of Religion and Society, Bangalore. (1958)-. English. Twelve times a year. $24.00 (one year); $38.00 (two years); $54.00 (three years). Rockford Institute, 934 North Main Street, Rockford IL 61103. **Tel** (815)964-5053, FAX (815)965-1826. **LC** BR1150; .C43. **DD** 261.1/06/25487.

US/0742-6984
**RELIGION & SOCIETY REPORT, THE.** [Relig. soc. rep.]. **Added/Corp** Center on Religion & Society (New York, N.Y.). **VFOAT** Religion and Society Report. Vol. 1, No. 1 (June 1984)-. Periodical. English. mo. $24.00 (one year), $44.00 (two year) US; $30.00 (one year), $48.00 (two year) other. Rockford Institute, 934 North Main Street, Rockford IL 61103. **Tel** (815)964-5053, FAX (815)965-1826. **ED** Harold O J Brown. **DD** 261. cum. index. **Bk Rev. Circ:** 5,300.
**Desc:** Reports on the intersection of religion and society and serves to reinvigorate religious sensibilities in 'The Public Square' by exemplifying Judeo/Christian traditions.
**Ind/Abst** Curr. Thoughts Trends.

GW
**RELIGION AND SOCIETY (THE HAGUE).** (RELIGION AND SOCIETY.). **VFOAT** RS. (1976)-. Monographic series. English. ir. Price varies per volume. Walter de Gruyter Inc., PO Box 303421, D 10728 Berlin Germany. **Tel** 011 49 30 260050, FAX 011 49 30 26005251. **LC** UNC.

US/1061-5210
**RELIGION AND THE SOCIAL ORDER.** [Relig. soc. order]. **Added/Corp** Association for the Sociology of Religion. Vol. 1 (1991)-. English. ir. $73.25. JAI Press Inc., 55 Old Post Road, Suite 2, PO Box 1678, Greenwich CT 06836-1678. **Tel** (203)661-7602, FAX (203)661-0792. **ED** David G. Bromley. **LC** IN PROCESS; BL60; .R42. **DD** 306.

US/0273-2556
**RELIGION (BOCA RATON).** (RELIGION.). [Religion]. V. 1, Article 1-. English. Social Issues Resources Series Inc, PO Box 2348, Boca Raton FL 33427. **Tel** (800)327-0513, (407)994-0079. **ED** Eleanor C Goldstein. **LC** BL1; .R34. **DD** 291/.05.
**Desc:** Interdisciplinary resource material consisting of reprinted articles from popular and professional journals, newspapers, magazines and government documents.

●US/1069-4781
**RELIGION IN EASTERN EUROPE.** (RELIGION IN EASTERN EUROPE / CHRISTIANS ASSOCIATED FOR RELATIONSHIPS WITH EASTERN EUROPE.). [Relig. East. Eur.]. **Added/Corp** Christians Associated for Relationships with Eastern Europe (U.S.). Vol. 13, No. 1 (Feb. 1993)-. Periodical. English. bm. $36.00. South Dakota Academy of Science, Department of Math, Augustana College, Sioux Falls SD 57107. **Tel** (605)336-4825. **LC** BR738.6; .O25. **DD** 274.7/082/05. ***Continues*** *Occasional Papers on Religion in Eastern Europe, 0731-5465.*
**Ind/Abst** Relig. Index One Period.

MW
**RELIGION IN MALAWI.** Vol. 1, No. 1 (Dec. 1987)-. English. sa. University of Malawi / Department of Religious Studies, Box 280, Zomba Malawi. **Tel** 011 265 522622.

RU
**RELIGION IN USSR.** **Added/Corp** Agenstvo Pechati "Novosti.". (19??)-. English. mo. Novosti Press Agency Publishing House, 4 Zubovski Boulevard, Moscow Russia. **Tel** 095-201-2424, FAX 095-201-2119, telex 411321. **LC** PAR.

US/0149-8428
**RELIGION INDEX ONE. PERIODICALS.** **See** Religion and Theology-Abstracting, Bibliographies and Statistics.

US/0149-8436
**RELIGION INDEX TWO : MULTI-AUTHOR WORKS.** (1976)-. English. an. $370.00. American Theological Library Association, 820 Church Street, 3rd Floor, Evanston IL 60201. **Tel** (708)869-7788, FAX (708)869-8513. **ED** Erica Treesh. **LC** Z7751; .R35; BL48. **DD** 016.2. **Bk Rev. Ad Acc. Circ:** 1,000 (ctrl). available on an online database; available on CD-ROM; available on microfilm.
**Desc:** Indexes 450+ books and their 5,500 essays with special emphasis placed on the indexing of Festschriften, conference proceedings, congresses and series.

UK/0048-721X
**RELIGION (LONDON. 1971).** (RELIGION.). [Religion]. Vol. 1 (Spring 1971)-. Academic Scholarly Publication. English. qt (4 issues). $155.00. Academic Press Ltd., A Division of Harcourt Brace & Company Ltd., 24-28 Oval Road, London NW1 7DX England. **Tel** 071 267 4466, FAX 071 482 2293, 071 485 4752, telex 25775 ACPRES G. **(Subscription address:** Harcourt Brace & Company, Ltd., Foots Cray, High Street, Sidcup Kent DA14 5HP England.) **ED** A. Cunningham and I. Strenski. **LC** BL1; .R37. **DD** 200/.5. **[CCC].** Documents available from The Genuine Article, UMI Article Clearinghouse.
**Desc:** Provides a regular survey of current work in major and specific areas of enquiry. Its swift reviewing and crossing of traditional frontiers to encompass such related studies as psychology and archaeology combine to make it a valued point of reference for a growing readership. Already well known for its strong and established interest in comparative and pioneering work, the journal has expanded its coverage of the varied disciplines that together embrace the history, structure, and general theory of religions of the world. Organized through two broads, one American and one European, thereby significantly increasing the scope of the journal and reinforcing its position as the international forum for debate and scholarship in the field.
**Ind/Abst** Acad. Search (Jan. 1994-); Arts Humanit. Citation Index [Full Cov.]; Curr. Contents Arts Humanit.; Expand. Acad. Index (1989-); Humanit. Index; Humanit. Source (Jul. 1993-); Index Book Rev. Relig.; INFO-SOUTH Abstr.; Int. Bibliogr. Sociol.; Mag. Search; New Testam. Abstr.; Newsp. Period. Abstr. (1991-); Old Testam. Abstr.; Relig. Index One Period. (1971-); Res. Alert [Full Cov.]; Soc. Sci. Cit. Index [Select. Cov.].

●UK/0963-7494
**RELIGION, STATE & SOCIETY : THE KESTON JOURNAL.** **Added/Corp** Keston College. **VFOAT** Religion, State, and Society; Keston Journal. Vol. 20, No. 1 (1992)-. Periodical. English. qt. £124.00. Carfax Publishing Company, PO Box 25 Abingdon, Oxfordshire OX14 3UE England. **Tel** 011 44 235 555335, FAX (0279)31067, telex 817484. **(Subscription address:** US and Canada/ PO Box 2025, Dunnellon, FL 34430-2025; telephone:(904)489-6996) **ED** Philip Walters. **LC** BR738.6; .R427. **DD** 261.7/2/091717. **[CCC].** Index available. available on microfiche. ***Continues*** *Religion in Communist Lands, 0307-5974.*
**Desc:** Covers the experiences of religious communities in communist and formerly communist countries throughout the world.
**Ind/Abst** Int. Bibliogr. Sociol.; Relig. Index One Period. (1992-).

US/0034-401X
**RELIGION TEACHER'S JOURNAL.** [Relig. teach. j.]. (1967)-. Periodical. English. Seven times a year (published Sept.- May with Apr./May & Nov./Dec. issues combined). $17.95 (US); $22.95 (including postage) other. Twenty Third Publications, 185 Willow Street, PO Box 180, Mystic CT 06355-0180. **Tel** (203)536-2611, (800)321-0411, FAX (203)572-0788. **ED** Gwen Costello. **Bk Rev. Ad Acc. Circ:** 40,000 (ctrl). available on microfilm and microfiche from University Microfilms International (UMI).
**Desc:** Practical and motivational articles for religion teachers.
**Ind/Abst** Med. Rev. Dig.; Abr. Cathol. Period. Lit. Index; Cathol. Period. Lit. Index.

US/0886-2141
**RELIGION WATCH.** [Relig. watch]. Vol. 1, No. 1 (Sept. 1985)-. Periodical. English. Eleven times a year. $19.95 (one year), $25.00 (two years) US; $21.45 (one year), $26.50 (two years) Canada; $22.45 (one year), $25.50 (two years) other. Religion Watch, PO Box 652, North Bellmore NY 11710. **Tel** (516)785-6765. **ED** Richard P Cimino. **LC** BL1; .R38. **DD** 291/.09/0405. Index available (bound in Dec. issue). **Bk Rev. Circ:** 700.
**Desc:** Monitors periodicals and books for trends in contemporary religion. The 8-10 page newsletter also notes new books and periodicals in religion.
**Ind/Abst** Curr. Thoughts Trends.

AT
**RELIGION, WISSENSCHAFT, KULTUR.** an.
**Ind/Abst** Am. Hist. Life (1955-1977,1979-).

SP
**RELIGION Y ESCUELA.** Spanish. mo. 1750.00ptas Spain; 2226.00ptas other. Promocion Popular Cristiana, Enrique Jardiel, Poncela 4, 28016 Madrid, Spain. **Tel** 011 34 1 3592300.

IT
**RELIGIONE E SCUOLA.** (19??)-. Italian. bm (6 issues). L40000.00 Italy; L58000.00 other. Editrice Queriniana, Casella Postale 403, 25100 Brescia Italy. **Tel** 39 30 294653.
**Desc:** Information on teaching, pedagogy, didactics, religion and art, international issues, history and more.

GW/0486-3585
**RELIGIONEN DER MENSCHHEIT, DIE.** Vol. 1 (1961)-. Monographic series. German. ir. Price varies per volume. W Kohlhammer Verlag GmbH, Postfach 800430, D 70549 Stuttgart Germany. **Tel** 011 49 711 78631, FAX 011 49 711 7863263, telex 7-255820. **ED** Peter Antes, Hubest Caucik, Burlehard Gladigow, and Mastin Greshat. Index available. **Bk Rev. Ad Acc.**
**Desc:** This encyclopedia intends to present, as well as possible, all religions of mankind, from the beginning until today.

IT
**RELIGIONI E SOCIETA (FLORENCE, ITALY).** (RELIGIONI E SOCIETA.). Yearly Vol. 1, No. 1, (Jan./June 1986)-. Periodical. Italian. sa. L38000 Italy; L50000 Europe; L68000 other. Rosenberg & Sellier, Via Andrea Doria 14, 10123 Turin Italy. **Tel** 011 39 11 8127808, telex 224202 ROSSELI.
**Ind/Abst** Soc. Plann. Policy Dev. Abstr.; Sociol. Abstr. (1986-) [Full Cov.].

GW
**RELIGIONSGESCHICHTLICHE VERSUCHE UND VORARBEITEN.** Vol. 1, (1903)-. Monographic series. German (English, Greek and Modern, Latin). ir. Price varies per volume. Walter de Gruyter Inc., PO Box 303421, D 10728 Berlin Germany. **Tel** 011 49 30 260050, FAX 011 49 30 26005251. **(Subscription address:** US and Canada/ 200 Saw Mill River Road, Hawthorne, NY 10532) **ED** Walter Burkert, Carshen Colpe. **Bk Rev. Ad Acc.**

DK/0108-1993
**RELIGIONSVIDENSKABELIGT TIDSSKRIFT.** No. 1 (Oct. 1982)-. Periodical. Danish (summaries and/or abstracts in English). sa. Kr90.00. Institut for Religions Studier Tedsskrift, Aarhus Universitet C Denmark. **Tel** (06)136711. **ED** Per Ingesman, Hans Jorgen Lundager Jensen, Jens Peter Schjodt. **Bk Rev. Ad Acc. Circ:** 350 (ctrl).
**Desc:** History of religions, science of religions, theology, philosophy of religion, sociology of religion, psychology of religion, anthropology, structuralism and semiotics.

US/0034-4044
**RELIGIOUS AND THEOLOGICAL ABSTRACTS.** **See** Religion and Theology-Abstracting, Bibliographies and Statistics.

UK/0305-960X
**RELIGIOUS BOOKS IN PRINT.** **Added/Corp** J. Whitaker & Sons. **VFOAT** Whitaker Religious Books in Print. (19??)-. Periodical. English. an. £35.00 UK; £44.00 other. J. Whitaker & Sons Ltd, 12 Dyott Street, London WC1A 1DF England. **Tel** 011 44 71 8368911, FAX 011 44 71 836 2909.

US/0034-4079
**RELIGIOUS BROADCASTING.** **See** Communication-Broadcasting.

US
**RELIGIOUS COALITION FOR ABORTION RIGHTS NEWSLETTER.** **See** Birth Control.

US/0034-4087
**RELIGIOUS EDUCATION.** [Relig. educ.]. **Added/Corp** Religious Education Association. Association of Professors and Researchers in Religious Education. Vol. 1 (Apr. 1906)-. Periodical. English. qt (4 issues). Free to members of the Religious Education Association. Religious Education Association, 409 Prospect Street, New Haven CT 06511. **Tel** (203)865-6141. **ED** Hanan Alexander. **LC** BV1460; .R3. **DD** 268.05. **CODEN** RLEDAN. cum. index. **Bk Rev. Ad Acc. Circ:** 3,500. available on microfilm and microfiche from University Microfilms International (UMI). Documents available from The Genuine Article.
**Desc:** Addresses issues in religious education from various faith perspectives. Contributors represent scholarship from Protestant, Jewish, Roman Catholic, and Orthodox Christian traditions. In each 160-page issue a particular thesis is presented, along with articles of general interest and book reviews. A yearly index is included.
**Ind/Abst** Acad. Search (July 1993-); Arts Humanit. Citation Index [Full Cov.]; Book Rev. Digest; Book Rev. Index; Contents Pages Educ.; Curr. Contents Arts Humanit.; Curr. Index J. Educ. (March 1990-); Educ. Index; Guide Soc. Sci. Relig.; Humanit. Source (Jul. 1993-); Index Book Rev. Relig.; Index Jew. Period. (19??-199?); INFO-SOUTH Abstr.; Mag. Search;

Psychol. Abstr. (1928-); Relig. Index One Period. (1974-); Relig. Theol. Abstr.; Res. Alert [Full Cov.]; Soc. Sci. Cit. Index [Select. Cov.].

AT/0815-3094
**RELIGIOUS EDUCATION JOURNAL OF AUSTRALIA.** **See** Education.

US/0275-3529
**RELIGIOUS FREEDOM REPORTER.** **See** Law-Constitutional Law.

US/0896-8187
**RELIGIOUS FUNDING MONITOR.** ***Ceased.*** [Relig. funding monit.]. Ceased August (1990). Periodical. English. mo. Taft Group, 835 Penobscott Building, Customer Service, Detroit MI 48226. **Tel** (800)877-8238, FAX (313)961-6083. **DD** 206.

US/0738-7318
**RELIGIOUS HERALD, THE.** [Relig. her.]. **Added/Corp** Baptist General Association of Virginia. Vol. 1 No. 1 (Jan. 11, 1828)-. Periodical. English. wk. $9.75. The Religious Herald, PO Box 8377, Richmond VA 23226-0377. **Tel** (804)672-1973, FAX (804)672-2051. **ED** Julian Pentecost. **DD** 286. Index available. **Ad Acc. Circ:** 40,000. ***Continues*** *Evangelical Inquirer;* ***Absorbed*** *South Carolina Baptist.*
**Desc:** Southern Baptist news journal for Virginia.

US/0034-4095
**RELIGIOUS HUMANISM.** [Relig. humanism]. **Added/Corp** Fellowship of Religious Humanists. Vol. 1 (Winter 1967)-. Periodical. English. qt (4 issues). $32.00 (one year), $55.00 (two year), $85.00 (three year). Fellowship of Religious Humanists, Inc., PO Box 597396, Chicago IL 60659. **Tel** (312)338-5493. **(Subscription address:** Religious Humanism / FRH, PO Box 278, Yellow Springs OH 45387-0278.**) ED** Mason Olds. **LC** BL2747.6; .R43. Index available (10-yr increments/$5 ea). cum. index. **Bk Rev. Pr Rev. Circ:** 700 (ctrl). available on microfilm and microfiche from University Microfilms International (UMI). Documents available from The Genuine Article.
**Desc:** To promote and encourage the religious, ethical and philosophical thought.
**Ind/Abst** Arts Humanit. Citation Index [Full Cov.]; Curr. Contents Arts Humanit.; Guide Soc. Sci. Relig.; Index Book Rev. Relig.; Philos. Index; Relig. Index One Period.; Relig. Theol. Abstr.; Res. Alert [Full Cov.].

US/1057-2961
**RELIGIOUS LEADERS OF AMERICA (DETROIT, MICH.).** (RELIGIOUS LEADERS OF AMERICA.). [Relig. lead. Am.]. **Added/Corp** Gale Research Inc. 1st Ed. (1991)-. English. te. $79.95. Gale Research Inc., 835 Penobscot Building, Detroit MI 48226. **Tel** (800)877-GALE, (313)961-2242, FAX (313)961-6083, telex TWX 810-221-7086. **LC** BL2525; .R47. **DD** 291/.092/2; B.

US/0279-0459
**RELIGIOUS LIFE (CHICAGO, ILL.).** (RELIGIOUS LIFE / INSTITUTE ON RELIGIOUS LIFE.). [Relig. life]. **Added/Corp** Institute on Religious Life (U.S.). (19??)-. Periodical. English. mo. $6.00 US; $8.00 (surface mail), $11.00 (airmail) other. Institute on Religious Life, PO Box 41007, Chicago IL 60641. **Tel** (312)267-1195. **ED** James Downey. **Bk Rev. Ad Acc. Circ:** 3,700.
**Desc:** Newsletter of news, talks of the Holy Father, book reviews, commentaries and reflections by noted writers on the church's teaching and on spiritual life.

IE
**RELIGIOUS LIFE REVIEW.** No. 88 (Jan./Feb. 1981)-. Periodical. English. bm. $19.93. Dominican Publications, 42 Parnell Square, Dublin 1 Ireland. **Tel** 11 353 1 8731355, FAX 731760, telex 725201. ***Continues*** *Supplement to Doctrine and Life, 0419-5078.*

US/0486-3658
**RELIGIOUS PERSPECTIVES.** (1960)-. Monographic series. English. ir. Price varies per volume. Harper Collins Publishers, Keystone Industrial Park, Scranton PA 18512. **Tel** (800)242-7737, (800)233-4727, FAX (800)822-4090.

US/0278-7784
**RELIGIOUS SOCIALISM.** **See** Political Science-Socialism, Communism, Anarchism, Utopianism.

UK/0034-4125
**RELIGIOUS STUDIES.** [Relig. stud.]. Vol. 1 (Oct. 1965)-. Academic Scholarly Publication. English. qt. $158.00 US, Canada and Mexico; £84.00 other. Cambridge University Press, The Edinburgh Building, Shaftesbury Road, Cambridge CB2 2RU United Kingdom. **Tel** 011 44 223 312393, FAX 011 44 223 325959. **(Subscription address:** Cambridge University Press / North America, 110 Midland Avenue, Port Chester NY 10573.**) ED** Peter Byrne and Keith Ward. **LC** BL1; .R43. **DD** 200/.5. **Bk Rev.** available on microfilm and microfiche from University Microfilms International (UMI). Documents available from The Genuine Article, UMI Article Clearinghouse.
**Desc:** An international journal for the philosophy of religion, it publishes material in other branches of religious studies such as methodology of the study of religion, history of religion and sociology of religion. Authors are encouraged to develop their ideas fully while maintaining the highest standards of precision and clarity. Encourages interchange and juxtapositions of views by publishing groups of articles on the same theme.
**Ind/Abst** Arts Humanit. Citation Index [Full Cov.]; Book Rev. Index; Br. Humanit. Index; Curr. Contents Arts Humanit.; Expand. Acad. Index (1989-); Humanit. Index; Humanit. Source (Jul. 1993-); Index Book Rev. Relig.; INFO-SOUTH Abstr.; Mag. Search; Middle East Abstr. Index; New Testam. Abstr.; Newsp. Period. Abstr. (1991-); Philos. Index; Relig. Index One Period. (1965-); Relig. Theol. Abstr.; Res. Alert [Full Cov.]; Soc. Sci. Cit. Index [Select. Cov.].

CN/0829-2922
**RELIGIOUS STUDIES AND THEOLOGY.** [Relig. stud. theol.]. **VFOAT** RS&T. Vol. 5, No. 1 (Jan. 1985)-. Periodical. English. Three times a year. 40.00Can$ Canada; $40.00 US; $45.00 other. Religious Studies and Theology, 11045 Saskatchewan Drive, Edmonton Alta T6G 2E5 Canada. **Tel** 403-492-2174. **ED** P J Cahill. **DD** 200/.5. **Bk Rev. Ad Acc. Circ:** 600 (ctrl). available on microfilm and microfiche from University Microfilms International (UMI). ***Continues*** *Religious Studies Bulletin (Calgary, Alta.), 0710-0655.*
**Desc:** Wide scope, major focus on contemporary issues across the field of religious studies and theology. Also addresses the traditional issues, interdisciplinary, and international.
**Ind/Abst** Index Book Rev. Relig.; New Testam. Abstr.; Relig. Index One Period.; Relig. Theol. Abstr.

RU
**RELIGIOUS STUDIES IN THE USSR SERIES / USSR ACADEMY OF SCIENCES.** **Added/Corp** Akademiia Nauk SSSR. (1986)-. Monographic series. English. ir. Price varies per volume. Social Sciences Today Editorial Board, Academy of Sciences, 33/12 Arbat, Moscow 121002 Russia. **Tel** 241-09-06.

US/0885-0372
**RELIGIOUS STUDIES NEWS.** [Relig. stud. news]. **Added/Corp** American Academy of Religion. Society of Biblical Literature. **VFOAT** RSN. (1985)-. Periodical. English. qt. $20.00. Religious Studies News, PO Box 15288, Atlanta GA 30333. **Tel** (404)636-4757. **ED** David J. Lull and Helen K. Kelley. **DD** 200. **Circ:** 8,500 (ctrl). available on microfilm and microfiche from University Microfilms International (UMI). ***Continues*** *Bulletin - Council on the Study of Religion, 0002-7170.* ***Continued in part by*** *Bulletin (Council of Societies for the Study of Religion), 1060-1635.*
**Desc:** Seeks to foster communication of announcements, dates and events to persons involved in the academic study of religion, especially those in learned societies in the field.
**Ind/Abst** Acad. Search (July 1993-); Relig. Index One Period. (1985-).

US/0319-485X
**RELIGIOUS STUDIES REVIEW.** [Relig. stud. rev.]. (Sept. 1975)-. Periodical. English. qt. $36.00 (institutions) US; $44.00 (institutions) other. Council of Societies for the Study of Religion, Valparaiso University, Valparaiso IN 46383. **Tel** (219)464-5515. **ED** Watson E Mills. **LC** BL1; .R44. **DD** 200/.5. Index available. cum. index. **Bk Rev. Ad Acc. Circ:** 6,000. available on microfilm.
**Desc:** Review of publications in the field of religion and related disciplines.
**Ind/Abst** Book Rev. Index; Index Islam. Lit.; Index Book Rev. Relig.; Middle East Abstr. Index; New Testam. Abstr.; Old Testam. Abstr.; Relig. Index One Period. (1975-); Relig. Theol. Abstr.

AT/0156-1650
**RELIGIOUS TRADITIONS.** [Relig. tradit.]. Vol. 1 (Apr. 1978)-. Periodical. English. an (May). $15.00. McGill University / Faculty of Religious Studies, 3520 University Street, Montreal QUE H3A 2A7 Canada. **Tel** (514)398-4121, telex 26169. **ED** Arvind Sharma. **Bk Rev. Ad Acc. Circ:** 300. available on microfilm from University Microfilms International (UMI). ***Absorbed*** *Journal of Studies in Mysticism.*
**Ind/Abst** Index Book Rev. Relig.; Relig. Index One Period. (1978-); Relig. Theol. Abstr.

NE
**REMONSTRANTS WEEKBLAD : RW.** **VFOAT** RW. Periodical. Dutch. sm. 37.50F. Remonstrants Weekblad, Nieuwe Gracht 27, 3512 LC Utrecht The Netherlands. **Tel** 030-316970. **Ad Acc.** ctrl circ.

FR/0992-9215
**RENCONTRE - MOUVEMENT CHRETIEN DE PROFESSIONS SOCIALES.** **See** Sociology-Social Services and Welfare.

UK
**RENEWAL MAGAZINE.** English. Twelve times a year. £21.00 UK; £26.00. Renewal Magazine, Broadway House Crowborough, East Sussex TN6 1HQ England. **Tel** 08921 or 652364. **ED** Rev. Wallace Boulton (phone: 0892 652364). **Bk Rev**, (Qty: 40/50). **Ad Acc, Adv Mgr:** P. Thomas. **Circ:** 11,000 (ctrl).

GW
**REPERTORIUM DER KIRCHENVISITATIONSKATEN.** Klett-Cotta Verlagsgemeinschft, PO Box 106016, D 70049 Stuttgart Germany. **Tel** 011 49 711 66720.

SZ
**REPORT AND RESOLUTIONS OF THE ... MEETING OF THE EXECUTIVE COMMITTEE.** **Main/Corp** World Alliance of YMCAS. Executive Committee. **VFOAT** Report and Resolutions of the Executive Committee. English. World Alliance of Young Men's Christian Associations, 37 Quai Wilson, CH-1201 Geneva, Switzerland. **Tel** 011 41 22 7323100, FAX 011 41 22 7384015. **LC** BV1032; .A35. **DD** 267/.33/05.

US/0364-6661
**REPORT FROM THE CAPITAL.** **Added/Corp** Baptist Joint Committee on Public Affairs. (19??)-. Periodical. English. Twenty-four times a year. $10.00 (one year); $18.00 (two years). Baptist Joint Committee, 200 Maryland Avenue Northeast, Washington DC 20002. **Tel** (202)544-4226. **ED** Larry Chesser and Pam Parry. Index Available in first issue of next volume--loose--separately paged. cum. index. **Bk Rev**, (Qty: 12/yr). **Circ:** 7,000 (ctrl).
**Desc:** Religious liberty and separation of church and state: in-depth coverage of court and legislative events in this field, especially at federal level.
**Ind/Abst** South. Baptist Period. Index.

US
**REPORT - MENNONITE CENTRAL COMMITTEE. PEACE SECTION TASK FORCE ON WOMEN IN CHURCH AND SOCIETY.** **Main/Corp** Mennonite Central Committee. Peace Section Task Force on Women in Church and Society. Periodical. English. bm. Peace Section MCC, 21 South 12th Street, Akron PA 17501.

CN/0829-3724
**REPORT TO THE PEOPLE / YOUTH FOR CHRIST KINGSTON.** [Rep. people - Youth Christ Kingst.]. Vol. 4 (Nov. 1, 1984)-. Periodical. English. bm. Kingston Youth for Christ, PO Box 2077, Kingston Ontario K7L 5J8 Canada. **DD** 267/.61/0971372. ***Continues*** *Youth for Christ Kingston (News), 0822-8345.*

CN/0228-8044
**REPORT TO THE PEOPLE / YOUTH FOR CHRIST/VANCOUVER.** [Rep. people - Youth Christ/Vanc.]. Vol. 1, No. 1 (March 1979)-. Periodical. English. mo. Free. Youth for Christ, Vancouver, PO Box 80267, Burnaby BC V5H 3X5 Canada. **DD** 267/.61/0971133.

UK
**REPORTS TO THE GENERAL ASSEMBLY OF THE UNITED FREE CHURCH OF SCOTLAND.** **Main/Corp** United Free Church of Scotland. (1929)-. Corporate Report. English. an. United Free Church of Scotland, 11 Newton Place, Glasgow G3 7PR Scotland. **Tel** (041)332-3435. **ED** Rev. J.O. Fulton. **LC** BX9089; .U54b. **DD** 262/.052411. **Circ:** 250 (ctrl).
**Desc:** Religion report of work of assembly committees throughout the preceding year; financial state of the denomination.

US
**RESEARCH IN MINISTRY.** **Added/Corp** American Theological Library Association. (1981)-. English. an. $56.50. American Theological Library Association, 820 Church Street, 3rd Floor, Evanston IL 60201. **Tel** (708)869-7788, FAX (708)869-8513. **ED** Thomas J. Davis. **LC** Z7751; .R43; BR118. **DD** 016.25. **Circ:** 100 (ctrl). available on CD-ROM.
**Desc:** Indexes doctor of ministry projects and thesis from ATS accredited seminaries and divinity schools. Author abstracts are included.

●US/1055-1158
**RESEARCH IN RELIGION AND FAMILY--BLACK PERSPECTIVES.** **See** Ethnic Interests.

US/1046-8064
**RESEARCH IN THE SOCIAL SCIENTIFIC STUDY OF RELIGION.** [Res. soc. sci. study relig.]. **VFOAT** Social Scientific Study of Religion. Vol. 1 (1989)-. English. an. $73.25. JAI Press Inc., 55 Old Post Road, Suite 2, PO Box 1678, Greenwich CT 06836-1678. **Tel** (203)661-7602, FAX (203)661-0792. **ED** Monty Lynn and David Moberg. **LC** BL60; .R48. **DD** 306.6.

CN/0704-0539
**RESEAU (MONTREAL).** (RESEAU.). **Added/Corp** Dominicains. Province Canadienne de Saint-Dominique. Sept. (1975)-. Periodical. French. Resau, 5353 Av Notre-Dame de Grace, Montreal Quebec H4A 7L2 Canada. **DD** 271/.2/071.

CN/0832-9354
**RESOURCE.** (RESOURCE : CHURCH MINISTRIES LEADERSHIP MAGAZINE.). [Resource]. Vol. 1, No. 1

(Sept./Oct. 1986)-. Periodical. English. bm. $15.00 US; $18.00 North America; $20.00 other. Church Ministries of the Pentecostal Assemblies of Canada, 10 Overlea Boulevard, Toronto Ontario M4H 1A5 Canada. **Tel** (416)425-1010, FAX (416)425-8308. **ED** Rick Hiebert. **DD** 253/.05. **Bk Rev. Ad Acc.** ctrl circ. ***Formed by the union of*** *Chivalry, 0700-6594.*
**Desc:** Issues for church leaders; both clergy and laity.

US/0744-0251
**RESPUESTA.** [Respuesta]. Periodical. Spanish (Spanish). qt. $4.25. Southern Baptist Convention, 901 Commerce, Suite 750, Nashville TN 37203. **Tel** (615)244-2355, FAX (615)742-8919. **(Subscription address:** Sunday School Board - Customer Service, 127 Ninth Avenue North, Nashville, TN 37234 USA; telephone: (800)458-2772**)**

US/0034-5830
**RESTORATION HERALD. Added/Corp** Christian Restoration Association. (1925)-. Periodical. English. mo. $8.00 (one year), $20.00 (three year). Christian Restoration Association, 5664 Cheviot Road, Cincatti OH 45247. **Tel** (513)385-0461. **ED** Lee Mason. **Circ:** 7,000 (ctrl).
**Desc:** Features, submitted articles and news related to Biblical teachings and the activities of Christian churches and churches of Christ.

US/0486-5642
**RESTORATION QUARTERLY.** [Restor. q.]. Vol. 1 (1957)-. Periodical. English. Four times a year. $10.00 (individuals), $20.00 (institutions) US; $15.00 (individuals), $25.00 (institutions) other. Restoration Quarterly Corporation, Box 8227, ACU Station, Abilene TX 79699. **Tel** (915)677-7897. **ED** James W. Thompson. **Bk Rev**, (Qty: 35-40). **Ad Acc. Pr Rev. Circ:** 700 (ctrl). available on microfilm and microfiche from University Microfilms International (UMI).
**Desc:** Biblical studies and history of the Restoration Movement.
**Ind/Abst** Index Book Rev. Relig.; New Testam. Abstr.; Old Testam. Abstr.; Relig. Index One Period. (1980-); Relig. Theol. Abstr.

US/1070-8073
**RESTORATION SERIALS INDEX.** (RESTORATION SERIALS INDEX : A PUBLICATION OF CHRISTIAN COLLEGE LIBRARIANS.). [Restor. ser. index]. **Added/Corp** Abilene Christian University. Christian College Librarians (Organization). (1984-1986)-. English. an (Summer). $47.50 (annual editions), $85.00 (three years cumulations). Abilene Christian University, PO Box 8177, ACU Station, Abilene TX 79699. **Tel** (915)674-2344, FAX (915)674-2202. **ED** Marsha Harper (phone: (915)674-2538), and Erma Jean Loveland, (phone: (915)674-2339). **DD** 205. Index available. cum. index. **Circ:** 50. ***Continues*** *Christian College Librarian's Index.*
**Desc:** A computer-produced author/subject index to periodicals and lectureships by members of the churches of Christ.

US/0191-0167
**RESTORATION WITNESS. Added/Corp** Reorganized Church of Jesus Christ of Latter Day Saints. (19??)-. Periodical. English. bm. $11.00. Herald Publishing House, Drawer HH, Independence MO 64055. **Tel** (816)252-5010, FAX (816)252-3976. **ED** Barbara Howard. Index available. cum. index. **Ad Acc, Adv Mgr:** G Booz, **Tel** (816)252-5010. **Circ:** 2,400.

US/0279-8042
**RESTORER (ROWLETT, TEX.), THE.** (THE RESTORER.). **Added/Corp** Rowlett Church of Christ. (198?)-. Periodical. English. mo (10 issues). $12.00. The Restorer, 1021 Via del Rey, Mesquite TX 75150. **Tel** (214)279-0667. **ED** Gary Workman. **Circ:** 5,000.
**Desc:** Articles taken from the Bible. Subscribed to by the members of the Church of Christ.

CN/0714-7686
**RESURRECTION BULLETIN, THE.** Bulletin. English. sa. Resurrection Bulletin, c/o Provincial Office, Resurrection College, Waterloo Ontario N2L 3G7 Canada. **Tel** (519)885-4370. **ED** Charles Westfall. **DD** 255/.79. **Circ:** 2,660 (ctrl).
**Ind/Abst** Relig. Theol. Abstr.

US/0749-0593
**RETREAT DIRECTORY, THE.** Directory. English. $3.00. Norma Down, 7201 16th Place, Hyattsville MD 20783. **LC** BV5068.R4; D68. **DD** 269/.6/02575.

US/0743-1244
**RETURN TO THE SOURCE.** [Return source]. Vol. 1, No. 1 (Mar. 1982)-. Periodical. English. mo. Return to the Source, 3249 West Roosevelt Road, Chicago IL 60624. **Tel** (312)762-3024. **ED** Shemuel B Israel. **LC** E185.5; .R44. **DD** 973/.0496073/005. **Bk Rev. Ad Acc. Circ:** 1,500 (ctrl).
**Desc:** Analytic essays presenting historic and esoteric material which serves to provide a link between man, both ancient and modern, and his source.

CN/0034-6284
**REVEIL MISSIONNAIRE.** [Reveil Mission.]. (1966)-. Periodical. French. bm. 3.00Can$. Missionnaires de la Consolata, 2381 Ouest Blvd Gouin, Montreal Quebec Canada. **Tel** (514)334-1910, FAX (514)332-1940. **DD** 266.2. **Circ:** 22,000 (ctrl).
**Desc:** This publication deals with religious missions in third world countries.

US/1050-7930
**REVIEW OF BOOKS ON THE BOOK OF MORMON.** [Rev. books Book Mormon]. Vol. 1 (1989)-. Periodical. English. an. Foundation for Ancient Research and Mormon Studies, PO Box 7131, University Station, Provo UT 84602. **Tel** (801)378-3295. **ED** Daniel C. Peterson. **LC** BX8627; .R37. **DD** 289.3/22. **Bk Rev. Ad Acc. Pr Rev. Circ:** 5,000 (ctrl).

PK/0034-6721
**REVIEW OF RELIGIOUS.** Began publication in 1902. Periodical. English. mo. Ahmadiyya Movement Islam Inc, 2141 Leroy Place NW, Washington DC 20008. **LC** BP1. available on microfilm and microfiche from University Microfilms International (UMI).

US/0034-673X
**REVIEW OF RELIGIOUS RESEARCH.** [Rev. relig. res.]. **Added/Corp** Religious Research Association. Vol. 1 (Summer 1959)-. Periodical. English. qt. $40.00. Religious Research Association Inc., Catholic University of America, Marist Hall, Room 108, Washington DC 20064. **Tel** (212)319-5447. **ED** Ed Lehman. **LC** BL1; .R485. **NLM** W1 RE254N. Index available. cum. index. **Bk Rev. Ad Acc. Pr Rev. Circ:** 1,200 (ctrl). available on microfilm and microfiche from University Microfilms International (UMI). Documents available from The Genuine Article.
**Desc:** Methods, research, findings, and uses of studies on religious behavior. Articles, book reviews, and reports of research projects: academic.
**Ind/Abst** Abstr. Anthropol.; Abstr. Res. Pastor. Care Couns. (19??-); Am. Hist. Life (1987-); Arts Humanit. Citation Index [Full Cov.]; Curr. Contents Arts Humanit.; Curr. Contents Soc. Behav. Sci.; Guide Soc. Sci. Relig.; Index Book Rev. Relig.; Middle East Abstr. Index; Relig. Index One Period. (1959-); Relig. Theol. Abstr.; Res. Alert [Full Cov.]; Soc. Plann. Policy Dev. Abstr.; Soc. Sci. Cit. Index [Full Cov.]; Sociol. Abstr. [Full Cov.].

SP/0210-5551
**REVISTA CATALANA DE TEOLOGIA.** [Rev. catalana teol.]. **Added/Corp** Facultat de Teologia de Barcelona. Seccio de St. Pacia. (1976)-. Periodical. Catalan (Spanish, French and English; summaries and/or abstracts in English). Twice a year (Feb. & July). $25.00. Barcelona Facultat Teologia, Barcelona/Diputacion 231, Barcelona 7 Spain. **Tel** 011 34 3 2534925. **LC** WMLC 93/665. Index available. cum. index. **Bk Rev. Circ:** 500 (ctrl).
**Ind/Abst** New Testam. Abstr.; Old Testam. Abstr.

SP/0034-9372
**REVISTA ESPANOLA DE DERECHO CANONICO.** [Rev. esp. derecho canon.]. V. 1- (No. 1- ); Jan./April 1946-. Periodical. Spanish (summaries and/or abstracts in English and Latin). Three times a year. 1,200ptas. Universidad Pontificia de Salamanca, Apartado de Correos 541, 37080 Salamanca Spain. **Tel** 011 34 23 215140. **LC** K19; .E8. **CODEN** REDCE4. Index available in last issue of volume--attached. cum. index.
**Ind/Abst** Am. Hist. Life (1958-1981); Bibliogr. Mission.; Canon Law Abstr.

SP/0210-7112
**REVISTA ESPANOLA DE TEOLOGIA.** (REVISTA ESPANOLA DE TEOLOGIA / CONSEJO SUPERIOR DE INVESTIGACIONES CIENTIFICAS, PATRONATO "RAIMUNDO LULIO", INSTITUTO "FRANCISCO SUAREZ".). [Rev. esp. teol.]. **Added/Corp** Instituto "Francisco Suarez.". Vol. 1, No. 1 (1940)-. Periodical. Spanish. an. 3200ptas Spain; 4400ptas other. Instituto Superior de Teologia, Calle San Buenaventura No 9, 28005 Madrid Spain. **Tel** 011 34 1 2652404, 011 34 1 2653404. **LC** BR7; .R5. **DD** 205.
**Desc:** Reports on activities from medieval history departments included in the Council of Higher Education. Includes collected articles from specialists in the field of Spanish theological and philosophical thought.
**Ind/Abst** Index Book Rev. Relig.; MLA Int. Bibl. Books Artic. Mod. Lang. Lit.; Relig. Index One Period.

ES
**REVISTA LATINOAMERICANA DE TEOLOGIA.** Vol. 1, 1 (Jan./April 1984)-. Periodical. Spanish. Three times a year. University of Centroamerica, Apartado 01 575, San Salvador El Salvador. **Tel** 240011. **LC** BT30.L37; R48. **DD** 230/.098.
**Ind/Abst** New Testam. Abstr.

CL
**REVISTA MENSAJE.** Spanish. mo (except Feb. and April). $45.00 (air mail) US; $35.00 (surface mail), $55.00 (air mail) other. Revista Mensaje, Casilla 10445, Almir Barosso 24, Santiago Chile. **Tel** 011 56 2 6960653.

CG/1016-2461
**REVUE AFRICAINE DE THEOLOGIE.** [Rev. afr. theol.]. No. 1, (April 1977)-. Periodical. French. sa. $20.00. Faculte Theologie Catholique Kinshasa, B P 1534, Kinshasa Limete Zaire. **LC** BR3; .R28. **DD** 230/.26/05. **Bk Rev. Circ:** 7,000.
**Desc:** Covers theology, philosophy, and religions.
**Ind/Abst** Bibliogr. Mission.; Missionalia; New Testam. Abstr.

BE/0035-0893
**REVUE BENEDICTINE.** [Rev. Benedict.]. **Added/Corp** Abbaye de Maredsous. Vol. 7, No. 1 (Jan. 1890)-. Periodical. French (English, German and Italian). sa. 2900.00F. Revue Benedictine, Abbaye de Maredsous, 5537 Denee Belgium. **Tel** 011 32 82 699155. **ED** Abbaye de Maredsous. **LC** BX3001; .R4. Index available. cum. index. **Bk Rev. Circ:** 1,000. ***Continues*** *Messager des Fideles.*
**Desc:** Church history with special interest for monasticism.
**Ind/Abst** BHA : Biblio. Hist. Art; MLA Int. Bibl. Books Artic. Mod. Lang. Lit.; New Testam. Abstr.; Old Testam. Abstr.

FR/0294-0965
**REVUE D'ARCHEOLOGIE MODERNE ET D'ARCHEOLOGIE GENERALE : RAMAGE.** See Archaeology.

FR/0556-7378
**REVUE DE DROIT CANONIQUE.** **Added/Corp** Centre National de la Recherche Scientifique (France). Vol. 1 (March 1951)-. Periodical. French (Italian). ir. 190.00F France; 270.00F other. Revue de Droit Canonique, 2 rue des Freres, 67081 Strasbourg Cedex France. **LC** K21; .D3. **DD** 262.9/05. Index available. **Bk Rev. Ad Acc.**
**Ind/Abst** Bibliogr. Mission.

FR/0035-1423
**REVUE DE L'HISTOIRE DES RELIGIONS.** [Rev. hist. relig.]. Vol. 1 (Jan./Feb. 1880)-. Periodical. French. qt. 390.00F France; 470.00F other. Presses Universitaires de France, Department des Revues, 14 Avenue du Bois de l'Epine, BP 90, 91003 Evry Cedex France. **Tel** (1)60 77 82 05, FAX (1) 60 79 20 45, telex PUF 600 474 F. **ED** Charles Amiel. **LC** BL3; .R4. **DD** 200/.9. **[CCC].** Documents available from The Genuine Article. ***Absorbed*** *Societe Ernest Renan. Bulletin.*
**Desc:** Considers general history of religion and details of specific religions, ancient or modern, highly civilized or primitive.
**Ind/Abst** Am. Hist. Life (1955-); Arts Humanit. Citation Index [Full Cov.]; BHA : Biblio. Hist. Art; Index Book Rev. Relig.; Int. Bibliogr. Sociol.; New Testam. Abstr.; Relig. Index One Period. (1949-); Res. Alert [Full Cov.]; Romant. Move.; Soc. Sci. Cit. Index [Select. Cov.].

SZ/0035-1784
**REVUE DE THEOLOGIE ET DE PHILOSOPHIE.** See Philosophy.

FR/0035-2012
**REVUE DES ETUDES AUGUSTINIENNES.** [Rev. etud. augustin.]. (1955)-. Periodical. French (English, German, Italian and Dutch). sa (2 issues). 2400.00F. Brepols Publishers, Steenweg OP Tielen 68, B-2300 Turnhout Belgium. **Tel** 011 32 14 402500. **LC** BX2901; .R4. **DD** 270.2. **Bk Rev. Ad Acc.** ***Supersedes*** *Annee Theologique Augustinienne.*
**Desc:** Learned studies about history, literature, philosophy, theology from the middle ages to our age.
**Ind/Abst** BHA : Biblio. Hist. Art; MLA Int. Bibl. Books Artic. Mod. Lang. Lit.; New Testam. Abstr.; Philos. Index.

FR/0035-2209
**REVUE DES SCIENCES PHILOSOPHIQUES ET THEOLOGIQUES (PARIS : 1947).** See Philosophy.

FR/0035-2217
**REVUE DES SCIENCES RELIGIEUSES.** [Rev. sci. relig.]. **Added/Corp** Universite des Sciences Humaines de Strasbourg. Faculte de Theologie Catholique. Vol. 1 (1921)-. Periodical. French. qt (Jan., Apr., July, Oct.). 190.00F Europe; 200.00F other. Palais Universite, 67084 Strasbourg Cedex France. **Tel** 011 33 88 259700. **ED** N.A. Vannier. **LC** BX802; .R43. cum. index. **Bk Rev**, (Qty: 4). **Ad Acc. Circ:** 1,000. ***Continues*** *Bulletin d'Ancienne Litterature et d'Archeologie Chretiennes.*
**Desc:** Theological information.
**Ind/Abst** Bibliogr. Mission.; BHA : Biblio. Hist. Art; Index Book Rev. Relig.; New Testam. Abstr.; Old Testam. Abstr.; Relig. Index One Period. (1949-); Romant. Move.

BE/0035-2381
**REVUE D'HISTOIRE ECCLESIASTIQUE.** **See** Religion and Theology-Abstracting, Bibliographies and Statistics.

FR/0035-2403
**REVUE D'HISTOIRE ET DE PHILOSOPHIE RELIGIEUSES.** [Rev. hist. philos. relig.]. **Added/Corp** Universite de Strasbourg. Faculte de theologie protestante. Faculte de theologie protestante (Montpellier, France) Faculte de theologie protestante de Paris. Vol. 1 (1921)-. Periodical. French. qt. 165.00F France; 200.00 other. Presses Universitaires de France, Department des Revues, 14 Avenue du Bois de l'Epine, BP 90, 91003 Evry Cedex France. **Tel** (1)60

77 82 05, FAX (1) 60 79 20 45, telex PUF 600 474 F. **ED** Marc Philonenko. **LC** BR3; .R33. **DD** 230/.05. **[CCC].** cum. index.
**Desc:** Concentrating on Protestant theology, and open to all religious and philosophical currents. The scientific objective is the study of problems inherited in Christian theology and its relationship with non-Christian thought.
**Ind/Abst** Am. Hist. Life (1963-); Index Book Rev. Relig.; New Testam. Abstr.; Relig. Index One Period. (1948-); Relig. Theol. Abstr.; Romant. Move.

CG
**REVUE DU CLERGE AFRICAIN.** V. 1, No. 1-Jan. 1946-. Periodical. French. $5.00. J de Cock Mayidi, BP 6, Inkisi Congo. **LC** BX802; .R45. **DD** 230/.2/05.

FR/0035-3620
**REVUE MABILLON.** [Rev. Mabillon]. **Added/Corp** Saint-Martin (Abbey : Liguge, France) Societe Mabillon pour le Developpement des Etudes d'Histoire Monastique en France. Vol. 1 No. 1 (May 1905)- Vol. 61 No. 315/318 (Jan./Dec. 1989); New Series, Vol. 1 (1990)-. Periodical. French (summaries and/or abstracts in English). an. 1700F. Brepols Publishers, Steenweg OP Tielen 68, B-2300 Turnhout Belgium. **Tel** 011 32 14 402500. **LC** BX2613; .A22. **DD** 271.
**Ind/Abst** BHA : Biblio. Hist. Art.

BE
**REVUE MABILLON: REVUE INTERNATIONAL D'HISTORIE ET DE LITERATURE RELIGIEUSES.** **See** History(General)-History of Europe.

BE/0080-2654
**REVUE THEOLOGIQUE DE LOUVAIN.** [Rev. theol. Louv.]. **Added/Corp** Universite Catholique de Louvain (1970-). Faculte de Theologie. Fondation Universitaire de Belgique. Vol. 1 (1970)-. Periodical. French (summaries and/or abstracts in English). Four times a year. $53.00. College Albert Descamps, Grand Place 45, 1348 Louvain-la-Neuve Belgium. **Tel** 32 10 174592, FAX 32 10 478740. Index available (Bound in 4th issue.). cum. index. **Bk Rev. Circ:** 1,200. Documents available from The Genuine Article.
**Desc:** Review dealing with various topics of the theological field.
**Ind/Abst** Arts Humanit. Citation Index [Full Cov.]; Bibliogr. Mission.; Curr. Contents Arts Humanit.; Index Book Rev. Relig.; New Testam. Abstr.; Old Testam. Abstr.; Res. Alert [Full Cov.]; Romant. Move.; Soc. Sci. Cit. Index [Select. Cov.]; Abr. Cathol. Period. Lit. Index; Cathol. Period. Lit. Index.

FR/0035-4295
**REVUE THOMISTE.** (REVUE THOMISTE; REVUE DOCTRINALE DE THEOLOGIE ET DE PHILOSOPHIE.). [Rev. thomiste]. **Added/Corp** St. Maximin, France. Ecole de Theologie Pour les Missions. Toulouse. Ecole de Theologie. Dominicans. Province de Toulouse. (1893)-. Periodical. French. qt. 380.00F France; 450.00F Europe; 480.00F other. Ecole de Theologie, 1 Avenue Lacordaire, F-31078 Toulouse Cedex France. **Tel** 33 62 173131, FAX 33 62 173117. **ED** Serge-Thomas Bonino (editor's phone: 33 62 173126). **LC** BX802; .R5. Index available. **Bk Rev. Ad Acc. Circ:** 1,000.
**Desc:** Thomist science and general theology and philosophy.
**Ind/Abst** Bibliogr. Mission.; MLA Int. Bibl. Books Artic. Mod. Lang. Lit.; New Testam. Abstr.; Philos. Index; Abr. Cathol. Period. Lit. Index; Cathol. Period. Lit. Index.

FR
**RIC; REPERTOIRE BIBLIOGRAPHIQUE DES INSTITUTIONS CHRETIENNES.** **Added/Corp** Cerdic. Vol. 3 (1969)-. Bibliography. English (French, German, Italian and Spanish). sa. CERDIC Publications, 2 rue Goethe, Palais Universitaire, F-67000 Strasbourg France. **Tel** 88 25 97 09. **ED** Marie Zimmermann and Jean Schlick. **Circ:** 800. ***Continues*** *Repertoire Bibliographique des Institutions Chretiennes.*
**Desc:** Analysis of international documentation in the field of christian and religious institutions, the different churches, their organization and their action, their legislation, ethical and theological thinking, their relations between them, as well as with society and governments.

FR
**RIC SUPPLEMENT.** **Added/Corp** Strasbourg. Universite. Centre de Recherche et de Documentation des Institutions Chretiennes. **VAT** Repertoire Bibliographique des Institutions Chretiennes Supplement. (1973)-. English (French, German, Italian and Spanish). ir (eight-ten issues per year). 75.00F. Cerdic Publications, 2 rue Goethe Palais Universitaire, 67000 Strasbourg France. **Tel** (88)355940. **ED** Jean Schlick and Marie Zimmermann. **Circ:** 600.
**Desc:** International bibliographical repertory about religion and Christian churches, their organization, relations with societies and governments, etc.

IT
**RICERCHE DI STORIA SOCIALE E RELIGIOSA.** **Added/Corp** Centro Studi per le Fonti Della Storia Della Chiesa nel Veneto. Centro Studi di Storia Sociale e Religiosa nel Mezzogiorno. Vol 1, (Jan./June 1972)-. Periodical. Italian. Twice a year (June, Dec.). L65000. Edizioni di Storia e Letteratura, Via Lancellotti 18, Rome 00186 Italy. **Tel** 011 39 6 68806556. **ED** Gabriele de Rosa. **LC** BL60; .R5. **Bk Rev.**
**Desc:** Original research articles on topics of religious and social history in the New and Old Worlds, with attention to culture, spirituality, and their impact on history.

SZ
**RISK BOOK SERIES.** **Added/Corp** World Council of Churches. No. 1 (1978)-. Monographic series. English (French, German and Spanish). Four times a year. $32.50. World Council of Churches, PO Box 2100, CH 1211 Geneva 2 Switzerland. **Tel** 011 41 22 7906076, FAX 011 41 22 7910361, telex 23 423 OIK CH. **Circ:** 4,000.
**Desc:** Tackles the livliest issues facing the Ecumenical movement around the world. Provides Ecumenical analysis for a general church readership.
**Ind/Abst** Index Book Rev. Relig.; Relig. Index One Period. (1978-).

US/8750-5703
**RITE IDEAS.** Vol. 1, No. 1 (Dec. 1984)-. Periodical. English. mo. $15.00. Rite Ideas, 628 South Main Street, Lima OH 45804. **Tel** (419)227-1818, FAX (419)228-9184. **ED** Michael L Sherer. **DD** 264. **Circ:** 1,600 (ctrl). ***Continues*** *In the Worship Workshop with Avery & Marsh.*
**Desc:** Hands-on ideas for enriching Christian worship. Includes a monthly 'instant worship resource' of ready-to-use material.

IT/0042-7586
**RIVISTA DEL CLERO ITALIANO, LA.** **Added/Corp** Universita Cattolica del Sacro Cuore. (1920)-. Periodical. Italian. Twelve times a year. $47.00. Vita e Pensiero, Pubblic University, Largo Gemelli 1, 20123 Milan Italy. **Tel** 011 39 2 72342310, 011 39 2 72342370.

IT/0035-6395
**RIVISTA DI PASTORALE LITURGICA.** [Riv. pastor. liturg.]. (1963)-. Periodical. Italian. bm. L35000 (Italy); L52000 (other). Editrice Queriniana, Casella Postale 403, 25100 Brescia Italy. **Tel** 39 30 294653. **UDC** 264.

IT/0035-6557
**RIVISTA DI STORIA DELLA CHIESA IN ITALIA.** [Riv. stor. chiesa Ital.]. Vol. 1 (Jan./April 1947)-. Periodical. Italian (Multiple languages). sa. L35000.00 Volume 47. Herder Editrice e Libreria SRL, Piazza Montecitorio 117-120, 00186 Rome Italy. **Tel** 011 39 6 679 4628, FAX 011 39 6 678 4751. **ED** M. Maccarrone. **LC** BR870; .R58.
**Ind/Abst** Am. Hist. Life (1955-); BHA : Biblio. Hist. Art.

IT/0035-6573
**RIVISTA DI STORIA E LETTERATURA RELIGIOSA.** [Riv. stor. lett. relig.]. **Added/Corp** Turin. Universita. Biblioteca di Studi Storico-Religiosi "Erik Peterson.". Vol. 1 (1965)-. Periodical. Italian. Three times a year (Apr., Aug., Dec.). L75000 Italy; L95000 others. Casa Editrice Leo S. Olschki, Viuzzo del Pozzetto, Casella Postale 66, 50126 Florence Italy. **Tel** 011 39 55 6530684, FAX 011 39 55 6530214. Documents available from The Genuine Article.
**Ind/Abst** Am. Hist. Life (1987-); Arts Humanit. Citation Index [Full Cov.]; Bibliogr. Mission.; Curr. Contents Arts Humanit.; MLA Int. Bibl. Books Artic. Mod. Lang. Lit.; New Testam. Abstr.; Res. Alert [Full Cov.]; Soc. Sci. Cit. Index [Select. Cov.].

IT
**RIVISTA DI TEOLOGIA MORALE.** **Added/Corp** Associazione Italiana Dei Teologi Moralisti. Associazione Teologica Italiana per lo Studio Della Morale. Vol. 1, (Jan./March 1969)-. Periodical. Italian. Four times a year. L51000.00 Europe, L52000.00 Mediterraneen Basin, L56000.00 Africa, L58000.00 US & Asia, L64000.00 others (airmail); L63000.00 Italy, L69000.00 others (surface mail). Centro Editoriale Dehoniano, Via Nosadella 6, Casella Postale 568, 40123 Bologna Italy. **Tel** 011 39 51 306811. **LC** BJ1188.5; .R57. **DD** 241/.05. Index available. cum. index. **Bk Rev. Ad Acc.** ctrl circ.
**Desc:** A forum for professors and students of moral theology. Endeavors to contribute to resurgence of moral theology and to the solution of the moral problems of our times.
**Ind/Abst** Bibliogr. Mission.

IT/0035-6638
**RIVISTA DI VITA SPIRITUALE.** **Added/Corp** Padri Carmelitani Scalzi. (1947)-. Periodical. Italian. Five times a year (Jan., Mar., May, Sept., Nov.). 32000L Italy; 40000 other. Rivista di Vita Spirituale, Via Anagnina 662-B, 00040 Morena Rome Italy. **Tel** 011 39 6 7984782. ***Supersedes*** *Vita Carmelitana.*
**Ind/Abst** Bibliogr. Mission.

CN/0712-1695
**RM MARIANNHILL.** [R M Mariannhill]. **VFOAT** Mariannhill. **VAT** Revue Missionnaire Mariannhill (1981); Mariannhill (Sherbrooke. 1981). Vol. 33, No. 1 (1981)-. Periodical. French. ir (Feb., April, June, Oct, and Dec.). $3.00. Mariannhill Missionaries, 2100 Chemin Ste-Catherine/CP 8000, Rock Forest Quebec J1N 1E7 Canada. **Tel** (819)562-4676. **DD** 266/.2/05. **Circ:** 7,500. ***Continues*** *Revue Missionnaire Mariannhill, 0705-1514.*
**Desc:** Sixteen pages about the missionary work of our conferences here in Canada and in any other country in the world, including formation and information about the mission of the Roman Catholic Church.

IT/0391-108X
**ROCCA.** [Rocca]. **VFOAT** Rocca. Rivista Delle pro Civitate Christiana. (1943)-. Periodical. Italian. bm. L60000 Italy; L90000 other. Pro Civitate Christiana, Casella Postale 94, 06081 Assisi Italy. **Tel** 011 39 75 813641, 011 39 75 813231. **UDC** 2.

●PO
**ROCZNIKI TEOLOGICZNE.** **Added/Corp** Katolicki Uniwersytet Lubelski. Towarzystwo Naukowe. **VFOAT** Annals of Theology; Annales de Theology. (1992)-. Periodical. Polish (summaries and/or abstracts in English, French, German and Russian). bm. **LC** BX806.P6; R6. ***Continues*** *Roczniki Teologiczno-Kanoniczne.*
**Desc:** Journal of theology.

IT/0035-7812
**ROEMISCHE QUARTALSCHRIFT FUER CHRISTLICHE ALTERTUMSKUNDE UND KIRCHENGESCHICHTE.** [Roem. Quart.schr. christl. Alter.kd. Kirchengesch.]. **Added/Corp** Camposanto Teutonico (Rome, Italy) Goerres-Gesellschaft. Roemisches Institut. (1887)-. Periodical. German (French, Italian and Latin). Twice a year. DM228.00. Verlag Herder Freiburg, Postfach 79080, Frieburg, Germany. **Tel** (0761)27-17-0, FAX (0761)27 17-520, telex 761489. **ED** E. Gatz. **LC** BX1881; .R65.
**Desc:** Publication covering Church history.
**Ind/Abst** Avery Index Archit. Period. Suppl. Colum. Univ. (19??-199?); BHA : Biblio. Hist. Art; MLA Int. Bibl. Books Artic. Mod. Lang. Lit.; New Testam. Abstr.

IT
**ROMANA : BOLLETTINO DELLA PRELATURA DELLA SANTA CROCE E OPUS DEI.** (19??)-. Italian. sa. $20.00. Bollettino Romana, Viale Bruno Buozzi 73, 00197 Rome Italy. **Tel** 011 39 6 878741.

NE/0035-8169
**ROND DE TAFEL.** Vol. 23 (1968)-. Periodical. Dutch. bm. Fl22.00 Netherlands and Belgium; Fl30.00 other. Abdij Van Berne, Abdijstraat 53, NL 5473 AC Heeswijk-Dinther Netherlands. **Tel** 04139-1330. **ED** N van Beijnen. **Bk Rev. Circ:** 6 (ctrl). ***Continues*** *Offer.*
**Desc:** Articles about liturgy and information about liturgical subjects and events.

IT
**ROTAE ROMANAE DECISIONES SEU SENTENTIA SACRA ROMANA ROTA.** (19??)-. Latin. ir. $150.00. Libreria Editrice Vaticana, Citta del Vaticano, 00120 Vatican City. **Tel** 011 39 6 6983529, FAX 011 39 6 6984716.

US
**ROUNDTABLE.** **Main/Corp** Association of North American Missions. Periodical. English. qt. Association of North American Missions, PO Box 9710, Madison WI 53175.

US/0893-5246
**ROYAL AMBASSADOR LEADERSHIP.** **Added/Corp** Southern Baptist Convention. Brotherhood Commission. **VFOAT** Leadership. Vol. 1, No. 1 (Oct./Nov./Dec. 1987)-. Periodical. English. qt. $6.16. Baptist Brotherhood Commission, 1548 Popular Avenue, Memphis TN 38104. **Tel** (901)272-2461. ***Formed by the union of*** *Crusader Counselor, 0162-2579* ***and*** *Pioneer Plans.*
**Ind/Abst** South. Baptist Period. Index.

CN/0713-3413
**ROYAUME (LIMOILOU, QUEBEC).** (LE ROYAUME.). [Royaume]. No. 1 (May 1982)-. Periodical. French (English). ir. $5.00. Royaume, CP 520, Limoilou Quebec G1L 4W3 Canada. **DD** 232.91/05. ***Continues*** *Etoile, 0706-6856.*

US
**RUACH SERIES.** **Added/Corp** Episcopal Women's Caucus. (1976)-. Periodical. English. qt (published seasonally). $50.00. Episcopal Women's Caucus Inc, PO Box 5172, Laurel MD 20726. **Tel** (301)725-6369. **Bk Rev. Circ:** 1,000.
**Desc:** The feminist/womanist voice of the Episcopal Church.

CN/0228-8095
**RUPERT'S LAND NEWS.** [Rupert's Land news]. Periodical. English. mo. $5.00. Anglican Centre, 935 Nesbitt Bay, Winnipeg Manitoba R3T 1W6 Canada. **Tel** (204)453-6130. **ED** Anita Schmitt. **DD** 283/.71274. **Circ:** 8,700.
**Desc:** Information pertaining to Anglican Diocese of Rupert's Land in central Canada.

CN/0700-3897
**RURAL GLEANINGS.** **Added/Corp** Christian Rural Research and Resource Service. Vol. 1 (Fall

1974)-. Periodical. English. qt. Free. Christian Rural Research and Resource Service, Rural Route 1, Debert Nova Scotia B0M 1G0 Canada. **DD** 254.24/05. ctrl circ.

IT/0036-2190
**SACRA DOCTRINA.** [Sacra doctrina]. **Added/Corp** Studio Domenicano di Bologna. (1956)-. Periodical. Italian. Six times a year. L50.000 Italy; L90.000 other. Studio Domenicano, Via Osservanza 72, 40136 Bologna Italy. **Tel** 011 39 51 582034. **ED** Ottorino Benetollo. Index available in last issue of volume--attached. cum. index.
**Ind/Abst** Bibliogr. Mission.; New Testam. Abstr.

US/0899-2061
**SACRAMENTAL LIFE.** [Sacram. life]. **Added/Corp** Order of St. Luke. Vol. 1, No. 1 (Feb./Mar. 1988)-. Periodical. English. Five times a year. $20.00 nonmembers; Free, members. Order of St. Luke, PO Box 22279, Akron OH 44302. **Tel** (607)962-3512. **ED** Michael J. O'Donnell. **DD** 287.
**Desc:** Deals with liturgics.

NE/0771-7776
**SACRIS ERUDIRI.** [Sacris erudiri]. **Added/Corp** Steenbrugge, Belgium (West Flanders: Arrondissement Administratif Bruges). Sint Pieter (Benedictine Abbey). (1948)-. English (French, German and Latin; summaries and/or abstracts in English, French and Latin). an. Fl144.00. Martinus Nijhoff Publishers, Subsidiary of Kluwer Academic Publishers, Koraalrood 50, 2718 SC Zoetermeer Netherlands. **Tel** 011 31 79 684400. **LC** BX800.A1; S3. cum. index.
**Desc:** Religious literature.
**Ind/Abst** BHA : Biblio. Hist. Art; MLA Int. Bibl. Books Artic. Mod. Lang. Lit.; Old Testam. Abstr.

SP
**SAL TERRAE.** Vol. 52 (Jan. 1964)-. Periodical. Spanish. Eleven times a year. $40.00. Editorial Sal Terrae, Apartado 77, 39080 Santander Spain. **Tel** 011 34 42 320528, 011 34 42 320529. Index available. **Bk Rev. Ad Acc. Circ:** 4,300. ***Continues*** *Sal Terrae. Parte Teorica.*
**Desc:** Journal on pastoral theology.
**Ind/Abst** Bibliogr. Mission.; Canon Law Abstr.

US/0036-3480
**SALESIAN. Added/Corp** Salesian Missions of St. John Bosco. (19??)-. Periodical. English (Spanish). qt. Free on request. Salesian Mission, Box 30, New Rochelle NY 10802. **Tel** (914)633-8344. **ED** E.J. Cappelletti, Joseph Ros, Kenneth Germaine. **Circ:** 1,000,000.
**Desc:** Features work of the Salesians in missionary countries.

CN/0838-7397
**SALLY ANN.** [Sally Ann]. Vol. 35, No. 7 (Jan. 1988)-. Periodical. English. mo. 6.50Can$ Canada; 9.50Can$ other. Salvation Army Home Printing and Publishing Department, 455 North Service Road East, Oakville Ontario L6H 1A5 Canada. **Tel** (416)844-2561, FAX (416)845-1966. **ED** Margaret Hammond. **DD** 267/.15/05. Index available. **Bk Rev. Ad Acc. Circ:** 11,000 (ctrl). ***Continues*** *Home Leaguer (1983), 0822-5079.*

US/0883-2587
**SALT (CHICAGO, ILL.).** (SALT.). [Salt]. **Added/Corp** Claretian Fathers and Brothers. Vol. 1, No. 1 (Jan. 1981)-. Periodical. English. ir (10 issues). $18.00 (one year), $33.00 (two year), $45.00 (three year). Claretian Publications, 205 West Monroe Street, Chicago IL 60606. **Tel** (312)236-7782, (800)328-6515. **ED** Mark J. Brummel. **DD** 261. **Bk Rev. Ad Acc. Circ:** 8,479 (ctrl).
**Desc:** Magazine for justice-hungry Christians. Profiles modern-day samaritans and reports on people who have successfully righted a wrong. Each issue is sprinkled with clearly written articles, quick illustrated glimpses of church social teachings through the centuries, strong opinion, excerpts of important new books, and more.
**Ind/Abst** Abr. Cathol. Period. Lit. Index; Cathol. Period. Lit. Index.

CN/0709-616X
**SALT (EDMONTON).** (SALT.). [Salt]. **Added/Corp** Alberta Teachers' Association. Religious Studies and Moral Education Council. **VFOAT** Journal of the Religious Studies and Moral Education Council. No. 1 (Spring 1979)-. Periodical. English. Twice a year. 22.95Can$ Comes with Religious Studies & Moral Education Council membership. Alberta Teachers Association, 11010-142 Street, Barnett House, Edmonton Alberta T5N 2R1 Canada. **Tel** (403)453-2411. **DD** 200.7. **Bk Rev.** ctrl circ.

US
**SALT / THE SISTERS OF CHARITY.** (19??)-. Periodical. English. Four times a year. $5.00. Sisters of Charity BVM, 1100 Carmel Drive, Dubuque IA 52004. **Tel** (319)588-2351, FAX (319)588-4832. **ED** Mira Mosle. **Circ:** 8,300.
**Desc:** Publication for friends of the Sisters of Charity. Contains articles on members of this religious community.

CN/0225-3313
**SAMA. SOCIETE D'AIDE MISSIONNAIRE ANTIPODE.** (SAMA : BULLETIN D'INFORMATION DE LA SAMA.). **VAT** Societe d'Aide Missionnaire Antipode. Vol. 1, No. 1 (Oct./Nov.)-. Bulletin. French. bm. Free. SAMA, 7596 Av Rolland, Charlesbourg Quebec G1H 6C3 Canada. **DD** 266/.023/71401724. ctrl circ.

II
**SANKAYA PATRIKA.** V. 1-. Periodical. English (Hindi, Pali, Prakrit languages and Sanskrit). an. 32.00. Sales Department, Sampurnanand Sanskrit, Vishvavidyalaya, 221002 Varanasi India. **LC** BL2003; .S26.

II
**SANTA SANDESA.** 1973-. Hindi (Hindi). 10.00. Sant Kabir Chauk, 358 Nana Peth, Poona 411002 India. **LC** BL1145; .S28.

IT/0391-7819
**SANTO, IL. Added/Corp** Basilica di Sant'Antonio (Padua, Italy) Centro Studi Antoniani (Padua, Italy). (1975)-. Periodical. Italian (English). Three times a year. L50000 Italy; L70000 other. Centro Studi Antoniani, Piazza del Santo 11, 35123 Padua Italy. **Tel** 39 49 663944. **ED** Luciano Bertazzo. Index available. cum. index. **Bk Rev**, (Qty: 40-50). **Circ:** 500 (ctrl).
**Desc:** Articles of history, art, theology and music concerning St. Anthony of Padua and Franciscanism.
**Ind/Abst** BHA : Biblio. Hist. Art.

IT/0036-4711
**SAPIENZA. See** Philosophy.

CN/0703-9433
**SASKATCHEWAN ANGLICAN.** [Sask. Angl.]. Began publication in 1972?. Periodical. English. mo (ten issues per year). 3.00Can$. Saskatchewan Anglican, 1501 College Avenue, Regina Saskatchewan S4P 1B8 Canada. **Tel** (306)522-1608. **ED** W P Tomalin. **DD** 283/.7124. **Bk Rev. Circ:** 7,800. available on microfilm from Saskatchewan Archives Board.
**Desc:** News and articles about the Anglican church with emphasis on the Saskatchewan scene.

CN/0714-8003
**SAT SANDESH (MONTREAL).** (SAT SANDESH.). Vol. 1, No. 1 (Mar. 1978)-. Periodical. French. qt. $7.00. Sat Sandesh, c/o Claire d'Allaire App 1014, 3555 rue Berri, Montreal Quebec H2L 4G4 Canada. **DD** 294.6/44/05.

UK/0036-5106
**SAVING HEALTH. Added/Corp** Medical Missionary Association. Vol. 1 (Mar. 1962)-. Periodical. English. qt (Mar., June, Sept., Dec.). $5.00. Medical Missionary Association, 244 Camden Road, London NW1 9HE England. **Tel** 011 44 71 485 2672. **ED** Dr. W.E. Hawes. **Bk Rev**, (Qty: 2). **Circ:** 1,000. ***Supersedes*** *Conquest by Healing.*
**Desc:** Articles by doctors and nurses serving overseas in church-related medical work in third world countries.

CN/0700-6802
**SCARBORO MISSIONS. Added/Corp** Scarboro Foreign Mission Society. (1919)-. English. Nine times a year (Sept.-May). 5.00Can$. Scarboro Foreign Mission Society, 2685 Kingston Road, Scarborough Ontario M1M 1M4 Canada. **Tel** (416)261-7135. **ED** Father Gerald Curry, SFM. **Circ:** 35,000.
**Desc:** Presents a global vision of faith, one which promotes within the Canadian church a dialogue and understanding of the , cultures and struggles of the people among whom our missionaries work.
**Ind/Abst** Bibliogr. Mission.

US/0558-8766
**SCHOLARS' CHOICE. See** Religion and Theology-Abstracting, Bibliographies and Statistics.

GW
**SCHRIFTENREIHE DES VEREINS FUER RHEINISCHE KIRCHENGESCHICHTE. Main/Corp** Verein fuer Rheinische Kirchengeschichte. **Added/Corp** Verein fuer Rheinische Kirchengeschichte. Veroffentlichungen. (1953)-. Monographic series. German. ir. Price varies per volume. Dr. Rudolf Habelt GmbH, Postfach 150104, D 53040 Bonn Germany. **Tel** 011 49 228 232015.

UK/0954-4194
**SCIENCE & CHRISTIAN BELIEF. Added/Corp** Christians in Science (Great Britain). Victoria Institute (Great Britain). **VFOAT** Science and Christian Belief. Vol. 1, No. 1 (April 1989)-. Periodical. English. Twice a year (April and October). £15.90 UK; £16.65 other. Paternoster Press, A division of Send the Light Ltd., PO Box 300, Kingstown Broadway, Cumbria CA3 0QS England. **Tel** 011 44 228 512512, FAX 011 44 228 514949. **LC** AS122; .L9. **DD** 261.5/5. available on microfilm and microfiche from University Microfilms International (UMI). ***Formed by the union of*** *Science and Faith* ***and*** *Faith and Thought, 0014-7028.*
**Ind/Abst** Index Book Rev. Relig.; Relig. Index One Period.

US/1048-8642
**SCIENCE & RELIGION NEWS.** [Sci. relig. news]. **Added/Corp** Institute on Religion in an Age of Science. **VFOAT** Science and Religion News. (Spring 1990)-. Periodical. English. Four times a year (Feb., May, Aug., Nov.). $9.50 US; $11.50 Canada & Mexico; $13.50 others. Institute Religion in and Age Science, 65 Hoit Road, Concord NH 03301. **Tel** (603)226-3328, FAX (603)226-1831. **ED** Kevin Sharpe. **DD** 261. **Bk Rev**, (Qty: 70). **Ad Acc. Circ:** 2,000.
**Desc:** Professors list science and religion as an area of specialization in departmental listings of courses. A few graduate programs offer degrees in science and religion and in science and theology.

CN/0316-5345
**SCIENCE ET ESPRIT. See** Philosophy.

US/0036-8458
**SCIENCE OF MIND. See** Philosophy.

US/0735-7443
**SCLC (ATLANTA, GA.).** (SCLC : THE SOUTHERN CHRISTIAN LEADERSHIP CONFERENCE NATIONAL MAGAZINE.). [SCLC]. **Added/Corp** Southern Christian Leadership Conference. **VFOAT** Southern Christian Leadership Conference National Magazine; S.C.L.C. **VAT** Southern Christian Leadership Conference. Vol. 6, No. 8 (Oct./Nov. 1977)-. Periodical. English. bm. free. Southern Christian Leadership, 334 Auburn Avenue Northeast, Atlanta GA 30303. **Tel** (404)522-1420. **ED** Quentin Bradford. **LC** E185.5; .S4. **Ad Acc. Circ:** 600,000. ***Continues*** *S.C.L.C. West.*
**Desc:** News of Southern Christian Leadership Conference activities, programs, and events that are of interest to black and poor people.

US/1074-5769
**SCORE (NASHVILLE, TENN.). See** Music.

UK/0265-4539
**SCOTTISH BULLETIN OF EVANGELICAL THEOLOGY, THE.** [Scott. bull. evang. theol.]. **Added/Corp** Scottish Evangelical Theology Society. Rutherford House. Vol. 1, (1983)-. Bulletin. English. Twice a year (Mar., Sept.). $19.00. Rutherford House, 17 Claremont Park, C/O J. Glover, Edinburgh EH6 7PJ Scotland. **Tel** 11 44 31 5541206, FAX 031 555 1002. **ED** N. M. De S. Cameron and David F. Wright. **LC** BR1; .S354. **DD** 230/.044. **Bk Rev. Circ:** 1,000. ***Continues*** *Scottish Evangelical Theology Society Bulletin, 0262-1053.*
**Ind/Abst** Index Book Rev. Relig.; Relig. Index One Period.

UK/0143-8301
**SCOTTISH JOURNAL OF RELIGIOUS STUDIES, THE.** [Scott. j. relig. stud.]. **Added/Corp** University of Stirling. Dept. of Philosophy/Religious Studies. Vol. 1, No. 1 (Spring 1980)-. Periodical. English. Twice a year. $14.00 (individual); $30.00 (institution). University of Stirling, Department of Religious Studies, Sterling FK9 4LA Scotland. **Tel** 11 44 786 73171 ext. 2341, FAX 011 44 786 63000, telex 44 786 63000. **ED** Glyn Richards. **LC** BL1; .S35. **DD** 200/.5. Index available (Bound in 2nd iss.). cum. index. **Bk Rev**, (Qty: 12). **Ad Acc. Pr Rev. Circ:** 250. available on microfilm from University Microfilms International (UMI).
**Desc:** Promotes a critical investigation of all aspects of the study of religion.
**Ind/Abst** Br. Humanit. Index; Index Book Rev. Relig.; Relig. Index One Period. (1980-); Relig. Theol. Abstr.

UK/0036-9306
**SCOTTISH JOURNAL OF THEOLOGY.** [Scott. j. theol.]. Vol. 1 June (1948)-. Periodical. English. qt. $49.95 (individuals), $99.95 (institutions) US; £24.95 (individuals), £49.95 (institutions) UK; 64.95Can$ (individuals), 129.95Can$ (institutions) Canada; £27.95 (individuals), £55.95 (institutions) other. T & T Clark Ltd., 59 George Street, Edinburgh EH2 2LQ Scotland. **Tel** 011 44 31 2254703, FAX 011 44 31 2204260. **ED** A.I.C. Heron and A. Lewis. **LC** BR1; .S356. **DD** 200/.5. **[CCC]. Bk Rev. Ad Acc. Circ:** 1,200 (ctrl). Documents available from The Genuine Article, UMI Article Clearinghouse.
**Desc:** Publishes contributions of major theological and philosophical interest. Also publishes articles on Biblical and applied theology.
**Ind/Abst** Acad. Search (Jan. 1994-); Arts Humanit. Citation Index [Full Cov.]; Br. Humanit. Index; Curr. Contents Arts Humanit.; Expand. Acad. Index (1989-); Humanit. Index; Humanit. Source (Jul. 1993-); Index Book Rev. Relig.; INFO-SOUTH Abstr.; Mag. Search; New Testam. Abstr.; Newsp. Period. Abstr. (1991-); Old Testam. Abstr.; Relig. Index One Period. (1948-); Relig. Theol. Abstr.; Res. Alert [Full Cov.]; Soc. Sci. Cit. Index [Select. Cov.].

US/0883-1300
**SCP JOURNAL.** [SCP j.]. **Added/Corp** Spiritual Counterfeits Project. **VAT** Spiritual Counterfeits Project Journal. Vol. 1, No. 1 (April 1977)-. Periodical. English. ir (4 issues of journal and 2 issues of newsletter). $25.00 (includes SCP Newsletter). Spiritual Counterfeits Project, PO Box 4308, Berkeley CA 94704. **Tel** (510)540-0300, FAX (510)540-1107. **ED** Tal Brooke, Brooks Alexander and Joe Busey. **LC** WMLC L 83/403. **DD** 290. **Bk Rev**, (Qty: varies). **Circ:** 3,000 journal, 7,000 newsletter. ***Continues*** *Journal of the Spiritual Counterfeits Project.*
**Desc:** Researches various religious groups and spiritual trends from a Christian perspective.
**Ind/Abst** Christ. Period. Index.

US/0883-1319
**SCP NEWSLETTER.** [SCP newsl.]. **Added/Corp** Spiritual Counterfeits Project. (Feb./Mar. 1980)-. Periodical. English. Four times a year. $25.00. Spiritual Counterfeits Project, PO Box 4308, Berkeley CA 94704. **Tel** (510)540-0300, FAX (510)540-1107. **DD** 239. **Bk Rev**. ctrl circ. available on microfilm and microfiche from University Microfilms International (UMI). ***Continues*** *Newsletter - Spiritual Counterfeits Project.*
**Desc:** Evaluation of religious pluralism and philosophy - especially mystical influence - from a historic Christian perspective.

SP/0036-9764
**SCRIPTA THEOLOGICA.** [Scr. theol.]. **Added/Corp** Universidad de Navarra. Facultad de Teologia. (1969)-. Spanish. Three times a year. $60.00. Universidad de Navarra, Apartado 170, 31080 Pamplona Spain. **Tel** 011 34 948 252700. **ED** Pedro Rodriguez. **LC** BR7; .S37. **Bk Rev**. **Ad Acc**. **Circ:** 1,000 (ctrl).
**Desc:** Goal is to disseminate reports on studies carried out by the Department of Theology at the Universidad de Navarra. It represents the work of three major methodologies: scripture, historical theology and systematic theology.
**Ind/Abst** Bibliogr. Mission.; Index Book Rev. Relig.; New Testam. Abstr.; Old Testam. Abstr.; Relig. Index One Period.; Relig. Theol. Abstr.

IE/0332-1150
**SCRIPTURE IN CHURCH.** [Script. church]. No. 1 (Spring 1971)-. Periodical. English. qt. $39.19. Dominican Publications, 42 Parnell Square, Dublin 1 Ireland. **Tel** 11 353 1 8731355, FAX 731760, telex 725201.
**Ind/Abst** Old Testam. Abstr.

FR/0245-7458
**SE COMPRENDRE PARIS.** (1980)-. Periodical. French. Twelve times a year. 150.00F France; 200.00F other. SMA / Societe des Missionaires d'Afrique, 20 rue du Printemps, 75017 Paris France. **UDC** 297.

US/0747-864X
**SEABURY JOURNAL, THE.** ***Ceased.*** [Seabury j.]. Vol. 1, No. 1/2 (April/May 1983)-?. Periodical. English. mo (except July and Aug.). The Seabury Journal, PO Box 1106 S M S, Fairfield CT 06430. **ED** Ross B Baxter. **LC** WMLC L 83/9140. **DD** 283.

IE/0332-0618
**SEARCH (DUBLIN).** (SEARCH.). [Search]. Vol. 1, No. 1 (Spring 1978)-. Periodical. English. sa. £5.00 Ireland and UK; £6.50 other. Religious Education Resource Centre, Holy Trinity Church, Church Avenue, Rathmines Dublin 6 Ireland. **Tel** 011 352 1 4972821, FAX 011 352 1 4972821. **ED** Rev. Michael Burrows. Index available. cum. index. **Bk Rev**. **Circ:** 600. ***Formed by the union of*** *New Divinity* ***and*** *Resources.*
**Desc:** Contains information about: Old and New Testament, religious education, women's ministry, adult education and more.
**Ind/Abst** New Testam. Abstr.

US/0276-7899
**SECOND CENTURY (ABILENE, TEX.), THE.** ***Title Change.*** (THE SECOND CENTURY.). [Second cent.]. Vol. 1 No. 1 (Spring 1981)-Vol. 9 No. 4 (Winter 1992). Periodical. English. qt. Prof. T H Olbricht, Pepperdine University, Religion Department, Malibu CA 90263. **Tel** (213)456-4352. **ED** Everett Ferguson. **LC** BR165; .S42. **Bk Rev**. **Ad Acc**. **Circ:** 650. available on microfilm and microfiche from University Microfilms International (UMI). Documents available from The Genuine Article. ***Continued by*** *Journal of Early Christian Studies, 1067-6341.*
**Desc:** A journal of early Christian studies.
**Ind/Abst** Arts Humanit. Citation Index (19??-19??) [Full Cov.]; Index Book Rev. Relig.; New Testam. Abstr.; Relig. Index One Period. (1981-); Relig. Theol. Abstr.; Res. Alert [Full Cov.].

US/0890-1570
**SECOND OPINION (PARK RIDGE, ILL.).** **See** Medical Science and Technology.

IT
**SEDOS BULLETIN.** (19??)-. Bulletin. English. Eleven times a year. L25000 Europe; L35000 other. SEDOS, Via Dei Verbiti 1, 00154 Rome Italy. **Tel** 011 39 6 5741350.
**Ind/Abst** Index Book Rev. Relig.; Relig. Index One Period.

US/0363-5074
**SEEDBED.** **Added/Corp** Society for the Arts, Religion and Contemporary Culture. **VFOAT** Seed Bed. Vol. 1, No. 2 (May 1973)-. Periodical. English. Four times a year. $6.00 (surface mail), $8.00 (air mail). Seedbed, PO Box 96, Upper Darby PA 19082. **Tel** (610)352-2003, FAX (610)352-2652. **ED** S. Schlorff. Index available. cum. index. **Bk Rev**, (Qty: varies). **Circ:** 300 (ctrl). ***Supersedes*** *ARC Newsletter.*
**Desc:** A forum and channel of ideas and information useful to those involved in church and mission in the Arab world.

CN/0843-5197
**SEEDS & SOWERS.** **See** Education-Teaching and Curriculum.

SP
**SELECCIONES DE FRANCISCANISMO.** **Added/Corp** Franciscans. Provincia de Valencia. Vol. 1, No. 1 (Jan./April 1972)-. Periodical. Spanish. Three times a year. $20.00 Spain; $25.00 other. Selecciones de Franciscanismo, Apartado 7017, Administracion, 46080 Valencia Spain. **Tel** 011 34 6 3312031. Index available. **Circ:** 1,500.
**Ind/Abst** Bibliogr. Mission.

SP/0037-119X
**SELECCIONES DE TEOLOGIA.** Vol. 1, No. 1 (Feb. 1962)-. Spanish. qt. $28.00. Selecciones de Teologia, Roger de Lluria 13, 08010 Barcelona Spain. **Tel** 011 34 3 3012350, FAX 011 34 3 3178704. **ED** Rafael de Sivatte. **LC** WMLC L 82/396. Index available. cum. index. **Pr Rev. Circ:** 4,000.
**Desc:** Abstracts of articles on theology published in the world.
**Ind/Abst** Bibliogr. Mission.

CN/0701-4260
**SELON SA PAROLE.** **Added/Corp** Eglise Catholique. Archidiocese de Quebec. Vol. 3 (Jan. 1977)-. Periodical. French. mo. $4.00. Service du Renouveau Charismatique, 2140 Chemin St-Louis, Sillery Quebec G1T 1P8 Canada. **DD** 269. ***Continues*** *Bulletin de Liaison des Groupes de Prieres du Diocese de Quebec, 0384-6164.*

FR
**SEMAINE RELIGIEUSE D'ANGERS, LA.** (19??)-. Periodical. French. wk. 320.00F France; 405.00F other. Eveche d'Angers, Secretariat, 8 Place Mgr Rumeau, BP 246, 49002 Angers Cedex France. **Tel** 011 33 41 880700.

SP
**SEMANAS ESPANOLAS DE MISIONOLOGIA.** Spanish. ir. 600.00ptas. Biblioteca Semanas Misionales, e Martinez del Campo 11-1, Izqda Apt, 400 Burgos Spain.

US/0745-5518
**SEMINARY NEWS (ENID, OKLA.).** (SEMINARY NEWS : NEWS ABOUT THE GRADUATE SEMINAR OF PHILLIPS UNIVERSITY.). **Main/Corp** Phillips University (Enid, Okla.). Graduate Seminary. (19??)-. Periodical. English. qt. Free. Phillips Graduate Seminary, PO Box 2335, University Station, Enid OK 73702. **Tel** (405)237-4433. ***Continues*** *Phillips University, Enid, Oklahoma. Graduate Seminary. Phillips Seminary News.*

US/0899-6199
**SEMINARY TIMES, THE.** ***Ceased.*** [Semin. times]. (1988)-?. Periodical. English. qt. Wyndham Hall Press Inc, PO Box 877, Bristol IN 46507. **Tel** (219)848-7920. **DD** 207.

FR/0154-6902
**SEMIOTIQUE ET BIBLE.** (SEMIOTIQUE ET BIBLE : BULLETIN D'ETUDES ET D'ECHANGES.). [Semiot. bible]. **VFOAT** Semiotique & Bible. No. 1 (Dec. 1975)-. Bulletin. French. Four times a year (Jan., June, Sept., Dec.). 175.00F France; 225.00F other. Centre pour l'Analyse, 25 rue du Plat, 6G 288 Lyon Cedex France. **Tel** 011 33 72325030.
**Ind/Abst** New Testam. Abstr.

●US/1065-3783
**SEMPER REFORMANDA.** **Added/Corp** Reformed Presbyterian Church of North America. Vol. 1, No. 1 (Spring 1992)-. Periodical. English. Three times a year. Free to Reformed Presbyterian Church Elders; $9.00 other. Semper Reformanda, 3217 College Avenue, Beaver Falls PA 15010. **ED** Jonathon M. Watt (editor's telephone: (412)843-4840). **DD** 285. **Bk Rev**, (Qty: 3-6). **Pr Rev. Circ:** 150.
**Desc:** Current articles on theology, history or languages of interest to reformed Presbyterians.

●US/1059-3381
**SENIOR ADULT STUDENT GUIDE.** **Added/Corp** Assemblies of God. General Council. (1992)-. Periodical. English. qt. $5.40. Gospel Publishing House, 1445 Boonville Avenue, Springfield MO 65802. **Tel** (417)862-2781, FAX (417)866-1146. ***Continues in part*** *Senior Adult Student, 0887-0632.*

US
**SENTINEL OF THE BLESSED SACRAMENT.** ***Ceased.*** Periodical. English. mo. Sentinel of the Blessed, 194 East 76th Street, New York NY 10021.

CN/0225-512X
**SENTINEL (RIDGEWAY).** (THE SENTINEL.). [Sentinel (Ridgeway)]. Jan. 1977-. Periodical. English. International Christian Communications, PO Box 339, Ridgeway Ontario L0S 1N0. **DD** 248.2/5.

GW
**SEPTUAGINTA : VETUS TESTAMENTUM GRACUM.** (19??)-. Monographic series. German. ir. Price varies per volume. Vandenhoeck & Ruprecht, Robert Bosch Breite 6, D-37079 Goettingen Germany. **Tel** 011 49 551 695911, FAX 011 49 551 695917, telex 965226 VAN d.

US/0199-8153
**SEQUOIA (SAN FRANCISCO).** (SEQUOIA.). **Added/Corp** Northern California Ecumenical Council. Vol. 1 (Mar./Apr. 1980)-. Periodical. English. Six times a year. $16.00. Northern California Ecumenical Church, 942 Market Street, Room 707, San Francisco CA 94102. **Tel** (415)434-0672. **ED** Mark MacNamara. cum. index. **Bk Rev**, (Qty: 12-20). **Ad Acc**, **Adv Mgr:** Robert Forsberg. **Circ:** 1,200. ***Continues*** *Church at Work.*
**Desc:** Bimonthly journal of religious (mostly Christian, largely Protestant) news and views on current social issues, with heavy emphasis on northern California. Covers issues of justice, peace, and environment.

US
**SERMON BUILDER, THE.** Periodical. English. mo. $7.00. Church Extension Service Inc, PO Box 552, Golden CO 80401. **Tel** (303)279-1011. **ED** Glenn Williamson. ***Continues*** *New Sermon Builder.*

CN/0705-6338
**SERVANT, THE.** Vol. 1 (Nov./Dec. 1977)-. Periodical. English. qt. free. Steinbach Bible College, Box 1420, Steinbach Manitoba R0A 2A0 Canada. **Tel** (204)326-6451, FAX (204)326-6908. **ED** Jake Ginter. **DD** 207/.7127/4. **Pr Rev. Circ:** 10,000 (ctrl). ***Supersedes*** *S B I Bulletin, 0705-632X.*
**Desc:** Religious education focusing on baptist theology for Steinbach Bible College.

CN/0848-1741
**SERVANT (THREE HILLS).** (SERVANT : A MINISTRY OF PRAIRIE BIBLE INSTITUTE.). [Servant]. **Added/Corp** Prairie Bible Institute. Vol. 1, No. 1 (Jan./Feb. 1989)-. Periodical. English. bm (6 issues). Free in North America; 20.00Can$ other. Priarie Bible Institute, Three Hills Alberta, T0M 2A0 Canada. **Tel** (403)443-5511, FAX (403)443-5540. **ED** Phil Callaway. **DD** 248.4/05. **Bk Rev**, (Qty: 24). **Circ:** 25,000. ***Continues*** *Prairie Overcomer., 0384-532X.*
**Desc:** Purpose is to edify, exhort and encourage today's Christian.

KE
**SERVICE TO REFUGEES; PROGRESS REPORT.** **Main/Corp** all Africa Conference of Churches. Refugee Dept. English. All Africa Conference of Churches, PO Box 20301, Nairobi Kenya. **LC** BV4470; .A44A. **DD** 259.

KE
**SERVICE TO REFUGEES; PROJECT LIST.** **Main/Conf** All Africa Conference of Churches. Refugee Dept. English. All Africa Conference of Churches, PO Box 20301, Nairobi Kenya. **LC** BV4470; .A44B. **DD** 259.

KE
**SERVICE TO REFUGEES : PROJECTS BOOK.** **Main/Conf** All Africa Conference of Churches. Refugee Dept. English. Refugee Department, All Africa Conference of Churches, Waiyaki Way, PO Box 14205, Nairobi Kenya. **LC** BV4470; .A44B. **DD** 362.8/7/096. ***Continues*** *Service to Refugees.*

SP/0326-6702
**SERVICIO DE INFORMACIONES RELIGIOSAS.** (1977)-. mo.
**Ind/Abst** Index Book Rev. Relig.; Relig. Index One Period.

IT/0037-2773
**SERVIZIO DELLA PAROLA.** [Serv. parola]. (1968)-. Periodical. Italian. Ten times a year. L55000 Italy; L75000 other. Editrice Queriniana, Casella Postale 403, 25100 Brescia Italy. **Tel** 39 30 294653. **UDC** 2.

IT
**SETTE E RELIGIONI.** Italian. qt. L30000 Italy; L50000 Europe; L60000 other. Studio Domenicano, Via Osservanza 72, 40136 Bologna Italy. **Tel** 011 39 51 582034.

II/0970-8324
**SEVARTHAM.** **Added/Corp** St. Albert's College (Ranchi, India). (1976)-. Periodical. English (Hindi). an (May/June). $8.00. Sevartham, St. Albert's College, PB 5, Ranchi 834001 India. **Tel** 315033. **ED** Fathers J. Feys and Sudhir Kujur. **LC** GN635.I4; S44. **DD** 306/.0954. ctrl circ.
**Ind/Abst** Index Book Rev. Relig.; Relig. Index One Period.

US/1059-9576
**SEWANEE THEOLOGICAL REVIEW.** [Sewanee theol. rev.]. **Added/Corp** University of the South. School of Theology. Vol. 34:4 (1991)-. Periodical. English. qt. $20.00 (one year), $37.00 (two year), $54.00 (three year) US; $26.00 (one year), $49.00 (two year), $72.00 (three year) other. Sewanee Theological Review,

School of Theology, University of the South, Sewanee TN 37375-4001. **Tel** (615)598-1475. **LC** BR1; .S33. **DD** 230/.3/05. available on microfilm. ***Continues*** *Saint Luke's Journal of Theology, 0036-309X.*
**Ind/Abst** Index Book Rev. Relig.; Old Testam. Abstr. (1957-); Relig. Index One Period.

US/0582-9348
**SHAKER QUARTERLY, THE.** [Shak. q.]. **Added/Corp** United Society (Poland, Me.). Vol. 1, (Spring 1961)-. Academic Scholarly Publication. English. Four times a year (No specific months). $15.00. The Shaker Quarterly, Rural Route 1, Box 640, Poland Springs ME 04274. **Tel** (207)926-4597. **ED** The United Society, (phone: (207)926-4597). **DD** 289. Index available (Separately). cum. index (Thru 1974). **Bk Rev. Circ:** 300.
**Desc:** Scholarly research and news from the last remaining active report of the Shaker's community.

US/0887-8897
**SHAMAN'S DRUM.** **Added/Corp** Cross-Cultural Shamanism Network. No. 1, (Summer 1985)-. Periodical. English. Four times a year (Jan., Apr., July, Oct.). $20.00 one year; $35.00 two years. Shamans Drum, PO Box 430, Willits CA 95490. **Tel** (707)459-0486. **ED** Timothy White. **LC** BL2370.S5; S524. **DD** 291. **Bk Rev. Ad Acc.**
**Desc:** Focus in experiential shamanism. Overall focus is cross cultural but editorial approach is culture specific. Intends to inspire people to explore shamanism in greater depth.
**Ind/Abst** Except. Hum. Exp.

US/0193-8274
**SHARING THE PRACTICE.** **Added/Corp** Academy of Parish Clergy. Vol. 1, (Jan/Feb. 1978)-. Periodical. English. Four times a year (Jan., Apr., July, Oct.). $25.00. Academy of Parish Clergy Inc, 13500 Shaker Blvd, Suite 601, Cleveland OH 44120. **Tel** (216)295-2006. **ED** Dr. Dennis R. Bolton ( editor's address: 2330 Rose Garden Drive, Gastonia, N.C. 28504, phone: (704)864-6491). **Bk Rev**, (Qty: 50). **Ad Acc. Circ:** 600 (ctrl). available on microfilm from University Microfilms International (UMI). ***Absorbed*** *News and Views - Academy of Parish Clergy, 0361-2406.*
**Desc:** News articles and book reviews on the practice of ministry by the ministers. Includes the list of news about the members.

US/0745-1245
**SHARING THE VICTORY.** **See** Recreation, Leisure-Sports.

IS
**SHEVILIN.** Year 1- (Galion 1- ). Periodical. Hebrew. qt. National Religious Party, 166 IBN Gabirol Street, Tel Aviv Israel.

CC
**SHIH CHIEH TSUNG CHIAO TZU LIAO.** **VFOAT** Shijie Zongjiao Ziliao. No. 1 (March 1980)-. Periodical. Chinese. Four times a year. $6.88. Science Press, 16 Donghuangchenggen North Street, Beijing 100707, People's Republic of China. **Tel** 011 86 1 4019821, 011 86 1 4010642, FAX 011 86 1 4012180, 011 86 1 4019810, telex 210147. **(Subscription address:** China International Book Trading Corporation, PO Box 399, Library Service Department, Beijing 100044 People's Republic of China.**)** **LC** BL9.C4; S48. **DD** 200/.5.

CC/1000-4289
**SHIH CHIEH TSUNG CHIAO YEN CHIU.** **Added/Corp** Chung-kuo She Hui Ko Hsueh Yuan. Shih Chieh Tsung Chiao Yen Chiu So. **VFOAT** Shijie Zongjiao Yanjiu. No. 1 (Aug. 1979)-. Periodical. Chinese (summaries and/or abstracts in English). qt. $15.04. Science Press, 16 Donghuangchenggen North Street, Beijing 100707, People's Republic of China. **Tel** 011 86 1 4019821, 011 86 1 4010642, FAX 011 86 1 4012180, 011 86 1 4019810, telex 210147. **(Subscription address:** China International Book Trading Corporation, PO Box 399, Library Service Department, Beijing 100044 People's Republic of China.**)** **LC** BL9.C4; S5.

US
**SHINING LIGHT.** English. Six times a year. $8.00 (one year); $12.50 (two years); $18.00 (three years). Shining Light, PO Box 1235, Anderson IN 46015. **Tel** (412)981-3901. **ED** Dr. Wilfred Jordan (editor's telephone: (317)644-1593). **Bk Rev**, (Qty: 6/year). **Pr Rev. Circ:** 2,800 (ctrl).
**Desc:** Publication for the National Association of the Church of God.

JA
**SHINTO KOTEN KENKYU : KAIHO / SHINTO KOTEN KENKYUKAI.** **VFOAT** Kaiho. 1 (Oct. 1979)-. Periodical. Japanese. Shinto Taikei Hansankai, c/o Nashonaru Building, 1-2 Shiba Koen 1, Minato-ku Tokyo-To 105 Japan. **LC** BL2216; .S48.

JA
**SHINTO SHUKYO.** **Added/Corp** Shinto Shukyo Gakkai. **VFOAT** Journal of Shinto Studies. (19??)-. Japanese (Japanese). Kokugakuin Daigaku, 10-28 Higashi 4-chome, Shiuya-ku, Tokyo Japan. **Tel** (03)409-0111. **LC** BL2216; .S56.

II
**SHREE GURUDEV-VANI.** English. 5.00. Shree Gurudev Ashram, PO Vajreshwari Dist Thana, Ganeshpuri India. **LC** BL25; .S46.

IT
**SIDIC (ENGLISH ED.).** (SIDIC.). **Added/Corp** Service International de Documentation Judeo-Chretienne. Vol. 1 (1968)-. Periodical. English (French). Three times a year (Feb., June & Oct.). L30000 (Italy); 30.50Can$ (Canada); $27.00 (airmail), $23.00 (surface mail) other. Sidic, Via del Plebiscito 112 Int 9, 00186 Rome Italy. **Tel** (396)679-5307, FAX (396)678-6280. **ED** R Le Deaut, M Gilles and M Kelly. Index available. **Bk Rev. Circ:** 1,600 (ctrl).
**Desc:** Contains articles by Jews and Christians on themes of interest to both. Includes documentation on dialogue, news, bibliography, and book reviews.
**Ind/Abst** Bibliogr. Mission.; Old Testam. Abstr.; Abr. Cathol. Period. Lit. Index; Cathol. Period. Lit. Index.

IS
**SIFRUT HA-TSIYONIT / ZIONIST LITERATURE, HA-.** **Main/Corp** Arkhiyon Ha-Tsiyoni Ha-Merkazi (Jerusalem). **VFOAT** Zionist Literature. (19??)-. Bibliography. Hebrew (English, French, German and Spanish). bm (6 issues). Free. World Zionist Organization, PO Box 92, Department of Education and Culture, Jerusalem Israel. **Tel** 011 972 2 513297. **ED** S. Palmor. **Circ:** 1,000.
**Desc:** Listing of publications on Israel and Zionism.

CN/0316-361X
**SIGNAL (QUEBEC).** (SIGNAL.). **Added/Corp** Service de Coordination de la Rencontre. (1970)-. Periodical. French. ir. Service de Coordination de la Rencontre, C P 1096, Quebec Quebec G1K 7B5 Canada. **DD** 269/.2/05.

SA
**SIGNPOSTS : A DIGEST OF RESEARCHED INFORMATION FOR CONCERNED CITIZENS.** (198?)-. Periodical. English. mo. R36.00. Signpost Publication, PO Box 26148, 0007 Arcadia, South Africa. **Tel** 11 27 12 982680.

CN/0821-1442
**SII VOUS INFORME.** (LE SII VOUS INFORME / SERVICE D'INFORMATION INTERCOMMUNAUTAIRE.). [SII inf.]. **Added/Corp** Service d'Information Intercommunautaire (Montreal, Quebec). **VAT** Service d'Information Intercommunautaire Vous Informe. Vol. 1, No. 1 (Feb. 1972)-. Periodical. French. bm. Le Service D'Information Intercommunautaire, Bureau 120, 1800 Ouest Boul., Dorchester Montreal Quebec H3H 2H2. **DD** 271/.009714/281.

UK
**SIKH COURIER, THE.** **Added/Corp** Sikh Cultural Society of Great Britain. (Oct. 1960)-. Periodical. English. qt (4 issues). £6.00, £50.00 (life membership). Sikh Cultural Society of Great Britain, 88 Mollison Way, Edgware Middx HA8 5QW United Kingdom. **Tel** 952 1215. **ED** A. S. Chatwal and S. S. Kapoor. **LC** BL2017; .S48. **DD** 294.6/05. **Bk Rev**, (Qty: 6). **Ad Acc, Adv Mgr:** B. S. Grewal, **Tel** same as publisher. **Circ:** 3,000.

US/0364-8206
**SIKH DHARMA BROTHERHOOD.** Periodical. English. qt. $6.00. Sikh Dharma Brotherhood, 1704 Q Street NW, Washington DC 20009. **LC** BL2017; .S486A. **DD** 294.6/05.

II/0037-5128
**SIKH REVIEW, THE.** **Added/Corp** Sikh Cultural Centre, Calcutta. Vol. 1 (1953)-. Periodical. English. Twelve times a year. $25.00 one year; $65.00 three years. Sikh Cultural Centre, Karnani Mans #116, 116 Park Street 25A, Calcutta 700 016 India. **Tel** 011/91/33/220939. **ED** Saran Singh. **LC** BL2017; .S5. **DD** 294.6/05. **Bk Rev**, (Qty: 24). **Ad Acc. Circ:** 5,000 (ctrl).
**Ind/Abst** Int. Bibliogr. Sociol.

CN/0711-6683
**SIM NOW.** [SIM now]. **Added/Corp** Sudan Interior Mission. **VAT** Sudan Interior Mission Now. No. 1 (Jan./Feb. 1982)-. Periodical. English (French, German, Italian and Chinese). Four times a year. Sudan Interior Mission / SIM International, 10 Huntingdale Boulevard, Scarborough Ontario M1W 2S5 Canada. **Tel** (905)497-2424. **ED** Kerry Lovering and Marjory Koop. **LC** BV3500; .A18. **DD** 266/.006/01. **Circ:** 130,000 (ctrl). available on microfilm from University Microfilms International (UMI). ***Continues*** *Africa Now (Cedar Grove, (N.J.), 0044-6513.*
**Desc:** A publication to inform constituency of work of SIM in Asia, South America and Africa.

BL
**SIMPOSIO.** **Added/Corp** ASTE (Organization). Vol. 1 No. 1 (May 1968)-. Periodical. Portuguese. Aste Rua Rego Freitas, 530 Conj F 13, Sao Paulo Brazil. **LC** BR7; .S54. **DD** 230/.05.
**Ind/Abst** Relig. Index One Period.

KO
**SINANG SEGYE.** Periodical. Korean. mo. W900 each issue. Sinang Segyesa, c/o YMCA, 9 2-ka Chongno, Seoul Korea. **LC** BV4485; .S54.

KO
**SINANGGYE.** (19??)-. Periodical. Korean. mo. W8000. Sinanggye, 1-20 Yoido-dong Yongdungpo-ku, Seoul 150 Korea. **LC** BV4485; .S56.

US/0887-1167
**SINGLE ADULT MINISTRY INFORMATION.** ***Title Change.*** (SINGLE ADULT MINISTRY INFORMATION. : S.A.M.I.). [Single adult minist. inf.]. **Added/Corp** Institute of Singles Dynamics (U.S.). **VFOAT** S.A.M.I.; SAMI. Vol. 13, No. 5 (Mar. 1986)-(199?). Periodical. English. mo. Singles and Leaders Newsletter, PO Box 842, Norman OK 73030. **DD** 259. **Bk Rev. Ad Acc.** ctrl circ. ***Continues*** *Single I, 0737-2078.* ***Continued by*** *Singles & Leaders Newsletter, 1077-0887.*

US/1077-0887
**SINGLES & LEADERS NEWSLETTER.** [Singles lead. newsl.]. (199?)-. Periodical. English. mo. $15.00. Singles and Leaders Newsletter, PO Box 842, Norman OK 73030. **DD** 259. ***Continues*** *Single Adult Ministry Information, 0887-1167.*
**Desc:** Designed to help single leaders and adults find encouragement in the process of becoming.

KO
**SINHAK KWA SONKYO.** **VFOAT** Theology and Mission. Periodical. English (Korean). W1,000. Soul Sinhak Taehak, 101 Sosa-dong, Puchon-si Seoul Korea. **LC** BR9.K6; S56.

SA/0257-8891
**SKRIF EN KERK.** [Skrif kerk]. **Added/Corp** Nederduitse Gereformeerde Kerk. (1980)-. Periodical. Afrikaans. Twice a year. R30.00. University of Pretoria / Faculty of Theology, Pretoria 0002 South Africa. **Tel** 011 27 12 4202358.
**Ind/Abst** Index Book Rev. Relig.; New Testam. Abstr.; Relig. Index One Period.

SW
**SKRIFTER UTGIVNA AV SVENSKA KYRKOHISTORISKA FOERENINGEN / PUBLICATIONS OF THE SWEDISH SOCIETY OF CHURCH HISTORY.** **Added/Corp** Svenska Kyrkohistoriska Foereningen. **VFOAT** Publications of the Swedish Society of Church History. (1950)-. Monographic series. Swedish. Price varies per volume. Scandinavian University Press, PO Box 2959 Toeyen, N 0608 Oslo 6 Norway. **Tel** 011 47 2 2575400, FAX 011 47 2 2575353, telex 71896 UROR N. **(Subscription address:** Scandinavian University Press, 200 Meacham Ave., Elmont NY 11003.**)** **LC** UNC.
**Ind/Abst** Index Book Rev. Relig.

UK/0037-7686
**SOCIAL COMPASS.** **See** Social Sciences.

CN/1183-4986
**SOCIAL ISSUES NEWS.** [Soc. issues news]. **Added/Corp** United Church of Canada. Division of Mission in Canada. Office of Church in Society. (Apr. 1991)-. Periodical. English. qt. Free. United Church of Canada, 85 Saint Clair Avenue East Room 711, Toronto Ontario M45 1M8 Canada. **Tel** (416)925-5931. **DD** 261.8. ***Continues*** *Social Issues, 0839-7813.*

US/0731-0234
**SOCIAL QUESTIONS BULLETIN (1981).** (SOCIAL QUESTIONS BULLETIN.). **Added/Corp** Methodist Federation for Social Action (U.S.). Vol. 71, No. 6 (Nov./Dec. 1981)-. Periodical. English. bm. $15.00 (one year), $40.00 (three years). Methodist Federation for Social Action, 76 Clinton Avenue, Staten Island NY 10301. **Tel** (718)273-6372, FAX (718)273-6372. **ED** Rev. George D. McClain. **Bk Rev**, (Qty: 12). **Circ:** 2,000 (ctrl). available on microfilm from University Microfilms International (UMI). ***Continues*** *SQB, 0274-5208.*
**Desc:** We provide issue analyses and social action suggestions for religious activists (especially Methodists) on key national and international questions.

●US
**SOCIAL THOUGHT: JOURNAL OF RELIGION IN THE SOCIAL SERVICES.** (Fall 1994)-. Periodical. English. qt. $36.00 (individual); $48.00 (institution); $75.00 (library). The Haworth Press Inc, 10 Alice Street, Binghamton NY 13904-1580. **Tel** (607)722-5857, (800)3-HAWORTH, FAX (607)722-1424. **ED** Joseph J. Shields, PhD. Documents available from Haworth Document Delivery Service. ***Continues*** *Social Thought., 0099183X.*
**Desc:** Scholarly papers which focus on topics pertaining to institutional and noninstitutional religion in relationship to the development and delivery of social services.

US/0099-183X
**SOCIAL THOUGHT (WASHINGTON, D.C.).** ***Title Change. Suspended.*** (SOCIAL THOUGHT.). [Soc. thought]. **Added/Corp** National Conference of Catholic Charities (U.S.) National Catholic

School of Social Service (U.S.). Vol. 1 (Spring 1975)-Suspended. Academic Scholarly Publication. English. qt. National Catholic School of Social Services / NCSSS, Washington University, Washington DC 20064. **Tel** (202)319-5781. **ED** Eleanor Hannon Judah, Alexandra Peeler. **LC** HN30; .S58. **DD** 261.8/3/0973. **[CCC]**. Index available. **Bk Rev**. **Ad Acc**. ***Continued by*** *Social Thought: Journal of Religion in the Social Services.*
**Desc:** A scholarly multi-disciplinary perspective on issues and problems, social welfare, social work practice, social ethics, and social policy. Particular attention is paid to the development of a society in which the principles of social justice and charity are incorporated.
**Ind/Abst** Appl. Soc. Sci. Index Abstr. (19??-19??); Guide Soc. Sci. Relig. (19??-19??); Soc. Plann. Policy Dev. Abstr. (19??-19??); Soc. Work Abstr. (Spring 1987-19??) [Select. Cov.]; Sociol. Abstr. (19??-19??); Abr. Cathol. Period. Lit. Index (19??-19??); Cathol. Period. Lit. Index (19??-19??).

US/0737-5778
**SOCIAL WORK AND CHRISTIANITY.** **See** Sociology-Social Services and Welfare.

US/0038-0210
**SOCIOLOGICAL ANALYSIS.** ***Title Change.*** (SA. SOCIOLOGICAL ANALYSIS.). [Sociol. anal.]. **Added/Corp** Association for the Sociology of Religion. **VFOAT** Sociological Analysis. Vol. 34-53 No. 4 (1973)-Vol. 33 (1992). Periodical. English. qt. Association for the Sociology of Religion, Marist Hall/Room 108, Catholic University of America, Washington DC 20064. **Tel** (202)319-5447. **ED** William Swatos. **LC** JN51; .A51. **DD** 261. Index available. cum. index. **Bk Rev**. **Ad Acc**. **Pr Rev**. **Circ:** 1,200 (ctrl). available on microfiche from University Microfilms International (UMI). Documents available from The Genuine Article, UMI Article Clearinghouse. ***Continues*** *Sociological Analysis, 0038-0210.* ***Continued by*** *Sociology of Religion, 1069-4404.*
**Desc:** Sociology of religion: theoretical and empirical issues, comparative, historical, behavioral studies.
**Ind/Abst** Am. Hist. Life (1973-); Arts Humanit. Citation Index (19??-19??) [Full Cov.]; Curr. Contents Arts Humanit.; Curr. Contents Soc. Behav. Sci.; Expand. Acad. Index (1989-); Index Book Rev. Relig.; INFO-SOUTH Abstr.; Int. Bibliogr. Sociol.; Mag. Search; Middle East Abstr. Index; Newsp. Period. Abstr. (1991-); Relig. Index One Period. (1973-); Relig. Theol. Abstr. (19??-); Res. Alert [Full Cov.]; Soc. Plann. Policy Dev. Abstr.; Soc. Sci. Source (Jul. 1993-); Soc. Sci. Cit. Index (19??-19??) [Full Cov.]; Soc. Sci. Index; Soc. Sci. Index Fulltext (Dec. 1988-) [Full Txt.]; Sociol. Abstr.; Women Stud. Abstr.

●US/1069-4404
**SOCIOLOGY OF RELIGION.** [Sociol. relig.]. **Added/Corp** Association for the Sociology of Religion. Vol. 54, No. 1 Spring (1993)-. Periodical. English. Four times a year (Mar., June, Sept., Dec.,). $50.00. Association Sociology of Religion, Marist Hall Room 108, Catholic University, Washington DC 20064. **Tel** (202)319-5447. **LC** IN PROCESS. **DD** 261. **CODEN** SRELE2. ***Continues*** *SA. Sociological Analysis, 0038-0210.*
**Ind/Abst** Acad. Search (July 1993-); Arts Humanit. Citation Index [Full Cov.]; Relig. Index One Period.; Soc. Sci. Cit. Index; Sociol. Abstr.

US/0364-2097
**SOJOURNERS.** [Sojourners]. **Added/Corp** Sojourners Fellowship. People's Christian Coalition. (Jan. 1976)-. Periodical. English. mo (Feb./Mar. and Aug./Sept. combined). $30.00; $45.00 (airmail). Sojourners, PO Box 29272, Washington DC 20017. **Tel** (202)636-3637. **LC** BR115.W6; S55. **DD** 261.8/05. available on microfilm and microfiche from University Microfilms International (UMI). ***Continues*** *Post American, 0361-2422.*
**Ind/Abst** Acad. Search (Dec. 1984-Apr. 1987); Altern. Press Index (199?-); Christ. Period. Index (19??-); Curr. Thoughts Trends; Guide Soc. Sci. Relig.; Hum. Rights Intern. Rep.; Index Book Rev. Relig.; INFO-SOUTH Abstr.; Mag. Artic. Summar. Select (Dec. 1984-April 1987); Mag. Artic. Summar. CD-ROM (Dec. 1984-April 1987); Mag. Search; Peace Res. Abstr. J. (1979-1983); Relig. Index One Period. (1976-); Relig. Theol. Abstr.

US/0038-1039
**SOLIA.** (SOLIA. THE HERALD.). **Added/Corp** Romanian Orthodox Episcopate of America. **VFOAT** Herald. (1935)-. Periodical. English (Romanian). Twelve times a year. $12.00 US; $14.00 Canada; $16.00 other. Romanian Orthodox Episcopate, Solia Building, 146 West Courtland Street, Jackson MI 49201-2208. **Tel** (517)789-9088. **ED** Nathaniel Popp. **Circ:** 5,000 (ctrl).
**Desc:** It is the official newspaper of the Romanian Orthodox Episcopate of America. It contains religious news and deals with the issues of faith.

CL
**SOLIDARIDAD.** **Added/Corp** Catholic Church. Archdiocese of Santiago (Chile). Vicaria de la Solidaridad. (1976)-. Periodical. Spanish. bw. **LC** HN291; .S64. **DD** 261.8/3/0983.
**Ind/Abst** Hum. Rights Intern. Rep.

CN/0383-6711
**SOLIDARITES.** Vol. 1 (Oct. 1976)-. Periodical. French. bm. 5.00Can$ Canada. Developpement et Paix, 5633 est Sherbrooke, Montreal Quebec H1N 1A3 Canada. **Tel** (514)257-8711, FAX (514)259-8497. **DD** 266/.2/05. **Circ:** 40,000. ***Formed by the union of*** *Mondes Nouveaux, 0318-8280* ***and*** *Developpement et Paix; Information, 0318-8299.*

US/0194-9179
**SONFLOWERS DISCIPLESHIP JOURNAL.** ***Title Change.*** **Added/Corp** Holy Order of Mans Discipleship Movement. Periodical. English. mo. ***Superseded by*** *Epiphany (San Francisco, Calif.), 0273-6969.*

KO
**SONGSO YONGU.** Periodical. Korean. mo. W6,000. Songso Yongusa, 501 Mok-dong Kangso-ku, Seoul Korea. **LC** BS410; .S68.

AT/0038-1527
**SOPHIA.** [Sophia]. **Added/Corp** University of Melbourne. Dept. of Philosophy. Vol. 1 (April 1962)-. Periodical. English. Three times a year. 15.00Aus$ (individuals), 20.00Aus$ (institutions) Australia; $18.00 (individuals), $25.00 (institutions) US, Canada, and Europe; $12.50 (individuals), $15.00 (institutions) other. Deakin University / Faculty of Humanities, Geelong Victoria 3217 Australia. **Tel** 011 61 52 271334, FAX 011 61 52 272018, telex AA35625. **ED** Purushottama Bilimoria. **LC** BL1; .S66. **DD** 200/.1. **Bk Rev**, (Qty: 3). **Ad Acc**. **Circ:** 400. available on microfilm from University Microfilms International (UMI).
**Desc:** A journal for discussion in philosophical theology.
**Ind/Abst** APAIS, Aust. Public Aff. Inf. Ser. (1972-); Philos. Index.

US/8756-8756
**SOUND WORDS (MIFFLINBURG, PA.).** (SOUND WORDS.). Vol. 1 No. 1 (Nov/Dec 1984)-. Periodical. English. qt. $5.00 US; $6.00 other. Sound Words, 1885 Oaks Boulevard, Naples FL 33999-1101.

US/0038-1861
**SOUNDINGS (KNOXVILLE, TENN.).** (SOUNDINGS.). [Soundings]. **Added/Corp** Society for Values in Higher Education. Vanderbilt University. Society for Religion in Higher Education. Vol. 51 (Spring 1968)-. Periodical. English. Four times a year (Mar., June, Sept., Dec.). $18.00 (individuals); $27.00 (institutions); $12.00 (students) US; $13.00 (others). Soundings, 306 Alumni Hall, University of Tennessee, Knoxville TN 37996-0530. **Tel** (615)974-8252. **ED** Ralph Norman. **LC** BV1460; .C6. **DD** 081. Index available. **Ad Acc**. **Circ:** 1,800. available on microfilm and microfiche from University Microfilms International (UMI). Documents available from The Genuine Article. ***Continues*** *Christian Scholar, 0361-8234.*
**Desc:** Publishes the work of many established scholars, but it also welcomes contributions from younger writers who may need to be encouraged to take risks in developing new connections among disciplines. Often two or three articles on a topic are published together, giving a range and depth which no single perspective can provide.
**Ind/Abst** Am. Hist. Life (1973-); Am. Bibliogr. Slavic East Europ. Stud.; Arts Humanit. Citation Index [Full Cov.]; Curr. Contents Arts Humanit.; Curr. Index J. Educ.; Hospit. Health Admin. Index; Index Book Rev. Relig.; Lit. Crit. Regist.; MLA Int. Bibl. Books Artic. Mod. Lang. Lit.; New Testam. Abstr.; Old Testam. Abstr.; Relig. Index One Period. (1968-); Relig. Theol. Abstr. (1968-); Res. Alert [Full Cov.]; Soc. Plann. Policy Dev. Abstr.; Soc. Sci. Cit. Index [Select. Cov.]; Sociol. Abstr. (1973-).

US
**SOUNDS OF GOSPEL RECORDINGS.** English. ir. Free on request. Gospel Recordings, 122 Glendale Boulevard, Los Angeles CA 90026. **Tel** (213)250-0207, FAX (213)250-0136. **ED** Colin Scott. **Bk Rev**. **Ad Acc**. **Circ:** 14,000 (ctrl).

CN/0704-6324
**SOURCE (MONTREAL, QUEBEC).** (SOURCE.). [Source]. Periodical. English (French). Church of Scientology of Montreal, 4489 Papineau, Montreal Quebec H2H 1T7 Canada. **DD** 299/.936/05. ***Continues in part*** *Source, 0704-6324.*

SZ
**SOURCES ET SUPPLEMENT VIE DOMINICAINE.** (19??)-. Periodical. French. Six times a year. 40.00F Switzerland; 45.00F Europe (except Belgium & France); 50.00F other. Sources & Vie Dominicaine, Botzet 8, 1700 Fribourg Switzerland. **Tel** 011 41 37 241865. Index available. cum. index. **Bk Rev**, (Qty: 30). **Circ:** 1,000 (ctrl).

MW
**SOURCES FOR THE STUDY OF RELIGION IN MALAWI.** No. 1-. Monographic series. English. Price varies per volume. University of Malawi / Department of Religious Studies, Box 280, Zomba Malawi. **Tel** 011 265 522622.

UK/0950-2742
**SOUROZH.** [Sourozh]. **Added/Corp** Russian Patriarchal Diocese of Sourozh. No. 1 (Aug. 1980)-. Periodical. English. qt. $25.00 US; $33.00 other. Sourozh, 13 Carver Road, Herne Hill, London SE24 9LS England. **Tel** 011 44 865 512701. **ED** Rev. Basil Osborne. **Bk Rev**, (Qty: 10). **Circ:** 600 (ctrl).
**Desc:** Contains articles on the Orthodox Christian faith and related matters.
**Ind/Abst** Index Book Rev. Relig.; Relig. Index One Period.

SA/0038-2523
**SOUTH AFRICAN OUTLOOK.** Vol. 52 (1922)-. Periodical. English. mo. R30.00 South Africa; R33.60 African Postal Unions; $24.00 other. South African Outlook, PO Box 245, 7700 Rondebosch South Africa. **Tel** 27 11 478139, FAX 27 11 478138. **ED** Francis Wilson. Index available. **Bk Rev**. **Circ:** 1,300. ***Continues*** *Christian Express.*
**Ind/Abst** Hum. Rights Intern. Rep.

US/0747-1130
**SOUTH CAROLINA NEWS (CLEVELAND, TENN.).** (SOUTH CAROLINA NEWS.). **Added/Corp** Church of God in South Carolina. Vol. 1, (1945)-. Periodical. English. bm. Church of God Publishing House, PO Box 2250, Cleveland TN 37320. **Tel** (615)476-4512.

US
**SOUTH DAKOTA CHURCHMAN.** 1919. Periodical. English. ir. $3.00. South Dakota Episcopal Church, 200 West 18th Street, Sioux Falls SD 57102. **Tel** (605)823-4346. **ED** Mary B Hobbs. **Bk Rev**. **Circ:** 4,500 (ctrl).
**Desc:** Newsletter and bulletin board for Episcopal Diocese of South Dakota.

US/0746-9276
**SOUTH DAKOTA EPISCOPAL CHURCH NEWS.** **Added/Corp** Episcopal Church. Diocese of South Dakota. **VFOAT** South Dakota, the Episcopal Churchnews; Church News; Episcopal Churchnews; Episcopal Church News; Churchnews; South Dakota Episcopal Churchnews. (19??)-. Periodical. English. Eleven times a year. $4.00. South Dakota Episcopal Church, 200 West 18th Street, Sioux Falls SD 57102. **Tel** (605)823-4346. **ED** John B. Davis. **Bk Rev**. **Circ:** 4,500 (ctrl).

II
**SOUTH INDIA CHURCHMAN, THE.** (Feb. 1948)-. Periodical. English. mo. $10.00. Church of South India, 222 Cathedral Road, Madras 600 086, South India. **Tel** 11 91 44 8271266, 8276168. available on microfilm from American Theological Library Association. ***Continues*** *Madras Diocesan Magazine.*

US/0887-0934
**SOUTHEASTERN OUTLOOK.** (SOUTHEASTERN OUTLOOK : SOUTHEASTERN BAPTIST THEOLOGICAL SEMINARY BULLETIN.). **Added/Corp** Southeastern Baptist Theological Seminary. **VFOAT** Outlook. (19??)-. Bulletin. English. bm. Free. Faith and Mission, PO Box 1889, Southeastern Seminary, Wake Forest NC 27587. **Tel** (919)556-3101. **Circ:** 18,000 (ctrl). ***Continues*** *Outlook (Wake Forest, N.C.).*
**Ind/Abst** South. Baptist Period. Index.

US/1058-319X
**SOUTHERN BAPTIST HANDBOOK (1991).** (SOUTHERN BAPTIST HANDBOOK.). [South. Baptist handb.]. **Added/Corp** Southern Baptist Convention. Sunday School Board. (1991)-. English. **DD** 286. ***Separated from*** *Quarterly Review, 0162-4334.*

US/0081-3028
**SOUTHERN BAPTIST PERIODICAL INDEX.** **See** Religion and Theology-Abstracting, Bibliographies and Statistics.

AT/0313-5861
**SOUTHERN CROSS SYDNEY. 1961.** [South. cross Syd.]. (1961)-. Periodical. English. Eleven times a year (except Jan.). 25.00Aus$ (one year), 45.00Aus$ (two year) Australia; 38.50Aus$ sea mail Asia and Oceania; 42.60Aus$ sea mail other; 42.60Aus$, 46.45Aus$ (airmail) economy air New Zealand and Papau New Guinea; 47.00Aus$, 50.30Aus$ (airmail) economy air Indonesia and Malaysia; 50.85Aus$, 55.25Aus$ (airmail) economy air India and Japan; 55.25Aus$, 59.65Aus$ (airmail) economy air US and Israel; 59.65Aus$, 65.15Aus$ (airmail) economy air UK and Europe. Anglican Information Office, PO Box Q190 Queen Victoria Boulevard, Sydney New South Wales 2000 Australia. **Tel** 011 61 2 2651536, FAX 011 61 2 2612864. **DD** _a283.944.

US/1078-2613
**SOUTHERN SEMINARY.** [South. semin.]. **Added/Corp** Southern Baptist Theological Seminary. **VFOAT** Southern Seminary Magazine. (199?)-. Periodical. English. qt. Southern Baptist Theological Seminary, 2825 Lexington Road, Louisville KY 40280. **Tel** (502)897-4141. **DD** 286. ***Continues*** *Tie, 0040-7232.*

US/0885-2421
**SOUTHERN TIDINGS.** [South. tidings]. **Added/Corp** Southern Union Conference of Seventh-Day Adventists. **VFOAT** Tidings. (19??)-. Periodical. English. mo. $5.00. Southern Union Conference of Seventh-Day Adventists, Box 849, Decatur GA 30031. **DD** 286. ***Continues in part*** *Southern Union Worker.*
**Ind/Abst** Seventh-Day Adventist Period. Index (19??-).

US/0038-4917
**SOUTHWESTERN NEWS.** **Main/Corp** Southwestern Baptist Theological Seminary, Fort Worth. (1941)-. Periodical. English. mo. Southwestern Baptist Theological Seminary, Fort Worth TX 76122.
**Ind/Abst** South. Baptist Period. Index.

FR/0769-1734
**SOUVENANCE ANABAPTISTE.** [Souvenance anabaptiste]. **VFOAT** Mennonitisches Gedachtnis. (1982)-. Periodical. French. an. 90.00F. Jean Hege, 3 rue A Daudet / Reichshoffen, 67110 Niederbronn France. **ED** Claude Jerome. **UDC** 286. Index available. **Bk Rev. Circ:** 650.

US/0278-1018
**SOVIET CHRISTIAN PRISONER LIST.** [Sov. Christ. prison. list]. 1981-. English. an. Society for Study of Religion Under Communism, PO Box 2310, Orange CA 92669. **LC** BR1608.S65; S66. **DD** 272/.9.

UK/0049-1772
**SOWER, THE.** ***Title Change.*** (1919)-(19??). Periodical. English. McCrimmon Publishing Co Ltd, 10-12 High Street, Wakering Essex SS30EQ England. ***Merged with*** *Christian Celebration* ***to form*** *New Sower (Great Wakering, Essex).*

US
**SPECTRUM (EXETER, DEVON).** (SPECTRUM / SPONSORED BY THE ASSOCIATION OF CHRISTIAN TEACHERS.). **Added/Corp** Association of Christian Teachers. (19??)-. English. Twice a year (January and July). £17.90 UK; £18.45 other. Paternoster Press, A division of Send the Light Ltd., PO Box 300, Kingstown Broadway, Cumbria CA3 0QS England. **Tel** 011 44 228 512512, FAX 011 44 228 514949. **LC** LC368; .S67. **DD** 377/.05.
**Ind/Abst** Index Book Rev. Relig.; Relig. Index One Period.

US/0890-0264
**SPECTRUM (TAKOMA PARK, MD.).** (SPECTRUM : JOURNAL OF THE ASSOCIATION OF ADVENTIST FORUMS.). **Added/Corp** Association of Adventist Forums. (196?)-. Periodical. English. Five times a year (Publishes every 10 weeks). $25.00 (one year); $48.00 (two years); $71.00 (three years). Association of Adventist Forums, PO Box 5330, Takoma Park MD 20913. **Tel** (301)270-0423, FAX (301)270-2814. **LC** BX6101; .S78. **DD** 286. Index available. **Bk Rev**, (Qty: 3). **Ad Acc**, **Adv Mgr:** Chip Cassano. **Circ:** 6,000.

●US/1061-6160
**SPECTRUM (WHEATON, ILL.).** (SPECTRUM: A NATIONWIDE MINISTRY OF CBA OF AMERICA.). **Added/Corp** Conservative Baptist Association of America. (1992)-. Periodical. English. bm. CBA of America, 252560 Geneva Road, Carol Stream IL 60188. ***Continues*** *Challenge of the '80s Update, 0746-0015.*

US/0894-6183
**SPICE.** (SPICE : A SUPPORT SYSTEM FOR WOMEN AND MEN WHOSE SPOUSES ARE CLERGY.). [Spice]. (1981)-. Periodical. English. mo (10 issues). $18.00. Spice, PO Box 10212, Lansing MI 48901. **Tel** (616)798-7727. **ED** Laura Deming (Editor's Address, 485 Wellesley Drive, Muskegon, MI 49441). **DD** 253 #2 11. cum. index. **Bk Rev**, (Qty: 5).

SZ/0561-6158
**SPICILEGIUM FRIBURGENSE.** Vol. 1- 1957-. Monographic series. German (French, English and Italian). ir. Price varies per volume. Universitatsverlag Freiburg, Perolles 36, 1700 Fribourg Switzerland. **Tel** 037-24 68 12. **Circ:** 400 (ctrl).
**Desc:** Furnishes tools for the research, identification, and study of texts informative of the history of the Christian life.

US/0038-7592
**SPIRIT & LIFE (CLYDE, MO.).** (SPIRIT & LIFE.). **Added/Corp** Benedictine Sisters of Perpetual Adoration. **VAT** Spirit and Life (Clyde, MO.). (19??)-. Periodical. English. Six times a year (Jan., Mar., May, July, Sept., Nov.). $10.00 (one year); $18.00 (two years). Benedictine Sisters Publications Center, 800 North Country Club Road, Tucson AZ 85716-4583. **Tel** (314)638-6427. **ED** Dolores Dowling, OSB, (phone: (602)325-6401). **Bk Rev**. **Pr Rev. Circ:** 5,000 (ctrl). available on microfilm from University Microfilms International (UMI). ***Continues*** *Tabernacle and Purgatory.*
**Desc:** Practical, simple, pithy articles inspiring readers to live out their Christian lives prayerfully on a day-to-day basis.

US/0885-0291
**SPIRIT (SISTERS, OR.).** (SPIRIT.). No. 1, Ed. 1, (Sept./Oct. 1985)-. Periodical. English. qt. Fulfillment, PO box 1231, Sisters OR 97759. **Bk Rev**. **Ad Acc. Circ:** 40,000. ***Continues*** *Solo, 0164-4734.*
**Desc:** Helps guide today's new generation of adults toward a more Biblical lifestyle and philosophical perspective. Provides a framework for making decisions and wise choices in an increasingly complicated, changing and challenging world.

US/0160-7367
**SPIRIT (WASHINGTON).** (SPIRIT.). V. 1-. Periodical. English. Three times a year. $3.00. J S Tinney, PO Box 386, Howard University, Washington DC 20059. **LC** BR1644; .S67. **DD** 269.

US/0038-7614
**SPIRITUAL FRONTIERS.** [Spirit. front.]. **Added/Corp** Spiritual Frontiers Fellowship. Spiritual Frontiers Fellowship International. Vol. 1 (Winter 1969)-. Periodical. English. qt. $12.00 (general), free (SFF members). Spiritual Frontiers Fellowship International, PO Box 7868, Philadelphia PA 19101. **LC** BR115.P85; S75. **DD** 201. ***Supersedes*** *Gate Way.*
**Ind/Abst** Except. Hum. Exp.

II
**SPIRITUAL INDIA.** V. 1- Jan. 1973-. Periodical. English. $4.00. Shanti Villa, 1615 Madarsa Road, Kashmere Gate, Delhi 110006 India. **LC** BL2001.2; .S64. **DD** 200/.954.

US/0744-6780
**SPREADING THE FAME OF CHRIST.** **Added/Corp** Fellowship of Associates of Medical Evangelism. (19??)-. Periodical. English. bm. Free. Fellowship of Associates of Medical Evangelism, PO Box 688, Columbus IN 47201. **Tel** (812)379-4351, FAX (812)379-1105. **ED** Robert E Reeves. **Circ:** 22,000 (ctrl).
**Desc:** Addresses current issues in medical missions and Biblical base of medical missions.

CN
**SR SUPPLEMENTS.** **Added/Corp** Corporation for the Publication of Academic Studies in Religion in Canada. Canadian Corporation for Studies in Religion. (1974)-. Monographic series. English. Humanities Press, 165 1st Avenue, Atlantic Highlands NJ 07716. **Tel** (908)872-1441, (800)221-3845, FAX (908)872-0717, telex 752233. Index available.

CE
**SRI AUROBINDO CENTENARY ANNUAL.** 1972-. English. 3.00. SRI Aurobindo Centenary Committee, 47 Galle Face Court Galle Road, Colombo -3 Ceylon. **LC** BL1270.G4; S68. **DD** 181/.45.

AT/0036-3103
**ST. MARK'S REVIEW.** [St. Mark's rev.]. **Added/Corp** St. Mark's Institute of Theology. **VAT** Saint Mark's Review. (1955)-. Academic Scholarly Publication. English. Four times a year (Jan., Apr., July, Oct.). 25.00Aus$ Australia; 32.00Aus$ (surface mail), 35.00Aus$ (airmail) other. St Marks Library, PO Box E67, Queen Victoria Terrace, Canberra ACT 2600 Australia. **Tel** 11 61 62 731572, FAX 11 61 62 734067. **ED** Dr. Graeme Garrett. Index available. cum. index. **Bk Rev**, (Qty: 40-50). **Ad Acc**. **Pr Rev. Circ:** 700 (ctrl). available on microfilm from Xerox; available on microfilm and microfiche from University Microfilms International (UMI).
**Desc:** Journal for general, scholarly but non-technical discussion of issues of importance to Christians in Australia and worldwide.
**Ind/Abst** APAIS, Aust. Public Aff. Inf. Ser. (1963-); Index Book Rev. Relig.; Relig. Index One Period. (1979-).

US/1059-8375
**ST. WILLIBRORD STUDIES IN PHILOSOPHY AND RELIGION.** [St. Willibrord stud. philos. relig.]. **VAT** Saint Willibrord Studies in Philosophy and Religion. No. 1 (1991)-. Monographic series. English. ir. Price varies per volume. Borgo Press, PO Box 2845, San Bernardino CA 92406. **Tel** (714)884-5813, (714)885-1161. **ED** Bishop Karl Pruter. **DD** 200.
**Desc:** This series features studies on all aspects of Christianity, including histories, treatises, and manuals.

US/0362-4692
**STANDARD BEARER (GRAND RAPIDS), THE.** (THE STANDARD BEARER; A REFORMED SEMI-MONTHLY MAGAZINE.). Vol. 1 (1924)-. Periodical. English. Twenty-one times a year. $12.00. Reformed Free Publication Association, PO Box 603, Business Office, Grand Rapids MI 49468. **Tel** (616)531-1490. **ED** Professor David J. Engelsma (editor's address: 4949 Ivanrest Avenue, Grandville, MI 49418). Index available. **Bk Rev**. **Circ:** 2,500 (ctrl). available on microfilm from University Microfilms International (UMI).
**Desc:** News and information about religious, church, and news.

US/0896-6095
**STARLIGHT (WILSON, N.C.).** (STARLIGHT.). **VFOAT** Star Light. (1987)-. Periodical. English. qt. $15.00. Star Books Inc., 408 Pearson Street, Wilson NC 27893. **Tel** (919)237-1591. **ED** Irene Burk Harrell. **DD** 243. **Circ:** 1,000.
**Desc:** Contains testimonies, devotions, prophecy, poetry, fiction (adult and juvenile) showing the reality of Jesus Christ.

US/0162-6841
**START (BIRMINGHAM, ALA.).** (START.). [Start]. **Added/Corp** Southern Baptist Convention. Woman's Missionary Union. (19??)-. Periodical. English. qt. $12.95. Woman's Missionary Union, PO Box 830010, Birmingham AL 35283. **Tel** (205)991-8100, (205)991-4933. **ED** Kathryn W. Kizer. **DD** 266. **Circ:** 32,500 (ctrl).
**Desc:** The magazine for leaders of Mission Friends (preschoolers, birth until first grade) in Woman's Missionary Union, SBC.
**Ind/Abst** Microcomput. Index (Oct. 1990-May 1991); South. Baptist Period. Index.

GW/0039-1492
**STIMMEN DER ZEIT (FREIBURG).** (STIMMEN DER ZEIT.). [Stimmen der Zeit (Freib.)]. **Added/Corp** Abtei Maria Laach. Vol. 88 (Oct. 1914)-. Periodical. German. mo. DM144.00. Verlag Herder Freiburg, Postfach 79080, Frieburg, Germany. **Tel** (0761)27-17-0, FAX (0761)27 17-520, telex 761489. **ED** W. Seibel. cum. index. ***Continues*** *Stimmen aus Maria-Laach.*
**Ind/Abst** Am. Hist. Life (1954-); Annu. Bibliogr. Engl. Lang. Lit.; ARTbibliogr. Mod.; Bibliogr. Mission.; BHA : Biblio. Hist. Art; Energy Res. Abstr. (Dec. 1979-); Int. Aerosp. Abstr.; MLA Int. Bibl. Books Artic. Mod. Lang. Lit.; New Testam. Abstr.; Abr. Cathol. Period. Lit. Index; Cathol. Period. Lit. Index.

US/0883-7678
**STORY (SAINT PAUL, MINN.).** (STORY.). **VFOAT** Luther Northwestern Story; Luther Northwestern Theological Seminary Story. Vol. 1, No. 1 (Winter 1985)-. Periodical. English. qt. Luther Northwestern Theological Seminary, 2481 Como Avenue, St Paul MN 55108. ***Continues*** *Semogram Bell, 0274-9939.*

AG/0049-2353
**STROMATA.** [Stromata]. **Added/Corp** San Miguel, Argentine Republic. Colegio Maximo de San Jose. Facultad de Filosofia. San Miguel, Argentine Republic. Colegio Maximo de San Jose. Facultad de Teologia. Buenos Aires. Universidad del Salvador. Faculdad de Filosofia. Buenos Aires. Universidad del Salvador. Facultad de Teologia. **VFOAT** Stromata; Ciencia y Fe. Vol. 21, No. 3/4 (July/Dec. 1965)-. Periodical. Spanish. Twice a year. $25.00 Latin America; $30.00 other. Asociacion Civil Facultades, Loyola, Av Mitre 3226, CC 10, 1663 San Miguel Argentina. **Tel** 011 54 1 6647992. **ED** Jorge Seibold. **LC** BX805; .C54. Index available ($17.00). cum. index. **Bk Rev**. **Ad Acc. Circ:** 1,000 (ctrl). ***Continues*** *Ciencia y Fe.*
**Desc:** Articles and notes on various subjects of religion, theology, and philosophy. Includes book reviews, bibliographical news, Latin American theology, and an index.
**Ind/Abst** HAPI Hisp. Am. Period. Index; New Testam. Abstr.; Old Testam. Abstr.; Philos. Index.

IT
**STUDI DI SCIENZE RELIGIOSE.** (1989)-. Monographic series. Italian. Price varies per volume. Edizioni Zara, Via Portillia 6, 43100 Parma Italy. **Tel** 011 39 521 45945. ***Continues*** *Pubblicazioni dell'Istituto di Scienze Religiose dell'Universita di Parma.*

IT
**STUDI DI TEOLOGIA.** **Added/Corp** Istituto di Formazione Evangelica e Documentazione. **VFOAT** Sdt. (19??)-. Periodical. Italian. Twice a year (Feb., Oct.). L22000.00 Italy; L35000.00 other. Istituto Formaz Evang Documen, Casella Postale 756, 35100 Padua Italy. **Tel** 049/613891, FAX 049/619623. **ED** Pietro Bolognesi. **LC** BR5; .S78. **DD** 230/.05. Index available. **Bk Rev**, (Qty: 60). **Pr Rev. Circ:** 1,000.
**Desc:** Every issue is a monograph giving evangelical perspectives on a particular topic. Many book reviews of theological books also in every issue.

IT
**STUDI DI TEOLOGIA DOGMATICA.** **Added/Corp** Pontificia Universita Salesiana. Istituto di Teologia Dogmatica. (1983)-. Monographic series. Italian. Price varies per volume. Editrice Las, Piazza dell Ateneo Salesiano 1, 00139 Rome Italy. **Tel** 011 872 90 626, FAX 06 872 90 629. **Ad Acc**, **Adv Mgr:** F. Zucchelli Giuseppe. Documents available.

IT
**STUDI E MATERIALI DI STORIA DELLE RELIGIONI (L'AQUILA, ITALY : 1983).** (STUDI E MATERIALI DI STORIA DELLE RELIGIONI / PUBBLICATI DALLA SCUOLA DI STUDI STORICO-RELIGIOSI DELL'UNIVERSITA DI ROMA.). **Added/Corp** Universita di Roma. Scuola di Studi Storico-Religiosi. **VFOAT** SMSR. Vol. 7, No. 1 (1983)-. Periodical. Italian (English, French and German). sa. L38000 (Italy); L45000 (other). Japadre Editore, C Postale 170, 67100 L Aquila Italy. **Tel** 011 39 86226025. ***Continues*** *Studi Storico-Religiosi, 0393-4128.*

IT/0393-3687
**STUDI ECUMENICI.** **Added/Corp** Istituto di Studi Ecumenici S. Bernadino (Verona, Italy). Vol. 1, No. 1/2 (Jan./June 1983)-. Periodical. Italian (summaries and/or abstracts in English). qt. L37000 Italy; L42000 other. Rivista Studi Ecumenici, Castello 2786, 30122 Venice Italy. **Tel** 011 39 41 5235341, FAX 011 39 41 5228323. Each issue contains an index to its own contents (no volume index)--loose. cum. index. **Bk Rev**, (Qty: 8-10). **Circ:** 1,000 (ctrl).
**Desc:** Information on the ecumenical movement.
**Ind/Abst** Bibliogr. Mission.; Index Book Rev. Relig.; Old Testam. Abstr.; Relig. Index One Period.

IT
**STUDI FRANCESCANI.** (1903)-. Periodical. Italian. Four times a year. Studi Francescani, P. Mazzoli Via Giacomini 3, 50132 Florence Italy. **Tel** 011 39 55 474246.
**Ind/Abst** BHA : Biblio. Hist. Art; MLA Int. Bibl. Books Artic. Mod. Lang. Lit.

IT
**STUDIA ANSELMIANA; PHILOSOPHICA, THEOLOGICA. See** Philosophy.

PL
**STUDIA EKUMENICZNE.** Vol. 1-. Periodical. Polish (summaries and/or abstracts in English, French and Italian). Dzia Administracyjno-Gospodarczy, Akademii Teologii Katolickiej, Dewajtis 3, 01-653 Warszawa UL Poland. **LC** BX1; .S87.

NE/0039-3207
**STUDIA LITURGICA.** [Stud. liturg.]. **Added/Corp** Liturgical Ecumenical Center Trust. Vol. 1 (March 1962)-. Periodical. English (Latin, French and German). Twice a year (two double issues per year). $25.00. Studia Liturgica, PO Box 90, 5360 AB Grave The Netherlands. **Tel** 08860-73792. **ED** Paul F. Bradshaw (editor's address: University of Notre Dame, Department of Theology, Notre Dame, IN 46556; editor's telephone number: (219)239-7811). Index available. **Bk Rev. Circ:** 1,100.
**Desc:** An international ecumenical review for liturgical research and renewal.
**Ind/Abst** Index Book Rev. Relig.; New Testam. Abstr.; Relig. Index One Period. (1962-); Relig. Theol. Abstr.

IT/0080-3987
**STUDIA MISSIONALIA.** [Stud. mission.]. **Added/Corp** Pontificia Universita Gregoriana. Faculta di Missiologia. Vol. 1 (1943)-. Monographic series. Italian (English, French, German and Latin). an. L65000 Italy; $60.00 US. Editrice Pontificio Istituto Biblico, Piazza della Pilotta 35, 00187 Rome Italy. **Tel** 011 39 6 6781567, FAX 011 39 6 6780588. **ED** Mariasusai Dhavamony. **DD** 266/.2/05. Index available. **Circ:** 200.
**Desc:** Each volume averages 300-350 pages, contains subjects such as: Islam, Buddhism, Hinduism, religious ethnology, revelation, worship and ritual, prayers, meditation, mystique, moral and religion, etc., in Christianity and other religions.
**Ind/Abst** Bibliogr. Mission.; Index Book Rev. Relig.; Missionalia; New Testam. Abstr.; Relig. Index One Period. (1976-); Relig. Theol. Abstr.; Abr. Cathol. Period. Lit. Index; Cathol. Period. Lit. Index.

SW/0585-5373
**STUDIA MISSIONALIA UPSALIENSIA.** 1-1956-. Monographic series. Multiple languages (English, Swedish and German). ir. Price varies per volume. Liber International, S-205 10 Malmo Sweden. **Tel** 46-40-70650.

SP/0039-3258
**STUDIA MONASTICA.** [Stud. monast.]. **Added/Corp** Montserrat (Abbey). Vol. 1 (1959)-. Periodical. Multiple languages (Latin, Catalan, English, French, Italian, German, Portuguese and Spanish). Twice a year. $105.00. Abadia de Montserrat, Ausias March 92 98 Interior, 08013 Barcelona Spain. **Tel** 34 3 2450303 or 2314001, FAX 34 3 4473594. **ED** Josep Massot Muntaner. **LC** BX2400; .S8. Index available. **Bk Rev. Circ:** 800. Documents available from The Genuine Article.
**Desc:** Articles, chronicles and book reviews on themes of monastic history and spirituality of all times, in all countries.
**Ind/Abst** Am. Hist. Life (1966-1975)(1966-); Arts Humanit. Citation Index [Full Cov.]; BHA : Biblio. Hist. Art; Curr. Contents Arts Humanit.; MLA Int. Bibl. Books Artic. Mod. Lang. Lit.; Res. Alert [Full Cov.]; Soc. Sci. Cit. Index [Select. Cov.].

IT/0081-6736
**STUDIA MORALIA. See** Ethics.

US/0161-7222
**STUDIA MYSTICA. See** Literature.

IT/0039-3304
**STUDIA PATAVINA.** [Stud. patavina]. Vol. 1 (Jan./April 1954)-. Periodical. Italian (English). Three times a year. L50000 Italy; L65000 other. Studia Patavina, Via del Seminario 29, 35122 Padua Italy. **Tel** 39 49 657099, FAX 39 49 8761934. Index available (bound in 3rd issue). cum. index. **Bk Rev**, (Qty: 100-120). **Pr Rev. Circ:** 600.
**Desc:** Encourages interdisciplinary encounter of themes relevant to philosophy and religious experience, with particular reference to Christianity.
**Ind/Abst** Bibliogr. Mission.; New Testam. Abstr.; Old Testam. Abstr.

GW
**STUDIA PATRISTICA : PAPERS PRESENTED TO THE ... INTERNATIONAL CONFERENCE ON PATRISTIC STUDIES HELD. Main/Conf** International Conference on Patristic Studies. (1955)-. English (French, German, Italian, Russian and Spanish). ir. 3150.00F. Editions Peeters SA, Bondgenotenlaan 153, BP 41, B-3000 Leuven Belgium. **Tel** 32 16 235170, FAX 32 16 228500, telex 65987 PUL B. **LC** BR45; .T4 subser. cum. index.

NE/0585-5500
**STUDIA POST-BIBLICA.** (1959)-. Monographic series. Multiple languages (English, French and German). ir. Price varies per volume. E. J. Brill, Postbus 9000, 2300 PA Leiden Netherlands. **Tel** 011 31 71 312624, FAX 011 31 71 317532, telex 39296 BRILL NL.

NO/0039-338X
**STUDIA THEOLOGICA.** [Stud. theol.]. **VFOAT** Scandinavian Journal of Theology. Vol. 1 (1947)-. Periodical. English (French and German). Twice a year. Kr295.00, $55.00. Scandinavian University Press, PO Box 2959 Toeyen, N 0608 Oslo 6 Norway. **Tel** 011 47 2 2575400, FAX 011 47 2 2575353, telex 71896 UROR N. **(Subscription address:** Scandinavian University Press, 200 Meacham Ave., Elmont NY 11003.**) ED** Carl-Henrik Grenholm. **LC** BR1; .S684. **DD** 230/.05. Index available. cum. index. **Bk Rev. Ad Acc. Circ:** 600. available on microfilm and microfiche from University Microfilms International (UMI).
**Desc:** Aims to present Scandinavian contributions to the field of international theology in the major languages. Publishes articles of current interest to all theological disciplines, as well as the annual Mowinckel lecture from the University of Oslo and summaries of Nordic dissertations in theology.
**Ind/Abst** Index Book Rev. Relig.; MLA Int. Bibl. Books Artic. Mod. Lang. Lit.; New Testam. Abstr.; Relig. Index One Period. (1949-); Relig. Theol. Abstr.

SW
**STUDIA THEOLOGICA LUNDENSIA; UTG. AV TEOLOGISKA FAKULTETEN I LUND.** (19??)-. Monographic series. Multiple languages (Swedish, English and Latin). ir. Price varies per volume. Lund University Press, Box 141, S-22100 Lund Sweden. **Tel** 011 46 46 312000, FAX 011 46 46 305338, telex 33345 EDUCATE S.

PL/0585-5594
**STUDIA THEOLOGICA VARSAVIENSIA.** [Stud. Theol. Vars.]. **Added/Corp** Warsaw. Akademia Teologii Katolickiej. Wydzia Teologiczny. Vol. 1 (1963)-. Periodical. Multiple languages (Polish and Latin; summaries and/or abstracts in English, French, German and Latin). Twice a year. $20.00. **(Subscription address:** ARS Polona, PO Box 1001, 00068 Warsaw Poland.**) LC** BR9.P6; S77.
**Ind/Abst** Bibliogr. Mission.; New Testam. Abstr.; Old Testam. Abstr.

PL
**STUDIA Z HISTORII KAZNODZIEJSTWA I HOMILETYKI. Added/Corp** Warsaw. Akademia Teologii Katolickiej. Katedra Homiletyki. Vol. 1- (1975)-. Polish (summaries and/or abstracts in French). DZIA, Administracyjno-Gospodarczy ATK, Ul Dewajtis, 01-653 Warsaw Poland. **LC** BV4205; .S77.

IT/0450-9250
**STUDIE. Main/Corp** Krestanska Akademia. Began in 1958. Periodical. Czech. $5.00. Academia Cristiana Administrace Studii, Via Concordial, Rome 00183 Italy. **LC** BX806.C9; K74.

AU/0579-7780
**STUDIEN UND ARBEITEN DER THEOLOGISCHEN FAKULTAT. Main/Corp** Innsbruck. Universitat. Theologische Fakultat. (1968)-. Monographic series. German (English and French). ir. Price varies per volume. University of Innsbruck, Faculty of Theology, Innsbruck Austria. **Tel** 05222 5078501, FAX 05222 579799. **ED** Hans Bernhard Meyer. **Circ:** 800.
**Desc:** Studies on philosophical and theological subjects.

GW/0081-7295
**STUDIEN ZUR GESCHICHTE DER KATH. MORALTHEOLOGIE.** Vol. 1- ; 1954-. Monographic series. German. ir. Price varies per volume. Verlag Friedrich Pustet, Gutenbergstrasse 8, D-93051 Regensburg. **Tel** 0941 9 20 22-0, FAX 0941 94 86 52, telex 6 56 72.

GW/0585-6272
**STUDIEN ZUR UMWELT DES NEUEN TESTAMENTS.** (1962)-. Monographic series. German. ir. Price varies per volume. Vandenhoeck & Ruprecht, Robert Bosch Breite 6, D-37079 Goettingen Germany. **Tel** 011 49 551 695911, FAX 011 49 551 695917, telex 965226 VAN d. **ED** C H Burchard, G Jeremias, H W Vuhn and H Stegenann. **Bk Rev. Ad Acc. Circ:** 700.

DK/0904-2431
**STUDIES IN CENTRAL AND EAST ASIAN RELIGIONS : JOURNAL OF THE SEMINAR FOR BUDDHIST STUDIES, COPENHAGEN & AARHUS. See** Religion and Theology-Buddhism.

UK
**STUDIES IN CHRISTIAN ETHICS. Added/Corp** Society for the Study of Christian Ethics. Vol. 1, No. 1 (1988)-. Periodical. English. sa. £19.95 UK; $39.95 US; £21.95 other. T & T Clark Ltd., 59 George Street, Edinburgh EH2 2LQ Scotland. **Tel** 011 44 31 2254703, FAX 011 44 31 2204260. **ED** Richard Franklin and Oliver O'Donovan. **Bk Rev. Ad Acc. Pr Rev. Circ:** 750 (ctrl).
**Desc:** Articles on the theory and application of christian ethics in current topical situations.

NE/0924-9389
**STUDIES IN CHRISTIAN MISSION.** [Stud. Christ. mission]. (1990)-. Monographic series. English. ir. Price varies per volume. E. J. Brill, Postbus 9000, 2300 PA Leiden Netherlands. **Tel** 011 31 71 312624, FAX 011 31 71 317532, telex 39296 BRILL NL. **UDC** 266.

CN/0711-5903
**STUDIES IN CHRISTIANITY AND JUDAISM. Added/Corp** Canadian Corporation for Studies in Religion. **VFOAT** Etudes sur le Christianisme et le Judaisme. (1981)-. Monographic series. English. Price varies per volume. Humanities Press, 165 1st Avenue, Atlantic Highlands NJ 07716. **Tel** (908)872-1441, (800)221-3845, FAX (908)872-0717, telex 752233. **ED** Charles Kannengiesser (University of Notre Dame, Notre Dame, IN 46556). Index available.
**Desc:** Scholarly theological studies of all aspects of Christianity and Judaism, with focus on gnosticism, ancient Judaism and anti-Judaism in early Christianity.

UK/0424-2084
**STUDIES IN CHURCH HISTORY (LONDON, ENGLAND).** (STUDIES IN CHURCH HISTORY.). **Added/Corp** Ecclesiastical History Society. Vol. 1 (1964)-. English. an. **LC** BR141; .S84. **DD** 270.

UK
**STUDIES IN CHURCH HISTORY: SUBSIDIA. Added/Corp** Ecclesiastical History Society. (1978)-. Monographic series. English. Westfield College, Department of History, c/o Dr. V Davies, London NW3 3ST England. **Tel** 011 44 71 4357141. **LC** UNC.

UK/0039-3622
**STUDIES IN COMPARATIVE RELIGION.** ***Ceased.*** [Stud. comp. relig.]. Vol. 1 (Winter 1967)- Vol.17, No. 1 (199?). Periodical. English. qt. Perennial Books Ltd, Pates Manor, Hatton Road, Bedfont Middlesex England. **ED** J Peter Hobson, Olive Clive-Ross and Ralph Smith. **LC** BL1; .S78. **Bk Rev. Ad Acc.** available on microfilm and microfiche from University Microfilms International (UMI). ***Supersedes*** *Tomorrow.*
**Desc:** Studies in comparative religion, metaphysics, cosmology and traditional symbolism.
**Ind/Abst** Acad. Abstr. Full Text Elite (July 1990-199?); Humanit. Index; Humanit. Source (Jul. 1990-); Index Book Rev. Relig. (19??-199?); INFO-SOUTH Abstr.; Mag. Search; Relig. Index One Period. (19??-199?).

NE
**STUDIES IN GREEK AND ROMAN RELIGION. See** Classical Studies.

US/0148-1029
**STUDIES IN ICONOGRAPHY.** [Stud. iconogr.]. Vol. 1 (1975)-. English. an. $35.00 (institutions), $15.00 (individuals). Medieval Institute Publishing, Western Michigan University, Kalamazoo MI 49008. **Tel** (616)387-8755. **ED** Anthony Gully. **LC** NX1; .S84. **DD** 700. **Bk Rev. Pr Rev. Circ:** 480 (ctrl). Documents available from The Genuine Article.
**Desc:** The journal is interdisciplinary in nature. Articles focus on problems of iconography in critical studies of art and literature. All periods are covered.
**Ind/Abst** Annu. Bibliogr. Engl. Lang. Lit.; ARTbibliogr. Mod.; Arts Humanit. Citation Index; Avery Index Archit. Period. Suppl. Colum. Univ. (19??-199?); BHA : Biblio. Hist. Art; Curr. Contents Arts Humanit.; Res. Alert.

NE/0926-2326
**STUDIES IN INTERRELIGIOUS DIALOGUE.** (1991)-. English. sa. Fl83.00. J H Kok Pharos Publishing House, Postbus 130, 8260 AC Kampen Netherlands. **Tel** 31 520292555. **ED** Henk Vroom. **Pr Rev.**
**Desc:** Designed for comparative studies of religious beliefs and philosophies.

UK
**STUDIES IN JEWISH/CHRISTIAN RELATIONS. VFOAT** Studies in Jewish Christian Relations. No. 1- 1986-. Monographic series. English. Price varies per volume.

NE/0585-6914
**STUDIES IN MEDIEVAL AND REFORMATION THOUGHT.** Vol. 1 (1966)-. Monographic series. English. ir. Price varies per volume. E. J. Brill, Postbus 9000, 2300 PA Leiden Netherlands. **Tel** 011 31 71 312624, FAX 011 31 71 317532, telex 39296 BRILL NL. **ED** M. A. Oberman.
**Desc:** Covers Medieval philosophy, doctrinal theology and more.

●US/1061-9380
**STUDIES IN MUSLIM-JEWISH RELATIONS.** **VFOAT** Studies in Muslim Jewish Relations. (1992)-. Periodical. English. Harwood Academic Publishers / New York, PO Box 786, Cooper Station, New York NY 10276. **Tel** (212)206-8900, (201)643-7500. **(Subscription address:** International Publishers Distributor at one of the following addresses: 820 Town Center Drive, Langhorne, PA 19047; or PO Box 90, Reading Berkshire RG1 8JL UK; or Kent Ridge PO Box 1180, Singapore 9111, Republic of Singapore)

●US/1056-4969
**STUDIES IN PHENOMENOLOGICAL THEOLOGY.** (1992)-. Monographic series. English. Price varies per volume. Peter Lang Publishing, 62 West 45th Street, 4th Floor, New York NY 10036. **Tel** (212)764-1471, (800)770-5264, telex 6973364 PLNY.

CN/0008-4298
**STUDIES IN RELIGION.** (STUDIES IN RELIGION. SCIENCES RELIGIEUSES). [Stud. relig.]. **Added/Corp** Corporation for the Publication of Academic Studies in Religion in Canada. Canadian Corporation for Studies in Religion. **VFOAT** Sciences Religieuses; SR. Vol. 1 (June 1971)-. Periodical. English (French). qt. 45.00Can$ Canada; $49.00 other. Wilfrid Laurier University Press, 75 University Avenue West, Waterloo Ontario N2L 3C5 Canada. **Tel** (519)884-1970, FAX (519)725-1399. **ED** Tom Sinclair-Faulkner and Elizabeth Lacelle. **LC** BL1; .S8. **DD** 200/.5. **[CCC].** Index available. **Bk Rev. Ad Acc. Pr Rev. Circ:** 1,300. available on microfilm and microfiche from University Microfilms International (UMI). Documents available from The Genuine Article. ***Supersedes*** *Canadian Journal of Theology, 0576-5579.*
**Desc:** Publishes articles and reviews in the various disciplines concerned with the scientific study of religion.
**Ind/Abst** Arts Humanit. Citation Index [Full Cov.]; Curr. Contents Arts Humanit.; Index Book Rev. Relig.; Middle East Abstr. Index; MLA Int. Bibl. Books Artic. Mod. Lang. Lit.; New Testam. Abstr.; Old Testam. Abstr.; Relig. Index One Period. (1971-); Relig. Theol. Abstr.; Res. Alert [Full Cov.]; Soc. Sci. Cit. Index [Select. Cov.].

US
**STUDIES IN RELIGION AND SOCIETY SERIES.** (1972)-. Monographic series. English. ir. Price varies per volume. Center for Scientific Study Religion, 5757 University Avenue, Chicago IL 60637.

II
**STUDIES IN SIKHISM AND COMPARATIVE RELIGION.** **Added/Corp** Guru Nanak Foundation. Vol. 1, No. 1 (Oct. 1982)-. Periodical. English. sa. $15.00. Guru Nanak Foundation, Near Qutab Hotel, New Delhi 110067 India. **Tel** 654353/652151. **(Subscription address:** Prints India, 11 Darya Ganj, New Delhi, 110002 India, (Phone: 011 91 11 3268645)) **ED** Mohinder Singh. **LC** BL2017; .S88. **DD** 294.6/05. **Bk Rev. Circ:** 750.
**Desc:** Religion history and philosophy with major focus on comparative study of religion and Sikhism.

NE
**STUDIES IN SPIRITUALITY.** (19??)-. English. an. Fl90.00 Vol. 3. J H Kok, Postbus 130, 8260 AC Kampen Netherlands. **Tel** 011 31 520292555, FAX 011 31 520227331.

NE/0081-8607
**STUDIES IN THE HISTORY OF CHRISTIAN THOUGHT.** Vol. 1 (1966)-. Monographic series. Multiple languages (English, French and German). ir. Price varies per volume. E. J. Brill, Postbus 9000, 2300 PA Leiden Netherlands. **Tel** 011 31 71 312624, FAX 011 31 71 317532, telex 39296 BRILL NL. **ED** H. A. Oberman.

NE/0169-8834
**STUDIES IN THE HISTORY OF RELIGIONS.** (1954)-. Monographic series. English (German). ir. Price varies per volume. E. J. Brill, Postbus 9000, 2300 PA Leiden Netherlands. **Tel** 011 31 71 312624, FAX 011 31 71 317532, telex 39296 BRILL NL.

US
**STUDIES IN THE REFORMATION.** 1- 1977-. Periodical. Multiple languages. ir. Harper Collins Publishers, Keystone Industrial Park, Scranton PA 18512. **Tel** (800)242-7737, (800)233-4727, FAX (800)822-4090. **DD** 230.3.

US
**STUDIES IN WOMEN AND RELIGION.** **See** Women's Interests.

MY
**SUARA.** **Main/Corp** Malaysia Inter-Religious Organisation. Vol. 1, (1970)-. Periodical. English. qt. Belangor Editorial Board M I R O, 16 Road 49E, Petaling Jaya Malaysia. **LC** BL1; .M34. **DD** 291/.05.

US/0898-3380
**SUFISM (SAN RAFAEL, CALIF.).** (SUFISM.). [Sufism]. **Added/Corp** International Association of Sufism. Vol. 1, No. 1 (Spring 1988)-. Periodical. English. Four times a year (Seasonally). $32.00 (institutions), $16.00 (individuals). International Association of Sufism, PO Box 2382, San Rafael CA 94912. **Tel** (415)472-6959, FAX (415)472-6959. **ED** Ali Kianfar Ph.D. and Nahid Angha Ph.D. **DD** 297. **Bk Rev**, (Qty: 12). **Ad Acc, Adv Mgr:** Blake Ross, **Tel** (415)472-6959. **Circ:** 2,000 (ctrl).
**Desc:** An artistic and intellectual journal dealing with indepth articles and essays related to Islam and Sufism. Subject categories include art, poetry, history, mysticism, science, philosophy as well as biographies of great saints.

US/0066-0868
**SUMMARY OF PROCEEDINGS. ANNUAL CONFERENCE / AMERICAN THEOLOGICAL LIBRARY ASSOCIATION.** **See** Library and Information Sciences.

US/0039-5161
**SUNDAY (ATLANTA, GA.).** (SUNDAY; THE MAGAZINE FOR THE LORD'S DAY.). **Added/Corp** Lord's Day Alliance of the United States. Vol. 55, No. 4 4th Qtr. (1969)-. Periodical. English. qt. Lords Day Alliance of the US, 2930 Flower Road South, Suite 16, Atlanta GA 30341. **Tel** (404)936-5377. available on microfilm from University Microfilms International (UMI). ***Continues*** *Lord's Day Leader.*

US/1057-3259
**SUNDAY BY SUNDAY.** (SUNDAY BY SUNDAY : LECTIONARY-BASED REFLECTION FOR ADULTS.). [Sunday Sunday]. **Added/Corp** Sisters of St. Joseph of Carondelet. Vol. 1, No. 1 (Oct. 6, 1991)-. Periodical. English. wk. $6.95. Sisters of St. Joseph of Carondelet, 1884 Randolph Avenue, St. Paul MN 55105. **DD** 242.

US/0736-9174
**SUNDAY SCHOOL YOUTH TEACHER.** Vol. 13, No. 2 (Jan./Feb./Mar. 1984)-. Periodical. English. qt. $7.75. Southern Baptist Convention, 901 Commerce, Suite 750, Nashville TN 37203. **Tel** (615)244-2355, FAX (615)742-8919. **(Subscription address:** Sunday School Board - Customer Service, 127 Ninth Avenue North, Nashville, TN 37234 USA; telephone: (800)458-2772) ***Continues*** *Youth Teacher, 0162-4865.*

US/0745-3558
**SUNDAY SERMONS.** (19??)-. Periodical. English. bm. $77.00 (1 year), $123.20 (2 year), $184.80 (3 year) US and Canada; $95.00 (1 year), $156.00 (2 year) other, including 1st class postage. Voicings Publications, PO Box 3102, Margate NJ 08402. **Tel** (609)822-9401.
**Desc:** Full text sermon resource for professional clergy. Non-denominational, this resource provides a full text sermon for each Sunday, plus New Year's Day, Good Friday, and Christmas. Texts follow ABC lectionary cycle.

CN/0827-312X
**SUNDIAL (TORONTO).** (THE SUNDIAL.). [Sundial]. March/April 1984-. Periodical. English. qt. Free with membership to Evangelical Fellowship of Canada. Evangelical Fellowship of Canada, PO Box 8800 Station B, Willowdale Ontario M2K 2R6 Canada. **Tel** (416)479-5885, FAX (416)479-4742. **ED** Anne R James. **DD** 269/.2. **Circ:** 11,000 (ctrl).
**Desc:** Commentary for members of the Evangelical Fellowship of Canada.

US/0562-6048
**SUNRISE (ALTADENA, CALIF.).** **See** Philosophy.

US/0363-1370
**SUNSTONE.** [Sunstone]. (1975)-. Periodical. English. Six times a year (Feb., Apr., June, Aug., Oct., Dec.). $32.00. Sunstone Foundation, 331 South Rio Grande Street, Suite 206, Salt Lake City UT 84101-1121. **Tel** (801)355-5926, (800)326-5926, FAX (801)355-4043. **ED** Elbert Peck. **LC** AP2; .S9755. **DD** 051. Index available. cum. index. **Bk Rev**, (Qty: 15-20). **Ad Acc, Adv Mgr:** K. Kolan, **Tel** (801)355-5926. **Pr Rev. Circ:** 10,000.
**Desc:** News and articles on mormons experiences, scholarships, issues and arts.

NE/0167-9732
**SUPPLEMENTS TO NOVUM TESTAMENTUM.** (1958)-. Monographic series. English (German and French). ir. Price varies per volume. E. J. Brill, Postbus 9000, 2300 PA Leiden Netherlands. **Tel** 011 31 71 312624, FAX 011 31 71 317532, telex 39296 BRILL NL. **ED** D. K. Barrett and A. F. J. Klyn. **Bk Rev. Ad Acc. Circ:** 1,350.
**Desc:** Covers the whole area of textual and literary criticism, the language, critical interpretation, theology, historical and literary background of the Novum Testamentum and early Christian literature.

NE/0083-5889
**SUPPLEMENTS TO VETUS TESTAMENTUM.** **Added/Corp** International Organization of Old Testament Scholars. International Organization for the Study of the Old Testament. **VFOAT** Vetus Testamentum. Supplements. Vol. 1 (1953)-. Monographic series. English (French and German). ir. Price varies per volume. E. J. Brill, Postbus 9000, 2300 PA Leiden Netherlands. **Tel** 011 31 71 312624, FAX 011 31 71 317532, telex 39296 BRILL NL. **ED** J. A. Emerton, W. L. Holladay. **Bk Rev. Ad Acc.** ctrl circ.
**Desc:** Covers the whole range of O.T. study, including history, literature, religion and theology, text, versions, language, etc.

NE/0920-623X
**SUPPLEMENTS TO VIGILIAE CHRISTIANAE.** Vol. 1 (1987)-. Monographic series. English (French, German and Latin). ir. Price varies per volume. E. J. Brill, Postbus 9000, 2300 PA Leiden Netherlands. **Tel** 011 31 71 312624, FAX 011 31 71 317532, telex 39296 BRILL NL. **LC** UNC. ***Continues*** *Philosophia Patrum.*
**Desc:** Covers early Christian literature, Church history, fathers of the Church and more.

US/0739-2419
**SUPPLIERS DIRECTORY (COLORADO SPRINGS, COLO.).** (SUPPLIERS DIRECTORY.). Directory. English. an. $64.95. CBA Service Corporation, PO Box 200, 2620 Venetucci Boulevard, Colorado Springs CO 80901. ***Continues*** *CBA Suppliers Directory.*

UK
**SURVEY OF CURRENT LITERATURE ON THE CHRISTIAN MISSION AND CHRISTIANITY IN THE NON-WESTERN WORLD (MICROFORM).** No. 1 (1982)-. Periodical. English. an. Scottish Institute of Missionary Studies, Aberdeen AB9 2 UB Scotland. ***Continues in part*** *Bulletin of the Scottish Institute of Missionary Studies.*

CN/0229-1975
**SURVIVE (VANCOUVER, B.C.).** (SURVIVE.). [Survive]. Periodical. English. mo. Free. Church of Scientology of British Columbia, 4857 Main Street, Vancouver British Columbia V5V 3R Canada. **DD** 299/.936. ctrl circ. Documents available from Ask*IEEE.
**Ind/Abst** INSPEC (Autumn 1991-).

SW/0346-217X
**SVENSK MISSIONSTIDSKRIFT.** [Sven. missionstidskr.]. **Added/Corp** Svenska Missionsrådet. (1913)-. Periodical. Swedish (summaries and/or abstracts in English; table of contents in English). qt (Mar., June, Sept., Dec.). Kr100.00 Scandinavia; Kr110.00 other. Swedish Institute of Missionary Research, Box 1767, S-11187 Stockholm Sweden. **Tel** 011 46 18 137525, FAX 011 46 18 215130, telex 19248. **ED** Carl Fredrik Hallencreutz. **LC** BV2355.S9; S9. Index available (published separately). cum. index. **Bk Rev. Ad Acc. Circ:** 1,000.
**Desc:** Religion, society and churches in the Third World Missionary research and reports.
**Ind/Abst** Bibliogr. Mission.; Index Book Rev. Relig.; Missionalia; Relig. Index One Period. (1967-); Relig. Theol. Abstr.

SW/0039-6761
**SVENSK TEOLOGISK KVARTALSKRIFT.** [Sven. teol. kvart.skr.]. **VFOAT** STK. (1925)-. Periodical. Swedish. qt. Kr310.00. Bloms Boktryckeri AB, Bytaregatan 6, 22221 Lund Sweden. **Tel** 46 46 111110, FAX 46 46 158594. **ED** G. Aulen. **LC** BR6; .S8. Index available (bound in fourth issue). cum. index. **Bk Rev. Circ:** 1,000.
**Desc:** Contains articles on actual theological and religious questions.
**Ind/Abst** Index Book Rev. Relig.; New Testam. Abstr.; Old Testam. Abstr.; Relig. Index One Period. (1971-); Relig. Theol. Abstr.

UK
**SWORD AND THE TROWEL, THE.** Vol. 1 (Jan. 1865)-. Periodical. English. Four times a year. £3.40 UK; £4.35. Metropolitan Tabernacle, Elephant & Castle, London SE1 6SD England. **Tel** 011 44 71 7357076, FAX 011 44 71 7357989.

US/0039-7547
**SWORD OF THE LORD, THE.** (1934)-. Periodical. English. bw. $12.00. The Sword of the Lord, PO Box 1099, Murfreesboro TN 37130. **Tel** (615)893-6700. **ED** Curtis Hutson, John A. Reynolds. Index available. cum. index. **Bk Rev. Ad Acc. Circ:** 125,000.

CN/0828-9131
**SWORD. SIKH WORLD ORGANIZATION'S REVIEW AND DIGEST.** (THE SWORD.). [SWORD, Sikh World Organ. rev. dig.]. **Added/Corp** World Sikh Organization of Canada. **VAT** Sikh World Organization's Review and Digest. Vol. 1, No. 1 (Apr. 1985)-. Periodical. English (summaries and/or abstracts in Panjabi). qt. Free to members. World Sikh Organization of Canada, PO Box L5830, Station F, Ottawa, Ontario, K2C 3S7 Canada. **DD** 294.6/05.
**Ind/Abst** Hum. Rights Intern. Rep.; SPORT Discus.

GW/0082-0660
**SYMBOLON.** ***Ceased.*** Vol. 1 (1960)-(1992). German. be. E J Brill, Antwerpener Str 6 12, W-5000 Koeln 1 Germany. **Tel** (221)516488, telex 22 14 304-ORBRI. **ED** Peter Gerlitz. **LC** BL600; .S94.

**Desc:** Articles on symbol research draw from the fields of comparative religion, ethnology, prehistory, early history, iconography, literature, sociology, psychology, etc.
**Ind/Abst** BHA : Biblio. Hist. Art (?-?).

CN/0710-1627
**SYNAXIS.** [Synaxis]. English. an. $6.00. Synaxis Press, PO Box 404, Chilliwack British Columbia V2P 6J7 Canada. **Tel** (604)858-7750. **DD** 230/.193. cum. index. **Bk Rev. Circ:** 1,700.
**Desc:** A traditionalist Orthodox Christian theological journal.
**Ind/Abst** Bibliogr. Mission.

FR/0294-7080
**SYSTEMES DE PENSEE EN AFRIQUE NOIRE.** **VFOAT** Sacrifice. Vol. 1 (1975)-. Periodical. English (French). **LC** BL2462.5. **DD** 299/.6/05.
**Ind/Abst** Anthropol. Lit.

●US/1059-6860
**SYZYGY (STANFORD, CALIF.).** (SYZYGY: JOURNAL OF ALTERNATIVE RELIGION AND CULTURE.). [Syzygy]. **Added/Corp** Center for Studies on New Religions (Torino, Italy) Institute for the Study of American Religion. (1992)-. Periodical. English (summaries and/or abstracts in French). Four times a year (Feb., May, Aug., Nov.). $30.00 (individual); $50.00 (institution). Center for Academic Publication, 160 North Fairview Avenue, Santa Barbara CA 93117. **Tel** (805)683-1676, FAX (805)683-4876. **LC** BP600; .S98. **DD** 299/.93.

UK/0039-8837
**TABLET (LONDON), THE.** (THE TABLET.). [Tablet]. V. 1- (No. 1- ); May 16, 1840-. English. wk. £40.00 UK; £102.00 (airmail) US. Tablet Publishing Company, 48 Great Peter Street, London SW1P 2HB England. **Tel** 222-7462, FAX 222-4967. **ED** John Wilkins. **LC** AP4; .T17. **DD** 052. **[CCC]**. Index available. **Bk Rev. Ad Acc. Circ:** 55,000. available on microfilm and microfiche from University Microfilms International (UMI).
**Desc:** Each week it seeks to instruct and entertain on religion, politics, society, ethics and the arts, considered in the light of Christian principles and beliefs.
**Ind/Abst** Abr. Cathol. Period. Lit. Index; Cathol. Period. Lit. Index.

US/1064-881X
**TABLETALK (LAKE MARY, FLA.).** (TABLE TALK.). [Tabletalk]. **Added/Corp** Ligonier Valley Study Center. Ligonier Ministries. **VFOAT** Tabletalk. Vol. 1, No. 1 (May 6, 1977)-. Periodical. English. mo. $24.00. Ligonier Ministries, P.O.Box 547500, Orlando FL 32854. **Tel** (800)435-4343, FAX (407)333-4233. **ED** R.C. Sproul, Jr. **DD** 268. **Circ:** 28,000 (ctrl).

CC
**TAIWAN CHURCH GROWTH BULLETIN.** Bulletin. English. ir. Taiwan Church Growth Society, PO Box 30-525, Taipei 107 Taiwan.

CH/0251-4788
**TAIWAN SHENXUE LUNKAN.** (TAI-WAN SHEN HSUEH LUN KAN.). [Taiwan shenxue lunkan]. **VFOAT** Taiwan Journal of Theology. Vol. 1, No. 1 (March 1979)-. Periodical. Chinese (English). $4.00. Taiwan Theological College, 20 Lane 2 Section 2 Yang Teh Ta Road, Shihlin Taipei Taiwan. **LC** BR118; .T35. **DD** 230/.05.
**Ind/Abst** Index Book Rev. Relig.; Relig. Index One Period. (1979-).

NE
**TALMON STUDIES IN BIBLICAL LITERATURE.** **See** Literature.

PH
**TAMBARA.** Vol. 1, No. 1 (March 1984)-. Periodical. English. an. $10.00. Ateneo de Davao University, PO Box 13, Davao City 8000 Philippines. **ED** Heidi K. Gloria. **LC** DS651; .T33. **DD** 959.9/005.

IS
**TANTUR NEWSLETTER.** No. 6- June 1974-. Newsletter. English. Ecumenical Institute, POB 19556, Jerusalem Israel. ***Continues*** *Newsletter - Ecumenical Institute for Advanced Theological Studies.*

CN/0712-2942
**TARGET (TORONTO).** (TARGET.). [Target]. **VFOAT** Piao Kan. Periodical. Chinese (English). bm. Ambassadors for Christ in Canada, 41 Cecil Street, Toronto Ontario M5T 1N1 Canada. **DD** 269/.2/05.

NR
**TCNN RESEARCH BULLETIN.** **Added/Corp** Theological College of Northern Nigeria. **VFOAT** T.C.N.N. Research Bulletin. No. 1 (July 1978)-. Periodical. English. Twice a year. $25.00. TCNN / Theological College of Northern Nigeria, PO Box 64, Bukuru Plateau State Nigeria. **ED** Roy Valencourt and Timothy Palmer. **LC** BR1463.N5; T25. **DD** 276.69/005. **Bk Rev. Circ:** 200 (ctrl).
**Desc:** Christian theology in the Nigerian context.

US/8755-8769
**TEACH (FORT WORTH, TEX.).** (TEACH / A NEWSLETTER FOR CHRISTIAN TEACHERS AND LEADERS.). [Teach]. **VFOAT** Teach Newsletter. Vol. 1, No. 1 (Jan./Feb. 1985)-. Newsletter. English. Four times a year (Mar., June, Sept., Dec.). $16.95. Sweet Publishing, Teach Newsletter, 3950 Fossil Creek Blvd, #201, Fort Worth TX 76137. **Tel** (800)531-5220, FAX (817)232-2030. **ED** Mary Hollingsworth. **DD** 268. **Bk Rev. Circ:** 5,000 (ctrl).
**Desc:** A newsletter for Christian teachers and church leaders. Practical, educational quick-read information and how-to-teach articles for all age levels. Non-denominational.

●US/1065-5182
**TEACHERS IN FOCUS.** **See** Education.

US/0894-7821
**TEACHERS INTERACTION.** [Teach. interact.]. **VFOAT** Interaction Newsletter; Teachers Interaction Newsletter. Vol. 28, No. 8 (Sept. 1987)-. Periodical. English. mo. $10.25. Concordia Publishing House, 3558 South Jefferson Avenue, St Louis MO 63118. **Tel** (314)268-1000, (800)325-3381, FAX (314)268-1329. **ED** Martha Streufer Jander. **DD** 284. **Circ:** 14,000. available on microfilm and microfiche from University Microfilms International (UMI); and Xerox. ***Continues*** *Interaction, 0020-5117.*
**Desc:** Designed with the volunteer church school teacher in mind. Includes educational, inspirational, theological and practical articles and helps.

US/0163-3422
**TEAM TORIZONS.** (TEAM HORIZONS.). **Main/Corp** Evangelical Alliance Mission. **VAT** The Evangelical Alliance Mission Horizons. Vol. 54, No. 3 (May/June 1978)-. Periodical. English. bm (Jan., Mar., May, July, Sept., Nov.). $2.00 (one year); $5.00 (three year). Evangelical Alliance Mission, PO Box 969, Wheaton IL 60187. **Tel** (708)653-5300. **ED** Jack Kilgore. **LC** BV2350; .M48. **DD** 266/.005. **Circ:** 40,000 (ctrl). ***Continues*** *Horizons.*

US/1076-9897
**TEEN LIFE (SPRINGFIELD, MO.).** (TEEN LIFE.). **Added/Corp** Assemblies of God. General Council. (1994)-. Periodical. English. qt. $3.60 (single issue). Gospel Publishing House, 1445 Boonville Avenue, Springfield MO 65802. **Tel** (417)862-2781, FAX (417)866-1146. **ED** Gary Legget. ***Continues*** *HiCall, 0018-120X.*
**Desc:** Paper designed to help build Christian character for teens.

●US/1059-3349
**TEEN STUDENT GUIDE (SPRINGFIELD, MO.).** **See** Children and Youth Interests.

●US/1059-3330
**TEEN TEACHER GUIDE (SPRINGFIELD, MO.).** (TEEN TEACHER GUIDE.). **Added/Corp** Assemblies of God. General Council. (1992)-. Periodical. English. qt. $9.20. Gospel Publishing House, 1445 Boonville Avenue, Springfield MO 65802. **Tel** (417)862-2781, FAX (417)866-1146. ***Continues*** *Teen Teacher, 0190-4574.*

US
**TEENAGE CHRISTIAN.** **See** Children and Youth Interests.

CG/1013-7769
**TELEMA (KINSHASA).** (TELEMA : LEVE-TOI ET MARCHE.). [Telema]. Vol. 5 No. 17 (Jan./Mar. 1979)-. Periodical. French. Four times a year (Jan., Apr., July, Oct.). $47.60 (surface mail); $62.60 (airmail). Revue Telema, Avenue P Boka 7, B P 3277, Kinshasa Gombe Zaire. **Tel** (204)945-3103. **ED** Boka di Mpasi Londi. **LC** BR3; .T44. **DD** 230/.2. **Bk Rev. Circ:** 2,500 (ctrl). ***Continues*** *Telema, 1013-7769.*
**Desc:** Christian (Ecumenical) reflections and creativity in Africa.
**Ind/Abst** Bibliogr. Mission.; New Testam. Abstr.; Old Testam. Abstr.

AT/1030-8768
**TELL.** Periodical. English. qt. 8.00Aus$. Fusion Australia, PO Box 105, Hornsby New South Wales, 2077 Australia. **Tel** 61 2 4777665, FAX 61 2 4764175. **ED** Mal Garvin and Richard Palmer. **Ad Acc. Circ:** 10,000.
**Desc:** Youth oriented magazine concerned with enhancing christian values in a way that is not alien to the youth culture.

●US/1063-9438
**TELL (CINCINNATI, OHIO).** (TELL : TEAM EXPANSION'S LOG OF LOVE.). [TELL]. **Added/Corp** Team Expansion (Organization). **VFOAT** Team Expansion's Log of Love. Vol. 10, No. 1 (June 1992)-. Periodical. English. qt (Mar., June, Sept., Dec.). $1.00 US; $8.00 other. Team Expansion, PO Box 4100, Cincinnati OH 45204. **Tel** (800)447-0800, FAX (513)244-8430. **DD** 266. ***Continues*** *Vital Signs.*

FI/0497-1817
**TEMENOS.** [Temenos]. **Added/Corp** Suomen Uskontotieteellinen Seura. Vol. 1 (1965)-. Periodical. English (French and German). an (Nov.). Fl187.00. Finnish Society for the Study of Comparative Religion, Henrikinkatu 3, 20500 Turku Finland. **(Subscription address:** Akateeminen Kirjakauppa, PO Box 23, SF-00371 Helsinki Finland**)** **ED** Lauri Honko. **LC** BL1.A1; T45. **DD** 291/.05. Index available. Documents available from The Genuine Article.
**Desc:** Studies in comparative religion presented by scholars in Denmark, Finland, Norway and Sweden.
**Ind/Abst** Anthropol. Index; Arts Humanit. Citation Index (19??-19??) [Full Cov.]; Curr. Contents Arts Humanit.; MLA Int. Bibl. Books Artic. Mod. Lang. Lit.; Res. Alert [Full Cov.]; Soc. Sci. Cit. Index [Select. Cov.].

FR
**TEMOIGNAGE MESSIANIQUE AU PEUPLE D'ISRAEL.** French. qt (4 issues). 60.00F. Centre Messianique, Boite Postale 161, 75523 Paris Cedex 11 France. **Tel** 011 33 1 48058973. **ED** Paul Ghennassia. **Circ:** 6,000 (ctrl).
**Desc:** Contains articles and information about messianic works in Israel and in the world.

US
**TENNESSEE ARCHIVISTS.** **Added/Corp** Tennessee Archivists. **VFOAT** TA. No. 2 (Fall 1977)-. Periodical. English. Four times a year. $10.00 (institutional membership). Disciples of Christ Historical Society, 1101 19th Avenue South, Nashville TN 37212. **Tel** (615)327-1444, FAX (615)327-1445. ***Continues*** *Tennessee Archivists News & Notes.*

JA/0495-1492
**TENRI JOURNAL OF RELIGION.** No. 1 (Mar. 1955)-. Periodical. English. an. Tenri University Press, Tenri Central Library, Tenri-Shi, Nara 632 Japan. **Tel** 07436-3-1515, FAX 07436-3-7723. **LC** BL1; .T4. **DD** 200/.5.
**Ind/Abst** Bibliogr. Mission.

JA/0040-3482
**TENRIKYO.** **Added/Corp** Tenrikyo. Kaigai Dendobu. No. 1 (January 1962)-. Periodical. English. Twelve times a year. $50.00. Tenrikyo Overseas Mission Dept, Translation Section, 271 Mishima, Tenri 632 Japan. **Tel** 67436 3-1511 ext. 6530, . **LC** BL2222.T4; T385. **DD** 299/.5619. ***Supersedes*** *Tenrikyo.*

JA
**TENRIKYO TOKEI NENKAN.** **VFOAT** Statistical Year Book of Tenrikyo. Vol. 1, No. 6- 1931-. Multiple languages (Japanese and English). Tenrikyo Kyokai Hombu, Mishima-cho Tenri-shi Nara-ken, Tenri Japan. **LC** BL2222.T4; T43.

SP/0495-1549
**TEOLOGIA ESPIRITUAL.** (TEOLOGIA ESPIRITUAL : REVISTA CUATRIMESTRAL DE LOS ESTUDIOS.). [Teol. espirit.]. **Added/Corp** Facultad de Teologia San Vicente Ferrer. Seccion Padres Dominicos. Estudios Generales Dominicanos de Espana. Vol. 1, No. 1 (Jan./April 1957)-. Periodical. Spanish. Three times a year. 3300.00ptas Spain; 4300.00ptas other. Teologia Espiritual, C Pouet de Sant Vicent 1, 46003 Valencia Spain. **Tel** 011 34 6 3528481. **LC** BX2350.65; .T46. **DD** 248/.05. Index available. cum. index. **Circ:** 500.
**Ind/Abst** MLA Int. Bibl. Books Artic. Mod. Lang. Lit.

CL/0049-3449
**TEOLOGIA Y VIDA.** [Teol. vida]. **Added/Corp** Universidad Catolica de Chile. Facultad de Teologia. Vol. 1, (Jan./March 1960)-. Periodical. Spanish. Four times a year (Mar., June, Sept., Dec.). 35,00Chil$. Facultad de Teologia UC, Casilla Postal 316, Correo 22, Santiago Chile. **Tel** 011 56 2 2744041 Ext. 2075. **ED** Marciano Barrios Valdes. cum. index (1960-1979). **Bk Rev. Ad Acc, Adv Mgr:** Marciano Barrios V., **Tel** 274.40.41. ax.2075. **Circ:** 1,000. available on microfilm from University Microfilms International (UMI).
**Desc:** Theological reflection for the world of today. Studies, reflections, church documents and reviews of books, and international and Latin-American journals.
**Ind/Abst** Bibliogr. Mission.; Canon Law Abstr.; New Testam. Abstr.; Old Testam. Abstr.; Abr. Cathol. Period. Lit. Index; Cathol. Period. Lit. Index.

FI/0040-3555
**TEOLOGINEN AIKAKAUSKIRJA. TEOLOGISK TIDSKRIFT.** **VFOAT** Teologisk Tidskrift. Vol. 1, (1896)-. Periodical. Finnish (Swedish). Six times a year (Jan., Mar., May, Sept., Nov., Dec.). Fmk150.00 Finland and Scandinavia; Fmk210.00 other. Teologinen Aikakauskirja, Fabianinkatn 7, SF-00130 Helsinki Finland. **Tel** 80-1913036, FAX 80-1913033. **ED** Juha Seppo. **LC** BR9.F5; T4. Index available (Bound in Jan. iss.). cum. index (Til 1983). **Bk Rev**, (Qty: 160). **Ad Acc. Circ:** 3,000 (ctrl).
**Desc:** Theological articles and book reviews.

NO
**TEOLOGISK FORUM.** (1987)-. Periodical. Norwegian, Danish and Swedish. sa. $20.00 Norway; $25.00 other. Methodist Theological Seminary, Vestlundveien 27, N-5033 Fyllingsdalen Norway. **Tel** 47 55 161727. **ED** Roar G Fotland. Index available. **Ad Acc. Circ:** 150.
**Desc:** Articles dealing with Methodism: its doctrine, history, etc, in Scandinavia.

NE
**TER HERKENNING.** Vol. 1 (Feb. 1973)-. Periodical. Dutch. bm. Fl14.00. SDU Uitgeverij, Postbus

20014, Christoffel Plan, 2500 EA Den Haag Netherlands. **Tel** 011 31 70 3789911. Index available. **Bk Rev. Ad Acc.** ***Formed by the union of*** *Christus en Israel* ***and*** *Kerk en Israel.*

IT
**TERESIANUM.** [Teresianum]. **Added/Corp** Teresianum. Vol. 33, No. 1/2 (1982)-. English (French, German, Italian, Latin and Spanish). sa (June & Dec.). L50000. Edizioni de Teresianum, Piazza San Pancrazio 5A, Rome 00152 Italy. **Tel** 011 39 6 582362, 011 39 6 5810140. **ED** P Virgilio Pasquetto. **Bk Rev. Circ:** 700 (ctrl). ***Continues*** *Ephemerides Carmeliticae.*
**Desc:** We publish all articles dealing with religious and Christian spirituality.
**Ind/Abst** Bibliogr. Mission.; BHA : Biblio. Hist. Art; New Testam. Abstr.; Old Testam. Abstr.

US/0743-572X
**TESTAMENT.** Vol. 1, No. 1 (Apr. 1984)-. Periodical. English. qt. Church of God, PO Box 46041, Denver CO 80201.

IT/0040-3989
**TESTIMONIANZE.** [Testimonianze]. (1957)-. Periodical. Italian. Twelve times a year. L60000 (regular subscribers) Italy; L120000 (others); L150000 (sustaining). Testimonianze, Via dei Roccettini 11, 50016 Domenico Fiesole Italy.
**Ind/Abst** Old Testam. Abstr.

US/1045-3989
**TESTIMONY OF TRUTH, THE.** [Testimony truth]. **Added/Corp** People of the Living God. No. 298 (Aug. 1988)-. Periodical. English. mo. People of the Living God, 2101 Prytania Street, New Orleans LA 70130. **DD** 261. ***Continues*** *Testimony (McMinnville, Tenn.).*

US/0746-9756
**TEXAS CHURCH WOMAN.** (TEXAS CHURCH WOMAN / CHURCH WOMEN UNITED IN TEXAS.). Periodical. English. bm. $2.00. Texas Church Woman, Route 3 Box 176, Hereford TX 79045.

GW/0082-3775
**TEXTUS PATRISTICI ET LITURGICI.** No. 1-1964-. Monographic series. German. ir. Price varies per volume. Verlag Friedrich Pustet, Gutenbergstrasse 8, D-93051 Regensburg. **Tel** 0941 9 20 22-0, FAX 0941 94 86 52, telex 6 56 72.

CN/0229-964X
**TFP INFORME.** ***Ceased.*** [TFP inf.]. **Added/Corp** Jeunes Canadiens Pour une Civilisation Chretienne. **VFOAT** Tradition, Famille, Propriete; TFP : Tradition, Famille, Propriete. **VAT** Tradition, Famille Propriete Informe. No. 1 (1980)-(199?). Periodical. French. Three times a year. Jeunes Canadiens pour une Civilisation Chretienne, CP 566 Succurslae Youville, Montreal Quebec H2P 2W1 Canada. **DD** 248.4/05.

CN/0229-9631
**TFP NEWSLETTER.** ***Ceased.*** [TFP newsl.]. **VFOAT** Tradition, Family, Property; TFP : Tradition, Family, Property. **VAT** Tradition, Family, Property Newsletter. No. 1 (1980)-(1992). Newsletter. English. Three times a year. Young Canadians For a Christian Civilization, PO Box 566, Youville Station, Montreal Quebec H2P 2W1 Canada. **DD** 248.4/05.

UK/0307-8388
**THEMELIOS.** [Themelios]. Vol. 1-11 No. 2 (Oct. 1962)-(Summer 1975) New Ser. Vol. 1 (Autumn 1975)-. Periodical. English. Three times a year. $10.00, $15.00 (airmail) one year; $18.00, $28.00 (airmail) two year; $26.00, $41.00 (airmail) three year. UCCF Subscription Department, 38 de Montfort Street, Leicester LE1 7GP England. **Tel** (0533)551700, FAX (0533)555672. **ED** Christopher Wright. **DD** 201/.1/05. Index available. cum. index. **Bk Rev. Circ:** 1,000. available on microfilm and microfiche from University Microfilms International (UMI). ***Absorbed*** *Theological Students Fellowship. TSF Bulletin.*
**Desc:** An international journal for theological students, expounding and defending the historic Christian faith.
**Ind/Abst** Index Book Rev. Relig.; New Testam. Abstr.; Old Testam. Abstr.; Relig. Index One Period.; Relig. Theol. Abstr.

GW/0720-9525
**THEMEN DER PRAKTISCHEN THEOLOGIE, THEOLOGIA PRACTICA.** **VFOAT** Theologia Practica. Vol. 16 No. 1/2 (1981)-. Periodical. German. Four times a year. DM65.80 Germany; DM69.00 other. Kaiser Verlag Zeitschriften, Quell Verlag Furtbachstr 12A, D 70178 Stuttgart Germany. **Tel** 011 49 711 6010057, FAX 011 49 711 6010076. **[CCC]. Bk Rev. Ad Acc. Circ:** 1,200. ***Continues*** *Theologia Practica, 0049-3643.*

US/0362-0085
**THEOLOGIA 21.** **VAT** Theologia Twenty-One. Vol. 6 (Jan. 1976)-. Periodical. English. ir. $15.00. Dominion Press / Oregon, PO Box 4608, Salem OR 97302. **ED** Friend Stuart. Index available. cum. index. **Circ:** 100 (ctrl). available on microfilm from University Microfilms International (UMI). ***Continues*** *Immortality Newsletter, 0019-2783.*
**Desc:** The official organ of the Affiliated Christian Imortalists, covering advanced metaphysical theology. An alternative interpretation of Christianity, completely Bible-based. A theology for the 21st century.

GR/1105-154X
**THEOLOGIA ATHENAI.** [TheologiaAthenai]. **VFOAT** Theologie (Athenes). (1923)-. Periodical. Greek, Modern. qt. **UDC** 281.9.
**Ind/Abst** BHA : Biblio. Hist. Art.

SA
**THEOLOGIA EVANGELICA.** (Apr. 1968)-. Periodical. Afrikaans (English). Three times a year. R12.00 South Africa; $9.00 other. University of South Africa, PO Box 392, Pretoria 0001 South Africa. **Tel** 011 27 12 4298468, FAX 011 (27)12 429 3321, telex (59)350068+. **LC** BR9.A34; T46. **DD** 230/.05. available on microfilm from University Microfilms International (UMI).
**Ind/Abst** Index Book Rev. Relig.; New Testam. Abstr.; Old Testam. Abstr.; Relig. Index One Period.; Relig. Theol. Abstr.

NE/0040-5612
**THEOLOGIA REFORMATA.** Began with Vol. 1 in 1957. Periodical. Dutch. qt. F57.50. Oosterbaan & Le Cointre B V, Postbus 25, 4460 AA Goes Netherlands. **Tel** (011)31-1100-15591, FAX (011)31-1100-16492. cum. index.

SA
**THEOLOGIA VIATORUM (PIETERSBURG, SOUTH AFRICA).** (THEOLOGIA VIATORUM.). **Added/Corp** University of the North (South Africa). Faculty of Theology. Vol. 1, No. 1 (Nov. 1973)-. Periodical. English (Afrikaans). sa. R1.24 South Africa; R1.50 other. Private Bag X1102, Sovenga Transvaal, Republic of South Africa. **LC** BR1; .T49. **DD** 230/.05.

HU/0133-7599
**THEOLOGIAI SZEMLE.** [Theol. szle.]. V. 1, No. 1 (Easter 1925)-1st Review, 1948. Periodical. Hungarian. mo. $41.00. Bekes Megyei Lapkiado Vallalat Bekescsaba, SZT Istvan Ter 3, 5601 Hungary. **Tel** 227-870. **LC** BR9.H8; T45. Index available. cum. index. **Bk Rev. Ad Acc. Circ:** 1,600.
**Desc:** Scientific theological periodical.
**Ind/Abst** Am. Hist. Life (1963-1972, 1987-).

UK/0954-2191
**THEOLOGICAL BOOK REVIEW.** [Theol. book rev.]. (1988)-. Periodical. English. Three times a year. $30.00. Feed the Minds, Robertson House, Leas Road, Guildford Surrey GU1 4QW England. **Tel** 011 44 483 577877, FAX 011 44 483 301387. **ED** Patrick Lambe. **DD** 016.2. **Bk Rev. Circ:** 500.
**Desc:** Current awareness journal containing notes and reviews of English language theology within six months of publication.

CN/1184-8901
**THEOLOGICAL DIGEST & OUTLOOK.** [Theol. dig. outlook]. **Added/Corp** Church Alive (Society). **VAT** Theological Digest and Outlook. Vol. 6, No. 1 (Jan. 1991)-. Periodical. English. Twice a year (Jan., July). 15.00Can$ Canada; 17.00Can$ US; 20.00Can$ other. Church Alive, 265 Linden Avenue, Burlington Ontario L7L 2P4 Canada. **Tel** (905)634-9834, FAX (905)634-9834. **ED** Graham Scott. **DD** 230/.792/05. cum. index (begins with 1994). **Bk Rev**, (Qty: 5). **Ad Acc. Circ:** 700. ***Continues*** *Theological Digest., 0847-0065.*
**Desc:** Attempts to make a clear, Biblical witness to Jesus Christ crucified, risen and exalted; to encourage rigorous theological enquiry and discussion; to challenge doctrinal inadequacies; to encourage spiritual growth through prayer, Bible learning sacramental worship and other means of grace; to encourage a truly prophetic approach to the culture.

US/0040-5620
**THEOLOGICAL EDUCATION.** [Theol. educ.]. **Added/Corp** Association of Theological Schools in the United States and Canada. American Association of Theological Schools in the United States and Canada. Vol. 1, (Autumn 1964)-. Periodical. English. Twice a year (May, Nov.). $7.00 US; $8.00 others. Association of Theological Schools, 10 Summit Park Drive, Pittsburgh PA 15275. **Tel** (412)788-6505, FAX (412)788-6510. **ED** David Schuller. **LC** BV4019; .A543. **DD** 207/.73. **Circ:** 3,200 (ctrl). available on microfilm and microfiche from University Microfilms International (UMI).
**Desc:** Only periodical in North America dealing with major issues of theological education.
**Ind/Abst** Index Book Rev. Relig.; Relig. Index One Period. (1964-); Relig. Theol. Abstr.

US/0198-6856
**THEOLOGICAL EDUCATOR, THE.** [Theol. educ.]. **Added/Corp** New Orleans Baptist Theological Seminary. (19??)-. Periodical. English. Twice a year (Spring and Fall). $8.00 (one year), $14.00 (two year), $18.00 (three year);. New Orleans Baptist Theological Seminary, 3939 Gentilly Boulevard, New Orleans LA 70126. **Tel** (504)286-3610, FAX (504)286-3639. **ED** Paul E. Robertson. **LC** BR1; .T574. **DD** 230/.05. Index available. cum. index. **Bk Rev**, (Qty: 75-100). **Ad Acc. Circ:** 2,500.
**Desc:** A journal of theology and ministry.
**Ind/Abst** Guide Soc. Sci. Relig.; New Testam. Abstr.; South. Baptist Period. Index.

UK
**THEOLOGICAL NEWS.** **Added/Corp** World Evangelical Fellowship. Theological Assistance Programme. World Evangelical Fellowship. Theological Commission. (1969?)-. Periodical. English. qt. $8.00 US. World Evangelical Fellowship, PO Box 94, Theological Comm., Seoul 120 650 Korea. **Tel** 011 82 2 3939895. cum. index. ***Absorbed*** *Theological Education Today.*

LE/0379-9557
**THEOLOGICAL REVIEW (BEIRUT, LEBANON).** (THEOLOGICAL REVIEW.). [Theol. rev.]. **Added/Corp** Near East School of Theology (Beirut, Lebanon). **VFOAT** Theological Review of the Near East School of Theology. Vol. 1 (April 1978)-. Periodical. English (Arabic, French and German). sa. $24.00 (one year), $46.00 (two year), $67.00 (three year). The Near East School of Theology, PO Box 13-5780, Chouran, Beirut Lebanon. **Tel** 346708, telex NEST LE V 44246. **ED** George Sabra. **LC** BR1; .T585. **DD** 205. **Bk Rev. Circ:** 300. available on microfilm from University Microfilms International (UMI). ***Continues*** *Quarterly (Near East School of Theology (Beirut, Lebanon)).*
**Ind/Abst** Index Book Rev. Relig.; New Testam. Abstr.; Old Testam. Abstr.; Relig. Index One Period. (1978-); Relig. Theol. Abstr.; Middle East J.

US/0040-5639
**THEOLOGICAL STUDIES (BALTIMORE).** (THEOLOGICAL STUDIES.). [Theol. stud.]. Vol. 1 (Feb. 1940)-. Periodical. English. qt. $20.00 (individual), $27.00 (institution) US; $27.00 (individual), $32.00 (institution) other. Sheridan Press, PO Box 465, Hanover PA 17331. **Tel** (800)352-2210, (717)632-3535, FAX (717)633-8900. **LC** BX801; .T45. **DD** 230.05. available on microfilm and microfiche from University Microfilms International (UMI). Documents available from The Genuine Article, UMI Article Clearinghouse.
**Desc:** Research articles in biblical, historical, systematic, pastoral, spiritual theology; annual survey of developments in ethics and moral theology.
**Ind/Abst** Acad. Search (July 1993-); Arts Humanit. Citation Index [Full Cov.]; Bibliogr. Mission.; BHA : Biblio. Hist. Art; Book Rev. Index; Canon Law Abstr.; Curr. Contents Arts Humanit.; Expand. Acad. Index (1989-); Humanit. Index; Humanit. Source (Jul. 1993-); Index Book Rev. Relig.; INFO-SOUTH Abstr.; Mag. Search; New Testam. Abstr.; Newsp. Period. Abstr. (1991-); Old Testam. Abstr.; Relig. Index One Period. (1949-); Relig. Theol. Abstr.; Res. Alert [Full Cov.]; Soc. Sci. Cit. Index [Select. Cov.]; Abr. Cathol. Period. Lit. Index; Cathol. Period. Lit. Index.

GW
**THEOLOGIE DER GEGENWART.** (Winter 1960)-. Periodical. German. Four times a year. DM32.00 Germany; DM44.00 other. Verlag Butzon Bercker GmbH, Postfach 215, D 47613 Kevelaer Germany. **Tel** 011 49 2832 9290. cum. index. **Bk Rev. Ad Acc.** ctrl circ. ***Continues*** *Theologischer Digest.*
**Desc:** International information about the actuality of theology.

GW/0939-5121
**THEOLOGIE FUER DIE PARXIS.** [Theol. Prax.]. (1975)-. Periodical. German. Twice a year (Spring and Fall). DM16.00. Christliches Verlagshaus GmbH, Postfach 311141, Motorstrasse 36, D-70471 Stuttgart Germany. **Tel** 011 49 711 830000, FAX 011 49 711 83000-10. **UDC** 22/28.

FR/0563-4253
**THEOLOGIE HISTORIQUE.** **Added/Corp** Institut Catholique de Paris. (1963)-. Monographic series. French. ir. Price varies per volume. Beauchesne Editeur, 72 rue des Saints Peres, 75007 Paris France. **Tel** 011 33 1 45488028. **LC** UNC.
**Desc:** History of Christianity in France-Roman Catholic Church, Reformation, Protestantism.

GW/0049-366X
**THEOLOGIE UND GLAUBE.** [Theol. Glaube]. Vol. 1 (1909)-. German. qt. DM66.00 Germany; DM68.00 other. Ferdinand Schoeningh Verlag, Postfach 2540, D 33055 Paderborn Germany. **Tel** 011 49 5251 127665. **LC** BR4; .T38. **[CCC].** Index available. **Ad Acc. Circ:** 750 (ctrl).
**Ind/Abst** Bibliogr. Mission.; Canon Law Abstr.; New Testam. Abstr.; Old Testam. Abstr.

GW/0040-5655
**THEOLOGIE UND PHILOSOPHIE.** [Theol. Philos.]. Vol. 41 (1966)-. Periodical. German. qt (4 issues). DM228.00. Verlag Herder Freiburg, Postfach 79080, Frieburg, Germany. **Tel** (0761)27-17-0, FAX (0761)27 17-520, telex 761489. ***Continues*** *Scholastik.*
**Ind/Abst** Annu. Bibliogr. Engl. Lang. Lit.; Bibliogr. Mission.; Canon Law Abstr.; Index Book Rev. Relig.; New Testam. Abstr.; Philos. Index.

GW/0342-2372
**THEOLOGISCHE BEITRAEGE.** [Theol. Beitr.]. (1970)-. Periodical. German. bm (Feb., Apr., June, Aug., Oct., Dec.). DM49.50. R Brockhaus Verlag,

Postfach 110152, W 5600 Wuppertal 11 Germany. **Tel** 011 49 2104 691134. **ED** Heinz D. Becker. **Bk Rev**. **Ad Acc**. ctrl circ.
**Ind/Abst** New Testam. Abstr.; Old Testam. Abstr.

GW/0563-430X
**THEOLOGISCHE BUCHEREI.** Vol. 1 (1953)-. Monographic series. German. ir. Price varies per volume. Christian Kaiser Verlag, Lilienstrasse 70, D-81669 Munich Germany. **Tel** 011 49 89 483014. **(Subscription address:** VVA Bertelsmann Distributors GmbH, Postfach 7777, D-33310 Guetersloh Germany.**)** **ED** Gerhard Sauter. **Circ:** 1,500.

GW/0040-5671
**THEOLOGISCHE LITERATURZEITUNG.** [Theol. Litztg.]. Vol. 1 (Jan. 1876)-. Periodical. German (English and French). Twelve times a year. DM198.00 Germany; DM228.00 other. Evangel Verlagsanstalt Gmbh, Postfach 1467, D 04025 Leipzig Germany. **Tel** 011 49 341 7114122, FAX 49 341 295383. **ED** Ernst-Heinz Amberg. **LC** Z7753; .T39. Index available. **Bk Rev. Circ:** 3,500. ***Absorbed** Theologisches Literaturblatt, 0323-6285.*
**Desc:** Book reviews on all fields of theology and religion, with summaries on special theological questions. Includes bibliography.
**Ind/Abst** BHA : Biblio. Hist. Art; Index Book Rev. Relig.; New Testam. Abstr.; Old Testam. Abstr.; Relig. Index One Period. (1963-); Relig. Theol. Abstr.

GW/0342-1430
**THEOLOGISCHE QUARTALSCHRIFT (MUNCHEN).** (THEOLOGISCHE QUARTALSCHRIFT.). [Theol. Quartalschr.]. **VFOAT** Tubingen Quartalschrift. (1819)-. Periodical. German. qt (Mar., June, Sept., Dec.). DM64.00. Erich Wewel Verlag, Anzinger Strasse 15, D 81671 Munich Germany. **Tel** 011 49 89 41300120, FAX 011 49 89 300138, telex FS 5-22504 MANZ D. **ED** Erich Wewel Verlag. **LC** BR4; .T45. **[CCC].** Index available (Bound in next issue). **Bk Rev**, (Qty: 50). **Ad Acc. Circ:** 500 (ctrl).
**Ind/Abst** Bibliogr. Mission.; Index Book Rev. Relig.; New Testam. Abstr.; Old Testam. Abstr.; Relig. Index One Period.; Relig. Theol. Abstr.

GW/0040-568X
**THEOLOGISCHE REVUE.** [Theol. Rev.]. **Added/Corp** Universitat Munster. Katholisch-Theologische Fakultat. (1902)-. Periodical. German. bm. DM96.00 Germany; $38.23 US. Aschendorffsche Verlagsbuchhandlung, Postfach 1124, D-48135 Muenster Germany. **Tel** 011 49 251 690132, telex 08-92 830 WN MS D. **LC** BR4; .T47. **DD** 230/.05. **[CCC].** Index available. **Bk Rev. Ad Acc. Circ:** 900.
**Desc:** Critical reviews of theological literature especially Roman Catholic church, current bibliography of important theological publications, international discussions of new works.
**Ind/Abst** Bibliogr. Mission.; BHA : Biblio. Hist. Art; New Testam. Abstr.

GW/0040-5698
**THEOLOGISCHE RUNDSCHAU.** [Theol. Rundsch.]. (1897)-(Dec. 1917); New Series, Vol. 1 (1918)-. Periodical. German. qt. DM138.00. JCB Mohr / Paul Siebeck, Postfach 2040, D 72010 Tuebingen Germany. **Tel** 011 49 7071 9230, FAX 011 49 7071 51104, telex 7/262872 mohr d. **ED** Jorg Baur and Lothar Perlitt. **LC** BR4; .T5. **DD** 230.05. **[CCC].** cum. index. **Bk Rev. Ad Acc. Circ:** 1,200. ***Absorbed** Deutsche Theologie.*
**Desc:** Aims to inform those interested in theological work by collective reports and sporadically by single reviews of important results and present problems in all theological fields.
**Ind/Abst** BHA : Biblio. Hist. Art; Index Book Rev. Relig.; New Testam. Abstr.; Old Testam. Abstr.; Relig. Index One Period. (1978-); Relig. Theol. Abstr.

SZ
**THEOLOGISCHE STUDIEN.** Vol. 1 (1938)-. German. Theologischer Verlag Zuerich, Raeffelstrasse 20, CH8045 Zuerich Switzerland. **Tel** 011 41 1 4617710.

SZ/0040-5701
**THEOLOGISCHE ZEITSCHRIFT.** [Theol. Z.]. **Added/Corp** Universitat Basel. Theologische Fakultat. (June 1945)-. Periodical. German. Four times a year (Feb., May, Sept., Dec.). 96.00F Switzerland; 97.00F Europe; 107.00F others. Verlag Friedrich Reinhardt AG, Missionstrasse 36, CH-4012 Basel Switzerland. **Tel** 011 41 61 2613390. **ED** K. Seybold. **LC** BR4; .T62. **DD** 230/.05. **Bk Rev. Ad Acc. Circ:** 800.
**Desc:** Lectures and articles on theological subjects.
**Ind/Abst** Annu. Bibliogr. Engl. Lang. Lit.; Index Book Rev. Relig.; New Testam. Abstr.; Old Testam. Abstr.; Relig. Index One Period. (1949-); Relig. Theol. Abstr.

GW
**THEOLOGISCHER HANDKOMMENTAR ZUM NEUEN TESTAMENT.** German. ir. Evangel Verlagsanstalt Gmbh, Postfach 1467, D 04025 Leipzig Germany. **Tel** 011 49 341 7114122, FAX 49 341 295383. **(Subscription address:** LKG Leipziger Komm & Grossbuch, Postfach 520, D 04005 Leipzig Germany**)**

GW
**THEOLOGISCHES WORTERBUCH ZUM ALTEN TESTAMENT.** (19??)-. Monographic series. German. ir. Price varies per volume. W Kohlhammer Verlag GmbH, Postfach 800430, D 70549 Stuttgart Germany. **Tel** 011 49 711 78631, FAX 011 49 711 7863263, telex 7-255820.

IT
**THEOLOGOS, HO.** **Added/Corp** Facolta Teologica di Sicilia "S. Giovanni Evangelista.". (19??)-. Periodical. Italian. Three times a year. L50000 Italy; L60000 others. Opera Universit Faculto Teologica, S. Giovanni Evangelista, Corso Vittorio Emanuele 463, 90134 Palermo Italy. **Tel** 011 39 91 6111839, FAX 011 39 91 611870. Index available. cum. index. **Bk Rev**, (Qty: 15-20). **Pr Rev. Circ:** 400 (ctrl).

HK/0253-3812
**THEOLOGY & LIFE (HONG KONG).** (THEOLOGY & LIFE.). [Theol. life]. **VFOAT** Theology and Life; Shen Hsueh Yu Sheng Huo. No. 1 (May 1977)-. Periodical. Chinese (English). an. HK$30.00 Hong Kong; HK$45.00 Asia and Africa; HK$65.00 other. Lutheran Theological Seminary / Hong Kong, PO Box 20, Shatin NT Hong Kong. **Tel** 6911520, 0615213, FAX 852 6918458. **ED** Andrew K H Hsiao and Thor Strandenaes. **Pr Rev. Circ:** 1,100 (ctrl).
**Ind/Abst** Index Book Rev. Relig.; Relig. Index One Period. (1977-).

US
**THEOLOGY AND LIFE SERIES.** **VFOAT** Theology & Life Series. Vol. 1 (1983)-. Monographic series. English. ir. Price varies per volume. Michael Glazier, 1935 West 4th Street, Wilmington DE 19805.

US/1052-9314
**THEOLOGY & PUBLIC POLICY.** [Theol. public policy]. **Added/Corp** Churches' Center for Theology and Public Policy (Washington, D.C.). **VFOAT** Theology and Public Policy. (Fall 1989)-. Periodical. English. sa. $10.00 US; $13.00 other. Churches Center for Theology and Public Policy, 4500 Massachusetts Avenue Northwest, Washington DC 20016-5690. **Tel** (202)885-8648. **ED** James A. Nash. **LC** BJ1188.5; .T48. **DD** 261.8/05. Index available. cum. index. **Circ:** 1,200.
**Desc:** Interpretations of the meaning of the Christian vision and mission for social policies, in order to enhance the churches' witness.

UK
**THEOLOGY AND SCIENCE AT THE FRONTIERS OF KNOWLEDGE.** No. 1 (1985)-. Monographic series. English. Price varies per volume. **(Subscription address:** US/ PO Box 620000, Orlando, FL 32891-8340; UK/ Foots Cray High Street, Sidcup, Kent DA14 5HP England; Aus-NZ/ Locked Bag 16, Marrickville NSW 2204 Australia; telephone: US/ (800)543-9534, FAX: (407)363-9661; UK/ 081-300-3322, FAX: 081-309-0807**)**

US/0040-5728
**THEOLOGY DIGEST.** [Theol. dig.]. **Added/Corp** St. Louis University (Mo.) St. Mary's College, St. Marys, Kan. St. Louis University. School of Divinity. Vol. 1 (Winter 1953)-. Periodical. English. qt. $12.00 (one year), $22.00 (two year) US; $16.00 (one year), $28.00 (two year) other. Theology Digest, 3634 Lindell Boulevard, St Louis MO 63108. **Tel** (314)658-2857, (314)658-2859, FAX (314)658-3874. **ED** Bernhard A Asen. **LC** BX801; .T48. **DD** 230.2. cum. index. **Bk Rev. Ad Acc. Circ:** 5,000 (ctrl). available on microfilm and microfiche from University Microfilms International (UMI).
**Desc:** Offers condensations of recent significant articles selected from theological journals originally appearing in eight different languages.
**Ind/Abst** Bibliogr. Mission.; Missionalia; Old Testam. Abstr.; Relig. Theol. Abstr.; Abr. Cathol. Period. Lit. Index; Cathol. Period. Lit. Index.

GW/0176-1439
**THEOLOGY IN CONTEXT.** **Added/Corp** Missionswissenschaftliches Institut Missio. **VFOAT** Theologie im Kontext. Vol. 1, No. 1 (1984)-. English (German and Spanish). sa (Feb. and July). $20.00 (surface mail); $28.00 (air mail). Missionswissensch Institut EV, Goethestrasse 43, Postfach 1110, D 52012 Aachen Germany. **Tel** 011 49 241 75071, telex 0832719. **LC** Z7753; .T38; BR118. **DD** 016.23/009172/4. **Circ:** 850.
**Ind/Abst** Bibliogr. Mission.

UK/0040-571X
**THEOLOGY (LONDON).** (THEOLOGY.). [Theol.]. **Added/Corp** Society for Promoting Christian Knowledge (Great Britain). (1920)-. Periodical. English. bm (Jan., Mar., May, July, Sept., Nov.). £15.00 UK; $30.00 US. Society for Promoting Christian Knowledge, Holy Trinity Church, Marylebone Road, London NW1 4DU England. **Tel** 011 44 71 3875282, FAX 011 44 71 3882352. **ED** P. Law. **LC** BR1; .T617. Index available. **Circ:** 5,000 (ctrl). available on microfilm.
**Desc:** A forum for all people who think about their faith and its relation to current theological study and everyday life.
**Ind/Abst** Br. Humanit. Index; Index Book Rev. Relig.; New Testam. Abstr.; Relig. Index One Period. (1967-); Relig. Theol. Abstr.

US
**THEOLOGY NEWS & NOTES.** **Added/Corp** Fuller Theological Seminary. **VFOAT** Theology News and Notes. **VAT** Theology News and Notes. (Apr. 1954)-. Periodical. English. qt. Free on request. Fuller Theological Seminary, 135 North Oakland Avenue, Pasadena CA 91182. **Tel** (818)584-5200.

US
**THEOLOGY TODAY.** (Apr. 1944)-. Periodical. English. ir. Hochman Associates, 950 Third Avenue, 16th Floor, New York NY 10022. **Tel** (212)371-4932. available in print.
**Ind/Abst** Book Rev. Index; Book Rev. Mon.; Guide Soc. Sci. Relig. Period. Lit.; Index Relig. Period. Lit.; New Testam. Abstr.; Old Testam. Abstr.; Relig. Theol. Abstr.; Subj. Index Sel. Period. Lit.

US/0040-5736
**THEOLOGY TODAY (EPHRATA, PA.).** (THEOLOGY TODAY. PRINT EDITION). [Theol. today]. Vol. 1 (April 1944)-. Periodical. English. qt. $21.00 (one year), $39.00 (two year). Hochman Associates, 950 Third Avenue, 16th Floor, New York NY 10022. **Tel** (212)371-4932. **(Subscription address:** Theology Today, PO Box 29, Princeton NJ 08542.**)** **ED** Hugh T. Kerr and Craig Dykstra. **LC** BR1; .T62. **DD** 205. cum. index. **Bk Rev. Ad Acc. Circ:** 14,000. available on microfilm and microfiche from University Microfilms International (UMI). Documents available from The Genuine Article, UMI Article Clearinghouse.
**Desc:** A non-denominational journal of religious opinion on Biblical, theological and social issues.
**Ind/Abst** Acad. Abstr. Full Text Elite (July 1990-); Acad. Abstr. (July 1990-); Acad. Search (July 1990-); Arts Humanit. Citation Index [Full Cov.]; Bibliogr. Mission.; Book Rev. Index; Curr. Contents Arts Humanit.; Curr. Thoughts Trends; Expand. Acad. Index (1989-); Guide Soc. Sci. Relig.; Humanit. Index; Humanit. Source (Jul. 1990-); Index Book Rev. Relig.; INFO-SOUTH Abstr.; Mag. Search; Middle East Abstr. Index; New Testam. Abstr.; Newsp. Period. Abstr. (1988-); Old Testam. Abstr.; Relig. Index One Period. (1949-); Relig. Theol. Abstr.; Res. Alert [Full Cov.]; Soc. Sci. Source (Jul. 1990-); Soc. Sci. Cit. Index [Select. Cov.].

GW/0342-7145
**THEORIE UND PRAXIS DER SOZIALPADAGOGIK.** **VFOAT** TPS. Theorie und Praxis der Sozialpadagogik. (1972)-. Periodical. German. bm. DM45.50. Luther Verlag GmbH, Postfach 140380, Cansteinstrasse 1, D-33623 Bielefeld, Germany. **Tel** 011 49 521 448638, FAX 011 49 521 448681. **UDC** 37.013.42.

US/0951-497X
**THEOSOPHICAL HISTORY.** [Theosoph. hist.]. **Added/Corp** Theosophical History Foundation. (1985)-. Periodical. English. qt. $14.00 US, Canada and Mexico; $16.00 other. Theosophical History Foundation, California State University, Religious Study, Fullerton CA 92634. **Tel** (714)773-2441, (714)773-3727, FAX (714)773-3990, (714)448-5820. **ED** James A. Santucci. Index available (published separately). cum. index. **Bk Rev**, (Qty: 12). **Pr Rev. Circ:** 250.
**Desc:** Purpose is to publish contributions specifically related to the modern theosophical movement, from the time of H.P. Blavatsky and her followers.

II/0040-5892
**THEOSOPHIST, THE.** Vol. 1 (Oct. 1879)-. Periodical. English. mo. $15.00. Theosophical Publishing House, Adyar, India. **(Subscription address:** Prints India, 11 Darya Ganj, New Delhi, 110002 India, (Phone: 011 91 11 3268645)**)** **ED** G. S. Arundale. **LC** BP500; .T6.

US/0040-6058
**THESE TIMES.** ***Title Change.*** Periodical. English. mo. Review and Herald Publishing Association, 55 West Oak Ridge Drive, Hagerstown MD 21740. **Tel** (301)791-7000 ext. 2534, FAX (301)790-9734. ***Absorbed by** Signs of the Times, 0037-5047.*

UK/0309-3492
**THIRD WAY.** (1977)-. Periodical. English. Ten times a year (July/Aug. and Dec/Jan. issues combined). £29.00 UK and EEC; £35.00 other. Third Way Ltd, Saint Peters Sumner Road, Harrow Middex HA2 4BX England. **Tel** 011 44 81 4238494, FAX 011 44 81 4235367. **ED** Huw Spanner, (Telephone: (081) 423 8494). **Bk Rev**, (Qty: 50). **Ad Acc. Circ:** 6,000. available on microfilm from University Microfilms International (UMI).
**Desc:** Christian perspectives on social, political and cultural issues in the contemporary world.

US/0273-6527
**THIS PEOPLE.** [This people]. (19??)-. Periodical. English. Four times a year. $11.95 US; $16.95 other. Utah Alliance, PO Box 2250, Salt Lake City UT 84110-2250. **Tel** (801)581-0881. **ED** Scot F. and Maurine Jo. Proctor (editors' phone: (801)943-1875). **LC** BX8601; .T54. **DD** 289.3/3. **Bk Rev. Ad Acc. Circ:** 20,000 (ctrl).
**Desc:** Deals with challenges and problems facing the Latterday Saints (Mormons).

US/1049-4561
**THIS ROCK.** (THIS ROCK : THE MAGAZINE OF PRACTICAL APOLOGETICS AND EVANGELIZATION.). [This rock]. (Jan. 1990)-.

Periodical. English. mo. $24.00 (one year), $42.00 (two year) US; $30.00 Canada and Mexico; $35.00 other. This Rock, PO Box 17490, San Diego CA 92177. **Tel** (619)541-1131, FAX (619)541-1154. **DD** 282.

US/0040-6325
**THOMIST, THE.** See Philosophy.

US/0040-6457
**THOUGHT (NEW YORK).** ***Ceased.*** (THOUGHT.). [Thought]. Vol. 1 No. 1 (June 1926)-(1992). Periodical. English. qt. Fordham University Press, Box L, Fordham University, Bronx NY 10458. **Tel** (718)817-4780, FAX (718)817-4785. **ED** Richard Dimler. **LC** AP2; .T333. **DD** 051. **[CCC].** Index available in last issue of volume--attached. cum. index. **Bk Rev. Ad Acc. Circ:** 1,100. available on microfilm and microfiche from University Microfilms International (UMI). Documents available from The Genuine Article, UMI Article Clearinghouse.
**Desc:** Articles on timely, contemporary issues in philosophy, theology, literature and the arts within the context of the Judeo-Christian tradition.
**Ind/Abst** Am. Hist. Life (1963-1976),(1980-); Annu. Bibliogr. Engl. Lang. Lit.; Arts Humanit. Citation Index (19??-19??) [Full Cov.]; Book Rev. Index; Expand. Acad. Index (1989-); Humanit. Index; Middle East Abstr. Index; MLA Int. Bibl. Books Artic. Mod. Lang. Lit.; New Testam. Abstr.; Newsp. Period. Abstr. (1991-); Old Testam. Abstr.; Philos. Index; Relig. Theol. Abstr. (199?-); Res. Alert [Full Cov.]; Soc. Sci. Cit. Index [Select. Cov.]; Abr. Cathol. Period. Lit. Index; Cathol. Period. Lit. Index.

CN/0840-5778
**THY KINGDOM COME (BURNABY, B.C.).** (THY KINGDOM COME / THE ASSOCIATION OF THE COVENANT PEOPLE.). [Thy kingd. come]. **Added/Corp** Association of the Covenant People. Vol. 1, No. 1 (Sept. 1988)-. Periodical. English. mo. $10.00. Association of the Covenant People, 7730 Edmonds Street, Burnaby British Columbia V3N 1B8 Canada. **Tel** (604)524-1170. **DD** 289.9. ***Continues*** *Identity, 0381-8691.*

II/0254-9808
**TIBETAN BULLETIN.** [Tibet. bull.]. (1970)-. Periodical. English. bm. $10.00. **(Subscription address:** Prints India, 11 Darya Ganj, New Delhi, 110002 India, (Phone: 011 91 11 3268645))
**Ind/Abst** Hum. Rights Intern. Rep.

CN/0710-5061
**TICKER TAPE (TORONTO).** (TICKER TAPE / TASKFORCE ON THE CHURCHES AND CORPORATE RESPONSIBILITY.). [Ticker tape]. No. 1-. Periodical. English. qt. $6.00. Ticker Tape, 600 Jarvis Street Canada. **DD** 261.8/5/05.

NO/0040-7194
**TIDSSKRIFT FOR TEOLOGI OG KIRKE.** [Tidsskr. teol. kirke]. (1930)-. Periodical. Norwegian. qt. Kr365.00, $64.00. Scandinavian University Press, PO Box 2959 Toeyen, N 0608 Oslo 6 Norway. **Tel** 011 47 2 2575400, FAX 011 47 2 2575353, telex 71896 UROR N. **(Subscription address:** Scandinavian University Press, 200 Meacham Ave., Elmont NY 11003.**) ED** Magne Saeboe. **LC** BX8001; .T63. Index available. **Bk Rev. Ad Acc. Circ:** 1,000.
**Desc:** Theological and ecclesiastical problems in Norway and internationally.
**Ind/Abst** New Testam. Abstr.; Old Testam. Abstr.

US/0040-7232
**TIE (LOUISVILLE), THE.** ***Title Change.*** (THE TIE.). [Tie]. **Added/Corp** Southern Baptist Theological Seminary. (1932)-(19??). Periodical. English. bm. Southern Baptist Theological Seminary, 2825 Lexington Road, Louisville KY 40280. **Tel** (502)897-4141. **DD** 286. ***Continued by*** *Southern Seminary, 1078-2613.*
**Ind/Abst** South. Baptist Period. Index.

CL
**TIERRA NUEVA.** **Added/Corp** Centro de Estudios para el Desarrollo e Integracion de America Latina. Vol. 1 No. 1 (Apr. 1972)-. Periodical. Spanish. Four times a year. $9.00. Centro de Estudios de Integracion de America Latina, Casilla 118 Correo 35 L Condes, Santiago Chile. **LC** BR600; .T53. Index available. cum. index. **Circ:** 4,000 (ctrl).

NE/0168-9959
**TIJDSCHRIFT VOOR THEOLOGIE.** [Tijdschr. theol.]. Vol. 1 (Jan. 1961)-. Periodical. Dutch (summaries and/or abstracts in English). qt. Fl67.50 Netherlands; Fl85.00 other. Tijdschrift Voor Theologie, Postbus 909, 6500 GK Nijmegen Netherlands. **Tel** 011 31 80 229844. **ED** T. M. Schoof. Index available. cum. index. **Bk Rev. Ad Acc. Circ:** 2,000. ***Supersedes*** *Studia Catholica.*
**Desc:** Treats actual religious problems on a theological level.
**Ind/Abst** New Testam. Abstr.; Old Testam. Abstr.; Relig. Theol. Abstr.

US/0163-1799
**TODAY'S CHRISTIAN WOMAN.** [Today's Christ. woman]. (Fall/Winter 1978/1979)-. Periodical. English. bm (6 issues). $17.95. Christianity Today Inc., 465 Gundersen Drive, Carol Stream IL 60188. **Tel** (708)260-6200. **(Subscription address:** CDS / SIFD Agency Control, 1901 Bell Avenue, Des Moines IA 50315.**) ED** Julie Talerico. **LC** BV4527; .T63. **DD** 248/.843/05. **Bk Rev. Ad Acc. Circ:** 180,000. available on microfilm and microfiche from University Microfilms International (UMI).
**Desc:** The magazine for women who want to put their faith to work in their daily lives at home, work, or in the community. Inspirational and practical. Contains interviews, fiction, how-to articles, marriage, parenting, and health advice.
**Ind/Abst** Christ. Period. Index (19??-); Curr. Thoughts Trends.

US/0563-637X
**TODAY'S MINISTRY (NEWTON CENTRE, MASS. : 1983).** (TODAY'S MINISTRY.). Vol. 1, No. 1 (Spring 1983)-. Periodical. English. Three times a year. Andover Newton Theological School, Newton Centre MA 02159. **ED** Joseph P Broughton. **Circ:** 8,000 (ctrl). ***Continues*** *Today's Ministry, 0563-637X.*

US/0040-8549
**TODAY'S PARISH.** [Today's parish]. (1969)-. Periodical. English. Seven times a year. $22.00 (US); $30.00 (including postage) Canada; $27.00 (including postage) other. Twenty Third Publications, 185 Willow Street, PO Box 180, Mystic CT 06355-0180. **Tel** (203)536-2611, (800)321-0411, FAX (203)572-0788. **ED** Carol Clark. **Bk Rev. Ad Acc.**
**Desc:** Proven ways to develop and renew vibrant faith communities. For professional and volunteer parish leaders and concerned parishioners.
**Ind/Abst** Abr. Cathol. Period. Lit. Index; Cathol. Period. Lit. Index.

JA
**TOHO SHUKYO.** **VFOAT** Journal of Eastern Religions. Periodical. Japanese (summaries and/or abstracts in English). Otemon Gakuin Daigaku, 230 Al 567, Ibaraki Japan. **LC** BL1899; .T64.

CN/0824-1422
**TON AMI.** (TON AMI : BULLETIN DE L'ASSOCIATION DES AUMONIERS D'HOPITAUX DU QUEBEC.). [Ton ami]. **Added/Corp** Association des Aumoniers d'Hopitaux du Quebec. (Febr. 1983)-. Bulletin. French. qttq. 28.00Can$. Association Aumoniers d'Hopitaux Quebec, Case Postale 350 Succ. H, Montreal Quebec H3G 2L1 Canada. **Tel** (819)821-5100, FAX (819)281-2065. **DD** 253.5/0880814.

KO
**TONGHAK SASANG NONCHONG.** v. 1-Series. Periodical. Korean. W5,000. Chondogyo Chungang Chongbu Chulpanbu, 88 Kyongun-dong Chongno-ku, Seoul Korea. **LC** BL2240.C5; T67.

US/1050-4745
**TORAH U-MADDA JOURNAL, THE.** [Torah u-madda journal]. **Added/Corp** Yeshiva University. Torah U-Madda Project. Vol. 1 (1989)-. Periodical. English (Hebrew). ir. $2.50. Max Stern Division Communal Services, Yeshiva University, 500 West 185th Street, New York NY 10033. **Tel** (212)960-5262. **LC** BM538.S3; T68. **DD** 296.3/87.
**Ind/Abst** Index Book Rev. Relig.; Relig. Index One Period.; Relig. Theol. Abstr. (199?-).

CN/0826-9831
**TORONTO JOURNAL OF THEOLOGY.** [Tor. j. theol.]. **Added/Corp** Toronto School of Theology (Ont.). Vol. 1 No. 1 (Spring 1985)-. Periodical. English. sa. 30.00Can$ Canada; $30.00 other. Wilfrid Laurier University Press, 75 University Avenue West, Waterloo Ontario N2L 3C5 Canada. **Tel** (519)884-1970, FAX (519)725-1399. **ED** Michael Steinhouser. **DD** 230/.05. **Bk Rev. Circ:** 600 (ctrl).
**Desc:** Journal of theological opinion and analysis.
**Ind/Abst** Index Book Rev. Relig.; Relig. Index One Period.; Relig. Theol. Abstr.

US/8756-7385
**TORONTO STUDIES IN RELIGION.** [Tor. stud. relig.]. (1985)-. Monographic series. English. ir. Price varies per volume. Peter Lang Publishing, 62 West 45th Street, 4th Floor, New York NY 10036. **Tel** (212)764-1471, (800)770-5264, telex 6973364 PLNY. **ED** Donald Weibe. **DD** 200.
**Desc:** Series of monographs and books designed as a contribution to the scholarly and academic understanding of religion.

US
**TORONTO STUDIES IN THEOLOGY. BONHOEFFER SERIES.** **VFOAT** Bonhoeffer Series. Monographic series. English. Price varies per volume. Edwin Mellen Press, PO Box 450, Lewiston NY 14092. **Tel** (716)754-2788. **ED** H Richardson. **Circ:** 1,000 (ctrl).
**Desc:** Monographs on contemporary theology, ethics, and philosophy of religion.

US
**TOUCHSTONE.** English. qt. $8.00 US; $12.00 other. National Federation of Priests Council, 1337 West Ohio Street, Chicago IL 60622. **Tel** (312)226-3334, FAX (312)829-8915. **ED** Rev. Thomas G. Simons. **Bk Rev,** (Qty: 8-10). **Circ:** 27,000 (ctrl).

US/0897-327X
**TOUCHSTONE (CHICAGO, ILL. 1986).** (TOUCHSTONE.). [Touchstone]. **Added/Corp** B'rith Christian Union. (1986)-. Periodical. English. Four times a year. $18.00 one year; $32.00 two years. The Fellowship of St. James, 3300 West Cullom Avenue, Chicago IL 60618. **Tel** (312)267-1440. **DD** 205.

CN/0827-3200
**TOUCHSTONE (WINNIPEG).** (TOUCHSTONE / HERITAGE AND THEOLOGY IN A NEW AGE.). [Touchstone]. **Added/Corp** Touchstone, Heritage and Theology in a New Age (Organization). University of Winnipeg. Faculty of Theology. **VFOAT** Touchstone, Heritage and Theology in a New Age. Vol. 1, No. 1 (Jan. 1983)-. Periodical. English. Three times a year. $17.00 (one year), $32.00 (two year), $45.00 (three year). Faculty of Theology, University of Winnipeg, Winnipeg Manitoba R3B 2E9 Canada. **Tel** (204)786-9855. **ED** A. McKibbin Watts. **DD** 230/.792/05. **Bk Rev. Circ:** 2,000 (ctrl).
**Desc:** To bring the heritage of theology and faith to bear on present life and witness, to engage issues in the light of the biblical message and Christian tradition.
**Ind/Abst** Index Book Rev. Relig.; Relig. Index One Period.

UK
**TOWARDS WHOLENESS.** **Added/Corp** Friends Fellowship of Healing. No. 1 (Spring 1972)-. Periodical. English. Three times a year. £1.00. Friends Fellowship of Heling, 20 Burnet Avenue, Burpham, Guilford, Surrey GU1 1YD England. **Tel** 011 44 31 48369257. **ED** Joanna Harris. **Bk Rev. Circ:** 1,250.

CN/0704-6421
**TRACES. TEACHERS OF RELIGION AND CHRISTIAN ETHICS IN SASKATCHEWAN.** (T R A C E S.). **Main/Corp** Teachers of Religion and Christian Ethics in Saskatchewan. **VAT** Teachers of Religion and Christian Ethics in Saskatchewan. Vol. 1, No. 3 (May 1977)-. Periodical. English. qt. $10.00 Comes with Teachers of Religion and Christian Ethnics membership. Saskatchewan Teachers Federation, PO Box 1108, Saskatoon Saskatchewan, S7K 3N3 Canada. **Tel** (306)373-1660. **DD** 268. ***Continues*** *Teachers of Religion and Christian Ethics. TRACES Newsletter., 0701-192X.*

US/0744-6128
**TRAI TIM DU'C ME.** **VFOAT** Immaculate Heart of Mary Magazine. Periodical. Vietnamese (English). mo. $24.00 US; $36.00 Canada; $48.00 other. Trai Tim Duc Me, PO Box 836, Carthage MO 64836. **Tel** (417)358-8296. **LC** BX806.V5; T73. **Bk Rev. Ad Acc. Circ:** 10,000.

CN/0225-7416
**TRAIT D'UNION JEUNESSE, LE.** ***Ceased.*** [Trait union jeun.]. **Added/Corp** Communaute R3 du Diocese de Valleyfield. Vol. 2 (Sept. 1979)-(199?). Periodical. French. ir. Communaute R3 du Diocese de Valleyfield, Secretariat R3, 31 rue Fabrique, Valleyfield Quebec J6T 4G9 Canada. **DD** 248/.05. ***Continues*** *Trait d'Union R P3 S, 0225-7408.*

UK/0265-3788
**TRANSFORMATION (EXETER).** (TRANSFORMATION.). [Transformation]. **Added/Corp** World Evangelical Fellowship. Theological Commission. Vol. 1, No. 1 (Jan./Mar. 1984)-. Periodical. English. Four times a year. £14.40 UK; £15.15 other. Paternoster Press, A division of Send the Light Ltd., PO Box 300, Kingstown Broadway, Cumbria CA3 0QS England. **Tel** 011 44 228 512512, FAX 011 44 228 514949. **ED** Tokunboh Adeyemo, Vinay Samuel, and Ronald Sider. Index available. cum. index. **Bk Rev. Ad Acc. Circ:** 2,200. available on microfilm and microfiche from University Microfilms International (UMI).
**Desc:** Provides a forum for international discussions on economics, development, violence, family life and other ethical issues.
**Ind/Abst** Christ. Period. Index (19??-); Index Book Rev. Relig.; Int. Bibliogr. Sociol.; Missionalia; Relig. Index One Period.; Relig. Theol. Abstr.

CN/0229-4362
**TRANSPORTEUR, LE.** [Transporteur]. **Added/Corp** Christian Transportation. No. 15 (Oct./Dec. 1980)-. Periodical. French. bm (6 issues). Free on request. Christian Transportation Inc., 2222 South Sheridan Way, Building 2, Unit 5, Mississauga Ontario L5J 2M4 Canada. **Tel** (416)822-2700. **DD** 248.8/8. ***Continues*** *Bonne Nouvelle pour le Transporteur., 0229-4354.*

US/1056-232X
**TREK, LIFE-CENTERED BIBLE STUDY FOR JUNIOR HIGHS. TEACHER IDEA BOOK.** **VFOAT** Teacher Idea Book; TREK. Teacher Idea Book. (1991)-. Periodical. English. qt. $14.75. United Methodist Publishing House, PO Box 801, 201 8th Avenue South, Nashville TN 37202. **Tel** (615)749-6732, (615)749-6615, FAX (615)749-6578, (615)749-6579.

GW
**TRIERER THEOLOGISCHE STUDIEN.** v. 1-. Monographic series. German. ir. Price varies per

volume. Paulinus Verlag, Postfach 3040 65, D 54220 Trier Germany. **Tel** 011 49 651 4604162, FAX 011 49 651 4604153, telex 472735. **Circ:** 400-500.
**Desc:** A collection of books edited by the theology department of the University of Trier; includes biographies of church fathers, essays on Christian thought and dogma and notes on modern and historical liturgical practices.

GW/0041-2945
**TRIERER THEOLOGISCHE ZEITSCHRIFT.** [Trierer theol. Z.]. **Added/Corp** Theologische Fakultaet Trier. Johannes Gutenberg-Universitaet. Katholisch-Theologische Fakultaet. Vol. 56 (1947)-. Periodical. German. Four times a year. DM64.80. Paulinus Verlag, Postfach 3040 65, D 54220 Trier Germany. **Tel** 011 49 651 4604162, FAX 011 49 651 4604153, telex 472735. **LC** BR4; .T77. **DD** 230/.2/05. **Bk Rev. Ad Acc. Circ:** 800 (ctrl). available on microfilm and microfiche from University Microfilms International (UMI). ***Continues** Theologie und Seelsorge.*
**Desc:** Articles and research on theology and philosophy.
**Ind/Abst** BHA : Biblio. Hist. Art; Canon Law Abstr.; New Testam. Abstr.; Old Testam. Abstr.

US/0145-9503
**TRIMENIAIO PERIODIKO TES CHRISTIANIKES EPISTEMES. BIBLIKA MATHEMATA.** **Added/Corp** Christian Science Publishing Society. **VFOAT** Christian Science Quarterly. Bible Lessons. (19??)-. Periodical. English (Greek, Modern). qt. Christian Science Publishing Society, One Norway Street, Boston MA 02115. **Tel** (617)450-2678, (617)450-2504.

CN/0318-0573
**TRINITE, LIBERTE.** No longer published after Dec. 1977?. French. te. Les Peres Trinitaires, 3449 Ave Ontario, Montreal Quebec H3G 2C8 Canada. **DD** 255/.79.

US/0360-3032
**TRINITY JOURNAL.** **Added/Corp** Trinity Evangelical Divinity School. (Spring 1980)-. Periodical. English. sa (May and Nov.). $10.00 US. Trinity Evangelical Divinity School, 2065 Half Day Road, Bannockburn, Deerfield IL 60015. **Tel** (708)945-8800. **ED** Douglas J. Moo. ***Continues** Trinity Journal, 0360-3032.*
**Ind/Abst** New Testam. Abstr.; Relig. Index One Period. (1980-).

US/0270-2533
**TRINITY SEMINARY REVIEW.** [Trinity Semin. rev.]. **Added/Corp** Trinity Lutheran Seminary (Columbus Ohio). Vol. 1, No. 1 (Spring 1979)-. Periodical. English. sa. Free. Trinity Lutheran Seminary, 2199 East Main Street, Columbus OH 43209. **Tel** (614)235-4136. **ED** Walter F Taylor Jr. cum. index. **Bk Rev. Circ:** 6,000.
**Desc:** Forum for interaction between theological disciplines and practice of ministry.
**Ind/Abst** Index Book Rev. Relig.; Relig. Index One Period. (1979-); Relig. Theol. Abstr.

SI
**TRINITY THEOLOGICAL COLLEGE ANNUAL.** **Main/Corp** Trinity Theological College. **Added/Corp** Trinity Theological College. Annual. Vol. 1 (1964)-. English (Chinese). an. Trinity Theological College, 7 Mount Sophia, Singapore 0922 Singapore.

US
**TRINITY'S WELLSPRING.** (19??)-. English. Three times a year. Trinity Evangelical Divinity School, 2065 Half Day Road, Bannockburn, Deerfield IL 60015. **Tel** (708)945-8800. **ED** Robert Moeller. **Circ:** 10,000 (ctrl). ***Continues** Voices.*
**Desc:** Written for alumni, donors, and friends of Trinity Evangelical Divinity School, to inform, challenge and educate individuals regarding the ministry and influence of the school.

HK
**TRIPOD.** Six times a year.
**Ind/Abst** Index Book Rev. Relig.; Relig. Index One Period.

HK
**TRIPOD. CHRISTIANITY AND CONTEMPORARY CHINA.** English (Chinese). bm (Feb., Apr., June, Aug., Oct., Dec.). $15.00 Hong Kong, Macau, & mainland China; $25.00 Asia; $30.00 other. Holy Spirit Study Centre, 6 Welfare Road, Aberdeen Hong Kong. **Tel** 011 852 5 5530141, FAX 011 852 5 8731545. **ED** Fr. John Tong. Index available.
**Ind/Abst** Hum. Rights Intern. Rep.

SW/0346-2803
**TRO OCH LIV.** (1942)-. Periodical. Swedish. Six times a year. Kr180.00 Sweden; Kr200.00 other. Tro Och Liv, Kottlavagen 116, S 181 41 Lidingo, Sweden. **Tel** 011 46 8 7675831, FAX 011 46 8 7670714. **ED** Lennart Molin. **Bk Rev**, (Qty: 50-60). **Ad Acc, Adv Mgr:** Stefan Claesson, **Tel** 011 46 8 7433172. **Circ:** 2,700.
**Desc:** Periodical dealing with different theological issues with an objective of reaching theologians as well as laymen with some theological training.

US/0041-3712
**TRUTH SEEKER (SAN DIEGO, CALIF.), THE.** (TRUTH SEEKER.). [Truth seek.]. Vol. 1 (Sept. 1873)-. Periodical. English. qt. $20.00 North America; $25.00 other. Truth Seeker Company Inc, PO Box 2832, San Diego CA 92112. **Tel** (619)239-9043, FAX (619)239-0734. **(Subscription address:** PO Box 2832, San Diego CA 92112-2832) **ED** William B. Lindley. **LC** BL2700; .T7. **DD** 051. **Bk Rev. Pr Rev.** available via electronic mail; available on microfilm from University Microfilms International (UMI).
**Desc:** Publication on free thought.

CH
**TSUNG CHIAO SHIH CHIEH.** **VFOAT** Religious World. Began with Oct. 1979 issue. Periodical. Chinese. qt. Tsung Chiao Shih Chieh Tsa Chih She 31 Chi-Nan Road, 2nd Section, Taipei Taiwan. **LC** BL9.C4; T88. **DD** 200/.5.

PH/0116-4260
**TUGON.** [Tugon]. Vol. 1 No. 1 (Nov. 1979)-. Periodical. English (English). Three times a year. $18.00. National Council of Churches in the Philippines, PO Box 1767, Manila 1099 Philippines. **Tel** 011 63 2 995311.
**Ind/Abst** Bibliogr. Mission.; Hum. Rights Intern. Rep.; Index Book Rev. Relig.; Index Philip. Period.; Relig. Index One Period.

II
**TULASI PRAJNA.** Jan./Mar. 1975-. Periodical. Hindi (Hindi). Jain Vishwa Bharati, Ladnun Rajasthan, Ladanum India. **LC** BL1300; .T84.

US/0745-8606
**TWIN CITIES CHRISTIAN, THE.** (TWIN CITIES CHRISTIAN.). **Added/Corp** Twin Cities Christian Publishing Company, Watertown, Minn. Greater Minneapolis Association of Evangelicals, Minneapolis, Minn. Greater St. Paul Association of Evangelicals, St. Paul, Minn. Vol. 1 (Sept. 1978)-. Periodical. English. bw. $19.95 (one year), $36.00 (two year). EP News Service, 1619 Portland Avenue South, Minneapolis MN 55404. **Tel** (612)339-9579, FAX (612)339-6973. **ED** Doug Trouten. **Bk Rev**, (Qty: 50 /yr). **Ad Acc. Circ:** 8,000 (ctrl).
**Desc:** Independent Christian newspaper serving Christian community in the St. Paul/Minneapolis area.

SA/1013-1116
**TYDSKRIF VIR CHRISTELIKE WETENSKAP.** [Tydskr. christelike wet.]. (1965)-. Periodical. Afrikaans. sa. R40.00 institutions; R20.00 individuals. Verenigine Christelike, PO Box 1824, Bloemfontein 9300 South Africa. **Tel** 011 27 51 489160.

UK/0082-7118
**TYNDALE BULLETIN (1966).** (TYNDALE BULLETIN.). [Tyndale bull.]. **Added/Corp** Tyndale Fellowship for Biblical and Theological Research. Tyndale House. No. 17 (1966)-. Bulletin. English. sa. £5.95 UK; (add £1.00 postage) other. Tyndale Bulletin, Tyndale House, 36 Selwyn Gardens, Cambridge CB3 9BA United Kingdom. **Tel** 0223 352159, FAX 0223 464230. **(Subscription address:** Norton Street, Nottingham, NG7 3HR United Kingdom) **ED** Bruce W Winter. **[CCC].** Index available. cum. index. **Circ:** 1,100. ***Continues** Tyndale House. Tyndale House Bulletin.*
**Ind/Abst** Index Book Rev. Relig.; New Testam. Abstr.; Old Testam. Abstr.; Relig. Index One Period. (1978-); Relig. Theol. Abstr.

GW/0342-1465
**UNA SANCTA (METTINGEN).** (UNA SANCTA.). [Una St.]. Vol. 1 (1946)-. Periodical. German. qt. DM39.70. Kyrios Verlag, Postfach 7545, W 8050 Freising Germany. **Tel** 08161/5527. Index available. **Ad Acc.**
**Ind/Abst** New Testam. Abstr.

DK
**UNDER AFRIKAS SOL.** **Main/Corp** Dansk Forenet Sudan Mission. Danish. an. Forlaget Savanne, Norregade 14, Box 57, 6070 Christiansfeld Denmark. **Tel** 04-56 22 33. **LC** BV3500; .A33A. Index available. **Bk Rev. Circ:** 3,300 (ctrl).

US/0097-6784
**UNDERGROUND EVANGELISM MAGAZINE.** (19??)-. Periodical. English. qt. Free. Underground Evangelism, PO Box 250, Glendale CA 91209. **Tel** (213)254-4371, telex 4720231 INTERAID. **ED** Rudolf Eastmann. **LC** BV3777.C62; U53. **DD** 269/.2/091717. **Circ:** 75,000.
**Desc:** Published in the interest of world evangelism and gospel outreach in Albania, Bulgaria, China, Czechoslovakia, East Germany, Hungary, Poland, Romania, the USSR and Yugoslavia.

US/1061-0871
**UNIFICATION NEWS.** (1982)-. Periodical. English. mo. $15.00 (one year), $28.00 (two year) US; $45.00 (one year), $86.00 (two year) includes postage other. HSA-UWC, 4 West 43rd Street, New York NY 10036. **Tel** (212)997-0050. **ED** R Lewis. **Bk Rev**, (Qty: 12). **Ad Acc. Circ:** 6,800 (ctrl).
**Desc:** Coverage of the unification movement.

FR
**UNITE CHRETIENNE.** **VFOAT** Pages Documentaires Unitas. No 19 Aug. (1970)-. Periodical. French. qt. 100.00F France; 110.00F other. Unite Chretienne, 2 rue Jean Carries, 69005 Lyon France. **Tel** 011 33 78 421167. **ED** Pere Pierre Michalon. **Bk Rev. Circ:** 2,000. ***Formed by the union of** Unitas **and** Pages Documentaires.*
**Desc:** Two or three basic articles on the subject matter of each issue. Book reviews and ecumenical news.

FR
**UNITE DES CHRETIENS.** (19??)-. French. qt (Jan., Apr., July, Oct.). 107.74F France; 125.00F other. Sec Natl des Chretiens, 80 rue de l'Abbe Carton, 75014 Paris, France. **Tel** 011 33 1 45420039, FAX 011 33 1 45420307. **ED** Guy Lourmande. **Circ:** 3,800 (ctrl).
**Desc:** Articles written by theologians and biblical scholars about subjects such as the Bible, ecumenical events, etc. The authors belong to different churches including Catholic and Lutheran.

CN/0041-7238
**UNITED CHURCH OBSERVER, THE.** [United Church obs.]. **Added/Corp** United Church of Canada. Vol. 1 (March 1, 1939)-. Periodical. English. mo. 18.69Can$ (1 year), 37.38Can$ (2 year), 56.07Can$ (3 year). United Church of Canada, 85 Saint Clair Avenue East Room 711, Toronto Ontario M4S 1M8 Canada. **Tel** (416)925-5931. **ED** Hugh McCullum. **LC** BX9881.A1; U6. **DD** 280. **Bk Rev. Ad Acc. Circ:** 155,000 (ctrl). available on microfilm and microfiche from University Microfilms International (UMI). ***Supersedes** New Outlook; United Church Record and Missionary Review; Christian Advance.*
**Desc:** Award-winning magazine written for United Church and general interest readers; covers church news, Canadian and international issues and a wide variety of topics. Features special sections for children and youth, book and film reviews and commentary from a number of monthly columnists.
**Ind/Abst** Can. Index (?-?); Can. Period. Index (19??-); Peace Res. Abstr. J. (1965-1966), (1975).

US/0041-7270
**UNITED EVANGELICAL ACTION.** ***Ceased.*** **VFOAT** Action. Vol.1 (Aug. 1, 1942)- (1992). Periodical. English. bm. National Association of Evangelicals, PO Box 28, Wheaton IL 60189. **Tel** (708)665-0500. **ED** Donald R Brown. **Bk Rev. Ad Acc. Circ:** 1,100 (ctrl). available on microfilm and microfiche from University Microfilms International (UMI).
**Desc:** Presents issues of interest to evangelical Christians.
**Ind/Abst** Guide Soc. Sci. Relig.

UK/0958-2789
**UNITED SOCIETY FOR THE PROPAGATION OF THE GOSPEL ISSUES.** English. qt. £4.00. United Society for the Propagation of the Gospel, 15 Tufton Street, London SW1 England.
**Desc:** Issues of justice, peace and mission with comment.

●US/1065-5913
**UNITED YOUTH DIGEST.** [United youth dig.]. **Added/Corp** First United Church of Jesus Christ Apostolic. Vol. 1, No. 1 (June 1992)-. Periodical. English. sa. $1.00 (single issue). United Youth Digest, 436 East 51st Street, Brooklyn NY 11203-4402. **DD** 289.

US/0162-3567
**UNITY (UNITY VILLAGE).** (UNITY, A WAY OF LIFE.). (1???)-. Periodical. English. mo. $7.00. Unity School of Christianity, Unity Village MO 64065. **Tel** 251-3571524-3550, FAX (816)251-3550. **ED** Philip White. **Circ:** 370,000.
**Desc:** Self-improvement and motivational material.

UK/0041-8226
**UNIVERSE MANCHESTER.** **See** Newspapers.

CK
**UNIVERSITAS CANONICA / PUBLICACION SEMESTRAL PREPARD A POR LA FACULTAD DE DERECHO CANONICO.** **Added/Corp** Pontificia Universidad Javeriana. Facultad de Derecho Canonico. Vol. 1 (Oct. 1980)-. Periodical. Spanish. sa. $30.00. Facultad de Derecho, University Javeriana, Cra 7 40 62, Bogota Colombia. **Tel** 011 57 1 2326554. **LC** K25; .N5636. **DD** 262.9/05.

US/0041-9524
**UNIVERSITY OF DAYTON REVIEW, THE.** **See** Literary and Political Reviews.

US
**UNIVERSITY OF NOTRE DAME. DEPARTMENT OF THEOLOGY. LITURGICAL STUDIES.** (1955)-. English. ir. University of Notre Dame Press, PO Box 635, South Bend IN 46624. **Tel** (219)239-6349, (800)677-3232, FAX (219)239-8148.

## Religion and Theology

**US**
**UNIVERSITY OF NOTRE DAME STUDIES IN THE PHILOSOPHY OF RELIGION.** Added/Corp University of Notre Dame. VFOAT Studies in the Philosophy of Religion. (1979)-. Monographic series. English. ir. Price varies per volume. University of Notre Dame Press, PO Box 635, South Bend IN 46624. Tel (219)239-6349, (800)677-3232, FAX (219)239-8148. ED Frederick Crosson. LC UNC.

US/0149-0230
**UNPUBLISHED WRITINGS ON WORLD RELIGIONS.** No. 1- Oct. 1977-. English. sa. $4.00. Institute for Advanced Studies on World Religions, Melville Memorial Library, SUNY, Stony Brook NY 11794-3383. Tel (516)632-6580.

**SZ**
**UPDATE.** English (German, French and Spanish). qt. 9.00F (1 year), 16.00F (2 year), 24.00F (3 year) Switzerland; $6.00 other. World Alliance of Reformed Churches, PO Box 2100-150, route de Ferney, 1211 Geneva 2 Switzerland. Tel (022)7916236, FAX (022)7916505, telex 415 730 OIK CH (WARC). Circ: 1,300.
 Desc: News of the World Alliance of Reformed Churches' member churches around the world.

DK/0906-7272
**UPDATE & DIALOG.** [Update dialog]. VFOAT Update and Dialog. (1991)-. Periodical. Danish (English and Latvian). sa. kr100.00. Dialog Centre International, Katrinebjergvej 46, DK 8200 Arhus N Denmark. Tel 011 45 86169202, FAX 011 45 86105416. ED Johannes Aagaard. DD 306.6. cum. index. Bk Rev. Ad Acc. Circ: 200 (ctrl).
 Desc: Covers new and emerging religions worldwide with a special interest into paganism, cults, and new age movements.

**US**
**UPDATE CENTRAL AMERICA / INTER-RELIGIOUS TASK FORCE ON CENTRAL AMERICA.** Added/Corp Inter-Religious Task Force on Central America. (19??)-. Periodical. English.
 Ind/Abst Hum. Rights Intern. Rep.

**US**
**UPDATE (EVANGELICAL WOMEN'S CAUCUS).** Title Change. (UPDATE : NEWSLETTER OF THE EVANGELICAL WOMEN'S CAUCUS.). Added/Corp Evangelical Women's Caucus. VFOAT EWC Update. Vol. 9, No. 1 (Spring 1985)-(19??)-. Newsletter. English. qt (Mar., Jun., Sep., Dec.). Evangelical Womens Caucus, Box 209, Hadley NY 12835. Continues EWC Update, 0738-5749. Continued by Update (Evangelical & Ecumenical Women's Caucus), 1064-0800.

US/0042-0735
**UPPER ROOM, THE.** [Upper room]. Added/Corp Methodist Episcopal Church, South. General Committee on Evangelism. Methodist Episcopal Church. Commission on Evangelism. Methodist Episcopal Church, South. Board of Missions. Methodist Church (U.S.). General Commission on Evangelism. Methodist Church (U.S.). General Board of Evangelism. Vol. 1 (Apr./June 1935)-. Periodical. English (French, Spanish and German). bm. $4.95 (one year), $8.95 (two years), $12.95 (three years). Upper Room, 1908 Grand Avenue, PO Box 189, Nashville TN 37202. Tel (800)925-6847, FAX (615)340-7275. LC BV4800; .U6. DD 242. available in braille.
 Desc: Christian devotional calendar with an interdenominational, interracial, and international format.

●US/1060-8583
**UPSIDEDOWN (WOBURN, MASS.).** (UPSIDEDOWN.). [UpsideDown]. Added/Corp Boston Church of Christ. VFOAT Upside Down. Issue 1 (Jan. 1992)-. Periodical. English. qt $16.00. Upsidedown, 1 Merrill Street, Woburn MA 01801. DD 248.

US/1056-7216
**URBAN MISSION.** [Urban mission]. Added/Corp Westminster Theological Seminary (Philadelphia, Pa.). Vol. 1, No. 1 (Sept. 1983)-. Periodical. English. qt. $16.00. Urban Mission, PO Box 27009, Philadelphia PA 19118. Tel (215)887-5511. DD 269. Index available (in last issue). available on microfilm and microfiche from University Microfilms International (UMI).
 Ind/Abst Christ. Period. Index (19??-); Index Book Rev. Relig. (1985-); Missionalia (19??-); Relig. Index One Period. (19??-); Relig. Theol. Abstr. (19??-).

**US**
**US PARISH.** (19??)-. English. mo $24.95. Claretian Publications, 205 West Monroe Street, Chicago IL 60606. Tel (312)236-7782, (800)328-6515.

US/0362-1545
**USQR, UNION SEMINARY QUARTERLY REVIEW.** (UNION SEMINARY QUARTERLY REVIEW.). [USQR, Union Semin. q. rev.]. Added/Corp Union Theological Seminary (New York, N.Y.). VFOAT USQR. Vol. 1 (Nov. 1945)-. Periodical. English. Four times a year. $40.00 (institutions), $21.00 (individuals) US; add $4.00 postage Canada and Mexico; add $5.00 postage other. Union Seminary Quarterly Review, 3041 Broadway, New York NY 10027. Tel (212)280-1361, FAX (212)280-1416. ED Pamela Eisenbaum. LC BV4070; .U6. DD 205. Bk Rev. Ad Acc. Pr Rev. Circ: 1,400. available on microfilm and microfiche from University Microfilms International (UMI). Formed by the union of Union Review, 0362-9031 and Alumni Bulletin - Union Theological Seminary.
 Desc: A journal dedicated to general issues of theology and culture.
 Ind/Abst Index Book Rev. Relig.; New Testam. Abstr.; Old Testam. Abstr.; Relig. Index One Period. (1948/1949-); Relig. Theol. Abstr.

**US**
**UTAH EVANGEL, THE.** (195?)-. Periodical. English. Nine times a year. free. Utah Missions Inc., Box 348, Marlow OK 73055. Tel (405)658-5631, 800 654-3992.

CN/0824-0388
**VAN (RIVIERE BEAUDETTE).** (LE VAN.). [Van]. (1980)-. Periodical. French. mo $2.95 Each Number. Le Van, CP 214 Succursale B, Longueuil Quebec J4L 4G7 Canada. DD 261.8/05.

US/0042-2568
**VANGUARD (VALPARAISO).** (VANGUARD.). (Feb. 1954)-. Periodical. English. bm $15.00 contribution. Lutheran Human Relations Association of America, 2703 North Sherman Boulevard, Milwaukee WI 53210. Tel (414)871-7300. ED Susan Ruehle and Charles Ruehle. LC BT734; .V3. DD 261.83. Bk Rev. Circ: 10,000. available on microfilm from University Microfilms International (UMI).
 Desc: News, resources and commentary to assist Christians to combat racism, sexism, and other forms of injustice in church and society.

●US/1061-8333
**VARIEGATED GOSPEL.** (VARIEGATED GOSPEL / /WRITTEN BY PEOPLE OF COLOR.). (1992)-. Periodical. English. qt. $10.00. Variegated Gospel, PO Box 23296, Pittsburgh PA 15222.

US/0361-8331
**VECTOR (BURLINGTON).** (VECTOR.). [Vector]. Periodical. English. Video Femmes, Bureau 3875, 10, McMahon, Quebec Quebec G1R 3S1 Canada.

US/0748-3406
**VENTURE INWARD / THE MAGAZINE OF THE ASSOCIATION FOR RESEARCH AND ENLIGHTENMENT.** Added/Corp Association for Research and Enlightenment. Vol. 1 No. 1 (Sept./Oct. 1984)-. Periodical. English. bm. $20.00. Association for Research and Enlightenment, PO Box 595, Virginia Beach VA 23451. Tel (804)428-3588, FAX (804)422-4631. ED A. Robert Smith. Index available. cum. index. Bk Rev. Circ: 75,000 (ctrl). Formed by the union of A.R.E. Journal and A.R.E. News.
 Desc: Information pertaining to spiritual growth, personal improvement, metaphysics, and parapsychology.

US/0895-9951
**VERDICT (FALLBROOK, CALIF. : 1987).** Title Change. (VERDICT.). [Verdict]. (1987)-?. Periodical. English. ir. Verdict Publications, PO Box 1311, Fallbrook CA 92028. Tel (619)728-5856. ED Robert D Brinsmead. DD 230. Continues Christian Verdict. Continued by Quest.
 Desc: Committed to the belief that God raised Jesus of Nazareth from the dead and that He is Lord.

GW/0342-2410
**VERKUNDIGUNG UND FORSCHUNG.** [Verkund. Forsch.]. (1940)-. Periodical. German. sa. DM45.00 Germany. Kaiser Verlag Zeitschriften, Quell Verlag Furtbachstr 12A, D 70178 Stuttgart Germany. Tel 011 49 711 6010057, FAX 011 49 711 6010076. ED Gerhard Sauter, Rudolf Bohren, Carsten Colpe, Walther Furst, Ferdin Hahn, Jorg Jeremias, Manfred Josuttis, Gunter Klein, Karl-Heinz zur Muhlen, Hans Werner H Schmidt, Grete Schneider, Theo Sundermeier and Michael Welker. LC BR4; .V4. [CCC]. Bk Rev. Ad Acc. Circ: 1,800.
 Desc: Evangelical theology.
 Ind/Abst New Testam. Abstr. (19??-).

GW/0537-7919
**VEROFFENTLICHUNGEN.** Main/Corp Institut fuer Europaische Geschichte (Mainz, Germany). Vol 1 (1953)-. Monographic series. German. ir. Price varies per volume. Franz Steiner Verlag GmbH, Postfach 101061, D 70009 Stuttgart Germany. Tel 011 49 0711 2582372, FAX 011 49 0711 2582290, telex 723636 daz d. ED Karl Otmar Freiherr von Aretin.
 Desc: Monographs dedicated to European and church history as well as to problems of theology.

US/0164-4211
**VERONA MISSIONS.** Title Change. (19??)-(19??). Periodical. English. bm. Verona Missions, 2104 St Michael Street, Cincinnati OH 45204. Tel (513)921-1400. Continues Verona Father Missions, 0042-4234. Continued by Comboni Missions, 0279-3652.

IT/1121-9696
**VETERA CHRISTIANORUM.** (19??)-. Italian (French, Spanish, English, German, Latin and Greek, Modern). sa. L600000 Italy; 800000 other. Edipuglia Srl., Via Dalmazia 22/B, 70050 Bari-S Spirito Italy. Tel 39 80 5333056, FAX 39 80 5333057.

CN/0226-7861
**VIATEURS EN MISSION.** [Viateurs mission]. Added/Corp Missions Saint-Viateur, Montreal, Quebec. No. 203 (Dec. 1979)-. Periodical. French. Missions Saint-Viateur, 450 Av Querbes, Montreal Quebec H2V 3W5 Canada. DD 266/.2/05. Continues Missions Saint-Viateur, 0226-7888.

US/8750-2534
**VICTORIA (SAN DIEGO, CALIF).** (VICTORIA.). [Victoria]. Added/Corp Morris Cerullo World Evangelism. (198?)-. Periodical. Spanish (Spanish). qt. $6.00. Victoria, PO Box 700, San Diego CA 92138. DD 266.

US/0745-9173
**VICTORY (SAN DIEGO, CALIF.).** (VICTORY.). [Victory]. Vol. 1, No. 1 (Apr. 1983)-. Periodical. English. bm. $6.00. World Evangelism Inc, PO Box 700, San Diego CA 92138. DD 266. Continues Deeper Life.

**SP**
**VIDA NEUVA.** (19??)-. Periodical. Spanish. wk (Sat.). 9250ptas Spain; 17500ptas other. Promocion Popular Cristiana, Enrique Jardiel, Poncela 4, 28016 Madrid, Spain. Tel 011 34 1 3592300. Index available (free).

**SP**
**VIDA RELIGIOSA.** Spanish. ir. 3900.00ptas. Vida Religiosa, Buen Suceso 22, 28008 Madrid Spain. Tel 011 34 1 2482102.
 Ind/Abst Canon Law Abstr.

**CR**
**VIDA Y PENSAMIENTO.** Added/Corp Seminario Biblico Latinoamericano. Departamento de Publicaciones. Vol. 1, No. 1 (Jan./June 1981)-. Periodical. Spanish. Twice a year (June, Dec.). $9.00 Costa Rica; $36.00 other. Seminario Biblico Latinoamericano, Americano Calle 3 AV 14 16, San Jose Costa Rica. Tel 011 506 227555 or 333830. Bk Rev. Ad Acc. Circ: 750.

FR/0382-0181
**VIE CHRETIENNE, LA.** Began publication in 1951. Periodical. French. mo (11 issues per year). 38.20Can$ surface mail, 51.10Can$ air mail. Periodica Inc, PO Box 444, Outremont Quebec H2V 4R6 Canada. Tel (514)274-5468, FAX (514)274-0201.

**BE**
**VIE CONSACREE.** Added/Corp Centre de Documentation et de Recherche Religieuses. Yearly Vol. 38 (Jan./Feb. 1966)-. Periodical. French. Six times a year. 585F EEC countries; 720F other. Columbo Plan Bureau, 12 Melbourne Avenue, Colombo 4 Sri Lanka Ceylon. ED Noelle Hausman. cum. index. Bk Rev. Circ: 6,500. Continues Revue des Communautes Religieuses.
 Desc: Addressed to religious men and women, to help them fulfill their consecration by theoretical and practical papers.
 Ind/Abst Canon Law Abstr.

**CN**
**VIE DES COMMUNAUTES RELIGIEUSES.** French. Five times a year (Jan., March, May, Sept., Nov.). 13.00Can$. Vie des Communautes, 5750 Boulevard Rosemont, Montreal QUE H1T 2H2 Canada. Tel (514)259-6911. Bk Rev. Circ: 3,300 (ctrl).

CN/0229-3803
**VIE OUVRIERE (MONTREAL, QUEBEC).** See Economics-Labor.

CN/0709-8812
**VIE SERVITE.** VFOAT Servite Life. V. 1- Fall 1958-. Periodical. French (English). qt. Free. Ordre des Servites de Marie, Maison Provinciale, 5705 East Boulevard Gouin, Montreal Nord Quebec H1G 5X1 Canada. DD 271/.79.

FR/0042-5613
**VIE SPIRITUELLE, LA.** [Vie spirit.]. Vol. 1, No. 1 (Oct. 1919)-. Periodical. French. Five times a year. $70.00. Editions du Cerf, BP 65, 77932 Perthes Cedex France. Tel 011 33 1 44181212. (Subscription address: US: Novalis, PO Box 990, Outremont H2V 4S7 Canada) cum. index.
 Ind/Abst Bibliogr. Mission.; Old Testam. Abstr.; Point Repere (1979-1980).

**UK**
**VIEWPOINT.** V. 1- Fall 1957-. Periodical. English. Three times a year. International School of Christian Fellow, 47 Marylebone Lane, London W1M 6AX England.

NE/0042-6032
**VIGILIAE CHRISTIANAE.** Ceased. See Literature.

US/0164-7288
**VIRTUE.** [Virtue]. **Added/Corp** Bethesda Christian Center. (Oct. 1978)-. Periodical. English. bm. $16.95 (one year), $24.95 (two year), $32.95 (three year). Good Family Magazines, PO Box 36630, Colorado Springs CO 80636. **Tel** (719)531-7776. **(Subscription address:** Kable Publishers Aide, 308 East Hitt Street, Subscription Department, Mt. Morris IL 61054-1473.**) ED** Becky Durost Fish. **LC** BJ1610; .V57. **DD** 248/.843/05. **Bk Rev. Ad Acc. Circ:** 130,000 (ctrl).
**Desc:** For the woman who desires to know God and be used by him as a woman, wife, mother and friend. Virtue's columns reveals the depth and variety of expression that can be given to femininity and faith.

NE/0169-5606
**VISIBLE RELIGION / INSTITUTE OF RELIGIOUS INCONOGRAPHY, STATE UNIVERSITY GRONINGEN.** ***Ceased.*** **Added/Corp** Rijksuniversiteit te Groningen. Instituut voor Godsdiensthistorische Beelddokumentatie. Vol. 1 (1982)-Series complete (199?). English. an. E. J. Brill, Postbus 9000, 2300 PA Leiden Netherlands. **Tel** 011 31 71 312624, FAX 011 31 71 317532, telex 39296 BRILL NL. **ED** H.G. Kippenberg. **LC** BL1; .V57. **DD** 291.3/05. **[CCC].**
**Desc:** Paper series covering genres in visual representation.
**Ind/Abst** Int. Bibliogr. Sociol.

US
**VISION.** (19??)-. English. Three times a year (Mar., July, Nov.). $10.00 (one year); $18.00 (two years). National Catholic Office for the Deaf, 814 Thayer Avenue, Silver Spring MD 20910. **Tel** (301)587-7992. **ED** Nora Letourneau. **Ad Acc. Circ:** 2,000. ***Continues*** *Listening.*

US
**VISION.** English. Ten times a year. $24.00. National Association of Catholic Chaplain, PO Box 07473, Milwaukee WI 53207-0473. **Tel** (414)483-4898, FAX (414)483-6712. **ED** Rebecca Evans. **Bk Rev**, (Qty: 30). **Circ:** 3,700.
**Desc:** News and information for the chaplains in the health careministry.

US/0274-6581
**VISION.** Vol. 1 (1943)-. Periodical. English. qt. New Orleans Baptist Theological Seminary, 3939 Gentilly Boulevard, New Orleans LA 70126. **Tel** (504)286-3610, FAX (504)286-3639.
**Ind/Abst** South. Baptist Period. Index.

US/0882-6609
**VISION (PASADENA, CALIF.).** (VISION / CHRISTIAN EDUCATORS ASSOCIATION INTERNATIONAL.). Periodical. English. bm. $15.00. Christian Educator Association International, PO Box 50025, Pasedena CA 91105. **Tel** (818)798-1124, FAX (818)398-2475. **ED** Forrest L Turpen. **Bk Rev. Ad Acc.** ctrl circ.
**Desc:** A ministry magazine for Christian educators in the public schools.

PR
**VISITANTE, EL. VFOAT** Visitante de Puerto Rico. Vol. 1, No. 1 (1975)-. Newspaper. Spanish. wk. $20.00 Puerto Rico; $36.00 other. El Visitante / Puerto Rico, PO Box 41305 Minillas Station, San Juan, Puerto Rico 00940. **Tel** (809)728-3710, FAX (809)728-3656. **ED** Father Efrain Zabala. **Ad Acc, Adv Mgr:** Carola Llompart. **Circ:** 60,000 (ctrl).

CN/0507-1690
**VITA EVANGELICA (ENGLISH EDITION).** (VITA EVANGELICA.). No. 1- 1966-. Monographic series. English. ir. Price varies per volume. Canadian Religious Conference, 324 Laurier Avenue East, Ottawa Ontario K1N 6P6 Canada. **Tel** (613)236-0824.

IT
**VITA MONASTICA.** (19??)-. Italian. Four times a year. L35000 Italy; L45000 other. Congreg Eremiti Camaldolesi, Edizioni Camaldoli, 52010 Camaldoli AR Italy. **Tel** 011 39 575 556012, FAX 011 39 575 560855. **Bk Rev**, (Qty: 30). **Circ:** 1,300.
**Desc:** Covers spirituality and liturgy.

US/1077-6982
**VITAL CHRISTIANITY (1994).** (VITAL CHRISTIANITY : PUBLICATION OF THE CHURCH OF GOD.). [Vital Christianity]. **Added/Corp** Church of God (Anderson, Ind.). (199?)-. Periodical. English. mo. Warner Press Inc, PO Box 2499, Anderson IN 46018. **Tel** (317)644-7721. **DD** 289. ***Continues*** *Journal of Vital Christianity, 1046-543X.*

FR/0291-1795
**VIVRE ENSEMBLE LILLE.** (1978)-. Periodical. French. Ten times a year. 100.00F France; 150.00F other. Communaute Chretienne, 111 rue des Stations, 59800 Lille France. **Tel** 011 33 20 572319. **UDC** 271.

CN/0226-7772
**VIVRE (GRANBY).** (VIVRE.). [Vivre]. **VFOAT** Revue Vocationnelle. V. 1- Nov./Dec. 1978-. Periodical. French. ir. Free. Centre Projet de Vie, CP 32, Granby Quebec J2G 8E3 Canada. **DD** 248/.05. ***Supersedes*** *Grandir.*

CN/0708-2479
**VOCE EVANGELICA. VFOAT** Evangel Voice. V. 13 (Jan./March 1974)-. Periodical. Italian (English). bm. Free. Voce Evangelica, Box 222 Station V, Toronto, Ontario M6R 3A5. **DD** 289.9. ctrl circ. ***Continues*** *Communicato Missionario, 0708-2460.*

●GT
**VOCES DEL TIEMPO : REVISTA DE RELIGION Y SOCIEDAD. Added/Corp** Sociedad Para el Estudio de la Religion en Guatemala. (Jan/Mar 1992)-. Periodical. Spanish (translations available in English). qt. SERGUA, Apartado Postal 1223, 01901 Guatemala, Guatemala.

US/0042-8116
**VOICE OF FREEDOM (DALLAS, TEX.).** (VOICE OF FREEDOM.). [Voice freed.]. 1952-. English. mo. $8.00 US; $8.50 other. Freedom Press, Inc., Box 24836, Dallas TX 75224.

US/0049-6669
**VOICE (WESTCHESTER).** (VOICE.). **Added/Corp** Independent Fundamental Churches of America. (19??)-. Periodical. English. bm (6 issues). $7.50. Independent Fundamental Churches of America, PO Box 810, 3520 Fairlanes, Grandville MI 49468. **Tel** (616)531-1840. **ED** Paul J. Dollaske. **Bk Rev. Ad Acc. Circ:** 10,000 (ctrl).
**Desc:** An in-house publication for member churches, with contributed articles, and news of interest to same. Specialized articles are included.

US/0891-3420
**VOICES (DEERFIELD, ILL.).** ***Ceased.*** (VOICES.). **Added/Corp** Trinity Evangelical Divinity School. (197?)-(19??). Periodical. English. qt. Trinity Evangelical Divinity School, 2065 Half Day Road, Bannockburn, Deerfield IL 60015. **Tel** (708)945-8800. **DD** 285.

II
**VOICES FROM THE THIRD WORLD. Added/Corp** Asian Theology Centre (Colombo, Sri Lanka) Ecumenical Association of Third World Theologians. (19??)-. Periodical. English. Twice a year (Jan. & Dec.). $7.00 Asia & Africa, $10.00 others (surface mail); $12.00 Asia & Africa, $14.00 others (airmail). Board of Theological Education Senate of Serampore College, PO Box 4635, 63 Miller's Road, Bangalore 560 046 India. **Tel** 011 91 812 3343385, FAX 011 91 812 215506. **ED** Dr. K. C. Abraham. **LC** BR1; .V58. **DD** 230/.09172/405.

FR/0241-6646
**VOIE D'AVALLON, LA.** (1980)-. Periodical. French. Four times a year. 20.00F. La Voie d'Avallon, Run Meno Vieux Marche, 22420 Plouaret France. **UDC** 28. ***Continues*** *Espoir (Plouaret), 0338-7453.*

CN/0700-9313
**VOIX DU SANCTUAIRE. Main/Corp** Sanctuaire de Notre-Dame de Lourdes, Rigaud, Quebec. Vol. 1 (1957)-. French (English). an. Free. Pere Directeur Sanctuaire de Norte-Dame-de-Lourdes, Rigaud Quebec J0P 1P0 Canada. **Tel** (514)451-4631. **ED** Reve Ladonceur. **DD** 263/.042/714263. **Ad Acc. Circ:** 10,000 (ctrl).

RU/0506-0044
**VOPROSY ISTORII RELIGII I ATEIZMA.** [Vopr. istor. relig. ateizma]. **Added/Corp** Institut Istorii (Akademiia Nauk SSSR). (1950)-. Academic Scholarly Publication. Russian. Izdatelstvo Nauka / Akademiia Nauk, Publishing House of the Russian Academy of Sciences, Leninskii Porspekt 14, 117901 Moscow Russia. **Tel** 011 95 954-21-53, FAX 011 95 938-21-44, telex 411964. **LC** BL80; .A522.
**Ind/Abst** Am. Hist. Life (1955-1956).

UK/0263-6786
**VOX EVANGELICA.** [Vox evang.]. **Added/Corp** London Bible College. Vol. 1 (1962)-. Periodical. English. an (April). £6.95 UK; £7.30 other. Paternoster Press, A division of Send the Light Ltd., PO Box 300, Kingstown Broadway, Cumbria CA3 0QS England. **Tel** 011 44 228 512512, FAX 011 44 228 514949. **[CCC].** available on microfilm and microfiche from University Microfilms International (UMI).
**Ind/Abst** Index Book Rev. Relig.; New Testam. Abstr.; Old Testam. Abstr.; Relig. Index One Period.; Relig. Theol. Abstr.

PL
**VOX PATRUM.** Academic Scholarly Publication. Polish (summaries and/or abstracts in English, French, German, Italian and Latin). sa. Z1,000 Poland; $20.00 US. Miedzywydzialowy Zaklad Badan nad Antykiem, Chrzescijanskim KUL ul Chopina 29/5A, 20-023 Lublin Poland. **Tel** 228-10. **ED** Stanislaw Longosz. **LC** BR162.2; .V66. Index available. **Bk Rev. Ad Acc. Circ:** 1,000 (ctrl).
**Desc:** Scholarly journal on Christian topics of literature, history and ethics. Prints papal church documents; specializes in articles on early church fathers, prints translations into Polish of historical church documents from Latin and Greek.

AT/0728-0912
**VOX REFORMATA.** [Vox reformata]. (1962)-. Periodical. English (Dutch). sa. 8.00Aus$ Australia; $7.00 North America; £4.50 UK. The Bursar Reformed Theological College, 55 Maud Street, Geelong Victoria 3220 Australia. **Tel** (052)222979. **ED** R. O. Zorn and H. de Waard. Index available (Bound in July issue). cum. index. **Bk Rev. Ad Acc. Circ:** 200 (ctrl). available on microfilm from University Microfilms International (UMI).
**Desc:** A theological journal, usually containing two essays or articles by either members of faculty, visiting lecturers, or ministers of reformed church, together with many book reviews.
**Ind/Abst** Missionalia (19??-); New Testam. Abstr. (19??-); Old Testam. Abstr. (19??-).

PL/0137-480X
**W DRODZE.** [W Drodze]. (1973)-. Periodical. Polish. mo. Price on Request. **(Subscription address:** ARS Polona, PO Box 1001, 00068 Warsaw Poland.**) UDC** 24.

CN/0043-0218
**WAR CRY (OAKVILLE).** ***Ceased.*** (THE WAR CRY.). **Added/Corp** Salvation Army (Canada). (1???)-?. Periodical. English. wk. Salvation Army Triumph Press, 455 North Service Road East, Oakville Ontario L6H 1A5 Canada. **Tel** (416)844-2561.
**Ind/Abst** Guide Soc. Sci. Relig.

UK
**WATCHING AND WAITING.** English. Four times a year (Jan., Apr., July, Oct.). £3.00. Sovereign Grace Advent Testimony, 1 Donald Way, Chelmsford ESX CM2 9JB England. **Tel** 011 44 245-268815. **ED** Stephen A. Tomi. Index available. **Bk Rev.**

US/0898-6606
**WATERWHEEL (SILVER SPRING, MD.).** (WATERWHEEL : A QUARTERLY NEWSLETTER OF THE WOMEN'S ALLIANCE FOR THEOLOGY, ETHICS AND RITUAL.). [Waterwheel]. **Added/Corp** Women's Alliance for Theology, Ethics and Ritual. Vol. 1, No. 1 (Spring 1988)-. Periodical. English. Four times a year. $35.00 US; $50.00 other. Waterwheel, 8035 13th Street, Silver Spring MD 20910. **Tel** (301)589-2509, FAX (301)589-3150. **ED** Mary E. Hunt and Diann L. Neu. **DD** 291. Index available. cum. index. **Bk Rev.** ctrl circ.

UK/0043-1575
**WAY, THE.** [Way]. Vol. 1 (Jan. 1961)-. Periodical. English. Four times a year (Jan., Apr., July, Oct.). £14.50 (individuals), £16.50 (institutions). The Way, 114 Mount Street, London W1Y 6AN England. **Tel** 011 44 71 499 7002. **LC** BX2350.A1; W3. **DD** 260. **Bk Rev. Ad Acc. Circ:** 6,000 (ctrl). available on microfilm and microfiche from University Microfilms International (UMI).
**Ind/Abst** Bibliogr. Mission.; New Testam. Abstr.; Old Testam. Abstr.; Abr. Cathol. Period. Lit. Index; Cathol. Period. Lit. Index.

US/0273-8295
**WAY OF ST. FRANCIS (1980).** (WAY OF ST. FRANCIS.). [Way St. Francis]. **Added/Corp** Franciscan Friars of California. **VFOAT** Way. **VAT** Way of Saint Francis (1980). (1980)-. Periodical. English. Six times a year (Jan., Mar., May, July, Sept., Nov.). $5.00 (one year); $8.00 (two year);. Way of St Francis, 107 Golden Gate Avenue, San Francisco CA 94102. **Tel** (415)621-3279. **ED** Simon Scanlon. **Bk Rev. Circ:** 4,500 (ctrl). ***Continues*** *Way.*

US/0890-6491
**WEAVINGS.** [Weavings]. Vol. 1, No. 1 (Sept./Oct. 1986)-. Periodical. English. bm. $19.00 (one year), $29.00 (two years), $39.00 (three years). Upper Room, 1908 Grand Avenue, PO Box 189, Nashville TN 37202. **Tel** (800)925-6847, FAX (615)340-7275. **DD** 205.
**Ind/Abst** Index Book Rev. Relig.; Relig. Index One Period.

GW/0043-2040
**WEGE ZUM MENSCHEN. Added/Corp** Evangelische Konferenz fur Familien- und Lebensberatung. Deutsche Gesellschaft fur Pastoralpsychologie. Konferenz fur Evangelische Krankenhausseelsorge. Vol. 6 (1954)-. Periodical. German. Eight times a year. DM124.00 Germany, $89.75 US. Vandenhoeck & Ruprecht, Robert Bosch Breite 6, D-37079 Goettingen Germany. **Tel** 011 49 551 695911, FAX 011 49 551 695917, telex 965226 VAN d. **[CCC].** ***Continues*** *Weg Zur Seele.*

GW/0723-6204
**WELTMISSION, DIE. Added/Corp** Evangelisches Missionswerk in Deutschland. (199?)-. German. bm. DM15.00. Missionshilfe Verlag, Normannenweg 17 21, D 20537 Hamburg Germany. **Tel** 011 49 40 25456143, FAX 001 49 40 252987, telex 402/6105429. **LC** BV2354; .W67. **DD** 226/.005. Index available. cum. index. **Bk Rev**, (Qty: 12-15). **Ad Acc, Adv Mgr:** Eike Rahn. ctrl circ. ***Continues*** *Weltmission (Evangelisches Missionswerk im Bereich der Bundesrepublik Deutschland und Berlin West).*

GW/0341-082X
**WELTMISSION (EVANGELISCHES MISSIONSWERK IN DER BUNDESREPUBLIK DEUTSCHLAND UND BERLIN WEST).** ***Title Change.*** (DIE WELTMISSION.). **Added/Corp** Evangelisches

Missionswerk im Bereich der Bundesrepublik Deutschland und Berlin West. Vol. 53, No. 1 (Feb. 1983)-(199?). Periodical. German. bm. Missionshilfe Verlag, Normannenweg 17 21, D 20537 Hamburg Germany. **Tel** 011 49 40 25456143, FAX 001 49 40 252987, telex 402/6105429. **ED** Herbert Meissner. **LC** BV2354; .W67. **DD** 266/.005. Index available. **Bk Rev. Ad Acc. Circ:** 18,500. ***Continues*** *Wort in der Welt (Deutsche Evangelische Missions-Rat Germany).* ***Continued by*** *Weltmission (Evangelisches Missionswerk in Deutschland).*

NE/0043-2695
**WENDING.** Volume 1, No. 1 (March 1946)-. Periodical. Dutch. bm. Fl70.50. Tijd and Taak, Postbus 15785, 101 NG Amsterdam Netherlands. **Tel** 011 31 20 6257921. **LC** BR2; .W4. ***Formed by the union of*** *Algemeen Weekblad voor Kerk en Christendom* ***and*** *Kouter.*

NE/0165-988X
**WERELD EN ZENDING.** [Wereld Zending]. (1972)-. Periodical. Dutch (summaries and/or abstracts in English). qt. Fl35.00 Netherlands; $38.11 other. Wereld en Zending, Postbus 130, 8260 AC Kampen Netherlands. **Tel** 011 31 20 7171654. **ED** J. van Slageren. **LC** BV3000; .W48. Index available (Bound in last issue). **Bk Rev. Circ:** 2,000 (ctrl). ***Formed by the union of*** *Missiewerk* ***and*** *Heerbaan.*
**Desc:** Ecumenical journal for missiology and missionary life, for the Netherlands and Belgium.
**Ind/Abst** Am. Hist. Life (1972-1977); Bibliogr. Mission. (19??-); Missionalia (19??-).

BE
**WERELDWIJD.** (19??)-. mo. 800.00F Belgium; 1050.00F other. Wereldwijd, Arthur Geomaere 69, 2018 Antwerp Belgium. **Tel** 011 03 216 29 35, FAX 011 03 237 77 57. **Ad Acc, Adv Mgr:** Anckaert Goedele. Full Page (B&W) 22,000F. Half Page (B&W) 13,500F. Full Page (Color) 44,000F. **Acid Free. Circ:** 30,000.
**Desc:** Covers North-South problems, religion and spirituality.
**Ind/Abst** Bibliogr. Mission.

US/0092-4245
**WESLEYAN THEOLOGICAL JOURNAL.** [Wesleyan theol. j.]. **Added/Corp** Wesleyan Theological Society. Vol. 1 (Spring 1966)-. English. sa. $10.00. Wesleyan Theological Society, PO Box 100, Wilmore KY 40390. **Tel** (606)858-4091. **LC** BR1; .W37. **DD** 287/.1. **Bk Rev. Ad Acc. Circ:** 1,600 (ctrl). available on microfilm and microfiche from University Microfilms International (UMI).
**Desc:** Historical theological biblical topics in the Wesleyan Armenian interpretation and tradition.
**Ind/Abst** Christ. Period. Index (19??-); Index Book Rev. Relig.; Relig. Index One Period. (1971-); Relig. Theol. Abstr.

US/0739-0440
**WESLEYAN WORLD.** (WESLEYAN WORLD / WESLEYAN CHURCH, GENERAL DEPARTMENT OF WORLD MISSIONS.). [Wesley. world]. **Added/Corp** Wesleyan Church. Wesleyan Church. General Dept. of World Missions. Vol. 50, No. 1 (Sept. 1968)-. Periodical. English. mo (July/Aug. and Nov/Dec. issues combined). $5.00. Wesleyan Publishing House, PO Box 50434, Indianapolis IN 46250-0434. **Tel** (317)842-0444, (317)576-0444, FAX (317)842-9188. **ED** Wayne W. Wright. **DD** 266. Index available (Bound in Dec. issue). **Bk Rev. Circ:** 16,500. ***Formed by the union of*** *Wesleyan Missionary and World Missions Bulletin.*
**Desc:** To inform North American readers of the Wesleyan Church's overseas missionary program and to promote that program.

US/0043-4132
**WESTERN RECORDER (MIDDLETOWN).** (WESTERN RECORDER.). (19??)-. Periodical. English. Fifty times a year. $10.50 Kentucky; $10.00 other. Kentucky Baptist Convention, 10701 Shelbyville Road, Middletown KY 40243. **Tel** (502)245-4101. **ED** E. Marvin Knox, P.O. Box 43969, Louisville, KY 40253, (502)244-6471. Index available. **Ad Acc, Adv Mgr:** Smith, **Tel** (502)244-6473. **Circ:** 50,000 (ctrl). available on audiocassette (for Blind subscribers); available on microfilm from University Microfilms International (UMI).
**Desc:** Contains news articles of the Southern Baptists around the world.

UK
**WESTMINSTER RECORD.** English. qt (Jan., April, July, Oct.). £5.00. Westminster Chapel, Buckingham Gate, London SW1E 6BS England. **Tel** 011 44 1 834 1731. **ED** K Bush. **Circ:** 800.

US/0043-4388
**WESTMINSTER THEOLOGICAL JOURNAL, THE.** [Westminst. theol. j.]. **Added/Corp** Westminster Theological Seminary, Philadelphia. Vol. 1, (Nov. 1938)-. Periodical. English. Twice a year (May, Oct.). $20.00 individuals; $30.00 institutions. Westminster Theological Seminary, Chestnut Hill, PO Box 27009, Philadelphia PA 19118. **Tel** (215)887-5511. **ED** Moises Silva. **LC** BR1; .W45. **DD** 205. Index available. cum. index. **Bk Rev. Pr Rev. Circ:** 1,200. available on microfilm and microfiche from University Microfilms International (UMI).
**Desc:** A journal with articles and book reviews in the areas of Biblical studies, theology, church history, apologetics and practical theology.
**Ind/Abst** Christ. Period. Index; Index Book Rev. Relig.; Index Relig. Period. Lit.; Int. Zeitschriftenschau Bibelwissenschaft Grenzgeb.; New Testam. Abstr.; Old Testam. Abstr.; Recent. Publ. Artic.; Relig. Index One Period. (1948-); Relig. Theol. Abstr.

US/0889-0781
**WHEREVER IN THE WORLD, FOR JESUS' SAKE.** **Added/Corp** Evangelical Alliance Mission. **VFOAT** Wherever; Wherever Magazine. Vol. 1, No. 1 (Spring 1976)-. Periodical. English. tq (Jan., Mar., Oct.). Free (US & Canada); $5.00 (others). Evangelical Alliance Mission, PO Box 969, Wheaton IL 60187. **Tel** (708)653-5300. **ED** Jack Kilgore. **DD** 266. **Circ:** 15,000 (ctrl).

US/0043-5007
**WHITE WING MESSENGER.** Periodical. English. bw. $4.50. White Wing Publishing House, PO Box 3000, Cleveland TN 37311. **Tel** (615)476-8536.

US/0361-1930
**WHOLE EARTH NEWSLETTER.** **Added/Corp** United Church Board for World Ministries. **VFOAT** New Missionary Herald Whole Earth Newsletter. Vol. 1 (1970)-. Periodical. English. tq. United Church Board for World Ministries, 475 Riverside Drive, New York NY 10027. **Tel** (212)870-2183. ***Supersedes*** *Missionary Herald Newsletter, 0544-4357.*

US/0160-3728
**WHO'S WHO IN RELIGION.** (1975/76)-. English. ir. $129.00. Marquis Who's Who, A Reed Reference Publishing Company, Part of Reed International PLC, 121 Chanlon Road, New Providence NJ 07974. **Tel** (908)464-6800, (800)521-8110, FAX (908)665-6688, telex 138 755. **LC** BL2530.U6; W48. **DD** 200/.92/2 B. available on magnetic tape and CD-ROM.

AU
**WIENER BEITRAGE ZUR THEOLOGIE.** **Added/Corp** Universitat Wien. Katholisch-Theologische Fakultat. Vol. 1 (1963)-. Monographic series. German. ir. Price varies per volume. Wiener Dom-Verlag, Strozzigasse 8, A-1080 Vienna Austria.

PL
**WIEZ.** **Added/Corp** RSW "Prasa-Ksiazka-Ruch.". (1958)-. Periodical. Polish. mo. $54.00. **(Subscription address:** ARS Polona, PO Box 1001, 00068 Warsaw Poland.**)**
**Ind/Abst** MLA Int. Bibl. Books Artic. Mod. Lang. Lit.

US/1056-0556
**WINDOWS (AUSTIN, TEX.).** (WINDOWS.). [Windows]. **Main/Corp** Austin Presbyterian Theological Seminary. **Added/Corp** Austin Presbyterian Theological Seminary. **VFOAT** Austin Seminary Windows. Vol. 105, No. 1 (Dec. 1989)-. Periodical. English. Twice a year (Apr. and Oct.). free on request. Austin Presbyterian Theological Seminary, 100 East 27th Street, Austin TX 78705. **Tel** (512)472-6736, FAX (512)479-0738. **ED** Terry Much. **DD** 285. **Circ:** 12,500 (ctrl). available on microfiche from University Microfilms International (UMI). ***Continues in part*** *Austin Seminary Bulletin, 0191-8613.*

US/0362-5648
**WISCONSIN LUTHERAN QUARTERLY.** **Added/Corp** Wisconsin Lutheran Seminary. Wisconsin Evangelical Lutheran Synod. Vol. 57 (1960)-. Periodical. English. qt. $10.00 (1 year), $18.00 (2 year) US; $17.00 (1 year), $32.00 (2 year) (surface mail), $31.00 (1 year) (air mail) other. Northwestern Publishing House, 1250 North 113th Street, Milwaukee WI 53226-3284. **Tel** (414)475-6600, FAX (414)475-7684. **ED** Prof. Wilbert R. Gawrisch. **Bk Rev**, (Qty: 40). **Circ:** 2,300. ***Continues*** *Quartalschrift, 0363-6615.*
**Desc:** Serves as a testimony of its theological convictions and a public witness to the Bible's truths.

GW/0043-678X
**WISSENSCHAFT UND WEISHEIT.** [Wiss. Weish.]. Vol. 1 (April 1934)-. Periodical. German. Three times a year. $39.46. JP Bachem Verlag GmbH, Ursulaplatz 1, Bachemhaus, W5000 Cologne 1 Germany. **Tel** 011 49 221 1619122, FAX (0221)3771-128. **ED** P. Johannes B. Freyer and P. Alexander Gerken. **LC** BR4; .W5. **DD** 230/.2/05. **Ad Acc.** ctrl circ.
**Ind/Abst** New Testam. Abstr.; Old Testam. Abstr.; Philos. Index.

GW/0512-1582
**WISSENSCHAFTLICHE MONOGRAPHIEN ZUM ALTEN UND NEUEN TESTAMENT.** Vol. 1 (1959)-. Monographic series. German. ir. Price varies per volume. Neukirchener Verlag Erziehungs, Andreas Braem Strasse 18 20, PO Box 1161, D 47506 Neukirchen VLU Germany. **Tel** 011 49 2845 392227. **LC** UNC.

GW/0179-0080
**WISSENSCHAFTLICHER BUCH BESPRECHUNGSDIENST : WIBB.** **VFOAT** WIBB; Wissenschaftlicher Buch-Besprechungsdienst. German. bm. Verlag Literarisches Buro, Uhlandstrasse 8, W-4500 Osnabruck Germany. **LC** Z7403; .W57; Q158.5. **DD** 016.5.

KO
**WOLGAN KOSIN.** **VFOAT** Kosin. Periodical. Korean. mo. W10,000. Wolgan Kosinsa, 34 Amnam-dong So-ku, Pusan Korea. **LC** BV4485; .W65.

KO
**WOLGAN MOKHOE.** **VFOAT** The Pastoral Monthly; Pastoral Monthly; Mokhoe. Began in 1976. Periodical. Korean. mo. W40000. The Pastoral Monthly, 547-5 Panpo-2 dong Socho-gu, Seoul 137-042 Korea. **Tel** 534-7196. **ED** Jong Koo Park. **LC** BV4000; .W64. **Circ:** 10,000.

UK/0962-2152
**WOMAN ALIVE.** **See** Women's Interests.

US/0043-7379
**WOMAN'S PULPIT, THE.** [Woman's pulpit]. **Added/Corp** International Association of Women Ministers. American Association of Women Ministers. Vol. 1 (1922)-. Periodical. English. qt. $15.00. International Association of Women Ministers, 579 Main Street, Stroudsburg PA 18360. **Tel** (717)421-7751. **ED** LaVonne Althouse. **LC** BV676; .W54. **DD** 262/.14. **Circ:** 400 (ctrl).

US/0890-3395
**WOMEN ALIVE.** (WOMEN ALIVE!). [Women alive]. (198?)-. Periodical. English. Six times a year. $13.95 US; $17.95 other. Women Alive, PO Box 4683, Overland Park KS 66204. **Tel** (913)649-8583. **ED** Aletha Hinthorn. **DD** 261. **Bk Rev**, (Qty: 6/year). **Circ:** 5,000 (ctrl).
**Desc:** Includes articles and Bible studies to encourage women to holy living.

CN/0827-2263
**WOMEN'S CONCERNS.** [Women's concerns]. Issue 25 (Mar. 1984)-. Periodical. English. Three times a year. 6.00Can$ Canada; $8.00 other. Women's Concerns Division of Mission in Canada, 85 St Clair Avenue East, Toronto Ontario M4T 1M8 Canada. **Tel** (416)925-5931, telex 06528224. **ED** Deborah Marshall and Lynda Newmarch. **DD** 261.8/344. **Bk Rev. Circ:** 5,000 (ctrl). ***Continues*** *Women's Concerns Newsletter, 0713-3693.*
**Desc:** A resource of the United Church of Canada. It keeps women aware of issues which affect their lives and how they impact Christian growth and wholeness.

SA/0257-8921
**WOORD EN DAAD / WORD AND ACTION.** **VFOAT** Word and Action. (Jan. 1954)-. Periodical. Afrikaans (English). qt. R30.00 South Africa; R40.00 other. REMSA, PO Box 20011, Noordbrug 2522, South Africa. **Tel** 011 27 148 992919, FAX 011 27 148 992799. **ED** Prof W. Du Plessis. **Bk Rev. Ad Acc, Adv Mgr:** E. M. Strydom. **Circ:** 600.

US/0049-7959
**WORD AND WAY.** **Added/Corp** Missouri Baptist Convention. (19??)-. Newspaper. English. wk. $9.15. Missouri Baptist Convention, 400 East High Street, Jefferson City MO 65101. **Tel** (314)635-7931, FAX (314)659-7436. **ED** Bob Terry. **Bk Rev. Circ:** 55,000 (ctrl). ***Continues*** *Word and Way and Central Baptist.*

US/0275-5270
**WORD & WORLD.** [Word world]. **Added/Corp** Luther-Northwestern Theological Seminaries. **VFOAT** Word and World. Vol. 1, No. 1 (Winter 1981)-. Periodical. English. qt. $18.00 (1 year), $33.00 (2 year), $45.00 (3 year) US; $20.00 (1 year), $37.00 (2 year), $51.00 (3 year) other. Word and World, 2481 Como Avenue, St Paul MN 55108. **Tel** (612)641-3482. **ED** Sylvia Ruud. **LC** BR1; .W67. **DD** 230/.41. cum. index. **Bk Rev. Ad Acc, Adv Mgr:** Ruth Taylor, **Tel** (207)799-4387. available on microfilm and microfiche from University Microfilms International (UMI).
**Desc:** Theology for Christian ministry.
**Ind/Abst** Index Book Rev. Relig.; New Testam. Abstr.; Old Testam. Abstr.; Relig. Index One Period. (1981-); Relig. Theol. Abstr.

US/0043-7964
**WORD (BROOKLYN), THE.** (THE WORD.). **Added/Corp** Antiochian Orthodox Christian Archdiocese of New York and All North America. Vol. 1 (1957)-. Periodical. English. Ten times a year (not published in July and August). $18.00 US; $24.00 (includes postage) other. The Word, 358 Mountain Road, Englewood NJ 07631. **Tel** (201)871-1355, FAX (201)871-7954. **ED** George S Corey (editor's address: 52-78th Street, Brooklyn, NY 11209; phone: (718)748-7940).

AT
**WORD IN LIFE.** English. qt. 20.00Aus$. Catholic College of Education, Sydney LTD POB 968 40 Edward St, N Sydney 2060 Australia. **Tel** 61 2 739 2368.
**Ind/Abst** Aust. Educ. Index.

US/0194-6684
**WORD OF LIFE LIFE LINES.** **Main/Corp** Word of Life Fellowship, inc. **VFOAT** Life Lines. (19??)-. Periodical. English. an (April). Free on request. Word of Life Fellowship Inc., C/O Mark Ward, Schroon Lake NY 12870. **Tel** (518)532-7111, FAX (518)532-7421. **Ad Acc, Adv Mgr:** Beverly Schmaker, **Tel** (518)532-7111. **Circ:**

100,000.
**Desc:** The articles in these issues are based on the gospels that engrave an impression on the reader that evangelism is to be a priority with every believer.

US/0888-1316
**WORD ON WORSHIP.** [Word worsh.]. **Added/Corp** Catholic Church. Archdiocese of Newark (N.J.). Worship Office. (198?)-. Periodical. English. qt. $10.00 US; $11.50 other. Worship Office, 100 Linden Avenue, Archdiocese of Newark, Irvington NJ 07111. **Tel** (201)596-4280. **ED** Rev. Robert G.Lafemera. **DD** 248. **Bk Rev**.
**Ind/Abst** Bibliogr. Mission.

US/1055-0909
**WORKS (ALTADENA, CALIF.).** (WORKS : JOURNAL OF THE CHURCH IN THE WORLD.). (1991)-. Periodical. English. mo. $42.00 US; $48.00 Canada. Telford Work / California, 657 East Mendocino Street, Altadena CA 91001. **DD** 261.

US/0888-157X
**WORLD (ASHEVILLE, N.C.). See** General Interest-General Interest-North America.

US/0892-2462
**WORLD (BOSTON, MASS.), THE.** (THE WORLD : JOURNAL OF THE UNITARIAN UNIVERSALIST ASSOCIATION.). [World]. **Added/Corp** Unitarian Universalist Association. Vol. 1, No. 1 (Jan./Feb. 1987)-. Periodical. English. bm (6 issues). $18.00 US; $25.00 other. Unitarian Universalist Association, 25 Beacon Street, Boston MA 02108. **Tel** (617)742-2100. **DD** 288. available on microfilm and microfiche from University Microfilms International (UMI). Documents available from UMI Article Clearinghouse. ***Continues*** *Unitarian Universalist World, 0041-7122.*
**Desc:** Publishes reviews, interviews, literature, analysis, on political, theological, human-interest themes from liberal religious perspective.
**Ind/Abst** ABI/INFORM Glob. Ed.; ABI Inform Ondisc (July 1985-).

US/0743-2399
**WORLD CHRISTIAN : TODAY'S MISSION MAGAZINE.** [World Christ.]. Vol. 2, No. 1 (Jan./Feb. 1983)-. Periodical. English. Seven times a year (6 bimonthly and 1 summer reader). $15.00. World Christian Incorporated, P.O.Box 3278, Ventura CA 93006. **Tel** (805)650-7871, FAX (805)650-7874. **ED** Martin Melvin. **Ad Acc. Circ:** 10,000. available on microfilm and microfiche from University Microfilms International (UMI). ***Continues*** *Today's Mission;* ***Absorbed*** *U (Downers Grove, Ill.), 0893-0201.*
**Desc:** A movement of dedicated Christians intent on expanding the Kingdom of God around the world. Informs the Body of Christ about "current events" in world missions and to challenge each and every believer to greater involvement in the "Great Commission" and "Great Commandment."

US
**WORLD EVANGELIZATION (CHARLOTTE, N.C.).** (WORLD EVANGELIZATION : A PUBLICATION OF THE LAUSANNE COMMITTEE FOR WORLD EVANGELIZATION.). **Added/Corp** Lausanne Committee for World Evangelization. Vol. 11, No. 40 (Sept. 1985)-. Periodical. English. qt. $25.00. Lausanne Committee for World Evangelization, 5970 Fairview Road, Suite 514, Charlotte NC 28210. **Tel** (704)554-6803. ***Continues*** *World Evangelization Information Bulletin.*

●UK
**WORLD FAITHS ENCOUNTER. Added/Corp** World Congress of Faiths. No. 1 (Mar. 1992)-. Periodical. English. Three times a yearTri-quarterly. $25.00. World Congress of Faiths, 28 Powis Gardens, London W11 1JG England. **Tel** 011 44 71 7272607. **ED** Rev. Alan Race. **LC** BL410; .W67. **Bk Rev. Ad Acc. Circ:** 1,000. ***Continues*** *World Faiths Insight, 0273-1266.*
**Desc:** Resource for dealing with the new questions of living in a multi-faith society.
**Ind/Abst** Christ. Period. Index (1992-).

US/0043-8804
**WORLD ORDER.** Vol. 1 (Fall 1966)-. Periodical. English. qt. $10.00 North America; $15.00 other. World Order, 536 Sheridan Road, Wilmette IL 60091. **Tel** (708)869-9039. **ED** Betty Fisher. Index available. cum. index. **Bk Rev. Circ:** 4,000. available on microfilm and microfiche from University Microfilms International (UMI). ***Continues*** *World Order, 0043-8804.*
**Desc:** Intended to stimulate, inspire, and serve thinking people in their search to find relationships between contemporary life and contemporary religious teachings and philosophy.
**Ind/Abst** Index Am. Period. Verse; Index Book Rev. Relig.; Relig. Index One Period.

US/0043-8839
**WORLD PARISH.** [World parish]. **Added/Corp** World Methodist Council. Vol. 1 (Oct. 1962)-. Periodical. English. bm. Free. World Methodist Council, Lake Junaluska NC 28745. **Tel** (704)456-9432, FAX (704)456-9433. **ED** Joe Hale. **LC** BX8201; .W75. **DD** 287/.05. **Circ:** 18,000. ***Supersedes in part*** *World Parish (1948), 0043-8839.*
**Desc:** International organ of the World Methodist Council, overall goal is to bring encouragement and hope to those churches in the tradition we serve.

US/1063-7931
**WORLD PULSE.** (WORLD PULSE / EVANGELICAL MISSIONS INFORMATION SERVICE.). [World pulse]. **Added/Corp** Evangelical Missions Information Service. (19??)-. Periodical. English. sm. $48.95 (one year), $92.95 (two year). Evangelical Missions Information Service, PO Box 794, Wheaton IL 60189. **Tel** (703)653-2158, FAX (708)653-0520. **ED** James Reapsome. **DD** 266. **Circ:** 5,000. available on microfiche from University Microfilms International (UMI); available on microfilm. ***Continues*** *Pulse (Wheaton, Ill. : 1984), 0747-8631.*
**Desc:** Newsletter covering world missions.

CN/0713-3391
**WORLD VIEW (TORONTO).** (WORLD VIEW.). [World view]. **VFOAT** Worldview. Vol. 1, No. 1 (July 1982)-. English. an. $1.00. Canec Publishing and Supply House, 85 St Clair Avenue East, Toronto Ontario M4T 1M8 Canada. **DD** 266/.023/05.

US/0746-9241
**WORLDWIDE CHALLENGE (SAN BERNARDINO, CALIF.).** (WORLDWIDE CHALLENGE.). [Worldw. chall.]. **Added/Corp** Campus Crusade for Christ. **VFOAT** Challenge. (19??)-. Periodical. English. Six times a year (Jan., Mar., May, July, Sept., Nov.). $12.95 one year; $22.95 two years. Campus Crusade for Christ International, 100 Sunport Lane, Department 2390, Orlando FL 32809. **Tel** (407)826-2383, (800)688-4992, FAX (407)826-2374. **ED** Diane McDougall. **Circ:** 100,000.
**Desc:** Practical articles on Christian growth, plus news and feature articles about Campus Crusade for Christ.

US/0199-0292
**WORLDWIDE MISSIONS. Added/Corp** World-wide Missions, Inc. **VAT** World Wide Missions. (19??)-. Periodical. English. mo. World-Wide Missions, Box G, Pasadena CA 91109.

US/0043-941X
**WORSHIP.** [Worship]. **Added/Corp** St. John's Abbey (Collegeville, Minn.). Vol. 26 (Dec. 1951)-. Academic Scholarly Publication. English. bm. $26.00 (one year), $51.00 (two year) US; $28.00 (one year), $55.00 (two year) other. Liturgical Press, St. Johns Abbey, Collegeville MN 56321. **Tel** (612)363-2213, (800)858-5450, FAX (612)363-3299, (800)445-5899. **ED** R. Kevin Seasoltz. **LC** BV175; .W67. Index available. **Bk Rev. Ad Acc. Circ:** 7,000 (ctrl). available on microfilm and microfiche from University Microfilms International (UMI). ***Continues*** *Orate Fratres, 0196-6898.*
**Desc:** A scholarly, ecumenical review exploring the structure of Christian worship and the problems of liturgical renewal.
**Ind/Abst** Bibliogr. Mission.; Canon Law Abstr.; Index Book Rev. Relig.; New Testam. Abstr.; Old Testam. Abstr.; Relig. Index One Period. (1951-); Relig. Theol. Abstr.; Abr. Cathol. Period. Lit. Index; Cathol. Period. Lit. Index.

US/0890-5754
**WORSHIP AND ARTS.** ***Ceased.*** [Worsh. arts]. (1956)-Vol. 30 No. 6 (Feb. 1987). Periodical. English. bm. Worship and Arts, 11392 Wallingsford Road, Los Alamitos CA 90720. **ED** E J Mero. **DD** 291. **Bk Rev. Ad Acc. Circ:** 1,000.
**Desc:** Non-denominational publication promoting worship arts in the church. Reviews of new music for adult, youth and childrens choirs and of organ music, books and records.

UK/0032-7407
**WORSHIP AND PREACHING.** V. 1 (1970)-. Periodical. English. bm. $20.00 (surface mail) U.S. Methodist Publishing House / US, PO Box 801, Nashville TN 37202. Index available. cum. index. **Bk Rev. Ad Acc.** ***Continues*** *Preacher's Quarterly, 0478-0264.*

II
**WORSHIP IN INDIA SERIES.** No. 1 (1979)-. Monographic series. English. ir. Price varies per volume. Books Today, 24-B5 Original Road, Karol Bagh New Delhi 110005 India. **Tel** 4721928. **ED** B.C. Sinha. **Circ:** 1,000.
**Desc:** Studies human nature in India since the pre-Vedic period; a socio-religious study.

US/0164-6303
**WORSHIP TIMES.** ***Ceased.*** Vol. 1 (Winter 1978/79)-?. Periodical. English. qt. Worship Times, PO Box 444, Saratoga CA 95070.

US/1051-9653
**WORSHIP WORKS.** [Worsh. works]. Vol. 1, No. 1 (Sept. 1988)-. Periodical. English. mo. $30.00 US; $35.00 Canada; $60.00 other. Worship Works, PO Box 58, Topeka KS 66601. **Tel** (913)232-0354. **ED** Robin Kash. **DD** 268. **Bk Rev. Ad Acc. Circ:** 1,000. available on diskette.

CN/0848-4449
**YEAR BOOK AND DIRECTORY - UNITED CHURCH OF CANADA.** (YEAR BOOK AND DIRECTORY / THE UNITED CHURCH OF CANADA.). [Year book dir. - United Church Can.]. **Main/Corp** United Church of Canada. **Added/Corp** United Church of Canada. Division of Communication. Dept. of Education and Information. **VFOAT** United Church of Canada Year Book. (1989)-. Directory. English. an. 29.95Can$. United Church of Canada, 85 Saint Clair Avenue East Room 711, Toronto Ontario M45 1M8 Canada. **Tel** (416)925-5931. **ED** Douglas L. Hunders (editor's phone: (416)925-5931 Ext. 1950). **DD** 287.9/2/05. cum. index. ctrl circ. ***Continues*** *Year Book - United Church of Canada, 0082-7886.*

UK/0069-3995
**YEAR BOOK ... (... YEAR OF ISSUE) / THE CHURCH OF SCOTLAND. Main/Corp** Church of Scotland. (1966)-. English. an. £11.31. Church of Scotland, 121 George Street, Edinburgh EH2 4YN Scotland. **Tel** 011 44 31 2255722, FAX 011 44 31 2203113, telex 727935. **ED** Andrew Herron and Roy M. Tuton. Index available. **Ad Acc. Circ:** 2,000. ***Continues*** *Church of Scotland. Church of Scotland Year-Book.*

US/0731-5392
**YEARBOOK & DIRECTORY OF THE CHRISTIAN CHURCH (DISCIPLES OF CHRIST). Main/Corp** Christian Church (Disciples of Christ). **VFOAT** Yearbook and Directory of the Christian Church (Disciples of Christ). Directory. English. an. General Office of the Christian Church, Disciples of Christ, 222 South Downy Avenue, Indianapolis IN 46206. **LC** BX7307; .C48A. **DD** 286.6/3.

US/0272-5339
**YEARBOOK - NATIONAL ASSOCIATION OF CONGREGATIONAL CHRISTIAN CHURCHES, THE. Main/Corp** National Association of Congregational Christian Churches. 1972/73-. English. an. $8.00. National Association of Congregational Christian Churches, Editorial Office, 87473 South Howell Avenue, Box 1620, Oak Creek WI 53154. **Tel** (414)764-1620. **ED** J Fred Rennebohm. **LC** BX7113; .N3. **DD** 285.8/33/02573. **Circ:** 2,400 (ctrl). ***Continues*** *National Association of Congregational Christian Churches. Handbook.*
**Desc:** A directory of membership of Congregational Christian Churches.

US/0195-9034
**YEARBOOK OF AMERICAN AND CANADIAN CHURCHES.** [Yearb. Am. Can. churches]. **Added/Corp** Office of Research, Evaluation, and Planning of the National Council of the Churches of Christ in the U.S.A. **VFOAT** Yearbook of American & Canadian Churches. 41st Edition (1973)-. English. an (Apr.). $29.95. Abingdon Press, PO Box 801, Nashville TN 37202. **Tel** (615)749-6451, (800)251-3320. **LC** BR513; .Y4. **DD** 277/.05. ***Continues*** *Yearbook of American Churches.*
**Ind/Abst** Stat. Ref. Index.

US/0084-3849
**YEARBOOK OF JEHOVAH'S WITNESSES.** English. an. Watch Tower Bible and Tract Society / Canadian Branch, PO Box 4100, Georgetown Ontario L7G 4Y4 Canada. **Tel** (718)625-3600.

US/0513-2096
**YEARS AHEAD, THE. Added/Corp** Southern Baptist Conference. Relief and Annuity Board. (1956)-. Periodical. English. qt (4 issues). Free. Relief and Annuity Board, Southern Baptist Convention, PO Box 2190, Dallas TX 75221. **Tel** (214)720-0511.
**Ind/Abst** South. Baptist Period. Index.

SP/0513-5311
**YERMO.** [Yermo]. **Added/Corp** Sociedad de Estudios Monasticos. Madrid. Santa Maria de El Paular (Monastery). **VFOAT** Revista de la Sociedad de Estudios Monasticos. Vol 1 (1963)-. Periodical. Spanish.
**Ind/Abst** Am. Hist. Life (1966-1977).

UK
**YES (LONDON, ENGLAND).** (YES : CMS MAGAZINE.). Periodical. English. Six times a year. £3.90. Church Missionary Society, 157 Waterloo Road, London SE1 8UU England. **Tel** 011 44 71 9288681, telex 8950907 ANGCOM G. **ED** Robin E Gurney. **Bk Rev. Circ:** 18,000 (ctrl).
**Desc:** Contains news of CMS activities in Africa, Asia, and the United Kingdom.

US/0746-861X
**YOUNG SALVATIONIST.** Periodical. English. mo (except bimonthly in July and August). $3.50 US; $5.00 Canada; $6.00 other. Salvation Army National Headquarters, 799 Bloomfield Avenue, Verona NJ 07044. **Tel** (201)239-0606. **DD** 267. **Circ:** 50,000. ***Continues*** *Young Soldier, 0744-5032.*

US/0049-8394
**YOUR CHURCH.** [Your church]. Vol. 1 (April/June 1955)-. Periodical. English. bm (6 issues). $15.00.

Christianity Today Inc., 465 Gundersen Drive, Carol Stream IL 60188. **Tel** (708)260-6200. **ED** Phyllis Mather Rice. **LC** BV652.A1; Y6. **DD** 254. **Bk Rev.** **Ad Acc.** **Circ:** 188,000 (ctrl). available on microfilm and microfiche from University Microfilms International (UMI). ***Absorbed*** *Protestant Church Buildings and Equipment, 0555-490X.*
**Desc:** Strives to provide pastors with information about all aspects of their work including building and equipment, counseling, administration, personal finances and to present a variety of thought provoking articles.
**Ind/Abst** Int. Index Multi Media Inf.

US/0044-1015
**YOUR EDMUNDITE MISSIONS NEWS LETTER.** **VFOAT** Edmundite Missions. Periodical. English. bm. Edmundite Mission, 1428 Broad Street, Selma AL 36701.

UK
**YOUR TOMORROW.** Vol. 1, No. 1 (April 1987)-. English. mo. £11.00. Prophetic Witness Movement International, 59 Baldwin Avenue, Eastborne Sussex BN21 3Y8 England. **Tel** 011 44 323-33650. ***Continues*** *Prophetic Witness, 0033-135X.*

CN/0713-3634
**YOUTH & ADULTS TOGETHER.** Periodical. English. ir. Free. Division of Mission in Canada, United Church of Canada, 85 St Clair Avenue East, Toronto Ontario M4T 1M8 Canada. **DD** 268/.433/05.

US/1053-1815
**YOUTH ILLUSTRATOR, THE.** [Youth illus.]. (1991)-. Periodical. English. bm. $19.50. The Youth Illustrator, MPO Box 0072, Oberlin OH 44074-0072. **DD** 243.

US/0190-4566
**YOUTH LEADER (SPRINGFIELD, MO.), THE.** (THE YOUTH LEADER.). **Added/Corp** Assemblies of God. General Council. Assemblies of God. National Youth Dept. (19??)-. Periodical. English. Eight times a year. $14.95 US; $16.95 other. The Youth Leader, 1445 Boonville Avenue, Springfield MO 65802. **Tel** (417)862-2781. **ED** Rich Percifield. **Bk Rev**, (Qty: 32/year). **Ad Acc**, **Adv Mgr:** Chuck Goldberg. **Circ:** 3,500 (ctrl).
**Desc:** How-to and programming help for leaders of Christian youth groups.

US/0279-6651
**YOUTH (PASADENA, CALIF.).** **See** Children and Youth Interests.

US
**YOUTHWALK.** **See** Children and Youth Interests.

US/0747-3486
**YOUTHWORKER JOURNAL.** [Youthworker]. **VFOAT** Youth Worker. (Spring 1984)-. Periodical. English. Four times a year. $25.95 US; $32.95 other. Youth Specialties Inc., 1224 Greenfield Drive, El Cajon CA 92021. **Tel** (619)440-2333. **ED** Tim McLaughlin. **Bk Rev.** **Ad Acc**, **Adv Mgr:** J. Hatcherian, **Tel** (813)822-0109.
**Desc:** Addresses the professional and personal needs of Christian, career youth workers in the church with articles on youth ministry.
**Ind/Abst** Christ. Period. Index; Curr. Thoughts Trends.

PL
**Z BIBLIA NA CO DZIEN.** Periodical. Polish. 5.00. Zwiastun Wydawnictow Koscioa Ewang-Ausgab W Prl, Ul Miodowa 21, 00-246 Warszawa Poland. **LC** BV4509.P6; Z18.

US/0514-2482
**ZEAL.** Periodical. English. qt. Zeal, St Elizabeth Mission Society, Allegheny NY 14706.

GW/0044-2038
**ZEICHEN DER ZEIT (BERLIN, GERMANY).** (DIE ZEICHEN DER ZEIT.). Vol. 1 (1947)-. Periodical. German. Six times a year (Feb., Apr., June, Aug., Oct., Dec.). DM60.00 Germany; DM75.00 other; DM14.00 (single issue). Evangel Verlagsanstalt Gmbh, Postfach 1467, D 04025 Leipzig Germany. **Tel** 011 49 341 7114122, FAX 49 341 295383. **LC** BR4; .Z693. **DD** 230/.05.

GW/0044-2615
**ZEITSCHRIFT FUER DIE NEUTESTAMENTLICHE WISSENSCHAFT UND DIE KUNDE DER ALTEREN KIRCHE.** [Z. Neutest. Wiss. Kunde alteren Kirche]. **VFOAT** Zeitschrift fuer die Neutestamentliche Wissenschaft und die Kunde der Alteren Kirche. (1900)-. Periodical. German (English). Twice a year (double issues). $104.80. Walter de Gruyter Inc., PO Box 303421, D 10728 Berlin Germany. **Tel** 011 49 30 260050, FAX 011 49 30 26005251. **LC** BS410; .Z6. **[CCC].** cum. index.
**Ind/Abst** Index Book Rev. Relig.; New Testam. Abstr.; Relig. Index One Period. (1949-); Soc. Sci. Cit. Index [Select. Cov.].

GW/0044-2925
**ZEITSCHRIFT FUER KIRCHENGESCHICHTE.** [Z. Kirchengesch.]. **Added/Corp** Gesellschaft fur Kirchengeschichte (Germany) Verband der Historiker Deutschlands. Sektion fur Kirchengeschichte. Vol. 1 (March 1876)-. Periodical. German. tq. DM244.00. W Kohlhammer Verlag GmbH, Postfach 800430, D 70549 Stuttgart Germany. **Tel** 011 49 711 78631, FAX 011 49 711 7863263, telex 7-255820. **LC** BR140; .Z4. **DD** 270/.05. **[CCC].** **Bk Rev.** **Ad Acc.** ctrl circ. Documents available from The Genuine Article.
**Desc:** Non-denominational publication which includes summarized descriptions of large complex questions on miscellaneous subjects. Also texts as well as reviews of important publications on church history from Germany to abroad.
**Ind/Abst** Am. Hist. Life (1954-1955,1961-); Arts Humanit. Citation Index [Full Cov.]; Bibliogr. Mission.; Curr. Contents Arts Humanit.; Index Book Rev. Relig. (1954-1955, 1961-); New Testam. Abstr.; Relig. Index One Period. (1950-); Relig. Theol. Abstr. (1954-1955, 1961-); Res. Alert [Full Cov.]; Romant. Move. (1954-1955, 1961-).

SZ/1017-7620
**ZEITSCHRIFT FUER KULTUR, POLITIK, KIRCHE.** (ZEITSCHRIFT: FUER KULTUR, POLITIK, KIRCHE / REFORMATIO.). [Z. Kult. Polit. Kirche]. **VFOAT** Zeitschrift Reformatio; Reformatio. (1990)-. Periodical. German. bm (6 issues). 66.00F. Laenggass Druck AG Bern, Laenggassstrasse 65, Postfach 1289, CH 3001 Bern Switzerland. **Tel** 011 41 31 242431. **(Subscription address:** Laenggass Druck AG, Postfach 7062, CH 3001 Bern Switzerland.**)** **UDC** 008. ***Continues*** *Reformatio (Bern), 0034-3021.*
**Ind/Abst** Index Book Rev. Relig.; Relig. Index One Period.

GW
**ZEITSCHRIFT FUER MISSION.** **Added/Corp** Deutsche Gesellschaft fur Missionswissenschaft. Basler Mission. (1975)-. Periodical. German. Four times a year (Feb., May, Aug., Nov.). DM39.80. Christliches Verlagshaus GmbH, Postfach 311141, Motorstrasse 36, D-70471 Stuttgart Germany. **Tel** 011 49 711 830000, FAX 011 49 711 83000-10. Index available. **Bk Rev.** **Ad Acc.** **Circ:** 1,300 (ctrl). ***Formed by the union of*** *Evangelisches Missions-Magazin* ***and*** *Evangelische Missions-Zeitschrift.*
**Desc:** Scientific and theological articles about the Christian missions worldwide. Including articles on the Third World problems.
**Ind/Abst** Bibliogr. Mission.; Index Book Rev. Relig.; Missionalia; Relig. Index One Period.

GW/0044-3123
**ZEITSCHRIFT FUER MISSIONSWISSENSCHAFT UND RELIGIONSWISSENSCHAFT.** [Z. Missionswiss. Religionswiss.]. **Added/Corp** Internationales Institut fur Missionswissenschaftliche Forschungen. Missionswissenschaftliches Institut Missio. Institut fur Missionswissenschaftliche Forschungen (Munster in Westfalen, Germany). Vol. 34 (1950)-. Periodical. German. qt. Aschendorffsche Verlags Buchhan, Postfach 1124, W-4400 Muenster FR Germany. **LC** BV2130; .Z4. **[CCC].** ***Continues*** *Missionswissenschaft und Religionswissenschaft.*
**Ind/Abst** Bibliogr. Mission.; Canon Law Abstr.; Index Book Rev. Relig.; Int. Bibliogr. Sociol.; Missionalia; Relig. Index One Period. (1950-); Relig. Theol. Abstr.

GW
**ZEITSCHRIFT FUER NEUERE THEOLOGIEGESCHICHTE.** Vol. 1 (1994)-. German. Twice a year. $101.70. Walter de Gruyter Inc., PO Box 303421, D 10728 Berlin Germany. **Tel** 011 49 30 260050, FAX 011 49 30 26005251.

GW/0044-3441
**ZEITSCHRIFT FUER RELIGIONS- UND GEISTESGESCHICHTE.** [Z. Relig.-Geistesgesch.]. Vol. 1 (1948)-. Periodical. German (English). qt. Fl150.00 (institutions) Netherlands; $85.75 (institutions) other. E. J. Brill, Postbus 9000, 2300 PA Leiden Netherlands. **Tel** 011 31 71 312624, FAX 011 31 71 317532, telex 39296 BRILL NL. **ED** H. J. Schoeps. **LC** BL4; .Z45. **[CCC].** **Bk Rev.** **Ad Acc.** **Circ:** 550. Documents available from The Genuine Article.
**Desc:** Aims to further all scientific efforts related to the history and comparison of religions. It is also the organ of German thought and as such deals with the history of ideas and ideologies in an attempt to present the spirit of a certain epoch, The Zetgeist. The journal is a platform where the great religions of our world meet and argue their problems past and present.
**Ind/Abst** Am. Hist. Life (1954-1956, 1965-); Annu. Bibliogr. Engl. Lang. Lit.; Arts Humanit. Citation Index [Full Cov.]; BHA : Biblio. Hist. Art; Curr. Contents Arts Humanit.; Index Book Rev. Relig.; New Testam. Abstr.; Philos. Index; Relig. Index One Period. (1949-); Relig. Theol. Abstr.; Res. Alert [Full Cov.]; Romant. Move.; Soc. Sci. Cit. Index [Select. Cov.].

GW/0044-3549
**ZEITSCHRIFT FUER THEOLOGIE UND KIRCHE.** [Z. Theol. Kirche]. (1891)-. Academic Scholarly Publication. German. qt. DM82.00. JCB Mohr / Paul Siebeck, Postfach 2040, D 72010 Tuebingen Germany. **Tel** 011 49 7071 9230, FAX 011 49 7071 51104, telex 7/262872 mohr d. **ED** Eberhard Jungel. **LC** BR4; .Z75. **DD** 230/.05. **[CCC].** cum. index. **Bk Rev.** **Ad Acc.** **Circ:** 2,600. Documents available from The Genuine Article.
**Desc:** A scholarly journal devoted to all areas of theological research and the teachings of the Church.
**Ind/Abst** Arts Humanit. Citation Index [Full Cov.]; BHA : Biblio. Hist. Art; Curr. Contents Arts Humanit.; Index Book Rev. Relig.; New Testam. Abstr.; Old Testam. Abstr.; Relig. Index One Period. (1950-); Relig. Theol. Abstr.; Res. Alert [Full Cov.].

GW
**ZEITSCHRIFT FUER THEOLOGIE UND KIRCHE. BEIHEFT.** (1959)-. Monographic series. German. ir. Price varies per volume. JCB Mohr / Paul Siebeck, Postfach 2040, D 72010 Tuebingen Germany. **Tel** 011 49 7071 9230, FAX 011 49 7071 51104, telex 7/262872 mohr d. **LC** BR4; .Z75 Suppl.
**Ind/Abst** BHA : Biblio. Hist. Art.

SZ/0044-3484
**ZEITSCHRIFT FUR SCHWEIZERISCHE KIRCHENGESCHICHTE. REVUE D'HISTOIRE ECCLESIASTIQUE SUISSE.** **Added/Corp** Arbeitsgemeinschaft Katholischer Historiker der Schweiz. **VFOAT** Revue d'Histoire Ecclesiastique Suisse. Vol. 1, (1907)-. Periodical. German (French). Four times a year. 50.00F Switzerland; 57.00F others. Editions St Paul Paulus Verlag, Boulevard de Perolles 42, Ch 1700 Fribourg Switzerland. **Tel** 011 41 37 864331. **ED** Urs Altermatt. **LC** BR1030; .Z48. Index available. **Bk Rev.** **Ad Acc.** **Pr Rev.** **Circ:** 500.
**Desc:** Articles on church history by eminent authors and book reviews.

GW/0340-8361
**ZEITSCHRIFTENINHALTSDIENST THEOLOGIE.** [ZID Theologie]. **Added/Corp** Universitat Tubingen. Bibliothek. Theologische Abteilung. **VAT** Zeitschriften Inhaltsdienst Theologie. (1975)-. Periodical. German (English, French, Spanish and Italian). Twelve times a year. DM28.00 Germany; DM40.00 (private), DM50.00 (libraries) other. Universitaetsbibliothek Tuebin Gen Theologische, ABT Postfach 2620, D 72016 Tubingen 1 Germany. **Tel** 011 49 7071 296499. Index available. cum. index (1980-1984). **Circ:** 950 (ctrl).
**Desc:** Contains current contents on approximately 400 periodicals.

JA
**ZEN BUNKA.** Periodical. English. qt. **(Subscription address:** Japan Publications Trading Company, Ltd., PO Box 5030, Tokyo International, Tokyo 100-31 Japan.**)**

PL/0044-488X
**ZNAK.** [Znak]. Vol. 1 (June 1946)-. Periodical. Polish. mo. $54.00. **(Subscription address:** ARS Polona, PO Box 1001, 00068 Warsaw Poland.**)** **LC** AP54; .Z6.
**Ind/Abst** Am. Hist. Life; MLA Int. Bibl. Books Artic. Mod. Lang. Lit.

FR/0984-8274
**ZNAKI CZASU.** (1986)-. Periodical. Polish. mo. Price on Request. **(Subscription address:** ARS Polona, PO Box 1001, 00068 Warsaw Poland.**)** **UDC** 26(438).

AT
**ZODAK CENTRE FOR RELIGIOUS RESEARCH PUBLICATIONS.** English. Four times a year (published Mar., June, Sept., and Dec.). $50.00 institutoins and libraries, $30.00 individuals. Zadok Institute for Christianity and Society, Locked Bag 23, Kew, Victoria, 3101 Australia. **Tel** 011 61 3 816 93674, FAX 011 61 3 816 9617. **ED** Diaby Hannah. Index available. cum. index. **Bk Rev**, (Qty: 20). **Circ:** 1,000 (ctrl).
**Desc:** Exists with the aim of encouraging thought and action by Christians on a wide range of social and religious issues.

PL/0514-4655
**ZWIASTUN.** **Added/Corp** Koscio-Ewangelicko-Augsburski w PRL. Vol. 16, No. 1 (1961)-. Periodical. Polish. sm. Price on Request. **(Subscription address:** ARS Polona, PO Box 1001, 00068 Warsaw Poland.**)** ***Continues*** *Straznica Ewangeliczna.*

SZ/0254-4407
**ZWINGLIANA.** (ZWINGLIANA : MITTEILUNGEN ZUR GESCHICHTE ZWINGLIS DER REFORMATION.). [Zwingliana]. (1897)-. Periodical. German. sa. SIGWERB AG, PF 173 Dorfmattenstr 26, CH 5612 Villmergen Switzerland. **Tel** 011 41 57 230505, FAX 011 41 57 231550. **LC** WMLC L 83/3819.
**Ind/Abst** Relig. Index One Period.

SZ
**ZWINGLIANA: BEITRAEGE ZUR GESCHICHTE ZWINGLIS DER REFORMATION UND DES PROTESTANTISMUS IN DER SEHWEIZ.** sa.
**Ind/Abst** Index Book Rev. Relig.; Relig. Index One Period.

PL/0044-5584
**ZYCIE I MYSL.** [Zycie mysl]. **Added/Corp** Instytut Zachodni. (May/June 1950)-. Periodical. Polish. mo. **(Subscription address:** ARS Polona, PO Box 1001, 00068 Warsaw Poland.**)** **LC** BX806.P6; Z9.
**Ind/Abst** Am. Hist. Life (1955-1963,1970-1972,1975).

PL
**ZYCIE KATOLICKIE W POLSCE.**
**Added/Corp** Stowarzyszenie "Pax.". (196?)-. Periodical. Polish. Twelve times a year. $30.00 (latest edition). **(Subscription address:** ARS Polona, PO Box 1001, 00068 Warsaw Poland.**)** **LC** BX1564.A1; Z94.

UK/0591-2385
**ZYGON.** [Zygon]. **Added/Corp** Institute on Religion in an Age of Science. Meadville Theological School. Meadville/Lombard Theological School. Center for Advanced Study in Religion and Science. Rollins College (Winter Park, Fla.). **VFOAT** Zygon Journal of Religion & Science. Vol. 1 (March 1966)-. Periodical. English. Four times a year. $62.50 North America; $82.50 other. Blackwell Publishers, 238 Main Street, Cambridge MA 02142. **Tel** (617)547-7110, (800)835-6770, FAX (617)547-0789. **ED** Philip Hefner. **LC** BL240.2; .Z9. **DD** 215. **[CCC]**. Index available in last issue of volume--attached. cum. index. **Bk Rev. Ad Acc. Circ:** 2,250. available on microfilm from University Microfilms International (UMI); available on microfiche. Documents available from The Genuine Article, UMI Article Clearinghouse.
**Desc:** A sourcebook of 20 years of exploring ways in which knowledge from the contemporary sciences and insights from the world's religious and philosophical heritage can be yoked together (zygon), so as to light the way in our human search for life's meaning and general moral direction.
**Ind/Abst** Acad. Search (July 1993-); Am. Hist. Life (1967-); Arts Humanit. Citation Index [Full Cov.]; Book Rev. Index; Curr. Contents Arts Humanit.; Curr. Contents Soc. Behav. Sci.; Except. Hum. Exp.; Expand. Acad. Index (1989-); Guide Soc. Sci. Relig.; Humanit. Index; Humanit. Source (Jul. 1993-); Index Book Rev. Relig.; Mag. Search; New Testam. Abstr.; Newsp. Period. Abstr. (1991-); Old Testam. Abstr.; Peace Res. Abstr. J. (1983,1985-1986); Philos. Index; Psychol. Abstr. (1979-); Relig. Index One Period. (1966-); Relig. Theol. Abstr.; Res. Alert [Full Cov.]; Soc. Plann. Policy Dev. Abstr.; Soc. Sci. Cit. Index [Full Cov.].

---

## ABSTRACTING, BIBLIOGRAPHIES AND STATISTICS

---

US/0737-3457
**ABRIDGED CATHOLIC PERIODICAL AND LITERATURE INDEX, THE.** [Abr. Cathol. period. lit. index]. **Added/Corp** Catholic Library Association. (1983)-. Abstracting/Indexing Service. English. bm. Catholic Library Association, 700 Terrace Heights, St. Mary's #26, Winona MN 55987. **Tel** (507)457-6935, (507)457-1563. **ED** Natalie A. Logan. **Bk Rev. Circ:** 350 (ctrl).
**Desc:** Indexes periodicals and selected books for adults by Catholic authors; it is intended for the smaller parish library and religious education center.

US/0733-2599
**ABSTRACTS OF RESEARCH IN PASTORAL CARE AND COUNSELING.** [Abstr. res. pastor. care couns.]. **Added/Corp** Joint Council on Research in Pastoral Care and Counseling. (1979)-. Abstracting/Indexing Service. English. an. $30.00. Commission on Pastoral Research, Loyola College in Maryland, Pastoral Counseling Department, 7135 Minstrel Way, Suite 101, Columbia MD 21045. **Tel** (410)290-5995. **ED** Joanne M. Greer Ph.D. **LC** BV4012.2; .A26. **DD** 253.5/05. Index available. cum. index. **Pr Rev. Circ:** 250 (ctrl). ***Continues*** *Pastoral Care and Counseling Abstracts.*
**Desc:** Collects data of research being done in the United States and abroad in the area of pastoral care and counseling, and to make that information available to interested individuals and institutions. This publication lists published and unpublished research during the preceding year. Also brief summaries or abstracts of each relevant research project from selected journals is included. In addition, pertinent PhD and D.Min. dissertations are listed.

KE/1013-171X
**AFRICAN CHRISTIAN STUDIES.** **See** Religion and Theology.

US
**ATLA BIBLIOGRAPHY SERIES.** **Main/Corp** American Theological Library Association. **Added/Corp** American Theological Library Association. **VFOAT** American Theological Library Association Bibliography Series; Bibliography Series. (1974)-. Bibliography. English. ir. Price varies per volume. Scarecrow Press Inc., 52 Liberty Street, PO Box 4167, Metuchen NJ 08840. **Tel** (908)548-8600, (800)537-7107.

VC/0394-9869
**BIBLIOGRAPHIA MISSIONARIA / PONTIFICAL MISSIONARY LIBRARY OF THE CONGREGATION FOR THE EVANGELIZATION OF PEOPLES.**
**Added/Corp** Pontificia Biblioteca Missionaria. Pontificia Universitas Urbaniana. **VFOAT** BM. No. 50 (1986)-. Abstracting/Indexing Service. English (Multiple languages). an (July). $45.00. Pontificia Biblioteca Missionaria, Pontificia Universita Urbaniana, V Urbano VIII 16, 00165 Rome Italy. **Tel** 011 39 6 68308361 2. **LC** Z7838.M6; B5; BV2180. **Circ:** 1,000. ***Continues*** *Bibliografia Missionaria.*

US/0065-8847
**BIBLIOGRAPHIC SERIES.** **Main/Corp** American Institute of Islamic Studies. No. 1 (1969)-. Monographic series. English. ir. Price varies per volume. American Institute of Islamic Studies, PO Box 10398, Denver CO 80210. **Tel** (303)936-0108.

UK/0081-1440
**BOOK LIST / SOCIETY FOR OLD TESTAMENT STUDY.** **Main/Corp** Society for Old Testament Study. English. an. Society for Old Testament Study, University of Manchester, ME Studies, Manchester M13 9RL England. **LC** Z7772.A1.

US/0360-6112
**BUDDHIST TEXT INFORMATION.** No. 1-Nov. 1974-. Periodical. English. qt. $10.00. Institute for Advanced Studies on World Religions, Melville Memorial Library, SUNY, Stony Brook NY 11794-3383. **Tel** (516)632-6580. **ED** Richard A Gard. **LC** Z7860; .B84; BQ1020. **DD** 016.2943. Index available. cum. index. **Circ:** 350.
**Desc:** Cumulative bibliographic information for the study of Buddhist texts. In addition, describes texts and their published editions, translations, and studies. Special attention given to projects planned in progress.

CN/0068-970X
**BULLETIN - CANADIAN SOCIETY OF BIBLICAL STUDIES.** [Bull. Can. Soc. Biblic. Stud.]. **Main/Corp** Canadian Society of Biblical Studies. **VFOAT** Bulletin de la Societe Canadienne des Etudes Bibliques; Bulletin of the Canadian Society of Biblical Studies; Abstracts. **VAT** Abstracts - Canadian Society of Biblical Studies. (1935)-. Multiple languages (English and French). an. 15.00Can$. St. Thomas More College, 1437 College Drive, Saskatoon Saskatchewan S7N 0W6 Canada. **Tel** (306)966-8900. **DD** 220/.07.

BE
**BULLETIN D'HISTOIRE CISTERCIENNE / BULLETIN OF CISTERICAN HISTORY.**
**VFOAT** Citeaux, Commentarii Cistercienses. Bulletin d'Histoire Cistercienne; Cistercian History Abstracts; Bulletin of Cistercian History. No. 1 (1987)-. Bulletin. French (Dutch, English, German, Italian and Spanish). ir (approx. every two years). Citeaux Commentarii Cistercienses, 17 rue Rabe, 89230 Pontigny France. **Tel** 011 33 1 86475821, FAX 011 33 1 86475518. **(Subscription address:** Brother Anthony Weber, Abbey of the Genesee, Piffard NY 14533.**)** **LC** BX3401; .C582.
**Ind/Abst** BHA : Biblio. Hist. Art.

UK/0008-5650
**CANON LAW ABSTRACTS.** [Canon law abstr.]. **Added/Corp** Canon Law Society of Great Britain and Ireland. No. 1 (1958)-. Abstracting/Indexing Service. English. sa. £16.00. Canon Law Society of Great Britain and Ireland, Cathedral House, Ingrave Road, Brentwood ESX CM15 8AT England. **Tel** 011 44 277 214821. **Circ:** 1,000. available on microfilm from University Microfilms International (UMI).
**Desc:** Review of periodical literature in Canon Law.
**Ind/Abst** Bibliogr. Mission.; Old Testam. Abstr.

US/0008-8285
**CATHOLIC PERIODICAL AND LITERATURE INDEX, THE.** [Cathol. period. lit. index]. **Added/Corp** Catholic Library Association. (July/August 1968)-. Abstracting/Indexing Service. English. qt. $130.00; $100.00 (cumulative edition). Catholic Library Association, 700 Terrace Heights, St. Mary's #26, Winona MN 55987. **Tel** (507)457-6935, (507)457-1563. **ED** Natalie A Logan. **LC** AI3; .C32. **DD** 011. **Circ:** 1,400 (ctrl). ***Continues*** *Catholic Periodical Index, 0363-6895;* ***Absorbed*** *Guide to Catholic Literature, 0145-191X.*
**Desc:** An author and subject index to over 158 periodicals and national Catholic newspapers, and to books for adults by Catholics and other authors whose work is of interest to Catholics.

US/0008-8307
**CATHOLIC PRESS DIRECTORY.** 1923-. Directory. English. an. $25.00. Catholic Press Association, 119 North Park Avenue, Rockville Centre NY 11570. **Tel** (516)766-3400. **ED** Regina Salzmann. **LC** Z6951; .C36. **DD** 071/.3. **Ad Acc. Circ:** 2,200 (ctrl).
**Desc:** A reference book of Catholic publications and publishers of the Catholic Press Association; membership information.

US/0069-3871
**CHRISTIAN PERIODICAL INDEX.** [Christ. period. index]. **Added/Corp** Christian Librarians' Fellowship. Association of Christian Librarians. (1956)-. Abstracting/Indexing Service. English. tq. $102.00 (tri-annual index with supplements). Association of Christian Libraries, PO Box 4, Cedarville OH 45314. **Tel** (513)766-2211 ext. 207. **ED** Douglas J Butler. cum. index. **Circ:** 500.
**Desc:** An author and subject index to selected Christian periodicals and periodicals of interest to the Christian conservative community.

US/1054-8688
**CURRENT THOUGHTS AND TRENDS.** [Curr. Thoughts Trends]. **VFOAT** Current Thoughts & Trends. Vol. 6, No. 8 (Aug. 1990)-. Abstracting/Indexing Service. English. mo. $36.00 (1 year), $59.00 (2 year), $76.00 (3 year) US; $42.00 (1 year), $71.00 (2 year), $94.00 (3 year) other. Current Thoughts and Trends, PO Box 35004, Colorado Springs CO 80935. **Tel** (719)548-9222, FAX (719)598-7128. **ED** Dennis Cone, Telephone: (719)531-3550. **LC** BR1; .C87. **DD** 205. Index available (Dec. issue). **Circ:** 8,000. available on diskette. ***Continues*** *Current Christian Abstracts, 0883-1440.*
**Desc:** Provides concise, timely summaries of current thoughts and trends in religious and secular periodicals.

US/0072-8241
**GUIDE TO BIBLES IN PRINT.** (1966)-. English. an. Shori Press, 1580 Maple Avenue, Evanston IL 60201. **LC** Z7770; .G8. **DD** 016.22.

US/1054-0946
**GUIDE TO SOCIAL SCIENCE AND RELIGION.** [Guide soc. sci. relig.]. **VFOAT** Guide to Social Science & Religion; Information Index. Vol. 24, No. 3/4 (1988)-. Abstracting/Indexing Service. English. sa. $89.00. National Periodical Library, PO Box 3278, Clearwater FL 34630. **ED** Albert M. Wells. **DD** 016. Index available. cum. index. **Circ:** 600. ***Continues*** *Guide to Social Science and Religion in Periodical Literature, 0017-5307.*
**Desc:** Indexes by subject the articles of more than 100 religious and sociological periodicals.

II/0970-1168
**HINDUSTAN YEAR-BOOK AND WHO'S WHO.** [Hindustan Year-B. Who's Who]. (1932)-. English. an. $10.00. MC Sakar & Sons Private Ltd, 14 Bankim Chatterjee St, Calcutta 700073 India. **Tel** 011 91 33 312490. **ED** S. Sakar. cum. index. **Bk Rev. Ad Acc.** ctrl circ.

CI
**HRVATSKA KRSCANSKA BIBLIOGRAFIJA.** **Added/Corp** Katolicki Bogoslovni Fakultet u Zagrebu. **VFOAT** Bibliographia Croatica Christiana. (1959)-. Bibliography. Serbo-Croatian (Roman). ir. Katolicki Bogoslovni Fakultet u Zagrebu, Facultas Theologica Catholica Zagrabiensis, 41001 Zagreb, Kaptol 29/11, p.p. 432 Croatia. **Tel** 385 041 271 343. **ED** Dr. Aldo Staric. **LC** Z7753; .H78; BL48. Index available. **Bk Rev.**
**Desc:** Information on Croatian Christian bibliograhy records, books, pamphlets, musical notes, essays, articles, and other contribution of the Croatian speaking areas. Covers area of treating religious or Christian topics from historical, theological, philosophical, artistic, psychological, sociological, or practical standpoint.

US/0161-5483
**ICUIS BIBLIOGRAPHY SERIES.** **Main/Corp** Institute on the Church in Urban-Industrial Society. **VAT** Institute on the Church in Urban-Industrial Society Bibliography Series. No. 1 (1974)-. Bibliography. English. qt. Price varies per volume. ICUIS, 5700 South Woodlawn Avenue, Chicago IL 60637. **ED** Clinton E Stockwell and L Dale Richesin. **Bk Rev. Circ:** 3,000.
**Desc:** Profiles urban ministries; lists resources and calendar items.
**Ind/Abst** Relig. Index One Period.

UK
**INDEX ISLAMICUS.** (1980)-. Abstracting/Indexing Service. English. ir (issued every six to seven years). $315.00. Bowker Saur Ltd., A Reed Reference Publishing Company, Part of Reed International PLC, 59-60 Grosvenor Street, London WIX 9DA England. **Tel** 011 44 71 4935841, FAX 011 44 71 4991590. **(Subscription address:** World-Wide Subscription Services, Unit 4, Gibbs Reed Farm Pashley Road, Ticehurst TN5 7HE England.**)** **LC** Z7835.M6; L62; BP166.2. **DD** 016.909/097671. **Circ:** 1,000. available on microfiche. ***Continues*** *Index Islamicus. Supplement, 0306-9524.*
**Desc:** Lists under subject headings books and articles on Islamic subjects, drawn sources published in all the major European languages, including Russian.

US/0887-1574
**INDEX TO BOOK REVIEWS IN RELIGION.** [Index book rev. relig.]. **Added/Corp** American Theological Library Association. **VFOAT** IBRR. (Feb. 1986)-. Abstracting/Indexing Service. English. qt. $325.00. American Theological Library Association, 820 Church Street, 3rd Floor, Evanston IL 60201. **Tel** (708)869-7788, FAX (708)869-8513. **ED** S Sue Horner. **LC** Z7753; .I5; BL1.A1. **DD** 016.2. cum. index. **Bk Rev.**

**Ad Acc. Circ:** 850 (ctrl). available on an online database; available on CD-ROM; available on microfilm. ***Continues in part*** *Religion Index One. Periodicals, 0149-8428.*
**Desc:** Indexes book reviews in religion; includes essential order information (publisher pagination) to be as helpful as possible to librarian as well as scholars. Was "Book Review Index" in Religion Index One: Periodicals.

US/0019-4050
**INDEX TO JEWISH PERIODICALS.** [Index Jew. period.]. Vol. 1 (June/Aug. 1963)-. Abstracting/Indexing Service. English. sa. $85.00 plus $2.50 postage US; $85.00 plus $3.50 postage OTHER. Index to Jewish Periodicals, PO Box 18570, Cleveland Heights OH 44118. **ED** Lenore P Koppel editors telephone (216)381-4846. **LC** Z6367; .I5. **Bk Rev. Circ:** 400.
**Desc:** An author and subject index to selected English language journals of general and scholarly interest.

GW/0074-9745
**INTERNATIONALE ZEITSCHRIFTENSCHAU FUER BIBELWISSENSCHAFT UND GRENZGEBIETE.** **Added/Corp** Katholisches Bibelwerk e.V. Stuttgart. **VFOAT** International Review of Biblical Studies. (1952)-. Abstracting/Indexing Service. German (German, English and French). an. DM158.00 (Vol. 37). Cornelsen Velhagen and Klasing, Postfach 100271, D 33502 Bielefeld 1 Germany. **Tel** 011 49 521 97190, FAX 05217872 260, telex 175218149 CORBI. **LC** Z7770; .I57. **Ad Acc. Circ:** 800.
**Desc:** Contains 3,000 abstracts and reviews of all materials relevant to biblical studies. Includes sections on religion in general, middle eastern archaeology, and theology.

US/0022-5754
**JUDAICA BOOK NEWS.** ***Ceased.*** [Jud. book news]. Vol. 1 (Fall 1970)-(1992). Periodical. English. sa. Book News Periodicals Inc, 303 West 10th Street, New York NY 10024. **Tel** (212)691-3817. **ED** Ernest Weiss. **LC** Z6367; .J8. **DD** 016.91003/924. **Bk Rev. Ad Acc. Circ:** 15,000. available on microfilm and microfiche from University Microfilms International (UMI).
**Desc:** Articles, critical book reviews, picture stories, comprehensive bibliography of news and forthcoming English language books of Jewish interest.
**Ind/Abst** Index Jew. Period. (199?-).

SA/0256-9507
**MISSIONALIA.** (MISSIONALIA / THE SOUTH AFRICAN MISSIOLOGICAL SOCIETY.). [Missionalia]. **Added/Corp** South African Missiological Society. Vol. 1, No. 1 (April 1973)-. Abstracting/Indexing Service. English. Three times a year. R25.00 (individuals), R30.00 (institutions) South Africa, Namibia; $12.00 (individuals), $15.00 (institutions) Southern Africa; $20.00 (individuals), $25.00 (institutions) Africa; $27.00 (individuals), $35.00 (institutions) Canada; $25.00 (individuals), $30.00 (institutions) other. Journal of the South African Missiological Society, PO Box 35704, Menlo Park 0102 South Africa. **Tel** 011 27 12 4294477, FAX 011 27 12 4293332. **ED** J.N.J. Kritzinger. Index available. cum. index. **Bk Rev**, (Qty: 45). **Ad Acc. Circ:** 1,400 (ctrl). available on microfilm and microfiche from University Microfilms International (UMI). ***Formed by the union of*** *Lux Mundi (Pretoria, South Africa)* ***and*** *Missionaria.*
**Desc:** Scholarly articles on Christian missions; about 1,000 abstracts annually of articles on missiological themes appearing in theological journals worldwide.
**Ind/Abst** Bibliogr. Mission.; Index Book Rev. Relig.; Relig. Index One Period. (1979-); Relig. Theol. Abstr. (1979-).

CN/0225-3801
**MISSIONNAIRES CATHOLIQUES CANADIENS, STATISTIQUES.** **VFOAT** Canadian Catholic Missionaries, Statistics. Began publication in 197-. English (French). be. Canadian Religious Conference, 324 Laurier Avenue East, Ottawa Ontario K1N 6P6 Canada. **Tel** (613)236-0824. **DD** 266/.2/0212.

US/0028-6877
**NEW TESTAMENT ABSTRACTS.** [New Testam. abstr.]. **Added/Corp** Weston School of Theology. Weston College of the Holy Spirit. Weston College School of Theology. Council on the Study of Religion. Vol. 1 (Fall 1956)-. Abstracting/Indexing Service. English. Three times a year. $30.00 US; $33.00 other. Catholic Biblical Association of America, Catholic University of America, Washington DC 20064. **Tel** (202)319-5519. **ED** Daniel Harrington, Christopher Matthews and Stanley Marrow. **LC** BS410; .N35. **DD** 220.05. Index available. cum. index. **Ad Acc. Circ:** 2,250.
**Desc:** A research and bibliographic aid for scholars, librarians, clergymen and students of the New Testament and its historical milieu.
**Ind/Abst** Bibliogr. Mission.

US/0078-3854
**OFFICIAL CATHOLIC DIRECTORY, THE.** (1886)-. Directory. English. an (mid-year supplement is available). $190.00. R R Bowker, A Reed Reference Publishing Company, Part of Reed International PLC, PO Box 31, 121 Chanlon Drive, New Providence NJ 07974. **Tel** (908)464-6800, (800)521-8110, FAX (908)665-6688, telex 138-755. **(Subscription address:** PJ Kennedy & Sons, 3004 Glenview Road, Wilmette, IL 60091; telephone: (800)323-6772**)** **LC** BX845; .C5.
**Desc:** Provides a serious overview of today's church. All information is confirmed and approved by each diocese before publication.

US/0364-8591
**OLD TESTAMENT ABSTRACTS.** [Old Testam. abstr.]. **Added/Corp** Catholic Biblical Association of America. Vol. 1 (Feb. 1978)-. Abstracting/Indexing Service. English. Three times a year. $26.00. Catholic Biblical Association of America, Catholic University of America, Washington DC 20064. **Tel** (202)319-5519. **ED** Thomas P McCreesh and Joseph Jensen. **LC** BS410; .O42. **DD** 221.6/05. Index available. **Bk Rev. Ad Acc. Circ:** 2,000 (ctrl).
**Desc:** English/abstracts of article and books on Old Testament and related areas (archeology, linguistics, biblical theology, etc.) from publications throughout the world in all languages (including Japanese and modern Hebrew).
**Ind/Abst** Bibliogr. Mission.; Abr. Cathol. Period. Lit. Index; Cathol. Period. Lit. Index.

UK/0308-7395
**QUARTERLY INDEX ISLAMICUS.** [Q. index Islam.]. **Added/Corp** Mansell (Firm). Vol. 1 (Jan. 1977)-. Abstracting/Indexing Service. English. qt. $295.00 US; £195.00 other. Bowker Saur Ltd., A Reed Reference Publishing Company, Part of Reed International PLC, 59-60 Grosvenor Street, London WIX 9DA England. **Tel** 011 44 71 4935841, FAX 011 44 71 4991590. **ED** G. J. Roper and C. H. Bleaney. **LC** Z3013; .Q34; DS44. **DD** 016.956. available on microfiche.
**Desc:** Bibliography of published materials on Islam and Middle Eastern studies, updating quinquennial supplements of Index Islamicus.

US/0149-8428
**RELIGION INDEX ONE. PERIODICALS.** [Relig. index one, Period.]. **Added/Corp** American Theological Library Association. (July/Dec. 1977)-. Abstracting/Indexing Service. English. sa (with 2nd issue every year being an annual cumulation). $450.00. American Theological Library Association, 820 Church Street, 3rd Floor, Evanston IL 60201. **Tel** (708)869-7788, FAX (708)869-8513. **ED** Don M Haymes. **LC** Z7753; .A5; BL1. **DD** 016.2. cum. index. **Bk Rev. Ad Acc. Circ:** 1,200 (ctrl). available on CD-ROM; available on microfilm; available on an online database. ***Continues*** *Index to Religious Periodical Literature, 0019-4107.* ***Continued in part by*** *Index to Book Reviews in Religion, 0887-1574.*
**Desc:** Indexes periodicals in and related to the field of religion. Includes both scholarly and more popular journals, which serve primarily as source documents for the study of religion.

US
**RELIGION INDEXES [COMPUTER FILE].** **Added/Corp** H.W. Wilson Company. (198?)-. Periodical. English. an. $1050.00. American Theological Library Association, 820 Church Street, 3rd Floor, Evanston IL 60201. **Tel** (708)869-7788, FAX (708)869-8513.
**Desc:** Includes citations from Religion Index One, Religion Index Two, and Index to Book Reviews in Religion.

US/0034-4044
**RELIGIOUS AND THEOLOGICAL ABSTRACTS.** Vol. 1 (March 1958)-. Abstracting/Indexing Service. English. qt (Mar., Jun., Sep., Dec.). $100.00 (institutions), $50.00 (individuals). Religious & Theological Abstracts Inc., PO Box 215, 121 South College Street, Myerstown PA 17067. **Tel** (717)866-6734, FAX (717)866-6734. **ED** William S. Sailer. **LC** BR1; .R286. **DD** 208.22. Index available. cum. index. **Circ:** 1,000 (ctrl). available on microfiche (all back issues); available on CD-ROM.
**Desc:** Contains abstracts classified by Bible, theological, historical, and practical. An objective summary of current religious thought. CD-ROM electronically searches 80,000 abstracts.

BE/0035-2381
**REVUE D'HISTOIRE ECCLESIASTIQUE.** [Rev. hist. eccles.]. Vol. 1 (1900)-. Periodical. French (English and German). Four times a year (Jan., Apr., July, Oct.). 3800F. Bibliotheque de l'Universite Coll-Erasme, PLC Blaise Pascal, 1348 Louvain La Neuve Belgium. **Tel** 011 32 10 472111. **LC** BX940; .R5. **DD** 282. Index available. cum. index. **Bk Rev. Ad Acc. Circ:** 1,800 (ctrl). Documents available from The Genuine Article.
**Desc:** History of the church from the beginnings to our days, with systematical bibliography.
**Ind/Abst** Am. Hist. Life (1954-1956, 1958-); Arts Humanit. Citation Index [Full Cov.]; Bibliogr. Mission. (1954-); BHA : Biblio. Hist. Art; Curr. Contents Arts Humanit.; Index Book Rev. Relig. (1954-); MLA Int. Bibl. Books Artic. Mod. Lang. Lit.; New Testam. Abstr.; Relig. Index One Period. (1949-); Relig. Theol. Abstr.; Res. Alert [Full Cov.]; Romant. Move. (1954-); Soc. Sci. Cit. Index [Select. Cov.]; Abr. Cathol. Period. Lit. Index; Cathol. Period. Lit. Index.

US/0558-8766
**SCHOLARS' CHOICE.** **Added/Corp** Union Theological Seminary in Virginia. Library. No. 1 (Jan. 1960)-. English (German, French, Spanish, Japanese and Indonesian). sa (published in July and December). $5.00. Union Theological Seminary, 3401 Brook Road, Richmond VA 23227. **Tel** (804)355-0671 Ext. 296, FAX (804)355-3919. **ED** John B. Trotti (editor's phone: (804)278-4311). **LC** Z7753; .S32. **Circ:** 250.
**Desc:** A bibliography of current titles in religion selected by scholars for American Theological Libraries.

US/0270-3599
**SEVENTH-DAY ADVENTIST PERIODICAL INDEX.** Vol. 1 (1971)-. Abstracting/Indexing Service. English. ir. $25.00 US. Andrews University, Seminary Studies, Berrien Springs MI 49104. **Tel** (616)471-6023, (616)471-7771, FAX (616)473-4472. **ED** Daniel J. Drazen, Gina Boyd. Index available. **Circ:** 300.
**Desc:** The aim is to provide easy access to material in Seventh- day Adventist periodicals for students, educators, ministers, and the general researcher. Indexes 34 periodicals.

US/0081-3028
**SOUTHERN BAPTIST PERIODICAL INDEX.** [South. Baptist period. index]. **Added/Corp** Southern Baptist Convention. Historical Commission. Southwest Baptist University (Bolivar, Mo.). Estep Library. **VFOAT** SBPI. (1965)-. Abstracting/Indexing Service. English. an. $95.00. Southern Baptist Periodical Index, c/o Estep Library, Southwest Baptist University, Bolivar MO 65613. **Tel** (417)326-1621. **ED** Eldonna DeWeese; (417)326-1625. **LC** Z7845.B2; S64; BX6462.7. **DD** 286/.132/05. **Circ:** 350.
**Desc:** Indexes articles and reviews in major publications of Southern Baptist Convention national agencies.

PP
**STATISTICS FROM RELIGIOUS ORGANIZATIONS.** **Main/Corp** Papua New Guinea. Bureau of Statistics. English. Bureau of Statistics / Papua New Guinea, PO Box 2032, Konedobu Papua New Guinea. **LC** BV3680.N5; P26A. **DD** 266/.00995/3.

US/0039-3568
**STUDIES IN BIBLIOGRAPHY AND BOOKLORE.** [Stud. bibliogr. booklore]. Vol. 1 (June 1953)-. Bibliography. English (Hebrew, German and French). ir. $12.00 (postage) other. Hebrew Union College, Library, 3101 Clifton Avenue, Cincinnati OH 45220-2488. **Tel** (513)221-1875, FAX (513)221-0321. **ED** Herbert C Zafren. **LC** Z7070; .S88. **DD** 010. Index available. cum. index. **Bk Rev. Pr Rev. Circ:** 1,000 (ctrl).
**Desc:** Judaic bibliography very broadly conceived.
**Ind/Abst** Am. Hist. Life (1954-); Child. Lit. Abstr. (19??-); Index Jew. Period. (19??-199?); Middle East Abstr. Index; Old Testam. Abstr.

## BIBLE

UK
**1 TO ONE (MARKHAM, ONT.).** (1 TO ONE.). **VFOAT** One to One. (Jan./March 1989)-. Periodical. English. Four times a year (Jan., Apr., July, Oct.). £12.00. Scripture Union / Pennsylvania, 7000 Ludlow Street, Upper Darby PA 19082. **Tel** (215)352-5400. **DD** J220.6/05. ***Continues*** *Keynotes, 0315-2006.*
**Desc:** Provides interest-catching comments on a large portion of the Bible. It teaches 11-14 year olds to rely on God's Word to solve the problems and temptations they are facing today.

SZ
**ABHANDLUNGEN ZUR THEOLOGIE DES ALTEN UND NEUEN TESTAMENTS.** (19??)-. Monographic series. German. ir. Price varies per volume. Theologischer Verlag Und Buchhandlungen AG, Raffelstrasse 20, Postfach 8045, Zurich Switzerland. **Tel** 011 41 1 4617710. **(Subscription address:** Schweizer Buchzentrum / Swiss Book Center, Postfach, CH 4601 Olten Switzerland.**)**

NE/0065-0382
**ABR-NAHRAIN.** (ABR-NAHRAIN : AN ANNUAL UNDER THE AUSPICES OF THE DEPARTMENT OF SEMITIC STUDIES, UNIVERSITY OF MELBOURNE.). [Abr-nahrain]. **Added/Corp** University of Melbourne. Dept. of Semitic Studies. University of Sydney. Dept. of Semitic Studies. University of Melbourne. Dept. of Middle Eastern Studies. **VAT** Abr -Nahrain; Abr Nahrain. Vol. 1 (1960)-. English (French and German). an. 1200F. Editions Peeters SA, Bondgenotenlaan 153, BP 41, B-3000 Leuven Belgium. **Tel** 32 16 235170, FAX 32 16 228500, telex 65987 PUL B. **ED** T. Muraoka. **LC** PJ3001; .A2. **Bk Rev.** available on an online database.
**Desc:** Aims to appeal to all university specialists in the fields of Arabic, Syriac and Hebrew, Semitic palaeography and linguistics, and archaeological and literary studies on biblical material.
**Ind/Abst** Index Islam. Lit.; Middle East Abstr. Index; MLA Int. Bibl. Books Artic. Mod. Lang. Lit.; Old Testam. Abstr.; Relig. Theol. Abstr. (199?-).

CN/1184-7204
**ACTUALITES BIBLIQUES.** [Actual. bibliques]. **Added/Corp** Societe Biblique Canadienne. Vol. 15, No 1

(Spring 1990)-. Periodical. French. qt. Free. Societe Biblique Canadienne / Canadian Bible Society, 10 Carnforth Road, Toronto, Ontario M4A 2S4 Canada. **Tel** (416)757-4171, FAX (416)757-3376, telex TOR 06 963696. **DD** 220. ***Continues*** *Bulletin de Nouvelles Bibliques., 0834-1842.*

US/0149-8347
**ADULT BIBLE STUDIES.** (ADULT BIBLE STUDIES.). **Added/Corp** United Methodist Church (U.S.). Board of Discipleship. Curriculum Resources Committee. (19??)-. Periodical. English. qt. $16.25 US; $17.25 other. Graded Press, 201 Eighth Avenue South, Box 801, Nashville TN 37202. **Tel** (615)749-6417. **ED** Victor J. Jacobs. **Bk Rev. Circ:** 700,000.
**Desc:** A systematic study of the Bible for adults designed to relate the authority, history, and relationship of its message to life.

IS/0303-1500
**ALON HA-ONATI - NEOT QEDUMIM, HA-.** (HA-ALON HA-ONATI - NEOT KEDUMIM.). **Main/Corp** Neot Kedumim Ltd. No. 1/2 (1966)-. Hebrew. Neot Kedwmin Ltd, PO Box 299, Kiryat Ono Israel. **LC** BS660; .N45A.

GW
**ALTER ORIENT UND ALTES TESTAMENT.** V. 1- 1969-. Monographic series. Multiple languages (English and German). ir. Price varies per volume. Neukirchener Verlag, Postfach 216, W-4133 Neukirchen Germany.

US/0006-0801
**AMERICAN BIBLE SOCIETY RECORD.** **Main/Corp** American Bible Society. **Added/Corp** American Bible Society. Record. Vol. 115, No. 6 (July/Aug. 1970)-. Periodical. English. Ten times a year (Except for June and Sept.). Free. American Bible Society, 1865 Broadway, New York NY 10023. **Tel** (212)408-1480. **ED** Clifford P. MacDonald. **LC** BV2370; .A4. **DD** 205. cum. index. **Circ:** 350,000 (ctrl). ***Continues*** *Bible Society Record.*
**Desc:** Stories and articles concerning the work and mission of the American Bible Society.

IT
**ANALECTA BIBLICA.** (19??)-. $40.00 US. Editrice Pontificio Istituto Biblico, Piazza della Pilotta 35, 00187 Rome Italy. **Tel** 011 39 6 6781567, FAX 011 39 6 6780588.

US
**ANCHOR BIBLE, THE.** (1964)-. Periodical. English (Undetermined). ir. Individually priced by each title in series. Anchor Bible Series, 6 Commercial Street, Hicksville NY 11801. **Tel** (516)433-3800, 800-347-7828.

JA/0912-9243
**ANNUAL OF THE JAPANESE BIBLICAL INSTITUTE.** [Annu. Jpn. Biblic. Inst.]. **Main/Corp** Nihon Seishogaku Kenkyujo. Vol. 1 (1975)-. Periodical. English (French and German). an. $55.00. Yamamoto Shoten Publishing House, 23 Ichigaya Honmuracho, Shinjuku-ku Tokyo 162 Japan. **(Subscription address:** Japan Publications Trading Company, Ltd., PO Box 5030, Tokyo International, Tokyo 100-31 Japan.**)**
**Ind/Abst** New Testam. Abstr.; Old Testam. Abstr.

US/0740-6401
**ANNUAL REPORT OF THE AMERICAN BIBLE SOCIETY.** [Annu. rep. Am. Bible Soc.]. **Main/Corp** American Bible Society. (1817)-. English. an. Free on request. American Bible Society, 1865 Broadway, New York NY 10023. **Tel** (212)408-1480. **ED** C.P. MacDonald. **LC** BV2370; .A5. **DD** 266.06273. Index available. **Circ:** 2,000 (ctrl).
**Desc:** Report of worldwide work of scripture translation, publication and distribution for the past year.

AT/0045-0308
**AUSTRALIAN BIBLICAL REVIEW.** [Aust. biblic. rev.]. **Added/Corp** Fellowship for Biblical Studies (Australia). Vol. 1 (Mar./June 1951)-. Periodical. English. an (Oct.). 9.25Aus$ Victoria in Australia; 9.50Aus$ Australia; 9.80Aus$ Asia and Oceania; 10.40Aus$ other (postage included). Fellowship Biblical Studies, JT Theological Library, Ormond College, Parkville Vic 3052 Australia. **ED** N. W. Watson and M. A. O'Brien. **LC** BS410; .A85. **DD** 220/.05. **Bk Rev**, (Qty: 20). **Circ:** 450.
**Ind/Abst** Index Book Rev. Relig.; New Testam. Abstr.; Old Testam. Abstr.; Relig. Index One Period. (1974-); Relig. Theol. Abstr.

GW/0408-8298
**BEITRAEGE ZUR GESCHICHTE DER BIBLISCHEN EXEGESE.** Vol. 2 (1959)-. Monographic series. German. ir. Price varies per volume. JCB Mohr / Paul Siebeck, Postfach 2040, D 72010 Tuebingen Germany. **Tel** 011 49 7071 9230, FAX 011 49 7071 51104, telex 7/262872 mohr d. ***Continues*** *Beitrage zur Geschichte der Neutestamentlichen Exegese.*

IT/0006-0585
**BIBBIA E ORIENTE.** [Bibbia oriente]. Yearly V. 1- Jan./Feb. 1959-. Periodical. Italian (French, English, German and Greek, Modern). qt. $85.00. Centro Studi Arti Grafiche, Sardini Editrice, 25040 Bornato BS Italy. **Tel** 39 30 725123. **ED** Fausto Sardini. **LC** BS410; .B42. **DD** 220. Index available. **Bk Rev.** ctrl circ.
**Ind/Abst** Bibliogr. Mission.; New Testam. Abstr.; Old Testam. Abstr.; Relig. Theol. Abstr.

GW/0006-0615
**BIBEL UND GEMEINDE.** **Added/Corp** Bibelbund. Yearly V. 44, No. 3, (1954)-. Periodical. German. qt (Jan., Apr., Jul., Oct.). $15.00. Verlag Bibel und Gemeinde, Postfach 1153, D 76333 Waldbronn Germany. Index available. **Bk Rev. Circ:** 3,500. ***Continues*** *Nach dem Gesetz und Zeugnis.*
**Desc:** Encourages understanding of the Bible and the value of its authority; publicizes scientific and general literature concerning inerrancy and absolute trustworthiness of scriptures, etc.

GW/0006-0623
**BIBEL UND KIRCHE.** [Bibel Kirche]. **Added/Corp** Katholisches Bibelwerk (Stuttgart, Germany) Schweizerisches Katholisches Bibelwerk. Osterreichisches Katholisches Bibelwerk. **VFOAT** Jahrbuch. (1946)-. Periodical. German. qt. DM25.00 Germany; $12.00 US. Kath Bibelwerk EV, Silberburgstrasse 121, W7000 Stuttgart 1 Germany. **Tel** 0711 626001, FAX 0711 616682. **ED** Franz-Josef Ortkemper. Index available. **Bk Rev. Ad Acc. Circ:** 25,000 (ctrl). ***Supersedes*** *Katholisches Bibelwerk.*
**Desc:** Includes four articles: biblical theology, archeological-biblical article; biblical literature reviews, news of biblical movement and Bible institutes.
**Ind/Abst** New Testam. Abstr.; Old Testam. Abstr.

AU/0006-064X
**BIBEL UND LITURGIE.** **Added/Corp** Pius Parsch Institut. Osterreichisches Katholisches Bibelwerk. Vol. 1 (1926)-. Periodical. German. Four times a year (Mar., June, Sept., Dec.). S376.00. Patmos Verlag Gmbh, AM Wehrhahn 100, D 40211 Duesseldorf Germany. **Tel** 011 49 211 167950. **(Subscription address:** Oesterreich Katholisches Bibel, Stiftsplatz 8 Postfach 48, A 3400, Klosterneuburg, Austria, telephone: 011 43 2243 2938**)** Index available. **Bk Rev. Circ:** 1,200 (ctrl).
**Desc:** Journal for Bible research, pastoral Bible studies, liturgical studies and practice.
**Ind/Abst** New Testam. Abstr.; Old Testam. Abstr.

US/0162-9220
**BIBLE ADVENTURES (ELGIN, ILL.).** (BIBLE ADVENTURES.). English. qt. $4.00. David C Cook Publishing Company, 850 North Grove Avenue, Elgin IL 60120. **DD** 220.

US/0746-0104
**BIBLE ADVOCATE (BROOMFIELD, COLO.).** (BIBLE ADVOCATE : A PUBLICATION OF THE CHURCH OF GOD (SEVENTH DAY)). **Added/Corp** Church of God (Seventh Day). (19??)-. Periodical. English. Eleven times a year (Except Aug.). Free on request. Bible Advocate Press, PO Box 33677, Denver CO 80233. **Tel** (303)452-7973. **ED** Roy A. Marrs. Index available. **Circ:** 12,000 (ctrl).

II/0970-2288
**BIBLE BHASHYAM (ENGLISH ED.).** (BIBLE BHASHYAM.). [Bible bhashyam]. **Added/Corp** St. Thomas Apostolic Seminary. Vol. 7, No. 1 (March 1981)-. Periodical. English (Malayalam). qt. $20.00. Bible Bhashyam, PO Box I Vadavathoor Kottayam, 686 010, Kerala India. **Tel** 011 91 83190481. **(Subscription address:** Prints India, 11 Darya Ganj, New Delhi 110002 India.**) ED** Mathew Vellanickal. **LC** BS410; .B64. **DD** 220/.05. **Bk Rev. Ad Acc. Circ:** 1,850. ***Continues*** *Biblebhashyam, 0970-2288.*
**Desc:** Personalities and themes in the Bible, with emphasis on the relevance of the theme in Indian context.
**Ind/Abst** Bibliogr. Mission.; New Testam. Abstr.; Old Testam. Abstr.

US/1057-0217
**BIBLE BOOK STUDY FOR YOUTH. BIBLE STUDY CARDS.** [Bible book study youth, Bible study cards]. **Added/Corp** Southern Baptist Convention. Sunday School Board. **VFOAT** Bible Study Cards. Vol. 1, No. 1 (Apr., May, June 1992)-. Periodical. English. qt. $3.60. Southern Baptist Convention, 901 Commerce, Suite 750, Nashville TN 37203. **Tel** (615)244-2355, FAX (615)742-8919. **(Subscription address:** Sunday School Board - Customer Service, 127 Ninth Avenue North, Nashville, TN 37234 USA; telephone: (800)458-2772**) DD** 268.

US/0162-4830
**BIBLE BOOK STUDY FOR YOUTH TEACHERS.** V. 1- Oct./Dec. 1978-. Periodical. English. qt. $5.50. Southern Baptist Convention, 901 Commerce, Suite 750, Nashville TN 37203. **Tel** (615)244-2355, FAX (615)742-8919. **(Subscription address:** Sunday School Board - Customer Service, 127 Ninth Avenue North, Nashville, TN 37234 USA; telephone: (800)458-2772**)**

US/0883-9204
**BIBLE COLLECTORS' WORLD.** [Bible collect. world]. **Added/Corp** International Society of Bible Collectors. Vol. 1, No. 1 (Jan./March 1985)-. Periodical. English. Four times a year (Jan., Apr., July, Oct.). $20.00. Bible Collectors' World - Don Heese, 12155 West 58th Place, Apartment E-103, Arvada CO 80004. **ED** Bill E. Paul, (editor's address: PO Box 30526, Seattle, WA 98103-0526, phone: (206)782-3992). **LC** BS410; .B53. **DD** 220/.075. Index available. cum. index. **Bk Rev**, (Qty: 25). **Ad Acc. Circ:** 250. available on microfilm from University Microfilms International (UMI). ***Continues*** *Bible Collector, 0006-0690.*
**Desc:** The purpose of the society is to exchange information and to encourage interaction between all those interested in discoveries and developments relating to the background and history if all Bible versions, including their translation, publication preservation display and distribution.

US/0162-4695
**BIBLE DISCOVERERS.** **Added/Corp** Southern Baptist Convention. Sunday School Board. (19??)-. Periodical. English. Four times a year. $7.20. Southern Baptist Convention, 901 Commerce, Suite 750, Nashville TN 37203. **Tel** (615)244-2355, FAX (615)742-8919. **(Subscription address:** Sunday School Board - Customer Service, 127 Ninth Avenue North, Nashville, TN 37234 USA; telephone: (800)458-2772**)**

US/0162-4687
**BIBLE DISCOVERERS TEACHER.** **Added/Corp** Southern Baptist Convention. Sunday School Board. (19??)-. Periodical. English. qt. Southern Baptist Convention, 901 Commerce, Suite 750, Nashville TN 37203. **Tel** (615)244-2355, FAX (615)742-8919. **(Subscription address:** Sunday School Board - Customer Service, 127 Ninth Avenue North, Nashville, TN 37234 USA; telephone: (800)458-2772**)**

US/0256-9361
**BIBLE DISTRIBUTOR. ENGLISH.** (THE BIBLE DISTRIBUTOR.). [Bible distrib.]. Periodical. English (Spanish and French). Three times a year. $9.00. United Bible Societies / New York, 1865 Broadway, New York NY 10023. **Tel** (212)408-1300. **ED** Kenneth J Thomas and Nancy Vazquez. **Circ:** 8,000 (ctrl).

US
**BIBLE EXPOSITOR AND ILLUMINATOR.** (19??)-. Periodical. English. qt. $13.00. Union Gospel Press, Box 6059, Cleveland OH 44101. **Tel** (216)749-2100. **ED** Julia P. Stabley. **Circ:** 200,000.

US/0162-9573
**BIBLE-IN-LIFE STORIES.** Periodical. English. qt. $3.50. David C Cook Publishing Company, 850 North Grove Avenue, Elgin IL 60120.

US/0747-3893
**BIBLE JOURNEYS FOR CHRISTIANS.** ***Ceased.*** (1984)-(Dec. 1994). Periodical. English. wk. ALT Publishing Company, PO Box 400, Green Bay WI 54305. **Tel** (414)432-1413. **ED** James L. Alt. **Circ:** varies (ctrl).
**Desc:** Sunday homily Service.

UK/0006-0763
**BIBLE LANDS.** **Added/Corp** Jerusalem and the East Mission. Vol. 1 (1903)-. Newsletter. English. sa. Jerusalem & Middle East Church Association, 1 Hart House, The Hart, Farnham Surrey GU9 7HA England. **Tel** 011 44 252 726994, FAX 011 44 252 735558. **ED** Mrs. V. Wells and C. Willianson. Index available. **Bk Rev. Ad Acc. Circ:** 3,500. available with illustrations.

UK
**BIBLE LEAGUE QUARTERLY.** **Added/Corp** Bible League, London. (1???)-. Periodical. English. Four times a year (Jan., Apr., July, Oct.). £5.00. The Bible League, 20 Thistlebarrow Road, Salisbury Wilts SP1 3RT England. **Tel** 0722-325581. **ED** Reverend J. P. Thackway (editor's address: "Fairlea", Front Parc Road, Holywell Clwyd CH8 7SP England). **Bk Rev**, (Qty: 6). **Circ:** 1,200.
**Desc:** Promotes the reverent study of the holy scriptures and to resist the varied attacks upon their inspiration, infallibility and sole sufficiency as the word of God.

US/0279-8069
**BIBLE NEWSLETTER, THE.** [Bible newsl.]. Vol. 1, No. 1 (Feb. 1981)-. Newsletter. English. mo. $15.95. Eternity Subscriber Services, PO Box 611, Holmes PA 19043. **Tel** (215)546-3696.

US/8755-6316
**BIBLE REVIEW (WASHINGTON, D.C.).** (BIBLE REVIEW.). [Bible rev.]. **Added/Corp** Biblical Archaeology Society. Vol. 1, No. 1 (Feb. 1985)-. Periodical. English. Six times a year. $24.00 US; $30.00 other. Biblical Archaeology Society, 3000 Connecticut Avenue Northwest, Suite 300, Washington DC 20008. **Tel** (202)387-8888. **(Subscription address:** CDS Agency Hard Copy, PO Box 4966, Des Moines IA 50340.**) LC** BS410; .B58. **DD** 220/.05.
**Desc:** Brings biblical scholarship to the layperson.
**Ind/Abst** Index Book Rev. Relig.; New Testam. Abstr.; Relig. Index One Period.

US/0164-5587
**BIBLE-SCIENCE NEWSLETTER.** (BIBLE SCIENCE NEWSLETTER.). **Added/Corp** Bible Science Association (U.S.). (19??)-. Newsletter. English. Nine times a year. $25.00 US; $35.00 other; $20.00 students and seniors. Bible-Science Association, PO Box 33220, Minneapolis MN 55433-0220. **Tel** (612)755-8606, (800)422-4253, (800)422-4253, FAX (612)755-8535. **ED** Paul A Bartz. **Circ:** 12,000 (ctrl).

**Desc:** Practical articles, news, features and book reviews for the Christian dealing with all areas of Bible and science relationships.

US/0006-0798
**BIBLE SEARCHERS : TEACHER.**
Periodical. English. qt. $8.50. Southern Baptist Convention, 901 Commerce, Suite 750, Nashville TN 37203. **Tel** (615)244-2355, FAX (615)742-8919. **(Subscription address:** Sunday School Board - Customer Service, 127 Ninth Avenue North, Nashville, TN 37234 USA; telephone: (800)458-2772**)**

US/0890-457X
**BIBLE TEACHING FOR CONFIDENT LIVING.** ***Ceased.*** **VFOAT** Confident Living. Vol. 44, No. 8 (Sept. 1986)-(1993). Periodical. English. ir. Back to the Bible Broadcast, PO Box 82808, Lincoln NE 68501. **Tel** (402)474-4567, (800)759-2425, FAX (402)474-4519. **ED** Jan E Reeser. **DD** 248. **Circ:** 95,000 (ctrl). ***Continues*** *Good News Broadcaster, 0017-2154.*
**Desc:** Promotes spiritual growth of believers by teaching the Word and applying it to Christian living.
**Ind/Abst** Guide Soc. Sci. Relig.

US/0006-0836
**BIBLE TODAY, THE.** [Bible today]. No. 1 (Oct. 1962)-. Periodical. English. bm. $22.00 (one year), $43.00 (two year) US; $26.00 (one year), $51.00 (two year) other. Liturgical Press, St. Johns Abbey, Collegeville MN 56321. **Tel** (612)363-2213, (800)858-5450, FAX (612)363-3299, (800)445-5899. **ED** Dianne Bergant. Index available. **Bk Rev. Ad Acc. Circ:** 12,000 (ctrl). available on microfilm and microfiche from University Microfilms International (UMI).
**Desc:** Strives to promote, understand and appreciate scripture for life and ministry; written especially for the non-specialist reader.
**Ind/Abst** Bibliogr. Mission.; New Testam. Abstr.; Old Testam. Abstr.; Abr. Cathol. Period. Lit. Index; Cathol. Period. Lit. Index.

UK/0260-0935
**BIBLE TRANSLATOR, THE. Added/Corp** United Bible Societies. **VFOAT** Technical Papers for the Bible Translator; Practical Papers for the Bible Translator. Vol. 1 (1950)-. Periodical. English. Four times a year (Jan., Apr., July, Oct.). $12.00. United Bible Societies / England, General Office, Reading Bridge House/7th Floor, Reading RG1 8PJ England. **(Subscription address:** Translation Services Coordinator, United Bible Societies, 1865 Broadway, New York, NY 10023, telephone: (212)408-1469 or (212)582-7245 Fax**) ED** Dr. P. Ellingworth. **LC** IN PROCESS. **DD** 220.05. Index available. cum. index. **Bk Rev. Ad Acc. Circ:** 2,800. available on microfilm and microfiche from University Microfilms International (UMI).
**Ind/Abst** Christ. Period. Index (19??-); Index Book Rev. Relig.; New Testam. Abstr.; Old Testam. Abstr.; Relig. Index One Period.; Relig. Theol. Abstr.; Soc. Plann. Policy Dev. Abstr.

FR
**BIBLIA PATRISTICA.** French. Editions du CNRS, 22 rue Saint Armand, F 75015 Paris France. **Tel** 011 33 1 45075050.

IT/0006-0879
**BIBLIA REVUO.** [Biblia rev.]. No. 1-8, 1964-66. Periodical. Esperanto. qt. Universala Esperanto-Asocio, Nieuwe Binnenweg 176, 3015 BJ Rotterdam Netherlands. **Tel** 011 31 10 4361044, FAX 011 31 10 4361751, telex 23721.
**Ind/Abst** New Testam. Abstr.; Old Testam. Abstr.

SP/0210-5209
**BIBLIA Y FE.** [Biblia fe]. (Jan./April 1975)-. Periodical. Spanish. Three times a year. $5.45 Spain; $11.00 others. Biblia Y Fe, Fermin Caballero 53, Madrid 3 Spain. **ED** Antonio Salas. **Circ:** 2,500.
**Desc:** Journal of Biblical theology. Consists of monograph numbers on key religious and humanistic themes seen from a Biblical perspective.
**Ind/Abst** Old Testam. Abstr.

IT/0006-0887
**BIBLICA.** [Biblica]. **Added/Corp** Pontificio Istituto Biblico. Vol. 1 (1920)-. Periodical. English (French, German, Italian and Spanish). qt. L75000 Italy; $70.00 other. Editrice Pontificio Istituto Biblico, Piazza della Pilotta 35, 00187 Rome Italy. **Tel** 011 39 6 6781567, FAX 011 39 6 6780588. **ED** H Simian-Yofre. **LC** BS410; .B7. **DD** 220/.05. Index available. cum. index. **Bk Rev. Circ:** 1,600. Documents available from The Genuine Article.
**Ind/Abst** Arts Humanit. Citation Index [Full Cov.]; Bibliogr. Mission.; Curr. Contents Arts Humanit.; Index Book Rev. Relig.; New Testam. Abstr.; Old Testam. Abstr.; Relig. Index One Period. (1949-); Relig. Theol. Abstr.; Res. Alert [Full Cov.].

IT
**BIBLICA ET ORIENTALIA. Added/Corp** Pontificio Istituto Biblico. No. 1 (1928)-. Monographic series. Italian (English and German). ir. Price varies per volume. Editrice Pontificio Istituto Biblico, Piazza della Pilotta 35, 00187 Rome Italy. **Tel** 011 39 6 6781567, FAX 011 39 6 6780588. **ED** J. Swetnam.

US/0006-0895
**BIBLICAL ARCHAEOLOGIST, THE.** **See** Archaeology.

US/0098-9444
**BIBLICAL ARCHAEOLOGY REVIEW, THE.** **See** Archaeology.

UK
**BIBLICAL ARCHAEOLOGY REVIEW.** (19??)-. Periodical. English. Six times a year. £23.70 UK; £26.35 other. Paternoster Press, A division of Send the Light Ltd., PO Box 300, Kingstown Broadway, Cumbria CA3 0QS England. **Tel** 011 44 228 512512, FAX 011 44 228 514949.

US/0749-9280
**BIBLICAL BULLETIN.** [Biblic. bull.]. Bulletin. English. ir (three to four issues per year). free. Biblical Seminary, 200 North Main Street, Hatfield PA 19440. **Tel** (215)368-5000, FAX (215)368-7002. **ED** Sherry Kull. **DD** 207. **Bk Rev. Pr Rev. Circ:** 13,000.
**Desc:** Articles on the Bible and christianity and their application to contemporary issues.

●NE
**BIBLICAL INTERPRETATION.** Vol. 1, No. 1 (Feb. 1993)-. Periodical. English. tq. Fl157.00 (institutions) Netherlands; $89.75 other. E. J. Brill, Postbus 9000, 2300 PA Leiden Netherlands. **Tel** 011 31 71 312624, FAX 011 31 71 317532, telex 39296 BRILL NL. **LC** BS410; .B53.

US/0067-6535
**BIBLICAL RESEARCH.** [Biblic. res.]. **Added/Corp** Chicago Society of Biblical Research. Vol. 1 (1956)- Vol. 38 (1993)-. Periodical. English. an (November). $10.00. Chicago Society of Biblical Research, 3225 West Foster, Professor C. Katter, Chicago IL 60625. **Tel** (312)583-2700. **ED** David Aune. **LC** BS410; .B76. **DD** 220/.05. Index available. **Ad Acc, Adv Mgr:** C. Katter, **Tel** (312)509-5840. **Circ:** 700 (ctrl). available on microfilm and microfiche from University Microfilms International (UMI).
**Desc:** Papers of the Chicago Society of Biblical Research, contributed by members of the society. History, literature and interpretation of documents: Old Testament, Intertestamental, and New Testament.
**Ind/Abst** Index Book Rev. Relig.; New Testam. Abstr.; Old Testam. Abstr.; Relig. Index One Period. (1956-); Relig. Theol. Abstr.

US/0746-4525
**BIBLICAL RESEARCH MONTHLY.** 1937. Periodical. English. bm. $15.00. Biblical Research Society, 4005 Verdugo Road, Los Angeles CA 90065. **Tel** (310)257-8162. **ED** Ronald L Cooper.

US/0277-0474
**BIBLICAL SCHOLARSHIP IN NORTH AMERICA.** (BIBLICAL SCHOLARSHIP IN NORTH AMERICA / SOCIETY OF BIBLICAL LITERATURE.). **Added/Corp** Society of Biblical Literature. (19??)-. Monographic series. English. ir. Price varies per volume. Scholars Press / Georgia, PO Box 15399, Atlanta GA 30333-0399. **Tel** (404)636-4757, (404)727-2320, FAX (404)727-2348. **ED** P Achtemeier, E Epp, E B Holifield, H Orlinsky, and K Richards.
**Desc:** Studies of schools of scholarship, individual scholars, and those subdisciplines to which Americans have made notable contributions.

US/0146-1079
**BIBLICAL THEOLOGY BULLETIN.** [Biblic. theol. bull.]. Vol. 1 (Feb. 1971)-. Bulletin. English. qt. $25.00. St Johns University / Theology, Department of Theology, Leland J White, Jamaica NY 11439. **Tel** (718)990-6161. **(Subscription address:** Biblical Theology Bulletin, St John's University, Jamaica, NY 11439**) ED** Leland J White and David M Bossman. **LC** BS410; .V42. **DD** 220/.05. **[CCC].** Index available. cum. index. **Bk Rev. Ad Acc. Pr Rev. Circ:** 1,500 (ctrl). available on microfilm and microfiche from University Microfilms International (UMI). ***Continues*** *Verbum Domini.*
**Desc:** Articles and reviews by senior and new scholars edited for non-specialized readers interested in multi-disciplinary approaches to Bible and theology.
**Ind/Abst** Bibliogr. Mission.; Book Rev. Index; Guide Soc. Sci. Relig.; Index Book Rev. Relig.; Int. Zeitschriftenschau Bibelwissenschaft Grenzgeb.; New Testam. Abstr.; Old Testam. Abstr.; Relig. Index One Period. (1971-); Relig. Theol. Abstr.; Abr. Cathol. Period. Lit. Index; Cathol. Period. Lit. Index.

US/0006-0925
**BIBLICAL VIEWPOINT. Added/Corp** Bob Jones University. Vol. 1, (Apr. 1967)-. Periodical. English. Twice a year (Apr., Nov.). $4.00 (one year); $7.50 (two years); $11.00 (three years). Bob Jones University / South Carolina, Greenville SC 29614. **Tel** (803)242-5100. **Circ:** 2,000. available on microfilm and microfiche from University Microfilms International (UMI).
**Desc:** A journal for the reverent exposition of the Bible, maintaining the view of a Bible-believing Christian.
**Ind/Abst** Christ. Period. Index; Relig. Theol. Abstr.

GW
**BIBLISCH-THEOLOGISCHE STUDIEN.** (1977)-. Monographic series. German. ir. Price varies per volume. Neukirchener Verlag des Erziehungsvereins GmbH, Andreas Braem Strasse 18 20, D 47506 Neukirchen-Vluyn Germany. **Tel** 011 49 2845 392227. ***Supersedes*** *Biblische Studien.*

GW/0178-2967
**BIBLISCHE NOTIZEN.** [Bibl. Not.]. Issue 1 (1976)-. Periodical. German (English). Three times a year. DM39.00 Germany; DM40.50 Europe; DM80.00 other. Institute Fuer Biblische Exegese, Geschwister Scholl Platz 1, D 80539 Munich Germany. **Tel** 011 49 89 21803215. **ED** Manfred Gorg. Index available (Bound in all issues).
**Ind/Abst** Index Book Rev. Relig.; New Testam. Abstr.; Old Testam. Abstr.; Relig. Index One Period. (1980-).

GW/0523-5154
**BIBLISCHE UNTERSUCHUNGEN.** Vol. 1, (1967)-. Monographic series. German. ir. Price varies per volume. Verlag Friedrich Pustet, Gutenbergstrasse 8, D-93051 Regensburg. **Tel** 0941 9 20 22-0, FAX 0941 94 86 52, telex 6 56 72.

GW/0006-2014
**BIBLISCHE ZEITSCHRIFT.** [Biblische Z.]. Vol. 1 (1903)-. Periodical. German (English). sa. DM60.00. Ferdinand Schoeningh Verlag, Postfach 2540, D 33055 Paderborn Germany. **Tel** 011 49 5251 127665. **ED** Josef Schreiner and Rudolf Schnackenburg. **LC** BS410; .B83. **DD** 220/.05. **[CCC].** Index available. **Ad Acc. Circ:** 900 (ctrl). available on microfilm and microfiche from University Microfilms International (UMI). Documents available from The Genuine Article.
**Ind/Abst** Arts Humanit. Citation Index [Full Cov.]; Curr. Contents Arts Humanit.; Index Book Rev. Relig.; New Testam. Abstr.; Old Testam. Abstr.; Relig. Index One Period. (1963-); Relig. Theol. Abstr.; Res. Alert [Full Cov.].

GW
**BONNER BIBLISCHE BEITRAEGE.** (19??)-. German. ir. Price varies. Verlag Anton Hain Athenaeum, Wormer Strasse 99, D 55294 Bodenheim Germany. **Tel** 011 49 6135 3057. **(Subscription address:** Prolit Verlagsauslieferung, Postfach 9, D 35461 Fernwald Germany.**)**

CN/0068-970X
**BULLETIN - CANADIAN SOCIETY OF BIBLICAL STUDIES.** **See** Religion and Theology-Abstracting, Bibliographies and Statistics.

US/1065-223X
**BULLETIN FOR BIBLICAL RESEARCH.** (BULLETIN FOR BIBLICAL RESEARCH / IBR.). [Bull. Biblic. res.]. **Added/Corp** Institute for Biblical Research (Winona Lake, Ind.). Vol. 1 (1991)-. Periodical. English. an. $12.50 (individuals); $17.50 (institutions). Institute for Biblical Research, PO Box 275, Winona Lake IN 46590-0275. **(Subscription address:** Eisenbrauns, PO Box 275, Winona Lake IN 46590.**) DD** 220.

UK/0041-719X
**BULLETIN - UNITED BIBLE SOCIETIES.** **Main/Corp** United Bible Societies. (1950)-. Bulletin. English. sa. $5.00. United Bible Societies / England, General Office, Reading Bridge House/7th Floor, Reading RG1 8PJ England. **(Subscription address:** 1865 Broadway, New York, NY 10023; Tel: (212)408-1312**) LC** BV2370; .U5. **Bk Rev. Ad Acc. Circ:** 200 (ctrl). available on microfilm and microfiche from University Microfilms International (UMI).
**Desc:** Information on the work of the United Bible Societies throughout the world.

UK
**CAMBRIDGE BIBLE COMMENTARY ON THE NEW ENGLISH BIBLE. OLD TESTAMENT.** Academic Scholarly Publication. English. ir. Cambridge University Press, The Edinburgh Building, Shaftesbury Road, Cambridge CB2 2RU United Kingdom. **Tel** 011 44 223 312393, FAX 011 44 223 325959.

JM/0008-6436
**CARIBBEAN CHALLENGE. Added/Corp** Christian Literature Crusade. (1957)-. Periodical. English. Eleven times a year. $7.00. Christian Literature Crusade Inc, Box 186, 55 Church Street, Kingston Jamaica. **Tel** (809)922-7878. **ED** John Keane. **Ad Acc. Circ:** 18,000.
**Desc:** A gospel magazine designed primarily for the English speaking masses of the West Indies. Distributed also to England, Canada, US and other parts of the world.

US/0008-7912
**CATHOLIC BIBLICAL QUARTERLY, THE.** [Cathol. Biblic. q.]. **Added/Corp** Catholic Biblical Association of America. Vol. 1 (Jan. 1939)-. Academic Scholarly Publication. English. qt. $25.00. Catholic Biblical Association of America, Catholic University of America, Washington DC 20064. **Tel** (202)319-5519. **ED** Aelred Cody. **LC** BS410; .C3. Index available. cum. index. **Bk Rev. Ad Acc. Circ:** 4,280 (ctrl). available on microfilm and microfiche from University Microfilms International (UMI). Documents available from The Genuine Article, UMI Article Clearinghouse.

**Desc:** Scholarly investigation of scripture and related fields including exegesis, biblical theology, archaeology, textual and literary criticism, Near Eastern history, comparative religion as related to the bible, quran, ugaritic, etc.
**Ind/Abst** Acad. Ind. [Computer File] (1992-); Acad. Search (Jan. 1994-); Arts Humanit. Citation Index [Full Cov.]; Bibliogr. Mission.; Curr. Contents Arts Humanit.; Expand. Acad. Index (1989-); Humanit. Index; Humanit. Source (Jul. 1993-); Index Book Rev. Relig.; INFO-SOUTH Abstr.; Mag. Search; Middle East Abstr. Index; New Testam. Abstr.; Newsp. Period. Abstr. (1991-); Old Testam. Abstr.; Relig. Index One Period. (1949-); Relig. Theol. Abstr.; Res. Alert [Full Cov.]; Soc. Sci. Cit. Index [Select. Cov.]; Abr. Cathol. Period. Lit. Index; Cathol. Period. Lit. Index.

US
**CATHOLIC BIBLICAL QUARTERLY. MONOGRAPH SERIES.** **Added/Corp** Catholic Biblical Association of America. Vol. 1, (1971)-. Monographic series. English. ir. Price varies per volume. Catholic Biblical Association of America, Catholic University of America, Washington DC 20064. **Tel** (202)319-5519. **ED** Robert J. Karris. Index available. **Circ:** 1,000 (ctrl).
**Desc:** Covers all areas of scripture and related fields (archaeology, biblical theology, linguistics and qumran).

US/0278-3746
**CHILDREN'S BIBLE STUDIES. ELEMENTARY B. STUDENT BOOK.** **VFOAT** Elementary B. Student. Vol. 1, No. 1 (Fall 1982)-. Periodical. English. qt. $7.75. Graded Press, 201 Eighth Avenue South, Box 801, Nashville TN 37202. **Tel** (615)749-6417. ***Continues*** *Middle Elementary Student, 0149-774X.*

CN/0710-099X
**CLAIRON (MONTREAL).** (LE CLAIRON.). [Clairon]. Periodical. French. ir. 10.00Can$. Publications GBU, Bureau 601, 455 Ouest rue St-Antoine, Montreal Quebec H2Z 1J1 Canada. **Tel** (514)861-5233. **DD** 220/.06/0714. **Bk Rev. Circ:** 800 (ctrl).

CN/0316-3040
**COME AND SEE.** V. 1- Aug. 1974-. Periodical. English. bm. Free. Nathaniel Literature Distributors, 64 Hills Road, Ajax Ontario L1S 2W4 Canada. **Tel** (416)683-6276. **ED** J Van Dijk. **DD** 220.6/05. **Circ:** 7,000 (ctrl).

US/0162-962X
**COMPREHENSIVE BIBLE STUDY.** Periodical. English. qt. $4.25. David C Cook Publishing Company, 850 North Grove Avenue, Elgin IL 60120.

●US/1061-673X
**CTVRTLETNIK KRESTANSKE VEDY. BIBLICKE LEKCE.** **Added/Corp** Christian Science Publishing Company. **VFOAT** Biblicke Lekce; Bible Lessons; Christian Science Quarterly. Bible Lessons. Vol. 104, No. 1 (1993)-. Periodical. Czech (English). qt. Christian Science Publishing Society, One Norway Street, Boston MA 02115. **Tel** (617)450-2678, (617)450-2504. **DD** 289.

SP
**CULTURA BIBLICA.** **Added/Corp** Asociacion para el Fomento de los Estudios Biblicos en Espana. Vol. 1, No. 1 (May 1944)-. Periodical. Spanish. Three times a year. Cultura Biblica, Julian Gayarre 1, Madrid 7 Spain.

US
**DAWN : A HERALD OF CHRIST'S PRESENCE, THE.** **Added/Corp** Dawn Bible Students Association. (19??)-. Periodical. English. mo. $1.00. Dawn Bible Students Association, 199 Railroad Avenue, East Rutherford NJ 07073. **Tel** (201)438-6421. **ED** George Jeuck. ctrl circ.

GR/1012-2311
**DELTION BIBLIKON MELETON.** [Delt. bibl. mel.]. **VFOAT** Bulletin of Biblical Studies. (1971)-. Periodical. English. Twice a year (June, Dec.). $10.00. Artos Zoes Publications, 12 Afronoros, Athens 11635 Greece. **Tel** 011 30 7015379.
**Ind/Abst** New Testam. Abstr.; Old Testam. Abstr.

FR
**DICTIONNAIRE DE LA BIBLE. SUPPLEMENT.** **VFOAT** Supplement au Dictionnaire de la Bible. Vol. 1 (1926)-. French. ir (6 updates per volume). Price varies per volume. Letouzey et Ane, 87 Boulevard Raspail, 75006 Paris France. **Tel** 011 33 1 45488014.

CN/0018-912X
**DISCOVER THE BIBLE.** (1964)-. Periodical. English (French). wk. 22.00Can$ US and Canada; 36.00Can$ other. Guided Study Program, PO Box 2400, London N6A 4G3 Ontario Canada. **Tel** (519)439-7211, FAX (519)439-0207. **ED** Guy Lajoie. **Circ:** 2,500 (ctrl).

FR
**DOSSIERS POUR L'ANIMATION BIBLIQUE.** Monographic series. French. Price varies per volume. Editions du Centurion, 17 rue de Babylone, 75007 Paris France.

US/8755-2175
**EARLITEEN (TEACHER'S ED.).** (EARLITEEN.). **VFOAT** Early Teen. Vol. 24, No. 1 (First Quarter 1985)-. Periodical. English. Four times a year. $16.64. Review and Herald Publishing Association, 55 West Oak Ridge Drive, Hagerstown MD 21740. **Tel** (301)791-7000 ext. 2534, FAX (301)790-9734. **Circ:** 21,000.
**Desc:** Sabbath school lesson material for Earliteen Bible lessons.

US
**EMMAUS JOURNAL, THE.** English. Twice a year. $7.00. Emmaus Bible College, 2570 Asbury Road, Dubuque IA 52001. **Tel** (319)588-8000. **ED** John H. Fish III.
**Desc:** Devoted to the exposition of the Bible, biblical doctrines, and practical issues from a biblical perspective.

SP/0014-1437
**ESTUDIOS BIBLICOS.** [Estud. biblic.]. (Nov. 29 1929)-. Academic Scholarly Publication. Spanish. qt. 2438ptas Spain; 3450ptas other. Estudios Biblicos, San Buenaventura 9, 28005 Madrid Spain. **LC** BS410; .E55. **DD** 220.02. **Bk Rev.**
**Desc:** Scholarly journal covering the field of Bible studies (Old and New Testaments) and literature from the ancient Middle East relating to the Bible. Format includes research, articles, and reviews of principal books in the field from publishers world-wide.
**Ind/Abst** Index Book Rev. Relig.; New Testam. Abstr.; Old Testam. Abstr.; Relig. Index One Period.

CN/0712-2667
**ETOILE DU MATIN.** (L'ETOILE DU MATIN.). [Etoile matin]. No. 1 Sept. 1980-. Periodical. French. qt. 12.00Can$ Canada; $10.00 US. Etoile du Matin, 45 William Street, Ottawa Ontario K1N 6Z9 Canada. **Tel** (613)234-8880. **DD** 220/.05. **Bk Rev. Circ:** 2,500.
**Desc:** Publication for the teaching and encouragement of its readers. Teaching is based on fundamental and historical theology.

US/0744-0448
**EXEGETICAL RESOURCE.** (198?)-. Periodical. English. qt. $36.00 (libraries), $18.00 (other). Logos Art Productions, PO Box 240, South St. Paul MN 55075. **Tel** (800)328-0200, (612)451-9945, FAX (612)457-4617. **DD** 251. **Circ:** 2,000 (ctrl). ***Continues*** *Pulpit Resource. Supplement, 0274-6344.*
**Desc:** Interpretive help on the Bible developed from variant readings and ancient texts.

US/0149-8584
**EXPLORING THE BIBLE. AGES 8-12. PACKET.** **VAT** Exploring the Bible. Ages Eight to Twelve. Packet. English. an. $5.95. Graded Press, 201 Eighth Avenue South, Box 801, Nashville TN 37202. **Tel** (615)749-6417.
**Desc:** Kit contains: picture, maps, photos, cards, etc.

UK/0014-5246
**EXPOSITORY TIMES, THE.** [Expo. times]. Vol. 1 (Oct. 1889)-. Periodical. English. mo. $29.95 US; £14.95 UK; 39.95Can$ Canada; 42.50Aus$ Australia; £17.50 other. T & T Clark Ltd., 59 George Street, Edinburgh EH2 2LQ Scotland. **Tel** 011 44 31 2254703, FAX 011 44 31 2204260. **ED** Cyril Rodd. **LC** BS410; .E8. Index available. cum. index. **Bk Rev. Ad Acc. Pr Rev. Circ:** 7,000 (ctrl). Documents available from The Genuine Article.
**Desc:** Periodical for ministers and laymen world-wide who wish to keep informed of recent biblical and theological studies.
**Ind/Abst** Arts Humanit. Citation Index [Full Cov.]; Br. Humanit. Index; Curr. Contents Arts Humanit.; Index Book Rev. Relig.; New Testam. Abstr.; Old Testam. Abstr.; Relig. Index One Period. (1948/1949-); Relig. Theol. Abstr.; Res. Alert [Full Cov.]; Soc. Sci. Cit. Index [Select. Cov.].

●US/1061-6721
**EZHEKVARTALNIK KHRISTIANSKOI NAUKI. BIBLEISKIE UROKI.** **Added/Corp** Christian Science Publishing Company. **VFOAT** Bibleiskie Uroki; Bible Lessons; Christian Science Quarterly. Bible Lessons. (1992)-. Periodical. Russian (English). qt. $3.00 (single issue). The Christian Science Publishing Society, 1 Norway Street, Boston MA 02115. **Tel** (800)225-7090.

US/0071-3597
**FACET BOOKS. BIBLICAL SERIES.** No. 1 (1963)-. English. Fortress Press, 2900 Queen Lane, Philadelphia PA 19129. **Tel** (215)848-6800. **DD** 220.

US
**FAITH.** English. qt. Free (after 18 months, donations are taken). Deborah Provencher Ed, PO Box 62970, Colorado Springs CO 80962-2970. **Tel** (719)488-9200, FAX (719)488-3840. **ED** Deborah Provencher. **Bk Rev. Circ:** 90,000.
**Desc:** Excerpts from Christian books and articles about scripture distribution around the world.

CN/0225-2112
**FEUILLET BIBLIQUE, LE.** [Feuill. biblique]. **Added/Corp** Eglise Catholique. Archidiocese de Montreal. Centre Biblique. No. 849 (Sept. 3, 1978)-. Periodical. French. Forty-three times a year (Except July & Aug.). 20.00Can$ Canada; 22.00Can$ US; 36.80Can$ other. Bible Center, 2000 rue Sherbrooke Quest, Montreal Quebec H3H 1G6 Canada. **Tel** (514)931-7311, FAX (514)931-3432. **ED** Yves Guillemette. **DD** 220/.05. **Circ:** 7,000 (ctrl). ***Continues*** *Parole Dimanche, 0225-2120.*
**Desc:** A lucid presentation of each Sunday's three biblical readings.

SP
**FILOLOGIA NEOTESTAMENTARIA.** **See** Linguistics.

GW
**FORSCHUNGEN ZUR RELIGION UND LITERATUR DES ALTEN UND NEUEN TESTAMENTS.** Vol. 1 (1903)-. Monographic series. German. ir. Price varies per volume. Vandenhoeck & Ruprecht, Robert Bosch Breite 6, D-37079 Goettingen Germany. **Tel** 011 49 551 695911, FAX 011 49 551 695917, telex 965226 VAN d. **Ad Acc.**

US/0883-4970
**FORUM (BONNER, MONT.).** (FORUM.). [Forum]. **VFOAT** Foundations & Facets Forum; Foundations and Facets Forum. Vol. 1, No. 1 (Mar. 1985)-. Periodical. English. qt. $30.00. Polebridge Press, 19678 8th Street East, Sonoma CA 95476. **Tel** (707)996-9228, FAX (707)996-5022. **ED** Culver H. Nelson. **LC** BS410; .F67. **DD** 220/.05. **Bk Rev. Ad Acc. Circ:** 700 (ctrl).
**Desc:** Provides a forum for focused discussion of the biblical and American traditions as reflected in scholarship, literature, cinema, art, myth, ethics and religion.
**Ind/Abst** Index Book Rev. Relig.; New Testam. Abstr.; Relig. Index One Period.; Relig. Theol. Abstr. (199?-).

US
**GIDEON, THE.** **Added/Corp** Gideons International. Vol. 3, No. 3, (1903)-. Periodical. English. Eleven times a year. $4.50. Gideons International, 2900 Lebanon Road, Nashville TN 37214. **Tel** (615)883-8533. ***Continues*** *Gideon Quarterly.*

US/0745-0788
**GODS REVIVALIST AND BIBLE ADVOCATE.** [ERROR IN DATA]. **VFOAT** God's Revivalist. (1901)-. Periodical. English. mo. $4.50. 1810 Young Street, Cincinnati OH 45210. **Tel** (513)721-7944. **ED** Hubert Hotchkiss. **DD** 269. **Bk Rev. Circ:** 21,000 (ctrl).
**Desc:** Articles pertaining to Christian growth, revival in the church, and the interests and happenings of God's Bible School.

US/0199-3429
**GOD'S WORD TODAY.** Vol. 1 (Oct. 1979)-. Periodical. English. Twelve times a year. $14.95 US; $21.95 other. Catholic Digest - Minnesota, PO Box 64088, St. Paul MN 55164. **Tel** (612)647-5298. **(Subscription address:** God's Word Today, 5615 West Cermark Road, Cicero IL 60650.**) ED** George Martin and Kevin Perrotta. **Bk Rev**, (Qty: 3). **Circ:** 57,000.
**Desc:** A daily guide to Bible reading for Catholics.

US
**GRACE SEMINARY SPIRE.** **Main/Corp** Grace Theological Seminary, Winona Lake, Indiana. 1974. Periodical. English. qt. Grace Theological Seminary, 200 Seminary Drive, Winona Lake IN 46590. **Tel** (219)372-5117, FAX (219)372-5265. **ED** Gerald H Twombly. **Circ:** 6,000.
**Desc:** Brief articles on themes relating to Biblical interpretation, ethical issues, answers to alumni questions and alumni news items.

GW
**GRUNDRISSE ZUM NEUEN TESTAMENT.** (19??)-. German. ir. Price varies per volume. Vandenhoeck & Ruprecht, Robert Bosch Breite 6, D-37079 Goettingen Germany. **Tel** 011 49 551 695911, FAX 011 49 551 695917, telex 965226 VAN d.

GW/0932-9706
**HANDBUCH ZUM NEUEN TESTAMENT.** (1912)-. Monographic series. German. ir. Price varies per volume. JCB Mohr / Paul Siebeck, Postfach 2040, D 72010 Tuebingen Germany. **Tel** 011 49 7071 9230, FAX 011 49 7071 51104, telex 7/262872 mohr d.

US
**HAPPY TIMES.** (19??)-. Periodical. English. mo. $7.50. Concordia Publishing House, 3558 South Jefferson Avenue, St Louis MO 63118. **Tel** (314)268-1000, (800)325-3381, FAX (314)268-1329.

US/0073-0637
**HARVARD SEMITIC MONOGRAPHS.**
**Added/Corp** Harvard University. Harvard Semitic Museum. **VFOAT** Harvard Semitic Monograph Series; Harvard Semitic Monograph. Vol. 1 (1968)-. Monographic series. English. ir. Price varies per volume. Scholars Press Customer Service, PO Box 6996, Alpharetta GA 30239. **Tel** (800)437-6692. **ED** Frank M. Cross Jr. **Bk Rev. Ad Acc.**
**Desc:** Biblical criticism and research.

UK/0017-8217
**HARVESTER, THE.** ***Title Change.*** Periodical. English. mo. Paternoster Press, A division of Send the Light Ltd., PO Box 300, Kingstown Broadway, Cumbria CA3 0QS England. **Tel** 011 44 228 512512, FAX 011 44 228 514949. **(Subscription address:** PO Box 11127, Birmingham, AL 35202) **ED** Jonathan Lamb. **[CCC]. Bk Rev. Ad Acc.** available on microfilm from University Microfilms International (UMI). ***Continued by*** *Aware.*
**Desc:** With an emphasis on Bible study, this journal seeks to inform readers of current worldwide issues. Provides an excellent book review service.

US/0193-7162
**HEBREW ANNUAL REVIEW.** ***Suspended.*** **See** Linguistics.

US/0146-4094
**HEBREW STUDIES.** **See** Religion and Theology-Judaism.

US
**HERMENEIA; A CRITICAL AND HISTORICAL COMMENTARY ON THE BIBLE.** (1971)-. English. ir. Fortress Press, 2900 Queen Lane, Philadelphia PA 19129. **Tel** (215)848-6800.

UK
**HISTORY OF THE GENEVA BIBLE.**
(19??)-. Monographic series. English. an. Price varies per volume. Olive Tree, 2 Milnthorpe Road, London W4 3DX England. **ED** L.F. Lupton. Index available. **Bk Rev. Pr Rev. Circ:** 500.
**Desc:** Contains the first part of the story of the authorised version of the English Bible of 1611. In the first third of the book there are brief accounts, with history links, of English versions of Scripture, specified by King James, from Tyndale to the Geneva Bible. This brings into a concise form much information which is scattered in other volumes and elsewhere.

US/0195-9085
**HORIZONS IN BIBLICAL THEOLOGY.**
[Horiz. biblic. theol.]. **Added/Corp** Clifford E. Barbour Library. Vol. 1, (1979)-. Academic Scholarly Publication. English. Twice a year (June and December). $15.00 (US & Canada) institution; $17.00 (other) institution; $12.00 (US & Canada) individual; $12.50 (other) individual;. Pittsburgh Theological Seminary, 616 North Highland Avenue, Pittsburgh PA 15206-2596. **Tel** (412)362-5610, FAX (412)363-3260. **ED** Ulrich Mauser. **LC** BS543.A1; H67. **DD** 230. **Bk Rev. Circ:** 600. available on microfilm and microfiche from University Microfilms International (UMI).
**Desc:** Dialogue between old and new testament theologies and scholarly work aimed at the achievement of canonical interpretation of scripture.
**Ind/Abst** Index Book Rev. Relig.; New Testam. Abstr.; Old Testam. Abstr.; Relig. Index One Period. (1979-); Relig. Theol. Abstr.

US/1057-0861
**HOW TO GET RICHES FROM GOD SCRIPTURALLY.** (1991)-. Periodical. English. How to Get Riches from God Scripturally, PO Box 2376, Hollywood CA 90078-2376.

US/0279-3172
**IN OTHER WORDS.** [In other words].
**Added/Corp** Wycliffe Bible Translators. (Feb. 1975)-. Periodical. English. Six times a year. Free on request. Wycliffe Bible Translators, PO Box 2727, Huntington Beach CA 92647. **Tel** (714)969-4600, FAX (714)969-4661. **ED** Roger L. Garland (editor's telephone: (714)969-4641). **Circ:** 220,000 (ctrl). available on microfilm from University Microfilms International (UMI). ***Continues*** *Translation (Glendale, Calif.), 0041-1221.*
**Desc:** Intended for evangelical Bible-oriented people with information fair on missions and missionaries.

BE
**INSTRUMENTA BIBLICA.** ir. Brepols Publishers, Steenweg OP Tielen 68, B-2300 Turnhout Belgium. **Tel** 011 32 14 402500.

●US
**INTERCESSION BIBLE STUDY LESSON.**
(1992)-. Periodical. English. mo. KD Ellis Publications, PO Box 13268, Oklahoma City OK 73113-1268.

AT
**INTERCHANGE (SYDNEY, AUSTRALIA).** (INTERCHANGE.). **Added/Corp** IVF Graduates Fellowship (Australia). Australian Fellowship of Evangelical Students. Graduates Fellowship. Vol. 1, No. 1 (1967)-. Periodical. English. Twice a year (Apr. & Oct.). 20.00Aus$ (one year), 35.00Aus$ (two years). AFES Graduates Fellowship Australia, 16 Mill Hill Road, Bondi Junction NSW 2022 Australia. **Tel** 61 2 3691688 02 690 1288. **ED** Dr. Bruce Langtry (editor's address: University of Melbourne, Department of Philosophy, Parkville Victoria 3052 Australia). **Bk Rev. Pr Rev. Circ:** 500 (ctrl).
**Desc:** Promotes discussion on the bearing of the teachings of the Bible on current questions.

GW/0074-9745
**INTERNATIONALE ZEITSCHRIFTENSCHAU FUER BIBELWISSENSCHAFT UND GRENZGEBIETE.** **See** Religion and Theology-Abstracting, Bibliographies and Statistics.

IE/0268-6112
**IRISH BIBLICAL STUDIES.** [Ir. Biblic. stud.]. **VFOAT** IBS. Issue 1 (Jan. 1979)-. Periodical. English. qt. $26.00. Union Theological College, 26 College Green, Belfast BT7 1LN North Ireland. **Tel** 011 353 232 325374, FAX 011 353 232 2325374. **ED** J C McGillough. **LC** BS543. cum. index. **Bk Rev**, (Qty: 20). **Ad Acc. Circ:** 400.
**Ind/Abst** New Testam. Abstr.; Old Testam. Abstr.; Relig. Theol. Abstr.

IS/0792-3910
**JEWISH BIBLE QUARTERLY, THE.**
**Added/Corp** World Jewish Bible Center (Jerusalem). **VFOAT** Dor le Dor. Vol. 18, No. 1 (Fall 1989)-. Periodical. English (Hebrew). qt (Jan., Apr., July, Oct.). $24.00. Jewish Bible Quarterly, PO Box 29002, Jerusalem Israel. **Tel** 011 972 2 759146, FAX 011 972 2 759144. **ED** Dr. Shimon Bakon. **LC** BS410; .D66. **DD** 22L.6/05. Index Available Received separately--bound from publisher (y). cum. index. **Bk Rev**, (Qty: 6). **Ad Acc. Circ:** 1,400. available on an online database. ***Continues*** *Dor le-Dor, 0334-2166.*
**Desc:** Provides studies on biblical themes. As the only Jewish-sponsored English-language journal devoted to the Bible. It is an essential source of information for anyone working in Bible and Old Testament studies. Publishes a original, translations from scholarly hebrew journals, book reviews, a triennal calendar of Bible reading and correspondence. All viewpoints are considered: Orthodox, Conservative, reform, and Secular-Humanistic.
**Ind/Abst** Index Jew. Period.; Int. Zeitschriftenschau Bibelwissenschaft Grenzgeb.; Old Testam. Abstr.

UK/0142-064X
**JOURNAL FOR THE STUDY OF THE NEW TESTAMENT.** [J. study New Testam.]. **Added/Corp** University of Sheffield. Dept. of Biblical Studies. **VFOAT** J.S.N.T.; JSNT. Iss. 1, (Oct. 1978)-. Periodical. English. Four times a year (Mar., June, Sept., Oct.). £14.50 (individuals), £40.00 (institutions) UK; $28.50 (individuals), $75.00 (institutions) US. Sheffield Academic Press Ltd, 343 Fulwood Road, Sheffield S10 3BP England. **Tel** 011 44 742 670044, 011 44 742 668431, FAX 011 44 742 660291. **ED** D. Hill, E. Bammel, B. Gerhardsson, A. Hansen and M. Wilcox. **LC** BS410; .J678. **DD** 225/.05. **Bk Rev. Ad Acc. Circ:** 950 (ctrl). available on microfilm and microfiche from University Microfilms International (UMI).
**Desc:** Critical scholarship in new testament studies.
**Ind/Abst** Index Book Rev. Relig.; New Testam. Abstr.; Relig. Index One Period. (1979-); Relig. Theol. Abstr.

UK/0143-5108
**JOURNAL FOR THE STUDY OF THE NEW TESTAMENT. SUPPLEMENT SERIES.** **Added/Corp** University of Sheffield. Dept. of Biblical Studies. (1980)-. Monographic series. English. Five times a year. Price varies per volume. Sheffield Academic Press Ltd, 343 Fulwood Road, Sheffield S10 3BP England. **Tel** 011 44 742 670044, 011 44 742 668431, FAX 011 44 742 660291.

UK/0309-0892
**JOURNAL FOR THE STUDY OF THE OLD TESTAMENT.** [J. stud. Old Testam.]. (Dec. 1976)-. Periodical. English. Four times a year (Mar., June, Sept., Oct.). £40.00 (institutions), £14.50 (individuals) UK; $75.00 (institutions), $28.50 (individuals) US. Sheffield Academic Press Ltd, 343 Fulwood Road, Sheffield S10 3BP England. **Tel** 011 44 742 670044, 011 44 742 668431, FAX 011 44 742 660291. **ED** D. J. A. Clines, P. R. Davies, David M. Gunn. **LC** BS410; .J68. **DD** 221/.05. Index available. cum. index. **Bk Rev. Ad Acc. Circ:** 1,500 (ctrl). available on microfilm and microfiche from University Microfilms International (UMI).
**Desc:** Critical scholarship in Old Testament studies.
**Ind/Abst** Index Book Rev. Relig.; New Testam. Abstr.; Old Testam. Abstr.; Relig. Index One Period. (1976-); Relig. Theol. Abstr.

UK/0309-0787
**JOURNAL FOR THE STUDY OF THE OLD TESTAMENT. SUPPLEMENT SERIES.** **Added/Corp** University of Sheffield. Dept. of Biblical Studies. **VFOAT** Supplement Series. Vol. 1 (1976)-. Monographic series. English. ir. Price varies per volume. Sheffield Academic Press Ltd, 343 Fulwood Road, Sheffield S10 3BP England. **Tel** 011 44 742 670044, 011 44 742 668431, FAX 011 44 742 660291.

US/0021-9231
**JOURNAL OF BIBLICAL LITERATURE.**
**Added/Corp** Society of Biblical Literature. Vol. 1 (June 1881)-. Periodical. English. qt. $50.00. Scholars Press / Georgia, PO Box 15399, Atlanta GA 30333-0399. **Tel** (404)636-4757, (404)727-2320, FAX (404)727-2348. **DD** 220.05.
**Ind/Abst** Soc. Sci. Cit. Index [Select. Cov.].

US/0021-9231
**JOURNAL OF BIBLICAL LITERATURE.**
[J. Biblic. lit.]. **Added/Corp** Society of Biblical Literature and Exegesis (U.S.) Society of Biblical Literature. Vol. 9 (1890)-. Periodical. English. qt. $50.00 (surface mail); $59.50 Canada and Mexico; $70.00 other. Scholars Press / Georgia, PO Box 15399, Atlanta GA 30333-0399. **Tel** (404)636-4757, (404)727-2320, FAX (404)727-2348. **ED** Victor P Furnish. **LC** BS410; .J86. **DD** 220.05. cum. index. **Circ:** 6,200. available on microfilm from University Microfilms International (UMI). Documents available from The Genuine Article, UMI Article Clearinghouse. ***Continues*** *Journal of the Society of Biblical Literature and Exegesis.*
**Desc:** Brings the highest level of technical expertise to bear on the canon, cognate literature and historical matrix of the Bible.
**Ind/Abst** Acad. Search (July 1993-); Arts Humanit. Citation Index [Full Cov.]; Book Rev. Index; Curr. Contents Arts Humanit.; Expand. Acad. Index (1989-); Guide Soc. Sci. Relig.; Humanit. Index; Humanit. Source (Jul. 1993-); Index Book Rev. Relig.; Index Jew. Period. (19??-199?); INFO-SOUTH Abstr.; Mag. Search; New Testam. Abstr.; Newsp. Period. Abstr. (1991-); Old Testam. Abstr.; Relig. Index One Period. (1949-); Relig. Theol. Abstr.; Res. Alert [Full Cov.].

US/1075-0347
**JOURNAL OF BIBLICAL STORYTELLING.** [J. Biblic. storytell.]. **Added/Corp** Network of Biblical Storytellers. Vol. 1, No. 1 (1989)-. Periodical. English. $9.00. United Theological Seminary, 1810 Harvard Boulevard, Dayton OH 45406. **Tel** (513)278-5817. **DD** 220.

US/0196-9072
**JOURNAL OF PASTORAL PRACTICE, THE.** ***Title Change.*** [J. pastor. pract.]. **Added/Corp** Christian Counseling & Educational Foundation. Vol. 1 (1977)-(1992). Periodical. English. sa. Christian Counseling and Education Foundation, 1790 East Willow Grove Avenue, Laverock PA 19118. **Tel** (215)884-7676. **ED** Jay E Adams. Index available. **Bk Rev. Circ:** 625 (ctrl). ***Continued by*** *Journal of Biblical Counseling, 1063-2166.*
**Desc:** Biblical insights and methods dealing with the counseling of troubled people, for pastors and lay people alike.
**Ind/Abst** Christ. Period. Index (19??-).

GT
**KAIROS : REVISTA PUBLICADA POR EL SEMINARIO TEOLOGICO CENTROAMERICANO.** **Added/Corp** Seminario Teologico Centroamericano. (1986)-. Periodical. Spanish. Twice a year. $12.50 US, Canada, Europe; $7.50 other. Seminario Teologico Centro Americano, Apartado 213, 01901 Guatemala Guatemala. **Tel** 502 2 710573, 502 2 721677. **ED** Lic. David Suazo (editor's phone: 502 2 715160). **Circ:** 500 (ctrl).
**Desc:** Contributes to the theological formation of pastors, seminarians, professors and lay leaders through articles about biblical themes, theology and ministries.

●US/1061-4958
**KEE PRODUCTIONS PRESENTS THE INTERCESSORY BIBLE JOURNAL.** [KEE Prod. presents intercess. Bible j.]. **Added/Corp** KEE Productions. **VFOAT** Intercessory Bible Journal. Vol. 1, No.1 March (1992)-. Periodical. English. bm. KD Ellis Publications, PO Box 13268, Oklahoma City OK 73113-1268. **DD** 248.

US/0145-739X
**KRISTEN VIDENSKABS KVARTALSHEFTE. BIBELSTUDIER.**
**Added/Corp** Christian Science Publishing Society. **VFOAT** Christian Science Quarterly. Bible Lessons. (19??)-. Periodical. Danish (English). qt. $19.50. Christian Science Publishing Society, One Norway Street, Boston MA 02115. **Tel** (617)450-2678, (617)450-2504.

US/0145-7381
**KRISTEN VITENSKAPS KVARTALSHEFTE. BIBELSTUDIER.**
**Added/Corp** Christian Science Publishing Society. **VFOAT** Christian Science Quarterly. Bible Lessons. (19??)-. Periodical. English (Norwegian). qt. Christian Science Publishing Society, One Norway Street, Boston MA 02115. **Tel** (617)450-2678, (617)450-2504.

IS
**LIBER ANNUUS - STUDIUM BIBLICUM FRANCISCANUM.** (LIBER ANNUUS.). [Liber annu. - Stud. Biblicum Francisc.]. **Main/Corp** Studium Biblicum Franciscanum. **VFOAT** Studii Biblici Franciscani. (1951)-. Periodical. Latin (English, French, German, Italian and Spanish). an. price varies per volume. Franciscan Printing Press, PO Box 14064, Jerusalem 91140 Israel. **Tel** 011 972 2 286594. **LC** BS410; .J4. **UDC** 22. cum. index. **Bk Rev**. **Ad Acc**. ctrl circ.
**Desc:** Theological, biblical, archaeological books.
**Ind/Abst** Bibliogr. Mission.; BHA : Biblio. Hist. Art; New Testam. Abstr.; Numis. Lit.; Old Testam. Abstr.

CN/0229-5261
**LIVING WORD (SWAN RIVER).** (THE LIVING WORD.). [Living word]. Periodical. English. qt. 1,672Can$ Canada; 357.00Can$ North America; 54.00Can$ other. Living Word Bible Institute, PO Box 969, Swan River Manitoba R0L 1Z0 Canada. **Tel** (204)734-3836. **DD** 269/.2. **Circ:** 2,000 (ctrl).
**Ind/Abst** Bibliogr. Mission.; Missionalia.

US/0145-7454
**LIVRETE TRIMESTRAL DA CIENCIA CRISTA. LICOES BIBLICAS. Added/Corp** Christian Science Publishing Society. **VFOAT** Christian Science Quarterly. Bible Lessons. (19??)-. Periodical. English (Portuguese). qt. Christian Science Publishing Society, One Norway Street, Boston MA 02115. **Tel** (617)450-2678, (617)450-2504.

US
**MASTER THOUGHTS.** qt. $15.00. Dominion Press, POB 37, San Marcos CA 92609. **Circ:** 100 (ctrl). available on microfilm.
**Desc:** Verse by verse analysis of all the words of Jesus recorded in red-letter Bibles. Project will not be finished until the year 2008. All back issues are available.

US/0194-7826
**MEGIDDO MESSAGE.** (MEGIDDO MESSAGE; DEVOTED TO THE CAUSE OF CHRIST.). **Added/Corp** Megiddo Mission Church. (1914)-. Periodical. English. mo (Except July). $5.00. Megiddo Church, 481 Thurston Road, Rochester NY 14619. **Tel** (716)235-4150, FAX (716)436-3627. **ED** Newton H. Payne (Editor's address: 98 W Sawyer Pl., Rochester, NY 14619; Telephone: (716)436-1614). Index available. cum. index. **Circ:** 12,000 (ctrl). available on diskette; available on microfilm from University Microfilms International (UMI); available on microfiche.
**Desc:** Encouraging Bible teaching/application, promoting inspirational and moral principles. Not affiliated with any other group. Upholds faith in God, Christ and the Bible.

US
**MEMBER'S HANDBOOK / SOCIETY OF BIBLICAL LITERATURE. Main/Corp** Society of Biblical Literature. (19??)-. English. $15.00. Scholars Press / Georgia, PO Box 15399, Atlanta GA 30333-0399. **Tel** (404)636-4757, (404)727-2320, FAX (404)727-2348. **LC** BS411; .S5816. **DD** 220/.06/01. **Circ:** 6,200.

US/0278-4432
**MENDY AND THE GOLEM. VFOAT** Adventures of Mendy and the Golem. Vol. 1, No. 1 (July 1981)-. Periodical. English. Five times a year (Jan., Mar., May, Sept., Nov.). $5.00. Mendy Enterprises, 450 Seventh Avenue, New York NY 10001. **Tel** (212)410-1155. **ED** Yankel Pinson. **Ad Acc**. **Circ:** 30,000 (ctrl).
**Desc:** Thirty two pages of fun and excitement in a comic format making stories of the Bible fun, and relating them to people of all ages.

US/1058-0565
**MISSION AND MINISTRY. See** Religion and Theology-Protestantism.

FR/0154-9049
**MONDE DE LA BIBLE, LE.** [Monde Bible]. (Nov./Dec. 1977)-. Periodical. French. Six times a year. $45.00. Bayard Presse, Svc Client, 3 rue Bayard/Dept 2, 75393 Paris Cedex 08 France. **Tel** 011 33 1 44356060, 011 33 1 44356262. **(Subscription address:** Novalis, PO Box 990, Outremont H2V 4S7 Canada.**)** Index available. **Ad Acc. Circ:** 10,000. ***Supersedes*** *Bible et Terre Sainte.*
**Desc:** Recent discoveries concerning archaeology in the Holy Land and new ways of studying the Bible.
**Ind/Abst** Old Testam. Abstr.

IT/1120-7353
**MONDO DELLA BIBBIA, IL.** [Mondo bibbia]. (1990)-. Periodical. Italian. Five times a year. L35000 (Italy); L43000 (other). Editrice Elle di Ci, Corso Francia 214, 10090 Rivoli Turin Italy. **Tel** 39 11 9591091, FAX (011)9574048. **UDC** 22.

UK
**MONOGRAPH SERIES. Main/Corp** Society for Old Testament Study. Vol. 1 (1971)-. Monographic series. English. ir. Price varies per volume. Cambridge University Press, The Edinburgh Building, Shaftesbury Road, Cambridge CB2 2RU United Kingdom. **Tel** 011 44 223 312393, FAX 011 44 223 325959. **(Subscription address:** North America/ Cambridge University Press, 40 West 20th Street, New York, NY 10011-4211; telephone: (212)924-3900**)**

PL
**NA STRAZY. Added/Corp** Zrzeszenie Wolnych Badaczy Pisma Swietego. (1958)-. Periodical. Polish. bm. Price on Request. **(Subscription address:** ARS Polona, PO Box 1001, 00068 Warsaw Poland.**)**

GW
**NEUTESTAMENTLICHE ABHANDLUNGEN.** Vol. 1- 1908; New Ser., Vol. 1 (1969)-. Monographic series. German. ir. Price varies per volume. Aschendorffsche Verlagsbuchhandlung, Postfach 1124, D-48135 Muenster Germany. **Tel** 011 49 251 690132, telex 08-92 830 WN MS D. **ED** Joachim Gnilka.
**Desc:** Monograph volumes of commentaries to the New Testament.

CN/0712-8096
**NEW DIRECTION (TORONTO).** (NEW DIRECTION.). [New dir.]. (Oct. 1979)-. Periodical. English. bm. $5.00. New Direction / Toronto, c/o 100 Huntley Street, Toronto Ontario M4Y 2L1 Canada. **DD** 220/.05.

US/0028-6877
**NEW TESTAMENT ABSTRACTS. See** Religion and Theology-Abstracting, Bibliographies and Statistics.

UK/0028-6885
**NEW TESTAMENT STUDIES.** [New Testam. stud.]. **Added/Corp** Society for New Testament Studies. Vol. 1 (Sept. 1954)-. Academic Scholarly Publication. English (French and German). qt (4 issues). $107.00 US, Canada and Mexico; £56.00 other. Cambridge University Press, The Edinburgh Building, Shaftesbury Road, Cambridge CB2 2RU United Kingdom. **Tel** 011 44 223 312393, FAX 011 44 223 325959. **(Subscription address:** Cambridge University Press / North America, 110 Midland Avenue, Port Chester NY 10573.**) ED** A. J. M. Wedderburn. **LC** BS410; .N4. **DD** 225.05. **[CCC]**. cum. index. available on microfilm and microfiche from University Microfilms International (UMI). Documents available from The Genuine Article, UMI Article Clearinghouse. ***Supersedes*** *Society for New Testament Studies. Bulletin - Studiorum Novi Testamenti Societas.*
**Desc:** Includes articles on all aspects of the text, exegesis and theology of the New Testament and of closely related writings. Each issue contains nine or ten scholarly articles. Contributors come from many different backgrounds and from all parts of the world. Articles are published in English, French and German.
**Ind/Abst** Acad. Search (Jan. 1994-); Arts Humanit. Citation Index [Full Cov.]; Bibliogr. Mission.; Curr. Contents Arts Humanit.; Expand. Acad. Index (1989-); Humanit. Index; Humanit. Source (Jul. 1993-); Index Book Rev. Relig.; INFO-SOUTH Abstr.; Mag. Search; New Testam. Abstr.; Newsp. Period. Abstr. (1991-); Relig. Index One Period. (1954-); Relig. Theol. Abstr.; Res. Alert [Full Cov.]; Abr. Cathol. Period. Lit. Index; Cathol. Period. Lit. Index.

NE/0077-8842
**NEW TESTAMENT TOOLS AND STUDIES.** (19??)-. Monographic series. English. ir. Price varies per volume. E. J. Brill, Postbus 9000, 2300 PA Leiden Netherlands. **Tel** 011 31 71 312624, FAX 011 31 71 317532, telex 39296 BRILL NL. **ED** P. J. Hartin.
**Desc:** New approaches in the criticism of the New Testament.

US/0737-2876
**NOTES ON SCRIPTURE IN USE.** [Notes scr. use]. **VFOAT** N.O.S.; NOS. (1981)-. Periodical. English. Four times a year. $24.95. Summer Institute of Linguistic, 7500 West Camp Wisdom Road, Dallas TX 75236. **Tel** (214)709-2404, FAX (214)709-2433, telex 9108614123. **ED** Doris Porter (phone: (214)709-2400 Ext. 2357). **DD** 220. **Bk Rev**. **Ad Acc**. **Circ:** 700 (ctrl). available on microfiche.
**Desc:** Occasional journal devoted to discussion of issues relating to promotion of scriptures in vernacular languages among native speakers of these languages.

US/0734-0788
**NOTES ON TRANSLATION.** [Notes transl.]. **Added/Corp** Wycliffe Bible Translators. (19??)-. Periodical. English. Four times a year. $19.95 US; $23.95 others. Summer Institute of Linguistic, 7500 West Camp Wisdom Road, Dallas TX 75236. **Tel** (214)709-2404, FAX (214)709-2433, telex 9108614123. **ED** Katharine Barnwell. **LC** BS449; .N67. **DD** 220.4. Index available (back issues). **Circ:** 1,000. available on microfiche.
**Desc:** A publication of the Wycliffe Bible Translators, with theoretical and practical articles on Bible translation and related topics.
**Ind/Abst** MLA Int. Bibl. Books Artic. Mod. Lang. Lit.; RILM Abstr.

NE/0048-1009
**NOVUM TESTAMENTUM.** [Novum Testam.]. Vol. 1 (Jan. 1956)-. Periodical. English (French and German). qt. Fl175.00 (institutions) Netherlands; $100.00 other. E. J. Brill, Postbus 9000, 2300 PA Leiden Netherlands. **Tel** 011 31 71 312624, FAX 011 31 71 317532, telex 39296 BRILL NL. **ED** H. J. de Jonge. **LC** BS410; .N6. **DD** 225.05. **[CCC]**. cum. index. **Circ:** 424. Documents available from The Genuine Article.
**Desc:** An international publication for New Testament and related studies.
**Ind/Abst** Arts Humanit. Citation Index [Full Cov.]; Curr. Contents Arts Humanit.; Index Book Rev. Relig.; New Testam. Abstr.; Relig. Index One Period. (1956-); Relig. Theol. Abstr.; Res. Alert [Full Cov.].

US/0364-8591
**OLD TESTAMENT ABSTRACTS. See** Religion and Theology-Abstracting, Bibliographies and Statistics.

SA/1010-9919
**OLD TESTAMENT ESSAYS.** (OLD TESTAMENT ESSAYS / BY THE DEPT. OF OLD TESTAMENT, UNIVERSITY OF SOUTH AFRICA.). [Old Testam. essays]. **Added/Corp** University of South Africa. Dept. of Old Testament. Old Testament Society of South Africa. Vol. 1 (1983)-. Academic Scholarly Publication. English (German). Three times a year. $50.00. Serva Publishers, PO Box 30043 Sunnyside, 0132 Preroria South Africa. **Tel** 011/27/12/4401675. **ED** J J Burden. **LC** BS410; .O43. **Bk Rev**. **Circ:** 300.
**Desc:** Scholarly reports on research into the old testament.
**Ind/Abst** Old Testam. Abstr.; Relig. Theol. Abstr.

US/1061-4796
**ONE TO ONE (UPPER DARBY, PA.).** (ONE TO ONE.). [One one]. **Added/Corp** Scripture Union. **VFOAT** 1 to One. (19??)-. Periodical. English. Four times a year (Jan., Apr., July, Oct.). $12.00. Scripture Union / Pennsylvania, 7000 Ludlow Street, Upper Darby PA 19082. **Tel** (215)352-5400. **DD** 268.
**Desc:** Information for the 11-14 year olds to rely on God's Word to solve the problems and temptations that they are facing in the world today. Life-related cartoons, issue oriented articles, and investigate questions that create many opportunities for personal discovery.

US/0890-8133
**ORIGINS (CHICAGO, ILL. 1984).** (ORIGINS.). [Origins]. **Added/Corp** Newberry Library. Family & Community History Center. Newberry Library. Local & Family History Section. (1984)-. Periodical. English. Four times a year. $9.00. Newberry Library, 60 West Walton Street, Chicago IL 60610. **Tel** (312)943-9090 ext. 472. **DD** 929.

US/0093-7495
**ORIGINS (LOMA LINDA). See** Science and Technology.

NE/0169-7226
**OUDTESTAMENTISCHE STUDIEN.** (OUDTESTAMENTISCHE STUDIEN : NAMENS HET OUDTESTAMENTISCH WERKGEZELSCHAP IN NEDERLAND.). [Oudtestam. stud.]. **Added/Corp** Oudtestamentisch Werkgezelschap in Nederland. (1942)-. Monographic series. Dutch (English, French and German). ir. Price varies per volume. E. J. Brill, Postbus 9000, 2300 PA Leiden Netherlands. **Tel** 011 31 71 312624, FAX 011 31 71 317532, telex 39296 BRILL NL. **ED** A. S. Van Der Woude. **LC** BS1192; .O87. **Bk Rev**. **Ad Acc**.
**Desc:** Covers Old Testament studies, mainly by Dutch scholars. Both, monographs and collective volumes are covered.
**Ind/Abst** Old Testam. Abstr.

CN/0709-0056
**PARABOLE.** V. 1- Oct. 1978-. Periodical. French. bm. Parabole, 212 Boulevard St Joseph Ouest, Montreal Quebec H2T 2P8 Canada. **Tel** (514)274-4381. **DD** 220/.05. ***Supersedes*** *Bulletin Biblique, 0709-0048.*

CN/0824-1821
**PARTAGE (MONTREAL).** (PARTAGE.). [Partage]. 2 (April/May/June 1984)-. Periodical. French. qt. 7.00Can$. Ligue pour la Lecture de la Bible, 1701 Belleville, Lemoyne QUE J4P 3M2 Canada. **Tel** (514)465-0445, FAX (514)923-8966. **DD** 220.6/05. **Circ:** 6,000. ***Continues*** *Pain du Jour, 0704-187X.*
**Desc:** Bible readings adapted to life every day.

US
**PELOUBET'S SELECT NOTES ON THE INTERNATIONAL BIBLE LESSONS FOR CHRISTIAN LIVING. UNIFORM SERIES. VFOAT** Uniform Series; Select Notes on the International Bible Lessons for Christian Teaching. 1875. English. an. $7.95. Baker Book House, PO Box 6287, Grand Rapids MI 49506. **Tel** (616)676-9185. **ED** Ralph Earle. ***Continues*** *Select Notes on the International Sunday School Lessons. Improved Uniform Series.*
**Desc:** A complete Sunday School teacher's aid for all denominations using the International Sunday School Lessons.

●US/1061-1010
**PICKING THE "RIGHT" BIBLE STUDY PROGRAM.** [Pick. right bible study program]. (1992)-. English. $14.95. ACTA Publications, 4848 North Clark Street, Chicago IL 60640. **DD** 220.

US/0032-4884
**PORTALS OF PRAYER.** (19??)-. Periodical. English. qt. $4.75 regular edition; $7.25 large print edition. Concordia Publishing House, 3558 South Jefferson Avenue, St Louis MO 63118. **Tel** (314)268-1000, (800)325-3381, FAX (314)268-1329. **Circ:** 737,716.
**Desc:** Quarterly daily devotions.

US/0273-5148
**PRIMARY ONE.** ***Title Change.*** Vol. 19, No. 1 (Sept., Oct., Nov. 1981)-(19??). Periodical. English. qt. Gospel Publishing House, 1445 Boonville Avenue, Springfield MO 65802. **Tel** (417)862-2781, FAX (417)866-1146. ***Continues*** *Bible Stories One, 0190-4256.* ***Continued by*** *Primary One Student Guide, 1059-3276.*

IE/0332-4427
**PROCEEDINGS OF THE IRISH BIBLICAL ASSOCIATION.** [Proc. Ir. Biblic. Assoc.]. **Main/Corp** Irish Biblical Association. No. 1 (1976)-. English. an. $10.95 Ireland; $12.70 other. The Columba Press, 93 The Rise, Mt Merrion Blackrock Co, Dublin Ireland. **Tel** 011 353 2832954. **ED** Wilfrid Harrington, K. J. Cathcart, Martin McNamara. **LC** UNC. **DD** 220/.05. **Bk Rev.** **Ad Acc.** **Circ:** 200.
**Desc:** Biblical, theological and ancient historical essays.
**Ind/Abst** New Testam. Abstr.; Old Testam. Abstr.; Relig. Theol. Abstr.

NE
**PSEUDEPIGRAPHA VETERIS TESTAMENTI GRAECE.** (1964)-. Monographic series. English. ir. Price varies per volume. E. J. Brill, Postbus 9000, 2300 PA Leiden Netherlands. **Tel** 011 31 71 312624, FAX 011 31 71 317532, telex 39296 BRILL NL. **ED** A. M. Denis and M. de Jonge.

PL/0867-8715
**QUMRAN CHRONICLE.** Polish (English, German and French). ir (two to three times a year). $75.00. Institute of Oriental Philology, c/o Z. Kapera, Ul Borsucza 3 58, 30 408 Krakow, Poloand. **Tel** 011 48 12 674124, FAX 011 48 12 22 6793. **ED** Dr. Z. Kapera. **Bk Rev**, (Qty: 5-10). **Ad Acc.** ctrl circ.

US/0034-303X
**REFORMATION REVIEW, THE.** ***Suspended.*** Vol. 1 (Oct. 1953)-Suspended Vol. 30, No. 1. Academic Scholarly Publication. English. ir. $15.00. International Council of Christian Churches, 756 Haddon Avenue, Collingswood NJ 08108. **Tel** (609)858-0700. **ED** Dr J C Maris and Dr William LeRoy. **Bk Rev.** **Circ:** 300.
**Desc:** Scholarly presentation of some of the finest fundamental Biblical messages and exegesis of our day taken mainly from essays ICCC affiliated publications and conferences.

CN/0225-3798
**RESEARCHER (SUDBURY).** ***Ceased.*** (THE RESEARCHER.). [Researcher]. Vol. 1 Spring (1971)-(1994). Periodical. English. qt. $2.00. Bible Lovers Fellowship, PO Box 232, Sudbury Ontario P3E 4N5 Canada. **ED** J R Boyd. **DD** 220.1/5/05.

AG/0034-7078
**REVISTA BIBLICA.** [Rev. biblica]. No. 1 (1939)-. Periodical. Spanish. qt. $16.00. Eduardo Bierzychudek, Casilla Postal 33, 1425 Buenos Aires Argentina. **Tel** 84-6066. **ED** Eduardo Bierzychudek. Index available. cum. index. **Bk Rev.** **Ad Acc.** **Pr Rev.** **Circ:** 500 (ctrl).
**Desc:** Biblical exegesis, theology and hermeneutical studies in an ecumenical fashion by Catholic and Protestant scholars.
**Ind/Abst** Index Book Rev. Relig.; New Testam. Abstr.; Relig. Index One Period.

CR
**REVISTA DE INTERPRETACAO BIBLICA LATINO-AMERICANA : RIBLA.** **VFOAT** RIBLA. (19??)-. Periodical. Portuguese. Three times a year (Apr., Aug., Dec.). $18.00 Latin America; $30.00 other. Editorial Dei, Apartado 390-2070 Sabanilla, San Jose Costa Rica. **Tel** 506 530229, FAX 506 531541, telex 3472. **Bk Rev.** **Circ:** 1,500 (ctrl).

CR/1018-5763
**REVISTA DE INTERPRETACION BIBLICA LATINOAMERICANA : RIBLA.** **Added/Corp** Departamento Ecumenico de Investigaciones (Costa Rica). **VFOAT** RIBLA. No. 1 (1988)-. Periodical. Spanish. Three times a year (Apr., Aug., Dec.). $18.00 Latin America; $30.00 other. Editorial Dei, Apartado 390-2070 Sabanilla, San Jose Costa Rica. **Tel** 506 530229, FAX 506 531541, telex 3472. **Ad Acc.**

FR/0035-0907
**REVUE BIBLIQUE.** (REVUE BIBLIQUE / PUBLIEE PAR L'ECOLE PRATIQUE D'ETUDES BIBLIQUES.). [Rev. biblique]. **VFOAT** Vivre et Penser. Vol. 24 (1915)-. Periodical. French (English). qt. 988.00F (France); 1030.00F (other). J Gabalda & Cie Editeurs, 18 rue Pierre et Marie Curie, 75005 Paris France. **Tel** 011 33 1 43265355. **LC** BS410. **DD** 220.05. cum. index. **Bk Rev.** Documents available from The Genuine Article. ***Continues*** *Revue Biblique Internationale.*
**Desc:** Includes Judaism, Bible, archeological, and analysis of Old and New Testament.
**Ind/Abst** Arts Humanit. Citation Index [Full Cov.]; Bibliogr. Mission.; BHA : Biblio. Hist. Art; Curr. Contents Arts Humanit.; Index Book Rev. Relig.; New Testam. Abstr.; Old Testam. Abstr.; Relig. Index One Period. (1949-); Relig. Theol. Abstr.; Res. Alert [Full Cov.].

IT/0394-980X
**RICERCHE STORICO BIBLICHE : RSB.** **Added/Corp** Associazione Biblica Italiana. **VFOAT** RSB. Vol. 1, No. 1 (Jan./June 1989)-. Periodical. Italian. sa (June & December). L58000 Itlay; L69000 other. Centro Editoriale Dehoniano, Via Nosadella 6, Casella Postale 568, 40123 Bologna Italy. **Tel** 011 39 51 306811. **LC** BS410; .R53. **DD** 220.9/5/005.

IT/0035-5798
**RIVISTA BIBLICA.** **Added/Corp** Associazione Biblica Italiana. Vol. 5 (Jan./March 1957)-. Periodical. Italian (English and French). qt. L49000 Italy; L56000 other. Centro Editoriale Dehoniano, Via Nosadella 6, Casella Postale 568, 40123 Bologna Italy. **Tel** 011 39 51 306811. **ED** Alfio Filippi. Index available in last issue of volume--attached. **Bk Rev.** **Ad Acc.** **Circ:** 2,000 (ctrl). ***Continues*** *Rivista Biblica Italiana.*
**Desc:** Informs the public about progress in research as it is being conducted by Italian Bible scholars.
**Ind/Abst** Bibliogr. Mission.; New Testam. Abstr.

DK/0901-8328
**SCANDINAVIAN JOURNAL OF THE OLD TESTAMENT : SJOT.** **Added/Corp** Aarhus Universitet. Institut for Gammel Testamente. **VFOAT** SJOT. Vol. 1 (1987)-. Academic Scholarly Publication. English (German). sa. Kr355.00, $67.00. Scandinavian University Press, PO Box 2959 Toeyen, N 0608 Oslo 6 Norway. **Tel** 011 47 2 2575400, FAX 011 47 2 2575353, telex 71896 UROR N. **(Subscription address:** Scandinavian University Press, 200 Meacham Ave., Elmont NY 11003.**)**
**Desc:** Publishes more entensive articles than is usually the case, thereby allowing more complete scholarly argumentation to appear.
**Ind/Abst** Index Book Rev. Relig.; Int. Bibliogr. Sociol.; Relig. Index One Period.; Relig. Theol. Abstr.

SA/0254-1807
**SCRIPTURA.** (SCRIPTURA : TYDSKRIF VIR BYBELKUNDE.). [Scriptura]. **Added/Corp** University of Stellenbosch. Dept. of Biblical Studies. No. 1 (July 1980)-. Periodical. Afrikaans (English). Four times a year. $40.00. University of Stellenbosch / Department of Biblical Studies, 7600 Stellenbosch South Africa. **Tel** 011 27 2231 772117, telex 520383 SA. **ED** B.C. Lategan. Index Available, published separately, free-automatically sent. **Bk Rev.** **Pr Rev.** **Circ:** 250-300 (ctrl).
**Desc:** Publishes refereed contributions on the Bible and theology. Special emphasis is given to contextual, theological, and ethical issues, in particular those relating to South Africa.
**Ind/Abst** Index Book Rev. Relig.; New Testam. Abstr.; Relig. Index One Period. (1980-); Relig. Theol. Abstr.

UK/0036-9780
**SCRIPTURE BULLETIN.** [Script. bull.]. **Added/Corp** Catholic Biblical Association of Great Britain. Bible Reading Fellowship. Society for Promoting Christian Knowledge (Great Britain). Vol. 1 (Jan./March 1969)-. Periodical. English. Twice a year. Membership: £4.00 UK; £4.50 Europe; £6.00 other. Catholic Bible Association of Great Britain, Maryville House Old O'Scott Hill, Birmingham B44 9AG England. **Tel** 011 44 21 3608118. **ED** J. McGuckin and S. Greenhalgh. **LC** BS410; .S36. **DD** 220/.05. **Bk Rev.** **Ad Acc.** **Circ:** 550. ***Supersedes*** *Scripture.*
**Desc:** Biblical comment, criticism and reviews.
**Ind/Abst** New Testam. Abstr.; Old Testam. Abstr.; Abr. Cathol. Period. Lit. Index; Cathol. Period. Lit. Index.

US/0747-0207
**SCRIPTURE COMES ALIVE.** (19??)-. Periodical. English. wk. $35.00. ALT Publishing Company, PO Box 400, Green Bay WI 54305. **Tel** (414)432-1413. **ED** James L. Alt. **Circ:** varies (ctrl). ***Continues*** *Fr. McBride Homily Service.*
**Desc:** Sunday Homily Service.

JA
**SEISHOGAKU RONSHU / NIHON SEISHOGAKU KENKYUJO HEN.** Began in 1962. Japanese. an. ¥2000. Yamamoto Shoten, 23 Ichigaya Honmura-cho Shinjuku-ku, Tokyo Japan. **LC** BS410; .S43 .

US/0095-571X
**SEMEIA.** [Semeia]. **Added/Corp** Society of Biblical Literature. (1974)-. Periodical. English. qt. $30.00 (subscribers to American Academy of Religion or the Journal of Biblical Literature), $35.00 other. Scholars Press / Georgia, PO Box 15399, Atlanta GA 30333-0399. **Tel** (404)636-4757, (404)727-2320, FAX (404)727-2348. **ED** Robert Colley. **LC** BS410; .S45. **DD** 220.6/05. **Circ:** 1,275. available on microfilm and microfiche from University Microfilms International (UMI). Documents available from The Genuine Article.
**Ind/Abst** Arts Humanit. Citation Index [Full Cov.]; Curr. Contents Arts Humanit.; Index Book Rev. Relig.; New Testam. Abstr.; Old Testam. Abstr.; Relig. Index One Period. (1979-); Relig. Theol. Abstr.; Res. Alert [Full Cov.]; Soc. Sci. Cit. Index [Select. Cov.].

CN/0228-670X
**SEMENCE, LA.** [Semence]. Periodical. French. qt. Free. La Semence, 230 rue Lupien, Cap-de-la-Madeleine Quebec G8T 6W4 Canada. **Tel** (819)378-4023. **DD** 220/.05. **Ad Acc.** **Circ:** 15,000 (ctrl).
**Desc:** A Christian outreach primarily to French speaking persons living in Canada and North America.

US/0199-5049
**SHARE THE WORD.** **Added/Corp** Paulist Fathers. Office for Evangelization. (Lent 1980)-. Periodical. English. Six times a year. $15.00. Share the Word, 3031 4th Street Northeast, Washington DC 20017. **Tel** (202)832-5022. **ED** Ms. Paula Diebl. **Circ:** 63,000 (ctrl). available on videocassette (VHS, Beta); available on audiocassette.
**Desc:** Home Bible study guide that follows the Sunday Liturgical readings.

IS
**SHENATON LE-MIKRA ULE-HEKER HA-MIZRAH HA-KADUM.** **VFOAT** Shnaton, An Annual for Biblical and Ancient Near Eastern Studies; Annual for Biblical and Ancient Near Eastern Studies. (19??)-. Hebrew (summaries and/or abstracts in English). an. IL49.00 Israel; $35.00 US. Hotsaat Tanakh Yistael, Rehov Hasharon 12 Tel-Aviv, Israel. **Tel** 03-370621. **ED** M Weinfeld. **LC** BS410; .S48. **Bk Rev.** **Circ:** 500.

US/0745-4430
**SHORE LINES.** (SHORE LINES / GULF SHORE BIBLE INSTITUTE.). **Added/Corp** Gulf Shore Bible Institute (Fort Myers, Fla.). Vol. 1, No. 1 (Nov./Dec.) 1982-. Periodical. English. qt. Gulf Shore Bible Institute, PO Box 2522, Fort Myers FL 33902.

US/0145-2770
**SOCIETY OF BIBLICAL LITERATURE DISSERTATION SERIES.** (DISSERTATION SERIES.). **Added/Corp** Society of Biblical Literature. **VFOAT** SBL Dissertation Series. No. 1 (1972)-. Monographic series. English. ir. Price varies per volume. Scholars Press / Georgia, PO Box 15399, Atlanta GA 30333-0399. **Tel** (404)636-4757, (404)727-2320, FAX (404)727-2348. **ED** C. Talbert and J. Roberts. **LC** UNC.
**Desc:** Dissertations which try to make scholarly contributions in any aspect of study in biblical or cognate fields.

US/0145-269X
**SOCIETY OF BIBLICAL LITERATURE MONOGRAPH SERIES.** **Added/Corp** Society of Biblical Literature. Society of Biblical Literature. Monograph Series. (1971)-. Monographic series. English. ir. Price varies per volume. Scholars Press / Georgia, PO Box 15399, Atlanta GA 30333-0399. **Tel** (404)636-4757, (404)727-2320, FAX (404)727-2348. **ED** Adela Yarbro Collins. **LC** UNC. ***Continues*** *Journal of Biblical Literature. Monograph Series.*
**Desc:** Scholarly investigations of any subject which pertains to biblical literature.

US/0145-2711
**SOCIETY OF BIBLICAL LITERATURE SEMINAR PAPERS.** [Soc. Biblic. Lit. semin. pap.]. **Main/Corp** Society of Biblical Literature. **Added/Corp** Society of Biblical Literature. Seminar Papers. (1973)-. English. an. $28.50 nonmembers; $21.00 members. Scholars Press / Georgia, PO Box 15399, Atlanta GA 30333-0399. **Tel** (404)636-4757, (404)727-2320, FAX (404)727-2348. **ED** Kent Richards. **LC** BS410; .S65a. **DD** 220.6. ***Continues*** *Society of Biblical Literature. Book of Seminar Papers, 0160-631X.*
**Desc:** A publication of the papers presented at the annual AAR/SBL meeting.
**Ind/Abst** Relig. Index One Period. (1978-).

NE
**STUDIA IN VETERIS TESTAMENTI PSEUDEPIGRAPHA.** Vol. 1 (1970)-. Monographic series. Latin (table of contents in English). ir. Price varies per volume. E. J. Brill, Postbus 9000, 2300 PA Leiden Netherlands. **Tel** 011 31 71 312624, FAX 011 31 71 317532, telex 39296 BRILL NL. **LC** BS1700; .S78.

IT
**STUDIA POHL; SERIES MAIOR.** **Added/Corp** Pontificio Istituto Biblico. (1969)-. Monographic series. English. ir. Price varies per volume. Editrice Pontificio Istituto Biblico, Piazza della Pilotta 35, 00187 Rome Italy. **Tel** 011 39 6 6781567, FAX 011 39 6 6780588. **ED** W. Mayer.

GW
**STUDIEN ZUM FRUHNEUHOCHDEUTSCHEN.** **See** Linguistics.

GW
**STUDIEN ZUM NEUEN TESTAMENT.** Vol. 1 (1969)-. Monographic series. German. ir. Price varies per volume. VVA Bertelsmann Dist GmbH, Postfach 7600, D 33310 Gutersloh Germany. **Tel** 011 49 5241 803294. **ED** Gunter Klein, Willi Marxsen and Wolfgang Schrage.
**Desc:** Monograph series on studies of the New Testament.

US/0894-6361
**STUDIES IN THE BIBLE AND EARLY CHRISTIANITY.** [Stud. Bible early Christ.]. Vol. 1 (1981)-. Monographic series. English. ir. Price varies per volume. Edwin Mellen Press, PO Box 450, Lewiston NY 14092. **Tel** (716)754-2788, FAX (716)754-4335. **LC** UNC. **DD** 220. Index available.

GW/0585-7961
**STUTTGARTER BIBELSTUDIEN.** (1965)-. Monographic series. German. ir. Price varies per volume. Katholisches Bibelwerk EV, Silberburgstrasse 121, D 70176 Stuttgart Germany. **Tel** 011 49 711 6192050.

SW/1100-2298
**SVENSK EXEGETISK ARSBOK.** [Sven. exeg. arsb.]. **Added/Corp** Uppsala Exegetiska Sallskap. (1936)-. Multiple languages (English and Swedish). an (Sept.). Kr100.00 Sweden; Kr150.00 others. Uppsala Exegetiska Sallskap Theologiska Institution, PO Box 1604, S 751 46 Uppsala Sweden. **LC** BS410; .S93. **Bk Rev.**
**Ind/Abst** New Testam. Abstr.; Old Testam. Abstr.; Relig. Theol. Abstr.

US/0040-0645
**TEACHING PICTURES FOR BIBLE SEARCHERS.** **Added/Corp** Southern Baptist Convention. Sunday School Board. (19??)-. English. Southern Baptist Convention, 901 Commerce, Suite 750, Nashville TN 37203. **Tel** (615)244-2355, FAX (615)742-8919. **(Subscription address:** Sunday School Board - Customer Service, 127 Ninth Avenue North, Nashville, TN 37234 USA; telephone: (800)458-2772**)**

IS/0082-3767
**TEXTUS.** (TEXTUS; ANNUAL OF THE HEBREW UNIVERSITY BIBLE PROJECT.). [Textus]. **Added/Corp** Universitah Ha-Ivrit Bi-Yerushalayim. Mifal Ha-Mikra. Vol. 1 (1960)-. Periodical. English (Hebrew). ir. Price varies per volume. Magnes Press, Hebrew University of Jerusalem, PO Box 7695, Jerusalem 91076 Israel. **Tel** 011 972 2 660341, 011 972 2 635291, FAX 011 972 2 633370, telex 25391. **ED** C. Rabin and S. Talmon. **LC** BS410; .T45. cum. index. **Circ:** 1,000.
**Ind/Abst** MLA Int. Bibl. Books Artic. Mod. Lang. Lit.

US/0744-7248
**THAILAND BIBLE LITERATURE.** Periodical. English. bm. Salem Church of Christ, Route 5 Box 216, Florence AL 35630.

US/1056-2311
**TREK, LIFE-CENTERED BIBLE STUDY FOR JUNIOR HIGHS. STUDENTS LEAFLETS.** **VFOAT** Students Leaflets; TREK. Students Leaflets. (1991)-. Periodical. English. qt. $14.75. United Methodist Publishing House, PO Box 801, 201 8th Avenue South, Nashville TN 37202. **Tel** (615)749-6732, (615)749-6615, FAX (615)749-6578, (615)749-6579.

US/1056-229X
**TREK, LIFE-CENTERED BIBLE STUDY FOR SENIOR HIGHS. STUDENTS LEAFLETS.** **VFOAT** Students Leaflets; TREK. Students Leaflets. (1991)-. Periodical. English. qt. $14.75. United Methodist Publishing House, PO Box 801, 201 8th Avenue South, Nashville TN 37202. **Tel** (615)749-6732, (615)749-6615, FAX (615)749-6578, (615)749-6579.

US/1056-2303
**TREK, LIFE-CENTERED BIBLE STUDY FOR SENIOR HIGHS. TEACHER IDEA BOOK.** **VFOAT** Teacher Idea Book; TREK. Teacher Idea Book. (1991)-. Periodical. English. qt. $14.75. United Methodist Publishing House, PO Box 801, 201 8th Avenue South, Nashville TN 37202. **Tel** (615)749-6732, (615)749-6615, FAX (615)749-6578, (615)749-6579.

US/0042-0476
**UNSEARCHABLE RICHES.** Vol. 1 (Jan. 1910)-. Periodical. English. bm. $1.00. Concordant Publishing Concern, 15570 West Knochaven Road, Canyon County CA 91351. **Tel** (805)252-2112. **ED** Dean Hough. Index available. cum. index. **Circ:** 2,000.
**Desc:** Contains expositions and commentary pertaining to scripture.

IT/0506-8126
**VETERA CHRISTIANORUM.** **Added/Corp** Universita di Bari. Istituto di Letteratura Cristiana Antica. (1964)-. Periodical. Italian (Latin, Greek, Modern, English, German and Spanish, French). sa. L60.000 Italy; L80.000 other. Edipuglia Srl., Via Dalmazia 22/B, 70050 Bari-S Spirito Italy. **Tel** 39 80 5333056, FAX 39 80 5333057. Index available. cum. index. **Bk Rev**, (Qty: 30). **Ad Acc, Adv Mgr:** Ceglie. **Circ:** 1,000.
**Desc:** Explores, in depth, the most ancient versions of Holy Scripture, the Biblical exegeses of the Church Fathers, and liturgical expression, as well as the educational validity of communication at all levels, widening the field to cover the various manifestations of ancient Christianity in the Apulia region of Italy.
**Ind/Abst** Bibliogr. Mission.; BHA : Biblio. Hist. Art; MLA Int. Bibl. Books Artic. Mod. Lang. Lit.; New Testam. Abstr.

GW/0571-9070
**VETUS LATINA. AUS DER GESCHICHTE DER LATEINISCHEN BIBEL.** [Vetus Lat., Gesch. lat. Bibel]. **VFOAT** Aus der Geschichte der Lateinischen Bibel. (1957)-. Monographic series. German. ir. Price varies per volume. Verlag Herder Freiburg, Postfach 79080, Frieburg, Germany. **Tel** (0761)27-17-0, FAX (0761)27 17-520, telex 761489. **(Subscription address:** Verlag Herder Freiburg / KNO, PF 800620 Koch, Neff & Oetinger, D 70506 Stuttgart Germany.**) UDC** 22.

GW
**VETUS LATINA DIE RESTE DER ALTLATEINISCHEN BIBEL.** (19??)-. Monographic series. German. ir. Price varies per volume. Verlag Herder Freiburg, Postfach 79080, Frieburg, Germany. **Tel** (0761)27-17-0, FAX (0761)27 17-520, telex 761489.

NE/0042-4935
**VETUS TESTAMENTUM.** [Vetus Testam.]. **Added/Corp** International Organization of Old Testament Scholars. International Organization for the Study of the Old Testament. Vol. 1 (1951)-. Periodical. English (French and German). qt. Fl185.00 (institutions) Netherlands; $105.75 (institutions) other. E. J. Brill, Postbus 9000, 2300 PA Leiden Netherlands. **Tel** 011 31 71 312624, FAX 011 31 71 317532, telex 39296 BRILL NL. **ED** J. A. Emerton. **LC** BS410; .V45. **[CCC]. Bk Rev. Ad Acc. Circ:** 2,650 (ctrl). Documents available from The Genuine Article.
**Desc:** Covers the whole range of Old Testament study, with articles, short notes, and book reviews, including history, literature, religion and theology, text, versions, language, and the bearing on the Old Testament of archaeology and the study of the ancient near east.
**Ind/Abst** Arts Humanit. Citation Index [Full Cov.]; Bibliogr. Mission.; Curr. Contents Arts Humanit.; Index Book Rev. Relig.; New Testam. Abstr.; Old Testam. Abstr.; Relig. Index One Period. (1951-); Relig. Theol. Abstr.; Res. Alert [Full Cov.]; Soc. Sci. Cit. Index [Select. Cov.].

US/0145-7411
**VIERTELJAHRSHEFT DER CHRISTLICHEN WISSENSCHAFT. BIBELLEKTIONEN.** **Added/Corp** Christian Science Publishing Society. **VFOAT** Christian Science Quarterly. Bible Lessons. (19??)-. Periodical. English (German). qt. Christian Science Publishing Society, One Norway Street, Boston MA 02115. **Tel** (617)450-2678, (617)450-2504.

US/0277-0431
**WAY MAGAZINE, THE.** **Added/Corp** Way International. (1953)-. Periodical. English. Six times a year (Jan., Mar., May, July, Sept., Nov.). $12.00 US; $15.00 other. American Christian Press, Box 328, New Knoxville OH 45871. **Tel** (419)753-2523, FAX (419)753-2903, telex 241275. **ED** Keith W. Jackson. Index available (Jan. iss.). cum. index. **Pr Rev. Circ:** 7,000 (ctrl). available on videocassette from the publisher.
**Desc:** Features Biblical research and the application of Biblical principles in such areas as health, prosperity and family matters.

GW/0512-1604
**WISSENSCHAFTLICHE UNTERSUCHUNGEN ZUM NEUEN TESTAMENT.** Vol. 1, (1950)-. Monographic series. German. ir. Price varies per volume. JCB Mohr / Paul Siebeck, Postfach 2040, D 72010 Tuebingen Germany. **Tel** 011 49 7071 9230, FAX 011 49 7071 51104, telex 7/262872 mohr d.

UK
**WORD IN ACTION.** **See** Newspapers.

US/1057-0209
**YOUTH IN ACTION. BIBLE STUDY CARDS.** [Youth action, Bible study cards]. **Added/Corp** Southern Baptist Convention. Sunday School Board. **VFOAT** Bible Study Cards. (1991)-. Periodical. English. qt. $3.60. Southern Baptist Convention, 901 Commerce, Suite 750, Nashville TN 37203. **Tel** (615)244-2355, FAX (615)742-8919. **(Subscription address:** Sunday School Board - Customer Service, 127 Ninth Avenue North, Nashville, TN 37234 USA; telephone: (800)458-2772**) DD** 268.

US/1057-0195
**YOUTH IN DISCOVERY. BIBLE STUDY CARDS.** [Youth discov., Bible study cards]. **Added/Corp** Southern Baptist Convention. Sunday School Board. **VFOAT** Bible Study Cards. (1991)-. Periodical. English. qt. $3.90. Southern Baptist Convention, 901 Commerce, Suite 750, Nashville TN 37203. **Tel** (615)244-2355, FAX (615)742-8919. **(Subscription address:** Sunday School Board - Customer Service, 127 Ninth Avenue North, Nashville, TN 37234 USA; telephone: (800)458-2772**) DD** 268.

GW/0044-2526
**ZEITSCHRIFT FUER DIE ALTTESTAMENTLICHE WISSENSCHAFT.** [Z. alttest. wiss.]. **Added/Corp** Deutsche Morgenlandische Gesellschaft. (1881)-. Periodical. German. Three times a year. $160.30. Walter de Gruyter Inc., PO Box 303421, D 10728 Berlin Germany. **Tel** 011 49 30 260050, FAX 011 49 30 26005251. **ED** Otto Kaises. **LC** BS410; .Z4. **DD** 221.6/05. **[CCC].** cum. index. **Bk Rev. Ad Acc. Circ:** 1,600. Documents available from The Genuine Article.
**Ind/Abst** Arts Humanit. Citation Index [Full Cov.]; Curr. Contents Arts Humanit.; Index Book Rev. Relig.; New Testam. Abstr.; Old Testam. Abstr.; Relig. Index One Period. (1950-); Relig. Theol. Abstr.; Res. Alert [Full Cov.]; Soc. Sci. Cit. Index [Select. Cov.].

GW
**ZEITSCHRIFT FUER DIE ALTTESTAMENTLICHE WISSENSCHAFT. BEIHEFTE.** (1896)-. Monographic series. German. ir. Price varies per volume. Walter de Gruyter Inc., PO Box 303421, D 10728 Berlin Germany. **Tel** 011 49 30 260050, FAX 011 49 30 26005251. **(Subscription address:** Walter de Gruyter Inc., 200 Saw Mill River Road, Hawthorne NY 10532.**) ED** O. Kaiser. **Bk Rev. Ad Acc. Circ:** 1,400.
**Desc:** Publishes papers in different languages concerning the interpretation of biblical scholars of the Old Testament.

## BUDDHISM

US/0747-900X
**AMERICAN BUDDHIST NEWSLETTER, THE.** [Am. Buddh. newsl.]. **Added/Corp** American Buddhist Movement. (198?)-. Periodical. English. mo. American Buddhist Movement, 301 West 45th Street, New York NY 10036. **Tel** (212)489-1075. **ED** Kevin O'Neil. **DD** 294. Index available. **Bk Rev. Ad Acc. Circ:** 6,000.

US/0147-4839
**ANNALS OF THE NYINGMA LINEAGE IN AMERICA.** V. 1- 1969/75-. English. ir. $12.00. Dharma Publishing, 2425 Hillside Avenue, Berkeley CA 94704. **Tel** (510)548-5407, FAX (510)548-2230. **ED** Michael Dow and Elizabeth Cook. **LC** BQ7662.2; .A56. **DD** 294.3/923.
**Desc:** Description and illustrations of purpose and development of the Nyingma Centers in America. Historical coverage 1969 through 1985, with introduction by the founder, Tarthang Tulku.

CN/1181-8360
**BUDDHISM AT THE CROSSROADS.** ***Suspended.*** [Buddh. crossroads]. **Added/Corp** Zen Lotus Society (Toronto, Ont.). Vol. 6, No. 4 (Fall 1990)-(199?). Periodical. English. qt. $20.00 per year. Zen Lotus Society, 1214 Packard Road, Ann Arbor MI 48104. **Tel** (313)761-6520. **DD** 294.3/927/05. ***Continues*** *Spring Wind (Toronto, Ont.), 0825-799X.*

US/0882-0945
**BUDDHIST-CHRISTIAN STUDIES.** [Buddh. Christ. stud.]. **Added/Corp** University of Hawaii at Manoa. East-West Religions Project. **VAT** Buddhist Christian Studies. Vol. 1 (1981)-. English. an. $20.00 (one year), $36.00 (two year) istitution, $17.00 (one year), $31.00 (two year) individual, US; $22.00 (one year), $40.00 (two year) institution, $19.00 (one year), $34.00 (two year), individual, other. University of Hawaii Press, 2840 Kolowalu Street, Honolulu HI 96822. **Tel** (808)956-8833, (808)948-8697, FAX (808)988-6052. **ED** David W. Chappell. **LC** BR128.B8; B83. **DD** 261.2/43. **Bk Rev. Ad Acc. Circ:** 350 (ctrl).
**Desc:** Buddhism and Christianity and their interrelationship based on historical materials and contemporary experience, offering articles, book review, and news items.
**Ind/Abst** Bibliogr. Mission.; Index Book Rev. Relig.; Relig. Index One Period.

II
**BUDDHIST STUDIES.** 1974-. English (Hindi and Sanskrit). an. Rs20.00. Department of Buddhist Studies, University of Delhi, Delhi-7 India. **Tel** 2521521-218. **ED** K K Mittal. **LC** BQ2; .B82. **DD** 294.3/05. **Bk Rev. Circ:** 400.

UK/0265-2897
**BUDDHIST STUDIES REVIEW.** [Buddh. stud. rev.]. **Added/Corp** Institut de recherche bouddhique Linh-Son. Pali Buddhist Union. Vol. 1, No. 1 (1984)-. Periodical. English (French). sa. £7.50 individuals, £12.50 institutions. Buddhist Studies Review, 31 Russell Chambers, Bury Place, London WC1A 2JX England. **ED** Russell Webb. **LC** IN PROCESS. Index available. cum. index. **Bk Rev. Ad Acc. Circ:** 400 (ctrl). ***Formed by the union of*** *Pali Buddhist Review, 0308-3756* ***and*** *Linh-Son Publication d'Etudes Bouddhologiques, 0294-619X.*
**Desc:** Academic periodical specializing in mainstream Buddhism (i.e. the Hinayana tradition and early Indian Mahayana)

MP
**BUDDHISTS FOR PEACE.** Vol. 1, No. 1 (1979)-. Periodical. English. qt. $8.00, $100.00 (lifetime). Asian Buddhist Conference for Peace, Gangdanthekchenling Monaster, Ulan Bator-51 Mongolia. **Tel** 53538. **ED** B Wangchindorj. **LC** BQ20.A74; B8. **DD** 294.3/37873/05.

JA
**BUKKYO SHIGAKU KENKYU. Added/Corp** Bukkyo Shigakukai. **VFOAT** Journal of the History of Buddhism. Vol. 1 No. 2 (June 1974)-. Japanese. sa. $65.00. Bukkyo Shigakukai, c/o Bukkyo Daigaku, 96 Murasakino Kita, Hananobo-cho Kita-ku, 603 Kyoto-shi Japan. **(Subscription address:** Japan Publications Trading Company, Ltd., PO Box 5030, Tokyo International, Tokyo 100-31 Japan.**) LC** BQ6; .B84. ***Continues** Bukkyo Shigaku.*

JA
**BUKKYO SHISO SHI. VFOAT** Journal of the History of Buddhist Thoughts. 1 (1979)-. Periodical. Japanese (Japanese). ¥1800. Heirakuji Shoten, Sanjo Noboru Kyoto Japan. **LC** BQ4066; .B84.

JA
**BUKKYOSHI KENKYU (RYUKOKU DAIGAKU. BUKKYOSHI KENKYUKAI).** (BUKKYOSHI KENKYU / HENSHUSHA, RYUKOKU DAIGAKU BUKKYOSHI KENKYUKAI.). **VFOAT** Journal of Studies in History of Buddhism. Japanese. Nagata Bunshodo Nishinotoin Nishi Iru Hanayacho, Shimogyo-ku, Kyoto-shi 600 Japan. **LC** BQ256; .B84.

CN/0822-0581
**CHAN NHU / VIETNAMESE-CANADIAN BUDDHIST ASSOCIATION.** [Chan nhu']. **VFOAT** Hoi Phat-Giao Viet-Nam Gia-Na-Dai. Periodical. Vietnamese. mo. Chan Nhu', PO Box 1536, Ottawa Ontario K1G 0M1. **DD** 294.3/05.

CN/0704-4909
**CHIMO (TORONTO).** (CHIMO.). [Chimo]. V. 1-Jan. 1975-. Periodical. English. mo. $20.00. Chimo Media Publishing Ltd, 250 Esplanade/5th Floor, Toronto Ontario M5A 1J2 Canada. **DD** 294.5/43/05.

II
**CHO-YANG / CHOS YANS. Added/Corp** Council for Religious and Cultural Affairs of H.H. the Dalai Lama. **VFOAT** Cho Yang. **VAT** Cho Yang. Vol. 1, No. 1 (Spring 1986)-. Periodical. English. Twice a year. $25.00. Council for Religious & Cultural Affairs, Cangchen Kyishong/Draramsala, Distt Kangra 176215 HP India. **LC** DS786; .C554.

US/0097-7209
**CRYSTAL MIRROR. Added/Corp** Tibetan Nyingma Meditation Center (Berkeley, Calif.). Vol. 1 (1971)-. English. an. $12.95. Dharma Publishing, 2425 Hillside Avenue, Berkeley CA 94704. **Tel** (510)548-5407, FAX (510)548-2230. **LC** BQ7662; .C78. **DD** 294.3/923/05.
**Desc:** Overview of Buddhist history with teachings on mind, consciousness, philosophy, practice and transmission.

JA
**DAIBYAKURENGE.** (1949)-. Periodical. Japanese. mo. Daibyakurenge Kankokai, 18 Shinanomachi Shinjuku-ku, Tokyo 160 Japan. **LC** BQ8400; .D34.

CE/0012-2181
**DIALOGUE (COLOMBO, SRI LANKA).** (DIALOGUE.). **Added/Corp** Ecumenical Institute for Study & Dialogue (Colombo, Sri Lanka) Christian Institute of Buddhist Studies (Colombo, Sri Lanka) Study Centre for Religion & Society (Colombo, Sri Lanka). No. 1 (Sept. 1963)-. Periodical. English. Three times a year (Apr., Aug., Dec.). $10.00 Sri Lanka; $14.00 other. Ecumenical Institute of Study & Dialogue, 490-5 Havelock Road, Colombo 6 Sri Lanka Ceylon. **Tel** 586998. **ED** Aloysius Pieris. Index available. cum. index. **Bk Rev. Circ:** 2,000.
**Desc:** Buddhist Christian dialogue with particular attention to Sri Lanka.
**Ind/Abst** Bibliogr. Mission.; Index Book Rev. Relig.; Relig. Index One Period.

JA
**DOHO DAIGAKU RONSO. Main/Corp** Doho Gakkai. **VFOAT** Journal of Buddhism and Cultural Science; Dohodaigaku Ronso. Japanese (Japanese). Doho Daigaku Ronso, 1 Inabajicho 7 Nakamura-ku, Nagoya Japan. **LC** AS552.D54; A2.

JA/0012-8708
**EASTERN BUDDHIST, THE. Added/Corp** Toho Bukkyo Kyokai (Kyoto, Japan). Vol. 1, No. 1 (May 1921); New Series, Vol. 1, No. 1 (Sept. 1965)-. Periodical. English. sa. $20.00. Scholars Press / Georgia, PO Box 15399, Atlanta GA 30333-0399. **Tel** (404)636-4757, (404)727-2320, FAX (404)727-2348. **DD** 294.3205. cum. index. **Circ:** 350. Documents available from The Genuine Article.
**Ind/Abst** Arts Humanit. Citation Index [Full Cov.]; Curr. Contents Arts Humanit.; Index Book Rev. Relig.; Int. Bibliogr. Sociol.; MLA Int. Bibl. Books Artic. Mod. Lang. Lit.; Relig. Index One Period. (1977-); Res. Alert [Full Cov.].

JA
**GEKKAN MIKKYO KOZA. THE MIKKYO KOZA. VFOAT** The Mikkyo Koza. (19??)-. Periodical. Japanese. ¥1200. Hirakawa Shuppan, 15-17 Hirakawacho 2-chome, Chiyoda-ku 102, Tokyo Japan. **LC** BQ8900; .G43.

US/0738-2294
**GESAR.** (GESAR : BUDDHIST PERSPECTIVES.). **Added/Corp** Nyingma Centers. **VFOAT** Buddhist Perspectives. (19??)-. Periodical. English. Four times a year. $12.00 (one year), $23.00 (two year) US; $15.00 (one year), $29.00 (two year) other. Dharma Publishing, 2425 Hillside Avenue, Berkeley CA 94704. **Tel** (510)548-5407, FAX (510)548-2230. **ED** Leslie Bradburn. Index available (bound in last issue). cum. index. **Bk Rev. Circ:** 1,000.

JA
**HOKKE BUNKA KENKYU. VFOAT** Journal of Institute for the Comprehensive Study of Lotus Sutra. 1975 Edition-. Multiple languages (Japanese and English). Rissho Daigako Hokekyo Bunka Kenkyujo, 2-16 Osaki 4-chome Shinagawa-ku, Tokyo 14 Japan. **LC** BQ2057; .H65.

HK/0073-3253
**HSIANG-KANG FO CHIAO. VFOAT** Buddhism in Hong Kong. (19??)-. Periodical. Chinese. mo.
**Ind/Abst** Health Plan. Adminis.

CH
**HUA FAN FO HSUEH NIEN KAN. VFOAT** Journal of Sino-Indian Buddhist Studies. First published in 1982-. Periodical. Chinese. an. $10.00. Hua Fan Fo Hsueh Yen Chiu So, 22 Lane 110 Yang Te Road Sec 2 Shih Lin, Taipei Taiwan. **LC** BQ3; .H79. **DD** 294.3/05.

II
**INDEX INTERNATIONALIS INDICUS. Added/Corp** Centre for Asian Dokumentation in Humanities. (19??)-. Abstracting/Indexing Service. English (Bengali, Hindi and Sanskrit). te. Rs1000.00. Centre for Asian Dokumentation, K 15 / CIT Building, Christopher Road, Calcutta 700014 India. **ED** S. Chaudhuri. cum. index. **Bk Rev. Ad Acc. Circ:** 400.
**Desc:** Cumulative list of articles on indological and buddhistic studies.

II
**INDIAN JOURNAL OF BUDDHIST STUDIES / BAUDDHA ADHYAYANA KI BHARATIYA PATRIKA, THE. Added/Corp** BJK Institute of Buddhist & Asian Studies (Varanasi, India). **VFOAT** IJBS; Bauddha Adhyayana ki Bharatiya Patrika; I.J.B.S.; Indian jl. Buddhist Studies. Vol. 1, No. 1 (Spring 1989)-. Periodical. English (Hindi). sa. $30.00. Tara Book Agency, Varanasi, India. **(Subscription address:** Prints India, 11 Darya Ganj, New Delhi, 110002 India, (Phone: 011 91 11 3268645)**) LC** IN PROCESS.

US/0741-2193
**JOURNAL OF BUDDHIST PHILOSOPHY.** [J. Buddh. philos.]. Vol. 1 (1983)-. Periodical. English. an. $30.00. Buddhist Philosophy, PO Box 2717, Bloomington IN 47402-2717.

US/0193-600X
**JOURNAL OF THE INTERNATIONAL ASSOCIATION OF BUDDHIST STUDIES, THE. Main/Corp** International Association of Buddhist Studies. **VFOAT** J.I.A.B.S. Vol. 1 (1978)-. Academic Scholarly Publication. English. sa. $50.00. IABS Department of Oriental Language, University of California, Berkeley CA 94702. **Tel** (510)642-3480. **ED** A K Narain. **LC** BQ2; .I55a. **DD** 294.3/05. **Bk Rev. Ad Acc. Circ:** 600 (ctrl). available on microfilm and microfiche from University Microfilms International (UMI).
**Desc:** Contains scholarly articles that deal with all possible aspects of Buddhist studies.
**Ind/Abst** Index Book Rev. Relig.; Relig. Index One Period.

US/0891-1177
**JOURNAL OF THE ORDER OF BUDDHIST CONTEMPLATIVES, THE.** [J. Order Buddh. Contempl.]. **Added/Corp** Order of Buddhist Contemplatives. Vol. 1, No. 1 (1986)- Vol. 8 (Spring 193-94)-. Periodical. English. Four times a year (Jan.,Apr., July, Oct.). $20.00 US; $23.00 Canada and Mexico; $23.00 (surface mail), $30.00 (airmail) other. Shasta Abbey, 3612 Summit Drive, PO Box 199, Mount Shasta CA 96067. **Tel** (916)926-4208. **ED** L B H Kinzan Learman. **LC** BQ9460; .J68. **DD** 294.3/657/05. **Circ:** 540. ***Continues** Journal of Shasta Abbey, 0732-8508.*
**Desc:** The Journal of the Order of Buddhist Contemplatives contains articles on Buddhist meditation and practice written by priests of the Order and lay members of the congregation.

JA
**KIKANSHI; BANKOKU BUKKYOTO REMMEI KEN SEITO KOKUGO UNDO. Main/Corp** Bankoku Bukkyoto Remmei. **Added/Corp** Bankoku Bukkyoto Remmei. Organ of the Universal Buddhist League and the Genuine Japanese Language Movement. **VFOAT** Organ for the Universal Buddhist League and the Genuine Japanese Language Movement, The Japanese-English. (19??)-. Periodical. English (Japanese). Universal Buddhist League, 1116 Nogayamachi, Machidashi Tokyo 194-01 Japan. **LC** BQ6; .B35a.

JA
**KOMAZAWA DAIGAKU BUKKYO GAKUBU RON SHU. Main/Corp** Komazawa Daigaku, Tokyo. Bukkyo Gakubu. **VFOAT** Journal of Buddhist Studies. Began with March 1971 issue. Japanese. Komazawa Daigaku Bukkyo Gakubu Kenkyoshitsu, 23-1 Komazawa 1-chome, Setagaya-ku, Tokyo Japan. **LC** BQ6; .K65A.

II/0025-0406
**MAHA BODHI, THE. Added/Corp** Maha Bodhi Society of India. (1924)-. Periodical. English. Six times a year. $12.00. Maha Bodhi Publications, 4A Bankim Chatterjee Street, Calcutta 700 073 India. **Tel** 011 91 33 316314. **ED** Wipulasara Mahathera. **Bk Rev. Ad Acc. Circ:** 2,000. ***Continues** Maha Bodhi and the United Buddhist World.*
**Desc:** One of the oldest international and widely read journals that is devoted to Buddhism, Buddhist literature, art, culture and Buddhist news and reviews.

BE
**MELANGES CHINOIS ET BOUDDHIQUES. Added/Corp** Institut Belge des Hautes Etudes Chinoises. (1932)-. Monographic series. French (English). ir (every two years). Price varies per volume. Institut Belge des Hautes Etudes Chinoises, Musees Royaux d'Art et d'Histoire, 10 Parc du Cinquantenaire, 1040 Bruxelles Belgium. **Tel** 011 02 733 96 10, FAX 011 02 733 77 35. **LC** BL1405; .M4. **DD** 294.304. **Circ:** 1,000.
**Desc:** Serial on Chinese classical studies and Buddhism.

UK/0026-3214
**MIDDLE WAY : JOURNAL OF THE BUDDHIST SOCIETY, THE. Added/Corp** Buddhist Society (London, England). (May/June 1943)-. Academic Scholarly Publication. English. Four times a year (Feb., May, Aug., Nov.). £8.50 UK; £10.50 Ireland, Denmark, Netherlands, Belgium, Luxemburg, Germany, France, Italy and Greece; £9.50 other. Buddhist Society, 58 Eccleston Square, London SW1 V1PH England. **Tel** 011 44 71 834 5858. **ED** Desmond Biddulph and John Swain. Index available. cum. index. **Bk Rev. Ad Acc.** Full Page (B&W) £110.00. Half Page (B&W) £60.00. **Circ:** 3,500 (ctrl). ***Continues** Buddhism in England.*
**Desc:** General and scholarly articles on Buddhism, Eastern culture, views and religion. News regarding Buddhist organizations worldwide.
**Ind/Abst** Index Book Rev. Relig.; Relig. Index One Period.

US/0896-8942
**MOUNTAIN RECORD.** [Mt. rec.]. **Added/Corp** Mountains and Rivers Order (Mount Tremper, N.Y.). Vol. 9, No. 2 (Fall 198?)-. Periodical. English. Four times a year. $14.00 (one year); $25.00 (two years); $35.00 (three years). Dharma Communications, PO Box 156, South Plank Road, Mt Tremper NY 12457-0156. **Tel** (914)688-2228. **ED** Amy S. Brown. **DD** 294. **Bk Rev. Ad Acc. Circ:** 5,000.
**Desc:** A journal of Zen Buddhist practice in America with essays and articles on Eastern and Western religious traditions, ethics and morality, science, business, social action and ecology. Reports the activities of Zen Mountain Monastery and the Society of Mountains and Rivers.

JA
**NARITASAN BUKKYO KENKYUJO KIYO. VFOAT** Journal of Naritasan Institute for Buddhist Studies. Japanese (Japanese). Naritasan Shinshoji, Narital 286, Narita Japan. **LC** BQ6; .N37A.

JA/0385-5805
**NIHON BUKKYO SHIGAKU / NIHON BUKKYO SHIGAKUKAI.** Japanese. Sankibo Busshorin, 28-4 Hongo 5, Bunkyo-ku Tokyo Japan. **LC** BQ670; .N535.

JA
**NIPPON BUKKYO GAKKAI NEMPO. Main/Corp** Nihon Bukkyo Gakkai. **VFOAT** Journal of the Nippon Buddhist Research Association. Japanese. an. Nippon Bukkyo Gakkai Seibu Jimusho, c/o Otani Daigaku, Koyama Kamifusacho, Kita-ku, Kyoto Japan. **LC** BQ6; .N56A.

BR
**PALI PARAGU BWE YA PUGGO MYA I HTEIRUPPATTI MYA. Main/Corp** Pali Takkatho Baho Ahpwe. Periodical. Burmese (Burmese). Pali Takkatho Baho Ahpwe, PO Box 1003, Yankonmyo Burma. **LC** BQ424; .P33A.

KO
**POMNYUN.** Periodical. Korean. W2,000. Pomnyun Sa, 74 Kwanhun-dong, Chongno-ku, Seoul South Korea. **LC** BQ8.K6; P65.

KO
**PULGWANG.** Periodical. Korean. mo. W8.000. Pulgwanghoe, 136 Pongik-dong Chongno-ku, Seoul 110 Korea. **LC** BQ8.K6; P79.

KO
**PULGYO MUNHWA. VFOAT** Buddhist Civilization. V. 1- Feb. 1974-. Periodical. Korean (Korean). 400 single issue. 382 Sonhwa-dong, Taejon Korea. **LC** DS901; .P84.

KO
**PULGYO (SEOUL, KOREA).** (PULGYO.). **VFOAT** Buddhism. (19??)-. Periodical. Korean. mo. 7,000. Pulgyosa, 1 Pongwon-dong Sodaemun-ku, Seoul Korea. **LC** BQ8.K6; P8.

UK
**SACRED BOOKS OF THE BUDDHISTS.** V. 1- 1895-. Monographic series. English. Price varies per volume. **LC** BQ1138.

NP
**SAMBODA.** Vol. 1, No. 1 (June/Aug. 1991)-. Periodical. English (Nepali). qt. Rs150.00 Nepal; $25.00 US single issue. Samboda, PO Box 4778, Panipokhari, Maharajgunj, Kathmandu Nepal. **LC** BQ7530; .S25. **Desc:** Chiefly on Tibetan Buddhism.

JA
**SEIKYO HODO SHASHINSHU. VFOAT** Best Press Photos: The Seikyo; Seikyo. 1973-. Japanese (Japanese). ¥850. Seikyo Shimbun Sha, 18 Shinanomachi Shinjuku-ku, Tokyo 160 Japan. **LC** BQ8400; .S43.

CH
**SHIH FANG YUEH KAN. VFOAT** Shih Fang; Universal Monthly; Shih Fang Tsa Chih. V. 1, (Oct. 1982)-. Periodical. Chinese. mo. NT$150.00. Shih Fang Tsa Chih She, PO Box 91-389, Taipei Taiwan. **LC** BQ620; .S5. **DD** 294.3/0951.

JA
**SHINSHUGAKU. Added/Corp** Ryukoku Daigaku Shinshu Gakkai. **VFOAT** Journal of Studies in Shin Buddhism. (19??)-. Periodical. Japanese (Japanese). sa. Ryukoku Daigaku Shinshu Gakkai, Kyoto 600 Japan. **LC** BQ8700; .S54.

JA/0286-4185
**SHITENNOJI KOKUSAI BUKKYO DAIGAKU BUNGAKUBU KIYO. VFOAT** Review of International Buddhist University, Faculty of Letters. Japanese. Shitennoji Kokusai Bukkyo, Daigaku 1308 Hanyuno, Habikino-shi Osaka-fu Japan. **LC** AS552.H52; A35.

JA/0385-6321
**SOKA GAKKAI NEWS, THE. Main/Corp** Soka Gakkai. **Added/Corp** Soka Gakkai. Kohoshitsu. Soka Gakkai. Kohoshitsu. Kokusaikyoku. **VFOAT** SokaGakkai News. No. 1 (Feb. 25, 1975)-. Periodical. Japanese. mo. Free on request. International Bureau Soka Gakkai, 32 Shinano-machi Shinjuku Ku, Tokyo 160 Japan. **Tel** 011 81 3 3530616, telex J33145SKG. **LC** BQ8400; .S64a. **DD** 294.3/65. Index available. **Desc:** Reports current activities of Soka Gakkai: individual experiences; programs of youth, women's education and other divisions; activities of SGI president Ikeda.

JA
**SOKA GAKKAI NYUSU / THE SOKAGAKKAI NEWS. Added/Corp** Soka Gakkai. **VFOAT** Sokagakkai News. (19??)-. Periodical. Japanese. mo. Free. Soka Gakkai Kohoshitsu, 32 Shinano-machi, Shinjuku-ku Tokyo-to 160 Japan. **Tel** 03(353)7111, FAX 03(355)0546, telex J33145SKG. **ED** Toshiyuki Mitsugi. **LC** BQ8400; .S650. **Circ:** 32,000.

DK/0904-2431
**STUDIES IN CENTRAL AND EAST ASIAN RELIGIONS : JOURNAL OF THE SEMINAR FOR BUDDHIST STUDIES, COPENHAGEN & AARHUS. Added/Corp** Seminar for Buddhist Studies, Copenhagen & Aarhus. **VFOAT** Journal of the Seminar for Buddhist Studies, Copenhagen & Aarhus; SCEAR. Vol. 1 (Autumn 1988)-. English (French and German). an (Nov.). $30.00. SBS Publications / CESEA, 5 Stokhusgade, 1st Floor, 1317 Copenhagen K Denmark. **Tel** 011 42 33 153106, FAX 011 31 35 322595. **ED** Henrik H. Sorensen and Jan Astley. **LC** BQ1; .S78. **Bk Rev**, (Qty: 10). **Ad Acc. Pr Rev. Circ:** 2,300 (ctrl).

US
**STUDIES IN EAST ASIAN BUDDHISM / KURODA INSTITUTE. Added/Corp** Kuroda Institute. (1983)-. Monographic series. English. ir. Price varies per volume. University of Hawaii Press, 2840 Kolowalu Street, Honolulu HI 96822. **Tel** (808)956-8833, (808)948-8697, FAX (808)988-6052. **Desc:** Scholarly research on Buddhist history and philosophy.

DK
**STUPA.** (1978)-. Periodical. Danish. **LC** BQ7549; .S78.

JA
**TAISHO DAIGAKU KENKYU KIYO. VFOAT** Taisho Daigaku Kenkyukiyo; Memoirs of Taisho University. Began in 1954; with issue 39. Periodical. English (Japanese). Taisho Daigaku Shuppanbu 20-1, Nishi Sugamo 3-chome, Toshima-ku Tokyo Japan. **LC** BQ6; .T3. ***Continues*** *Taisho Daigaku Gakuho.*

JA
**TAISHO DAIGAKU SOGO BUKKYO KENKYUJO NENPO. Added/Corp** Taisho Daigaku. Sogo Bukkyo Kenkyujo. **VFOAT** Annual of the Institute for Comprehensive Studies of Buddhism, Taisho University. (1979)-. English (Japanese). an. Taisho Daigaku Sogo Bukkyo Kenkyujo, 20-1 Nishi Sugamo 3-chome, Toshima-ku, Tokyo Japan. **LC** BQ6; .T34.

US
**TEN DIRECTIONS, THE.** English. sa (May and Nov.). Free on request. Zen Center of Los Angeles, 923 South Normandie Avenue, Los Angeles CA 90006. **Tel** (213)387-2351, FAX (213)387-2377.

JA
**TOHOKAI. Added/Corp** Toyo Bunka Suishinkai. No. 1- (Dec. 1973-1978)-. Periodical. Japanese. mo. ¥1200. Tohokai Inc, 6-2-17 Nishitemma Kita-U, Osaka 530 Japan. **Tel** (03)365-5131. **LC** BQ6; .T64.

US/1055-484X
**TRICYCLE (NEW YORK, N.Y.).** (TRICYCLE : THE BUDDHIST REVIEW.). [Tricycle]. **Added/Corp** Buddhist Ray, Inc. Vol. 1, No. 1 (Fall 1991)-. Periodical. English. qt. $20.00 (1 year), $38.00 (2 year), $57.00 (3 year) US; $25.00 (1 year), $48.00 (2 year), $72.00 (3 year) other. Buddhist Ray Incorporated, 163 West 22nd Street, New York NY 10011. **Tel** (212)645-1143, FAX (212)645-1493. **ED** Helen Tworkov. **LC** BQ2; .T75. **DD** 294.3/05. **Bk Rev**, (Qty: 20). **Ad Acc. Circ:** 30,000. **Desc:** America's largest independent Buddhist publication.

US
**UOC TUE. VFOAT** Torch of Wisdom. So Ramat- April 5, 1976-. Periodical. English (Vietnamese). $0.85 each issue. 5333 16th Street NW, Washington DC 20011. **LC** BQ120; .D86. **DD** 294.3.

US/0507-6986
**VAJRA BODHI SEA. Added/Corp** Sino-American Buddhist Association. **VFOAT** Hai Ti Pu Kang Chin. (Apr. 1970)-. Periodical. English (Chinese; summaries and/or abstracts in Chinese). Twelve times a year. $60.00. Buddhist Text Translation Association, 800 Sacramento Street, San Francisco CA 94108. **Tel** (415)421-6117. **LC** BQ2; .V34. Index available. **Bk Rev. Circ:** 3,500. **Desc:** English translations of major Buddhist scriptures, biographical sketches of ancient masters, Sanskrit language lessons and contemporary articles by practitioners. Bilingual in English and Chinese.

US/0882-0813
**VAJRADHATU SUN, THE.** [Vajradhatu sun]. Periodical. English (Spanish). bm. $18.00 US; $20.00 Canada; $28.00 other. The Vajradhatu Sun, 1345 Spruce Street, Boulder CO 80302. **Tel** (303)444-0190, FAX (303)443-2975. **ED** Rick Fields and Linda Cressman. **LC** BQ2; .V36. **DD** 294.3/05. Index available. cum. index. **Bk Rev. Ad Acc. Circ:** 5,000. **Desc:** Covers the growth of Buddhism in the west.

CE/0049-7541
**WHEEL, THE. Added/Corp** Buddhist Publication Society. (1958)-. Periodical. English. Three times a year. $15.00. The Buddhist Publications Society, PO Box 61, Kandy Sri Lanka Ceylon. **Tel** (08)03679. **LC** BL1400; .W45. **Circ:** 45,000. **Desc:** Publications relating to Buddhism, its philosophy, and its practice. Including translations of selected Pali texts, with notes, as found in the oldest and most reliable Buddhist tradition, the "Theravada Pali Canon".

CE/0043-8286
**WORLD BUDDHISM. Added/Corp** World Fellowship of Buddhists. Vol. 1 (Aug. 1952)-. Periodical. English. mo. $4.00. Paramadhamma Buddhist Institut Ratmalana, Sri Lanka Ceylon. **LC** BL1400; .W6. available on microfilm and microfiche from University Microfilms International (UMI).

CE/0084-1447
**WORLD BUDDHISM.** (VESAK ANNUAL.). English. 153-3 Dutugemunu Street, Nugegoda Sri Lanka Ceylon. **LC** BL1400. **DD** 294.3/05. Index Available in first issue of next volume--loose-unpaged.

SI/0377-8088
**YOUNG BUDDHIST, THE.** Multiple languages (English and Chinese). 83 Silat Road, 3 Singapore Republic of Singapore. **LC** BQ3; .Y67. **DD** 294.3/05.

JA/0513-5974
**YOUNG EAST. *Ceased.*** Vol. 1-15 No. 1-60 (1952)-?. Periodical. English. qt. Tohokai Inc, 6-2-17 Nishitemma Kita-U, Osaka 530 Japan. **Tel** (03)365-5131. **ED** Bando Slojun. **LC** BL1400; .Y62. **Bk Rev. Ad Acc. Circ:** 1,200 (ctrl). ***Supersedes*** *Young East.* **Desc:** A journal on Buddhism and Japanese culture. First published in 1925.

US/0360-991X
**ZCLA JOURNAL. Main/Corp** Zen Center of Los Angeles. **VAT** Zen Centre of Los Angeles Journal. Periodical. English. Three times a year. $6.00. Zen Center of Los Angeles, 923 South Normandie Avenue, Los Angeles CA 90006. **Tel** (213)387-2351, FAX (213)387-2377. **LC** BQ9250; .Z463A. **DD** 294.3/927.

## CATHOLICISM

FR
**30 JOURS DANS L'EGLISE ET DANS LE MONDE. VFOAT** Trente Jours dans l'Eglise et dans le Monde; Trente J; 30 J. No. 1 (Oct. 1987)-. Periodical. French. mo. 420.00F. ETG Media, 12 rue Florentin, 75001 Paris France. **Tel** 011 33 42 961841. **LC** BX802; .A17. **DD** 282/.05. **Ad Acc, Adv Mgr:** Ehrica Biondi. **Circ:** 10,000.

US/0737-3457
**ABRIDGED CATHOLIC PERIODICAL AND LITERATURE INDEX, THE. See** Religion and Theology-Abstracting, Bibliographies and Statistics.

VC/0001-5199
**ACTA APOSTOLICA SEDIS, COMMENTARIUM OFFICIALE.** (ACTA APOSTOLICAE SEDIS.). [Acta apostol. sedis, Comment. off.]. **Main/Corp** Catholic Church. Pope. **Added/Corp** Vatican City. Laws, etc. Vol. 1 (Jan. 1, 1980)-. Periodical. Latin (English, French, German, Italian and Polish). mo. $112.00. Liberia Editrice Vaticana, Citta del Vaticano, 00120 Vatican City. **Tel** 011 39 6 69883529, telex 2024 DIRGENTEL VA. **LC** BX850; .A32. Index Available Published separately--free--upon request. available on microfilm and microfiche from University Microfilms International (UMI). ***Supersedes*** *Acta Santae Sedis.* **Desc:** Official record of transactions and proceedings from the Apostolic See in Vatican City under the direction of the Pope. **Ind/Abst** Bibliogr. Mission.; Abr. Cathol. Period. Lit. Index; Cathol. Period. Lit. Index.

IT/0065-1443
**ACTA NUNTIATURAE GALLICAE.** 1-. Monographic series. French. ir. Price varies per volume. Universita Gregoriana Editrice, 00187 Rome Italy. **Tel** (06)6781567. **ED** Pierre Blet. **LC** BX1528.

IT/0001-6411
**ACTA ORDINIS FRATRUM MINORUM. Added/Corp** Regula Ordinis Franciscani Saecularis. Vol. 1 (1982)-. Periodical. Latin. bm (6 issues). L30000 Italy; L40000 other. Curia Generalis OFM, Via South Maria Mediatrice 25, 00165 Rome Italy. **Tel** 011 39 6 684919. cum. index. **Ind/Abst** Bibliogr. Mission.

AG
**ACTUALIDAD PASTORAL.** (19??)-. Periodical. Spanish. Six times a year. $50.00. Actualidad Pastoral, Abel Costa 261, C. C. 140, 1708 Moron Buenos Aires Argentina. **Tel** 011 54 627 2806, FAX 011 54 627 2806. **ED** Vicente Oscar Vetrano. **LC** BX1425.A1; A27. Index available. cum. index. **Bk Rev**, (Qty: 20). **Ad Acc. Circ:** 4,000.

US/0272-7250
**ALBANIAN CATHOLIC BULLETIN.** (ALBANIAN CATHOLIC BULLETIN. BULETINI KATHOLIK SHQIPTAR.). **Added/Corp** Albanian Catholic Information Center. **VFOAT** Buletini Katholik Shqiptar. Vol. 1 (1980)-. Bulletin. English (Albanian). an. $10.00 donation. Albanian Catholic Information Center, 1032 Irving Street/Suite 518, San Francisco CA 94122. **Tel** (415)666-6966. **ED** Gjon Sinishta. Index available. **Bk Rev. Circ:** 1,500 (ctrl). **Desc:** Promoting religious freedom and information about historical and cultural heritage of Albanian people. **Ind/Abst** Hum. Rights Intern. Rep.; Index Book Rev. Relig.; Relig. Index One Period.

CN/0316-473X
**ALBERTA CATHOLIC DIRECTORY. VFOAT** Official Alberta Catholic Directory. 1971-. Directory. English. an. 7.00Can$. Alberta Catholic Directory, 10562 109th Street, Edmonton Alberta T5H 3B2 Canada. **Tel** 420-1330. **DD** 282/.025/7123. **Ad Acc. Circ:** 1,500 (ctrl). ***Formed by the union of*** *Alberta Catholic Directory Edmonton Ed., 0316-4748* ***and*** *Alberta Catholic Directory Calgary Ed, 0316-4756.* **Desc:** Official ecclesiastical directory for Province of Alberta and Diocese of Mackenzie, Ft Smith.

PE/0252-8835
**ALLPANCHIS.** (ALLPANCHIS : REVISTA DEL INSTITUTO DE PASTORAL ANDINA.). [Allpanchis]. **Added/Corp** Instituto de Pastoral Andina. **VFOAT** Allpanchis Phuturinqa; Orakesajj Achukaniwa; Nuestra

sa. Free for members. Societe Canadienne D'Histoire de L'Eglise Catholique, 175 Rue Main, Ottawa Ontario K1S 1C3 Canada. **DD** 282/.71/05.

FR/0007-4322
**BULLETIN DE LITTERATURE ECCLESIASTIQUE.** [Bull. litt. eccles.]. Vol. 1 (Jan. 1899)-. Bulletin. French. qt. $55.00. Institut Catholique de Toulouse, 31 rue de la Fonderie, F 31068 Toulouse Cedex France. **Tel** 011 33 61 368117. **Circ:** 700. ***Continues*** *Bulletin Theologique, Scientifique et Litteraire de l'Institut Catholique de Toulouse.*
**Desc:** Articles concerning the history of theology and religious literature in the epochs of the two testaments, the patristic and the scholastic with some more speculative articles of theology or philosophy.
**Ind/Abst** BHA : Biblio. Hist. Art; MLA Int. Bibl. Books Artic. Mod. Lang. Lit.; New Testam. Abstr.; Old Testam. Abstr.; Romant. Move.

CN/0703-1963
**BULLETIN DE NOUVELLES - SOCIETE CANADIENNE DE DROIT CANONIQUE.** **Main/Corp** Canadian Canon Law Society. **VFOAT** Newsletter - Canadian Canon Law Society. V. 1- Mar. 1974-. Bulletin. English (French). Twice a year. Free to members. Canadian Canon Law Society, 223 Main Street, Ottawa Ontario K1S 1C4 Canada. **Tel** (613)230-7330. **ED** Alexandre Tache. **DD** 262.9/05. **Circ:** 425 (ctrl).
**Desc:** Contains news, reports and selected texts of canonical interest, pertaining mainly to Canadian context.

GW
**BULLETIN DEI VERBUM.** Bulletin. German (English, French and Spanish). Four times a year. $17.00 regular; $30.00 supporting; $10.00 Third World; $10.00 students. Catholic Biblical Federation, General Secretariat, Postfach 10 52 22, D 70045 Stuttgart Germany. **Tel** 011 49 0711 169240, FAX 011 49 0711 1692424.

BE
**BULLETIN D'HISTOIRE CISTERCIENNE / BULLETIN OF CISTERICAN HISTORY.** **See** Religion and Theology-Abstracting, Bibliographies and Statistics.

US/0547-7115
**BULLETIN OF THE NATIONAL GUILD OF CATHOLIC PSYCHIATRISTS, INC, THE.** ***Suspended.*** **See** Medical Science and Technology-Psychiatry.

CN/0226-5923
**C. H. A. C. REVIEW.** **See** Medical Science and Technology-Hospital Administration and Medical Centers.

CN/0007-9774
**CAHIERS DE JOSEPHOLOGIE.** [Cah. Josephol.]. **Added/Corp** Oratoire Saint-Joseph (Montreal, Quebec). Centre de Recherche et de Documentation. Vol. 1, No. 1 (Jan./June 1953)- Vol.41 (Jan. 1993)-. Periodical. French (English). Twice a year (January and December). 25.00Can$. Centre de Recherche, 3800 Chemin Queen Mary, Montreal Quebec H3V 1H6 Canada. **Tel** (514)733-8211 ext. 2331. **ED** Roland Gauthier. **LC** BT690; .C3. Index available. **Bk Rev. Circ:** 500.
**Desc:** Everything in relation with the theology of St. Joseph and the history of the devotion to St. Joseph.
**Ind/Abst** Index Book Rev. Relig.; New Testam. Abstr.; Old Testam. Abstr.; Abr. Cathol. Period. Lit. Index; Cathol. Period. Lit. Index.

FR
**CAHIERS SAINT DOMINIQUE.** French. qt (4 issues). 135.00F France; 180.00F other. Cahiers Saint Dominique, 29 Boulvard Latour Maubourg, 75340 Paris Cedex 07 France. **Tel** 011 33 1 44181212. **ED** Isabella Paria Rioux. **Bk Rev**, (Qty: 4). **Ad Acc. Circ:** 2,000 (ctrl).

CN/0714-7724
**CANADIAN CATHOLIC REVIEW, THE.** [Can. cathol. rev.]. Vol. 1, No. 1 (Jan. 1983)-. Periodical. English. Eleven times a year (monthly with July/Aug. issues combined). 25.00Can$ (one year) 40.00 Can$ (two years). Canadian Catholic Review, 1437 College Drive, Saskatoon Saskatchewan, S7N 0W6 Canada. **Tel** (306)966-8900, (306)966-8959, FAX (306)966-8904. **ED** Daniel Callam. **DD** 282/.05. Index available. cum. index. **Bk Rev**, (Qty: 90). **Ad Acc, Adv Mgr:** Don Ward, **Tel** (306)966-8959. **Circ:** 1,000.
**Desc:** Contains gospel of Jesus, articles on Saints, scholars and founders of spiritual insights, justice, community, church in other countries, scripture, liturgy, columns on movies, television, American notes, and Eastern church. This publication is devoted to the examination of religious and social issues from a Catholic viewpoint; also contains articles on literature, culture, saints, Scripture, media; book reviews; columns. It is faithful to the teachings of the Magisterium.
**Ind/Abst** Guide Soc. Sci. Relig.; Abr. Cathol. Period. Lit. Index; Cathol. Period. Lit. Index.

BL
**CANCHIM : RESUMOS INFORMATIVOS.** **Added/Corp** Empresa Brasileira de Pesquisa Agropecularia. (19??)-. Periodical. Portuguese.

US
**CARING COMMUNITY, THE.** (19??)-. Newsletter. English. Twelve times a year. $12.00. National Catholic Reporter Publishing Company, PO Box 419281, 115 East Armour Boulevard, Kansas City MO 64141-6281. **Tel** (816)531-0538, (800)444-8910, (800)333-7373, FAX (816)531-7466. **ED** Carolyn Hoff.

IT/0008-6673
**CARMELUS.** V. 1-. Periodical. English (French, German, Italian, Latin and Spanish). sa. L40000 Italy; $30.00 other. Institutum Carmelitanum, Via Sforza Pallavicini 10, 00193 Rome Italy. **Tel** (06)6543-513. **ED** Joachim Smet. **LC** BX3201; .C35. **DD** 255/.73/005. **Bk Rev. Ad Acc. Circ:** 600. ***Supersedes*** *Analecta Ordinis Carmelitaram.*
**Desc:** Theological, philosophical, bibliographical and historical studies, especially as these relate to the Carmelite Order.
**Ind/Abst** Bibliogr. Mission.

BL
**CATALOGO DAS INSTITUICOES CATOLICAS DE ENSIO SUPERIOR NO BRASIL.** **See** Education.

FR
**CATECHESE.** (1960)-. Periodical. French. qt. 200.00F France; 230.00F other. Catechese, 6 Avenue Vavin, 75006 Paris France. **Tel** 011 33 1 43252375, FAX 011 33 1 40468069.
**Ind/Abst** Bibliogr. Mission.

US/0008-7726
**CATECHIST.** [Catechist]. **Added/Corp** National Catholic Catachists Society. (1967)-. Periodical. English. Seven times a year. $18.95. Peter Li Education Group, 330 Progress Road, Dayton OH 45449. **Tel** (513)847-5900, (800)543-4383. **ED** Patricia Fischer. **Bk Rev. Ad Acc. Circ:** 46,000. available on microfilm and microfiche from University Microfilms International (UMI).
**Desc:** Presents and provides teaching ideas, student activities, insights and information in a way that's beneficial to veteran catechists, religion teachers, and DRE's. Editorial is tied into the Church year and teaches readers how to present materials at different stages of child development.
**Ind/Abst** Med. Rev. Dig.; Abr. Cathol. Period. Lit. Index; Cathol. Period. Lit. Index.

US
**CATECHIST'S CONNECTION, THE.** (19??)-. Newsletter. English. Ten times a year. $12.00. National Catholic Reporter Publishing Company, PO Box 419281, 115 East Armour Boulevard, Kansas City MO 64141-6281. **Tel** (816)531-0538, (800)444-8910, (800)333-7373, FAX (816)531-7466. **ED** Jean Marie Hiesberger.

PY
**CATEQUESIS LATINOAMERICANO.** Began 1969?. Periodical. Spanish. Instituto Teologico Pastoral del Celam, Revista Medellin, Apartado Aereo 51086, Bogota 2 Colombia. **Tel** 011 57-91-2357046.

SP
**CATEQUETICA.** No. 4 (Jan./April 1961)-. Periodical. Spanish. Four times a year. $25.00. Editorial Sal Terrae, Apartado 77, 39080 Santander Spain. **Tel** 011 34 42 320528, 011 34 42 320529. cum. index. **Circ:** 4,000. ***Continues*** *Sal Terrae. Parte Catequetica.*
**Desc:** Covers religious celebrations, solutions for difficulties and religious instruction. Includes informal expositions on scripture for baptisms, first communion, weddings, funerals, etc., plus admonitions to the faithful and instructions from the Pope.

US/0745-399X
**CATHOLIC ACCENT, THE.** **Added/Corp** Catholic Church. Diocese of Greensburg (Pa.). Vol. 1, No. 1 (June 1, 1961)-. Newspaper. English. Fifty-two times a year (Thursdays). $13.25. Catholic Accent, PO Box 850, Greensburg PA 15601. **Tel** (412)837-0901. **ED** Alice Laurich and Carol Kalich. **Ad Acc. Circ:** 51,000. available on microfiche.

US/0008-7904
**CATHOLIC ADVANCE, THE.** **Added/Corp** Catholic Church. Diocese of Wichita (Kan.) Catholic Church. Diocese of Concordia (Kan.). (1901)-. Newspaper. English. wk. $10.00 Kansas; $12.00 other US; $13.00 other. Catholic Advance, 424 North Broadway, Wichita KS 67202. **Tel** (316)263-8191. **ED** M. Cecilia Bush. **Bk Rev. Ad Acc. Circ:** 27,000 (ctrl).
**Desc:** Publishes news of Catholic and religious interest of the Diocese of Wichita, and national and international scenes.

US/0069-1208
**CATHOLIC ALMANAC.** **Added/Corp** Saint Anthony's Guild. 65th (1969)-. English. an. $19.95 paperback; $22.95 clothbound. Our Sunday Visitor Inc., 200 Noll Plaza, Box 920, Huntington IN 46750. **Tel** (219)356-8400, (800)348-2440, FAX (219)356-8472. **ED** Felician Foy and Rose Avato. **LC** AY81.R6; N3. **DD** 282. ***Continues*** *National Catholic Almanac.*
**Desc:** Single-volume encyclopedic reference on the Catholic Church.
**Ind/Abst** Stat. Ref. Index.

UK
**CATHOLIC ANCESTOR.** **See** Genealogy and Heraldry.

US/1044-1581
**CATHOLIC ANSWER, THE.** [Cathol. answ.]. **Added/Corp** Our Sunday Visitor, Inc. (1987)-. Periodical. English. Six times a year. $18.00 US; $20.00 other. Our Sunday Visitor Inc., 200 Noll Plaza, Box 920, Huntington IN 46750. **Tel** (219)356-8400, (800)348-2440, FAX (219)356-8472. **DD** 282.

UK/0261-4316
**CATHOLIC ARCHIVES : THE JOURNAL OF THE CATHOLIC ARCHIVES SOCIETY.** **Added/Corp** Catholic Archives Society. No. 1 (1981)-. English. an (April). £4.00 UK; £4.50 other. Catholic Archives Society, c/o R. M. Gard, 21 Larchwood Avenue, N Gosforth, Newcastle upon Tyne NE13 6PY England. **Tel** 011 44 091 236 6043. **ED** R. M. Gard. cum. index. **Bk Rev. Circ:** 500.
**Desc:** Describes the character, arrangement, and historical interest of the archives of the Roman Catholic Church in the UK, with occasional articles in other countries.

US
**CATHOLIC BULLETIN, THE.** Vol. 1, No. 1 (Jan. 7, 1911)-. Newspaper. English. Fifty-two times a year. $26.95. Catholic Bulletin Publishing Company, 244 Dayton Avenue, St. Paul MN 55102. **Tel** (612)291-4444, FAX (612)291-4460. **ED** Robert Zuskowski. **Ad Acc, Adv Mgr:** Terri Broderick, **Tel** (612)290-1630. **Circ:** 25,000. available on microfilm. ***Continues*** *Weekly Bulletin (Saint Paul, Minn.).*
**Desc:** Catholic news, information, and commentary. Official publication of the Archdiocese of St. Paul and Minneapolis.

US/8756-7482
**CATHOLIC CHALLENGE, THE.** [Cathol. chall.]. Vol. 1, No. 1, (Summer 1985)-. Periodical. English. qt. $15.00. Sanderleaf Publishing Inc, 182 109th Avenue, Elmont NY 11003. **DD** 282.

US/0008-7971
**CATHOLIC CHRONICLE, THE.** Periodical. English. bw. $17.00. Catholic Chronicle, PO Box 1866, Toledo OH 43603. **Tel** (419)243-4178, FAX (419)-243-4235. **ED** Richard S Meek. Index available. **Bk Rev. Ad Acc. Circ:** 39,000 (ctrl).
**Desc:** Report on news of interest to Catholics in Northwestern Ohio.

US/0746-0511
**CATHOLIC COMMENTATOR, THE.** Periodical. English. bw. $10.00. Catholic Diocese of Baton Rouge, 1800 South Acadian Thruway, Baton Rouge LA 70808. **Tel** (504)387-0983. **ED** Laura G Deavers.

US/1054-2728
**CATHOLIC COURIER (1989).** (CATHOLIC COURIER.). **Added/Corp** Catholic Church. Diocese of Rochester (N.Y.). (1989)-. Newspaper. English. wk. $20.00. Catholic Courier, 1150 Buffalo Road, Rochester NY 14624. **Tel** (716)328-4340. **ED** Karen M. Franz, Richard A. Kiley (Managing Editor). **Photos. Ad Acc.** Full Page (B&W) $1302.00. Half Page (B&W) $713.00. **Pub. Size:** Tabloid. **Wire Svcs.:** CS. **Circ:** 50,150. available in microform. ***Continues*** *Courier-Journal.*

US/0008-7998
**CATHOLIC DIGEST (SAINT PAUL, MINN.).** (CATHOLIC DIGEST.). [Cath. dig.]. **Added/Corp** College of St. Thomas (Saint Paul, Minn.). **VFOAT** Catholic Readers' Digest. Vol. 2, No. 2 (Dec. 1937)-. Periodical. English. mo. $16.97 (one year), $33.94 (two year). Catholic Digest, 475 Riverside Drive, Suite 1268, New York NY 10115. **Tel** (212)870-2552. **(Subscription address:** Neodata / Colorado, PO Box 2606, Boulder Boulder CO 80322.) **LC** BX801; .C34. **DD** 282/.05. **Ad Acc.** available on microfilm and microfiche from University Microfilms International (UMI). ***Continues*** *Catholic Digest of Catholic Books and Magazines.*
**Desc:** A general family magazine of original and reprinted stories about religion, family life, inspiration, health and fitness, humor, and self-help.
**Ind/Abst** Abr. Cathol. Period. Lit. Index; Cathol. Period. Lit. Index.

UK/0306-5677
**CATHOLIC DIRECTORY FOR SCOTLAND, THE.** [Cathol. dir. Scotl.]. Directory. English. an. J S Burns, 25 Finlas Street, Glasgow G22 5DS Scotland. **LC** BX1497.A3; C3. **DD** 282/.025/41. ***Continues*** *Catholic Directory for the Clergy and Laity in Scotland, 0069-1232.*

UK
**CATHOLIC DIRECTORY OF ENGLAND AND WALES, THE.** Directory. English. an. The Universe, 18 Crosby Road North, Waterloo Liverpool L22 4QF England. **LC** BX1491.A1; C25. **DD** 282/.42/025. ***Continues*** *Catholic Directory.*

US/0162-7031
**CATHOLIC EXPONENT, THE.** Periodical. English. wk. $15.00 US; $25.00 other. The Catholic Exponent, Ohio One Building/Room 330, 25 East Boardman Street, Youngstown OH 44503. **Tel** (216)744-5251. **ED** Denny Finneran and Elaine Polomsky Soos. **Bk Rev. Ad Acc. Circ:** 35,000. available on microfilm and microfiche.
**Desc:** News, features, commentary which appeal to Catholics in six county area of northeastern Ohio from Lake Erie to Ohio River. Special monthly entertainment section. Other special sections on marriage, retirement, careers, health, football, death and dying, respect life, senior rec/fun.

US/0008-8056
**CATHOLIC FREE PRESS, THE. Added/Corp** Catholic Church. Diocese of Worcester (Mass.). Bishop. Vol. 1, No. 1 (May 4, 1951)-. Periodical. English. wk. $19.00 (US); $22.00 (other). Catholic Free Press, 47 Elm Street, Worcester MA 01692. **Tel** (508)757-6387, FAX (508) 753-7180. **ED** Gerard E. Goggins. **Bk Rev**, (Qty: 1 /wk). **Ad Acc, Adv Mgr:** R.C. Ballantine. **Circ:** 21,000 (ctrl). ***Continues*** *Catholic Messenger.*
**Desc:** Serving primarily the catholic population of central Massachusetts.

UK/0008-8064
**CATHOLIC GAZETTE.** Began in 1910. Periodical. English. mo. £7.00. Catholic Missionary Society, Mission House, 114 West Heath Road, London NW3 7TX England. **Tel** 458 3316. **ED** Kevin O'Connell. **Bk Rev. Ad Acc. Circ:** 2,500.
**Desc:** Primarily concerned with evangelization through parish renewal, outreach to the unchurched and personal growth in faith.

UK/0008-8072
**CATHOLIC HERALD.** (1894)-. Periodical. English. Fifty-two times a year (Fri.). £26.90 UK, Northern Ireland & Channel Islands; £38.38 Europe; £41.49 others. Catholic Herald / England, Herald House, Lambs Passage, Bunhill Row, London EC1Y 8TQ England. **Tel** 011 44 71 588 3101, FAX 011 44 71 256 9728, telex 88134723. **ED** Peter Stanford. **Bk Rev. Ad Acc. Circ:** 22,000. ***Absorbed*** *Weekly Herald; South Coast Catholic Herald.*
**Desc:** A religious journal of opinions giving news from home and abroad.

US/0746-4185
**CATHOLIC HERALD (SACRAMENTO, CALIF.).** (CATHOLIC HERALD.). (19??)-. Periodical. English. ir (weekly in Jan. and Dec., bi-weekly in June, July, Aug.). $15.00. Catholic Herald, 5890 Newman Court, Sacramento CA 95819. **Tel** (916)452-3344. **ED** George Schuster. Index available. **Bk Rev. Ad Acc. Circ:** 38,500 (ctrl).
**Desc:** Church news and commentary on local, national and international levels.

US/0008-8080
**CATHOLIC HISTORICAL REVIEW, THE.** [Cathol. hist. rev.]. **Added/Corp** American Catholic Historical Association. Vol. 1 (April 1915)-. Periodical. English. qt (4 issues). $32.00 (institution). Catholic University of America Press, 620 Michigan Avenue Northeast, Administration Building/Room 303, Washington DC 20064. **Tel** (202)319-5052, FAX (202)319-5802. **ED** Robert Trisco. **LC** BX1404; .C3. **DD** 282/.73. Index available (bound in Oct. issue). cum. index. **Bk Rev. Ad Acc. Circ:** 2,200. available on microfilm and microfiche from University Microfilms International (UMI). Documents available from The Genuine Article, UMI Article Clearinghouse.
**Desc:** Publishes articles, review articles and lists of books received in all areas of church history.
**Ind/Abst** Acad. Search (July 1993-); Am. Hist. Life (1954-); Am. Bibliogr. Slavic East Europ. Stud.; Annu. Bibliogr. Engl. Lang. Lit.; Arts Humanit. Citation Index [Full Cov.]; Bibliogr. Mission.; Book Rev. Index; Curr. Contents Arts Humanit.; Expand. Acad. Index (1989-); Hist. Source (July 1993-); Humanit. Index; Humanit. Source (Jul. 1993-); Index Book Rev. Relig.; INFO-SOUTH Abstr.; Mag. Search; Middle East Abstr. Index; Newsp. Period. Abstr. (1991-); Old Testam. Abstr.; Relig. Theol. Abstr.; Res. Alert [Full Cov.]; Romant. Move.; Soc. Sci. Cit. Index [Select. Cov.]; Abr. Cathol. Period. Lit. Index; Cathol. Period. Lit. Index; West. Hist. Q.

US
**CATHOLIC INSIGHT.** ***Ceased.*** (19??)-(Jan. 1994). English. Six times a year. Our Sunday Visitor Inc., 200 Noll Plaza, Box 920, Huntington IN 46750. **Tel** (219)356-8400, (800)348-2440, FAX (219)356-8472.

FR
**CATHOLIC INTERNATIONAL. Added/Corp** Augustinians of the Assumption. North American Province. Vol. 1, No. 1 (Oct. 1990)-. Periodical. English (translations available in Multiple languages). mo. $49.95 US; $70.00 Mexico; $73.00 Europe; $78.00 other. Assumption Communications, 101 Barry Road, Worcester MA 01609. **Tel** (508)756-2893.

US/0008-8129
**CATHOLIC JOURNALIST.** See Journalism.

US/0008-8137
**CATHOLIC LAWYER, THE.** See Law.

US/0008-820X
**CATHOLIC LIBRARY WORLD, THE.** See Library and Information Sciences.

UK/0008-8226
**CATHOLIC MEDICAL QUARTERLY : JOURNAL OF THE GUILD OF CATHOLIC DOCTORS.** See Medical Science and Technology.

US/0008-8234
**CATHOLIC MESSENGER.** Periodical. English. $20.00 US and Latin America; $22.00 other. Catholic Messenger, PO Box 460, Davenport IA 52805. **Tel** (319)323-9959, FAX (319)323-6612. **ED** Francis C Henricksen. cum. index. **Bk Rev. Ad Acc, Adv Mgr:** Kathy. **Circ:** 24,000.

US/0164-0674
**CATHOLIC NEAR EAST MAGAZINE. Added/Corp** Catholic Near East Welfare Association. Pontifical Mission for Palestine. Vol. 1 (Winter 1974)-. Periodical. English. Four times a year. $5.00. Catholic Near East Welfare Association, 1011 First Avenue, NY NY 10022. **Tel** (212)826-1480, 52726922 (Paris, France). **ED** Christian Molidor and Michael Healy. **LC** BX1617; .C37. **DD** 282/.56.
**Desc:** Articles and photographs to generate a spirit of concern, understanding, and brotherhood with people of the Near East.

CN/0701-0788
**CATHOLIC NEW TIMES.** [Cathol. new times]. Vol. 1 (Jan. 16, 1977)-. Periodical. English. Twenty-two times a year. 20.00Can$ (one year), 37.00Can$ (two years) Canada; $30.00 other. Catholic New Times, 80 Sackville Street, Toronto Ontario M5A 3E5, Canada. **Tel** (416)361-0761. **ED** Anne O'Brien. **DD** 282.71. **Bk Rev**, (Qty: 40). **Ad Acc, Adv Mgr:** Noreen Zarand. **Circ:** 10,000. available on microfiche.
**Desc:** Independent, national Catholic newspaper, with emphasis on social and economic justice world news, original reports and analysis, reviews of books and media, etc.
**Ind/Abst** Can. Index; Can. Period. Index (19??-).

US/0278-1174
**CATHOLIC NEW YORK. Added/Corp** Catholic Church. Archdiocese of New York (N.Y.). Vol. 1, No. 1 (Sept. 27, 1981)-. Periodical. English (Spanish). Fifty-one times per year. $20.00 (one year), $36.00 (two year), $52.00 (three year). Ecclesiastical community Corp., PO Box 5133, New York NY 10150. **Tel** (212)688-2399. **LC** Discard.

US/1060-0159
**CATHOLIC NEWS & HERALD, THE.** [Cathol. news her.]. **VFOAT** Catholic News and Herald. Vol. 1, No. 1 (Sept. 6, 1991)-. Periodical. English. wk. Catholic News & Herald, PO Box 37267, Charlotte NC 28237. **DD** 282.

●US/1069-4862
**CATHOLIC PARENT (HUNTINGTON, IND.).** (CATHOLIC PARENT.). (1993)-. Periodical. English. Six times a year. $18.00 US; $24.00 other. Our Sunday Visitor Inc., 200 Noll Plaza, Box 920, Huntington IN 46750. **Tel** (219)356-8400, (800)348-2440, FAX (219)356-8472.

US/0008-8285
**CATHOLIC PERIODICAL AND LITERATURE INDEX, THE.** See Religion and Theology-Abstracting, Bibliographies and Statistics.

CN/0383-1620
**CATHOLIC REGISTER, THE.** [Cathol. regist.]. (April 15, 1972)-. Periodical. English. Forty-seven times a year. 21.79Can$ Canada; 39.95Can$ others. Catholic Register, 67 Bond Street, Suite 303, Toronto ONT M5B 1X6 Canada. **Tel** (416)362-6822, FAX (416)362-8652. **ED** Bernard Daly. **Bk Rev. Ad Acc, Adv Mgr:** S. Tyson, **Tel** same as publisher. **Circ:** 45,000 (ctrl). ***Supersedes*** *Canadian Register National Ed., 0008-4913.*
**Desc:** This is a Catholic newspaper giving news and features of the Catholic church and its challenges in the modern world.

US/8756-9698
**CATHOLIC RESOURCE NEWSLETTER.** [Cathol. resour. newsl.]. (198?)-. Newsletter. English. $15.00 US; $18.00 Canada. Thalassa Resources, Box 273575, Boca Raton FL 33427-3575. **DD** 261.

US/0008-8315
**CATHOLIC REVIEW (BALTIMORE, MD.), THE.** (THE CATHOLIC REVIEW.). [Cathol. rev.]. Periodical. English. wk. $22.00 US; $36.00 other. Catholic Review, 320 Cathedral Street, Box 777, Baltimore MD 21203. **ED** Daniel Medinger. **Ad Acc, Adv Mgr:** John McNulty, **Tel** (410)547-5562. **Circ:** 70,000.

AT
**CATHOLIC SCHOOL STUDIES: A JOURNAL OF EDUCATION FOR AUSTRALIAN & NEW ZEALAND CATHOLIC SCHOOLS.** See Education-Teaching and Curriculum.

US/0162-0363
**CATHOLIC SENTINEL - CATHOLIC CHURCH. DIOCESE OF BAKER (OR.).** (CATHOLIC SENTINEL - DIOCESE OF BAKER.). **Added/Corp** Catholic Truth Society of Oregon, Inc. Catholic Church. Diocese of Baker (Or.). (19??)-. Periodical. English. wk. $22.00 (1 year), $40.00 (2 year). Catholic Sentinel, PO Box 18030, Portland OR 97218. **Tel** (503)281-1191, FAX (503)282-3486. **Bk Rev. Ad Acc. Circ:** 17,000 (ctrl).

US/0886-8190
**CATHOLIC SINGLES.** ***Ceased.*** See Sociology.

US/0896-2715
**CATHOLIC SPIRIT (AUSTIN, TEX.).** (CATHOLIC SPIRIT : OFFICIAL PUBLICATION OF THE DIOCESE OF AUSTIN.). **Added/Corp** Catholic Church. Diocese of Austin (Tex.). (198?)-. Periodical. English. mo. $4.00 (members); $9.00 (non-members). Catholic Spirit, Box 13327, Austin TX 78711. **Tel** (512) 476-4888. ***Continues*** *Catholic Journal (Austin, Tex.).*

US/0411-2741
**CATHOLIC STANDARD (WASHINGTON, D.C.).** (CATHOLIC STANDARD / ARCHDIOCESE OF WASHINGTON.). **Added/Corp** Catholic Church. Archdiocese of Washington (D.C.). (19??)-. Periodical. English. Four times a year. Free. Carroll Publishing Company Inc., 5001 Eastern Avenue, PO Box 4464, Washington DC 20017. **Tel** (301)853-4504. **ED** Thomas Rowan. **Bk Rev. Ad Acc. Circ:** 54,000. available on microfilm.
**Desc:** A Catholic newspaper which publishes international, national, and metropolitan religious news.

US/0744-267X
**CATHOLIC SUN (SYRACUSE, N.Y.), THE.** (THE CATHOLIC SUN.). **VFOAT** Sun. (1892)-. Periodical. English. wk (except last week in Dec., first week in Jan., and first 2 weeks in July). $18.00. Catholic Sun, 257 East Onondaga Street, Syracuse NY 13202. **Tel** (315)422-8153. **ED** Wesley J. Brush. **Bk Rev. Ad Acc. Circ:** 46,300.
**Desc:** News and features relating activities, policies and teachings of Roman Catholic Diocese of Syracuse in Central New York.

US/0147-5959
**CATHOLIC TELEPHONE GUIDE.** English. an. $15.00. Catholic News Publishing, 210 North Avenue, New Rochelle NY 10801-6402. ***Continues*** *Catholic Telephone Guide and Directory for the Archdiocese of New York and the Diocese of Brooklyn.*

US/0745-6050
**CATHOLIC TIMES (COLUMBUS, OHIO), THE.** (THE CATHOLIC TIMES.). **Added/Corp** Catholic Church. Diocese of Columbus (Ohio). (1951)-. Newspaper. English. wk (except certain holidays). $18.00. Catholic Times Inc, PO Box 636, Columbus OH 43216. **Tel** (614)224-5195. **ED** Mike Collins. **Bk Rev**, (Qty: 50). **Ad Acc, Adv Mgr:** Jim Fath, **Tel** (614)224-5115. **Circ:** 34,000.

CN/0703-1521
**CATHOLIC TIMES (MONTREAL).** (THE CATHOLIC TIMES.). Vol. 1, (Dec. 1976)-. Periodical. English. Ten times a year. 11.66Can$. Catholic Times, 2005 St Mark Street West, Montreal Quebec H3H 2G8 Canada. **Tel** (514)937-2301. **ED** Eric Durocher. **DD** 282/.714/281005. **Bk Rev. Ad Acc. Circ:** 12,500 (ctrl).
**Desc:** An English language newspaper for Roman Catholics of the province of Quebec.

US
**CATHOLIC TRENDS. Added/Corp** United States Catholic Conference. (19??)-. Periodical. English. Twenty-six times a year. $33.00 (one year), $59.00 (two year), $88.00 (three year). Catholic News Service, 3211 4th Street Northeast, Washington DC 20017. **Tel** (202)541-3289, (202)541-3250, FAX (202)541-3255, telex 892589. **ED** David Gibson, (phone: (202)541-3284). **Circ:** 4,500. available on an online database from NEWSNET.
**Desc:** Provides current news and analysis of Catholic church activities through brief reports on such areas as public policy, ecumenism, court decisions, education and ministries.

US/0273-6136
**CATHOLIC TWIN CIRCLE.** [Cathol. twin circ.]. (19??)-. Periodical. English. wk (52 issues). $49.95. Twin Circle Publishing Company, 15760 Ventura Boulevard, Suite 1201, Encino CA 91436. **Tel** (818)382-1868, (800)421-3230, FAX (818)382-3677. **ED** Loretta Seyer. **Bk Rev. Ad Acc, Adv Mgr:** Frank Wright. **Circ:** 56,878 (ctrl). ***Continues*** *Twin Circle, 0041-4654.*

**Desc:** National Catholic tabloid, publishes articles 400-2,000 words long which examine issues of interest to Catholics of all ages.

US/0162-7023
**CATHOLIC UNIVERSE-BULLETIN, THE.** **VFOAT** Catholic Universe Bulletin. Vol. 52, No. 48 (May 28, 1926)-. Newspaper. English. Twenty-five times a year. $19.00. Catholic Universe Bulletin Publishing Co., 1027 Superior Avenue, Cleveland OH 44114. **Tel** (216)696-6525 ext 451, (800)869-6525, FAX (216)696-6519. **ED** Michael Dimingo and Pat Hyland (Managing Editor). **Bk Rev. Photos. Ad Acc. Adv Mgr:** David Sarosy. Full Page (B&W) $930.00. Half Page (B&W) $545.00. **Pub. Size:** Tabloid. **Circ:** 40,000. available in microform. ***Formed by the union of*** *Catholic Universe* ***and*** *Catholic Bulletin.*

US
**CATHOLIC UPDATE.** English. mo. $9.00. Saint Anthony Messenger, 1615 Republic Street, Cincinnati OH 45210. **Tel** (513)241-5615, (800)488-0488, FAX (513)241-0399.

US/0008-8404
**CATHOLIC VIRGINIAN.** **Added/Corp** Richmond, Va. (Diocese). (19??)-. Periodical. English. Twenty-six times a year. $12.50. Catholic Virginian Press Inc, PO Box 26843, Richmond VA 23261. **Tel** (804)359-5654.

US/0279-0645
**CATHOLIC VOICE (OAKLAND, CALIF.), THE.** (THE CATHOLIC VOICE / DIOCESE OF OAKLAND.). **Added/Corp** Catholic Church. Diocese of Oakland (Calif.). (19??)-. Periodical. English. Twenty-six times a year. $18.00. Catholic Voice, 2918 Lakeshore Avenue, Oakland CA 94610. **Tel** (510)893-4711. **ED** Monica Clark, (phone: (510)893-5339). **Bk Rev**, (Qty: 12+). **Ad Acc, Adv Mgr:** Tim Holden. **Circ:** 102,000 (ctrl).

US/0008-8463
**CATHOLIC WORKER, THE.** [Cathol. work.]. Vol. 1; May 1933-. Periodical. English. bm. $.25. Catholic Worker, 36 East First Street, New York NY 10003. **Tel** (212)777-9617. **LC** BX801; .C36965. **DD** 282/.05. available on microfilm and microfiche from University Microfilms International (UMI).
**Ind/Abst** Peace Res. Abstr. J. (1976-1983); Abr. Cathol. Period. Lit. Index; Cathol. Period. Lit. Index.

US/1042-3494
**CATHOLIC WORLD (1989), THE.** (THE CATHOLIC WORLD.). [Cathol. world]. **Added/Corp** Paulist Fathers. Vol. 232, No. 1387 (Jan./Feb. 1989)-. Periodical. English. bm (6 issues). $12.00 (one year), $21.00 (two year), $29.00 (three year). Paulist Press, 997 McArthur Boulevard, Mahwah NJ 07430. **Tel** (201)825-7300, FAX (201)825-8345. **ED** Laurie Felknor. **LC** AP2; .C3. **DD** 282/.05. Index available. **Bk Rev.** available on microfilm and microfiche from University Microfilms International (UMI); available on CD-ROM from University Microfilms International (UMI). Documents available from UMI Article Clearinghouse, Magazine Collection. ***Continues*** *New Catholic World, 0363-5066.*
**Desc:** A thematic magazine dealing with current religious, cultural and social issues from a religious point of view.
**Ind/Abst** Acad. Search (July 1993-); Access (1980-); Am. Hist. Life (1966-1971); Annu. Bibliogr. Engl. Lang. Lit.; Book Rev. Index; Gen. Period. Index (1989-); INFO-SOUTH Abstr.; Mag. Index Plus (1989-); Newsp. Period. Abstr. (1988-); Read. Guide Period. Lit.; Abr. Cathol. Period. Lit. Index; Cathol. Period. Lit. Index; Mag. Index (1977-).

US/1058-8159
**CATHOLIC WORLD REPORT, THE.** [Cathol. world rep.]. (Nov. 1991)-. Periodical. English. Eleven times a year (Aug./Sept. issues combined). $39.95 US; $40.65 Canada; $50.95 others. Ignatius Press Publishing, 2515 McAllister Street, San Francisco CA 94118. **Tel** (415)387-2324, FAX (415)387-0896. **ED** Joseph Fressio. **LC** BX801; .C3696525. **DD** 282/.05. **Bk Rev. Ad Acc, Adv Mgr:** Mary Jennett. **Circ:** 20,000.
**Desc:** International news monthly, providing news on the life of the Catholic Church and a Christian perspective on world events.

US/0277-8165
**CATHOLIC YOUTH MINISTRY.** ***Title Change.*** Periodical. English. qt. Youth Ministry Quarterly, RFD 1 Box 142, New Hampton NH 03256. **Tel** (603)744-6316, FAX (603)744-6318. **ED** Patty R Coleman. **Bk Rev. Circ:** 1,300 (ctrl). ***Continued by*** *Youth Ministry Quarterly, 1054-7126.*
**Desc:** A publication of youth ministry ideas, things to do, magazines, and video newsletter ideas.

GW/0008-8501
**CATHOLICA (MUNSTER).** (CATHOLICA.). [Catholica]. Vol. 1 (Jan. 1932)-. Periodical. German. qt. DM68.00 Germany; $29.87 US. Aschendorffsche Verlagsbuchhandlung, Postfach 1124, D-48135 Muenster Germany. **Tel** 011 49 251 690132, telex 08-92 830 WN MS D. **[CCC]**. Index available. cum. index. **Bk Rev. Ad Acc. Circ:** 800.
**Desc:** Journal for ecumenical theology. Helps to further understanding among different faiths, unity of the church and open theological discussions.
**Ind/Abst** Bibliogr. Mission.; Index Book Rev. Relig.; New Testam. Abstr.; Relig. Index One Period.; Relig. Theol. Abstr.; Abr. Cathol. Period. Lit. Index; Cathol. Period. Lit. Index.

US
**CATHOLICISM TODAY.** English. qt. $8.00. C E C, PO Box 99141, Louisville KY 40269.

US/0094-2421
**CELEBRATION (KANSAS CITY, MO.).** (CELEBRATION.). [Celebration]. (1972)-. Periodical. English. Twelve times a year. $64.95. National Catholic Reporter Publishing Company, PO Box 419281, 115 East Armour Boulevard, Kansas City MO 64141-6281. **Tel** (816)531-0538, (800)444-8910, (800)333-7373, FAX (816)531-7466. **(Subscription address:** Celebration, PO Box 419493, Circulation Manager, Kansas City MO 64141.**) ED** Bill Freburger.
**Desc:** An ecumenical worship resource.

CN/0822-8426
**CHAC INFO.** **See** Public Health and Safety.

US/0009-3718
**CHICAGO STUDIES.** [Chic. stud.]. **Added/Corp** Civitas Dei Foundation. Vol.1 (Spring 1962)-. Periodical. English. Three times a year (Apr., Aug., Nov.). $17.50 US; $21.50 other. Chicago Studies, Box 665, Mundelein IL 60060. **Tel** (708)566-1462. **ED** George J Dyer. **LC** BX801; .C36995. **DD** 230/.2/05. Index available. cum. index. **Circ:** 10,000 (ctrl). available on microfilm and microfiche from University Microfilms International (UMI).
**Desc:** Attempts to fill the gap between the technical theological journal and the popular religious periodical. It asks scholars to speak on pastoral issues but without the apparatus appropriate to a technical journal. They address themselves to priests, religious educators and other Catholics.
**Ind/Abst** Canon Law Abstr.; New Testam. Abstr.; Old Testam. Abstr.; Relig. Theol. Abstr.; Abr. Cathol. Period. Lit. Index; Cathol. Period. Lit. Index.

GW/0173-3028
**CHRIST UND WELT / RHEINISCHER MERKUR.** **VFOAT** Rheinischer Merkur; Christ und Welt Rheinischer Merkur; Rheinischer Merkur/Christ und Welt. 1980-. Periodical. German. wk. Verlag Rheinischer Merkur GmbH 2309, W-5400 Koblenz 40 Germany. **Tel** 011 49 261 13930. ***Formed by the union of*** *Deutsche Zeitung* ***and*** *Rheinischer Merkur.*

●US
**CHRISTIAN INITIATION.** (1994)-. Newsletter. English. Six times a year. $12.00. National Catholic Reporter Publishing Company, PO Box 419281, 115 East Armour Boulevard, Kansas City MO 64141-6281. **Tel** (816)531-0538, (800)444-8910, (800)333-7373, FAX (816)531-7466. **ED** Bill Freburger.

FR/0009-5834
**CHRISTUS.** Vol. 1, No. 1 (Jan. 1954)-. Periodical. French. qt. $16.63. Assas Editions, 14 rue d'Assas, 75006 Paris France. **Tel** 011 33 1 44394848, FAX 011 33 1 40490192. **ED** Bernard Merdilous. **Ad Acc. Circ:** 5,000.
**Desc:** Spirituality and action according to the Jesuits.

US/0730-7349
**CHRONICLE OF THE CATHOLIC CHURCH IN LITHUANIA (CHICAGO, ILL.), THE.** (THE CHRONICLE OF THE CATHOLIC CHURCH IN LITHUANIA.). [Chron. Cathol. Church Lith.]. No. 1 (1974)-. Periodical. English. Loyola University Press, 3441 North Ashland, Chicago IL 60657. **LC** BX1559.L5; L532. **DD** 282/.475.
**Ind/Abst** Hum. Rights Intern. Rep.

PL
**CHRZESCIJANIE.** Began in 1974. Periodical. Polish. 460.00. Akademia Teologii Katolickiej, Ul Dewajtis 3, 01-653 Warsawa Poland. **LC** BX4690.P6; C48.

PL
**CHRZESCIJANIN W SWIECIE.** **Added/Corp** Osrodek Dokumentacji i Studiow Spoecznych. (1969)-. Periodical. Polish. mo. $47.00. **(Subscription address:** ARS Polona, PO Box 1001, 00068 Warsaw Poland.**) LC** BX806.P6; C53.

US
**CHUONG VIET.** **Added/Corp** Hoi Sinh Vien Cong Giao Viet Nam tai My. (19??)-. Periodical. Vietnamese. qt. $6.00. Vietnamese Catholic Students, 5621 South Blackstone Avenue, Chicago IL 60637.

US/0009-6601
**CHURCH WORLD.** [Church world]. (1930)-. Periodical. English. Forty-eight times a year. $25.00. Church World, PO Box 698, Brunswick ME 04011. **Tel** (207)729-8753. **ED** Henry Gosselin. **DD** 282. **Bk Rev. Ad Acc. Circ:** 10,000.
**Desc:** Local, National and international religious news about Catholicism.

SP/0210-0398
**CIENCIA TOMISTA.** [Cienc. tomista]. No. 1, Vol. 1, (March/April 1910)-. Periodical. Spanish. Three times a year. 4100ptas (Spain); 5500ptas (other). Ciencia Tomista, Pza Concilio de Trento, Apt 17, 37080 Salamanca Spain. **Tel** 011 34 23 215000, FAX 011 34 23 265480. **ED** Luis Lago Alba. **LC** BX805; .C5. Index available. cum. index (from 1910 till 1960). **Bk Rev. Circ:** 750.
**Desc:** Studies made with methodological strictness and criticism of theological themes. Notes and comments on theological works, contemporary movements. Bibliographical reviews.
**Ind/Abst** Bibliogr. Mission.; MLA Int. Bibl. Books Artic. Mod. Lang. Lit.; Abr. Cathol. Period. Lit. Index; Cathol. Period. Lit. Index.

CN/0227-552X
**CIRCULAIRE AUX PRETRES ET AUTRES AGENTS DE PASTORALE.** (CIRCULAIRE AUX PRETRES ET AUTRES AGENTS DE PASTORALE : PRINCIPAUX DOCUMENTS PUBLIES EN ...). [Circ. pretres autre agents pastor.]. **Main/Corp** Eglise Catholique. Diocese de Trois-Rivieres. Eveque (1975- : Noel). No. 1 (1975/76)-. French. an (occasionally two issues per year). Free to Priests and Pastors. l'Eveche de Trois-Rivieres, 362 rue Bonaventure, Trois-Rivieres Quebec G9A 5J9 Canada. **Tel** (819)374-2409, FAX (819)379-2496. **DD** 262/.0271445/05. Index available. cum. index. **Pr Rev. Circ:** 500 to 600 (ctrl). ***Continues*** *Circulaires au Clerge.*

US
**CISTERCIAN FATHERS SERIES.** No. 1 (1970)-. Periodical. English. ir (1 or 2 per year). Cistercian Publications, St. Joseph's Abbey, Spencer MA 01562. **Tel** (508)885-7011. **DD** 282.

US/1062-6549
**CISTERCIAN STUDIES QUARTERLY.** [Cistercian stud. q.]. **VFOAT** CSQ. Vol. 26, No. 1 (1991)-. Periodical. English. Four times a year (Mar., June, Sept., Dec.). $25.00. Santa Rita Abbey, HC 1 Box 929, Sonoita AZ 85637-9705. **Tel** (602)455-5595, FAX (602)455-5595. **ED** Fr. John Baptist Porter, (editor's address: 3401 Golden Rain Road, Apartment 7, Walnut Creek, CA 94595, phone: (510)939-9710). **LC** BX3401; .C57. **DD** 271. Index available. cum. index. **Bk Rev. Circ:** 1,500. available on microfilm from University Microfilms International (UMI). ***Continues*** *Cistercian Studies, 0578-3224.*
**Desc:** Contains articles which combine historical and critical studies with contemporary writings on spirituality. The journal is dedicated to maintaining dialogue on such subjects as Western and Eastern Monastic Spirituality, contemplative lifestyles, ecumenism, issues concerning peace and justice and pastoral issues dealing with the many facets of religious and lay commitment to Christ.

BE/0774-4919
**CITEAUX, COMMENTARII CISTERCIENSES.** [Citeaux comment. cist.]. **Added/Corp** Abbaye des Trappistes de Westmalle. **VFOAT** Citeaux. (1959)-. Periodical. French (Dutch, English, German, Latin, Italian and Spanish; summaries and/or abstracts in French, English and German). Twice a year. 220.00F. Citeaux Commentarii Cistercienses, 17 rue Rabe, 89230 Pontigny France. **Tel** 011 33 1 86475821, FAX 011 33 1 86475518. **(Subscription address:** Brother Anthony Weber, Abbey of the Genesee, Piffard NY 14533.**) ED** Terryl N. Kinder. **LC** BX3401; .C58. Index available. cum. index. **Bk Rev**, (Qty: approx. 20). **Pr Rev. Acid Free. Circ:** 500. ***Continues*** *Citeaux in de Nederlanden.*
**Ind/Abst** Am. Hist. Life (1959-1969); BHA : Biblio. Hist. Art; MLA Int. Bibl. Books Artic. Mod. Lang. Lit.

IT/0009-8167
**CIVILTA CATTOLICA, LA.** [Civ. cattol.]. Vol. 1 (April 1850)-. Periodical. Italian. Twenty-four times a year. L80000 (one year), L140000 (two years), L200000 (three years) Italy; $100.00 (one year), $180.00 (two years), $250.00 (three years) other. La Civilta Cattolica, Via di Porta Pinciana 1, 00187 Rome Italy. **Tel** 39 6 6798351, FAX 39 6 6840997. **LC** AP37; .C5. Index available. cum. index. **Bk Rev. Ad Acc. Circ:** 18,000.
**Desc:** Contains 140 articles, notes, comments and reviews of the press; 70 political and cultural commentaries of current interest.
**Ind/Abst** Am. Hist. Life (1955-1958); Bibliogr. Mission.; Int. Polit. Sci. Abstr.; New Testam. Abstr.; Abr. Cathol. Period. Lit. Index; Cathol. Period. Lit. Index.

BE
**COLLECTANEA CISTERCIENSIA.** **Added/Corp** Trappists. **VFOAT** Nova et Vetera. Vol. 27 (1965)-. Periodical. French (Dutch, English and German). Four times a year. $24.00. St Josephs Abbey, Spencer MA 01562. **Tel** (508)885-3901. **LC** BX3401; .C6. ***Continues*** *Collectanea Ordinis Cisterciensium Reformatorum.*

IT/0010-0749
**COLLECTANEA FRANCISCANA.** **Added/Corp** Istituto Storico dei Frati Minori Cappuccini. Collegio San Lorenzo da Brindisi dei Minori Cappuccini. Vol. 1 (1931)-. Periodical. Latin (French, German, Italian and Latin). Four times a year. $70.00. Istituto Storico del Cappuccini, Circonv Occidentale 6850, I-00163 Rome Italy. **Tel** 011 39 6 6251949. **ED** Isidoro de Villapadierna and Salezy Kafel. Index available. cum. index. **Bk Rev.**
**Desc:** Lists publications (including reviews) on Francis

and Clare of Assisi and their followers, also includes life, doctrine, history and art issues.
**Ind/Abst** Bibliogr. Mission.

PL/0137-6985
**COLLECTANEA THEOLOGICA.** [Collect. theol.]. **Added/Corp** Polskie Towarzystwo Teologiczne. Akademia Teologii Katolickiej (Warsaw, Poland). (1920)-. Periodical. Polish (Latin, English, French and German). qt. **(Subscription address:** ARS Polona, PO Box 1001, 00068 Warsaw Poland.**)** **LC** BX880; .C597.
**Ind/Abst** Bibliogr. Mission.; New Testam. Abstr.; Old Testam. Abstr.

FR
**COLLECTION - UNIVERSITE DE LYON II. CENTRE D'HISTOIRE DU CATHOLICISME. Main/Corp** Universite de Lyon II. Centre d'Histoire du Catholicisme. (19??)-. Monographic series. French. ir. Price varies per volume. Letouzey et Ane, 87 Boulevard Raspail, 75006 Paris France. **Tel** 011 33 1 45488014.

US/0010-1869
**COLUMBIA (NEW HAVEN).** (COLUMBIA.). [Columbia]. **Added/Corp** Knights of Columbus. Vol. 1 (Aug. 1921)-. Periodical. English (French and Spanish). mo. $6.00. Knights of Columbus, PO Drawer 1670, New Haven CT 06507. **Tel** (203)772-2130. **ED** Richard McMunn. **LC** AP2; .C67. Index available. **Bk Rev. Circ:** 1,402,000 (ctrl).
**Desc:** Covers current events, social problems, apostolic activities, education, rearing a family, patriotic endeavors, and profiles of triumph over handicaps.
**Ind/Abst** Abr. Cathol. Period. Lit. Index; Cathol. Period. Lit. Index.

US/0746-5114
**COMMON GROUND (DES MOINES, IOWA).** (COMMON GROUND : NEWSLETTER OF THE NATIONAL CATHOLIC RURAL LIFE CONFERENCE.). [Common ground]. **Added/Corp** National Catholic Rural Life Conference (U.S.). (19??)-. Newsletter. English. Nine times a year. Membership: $100.00 institutions; $25.00 individuals. National Catholic Rural Life Conference, 4625 Northwest Beaver Avenue, Des Moines IA 50310. **Tel** (515)270-2634. ***Continues*** *Earth Matters, 1041-9276.*

CN/0847-2939
**COMMUNION, EN.** (EN COMMUNION : REVUE DU DIOCESE DE NICOLET.). [En communion]. **Added/Corp** Eglise Catholique. Diocese de Nicolet. (Nov. 1989)-. Periodical. French. Twelve times a year. 15.00Can$. En Communion, C P 250, Nicolet Quebec J0G 1E0 Canada. **DD** 282/.71455. ***Formed by the union of*** *A L'Ecoute (Nicolet, Quebec)., 0823-1451* ***and*** *Quinzaine Diocesaine (Nicolet, Quebec)., 0319-0854.*

FR/0042-370X
**COMMUNION. Added/Corp** Communaute de Taize. (1970)-. Periodical. French (French). qt. Liberal Catholic Church in Australia, 300 Blaxland Road, North Ryde New South Wales 2112 Australia. **Tel** 02 808 1110. **ED** William Hill and Ronald Rivett (editor's address: 69 St John' John's Road, The Glebe Sydney New South Wales Australia). **LC** BR3; .V42. cum. index. **Bk Rev. Circ:** 400 (ctrl). available on microfilm and microfiche from University Microfilms International (UMI). ***Continues*** *Verbum Caro.*
**Desc:** Provincial Church News. Articles by clergy and members on all aspects of the religious experience.

CN/0010-3985
**COMPANION (TORONTO).** (THE COMPANION.). **Added/Corp** Franciscans. **VFOAT** Companion of St. Francis and St. Anthony. (1???)-. Periodical. English. mo. 14.02Can$ (one year), 25.23Can$ (two year) Canada; 17.00Can$ (one year), 30.00Can$ (two year) other. Companion of Saint Francis, PO Box 535, Station F, Toronto ONT M4Y 2L8 Canada. **Tel** (416)463-5442, (416)463-6318, FAX (416)463-4392. **ED** Richard Riccioli. **Bk Rev. Ad Acc. Circ:** 4,500.
**Desc:** Catholic family devotional.

SP/0573-2018
**COMPOSTELLANUM.** [Compostellanum]. **Added/Corp** Chidiocesis de Santiago de Compostela. Seccion de Ciencias Eclesiasticas y Estudios Jacobeos. (1956)-. Periodical. Multiple languages. ir. 3200ptas Spain; 3700ptas other. Compostellanum, Plaza de la Inmaculada 5, 15704 Santiago Spain. **Tel** 011 34 81 586277. **UDC** 2.
**Ind/Abst** BHA : Biblio. Hist. Art.

BL
**COMUNICADO MENSAL DA CONFERENCIA NACIONAL DOS BISPOS DO BRASIL. Main/Corp** Catholic Church. Conferencia Nacional dos Bispos do Brasil. Portuguese. Rua do Russell 76, CP 16085, Rio de Janeiro Brazil. **LC** BX805; .C58A.
**Ind/Abst** Bibliogr. Mission.

PL
**CONCILIUM.** Periodical. Polish. Pallottinum, Ul Przebyszewskiego 30, Poznan Poland. **LC** BX806.P6; C74.

FR
**CONCILIUM (PARIS, FRANCE).** (CONCILIUM : REVUE INTERNATIONALE DE THEOLOGIE.). (19??)-. Periodical. French. bm. Beauchesne Editeur, 72 rue des Saints Peres, 75007 Paris France. **Tel** 011 33 1 45488028. cum. index.
**Desc:** Covers latest research in religious science and thought, problems of contemporary church and discrimination within the church and society.

GW
**CONCILIUM TRIDENTINUM.** (19??)-. Monographic series. Latin. ir. Price varies per volume. Verlag Herder Freiburg, Postfach 79080, Frieburg, Germany. **Tel** (0761)27-17-0, FAX (0761)27 17-520, telex 761489.

SZ/0010-8154
**CONVERGENCE (FRIBOURG).** ***Ceased.*** (CONVERGENCE.). (1968)-?. Periodical. English. ir. Pax Romana, BT 1062, CH-1701 Fribourg Switzerland. **Tel** (037)262649. **ED** R J Rajkumar. **LC** BX801; .C68. **DD** 282/.05. **Circ:** 2,500 (ctrl). ***Continues*** *Pax Romana Journal.*
**Desc:** Intellectual review on themes, women and development, spirituality, human rights, socio-cultural affairs, development, and theology.
**Ind/Abst** Educ. Index; Middle East Abstr. Index.

US/0010-8685
**CORD (ST. BONAVENTURE, N.Y.), THE.** (THE CORD; A FRANCISCAN SPIRITUAL REVIEW.). [Cord]. **Added/Corp** Franciscan Institute (St. Bonaventure University). (1951)-. Periodical. English. Eleven times a year (July/Aug. issue combined). $16.00. Franciscan Institute, St Bonaventure University, St Bonaventure NY 14778. **Tel** (716)375-2105, FAX (716)375-2389. **ED** Joseph Doino. **DD** 248. Index available. **Bk Rev. Circ:** 1,500 (ctrl).
**Desc:** Review of Franciscan scriptural and doctrinal topics also biographical and factual accounts of movements affecting day to day spirituality.

GW/0070-0320
**CORPUS CATHOLICORUM.** No. 1 (1919)-. Monographic series. German. ir. Price varies per volume. Aschendorffsche Verlagsbuchhandlung, Postfach 1124, D-48135 Muenster Germany. **Tel** 011 49 251 690132, telex 08-92 830 WN MS D. **ED** Erwin Iserloh. **LC** BR302; .C6.
**Desc:** Works of Catholic authors during the reformation. Monograph series on the issues, theologians and important personalities of that era.

FR/0395-9112
**COURRIER DE L'A.C.I. VFOAT** Courrier des Militants; Courrier de l'Action Catholique des Milieux Independants. (1959)-. Periodical. French. bm (6 issues). 90.00F France; 121.25F other. Le Courrier ACI Action, 3 Bis rue Francois Ponsard, 75116 Paris France. **UDC** 282.

CN/0823-7808
**COURRIER MARGUERITE BOURGEOYS (ENGLISH ED.).** (COURRIER MARGUERITE BOURGEOYS.). [Courr. Marguerite Bourgeoys]. **Added/Corp** Congregation of Notre-Dame. Centre Marguerite-Bourgeoys (Montreal, Quebec). No. 1 (1971)-. Periodical. English. Free. Congregation De Notre-Dame, 3040 Sherbrooke Street West, Montreal Quebec H3Z 1A4. **DD** 282/.092/4.

US
**CRISIS (NOTRE DAME, IND.).** (CRISIS.). Vol. 4, No. 7 (July/Aug. 1986)-. Periodical. English. Eleven times a year. $25.00 (one year), $45.00 (two year), $61.00 (three year). Brownson Institute, PO Box 1006, Notre Dame IN 46556. **Tel** (219)239-5825, (800)852-9962. **LC** BX801; .C3697. **DD** 282/.05. **Bk Rev. Ad Acc.** ***Continues*** *Catholicism in Crisis, 0884-1705.*
**Desc:** A journal of Lay Catholic opinion examining the interplay between Catholicism and public policy issues such as economics, human rights, defense and foreign policy, and the arts.
**Ind/Abst** Abr. Cathol. Period. Lit. Index; Cathol. Period. Lit. Index.

AG/0011-1473
**CRITERIO.** (1928)-. Periodical. Spanish. Twenty-two times a year. $80.00. Kriterion S.A., Junin 627, 1026 Buenos Aires Argentina. **Tel** 011 54 467975. **LC** AP63; .C66. Index available. **Bk Rev. Ad Acc. Circ:** 2,500. available on microfilm from University Microfilms International (UMI).
**Desc:** Catholic journal of culture and current events. Themes are cultural, scientific, educational, moral, and religious.
**Ind/Abst** HAPI Hisp. Am. Period. Index (19??-).

US/0011-149X
**CRITIC; A CATHOLIC REVIEW OF BOOKS AND THE ARTS, THE. Added/Corp** Thomas More Association. Vol. 1 (Apr. 1942)-. Periodical. English. qt. $20.00 US and Canada. Thomas More Association, 205 West Monroe Street/6th Floor, Chicago IL 60606. **Tel** (312)609-8880, (800)835-8965, FAX (312)609-8891.
**Ind/Abst** Abr. Cathol. Period. Lit. Index; Cathol. Period. Lit. Index.

US
**CRITICAL GUIDE TO CATHOLIC REFERENCE BOOKS.** (199?)-. English. an. $47.00. Libraries Unlimited Inc., PO Box 6633, Department 920, Englewood CO 80155. **Tel** (800)237-6124. **ED** James P. McCabe.
**Desc:** Supports scholarly research on Catholicism.

FR/0223-4734
**CROIRE AUJOURD'HUI.** Began in 1971. Periodical. French. ir. $23.95. Croire Aujourd'Hui, Surface 12 rue d'Assas, 75006 Paris France.

FR/0336-8106
**D.S (DICTIONNAIRE DE SPIRITUALITE). VFOAT** Dictionnaire de Spiritualite. (1975)-. Monographic series. French. ir. Price varies per volume. Beauchesne Editeur, 72 rue des Saints Peres, 75007 Paris France. **Tel** 011 33 1 45488028. **UDC** 282.

US/0747-2315
**DAN CHUA. Added/Corp** Viet-Chau. (Feb. 15, 1977)-. Periodical. Vietnamese. Twelve times a year. $30.00 US; $40.00 Canada; $70.00 other. Nguyet San Cong Giao, PO Box 1419, Gretna LA 70053-1419. **Tel** (504)392-1630, FAX (504)391-9793. **LC** BX806.V5; D36. **Bk Rev**, (Qty: 4,000). **Ad Acc, Adv Mgr:** Ann Mary. **Circ:** 2,500 (ctrl).

US/0045-978X
**DEAF CATHOLIC, THE.** (THE DEAF CATHOLIC / INTERNATIONAL CATHOLIC DEAF ASSOCIATION.). Periodical. English. qt. The Deaf Catholic, 814 Thayer Avenue, Silver Spring MD 20910.

VC
**DECISIONES SEU SENTENTIAE. Main/Corp** Catholic Church. Rota Romana. Tribunal Apostolicum. Vol. 1 (1909)-. Latin. an. $100.00. Liberia Editrice Vaticana, Citta del Vaticano, 00120 Vatican City. **Tel** 011 39 6 69883529, telex 2024 DIRGENTEL VA. ctrl circ.
**Desc:** Descriptive listing of the sentences or decisions given or made by the Apolistic Tribunal of the Roman Rota.

CN/0381-8950
**DEUTSCHE KATHOLIK IN KANADA, DER.** Began publication in May 1964. Periodical. German. ir. Catholic in Canada, 131 McCaul Street, Toronto Ontario 130 Canada. **DD** 282/.05.

AG
**DIDASCALIA (ROSARIO, SANTA FE, ARGENTINA).** (DIDASCALIA.). Periodical. Spanish. mo. $20.00. Didascalia, Presidente Roca 150, Rasario Argentina.

FR/0180-9288
**DIEU EST AMOUR SAINT-CENERE.** (DIEU EST AMOUR.). (1978)-. Periodical. French. Eight times a year. 250.00F France; 244.86F other. Librairie Tequi, 53150 St Cenere France. **Tel** 011 33 1 43010181, FAX 43 90 15 52. **UDC** 231. Index available. ctrl circ.

GW/0341-9975
**DIOZESE HILDESHEIM IN VERGANGENHEIT UND GEGENWART, DIE. Added/Corp** Verein fur Heimatkunde im Bistum Hildesheim. (1972)-. German. **LC** BX1538.H5; D55.
**Ind/Abst** BHA : Biblio. Hist. Art.

BL
**DIRETORIO LITURGICO. Main/Corp** Catholic Church. Conferencia Nacional dos Bispos do Brasil. Portuguese. Comissao Nacional de Liturgia, Caixa Postal 13-2067, 70401 Brasilia DF Brazil. **LC** BX1466.A4; C37A. **DD** 264/.021.

IT/0012-3455
**DIRITTO ECCLESIASTICO E RASSEGNA DI DIRITTO MATRIMONIALE, IL.** ***Title Change.*** **See** Law.

VC/0012-4443
**DOCTOR COMMUNIS.** [Dr. communis]. **Added/Corp** Accademia Romana di S. Tommaso d'Aquino e di Religione Cattolica. (Jan./April 1948)-. Periodical. Italian (French, Latin and Spanish). Three times a year. $35.00. Doctor Communis, Palazzo Cononici, 00120 Vatican City Italy. ***Supersedes*** *Acta Pont. Academiae Romanae S. Thomae Aq. et Religionis Catholicae.*
**Ind/Abst** Bibliogr. Mission.; New Testam. Abstr.; Philos. Index; Abr. Cathol. Period. Lit. Index; Cathol. Period. Lit. Index.

FR/0012-4613
**DOCUMENTATION CATHOLIQUE, LA.** [Doc. cathol.]. (1919)-. Periodical. French. sm. $80.00 US; 84.00Can$. Bayard Presse, Svc Client, 3 rue Bayard/Dept 2, 75393 Paris Cedex 08 France. **Tel** 011 33 1 44356060, 011 33 1 44356262. **(Subscription address:** Novalis, PO Box 990, Outremont H2V 4S7 Canada.**)** **LC** BX802; .D6. Index available. cum. index. **Bk Rev. Ad Acc. Circ:** 23,000 (ctrl). ***Continues***

*Questions Actuelles.*
**Ind/Abst** Bibliogr. Mission.; Abr. Cathol. Period. Lit. Index; Cathol. Period. Lit. Index.

UK/0012-5806
**DOWNSIDE REVIEW, THE.** **See** Literature.

SP/0012-9038
**ECCLESIA MADRID.** [EcclesiaMadr.]. (1941)-. Periodical. Spanish. wk. 5.100ptas Spain; $113.00 Japan; $96.00 Africa; $91.00 other. Revista Ecclesia, Conferencia Episcopal Esp, Alfonso XI 4, 28014 Madrid Spain. **Tel** 011 34 1 531-5407, 531-5408. **UDC** 25. Index available. **Bk Rev. Ad Acc. Circ:** 20,000.
**Desc:** Editorial on opinions, culture, the world, Latin America, Vatican and specific documentation.

CN/1184-6186
**ECOLES SECONDAIRES DE LA CECM, LES.** **See** Education.

CN/0710-6238
**EGLISE DE CHICOUTIMI ... ANNUAIRE DIOCESAIN.** [Eglise Chicoutimi, Annu. dioc.]. **Main/Corp** Eglise Catholique. Diocese de Chicoutimi. **VAT** Annuaire Diocesain (Chicoutimi. 1981). 1981-. French. an. $5.00 per volume. Eveche de Chicoutimi, 602 Racine Est, Chicoutimi Quebec G7H 6J6 Canada. **Tel** (418)543-0783. **DD** 282/.025/71416. ***Continues*** *Eglise Catholique. Diocese de Chicoutimi. Repertoire, 0381-6710.*

CN/0838-6226
**EGLISE DE NICOLET, ANNUAIRE.** (QUINZAINE DIOCESAINE.). [Eglise Nicolet annu.]. **Main/Corp** Eglise Catholique. Diocese de Nicolet. (1979)-. French. En Communion, C P 250, Nicolet Quebec J0G 1E0 Canada. **DD** 282/.025/71455. ***Continues*** *Diocese de Nicolet; Annuaire Diocesain., 0318-9848.*

CN/1184-1990
**EGLISE DE SAINT-JEROME.** (EGLISE DE SAINT-JEROME : [BULLETIN].). [Eglise St.-Jerome]. **Added/Corp** Eglise Catholique. Eveche de Saint-Jerome. Vol. 27, No. 4 (Sept./Oct. 1990)-. Bulletin. French. bm. Limited free distribution. Diocese de Saint-Jerome, CP 580, Saint-Jerome Quebec J72 5A9 Canada. **DD** 262/.0271424/05. ***Continues*** *Informations (Eglise Catholique. Diocese de Saint Jerome)., 0712-6999.*

CN/0227-6364
**EGLISE DE TROIS--RIVIERES.** ***Title Change.*** (EGLISE DE TROIS-RIVIERES : BULLETIN.). [Eglise de Trois-Rivieres]. Bulletin. French. mo. Eglise de Trois-Rivieres, CP 1480, Trois-Rivieres Quebec G9A 5L6 Canada. **DD** 282/.71445. ***Continues*** *Bulletin d'Information Pastorale, 0227-6356.* ***Continued by*** *Eglise de Trois-Rivieres : Bulletin. Document, 0227-6372.*

CN/0227-6372
**EGLISE DE TROIS-RIVIERES. DOCUMENT.** (EGLISE DE TROIS-RIVIERES : BULLETIN. DOCUMENT.). [Eglise de Trois-Rivieres, Doc.]. 1 (2 Oct. 1977)-. Bulletin. French. bw. Free. Eglise de Trois-Rivieres, CP 1480, Trois-Rivieres Quebec G9A 5L6 Canada. **DD** 282/.71445. ***Separated from*** *Eglise de Trois-Rivieres : Bulletin, 0227-6364.*

AU
**EINFUHRUNG IN DIE PERIKOPEN.** (19??)-. German. Four times a year. S658.00. Osterreichisches Katholisches Bibelwerk, Stiftsplatz 8, A-3400 Klosterneuburg Austria. **Tel** 011 43 2243 293882, 293883.

DR
**EME EME; ESTUDIOS DOMINICANOS.** **Added/Corp** Universidad Catolica Madre y Maestra. Universidad Catolica Madre y Maestra. Centro de Estudios Dominicanos. (June/July 1972)-. Periodical. Spanish. Six times a year. Universidad Catolica Madre y Maestra, Departamento de Publicaciones, Santiago de los Caballeros Dominican Republic. **LC** BX3501; .E46.
**Ind/Abst** Geogr. Abstr. Human Geogr. (?-?).

●US
**ENNEIGRAM EDUCATOR.** **See** Psychology.

IT/0013-9491
**EPHEMERIDES IURIS CANONICI.** Vol. 1 (1945)-. Periodical. English (French, Italian, Latin and Spanish). Three times a year. $100.00. Libreria Sole, Via dei Lucchesi 20, 00187 Rome Italy. **Tel** 011 39 6 6790675. cum. index.
**Ind/Abst** Bibliogr. Mission.; Canon Law Abstr.

GW/0013-9963
**ERBE UND AUFTRAG (BEURON).** (ERBE UND AUFTRAG / HERAUSGEGEBEN VON DER ERZABTEI BEURON.). [Erbe Auftr.]. **Added/Corp** Benediktinerkloster Beuron. (1958)-. German. bm (Feb., Apr., June, Aug., Oct., Dec.). DM28.00 (latest edition). Beuroner Kunstverlag, Erzabtei St Martin, D-88631 Beuron Germany. **Tel** 011 49 7466 264. **ED** Benedikt Schwank. **LC** BX3001; .B46. Index available. cum. index. **Bk Rev. Ad Acc. Circ:** 2,000 (ctrl). ***Continues*** *Benediktinische Monatsschrift zur Pflege Religiosen und Geistigen Lebens.*
**Ind/Abst** New Testam. Abstr.; Old Testam. Abstr.

CN/0318-7551
**ESKIMO; COUNTRY, INHABITANTS, CATHOLIC MISSIONS.** **Added/Corp** Oblates of Mary Immaculate. Hudson Bay Diocese. Vol. 1-84, Oct. (1944-1970) (New Series) No. 1- Spring/Summer (1971)-. Periodical. English (French). sa (Spring and Fall). 5.00Can$. Oblate Fathers of Hudson Bay Vicariate, PO Box 10, Churchill Manitoba R0B 0E0 Canada. **Tel** (204)675-2252. ctrl circ.

UK/0423-4456
**ESSEX RECUSANT.** ***Ceased.*** Vol. 1 (Apr. 1959)-?. Periodical. English. Three times a year. Essex Recusant Society, 1 Cliffsea Grove, Rev Hanahan, Leigh on Sea SS9 1NG England. cum. index.

BL
**ESTATISTICA DO CULTO CATOLICO.** Began in 1956. Portuguese. $0.20. Ministerio da Justica, Esplanada dos Ministerios, Ed Sede do MJ-Bloco, 10 Brasilia DF CEP 70064 Brazil. **LC** BX1466.A1; E85.

SP/0210-1610
**ESTUDIOS ECLESIASTICOS.** [Estud. ecles.]. Vol. 1 No. 1 (1922)-. Periodical. Spanish. qt. $50.00. Centro Loyola, Pablo Aranda 3, 28006 Madrid Spain. **Tel** 011 34 1 565-4930, 562-6604, FAX 011 34 1 563-4073. **ED** A Vargas-Machuca. Index available. **Bk Rev. Ad Acc. Circ:** 700.
**Desc:** Investigation and information on all subjects of theology, especially on Catholic theology and Bible.
**Ind/Abst** Am. Hist. Life (1969-); Bibliogr. Mission.; Canon Law Abstr.; Index Book Rev. Relig.; New Testam. Abstr.; Old Testam. Abstr.; Relig. Index One Period. (1984-).

US/0743-524X
**EUCHARISTIC MINISTER.** No. 1 (Apr. 1984)-. Newsletter. English. Twelve times a year. $12.00 US; $17.50 other. National Catholic Reporter Publishing Company, PO Box 419281, 115 East Armour Boulevard, Kansas City MO 64141-6281. **Tel** (816)531-0538, (800)444-8910, (800)333-7373, FAX (816)531-7466. **ED** Beatrice Fleo.

US/0738-8489
**EVANGELIST (ALBANY, N.Y.), THE.** (THE EVANGELIST : OFFICIAL PUBLICATION OF THE DIOCESE OF ALBANY.). **Added/Corp** Catholic Church. Diocese of Albany (N.Y.). (1926)-. Newspaper. English. Fifty times a year (Except one week in July & one week in Dec.). $20.00 US, $35.00 others (one year); $30.00 US, $70.00 other (two years). Albany Catholic Press Association, Inc., 40 North Main Avenue, Albany NY 12203. **Tel** (518)453-6688, FAX (518)453-6793. **ED** James Breig. **Bk Rev**, (Qty: 5). **Ad Acc. Circ:** 60,000.
**Desc:** The publication of the Roman Catholic Diocese of Albany, New York.

IT/0014-7095
**FAMIGLIA CRISTIANA.** (19??)-. Italian. wk. L129900 Italy; L248000 other. Societa San Paolo Gruppo Periodici, Via Liberazione 4, 12051 Alba Cuneo Italy. **Tel** 011 39 173 296356, FAX 011 39 173 317423.

MX
**FAMILIA CRISTIANA.** (19??)-. Spanish. mo. Ediciones Paulinas SA, Apdo 69-766, 04460 Coyoacan Mexico DF Mexico. **ED** G. Emmanuel Hidalgo. **UDC** 24. **Ad Acc. Circ:** 80,000.

CN/0318-0581
**FAMILLE QUEBEC.** **See** Family and Marriage.

US/0899-1529
**FAMILY (BOSTON, MASS.), THE.** (THE FAMILY.). [Family]. **Added/Corp** Daughters of St. Paul. (19??)-. Periodical. English. mo (11 issues). $12.00 (one year), $21.00 (two year), $30.00 (three year) US; $20.00 (one year) other. Daughters of St. Paul, 50 St. Pauls Avenue, Boston MA 02130. **Tel** (617)522-8911, FAX (617)524-8035. **ED** Sister M. Leahill and Sister Theresa Francis Myers. **DD** 248. Index available. cum. index. **Bk Rev. Circ:** 7,000.
**Desc:** Committed to helping families grow in the awareness of their heritage, in understanding of Catholic teaching, in reverence for the dignity of others, and in holiness of purpose.

FR/0760-5099
**FEU ET LUMIERE SAINT-BROLADRE.** (1983)-. Periodical. French. Twelve times a year. 33.00F. Feu et Lumiere, BP 8, 50140 Mortain France. **Tel** 011 33 33 593297. **ED** F. Ephrain. **UDC** 258. **Bk Rev. Circ:** 35,000.
**Desc:** Information and news about the Catholic education, christian law, and the spiritual life.

US/0273-7280
**FILIPINO CATHOLIC.** (1980)-. Periodical. English. sm. $10.00 Canada and Mexico; $20.00 other. Filipino Catholic, 1725 Silverlake Road, Los Angeles CA 90026. **Tel** (213)660-2802. **ED** Ping Bayani. **Ad Acc. Circ:** 10,000. ***Continues*** *Filipino Catholic News-Magazine, 0199-6355.*

US/0746-4584
**FLORIDA CATHOLIC, THE.** [Fla. Cathol.]. Vol. 1 (1939)-. Periodical. English. Forty-Five times a year. $15.00 Florida; $18.00 other. Florida Catholic, PO Box 609512, Orlando FL 32860. **Tel** (407)660-9141. **ED** David P. Page and Henry P. Libersat. **DD** 280. **Bk Rev. Ad Acc. Circ:** 90,000. ***Absorbed*** *Southern Catholic, 0745-1121* ***and*** *Voice (Miami, Fla.).*

FR/0152-139X
**FOI AUJOURD HUI.** ***Title Change.*** (19??)-(199?). French. Bayard Presse, Svc Client, 3 rue Bayard/Dept 2, 75393 Paris Cedex 08 France. **Tel** 011 33 1 44356060, 011 33 1 44356262. ***Merged with*** *Panorama, 0299-6898.*

GW/0178-1626
**FORUM KATHOLISCHE THEOLOGIE.** Vol. 1, No. 1 (1985)-. Periodical. German. qt. DM45.50 Germany; DM53.50 other. B. Pattloch Buchhandlung, Herstallstr 17, PF 549, W-8750 Aschaffenburg Germany. **Tel** 011 49 6021 21277, FAX 49 6021 23778. **ED** Leo Scheffczyk, Kurt Krenn, and Anton Ziegenaus. ***Continues*** *Munchener Theologische Zeitschrift.*
**Ind/Abst** Bibliogr. Mission.; New Testam. Abstr.

US
**FRANCE CATHOLIQUE-ECCLESIA.** No. 1358 (Dec. 1972)-. French. France Catholique Ecclesia, 12 rue Edmond Valenti, 75007 Paris France. **LC** MICROFILM 01350 BX; BX802. ***Continues*** *France Catholique.*

UK
**FRANCISCAN, THE.** **Added/Corp** Society of Saint Francis. (1959)-. Periodical. English. Three times a year. $7.00 US. Sport Medicine Council Alberta, 11759 Groat Road, Edmonton Alta T5M 3K6 Canada. **Tel** (403)453-8636, FAX (403)422-3093. **Bk Rev. Ad Acc. Circ:** 5,000 (ctrl).
**Desc:** News of the Society of St. Francis and comments, reflections and thoughts on issues affecting the Church today.

CN/0319-6739
**FRANCISCAN MISSIONARY.** **VFOAT** Reporter. Fall 1972-. Periodical. English. qt. Franciscan Missionary Union, PO Box 220, Lumsden Saskatchewan S0G 3C0 Canada. **DD** 266/.2/85. ***Supersedes*** *Franciscan Missionary Reporter, 0319-6720.*

US/0080-5459
**FRANCISCAN STUDIES.** [Francisc. stud.]. Vols. 1-21, (Jan. 1924-40); New Series, Vol. 1 (Mar. 1941)-. Periodical. English. an. $20.00. Franciscan Institute, St Bonaventure University, St Bonaventure NY 14778. **Tel** (716)375-2105, FAX (716)375-2389. **ED** Conrad L Harkins. **LC** BX3601; .F7. **DD** 255/.3. **Circ:** 1,000. available on microfilm and microfiche from University Microfilms International (UMI).
**Ind/Abst** Bibliogr. Mission.; MLA Int. Bibl. Books Artic. Mod. Lang. Lit.; Philos. Index; Abr. Cathol. Period. Lit. Index; Cathol. Period. Lit. Index.

BE/0015-9840
**FRANCISCANA.** [Franciscana]. **Added/Corp** Instituut voor Franciscaanse Geschiedenis (Sint-Truiden, Belgium). (1946)-. Periodical. Dutch. Four times a year. 500F. Instiuut Franciskaanse Geschiedeni, Minderbroedersstraat 5, 3800 Sint Truiden, Belgium. **ED** Rev. Father Heribert Roggen O. F. M. Index available. **Ad Acc.**
**Ind/Abst** Am. Hist. Life (1955-1964).

GW/0016-0067
**FRANZISKANISCHE STUDIEN.** [Franziskan. Stud.]. Vol. 1 (1914)-. Periodical. German (English and French). Four times a year. DM48.00 Germany; DM58.00 others. Dietrich Coelde Verlag AG, Walburgisstr 41, D 59457 Werl Germany. **Tel** 011 49 29224011. **LC** BX3601; .F76.
**Desc:** Studies on Franciscan philosophy and theology.
**Ind/Abst** BHA : Biblio. Hist. Art; MLA Int. Bibl. Books Artic. Mod. Lang. Lit.

GW
**FREIBURGER DIOEZESAN-ARCHIV.** **Added/Corp** Kirchengeschichtlicher Verein fuer Geschichte, Christliche Kunst, Altertums- und Literaturkunde des Erzbistums Freiburg. (1865)-. German. an. Verlag Herder Freiburg, Postfach 79080, Frieburg, Germany. **Tel** (0761)27-17-0, FAX (0761)27 17-520, telex 761489. **ED** H. Ott. **LC** BX1538.F65; F73.
**Ind/Abst** BHA : Biblio. Hist. Art.

IE/0016-3120
**FURROW, THE.** [Furrow]. V. 1- Feb. 1950-. Periodical. English. mo. £21.00 Ireland; $32.00, $45.00 (airmail) US. Saint Patricks College / Ireland, Maynooth County, Kildare Ireland. **Tel** 011 353 286215. **ED** Ronan Drury. Index available. cum. index. **Bk Rev. Ad Acc. Circ:** 8,000. available on microfilm from Xerox; available on microfilm and microfiche from University Microfilms International (UMI).
**Desc:** A pastoral review dealing with the religious concerns of the Roman Catholic Church, especially the various ministries within it and its wider outreach to the churches and the arts.

**Ind/Abst** Canon Law Abstr.; New Testam. Abstr.; Old Testam. Abstr.; Abr. Cathol. Period. Lit. Index; Cathol. Period. Lit. Index.

US
**GEORGIA BULLETIN.** Bulletin. English. ir. $16.00. Georgia Bulletin, 680 West Peachtree Street NW, Atlanta GA 30308. **Tel** (404) 888-7832, FAX (404) 888-7849. **ED** Gretchen Keiser. **Bk Rev. Ad Acc, Adv Mgr:** Leonard Markum. **Circ:** 47,000.
**Desc:** Catholic newpaper.

GW
**GERMANIA SACRA. Added/Corp** Berlin. Kaiser-Wilhelm-Institut fuer Deutsche Geschichte. Gottingen. Max-Planck-Institut fuer Geschichte. (1929)-. Monographic series. German. ir. Price varies per volume. Walter de Gruyter Inc., PO Box 303421, D 10728 Berlin Germany. **Tel** 011 49 30 260050, FAX 011 49 30 26005251. **LC** BX1534.A1; G53.
**Desc:** Information on the Catholic church in Germany.

US/0738-6419
**GOOD NEWS LETTER (WASHINGTON, D.C.), THE.** (THE GOOD NEWS LETTER / THE NATIONAL INSTITUTE FOR THE WORD OF GOD, WORD OF GOD INSTITUTE.). [Good news letter]. **Added/Corp** Word of God Institute (Washington, D.C.). No. 1 (Dec. 1972)-. Newsletter. English. sa. Free. National Institute for the Word of God, 487 Michigan Avenue Northeast, Washington DC 20017. **Tel** (202)529-0001. **ED** Mary Ann McGuire. **DD** 282. **Bk Rev**, (Qty: 3). **Circ:** 1,600 (ctrl).

FR/0993-0787
**GRAIN DE SOLEIL PARIS.** (GRAIN DE SOLEIL.). **VFOAT** Collection Grain de Soleil (Paris). (1988)-. Periodical. French. Eleven times a year. 56.92Can$. Bayard Presse, Svc Client, 3 rue Bayard/Dept 2, 75393 Paris Cedex 08 France. **Tel** 011 33 1 44356060, 011 33 1 44356262. **(Subscription address:** Novalis, PO Box 990, Outremont H2V 4S7 Canada.**) UDC** 084.12 - 053.5 : 26.

US/8755-9323
**GREEN BAY CATHOLIC COMPASS, THE.** (THE GREEN BAY CATHOLIC COMPASS : SERVING THE DIOCESE OF GREEN BAY.). **VFOAT** Compass. Periodical. English. wk. Green Bay Register Inc, 1825 Riverside Drive, Box 1825, Green Bay WI 54305. ***Continues** Spirit.*

CK
**GUIA ECLESIASTICA LATINOAMERICANA.** Spanish. Secretariado General del Celam Aereo 51086, Bogota Colombia. **LC** BX1425.A4; G84.

CN/0317-7203
**GUIDELINES FOR PASTORAL LITURGY. Main/Corp** Catholic Church. Canadian Conference of Catholic Bishops. National Liturgical Office. **VFOAT** Liturgical Calendar. 1977-. English. an. $5.50. Office National de Liturgie, Conference des Eveques Catholiques du Canada, 90 Av Parent, Ottawa Ontario K1N 7B1 Canada. **Tel** (613)236-9461, FAX (613)236-8117. **DD** 264/.021. **Circ:** 9,000. ***Continues** Guidelines for Pastoral Liturgy, 0317-7203.*
**Desc:** Guidelines for pastoral liturgy, liturgical calendar tool for preparing and celebrating liturgy.

IE/0791-1513
**HALLEL CAPPOQUIN.** (HALLEL.). [Hallel Cappoquin]. (196?)-. Periodical. English. sa (April and October). 8.00p Ireland; £3.00 Europe; $3.19 US;. Hallel, Mount Saint Joseph Abbey, Roscrea Eire Ireland. **Tel** 011 505 21711, FAX 011 505 22198. **ED** Rev. Ciarain O. Sabhaois. **DD** 248.894 255. **Bk Rev**, (Qty: 10-12). **Circ:** 300.
**Desc:** Reviews monastic spirituality and liturgy.

US/0893-536X
**HEARTS AFLAME. Added/Corp** Blue Army of Our Lady of Fatima. (June/July 1987)-. Periodical. English. qt (published seasonally). $2.00 one year; $5.00 three years. World Apostolate of Fatima, Box 976, Mountain View Road, Washington NJ 07882. **Tel** (201)689-1700, FAX (201)689-6279. **ED** Mary Celeste. **DD** 248.
**Desc:** A Catholic teen magazine.

GW/0018-0645
**HERDER-KORRESPONDENZ.** [Herder-Korrespondenz]. **VFOAT** Herder Korrespondenz. Vol. 1 (1946)-. Periodical. German. mo. DM178.80. Verlag Herder Freiburg, Postfach 79080, Frieburg, Germany. **Tel** (0761)27-17-0, FAX (0761)27 17-520, telex 761489. **ED** U. Ruh, K. Nientiedt, A. Foitzik. **LC** BX803; .H4.
**Desc:** Monthly publication covering religion.
**Ind/Abst** Bibliogr. Mission.; Energy Res. Abstr. (Oct. 1979-).

UK/0018-1196
**HEYTHROP JOURNAL.** [Heythrop j.]. Vol. 1 (Jan. 1960)-. Academic Scholarly Publication. English. Four times a year. £50.00 UK and Europe; $84.00 North America; £54.50 other. Basil Blackwell Publishers Ltd, 108 Cowley Road, Oxford 0X4 1JF England. **Tel** 011 44 865 791100, FAX 011 44 865 791347, telex 837022 OXBOOK G. **(Subscription address:** Blackwell Publishers / UK, Marston Book Services, PO Box 87, Oxford OX2 0DT England.**) ED** T J Deidun. **LC** BX801; .H4. **[CCC].** Index available. cum. index. **Bk Rev. Ad Acc. Circ:** 900. available on microfilm and microfiche from University Microfilms International (UMI). Documents available from The Genuine Article.
**Desc:** Articles and book reviews on religious dogma, history, philosophy and related topics; broad Catholic ecumenical slant. University research level.
**Ind/Abst** Arts Humanit. Citation Index [Full Cov.]; Bibliogr. Mission.; Canon Law Abstr.; Curr. Contents Arts Humanit.; Index Book Rev. Relig.; New Testam. Abstr.; Old Testam. Abstr.; Philos. Index; Relig. Theol. Abstr.; Res. Alert [Full Cov.]; Romant. Move.; Soc. Sci. Cit. Index [Select. Cov.]; Abr. Cathol. Period. Lit. Index; Cathol. Period. Lit. Index.

IO/0377-9610
**HIDUP.** [Hidup]. Vol. 24, No. 25- July 5, 1970-. Periodical. Indonesian. wk. $24.00. Yayasan Hidup Katolik, Kotakpos 2197, Jakarta 10001 Indonesia. **Tel** 365307/372170. **ED** Subroto Widjojo. **LC** BX1653.A1; H5. **Bk Rev. Ad Acc. Circ:** 50,000 (ctrl). ***Continues** Hidup Katolik, 0376-6330.*
**Desc:** Deepens and broadens the Christian faith and vision among the Catholics in Indonesia; it commits itself to evangelization, inculturation and ocumenism.

SP/0018-215X
**HISPANIA SACRA.** [Hisp. sacra]. **Added/Corp** Instituto Enrique Florez. Centro de Estudios Historicos (Spain). Departamento de Historia de la Iglesia. Centro de Estudios Historicos (Spain). **VFOAT** HS; H.S. Vol. 1, No. 1 (Jan./June 1948)-. Periodical. Spanish (French and English; summaries and/or abstracts in English). sa. 4500ptas Spain; 6000ptas other. Consejo Superior Investigacion Cientificas (CSIC), Vitruvio 8, 28006 Madrid Spain. **Tel** 011 34 1 5612833, FAX 011 34 1 4113077, telex 42182. **Bk Rev.**
**Desc:** Central theme is the history of the Roman Catholic Church in Spain; its origin and development, with research on biographies, institutions, and socio-economic statistics. Prints codices and documents, and liturgical histories.
**Ind/Abst** Am. Hist. Life (1955-1961, 1975-); BHA : Biblio. Hist. Art; Index Book Rev. Relig.; Relig. Index One Period.

US/0018-4268
**HOMILETIC & PASTORAL REVIEW.** **VFOAT** HPR. Vol. 21 (Oct. 1920)-. Periodical. English. mo (except bimonthly August and September). $24.00 (1 year), $44.00 (2 year) US; $25.00 (1 year), $45.00 (2 year) other. Catholic Polls Inc, 86 Riverside Drive, New York NY 10024. **Tel** (212)799-2600, FAX (212)787-0351. **ED** Kenneth Baker. **LC** BX801; .H7. Index available in last issue of volume--attached. cum. index. **Bk Rev. Ad Acc. Circ:** 15,000. available on microfilm and microfiche from University Microfilms International (UMI). ***Continues** Homiletic Monthly and Pastoral Review.*
**Desc:** For Catholic priest, religious and lay theologians concerned with current issues of both dogmatic and moral nature which are of practical concern to the priest.
**Ind/Abst** Bibliogr. Mission.; Canon Law Abstr.; Index Book Rev. Relig.; New Testam. Abstr.; Old Testam. Abstr.; Abr. Cathol. Period. Lit. Index; Cathol. Period. Lit. Index.

SP/0439-4208
**HOMILETICA.** No.20 (1961)-. Periodical. Spanish. tq. 3.100ptas Spain; $40.00 Europe; $45.00 other. Editorial Sal Terrae, Apartado 77, 39080 Santander Spain. **Tel** 011 34 42 320528, 011 34 42 320529. **Circ:** 5,000. ***Continues** Sal Terrae. Parte Practica.*
**Desc:** An informal exposition of scripture for each Sunday and holiday for the Roman Catholic Church.

IT
**HUMANITAS (BRESCIA, ITALY). See** Philosophy.

PE
**ICLA BOLETIN. Added/Corp** Centro de Documentaci'on MIEC, JECI. **VFOAT** Boletin Informativo Catolico Latinoamericano. **VAT** Informativo Catolico Latinoamericano Boletin. No. 1 (Oct. 1979)-. Periodical. Spanish. mo. Secretariado Latinoamericano Pax Romana Miec-Jeci Centro de Documentation, Apartado 3564, Lima 100 Peru.
**Ind/Abst** Hum. Rights Intern. Rep.

US/8755-6871
**IDEA INK.** [Idea ink]. Periodical. English. qt. $5.95. Idea Ink, PO Box 4010, Madison WI 53711. **Tel** (608)273-0330. **ED** Charles Fiore. **DD** 261. **Ad Acc. Circ:** 70,000.
**Desc:** An authentically Catholic opinion quarterly, with emphasis on the family and personal morality, spirituality, social issues, and matters of current public concern.

SP/0211-5441
**IMAGENES DE LA FE.** [Imagenes fe]. **VFOAT** Fetes et Saisons en Espanol. (1966)-. Periodical. Spanish. mo (10 issues per year). 3400ptas Spain; 3675ptas other. Promocion Popular Cristiana, Enrique Jardiel, Poncela 4, 28016 Madrid, Spain. **Tel** 011 34 1 3592300. **UDC** 2.

II
**IN CHRISTO : A QUARTERLY FOR RELIGIOUS.** (19??)-. Periodical. English. qt. $5.00. The Manager in Christo, Xavier Publications Ranchi, PO Box 8, Ranchi-834001 India. **LC** BX2400; .I5. **DD** 255/.005.

IT
**INFORMATIONES SACRA CONGREGATIO PRO RELIGIOSIS ET INSTITUTIS SAECULARIBUS.** (19??)-. Italian. sa. L25000.00 Italy; L30000.00 Europe; L35000.00 Mediterranean Basin; L40000.00 other. SCRIS, Piazza Pio XII 3, 00193 Rome Italy.

US/0897-229X
**INNER HORIZONS.** ***Ceased.*** [Inner horiz.]. **Added/Corp** Daughters of St. Paul. Vol. 1, No. 1 (Winter 1988)-Vol. 5 (April 1992). Periodical. English. qt ((by seasons)). Daughters of St. Paul, 50 St. Pauls Avenue, Boston MA 02130. **Tel** (617)522-8911, FAX (617)524-8035. **ED** Sister Mary Paula Kolar. **DD** 282. Index available ((bound in each issue)). **Bk Rev**, (Qty: (approx. 50-70)). **Ad Acc, Adv Mgr:** Sister Mary Paula Kolar. **Circ:** 1100. ***Continues** Strain Forward.*
**Desc:** Contains articles by various authors, many well known, which are meant to be of spiritual enrichment for the growth of Catholic adults and a strengthening in Catholic teaching with suggested reading, advertised on the topics in each issue.

UK/0020-157X
**INNES REVIEW, THE.** [Innes rev.]. **Added/Corp** Scottish Catholic Historical Association. Vol. 1 (1950)-. Periodical. English. Twice a year (Spring & Autumn). £14.00 UK & Europe; £15.00 others. Scottish Catholic Historical Association, John Burns and Sons, 25 Finlas Street, Glasgow G22 5DS Scotland. **Tel** 011 41 336 8678. **ED** David Brown and Alastair Roberts, (editor's address: Department of Scottish History, University of Glasgow, G12 8QH England, phone: 011 41 339 8855 ext. 4148). **LC** BX2597; .A3. **Bk Rev. Circ:** 500 (ctrl).
**Desc:** Religious and cultural history of Scotland with special attention to the part played in it by the Catholic Church.
**Ind/Abst** Am. Hist. Life (1955-); Br. Archaeol. Bibliogr.

US
**INTERFACE.** Issue 1 (Spring 1979)-. Periodical. English. qt. 1312 Massachusetts Avenue NW, Washington DC 20005. ***Supersedes** Catholic Church. National Conference on Catholic Bishops. Bishops' Committee for Ecumenical and Interreligious Affairs. Newsletter.*

US/0273-6187
**INTERMOUNTAIN CATHOLIC. See** Religion and Theology.

GW/0341-8693
**INTERNATIONALE KATHOLISCHE ZEITSCHRIFT.** [Int. kathol. Z.]. **VFOAT** Internationale Katholische Zeitschrift Communio. Vol. 1 (Jan./Feb. 1972)-. Periodical. German (English, Italian and Spanish). bm (Jan., Mar., May, July, Sept., Nov.). DM54.00. Verlad Bonifatius Druckerei, Liboristrasse 1 3, D 33098 Paperborn Germany. **Tel** 011 49 5251 297171. **(Subscription address:** Communio Verlagsges, Friesentrasse 50, D 56077 Cologne Germany.**) ED** Maximilian Greiner. **LC** BX803; .I58. Index available. **Bk Rev. Ad Acc. Circ:** 3,000 (ctrl).
**Ind/Abst** Index Book Rev. Relig.; New Testam. Abstr.; Old Testam. Abstr.; Relig. Index One Period. (1973-).

IE/0075-0735
**IRISH CATHOLIC DIRECTORY, THE.** (IRISH CATHOLIC DIRECTORY / COMPILED AND EDITED BY THE UNIVERSE.). (1960)-. Directory. English. an (Dec.). £17.50 UK; £21.20 Europe; £24.00 others. Gabriel Communications Ltd, 1st Floor, St. James Building, Oxford M1 8PS England. **Tel** 011 44 71 278 7321. **LC** BX1503.A3; I6. **DD** 282/.415/025. ***Continues** Irish Catholic Directory and Almanac.*

●IE
**IRISH CATHOLIC DIRECTORY & DIARY. VFOAT** Irish Catholic Directory and Diary. (1992)-. Directory. English. **LC** BX1503.A3; I6. **DD** 282/.415/025. ***Continues** Irish Catholic Directory.*

NE
**JAARBOEK VAN HET KATHOLIEK DOCUMENTATIE CENTRUM. Main/Corp** Katholiek Documentatie Centrum. 1971-. Dutch (English). an. Fl30.00. Katholiek Documentatie Centrum, Erasmuslaan 36, 6525 GG Nijmegen Netherlands. **Tel** 080-512412. **LC** BX1549.A1; K3A. **Circ:** 500 (ctrl).
**Desc:** Report of activities by the Katholiek Documentatie Centrum. Scientific articles about the history of the Catholic life, Catholic people and the Catholic church in the Netherlands in the 19th and 20th century.

GW/0454-0158
**JAHRBUCH DES STIFTES KLOSTERNEUBURG. NEUE FOLGE. Main/Corp** Klosterneuburg, Austria (Monastery of Augustinian Canons). (1961)-. German. be. **LC**

BX2609.K55; K52. ***Continues*** *Klosterneuburg, Austria (Monastery of Augustinian Canons). Jahrbuch.*
**Ind/Abst** BHA : Biblio. Hist. Art.

GW/0341-9916
**JAHRBUCH DES VEREINS FUER AUGSBURGER BISTUMSGESCHICHTE E. V.** [Jahrb. Ver. Augsbg. Bistumsgesch. e.V.]. (1967)-. Periodical. German. an. **UDC** 262.3(430.1-35.68)(091).
**Ind/Abst** BHA : Biblio. Hist. Art.

AU
**JAHRBUCH FUER KATHOLISCHE ERZIEHUNG IN OSTERREICH.** Vol. 1 (1933)-. German. an.

UK
**JESUITS AND FRIENDS.** (19??)-. English. Three times a year. Free. Jesuit Missions, 11 Edge Hill, London SW19 4LR England. **Tel** 11 44 81 9460466, FAX 11 44 81 9462292. **ED** D. Birchall SJ. **Circ:** 25,000.
**Desc:** News of British Jesuits at home and abroad.

US/1048-2431
**JOURNAL OF TEXAS CATHOLIC HISTORY AND CULTURE / TEXAS CATHOLIC HISTORICAL SOCIETY, THE.** [J. Tex. Cathol. hist. cult.]. **Added/Corp** Texas Catholic Historical Society. Vol. 1, No. 1 (Mar. 1990)-. Periodical. English. $6.00 (single issue). Texas Catholic Conference, 3001 South Congress Avenue, Austin TX 78704. **Tel** (512)447-4132, FAX (512)441-5055. **ED** Dr. Patrick Foley. **LC** BX1415.T4; J68. **DD** 282/.764/05. cum. index. **Bk Rev**, (Qty: 20). **Ad Acc. Pr Rev. Circ:** 750 (ctrl).
**Desc:** A scholarly journal devoted to the study and presentation of Roman Catholic history and culture as such has developed over the centuries in Texas and the American Southwest.

AT/0084-7259
**JOURNAL OF THE AUSTRALIAN CATHOLIC HISTORICAL SOCIETY.** [J. Aust. Cathol. Hist. Soc.]. **Added/Corp** Australian Catholic Historical Society. (196?)-. Periodical. English. an. comes with Australian Catholic Historical Society membershhip. Australian Catholic Historical Society, PO Box A 621, Sydney South New South Wales, Australia. **Tel** 011 61 2 7596980. **ED** A. E. Cahill. **Bk Rev. Ad Acc. Circ:** 400.
**Desc:** Contains papers on the history of the Roman Catholic Church in Australia.
**Ind/Abst** Am. Hist. Life; APAIS, Aust. Public Aff. Inf. Ser. (1963-).

CN/0826-3205
**JOURNAL OF THE ... GENERAL SYNOD / ANGLICAN CHURCH OF CANADA.** **See** Religion and Theology-Protestantism.

CN/0848-9025
**JOURNAL - PROVINCIAL ASSOCIATION OF CATHOLIC TEACHERS.** **See** Education.

US/0022-6858
**JURIST (WASHINGTON), THE.** (THE JURIST.). [Jurist]. **Added/Corp** Catholic University of America. School of Canon Law. Catholic University of America. Dept. of Canon Law. Vol. 1, No. 1 (Jan. 1941)-. English. Twice a year. $35.00. The Catholic University of America, 413 Caldwell Hall, Washington DC 20064. **Tel** (202)319-5439, FAX (209)319-4967. **ED** James H. Provost. Index available in last issue of volume--attached. **Bk Rev. Pr Rev. Circ:** 2,000. available on microfilm and microfiche from University Microfilms International (UMI).
**Desc:** Studies in church law and ministry.
**Ind/Abst** Bibliogr. Mission.; Canon Law Abstr.; Curr. Law Index (1980-); Index Leg. Period.; Leg. Resour. Index (1980-); LegalTrac (1980-); Abr. Cathol. Period. Lit. Index; Cathol. Period. Lit. Index.

CN/0380-0962
**KALENDAR SVITLA.** **VFOAT** Light Almanac. Began publication in 1951?. Ukrainian. an. 8.00Can$ Canada; $8.00 other. Basilian Press, 265 Bering Avenue, Toronto, Ontario M8Z 3A5 Canada. **Tel** (905)234-1212. **ED** Nicon Svirsky Osbm. **DD** 282/.05. **Bk Rev. Circ:** 3,500 (ctrl).

IO
**KARYA-KARYA GEREJA KATOLIK INDONESIA.** Indonesian. Bagian Dokumentasi Penerangan, Kantor Waligeneja Indonesia, Taman Cut Mutiah 10, Jakarta Indonesia. **LC** BX1653.A1; K36.

GW
**KATHOLISCHEN MISSIONEN, DIE.** **VFOAT** KM. (1947)-. Periodical. German. bm (6 issues). DM23.40. Verlag Herder Freiburg, Postfach 79080, Frieburg, Germany. **Tel** (0761)27-17-0, FAX (0761)27 17-520, telex 761489. **ED** L. Wiedenmann. cum. index. ***Continues*** *Katholischen Missionen, Illustrierte Monatsschrift des Vereins der Glaubensverbreitung in den Landern Deutscher Zunge Mit den Zentralen Aachen, Munchen, Wien und Teplitz-Schonau, 0022-9407.*
**Desc:** Journal covering Catholic missions.
**Ind/Abst** Bibliogr. Mission.

GW
**KATHOLISCHES LEBEN UND KIRCHENREFORM IN ZEITALTER DER GLAUBENSSPALTUNG.** Monographic series. German. ir. Price varies per volume. Aschendorffsche Verlagsbuchhandlung, Postfach 1124, D-48135 Muenster Germany. **Tel** 011 49 251 690132, telex 08-92 830 WN MS D. **ED** Erwin Iserloh. ***Continues*** *Katholisches Leben und Kaempfen in Zeitalter Der Glaubensspaltung.*
**Desc:** Monograph series on Catholic life and church reform during the period of reformation and counter-reformation, Martin Luther and the Pope, theologians and important personalities of that era.

XR
**KATOLICKY TYDENIK.** **Added/Corp** Ceska Katolicka Charita. 1990-. Periodical. Czech. wk. **(Subscription address:** Artia Pegas Press Ltd., Palac Metro Narodni Trida 25, 11210 Prague 1 Czech Republic.**) LC** BX806.C9; K33. ***Continues*** *Katolicke Noviny.*

JA
**KATORIKKU KENKYU.** **Added/Corp** Jochi Daigaku Shingakukai. **VFOAT** Catholic Studies. (19??)-. Japanese (summaries and/or abstracts in English). sa. ¥2146 Japan; $15.00 US. Jochi Daigaku Shingakukai, Kamishakujii 4-32-11, Nerima-ku Tokyo 177 Japan. **Tel** 03-929-0848. **ED** Peter Nemeshegyi. **LC** BX806.J36; K37. Index available. cum. index. **Bk Rev. Circ:** 1,000. ***Continues*** *Katorikku Shingaku.*
**Desc:** Articles on biblical science, history of theology, modern theology, Christian philosophy, church history, inculturation of Christianity, ecumenism and science of religion.
**Ind/Abst** Bibliogr. Mission.; Old Testam. Abstr.

UK/0044-4018
**KENT RECUSANT HISTORY.** No. 1 (Spring 1979)-. Periodical. English. sa. £5.00 (individuals), £7.50 (per household), £4.00 (institutions), £1.50 (per copy); £5.50 other. Kent Recusant History Society, 2 Sea Street, Whitstable Kent England. **Tel** 0227.453490. **(Subscription address:** 30 Castle Row, Canterbury Kent England**) ED** Antony C W Ryan, Christopher Buckingham. **LC** BX1494.K46; K46. **DD** 282/.4223. cum. index. **Bk Rev. Circ:** 120.
**Desc:** Articles containing the results of research on recusant and post-Reformation non-conformist history.

CN/0700-9496
**KHAOUA.** V. 1- Nov. 1967-. Periodical. French. qt. 20.00Can$. Service Preparation a la Vie, 10215 rue Sacre Coeur, Montreal Quebec H2C 2S6 Canada. **Tel** (514)387-6475. **DD** 248/.4/05. Index available. ***Continues*** *Khaoua, 0700-9496.*
**Desc:** Covers religion, theology, and Roman Catholic Church.

GW
**KIRCHE IN NOT.** 1- 1953-. Periodical. German. Ostpriesterhilfe E V und Haus der Begegnung, 624 Konigstein-Tns IM Taunus Germany. **LC** BR738.6.

GW/0942-136X
**KONTRASTE FREIBURG. 1992.** [Kontraste Freibg., 1992]. (1992)-. Periodical. German. qt. Verlag Herder Freiburg, Postfach 79080, Frieburg, Germany. **Tel** (0761)27-17-0, FAX (0761)27 17-520, telex 761489. **ED** Christian Dau. **UDC** 32(569.4). ***Continues*** *Kontraste, Impuls, 0344-5984.*

PL
**KROLOWA APOSTOOW.** **Added/Corp** Stowarzyszenie Apostolstwa Katolickiego (Poland). (19??)-. Periodical. Polish. mo. Price on Request. **(Subscription address:** ARS Polona, PO Box 1001, 00068 Warsaw Poland.**) LC** BX1564.A1; K76.

KO
**KYOHOESA YON'GU.** **VFOAT** Research Journal of Korean Church History. V. 1- Series; 1977-. Periodical. French (Korean). 2.000 single issue. Hanguk Kyohoesa Yonguso, 367-27 Hapchong-dong Mapo-ku, Seoul Korea. **LC** BX1670.5; .K9. **DD** 282/.519.

KO
**KYONGHYANG CHAPCHI.** Periodical. Korean. W3,000. Hanguk Chonjugyo Chungang Hyobuihoe, CPO Box 16, Seoul South Korea. **LC** BX806.K67; K9.

●US/1064-556X
**LATIN MASS, THE.** [Latin Mass]. **Added/Corp** Foundation for Catholic Reform. Vol. 1, No. 1 (Mar./Apr. 1992)-. Periodical. English. bm. $25.00. Foundation for Catholic Reform, Box 255, Harrison NY 10528. **DD** 282.

IT/0023-902X
**LAURENTIANUM.** (LAURENTIANUM : COMMENTARII TRIMESTRES CURA COLLEGII INTERNATIONALIS LAURENTII A BRINDISI, FRATRUM MINORUM CAPUCCINORUM IN URBE.). **Added/Corp** Collegio Internazionale di S. Lorenzo a Brindisi. (1960)-. Periodical. Italian (English, French, German and Spanish). Three times a year. L40000 Itlay; L45000 other. Laurentianum, Coll S Lorenzo, Circonvallazione Occidentale 6850, 00163 Rome Aurelio Italy. **Tel** 011 39 329934, FAX 011 39 329934. **ED** Ettore Covi. cum. index. **Bk Rev. Ad Acc. Circ:** 500 (ctrl). ***Continues*** *Ius Seraphicam, (OCLC)12579793.*
**Desc:** Theology, philosophy, Canon Law, history, Bible, spirituality, Franciscan history, and spirituality.
**Ind/Abst** Bibliogr. Mission.; Canon Law Abstr.; MLA Int. Bibl. Books Artic. Mod. Lang. Lit.; New Testam. Abstr.; Old Testam. Abstr.

●US
**LECTOR.** (1994)-. Newsletter. English. Twelve times a year. $12.00. National Catholic Reporter Publishing Company, PO Box 419281, 115 East Armour Boulevard, Kansas City MO 64141-6281. **Tel** (816)531-0538, (800)444-8910, (800)333-7373, FAX (816)531-7466.
**Desc:** Published for those who deliver scripture readings in worship services.

US/0740-9613
**LET'S PRAY TOGETHER.** ***Ceased.*** (LET'S PRAY TOGETHER : A PUBLICATION OF FAMILIES FOR PRAYER.). **VFOAT** Together. Ceased (Sept. 1989). Periodical. English. wk. Families for Prayer, 775 Madison Avenue, Albany NY 12208. **Tel** (518)462-6458. **ED** John Gurley, Angelita Fenker, James Breig. **Circ:** 70,000 (ctrl).
**Desc:** A publication to foster, encourage and facilitate prayer in the home.

CN/0820-6945
**LETTRES MANUSCRITES OU COMMUNIQUES PUBLIES DANS L'ARCHIDIOCESE D'OTTAWA.** **Main/Corp** Eglise Catholique. Archidiocese d'Ottawa. Archeveque (1967- : Plourde). Vol. 1, No. 1 (1967)-. French. an. L'Archidiocese D'Ottawa, 256 Rue King Edward, Ottawa Ontario K1N 7M1 Canada. **DD** 262/.0271384/05.

UK/0024-1792
**LIBERAL CATHOLIC.** **Added/Corp** Liberal Catholic Church. Vol. 1 (1921)-. Periodical. English. Three times a year. £6.00. Liberal Catholic Church, 30 Gordon Street, London WC1H 0BE England.

PH
**LIFE FORUM.** Vol. 14, No. 1-. Periodical. English. bm. P50.00 Philippines; $25.00 North America; $20.00 other. Life Forum, Caritas Manila Otis Cor Santiago/Room 6, Pandacan Manila Philippines. **Tel** 506332. **ED** Mary Pilar Verzosa. **LC** BX1912; .P47. **Bk Rev. Ad Acc. Circ:** 2,000. ***Continues*** *Philippine Priests' Forum.*

US/0024-3450
**LIGUORIAN.** [Liguorian]. **Added/Corp** Redemptorists. (1913)-. Periodical. English. mo. $15.00 US; $21.00 other. Liguori Publications, One Liguori Drive, Liguori MO 63057. **Tel** (314)464-2500, FAX (314)464-8449. **ED** Allan Weinert. **LC** BX4020.A1; L5. **DD** 271.6. Index available. **Bk Rev. Circ:** 500,000 (ctrl). available on microfilm and microfiche from University Microfilms International (UMI).
**Desc:** Leading Catholic family magazine. Ideas mixed with ideals, informative and inspiring. For Christians of all ages.
**Ind/Abst** Abr. Cathol. Period. Lit. Index; Cathol. Period. Lit. Index.

US/0196-7258
**LISTENING (WASHINGTON).** ***Title Change.*** **See** Physically Impaired.

US/1046-9990
**LITURGY 90.** [Liturgy 90]. **Added/Corp** Catholic Church. Archdiocese of Chicago (Ill.). Office for Divine Worship. Vol. 21, No. 1 (Jan. 1990)-. Periodical. English. Eight times a year. $18.00 US; $25.00 other. Liturgy Training Publications, 1800 North Hermitage Avenue, Chicago IL 60622. **Tel** (312)486-8970, (800)933-1800, FAX (800)933-7094. **ED** David Philippart. **DD** 264. ***Continues*** *Liturgy 80, 1040-6603.*

US/0024-5275
**LIVING LIGHT, THE.** [Living light]. **Added/Corp** United States Catholic Conference. Dept. of Education. National Center of the Confraternity of Christian Doctrine. National Center of Religious Education--CCD. Vol. 1, No. 1 (Spring 1964)-. Periodical. English. Four times a year. $29.95 US & Canada; $39.95 other. US Catholic Conference, 3211 4th Avenue Northeast, Publishing Services, Washington DC 20017-1194. **Tel** (202)541-3090, FAX (202)541-3089, telex 7400424. **ED** Elaine McCarron, (phone: (202)541-3097). **LC** BX923; .L5. Index available (published in May). **Bk Rev. Ad Acc, Adv Mgr:** Chuck Bugge. **Circ:** 1200. available on microfilm and microfiche from University Microfilms International (UMI).
**Desc:** Provides a forum for catechists and professional educators. Designed to present developments and trends, identify problems and issues, report on research, encourage critical thinking, and to contribute to decision-making in the field of religious education and pastoral action.
**Ind/Abst** Old Testam. Abstr.; Abr. Cathol. Period. Lit. Index; Cathol. Period. Lit. Index.

US
**LOOSE LEAF LECTIONARY.** English. Three times a year. $54.50 US; $61.00 other. Liturgical Press, St. Johns Abbey, Collegeville MN 56321. **Tel** (612)363-2213, (800)858-5450, FAX (612)363-3299, (800)445-5899.

CN
**MAGISTRA.** (19??)-. English. sa. $30.00 institutions; $20.00 individuals. Dekalb College Social Sciences Dept., North Campus, 2101 Womack Road, Dunwoody GA 30338-4497. **Tel** (404)551-3234, FAX (404)604-3798. **ED** Deborah Vess and Judith Sutera. Index available. cum. index. **Bk Rev**, (Qty: 10). **Ad Acc. Circ:** 400. ***Continues*** *Vox Benedictina.*

FR/0025-0937
**MAISON-DIEU, LA.** [Maison-Dieu]. **Added/Corp** Centre de Pastorale Liturgique. Centre National de Pastorale Liturgique. No. 1 (Jan. 1945)-. Periodical. French. Four times a year. 225.27F France; 230.00F EEC Countries; 285.00F others. Editions du Cerf, BP 65, 77932 Perthes Cedex France. **Tel** 011 33 1 44181212. **(Subscription address:** PO Box 990, Outremont, H2V 4S7 Canada, telephone: (514)948-1222 or (514)278-3025**)** cum. index.
**Ind/Abst** Bibliogr. Mission.; New Testam. Abstr.; Abr. Cathol. Period. Lit. Index; Cathol. Period. Lit. Index.

IO
**MAJALAH BIMAS KATOLIK. Main/Corp** Indonesia. Direktorat Jenderal Bimas Katolik. **VAT** Majalah Bimbingan Masyarakat Katolik. Indonesian. Direktorat Jenderal Bimas Katolik, Jln Moh Husni Thamrin 6, Jakarta Indonesia. **LC** BX1653.A1; A25. ***Continues*** *Indonesia. Direktorat Jenderal Bimas Katolik. Madjalah.*

CN/0820-6937
**MANUSCRIPT LETTERS OR COMMUNIQUES PUBLISHED IN THE ARCHDIOCESE OF OTTAWA. Main/Corp** Catholic Church. Archdiocese of Ottawa. Archbishop (1967- : Plourde). English. an. Archdiocese of Ottawa, 256 King Edward Street, Ottawa Ontario K1N 7M1. **DD** 262/.0271384/05.

US/0464-9680
**MARIAN STUDIES.** (MARIAN STUDIES : PROCEEDINGS OF THE ... NATIONAL CONVENTION OF THE MARIOLOGICAL SOCIETY OF AMERICA HELD IN ... ON ...). [Marian stud.]. **Main/Corp** Mariological Society of America. National Convention. Vol. 1, (1950)-. Proceedings. English. an (December). $12.00. Marianological Society of America, University of Dayton, Marian Library, Box 1390, Dayton OH 45469. **Tel** (513)229-4214, FAX (513)229-4590. **ED** Rev. Thomas A. Thompson S. M. **LC** BT596; .M33. **DD** 232. Index available (Bound in next issue). cum. index ((1950-1980)). **Circ:** 700 (ctrl). available on microfilm from University Microfilms International (UMI).
**Desc:** A Catholic theological association dedicated to studying and making known the role of the Blessed Virgin Mary in the mystery of Christ, the Church and in the history of salvation.
**Ind/Abst** New Testam. Abstr.; Cathol. Period. Lit. Index.

US/0025-4142
**MARYKNOLL.** [Maryknoll]. **Added/Corp** Catholic Foreign Mission Society of America. Vol. 33, No. 5 (May 1939)-. Periodical. English (Spanish). mo (July/Aug. issues combined). $10.00. Catholic Foreign Mission Society, PO Box 301, Maryknoll NY 10545. **Tel** (914)941-7590, FAX (914)945-0670. **ED** Joseph R. Veneroso, M.M. **DD** 266. Index available. cum. index. **Bk Rev**, (Qty: 11). **Circ:** 600,000 (ctrl). available on audiocassette; available on microfilm and microfiche from University Microfilms International (UMI). ***Continues*** *Field Afar, 0271-7204.*
**Desc:** Focus is on the work of missionaries in Asia, South America, Central America, Bangladesh, Thailand, and Vietnam.
**Ind/Abst** Bibliogr. Mission.

CK
**MEDELLIN.** Vol.1 (March 1975). Periodical. Spanish. qt. $35.00. Instituto Teologico Pastoral del Celam, Revista Medellin, Apartado Aereo 51086, Bogota 2 Colombia. **Tel** 011 57-91-2357046. **ED** Alfred Morin. **LC** BX1751.2; .M43. Index available. **Bk Rev. Circ:** 1700.
**Desc:** Concerns pastoral studies, Bible, theology, spirituality, catechetics, social studies and philosophy.
**Ind/Abst** Bibliogr. Mission.; Abr. Cathol. Period. Lit. Index; Cathol. Period. Lit. Index.

US/0026-2927
**MID-AMERICA (CHICAGO).** (MID-AMERICA; AN HISTORICAL REVIEW.). [Mid-Am.]. **Added/Corp** Loyola University of Chicago. Institute of Jesuit History. Illinois Catholic Historical Society. Loyola University of Chicago. Vol. 12 (July 1929)-. Periodical. English. Three times a year. $15.00 US; $16.00 other. Loyola University / Department of History, 6525 North Sheridan Road, Chicago IL 60626. **Tel** (312)508-2221. **ED** Louise Kerr. **Bk Rev. Circ:** 1,500. available on microfilm and microfiche from University Microfilms International (UMI). Documents available from The Genuine Article. ***Continues*** *Illinois Catholic Historical Review, 0146-549X.*
**Desc:** Covers American history, particularly the Progressive Era.
**Ind/Abst** Am. Hist. Life (1954-); Arts Humanit. Citation Index [Full Cov.]; Bibliogr. Mission.; Book Rev. Index (1954-); Humanit. Index; Lit. Crit. Regist.; Res. Alert [Full Cov.]; Soc. Sci. Cit. Index [Select. Cov.]; Soc. Work Abstr. (?-?); Abr. Cathol. Period. Lit. Index; Cathol. Period. Lit. Index.

CN/0228-1171
**MILITANT CHRETIEN INTERNATIONAL, LE.** [Milit. chretien int.]. **VAT** Militant Catholique International (1980). No. 14 (May 1980)-. Periodical. French. qt. 0.25Can$ per no. Le Militant Chretien International, CP 5130 Succursale Beauport, Quebec Quebec G1E 6B5 Canada. **DD** 248/.05. ***Continues*** *Militant Catholique International, 0701-0613.*

US/0275-6250
**MINUTES OF THE SEMI-ANNUAL MEETING OF THE BOARD OF DIRECTORS OF THE FIRST CATHOLIC SLOVAK UNION OF THE UNITED STATES AND CANADA.** [Minutes semi-annu. meet. Board Dir. First Cathol. Slovak Union U. S. Can.]. **Main/Corp** First Catholic Slovak Union of America. Board of Directors. English. sa. First Catholic Slovak Union, 6611 Rockside Road, Cleveland OH 44131-2398. **LC** E184.S64; F57A. **DD** 973/.049187.

IT
**MISCELLANEA FRANCESCANA.** (19??)-. Periodical. Italian. qt. L55000.00 Italy. Miscellanea Francescana, Via del Serafico 1, 00142 Rome Italy. **Tel** 011 39 6 5017419, 011 39 6 5191586. **Bk Rev.** ***Continues*** *Miscellanea Francescana di Storia, di Lettere, di Arti.*
**Ind/Abst** Am. Hist. Life (1963-1976); Bibliogr. Mission.; BHA : Biblio. Hist. Art; MLA Int. Bibl. Books Artic. Mod. Lang. Lit.

CN/0708-9813
**MISSION (QUEBEC).** (MISSION.). [Mission]. **Added/Corp** Peres Blancs. **VAT** Mission (Montreal. Ed. Francaise). Vol. 72, No. 4 (July/Aug. 1976)-. French. ir. 5.00Can$ (one year), 9.00Can$ (two year) Canada; 10.00Can$ (one year), 20.00Can$ (two year) other. Mission, 1640 St-Hubert, Montreal Quebec H2L 4K3 Canada. **Tel** (514)849-1167. **ED** Yvon Lavoie. **DD** 266/.2/05. **Bk Rev. Circ:** 48,000 (ctrl). ***Continues*** *Missions d'Afrique, 0708-9805.*
**Desc:** Roman Catholic missionary work in Africa.
**Ind/Abst** Bibliogr. Mission.

US
**MISSION UPDATE.** (19??)-. Periodical. English. Five times a year. $30.00. US Catholic Mission Association, 3029 4th Street Northeast, Washington DC 20017. **Tel** (202)823-3112, FAX (202)832-3688. **ED** Lou McNeil. **Circ:** 1,000 (ctrl).

SP/0211-5492
**MISSIONALIA HISPANICA.** ***Ceased.*** [Mission. hisp.]. Vol. 1 (No. 1/2) 1944-?. Periodical. Spanish. sa. Consejo Superior Investigacion Cientificas (CSIC), Vitruvio 8, 28006 Madrid Spain. **Tel** 011 34 1 5612833, FAX 011 34 1 4113077, telex 42182. **LC** BV2130; .M38. **DD** 266.2.
**Desc:** Offers sources and studies on the Spanish missionaries to the Indies, their movements, and pan-cultural historic ramifications.
**Ind/Abst** Am. Hist. Life (1959-1964, 1967-); Bibliogr. Mission.

CN/0225-3801
**MISSIONNAIRES CATHOLIQUES CANADIENS, STATISTIQUES. See** Religion and Theology-Abstracting, Bibliographies and Statistics.

CN/0700-4192
**MISSIONS DES FRANCISCAINS.** [Missions francisc.]. **Added/Corp** Franciscans. (1???)-. Periodical. French. Four times a year. $10.00. Missions des Franciscains, 2080 Ouest Boulevard Rene-Levesque, Montreal Quebec H3H 1R6 Canada. **Tel** (514)932-6094, FAX (514)259-7407. **ED** Raymond R. Lagace. **DD** 266/.2/85. **Circ:** 7,000 (ctrl).

RM/1013-4204
**MITROPOLIA ARDEALULUI.** [Mitrop. ardeal.]. (19??)-. Periodical. Romanian. bm.
**Ind/Abst** BHA : Biblio. Hist. Art.

RM
**MITROPOLIA MOLDOVEI SI SUCEVEI : REVISTA OFICIALA A ARHIEPISCOPIEI IASILOR SI A EPISCOPIEI ROMANULUI SI HUSILOR. Added/Corp** Biserica Ortodoxa Romana. Arhiepiscopia Iasilor. Biserica Ortodoxa Romana. Episcopia Romanului si Husilor. (19??)-. Periodical. Romanian. mo. **LC** WMLC L 83/9810.
**Ind/Abst** BHA : Biblio. Hist. Art.

CN/0026-9190
**MONASTIC STUDIES.** [Monast. stud.]. **Added/Corp** Mount Saviour Monastery (Pine City , N.Y.). Our Lady of the Holy Cross Abbey (Berryville, Va.). Benedictine Priory of Montreal. No. 1 (1963)-. English. an. 25.00Can$. Monastic Studies, PO Box 52, Stn Cote St Luc, Montreal Quebec H4V 1H8 Canada. **Tel** (514)485-7127, FAX (514)849-4417. **ED** Laurence Freeman. **LC** BX2400; .M6. **DD** 255/.01/05. cum. index. **Bk Rev. Ad Acc. Circ:** 500-1000 (ctrl). available on microfilm and microfiche from University Microfilms International (UMI); available on diskette. ***Continues*** *Cistercian Studies.*
**Desc:** Journal of topics on monasticism, monastic history, theology, and monastic spirituality.
**Ind/Abst** Br. Archaeol. Bibliogr.

IT/0026-6094
**MONDO E MISSIONE. Added/Corp** Pontificio istituto missioni estere. (19??)-. Italian. Ten times a year (d). L30000 Italy; L42000.00 other. Centro Missionario Pime, Via Mose Bianchi 94, 20149 Milan Italy. **Tel** 011 39 2 4980741, FAX 011 39 2 4812889. **ED** Piero Gheddo. **LC** BV2130; .M47. **DD** 266/.2/05. Index available in last issue of volume--attached. **Bk Rev. Ad Acc, Adv Mgr:** Ferrari Andrea. **Circ:** 25,000. ***Continues*** *Missioni Cattoliche.*
**Desc:** International Third World missionary and churches information. Social and political problems, economics and dialogue with other religions.
**Ind/Abst** Bibliogr. Mission.; Missionalia.

US/0883-7899
**MONTANA CATHOLIC, THE.** Vol. 1, No. 1 (Apr. 17, 1985)-. Periodical. English. bw. The Montana Catholic, PO Box 1729, Helena MT 59620. ***Continues*** *Westmont Word, 8750-4715.*

IT
**MONUMENTA HISTORICA SOCIETATIS IESU. Added/Corp** Institutum Historicum Societatis Iesu, Rome. (1???)-. Monographic series. Latin (Spanish, Portuguese and English). ir. Price varies per volume. Institutum Historicum Societatis Iesu, Via dei Penitenzieri 20, 00193 Rome Italy. **Tel** 686 93 57. **LC** BX3701; M7.
**Desc:** Contains editions of documents relating to the foundation of the Society of Jesus, the first generation of Jesuits, and Jesuit missions.

US
**MONUMENTA IURIS CANONICI. SERIES A : CORPUS GLOSSATORUM.** V. 1- 1969-. Periodical. English. ir. Bibliotecha Apostolica Vaticana, Citta del Vaticano, 00120 Vatican City. **Tel** 011 396 6 69885051.

GW/0544-9987
**MONUMENTA MONODICA MEDII AEVI. HRSG. IM AUFTRAG DES INSTITUTS FUER MUSIKFORSCHUNG REGENSBURG MIT UNTERSTUTZUNG DER MUSIKGESCHICHTLICHEN KOMMISSION VON BRUNO STABLEIN. See** Music.

GW/0580-1400
**MUENCHENER THEOLOGISCHE ZEITSCHRIFT.** [Munch. theol. Z.]. (Jan. 1950)-. Periodical. German. qt. DM56.00. EOS Verlag, Erzabtei St Ottilien, D 86941 St Ottilien Germany. **Tel** 011 49 8193 71261, FAX 011 49 8193 6844. **LC** BR4; .M85. cum. index. **Bk Rev.** ctrl circ.
**Ind/Abst** MLA Int. Bibl. Books Artic. Mod. Lang. Lit.; New Testam. Abstr.

SP/0027-3252
**MUNDO CRISTIANO.** (REVISTA MUNDO CRISTIANO.). [Mundo crist.]. **VFOAT** M.C. Mundo Cristiano. (1963)-. Periodical. Spanish. Twelve times a year. 3700ptas Spain and Portugal; 4450ptas other. Ediciones Palabra SA, PO Castellana 210 2B, 28046 Madrid Spain. **Tel** 011 34 1 3507739, 011 34 1 3508311. **UDC** 2. **Bk Rev. Ad Acc. Circ:** 31,000 (ctrl).

IT
**MUSICAE SACRAE MINISTERIUM (ROME). See** Music.

PL
**MUZYKA RELIGIJNA W POLSCE : MATERIAY I STUDIA. See** Music.

US
**MY DAILY VISITOR.** (19??)-. English. Six times a year. $9.00 US; $11.00 other. Our Sunday Visitor Inc., 200 Noll Plaza, Box 920, Huntington IN 46750. **Tel** (219)356-8400, (800)348-2440, FAX (219)356-8472.

US/0164-3568
**MY FRIEND. See** Children and Youth Interests.

US/0027-7894
**NAROD POLSKI. Added/Corp** Polish Roman Catholic Union of America. **VFOAT** Polish Nation; Narod. Vol. 1, No. 1 (1897)-. Newspaper. Polish (English). sm. $10.00. Polish Roman Catholic Union, 984 Milwaukee Avenue G, Chicago IL 60622. **Tel** (212)533-0250. **ED** Joseph W. Zurawski. **LC** Newspaper 7002. **Bk Rev. Circ:** 31,000 (ctrl). available on microfilm.
**Desc:** Polish-American journal describing official activities of the Polish Roman Catholic Union of America: fraternal, religious, sports, cultural, historical, literary and social.

US/0745-5127
**NATIONAL CATHOLIC FORESTER.** (NATIONAL CATHOLIC FORESTER / NATIONAL CATHOLIC SOCIETY OF FORESTERS.). Periodical. English. qt. National Catholic Society of Foresters, 35 East Wacker Drive, Chicago IL 60601.

US/0027-8920
**NATIONAL CATHOLIC REGISTER.** [Natl. Cathol. regist.]. **VFOAT** Register. Vol. 46, No. 40 (Aug. 30, 1970)-. Periodical. English. wk (52 issues). $49.95 (one year), $74.50 (two year). Twin Circle Publishing Company, 15760 Ventura Boulevard, Suite 1201, Encino CA 91436. **Tel** (818)382-1868, (800)421-3230, FAX (818)382-3677. **ED** Joop Koopman. **DD** 282. **Bk Rev. Ad Acc, Adv Mgr:** Frank Wright, **Tel** same as publisher. **Circ:** 53,500. ***Continues*** *National Register.*
**Desc:** National Catholic newsweekly.
**Ind/Abst** Curr. Lit. Fam. Plan. (19??-199?); Abr. Cathol. Period. Lit. Index; Cathol. Period. Lit. Index.

US/0027-8939
**NATIONAL CATHOLIC REPORTER.** [Natl. Cathol. report.]. Vol. 1 (1964)-. Periodical. English. Forty-Four times a year. $32.95. National Catholic Reporter Publishing Company, PO Box 419281, 115 East Armour Boulevard, Kansas City MO 64141-6281. **Tel** (816)531-0538, (800)444-8910, (800)333-7373, FAX (816)531-7466. **ED** Tom Fox. **LC** UNC. **Bk Rev. Ad Acc. Circ:** 52,000. available on microfilm and microfiche from University Microfilms International (UMI); available on an online database (file 647/Full-Text) from DIALOG. Documents available from UMI Article Clearinghouse, Magazine Collection.
**Desc:** Progressive lay-edited independent newsweekly for U.S. Catholics. It covers the political, social and economic communities. It also covers the church as an institution engaged in society.
**Ind/Abst** Acad. Search (July 1993-); Access (1975-1987); Curr. Lit. Fam. Plan.; Gen. Period. Index (1985-); INFO-SOUTH Abstr.; Mag. Index Plus (1989-); Mag. Search; Newsp. Period. Abstr. (1988-); Abr. Cathol. Period. Lit. Index; Cathol. Period. Lit. Index; Mag. Index (1977-).

US/0736-9476
**NATIONAL DIRECTORY OF CATHOLIC HIGHER EDUCATION.** **See** Education-Higher Education.

CN/1183-1863
**NAZARETH (COMBERMERE).** (NAZARETH : A CATHOLIC FAMILY JOURNAL.). [Nazareth]. (1991)-. Periodical. English. qt (Feb., May, Sep., Nov.). 20.00Can$ (one year), 35.00Can$ (two year) Canada; £15 (one year), £25 (two year) UK and Ireland; $20.00 (one year), $35.00 (two year) US. Nazareth Journal, PO Box 106, Combermere Ontario K0J 1L0 Canada. **Tel** (613)756-2067, FAX (613)757-3486. **ED** Michael O'Brien. **DD** 248.4/82/05. **Bk Rev**, (Qty: 10-12). **Ad Acc, Adv Mgr:** J. Nordholt. **Circ:** 3,000 (ctrl).
**Desc:** Our mission is to strengthen and inspire Catholic families to live the Gospels in simplicity, truth and holiness, as exemplified by the Holy Family.

US/0147-8044
**NCEA-GANLEY'S CATHOLIC SCHOOLS IN AMERICA.** (CATHOLIC SCHOOLS IN AMERICA.). **Added/Corp** Curriculum Information Center. National Catholic Educational Association. **VAT** National Catholic Educational Association-Ganley's Catholic Schools in America. (19??)-. Periodical. English. an (published Mar., or Apr.). $40.00. Fisher Publishing Company / CO, PO Box 1073, Montrose CO 81402. **Tel** 800 766-5151 or, (302)249-1303. **ED** Mary Mahar. **LC** LC501; .N296a. **DD** 377/.82/73. ***Continues*** *National Catholic Educational Association. Research Dept. Catholic Schools in the United States, 0091-9527.*

US/1044-8322
**NEW CATHOLIC EXPLORER.** (NEW CATHOLIC EXPLORER / DIOCESE OF JOLIET, ILLINOIS.). **Added/Corp** Catholic Church. Diocese of Joliet (Ill.). (198?)-. Periodical. English. Fifty times a year. $15.00 (one year), $28.00 (two year), $42.00 (three year). New Catholic Explorer, 402 South Independence Boulevard, Romeoville IL 60441-2299. **Tel** (815)838-6475. **ED** Patricia L. Morrison. **Bk Rev. Ad Acc. Circ:** 25,000. ***Continues*** *Joliet Catholic Explorer, 0273-6217.*
**Desc:** Official newspaper of the Roman Catholic Diocese of Joliet, Illinois. National, international and local news.

US/0744-8589
**NEW COVENANT (ANN ARBOR, MICH.).** (NEW COVENANT.). [New covenant]. **Added/Corp** Catholic Charismatic Renewal of the United States. National Service Committee. Charismatic Renewal Services. (July 1971)-. Periodical. English. Twelve times a year. $18.00 US; $24.00 other. Our Sunday Visitor Inc., 200 Noll Plaza, Box 920, Huntington IN 46750. **Tel** (219)356-8400, (800)348-2440, FAX (219)356-8472. **ED** Jim Manney. **LC** BX2350.57; .N46. **DD** 248/.48/205. Index available. **Bk Rev. Ad Acc. Circ:** 50,000. available on microfilm and microfiche from University Microfilms International (UMI). ***Supersedes*** *Pastoral Newsletter.*
**Desc:** The magazine of Catholic renewal.
**Ind/Abst** Abr. Cathol. Period. Lit. Index; Cathol. Period. Lit. Index.

IE
**NEW LITURGY. BULLETIN OF THE NATIONAL SECRETARIAT, IRISH EPISCOPAL COMMISSION FOR LITURGY.** (1974)-. Periodical. English. qt. 5.00p Ireland; 6.00p other. Irish Institute of Pastoral Liturgy, College Street, Carlow Ireland. **Tel** 011 353 503 42942, FAX 011 353 503 42800. **ED** Patrick Jones. **Bk Rev. Circ:** 1,400 (ctrl).
**Desc:** Contains articles of practical and pastoral interest on liturgy.

US/1043-3538
**NEW WORLD (1989), THE.** (THE NEW WORLD.). [New world]. **Added/Corp** Catholic Church. Archdiocese of Chicago (Ill.). Vol. 97, No. 6 (Feb. 10, 1989)-. Periodical. English. wk. $25.00 (1 year), $40.00 (2 year). New World Publications, 1144 West Jackson, Chicago IL 60607. **Tel** (312)243-1300, FAX (312)243-1526. **ED** Rev. Thomas Widner. **LC** BX801; .N44. **DD** 282/.773/05. **Bk Rev**, (Qty: 12). **Ad Acc, Adv Mgr:** Joyce Peterson. **Circ:** 32,500 (ctrl). available on microfilm. ***Continues*** *Chicago Catholic, 0149-970X.*
**Desc:** Articles of interest to Roman Catholics in the Cook and Lake counties of Illinois.

CN/0227-6291
**NEWSLETTER / FEDERATION OF CATHOLIC PARENT-TEACHER ASSOCIATIONS OF ONTARIO.** **See** Education.

CN/0227-0021
**NOEUD.** (LE NOEUD : LAMORANDIERE SIC & LAC CASTAGNIER.). [Noeud]. Periodical. French. mo. Free. Le Noeud, c/o RR No 1, Rochebeaucourt Quebec J0Y 2J0 Canada. **DD** 282/.71413. ctrl circ.

UK/0307-4455
**NORTHERN CATHOLIC HISTORY.** Spring 1975-. Periodical. English. an. £4.00 UK; £5.00 other. North East Catholic History Society, 21 Larchwood Avenue, Wideopen, Newcastle Tyne NE13 6PY UK. **Tel** 091 236 6043. **ED** Rubin Martin Gard. **LC** BX1491.A1; N67. **DD** 282./.428. **Bk Rev. Circ:** 400 (ctrl).
**Desc:** Contains articles on the history of the Roman Catholic Church in Northeast England from the earliest times to the present century.

CN/0229-110X
**NOS ECOLES (OTTAWA).** (NOS ECOLES / LE CONSEIL DES ECOLES SEPAREES CATHOLIQUES D'OTTAWA.). Vol. 1, No. 1 (June 1974)-. Periodical. French. Conseil des Ecoles Separes Catholique d'Ottawa, 140 rue Cumberland, Ottawa Ontario K1N 7G9 Canada. **DD** 371.97/114/07138405.

VC/0029-4306
**NOTITIAE.** [Notitiae]. Vol. 1, (1965)-. Periodical. Latin (French, German, Italian and Spanish; summaries and/or abstracts in English). Twelve times a year. $45.00. Liberia Editrice Vaticana, Citta del Vaticano, 00120 Vatican City. **Tel** 011 39 6 69883529, telex 2024 DIRGENTEL VA. Index available in last issue of volume--attached.
**Ind/Abst** Bibliogr. Mission.; Canon Law Abstr.; Abr. Cathol. Period. Lit. Index; Cathol. Period. Lit. Index.

CN/0700-6500
**NOTRE-DAME DU CAP.** **Added/Corp** Oblates of Mary Immaculate. **VFOAT** Annales de Notre-Dame du Cap. (Jan. 1945)-. French. Ten times a year (Except for Feb. & Aug.). 8.00Can$ Canada; 10.00Can$ US; 11.50Can$ other. Revue Notre Dame du Cap, 626 Rue Notre Dame, Cap D Madeleine G8T 4G9 Canada. **Tel** (819)374-2441, FAX (819)374-2441. **Bk Rev**, (Qty: 9). **Ad Acc. Circ:** 95,000. ***Supersedes*** *Annales de Notre-Dame du Cap, 0700-6497.*
**Desc:** This report is with interviews features, spirituality, and news reflection within the church.

US
**NOTRE DAME STUDIES IN AMERICAN CATHOLICISM.** **VFOAT** Studies in American Catholicism. (1979)-. Monographic series. English. ir. Price varies per volume. University of Notre Dame Press, PO Box 635, South Bend IN 46624. **Tel** (219)239-6349, (800)677-3232, FAX (219)239-8148.

CN/0029-4578
**NOTRES.** (LES NOTRES.). **Added/Corp** Montfortains. Filles de la sagesse. No. 5 (Feb. 1962)-. Periodical. French. qt. Procure des Missions, 665 Church Street, Dorval Lachine Quebec Canada. ***Continues*** *Montfortains. Bulletin Missionnaire Montfortain., 0383-2716.*

BE/0378-2735
**NOUVELLES - CICIAMS.** (NOUVELLES - COMITE INTERNATIONAL CATHOLIQUE DES INFIRMIERES ET ASSISTANTES MEDICO-SOCIALES. NEWS - INTERNATIONAL COMMITTEE OF CATHOLIC NURSES AND MEDICO-SOCIAL WORKERS.). [Nouv. - CICIAMS]. **Added/Corp** International Committee of Catholic Nurses and Medico-Social Workers. **VFOAT** News - International Committee of Catholic Nurses and Medico-Social Workers. (1975)-. Periodical. Multiple languages (English and French). qt. **NLM** W1 NO836. ***Formed by the union of*** *C.I.C.I.A.M.S. Nouvelles* ***and*** *C.I.C.I.A.M.S. News, 0007-8417.*
**Ind/Abst** Int. Nurs. Index.

US/1047-2398
**NOVA (BROOKFIELD, WIS.).** (NOVA.). (19??)-. Periodical. English. bm (6 issues). $56.00. Liturgical Publications Inc, 2875 South James Drive, New Berlin WI 53151. **Tel** (414)785-1188, (800)876-4574. **ED** Rev. Albert J Nevins (editor's address: PO Box 19113, Tampa, FL 33686). **DD** 251. **Circ:** 1,500. ***Continues*** *Nova Et Vetera.*
**Desc:** A Roman Catholic homily resource which includes "Voice of Ministry," a scripture commentary for lectors, homilies, ministerial reflections and "Rejoice Today" art for religious and educational bulletins.

IT
**NOVARIEN.** **Added/Corp** Associazione di Storia Ecclesiale Novarese. (1967)-. Periodical. Italian. an (Feb. or Mar). Free. Association Storia Chiesa Novarese, Archiv Diocesano Pal Vescovile, 28100 Novaro Italy. **Tel** 011 39 321 393031.
**Ind/Abst** BHA : Biblio. Hist. Art.

VC
**NUNTIA.** ***Ceased.*** (1975)-Issue 31 (Dec. 1989). Periodical. Latin. sa. Liberia Editrice Vaticana, Citta del Vaticano, 00120 Vatican City. **Tel** 011 39 6 69883529, telex 2024 DIRGENTEL VA.
**Ind/Abst** Bibliogr. Mission. (?-?); Canon Law Abstr.

US/0029-7739
**OBSERVER (ROCKFORD), THE.** (THE OBSERVER.). **Added/Corp** Catholic Church. Diocese of Rockford. (19??)-. Periodical. English. sm. $16.00. Observer, 921 West State Street, Rockford IL 61102. **Tel** (815)-963-3471, FAX (815)968-2808. **ED** Owen Phelps Jr. **Bk Rev**, (Qty: 6). **Ad Acc, Adv Mgr Tel** (815)963-3471. **Circ:** 30,000. available on microfilm from the publisher.
**Desc:** Religious non-profit printing world, national, local news of interest to the Catholics.

US/1059-3144
**ODAN NEWSLETTER.** [ODAN newsl.]. **Added/Corp** Opus Dei Awareness Network. **VFOAT** Opus Dei Awareness Network Newsletter. Vol. 1, No. 11 [i.e. 1] (Nov. 1991)-. Newsletter. English. mo. $15.00. Opus Dei Awareness Network, PO Box 4333, Pittsfield MA 01202. **DD** 282.

CN/1181-9219
**ORATOR (OTTAWA).** (THE ORATOR.). [Orator]. **Added/Corp** Saint Brigid's Association. Vol. 1, No. 1 (July/Aug. 1990)-. Periodical. English. bm. Free to members (membership $12.00 per year). Saint Brigid's Association, PO Box 71022, Ottawa, Ontario K2P 2L9 Canada. **DD** 282/.71384/05.

BL
**ORDEM, A.** **Added/Corp** Centro Dom Vital. (1921)-. Periodical. Portuguese. Three times a year. **LC** BX805; .O7.

CN/0708-711X
**ORDO (1977).** (ORDO.). **Main/Corp** Catholic Church. Canadian Conference of Catholic Bishops. National Liturgical Office. **VFOAT** Notes Pastorales, Calendrier pour l'Annee Liturgique. (1977)-. French. an. $5.50. Office National de Liturgie, Conference des Eveques Catholiques du Canada, 90 Av Parent, Ottawa Ontario K1N 7B1 Canada. **Tel** (613)236-9461, FAX (613)236-8117. **DD** 264/.021. **Circ:** 9,000. ***Continues*** *Canadian Catholic Conference. National Liturgical Office. Notes Pastorales, Calendrier Liturgique, Supplements Diocesains., 0317-722X.*
**Desc:** Guidelines for pastoral liturgy, liturgical calendar tool for preparing and celebrating liturgy.
**Ind/Abst** Leis. Recreat. Tour. Abstr.; World Agric. Econ.

US/0093-609X
**ORIGINS (WASHINGTON).** (ORIGINS.). [Origins]. Vol. 1, (May 24, 1971)-. Periodical. English. Forty-eight times a year (Every other Fridays (except July/Aug)). $97.00 US; $123.00 Canada & Mexico; $134.00 Pacific Islands; $146.00 Europe & South America; $159.00 other. Catholic News Service, 3211 4th Street Northeast, Washington DC 20017. **Tel** (202)541-3289, (202)541-3250, FAX (202)541-3255, telex 892589. **ED** David Gibson, (phone: (202)541-3284). **LC** BX801; .O7. **DD** 282/.73. Index available (Bound in next iss.). cum. index (20 yr. index at $12.95). **Circ:** 8,000. available on an online database from NEWSNET.
**Desc:** Covers priesthood, laity, church and public affairs, religious life, pope's travels, US bishops, court decisions, spirituality, pastoral planning, parish life, legislation and more.
**Ind/Abst** Seventh-Day Adventist Period. Index (19??-); Abr. Cathol. Period. Lit. Index; Cathol. Period. Lit. Index.

CN/0823-7069
**OUR DIOCESE (GRAND FALLS).** (OUR DIOCESE.). [Our dioc.]. V. 1, No. 1 (Oct. 1982)-. Periodical. English. bm. Free to members. Our Diocese, c/o V Blackmore, Chancery Office, PO Box 397, Grand Falls Newfoundland A2A 2J8 Canada. **DD** 282/.718/05.

CN/0229-1096
**OUR SCHOOLS (OTTAWA).** (OUR SCHOOLS / THE OTTAWA ROMAN CATHOLIC SEPARATE SCHOOL BOARD.). Periodical. English. Ottawa Roman Catholic Separate School Board, 140 Cumberland Street, Ottawa Ontario K1N 7G9 Canada. **DD** 377/.8271384.

US/0030-6967
**OUR SUNDAY VISITOR.** [Our Sunday visit.]. (1912)-. Periodical. English. Fifty-two times a year. $36.00 US; $48.00 other. Our Sunday Visitor Inc., 200 Noll Plaza, Box 920, Huntington IN 46750. **Tel** (219)356-8400, (800)348-2440, FAX (219)356-8472. **ED** Robert P. Lockwood and Greg Erlandson. **Bk Rev. Ad Acc. Circ:** 180,000. available on microfilm.
**Desc:** Spiritual guidance and news reporting for Catholics. Pinpoints Catholic perspective on world events. Explains precepts of Catholic Faith.
**Ind/Abst** Abr. Cathol. Period. Lit. Index; Cathol. Period. Lit. Index.

US/1057-929X
**OUR SUNDAY VISITOR'S CATHOLIC HERITAGE.** [Our Sunday Visit. Cathol. herit.]. **VFOAT** Catholic Heritage. Vol. 1, No. 1 (Sept./Oct. 1991)-. Periodical. English. Six times a year. $15.00 US; $17.00 other. Our Sunday Visitor Inc., 200 Noll Plaza, Box 920, Huntington IN 46750. **Tel** (219)356-8400, (800)348-2440, FAX (219)356-8472. **DD** 282.

US/0030-7564
**OVERVIEW. Added/Corp** Thomas More Association. (Oct. 1966)-. Periodical. English. Eleven times a year. $15.95 US and Canada. Thomas More Association, 205 West Monroe Street/6th Floor, Chicago IL 60606. **Tel** (312)609-8880, (800)835-8965, FAX (312)609-8891. **ED** Sara Miller. **Circ:** 4,000 (ctrl).
**Desc:** A continuing survey of issues, events, trends and opinions affecting Catholics, as reported in journals and newspapers from around the world.

FR/0299-6898
**PANORAMA PARIS. 1986.** [Panorama Paris, 1986]. (1986)-. Periodical. French. mo. $60.00. Bayard Presse, Svc Client, 3 rue Bayard/Dept 2, 75393 Paris Cedex 08 France. **Tel** 011 33 1 44356060, 011 33 1 44356262. **UDC** 070.482(44). ***Continues** Panorama Aujourd'hui (Paris), 0048-2838.*

GW
**PAPSTE UND PAPSTTUM.** Bd. 1- 1971-. Periodical. German. ir. Anton Hiersemann Verlag, Rosenbergstrasse 113, D 70193 Stuttgart Germany. **Tel** 011 49 711 638264 5.

US
**PASAULIO LIETUVIU KATALIKU ZINYNAS. VFOAT** World Lithuanian Roman Catholic Directory. Multiple languages (English and Lithuanian). 213 South 4th Street, Brooklyn NY 11211. **LC** BX845; .P37. **DD** 282/.025/73.

AT
**PASTORAL HORIZONS. *Ceased.*** (19??)-(Nov. 1994). English. Four times a year. Catholic Research Office, Pastoral Planning, 390 Albert Street, East Melbourne 3002 Australia. **Tel** 011 61 3 6670370, FAX 011 61 3 6670317. **ED** R. Dixon. **Bk Rev**, (Qty: 1-2). ctrl circ.

CN/0383-2236
**PASTORALE-QUEBEC.** V. 83- Jan. 14, 1971-. Periodical. French. ir. $15.48. Romain de Quebec, 1073 Ouest Boulevard Saint Cyrille, Sillery Quebec G1S 4R5 Canada. **Tel** (418)688-1211. ***Continues** Eglise de Quebec.*

US/0895-8165
**PENINSULA HERITAGE.** [Penins. herit.]. **Added/Corp** Upper Peninsula Catholic Historical Association. Vol. 1, No. 1 (Winter 1987)-. Periodical. English. qt. $6.00 (one year), $10.00 (two year) individuals. Upper Peninsula Catholic Historical Association, PO Box 1145, Marquette MI 49855. **ED** Regis Walling. **DD** 280. **Bk Rev. Ad Acc. Circ:** 225 (ctrl).

FR/0031-4781
**PENSEE CATHOLIQUE, LA.** (1946)-. Periodical. French. bm. 500.00F. Pensee Catholique, BP 39, F 92370 Chaville, Paris France. **LC** BX802; .P43. **DD** 282/.05. cum. index. **Bk Rev.**
**Desc:** History, theology, philosophy, literature, etc.
**Ind/Abst** Bibliogr. Mission.

US
**PEOPLE OF GOD/ SERVING THE MULTI-CULTURED PEOPLE OF THE ARCHDIOCESE OF SANTA FE.** English. Eleven times a year. $9.00. People of God, 1800 Martha NE, Albuquerque NM 87112. **Tel** (505)298-7557. **ED** Rev. Arthur J. Perrault.
**Desc:** Serves multi-cultural people of the Archdiocese of Sante Fe with religious articles of local, natural and international concerns.

IO
**PERABA.** Vol. 19, No. 15- June 1968-. Periodical. Multiple languages. ir. 150 per month. Yayasan Badan Penerbit Peraba, Bintaran Kidul 5, Jogjakarta Indonesia. **LC** BX1653.A1; P7. ***Continues** Praba.*

CN/1187-5429
**PERE MARIE-CLEMENT STAUB, A., SON EXEMPLE, SA PAROLE, SON OEUVRE.** [Pere Marie-Clement Staub A.A. ex. parole oeuvre]. **Added/Corp** Soeurs de Sainte-Jeanne d'Arc. Secretariat Pere Marie-Clement. Soeurs de Sainte-Jeanne d'Arc. No 1 (Oct. 1991)-. Periodical. French. sa. Free. Soeurs de Sainte-Jeanne D'Arc, Secretariat-Father Marie-Clement, 1505 de L'Assomption, Sillery Quebec G1S 4T3 Canada. **DD** 271. ***Continues** Echo de la Cause du Pere Marie-Clement., 1187-5410.*

CG
**PERSONNEL ECCLESIASTIQUE / ARCHDIOCESE DE KINSHASA. Main/Corp** Catholic Church. Archdiocese of Kinshasa (Zaire). French. Secretariat et Chancellerie Archidiocese de Kinshasa, BP 8431, Kinshasa 1 Zaire. **LC** BX1682.C6; C38A. **DD** 282/.675114/025.

UY
**PERSPECTIVAS DE DIALOGO.** Periodical. Spanish. $6.00. Centro Pedro Fabro, Cerrito 400, Montevideo Uruguay. **LC** BX805; .P47. **DD** 282/.05.

GW
**PERSPECTIVE (MUNCHEN).** (PERSPECTIVE; BULETINUL MISIUNII ROMANE UNITE DIN GERMANIA.). **Added/Corp** Misiunea Romana Unita din Germania. (July/Oct. 1978)-. Periodical. Romanian. Rumanisch-Katolische Mission in Deutschland, Kreittmayrstr 28, 8000 Munchen 2 Germany. **LC** Discard.

SP
**PHASE.** (1961)-. Periodical. Spanish. Six times a year. $35.00. Centre de Pastoral Liturgica, Rivadeneyra 6 7, 08002 Barcelona Spain. **Tel** 011 34 3 3022235. **LC** BX1970.A1; P43. Index available. **Bk Rev. Ad Acc. Circ:** 2,000.
**Desc:** All subjects related to the the liturgy of the Roman Catholic Church.

IT
**PICENUM SERAPHICUM.** Italian (Italian). 3.500. Biblioteca Francescana, Conto Corrente Postale 15/27009, 60015 Falconara Italy. **LC** BX3601; .P5.

CN/0226-3572
**PIERRES VIVANTES.** [Pierres vivantes]. April 1974-. French. an. Free. Comite des Fondateur de l'Eglise du Canada, Pierres Bibantes, 1085 rue de la Cathedrale, Montreal Quebec H3B 2V4 Canada. **DD** 261.7/0971. ctrl circ.

US/0032-4353
**POPE SPEAKS, THE.** [Pope speaks]. **Added/Corp** Catholic Church. Pope. Vol. 1, 1st Quarter (1954)-. Periodical. English. Six times a year. $18.00 US; $21.00 other. Our Sunday Visitor Inc., 200 Noll Plaza, Box 920, Huntington IN 46750. **Tel** (219)356-8400, (800)348-2440, FAX (219)356-8472. **ED** Albert J. Nevins and Phillip Carl. **LC** BX850; .P6. **DD** 282.05. Index available in last issue of volume--attached. cum. index (printed only in Spring issue). **Circ:** 9,000. available on microfilm and microfiche from University Microfilms International (UMI).
**Desc:** Journal of recent papal letters, addresses, and other major church documents.
**Ind/Abst** Abr. Cathol. Period. Lit. Index; Cathol. Period. Lit. Index.

UK
**POPE TEACHES, THE. Added/Corp** Catholic Truth Society (Great Britain). Vol. 1 (Oct./Dec. 1978)-. Periodical. English. mo. £6.00 UK; £16.00 other. Catholic Truth Society, PO Box 422, London SW1V 1PO England. **Tel** 011 441 834 4392, telex 295542 PAVIS G. **ED** David Murphy. **LC** BX801; .P77. Index available. cum. index. **Circ:** 3,000.
**Desc:** A selection from the homilies and addresses of the pope in new English translation. A compendium of spiritual insight, gospel teaching and social guidance.

CN/0701-0192
**POSOL. *Ceased.*** 1/2 (Jan./Feb. 1974)-(1992). Periodical. Slovak (English). mo. Posol, PO Box 600, 147 Elgin Street North, Cambridge Ontario N1R 5W3 Canada. **Tel** (519)621-7692. **ED** Rajmund Ondrus. **DD** 282/.71. **Circ:** 2,500.

US
**PRAY TOGETHER MISSALETTE.** Periodical. English. Five times a year. $12.50. Sunday Missal Service, 1012 Vermont Street, Quincy IL 62301. **Tel** (217)222-4030, FAX (217)222-6808. **Circ:** 252,000.
**Desc:** Missalette sent to Catholic churches throughout the country.

US/0747-5748
**PRAYER GROUP DIRECTORY.** Began publication in 1971. Directory. English. an. Charismatic Renewal Services, 237 North Michigan Street, South Bend IN 46601. **LC** BX2350.57; .P73. **DD** 248/.025/73.

US/0895-4968
**PRAYING (KANSAS CITY, MO.).** (PRAYING.). [Praying]. No. 1 (1984)-. Periodical. English. bm (6 issues). $18.00. National Catholic Reporter Publishing Company, PO Box 419281, 115 East Armour Boulevard, Kansas City MO 64141-6281. **Tel** (816)531-0538, (800)444-8910, (800)333-7373, FAX (816)531-7466. **(Subscription address:** Praying Magazine, PO Box 419335, Kansas City MO 64141.**) ED** Art Winter. **Circ:** 18,000.
**Desc:** Provides contemporary spirituality for daily living.

IT/0032-7727
**PRESENZA PASTORALE.** [Presenza past.]. (1968)-. Periodical. Italian. Ten times a year. L42000.00 Italy; L53000.00 other. Editrice A V E, Via Aurelia 481, 00165 Rome Italy. **Tel** 011 39 6 6633041, FAX 011 39 6 6620207. **UDC** 2. ***Continues** Assistente Ecclesiastico.*

FR
**PRETRES DIOCESAINS.** (19??)-. French. mo (June/July & Aug./Sept. issues combined). 230.00F France; 300.00F other. Pretres Diocesains, 179 Rue de Tolbiac, 75013 Paris France. **Tel** 011 33 1 45893253. **ED** Alexander Rouille.

US/0032-8200
**PRIEST, THE.** [Priest]. Vol. 1 (Jan. 1945)-. Periodical. English. Eleven times a year. $30.00 US; $35.00 other. Our Sunday Visitor Inc., 200 Noll Plaza, Box 920, Huntington IN 46750. **Tel** (219)356-8400, (800)348-2440, FAX (219)356-8472. **ED** Owen F. Campion. **LC** BX803; .P73. **DD** 250.5. Index available in last issue of volume--attached. cum. index. **Bk Rev. Ad Acc. Circ:** 12,000. available on microfilm and microfiche from University Microfilms International (UMI). ***Supersedes** Acolyte.*
**Desc:** Magazine written for and about the priesthood. Includes homily backgrounds, features, etc.
**Ind/Abst** Abr. Cathol. Period. Lit. Index; Cathol. Period. Lit. Index.

UK/0952-6390
**PRIESTS & PEOPLE.** [Priests people]. **VFOAT** Priests and People. Vol. 1, No. 1 (April 1987)-. Periodical. English. Eleven times a year. $37.00 (surface mail), $48.00 (airmail). Tablet Publishing Company, 48 Great Peter Street, London SW1P 2HB England. **Tel** 222-7462, FAX 222-4967. **ED** Bernard Bickers. **LC** BX801; .P87. **DD** 282/.05. Index available. **Bk Rev. Ad Acc. Circ:** 18,000. available on microfilm and microfiche from University Microfilms International (UMI). ***Continues** Clergy Review, 0009-8736.*
**Desc:** A ready source of information on theology, scripture, philosophy, history, law, psychology, sociology and pastoral studies.
**Ind/Abst** Canon Law Abstr.; New Testam. Abstr.; Abr. Cathol. Period. Lit. Index; Cathol. Period. Lit. Index.

BE/1012-4543
**PRO MUNDI VITA STUDIES. *Ceased.*** **Added/Corp** Pro Mundi Vita (Society). **VFOAT** PMV Studies; P.M.V. Studies. No. 1 (Jan. 1988)-(Dec. 1990). Monographic series. English. bm. Abdij Vant Park, Abdijdreef 7 A, 3030 Leuven Belgium. **Tel** 32 16 20 71 91. **LC** BX801; .P89. **DD** 282/.05. available on microfilm and microfiche from University Microfilms International (UMI). ***Formed by the union of** Pro Mundi Vita Dossiers. Africa Dossier, 0378-3413; Pro Mundi Vita Dossiers. Europe/North America Dossier, 0379-4113; Pro Mundi Vita Dossiers. Asia-Australasia Dossier, 0379-3427 **and** Bulletin (Pro Mundi Vita (Society)), 0378-3405.*
**Ind/Abst** Bibliogr. Mission.; Relig. Theol. Abstr.

US/0065-7638
**PROCEEDINGS OF THE AMERICAN CATHOLIC PHILOSOPHICAL ASSOCIATION.** **See** Philosophy.

US/0277-9889
**PROCEEDINGS OF THE ANNUAL CONVENTION - CANON LAW SOCIETY OF AMERICA.** (PROCEEDINGS OF THE ... ANNUAL CONVENTION.). [Proc. annu. conv. - Canon Law Soc. Am.]. **Main/Conf** Canon Law Society of America. Convention. (19??)-. Proceedings. English. an. $16.00. Canon Law Society of America, Catholic Universit, 431 Caldwell, Washington DC 20064. **Tel** (202)269-3491, FAX (202)319-5718. **LC** LAW. **DD** 262.9.
**Ind/Abst** Abr. Cathol. Period. Lit. Index; Cathol. Period. Lit. Index.

US/0739-6023
**PROGRESS (SEATTLE, WASH.), THE.** (THE PROGRESS.). **Added/Corp** Catholic Church. Archdiocese of Seattle (Wash.). (19??)-. Periodical. English. Forty-six times a year. $25.00. Catholic Archdiocese / Seattle Washington, 910 Marion Street, Seattle WA 98104. **Tel** (206)382-4850. **Bk Rev. Ad Acc. Circ:** 21,000. ***Continues** Catholic Northwest Progress.*

US/8750-5452
**PROVIDENCE VISITOR (1984), THE.** **See** Newspapers.

PL/0239-7471
**PRZEGLAD KATOLICKI. Added/Corp** Catholic Church. Archdiocese of Warsaw (Poland). (19??)-. Newspaper. Polish. Twenty-six times a year. $39.00. **(Subscription address:** ARS Polona, PO Box 1001, 00068 Warsaw Poland.**)**

PL
**PRZEWODNIK KATOLICKI.** (1895)-. Periodical. Polish. wk. $52.00. **(Subscription address:** ARS Polona, PO Box 1001, 00068 Warsaw Poland.) **LC** BX806.P6; P7.

US/1059-6801
**PUBLICATIONS IN PRINT (WASHINGTON, D.C.).** (PUBLICATIONS IN PRINT.). [Publ. print]. **Main/Corp** United States Catholic Conference. **Added/Corp** Catholic Church. National Conference of Catholic Bishops. Spring (1991)-. English. $2.95. United States Catholic Conference / Office for Publishing and Promotion Services, 3211 4th Street Northeast, Washington DC 20017-1194. **LC** BX1404; .P82. **DD** 016.

UK/0576-9515
**PUBLICATIONS. (MONOGRAPH SERIES).** **Main/Corp** Catholic Record Society, London. Vol. 1 (1968)-. Monographic series. English. ir (4 issues per year). Price varies per volume. Catholic Record Society, 12 Melbourne Place, Wolsingham Company, CO Durham DL13 3EH England. **ED** J A Williams. **DD** 282. **Circ:** 1,000.
**Desc:** Postreformation of English Catholic history.

IT
**QUADERNI PER LA SCUOLA CATTOLICA.** **Added/Corp** Federazione Istituti Dipendenti dalla Autorita Ecclesiastica. **VFOAT** Problemi della Scuola Cattolica. Monographic series. Italian. Price varies per volume. **LC** WMLC 91/260.

FR
**QUATRE FLEUVES, LES.** ***Suspended.*** Vol. 1-Suspended. Monographic series. French. sa. Price varies per volume. Beauchesne Editeur, 72 rue des Saints Peres, 75007 Paris France. **Tel** 011 33 1 45488028.
**Desc:** Journal of religious research and reflection.
**Ind/Abst** Bibliogr. Mission.

CN/0035-3795
**R N D REVUE NOTRE DAME.** [R N D, Rev. Notre Dame]. **Added/Corp** Missionaries of the Sacred Heart. (1970)-. Periodical. French. Eleven times a year. 10.00Can$ one year, 18.00Can$ two year. Revue Notre Dame, 2215 Marie-Victorin, Sillery Quebec, G1T 1J6 Canada. **Tel** (418)681-3581 (French only), FAX (418)681-1139. **ED** Yvon Labbe. **DD** 248/.05. **Circ:** 150,000. ***Supersedes*** *R N D Revue Notre-Dame du Sacre-Coeur, 0382-6961.*
**Desc:** A Catholic magazine for social and religious formation.
**Ind/Abst** Point Repere (1983-).

IE/0034-0960
**REALITY DUBLIN.** (REALITY.). [Reality Dublin]. (1966)-. Periodical. English. mo. 11.50p Ireland and UK; 9.25p other. Redemptorist Publ, 75 Orwell Road, Rathgar, Dublin 6 Ireland. **Tel** 01 961488 OR 961688. **DD** 282. ***Continues*** *The Redemptorist Record, 0791-153X.*

BL/0101-8434
**REB. REVISTA ECLESIASTICA BRASILEIRA.** (REVISTA ECLESIASTICA BRASILEIRA.). [REB, Rev. ecles. bras.]. **VFOAT** REB. Vol. 1 (1941)-. Periodical. Portuguese. qt. $80.00. Editora Vozes Ltda, R Frei Luis, 100 CP 90023, 25689 Petropolis RJ Brazil. **Tel** 11 55 242 435112. **LC** BX805; .R37. **DD** 282.05. cum. index. **Bk Rev. Circ:** 2,500.
**Desc:** Catholic theology, pastoral work in a country where the majority of population is Christian but oppressed by poverty.
**Ind/Abst** Bibliogr. Mission.; New Testam. Abstr.; Old Testam. Abstr.; Abr. Cathol. Period. Lit. Index; Cathol. Period. Lit. Index.

FR
**RECHERCHES ACTUELLES - INSTITUT CATHOLIQUE DE PARIS.** **Main/Corp** Institut Catholique de Paris. 1-. French. Beauchesne Editeur, 72 rue des Saints Peres, 75007 Paris France. **Tel** 011 33 1 45488028. **LC** BR45; .P29A. **DD** 230/.08 S.

US/0002-7790
**RECORDS OF THE AMERICAN CATHOLIC HISTORICAL SOCIETY OF PHILADELPHIA.** [Rec. Am. Cathol. Hist. Soc. Phila.]. Vol. 1 (1886)-. Periodical. English. qt (Mar., June, Sep., Dec.). $15.00 US; $16.00 Canada; $16.50 other. American Catholic Historical Society of Philadelphia, 263 South 4th Street, PO Box 84, Philadelphia PA 19106. **Tel** (215)925-5752. **ED** Thomas R Greene (editor's address: History Dept, Villanova University, Villanova, PA 19085). **LC** E184.C3; A4. Index available in last issue of volume--attached. **Bk Rev. Ad Acc, Adv Mgr:** Dr Greene, **Tel** (215)645-4677. **Circ:** 1,000. ***Absorbed*** *American Catholic Historical Researches.*
**Desc:** Founded for the purpose of collecting and preserving materials relating to American history and the contributions of Catholics to the building of the Americas, as well as the Catholic church in the United States.
**Ind/Abst** Am. Hist. Life (1954-); Abr. Cathol. Period. Lit. Index; Cathol. Period. Lit. Index.

FR
**RECUEIL DES HISTORIENS DE LA FRANCE. POUILLES.** **Main/Corp** Academie des Inscriptions et Belles-Lettres, Paris. (1904)-. French. ir. Price varies per volume. Diffusion de Boccard, 11 rue de Medicis, 75006 Paris France. **Tel** 011 33 1 43260037. **LC** BX1528.A1; A3.

GW/0080-0473
**REFORMATIONSGESCHICHTLICHE STUDIEN UND TEXTE.** No. 1 (1906)-. Monographic series. German. ir. Price varies per volume. Aschendorffsche Verlagsbuchhandlung, Postfach 1124, D-48135 Muenster Germany. **Tel** 011 49 251 690132, telex 08-92 830 WN MS D. **ED** Erwin Iserloh.
**Desc:** History of the reformation of the Roman Catholic Church, texts and research, monograph series, theologians and important personalities of that era, counter-reformation, state and church reform.

IT/0034-3498
**REGNO, IL.** **VFOAT** Regno, Documento; Regno, Attualita. (1941)-. Periodical. Italian. Twenty-four times a year. L56000.00 Italy; L83000.00 others. Centro Editoriale Dehoniano, Via Nosadella 6, Casella Postale 568, 40123 Bologna Italy. **Tel** 011 39 51 306811. **ED** Alfio Filippi. Index available. cum. index. **Circ:** 12,000 (ctrl).
**Desc:** Reports on current events worldwide in the life of the Roman Catholic Church.

US/0048-7155
**REIGN OF THE SACRED HEART.** Periodical. English. mo. Reign of the Sacred Heart, 6889 South Lovers Lane, Hales Corner WI 53130.

CN/0034-3781
**RELATIONS (MONTREAL).** ***Title Change.*** (RELATIONS.). [Relations]. Vol. 1, No. 1; Jan. 1941-. Periodical. French. Ten times a year (Jan./Feb. and July/Aug issues combined). Maison Bellarmin, 25 ouest, rue Jarry, Montreal, Quebec, H2P 1S6 Canada. **Tel** (514)387-2541. **LC** BX802; .R23. **DD** 282.05. available on microfilm and microfiche from University Microfilms International (UMI). ***Superseded by*** *Ordre Nouveau.*
**Ind/Abst** Can. Period. Index; Point Repere (1983-); Soc. Work Abstr. [Select. Cov.].

IT/0484-4823
**RERUM ECCLESIASTICARUM DOCUMENTA. SERIES MAIOR: FONTES.** **Added/Corp** Rome (City). Pontificio Ateneo di Sant'Anselmo. (1956)-. Latin. ir. Herder Editrice e Libreria SRL, Piazza Montecitorio 117-120, 00186 Rome Italy. **Tel** 011 39 6 679 4628, FAX 011 39 6 678 4751.

CN
**RESTORATION.** (19??)-. Periodical. English. Ten times a year. 6.00Can$. Restoration, Combermere Ontario KOJ 1LO Canada. **Tel** (613)756-3713. **ED** David May. **Circ:** 9,700. available in microform from University Microfilms International (UMI).

FR/0484-5854
**RESURRECTION PARIS.** (1956)-. Periodical. French. bm. 220.00F France; 260.00F other. Resurrection, 2 Place de Louvre, 75001 Paris France. **Tel** 011 33 1 42511702. **UDC** 23. **CODEN** 25. **Bk Rev. Circ:** 1,000.
**Desc:** All topics concerned with religious matters.

US/0034-639X
**REVIEW FOR RELIGIOUS.** [Rev. relig.]. **Added/Corp** Missouri Province Educational Institute. St. Louis University (Mo.). Dept. of Theology St. Mary's College, St. Marys, Kan. Vol. 1 (Jan. 1942)-. Periodical. English. bm. $20.00 (one year), $35.00 (two year) US; $24.00 (surface mail), $46.00 (two years), surface mail, $43.00 (airmail), $84.00 (airmail) other; $5.00 (single issue). Review for Religious, 3601 Lindell Boulevard, St Louis MO 63108-3393. **Tel** (314)535-3048. **LC** BX2400; .R4. **DD** 271.05. Index available in last issue of volume--attached. **Bk Rev. Circ:** 16,500 (ctrl). available on microfilm and microfiche from University Microfilms International (UMI).
**Desc:** Intended for Roman Catholic priests, brothers and sisters, it deals with their personal lives and vowed commitments.
**Ind/Abst** Bibliogr. Mission.; Book Rev. Index; New Testam. Abstr.; Abr. Cathol. Period. Lit. Index; Cathol. Period. Lit. Index.

SP
**REVISTA AGUSTINIANA.** (1980)-. Periodical. Spanish (French). Three times a year (Feb., June, Oct.). $50.00. Revista Agustiniana, Ramonet 3, 28033 Madrid Spain. **Tel** 011 34 1 3021115. **LC** BX805; .R34. **Circ:** 1,000. ***Continues*** *Revista Agustiniana de Espiritualidad.*

BL
**REVISTA BIBLICA BRASILEIRA.** Portuguese (summaries and/or abstracts in French, German and English). qt. $25.00. Revista Biblica Brasileira, Caixa Postal 1577, 60-001 Fortaleza Ceara Brazil. **Tel** 011 55 85 2281837.

SP/0034-8147
**REVISTA DE ESPIRITUALIDAD.** [Rev. espirit.]. **Added/Corp** Carmelites. No. 1 (Oct./Dec. 1941)-. Periodical. Spanish. Four times a year (Jan., Apr., June, Oct.). Revista de Espiritualidad, Triana 9, 28016-Madrid Spain. **Tel** 011 34 1 2591661. **LC** BX805; .R358. **Circ:** 1,000.
**Ind/Abst** New Testam. Abstr.

PE
**REVISTA DE INVESTIGACION.** **Main/Corp** Universidad Nacional de San Agustin. V. 1- Dec. 1970-. Spanish. Direccion Universitaria de Investigacion, Casilla 23, Arequipa Peru. **LC** AS88.U55; A34.

SP
**REVISTA DE PASTORAL JUVENIL.** Spanish. mo. 2.250ptas Spain; 4.800ptas other. Inst Calasanz de Ciencias Educ, Eraso 3, Madrid 28 Spain. **Tel** 91-2557200, FAX 91-3611052. Index available. **Circ:** 4,000 (ctrl).
**Desc:** Studies and activites about pastoral actions with youth and adolescents.

PE
**REVISTA TEOLOGICA LIMENSE.** **Added/Corp** Facultad de Teologia Pontificia y Civil de Lima. (19??)-. Periodical. Spanish. Three times a year. $20.00 Peru; $35.00 Latin America; $45.00 other. Revista Teologica Limense, Apartado 21-0135, Lima 21 Peru. **Tel** 011 51 14 636125, FAX 011 51 14 610245. **LC** BX1751.2; .R457. Index available. cum. index. **Bk Rev. Ad Acc, Adv Mgr:** P. Ulrich Berges. **Circ:** 1,000 (ctrl). ***Continues*** *Revista Teologica.*
**Desc:** Articles are always about theology with some articles on philosophy.
**Ind/Abst** Bibliogr. Mission.

CN/0226-5931
**REVUE A. C. C. S.** **See** Medical Science and Technology-Hospital Administration and Medical Centers.

FR/0300-9505
**REVUE D'HISTOIRE DE L'EGLISE DE FRANCE.** [Rev. hist. Eglise France]. Vol. 1- (No. 1- ); Jan. 1910-. French. sa. 285.00F (French), 1.725.00F (Belgian). Brepols Publishers, Steenweg OP Tielen 68, B-2300 Turnhout Belgium. **Tel** 011 32 14 402500. **ED** Marc Venard. **LC** BR840; .R46. **DD** 274.4. Index available. cum. index. ctrl circ.
**Desc:** History of church in France.
**Ind/Abst** Am. Hist. Life (1954-); BHA : Biblio. Hist. Art; Romant. Move.

FR
**REVUE DU ROSAIRE.** (19??)-. Periodical. French. Twelve times a year. 105.00F France; 130.00F other. Editions du CERF, BP 65, 77932 Perthes Cedex France. **Tel** 011 33 1 44181212.

FR/0035-3620
**REVUE MABILLON.** **See** Religion and Theology.

CN/0831-0777
**REVUE SAINTE ANNE, LA.** [Rev. Ste Anne.]. **VAT** Sainte Anne de Beaupre (1985). Vol. 113, No. 1 (Jan. 1985)-. Periodical. French. mo. 100.00Can$. Revue Sainte Anne, CP 1000, Ste-Anne-de-Beaupre, Quebec G0A 3C0 Canada. **DD** 282/.714/05. ***Continues*** *Sainte Anne de Beaupre, 0318-4366.*
**Ind/Abst** Bibliogr. Mission.

IT
**RICERCHE STORICHE SALESIANA / A CURA DELL'ISTITUTO STORICO SALESIANO.** Yearly V. 1, No. 1, (July/Dec. 1982)-. Periodical. Italian (Spanish, French, Portuguese and German). sa. L14000 (per issue) Italy; L25000 (per issue) US. Piazza dell'Ateneo Salesiano 1, 00139 Rome Italy. **LC** BX4045.A1; R52. **DD** 255/.79. Index available. **Bk Rev. Circ:** 700.
**Desc:** Review of religious and civil history; especially about St. John Bosco and the Salesian Congregation.
**Ind/Abst** Bibliogr. Mission.

IT/0394-3275
**RIVISTA CISTERCENSE.** [Riv. cistercen.]. **Added/Corp** Abbazia di Casamari. Vol. 1, No. 1 (Jan./Apr. 1984)-. Periodical. Italian. qt. ***Continues*** *Notizie Cistercensi, 0394-333X.*
**Ind/Abst** BHA : Biblio. Hist. Art.

IT/0035-6956
**RIVISTA LITURGICA.** (1914)-. Periodical. Italian. bm. L38000 (Italy); L50000 (other). Editrice Elle di Ci, Corso Francia 214, 10090 Rivoli Turin Italy. **Tel** 39 11 9591091, FAX (011)9574048. **Bk Rev. Circ:** 2,000.
**Desc:** Devoted to a bibliographical bulletin which is unique in Italy.
**Ind/Abst** Bibliogr. Mission.

US/0272-0418
**RSCJ: A JOURNAL OF REFLECTION.** [RSCJ: j. reflect.]. V. 1- Apr. 1979-. Periodical. English. sa. $3.00 US and Canada, $4.00 others. Sacred Heart Higher Education Association, Religious of the Scared Heart, 4535 Maryland Avenue, St. Louis MO 63108. **LC** BX4435; .R25. **DD** 255/.93/005.

US/0036-2255
**SACRED MUSIC.** [Sacred music]. **Added/Corp** Church Music Association of America. Vol. 92 (Spring

1965)-. Periodical. English. qt. $10.00. Church Music Association of America, 548 Lafond Avenue, Saint Paul MN 55103. **Tel** (612)293-1710. **ED** Richard J Schuler. Index available. **Bk Rev. Ad Acc. Circ:** 1,000. available on microfilm and microfiche from University Microfilms International (UMI). Documents available from The Genuine Article. ***Formed by the union of*** *Catholic Choirmaster, 0197-551X* ***and*** *Caecilia.*
**Desc:** Sacred music for the Catholic Church in accord with directives of the Vatican Council, in theory and practice.
**Ind/Abst** Arts Humanit. Citation Index [Full Cov.]; Curr. Contents Arts Humanit.; Music Artic. Guide; Music Index; Ref. Sources; Res. Alert [Full Cov.]; Abr. Cathol. Period. Lit. Index; Cathol. Period. Lit. Index.

KO
**SAEBYOK (CATHOLIC CHURCH. ARCHDIOCESE OF SEOUL (KOREA). HANGBOGUK).** (SAEBYOK ). Periodical. Korean. mo. Chonjugyo Soul Tae Kyogu Hongboguk, 1 2-Ka Myong-Dong Chung-ku, Seoul Korea. **LC** BX1670.7.S46; S23.

CN/0710-023X
**SALAM (MONTREAL).** (SALAM : BULLETIN MISSIONNAIRE DE SAINTE-CROIX.). Bulletin. French. qt. $1.00. Salam, 3800 rue Jean-Brillant, Montreal Quebec H3T 1P1 Canada. **Tel** (514)737-8332. **ED** Julien Heto. **DD** 266/.2/05. **Circ:** 2,500. ***Continues*** *Bulletin Missionnaire des Freres de Sainte-Croix.*
**Desc:** Informs readers of the work of our missionaries in various countries; serves as a link between missionaries and their relatives, friends and benefactors.

IT/0036-3502
**SALESIANUM.** [Salesianum] **Added/Corp** Pontificio Ateneo salesiano. Vol. 1 (1939)-. Periodical. Italian (German, French, English, Latin and Spanish; summaries and/or abstracts in English). qt. L50000.00 Italy; L60000.00 other. Editrice Las, Piazza dell Ateneo Salesiano 1, 00139 Rome Italy. **Tel** 011 872 90 626, FAX 06 872 90 629. **LC** BX800.A1; S34. Index available. cum. index. **Bk Rev. Pr Rev. Circ:** 750 (ctrl).
**Desc:** Covers humanities and canon law.
**Ind/Abst** Bibliogr. Mission.; Canon Law Abstr.; MLA Int. Bibl. Books Artic. Mod. Lang. Lit.; New Testam. Abstr.; Relig. Theol. Abstr.

SP/0036-3537
**SALMANTICENSIS.** [Salmanticensis]. **Added/Corp** Universidad Pontificia de Salamanca. Vol. 1 (Jan. 1954)-. Periodical. Spanish (Latin). ir. $45.00. Revista Univ Pontificia, Compania 1, Salamanca Spain. **ED** JRE Ramin Trevijuno. **Bk Rev. Circ:** 600.
**Ind/Abst** Am. Hist. Life (1966-1972); Bibliogr. Mission.; Index Book Rev. Relig.; Indice Hist. Esp. (1966-1972); New Testam. Abstr.; Relig. Index One Period.

US/1061-2165
**SANCTUARY (DENVER, COLO.).** (SANCTUARY.). [Sanctuary]. (Dec. 1, 1991)-. Periodical. English. wk. Sister Mary Paraclete Young, Lamb of God Sanctuary, 5243 Martin L King Boulevard, Denver CO 80207. **DD** 282.

IT/0036-9810
**SCUOLA CATTOLICA, LA.** [Sc. cattol.]. **Added/Corp** Seminario Arcivescovile di Milano. Milan. Pontificia Facolta Teologia. 4th Ser., Vol. 1 (Jan. 1902)-. Periodical. Italian. Five times a year. L50000 (Italy); L83000 (other). Editrice Ancora Milano, Via G B Niccolini 8, 20154 Milan Italy. **Tel** 39 2 3189941. **ED** Ed Ancora. Index available. cum. index. **Bk Rev. Ad Acc. Circ:** 1,000 (ctrl). ***Supersedes*** *Scuola Cattolica e la Scienza Italiana.*
**Ind/Abst** Bibliogr. Mission.; New Testam. Abstr.

FR/0751-6681
**SEDES SAPIENTIAE.** [Sedes sapientiae]. (1968)-. Periodical. French. qt. 150.00F. Societe Saint Thomas d'Acquin, Chemere Le Roi, 53340 Chemere Le Roi France. **Tel** 011 33 43906425. **UDC** 248.

VC/0582-6314
**SEMINARIUM.** [Seminarium]. **Added/Corp** Catholic Church. Congregatio Pro Institutione Catholica. Catholic Church. Congregatio de Seminariis et Studiorum Universitatibus. Pontificia Opera Delle Vocazioni Ecclesiastiche. Vol. 1, (1950)-. Periodical. Italian (German, Italian, Latin and Spanish; table of contents in English and Portuguese). Four times a year (Mar., June, Sept., Dec.). $40.00. Liberze Editrize Vaticana, Citta del Vaticano, 00120 Vatican City. **Tel** 011 39 6 69883529. Index available in last issue of volume--attached. **Bk Rev. Circ:** 950 (ctrl).
**Desc:** Provides ample religious material which serves for seminaries, universities and other ecclesiastical fields.
**Ind/Abst** Bibliogr. Mission.; Abr. Cathol. Period. Lit. Index; Cathol. Period. Lit. Index.

PY
**SENDERO : ORGANO DE LA CONFERENCIA EPISCOPAL PARAGUAYA.** **Added/Corp** Catholic Church. Conferencia Episcopal Paraguaya. (19??)-. Periodical. Spanish. wk. **LC** BX1482.A1; S46. **DD** 282/.892/05.
**Ind/Abst** Hum. Rights Intern. Rep.

BL
**SERVICO DE DOCUMENTACAO.** Portuguese. ir. Editora Vozes Ltda, R Frei Luis, 100 CP 90023, 25689 Petropolis RJ Brazil. **Tel** 11 55 242 435112. **LC** BX805; .S45.

US/0199-5049
**SHARE THE WORD.** **See** Religion and Theology-Bible.

FR/0338-2052
**SIGNES D'AUJOURD'HUI PARIS.** (1975)-. Periodical. French. Six times a year. 83.20F France. Bayard Presse, Svc Client, 3 rue Bayard/Dept 2, 75393 Paris Cedex 08 France. **Tel** 011 33 1 44356060, 011 33 1 44356262. **UDC** 282.

KO
**SINHAK CHONMANG.** **Added/Corp** Taegon Sinhak Taehak. Chonmang Pyonjipbu. **VFOAT** Theological Perspective. (19??)-. Periodical. Korean. qt. **LC** BX1751.2.A1; S53.

US/0037-590X
**SISTERS TODAY.** [Sisters today]. (19??)-. Periodical. English. bm. $19.00 (one year), $37.00 (two year) US; $21.00 (one year), $41.00 (two year) other. Liturgical Press, St. Johns Abbey, Collegeville MN 56321. **Tel** (612)363-2213, (800)858-5450, FAX (612)363-3299, (800)445-5899. **ED** Mary Anthony Wagner, Mary E Mason, Stefanie Weisgram, and M Audrey Synnott. **LC** BX4200; .S57. **DD** 255/.9/005. Index available. **Bk Rev. Ad Acc. Circ:** 6,200 (ctrl). available on microfilm and microfiche from University Microfilms International (UMI). ***Continues*** *Sponsa Regis.*
**Desc:** Seeks to explore the vision of women and the church in our time through essays, interviews, and poetry.
**Ind/Abst** Abr. Cathol. Period. Lit. Index; Cathol. Period. Lit. Index.

US/0897-8107
**SLOVAK CATHOLIC FALCON.** (SLOVAK CATHOLIC FALCON : OFFICIAL PUBLICATION OF THE SLOVAK CATHOLIC SOKOL / SLOVENSKY KATOLICKY SOKOL.). **Added/Corp** Slovak Catholic Sokol (U.S.). **VFOAT** Falcon. (198?)-. Periodical. English (Slovak). wk. $20.00. Slovak Catholic Sokol, 205 Madison Street, Passaic NJ 07055. **Tel** (201)777-4010, FAX (201)779-8245. **ED** Daniel F. Tanzone. **DD** 377. **Bk Rev. Circ:** 10,000. available with illustrations. ***Continues*** *Catholic Falcon, 0745-1571.*

US/0037-7767
**SOCIAL JUSTICE REVIEW.** [Soc. justice rev.]. **Added/Corp** Catholic Central Union of America. Vol. 33 (April 1940)-. Periodical. English (German). bm. $15.00 US; $18.00 (surface mail), $25.00 (airmail) other. Central Bureau Catholic Verein America, 3835 Westminster Place, St Louis MO 63108. **Tel** (314)371-1653. **ED** John H. Miller. **Bk Rev. Circ:** 3,000. available on microfilm from University Microfilms International (UMI). ***Continues*** *Central-Blatt and Social Justice.*
**Desc:** Primary aim is Catholic social action, stressing the Roman Catholic viewpoint in social, economic, religious, intellectual and political problems affecting contemporary society.
**Ind/Abst** Appl. Soc. Sci. Index Abstr.; Abr. Cathol. Period. Lit. Index; Cathol. Period. Lit. Index.

US/0038-187X
**SOUNDS OF TRUTH AND TRADITION.** **Added/Corp** Catholic Traditionalist Movement. (19??)-. Periodical. English. qt. Catholic Traditionalist Movement, East Pan Am Building, 200 Park Avenue/Suite 303, New York NY 10017. **LC** BX1752; .S66. **DD** 282/.05.

UK/0269-8390
**SOUTH WESTERN CATHOLIC HISTORY.** **VFOAT** Southwestern Catholic History. (1983)-. English. an.

US/0745-0257
**SOUTHERN CROSS (SAN DIEGO, CALIF.).** (SOUTHERN CROSS.). **Added/Corp** Catholic Church. Diocese of San Diego. (19??)-. Periodical. English (Spanish). Twenty-three times a year. $18.00. Southern Cross, PO Box 81869, San Diego CA 92138. **Tel** (619)490-8266. **ED** Lawrence Montali. **Bk Rev. Ad Acc. Circ:** 20,000 (ctrl).
**Desc:** A newspaper of the Roman Catholic Diocese of San Diego.

US/0038-7630
**SPIRITUAL LIFE (WASHINGTON).** (SPIRITUAL LIFE.). [Spirit. life]. **Added/Corp** Discalced Carmelites. Washington Province. (1955)-. Periodical. English. Four times a year (Mar., June, Sept., Dec.). $12.00 one year; $22.00 two years;. Spiritual Life, 2131 Lincoln Road Northeast, Washington DC 20002. **Tel** (800)832-8489 or (202)832-8489, FAX (202)832-8967. **ED** Steven Payne. **LC** BX2350.A1; S6. **DD** 248.05. Index available. **Bk Rev. Circ:** 18,000. available on microfilm and microfiche from University Microfilms International (UMI).
**Desc:** A Catholic publication of contemporary spirituality.
**Ind/Abst** Abr. Cathol. Period. Lit. Index; Cathol. Period. Lit. Index.

US/0162-6760
**SPIRITUALITY TODAY.** ***Ceased.*** [Spiritual. today]. Vol. 30 (Mar. 1978)-(1992). Periodical. English. qt. Spirituality Today, 1909 South Ashland Avenue, Chicago IL 60608. **Tel** (314)658-3873. **(Subscription address:** Aquinas Institute, 3642 Lindell Boulevard, St Louis, MO 63108-3396) **ED** Regina Siegfried. **LC** BX2350.A1; C7. **DD** 205. Index available. cum. index. **Bk Rev. Ad Acc. Circ:** 4,000. available on microfilm and microfiche from University Microfilms International (UMI). ***Continues*** *Cross and Crown, 0011-1910.*
**Desc:** A journal dedicated to a thoughtful but not academic exploration of contemporary spirituality. Ecumenical and international in scope and readership, we are interested in Third World concerns.
**Ind/Abst** Old Testam. Abstr.; Abr. Cathol. Period. Lit. Index; Cathol. Period. Lit. Index.

FR/0038-7665
**SPIRITUS.** (May 1959)-. Periodical. French. qt. 160.00F North America, Europe, Japan; 130.00F other. Revue Spiritus, 40 rue la Fontaine, 75781 Paris Cedex 16 France. **Tel** 011 33 1 42888264, FAX 011 33 1 42884175. cum. index. **Circ:** 2,000 (ctrl).
**Desc:** Tri-mester magazine of studies in experience and missionaries reflections in the Catholic Church.
**Ind/Abst** Bibliogr. Mission.; Missionalia.

US/0036-276X
**ST. ANTHONY MESSENGER.** (SAINT ANTHONY MESSENGER; A NATIONAL CATHOLIC FAMILY MAGAZINE.). [St. Anthony messenger]. **Added/Corp** Franciscan Friars of St. John Baptist Province. Vol. 1 (1892)-. Periodical. English. mo. $16.00 (one year), $31.00 (two year), $46.00 (three year). Saint Anthony Messenger, 1615 Republic Street, Cincinnati OH 45210. **Tel** (513)241-5615, (800)488-0488, FAX (513)241-0399. **ED** Norman Perry. **DD** 255. cum. index. **Circ:** 380,000. available on microfilm and microfiche from University Microfilms International (UMI).
**Desc:** A family oriented, general-interest Catholic magazine. Helps readers better understand the teachings of the gospel and Catholic church and how they apply to life.
**Ind/Abst** Abr. Cathol. Period. Lit. Index; Cathol. Period. Lit. Index.

US/0036-3022
**ST. LOUIS REVIEW.** **Added/Corp** Catholic Church. Archdiocese of St. Louis (Mo.). **VFOAT** Saint Louis Review. **VAT** Saint Louis Review. Vol. 17, No. 1 (Feb. 1, 1957)-. Newspaper. English. Fifty times a year (Except the week of Christmas & July 4th). $15.00. St Louis Review, 462 North Taylor Avenue, St Louis MO 63108. **Tel** (314)531-9700. **ED** Edward J. Sudekum. **Bk Rev. Ad Acc. Circ:** 96,500 (ctrl). ***Continues*** *St. Louis Register (St. Louis, Mo. : 1941).*
**Desc:** Catholic news, views and features of interest in the St. Louis area, nationally and internationally.

CG
**STATISTIQUES DE L'ENSEIGNEMENT PRIMAIRE ET SECONDAIRE.** **Main/Corp** Bureau de l'Enseignement National Catholique. French. Enseignement National Catholique, BP 3258, Kinshasa-Gombe Zaire. **LC** LC508.Z35; B8C. **DD** 377/.8/26751.

IT/0039-2901
**STUDI CATTOLICI.** **Added/Corp** Associazione Ricerche e Studi (Italy). (June 1957)-. Periodical. Italian. mo (10 issues). L70000.00. Edizioni Ares, Via a Stradivari 7, 20131 Milan Italy. **Tel** 011 39 2 29526156, FAX 011 39 2 29514202. **ED** Cesare Cavalleri. **LC** BX804; .S84. Index available. cum. index. **Bk Rev. Ad Acc. Pr Rev. Circ:** 20,000.
**Desc:** Topics include theology, literature, arts, sociology, philosophy, history, and actuality.

IT
**STUDI E RICERCHE FRANCESCANE.** (1972)-. Periodical. Italian. Four times a year. L45000.00 Italy; L55000.00 other. Studi e Ricerche Francescane, Piazza S Efra, P Vecchio 21, 80137 Naples Italy. **Tel** 011 39 81 444425.

IT/0039-3045
**STUDI STORICI DELL'ORDINE DEI SERVI DI MARIA.** **Added/Corp** Servites. Istituto Storico O.S.M. (19??)-. Periodical. English (Italian and Spanish). sa. $15.00. Viale Trenta Aprile 6, 00153 Rome Italy. **LC** BX4055.A1; S78. **DD** 271/.47/005. ***Continues*** *Studi Storici Sull'Ordine dei Servi di Maria.*
**Ind/Abst** Bibliogr. Mission.; BHA : Biblio. Hist. Art.

CN/0039-310X
**STUDIA CANONICA.** [Stud. canon.]. **Added/Corp** Universite Saint-Paul, Ottawa, Ont. Faculte de Droit Canonique. Vol. 1 (1967)-. Periodical. English (French). sa. 45.00Can$ Canada; $45.00 other. Saint Paul University, 223 Main Street, Ottawa Ontario K1S 1C4 Canada. **Tel** (613)236-1393 ext. 2294, FAX (613)782-3005. **ED** Francis G Morrisey, Michel Theriault and Jean Thorn. **LC** K23; .T83. **DD** 262.9/05. Index available. cum. index. **Bk Rev. Circ:** 1,300 (ctrl). available on microfilm from University Microfilms International (UMI).
**Desc:** Only one of the two canonical serials in North America, one of the few in the world. Bilingual

(English-French). Contains selected judgments from matrimonial courts.
**Ind/Abst** Bibliogr. Mission.; Canon Law Abstr.; Index Can. Leg. Period. Lit.; Abr. Cathol. Period. Lit. Index; Cathol. Period. Lit. Index.

IT
**STUDIA ET DOCUMENTA IURIS CANONICI.** 1 (1970)-. Monographic series. Italian. ir. Price varies per volume. Libreria Sole, Via dei Lucchesi 20, 00187 Rome Italy. **Tel** 011 39 6 6790675.

GW
**STUDIEN UND MITTEILUNGEN ZUR GESCHICHTE DES BENEDIKTINER-ORDENS UND SEINER ZWEIGE.** **Added/Corp** Bayerische Benediktinerakademie Munich. Vol. 1 (1880)-. Periodical. German. ir (4 per year, delivered twice a year). DM176.00. EOS Verlag, Erzabtei St Ottilien, D 86941 St Ottilien Germany. **Tel** 011 49 8193 71261, FAX 011 49 8193 6844. **ED** Aegidius Kolb. **Ad Acc. Circ:** 400 (ctrl).
**Ind/Abst** BHA : Biblio. Hist. Art.

US/0193-2748
**STUDIES IN FORMATIVE SPIRITUALITY.** ***Title Change.*** [Stud. form. spiritual.]. **Added/Corp** Duquesne University. Institute of Formative Spirituality. Vol. 1, No. 1 (Feb. 1980)-Vol. 14, No. 3 (Nov. 1993). Periodical. English. Three times a year. Institute of Formative Spirituality, 906 Rockwell Hall, Duquesne University, Pittsburgh PA 15282. **Tel** (412)396-6026. **ED** Helen Douglas. **LC** BX2350.2; .S74. **DD** 248. **Bk Rev**, (Qty: 3-5). **Circ:** 4,000. available on microfilm and microfiche from University Microfilms International (UMI). Documents available from UMI Article Clearinghouse. ***Continues*** *Humanitas, 0018-7496.* ***Continued by*** *Journal of Spiritual Formation.*
**Desc:** A discipline-related approach to the issues of formation and human experience designed to integrate the transcendent, functional, vital and socio-historical dimensions of life.
**Ind/Abst** Abstr. Res. Pastor. Care Couns. (19??-); Acad. Search (July 1993-); Except. Hum. Exp.; Expand. Acad. Index (1989-); Humanit. Index; Humanit. Source (Jul. 1993-); INFO-SOUTH Abstr.; Mag. Search; Newsp. Period. Abstr. (1991-); Philos. Index; Psychol. Abstr. (1983-); PsycINFO; PsycLit; Relig. Theol. Abstr.; Abr. Cathol. Period. Lit. Index; Cathol. Period. Lit. Index.

US
**STUDIES IN THE SPIRITUALITY OF JESUITS.** **Added/Corp** American Assistancy Seminar on Jesuit Spirituality. Vol. 1, No. 1 Sept. (1969)-. Periodical. English. Five times a year (Jan., March, May, September, Nov.). $12.00 (US); $17.00 (other). The Seminar on Jesuit Spirituality, 3700 West Pine Boulevard, St Louis MO 63108. **Tel** (314)652-5737. **(Subscription address:** PO Box 14561, St Louis, MO 63178**) ED** John W. Padberg. cum. index. **Circ:** 7,500 (ctrl).
**Desc:** Published especially but not exclusively for Jesuits.

BE
**SUBSIDIA HAGIOGRAPHICA.** **Added/Corp** Bollandists. (1886)-. Monographic series. French (English, Italian and German). ir. Price varies per volume. Societe des Bollandistes, 24 Boulevard Saint-Michel, B-1040 Bruxelles Belgium. **Tel** 011 32 2 7393338, FAX 011 32 2 7393338. Index available. **Circ:** 600.

US
**SUNDAY HOMILY HELPS.** English. mo. $30.00. Saint Anthony Messenger, 1615 Republic Street, Cincinnati OH 45210. **Tel** (513)241-5615, (800)488-0488, FAX (513)241-0399. ***Separated from*** *Homily Helps.*

CN/0820-9669
**SUPPLEMENT / DIOCESE DE SAINTE-ANNE-DE-LA-POCATIERE.** **Main/Corp** Eglise Catholique. Diocese de Sainte-Anne-de-la-Pocatiere. 1982/83-. French. an. Eveche de Sainte-Anne, C P 430 Canada, La Pocatiere Quebec G0R 1Z0 Canada. **DD** 282/.025/71475. ***Continues*** *Eglise Catholique. Diocese de Sainte-Anne-de-la-Pocatiere. Annexe a l'Annuaire Diocesain, 0820-9650.*

BE
**SYLLOGE EXCERPTORUM E DISSERTATIONIBUS AD GRADUM DOCTORIS IN SACRA THEOLOGIA VEL IN IURE CANONICO CONSEQUENDUM CONSCRIPTIS.** **Main/Corp** Louvain. Universite Catholique. Vol. 1- 1932/33-. Periodical. Multiple languages (Latin and French). University Catholique de Louvain, Faculte de Theologie, Grand Place 45, 1348 Louvain la Neuve Belgium. **LC** BX1751.A1; L6. **DD** 208.2.

US/0279-781X
**SYNTHESIS.** ***Ceased.*** Vol. 1, No. 1, March (1981)-Ceased Nov. (1991). Periodical. English. qt. Growth Associates / New Hampshire, PO Box 142, New Hampton NH 03256. **Tel** (800)637-9144, (508)779-6142. **ED** William V Coleman. **Bk Rev. Ad Acc. Circ:** 1,000 (ctrl).
**Desc:** Abstracts of current literature of interest to church leaders plus, weekly liturgy aids.

US/0039-8845
**TABLET, THE.** Periodical. English. wk. $20.00 (one year), $36.00 (two year), $50.00 (three year) US; $35.00 (one year), $66.00 (two year), $95.00 (three year) other. The Tablet Publishing Company, 653 Hicks Street, Brooklyn NY 11231. **Tel** (800)486-3838, (718)858-3838. **ED** Ed Wilkinson. **LC** BX801; .T3. **DD** 070.482. **Bk Rev. Ad Acc. Circ:** 93,000.
**Desc:** Catholic weekly newspaper.

GW/0492-1283
**TAG DES HERRN.** (19??)-. Periodical. German. Twenty-six times a year. LKG Leipziger Kommissions & Grossbuchhandel, Leninstrasse 16, Postfach 520, D 04005 Leipzig, Germany. **Tel** 011 49 341 71370. **Circ:** 100,000 (ctrl).
**Desc:** Bulletin of the Catholic Church in East Germany. Pastoral and cathecistic concepts and information concerning the World Church and the Catholic Church in East Germany.

US
**TALKS OF POPE JOHN PAUL II.** **Added/Corp** Pro Ecclesia Foundation. Vol. 14, No. 5 (Mar. 1979)-. Periodical. English. Twelve times a year. $25.00 (one year); $45.00 (two year) Only Available with Pro Ecclesia. Center for Catholic and Evangelical Theology, 5642 Endwood Trail, Northfield MN 55057. **ED** Timothy A. Mitchell. **Bk Rev. Ad Acc. Circ:** 1,500 (ctrl). ***Continues*** *Talks of the Pope.*
**Desc:** Reproduces talks of our Holy Father.

AU/1215-282X
**TAVLATOK.** **Added/Corp** Unio Cleri Hungarici. Tragerverein. (1991)-. Periodical. Hungarian. qt. **LC** BX880; .S94. ***Continues*** *Szolgalat.*

US/1041-1569
**TENNESSEE REGISTER, THE.** **See** Newspapers.

BL
**TEOCOMUNICACAO.** Portuguese. Diretorio Academico Instituto de Teologia, Caixa Postal 1429 Alegre Brazil. **LC** BX805; .T35. **DD** 301.5/8.

IT
**TEOLOGIA (BRESCIA, ITALY).** (TEOLOGIA.). Vol. 1, No. 1 (Jan. 1976)-. Periodical. Italian. qt. $48.00. Glossa Srl, Via Cavalieri S Sepolcro 3, 20121 Milan Italy. **Ad Acc, Adv Mgr:** Lovati Claudio. **Circ:** 1500.
**Ind/Abst** New Testam. Abstr.; Old Testam. Abstr.

IT
**TETTO, IL.** (1964)-. Periodical. Italian. Six times a year. L50000 (institution); L45000 (individual) Italy; L50000 (other). Il Tetto, Piazzetta Cariati 2, 80132 Naples Italy. **Tel** 11 39 81 414946. **LC** AP37; .T48. ***Supersedes in part*** *Quarta Generazione.*

CK
**THEOLOGICA XAVERIANA.** **Added/Corp** Pontificia Universidad Javeriana. Facultad de Theologia. (1975)-. Periodical. Spanish. qt (Mar., June, Sept., Dec.). $40.00. Universidad Javeriana, Apartado Aereo 54953, Bogota 2 Colombia. **Tel** 011-57-1-212-4846, FAX 310-5163. **ED** German Neira Fernandez, S.J. Index available. **Bk Rev. Ad Acc. Circ:** 600 (ctrl). ***Continues*** *Ecclesiastica Xaveriana.*
**Desc:** Doctrinal and practical theology in the Roman Catholic Church especially in Latin America; Biblical, pastoral and moral subjects.
**Ind/Abst** Bibliogr. Mission.; Canon Law Abstr.

AU/0040-5663
**THEOLOGISCH-PRAKTISCHE QUARTALSCHRIFT.** **Added/Corp** Philosophisch-Theologische Hochschule der Diozese Linz. Philosophisch-Theologische Diozesan-Lehranstalt. Bischofliche Philosophisch-Theologische Diozesan-Lehranstalt. (1848)-. Periodical. German. qt. DM58.00 Austria; DM66.00 (surface mail), DM81.00 (air mail) other. Verlag Friedrich Pustet, Gutenbergstrasse 8, D-93051 Regensburg. **Tel** 0941 9 20 22-0, FAX 0941 94 86 52, telex 6 56 72. **ED** Kath. Theol. Hochshule. **LC** BX803; .T47. Index available. cum. index. **Bk Rev. Ad Acc. Circ:** 2,500.
**Desc:** Gives information on the various topics of Roman Catholic theology for both students, ministers and others interested in theology.
**Ind/Abst** Canon Law Abstr.; New Testam. Abstr.

HK
**THEOLOGY ANNUAL.** **Added/Corp** Holy Spirit Seminary College. Theology Division. (197?)-. Periodical. Chinese (English). an. $5.00. Holy Spirit Seminary College, 6 Welfare Road Theology Division, Aberdeen Hong Kong. **Tel** 011 852 5 5530265, FAX 011 852 5 8732720. **ED** Sr. Maria Goretti LAU, SPB. **Circ:** 500.
**Desc:** Articles in English and Chinese in the general areas of Catholic Theology and philosophy, written by members of the faculty and students.
**Ind/Abst** Bibliogr. Mission.

US/0040-6791
**TIDINGS (LOS ANGELES).** (TIDINGS.). **Added/Corp** Catholic Church. Archdiocese of Los Angeles. (1???)-. Periodical. English. Fifty-two times a year. $16.24. Tidings Publishing Company, 1530 West 9th Street, Los Angeles CA 90015. **Tel** (310)251-3360. **ED** Al Antczak. **Bk Rev. Ad Acc. Circ:** 47,500.
**Desc:** Official publication of the Roman Catholic Archdiocese of Los Angeles.

AT
**TJURUNGA; AN AUSTRALASIAN BENEDICTINE REVIEW.** No. 1- Sept. 1971- . Periodical. English. sa. 12.00Aus$ Australia; 14.00Aus$ other. St Benedict's Monastery, Arcadia New South Wales 2159 Australia. **Tel** 02-653-1159. **ED** BR Terence Kavenagh. Index available. cum. index. **Bk Rev. Ad Acc. Circ:** 286.
**Desc:** Studies on the rule of St Benedict and its present relevance, on monastic spirituality and history in general.

US/0745-3612
**TODAY'S CATHOLIC (SAN ANTONIO, TEX.).** (TODAY'S CATHOLIC : OFFICIAL PUBLICATION OF THE ARCHDIOCESE OF SAN ANTONIO AND THE DIOCESE OF VICTORIA.). **Added/Corp** Catholic Church. Archdiocese of San Antonio (Tex.) Catholic Church. Diocese of Victoria (Texas). Vol. 83, No. 30 (Aug. 3, 1972)-. Newspaper. English (Spanish). Twenty-six times a year. $20.00. Today's Catholic, PO Box 28410, San Antonio TX 78228. **Tel** (512)734-2620. **ED** Martha Brinkmann. **Bk Rev. Ad Acc. Circ:** 23,000 (ctrl). available in microform. ***Continues*** *Alamo Messenger.*
**Desc:** For the catholics which offers information on all phases of life.

US/0199-8803
**TODAY'S MISSAL.** Periodical. English. bm. $1.98. Oregon Catholic Press, PO Box 18030, Portland OR 97218. **Tel** (503)281-1191. **ED** Randall DeBruyn.
**Desc:** Providing liturgy and music for Catholic worship, including 7 seasonal missals and a music issue/hymnal.

●BE/0778-8304
**TRAJECTA.** **Added/Corp** Redactie Trajecta vzw. (1992)-. Periodical. Dutch (summaries and/or abstracts in English and German). Four times a year. Fl80.00 Europe; Fl90.00 other. Trajecta vzm, Postbus 9100, 6500 HA Nijmegen, the Netherlands. **Tel** 011 31 80 612412. **LC** BX1549.A1; T73. ***Continues*** *Archief voor de Geschiedenis van de Katholieke Kerk in Nederland, 0003-8326.*
**Desc:** History of Catholic life in the Low Countries of Europe.
**Ind/Abst** Am. Hist. Life (1992-).

US
**TSERKOVNYI VISNYK / UKRAINSKA KATOLYTSKA PARAFIIA SVIATYKH VOLODYMYRA I OLHY V CHIKAGO.** V. 4, No. 57 (Jan. 24, 1971)-. Periodical. Ukrainian. bw. $7.00. Cerkovnyi Visnyk, 2247 West Chicago Avenue, Chicago IL 60622. **LC** BX4711.736.C5; S248. ***Continues*** *Visnyk Ukrainskoi Katolytskoi Parafii Sviatykh Volodymyra I Olhy V Chikago.*

US/0041-7548
**U.S. CATHOLIC.** [U.S. Cathol.]. **Added/Corp** Claretian Missionaries. (Jan. 1972)-. Periodical. English. mo. $18.00 (one year), $33.00 (two year), $45.00 (three year). Claretian Publications, 205 West Monroe Street, Chicago IL 60606. **Tel** (312)236-7782, (800)328-6515. **ED** Mark J. Brummel. **LC** BX801; .U44. **DD** 282/.73. **Bk Rev. Ad Acc. Circ:** 54,346 (ctrl). available on microfilm and microfiche from University Microfilms International (UMI). Documents available from UMI Article Clearinghouse. ***Continues*** *U.S. Catholic and Jubilee.*
**Desc:** A magazine of dialogue. Prefers to raise significant questions rather than supply easy answers. Explores issues affecting catholics and invites reader response. By reading the voices across America, subscribers feel a sense of unity as they integrate faith into their daily lives.
**Ind/Abst** Acad. Abstr. Full Text Elite (June 1984-); Acad. Abstr. (June 1984-); Acad. Search (June 1984-); Curr. Thoughts Trends; Gen. Period. Index (1985-); Guide Soc. Sci. Relig.; INFO-SOUTH Abstr.; Mag. Artic. Summar. Elite (June 1984-); Mag. Artic. Summar. Select (June 1984-); Mag. Artic. Summar. CD-ROM (June 1984-); Mag. Index Plus (1989-); Mag. Index. Sel. (1986-); Mag. Search; Newsp. Period. Abstr. (1988-); Read. Guide Abstr. Select Ed.; Read. Guide Period. Lit.; Abr. Cathol. Period. Lit. Index; Cathol. Period. Lit. Index; Mag. Index (1977-); Vocat. Search (June 1984-).

US/0735-8318
**U.S. CATHOLIC HISTORIAN.** **Added/Corp** United States Catholic Historical Society. **VFOAT** US Catholic Historian; United States Catholic Historian. Vol. 1, No. 1 (Fall 1980)-. Periodical. English. Four times a year. $40.00 US; $50.00 other. Our Sunday Visitor Inc., 200 Noll Plaza, Box 920, Huntington IN 46750. **Tel** (219)356-8400, (800)348-2440, FAX (219)356-8472. **LC** BX1404; .U23. **DD** 282/.0973.
**Ind/Abst** Am. Hist. Life (1986-); Abr. Cathol. Period. Lit. Index; Cathol. Period. Lit. Index.

US
**UNIREA. ALMANAC. CALENDARUL. UNIREA.** **Added/Corp** Association of Romanian Catholics of America. **VFOAT** Calendarul. Unirea. (19??)-. English (Romanian). Ten times a year. $10.00 US; $11.00 other. UNIREA / Association of Romanian Catholics, 1101 44th Street Northeast, Canton OH 44714. **Tel** (216)493-8056, (216)492-8413, FAX (216)493-8428. **ED** Rev. George D. Gage (editor's address: 7782 Glenwood Avenue, Boardman, OH 44512; phone: (216)726-8509). **LC** BX4711.41; .J48. **DD** 281/.5.

CN/0381-9876
**UNIVERS (LIMOILOU).** (UNIVERS.). **Added/Corp** Society for the Propagation of the Faith. **VFOAT** Cahier d'Animation Missionnaire. 48th Vol. (Jan./Feb. 1971)-. Periodical. French. bm (Feb., Apr., June, Oct., Dec.). 8.00Can$ (one year), 15.00Can$ (two year) Canada; 12.00Can$ other. Univers, 2269 Chemin Street, St Louis Quebec G1T IR5 Canada. **Tel** (418)687-9531, FAX (418)687-9051. **DD** 266/.2/05. ***Continues*** *Propagation de la Foi.*
**Desc:** Information concerning the missionary action of the Catholic Church in the world.

US/0731-4809
**UPDATE (WILMINGTON, N.C.).** (UPDATE.). [Update]. **VFOAT** Official Catholic Teachings; Official Catholic Teachings, Update. 1977-. English. an. McGrath Publishing Company, PO Box 9001, Wilmington NC 28402. **LC** BX850; .U63. **DD** 262.9/1. cum. index.
**Desc:** Each volume contains a cumulative subject index to the Official Catholic teachings series and to all Update volumes.

US/0747-1440
**UPPER PENINSULA CATHOLIC, THE.** (THE UPPER PENINSULA CATHOLIC : THE NEWSPAPER OF THE DIOCESE OF MARQUETTE.). **VFOAT** U.P. Catholic; UP Catholic. Periodical. English. bw. U P Catholic, PO Box 548, Marquette MI 49855.

US/8750-6238
**VALLEY CATHOLIC, THE.** (THE VALLEY CATHOLIC / DIOCESE OF SAN JOSE.). **Added/Corp** Catholic Church. Diocese of San Jose. (198?)-. Periodical. English. Eleven times a year. $15.00 Santa Clara; $16.00 other. VAlley Catholic, 900 LaFayette Street Suite 301, Santa Clara CA 95050. **Tel** (408)983-0260. **ED** Roberta Ward. **Bk Rev**, (Qty: 1). **Ad Acc**, **Adv Mgr:** M. Hawkins. **Circ:** 25,000 (ctrl).

SP/0042-3718
**VERDAD Y VIDA.** (VERDAD Y VIDA, REVISTA DE LAS CIENCIAS DEL ESPIRITU.). [Verdad vida]. **Added/Corp** Madrid. San Francisco el Grande (Church). (1943)-. Periodical. Spanish. qt. **LC** BX3601; .V4.
**Ind/Abst** Am. Hist. Life (1959-1960,1964); MLA Int. Bibl. Books Artic. Mod. Lang. Lit.

US/0042-4145
**VERMONT CATHOLIC TRIBUNE.** **VFOAT** Catholic Tribune. Periodical. English. ir. $7.00 US; $8.00 other. Vermont Catholic Tribune, 351 North Avenue, Burlington VT 05401.

GW
**VEROFFENTLICHUNGEN DER KOMMISSION FUER ZEITGESCHICHTE. REIHE B: FORSCHUNGEN.** **Main/Corp** Kommission fuer Zeitgeschichte. Vol. 18 (1975)-. Monographic series. German. ir. Price varies per volume. Matthias Grunewald Verlag Gmbh, Postfach 3080, D 55020 Mainz Germany. **Tel** 011 49 6131 839055. **Circ:** 1,500 (ctrl). ***Continues*** *Katholische Akademie in Bayern. Kommission fuer Zeitgeschichte. Veroffentlichungen. Reihe B: Forschungen.*
**Desc:** Historical analysis of the Catholic church in Germany in relation to German society and state from the 19th Century up to contemporary times, especially during Hitler's regime.

GW
**VEROFFENTLICHUNGEN DER KOMMISSION FUR ZEITGESCHICHTE. REIHE A : QUELLEN.** **Main/Corp** Kommission fur Zeitgeschichte. Vol. 18 (1975)-. Monographic series. German. ir. Price varies per volume. Matthias Grunewald Verlag Gmbh, Postfach 3080, D 55020 Mainz Germany. **Tel** 011 49 6131 839055. **Circ:** 1,500 (ctrl). ***Continues*** *Katholische Akademie in Bayern. Kommission fur Zeitgeschichte. Veroffentlichungen. Reihe A: Quellen.*
**Desc:** Documentation of the Catholic Church in Germany in relation to German society and state from the 19th Century up to contemporary times, especially during Hitler's regime.

CL
**VICARIA DE LA SOLIDARIDAD.** **Main/Corp** Catholic Church. Archdiocese of Santiago (Chile). Vicaria de la Solidaridad. Began with: Yearly V. (Jan. '77). Spanish. an. Plaza de Armas 444 Casilla 30 D, Santiago de Chile. **LC** HN39.C5; C33A. **DD** 261.8/3/098331. ctrl circ.

II/0970-1222
**VIDYAJYOTI (DELHI).** (VIDYAJYOTI.). [Vidyajyoti]. Vol. 39 (Jan. 1975)-. Periodical. English. mo. $18.00. Views, 4A Raj Nivas Marg, Delhi 110054 India. **Tel** 2524707. **ED** S Arokiasamy, T K John, P M Meagher, G Gispert-Sauch. **LC** BX801; .C58. **DD** 230/.2/05. **CODEN** PUZBAR. Index available. cum. index. **Bk Rev**. **Ad Acc**. **Circ:** 2,900. ***Continues*** *Clergy Monthly.*
**Desc:** Specially interested in Indian theology and church work in India and Asia, in dialogue with other religions and the meaning of mission today. Also concerned with social problems.
**Ind/Abst** Missionalia; New Testam. Abstr.; Old Testam. Abstr.

CN/0380-8254
**VIE LITURGIQUE.** **Added/Corp** Eglise Catholique. Archidiocese de Quebec. Commission de Liturgie. (1968)-. Periodical. French. ir (10 issues). 35.00Can$ Canada; 62.00Can$ other. La Revue Vie Liturgique Inc., 1073 Boul St Cyrille Ouest, Sillery Quebec G1S 4R5 Canada. **Tel** (418)688-1211. **DD** 264/.02/005.

CN/0318-9392
**VIE OBLATE.** **Added/Corp** Oblates of Mary Immaculate. St. Joseph's Province. **VFOAT** Oblate Life. Vol. 33, No. 1 (March 1974)-. French (English). Three times a year. 10.00F France; $7.97 US. Vie Oblate Life, 175 Main Street, Ottawa Ontario K1S 1C3 Canada. **Tel** (613)237-0580. **ED** Romuald Boucher. **DD** 255/.76/005. Index available (Free on request). cum. index. **Bk Rev**. **Circ:** 500 (ctrl). ***Continues*** *Etudes Oblates, 0318-9384.*
**Desc:** Mostly on oblate of Mary Immaculate (Order): founder, spirituality of the order, history of the order and their works in all parts of the world.

FR/0151-2323
**VIE PARIS. 1976, LA.** [Vie Paris, 1976]. (1976)-. Periodical. French. wk. 651.32F. Malesherbes Publications, 163 Boulevard Malesherbes, 75859 Paris France. **Tel** 011 33 1 48884600, FAX 011 33 1 48884601. **UDC** 08. ***Continues*** *La Vie Catholique, 0042-5354.*

HU/0042-6024
**VIGILIA.** Periodical. Hungarian (Hungarian). mo. $25.00 US. Uigilia Kiadohivatala, Budapest V, Kossuth Lojos U-1 1053 Hungary. **Tel** 177-246. **(Subscription address:** Kultura, PO Box 149, H-1389, Budapest 62 Hungary**) ED** laszlo lukacs. **LC** BX806.H8. cum. index. **Circ:** 11,000.
**Desc:** Periodical on Christian culture; deals with theology, the life of Christianity, primarily Catholicism, arts and literature. Publishes essays, short stories and poems.

US/0277-2205
**VINCENTIAN HERITAGE.** [Vincent. herit.]. **Added/Corp** Vincentian Studies Institute (U.S.) Vincentians. Daughters of Charity of St. Vincent de Paul. Vol. 1 (1980)-. Periodical. English. sa. $15.00 North America; $16.00 other. Vincentian Studies Institute, 1701 West St Joseph Street, Perryville MO 63775. **Tel** (314)547-6533, FAX (314)547-2204. **ED** Stafford Poole (editor's address: 641 West Adams Boulevard, Los Angeles CA 90007). **LC** BX3770.A1; V56. **DD** 255/.77/005. Index available. cum. index. **Pr Rev**. **Circ:** 1,050 (ctrl).
**Desc:** Dedicated to maintaining a living interest in the historical and spiritual heritage of the congregation of the mission and the company of the Daughters of Charity, both founded by Saint Vincent de Paul (1581-1660) and often called the Double Family.

US/0744-9178
**VISIONS (MORAINE, OHIO).** (VISIONS.). (19??)-. Periodical. English. wk. $22.00. Peter Li Education Group, 330 Progress Road, Dayton OH 45449. **Tel** (513)847-5900, (800)543-4383. **ED** Therese Sherlock and Joan Mitchell. **Circ:** 56,000.
**Desc:** Strives to help make the connection between the Sunday Gospel and everyday life for students.

US/0194-9160
**VISITANTE DOMINICAL, EL.** [Visit. dominic.]. Vol. 1 (1974)-. Newspaper. Spanish (Multiple languages). Fifteen times a year. $23.00 US; $24.50 other. El Visitante, PO Box 1130, San Antonio TX 78294. **Tel** (512)736-1685. **ED** Fernando Pinon (editor's phone: (210)736-1916). **DD** 205. **Bk Rev**. **Ad Acc**. **Circ:** 16,000. available on CD-ROM.

IT/0042-7365
**VITA SOCIALE.** (19??)-. Periodical. Italian. bm. L30000.00 Italy; L35000.00 other. Centro Riviste Provincia Romana, Piazza S Domenico 1, 51100 Pistoia Italy. **Tel** 011 39 573 28158, 25004. Index available. cum. index. **Bk Rev**. **Ad Acc**. **Circ:** 800.
**Desc:** Treats social problems in a theological interpretation.

CN/0715-8726
**VOX BENEDICTINA.** ***Title Change.*** [Vox benedict.]. Vol. 1, No. 1 (Jan. 1984)-(1994). Periodical. English. sasa. Dekalb College Social Sciences Dept., North Campus, 2101 Womack Road, Dunwoody GA 30338-4497. **Tel** (404)551-3234, FAX (404)604-3798. **ED** Deborah Vess. **LC** BX4275; .V6. **DD** 282/.088042. Index available (Each volume contains index for that year in the Dec. issue - $4.25). cum. index. **Bk Rev**, (Qty: 10). **Ad Acc**. **Pr Rev**. **Circ:** 400. ***Continued by*** *Magistra.*
**Desc:** Articles about and translations of the lives and writings of women whose lives have been informed by monastic spirituality.

US
**WEEKDAY HOMILY HELPS.** English. mo. $55.00. Saint Anthony Messenger, 1615 Republic Street, Cincinnati OH 45210. **Tel** (513)241-5615, (800)488-0488, FAX (513)241-0399. ***Separated from*** *Homily Helps.*

CN/0512-5235
**WESTERN CATHOLIC REPORTER.** Vol.1 (Sept. 9, 1965)-. English. wk. 20.56Can$ Canada; 50.00Can$ other. Western Catholic Reporter, 8421 100 1st Avenue, Edmonton Alberta T6A O1L Canada. **Tel** (403)465-8030. **ED** Glen Argan. **Bk Rev**. **Ad Acc**. **Circ:** 36,000. ***Supersedes*** *Western Catholic, 0384-7551.*
**Desc:** A newspaper dealing with what's going on in the Catholic Church everywhere, but principally in Alberta.

US/0742-4639
**WORD AMONG US, THE.** (198?)-. Periodical. English (Japanese, Spanish and Portuguese). Twelve times a year. 23.00Can$ Canada; $18.00 US; $28.00 other. The Word Among US, Box 6003, Gaithersburg MD 20884. **Tel** (301)990-2090, FAX (301)990-2087. **ED** Tony Bosnick. **LC** Discard. Index available (published separately). cum. index. **Bk Rev**. **Circ:** 200,000.
**Desc:** A practical guide to living the Christian life - designed to help Catholics draw closer to Jesus Christ through daily personal prayer and scripture reading.

US/0193-9211
**WORD AND SPIRIT.** [Word spirit]. **VFOAT** Word & Spirit. (1979)-. Periodical. English. an. Price varies. St Bedes Publications, PO Box 545, 545 North Main Street, Petersham MA 01366. **Tel** (508)724-3407. **ED** Mary Joseph. **LC** BX801; .W67. **DD** 282. **Circ:** 250. available on microfilm from University Microfilms International (UMI).
**Desc:** A monastic journal which deals with a different theme each year focusing on topics of monastic, theological, or spiritual interest or celebrating an anniversary of some (religious or church-oriented) historical event.
**Ind/Abst** Old Testam. Abstr.; Relig. Theol. Abstr.

US/0746-5580
**WYOMING CATHOLIC REGISTER, THE.** (19??)-. Periodical. English. mo. $7.50. Wyoming Catholic Register, Box 1308, Cheyenne WY 82003. **Tel** (307)638-1530, FAX (307)637-7936. **Bk Rev**. **Ad Acc**. **Pr Rev**. **Circ:** 16,000 (ctrl).
**Desc:** Catholic newspaper which reports and editorializes on news matters and issues concerning the Catholic church. It also defends and promotes the Catholic faith.

US/1064-8682
**YOU! (AGOURA HILLS, CALIF.).** (YOU! : VERITAS CATHOLIC YOUTH MAGAZINE.). [You!]. **Added/Corp** Veritas Communications. Vol. 91, No. 1 (Jan. 1991)-. Periodical. English. mo. $19.95 US; $25.95 other. Veritas Communication Inc, 29800 Agoura Road, Suite 102, Agoura Hills CA 91301. **Tel** (818)991-1813, FAX (818)991-2024. **ED** Paul Lauer. **DD** 248. **Bk Rev**. **Ad Acc**, **Adv Mgr:** Anita Birsa. **Circ:** 35,000 (ctrl). ***Continues*** *Veritas.*

US/1054-7126
**YOUTH MINISTRY QUARTERLY.** [Youth minist. q.]. Periodical. English. qt. $23.00. Youth Ministry Quarterly, RFD 1 Box 142, New Hampton NH 03256. **Tel** (603)744-6316, FAX (603)744-6318. ***Continues*** *Catholic Youth Ministry, 0277-8165.*

US
**YOUTH UPDATE.** English. mo. $12.00 US; $15.60 Canada, postage included; $18.00 other, postage included. Saint Anthony Messenger, 1615 Republic Street, Cincinnati OH 45210. **Tel** (513)241-5615, (800)488-0488, FAX (513)241-0399.

CN/0318-1642
**ZA RIDNU CERKVU.** (ZA RIDNU TSERKVU.). **VFOAT** Bulletin Za Ridnu Cerkwu. Vol. 1- July 1966-. Periodical. Ukrainian. $3.00. Bulletin Za Ridnu Cerkwu, PO Box 874 Terminal A, Toronto Ontario M5W 1G3 Canada. **DD** 282/.71.

AU/0044-2895
**ZEITSCHRIFT FUER KATHOLISCHE THEOLOGIE.** [Z. kathol. Theol.]. **Added/Corp** Universitaet Innsbruck. Theologische Fakultaet. Vol. 1 (1877)-. Periodical. German. qt (Feb., Apr., July, Nov.). S924.00. Verlag Herder Wien, Postfach 248 Wollezeile 33, A 1011 Vienna Austria. **Tel** 011 43 1 5121413. **ED** H.B. Meyer. **LC** BX803; .Z5. **DD** 230/.2/05. cum. index.
**Ind/Abst** Am. Hist. Life (1955-1959); Canon Law Abstr.; Index Book Rev. Relig.; New Testam. Abstr.; Old Testam. Abstr.; Relig. Index One Period.

AU
**ZEITZEICHEN ZEITUNG DER KATHOLISCHEN ARBEITERBEWEGUNG OESTERREICHS.** (19??)-. German. mo. S55.00 Austria; S70.00 Europe; S100.00 other. Katholischer Arbeiterverein, Postfach 977, Stephansplatz 6V34, A-1010 Vienna Austria.

CN/0820-6449
**ZUPNI VJESNIK NASE GOSPE KRALJICE HRVATA, TORONTO, HRVATSKIH MUCENIKA, MISSISSAUGA.** **VFOAT** Zupski Vjesnik. No. 33 (13 Edition 1978)-. Periodical. Serbo-Croatian (Roman) (English). wk. Free. Zupni Vjesnik, 7 Croatia Street, Toronto Ontario M6H 1K8 Canada. **Tel** (416)536-3669. **ED** Josip D Gjuran. **DD** 282/.05. **Ad Acc. Circ:** 2,000. ***Continues*** *Zupski Vjesnik Nase Gospe Kraljice Hrvata, Toronto, Hrvatskih Mucenika, 0820-6430.*
**Desc:** Journal of Catholic religion in Canada.

## EASTERN CHRISTIAN CHURCHES

RM
**BISERICA ORTODOXA ROMANA.** **Added/Corp** Institutul Biblic si de Misiune Ortodoxa Romanian Orthodox Eastern Church. **VFOAT** Eglise Orthodoxe Roumaine; Buletinul Oficial al Patriarhiei Romine. (18??)-. Periodical. Romanian. mo. DM104.00. **(Subscription address:** Kubon & Sagner, ABT Zeitschriftenimport, D 80328 Munich Germany.**)** **LC** BX690; .B5.
**Desc:** Publishes the correspondence of the Romanian Orthodox Church with other Orthodox churches, as well as information, studies, and instructions.
**Ind/Abst** BHA : Biblio. Hist. Art.

US/0893-7796
**CANADIAN ORTHODOX MISSIONARY, THE.** [Can. orthodox mission.]. July/Aug. 1986-. Periodical. English. bm. $10.00. Synaxis Press, PO Box 404, Chilliwack British Columbia V2P 6J7 Canada. **Tel** (604)858-7750. **DD** 281. ***Continues*** *Orthodoxy Canada, 0710-1635.*

US/0732-9245
**CAREE COMMUNICATOR.** **See** Religion and Theology-Protestantism.

II/0258-1744
**CHRISTIAN ORIENT.** [Christ. Orient]. **Added/Corp** St. Thomas Apostolic Seminary. Oriental Study Forum (Kottayam, India). Vol. 1, No. 1 (March 1980)-. Periodical. English. qt. $30.00. Christian Orient Trust, PB No 1 Vadavathoor, Kottayam Kerala 686010 India. **(Subscription address:** Prints India, 11 Darya Ganj, New Delhi, 110002 India, (Phone: 011 91 11 3268645)**)** **LC** BX4710.1; .C47. **DD** 281/.5.
**Ind/Abst** Index Book Rev. Relig.; Relig. Index One Period.; Relig. Theol. Abstr.

US/0273-3269
**COPTIC CHURCH REVIEW.** [Copt. Church rev.]. **Added/Corp** Society of Coptic Church Studies (N.J.). Vol. 1 (Spring 1980)-. Periodical. English. qt. $10.00 US. Society of Coptic Church Studies, PO Box 714, East Brunswick NJ 08816. **Tel** (717)273-9817. **ED** Dr. Rodolph Yanney. **LC** BX130; .C66. **DD** 281/.7. Index available (included in Dec. issue). cum. index. **Circ:** 1,000. available on microfilm from University Microfilms International (UMI).
**Desc:** Biblical studies with emphasis on spiritual exegesis, liturgical life of Church, lives and writings of the Church Fathers, ascetic and mystic spirituality.
**Ind/Abst** Index Book Rev. Relig.; Relig. Index One Period. (1980-); Relig. Theol. Abstr.

US/0012-1959
**DIAKONIA (BRONX, N.Y.).** (DIAKONIA.). [Diakonia]. **Added/Corp** University of Scranton, John XXIII Center for Eastern Christian Studies. Vol. 1, No. 1 (Jan. 1966)-. Periodical. English. Three times a year. $16.00 (1 year), $31.00 (2 year) US; $20.00 (1 year), $39.00 (2 year) other. Diakonia, University of Scranton, Scranton PA 18510. **Tel** (717)941-6141. **LC** WMLC L 83/3021. **DD** 280. available on microfilm and microfiche from University Microfilms International (UMI).
**Ind/Abst** Am. Bibliogr. Slavic East Europ. Stud.; Index Book Rev. Relig.; Relig. Index One Period.; Relig. Theol. Abstr.; Abr. Cathol. Period. Lit. Index; Cathol. Period. Lit. Index.

GR
**EKKLESIA KAI THEOLOGIA : EKKLESIASTIKE KAI THEOLOGIKE EPETERIS TES HIERAS ARCHIEPISKOPES THYATEIRON KAI MEGALES VRETANNIAS.** **Added/Corp** Hiera Archiepiskope Thyateiron kai Megales Vretannias. **VFOAT** Church and Theology. Vol. 1 (1980)-. Academic Scholarly Publication. Greek, Ancient (French, German and English). an. £50.00 UK; £80.00 others. Ekklesia kai Theologia, 9 R Ferraiou Str., Khalandni 15232, Athens Greece. **ED** Methodios Fouyas. **LC** BX200; .E37. Index available. cum. index. **Bk Rev. Ad Acc. Circ:** 1,000 (ctrl).
**Desc:** An academic theological review including scholarly articles, dissertations, reviews and other related material by Orthodox and non-Orthodox scholars from all over the world.

ET
**EKKLESIASTIKOS PHAROS.** **Added/Corp** Alexandria, Egypt (Patriarchate, Greek). Vol. 1 (1907)-. Periodical. Greek, Modern (English, French and German). qt. $20.00. Archbishop Methodos Fouyas, PO Box 571, Addis Ababa Ethiopia. cum. index.

SZ
**EPISKEPSIS (FRENCH ED.).** (EPISKEPSIS.). **Added/Corp** Orthodoxon Kentron tou Oikoumenikou Patriarcheiou. (1970)-. Periodical. French (French). Six times a year. $14.84. Center of Orthodoxe Patriarcat Oecum, 37 Chemin de Chambesy, 1292 Geneva Switzerland.

RM
**GLASUL BISERICII.** **Added/Corp** Biserica Ortodoxa Romana. Mitropolia Ungrovlahiei. (19??)-. Periodical. Romanian. Four times a year. DM118.00. **(Subscription address:** Kubon & Sagner, ABT Zeitschriftenimport, D 80328 Munich Germany.**)** **LC** BX690; .G57.
**Ind/Abst** BHA : Biblio. Hist. Art.

GR
**HO EPHEMERIOS.** Periodical. Greek, Modern. sm. **LC** BX618; .E63.

II
**INTERACTION : MONTHLY NEWSLETTER OF THE HENRY MARTYN INSTITUTE.** **See** Religion and Theology-Islam, Bahaism, Theosophy.

RU/0201-7318
**JOURNAL OF THE MOSCOW PATRIARCHATE, THE.** [J. Mosc. Patriarchate]. **Main/Corp** Russkaia Pravoslavnaia Tserkov. Moskovskaia Patriarkhiia. (1971)-. Periodical. Russian (English). mo. $51.00. Moscow Patriarchate, PO Box 624, Novodevichi Pr., 1, G-435, Moscow 119435 Russia. **Tel** 246 98 48, FAX 230 27 35. **(Subscription address:** Victor Kamkin, 4956 Boiling Brook Parkway, Rockville MD 20852.**)** **LC** BX460; .O725a. **DD** 281.9/47. **[CCC].**
**Ind/Abst** Index Book Rev. Relig.; Relig. Index One Period. (1980-); Relig. Theol. Abstr.

CN/0381-5110
**KALENDAR HOLOSU SPASYTELJA.** (KALENDAR HOLOSU SPASYTELIA.). **VFOAT** Redeemer's Voice Almanac; Holosu Spasytelia; Redeemer's Voice; Redeemer's Voice Calendar; Redeemer's Voice Calendar-Almanac. 1939-. Ukrainian (English). an. 6.00Can$. Redeemer's Voice Press, Yorkton Saskatchewan S3N 3V7 Canada. **Tel** (306)783-4487. **ED** Roman Chomiak. **DD** 281.9/71. **Bk Rev. Ad Acc. Circ:** 1,200.
**Desc:** Interspersed with English and Ukrainian; has Ukrainian Catholic liturgical calendar.

AU
**KANON : YEARBOOK OF THE SOCIETY OF THE LAW OF THE ORIENTAL CHURCHES.** **Added/Corp** Society of the Law of the Oriental Churches. Society for the Law of the Oriental Churches. (1973)-. Monographic series. German (English, French, Italian and Latin). ir. Price varies per volume. Verband der Wissenschaftlichen Gesellschaften Osterreichs, Lindengasse 37, A-1070 Vienna Austria. **Tel** 011 43 1 932166, 011 43 1 934756, telex 847/134981. **ED** Richard Potz. **LC** UNC. **Circ:** 200.
**Desc:** Publishes the main lectures and speeches of the bi-annual congress of the Society for the Law of the Eastern Christian Churches.

GW/0453-9273
**KIRCHE IM OSTEN.** (KIRCHE IM OSTEN : STUDIEN ZUR OSTEUROPAISCHEN KIRCHENGESCHICHTE UND KIRCHENKUNDE.). [Kirche im Osten]. **Added/Corp** Universitat Munster. Ostkirchen-Institut. Vol. 1 (1958)-. German. an. DM80.00. Vandenhoeck & Ruprecht, Robert Bosch Breite 6, D-37079 Goettingen Germany. **Tel** 011 49 551 695911, FAX 011 49 551 695917, telex 965226 VAN d. **Ad Acc.**
**Ind/Abst** BHA : Biblio. Hist. Art; Index Book Rev. Relig.; Relig. Index One Period. (1958-).

US/0279-8433
**LIVING ORTHODOXY.** (1979)-. Periodical. English. bm. $18.00 US; $21.00 other. St John of Kronstadt Press, Agape Community, Liberty TN 37095. **Tel** (615)536-5239. **ED** Gregory Williams. Index available. cum. index. **Bk Rev. Circ:** 500. available on diskette (Macintosh).
**Desc:** Traditional Orthodox Christian material in English: Saints' lives, short articles of spiritual guidance, explanations of Orthodox liturgical practice, book reviews of interest to strugglers in the faith, and occasional news of the publishing community.
**Ind/Abst** Index Book Rev. Relig.; Relig. Index One Period.

PO
**LOOKING EAST.** Periodical. English. Byzantine Center, Fatima Portugal. **LC** BX106.3; .L65. **DD** 281.9. **UDC** 281.9.

LE
**MAJALLAT AL-NUR AL-URTHUDHUKSIYAH.** **VFOAT** Nur Al-Urthudhuksiyah. Periodical. Arabic. ir. 30.00. Shafiq Haydar Mina Tarabulus Hayy Mar Ilyas, Box 11-2966, Beirut Lebanon. **LC** BX200; .M33.

US/0882-9756
**MAJALLAT AL-SALAM.** **VFOAT** Salam; Peace News. Began in 1978. Periodical. Arabic (English). mo. PO Box 3309, Detroit MI 48203. **LC** BX130; .M25.

SZ
**MECC PERSPECTIVES - MIDDLE EAST COUNCIL OF CHURCHES.** **Main/Corp** Middle East Council of Churches. **Added/Corp** Majlis Kanais al-Sharq al-Awsat. No. 1 (April/May 1984)-. Periodical. English. **LC** BR1070; .M44. **DD** 275.6/082/05.
**Ind/Abst** Hum. Rights Intern. Rep.

GR
**MONASTERIOLOGIA.** (1980)-. Periodical. Greek, Modern. **LC** BX385.G8; M66.

US/0030-2503
**ONE CHURCH.** (ONE CHURCH / EDINAIA TSERKOV.). **Added/Corp** Russkaia Pravoslavnaia Tserkov. Exarchate of North and South America. Russkaia Pravoslavnaia Tserkov. Patriarchal Parishes in the United States. **VFOAT** Edinaia Tserkov. (1947)-. Periodical. English. Six times a year. $7.50. One Church Circulation Department, 158 Stiles Street, Elizabeth NJ 07208-1811. **Tel** (201)352-1192. **ED** F. Kovulchuk. Index available. **Bk Rev. Circ:** 1,600 (ctrl). available on microfilm and microfiche from University Microfilms International (UMI).
**Desc:** Official publication of the Patriarchal Parishes of the Russian Orthodox Church in the USA, also includes Orthodox interest to all concerned with Church life in the Soviet Union.

GW/0340-6407
**ORIENS CHRISTIANUS.** [Oriens Christ.]. **Added/Corp** Gorres-Gesellschaft. Vol. 1, No. 8 (1901/1908)-. German. an. Otto Harrassowitz Verlag, Taunusstrasse 14, Postfach 2929, D-65019 Wiesbaden Germany. **Tel** 011 49 611 5300, FAX 530570, telex 4186 135 OH D. cum. index.
**Ind/Abst** BHA : Biblio. Hist. Art; Index Book Rev. Relig.; Relig. Index One Period. (1980-).

IT
**ORIENTALIA CHRISTIANA ANALECTA.** **Added/Corp** Pontificium Institutum Orientalium Studiorum. No. 101 (1935)-. Monographic series. English (French, German, Italian and Spanish). ir. Price varies per volume. Pontificio Istituto Orientale, Piazza S, Maria Maggiore 7, 00185 Rome Italy. **Tel** 011 39 6 4465589. **ED** Robert F. Taft and James Lee Dugan. Index available. cum. index. **Bk Rev. Circ:** 500. ***Continues*** *Orientalia Christiana.*
**Desc:** A scholarly journal containing editions of oriental texts and book-length monographs about the Christian East, its theology, history, patrology, liturgy archeology and canon law.

IT/0030-5375
**ORIENTALIA CHRISTIANA PERIODICA.** [Orient. christ. period.]. Vol. 1 (1935)-. Periodical. Italian (English, French, German and Spanish). sa. L50000 Italy; $50.00 US; L60000 other. Pontificio Istituto Orientale, Piazza S, Maria Maggiore 7, 00185 Rome Italy. **Tel** 011 39 6 4465589. **ED** Vincenzo Poggi and James Lee Dugan. **LC** BX100; .O74. **DD** 281.05. **UDC** 281.9. Index available. cum. index. **Bk Rev. Circ:** 1,000. available on photocopies.
**Desc:** Articles and book reviews about whatever concerns theology, history, patrology, liturgy, archaeology, and Canon Law of the Christian East.
**Ind/Abst** Bibliogr. Mission.; BHA : Biblio. Hist. Art; Index Islam. Lit.; Index Book Rev. Relig.; New Testam. Abstr.; Relig. Index One Period. (1949-).

US
**ORTHODOX CATHOLIC VOICE, THE.** **Added/Corp** Orthodox Catholic Church of North and South America. **VFOAT** Voice; O.C. Voice. (19??)-. Periodical. English. bm (6 issues). $4.00 US; $5.00 other. Orthodox Catholic Church of North and South America, PO Box 1213, Akron OH 44309. **Tel** (216)753-1155. **ED** Bishop Roman (Editor's Address: 594 Fifth Street NE, Barberton, OH 44203; Phone: (216)753-1155). **Bk Rev** (Qty: 4-5). **Ad Acc. Circ:** 400.

US/0048-2269
**ORTHODOX CHURCH, THE.** [Orthodox Church]. **Added/Corp** Russian Orthodox Greek Catholic Church of America. Metropolitan Council. Orthodox Church in America. Executive Council. (19??)-. Periodical. English. mo. $10.00 US; $15.00 Canada; $20.00 other. Orthodox Church in America, PO Box 675, Syosset NY 11791. **Tel** (516)922-0550. **ED** Leonid Kishkovsky. **LC** BX496.A1; O5. **DD** 281.9/73. **Circ:** 31,500.
**Desc:** Varied religious news covering both national and international events and information.

US/0744-1495
**ORTHODOX HERALD, THE.** Periodical. English. mo. $4.00. The Orthodox Herald, PO Box 9, Hunlock Creek PA 18621. **Tel** (717)256-7232. **ED** W Basil Stroyen and Nina Stroyen. **UDC** 281.93. **Bk Rev. Circ:** 5,000.
**Desc:** Living the Eastern Orthodox faith in the 20th century. Some ethnic traditions are given, mainly those of the Russian and Carpatho-Russian people, and their bearing on the faith.

US/0030-5820
**ORTHODOX LIFE.** [Orthodox life]. **Added/Corp** Holy Trinity Monastery (Jordanville, N.Y.). Vol. 1 (Jan./Feb. 1950)-. Periodical. English (Russian). bm. $12.00 (one year); $20.00 (two year); $30.00 (three year). Holy Trinity Monastery, PO Box 36, Jordanville NY 13361. **Tel** (315)858-0940. **ED** Bishop Hilarion. **LC** BX460; .073. **DD** 281.9/3. **Bk Rev. Circ:** 1,800 (ctrl).
**Desc:** Regularly featured are original and translated lives of Saints and articles on the history and doctrine of the Orthodox Church.
**Ind/Abst** Am. Bibliogr. Slavic East Europ. Stud.

US/0030-5839
**ORTHODOX WORD, THE.** **Added/Corp** Saint Herman of Alaska Brotherhood. Russkaia Pravoslavnaia Tserkov Zagranitsei. Vol. 1, (1965)-. Periodical. English. Six times a year (Jan., Mar., may, July, Sept., Nov.). $12.00 US & Canada & Mexico; $15.00 others. Orthodox Word, PO Box 70, Platina CA 96076. **ED** Father Herman and Father Damasiene, (phone: (707)887-9740). Index available (Last iss.). **Bk Rev**, (Qty: 2). **Ad Acc. Circ:** 3,000. available on microfilm and microfiche from University Microfilms International (UMI).
**Desc:** Presents Eastern Othordox spirituality with special emphasis on the institution of eldership and authentic spiritual guides in the Greek Russian and Roomanian traditions as well as explanations of the Christian faith and monastic life.

GW/0931-0347
**ORTHODOXIE HEUTE.** (19??)-. German. qt. DM30.00. Sergius Heitz, Pattscheider Strasse 30, 4000 Dusseldorf 13 Germany. **ED** Erzpriester Sergius Heitz. **Bk Rev. Pr Rev.** ctrl circ.
**Desc:** Covers Orthodox theology, actual news of the Orthodox world, comments on ecumenical events and book reviews.

RM
**ORTODOXIA.** **Added/Corp** Orthodox Eastern Church, Romanian. Patriarch. Romanian Orthodox Eastern Church. Patriarch. (1949)-. Periodical. Romanian. qt. DM164.00. Institutul Biblic si de Misiune Ortodoxa, Intrarea Patriarhiei Nr 9 Secrotul 5, Bucuresti Romania. **(Subscription address:** Kubon & Sagner, ABT Zeitschriftenimport, D 80328 Munich Germany.**)** **LC** BX690; .O7.

GW/0030-6487
**OSTKIRCHLICHE STUDIEN.** [Ostkirchl. Stud.]. (Jan. 1952)-. Periodical. German (English and French). Four times a year (Mar., June, Sept., Dec.). DM98.00 Germany; DM105.00 others. Augustinus-Verlag, Grabenberg 2, Postfach 110252, W 97029 Wuerzburg F R Germany. **Tel** 011/49/931/51157. **ED** Professor H. M. Biedermann (phone: 011 49 931 71085). **LC** BX100; .O765. **DD** 281/.5. Index available (Bound in 4th iss.). **Circ:** 620.
**Desc:** These articles are by outstanding scholars on eastern church's history and theology. Documentation, comments, reviews, and summaries of eastern periodicals are included.
**Ind/Abst** Am. Hist. Life (1954-1957, 1960-); BHA : Biblio. Hist. Art; Index Book Rev. Relig.; New Testam. Abstr.; Relig. Index One Period. (1980-); Relig. Theol. Abstr.

YU
**PRAVOSLAVLJE.** (No. -19). Periodical. Serbo-Croatian (Cyrillic). sm. **(Subscription address:** Jugoslovenska Knjiga, PO Box 36, YU 11001 Belgrade Yugoslovia.**)** **LC** BX710; .P76. **UDC** 281.9.

US/0032-6992
**PRAVOSLAVNAJA ZIZN.** (PRAVOSLAVNAIA ZHIZN. ORTHODOX LIFE.). **Added/Corp** Holy Trinity Monastery (Jordanville, N.Y.). **VFOAT** Orthodox Life. Vol. 1 (Jan. 1950)-. Periodical. Russian. mo. $10.00. Holy Trinity Monastery, PO Box 36, Jordanville NY 13361. **Tel** (315)858-0940. **ED** Bishop Hilarion. **LC** BX460; .P683. **DD** 281.9/3. **Bk Rev. Circ:** 1,600.
**Desc:** Orthodox life publishes articles of a wide variety-all concerning the orthodox church. Frequent topics include lives of saints, liturgics, church history, the tenor is solid and sober.

CN/0225-0292
**PRAVOSLAVNOE OBOZRENIE.** (PRAVOSLAVNOE OBOZRIENIE.). [Pravosl. obozr.]. **VFOAT** Orthodox Observer. Began publication in 1953?. Periodical. Russian. bm. Orthodox Observer, 8011 Champagneur Avenue, Montreal Quebec H3N 2K4 Canada. **DD** 281.9/05. **UDC** 281.9.

IS/0032-9622
**PROCHE-ORIENT CHRETIEN.** **Added/Corp** Seminaire Sainte-Anne de Jerusalem. Vol.1 (1951)-. Periodical. French (English). sa. $20.00. Editions Proche-Orient Chretie, Sainte-Anne PO Box 19079, Jerusalem Israel. **Tel** 011 972 2 281992, FAX 011 972 2 280764. **ED** White Fathers. **LC** BR1070; .P74. Index available. cum. index (1951-1970). **Bk Rev**, (Qty: 20). **Circ:** 1,000.
**Desc:** Research and information periodical on Eastern Christian churches and ecumenism in dialogue with the other monotheistic religions in the Middle-East.
**Ind/Abst** Index Book Rev. Relig.; Relig. Index One Period.; Relig. Theol. Abstr.

US/0036-0317
**RUSSIAN ORTHODOX JOURNAL, THE.** **Added/Corp** Federated Russian Orthodox Clubs. Vol. 1 (May 1927)-. Periodical. English. Ten times a year. $12.00. Federated Russian Orthodox Clubs, 10 Downs Drive Plains, Wilkes Barre PA 18705. **Tel** (717)825-3158. **(Subscription address:** Federated Russian Orthodox Clubs, 21 Hoeffer Street, Latham NY 12110.**)** **ED** Mark Soroka. **LC** BX496.A1; R8. **DD** 281.973. **Bk Rev. Ad Acc. Circ:** 3,500 (ctrl).
**Desc:** Fraternal activities of federated Russian Orthodox clubs including religious, cultural, sports, and educational topics.

US/0222-1543
**RUSSKOE VOZROZHDENIE.** (RUSSKOE VOZROZHDENIE / LA RENAISSANCE RUSSE.). **Added/Corp** Russkaia Pravoslavnaia Tserkov Zagranitsei. Kommissiia po Podgotovke Prazdnovaniia 1000-Letiia Kreshcheniia Russkogo Naroda pri Arkhiereiskom Sinode. **VFOAT** Russian Renascence. (1978)-. Periodical. Russian. qt. 1000 Anniversary Committee, 322 West 108 Street, New York NY 10025. **Tel** (212)663-9093. **ED** Miliza K. Holoduy. **LC** BX598.A1; R87. **DD** 947. cum. index. **Bk Rev. Pr Rev. Circ:** 1,500.
**Desc:** Topics dealing with Russian Orthodoxy, literature, philosophy and history.

US/0741-9163
**SACRED ART JOURNAL.** **See** The Arts-Art.

UK/0144-8722
**SOBORNOST.** [Sobornost]. **Added/Corp** Fellowship of St. Alban and St. Sergius. Vol. 1 (1979)-. Periodical. English. sa. £8.00 UK; £10.00 other. Fellowship of St Alban and St Sergius, St Basil House, 52 Ladbrove Grove, London W11 2PB England. **Tel** 44 71 7277713. **ED** Sergei Hackel. **LC** BX100; .S6. **DD** 281.9/05. **Bk Rev. Ad Acc. Circ:** 2,300 (ctrl). available on microfilm and microfiche from University Microfilms International (UMI). Documents available from The Genuine Article. ***Formed by the union of** Sobornost, 0144-8722 **and** Eastern Churches Review.*
**Desc:** Articles on Eastern Christian churches and east-west ecumenism, reports, news items, book reviews, and fellowship affairs.
**Ind/Abst** Arts Humanit. Citation Index [Full Cov.]; Bibliogr. Mission.; Br. Humanit. Index; Index Book Rev. Relig.; Relig. Index One Period. (1980-); Relig. Theol. Abstr.; Res. Alert [Full Cov.]; Soc. Sci. Cit. Index [Select. Cov.].

GW/0584-1259
**SOPHIA.** Vol. 1- 1961-. Monographic series. German. ir. Price varies per volume. Paulinus Verlag, Postfach 3040 65, D 54220 Trier Germany. **Tel** 011 49 651 4604162, FAX 011 49 651 4604153, telex 472735. **ED** Julius Tyciak and Wilhelm Nyssen. **UDC** 281.
**Desc:** Book series concentrating on Eastern Christianity and its sources, evolution, symbolism and liturgy. Includes original source material for study, as well as essays.

FR/0750-1978
**SOURCES CHRETIENNES.** [Sources chret.]. No. 1 (1941)-. Monographic series. French (Greek, Modern and Latin). ir. Price varies per volume. Editions du CERF, BP 65, 77932 Perthes Cedex France. **Tel** 011 33 1 44181212. **LC** UNC. **Bk Rev. Ad Acc. Circ:** 2,500 (ctrl).
**Desc:** Ancient manuscripts for the modern reader. The first text of Christian culture from the I-XII Century.
**Ind/Abst** MLA Int. Bibl. Books Artic. Mod. Lang. Lit.

US/0036-3227
**ST. VLADIMIR'S THEOLOGICAL QUARTERLY.** [St. Vladmir's theol. q.]. **Added/Corp** St. Vladimir's Orthodox Theological Seminary (Crestwood, Tuckahoe, Westchester County, N.Y.). Vol. 13 (1969)-. Periodical. English. qt (Mar., June, Oct., Dec.). $25.00 US; $35.00 other. St Vladimirs Orthodox Theological Seminary, 575 Scarsdale Road, Crestwood, Tuckahoe NY 10707. **Tel** (914)961-8313. **ED** John Breck. **LC** BX460; .S3. **DD** 230/.1/93. cum. index. **Bk Rev. Ad Acc. Circ:** 1,500 (ctrl). available on microfilm and microfiche from University Microfilms International (UMI). ***Continues** St. Vladimir's Seminary Quarterly, 0360-6481.*
**Desc:** Publishes articles and brief notes on subjects of particular interest to Orthodox Christians and those interested in Orthodoxy on: scripture, doctrine, ethics, church history, liturgics, iconography, etc.
**Ind/Abst** Index Book Rev. Relig.; New Testam. Abstr. (-19??); Old Testam. Abstr.; Relig. Index One Period. (1969-); Relig. Theol. Abstr. (19??-).

GW/0562-0694
**STIMME DER ORTHODOXIE.** **VFOAT** Golos Pravoslaviia. Periodical. German. mo. 1.30M each issue. Wildensteiner Strasse 10, 1157 Berlin Germany. **LC** BX460; .S77. **UDC** 281.9.
**Ind/Abst** Bibliogr. Mission.

IT
**STUDI E RICERCHE SULL'ORIENTE CRISTIANO.** (Jan./April 1978)-. Periodical. Italian. L25000 Italy; L40000 other. Studi Ric Oriente Cristiano, Via Panaro 11, 00199 Rome Italy. **LC** BX100; .S85. **UDC** 281.9.
**Ind/Abst** Bibliogr. Mission.; BHA : Biblio. Hist. Art.

RM/1011-8845
**STUDII TEOLOGICE.** (STUDII TEOLOGICE : REVISTA INSTITUTELOR TEOLOGICE DIN PATRIARHIA ROMANA.). [Stud. teol.]. **Added/Corp** Institutul Biblic si de Misiune Ortodoxa. **VFOAT** Etudes Theologiques. (195?)-. Periodical. Romanian. Six times a year. DM215.00. **(Subscription address:** Kubon & Sagner, ABT Zeitschriftenimport, D 80328 Munich Germany.**)** **LC** BX690; .S75.
**Desc:** Publishes theological studies.
**Ind/Abst** MLA Int. Bibl. Books Artic. Mod. Lang. Lit.

US/1043-7878
**TRUE VINE.** [True vine]. **Added/Corp** Holy Orthodox Church in North America. (Spring 1989)-. Periodical. English. Four times a year. $17.00 (one year); $30.00 (two year); $42.00 (three year). True Vine, PO Box 129, Roslindale MA 02131. **Tel** (617)734-0608. **DD** 281.

PL
**TSERKOVNYI VESTNIK : CERKIEWNY WIESTNIK.** **Added/Corp** Polskaia Avtokefalnaia Pravoslavnaia Tserkov. Varshavskaia Pravoslavnaia Mitropoliia. **VFOAT** Cerkiewny Wiestnik. (19??)-. Periodical. Russian. mo. Price on Request. **(Subscription address:** ARS Polona, PO Box 1001, 00068 Warsaw Poland.**)** ***Continues** Tserkovnyi Vestnik (Pravoslavnaia Tserkv v Polshe).*

US/0147-1015
**UKRAINIAN ORTHODOX WORD.** ***Suspended.*** Periodical. English. bm. $3.00. Ukrainian Orthodox Church of the USA, Box 495, South Bound Brook NJ 08880. **LC** BX738.U4; U47. **DD** 281.9/73. **UDC** 281.9(73).

US/0041-7262
**UNITED EVANGELICAL.** ***Title Change.*** (19??0-(19??). Periodical. English. mo. Church Center Press, PO Box 186, Myerstown PA 17067. **Tel** (717)866-7581. **Bk Rev. Ad Acc. Circ:** 2,800 (ctrl). ***Continued by** EC Doors and Windows.*
**Desc:** Religious articles and news about the E. C. Churches.

US/0145-7950
**YEARBOOK AND CHURCH DIRECTORY OF THE ORTHODOX CHURCH IN AMERICA.** **Main/Corp** Orthodox Church in America. 22nd Ed. (1971)-. Directory. English. an. $9.50. Route 25A, PO Box 675, Syosset NY 11791. **Tel** (516)922-0550. **LC** BX496.A5; R8. **DD** 281.9/025/1812. **UDC** 281.98(058). **Ad Acc.** ***Continues** Russian Orthodox Greek Catholic Church of America. Year Book and Church Directory.*
**Desc:** Directory of dioceses, parishes, organizations, institutions and clergy, organized geographically by states. Covers US and Canada, plus foreign OCA parishes.

RU/0132-862X
**ZURNAL MOSKOVSKOJ PATRIARHII.** (ZHURNAL MOSKOVSKOI PATRIARKHII.). [Z. Mosk. patriarhii]. **Main/Corp** Russkaia Pravoslavnaia Tserkov. Moskovskaia Patriarkhiia. **Added/Corp** Russkaia Pravoslavnaia Tserkov. Moskovskaia Patriarkhiia. (1931)-. Periodical. Russian. mo. $89.95. **(Subscription address:** East View Publications Inc., 3020 Harbor Lane North, Suite 110, Minneapolis MN 55447.**)** **LC** BX460; .O7.
**Ind/Abst** Am. Hist. Life (1955).

## HINDUISM

II
**ANANDA SANDESA.** Hindi (Hindi). 10.00. Sri Anandapura Trasta, Karyalaya Ananda Sandesa, Dist Guna MP, Sri Anandapura India. **LC** BL1100; .A5.

II/0304-9272
**BRAHMANA-GAURAVA.** Hindi (Hindi). 3.00. Moti Katra 3, Agara India. **LC** BL1100; .B7.

II
**CINTAMANI.** (19??)-. Periodical. Multiple languages (Hindi, Sanskrit and English). qt. 4.00. 28/16 V G Kher Road, 40006 Bombai India. **LC** BL1100; .C55.

II
**DHARMA MARGA.** April/June 1982-. Periodical. Hindi. qt. Rs12.00. Ramayana Vidyapeeth, 15 Institutional Area/Lodi Road, New Delhi 1100 India. **LC** BL1100; .D515.

# Religion and Theology —Islam, Bahaism, Theosophy

II
**DIVINE LIFE, THE.** See New Age Publications.

II
**DIVYAJYOTIH.** Sanskrit (Sanskrit). 12.00. Divyajyoti Office, Simala India. **LC** PK401; .D58.

CN/0844-4587
**HINDU-CHRISTIAN STUDIES BULLETIN.** [Hindu-Christ. stud. bull.]. **Added/Corp** Calgary Institute for the Humanities. Vol. 1 (Autumn 1988)-. Bulletin. English. an (July). 12.00Can$. Centre for Studies in Religion & Society, University of Victoria, PO Box 3045, Victoria, British Columbia V8W 3P4 Canada. **Tel** (604)721-6271, FAX (604)721-6234. **ED** Harold Coward. **DD** 294.5/172. **Bk Rev**, (Qty: 8-15). **Pr Rev. Circ:** 400 (ctrl).
**Desc:** Offers a world-wide forum for the presentation of Hindu-Christian scholarly studies and dialogue. Each issue presents articles, viewpoint essays and news items on Hinduism and Christianity and their interrelationship based upon historical materials and contemporary experience.

II
**HINDU REGENERATION.** Periodical. English. Rs6.00. Henry Martyn Institute, PO Box 153, Hyderabad 500001 AP India. **Tel** 268645. **LC** BL1100; .H53. **DD** 294.5/05.

II
**HINDU VISVA.** Periodical. Hindi (Hindi). 12.00. Vishva Hindu Parishad, 6/10 Arya Samaj Road, Karol Bagh, New Delhi 110005 India. **LC** BL1100; .H544.

US/0896-0801
**HINDUISM TODAY.** Vol. 7, No. 3 (Sept. 1985)-. Periodical. English. Twelve times a year. $29.00. Hinduism Today, 107 Kaholaiele Road, Kapaa HI 96746. **Tel** (808)890-1008. **DD** 294. *Continues New Saivite World.*
**Desc:** Includes information on karma, dharma, reincarnation, transformation, Bhakti, yoga, meditation, astrology, Ayurveda, and the path of the Rishis.

II
**HINDUTVA.** (19??)-. Periodical. English. mo. $3.00. A-14 Green Park Extension, New Delhi 16 India. **LC** BL1100; .H57. **DD** 294.5/05.

II
**JAKATKURU.** **VFOAT** Jagath Guru; Jagathguru. Periodical. English (Tamil). mo. Rs18.00. 3 Satyanarayana Street, West Mambalam, Madras 600033 India. **LC** BL1100; .J34.

NP
**JIJNASA (KATHMANDU, NEPAL).** (JIJNASA : GUNARAJA SMARAKA SAMITIKO MUKHAPATRA.). Sept./Oct. 1983-. Periodical. Nepali (Nepali). an Rs5.00. Mahakal Sthan, Post Box No 162, Kathmandu Nepal. **LC** BL1100; .J55.

CN/0706-6449
**JOURNAL OF STUDIES IN THE BHAGAVADGITA, THE.** **Added/Corp** University of Sydney. Dept. of Religious Studies. Vol. 1 (1981)-. English. an. $15.00.
**Ind/Abst** Index Book Rev. Relig.; Relig. Index One Period.

II/0377-9505
**MANASAMANI.** [Mana samani]. Hindi (Hindi). mo. 5.00. Ramvan Satna, Madhya Pradesh, Ramavana India. **LC** BL1100; .M35.

II
**NIRMALYA : SRI JAGANNATHA MISANA MUKHAPATRA.** Vol. 1, No. 1 (Aug. 1982)-. Periodical. Oriya (Oriya). qt. Rs3.00. Sri Jagannath Mission, Kacheri Road, Puri 752001 India. **LC** BL1225.J3; N57.

II
**PAROPAKARI.** Hindi (Hindi). Rs10.00. Surendra Prakassa Sarma, Srikarana Sarada Mantri Paropakarini Sabha, Ajamera India. **LC** BL1100; .P38.

II/0032-6178
**PRABUDDHA BHARATA.** **Added/Corp** Advaita Ashrama. **VFOAT** Awakened India. Vol. 1 (July 1896)-. Periodical. English. mo. $20.00. Prabuddha Bharata, 5 Dehi Entally Road, Calcutta 700 014 India. **Tel** 11 91 33 2440898. **ED** Swami Swananda. **LC** BL1100; .P7. **DD** 294.05. Index available. **Bk Rev. Ad Acc. Circ:** 5,000 (ctrl).
**Ind/Abst** Bibliogr. Mission.

SI
**REPORT - SINGAPORE HINDUS RELIGIOUS AND CULTURAL SEMINAR.** **Main/Conf** Singapore Hindus Religious and Cultural Seminar. 1969/71-. Multiple languages (English and Tamil). **LC** BL1157.S55; S55A. **DD** 294.5/05.
**Desc:** First vol. covers the 1st-3d seminar.

II
**SIDDHA VANI.** **Added/Corp** Siddha Yoga Dham. (19??)-. English. an. $1.50. Siddha Yoga Dham, S-174 Panch Shila Park, New Delhi 110017 India. **ED** Janak Nanda. **LC** BL1100; .S53. **DD** 294.5/05. **Ad Acc. Circ:** 2,000. available with illustrations.

II
**TATTVALOKAH / TATTVALOKA.** **Added/Corp** Sri Abhinava Vidyatheertha Educational Trust. **VFOAT** Tattvaloka. (19??)-. Periodical. English (Sanskrit). bm. Rs60.00 India; $25.00 other. Tattvaloka, 5 Sradhananda House, Sradhananda Road, Matunga Bombay 400019 India. **Tel** 4374699. **ED** T. R. Ramachandran. **LC** B132.V3; T39. **DD** 181/.48/05. Index available. **Bk Rev. Ad Acc. Circ:** 5,000 (ctrl).
**Desc:** Dedicated to truth and moral excellence under the guidance of the Holy Sankaracharya Jagadguru of Sri Sarada Pitham, Sringeri, Karnataka, India.

II
**VEDIC LIGHT.** Periodical. English (Sanskrit). mo. Rs30.00 India; $12.00 other. Sarvadeshik Arya Pratinidhi Sabha, Maharshi Dayananda Bhawan, 3/5 Asaf Alit Road, New Delhi 110002 India. **Tel** 274771, 260985. **ED** S C Pathak. **LC** BL1100; .V43. **DD** 294.5/05. **Bk Rev. Ad Acc. Circ:** 750.
**Desc:** Mainly touching on religion, sociology, Indian culture and traditions based on vedas.

IO
**WARTA HINDU DHARMA.** Indonesian. 60. Jln Nangka-7A, Denpasar Indonesia. **LC** BL1100; .W36.

II
**YUKRANDA.** Periodical. Hindi (Hindi). Rs12.00. Directorate of Employment and Training, 790 Wright Town, Madhya Pradesh India. **LC** BL1100; .Y84.

## ISLAM, BAHAISM, THEOSOPHY

TI
**15-21.** **VFOAT** Khamis Ashar-Al-Wahid Wa-Al-Ishrun. No. 1 (November 1982)-. Periodical. Arabic. mo. 160.00. 3 Nahj Al-Hijab, S B 1024, Tunis Tunisia. **LC** BP1; .A15.

US/8755-1780
**ABRAXAS (HOLLYWOOD, LOS ANGELES, CALIF.).** (ABRAXAS.). [Abraxas]. **Added/Corp** Ecclesia Gnostica (Hollywood, Los Angeles, Calif.) Gnostic Society (Hollywood, Los Angeles, Calif.). (19??)-. Periodical. English. an. $4.00. The Gnostic Society, PO Box 3993, Hollywood CA 90078. **LC** BP600; .A27. **DD** 299/.932/05.

II/0001-902X
**ADYAR LIBRARY BULLETIN, THE.** [Adyar libr. bull.]. **Added/Corp** Adyar Library. Vol. 22, No. 1/2 (May 1958)-. Bulletin. English (Sanskrit). an. $20.00. Adyar Library & Research Center, The Theosophical Society, Adyar Madras 600020 India. **Tel** 413528. **(Subscription address:** Prints India, 11 Darya Ganj, New Delhi 110002 India.**) LC** BP500; .B7. Index available. **Bk Rev. Circ:** 500. available on microfilm. *Continues Brahmavidya, The Adyar Library Bulletin.*
**Ind/Abst** MLA Int. Bibl. Books Artic. Mod. Lang. Lit.

KE
**AFRICA ISMAILI.** Periodical. Multiple languages (English and Gujarati). $0.60. Shia Imami Ismaila Association for Kenya, PO Box 30606, Nairobi Kenya. **LC** BP195.I8; A36. **DD** 297/.822/05. **UDC** 297(676.2).

CN/0229-5644
**AHMADIYYA GAZETTE.** (AHMADIYYA GAZETTE (CANADA).). [Ahmadiyyah gaz. Can.]. **VFOAT** Ahmadiyyah Gazit. Jan. 1978-. Periodical. English (Urdu). mo. Free. Ahmadiyyah Movement, Suite 311, 15 Thorncliffe Park Drive, Toronto Ontario M4H 1H6 Canada. **DD** 297/.86/05. **UDC** 297(71). ctrl circ.

PK
**AL-ATASH.** **VFOAT** Atash; Communicating the Uncommunicated. V. 1- Dec. 1977-. Periodical. English (Urdu). mo. Taha Turabi, PO Box 8976, Karachi Pakistan. **LC** BP193.5; .A85. **DD** 297/.82/05. **UDC** 297.

KU
**AL-BALAGH.** Periodical. Arabic. $100.00 (governmental institutions), $35.00 (individuals) Arab countries; $50.00 other. Muassasat Al-Balagh Lil-Sihafah Wa-Al-Tibaah, Shari Al-Matar Al-Dawli, PO Box 4558, Al-Kuwayt Kuwait. **Tel** 481-9008, telex 44389. **ED** Abdul Rahman. **LC** BP1; .B33. **UDC** 297. **Bk Rev. Ad Acc. Circ:** 15,000.
**Desc:** Islamic political issues

PK
**AL-BASHIR.** V. 1- Mar./Apr. 1972-. Periodical. Urdu (Urdu). Mir Najaf Ali, 288 Khamosh Kalony Tard Chaurangi 1, Karachi Pakistan. **LC** BP1; .B35. **UDC** 297.

SJ
**AL-BAYAN.** Arabic. £s0.10. PO Box 1458, Al-Khartum Sudan. **LC** BP1; .B37. **UDC** 297.

UA
**AL-DAWAH.** Periodical. Arabic. mo. $18.00. PO Box 1636, Al-Qahirah United Arab Republic. **LC** BP1; .D393. **UDC** 297.

PK/0002-399X
**AL-DIRASAT AL-ISLAMIYAH.** **VFOAT** Arabic Quarterly of the Islamic Research Institute, Islamabad, Pakistan; Dirasat Al-Islamiyah. qt. $20.00. Islamic Research Institute, PO Box 1035, Islamabad Pakistan. **Tel** 011 92 51 8507515, FAX 011 92 51 853360, telex 54068 IIU PK. **ED** Muhammad Al-Gazali. **LC** BP1; .D5. Index available. **Bk Rev. Ad Acc. Circ:** 3,000.

TI
**AL-ILM WA-AL-IMAN.** (19??)-. Periodical. Arabic. mo. **LC** BP190.5.S3; I44.

MR
**AL-IRSHAD.** **VFOAT** Irchad. Periodical. Arabic (French). ir. 30.00. Al-Mamlakah Al-Maghribiyah Mudiriyat Al-Shuun Al-Islamiyah Al-Tabiah Li-Wizarat Al-Awqaf Wa-Al-Shuun Al-Islamiyah, Al Irchad, C C P 37-50, Al-Rabat Morocco. **LC** BP1; .I63. **UDC** 297.

MY
**AL ISLAM.** Periodical. Malay (Malay). $1.00 single issue. Kumpulan Syarikat Utusan Melay Bhd, No 46 M Jl Lima Dif Jl, Chan Saw Lin, Kuala Lumpur Malaysia. **LC** BP1; .I65. **UDC** 297.

UA
**AL-ITISAM.** Periodical. Arabic. mo. PO Box 1707, Al-Qahirah United Arab Republic. **LC** BP1; .I8. **UDC** 297.

KE
**AL MOMIN.** **VFOAT** Mumin. Began in 1980. Periodical. English (English). Jamia Mosque Railway Landhies and Islamia Primary School Association, PO Box 72624, Nairobi Kenya. **LC** BP1; .M57. **DD** 297/.05. **UDC** 297.

LE
**AL-MUNTALAQ.** Periodical. Arabic. 13.00 single issue. PO Box 25105, Al-Ghubayri Lebanon. **LC** BP1; .M773. **UDC** 297.

PK
**AL-MUSLIH.** July 1- August 23, 1973-. Periodical. Urdu. 12.00. Mirza Abdurrahim Beg, Ahmadia Mall Magazine Lane, Karachi Pakistan. **LC** BP195.A5; M79. **UDC** 297.

LE
**AL-MUSLIM AL-MUASIR.** **VFOAT** Majallat Al-Muslim Al-Muasir; Contemporary Muslim. Periodical. Arabic. qt. £L15.00. PO Box 119429, Beirut Lebanon. **LC** BP1; .M776. **UDC** 297.

MY/0127-2284
**AL-NAHDAH.** **Added/Corp** Regional Islamic Dawah Council of Southeast Asia and the Pacific. Vol. 1, No. 1 (Mar. 1981)-. Periodical. English. Four times a year (Jan., Apr., July, Oct.). $5.00 (one year), $8.00 (two years), $12.00 (three years) surface mail; $13.00 Europe & Middle East & Egypt, $14.00 US & Africa, $2.87 Malaysia & Singapore & Brunei, $10.00 Southeast Asia & Hong Kong, $12.00 others (airmail). Al Nahdah, 5th Floor Perkim Building, Jalan Ipoh, 51200 Kuala Lumpur Malaysia. **Tel** 60 3 44 28 166. **ED** Fudlullah Wilmot. **LC** BP1; .N35. **DD** 297/.05. **Bk Rev. Ad Acc. Circ:** 5,000.
**Desc:** General information on activities and problems of Muslims in the sea and Pacific region as well as articles by contemporary Muslim thinkers.

GW
**AL-RAID / YUSDIRUHA AL-MARKAZ AL-ISLAMI FI AKHIN (MASJID BILAL) WA-ITTIHAD AL-TALABAH AL-MUSLIMIN FI URUBBA.** **Main/Corp** Raid (Aachen, Germany). Arabic. mo (ten issues per year). DM40.00 (individuals), DM70.00 (institutions) Germany; $24.00 (individuals), $36.00 (institutions) US. Al-Raid, PO Box 120263, 4060 Viersen 12 Germany. **Tel** (0261)874175. **ED** Nabil Chbib. **LC** BP1; .R34. **UDC** 297. **Bk Rev. Circ:** 7,000.

LE
**AL-RISALAH AL-ISLAMIYAH.** Periodical. Arabic. 1.50 single issue. PO Box 155063, Beirut Lebanon. **LC** BP1; .R54. **UDC** 297.

IQ
**AL-RISALAH AL-ISLAMIYAH / TASDURUAN WIZARAT AL-AWQAF WA-AL-SHUUN AL-DINIYAH.** Arabic. 6. Kurnish Al-Azamiayh, Qurb Al-Mathaf Al-Harbi, Baghdad Iraq. **LC** BP1; .R545A. **UDC** 297.

LE
**AL-TAQRIR AL-ISLAMI.** No. 1 (1979)-. Periodical. Arabic. ir. Al-Markaz Al-Islami Lil-Tarbiyah Bayrut Lubnan, PO Box 14/5355, Beirut Lebanon. **Tel** 317708. **LC** BP63.L4; T36. **UDC** 297. **Circ:** 5,000.
**Desc:** Covers the general problems in the Muslim world.

# Religion and Theology —Islam, Bahaism, Theosophy

LE
**AL-TARBIYAH AL-ISLAMIYAH.** Periodical. Arabic. 1.25. PO Box 34, Baghdad Lebanon. **LC** BP1; .T28. **UDC** 297.

UA
**AL-TASAWWUF AL-ISLAMI : SHARIAH WA-TARIQAH WA-HAQIQAH.** VFOAT Majallat Al-Tasawwuf Al-Islami. Periodical. Arabic. Majallat Al-Tasawwuf Al-Islami Al-Ghulam, PO Box 992, Cairo Egypt. **LC** BP188.45; .T38. **UDC** 297.

UA
**AL-TAWHID.** **Added/Corp** Jamaat Ansar Al-Sunah Al-Muhammadiyah (Egypt). (19??)-. Periodical. Arabic (Urdu and English). Four times a year (Jan., Apr., July, Oct.). $40.00 (individuals); $50.00 (institutions). Publilink, PO Box 19395, 4443 Tehran Iran. **Tel** FAX 011 98 21 769432. **LC** BP1; .T34. **Circ**: 67,000.

IO
**ALMANAK MUHAMMADIYAH.** **Main/Corp** Muhammadiyah (Organization). Indonesian. Pimpinan Pusat Muhammadiyah Majlis Pustaka, Jl Kha Dahlan 99, Jogyakarta Indonesia. **LC** BP10; .M813. **UDC** 297. **Continues** Almanak Muhammadijah.

US/0887-7653
**AMERICAN JOURNAL OF ISLAMIC SOCIAL SCIENCES, THE.** See Social Sciences.

NE/0066-1554
**ANATOLICA.** See Linguistics.

UA
**ANNALES ISLAMOLOGIQUES.** **Added/Corp** Institut Francais d'Archeologie Orientale du Caire. (195?)-. Periodical. Arabic (French and English). ir (1-2 times per year / one issue per volume). $75.00. Leila Bookshop, PO Box 31 El-Daher, 11271 Cairo Egypt. **Tel** 011 202 3924475, 011 202 3507399. **LC** BP1; .A65. **Continues** Melanges Islamologiques.
**Desc:** Ideas in the areas of Islamic arts, architecture, and archeology.
**Ind/Abst** BHA : Biblio. Hist. Art; Index Islam. Lit.; Middle East J.

US/0195-9212
**BAHAI NEWS (WILMETTE).** (BAHA'I NEWS.). Periodical. English. mo. $8.00. National Spiritual Assembly of the Bahais of the United States, 112 Linden Avenue, Wilmette IL 60091. **Tel** (312)869-9039. **ED** John Bowers. **LC** BP300; .B25. **DD** 297/.09/.05. **UDC** 298.8. Index available. **Circ**: 5,000 (ctrl).

PK
**BASIR.** VFOAT Baseer. Periodical. Urdu. mo. 10.00. Zafar Hamid, Hamid Manzil Basir Istrit Nazim Abad No 2, Karachi Pakistan. **LC** BP1; .B355.

GW
**BIBLIOTHECA ISLAMICA.** **Added/Corp** Deutsche Morgenlandische Gesellschaft. (1929)-. Monographic series. German. ir. Price varies per volume. Franz Steiner Verlag GmbH, Postfach 101061, D 70009 Stuttgart Germany. **Tel** 011 49 0711 2582372, FAX 011 49 0711 2582290, telex 723636 daz d. **ED** Ulrich Haarmann, Erika Glassen.

UA/0259-7373
**BULLETIN CRITIQUE DES ANNALES ISLAMOLOGIQUES.** **Added/Corp** Institut Francais d'Archeologie Orientale du Caire. (1986)-. Bulletin. French. an. **LC** BP1; .B8.
**Ind/Abst** BHA : Biblio. Hist. Art.

II
**BULLETIN OF THE HENRY MARTYN INSTITUTE OF ISLAMIC STUDIES (HYDERABAD, INDIA).** (THE BULLETIN OF THE HENRY MARTYN INSTITUTE OF ISLAMIC STUDIES.). **Added/Corp** Henry Martyn Institute of Islamic Studies. VFOAT Bulletin. Vol. 3, No. 3 (July/Sept. 1985)-. Bulletin. English. Four times a year (Jan., Apr., July, Oct.). Henry Martyn Institute, PO Box 153, Hyderabad 500001 AP India. **Tel** 268645. (**Subscription address:** Prints India, 11 Darya Ganj, New Delhi 110002 India.) **LC** BP1; .B84. **DD** 297/.05. Index available. cum. index. **Bk Rev. Circ**: 500. **Continues** Bulletin of Christian Institutes of Islamic Studies (Hyderabad, India), 0970-4698.
**Desc:** Concerns comparative religion, Islamic studies, and Christian-Muslim relations.
**Ind/Abst** Bibliogr. Mission.; Index Book Rev. Relig.; Relig. Index One Period.

CN/0707-2945
**CANADIAN MUSLIM, THE.** V. 1- July 1977-. Periodical. English (Arabic). qt. Free. Ottawa Muslim Association, PO Box 2952 Station D, Ottawa Ontario K1P 5W9 Canada. **ED** Saeed Bokhari, Khalifah Ihsanullah and Zohaiv Hassan. **DD** 297/.65. **UDC** 297(71). **Bk Rev. Ad Acc.** ctrl circ.

●UK/0966-3452
**CENTRAL ASIA BRIEF.** **Added/Corp** Islamic Foundation (Great Britain). No. 1 (1992)-. Periodical. English. bm. Islamic Foundation Publishing Unit, Unit 9/Old Dunlop Factory, 62 Evington Valley Road, Leicester LE5 5LJ England. **Tel** 011 44 533 734860, FAX 011 44 533 244946, telex 341539 ISLAMF G. **LC** DK845; .C46. **Continues** Soviet Muslims Brief.

GW
**CIBEDO BEITRAEGE ZUM GESPRACH ZWISCHEN CHRISTEN UND MUSLIMEN.** **Added/Corp** Christlich-Islamische Begegnung "Dokumentationsleitstelle" (Cologne, Germany). VFOAT C.I.B.E.D.O. Beitrage zum Gesprach Zwischen Christen und Muslimen. Vol. 1, No. 1 (1987)-. Periodical. German. Four times a year. DM25.58 Germany; DM27.50 other. CIBEDO, Postfach 17 04 27, D 60078 Frankfurt Germany. **Tel** 011 49 69 726491. **Formed by the union of** CIBEDO-Dokumentation, 0721-0027 **and** CIBEDO-Texte, 0721-0035.

PK
**CONCEPT (ISLAMABAD, PAKISTAN).** See History(General)-History of Asia.

MY/0126-5938
**DAKWAH.** [Dakwah]. Periodical. Malay. $1.00 single issue. Yayasan Dakwah Islamiah Malaysia, Tingkat 11 Wisma Batik Jalan Tun Perak, Kuala Lumpur Malaysia. **LC** BP1; .D34. **UDC** 297.

IR
**DARSHAI AZ MAKTAB-I ISLAM.** VFOAT Maktab-I Islam. Periodical. Persian. mo. 1000.00IR. **LC** BP193.3; .D36. **UDC** 297.

PK
**DIN O DANISH.** VFOAT Din-W-Danish Quarterly. 1970-. Periodical. Multiple languages (Urdu and English).

US/1053-2951
**EDUCATION IN ISLAM.** (1991)-. English. AD Publisher, PO Box 32330, Washington DC 20007.

NE
**ENCYCLOPAEDIA OF ISLAM. NEW ED., PREPARED BY A NUMBER OF LEADING ORIENTALISTS. EDITED BY AN EDITORIAL COMMITTEE CONSISTING OF H.A.R. GIBB [AND OTHERS], THE.** (19??)-. English. ir. $371.50 (Volume VII). E. J. Brill, Postbus 9000, 2300 PA Leiden Netherlands. **Tel** 011 31 71 312624, FAX 011 31 71 317532, telex 39296 BRILL NL.
**Desc:** Sets out in detail the present state of our knowledge of the Islamic world. Articles present original, pioneering research, with extensive bibliographical references to primary and secondary literature. Serves as a reference source for every facet of Islamic culture.

FR/0531-1888
**ETUDES MUSULMANES.** Vol. 1 (1954)-. Monographic series. French. ir. Price varies per volume. Librairie Philosophique J Vrin, 6 Place de la Sorbonne, 75005 Paris France. **Tel** 011 33 1 43540347. **ED** J. Jolivet, A. de Libera and M. Cristiani.
**Desc:** We publish without periodicity, new titles in this area: Islamic philosophy, agreed by the director's collection.

SI
**FAJAR ISLAM (MUSLIM RELIGIOUS COUNCIL OF SINGAPORE).** (FAJAR ISLAM : JOURNAL OF MUSLIM ISSUES IN SINGAPORE.). **Added/Corp** Muslim Religious Council of Singapore. Community Relations and Information Committee. Vol. 1, No. 1 (1988)-. Periodical. English (summaries and/or abstracts in Chinese, Malay and Tamil). an. Majlis Ugama Islam Singapura, Singapore 6 Singapore. **LC** BP63.S55; F34. **DD** 297/.095957/05. **Continues** Fajar Islam, 0046-3183.

PK/0430-4055
**FIKR O NAZAR.** Vol. 1 (1964)-. Periodical. Urdu (Urdu). qt. $15.00. Islamic Research Institute, PO Box 1035, Islamabad Pakistan. **Tel** 011 92 51 8507515, FAX 011 92 51 853360, telex 54068 IIU PK. **ED** Sahibzada Sajidur-Rehman. **LC** BP1. Index available. **Bk Rev. Ad Acc. Circ**: 3,000.

GW
**FREIBURGER ISLAMSTUDIEN.** (1968)-. Monographic series. German. ir. Price varies per volume. Franz Steiner Verlag GmbH, Postfach 101061, D 70009 Stuttgart Germany. **Tel** 011 49 0711 2582372, FAX 011 49 0711 2582290, telex 723636 daz d. **ED** Hans Robert Roemer, Werner Ende.

MR
**FURQAN (CASABLANCA, MOROCCO).** (AL-FURQAN.). Periodical. Arabic. bm. 50MD. Al-Shaykh Muhammad Zahl, Maktabat Shaykh Al-Islam Ibn Taymiyah 91 Mukarpar, Zanqat 65 Bayna Al-Mudun, Al-Dar Al-Bayda Morocco. **LC** BP1; .F85. **UDC** 297.

UK
**HAJJ RESEARCH CENTRE STUDIES.** Vol. 1 (1978)-. Monographic series. English. Price varies per volume. Croom Helm Ltd, 2-10 St John's Road, London SW11 England.

PK/0250-7196
**HAMDARD ISLAMICUS.** (HAMDARD ISLAMICUS : QUARTERLY JOURNAL OF THE HAMDARD NATIONAL FOUNDATION, PAKISTAN.). [Hamdard Islam.]. **Added/Corp** Hamdard National Foundation, Pakistan. Vol. 1, No. 1 (Summer 1978)-. Periodical. English. qt (Mar., June, Sep., Dec.). $28.00. Hamdard Foundation Press, Nazimabad Mandard Center, Karachi 18 Pakistan. **Tel** 616001. **ED** Ansar Zahid Khan. **LC** BP1; .H344. **DD** 297/.05. **Bk Rev. Ad Acc. Circ**: 2,000 (ctrl).
**Desc:** Seeks to build a bridge between Islam and the West. Publishes articles on every branch of Islamic sciences such as Quran, Hadith, jurisprudence and law, etc.
**Ind/Abst** Am. Hist. Life (1980-); Index Islam. Lit.; Index Book Rev. Relig.; Middle East Abstr. Index; Relig. Index One Period. (1981-); Relig. Theol. Abstr.

BG
**I.F. PUBLICATIONS.** **Added/Corp** Isalamika Phaundesana (Bangladesh). VFOAT I.F. Publications; Ipha Prakasana; I. Pha. Prakasana. (19??)-. Monographic series. English. ir. Price varies per volume. Islamic Foundation Bangladesh, Dacca Bangladesh.

UK
**INDEX ISLAMICUS.** See Religion and Theology-Abstracting, Bibliographies and Statistics.

UK
**INDEX OF ISLAMIC LITERATURE.** See Literature-Abstracting, Bibliographies and Statistics.

II
**INTERACTION : MONTHLY NEWSLETTER OF THE HENRY MARTYN INSTITUTE.** **Added/Corp** Henry Martyn Institute. VFOAT Christian Muslim Interaction; Muslim Christian Interaction; A.HMI newsletter. Vol. 1, No. 1 (July 1979)-. Newsletter. English. sa. $25.00. Henry Martyn Institute, PO Box 153, Hyderabad 500001 AP India. **Tel** 268645. (**Subscription address:** Prints India, 11 Darya Ganj, New Delhi, 110002 India, (Phone: 011 91 11 3268645)) **Continues** Interaction (Hyderabad, India : 1975).

PK/0021-0773
**IQBAL REVIEW.** See Literature.

YE
**IRSHAD (SANA, YEMEN).** (AL-IRSHAD.). Periodical. Arabic. mo. 20.00. Maktab Al-Tawjih Wa-Al-Irshad Al-Amm Al-Wizarat Al-Awqaf Bi-Al-Jumhuriyah Al-Arabiyah Al-Yamaniyah, S B 852, Sana Yemen. **LC** BP1; .I62. **UDC** 297.

UK
**ISLAM.** VFOAT Islam Journal. No. 1-. Periodical. English. qt. $12.00. Diwan Press, The Annex Wood, Dalling Hall, Norwich NR11 6SG Norfolk England. **UDC** 297.
**Ind/Abst** Bibliogr. Mission.

UK/0959-6410
**ISLAM & CHRISTIAN MUSLIM RELATIONS.** VFOAT Islam and Christian Muslim Relations Journal; ICMR; Islam and Christian-Muslim Relations; I.C.M.R.; Islam & Christian-Muslim Relations Journal. Vol. 1, No. 1 (June 1990)-. Periodical. English. Twice a year (June and December). £48.00. Carfax Publishing Company, PO Box 25 Abingdon, Oxfordshire OX14 3UE England. **Tel** 011 44 235 555335, FAX (0279)310015, telex 817484. (**Subscription address:** US and Canada/ PO Box 2025, Dunnellon, FL 34430-2025; telephone:(904)489-6996) **ED** Christian W. Troll. **LC** BP172; .I787. **DD** 297/.1972. Index available. available on microfiche. **Continues** Bulletin on Islam and Christian-Muslim Relations in Africa, 0264-1356.
**Desc:** Invites scholarly contributions concerning both Islam and Christian-Muslim relations worldwide. It will deal with a wide range of subjects in these areas and especially seeks to encourage research into specific historical, regional or sociological themes. Articles are welcome which deal with the role of Muslim interaction with Christian and other societies and cultures whether minorities or majorities.
**Ind/Abst** Index Book Rev. Relig.; Relig. Index One Period.; Soc. Plann. Policy Dev. Abstr.; Middle East J.

II/0021-1826
**ISLAM AND THE MODERN AGE.** **Added/Corp** Islam and the Modern Age Society. (May 1970)-. Periodical. English. qt. $30.00. Zakir Husain Institute of Islamic Studies, Jamia Millia Islamia, 110025 New Delhi India. **Tel** 011 9 11 630258. (**Subscription address:** Prints India, 11 Darya Ganj, New Delhi, 110002 India, (Phone: 011 91 11 3268645)) **ED** D.S. Jamaluddin. **LC** D199.3; .I78. Index available. **Circ**: 1,500.
**Desc:** Articles on Islam and other religions are published in this journal. Moreover, historical and philosophical aspects of religions are also studied through articles.
**Ind/Abst** Bibliogr. Mission.; Index Islam. Lit.; Int. Polit. Sci. Abstr.; Middle East J.

BG/0379-4032
**ISLAM AND THE MODERN WORLD.** V. 1- Mar. 1977-. Periodical. English. qt. $8.00. GPO Box 351, 16-A Larmini, Dacca Bangladesh. **LC** BP1; .I655. **DD** 297/.05. **UDC** 297.

GW/0021-1818
**ISLAM (BERLIN), DER.** (DER ISLAM.). [Islam]. Vol. 1 (1910)-. Periodical. German. sa. $123.35. Walter de Gruyter Inc., PO Box 303421, D 10728 Berlin Germany. **Tel** 011 49 30 260050, FAX 011 49 30 26005251. **LC** DS36; .I7. **[CCC].** Documents available from The Genuine Article.
**Ind/Abst** Index Book Rev. Relig.; MLA Int. Bibl. Books Artic. Mod. Lang. Lit.; Numis. Lit.; Relig. Index One Period.; Res. Alert [Full Cov.]; Soc. Sci. Cit. Index [Select. Cov.]; Middle East J.

FR/0984-7685
**ISLAM ET SOCIETES AU SUD DU SAHARA.** (May 1987)-. French (English and German). an. 50.00F. Maison des Sciences de l Homme, Bureau 413, 54 Boulevard Raspail, 75270 Paris Cedex 06 France. **Tel** 011 33 1 49542013, 011 33 1 49542236. **(Subscription address:** CID, 131 Boulevard Saint Michel, 75005 Paris France.**) LC** BP64.A4; S824.
**Ind/Abst** Am. Hist. Life (1987-); Int. Bibliogr. Sociol. (19??-); PAIS Int. Print (19??-).

GW/0393-246X
**ISLAM, STORIS E CIVILTA.** (ISLAM.). [Islam stor. civilta]. **Added/Corp** Accademia Della Cultura Islamica. (1982)-. Periodical. German. Four times a year (Mar., June, Sept., Dec.). 30.00F Switzerland; 35.00F others. Der Islam, Forchstrasse 323, 8008 Zurich Switzerland.
**Ind/Abst** Middle East J.

TU
**ISLAM TETKIKLERI ENSTITUSU DERGISI.** **Main/Corp** Istanbul. Universite. Islam Tetkikleri Enstitusu. **Added/Corp** Istanbul. Universite. Islam Tetkikleri Enstitusu. Review of the Institute of Islamic Studies. **VFOAT** Review of the Institute of Islamic Studies. Vol. 1 (1953)-. Multiple languages (Turkish, English and French). qt. Ayniyat Burosu, Istanbul University, Faculty of Letters, Istanbul Turkey. **LC** BP20; .I76a.
**Ind/Abst** Am. Hist. Life (1953, 1964-).

US/0748-0482
**ISLAMIC AFFAIRS.** Periodical. English (Arabic). mo. $15.00. Islamic Affairs, POB 5132, Falls Church VA 22044. **Tel** (703)536-6728. **ED** Yasin T Aljibouri. **UDC** 297. **Bk Rev**. **Ad Acc. Circ:** 6,000 (ctrl).
**Desc:** Covers non-sectarian, non-political Islamic information.

UK
**ISLAMIC AFFAIRS ANALYST.** **See** Political Science.

II/0021-1834
**ISLAMIC CULTURE.** [Islam. cult.]. **Added/Corp** Islamic Culture Board. Vol. 1, No. 1 (Jan. 1927)-. Periodical. English. qt. $40.00. **(Subscription address:** Prints India, 11 Darya Ganj, New Delhi 110002 India.**) LC** DS36; .I74. **DD** 950. available on microfilm.

MY/0126-852X
**ISLAMIC HERALD.** [Islam. her.]. **Added/Corp** Pertubuhan Kebajikan Islam Malaysia. Vol. 1 (May 1975)-. English. Six times a year. $3.00. Islamic Herald, 250 D Tingkat 2, Jalan Ipoh Kuala Lumpur Malaysia. **LC** BP1; .I675. **DD** 297/.05.
**Ind/Abst** Index Islam. Lit.

US/8756-2367
**ISLAMIC HORIZONS.** [Islam. horiz.]. **Added/Corp** Islamic Society of North America. Muslim Students' Association of the United States and Canada. Vol. 5, No. 4, (1976)-. Periodical. English. qt. $24.00 US; $28.00 Canada; $36.00 other. Islamic Horizons, PO Box 38, Plainfield IN 46168. **Tel** (317)839-1803, (317)839-8157. **LC** BP1; .I676. **DD** 297/.05. ***Continues*** *MSA News.*

NE/0928-9380
**ISLAMIC LAW AND SOCIETY.** (19??)-. English. Three times a year. Fl220.00 (institutions) Netherlands; $125.75 other. E. J. Brill, Postbus 9000, 2300 PA Leiden Netherlands. **Tel** 011 31 71 312624, FAX 011 31 71 317532, telex 39296 BRILL NL.

PK
**ISLAMIC ORDER.** V. 1- Jan. 1979-. Periodical. English. $20.00. Ismail, Ahmad Minai 218, Bahadurabad Karachi Pakistan. **LC** BP1; .I686. **DD** 297/.05. **UDC** 297.
**Ind/Abst** Index Islam. Lit.

II
**ISLAMIC PERSPECTIVE.** **Added/Corp** Institute of Islamic Studies (Bombay, India). Vol. 1, Issue 1 (Jan. 1984)-. Periodical. English. sa. $30.00. Institute of Islamic Studies, Bombay, India. **(Subscription address:** Prints India, 11 Darya Ganj, New Delhi, 110002 India, (Phone: 011 91 11 3268645)**) LC** BP1; .I688. **DD** 297/.05.

US/0730-613X
**ISLAMIC REVOLUTION.** [Islam. revolut.]. Vol. 1 Apr. 1979-. Periodical. English. mo. $12.00 US; $14.00 Canada. Research and Publication, PO Box 2556, Falls Church VA 22042. **UDC** 297.

PK/0578-8072
**ISLAMIC STUDIES.** **Added/Corp** Islamic Research Institute (Pakistan) Central Institute of Islamic Research (Pakistan). Vol. 1 (Mar. 1962)-. Periodical. English. qt (Jan., Apr., July, Oct.). $30.00. Islamic Research Institute, PO Box 1035, Islamabad Pakistan. **Tel** 011 92 51 8507515, FAX 011 92 51 853360, telex 54068 IIU PK. **ED** Zafar-Ishop Ansari. **LC** BP1; .I72. **DD** 297/.05. Index available. cum. index. **Bk Rev**, (Qty: 4). **Ad Acc. Circ:** 3,000 (ctrl).
**Desc:** Publishes articles on Islamic history, law, jurisprudence, politics, economics, literature, culture, science, religion, and other Islamic subjects.
**Ind/Abst** Index Islam. Lit.; Middle East J.

IR
**ITISAM (TEHRAN, IRAN).** (ITISAM.). Periodical. Persian. mo. 600.00IR. Khiyaban-I Talaqani, Tehran Iran. **LC** BP192.7.I68; I86.

TI
**JAWHAR AL-ISLAM.** **VFOAT** Jaoqhar el Islam. Periodical. Multiple languages (Arabic and French). mo. 28 Jamal Abdul Nasser Street, Tunis Tunisia. **LC** BP1; .J38. **UDC** 297.

MY
**JERNAL JIHAD.** **Added/Corp** Universiti Kebangsaan. Fakulti Pengajian Islam. Persatuan Mahasiswa. **VFOAT** Jihad. Vol. 1 (1972/73)-. Malay (English). ir. Persatuan Mahasiswa Fakulti Pengajian Islam, Jalan University, Petaling Jaya Malaysia. **LC** BP1; .J46.

UK/0955-2340
**JOURNAL OF ISLAMIC STUDIES (OXFORD, ENGLAND).** (JOURNAL OF ISLAMIC STUDIES.). **Added/Corp** Oxford Centre for Islamic Studies. Vol. 1 (1990)-. Periodical. English. sa. £54.00 UK and Europe; $98.00 other. Oxford University Press, Walton Street, Oxford OX2 6DP England. **Tel** 011 44 865 56767, FAX 011 44 865 267773, telex 837330 OXPRES G. **(Subscription address:** Oxford University Press / USA, Journals Marketing Department, Oxford University Press, 2001 Evans Road, Cary NC 27513.**) ED** Farhan Ahmad Nizami. **LC** DS35.3; .J68. **DD** 909/.097671. **[CCC].** available on microfilm and microfiche from University Microfilms International (UMI).
**Desc:** Dedicated to the scholarly study of any aspect of Islam and of the Islamic world. Particular emphasis in the fields of history, geography, political science, economics, anthropology, sociology, law literature, religion, philosophy, international relations, and environmental and development issues.

II
**JOURNAL OF OBJECTIVE STUDIES.** **Added/Corp** Institute of Objective Studies (New Delhi, India). Vol. 1, No. 1 & 2 (July-Oct. 1989)-. Periodical. English. qt. $40.00. Institute of Objective Studies, PO Box 9725, Jamia Nagar, New Delhi 110025 India. **Tel** 630989, FAX 6841104. **(Subscription address:** Prints India, 11 Darya Ganj, New Delhi, 110002 India, (Phone: 011 91 11 3268645)**) ED** F.R. Faridi. **LC** IN PROCESS. **Bk Rev. Ad Acc.**

UK/0266-2183
**JOURNAL OF THE MUHYIDDIN IBN ARABI SOCIETY.** **Added/Corp** Muhyiddin Ibn Arabi Society. Vol. 1 (1982)-. English. Twice a year (July and Dec.). £16.50. Muhyiddin Ibn Arabi Society, 23 Oakthorpe Road, Oxford OX2 7BD England. **Tel** 011 44 865 511963. **ED** Mr. S. Hirtenstein. **Bk Rev. Ad Acc.**
**Desc:** Articles, translations, and book reviews.

IR
**KAYHAN-I FARHANGI.** (March/April 1984)-. Periodical. Persian. mo. $222.00 (US & Oceania); $178.00 (Middle East); $202.00 (Europe); $215.00 (other). Kayhan Publications Institute, Martyr Shahcheraghi Avenue, Tehran, Iran. **Tel** 3110251-60, telex 212467. **LC** BP193.5; .K4.

US/1053-2943
**LIFE AFTER DEATH, AN ISLAMIC PERSPECTIVE.** **VFOAT** Life After Death. (1991)-. English. AD Publisher, PO Box 32330, Washington DC 20007.

●US/1060-4596
**LIGHT & ISLAMIC REVIEW, THE.** **Added/Corp** Ahmadiyya Anjuman Ishaat Islam, Lahore. **VFOAT** Light and Islamic Review. Vol. 69, No. 1 (Jan.-Feb. 1992)-. Periodical. English. bm. $15.00 US; $18.00 other. Ahmadiyya Anjuman Ishaat Islam Lashore Inc, 1315 Kingsgate Road, Columbus OH 43221. **Tel** (614)457-8504. **LC** BP1; .L54. ***Continues*** *Light (Columbus, Ohio).*

CN/0229-5636
**LIGHT (TORONTO. 1978).** (THE LIGHT.). [Light]. Vol. 1, No. 1 (1978)-. Periodical. English. ir. Ahmadiyyah Movement, Suite 311, 15 Thorncliffe Park Drive, Toronto Ontario M4H 1H6 Canada. **DD** 297/.86/05. **UDC** 297.

IR
**LUQMAN.** **Added/Corp** Presses Universitaires d'Iran. Vol. 1, No 1 (Fall/Winter 1984/1985)-. Academic Scholarly Publication. French (summaries and/or abstracts in Persian). sa. £10.00 Middle East; £11.00 Europe & Asia; £14.00 America & Far East. Iran University Press, 85 Park Avenue, PO Box 15875/4748, Tehran Iran. **Tel** 623232, FAX (008921)4661749, telex 213636-8-D5300. **ED** Djavad Hadidi. **Bk Rev. Circ:** 1,000.
**Desc:** Presents academic reviews and findings in the fields of literature, theology, philosophy and social sciences.

II/0970-1672
**MAAS JOURNAL OF ISLAMIC SCIENCE.** [MAAS j. Islam. sci.]. **Added/Corp** Muslim Association for the Advancement of Science. **VFOAT** Journal of Islamic Science. **VAT** Muslim Association for the Advancement of Science Journal of Islamic Science. Vol. 1, No. 1 (Jan. 1985)-. Periodical. English (Urdu). Twice a year. $20.00. Muslim Association for the Advancement of Science, Al Homera Muzammil Manzil Corp, Civil Lines Alig 202 002 India. **Tel** 011 571 29209. **(Subscription address:** Prints India, 11 Darya Ganj, New Delhi 110002 India.**) ED** M Zaki Kirmani. **LC** BP190.5.S3; M33. **DD** 297/.1975. **NLM** W1; M103. **CODEN** MJISEN. Index available. **Bk Rev. Ad Acc. Pr Rev. Circ:** 1,000.
**Ind/Abst** Index Islam. Lit.

IR
**MAHJUBAH.** (19??)-. Periodical. English. Twelve times a year. $30.00. Islamic Thought Foundation, PO Box 14155 3987, Tehran Iran. **LC** BP193.5; .M325. **DD** 297/.05.

IR
**MAHNAMAH-I PASDAR-I ISLAM / DAFTAR-I TABLIGHAT-I ISLAMI.** **VFOAT** Pasdar-I Islam. Periodical. Persian. mo. 900.00IR Iran; $10.00 (per issue) US. Daftar-I Tablighat-I Islami, PO Box 320, Qum Iran. **Tel** 0251-24803. **ED** M Rahimian. **LC** BP1927.I68; M34. **UDC** 297.
**Desc:** Interpretation of the Holy Qoran, traditions of Holy prophets and Imams, analysis of daily political events, consideration of the society's problems, consideration of different Islamic subjects and interviews with important persons. Its essential policy is influenced by Islam, with the cooperation and sympathy of outstanding Islamic scholars; not affiliated with any party.

II
**MAHNAMAH RAH-I ISLAM.** **Added/Corp** Khanah-yi Farhang Jamhuri Islami Iran (New Delhi, India). **VFOAT** Rah-e-Islam Urdu Monthly; Rah-I Islam. (1991)-. Periodical. Urdu. mo. Rs5.00 (single issue). Khanah-Yi Farhang-I Jamhuri Islami Iran, 18 Tilak Marg, Na'l Dihli India.

IR
**MAJALLAH-I NUR-I ILM : NASHRIYAH-I JAMIAH-I MUDARRISIN-I HAWZAH-I ILMIYAH-I QUM.** Periodical. Persian. **LC** BP193.5; .M329. **UDC** 297.

SJ
**MAJALLAT AL-FIKR AL-ISLAMI / TUSDIRUHA JAMAAT AL-FIKR WA-AL-THAQAFAH AL-ISLAMIYAH BI-AL-KHARTUM.** V. 1, No. 1, (September 1983)-. Periodical. Arabic. qt. $2.00 single issue. Slkritir Tahrir Majallat, Al-Fikr Al-Islami, PO Box 2469 Al-Khartum Sudan. **LC** BP1; .M3178. **UDC** 297.

UA
**MAJALLAT KULLIYAT AL-SHARIAH.** **See** Law.

SU
**MAJALLAT KULLIYAT USUL AL-DIN / TUSDIRUHA KULLIYAT USUL AL-DIN.** Periodical. Arabic. an. Amid Kulliyat Usul Al-Din, Shari Al-Zahran S B 5446, Al-Riyad Saudi Arabia. **LC** BP1; .M3245.

UA
**MAKARIM AL-AKHLAQ AL-ISLAMIYAH.** Began in 1900. Periodical. Arabic. Jamiyat Makarim Al-Akhlaq Al-Islamiyah, 61 Shari Jazirat Badran Shubra, Al-Qahirah United Arab Republic (Egypt). **LC** BP1; .M325. **UDC** 297.

TS
**MANAR AL-ISLAM.** V. 1- Jan. 1976-. Periodical. Arabic. $30.00 Egypt; $20.00 North America; $12.00 to $15.00 other. Ministry of Justice and Islamic Affairs, PO Box 2922, Abu Zaby Trucial States, Abu Dhabi United Arab Emirates. **Tel** 212300. **ED** Ali Mohamed Al Egla. **LC** BP1; .M353. **UDC** 297. Index available. cum. index. **Bk Rev. Circ:** 30,000 (ctrl).

●US/1071-5215
**MESSAGE (1993).** (THE MESSAGE.). [Message]. **Added/Corp** Islamic Circle of North America. Vol. 16, No.

●9 (Feb. 1993)-. Periodical. English. mo. $25.00 (one year), $45.00 (two year), $54.00 (three year). Islamic Circle of North America, 166-26 89th Avenue, Jamaica NY 11432. **Tel** (718)658-5163, FAX (718)523-3645. **ED** Muhammad F. Khan. **DD** 297. **Bk Rev. Ad Acc, Adv Mgr:** Tariq Kahn. **Circ:** 6,275 (ctrl). ***Continues*** *Message International (Jamaica, New York, N.Y.), 1046-1019.*

IO
**MIMBAR AGAMA & BUDAYA / DIASUH OLEH LEMBAGA PENELITIAN IAIN JAKARTA.** **VFOAT** Mimbar Agama Dan Budaya. V. 1, No. (April 1983)-. Periodical. Indonesian. qt. Rp4,000. Institut Agama Islam Negeri, Syarif Hidayatullah, Jl Ciputat Raya, Jakarta Selatan Indonesia. **Tel** 741925. **ED** H Mastuhu, Rusaini Rusin, H Hisyam Maksum, Roswen Dja'far, Husni Thoyyar, M Dien Madjid, Faridal Arkam. **LC** BP1; .M468. **UDC** 297(594).

UK
**MINARET, THE.** **VFOAT** Minaret Educational Review. Vol. 1 (Jan./Mar. 1977)-. Periodical. English (Arabic). qt. £2.00 UK; £3.00 other. Minaret House, 9 Leslie Park Road, Surrey CR0 6TN Croydon England. **LC** LC901; .M56. **DD** 370/.917/671.

PK/0026-4415
**MINARET, THE.** **Added/Corp** World Federation of Islamic Missions. **VFOAT** Minaret Monthly International. (1964)-. Periodical. English. mo. **LC** BP1; .M48.

US/0892-0559
**MINARET (LOS ANGELES, CALIF.), THE.** (THE MINARET.). [Minaret]. **Added/Corp** Islamic Center of Southern California. (19??)-. Periodical. English. Four times a year. $10.00 US; $40.00 others. Islamic Information Service, 434 South Vermont Avenue, Los Angeles CA 90020. **Tel** (213)384-4570. **DD** 297.

UA
**MINBAR AL-ISLAM.** **Added/Corp** United Arab Republic. Majlis al-Ala lil-Shuun al-Islamiyah. Vol. 1 (July 1961)-. Periodical. English. qt. Miss Linda Fawzi, 3 Kobessi Str Fagallah, Cairo Egypt. **LC** BP1; .M5.

UK
**MUSLIM HERALD.** English. Muslim Herald, 16 Gressenhall Road, London SW18 5QL England.

II
**MUSLIM INDIA.** Vol. 1, No. 1 (Jan. 1983)-. Periodical. English. mo. $25.00. Muslim India, New Delhi, India. **(Subscription address:** Prints India, 11 Darya Ganj, New Delhi, 110002 India, (Phone: 011 91 11 3268645)) **LC** DS432.M84; M87. **DD** 954/.00882971.

TR
**MUSLIM (JAMAAH AL-ISLAMIYAH (LIBIYA)).** (AL-MUSLIM.). Periodical. Arabic. $15.00. Al-Muslim, PO Box 1147, Port of Spain Trinidad West Indies. **LC** DS35.3; .M87. **UDC** 297.

US/0883-816X
**MUSLIM JOURNAL.** [Muslim j.]. **VFOAT** World News Examiner. Vol. 10, No. 28 (May 10, 1985)-. Newspaper. English. wk. $39.00 (one year), $65.00 (two year) US; $50.00 (one year), $86.00 (two year) other. Mulsim Journal, 910 West Van, Suite 100, Chicago IL 60607. **Tel** (312)243-7600, FAX (312)243-9778. **ED** Ayesha K. Mustafaa. **DD** 297. **Bk Rev. Ad Acc. Circ:** 15,000 (ctrl). ***Continues*** *A.M. Journal.*
**Desc:** World and local current events evolving out of truth and righteousness.

UK/0260-3063
**MUSLIM WORLD BOOK REVIEW, THE.** Vol. 1, No. 1 (Autumn 1980)-. Periodical. English. qt. £20.00 (individuals), £30.00 (institutions), UK; £28.00 (individuals), £38.00 (institutions) other. Islamic Foundation Publishing Unit, Unit 9/Old Dunlop Factory, 62 Evington Valley Road, Leicester LE5 5LJ England. **Tel** 011 44 533 734860, FAX 011 44 533 244946, telex 341539 ISLAMF G. **ED** M.M/ Attan and A.R. Kidwai. **LC** DS35.3; .M88. **DD** 909/.097671. **UDC** 297(048.4). Index available. cum. index. **Bk Rev. Ad Acc. Circ:** 1,000.
**Desc:** Aspires both to inform and stimulate the lay readers as well as the scholars through in-depth reviews, short introductions and select bibliographies.
**Ind/Abst** Index Book Rev. Relig.; Middle East J.

US/0027-4909
**MUSLIM WORLD (HARTFORD), THE.** (THE MUSLIM WORLD.). [Muslim world]. **Added/Corp** Hartford Seminary Foundation. Duncan Black Macdonald Center. Vol. 38 (Jan. 1948)-. Periodical. English. qt (January, April, July, October). $30.00 (institutions), $20.00 (individuals). Hartford Seminary, 77 Sherman Street, Hartford CT 06105. **Tel** (203)232-4451, FAX (203)231-0648. **ED** Ibrahim Abu-Rabi, David A. Kerr. Index available. cum. index. **Bk Rev. Ad Acc. Circ:** 1,400 (ctrl). available on microfilm and microfiche from University Microfilms International (UMI); available on CD-ROM. Documents available from The Genuine Article, UMI Article Clearinghouse. ***Continues*** *Moslem World, 0362-4641.*
**Desc:** Study of Islam and Christian-Muslim relations in the past and present.
**Ind/Abst** Acad. Search (July 1993-); Am. Hist. Life (1971-); Arts Humanit. Citation Index [Full Cov.]; Bibliogr. Mission.; Curr. Contents Arts Humanit.; Expand. Acad. Index (1989-); Humanit. Index; Humanit. Source (Jul. 1993-); Index Islam. Lit.; Index Book Rev. Relig.; INFO-SOUTH Abstr.; Mag. Search; Middle East Abstr. Index; MLA Int. Bibl. Books Artic. Mod. Lang. Lit.; Newsp. Period. Abstr. (1991-); Relig. Index One Period. (1949-); Relig. Theol. Abstr.; Res. Alert [Full Cov.]; Soc. Sci. Cit. Index [Select. Cov.]; Middle East J.

SU
**MUSLIM WORLD LEAGUE JOURNAL, THE.** **Added/Corp** Muslim World League. **VFOAT** M.W.L. Journal; MWL Journal. (198?)-. Periodical. English (Arabic). mo. 36riyals (individuals), 100riyals (institutions) Saudi Arabia; $20.00 (individuals), $26.00 (institutions) other. Muslim World League, PO Box 537 & 538, Makkah Al-Mukkarramah, Mecca, Saudi Arabia. **Tel** 011 966 2 544-5335, FAX 011 966 2 543-1688. **ED** Abdulahi Sheikh Muhammad & Muhammad Nasir. **LC** BP1; .R32a. **DD** 2997/.05. **Bk Rev. Ad Acc. Pr Rev. Circ:** 30,000 (ctrl). ***Continues*** *Journal of Muslim World League.*
**Desc:** This publication focuses on the Muslim world, Islamic history, and current affairs. It a cover story and guidance form the Quran and Sunnah of Prophet Muhammed.

IR/0259-9090
**NASHR-I DANISH.** **Added/Corp** Sitad-i Inqilab-i Farhangi (Iran). Vol. 1, (Nov./Dec. 1980)-. Academic Scholarly Publication. Persian. bm (6 issues). £26.00 Middle East; £30.00 Europe & Asia; £34.00 America & Far East. Iran University Press, 85 Park Avenue, PO Box 15875/4748, Tehran Iran. **Tel** 623232, FAX (008921)4661749, telex 213636-8-D5300. **ED** Nasrollah Pourjavady. **LC** DS266; .N319. Index available. **Bk Rev. Ad Acc. Pr Rev. Circ:** 12,000.
**Desc:** Contains literary articles, book reviews, bibliographic listings, and news about books related to the field of scholarly publishing in Iran and elsewhere.

SU
**NASHRAT MAHAD SHUUN AL-AQALLIYAT AL-MUSLIMAH, JAMIAT AL-MALIK ABD AL-AZIZ BI-JIDDAH.** **Main/Corp** Jamiat Al-Malik Abd Al-Aziz. Mahad Shuun Al-Aqalliyat Al-Muslimah. **Added/Corp** Jamiat al-Malik Abd al-Aziz al-Ahliyah. Mahad Shuun al-Aqalliyat al-Muslimah. Bulletin. **VFOAT** Bulletin - Institute of Muslim Minority Affairs (IMMA), King Abdul Aziz University, Jeddah. (19??)-. Arabic (English). bm. $17.00. Institute of Muslim Minority Affairs, 46 Goodge Street/1st Floor, London W1P 1FJ United Kingdom. **Tel** 11 44 71 636 6740, FAX 11 44 71 255 1473, telex 296182. **ED** Syed Z Abedin. **LC** BP52.5; .J35a. cum. index. **Bk Rev. Ad Acc.**
**Desc:** An investigation into the conditions of life of Muslim minorities all over the world.

US/1054-3880
**NETWORK (NEWARK, N.J.), THE.** (THE NETWORK : THE NEWSLETTER OF THE AFRICAN-AMERICAN INSTITUTE OF ISLAMIC RESEARCH.). [Network]. **Added/Corp** African-American Institute of Islamic Research. Vol. 1, No. 1 (Jan. 1991)-. Newsletter. English. bm. $12.00. African-American Institute of Islamic Research, PO Box 1235, Newark NJ 07101. **DD** 297.

UK/0955-095X
**NEW HORIZON (LONDON, ENGLAND).** (NEW HORIZON.). Periodical. English. mo. £10.00 England; $40.00 North America; £18.00 Middle East and Africa, India, Pakistan, and Bangladesh; £15.00 Europe; £20.00 other. New Horizon, 144-146 King's Cross Road, London WC1X 9DH England. **Tel** (01)833-8275, FAX (01)278-4797, telex (01)893-578 ISLAMI. **ED** S Ghazanfar Ali, Asma Siddiqi, and Karen Dabrowska. **Bk Rev. Ad Acc. Circ:** 7,000 (ctrl).
**Desc:** Muslim world review.

US/0732-1848
**NEW TREND (BALTIMORE, MD.).** **See** Political Science-International Relations.

UK/0143-9774
**NEWS OF MUSLIMS IN EUROPE.** ***Ceased.*** (March 7, 1980)-?. Periodical. English. qt. The Centre Selly Oak Colleges, Birmingham B29 6LE United Kingdom. **Tel** 021-472 0063. **ED** Jorgen S Nielsen. **UDC** 297(4). Index available. **Circ:** 500.
**Desc:** Mimeographed, eight-to-ten pages; supplements "Research Papers," publishing short accounts of developments relating to Muslims and Christian-Muslim relations in Europe on topics of current interest.

UA
**NIDA AL-ISLAM.** **VFOAT** Mawsuat Nida Al-Islam. (19??)-. Periodical. Arabic. mo. 0.60 (single issue). Dar Al-Fikr, 58 Shari 26 Yuliyu, Al-Qahirah United Arab Republic Egypt. **LC** BP1; .N52.

II
**NUR-I HAYAT.** **VFOAT** Noor-E-Hyat. Periodical. Urdu (Urdu). 8.00. Markazi Anjiman-I Mahdviyyah Building, Chancalguda, Haidrabad India. **LC** BP193.5; .N86. **UDC** 297.

US/8756-4637
**NURADEEN.** [Nuradeen]. Periodical. English. qt. $16.00. Zahra Publications, PO Box 730, Blanco TX 78606. **Tel** (512)833-5334. **DD** 297. **UDC** 297. **Bk Rev. Ad Acc. Circ:** 5,000 (ctrl).

MY/0128-3715
**PERIODICA ISLAMICA : AN INTERNATIONAL CONTENTS JOURNAL.** Vol. 1, No. 1 (1991)-. Periodical. English. qt. £120.00; $70.00 (institution), $35.00 (individual) US & Canada. Berita Publishing Company, 22 Jalan Liku, 59100 Kuala Lumpur Malaysia. **Tel** 60 3 2825286, FAX 60 3 2821605, telex 30259. **(Subscription address:** US and Canada/ PO Box 2025, Dunnellon, FL 34430-2025; telephone:(904)489-6996) **ED** Ahmad Kushairi Darus and Hashim M. Isa. **LC** IN PROCESS. **[CCC].** Index available. cum. index. **Ad Acc. Circ:** 750. available on microfilm and microfiche.

KE
**PRISM (NAIROBI, KENYA).** (PRISM.). Began with 1978 vol. Periodical. English. an. Prism, PO Box 40190, Nairobi Kenya. **LC** BP195.I8; P75. **DD** 297/.822/05. **UDC** 297(676.2).

UK/0308-7395
**QUARTERLY INDEX ISLAMICUS.** **See** Religion and Theology-Abstracting, Bibliographies and Statistics.

●US/1064-0770
**QURANIC GUIDANCE.** (QURANIC GUIDANCE : QURANIC VERSES WITH THEIR ENGLISH AND BENGALI TRANSLATION.). (1992)-. English. Belal-E-Islam Rokonuddin, 6907 Riggs Road, Hyattsville MD 20783.

II
**RAID (LUCKNOW, INDIA).** (AL-RAID.). **VFOAT** Sahifat Al-Raid, Al-Hind. Periodical. Arabic. sm. Rs25.00. Al-Raid Nadwa, PO Box 93, Lucknow India. **LC** BP1; .R35.

UK/0260-3772
**RESEARCH PAPERS (CENTRE FOR THE STUDY OF ISLAM AND CHRISTIAN-MUSLIM RELATIONS (BIRMINGHAM, WEST MIDLANDS, ENGLAND)).** ***Ceased.*** (RESEARCH PAPERS : MUSLIMS IN EUROPE.). **VFOAT** Muslims in Europe. March 1979-?. Periodical. English. qt. The Centre Selly Oak Colleges, Birmingham B29 6LE United Kingdom. **Tel** 021-472 0063. **ED** Jorgen S Nielsen. **UDC** 297. **Ad Acc. Circ:** 600.
**Desc:** Contains one or more articles on a chosen theme; covers law, immigration, women's status, dialogue and education. Unique resource for researchers on Muslims in Europe.
**Ind/Abst** Br. Humanit. Index.

SP
**REVISTA DEL INSTITUTO DE ESTUDIOS ISLAMICOS.** Spanish. be. 2000.00ptas. Institut Francisco de Asis Mendez, Casariego 10 Matias Montero 14, Madrid 2 Spain. **Tel** 011 34 1 5639468.

FR/0336-156X
**REVUE DES ETUDES ISLAMIQUES.** [Rev. etud. islam.]. Vol. 1 (1927)-. Periodical. French. ir. 640.00F (latest volume). Librairie Orientaliste Paul Geuthner, 12 rue Vavin, 75006 Paris France. **Tel** 011 33 1 46347130. **ED** L. Massignon. **LC** BP1; .R53. **DD** 297.05. ***Supersedes*** *Revue du Monde Musulman.*
**Ind/Abst** MLA Int. Bibl. Books Artic. Mod. Lang. Lit.

FR/0997-1327
**REVUE DU MONDE MUSULMAN ET DE LA MEDITERRANEE.** **Added/Corp** Association pour l'Etude des Sciences Humaines en Afrique du Nord et au Proche-Orient. (1988)-. Periodical. English (French). qt. 303.32F France; 320.00F other. Editions Edisud, La Calade RN 7, 13090 Aix En Provence France. **Tel** 011 33 42 216144, FAX 011 33 42 215620. **ED** Baduel Pierre and Panzac Daniel. **LC** DT160; .R44. **DD** 909/.097671/05. Index available. **Bk Rev.** ctrl circ. ***Continues*** *Revue de l'Occident Musulman et de la Mediterranee, 0035-1474.*
**Desc:** Journal of the Arab world and the Mediterranean.
**Ind/Abst** Am. Hist. Life (1974-); Int. Bibliogr. Sociol.; Middle East J.

MR
**RISALAH (RABAT, MOROCCO).** (AL-RISALAH.). **VFOAT** Arrisala. Periodical. Arabic. sm. 1.00 single issue. B P 356, Rabat Morocco. **LC** BP1; .R538. **UDC** 297.

UA
**RISALAT AL-AZHAR.** No. 1- (July 3, 1981). Periodical. Arabic. wk. Idarat Al-Azhar Bi-Al-Qahirah Egypt, Majma Al-Buhuth, Al-Islamiyah Bi-Al-Azhar, Al-Qahirah Egypt. **LC** BP1; .C3 SUPPL. **UDC** 297.

# Religion and Theology —Judaism

UA
**RISALAT AL-ISLAM (CAIRO, EGYPT : 1983).** (RISALAT AL-ISLAM / YUSDIRUHA AL-MARKAZ AL-AMM LI-JAMIYAT AL-SHUBBAN AL-MUSLIMIN AL-ALAMIYAH.). No. 1 (December 1983)-. Periodical. Arabic. mo. £E0.25 single issue. 12 Shari Ramsis, Al-Qahirah Egypt. **LC** BP1; .R562. **UDC** 297.

SU
**RISALAT AL-MAAHID AL-ILMIYAH / TASDURU AN MAHAD AL-RIYAD AL-ILMI.** **VFOAT** Message Magazine. Periodical. Arabic. Al-Batha Mahad Al-Riyad Al-Ilmi, Al-Riyad Saudi Arabia. **LC** BP1; .R565. **UDC** 297.

LY
**RISALAT SL-JIHAD.** **Added/Corp** Jamiyat Al-Dawah Al-Islamiyah (Libya). **VFOAT** Rissalat Al-Jihad. (19??)-. Periodical. English (English). mo. $1.00 single issue. PO Box 2682, Tripoli Libya. **LC** BP1; .R564. **DD** 297/.05.

TU
**SELCUK UNIVERSITESI ILAHIYAT FAKULTESI DERGISI.** **VFOAT** Ilahiyat Fakultesi Dergisi. Periodical. Turkish (English). **LC** BP1; .S45. **Ind/Abst** Index Vet.

IO
**SINAR DARUSSALAM.** Vol. 1.- (No. 1- ); Mar. 1968-. Periodical. Multiple languages (English and Indonesian). 100 each issue. Kopelma Darussalam, Kotak Pos 29, Banda ACEH Indonesia. **LC** BP1; .S56.

IO
**SINAR ISLAM.** Began with Sept. 1932 issue. Periodical. Indonesian. 150 each issue. Jemaat Ahmadiyah Indonesia, JI Tawakkal Ujung Raya 7, Jakarta Barat, Jakarta Indonesia. **LC** BP195.A5; S55.

FR/0585-5292
**STUDIA ISLAMICA.** [Stud. islam.] (1953)-. Periodical. French (English). sa (2 issues). 203.00F France; 214.00F other. Editions Maisonneuve et Larose, 15 rue Victor Cousin, 75005 Paris France. **Tel** 011 33 1 43543270, **FAX** 011 33 1 43257741. **ED** R. Brunschvig and J. Schacht. **LC** BP1; .S8. cum. index.
**Ind/Abst** Am. Hist. Life (1962-); Index Islam. Lit.; MLA Int. Bibl. Books Artic. Mod. Lang. Lit.

IO/0125-0492
**STUDIA ISLAMIKA.** V. 1.- July/Sept. 1976-. Periodical. English (Indonesian). qt. Rp4,000. Institut Agama Islam Negeri, Syarif Hidayatullah, JI Ciputat Raya, Jakarta Selatan Indonesia. **Tel** 741925. **ED** H Chatibul Umam, H Mastuhu, Djabal Noor, Amru Ichwan, Ubaid Madona. **LC** BP1; .S82. **UDC** 297.

UK
**SUFI.** (Fall 1988)-. Periodical. Persian. qt.
**Ind/Abst** Middle East J.

II
**TAHQIQAT-I ISLAMI.** Periodical. Urdu (Urdu). qt. Rs30.00 India; $25.00 other. Idarah-Yi Tahqiq Va Tasnif-I, Islami Panvali Kothi, Dudhpur 202001 Aligarh India. **Tel** 9878. **(Subscription address:** Idara e Tahqeeq o Tasneef e Islami, Panwali Kothi Dodhpur Aligarh UP 202001 India**) ED** Syed Jalaluddin Umri. **LC** BP1; .T25.
**Bk Rev. Ad Acc. Circ:** 1,500 (ctrl).

II
**TAHZIB AL-AKHLAQ.** **VFOAT** Tahzibul Akhlaq Fortnightly; Mohammedan Social Reformer. Periodical. Urdu (Urdu). sm. Rs20.00 India; $15.00 US. Department of Urdu, Aligarh Muslim University, Aligarh India. **LC** BP1; .T253. **UDC** 297.

IR
**TAWHID (TEHRAN, IRAN).** (AL-TAWHID.). **Added/Corp** Sazman-i Tablighat-i Islami (Tehran, Iran). Vol. 1, No. 1 (Oct. 1983)-. Periodical. English. qr. $40.00 (individual); $50.00 (institution). Publilink, PO Box 19395, 4443 Tehran Iran. **Tel FAX** 011 98 21 769432. **LC** BP1; .T38. **DD** 297/.05.
**Ind/Abst** Middle East J.

II/0040-5884
**THEOSOPHICAL MOVEMENT, THE.** **Added/Corp** United Lodge of Theosophists (Bombay, India). Vol. 1 (Nov. 1930)-. Periodical. English. mo. $15.00. Theosophy Company India Private Ltd, Theosophy Hall, 40 New Marine Lines, Bombay 400-020 India. **Tel** 299024. **(Subscription address:** Prints India, 11 Darya Ganj, Delhi, 110002 India, (Phone: 011 91 11 3268645)**) ED** M Dastur. **LC** BP500; .T435. **DD** 212. Index available. **Bk Rev. Circ:** 320.
**Desc:** Devoted to the living of the higher life. Disseminates theosophy as in works of H.P. Blavatsky and William Q. Judge.

BG
**THOUGHTS ON ECONOMICS.** See Economics-Economic History, Conditions.

IR
**TURATHUNA.** **Added/Corp** Muassasat Al-bayt li-Ihya al-Turath,. (1985)-. Periodical. Arabic. Four times a year. Bank Melli Iran QUM, PO Box 996, QUM Iran. **LC** BP193.5; .T87.

II
**UHUD.** **VFOAT** Ohad. Periodical. Urdu (Urdu). 6.50. Ilyas Husain Arzu, Bazaria Fath Ali, Rampur India. **ED** Ilyas Husain Arzu. **LC** BP1; .U36.

QA
**UMMAH (DAWHAH, QATAR).** (AL-UMMAH.). V. 1, No. 1, (Nov. 1980)-. Arabic. mo. $16.00. SB 893, Al-Dawhah Qatar. **LC** BP1; .U39.

PK
**UNIVERSAL MESSAGE, THE.** **Added/Corp** Islamic Research Academy. (June 1979)-. Periodical. English. Twelve times a year. Islamic Research Academy, C-163/10 Mansoora, Karachi 3805 Pakistan. **Tel** 681157. **ED** Qadid Sharif. **LC** BP1; .U54. **DD** 909/.097671. **Bk Rev. Ad Acc.** ctrl circ.
**Desc:** Discussing social, historical, political, and economic subjects as enunciated by Islam.

SZ
**URWAH AL-WUTHQA (GENEVA, SWITZERLAND).** (FIRMEST BOND.). **VFOAT** Le Lien Indeliable; Lien Indeliable. Periodical. English. qt. $50.00 organizations and governments, $25.00 students and scholars. Al-Urwa Al-Wathqa, PO Box 1894, CH-1218 Geneva Switzerland. **Tel** (022)44.22.68, telex 415877 BOND CH. **ED** Abdul H Tabibi. **LC** BP1; .U753. **DD** 297/.05. **UDC** 297. **Bk Rev. Circ:** 2,000.
**Desc:** Comment of world affairs, interreligious, dialogue, history, cultural, etc.

IR
**VAHDAT : NASHRIYAH-I DAFTAR-I TAHKIM-I VAHDAT.** Periodical. Persian. ir. 240.00IR. Khiyaban-I Inqilab Khiyaban-I Kharak Block 52, Tehran Iran. **LC** BP192.7.I68; V34.

US/1049-2526
**VIDYA (SANTA BARBARA, CALIF.).** (VIDYA.). [Vidya]. **Added/Corp** Universal Theosophy Fellowship. Vol. 1, No. 1 (Nov. 1, 1989)-. Periodical. English. Six times a year (Jan., Mar., May, July, Sept., Nov.). $12.00. Vidya, 1407 Chapala Street, Santa Barbara CA 93101. **Tel** (805)966-3941. **LC** BP500; .H43. **DD** 299/.934/05. **Continues** Hermes (Santa Barbara, Calif.), 0736-0940.

PK/0042-8132
**VOICE OF ISLAM, THE.** **Added/Corp** Jamiyat-ul-Falah. (19??)-. Periodical. English. ir. $7.00. Voice of Islam, Box 7141 Akbar Road Sadar, Karachi 3 Pakistan. **Tel** 721391. **LC** BP1; .V6.

IO
**WAHYU.** Ed. 1.- Oct. 1978-. Periodical. Indonesian. mo. 400 single issue. Yayasan Wahyu, JI Kebon Dacang 30 No 9, Jakarta Indonesia. **LC** BP63.I5; W33.

NE/0043-2539
**WELT DES ISLAMS, DIE.** [Welt Islam.]. **Added/Corp** Deutsche Gesellschaft fuer Islamkunde. **VFOAT** World of Islam; Monde de l'Islam. (1913)-. German (English and French). sa. Fl134.00 Netherlands; $76.75 other. E. J. Brill, Postbus 9000, 2300 PA Leiden Netherlands. **Tel** 011 31 71 312624, **FAX** 011 31 71 317532, telex 39296 BRILL NL. **ED** S. Wild. **LC** DS36; .W4. **[CCC]**. cum. index. **Bk Rev. Ad Acc. Circ:** 500 (ctrl).
**Desc:** Focuses on the history and culture of the peoples of Islam from the end of the 18th Century. Special attention is given to literature. In addition to articles, each issue includes a section of short notes.
**Ind/Abst** Am. Hist. Life (1968-); Index Book Rev. Relig.; MLA Int. Bibl. Books Artic. Mod. Lang. Lit.; Relig. Index One Period.; Middle East J.

PK
**WORLD ISLAMIC TIMES.** (1981)-. Periodical. English. Forty-eight times a year. World Islamic Times, Municipal Road G-6/2, Islamabad Pakistan. **LC** BP1; .W66. **DD** 909/.0976710828.

---

# JUDAISM

CN/0711-2092
**ACTUALITE JUIVE.** [Actual. juive]. **VFOAT** Canadian Jewish Digest. **VAT** Canadian Jewish Digest (1978). Vol. 19, No. 4-. Periodical. English (French). sa. $1.00. Canadian Jewish Congress, 1590 Avenue Docteur Penfield, Montreal Quebec H3G 1C5 Canada. **Tel** (514)931-7531. **DD** 971/.004924. **UDC** 971(=924).
**Continues** Selections de Canadian Jewish Digest, 0711-2084.

US/1061-5202
**ADL ON THE FRONTLINE.** See Ethnic Interests.

US/0740-2392
**AGADA.** **VFOAT** Agadah. Vol. 1 No. 1 (Summer 1981)-. Periodical. English. Twice a year (Summer & Winter). $12.00. Agada, 2020 Essex Street, Berkeley CA 94703. **Tel** (510)848-0965. **ED** Reuven Goldfarb. **LC** BM1; .A37. **DD** 296/.05. **Bk Rev. Circ:** 1,000 (ctrl).
**Desc:** An illustrated Jewish literary magazine, featuring the finest available fiction, poetry, memoir, midrash, and commentary reflective of Jewish values, concerns, and sensibility.
**Ind/Abst** Am. Humanit. Index.

US/0747-6175
**AJL NEWSLETTER.** See Library and Information Sciences.

SZ
**AJS BULLETIN.** **Added/Corp** Aktionsgemeinschaft feur die Juden in der Sowjetunion. (Mar./Apr. 1991)-. Bulletin. German. te. **Continues** Juden in der UdSSR.

US/0364-0094
**AJS REVIEW.** [AJS rev.]. **Main/Corp** Association for Jewish Studies. **VAT** Association for Jewish Studies Review. Vol. 1 (1976)-. Academic Scholarly Publication. English (German and Hebrew). Twice a year. $15.00 (latest volume). KTAV Publishing House, Inc., 900 Jefferson Street, PO Box 6249, Hoboken NJ 07030-7205. **Tel** (201)963-9524, **FAX** (201)963-0102. **ED** Norman Stillman. **LC** BM1; .A78a. **DD** 296. cum. index. **Bk Rev. Ad Acc. Circ:** 1,000 (ctrl).
**Desc:** Scholarly studies of any subject relating to Jews and Judaism.
**Ind/Abst** Am. Hist. Life (1980-).

CN/0316-5256
**AL MITZPE HAHINUCH.** V. 1- Nov. 1972-. Periodical. English (Hebrew). Free. Canadian Zionist, 1310 Greene Avenue/Suite 822, B Brodwin, Montreal Quebec H3Z 2B2 Canada. **Tel** (514)934-0804, telex 05-24345. **DD** 377/.9/60971.

IS
**ALE SEFER.** **Added/Corp** Ramat-Gan, Israel. Bar-Ilan University. Dept. of Bibliography and Librarianship. **VFOAT** Alei Sefer. (June/July 1975)-. Hebrew. Twice a year. $15.00. Universitat Bar-Ilan, Department of Philosophy, Ramat Gan 52900 Israel. **Tel** 11 972 3 5318575, 11 972 3 5318401, telex 342290 BARIL IL. **ED** S. Haulin. **LC** Z228.H4; A57. **Bk Rev. Circ:** 700.
**Desc:** Innovative, comprehensive journal devoted to the scientific examination of bibliographies and to the study of the Hebrew book.

IS/0736-8518
**ALEF.** See Ethnic Interests.

US/0164-0178
**AMERICAN JEWISH HISTORY.** See Ethnic Interests.

US/0002-9084
**AMERICAN JEWISH WORLD, THE.** (1915)-. Newspaper. English. Fifty-two times a year. $19.00 (one year); $33.00 (two years). The American Jewish World, 4509 Minnetonka Boulevard, Minneapolis MN 55416. **Tel** (612)920-7000, **FAX** (612)920-6205. **ED** Marshall Hoffman. **Bk Rev,** (Qty: 26). **Ad Acc. Circ:** 7,000. **Continues** Jewish weekly.
**Desc:** Provides news and features of interest to the Jewish community, primarily of the upper midwest.

US/0065-8987
**AMERICAN JEWISH YEAR BOOK.** [Am. Jew. year b.]. **VFOAT** American Jewish Yearbook. Vol. 1 (1899/1900)-. English. an. $30.00. Jewish Publication Society, O' Neill Highway, Dunmore PA 18512. **Tel** (800)355-1165, (717)969-4047. **LC** E184.J5; A6. **DD** 296. **UDC** 296(058)(73). **NLM** E 184.J5 A512. cum. index.
**Desc:** Issues include reports of the year for the Jewish Publication Society of America.
**Ind/Abst** Am. Bibliogr. Slavic East Europ. Stud. (19??-19??); Linguist. Lang. Behav. Abstr. (1992-); Soc. Plann. Policy Dev. Abstr. (1992-); Sociol. Abstr. (1992-); Stat. Ref. Index.

US/0164-3916
**AMERICAN RABBI (CANOGA PARK, LOS ANGELES, CALIF.), THE.** (THE AMERICAN RABBI.). [Am. rabbi]. (1978)-. Periodical. English. Six times a year (Feb., Apr., June, Oct., Dec.). $36.00. Pastoral Services, 7507 Melba Avenue, Dr. Harry Essrig, Canoga Park CA 91304. **Tel** (818)346-4049. **ED** Rabbi Harry Essrig, (phone: (818)346-4049). **LC** BM730.A1; .A44. **DD** 296.4/2. Index available (Bi-annual). cum. index. **Bk Rev,** (Qty: 12-15). **Ad Acc. Circ:** 900 (ctrl). **Continues** Pastoral Services.
**Desc:** Homiletical publication for Rabbi's, of all branches of Judaism.

US/0003-102X
**AMERICAN SEPHARDI, THE.** Ceased. **Added/Corp** Yeshiva University. Sephardic Studies Program. Vol. 1, No. 1 (Dec. 1966)-(19??). Periodical. English (Hebrew and Ladino). sa. **LC** DS101; .A62. **DD** 973/.04924.
**Ind/Abst** MLA Int. Bibl. Books Artic. Mod. Lang. Lit. (?-?).

US/0747-0258
**AMIT WOMAN, THE. Added/Corp** AMIT Women. Vol. 56 No. 3 (Jan. 1984)-. Periodical. English. bm. $15.00 membership. Amit Women, 817 Broadway, New York NY 10003. **Tel** (212)477-4720. **ED** Micheline Ratzersdorfer. **LC** DS150.R3; A47. **DD** 956.94/001/05. **Bk Rev. Ad Acc. Circ:** 32,500 (ctrl). ***Continues*** *American Mizrachi Woman, 0161-3952.*
**Desc:** Concerned with Jewish, Zionist and Israeli topics, Jewish art, sociology, travel. Audience with above average educational level committed to Jewish tradition and Zionism.
**Ind/Abst** Index Jew. Period. (19??-).

AG
**ARCA DEL SUR.** No. 1 (August 1991)-. Periodical. Spanish.

FR/0518-2840
**ARCHE (1957).** (L'ARCHE.). (Jan. 1957)-. Periodical. French. ir. 330.00F (1 year), 610.00F (2 year). L'Arche, 36 rue de Picpus, 75012 Paris France. **Tel** 011 33 1 43425800. **LC** DS101. **UDC** 296. **Bk Rev. Ad Acc, Adv Mgr:** Y Level, **Tel** 46228055. **Circ:** 25,000. ***Continues*** *Revue du F.S.J.U.*

AU
**ASCHKENAS.** (1991)-. German. Boehlau Verlag GmbH & Cie / Koeln, Theodor Heuss STR 76, D-51149 Cologne Germany. **Tel** 011 49 2203 307021, FAX 011 49 2203 307349.

US
**ATERET ZEKENIM.** 1-. Hebrew. Simcha-Graphic Association, 4311 15th Avenue, Brooklyn Ny 11219. **LC** BM520; .A83.

AT
**AUSTRALIAN JEWISH DEMOCRAT.** (19??)-. English. Four times a year (Seasonally). 15.00Aus$ Australia; 18.00Aus$ others. Australian Jewish Democrat, PO Box 35, Fairfield Victoria 3078 Australia. **Tel** 011 61 3 5573466. **Bk Rev. Circ:** 400.

US
**AVI AVOT.** ***Ceased.*** **See** Genealogy and Heraldry.

US/0882-6501
**AVOTAYNU. See** Genealogy and Heraldry.

GW
**BABYLON.** No. 1 (Oct. 1986)- Periodical. German. sa. Verlag Neue Kritik KG, Kettenhofweg 53, W 6000 Frankfurt 1 F R Germany. **Tel** 49 69 490759. **LC** DS101; .B28. **DD** 909/.04924/005.

US/0005-450X
**BALTIMORE JEWISH TIMES.** Vol. 86, No. 11 (May 4, 1962)-. Newspaper. English. wk. $42.00. Baltimore Jewish Times, 2104 North Charles Street, Baltimore MD 21218. **Tel** (410)752-3504, FAX (313)354-1210. **ED** Micheal Davis. Index available (every issue). cum. index. **Ad Acc. Circ:** 20,000 (ctrl). ***Continues*** *Jewish Times (Baltimore, Md.).*
**Desc:** Contains Baltimore Jewish Community, worldwide events about Jewish community.

IS
**BE-OR HA-TORAH (JERUSALEM).** (BE-OR HA-TORAH.). **Added/Corp** Agudat Akademaim Shomre Mitsvot Yotse Rusyah u-Mizrah Eropah (Israel). **VFOAT** Bor Hatorah. Vol. 1 (1982)-. Periodical. English (Hebrew). sa. $9.00. Bor Hatorah, c/o Dr Yaacov Hanoka, 107 York Terrace, Brookline MA 02146. **LC** BM1; .B39. **DD** 296.8/32/05.

IS/0005-979X
**BETH MIKRA : KETAV-ET SHEL HA-HEVRAH LE-HEKER HA-MIKRA BE-YISRAEL.** [BeitMiqra]. **VFOAT** Beth Mikra. Vol. 1 (Mar. 1956)-. Academic Scholarly Publication. Hebrew. qt. $38.00. World Jewish Bible Society, PO Box 7024, Jerusalem 91070 Israel. **Tel** 011 972 0 255965. **ED** David Hacohen. **LC** BS410; .B4. **Bk Rev. Circ:** 1,500.
**Desc:** Dedicated entirely to Bible studies, featuring articles based on the Jewish Bible, language, geography, history, beliefs and archaeology.
**Ind/Abst** Old Testam. Abstr.; Relig. Theol. Abstr.

US/0006-3932
**BITZARON.** ***Ceased.*** [Bitsaron]. Vol. 1 (1939)-Vol. 6, No. 49 (Aug. 1992). Periodical. Hebrew (summaries and/or abstracts in English). qt. Bitsaron, PO Box 623 Cooper Station, New York NY 10003. **Tel** (212)598-3987. **ED** Hayin Leat. **LC** DS101; .B53. **DD** 059. **Bk Rev. Ad Acc.** ctrl circ.
**Desc:** Literary criticism: biblical, medieval, and modern studies of Jewish interest.
**Ind/Abst** Am. Hist. Life (1966-1972); MLA Int. Bibl. Books Artic. Mod. Lang. Lit.

PL/0006-4033
**BIULETYN ZYDOWSKIEGO INSTYTUTU HISTORYCZNEGO W POLSCE.** (BIULETYN ZYDOWSKIEGO INSTYTUTU HISTORYCZNEGO.). [Biul. Zyd. Inst. Hist. Pol.]. **Main/Corp** Zydowski Instytut Historyczny W Polsce. **Added/Corp** Zydowski Instytut Historyczny w Polsce. **VFOAT** Biuletyn Zydowskiego Instytutu Historycznego w Polsce. No. 1 ( Jan./June 1951)-. Periodical. Polish (summaries and/or abstracts in English, French, Russian and Yiddish). qt. $42.00. **(Subscription address:** ARS Polona, PO Box 1001, 00068 Warsaw Poland.**) LC** DS135.P6; Z9. cum. index.
**Ind/Abst** Am. Hist. Life (1954-); BHA : Biblio. Hist. Art (1954-); Numis. Lit. (1954-).

PL
**BIULETYN ZYDOWSKIEGO INSTYTUTU HISTORYCZNEGO [MICROFORM]. Added/Corp** Zydowski Instytut Historyczny w Polsce. No. 1 (Jan./June 1951)-. Periodical. Polish. **(Subscription address:** ARS Polona, PO Box 1001, 00068 Warsaw Poland.**)** cum. index.

US/0279-3415
**B'NAI B'RITH INTERNATIONAL JEWISH MONTHLY, THE.** [B'nai B'rith int. Jewish mon.]. **Added/Corp** B'Nai B'Rith. **VFOAT** International Jewish Monthly; Jewish Monthly. Vol. 96, No. 1 (Aug./Sept. 1981)-. Periodical. English. Eight times a year. $12.00 nonmembers; $7.50 members. B'Nai B'Rith Inc., 1640 Rhode Island Avenue NW, Washington DC 20036. **Tel** (202)857-6645, FAX (202)296-1092. **ED** Jeff Rubin. **LC** HS2228.B4; N3. **DD** 369. **Bk Rev. Ad Acc. Circ:** 180,000. available on microfilm and microfiche from University Microfilms International (UMI). ***Continues*** *National Jewish Monthly, 0027-9552.*
**Desc:** A Jewish family publication that covers Israel, politics, religion, current events, history, culture and lifestyles.
**Ind/Abst** Index Jew. Period. (19??-199?); PAIS Int. Print.

US/0006-5277
**B'NAI B'RITH MESSENGER.** [B'nai B'rith messenger]. Vol. 2, No. 2 (Apr. 29, 1898)-. Periodical. English. wk (also monthly editions). $27.00 US; $38.00 Canada and Mexico; $52.00 other. B'nai B'rith Messenger, 2510 West 7th Street, Los Angeles CA 90057. **Tel** (310)380-5000. **ED** Yale Butler. **Bk Rev. Ad Acc. Circ:** 67,000. ***Continues*** *Emanu-el;* ***Absorbed*** *California Jewish Review; Jewish Community Press; California Jewsih Voice.*
**Desc:** The "newspaper of record" of the Jewish community of California. Founded in 1897 and publishes a weekly Southern California edition and a monthly North California edition.

US/1046-8358
**BRIDGES (SEATTLE, WASH.). See** Women's Interests.

NE/0926-2261
**BRILL'S SERIES IN JEWISH STUDIES.** [Brill's ser. Jew. stud.]. (1991)-. Monographic series. English. ir. Price varies per volume. E. J. Brill, Postbus 9000, 2300 PA Leiden Netherlands. **Tel** 011 31 71 312624, FAX 011 31 71 317532, telex 39296 BRILL NL. **UDC** 933 296.
**Desc:** Series covering Jewish studies. Topics have included Judea and Mediterranean politics and Judaism in the writings of W.M. Thackeray.

US/0147-927X
**BROWN JUDAIC STUDIES.** [Brown Jud. stud.]. **Added/Corp** Brown University. No. 1 (1976)-. Academic Scholarly Publication. English. ir. Price varies per volume. Scholars Press Customer Service, PO Box 6996, Alpharetta GA 30239. **Tel** (800)437-6692. **ED** Jacob Neusner. **LC** UNC. **DD** 181. ***Absorbed*** *Studia Philonica.*
**Desc:** Scholarly monographs on all aspects of the history of Judaism and on the study of Judaism from the history of religions perspective accommodating diverse methods and issues.

FR
**BULLETIN D'ETUDES KARAITES.** (I983)-. Bulletin. French. an. 1000F. Editions Peeters SA, Bondgenotenlaan 153, BP 41, B-3000 Leuven Belgium. **Tel** 32 16 235170, FAX 32 16 228500, telex 65987 PUL B. **ED** S. Szyszman, D. Barthelemy, H. Inalcik, G. Tamani, H. Z. Kosay, J. Margain, A. de Pury, P. Ruger, P. Sacchi, C. Perrot, T. Willi. **Bk Rev.**

US/1065-223X
**BULLETIN FOR BIBLICAL RESEARCH. See** Religion and Theology-Bible.

UK/0954-1179
**BULLETIN OF JUDAEO-GREEK STUDIES.** (Autumn 1987)-. Bulletin. English (summaries and/or abstracts in French, Spanish, Greek and Modern, Hebrew). bm. £7.00. Bulletin of Judaeo-Greek Studies, University of Cambridge, Faculty Oriental/ Sidgwick Avenue, Cambridge CB3 9DA England. **ED** Nichola de Lange and Judith Humphrey. **Bk Rev. Ad Acc. Circ:** 150.
**Desc:** History and culture of Greek-speaking Jews and Jews in Greek-speaking lands through history.

US/0145-3890
**BULLETIN OF THE INTERNATIONAL ORGANIZATION FOR SEPTUAGINT AND COGNITE STUDIES.** [Bull. Int. Organ. Septuagint Cogn. Stud.]. **Main/Corp** International Organization for Septuagint and Cognate Studies. **VFOAT** Bulletin IOCOS. No. 1, (June 1968)-. Bulletin. Multiple languages (English, French and German). an. $8.00. Clemson University / Philosophy & Religion, c/o Leonard Greenspoon, Department of Philosophy & Religion, Clemson SC 29634-1508. **Tel** (803)656-5358. **ED** Melvin K. H. Peters and Walter R. Bodine. **Bk Rev. Pr Rev. Circ:** 500 (ctrl).
**Desc:** Publishes articles and notes on the critical study of Jewish Greek Scriptures and related subjects.
**Ind/Abst** Index Book Rev. Relig.; New Testam. Abstr.; Old Testam. Abstr.; Relig. Index One Period. (1980-).

UK
**BULLETIN OF THE JEWISH HISTORICAL SOCIETY OF ENGLAND. Main/Corp** Jewish Historical Society of England. (1982)-. Bulletin. English. an. Free to members. Honorary Secretary / Jewish Historical Society of England, 33 Seymour Place, London W1H 5AP England. **Tel** 01-723-4404. **LC** DS135.E5; A24. **DD** 942/.004924/006. **Bk Rev. Ad Acc. Circ:** 1,000 (ctrl). ***Continues*** *Jewish Historical Society of England. Annual Report and Accounts for the Session, 0306-7998.*
**Desc:** Annual report and accounts of the society and its branches and Anglo-Jewish archives.

IS/0333-6298
**BWR TWRH.** [Bwr twrh]. **VFOAT** B'or Ha'torah. (1982)-. Periodical. Hebrew. an. $7.50. Shamir, PO Box 5749, Jerusalem Israel. **Tel** 011 972 02 223702, FAX 011 972 02 385118. **ED** Herman Branover. **UDC** 296. Index available. **Bk Rev. Ad Acc. Circ:** 1,500.
**Desc:** Forum for students, teachers, scientists, artists, and wondering Jews. Examines personal and intellectual conflicts of modern Jews through the perspective of the scientist, the philosopher, the artist, poet, and photographer, and the tested faith of the Torah-keeping Jew.

FR
**CAHIERS BERNARD LAZARE.** 1957. Periodical. French. ir. $19.96. Cahiers Bernard Lazare, 10 rue St Claude, 75003 Paris France. **ED** Cercle Bernard Lasar. **LC** DS101; .C32. **DD** 956.94/005. **Bk Rev. Ad Acc. Circ:** 2,000.
**Desc:** Information, articles on Israel, Jewish diaspora and left wing ideas.

US
**CANADA JEWISH TRAVEL GUIDE. See** Travel and Tourism.

CN
**CANADIAN JEWISH NEWS MONTREAL ED.** (THE CANADIAN JEWISH NEWS). [Can. Jew. news Montr. ed.]. (19??)-. Periodical. English. wk (50 issues). 25.00Can$. Canadian Jewish News, 10 Gateway Boulevard, Suite 420, Don Mills, Ontario M3C 3A1 Canada. **Tel** (416)422-2331, FAX (416)424-1886. **ED** Mrs. Patricia Rucker. **Bk Rev. Ad Acc, Adv Mgr:** V. Gillman, **Tel** 422-2331. **Circ:** 29,500 (Toronto ed.0, 21,500 (Montreal ed.).
**Desc:** Presents international, national and local news, including arts and business, of interest to the Canadian Jewish community.

AT
**CASUAL BULLETIN / ARCHIVE OF AUSTRALIAN JUDAICA. Main/Corp** University of Sydney. Archive of Australian Judaica. No. 1 (Aug. 1983)-. Bulletin. English. Twice a year (March and Dec.). Free. University of Sydney Fisher Library, Rare Books, Sydney 2006 New South Wales Australia. **Tel** 011 61 2 6924162, FAX 011 61 2 6922890. **ED** Marianne Dacy. **LC** CD2529.S9; U5. **Circ:** 500 (ctrl).
**Desc:** Outlines papers received, research projects in bibliography, filming carried out, plans for future acquisitions; Australian Jews and research.

US/1058-8760
**CCAR JOURNAL (1991).** (CCAR JOURNAL : A REFORM JEWISH QUARTERLY.). [CCAR j.]. **VAT** Central Conference of American Rabbis Journal. Vol. 38, No. 3 (Summer 1991)-. Periodical. English. Three times a year. $18.00 (1 year), $32.00 (2 year), $45.00 (3 year). Central Conference of American Rabbis, 192 Lexington Avenue, New York NY 10016. **Tel** (212)684-4990, FAX (212)689-1649. **LC** BM197.A1; C2. **DD** 296.8/346/05. available on microfilm and microfiche from University Microfilms International (UMI).
**Desc:** Contains articles of contemporary interest by leading members of the rabbinic, scholarly and lay communities.
**Ind/Abst** Index Jew. Period.

RH
**CENTRAL AFRICAN ZIONIST DIGEST.** V. 1- April 1958-. Periodical. English. Central Africa Zionist Organization, PO Box 1162, Bulawayo Rhodesia. **LC** DS149.A1; C44. **DD** 956.94/001.

US/0069-1607
**CENTRAL CONFERENCE OF AMERICAN RABBIS ANNUAL CONVENTION. Main/Corp** Central Conference of American Rabbis. **VFOAT** Central Conference of American Rabbis Yearbook; Yearbook - Central Conference American Rabbis. (19??)-. Monographic series. English. ir. Price varies per volume. Central

Conference of American Rabbis, 192 Lexington Avenue, New York NY 10016. **Tel** (212)684-4990, FAX (212)689-1649. **ED** Elliot Stevens. Index available. cum. index. **Circ:** 1,650 (ctrl).
**Desc:** Substantial, indexed reference on reform thought including the annual summary of proceedings of the Central Conference of American Rabbis Convention, conferences, papers and addresses.
**Ind/Abst** Index Jew. Period. (199?-).

IS
**CHALLENGE; SUPPLEMENT OF BA-MAARAKHAH.** V. 1, No. 2/3- ; March/April 1976-. Periodical. English. qt. $10.00. Sephardic Council of Jerusalem, PO Box 10, Jerusalem Israel.

CN/0225-5375
**CHRISTIANS, JEWS TODAY (FRENCH EDITION).** (CHRISTIANS, JEWS TODAY.). **VFOAT** Chretiens, Juifs Aujourd'hui. **VAT** Chretiens, Juifs Aujourd'Hui (Edition Anglaise). V. 6, No. 1- Oct. 1979-. Periodical. French. ir. Ligue pur les Droits de l'Homme des Bnai Brith, Bureau 200/7881 Boulevard Decarie, Montreal Quebec H4P 2H2 Canada. **DD** 296.3/872. ***Continues*** *Chretiens et Juifs Aujourd'Hui.*

US/1066-2863
**CINCINNATI JUDAICA REVIEW.** [Cincinnati Jud. rev.]. **Added/Corp** University of Cincinnati. Judaic Studies Program. Vol. 1 (Spring 1990)-. English. an. $6.50. Judaic Studies Program, ML 169, University of Cincinnati, Cincinnati OH 45221. **Tel** (513)556-2297. **DD** 296.

UK
**CLAUDE MONTEFIORE LECTURES.** ***Ceased.*** **Added/Corp** Liberal Jewish Synagogue (London, England). (1950)-(19??). Monographic series. English. an.

AG
**COLOQUIO (CONGRESO JUDIO LATINOAMERICANO).** (COLOQUIO : PUBLICACION PERIODICA DEL CONGRESO JUDIO LATINOAMERICANO, RAMA DEL CONGRESO JUDIO MUNDIAL.). **Added/Corp** Congreso Judio Latinoamericano. Vol. 1, No. 1 (April 1979)-. Periodical. Spanish (summaries and/or abstracts in English). ir (three or four issues per year). Free (libraries and academic institutions), $10.00 single issue (individuals). Congreso Judio Latinoamericano, Larrea 744, 1030 Buenos Aires Argentina. **Tel** 01-961-4534 OR 01-962-5028, FAX 963-7056. **ED** Pedro J Olschansky. **LC** DS101; .C5696. **DD** 909/.04924. Index available. cum. index. **Circ:** 1,500.

US/0069-6366
**COLUMBIA UNIVERSITY STUDIES IN JEWISH HISTORY, CULTURE, AND INSTITUTIONS.** **Main/Corp** Columbia University. Center of Israel and Jewish Studies. **Added/Corp** Center of Israel and Jewish Studies. Columbia University Studies in Jewish History, Culture, and Institutions. No. 1 (1971)-. English. ir. Columbia University Press, 136 South Broadway, Irvington NY 10533. **Tel** (914)591-9111. **DD** 296; 956.94.

US/0010-2601
**COMMENTARY (NEW YORK).** (COMMENTARY.). [Comment.]. **Added/Corp** American Jewish Committee. Vol. 1 (Nov. 1945)-. Periodical. English. mo. $39.00. Commentary, 165 East 56th Street, New York NY 10022. **Tel** (212)751-4000, (800)829-6270. **ED** Neal Kozodoy. **LC** DS101; .C63. **DD** 296.05. Index available. **Bk Rev. Ad Acc. Pr Rev. Circ:** 37,000 (ctrl). available on microfilm and microfiche from University Microfilms International (UMI). Documents available from The Genuine Article, UMI Article Clearinghouse. ***Continues*** *Contemporary Jewish Record, 0363-6909.*
**Desc:** Commentary explores the pressing issues of the day with uncommon depth, perception, and courage.
**Ind/Abst** ABC POL SCI (19??-19??); Acad. Abstr. Full Text Elite (Jan. 1984-); Acad. Abstr. (Jan. 1984-); Acad. Ind. [Computer File] (1984-); Acad. Search (Jan. 1984-); Am. Hist. Life (1955-); Am. Bibliogr. Slavic East Europ. Stud.; Arts Humanit. Citation Index [Select. Cov.]; Book Rev. Digest; Book Rev. Index; Curr. Contents Soc. Behav. Sci.; Curr. Index J. Educ.; Energy Res. Abstr. (March 1981-); Film Lit. Index; Gen. Period. Index (1985-); Guide Soc. Sci. Relig. (1959-); Hum. Rights Intern. Rep.; Humanit. Index; Index Book Rev. Relig.; Index Jew. Period.; Index Period. Artic. Relat. Law (1955-); INFO-SOUTH Abstr.; Infobank (Jan. 1969-); Int. Bibliogr. Sociol.; Int. Polit. Sci. Abstr.; Mag. Artic. Summar. Elite (Jan. 1984-); Mag. Artic. Summar. Select (Jan. 1984-); Mag. Artic. Summar. CD-ROM (Jan. 1984-); Mag. Express (1986-) [Full Txt.]; Mag. Index Plus (1989-); Mag. Index. Sel. (1986-); Mag. Search; MLA Int. Bibl. Books Artic. Mod. Lang. Lit.; Newsp. Period. Abstr. (1986-); Read. Guide Abstr. Select Ed.; Read. Guide Period. Lit.; Relig. Index One Period.; Res. Alert [Full Cov.]; Resource/One Ondisc; Soc. Sci. Cit. Index [Full Cov.]; Mag. Index (1977-); TOM Gen. Index (1992-) [Full Txt.]; Vocat. Search (Jan. 1984-).

US
**COMPLETE UNITED STATES JEWISH TRAVEL GUIDE.** **See** Travel and Tourism.

US/0010-6542
**CONSERVATIVE JUDAISM.** **Added/Corp** Rabbinical Assembly of America. Rabbinical Assembly. Jewish Theological Seminary of America. Vol. 1, No. 1 (Jan. 1945)-. Periodical. English (Hebrew). qt (Mar., Jun., Sep., Dec.). $20.00 (individual); $15.00 (students). The Rabbinical Assembly, 3080 Broadway, New York NY 10027. **Tel** (212)678-8060, FAX (212)749-9166. **ED** Lisa Stein (managing editor). **LC** BM197.5; .C66. **DD** 296.8/342/05. **Bk Rev**, (Qty: 15). **Ad Acc. Circ:** 2,000 (ctrl). available on microfilm and microfiche from University Microfilms International (UMI).
**Desc:** Serious critical inquiry of Jewish texts and traditions, and contemporary Jewish issues with a particular focus on conservative theology and ideology.
**Ind/Abst** Index Book Rev. Relig.; Index Jew. Period.; New Testam. Abstr.; Relig. Index One Period.; Relig. Theol. Abstr.

IS/0334-2336
**DAAT.** **Added/Corp** Universitat Bar-Ilan. Mahlakah le-filosofyah. Vol.1 (Winter 1978)-. Periodical. Hebrew (English). sa. $30.00. Universitat Bar-Ilan, Department of Philosophy, Ramat Gan 52900 Israel. **Tel** 11 972 3 5318575, 11 972 3 5318401, telex 342290 BARIL IL. **ED** Moshe Hallamish. **LC** B154; .D3. **DD** 296. Index available. cum. index. **Bk Rev. Circ:** 600 (ctrl).

US
**DIRECTORY & RESOURCE GUIDE / UNITED SYNAGOGUE OF AMERICA.** **Main/Corp** United Synagogue of America. **VFOAT** Directory and Resource Guide. (1991)-. Directory. English. United Synagogue Conservative Judaism, 155 5th Avenue, New York NY 10010. **Tel** (212)533-7800. **LC** BM197.5; .U49a. **DD** 296.6/7/05. ***Continues*** *Yearbook, Directory & Buyers' Guide, 0747-5152.*

US/0017-6524
**DOAR, HA-.** **Added/Corp** Histadruth Ivrith of America. **VFOAT** Hadoar. (July 1922)-. Academic Scholarly Publication. Hebrew. Twenty-six times a year (October through June). $36.00. Hadoar Association Inc., 47 West 34th Street, Room 609, New York NY 10001. **Tel** (212)629-9443. **ED** Shlomo Shamir and Yael Feldman. **LC** DS101; .D6. Index available. cum. index. **Bk Rev. Ad Acc.** ***Continues*** *Doar.*
**Desc:** Hebrew articles about Jews and Judaism with concentration on United States and Israel. Scholarly and literary works are included.

●UK
**EAST EUROPEAN JEWISH AFFAIRS.** **Added/Corp** Institute of Jewish Affairs. World Jewish Congress. Vol. 22, No. 1 (Summer 1992)-. Periodical. English. sa (2 issues). $60.00. Institute of Jewish Affairs, 79 Wimpole Street, London W1M 7DD England. **Tel** 011 44 71 9358266, FAX 011 44 71 9353252, telex 21633. **LC** DS135.R92; S65. **DD** 947/.004924. ***Continues*** *Soviet Jewish Affairs, 0038-545X.*

IS
**EDUT.** **See** History(General).

IS/0303-1497
**EMEQ, HA-.** (HA-EMEK.). [Emeq]. **Added/Corp** Kollel Yireai Hashem. **VFOAT** Torah Journal Ho'Ameck. No. 1 (April 1971)-. Hebrew. Kolel Yire Ha-Shem, 8 Baal Hatanye Street, PO Box 5181, Yerushalagim Israel. **LC** BM520; .E46.

IS/0303-7819
**ENCYCLOPAEDIA JUDAICA YEAR BOOK.** **VFOAT** Encyclopedia Judaica Yearbook. (1973)-. English. an. Keter Publishing, PO Box 7145, Jerusalem Israel. **Tel** 972 2 521201. **LC** DS102.8; .E498. **DD** 909/.04/924. **NLM** DS 102.8 E561.
**Desc:** Updates the 16 volumes Encyclopaedia Judaica with articles and major events.

CN/0827-8687
**ETHIOPIAN JEWRY REPORT.** (ETHIOPIAN JEWRY REPORT / CANADIAN ASSOCIATION FOR ETHIOPIAN JEWS.). [Ethiop. Jewry rep.]. **Added/Corp** Canadian Association for Ethiopian Jews. Vol.1, No. 1 (Spring 1982)-. Periodical. English. ir. Free. Canadian Association for Ethiopian Jews, 788 Marlee Avenue, Toronto Ontario M5R 9Z9 Canada. **DD** 963/.004924. ctrl circ.
**Ind/Abst** Hum. Rights Intern. Rep.

NE
**ETUDES SUR LE JUDAISME MEDIEVAL.** (1969)-. Monographic series. French. ir. Price varies per volume. E. J. Brill, Postbus 9000, 2300 PA Leiden Netherlands. **Tel** 011 31 71 312624, FAX 011 31 71 317532, telex 39296 BRILL NL.

UK/0014-3006
**EUROPEAN JUDAISM.** [Eur. Jud.]. **Added/Corp** World Union for Progressive Judaism. European Board. Leo Baeck College. Michael Goulston Educational Foundation. Vol. 1 (1966)-. Periodical. English. Twice a year. $86.00. Berghahn Books, Bush House Merewood, Sandhills OXF OX3 8EP United Kingdom. **(Subscription address:** Carfax Publishing Co., PO Box 25, Abingdon, Oxfordshire OX14 3UE United Kingdom.) **LC** BM1; .E86. **DD** 296/.05. **[CCC].** Index available. cum. index. **Bk Rev. Ad Acc. Circ:** 500. available on microfilm and microfiche from University Microfilms International (UMI).
**Desc:** Serves as a link between European Jewish communities which survived the Holocaust. A focal point for American and Israeli influences, etc.
**Ind/Abst** Index Jew. Period. (19??-199?); Middle East Abstr. Index.

IS/0334-4436
**EVREI I EVREISKII NAROD. MATERIALY IZ SOVETSKOI PECHATI.** ***Ceased.*** **VFOAT** Materialy iz Sovetskoi Pechati; Excerpts from the Soviet Press; Likutim Meha-Itonut ha-Sovyetit; Jews and the Jewish People. Excerpts from the Soviet Press; Yehudim Veha-am ha-Yehudi. Lkutim Meha-Itonut ha-Sovyetit. (197?)-(19??). Periodical. Russian. ir. Hebrew University of Jerusalem / Centre for Research and Documentation in East European Jewry, Jerusalem 91904 Israel. **Tel** 011 972 2 584271, 584262. **LC** DS135.R9; E84. ***Continues*** *Evrei i Evreiskii Narod. Ezhekvartalnyi Sbornik iz Sovetskoi Pechati.*

GW/0939-5369
**EVREISKII ZHURNAL.** **VFOAT** Jewish Magazine; Yidisher Zshurnal. No. 1 (1991)-. Periodical. Russian (summaries and/or abstracts in English). qt.

UK
**EYLAH, L'.** **VFOAT** L'Eylah. (19??)-. Periodical. English. sa. £6.00 UK; $12.50 other. Jews' College, 44A Albert Road, London NW4 2SJ England. **Tel** 01 203 6427, FAX 01 203 6420. **ED** Philip Ginsbury. **LC** BM1; .L43. **DD** 296/.05. Index available. cum. index. **Bk Rev. Ad Acc. Circ:** 4,500 (ctrl).
**Desc:** Discussion of contemporary orthodox Jewish issues.
**Ind/Abst** Index Jew. Period. (199?-).

IS
**FORUM FOR THE PROBLEMS OF ZIONISM, WORLD JEWRY AND THE STATE OF ISRAEL.** **Added/Corp** World Zionist Organization. **VFOAT** Forum. (19??)-. Periodical. English. World Zionist Organization / New York, 110 East 59th Street, New York NY 10022. **Tel** (212)339-6000.
**Ind/Abst** Index Jew. Period.; Middle East Abstr. Index.

UK
**FWZ REVIEW.** ***Title Change.*** **See** Women's Interests.

US/0191-6939
**GENERATIONS (BALTIMORE).** (GENERATIONS.). Vol. 1 (Dec. 1978)-. Periodical. English. an. $6.00. Jewish Historical Society of Maryland, 15 Lloyd Street, Baltimore MD 21202. **Tel** (410)732-6400. **ED** Bernard Fishman. **LC** F190.J5; G44. **DD** 975.2/004/924. **Pr Rev. Circ:** 2,000 (ctrl).
**Desc:** Articles, oral histories, and other studies relating to the history, development and character of Jewish communities in Maryland.
**Ind/Abst** Abstr. Anthropol.; Abstr. Res. Pastor. Care Couns. (19??-); PsycINFO (1990-); PsycLit.

US/0016-6669
**GENESIS 2.** ***Ceased.*** [Genes. 2]. **VAT** Genesis Two. (19??)-(19??). Periodical. English. qt. Genesis 2, 30 Old Whitfield Road, Accord NY 12404. **Tel** (914)626-4110. **ED** Lawrence Bush. **Bk Rev. Ad Acc. Circ:** 2,500 (ctrl). available on microfilm from University Microfilms International (UMI).
**Desc:** A progressive Jewish news journal devoted to changing Jewish politics, religion, and culture.
**Ind/Abst** Altern. Press Index (-199?).

US
**GESHER (NEW YORK, N.Y.).** (GESHER.). **Added/Corp** Rabbi Isaac Elchanan Theological Seminary. Student Organization. (19??)-. Periodical. English (English). ir. $5.00. Gesher, 500 West 185 Street, New York NY 10033. **LC** BM1; .G47. **DD** 296/.05.

IS/0435-8406
**GESHER (WORLD JEWISH CONGRESS. ISRAEL EXECUTIVE).** (GESHER : RIVON LI-SHEELOT HAYE HA-UMAH.). **Added/Corp** World Jewish Congress. Israel Executive. (June 1954)-. Periodical. Hebrew. Twice a year. $25.00. World Jewish Congress, PO Box 4293, Jerusalem Israel. **Tel** 011 972 2 635544 46, FAX 011 972 2 635262. **ED** Shlomo Shafir. **LC** DS101; .G45. **Bk Rev**, (Qty: 100/yr). **Ad Acc. Circ:** 2,000 (ctrl).
**Desc:** Contemporary Judaism and Zionism.

US/0747-444X
**GREATER PHOENIX JEWISH NEWS.** ***Title Change.*** (1983)-(1993). Newspaper. English. wk. Phoenix Jewish News, Inc., PO Box 26590, Phoenix AZ 85068. **Tel** (602)870-9470, FAX (602)870-9470. **ED** Flo

Eckstein. **Bk Rev**. **Ad Acc**. **Circ:** 6,000. ***Continues*** *Phoenix Jewish News, 0031-8353.* ***Continued by*** *Jewish News of Greater Phoenix, 1070-5848.*
**Desc:** News and feature stories of special interest to Jewish readers including local and world events, social milestones, politics and community business news.

AG
**GUIA ANUAL ISRAELITA.** (19??)-. Spanish. an. Editorial Promocion, Pueyrredon 468 40 Piso Of 16, Buenos Aires Argentina. **LC** F3001.9.J5; G83.

US
**GUIDE TO JEWISH CANADA & USA. VAT** Oscar Israelowitz's Guide to Jewish Canada & USA. (1990)-. Periodical. English. $14.45. Israelowitz Publishing, Box 228, Brooklyn NY 11229. **Tel** (718)951-7072, FAX (718)951-7072. **ED** Oscar Israelowitz.

US
**GUIDE TO THE JEWISH WEST. See** Travel and Tourism.

US/0017-6516
**HADASSAH MAGAZINE.** [Hadassah mag.]. **Added/Corp** Hadassah, the Women's Zionist Organization of America. Vol. 41 No. 8 (Apr. 1961)-. Periodical. English. Ten times a year. $25.00 US; $23.00 other. Womens Zionist Organization of America, 50 West 58th Street, New York NY 10019. **Tel** (212)355-7900, FAX (212)303-8282, telex 425191. **ED** Alan Tigay. **LC** DS101; .H23. **DD** 956.94/005. Index available. cum. index. **Bk Rev**. **Ad Acc**. **Circ:** 338,000 (ctrl). available on microfilm and microfiche from University Microfilms International (UMI). ***Continues*** *Hadassah Newsletter.*
**Desc:** Articles on Jewish life in Israel, America and around the world.
**Ind/Abst** Index Jew. Period.

US
**HARVARD JUDAIC MONOGRAPHS.** 1-. Monographic series. English. ir. Price varies per volume. Harvard University Press, 79 Garden Street, Cambridge MA 02138. **Tel** (617)496-1344, (800)448-2242.

US/0147-9342
**HARVARD SEMITIC STUDIES.** [Harv. Semit. stud.]. **Added/Corp** Harvard Semitic Museum. (1977)-. Monographic series. English. ir. Price varies per volume. Scholars Press / Georgia, PO Box 15399, Atlanta GA 30333-0399. **Tel** (404)636-4757, (404)727-2320, FAX (404)727-2348. ***Continues*** *Harvard Semitic Series, 0073-0645.*

US/0146-4094
**HEBREW STUDIES.** [Hebr. stud.]. **Added/Corp** National Association of Professors of Hebrew in American Institutions of Higher Learning. Vol. 17 (1976)-. Multiple languages (English and Hebrew). an (Nov.). $25.00. University of Wisconsin / National Association of Professors of Hebrew, 1220 Linden Drive, 1358 Van Hise, Madison WI 53706. **Tel** (608)262-3204, FAX (608)262-9417. **ED** Michael V Fox. **LC** PJ4501; .H4. **DD** 492.4/05. **Bk Rev**, (Qty: 30-50). **Ad Acc**. **Pr Rev. Circ:** 675. available on microfilm and microfiche from University Microfilms International (UMI). ***Continues*** *Hebrew Abstracts, 0438-895X.*
**Desc:** Devoted to Hebrew language, literature, the Bible and related areas of scholarship.
**Ind/Abst** Index Book Rev. Relig.; Middle East Abstr. Index; Old Testam. Abstr.; Relig. Index One Period.; Relig. Theol. Abstr. (199?-).

US/0360-9049
**HEBREW UNION COLLEGE ANNUAL.** [Heb. Union Coll.]. **Main/Corp** Hebrew Union College. **Added/Corp** Hebrew Union College. Annual. Vol. 1 (1924)-. Academic Scholarly Publication. English (Hebrew, French and German). an. $30.50. Jewish Institute of Religion, 3101 Clifton Avenue, Cincinnati OH 45220. **Tel** (513)221-1875, FAX (513)221-1847. **ED** Herbert H Paper. **LC** BM11; .H4. **DD** 296/.05. cum. index. **Circ:** 2,500. available on microfiche from University Microfilms International (UMI); available on microfilm. Documents available from The Genuine Article. ***Supersedes*** *Journal of Jewish Lore and Philosophy, 0190-4361.*
**Desc:** Scholarly essays in the several areas of Jewish and cognate studies, ancient and modern: Bible, rabbinics, language and literature, history, philosophy, and religion.
**Ind/Abst** Am. Hist. Life (1955-); Arts Humanit. Citation Index [Full Cov.]; Index Book Rev. Relig.; New Testam. Abstr.; Old Testam. Abstr.; Relig. Index One Period. (1949-); Relig. Theol. Abstr.; Res. Alert [Full Cov.]; Soc. Sci. Cit. Index [Select. Cov.].

US/0275-9993
**HEBREW UNION COLLEGE ANNUAL. SUPPLEMENTS.** **Added/Corp** Hebrew Union College-Jewish Institute of Religion. No. 1 (1976)-. Monographic series. English (Hebrew, French and German). ir. Price varies per volume. Jewish Institute of Religion, 3101 Clifton Avenue, Cincinnati OH 45220. **Tel** (513)221-1875, FAX (513)221-1847. **ED** Sheldon H. Blank. **Circ:** 2,400.
**Desc:** Scholarly essays in Jewish and Cognate studies ancient and modern: Bible, rabbinies, language and literature, history, philosophy and religion.

BL
**HERANCA JUDAICA.** 19??)-. Portuguese. qt. $10.00. Heranca Judaica, Rua Cacapava 105, CEP 01408 Sao Paulo Brazil. **Tel** (011)282-5844, FAX (011)282-5885. **LC** F2659.J5; H47. **DD** 981/.004924/005. **Bk Rev**. **Ad Acc**, **Adv Mgr:** Ernesto Strauss, **Tel** 282-5844. Full Page (B&W) $360.00. Half Page (B&W) $180.00. **Circ:** 3,000 (ctrl).
**Desc:** Cultural Jewish themes or any subject connected with Judaism.

UK
**HERITAGE (LONDON).** (HERITAGE.). Began in 1982. English.

US/0441-4195
**HUMANISTIC JUDAISM.** **Added/Corp** Society for Humanistic Judaism. (1967)-. Periodical. English. qt. $25.00 (institutions), $18.00 (individuals) US; $31.00 (institutions), $24.00 (individuals) Canada; $43.00 (institutions), $36.00 (individuals) other. Society for Humanistic Judaism, 28611 West 12 Mile Road, Farmington Hill MI 48334. **Tel** (313)478-7610, FAX (313)377-9014. **ED** M Bonnie Cousens and Ruth Duskin Feldman. **LC** BM1; .H85. **DD** 296.8/3. **Bk Rev**. **Circ:** 2,100.
**Desc:** Contains philosophical, informational, educational, creative, and celebratory materials that reflect the philosophy of humanistic Judaism. A reasoned, secular, and humanistic approach directed at contemporary issues and concerns.
**Ind/Abst** Index Jew. Period.

US/0513-5419
**IDISHE VORT, DOS.** (DOS IDISHE VORT. DOS YIDDISHE VORT.). **Added/Corp** Agudath Israel of America. **VFOAT** Yiddishe Vort. Vol. 1 (1953)-. Periodical. Yiddish (English). mo. $9.00. Dos Yiddishe Vort, 84 William Street, New York NY 10038. **Tel** (212)791-1812. **LC** BM1.; I48 (Hebr). **DD** 296. ***Continues*** *Yiddishe Vort.*

IS/0302-8127
**IMANUEL.** [Immanuel]. **VFOAT** Immanuel. No. 1 (Summer 1972)-. English. an (Once a year in a double issue). $19.00 Israel; $21.00 other. Ecumenical Theological Research Frat, PO Box 249, Jerusalem 91022 Israel. **Tel** 011 972 2 254941, FAX 011 972 2 254961. **ED** Malcolm F. Lowe, (phone: 972-2-254-961). **LC** BM1; .I53. **DD** 296/.05. Index available. **Bk Rev**. **Circ:** 2,000. Documents available from The Genuine Article.
**Desc:** An organ of religious research in Israel, dedicated to promoting dialogue between Christians and Jews and to disseminating abroad the experience gained in the dialogue.
**Ind/Abst** Arts Humanit. Citation Index (19??-19??) [Full Cov.]; Index Book Rev. Relig.; New Testam. Abstr. (-19??); Old Testam. Abstr.; Relig. Index One Period. (1979-); Relig. Theol. Abstr. (199?-); Res. Alert [Full Cov.].

US/0019-4050
**INDEX TO JEWISH PERIODICALS. See** Religion and Theology-Abstracting, Bibliographies and Statistics.

CN/1183-9937
**IOUDAIOS REVIEW.** [Ioudaios rev.]. **VFOAT** Ioudaios. Vol. 1.001 (July 1991)-. Periodical. English. Free to members. Ioudaios Review, c/o Ioudaios Yorkvl Bitnet, c/o D Reimer, Editor, Department of Religion and Culture, Wilfrid Laurier University, Waterloo Ontario N2L 3C5 Canada. **DD** 296/.09/015.

US/0021-2083
**ISRAEL HORIZONS.** [Isr. horiz.]. **Added/Corp** Americans for Progressive Israel-Hashomer Hatzair. **VFOAT** Israel Horizons and Labour Israel. Vol. 1 (Nov. 1952)-. Periodical. English. Four times a year. $15.00. Americans for Progressive Israel, 224 West 35th Street, Suite 403, New York NY 10011. **Tel** (212)868-0386, FAX (212)627-1287. **ED** Arieh Lebowitz. **LC** DS101; .I639. **DD** 915.694/005. Index available. **Bk Rev**. **Ad Acc**. **Circ:** 4,000 (ctrl). available on microfilm. ***Absorbed*** *Labour Israel.*
**Desc:** A socialist, Zionist exploration of the Jewish United States and other communities.
**Ind/Abst** Hum. Rights Intern. Rep.; Left Index; Middle East Abstr. Index; PAIS Int. Print (1991-?).

IS/0021-2237
**ISRAEL LAW REVIEW. See** Law.

US/0199-7424
**ISRAEL SCENE (AMERICAN EDITION).** ***Title Change.*** (ISRAEL SCENE.). [Isr. scene]. **Added/Corp** World Zionist Organization. American Section. (Feb. 1980)-(1993). Periodical. English. mo. World Zionist Organization / New York, 110 East 59th Street, New York NY 10022. **Tel** (212)339-6000. **LC** DS101; .I646. **DD** 956.94/005. **Circ:** 10,000. ***Supersedes*** *Israel Digest. American Edition, 0021-2024.* ***Merged into*** *Jerusalem Post International Edition.*
**Desc:** News and interests of Israel and the Middle East.
**Ind/Abst** Index Jew. Period. (19??-199?).

US/0741-465X
**ISSUES OF THE AMERICAN COUNCIL FOR JUDAISM.** [Issues Am. Counc. Jud.]. **Added/Corp** American Council for Judaism. **VFOAT** Issues. Autumn 1979-. Periodical. English. qt. Free. American Council for Judaism / New York, 307 Fifth Avenue, New York NY 10016. ***Continues*** *Brief, 0006-9922.*

US
**ITALY JEWISH TRAVEL GUIDE. See** Travel and Tourism.

●US
**JDL NEWS & VIEWS : AN OFFICIAL PUBLICATION OF THE JEWISH DEFENSE LEAGUE.** **Added/Corp** Jewish Defense League. **VFOAT** JDL News and Views; Jewish Defense League News and Views. (Spring 1992)-. Periodical. English. **LC** E184.J5; J49.

IS
**JERUSALEM LETTER.** **Added/Corp** Merkaz le-Heker ha-Kehilah ha-Yehudit (Jerusalem) Mekhon Yerushalayim le-Limudim Federaliyim. Merkaz ha-Yerushalmi le-Inyene Tsibur u-Medinah. (1977)-. Periodical. English. bw. (Includes Viewpoints) $55.00 institutions; $40.00 individuals. Jerusalem Center for Public Affairs, 13 Tel Hai, 92107 Jerusalem Israel. **Tel** 011 972 2 619281, FAX 011 972 2 619112. **(Subscription address:** Center for Jewish Community Studies, 1616 Walnut Street, Suite 513, Philadelphia, PA 19103; telephone: (215)787-1859**) LC** DS140; .J46. **DD** 956.9405/05.

US/0447-7049
**JEWISH ACTION.** **Added/Corp** Union of Orthodox Jewish Congregations of America. (19??)-. Periodical. English. Four times a year. $18.00 US; $25.00 Canada; $35.00 other. Union of Orthodox Jewish Congregations of America, 333 7th Avenue, New York NY 10001. **Tel** (212)563-4000. **LC** BM1; .J48.
**Ind/Abst** Index Jew. Period. (199?-).

SA
**JEWISH AFFAIRS.** **Added/Corp** South African Jewish Board of Deputies. Vol. 1, (June 1946)-. Periodical. English. Four times a year (Feb., May, Sept., Dec.). $40.00. Jewish Affairs, PO Box 87557, Houghtoix 2041 South Africa. **Tel** 011 27 486-1434, FAX 011 27 656-4940. **ED** Dr. J. Sherman. **LC** DS101; .S69. **DD** 296. **Bk Rev**. **Ad Acc**. **Circ:** 2,000 (ctrl).
**Desc:** A cultural magazine with articles of Jewish interest in the fields of literature, art, history, and Judaism and reflecting the contemporary Jewish situation in South Africa and worldwide.

US/8755-299X
**JEWISH BOOK NEWS.** [Jew. book news]. English. bm. Free. Jewish Book Club, 230 Livingston Street, Northvale NJ 07647. **Tel** (201)767-4093. **ED** Arthur Kurzweil. **LC** DS101; .J385. **DD** 909/.04924. **Bk Rev**. **Circ:** 15,000 (ctrl).
**Desc:** A 64 page journal devoted to current books of judaica; sent to members of the Jewish Book Club.

UK/0269-4662
**JEWISH BOOK NEWS & REVIEWS.** **VFOAT** Jewish Book News and Reviews. Vol. 1, No. 1 (Summer 1986)-. Periodical. English. Three times a year. £7.50. Jewish Book Council of Great Britain, 138 Middle Lane, Crouch End, London N8 7JP England. **ED** S.W. Massil. **LC** PAR.

UK/0021-633X
**JEWISH CHRONICLE (LONDON, ENGLAND : 1845).** (THE JEWISH CHRONICLE.). Vol. 1, No. 21 (June 27, 1845)-. Newspaper. English. wk. £45.00 UK; £65.00 Europe; £60.00 other. Jewish Chronicle / London, 25 Furnival Street, London EC4A 1JT England. **Tel** 011/44/71/4059252, FAX 011/44/71/4059040, telex 94011415. **(Subscription address:** Jewish Chronicle, 127 Sandgate Road Folkestone Kent, CT20 2BL England**) ED** Ned Temko. **LC** AP92; .J3. Index available. **Ad Acc**. **Circ:** 47,250. available on microfilm; available on microfiche; available on CD-ROM. ***Continues*** *Jewish Chronicle and Working Man's Friend;* ***Absorbed*** *Hebrew Observer; Jewish World.*
**Desc:** News from Jewish communities all around the world with accent from the United Kingdom, Israel, and the Middle East.

US/0021-6380
**JEWISH CURRENT EVENTS (ELMONT, N.Y.).** (JEWISH CURRENT EVENTS.). (19??)-. Periodical. English. Fifteen times a year. $8.95 (1 to 4 copies) US; $10.00 (1 to 4 copies) Canada; $7.95 (5 to 14 copies) US; $8.95 (5 to 14 copies) Canada. Jewish Current Events, PO Box 19637, San Diego CA 92159. **Tel** (619)698-6430. **ED** Samuel Deutsch. **DD** 296. ctrl circ.
**Desc:** An ideal supplement for the social studies and Jewish history curriculum. It is designed to educate and inform the Jewish youth of today.

US/0021-6399
**JEWISH CURRENTS.** [Jew. curr.]. **Added/Corp** Morning Freiheit Association. Vol. 1 No. 1 (Nov. 1946)-.

Periodical. English. Eleven times a year. $20.00 (one year), $35.00 (two years), $50.00 (three years) US; $25.00 (one year), $45.00 (two years), $60.00 (three years) other. Association for the Promotion of Jewish Secularism, 22 East 17th Street, Suite 601, New York NY 10003. **Tel** (212)924-5740. **ED** Morris Schappes. **DD** 296. Index available. cum. index. **Bk Rev. Ad Acc.** available on microfilm and microfiche from University Microfilms International (UMI). ***Continues*** *Jewish life.*
**Desc:** Broad coverage stressing Israel's survival in a peaceful middle east, problems of American jewry, black-jewish relations, Soviet Jewish situation, progressive Jewish culture including translations from Yiddish - stories, poems, reviews of books, plays, films, records, concerts, and dance.

US/0021-6429
**JEWISH EDUCATION.** ***Title Change.*** [Jew. Educ.]. **Added/Corp** National Council for Jewish Education. American Association for Jewish Education. Council for Jewish Education. Vol. 1 (Jan. 1929)-(1993)-. Periodical. English. qt. Council for Jewish Education, 730 Brondway, 2nd Floor, New York NY 10019. **Tel** (212)529-2000, FAX (212)586-9579. **ED** Alvin L Schitt. **LC** LC701; .J35. **DD** 370. cum. index. **Bk Rev. Ad Acc. Circ:** 1,500. available on microfilm and microfiche from University Microfilms International (UMI). ***Continued by*** *Journal of Jewish Education.*
**Ind/Abst** Contents Pages Educ. (?-?); Educ. Index (?-?); Index Jew. Period. (?-?); Relig. Theol. Abstr. (?-?).

US/0276-6310
**JEWISH EDUCATION DIRECTORY.** **Added/Corp** American Association for Jewish Education. Dept. of Statistical Research and Information. (1971)-. Directory. English. ir. $8.50. Jewish Education Service of North America Inc., 730 Broadway, New York NY 10003. **Tel** (212)529-2000. **LC** LC741; .J47. **DD** 370/.89924073. ***Continues*** *Jewish Education Register and Directory.*

US/0021-6437
**JEWISH EXPONENT, THE.** [Jew. expon.]. **Added/Corp** Federation of Jewish Charities. Allied Jewish Appeal of Philadelphia. Federation of Jewish Agencies of Greater Philadelphia. Vol. 1, No. 1 (April 15, 1887)-. Newspaper. English. Fifty-two times a year. $32.95. Jewish Exponent, 226 South 16th Street, Philadelphia PA 19102. **Tel** (215)893-5790.

US/0890-9113
**JEWISH FOLKLORE AND ETHNOLOGY REVIEW.** **See** Folklore.

●US
**JEWISH HISTORICAL SOCIETIES' NETWORK : A PUBLICATION OF THE AMERICAN JEWISH HISTORICAL SOCIETY.** **Added/Corp** American Jewish Historical Society. Vol. 4 No. 1 (Winter 1992)-. Periodical. English. American Jewish Historical Society, 2 Thornton Road, Waltham MA 02154. **Tel** (617)891-8110, FAX (617)899-9208. ***Continues*** *Local Jewish Historical Society News (Denver, Colo.).*

UK
**JEWISH HISTORICAL STUDIES : TRANSACTIONS OF THE JEWISH HISTORICAL SOCIETY OF ENGLAND.** **Added/Corp** Jewish Historical Society of England. **VFOAT** Transactions of the Jewish Historical Society of England. Vol. 29 (1986)-. English. Jewish Historical Society of England, 33 Seymour Place, London W1H 5AP England. **ED** Jeremy Schonfield. **LC** DS135.E5; A2. **DD** 941/.004924. Index available. cum. index. **Bk Rev. Ad Acc. Circ:** 1,000 (ctrl). ***Continues*** *Jewish Historical Society of England. Transactions - The Jewish Historical Society of England.*
**Desc:** Lectures delivered to The Society, plus other short articles and reviews of interest to members.
**Ind/Abst** Am. Hist. Life (1981-).

IS/0334-701X
**JEWISH HISTORY.** **VFOAT** Historyah Yehudit. Vol. 1, No. 1 (Spring 1986)-. Periodical. English (Hebrew). Twice a year. $40.00 (institutions), $25.00 (individuals) US; $45.00 (institutions), $30.00 (individuals) other. University of Haifa / Department of Jewish History, Haifa 31999 Israel. **Tel** 011 972 4 240947. **(Subscription address:** University Press of New England, 23 South Main Street, Hanover NH 03755.**)** **ED** K.R. Stow and R. Cohen. **LC** DS101; .J46556. **DD** 909/.04924/005. **[CCC].**
**Desc:** Jewish history covering the full chronological and geographical range of the Jewish historical experience. Meant to be a meeting place in print for historians of the Jews, and a focus for Jewish historical writing.
**Ind/Abst** Am. Hist. Life (1986-).

US/0888-0468
**JEWISH JOURNAL OF GREATER LOS ANGELES, THE.** **VFOAT** Jewish Journal. Vol. 1, No. 1 (Feb. 28-Mar. 6, 1986)-. Newspaper. English. Fifty-two times a year. $23.50 California; $36.00 others. Jewish Journal, 3660 Wilshire Boulevard, Suite 204, Los Angeles CA 90010. **Tel** (213)738-7778, FAX (213)386-9501. **ED** Gene Lichtenstein (Editor-in-Chief) and Marlene Marhn (Managing Editor). **Bk Rev**, (Qty: 24). **Photos. Ad Acc, Adv Mgr:** Toni Van Ness. Full Page (B&W) $1,960.00. Half Page (B&W) $1,008.00. Full Page (Color) $2,960.00. Half Page (Color) $2,008.00. **Pub. Size:** Tabloid. **Circ:** 52,000 (mailed) (ctrl). ***Continues*** *Los Angeles Jewish Community Bulletin, 0194-4983.*

UK/0021-6534
**JEWISH JOURNAL OF SOCIOLOGY, THE.** **See** Sociology.

SZ/1045-6015
**JEWISH LAW IN CONTEXT.** [Jew. law context]. **Added/Corp** Boston University. Institute of Jewish Law. Vol. 1 (1991)-. Monographic series. English. ir. Price varies per volume. Harwood Academic Publishers, PO Box 90, Reading RG1 8JL England. **Tel** 011 44 734 560080. **(Subscription address:** Harwood Academic Publishers, PO Box 786, Cooper Station, New York NY 10276.**)** **DD** 296.

US/0021-6550
**JEWISH LEDGER (ROCHESTER NY).** **See** Newspapers.

US/0732-4855
**JEWISH LIFE IN GREATER WASHINGTON.** (JEWISH LIFE IN GREATER WASHINGTON : A SPECIAL PROJECT OF THE JEWISH WEEK NEWSPAPER.). (1979/80)-. English. wk. $15.00. **LC** F205.J5; .J48. **DD** 975.3/004924/025.

US/0744-6632
**JEWISH NEWS (RICHMOND, VA.), THE.** (THE JEWISH NEWS.). [Jew. news]. **VFOAT** Richmond Jewish News. Periodical. English. wk (except last week in July, the first week in Aug., and major Jewish holidays). $22.00 US. The Jewish News, PO Box 29917, Richmond VA 23233. **Tel** (804)740-2000. **ED** Fay Kranz. **Bk Rev. Ad Acc.** ctrl circ.

US/0021-6615
**JEWISH OBSERVER, THE.** [Jew. obs.]. **Added/Corp** Agudath Israel of America. (Sept. 1963)-. Periodical. English. Ten times a year. $22.00 US; $34.00 other. Agudath Israel of America, 84 William Street, New York NY 10038. **Tel** (212)797-9000, 797-7399, FAX (212)269-2843. **ED** Nisson Wolpin. **LC** BM1; .J44. **Bk Rev. Ad Acc. Circ:** 15,000 (ctrl). available on microfilm and microfiche from University Microfilms International (UMI).
**Desc:** Comments on contemporary issues and events from a religious Jewish perspective - biographical sketches, book reviews, essays on Jewish festivals, interviews and letters to the editor.
**Ind/Abst** Index Jew. Period.

UK/0449-010X
**JEWISH QUARTERLY, THE.** [Jew. q.]. **Added/Corp** Jewish Literary Trust (London, England). Vol. 1, No. 1 (Spring 1953)-. Periodical. English. qt. £12.50 UK; £17.50 Europe; £35.00 other. Jewish Quarterly, PO Box 1148, London NW5 2A2 England. **Tel** 011 44 71 485 4062, telex 266763. **ED** Elena Lappin. **LC** DS101; .J478. Index available. **Bk Rev. Ad Acc. Circ:** 3,000. available on microfilm and microfiche from University Microfilms International (UMI).
**Ind/Abst** Abstr. Engl. Stud. (1985-).

US/0021-6682
**JEWISH QUARTERLY REVIEW (PHILADELPHIA, PA.).** (THE JEWISH QUARTERLY REVIEW.). [Jew. q. rev.]. **Added/Corp** Dropsie University. Dropsie College for Hebrew and Cognate Learning. Vol. 1 (July 1910)-. Periodical. English (Hebrew). qt. $35.00 (individuals), $50.00 (institutions) US; $39.00 (individuals), $54.00 (institutions) other. Center for Judaic Studies, 420 Walnut Street, Philadelphia PA 19106. **Tel** (215)238-1290, FAX (215)238-1540. **ED** David M. Goldenberg. **LC** DS101; .J5. **DD** 296.05. Index available. **Bk Rev**, (Qty: 40-50). **Ad Acc. Pr Rev. Circ:** 800. available on microfilm from University Microfilms International (UMI). Documents available from The Genuine Article. ***Continues*** *Jewish Quarterly Review (London, England), 0021-6682.*
**Desc:** Publishes ancient and medieval texts, articles on the history of Jewish language and culture, and critical reviews of relevant books.
**Ind/Abst** Am. Hist. Life (1960-1971); Anthropol. Index; Arts Humanit. Citation Index [Full Cov.]; BHA : Biblio. Hist. Art; Curr. Contents Arts Humanit.; Index Book Rev. Relig.; Index Jew. Period. (19??-199?); Int. Bibliogr. Sociol.; Middle East Abstr. Index (1960-1971); MLA Int. Bibl. Books Artic. Mod. Lang. Lit.; New Testam. Abstr.; Old Testam. Abstr.; Relig. Index One Period. (1949-); Relig. Theol. Abstr.; Res. Alert [Full Cov.]; Soc. Sci. Cit. Index [Select. Cov.]; Middle East J.

US/0021-6704
**JEWISH SOCIAL STUDIES.** [Jew. soc. stud.]. Vol. 1, No. 1 (Jan. 1939)-. Academic Scholarly Publication. English. Three times a year. $65.00. Indiana University Press, 601 North Morton Street, Bloomington IN 47404. **Tel** (812)855-3830, (800)842-6796. **ED** Tobey B. Gitelle. **LC** DS101; .J555. **DD** 909/.04924. cum. index. **Bk Rev. Circ:** 1,300.
**Desc:** Devoted to contemporary and historical aspects of Jewish life. Scholarly articles on Jewish topics in social science.
**Ind/Abst** Abstr. Anthropol.; Acad. Search (July 1994-); Am. Hist. Life (1954-); Am. Bibliogr. Slavic East Europ. Stud. (19??-19??); Appl. Soc. Sci. Index Abstr.; Arts Humanit. Citation Index (19??-19??) [Full Cov.]; Book Rev. Index (?-Oct. 1990); Commun. Abstr. (?-?); Humanit. Source (Jul. 1993-); Index Jew. Period.; INFO-SOUTH Abstr.; Int. Bibliogr. Sociol.; Int. Polit. Sci. Abstr.; Mag. Search; Middle East Abstr. Index; Soc. Plann. Policy Dev. Abstr.; Soc. Sci. Index; Sociol. Abstr.

US/0021-6720
**JEWISH SPECTATOR.** **Added/Corp** New York. School of the Jewish Woman. Vol. 1 (Nov./Dec. 1935)-. Periodical. English. qt. $24.00 (one year), $44.00 (two year), $60.00 (three year) US; $28.00 (one year), $52.00 (two year), $72.00 (three year) other. Jewish Spectator, 4391 Park Milano, Calabasas CA 91302. **Tel** (818)591-7481, FAX (818)591-7267. **ED** Robert Bleiweiss. **Bk Rev. Circ:** 8,000 (ctrl). available on microfilm and microfiche from University Microfilms International (UMI).
**Desc:** Journal of Jewish and world affairs with a liberal orientation.
**Ind/Abst** Am. Bibliogr. Slavic East Europ. Stud.; Guide Soc. Sci. Relig.; Index Jew. Period.; Middle East Abstr. Index.

CN/0021-6739
**JEWISH STANDARD (TORONTO).** (THE JEWISH STANDARD.). Began publication in 1930?. Periodical. English. sm. 14.00Can$ Canada; 20.00Can$ other. Julius Hayman Ltd, 77 Mowat Avenue, Suite 016, Toronto Ontario M6K 3E3 Canada. **Tel** (416)537-2696. **ED** Julius Hayman, Michael Hayman. **Bk Rev. Ad Acc. Circ:** 9,500.

●GW/0944-5706
**JEWISH STUDIES QUARTERLY.** Vol. 1 (1993)-. English (French and German). Four times a year. DM148.00. JCB Mohr / Paul Siebeck, Postfach 2040, D 72010 Tuebingen Germany. **Tel** 011 49 7071 9230, FAX 011 49 7071 51104, telex 7/262872 mohr d. **ED** Joseph Dan and Peter Schafer.
**Desc:** Presents studies on all aspects of Jewish history and culture while aiming to increase the element of debate in Jewish studies and find better understanding of Judaism in the widest sense.

US/1056-3342
**JEWISH TELEVIMAGE REPORT.** [Jew. televimage rep.]. **Added/Corp** Jewish Televimages Resource Center. **VFOAT** JTVR. Premiere Issue (May 1991)-. Periodical. English. Nine times a year. $45.00 (one year), $79.00 (two year). The Jewish Televimage Report, 78-46 265th Street, Floral Park NY 11004. **Tel** (718)962-1730. **ED** Jonathon Pearl. **DD** 791. **Bk Rev.**
**Desc:** Guide to television's Jewish themes and characters. Provides news, analysis, commentary, advance notice, interviews, and behind-the-scenes information about TV's Jewish images.

CN/0382-0254
**JEWISH TIMES (DOWNSVIEW).** ***Ceased.*** (THE JEWISH TIMES.). Vol. 1 (Feb. 14, 1975)-(19??). Periodical. English. Fourteen times a year. Jewish Times, 2828 Bathurst Street, Toronto Ontario M6B 3A7 Canada. **Tel** (416)789-4503. **DD** 301.45/1/924.

US/0883-1904
**JEWISH VEGETARIANS OF NORTH AMERICA : NEWSLETTER.** **See** Nutrition and Dietetics.

US/0021-6828
**JEWISH VOICE, THE.** Periodical. English. bw. $7.50 North America; $15.00 other. Jewish Federation of Delaware, 101 Garden of Eden Road, Wilmington DE 19803. **Tel** (302)478-6200, FAX (302)478-5374. **ED** Paula Berengut. **Bk Rev. Ad Acc. Circ:** 3,200 (ctrl).
**Desc:** Local, national and international articles concerning American and worldwide Jewry.

US/0021-6860
**JEWISH WEEKLY NEWS.** **See** Ethnic Interests.

IS
**JEWISH WOMAN'S OUTLOOK, THE.** **VFOAT** Outlook. No. 1 (May-June 1980)-. Periodical. English. bm. The Jewish Womans Outlook, 690 Eighth Street, Lakewood NJ 08701. **Tel** (201)367-1164. **LC** BM729.W6; J48. **DD** 296/.088042.

US/0199-4441
**JEWISH WORLD (ALBANY), THE.** **See** Ethnic Interests.

UK/0075-3769
**JEWISH YEAR BOOK, THE.** (1896/97)-. English. an (Jan.). Jewish Chronicle / London, 25 Furnival Street, London EC4A 1JT England. **Tel** 011/44/71/4059252, FAX 011/44/71/4059040, telex 94011415. **(Subscription address:** Frank Cass & Company Ltd., Newbury House, 890 900 Eastern Avenue, Ilford Essex IG2 7HH England.**)**

CN/0711-026X
**JONATHAN (MONTREAL).** ***Suspended.*** (JONATHAN.). [Jonathan]. No. 1 (Oct. 1981)-?. Periodical. French. ir. $9.67. Jonathan, 1310 Avenue Green/Bureau 710, Montreal Quebec H3Z 2B2 Canada.

**Tel** (514)934-0772. **ED** Victor Teboul. **DD** 305.8/924/0714. **Bk Rev. Ad Acc. Circ:** 5,000.
**Desc:** Jewish cultural magazine in French on French Canada, the US, Europe and Israel.

NE/0047-2212
**JOURNAL FOR THE STUDY OF JUDAISM IN THE PERSIAN, HELLENISTIC AND ROMAN PERIOD.** [J. Study Jud. Persian, Hell., Roman period]. Vol. 1 (Mar. 1970)-. Academic Scholarly Publication. Multiple languages (English, French and German). sa (2 issues bi-annually). Fl178.00 (institutions) Netherlands; $101.75 (institutions) other. E. J. Brill, Postbus 9000, 2300 PA Leiden Netherlands. **Tel** 011 31 71 312624, FAX 011 31 71 317532, telex 39296 BRILL NL. **ED** A.S. Van der Woude. **LC** BM176; .J6. **[CCC]. Circ:** 352.
**Desc:** An international forum of scholarly discussions on the history, literature and religious ideas of Judaism in the Persian, Hellenistic and Roman periods. It provides biblical scholars, students of rabbinic literature, and classics and historians of the Hellenism of the ancient near east with information.
**Ind/Abst** Index Book Rev. Relig.; Int. Bibliogr. Sociol.; New Testam. Abstr.; Old Testam. Abstr.; Relig. Index One Period. (1970-); Relig. Theol. Abstr.

US/0730-2614
**JOURNAL OF HALACHA AND CONTEMPORARY SOCIETY. Added/Corp** Yeshiva Rabbi Jacob Joseph. **VFOAT** Journal of Halacha. Vol. 1, No. 1 (Spring 1981)-. Periodical. English. sa. $12.00 US. Rabbi Jacob Joseph School, 3495 Richmond Road, Staten Island NY 10306. **Tel** (718)979-6333, FAX (212)334-9146. **ED** Rabbi Alfred Cohn (editor's address and telephone: 5 Fox Lane, Spring Valley, NY 10977; (914)425-9270). **LC** BM520; .J68. **DD** 296.1/8/05. Index available. cum. index. **Pr Rev. Circ:** 3,000.
**Desc:** Concerns modern life issues and problems analyzed in terms of Jewish Law.

●US
**JOURNAL OF JEWISH EDUCATION. Added/Corp** Council for Jewish Education. Jewish Education Service of North America. **VFOAT** Jewish Education. Vol. 61, No. 1 (1994)-. Periodical. English. tq. $20.00. Council for Jewish Education, 730 Brondway, 2nd Floor, New York NY 10019. **Tel** (212)529-2000, FAX (212)586-9579. **ED** Alvin L. Schitt. **LC** LC701; .J35. **DD** 370. cum. index. **Bk Rev. Ad Acc. Circ:** 1,500. available on microfilm and microfiche from University Microfilms International (UMI). ***Continues** Jewish Education, 0021-6429.*
**Ind/Abst** Educ. Index.

US/0197-0100
**JOURNAL OF JEWISH MUSIC AND LITURGY. See** Music.

UK/0022-2097
**JOURNAL OF JEWISH STUDIES, THE.** [J. Jew. stud.]. Vol. 1 (1948)-. English. sa (Apr. & Oct.). $40.00 US & Canada; £21.00 other. Journal of Jewish Studies, Oriental Institute, Pusey Lane, Oxford OX1 2LE England. **Tel** 011 44 865 727075. **ED** Geza Vermes. **LC** BM1; .J63. **DD** 296.05. Index available. cum. index. **Bk Rev**, (Qty: 40). **Ad Acc. Circ:** 1,000. Documents available from The Genuine Article.
**Desc:** A periodical concerned with Jewish civilization, in particular in the second temple and the Mishnaic-Talmudic eras. Full bibliographical coverage.
**Ind/Abst** Acad. Search (July 1993-); Am. Hist. Life (1959-); Arts Humanit. Citation Index [Full Cov.]; Br. Humanit. Index; Curr. Contents Arts Humanit.; Humanit. Source (Jul. 1993-); Index Book Rev. Relig.; Index Jew. Period. (19??-199?); INFO-SOUTH Abstr.; Int. Bibliogr. Sociol.; Mag. Search; Middle East Abstr. Index; New Testam. Abstr.; Old Testam. Abstr.; Relig. Index One Period. (1948/1949-); Relig. Theol. Abstr.; Res. Alert [Full Cov.].

SZ/1053-699X
**JOURNAL OF JEWISH THOUGHT & PHILOSOPHY, THE.** [J. Jew. thought philos.]. **VFOAT** Journal of Jewish Thought and Philosophy; Jewish Thought & Philosophy; Jewish Thought and Philosophy. Vol. 1, No. 1 (1991)-. English (Hebrew). Twice a year. $106.00 (academic institutions), $165.00 (corporate institutions). Harwood Academic Publishers, PO Box 90, Reading RG1 8JL England. **Tel** 011 44 734 560080. **(Subscription address:** International Publishers Distributor at one of the following addresses: 820 Town Center Drive, Langhorne, PA 19047; or PO Box 90, Reading Berkshire RG1 8JL UK; or Kent Ridge PO Box 1180, Singapore 9111, Republic of Singapore**) LC** BM1; .J64. **DD** 181/.06/05. **CODEN** JJTPE2. **[CCC].**
**Ind/Abst** Int. Bibliogr. Sociol.

US/0700-9801
**JOURNAL OF PSYCHOLOGY AND JUDAISM. See** Psychology.

US/0449-5128
**JOURNAL OF SYNAGOGUE MUSIC. See** Music.

US/0021-3772
**JTA DAILY NEWS BULLETIN. Added/Corp** Jewish Telegraphic Agency (New York, N.Y.) Jewish Telegraphic Agency (New York, N.Y.) News Bulletin. (19??)-. Periodical. English. da. $265.00. Jewish Telegraph Agency Inc, 330 Seventh Avenue, 11th Floor, New York NY 10001. **Tel** (212)643-1890, FAX (212)643-8498, telex 12-6978. **ED** Mark J. Joffe. **LC** DS101; .J14. **DD** 296. **Bk Rev. Circ:** 2,500 (ctrl).
**Desc:** News of Jewish concern and interest from international news agency.

SZ/0022-572X
**JUDAICA.** [Judaica]. Vol. 1- ; 31 Mar. 1945-. Periodical. German. qt. $30.00. Redaktion der Judaica, Etzelstrasse 19, CH-8038 Zurich Switzerland. **Tel** 01 482 64 23. **ED** K Hruby and Mastin Cunz. **LC** DS101; .J75. **Bk Rev. Ad Acc. Circ:** 1,000.
**Desc:** Information and research on Jewish-Christian subjects; Bible, dialogue, book reviews.
**Ind/Abst** Am. Hist. Life (1973-); Index Book Rev. Relig.; Old Testam. Abstr.

XR/0022-5738
**JUDAICA BOHEMIAE.** [Jud. Bohem.]. **Added/Corp** Statni Zidovske Muzeum (Czech Republic). (1965)-. Periodical. English (French, German and Russian). Twice a year. $39.40. **(Subscription address:** Artia Pegas Press Ltd., Palac Metro Narodni Trida 25, 11210 Prague 1 Czech Republic.**) LC** DS135.C95; J82.
**Ind/Abst** Am. Hist. Life (1985-).

US/0022-5762
**JUDAISM.** [Judaism]. **Added/Corp** American Jewish Congress. Vol. 1, (Jan. 1952)-. Periodical. English. qt (4 issues). $35.00 (institutions), $20.00 (individuals). American Jewish Congress, 15 East 84th Street, New York NY 10028. **Tel** (212)879-4500 Ext.200/212, FAX (212)249-3672. **ED** Ruth B. Waxman. **LC** BM1; .J8. **DD** 296.05. Index available. cum. index. **Bk Rev. Ad Acc. Circ:** 6,500 (ctrl). available on microfilm and microfiche from University Microfilms International (UMI). Documents available from The Genuine Article, UMI Article Clearinghouse.
**Desc:** Creative discussion and exposition of the religious, moral and philosophical concepts of Judaism and their relevance to the problems of modern society.
**Ind/Abst** Abstr. Engl. Stud.; Acad. Abstr. Full Text Elite (July 1990-) [Full Txt.]; Acad. Abstr. (July 1990-); Acad. Ind. [Computer File] (1987-); Acad. Search (July 1990-); Am. Bibliogr. Slavic East Europ. Stud.; Annu. Bibliogr. Engl. Lang. Lit.; Arts Humanit. Citation Index [Full Cov.]; Curr. Contents Arts Humanit.; Expand. Acad. Index (1987-); Guide Soc. Sci. Relig.; Humanit. Index; Humanit. Source (Jul. 1990-); Index Book Rev. Relig.; Index Jew. Period.; INFO-SOUTH Abstr.; Mag. Artic. Summar. Elite (July 1990-) [Full Txt.]; Mag. Artic. Summar. CD-ROM (July 1990-); Mag. Search; Middle East Abstr. Index; MLA Int. Bibl. Books Artic. Mod. Lang. Lit.; New Testam. Abstr.; Newsp. Period. Abstr. (1988-); Relig. Index One Period. (1952-); Relig. Theol. Abstr.; Res. Alert [Full Cov.]; Soc. Sci. Cit. Index [Select. Cov.].

FR
**JUIFS EN URSS, LES. Added/Corp** Biblioth·eque Juive Contemporaine (Paris, France). No. 1 (Feb. 1989)-. Periodical. French. mo. ***Continues** Mois Avec les Juifs d'U.R.S.S., 0245-6494.*

US/0163-352X
**KEEPING POSTED. TEACHER'S/LEADER'S EDITION (NEW YORK). See** Education.

US
**KEFAR HABAD : SHEVUON TSEIRE AGUDAT HABAD BE-E. HA-K.** Periodical. Hebrew. wk. $68.00. Kfar Chabad Weekly Magazine, 648 Lefferts Avenue, Brooklyn NY 11203. **LC** BM1; .K43.

GW/0179-7239
**KIRCHE UND ISRAEL. VFOAT** Kirche und Israel (KUI). Vol. 1. (1986)-. Periodical. German. Twice a year. DM42.00. Neukirchener Verlag des Erziehungsvereins GmbH, Andreas Braem Strasse 18 20, D 47506 Neukirchen-Vluyn Germany. **Tel** 011 49 2845 392227.

IS/0023-1851
**KIRYAT SEFER.** (KIRYAT SEFER : RIVON BIBLIYOGRAFI SHEL BET HA-SEFARIM HA-LEUMI VEHA-UNIVERSITAI BI-YERUSHALAYIM.). [Qiryat sepr]. **Added/Corp** Bet Ha-Sefarim Ha-Leumi Veha-Universitai Bi-Yerushalayim. **VFOAT** Kirjath Sepher. Vol. 1, (Apr. 1924)-. Hebrew (English). Four times a year (Mar., June, Sept., Dec.). $50.00. Jewish National and University Library, PO Box 34165, Jerusalem 91341 Israel. **Tel** 011 972 2 585039, 585019, FAX 011 972 2 586315, telex 25307. **ED** Dr. Avigdor Shinan. **LC** Z6367; .K57; DS102.5. **DD** 016.8924. **NLM** Z 7070 K58. Index Available, published separately, free-automatically sent. **Bk Rev. Circ:** 1,000 (ctrl).
**Desc:** Contains a complete list of new Israeli publications and books related to Jewish studies published outside Israel in different languages.

IS/0334-472X
**KIYWWNIYM.** (KIVUNIM.). **Added/Corp** World Zionist Organization. Information Dept. No. 1 (Nov. 1978)-. Periodical. Hebrew. qt (Feb., May, Aug., Nov.). $25.00. World Zionist Organization, PO Box 92, Department of Education and Culture, Jerusalem Israel. **Tel** 011 972 2 513297. **ED** Lifsha Ben-Shach, Amos Yovel. **LC** BM1; .K54. ***Continues** Bi-Tefutsot Ha-Golah, 0520-2248.*
**Desc:** Journal of Zionism and Judaism.

CN/0228-2577
**KOL YAAKOV.** [Kol yaakov]. Published since Sept. 1979?. Periodical. French. bm. Free. Rabbinat Sepharade du Quebec, Kol Yaakov, 5850 Victoria Avenue, Montreal Quebec H3W 2R5 Canada. **DD** 296/.09714/281.

IS
**KOL YISRAEL. VFOAT** Kol Israel Jerusalem. Periodical. Hebrew. IL3.00 single issue. Kol Israel, POB 513, Jerusalem Israel. **LC** BM390; .K58.

US
**KOVETS KEREM SHELOMOH. VFOAT** Kerem Shelomoh. Vol. 1, No. 1, (Nov. 1977)-. Periodical. Hebrew. mo. $15.00. Kerem Shlomo M E CH of Bobov, 1577 48th Street, Brooklyn NY 11219. **Tel** (718)871-6623. **ED** Shmerel Zitronenbaum. **LC** BM520; .K677. Index available. **Circ:** 2,000 (ctrl).
**Desc:** Commentary and sermons on the Bible and talmud historical documents regarding rabbinical society and hasidim.

US
**KOVETS NOAM HA-TORAH. Added/Corp** Kolel Noam Elimelekh (Brooklyn, New York, N.Y.). **VFOAT** Noam ha-Torah. (April 1991)-. Hebrew. **LC** BM520; .K6844.

US
**KOVETS YAGDIL TORAH (BROOKLYN, NEW YORK, N.Y. : 1976).** (KOVETS YAGDIL TORAH.). **VFOAT** Yagdil Torah. V. 1., No. 1-. Periodical. Hebrew. bm. Yagdil Torah, 770 Eastern Parkway, Brooklyn NY 11213. **LC** BM520; .K69.

US/0894-9816
**LAM-MISPAHA.** (LA-MISHPAHAH.). [Lam-mispaha]. **Added/Corp** Histadruth Ivrith of America. **VFOAT** Lamishpaha; Hebrew Monthly. (1963)-. Periodical. Hebrew (English). Ten times a year (Except July and Aug.). $15.00 US; $16.50 other. Hadoar Association Inc., 47 West 34th Street, Room 609, New York NY 10001. **Tel** (212)629-9443. **LC** PJ4569; .L27. **DD** 892. **Bk Rev. Ad Acc. Circ:** 6,500.
**Desc:** A magazine, in simple Hebrew, for students of Hebrew, youngsters as well as adults.

US/0738-1379
**LATIN AMERICAN JEWISH STUDIES NEWSLETTER (1983).** (LATIN AMERICAN JEWISH STUDIES NEWSLETTER.). [Latin Am. Jew. stud. newsl.]. **Main/Corp** Latin American Jewish Studies Association. **VFOAT** Newsletter. Vol. 4, No. 1 (July 1983)-. Newsletter. English (Spanish). Twice a year (Jan. and Aug.). Free to Latin American Jewish Studies Association members; Membership: $20.00 (individuals); $30.00 (institutions). Latin American Jewish Studies Association, 2104 Georgetown Boulevard, Ann Arbor MI 48105. **Tel** (313)996-2880, FAX (313)665-7880. **ED** Judith Elkin. **DD** 323. **Bk Rev**, (Qty: 10). **Ad Acc. Circ:** 500. ***Continues** Latin American Jewish Studies Associaton. Latin American Jewish Studies Association Newsletter.*
**Desc:** Newsletter carries professional notes, news of conferences, and current bibliography.

US/0094-5625
**LE-TORAH VE-HORA AH.** Hebrew. 145 East Broadway, New York NY 10002. **LC** BM520; .L47.

US/0898-6444
**LEGACY (LOS ANGELES, CALIF.).** (LEGACY : JOURNAL OF THE SOUTHERN CALIFORNIA JEWISH HISTORICAL SOCIETY.). [Legacy]. **Added/Corp** Southern California Jewish Historical Society. Vol. 1, No. 1 (1987)-. Periodical. English. an. $13.95 (latest volume). Southern California Jewish Historical Society, 6505 Wilshire Boulevard, Room 502, Los Angeles CA 90048. **Tel** (213)653-7740. **LC** F855.2.J5; L45. **DD** 979.4/9004924.

IS
**LEOM, LEOM U-MASORET. VFOAT** Leom U-Masoret. 1- No. 727- Jan. 1966-. Periodical. Hebrew. bm. $2.50. Adhut Yisrael Be-Erets, Yisrael Israel. **LC** BM390; .L4.

US/0146-2334
**LILITH (NEW YORK).** (LILITH.). [Lilith]. Vol. 1, No. 1 (Fall 1976)-. Periodical. English. qt. $26.00. Lilith Magazine, 250 West 57th Street, New York NY 10107. **Tel** (212)757-0818. **(Subscription address:** PO Box 3000, Department LIL, Denville, NJ 07834**) ED** Susan Weidman Schneider. **LC** BM729.W6; L54. **DD** 296.3/878344/05. **Bk Rev. Ad Acc. Circ:** 10,000. available on microfiche.
**Desc:** Focus on Jewish women's issues all over the world.
**Ind/Abst** Index Jew. Period. (19??-); Middle East Abstr. Index; Women Stud. Abstr.

# Religion and Theology —Judaism

**US**
**LOCAL JEWISH HISTORICAL SOCIETY NEWS / AMERICAN JEWISH HISTORICAL SOCIETY.** *Title Change.* **Added/Corp** American Jewish Historical Society. University of Denver. Center for Judaic Studies. Rocky Mountain Jewish Historical Society. Vol. 1, Issue 1 (Fall 1987)-(199?). Periodical. English. American Jewish Historical Society, 2 Thornton Road, Waltham MA 02154. **Tel** (617)891-8110, FAX (617)899-9208. *Continued by Jewish Historical Societies' Network.*

**US/0745-5607**
**LONG ISLAND JEWISH WEEK, THE.** **VFOAT** Jewish Week. (1???)-. Periodical. English. wk. $22.00. The Jewish Week, 1457 Broadway, NY NY 10036. **Tel** (212)686-2320. **Bk Rev. Ad Acc. Circ:** 110,000.

**IS**
**MABUE HA-NAHAL.** Year 1- (1- ); 738- Jan. 1977-. Periodical. Hebrew. mo. $2.00. Mabue Ha-Nahal, PO Box 5404, Jerusalem Israel. **Tel** 2 822853. **ED** Mordechai Turetz. **LC** BM198; .M23. **Ad Acc. Circ:** 2,000.
**Desc:** Thoughts and stories, historical articles on Torah and chassidism in accordance to the approach of the Rabbi of Braslov.

**US**
**MADRIKH LA-KASHRUT.** **VFOAT** Madrich Lakashrus. Periodical. Multiple languages (English, Hebrew and Yiddish). bm. $4.00. **LC** BM710.

**IS**
**MAHASHEVET.** (19??)-. Periodical. Hebrew. Mahashevet, PO Box 363, Bene Berak Israel. **LC** BM1; .M344.

**IS/0333-838X**
**MAHUT.** See Literature.

**US**
**MAOR, HA-.** **VFOAT** Hamaor. (19??)-. Periodical. Hebrew. bm. $7.00 US; $9.00 other. Hamaor, 5002 18th Avenue, Brooklyn NY 11204. **LC** BM520; .M35.

**US/1063-0015**
**MASORET (NEW YORK, N.Y.).** (MASORET: THE MAGAZINE OF THE JEWISH THEOLOGICAL SEMINARY OF AMERICA.). [Masoret]. **Added/Corp** Jewish Theological Seminary of America. Issue 1, No. 1 (Fall 1991)-. Periodical. English. Three times a year. Jewish Theological Seminary of America, Communication Department, 3080 Broadway, New York NY 10027-4649. **DD** 296.

**IS/0333-7081**
**MEHKERE YERUSHALAYIM BE-MAHASHEVET YISRAEL / HA-UNIVERSITAH HA-IVRIT BI-YERUSHALAYIM, HA-FAKULTAH LE-MADAE HA-RUAH, HA-MAKHON LE-MADAE HA-YAHADUT.** **Added/Corp** Universitah Ha-Ivrit Bi-Yerushalayim. Makhon Le-Madae Ha-Yahadut. **VFOAT** Jerusalem Studies in Jewish Thought. (1981)-. Periodical. Hebrew. ir. Jewish National and University Library, PO Box 34165, Jerusalem 91341 Israel. **Tel** 011 972 2 585039, 585019, FAX 011 972 2 586315, telex 25307. **LC** BM1; .M43.

**US/0891-7116**
**MELTON JOURNAL, THE.** See Education.

**US/0278-2782**
**MESSIANIC OUTREACH, THE.** Vol. 1 (Sept. 1981)-. Periodical. English. qt (4 issues). $6.00. Messianic Literature Outreach, PO Box 37062, Cincinnati OH 45222. **Tel** (614)436-7746. **ED** Elliot Klayman. **LC** Discard. Index available. cum. index. **Bk Rev**, (Qty: 2). **Pr Rev. Circ:** 3,000 (ctrl). Documents available.
**Desc:** Messianic Jewish oriented containing articles of interest to believers in Messiah.

**US/0094-9701**
**METIVTA, HA-.** **Added/Corp** Metivta Torah Va-Daat. **VFOAT** Hamesivta. (19??)-. Hebrew. 452 East 9th Street, Brooklyn NY 11218. **LC** BM520; .M47.

**US/0543-9833**
**MICHIGAN JEWISH HISTORY.** [Mich. Jew. hist.]. V. 1- Mar. 1960-. English. sa. $10.00. Jewish Historical Society, 29629 Southfield Road/Room 217, Southfield MI 48076. **Tel** (313)557-8315. **LC** F575.J5; M5. **DD** 977.4/004924.
**Ind/Abst** Am. Hist. Life (1973-).

**US/0026-332X**
**MIDSTREAM (NEW YORK).** (MIDSTREAM : A MONTHLY JEWISH REVIEW.). [Midstream]. **Added/Corp** Theodore Herzl Foundation. Vol. 1 (Autumn 1955)-. Periodical. English. mo. $21.00. **(Subscription address:** Midstream Magazine, 110 East 59 Street, Suite 4100, New York NY 10022.**) ED** Joel Carmichael. **LC** DS149; .A336. **DD** 296.05. Index available. cum. index. **Bk Rev. Ad Acc. Circ:** 10,000. available on microfilm and microfiche from University Microfilms International (UMI).
**Desc:** A guide to a better understanding of the fateful changes confronting world jewry today.
**Ind/Abst** Am. Hist. Life (1971-1987); Am. Bibliogr. Slavic East Europ. Stud.; Film Lit. Index; Guide Soc. Sci. Relig.; Hum. Rights Intern. Rep.; Index Jew. Period.; Middle East Abstr. Index; PAIS Int. Print.

**US/1062-9521**
**MIDWEST JEWISH WEEK, THE.** [Midwest Jew. week]. (1991)-. Periodical. English. wk. $21.00. The Midwest Jewish Week, PO Box 597349, Chicago IL 60659. **DD** 305.

**US/1050-9348**
**MISHPACHA (VIENNA, VA.).** (MISHPACHA.MISHPAHAH.). [Mishpacha]. **Added/Corp** Jewish Genealogy Society of Greater Washington. **VFOAT** Mishpahah. (19??)-. Periodical. English. Four times a year (Jan., Apr., July, Oct.). $10.00. Jewish Genealogy Society Great Washington, PO Box 412, Vienna VA 22183. **Tel** (301)657-3389. **ED** Susan Wynne (editor's address: 3128 Brooklawn Terrace, Chevy Chase, MD 20815). **LC** CS31; .M57. **DD** 929/.1/089924. cum. index. **Bk Rev**, (Qty: each issue). **Ad Acc. Adv Mgr:** Susan Wynne, **Tel** (301)657-3389. **Circ:** 500 (ctrl) available on microfiche from Avotaynu, Inc.
**Desc:** This publication is a mixture of news items and substantive articles about Jewish family and history research.

**US/0276-1114**
**MODERN JUDAISM.** [Mod. Jud.]. Vol. 1, No. 1 (May 1981)-. Periodical. English. Three times a year (Feb., May, and Oct.). $57.00 US; $61.00 Canada and Mexico; $62.10 other. Johns Hopkins University Press, 2715 North Charles Street, Baltimore MD 21218-4319. **Tel** (410)516-6987, FAX (410)516-6968. **ED** Steven T. Katz. **LC** BM195; .M63. **DD** 296/.09/03. **[CCC]**. **Bk Rev. Ad Acc. Circ:** 650. available on microfilm and microfiche from University Microfilms International (UMI). Documents available from The Genuine Article.
**Desc:** Examines topics relative to the Jewish experience since the Haskalah, including the Zionist movement and the establishment of the State of Israel, the rise of modern anti-Semitism and its climax in the holocaust, and the implications of Jewish emancipation in Europe.
**Ind/Abst** Abstr. Engl. Stud.; Am. Hist. Life (1981-); Arts Humanit. Citation Index [Full Cov.]; Curr. Contents Arts Humanit.; Index Book Rev. Relig.; Index Jew. Period.; Middle East Abstr. Index; Relig. Index One Period. (1981-); Relig. Theol. Abstr.; Res. Alert [Full Cov.]; Soc. Sci. Cit. Index [Select. Cov.].

**US/0099-0280**
**MOMENT (NEW YORK).** (MOMENT.). [Moment]. Vol. 1 (May/June 1975)-. Periodical. English. Six times a year. $27.00 US; $33.00 other. Moment, 3000 Connecticut Avenue NW, Suite 300, Washington DC 20008. **Tel** (202)387-8888. **(Subscription address:** CDS Agency Hard Copy, PO Box 4966, Des Moines IA 50340.**) ED** Hershel Shanks. **LC** DS101; .M59. **DD** 909/.04/92408. **Bk Rev. Ad Acc. Circ:** 30,000. available on microfilm and microfiche from University Microfilms International (UMI).
**Desc:** Independent Jewish magazine containing pieces on Israel, Judaism, politics (American and Israeli), fiction and sociology.
**Ind/Abst** Guide Soc. Sci. Relig.; Index Jew. Period.; Middle East Abstr. Index.

**US/0190-5627**
**MONOGRAPHS OF THE HEBREW UNION COLLEGE.** **Main/Corp** Hebrew Union College. No. 1 (19??)-. Monographic series. English. ir. Price varies per volume. Jewish Institute of Religion, 3101 Clifton Avenue, Cincinnati OH 45220. **Tel** (513)221-1875, FAX (513)221-1847. **Bk Rev. Ad Acc.**
**Desc:** Scholarly studies of any subject relating to Jews or Judaism, including but not limited to history, theology, philosophy, art, literature, etc.

**US/0147-7536**
**MUSICA JUDAICA.** See Music.

**US/1043-2795**
**NATIONAL JEWISH NEWS, THE.** [Ntl. Jew. news]. **VFOAT** Jewish News. Periodical. English. mo. International Jewish Life Media Group, 4211 Laurel Canyon Boulevard, Studio City CA 91604. *Continues National Jewish Daily, 0893-4320.*

●**US/1058-8213**
**NEFESH.** **VFOAT** Nefesh, the Jewish Soul. (1991)-. Periodical. English. sa. Free. Nefesh, PO Box 1996, Morristown NJ 07962-1996. *Continues Nefesh, 1058-8213.*

**US**
**NEW YORK CITY JEWISH TRAVEL GUIDE.** See Travel and Tourism.

**US/0737-8092**
**NEWSLETTER - CENTER FOR HOLOCAUST STUDIES (BROOKLYN, NEW YORK, N.Y.).** See History(General)-History of Europe.

**IS/0377-1784**
**NEWSLETTER - CENTRAL ARCHIVES FOR THE HISTORY OF THE JEWISH PEOPLE.** See Genealogy and Heraldry-Archives.

**UK/0952-8997**
**NEWSLETTER OF THE JEWISH LAW ASSOCIATION.** No. 1 (Autumn 1987)-. Newsletter. English. $10.00 (membership). Jewish Law Association, Central Conference of American Rabbis, 192 Lexington Avenue, New York NY 10016.

**US/0892-4945**
**NOAH'S ARK.** See Children and Youth Interests.

●**RU**
**NOI.** (1992)-. Russian. mo. $109.95. **(Subscription address:** East View Publications Inc., 3020 Harbor Lane North, Suite 110, Minneapolis MN 55447.**)**

**SW/0348-1646**
**NORDISK JUDAISTIK / SCANDINAVIAN JEWISH STUDIES.** **VFOAT** Scandinavian Jewish Studies. Vol. 1, No. 1 (Dec. 1975)-. Periodical. Swedish (Danish, English and Norwegian; summaries and/or abstracts in English and German). Twice a year. Fmk100.00 Finland; $35.00 other. Nordisk Judaistik, c/o Karl-Johan Illman, Biskopsgatan 16A, SF-20500 ABO Finland. **Tel** (9)21-654283, FAX (9)21-654835. **ED** Karl-Johan Illman. **Bk Rev.** ctrl circ.
**Desc:** Judaism and history of Jews, always and everywhere, but with special emphasis on the Scandinavian countries, including Finland.
**Ind/Abst** Am. Hist. Life (1985-).

**US/0745-0664**
**NORTHERN CALIFORNIA JEWISH BULLETIN.** *Title Change.* (1981)-(19??). Bulletin. English. wk. Northern California Jewish Bulletin, 88 First Street/Suite 300, San Francisco CA 94105. **Tel** (415)957-9340. *Continues San Francisco Jewish Bulletin, 0021-6364. Continued by Jewish Bulletin of Northern California, 1067-8883.*

**FR/0550-1350**
**NOUVEAUX CAHIERS, LES.** 1. - Year. (No. 1-); Jan./Mar. 1965-. Periodical. French. qt. 160.00F, 120.00F (students) France; 200.00F, 140.00F (students) other. Alliance Israelite Universelle, 45 Rue de la Bruyere, 75009 Paris France. **Tel** 011 33 1 42803500. **ED** Gerard Israel and Colette Baer. **LC** DS101; .N68. **UDC** 951.9. Index available. cum. index. **Bk Rev. Ad Acc.** ctrl circ.
**Desc:** Jewish and Israeli literature, poetry, human rights, sociology, books movies and exhibitions review, Zionism, and Judeo-Christian relations.

**US**
**OJC THE OHIO JEWISH CHRONICLE, THE.** See Newspapers.

**US/0030-2139**
**OLAMENU.** See Education-Early Childhood and Primary Education.

**US/0882-1933**
**OLSCHWANGER JOURNAL.** See Genealogy and Heraldry.

**US/0362-2770**
**OPTIONS (WAYNE, N.J.).** See Ethnic Interests.

**IS**
**OR-TORAH.** **Added/Corp** Hevrat Or-Torah. Irgun Ole Gerbah u-derom Tunisiyah be-Yisrael. Vol. 1 (June/July 1968)-. Periodical. Hebrew. Six times a year. $5.00. Or Torah, PO Box 18, Ashkelon Israel. **Tel** 011 972 51 37441.

**IS**
**ORAITA.** Periodical. Hebrew. IL12.00. Orayta, PO Box 245, Netanyah Israel. **Tel** (053)44864. **ED** Robbi Amihud Levin. **LC** BM520; .O7. **Bk Rev. Circ:** 2,500 (ctrl).
**Desc:** Rabbinical publication for Jewish thought and Halacha.

**CN/0834-0242**
**OUTLOOK - CANADIAN JEWISH OUTLOOK SOCIETY.** (OUTLOOK.). [Outlook - Can. Jew. Outlook Soc.]. **Added/Corp** Canadian Jewish Outlook Society. Vol. 24, No. 1/2 (Jan./Feb. 1986)-. Periodical. English. Ten times a year (Jan./Feb. & July/Aug. issues combined). 25.00Can$ (individuals), 35.00Can$ (institutions) Canada; 31.00Can$ (individuals), 41.00Can$ (institutions) others. Canadian Jewish Outlook Society, 6184 Ash Street 3 Street, Vancouver BC V5Z 3G9 Canada. **Tel** (604)324-5101. **DD** 909/.04924/005. *Continues Canadian Jewish Outlook, 0045-5059.*

**US**
**PARDES, HA-.** **VFOAT** Hapardes. Vol. 1 (April 1927)-. Periodical. Hebrew. mo. $8.00. **ED** S A Pardes. **LC** BM520; .P35. *Supersedes Pardes Poland; Pardes.*

US
**PEER MORDEKHAI.** 1- Feb. 1969-. Hebrew. an. 28400 Euclid Avenue, Viklif OH 44092. **LC** BM504.2; .P43.

US/1063-6269
**POINTS EAST.** [Points east]. **Added/Corp** Sino-Judaic Institute. Vol. 1, No. 1 (Jan. 1986)-. Periodical. English. Three times a year. $50.00 Comes with Sino-Judaic Institute Membership. Sino Judaic Institute, 2316 Blueridge Avenue, Menlo Park CA 94025. **Tel** (415)854-5283, FAX (415)854-5393. **LC** DS135.C5; P64. **DD** 950. **Circ:** 400.

UK/0268-1056
**POLIN.** ***Ceased.*** **Added/Corp** Institute for Polish-Jewish Studies (Oxford, England). Vol. 1 (1986)-(1992). English. Twice a year. Basil Blackwell Publishers Ltd, 108 Cowley Road, Oxford 0X4 1JF England. **Tel** 011 44 865 791100, FAX 011 44 865 791347, telex 837022 OXBOOK G. **(Subscription address:** Marston Book Services, PO Box 87, Oxford OX2 0DT England**) ED** Antony Polonsky. **LC** DS135.P6; P56. **DD** 943.8/004924. **CODEN** POLNEN. **Bk Rev. Ad Acc. Circ:** 1,000. available in microform from University Microfilms International (UMI).
**Desc:** Provides a leading forum for authoritative historical and cultural material on Polish and East European Jewry.
**Ind/Abst** Int. Bibliogr. Sociol.; Soc. Plann. Policy Dev. Abstr.

US/0146-888X
**POLYDOXY.** V. 1- Autumn 1975-. Periodical. English. Three times a year. $25.00. Polydoxy, PO Box 2044, Cincinnati OH 45201. **LC** BM1; .P64. **DD** 296.8/346/05.

IS
**PRAKLIT, HA-.** **Added/Corp** Universitah Ha-Ivrit Bi-Yerushalayim. Faculty of Law. Vol. 1 (1943)-. Periodical. Hebrew (summaries and/or abstracts in English). Hapraklit, 50 Baffin, PO Box 788, Tel Aviv Israel.

US/0065-6798
**PROCEEDINGS - AMERICAN ACADEMY FOR JEWISH RESEARCH.** **Main/Corp** American Academy for Jewish Research. **VFOAT** Proceedings of the American Academy for Jewish Research. Vol. 1 (1930)-. English (Hebrew, Arabic, German and French). an. $30.00 (one year) Comes with American Academy for Jewish Research membership. American Academy for Jewish Research, 3080 Broadway, New York NY 10027. **Tel** (212)678-8864, FAX (212)678-8947. **ED** Professor N. Garna. **LC** DS101; .A34. **DD** 296.
**Desc:** Includes a list of members.
**Ind/Abst** BHA : Biblio. Hist. Art.

US/0145-4366
**PROCEEDINGS OF THE ANNUAL CONVENTION OF THE NATIONAL ASSOCIATION OF SYNAGOGUE ADMINISTRATORS.** **Main/Corp** National Association of Synagogue Administrators. Proceedings. English. an. National Association of Synagogue Administrators, 3080 Broadway, New York NY 10027. **LC** BM653; .N38A. **DD** 296.6/0973.

US/0571-6489
**PROCEEDINGS OF THE ASSOCIATIONS OF ORTHODOX JEWISH SCIENTISTS.** **Main/Corp** Association of Orthodox Jewish Scientists. Vol. 1 (1966)-. Periodical. English (Hebrew). ir. $5.00. Association of Orthodox Jewish Scientists, 3 West 16th Street, New York NY 10016. **Tel** (212)229-2340. **LC** BM1; .P77. **DD** 215.

US/0887-4913
**PROCEEDINGS OF THE CENTER FOR JEWISH-CHRISTIAN LEARNING.** **See** Religion and Theology.

●US/1066-0585
**RABBINICS TODAY.** [Rabbin. today]. (1992)-. Periodical. English. Ten times a year (Except July/Aug.). $65.00. Rabbinics Today, PO Box 323, Atlantic Beach NY 11509. **Tel** (506)371-3447. **ED** Rabbi Basil Herring. **DD** 296. **Bk Rev**, (Qty: 10). **Ad Acc. Circ:** 500.
**Desc:** News and articles for the professionals rabbinic of today.

AG
**RAICES : JUDAISMO CONTEMPORANEO.** **Added/Corp** Asociacion Mutual Israelita Argentina. Vol. 1 No. 1 Spring (1991)-. Periodical. Spanish. qt.

IT/0033-9792
**RASSEGNA MENSILE DI ISRAEL, LA.** [Rass. mens. Israel]. **Added/Corp** Unione Delle Comunita Israelitiche Italiane. Vol. 1 (Oct. 1925)-. Periodical. Italian. ir. $65.00 US. Unione Delle Comunita Israelitiche Italiane, Lungotevere Sanzio 9, 00153 Rome Italy. **Tel** 011 39 6 5803667, 011 39 6 5803670. **LC** DS101; .R37. Index available (free). cum. index.
**Ind/Abst** MLA Int. Bibl. Books Artic. Mod. Lang. Lit.

US/0034-1495
**RECONSTRUCTIONIST.** [Reconstructionist]. **Added/Corp** Jewish Reconstructionist Foundation. Federation of Reconstructionist Congregations and Havurot. Federation of Reconstructionist Congregations and Havurot. Newsletter - Federation of Reconstructionist Congregations and Havurot. Began in (1935). Periodical. English. qt. $20.00 (one year), $35.00 (two year), $50.00 (three year) US; $25.00 (one year), $45.00 (two year), $65.00 (three year) other. FRCH Reconstruction, Church Road & Greenwood Avenue, Wyncote PA 19095. **Tel** (215)887-1988. **ED** Joy Levitt (address: PO Box 1336, Roslyn Hights NY 11577). **LC** DS133; .R4. **DD** 296. **Bk Rev. Ad Acc. Circ:** 8,500 (ctrl). available on microfilm and microfiche from University Microfilms International (UMI). ***Absorbed*** *Newsletter (Federation of Reconstructionist Congregations and Havurot).*
**Desc:** A review of the contemporary Jewish world--its cultural expression, religious and social issues, middle east, philosophy, synagogue life, and ritual observance.
**Ind/Abst** Index Jew. Period.; Middle East Abstr. Index.

US/0482-0819
**REFORM JUDAISM.** **Added/Corp** Union of American Hebrew Congregations. (Sept. 1972). Periodical. English. qt. $10.00 (one year), $18.00 (two years). Union of American Hebrew Congregation, 838 Fifth Avenue, New York NY 10021. **Tel** (212)249-0100, FAX (212)734-2857. **ED** Aron Hirt-Manheimer. **Bk Rev. Ad Acc. Circ:** 285,000 (ctrl).
**Desc:** In-depth articles about current issues of interest to the Jewish community and articles about the Reform Jewish movement.
**Ind/Abst** Index Jew. Period.

UK
**RESEARCH REPORT (INSTITUTE OF JEWISH AFFAIRS).** (RESEARCH REPORT / INSTITUTE OF JEWISH AFFAIRS, IN ASSOCIATION WITH THE WORLD JEWISH CONGRESS.). **Added/Corp** Institute of Jewish Affairs. World Jewish Congress. **VFOAT** IJA Research Reports; I.J.A. Research Reports. **VAT** Institute of Jewish Affairs Research Reports. (Dec. 1968)-. English. Six times a year. $50.00. Institute of Jewish Affairs, 79 Wimpole Street, London W1M 7DD England. **Tel** 011 44 71 9358266, FAX 011 44 71 9353252, telex 21633. **Circ:** 1,000.
**Desc:** Background surveys and analyses of topical political, social, economic, and legal issues particularly relevant to world Jewry.

US/0034-5709
**RESPONSE (NEW YORK. 1967).** (RESPONSE; A CONTEMPORARY JEWISH REVIEW.). (Summer 1967)-. Periodical. English. qt (Feb., May, Aug., Nov.). $16.00 (individuals), $20.00 (institutions) US; $17.00 (individuals), $21.00 (institutions) other. Response, 27 West 20th Street, 9th Floor, New York NY 10011. **Tel** (212)675-1168, FAX (212)929-3459. **ED** Yigal Schleifer. **LC** BM1; .R45. cum. index. **Bk Rev. Ad Acc. Circ:** 1,600. available on microfilm and microfiche from University Microfilms International (UMI).
**Ind/Abst** Index Jew. Period. (199?-).

FR/0035-1725
**REVUE DE QUMRAN.** [Rev. Qumran]. Vol. 1 No. 1 (July 1958)-. Periodical. English (French, German, Italian and Latin). sa. 598.00F France; 710.00F other. J Gabalda & Cie Editeurs, 18 rue Pierre et Marie Curie, 75005 Paris France. **Tel** 011 33 1 43265355. **ED** Abbe Puech. **LC** BM487.A62; R4. **DD** 296.1/55. **Bk Rev.**
**Desc:** Articles about the Dead Sea Scrolls and proof of the Grottos of Qumran.
**Ind/Abst** Index Book Rev. Relig.; New Testam. Abstr.; Old Testam. Abstr.; Relig. Index One Period. (1958-); Relig. Theol. Abstr.

FR/0484-8616
**REVUE DES ETUDES JUIVES.** [Rev. etud. juives]. **Added/Corp** Societe des Etudes Juives (France) Ecole Pratique des Hautes Etudes (France). Section des Sciences Economiques et Sociales. Ecole des hautes Etudes en Sciences sociales. Societe des Etudes Juives (France) Actes et Conferences. Vol. 1, No. 100 (July/Sept. 1880)-. Periodical. French (English). Twice a year. 3000.00F Belgium; 3151.00F other. Societe Des Etudes Juives, 19 Rue de Teheran, 75008 Paris France. **Tel** 011 33 1 45641728. **(Subscription address:** Editions Peeters SA, Bondgenotenlaan 153, 3000 Leuven Belgium**) ED** G. Nahon and C. Touati. **LC** DS101; .R45. **DD** 909/.04924/005. Index available in last issue of volume--attached. cum. index. **Bk Rev. Ad Acc.** Documents available from The Genuine Article. ***Absorbed*** *Historia Judaica, 1054-1330.*
**Desc:** Studies on history, philosophy and theology of Judaism.
**Ind/Abst** Am. Hist. Life (1955-); Arts Humanit. Citation Index [Full Cov.]; BHA : Biblio. Hist. Art; Curr. Contents Arts Humanit.; Index Book Rev. Relig.; New Testam. Abstr.; Relig. Index One Period.; Res. Alert [Full Cov.]; Romant. Move.; Soc. Plann. Policy Dev. Abstr.; Soc. Sci. Cit. Index [Select. Cov.]; Sociol. Abstr.

US
**ROCKY MOUNTAIN JEWISH HISTORICAL NOTES.** **Added/Corp** Rocky Mountain Jewish Historical Society. Ira M. Beck Memorial Collection of Rocky Mountain Jewish History. Vol. 1, (Oct. 1977)-. Periodical. English. Four times a year. $30.00. Rocky Mountain Jewish Historical Society, University of Denver, Denver CO 80208. **Tel** (303)871-3020. **ED** John Livingston. **Circ:** 800.

US/0733-9062
**SAFRA.** (SAFRA / SPONSORED BY THE AMERICAN ASSOCIATION FOR JEWISH EDUCATION AND THE BOARD OF JEWISH EDUCATION OF METROPOLITAN CHICAGO.). Vol. 1, No. 1 (Fall 1980)-. Periodical. English. sa. $3.00 US; $4.50 Canada. Jewish Education Service of North America Inc., 730 Broadway, New York NY 10003. **Tel** (212)529-2000. **LC** BM100; .S37. **DD** 377/.96/0973.

SP/0037-0894
**SEFARAD.** [Sefarad]. **Added/Corp** Instituto "Arias Montano". Vol. 1 (1941)-. Periodical. Spanish. Twice a year. 5000ptas Spain; 7000ptas other. Consejo Superior Investigacion Cientificas (CSIC), Vitruvio 8, 28006 Madrid Spain. **Tel** 011 34 1 5612833, FAX 011 34 1 4113077, telex 42182. **LC** DS101; .S4. cum. index. **Bk Rev.** ***Absorbed*** *Estudios Sefardies.*
**Desc:** This journal of Hebraic, Sephardic and Near Eastern studies considers philology and textual exegesis of the Hebrew Bible and its ancient versions, the history and culture of Jews in Spain, as well as Sephardic literature, history and cultural achievements. Also prints research on Hebrew and Aramaic linguistics.
**Ind/Abst** Am. Hist. Life (1955-1977, 1979-); BHA : Biblio. Hist. Art; MLA Int. Bibl. Books Artic. Mod. Lang. Lit.; New Testam. Abstr.; Numis. Lit.; Old Testam. Abstr.

NE
**SEMITIC STUDY SERIES.** New. No. 1 (1952)-. Monographic series. English. ir. Price varies per volume. E. J. Brill, Postbus 9000, 2300 PA Leiden Netherlands. **Tel** 011 31 71 312624, FAX 011 31 71 317532, telex 39296 BRILL NL.

FR/0373-630X
**SEMITICA.** **See** Linguistics.

IS
**SERIDIM.** **VFOAT** Sridim. No. 1 (October 1981)-. Periodical. Hebrew (English). sa. IL5.00 Israel; IL8.00 other. Sridim, PO Box 5324, Jerusalem 91052 Israel. **Tel** (02)812859. **ED** Moshe Rose. **LC** BM520; .S46. **Ad Acc. Circ:** 700 (ctrl).
**Desc:** Essays, lectures, and response on rabbinic themes.

UK
**SHALOM.** **Added/Corp** Church's Ministry Among the Jews. (1974)-. Periodical. English. Three times a year (Mar., July, Nov.). £4.00. Church's Ministry Among Jews, 30C Clarence Road, St. Albans Hts. AL1 4JJ England. **Tel** 011 44 72733114, FAX 011 44 72748312. **ED** M. Perry. **Circ:** 7,000 (ctrl). ***Continues CMJ Quarterly.***

US/0037-3656
**SHEVILEY HA-HINNUKH.** ***Suspended.*** **Added/Corp** National Council for Jewish Education (U.S.). (1925)-(19??). Periodical. Hebrew (English). qt. Council for Jewish Education, 730 Brondway, 2nd Floor, New York NY 10019. **Tel** (212)529-2000, FAX (212)586-9579.
**Ind/Abst** Relig. Index One Period.

US/0894-606X
**SHIRIM.** **See** Literature-Poetry.

US/0748-9706
**SHOFAR (MELVILLE, N.Y.).** **See** Children and Youth Interests.

US/0745-9327
**SHOFAR (WASHINGTON, D.C.), THE.** (THE SHOFAR / B'NAI B'RITH YOUTH ORGANIZATION.). [Shofar]. Periodical. English. bm. B'nai B'rith Youth Organization, Circulation Manager, 1640 Rhode Island Avenue NW, Washington DC 20036. **Tel** (202)857-6633. **DD** 296. **Circ:** 35,000 (ctrl).

US/0882-8539
**SHOFAR (WEST LAFAYETTE, IND.).** (SHOFAR.). [Shofar]. **Added/Corp** Purdue University. Jewish Studies Program. Midwest Jewish Studies Association. Vol. 1, No. 1 (Fall 1982)-. Periodical. English. Four times a year. $20.00 US; $25.00 other. Jewish Studies Program, 1363 LAEB, Room 2263, Purdue University, West Lafayette IN 47907-1363. **Tel** (317)494-7965, FAX (317)494-3660. **ED** Joseph Haberer; (317)494-4172; Nancy Lein; (317)494-7763. **LC** IN PROCESS. **DD** 296. **Bk Rev**, (Qty: 60/yr). **Pr Rev. Circ:** 350.
**Desc:** Dealing with Jewish studies, it is primarily for teachers, scholars and librarians of Jewish studies at universities and colleges. Includes articles, book-notes, film/media, news and information.
**Ind/Abst** Old Testam. Abstr.; Relig. Theol. Abstr. (199?-).

IS
**SINAI.** Vol. 1 (June 1937)-. Periodical. Hebrew. bm. $15.00. Sinai, PO Box 642, Jerusalem Israel. **Tel** 011 972 2 526231. **ED** Dr. Yitzchak Raphael. **LC** BM1; .S52. cum. index. **Bk Rev. Circ:** 1,000 (ctrl).
**Desc:** Studies in Jewish religious life, history and literature.

IS/0044-4758
**SIYYON.** (ZION.). [Siyyon]. Vol. 1 (1949)-. Hebrew (English; summaries and/or abstracts in English). Four times a year. $70.00. Historical Society of Israel, PO Box 4179, 22 Rashba Street, Jerusalem 91 041 Israel. **Tel** (02)637171, FAX 02-662135. **ED** I. Gutman, I. Efal, S. Almog and Y. Hacker. Index available. cum. index. **Bk Rev**, (Qty: 20-25). **Ad Acc. Circ:** 800 (ctrl). ***Supersedes*** *New Judea.*
**Desc:** Journal for research in Jewish history from the biblical period to our days in Israel and abroad.
**Ind/Abst** Am. Hist. Life; Relig. Theol. Abstr.

UK
**SONCINO HEBREW ENGLISH TALMUD.** English. ir. $995.00. Soncino Press Ltd, 123 Ditmas Avenue, Brooklyn NY 11218. **Tel** (718)972-6200, FAX (718)972-6204.
**Desc:** English translation of the Babylonian Talmud.

US/0740-8528
**SPECIAL INTEREST REPORT / THE AMERICAN COUNCIL FOR JUDAISM.** **Main/Corp** American Council for Judaism. (19??)-. Periodical. English. Ten times a year. Free. American Council for Judaism / Virginia, PO Box 9009, Alexandria VA 22304. **Tel** (703)836-2546.

GW/0585-5306
**STUDIA JUDAICA; FORSCHUNGEN ZUR WISSENSCHAFT DES JUDENTUMS.** Vol. 1 (1961)-. Monographic series. Multiple languages (German and English). ir. Price varies per volume. Walter de Gruyter Inc., PO Box 303421, D 10728 Berlin Germany. **Tel** 011 49 30 260050, FAX 011 49 30 26005251. **(Subscription address:** US and Canada/ 200 Saw Mill River Road, Hawthorne, NY 10532**)**

US/0740-8625
**STUDIES IN CONTEMPORARY JEWRY.** (STUDIES IN CONTEMPORARY JEWRY / INSTITUTE OF CONTEMPORARY JEWRY, THE HEBREW UNIVERSITY OF JERUSALEM.). [Stud. contemp. Jew.]. **Added/Corp** Universitah Ha-Ivrit Bi-Yerushalayim. Makhon Le-Yahadut Zemanenu. (1984)-. Monographic series. English. ir. Price varies per volume. Oxford University Press / New York, 200 Madison Avenue, New York NY 10016. **Tel** (212)679-7300, (919)677-0977, (800)451-7556, (800)445-9714, FAX (919)677-1303. **LC** DS125; .S75. **DD** 909/.04924; 909.

IS/0333-9661
**STUDIES IN JEWISH EDUCATION / THE HEBREW UNIVERSITY OF JERUSALEM, THE MELTON CENTRE FOR JEWISH EDUCATION IN THE DIASPORA. See** Education.

US/0884-6952
**STUDIES IN JUDAICA AND THE HOLOCAUST.** [Stud. Jud. Holocaust]. (198?)-. Monographic series. English. ir. Price varies per volume. Borgo Press, PO Box 2845, San Bernardino CA 92406. **Tel** (714)884-5813, (714)885-1161. **DD** 305.
**Desc:** Monographs on all aspects of Jewish civilization, history, and culture, including the Jewish holocaust of the 1940s.

IS/0334-1771
**STUDIES IN ZIONISM.** ***Title Change.*** [Stud. Zion.]. **Added/Corp** Makhon le-Heker ha-Tsiyonut al shem Hayim Vaitsman. (Autumn 1981)-(19??). Academic Scholarly Publication. English. Three times a year. Frank Cass & Company Ltd, Newbury House, 890-900 Eastern Avenue, Newbury Park, Ilford, Essex IG2 7HH United Kingdom. **Tel** 011 44 81 599 8866, FAX 011 44 81 599 0984, telex 897719. **ED** Ronald Zweig and Matityahu Mintz. **LC** DS149.A1; S78. **DD** 956.94/001/05. **Bk Rev. Ad Acc, Adv Mgr:** Anne Kidson. **Circ:** 305. available on microfilm from University Microfilms International (UMI). ***Continues*** *Zionism (Makhon Le-Heker Ha-Tsiyonut Al Shem Hayim Vaitsman : 1980), 0333-7510.* ***Continued by*** *Journal of Israeli History.*
**Desc:** An international journal concentrating on Zionism's social, political, and intellectual history. Publishes in-depth scholarly articles and book reviews. It is essential reading for scholars, historians, and educators concerned with the Zionist movement and its worldwide political implications.
**Ind/Abst** Am. Hist. Life (1981-?); Index Book Rev. Relig.; Index Jew. Period.; Middle East Abstr. Index; Relig. Index One Period.; Relig. Theol. Abstr.; Middle East J.

US/0585-7457
**STUDIES ON THE TEXTS OF THE DESERT OF JUDAH.** Vol. 1 (1957)-. Monographic series. Multiple languages (English, French and German). ir. Price varies per volume. E. J. Brill, Postbus 9000, 2300 PA Leiden Netherlands. **Tel** 011 31 71 312624, FAX 011 31 71 317532, telex 39296 BRILL NL.

IS
**SURVEY OF ARAB AFFAIRS. Added/Corp** Merkaz ha-Yerushalmi le-Inyene Tsibur u-Medinah. **VFOAT** SAA. (Aug. 12, 1985)-. Periodical. English. Four times a year. $25.00 institutions; $18.00 individuals. Jerusalem Center for Public Affairs, 13 Tel Hai, 92107 Jerusalem Israel. **Tel** 011 972 2 619281, FAX 011 972 2 619112. **(Subscription address:** Center for Jewish Community Studies, 1616 Walnut Street, Suite 513, Philadelphia, PA 19103; telephone: (215)787-1859**) LC** DS36; .S9.

US/1044-0011
**S'VARA (NEW YORK, N.Y.).** ***Suspended.*** **See** Philosophy.

RU/0731-3993
**SVET (BROOKLYN, NEW YORK, N.Y.).** (SVET.). (Oct. 1981)-. Periodical. Russian. mo. $18.00. Svet, 1383 President Street, Brooklyn NY 11213. **LC** BM1; .S9.

IS
**TARBIZ; RIVON LE-MADE HA-YAHADUT. Added/Corp** Universitah Ha-Ivrit Bi-Yerushalayim. **VFOAT** Tarbiz; a Quarterly for Jewish Studies. Vol. 1 (1929)-. Periodical. Hebrew (summaries and/or abstracts in English; table of contents in English). be. $25.00. Magnes Press, Hebrew University of Jerusalem, PO Box 7695, Jerusalem 91076 Israel. **Tel** 011 972 2 660341, 011 972 2 635291, FAX 011 972 2 633370, telex 25391. cum. index.
**Ind/Abst** Am. Hist. Life (1955-1971); MLA Int. Bibl. Books Artic. Mod. Lang. Lit.; Relig. Theol. Abstr.

IS/0334-3650
**TARBIZS.** [Trbys]. **Added/Corp** Universitah Ha-Ivrit Bi-Yerushalayim. (Oct. 1929)-. Periodical. Hebrew (English; summaries and/or abstracts in English). Four times a year. $38.00. Magnes Press, Hebrew University of Jerusalem, PO Box 7695, Jerusalem 91076 Israel. **Tel** 011 972 2 660341, 011 972 2 635291, FAX 011 972 2 633370, telex 25391. **ED** Professors I. Ta-Shma Y. Kaplan. **LC** DS101; .T35. cum. index. **Bk Rev.** ctrl circ.
**Ind/Abst** Am. Hist. Life (1955-1971); MLA Int. Bibl. Books Artic. Mod. Lang. Lit. (19??-).

IS
**TEL AVIV REVIEW (TEL AVIV, ISRAEL : 1988).** ***Suspended.*** (TEL AVIV REVIEW.). **VFOAT** TR. Vol. No. 1 (Jan. 1988)-Suspended. English. an (Winter). $28.00 (institutions), $14.00 (individuals), $19.95 (single issue) US; (add $2.00 for postage) other. Duke University Press, PO Box 90660, Durham NC 27708-0660. **Tel** (919)687-3600, (919)688-5134 (orders), FAX (919)688-4574, telex 802829. **ED** Gabriel Moked. **LC** PJ5059.E1; T45. **DD** 892.4/080005.
**Desc:** Devoted to translations (into English) from ancient and modern Hebrew literature; to poetry, fiction and drama of non-Israeli Jewish writers and to essays on aspects of Judaism, Israel, and the Middle East and issues.

IS/0932-8408
**TEL AVIVER JAHRBUCH FUR DEUTSCHE GESCHICHTE / HERAUSGEGEBEN VOM INSTITUT FUR DEUTSCHE GESCHICHTE. VFOAT** TAJB. Vol. 16 (1987)-. Periodical. German. an. Bleicher Verlag, Holderackerstr. 14, W-7016 Gerlingen Germany. **LC** DD4; .T46A. **DD** 943. ***Continues*** *Jahrbuch des Instituts fur Deutsche Geschichte, 0334-4606.*
**Ind/Abst** Am. Hist. Life (1972-).

IS
**TELEM.** Periodical. Hebrew. Tenuah Le-Yahadut Mitkademet Be-Yisrael, Rehov David Ha-Melekh 13, Jerusalem Israel. **LC** BM197; .T44.

IT
**TESTIMONIANZE SULL'EBRAISMO.** 1978-. Monographic series. Italian. Price varies per volume.

●US/1056-8492
**TODAY'S JEWISH FAMILY.** (1991)-. Periodical. English. bm. $6.00. YAZZ Publishing Co., PO Box 463, Island Park NY 11558.

US
**TORAH EDUCATION.** V. 1- Sept. 1969-. English. World Zionist Organization / New York, 110 East 59th Street, New York NY 10022. **Tel** (212)339-6000. **LC** BM100; .T65. **DD** 377/.9/605.

US/1050-4745
**TORAH U-MADDA JOURNAL, THE. See** Religion and Theology.

US/0041-0608
**TRADITION (NEW YORK).** (TRADITION.). [Tradition]. **Added/Corp** Rabbinical Council of America. Vol. 1 (Fall 1958)-. Periodical. English. Four times a year. $25.00 US; $31.00 Canada; $54.00 others. Rabbinical Council of America, 275 7th Avenue, New York NY 10001. **Tel** (212)807-7888. **LC** BM1; .T7. **CODEN** TRADD2. cum. index. available on microfilm and microfiche from University Microfilms International (UMI). Documents available from The Genuine Article.
**Ind/Abst** Arts Humanit. Citation Index [Full Cov.]; Index Book Rev. Relig.; Index Jew. Period. (19??-199?); Middle East Abstr. Index; MLA Int. Bibl. Books Artic. Mod. Lang. Lit.; New Testam. Abstr.; Relig. Index One Period.; Relig. Theol. Abstr.; Res. Alert [Full Cov.]; Soc. Sci. Cit. Index [Select. Cov.].

IS
**TSOFAR.** (19??)-. Periodical. Hebrew. wk. $40.00 (surface mail), $80.00 (airmail). **LC** BM1; .T78.

US/0888-3440
**ULTIMATE ISSUES.** (ULTIMATE ISSUES : A REPORT / BY DENNIS PRAGER.). [Ultim. issues]. Vol. 1, No. 1 (Winter 1985)-. Periodical. English. qt. $24.00 (US), $26.00 (Canada), $28.00 (other) surface mail; $30.00 (Canada), $34.00 (other) air mail. Ultimate Issues, 6020 Washington Boulevard, Suite 2, Culver City CA 90232. **Tel** (310)558-3958, (800) 225-8584, FAX (310)558-4241. **ED** Dennis Prager. **DD** 303. Index available. cum. index. **Bk Rev. Circ:** 8,500.

US
**UNITED STATES HOLOCAUST MEMORIAL MUSEUM GUIDE. See** Travel and Tourism.

US/0041-8153
**UNITED SYNAGOGUE REVIEW.** **Added/Corp** United Synagogue of America. **VFOAT** Review. (19??)-. Periodical. English. Twice a year. $3.00. United Synagogue Conservative Judaism, 155 5th Avenue, New York NY 10010. **Tel** (212)533-7800. **ED** Lois Goldrich. **Bk Rev. Ad Acc. Circ:** 255,000. available on microfilm from University Microfilms International (UMI).

FR
**UNZER SHTIME / NOTRE VOIX. VFOAT** Notre Voix. (19??)-. Periodical. Yiddish. ir. 70.00F France; 120.00F others. Notre Voix, 52 rue Rene Boulanger, 75010 Paris France.

UK
**VISION. See** Women's Interests.

RU
**VREMIA I MY.** (1990)-. Russian. Four times a year. $86.00. Publishing House Russian Language, 409 Highwood Avenue, Leonia NJ 07605. **Tel** (201)592-6155. **ED** Victor Perelman. **LC** DS101; .V742. ***Continues*** *Vremia i My (DLC) 76647044, 0737-7061.*

US/0746-9373
**WASHINGTON JEWISH WEEK.** [Washington Jew. week]. (Nov. 3, 1983)-. Periodical. English. Fifty-two times a year. $26.00 Maryland, DC and Virginia, $30.00 other US; $57.00 other. Washington Jewish Week, 12300 Twinbrook Parkway #250, Rockville MD 20852. **Tel** (301)230-2222. **ED** Eric Rozeman. **LC** AP92; .J73. **DD** 071/.53. **Ad Acc. Circ:** 20,000 (ctrl). ***Continues*** *Jewish Week (Washington, D.C.: 1975), 0272-7781.*
**Desc:** A paper concerned with the Jewish community and anything relating to Judaism.

US/0749-5471
**WESTERN STATES JEWISH HISTORY. See** Ethnic Interests.

US/0043-6488
**WISCONSIN JEWISH CHRONICLE, THE.** **Added/Corp** Wisconsin Jewish Publications Foundation. Vol. 1, No. 1 (Dec. 16, 1921)-. Newspaper. English (Russian). Fifty times a year. $30.00. The Wisconsin Jewish Chronicle, 1360 North Prospect Avenue, Milwaukee WI 53202. **Tel** (414)271-2992, FAX (414)271-0487. **ED** Andrew Muchin. **Bk Rev. Ad Acc, Adv Mgr:** Joni Oxmoor. **Circ:** 5,500.
**Desc:** Emphasis on the local Jewish news and analysis of national and international Jewish developments. Also includes special sections on party, business, health, etc.

●US
**WJC REPORT : WORLD JEWISH CONGRESS PUBLICATION, THE.** **Added/Corp** World Jewish Congress. **VFOAT** World Jewish Congress Report. Vol. 16, No. 3 (Feb./Mar. 1992)-. Periodical. English. ***Continues*** *News & Views (World Jewish Congress).*

US/0043-7557
**WOMEN'S LEAGUE OUTLOOK.** **Added/Corp** Women's League for Conservative Judaism. United Synagogue of America. National Women's League. **VFOAT** Outlook. (1930)-. Periodical. English. qt. $8.00 US; $10.00 other. Womens League for Conservative Judaism, 48 East 74th Street, New York NY 10021. **Tel** (212)628-1600, FAX (212)772-3507. **ED** Lynne Heller. **Bk Rev. Ad Acc. Circ:** 140,000 (ctrl).
**Desc:** A publication of the women's arm of conservative synagogues functioning all over the US, Canada and overseas.

US/0043-759X
**WOMEN'S WORLD (WASHINGTON, D.C.). See** Women's Interests.

CN/0824-7420
**WORLD OF LUBAVITCH.** (THE WORLD OF LUBAVITCH : PUBLICATION OF THE LUBAVITCH YOUTH ORGANIZATION, TORONTO.). [World Lubavitch]. Vol. 1, No. 1 (Jan. 1980)-. Periodical. English.

bm. Free. Chabad-Lubavitch, 770 Chabad Gate, Thornhill Ontario L4J 3V9 Canada. **Tel** (416)731-7000. **ED** J Gansburg. **DD** 296.8/33. **UDC** 296. **Ad Acc. Circ:** 5,000 (ctrl).
**Desc:** Jewish religion, Hasidic viewpoint, and community affairs.

IS
**YAHADUT.** Periodical. Hebrew. Mekhon Yisrael Sava, PO Box 11 Kiryath Sanz, Netanyah Israel. **LC** BM1; .Y33. **UDC** 296.

US/0084-3369
**YALE JUDAICA SERIES.** Vol. 1 (1948)-. Monographic series. English. ir. Price varies per volume. Yale University Press, PO Box 209040, New Haven CT 06520. **Tel** (203)432-0940, (800)987-7323, FAX (203)432-0948.

IS/0513-4617
**YALKUT MORESHET.** (1963)-. Hebrew (English). Six times a year. Yalkut Moreshet, PO Box 400009, 9 ME Esafim St, Tel Aviv Israel.
**Ind/Abst** Am. Hist. Life (1975-).

US
**YEARBOOK (WORLD CONFEDERATION OF JEWISH COMMUNITY CENTERS).** (YEARBOOK / WORLD CONFERENCE OF JEWISH COMMUNITY CENTERS.). **VFOAT** Year Book; Rapport Annuel; Shenaton. English (French, Hebrew and Spanish). an. **LC** DS102.9; .Y4. **DD** 305.8/924.

IS/0513-5230
**YEDI'OT GENAZIM.** **Added/Corp** Tel-Aviv. Genazim, Makhon Biyo-Bibliografi al Shem Asher Barash. (1962)-. Hebrew. ir. Yeduit Gnazim, 6 Rehov Kaplan, Tel Aviv Israel. cum. index

IS/0792-044X
**YIDDISHKEIT.** [Yiddishkeit]. (1986)-. Periodical. English. Four times a year. $10.00 surface mail; $14.00 airmail. Yiddishkeit, PO Box 5737, Jerusalem Israel. **Tel** 011 972 2 823933. **UDC** 296. **Bk Rev. Ad Acc. Circ:** 1,000.

US/1050-8864
**YIVO ANNUAL.** [Yivo annu.]. **Added/Corp** Yivo Institute for Jewish Research. Vol. 19 (1990)-. English. an. $17.00, member Yivo Institute of Jewish Research; $20.00 other. Yivo Institute for Jewish Research, 1048 Fifth Avenue, New York NY 10028. **Tel** (212)535-6700. **LC** DS101; .Y52. **DD** 305. ***Continues** Yivo Annual of Jewish Social Science, 0084-4209.*

US/0898-8358
**YIVO NEWS.** [Yivo news]. **Added/Corp** Yivo Institute for Jewish Research. **VFOAT** Yivo; Yedies Fun Yivo. No. 169 (Autumn 1986)-. Periodical. English (Yiddish). sa. Free; $50.00 (membership Yivo Institute of Jewish Research). Yivo Institute for Jewish Research, 1048 Fifth Avenue, New York NY 10028. **Tel** (212)535-6700. **LC** DS101; .N43. **DD** 909/.04924006. ***Continues** News of the Yivo, 0028-9302.*

SA
**YONTEV BLETER.** **VFOAT** Yomtov Bletter. (19??)-. English (Yiddish). $6.00. PO Box 7690, Johannesburg 2000 South Africa. **LC** BM690; .Y66.

US/0044-0817
**YOUNG JUDAEAN.** (THE YOUNG JUDAEAN.). [Young Jud.]. **Added/Corp** Hadassah Zionist Youth Commission. Hadassah, the Women's Zionist Organization of America. (19??)-. Periodical. English. qt. National Young Judaea, 50 West 58th Street, New York NY 10019. **LC** AP222; .Y73. **DD** 296.
**Ind/Abst** Index Jew. Period. (19??-199?).

IS/0084-439X
**YUBAL GOBES MEHQARIM SEL HA-MERKAZ LE-HEQER HA-MUSIQAH HA-YHUDIT.** **See** Music.

US/0098-3640
**YUGNTRUF.** **See** Literature.

IS
**ZIONIST IDEAS.** **VFOAT** Mahashavot Tsiyoniyot. Monographic series. English. sa. Price varies per volume. Department of Development and Services, World Zionist Organization, PO Box 92, Jerusalem 91920 Israel. **Tel** (02)635733. **ED** Geoffrey Wigoder. **LC** DS149.A1; Z55. **UDC** 296. **Bk Rev. Circ:** 1,000 (ctrl).
**Desc:** Articles on Zionist thought, reports of discussions of Zionist seminars, and reviews of new books on Zionism.

SA
**ZIONIST RECORD AND SA JEWISH CHRONICLE.** **VAT** Zionist Record and South African Jewish Chronicle. (Aug. 14, 1959)-. Periodical. English. wk. R15.00. Zionist Centre, PO Box 150, 84 de Villiers Street, 2000 Johannesburg South Africa. **LC** DS133; .Z49. **DD** 968/.004/924. ***Formed by the union of** Zionist Record **and** SA Jewish Chronicle.*

## PROTESTANTISM

US/0360-3717
**A.M.E. ZION QUARTERLY REVIEW, THE.** [A. M. E. Zion q. rev.]. **Main/Corp** African Methodist Episcopal Zion Church. **VAT** African Methodist Episcopal Zion Quarterly Review. (1???)-. Periodical. English. qt. $10.00. AME Zion Quarterly Review, PO Box 146, Bedford PA 15522. **DD** 287. ***Continues** Church Quarterly.*
**Ind/Abst** Index Book Rev. Relig.; Relig. Index One Period. (1981-).

US
**AB TOUCH.** English. Divinity Board of the Southern Baptist Convention, PO Box 2190, Dallas TX 75221-2190.
**Ind/Abst** South. Baptist Period. Index (1987-).

CN/0821-0209
**ACCENT ON ARTS.** (ACCENT ON ARTS : NEWS HIGHLIGHTS FROM ADVENTIST RADIO TELEVISION SERVICES.). [Accent ARTS]. **VAT** Accent on Adventist Radio Television Services. Periodical. English. qt. Free. Adventist Radio Television Services, Unit N, 500 Dufferin Street, Downsview Ontario M3H 5T5 Canada. **DD** 269/.2. **UDC** 269; 286.3. ctrl circ.

US/0731-2687
**ACCION (EL PASO, TEX.).** (ACCION.). Spanish. qt. $2.50. Southern Baptist Convention, 901 Commerce, Suite 750, Nashville TN 37203. **Tel** (615)244-2355, FAX (615)742-8919. **(Subscription address:** Sunday School Board - Customer Service, 127 Ninth Avenue North, Nashville, TN 37234 USA; telephone: (800)458-2772**)** **UDC** 286.1.

US/0883-8933
**ACCORD (NEW YORK, N.Y.).** (ACCORD.). [Accord]. Vol. 1, No. 1 (Dec. 1984)-. Periodical. English. mo. $28.00 US; $35.00 Canada. Accord Inc, 481 8th Avenue, New York NY 10001. **LC** BX9750; .S403. **DD** 289.9. **UDC** 289.9.

CN/0079-4996
**ACTS AND PROCEEDINGS OF THE GENERAL ASSEMBLY OF THE PRESBYTERIAN CHURCH IN CANADA.** (THE ACTS AND PROCEEDINGS OF THE GENERAL ASSEMBLY OF THE PRESBYTERIAN CHURCH IN CANADA.). **Main/Corp** Presbyterian Church in Canada. General Assembly. (1875)-. Proceedings. English. an. 10.00Can$. Presbyterian Church in Canada, 50 Wynford Drive, Don Mills Ontario M3C 1J7 Canada. **Tel** (905)441-1111. **ED** E.F. Roberts. **LC** WMLC L 83/4918. **DD** 285/.2/71. **Circ:** 5,000 (ctrl).
**Desc:** Yearbook containing reports, statistics and minutes of the meeting of the general assembly.

US/0731-2733
**ADELANTE (EL PASO, TX.).** (ADELANTE.). **Added/Corp** Southern Baptist Convention. Sunday School Board. (19??)-. Periodical. Spanish. qt. $2.75. Southern Baptist Convention, 901 Commerce, Suite 750, Nashville TN 37203. **Tel** (615)244-2355, FAX (615)742-8919. **(Subscription address:** Sunday School Board, Customer Service, 127 9th Avenue North, Nashville TN 37234.**)** **LC** Discard.

●US/1071-4383
**ADULT LIFE AND WORK STUDY GUIDE.** (1994)-. Periodical. English. qt. $2.50 (single issue).

US/0747-1564
**ADULT SABBATH SCHOOL LESSONS (EASY ENGLISH ED.).** (ADULT SABBATH SCHOOL LESSONS.). **Added/Corp** General Conference of Seventh-Day Adventists. Sunday School Dept. Christian Record Braille Foundation. (19??)-. Periodical. English. Four times a year. $6.75. Pacific Press Publishing Association, PO Box 7000, Boise ID 83707. **Tel** (208)465-2500, FAX (208)465-2531.
**Ind/Abst** Seventh-Day Adventist Period. Index (19??-).

US/0001-8589
**ADVANCE (SPRINGFIELD).** (ADVANCE.). **Added/Corp** Assemblies of God. General Council. Vol. 1- (Oct. 1965)-. Periodical. English. mo. $14.75 (one year), $28.00 (two year) US; $22.00 (one year), $43.50 (two year) other. Gospel Publishing House, 1445 Boonville Avenue, Springfield MO 65802. **Tel** (417)862-2781, FAX (417)866-1146. **ED** Gwen Jones. Index available. cum. index. **Bk Rev. Ad Acc.** ctrl circ.
**Desc:** Magazine for Assemblies of God ministers and church leaders.

US/0741-4307
**ADVENT CHRISTIAN WITNESS (1983), THE.** (THE ADVENT CHRISTIAN WITNESS.). April 1983-. Periodical. English. mo (July/Aug. combined). $11.00. Advent Christian Witness Publications, Box 23152, Charlotte NC 28212. **Tel** (704)545-6161. **ED** Robert J Mayer. **UDC** 286.3. **Bk Rev. Circ:** 5,000. ***Continues** Advent Christian Witness to the World, 0274-9289.*
**Desc:** A magazine that serves members and friends of the Advent Christian Church.

US/0360-389X
**ADVENTIST HERITAGE.** [Advent. herit.]. **Added/Corp** Loma Linda University. Division of Religion. Loma Linda University. Dept. of Archives and Research. Vol. 1 (Jan. 1974)-. Periodical. English. Three times a year. $12.00. La Sierra University, Department of English, 4700 Pierce Street, Riverside CA 92515. **Tel** (714)785-2241. **ED** Ron Gragbill, Gary Chartiev. **LC** BX6101; .A47. **DD** 286/.7/09. Bound Index published separately, free upon request. **Bk Rev**, (Qty: 2-5). **Ad Acc. Circ:** 1,600. available on microfilm and microfiche from University Microfilms International (UMI).
**Desc:** Solely dedicated to recounting the history of the Adventist Church around the world.
**Ind/Abst** Am. Hist. Life (1974-); Seventh-Day Adventist Period. Index (1971-).

US/0163-8866
**ADVENTIST REVIEW (MONTHLY, INTER-AMERICAN EDITION).** (ADVENTIST REVIEW.). [Adventist rev.]. (19??)-. Periodical. English. mo. $11.95. Manager Periodical Department, Review and Herald, 6856 Eastern Avenue NW, Washington DC 20012.
**Ind/Abst** Seventh-Day Adventist Period. Index (19??-).

US/0161-1119
**ADVENTIST REVIEW (WEEKLY).** (ADVENTIST REVIEW.). [Adventist rev.]. **Added/Corp** General Conference of Seventh-Day Adventists. Vol. 155 (Jan 5, 1978)-. Periodical. English. Fifty-two times a year. $48.97 US; $59.17 other. Review and Herald Publishing Association, 55 West Oak Ridge Drive, Hagerstown MD 21740. **Tel** (301)791-7000 ext. 2534, FAX (301)790-9734. **ED** William G. Johnson. **LC** BX6101; .A3. **DD** 286/.73. **Ad Acc. Circ:** 78,000. ***Continues** Advent Review and Sabbath Herald, 0095-2397.*
**Desc:** General magazine for Seventh-Day Adventist Church membership. A variety of topics are covered to inform and inspire church members.
**Ind/Abst** Seventh-Day Adventist Period. Index (1971-).

US/0745-6441
**ADVENTIST REVIEW (WEEKLY, SOUTHWESTERN EDITION).** (ADVENTIST REVIEW : GENERAL ORGAN OF THE SEVENTH-DAY ADVENTIST CHURCH.). [Adventist rev.]. **Added/Corp** General Conference Seventh-Day Adventists. (19??)-. Periodical. English. Fifty-two times a year. $48.97 US; $59.17 other. Review and Herald Publishing Association, 55 West Oak Ridge Drive, Hagerstown MD 21740. **Tel** (301)791-7000 ext. 2534, FAX (301)790-9734. **DD** 286.7/32/05. **Ad Acc.**

CN/0823-0315
**AGLOW NEWSLETTER (MELVILLE).** (AGLOW NEWSLETTER.). [Aglow newsl.]. **Added/Corp** Women's Aglow Fellowship (Melville, Sask.). (1982)-. Newsletter. English. mo. Limited free distribution. Women's Aglow Fellowship, PO Box 2675, Melville Saskatchewan S0A 2P0 Canada. **DD** 248.4/05. ctrl circ.

US/0731-2679
**AHORA (EL PASO, TEX.).** (AHORA.). **Added/Corp** Southern Baptist Convention. Sunday School Board. (19??)-. Spanish. qt. $2.50. Southern Baptist Convention, 901 Commerce, Suite 750, Nashville TN 37203. **Tel** (615)244-2355, FAX (615)742-8919. **(Subscription address:** Sunday School Board - Customer Service, 127 Ninth Avenue North, Nashville, TN 37234 USA; telephone: (800)458-2772**)** **LC** Discard.

US
**AL-MASHAL.** **VFOAT** Arabic Baptist Church Bulletin, Washington D.C. Periodical. Arabic. bm. Free. 4605 Massachusetts Avenue NW, Washington DC 20016. **Tel** 363-3911. **ED** Esper Ajaj. **LC** BX6480.W3; A75. **UDC** 286.1.

US/0002-4147
**ALABAMA BAPTIST HISTORIAN, THE.** [Ala. Baptist Hist.]. **Added/Corp** Alabama Baptist Historical Society. Vol. 1 No. 1 (Nov. 1964)-. Periodical. English. Twice a year (January and July). $5.00. Alabama Baptist Historian, Samford University, 800 Lakeshore Drive, Birmingham AL 35209. **Tel** (205)870-2749, FAX (205)870-2642. **ED** Dr. Lee N. Allen, (phone: (205)870-2675). **Bk Rev. Circ:** 200.
**Desc:** History on Alabama Baptist.
**Ind/Abst** Am. Hist. Life (1986-).

US/0194-7834
**ALASKA BAPTIST MESSENGER.** **Added/Corp** Alaska Baptist Convention. (1945)-. Periodical. English. Twelve times a year. Free for schools, libraries, and ministers; $5.00 other. Alaska Baptist Convention, 1750 O Malley Road, Anchorage AK 99516. **Tel** (907)344-9627, FAX (907)344-7044. **ED** Bill Duncan. **Ad Acc. Circ:** 2,500 (ctrl).

US/0742-7735
**ALASKAN EPIPHANY.** **Added/Corp** Protestant Episcopal Church in the U.S.A. Alaska (Diocese). Vol. 1 (April 1980)-. Periodical. English. Four times a year (Apr., June, Sept., Dec.). $10.00. Alaskan Epiphany, 1030

Second Avenue, Fairbanks AK 99701. **Tel** (907)452-3349. **ED** Mary Parsons, (editor's address: 1205 Denali Way, Fairbanks, AK 99701-4178, phone: (907)452-3040). **Bk Rev**, (Qty: 1-5). **Circ:** 3,000. ***Formed by the union of*** *Alaskan Churchman* ***and*** *Epiphany.*
**Desc:** Presents the activities, past and present, of the Episcopal Church in Alaska, with coverage of Alaskan and national issues.

UK
**ALCUIN. Main/Corp** Alcuin Club. (1973/74)-. English. an. £10.00 UK; $20.00 US; £11.00 other. The Alcuin Club, Norton Vicarage, Windmill Hill, Runcorn, Cheshire WA7 6QE Great Britain. **Tel** 0928 715+54, telex 580616. **(Subscription address:** All Saints Vicarage, Highlands Road, Runcorn, Cheshire WA7 4PS United Kingdom**) ED** M F Perham. **LC** BX5141.A1; A55. **DD** 264/.03/005. **UDC** 264. **Bk Rev. Circ:** 1,000. ***Continues*** *Alcuin Club. Report.*

NE
**ALGEMEEN DOOPSGEZIND WEEKBLAD. Added/Corp** Algemene Doopsgezinde Societeit (Netherlands). (19??)-. Periodical. Dutch. wk. Fl79.25 Netherlands; Fl119.25 other. ADW Algemeen Doopsgezind Soc, Singel 454, 1017 Aw Amsterdam Netherlands. **Tel** 011 31 20 6230914.

US/0002-757X
**AMERICAN BAPTIST, THE.** ***Title Change.*** [Am. Baptist]. Vol. 168, No. 4- (April 1970)-(July/August 1992). Periodical. English. mo. American Baptist Center, PO Box 871, Valley Forge PA 19482. **Tel** (800)334-1427. **LC** BX6201; .A48. **DD** 286/.131/05. available on microfilm and microfiche from University Microfilms International (UMI). ***Formed by the union of*** *Crusader* ***and*** *Mission.* ***Merged with*** *American Baptist Churches in the U.S.A. Division of Communication. AB Input, 0364-2089* ***to form*** *American Baptists in Mission.*
**Desc:** Offers encouragement and spiritual refreshment to the 1.56 million members of the American Baptist Churches as well as insightful and informative feature stories, news and reviews of missions and ministries.

US/0745-3698
**AMERICAN BAPTIST QUARTERLY.** [Am. Baptist q.]. **Added/Corp** American Baptist Historical Society. Vol. 1, No. 1, Oct. (1982)-. Periodical. English. Four times a year (Mar., June, Sept., Dec.). $27.05 one year; $49.50 two years; $68.23 three years. American Baptist Historical Society, PO Box 851, Valley Forge PA 19482-0851. **Tel** (215)768-2378. **ED** Dr. William R. Miller. **LC** BX6201; .A53. **DD** 286/.05. Index available. cum. index. **Bk Rev. Circ:** 1,000. available on microfilm and microfiche from University Microfilms International (UMI). ***Continues*** *Foundations, 0015-8992.*
**Desc:** Matters of interest to Baptists, biblical, historical and theological. Organized around themes of archival resources and cultural mythologies.
**Ind/Abst** Am. Hist. Life (1982-); Hist. Abstr.; Index Book Rev. Relig. (1982-); Recent. Publ. Artic.; Relig. Index One Period. (1982-); Relig. Theol. Abstr.

US/0191-0183
**AMERICAN BAPTIST WOMAN, THE. Added/Corp** American Baptist Women. (19??)-. Periodical. English. Three times a year (Winter, Spring & Fall). $6.00. American Baptist Women's Ministries, PO Box 851, Valley Forge PA 19482-0851. **Tel** (215)768-2283. **Bk Rev.** ctrl circ.

●US
**AMERICAN BAPTISTS IN MISSION. Added/Corp** American Baptist Churches in the U.S.A. **VFOAT** In Mission. (Sept. 1992)-. Periodical. English. bm. Free on request. American Baptist Center, PO Box 871, Valley Forge PA 19482. **Tel** (800)334-1427. **LC** IN PROCESS. ***Formed by the union of*** *American Baptist Churches in the U.S.A. Division of Communication. AB Input, 0364-2089* ***and*** *American Baptist, 0002-757X.*

US/0886-5159
**AMERICAN PRESBYTERIANS.** [Am. Presbyt.]. **Added/Corp** Presbyterian Historical Society. Historical Foundation of the Presbyterian and Reformed Churches. Cumberland Presbyterian Church. Historical Foundation. Vol. 63, No. 3 (Fall 1985)-. Periodical. English. Four times a year (Mar., June, Sept., Dec.). $15.00 Comes with Presbyterian Historical Association Membership. Journal of Presbyterian History, 425 Lombard Street, Philadelphia PA 19147-1516. **Tel** (215)627-1852, FAX (215)627-0509. **ED** James H. Smylie. **LC** BX8935; .A46. **DD** 285/.173. Index available. cum. index. **Bk Rev.** available on microfilm and microfiche from University Microfilms International (UMI). Documents available from The Genuine Article. ***Continues*** *Journal of Presbyterian History, 0022-3883.*
**Ind/Abst** Am. Hist. Life (1954-); Annu. Bibliogr. Engl. Lang. Lit.; Arts Humanit. Citation Index [Full Cov.]; Curr. Contents Arts Humanit.; Index Book Rev. Relig.; Relig. Index One Period.; Relig. Theol. Abstr.; Res. Alert [Full Cov.]; Soc. Sci. Cit. Index [Select. Cov.]; West. Hist. Q.

CL
**ANALISIS. Added/Corp** Academia de Humanismo Cristiano (Santiago, Chile). No. 1 No. 2 (Feb. 1978)-. English. mo. $50.00 single issue. Academia de Humanismo Cristiano, Catedral 1063, Piso 5, Santiago Chile. **Tel** 011 56 2 6980864. **LC** AS81.A1; A25. ***Continues*** *Academia.*

CN/0517-7731
**ANGLICAN, THE. Added/Corp** Anglican Church of Canada. Diocese of Toronto. Vol. 1 (Easter 1958)-. English. mo (except July and Aug.). 5.00Can$ Canada; 10.00Can$ other. Anglican Diocese of Toronto, 135 Adelaide Street East, Toronto Ontario M5C 1L8 Canada. **Tel** (416)363-6021, FAX (416)363-7678. **ED** Debbie Dimmick. **Bk Rev. Ad Acc. Circ:** 44,000 (ctrl). ***Absorbed*** *Anglican Church of Canada. Anglican Church Women. Diocese of Toronto. News and Views, 0700-7582.*
**Desc:** Serves the clergy and laity of the Anglican Diocese of Toronto. Includes national publication 'Canadian Churchman'.

US/0896-8039
**ANGLICAN AND EPISCOPAL HISTORY.** [Angl. Episcop. hist.]. **Added/Corp** Historical Society of the Episcopal Church. Vol. 56, No. 1 (March 1987)-. Periodical. English. Four times a year (Mar., June, Sept., Dec.). $25.00. Historical Society of the Episcopal Church, 606 Rathervue Place, PO Box 2247, Austin TX 78768. **Tel** (512)472-6816. **LC** BX5800; .H5. **DD** 283/.73/05. Index available. **Pr Rev.** available on microfilm and microfiche from University Microfilms International (UMI). ***Continues*** *Historical Magazine of the Protestant Episcopal Church, 0018-2486.*
**Ind/Abst** Am. Hist. Life (March 1987-); Annu. Bibliogr. Engl. Lang. Lit.; Index Book Rev. Relig.; Relig. Index One Period. (March 1987-); West. Hist. Q.

US/0003-3278
**ANGLICAN DIGEST, THE.** V. 1- 1959-. Periodical. English. bm. $15.00. Speak Inc, Hillspeak, Eureka Springs AR 72632-9705. **Tel** (501)253-9701. **ED** C Frederick Barbee. **UDC** 283. **Bk Rev. Ad Acc. Circ:** 115,000.
**Desc:** A miscellany relecting the words and work of the faithful throughout the Anglican Communion.

CN/0823-8308
**ANGLICAN MESSENGER (EDMONTON).** (ANGLICAN MESSENGER / DIOCESE OF EDMONTON, DIOCESE OF ATHABASCA.). **Added/Corp** Anglican Church of Canada. Diocese of Edmonton. Vol. 53, No. 1 (Jan. 1984)-. English. mo (10 issues). 5.00Can$ Canada; 15.00Can$ other. Anglican Church of Canada, 1003 84th Avenue, Edmonton Alberta T6E 2G6 Canada. **Tel** (403)439-7344. **DD** 283/.71231. ***Continues*** *Peace Messenger, Edmonton Anglican, 0229-1800.*

FR
**ANNUAIRE DE LA FRANCE PROTESTANTE. Main/Corp** Federation Protestante de France. (1979)-. French. an. Imprimerie Lormond S A, Boite Postale No 347, 62 Avenue Gambetta, 82003 Montauban France. **ED** J R Graff. **LC** BX4843.A2; F7. **DD** 280/.4/02544. ***Continues*** *France Protestante.*

CN/0705-9590
**APPEL DU SACRE-COEUR, L'. Added/Corp** Assomptionistes. (Jan. 1948)-. Periodical. French. Ten times a year. 7.50Can$. Montmartre Canadien, 1679 Ch St Louis, Quebec Province of Quebec G1S 1G5 Canada. ***Absorbed*** *Message du Coeur de Jesus, 0704-0105.*

US/8750-4723
**ARAUTO DA SANTIDADE, O.** Vol. 1, No. 1 (Aug. 1972)-. Periodical. Portuguese. mo. $4.00. Casa Nazarena de Publicaciones, 6401 The Paseo, Kansas City MO 64131. **Tel** (816)333-7000. **DD** 289. **Circ:** 2,000.

CN/0229-2807
**ARC (MONTREAL).** (ARC.). [Arc]. **Added/Corp** McGill University. Faculty of Religious Studies. (1973)-. Periodical. English. an. $12.00. Faculty of Religious Studies, McGill University, 3520 University Street, Montreal Quebec H3A 2A7 Canada. **Tel** (514)392-4826. **ED** Bruce Guenther. **DD** 205. **Bk Rev**, (Qty: 12-20/yr). **Ad Acc. Circ:** 600-700 (ctrl).
**Desc:** A journal devoted to Christian theology and ethics, the comparative study of religion, and religion and culture.
**Ind/Abst** Can. Period. Index (19??-); Index Book Rev. Relig.; Relig. Index One Period.

GW/0066-6491
**ARCHIV FUER SCHLESISCHE KIRCHENGESCHICHTE.** [Arch. schles. Kirchengesch.]. (19??)-. German. an. Jan Thorbecke Verlag GmbH and Company, Karlstrasse 10, Postfach 546, D 72482 Sigmaringen Germany. **Tel** 011 49 7571 728100, FAX 011 07571-728-280, telex 732534. **LC** BR857.S6; A72.
**Ind/Abst** BHA : Biblio. Hist. Art; Numis. Lit.

US/1047-1936
**ARIZONA EPISCOPALIAN, THE.** (ARIZONA EPISCOPALIAN.). **Added/Corp** Episcopal Church. Diocese of Arizona. Vol. 9, No. 5 (Sept. 1989)-. Periodical. English. mo. The Arizona News, PO Box 13647, Phoenix AZ 85002-3647. ***Continues*** *Arizona News of the Episcopal Church, 0279-0475.*

US/1040-6506
**ARKANSAS BAPTIST (1987).** (ARKANSAS BAPTIST.). **VFOAT** Arkansas Baptist Newsmagazine. Vol. 86, No. 19 (May 14, 1987)-. Periodical. English. Twenty-six times a year. $8.85 (one year), $17.70 (two year), $26.00 (three year). Arkansas Baptist State Convention, PO Box 552, Little Rock AR 72203. **Tel** (501)376-4791, FAX (501)374-2754. **ED** Trennis G. Henderson. **Ad Acc, Adv Mgr:** Nelle O'Bryan. **Circ:** 40,000. ***Continues*** *Arkansas Baptist Newsmagazine, 0004-1734.*

US/0890-5258
**ARKANSAS EPISCOPALIAN, THE. Added/Corp** Episcopal Church. Diocese of Arkansas. Vol. 59, No. 6 (Sept. 1985)-. Newspaper. English. Nine times a year. $3.00 (donation). Episcopal Diocese of Arkansas, PO Box 164668, Little Rock AR 72216-4668. **Tel** (501)372-2168. **ED** Julie Keller. **Bk Rev. Circ:** 8,200 (ctrl). ***Continues*** *Arkansas Churchman, 0199-4611.*

HK
**ASIA LUTHERAN NEWS : ALN. VFOAT** ALN. Periodical. English. mo. $12.00. Asia Lutheran News, 29A Melder Place, Nugegoda Sri Lanka Ceylon. **UDC** 284(548.7).

US/0362-0816
**ASSOCIATE REFORMED PRESBYTERIAN, THE. Added/Corp** Associate Reformed Presbyterian Church. General Synod. Vol. 1 (Jan. 1976)-. Periodical. English. Twelve times a year. $15.00 (one year), $28.00 (two years), $39.00 (three years). Associate Reformed Presbyterian Center, One Cleveland Street, Greenville SC 29601. **Tel** (803)232-8297. **ED** Ben Johnston. **Bk Rev**, (Qty: 15-20). **Ad Acc. Circ:** 6,200. available on microfilm from University Microfilms International (UMI); available on audiocassette. ***Formed by the union of*** *Associate Reformed Presbyterian, 0362-0816* ***and*** *Associate Reformed Presbyterian Synodical Journal Christian Education.*
**Desc:** Official publication of the Associate Reformed Presbyterian Church, reflecting the special programs and emphases of all arms of the denomination.

SZ
**AT MI (SAINT GALLEN, SWITZERLAND).** (AT MI : TIENG NOI CA HOI THANH TIN-LANH VN TAI AU-CHAU.). Vol. 1, No. 1 (1987)-. Periodical. Vietnamese. qt. At Mi, Schorenstr 71, CH-9000 St Gallen Switzerland. **LC** BX4837; .D37.

CN/0004-6752
**ATLANTIC BAPTIST, THE.** [Atl. Baptist]. **Added/Corp** United Baptist Convention of the Atlantic Provinces. Board of Publication. Vol. 1 (Jan. 1, 1965)-. Periodical. English. mo (July/Aug. issue combined). 16.12Can$ Canada; 27.50Can$ others. Atlantic Baptist, PO Box 756, Kentville Nova Scotia B4N 3X9 Canada. **Tel** (902)678-6868, FAX (902)681-0315. **ED** Rev. Michael A. Lipe. **Bk Rev. Ad Acc. Circ:** 7,500. ***Supersedes*** *Maritime Baptist, 0315-4084.*
**Desc:** News and features of interest to persons of all ages. Directed specifically to members of churches in the United Baptist Convention of the Atlantic Provinces of Canada.

AT/0812-4353
**AUSTRALIAN EVANGEL.** **See** Religion and Theology.

AT
**AUSTRALIAN PRESBYTERIAN LIFE. Added/Corp** Presbyterian Church of Australia. (Feb. 5, 1966)-. Periodical. English. mo (except January). 27.00Aus$ Australia; 43.00Aus$ other. Australian Presbyterian Living Today, 156 Collins Street, Melbourne 3000 Australia. **Tel** 011 61 3 6542765. **ED** Neville Sandon. **Bk Rev. Ad Acc. Circ:** 5,500 (ctrl). ***Supersedes*** *Presbyterian Life.*
**Desc:** News and features to aid Christian growth.

CN/0227-2962
**B. C. AREA ANNUAL DOCKET.** [B.C. area annu. docket]. **Main/Corp** Baptist Union of Western Canada. B.C. Area. Assembly. **VAT** British Columbia Area Annual Docket; Annual Docket of the B.C. Area. Began publication in 1975 or 1976. English. an. Free. Baptist Union of Western Canada B C Area, 8411 Rosebank Crescent, Richmond British Columbia V7A 2K8 Canada. **DD** 286/.1711. **UDC** 286.1(711). ctrl circ. ***Continues*** *Baptist Union of Western Canada. B. C. Area. Assembly. Annual Assembly of the B.C. Area, 0227-2954.*

US
**B.M.A.A. DIRECTORY AND HANDBOOK. Main/Corp** Baptist Missionary Association of America. **VFOAT** Directory & Handbook. Directory. English. Baptist News Service, PO Box 97, Jacksonville TX 75766. **Tel** (214)586-2501. **ED** James C Blaylock. **LC** BX6209.B37; B36B. **DD** 266/.61/02573. **UDC** 266.1(035); 286.1. **Circ:** 5,000.
**Desc:** Directory of churches, ministers and missionaries of the Baptist Missionary Association of America. Statistics included on these churches.

US
**BAPTIST & REFLECTOR.** English. $7.50. Tennessee Baptist Board, PO Box 728, Brentwood TN 37027. **Tel** (615)373-2255. **ED** William Fletcher Allen (Editor's Address: 5001 Maryland Way, Brentwood, TN 37027; Phone: (615)371-2003). **Ad Acc. Circ:** 60,000.

US/0745-5836
**BAPTIST BIBLE TRIBUNE.** [Baptist Bible trib.]. **Added/Corp** Baptist Bible Fellowship. Baptist Bible Fellowship International. (1950)-. Periodical. English. Twelve times a year. $9.00. Baptist Bible Tribune, PO Box 309 HSJ, Springfield MO 65801. **Tel** (417)831-3996. **ED** James O Combs. **DD** 248. **Bk Rev**, (Qty: 50-100). **Ad Acc, Adv Mgr:** Michelle Dove. **Circ:** 35,000. available on microfilm.
**Desc:** Baptist Bible fellowship church news, sermons, book reviews and family articles of interest to conservative Christians.

US/0005-5689
**BAPTIST BULLETIN, THE. Added/Corp** General Association of Regular Baptist Churches (North) General Association of Regular Baptist Churches. **VFOAT** Baptist Bulletin for Bible-Believing Baptists. (June/July 1935)-. Bulletin. English. mo (Aug./Sept. issue combined). $10.00 one year, $25.00 three year. Regular Baptist Press, 1300 North Meacham Road, Schaumburg IL 60173. **Tel** (708)843-1600, FAX (708)843-3757. **ED** Vernon D. Miller. **Bk Rev. Ad Acc. Circ:** 27,700.
**Desc:** Official organ of the General Association of Regular Baptist Churches.
**Ind/Abst** Guide Soc. Sci. Relig.

US/8756-9612
**BAPTIST CHALLENGE, THE. VFOAT** Challenge. Vol. 1, No. 1 (Jan./Feb./Mar. 1961)-. Periodical. English. mo. Free on request. The Baptist Challenge, PO Box 5567, Little Rock AR 72215-5567. **Tel** (501)664-3225. **ED** M. L. Moser Jr. **Bk Rev. Ad Acc. Circ:** 5,300 (ctrl).

US/0744-6985
**BAPTIST COURIER.** (1878)-. Periodical. English. Forty-Five times a year. $8.50. Baptist Courier, PO Box 2168, 100 Manly Street, Greenville SC 29602. **Tel** (803)232-8736. **ED** John E Roberts. **Ad Acc. Circ:** 113,000. ***Continues** Working Christian.*
**Desc:** News journal for the South Carolina Baptist Convention.

US/0408-506X
**BAPTIST DIGEST.** (1954)-. Periodical. English. mo. $2.50. Kansas Nebraska Convention SB, 5410 South West Seventh Street, Topeka NE 66606. **Tel** (913)273-4880.

CN
**BAPTIST HERITAGE IN ATLANTIC CANADA.** V. 1-. Monographic series. English. Price varies per volume. Lancelot Press, PO Box 425, Hantsport Nova Scotia B0N 2T0 Canada. **UDC** 286.1(71).

US
**BAPTIST HERITAGE UPDATE.** English. qt. Free to members; $14.95 (one year), $28.95 (two year), $42.95 (three year) membership US; $21.95 (one year), $42.95 (two year), $63.95 (three year) membership Canada and Mexico. Historical Commission of the Southern Baptist Convention, 901 Commerce/Suite 400, Nashville TN 37203-3630. **Tel** (615)244-0344, FAX (615)242-2153. **ED** Kim Medley. cum. index. **Bk Rev**, (Qty: 10). **Circ:** 1,113.
**Desc:** Newsletter including features on the history and works of Southern Baptists.

US/0005-5719
**BAPTIST HISTORY AND HERITAGE.** [Baptist hist. herit.]. **Added/Corp** Southern Baptist Historical Society. Southern Baptist Convention. Historical Commission. Vol. 1 (Aug. 1965)-. Periodical. English. qt (Jan., Apr., July, Oct.). $10.95 (1 year), $20.95 (2 year), $31.95 (3 year) US; $13.45 (1 year), $25.95 (2 year), $39.50 (3 year) other (includes postage). Historical Commission of the Southern Baptist Convention, 901 Commerce/Suite 400, Nashville TN 37203-3630. **Tel** (615)244-0344, FAX (615)242-2153. **ED** Carol Woodfin. **LC** BX6207; .S6. Index available (bound in 4th issue). cum. index. **Bk Rev. Circ:** 2,500 (ctrl). available on microfilm and microfiche from University Microfilms International (UMI).
**Desc:** Includes special issues on women's roles, ethnics, the Bible, missions, the family, Sunday Schools, and other vital topics. Dedicated to interpreting the Baptist story so that Baptists can understand and appreciate their past and discover historical perspective for the present and future.
**Ind/Abst** Am. Hist. Life (1972-); Christ. Period. Index (19??-); Index Book Rev. Relig. (1972-); Relig. Index One Period. (1977-); Relig. Theol. Abstr.; South. Baptist Period. Index.

US/0740-2104
**BAPTIST MESSAGE.** Periodical. English. wk. $10.25. Louisiana Baptist Convention, PO Box 311, Alexandria LA 71301. **Tel** (318)442-7728. **ED** Lynn P Clayton. **UDC** 286.1. **Circ:** 65,000. ***Continues** Baptist Chronicle.*
**Desc:** Primarily about Louisiana Baptists and Southern Baptists.

US/0744-9518
**BAPTIST MESSENGER (OKLAHOMA CITY, OKLA.).** (BAPTIST MESSENGER.). **Added/Corp** Baptist General Convention of the State of Oklahoma. (1912)-. Periodical. English. Fifty times a year. $6.00 (one year). Baptist General Convention of Oklahoma, 3800 North May Avenue, Oklahoma City OK 73112. **Tel** (405)942-3800, FAX (405) 947-7170. **ED** Glenn A Brown. **Ad Acc. Circ:** 115,000 (ctrl).
**Desc:** Information of interest to or about Oklahoma Southern Baptists.

US/0735-5815
**BAPTIST PEACEMAKER.** [Baptist peacemak.]. **Added/Corp** Deer Park Baptist Church (Louisville, Ky.) Baptist Peace Fellowship of North America. **VFOAT** Baptist Peace Maker. Vol. 1, No. 1 (Dec. 1980)-. Periodical. English. Four times a year (Jan., Apr., July, Oct.). $20.00 (individuals), $25.00 (institutions) Comes with Baptist Peace Fellowship membership. Baptist Peace Fellowship, 499 Patterson Street, Memphis TN 38111. **Tel** (901)324-7675. **ED** Glen Hinson and Carman Sharp. **DD** 261. **Bk Rev. Circ:** 20,000.
**Desc:** Articles on peacemaking, biblical studies, reviews and editorials issues.

US
**BAPTIST PRESS.** Periodical. English. da (Monday-Friday). $150.00. Southern Baptist Convention, 901 Commerce, Suite 750, Nashville TN 37203. **Tel** (615)244-2355, FAX (615)742-8919. **(Subscription address:** Sunday School Board - Customer Service, 127 Ninth Avenue North, Nashville, TN 37234 USA; telephone: (800)458-2772) **ED** Herb Hollinger. **Circ:** 550. available on an online database from Compuserve.
**Desc:** This is the news service for the Southern Baptist Convention.

US/0005-5743
**BAPTIST PROGRAM, THE. Added/Corp** Southern Baptist Convention. Executive Committee. (1927)-. Periodical. English. Twelve times a year. Southern Baptist Convention, 901 Commerce, Suite 750, Nashville TN 37203. **Tel** (615)244-2355, FAX (615)742-8919. **LC** BX6207; .A4075. **DD** 286/.132/05.
**Ind/Abst** South. Baptist Period. Index.

US/0005-5751
**BAPTIST PROGRESS. Added/Corp** Baptist Missionary Association of Texas. (1912)-. Periodical. English. wk. $15.00. Baptist Progress / Texas, PO Box 2085, Waxahachie TX 75165. **Tel** (214)923-0756. **ED** Danny W. Pope. **Bk Rev. Ad Acc. Circ:** 15,500 (ctrl).
**Desc:** Promotes interest in missions, evangelism, benevolence and Christian education among the churches of the Baptist Missionary Association of Texas.

US/0164-7423
**BAPTIST PROGRESS (BROOKLYN).** (BAPTIST PROGRESS.). Periodical. English. bm. $2.00. Baptist Progress / New York, 712-714 Quincy Street, Brooklyn NY 11221. **UDC** 286.1.

UK/0005-576X
**BAPTIST QUARTERLY (LONDON).** (THE BAPTIST QUARTERLY.). [Baptist q]. **Added/Corp** Baptist Historical Society. New Series, Vol. 1 (Jan. 1922)-. Periodical. English. Four times a year (Jan., Apr., July, Oct.). £20.00. Baptist Historical Society, 28 Dowthorpe Hill, Northhampton NN6 0PB England. **Tel** 011 44 604 811170. **ED** J. H. Y. Briggs. **LC** BX6276.A1; B32. Index available. cum. index. **Bk Rev. Ad Acc. Circ:** 650 (ctrl). available on microfilm and microfiche from University Microfilms International (UMI). ***Supersedes** Baptist Historical Society. Transactions of the Baptist Historical Society.*
**Desc:** Seeks to advance awareness of Baptist history and principles.
**Ind/Abst** Am. Hist. Life (1955-); Br. Humanit. Index; Index Book Rev. Relig.; Relig. Index One Period. (1949-); Relig. Theol. Abstr.

US/0005-5778
**BAPTIST RECORD (JACKSON, MISS.), THE.** (THE BAPTIST RECORD.). **Added/Corp** Mississippi Baptist Convention. (1877)-. Periodical. English. wk (Weekly except Independence Day and Christmas). $7.35. Mississippi Baptist Convention, Box 530, Jackson MS 39205. **Tel** (601)968-3800. **ED** Guy Henderson. **Bk Rev**, (Qty: 50). **Ad Acc, Adv Mgr:** Teresa Dickens. **Circ:** 110,000. ***Continues** Baptist (Jackson, Miss.).*
**Desc:** Provides information to readers about the denomination, both state and national, and provides inspiration and challenge through articles on missions involvement and issues related to everyday life.

US
**BAPTIST STANDARD.** (1898)-. Periodical. English. Fifty-one times per year (weekly except the last week of the year.). $10.05. Baptist Standard Publishing Company, Box 660267, Dallas TX 75266-0267. **Tel** (214)630-4571, FAX (214)638-8535. **ED** Presnall H. Wood. Index available. **Bk Rev. Ad Acc, Adv Mgr:** Doug Hylton. **Circ:** 217,148.
**Desc:** Baptist news in the state of Texas and the activities of the Southern Baptist Convention.

UK/0005-5786
**BAPTIST TIMES.** No. 4583, (Sept. 1925)-. Periodical. English. wk. £41.60 Europe; £39.00 other. Baptist Times Ltd, Baptist Church House, 129 Broadway Didcot, Oxon OX11 8RT England. **Tel** 011 44 235 512077. **ED** G Locks. **Bk Rev. Ad Acc.** ctrl circ. ***Continues** Baptist Times and Freeman.*
**Desc:** Baptist and other news for British readers.

US/0883-7864
**BAPTIST TRUE UNION. Added/Corp** Baptist Convention of Maryland/Delaware. **VFOAT** True Union. Vol. 68, No. 14 (Apr. 4, 1985)-. Periodical. English. Forty-eight times a year. $7.50. Baptist True Union, 10255 Old Columbia Road, Columbia MD 21046-1716. **Tel** (410)290-5290, FAX (410)290-7040. **ED** Ron Chaney. **Bk Rev. Ad Acc. Circ:** 10,000. ***Continues** Maryland Baptist, 0025-4169.*
**Desc:** We are the official news journal for Southern Baptists in Maryland and Delaware. News is about our convention and related Christian topics.

US/0888-9074
**BAPTIST TRUMPET (LITTLE ROCK, ARK.).** (BAPTIST TRUMPET.). [Baptist trumpet]. **Added/Corp** Baptist Missionary Association of Arkansas. (Feb. 13, 1952)-. Newspaper. English. Forty-six times a year. $12.50. Baptist Trumpet, Box 192208, Little Rock AR 72219-2208. **Tel** (501)565-4601. **ED** David Tidwell. **Bk Rev. Ad Acc. Circ:** 13,110 (ctrl). ***Continues** Temple Trumpet.*
**Desc:** Devotional materials and news of Baptist Missionary Association of America and general religious news.

UK/0302-3184
**BAPTIST UNION DIRECTORY, THE.** [Baptist Union dir.]. **Added/Corp** Baptist Union of Great Britain and Ireland. Council. (19??)-. Directory. English. an. £5.50. Baptist Church House, 4 Southampton Row, London WC1B 4AB England. **LC** BX6276.A1; B43. **DD** 286/.1/06242. **Ad Acc.**

US/0005-5808
**BAPTIST WORLD (WASHINGTON, D.C.).** (BAPTIST WORLD.). [Baptist world]. V. 1- 1954-. Periodical. English. qt. $6.00, $15.00 (three year). Baptist World Alliance, 6733 Curran Street, McLean VA 22101. **Tel** (703)790-8980, FAX (703)893-5160. **ED** Wendy Ryan. **DD** 286. **UDC** 286.1. **Bk Rev. Ad Acc. Circ:** 10,000 (ctrl). available on microfilm and microfiche from University Microfilms International (UMI). ***Absorbed** BWA Youth News.*
**Desc:** Provides news of baptists in over 140 countries of the world.

SZ
**BARTH KARL GESAMTAUSGABE.** German. ir. 69.00F. Theologischer Verlag Zuerich, Raeffelstrasse 20, CH8045 Zuerich Switzerland. **Tel** 011 41 1 4617710.

CN/0849-3103
**BCOQ DIRECTORY.** [BCOQ dir.]. **Main/Corp** Baptist Convention of Ontario and Quebec. **VAT** Baptist Convention of Ontario and Quebec Directory. (1991)-. Directory. English. Baptist Convention of Ontario and Quebec, 217 St George Street, Toronto Ontario M5R 2M2 Canada. **Tel** (416)922-5163. **DD** 286/.1713. ***Continues** Directory., 0848-9149.*

BE
**BELGISCHE PROTESTANTSE.** (19??)-. Dutch (French, German and English). qt. 425.00F. University Faculty Protestantse Godgel, Bollandistenstraat 40, B-1040 Brussels Belgium. **Tel** 011 32 2 7356746. Index available. cum. index. **Ad Acc.** ctrl circ.

CN/0227-5554
**BEREAN AMBASSADOR, THE.** [Berean ambassador]. No. 1-. Periodical. English. mo. Free. Reverend J R Boyd, PO Box 232, Sudbury Ontario P3E 4N5 Canada. **DD** 286/.05. **UDC** 286.1. ctrl circ.

GW
**BERICHT UBER DIE VERHANDLUNGEN DER ORDENTLICHEN SYNODE DE NORDELBISCHEN EV.-LUTH. KIRCHE.** **Main/Corp** Nordelbische Evangelisch-Lutherische Kirche. Synod. (19??)-. German. Nordelisch-Lutherische Kirche, Danische Strasse 21/35, 2300 Kiel 1 Germany. **Tel** (0431)991250. **LC** BX8022.N67; N66a.
**Desc:** Includes vote count, question and answer periods. Appendices show church law extracts, invitees, seating charts, and speakers.

UK/0965-531X
**BIBLE PUZZLER.** (1987)-. Periodical. English. qt. £7.50 UK; £9.00 Europe; £10.50 (air mail) other. Herald House Publishing, 96 Dominion Road, Worthing West Sussex, BN14 8JP England. **Tel** 011 44 903 821082, FAX 011 44 903 821081. **ED** Heather Thompson. **Ad Acc, Adv Mgr:** Paul Slide. **Circ:** 3,500. ***Continues***

*Christian Puzzler, 0958-3858.*
**Desc:** Bible-based puzzles and word games for the family.

US/0006-0909
**BIBLICAL MISSIONS.** ***Suspended.*** **Added/Corp** Independent Board for Presbyterian Foreign Missions, Philadelphia. (1935)-Vol. 57 No. 1 (1991). Periodical. English. bm. $6.00. Independent Board for Presbyterian Foreign Missions, 246 Walnut Lane, Philadelphia PA 19144. **Tel** (215)438-0511. **ED** Earle R. White. **Circ:** 2,500 (ctrl).
**Desc:** Presentation of foreign missions and work of Independent Board for Presbyterian Foreign Missions.

US/0279-8182
**BIBLICAL RECORDER.** [Biblic. rec.]. **Added/Corp** Baptist State Convention of North Carolina. (1833)-. Periodical. English. wk. $8.48 (North Carolina residents add 6% sales tax) Also available on cassette tape for vision impaired. Biblical Recorder, Box 26568, Raleigh NC 27611. **Tel** (919)847-2128, (919)847-2127. **ED** R G Puckett. **Ad Acc.**
**Desc:** Religious publication of the Baptist State Convention of North Carolina.

US/0279-9111
**BOND (MINNEAPOLIS, MINN.).** (BOND / LUTHERAN BROTHERHOOD.). [Bond]. **Added/Corp** Lutheran Brotherhood. **VFOAT** Lutheran Brotherhood Bond. (19??)-. Periodical. English. qt. Lutheran Brotherhood, 625 4th Avenue South, Minneapolis MN 55415. **LC** BX8001; .B6. **DD** 284.1/05. ***Continues*** *Lutheran Brotherhood Bond.*

CN/0701-0648
**BONNE NOUVELLE DE L'ALLIANCE.** First issue in 1974. Periodical. French. ir. Free. Bonne Nouvelle de l'Alliance, 7505 Boulevard Parent, Trois-Rivieres Quebec G9A 5E1 Canada. **DD** 234/.1/05. **UDC** 234.1.

RU/0203-5839
**BRATSKII VESTNIK.** **Added/Corp** Vsesoiuznyi Sovet Evangelskikh Khristian-Baptistov (Soviet Union). (194?)-. Periodical. Russian. bm. $40.00. Union Evangelical Christians, Baptists of the USSR, PO Box 520, Moscow 101000 Russia. **Tel** 011 7 095 2979626. **LC** BX6310.R9; B7.

US/1071-4200
**BRETHREN IN CHRIST HISTORY AND LIFE.** [Brethr. Christ hist. life]. **Added/Corp** Brethren in Christ Historical Society. **VFOAT** History and Life. Vol. 1, No. 1 (June 1978)-. Periodical. English. Three times a year (Apr., Aug., Dec.). $10.00. Brethren in Christ Historical Society, Messiah College, Grantham PA 17027. **Tel** (717)691-6048 Ext. 6048, FAX (717)691-6042. **ED** E. Morris Sider. **LC** BX9675.A1; B74. **DD** 289.9. Index available (Free). cum. index. **Bk Rev**, (Qty: 12-20). **Pr Rev. Circ:** 600.
**Desc:** Articles, reviews, and news on the history and current life of the Brethren in Christ Church.
**Ind/Abst** Index Book Rev. Relig.; Relig. Index One Period.

US/0197-3045
**BRIDE OF CHRIST, THE.** (THE BRIDE OF CHRIST / LUTHERAN LITURGICAL RENEWAL.). [Bride Christ]. **Added/Corp** Lutheran Liturgical Renewal (Society) Trinity Evangelical Lutheran Church (Henderson, Ky.). (197?)-. Periodical. English. qt. $11.50 (regular delivery), $15.00 (first class). Lutheran Liturgical Renewal, Box 21201, Lehigh Valley PA 18002-1201. **Tel** (610)868-5229. **ED** Aubrey Bougher. **LC** BX8067.A1; B69. **DD** 264/.041. Index available (Dec.). **Bk Rev**, (Qty: 6-8). **Ad Acc**, **Adv Mgr:** Charles Shoemaker. **Circ:** 1,000.
**Desc:** Covers liturgy, liturgiology, theology-primarily, but not exclusively Lutheran.

FR/0037-9050
**BULLETIN DE LA SOCIETE DE L'HISTOIRE DU PROTESTANTISME FRANCAIS (1981).** (BULLETIN DE LA SOCIETE DE L'HISTOIRE DU PROTESTANTISME FRANCAIS.). [Bull. Soc. hist. protestant. fr.]. **Added/Corp** Societe de l'Histoire du Protestantisme Francais (France). **VFOAT** Bulletin Historique et Litteraire de la Societe de l'Histoire du Protestantisme Francais. Vol.127 (Jan/Mar 1981)-. Bulletin. French. qt (4 issues). 220.00F France; 300.00F other. Societe de L'Histoire du Protestantisme Francais, 54 rue de Saints-Peres, 75007 Paris France. **Tel** 011 33 1 45486207. **ED** Andre Encreve. Index available. cum. index. **Bk Rev. Pr Rev.** ctrl circ. ***Continues*** *Bulletin (Societe de l'Histoire du Protestantisme Francais (France)).*
**Ind/Abst** Am. Hist. Life (1963-); BHA : Biblio. Hist. Art; Index Book Rev. Relig.; Relig. Index One Period.; Romant. Move.

SZ
**BULLETIN DU CENTRE PROTESTANT D'ETUDES.** **Main/Corp** Centre Protestant d'Etudes. No. 1- Oct. 1948-. Bulletin. French. ir. 30.00F Switzerland; $20.00 US. Centre Protestant d'Etudes, 7 rue Tabazan, 1204 Geneva Switzerland. **Tel** 29 70 07. **ED** Isabelle Graessle, Marc Faesser, and Bernard Rordorf. **UDC** 284. Index available. cum. index. **Ad Acc.** ctrl circ.
**Desc:** Created with the intention of making theological and ethical research (made in the CPE).
**Ind/Abst** New Testam. Abstr.; Old Testam. Abstr.

US/0362-0581
**BULLETIN - LUTHERAN THEOLOGICAL SEMINARY, GETTYSBURG.** **Main/Corp** Lutheran Theological Seminary, Gettysburg, Pa. **Added/Corp** Lutheran Theological Seminary, Gettysburg, Pa. Gettysburg Seminary Bulletin. **VFOAT** Gettysburg Seminary Bulletin. Vol. 20 (Nov. 1941)-. Bulletin. English. Four times a year. Free on request. Lutheran Theological Seminary / Gettysburg, PA, Bulletin 61, NW Confederate Avenue, Gettysburg PA 17325. **Tel** (717)334-6286. **ED** Richard D. Nelson. **Circ:** 3,000. available on microfilm from University Microfilms International (UMI). ***Continues*** *Gettysburg Seminary Bulletin, 0016-9366.*
**Desc:** An organ of the seminary for the dissemination of material of interest and value primarily of interest to alumni, students, and friends, but also to a broader readership including pastors and theologians.
**Ind/Abst** Index Book Rev. Relig.; Relig. Index One Period.; Relig. Theol. Abstr.

BE
**BULLETIN - SOCIETE D'HISTOIRE DU PROTESTANTISME BELGE.** **Main/Corp** Societe d'Histoire du Protestantisme Belge. Ser. 6, Issue 4- Jan./Mar. 1975-. Bulletin. French. ir. $9.88. Rue Leys 52, 1040 Bruxelles Belgium. **UDC** 284(09)(493). ***Continues*** *Societe d'Histoire du Protestantisme Belge. Annales.*

UK/0045-3536
**BULWARK, THE.** **Added/Corp** Scottish Reformation Society. (19??)-. Periodical. English. bm. £2.00 UK; $4.00 US. Scottish Reformation Society, The Magdalenchapel, 41 Cowgate, Edinburgh EH1 1EE Scotland. **Tel** 44 31 2201450. **ED** A Sinclair Horne. **LC** BX4800; .B8. **Bk Rev. Circ:** 5,000 (ctrl). ***Continues*** *Bulwark, or, Reformation Journal in Defence of the True Interests of Man and of Society, especially in Reference to the Religious, Social and Political Bearings of Popery.*
**Desc:** Traditional, biblical Protestant witness emphasizing reformed theology and history of reformation.

US/0007-6309
**BURNING BUSH.** English. bm. $3.00 US; $3.50 other. Metropolitan Church Association, 323 Broad Street, Lake Geneva WI 53147. **Tel** (414)248-6786. **(Subscription address:** Metropolitan Church Association, PO Box 156, Dundee IL 60118.) **ED** Eva L. Adams.

US/0892-6646
**CALIFORNIA-NEVADA UNITED METHODIST REPORTER, THE.** ***Title Change.*** [Calif.-Nev. United Methodist report.]. **Added/Corp** United Methodist Church (U.S.). California-Nevada Conference. **VFOAT** California Nevada United Methodist Reporter; United Methodist Reporter. (19??)-(19??). Periodical. English. bw (26 issues per year). California-Nevada Conference United Methodist Church, PO Box 420 467, San Francisco CA 94142. **Tel** (415)474-3101, FAX (415)775-9705. **ED** Charles Lerrigo. **DD** 287. ***Continued by*** *California Nevada United Methodist Review.*

US
**CALIFORNIA NEVADA UNITED METHODIST REVIEW.** (19??)-. English. bw (26 issues). $12.00 all. California-Nevada Conference United Methodist Church, PO Box 420 467, San Francisco CA 94142. **Tel** (415)474-3101, FAX (415)775-9705. ***Continues*** *California Nevada United Methodist Reporter, 0892-6646.*

US/0008-1558
**CALIFORNIA SOUTHERN BAPTIST, THE.** [Calif. South. Baptist]. **Added/Corp** California Southern Baptist Convention. (1941)-. Periodical. English. bw. $9.50. The Southern Baptist, 678 East Shaw Avenue, Fresno CA 93710. **Tel** (209)229-9533. **ED** Mark A. Wyatt (phone: ext. 226). **DD** 286. **Bk Rev. Ad Acc. Circ:** 13,000.
**Desc:** News for and about Southern Baptist churches and state, national and international news affecting them. Includes promotion of denominational work locally, nationally and internationally.

US/8756-0429
**CALVARY BAPTIST THEOLOGICAL JOURNAL.** **Added/Corp** Calvary Baptist Theological Seminary (Lansdale, Pa.). Vol. 1, No. 1 (Spring 1985)-. Periodical. English. sa (May & Oct.). $12.00 (1 year), $20.00 (2 year) US; $14.00 (1 year), $24.00 (2 year) other. Calvary Baptist Theological Seminary, 1380 Valley Forge Road, Lansdale PA 19446. **Tel** (215)368-7538, FAX (215)368-1003. **ED** Clint Banz. **DD** 286. cum. index. **Bk Rev. Circ:** 300.
**Desc:** A research and writing ministry of Calvary Baptist Theological Seminary designed to provide practical and academic articles to pastors and students.
**Ind/Abst** Guide Soc. Sci. Relig.; Relig. Theol. Abstr. (199?-).

CN/0410-3882
**CALVINIST CONTACT.** ***Title Change.*** [Calvin. contact]. **Added/Corp** Christian Reformed Immigration Societies in Canada. No. 26 (Oct. 16, 1951)-(1992). Periodical. English (English and Dutch). wk. Calvinist Contact Publishing Ltd, 261 Martindale Road, St Catharines Ontario, L2W 1A1 Canada. **Tel** (416)682-8311, FAX (416)682-8313. **ED** Bert Witvoet, Stan de Jong. **Bk Rev. Ad Acc. Circ:** 7,000 (ctrl). ***Continues*** *Contact, 0382-5949.* ***Continued by*** *Christian Courier, 1192-3415.*
**Desc:** News, idea and contact paper distributed weekly to the reformed community in Canada and USA.

CN/0832-0179
**CANADA LUTHERAN (NATIONAL ED.).** (CANADA LUTHERAN.). [Can. Lutheran]. **Added/Corp** Evangelical Lutheran Church in Canada. Vol. 1 No. 1 (Jan. 1986)-. Periodical. English. Eleven times a year (Except July). $17.00 one year; $31.00 two year; $44.50 three year. Evangelical Lutheran Church in Canada, 1512 Saint James Street, Winnipeg MB R3H 0I2 Canada. **Tel** (204)786-6707. **ED** Kenn Ward, (phone: (204)786-6707). **DD** 284.1/71/05. **Bk Rev**, (Qty: 8-15). **Ad Acc**, **Adv Mgr:** Liz Olson. **Circ:** 26,000. ***Formed by the union of*** *Shepherd, 0383-8544; Western Canada Lutheran, 0382-0793; Central Canada Lutheran, 0708-7969; Canada Lutheran, 0008-2716.*
**Desc:** Providing information inspiration and intepretation for members of the Evangelical Lutheran church in Canada.

CN/0702-5084
**CANADIAN ADVENTIST MESSENGER.** **Added/Corp** Seventh-day Adventist Church in Canada. Vol. 46, No. 13 (July 7, 1977)-. Periodical. English. sm. $2.00. Seventh-Day Adventist Church in Canada, Canadian Adventist Messenger, 1148 King Street East, Oshawa Ontario L1H 1H4 Canada. **Tel** (416)433-0011. **ED** G E Maxson. **DD** 286/.771. **Ad Acc. Circ:** 13,400 (ctrl). ***Continues*** *Canadian Union Messenger, 0383-252X.*
**Desc:** Church journal aimed at sharing with our members what is happening in our denomination across Canada and questions that might affect them or the church.
**Ind/Abst** Seventh-Day Adventist Period. Index (1971-).

US/0528-0559
**CAPITAL BAPTIST.** (1954)-. Periodical. English. Sixteen times a year (monthly). $5.00 (one year); $9.00 (two years); $12.00 (three years). District of Columbia Baptist, 1628 16th Street Nothwest, Washington DC 20009. **Tel** (202)265-1526, FAX (202)667-8258. **ED** Victor Tupitza. **Bk Rev. Ad Acc. Circ:** 9,000.
**Desc:** News of American Baptist Churches USA, Southern Baptist Convention, District of Columbia Baptist Convention and religion in general. Articles on theology and inspiration are included.

US/0732-9245
**CAREE COMMUNICATOR.** (CAREE COMMUNICATOR / CHRISTIANS ASSOCIATED FOR RELATIONSHIPS WITH EASTERN EUROPE.). [Caree commun.]. **Added/Corp** Christians Associated for Relationships with Eastern Europe (U.S.). **VAT** Christians Associated for Relationships with Eastern Europe Communicator. (19??)-. English. ir. Free with membership. CAREE Communicator, c/o Dr William Luther White, Illinois Wesleyan University, Bloomington IL 61701. **Tel** (309)556-3005. **ED** William L. White. **Circ:** 300. ***Continues*** *CAREE Newsletter.*
**Desc:** Occasional publication (three or four annually) of "Christians Associated for Relations with Eastern Europe," a special interest group connected with the National Council of Churches.

US/0887-1094
**CELEBRATION (HAGERSTOWN, MD.).** (CELEBRATION.). **Added/Corp** General Conference of Seventh-Day Adventists. North American Division. Church Ministries Dept. (198?)-. Periodical. English. Twelve times a year. $22.97. Review and Herald Publishing Association, 55 West Oak Ridge Drive, Hagerstown MD 21740. **Tel** (301)791-7000 ext. 2534, FAX (301)790-9734. **DD** 286.

US/8750-4308
**CENTINELA (NAMPA, IDAHO), EL.** (EL CENTINELA.). [Centinela]. **Added/Corp** General Conference of Seventh-Day Adventists. (19??)-. Periodical. Spanish. Twelve times a year. $9.99. Pacific Press Publishing Association, PO Box 7000, Boise ID 83707. **Tel** (208)465-2500, FAX (208)465-2531. **ED** Tulio N. Peverini. **DD** 286. Index available (bound in Dec issue). **Acid Free. Circ:** 100,000 (ctrl).
**Desc:** A missionary magazine of the Seventh-Day Adventist Church for the Spanish-speaking population of the North American and Inter-American divisions of the world-wide church. Each issue contains an editorial and articles on current issues, religion and doctrines, the family, health and psychology, true stories, question and answer columns and other religion/health columns on a regular basis.

US
**CHALLENGE (MEMPHIS).** (CHALLLENGE.). English. Baptist Brotherhood Commission, 1548 Popular Avenue, Memphis TN 38104. **Tel** (901)272-2461.
**Ind/Abst** South. Baptist Period. Index (1990-).

US/0745-2918
**CHALLENGE OF CONSERVATIVE BAPTIST HOME MISSIONS, THE.** ***Title Change.*** [Chall. Conserv. Baptist home missions]. **Added/Corp** Conservative Baptist Home Mission Society. **VFOAT** Challenge. (19??)-(1992). Periodical. English. qt. Conservative Baptist Home Mission Society, 25W560 Geneva Road, Wheaton IL 60187. **Tel** (312)653-4900. **ED** Jack Estep. **DD** 266. **Circ:** 95,000 (ctrl). ***Continued by** Challenge of CBHMS, 1065-1845.*
**Desc:** Provides information about Conservative Baptist missionary activity in North and Central America.

CN/0821-7688
**CHAN LY.** (CHAN LY : NGUYET-SAN CUA HOI-THANH TIN-LANH VIET-NAM.). [Chan ly]. **VAT** Chanly. V. 1 (April, 1976)-. Periodical. Vietnamese. mo. Chanly, c/o Vietnamese Alliance Church, 11 West 10th Avenue, Vancouver British Columbia V5Y 1R5 Canada. **DD** 248/.4/89905.

US/0009-1723
**CHARITY AND CHILDREN. See** Sociology-Social Services and Welfare.

HK
**CHINA PRAYER LETTER.** (19??)-. English (Chinese). mo. Free on request. Chinese Church Research Center, PO Box 312, Shatin NT Hong Kong. **Tel** 011 852 0 6044456. **ED** Thomas Lawrence and Brent Fulton. **Bk Rev. Circ:** 7,000. ***Continues** China and Church Today.*
**Desc:** A monthly newsletter featuring current information on the state of Protestant Christianity in China.

US/0890-6793
**CHRISTIAN CHALLENGE, THE.** [Christ. chall.]. **Added/Corp** Foundation for Christian Theology (U.S.). (January 1962)-. Periodical. English. Nine times a year. $20.00 (one year), $37.00 (two year), $55.00 (three year) US; $25.00 Canada; $30.00 other. The Foundation for Christian Theology, Christian Challenge, 1215 Independence Avenue SE, Washington DC 20003. **Tel** (202)547-5409, FAX (202)543-8704. **ED** Auburn Faber Traycik. **LC** BX5800; .C195. **DD** 283/.05. **Ad Acc. Circ:** 5,000. available on microfilm.

●CN/1192-3415
**CHRISTIAN COURIER.** [Christ. cour.]. (1992)-. Periodical. English. Forty-seven times a year. 32.00Can$ (one year), 60.00Can$ (two years), 90.00Can$ (three years). Calvinist Contact Publishing Ltd, 261 Martindale Road, St Catharines Ontario, L2W 1A1 Canada. **Tel** (416)682-8311, FAX (416)682-8313. **ED** Bent Witvoet. **DD** 284/.271/05. **Bk Rev**, (Qty: 40). **Ad Acc, Adv Mgr:** Stan De Jong. ctrl circ. ***Continues** Calvinist Contact, 0410-3882.*
**Desc:** An independent weekly that seeks that truth, care and rule of Jesus Christ as it; reports on significant happenings in the Christian community and the world; espresses opinions expresses are infused by Scripture and Spirit and rooted in a reformed perspective; provides opportunities for contact and discussion for the Christian community

●US/1072-1436
**CHRISTIAN EDUCATION COUNSELOR.** **Added/Corp** Assemblies of God. General Council. (1994)-. Periodical. English. mo. $12.00 (leader edition). Gospel Publishing House, 1445 Boonville Avenue, Springfield MO 65802. **Tel** (417)862-2781, FAX (417)866-1146. ***Continues** Sunday School Counselor, 0039-5285.*

UK/0953-4385
**CHRISTIAN HERALD WORTHING.** (CHRISTIAN HERALD.). [Christ. her.Worthing]. (1985)-. Newspaper. English. wk. £46.00. Herald House Publishing, 96 Dominion Road, Worthing West Sussex, BN14 8JP England. **Tel** 011 44 903 821082, FAX 011 44 903 821081. **ED** Bruce Hardy. **Bk Rev**, (Qty: 350). **Ad Acc, Adv Mgr:** Ann Terry. **Circ:** 22,000. ***Continues** Christian Herald and Signs of our Times.*
**Desc:** Interdenominational evangelical newspaper including news, devotional, and family articles.

US/0362-0832
**CHRISTIAN INDEX, THE. Added/Corp** Georgia Baptist Convention. Vol. 1 (July 4, 1829)-. Periodical. English. ir. $9.00 (one year), $16.00 (two year), $22.00 (three year). GA Baptist Convention Publishing, 2930 Flowers Road South, Atlanta GA 30341. **Tel** (404)455-0404, FAX (404) 936-5160. **ED** Dr. R. Albert Mohler. **LC** BX6201; .C46. **Bk Rev. Circ:** 100,000 (ctrl). ***Supersedes** Columbian Star.*
**Desc:** Georgia Southern Baptist state paper, with news about Baptist churches and the Georgia Baptist Convention. Includes news of the Southern Baptist Convention.

US/0744-4060
**CHRISTIAN INDEX (MEMPHIS, TENN.), THE.** (THE CHRISTIAN INDEX : OFFICIAL PUBLICATION, CHRISTIAN METHODIST EPISCOPAL CHURCH.). [Christ. index]. **Added/Corp** Christian Methodist Episcopal Church. (1???)-. Periodical. English. sm. $15.00 (one year), $28.00 (two years), $40.00 (three years). CME Church, 4466 Elvis Presley Boulevard, PO Box 191, Memphis TN 38116. **Tel** (901)345-1173. **ED** Lawrence L Reddick III, PO Box 665, Memphis, TN 38101. **DD** 287. **Circ:** 6,000 (ctrl).
**Desc:** Denominational news items and relevant issues facing members of the Christian Methodist Episcopal church, a predominantly black denomination founded in 1870.

US/0009-5419
**CHRISTIAN LEADER (HILLSBORO).** (CHRISTIAN LEADER.). **Added/Corp** United States Conference of Mennonite Brethren Churches. (19??)-. Periodical. English. Twenty-two times a year. $19.00. US Conference of Mennonite Brethren Churches Board Publishers, Box L, Hillsboro KS 67063. **Tel** (316)947-5543. **ED** Wally Kroeker. **Bk Rev. Ad Acc. Circ:** 9,500 (ctrl).
**Desc:** Devoted to the interests of the Mennonite Brethren Conference and the cause of Christ in general.

US/0146-9924
**CIRCUIT RIDER (NASHVILLE), THE.** (THE CIRCUIT RIDER.). Vol. 1, No. 1 (Oct. 1976)-. Periodical. English. mo. $8.00 (1 year), $15.00 (2 year), $20.00 (3 year). United Methodist Publishing House, PO Box 801, 201 8th Avenue South, Nashville TN 37202. **Tel** (615)749-6732, (615)749-6615, FAX (615)749-6578, (615)749-6579. **ED** Keith I. Pohl. **LC** BX8382.2.A1; C57. **DD** 287/.673. Index available. cum. index. **Bk Rev. Circ:** 46,000 (ctrl).
**Desc:** A professional journal for the applied practice of Christian ministry for United Methodist clergy.
**Ind/Abst** Curr. Thoughts Trends.

CN/0823-2725
**CMBC ALUMNI BULLETIN. See** College and School Publications-Alumni.

CN/1184-0420
**CMC YEARBOOK.** [CMC yearb.]. **Main/Corp** Conference of Mennonites in Canada. **VAT** Conference of Mennonites in Canada Yearbook. (1989)-. English. an. 6.00Can$ Canada; 7.00Can$ other. Conference of Mennonites in Canada, 600 Shaftesbury Boulevard, Winnipeg Manitoba R3P 0M4 Canada. **Tel** (204)888-6781, FAX (204)831-5675. **ED** Margaret Franz. **DD** 289.7/71. **Circ:** 800. ***Continues** Yearbook - Conference of Mennonites in Canada., 0543-467X.*

BE/0530-7848
**COLLECTION ESSAIS SUR L'HISTOIRE DU PROTESTANTISME FRANCAIS.** V. 1- 1963-. Periodical. French. Belge rue Leys 52, 1040 Bruxelles Belgium. **UDC** 284.5(44).

US/0744-2939
**COLLEGIATE QUARTERLY.** [Coll. q.]. **VFOAT** Collegiate Quarterly. (19??)-. Periodical. English. Four times a year (Jan., Apr., July, Oct.). $12.50. Pacific Press Publishing Association, PO Box 7000, Boise ID 83707. **Tel** (208)465-2500, FAX (208)465-2531. **DD** 268.
**Ind/Abst** Seventh-Day Adventist Period. Index (1971-).

US/0883-6728
**COLORADO EPISCOPALIAN, THE.** **Added/Corp** Episcopal Church. Diocese of Colorado. (194?)-. Periodical. English. Ten times a year. Free on request. Diocese of Colorado, Box 18M Capitol Hill Station, Denver CO 80218. **Tel** (303)837-1173. **ED** Barbara Benedict. **Circ:** 16,200.

US/1049-9962
**COMMON LOT.** (THE COMMON LOT.). [Common lot]. **Added/Corp** United Church of Christ. Advisory Commission on Women. United Church of Christ. Task Force on Women in Church and Society. Coordinating Center for Women in Church and Society. No. 1 (Jan. 1974)-. Periodical. English. Four times a year. $18.00. United Church of Christ / Ohio, 700 Prospective Avenue, Cleveland OH 44115. **Tel** (216)736-2150. **DD** 305.

US/0010-5260
**CONCORDIA HISTORICAL INSTITUTE QUARTERLY.** [Concordia Hist. Inst., St. Louis]. **Main/Corp** Concordia Historical Institute. Vol. 1 (1928)-. Academic Scholarly Publication. English. qt. $20.00 US; $23.00 other. Concordia Historical Institute, Dept Arch & Hist, 801 De Mun Avenue, St Louis MO 63105. **Tel** (314)721-5934. **ED** Leroy E Vogel. **LC** BX8001; .C535. **DD** 284.105. Index available in last issue of volume--attached. cum. index. **Bk Rev**, (Qty: 10). **Ad Acc, Adv Mgr:** Aug. R. Suelflow. **Circ:** 2,000. available on microfilm and microfiche from University Microfilms International (UMI).
**Desc:** First to be devoted to the history of Lutheranism in America. Articles cover a broad range of subjects and interests. Scholarly and popular studies, personal reminiscences, book reviews, reports of research and historical activities.
**Ind/Abst** Am. Hist. Life (1962-); Genealogical Period. Annu. Index; Index Book Rev. Relig.; Recent. Publ. Artic.; Relig. Index One Period. (1975-); Relig. Theol. Abstr. (199?-); Writ. Am. Hist.

US/0361-8862
**CONGREGATION, THE.** V. 1- Jan./Feb. 1972-. Periodical. English. bm. Free. Lutheran Church in America, 2900 Queen Lane, Philadelphia PA 19129. **Tel** (215)849-5800.

US/0361-2376
**CONGREGATIONAL JOURNAL.** ***Ceased.*** **Added/Corp** Hollywood Congregational Center for Study and Service. Vol.1 Sept. (1975)-Vol. 19, No. 1/2 (Dec. 1993). Periodical. English. Twice a year. American Congregational Center, 298 Fairfax Avenue, Ventura CA 93003. **Tel** (805)644-3397.
**Ind/Abst** Index Book Rev. Relig.

US/0731-2717
**CONQUISTADORES. ALUMNOS.** (CONQUISTADORES.). Periodical. Spanish. qt. $2.50. Southern Baptist Convention, 901 Commerce, Suite 750, Nashville TN 37203. **Tel** (615)244-2355, FAX (615)742-8919. **(Subscription address:** Sunday School Board - Customer Service, 127 Ninth Avenue North, Nashville, TN 37234 USA; telephone: (800)458-2772**)** **UDC** 286.1(768).

US/0731-2725
**CONQUISTADORES. MAESTROS.** (CONQUISTADORES.). Spanish. qt. $4.50. Southern Baptist Convention, 901 Commerce, Suite 750, Nashville TN 37203. **Tel** (615)244-2355, FAX (615)742-8919. **(Subscription address:** Sunday School Board - Customer Service, 127 Ninth Avenue North, Nashville, TN 37234 USA; telephone: (800)458-2772**)** **UDC** 286.1(768).

US/0573-7796
**CONTACT - NATIONAL ASSOCIATION OF FREE WILL BAPTISTS.** (CONTACT : OFFICIAL PUBLICATION OF THE NATIONAL ASSOCIATION OF FREE WILL BAPTISTS.). **Added/Corp** National Association of Free Will Baptists (U.S.). (1953)-. Periodical. English. mo. $12.00. National Association of Free Will Baptists, 5233 Mt. View Road, Antioch TN 37013-2306. **Tel** (615)731-6812, FAX (615)731-0771. **(Subscription address:** National Association of Free Will Baptists, PO Box 5002, Antioch, TN 37011-5002**)** **ED** Jack Williams. Index available (December issue). **Bk Rev**, (Qty: 12). **Circ:** 5,000 (ctrl).
**Desc:** To provide news of interest and related articles for the Free Will Baptist denomination.

US/1046-3801
**CONTEMPORARY PRAISE.** [Contemp. praise]. **Added/Corp** Southern Baptist Convention. Sunday School Board. Vol. 1, No. 1 (Oct.-Nov.-Dec. 1990)-. Periodical. English. qt. $7.50. Materials Services Department, 127 9th Avenue North, Nashville TN 37234. **Tel** (615)251-2000. **DD** 783. ***Continues** Gospel Choir, 0362-0417.*

US/0011-0671
**COVENANT COMPANION. Added/Corp** Evangelical Covenant Church of America. Vol. 48 (1959)-. Periodical. English (Spanish). mo. $26.00. Covenant Companion, 3200 West Foster, Chicago IL 60625. **Tel** (312)784-3000, FAX (312)478-2622. **ED** James R Hawkinson. Index available. **Bk Rev. Ad Acc. Circ:** 24,500. available on audiocassette. ***Continues** Covenant Weekly.*
**Desc:** The official organ of the Evangelical Covenant Church. Seeks to stimulate, gather, and build up the church it serves, as well as put it in touch with the wider Christian world.

US/0163-8688
**CRADLE ROLL PROGRAM HELPS.** (197?)-. English. Four times a year. $16.36. Review and Herald Publishing Association, 55 West Oak Ridge Drive, Hagerstown MD 21740. **Tel** (301)791-7000 ext. 2534, FAX (301)790-9734. **Circ:** 3,400.
**Desc:** Sabbath school aids for the leader of the Cradle Roll Department.

CN/0845-4795
**CROSSTALK AND ANGLICAN JOURNAL EPISCOPAL.** [Crosstalk Angl. j. episcop.]. **VFOAT** Anglican Journal Episcopal. Vol. 12, No. 1 (Jan. 1989)-. Periodical. English (French). mo. 4.00Can$ Canada; 8.00Can$ US; 10.00Can$ other. Anglican Church of Canada Diocese of Ottawa, 71 Bronson Avenue, Ottawa Ontario K1R 6G6 Canada. **Tel** (416)924-9192, FAX (416)924-7904. **ED** Jerrold F Hames. **DD** 283/.713/84. **Bk Rev. Ad Acc. Circ:** 273,000 (ctrl). ***Continues** Canadian Churchman and Crosstalk for the Anglican Diocese of Ottawa, 0706-8069.*
**Desc:** Published for Anglicans across Canada. Contains reports of current news events and human interest features from across the country and overseas, recognizing the wide diversity and interest of its readers.

US/0011-2151
**CRUSADER (MEMPHIS).** (CRUSADER.). **Added/Corp** Southern Baptist Convention. Brotherhood Commission. Vol. 1, (Oct. 1970)-. Periodical. English. Twelve times a year. $10.20. Baptist Brotherhood Commission, 1548 Popular Avenue, Memphis TN 38104. **Tel** (901)272-2461. **ED** James D. Warren. Index available. **Pr Rev. Circ:** 80,000. available on microfilm.
**Desc:** Missions education for boys grades 4-6 in Southern Baptist Churches.
**Ind/Abst** South. Baptist Period. Index.

US/0011-2976
**CUMBERLAND PRESBYTERIAN, THE.** [Cumberl. Presbyt.]. (1874)-. Periodical. English. sm (22

no. a year). $10.00. Cumberland Presbyterian, 1978 Union, Memphis TN 38104. **Tel** (901)276-4572. **ED** J Richard Magrill Jr. **DD** 285. **UDC** 285.3. **Bk Rev.** **Ad Acc. Circ:** 7,400.

US/0160-0885
**CURRICULUM PLANS.** English. an. $6.00. Curriculum Resources Committee, United Methodist Church, 201-8th Avenue South, Nashville TN 37202. **Tel** (615)749-6439. **ED** Dal Joon Won. **LC** BX8225.A1; U54A. **DD** 268/.6. **UDC** 287. **Circ:** 400 (ctrl).
**Desc:** Contains approved unit descriptions for use in developing United Methodist study resources for Christian education settings.

US/0045-9771
**DEACON.** **Added/Corp** Southern Baptist Convention. Sunday School Board. (1970)-. Periodical. English. qt. $11.80 (one year), $23.00 (two years). Southern Baptist Convention, 901 Commerce, Suite 750, Nashville TN 37203. **Tel** (615)244-2355, FAX (615)742-8919. **(Subscription address:** Sunday School Board, Customer Service, 127 9th Avenue North, Nashville TN 37234.**)** Index available. cum. index (every three years).
**Ind/Abst** South. Baptist Period. Index.

US/0093-786X
**DESERET NEWS CHURCH ALMANAC.** 1974-. English. an. Newspaper Agency Corporation, 143 South Main Street, Salt Lake City UT 84110. **Tel** (801)237-2950, FAX (801)237-2121. **LC** BX8606; .D47. **DD** 289.3/3. **UDC** 289.3.

GW/0012-0294
**DEUTSCHE HUGENOTT, DER.** [Dtsch. Hugenott]. **Added/Corp** Deutscher Hugenotten-Verein. Vol. 1 (1929)-. Periodical. German. qt. DM50.00. Deutscher Hugenotten Verein EV, Hafenplatz 9A, D 34385 Bad Karlshafen Germany. **Tel** 011 49 5672 1433.
**Ind/Abst** Am. Hist. Life.

US/0160-6654
**DEVOTIONAL SPEECHES OF THE YEAR.** English. $4.95. Brigham Young University Press / Print Services, 205 VPB, Provo UT 84602. **LC** BX8639.A1; D48. **DD** 252/.09/33. **UDC** 252.

US
**DIALOGO TEOLOGICO.** Began in 1973. Periodical. Spanish. sa. Dialogo Teologico, Box 5671, El Paso TX 79955. **Tel** (615)251-2613. **LC** BX6201; .D52. **DD** 230/.6/105. **UDC** 23.

US/0012-2157
**DIALOGUE (LOS ANGELES).** (DIALOGUE.). [Dialogue]. Vol. 1, (Spring 1966)-. Periodical. English. qt. $30.00. Dialogue / Utah, PO Box 658, Salt Lake City UT 84110-0658. **Tel** (801)750-1154. **ED** F. Ross and Mary Kay Peterson. **LC** BX8601; .D5. **DD** 289.3/05. **UDC** 289.3. **Bk Rev**, (Qty: 22). **Circ:** 4,500. available on microfilm and microfiche from University Microfilms International (UMI).
**Desc:** An independent journal established to express Mormon culture and examine the relevance of religion to secular life.
**Ind/Abst** Am. Hist. Life (1966-); Index Book Rev. Relig.; Relig. Index One Period.

CN/0846-3301
**DIOCESAN POST.** [Dioc. post]. **Added/Corp** Anglican Church of Canada. Diocese of British Columbia. Vol. 26, No. 1 (Jan. 1991)-. Periodical. English. ir. Limited free distribution. Diocese of British Columbia, Anglican Church of Canada, 912 Vancouver Street, Victoria British Columbia V8V 3V7 Canada. **DD** 283. ***Continues*** *British Columbia Diocesan Post., 0007-0491.*

CN/0316-800X
**DIRECTORY: LUTHERAN CHURCHES IN CANADA.** **Added/Corp** Lutheran Council in Canada. Division of Information Services. Canadian Lutheran Council. **VFOAT** Lutheran Churches in Canada. (19??)-. Directory. English. an (Aug). 5.00Can$. Evangelical Lutheran Church in Canada, 1512 Saint James Street, Winnipeg MB R3H 0L2 Canada. **Tel** (204)786-6707. **LC** BX8063.C2; D56. **DD** 284/.1/02571.

CN/1182-1701
**DIRECTORY / MENNONITE CONFERENCE OF EASTERN CANADA.** [Dir. - Mennon. Conf. East. Can.]. **Main/Corp** Mennonite Conference of Eastern Canada. **VFOAT** Directory - Conference des Mennonites de l'Est du Canada. 1st Ed. (1989)-. Directory. English (French). an. $3.00. Mennonite Conference of Eastern Canada, 60 New Dundee Road, Kitchener Ontario N2G 3W5 Canada. **Tel** (519)748-2162, FAX (519)748-6684. **DD** 289.7/713/025. **Circ:** 300 (ctrl).
**Desc:** Directory of organizations, conferences and congregations.

US/0740-9915
**DIRECTORY OF SOUTHERN BAPTIST CHURCHES.** [Update dir. South. Baptist churches]. Directory. English. $19.95. Southern Baptist Convention, 901 Commerce, Suite 750, Nashville TN 37203. **Tel** (615)244-2355, FAX (615)742-8919. **(Subscription address:** Sunday School Board - Customer Service, 127 Ninth Avenue North, Nashville, TN 37234 USA; telephone: (800)458-2772**)** **LC** BX6462; .D57. **DD** 286/.132/02573. **UDC** 286.1(036)(73).

US/0091-9381
**DIRECTORY OF THE AMERICAN BAPTIST CHURCHES IN THE U.S.A.** **Main/Corp** American Baptist Churches in the U.S.A. **VAT** Directory of the American Baptist Churches in the United States of America. (1973)-. Directory. English. an. $6.50. American Baptist Center, PO Box 871, Valley Forge PA 19482. **Tel** (800)334-1427. **ED** Patricia Schlosser. **LC** BX6207; .A316. **DD** 286/.131/02573. **Circ:** 6,000 (ctrl).
**Desc:** Contains official lists, registry of churches and information on their professional staffs and statistics.

US/0503-2636
**DIRECTORY (UNITARIAN UNIVERSALIST ASSOCIATION : 1965).** (DIRECTORY, UNITARIAN UNIVERSALIST ASSOCIATION.). **Main/Corp** Unitarian Universalist Association. **VFOAT** Unitarian Universalist Association Directory. (1961/1962)-. English. an. $18.95. Unitarian Universalist Association, 25 Beacon Street, Boston MA 02108. **Tel** (617)742-2100. **ED** Mark W. Harris. **LC** BX9811; .U46a. **DD** 288/.32/025. Index available. **Ad Acc. Circ:** 2,000 (ctrl). available on microfilm. ***Formed by the union of*** *Unitarian Year Book ... and Annual Report* ***and*** *Universalist Directory and Handbook.*
**Desc:** A directory of all Unitarian Universalist churches, ministers, offices and related organizations.

US/0092-8372
**DISCIPLE (ST. LOUIS, MO.).** (THE DISCIPLE.). [Disciple]. Began with Jan. 6, 1974 issue. Periodical. English. mo. $1.50 single copy, $10.00 one year, $19.00 two years. Christian Board of Publication, Beaumont & Pine Boulevard, Box 179, St Louis MO 63166. **Tel** (314)231-8500. **ED** James L Merrell. **LC** BX7301; .D48. **DD** 286/.63. **UDC** 289.2. Index available. cum. index. **Bk Rev.** **Ad Acc. Circ:** 58,000. available on microfilm and microfiche from University Microfilms International (UMI). ***Formed by the union of*** *Christian* ***and*** *Word Call.*
**Desc:** Journal of the Christian Church (Disciples of Christ), a 1.1 million member mainline Protestant denomination in the U.S. and Canada, with contacts around the world.

US/0162-198X
**DISCOVERY (BIRMINGHAM, ALA.).** (DISCOVERY.). [Discovery]. **Added/Corp** Southern Baptist Convention. Woman's Missionary Union. (19??)-. Periodical. English. mo. $10.95. Woman's Missionary Union, PO Box 830010, Birmingham AL 35283. **Tel** (205)991-8100, (205)991-4933. **ED** Barbara Massey. **DD** 266. **Circ:** 209,000 (ctrl).
**Desc:** A magazine for members of Girls in Action, a Woman's Missionary Union organization for girls, ages 6 through 11, or in grades 1 through 6.
**Ind/Abst** Acad. Search (July 1993-); INFO-SOUTH Abstr.; Mag. Search; South. Baptist Period. Index.

CG
**DOCUMENTATION ET INFORMATION PROTESTANTES : DIP.** **Added/Corp** Eglise du Christ au Zaire. **VFOAT** DIP. (19??)-. Periodical. English. mo. $25.00. Eglise du Christ Au Zaire, BP 3094, Kinshasa Republic of Zaire.

CN/0827-2395
**DOMINION (TORONTO).** (THE DOMINION / MARANATHA CAMPUS MINISTRIES INTERNATIONAL.). [Dominion]. **Added/Corp** Maranatha Campus Ministries International. Vol. 1, No. 1 (Fall 1982)-. Periodical. English. Maranatha Christian Fellowship, Toronto Ontario MS5 2Y4 Canada. **DD** 289.9.

US/0163-8769
**EARLITEEN-JUNIOR PROGRAM HELPS.** (197?)-. Periodical. English. Four times a year. $16.36. Review and Herald Publishing Association, 55 West Oak Ridge Drive, Hagerstown MD 21740. **Tel** (301)791-7000 ext. 2534, FAX (301)790-9734. **Circ:** 6,400.
**Desc:** Sabbath school aids for the leaders of the Earliteen.

CN
**EASTERN JOURNAL OF PRACTICAL THEOLOGY.** (19??)-. English. Twice a year (April & October). Free on request. Eastern Pentecostal Bible College, 780 Argyle Street, Peterborough Ontario K9H 5T2 Canada. **Tel** (705)748-9111, FAX (715)748-3931. **ED** Ronald Kydd. **Bk Rev. Circ:** 1,000 (ctrl).
**Desc:** Exists to serve the constituency of the Eastern Pentecostal Bible College and the wider church world, by publishing material which will be of practical benefit to people engaged in active ministry.

US/0884-1136
**ENSIGN (SALT LAKE CITY, UTAH).** (ENSIGN : THE ENSIGN OF THE CHURCH OF JESUS CHRIST OF LATTER-DAY SAINTS.). [Ensign]. Periodical. English. mo. $9.00. Ensign, 50 East North Temple Street, Salt Lake City UT 84150. **LC** BX8601; .C5. **DD** 289.3/32/05. **UDC** 289.3. ***Continues*** *Ensign of the Church of Latter-Day Saints, 0013-8606.*

US/0071-1012
**EPISCOPAL CHURCH ANNUAL, THE.** **Added/Corp** Episcopal Church. (1953)-. English. an. $27.95. Morehouse Publishing Company, 5480 Linglestown Road, Box 1321, Harrisburg PA 17105. **Tel** 800-877-0012. **ED** E Allen Kelley. Index available. **Ad Acc. Circ:** 6,000. ***Continues*** *Living Church Annual.*
**Desc:** Full listing of Episcopal Church's parishes, clergy, organizations, officers, administrative staff and statistics.

US
**EPISCOPAL CLERICAL DIRECTORY.** 25th- Ed. Directory. English. be. Church Hymnal Corporation, 800 Second Avenue, New York NY 10017. **LC** BX5990; .E5. **UDC** 283:262(036). ***Continues*** *Episcopal Clergy Directory.*

US/1050-0057
**EPISCOPAL LIFE.** [Episcop. life]. **Added/Corp** Episcopal Church. Domestic and Foreign Missionary Society. Vol. 1, No. 1 (Apr. 1990)-. Periodical. English. Twelve times a year. $7.00 one year; $13.00 two years; $16.00 three years. Episcopalian Inc., 1201 Chestnut Street, Suite 1200, Philadelphia PA 19107. **Tel** (215)564-2010, FAX (215)564-6336. **ED** Jerrold Hames (phone: (800)344-7626). **DD** 283. cum. index. **Ad Acc, Adv Mgr:** D. Kelso, **Tel** (215)564-2010. **Circ:** 180,000 (ctrl). ***Continues*** *Episcopalian, 0013-9629.*
**Ind/Abst** Curr. Thoughts Trends.

US/0013-9610
**EPISCOPAL RECORDER.** **Added/Corp** Reformed Episcopal Church. (18??)-. Periodical. English. mo. $2.00. Episcopal Recorder, 4225 Chestnut Street, Philadelphia PA 12104. available on microfilm from University Microfilms International (UMI). ***Continues*** *Philadelphia Recorder.*
**Ind/Abst** Guide Soc. Sci. Relig.

US/0895-0830
**EPISCOPAL TEACHER.** (EPISCOPAL TEACHER : A PUBLICATION OF THE CENTER FOR THE MINISTRY OF TEACHING.). **Added/Corp** Center for the Ministry of Teaching (Alexandria, Va.). **VFOAT** CMT Episcopal Teacher. (198?)-. Periodical. English. Ten times a year (Monthly except July and December). $10.00. Episcopal Teacher, 3737 Seminary Road, Alexandria VA 22304. **Tel** (703)370-6600 Ext. 1750. **ED** Locke E. Bowman Jr. **DD** 283. **Circ:** 3,700.

US/0749-9574
**EPISCOPAL WOMEN'S HISTORY PROJECT, THE.** (THE EPOSCOPAL WOMEN'S HISTORY PROJECT : NEWSLETTER.). [Episcop. Women Hist. Proj.]. Vol. 1, No. 1 (Fall 1981)-. Newsletter. English. qt. $35.00. Episcopal Women's History Project, General Theological Seminary, 175 Ninth Avenue, New York NY 10011. **Tel** (212)243-5150. **ED** Sandra H Boyd. **DD** 283. **UDC** 283-055.2. Index available. **Bk Rev.**
**Desc:** Research and oral history notes, photos and primary source material documenting work of women in Episcopal Church, project news and plans.

BE
**EPTA BULLETIN.** (1981)-. Bulletin. English. Twice a year. $15.00. Elim Bible College, London Road, Malcom Hathaway, Nantwich CW5 6LW England. **Tel** 011 44 270 627043, FAX 011 44 270 610013. **ED** Jean-Daniel Pluss (editor's address: Heuelstrasse 45, 8032 Zurich Switzerland). Index available. **Bk Rev**, (Qty: 10-12). **Pr Rev. Circ:** 350.
**Desc:** Provides information on the Pentecostal Church history.
**Ind/Abst** Index Book Rev. Relig.; Relig. Index One Period.

UK/0308-0382
**EPWORTH REVIEW.** [Epworth rev.]. (1974)-. Periodical. English. Three times a year. £6.00 UK; £8.00 other. Methodist Publishing House / UK, 20 Ivatt Way, Peterborough PE3 7PG United Kingdom. **Tel** 011 44 733 332202. **LC** BR1; .E54. **DD** 230/.7/05. **Ad Acc.**
**Ind/Abst** Index Book Rev. Relig.; New Testam. Abstr.; Old Testam. Abstr.; Relig. Index One Period.; Relig. Theol. Abstr.

US/0090-3817
**ESSAYS AND REPORTS - LUTHERAN HISTORICAL CONFERENCE.** [Essays rep.- Lutheran Hist. Conf.]. **Main/Conf** Lutheran Historical Conference. (1964)-. English. be. $9.25 (two years). Lutheran Historical Conference, 801 De Mun Avenue, St. Louis MO 63105. **Tel** (314)721-5934 ext. 320. **ED** Aug R Suelflow. **LC** BX8011.A1; L83. **Pr Rev. Circ:** 500.
**Ind/Abst** Index Book Rev. Relig. (-19??); Relig. Index One Period. (1974-); Relig. Theol. Abstr. (1974-).

CN/0014-3324
**EVANGELICAL BAPTIST.** **Added/Corp** Fellowship of Evangelical Baptist Churches in Canada. Evangelical Baptist. Vol. 10 (Nov. 1962)-. Periodical. English. mo (11 issues per year). 13.95Can$ Canada; 16.95Can$ other. Fellowship Evangelical Baptist Churches of Canada, 679 Southgate Drive, Guelph Ontario, N1G 4S2 Canada. **Tel** (519)821-4830, FAX (519)821-9829. **ED** Roy Lawson and Sarah Abraham. **Bk Rev.** **Ad Acc. Circ:** 7,000. ***Continues*** *Fellowship*

*Baptist.*
**Desc:** Official publication of the fellowship of Evangelical Baptist churches in Canada.

US/0745-8495
**EVANGELICAL METHODIST, THE.** (THE EVANGELICAL METHODIST : VOICE OF BIBLE-BELIEVING METHODISM.). **Added/Corp** Evangelical Methodist Church. (19??)-. Periodical. English. Ten times a year (Except July and August). $3.00. Evangelical Methodist Church, 3036 North Meridian, Wichita KS 67024. **Tel** (301)457-5101. **ED** Donald McKnight. **Circ:** 2,500.

UK
**EVANGELICAL TIMES.** English. Twelve times a year. £8.20 UK; £10.20 other. Evangelical Times, 12 Wooler Street, Darlington Dur DL1 1RQ England. **Tel** 011 44 325 380232, FAX 011 44 325 466153. **Bk Rev. Ad Acc. Circ:** 11,000.
**Desc:** News and views for Evangelical Churches.

US/0745-4074
**EVANGELIZE (MINNEAPOLIS, MINN.).** (EVANGELIZE.). **Added/Corp** Lutheran Evangelistic Movement. (May 1945)-. Periodical. English. mo. Lutheran Evangelical Movement, 2721 East 42nd Street/Suite C, Minneapolis MN 55406. **Tel** (612)332-5677.

CN/0700-7949
**EXCHANGE (TORONTO).** (EXCHANGE.). V. 1- Nov. 1976-. Periodical. English. Three times a year. Free to congregations of the United Church of Canada. United Church of Canada, 85 Saint Clair Avenue East Room 711, Toronto Ontario M45 1M8 Canada. **Tel** (416)925-5931. **ED** Lynda Newmarch. **DD** 287/.92/05. **UDC** 287.9. **Circ:** 12,800.
**Desc:** Presents programs and outlines on a variety of Christian development and social concerns, support resources, and news of events and of groups.

US/0745-0346
**EXPLORING 1 FOR LEADERS. VFOAT** Exploring One for Leaders. Periodical. English. qt. $7.25. Southern Baptist Convention, 901 Commerce, Suite 750, Nashville TN 37203. **Tel** (615)244-2355, FAX (615)742-8919. **(Subscription address:** Sunday School Board - Customer Service, 127 Ninth Avenue North, Nashville, TN 37234 USA; telephone: (800)458-2772**)** **UDC** 286.1. ***Continues*** *Exploring A for Leaders, 0162-4423.*

US/0162-4431
**EXPLORING B.** V. 1- 1969-. Periodical. English. qt. $3.75. Southern Baptist Convention, 901 Commerce, Suite 750, Nashville TN 37203. **Tel** (615)244-2355, FAX (615)742-8919. **(Subscription address:** Sunday School Board - Customer Service, 127 Ninth Avenue North, Nashville, TN 37234 USA; telephone: (800)458-2772**)** **ED** Neal C Buchanan. **UDC** 286.1. **Bk Rev. Ad Acc. Circ:** 140,000 (ctrl).
**Desc:** Religious education material for children who are in grades four, five, and six.

SZ
**FACTUM.** (19??)-. German. Ten times a year. DM46.20. Forderung Christlicher Publzsk, Post Box 263, CH 9435 Heerbrugg Switzerland. **Tel** 011 41 71 724358, FAX 011 41 71 725665. **Bk Rev**, (Qty: 12). **Ad Acc. Circ:** 7,000 (ctrl).

US
**FAITH AND FELLOWSHIP. Added/Corp** Church of the Lutheran Brethren of America. **VFOAT** Faith & Fellowship. (1934)-. Periodical. English. Seventeen times a year (every three weeks). $12.00 (one year), $21.00 (two year). Faith and Fellowship, Box 655, Fergus Falls MN 56537. **Tel** (218)736-7357. **ED** David R. Rinden. Index available. cum. index. **Bk Rev**, (Qty: 25). **Circ:** 5,150 (ctrl).
**Desc:** A publication of the Lutheran Brethren synod which provides news and articles of current interest within the denomination.

US/0360-9065
**FAITH-LIFE. Added/Corp** Protestant Conference. Vol. 1 (1928)-. Periodical. English. bm (6 issues). $6.00. Protestant Conference, 1023 Colan Boulevard, Rice Lake WI 54868. **Tel** (715)234-4164.

US/0745-8215
**FE Y VIDA.** Periodical. Spanish. qt. American Baptist Center, PO Box 871, Valley Forge PA 19482. **Tel** (800)334-1427. **UDC** 286.1.

CN/0317-266X
**FELLOWSHIP YEARBOOK.** (THE FELLOWSHIP YEAR BOOK.). **Added/Corp** Fellowship of Evangelical Baptist Churches in Canada. (1969)-. English. an (Published in November). 12.00Can$. Fellowship of Evangelical Baptist Churches in Canada, 679 Southgate Drive, Guelph Ontario N1G 4S2 Canada. **Tel** (519)821-4830. **DD** 286/.1/06271. Index available. ***Supersedes*** *Missions Digest and Year Book, 0544-439X.*
**Desc:** Annual report of the Executive Council and Boards presented to the annual convention.

PH/0430-4144
**FILIPINO METHODIST MAGAZINE, THE. Added/Corp** Methodist Church in the Philippines. Vol. 1 (March 1965)-. Periodical. English. mo. Filipino Methodist, PO Box 756, Manila Philippines. **Tel** 521 11 14.

US/8750-9377
**FIRM FOUNDATION.** (1884)-. Newspaper. English. mo. $15.00. Firm Foundation, PO Box 210876, Bedford TX 76095-7876. **Tel** (904)456-0222. **ED** H. A. Dobbs (phone: (713)469-3102). Index available (bound in December issue). **Ad Acc. Circ:** 8,000 (ctrl).
**Desc:** Religious orientation primarily for the Church of Christ.

US/0890-7277
**FIRST THINGS (RUSH CITY, MINN.).** (FIRST THINGS.). **Added/Corp** First Evangelical Lutheran Church (Rush City, Minn.). (199?)-. Periodical. English. wk. First Evangelical Lutheran Church, 580 West 5th Street Box 73, Rush City MN 55069.

US/1064-136X
**FIVE STONES, THE.** (THE FIVE STONES : A SMALL CHURCH NETWORK OF THE AMERICAN BAPTIST CONVENTION.). [Five stones]. **Added/Corp** American Baptist Convention. (1983)-. Periodical. English. qt (Jan., April, July, Oct.). $12.50. Five Stones, PO Box D-2, Rock Island RI 02807. **Tel** (401)466-5940. **ED** Anthony G. Pappas. **DD** 259. **Bk Rev**, (Qty: varies). **Circ:** 750.
**Desc:** Newsletter for people of small churches.

US
**FLORIDA BAPTIST WITNESS / ORGAN OF THE FLORIDA BAPTIST STATE CONVENTION. Added/Corp** Florida Baptist State Convention. (19??)-. Periodical. English. wk (except weeks of Christmas & 4th of July). $8.50. Florida Baptist Witness, 1230 Hendricks Avenue, Jacksonville FL 32207. **Tel** (904)396-2351. **ED** Jack E Brymer Sr. **Bk Rev. Ad Acc. Circ:** 81,000 (ctrl).
**Desc:** News and information concerning the work of the Florida and Southern Baptist convention featuring outstanding contributions of people and churches in ministry.

US
**FLORIDA UNITED METHODIST.** Vol. 29 (Sept. 1970)-. English. Fifty-two times a year. $12.00. Florida Annual Conference, PO Box 3767, Lakeland FL 33802. **Tel** (813)688-5563. **ED** Barbara B. Wilcox. **Circ:** 30,000. ***Continues*** *The Florida Methodist.*

US/0279-8840
**FOCAL POINT (ENGLEWOOD, COLO.).** (FOCAL POINT.). **Added/Corp** Denver Conservative Baptist Seminary. Vol. 1, No. 1 (Jan./Mar. 1981)-. Periodical. English. Four times a year. Free on request. Denver Conservative Baptist Seminar, PO Box 10000, Denver CO 80210. **Tel** (303)761-2482. **ED** Cheryl A. Smith. **Bk Rev. Circ:** 33,000. ***Continues*** *Conservative Seminarian.*
**Desc:** Provides practical, immediately usable articles for effective daily living.

US/0741-1537
**FOLIO (LOUISVILLE, KY.).** (FOLIO : A NEWSLETTER FOR SOUTHERN BAPTIST WOMEN IN MINISTRY.). Vol. 1, No. 1 (June 1983)-. Newsletter. English. qt (Jan., Apr., June, Sept.). $15.00. Folio Southern Baptist, 2800 Frankfort Avenue, Louisville KY 40206. **Tel** (502)896-4425. **ED** Amanda Hiley. **LC** BX6345; .F64. **DD** 262/.14632/088042. Index available. cum. index. **Bk Rev**, (Qty: 2). **Circ:** 3,000.

US/0046-4732
**FORUM LETTER. Added/Corp** American Lutheran Publicity Bureau. Vol. 1 (Jan. 1972)-. Periodical. English. Sixteen times a year (Four quarterly magazines & twelve monthly newsletters). $22.50 (individuals), $25.00 (institutions) US; $26.00 (individuals), $28.50 (institutions) Canada; $30.00 (individuals), $32.50 (institutions) others. American Lutheran Publicity Bureau, PO Box 327, Delhi NY 13753. **Tel** (607)746-7511.

UK
**FOUNDATIONS (ST. ALBANS, HERTS).** (FOUNDATIONS.). **Added/Corp** British Evangelical Council. (197?)-. Periodical. English. Twice a year (May & Nov.). £4.00 UK; £5.00 other. British Evangelical Council, 113 Victoria Street, St Albans A1 3TJ England. **Tel** 011 44 1727 855655, FAX 011 44 1727 855655. **ED** Dr. Eryl Davies. Index available. **Bk Rev**, (Qty: 5). **Circ:** 1,000.
**Desc:** Contemporary theology with particular attention to evangelical churches outside pluralist ecumenical bodies.
**Ind/Abst** Relig. Theol. Abstr. (199?-).

CN/0823-4590
**FREE METHODIST HERALD.** (THE FREE METHODIST HERALD.). [Free Methodist her.]. **Added/Corp** Free Methodist Church in Canada. Jurisdictional Conference. Vol. 60 No. 8 (Sept. 1982)-. Periodical. English. mo. $6.75. Free Methodist Church of Canada, Jurisdictional Conference, 371 Delaware Avenue, Toronto Ontario M6H 2T7. **DD** 287/.97/05. ***Continues*** *Canadian Free Methodist Herald, 0383-0136.*

UK/0016-1268
**FRIEND (LONDON), THE.** (THE FRIEND.). (Jan. 1843)-. Periodical. English. wk. $79.00. Headley Brothers Ltd., The Invicta Press, Queens Road, Ashford Kent TN24 8HH England. **Tel** 011 44 233 623131. **ED** David Firth. **LC** BX7601; .F48. **DD** 289.605.
**Ind/Abst** Peace Res. Abstr. J. (1970).

US/0739-5418
**FRIENDLY LETTER, A. *Ceased.*** Issue No. 1 (1981)-(1993). Periodical. English. mo. A Friendly Letter, PO Box 1361, Falls Church VA 22041. **Tel** (703)845-0427. **ED** Chuck Fager. Index available. cum. index. **Bk Rev. Ad Acc. Circ:** 750.
**Desc:** An independent Quaker newsletter, reporting and analyzing Quaker news and issues neglected by other Quaker publications. Also includes Quaker humor and history.

US/0740-5618
**FRIENDLY WOMAN, THE. See** Women's Interests.

IE/0790-3642
**FRIENDLY WORD, THE.** (THE FRIENDLY WORD : IRELAND'S QUAKER NEWS JOURNAL.). [Friendly word]. (1984)-. Periodical. English. bm. $10.00. Friendly Word, 3 Lakelands Road Des King, Black Rock Co Dublin Ireland. **Tel** 886530. **ED** Felicity McCartney (editor's address: 621 Sea Coast Road, Limavady, BT49 OLH, Northern Ireland). **DD** 289.6415. **Bk Rev. Pr Rev. Circ:** 500 (ctrl). ***Continues*** *Irish Friends' Newsletter.*
**Desc:** Theological, social, human rights, peace and international issues of interest to Quakers in Ireland and abroad.

US
**GATEWAY. See** College and School Publications-Alumni.

US/0360-571X
**GAY LUTHERAN, THE. See** Homosexuality.

US/0503-3551
**GENERAL MINUTES OF THE ANNUAL CONFERENCES OF THE UNITED METHODIST CHURCH. Main/Corp** Methodist Church (U.S.). (1968)-. English. an. $15.85 (paperbound), $21.60 (clothbound). GCFA United Methodist Church, 1200 Davis Street, Evanston IL 60201. **Tel** (312)869-3345. **ED** Daniel A. Nielsen. **LC** BX8382.2.A1; U57b. **DD** 287/.673. **Circ:** 3,000. ***Continues*** *General Minutes of the Annual Conferences of the Methodist Church in the United States, Territories, and Cuba.*
**Desc:** Includes names and mailing addresses of Bishops; general jurisdictional conference secretaries and treasurers; annual conference secretaries, statisticians and treasurers, judicial council decisions, pastoral appointments, statistical information and lists and indexes.

SZ/0323-8202
**GLAUBE UND HEIMAT.** Periodical. German. wk. Deutscher Judo Verband, Redaktion Ippon Segewaldweg 40, D 12557 Berlin Germany. **Tel** 011 49 711 210770, telex 051 678. **LC** BX9798.U5; G55. **DD** 284.1/4322/05. **UDC** 284.1.

US/0436-1563
**GOOD NEWS (WILMORE).** (GOOD NEWS.). **Added/Corp** Forum for Scriptural Christianity. Vol. 1 (Winter 1967)-. Periodical. English. Six times a year. $14.95 North America; $16.95 other. Good News, 308 East Main Street, Wilmore KY 40390. **Tel** (606)858-4661. **ED** James V. Heidinger II. **Bk Rev. Ad Acc. Circ:** 20,000.
**Desc:** News and features about evangelical renewal within the UM Church.
**Ind/Abst** Curr. Thoughts Trends.

US/0745-7618
**GOSPEL TIDINGS (OMAHA, NEB.).** (GOSPEL TIDINGS.). Periodical. English. bm. $6.75. Evangelical Mennonite Brethren, Conference Central Office, 5800 South 14th Street, Omaha NE 68107. **Tel** (402)731-4780. **ED** Lyle Wahl. **UDC** 289.7. **Bk Rev. Ad Acc. Circ:** 2,400 (ctrl).
**Desc:** Educational inspirational content, directed to members in our fellowship of churches.

US/1045-8948
**GROWING CHURCHES.** [Grow. churches]. **Added/Corp** Southern Baptist Convention. Sunday School Board. Vol. 1, No. 1 (Oct./Nov./Dec. 1990)-. Periodical. English. qt. $16.25 (one year), $32.25 (two year). Southern Baptist Convention, 901 Commerce, Suite 750, Nashville TN 37203. **Tel** (615)244-2355, FAX (615)742-8919. **(Subscription address:** Sunday School Board - Customer Service, 127 Ninth Avenue North, Nashville, TN 37234 USA; telephone: (800)458-2772**)** **LC** BV652.25; .G73. **DD** 254/.5/05.
**Ind/Abst** South. Baptist Period. Index (1990-).

US/0017-5226
**GUIDE (WASHINGTON).** (GUIDE.). **Added/Corp** Seventh-Day Adventist Church. (19??)-. Periodical. English. wk. $35.97. Review and Herald Publishing Association, 55 West Oak Ridge Drive, Hagerstown MD 21740. **Tel** (301)791-7000 ext. 2534,

FAX (301)790-9734. **ED** Jeannette Johnson. Index available. **Circ:** 50,000. available on microfilm from University Microfilms International (UMI).
**Desc:** A journal written for 10-14 year-olds who want true stories relevant to the needs of today's Christian young person that emphasize the positive aspects of Christian living.

UK/0082-7908
**HANDBOOK OF THE UNITED FREE CHURCH OF SCOTLAND, THE. Main/Corp** United Free Church of Scotland. (1929)-. Directory. English. be. £3.00. United Free Church of Scotland, 11 Newton Place, Glasgow G3 7PR Scotland. **Tel** (041)332-3435. **ED** D.R. Beatty. **LC** BX9089; .A2. **DD** 285.241. **Circ:** 650.
**Desc:** Directory of officials, congregations, ministers and office-bearers of the United Free Church of Scotland.

KO
**HANGUK KIDIKKYO CHANGNOHOE HOEBO. VFOAT** The Presbyterian Life; Presbyterian Life; Changnohoe Po. Periodical. Korean. ir (ten issues per year). W6000. Hanguk Kidokkyo Changnohoe, Chonghoe 136-46 Yonji-dong Chongno-ku, Seoul Korea. **ED** Kim Sang Keun. **LC** BX9151.K6; H36. **UDC** 285.1. **Bk Rev. Ad Acc. Circ:** 3,000 (ctrl).
**Desc:** Sermons, theological articles, church news, column on peace and unification, church and society issues, statements, declarations, occasionally overseas church news, etc.

KO
**HANGUK KIDOKKYO KYOHOE CHUSOROK.** ***Title Change.*** (1986)-(198?). Korean (English). an. Kurisuchyan Raipusa, 19-1 1-ka To-dong, Yongsan-ku, Seoul Korea. **LC** BR1320; .H356.
***Continues*** *Hanguk Kyohoe Chonhwa Ponhobu.*
***Continued by*** *Hanguk Kyohoe Chusorok.*

KO
**HANGUK KYOHOE CHUSOROK. VFOAT** Kyohoe Chusorok; Kidokkyo Hanguk Kyohoe Chusorok. (198?)-. Korean (English). Kurisuchyan Raipusa, 19-1 1-ka To-dong, Yongsan-ku, Seoul Korea. **LC** BR1320; .H356. ***Continues*** *Hanguk Kidokkyo Kyohoe Chusorok.*

US
**HARVEST, THE.** Periodical. English. Three times a year. Free upon request. Baptist Mid-Missions, PO Box 308011, 7749 Webster Road, Cleveland OH 44130-8011. **Tel** (216)826-3930, FAX (216)826-4457. **ED** William H. Smallman, Lonnie Rochards & Nancy Freund. **Circ:** 80,000.
**Desc:** Report to churches and individuals on activity of fundamental Baptist Missionaries around the world.

US/1056-1986
**HELP FOR LIVING.** [Help living]. **Added/Corp** Southern Baptist Convention. Sunday School Board. (1991)-. Periodical. English. qt. $3.90. Southern Baptist Convention, 901 Commerce, Suite 750, Nashville TN 37203. **Tel** (615)244-2355, FAX (615)742-8919. **(Subscription address:** Sunday School Board - Customer Service, 127 Ninth Avenue North, Nashville, TN 37234 USA; telephone: (800)458-2772**)** **DD** 248.

US/0018-0513
**HERALD OF HOLINESS. Added/Corp** Church of the Nazarene (1919- ). Vol. 1 (April 17, 1912)-. Periodical. English. mo. $10.00 (one year); $19.00 (two year); $28.00 (three year). Nazarene Publishing House, PO Box 419527, Kansas City MO 64141. **Tel** (816)931-1900. **LC** BX8699.N3; H35. **DD** 289.9.
**Ind/Abst** Guide Soc. Sci. Relig.

US/0270-4919
**HISTORICAL INTELLIGENCER.** (HISTORICAL INTELLIGENCER : HISTORICAL JOURNAL OF THE UNITED CHURCH OF CHRIST.). [Hist. intell.]. Vol. 1, No. 1 (Fall 1980)-. Periodical. English. an. $20.00. United Church of Christ / New York, 287 Park Avenue South, New York NY 10010. **LC** BX9884; .H57. **DD** 285.8/34.

US
**HISTORIOGRAPHER, THE. Added/Corp** Church Historical Society. Vol. 1 (1938)-. English. an. Church Historical Society, PO Box 2247, Austin TX 78767. **LC** BX5810; .C53. **DD** 283.73.
**Desc:** Includes reports of the president, librarian, etc. of the society.

SZ/0379-7465
**HOKHMA.** [Hokhma]. No.1 (1976). Periodical. French. Three times a year. $13.00 Switzerland; $15.00 other. Effigie Communication, BP 62, F 78250 Meulan France. **ED** Fabrice Lengronne. **LC** BR3; .H64. **DD** 230/.05. Index available. cum. index. **Bk Rev. Ad Acc. Circ:** 1,300.
**Desc:** Articles written by professors, pastors and students; tries to approach the Bible unbiased and relate it to the church and the world of today.
**Ind/Abst** New Testam. Abstr.

US/0018-4071
**HOME LIFE (NASHVILLE).** (HOME LIFE.). **Added/Corp** Southern Baptist Convention. Sunday School Board. Vol. 1 (Jan. 1947)-. Periodical. English. mo. $10.70 (one year), $21.10 (two year), $31.50 (three year). Materials Services Department, 127 9th Avenue North, Nashville TN 37234. **Tel** (615)251-2000. **ED** Reuben Herring. **Bk Rev. Ad Acc. Circ:** 750,000 (ctrl).
**Desc:** Popular reading publication on Christian marriage and Christian family life distributed mainly through Southern Baptist churches.
**Ind/Abst** Index Philip. Period. (-199?); South. Baptist Period. Index.

HK
**HONG KONG PEAK. Added/Corp** American Baptist Mission in Hong Kong. (19??)-. Periodical. English. ir. World Publications / San Francisco, 100 Spear Street/Suite 220, San Francisco CA 94105. **Tel** (415)777-1171. **Circ:** 6,000 (ctrl).
**Desc:** Read by affluent individuals in Hong Kong. Heavy concentration of corporate executives, directors, and government officials.

US/1056-4624
**HOOSIER UNITED METHODIST NEWS. Added/Corp** Indiana Area United Methodist Communications (Organization). Vol. 21, No. 4 (April 1991)-. Periodical. English. mo. Hoosier United Methodist News, 1100 West 42nd Street, Indianapolis IN 46200.
***Continues*** *Hoosier United Methodist, 0888-3696.*

HK/0367-5920
**HSIANG-KANG CH'IN HUI HSUEH YUAN HSUEH PAO. See** College and School Publications.

GW
**IDEA.** (IDEA. (ENGLISH EDITION).). English. ir. DM4.00. Informationsdienst Ev Allianz, Moritz Hensoldt Str 22, PF 1820, W 6330 Wetzlar 1 Germany. **Tel** 011 49 6441 90140.

US/1051-5143
**IEVANHELSKYI RANOK.** [Evang. ranok]. **VFOAT** Evangelical Morning. Ukrainian. mo. Ukrainske Ievanhelske Obiednannia, PO Box 185, Postal Station East, Toronto 4 Ontario Canada. **LC** BX4800; .I35. **DD** 267. ***Continues*** *Kanadiiskyi Ranok.*
**Desc:** Issues for 1961-71 include separately titled section: The Ukrainian Christian Herald ... .

US/0019-1868
**ILLINOIS BAPTIST.** [Ill. Baptist]. **Added/Corp** Illinois Baptist State Association. (1905)-. Periodical. English. Twenty-six times a year (weekly except the last week of the month). $6.50 (one year), $12.50 (two years). Illinois Baptist State Association, Box 19247, Springfield IL 62794. **Tel** (217)786-2600. **ED** Bill Webb (phone: (217)786-2600 ext. 37). **DD** 286. **Bk Rev.**

US/0019-2821
**IMPACT (CONSERVATIVE BAPTIST FOREIGN MISSION SOCIETY).** (IMPACT.). **Added/Corp** Conservative Baptist Foreign Mission Society. **VFOAT** Conservative Baptist Impact. Vol. 26 (Jan. 1969)-. Periodical. English. Six times a year. $3.00. Conservation Baptist for Mission, PO Box 5, Wheaton IL 60187. ***Continues*** *Conservative Baptist Impact.*

US/8756-1816
**INDEPENDENT BAPTIST VOICE, THE.** (198?)-. Periodical. English. wk. $17.00 (one year), $33.00 (two year) Broome County; $19.00 (one year), $47.00 (two year) other. Masthead Publications, PO Box 208, Conklin NY 13748. **Tel** (607)775-0472. **ED** Elizabeth Einstein. **Ad Acc.**

US/0744-4087
**INDEPENDENT METHODIST BULLETIN, THE.** (THE INDEPENDENT METHODIST BULLETIN / ASSOCIATION OF INDEPENDENT METHODISTS.). **Added/Corp** Association of Independent Methodists. Executive Committee. Vol. 2, No. 10 & 11 (Oct./Nov. 1980)-. Periodical. English. bm. Free. Association of Independent Methodists, PO Box 4274, Jackson MS 39296. **Tel** (601)362-1301. **ED** Gary Thornton. **Bk Rev. Circ:** 2,000. ***Continues*** *Independent Methodist.*
**Desc:** Contains news reports from individual churches, reports on Association of Independent Methodist events, sermons, missionary reports and warning reports of liberal activities in our world.

US/0892-6654
**INDIAN HIGHWAYS (TEMPE, ARIZ.). See** Ethnic Interests.

US/8750-8176
**INDIANA APOSTOLIC TRUMPET.** (INDIANA APOSTOLIC TRUMPET : OFFICIAL PUBLICATION, INDIANA DISTRICT, UNITED PENTECOSTAL CHURCH.). Periodical. English. mo. $4.00. Indiana Apostolic Trumpet, c/o S Young, PO Box 2125, Terre Haute IN 47802. **UDC** 289.9.

SZ
**INFORMATION - LUTHERAN WORLD FEDERATION NEWS SERVICE. Main/Corp** Lutheran World Federation. News Service. **VFOAT** LWF Information; LWB Information. Periodical. English (German). wk. $30.00. Lutheran World Federation, 150 Route de Ferney, CP 2100, Geneva 20 Switzerland. **Tel** 011 41 22 7916111. **ED** Norman Hjelm. **UDC** 284.1. **Bk Rev. Circ:** 3,000 (ctrl). ***Continues*** *Press Service - News Bureau, Lutheran World Federation.*
**Desc:** International news service covering Lutheranism in particular and relief/development issues and ecumenism in general. Noted for coverage of Southern Africa and anti-apartheid movement.

US/0020-1944
**INSIGHT (WASHINGTON).** (INSIGHT.). (19??)-. Periodical. English. wk. $36.97. Review and Herald Publishing Association, 55 West Oak Ridge Drive, Hagerstown MD 21740. **Tel** (301)791-7000 ext. 2534, FAX (301)790-9734.
**Ind/Abst** Seventh-Day Adventist Period. Index (19??-).

CN/0383-6061
**INTERCOM (WILLOWDALE).** (INTERCOM.). V. 1- Oct. 1968-. Periodical. English. Fellowship Evangelical Baptist Churches of Canada, 679 Southgate Drive, Guelph Ontario, N1G 4S2 Canada. **Tel** (519)821-4830, FAX (519)821-9829. **UDC** 286.1(71).

US/0145-6970
**INTERNATIONAL PENTECOSTAL HOLINESS ADVOCATE, THE. Added/Corp** Pentecostal Holiness Church. International Pentecostal Holiness Church. Vol. 59, No. 20 (Feb. 8, 1976)-. Periodical. English. Twelve times a year. $9.75. International Pentecostal Holiness Church, Advocate Press, Box 98, Franklin Springs GA 30639. **Tel** (404)245-7272. **ED** Shirley Spencer, PO Box 12609, Oklahoma City, OK 73157; Telephone:(405)787-7110. **LC** BX8795.P25; A2. **DD** 289.9. **Bk Rev,** (Qty: 16-18).
***Continues*** *Pentecostal Holiness Advocate.*

US/0020-9678
**INTERPRETER (EVANSTON, ILL.), THE.** (THE INTERPRETER.). [Interpreter]. **Added/Corp** United Methodist Church (U.S.). Division of Interpretation. United Methodist Communications (Organization). Vol. 13 (Jan. 1969)-. Periodical. English. Eight times a year. $8.00. The Interpreter, 810 12th Avenue South, PO Box 320, Nashville TN 37203. **Tel** (615)742-5400, FAX (615)742-5460. **ED** Ralph E. Baker (editor's phone: (615)742-5476). **DD** 287. Index available. **Ad Acc, Adv Mgr:** Laura O'Kumu, **Tel** (615)742-5104. **Circ:** 285,000 (ctrl). available on microfilm from University Microfilms International (UMI). ***Continues*** *Methodist Story-Spotlight.*
**Desc:** The official program publication for all United Methodist clergy and local church leaders in the 50 states.
**Ind/Abst** Comput. Lit. Index.

IE
**IRISH BAPTIST.** (1930)-. Periodical. English. Eleven times a year (July/Aug. issues combined). $12.60. Baptist Union of Ireland, 117 Lisburn Road, Belfast BT9 7AW, North Ireland. **Tel** 44 232 663108, FAX 44 232 663616. **ED** S. Crowe. Index available. cum. index. **Circ:** 3,000.
**Desc:** News of local churches and missions, home and abroad. Devotional articles and controversial subjects are included also.

IE/0075-0727
**IRISH BAPTIST HISTORICAL SOCIETY JOURNAL. Main/Corp** Irish Baptist Historical Society. **Added/Corp** Irish Baptist Historical Society. Journal. Vol. 1 (1968/69)-. Periodical. English. an. $10.00. Baptist Union of Ireland, 117 Lisburn Road, Belfast BT9 7AW, North Ireland. **Tel** 44 232 663108, FAX 44 232 663616. **ED** Dr. Joshua Thompson (editor's address: 17 Strangford Avenue, Belfast BT9 6PG England; editor's phone: 44 232 669157). **LC** BX6281.A1; I7. **DD** 286.1/415. **Bk Rev.**
**Desc:** Historical accounts of churches in Ireland and also prominent readers in Baptist circles.

AU/1013-6991
**JAHRBUCH FUER DIE GESCHICHTE DES PROTESTANTISMUS IN OSTERREICH.** [Jahrb. Gesch. Protestant. Osterr.]. **Added/Corp** Gesellschaft fur die Geschichte des Protestantismus in Osterreich. (1980)-. German. an.
***Continues*** *Jahrbuch der Gesellschaft fur die Geschichte des Protestantismus in Osterreich.*
**Ind/Abst** Am. Hist. Life (1980-).

US/0272-0922
**JD (WASHINGTON). See** Law.

PL
**JEDNOTA. Added/Corp** Koscio Ewangelicko-Reformowany Polski. Vol. 1 (1957)-. Periodical. Polish. mo. Price on Request. **(Subscription address:** ARS Polona, PO Box 1001, 00068 Warsaw Poland.**)** **LC** BX9480.P7; J4. ***Continues*** *Jednota.*

CS
**JEDNOTA BRATRSKA. Added/Corp** Moravian Church. (19??)-. Periodical. Czech. mo. **(Subscription address:** Artia Pegas Press Ltd., Palac Metro Narodni Trida 25, 11210 Prague 1 Czech Republic.**)** **LC** BX4922; .J42.
**Desc:** Information on the Moravian Church.

US/0739-7852
**JOHN WHITMER HISTORICAL ASSOCIATION JOURNAL, THE.** [John Whitmer Hist. Assoc. j.]. **Added/Corp** John Whitmer

Historical Association. **VFOAT** Journal. Vol. 1 (1981)-. Academic Scholarly Publication. English. an (Sept.). $15.00. Graceland College, c/o Alma Blair, 700 College Avenue, Lamoni IA 50140. **Tel** (515)784-5171, (515)784-6408. **ED** William Russell. **Bk Rev. Circ:** 600. **Desc:** Publication dealing with Latter Day Saint history as a means of encouraging serious research and exchange of various scholarly viewpoints.

●UK/0966-7369
**JOURNAL OF PENTECOSTAL THEOLOGY.** [J. pentecostal theol.]. **Added/Corp** Church of God (Cleveland, Tenn.). School of Theology. Issue 1 (Oct. 1992)-. Periodical. English. sa (Oct., Apr.). £15.00 individuals; £20.00 institutions. Sheffield Academic Press Ltd, 343 Fulwood Road, Sheffield S10 3BP England. **Tel** 011 44 742 670044, 011 44 742 668431, FAX 011 44 742 660291. **ED** Rick D. Moore, John Christopher Thomas, & Steven J. Land. **DD** 289. **Bk Rev. Ad Acc, Adv Mgr:** Anne Dolling, **Tel** 670043. **Desc:** Information on penetecostalism and pentecostal churches. Articles cover the areas of biblical studies, modern theology, ethics, and practical theology.

US/0730-6938
**JOURNAL OF THE ANNUAL CONVENTION - EPISCOPAL CHURCH. DIOCESE OF BETHLEHEM.** (JOURNAL OF THE ... ANNUAL CONVENTION / THE DIOCESE OF BETHLEHEM, THE EPISCOPAL CHURCH.). **Main/Corp** Episcopal Church. Diocese of Bethlehem. English. an. Diocese of Bethlehem, 826 Delaware Avenue, Behlehem PA 18015. **LC** BX5918.B5; A3. **DD** 283/.7482/05. **UDC** 283(748). ***Continues*** *Journal of the Proceedings of the ... Annual Convention of the Protestant Episcopal Church in the Diocese of Bethlehem.*

UK/0071-9587
**JOURNAL OF THE FRIENDS' HISTORICAL SOCIETY, THE.** [J. Friends Hist. Soc.]. **Main/Corp** Friends' Historical Society. **Added/Corp** Friends' Historical Society. Vol. 1, No. 1 (Nov. 1903)-. Periodical. English. £6.00 UK; $11.00 other. Friends Historical Society, Euston Road, London NW1 2BJ England. **ED** Gerald A J Hodgett. **LC** BX7676.A1; F6. **Circ:** 425.
**Ind/Abst** Am. Hist. Life (1957-).

US
**JOURNAL OF THE GENERAL CONVENTION OF THE NEW JERUSALEM.** **Main/Corp** General Convention of the New Jerusalem in the United States of America. 1817-. English. an. General Convention of the New Jerusalem in the United States of America, 48 Sargent Street, Newton MA 02158. **Tel** (617)969-4240. **LC** BX8705; .A3. **UDC** 283(71).

CN/0826-3205
**JOURNAL OF THE ... GENERAL SYNOD / ANGLICAN CHURCH OF CANADA.** **Main/Corp** Anglican Church of Canada. General Synod. (1983)-. English. ir (Publishes every three years). 25.00Can$. Anglican Church of Canada / Toronto, 600 Jarvis Street, Toronto Ontario M4Y 2J6 Canada. **Tel** (416)924-9192. **LC** BX5603; .A3. **DD** 283/.71. **Ad Acc.** ctrl circ. ***Continues*** *Anglican Church of Canada. General Synod. Journal of Proceedings - Anglican Church of Canada, General Synod., 0380-2469.*

US
**JOURNAL OF THE NORTH MISSISSIPPI CONFERENCE OF THE UNITED METHODIST CHURCH ... : SESSION SINCE MERGER OF THE UPPER MISSISSIPPI CONFERENCE (ORGANIZED IN 1891) AND THE NORTH MISSISSIPPI CONFERENCE (ORGANIZED IN 1870).** **Main/Corp** United Methodist Church (U.S.). North Mississippi Conference. **VFOAT** Journal, North Mississippi Conference of the United Methodist Church. 3rd (1975)-. English. an. **UDC** 287. ***Continues*** *Journal of the New North Mississippi Conference.*

US/0146-0196
**JOURNAL OF THE SOUTH CAROLINA BAPTIST HISTORICAL SOCIETY.** **Main/Corp** South Carolina Baptist Historical Society. Vol. 1 (Nov. 1975)-. English. an (November). $3.00. Baptist Historical Collection, Furman University Library, Greenville SC 29613. **Tel** (803)294-2194. **ED** J. Glenwood Clayton. **LC** BX6248.S6; S68a. **DD** 286/.1757. **Bk Rev. Ad Acc. Circ:** 150. **Desc:** Articles about South Carolina Baptist history. Reprints some original documents.

UK/0049-5433
**JOURNAL - UNITED REFORMED CHURCH HISTORY SOCIETY.** [J. United Reform. Church Hist. Soc.]. **Main/Corp** United Reformed Church History Society. Vol. 1 (May 1973)-. Periodical. English. sa. £6.49. United Reformed Church, 86 Tavistock Place, London WC1H 9RT England. **Tel** 011 44 71 9162020. **ED** Clyde Binfield. **LC** BX9890.U25; U55A. **DD** 285/.2. **UDC** 285.5. **Bk Rev.** available on microfilm from University Microfilms International (UMI). ***Supersedes*** *Congregational Historical Society. Transactions; Journal - Presbyterian Historical Society of England, 0079-5011.*
**Desc:** Historical material relating to congregational and presbyterian worthies, practices and theological teaching. **Ind/Abst** Am. Hist. Life (1973-).

US
**JUNIOR TRAIL.** English. qt. $4.50. Gospel Publishing House, 1445 Boonville Avenue, Springfield MO 65802. **Tel** (417)862-2781, FAX (417)866-1146.

RU
**KHRISTIANIN.** (1990)-. Periodical. Russian. Four times a year. $79.95. **(Subscription address:** East View Publications Inc., 3020 Harbor Lane North, Suite 110, Minneapolis MN 55447.**)**

US/0163-8718
**KINDERGARTEN PROGRAM HELPS.** (197?)-. English. Four times a year. $16.36. Review and Herald Publishing Association, 55 West Oak Ridge Drive, Hagerstown MD 21740. **Tel** (301)791-7000 ext. 2534, FAX (301)790-9734.
**Desc:** Program aids for leaders in Kindergarten Sabbath School.

US/0746-6889
**KINGDOM BUILDER / BAPTIST TRAINING UNION, THE.** **VFOAT** B.T.U. Young People's Quarterly. The Kingdom Builder; BTU Young People's Quarterly. The Kingdom Builder. Periodical. English. qt. National Baptist Publishing Board, 7145 Centennial Boulevard, Nashville TN 37209. **UDC** 377.8:286.1. ***Continues*** *Baptist Training Union Young People's Quarterly.*

GW/0453-9281
**KIRCHE IM OSTEN. MONOGRAPHIENREIHE.** **Added/Corp** Munster. Universitat. Ostkircheninstitut. Vol. 1 (1959)-. Monographic series. German. Price varies per volume. Vandenhoeck & Ruprecht, Robert Bosch Breite 6, D-37079 Goettingen Germany. **Tel** 011 49 551 695911, FAX 011 49 551 695917, telex 965226 VAN d.

GW/0075-6210
**KIRCHLICHES JAHRBUCH FUER DIE EVANGELISCHE KIRCHE IN DEUTSCHLAND.** **Added/Corp** Evangelische Kirche in Deutschland. Beckmann, Joachim. Hauschild, Wolf-Dieter. Wilkens, Erwin. **VFOAT** Kirchliches Jahrbuch. Vol. 60 (1933)-. German. an. DM42.00. VVA Bertelsmann Dist GmbH, Postfach 7600, D 33310 Gutersloh Germany. **Tel** 011 49 5241 803294. **ED** Wolf D. Hauschild, Erwin Wilkins, Georg Kretschmar, and Eduard Lonse. **Circ:** 500. ***Continues*** *Kirchliches Jahrbuch fuer die Evangelischen Landeskirchen Deutschlands).*
**Desc:** Church annual of the Protestant church in West German.

US
**KIRCHLICHES MONATSBLATT FUER DAS EVANGELISCH-LUTHERISCHE HAUS.** **Added/Corp** Lutheran Church in America. German Conference. Editorial Committee. Lutheran Church in America. German Conference. (19??)-. Periodical. German. mo. 12.00Can$. Kirchliches Monatsblatt, 29 Morris Court SE, Medicine Hat Alberta T1A 7P5 Canada. **Tel** (403)529-2679, FAX (403)527-4621. **ED** Jakob Pillibeit. **Ad Acc. Circ:** 1,500 (ctrl).

US/0145-7527
**KIRISUTOKYO KAGAKU KOTARI. SEISHO KYOKA.** **VFOAT** Seisho Kyoka; Christian Science Quarterly. Japanese Edition. Periodical. Japanese (English). qt. $3.25. 1 Norway Street, Boston MA 02115. **UDC** 289.94.

US/0893-5262
**LAD (MEMPHIS, TENN.).** (LAD.). Vol. 1, Issue 1 (Oct. 1987)-. Periodical. English. mo. $9.48. Baptist Brotherhood Commission, 1548 Poplar Avenue, Memphis TN 38104. **Tel** (901)272-2461. **ED** Tim Seanor. **UDC** 286.1. **Circ:** 70,000.
**Desc:** Mission education for boys grades 1-3 in southern Baptist churches.
**Ind/Abst** South. Baptist Period. Index.

US/0194-908X
**LAKE UNION HERALD.** **Added/Corp** Lake Union Conference of Seventh-Day Adventists. (19??)-. Periodical. English. wk. Lake Union Conference of Seventh-Day Adventists, Box C, Berrien Springs MI 49103. **LC** BX6101; .L3.
**Ind/Abst** Seventh-Day Adventist Period. Index (19??-).

US/0747-2706
**LANCASTER CONFERENCE NEWS.** Began in 1984?. Periodical. English. sm. $4.00. Lancaster Conference News, PO Box 128, Salunga PA 17538-0628. **Tel** (717)898-2411. **ED** Glenn Lehman. **UDC** 289.7. ctrl circ. ***Continues*** *Lancaster Mennonite Conference News, 0273-981X.*

CN/0380-0946
**LETTRE DE L'ABBE GRAVEL, LA.** No. 41-; Mar. 1974-. Periodical. French. ir. L'Abbe Pierre Gravel, Presbytere de Boischatel, Boischatel Quebec G0A 1H0 Canada. **DD** 205. ***Continues*** *Lettre de Michelle de St. -Antoine.*

US/0024-2055
**LIBERTY (WASHINGTON. 1906).** (LIBERTY.). **Added/Corp** General Conference of Seventh-Day Adventists. Religious Liberty Bureau. Religious Liberty Association. International Religious Liberty Association. Religious Liberty Association of America. Vol. 1 (Apr. 1906)-. Periodical. English. Six times a year. $6.95. Review and Herald Publishing Association, 55 West Oak Ridge Drive, Hagerstown MD 21740. **Tel** (301)791-7000 ext. 2534, FAX (301)790-9734. **ED** Roland R. Hegstad. **LC** BX6101; .L7. **DD** 286/.73. **Circ:** 250,000. available on microfilm and microfiche from University Microfilms International (UMI).
**Desc:** Deals with Church-State separation or religious liberty issues.
**Ind/Abst** Seventh-Day Adventist Period. Index (19??-).

FR/1157-7452
**LIBRESENS PARIS.** **VFOAT** Libres Sens (Paris). (1991)-. Periodical. French. Ten times a year (July/Aug. & Sept./Oct. issues combined). 240.00F. CTR Protestant d Etudes de Doc, 46 rue de Vaugirard, 75006 Paris France. **Tel** 011 33 1 46337724. **ED** M. Geoffroy de Turckheim. **UDC** 284. **Bk Rev. Circ:** 300. ***Continues*** *Bulletin du Centre Protestant d'Etudes et de Documentation, 0181-7671.*

UK/0024-306X
**LIFE AND WORK.** New Ser., No. 1, (Jan. 1930)-. Periodical. English. mo. £9.00. Church of Scotland, 121 George Street, Edinburgh EH2 4YN Scotland. **Tel** 011 44 31 2255722, FAX 011 44 31 2203113, telex 727935. **ED** Robert D Kernohan. **UDC** 283(411). **Bk Rev. Ad Acc. Circ:** 100,000. ***Absorbed*** *Church of Scotland Home and Foreign Mission Record; Record of the Church of Scotland.*
**Desc:** News magazine and review of the church of Scotland (Presbyterian).

US/0024-3299
**LIGHT AND LIFE (WINONA LAKE).** (LIGHT AND LIFE.). **Added/Corp** Free Methodist Church of North America. Vol. 103, No. 13 (July 14, 1970)-. Periodical. English. mo. $15.00. Free Methodist Church of North America, PO Box 535002, Indianapolis IN 46253. **Tel** (317)244-3660, FAX (317)244-1247. **ED** Robert Haslam. Index available. **Bk Rev. Ad Acc. Circ:** 30,000. ***Continues*** *Free Methodist.*
**Desc:** All articles are devoted to helping persons live as Christians in a secular world.

UK
**LIGHTBEARER.** **VFOAT** Light Bearer. Vol. 1 (1905)-. Periodical. English. Six times a year. £4.30. Sudan United Mission, 75 Granville Road, Sidcup Kent England. **Tel** 01 300 1109. **ED** D. Calcott. Index available. **Bk Rev. Ad Acc. Circ:** 5,000.
**Desc:** A missionary magazine of the SUM fellowship. Covers missionary work in the Sudan and northern Nigeria. The mission is Protestant Evangelical.

US/0885-4378
**LUCHA STRUGGLE.** **See** Social Sciences.

GW/0340-6210
**LUTHER.** (LUTHER : MITTEILUNGEN DER LUTHERGESELLSCHAFT.). [Luther]. **Added/Corp** Luthergesellschaft. Vol. 1 (1919)-. Periodical. German. Three times a year. DM42.00. Vandenhoeck & Ruprecht, Robert Bosch Breite 6, D-37079 Goettingen Germany. **Tel** 011 49 551 695911, FAX 011 49 551 695917, telex 965226 VAN d. **LC** BR323.5; .L8. **[CCC].**
**Ind/Abst** Index Book Rev. Relig.; MLA Int. Bibl. Books Artic. Mod. Lang. Lit.; Relig. Index One Period.

AT
**LUTHERAN, THE.** V. 1- Jan. 21, 1967-. Periodical. English. ir (issued every three weeks). $18.00 church workers; $22.00 groups; $26.00 individuals. Lutheran Publishing House, Box 1368, Government Printing Office, Adelaide 5001 Australia. **Tel** (08)223 4552. **ED** R J Wiebusch. **UDC** 284.1(93/94). Index available. **Bk Rev. Ad Acc. Circ:** 11,700 (ctrl). ***Formed by the union of*** *Lutheran Herald* ***and*** *Australian Lutheran.*
**Desc:** Devotional, informative, promotional, and inspirational feature articles, Church reports, and news of the Lutheran Church in Australia, New Zealand, and overseas.

US/0746-3413
**LUTHERAN AMBASSADOR, THE.** **Added/Corp** Association of Free Lutheran Congregations (U.S.). (1963)-. Periodical. English. bw. $15.00. The Lutheran Ambassador, 3110 East Medicine Lake Boulevard, Minneapolis MN 55441. **Tel** (612)545-5631. **ED** Raynard Huglen and Robert Lee. **Bk Rev. Circ:** 5,000.

US/0024-743X
**LUTHERAN (CHICAGO, ILL. : 1988).** (THE LUTHERAN.). [Lutheran]. Vol. 1, No. 1 (Jan. 6, 1988)-. Periodical. English. ir. $10.00 US; $19.20 other.

Evangelical Lutheran Church in America, 426 Fifth Street, Box 1209, Minneapolis MN 55440. **LC** BX8001; .L42. **DD** 284.1/3. ***Formed by the union of*** *Lutheran, 0024-743X; Lutheran Standard, 0024-7545* ***and*** *Lutheran Perspective (Chicago, Ill.).*

US/0363-4051
**LUTHERAN CHURCH DIRECTORY FOR THE UNITED STATES.** **Added/Corp** Lutheran Council in the USA. (1971)-. Directory. English. ir. $3.00. Lutheran Council in the USA, 122 C Street NW/Suite 300, Washington DC 20001. **Tel** (212)532-6350. **ED** Benjamin A Bankson. **LC** BX8009; .L838. **DD** 284/.1/02573. **Circ:** 25,000 (ctrl). ***Continues in part*** *Lutheran Church Directory for the United States and Canada, 0460-0096.*
**Desc:** The directory contains a state-by-state listing of the names and addresses of all US Lutheran congregations and Inter-Lutheran organizations.

US/0361-8757
**LUTHERAN COUNCIL IN THE U.S.A. NEWS BUREAU (NEWS RELEASE).** (NEWS RELEASES - NEWS BUREAU, LUTHERAN COUNCIL IN THE USA.). **Main/Corp** Lutheran Council in the United States of America. News Bureau. **Added/Corp** National Lutheran Council. News Releases. Vol. 1 (1914)-. English. News Bureau, Lutheran Council in the USA, 315 Park Avenue South, New York NY 10010.

US/0458-497X
**LUTHERAN DIGEST, THE.** Vol. 1 (Summer 1953)-. Periodical. English. Four times a year (Mar., June, Sept., Dec.). $20.00 (two years). Lutheran Digest, PO Box 4250, Hopkins MN 55343. **Tel** (612)933-2820. **ED** Russell A. Peterson and T. A. Radaeke. **LC** BR1; .L89. **DD** 205. **Ad Acc. Circ:** 185,000 (ctrl).
**Desc:** Directed at the family; its contents are designed to have something for all ages of readers, providing poetry, scripture, cartoons, pictures, and articles of devotional type, humor, and articles of self-help.

US/0024-7448
**LUTHERAN EDUCATION.** [Lutheran educ.]. **Added/Corp** Lutheran Church--Missouri Synod. Concordia Teachers College (River Forest, Ill.). (1947)-. Periodical. English. Five times a year. $9.00 (one year), $16.00 (two year) US, add $3.00 (surface mail), $15.00 (airmail) for postage other. Concordia University, 7400 Augusta Street, % Jo Ann Kiefer, River Forest IL 60305-1499. **Tel** (708)771-8300, FAX (708)209-3176. **ED** Wayne Lucht. **LC** LC573; .L8. **DD** 377/.841/73. Index available. **Bk Rev. Ad Acc. Circ:** 5,000. available on microfilm and microfiche from University Microfilms International (UMI). ***Continues*** *Lutheran School Journal, 0362-465X.*
**Desc:** A journal designed for/by teachers especially in Lutheran schools.
**Ind/Abst** Educ. Index.

US/0458-4988
**LUTHERAN EDUCATOR.** **See** Education.

US/0024-7456
**LUTHERAN FORUM.** Vol. 1 (Jan. 1967)-. Periodical. English. Sixteen times a year (Four quarterly magazines & twelve monthly newsletters). $22.50 (individuals), $25.00 (institutions) US; $26.00 (individuals), $28.50 (institutions) Canada; $30.00 (individuals), $32.50 (institutions) others. American Lutheran Publicity Bureau, PO Box 327, Delhi NY 13753. **Tel** (607)746-7511. **LC** BX8001; .L468. **Circ:** 3,600. available on microfilm and microfiche from University Microfilms International (UMI). ***Supersedes*** *American Lutheran.*
**Ind/Abst** Index Book Rev. Relig.; Relig. Index One Period.; Relig. Theol. Abstr.

US/0360-6945
**LUTHERAN JOURNAL, THE.** [Lutheran j.]. (194?)-. Periodical. English. qt (Jan., April, June, Oct.). $4.00 (one year), $10.00 (two year) US; $8.00 (one year), $19.00 (two year) Canada; $11.00 (one year), $28.00 (two year) other. Outlook Publications Inc., 7317 Cahill Road, Edina MN 55435. **Tel** (612)941-6830. **ED** Armin U Deye. **LC** BX8001; .L475. **DD** 284.1/05. **Bk Rev. Ad Acc. Circ:** 136,000. ***Continues*** *Northwest Lutheran Journal.*
**Desc:** Wholesome and inspirational material for the enjoyment and enrichment of Lutherans.

US/0024-7464
**LUTHERAN LAYMAN, THE.** **See** Religion and Theology.

US/0024-7472
**LUTHERAN LIBRARIES.** **See** Library and Information Sciences.

US/0885-9922
**LUTHERAN PARTNERS.** [Lutheran partn.]. **Added/Corp** Lutheran Church in America. American Lutheran Church (1961- ) Association of Evangelical Lutheran Churches (U.S.). **VFOAT** Partners. Vol. 1, No. 1 (May/June 1985)-. Periodical. English. Six times a year (Jan., Mar., May, July, Sept., Nov.). $10.00. Augsburg Fortress, 426 South Fifth Street, Box 1209, Minneapolis MN 55440. **Tel** (612)330-3300, (800)328-4648. **ED** Carl E. Linder. **LC** BX8001; .L54. **DD** 284.1/3. **Bk Rev. Ad Acc. Circ:** 23,000 (ctrl). ***Continues*** *LCA Partners.*
**Desc:** The magazine of those in the public ministries of the ELCA.

US/0279-4462
**LUTHERAN PERSPECTIVE.** ***Ceased.*** Vol. 9, No. 1 (Oct. 19, 1981)-Ceased 1988. Periodical. English. bw. Lutheran Perspective, PO Box 578 555, Chicago IL 60657-8555. **Tel** (312)753-0785. **ED** Randall R Lee. **UDC** 284.1(7). **Circ:** 15,000. available in microform from University Microfilms International (UMI). ***Continues*** *Missouri in Perspective, 0194-9705.*
**Desc:** Provides news and information affecting all Lutherans in the U.S. and Canada from an unbiased point of view.

US/0024-7510
**LUTHERAN SENTINEL.** **Added/Corp** Norwegian Synod of the American Evangelical Lutheran Church. Evangelical Lutheran Synod. Vol. 1 (1918)-. Periodical. English. Twelve times a year. $7.00 (one year), $18.00 (three years). Lutheran Sentinel, 204 North Second Avenue West, Lake Mills IA 50450. **Tel** (605)334-4225. **ED** Paul G Madson. **Bk Rev. Circ:** 5,800 (ctrl). available on microfilm.
**Desc:** The official church organ of the evangelical Lutheran synod with articles of a devotional and doctrinal nature, others of church news and information.

US/0024-7537
**LUTHERAN SPOKESMAN.** **Added/Corp** Church of the Lutheran Confession. Vol. 1 (1958)-. Periodical. English. Twelve times a year. $7.50 one year; $14.00 two year; $21.00 three year. Lutheran Spokesman, Bus Manager, 2750 North Oxford Street, Roseville MN 55113. **Tel** (612)484-4043. **ED** Paul Fleischer. Index available. cum. index. **Bk Rev. Circ:** 2,500 (ctrl).
**Desc:** Official organ of the church of the Lutheran confession. Religious articles, Bible study, book reviews, devotions, and current events are included.

US/0360-9685
**LUTHERAN SYNOD QUARTERLY, THE.** **Added/Corp** Evangelical Lutheran Synod. Vol. 1-20, (1940-1960); New Series, Vol . 1 (1961)-. Periodical. English. Four times a year (Mar., June, Sept., Dec.). $8.00. Bethany Lutheran Seminary, 734 Marsh Street, Mankato MN 56001. **Tel** (507)625-2977 Ext.27. **ED** Wilhelm W. Petersen. **Bk Rev. Circ:** 350. available on microfilm.
**Desc:** Articles on theological issues of the day, and on our doctrinal heritage based on the Lutheran reformation.
**Ind/Abst** Relig. Theol. Abstr.

AT/0024-7553
**LUTHERAN THEOLOGICAL JOURNAL.** [Lutheran theol. j.]. **Added/Corp** Luther Seminary, North Adelaide, Australia. Vol 1 (1967)-. Periodical. English. Three times a year. 19.00Aus$. Open Book Publishers, 205 Halifax Street, Adelaide 5000 South Australia. **Tel** 011 61 8 2235468. **ED** J.G. Strelan. **[CCC]. Bk Rev. Circ:** 600 (ctrl). available on microfilm and microfiche from University Microfilms International (UMI). ***Supersedes*** *Australasian Theological Review.*
**Desc:** Contains theological articles.
**Ind/Abst** Index Book Rev. Relig.; New Testam. Abstr.; Old Testam. Abstr.; Relig. Index One Period. (1980-).

US
**LUTHERAN VISTAS.** Periodical. English. qt. $5.00. Lutheran Vistas, 16105 Elmwood Station, Minneapolis MN 55416. **Tel** (612)926-5949. **ED** P A Engfer. **UDC** 284.1. **Bk Rev. Circ:** 48,000 (ctrl).
**Desc:** Religious articles by nationally known authors.

US/0024-7588
**LUTHERAN WITNESS REPORTER.** (1882)-. English. mo. $7.50. Lutheran Church, 1333 S Kirkwood Road, St Louis MO 63122-7295. **Tel** (314)965-9000. **(Subscription address:** 3558 S Jefferson Avenue, St Louis, MO 63118**) ED** David Mahsman. **Ad Acc. Circ:** 400,000 (ctrl).
**Desc:** Religious articles on missions, doctrine, people and places, current issues, letters, opinions, and editorials.

US/0024-757X
**LUTHERAN WITNESS (ST. LOUIS), THE.** (THE LUTHERAN WITNESS.). **Added/Corp** General English Lutheran Conference of Missouri and Other States. English Evangelical Lutheran Synod of Missouri and Other States. Evangelical Lutheran Synod of Missouri & Other States. Evangelical Lutheran Synod of Missouri, Ohio, and Other States. Lutheran Church--Missouri Synod. Vol. 1, No. 1 (May 21, 1882)-. Periodical. English. mo. $7.50. Concordia Publishing House, 3558 South Jefferson Avenue, St Louis MO 63118. **Tel** (314)268-1000, (800)325-3381, FAX (314)268-1329. **ED** Rev. David L. Mahsman. **LC** BX8001; .L7. Index available. **Ad Acc, Adv Mgr:** Roberta Hipenbecker, **Tel** (314)268-1129. **Circ:** 350,000 (ctrl). available on microfilm from Xerox; available on microfilm and microfiche from University Microfilms International (UMI).
**Desc:** Articles related to the church's mission and issues of the day, features on people, places, news and opinion columns.
**Ind/Abst** Curr. Thoughts Trends; Guide Soc. Sci. Relig.

US/0896-209X
**LUTHERAN WOMAN TODAY.** [Lutheran woman today]. **Added/Corp** Women of the Evangelical Lutheran Church in America. Vol. 1, No. 1 (Jan. 1988)-. Periodical. English. Eleven times a year (monthly except Aug.). $10.00 North America; $15.00 others. Lutheran Woman Today, 426 South Fifth Street, PO Box 1209, Minneapolis MN 55440. **ED** Nancy J. Stelling. **DD** 248. **Circ:** 288,000. available on audiocassette. ***Continues*** *Lutheran Women, 0024-7596.*

US/8750-5207
**LUTHERAN WOMEN'S MISSIONARY LEAGUE QUARTERLY ECHO / NEBRASKA DISTRICT SOUTH.** ***Title Change.*** **Added/Corp** Lutheran Women's Missionary League. Nebraska District South. **VFOAT** Quarterly Echo. (19??)-(1992). Periodical. English. qt. LWML Quarterly Echo, 537 E Memorial Drive, Grand Island NE 68801. ***Continued by*** *LWML Quarterly Echo, 1066-5749.*

US/0361-2392
**LUTHERANS ALERT, NATIONAL.** ***Ceased.*** (LUTHERANS ALERT.). [Lutherans alert natl.]. Vol. 1, (1966)-Vol. 25, (1992). Periodical. English. qt. Lutherans-Alert-National, PO Box 7186, Tacoma WA 98407. **UDC** 284.1.

GW
**LUTHERISCHE KIRCHE.** 1.- Yearly volume; March 1970-. Periodical. German. mo. Lutherische Kirche, Dietesheimer Str 139, 6052 Muehlheim Germany. **UDC** 284.1(43). ***Formed by the union of*** *Kirchenblatt der Evangelisch-Lutherischen (Altluth.) Kirche Mit Amtlichen Mitteilungen; Lutheraner* ***and*** *Unter der Kreuze.*

NO/0332-5431
**LUTHERSK KIRKETIDENDE.** V. 1-12 July 5, 1863-27. June 1869. Periodical. Norwegian. sm. Lutherstiftelsen Sog Forlag, Akerscate 47, Oslo 1 Norway. **UDC** 284.1(481).

US/0745-0273
**MAINE UNITED METHODIST, THE.** Periodical. English. bm. Free. Maine Annual Conference, Council on Ministries, POB 277, Winthrop ME 04364-0277. **Tel** (207)377-2912. **ED** Beverly J Abbott. **UDC** 287(741). **Bk Rev. Circ:** 5,200 (ctrl).

KO
**MANNAM.** **VFOAT** The Monthly Young Nak; Monthly Young Nak. Periodical. Korean (Korean). mo. Yongnak Kyohoe Hongbo Chulpanbu, 69 Cho-dong 2-ka Chung-ku, Seoul Korea. **LC** BX9215.S4; Y665.

CN/0824-5673
**MENNOGESPRACH (WATERLOO).** ***Title Change.*** (MENNOGESPRACH / MENNONITE HISTORICAL SOCIETY OF ONTARIO.). [MennogesprÈach]. **Added/Corp** Mennonite Historical Society of Ontario. Vol. 1, No. 1 (Mar. 1983)-Vol. 10, No. 2 (Sept. 1992). Periodical. English. sa. Mennonite Historical Society of Ontario, Conrad Grebel College, Waterloo Ontario N2L 3G6 Canada. **Tel** (519)885-0220. **ED** Samuel Steiner. **DD** 289.7/713/09. **Bk Rev. Circ:** 150. ***Continued by*** *Ontario Mennonite History, 1192-5515.*
**Desc:** Devoted to history and genealogy of Mennonites and Amish in Ontario, Canada.

US/0025-9330
**MENNONITE (1936), THE.** (THE MENNONITE.). [Mennonite]. **Added/Corp** General Conference Mennonite Church. Mennonite General Conference of North America. Vol. 51, No. 1 (Jan. 7, 1936)-. Periodical. English. sm. $23.30 (1 year), $40.77 (2 year), $56.13 (3 year) Kansas; $22.00 (1 year), $38.50 (2 year), $53.00 (3 year) US; $25.50 (1 year), $45.00 (2 year), $62.00 (3 year) Canada; $24.00 (surface mail) other; $46.00 airmail Mexico; $60.00 airmail South America; $70.00 airmail Europe; $84.00 airmail Asia. General Board, 722 Main Street, PO Box 347, Newton KS 67114. **Tel** (316)283-5100, FAX (316)283-0454. **ED** Gordon Houser. **DD** 289. Index available. **Bk Rev. Ad Acc. Circ:** 10000. available on microfilm and microfiche from University Microfilms International (UMI). ***Continues in part*** *Mennonite and the Christian Evangel.*
**Desc:** Features articles that teach Christian discipleship from a Mennonite perspective and news about the Christian world, particularly about the General Conference Mennonite Church.
**Ind/Abst** Guide Soc. Sci. Relig.

CN/0025-9349
**MENNONITE BRETHREN HERALD.** [Mennon. Brethren her.]. **Added/Corp** Canadian Conference of the Mennonite Brethren Church of North America. Vol. 1 (Jan. 19 1962)-. Periodical. English. Twenty-four times a year (Published on Friday). 24.00Can$ Canada: 30.00Can$ other. Mennonite Brethren Herald, 3 169 Riverton Avenue, Winnipeg Manitoba R2L 2E5 Canada. **Tel** (204)669-6575, FAX (204)654-1865. **ED** Ron Geddert. **DD** 289.7/71. Index available (Bound in 24th issue, in December). **Bk Rev,** (Qty: 50). **Ad Acc, Adv Mgr:** S. Brandt. **Circ:** 15,000 (ctrl).
**Desc:** Information for members of Mennonite Brethren

Churches, events in the church and the world at large, to meet the personal and corporate spiritual needs of members.

CN/0700-8066
**MENNONITE HISTORIAN. Added/Corp** Conference of Mennonites in Canada. History Archives Committee. Vol. 1 (Sept. 1975)-. Periodical. English. qt. 6.50Can$. Mennonite Heritage Centre, 600 Shartesbury Boulevard, Winnipeg Manitoba R3P 0M4 Canada. **Tel** (204)888-6781. **ED** Lawrence Klippenstein and Ken Reddig. **DD** 289.7/71. Index available. cum. index. **Bk Rev. Ad Acc. Circ:** 3,300 (ctrl).
**Desc:** A publication of historical articles and reports written in semi-popular style pertinent particularly to Mennonites of Canadian-Russian background.

US/0025-9357
**MENNONITE HISTORICAL BULLETIN.** [Mennon. hist. bull.]. **Added/Corp** Mennonite General Conference. Historical and Research Committee. Mennonite General Conference. Historical Committee. Vol. 1, Apr. (1940)-. Bulletin. English. qt (Jan., Apr., July, Oct.). $20.00. Mennonite Historical Bulletin, 1700 South Main Street, Goshen IN 46526. **Tel** (219)535-7477. **ED** Levi Miller. **LC** BX8101; .M38. Index available. cum. index. **Bk Rev**, (Qty: 16/yr). **Circ:** 400. available on microfilm and microfiche from University Microfilms International (UMI).
**Desc:** A publication which covers all aspects of Mennonite and Anabaptist history including book reviews, recent publications, interpretive and descriptive articles.
**Ind/Abst** Am. Hist. Life (1969-1978).

US/0025-9365
**MENNONITE LIFE.** [Mennon. life]. **Added/Corp** Bethel College (North Newton, Kan.). Vol. 1, (Jan. 1946)-. Periodical. English. Four times a year (Mar., June, Sept., Dec.). $15.00 (one year); $22.00 (two years). Bethel College Mennonite Library & Archives, North Newton KS 67117. **Tel** (316)283-2500, FAX (316)284-5286. **ED** James C. Juhnke. **LC** BX8101; .M39. **DD** 289.705. Index available. cum. index. **Bk Rev**, (Qty: 20). **Circ:** 700 (ctrl). available on microfilm and microfiche from University Microfilms International (UMI).
**Desc:** Illustrated articles related to Mennonite/Anabaptist history, faith, life and culture
**Ind/Abst** Am. Hist. Life (1963-); Am. Bibliogr. Slavic East Europ. Stud.; ARTbibliogr. Mod.; Index Book Rev. Relig.; Relig. Index One Period. (1980-); Relig. Theol. Abstr.

US/0025-9373
**MENNONITE QUARTERLY REVIEW, THE.** [Mennon. q. rev.]. **Added/Corp** Goshen College, Goshen, Ind. Goshen College, Goshen, Ind. Mennonite Historical Society. Mennonite Historical Society. Vol 1 (Jan 1927)-. Periodical. English. qt (Jan., Apr., July, Oct.). $19.00 (clergy), $24.00 (other) US & Canada; $20.00 (clergy), $25.00 (other) other. Mennonite Quarterly Review, Goshen College, Goshen IN 46526. **Tel** (219)535-7111. **ED** John D. Roth. **LC** BX8101; .M4. **DD** 289.7/05. Index available (bound in Oct. issue). cum. index. **Bk Rev**, (Qty: 40-45). **Circ:** 950. available on microfilm from AMS Press, Inc. ***Supersedes*** *Goshen College Record. Review Supplement.*
**Desc:** Promotes interest in and dissemination of information concerning Anabaptist-Mennonite as well as Amish and Hutterite history, thought, life, and current affairs.
**Ind/Abst** Am. Hist. Life (1954-); Am. Bibliogr. Slavic East Europ. Stud.; Index Book Rev. Relig.; Recent. Publ. Artic.; Ref. Sources; Relig. Index One Period. (1949-); Relig. Theol. Abstr.; Sage Race Relat. Abstr.; Writ. Am. Hist.

US/0275-1178
**MENNONITE YEARBOOK & DIRECTORY. VFOAT** Mennonite Yearbook. **VAT** Mennonite Year Book and Directory; Mennonite Yearbook and Directory. V. 1 (1910)-. Directory. English. be. $7.95. Mennonite Publishing House, 616 Walnut Avenue, Scottsdale PA 15683-1999. **Tel** (412)887-8500, FAX (412)887-3111. **ED** James E Horsch. **LC** BX8107; .M4. **DD** 289.7. **UDC** 289.7(058). **Circ:** 5,000.
**Desc:** Information concerning the ministers, congregations, boards and institutions of the Mennonite Church (MC) in North America, worldwide and inter Mennonite relationships noted.

GW/0342-1171
**MENNONITISCHE GESCHICHTSBLATTER.** [Mennon. Geschichtsbl.]. **Added/Corp** Mennonitischer Geschichtsverein (Germany). (Nov. 1936)-. Periodical. German. an. DM53.50. Mennonitischer Geschichtsverei, Christel Schultz Blumenweg 28, 63128 Dietzenbach Germany. **Tel** 011 49 6074 3546. **LC** BX8101; .M46.

CN/0705-4041
**MENNONITISCHE POST.** (DIE MENNONITISCHE POST.). [Mennon. Post]. Vol. 1 (April 21, 1977)-. Newspaper. German (English). sm. $20.00. Die Mennonitische Post, PO Box 1120, Steinbach Manitoba R0A 2A0 Canada. **Tel** (204)326-6790. **ED** Abe Wankertin. **DD** 289.7/05. **Circ:** 5,500.
**Desc:** A paper for Mennonite colonists in Latin America and their 'kin' in North America. Content is letters and news and religious articles.

US/0026-0231
**MESSAGE (NASHVILLE, TENN.).** (MESSAGE.). [Message]. **Added/Corp** Southern Publishing Association. Review and Herald Publishing Association. Vol. 44, No. 3 (May/June 1978)-. Periodical. English. Six times a year. $8.97 US; $14.07 other. Review and Herald Publishing Association, 55 West Oak Ridge Drive, Hagerstown MD 21740. **Tel** (301)791-7000 ext. 2534, FAX (301)790-9734. **ED** Delbert W. Baker. **LC** BX6101; .M4. **DD** 286.7/3. **Bk Rev. Circ:** 100,000. ***Continues*** *Message Magazine, 0162-6019.*
**Desc:** A Christian magazine of contemporary issues primary focus is a black minority readership. It appeals to an interdenominational audience with readers mainly in the US and also abroad.
**Ind/Abst** Seventh-Day Adventist Period. Index (1971-).

US/0026-1238
**METHODIST HISTORY.** [Methodist hist.]. **Added/Corp** United Methodist Church (U.S.). Commission on Archives and History. Association of Methodist Historical Societies. United Methodist Church (U.S.). General Commission on Archives and History. Vol. 1 (Oct. 1962)-. Periodical. English. qt. $10.00 (one year) students, $15.00 (one year), $25.00 (two year), $45.00 (four year) US; $12.00 (one year) students, $17.00 (one year), $29.00 (two year), $ 51.00 (four year) other. General Commission on Archives and History, The United Methodist Church, PO Box 127, 36 Madison Avenue, Madison NJ 07940. **Tel** (201)822-2787, FAX (201)408-3909. **ED** Charles Yrigoyen (201)408-3189. **LC** BX8235; .M44. **DD** 287/.05. Index available. cum. index. **Bk Rev**, (Qty: 15-20). **Ad Acc. Circ:** 1,000 (ctrl). available on microfilm and microfiche from University Microfilms International (UMI). ***Supersedes in part*** *World Parish, 0510-9272.*
**Desc:** Articles, book reviews and news on the history of the United Methodist Church and its antecedent bodies and the Wesleyan-Methodist heritage.
**Ind/Abst** Am. Hist. Life (1962-); Index Book Rev. Relig.; Index Relig. Period. Lit.; Relig. Index One Period. (1964-); Relig. Theol. Abstr.; United Methodist Period. Index; Writ. Am. Hist.

UK
**METHODIST RECORDER.** No. 1 (April 4, 1861)-. Periodical. English. wk. £27.50 UK; £41.50 Europe; £43.50 US & Canada; £57.00 other. Methodist Newspaper Company Ltd, 122 Golden Lane, London EC1Y 0TL England. **Tel** 01-251 8414, FAX 01-608 3490. **ED** Michael Taylor. **Bk Rev. Ad Acc, Adv Mgr:** R. Blanchard. **Circ:** 25,317. available on microfilm from World Microfilm Publications Ltd. ***Absorbed*** *United Methodist* ***and*** *Methodist Times and Leader.*
**Desc:** British and world Methodist Church news with articles on religious and social issues. Also general church interest features and advertising.

SW
**METODISTKYRKANS I SVERIGE ARSBOK. Main/Corp** Methodist Church (Sweden). Swedish. NYA Bokforlaags AB, Sibyllegatan 18 III, 114 42 0, Stockholm Sweden. **LC** BX8310.S87; M39A. **UDC** 287(485).

CN/0823-2555
**MINISTERE DU ROYAUME POUR LE CANADA, LE.** [Minst. roy. Can.]. Vol. 25, No. 1 (Jan. 1982)-. Periodical. French. mo. Temoins de Jehova, Canadian Branch, C P 4100, Georgetown Ontario L7G 4Y4 Canada. **DD** 289.9/2/05. **UDC** 289.9(71). ***Continues*** *Service du Royaume, 0710-1473.*

CN/0823-2571
**MINISTERO DEL REGNO PER IL CANADA, IL.** Vol. 25, No. 1 (Jan. 1982)-. Periodical. Italian. mo. Watch Tower Bible and Tract Society / Canadian Branch, PO Box 4100, Georgetown Ontario L7G 4Y4 Canada. **Tel** (718)625-3600. **DD** 289.9/2/05. **UDC** 289.9(71). ***Continues*** *Servizio del Regno, 0382-4802.*

US/0895-9056
**MINISTRY DEVELOPMENT JOURNAL.** ***Ceased.*** [Minist. dev. j.]. **Added/Corp** Episcopal Church. Education for Mission and Ministry. (Spring 1983)-(199?). Periodical. English. qt. Episcopal Church Center, 815 Second Avenue, New York NY 10017. **DD** 283.

CN/0317-9583
**MINUTES - ANNUAL CONVENTION OF THE EASTERN CANADA SYNOD, LUTHERAN CHURCH IN AMERICA. Main/Corp** Lutheran Church in America. Eastern Canada Synod. Convention. **VAT** Minutes - Eastern Canada Synod; Minutes. Annual Convention - Easter Canada Synod. Lutheran Church in America. 1st- 1962-. English. an. Eastern Canada Synod, Luthern Church in America, 251 King Street, Kitchener Ontario N2G 1B5. **DD** 284/.1/71. **UDC** 284.1(71).

US
**MINUTES / THE ... GENERAL SYNOD OF THE UNITED CHURCH OF CHRIST. Main/Corp** United Church of Christ. General Synod. 2nd (1959)-. English. be. $3.00. Office of the Secretary UCC, 287 Park Ave. South, New York NY 10010. **LC** WMLC L 83/3516. **UDC** 289.94. ***Continues*** *United Church of Christ. Uniting General Synod. Minutes.*

US/0082-8548
**MINUTES - UNITED PRESBYTERIAN CHURCH IN THE U.S.A. Main/Corp** United Presbyterian Church in the U.S.A. General Assembly. New Ser. V. 1-23, 1870-1900. English. an. United Presbyterian Church in US, 475 Riverside Drive/Room 1244, New York NY 10027. **Tel** (212)870-2040. **LC** BX895L; .A4. **DD** 285.1. **UDC** 285. ***Continues*** *Minutes of the General Assembly of the Presbyterian Church in the U.S.A.*
**Desc:** Vol. for 1958 includes also the Minutes of the final General Assembly of the United Presbyterian Church of North America and the minutes of the final General Assembly of the Presbyteruan.

AT
**MISSION.** English. qt. 5.00Aus$ Australia; 8.00Aus$ (surface mail), 9.00Aus$ (air mail) other. Australian Churches of Christ, 180A Gray Street, Adelaide 5000 Australia. **Tel** 011 61 8 2124446, FAX 011 61 8 2126388. **Circ:** 3,800. ***Continues*** *Missionary News.*

US/1058-0565
**MISSION AND MINISTRY.** [Mission minist.]. **Added/Corp** Episcopal Church. Fellowship of Witness. Trinity Episcopal School for Ministry. Vol. 1, No. 1, (1982)-. Periodical. English. qt. $12.00 US; $20.00 other. Trinity Episcopal School for Ministry, 311 Eleventh Street, Ambridge PA 15003. **Tel** (412)266-3838, FAX (412)266-4617. **ED** David Mills. **LC** BX5925; .M58. **DD** 283/.05. **Bk Rev. Pr Rev. Circ:** 1,500. ***Continues*** *Kerygma.*
**Desc:** Theological reflection and pastoral instruction for clergy and laity.

FR/0760-2626
**MISSION (DEPARTEMENT EVANGELIQUE FRANCAIS D'ACTION APOSTOLIQUE).** (MISSION.). **Added/Corp** Departement Evangelique Francais d'Action Apostolique. (March 15, 1990)-. Periodical. French. Ten times a year. 165.00F France; 200.00F other. Dept Evangelique Francais Act, 102 Boulevard Arago, Paris 75014 France. **Tel** 011 33 1 43207095, FAX 011 33 1 43350055, telex 206959F. **ED** Jean Alexandre. cum. index. **Bk Rev**, (Qty: 5). **Ad Acc. Circ:** 4,100. ***Continues*** *Journal des Missions Evangeliques, 0760-2626.*
**Desc:** Information and news about the Protestant missionary.

US/0164-4696
**MISSION-FOCUS.** ***Ceased.*** **Added/Corp** Mennonite Church. Board of Missions. Vol. 1 (Sept. 1972)-. Periodical. English. qt. Mennonite Board of Missions, 500 South Main Street, Box 370, Elkhart IN 46515. **Tel** (219)294-7523, telex 6503231818 MCIUW. **ED** Wilbert R Shenk. Index available. **Bk Rev. Circ:** 1,700.
**Desc:** To provide an inter-Mennonite tool, review missionary experience and practice from a believers' free church perspective and stimulate serious reflection on the mission of the church.

UK
**MISSIONARY HERALD (LONDON, ENGLAND : 1921).** (MISSIONARY HERALD : THE MONTHLY MAGAZINE OF THE BAPTIST MISSIONARY SOCIETY.). **Added/Corp** Baptist Missionary Society. Vol. 103 (Jan. 1921)-. Periodical. English. Ten times a year (monthly with July/Aug. and Nov./Dec. issues combined). £9.40 UK; £15.90 others. Baptist Missionary Society, PO Box 49 Baptist House, Didcot Oxon. 0X11 8XA England. **Tel** 011 44 235 512077, FAX 011 44 235 511265. **ED** David Pountain. **Ad Acc.** ctrl circ. ***Continues*** *Herald (Baptist Missionary Society).*
**Desc:** Baptist world mission Third World issues including agriculture, rural development, education, preventive medicine, health education, and relations with churches overseas.

US/0279-5345
**MISSIONS USA.** [Missions USA]. **Added/Corp** Southern Baptist Convention. Home Mission Board. **VAT** Missions United States of America. Vol. 52, No. 1 (Jan.-Feb. 1981)-. Periodical. English. Six times a year. Southern Baptist Convention / Georgia, 1350 Spring NW, Atlanta GA 30309. **Tel** (404)873-4041. **LC** BV2520.A1; H6. **DD** 266/.6173. ***Continues*** *Home Missions, 0018-408X.*
**Ind/Abst** South. Baptist Period. Index.

GW
**MITTEILUNGEN : DER STUDIENGEMEINSCHAFT FUER GESCHICHTE DER EVANGELISCH METHODISTISCHEN KIRCHE.** German. ir. DM19.80. Christliches Verlagshaus GmbH, Postfach 311141, Motorstrasse 36, D-70471 Stuttgart Germany. **Tel** 011 49 711 830000, FAX 011 49 711 83000-10.

GW
**MITTEILUNGSBLATT DES BUNDES DER EVANGELISCHEN KIRCHEN IN DER DEUTSCHEN DEMOKRATISCHEN REPUBLIK.** **Main/Corp** Bund der Evangelischen Kirchen in der DDR. (19??)-. German. Six times a year. DM6.00. Verlag Evangelische Verlagsanstalt GmbH, Auguststrasse 80, 1040 Berlin Germany. **Tel** 2886-242. **ED** Werner Leich. **LC** BX8018; .B85a. **DD** 284/.143/1. **Circ:** 2,800 (ctrl).
**Desc:** Official statements, laws and orders of the Protestant church in East Germany.

US
**MODERN REFORMATION.** English. Six times a year. $18.00 (one year); $36.00 (two year). Christians United Reformation, 2034 East Lincoln Avenue, Suite 209, Anaheim CA 92806. **Tel** (714)956-2873. **ED** Sara McReynolds.

US/0360-6171
**MONDAY MORNING (INDIANAPOLIS, IND.).** (MONDAY MORNING.). [Monday morning]. (1936)-. Periodical. English. Twenty-one times a year (Twice monthly except monthly June-Aug.). $12.00. Monday Morning / Kentucky, 100 Witherspoon Street, Louisville KY 40202. **Tel** (502)569-5755, FAX (502)569-5018. **ED** Kevin Piecuh. **DD** 253. **Bk Rev. Ad Acc. Circ:** 23,000 (ctrl).
**Desc:** A magazine for Presbyterian leaders. A free and open forum for all.

UK
**MONTHLY RECORD OF THE FREE CHURCH OF SCOTLAND, THE.** **Main/Corp** Free Church of Scotland. (1901)-. Periodical. English. mo. £10.00. Free Church of Scotland, 15 North Bank Street, The Mound, Edinburgh EH1 2LS Scotland. **Tel** 011 44 31 2265286, FAX 011 44 31 2200597. **ED** Rev R. C. Christie. **Bk Rev. Circ:** 7,000. ***Supersedes in part** Free Church of Scotland Monthly.*
**Desc:** Official magazine of the Free Church of Scotland, committed to the reformed, evangelical, protestant faith.

US/0273-2114
**MOTIF (SPRINGFIELD).** **See** Music.

JA
**MUKYOKAISHUGI NO JIKO TENKEN.** No. 1 (1978)-. Periodical. Japanese. Okawara Reizo, 5-16 Higashi Gotanda 5, Shinagawa-ku 141, Tokyo Japan. **LC** BX8699.M8; M79.

CN/0711-1843
**MUSTARD SEED.** (THE MUSTARD SEED / THE DIOCESE OF BRANDON OF THE ANGLICAN CHURCH.). **Added/Corp** Anglican Church of Canada. Diocese of Brandon. (19??)-. Periodical. English. Ten times a year. 5.00Can$. Diocese of Brandon, 341 13th Street, Brandon Manitoba R7A 4P8 Canada. **Tel** (204)727-7142. **DD** 283/.71273/05.

US/1058-5907
**NATIONAL BAPTIST PREACHERWOMAN SERMON SERIES, THE.** [Natl. Baptist preacherwoman sermon ser.]. **VFOAT** Preacherwoman Sermon Series. Vol. 1 (1991)-. Periodical. English. be. $6.00. Mays Commercial Services, c/o P. A. Singletary, 122-59 Nellis Street, Springfield Gardens NY 11413. **DD** 252.

US/1061-6225
**NATIONAL BAPTIST WOMEN CLERGY DIRECTORY, THE.** (THE NATIONAL BAPTIST WOMEN CLERGY ... DIRECTORY / SPIRITUAL LIFE COMMISSION, WOMEN'S AUXILIARY, NATIONAL BAPTIST CONVENTION, U.S.A., INC.). [Natl. Baptist women clergy dir.]. **Main/Corp** National Baptist Convention of the United States of America. Spiritual Life Commission. (1991)-. Directory. English. Reverend E Miller, 10728 Worden Street, Detroit MI 48224. **LC** BX6453; .N37. **DD** 286.

US/1061-4486
**NEBRASKA EPISCOPALIAN, THE.** [Neb. Episcop.]. **Added/Corp** Episcopal Church. Diocese of Nebraska. (1991)-. Periodical. English. mo. Episcopalian Diocese of Nebraska, Nancy Hansen, Nebraska Episcopalian, 200 North 62 Street, Omaha NE 68132. **DD** 283. ***Continues** Nebraska Churchman.*

US/0745-2705
**NEBRASKA LUTHERAN.** (NEBRASKA LUTHERAN / NEBRASKA SYNOD.). **Added/Corp** Lutheran Church in America. Nebraska Synod. (19??)-. Periodical. English. qt. Nebraska Lutheran, Waterloo NE 68069. **Tel** (402)341-4155. **ED** Roger Bruns. **Circ:** 31,000.

US/0745-418X
**NETWORK NEWS (BLUFFTON, OHIO).** (NETWORK NEWS : OFFICIAL PUBLICATION OF THE WITHERSPOON SOCIETY OF PRESBYTERIANS.). **Added/Corp** Witherspoon Society (Fort Wayne, Ind.). (19??)-. Periodical. English. Six times a year. $20.00. Witherspoon Society, 4355 Kenyon Road, c/o Hank Bremer, Los Angeles' CA 90066. **ED** Willem Bodisco Massink. **Bk Rev. Circ:** 1,100.
**Desc:** Seeks to assist and report efforts of the Society's members to confess their loyalty to God in Jesus Christ by bearing witness to him through the Presbyterian Church in areas of peace and justice.
**Ind/Abst** Music Artic. Guide.

US/0275-0805
**NEW CHURCH LIFE.** [New church life]. **Added/Corp** General Church of the New Jerusalem. Vol. 1 (Jan. 1881)-. Periodical. English. mo. $12.00 US; $36.72 other. General Church of the New Jerusalem, Box 278, Bryn Athyn PA 19009. **Tel** (215)947-6225. **ED** Donald L Rose. **LC** BX8701; .N5. **DD** 289.4/05. Index available. cum. index. **Bk Rev. Circ:** 2,000.
**Desc:** Presents the religious works of Emanuel Swedenborg, the focus of this journal for more than 100 years, and the church founded thereon.

US/0746-7702
**NEW DISCIPLES TEACHER, THE.** Vol. 1, No. 1 (1st Quarter, Jan./Feb./Mar. 1984)-. Periodical. English. qt. National Baptist Publishing Board, 7145 Centennial Boulevard, Nashville TN 37209. **UDC** 286.1.

US/0891-3137
**NEW ENGLAND BAPTIST (NORTHBOROUGH, MASS.), THE.** (THE NEW ENGLAND BAPTIST : SERVING SOUTHERN BAPTISTS IN NEW ENGLAND.). [N. Engl. Baptist]. **Added/Corp** Baptist Convention of New England. Baptist General Association of New England. Vol. 1, No. 1 (197?)-. Periodical. English. Twelve times a year. Free to New England; $2.50 others. The New England Baptist, PO Box 688, 5 Oak Avenue, Northborough MA 20688. **Tel** (6170393-6013. **ED** James H. Currin. **DD** 286.

US/0363-6968
**NEW LIFE (DENVER).** ***Suspended.*** (NEW LIFE.). **Added/Corp** Anchor Society. Vol. 1 (July 1973)-(19??). Periodical. English. mo. Korean Community Service, 6125 Carlos Avenue, Hollywood CA 90028. **Tel** (213)466-4145 ext. 8. **LC** BX5800; .N49. **DD** 283/.05.

US/0043-8812
**NEW WORLD OUTLOOK.** [New world outlook]. **Added/Corp** United Methodist Church (U.S.). Joint Commission on Education and Cultivation. United Methodist Church (U.S.). Board of Global Ministries. Education and Cultivation Division. United Methodist Church (U.S.). Mission Education and Cultivation Program Dept. Vol. 60, No. 2 (Feb. 1970)-. Periodical. English. Six times a year (Jan., Mar., May, July, Sept., Nov.). $12.00. Board of Global Ministries, 475 Riverside Drive, Room 1351, New York NY 10115. **Tel** (212)870-3765, FAX (212)870-3940. **ED** Alma Graham. **LC** BV2550; .N45. **DD** 287. **Bk Rev**, (Qty: 2-4). **Ad Acc, Adv Mgr:** Ruth Kurtz. **Circ:** 35,000. ***Formed by the union of** New and World Outlook.*
**Desc:** Features articles and photos on the US and world missions, missionaries, and mission projects.
**Ind/Abst** Middle East Abstr. Index.

CN/0703-5888
**NIAGARA ANGLICAN, THE.** V. 1- Jan. 1955-. Periodical. English. mo (except July and August). 5.00Can$ Canada; 10.00Can$ US. Synod Office / Diocese of Niagara, Diocese of Niagara, 67 Victoria Avenue South, Hamilton Ontario L8N 2S8 Canada. **Tel** (416)527-1117. **ED** Larry Perks. **DD** 283/.713/52. **UDC** 283(73). **Circ:** 20,500.
**Desc:** Award winning member of the Canadian Church Press. One of 19 diocesan papers. Independently edited.

US/0745-2195
**NORTHWEST BAPTIST WITNESS.** (19??)-. Periodical. English. ir (18 to 21 per year). $5.00 (one year), $12.00 (three year). Northwest Baptist Witness, 1033 Northeast 6th Avenue, Portland OR 97232. **Tel** (503)238-4545. **ED** James L. Watters. **Bk Rev. Circ:** 15,000 (ctrl).
**Desc:** Publishes to inform readers of issues and events related to Baptists' life and work around the world.

CN/1180-5323
**NORTHWEST EVANGELICAL BAPTIST JOURNAL.** [Northw. Evang. Baptist j.]. **Added/Corp** Northwest Baptist Theological College and Seminary. Vol. 1, No. 1 (Feb. 1991)-. Periodical. English. sa. Limited free distribution. Northwest Baptist Theological College and Seminary, PO Box 790, Langley British Columbia V3A 8B8 Canada. **DD** 286.

US/0029-3512
**NORTHWESTERN LUTHERAN (MILWAUKEE, WIS.), THE.** (THE NORTHWESTERN LUTHERAN.). **Added/Corp** Wisconsin Evangelical Lutheran Synod. Vol. 1 (1914)-. Periodical. English. sm (except monthly in July, Aug., and Dec.). $8.50. Northwestern Publishing House, 1250 North 113th Street, Milwaukee WI 53226-3284. **Tel** (414)475-6600, FAX (414)475-7684. **ED** Rev. James P. Schaeffer. Index available. **Circ:** 60,000. available on audiocassette.

CN/0823-2598
**NOSSO MINISTERIO DO REINO PARA O CANADA.** [Nosso minist. reino Can.]. Vol. 25, N. 1 (Jan. 1982)-. Periodical. Portuguese. mo. Watch Tower Bible and Tract Society / Canadian Branch, PO Box 4100, Georgetown Ontario L7G 4Y4 Canada. **Tel** (718)625-3600. **DD** 289.9/2/05. **UDC** 289.954(71).

CN/0823-258X
**NUESTRO MINISTERIO DEL REINO PARA EL CANADA.** [Nuestro minist. reino Can.]. V. 25, No. 1 (Jan. 1982)-. Periodical. Spanish. mo. Watch Tower Bible and Tract Society / Canadian Branch, PO Box 4100, Georgetown Ontario L7G 4Y4 Canada. **Tel** (718)625-3600. **DD** 289.9/2/05. **UDC** 289.954(71).

US
**OFFICIAL REPORT OF THE ... CONGRESS.** **Main/Conf** Baptist World Congress. **VFOAT** Truth That Makes Men Free; Celebrating Christs's Presence Through the Spirit. 11th (1965)-. English. ir. Baptist World Alliance, 6733 Curran Street, McLean VA 22101. **Tel** (703)790-8980, FAX (703)893-5160. **UDC** 286.01(063). ***Continues** Baptist World Congress (5th-10th : 1934-1960). Official Report.*

BE/0772-3326
**ONDERNEMEN.** [Ondernemen]. (1968)-. Periodical. Dutch. Ten times a year (Except July & Aug.). 1400F. Orgaan VH Verbond Christelijke Werkgevers, Kaderleden Tervuren, 463 1160 Brussels Belgium. **Tel** 02/773 16 90, FAX 02/773 16 00. **UDC** 335. Index available. **Bk Rev. Ad Acc. Pr Rev.** ***Continues** De Christelijke Werkgever (1945), 0772-3369.*

US/8750-5754
**OUTLOOK (GRAND RAPIDS, MICH.), THE.** (THE OUTLOOK.). Vol. 21, No. 6 (June 1971)-. Periodical. English. mo. $15.00 US; $17.00 Canada. Reformed Fellowship Inc, 4855 Starr Street SE, Grand Rapids MI 49546. **Tel** (616)949-5421. **ED** Peter de Jong. **DD** 200. **UDC** 284. Index available. **Bk Rev. Circ:** 4,500 (ctrl). ***Continues** Christian Reformed Outlook, 0732-5177; Torch and Trumpet.*
**Desc:** Gives sharpened expression to the reformed faith, to promote the spiritual welfare and purity of the Christian.

CN/0826-0877
**PAPERS / CANADIAN METHODIST HISTORICAL SOCIETY.** [Pap. - Can. Methodist Hist. Soc.]. **Main/Corp** Canadian Methodist Historical Society. Began with V. 1 (1978). Periodical. English. an. 10.00Can$ Canada; $8.00 US. Canadian Methodist Historical Society, c/o United Church Archives, Victoria University, 73 Queen's Park Crescent, Toronto Ontario M5S 1K7 Canada. **Tel** (416)585-4563. **ED** James Dale. **DD** 287/.0971. **UDC** 287(71). **Circ:** 40 (ctrl).
**Desc:** Papers presented to annual conference of Canadian Methodist Historical Society related to social, religious, and theological history of Methodism especially in Canada.

US/0190-4639
**PARACLETE (SPRINGFIELD, MO.).** (PARACLETE.). **Added/Corp** Assemblies of God. Spritual Life-Evangelism Commission. Assemblies of God. General Council. (1967)-. Periodical. English. qt (Jan., Apr., July, Oct.). $7.50 US; $9.50 other. Gospel Publishing House, 1445 Boonville Avenue, Springfield MO 65802. **Tel** (417)862-2781, FAX (417)866-1146. **ED** David R Bundrick. Index available. cum. index. **Bk Rev. Ad Acc. Circ:** 3,650 (ctrl). available on microfilm and microfiche from University Microfilms International (UMI).
**Desc:** Journal concerning the person and work of the Holy Spirit.
**Ind/Abst** Christ. Period. Index; Guide Soc. Sci. Relig.; Index Book Rev. Relig.; Relig. Index One Period.; Relig. Theol. Abstr.

US
**PATHWAY OF TRUTH.** English. Twelve times a year. $3.00. Pathway of Truth, Route 2 / Box 78, Holly Pond AL 35083. **Tel** (205)796-2232. **ED** Guy Hunt (editor's address: 285 County Road 1711, Holly Pond, AL 35083). **Circ:** 400.
**Desc:** A Primitive Baptist publication.

US/0195-1815
**PENN JERSEY BAPTIST.** **Added/Corp** Baptist Convention of Pennsylvania/South Jersey. (1970)-. Periodical. English. mo (with Jun/Jul and Nov/Dec issues combined). $7.00. Penn-Jersey Baptist, 4620 Fritchey Street, Harrisburg PA 17109. **Tel** (717)652-5856. **Circ:** 6,500.
**Desc:** Articles pertaining to life and work of Southern Baptists and around the world.

US/0360-9782
**PENSION BOARDS.** (PENSION BOARDS - UNITED CHURCH OF CHRIST.). **Main/Corp** United Church of Christ. (1967)-. English. an. United Church of Christ / New York, 287 Park Avenue South, New York NY 10010. **LC** BX7245.5; .U53A. **DD** 658.32/53.

CN/0226-9848
**PENTECOSTAL ASSEMBLIES OF CANADA. YOUTH DEPT. WESTERN ONTARIO DISTRICT.** (LOOK INSIDE.). [Look inside]. Vol. 1, No. 1 (Winter 1975)-. Periodical. English. qt. Free. Look Inside, 3419 Mainway, Burlington Ontario L7M 1A9 Canada. **DD** 259/.2. **UDC** 289.9(713). ctrl circ.

US/0031-4897
**PENTECOSTAL EVANGEL. Added/Corp** Assemblies of God. General Council. (1913)-. Periodical. English. wk. $15.95 US; $29.95 other. Gospel Publishing House, 1445 Boonville Avenue, Springfield MO 65802. **Tel** (417)862-2781, FAX (417)866-1146. **ED** Richard Champion. **LC** BX6198.A7; P45. **DD** 289.9. Index available. **Bk Rev**. **Ad Acc. Circ:** 275,000. available on microfilm.
**Desc:** Official magazine of the Assemblies of God.
**Ind/Abst** Guide Soc. Sci. Relig.

US/0745-2330
**PENTECOSTAL FREE-WILL BAPTIST MESSENGER. VFOAT** Messenger. V. 1- 1938-. Periodical. English. mo. $4.20. Pentecostal Free Will Baptist Church Inc, PO Box 1568, Dunn NC 28334. **Tel** (919)892-4161. **ED** Donna Hammond. **UDC** 289.9. **Bk Rev. Circ:** 15,000.
**Desc:** Informative, devotional and promotional magazine for the Pentecostal Free Will Baptist denomination.

US/0031-4919
**PENTECOSTAL MESSENGER, THE. Added/Corp** Pentecostal Church of God of America. (1926)-. Periodical. English. mo (except July). $11.00 (one year), $19.00 (two year), $26.00 (three year) US; $18.00 (one year), $33.00 (two year), $47.00 (three year) other. Messenger Publishing House, PO Box 850, Joplin MO 64802. **Tel** (417)624-7050. **ED** Don Allen. **Bk Rev. Ad Acc, Adv Mgr:** P. Allen. **Circ:** 7,500.
**Desc:** Inspirational and devotional articles and reports. For ministers and adult church members. Exists to encourage spiritual growth in the members while inspiring, informing, and challenging.

PL
**PIELGRZYM POLSKI.** (1926)-. Periodical. Polish. mo. Price on Request. **(Subscription address:** ARS Polona, PO Box 1001, 00068 Warsaw Poland.**) LC** BX8201; .P54.

US/0272-0965
**PNEUMA (SPRINGFIELD).** (PNEUMA; THE JOURNAL OF THE SOCIETY FOR PENTECOSTAL STUDIES.). [Pneuma]. **Added/Corp** Society for Pentecostal Studies. Vol. 1 (Spring 1979)-. Periodical. English. sa. $24.00 (one year), $48.00 (two year), $72.00 (three year) institutions US, Canada and Mexico; $28.00 (one year), $56.00 (two year), $84.00 (three year) institutions other; $18.00 (one year), $36.00 (two year), $54.00 (three year) individuals US, Canada and Mexico; $22.00 (one year), $44.00 (two year), $66.00 (three year) individuals other. Society for Pentecostal Studies, PO Box 2671, Gaithersburg MD 20886. **Tel** (301)990-2060, FAX (301)990-2087. **ED** Murray W Dempster (Editor's Address: Southern California College, 55 Fair Drive, Costa Mesa, CA 92626). **LC** BR1644; .P57. **DD** 270.8/2. **Bk Rev. Circ:** 500. available on microfilm from TREN; available on microfilm and microfiche from University Microfilms International (UMI).
**Desc:** Biblical, theological, historical, and sociological studies related to the Pentecostal and Charismatic movements.
**Ind/Abst** Index Book Rev. Relig.; Relig. Index One Period. (1980-).

FR/0032-5228
**POSITIONS LUTHERIENNES.** (1953)-. Periodical. French. Four times a year. 170.62F France; 250.00F others. Positions Lutheriennes, 16 rue Chauchat, 75009 Paris France. **Tel** 011 33 1 45821999. **Bk Rev.**
**Desc:** Religious sciences - church history, ethics, ecumenism, explanation and critical interpretations of text, musicology.

IE/0032-7530
**PRESBYTERIAN HERALD : THE RECORD OF THE PRESBYTERIAN CHURCH IN IRELAND, THE. Added/Corp** Presbyterian Church in Ireland. No. 1 (Jan. 1944)-. Periodical. English. mo. 7.80p (UK including Northern Ireland); 9.50p (other). Presbyterian Church in Ireland Fisherwick, Publs Bd Church House, Fisherwick, Belfast BT1 6DW Ireland. **Tel** 11 353 1 225777. **ED** Robert Cobain. available on microfilm from University Microfilms International (UMI). ***Absorbed** Missionary Herald of the Presbyterian Church in Ireland; Witness (Belfast); Irish Presbyterian.*

US/0361-2724
**PRESBYTERIAN KEY, THE. Added/Corp** Presbyterian Historical Society. V. 1 (1945)-. English. ir. Presbyterian Historical Society, 425 Lombard Street, Philadelphia PA 19147. **Tel** (215)627-1852.

US/0555-0572
**PRESBYTERIAN LAYMAN, THE. Added/Corp** Presbyterian Lay Committee. Vol. 1 (Jan. 1968)-. Periodical. English. Six times a year. Free. Presbyterian Layman, 1489 Baltimore Pike, Suite 301, Spring Field PA 19064-3989. **Tel** (215)543-0227. **ED** James J. Cochran. **Bk Rev. Circ:** 560,000 (ctrl).
**Desc:** Presbyterian church (USA) related, independent, evangelical, advocacy publication.

US/0032-7565
**PRESBYTERIAN OUTLOOK (RICHMOND, VA.).** (PRESBYTERIAN OUTLOOK.). [Presbyt. outl.]. Periodical. English. ir (44 no. a year). Outlook Publishers Inc, 512 East Main Street, Richmond VA 23219. **Tel** (804)649-1371. **DD** 285. **UDC** 285.1. available on microfilm and microfiche from University Microfilms International (UMI). ***Continues** Presbyterian of the South and the Presbyterian Standard; **Absorbed** Presbyterian Tribune.*

CN/0032-7573
**PRESBYTERIAN RECORD (MONTREAL).** ***Title Change.*** (THE PRESBYTERIAN RECORD.). [Presbyt. rec. (Montr.)]. **Added/Corp** Presbyterian Church in Canada. General Assembly. Presbyterian Church in Canada. **VFOAT** Record. Vol. 25, No. 1 (Jan. 1899)-?. Periodical. English. mo (except August). Presbyterian Record, 50 Wynford Drive, Don Mills Ontario M3C 1J7 Canada. **Tel** (416)441-1111. **ED** John Congram. **LC** BX8901; .P79. **DD** 285.171. Index available. **Bk Rev. Ad Acc. Circ:** 70,000. ***Continues** Record (Presbyterian Church in Canada). **Continued by** Presbyterian Record (Montreal, Quebec), 0032-7573.*
**Desc:** The national magazine of the Presbyterian church in Canada. Unsubsidized, independent editorial policy. Pays contributors.
**Ind/Abst** Can. Index; Can. Period. Index (19??-); Peace Res. Abstr. J. (1965-1966).

US/0032-759X
**PRESBYTERIAN SURVEY. Added/Corp** Presbyterian Church in the U.S. Vol. 1 (Nov. 1911)-. Periodical. English. Ten times a year (Jan/Feb. and July/Aug. issue combined). $11.00. Presbyterian Church (USA), 100 Witherspoon St, Room 5628, Louisville KY 40202. **Tel** (502)569-5637, FAX (502)569-8073. **ED** Catherine Cottingham. **LC** BV2570.A1; P64. **DD** 266.51. Index available. **Bk Rev**, (Qty: 15). **Ad Acc, Adv Mgr Tel** (502)569-5634. **Circ:** 95,000 (ctrl). available on microfilm and microfiche from University Microfilms International (UMI). ***Formed by the union of** Missionary, 0362-9007 **and** Home Mission Herald.*
**Desc:** This magazine focuses primarily on the Presbyterian Church. Offering broad coverage and interpretation of the work of the church and other religious news.
**Ind/Abst** Curr. Thoughts Trends.

US/0193-6212
**PRESBYTERION.** [Presbyterion]. **Added/Corp** Covenant Theological Seminary. Vol. 1 (Spring 1975)-. Periodical. English. sa. $8.50. Covenant Theological Seminary, 12330 Conway Road, St Louis MO 63141. **Tel** (314)434-4044. **ED** Phil Long. **DD** 285. Index available. **Bk Rev. Circ:** 600. available on microfilm and microfiche from University Microfilms International (UMI).
**Desc:** A conservative Presbyterian theological journal for educated laymen and ministers.
**Ind/Abst** Christ. Period. Index; Index Book Rev. Relig.; New Testam. Abstr.; Old Testam. Abstr.; Relig. Index One Period.; Relig. Theol. Abstr.

●US/1059-3276
**PRIMARY ONE STUDENT GUIDE. Added/Corp** Assemblies of God. General Council. **VFOAT** Primary One. (1992)-. Periodical. English. qt. $5.20. Gospel Publishing House, 1445 Boonville Avenue, Springfield MO 65802. **Tel** (417)862-2781, FAX (417)866-1146. ***Continues** Primary One, 0273-5148.*

●US/1059-3268
**PRIMARY TEACHER GUIDE. Added/Corp** Assemblies of God. General Council. (1992)-. Periodical. English. qt. $9.20. Gospel Publishing House, 1445 Boonville Avenue, Springfield MO 65802. **Tel** (417)862-2781, FAX (417)866-1146. ***Continues** Primary Teacher, 0277-9188.*

●US/1059-3284
**PRIMARY TWO STUDENT GUIDE. Added/Corp** Assemblies of God. General Council. **VFOAT** Primary Two. (1992)-. Periodical. English. qt. $5.20. Gospel Publishing House, 1445 Boonville Avenue, Springfield MO 65802. **Tel** (417)862-2781, FAX (417)866-1146. ***Continues** Primary Two, 0273-5164.*

US/0092-4415
**PRIMITIVE BAPTIST YEARBOOK.** Vol. 1, (1972)-. English. PO Box 235, Rainsville AL 35986. **LC** BX6380; .P72. **DD** 286/.4.

UK
**PROCEEDINGS OF THE HUGUENOT SOCIETY OF GREAT BRITAIN AND IRELAND. Main/Corp** Huguenot Society of Great Britain and Ireland. **VFOAT** Huguenot Society Proceedings. Proceedings. English. **LC** BX9450; .H7. **DD** 284/.5/0941. ***Continues** Proceedings of the Huguenot Society of London, 0309-8346.*
**Ind/Abst** Am. Hist. Life (1975-); BHA : Biblio. Hist. Art.

US/0731-4078
**PROCEEDINGS OF THE UNITARIAN UNIVERSALIST HISTORICAL SOCIETY, THE.** Vol. 19, Pt. 1 (1980-1981)-. Proceedings. English. ir. $8.00 (per issue). Prof C Wright, Harvard Divinity School, Cambridge MA 02138. **ED** Richard Myers. **UDC** 288. **Bk Rev. Ad Acc. Circ:** 350. ***Continues** Proceedings of the Unitarian Historical Society, 0082-7819.*
**Desc:** Scholarly articles on Unitarianism, Universalism, and related movements in liberal religion.
**Ind/Abst** Am. Hist. Life (1982-).

US/0147-3336
**PROGRAM-CURRICULUM PLANS. Main/Corp** United Methodist Church (United States). Program-Curriculum Committee. English. PO Box 801, Nashville TN 37202. **Tel** (615)749-6463. **LC** BV1559; .U54A. **DD** 208.

CN/0826-533X
**PROMISE (REGINA).** (THE PROMISE.). [Promise]. Vol. 1, Issue 1 (June 1983)-. Periodical. English. qt. Promise, c/o Barbara Thompson, St Luke's Anglican Church, 3233 Argyle Road, Regina Saskatchewan S4S 2B5 Canada. **Tel** (306)586-9355. **ED** Dennis E Walter. **DD** 283/.7124/4. **UDC** 283(712). **Bk Rev. Ad Acc. Circ:** 325 (ctrl).
**Desc:** Covers christian messages and parish news.

US/1070-8138
**PROTESTANT REFORMED THEOLOGICAL JOURNAL.** [Protestant Reform. theol. j.]. **Added/Corp** Theological School of the Protestant Reformed Churches. (1967)-. Periodical. English. Twice a year (Apr., Nov.). Free. Theology School Protest Reform Church, 4949 Ivanrest Avenue, Grandville MI 49418. **Tel** (616)531-1490. **ED** Professor Herman Hanks. **DD** 285. Index available. cum. index. **Bk Rev**, (Qty: 10). **Circ:** 500 (ctrl).

IT/0033-1767
**PROTESTANTESIMO.** [Protestantesimo]. (1946)-. Periodical. Italian. Four times a year (Feb., Apr., July, Oct.). L42000 Italy; L45000 others. Facolta Valdese di Teologia, Via Pietro Cossa 42, 00193 Rome Italy. **Tel** 011 39 6 3225493. **ED** Bruno Corsani. **LC** BR5; .P7. Index available in last issue of volume--attached. **Bk Rev. Ad Acc. Circ:** 1,000 (ctrl).
**Desc:** The magazine tends to put the readers in contact with the thought-world issued from the reformation and with the leading motifs of the ecumenical movement.
**Ind/Abst** Am. Hist. Life (1973-1976); Bibliogr. Mission.; Index Book Rev. Relig.; Relig. Index One Period. (1980-).

CN/0229-1916
**QUAKER CONCERN. Added/Corp** Society of Friends. Canadian Friends Service Committee. Vol. 2, No. 3 (Nov./Dec. 1976)-. Periodical. English. qt. $4.00 (recommended minimum donation) US. Canadian Friends Historical Association, 60 Lowther Avenue, Toronto Ontario M5R 1C7 Canada. **Tel** (416)839-4328. **ED** Elaine Bishop. **DD** 289.6/71. **Circ:** 3,100. ***Continues** Society of Friends. Canadian Friends Service Committee. Quaker Service Report., 0703-9425.*
**Desc:** Reports on projects of Canadian Friends Service Committee on issues of concern to Friends: disarmament, development, social justice and Native Peoples' rights.

US/0033-5088
**QUAKER RELIGIOUS THOUGHT. Added/Corp** Quaker Theological Discussion Group. **VFOAT** QRT. Vol. 1 (Spring 1959)-. Periodical. English. Three times a year. Price varies. Quaker Religious Thought, 128 Tate Street, Greensboro NC 27403. **Tel** (910)274-8707. **ED** Dean Freiday. **LC** BX7601; .Q35. **Bk Rev. Circ:** 500. available on microfilm from University Microfilms International (UMI).
**Desc:** Historical and theological studies of Quakerism and its relevance to contemporary life.

US/0270-9287
**QUARTERLY REVIEW - UNITED METHODIST BOARD OF HIGHER EDUCATION AND MINISTRY (U.S.).** (QUARTERLY REVIEW : QR.). [Q. rev. - United Methodist Board High. Educ. Minist. (U.S.)]. **Added/Corp** United Methodist Board of Higher Education and Ministry (U.S.) United Methodist Publishing House. **VFOAT** QR. Vol. 1, No. 1 (Fall 1980)-. Periodical. English. qt (Mar., June, Sept., Dec.). $16.00 (1 year), $28.00 (2 year), $36.00 (3 year) US; $18.00 (1 year), $32.00 (2 year), $42.00 (3 year) other. Graded Press, 201 Eighth Avenue South, Box 801, Nashville TN 37202. **Tel** (615)749-6417. **ED** Sharon Hels. **LC** BX8201; .Q37a. **DD** 287/.6/05. Index available. **Bk Rev. Ad Acc.** available on microfilm and microfiche from University Microfilms International (UMI). ***Continues** Religion in Life, 0034-3986.*
**Ind/Abst** Index Book Rev. Relig.; Relig. Index One Period. (1980-); Relig. Theol. Abstr.

CN/0082-7878
**RECORD OF PROCEEDINGS - GENERAL COUNCIL. UNITED CHURCH OF CANADA.** (RECORD OF PROCEEDINGS - UNITED CHURCH OF CANADA, GENERAL COUNCIL. COMPTE RENDU.). **Main/Corp** United Church of Canada. General Council. **VFOAT** Compte Rendu. 1st-1925-. Proceedings. English. be. United Church of

Canada, 85 Saint Clair Avenue East Room 711, Toronto Ontario M45 1M8 Canada. **Tel** (416)925-5931. **ED** Douglas L Flanders. **DD** 287/.92. **UDC** 287.9. Index available. **Circ:** 5,000.
**Desc:** Covers compilation of reports, minutes and other documentation pertaining to the biennial meetings of the national administrative body of The United church of Canada, known as the General council.

UK/0306-7262
**REFORM.** **Added/Corp** United Reformed Church in England and Wales. United Reformed Church in the United Kingdom. (Nov. 1972)-. Periodical. English. Eleven times a year. £8.25 UK; £9.20 other. United Reformed Church, 86 Tavistock Place, London WC1H 9RT England. **Tel** 011 44 71 9162020. **ED** Norman Hart. **Bk Rev. Ad Acc. Circ:** 18,000. available on microfilm from University Microfilms International (UMI). ***Formed by the union of*** *Congregational Monthly; Outlook **and** Enterprise.*
**Desc:** Magazine of the United Reformed Church for the exchange of news and ideas.

HU
**REFORMATUSOK LAPJA.** V. 1, No. 1, (March 31, 1957)-. Periodical. Hungarian. wk. 300.00ft Hungary; $15.00 other. Reformatusok Lapja, PO Box 424, H-1395 Budapest 62 Hungary. **Tel** 1/176-809. **ED** Attila P Komlos. **UDC** 285.1. **Bk Rev. Ad Acc. Circ:** 35,000.
**Desc:** For Presbyterian church-related people, dealing with question of religion, church-policy, ecumenism and social activity of believers, dialog between christians and marxists.

US/0745-1164
**RESOURCE (KANSAS CITY, MO.).** (RESOURCE.). Vol. 1, No. 1 (Dec., Jan., Feb. 1982/1983)-. Periodical. English. qt. $7.25. Nazarene Publishing House, PO Box 419527, Kansas City MO 64141. **Tel** (816)931-1900.

US/0034-5725
**RESPONSE (CINCINNATI).** (RESPONSE.). Vol. 1 (Jan. 1969)-. Periodical. English. Eleven times a year (July/Aug. issues combined). $10.00. Board of Global Ministries, 475 Riverside Drive, Room 1351, New York NY 10115. **Tel** (212)870-3765, FAX (212)870-3940. ***Formed by the union of*** *Methodist Woman **and** World Evangel.*

US/0034-6373
**REVIEW AND EXPOSITOR (BERNE).** (REVIEW AND EXPOSITOR.). **Added/Corp** Southern Baptist Theological Seminary. Vol. 1 (Apr. 1904)-. Periodical. English. qt (Jan., Apr., July, Oct.). $20.00 US; $22.00 others. Theological Seminary/Fac SO BA, 2825 Lexington Road, Louisville KY 40280. **Tel** (502)897-4407. **ED** Dr. Charles J. Scalise and Dan Striver. **LC** BX6201; .R5. **DD** 286.105. Index available (Oct.). **Bk Rev. Ad Acc, Adv Mgr:** Joel Drinkard Jr. **Circ:** 3,500. available on microfilm and microfiche from University Microfilms International (UMI).
**Desc:** Since the year of 1904, this magazine has sought to participate both in continuing biblical and theological inquiry and in the ongoing ministry of the church. It seeks both academic competence and enrichment in Christian life and ministry.
**Ind/Abst** Index Book Rev. Relig.; Int. Zeitschriftenschau Bibelwissenschaft Grenzgeb.; New Testam. Abstr.; Relig. Index One Period.; Relig. Theol. Abstr.; South. Baptist Period. Index.

FR/0035-3884
**REVUE REFORMEE, LA.** (LA REVUE REFORMEE.). [Rev. reform.]. **Added/Corp** Societe Calviniste de France. (April 1950)-. Periodical. French. Five times a year. 152.00F France; 210.00F (air mail), 180.00F (surface mail) other. Editions Kerygma, 33 Avenue Jules Ferry, 13100 Aix en Provece France. **Tel** 011 33 42 261355. **ED** Paul Wells. **LC** BX9401; .R48. **DD** 284/.2/05. cum. index. **Circ:** 1,300 (ctrl).
**Ind/Abst** New Testam. Abstr.; Old Testam. Abstr.

US/0745-3884
**ROCKY MOUNTAIN AMERICAN BAPTIST.** Periodical. English. bm. Rocky Mountain American Baptist, 1344 Pennsylvania Street, Denver CO 80203. **UDC** 286.1. ***Formed by the union of*** *Colorado Baptist **and** Wyoming Baptist News.*

US/0485-294X
**ROCKY MOUNTAIN BAPTIST.** [Rocky Mt. Baptist]. **Added/Corp** Colorado Baptist General Convention. (1952)-. Periodical. English. ir (24 issues per year). $5.00. Colorado Baptist General Convention, 7393 South Alton Way, Englewood CO 80112. **Tel** (303)771-2480. **ED** Charles E Sharp. **Ad Acc. Circ:** 8,500.
**Desc:** Carries news of local state churches, national news of interest to Southern Baptists, Sunday school lessons, editorials, pictures, letters and columns of specialties.

NE
**RONDOM HET WOORD.** **Added/Corp** Nederlandse Christelijke Radio-Vereniging. Vol. 1 (1958)-. Periodical. Dutch. qt. Fl15.00 (per half year), Free (institutions). Rondom Het Woord, PO Box 208, 3770 AE Barneveld Netherlands. **Tel** (03418)51102. **Circ:** 2,750.

US/0035-9084
**ROYAL SERVICE.** Periodical. English. mo. $11.00 US; $15.50 other. Woman's Missionary Union, PO Box 830010, Birmingham AL 35283. **Tel** (205)991-8100, (205)991-4933. **ED** Edna M Ellison. **LC** BV2520.A1; R6. **DD** 266.61. **UDC** 286.3. **Bk Rev. Circ:** 310,000 (ctrl). available on audiocassette. ***Continues*** *Our Mission Fields.*
**Desc:** Magazine for the Baptist Women organization. Each issue contains a Bible study, current mission study, suggestions for mission action, a prayer calendar of missionaries and a list of resources for christian living.
**Ind/Abst** South. Baptist Period. Index.

US/0036-214X
**SABBATH RECORDER, THE.** (SABBATH RECORDER. A SEVENTH-DAY BAPTIST WEEKLY.). **Added/Corp** American Sabbath Tract Society. (19??)-. Periodical. English. Eleven times a year (July/Aug. issues combined). Free on request. Seventh Day Baptist Center, PO Box 1678, Janesville WI 53547. **Tel** (608)752-5055, FAX (608)752-7711. **ED** Rev. Kevin J. Bulter. **Circ:** 4,600 (ctrl). available on microfilm. ***Continues*** *Sabbath Recorder (New York, N.Y.).*
**Desc:** Inspirational and information news for and about the Seventh-Day Baptists.

US/0098-9517
**SABBATH WATCHMAN, THE.** Periodical. English (German). bm. $8.00 US; $10.00, $20.00 (airmail) other. Religious Liberty Publishing, 9999 E Mississippi Avenue, Denver CO 80231-1927. **Tel** (303)363-9853. **ED** L Watts. **LC** BX6101; .S23. **DD** 286/.73. **UDC** 289.3. **Circ:** 500 (ctrl).
**Desc:** The official organ of the Seventh-Day Adventist Church Reform Movement, North American union, International Missionary Society.

US
**SAINT LOUIS LUTHERAN.** English. mo. $6.00. Saint Louis Lutheran, 3558 South Jefferson Avenue, St Louis MO 63118. **Tel** (314)664-7000.

US/0036-3251
**SAINTS HERALD.** [St. her.]. **Added/Corp** Reorganized Church of Jesus Christ of Latter Day Saints. **VFOAT** Herald. Vol. 1, (187?)-. Periodical. English. Twelve times a year. $21.80. Herald Publishing House, Drawer HH, Independence MO 64055. **Tel** (816)252-5010, FAX (816)252-3976. **ED** Roger Yarrington (editor's address: PO Box 1770, Independence MO 64055). **DD** 289. **Bk Rev**, (Qty: 6-8 per year). **Ad Acc, Adv Mgr:** G Booz, **Tel** (816)252-5010. **Pr Rev. Circ:** 36,000. ***Absorbed*** *Vision (Independence, MO.);* ***Continues*** *True Latter-Day Saints' Herald.*

US/0036-8032
**SCHWENKFELDIAN, THE.** **Added/Corp** Schwenkfelder Church. General Conference. (1903)-. Periodical. English. Three times a year (Feb., June, & Oct.). $4.00. General Conference of the Schwenkfelder Church, 1 Seminary Street, Pennsburg PA 18073. **Tel** (215)679-3103. **ED** Nancy MacQueen Byron. **LC** UNC. cum. index. **Bk Rev. Circ:** 1,750 (ctrl).
**Desc:** Report of the activities, events, and scholarship of the Schwenkfelder Churches of America.

UK/0036-9136
**SCOTTISH BAPTIST MAGAZINE.** (1875)-. Periodical. English. ir. £7.50. Baptist Union of Scotland, 14 Aytoun Road, Glasgow G41 5RT Scotland. **Tel** 041 423 6169. **ED** Robert M. Armstrong. **Bk Rev. Ad Acc. Circ:** 3,500.
**Desc:** Features and news of interest and relating to Baptists in Scotland. Nider church science and Christian involvement in and comment on social and moral issues.

US/0048-9913
**SEARCH (NASHVILLE).** ***Ceased.*** (SEARCH.). **Added/Corp** Southern Baptist Convention. Sunday School Board. (1970)-(1993). Periodical. English. qt. Materials Services Department, 127 9th Avenue North, Nashville TN 37234. **Tel** (615)251-2000. **ED** Judith Slayden Hayes. **Bk Rev. Ad Acc. Circ:** 11,500 (ctrl).
**Desc:** Professional journal for Southern Baptist Ministers. Contemporary issues: theology, education, music, administration.
**Ind/Abst** Predicasts F&S Index, U. S. Annu. Ed.; South. Baptist Period. Index.

US/0739-2281
**SEARCHING TOGETHER.** [Search. together]. **Added/Corp** Baptist Reformation Educational Ministries. Vol. 11 No. 3 (Autumn 1982)-. Periodical. English. Four times a year. $10.00. Word of Life Church, PO Box 548, St. Croix Falls WI 54024. **Tel** (715)755-3560. **ED** Jon Zens. **DD** 248. Each issue contains an index to its own contents (no volume index)--loose. **Bk Rev. Ad Acc. Circ:** 3,000. available on microfilm and microfiche from University Microfilms International (UMI). ***Continues*** *Baptist Reformation Review, 0276-7945.*
**Desc:** Deals with contemporary issues facing the church in light of the Bible.
**Ind/Abst** Index Book Rev. Relig.; Relig. Index One Period. (1982-); Relig. Theol. Abstr.

US
**SENIOR MUSICIAN.** **See** Music.

CN/0037-2307
**SENTINEL (POINTE CLAIRE).** (THE SENTINEL.). **Added/Corp** Provincial Association of Protestant Teachers of Quebec. (Nov. 1966)-. Periodical. English (French). Four times a year. 6.00Can$ Canada; 7.50Can$ US; 11.00Can$ other. Provincial Association of Protestant Teachers of Quebec, 17035 Brunswick Boulevard 1, Kirkland Quebec H9H SG6 Canada. **Tel** (514)694-9779.

CN/0049-0202
**SENTINEL (TORONTO. 1957).** (THE SENTINEL.). **Added/Corp** Loyal Orange Association of British America. Vol. 82 (Oct. 1957)-. Periodical. English. Six times a year. 7.48Can$ Canada; 8.41Can$ other. British America Publishing Company Ltd., 94 Sheppard Avenue West, Willowdale Ontario M2N 1M5 Canada. **Tel** (905)223-1690. **ED** Norman R. Ritchie. **Bk Rev. Ad Acc. Circ:** 8,000 (ctrl). ***Continues*** *Sentinel and Orange and Protestant Advocate, 0381-5358.*
**Desc:** Religious news, patriotic items, and lodge events - the official publication of the Loyal Orange Association.

US/0270-3599
**SEVENTH-DAY ADVENTIST PERIODICAL INDEX.** **See** Religion and Theology-Abstracting, Bibliographies and Statistics.

US
**SHABBAT SHALOM.** **Added/Corp** General Conference of Seventh-Day Adventists. North American Division. (Apr./June 1986)-. Periodical. English. Four times a year. $6.00 US; $8.00 other. Review and Herald Publishing Association, 55 West Oak Ridge Drive, Hagerstown MD 21740. **Tel** (301)791-7000 ext. 2534, FAX (301)790-9734. ***Continues*** *New Israelite.*
**Ind/Abst** Seventh-Day Adventist Period. Index (19??-).

US/0037-5047
**SIGNS OF THE TIMES (MOUNTAIN VIEW).** (SIGNS OF THE TIMES.). (1874)-. Periodical. English. Twelve times a year. $12.95. Pacific Press Publishing Association, PO Box 7000, Boise ID 83707. **Tel** (208)465-2500, FAX (208)465-2531. **ED** Kenneth J. Holland. **LC** BX6101; .S7. **Circ:** 375,000 (ctrl). ***Absorbed*** *These Times, 0040-6058.*
**Desc:** Practical Christianity showing that Bible principles are relevant today.
**Ind/Abst** Seventh-Day Adventist Period. Index (1971-).

CN/0700-5202
**SLAVNA NADEJE.** (GLORIOUS HOPE.). [Slavna nadeje]. **Added/Corp** Czechoslovak Baptist Convention of USA and Canada. Vol. 6, Issue 1 (1978/1979)-. Periodical. Czech (summaries and/or abstracts in English). bm. Czechoslovak Baptist Convention of USA and Canada, 3059 Grandview Street, Windsor, Ontario N8T 2M1 Canada. **DD** 286/.5. ***Continues*** *Slavna Nadeje., 0700-5202.*

US/0038-3848
**SOUTHERN BAPTIST EDUCATOR, THE.** **Added/Corp** Southern Baptist Convention. Education Commission. (1919)-. Periodical. English. Ten times a year (published monthly except July and Dec.). $8.00 (one year), $15.00 (two years), $21.50 (three years). Education Commission SBC, 901 Commerce Street, suite 600, Nashville TN 37203. **Tel** (615)244-2362, FAX (615)242-2153. **ED** Tim Fields. **Bk Rev. Pr Rev. Circ:** 12,000.
**Desc:** News and feature articles related to Southern Baptist educational institutions.
**Ind/Abst** South. Baptist Period. Index.

US/0199-8269
**SOUTHERN BAPTIST JOURNAL.** **Added/Corp** Baptist Faith and Message Fellowship. (1973)-. Periodical. English. Four times a year. $9.00. Southern Baptist Journal, 6145 Old Highway 290 Loop, Austin TX 78749. **Tel** (512)892-0358.

US/0743-7439
**SOUTHERN FRIEND, THE.** (THE SOUTHERN FRIEND : JOURNAL OF THE NORTH CAROLINA FRIENDS HISTORICAL SOCIETY.). **Added/Corp** North Carolina Friends Historical Society. Vol. 1, No. 1 (Spring 1979)-. Periodical. English. Twice a year (May, Nov.). $15.00. North Carolina Friends Historical Society, Box 8502, Greensboro NC 27419-0502. **Tel** (919)274-8707. **ED** Damon D. Hickey and Herbert Poole. **LC** BX7648.N8; S68. **DD** 289.6/756. **Bk Rev. Circ:** 400 (ctrl).
**Desc:** History of friends (Quakers) in the Southeastern United States.
**Ind/Abst** Am. Hist. Life (1981-).

US/0038-4828
**SOUTHWESTERN JOURNAL OF THEOLOGY.** [Southwest. j. theo]. **Added/Corp** Fort Worth, Tex. Southwestern Baptist Theological Seminary. School of Theology. Vol. 1, Oct. (1958)-. Periodical. English. Three times a year (Jan., May, Aug.). $13.00 (1 year); $24.00 (2 year); $33.00 (3 year). Southwestern Journal of Theology, Box 22000 2E, Fort Worth TX 76122-0490. **Tel** (817)923-1921 Ext 2820. **ED** William M. Tillman Jr., telephone: (817)923-1921 Ext. 6960. **LC** BX6201; .S65. **DD** 286/.1/05. **Bk Rev**, (Qty: 150). **Ad Acc. Circ:** 3,000. available on microfilm and microfiche from University Microfilms International (UMI).
**Desc:** Academic journal containing several articles along a common theme and book reviews.
**Ind/Abst** Christ. Period. Index (19??-); Index Book Rev. Relig.; New Testam. Abstr.; Old Testam. Abstr.; Relig. Index One Period. (1958-); Relig. Theol. Abstr.; South. Baptist Period. Index.

US
**SPIRE.** **See** College and School Publications-Alumni.

US/0038-9382
**STANDARD (EVANSTON, ILL.), THE.** (THE STANDARD.). [Standard]. **Main/Corp** Baptist General Conference. (19??)-. Periodical. English. Ten times a year (monthly with Jan./Feb. and Aug./Sep. issues combined). $15.75. Baptist General Conference, 2002 South Arlington Heights Road, Arlington Heights IL 60005. **Tel** (708)228-0200. **ED** Gary Marsh. **DD** 286. **Bk Rev**, (Qty: Varies). **Ad Acc**, **Adv Mgr:** Pam Nelsen. **Circ:** 23,000.
**Desc:** Promotion for the Baptist General Conference (BGC), information and inspiration for members of BGC churches.

US/0039-2685
**STUDENT (NASHVILLE), THE.** (THE STUDENT.). V. 1- 1922-. Periodical. English. mo. $16.75. Materials Services Department, 127 9th Avenue North, Nashville TN 37234. **Tel** (615)251-2000. **LC** BX6205.B27. **DD** 248/.83. available on microfilm and microfiche from University Microfilms International (UMI).
**Ind/Abst** South. Baptist Period. Index.

US/0039-5285
**SUNDAY SCHOOL COUNSELOR.** ***Title Change.*** **Added/Corp** Assemblies of God, Springfield, Mo. Sunday School Dept. **VFOAT** Counselor. (19??)-(1993). English. mo. Gospel Publishing House, 1445 Boonville Avenue, Springfield MO 65802. **Tel** (417)862-2781, FAX (417)866-1146. **ED** Sylvia Lee. Index available. cum. index. **Bk Rev**. **Circ:** 37,000. ***Continued by*** *Christian Education Counselor, 1072-1436.*
**Desc:** Provides information and inspiration to Sunday school teachers and administrators, primarily in Assemblies of God churches. Communicates the Sunday school program of the Assemblies of God to local churches.

US/1056-201X
**SUNDAY SCHOOL LEADER (LARGER CHURCH ED.), THE.** (THE SUNDAY SCHOOL LEADER.). [Sunday sch. lead.]. **Added/Corp** Southern Baptist Convention. Sunday School Board. **VFOAT** Sunday School Leader, Larger Church Edition. Vol. 1, No. 1 (Oct. 1991)-. Periodical. English. mo. $16.20 (one year), $32.10 (two year). Southern Baptist Convention, 901 Commerce, Suite 750, Nashville TN 37203. **Tel** (615)244-2355, FAX (615)742-8919. **(Subscription address:** Sunday School Board, Customer Service, 127 9th Avenue North, Nashville TN 37234.**)** **DD** 268.
**Ind/Abst** South. Baptist Period. Index (1991-).

US/1056-2001
**SUNDAY SCHOOL LEADER. SMALLER CHURCH ED, THE.** (THE SUNDAY SCHOOL LEADER.). **Added/Corp** Southern Baptist Convention. Sunday School Board. (1991)-. Periodical. English. qt. $4.50. Southern Baptist Convention, 901 Commerce, Suite 750, Nashville TN 37203. **Tel** (615)244-2355, FAX (615)742-8919. **(Subscription address:** Sunday School Board - Customer Service, 127 Ninth Avenue North, Nashville, TN 37234 USA; telephone: (800)458-2772**)**
**Ind/Abst** South. Baptist Period. Index (1991-).

US/0731-6518
**SUNSTONE REVIEW (SALT LAKE CITY, UTAH).** (THE SUNSTONE REVIEW.). [Sunstone rev.]. **Added/Corp** Sunstone Foundation. Vol. 1, No. 1 (July/August 1981)-. Periodical. English. mo. Sunstone Foundation, 331 South Rio Grande Street, Suite 206, Salt Lake City UT 84101-1121. **Tel** (801)355-5926, (800)326-5926, FAX (801)355-4043. **LC** BX8601; .S88. **DD** 289.3/32/05.

US/0090-9459
**SUPPLEMENTARY DIRECTORY OF THE AMERICAN BAPTIST CHURCHES IN THE U.S.A.** (SUPPLEMENTARY DIRECTORY.). **Main/Corp** American Baptist Churches in the U.S.A. (1972/73)-. Directory. English. Judson Press, Box 851, Valley Forge PA 19481. **LC** BX6207; .A32. **DD** 286/.173. **UDC** 286.1(73). ***Supersedes in part*** *American Baptist Convention. Year Book, Containing Historical Documents and Tables.*

US/0890-4006
**TEENQUEST.** **See** Children and Youth Interests.

US/0732-4324
**TEXAS BAPTIST HISTORY.** (TEXAS BAPTIST HISTORY : JOURNAL OF THE TEXAS BAPTIST HISTORICAL SOCIETY.). **Added/Corp** Texas Baptist Historical Society. Vol. 1 (1981)-. Periodical. English. an (Oct.). $10.00 Comes with Texas Baptist Historical Society membership. Texas Baptist Historical Society, Box 22000-2E, Fort Worth TX 76122. **Tel** (817)923-1921 Ext. 3330. **ED** Eugene Baker. **LC** BX6248.T4; T49. **DD** 286/.1764/05. **Bk Rev**. **Circ:** 200 (ctrl).
**Desc:** Devoted to the study of Baptists in Texas.

UK
**TODAY.** News (UK) Ltd, 70 Vauxhall Bridge Road, London SW1V 2RP England.

UK
**TOGETHER.** **Added/Corp** Church Pastoral Aid Society. Vol. 102 (Sept./Oct. 1974)-. Periodical. English. ir (nine issues per year). £6.50 UK; £9.00 Europe; £11.50 other. General Synod Board of Ed, 118 Duxford Road D, Whittlesford Cambridge CB2 4NA England. **Tel** (0223)832331. ***Supersedes*** *Church and People.*
**Ind/Abst** Bibliogr. Mission.

KO
**TONGIL SEGYE.** Periodical. Korean. mo. W10,000. Segye Kidokkyo Tongil Sillyong Hyophoe, 9-1 2-ka Chongpa-dong Yongsan-ku, Seoul Korea. **LC** BX9750.S4; T664.

CN/0710-2135
**TOPIC (VANCOUVER).** (TOPIC / DIOCESE OF NEW WESTMINSTER.). [Topic]. Periodical. English. mo. $2.00. Diocese of New Westminster, 692 Burrard Street, Vancouver BC V6L 2L1 Canada. **DD** 283/.71133. **UDC** 283(711).

CN/0714-8100
**TRANSACTION.** (TRANSACTION.). [TransAction]. No. 437 (Jan./Feb. 1982)-. Periodical. English. bm. Free. Christian Transportation, 2222 South Sheridan Way, Unit 5 Building 2, Mississauga Ontario L5J 2M4 Canada. **Tel** (416)822-2700. **ED** Louis G. Voyer. **DD** 248.8/8. **Circ:** 29,000. ***Formed by the union of*** *Postal Christian Witness, 0700-7787; Christian Airman, 0381-0275; Christian Bus Driver, 0382-8727; Automotive Christian, 0382-5299; Christian Sailor, 0714-8089* ***and*** *Christian Railroader, 0714-8097.*

US/0886-1730
**TRANSACTIONS OF THE MORAVIAN HISTORICAL SOCIETY.** [Trans. Morav. Hist. Soc.]. **Main/Corp** Moravian Historical Society. (1857/1858)-. Monographic series. English. an (Oct.). Price varies per volume. Moravian Historical Society Inc, Whitefield House, 214 East Center, Nazareth PA 18064. **Tel** (215)759-5070. **ED** David Schattschneider. **LC** BX8553; .M7. **DD** 284.6. Index available. cum. index. **Circ:** 500 (ctrl).
**Desc:** Articles on history of the Moravian church as well as minutes of the society's annual meetings.
**Ind/Abst** Am. Hist. Life (1963-).

UK/0082-7800
**TRANSACTIONS OF THE UNITARIAN HISTORICAL SOCIETY.** [Trans. Unit. Hist. Soc.]. **Main/Corp** Unitarian Historical Society, London. Vol. 1 (1916)-. English. an (April). £7.50. Unitarian Historical Society, 58 Stoneygate Court, London Road, Leicester LE2 2AJ England. **Tel** 703976. **ED** Alan Ruston. **LC** BX9803; .U8. **DD** 288. Index available. cum. index. **Bk Rev**, (Qty: 5-6). **Ad Acc**. **Circ:** 350 (ctrl).
**Desc:** Covers the history and the Unitarian churches, societies, individuals and Unitarian thought.
**Ind/Abst** Am. Hist. Life (1955-).

US
**TRINITY WORLD FORUM.** **Added/Corp** Trinity Evangelical Divinity School. School of World Mission and Evangelism. (197?)-. Periodical. English. Three times a year. $2.00. Trinity Evangelical Divinity School, 2065 Half Day Road, Bannockburn, Deerfield IL 60015. **Tel** (708)945-8800. **Bk Rev**. **Circ:** 3,500.
**Desc:** Seeks to relate important and current issues in mission and evangelism to the missionary, pastor, and the mission-minded layman.

US/0149-6468
**TRUST FUNDS.** (TRUST FUNDS - PROTESTANT EPISCOPAL CHURCH IN THE U.S.A. COMMITTEE ON TRUST FUNDS.). [Trust funds]. **Main/Corp** Protestant Episcopal Church in the U.S.A. Committee on Trust Funds. English. Protestant Episcopal Church in the USA, 815 Second Avenue, New York NY 10017. **LC** BX5961; .P76A. **DD** 254.8. **UDC** 283.

US/0276-6604
**TWENTIETH CENTURY WATCH.** **Added/Corp** Church of God, International. Vol. 1, No. 1 (May-June 1980)-. Periodical. English. bm. $7.50. Twentieth Century Watch Subscriber Services Department. **LC** BX6178; .T86. **DD** 289.9.

UK
**UK CHRISTIAN HANDBOOK.** **Added/Corp** Evangelical Alliance. MARC Europe. **VFOAT** Christian Handbook. **VAT** United Kingdom Christian Handbook. Began in (1980)-?. English. $40.00 US; $43.00 Canada; $44.00 other. Marc Publications, 121 East Huntington Drive, Monrovia CA 91016. **Tel** (818)303-8811, (800)777-7752, FAX (818)301-7786. **ED** P Brierley. **LC** BV2420; .U3. **DD** 274.1/0828/025. ***Continues*** *UK Protestant Missions Handbook.*

US/0882-4029
**UNITARIAN UNIVERSALISM.** [Unit univers.]. 1984-. Periodical. English. an. Unitarian Universalist Ministers Association, 25 Beacon Street, Boston MA 02108. **DD** 288. **UDC** 288.

US/0362-0492
**UNITARIAN UNIVERSALIST CHRISTIAN, THE.** [Unit. Univers. Christ.]. **Added/Corp** Unitarian Universalist Christian Fellowship. Vol. 25, Spring (1969)-. Periodical. English. qt. $30.00 US; $35.00 Canada; $40.00 other. Unitarian Universalist Christian, 110 Arlington Street, Boston MA 02116. **Tel** (617)482-2957. **ED** Thomas D Wintle. **LC** BX9801; .U74. **DD** 288/.32/05. Index available. cum. index. **Bk Rev**. **Ad Acc**. **Circ:** 1,200 (ctrl). available on microfilm from University Microfilms International (UMI). ***Continues*** *Unitarian Christian, 0364-3506.*
**Desc:** Journal of liberal Christian thought and opinion, with attention to theology, worship, spirituality, history and ecumenical developments; book reviews, poetry.
**Ind/Abst** Index Book Rev. Relig. (1980-); Relig. Index One Period. (1980-); Relig. Theol. Abstr.

GW/0344-9254
**UNITAS FRATRUM.** (UNITAS FRATRUM; BEITRAEGE AUS DER BRUDERGEMEINE.). [Unitas fratr.]. (1978)-. Periodical. German (summaries and/or abstracts in English). ir. $22.00. Moravian College, Reeves Library, Bethlehem PA 18018. **Tel** (215)861-1541. **ED** Hans Schneider and Winfred Kohls. **[CCC]**. **Bk Rev**. **Ad Acc**. **Circ:** 300 (ctrl).
**Desc:** Journal devoted to the history, present life and work of the Moravian church.
**Ind/Abst** Am. Hist. Life (1986-); Index Book Rev. Relig.; Relig. Index One Period.

US/0882-7214
**UNITED CHURCH NEWS (NATIONAL EDITION).** **See** Newspapers.

US/8750-7668
**UNITED METHODIST CHRISTIAN ADVOCATE, THE.** **Added/Corp** United Methodist Church (U.S.). Alabama-West Florida Conference. United Methodist Church (U.S.). Birmingham Area Board of Communications and Christian Advocate. United Methodist Church (U.S.). Joint Board of Communication/Advocate of the North Alabama and Alabama-West Florida Conferences. United Methodist Communications Council (U.S.). Newspaper Division. **VFOAT** Christian Advocate. (19??)-. Periodical. English. bw. $10.00 (one year). United Methodist Christian Advocate, 898 Arkadelphia Road, Birmingham AL 35204-3498. **Tel** (205)226-7971, FAX (205)226-7991. **ED** Charles Roundtree. Index available. **Bk Rev**, (Qty: 12 /yr). **Ad Acc**. **Circ:** 10,000 (ctrl).

US
**UNITED METHODIST NEWSCOPE, THE.** **VFOAT** Newscope. (Apr. 6, 1973)-. Periodical. English. wk. $24.95 (first class), $19.50 (surface mail). United Methodist Publishing House, PO Box 801, 201 8th Avenue South, Nashville TN 37202. **Tel** (615)749-6732, (615)749-6615, FAX (615)749-6578, (615)749-6579.

US/0737-5581
**UNITED METHODIST REPORTER (DALLAS, TEX.), THE.** (THE UNITED METHODIST REPORTER.). Vol. 1 (Dec. 8, 1972)-. Periodical. English (Spanish). wk. $18.00. United Methodist Church / Dallas, PO Box 660275, Dallas TX 75266. **Tel** (214)630-6495, FAX (214)630-0079. **ED** Spurgeon M Dunnam III. **UDC** 284(73); 287. **Bk Rev**. **Ad Acc**. **Circ:** 475,000 (ctrl). ***Continues*** *Southern New England Reporter; The Texas Methodist.*
**Desc:** News and commentary, primarily on mainline protestantism in the United States.

US
**UNITED METHODIST RURAL FELLOWSHIP BULLETIN.** **Main/Corp** United Methodist Rural Fellowship. Vol. 24, No. 3 (Sept. 1967)-. Bulletin. English. Four times a year. $10.00. United Methodist Rural Fellowship, PO Box 514, Filer ID 83328. **Tel** (208)326-5812. **ED** Roger Armstrong (editor's address: 715 Center, Little Rock, AR 72201 USA; telephone: (501)324-8027). ***Continues*** *Methodist Rural Fellowship Bulletin.*

US
**UNIVERSALIST FRIENDS.** (19??)-. Periodical. English. sa. $10.00. Quaker Universalist Fellowship, 121 Watson Mill Road, Landenberg PA 19350-9344. **Tel** (215)274-8856. **ED** Emily Conlon. **Bk Rev**. **Ad Acc**. **Pr Rev.**

UK/0267-6648
**UNIVERSALIST - QUAKER UNIVERSALIST GROUP.** (UNIVERSALIST.). [Universalist - Quaker Universalist Group]. (1979)-. Periodical. English. Three times a year. $7.50. Quaker Universalist Fellowship, 121 Watson Mill Road, Landenberg PA 19350-9344. **Tel** (215)274-8856. **ED** Jean Hardy. **Bk Rev**. **Ad Acc**. **Pr Rev**. available on microfilm from University Microfilms International (UMI).

US/0746-0228
**UTAH-IDAHO SOUTHERN BAPTIST WITNESS.** **Added/Corp** Utah-Idaho Southern Baptist Convention. **VFOAT** Utah-Idaho Witness; Witness; Utah Idaho Southern Baptist Witness; Utah-Idaho SBC Witness. (19??)-. Periodical. English. ir. $4.00. Southern Baptist, PO Box 1039, Sandy UT 84091. **Tel** (801)255-3565, FAX (801)255-3622. **ED** C.C. Billingsley. **Bk Rev**, (Qty: 2/yr). **Circ:** 2300 (ctrl).

NO
**UTSYN.** (1891)-. Periodical. Norwegian. ir. Norsk Lithersk Misjonssanland, Grensen 19, Oslo 1 Norway.

NE
**VAN ALPHEN'S NIEUW KERKELIJK HANDBOEK.** **Added/Corp** Bond van Nederlandse Predikanten. **VFOAT** Nieuw Kerkelijk Handboek. (19??)-. Dutch. an. De Boer Mailingservice, Postbus 507, 1200 AM Hiversum Netherlands. **Tel** 011 31 30 258611. **LC** BR901; .V3. **DD** 280/.4/09492. ***Continues*** *Nieuw Kerkelijk Handboek.*

SW
**VAR LOSEN.** (1910)-. Periodical. Swedish. Nine times a year. Kr180.00 Sweden; Kr210.00 other. Var Losen, Box 57, S193 00 Sigtuna Sweden. **Tel** 011 46 76 051610. **LC** BX8001; .V3.

US/0749-3509
**VIBRANT LIFE.** **See** Health and Personal Fitness.

US/1064-5063
**VIEWPOINTS (ATLANTA, GA.).** (VIEWPOINTS : GEORGIA BAPTIST HISTORY.). [Viewp.]. **Added/Corp** Georgia Baptist Historical Society. **VFOAT** Viewpoints Georgia Baptist History. Vol. 1 (1968)-. Periodical. English. be. $5.00 (membership). Georgia Baptist Historical Society, 2170 Thomson Road, Washington GA 30673. **Tel** (706)678-1037. **ED** Robert Gardner (editor's phone: (706)291-2121 or (800)868-6980). **DD** 277. Index available. cum. index. **Bk Rev**. **Circ:** 500. available on microfilm.
**Desc:** Compilation of essays and lectures given at annual meetings of the Georgia Baptist Historical Society. Essays are usually the result of extensive research on various subjects of historical interest.
**Ind/Abst** Am. Hist. Life (1968-).

US/0083-6311
**VIRGINIA BAPTIST REGISTER, THE.** [Va. Baptist regist.]. **Added/Corp** Virginia Baptist Historical Society. No. 1 (1962)-. English. an (November). $4.50. Virginia Baptist Historical Society, University of Richmond, Richmond VA 23173. **Tel** (804)289-8434. **ED** John S. Moore Jr. **LC** BX6248.V8; V56. **DD** 286/.1755. Index available. **Bk Rev**. **Circ:** 750 (ctrl).
**Desc:** Includes previously unpublished articles, diaries, journals, and documents related to early baptist history in Virginia.
**Ind/Abst** Am. Hist. Life.

US/0891-5598
**VIRGINIA UNITED METHODIST ADVOCATE.** ***Title Change.*** [Va. United Methodist advocate]. Periodical. English. Two issues per month (second and fourth Thursday of each month). Virginia United Methodist Advocate, PO Box 11367, Richmond VA 23230. **Tel** (804)359-9451, (800)768-6040, FAX (804)359-5427. **ED** Alvin J Horton. **DD** 287. **UDC** 287. Index available. **Bk Rev**. **Ad Acc**. **Circ:** 18,000 (ctrl). ***Continued by*** *Virginia Advocate, 0042-6458.*
**Desc:** Methodist-related stories and ads.

US/0164-3606
**VOICE OF EVANGELICAL METHODISM, THE.** Periodical. English. mo. $5.00. Evangelical Methodist Church, 3036 North Meridian, Wichita KS 67024. **Tel** (301)457-5101. **UDC** 287.

US/0042-8175
**VOICE OF MISSIONS.** **Added/Corp** African Methodist Episcopal Church. Missionary Dept. Vol. 1 (Jan. 1893)-. Periodical. English. mo. $10.00. African Methodist Episcopal Church, 475 Riverside Drive/Room 1926, New York NY 10115. **Tel** (212)864-2471. **ED** Frederick C. Harrison. **Bk Rev**. **Circ:** 4,100.
**Desc:** News from 29 countries which the African Methodist Episcopal Church serves. Mission trends and activities plus promotional material in missions.

US/0043-1087
**WATCHTOWER, THE.** [Watchtower]. **Added/Corp** Watchtower Bible and Tract Society, Canadian Branch. Watchtower Bible and Tract Society of New York. **VFOAT** Watchtower Announcing Jehovah's Kingdom. (1???)-. Periodical. English. sm (24 issues). Watchtower Bible & Tract Society, 25 Columbia Heights, Walkill NY 12589. **Tel** (914)744-2041. **ED** F. W. Franz. **Circ:** 11,150,000 (ctrl).
**Desc:** Announces Jehovah God's heavenly kingdom. It is the principal publication of Jehovah's Witnesses. Discusses prophecy and gives counsel.

US
**WELLSPRING: A JOURNAL FOR UNITED METHODIST CLERGYMAN.** English. sa. $7.00. First Publishing Inc., 2100 Riverchase Center, Suite 110, Birmingham AL 35244. **Tel** (205)733-1970, FAX (205)733-1974.

US/0275-6528
**WELLWOMAN.** (WELL WOMAN.). **Added/Corp** Lutheran Women's Caucus. **VFOAT** Wellwoman. (June 1978)-. Periodical. English. Four times a year. Lutheran Women's Caucus, 1124 South Ashland Avenue, Chicago IL 60607. ***Continues*** *Adam's Rib.*

US/0043-289X
**WESLEYAN ADVOCATE, THE.** [Wesley. advocate]. **Added/Corp** Wesleyan Church. Vol. 127- (July 15, 1968)-. Periodical. English. mo. $12.50. Wesleyan Publishing House, PO Box 50434, Indianapolis IN 46250-0434. **Tel** (317)842-0444, (317)576-0444, FAX (317)842-9188. **ED** Norman Wilson and Jerry Brecheisen. **DD** 287.1. Index available. **Bk Rev**. **Ad Acc**. **Circ:** 17,000 (ctrl). ***Formed by the union of*** *Wesleyan Methodist, 0190-6100* ***and*** *Pilgrim Holiness Advocate.*
**Desc:** The official publication of the Wesleyan Church and carries news and articles of interest to members and friends of the denomination.
**Ind/Abst** Guide Soc. Sci. Relig.

US/0190-6097
**WESLEYAN CHRISTIAN ADVOCATE.** **Added/Corp** United Methodist Church (United States). North Georgia Conference. United Methodist Church (United States). South Georgia Conference. Vol. 1 (1836)-. Periodical. English. wk. $14.00. Wesleyan Christian Advocate, PO Box 54455, Atlanta GA 30308. **Tel** (404)659-8809, FAX (404)659-1727. **ED** Mark A. Westmoreland. **Bk Rev**. **Ad Acc**. **Circ:** 29,000 (ctrl).
**Desc:** Newspaper of the United Methodist Church in Georgia.

US/1049-8443
**WEST VIRGINIA SOUTHERN BAPTIST, THE.** **Added/Corp** West Virginia Convention of Southern Baptists. (19??)-. Periodical. English. Ten times a year (monthly except July & Dec.). Free on request. West Virginia Convention of South Baptists, 1 Mission Way, Scott Depot WV 25560-9604. **ED** Tom Young (editor's phone: (304)757-0944). **Circ:** 7,800.

US/0197-8896
**WITNESS (AMBLER), THE.** (THE WITNESS.). [Witness]. **Series/Conf** American Theological Library Association, Princeton NJ. (Jan. 6, 1917)-. Periodical. English. Ten times a year (Jan/Feb. & June/July issue combined). $20.00 US; $25.00 other. The Witness, 1249 Washington Blvd, Suite 3115, Detroit MI 48226. **Tel** (313)962-2650, FAX (313)962-1012. **ED** Jeanie Wylie-Kellermann. **LC** BX5800; .W5. Index available in last issue of volume--attached. **Bk Rev**, (Qty: 10/year). **Circ:** 5,500. available on microfilm and microfiche from University Microfilms International (UMI).
**Desc:** Ecumenical social justice journal with articles including art, poetry and personal profiles.
**Ind/Abst** Index Book Rev. Relig.; Relig. Index One Period. (1980-); Relig. Theol. Abstr.

US/0190-4620
**WOMAN'S TOUCH.** **See** Women's Interests.

US/1047-2339
**WORD & WITNESS.** [Word witn.]. **VAT** Word and Witness. (1976)-. Periodical. English. Six times a year. $49.00. Liturgical Publications Inc, 2875 South James Drive, New Berlin WI 53151. **Tel** (414)785-1188, (800)876-4574. **ED** Rev. Paul Wilson (editor's address: Emmanuel College, 75 Queens Park Cres., East, Toronto, ON Canada M5S 1K7). **DD** 251. **Circ:** 2,000.
**Desc:** Assists the lay, cleric and educator in applying the gospel to social conditions. Its social orientation has emphasis on daily events in light of the gospel. It also includes the helpful "Children's Message Resources." It is Protestant in slant.

UK
**WORKS OF JOHN WESLEY, THE.** Monographic series. English. ir. Price varies per volume. Abingdon Press, PO Box 801, Nashville TN 37202. **Tel** (615)749-6451, (800)251-3320.

UK
**WORLD PENTECOST.** **Added/Corp** World Conference of Pentecostal Churches. Vol. 1 (1971)-. Periodical. English. Four times a year (Mar., June, Sept., Dec.). $10.00. World Pentecost, PO Box 98, C/O Rev. Jakob Zopfi, 6376 Emmetten NW Switzerland. **Tel** 011 41 41 642555, FAX 011 41 41 643255. **ED** Rev. Jakob Zopfi. **LC** BX8762.A1; W67a. **DD** 289.9. **Bk Rev**. **Circ:** 1,500.
**Desc:** Publishes reports from Pentecostal churches all over the world. There well doctrinal teaching, reports from conferences and book reviews.

US/1046-381X
**WORSHIP (NASHVILLE, TENN.).** (WORSHIP : RESOURCES FOR THE CHURCH MUSICIAN.). [Worship]. **Added/Corp** Southern Baptist Convention. Sunday School Board. Vol. 1, No. 1 (Oct./Nov./Dec. 1990)-. Periodical. English. qt. $27.25. Southern Baptist Convention, 901 Commerce, Suite 750, Nashville TN 37203. **Tel** (615)244-2355, FAX (615)742-8919. **(Subscription address:** Sunday School Board - Customer Service, 127 Ninth Avenue North, Nashville, TN 37234 USA; telephone: (800)458-2772**)** **DD** 783. ***Continues*** *Opus Two, 0147-1597.*
**Ind/Abst** South. Baptist Period. Index (1990-).

NZ/0110-0416
**YEAR BOOK AND PROCEEDINGS OF THE GENERAL ASSEMBLY - PRESBYTERIAN CHURCH OF NEW ZEALAND.** (YEAR BOOK AND PROCEEDINGS OF THE GENERAL ASSEMBLY.). [Year book proc. Gen. Assem. - Presbyt. Church N. Z.]. **Main/Corp** Presbyterian Church of New Zealand. General Assembly. 1970-. Proceedings. English. an. $1.00. Otago Daily Times, Dunedin Cl, New Zealand. **LC** BX9165; .P68B. **DD** 285/.2931. **UDC** 285.1(063)(931). ***Formed by the union of*** *Proceedings of the General Assembly of the Presbyterian Church of New Zealand, 0551-9845* ***and*** *Year Book - Presbyterian Church of New Zealand, 0551-9853.*

CN/0082-7843
**YEAR BOOK OF THE UNITED BAPTIST CONVENTION OF THE ATLANTIC PROVINCES.** **Main/Corp** United Baptist Convention of the Atlantic Provinces. **VFOAT** United Baptist Yearbook; A.U.B.C. Year Book. 1963-. Periodical. English. Lingley Print, PO Box 1053, Saint John NB E2L 4E7 Canada. **DD** 286/.1/715. ***Continues*** *United Baptist Convention of the Maritime Provinces. Year Book, 0315-5250.*

UK
**YEAR BOOK - UNITED REFORMED CHURCH.** **Main/Corp** United Reformed Church. (1973/74)-. English. an. £7.50 UK; £12.00 North America. United Reformed Church, 86 Tavistock Place, London WC1H 9RT England. **Tel** 011 44 71 9162020. **ED** Sheila Lowden. **LC** BX9890.U25; U54a. **DD** 285/.2. **Ad Acc**. **Circ:** 2,000.

CN/0710-4707
**YEARBOOK.** [Yearb. - Inter-Mennon. Conf., Ont.]. **Main/Corp** Inter-Mennonite Conference (Ontario). 8th Ed. (1981)-. English. an. $10.00. Mennonite Conference of Eastern Canada, 60 New Dundee Road, Kitchener Ontario N2G 3W5 Canada. **Tel** (519)748-2162, FAX (519)748-6684. **DD** 289.7/713. **Circ:** 1,500 (ctrl). ***Continues*** *Conference of the United Mennonite Churches of Ontario. Yearbook, 0319-0218.*
**Desc:** Pictorial book of congregational nature.

US/0092-4660
**YEARBOOK AND MINUTES OF THE ANNUAL CONFERENCE - EVANGELICAL FREE CHURCH OF AMERICA.** ***Title Change.*** (YEARBOOK AND MINUTES OF THE ANNUAL CONFERENCE.). **Main/Corp** Evangelical Free Church of America. English. an. Evangelical Free Church of America, 1515 East 66th Street, Minneapolis MN 55423. **LC** BX7548.A1; E93A. **DD** 289.9. ***Continued by*** *Yearbook (Evangelical Free Church of America), 1049-8591.*

CN/0067-4087
**YEARBOOK - BAPTIST UNION OF WESTERN CANADA.** (YEARBOOK.). **VFOAT** A.Year book. (1907)-. English. an. 20.00Can$. Baptist Union of Western Canada, 838 11th Avenue SW, Suite 202, Calgary Alberta T2R 0E5 Canada. **Tel** (403)234-9044, FAX (403)269-6755. **ED** Rev. William Cram. **LC** BX6252.W47; B37a. **DD** 286/.1/712. Index available. **Circ:** 500 (ctrl).
**Desc:** Yearbook containing reports to annual meetings, statistics and directory of officers and churches.

US/1049-8591
**YEARBOOK / EVANGELICAL FREE CHURCH OF AMERICA.** [Yearb. - Evang. Free Church Am.]. **Main/Corp** Evangelical Free Church of America. (19??)-. English. Evangelical Free Church of America, 1515 East 66th Street, Minneapolis MN 55423. **LC** BX7548.A1; E93a. **DD** 289.9/5. ***Continues*** *Evangelical Free Church of America.; Yearbook and Minutes of the Annual Conference - Evangelical Free Church of America, 0092-4660.*

US
**YEARBOOK / EVANGELICAL LUTHERAN CHURCH IN AMERICA.** **Main/Corp** Evangelical Lutheran Church in America. (1988)-. Periodical. English. an. $13.95. Augsburg Fortress Publishers, 426 South Fifth Street, Box 1209, Minneapolis MN 55440. **Tel** (800)328-4648, (612)330-3300. ***Formed by the union of*** *The American Lutheran Church; The Directory of the Association of Evangelical Lutheran Churches* ***and*** *LCA Yearbook.*

US
**YEARBOOK / LUTHERAN CHURCH IN AMERICA.** **Main/Corp** Lutheran Church in America. English. an. $7.95. Fortress Press, 2900 Queen Lane, Philadelphia PA 19129. **Tel** (215)848-6800. **ED** R T Swanson. Index available. **Ad Acc**. **Circ:** 15,000 (ctrl).
**Desc:** Directory of clergy, congregations, and church wide in America including colleges, seminaries and institutions.

US/0148-3013
**YEARBOOK - NEW YORK YEARLY MEETING, RELIGIOUS SOCIETY OF FRIENDS.** [Yearb., Proc. appointm., N. Y. Yrly. Meet. Relig. Soc. Friends]. **Main/Corp** Society of Friends. New York Yearly Meeting. **Added/Corp** Society of Friends. New York Yearly Meeting. Proceedings and Appointments, New York Yearly Meeting, Religious Society of Friends. (19??)-. English. an. Society of Friends, 15 Rutherford Place, New York NY 10003. **LC** BX7607.N5; A35. **DD** 289.6/05.

# Religion and Theology—Protestantism

**US/0092-3478**
**YEARBOOK OF THE AMERICAN BAPTIST CHURCHES IN THE U.S.A.** (YEARBOOK.). **Main/Corp** American Baptist Churches in the U.S.A. (19??)-. Periodical. English. ir. Free on request. American Baptist Churches USA, PO Box 851, Valley Forge PA 19481. **Tel** (215)768-2000. **LC** BX6207; .A3. **DD** 286/.173. **Continues** Yearbook, Containing Historical Documents and Tables.

**US/1047-1642**
**YOUTH MINISTRY QUARTERLY.** *Ceased.* See Children and Youth Interests.

**GW**
**ZEITSCHRIFT FUER BAYERISCHE KIRCHENGESCHICHTE.** **Added/Corp** Verein fuer Bayerische Kirchengeschichte. Jahresberichte. Verein fuer Bayerische Kirchengeschichte. Vol. 1 (1926)-. German. an (Nov.). DM27.00. Zeitschrift fuer Bayerische Kirchengeschichte, Veilhofstrasse 28, D 90489 Nuernberg Germany. **Tel** 0911/550269 OR 550296. **ED** Horst Weigelt. **LC** BR857.B37; Z4. **Bk Rev. Circ:** 700 (ctrl). **Continues** Beitraege zur Bayerischen Kirchengeschichte.
 **Desc:** Ecclesiastical history of Bavaria, and history of protestantism in Bavaria.

**GW/0044-2674**
**ZEITSCHRIFT FUER EVANGELISCHE ETHIK.** [Z. evang. Ethik]. Vol. 1 (Jan. 1957)-. Periodical. German. qt. DM88.40 (one year), DM50.40 (students), DM26.10 single issue. Guetersloher Verlagshaus, Postfach 450, D 33311 Guetersloh Germany. **Tel** 011 49 5241 74050. **(Subscription address:** VVA Bertelsmann Distributors GmbH, Postfach 7777, D-33310 Guetersloh Germany.) **ED** Ellen Strathmann-Von Soosteu. **LC** BJ1188.5. Index available. cum. index. **Circ:** 1,400. Documents available from The Genuine Article.
 **Desc:** Commentaries, studies, reports and discussions on protestant ethics.
 **Ind/Abst** Arts Humanit. Citation Index [Full Cov.]; Curr. Contents Arts Humanit.; Index Book Rev. Relig.; Relig. Index One Period. (1957-); Res. Alert [Full Cov.].

**GW/0044-2690**
**ZEITSCHRIFT FUER EVANGELISCHES KIRCHENRECHT.** Vol. 1, (April 1951)-. Periodical. German. qt. DM152.00. JCB Mohr / Paul Siebeck, Postfach 2040, D 72010 Tuebingen Germany. **Tel** 011 49 7071 9230, FAX 011 49 7071 51104, telex 7/262872 mohr d. **ED** Axel Frhr von Campenhausen, Christopher Link, Hans Martin Muller, Dietrich Pirson, and Peter von Tiling. **LC** LAW. **[CCC]. Bk Rev. Ad Acc. Circ:** 700.
 **Desc:** Deals with all problems of protestant ecclesiastical law and the relation between state and church, mainly in Germany.
 **Ind/Abst** Index Foreign Leg. Per.

**SW**
**ZEITSCHRIFT FUR KULTUR, POLITIK, KIRCHE.** German. Six times a year. 66.00F (add postage). Langgassdruck AG, Administration Zeitschrift, Postfach 7062, CH-3001 Bern Switzerland. **Tel** 31 24 24 31. **ED** Hektor Leibundgut. Index available. cum. index. **Bk Rev. Ad Acc. Pr Rev. Circ:** 2,000 (ctrl).
 **Desc:** Protestant publication for culture, politics, religion and theology.

**US/0098-9282**
**ZION'S HERALD (1975).** (ZION'S HERALD.). **Added/Corp** United Methodist Area Services Committee. Boston Wesleyan Association. Vol. 153, No. 6 (June/July 1975)-. Periodical. English. bw. $15.00. United Methodist Church South New England, 566 Commonwealth Avenue, Boston MA 02215. **Tel** (617)266-3900, FAX (617)266-4619. **ED** Ann Whiting. **LC** BX8201; .Z6. **DD** 287/.674. **Bk Rev. Ad Acc. Circ:** 7,000 (ctrl). **Continues** Methodist Churchman.
 **Desc:** Focuses on news and features about New England United Methodists.

# RESTAURANTS

**US/1049-782X**
**AERODINE'S FLY-IN RESTAURANT GUIDE.** [Aerodine's fly-in restaur. guide]. **VFOAT** Fly-In Restaurant Guide. English. an. Aerodine Magazine, PO Box 247, Palatine IL 60078. **LC** TL726.2; .A5596. **DD** 647.9577.

**CN/0848-631X**
**ALBERTA RESTAURANT NEWS.** *Ceased.* [Alta. restaur. news]. **Added/Corp** Alberta Restaurant & Foodservices Association. Vol. 1, No. 1 (Summer 1990)-(1992). Periodical. English. qt. Association Publications Ltd, 209-65 Dewdney Avenue, Winnipeg Man R3B 0E1 Canada. **Tel** (800)642-3891, (403)426-6263. **DD** 647.957123/068/8.

**GW/0002-5895**
**ALLGEMEINE HOTEL- UND GASTSTATTEN-ZEITUNG.** See Hotels/Motels.

**US**
**... ANALYSIS OF IMPULSE SNACK BAR OPERATIONS : A STUDY PRESENTED TO THE GOLD MEDAL PRODUCTS COMPANY OF CINCINNATI, OHIO / BY WENDELL G. EARLE AND GEORGE S. HAYWARD, THE.** **Added/Corp** Gold Medal Products Company. **VFOAT** Biennial Analysis of Impulse Snack Bar Operations. (19??)-. English. be. Gold Medal Products Company, 1825 Freeman Avenue, Cincinnati OH 45214. **LC** TX945; .A655. **DD** 338.4/7647/9573.

**US**
**ANNUAL TABLESERVICE RESTAURANT OPERATIONS REPORT ... FOR THE UNITED STATES / NATIONAL RESTAURANT ASSOCIATION.** **VFOAT** Tableservice Restaurant Operations Report. 1st (1976)-. English. an. National Restaurant Association, 1200 17th Street NW, Washington DC 20036. **Tel** (202)331-5900.

**US/0044-9881**
**ATLANTIC CONTROL STATES BEVERAGE JOURNAL.** *Title Change.* (19??)-(19??). Periodical. English. mo. Arnold Lazarus, 3 Twelfth Street, Wheeling WV 26003. **Tel** (304)232-7620, FAX (304)233-1236. **ED** Arnold Lazarus. **Bk Rev. Ad Acc. Circ:** 7,450 (ctrl). **Split into** Atlantic Control States/West Virginia Beverage Journal, 1054-6553; Atlantic Control States/Virginia Beverage Journal, 1054-6561 **and** Atlantic Control States/North Carolina Beverage Journal, 1054-657X.
 **Desc:** Trade journal serving the food/drink service industry.

**US**
**BALTIMORE EPICURE.** (19??)-. English. Peanut Butter Publishing, 329 2nd West, Seattle WA 98119-4105. **Tel** (206)628-6200. **Circ:** 250,000.
 **Desc:** Reproduction of the menus from 75 popular restaurants in major cities across the country. Series of 20 epicures.

**US/0893-1194**
**BED & BREAKFAST AMERICAN STYLE.** *Suspended.* See Travel and Tourism.

**US/0887-7505**
**BED & BREAKFAST UPDATE.** *Ceased.* See Travel and Tourism.

**UK**
**BHRCA OFFICIAL GUIDE TO HOTELS AND RESTAURANTS IN GREAT BRITAIN, IRELAND AND OVERSEAS.** See Hotels/Motels.

**US/0892-5399**
**BILL OF FARE.** *Title Change.* (BILL OF FARE / TENNESSEE RESTAURANT ASSOCIATION.). Periodical. English. bm. Images Publications, PO Box 474, Loudon TN 37774. **Tel** (615)458-3560. **Continued by** Tennessee Restauranteurs.

**US/0731-1923**
**... BOSTON RESTAURANT GUIDE, THE.** [Boston restaur. guide]. 1980-. English. an. $3.95. Jubilee Publications, Inc., 227 Statler Office Building, Boston MA 02116.

**UK**
**BRITISH HOTELIER & RESTAURATEUR : OFFICIAL MAGAZINE OF THE BRITISH HOTELS, RESTAURANTS & CATERERS ASSOCIATION.** *Title Change.* See Hotels/Motels.

**CN/0711-6322**
**CAFES ET RESTAURANTS CHOUETTES.** **VAT** Restaurants Chouettes (1981). 1981-. French. an. $2.50 per number. Cafes et Restaurants Chouettes, 1026 East rue Mont-Royal, Montreal Quebec H2J 1X2 Canada. **DD** 647/.95714281. **Continues** Restaurants Chouettes de Montreal, 0711-6314.

**US/0735-5548**
**CAMERON'S FOODSERVICE PROMOTIONS REPORTER.** *Title Change.* See Business-Advertising and Public Relations.

**CN/1182-9923**
**CANADIAN HOTEL AND RESTAURANT (1990).** *Title Change.* See Hotels/Motels.

**CN**
**CANADIAN HOTEL & RESTAURANT SOURCES DIRECTORY.** See Hotels/Motels.

**US/0148-4516**
**CAPITAL FEASTS.** 1970-. English. an. $4.50. Rock Creek Publishing Company, PO Box 19273, Washington DC 20036. **LC** TX907; .C33. **DD** 647/.95753.

**CN/0830-0895**
**CHEF DU SERVICE ALIMENTAIRE, LE.** [Chef serv. aliment.]. **VFOAT** Chef. Vol. 4, No. 1 (Sept./Oct. 1985)-. Periodical. French (English). Six times a year. 30.00Can$. Le Chef du Service Alimentaire, 252 Route 171, St. Etienne Lauz QOS 2L0 Canada. **Tel** (418)831-5317, FAX (418)831-5172. **ED** Maurice LeBlanc. **DD** 647/.94714. **Ad Acc. Circ:** 18,000 (ctrl). **Continues** Restaurateur (Saint-Etienne-de-Lauzon, Quebec), 0821-2775.
 **Desc:** Covers hospitality and food service industry.

**FR/0980-8396**
**CHEF PARIS, LE.** See Home Economics.

**US/0091-861X**
**COOKING FOR PROFIT.** See Food and Food Industry.

**US/0010-8804**
**CORNELL HOTEL AND RESTAURANT ADMINISTRATION QUARTERLY, THE.** See Hotels/Motels.

**US/0411-7085**
**DIRECTORY OF CHAIN RESTAURANT OPERATORS.** **Added/Corp** Business Guides, Inc. **VFOAT** Chain Restaurant Operators; Chain Store Guide; Chain Restaurants; Restaurants. (19??)-. Directory. English. an. $284.00 continental US; $294.00 Alaska, Hawaii, Puerto Rico, Canada, & Mexico; $309.00 other. Lebhar Friedman Inc., 3922 Coconut Palm Drive, Tampa FL 33619. **Tel** (800)927-9292, (813)664-6707. **ED** Jim Ticrney. **LC** TX907; .D49. **DD** 647/.9573/05.
 **Desc:** Provides company profiles on 3,000 or more unit chain restaurant companies operating or franchising 160,000 restaurants, drive-ins, cafeterias, etc.

**US/0888-0166**
**DIRECTORY OF HIGH-VOLUME INDEPENDENT RESTAURANTS.** [Dir. high-vol. indep. restaur.]. **VFOAT** Directory of High Volume Independent Restaurants; High-Volume Independent Restaurants; High Volume Independent Restaurants; Chain Store Guide. (1987)-. Directory. English. be. $229.00. Chain Store Guide Information Services, 425 Park Avenue, New York NY 10022. **Tel** (212)371-9400, FAX (212)826-6390. **ED** Lars Jacobsen. **LC** TX907; .D495. **DD** 338.7/61647/9573. Index available.
 **Desc:** Profiles on more than 7,000 one-or-two unit independents operating nearly 8,000 restaurants in the US each with a minimum of $1,000,000 in annual sales. Identifies type of food service, liquor served, type of menu, sales volume, number of seats, on-or-off site catering, the names/titles of more than 17,000 key executives and more.

**CN/0227-4302**
**DIRECTORY OF RESTAURANT AND FAST FOOD CHAINS IN CANADA.** [Dir. restaur. fast food chains Can.]. **VFOAT** Restaurant and Fast Food Chains in Canada. (1980)-. Directory. English. an. 200.00Can$. MacLean Hunter Publ. Limited / Toronto, 777 Bay Street, 8th Floor Agency Control, Toronto Ontario M5W 1A7 Canada. **Tel** (416)596-5000, (800)268-6811, FAX (416)596-5526. **DD** 642/.5/0971.
 **Desc:** A directory listing all restaurant chains with three or more outlets.

**US**
**DYNAMICS OF THE CHAIN RESTAURANT MARKET.** **Added/Corp** Technomic Consultants. International Foodservice Manufacturers Association. **VFOAT** Chain Restaurant Market. (19??)-. English. an. $328.50 (members), $478.50 (nonmembers). International Food Service Manufacturers Association, 875 North Michigan Avenue, Suite 3460, Chicago IL 60610. **Tel** (312)467-0810.
 **Desc:** Comprehensive source of current information for marketers to the chain restaurant foodservice market. Includes executive summary, and is available on data disk.

**CN/0704-5999**
**EDITION QUEBECOISE.** V. 2- Jan. 1977-. Periodical. French. mo. $2.00 per no. Infhotel Presse, CP 6053, Montreal 101, Quebec H3C 3A7 Canada. **DD** 641.5/72/09714. **Continues** Special Canada, 0700-799X.

**UK**
**EGON RONAY'S GUIDE TO HOTELS, RESTAURANTS, PUBS, INNS IN GREAT BRITAIN AND IRELAND AND LONDON PENSIONS.** See Hotels/Motels.

**US/0882-0376**
**EGON RONAY'S TWA GUIDE ... TO GOOD RESTAURANTS IN 35 EUROPEAN BUSINESS CITIES.** [Egon Ronay's TWA guide good restaur. 35 Eur. bus. cities].

# Restaurants

**VFOAT** TWA Guide ... to Good Restaurants in 35 European Business Cities. 1983-. English. an. $1.00. Harmony Books, 225 Park Avenue South, New York NY 10003. **Tel** (212)254-1600, telex 427195. **LC** TX910.A1; E37. **DD** 647/.954.

US/0747-2560
**FINE DINING.** (198?)-. Periodical. English. bm. $13.50. Fine Dining, PO Box 012259, Miami FL 33101. *Formed by the union of Fine Dining, South Florida, 0194-875X and Fine Dining, New York.*

GW/0939-8414
**FIRST CLASS ALFELD.** See Hotels/Motels.

US/0192-348X
**FLORIDA RESTAURATEUR.** [Fla. restaur.]. **Added/Corp** Florida Restaurant Association. (19??)-. Periodical. English. ir. Florida Restaurant Association, 2441 Hollywood Boulevard, Hollywood FL 33020. **Tel** (305)921-6300. **ED** Hugh Mickey McLinden. **DD** 642. **Ad Acc. Circ:** 7,000 (ctrl).
**Desc:** Service articles and news for Florida foodservice operators. Covers business ideas, new products and developments, and changes in the restaurant and hospitality industry.

US/0046-418X
**FLORIDA RESTAURATEUR & PURVEYOR NEWS.** (1956)-. Periodical. English. bm. $15.00. Florida Restaurant Association, 2441 Hollywood Boulevard, Hollywood FL 33020. **Tel** (305)921-6300. **ED** Angela Pyke. **DD** 642.5. **Ad Acc. Circ:** 7,000 (ctrl).
**Desc:** Service articles and news for Florida foodservice operators. New products, changes in industry, employee relations, trends, energy, food, economics, alcohol, and wages.

US/0891-0154
**FOOD & SERVICE / TEXAS RESTAURANT ASSOCIATION.** See Food and Food Industry.

CN/0007-8972
**FOODSERVICE & HOSPITALITY.** [Foodserv. hosp.]. **Added/Corp** Canadian Federation of Chefs de Cuisine. Canadian Restaurant Association. Ontario Hotel & Motel Association. Vol. 6, No. 1 (Jan. 1973)-. Periodical. English. Eleven times a year (monthly with July/Aug. issues combined). 42.06Can$ (one year); 60.75Can$ (two years); 70.09Can$ (three years) Canada; 60.00Can$ other. Food Service and Hospitality, 980 Yonge Street, Suite 400, Toronto Ontario M4W 2J8, Canada. **Tel** (416)923-8888, FAX (416)923-6114. **ED** Rosanna Caira. **[CCC]. Ad Acc. Circ:** 30,000 (ctrl).
*Continues Foodservice/Hospitality Canada, 0317-5162.*
**Desc:** Focuses on business and food trends; also hotel and restaurant operator profiles covering the food service and hospitality industry in Canada.
**Ind/Abst** Can. Bus. Index; F&S Index Plus Text, Int. [Select. Cov.]; PROMT.

US/1040-4546
**FOODSERVICE OPERATORS GUIDE.** See Food and Food Industry.

US/0739-9502
**GALLUP MONTHLY REPORT ON EATING OUT, THE. Ceased.** Ceased (March 1988). Periodical. English. mo. The Gallup Organization Inc, 53 Bank Street, Princeton NJ 08540. **Tel** (609)924-9600. **ED** Valerie Sinclair. Index available. **Circ:** 1,000. *Continues Gallup Monthly Report on Eating Out Attitudes and Behavior.*
**Desc:** Market research measuring the incidence of eating out, consumer's attitudes toward pricing, menu items beverages; information on take-out food and other relevant restaurant data.

US/0895-3910
**GASTRONOME (NEW YORK, N.Y.).** (GASTRONOME.). [Gastronome]. **Added/Corp** Chaine des Rotisseurs. (19??)-. Periodical. English. Three times a year. $30.00. Confrerie Chaine Des Rotisseurs USA, 980 Madison Avenue, Suite 202, New York NY 10021. **Tel** (212)570-1302. **ED** Marion Gorman. **DD** 641. *Continues Chaine Letter.*
**Desc:** Reviews restaurants, wine and food.

CN/0705-7520
**GITE (ST-JOSEPH).** See Hotels/Motels.

FR
**GUIDE FRANCE ... / GAULT ET MILLAU.** **VFOAT** Gault Millau Guide France. French (French). an. $125.00. Societe Anonyme Jour-Azur, 4 rue de Presbourg, 75116 Paris France. **LC** TX907; .G798. **DD** 647/.9444/05.

US/1059-583X
**GUIDE TO RESTAURANTS AND BARS.** [Guide restaur. bars]. **VFOAT** Restaurants and Bars. 1st Edition (Sept. 1991)-. English. ir. Practitioners Publishing Company, PO Box 966, Ft. Worth TX 76101-0966. **Tel** (800)323-8724, (817)322-3709. **LC** TX911.3.M27; G83. **DD** 647.95/068.

SP
**HORECO.** Spanish. mo. 10.000ptas 12100.00ptas other. Ediciones Alfil SA, Horeco Calle, 9 Zancotta 9-5, 48013 Bilbao Spain. **Tel** 34 4 4410766, FAX 34 4 4425116. **ED** Ignacio Echevarria. **UDC** 68. **Bk Rev. Ad Acc. Pr Rev. Circ:** 10,000 (ctrl).
**Desc:** Magazine on restaurants, hotels, and catering.

CN/0704-6359
**HOSPITALITE (TORONTO).** (L'HOSPITALITE.). [Hospitalite]. (1977)-. Periodical. French. bm. 37.00Can$ Canada; 59.00Can$ US; 68.00Can$ other. Communications Vero Inc, 1600 Henri Bourassa Boulevard, Montreal Quebec H3M 3E2 Canada. **Tel** (514)332-8376, FAX (541)332-2666. **ED** Pierre-Yves Verronneau. **DD** 647/.95714. **Ad Acc. Circ:** 15537 (ctrl). available on microfilm from University Microfilms International (UMI).
**Desc:** Articles about restaurants' quality and recipes.

US
**HOSPITALITY DIRECTIONS.** English. qt. $295.00 (one year); $590.00 (two year). Coopers & Lybrand (USA), Communications Department, 1301 Avenue of the Americas, New York NY 10019. **Tel** (212)259-3095.
**Ind/Abst** Leis. Recreat. Tour. Abstr.

US
**HOSPITALITY MANAGEMENT.** Vol. 1, No. 1 (Aug./Sept. 1988)-. Periodical. English. bm. $18.00. Roedler & Delmont, 1700 Livingston Avenue, St Paul MN 55118. **Tel** (612)457-2289. **CODEN** HOMAE3. *Formed by the union of Hospitality Scene and Today's Restaurant Manager.*
**Ind/Abst** Foods Adlibra.

US/0332-4400
**HOTEL & CATERING REVIEW (BLACKROCK, DUBLIN).** See Hotels/Motels.

II
**HOTEL AND RESTAURANT GUIDE INDIA.** See Hotels/Motels.

NE
**HOTEL- EN RESTAURANTGIDS NEDERLAND.** See Hotels/Motels.

GW
**HOTEL RESTAURANT.** German. mo. DM30.80 Germany; DM33.20 other. Hugo Matthaes Druckerei Verlag, Postfach 103144, W-7000 Stuttgart 10 Germany. **Tel** 011 49 711 21331. **ED** A M Mattlaes. Index available. **Bk Rev. Ad Acc. Circ:** 8,400 (ctrl).

SZ
**HOTEL- UND GASTGEWERBE RUNDSCHAU.** See Hotels/Motels.

FR
**HOTELS, CAFES, RESTAURANTS EN ... .** See Hotels/Motels.

US/0272-6602
**HOUSTON MONTHLY.** (HOUSTON MONTHLY'S RESTAURANT & ENTERTAINMENT GUIDE.). **VFOAT** Restaurant & Entertainment Guide. **VAT** Houston Monthly's Restaurant and Entertainment Guide. (1980)-. English. an. Party Line Publishing Co Inc, 6603 Rookin, Houston TX 77074. **Tel** (713)772-1039.

US/0279-9618
**ILLINOIS FOODSERVICE NEWS.** (ILLINOIS FOODSERVICE NEWS : THE MAGAZINE OF THE ILLINOIS RESTAURANT ASSOCIATION.). Vol. 69, No. 3 (Apr. 1981)-. Periodical. English. mo. Illinois Restaurant Association, 350 West Ontario/#7, Chicago IL 60610-4017.

US/8750-5525
**INDUSTRY NEWS (RICHMOND, VA.).** (INDUSTRY NEWS / VRA, VIRGINIA RESTAURANT ASSOCIATION.). Periodical. English. mo. $15.00. VRA, 2101 Libbie Avenue, Richmond VA 23230. **Tel** (804)288-3065. **ED** Elizabeth Parchoc. **Ad Acc. Circ:** 1,400 (ctrl). *Continues VRA News, 0745-3876.*
**Desc:** Articles and features on foodservice topics and foodservice people and places.

AT/0814-5806
**INSIDE DINING.** [Inside dining]. (1984)-. Periodical. English. mo. 38.00Aus$ Australia; 105.00Aus$ other. Yaffa Publishing Group Pty Ltd., GPO Box 606, Sydney NSW 2001 Australia. **Tel** 011 61 2 2812333, FAX 011 61 2 2812750. **DD** 647.95945. *Continues Restaurateur and Caterer, 0812-9878.*

US/0361-4220
**INTERNATIONAL GUILD GUIDE, THE.** English. $6.00. Guild Book Service, PO Box 14064, Norfolk VA 23518. **LC** TX950.53; .I57. **DD** 647/.95.

IO
**INVENTARISASI AKOMODASI PROPINSI MALUKU. Main/Corp** Maluku, Indonesia. Kantor Sensus Dan Statistik. Indonesian. Kantor Sensus and Statistik Propinsi Maluku, Jl Pattimora, Ambon Indonesia. **LC** TX910.I6; M34A.

●US/1052-214X
**JOURNAL OF RESTAURANT & FOODSERVICE MARKETING.** [J. restaur. foodserv. mark.]. **VFOAT** Journal of Restaurant and Foodservice Marketing. Vol. 1, No. 1 (1994)-. Periodical. English. qt. $60.00 US; $84.00 other. The Haworth Press Inc, 10 Alice Street, Binghamton NY 13904-1580. **Tel** (607)722-5857, (800)3-HAWORTH, FAX (607)722-1424. **ED** Simon Crawford-Welch. **DD** 647. **Acid Free.** Documents available from Haworth Document Delivery Service.
**Desc:** Features state-of-the-art knowledge on restaurant and foodservice marketing.

UK
**JUST A BITE.** 1979-. English. an. £1.50 UK; $3.95 US. Egon Ronay Organisation, Greencoat House, Francis Street, London SW1P 1 England. **LC** TX910.G7; J87. **DD** 647/.9541.

US/0022-8753
**KANSAS RESTAURANT. Added/Corp** Kansas Restaurant Association. (19??)-. Periodical. English. Four times a year. $100.00 Comes with Kansas Restaurant Association membership. Kansas Restaurant, 359 South Hydraulic, Wichita KS 67211. **Tel** (316)267-8383. **ED** Trish Phelps. **Bk Rev. Ad Acc. Circ:** 1,200 (ctrl).
**Desc:** All things of interest to to the foodservice and hospitality industry on both a national and state level.

CN/0846-2992
**LITT RESTAURANT GUIDE, THE.** [Litt restaur. guide]. (1991)-. English. $4.95 per v. Litt Publications, PO Box 215, Station C, 75 Ingleside Drive, Kitchener, Ontario N2G 3X9 Canada. **DD** 647.95713/05. *Continues Litt Report (Toronto edition)., 0846-2976.*

CN/0846-2984
**LITT RESTAURANT GUIDE (NATIONAL ED.).** (THE LITT RESTAURANT GUIDE : CANADIAN RESTAURANTS FROM COAST TO COAST.). [Litt restaur. guide]. (1991)-. English. $14.95 per volume. Litt Publications, PO Box 215, Station C, 75 Ingleside Drive, Kitchener, Ontario N2G 3X9 Canada. **DD** 647.9571/05. *Continues The Litt Report., 0848-1253.*

CN/0846-300X
**LITT RESTAURANT GUIDE (QUEBEC ED.).** (THE LITT RESTAURANT GUIDE.). [Litt. restaur. guide]. (1991)-. English. $4.95 per volume. Litt Publications, PO Box 215, Station C, 75 Ingleside Drive, Kitchener, Ontario N2G 3X9 Canada. **DD** 647.95714/05.

CN/0846-3018
**LITT RESTAURANT GUIDE (WESTERN ED.).** (THE LITT RESTAURANT GUIDE.). [Litt restaur. guide]. (1991)-. English. $4.95 per volume. Litt Publications, PO Box 215, Station C, 75 Ingleside Drive, Kitchener, Ontario N2G 3X9 Canada. **DD** 647.95712/05.

FI
**MAJOITUSLIIKKEIDEN KAPASITEETTI.** **VFOAT** Harbargeringsstallenas Kapasitet; Capacity of Accommodation Facilities. 1977-. Multiple languages (English, Finnish and Swedish). Tilastokeskus, PL 504, Annankatu 44, 00101 Helsinki Finland. **Tel** 358-0-17341, FAX 358-0-17342474, telex 1002111 TILASTO SF. **LC** TX901; .M338. *Continues Majoitustilasto, Majoitusliikkeiden Kapasiteetti.*

US/0197-5099
**MANHATTAN MENUS.** [Manhattan menus]. (19??)-. English. an. Restaurant Publishing, 265 West 37th Street/8th Floor, New York NY 10018. **Tel** (212)719-5896. **LC** TX907; .M323. **DD** 647/.95747/105.

CN/1184-1605
**MANITOBA RESTAURANT NEWS.** [Manit. restaur. news]. Vol. 1, No. 1 (Fall 1989)-. Periodical. English. qt. Limited free distribution. Manitoba Restaurant and Foodservices Association, 203-897 Corydon Avenue, Winnipeg Manitoba R3M 0W7 Canada. **DD** 647.957127/068. *Continues Manitoba Restaurant & Foodservices Association.; Membership Directory and Buyers' Guide, 0824-0930.*

US/0887-9214
**MEAT SOURCE. Ceased.** See Food and Food Industry.

US/0148-4133
**MENUS OF THE VALLEY'S FINEST RESTAURANTS.** English. an. $4.75. Quail Run Publications Inc, 5221 Quail Run Place, Paradise Valley AZ 85253. **Tel** (602)955-5953. **ED** John V Long. **Circ:** 10,000 (ctrl).
**Desc:** Restaurant menus as they actually appear from select dining establishments in the Phoenix Arizona metro area, cross referenced by location and food classification.

# Restaurants

UK
**MICHELIN GREAT BRITAIN AND IRELAND.** See Hotels/Motels.

UK
**MICHELIN GREATER LONDON.** See Hotels/Motels.

US/0892-8231
**MICHIGAN RESTAURATEUR (1987).** (MICHIGAN RESTAURATEUR.). [Mich. restaur.]. **Added/Corp** Michigan Restaurant Association. Vol. 52, No. 1 (Jan./Feb. 1987)-. Periodical. English. bm. $6.00 (members). Michigan Restaurant Association, 10214 East Warren, Detroit MI 48214. **DD** 338. **Continues** Michigan Hospitality, 0161-6447.

US/0888-7829
**MODERN FOOD SERVICE NEWS.** [Mod. food serv. news]. Vol. 1, No. 1 (Oct. 1989)-. Periodical. English. Twelve times a year. $30.00. Grocers Publishing Company, 15 Emerald Street, Hackensack NJ 07601. **Tel** (201)488-1800. **ED** John Strovinsky. **DD** 642. **Bk Rev**. **Ad Acc**. **Circ**: 24,000 (ctrl). **Continues** Modern Food Service News, 0888-7829.
 **Desc**: Newspaper for restaurants, institutions, chefs, purchasing agents, hotel/motels with on premises feeding capabilities.

CN/0823-2857
**MONTREAL CUISINE.** **VFOAT** Cuisine de Montreal. English (French). an. 12.95Can$ Canada. Montreal Cuisine, PO Box 1471 Place Bonaventure, Montreal Quebec H5A 1H5 Canada. **Tel** (514)871-9122, **FAX** (514)866-0578, telex 055-61811. **ED** John R McCann. **DD** 647/.95714281. Index available. **Bk Rev**. **Ad Acc**. **Circ**: 50,000.
 **Desc**: A guide to the restaurants and nightclubs in Montreal.

US/0196-0032
**MYRA WALDO'S RESTAURANT GUIDE TO NEW YORK CITY AND VICINITY.** **VFOAT** Restaurant Guide to New York City and Vicinity. English. $5.95 per copy. Macmillan Publishing Company, 866 3rd Avenue, New York NY 10022. **Tel** (212)702-2000, (800)257-5755. **(Subscription address:** Front and Brown Street, Riverside, NJ 08370) **LC** TX907; .W34. **DD** 647/.95747/1.

US/0028-0518
**NATION'S RESTAURANT NEWS.** [Nation's restaur. news]. **VFOAT** Restaurant News. (19??)-. Periodical. English. Fifty times a year. $59.00 (architects, consultants, manufacturers), $89.00 (other) (nontrade) $34.50 (trade) US; $69.00 (architects, consultants, manufacturers), $99.00 (other) (nontrade) $44.50 (trade) Canada; $295.00 other. Lebhar Friedman Inc., 3922 Coconut Palm Drive, Tampa FL 33619. **Tel** (800)927-9292, (813)664-6707. **DD** 642. **[CCC.]** available on microfilm and microfiche from University Microfilms International (UMI); available on an online database (files 16,570,648/Full-Text) from DIALOG. **Continues** National Restaurant News.
 **Desc**: Helps readers understand the forces shaping the market. Includes special reports, forecasts and trends, the Top 100, annual company profile, and the year in review.
 **Ind/Abst** Acad. Search (July 1993-); Bus. ASAP (1990-) [Full Txt.]; Bus. Index (1985-); Bus. Source (Jul. 1993-); F&S Index Plus Text, Int. [Full Txt.] [Select. Cov.]; Foods Adlibra; Gen. BusinessFile (1985-); Gen. Period. Index (1985-); Infobank (1979-); Infomat Int. Bus.; Mark. Advert. Ref. Serv. [Full Txt.]; PROMT [Full Txt.]; Stat. Ref. Index; Trade Ind. ASAP [Full Txt.]; Trade Ind. Index (1981-) [Full Txt.].

US
**NEW JERSEY RESTAURANT GUIDE.** English. $5.95 (plus $1.00 shipping and handling). John Bakie, 35 North Avenue, Bridgewater NJ 08807. **ED** John Bakie. **Ad Acc**.
 **Desc**: Listings of New Jersey restaurants and articles about dining in New Jersey.

US/8756-498X
**NEW ORLEANS MENU, THE.** See Food and Food Industry.

RU
**OBSHCHESTVENNOE PITANIE.** (1933)-. Periodical. Russian. mo. $21.50. Izdatelstvo Ekonomika, Berezhkovskaia Nab., 6, 121864 Moscow Russia. **LC** TX1; .O25.

US
**OFFICERS' REPORT & DAILY CONVENTION PROCEEDINGS - HOTEL AND RESTAURANT EMPLOYEES AND BARTENDERS INTERNATIONAL UNION.** See Hotels/Motels.

UK
**OFFICIAL GUIDE, HOTELS AND RESTAURANTS IN GREAT BRITAIN AND IRELAND, THE.** See Hotels/Motels.

US
**OFFICIAL GUIDE TO FOOD SERVICE AND HOSPITALITY MANAGEMENT CAREERS, THE.** See Occupations and Careers.

US/1060-6114
**OHIO RESTAURANT HOTLINE.** (OHIO RESTAURANT HOTLINE / THE OHIO RESTAURANT ASSOCIATION.). **Added/Corp** Ohio Restaurant Association. Vol. 1, Issue 1 (1990)-. Periodical. English. bm. Ohio State Restaurant Association, 1061 Country Club Road, Columbus OH 43227. **Continues** Legislative Bulletin (Ohio Restaurant Association), 1060-6122.

US/0746-5270
**OHIO RESTAURANT JOURNAL.** Vol. 1, No. 1 (Sept./Oct. 1983)-. Periodical. English. bm. $5.00 members. Ohio State Restaurant Association, 1061 Country Club Road, Columbus OH 43227. **Continues** OSRA Food Service Digest, 0745-1016.

US/0030-1183
**OHIO TAVERN NEWS.** Periodical. English. sm. $12.00 (one year), $20.00 (two years). Columbus Daily Reporter, 329 South Front Street, Columbus OH 43215-5094. **Tel** (614)224-4835, **FAX** (614)224-8649. **ED** Chris Bailey. **Ad Acc**, **Adv Mgr**: Tom Weeks, **Tel** (614)224-4835. **Circ**: 13,500 (ctrl).
 **Desc**: Industry news, changes in laws and regulations governing industry, meetings, columns on personnel changes, coming events and legislative activities.

CN/0714-8232
**OTTAWA-HULL GASTRONOMIC.** [Ottawa-Hull gastron.]. **VFOAT** Gastronomique d'Ottawa-Hull; Le Gastronomique d'Ottawa-Hull. 1st Ed. English (French). an. $3.95 each volume. Ottawa-Hull Gastronomic, c/o Apogee Enterprises, PO Box 48525 Station Bentall, Vancouver British Columbia V7X 1A2 Canada. **DD** 642/.5/02571384.

PK/0250-4359
**PAKISTAN HOTEL & RESTAURANT GUIDE.** See Hotels/Motels.

FR
**PARIS AND ENVIRONS : HOTELS AND RESTAURANTS.** See Hotels/Motels.

CN/0824-779X
**PASSEPORT GASTRONOMIQUE. LE QUEBEC.** **VFOAT** Gourmet Passport. Le Quebec. (1981)-. English (French). an. $6.95. Gourmet Passport, 2401 De La Province, Longueuil Quebec J4G 1G3. **DD** 647/.9571427.

CN/0226-7292
**PASSEPORT GASTRONOMIQUE. MONTREAL ET ALENTOURS.** **VFOAT** Gourmet Passport. Montreal and Vicinity. 1980-. English (French). an. Gourmet Passport, 2401 De La Province, Longueuil Quebec J4G 1G3. **DD** 647/.95714281.

CN/0710-040X
**PASSEPORT GASTRONOMIQUE. QUEBEC ET ALENTOURS.** **VFOAT** Gourmet Passport. Quebec and Vicinity. 1982-. English (French). an. Gourmet Passport, 2401 De La Province, Longueuil Quebec J4G 1G3. **DD** 647/.9571447.

CN/1185-2151
**PATRONS PICK TORONTO'S FAVOURITE RESTAURANTS.** [Patrons Pick Tor. favor. restaur.]. **VFOAT** Toronto's Favourite Restaurants. (1991)-. English. $8.95 per volume. Baby Boomer Press, Inc., PO Box 272, Markham Ontario L3P 3J7 Canada. **DD** 647.95/025713541. **Continues** The Patrons' Pick Toronto Restaurant Survey., 0844-4749.

FR
**PETIT LEBEY ... DES BISTROTS PARISIENS, LE.** **VFOAT** Lebey Guide to Parisian Bistros. 1987-. English (English). Editions R Laffont, 6 Place Saint Sulpice, 75006 Paris France. **LC** PAR.

US/0739-9340
**PRO-MOTION.** See Business-Marketing.

UK/0959-2687
**PROFESSIONAL HOTEL & RESTAURANT INTERIORS.** See Interior Design.

CN/0704-6561
**PROFESSOR DIVINSKY'S SELECT RESTAURANT GUIDE.** 4th- Ed.; 1976/1977-. English. an. $2.00 each number. N Divinsky, 2909-1733 Comox Street, Vancouver British Columbia V6G 1P6 Canada. **DD** 647/.95711/33. **Continues** Professor Divinsky's Guide to Good Food in Metro Vancouver, 0315-3592.

US/1059-7204
**RAM UPDATE.** **Main/Corp** Restaurant Association of Maryland. **VAT** Restaurant Association of Maryland Update. Vol. 1, No. 1 (Jan. 1991)-. Periodical. English. mo. Restaurant Association of Maryland, 7113 Ambassador Road, Baltimore MD 21207-2708.

US
**RESTAURANT AND FOOD BUSINESS PUBLICATIONS, NEWSLETTERS, ETC. - A REFERENCE.** English. be. $7.50 North America; $10.50 other. Restaurant Publishing / Houston, Box 570213, Houston TX 77257. **ED** A C Doyle. **Circ**: 1,500.
 **Desc**: References on restaurant and food businesses.

GW/0344-4422
**RESTAURANT- & HOTEL-MANAGEMENT.** See Hotels/Motels.

US/0097-8043
**RESTAURANT BUSINESS.** [Restaur. bus.]. Vol. 73, No. 4 (April 1974)-. Periodical. English. ir (18 issues per year). $79.00. Bill Communications Inc., 355 Park Avenue South, New York NY 10010-1789. **Tel** (800)821-6897, (212)592-6262, **FAX** (212)592-6209. **ED** Peter Berhuski. **LC** TP628; .S7. **DD** 642/.5. **CODEN** RSBSAY. **Bk Rev**. **Ad Acc**. **Circ**: 120,000. available on microfilm and microfiche from University Microfilms International (UMI). **Continues** Fast Food.
 **Desc**: Serves the information needs of commercial foodservice locations, including restaurants, hotels, motels, resorts, recreation/amusement places, clubs, industrial catering, plant/factory/office and in-transit. Articles cover every facet of labor, taxes, menu planning, food preparation, automation, product, equipment, industry trends, etc.
 **Ind/Abst** Acad. Search (Jan. 1993-); AGRICOLA [Select. Cov.]; BioBusiness (1988-); Bus. ASAP (1990-) [Full Txt.]; Bus. Index (1985-); Bus. Period. Index; Bus. Source (Jan. 1993-); Foods Adlibra; Gen. BusinessFile (1985-); Gen. Period. Index (1985-); INFO-SOUTH Abstr.; Mag. Search; Mark. Advert. Ref. Serv.; Stat. Ref. Index; Trade Ind. ASAP [Full Txt.]; Trade Ind. Index [Full Txt.]; UMI ABI/Inform--Bus. Period. Ondisc (Jan. 1991-) [Full Txt.]; Vocat. Search (Jan. 1993-); Wilson Bus. Abstr.

US/0270-4161
**RESTAURANT BUYERS GUIDE.** See Business-Purchasing.

US/0095-5159
**RESTAURANT EXECUTIVE.** Periodical. English. mo. $25.00. Morken/Grewe Communications, Inc., 645 North Michigan Avenue, Chicago IL 60611. **LC** TX945; .Q53. **DD** 647/.95/05. **Continues** Quickservice Operations Management.

US/0147-9989
**RESTAURANT HOSPITALITY.** [Restaur. hospit.]. Vol. 58, No. 6 (June 1974)-. Periodical. English. Twelve times a year. $60.00 US; $80.00 Canada; $110.00 Mexico; $130.00 other. Penton Publishing, 1100 Superior Avenue, Cleveland OH 44114-2543. **Tel** (216)696-7000, **FAX** (216)696-0836. **(Subscription address:** Penton Publishing, PO Box 96732, Chicago IL 60693.) **ED** Stephen Michaelides, Michael Deluca, Gail Ghetia, and David Farkas. **LC** TX901; .R43. **DD** 642/.56/05. **CODEN** RHOSDP. **[CCC.]** **Bk Rev**. **Ad Acc**. **Circ**: 140,000 (ctrl). available on microfilm from University Microfilms International (UMI); available on an online database (files 15,648/Full-Text) from DIALOG. Documents available from UMI Article Clearinghouse. **Continues** Hospitality, Restaurant, 0098-3292; **Absorbed** Restaurant Management (Cleveland, Ohio).
 **Desc**: Written for commercial food service executives. Topics include new food and equipment products and trends, menu/recipe ideas, marketing strategies, industry news, design and decorating, and operating costs.
 **Ind/Abst** ABI/INFORM Glob. Ed.; ABI Inform Ondisc (March 1988-); Acad. Search (July 1993-); BioBusiness (1990-); Bus. ASAP (1990-) [Full Txt.]; Bus. Index (1985-); Foods Adlibra; Gen. BusinessFile (1985-); Gen. Period. Index (1985-); INFO-SOUTH Abstr.; Mag. Search; Trade Ind. ASAP [Full Txt.]; Trade Ind. Index (1981-) [Full Txt.]; UMI ABI/Inform--Bus. Period. Ondisc (Mar. 1988-) [Full Txt.]; Vocat. Search (July 1993-).

US/1041-2840
**RESTAURANT INDEX.** (1991)-. English. an. $40.00. John Gordon Burke Publisher Inc., PO Box 1492, Evanston IL 60204. **Tel** (708)866-8625, **FAX** (708)866-8625.
 **Desc**: This information service locates award winning restaurants around the United States.

US/1052-4088
**RESTAURANT MANAGEMENT INSIDER.** [Restaur. manage. insid.]. (19??)-. Periodical. English. bw. $225.00 (one year), $420.00 (two year), $610.00 (three year) US, Canada and Mexico; $250.00 (one year), $470.00 (two year), $685.00 (three year) other. Walker Communications Inc., 1541 Morris Avenue, Bronx NY 10457. **Tel** (800)524-3785, (212)583-8060, **FAX** (212)583-8258, . **ED** Michael Schal. **DD** 647. **Bk Rev**. **Circ**: 500. **Continues** Restaurant Management Today, 1040-3434.
 **Desc**: Provides business management information for restaurant owners or managers.
 **Ind/Abst** Mark. Advert. Ref. Serv.

●US/1063-942X
**RESTAURANT MARKETING STRATEGIES.** [Restaur. mark. strateg.]. Vol. 1, No. 1 (Apr. 1992)-. Periodical. English. mo. $75.00. Walker Communications Inc., 1541 Morris Avenue, Bronx NY 10457. **Tel** (800)524-3785, (212)583-8060, FAX (212)583-8258, . **DD** 658.

●US/1062-2322
**RESTAURANT SERVICE REPORT.** VFOAT RSR. (1992)-. Periodical. English. mo. $119.00. Restaurant Service Report, PO Box 3306, Champaign IL 61826-3306.

US/1040-7030
**RESTAURANT WINE.** [Restaur. wine]. Vol. 1, No. 1 (Nov. 1988)- Vol. 6 (Nov/Dec. 1993)-. Periodical. English. Six times a year. $99.00. Restaurant Wine, PO Box 222, Napa CA 94559. **Tel** (707)224-4777, FAX (707)224-6740. **ED** Brenda Bablitt. **DD** 642. **Bk Rev**. **Circ:** 1600.

US/0273-5520
**RESTAURANTS & INSTITUTIONS (CHICAGO, ILL.).** (RESTAURANTS & INSTITUTIONS.). [Restaur. inst.]. VFOAT Restaurants and Institutions. VAT Restaurants and Institutions (Chicago, Ill.). Vol. 88, No. 1 (Jan. 1, 1981)-. Periodical. English. Twenty-four times a year. $110.00 US; $164.00 Canada; $153.00 Mexico; $185.00 (surface mail). Cahners Publishing Company, 249 West 17th Street, New York NY 10011. **Tel** (212)645-0067, FAX (212)242-6987. **(Subscription address:** Cahners Publishing Company / Colorado, Paid Subscription Service Center, PO Box 7610, Highlands Ranch CO 80126-7610.) **ED** Howard Schlossberg. **LC** TX1; .I58. **DD** 642/.5/05. **CODEN** RINSDR. **[CCC]**. **Ad Acc. Circ:** 500,000 (ctrl). available on microfilm and microfiche from University Microfilms International (UMI); available on an online database (file 648/Full-Text) from DIALOG. *Continues* Institutions (Chicago, Ill.)
**Desc:** Features news, new products, recipes, menu concepts and merchandising ideas from the most successful foodservice operations around the nation.
**Ind/Abst** Acad. Search (Jan. 1993-); AGRICOLA [Select. Cov.]; BioBusiness; Bus. Index (1985-); Foods Adlibra; Gen. BusinessFile (1985-); Gen. Period. Index (1985-); Hospit. Health Admin. Index; INFO-SOUTH Abstr.; Leis. Recreat. Tour. Abstr.; Mag. Search; Mark. Advert. Ref. Serv.; Nutr. Abstr. Rev., Ser. A, Hum. Exp.; Stat. Ref. Index; Trade Ind. ASAP [Full Txt.]; Trade Ind. Index [Full Txt.]; Vocat. Search (Jan. 1993-).

US
**RESTAURANTS & INSTITUTIONS MARKETPLACE.** (19??)-. English. bm (6 issues). $50.00 US; $75.00 Canada; $70.00 Mexico; $85.00 (surface mail) other. Cahners Publishing Company, 249 West 17th Street, New York NY 10011. **Tel** (212)645-0067, FAX (212)242-6987. **(Subscription address:** Cahners Publishing Company / Colorado, Paid Subscription Service Center, PO Box 7610, Highlands Ranch CO 80126-7610.)
**Desc:** Product news tabloid delivering issues full of new ideas, product information, recipes, coupons and more.

CN/0849-0538
**RESTAURANTS (QUEBEC).** *Title Change.* (LES RESTAURANTS : LA GASTRONOMIE QUEBECOISE.). [Restaurants]. **Added/Corp** Communaute Urbaine de Quebec (Quebec). Service du Tourisme et des Congres. VFOAT Restaurants. (1989)-(1991)-. French (English). PO Box 1119, Bureau 1919, Montreal Quebec H2W 2P4 Canada. **Tel** (514)288-8875, FAX (514)288-9125. **DD** 647.95714/471. *Continued by* Quoi d'Autre!., 0849-0546.

US/0890-5584
**RESTAURANTS USA.** (RESTAURANTS USA : THE MONTHLY MAGAZINE OF THE NATIONAL RESTAURANT ASSOCIATION.). [Restaur. USA]. **Added/Corp** National Restaurant Association (U.S.). VAT Restaurants United States of America. Vol. 6, No. 7 (Aug. 1986)-. Periodical. English. mo. Free (members), $125.00 (non-members). National Restaurant Association, 1200 17th Street NW, Washington DC 20036. **Tel** (202)331-5900. **LC** TX901; .N75. **DD** 647/.9573. *Continues* NRA News (Washington, D.C. : 1981), 0465-7004.
**Ind/Abst** Foods Adlibra.

US/0162-1319
**ROBERT FINIGAN'S PRIVATE GUIDE TO RESTAURANTS.** *Suspended.* VFOAT Private Guide to Restaurants. (1967)-?. Periodical. English. mo. $24.00. Winecom Inc, 2040 Polk Street/Suite 344, San Francisco CA 94109. **Tel** (415)474-3064. **ED** Robert Finigan. **Circ:** 3,500.
**Desc:** Criticism of northern California restaurants and others in major U.S. cities and abroad.

CN/0714-315X
**ROSTER / RESTAURANTS & FOODSERVICES ASSOCIATION OF BRITISH COLUMBIA.** [Roster - Restaur. & Foodserv. Assoc. B.C.]. **Main/Corp** Restaurant & Foodservices Association of British Columbia. English. an. Free to members. Naylor Communications Ltd, 100 Sutherland Avenue, Winnipeg Manitoba R2W 3C7 Canada. **Tel** (204)947-0222, FAX (604)985-7399. **ED** John Doyle and Will Oliver. **DD** 642/.5/025711. **Circ:** 2,200.

CN/0714-6116
**SEL & POIVRE.** [Sel poivre]. No. 1 (May/June 1981)-. Periodical. French. bm (6 issues). 12.00Can$ Canada; 24.00Can$ other. Publications Quebecor le Nordais, 5800 rue St. Denis, Bar 605, Montreal Quebec H2S 3L5 Canada. **Tel** (514)272-6330. **ED** Claude Durocher. **DD** 641.5/05. **Bk Rev**. **Ad Acc. Circ:** 47,608 (ctrl).
**Desc:** Recipes from good restaurants, tableware, and information about wine.

US/0196-5220
**SEYMOUR BRITCHKY'S RESTAURANT LETTER.** *Ceased.* No. 1 (1980)-?. Periodical. English. mo. Seymour Britchkys Restaurant Letter, PO Box 155, New York NY 10003. **ED** Seymour Britchky. **Circ:** 4,000.
**Desc:** A private guide to New York's newest restaurants and an ongoing review of established ones, in the form of detailed, literate reviews.

US/1053-0185
**STURM DIETER'S RESTAURANT GUIDE, OKLAHOMA CITY.** VFOAT Dieter's Restaurant Guide, Oklahoma City. (1991)-. English. $8.95. Sturm Guides, Inc., PO Box 540001, Oklahoma City OK 73154. **DD** 647.

PK
**SURVEY OF WHOLESALE & RETAIL TRADE & RESTAURANTS.** *See* Business-Retail.

CN/1187-2691
**TABLES CHAMPETRES ET PROMENADES A LA FERME AU QUEBEC.** [Tables champ. promen. ferme Que.]. **Added/Corp** Federation des Agricoteurs du Quebec. VFOAT Quebec Rural Cuisine. (1991)-. French (English). Limited free distribution. Federation des Agricoteurs du Quebec, 4545 Avenue Pierre-du-Coubertin, Montreal, Quebec H1V 3R2. **DD** 647.95714. *Continues* Les Tables Champetres au Quebec., 0848-1393.

CN/1187-2691
**TABLES CHAMPETRES ET PROMENADES A LA FERME AU QUEBEC.** [Tables champ. promen. ferme Que.]. **Added/Corp** Federation des Aagricoteurs du Quebec. VFOAT Quebec Rural Cuisine. (1991)-. English (French). Limited free distribution. Federation des Agricoteurs du Quebec, 4545 Avenue Pierre-du-Coubertin, Montreal, Quebec H1V 3R2. **DD** 647.95714. *Continues* Les Tables Champetres au Quebec.

US
**TENNESSEE RESTAURANTEUR.** English. Four times a year. $8.00. Images Publications, PO Box 474, Loudon TN 37774. **Tel** (615)458-3560. **ED** Ronnie Harb and Judy Mcgiel. **Ad Acc. Circ:** 1,200 (ctrl). *Continues* Bill of Fare / Tennessee, 0892-5399.
**Desc:** Education and state news for members of the Tennessee Restaurant Association.

US/1040-0885
**TOP SHELF.** *Ceased.* (198?)-Jan. (1993). Periodical. English. bm. Top Shelf Inc, 199 Ethan Allen Highway, Ridgefield CT 06877-6207. **Tel** (203)431-0124. **ED** Jack Kenny. **DD** 641. **Ad Acc. Circ:** 300,000 (ctrl).
**Desc:** Covers bar and beverage management.

FR/0150-7540
**TOUTES LES NOUVELLES DE L'HOTELLERIE ET DU TOURISME.** *See* Hotels/Motels.

US/0894-962X
**TRUCKSTOP WORLD.** *See* Transportation.

IT
**TURISMO D'ITALIA.** *See* Hotels/Motels.

FI/0357-749X
**VITRIINI.** *See* Hotels/Motels.

UK
**VOICE OF THE HOSPITALITY ASSOCIATION.** *See* Hotels/Motels.

US/0747-7996
**VRA ECONOMIC DIGEST.** [VRA econ. dig.]. VFOAT V.R.A. Economic Digest; Economic Digest. VAT Virginia Restaurant Association Economic Digest. English. an. Virginia Restaurant Association, 2102 Libbie Avenue, Richmond VA 23230. **LC** TX945; .V72. **DD** 338.4/764795755.

US/1054-1683
**WASHINGTON WEEKLY (WASHINGTON, D.C. 1989).** (WASHINGTON WEEKLY / NATIONAL RESTAURANT ASSOCIATION.). [Wash. wkly.]. **Added/Corp** National Restaurant Association (U.S.). (1989)-. Periodical. English. wk. $25.00 (members), $90.00 (nonmembers). National Restaurant Association, 1200 17th Street NW, Washington DC 20036. **Tel** (202)331-5900. **DD** 647. *Continues* NRA Washington Weekly, 0279-3350.

CN/0315-3088
**WHERE TO EAT IN CANADA.** (1972)-. Periodical. English. an (June). $14.95. Oberon Press, 400 350 Sparks Street, Ottawa Ontario K1R 7S8 Canada. **Tel** (613)238-3275. **ED** Anne Hardy. **DD** 647/.9571. **Bk Rev**. **Circ:** 5,000.
**Desc:** A guide to Canadian restaurants from coast to coast with over 500 listings in every part of Canada. It's the only one of its kind on the market today.

UK
**WHERE TO EAT IN HAMPSHIRE.** English. Kingsclere Publications Ltd, Highfield House, 2 Highfield Avenue, Newbury Berkshire RG14 5DS England. **DD** 647/.954227.

UK
**WHERE TO EAT IN SCOTLAND.** English. Kingsclere Publications Ltd, Highfield House, 2 Highfield Avenue, Newbury Berkshire RG14 5DS England. **DD** 647/.95411.

US/0274-7472
**WISCONSIN RESTAURATEUR, THE.** **Added/Corp** Wisconsin Restaurant Association. (1933)-. Trade Publication. English. Six times a year. $17.50. Wisconsin Restaurant Association, 31 South Henry Street / Suite 300, Madison WI 53703. **Tel** (608)251-3663, FAX (608)251-3666. **ED** Sonya K. Bice. **Ad Acc, Adv Mgr:** Kerry Koppen. **Circ:** 4,000.
**Desc:** A trade publication for the promotion, protection and improvement of Wisconsin's food service industry.

US/1062-2403
**ZAGAT LOS ANGELES, SO. CALIFORNIA RESTAURANT SURVEY.** [Zagat Los Angel. So. Calif. restaur. surv.]. **Added/Corp** Zagat Survey (Firm). VFOAT Zagat Los Angeles, Southern California Restaurant Survey; Los Angeles, So. California Restaurant Survey; A.Los Angeles, Southern California restaurant survey. (1991)-. English. $9.95. Zagat Survey, 4 Columbus Circle, New York NY 10019. **LC** TX907.3.C22; L679. **DD** 647/.95794/94. *Continues* Zagat Los Angeles Restaurant Survey.

---

## ABSTRACTING, BIBLIOGRAPHIES AND STATISTICS

---

CN/0226-2320
**RESTAURANT, CATERER AND TAVERN STATISTICS.** [Restaur. cater. tavern stat.]. **Added/Corp** Statistics Canada. Merchandising and Services Division. Statistics Canada. Services Division. Statistics Canada. Services, Science and Technology Division. VFOAT Statistiques des Restaurants, Traiteurs et Tavernes. Vol. 14, No. 1 (Jan. 1981)-. English (French). mo. 70.00Can$ Canada; $84.00 US; $98.00 other. Statistics Canada, Publications Sales & Services, Main Building Room 1710, Ottawa Ontario K1A 0T6 Canada. **Tel** (613)951-5078, (800)267-6677, FAX (613)951-1584, telex 053-3585. **LC** TX910.C2; A26. **DD** 338.4/7647/9571. *Continues* Statistics Canada. Merchandising and Services Division. Restaurant Statistics, 0008-2627.
**Desc:** Contains estimated restaurant, caterer and tavern statistics for Canada and the provinces, by chains and independents and and by kind of business. Includes revised figures for the previous month and cumulative-to-date estimates for chains and independents.

IO
**STATISTIK RESTORAN : HASIL PELAKSANAAN SURVEI KHUSUS RESTORAN DI 12 PROPINSI.** Indonesian. an. Rp1,000 Indonesia; $.75 US. Central Bureau of Statistics / Indonesia, c/o Dr. Sutomo, 8 Jalan, PO Box 3, Jakarta Indonesia. **Tel** 372808 374908 Ext.342. **LC** TX945; .S7617. ctrl circ.

---

## ROMANCE AND ADVENTURE

---

US/0739-3881
**AFFAIRE DE COEUR.** (19??)-. Periodical. English. Twelve times a year. $30.00 US; $56.00 other. Affaire de Coeur, 3976 Oak Hill Road, Oakland CA 94605. **Tel** (510)569-5675. **ED** Louise B. Snead. **Bk Rev**. **Ad Acc**.

US/1045-4497
**AGE OF REVOLUTION AND ROMANTICISM, THE.** (1992)-. Periodical. English. Peter Lang Publishing, 62 West 45th Street, 4th Floor, New York NY 10036. **Tel** (212)764-1471, (800)770-5264, telex 6973364 PLNY.

US/0002-5224
**ALFRED HITCHCOCK'S MYSTERY MAGAZINE.** (1956)-. Periodical. English. Fifteen times a year. $34.97 (one year), $69.94 (two year), $104.91 (three year). Dell Publishing Company Inc., 1540 Broadway, 9th Floor, New York NY 10036-4021. **Tel** (212)782-8532, FAX (212)782-8338. **(Subscription address:** CDS Agency Hard Copy, PO Box 4966, Des Moines IA 50340.**) ED** Cathleen Jordan. **Bk Rev. Ad Acc. Circ:** 225,000. available on microfilm from University Microfilms International (UMI).
**Desc:** Contains a mix of mystery and suspense. The magazine seeks and develops the newest talent in the mystery field, and has published the work of mystery writers such as John Lutz and Charlotte MacLeod.

US/0732-8923
**ANTITHESIS (MARIETTA, PA.).** (ANTITHESIS.). Began with Jan. 1978?. Periodical. English. qt. $18.00. Triad Publications, 687 East Market Street, Marietta PA 17547.

US/0737-6545
**ARES. SPECIAL ED.** (ARES.). **VFOAT** Ares Magazine. No. 1 (Summer 1983)-. Periodical. English. sa. $24.00 US; $32.40 Canada. Dragon Publishing, Division of TSR Hobbies Inc, PO Box 110, Lake Geneva WI 53147. **Tel** (414)248-3625.

US/0197-3363
**CAMEO (NEW YORK).** (CAMEO.). [Cameo]. Vol. 1 (Dec. 1979)-. Periodical. English. mo. $12.00. Public Enterprises Inc, 50 Rockefeller Plaza, New York NY 10020. **LC** PZ1; .C129; PS648.L6. **DD** 823/.008/0354.

SZ/0008-896X
**CENOBIO.** [Cenobio]. Vol. 1 (1952)-. Periodical. Multiple languages (French and Italian). Four times a year. 35.00F Switzerland; 55.00F other; 80.00F other overseas. Cenobio, Via Streccia 4, Ch-6943 Vezia Switzerland. **Tel** 011 41 91 568508, FAX 011 41 91 565156.
**Ind/Abst** MLA Int. Bibl. Books Artic. Mod. Lang. Lit.

IT/1120-4966
**CLASSICI URANIA.** [Class. urania]. (1984)-. Periodical. Italian. mo. L57600 Italy; L72000 other. Arnoldo Mondadori Editore, UFF Cont Abbonamenti, 20090 Segrate MI Italy. **Tel** 011 39 2 75422015, telex 320457 MONDMI I. **UDC** 82-912.9. ***Continues*** *Classici Fantascienza, 1120-7442.*

US/0742-4248
**CLUES (BOWLING GREEN, OHIO).** (CLUES.). [Clues]. Vol. 1:1 (Spring 1980)-. Periodical. English. sa. $15.00 (one year), $28.00 (two years). Popular Press Journals Area, Bowling Green State University, Bowling Green OH 43403. **Tel** (419)372-7866, (419)372-7865. **ED** Pat Browne. **LC** IN PROCESS. cum. index. **Bk Rev. Ad Acc. Circ:** 800.
**Desc:** Discusses all aspects of mystery fiction including film and television.
**Ind/Abst** Am. Humanit. Index (?-199?); Annu. Bibliogr. Engl. Lang. Lit.; MLA Int. Bibl. Books Artic. Mod. Lang. Lit.

US/1049-0892
**DEAD OF NIGHT.** [Dead night]. No. 1 (Jan. 1989)-. Periodical. English. qt. $15.00. Dead of Night Publications, 916 Shaker Road Suite 143, Longmeadow MA 01106-2416. **DD** 810.

US/0893-0252
**DROOD REVIEW OF MYSTERY, THE.** [Drood rev. myster.]. (198?)-. Periodical. English. mo. $20.00 (one year), $36.00 (two year). The Drood Review of Mystery, PO Box 1293, Brookline MA 02146. **Tel** (617)232-0411. **LC** PN3448.D4; D76. **DD** 823/.087209/005.
**Desc:** Offers reviews, commentary and news on the latest in mystery and suspense.

US/1054-8122
**ELLERY QUEEN'S MYSTERY MAGAZINE.** [Ellery Queen's mystery mag.]. **VFOAT** Ellery Queen. Vol. 92, No. 5 Nov. (1988)-. English. Fifteen times a year. $34.97 (one year); $69.94 (two years); $104.91 (three years). Dell Publishing Company Inc., 1540 Broadway, 9th Floor, New York NY 10036-4021. **Tel** (212)782-8532, FAX (212)782-8338. **(Subscription address:** CDS Agency Hard Copy, PO Box 4966, Des Moines IA 50340.**)** ***Continues*** *Ellery Queen, 0744-0022.*

US/0748-1101
**ELLERY QUEEN'S PRIME CRIMES.** **VFOAT** Prime Crimes. (Winter 1983)-. Periodical. English. an. $2.95. Dell Publishing Company Inc., 1540 Broadway, 9th Floor, New York NY 10036-4021. **Tel** (212)782-8532, FAX (212)782-8338. **(Subscription address:** CDS Agency Hard Copy, PO Box 4966, Des Moines IA 50340.**) LC** PR1309.D4; E44. **DD** 823/.0872/08.

US/8756-8535
**ESPIONAGE MAGAZINE.** [Espion. mag.]. **VFOAT** Espionage. Periodical. English. bm. $15.00. Curtis Circulation Company, PO Box 10170, Des Moines IA 50340. **ED** Jackie Lewis. **LC** PN6071.S64; E84. **DD** 808.83/872. **Bk Rev. Ad Acc. Circ:** 60,000 (ctrl).
**Desc:** Espionage stories on international intrigue, suspense, blackmail. Fiction and non-fiction. Issue contains biographies, short stories, humor, games, movie and book reviews, and interviews of spy authors.

US/0363-0560
**FAMOUS PULP CLASSICS.** **See** Literature.

US/0094-2375
**FANTASIAE.** ***Ceased.*** (FANTASIAE; MONTHLY NEWSLETTER OF THE FANTASY ASSOCIATION.). Vol. 1 (April 1973)-Ceased (1981). Newsletter. English. mo. Fantasy Association, PO Box 24560, Los Angeles CA 90024.

US/0277-0717
**FANTASY BOOK.** **See** Literature.

US/0271-7808
**FANTASY VOICES.** **See** Literature.

US/0016-2043
**FRONT PAGE DETECTIVE.** [Front page detect.]. (19??)-. Periodical. English. Seven times a year (Except Feb., Mar., May, July, Oct.). $12.00 one year; $23.00 two year; $33.00 three year;. RGH Publishing Corporation, 460 West 34th Street, New York NY 10001. **Tel** (212)947-6500. **ED** Rose Mandelsberg-Weiss. **DD** 364. **Bk Rev**, (Qty: varies).
**Desc:** It contains factual, yet suspenseful narratives of recent crimes. Although most of the crimes have been solved, and the defendants convicted, the focus of each story is on the detectives efforts to unravel the facts of the crime and the suspect. Printed in unbroken story format.

●US/1062-015X
**GASLIGHT (CLEVELAND, MINN.).** **See** Literature.

US/1183-5044
**HARLEQUIN WORLD'S BEST ROMANCES.** [Harlequin world's best roman.]. **VFOAT** World's Best Romances. Vol. 1, No. 1 (July/Aug. 1991)-. Periodical. English. bm. $10.96. Harlequin Books, PO Box 9052, Buffalo NY 14269. **Tel** (716)684-1500. **DD** 813.

US/1045-201X
**HEPCATS.** [Hepcats]. No. 1 (May 1989)-. Periodical. English. bm. $15.00 US; $18.00 Canada; $21.00 other. Double Diamond Press, 3600 North Hills Drive, #255, Austin TX 78731-3059. **ED** Martin Wagner. **DD** 741. **Circ:** 3,500.
**Desc:** Contains comics and graphic fiction.

FR/0338-8190
**INCONNU PARIS, L'.** (INCONNU : LE MAGAZINE DE L'ACTUALITE MYSTERIEUSE ET DES SCIENCES DU FUTUR.). (1975)-. Periodical. French. mo. 153.55F France; 237.00F other. Editions Presses Reunies, 18 20 rue Claude Tillier, 75012 Paris France. **Tel** 011 33 1 43726102. **UDC** 1.

US/0020-1847
**INSIDE DETECTIVE.** ***Ceased.*** [Inside detect.]. (19??)-(19??). Periodical. English. mo. RGH Publishing Corporation, 460 West 34th Street, New York NY 10001. **Tel** (212)947-6500. **DD** 051.

US/0747-380X
**INTIMACY.** **Added/Corp** Lexington Library, Inc. (198?)-. Periodical. English. mo. $19.00 (one year), $34.00 (two year). Sterling Macfadden, 233 Park Avenue South, New York NY 10003. **Tel** (212)979-4800. ***Continues*** *Bronz Thrills, 0277-8106.*

US/0161-2735
**KISS.** ***Ceased.*** Vol. 1 (1978)-(1991). Periodical. English. mo. Lancio USA Inc, 630 Third Avenue, New York NY 10017.

US/0195-2692
**LOST TREASURE.** [Lost treas.]. (197?)-. Periodical. English. mo. $19.92 (US); $27.42 (Canada). Lost Treasure Inc, PO Box 1589, Grove OK 74344. **Tel** (918)496-8169. **ED** Jim Watts. **LC** G521; .L67. **DD** 973/.05. **Bk Rev. Ad Acc, Adv Mgr Tel** (918)786-2182. **Circ:** 40,000.
**Desc:** The treasure hunter's guide to adventure and fortune.
**Ind/Abst** GeoRef.

UK
**LOVE STORY.** Periodical. English. Twelve times a year. Argus Specialist Publications, Queensway House, 2 Queensway Redhill, Surrey RH1 1QS England. **Tel** 0737 768611, FAX 0737 773993, telex 948669 TOPJNL G.
**Desc:** Stories of love and life.

US/0026-3621
**MIKE SHAYNE MYSTERY MAGAZINE.** 1936. Periodical. English. mo. $18.00. Renown Publications, PO Box 69150, Los Angeles CA 90069. **Tel** (818)343-2992. **ED** Charles Fritch. **Bk Rev. Ad Acc.**

US/0026-8399
**MODERN ROMANCES.** (19??)-. Periodical. English. mo. $17.97. MacFadden Women's Group, 233 Park Avenue South, New York NY 10003. **Tel** (212)979-4800, (800)666-8783.

IT
**MONDO LADINO : BOLLETTINO DELL'ISTITUTO CULTURALE LADINO.** **See** Linguistics.

US/0826-2586
**MS. TREE.** [Ms. Tree]. **VFOAT** Max Collins and Terry Beatty's Ms. Tree. Began with No. 4, (Oct. 1983). Periodical. English. mo. $24.00 US. Renegade Press, 2705 E 7th Street, Long Beach CA 90804-4708. **Tel** (310)433-4874. **DD** 741.5/971. **Bk Rev. Ad Acc. Circ:** 12,000. ***Continues*** *Ms. Tree's Thrilling Detective Adventure.*
**Desc:** Fictional account of female detective's search for her husband's killer in a modern setting. Told in graphic art format. Contains some violent adult material.

US
**MYSTERY SCENE.** English. bm. $35.00. Mystery Scene, 3840 Clark Road SE, Cedar Rapids IA 52403. **Tel** (310)363-9868.

US/0894-1211
**OFFICIAL DETECTIVE.** [Off. detect.]. (198?)-. Periodical. English. Seven times a year (Except Mar., May, July, Sept., Nov.). $12.00 one year; $23.00 two year; $33.00 three year. RGH Publishing Corporation, 460 West 34th Street, New York NY 10001. **Tel** (212)947-6500. **ED** Rose Mandelsberg-Weiss. **LC** WMLC 93/950. **DD** 364. **Bk Rev**, (Qty: varies). **Ad Acc, Adv Mgr:** J. Burriesci, **Tel** (212)947-6500. available on microfilm from University Microfilms International (UMI). ***Continues*** *Official Detective Stories, 0030-0306.*
**Desc:** Contains factual, yet suspenseful narratives of recent crimes. Although most of the crimes have been solved, and the defendants convicted, the focus of each story is on the detectives efforts to unravel the facts of the crime and apprehend the suspect. Printed in unbroken story format.

US/0031-5613
**PERSONAL ROMANCES.** Periodical. English. bm. $12.00. Dynasty Media Publishing Corporation, PO Box 1629, Englewood Cliff NJ 07632. **Tel** (212)371-4932.

●US/1074-4223
**POSTMODERNIST'S JOURNAL OF HORROR, THE.** **VFOAT** Post modernist's Journal of Horror; Industrial Gothic. (1995)-. English. $8.00. Glass Goldin Press, PO Box 590133, Birmingham AL 35259.

CN/0228-0205
**ROMANCE.** [Romance]. V. 1- 1980-. Periodical. French. 4.50Can$ per no. Canada; $1.25 per no. US. Les Productions Amerique Francaise, Bureau 203, 4920 Ouest Boul., De Maisonneuve, Westmount Quebec H3Z 1N1 Canada. **DD** 843/.08505.

US
**ROMANCE PACKAGE / SPANISH LANGUAGE POPULAR FICTION.** English. mo. $485.50. Hispanic Books Distributors Inc, 1665 West Grant Road, Tucson AZ 85745. **Tel** (602)882-9484, (800)634-2124, FAX (602)882-7696.

US/0747-3370
**ROMANTIC TIMES.** (ROMANTIC TIMES : FOR READERS OF ROMANTIC FICTION.). Vol. 1, No. 1 (July/Aug. 1981)-. Newspaper. English. bm. $60.00 US; $66.00 Canada. Romantic Times Publishing Group, 55 Bergen Street, Brooklyn Heights NY 11201. **Tel** (718)237-1097, FAX (718)624-4231. **ED** Kathryn Falk. **Bk Rev. Ad Acc. Circ:** 70,000 (ctrl).
**Desc:** Includes book reviews of all romance titles in advance of publication, author profiles, and writing tips.

GR
**ROMANTZO.** wk. $110.00. Theofanidis N Publ Company SA, 9 Panepistimioy Av, 105 64 Athens Greece. **Tel** 011 30 1 32 39 884. **(Subscription address:** US: The Greek House, Inc., 21 77 31st Street, Long Island, NY 11105)

US/0882-1348
**SCIFANT.** Periodical. English. mo. $24.00 (individuals), $20.00 (institutions) US, Canada and Mexico; $30.00 (individuals), $26.00 (institutions) other. Luna Ventures, PO Box 398, Suisun CA 94585-0398. **ED** Paul Doerr. **DD** 813. **Bk Rev. Ad Acc.** available on microfiche.
**Desc:** Fiction and non-fiction; science fiction, fantasy, space, horror.

SA/0559-9202
**SHOSETSU GENDAI.** **VFOAT** Shosetugendai Magazine. Vol. 1, No. 1 (1963)-. Periodical. Japanese.

mo. $158.00 California, $164.00 other US. **(Subscription address:** Kinokuniya Company Ltd., 38-1 Sakuragaoka 5, chome Setagaya-ku, Tokyo 156 Japan.**)**

US
**SILHOUETTE DESIRE.** English. $179.28. Silhouette Books, 3010 Walden Ave., Depew NY 14043. **Tel** (716)684-1800.

US
**SILHOUETTE INTIMATE MOMENTS.** English. $142.08. Silhouette Books, 3010 Walden Ave., Depew NY 14043. **Tel** (716)684-1800.

US
**SILHOUETTE ROMANCE.** English. $162.00. Silhouette Books, 3010 Walden Ave., Depew NY 14043. **Tel** (716)684-1800.

US
**SILHOUETTE SPECIAL EDITIONS.** English. $213.12. Silhouette Books, 3010 Walden Ave., Depew NY 14043. **Tel** (716)684-1800.

BE/0771-8071
**SPIROU.** [Spirou]. (1938)-. Periodical. French. wk. 469.00F France; 679.00F other. Editions Jean Dupuis, Service Abonnements B 250, 67232 S Genvieve, Cedex 09 France. **Tel** 11 33 44 074707, **FAX** 011 33 44 074534, telex 51132. **UDC** 084.12.

US
**STAR TREK : THE NEW VOYAGES.** No. 1- 1976-. English. Bantam Books Inc, 666 Fifth Avenue, New York NY 10019. **Tel** (212)340-7500. **ED** Sondra Marshak and Myrna Culbreath.

US/0038-996X
**STARTLING DETECTIVE.** Periodical. English. bm. $11.00. Globe Communications Corporation, 441 Lexington Avenue, New York NY 10017. **Tel** (212)949-4040, **FAX** (212)286-0072.

IT/0585-4962
**STUDI MEDIOLATINI E VOLGARI.** See Literature.

PL/0137-2475
**STUDIA ROMANICA POSNANIENSIA.** [Stud. Rom. Posnan.]. **Added/Corp** Uniwersytet im. Adama Mickiewicza w Poznaniu. (1971)-. Periodical. French (Polish). **LC** PC5; .S78.
**Ind/Abst** Soc. Plann. Policy Dev. Abstr.

US/0041-350X
**TRUE DETECTIVE.** [True detect.]. (19??)-. Periodical. English. Seven times a year (Jan. Mar., Apr., June, Aug., Oct., Dec.). $12.00 (one year); $23.00 (two years); $33.00 (three years). RGH Publishing Corporation, 460 West 34th Street, New York NY 10001. **Tel** (212)947-6500. **ED** Rose Mandelsberg-Weiss. **DD** 364. **Bk Rev** (Qty: varies). **Ad Acc, Adv Mgr:** J Burriesci.
**Desc:** Contains factual, but suspenseful, narratives of recent crimes. Although in the main, the crimes have already been solved, and the defendants convicted, the focus of each story is on the detectives' work in unraveling the crime and apprehending the suspect. Printed in unbroken story format.

US/0199-0004
**TRUE LOVE (NEW YORK).** (TRUE LOVE.). (19??)-. Periodical. English. mo. $17.97. MacFadden Women's Group, 233 Park Avenue South, New York NY 10003. **Tel** (212)979-4800, (800)666-8783.

US/0199-0020
**TRUE ROMANCE (NEW YORK).** (TRUE ROMANCE.). (19??)-. Periodical. English. mo. $17.97. MacFadden Women's Group, 233 Park Avenue South, New York NY 10003. **Tel** (212)979-4800, (800)666-8783.

UK/0262-415X
**TRUE ROMANCES.** (197?)-. English. Twelve times a year. Argus Consumer Publications, 2 4 Leigham Court Road, London SW16 2PD England. **Tel** 011 44 442 234303.
**Desc:** Stories aimed at contemporary young romantics.

US/0195-3117
**TRUE STORY (NEW YORK).** (TRUE STORY.). (19??)-. Periodical. English. mo. $14.95 (one year), $28.95 (two year). MacFadden Women's Group, 233 Park Avenue South, New York NY 10003. **Tel** (212)979-4800, (800)666-8783. **(Subscription address:** CDS Agency Hard Copy, PO Box 4966, Des Moines IA 50340.**)**

US/8755-7452
**WEIRDBOOK.** [Weirdbook]. **VFOAT** Weird Book. Periodical. English. ir. $22.50. W Paul Ganley, Box 149 Amherst Branch, Buffalo NY 14226-0149. **Tel** (716)839-2415. **ED** W Paul Ganley. **LC** WMLC L 83/7982. **DD** 813. **Circ:** 900 (ctrl).
**Desc:** Fantasy/horror fiction for the afficionado.

KO
**YADAM KWA SIRHWA.** **VFOAT** Historical Romance & True Story. (197?)-. Periodical. Korean. mo. W700 each issue. Popchisa, 10-26 Jongam-dong, Seongbuk-ku, Seoul South Korea. **LC** AP95.K6; Y33.

# RUBBER

US/0146-3977
**ANNUAL MEETING PROCEEDINGS - INTERNATIONAL INSTITUTE OF SYNTHETIC RUBBER PRODUCERS, INC.** *Title Change.* [Annu. meet. proc., Int. Inst. Synth. Rub. Prod.]. **Main/Corp** IISRP (Organization). (1969)-(199?). Proceedings. English. an. IISRP, 2077 South Gessner Road, Suite 133, Houston TX 77063. **Tel** (713)783-7511. **LC** TS1871; .I64. **DD** 338.4/7/67872. **CODEN** APIPDP. Documents available from CASDDS. *Continued by IISRP (Organization) Proceedings ... Annual General Meeting, 1070-6488.*
**Ind/Abst** Chem. Abstr.

US
**BLUE BOOK (NEW YORK, N.Y.).** (BLUE BOOK : MATERIALS, COMPOUNDING INGREDIENTS, AND MACHINERY FOR RUBBER). **VFOAT** Rubber World Blue Book. (1981)-. English. an. $112.00 (print), $160.00 (CD-ROM) US and Canada; $135.00 (print), $165.00 (CD-ROM) other. Rubber World, PO Box 5451, 1867 West Narjet Street, Akron OH 44334-0451. **Tel** (216)864-2122, **FAX** (216)864-5298, telex 297690 RWMAG UR. **LC** TS1893; .B58. **DD** 678/.21/0294. available on CD-ROM. *Continues Materials, Compounding Ingredients and Machinery for the Rubber Industry.*

UK/0307-6164
**BP&R BRITISH PLASTICS AND RUBBER.** See Plastics.

MY
**BUKU MAKLUMAT PERANGKAAN GETAH BAGI MALAYSIA. RUBBER STATISTICS HANDBOOK OF MALAYSIA.** See Rubber-Abstracting, Bibliographies and Statistics.

FR/1154-1105
**CAOUTCHOUCS & PLASTIQUES PARIS.** (CAOUTCHOUCS & PLASTIQUES.). **VFOAT** Revue Generale des Caoutchoucs & Plastiques (1989); Caoutchoucs et Plastiques (Paris). (1989)-. Periodical. French. mo. Societe d Expansion Technique et Economique, 5 rue de Seze, 75009 Paris France. **Tel** 011 33 16 44945060, telex 650 896 F. **UDC** 66. *Continues Revue Generale du Caoutchouc et des Plastiques, 0035-3175.*
**Ind/Abst** Hortic. Abstr.; Rev. Plant Pathol.

AG/0528-3280
**CAUCHO.** [Caucho]. **Added/Corp** Federacion Argentina de la Industria del Caucho. (Jan./Feb. 1958)-. Academic Scholarly Publication. Spanish. bm. Free on request. Federacion Argentina de la Industria del Caucho, Av Leandro N Alem 1069, 1001 Buenos Aires Argentina. **Tel** 313-2009/2140/2192. **LC** TS1870; .C38. **CODEN** CAUCDV. Index available. **Ad Acc. Circ:** 2,000 (ctrl). Documents available from CASDDS.
**Ind/Abst** Chem. Abstr.

HK
**CHINA PLASTIC & RUBBER JOURNAL.** See Plastics.

US
**CURRENT INDUSTRIAL REPORTS. MA-30B, RUBBER AND PLASTICS HOSE AND BELTING.** **VFOAT** Rubber and Plastics Hose and Belting. Began with 1973 issue. Government Publication. English. an. $1.00. US Department of Commerce / Bureau of the Census, Data User Services Division, Customer Services, Washington DC 20233-0800. **Tel** (301)763-4100. **(Subscription address:** Superintendent of Documents, US Government Printing Office, Washington DC 20402.**) LC** HD9999.H7183; U63.
**Desc:** Presents timely data on the production, inventories, and orders of approximately 5,000 products, which represents 40 percent of all US manufacturing.

UK/0262-1592
**DEVELOPMENTS IN RUBBER AND RUBBER COMPOSITES.** [Dev. rubber rubber compos.]. (1980)-. Academic Scholarly Publication. English. Elsevier Science Publishers BV, PO Box 211, 1000 AE Amsterdam Netherlands. **Tel** 011 31 20 5803642, **FAX** 011 31 20 5862696, telex 15682. **LC** TS1870; .D47. **DD** 678/.2/05. **CODEN** DRRCDA. Documents available from CASDDS.
**Ind/Abst** Chem. Abstr. (-1985).

IT
**ELASTICA.** L250.000 Italy; L400.000 other. Svilupo Industria Gomma, Via San Vittore 36, 20123 Milan Italy.
**Desc:** Technical - scientific journal for the rubber technologists.

US/0146-0706
**ELASTOMERICS.** *Ceased.* [Elastomerics]. Vol. 109 (Jan. 1977)-(1992). Academic Scholarly Publication. English. mo. Argus Business, 6151 Powers Ferry Road, Atlanta GA 30339. **Tel** (404)995-2500, (800)233-3359. **LC** TS1870; .R6. **DD** 338.4/7/678205. **CODEN** ELASDA. **[CCC].** available on microfilm and microfiche from University Microfilms International (UMI). Documents available from Article Express International, CASDDS. *Continues Rubber Age, 0035-9440.*
**Ind/Abst** Appl. Sci. Technol. Index (?-?); Bioeng. Abstr. (?-?); Chem. Abstr. (?-?); Chem. Bus. Bull. (?-?); Chem. Bus. NewsBase (1985-); Chem. Bus. Update (?-?); Chem. Ind. Notes (?-?); Coal Abstr. (?-?); Ei Page One (?-?); EMBASE (?-?); Eng. Mater. Abstr. (?-?); Eng. Index Annu.; F&S Index Plus Text, Int. [Select. Cov.]; Infomat Int. Bus.; Predicasts F&S Index, U. S. Annu. Ed. (?-?); PROMT; Text. Technol. Dig. (?-?); Trade Ind. ASAP [Full Txt.]; Trade Ind. Index [Full Txt.].

US/0146-0714
**ELASTOMERICS NEWS-LOG.** (NEWS LOG). V. 1, No. 8- Jan. 1977-. Academic Scholarly Publication. English. mo. $7.50 (libraries), $10.00 (individuals), $25.00 (societies). Palmerton Publishing Company, 461 Eighth Avenue, New York NY 10001. **LC** TS1870; .N44. **DD** 338.4/7/678205. **CODEN** ENLODX. Documents available from CASDDS. *Continues Rubber Age News-Log, 0363-8650.*
**Ind/Abst** Chem. Abstr.

US
**ELASTOMERS.** See Plastics.

UK/0306-414X
**EUROPEAN RUBBER DIRECTORY.** [Eur. rubber dir.]. 1st- Ed.; 1974-. Directory. Multiple languages (English, French, German and Italian). an. £27.00. **ED** Robert C Grace. **LC** TS1877; .E95. **DD** 338.4/7/67830254. **Bk Rev. Ad Acc. Circ:** 8,000 (ctrl).
**Desc:** Provides news and analyses of technical and commercial developments in the rubber and related end-user industries. Also, details new equipment materials, processes and applications.

UK/0266-4151
**EUROPEAN RUBBER JOURNAL (LONDON, ENGLAND : 1982).** (EUROPEAN RUBBER JOURNAL). [Eur. rubber j.]. Vol. 164, No. 1 (Feb. 1982)-. Academic Scholarly Publication. English (French, German and Italian). mo (except Aug.). £60.00 UK and Europe; $99.00 US and Canada. Crain Communications Ltd., 75-77 Cowcross Street, Cowcross Court, London EC1M 6BP England. **Tel** 011 44 71 6082774. **(Subscription address:** UK/ 120-126 Lavender Avenue, Mitcham Surrey CR4 3HP England; US/ 965 E Jefferson Avenue, Detroit, MI 48207-3187**) ED** David Shaw. **LC** TS1870; .I27. **DD** 338.4/76782/094. **CODEN** ERJODH. **[CCC]. Bk Rev. Ad Acc. Circ:** 6,739 (ctrl). available on microfilm and microfiche from University Microfilms International (UMI); available on an online database (files 16,648/Full-Text) from DIALOG. Documents available from Article Express International, CASDDS. *Continues European Rubber Journal + Urethanes Today, 0260-5317.*
**Desc:** Provides analyses of technical developments in the rubber and related industries. Details new equipment, materials, processes and applications. Also traces market trends and publishes up-to-the-minute industry news as well as information on personnel changes, forthcoming meetings and available literature throughout Europe and the leading non-European countries.
**Ind/Abst** Bioeng. Abstr.; Chem. Abstr. (1982-1983); Chem. Bus. Bull.; Chem. Bus. NewsBase (1985-); Chem. Bus. Update; Curr. Technol. Index; Ei Page One; Eng. Mater. Abstr.; Eng. Index Annu.; F&S Index Plus Text, Int. [Full Txt.] [Select. Cov.]; Fluid Abstr., Civil Eng.; Fluid Abstr. Proc. Eng.; FLUIDEX (1982-); Infomat Int. Bus.; PROMT [Full Txt.]; Trade Ind. ASAP [Full Txt.]; Trade Ind. Index [Full Txt.].

KO/0253-3138
**GOMU HAGHOI JI.** (KOMU HAKHOE CHI.). [Gomu haghoi ji]. **Added/Corp** Hanguk Komu Hakhoe. **VFOAT** Journal of the Korean Institute of Rubber Industry. (19??)-. Periodical. Korean. Hanguk Komu Hakhoe, Seoul Tukpyolsi, Seoul Korea. **LC** TS1870; .K65. **CODEN** KHAKDO. Documents available from CASDDS.
**Ind/Abst** Chem. Abstr.

US/0432-0905
**GOODYEAR CHEMICAL REVIEW.** Vol. 1 (?)-. English. Goodyear Tire & Rubber Company, 1144 East Market Street, Akron OH 44316. **Tel** (216)796-4143. **DD** 661; 668.

JA
**GOSEI GOMU.** [Gosei gomu]. **VFOAT** The Synthetic Rubber; Synthetic Rubber. Began in 1959. Academic Scholarly Publication. Japanese. sa. Nihon Gosei Gomu K.K., (Japan Synthetic Rubber, Ltd.), 11-24, Tsukiji 2 Chome, Chuoku, Tokyoto 104 Japan. **(Subscription address:** Maruzen Company Ltd., PO Box 5050, Import & Export Department, Tokyo 100 31 Japan.**) CODEN** GOGOD3. ctrl circ. Documents available from CASDDS.
**Ind/Abst** Chem. Abstr.

GW
**GUMMI BEREIFUNG.** 1 (1921)-. Periodical. German (summaries and/or abstracts in English). mo. DM190.00. Bielefelder Verlagsanstalt KG, Niederwall 53, D 33602 Bielefeld Germany. **Tel** 011 49 521 595520. Index available. **Bk Rev. Ad Acc. Circ:** 6,000 (ctrl). **Desc:** Trade paper for vulkanizers, tyre-dealers and accessories.
**Ind/Abst** Saf. Health Work.

GW/0176-1625
**GUMMI, FASERN, KUNSTSTOFFE.** [Gummi Fasern Kunstst.]. Vol. 37, 1 (Jan. 1984)-. Academic Scholarly Publication. German. Twelve times a year. DM248.60 Germany; DM252.80 others. AW Gentner Verlag, Postfach 101742, D-70015 Stuttgart Germany. **Tel** 011 49 711 636720, FAX 011 49 711 6367247, telex 841 722244. **ED** Dr. H. Gupta. **LC** TS1870; .G79. **DD** 678/.2/05. **CODEN** GFKUED. Index available. cum. index. **Bk Rev. Ad Acc. Circ:** 2,000. Documents available from Article Express International, CASDDS. ***Continues*** *Gummi, Asbest, Kunststoffe, 0017-5595.*
**Desc:** Processing and application of rubber, plastics, and fibers.
**Ind/Abst** Chem. Abstr. (1984-); Coal Abstr.; Ei Page One; EMBASE; Eng. Index Annu.; F&S Index Plus Text, Int. [Select. Cov.]; Fluid Abstr., Civil Eng.; Fluid Abstr. Proc. Eng.; FLUIDEX (1984-); Int. Packag. Abstr.; Int. Polym. Sci. Tech.; Nonwovens Abstr.; PROMT; Shock Vibr. Dig.

II/0970-2431
**INDIAN JOURNAL OF NATURAL RUBBER RESEARCH.** [Indian j. nat. rubber res.]. **Added/Corp** Rubber Research Institute of India. Vol. 1, No. 1 (1988)-. Periodical. English. sa. $30.00. Rubber Research Institute of India, Kottayam 686 009 India. **(Subscription address:** Prints India, 11 Darya Ganj, New Delhi 110002 India.**) LC** IN PROCESS. **CODEN** IJNREZ. Documents available from BIOSIS Document Express.
**Ind/Abst** Agric. Eng. Abstr.; Biol. Abstr.; Hortic. Abstr.; Plant Breed. Abstr.; Rev. Plant Pathol.; Seed Abstr.; Soils Fert.

IT/0019-7556
**INDUSTRIA DELLA GOMMA, L'.** [Ind. gomma]. **Added/Corp** Associazione Nazionale fra le Industrie Della Gomma, Cavi Elettrici ed Affini. (1963)-. Academic Scholarly Publication. Italian. mo. L12.100 Italy; L16.000 others. Gesto Srl, Via C Battisti 21, 20122 Milan Italy. **Tel** 011 39 2 55187581, FAX 011 39 2 5465310. **CODEN** INGOAF. Index available. **Bk Rev. Ad Acc. Circ:** 3,000 (ctrl). Documents available from CASDDS. ***Continues*** *Notizie per l'Idustria della Gomma, 0394-0780.*
**Desc:** Technology and economics of the rubber industry.
**Ind/Abst** Chem. Abstr.; F&S Index Plus Text, Int. [Select. Cov.]; PROMT.

NE/0922-4122
**INFORMATIEF NVR. See** Plastics.

UK
**INTERNATIONAL RUBBER DIGEST.** **Added/Corp** International Rubber Study Group. (19??)-. Periodical. English. mo. $126.00. International Rubber Study Group, 8th Floor York House, Empire Way, Wembley, HA9 0PA England. **Tel** 011 44 81 9037727. **ED** J.D. Carr. **Circ:** 1,000. ***Continues*** *Rubber Statistical News Sheet.*
**Desc:** Contains report on natural rubber market, topical items on all matters affecting the rubber industry.

US/0095-2443
**JOURNAL OF ELASTOMERS AND PLASTICS, THE. See** Plastics.

MY/0127-7065
**JOURNAL OF NATURAL RUBBER RESEARCH.** [J. nat. rubber res.]. **Added/Corp** Rubber Research Institute of Malaysia. Vol. 1, No. 1 (Mar. 1986)-. Periodical. English. Four times a year (Mar., June, Sept., Dec.). 58.00Mal$. Rubber Research Institute of Malaysia, PO Box 10150, 50908 Kuala Lumpur Malaysia. **Tel** 011 60 3 45607033, FAX 011 60 3 4573512, telex MA 30369. **LC** SB290; .K83. **DD** 678/.2. **CODEN** JNRREQ. **Circ:** 1,100. Documents available from BIOSIS Document Express, CASDDS. ***Continues*** *Rubber Research Institute of Malaysia. Journal of the Rubber Research Institute of Malaysia, 0127-0567.*
**Desc:** Publishes the results of research and authoritative reviews on all aspects of natural rubber.
**Ind/Abst** Agrofor. Abstr.; Biol. Abstr. (1986-); Chem. Abstr.; Crop Physiol. Abstr.; For. Prod. Abstr.; Grasslands For. Abstr.; Hortic. Abstr.; Plant Breed. Abstr.; Rev. Plant Pathol.; SEA Abstr.; Seed Abstr.; Soils Fert.; World Agric. Econ.

GW/0177-0608
**K-PLASTIC- & KAUTSCHUK-ZEITUNG EXPORT ISSUE.** [K-Plast.- & Kautsch.-Ztg. Export issue]. **VFOAT** K-Plastic- & Kautschuk-Zeitung (Export-Ausg.); K-Plastic- und Kautschuk-Zeitung (Export Issue). (19??)-. Periodical. English. sm. DM179.00 Germany; DM185.00 other. Umschau Verlag, Postfach 110262, D-60037 Frankfurt Germany. **Tel** 011 49 69 2600692, FAX 011 49 69 2600223, telex 411964. **UDC** 678.

RU/0022-9466
**KAUCHUK I REZINA.** [Kaucuk rezina]. (1949)-. Russian. Six times a year. $69.95. **(Subscription address:** East View Publications Inc., 3020 Harbor Lane North, Suite 110, Minneapolis MN 55447.**) LC** TS1870; .K35115. **[CCC].** Documents available from CASDDS.
**Ind/Abst** Chem. Abstr.; Coal Abstr.; Energy Res. Abstr.; Eng. Mater. Abstr.; Int. Polym. Sci. Tech.

GW/0022-9520
**KAUTSCHUK + GUMMI KUNSTSTOFFE.** [Kautsch. Gummi. Kunstst.]. **VAT** Kautschuk und Gummi Kunststoffe. (1964)-. Academic Scholarly Publication. English (German). mo. $269.00 North America. Dr. Alfred Huethig Verlag GmbH, Postfach 102869, D 69018 Heidelberg Germany. **Tel** 011 49 6221 489281. **(Subscription address:** Huethig Publishing Inc., 29 Macintosh Drive, Oxford CT 06478.**) CODEN** KGUKAC. **[CCC]. Pr Rev. Circ:** 6,350. Documents available from Article Express International, The Genuine Article, CASDDS. ***Continues*** *Kautschuk und Gummi Kunststoffe. Plastomere. Elastomere. Duromere, 0368-5446.*
**Desc:** Journal for high polymer materials, auxiliary materials, and machines for the rubber and plastics industry.
**Ind/Abst** Bioeng. Abstr.; Chem. Abstr.; Chem. Bus. Bull.; Chem. Bus. NewsBase (1985-); Chem. Bus. Update; Curr. Contents Eng. Tech. Appl. Sci.; Ei Page One; EMBASE; Energy Res. Abstr. (June 1971-); Eng. Index Annu.; F&S Index Plus Text, Int. [Select. Cov.]; Infomat Int. Bus.; PROMT; Res. Alert [Full Cov.]; SCISEARCH.

KO
**KOMU KONGHAKHOE CHI. Main/Corp** Han'Guk Komu Konghakhoe. **VFOAT** Journal of the Korean Institute of Rubber Industry. Periodical. Korean (Korean). **LC** TS1870; .H35.

NE/0167-9597
**KUNSTSTOF EN RUBBER.** [Kunstst. rubber]. **Added/Corp** Kunststoffen en Rubber Instituut TNO te Delft (Netherlands). Vol. 36, No. 4 (Apr. 1983)-. Academic Scholarly Publication. Dutch. mo. Fl111.75 Netherlands; Fl132.50 other. Tijl Tijdschriften BV, Postbus 9943, 1006 AP Amsterdam Netherlands. **Tel** (0)20-518 28 28. **CODEN** KRUBDV. Documents available from Article Express International, CASDDS. ***Continues*** *Plastica.*
**Ind/Abst** Chem. Abstr. (1983-); Ei Page One; Eng. Index Annu. [Select. Cov.]; F&S Index Plus Text, Int. [Select. Cov.]; PROMT.

GW
**KUNSTSTOFF INFORMATION.** Kunststoff Information, Victor Achard Strasse 17, D6380 Bad Homeburg Germany.

GW
**KUNSTSTOFF WOCHENDIENST.** German. Forty times a year. DM240.00. Info Zentral Kunststoffe, c/o Hamich Verlagsbuero, Jahnstr 57, D 64285 Darmstadt Germany. **Tel** 011 49 6151 61848.

GW/0932-6138
**KUNSTSTOFFE FEUR DIE ELEKTRONIK UND OPTIK.** [Kunstst. Elektron. Opt.]. (1988)-. Periodical. German. bm. DM163.20 Germany; DM166.00 other. Politec, WL Poley, Am Beisenbusch 37, W-4270 Dorsten 1 FR Germany. **Tel** 011 49 2362 3286. **UDC** 66/68.

MY/0126-8309
**LAPURAN TAHUNAN - MAJLIS PENGELUAR-PENGELUAR GETAH MALAYSIA. Main/Corp** Majlis Pengeluar-Pengeluar Getah Malaysia. **VFOAT** Annual Report - Rubber Producers' Council of Malaysia. 1973-. English (Malay). an. 120.00Mal$. Majlis Pengeluar-Pengeluar Getah Malaysia, Peti Surat 12688, 50786 Kuala Lumpur, Malaysia. **Tel** 2482677. **LC** HD9161.M32; M26A. **Circ:** 220. ***Continues*** *Laporan Tahunan - Majlis Pengeluar P2 S Getah Tanah Melayu.*
**Desc:** Lists names and publishers of all periodicals abstracted at least once by information center since 1960.

UK
**LMC COMMODITY BULLETINS ON RUBBER.** English. mo. £475.00. Landell Mills Commodities, 14 16 George Street, Oxford 0X1 2AF England. **Tel** 011 44 865 791737, FAX 011 44 865 791739, telex 827206.

UK
**LMC QUARTERLY RUBBER REPORTS SERVICE.** English. Four times a year. £2400.00. Landell Mills Commodities, 14 16 George Street, Oxford 0X1 2AF England. **Tel** 011 44 865 791737, FAX 011 44 865 791739, telex 827206.

MY
**MAJALAH RISDA. Main/Corp** Malaysia. Pihak Berkuasa Kemajuan Pekebun Kecil Perusahaan Getah. Vol. 1- Apr. 1973-. Periodical. Malay. qt. Bangunan Getah Asli, Petit Surat 1067 Jalan Ampang, Kuala Lumpur Malaysia. **LC** HD9161.M32; P54A.

MY/0127-2969
**MALAYSIAN RUBBER REVIEW.** [Malays. rubber rev.]. **Added/Corp** Lembaga Penyelidikan dan Kemajuan Getah Malaysia. Vol. 4 (1st quarter, 1983)-. Periodical. English. qt. £16. Malaysian Rubber Research Development Board, PO Box 10508, Kuala Lumpur 01-02 Malaysia. **Tel** (03)2614422, telex MA 30953 MRRDB. ***Continues*** *Ulasan Getah Malaysia, 0126-9089.*
**Desc:** Contains economic news, information, and statistics for investors and decision makers.

MY/0126-5865
**MONTHLY BULLETIN. Added/Corp** Majlis Pengeluar-Pengeluar Getah Malaysia. Vol. 32, No. 7 (July 1983)-. Bulletin. English. mo. £29.00. Malaysian Rubber Producers Research Association, Tun Abdul Razak Laboratory, Brickendonbury, Hertford SG13 8NL, United Kingdom. **Tel** 011 44 992 584966, FAX 011 44 992 554837. ***Continues*** *Monthly Statistical Bulletin (Majlis Pengeluar-Pengeluar Getah Malaysia).*

HU/0027-2914
**MUANYAG ES GUMI. See** Plastics.

US/0028-0755
**NATURAL RUBBER NEWS.** ***Ceased.*** [Nat. rubber news]. (Jan./Feb. 1951)-(1988). Periodical. English. mo. Malaysian Rubber Bureau, 1925 K Street NW, Washington DC 20006. **Tel** (202)452-0544. **LC** HD9161.A1; N3.
**Ind/Abst** AGRICOLA (?-?); Fluid Abstr., Civil Eng. (?-?); Fluid Abstr. Proc. Eng. (?-?); FLUIDEX (1973-); Predicasts F&S Index, U. S. Annu. Ed. (?-?).

UK/0747-4954
**NEW TRADE NAMES IN THE RUBBER AND PLASTICS INDUSTRIES.** (NEW TRADE NAMES IN THE RUBBER AND PLASTICS INDUSTRIES / RUBBER AND PLASTICS RESEARCH ASSOCIATION OF GREAT BRITAIN.). [New trade names rubber plast. ind.]. **Added/Corp** Rubber and Plastics Research Association of Great Britain. Rapra Technology Limited. **VFOAT** Trade Names in the Rubber and Plastics Industries; New Trade Names. (1962)-. English. an. £130.00. RAPRA Technology Ltd., Shawbury Shrewsbury, Shropshire SY4 4NR England. **Tel** 011 44 939 250383, FAX 011 44 939 251118, telex 35134 RAPRA G. **ED** Elaine Davison. **LC** HD9161.A1; N43. **DD** 668.4/0275. **[CCC]. Circ:** 750. available on an online database (through Pergamon Orbit Search Service as Rapra Database); available on microfilm and microfiche from University Microfilms International (UMI). ***Continues*** *Trade Names of Rubbers, Resins, and Plastics.*
**Desc:** Contains records of all the registered and non-registered trade names found in published literature from around the world. Company addresses, telephone and FAX numbers are provided too, making the database invaluable to buyers in particular.

JA/0029-022X
**NIPPON GOMU KYOKAISHI.** [Nippon Gomu Kyokaishi]. **VFOAT** Journal of the Society of the Rubber Industry. (1932)-. Academic Scholarly Publication. Japanese. mo. ¥9600 Japan; ¥10800 other. Society of the Rubber Industry / Japan, 5 26 1 Chome Motoakasaka, Minato ku Tokyo 107 Japana. **CODEN** NGOKAF. **[CCC].** Documents available from CASDDS. ***Continues*** *Gomu, 0367-4924.*
**Ind/Abst** Chem. Abstr.; Int. Polym. Sci. Tech.

US/0027-7045
**NTDRA DEALER NEWS.** [NTDRA deal. news]. **Main/Corp** National Tire Dealers and Retreaders Association. **VAT** National Tire Dealers and Retreaders Association dealer news. (19??)-. Periodical. English. mo. $13.00 US; $22.00 other. National Tire Dealers and Retreaders Association, 1250 I Street NW/Suite 400, Washington DC 20005. **Tel** (202)789-2300, FAX (202)682-3999. **ED** C.D. "Tony" Hylton. **Bk Rev**, (Qty: 3/yr). **Ad Acc, Adv Mgr:** Joan Senn. **Circ:** 7,000 (ctrl).
**Desc:** Features information to help independent tire dealers and retreaders improve profits, understand industry trends and keep abreast of association programs, and services.

US/0744-5679
**NTDRA MEMBERGRAM. Added/Corp** National Tire Dealers and Retreaders Association (U.S.). **VFOAT** N.T.D.R.A. Membergram; Membergram. **VAT** National Tire Dealers and Retreaders Association Membergram. Vol. 1, No. 1 (Mar. 1982)-. Periodical. English. mo. $6.00. National Tire Dealers and Retreaders Association, 1250 I Street NW/Suite 400, Washington DC 20005. **Tel** (202)789-2300, FAX (202)682-3999.

US/0077-5886
**NTDRA TIRE DEALERS SURVEY.** English. $3.00. National Tire Dealers and Retreaders Association, 1250 I Street NW/Suite 400, Washington DC 20005. **Tel** (202)789-2300, FAX (202)682-3999. **LC** HD9161.U5; L45. **DD** 380.1/45/6783202573.

MY/0032-096X
**PLANTER'S BULLETIN (RUBBER RESEARCH INSTITUTE OF MALAYSIA).** (PLANTER'S BULLETIN OF THE RUBBER RESEARCH INSTITUTE OF MALAYSIA.). [Plant. bull. Rubber Res.

Inst. Malays.]. **Main/Corp** Rubber Research Institute of Malaysia. **VFOAT** Plrs' Bull. Rubb. Res. Inst. Malaysia. No. 128 (Sept. 1973)-. English. Four times a year (Mar., June, Sept., Dec.). 28.00Mal$. Rubber Research Institute of Malaysia, PO Box 10150, 50908 Kuala Lumpur Malaysia. **Tel** 011 60 3 45607033, FAX 011 60 3 4573512, telex MA 30369. **LC** SB290; .R8a. **DD** 633/.8952/05. **CODEN** RRMPA5. **Circ:** 3,500. Documents available from BIOSIS Document Express. ***Continues*** *Planters' Bulletin of the Rubber Research Institute of Malaysia.*
**Ind/Abst** Agric. Eng. Abstr.; Biol. Abstr.; Hortic. Abstr.; Rev. Plant Pathol.; Soils Fert.; Weed Abstr.

BL
**PLASTICOS & I.E. E BORRACHA. See** Plastics.

UK/0309-4561
**PLASTICS AND RUBBER INTERNATIONAL.** ***Title Change.*** **See** Plastics.

UK/0307-9414
**PLASTICS AND RUBBER: MATERIALS AND APPLICATIONS.** ***Title Change.*** [Plast. rubber. Mater. appl.]. **Added/Corp** Plastics and Rubber Institute. Vol. 1- (Feb. 1976)-. Academic Scholarly Publication. English. qt. Station House, Nightgale Road, Hitchin, Herts SG5 1RJ. **LC** TP1101; .P48. **DD** 668.4/05. **CODEN** PRMAD9. Documents available from CASDDS. ***Merged with*** *Plastics and Rubber Processing and Applications, 0144-6045* ***to form*** *Plastics and Rubber: Processing, 0307-9422.*
**Ind/Abst** Chem. Abstr.

UK/0032-1168
**PLASTICS & RUBBER WEEKLY. See** Plastics.

UK/0959-8111
**PLASTICS, RUBBER AND COMPOSITES PROCESSING AND APPLICATIONS. See** Plastics.

FR/0032-1303
**PLASTIQUES MODERNES ELASTOMERES. See** Plastics.

FR/0296-9386
**PNEUMATIQUE PARIS, LE.** [Pneu-matique Paris]. **VFOAT** Pneumatique (Garches); Pneumatique (Paris). (1929)-. Periodical. French. Five times a year. 300.00F France; 350.00F other. VB Promotion, 15 Rue du 19 Janvier, 92380 Garches France. **Tel** 011 33 1 47014474. **UDC** 622. ***Continues*** *Le Pneu (Bruxelles), 0771-0372.*

UK/0883-153X
**POLYMER CONTENTS. See** Plastics-Abstracting, Bibliographies and Statistics.

UK/0142-9418
**POLYMER TESTING. See** Plastics.

•US/1070-6488
**PROCEEDINGS ... ANNUAL GENERAL MEETING.** (PROCEEDINGS ... ANNUAL GENERAL MEETING / INTERNATIONAL INSTITUTE OF SYNTHETIC RUBBER PRODUCERS, INC.). [Proc. annu. gen. meet.]. **Main/Corp** IISRP (Organization). **VFOAT** Annual General Meeting; Annual Meeting; Proceedings ... Annual Meeting. 33rd (1992)-. Proceedings. English. an. IISRP, 2077 South Gessner Road, Suite 133, Houston TX 77063. **Tel** (713)783-7511. **DD** 678. ***Continues*** *IISRP (Organization). Annual Meeting Proceedings - International Institute of Synthetic Rubber Producers, Inc.*
**Desc:** Provides news and information of interest to those involved in the artificial rubber industry and trade.

UK
**PROCEEDINGS OF THE ... ASSEMBLY OF THE INTERNATIONAL RUBBER STUDY GROUP. Main/Corp** International Rubber Study Group. Proceedings. English. International Rubber Study Group, 8th Floor York House, Empire Way, Wembley, HA9 0PA England. **Tel** 011 44 81 9037727. **LC** HD9161.A2; I532B. **DD** 338.4/76782.

US/0271-9312
**PROCEEDINGS OF THE CALIFORNIA CONFERENCE ON RUBBER-TOUGHENED PLASTICS. See** Plastics.

UK
**PROCEEDINGS OF THE ... MEETING OF THE INTERNATIONAL RUBBER STUDY GROUP. Main/Corp** International Rubber Study Group. Proceedings. English. International Rubber Study Group, 8th Floor York House, Empire Way, Wembley, HA9 0PA England. **Tel** 011 44 81 9037727. **LC** HD9161 .A2; I532C. **DD** 338.4/76782.

UK/0266-7320
**PROGRESS IN RUBBER AND PLASTICS TECHNOLOGY.** [Prog. rubber plast. technol.]. **Added/Corp** Plastics and Rubber Institute. Rapra Technology Limited. Rubber and Plastics Research Association of Great Britain. Vol. 1, No. 1 (Jan. 1985)-. Academic Scholarly Publication. English. qt (4 issues). £185.00 UK; $350.00 US; £205.00 other. RAPRA Technology Ltd., Shawbury Shrewsbury, Shropshire SY4 4NR England. **Tel** 011 44 939 250383, FAX 011 44 939 251118, telex 35134 RAPRA G. **ED** Jack Buist. **LC** TS1870; .I456. **DD** 678/.2/05. **CODEN** PRPTEE. **[CCC]. Bk Rev. Ad Acc. Pr Rev. Circ:** 250 (ctrl). Documents available from Article Express International, CASDDS. ***Continues*** *Progress of Rubber Technology, 0306-3542.*
**Desc:** Reviews of major recent developments in the rubber and plastics industries.
**Ind/Abst** Chem. Abstr. (1985-); Eng. Index Annu.

UK/0033-6750
**RAPRA ABSTRACTS. See** Rubber-Abstracting, Bibliographies and Statistics.

UK/0140-041X
**RAPRA NEWS.** [RAPRA news]. **Added/Corp** Rubber and Plastics Research Association of Great Britain. Vol. 1, No. 1 (May/June 1977)-. Periodical. English. Four times a year. Free. RAPRA Technology Ltd., Shawbury Shrewsbury, Shropshire SY4 4NR England. **Tel** 011 44 939 250383, FAX 011 44 939 251118, telex 35134 RAPRA G. ***Supersedes*** *RAPRA Members Journal; RAPRA in Brief.*
**Ind/Abst** BMT Abstr.; Int. Packag. Abstr.

US/0482-430X
**RETREADER'S JOURNAL.** ***Title Change.*** **See** Business.

FR/0035-3175
**REVUE GENERALE DES CAOUTCHOUCS & PLASTIQUES. Added/Corp** Societe d'Expansion Technique et Economique. **VFOAT** Revue Generale des Caoutchoucs et Plastiques; Caoutchoucs & Plastiques; Caoutchoucs et Plastiques. (1983)-. Periodical. French (summaries and/or abstracts in English). mo. Societe d Expansion Technique et Economique, 5 rue de Seze, 75009 Paris France. **Tel** 011 33 16 44945060, telex 650 896 F. **LC** TS1870; .R4. **DD** 668.9/05. **CODEN** CATPEW. **[CCC]. *Continues*** *Caoutchoucs & Plastiques.*
**Ind/Abst** Infomat Int. Bus.; Plant Breed. Abstr.; PROMT.

CN/0835-0027
**RUBBER AND PLASTIC PRODUCTS INDUSTRIES.** (RUBBER AND PLASTIC PRODUCTS INDUSTRIES / STATISTICS CANADA, INDUSTRY DIVISION, CENSUS OF MANUFACTURES SECTION.). [Rubber plast. prod. ind.]. **Added/Corp** Statistics Canada. Census of Manufactures Section. Statistics Canada. Industry Division. **VFOAT** Industries des Produits en Caoutchouc et en Matiere Plastique. (1985)-. English (French). an. 38.00Can$ Canada; $46.00 US; $54.00 other. Statistics Canada, Publications Sales & Services, Main Building Room 1710, Ottawa Ontario K1A 0T6 Canada. **Tel** (613)951-5078, (800)267-6677, FAX (613)951-1584, telex 053-3585. **LC** HD9161.C2; R8. **DD** 338.4/76684/0971021. ***Formed by the union of*** *Rubber Products Industries (Final), 0300-0214* ***and*** *Plastics Industries, 0319-9053.*
**Desc:** An annual census of manufacturers.

US/0300-6123
**RUBBER & PLASTICS NEWS.** [Rubber plast. news]. **VFOAT** Rubber and Plastics News. **VAT** Rubber and Plastics News. (1971)-. Trade Publication. English. Twenty-six times a year. Comes with Rubber & Plastics News II. Crain Communications Inc., 1400 Woodbridge, Detroit MI 48207. **Tel** (313)446-6000, (800)992-9970. **(Subscription address:** Crain Communications, 965 East Jefferson Avenue, Detroit, MI 48207-3187**) ED** Edward Noga. **[CCC].** Index available. **Ad Acc. Circ:** 15,910. available in microform from University Microfilms International (UMI); available on an online database (file 16/Full-Text) from DIALOG.
**Desc:** This magazine is for rubber product manufacturers and related industries in the United States and Canada. Including tires and inner tubes, mechanical and industrial rubber goods, synthetic and natural rubber, rubber footwear, reclaimed rubber and plastic products made by rubber companies. Covers research and design, engineering, machinery and general industry news.
**Ind/Abst** Chem. Bus. Bull.; Chem. Bus. NewsBase (1985-); Chem. Bus. Update; Eng. Mater. Abstr.; F&S Index Plus Text, Int. [Full Txt.] [Select. Cov.]; Infomat Int. Bus.; PROMT [Full Txt.].

US/0197-2219
**RUBBER & PLASTICS NEWS II.** [Rubber plast. news II]. **VAT** Rubber and Plastics News Two. Vol. 1 (Oct. 8, 1979)-. Periodical. English. bw. $28.00 US and possessions; $60.00 other. Crain Communications Inc., 1400 Woodbridge, Detroit MI 48207. **Tel** (313)446-6000, (800)992-9970. **[CCC].** available on microfilm and microfiche from University Microfilms International (UMI); available on an online database (file 16/Full-Text) from DIALOG.
**Ind/Abst** Chem. Bus. Bull.; Chem. Bus. NewsBase (1985-); Chem. Bus. Update; Eng. Mater. Abstr.; F&S Index Plus Text, Int. [Full Txt.] [Select. Cov.]; PROMT [Full Txt.].

US
**RUBBER & RUBBER PRODUCTS.** (19??)-. English. mo. $225.00. Predicasts Inc., A Ziff Communications Company, 11001 Cedar Avenue, Cleveland OH 44106. **Tel** (800)321-6388, (216)795-3000, FAX (216)229-9944, telex 985 604.

II/0537-0507
**RUBBER BOARD BULLETIN. Main/Corp** India (Republic). Rubber Board. **VFOAT** Bulletin. Vol. 1 (Jan./Mar. 1951)-. Bulletin. English. Four times a year (Jan., Apr., July, Oct.). Rs35.00. The Rubber Board, PB No 280, Sastri Road, Kottyam, 686001 Kerala State India. **Tel** 011 91 3231. **ED** PK. Narayanan. **LC** SB290; .I46. **Bk Rev. Ad Acc. Circ:** 1,000. Documents available from CASDDS.
**Desc:** Promotion of rubber cultivation and rubber research on various aspects of cultivation.
**Ind/Abst** Agrofor. Abstr.; Biodeter. Abstr. (1991-); Chem. Abstr.; For. Prod. Abstr. (1991-); For. Abstr.; Hortic. Abstr.; Plant Breed. Abstr.; Rev. Plant Pathol.; World Agric. Econ.

II/0970-4124
**RUBBER BOARD BULLETIN.** [Rubber Board Bull.]. (1956)-. Periodical. English. qt. $20.00. **(Subscription address:** Prints India, 11 Darya Ganj, New Delhi 110002 India.**) UDC** 633.91. ***Continues*** *Indian Rubber Board Bulletin, 0537-0507.*

US/0035-9475
**RUBBER CHEMISTRY AND TECHNOLOGY.** [Rubber chem. technol.]. **Added/Corp** American Chemical Society. Division of Rubber Chemistry. American Chemical Society. Rubber Division. Vol. 1 (April 1928)-. Periodical. English. ir (5 issues). $120.00 US; $132.50 other (Comes also with membership). American Chemical Society, 1155 Sixteenth Street Northwest, Washington DC 20036. **Tel** (800)333-9511, (800)227-5558, (614)447-3776, FAX (202)833-7736. **(Subscription address:** American Chemical Society / Rubber Division, PO Box 499, Akron OH 44309.**) ED** Gary Hamed. **LC** TS1870; .R75. **CODEN** RCTEA4. (bound in Nov. issue). cum. index. **Bk Rev. Ad Acc. Pr Rev. Circ:** 5,500. available on microfilm and microfiche from University Microfilms International (UMI). Documents available from Article Express International, The Genuine Article, CASDDS.
**Desc:** Publishes major technical papers relating to rubber and polymer chemistry published anywhere in the world.
**Ind/Abst** Appl. Sci. Technol. Index; Art Archaeol. Tech. Abstr.; Bioeng. Abstr.; Chem. Abstr.; Curr. Contents Eng. Tech. Appl. Sci.; Curr. Contents Phys. Chem. Earth Sci.; Ei Page One; Eng. Index Annu.; Fluid Abstr., Civil Eng.; Fluid Abstr. Proc. Eng.; FLUIDEX (1973-); Int. Aerosp. Abstr.; Polymer Contents; Res. Alert [Full Cov.]; Sci. Cit. Index; SCISEARCH; Surf. Treat. Technol. Abstr.; Text. Technol. Dig.

UK/0035-9483
**RUBBER DEVELOPMENTS.** [Rubber dev.]. **Added/Corp** Malaysian Rubber Producers' Research Association. British Rubber Development Board. Natural Rubber Development Board, London. Natural Rubber Bureau (Gt. Brit.) Natural Rubber Producers' Research Association. Lembaga Penyelidikan dan Kemajuan Getah Malaysia. Vol. 1 (1947)-. Periodical. English. qt. Free. Malaysian Rubber Bureau, 1925 K Street NW, Washington DC 20006. **Tel** (202)452-0544. **LC** TS1870; .B6. **DD** 678. **CODEN** RUDVAX. available on microfilm and microfiche from University Microfilms International (UMI). Documents available from CASDDS. ***Absorbed*** *NR Technology, 0307-9007.*
**Ind/Abst** Abstr. Bull. Inst. Pap. Sci. Tech.; Chem. Abstr.; Chem. Bus. Bull.; Chem. Bus. NewsBase (1988-); Chem. Bus. Update; Coal Abstr.; Ei Page One; Fluid Abstr., Civil Eng.; Fluid Abstr. Proc. Eng.; FLUIDEX; Leadscan; Pap. Board Abstr.; World Surf. Coat. Abstr.; World Text. Abstr.

II/0035-9491
**RUBBER INDIA. Added/Corp** Indian Rubber Industries Association. Vol. 1 (Jan. 1949)-. Academic Scholarly Publication. English. mo. $40.00. All India Rubber Industry Association, Lamington Road/Building 3, Bombay 8 India. **Tel** 395032/892174, telex 75033. **(Subscription address:** Prints India, 11 Darya Ganj, New Delhi, 110002 India, (Phone: 011 91 11 3268645)**) ED** M Noorani. **LC** TS1885.I5; R8. **DD** 678.05. **CODEN** RUIDA4. **Bk Rev. Ad Acc. Circ:** 1,250 (ctrl). Documents available from CASDDS.
**Desc:** Intended to serve technical and non-technical information needs of the Indian rubber industry and to act as a spokesman for the Indian rubber industry.
**Ind/Abst** Chem. Abstr.

II/0035-9513
**RUBBER NEWS.** Vol. 1 (Oct. 1961)-. Academic Scholarly Publication. English. mo. $20.00. Polymer Publications, 41/1191 Adarsh Nagar Prabhadev, Bombay 400 025 India. **Tel** 011 91 22 4300696, 011 91 22 4373813, FAX 011 91 22 4300696, telex RUBBERFLO. **(Subscription address:** Prints India, 11 Darya Ganj, New Delhi, 110002 India, (Phone: 011 91 11 3268645)**) ED** D.S. Kulkarni. **CODEN** RUBNAX. **Bk Rev. Ad Acc,**

**Adv Mgr:** Lalitha Eswaran. **Circ:** 1,500 (ctrl). Documents available from CASDDS.
**Ind/Abst** Chem. Abstr. (1961-1983).

US/0738-033X
**RUBBER, PRODUCTION, SHIPMENTS, AND STOCKS.** (CURRENT INDUSTRIAL REPORTS. MA-30A, RUBBER, PRODUCTION, SHIPMENTS, AND STOCKS / U.S. DEPARTMENT OF COMMERCE, BUREAU OF THE CENSUS.). [Rubber, prod., shipm., and stocks]. 1980-. Government Publication. English. an. $1.50. US Department of Commerce / Bureau of the Census, Data User Services Division, Customer Services, Washington DC 20233-0800. **Tel** (301)763-4100. **(Subscription address:** Superintendent of Documents, US Government Printing Office, Washington DC 20402.**) ED** Robert Marske. **LC** HD9161.U5; C87. **DD** 338.4/76782/0973. **Circ:** 500. ***Continues*** *Current Industrial Reports. MA-30A, Rubber, Production, Consumption, and Stocks, 0278-9310.*
**Desc:** Reports on manufacturers production of synthetic rubber elastomers, by type of elastomer.

US
**RUBBER PRODUCTS GUIDE.** English. ir. Rubber Products Guide, 33-61 190th Street, Flushing NY 11358. **LC** TS1877; .R845. **DD** 338.4/76782/02573.

US/0361-0640
**RUBBER RED BOOK.** 1st Ed. (1937)-. English. an. $89.95. Argus Business, 6151 Powers Ferry Road, Atlanta GA 30339. **Tel** (404)995-2500, (800)233-3359. **LC** TS1877; .R85. **DD** 338.4/7/6782. **Circ:** 4,300.
**Desc:** Directory of the rubber industry.

UK/0035-9564
**RUBBER TRENDS.** [Rubber trends]. **Added/Corp** Economist Intelligence Unit (Great Britain). (19??)-. Periodical. English. qt. £281.25 (schools and educational libraries), £375.00 (other) Europe, Africa and Middle East. The Economist Intelligence Unit, 40 Duke Street, London W1A 1DW England. **Tel** 011 44 71 8301000. **(Subscription address:** Economist Intelligence Unit / North America Subscriptions, 111 West 57th Street, New York NY 10019.**) ED** Arthur Way. **LC** HD9161.A1; R83. **[CCC].** available on microfilm from World Microfilm Publications Ltd.
**Desc:** Emphasizes the study of long-term developments. Analyzes the outlook for the main consuming countries and reports on trends in the rubber-using industries.
**Ind/Abst** Chem. Bus. Bull.; Chem. Bus. NewsBase (1985-); Chem. Bus. Update; F&S Index Plus Text, Int. [Select. Cov.]; Hortic. Abstr.; Predicasts; PROMT; Trade Ind. ASAP [Full Txt.]; Trade Ind. Index [Full Txt.]; World Agric. Econ.

US/0035-9572
**RUBBER WORLD.** Vol. 1 (Oct. 15, 1889)-. Periodical. English. Twelve times a year (plus 4 issues of Rubber World Product News). $29.00 US; $34.00 Canada; $45.00 other. Rubber World, PO Box 5451, 1867 West Narjet Street, Akron OH 44334-0451. **Tel** (216)864-2122, FAX (216)864-5298, telex 297690 RWMAG UR. **(Subscription address:** Rubber World, Subscription Department, PO Box 16004, St. Louis MO 63105-0705.**) ED** Don Smith, Walt Warner and Jill Wrigley. **LC** TS1870; .I4. **DD** 338.4/7/678205. **CODEN** RUBWAQ. **[CCC]. Circ:** 12,000. available on microfilm and microfiche from University Microfilms International (UMI); available on an online database (file 648/Full-Text) from DIALOG. Documents available from Article Express International, CASDDS.
**Desc:** Contains information pertaining to chemistry, compounding and engineering.
**Ind/Abst** Acad. Search (Jan. 1993-); Anal. Abstr.; Bus. ASAP (1990-) [Full Txt.]; Bus. Index (1985-); Chem. Abstr.; Chem. Ind. Notes; Ei Page One; Eng. Mater. Abstr.; Eng. Index Annu. [Select. Cov.]; F&S Index Plus Text, Int. [Select. Cov.]; Gen. BusinessFile (1985-); Gen. Period. Index (1985-); INFO-SOUTH Abstr.; Infomat Int. Bus.; Mag. Search; PROMT; Stat. Ref. Index; Trade Ind. ASAP [Full Txt.]; Trade Ind. Index [Full Txt.]; Vocat. Search (Jan. 1993-).

NE/0168-4965
**RUBBERVERWERKENDE INDUSTRIE / CENTRAAL BUREAU VOOR DE STATISTIEK, HOOFDAFDELING STATISTIEKEN VAN INDUSTRIE EN BOUWNIJVERHEID.** **See** Manufacturing.

US
**RUBBICANA. VFOAT** Rubber Directory & Buyer's Guide. **VAT** Rubber Directory and Buyer's Guide. (1978)-. English. an (June). £75.00 UK; £80.00 other. RAPRA Technology Ltd., Shawbury Shrewsbury, Shropshire SY4 4NR England. **Tel** 011 44 939 250383, FAX 011 44 939 251118, telex 35134 RAPRA G.
**Desc:** Information on the rubber industry and trade.

UK
**RUBBICANA. EUROPE.** (1984)-. English. an. $135.00 US. RAPRA Technology Ltd., Shawbury Shrewsbury, Shropshire SY4 4NR England. **Tel** 011 44 939 250383, FAX 011 44 939 251118, telex 35134 RAPRA G. **(Subscription address:** 965 East Jefferson, Detroit MI 48207-3187**)**
**Desc:** Directory of North American rubber product manufacturers and rubber industry suppliers, including an alphabetical list of companies, who's who, trade name index, and geographical list of rubber product manufacturers.
**Ind/Abst** PROMT.

UK
**SUMMARY OF PROCEEDINGS OF THE ... ASSEMBLY / INTERNATIONAL RUBBER STUDY GROUP. Main/Corp** International Rubber Study Group. Proceedings. English. ir. 20.00F or $40.00 surface mail, 25.00F or $50.00 air mail. International Rubber Study Group, 8th Floor York House, Empire Way, Wembley, HA9 0PA England. **Tel** 011 44 81 9037727. **ED** J D Carr. **LC** HD9161.A2; I532A. **DD** 338.4/76782. ***Continues*** *International Rubber Study Group. Summary of Proceedings of the Meeting.*
**Desc:** Collection of papers on worldwide trends in rubber production/consumption and transport given at International Rubber Study Group Assembly.

US
**TIRE BUSINESS. Added/Corp** Crain Communications Inc. (19??)-. Periodical. English. bw. $48.00 US; $63.55 Canada; $63.00 other. Crain Communications Inc., 1400 Woodbridge, Detroit MI 48207. **Tel** (313)446-6000, (800)992-9970. available on an online database (file 16/Full-Text) from DIALOG. ***Continues*** *Crain's Tire Business, 0746-9071.*
**Ind/Abst** F&S Index Plus Text, Int. [Full Txt.] [Select. Cov.]; PROMT [Full Txt.].

US/1046-7157
**TIRE RETREADING/REPAIR JOURNAL, THE. VFOAT** Tire Retreading Repair Journal. (1989)-. Periodical. English. mo. $50.00 US & Canada; $60.00 other. TIPS - Tire Industry Publication Service, PO Box 37203, Louisville KY 40233-7203. **Tel** (800)426-8835, (502)968-8900, FAX (502)964-7859. **ED** Marvin Bozarth. **DD** 629. ***Formed by the union of*** *Tire Repair Journal, 0731-7298* ***and*** *Retreader's Journal, 0482-430X.*

US/0040-8085
**TIRE REVIEW (1966).** (TIRE REVIEW.). [Tire rev.]. (June 1966)-. Periodical. English. Thirteen times a year. $48.00 US, Canada & Mexico; $96.00 others. Babcox Publications Inc., 11 South Ford Street, Akron OH 44304. **Tel** (216)535-7011. **ED** Bill Whitney. **LC** TS1870; .I3. **DD** 381/.4567832/068. **Ad Acc. Circ:** 32,800 (ctrl). available on an online database (file 648/Full-Text) from DIALOG. ***Continues*** *Tire and TBA Review.*
**Desc:** Delivers current business information relating to tire, wheel and automotive service industries.
**Ind/Abst** F&S Index Plus Text, Int. [Select. Cov.]; PROMT.

MY/0126-9089
**ULASAN GETAH MALAYSIA.** ***Title Change.*** [Ulasan getah Malays.]. **Added/Corp** Lembaga Penyelidikan dan Kemajuan Getah Malaysia. **VFOAT** Malaysian Rubber Review. Vol. 1 (July 1976)-(19??). English (Malay). ir. Malaysian Rubber Research Development Board, PO Box 10508, Kuala Lumpur 01-02 Malaysia. **Tel** (03)2614422, telex MA 30953 MRRDB. **ED** Ahmad Farouk, Bin Haji and S M Ishak. **LC** TS1870; .U42. **DD** 338.1/7/3895209595. **Bk Rev. Circ:** 1,500 (ctrl). ***Continued by*** *Malaysian Rubber Review, 0127-2969.*
**Desc:** A general assessment of the rubber industry in Malaysia and the world with emphasis on current economic and technical information.

US/0162-3869
**UNITED RUBBER WORKER: URW, THE.** [URW. United rubber work.]. **Main/Corp** United Rubber, Cork, Linoleum and Plastic Workers of America. **VFOAT** United Rubber Worker. (1935)-. Periodical. English. bm. Free (institutions), $10.00 (individuals). United Rubber Cork Linoleum and Plastic Workers of America Street, 570 White Pond Drive, Akron OH 44320. **Tel** (216)869-0320, FAX (216)434-5230. **ED** Milan Stone and J. Curtis Brown Sr. Index available. **Circ:** 160,000 (ctrl). ***Continues*** *United Rubber Worker, 0041-7475.*
**Ind/Abst** Work Relat. Abstr.

US/0043-5872
**WING FOOT CLAN, THE. VFOAT** Wingfoot Clan. Periodical. English. wk. Free. Goodyear Tire & Rubber Company, 1144 East Market Street, Akron OH 44316. **Tel** (216)796-4143. **ED** Dotti Eitel. **Circ:** 21,000 (ctrl).
**Desc:** Company policy and procedure information, economic information, subjects impacting rubber industry and general interest employee stories.

UK
**WORLD PLASTICS & RUBBER TECHNOLOGY.** **See** Plastics.

US/1051-4155
**X MAGAZINE.** **See** General Interest.

## ABSTRACTING, BIBLIOGRAPHIES AND STATISTICS

MY
**BUKU MAKLUMAT PERANGKAAN GETAH BAGI MALAYSIA. RUBBER STATISTICS HANDBOOK OF MALAYSIA. Main/Corp** Malaysia. Jabatan Perangkaan. **Added/Corp** Malaysia. Jabatan Perangkaan. Rubber Statistics Handbook of Malaysia. **VFOAT** Rubber Statistics Handbook of Malaysia. (1967)-. Multiple languages (English and Malay). an. 60.00Mal$. Department of Statistics / Malaysia, Jalan Cenderasari, 50514 Kuala Lumpur Malaysia. **Tel** 011 60 3 2922133. **LC** HD9161.M32; A3. **DD** 338.4/7/678209595. **Circ:** 180 (ctrl). ***Continues*** *Malaysia. Dept. of Statistics. Rubber Statistics Handbook of Malaysia.*

MY/0126-5865
**MONTHLY STATISTICAL BULLETIN / MAJLIS PENGELUAR-PENGELUAR GETAH MALAYSIA. Added/Corp** Majlis Pengeluar-Pengeluar Getah Malaysia. (Sept. 1973)-. Statistical Publication. English. mo. £24.00. Malaysian Rubber Production Council, Tunab Ruzak Lab Brickendonbury, Hertford SG13 8NL England. **Tel** 011 44 992 584966, FAX 011 44 992 554837. **LC** HD9161.M32; R8. **DD** 338.1/738952/09795. **Circ:** 130 (ctrl). ***Continues*** *Monthly Statistical Bulletin (Majlis Pengeluarp2s Getah Tanah Melayu), 0303-1640.*

UK/0033-6750
**RAPRA ABSTRACTS.** (RAPRA ABSTRACTS / RUBBER AND PLASTICS RESEARCH ASSOCIATION OF GREAT BRITAIN.). [RAPRA abstr.]. **Added/Corp** Rapra Technology Limited. Rubber and Plastics Research Association of Great Britain. **VAT** Rubber and Plastics Research Association of Great Britain Abstracts. Vol. 1, No. 1 (Jan. 1968)-. Abstracting/Indexing Service. English. mo (12 issues). £1,050.00 UK; $2,000.00 US; £1,150.00 other. RAPRA Technology Ltd., Shawbury Shrewsbury, Shropshire SY4 4NR England. **Tel** 011 44 939 250383, FAX 011 44 939 251118, telex 35134 RAPRA G. **ED** Christine Wright. **LC** TS1870; .R68. **[CCC]. Circ:** 700. available on microfilm and microfiche from University Microfilms International (UMI); available on CD-ROM. ***Formed by the union of*** *Plastics. RAPRA Abstracts* ***and*** *Rubbers. RAPRA Abstracts.*
**Desc:** Journal provides a comprehensive and up to date survey of current information relevant to engineering and advanced materials producers, processors and users.
**Ind/Abst** World Surf. Coat. Abstr.; World Text. Abstr.

UK/0035-9548
**RUBBER STATISTICAL BULLETIN.** (RUBBER STATISTICAL BULLETIN / IRSG.). [Rubber stat. bull.]. **Added/Corp** International Rubber Study Group. Vol. 1 (July 1946)-. Statistical Publication. English. mo. $270.00. International Rubber Study Group, 8th Floor York House, Empire Way, Wembley, HA9 0PA England. **Tel** 011 44 81 9037727. **ED** J D Carr. **LC** HD9161.A1; I55. **Circ:** 1,000. ***Continues*** *International Rubber Regulation Committee. Statistical Bulletin.*
**Desc:** Complete statistics on the world's rubber industry: production, consumption, trade, stocks, prices and uses.

IO
**STATISTIK INDUSTRI KARET REMAH (CRUMB RUBBER) ... INDONESIA.** 1980 and 1981-. English (Indonesian). an. Rp1500 Indonesia; $1.00 US. Central Bureau of Statistics / Indonesia, c/o Dr. Sutomo, 8 Jalan, PO Box 3, Jakarta Indonesia. **Tel** 372808 374908 Ext.342. **LC** HD9161.I6; S73. ctrl circ.

UK/0041-4859
**TYRES AND ACCESSORIES.** [Tyres Accessories]. (1946)-. Periodical. English. mo. £38.00 UK; £47.00 other. Tyre Industry Publications Ltd, Unit I Magnolia Centre, Telford Road, Clacton-on-Sea Essex, CO15 4LP England. **Tel** 44 255 222233, FAX 44 255 222234. **CODEN** TYACAB.

## SCIENCE AND TECHNOLOGY

IT
**21MO : SECOLO SCIENZA E TECNOLOGIA.** (19??)-. Italian. qt. L50000. Vita Nova Arl, Via Muzio Scevola 26, 00181 Rome Italy. **Tel** 011 39 6 71543915.

US/0895-6820
**21ST CENTURY SCIENCE & TECHNOLOGY.** [21st century sci. technol.]. **VFOAT** 21 Century; 21st Century Science and Technology; Twenty-First Century Science and Technology; Twenty-First Century Science & Technology. Vol. 1, No. 1 (Mar.-Apr. 1988)-. Periodical. English. Four times a year. $20.00 North America; $40.00 others. 21st

Century Science Associates, PO Box 16285, Washington DC 20041. **Tel** (703)777-7473. **ED** Marjorie Mazel Hecht. **LC** Q1; .A17. **DD** 505.
**Desc:** Dedicated to providing accurate and comprehensive information on advanced technologies and science policy.
**Ind/Abst** Access (1992-?).

FR/0397-829X
**A.F.P. SCIENCES.** [A.F.P. Sci.]. **VFOAT** Agence France Presse Sciences. (1976)-. Periodical. French. wk. 6993.14F France; 7800.00F other. Agence France Presse, 13 Place de la Bourse, BP 20, 75061 Paris Cedex 02 France. **Tel** 011 33 1 40414646. **UDC** 50. Index available. cum. index. ctrl circ.

US/0735-1488
**A.I.D. EVALUATION SPECIAL STUDY.** (A.I.D. EVALUATION SPECIAL STUDY / AGENCY FOR INTERNATIONAL DEVELOPMENT.). [A.I.D. eval. spec. study]. **VFOAT** Aid Evaluation Special Study. No. 1-. Monographic series. English. ir. Price varies per volume. Bureau for Science and Technology, Agency for International Development, Washington DC 20523.
**Ind/Abst** Agrofor. Abstr.

US/1062-2195
**AAAS HANDBOOK.** [AAAS handb.]. **Main/Corp** American Association for the Advancement of Science. **VFOAT** Handbook. (1991)-. English. an (published in May). $11.50. American Association for the Advancement of Science, 1333 H Street Northwest, Washington DC 20005. **Tel** (202)326-6400, (203)326-6417, (202)326-6430, FAX (202)842-1065. **(Subscription address:** AAAS Books, PO Box 753, Waldorf MD 20604.**)** **LC** Q11; .A511. **DD** 506. **NLM** Q 11; A512d. ***Continues*** *American Association for the Advancement of Science. Handbook, 0361-7874.*

●US
**AAAS PROGRAM/ABSTRACTS / AMERICAN ASSOCIATION FOR THE ADVANCEMENT OF SCIENCE.** (1992)-. Periodical. English. an.

US/0271-2229
**AAAS PUBLICATION.** [AAAS publ.]. **Added/Corp** American Association for the Advancement of Science. **VAT** American Association for the Advancement of Science Publication. (197?)-. Monographic series. English. ir. Price varies per volume. American Association for the Advancement of Science, 1333 H Street Northwest, Washington DC 20005. **Tel** (202)326-6400, (203)326-6417, (202)326-6430, FAX (202)842-1065. **LC** Q181.A1; A68. **DD** 508/.1. **CODEN** AAAPEH. Documents available from BIOSIS Document Express. ***Continues*** *Miscellaneous Publication (American Association for the Advancement of Science), 0569-2342.*
**Ind/Abst** Biol. Abstr. (1988-); GeoRef.

US
**AAAS SCIENCE AND TECHNOLOGY POLICY YEARBOOK.** **Added/Corp** American Association for the Advancement of Science. AAAS Committee on Science, Engineering, and Public Policy. **VFOAT** Science and Technology Policy Yearbook. (1991)-. English. an. $19.95 (member of AAAS), $23.95 (non-member). American Association for the Advancement of Science, 1333 H Street Northwest, Washington DC 20005. **Tel** (202)326-6400, (203)326-6417, (202)326-6430, FAX (202)842-1065. **(Subscription address:** AAAS Books, PO Box 753, Waldorf MD 20604.**)** **LC** Q11.A53; A13.

US/0164-0429
**AAAS SELECTED SYMPOSIA SERIES.** ***Ceased.*** (AAAS SELECTED SYMPOSIUM.). [AAAS sel. symp. ser.]. **Added/Corp** American Association for the Advancement of Science. **VFOAT** A.A.A.S. Selected Symposium; A.A.A.S. Selected Symposium Series; AAAS Selected Symposium Series. **VAT** American Association for the Advancement of Science Selected Symposia Series. (1977)-Series complete with 113. Academic Scholarly Publication. English. ir. Westview Press Inc, 5500 Central Avenue, Boulder CO 80301. **Tel** (303)444-3541, FAX (303)449-3356. **LC** UNC. **NLM** W3 A101S. **CODEN** ASSYDL. Documents available from BIOSIS Document Express, CASDDS.
**Ind/Abst** Biol. Abstr.; Chem. Abstr. (1978-1979); Ei Page One; GeoRef.

NO/0522-9189
**AARBOK FOR UNIVERSITETET I BERGEN., MATEMATISK-NATURVITENSKAPELIG SERIE.** (AARBOK FOR UNIVERSITETET I BERGEN. MAT.-NATURV. SERIE / ACTA UNIVERSITATIS BERGENSIS. SERIES MATHEMATICA RERUMQUE NATURALIUM.). [Aarbok Univ. Bergen., Mat.-Naturvitensk. ser.]. **Added/Corp** Universitetet i Bergen. **VFOAT** Aarbok for Universitetet i Bergen. Matematisk-naturvitenskapelig serie.; Matematisk-naturvitenskapelig Serie; Acta Universitatis Bergensis. Series Mathematica Rerumque Naturalium. (1960)-. Norwegian (English and Norwegian). ir. Scandinavian University Press, PO Box 2959 Toeyen, N 0608 Oslo 6 Norway. **Tel** 011 47 2 2575400, FAX 011 47 2 2575353, telex 71896 UROR N. **(Subscription address:** Scandinavian University Press, 200 Meacham Ave., Elmont NY 11003.**)** **LC** Q1; .B455. **DD** 505. **CODEN** ARBMAQ. ***Continues in part*** *Universitetet i Bergen. Aarbok. Naturvitenskapelig Rekke.*
**Ind/Abst** GeoRef; Math. Rev.

NE/0166-4786
**AARDE & I.E. EN KOSMOS.** [Aarde & kosmos]. Periodical. Dutch. mo. Fl52.50. Stichting Mens en Wetenschap, Postbus 108, 1270 AC Huizen Netherlands. **LC** Q4; .A22.
**Ind/Abst** EMBASE.

GW/0302-8054
**ABHANDLUNGEN DER AKADEMIE DER WISSENSCHAFTEN DER DDR.** (ABHANDLUNGEN.). [Abh. Akad. Wiss. DDR]. **Main/Corp** Akademie der Wissenschaften der DDR. (19??)-. German. Akademie-Verlag GmbH, Muehlenstrasse 33 34, D 13162 Berlin Germany. **Tel** 011 49 30 47889300, FAX 011 49 30 47889357. **(Subscription address:** VCH Publishers Inc., 303 Northwest 12th Avenue, Journals Department, Deerfield FL 33442.**)** **LC** Q49; .A39a.
**Ind/Abst** Life Sci. Collect.; Zentralbl. Math. Ihre Grenzgeb.

GW/0068-0737
**ABHANDLUNGEN DER BRAUNSCHWEIGISCHEN WISSENSCHAFTLICHEN GESELLSCHAFT.** [Abh. Braunschweig. Wiss. Ges.]. **Main/Corp** Braunschweigische Wissenschaftliche Gesellschaft. Vol. 1 (1949)-. Academic Scholarly Publication. German. ir. Verlag Erich Goltze KG, Stresemannstrasse 28, D 37079 Goettingen Germany. **Tel** 011 49 551 63078. **CODEN** ABWGAZ. Documents available from BIOSIS Document Express, Ask*IEEE, CASDDS.
**Ind/Abst** Biol. Abstr.; Chem. Abstr.; GeoRef; INSPEC (1968-Vol. 21, 1970); Int. Aerosp. Abstr.; Math. Rev.; Zentralbl. Math. Ihre Grenzgeb.

GW/0002-2993
**ABHANDLUNGEN DER MATHEMATISCH-NATURWISSENSCHAFTLICHEN KLASSE - AKADEMIE DER WISSENSCHAFTEN UND DER LITERATUR.** (ABHANDLUNGEN DER MATHEMATISCH- NATURWISSENSCHAFTLICHEN KLASSE.). [Abh. Math.-Nat.wiss. Kl. - Akad. Wiss. Lit.]. **Main/Corp** Akademie der Wissenschaften und der Literatur, (Germany). **Added/Corp** Akademie der Wissenschaften und der Literatur (Germany). Mathematisch-Naturwissenschaftliche Klasse. (1950)-. Monographic series. German. ir. Price varies per volume. Franz Steiner Verlag GmbH, Postfach 101061, D 70009 Stuttgart Germany. **Tel** 011 49 0711 2582372, FAX 011 49 0711 2582290, telex 723636 daz d. **LC** Q49; .M22. **NLM** W1 AK324. **CODEN** AWLMA9.
**Desc:** Mostly short monographs dedicated to all natural sciences, medicine, and mathematics.
**Ind/Abst** GeoRef; Math. Rev.; Life Sci. Collect.

●GW
**ABHANDLUNGEN DER NORDRHEIN-WESTFAELISCHEN AKADEMIE DER WISSENSCHAFTEN. SONDERREIHE PAPYROLOGICA COLONIENSIA.** **Added/Corp** Nordrhein-Westfaelische Akademie der Wissenschaften. **VFOAT** Sonderreihe Papyrologica Coloniensia; Papyrologica Coloniensia. Vol. 21 (1994)-. Monographic series. German. ir. Price varies per volume. Westdeutscher Verlag GmbH, Postfach 5829, D 65048 Wiesbaden Germany. **Tel** 011 49 611 160220. ***Continues*** *Abhandlungen der Rheinisch-Westfaelischen Akademie der Wissenschaften. Sonderreihe Papyrologica Coloniensia.*
**Ind/Abst** Numis. Lit.

GW/0078-9410
**ABHANDLUNGEN DER RHEINISCH-WESTFAELISCHEN AKADEMIE DER WISSENSCHAFTEN. SONDERREIHE PAPYROLOGICA COLONIENSIA.** ***Title Change.*** **Added/Corp** Rheinisch-Westfaelische Akademie der Wissenschaften. **VFOAT** Sonderreihe Papyrologica Coloniensia; Papyrologica Coloniensia. Vol. 5 (1974)-Vol. 20 (1992). Monographic series. German. ***Continues*** *Wissenschaftliche Abhandlungen der Arbeitsgemeinschaft fuer Forschung des Landes Nordrhein-Westfalen. Sonderreihe Papyrologica Coloniensia.* ***Continued by*** *Abhandlungen der Nordrhein-Westfaelischen Akademie der Wissenschaften. Sonderreihe Papyrologica Coloniensia.*
**Ind/Abst** Numis. Lit. (?-?).

GW/0365-6470
**ABHANDLUNGEN DER SACHSISCHEN AKADEMIE DER WISSENSCHAFTEN ZU LEIPZIG. MATHEMATISCH-NATURWISSENSCHAFTLICHE KLASSE.** [Abh. Sachs. Akad. Wiss. Leipzig, Math.-Nat.wiss. Kl.]. **Main/Corp** Sachsische Akademie der Wissenschaften zu Leipzig. (194?)-. Academic Scholarly Publication. German. ir. Price varies per volume. Akademie-Verlag GmbH, Muehlenstrasse 33 34, D 13162 Berlin Germany. **Tel** 011 49 30 47889300, FAX 011 49 30 47889357. **(Subscription address:** VCH Publishers Inc., 303 Northwest 12th Avenue, Journals Department, Deerfield FL 33442.**)** **CODEN** ASAWAO. Documents available from CASDDS. ***Continues*** *Abhandlungen der Mathematisch-Naturwissenschaftliche Klasse der Sachsischen Akademie der Wissenschaften.*
**Ind/Abst** Chem. Abstr. (1950-1981); GeoRef; Math. Rev.; Zentralbl. Math. Ihre Grenzgeb.

HU/0238-6178
**ABSTRACT REVIEW IN SCIENCE EXTENSION.** [Abstr. rev. sci. ext.]. (1988)-. English. mo. $60.00. Interbright, PO Box 225, Budapest H-1476 Hungary. **Tel** 001 36 1 156-0498, FAX 011 36 1 155-3779. **ED** Csilla Szentirmay. **UDC** 019.9. Index available. **Bk Rev. Ad Acc. Pr Rev. Circ:** 1,000 (ctrl).
**Desc:** A monthly review containing bibliographical information plus a brief outline and up-to-date results on sciences, arts and humanities.

US
**ABSTRACTS OF PUBLICATIONS - NATIONAL SCIENCE FOUNDATION U.S.** **Main/Corp** National Science Foundation (U.S.). Division of Intergovernmental Science & Public Technology. 1967/75-. English. National Science Foundation, 1800 G Street Northwest, Washington DC 20550. **Tel** (202)357-9859, (202)357-9498. ***Continues*** *Publications Abstracts.*
**Desc:** Summarizes the publications that have resulted from the activities that have been sponsored in State and Local governments and in technologically-oriented institutions around the country.

RM/0365-6330
**ABSTRACTS OF ROMANIAN SCIENTIFIC AND TECHNICAL LITERATURE.** (ABSTRACTS OF ROMANIAN SCIENTIFIC AND TECHNICAL LITERATURE / INSTITUTUL NATIONAL DE INFORMARE SI DOCUMENTARE.). [Abst. Rom. sci. tech. lit.]. **Added/Corp** Institutul Central de Documentare Tehnica (Romania) Institutul National de Informare si Documentare Stiintifica si Technica (Romania) Institutul National de Informare si Documentare (Romania). Vol. 7, No. 1 (Jan./Mar. 1971)-. Periodical. Multiple languages (English, French and Russian). sa. DM307.00. **(Subscription address:** Kubon & Sagner, ABT Zeitschriftenimport, D 80328 Munich Germany.**)** **LC** T4; .A15. **DD** 608. **CODEN** ARSTCW. Documents available from CASDDS. ***Continues*** *Abstracts of Romanian Technical Literature.*
**Desc:** Documentary information publication.
**Ind/Abst** Anal. Abstr.; Chem. Abstr.; Coal Abstr.; Concr. Abstr.; Corros. Abstr. (199?-); World Surf. Coat. Abstr.; World Text. Abstr.

SW
**ABSTRACTS OF UPPSALA DISSERTATIONS FROM THE FACULTY OF SCIENCE.** **Added/Corp** Uppsala Universitet. **VFOAT** Abstracts of Uppsala Dissertations in Science. Vol. 1 (1961)-. Monographic series. English. ir. Price varies per volume. Almqvist & Wiksell International, PO Box 4627, S-11691 Stockholm Sweden. **Tel** 011-46-8-6408800.

BE/0373-7063
**ACADEMIE ROYALE DES SCIENCES D'OUTRE-MER. CLASSE DES SCIENCES TECHNIQUES.** **See** Education.

GW/0940-225X
**ACADEMIE SPECTRUM.** **Added/Corp** Akademie der Wissenschaften in Berlin (1991-). (1991)-. Academic Scholarly Publication. German. mo. **LC** Q49; .S83. **DD** 505. **CODEN** ASPUET. Documents available from CASDDS. ***Continues*** *Spektrum (Berlin, Germany : 1970), 0049-1861.*
**Ind/Abst** Chem. Abstr. (1991).

US/0897-5523
**ACADEMY NEWSLETTER, THE.** [Acad. newsl.]. Newsletter. English. mo. $30.00. California Academy of Sciences, Golden State Park, San Francisco CA 94181-9961. **Tel** (415)221-5100. **ED** Pam McCosker and David Shaw. **LC** Q1; .C15. **DD** 506/.0794/61. Index available. cum. index. **Circ:** 25,000 (ctrl). ***Continues*** *Newsletter - California Academy of Sciences, 0271-020X.*
**Desc:** A newsletter describing the monthly activities and news of the California Academy of Sciences for its members.

US/0898-9621
**ACCOUNTABILITY IN RESEARCH.** [Account. res.]. **VFOAT** Research; Research, Policies, Audit, and Quality Assurance. Vol. 1, No. 1 (1989)-. Periodical. English. ir. Price varies. Gordon & Breach Science Publishers, Inc., PO Box 786, Cooper Station, New York NY 10276. **Tel** (212)206-8900, FAX (212)645-2459. **LC** Q180.55.E9; A23. **DD** 001.4. **NLM** W1; AC727. **CODEN** ARQAEZ. **[CCC].**
**Ind/Abst** Soc. Work Abstr. [Select. Cov.].

VE/0001-5504
**ACTA CIENTIFICA VENEZOLANA.** [Acta cient. venez.]. **Added/Corp** Asociacion Venezolana para el Avance de la Ciencia. Vol. 1, No. 1 (May/June 1950)-. Periodical. Spanish (English and French). Six times a year. $150.00 (institutions), $50.00 (individuals). Acta Cientifica Venezolana, Apartado Postal 47286, Caracas 1041 Venezuela. **Tel** (02)752-1002, 751-1420. **ED** V. Rodriguez Lemoine. **LC** Q22; .A343. **NLM** W1 AC783. **CODEN** ACVEAU. cum. index. **Bk Rev. Ad Acc. Circ:** 21,000 (ctrl). available on an online database. Documents available from BIOSIS Document Express, CASDDS.
**Desc:** Full papers on multidisciplinary science including medicine, physics, chemistry, engineering, mathematics, biology, earth sciences.
**Ind/Abst** AGRICOLA (?-1987); Biol. Abstr.; Chem. Abstr.; EMBASE; GeoRef; Health Plan. Adminis.; Hortic. Abstr.; Index Med.; Math. Rev.; Nutr. Abstr. Rev., Ser. A, Hum. Exp.; Life Sci. Collect.; PESTDOC; Rev. Med. Vet. Mycology.

XR/0231-6005
**ACTA HISTORIAE RERUM NATURALIUM NECNON TECHNICARUM. SPECIAL ISSUE.** [Acta hist. rer. nat. nec non tech.]. **Added/Corp** Ceskoslovenska Akademie Ved. Komise pro Dejiny Prirodnich Ved a Techniky. (1965)-. English (French and German; summaries and/or abstracts in Russian). ir. exchange basis only. Ceskoslovenskia Akademie Ved, Ustav Teorie a Dejin Vedy, Jilska 1, 110 00, Prague 1, Czech Republic. **(Subscription address:** Kubon & Sagner, ABT Zeitschriftenimport, D 80328 Munich Germany.**)** ***Continues in part*** *Sbornik Pro Dejiny Prirodnich Ved a Techniky.*
**Ind/Abst** Math. Rev.; Zentralbl. Math. Ihre Grenzgeb.

GW/0001-5857
**ACTA HISTORICA LEOPOLDINA.** [Acta hist. Leopold.]. **Added/Corp** Deutsche Akademie der Naturforscher Leopoldina. No. 1 (1963)-. Monographic series. German. ir. Price varies per volume. Johann Ambrosius Barth, Prager Strasse 16 B, D 04103 Leipzig Germany. **Tel** 011 49 341 7137570. **NLM** W1 AC809G. **CODEN** ACHLAG. Documents available from BIOSIS Document Express.
**Ind/Abst** Biol. Abstr.; Energy Res. Abstr. (Feb. 1982-); Math. Rev. (1985-); Zentralbl. Math. Ihre Grenzgeb.

DK/0065-1311
**ACTA HISTORICA SCIENTIARUM NATURALIUM ET MEDICINALIUM.** (ACTA HISTORICA SCIENTIARIUM NATURALIUM ET MEDICINALIUM / EDIDIT BIBLIOTHECA UNIVERSITATIS HAUNIENSIS.). [Acta hist. sci. nat. med.]. **Added/Corp** Kbenhavns Universitet. Universitetsbiblioteket. (1942)-. Monographic series. English (Danish, French and German). an. kr590.00. Danish National Library of Science and Medicine, 49 Norre Alle, DK-2200 Copenhagen N Denmark. **Tel** 01 396523, FAX 44.31.398533, telex 15 097. **ED** Poulel Christiansen. **NLM** W1 AC81G. **CODEN** AHSMA7.
**Desc:** History of science and medicine.
**Ind/Abst** GeoRef (19??-).

PH
**ACTA MANILANA.** No. 34 (Dec. 1985)-. English. an. Research Center for the Natural Sciences, University of Santo Tomas, Manila Philippines. **CODEN** ACTMEF. available in microform. Documents available from BIOSIS Document Express, Ask*IEEE. ***Continues*** *Acta manilana. Series A, Natural and Applied Sciences, 0567-7688.*
**Ind/Abst** Biol. Abstr. (1988-); Index Philip. Period.; INSPEC (1985-); Philip. Sci. Technol. Abstr.

CC/0894-9166
**ACTA MECHANICA SOLIDA SINICA.** (ACTA MECHANICA SOLIDA SINICA : THE OFFICIAL JOURNAL OF THE CHINESE SOCIETY OF THEORETICAL AND APPLIED MECHANICS.). [Acta mech. solida Sin.]. **Added/Corp** Chung-kuo li Hsueh Hsueh hui. Hua Chung Kung Hsueh Yuan. **VFOAT** Mechanica Solida; Ku ti li Hsueh Hsueh Pao. Vol. 1, No. 1 (Jan. 1988)-. Periodical. English. Four times a year. £147.00. Institute of Engineering Mechanics / Shanghai, Shanghai Jiaotong University, Shanghai 200030, People's Republic of China. **ED** Zudao Luo. **LC** TA349; .K82. **DD** 620.1/05. **CODEN** ASSIE8. available on microfilm and microfiche from University Microfilms International (UMI). Documents available from The Genuine Article, Ask*IEEE.
**Desc:** A comprehensive academic journal that provides a forum for important research papers which reflect current advances in solid state mechanics in China, and for the dissemination of this information on a world-wide basis.
**Ind/Abst** Acoust. Abstr.; INSPEC (1980-); Res. Alert [Full Cov.].

MX/0567-7785
**ACTA MEXICANA DE CIENCIA Y TECNOLOGIA.** ***Suspended.*** [Acta mex. cienc. tecnol.]. **Added/Corp** Instituto Politecnico Nacional (Mexico). Vol. 1 (1967)-Suspended (1992). Academic Scholarly Publication. Spanish. qt. Acta Mexicana de Ciencia Tecno, Apartado 42161, Mexico 17 DF Mexico. **CODEN** AMXCB4. Documents available from CASDDS.
**Ind/Abst** Chem. Abstr. (-1987); Math. Rev.; Zentralbl. Math. Ihre Grenzgeb.

IT/0392-419X
**ACTA NATURALIA DE L'ATENEO PARMENSE.** [Acta nat. Ateneo parm.]. **Added/Corp** Societa di Medicina e Scienze Naturali di Parma. (1981)-. Academic Scholarly Publication. Italian (French and English). qt. L25.000. Soc Medicina Scienze Naturale, Via Gramsci 14, 43100 Parma Italy. **Tel** 011 39 521 290370. **ED** F. Barbieri and P. Bobbio. **NLM** W1; AC8652. **CODEN** ANPMD3. Index available. **Bk Rev. Circ:** 350 (ctrl). Documents available from BIOSIS Document Express, CASDDS. ***Continues*** *Ateneo Parmense. Acta Naturalia.*
**Ind/Abst** Biol. Abstr. 919??-); Chem. Abstr. (19??-); GeoRef (19??-).

FR/0998-4364
**ACTA PALYNOLOGICA : AP.** ***Ceased.*** **VFOAT** AP. Vol. 1 (1989)-?. Periodical. English (French). qt. J Sivak, 4 rue Fournarie, 34000 Montpellier France. **Tel** 67 412819.

PL
**ACTA POLYTECHNICAE WRATISLAVIENSIS.** **Main/Corp** Breslau. Politechnika. No. 1 (1972)-. English (English). qt. Price on Request. **(Subscription address:** ARS Polona, PO Box 1001, 00068 Warsaw Poland.**) LC** T1; .B76a. **DD** 608.

HU/0001-7035
**ACTA TECHNICA / ACADEMIAE SCIENTIARUM HUNGARICAE.** [Acta techn., acad. scient. Hung.]. **Added/Corp** Magyar Tudomanyos Akademia. **VFOAT** Conference on Dimensioning and Strength Calculation. Vol. 1, No. 1 (1950)-. Academic Scholarly Publication. English (French, German and Russian). Four times a year. $92.00. Akademiai Kiado, Publishing House of the Hungarian Academy of Sciences, Prielle Kornelia u. 19-35, H-1117 Budapest Hungary. **Tel** 011 36 1 1811991, FAX 011 36 1 1811991, telex 22-6228 AKNYO H. **ED** Pal Michelberger (editor's address: Acta Technica, Munnich F u 7, H-1051 Budapest Hungary). **LC** T4; .M323. **CODEN** ATSHA8. **[CCC].** cum. index. **Bk Rev. Ad Acc. Circ:** 700. Documents available from Article Express International, Ask*IEEE.
**Desc:** Publishes papers written by Hungarian and other scientists dealing with mechanics, material testing, architecture, building technology, highway, railway and hydraulic constructions, thermodynamics, mechanical engineering, mechanical technology, metallurgy, electrical engineering, electronics, automation, and telecommunication.
**Ind/Abst** AGRICOLA; Alum. Ind. Abstr.; Bioeng. Abstr.; Ceram. Abstr. (19??-); Concr. Abstr.; Ei Page One; Eng. Mater. Abstr.; Eng. Index Annu.; GeoRef; INSPEC (1968-); Int. Aerosp. Abstr.; Math. Rev.; Met. Abstr.; Zentralbl. Math. Ihre Grenzgeb.

XR/0001-7043
**ACTA TECHNICA CSAV.** [Acta tech. CSAV]. **Added/Corp** Ceskoslovenska Akademie Ved. Vol. 7 (1961)-. Periodical. English. bm (6 issues). DM433.00 Germany; DM483.00 other. **(Subscription address:** Kubon & Sagner, ABT Zeitschriftenimport, D 80328 Munich Germany.**) LC** TA4.C34; A18. **CODEN** ATCVA4. cum. index. Documents available from Article Express International, Ask*IEEE, CASDDS. ***Continues*** *Ceskoslovenska Akademie Ved. Acta Technica.*
**Desc:** Main results of fundamental research in mechanical, electrical and civil engineering (mechanics of solids, thermodynamics, hydrodynamics, theory of materials, theory of structures, electrotechnics).
**Ind/Abst** Alum. Ind. Abstr.; Bioeng. Abstr.; Chem. Abstr.; Ei Page One; Eng. Mater. Abstr.; Eng. Index Annu.; Fluid Abstr., Civil Eng.; Fluid Abstr. Proc. Eng.; FLUIDEX (1973-1989); INSPEC (1968-); Int. Aerosp. Abstr. (1991-); Math. Rev.; Met. Abstr.; Zentralbl. Math. Ihre Grenzgeb.

FR
**ACTES.** ***Ceased.*** **Main/Conf** International Congress on the History of Science. (19??)-Vol. 3, No. 83 (1993). Multiple languages (English, French, German and Russian). ir. Actes, 39 rue Bobillot, 75013 Paris France. **Tel** 011 33 1 45806122. **LC** Q101; .I65. **DD** 509.
**Desc:** Actes for 5th-11th Congress issued as Collection of International Academy of the history of science.

FR/0300-8010
**ACTES DU ... CONGRES NATIONAL DES SOCIETES SAVANTES. SECTION DES SCIENCES.** **Main/Corp** Congres National des Societes Savantes. **VFOAT** Actes Section des Sciences. 110E (1985)-. French. an. Editions de CTHS, 3-5 bd Pasteur, F-75015 Paris France. **LC** AS153; .P2. **DD** 505. ***Continues*** *Comptes Rendus du ... Congres National des Societes Savantes. Section des Sciences, 0300-8010.*
**Ind/Abst** Geogr. Abstr. Phys. Geogr.; Geogr. Abstr. Human Geogr.; GeoRef.

US/0149-2829
**ACTIVITIES OF THE FEDERAL COUNCIL FOR SCIENCE AND TECHNOLOGY AND THE FEDERAL COORDINATING COUNCIL FOR SCIENCE, ENGINEERING AND TECHNOLOGY.** **Main/Corp** United States. Federal Coordinating Council for Science, Engineering and Technology. 1975/76-. English. Executive Office of the President Office of Science & Technology, Washington DC 20402. ***Continues*** *Activities of the Federal Council for Science and Technology.*

SP/0213-9693
**ACTUALIDAD... EN EL LABORATORICO CLINICO F. SUNER CASADEVALL, LA.** (1986)-. Periodical. Spanish. an. Editorial Garsi SA, Juan Bravo 46, 28006 Madrid, Spain. **Tel** 011 34 1 4021212, telex 98358 GARSI E. **UDC** 615. ***Continues*** *Actualidades en el Laboratorio Clinico, 0212-4564.*

FR/0365-6861
**ACTUALITES SCIENTIFIQUES ET INDUSTRIELLES.** [Actual. sci. ind.]. (19??)-. Monographic series. French. ir. price varies per volume. Hermann Editeurs Sciences Arts, 293 rue Lecourbe, F 75015 Paris France. **Tel** 011 33 1 45574540, telex 200595. **LC** Q111; .A3. ***Continues*** *Conferences d'Actualites Scientifiques et Industrielles.*
**Ind/Abst** Math. Rev.; Zentralbl. Math. Ihre Grenzgeb.

IT
**ADESIONE.** (19??)-. Italian (English and French). bm (6 issues). L45000 Italy; L87000 Europe; L180000 other. Onedit, Via Natale Battaglia 19, 20127 Milan Italy. **Tel** 011 39 2 26140708.
**Ind/Abst** Fluid Abstr., Civil Eng.; Fluid Abstr. Proc. Eng.; FLUIDEX (199?-).

UK
**ADVANCED HOSPITAL TECHNOLOGY.** English. mo. £240.00. SF Publications Ltd, 120 126 Lavender Avenue, Mitcham Surrey, CR4 3HP England. **Tel** 011 44 81 687-0993, FAX 011 44 81 547-1201.

US/0885-5684
**ADVANCED MANUFACTURING TECHNOLOGY.** **See** Computers-Automation.

●UK/1057-9257
**ADVANCED MATERIALS FOR OPTICS AND ELECTRONICS.** [Adv. mat. optics elec.]. (1992)-. Academic Scholarly Publication. English. Six times a year. $495.00. John Wiley & Sons Ltd., Baffins Lane, Chichester West Sussex PO19 1UD England. **Tel** 0243 779777, FAX 0243 776128 BTG:JWP001, telex 86290 WIBOOKG. **(Subscription address:** John Wiley / Philadelphia, PO Box 7247, Philadelphia PA 19170.**) ED** D.J. Cole-Hamilton. **LC** TK7874.8; .A33. **DD** 621.381. **CODEN** AMELE7. **[CCC].** Documents available from CASDDS. ***Formed by the union of*** *Journal of Molecular Electronics, 0748-7991* ***and*** *Chemtronics, 0267-5900.*
**Desc:** Provides a forum for the emerging knowledge of those advanced materials whose focus of interest is the growing discipline of information technology. Its purpose is to integrate the science and technology of advanced materials. This will range from the synthesis of precursor materials, their preparation in terms of processes and structures, through to their characterization and applications, thus highlighting the importance of these related areas in the development of such materials.
**Ind/Abst** Chem Inform; Chem. Abstr.; Curr. Contents Eng. Tech. Appl. Sci.; Curr. Contents Phys. Chem. Earth Sci.; SCISEARCH.

UK/0957-4778
**ADVANCED MATERIALS TECHNOLOGY.** ***Ceased.*** (19??)-(1992 Edition in 1993). English. an. Sterling Publications Ltd., PO Box 799, Brunel House, London W2 1XR England. **Tel** 011 44 71 2580066, FAX 011 44 71 4026441, telex 295819 ESPEEL G. **ED** Greville B Brook. **Ad Acc. Circ:** 15,000 (ctrl).
**Desc:** Contains information on advanced materials in the transportation, defense, and energy sectors.

NE/0921-8831
**ADVANCED POWDER TECHNOLOGY.** [Adv. powder technol.]. (1990)-. Periodical. English. qt. DM340.00. VSP International Science Publishers, Godfried van Seystlaan 47, 3703 BR Zeist Netherlands. **Tel** 011 31 3404 25790, FAX 011 31 3404 32081, telex 40217 USP NL. **(Subscription address:** VSP International Science Publishers, PO Box 346, 3700 AH Zeist Netherlands.**) ED** Y. Morikawa. **UDC** 62 :53. **Ad Acc.**
**Desc:** Integrating all aspects of research on powder engineering and technology. Publishes original research papers, rapid communications, short reviews and reports concerning particle characterization, mechanical powder

properties, storage, conveying, communition, classification, agglomeration, mixing and kneading, dispersion, reactor design, dust, separation and filtration.

UK
**ADVANCED RUSSIAN TECHNOLOGIES.** English. mo. Newmedia International Japan, AV Infanta Carlota 123 5 A, 08029 Barcelona Spain. **Tel** 011 34 3 4195690, FAX 414 42 13. ***Continues*** *Soviet Technology Alert, 0953-4016.*

US/8755-7258
**ADVANCED TECHNOLOGY IN THE PACIFIC NORTHWEST.** [Adv. technol. Pac. Northwest]. **Added/Corp** Quanix Data Services (Portland, Or.). **VFOAT** Directory and Guide to Advanced Technology in the Pacific Northwest; Directory & Guide to Advanced Technology in the Pacific Northwest; Quanix Directory and Guide to Advanced Technology in the Pacific Northwest. Vol. 1, (Winter 1985)-. English. sa. Quanix Data Services Inc, 2545 Southwest Spring Garden Street, Portland OR 97219. **Tel** (503)245-7665. **ED** D. E. Smith. **LC** T12.3.N94; A38. **DD** 338. Index available. **Ad Acc. Circ:** 2,000.
**Desc:** Directory of advanced technology in the Pacific Northwest. Covers more than 1,000 firms detailed in Oregon, Washington and Idaho in five categories.

US/0749-4874
**ADVANCED TECHNOLOGY IN WASHINGTON STATE.** ***Title Change.*** [Adv. technol. Wash. state]. **Added/Corp** Economic Development Council of Puget Sound. Research Dept. Economic Development Partnership for Washington. Economic Development Alliance for Washington. **VFOAT** Advanced Technology in Washington State Directory. (1983)-(1992). English. an. Commerce Publishing Corporation / Seattle, PO Box 9805, Seattle WA 98109. **(Subscription address:** Building 1, Suite 400, 18000 Pacific Highway South, Seattle, WA 98188) **LC** T12.3.W2; A38. **DD** 338.7/616/025797. **Circ:** 10,000. available on diskette. ***Continued by*** *Washington State Advanced Technology.*
**Desc:** Lists computer hardware, software and allied businesses, plus electronic, aerospace, biotechnology and other high tech firms in the state. The almost 2,000 listings include key personnel, product descriptions, sales volume, number of employees, facilities size, market area and SIC. Data on the size and impact of the high tech industry in the state is also included.

SZ/0142-5889
**ADVANCES IN DESERT AND ARID LAND TECHNOLOGY AND DEVELOPMENT.** [Adv. desert arid land technol. dev.]. (1979)-. Monographic series. English. ir. Price varies per volume. Harwood Academic Publishers / New York, PO Box 786, Cooper Station, New York NY 10276. **Tel** (212)206-8900, (201)643-7500. **ED** A. Bishay and W. G. McGinnies. **DD** 333.
**Ind/Abst** AGRICOLA [Full Cov.]; GeoRef.

●US
**ADVANCES IN GLOBAL HIGH-TECHNOLOGY MANAGEMENT.** **See** Business-General Management.

US/0890-2771
**ADVANCES IN HIGH-TECH MATERIALS.** ***Ceased.*** [Adv. high-tech mater.]. **VFOAT** Advances in High Tech Material. Vol. 1 (1987)-?. English. an. Technical Insights Inc., PO Box 1304, Fort Lee NJ 07024-9967. **Tel** (201)568-4744, FAX (201)568-8247, telex 425900 SWIFT UI. **DD** 620. ***Continues*** *Annual Report on High-Tech Materials, 8755-9978.*
**Desc:** Contains new methods of improving material performance, cutting costs in production and discoveries made in industrial R & D centers throughout the world.

●US/1054-0032
**ADVANCES IN INSTRUMENTATION AND CONTROL.** **Added/Corp** Instrument Society of America. Vol. 48 (1993)-. Monographic series. English. ir. Price varies per volume. Instrument Society of America, 67 Alexander Drive, Research Triangle NC 27709. **Tel** (919)549-8411, FAX (919)549-8288, telex 802 540. **[CCC].** ***Continues*** *ISA International Conference and Exhibit. Advances in Instrumentation and Control : Proceedings of the ISA ... International Conference and Exhibit.*

US/1054-0032
**ADVANCES IN INSTRUMENTATION AND CONTROL.** ***Title Change.*** (ADVANCES IN INSTRUMENTATION AND CONTROL : PROCEEDINGS OF THE ISA ... INTERNATIONAL CONFERENCE AND EXHIBIT.). [Adv. instrum. control]. **Added/Corp** Instrument Society of America. **VFOAT** Proceedings of the ISA ... International Conference and Exhibit. Vol. 44 (1989)-(1992). Academic Scholarly Publication. English. Instrument Society of America, 67 Alexander Drive, Research Triangle NC 27709. **Tel** (919)549-8411, FAX (919)549-8288, telex 802 540. **LC** TA165; .I594. **DD** 681/.2. **CODEN** AINCEV. **[CCC].** Documents available from BIOSIS Document Express, CASDDS. ***Continues*** *ISA International Conference and Exhibit. Advances in Instrumentation, 0065-2814.* ***Continued by*** *ISA International Conference, Exhibition and Training Program. Advances in Instrumentation and Control, 1054-0032.*
**Ind/Abst** Biol. Abstr.; Chem. Abstr. (1989-).

US/0890-2763
**ADVANCES IN R&D.** ***Title Change.*** [Adv. RD]. **Added/Corp** Technical Insights, Inc. **VFOAT** Advances in R and D. **VAT** Advances in Research & Development. (1987)-(19??). English. ir. Technical Insights Inc., PO Box 1304, Fort Lee NJ 07024-9967. **Tel** (201)568-4744, FAX (201)568-8247, telex 425900 SWIFT UI. **LC** T175; .T44a. **DD** 607/.2. ***Continues*** *Annual Report on Research & Development, 0739-6325.* ***Continued by*** *Research and Development.*
**Desc:** Provides comprehensive information on research and development achievements worldwide in 1986.

●US/1068-4883
**ADVANCES IN STRAWBERRY RESEARCH.** **See** Agriculture.

UK/0267-680X
**ADVANCES IN ULTRAHARD MATERIALS APPLICATION TECHNOLOGY.** **VFOAT** Ultrahard Materials Applications Technology. 1982-. English.

US/0044-6378
**ADVANCES IN URETHANE SCIENCE AND TECHNOLOGY.** [Adv. urethane sci. technol.]. **Added/Corp** University of Detroit. Polymer Institute. Vol. 1 (1971)-. Academic Scholarly Publication. English. ir. price varies per volume. Technomic Publishing Company, Inc., 851 New Holland Avenue, Box 3535, Lancaster PA 17604. **Tel** (717)291-5609, (800)233-9936, FAX (717)295-4538. **ED** Kurt C. Frisch and Daniel Klempner. **LC** TP1180.P8; A32. **DD** 668.4/239/05. **CODEN** AUSTCJ. Documents available from CASDDS.
**Desc:** Technology, chemistry, synthesis, properties, and applications of urethane foams, elastomers, adhesives, and coatings and their constituent materials.
**Ind/Abst** Chem. Abstr.

US
**AETS YEARBOOK.** **Main/Corp** Association for the Education of Teachers in Science. **Added/Corp** Association for the Education of Teachers in Science. ERIC Information Analysis Center for Science, Mathematics, and Environmental Education. ERIC Clearinghouse for Science, Mathematics, and Environmental Education. **VAT** Association for the Education of Teachers in Science Yearbook. 1st (1974)-. English. an. Prices varies. CSMEE, 1929 Kenny Road, Columbus OH 43210. **Tel** (800)276-0462, (614)292-6717. **Circ:** 1,000 (ctrl). available on microfiche (Vols. for (1983-) distributed to depository libraries).
**Desc:** This is an annual publication produced on a topic related to science education.

US
**AFOSR TECHNICAL REPORT SUMMARIES / PREPARED BY: ... CHIEF, TECHNICAL DOCUMENTS SECTION.** **Added/Corp** United States. Air Force. Office of Scientific Research. Technical Documents Section. **VFOAT** Technical Report Summaries. **VAT** Air Force Office of Scientific Research Technical Report Summaries. (19??)-. Periodical. English. qt. Documents available from CASDDS.
**Ind/Abst** Chem. Abstr.

UK/0954-6782
**AFRICAN REVIEW OF BUSINESS AND TECHNOLOGY.** [Afr. rev. bus. technol.]. **VFOAT** African Review. (1988)-. Periodical. English. Eleven times a year (Dec./Feb. issues combined). $93.50. Alain Charles Publishing Ltd., 27 Wilfred Street, London SW1E 6PR England. **Tel** 011 44 71 834 7676, FAX 011 44 71 973 0076, telex 297166/7. **LC** T1; .W47. **DD** 609.6. ***Continues*** *African Technical Review, 0266-6677.*

US/1050-0014
**AFRICAN TECHNOLOGY FORUM.** [Afr. technol. forum]. **VFOAT** ATF. (1988)-. Periodical. English. qt. $12.00 Africa; $24.00 other. African Technology Forum, PO Box 171, MIT Branch, Cambridge MA 02139. **Tel** (617)225-0339, FAX (617)252-3330. **ED** Mawuli Tse. **LC** T174.3; .A35. **DD** 960. cum. index. **Bk Rev**, (Qty: 8). **Ad Acc, Adv Mgr:** K.Wasiyo. **Circ:** 3,000.
**Desc:** Information source for science and technology in Africa.

●SA
**AFRIKA 2001.** **Added/Corp** Centre for Science Development. **VFOAT** Symposium on Science Policy and Research Management; Putting the Case for the Humanities. **VAT** Afrika Two Thousand and One. Vol. 1 (1992)-. Periodical. English. Twice a year (Apr. & Aug.). R20.00. Center for Science & Development, PO Box 270, 0001 Pretoria South Africa. **Tel** 011 27 12 2022714. ***Continues*** *RSA 2000.*

TH
**AGE REFDEX.** Vol. 5 (1986)-. English. an. Asian Geotechnical Engineering Information Center, c/o Asian Institute of Technology, Box 2754, Bangkok Thailand. **Tel** 529 0100-13 OR 529 0091-93, FAX (66-2)529 0374, telex 84276TH. Index available. ctrl circ. ***Continues*** *AGE Digest.*

JA
**AGENCY OF INDUSTRIAL SCIENCE AND TECHNOLOGY : AIST.** **Main/Corp** Kogyo Gijutsuin (Japan). **VFOAT** AIST; A.I.S.T. English. Agency of Industrial Science and Technology, Technology Research and Information Division, 1-3-1 Kasumigaseki, Chiyoda-ku, Tokyo Japan. **LC** T177.J3; K648A. **DD** 607/.2/52.

CN/0706-2613
**AGENDA (OTTAWA).** (AGENDA.). **VFOAT** Agenda. V. 1- Aug. 1978-. Periodical. English (French). qt. Science Council of Canada, 100 Metcalfe Street, Ottawa Ontario K1P 5M1 Canada. **Tel** (819)997-2560.

PH/0115-5679
**AGHAM.** [AGHAM]. Academic Scholarly Publication. English. qt. De La Salle University, 2401 Taft Avenue, Manila Philippines. **CODEN** AGHADE. Documents available from CASDDS.
**Ind/Abst** Chem. Abstr. (1973-1977); Index Philip. Period.; Philip. Sci. Technol. Abstr.

II/0002-1032
**AGRA UNIVERSITY JOURNAL OF RESEARCH. SCIENCE.** [Agra univ. j. res., sci.]. **Main/Corp** Agra University. **Added/Corp** Agra University. Journal of Research. **VFOAT** Journal of Research. Science. Vol. 1 (Nov. 1952)-. Periodical. English. tq. **LC** Q73; .A65. **CODEN** AURSA9. Documents available from CASDDS.
**Ind/Abst** Chem. Abstr.

JA/0286-262X
**AICHI-KEN KOGYO GIJUTSU SENTA HOKOKU.** [Aichi-ken Kogyo Gijutsu Senta hokoku]. **Added/Corp** Aichi-Ken Kogyo Gijutsu Senta. **VFOAT** Reports of Industrial Research Institute, Aichi Prefectural Government. (1982)-. Japanese (summaries and/or abstracts in English). Aichiken Kogyo Gijutsu Senta, (Industrial Research Institute, Aichi Prefectural Government), Nishishinwari, Hitotsugicho, Kariyashi, Aichiken 448 Japan. **CODEN** AKGHDO. Documents available from CASDDS. ***Continues*** *Aichi-Ken Kogyo Shidosho Hokoku, 0365-3765.*
**Ind/Abst** Chem. Abstr.

JA/0387-0812
**AICHI KOGYO DAIGAKU KENKYU HOKOKU, B, SENMON KANKEI RONBUNSHU.** (AICHI KOGYO DAIGAKU KENKYU HOKOKU.). [Aichi Kogyo Daigaku Kenkyu Hokoku, B, Senmon Kankei Ronbunshu]. **Added/Corp** Aichi Kogyo Daigaku. **VFOAT** Bulletin of Aichi Institute of Technology.; Kenkyu Hokoku. (1966)-. Japanese (English). Aichi Kogyo Daigaku, (Aichi Institution of Technology), 1247 Yachigusa, Yakusacho, Toyotashi, Aichiken 470-08 Japan. **LC** T4; .A34. **CODEN** AKDBDP. Documents available from CASDDS.
**Ind/Abst** Chem. Abstr.

JA/0388-7367
**AICHI KYOIKU DAIGAKU KENKYU HOKOKU. GEIJUTSU, HOKEN TAIIKU, KASEI, GIJUTSU KAGAKU.** **Added/Corp** Aichi Kyoiku Daigaku. (19??)-. Periodical. Japanese (English). an. Available on an exchange basis. Aichi Kyoiku Daigaku, Hirosawa 1 Igaya-cho, Kariya-shi Aichi-ken 448 Japan. **LC** AS552.K343; A2. cum. index. **Circ:** 600.

US/0895-3155
**AIMS NEWSLETTER.** (AIMS NEWSLETTER : A PUBLICATION OF THE AIMS EDUCATION FOUNDATION.). [AIMS newsl.]. **Added/Corp** AIMS Education Foundation. **VAT** Activities That Integrate Mathematics and Science Newsletter. Vol. 1, No. 1 (Aug. 1986)-. Newsletter. English. mo (10 issues). $27.50 (one year), $45.00 (two year). AIMS Education Foundation, PO Box 8120, Fresno CA 93747. **Tel** (209)255-4094. **DD** 507.

UA
**A'IN SHAMS SCIENCE BULLETIN.** **VFOAT** Nashra Al-Ilmiyah Li-Jamiat Ayn Shams. No. 1- 1956-. Bulletin. English (English). **LC** Q1. **NLM** W1 AI699V.

UA
**AKHBAR AL-AKADIMIYAH / TUSDIRUHA AKADIMIYAT AL-BAHTH AL-ILMI WA-AL-TIKNULUJIYA.** Periodical. Arabic. mo. Akadimiyat Al-Bahth Al-Ilmi Wa-Al-Tiknulujiya, 101 Shari Qasr Al-Ini, Cairo United Arab Republic Egypt. **LC** Q180.E3; A64.

TA/0002-3485
**AKHBOROTI AKADEMIAI FANHOI RSS TOJIKISTON. SHUBAI FANHOI FIZIKAIU MATEMATIKA, KHIMIIA VA GEOLOGIIA.** **Added/Corp** Akademiiai Fanhoi RSS Tojikiston. Shubai Fanhoi Fizikaiu Matematika, Khimiia va Geologiia. **VFOAT** Shubai Fanhoi Fizikaiu Matematika, Khimiia va Geologiia; Otdelenie Fiziko-Matematicheskikh,

Khimicheskikh i Geologicheskikh Nauk; Izvestiia Akademii Nauk Tadzhikskoi SSR. Otdelenie Fiziko-Matematicheskikh, Khimicheskikh i Geologicheskikh Nauk. (1980)-. Periodical. Russian (summaries and/or abstracts in Tajik). qt. **(Subscription address:** Victor Kamkin, 4956 Boiling Brook Parkway, Rockville MD 20852.) **LC** Q60; .A77. **CODEN** IANNES. Documents available from CASDDS. ***Continues*** *Akhboroti Akademiiai Fanhoi RSS Tojikiston. Shubai Fanhoi Fizikaiu Matematika va Geologiiaiu Khimiia.*
**Ind/Abst** Chem. Abstr.

UN/0321-477X
**AKUSTIKA I ULTRAZVUKOVAJA TEHNIKA (KIEV).** (AKUSTIKA I ULTRAZVUKOVAIA TEKHNIKA / MINISTERSTVO VYSSHEGO I SREDNEGO SPETSIALNOGO OBRAZOVANIIA USSR.). [Akust. ultrazvuk. teh.]. **Added/Corp** Ukraine. Ministerstvo Vyshchoi I Serednoi Spetsialnoi. (1966)-. Periodical. Russian. **CODEN** AKIUA2. Documents available from CASDDS.
**Ind/Abst** Chem. Abstr.

UA
**AL-ILM. Added/Corp** Akadimiyat Al-Bahth Al-Ilmi Wa-al-Tiknulujiya. Dar Al-Tahrir Lil-Tab Wa-al-Nashr "Al-Jumhuriyah". (1976)-. Periodical. Arabic. mo. $6.00. Sharikat Al-Tawzi Al-Muttahidah, 21 Shari Qasr Al-Nil, Al-Qahirah Egypt. **LC** Q4; .I547.

LE/1013-2392
**AL-'ILM WA-AL-TIKNULUGIYA. VFOAT** Science & Technology. (1982)-. Periodical. Arabic (English; summaries and/or abstracts in Arabic). bm. $40.00. Arab Development Institute, Science and Technology Department, PO Box 5300-14, Beirut Lebanon. **Tel** 831025/6/7/8, telex 22234 EMARAB LE. **ED** Dr. Mohamed Debs. **Bk Rev. Ad Acc. Circ:** 10,000.

UA
**AL-SHABAB WA-ULUM AL-MUSTAQBAL. See** Children and Youth Interests.

IQ
**AL-TURATH AL-ILMI AL-ARABI. Added/Corp** Markaz Ihya Al-Turath Al-Ilmi Al-Arabi (Baghdad, Iraq). (1977)-. Periodical. Arabic. Riasat Markaz Ihya Al-Turath Al-Ilmi Al-Arabi Al-Waziriyah, Shari Al-Sahib Bin Abbad, Baghdad Iraq. **LC** Q127.A5; T87.

US/1059-4280
**ALBANY LAW JOURNAL OF SCIENCE & TECHNOLOGY. See** Law.

CN/0701-1024
**ALBERTA SCIENCE EDUCATION JOURNAL.** [Alta. sci. educ. j.]. **Added/Corp** Alberta Teachers' Association. Science Council. Vol. 14, No. 3 (Aug. 1976)-. Periodical. English. Twice a year. 30.00Can$ membership. Alberta Teachers Association, 11010-142 Street, Barnett House, Edmonton Alberta T5N 2R1 Canada. **Tel** (403)453-2411. **ED** Gary Gay. **DD** 507. **Bk Rev. Circ:** 800 (ctrl). ***Continues*** *Alberta Science Education, 0317-8730.*
**Desc:** Contains articles of interest to science teachers interested in expanding their knowledge and in improving their practices.

CN/0229-3099
**ALBERTA SCIENCE TEACHER, THE.** [Alta. sci. teach.]. Vol. 1, No. 1 (Dec. 1980)-. Periodical. English. qt. 20.00Can$. Alberta Teachers Association, 11010-142 Street, Barnett House, Edmonton Alberta T5N 2R1 Canada. **Tel** (403)453-2411. **DD** 507. **Circ:** 820 (ctrl). ***Continues*** *Science Newsletter, 0384-1847.*

EG/1010-1098
**ALEXANDRIA SCIENCE EXCHANGE.** [Alexandria sci. exch.]. **Added/Corp** Jamiat Al-Iskandariyah. Prof. Dr. A.M. Balba Group for Soil and Water Research. (1980)-. Periodical. English. tq. **CODEN** ALSEEF. Documents available from CASDDS.
**Ind/Abst** Chem. Abstr.; Nutr. Abstr. Rev., Ser. A, Hum. Exp.

GW
**ALGORISMUS. See** Mathematics.

NZ/0111-1957
**ALPHA (WELLINGTON, N.Z.).** (ALPHA.). Vol. 1 (June 1980)-. Periodical. English. mo. Science Information Publishing Center, Box 9741, Wellington New Zealand. **Tel** 011 64 4 858939, FAX 011 64 4 850631, telex NZ 32076 RESERCH.

CK
**AMERICA LATINA 2001 I.E. DOS MIL UNO. VFOAT** America Latina 2001. **VAT** America Latina dos Mil Uno. No. 1- Jan./Feb. 1976-. Periodical. Spanish. $33.00. Bogota Anif Etc, Asociacion Nacionel de Institucions Financireras, Cale 35 No 4-8A Apartado Aero 29765, Bogota Colombia. **LC** T24.A1; A53.

US/8756-7296
**AMERICAN HERITAGE OF INVENTION & TECHNOLOGY. VFOAT** American Heritage of Invention and Technology. Vol. 1, No. 1 (Summer 1985)-. Periodical. English. qt (within the seasons). $15.00. American Heritage, Forbes Building, 60 Fifth Avenue, New York NY 10011. **Tel** (212)206-5512, (212)620-1804. **LC** T1; .A455. **DD** 605. **NLM** W1; AM423F. **[CCC].** available on microfilm and microfiche from University Microfilms International (UMI).
**Ind/Abst** Am. Hist. Life (1988-).

US/1042-1890
**AMERICAN INVENTOR (BLOOMINGTON, IND.).** (AMERICAN INVENTOR.). [Am. invent.]. **Added/Corp** Biogeron Laboratories, Inc. Vol. 1, No. 1 (Jan./Feb. 1989)-. Periodical. English. Six times a year. Biogeron Laboratories Inc, 1821 West Third Street, Suite 202, PO Box 5277, Bloomington IN 47403. **Tel** (812)336-2002, FAX (812)332-5580. **ED** John Warren and Patricia Warren. **DD** 608. **Bk Rev. Ad Acc. Pr Rev. Circ:** 5,000 (ctrl).
**Desc:** Covers topics of interest to inventors, entrepreneurs, and scientists. A forum for technology exchange.

US/0002-9599
**AMERICAN JOURNAL OF SCIENCE (1880).** (THE AMERICAN JOURNAL OF SCIENCE.). [Am. j. sci.]. Vol. 119, No. 109 (Jan. 1880)-. Academic Scholarly Publication. English. Ten times a year. $125.00 (institutions), $60.00 (individuals) US; $140.00 (institutions), $75.00 (individuals) other. Kline Geology Laboratory, Yale University, Room 217, PO Box 208109, New Haven CT 06520-8109. **Tel** (203)432-3131, (203)432-5668, FAX (203)432-5668. **ED** Marie C. Casey. **LC** Q1; .A5. **DD** 505. **NLM** W1 AM522D. **CODEN** AJSCAP. cum. index. **Pr Rev. Circ:** 3,000. available on microfilm from University Microfilms International (UMI). Documents available from Article Express International, The Genuine Article, Ask*IEEE, UMI Article Clearinghouse, Petroleum Abstracts Document Delivery Service, CASDDS, Documents on Demand. ***Continues*** *American Journal of Science and Arts, 0099-5363.*
**Desc:** Devoted to geology and related sciences and publishes articles presenting results of major research from all the earth sciences.
**Ind/Abst** Acad. Search (Jan. 1994-); AESIS Q.; Appl. Sci. Technol. Index; Bioeng. Abstr.; Ceram. Abstr.; Chem. Abstr.; Chem. Titles; Coal Abstr.; Curr. Contents Phys. Chem. Earth Sci.; Ecol. Abstr.; Ei Page One; EMBASE; Energy Inf. Abstr.; Energy Res. Abstr.; Eng. Index Annu.; Environ. Abstr.; Expand. Acad. Index (1989-); Gen. Sci. Index; Gen. Sci. Source (Jul. 1993-); Geogr. Abstr. Phys. Geogr.; Geol. Abstr.; GeoRef; INIS Atomindex [Micro.]; INSPEC (Jan. 1972-); Int. Aerosp. Abstr.; Leadscan; Mag. Search; Newsp. Period. Abstr. (1992-); Pet. Abstr.; Res. Alert [Full Cov.]; Sci. Cit. Index; SCISEARCH; Soc. Sci. Cit. Index [Select. Cov.]; Soils Fert.; Stat. Theory Method Abstr. (1959-1963); World Ceram. Abstr.

US/0003-0996
**AMERICAN SCIENTIST.** [Am. sci.]. **Added/Corp** Sigma Xi, the Scientific Research Society. Society of the Sigma Xi. Scientific Research Society of America. Sigma Xi, the Scientific Research Society of North America. Vol. 30, No. 2 (April 1942)-. Periodical. English. bm (6 issues). $45.00 (institutions), $28.00 (individuals). American Scientists, 99 Alexander Drive, PO Box 13975, Research Triangle Park NC 27709. **Tel** (919)549-0097, (800)282-0444. **ED** Rosalind Reid. **LC** LJ85; .S502. **DD** 378/.1985450973. **NLM** W1 AM756. **CODEN** AMSCAC. **[CCC].** cum. index. **Bk Rev. Ad Acc. Pr Rev. Circ:** 125,000. available on microfilm and microfiche from University Microfilms International (UMI). Documents available from The Genuine Article, Ask*IEEE, UMI Article Clearinghouse, Documents on Demand. ***Continues*** *Society of the Sigma Xi. Sigma Xi Quarterly.*
**Desc:** Believes that scientists want to know what is happening in disciplines outside their own. Articles cover all areas of science and endeavor to provide comprehensive and authoritative explanations of research.
**Ind/Abst** Acad. Abstr. Full Text Elite (March 1984-June 1989); Acad. Abstr. (March 1984-June 1989); Acad. Ind. [Computer File] (1987-); Acad. Search (Mar. 1984-June 1989); AGRICOLA [Select. Cov.]; Alum. Ind. Abstr.; Annu. Bibliogr. Engl. Lang. Lit.; Appl. Sci. Technol. Index; Art Archaeol. Tech. Abstr.; Biogr. Index; Biol. Dig.; Book Rev. Index; Br. Archaeol. Bibliogr.; Ceram. Abstr.; Comput. Rev.; Curr. Aware. Biol. Sci., CABS; Curr. Contents Life Sci.; Curr. Contents Phys. Chem. Earth Sci.; Curr. Ref. Fish Res.; Ecol. Abstr.; Energy Res. Abstr.; Eng. Mater. Abstr.; Environ. Abstr.; Environ. Period. Bibliogr.; Expand. Acad. Index (1987-); Field Crop Abstr.; Fish Rev.; Garden Lit. (1992-); Gen. Sci. Index; Gen. Sci. Source (Jan. 1988-June 1989); Geogr. Abstr. Phys. Geogr.; Geogr. Abstr. Human Geogr.; Geol. Abstr.; GeoRef; Grasslands For. Abstr.; Health Plan. Adminis.; Helminthol. Abstr.; Highw. Res. Abstr.; INFO-SOUTH Abstr.; INIS Atomindex [Micro.]; INSPEC (May-June 1970-); Int. Aerosp. Abstr.; Key Word Index Wildl. Res.; Leadscan; Linguist. Lang. Behav. Abstr.; Mag. Artic. Summar. Elite (March 1984-June 1989); Mag. Artic. Summar. Select (March 1984-June 1989); Mag. Artic. Summar. CD-ROM (March 1984-June 1989); Mag. Search; Math. Rev.; Met. Abstr.; Middle East Abstr. Index; Newsp. Period. Abstr. (1989-); Nutr. Abstr. Rev., Ser. B, Live Feeds and Feed.; Nutr. Abstr. Rev., Ser. A, Hum. Exp.; Nutr. Res. Newsl.; Plant Breed. Abstr.; Protozoolog. Abstr.; Psychol. Abstr. (May/June 1942-); PsycINFO; PsycLit; Ref. Upd. Deluxe Ed.; Res. Alert [Full Cov.]; Rev. Med. Vet. Entomol.; Sci. Cit. Index; SCISEARCH; Soc. Plann. Policy Dev. Abstr.; Soc. Sci. Cit. Index [Select. Cov.]; Sociol. Abstr.; Surf. Treat. Technol. Abstr.; Wildl. Rev.

BL/0001-3765
**ANAIS DA ACADEMIA BRASILEIRA DE CIENCIAS.** [An. Acad. Bras. Cienc.]. **Added/Corp** Academia Brasileira de Ci„encias. Vol. 13, No. 3 (Sept. 30, 1941)-. Periodical. English (Portuguese, French and Spanish). qt (Mar., June, Sept., Dec.). $100.00. Academia Brasileira de Ciencia, CAIXA Postal 229, 20001 Rio de Janeiro RJ Brazil. **LC** Q33; .R52. **DD** 506.281. **NLM** W1 AN108B. **CODEN** AABCAD. **Circ:** 1,000. Documents available from Article Express International, BIOSIS Document Express, Ask*IEEE, CASDDS. ***Supersedes*** *Annaes da Academia Brasileira de Sciencias.*
**Ind/Abst** AGRICOLA; Art Archaeol. Tech. Abstr.; Biol. Abstr.; Chem. Abstr.; Eng. Index Annu. [Select. Cov.]; Field Crop Abstr.; GeoRef; Grasslands For. Abstr.; Index Med.; INSPEC (1968-); Math. Rev.; Life Sci. Collect.; Protozoolog. Abstr.; Trop. Dis. Bull.; Zentralbl. Math. Ihre Grenzgeb.

PO
**ANAIS DA FACULDADE DE CIENCIAS. Main/Corp** Oporto, Portugal. Universidade. Instituto de Zoologia. V. 1 (1905/06)-. Periodical. Portuguese. qt. **LC** Q65. **CODEN** AFPOAI. Documents available from BIOSIS Document Express. ***Continues in part*** *Jornal de Sciencias Mathematicas e Astronomicas.*
**Ind/Abst** Biol. Abstr. (-1983); Zentralbl. Math. Ihre Grenzgeb.

RM/1011-4025
**ANALELE UNIVERSITATII DIN GALATI. FASCICULA VI, TEHNOLOGIA SI CHIMIA PRODUSELOR ALIMENTARE.** [An. Univ. Galati, Fasc. VI Tehnol. chim. prod. aliment.]. **Added/Corp** Universitatea din Galati. **VFOAT** Tehnologia si Chimia Produselor Alimentare. (1983)-. Periodical. Romanian (table of contents in English, French and German). an. Price varies. Redactia Analelor, 6200 Galati, Str Domneasca Nr. 47 Romania. **Tel** 40 93 413602, FAX 40 93 412328. **CODEN** AUFAEZ. Documents available from CASDDS. ***Continues*** *Buletinul Universitatii din Galati. Fascicula VI, Tehnologia si Chimia Produselor Alimentare, 0254-5608.*
**Ind/Abst** Chem. Abstr.

AG/0325-4186
**ANALES - CIDEPINT.** [An. - CIDEPINT]. **VFOAT** Anales - Centro de Investigacion y Desarrollo en Tecnologia de Pinturas. (1977)-. Periodical. Spanish. an. **UDC** 667.6. Documents available from CASDDS.
**Ind/Abst** Chem. Abstr.

PE
**ANALES CIENTIFICOS - UNIVERSIDAD NACIONAL DEL CENTRO DEL PERU. Main/Corp** Universidad Nacional del Centro del Peru. 1-1971-. Spanish. Departamento de Publicaciones e Impresiones, Calle Ferrocarril 469, Huancago Peru. **LC** Q183.4.P5; U55A. **DD** 505.

AG/0037-8437
**ANALES DE LA SOCIEDAD CIENTIFICA ARGENTINA.** [An. Soc. Cient. Argent.]. **Main/Corp** Sociedad Cientifica Argentina. Vol. 1 (1876)-. Periodical. Spanish (summaries and/or abstracts in English). ir. Library SRL, Department de Public AC, Cientifica Argentina, 127 Corrientes, Buenos Aires Argentina. **LC** Q33; .A6. **DD** 505. **NLM** W1 AN149T. **CODEN** ASCAA2. cum. index. Documents available from CASDDS.
**Ind/Abst** Chem. Abstr. (1876-1980); Field Crop Abstr.; GeoRef; Grasslands For. Abstr.; Helminthol. Abstr.; Rev. Med. Vet. Entomol.; Rev. Med. Vet. Mycology; Rev. Plant Pathol.; Stat. Theory Method Abstr. (1959-1963); Zentralbl. Math. Ihre Grenzgeb.

AG/0365-1185
**ANALES DE L'ACADEMIA NACIONAL DE CIENCIAS EXACTAS, FISICAS Y NATURALES, BUENOS AIRES.** (ANALES.). [An. acad. nac. cienc. exactas, fis. nat., B. Aires]. **Main/Corp** Academia Nacional de Ciencias Exactas, Fisicas y Naturales (Argentina). Began in 1928. Academic Scholarly Publication. Spanish. **LC** Q33; .B77. **DD** 506.282. **CODEN** ACFBAA. Documents available from CASDDS. ***Absorbed in part by*** *Academia Nacional de Ciencias Exactas, Fisicas y Naturales. Anales. Suplemento.*
**Ind/Abst** Chem. Abstr.; Crop Physiol. Abstr.; Energy Res. Abstr. (April 1983-); Field Crop Abstr.; GeoRef; Seed Abstr.; Soils Fert.

AT
**ANARE NEWS (AUSTRALIAN NATIONAL ANTARCTIC RESEARCH EXPEDITIONS).** (ANARE NEWS.). **Added/Corp** Australian National Antarctic Research Expeditions. **VFOAT** Newsletter. (19??)-. Periodical. English. qt. Free. Australia Antarctic Division, Channel Highway, Kingston 1050 Australia. **Tel** (002)290209, FAX (002)293335. **ED** S.E. Stallman. **Bk Rev. Circ:** 1,000.

AT
**ANARE SCIENTIFIC REPORTS. SERIES A (3), GEOLOGY.** **Added/Corp** Australian National Antarctic Research Expeditions. **VFOAT** Geology. (1966)-. Monographic series. English. ir. Price varies per volume. Australia Antarctic Division, Channel Highway, Kingston 1050 Australia. **Tel** (002)290209, FAX (002)293335. **ED** S A Potter. **CODEN** ANANBV. ***Continues*** *A.N.A.R.E. Reports. Series A, Volume III, Geology, 0567-080z.*
**Ind/Abst** GeoRef.

AT
**ANARE SCIENTIFIC REPORTS. SERIES B (1), ZOOLOGY.** **VFOAT** Zoology. **VAT** Australian National Antarctic Research Expeditions Scientific Reports. Series B (1), Zoology. (1966)-. Monographic series. English. ir. Price varies per volume. Australia Antarctic Division, Channel Highway, Kingston 1050 Australia. **Tel** (002)290209, FAX (002)293335. **ED** S A Potter. **CODEN** ANBZA3. **Circ:** 400. Documents available from BIOSIS Document Express. ***Continues in part*** *ANARE Reports. Series B, Volume I, Zoology, 0567-0810.*
**Ind/Abst** Biol. Abstr. (-1976).

FI/0066-197X
**ANNALES ACADEMIAE SCIENTIARUM FENNICAE. SERIES A. III : GEOLOGICA-GEOGRAPHICA.** **Main/Corp** Suomalainen Tiedeakatemia. **VFOAT** Toimituksia. III: Geologica-Geographica; Geologica Geographica. Vol. 1 (1942)-. Monographic series. English (French and German). ir. Price varies per volume. Bookstore Tiedekirja, Kirkkokatu 14, Helsinki 00170 Finland. **Tel** 011 358 0 635177. **LC** Q60; .H525. ***Supersedes in part*** *Suomalainen Tiedeakatemia. Toimituksia. Sarja A.*
**Ind/Abst** Geogr. Abstr. Phys. Geogr.; Geol. Abstr.; GeoRef.

CN/0066-8842
**ANNALES DE L'A C F A S.** **Main/Corp** Association Canadienne-Francaise pour l'Avancement des Sciences. **VFOAT** Resumes des Communications. Vol. 1 (1935)-. Periodical. French. an. 20.00Can$. Association Canadienne-Francaise pour l'Avancement des Sciences, 425 de la Gauchetiere Est, Montreal Quebec H2L 2M7 Canada. **Tel** (514)849-0045, FAX (514)849-5558. **DD** 016.084/1. **Bk Rev. Ad Acc. Circ:** 6,000 (ctrl).
**Desc:** General information concerning Canadian research.

SG/0418-2952
**ANNALES DE LA FACULTE DES SCIENCES, UNIVERSITE DE DAKAR.** (ANNALES DE LA FACULTE DES SCIENCES.). [Ann. Fac. sci., Univ. Dakar]. **Main/Corp** Universite de Dakar. Faculte des Sciences. V. 4- 1959-. French. an. Universite de Dakar / Faculte des Sciences, Dakar Fann Senegal. **DD** 600. **CODEN** AFSDAY. Documents available from BIOSIS Document Express. ***Continues*** *Annales de l'Ecole Superieure des Sciences, Institut des Hautes Etudes de Dakar.*
**Ind/Abst** Biol. Abstr. (-1980); GeoRef.

FR/0924-4204
**ANNALES DE L'INSTITUT PASTEUR ACTUALITES.** [An. Inst. Pasteur, Actual.]. (1990)-. Academic Scholarly Publication. French. Four times a year (1 volume). 515.00F France; 570.00F other. Editions Scientifique Elsevier, 141 rue de Javel, 75747 Paris Cedex 15 France. **Tel** 011 33 1 47 07 11 22, FAX 011 33 1 43 36 80 93. **(Subscription address:** Editions Scientifiques Elsevier / for North America, PO Box 7247-7576, Philadelphia PA 19170-7576.**) UDC** 664.8.036.3. **[CCC].**

IT
**ANNALI SCIENTIFICI.** (19??)-. Italian. an. L25000.00. Manfrini Editori, Via Brennero #2, 38060 Calliano Italy. **Tel** 011 39 464 84156, FAX 011 39 464 85086.

JA
**ANNALS - JAPAN ASSOCIATION FOR PHILOSOPHY OF SCIENCE.** **Main/Corp** Japan Association for Philosophy of Science. V. 1- 1956-. Periodical. English (French and German). an. ¥2,400. Japan Association for Philosophy of Science, c/o Keio University, 2-15-45 Minta Minato-ku, Tokyo 108 Japan. **Tel** (03)453-4511, FAX (03)798-7480. **ED** Hiroshi Kurosaki. Index available. cum. index. **Circ:** 600 (ctrl).
**Desc:** Concerned with the logic and philosophy of mathematics; includes foundational studies on natural and social sciences and the philosophy of science.

NE/0254-5330
**ANNALS OF OPERATIONS RESEARCH.** [Ann. oper. res.]. Vol. 1, No. 1-4 (Aug. 1984)-. English. Twenty-eight times a year. 1785.00F (includes distribution costs). Baltzer Science Publishers BV, Asterweg 1A, 1031 HL Amsterdam Netherlands. **Tel** 011 31 20 6370061, FAX 011 31 20 6323651. Documents available from Ask*IEEE.
**Ind/Abst** ACM Guide Comput. Lit.; Comput. Rev.; INSPEC (1984-); Int. Abstr. Oper. Res. [Full Cov.]; Math. Rev.; Oper. Res./Manag. Sci.; Zentralbl. Math. Ihre Grenzgeb.

UK/0003-3790
**ANNALS OF SCIENCE.** [Ann. sci.]. **Added/Corp** British Society for the History of Science. Bulletin. Vol. 1 (Jan. 1936)-. Periodical. English. bm. $465.00 North America; £282.00 UK. Taylor & Francis Ltd., Rankine Road, Basingstoke Hampshire, RG24 8PR United Kingdom. **Tel** 011 44 256 840366, FAX 011 44 256 479438, telex 858540. **(Subscription address:** Taylor & Francis Inc., 1900 Frost Road, Suite 101, Bristol PA 19007-1598.**) ED** G. Turner. **LC** Q1; .A616. **DD** 509. **NLM** W1 AN625. **CODEN** ANNSA8. **[CCC].** cum. index. **Pr Rev.** available on microfilm and microfiche from University Microfilms International (UMI). Documents available from The Genuine Article, BIOSIS Document Express, Ask*IEEE, CASDDS.
**Desc:** Deals with the development of science since the Renaissance. Now firmly established, its field of interest has widened to cover developments since the 13th Century and to include articles in French and German. Each issue includes a comprehensive book reviews section and essay reviews on a group of books on a broader level.
**Ind/Abst** Am. Hist. Life (1955-); Arts Humanit. Citation Index [Full Cov.]; Biol. Abstr.; Br. Humanit. Index; Chem. Abstr.; Curr. Contents Arts Humanit.; Curr. Contents Soc. Behav. Sci.; Ei Page One; GeoRef; INSPEC (Feb. 1972-); Leadscan; Math. Rev.; Protozoolog. Abstr.; Res. Alert [Full Cov.]; Romant. Move.; Soc. Sci. Cit. Index [Full Cov.]; Zentralbl. Math. Ihre Grenzgeb.

US/0077-8923
**ANNALS OF THE NEW YORK ACADEMY OF SCIENCES.** [Ann. N.Y. Acad. Sci.]. **Added/Corp** New York Academy of Sciences. Vol. 1 (July 1877)-. Academic Scholarly Publication. English. Thirty times a year. £2,950.00. New York Academy of Sciences, 2 East 63rd Street, New York NY 10021. **Tel** (212)838-0230, (800)843-6927, FAX (212)888-2894. **(Subscription address:** Eurospan Ltd., Journals and Serials Division, 3 Henrietta Street, Covent Garden, London WC2E 8LU England.**) LC** Q11; .N5. **DD** 500. **NLM** W1 AN626YL. **CODEN** ANYAA9. **[CCC].** Index available. **Pr Rev.** available on microfilm and microfiche from University Microfilms International (UMI). Documents available from The Genuine Article, BIOSIS Document Express, Ask*IEEE, CASDDS. ***Supersedes*** *Annals of the Lyceum of Natural History of New York, 0890-6564.*
**Desc:** Publishes significant research in all areas of science and medicine based on timely conference proceedings.
**Ind/Abst** AgBiotech News Inf.; AGRICOLA [Select. Cov.]; Anim. Behav. Abstr.; Anim. Breed. Abstr.; Biocont. News Inf. (1991-); Biol. Abstr.; Calcium Calcif. Tissue Abstr.; Ceram. Abstr. (19??-); Chem. Abstr.; Chemorecept. Abstr.; CSA Neuro. Abstr.; Curr. Aware. Biol. Sci., CABS; Dairy Sci. Abstr.; Ecology Abstr.; Ei Page One; EMBASE; Energy Inf. Abstr.; Energy Res. Abstr.; Field Crop Abstr.; Fish Rev.; Genet. Abstr.; GeoRef; Grasslands For. Abstr.; Health Plan. Adminis.; Helminthol. Abstr. (1991-); Hortic. Abstr.; Immunol. Abstr.; Index Med.; Index Vet.; INSPEC; Int. Aerosp. Abstr.; Leadscan; Maize Abstr.; Math. Rev.; Microbiol. Abstr. Sect. B; Microbiol. Abstr. Sect. C; MLA Int. Bibl. Books Artic. Mod. Lang. Lit.; Nutr. Abstr. Rev., Ser. B, Live Feeds and Feed.; Nutr. Abstr. Rev., Ser. A, Hum. Exp.; Oncog. Growth Factors Abstr.; PESTDOC; Pig News Inf.; Pollut. Abstr. Indexes; Poult. Abstr.; Protozoolog. Abstr.; Psychol. Abstr. (1932-); PsycINFO; PsycLit; Ref. Upd. Basic Ed.; Ref. Upd. Deluxe Ed.; Res. Alert [Full Cov.]; Rev. Agric. Entomol.; Rev. Med. Vet. Entomol.; Rev. Med. Vet. Mycology; Risk Abstr.; Saf. Health Work; Sci. Cit. Index; SCISEARCH; Small Anim. Abstr. Bibliogr.; Soc. Sci. Cit. Index [Select. Cov.]; Soils Fert.; SportSearch; Stat. Theory Method Abstr. (1959-1963); Sug. Indus. Abstr.; Vet. Bull.; Virol. AIDS Abstr.; Weed Abstr.; Wildl. Rev.; Zentralbl. Math. Ihre Grenzgeb.

SA/0303-2515
**ANNALS OF THE SOUTH AFRICAN MUSEUM.** **See** Museums and Galleries.

PH/0116-0710
**ANNALS OF TROPICAL RESEARCH.** (ANNALS OF TROPICAL RESEARCH : TECHNICAL JOURNAL OF THE VISAYAS STATE COLLEGE OF AGRICULTURE.). [Ann. trop. res.]. **Added/Corp** Visayas State College of Agriculture. Vol. 1, No. 1 (July-Sept. 1979)-. Periodical. English. qt. $25.00 (libraries); $30.00 other. Visayas State College of Agriculture, Visca Leyte 7127 A Philippines. **ED** Rolinda L. Talatala Sanico. **LC** Discard. **CODEN** ATREDV. Index available. **Circ:** 500. Documents available from BIOSIS Document Express.
**Desc:** Research results covering biology, plant and animal, and physical and social sciences.
**Ind/Abst** Biocont. News Inf.; Biodeter. Abstr.; Biol. Abstr.; Dairy Sci. Abstr.; Food Sci. Technol. Abstr.; Index Philip. Period.; Irr. Drain. Abstr.; Maize Abstr.; Nutr. Abstr. Rev., Ser. B, Live Feeds and Feed.; Philip. Sci. Technol. Abstr.; Soyabean Abstr.

FR
**ANNEE DE LA RECHERCHE EN SCIENCES DE L'EDUCATION.** **See** Education.

FR/0065-0552
**ANNUAIRE - ACADEMIE DES SCIENCES.** **Main/Corp** Academie des Sciences (France). Vol. 1 (1917)-. French. an. price varies per volume. Academie des Sciences, 23 Quai de Conti, 75006 Paris France. **Tel** 33 1 43 26 66 21, telex 206521F. **(Subscription address:** Centrale des Revues, 11 rue Gossin, Gauthier Villars, 92543, Montrouge Cedex France**) LC** Q46; .A138. **DD** 506.044.

CN/0229-6616
**ANNUAIRE DES LOISIRS SCIENTIFIQUES.** [Annu. loisirs sci.]. **Main/Corp** Federation Quebecoise du Loisir Scientifique. 1981-. French. an. Federation Quebecoise du Loisir Scientifique, 5955 Labreche 292, St-Francois-Laval Quebec H0A 1G0, Canada. **DD** 502.3/714.

FR
**ANNUAIRE INTERNATIONAL DES FOIRES-EXPOSITIONS & I.E. ET SALONS SPECIALISES, L'.** **VFOAT** Exposant International. French. ir. 72.00F. Societe Europeenne d'Etudes et de Relations Internationales, C C P, Paris 7002-76 France. **LC** T391; .A56. **DD** 607/.34.

FR/0077-6270
**ANNUAIRE NAVIS.** French. be. 500.00F. Ste Rene Moreux et Cie, 190 Boulevard Haussmann, 75008 Paris France. **Tel** 011 33 1 33310613.

II/0469-6786
**ANNUAL NUMBER / NATIONAL ACADEMY OF SCIENCES, INDIA.** **Main/Corp** National Academy of Sciences, India. Academic Scholarly Publication. English. an. Rs25.00 India; $8.00 US. General Secretary, National Academy of Sciences India, 5 Lajpatrai Road, Allahabad 211002 India. **Tel** 55224. **ED** H C Khare. **CODEN** NASAAV. Index available. **Circ:** 800. Documents available from CASDDS.
**Desc:** Publishes presidential addresses of physical and biological sciences and abstract of research papers presented at the annual session of the Academy in Physical and Biological Sciences.
**Ind/Abst** Chem. Abstr.

SA/0373-4250
**ANNUAL PROCEEDINGS / THE ASSOCIATED SCIENTIFIC AND TECHNICAL SOCIETIES OF SOUTH AFRICA, THE.** [Ann. proc. - Assoc. Sci. Tech. Soc. S. Afr.]. Proceedings. English. an. Associated Scientific and Technical Societies of SA, Kelvin House, 2 Holland Street, Johannesburg South Africa. **CODEN** ATSAAL. Documents available from Ask*IEEE.
**Ind/Abst** INSPEC (1968-).

US/8756-0518
**ANNUAL PROGRESS REPORT, TRACT C-A.** (ANNUAL PROGRESS REPORT : TRACT C-A / RIO BLANCO OIL SHALE COMPANY.). [Annu. progr. rep., tract C-a]. 1977/1978-. English. an. Gulf Oil/Standard Oil, 9725 East Hampden Avenue, Denver CO 80231. **DD** 665.
**Ind/Abst** GeoRef.

US/1067-7267
**ANNUAL QUALITY CONGRESS TRANSACTIONS.** [Annu. Qual. Congr. trans.]. **Main/Corp** American Society for Quality Control. **Added/Corp** American Society for Quality Control. **VFOAT** Annual ASQC Quality Congress & Exposition; Annual A.S.Q.C. Quality Congress and Exposition; ASQC Quality Congress Transactions; A.S.Q.C. Quality Congress Transactions. 35th (May 27-29, 1981)-. English. an. $51.25 member, $56.25 non-member. American Society for Quality Control, 611 East Wisconsin Avenue, PO Box 3005, Milwaukee WI 53201. **Tel** (414)272-8575, (800)248-1946, FAX (414)272-1734, telex 316567. **LC** TP149; .A57. **DD** 658. Documents available from Article Express International. ***Continues*** *Annual Technical Conference Transactions (American Society for Quality Control), 0360-6929.*
**Ind/Abst** Eng. Index Annu.

TZ
**ANNUAL REPORT AND ACCOUNTS / TANZANIA INDUSTRIAL RESEARCH AND DEVELOPMENT ORGANIZATION.** **Main/Corp** TIRDO (Organization). English. an. TIRDO, PO Box 23235, Dar Es Salaam Tanzania. **Tel** 68822, telex 41409 TIRDO. **Circ:** 600. ***Continues*** *TIRDO (Organization). Annual Report and Accounts for the Period ... .*

NZ
**ANNUAL REPORT / AUCKLAND INSTITUTE AND MUSEUM.** **Main/Corp** Auckland Institute and Museum. (1968)-. English. an. Auckland Institute & Museum, N Gardner, 6 Tuj Glen Road, Birkenhead Auckland 10 New Zealand. **LC** Q93; .A8. **DD** 069/.099312/2. ***Continues*** *Auckland Institute and Museum. Annual Report of the Auckland Institute and Museum.*

AT/0313-6736
**ANNUAL REPORT - AUSTRALIAN ACADEMY OF TECHNOLOGICAL SCIENCES.** (197?)-. English. an. Australian Academy of Technological Sciences, Ian McLennan House, 197 Royal Parade, Parkville, Victoria Australia 3052. **Tel** 61 3 3470622, FAX 61 3 3478237. ctrl circ.
**Ind/Abst** AESIS Q.

US/0736-6159
**ANNUAL REPORT / BATTELLE MEMORIAL INSTITUTE.** [Annu. rep. - Battelle Meml. Inst.]. **Main/Corp** Battelle Memorial Institute. (1981)-. English. an. Free on request. Battelle Memorial Institute, 505 King Avenue, Columbus OH 43201. **Tel** (614)424-7818, telex 24-5454. **LC** Q11; .B27. **DD** 506/.077157. **Circ:** 23,000 (ctrl). ***Continues*** *President's Report and Annual Review, 0163-0814.*

AT/1031-1378
**ANNUAL REPORT / CURTIN UNIVERSITY OF TECHNOLOGY.** **Main/Corp** Curtin University of Technology. (19??)-. English. an. Curtin University of Technology, GPO Box U 1987, Perth Western Australia 6001 Australia. **Tel** 61 09 351-7896, FAX 61 09 351-2503, telex AA92983. **LC** T173.P4776; A15. **DD** 607.1/1941/1. Index available. **Circ:** 2000 (ctrl).

FR
**ANNUAL REPORT / EUROPEAN SCIENCE FOUNDATION.** **Main/Corp** European Science Foundation. English (French). an. free. European Science Foundation, 1 Quai Lezay-Marnesia, 67080 Strasbourg France. **Tel** 88353063, FAX 88370532. **LC** Q180.E9; E924A. **DD** 001.4/094. **Ad Acc. Circ:** 1,500 (ctrl).
**Desc:** Annual Report on European Science Foundation's activities.

IO
**ANNUAL REPORT - INDONESIAN NATIONAL SCIENTIFIC DOCUMENTATION CENTER.** **Main/Corp** Pusat Dokumentasi Ilmiah Nasional (Indonesia). English. Centre for Scientific Documentation and Information, Jl Jenderal Gatot Subroto 10, PO Box 269/JKSMG/88, Jakarta 12790 Indonesia. **Tel** (021)583465, 510719, 511063, telex 62875 IA. **LC** Q224.3.I5; P87b. **DD** 354/.598/0081. **NLM** W2 LI4 P9A. **Bk Rev. Ad Acc. Circ:** 500 (ctrl).
**Desc:** Report of the Centre for Scientific Documentation Indonesian Institute of Sciences.

US/0275-1917
**ANNUAL REPORT / MASSACHUSETTS TECHNOLOGY DEVELOPMENT CORPORATION.** [Annu. rep. - Mass. Technol. Dev. Corp.]. **Main/Corp** Massachusetts Technology Development Corporation. Fiscal year 1979-. English. an. Massachusetts Technology Development Corporation, 131 State Street, Suite 620, Boston MA 02109. **LC** HG3729.U49; M387A. **DD** 332.7/42.

CN/1187-3728
**ANNUAL REPORT - NATIONAL MUSEUM OF SCIENCE AND TECHNOLOGY (OTTAWA).** **See** Museums and Galleries.

US/0083-2332
**ANNUAL REPORT - NATIONAL SCIENCE FOUNDATION.** (ANNUAL REPORT FOR FISCAL YEAR ... / NATIONAL SCIENCE FOUNDATION.). [Annu. rep. Natl. Sci. Found.]. **Main/Corp** National Science Foundation (U.S.). **VFOAT** N.S.F Annual Report; NSF Annual Report; Annual Report. **VAT** National Science Foundation annual report. 4th Ed. (1954)-. Government Publication. English. an. Superintendent of Documents, US Government Printing Office, Washington DC 20402. **Tel** (202)275-3328, FAX (202)786-2377. **LC** Q11; .U82. **DD** 353.0085/5. **NLM** W2 A N37A. **CODEN** NSFAAO. Documents available from BIOSIS Document Express. ***Continues*** *Annual Report of National Science Foundation.* ***Continued in part by*** *Grants and Awards for Fiscal Year ..., 0565-825X.*
**Ind/Abst** Biol. Abstr.

US
**ANNUAL REPORT OF AD HOC COMMITTEE ON GEODYNAMICS TO THE FEDERAL COUNCIL FOR SCIENCE AND TECHNOLOGY.** **Main/Corp** United States. Federal Council for Science and Technology. Ad Hoc Committee on Geodynamics. 1st (June 1976)-. English. an. National Science Foundation, 1800 G Street Northwest, Washington DC 20550. **Tel** (202)357-9859, (202)357-9498.

CN/0080-7478
**ANNUAL REPORT - SCIENCE COUNCIL OF CANADA.** **Main/Corp** Science Council of Canada. **VFOAT** Rapport Annuel. 1st (1966/67)-. Periodical. English (French). an. Science Council of Canada, 100 Metcalfe Street, Ottawa Ontario K1P 5M1 Canada. **Tel** (819)997-2560. **ED** Jane Whitney. **LC** Q21; .S3. **DD** 506/.1/71. **NLM** W1 SC691K. **Circ:** 3,000. ***Absorbed*** *Science Council of Canada. Rapport Annuel., 0582-2017.*
**Desc:** Report of the Science Council of Canada; includes information on research program, mandate members and budget.

US/0361-6452
**ANNUAL REPORT - SOUTHERN RESEARCH INSTITUTE.** **Main/Corp** Southern Research Institute (Birmingham, Ala.). (1945)-. English. an (April). free on request. Southern Research Institute, PO Box 55305, Birmingham AL 35255. **Tel** (205)323-6592, telex 5-9812 SRL BHM. **LC** T176; .S6. **DD** 607. **Circ:** 6,000.

AT/0158-4030
**ANNUAL REPORT - SUPERVISING SCIENTIST FOR THE ALLIGATOR RIVERS REGION.** [Annu. rep. - Superv. Sci. Alligator Rivers Reg.]. (1979)-. English. an. Australian Bureau of Statistics, PO Box 10, Belconnen Australian Capital Territory, 2616 Australia. **Tel** 011 61 6 2527911, FAX 011 61 6 2516009. **DD** _a333.720994295.
**Ind/Abst** AESIS Q.

NE
**ANNUAL REPORT - TECHNISCHE HOGESCHOOL DELFT.** **Main/Corp** Technische Hogeschool Delft. Centre for International Co-Operation and Appropriate Technology. **VFOAT** Annual Report CICAT. **VAT** Annual Report Centre for International Co-Operation and Appropriate Technology. English. an. Centre for International Co-Operation and Appropriate Technology, Building for Civil Engineering/Room 493, Stevinweg 1 Postbus 6048, 2600 GA Delft Netherlands. **LC** T1; .T254A. **DD** 361.7/7.

US/0095-2109
**ANNUAL REPORT TO THE CONGRESS BY THE OFFICE OF TECHNOLOGY ASSESSMENT.** (ANNUAL REPORT TO THE CONGRESS FOR ...). **Main/Corp** United States. Congress. Office of Technology Assessment. (1974)-. Periodical. English. an. Free on request. Office of Technology Assessment, US Congress Publications Office, 600 Pennsylvania Avenue SE, Washington DC 20510. **Tel** (202)228-6150. **LC** T174.5; .U56a. **DD** 328.73/07/6. **NLM** W2 A C83A.

US
**ANNUAL REPORT YEAR ENDING SEPT. 30 ... / ACCREDITATION BOARD FOR ENGINEERING AND TECHNOLOGY.** **Main/Corp** Accreditation Board for Engineering & Technology U.S.). 48th (1980)-. English. an. Accreditation Board for Engineering and Technology, 345 East 47th Street, New York NY 10017. ***Continues*** *Annual Report of the Engineers' Council for Professional Development.*

CN/0228-6246
**ANNUAL REVIEW - SCIENCE COUNCIL OF CANADA.** (EXPOSE ANNUEL ... / CONSEIL DES SCIENCES DU CANADA.). [Annu. rev. - Sci. Counc. Can.]. **Main/Corp** Science Council of Canada. **VFOAT** Annual Review ... . (1980)-. Periodical. French (English). an. Science Council of Canada, 100 Metcalfe Street, Ottawa Ontario K1P 5M1 Canada. **Tel** (819)997-2560. **DD** 354.710085/5. ***Separated from*** *Rapport Annuel - Conseil des Sciences du Canada.*

US/0734-5526
**ANNUAL SCIENCE AND TECHNOLOGY REPORT TO THE CONGRESS.** ***Title Change.*** [Annu. sci. technol. rep. Congr.]. **Main/Corp** National Science Foundation (U.S.). 1980-?. Government Publication. English. an. Superintendent of Documents, US Government Printing Office, Washington DC 20402. **Tel** (202)275-3328, FAX (202)786-2377. **LC** Q180.U5; U54K. **DD** 353.0085/5. available on microfiche (Vol. for (1981) distributed to depository libraries). Documents available from Documents on Demand. ***Continues*** *National Science Foundation (U.S.). Science and Technology Report, 0163-6421.* ***Continued by*** *Biennial Science and Technology Report to the Congress.*
**Ind/Abst** Am. Stat. Index.

US
**ANNUAL TECHNICAL REPORT / UNITED STATES DEPARTMENT OF AGRICULTURE, SOIL CONSERVATION SERVICE, BISMARCK PLANT MATERIALS CENTER.** **Added/Corp** Bismarck Plant Materials Center (U.S.). (19??)-. English. an. Director of Institutions, c/o Bob Mann, 10th Floor/Capitol, Bismarck ND 58505. Index available. **Bk Rev. Ad Acc.** ctrl circ.

IT
**ANNUARIO SEAT. VOL. B, ELETTROTECNICA, TERMOTECNICA E ATTREZZATURE INDUSTRIALI.** **VFOAT** Annuario S.E.A.T. Vol. B, Elettrotecnica, Termotecnica e Attrezzature Industriali; Elettrotecnica, Termotecnica e Attrezzature Industriali. Italian. an. Free. Via Aurelio Saffi 18, 10138 Turin Italy. **Tel** 011-33301, FAX 4472953, telex 212248 I. **LC** TK12; .A56. **DD** 621.3/025/45. Index available. cum. index. **Ad Acc. Circ:** 30,100 (ctrl).
**Desc:** Yearbook of Italian companies operating in electrotechnics, electronics, telecommunications, heating, air conditioning, environment saving, miscellaneous industrial equipment; includes information on the market in Italy.

AT/1030-7745
**ANSTO/E.** [ANSTO/E]. **Added/Corp** Australian Nuclear Science and Technology Organisation. (1987)-. Monographic series. English. ir. Australian Nuclear Science and Technology Organisation, Private Mailbag 1, Menai 2234 New South Wales Australia. **DD** 539.705. Documents available from CASDDS. ***Continues*** *AAEC/E, 1030-7737.*
**Ind/Abst** Chem. Abstr.

GW/0518-066X
**ANT. ANTRIEBSTECHNIK (1962).** (DIE ANTRIEBSTECHNIK : ANT.). [ANT. Antritech.]. **VFOAT** ANT. Vol. 1 No. 1 (Apr. 1962)-. Periodical. German (translations available in English and French). mo. Vereinigte Fachverlage, Postfach 4068, D 55030 Mainz Germany. **Tel** 011 49 6131 992150.
**Ind/Abst** Coal Abstr.; EMBASE (1973-); Fluid Abstr., Civil Eng.; Fluid Abstr. Proc. Eng.; FLUIDEX (197?-).

UK/0954-1020
**ANTARCTIC SCIENCE.** (ANTARCTIC SCIENCE / BLACKWELL SCIENTIFIC PUBLICATIONS.). [Antarct. sci.]. **Added/Corp** Blackwell Scientific Publications. Vol. 1, No. 1 (March 1989)-. Academic Scholarly Publication. English. qt (4 issues). $178.00 (institutions), $90.00 (individuals) US & Canada; £104.00 (institutions), £52.00 (individuals) Europe; £114.50 (institutions), £58.00 (individuals) other. Blackwell Scientific Publications Ltd, Marston Book Services, PO Box 87, Oxford OX2 ODT UK. **Tel** 011 44 865 791155, FAX 011 44 865 791927, telex 837 515 MARDIS G. **ED** D. W. H. Walton. **LC** Q127.A48; A58. **DD** 509.98/9. **CODEN** ANTSE8. **[CCC]. Pr Rev.** available on microfilm and microfiche from University Microfilms International (UMI). Documents available from The Genuine Article, BIOSIS Document Express. ***Continues*** *British Antarctic Survey Bulletin.*
**Desc:** For all scientists actively involved in Antarctica, as well as many others interested in the polar dimensions of science. Original and topical in its treatment of primary scientific data.
**Ind/Abst** Biol. Abstr. (1989-); Curr. Aware. Biol. Sci., CABS; Curr. Contents, Agric. Biol. Environ. Sci.; Curr. Contents Phys. Chem. Earth Sci.; Ecol. Abstr.; Environ. Period. Bibliogr.; Fish Rev.; Geogr. Abstr. Phys. Geogr.; GeoRef; Meteorol. Geoastrophys. Abstr. (199?-); Res. Alert [Select. Cov.]; Rev. Agric. Entomol.; SCISEARCH; Wildl. Rev.

RU/0570-2844
**ANTARKTIKA.** [Antarktika]. **Added/Corp** Akademiia Nauk SSSR. Mezhduvedomstvennaia Komissiia po Izucheniiu Antarktiki. **VFOAT** Antarctic. (1960)-. Academic Scholarly Publication. Russian (table of contents in English). Izdatelstvo Nauka / Akademiia Nauk, Publishing House of the Russian Academy of Sciences, Leninskii Porspekt 14, 117901 Moscow Russia. **Tel** 011 95 954-21-53, FAX 011 95 938-21-44, telex 411964. **(Subscription address:** Victor Kamkin, 4956 Boiling Brook Parkway, Rockville MD 20852.**)** **LC** G576; .A65. **CODEN** ARKTAO. Documents available from CASDDS.
**Ind/Abst** Chem. Abstr. (1960-1981); GeoRef; Int. Aerosp. Abstr.

BL
**ANUARIO - ABDIB.** **Main/Corp** Associacao Brasileira Para o Desenvolvimento das Industrias de Base. **VFOAT** Annual - ABDIB. **VAT** Anuario - Associacao Brasileira Para o Desenvolvimento das Industrias de Base. Portuguese (English, French and Spanish). **LC** T12.5.B7; A88A.

CK
**ANUARIO CIENTIFICO (BARRANQUILLA, COLOMBIA).** (ANUARIO CIENTIFICO / UNIVERSIDAD DEL NORTE.). Periodical. Spanish. an. Universidad del Norte / Investigaciones, Centro de Investigaciones, Apartado Aereo 1569, Barranquilla Colombia S A. **LC** Q180.C67; A58. **DD** 507/.2086115.

II
**ANUDANOM KI MANGEM (INDIA. DEPT. OF SCIENCE AND TECHNOLOGY).** **Main/Corp** India. Dept. of Science and Technology. **VFOAT** Demands for Grants. 1971/72-. Multiple languages (English and Hindi). an. Government of India Press, Minto Road, New Delhi 111054 India. **LC** Q127.I4; I47B.

AU/0376-1606
**ANZEIGER (OSTERREICHISCHE AKADEMIE DER WISSENSCHAFTEN).** (ANZEIGER / OSTERREICHISCHE AKADEMIE DER WISSENSCHAFTEN, MATHEMATISCH-NATURWISSENSCHAFTLICHE KLASSE.). [Anz.

Osterr. Akad. Wiss., Math.-naturwiss. kl.]. VOL. 84, NO. 1 (1947)-. German. ir (8 issues). DM240.00. Springer-Verlag GmbH & Company KG, Heidelberger Platz 3, D 14197 Berlin Germany. **Tel** 011 49 30 8207223, FAX 011 49 30 8214091, telex 183 319 SPBLN D. **(Subscription address:** Springer Verlag New York Inc. / for North America, 44 Hartz Way, Secaucus NJ 07096.**)** **LC** AS142; .V315. **DD** 505. **CODEN** OSAWA8. Documents available from BIOSIS Document Express. ***Continues*** *Anzeiger (Akademie der Wissenschaften in Wein).*
**Ind/Abst** Biol. Abstr.; Energy Res. Abstr.; GeoRef; Math. Rev.; Life Sci. Collect.; Zentralbl. Math. Ihre Grenzgeb.

●US/1062-3760
**APPLICATIONS AND SOLUTIONS.** (APPLICATIONS AND SOLUTIONS: THE JOURNAL OF HIGH-TECHNOLOGY APPLICATIONS.). (1992)-. Periodical. English. qt. $49.95. Phone Strategies, Inc., 415 RTE. 18, Suite 132, East Brunswick NJ 08816.

US/0093-8815
**APPLICATIONS OF CRYOGENIC TECHNOLOGY.** [Appl. cryog. technol.]. Vol. 1; 1968-. English. an. Scholiom International, 99 Seaview Boulevard/#310, Port Washington NY 11050-4610. **Tel** (212)445-8700. **LC** TP480; .A6. **DD** 621.5/9/05. **CODEN** ACGTAZ. Documents available from CASDDS.
**Desc:** A compilation of selected papers presented at the annual conference of the Cryogenic Society of America.
**Ind/Abst** Chem. Abstr. (1968-1979).

NE/0169-1317
**APPLIED CLAY SCIENCE.** [Appl. clay sci.]. Vol. 1, No. 1/2 (July 1985)-. Academic Scholarly Publication. English. bm (1 volume). Fl620.00. Elsevier Science Publishers BV, PO Box 211, 1000 AE Amsterdam Netherlands. **Tel** 011 31 20 5803642, FAX 011 31 20 5862696, telex 15682. **ED** F J Eckhardt, J E Gillott and R Kuhnel. **CODEN** ACLSER. **[CCC].** available on microfilm and microfiche from University Microfilms International (UMI). Documents available from Article Express International, CASDDS.
**Desc:** An international publication medium for research papers, reviews and short communications in the field of applied clay science.
**Ind/Abst** Chem. Abstr. (1985-); Eng. Index Annu.; Geogr. Abstr. Phys. Geogr.; Geol. Abstr.; GeoRef; Soils Fert.

US/0275-939X
**APPLIED RESEARCH SUMMARY OF AWARDS.** [Appl. res. summ. awards]. Began with fiscal year 1979. English. an. National Science Foundation, 1800 G Street Northwest, Washington DC 20550. **Tel** (202)357-9859, (202)357-9498. **LC** T176; .A67. **DD** 338.973.

US/0003-6986
**APPLIED SCIENCE & TECHNOLOGY INDEX.** **See** Science and Technology-Abstracting, Bibliographies and Statistics.

US/0003-7052
**APPRAISAL.** [Appraisal]. **Added/Corp** Children's Science Book Review Committee (U.S.). Vol. 1, No. 1 (Winter 1967)-. Periodical. English. qt (4 issues). $44.00 US; $56.00 other. Children Science Book Review Committee, Science Education Program, 605 Commonwealth Avenue, Boston MA 02215. **Tel** (617)353-4150. **ED** Diane Holzheimer. **LC** Z7401; .A63. **DD** 016.5. Index available (bound in last issue). **Bk Rev. Circ:** 2,300.
**Desc:** Detailed evaluative book reviews by both practicing children's librarians and subject specialists of all new children's and young adult science trade books.
**Ind/Abst** Book Rev. Digest; Book Rev. Index; Child. Lit. Abstr. (19??-).

UK/0305-0920
**APPROPRIATE TECHNOLOGY.** [Appropriate technol.]. Vol. 1 (1974)-. Periodical. English. qt. £20.00. Intermediate Technology Publishing Ltd., 103-104 Southampton Row, London WC1B 4HH England. **Tel** 011 44 71 436 9761, FAX 011 44 71 436 2013, telex 268312. **ED** Corwen McCutcheon. **LC** T1; .A66. **DD** 609/.172/4. **[CCC].** Index available (free). cum. index. **Bk Rev. Ad Acc. Pr Rev. Circ:** 3,500. Documents available from The Genuine Article, Documents on Demand.
**Desc:** Features simple, proven technologies appropriate to the developing world. Contains articles by field workers in developing countries and their technologies assessed by technical experts.
**Ind/Abst** Abstr. AIT Rep. Publ. Energy; Agric. Eng. Abstr. (19??-19??); Curr. Contents Eng. Tech. Appl. Sci.; Curr. Technol. Index; Educ. Technol. Abstr.; EMBASE; Environ. Abstr.; Environ. Period. Bibliogr.; Field Crop Abstr.; Fluid Abstr., Civil Eng.; Fluid Abstr. Proc. Eng.; FLUIDEX (1974-); For. Prod. Abstr.; For. Abstr.; Geogr. Abstr. Human Geogr.; Grasslands For. Abstr.; Int. Dev. Abstr.; J. Ferrocement; Leis. Recreat. Tour. Abstr.; Postharvest News Inf.; Res. Alert [Select. Cov.]; Rice Abstr.; Rural Dev. Abstr.; SCISEARCH; Soils Fert.; Stud. Women Abstr.; World Agric. Econ.

II
**APPROPRIATE TECHNOLOGY DOCUMENTATION BULLETIN.** **Added/Corp** Small Industry Extension Training Institute (India). (1973)-. Bulletin. English. bm. $10.00. Siet (Small Industry Extension Training) Institute, Yousufguda, Hyderabad 500045 India. **(Subscription address:** Prints India, 11 Darya Ganj, New Delhi 110002 India.**)** **LC** T27.I4; A76. **DD** 338.4/7/0954.

AT
**APPROPRIATE TECHNOLOGY INDEX.** **VFOAT** Atindex. Vol. 7, No. 1 (1986)-. Periodical. English. qt. 330.00Aus$. Noyce Publishing, GPO Box 2222T, Melbourne Victoria, 3001 Australia. **Tel** 11 61 03 8022749. ***Continues*** *Atindex, 0143-3938.*

SU/1015-4442
**ARAB GULF JOURNAL OF SCIENTIFIC RESEARCH.** **Added/Corp** Arab Bureau of Education for the Gulf States. **VFOAT** Majallat Al-Khalij Al-Arabi Lil-Buhuth Al-Ailmiyah. Vol. 7, No. 2 (Aug. 1989)-. Academic Scholarly Publication. English (Arabic; summaries and/or abstracts in Arabic). Three times a year. $25.00 (personal), $50.00 organizations. Arab Bureau of Education for the Gulf States, PO Box 3908, Riyadh 11481 Saudi Arabia. **Tel** 4774644, FAX 4783165, telex 401441 TARBIA SJ. **CODEN** AGSREJ. **Ad Acc. Pr Rev.** ctrl circ. Documents available from CASDDS. ***Formed by the union of*** *Arab Gulf Journal of Scientific Research. A, Mathematical and Physical Sciences, 0259-8930* ***and*** *Arab Gulf Journal of Scientific Research. B, Agricultural and Biological Sciences, 0259-8949.*
**Desc:** Deals with original works in pure and applied sciences concerning the Arab Gulf area.
**Ind/Abst** Chem. Abstr.; Curr. Aware. Biol. Sci., CABS; Ei Page One; Environ. Period. Bibliogr.; GeoRef; Hortic. Abstr.; Math. Rev.; NAPRALERT; Ocean. Abstr.; Plant Grow. Reg. Abstr.; Rev. Plant Pathol.

UK/0377-9211
**ARABIAN JOURNAL FOR SCIENCE AND ENGINEERING.** (AL-MAJALLAH AL-ARABIYAH LIL-ULUM WA-AL-HANDASAH. THE ARABIAN JOURNAL FOR SCIENCE AND ENGINEERING.). [Arab. j. sci. eng.]. **Added/Corp** Jamiat Al-Bitrul Wa-Al-Maadin. **VFOAT** Arabian Journal for Science and Engineering. (Nov. 1975)-. Academic Scholarly Publication. English (summaries and/or abstracts in Arabic). Four times a year. $62.00. King Fahd University of Petroleum and Mining, KFUPM Box 8, Dhahran 31261 Saudi Arabia. **Tel** 011 966 3 8605418. **ED** Fahd H. Dakhil. **LC** Q80.S2; M34. **DD** 505. **CODEN** AJSEDY. **[CCC]. Ad Acc. Pr Rev. Circ:** 800. available on microfilm and microfiche from University Microfilms International (UMI). Documents available from The Genuine Article, Ask*IEEE, CASDDS.
**Ind/Abst** Chem. Abstr.; Curr. Contents Eng. Tech. Appl. Sci.; Ei Page One; GeoRef; INSPEC (Jan. 1981-); Int. Aerosp. Abstr.; Math. Rev.; Res. Alert [Select. Cov.]; Zentralbl. Math. Ihre Grenzgeb.

UK/0957-4239
**ARABIC SCIENCES AND PHILOSOPHY : A HISTORICAL JOURNAL.** **VFOAT** Arabic Sciences and Philosophy. Vol. 1, No. 1 (Mar. 1991)-. Academic Scholarly Publication. English (French; summaries and/or abstracts in French and English). Twice a year. $87.00 US, Canada & Mexico; £56.00 other. Cambridge University Press, The Edinburgh Building, Shaftesbury Road, Cambridge CB2 2RU United Kingdom. **Tel** 011 44 223 312393, FAX 011 44 223 325959. **(Subscription address:** Cambridge University Press / North America, 110 Midland Avenue, Port Chester NY 10573.**)** **ED** Basim Musallam, Roshdi Rashed, Jean Jolivet, Muhsin Mahdi and George Saliba. **LC** DS36.8; .A69. **DD** 001.2/09174927. **Bk Rev. Ad Acc.** available on microfilm and microfiche from University Microfilms International (UMI).
**Desc:** An international journal devoted to the history of the Arabic sciences, mathematics and philosophy in the world of Islam between the eighth and eighteenth centuries in a cross-cultural context. Publishes original studies on the history of these disciplines as well as studies of the inter-relations between the Arabic, Greek, and Indian sciences and philosophy, and Latin, Byzantine, Hebrew, Italian and other European sciences and philosophy.

SP/0210-1963
**ARBOR.** [Arbor]. **Added/Corp** Consejo Superior de Investigaciones Cientificas (Spain). Vol. 1, No. 1 (Jan/Feb. 1944)-. Periodical. Spanish. Ten times a year. 7000ptas Spain; 10000ptas other. Consejo Superior Investigacion Cientificas (CSIC), Vitruvio 8, 28006 Madrid Spain. **Tel** 011 34 1 5612833, FAX 011 34 1 4113077, telex 42182. **LC** AP60; .A6. **DD** 056/.1. Documents available from The Genuine Article.
**Desc:** Goal is to facilitate society's understanding and support of scientific and technological enterprise, to assure the scientific community's recognition of the needs of the society that maintains it, and above all to ensure that both partners contribute to building the new culture that today's reality demands.
**Ind/Abst** Am. Hist. Life (1955-1975); Annu. Bibliogr. Engl. Lang. Lit.; Arts Humanit. Citation Index [Full Cov.]; BHA : Biblio. Hist. Art; Indice Hist. Esp. (1955-1975); MLA Int. Bibl. Books Artic. Mod. Lang. Lit.; Res. Alert [Full Cov.]; Romant. Move.; Soc. Sci. Cit. Index [Select. Cov.].

CN/0846-8583
**ARCHITECTURAL, ENGINEERING AND SCIENTIFIC SERVICES.** (ARCHITECTURAL, ENGINEERING, AND SCIENTIFIC SERVICES / STATISTICS CANADA, MERCHANDISING AND SERVICES DIVISION, RETAIL TRADE SECTION.). [Archit. eng. sci. serv.]. **Added/Corp** Statistics Canada. Retail Trade Section. **VFOAT** Bureaux d'Architectes, d'Ingenieurs-Conseils et de Services Scientifiques. (19??)-. English (French). ir. 33.00Can$ Canada; $40.00 US; $47.00 other. Statistics Canada, Publications Sales & Services, Main Building Room 1710, Ottawa Ontario K1A 0T6 Canada. **Tel** (613)951-5078, (800)267-6677, FAX (613)951-1584, telex 053-3585. **LC** TA26; .A7. **DD** 338.4/362/000971.

AU/0253-7400
**ARCHIV DER GESCHICHTE DER NATURWISSENSCHAFTEN.** No. 1 (1980/81)-. Periodical. German. Three times a year. Brueder Hollinek & Company, Feldgasse 13, A1238 Vienna Austria. **Tel** 011 43 1 8893646, 8893647. **NLM** W1; AR162M.

GW/0365-8406
**ARCHIV FUER ZUCHTUNGSFORSCHUNG.** ***Ceased.*** [Arch. Zuchtungsforsch.]. **Main/Corp** Deutsche Akademie der Landwirtschaftswissenschaften. Academic Scholarly Publication. German. qt. Deutscher Judo Verband, Redaktion Ippon Segewaldweg 40, D 12557 Berlin Germany. **Tel** 011 49 711 210770, telex 051 678. **CODEN** AVZFAH. Documents available from CASDDS.
**Ind/Abst** AgBiotech News Inf.; Chem. Abstr. (1971-1982); Crop Physiol. Abstr.; Field Crop Abstr.; Grasslands For. Abstr.; Hortic. Abstr.; Maize Abstr.; Nematol. Abstr.; Plant Breed. Abstr.; Plant Grow. Reg. Abstr.; Potato Abstr.; Rev. Plant Pathol.; Seed Abstr.; Soyabean Abstr.; Vitis Vitic. Enol. Abstr.; Wheat Barley Trit. Abstr.

GW/0003-9519
**ARCHIVE FOR HISTORY OF EXACT SCIENCES.** [Arch. hist. exact sci.]. Vol. 1 (1960)-. Periodical. English (French, German, Italian, Latin and Spanish). Eight times a year. DM1072.00. Springer-Verlag GmbH & Company KG, Heidelberger Platz 3, D 14197 Berlin Germany. **Tel** 011 49 30 8207223, FAX 011 49 30 8214091, telex 183 319 SPBLN D. **(Subscription address:** Springer Verlag New York Inc. / for North America, 44 Hartz Way, Secaucus NJ 07096.**)** **ED** C Truesdell. **LC** Q125; .A75. **DD** 509. **NLM** W1 AR301E. **CODEN** AHESAN. **[CCC].** cum. index. **Pr Rev.** available on microfilm and microfiche from University Microfilms International (UMI). Documents available from The Genuine Article.
**Desc:** Nourishes historical research meeting the standards of the mathematical sciences. Its aim is to give rapid and full publication to writings of exceptional depth, scope, and permanence.
**Ind/Abst** Am. Hist. Life (1985-); Br. Archaeol. Bibliogr.; Compumath Citation Index [Full Cov.]; Curr. Contents Phys. Chem. Earth Sci.; Index Sci. Rev.; Math. Rev.; Res. Alert [Full Cov.]; Sci. Cit. Index; SCISEARCH; Soc. Sci. Cit. Index [Select. Cov.]; Stat. Theory Method Abstr. (1969, 1972, 1974-1975, 1977-1981, 1983, 1986-1987); Zentralbl. Math. Ihre Grenzgeb.

SZ/0252-9289
**ARCHIVES DES SCIENCES ET COMPTE RENDU DES SEANCES DE LA SOCIETE.** **See** Natural History.

GW/0003-9810
**ARCHIVES INTERNATIONALES D'HISTOIRE DES SCIENCES.** [Arch. int. hist. sci.]. **Added/Corp** Academie Internationale d'Histoire des Sciences. International Union of the History of Science. International Union of the History and Philosophy of Science. Division of the History of Science. Vol. 1, No. 1 (1947)-. Periodical. English (French, German and Italian). Twice a year. L64903.00. Institutio Enciclopedia Italiana, Piazza Enciclopedia Italiana 4, 00186 Rome Italy. **Tel** 011 39 6 68982464. **NLM** W1 AR3965. **CODEN** AIHSAB. Documents available from CASDDS. ***Supersedes*** *Archeion.*
**Ind/Abst** Am. Hist. Life (1967-); Chem. Abstr.; GeoRef; Math. Rev.; Zentralbl. Math. Ihre Grenzgeb.

IT
**ARCHIVIO DELLA CORRISPONDENZA DEGLI SCIENZIATI ITALIANI.** (1985)-. Monographic series. Italian. ir. Price varies per volume. Casa Editrice Leo S. Olschki, Viuzzo del Pozzetto, Casella Postale 66, 50126 Florence Italy. **Tel** 011 39 55 6530684, FAX 011 39 55 6530214.
**Ind/Abst** Math. Rev. (1988-).

US/0004-0851
**ARCTIC AND ALPINE RESEARCH.** **See** Geography.

GW
**ARGENTINIEN, FORSCHUNGSPOLITIK UND FORSCHUNGSPRAXIS / BUNDESSTELLE FUR AUSSENHANDELSINFORMATION.** German. an. 3.00. Bundesstelle fuer Aussenhandelsinformation, Agrippastr 87 93, D 50676 Cologne Germany. **Tel** 011 49 221 2057316, FAX 011 49 221 2057212. **LC** Q180.A7; A75. **DD** 001.4/0982.

JA/0385-6844
**ARIAKE KOGYO KOTO SEMMON GAKKO KIYO.** **Main/Corp** Ariake Kogyo Koto Semmon Gakko. **Added/Corp** Ariake Kogyo Koto Semmon Gakko. Research Reports of the Ariake Technical College. (19??)-. Japanese. Ariake Kogyo Koto Senmon Gakko, (Ariake National College of Technology), 150, Higashihagiocho, Omutashi, Fukuokaken 836 Japan. **LC** AS552.A73; A73a. **CODEN** AKKKDJ. Documents available from CASDDS.
**Ind/Abst** Chem. Abstr.

US/0747-9921
**ARIS FUNDING REPORT. SOCIAL AND NATURAL SCIENCES REPORT.** **See** Social Sciences.

RU
**ARKHIV AKADEMII NAUK SSSR.** **Added/Corp** Akademiia Nauk SSSR. Arkhiv. (1933)-. Russian (summaries and/or abstracts in French).

US
**AROMA-CHOLOGY REVIEW.** (19??)-. English. ir (Summer and Winter). $35.00. Olfactory Research Fund, 145 East 32nd Street, New York NY 10016. **Tel** (212)725-2755, FAX (212)779-9058.
**Desc:** Reports on the results of current scientific work, being supported by the Olfactory Research Fund, in the new field of aroma-chology. Expanded to track international sources of information that provide current news in the medical, physical and social sciences which may be applied to the study of the sense of smell and psychological benefits of fragrance.

SW
**ARSBERATTELSE - NORDFORSK.** **Main/Corp** Scandinavian Council for Applied Research. Multiple languages (Danish, Norwegian and Swedish). Nordforsk, Huvudsekretariatet, Box 5103, S-102 43 5 Stockholm Sweden. **LC** T177.S33; S24C.

NO
**ARSRAPPORT FRA AVDELINGER OG INSTITUTTER / UNIVERSITETET I TRONDHEIM, NORGES TEKNISKE HGSKOLE.** Norwegian. an. **LC** T173; .T8435. ***Continues*** *Arsrapport Fra Instituttene.*

●US/1064-5462
**ARTIFICIAL LIFE.** [Artif. life]. (1992)-. Periodical. English. qt. $45.00 (individuals), $135.00 (institutions). Massachusetts Institute of Technology (MIT) Press, 55 Hayward Street, Cambridge MA 02142-1399. **Tel** (617)253-2889, (617)625-8481, FAX (617)258-6779. **ED** Christopher G. Langton. **DD** 589.
**Desc:** Forum for the dissemination of scientific research in the field of artificial life. Spans biological organization, including studies of the origin of life, self-assembly, growth and development, evolutionary and ecological dynamics, animal and robot behavior, social organization, and cultural evolution.

FR/0004-4008
**ARTS & METIERS.** No. 1 (Jan. 1951)-. Periodical. French. mo (ten issues per year). 280.00F France; 535.00F other. Arts et Metiers, 9 Bis Av D Iena, F 75783 Paris Cedex 16 France. **Tel** (1)47.23.61.64, FAX (1)47.20.58.48, telex 614321 F. **Bk Rev. Ad Acc. Circ:** 19,000 (ctrl). ***Continues*** *Ingenieurs Arts & Metiers.*

JA/0389-9306
**ASAHIKAWA KOGYO KOTO SENMON GAKKO KENKYU HOBUN.** (KENKYU HOBUN / ASAHIKAWA KOGYO KOTO SENMON GAKKO.). [Asahikawa Kogyo Koto Senmon Gakko kenkyu hobun]. **Added/Corp** Asahikawa Kogyo Koto Senmon Gakko. **VFOAT** Journal of the Asahikawa Technical College; Journal of the Asahikawa National College of Technology; Asahikawa Kogyo Koto Senmon Gakko Kenkyu Hobun. (1964)-. Periodical. Japanese (summaries and/or abstracts in English). an. **LC** T4; .K43. **CODEN** AKKHDA. Documents available from CASDDS.
**Ind/Abst** Chem. Abstr.

AT
**ASCENT TECHNOLOGY MAGAZINE : ATM.** **Added/Corp** Australia. Dept. of Industry, Technology, and Commerce. **VFOAT** ATM. (1991)-. Government Publication. English. Four times a year. 15.00Aus$. Australian Government Publishing Service, GPO Box 84, Canberra ACT 2601 Australia. **Tel** 011 61 6 2954411, FAX 011 61 6 2954455. **LC** T29.A1; A83. **DD** 609.94.
**Ind/Abst** AESIS Q.

SZ/1015-5481
**ASCOM TECHNICAL REVIEW.** [Ascom tech. rev.]. (1989)-. Periodical. English. qt. Free. Ascom Tech Ltd, Morganstrasse 129, CH-3018 Bern 14 Switzerland. **Tel** 011 41 31 9993918. **CODEN** ATAGEL. Documents available from Article Express International, Ask*IEEE. ***Continues*** *Hasler Review, 0374-3306.*
**Ind/Abst** Bioeng. Abstr. (1989-); Ei Page One (1989-); Eng. Index Annu.; INSPEC (1989-).

SI/0217-5460
**ASEAN JOURNAL ON SCIENCE & TECHNOLOGY FOR DEVELOPMENT.** [ASEAN j. sci. technol. dev.]. **VFOAT** Association of South East Asian Nations Journal on Science & Technology for Development. (1984)-. Periodical. English. sa. **DD** 509.59 609.59. Documents available from Documents on Demand.
**Ind/Abst** Abstr. AIT Rep. Publ. Energy; Environ. Abstr.

HK
**ASIA 2000.** **VFOAT** Asia Two Thousand. Periodical. English. bm. $18.00 (Introductory Rate), $24.00 (Regular Rate). Asia 2000, 10th Floor/146 Prince Edward Road W, Kowloon Hong Kong. **LC** T27.A1; A84. **DD** 609/.5.

II/0256-9957
**ASIA PACIFIC TECH MONITOR.** [Asia Pac. tech monit.]. (1984)-. Periodical. English. bm. $30.00. Asian and Pacific Centre for Transfer of Technology, 49 Palace Road, PO Box 115, Bangalore 560052 India. **UDC** 347.77. **CODEN** NU003.
**Ind/Abst** Abstr. BioCommer.

US
**ASIAN INTERNATIONAL LABORATORY.** bm. Free to qualified readers. International Scientific Communications Inc, PO Box 870, 30 Controls Drive, Shelton CT 06484-0870. **Tel** (203)926-9300, FAX (203)926-9310, telex 964292.
**Ind/Abst** Abstr. BioCommer.

US/0731-2350
**ASK (BETHESDA, MD.).** ***Ceased.*** (ASK.). [Ask]. Vol. 1, No. 1 (Feb. 1982)-?. Periodical. English. mo. Accurate Information Service, 9711 MacArthur Boulevard, Bethesda MD 20817. **Tel** (301)365-0412. **ED** Louis V Lombardo. **Bk Rev.**
**Desc:** Loose-leaf information service covering business and government information sources, products, and services for executives, information managers and librarians.

●UK
**ASLIB BOOK GUIDE / ASLIB.** **Added/Corp** Aslib. **VFOAT** Book Guide. Vol. 57, No. 1 (Jan. 1992)-. English. mo. £77.00 (member), £95.00 (non-member) Europe; £85.00 (member), £105.00 (non-member) other. ASLIB, Information House, 20-24 Old Street, London EC1V 9AP England. **Tel** 011 44 71 253 4488, FAX 011 44 71 430 0514, telex 23667 AJLIB G. **(Subscription address:** North America: 143 Old Marlton Pike, Medford, NJ 08055-8750**) LC** Z7403; .A84. **DD** 016.5. ***Continues*** *Aslib Book-List, 0001-2521.*

US
**ASSESSMENT ACTIVITIES.** **Main/Corp** United States. Congress. Office of Technology Assessment. English. Congress of the United States, Office of Technology Assessment, Washington DC 20510.

US/0895-7371
**ASTC NEWSLETTER.** [ASTC newsl.]. **Added/Corp** Association of Science-Technology Centers. **VFOAT** Association of Science Technology Centers Newsletter. **VAT** Association of Science-Technology Centers Newsletter. (19??)-. Newsletter. English. Six times a year (Jan., Mar., May, July, Sept., Nov.). $15.00 Members of Association of Science Technology Centers; $30.00 non-member. Science Technology Centers, 1025 Vermont Avenue Northwest, Suite 500, Washington DC 20005. **Tel** (202)783-7200, FAX (202)783-7207. **DD** 507. **Bk Rev**, (Qty: 6-10/ yr). **Circ:** 3,000.
**Ind/Abst** Museum Abstr.

CN/0226-1685
**ASTIS BIBLIOGRAPHY.** **See** Science and Technology-Abstracting, Bibliographies and Statistics.

UK
**ASTMS JOURNAL.** **VAT** Association of Scientific, Technical, and Managerial Staffs Journal. 1968-. Periodical. English. bm. ***Formed by the union of*** *AScW Journal* ***and*** *ASSET Journal.*

NE/0920-7996
**AT SOURCE : A QUARTERLY FOR DEVELOPMENT.** **VFOAT** Appropriate Technology Source. Vol. 15, No. 1 (March 1987)-. Periodical. English. qt. ***Continues*** *Vraagbaak.*
**Ind/Abst** Agric. Eng. Abstr. (1991-); Postharvest News Inf.; Rice Abstr.; Rural Dev. Abstr.

PR/0885-6079
**ATENEA (MAYAGUEZ, P.R.).** **See** The Arts-Art.

BL
**ATIVIDADES DESENVOLVIDAS.** **Main/Corp** Instituto de Pesquisas Technologicas. Portuguese. Cidade Universitaria Armando de Salles Oliveria, Caixa Postal 7141, Sao Paulo Brazil. **LC** T173.S255; A13. **DD** 607/.1181/6.

US
**ATMOSPHERIC PROGRAMS BULLETIN.** **Added/Corp** United States. Federal Aviation Administration. Office of Environment and Energy. United States. National Aeronautics and Space Administration. Upper Atmosphere Research Program. (Aug. 1991)-. Bulletin. English. ***Continues*** *Upper Atmospheric Programs, Bulletin, 0276-5411.*

AT/0727-3096
**ATS FOCUS.** **VFOAT** Academy of Technological Sciences Focus. (1978)-. Periodical. English. Five times a year. On exchange. Australian Academy of Technological Sciences, Ian McLennan House, 197 Royal Parade, Parkville, Victoria Australia 3052. **Tel** 61 3 3470622, FAX 61 3 3478237. **Bk Rev**, (Qty: 3-4). **Acid Free. Circ:** 1,000 (ctrl). ***Continues*** *Newsletter - Australian Academy of Technological Sciences, 0156-3033.*
**Ind/Abst** AESIS Q.

IT/0001-4419
**ATTI DELLA ACCADEMIA DELLE SCIENZE DI TORINO. CLASSE DI SCIENZE FISICHE, MATEMATICHE E NATURALI.** (ATTI DELLA ACCADEMIA DELLE SCIENZE DI TORINO. TOMO I, CLASSE DI SCIENZE FISICHE, MATEMATICHE E NATURALI.). [Atti Accad. sci. Torino, Cl. sci. fis., mat. nat.]. **VFOAT** Atti della Accademia delle Scienze di Torino. Classe di Scienze Fisiche, Matematiche e Naturali. (1945)-. Periodical. Italian. ir. Price varies. Accademia delle Scienze Torino, via Maria Vittoria 3, 10123 Turin Italy. **Tel** 011 39 11 510047. **(Subscription address:** Rosenberg & Sellier SRL, via Andrea Doria 14, 10123 Turin Italy.**) CODEN** AATFAA. Documents available from BIOSIS Document Express, Ask*IEEE, CASDDS. ***Continues*** *Atti della Reale Accademia delle Scienze di Torino.*
**Ind/Abst** Bibliogr. Mission. (1968-); Biol. Abstr. (-1988); Chem. Abstr.; INSPEC (1968-); Int. Aerosp. Abstr. (1983-); Math. Rev.; Life Sci. Collect.

IT/0392-2219
**ATTI DELLA ACCADEMIA LIGURE DI SCIENZE E LETTERE.** [Atti Accad. ligure sci. lett.]. Began in 1941. Italian (summaries and/or abstracts in English and French). an. Societa Ligure Storia Patria, Via Albaro 11, 16145 Genoa Italy. **Tel** 39 10 308683. **CODEN** AALGA7. Documents available from Ask*IEEE. ***Continues*** *Atti della Societa di Scienze e Lettere di Genova.*
**Ind/Abst** GeoRef; INSPEC (1969-); Math. Rev.; Zentralbl. Math. Ihre Grenzgeb.

IT/1120-6349
**ATTI DELLA ACCADEMIA NAZIONALE DEI LINCEI. RENDICONTI LINCEI. SCIENZE FISICHE E NATURALI.** (RENDICONTI LINCEI. SCIENZE FISICHE E NATURALI.). [Atti Accad. naz. Lincei, Rend. Lincei, Sci. fis. nat.]. **Added/Corp** Accademia Nazionale dei Lincei. Classe di Scienze Fisiche, Matematiche e Naturali. **VFOAT** Scienze Fisiche e Naturali. Vol. 1, No. 1 (1990)-. Periodical. English (Italian). qt. L70000.00 (Italy); L90000.00 (other). Accademia Nazionale dei Lincei, Via Lungara 10 Uff Diff Pubbl., 00165 Rome Italy. **Tel** 011 39 6 6838831. **LC** Q4; .R46. **CODEN** ANLNEL. Documents available from Ask*IEEE. ***Continues in part*** *Rendiconti (Accademia Nazionale dei Lincei. Classe di Scienze Fisiche, Matematiche e Naturali), 0392-7881.*
**Ind/Abst** INSPEC (1990-).

IT
**ATTI DELLA SOCIETA DEI NATURALISTI E MATEMATICI DI MODENA.** **Main/Corp** Societa dei Naturalisti e Matematici di Modena. Vol. 1 (1866)-. Italian. an. **LC** Q54; .M7. cum. index. Documents available from CASDDS.
**Ind/Abst** Chem. Abstr.

IT
**ATTI DELLA SOCIETA PELORITANA DI SCIENZE.** **Main/Corp** Societa Peloritana di Scienze. Vol. 29 (1983)-. Italian. an. **CODEN** APSCE3. Documents available from BIOSIS Document Express. ***Continues*** *Atti della Societa Peloritana di Science Fisiche, Matematiche e Naturali, 0037-8860.*
**Ind/Abst** Biol. Abstr. (1987-); Math. Rev.

IT/0392-6680
**ATTI - INSTITUTO VENETO DI SCIENZE, LETTRE ED ARTI. CLASSE DI SCIENZE FISICHE, MATEMATICHE E NATURALI.** (ATTI. CLASSE DI SCIENZE FISICHE, MATEMATICHE E NATURALI / ISTITUTO VENETO DI SCIENZE, LETTERE ED ARTI.). [Atti - Ist. ven. sci. lett. arti, Cl. sci. fis. mat. nat.]. **VFOAT** Classe di Scienze Fisiche, Matematiche e Naturali. Vol. 137-141- School Year (1978-79)-. Academic Scholarly Publication. Italian (English). an. **NLM** W1 AT752H. **CODEN** AIVNDZ.

Documents available from CASDDS. ***Continues*** *Atti. Classe di Scienze Matematiche e Naturali, 0373-255X.*
**Ind/Abst** Chem. Abstr.; GeoRef; Numis. Lit. (?-?).

AT/1036-0875
**AUSTRALASIAN SCIENCE MAG.**
[Australas. sci. mag.]. (1990)-. Periodical. English. qt. 20.00Aus$. USQ Press, University of Southern Queensland, PO Box 58, Darling Heights, Toowoomba QLD 4350 Australia. **DD** 507.1294. ***Continues*** *Australian Science Mag., 0729-6924.*

AT/0045-0855
**AUSTRALIAN SCIENCE TEACHERS' JOURNAL, THE.** [Aust. sci. teach. j.]. **Added/Corp** Australian Science Teachers' Association. (19??)-. Periodical. English. Four times a year (Mar., May, Aug., Nov.). 32.00Aus$ (individuals), 36.00Aus$ (institutions) Australia; 40.00Aus$ others. Australian Science Teachers Association, PO Box 2682, Canberra ACT 2601 Australia. **Tel** 011 61 6 258 9250, FAX 011 61 6 258 9565. **ED** Ian Pattle, (editor's address: 22 Balfour Street, Launceston 7250 Australia, phone: 003 314 048). **LC** Q183.43.A8; A8. **DD** 507. Index available. **Bk Rev. Ad Acc. Circ:** 5,200 (ctrl). available on microfilm and microfiche from University Microfilms International (UMI).
**Desc:** Science teaching in primary and secondary schools. Articles for physics, chemistry, biology, earth science and interdisciplinary senior science teachers.
**Ind/Abst** Aust. Educ. Index (1978-); Curr. Index J. Educ.; Tech. Educ. Train. Abstr.

IT/0393-3911
**AUTOMAZIONE INTEGRATA.** [Autom. int.]. **VFOAT** CN Automazione Integrata. (1985)-. Periodical. Italian. mo (11 issues per year). L75000 Italy; L140000 Europe; L185000 other. Tecniche Nuove SPA, Via Ciro Menotti 14, 20129 Milan Italy. **Tel** 011 39 2 75701, FAX 011 39 2 7610351, telex 334647 TECHS I. **UDC** 681.3. ***Continues*** *Controlli Numerici, Macchine a CN, Robot Industriali, 0392-6036.*

GW/0003-780X
**AV. DIE ARBEITSVORBEREITUNG.** [AV, Arbeitsvorbereit.]. **VFOAT** Die Arbeitsvorbereitung (Munchen). (1963)-. Periodical. German. bm (6 issues). DM107.40. Carl Hanser Verlag, Postfach 860420, D 81631 Munich Germany. **Tel** 011 49 89 998300, FAX 011 49 89 984809. **[CCC].**

US/1057-5839
**AWIS MAGAZINE.** (AWIS MAGAZINE / ASSOCIATION FOR WOMEN IN SCIENCE.). [AWIS mag.]. **Added/Corp** Association for Women in Science. **VAT** Association for Women in Science Magazine. Vol. 20, No. 1 (Jan./Feb. 1991)-. Periodical. English. bm (6 issues). $60.00. Association for Women in Science, 1522 K Street NW/Suite 820, Washington DC 20005. **Tel** (202)408-0742, FAX (202)408-8321. **ED** Barbara Mandula. **LC** Q149.U5; A88a. **DD** 331.4/815/0973. **Bk Rev**, (Qty: 6). **Ad Acc, Adv Mgr:** Annette Duplinsky. **Circ:** 4,000 (ctrl). ***Continues*** *Association for Women in Science. AWIS Newsletter, 0160-256X.*
**Desc:** Bi-monthly publication which features articles on the status of women in science and important policy issues, as well as interview, listings of grant and employment opportunities, etc.

CN/0711-4974
**B.C. SCIENCE TEACHERS NEWS UPDATE.** [B.C. Sci. Teach. news update]. Vol. 1, No. 1 (Mar. 1980)-. Periodical. English. Free to members. British Columbia Teachers Federation, 100-550 West 6th Avenue, Vancouver British Columbia V5Z 4P2 Canada. **Tel** (604)871-2283, (800)663-9163, FAX (604)871-2294, (604)871-2290. **DD** 506/.0711.

CN/0705-4769
**BACKGROUND STUDY / SCIENCE COUNCIL OF CANADA.** ***Ceased.*** [Sci. Counc. Can. backgr. study]. **Added/Corp** Science Council of Canada. (1978)-(1992). Periodical. English. ir. Science Council of Canada, 100 Metcalfe Street, Ottawa Ontario K1P 5M1 Canada. **Tel** (819)997-2560. **DD** 354.710085/5. ***Continues*** *Science Council of Canada Background Study, 0705-4769.*

BG/0304-9809
**BANGLADESH JOURNAL OF SCIENTIFIC AND INDUSTRIAL RESEARCH.** [Bangladesh j. sci. ind. res.]. **Added/Corp** Bangladesh Council of Scientific and Industrial Research. Vol. 8 (Jan./Oct. 1973)-. Periodical. English. qt. $24.00. Council of Scientific & Industrial Research / Bangladesh, Dlaumondi Mirpur Road, Dacca 1205 Bangladesh. **LC** Q1; .S829. **DD** 505. **NLM** W1 BA643. **CODEN** BJSIBL. Documents available from BIOSIS Document Express, Ask*IEEE, CASDDS. ***Continues*** *Scientific Researches.*
**Ind/Abst** Biodeter. Abstr.; Biol. Abstr.; Chem. Abstr.; Dairy Sci. Abstr.; Field Crop Abstr.; Fish Rev.; Food Sci. Technol. Abstr.; Grasslands For. Abstr.; Hortic. Abstr.; Index Vet.; INSPEC (Jan./Oct. 1973-); Nutr. Abstr. Rev., Ser. B, Live Feeds and Feed.; Nutr. Abstr. Rev., Ser. A, Hum. Exp.; Plant Breed. Abstr.; Rice Abstr.; Seed Abstr.; Soils Fert.; Soyabean Abstr.; Wildl. Rev.

US/1061-5555
**BANK TECHNOLOGY REPORT.** ***Ceased.*** [Bank technol. rep.]. (1992)-(Feb. 1993). Periodical. English. mo. Warren Gorham & Lamont Inc., Park Square Building, 31 St. James Avenue, Boston MA 02116-4112. **Tel** (617)423-2020, (800)950-1207, FAX (617)423-2026. **DD** 332. ***Continues*** *Bank Operations Report, 0045-1487.*

UK/0959-6488
**BARANOOSH SCIENTIFIC QUARTERLY.** Persian (English). qt. £22.00 UK; $66.00 other. Baranoosh Scientific, PO Box 311, Cambridge CB2 3AA England. **Tel** 011 44 223 424425. **ED** N Farahati. Index available. cum. index. **Bk Rev. Ad Acc. Pr Rev. Circ:** 500.
**Desc:** A general science an technology journal with articles, reports, book reviews and research notes in Farsi (Persian).

US/0732-7706
**BASE (BERKELEY, CALIF.).** (BASE.). [Base]. Vol. 1, No. 1 (Oct. 1982)-. Periodical. English. ir. $26.00 (four issues). Alin Foundation Press, 2107 Dwight Way, Berkeley CA 94704. **Tel** (510)664-3366. **ED** K. N. Matsumura. **DD** 605. Index available. **Bk Rev. Ad Acc.** ctrl circ.
**Desc:** Publishes original research work of scientists and scientists in training under the age of 23.

FR
**BASIC SCIENCE AND TECHNOLOGY STATISTICS.** **Added/Corp** Organisation for Economic Co-Operation and Development. Scientific, Technological and Industrial Indicators Division. **VFOAT** Statistiques de Base de la Science et de la Technologie. (1991)-. English (French). be. OECD Publications and Information Center, 2 rue Andre-Pascal, 75775 Paris Cedex 16 France. **Tel** 011 33 1 45248167, US:(202)785-6323, FAX 011 33 1 45248500 OR 45248176, telex 620 160 OCDE. **LC** Q172.5.S34; B37. **DD** 338.9/26/021.

US/0145-8477
**BATTELLE TODAY.** [Battelle today]. **Added/Corp** Battelle Memorial Institute. No. 1 (Aug. 1976)-. Periodical. English. qt. Free. Battelle Office of Corporate Communications, 505 King Avenue, Columbus OH 43201. **Tel** (614)424-7818, (614)424-3889, telex 24-5454. **ED** Harry R Templeton. **CODEN** BATODH. **Bk Rev. Circ:** 35,000 (ctrl). ***Supersedes*** *Research Outlook (Columbus), 0092-1122.*
**Desc:** Focuses on advanced materials, decontamination and decommissioning, defense systems and technology, design and manufacturing engineering, electronic systems, health and environment, information systems, manufacturing systems, nuclear systems, and technical services.
**Ind/Abst** AESIS Q.; Alum. Ind. Abstr.; Bibliogr. Mission. (1990-); BioBusiness; Eng. Mater. Abstr.; Fluid Abstr., Civil Eng.; Fluid Abstr. Proc. Eng.; FLUIDEX; GeoRef; Int. Packag. Abstr.; Met. Abstr.; Nonwovens Abstr.; Pap. Board Abstr.; Pollut. Abstr. Indexes; Print. Abstr.

US
**BATTERY AND EV TECHNOLOGY NEWS.** (19??)-. English. mo. $375.00. Business Communications Inc., 25 Van Zant Street, Suite 13, Norwalk CT 06855. **Tel** (203)853-4266. available on an online database (file 636/Full-Text) from DIALOG.
**Ind/Abst** PTS Newsl. Database [Full Txt.].

US
**BEE SCIENCE REVIEW.** English. qt. $20.00. WICWAS Press, PO Box 817, Cheshire CT 06410. **Tel** (203)250-7575.

UK/0144-929X
**BEHAVIOUR & INFORMATION TECHNOLOGY.** [Behav. inf. technol.]. **VFOAT** Behaviour and Information Technology. Vol. 1, No. 1 (Jan.-Mar. 1982)-. Periodical. English. bm. $283.00 North America; £172.00 UK. Taylor & Francis Ltd., Rankine Road, Basingstoke Hampshire, RG24 8PR United Kingdom. **Tel** 011 44 256 840366, FAX 011 44 256 479438, telex 858540. **(Subscription address:** Taylor & Francis Inc., 1900 Frost Road, Suite 101, Bristol PA 19007-1598.**) ED** T. F. M. Stewart, S. J. Payne and Ahmet Cakir. **LC** QA75.5. **DD** 004/.05. **CODEN** BEITD5. **[CCC]. Pr Rev.** available on microfilm from University Microfilms International (UMI). Documents available from The Genuine Article, Ask*IEEE.
**Desc:** Deals with the human aspects of information technology in three broad areas: computing, telecommunications and office automation. Covers research and development related to the design, use and impact of information technology.
**Ind/Abst** Abstr. Hum. Comput. Interact.; Anbar Account. Finan. Abstr. [Full Txt.]; Anbar Mark. Distr. Abstr. [Full Txt.]; Anbar Top Manage. Abstr. [Full Txt.]; Compumath Citation Index [Full Cov.]; Comput. Abstr.; Comput. Rev.; Curr. Contents Soc. Behav. Sci.; Ei Page One; Ergon. Abstr.; HILITES; Inf. Sci. Abstr.; INSPEC (Jan.-March 1982); Manage. Market. Abstr.; Manage. Bibliogr. Rev.; Oper. Prod. Manage. Abstr. [Full Txt.]; Person. Train. Abstr. [Full Txt.]; Pollut. Abstr. Indexes; Psychol. Abstr. (1982-); PsycINFO (1990-); PsycLit; Res. Alert [Full Cov.]; Soc. Sci. Cit. Index [Full Cov.]; Women Manage. Rev. [Full Txt.]; World Publ. Monit.

CC/0254-0037
**BEIJING GONGYE DAXUE XUEBAO.** (PEI-CHING KUNG YEH TA HSUEH HSUEH PAO.). [Beijing gongye daxue xuebao]. **Added/Corp** Pei-Ching Kung Yeh Ta Hsueh. **VFOAT** Journal of Beijing Polytechnic University. (1975)-. Periodical. Chinese (English). **CODEN** BGDXD6. Documents available from CASDDS.
**Ind/Abst** Chem. Abstr.

CC/1001-0645
**BEIJING LIGONG DAXUE XUEBAO.** **VFOAT** Journal of Beijing Institute of Technology. (1989)-. Periodical. Chinese. qt (4 issues). $43.75 surface mail, $57.00 airmail. Beijing Ligong Daxue, (Beijing Institute of Technology), Beijing, People's Republic of China. **(Subscription address:** China Books & Periodicals Inc., 2929 24th Street, San Francisco CA 94110.**) DD** 620. Documents available from Article Express International. ***Continues*** *Pei Ching K'uang Yeh Hsueh Yuan Hsueh Pao, 0476-028X.*
**Ind/Abst** Ei Page One; Eng. Index Annu.

GW
**BEITRAEGE ZUR ALEXANDER-VON-HUMBOLDT-FORSCHUNG.** **Added/Corp** Akademie der Wissenschaften der DDR. Alexander-von-Humboldt-Forschungsstelle. (1968)-. Monographic series. German. ir. Price varies per volume. Akademie-Verlag GmbH, Muehlenstrasse 33 34, D 13162 Berlin Germany. **Tel** 011 49 30 47889300, FAX 011 49 30 47889357. **(Subscription address:** VCH Publishers Inc., 303 Northwest 12th Avenue, Journals Department, Deerfield FL 33442.**)**
**Desc:** Results from the research institute on Alexander von Humboldt of the Academy of Sciences are published, namely editions of his diaries, letters, as well as chronologies and bibliographies.

GW/0522-6570
**BEITRAEGE ZUR GESCHICHTE DER WISSENSCHAFT UND DER TECHNIK.** Vol. 1 (1961)-. Monographic series. German. ir. Price varies per volume. Franz Steiner Verlag GmbH, Postfach 101061, D 70009 Stuttgart Germany. **Tel** 011 49 0711 2582372, FAX 011 49 0711 2582290, telex 723636 daz d. **ED** Bernhard Sticker. **DD** 500; 600. ***Continues*** *Mitteilungen zur Geschichte der Medizin, der Naturwissenschaften und der Tecknik.*

HU/0522-7232
**BEKESI ELET.** (Jan. 1966)-. Periodical. Hungarian. qt. $15.50. Bekescsaba 5600, PO Box 38, Budapest Hungary. **Tel** 36 66 28 182. **ED** Andras Krupa. **DD** 943.9. Index available. cum. index. **Bk Rev. Ad Acc. Circ:** 2,000.
**Desc:** Primarily Bekes county's scientific life; historical, ethnical, geographical and educational politics are presented. Has views on the county's and neighboring county's researchers.

AU
**BERICHT.** **Main/Corp** Hohere Technische Bundes-Lehr-und Versuchsanstalt Wien I. (19??)-. German. ir. L Schellinggrasse 13, 1010 Vienna Austria. **LC** T173.V65; A2.

AU
**BERICHT DER BUNDESREGIERUNG AN DEN NATIONALRAT.** **Main/Corp** Austria. Bundesministerium fur Wissenschaft und Forschung. German. **LC** Q180.A85; A26. **DD** 338.943606. ***Continues*** *Bericht der Bundesregierung an den Nationalrat.*

GW
**BERICHT - FORSCHUNGSFORDERUNGSFONDS FUR DIE GEWERBLICHE WIRTSCHAFT.** **Main/Corp** Forschungsforderungsfonds fur die Gewerbliche Wirtschaft. German. an. Forschungsforderungsfonds der Gewerbliche Wirtschaft, Karntner Strasse 21-23, 1015 Vienna Austria. **LC** T177.A9; F682A. **DD** 330/.06/043613.

GW
**BERICHT / STIFTERVERBAND FUR DIE DEUTSCHE WISSENSCHAFT.** **Main/Corp** Stifterverband Fur die Deutsche Wissenschaft. German. an. Stifterverband fur die Deutsche Wissenschaft, Brucker Holt 56-60 Postfach 23 03 60, 4300 Essen 1 Germany. **LC** AZ664; .S82. **DD** 063/.56. ***Continues*** *Tatigkeitsbericht / Stiftenverband fur die Deutsche Wissenschaft.*

GW/0942-332X
**BERICHTE AUS TECHNIK UND WISSENSCHAFT / LINDE.** **Added/Corp** Linde Aktiengesellschaft. (1991)-. Periodical. German. Linde AG, Lincolnstrasse 21, Wiesbaden Germany. **Tel** 011 49 6112200. **LC** TP242; .L54. Documents available from CASDDS. ***Continues*** *Linde Berichte aus Technik und Wissenschaft, 0024-3728.*
**Ind/Abst** Chem. Abstr.

GW/0722-7728
**BERICHTE AUS WASSERGUTEWIRTSCHAFT UND GESUNDHEITSINGENIEURWESEN.** (BERICHTE AUS WASSERGUTEWIRTSCHAFT UND GESUNDHEITSINGENIEURSWESEN / [INSTITUT FUER BAUWESEN V] TECHNISCHE UNIVERSITAT MUNCHEN.). [Ber. Wassergutewortsch. Gesundheitsingenieurwes.]. **Added/Corp** Technische Universitat Munchen. Institut fur Bauingenieurwesen V. (1974)-. Monographic series. German. **CODEN** BWGMDW. Documents available from CASDDS.
**Ind/Abst** Chem. Abstr.

GW/0028-0917
**BERICHTE DER NATURFORSCHENDEN GESELLSCHAFT ZU FREIBURG I. BR.** [Ber. Naturforsch. Ges. Freib. i. Br]. **Main/Corp** Naturforschende Gesellschaft zu Freiburg i. B. Vol. 1 (1886)-. German. an. DM30.00. Naturforschende ges Freiburg, Universitatsbilbiothek, PF 1629, D 79016 Freiburg Germany. **ED** Narurforschende Gesellschaft zu Freiburg/Brsg. **LC** Q49; .F861. **CODEN** BEFBAZ. **Bk Rev.** ***Supersedes*** *Berichte Uber die Verhandlungen der Naturforschenden Gesellschaft zu Freiburg i. B.*
**Ind/Abst** Energy Res. Abstr. (Feb. 1982-); Life Sci. Collect.

AU/0379-1416
**BERICHTE DES NATURWISSENSCHAFTLICH-MEDIZINI SCHEN VEREINS IN INNSBRUCK.** [Ber. Naturwiss.-med. Ver. Innsb.]. **Main/Corp** Naturwissenschaftlich-Medizinischer Verein in Innsbruck. (1870)-. German (English). **LC** Q44; .I6. **DD** 574/.05. **NLM** W1 NA932. **CODEN** BNMVAN. Documents available from BIOSIS Document Express.
**Ind/Abst** Biol. Abstr.; Entomol. Abstr.; Life Sci. Collect.

GW/0170-6233
**BERICHTE ZUR WISSENSCHAFTSGESCHICHTE.** [Ber. Wissenschaftgesch.]. **Added/Corp** Gesellschaft fuer Wissenschaftsgeschichte (Germany). Vol. 1 (1978)-. Academic Scholarly Publication. German. qt. $110.00. VCH Gesellschaft GmbH, Postfach 101161, D 69451 Weinheim Germany. **Tel** 011 49 6201 606459, FAX 011 49 6201 606184. **(Subscription address:** VCH Publishers Inc., 303 Northwest 12th Avenue, Journals Department, Deerfield FL 33442.**)** **LC** Q124.6; .B45. **DD** 509. **NLM** W1 BE653. **CODEN** BEWID8. **[CCC].** Documents available from CASDDS.
**Ind/Abst** Am. Hist. Life (1988-); Chem. Abstr.; Math. Rev.; Zentralbl. Math. Ihre Grenzgeb.

IO
**BERITA ILMU PENGETAHUAN DAN TEKNOLOGI.** ***Title Change.*** **Added/Corp** Lembaga Ilmu Pengetahuan Indonesia. (19??)-(19??). Periodical. Indonesian. qt. Lembaga Ilmu Pengetahuan Indonesia, Biro Publikasi Ilmiah Lipi, Medan Merdeka Selatan No 11, Jakarta Indonesia. **LC** Q4; .L47. ***Continues*** *Lembaga Ilmu Pengetahuan Indonesia. Berita L.I.P.I.* ***Continued by*** *Berita IPTEK.*

IO/0125-9156
**BERITA IPTEK.** **Added/Corp** Lembaga Ilmu Pengetahuan Indonesia. Th. 34 No. 1 (1990)-. Periodical. Indonesian. qt. ***Continues*** *Berita ilmu Pengetahuan dan Teknologi.*

IO
**BERKALA ITB.** **Main/Corp** Institut Teknologi Bandung. Periodical. Indonesian. wk. Institut Teknologi Bandung, Jl Tamansari 64, Bandung Indonesia. **LC** T173.B127; A253. ***Continues*** *ITB.*

US/0145-0379
**BERKELEY PAPERS IN HISTORY OF SCIENCE.** [Berkeley pap. hist. sci.]. **Added/Corp** University of California, Berkeley. Office for History of Science and Technology. (1977)-. Monographic series. English. ir. Price varies per volume. Office for History of Science and Technology, University of California, 470 Stephens Hall, University of California at Berkeley, Berkeley CA 94720. **Tel** (510)642-4581, FAX (510)643-5321, telex 910 366 7114. **ED** J. L. Heilbron. **LC** UNC.
**Desc:** Bibliographical sources for historians of science.
**Ind/Abst** Math. Rev.; Zentralbl. Math. Ihre Grenzgeb.

FR/0249-762X
**BIBLIOGRAPHIE PALYNOLOGIE.** [Bibliogr. palynol.]. **VFOAT** References Bibliographiques. (1974)-. French. an. Revue Pollen et Spores, BP 2015, 34024 Montpellier Cedex 1 France. **Tel** 67 41 28 19. **LC** Z6033.P2; B476; QE993. **DD** 016.582/016.
**Ind/Abst** GeoRef.

US/0888-7551
**BIBLIOGRAPHIES AND INDEXES IN SCIENCE AND TECHNOLOGY.** [Bibliogr. indexes sci. technol.]. (1986)-. Monographic series. English. ir. Price varies per volume. Greenwood Press Inc., PO Box 5007, Westport CT 06881-5007. **Tel** (203)226-3571, FAX (203)222-1502. **DD** 500. **CODEN** BSTEEC. Documents available from BIOSIS Document Express.
**Ind/Abst** Biol. Abstr. (1988-).

US/0149-3825
**BIBLIOGRAPHY ON COLD REGIONS SCIENCE AND TECHNOLOGY.** **Added/Corp** Library of Congress. Science and Technology Division. Cold Regions Bibliography Section. Library of Congress. Science and Technology Division. Cold Regions Bibliography Project. U.S. Army Cold Regions Research and Engineering Laboratory. **VFOAT** CRREL Bibliography. Vol. 23 (1969)-. Bibliography. English. an. National Technical Information Service - NTIS, Room 2027S, 5285 Port Royal Road, Springfield VA 22161. **Tel** (703)487-4630, (703)487-4660, (703)487-4650, FAX (703)321-8547, telex 89-9405. **LC** GB2401; .U53. **DD** 016.551/0911. available on CD-ROM (Arctic and Antarctic Regions) from Department of the Army. ***Continues*** *Bibliography on Snow, Ice and Frozen Ground, with Abstracts, 0149-3817.*

US
**BIENNIAL REPORT / MONTANA SCIENCE & TECHNOLOGY ALLIANCE.** **Main/Corp** Montana Science & Technology Alliance. (1991)-. English. be. **LC** WMLC 91/671.

US/0883-1548
**BIENNIAL REPORT OF THE NEW YORK STATE SCIENCE SERVICE.** [Bienn. rep. N.Y. State Sci. Serv.]. **Main/Corp** New York (State). State Science Service. English. ir. New York State Museum, 3140 Cultural Education Center, Albany NY 12230. **Tel** (518)474-3505. **LC** Q224.3.U62; A46. **DD** 353.97470085/5. **Circ:** 1,000.

US
**BIENNIAL REPORT / UNITED STATES-ISRAEL BINATIONAL SCIENCE FOUNDATION.** **Main/Corp** United States-Israel Binational Science Foundation. 1979/1980-. Periodical. English. be. National Science Foundation, 1800 G Street Northwest, Washington DC 20550. **Tel** (202)357-9859, (202)357-9498. **LC** Q180.I78; U54A. **DD** 507.205694. ***Continues*** *United States-Israel Binational Science Foundation. Annual Report.*

GW/0006-2375
**BILD DER WISSENSCHAFT.** [Bild Wiss.]. Vol. 1 (Jan./March 1964)-. Academic Scholarly Publication. German. mo. DVA Deutsche Verlagsanstalt, Neckarstrasse 121, D-70190 Stuttgart Germany. **Tel** 011 49 711 26310. **LC** Q3; .B55. **CODEN** BIWIAX. **[CCC].** Documents available from CASDDS.
**Ind/Abst** Chem. Abstr.; Coal Abstr.; EMBASE; Energy Res. Abstr.; GeoRef; Numis. Lit.

GW/0177-4212
**BILDUNG UND WISSENSCHAFT.** **Added/Corp** Inter Nationes. **VFOAT** Education and Science in the Federal Republic of Germany. (1972)-. Periodical. English (German). Four times a year. Free on request. Inter Nationes EV, Postfach 200749, D 53137 Bonn Germany. **Tel** 11 49 2288801, FAX 11 49 228 880355, telex 228308. **ED** Ivan Tapia. **LC** L31; .B542. **Bk Rev. Circ:** 10,000 (ctrl). ***Continues*** *Education in Germany.*
**Desc:** Publication covering education and science.

JA/0910-6545
**BIO INDUSTRY.** [Bio ind.]. **VFOAT** Baio Indasutori. (198?)-. Periodical. mo. $823.50. Shi Emu Shi, (CMC Co., Ltd.), Miyako Biru, 5-4, Uchikanda, 1 Chome, Chiyodaku, Tokyoto 101 Japan. **CODEN** BIINEG. Documents available from CASDDS.
**Ind/Abst** Chem. Abstr.

US/0733-222X
**BIO/TECHNOLOGY (NEW YORK, N.Y. 1983).** (BIO/TECHNOLOGY.). [Bio/technology]. **Added/Corp** Nature Publishing Company. **VFOAT** Biotechnology; Bio Technology. Vol. 1, No. 1 (March 1983)-. Academic Scholarly Publication. English (Japanese). Twelve times a year (plus annual Buyer's Guide). $195.00 US; £125.00 other. Nature Publishing Company, 65 Bleecker Street, 12th Floor, New York NY 10012. **Tel** (212)477-9600, (800)524-0328, FAX (212)477-8020. **(Subscription address:** Bio Technology, PO Box 1721, Riverton NJ 08077.**)** **ED** Douglas K. McCormick Biauy, Jennifer van Brunt, and Arthur Klavsner. **LC** TP248.3; .B557. **DD** 660/.6/05. **CODEN** BTCHDA. **[CCC].** Index available. cum. index. **Bk Rev. Ad Acc. Pr Rev. Circ:** 20,000 (ctrl). available on microfilm and microfiche from University Microfilms International (UMI); available on an online database (file 16/Full-Text) from DIALOG. Documents available from The Genuine Article, BIOSIS Document Express, CASDDS.
**Desc:** International journal with original research papers specifically-designed for biotechnologists. It also contains news, features, evaluations and original research by top experts.
**Ind/Abst** Abstr. Bull. Inst. Pap. Sci. Tech.; AgBiotech News Inf.; AGRICOLA [Select. Cov.]; Anim. Breed. Abstr.; Biodeter. Abstr. (19??-19??); Biol. Abstr.; Biotechnol. Res. Abstr.; Chem. Abstr. (1983-); Chem. Ind. Notes; CSA Neuro. Abstr. (?-?); Curr. Aware. Biol. Sci., CABS; Curr. Biotechnol.; Dairy Sci. Abstr.; EMBASE; Energy Res. Abstr. (March 1983-); F&S Index Plus Text, Int. [Select. Cov.]; Field Crop Abstr.; Food Sci. Technol. Abstr.; Foods Adlibra; For. Abstr.; Genet. Abstr.; Immunol. Abstr.; Index Vet.; INIS Atomindex [Micro.]; Maize Abstr.; Microbiol. Abstr. Sect. B; Microbiol. Abstr. Sect. A; Microbiol. Abstr. Sect. C; Nutr. Abstr. Rev., Ser. A, Hum. Exp.; Life Sci. Collect. (1985-); PESTDOC; Plant Breed. Abstr.; Plant Grow. Reg. Abstr.; Potato Abstr.; Poult. Abstr.; PROMT [Full Txt.]; Protozoolog. Abstr.; Res. Alert [Full Cov.]; Rev. Agric. Entomol.; Rev. Med. Vet. Entomol.; Rev. Plant Pathol.; Rice Abstr.; Sci. Cit. Index; SCISEARCH; Soc. Sci. Cit. Index [Select. Cov.]; Soyabean Abstr.; Weed Abstr.; Wheat Barley Trit. Abstr.

US/0077-2933
**BIOGRAPHICAL MEMOIRS.** **See** Biographies.

II/0376-6632
**BIOGRAPHICAL MEMOIRS OF FELLOWS OF THE INDIAN NATIONAL SCIENCE ACADEMY.** **See** Biographies.

BE
**BIOGRAPHIE NATIONALE. SUPPLEMENT : PUBLIEE PAR L'ACADEMIE ROYALE DES SCIENCES, DES LETTRES ET DES BEAUX-ARTS DE BELGIQUE.** **See** Biographies.

UK/0272-054X
**BIOLOGICAL SCIENCE TEXTS.** [Biol. sci. texts]. English. John Wiley & Sons Ltd., Baffins Lane, Chichester West Sussex PO19 1UD England. **Tel** 0243 779777, FAX 0243 776128 BTG:JWP001, telex 86290 WIBOOKG. **(Subscription address:** North, South and Central America/ John Wiley & Sons, Inc., Subscription Department, 605 Third Avenue, New York, NY 10158-0012, USA; telephone: (212)850-6645; FAX: (212)850-6021**)**

US/1064-251X
**BIOPROBES (EUGENE, OR.).** (BIOPROBES.). [Bioprobes]. **Added/Corp** Molecular Probes, Inc. (1985)-. Newsletter. English. Three times a year. Free on request. Molecular Probes, Inc., PO Box 22010, Eugene OR 97402-0414. **Tel** (503)465-8300, FAX (503)344-6504. **ED** Iain Johnson. **DD** 574. **Ad Acc. Circ:** 40,000 (ctrl).
**Desc:** Contains technical information on research products.

BE/1016-6505
**BIOTECH PRODUCTS INTERNATIONAL.** **VFOAT** BPI. Biotech Products International. (1989)-. Periodical. English. ir (7 issues per year). $95.00. Pan European Publishing Company, rue Verte 216, 1210 Brussels 21 Belgium. **Tel** 011 32 2 2420611. **(Subscription address:** Elsevier Librico NV, Div Pepco Groenstraat 216, 1210 Brussels 21 Belgium**)** **ED** Bas van Oosterhout and Sarah Soukias-Meredith. **UDC** 578. **Bk Rev. Ad Acc. Circ:** 30,000.
**Ind/Abst** Abstr. BioCommer.

US/1058-0239
**BIOTREATMENT NEWS.** [Biotreat. news]. (1990)-. Periodical. English (summaries and/or abstracts in Japanese). mo. $170.00 US; $180.00 Canada and Mexico; $195.00 other. Devo Enterprise Inc., 1003 K Street Northwest, Suite 501, Washington DC 20001-4425. **Tel** (202)393-7545, FAX (202)393-7546. **ED** Katherine Devine. **DD** 604. **Ad Acc, Adv Mgr:** E. Card, **Tel** same as publisher. **Circ:** 500.
**Desc:** Industry, government , and academic information on full scale, pilot, and research activities concerning the use of microorganisms and other biologicals, for treatment of hazardous, petroleum and industrial waste.

IS
**BIRZEIT RESEARCH REVIEW.** **VFOAT** Nashrat Abhath Bir Zayt. Vol. 1, No. 1 (Spring 1985)-. Periodical. English (Arabic). qt. Birzeit University Research Centre, PO Box 14, Birzeit West Bank Via Israel.
**Ind/Abst** Middle East J. (?-?).

US/0893-1348
**BISHOP MUSEUM OCCASIONAL PAPERS.** [Bishop Mus. occas. pap.]. **Added/Corp** Bernice Pauahi Bishop Museum. Vol. 26 (May 1986)-. Monographic series. English. an. Price varies per volume. Bishop Museum Press, PO Box 19000-A, Honolulu HI 96817. **Tel** (808)847-3511. **LC** QH198.H3; B45. **DD** 996.9/005. **CODEN** BMOPEC. Index available. Documents available from BIOSIS Document Express. ***Continues*** *Occasional Papers of Bernice P. Bishop Museum, 0067-6160.*
**Desc:** Presents original contributions in all phases of anthropology, history, botany, entomology, and zoology.
**Ind/Abst** Biol. Abstr. (1986-); GeoRef (1986-); Rev. Agric. Entomol.

RU/0202-5442
**BIULLETEN MEZHDUNARODNYKH NAUCHNYKH SEZDOV, KONFERENTSII, KONGRESSOV, VYSTAVOK / VSESOIUZNYI INSTITUT NAUCHNOI I TEKHNICHESKOI INFORMATSII, MEZHDUNARODNYI TSENTR NAUCHNOI I TEKHNICHESKOI INFORMATSII.** **Added/Corp** Vsesoiuznyi Institut Nauchnoi i Tekhnicheskoi Informatsii (Soviet Union) International Centre for Scientific and Technical Information. (1977)-. Periodical. Russian. bm. $17.00. VINITI - Vsesoyuznyi Institut Nauchno-Tekhnicheskoi Informatsii, All-Union Scientific and Technical Information Institute, Baltiiskaia Ulitsa 14, 125219 Moscow Russia. **Tel** 238-46-00, FAX 9430060, telex 411160. **(Subscription address:** Victor Kamkin, 4956 Boiling Brook Parkway, Rockville MD 20852.) **LC** AS8; .B56. ***Continues*** *Biulleten Mezhdunarodnykh Nauchnykh Sezdov, Konferentsii i Kongressov.*

AU/0067-9127
**BLAETTER FUER TECHNIKGESCHICHTE.** [Bl. Tech.gesch.]. **Main/Corp** Vienna. Forschungsinstitut fuer Technikgeschichte. **Added/Corp** Forschungsinstitut fuer Technikgeschichte in Wien. Vol. 6 (1939)-. Monographic series. German. ir. Price varies per volume. Springer-Verlag New York Inc., 175 5th Avenue, New York NY 10010. **Tel** (212)460-1500, telex 232 235 SPB UR. **(Subscription address:** Springer Verlag New York Inc. / for North America, 44 Hartz Way, Secaucus NJ 07096.) **LC** T15.A1; V54. ***Continues*** *Blaetter fuer Geschichte der Technik, 0178-143X.*
**Ind/Abst** Am. Hist. Life (1963-).

●US
**BLAST : THE BULLETIN OF LAW/SCIENCE & TECHNOLOGY / AMERICAN BAR ASSOCIATION, SECTION OF SCIENCE AND TECHNOLOGY.** **See** Law.

GW
**BMFT FORDERUNGSKATALOG.** **Main/Corp** Germany (West). Bundesministerium fur Forschung und Technologie. German. Deutscher Bundesverlag GmbH, Postfach 12 03 80, 5300 Bonn 1 Germany. **LC** T177.G4; G47A.

GW/0724-0856
**BMFT-JOURNAL.** **VFOAT** Bundesministerium fuer Forschung und Technologie Journal. (1983)-. Periodical. German. Free. Deutscher Bundesverlag GmbH, Postfach 12 03 80, 5300 Bonn 1 Germany. **UDC** 354.32(430.1)001.
**Desc:** Government publication covering events, information on research and technology.

UK/0263-3167
**BOILING POINT.** **Added/Corp** Intermediate Technology Development Group. Fuel for Food Programme. Intermediate Technology Development Group. German Appropriate Technology Exchange. Deutsche Gesellschaft fuer Technische Zusammenarbeit. (19??)-. Periodical. English. qt. £12.00. Intermediate Technology Publishing Ltd., 103-104 Southampton Row, London WC1B 4HH England. **Tel** 011 44 71 436 9761, FAX 011 44 71 436 2013, telex 268312.

PO/0304-5196
**BOLETIM - INSTITUTO DO AZEITE E PRODUTOS OLEAGINOSOS.** [Bol. - inst. azeite prod. oleaginosos]. **Main/Corp** Instituto do Azeite e Produtos Oleaginoso. Yearly V. 1- Jan./June 1973-. Bulletin. Portuguese. Instituto do Azeite e Produtos Oleaginosos, Av de Sidonio Pais 10 10 1, Lisbon Portugal. **LC** TP670; .I636A.
**Ind/Abst** Food Sci. Technol. Abstr.

BL/0100-1949
**BOLETIM TECNICO CEPED.** (BOLETIM TECNICO.). [Bol. tec. CEPED]. Began in 1974. Academic Scholarly Publication. Portuguese. sa. Centro de Pesquisas e Desenvolvimento Ceped Gerencia de Desenvolvimento, Caixa Postal 09, Camacari Bahia Brazil. **LC** T4; .B59. **CODEN** BTCPDY. Documents available from CASDDS.
**Ind/Abst** Chem. Abstr.

EC
**BOLETIN DE INFORMACIONES CIENTIFICAS NACIONALES.** ***Suspended.*** **Added/Corp** Casa de la Cultura Ecuatoriana. Secciones Cientificas. (1947)-(19??). Periodical. Spanish. mo. Casa de la Cultura Ecuatoriana, Nucleo del Azuay, Aptdo. 01-01-4907, Cuenca, Ecuador. **Tel** 593 2 565808, 565721. **LC** Q4; .B6. **NLM** W1 BO236.

SP/0212-9051
**BOLETIN DE LA ACADEMIA GALEGA DE CIENCIAS.** ***Title Change.*** [Bol. Acad. Galega Cienc.]. **Added/Corp** Academia Galega de Ciencias. (1982)-(19??). Periodical. Spanish (English and Romance). **CODEN** BAGCEJ. Documents available from CASDDS. ***Continued by*** *Revista (Santiago de Compostela, Spain).*
**Ind/Abst** Chem. Abstr. (?-?).

AG/0325-2051
**BOLETIN DE LA ACADEMIA NACIONAL DE CIENCIAS.** [Bol. Acad. nac. cienc.]. **Main/Corp** Academia Nacional de Ciencias (Argentina). Vol. 1 (1874)-. Academic Scholarly Publication. Spanish. Four times a year. $15.00 Argentina; $35.00 other. Acad Nacional Ciencias Argentina, Casilla de Correo 36, 5000 Cordoba Argentina. **Tel** 29687. **NLM** W1 AC222. **CODEN** BANCAG. cum. index. Documents available from CASDDS.
**Ind/Abst** Chem. Abstr.; Coal Abstr.; GeoRef; Life Sci. Collect.

UY
**BOLETIN ORCYT / OFICINA REGIONAL DE CIENCIA Y TECNOLOGIA DE LA UNESCO PARA AMERICA LATINA Y EL CARIBE.** **Added/Corp** Unesco. Regional Office for Science and Technology for Latin America and the Caribbean. (198?)-. Periodical. Spanish. Oficina Regional de Ciencia y Tecnologia Para America, Latina y el Caribe, Bulevar Artigas 1320-24, Casilla de Correo 859, Montevideo Uruguay. ***Continues*** *Boletin ROSTLAC.*

UY
**BOLETIN ROSTLAC / OFICINA REGIONAL DE CIENCIA Y TECNOLOGIA DE LA UNESCO PARA AMERICA LATINA Y EL CARIBE.** ***Title Change.*** **Added/Corp** Unesco. Regional Office for Science and Technology for Latin America and the Caribbean. No. 21 (1981)-(198?). Periodical. Spanish (English). Oficina Regional de Ciencia y Tecnologia Para America, Latina y el Caribe, Bulevar Artigas 1320-24, Casilla de Correo 859, Montevideo Uruguay. **LC** Q33; .U47. **DD** 509.8. ***Continues*** *Unesco. Regional Office for Science and Technology for Latin America and the Caribbean. Boletin.* ***Continued by*** *Boletin ORCYT.*

CR/0574-203X
**BOLETIN TECNICO / INTER-AMERICAN INSTITUTE OF AGRICULTURAL SCIENCES.** **See** Agriculture.

CK
**BOLETIN - UNIVERSIDAD LIBRE, SECCIONAL DE PEREIRA, CENTRO DE INVESTIGACIONES.** **Main/Corp** Colombia. Universidad Libre, Pereira. Centro de Investigaciones. Periodical. Spanish. Universidad Libre Seccional de Pereira, Centro de Investigaciones, Apartado Aereo 1330, Pereira Colombia.

IT
**BOLLETTINO DELL'ACCADEMIA GIOENIA DI SCIENZE NATURALI.** **Added/Corp** Accademia Gioenia di Scienze Naturali in Catania. Vol. 15 No. 319 (1982)-. Periodical. Italian (summaries and/or abstracts in English). sa. **CODEN** BAGNEI. Documents available from BIOSIS Document Express. ***Continues*** *Accademia Gioenia di Scienze Naturali in Catania. Bollettino Delle Sedute Della Accademia Gioenia di Scienze Naturali in Catania.*
**Ind/Abst** Biol. Abstr. (1985-1988).

IT/0392-3789
**BOLLETTINO DI LEGISLAZIONE TECNICA.** [Boll. legis. tec.]. (1933)-. Periodical. Italian. Nine times a year. L150,000 (includes supplement), L100,000 (without supplement), L180,000 (comes with Edizioni Legislazione Tecnica). Bollettino Legislazione Tec, Via Dell Architettura 16, 00144 Rome Italy. **Tel** 011 39 6 5911803, FAX 39 6 5921068. **UDC** 34:62. Index available (Dec.). cum. index. **Ad Acc. Circ:** 25,000. ***Absorbed*** *Legislazione e Normativa delle Costruzioni, 0392-503X.*
**Desc:** Contains law, decrees, norms, regulations civil engineers jurisprudence.

NE/0068-0346
**BOSTON STUDIES IN THE PHILOSOPHY OF SCIENCE.** [Boston stud. philos. sci.]. (1961/62)-. Monographic series. English. ir. Price varies. Kluwer Academic Publishers, Postbus 322, 3300 AH Dordrecht, The Netherlands. **Tel** 011 (31) 78 524400, FAX 011 31 78 183273, telex 20083. **LC** Q174; .B67. **CODEN** BPSCDD. Documents available from BIOSIS Document Express.
**Ind/Abst** Biol. Abstr. (-1980); Math. Rev.

GW
**BOUNDARY ELEMENTS.** (19??)-. Monographic series. English. ir. Price varies per volume. Springer-Verlag GmbH & Company KG, Heidelberger Platz 3, D 14197 Berlin Germany. **Tel** 011 49 30 8207223, FAX 011 49 30 8214091, telex 183 319 SPBLN D. **(Subscription address:** Springer Verlag New York Inc. / for North America, 44 Hartz Way, Secaucus NJ 07096.) **ED** Carlos A. Brebbia.
**Ind/Abst** Zentralbl. Math. Ihre Grenzgeb.

NE/0166-6363
**BOUWEN MET STAAL.** [Bouwen staal]. (1967)-. Periodical. Dutch. qt (Mar., June, Sept., Dec.). Fl77.50. Centrum Staal, Postbus 29076, 3001 GB Rotterdam Netherlands. **Tel** 011 31 10 4110433. **UDC** 669.14 + 693.8.

GW/0934-683X
**BR. BAUSTOFF-RECYCLING + DEPONIETECHNIK.** **VFOAT** BR. Baustoff-Recycling und Deponietechnik; Baustoff-Recycling + Deponietechnik. (1987)-. Periodical. German. bm (6 regular issues, 1 international issue and 1 special issue). DM162.00. Stein Verlag GmbH, Josef Herrmann Strasse 1-3, W-7557 Iffezheim FR Germany. **Tel** 011 49 7229 6060. **UDC** 69 :628.477.6.

US/1049-5312
**BRADYLINE.** (BRADYLINE : INSIGHTS INTO TOMORROW'S TECHNOLOGY FROM THE AUTHORS AND EDITORS OF BRADY BOOKS.). [BradyLine]. **VFOAT** Brady Line. (1990)-. Periodical. English. qt. Free. Prentice-Hall General Reference and Travel, 200 Old Tappan Road, Old Tappan NJ 07675. **Tel** (800)922-0579. **DD** 004.

UK
**BRAILLE SCIENCE JOURNAL.** **See** Physically Impaired.

GW
**BRASILIEN, FORSCHUNGSPOLITIK UNE FORSCHUNGSPRAXIS / BUNDESSTELLE FUER AUSSENHANDELSINFORMATION.** German. an. 3.00. Bundesstelle fuer Aussenhandelsinformation, Agrippastr 87 93, D 50676 Cologne Germany. **Tel** 011 49 221 2057316, FAX 011 49 221 2057212. **LC** Q180.B7; B66. **DD** 507/.2081.

UK/0007-0874
**BRITISH JOURNAL FOR THE HISTORY OF SCIENCE, THE.** [Br. j. hist. sci.]. **Added/Corp** British Society for the History of Science. **VFOAT** BJHS. Vol. 1 (June 1962)-. Academic Scholarly Publication. English. Four times a year (March, June, September and December). $140.00 US, Canada & Mexico; £80.00 other. Cambridge University Press, The Edinburgh Building, Shaftesbury Road, Cambridge CB2 2RU United Kingdom. **Tel** 011 44 223 312393, FAX 011 44 223 325959. **(Subscription address:** Cambridge University Press / North America, 110 Midland Avenue, Port Chester NY 10573.) **ED** John Brooke. **LC** Q125; .B77. **NLM** W1 BR472. **CODEN** BJHSAT. **[CCC]. Bk Rev. Ad Acc. Pr Rev. Circ:** 1,470. available on microfilm and microfiche from University Microfilms International (UMI). Documents available from The Genuine Article, BIOSIS Document Express, Ask*IEEE, UMI Article Clearinghouse, CASDDS. ***Continues*** *Bulletin of the British Society for the History of Science, 0950-5636.*
**Desc:** The official journal of the British Society for the History of Science. Publishes papers and review articles on all aspects of the history of science. Coverage is not restricted to any particular period or branch of science, and the importance of philosophical, socio-economic and political factors in scientific development is given full weight. There are regular special issues.
**Ind/Abst** Acad. Search (Jan. 1994-); Am. Hist. Life (1962-); Arts Humanit. Citation Index [Full Cov.]; Biol. Abstr.; Br. Humanit. Index; Chem. Abstr.; Curr. Contents Arts Humanit.; Curr. Contents Soc. Behav. Sci.; Expand. Acad. Index (1989-); Gen. Sci. Source (Jul. 1993-); GeoRef; Humanit. Index; Humanit. Source (Jul. 1993-); INFO-SOUTH Abstr.; INSPEC (March 1974-); Math. Rev.; Middle East Abstr. Index; Newsp. Period. Abstr. (1991-); Life Sci. Collect.; Res. Alert [Full Cov.]; Romant. Move.; Soc. Sci. Cit. Index [Full Cov.]; Zentralbl. Math. Ihre Grenzgeb.

UK/0007-0882
**BRITISH JOURNAL FOR THE PHILOSOPHY OF SCIENCE, THE.** [Br. j. philos. sci.]. **Added/Corp** British Society for the Philosophy of Science. British Society for the History of Science. Philosophy of Science Group. Vol. 1, No. 1 (May 1950)-. Periodical. English. qt. £35.00 UK and Europe; $72.00 other. Oxford University Press, Walton Street, Oxford OX2 6DP England. **Tel** 011 44 865 56767, FAX 011 44 865 267773, telex 837330 OXPRES G. **(Subscription address:** Oxford University Press, PO Box 417, Oxford OX2 6YS England; telephone: 011 44 865 56767) **ED** Greg Hunt. **LC** Q175; .B787. **DD** 501. **NLM** W1 BR475. **CODEN** BJPIA5. **[CCC].** Index available. cum. index. **Bk Rev. Ad Acc. Pr Rev. Circ:** 1,600. available on microfilm and microfiche from University Microfilms International (UMI). Documents available from The Genuine Article, Ask*IEEE, UMI Article Clearinghouse.
**Desc:** Study of the logic, the method, and the philosophy of science as well as those of the various special sciences, including the social sciences.
**Ind/Abst** Acad. Search (July 1993-); Arts Humanit. Citation Index [Full Cov.]; Br. Humanit. Index; Contents Pages Manage.; Curr. Contents Arts Humanit.; Curr. Contents Life Sci.; Curr. Contents Phys. Chem. Earth Sci.; Curr. Contents Soc. Behav. Sci.; Curr. Lit. Sci. Sci.; Expand. Acad. Index (1989-); Gen. Sci. Source (Jul.

1993-); Humanit. Index; Humanit. Source (Jul. 1993-); INFO-SOUTH Abstr.; INSPEC (Dec. 1973-); Math. Rev.; Newsp. Period. Abstr. (1991-); Life Sci. Collect.; Philos. Index; Res. Alert [Full Cov.]; Sci. Cit. Index; SCISEARCH; Soc. Sci. Cit. Index [Full Cov.]; Stat. Theory Method Abstr. (1967-1970); Zentralbl. Math. Ihre Grenzgeb.

US
**BROOKHAVEN BULLETIN / BROOKHAVEN NATIONAL LABORATORY.** **Added/Corp** Brookhaven National Laboratory. (19??)-. Bulletin. English. wk. Brookhaven National Laboratory, Associated Universities Inc., Upton NY 11973. **Tel** (212)620-8000.
**Ind/Abst** Energy Inf. Abstr.

US/0896-3045
**BROWNING NEWSLETTER (BURLINGTON, VT.), THE.** (THE BROWNING NEWSLETTER.). [Browning newsl.]. (197?)-. Newsletter. English. mo. $225.00. Fraser Management Association, PO Box 494, Burlington VT 05402. **Tel** (802)658-0322, FAX (802)658-0260. **DD** 304.

US/1053-7430
**BROWN'S DIRECTORY OF INSTRUCTIONAL PROGRAMS (7-12). SCIENCE/HEALTH.** (BROWN'S DIRECTORY OF INSTRUCTIONAL PROGRAMS (7-12). SCIENCE/HEALTH / PREPARED AND COMPILED BY BROWN PUBLISHING NETWORK.). [Brown's dir. instr. programs (7-12), Sci./health]. **Added/Corp** Brown Publishing Network. **VFOAT** Directory of Instructional Programs (7-12). Science/Health; Science/Health; Science, Health. (1991)-. Directory. English. an. $99.75. Association for Supervision and Curriculum Development, 1250 North Pitt Street, Alexandria VA 22314-1453. **Tel** (703)549-9110, FAX (703)549-3891, (703)836-7921. **LC** Q183.3.A1; B77. **DD** 507.1/2.

US/1053-7384
**BROWN'S DIRECTORY OF INSTRUCTIONAL PROGRAMS (K-8). SCIENCE/HEALTH / PREPARED AND COMPILED BY BROWN PUBLISHING NETWORK.** **See** Education-Teaching and Curriculum.

UK
**BSHS MONOGRAPHS.** **Main/Corp** British Society for the History of Science. **VFOAT** B.S.H.S. Monographs. (1979)-. Monographic series. English. ir. Price varies per volume. British Society for the History of Science, 31 High Street, Stanford in the Vale, Faringdon, Oxon SN7 8LH England. **ED** Paul Weindling (Address: Wellcome Institute for the History of Medicine, 45-47 Banbury Road, Oxford, OX2 6PE England).
**Desc:** Aims to promote and further the study of the history and philosophy of science.

UK/0144-6347
**BSHS NEWSLETTER.** [BSHS newsl.]. **VFOAT** British Society for the History of Science Newsletter. (1980)-. Newsletter. English. tq (Feb., Jun., Oct.). £6.00. British Society for the History of Science, 31 High Street, Stanford in the Vale, Faringdon, Oxon SN7 8LH England.
**Desc:** Reports on meetings, scientific anniversaries, appointments and awards, exhibitions, new journals, etc.

TH/0857-1554
**BUFFALO JOURNAL.** [Buffalo J.]. (1985)-. Periodical. English. Three times a year (Apr., Aug., Dec.). $45.00 Southeast Asia; $55.00 others. Research Centre for Bioscience in Animal Reproduction/ Faculty of Veterinary Science, Chulalongkorn University, Bangkok 10500 Thailand. **Tel** 011 66 2518936, FAX 011 66 2553910, telex 20217. **ED** Professor Maneewan Kamonpatana. **DD** 636.293. Index available. cum. index. ctrl circ.
**Desc:** Information related to buffalo science.
**Ind/Abst** Helminthol. Abstr. (1991-); Index Vet.; Sug. Indus. Abstr.; Vet. Bull.

SJ
**BUHUTH, EL.** **VFOAT** Periodical Review. V. 1-. English (English). National Council for Research, PO Box 321, Khartoum Sudan. **LC** Q91.S73; B84. **DD** 505.

RM
**BULETINUL SIINTIFIC SI TEHNIC AL INSTITUTULUI POLITEHNIC "TRAIAN VUIA" TIMISOARA. SERIA ELECROTEHNICA.** **Added/Corp** Institutul Politehnic "Traian Vuia" Timisoara. **VFOAT** Buletinul Stiintific Si Tehnic Al Institutului Politehnic Traian Vuia Timisoara. Electrotehnica; Seria Electrotehnica. (19??)-. Periodical. English (French and German; summaries and/or abstracts in French, German and Romanian). **(Subscription address:** Ilexim Press Department, PO Box 1, 136-1-137, Bucharest, Romania.**)** **LC** TK4; .B7625.

RM
**BULETINUL UNIVERSITATII DIN BRASOV. SERIA C : MATEMATICA, FIZICA, CHIMIE, STIINTE NATURALE.** **Main/Corp** Universitatea Din Brasov. (19??)-. Academic Scholarly Publication. Multiple languages (English, French and Romanian). an. $68.00 US. **(Subscription address:** Rodipet SA, Societatea Romana de Difuzare a Presei si Tipariturilor, Bucuresti Piata Pressei Libere Nr. 1 Sector 1, PO Box 33-57, Bucharest Romania.**)** **LC** Q49; .U5a. **DD** 505. **CODEN** BUBCDV. Documents available from CASDDS.
**Ind/Abst** Chem. Abstr.; Math. Rev.; Zentralbl. Math. Ihre Grenzgeb.

IO
**BULLETIN.** **Main/Corp** Lembaga Ilmu Pengetahuan Indonesia. (19??)-. Bulletin. English. Djalan Raden Saleh 43, Djakarta Indonesia. **LC** AS522.M3; A15. ***Continues*** *Bulletin (Madjelis Ilmu Pengetahuan).*

YU/0352-5740
**BULLETIN - ACADEMIE SERBE DES SCIENCES ET DES ARTS, CLASSE DES SCIENCES NATURELLES ET MATHEMATIQUES. SCIENCES NATURELLES.** [Bull. - Acad. serbe sci. arts, Cl. sci. nat. math., Sci. nat.]. **Main/Corp** Srpska Akademija Nauka i Umetnosti. Odeljenje Prirodno-Matematickih Nauka. **VFOAT** Sciences Naturelles. No 16 (1977)-. Bulletin. French (English, German and Serbo-Croatian (Roman)). **NLM** W1 BU478P. **CODEN** BASNA6. Documents available from BIOSIS Document Express, CASDDS. ***Continues*** *Srpska Akademija Nauka i Umetnosti. Odeljenje Prirodno-Matematickih Nauka. Bulletin - Academie Serbe des Sciences et des Arts, Classe des Sciences Mathematiques et Naturelles. Sciences Naturelles.*
**Ind/Abst** Biol. Abstr.; Chem. Abstr.

CN/0383-5359
**BULLETIN / ALBERTA RESEARCH COUNCIL.** ***Suspended.*** [Bull. - Alta. Res. Counc.]. **Added/Corp** Alberta Research Council. **VFOAT** Alberta Research Council Bulletin. 31 (1975)-Suspended (19??). Monographic series. English. ir. Research Council of Alberta, 303A Provincial Building, Red Deer Alberta T4N6K8 Canada. **Tel** (403)450-5111, (403)450-5408, FAX (403)450-5477. **LC** Q180.C2; R34. **DD** 557.123. **CODEN** BARCD5. ctrl circ. Documents available from Petroleum Abstracts Document Delivery Service. ***Continues*** *Research Council of Alberta. Bulletin, 0034-5172.*
**Ind/Abst** Ei Page One; GeoRef; Pet. Abstr.

CN/0820-7941
**BULLETIN (ALBERTA TEACHERS' ASSOCIATION. SCIENCE COUNCIL).** (BULLETIN / SCIENCE COUNCIL OF THE ALBERTA TEACHERS' ASSOCIATION.). [Bull. - Sc. Counc. Alta. Teach. Assoc.]. Bulletin. English. Three times a year. 20.00Can$ with Alberta Science Teacher subscription. Alberta Teachers Association, 11010-142 Street, Barnett House, Edmonton Alberta T5N 2R1 Canada. **Tel** (403)453-2411. **DD** 507/.107123. **Bk Rev.** **Circ:** 820 (ctrl).

CN/0708-1502
**BULLETIN CAN/OLE.** ***Title Change.*** [Bull. CAN/OLE]. **Main/Corp** Canada Institute for Scientific and Technical Information. **VFOAT** Bulletin CAN/OLE. **VAT** Bulletin Canadian on Line Enquiry. Vol. 1 (Jan. 1976)-Vol. 4, No. 1 (Feb. 1984). Bulletin. English (French). Six times a year. Canada Institute for Scientific and Technical Information, National Research Council of Canada, Ottawa Ontario K1A 0S2 Canada. **Tel** (613)993-3736, telex 053-3115. ***Continued by*** *CAN/OLE Bulletin, 0838-2883.*

CN/0381-5838
**BULLETIN - CANADIAN SOCIETY OF LABORATORY TECHNOLOGISTS.** [Bull. - Can. Soc. Lab. Technol.]. **Main/Corp** Canadian Society of Laboratory Technologists. Vol. 4, No. 1 (Jan./Feb. 1976)-. Bulletin. English (French). qt. 18.00Can$ Canada; 20.00Can$ other. Canadian Society of Laboratory Technologists, Box 2830 LCD 1, Hamilton Ontario L8N 3N8 Canada. **Tel** (905)528-8642, FAX (905)528-4968. **ED** Kurt Davis. **DD** 610.69/53/05. **Ad Acc.** **Circ:** 22,500 (ctrl). ***Continues*** *Canadian Society of Laboratory Technologists. News Bulletin, 0381-5846.*
**Desc:** Professional organization newsletter - applicable to Canadian Society of Laboratory Technologist members only.

JA/0578-2228
**BULLETIN - CHUO DAIGAKU, TOKYO. FACULTY OF SCIENCE AND ENGINEERING.** **See** Engineering.

US/0070-1416
**BULLETIN (CRANBROOK INSTITUTE OF SCIENCE).** ***Suspended.*** (BULLETIN.). **Added/Corp** Cranbrook Institute of Science. No. 1 (1931)-(19??). Bulletin. English. ir. Price varies per volume. Cranbrook Institute of Science, 500 Lone Pine Road, Bloomfield Hills MI 48013. **Tel** (313)645-3203, FAX (313)645-6545. **ED** C Jeryan. **LC** Q11; .C95. **DD** 505. ctrl circ. Documents available from BIOSIS Document Express.
**Desc:** A monographic series for both a scholarly and popular audience. Topics covered focus on the natural sciences and archaeology of the Great Lakes region.
**Ind/Abst** Biol. Abstr.

BE/0001-4141
**BULLETIN DE LA CLASSE DES SCIENCES. ACADEMIE ROYALE DE BELGIQUE.** (BULLETIN DE LA CLASSE DES SCIENCES.). [Bull. Cl. sci., Acad. r. Belg.]. **VFOAT** Bulletins de la Classe des Sciences; Mededelingen van de Afdeeling Wetenschappen; Mededelingen van de Klasse der Wetenschappen; Mededelingen van de Klasse der Wetenschappen. Series 4, 1899-1910; Series 5, Vol. 1-. Bulletin. French. mo. **LC** AS242; .B311. **NLM** W1 AC443D. **CODEN** BCSAAF. Index available in last issue of volume--attached. cum. index. **Circ:** 500 (ctrl). Documents available from BIOSIS Document Express, Ask*IEEE. ***Continues in part*** *Bulletins de l'Academie Royale des Sciences, des Lettres et des Beaux-Arts de Belgique.*
**Ind/Abst** Biol. Abstr.; GeoRef; INSPEC (1968-1969, 1983-); Int. Aerosp. Abstr.; Math. Rev.; Surf. Treat. Technol. Abstr.; Zentralbl. Math. Ihre Grenzgeb.

FR/0989-3059
**BULLETIN DE LA SOCIETE DES AMIS DE LA BIBLIOTHEQUE DE L'ECOLE POLYTECHNIQUE.** (1987)-. Bulletin. French. **UDC** 02.
**Ind/Abst** Zentralbl. Math. Ihre Grenzgeb.

FR/0153-9175
**BULLETIN DE LA SOCIETE D'ETUDES SCIENTIFIQUES DE L'AUDE.** [Bull. Soc. etud. sci. Aude]. (1890)-. Periodical. French. **UDC** 5.
**Ind/Abst** BHA : Biblio. Hist. Art.

FR/0037-9441
**BULLETIN DE LA SOCIETE INDUSTRIELLE DE MULHOUSE.** [Bull. Soc. ind. Mulhouse]. **Added/Corp** Societe Industrielle de Mulhouse (France). (1828)-. Bulletin. French. qt. 330.00F France; 360.00F other. Societe Industrielle de Mulhouse, 10 rue de la Bourse, 68056 Mulhouse France. **Tel** 011 33 89 457351. **ED** Valerie Perain. **LC** T2; .S75. cum. index. **Circ:** 2,000.

BE/0037-9565
**BULLETIN DE LA SOCIETE ROYALE DES SCIENCES DE LIEGE.** [Bull. Soc. R. sci. Liege]. **Main/Corp** Societe Royale des Sciences de Liege. Vol. 1 (1932)-. Periodical. French (English). Six times a year. 3392F Europe; 3642F other. Societe Royale des Science de Liege, 15 Avenue des Tilleuls, B-4000 Liege Belgium. **Tel** 011 32 41 520180 ext 391, FAX 011 32 41 669547. **ED** J. Godeaux. **LC** Q56; .L47. **NLM** W1 BU523. **CODEN** BSRSA6. Index available. cum. index. **Circ:** 700 (ctrl). Documents available from Ask*IEEE, CASDDS.
**Desc:** University research papers in mathematics, physics, chemistry and the natural sciences.
**Ind/Abst** Chem. Abstr.; Ei Page One; Energy Res. Abstr.; GeoRef; INSPEC (1968-); Int. Aerosp. Abstr.; Math. Rev.; Stat. Theory Method Abstr. (1966); Zentralbl. Math. Ihre Grenzgeb.

FR/0037-9581
**BULLETIN DE LA SOCIETE SCIENTIFIQUE DE BRETAGNE.** [Bull. Soc. sci. Bretagne]. **Main/Corp** Societe Scientifique de Bretagne. Vol. 1 (1924)-. Bulletin. French. qt. Entreprises RSP, CP 1564, Cap-Rouge, Quebec G0A 1K0. **LC** Q46; .R45. **CODEN** BSSBAS. Documents available from BIOSIS Document Express, Ask*IEEE, CASDDS.
**Ind/Abst** Biol. Abstr.; Chem. Abstr.; INSPEC (1977-1980); Life Sci. Collect.

BE
**BULLETIN DE L'ACADEMIE ROYALE DE BELGIQUE CLASSE DES SCIENCES.** Bulletin. French. ir. Libraire Alain Ferraton, Chausse de Charleroi 162, B-1060 Brussels Belgium. **Tel** 011 32 2 5386917.

CN/0317-9273
**BULLETIN DE LIAISON DU CONSEIL DE LA JEUNESSE SCIENTIFIQUE.** **Main/Corp** Conseil de la Jeunesse Scientifique. V. 1- Mar. 1971-. Bulletin. French. Free. Conseil De La Jeunesse Scientifique, Bureau 14, 230 Est Boul., Henri-Bourassa, Montreal Quebec H3L 1B8 Canada. **DD** 505.

MR/0253-3243
**BULLETIN DE L'INSTITUT SCIENTIFIQUE (RABAT).** (BULLETIN DE L'INSTITUT SCIENTIFIQUE.). [Bull. Inst. Sci.]. **Main/Corp** Jamiat Muhammad Al-Khamis. Mahad Al-Ilmi. **Added/Corp** Jamiat Muhammad Al-Khamis. Mahad Al-Ilmi. Nashrat Al-Mahad Al-Ilmi. **VFOAT** Nashrat Al-Mahad Al-Ilmi. No 1 (1976)-. Bulletin. French (summaries and/or abstracts in Arabic). **LC** Q91.M55;

R3a. **DD** 505. **CODEN** BISMDS. Documents available from BIOSIS Document Express.
**Ind/Abst** Agrofor. Abstr.; Biol. Abstr. (-1980); For. Abstr.; GeoRef; Rev. Agric. Entomol.

CN/0848-7510
**BULLETIN DE MATHEMATIQUES ET SCIENCES.** **See** Mathematics.

BE/0001-4176
**BULLETIN DES SEANCES - ACADEMIE ROYALE DES SCIENCES D'OUTRE-MER.** **Main/Corp** Academie Royale des Sciences d'Outre-Mer. **VFOAT** Mededelingen der Zittingen. Vol. 1-20, 1955-74; (1975)-. Bulletin. French (Dutch and English). ir. 2650F. Academie Royale des Sciences d'Outre-Mer, BP 3, 1 rue Defacqz, B-1050 Brussels, Belgium. **ED** J.J. Symoens. Index available. cum. index. **Bk Rev**. **Ad Acc**. available with illustrations; available with charts. Documents available from CASDDS, BLDSC. ***Supersedes*** *Brussels. Institut Royal Colonial Belge. Bulletin des Seances.*
**Ind/Abst** Am. Hist. Life (1954-); Bibliogr. Mission.

FR/0074-2783
**BULLETIN D'INFORMATION - COMITE INTERNATIONAL DES SCIENCES HISTORIQUES.** **Main/Corp** International Committee of Historical Sciences. No. 1 (1953)-. Bulletin. French.

FR/0243-3664
**BULLETIN D'INFORMATION - M.I.D.I.S.T.** (MIDIST BULLETIN D'INFORMATION.). [Bull. inf. - M.I.D.I.S.T.]. **VFOAT** M.I.D.I.S.T. Bulletin d'Information. **VAT** Mission Interministerielle de l'Information Scientifique et Technique Bulletin d'Information. Bulletin. French. qt. Ministere de l'Industrie et de la Recherche, 280, BD Saint-Germain, Paris 75700 France. ***Continues*** *Bulletin d'Information - B.N.I.S.T., 0183-3235.*
**Ind/Abst** Libr. Inf. Sci. Abstr.

FR/1144-3464
**BULLETIN D'INFORMATIONS SCIENTIFIQUES - INSTITUT PASTEUR.** [Bull. inf. sci. - Inst. Pasteur]. **VFOAT** Institut Pasteur Bulletin d'Informations Scientifiques. (19??)-. Periodical. French. wk (Except August). 130.00F. Institut Pasteur, 28 rue du Docteur Roux, 75724 Paris Cedex 15 France. **Tel** 011 33 1 45688272. **ED** C. Volkerick. **UDC** 061.62. cum. index. **Bk Rev**. **Ad Acc**. ctrl circ.

US/1073-5976
**BULLETIN / INSTITUTE FOR THEOLOGICAL ENCOUNTER WITH SCIENCE AND TECHNOLOGY.** **See** Religion and Theology.

FR
**BULLETIN MENSUEL DES AVIS TECHNIQUES.** **Added/Corp** Centre Scientique et Technique du Batiment (France). (Jan./Feb. 1984)-. French. mo. Centre Scientifique et Technique du Batiment, 84 Avenue Jean Jaures, BP 2, 77421 Marne la Vallee Cedex 2 France. **Tel** 011 31 1 64688282.

US/0145-0670
**BULLETIN (NATIONAL SCIENCE FOUNDATION (U.S.)).** (BULLETIN / NATIONAL SCIENCE FOUNDATION.). **Added/Corp** National Science Foundation (U.S.). **VFOAT** NSF Bulletin. (197?)-. Bulletin. English. mo (except July and Aug.). Free on request. National Science Foundation, 1800 G Street Northwest, Washington DC 20550. **Tel** (202)357-9859, (202)357-9498.

US/0028-5455
**BULLETIN - NEW JERSEY ACADEMY OF SCIENCE, THE.** [Bull. - N. J. Acad. Sci.]. **Main/Corp** New Jersey Academy of Science. **Added/Corp** New Jersey Academy of Science. **VFOAT** Bulletin . Vol. 1 (May 1955)-. Bulletin. English. sa (March and October). $30.00 US; add $3.00 for surface mail, add $8.00 for airmail, other. New Jersey Academy of Science, Beck Hall #216, Livingston Campus, Piscataway NJ 08854. **Tel** (908)463-0511. **ED** Robert Evans. **LC** Q11; .N425. **DD** 505. **CODEN** BJASAS. **Ad Acc**. **Pr Rev. Circ:** 800. available on microfilm and microfiche from University Microfilms International (UMI). Documents available from BIOSIS Document Express, CASDDS.
**Desc:** Peer-reviewed scientific research journal reporting results of fundamental study, chiefly in the areas of biology and earth sciences, reflecting efforts of university and college faculty.
**Ind/Abst** Biol. Abstr.; Chem. Abstr. (1955-1981); EMBASE (1955-1981); GeoRef; Int. Aerosp. Abstr.

US/0362-3769
**BULLETIN OF LAW, SCIENCE & TECHNOLOGY.** ***Title Change.*** **See** Law.

II/0250-4707
**BULLETIN OF MATERIALS SCIENCE.** [Bull. mater. sci.]. **Added/Corp** Indian Academy of Sciences. Indian National Science Academy. (1979)-. Academic Scholarly Publication. English. Six times a year. $100.00. Indian Academy of Sciences Circulation, PO Box 8005, Department of Sadashivanagar, Bangalore 560 080 India. **Tel** 011 91 812 342546, 342310, telex 0845-2178 ACAD IN. **(Subscription address:** Prints India, 11 Darya Ganj, New Delhi, 110002 India, (Phone: 011 91 11 3268645)) **ED** C N R Rao. **CODEN** BUMSDW. Index available. **Pr Rev. Circ:** 500. Documents available from The Genuine Article, Ask*IEEE, CASDDS.
**Desc:** Devoted to research in materials science and technology containing original research articles, topical reviews, reports on research and development in materials science, technology, and notes and news.
**Ind/Abst** Alum. Ind. Abstr.; Ceram. Abstr. (19??-); Chem. Abstr.; Curr. Contents Eng. Tech. Appl. Sci.; Curr. Titles Electrochem.; Eng. Mater. Abstr.; INSPEC (May 1979-); Met. Abstr.; Res. Alert [Full Cov.].

US/0270-4676
**BULLETIN OF SCIENCE, TECHNOLOGY & SOCIETY.** [Bull. sci. technol. soc.]. **VFOAT** Bulletin of Science, Technology and Society. (1981)-. Academic Scholarly Publication. English. Six times a year. $95.00 institutions, $30.00 individuals. STS Press / Pennsylvania, Materials Research Laboratory, University Park PA 16802. **Tel** (814)865-1137, FAX (814)865-2326, telex 13-7328. **ED** Rustum Ray. **LC** Q175.4; .B84. **DD** 303.4/83/05. **CODEN** BSTSDJ. **[CCC]**. Index available. **Bk Rev**, (Qty: 6). **Circ:** 300. available on microfilm and microfiche from University Microfilms International (UMI). Documents available from Article Express International, The Genuine Article.
**Ind/Abst** Arts Humanit. Citation Index [Select. Cov.]; Curr. Contents Soc. Behav. Sci.; EMBASE; Eng. Index Annu. [Select. Cov.]; Geogr. Abstr. Human Geogr.; Int. Dev. Abstr.; Linguist. Lang. Behav. Abstr.; Res. Alert [Full Cov.]; Soc. Plann. Policy Dev. Abstr.; Soc. Sci. Cit. Index [Full Cov.]; Soc. Welf. Soc. Plan./Policy Soc. Dev.; Sociol. Abstr.

US/0096-3402
**BULLETIN OF THE ATOMIC SCIENTISTS.** [Bull. at. sci.]. **Added/Corp** Educational Foundation for Nuclear Science (Chicago, Ill.) Atomic Scientists of Chicago. **VFOAT** Science and Public Affairs. Vol. 1, No. 7 (March 15, 1946)-. Bulletin. English. bm (6 issues per year). $30.00 US; $34.50 Canada & Mexico; $37.50 other. Educational Foundation for Nuclear Science, 6042 South Kimbark Avenue, Chicago IL 60637. **Tel** (312)702-2555, FAX (312)702-0725. **ED** Mike Moore. **LC** TK9145; .A84. **DD** 621.48/05. **NLM** W1 BU843J. **CODEN** BASIAP. **[CCC]**. Index available. cum. index. **Bk Rev**. **Ad Acc**. **Pr Rev. Circ:** 25,000. available on microfilm and microfiche from University Microfilms International (UMI); available on CD-ROM. Documents available from The Genuine Article, UMI Article Clearinghouse, Magazine Collection. ***Continues*** *Bulletin of the Atomic Scientists of Chicago, 0742-3829.*
**Desc:** A science and world affairs magazine for scientists and non-scientists. Articles and reviews cover topics such as: arms control, energy, technology and development, science and the citizen, environment, and international relations. Recognized as the authoritative source on science and public policy.
**Ind/Abst** ABC POL SCI; Acad. Abstr. Full Text Elite (Jan. 1984-) [Full Txt.]; Acad. Abstr. (Jan. 1984-); Acad. Ind. [Computer File] (1984-); Acad. Search (Jan. 1984-); Alum. Ind. Abstr.; Am. Hist. Life (1969-); Am. Bibliogr. Slavic East Europ. Stud.; Biol. Dig.; Book Rev. Digest; Book Rev. Index (1965-); Curr. Contents Soc. Behav. Sci.; Curr. Index J. Educ.; Curr. Mil. Pol. Lit.; Energy Inf. Abstr.; Energy Res. Abstr. (June 1971-); Eng. Mater. Abstr.; Environ. Period. Bibliogr.; Expand. Acad. Index (1992-); Gen. Period. Index (1985-); Gen. Sci. Index; Gen. Sci. Source (Jan. 1988-) [Full Txt.]; GeoRef; Health Saf. Sci. Abstr.; Index Period. Artic. Relat. Law; INFO-SOUTH Abstr.; Infobank (Jan. 1969-); INIS Atomindex [Micro.]; Int. Aerosp. Abstr.; Linguist. Lang. Behav. Abstr.; Mag. Artic. Summar. Elite (Jan. 1984-) [Full Txt.]; Mag. Artic. Summar. Select (Jan. 1984-); Mag. Artic. Summar. CD-ROM (Jan. 1984-); Mag. Express (1986-) [Full Txt.]; Mag. Index Plus (1989-); Mag. Index. Sel. (1986-); Mag. Search; Middle East Abstr. Index; Newsp. Period. Abstr. (1986-); PAIS Int. Print; Peace Res. Abstr. J. (1945-1981, 1984, 1987-); Pollut. Abstr. Indexes; Read. Guide Abstr. Select Ed.; Read. Guide Period. Lit.; Res. Alert [Full Cov.]; Resource/One Ondisc; Soc. Plann. Policy Dev. Abstr.; Soc. Sci. Cit. Index [Full Cov.]; Sociol. Abstr.; Mag. Index (1977-); Vocat. Search (Jan. 1984-) [Full Txt.].

US/0009-3491
**BULLETIN OF THE CHICAGO ACADEMY OF SCIENCES.** **Main/Corp** Chicago Academy of Sciences. **VFOAT** Chicago Academy of Sciences Bulletin. Vol. 1 (1883)-. Monographic series. English. ir. Price varies per volume. Chicago Academy of Sciences, Lincoln Park, 2001 North Clark Street, Chicago IL 60614. **Tel** (312)549-0606. **LC** Q11; .C45. **DD** 574/.05. **Circ:** 2,500. available on microfilm and microfiche from University Microfilms International (UMI).

UA/0366-4740
**BULLETIN OF THE FACULTY OF SCIENCE, ASSIUT UNIVERSITY.** (BULLETIN OF THE FACULTY OF SCIENCE.). [Bull. Fac. Sci., Assiut Univ.]. **Main/Corp** Jami'at Asyut. Kulliyat al-Ulum. **Added/Corp** Jami'at Asyut. Kulliyat al-Ulum. Majallah al-Ilmiyah li-Kulliyat al-Ulum, Jamiat Asyut. **VFOAT** Majallah al-Ilmiyah li-Kulliyat al-Ulum, Jamiat Asyut. Vol.1 (1972)-. Bulletin. English (summaries and/or abstracts in Arabic). **LC** Q87; .A87a. **DD** 505. **CODEN** BSAUDW. Documents available from BIOSIS Document Express, CASDDS.
**Ind/Abst** Biol. Abstr.; Chem. Abstr.

KO/0253-2964
**BULLETIN OF THE KOREAN CHEMICAL SOCIETY.** **See** Chemistry.

JA/0387-8511
**BULLETIN OF THE NATIONAL SCIENCE MUSEUM. SERIES E, (PHYSICAL SCIENCES & ENGINEERING).** [Bull. Natl. Sci. Mus., Ser. E, Phys. sci. eng.]. **Added/Corp** Kokuritsu Kagaku Hakubutsukan (Japan). **VFOAT** Kokuritsu Kagaku Hakubutsukan Kenkyu Hokoku. E-Rui, (Rikogaku); Physical Sciences & Engineering; Physical Sciences and Engineering; Rikogaku. Vol. 1 (1978)-. Bulletin. English (Japanese). an. National Science Museum, Ueno Park, Tokyo 110 Japan. **LC** Discard. **CODEN** BNSED5. Documents available from CASDDS.
**Ind/Abst** Chem. Abstr.

PL/0239-7528
**BULLETIN OF THE POLISH ACADEMY OF SCIENCES. TECHNICAL SCIENCES.** [Bull. Pol. Acad. Sci. Tech. sci.]. **Added/Corp** Polska Akademia Nauk. **VFOAT** Technical Sciences. Vol. 31, No. 1/12 (1983)-. Academic Scholarly Publication. English (summaries and/or abstracts in Russian). mo. $100.00. **(Subscription address:** ARS Polona, PO Box 1001, 00068 Warsaw Poland.) **CODEN** BASSEP. Documents available from Article Express International, Ask*IEEE, CASDDS. ***Continues*** *Bulletin de l'Academie Polonaise des Sciences. Serie des Sciences Techniques, 0001-4125.*
**Ind/Abst** Bioeng. Abstr.; Chem. Abstr. (1983-); Ei Page One; Eng. Index Annu.; Geotech. Abstr.; INSPEC (1983-); Wildl. Rev.; Zentralbl. Math. Ihre Grenzgeb.

TU/0254-4121
**BULLETIN OF THE TECHNICAL UNIVERSITY OF ISTANBUL.** [Bull. Tech. Univ. Istanbul]. **Added/Corp** Istanbul Teknik Universitesi. **VFOAT** Istanbul Teknik Universitesi Bulteni. (1982)-. Bulletin. English (German and Turkish). Istanbul Technical University, Faculty of Science and Letters, Room 409, Maslak, Istanbul Turkey. **CODEN** BTUIDZ. Documents available from Ask*IEEE, CASDDS. ***Continues*** *Istanbul Teknik Universitesi. Istanbul Teknik Universitesi Bulteni.*
**Ind/Abst** Chem. Abstr.; INSPEC (1968-); Math. Rev.; Zentralbl. Math. Ihre Grenzgeb.

JA/0495-8020
**BULLETIN OF THE TOKYO INSTITUTE OF TECHNOLOGY.** **Main/Corp** Tokyo Kogyo Daigaku. **Added/Corp** Tokyo Kogyo Daigaku. Bulletin. Series B. (1950)-. Bulletin. English.
**Ind/Abst** Ceram. Abstr. (19??-).

KE/0304-9590
**BULLETIN OF THE UNESCO REGIONAL OFFICE OF SCIENCE AND TECHNOLOGY FOR AFRICA.** **Main/Corp** UNESCO. Regional Office of Science and Technology for Africa. Office of Science and Technology for Africa. Vol. 9, (Jan./March 1974)-. Bulletin. English (French). Twice a year (Jan., July). Free. UNESCO / Kenya, PO Box 30592, Nairobi Kenya. **Tel** 011 254 2 333930, 011 254 2 520600. **LC** Q10; .U472a. **DD** 509/.6. **CODEN** BROADZ. **Bk Rev. Circ:** English 1,000, French 650 (ctrl). ***Continues*** *United Nations Educational, Scientific, and Cultural Organization. Field Science Office for Africa. Bulletin.*
**Desc:** News on office activities in promotion, planning, execution and supervision of Unesco's regional science programmes in Africa. Announcement of meetings, seminars and conferences.

NZ/0370-6559
**BULLETIN - ROYAL SOCIETY OF NEW ZEALAND.** [Bull. - R. Soc. N.Z.]. **Main/Corp** Royal Society of New Zealand. No. 4- 1954-. Bulletin. English. ir. Royal Society of New Zealand, PO Box 598, Wellington New Zealand. **Tel** 011 64 4 727421, FAX 011 64 4 731841. **CODEN** RNZBAY. **[CCC]**. **Bk Rev**. **Ad Acc. Circ:** 300 (ctrl). ***Continues*** *New Zealand Institute. Bulletin.*
**Desc:** Monographs or any work of science that is too large for publication in the society's journal.
**Ind/Abst** GeoRef.

FR
**BULLETIN SIGNALETIQUE. 900.** **Added/Corp** France. Centre National de la Recherche Scientifique. Centre de Documentation Scientifique et Technique. (197?)-. Bulletin. French. mo. 360.00F. Centre National de la Recherche Scientifique, Informascience, 26 rue Boyer, 75971 Paris France. **Tel** 61.41.11.05, telex CNRSDOC 220880 F. **LC** Z7913; .B824; T45. **DD** 016.5. **NLM** ZQ 1 B936SLX. ***Continues*** *Bulletin des Traductions - Centre National de la Recherche Scientifique. 900. Traductions Effectuees dans les Services et Centres Francais et Canadiens de Documentation, 0301-3502.*

FR
**BULLETIN SIGNALETIQUE (CENTRE D'INFORMATION ET DE DOCUMENTATION SUR LE VIETNAM CONTEMPORAIN).** (BULLETIN SIGNALETIQUE - CENTRE D'INFORMATION ET DE DOCUMENTATION SUR LE VIETNAM CONTEMPORAIN, C.I.D. VIETNAM.). No. 1 (Dec. 1986)-. Bulletin. French (English and Vietnamese). bm. C.I.D. Vietnam, 37 rue Ballu, 75009 Paris France.

US/0038-3872
**BULLETIN / SOUTHERN CALIFORNIA ACADEMY OF SCIENCES.** [Bull. - South. Calif. Acad. Sci.]. **Added/Corp** Southern California Academy of Sciences. **VFOAT** Bulletin of the Southern California Academy of Sciences. Vol. 70, No. 1 (Apr. 1971)-. Periodical. English. Three times a year (Apr., Aug., Dec.). $30.00 US and Canada; $35.00 other. Southern California Academy of Science, 900 West Exposition Boulevard, Los Angeles CA 90007. **Tel** (213)744-3384, FAX (213)746-2999. **ED** Daniel A. Guthrie (editor's address: W. M. Keck Science Center, 925 North Mills Avenue, Claremont, CA 91711, phone: (909)621-8000). **LC** Q11; .S85. **DD** 505. **CODEN** BCASAD. Index available. **Bk Rev. Pr Rev. Circ:** 600 (ctrl). Documents available from BIOSIS Document Express. ***Continues*** *Bulletin of the Southern California Academy of Sciences.*
**Desc:** Receptive to articles and research notes in any field of science with emphasis on the Southern California area.
**Ind/Abst** AGRICOLA [Select. Cov.]; Biol. Abstr.; Life Sci. Collect.

FR/1149-0306
**BULLETIN TECHNIQUE - GATTEFOSSE REPORT.** (1979)-. Periodical. Multiple languages. an. **UDC** 62. Documents available from CASDDS. ***Formed by the union of*** *Bulletin Technique - Gattefosse, 0397-7617* ***and*** *Gattefosse Report, 0397-7625.*
**Ind/Abst** Chem. Abstr.

US
**BUSINESS, INDUSTRY, TECHNOLOGY SERVICES.** **Added/Corp** Dayton, Ohio. Dayton and Montgomery County Public Library. Dayton, Ohio. Public Library. (19??)-. Periodical. English. Ten times a year. Free. Dayton & Montgomery County Public Library, 215 East 3rd Street, Dayton OH 45402. **Tel** (513)227-9500. **ED** Tamara A. Butcher. **DD** 027. **Circ:** 250.
**Desc:** Summarizations of new and current books in business, trade, and applied arts and sciences.

●US
**BY THE YEAR 2000: REPORT OF THE FCCSET COMMITTEE ON EDUCATION AND HUMAN RESOURCES.** **See** Education.

US/1049-1317
**C2C ABSTRACTS JAPAN. MATERIALS SCIENCES.** **See** Science and Technology-Abstracting, Bibliographies and Statistics.

BL
**CADERNOS DE HISTORIA E FILOSOFIA DA CIENCIA.** Periodical. Portuguese. Unicamp, CP 6133, 13.081 Campinas, Sao Paulo Brazil. **LC** Q124.6; .C33. **DD** 509.
**Ind/Abst** Philos. Index.

BL
**CADERNOS DE HISTORIA E FILOSOFIA DA CIENCIA. SUPLEMENTO.** Periodical. Portuguese. Unicamp, CP 6133, 13.081 Campinas, Sao Paulo Brazil. **LC** Q124.6; .C34. **DD** 509.

BL/0101-2991
**CADERNOS DE TECNOLOGIA E CIENCIA.** [Cad. tecnol. cienc.]. V. 1, No. 1, (June 1978)-. Periodical. Portuguese. mo. Editora Tama Ltda, rua Voluntarios da Patria 34 Casa 1, Caixa Postal 44.140, CEP 22.180 Rio de Janeiro RJ Brazil. **LC** T4; .C23. **DD** 605.

FR/0221-3664
**CAHIERS D'HISTOIRE ET DE PHILOSOPHIE DES SCIENCES.** [Cah. hist. philos. sci.]. **Added/Corp** Centre de Documentation Sciences Humaines (France). (1977)-. Monographic series. French. ir. Price varies per volume. Librairie Albert Blanchard, 9 rue de Medicisf, 75006 Paris France. **Tel** 011 33 1 43269034. **Ad Acc. Circ:** 500.
**Desc:** To give commentaries on essential texts in the sciences in an historical and epistemological perspective.
**Ind/Abst** Math. Rev.; Zentralbl. Math. Ihre Grenzgeb.

FR/0008-9850
**CAHIERS DU CENTRE SCIENTIFIQUE ET TECHNIQUE DU BATIMENT.** [Cah. Cent. sci. tech. batim.]. **Main/Corp** Centre Scientifique et Technique du Batiment (France). No. 1 (July 1948)-. French. mo (except bimonthly Jan./Feb. and July/Aug.). 1,596.47F. Centre Scientifique et Technique du Batiment, 84 Avenue Jean Jaures, BP 2, 77421 Marne la Vallee Cedex 2 France. **Tel** 011 31 1 64688282. Index available. cum. index. **Bk Rev. Ad Acc. Circ:** 3,500 (ctrl).
**Ind/Abst** Archit. Period. Index; Int. Build. Serv. Abstr.; Int. Civil Eng. Abstr.; Saf. Health Work; Soft. Abstr. Eng.; World Ceram. Abstr.

FR
**CAHIERS RATIONALISTES, LES.** Began in 1930. Periodical. French. Nine times a year. 300.00F France; 310.00F other. Union Rationaliste, 14 rue de l'Ecole-Polytechnique, 75005 Paris 5E France. **Tel** 46330350. **LC** AP20; .C165. **Bk Rev. Ad Acc. Circ:** 2,500.
**Desc:** Essays on religion, philosophy, science, and against parapsychology or other dubious sciences.

FR/0243-6299
**CAHIERS - SYSTEMA.** [Cah. - Syst.]. (1973)-. Periodical. French. **UDC** 51.
**Ind/Abst** Zentralbl. Math. Ihre Grenzgeb.

●US/1061-3552
**CAL SCIENCES.** (CAL SCIENCES: THE BERKELEY UNDERGRADUATE SCIENCE JOURNAL.). [Cal sci.]. (1992)-. Periodical. English. $10.00 (institutions). University of California, Berkeley, 700 Eshleman Hall, Berkeley CA 94720. **DD** 500.

GW
**CALENDAR OF EVENTS. TRADE FAIRS AND EXHIBITIONS.** **Main/Corp** Deutsche Lufthansa (1953- ). **VFOAT** Trade Fairs and Exhibitions. English. Deutsche Lufthansa AG, Special Business-Travel 75 Airport, 6000 Frankfurt Main Germany. **LC** T394; .D48A. **DD** 380.1/4567/074.

US/1041-0260
**CALIFORNIA SALES GUIDE TO HIGH-TECH COMPANIES.** [Calif. sales guide high tech co.]. **VFOAT** California Region; Sales Guide to High Tech Companies. California Region. English. qt. $145.00. Corporate Technology Information Services Inc, 12 Alfred Street, Suite 200, Woburn MA 01801-9998. **Tel** (617)932-3939, (800)333-8036, FAX (617)932-6335, telex 497-2961 CRPTECH. **ED** Steven W Parker. **LC** HC107.C23; H533. **DD** 338.7/62/00025794. Index available. cum. index. **Bk Rev. Circ:** 3,000. available on diskette.
**Desc:** Regional directory of over 3,000 technology manufacturers and developers.

●US/1059-7085
**CALIFORNIA TECHNOLOGY REGISTER.** [Calif. technol. registe.]. (1992)-. Directory. English. an. $145.00 (print); $495.00 (diskette). Database Publishing Company, PO Box 7440, Newport Beach CA 92658. **Tel** (714)646-1623, (800)-888-8434, FAX (714)631-8471. **LC** HF5065.C2; C28. **DD** 338.7/62/000294794.

US/0160-502X
**CALTECH.** [CALTECH]. **Main/Corp** California Institute of Technology. **VAT** California Institute of Technology. Periodical. English. bm. Caltech, 1201 East California Boulevard, Pasadena CA 91109. **CODEN** CALTD3.

UK/0963-7141
**CAMBRIDGE NONLINEAR SCIENCE SERIES.** [Camb. nonlinear sci. ser.]. (1991)-. Monographic series. English. ir. Price varies per volume. Cambridge University Press, The Edinburgh Building, Shaftesbury Road, Cambridge CB2 2RU United Kingdom. **Tel** 011 44 223 312393, FAX 011 44 223 325959.
**Ind/Abst** Zentralbl. Math. Ihre Grenzgeb.

●AG
**CAMPO Y TECNOLOGIA.** **Main/Corp** Instituto Nacional de Tecnologia Agropecuaria (Argentina). **Added/Corp** Instituto Nacional de Tecnologia Agropecuaria (Argentina). No. 1 (1992)-. Periodical. Spanish.

CN/0712-4848
**CANADIAN SCIENCE (DOWNSVIEW, ONT.).** ***Ceased.*** (CANADIAN SCIENCE.). [Can. sci.]. Vol. 1, No. 1 (Sept. 16, 1982)-(1992). Periodical. English. Forty-eight times a year. Canadian Science News Service, University of Toronto, Room 45/University College, Toronto Ontario M5S 1A1 Canada. **Tel** (416)595-7153, FAX (416)595-7153. **ED** 3543435435. **DD** 509/.71. **Bk Rev. Ad Acc.** ctrl circ.
**Desc:** Combination newsletter and camera-ready copy of stories on current Canadian scientific research and development.

PR/0008-6452
**CARIBBEAN JOURNAL OF SCIENCE.** [Caribb. j. sci.]. **Added/Corp** University of Puerto Rico (Mayaguez Campus). Institute of Caribbean Science. University of Puerto Rico (Mayaguez Campus). College of Arts and Sciences. University of Puerto Rico (Rio Piedras Campus). Institute of Caribbean Studies. Vol. 1 (Feb. 1961)-. Periodical. English (Spanish and French). sa (June & December). $13.00 student; $20.00 individual; $35.00 institution. University of Puerto Rico / Facultad de Artes y Ciencias, RUM-UPR, PO Box 5000, Mayaguez Puerto Rico 00681-5000. **Tel** (809)834-4040 ext. 3595, FAX (809)265-1225. **ED** Allen Lewis. **LC** Q1; .C32. **DD** 500. **CODEN** CRJSA4. **Circ:** 1,000 (ctrl). Documents available from BIOSIS Document Express, CASDDS.
**Desc:** Publishes papers relating to all fields of natural science in the Caribbean.
**Ind/Abst** Biol. Abstr.; Chem. Abstr.; Ecol. Abstr. (?-?); Fish Rev.; Geogr. Abstr. Human Geogr. (?-?); GeoRef; Meteorol. Geoastrophys. Abstr. (199?-); Life Sci. Collect.; Wildl. Rev.

US/0008-6460
**CARIBBEAN JOURNAL OF SCIENCE AND MATHEMATICS, THE.** ***Suspended.*** [Carib. j. sci. math.]. Vol. 1 (May 1968)-Suspended. Academic Scholarly Publication. English. ir. Western Carolina University Press, Western Carolina University, Callowhie NC 28723. **LC** Q1; .C33. **DD** 505. **CODEN** CJSCAD. Documents available from CASDDS.
**Ind/Abst** Chem. Abstr.; Math. Rev.

TR
**CARIRI.** **Main/Corp** Caribbean Industrial Research Institute. English. Caribbean Industrial Research Institute, University Post Office, St Augustine Trinidad. **LC** T177.T7; C3A. **DD** 607/.2/72983.

US/0045-5865
**CAROLINA TIPS.** [Carol. tips]. **Added/Corp** Carolina Biological Supply Company. Vol. 1 (1938)-. Periodical. English. Four times a year. free on request. Carolina Biological Supply Co, 2700 York Road, Burlington NC 27215. **Tel** (919)584-0381, FAX (919)584-3399, telex 574-354. **ED** Barbara Kuyper. **DD** 574. **Circ:** 125,000 (ctrl).
**Desc:** Articles for science teachers.

XR/0521-2359
**CASOPIS MORAVSKEHO MUZEA. VEDY PRIRODNI.** **See** Museums and Galleries.

UK/0264-3138
**CASTME JOURNAL.** **See** Education-Teaching and Curriculum.

US
**CATALOG OF PRODUCTS & SERVICES.** **Added/Corp** United States. National Technical Information Service. **VFOAT** Catalog of Products and Services; NTIS Products and Services Catalog. (1991)-. Catalog. English. National Technical Information Service - NTIS, Room 2027S, 5285 Port Royal Road, Springfield VA 22161. **Tel** (703)487-4630, (703)487-4660, (703)487-4650, FAX (703)321-8547, telex 89-9405.

US
**CATALOG OF PROFESSIONAL DEVELOPMENT SEMINARS / INSTITUTE FOR ADVANCED TECHNOLOGY, CONTROL DATA CORPORATION.** **Main/Corp** Control Data Corporation. Institute for Advanced Technology. (19??)-. Catalog. English. ir. Free. Institute of Advanced Technology, 6003 Executive Boulevard, Rockville MD 20852. **Tel** (800)638-6590. **LC** Discard. **Circ:** 500,000 (ctrl).
**Desc:** A collection of technical and management seminars designed for the professional community. All seminars are real world skill oriented. Seminars are regularly scheduled in major cities.

FR
**CATALOGUE COLLECTIF DES LIVRES FRANCAIS DE SCIENCES ET TECHNIQUES.** **VFOAT** Catalogue Collectif des Livres Francais de Sciences & Techniques. Began publication with 1965/66 issue. French. ir. Cercle de la Librairie, 35 rue Gregoire de Tours, F-75279 Paris Cedex 06 France. **Tel** 011 33 1 43291000, FAX 011 33 1 43296895, telex LIFRAN 270 838.

FR
**CATALOGUE DU SERVICE DU FILM DE RECHERCHE SCIENTIFIQUE.** **Main/Corp** Centre National de Documentation Pedagogique (France). Service du Film de Recherche Scientifique. **VFOAT** Catalogue du SFRS. (19??)-. French. te. Le Service, 366 Avenue Napoleon Bonaparte, 92501 Rueil-Malmaison France. **LC** Q192; .C44a. **DD** 016.5.

UK/0958-3629
**CATALYST OXFORD.** [CatalystOxf.]. (1990)-. Periodical. English. Four times a year (Sept., Nov., Feb., Apr.). £14.95 UK; £23.00 Europe; £28.50 (airmail) other. Philip Allan Publishers Ltd, Market Place, Deddington Oxford, OX15 0SE England. **Tel** 011 44 869 38652, FAX 011 44 869 38803. **DD** 500.

CN/0834-2466
**CATALYST (VANCOUVER. 1986).** (CATALYST : NEWSLETTER/JOURNAL OF THE BRITISH COLUMBIA SCIENCE TEACHERS' ASSOCIATION OF THE BRITISH COLUMBIA TEACHERS' FEDERATION.). [Catalyst]. **Added/Corp** British Columbia Science Teachers' Association. **VFOAT** BC Catalyst. Vol. 29, No. 3 (Spring 1986)-. Periodical. English. ir. 50.00Can$. British Columbia Teachers Federation, 100-550 West 6th Avenue, Vancouver British

Columbia V5Z 4P2 Canada. **Tel** (604)871-2283, (800)663-9163, FAX (604)871-2294, (604)871-2290. **DD** 507/.10711. ***Continues*** *Catalyst B.C., 0834-0196.*

UK
**CATCHWORD AND TRADE NAME INDEX : CATNI.** **See** Science and Technology-Abstracting, Bibliographies and Statistics.

SI
**CB MAGAZINE : TRAINING TECHNOLOGISTS FOR TOMORROW.** Singapore Polytechnic Department of Civil Engineering and Building, Civil Engineering and Building Club, Dover Road, 0513 Singapore.

UK/0261-6661
**CBI NEWS.** [CBI news]. **VFOAT** Confederation of British Industry News. (1981)-. English. Eleven times a year (July/Aug. issues combined). Free, members of the Confederation of British Industry, Universities, Academic Libraries & Polytechnics, £25.00 (non-members) UK; £49.00 (non-members) Europe; £59.00 (non-members) others. Confederation British Industry, 103 New Oxford Street, London WC1A 1DU England. **Tel** 011 47 22 950630, FAX 011 47 22 950719, telex 21332. **DD** _a338.006041. ***Continues*** *CBI Members Bulletin, 0140-2188.*

DK/0904-4701
**CDR WORKING PAPERS.** (1988)-. Centre for Development Research, NY Kongensgade 9, DK-1472 Copenhagen K Denmark. **Tel** 45 114 5700, FAX 45 33 140125.
**Ind/Abst** Rural Dev. Abstr.; World Agric. Econ.

DK/0008-8994
**CENTAURUS.** [Centaurus]. Vol. 1, No. 1 (Jan./Mar. 1950)-. Periodical. English (French and German). qt. kr1150.00. Munksgaard International Publishers Ltd, PO Box 2148, DK-1016 Copenhagen K Denmark. **Tel** 011 45 33 12 70 30, FAX 011 45 33 12 93 87, telex 19431 MUNKS DK. **ED** Kurt Moller Pedersen, Ole Knudsen and Olaf Pedersen. **DD** 610; 500. **NLM** W1 CE181. **CODEN** CENTA4. **[CCC]. Pr Rev.**
**Ind/Abst** Am. Hist. Life (1963-); Arts Humanit. Citation Index (19??-19??) [Full Cov.]; GeoRef; Math. Rev.; Middle East Abstr. Index; Zentralbl. Math. Ihre Grenzgeb.

VE
**CENTRAL UNIVERSITY OF VENEZUELAU TECHNICAL BULLETINS.** Universidad de Materiales y Modelos Estructurales, Apartado 50361-Sabana Grande 105, Caracas 1050 Venezuela.
**Ind/Abst** Concr. Abstr.

XR
**CESKOSLOVENSKE VYZKUMNE ZPRAVY A DISERTACE.** Czech. bm. kcs260.00. Narodni Informacni Stredisko, Havelkova 22, 130 00 Prague 3, Czech Republic. **Tel** PRAQUE 26 63 41, FAX (02)264775, telex 122214. **ED** J Pavlu. **LC** Z7403; .C46; Q158.5. Index available. **Circ:** 660.
**Desc:** List of Czechoslovakian research reports and dissertation.

●US/1063-1615
**CFC REPORT.** **VAT** Chlorofluorocarbons Report. (1992)-. Periodical. English. mo. $325.00. IAQ Publications, Inc., 2 Wisconsin Circle, Suite 430, Chevy Chase MD 20815. **Tel** (800)394-0115, (301)913-0115.

SZ
**CH-FORSCHUNG.** **VFOAT** CH Forschung. Periodical. German. mo. 80.00F. Gesellschaft Schweizer Forschungsinformation, St Urbangasse 2, CH-8001 Zurich Switzerland. **LC** Q67; .C45. **DD** 505.

KO
**CHAEMI KWAGIHYOP HOEBO.** **VFOAT** K.S.E.A. Letters; KSEA Letters. Periodical. English (Korean). bm. Korean Scientists and Engineers Association in America Inc, 6261 Executive Boulevard, Rockville MD 20852. **LC** AS36.C338; A16.

KO
**CHAYON KWAHAK YONGU.** **VFOAT** Natural Science Research. Periodical. Korean (summaries and/or abstracts in English). Choson Taehakkyo Chayon, Kwahak Yonguso 17 Pullo-dong, Tong-ku Kwangju-si Korea. **LC** Q80.K6; C55.
**Ind/Abst** Energy Res. Abstr. (April 1983-).

KO
**CHAYON KWAHAK YONGUSO HAKSUL NONMUNJIP.** **VFOAT** Haksul Nonmunjip; Journal of the Natural Science Research Institute. Periodical. English (Korean). Yonse Taehakkyo Chayon Kwahak Yonguso, 134 Sinchon-dong Sodaemun-ku, Seoul 120 Korea. **LC** Q4; .C398.
**Ind/Abst** Energy Res. Abstr. (Sept. 1980-).

CC
**CHE-CHIANG TA HSUEH HSUEH PAO.** **Added/Corp** Che-Chiang ta Hsueh. **VFOAT** Journal of Zhejiang University. (198?)-. Periodical. Chinese (English; summaries and/or abstracts in English). Six times a year. $22.98 surface mail; $43.57 airmail. **(Subscription address:** China International Book Trading Corporation, PO Box 399, Library Service Department, Beijing 100044 People's Republic of China.**) ED** Zong Xianjun. **Bk Rev. Ad Acc.** ***Continues*** *Hsueh Pao (Che-Chiang Ta Hsueh).*
**Desc:** Covers mathematics, physics, chemistry, geology, mechanics, mechanical engineering, electrical engineering, chemical engineering, electronic engineering, optical instruments, and biomedical instrumentation.

II/0009-2320
**CHEMICAL AGE OF INDIA.** **See** Chemistry.

LI/0235-7216
**CHEMIJA / LIETUVOS MOKSLU SKADEMIJA.** **Added/Corp** Lietuvos Mokslu Akademija. Chemijos ir Chemines Technologijos Institutas (Lietuvos TSR Mokslu Akademija). **VFOAT** Khimiia; Chemistry. (1990)-. Periodical. English (Russian; summaries and/or abstracts in Lithuanian). qt. **(Subscription address:** Victor Kamkin, 4956 Boiling Brook Parkway, Rockville MD 20852.**) LC** IN PROCESS. **CODEN** CHMJES. Documents available from CASDDS. ***Continues in part*** *Lietuvos TSR Mokslu Akademijos Darbai. Serija B, 0132-2729.*
**Ind/Abst** Chem. Abstr.

CH
**CHENG-KUNG TA HSUEH HSUEH PAO. JEN WEN, SHE HUI, KO CHI, I HSUEH PIEN.** **See** Humanities.

CC/0253-2263
**CHENGDU KEJI DAXUE XUEBAO.** (CHENGTU KUO CHI TA HSUEH HSUEH PAO / CHENG-TU KUO CHI TA HSUEH.). [Chengdu keji daxue xuebao]. **Added/Corp** Cheng-tu kuo chi ta Hsueh. **VFOAT** Journal of Chengdu University of Science and Technology; Cheng du Kejidaxue Xuebao. (1979)-. Academic Scholarly Publication. Chinese (English). bm. Chengdu Keji Daxue, Xuebao Bianjibu Chengdu, Sichuan 610065, People's Republic of China. **Tel** 581554. **LC** Q4; .C399. **DD** 505. **CODEN** CKDXDB. Documents available from CASDDS.
**Ind/Abst** Chem. Abstr.; Math. Rev.

US/0891-3862
**CHI KO HSUEH, TA.** (CHINESE JOURNAL OF ATMOSPHERIC SCIENCES.). [Chin. j. atmos. sci.]. **Added/Corp** Chung-Kuo Ko Hsueh Yuan. Ta Chi Wu Li Yen Chiu So. **VFOAT** Ta Chi Ko Hsueh; Scientia Atmospherica Sinica. Vol. 11, No. 1 (1987)-. Periodical. English (summaries and/or abstracts in Chinese; translations available in Chinese). qt. $460.00. Allerton Press, Inc., 150 Fifth Avenue, New York NY 10011. **Tel** (212)924-3950, FAX (212)463-9684, telex 427441 ALPRES. **LC** QC851; .T223. **DD** 551.5.
**Ind/Abst** Meteorol. Geoastrophys. Abstr.

CC/0529-0279
**CHI-LIN TA HSUEH TZU JAN KO HSUEH HSUEH PAO.** **Added/Corp** Chi-lin ta Hsueh. **VFOAT** Acta Scientiarum Naturalium Universitatis Jilinensis. (Feb. 1979)-. Academic Scholarly Publication. Chinese (summaries and/or abstracts in English). qt. $4.40. Jilin University Press, (Jilin Daxue Chubanshe), Changchun, Jilin People's Republic of China. **Tel** 23189. **(Subscription address:** China International Book Trading Corporation, PO Box 399, Library Service Department, Beijing 100044 People's Republic of China.**) LC** Q4.; .T85a. **DD** 505. **CODEN** CLTTDI. Documents available from CASDDS, BLDSC, CASDDS. ***Continues*** *Chi-lin ta Hsueh Hsueh Pao. Tzu Jan ko Hsueh Pan, 0529-0279.*
**Ind/Abst** Chem. Abstr.; Math. Rev.; Zentralbl. Math. Ihre Grenzgeb.

CH
**CHIAO HSUEH TUNG HSUN. LI KO PAN.** **VFOAT** Jiaoxuetongxun. Periodical. Chinese. mo. NT$0.36. Post Office, Cheng-chou Shih, People's Republic of China. **LC** Q183.4.C5; C44. **DD** 507/.1251.

CH
**CHIAO HSUEH YUEH KAN. CHUNG HSUEH LI KO PAN.** **VFOAT** Jiaoxueyuekan; Jiaoyuyuekan i.e. Jiaoxueyuekan. Periodical. Chinese. mo. NT$0.30. Post Office Hang-Chou Shih, Hang-Chou Shih, People's Republic of China. **LC** Q181.A1; C48. **DD** 607/.12.

JA/0577-6848
**CHIBA DAIGAKU KOGAKUBU KENKYU HOKOKU.** [Chiba Daigaku Kogakubu kenkyu hokoku]. **Added/Corp** Chiba Daigaku. Kogakubu. **VFOAT** Journal of the Faculty of Engineering, Chiba University; Research Reports of Faculty of Technology, Chiba University. No. 2 (1951)-. Periodical. Japanese (summaries and/or abstracts in English). sa. Chiba Daigaku Kogakubu, (Faculty of Engineering, Chiba University), 1-33, Yayoicho, Chibashi, Chibaken 260 Japan. **LC** T4; .C465. **CODEN** CDKKAN. Documents available from CASDDS. ***Continues*** *Chiba Daigaku Kogei Gakubu Kenkyu Hokoku.*
**Ind/Abst** Chem. Abstr.

JA/0385-7026
**CHIBA KOGYO DAIGAKU KENKYU HOKOKU. RIKO HEN.** [Chiba Kogyo Daigaku kenkyu hokoku, Riko hen]. **Added/Corp** Chiba Kogyo Daigaku. **VFOAT** Report of Chiba Institute of Technology. (19??)-. Japanese (summaries and/or abstracts in English). an. Chiba Kogyo Daigaku, 17-1 Tsudanuma 2, Narashino-shi, Chiba-ken 275 Japan. **LC** T4; .C4655. **CODEN** RPCTAL. Documents available from CASDDS.
**Ind/Abst** Chem. Abstr.

JA
**CHIHO KOKYO DANTAI SHIKEN KENKYU KIKAN SORAN.** **Added/Corp** Tokyo-to Doboku Gijutsu Kenkyujo. (1976)-. Periodical. Japanese. Tokyo-to Doboku Gijutsu Kenkyujo, 1-18 Konan 1-chome Minato-ku, Tokyo Japan. **LC** T177.J3; C5.

UK/0894-2536
**CHINA CENTER OF ADVANCED SCIENCE AND TECHNOLOGY (WORLD LABORATORY) SYMPOSIUM/WORKSHOP PROCEEDINGS.** [China Cent. Adv. Sci. Technol. World Lab. Symp./Workshop proc.]. **Main/Conf** CCAST (World Laboratory). **VFOAT** CCAST (World Laboratory) Symposium Workshop Proceedings; Proceedings of the CCAST (World Laboratory) Symposium/Workshop; Proceedings of the China Center of Advanced Science and Technology (World Laboratory); Symposium/Workshop; CCAST (World Laboratory); Symposium/Workshop Proceedings. (1987)-. Monographic series. English. ir. Price varies per volume. Gordon & Breach Science Publishers, PO Box 90, Reading RG1 8JL England. **Tel** 011 44 734 560080, FAX 011 44 734 568211. **(Subscription address:** Gordon & Breach Science Publishers / US, 820 Town Center Drive, Langhorne PA 19047.**) LC** UNC. **DD** 505. **CODEN** CCTPEC.

CC
**CHINA SCIENCE & TECHNOLOGY ABSTRACTS. SERIES II, CHEMISTRY, EARTH SCIENCE, ENERGY SOURCES.** ***Ceased.*** **VFOAT** Chemistry, Earth Science, Energy Sources; Chung-Kuo Ko Chi Wen Chai. **VAT** China Science and Technology Abstracts. Series II, Chemistry, Earth Science, Energy Sources. Vol. 2, No. 2 (April 1981)-?. Periodical. English. bm. International Information Service, GPO Box 3905, Room 103 Wing On Plaza, Tsimshatsui East, Kowloon Hong Kong. **Tel** 3-7391818, FAX 3-7213692, telex 30431 NTEDL HX. **ED** Chiu Nam Shum. **Circ:** 2,000. ***Continues*** *China Science & Technology Abstracts. Series II, Chemistry, Earth Science.*
**Desc:** Each issue collects about 400 abstracts and indexes from the papers published in the highly reputed journals of China.

US/0361-9001
**CHINESE SCIENCE.** V. 1- May 1975-. English. ir. $1.50 single issue. Technology Studies Program, Room 20D/212 Massachusetts Institute of Technology, Cambridge MA 02139. **ED** N Sivin. **LC** Q145; .C48. **DD** 509/.51. **NLM** Q 145 C539.

CC/0254-5179
**CHINESE SCIENCE ABSTRACTS. PART A.** [Chin. sci. abstr., Part A]. Vol. 1, No. 1 (July 1982)-. Periodical. English. bm. $470.00 (regular subscription), $783.00 (combination subscription with Chinese Science Abstracts Part B) The Americas; £315.00 (regular subscription), £525.00 (combination subscription with Chinese Science Abstracts Part B) other. Pergamon Press, An Imprint of Elsevier Science Ltd., The Boulevard, Langford Lane, Kidlington, Oxford OX5 1GB United Kingdom. **Tel** 011 44 865 843000, 011 44 865 843699, FAX 011 44 865 843010. **(Subscription address:** Elsevier Science Ltd. Oxford Fulfillment Centre, PO Box 800, Kidlington, Oxford OX5 1DX United Kingdom.**) ED** Fu Guoqiang, Wang Xiaohua, Sun Yanming, Xing Xiaochen, Huang Lianyou, Yan Mingwen. **LC** QA1; .C466. **DD** 505. Index available. **Ad Acc. Circ:** 1,500. available on microfilm and microfiche from University Microfilms International (UMI).
**Desc:** Provides abstracts of all important scientific articles from Chinese scientific periodicals.
**Ind/Abst** Math. Rev.

CC/0254-4903
**CHINESE SCIENCE ABSTRACTS. PART B.** **VFOAT** CSA. Vol. 1, No. 1 (Aug. 1982)-. Periodical. English. bm. $470.00 (regular subscription), $783.00 (combination subscription with Chinese Science Abstracts Part A) The Americas; £315.00 (regular subscription), £525.00 (combination subscription with Chinese Science Abstracts Part A) other. Pergamon Press, An Imprint of Elsevier Science Ltd., The Boulevard, Langford Lane, Kidlington, Oxford OX5 1GB United Kingdom. **Tel** 011 44 865 843000, 011 44 865 843699, FAX 011 44 865 843010. **(Subscription address:** Elsevier Science Ltd. Oxford Fulfillment Centre, PO Box 800, Kidlington, Oxford OX5 1DX United Kingdom.**) ED** Yan Mingwen, Fu Guoqiang, Wang Xiaohua, Sun Yanming, Xing Xiaochen, Huang Lianyou. **LC** QD1; .C783. **DD** 505. **NLM** Z 7403;

C539. Index available. **Ad Acc. Circ:** 1,500. available on microfilm and microfiche from University Microfilms International (UMI).
**Desc:** Provides abstracts of all important scientific articles from Chinese scientific periodicals.

CC/1001-6538
**CHINESE SCIENCE BULLETIN.** [Chin. sci. bull.]. **Added/Corp** Chung-Kuo ko Hsueh Yuan. **VFOAT** Kexue Tongbao; Ko Hsueh Tung Pao. Vol. 34, No. 1 (Jan. 1989)-. Bulletin. English (translations available in Chinese). Twenty-four times a year. $684.00. Science Press, 16 Donghuangchenggen North Street, Beijing 100707, People's Republic of China. **Tel** 011 86 1 4019821, 011 86 1 4010642, FAX 011 86 1 4012180, 011 86 1 4019810, telex 210147. **ED** Yan Dongsheng. **LC** Q4; .K5942. **DD** 505. **NLM** W1; KO279G. **CODEN** CSBUEF. **Pr Rev.** available on CD-ROM; available on microfilm and microfiche from University Microfilms International (UMI). Documents available from The Genuine Article, CASDDS. ***Continues*** *Ko Hsueh Tung Pao. English. Ko Hsueh Tung Pao, 0250-7862.*
**Desc:** Provides regular, rapid and authoritative reviews of current important developments in scientific research in China for scientific workers in both China and other countries. Presents concise reports on the latest research in basic and applied sciences and briefly covers the most recent research news.
**Ind/Abst** Ceram. Abstr. (199?-); Chem. Abstr.; Curr. Contents Phys. Chem. Earth Sci.; Math. Rev.; Meteorol. Geoastrophys. Abstr.; Res. Alert [Select. Cov.]; SCISEARCH; SEA Abstr.; Seed Abstr.; Soc. Sci. Cit. Index [Select. Cov.]; Wheat Barley Trit. Abstr.; Zentralbl. Math. Ihre Grenzgeb.

●JA/0577-9316
**CHIRIBOTAN.** Japanese (Multiple languages; summaries and/or abstracts in English). Four times a year. ¥3000. Natl. Sci. Mus Malacological Society, 3-23-1 Hyakunin-Cho Shinjuku, Tokyo 169 Japan. **Tel** 011 81 3 33642311 Ext. 521. **ED** Tsuchida, Eiji, (editor's address: Ocean Research Institute, Tokyo University, 1-15-1 Minamidai, Nakano-ku, Tokyo 164 Japan (phone: 03-3351-6470). Index Bound in First Issue. cum. index. **Bk Rev**, (Qty: 6). **Pr Rev. Circ:** 800.

US/0564-478X
**CHISPA.** **See** Children and Youth Interests.

BG/0253-5459
**CHITTAGONG UNIVERSITY STUDIES. PART II, SCIENCE.** [Chittagong Univ. stud., Part II: sci.]. **Added/Corp** Cattagrama Bisvabidyalaya. **VFOAT** Science; Cattagrama Bisvabidyalaya Stadija. Vol. 1 (1977)-. Periodical. Bengali (English). **LC** Q80.B3; C5. **DD** 505. **CODEN** CUSCDP. Documents available from BIOSIS Document Express, Ask*IEEE, CASDDS.
**Ind/Abst** Biol. Abstr.; Chem. Abstr.; INSPEC (1983-); Math. Rev.

KO
**CHONGUK TAEHAKSAENG HAKSUL YONGU PALPYO NONMUNJIP : KICHO KWAHAK PUNYA.** Korean (English). Sogang Taehakkyo Hakto Hoguktan, 1 Sinsu-dong, Mapo-ku Seoul Korea. **LC** Q4; .C4218. **DD** 505.

KO/0366-6662
**CHOSON MINJUJUUI INMIN KONGHWAGUK KWAHAGWON TONGBO.** [Choson Minjujuui Inmin Konghwaguk Kwahagwon tongbo]. **Main/Corp** Choson Minjujuui Inmin Konghwaguk Kwahagwon. (19??)-. Periodical. Korean. bm. **LC** Q4; .C4222a. **CODEN** CKWTAN. Documents available from CASDDS. ***Continues*** *Choson Minjujuui Inmin Konghwaguk Kwahagwon. Choson Kwahagwon Tongbo.*
**Ind/Abst** Chem. Abstr.

US/0012-8147
**CHRONICLE OF THE EARLY AMERICAN INDUSTRIES ASSOCIATION, INC, THE.** [Chron. Early Am. Ind. Assoc. Inc.]. **Added/Corp** Early American Industries Association. **VFOAT** Chronicle. Vol. 4, No. 1 (Jan. 1951)-. Periodical. English. qt. $25.00 US; $34.00 other. Early American Industries Association / New York, PO Box 2128 Empire State Plaza Station, Albany NY 12220. **Tel** (518)439-2215. **ED** Daniel B. Rerbel (editor's address: 1234 Linden Avenue, Yardley, PA 19067-7416, phone (215)428-0399). **LC** T1; .E2. **DD** 609.73. **Circ:** 3,300 (ctrl). available on microfilm and microfiche from University Microfilms International (UMI). ***Continues*** *Chronicle of Early American Industries, 0735-6110.*
**Desc:** Composed of collectors of tool and other artifacts related to early American crafts and industries. Deals with early technology, crafts, manufacturing, collecting, preserving tools and many other subjects.
**Ind/Abst** Am. Hist. Life.

FR/1168-1209
**CHRONIQUES - GRET.** (CHRONIQUES.). **VFOAT** Chroniques - Groupe de Recherche et d'Echanges Technologiques; Chroniques (Paris. 1990). (1990)-. Periodical. French. qt. 95.00F individuals; 165.00F institutions. Groupe Recherche Dechanges Tec, 213 rue La Fayette, 75010 Paris France. **Tel** 011 33 1 40351314, FAX 011 33 1 40350839, telex 212890. **UDC** 62(1-773). ***Continues*** *Chroniques, 0296-9114.*

JA/0910-8629
**CHUBU DAIGAKU KOGAKUBU KIYO.** **See** Engineering.

JA
**CHUGOKU KOGYO GIJUTSU.** **Main/Corp** Chugoku Kogyo Gijutsu Shikenjo. Oct. 1973-. Japanese. Chugoku Chiiki Gijutsu Shinko Senta, (Chugoku Technology Promotion Center), 4-33, Komachi, Nakaku, Hiroshimashi, Hiroshimaken 370 Japan. **LC** T178.C48; C48A.

JA
**CHUGOKU KOGYO GIJUTSU SHIKENJO NEMPO.** **Main/Corp** Chugoku Kogyo Gijutsu Shikenjo. Japanese. 15000 Hiromachi, 737-01 Kure Japan. **LC** T178.C48; C48B.

CC
**CHUNG-HUA KO HSUEH HUA PAO.** **VFOAT** Chung Hwa Popular Science. Vol. 1, (March 1954)-. Periodical. Chinese. bm. $4.86. Science Press, 16 Donghuangchenggen North Street, Beijing 100707, People's Republic of China. **Tel** 011 86 1 4019821, 011 86 1 4010642, FAX 011 86 1 4012180, 011 86 1 4019810, telex 210147.

CC
**CHUNG-KUO KO CHI SHIH LIAO.** **VFOAT** China Historical Materials of Science and Technology. (19??)-. Periodical. Chinese. bm. RMBY0.70. Post Office Beijing, Beijing, People's Republic of China. **LC** Q127.C5; C564. **DD** 505.
**Ind/Abst** Am. Hist. Life (1991-).

KO
**CHUNGNAM KWAHAK YONGUJI / CHAYON KWAHAK YONGUSO.** **VFOAT** Chungnam Journal of Sciences. Academic Scholarly Publication. English (Korean). sa. **LC** Q4; .C42275. **CODEN** CJOSDA. Documents available from CASDDS.
**Ind/Abst** Chem. Abstr.; Energy Res. Abstr. (Jan. 1982-).

KO
**CHUNGSO KIOP CHONGBO MONGNOK.** Korean. Chungso Kiop Chinhung Kongdan, 1-1040 Youido-dong Yongdungpo-ku, Seoul 150 Korea. **LC** Z7913; .C497; T45.

JA
**CHUO DAIGAKU RIKOGAKUBU KIYO.** **Main/Corp** Chuo Daigaku, Tokyo. Rikogakubu. **VFOAT** Bulletin of the Faculty of Science and Engineering, Chuo University. Academic Scholarly Publication. Japanese (English; summaries and/or abstracts in English). 1-13-27 Kasuga Bunkyo-ku, Tokyo Japan. **LC** Q1.A1; C48A. **CODEN** CDSEAB. Documents available from CASDDS.
**Ind/Abst** Chem. Abstr.

JA
**CHUSHO KIGYO GIJUTSU JITTAI CHOSA: GIJUTSU KAIHATSU KADAI HOKOKUSHO.** **Main/Corp** Chusho Kigyo Shinko Jigyodan. **VFOAT** Gijutsu Kaihatsu Kadai Hokokusho. (1972)-. Japanese. Sankaido Building, 9-13 Akasaka 1-chome, Minato-ku 107 Tokyo Japan. **LC** T4; .C54A.

AG
**CICLO DE CONFERENCIAS.** **Main/Corp** Sociedad Cientifica Argentina. Spanish. Comision de Cursos y Conferencias, Av Santa Fe 1145, Buenos Aires Argentina. **LC** Q33; .S21813.

VE/0529-7281
**CIENCIA AL DIA.** [Ciencia dia]. Began in 1961. Periodical. Spanish. qt. 1200ptas. Sociedad Venezolana Cinen Nat, Calle Arichuna Con, Cumaco 1521, Caracas Venezuela. **LC** Q4; .C424.

BL/0009-6725
**CIENCIA E CULTURA (SAO PAULO).** (CIENCIA E CULTURA.). [Cienc. cult.]. **Added/Corp** Sociedade Brasileira para o Progresso da Ciencia. Vol. 1, No. 1/2 (Jan./April 1949)-. Academic Scholarly Publication. English (French, Italian, Portuguese and Spanish). mo. Soc Brasileira Progresso Ciencia, Rua Maria Antonia 294 40 Andar, Sao Paulo Brazil. **Tel** 011 55 11 34-7998. **LC** Q4; .C425. **NLM** W1 CI221. **CODEN** CCUPAD. cum. index. Documents available from BIOSIS Document Express, CASDDS.
**Ind/Abst** Agrofor. Abstr. (1991-); Anim. Behav. Abstr.; Biodeter. Abstr. (1991-); Biol. Abstr.; Chem. Abstr.; Curr. Biotechnol.; Ecology Abstr.; EMBASE; Field Crop Abstr.; For. Abstr.; Helminthol. Abstr. (1991-); Hortic. Abstr.; Math. Rev.; Nutr. Abstr. Rev., Ser. A, Hum. Exp.; Ocean. Abstr.; Life Sci. Collect.; Plant Breed. Abstr.; Protozoolog. Abstr.; Rev. Agric. Entomol.; Rev. Med. Vet. Mycology; Rural Dev. Abstr.; Soils Fert.; Soyabean Abstr.

AG/0009-6733
**CIENCIA E INVESTIGACION.** [Cienc. invest.]. **Added/Corp** Asociacion Argentina para el Progreso de las Ciencias. Vol. 1, No. 1 (Jan. 1945)-. Academic Scholarly Publication. Spanish. ir. Associacion Argent Progreso, Avenida Alvear 1711 4 Piso, 1014 Buenos Aires Argentina. **LC** Q4; .C48. **NLM** W1 CI223. **CODEN** CIBAAH. available on microfilm from University Microfilms International (UMI). Documents available from BIOSIS Document Express, CASDDS.
**Ind/Abst** Biol. Abstr.; Chem. Abstr. (1945-1980).

BL/0100-8307
**CIENCIA E NATURA.** (CIENCIA E NATURA : REVISTA DO CENTRO DE CIENCIAS NATURAIS E EXATAS / MINISTERIO DA EDUCACAO E CULTURA, UNIVERSIDADE FEDERAL DE SANTA MARIA.). [Cienc. nat.]. **Added/Corp** Universidade Federal de Santa Maria. Centro de Ciencias Naturais e Exatas. No. 1 (Dec. 1979)-. Periodical. Portuguese. **CODEN** CNATD5. Documents available from CASDDS.
**Ind/Abst** Chem. Abstr.

PO/0254-0223
**CIENCIA E TECNICA VITIVINICOLA.** [Cienc. tec. vitivinic.]. **Added/Corp** Estacao Vitivinicola Nacional (Portugal). Vol. 1, No. 1 (1982)-. Periodical. Portuguese. sa. **CODEN** CTVIEI. Documents available from CASDDS.
**Ind/Abst** Chem. Abstr.

BL/0101-8515
**CIENCIA HOJE : REVISAT DE DIVULGACAO CIENTIFICA DA SOCIEDADE BRASILEIRA PARA O PROGRESSO DA CIENCIA.** Yearly V. 1, No. 1 (July/Aug. 1982)-. Periodical. Portuguese. bm. $20.00 US; $50.00, $100.00 (airmail) other. Av Venceslau Braz, 71 Fundos Casa 27, Rio de Janeiro RJ CEP 222 Brazil. **Tel** (021)295-4846, 295-4442, FAX (021)541-5342, telex (21)36952. **ED** Ennio Candotti, Roberto Lent, Otavio Velho and Cesar Queiroz. **LC** Q4; .C428. **DD** 505. **CODEN** CIHOEP. Index available. cum. index. **Bk Rev. Ad Acc. Circ:** 40,000 (ctrl).
**Desc:** A multidisciplinary magazine dedicated to the dissemination of scientific news in various areas of the exact sciences, biology, and the humanities.

US/0009-675X
**CIENCIA INTERAMERICANA.** ***Suspended.*** [Cienc. interam.]. Vol. 1, No. 1 (Jan./Feb. 1960)-Suspended with Vol. 27. Academic Scholarly Publication. Spanish. qt. $4.00. Organization of American States, 19th Street & Constitution Avenue NW, Suite 300, Washington DC 20006. **Tel** (202)458-6256. **LC** Q4.C43. **NLM** W1 CI223J. **CODEN** CIIABJ. Documents available from CASDDS.
**Ind/Abst** Chem. Abstr.; GeoRef.

MX/0185-075X
**CIENCIA (MEXICO CITY, MEXICO).** (CIENCIA.). **Added/Corp** Patronato de Ciencia (Mexico) Academia de la Investigacion Cientifica (Mexico). Vol. 1 (March 1940)-. Periodical. Spanish (summaries and/or abstracts in English; table of contents in English). qt. $78.00 (individuals), $156.00 (institutions). Academia Investigaciones Cientifica, Av San Jeronimo 260, 04500 Mexico DF Mexico. **Tel** 011 52 5 556278. **ED** Fernando del Rio. **LC** Q4; .C47. **DD** 505. **NLM** W1 CI226L. **CODEN** CIENA3. cum. index. **Bk Rev. Ad Acc. Circ:** 2,000 (ctrl). Documents available from BIOSIS Document Express, Ask*IEEE, CASDDS.
**Desc:** Review articles in all scientific fields.
**Ind/Abst** Biol. Abstr.; Chem. Abstr.; INSPEC (1968-).

MX/0185-0008
**CIENCIA Y DESARROLLO.** [Cienc. desarro.]. **Added/Corp** Consejo Nacional de Ciencia y Tecnologia (Mexico). No. 1 (March/April 1975)-. Academic Scholarly Publication. Spanish. bm (6 issues). $33.00 The Americas; $44.00 Europe; $60.00 Africa; $66.00 Asia. Consejo Nacional Ciencia y Tecno, Av Constituyentes 1046 Lomas A, CP 11950 Mexico DF Mexico. **Tel** 011 52 5 3277400. **(Subscription address:** Dirreccion Adj Inv Cientifica, Constituyentes 1046 Lomas Alta, CP 11950 Mexico DF Mexico.**) ED** Mauricio Fortes. **LC** Q4; .C4716. **CODEN** CIDED8. cum. index. **Bk Rev. Ad Acc. Circ:** 50,000 (ctrl). Documents available from CASDDS.
**Desc:** Bridging the gap between basic science and technology and the layman. Forum for establishing official scientific planning.
**Ind/Abst** Chem. Abstr. (1975-1983).

EC/0009-6768
**CIENCIA Y NATURALEZA.** [Cienc. nat.]. **Added/Corp** Universidad Central del Ecuador. Instituto de Ciencias Naturales. Vol. 1 (June 1957)-. Periodical. Spanish. an. Free on request. Universidad Central / Ecuador, Instituto de Ciencias Naturales, POB 633, Quito Canje Ecuador. **CODEN** CINQAN. Documents available from BIOSIS Document Express. ***Supersedes*** *Universidad Central del Ecuador. Instituto de Ciencias Naturales. Boletin del Instituto de Ciencias Naturales.*
**Ind/Abst** Biol. Abstr.; Field Crop Abstr.; GeoRef; Grasslands For. Abstr.

CU/0259-2932
**CIENCIA Y TECNICA EN LA AGRICULTURA. GANADO PORCINO.** [Cienc. tec. agric., Ganado porc.]. **Added/Corp** Centro de Informacion y Documentacion Agropecuario (Cuba) Centro de Investigaciones Porcinas (Cuba). **VFOAT** Ganado Porcino. (1978)-. Spanish (summaries and/or

abstracts in English; table of contents in English). be. Ediciones Cubanas, Obispo 527, Altos ESQ Bernaza, CP 10100 Havana Cuba. **Tel** 011 632980, 631942, FAX 011 631011, telex 512337, 6540. **CODEN** CAGPDY.
**Ind/Abst** Index Vet.; Pig News Inf.

SP/0009-6776
**CIENCIAS (MADRID), LAS.** (LAS CIENCIAS.). [Ciencias]. **Added/Corp** Asociacion Espanola para el Progreso de las Ciencias. Asociacion Espanola para el Progreso de las Ciencias. Anales. **VFOAT** Anales de la Asociacion Espanola para el Progreso de las Ciencias. (1934)-. Periodical. Spanish. **LC** Q65; .A67. **DD** 505. **NLM** W1 CI259. **CODEN** CINSAT. Documents available from CASDDS.
**Ind/Abst** Am. Hist. Life (1955-1962); Chem. Abstr.; Coal Abstr.

SX/1012-4926
**CIMBEBASIA : JOURNAL OF THE STATE MUSEUM, WINDHOEK. Added/Corp** Namibia. State Museum. Vol. 10 (Dec. 1988)-. English. an. State Museum of Namibia, PO Box 1203, Windhoek Namibia. **Tel** (061)293911, FAX (061)222005. **ED** C Roberts, J B Kinahan. **LC** Q85.8; .C55. **DD** 508. **CODEN** CIMBEB. Index available. **Bk Rev. Pr Rev. Circ:** 350 (ctrl). Documents available from BIOSIS Document Express. ***Formed by the union of** Cimbebasia. Ser. A, 0590-6342 **and** Cimbebasia. Ser. B, 0590-6350.*
**Desc:** Articles by specialists on the cultural and natural history of Southwestern Africa.
**Ind/Abst** Biol. Abstr. (1991-).

US/0896-3444
**CIMLINC TECHNICAL UPDATE. *Ceased.*** [CIMLINC tech. update]. Vol. 3, No. 1 (Jan. 15, 1988)-(1989). Periodical. English. mo. CIMLIMC Inc, 1957 Crooks Road, Troy MI 48084. **DD** 006. ***Continues** Technical Update (CIMLINC, Inc.), 0896-3436.*

CN/1191-1255
**CIRCUMPOLAR NOTES.** (INFORMATION CIRCUMPOLAIRE / DIRECTION DES AFFAIRES CIRCUMPOLAIRES ET SCIENTIFIQUES, PROGRAMME DU NORD, AFFAIRES INDIENNES ET DU NORD.). [Circumpolar notes]. **Added/Corp** Programme des Affaires du Nord (Canada). Direction des Affaires Circumpolaires et Scientifiques. Vol. 1, No 1 (Nov./Dec. 1991)-. Periodical. French (English). bm. **DD** 508.311/3/05.

CN/1191-1255
**CIRCUMPOLAR NOTES / CIRCUMPOLAR AND SCIENTIFIC AFFAIRS DIRECTORATE, NORTHERN AFFAIRS PROGRAM, DEPARTMENT OF INDIAN AFFAIRS AND NORTHERN DEVELOPMENT.** [Circumpolar notes]. **Added/Corp** Northern Affairs Program (Canada). Circumpolar & Scientific Affairs Directorate. **VFOAT** Information Circumpolaire. Vol. 1, No. 1 (Nov./Dec. 1991)-. Periodical. English (French). bm. **DD** 508.311/3/05.

AT/1032-3007
**CIT TASK FORCE REPORT.** [CIT task force rep.]. **VAT** Computing and Information Technology Task Force Report. No. 1; 1988-. Monographic series. English. ir. Price varies per volume. Bond University, Gold Coast Law School, Queensland 4229 Australia. **Tel** 011 61 75 925011, FAX 011 61 75 952246.

SM/0258-5308
**CIVILTA CIBERNETICA. *Suspended.*** [Civilta cibern.]. (1981)-(April 1992). Periodical. Italian. qt. IST Sammarinese Cibernetica, Via Cappuccini, 47031 San Marino. **Tel** 011 39 549 882808. **UDC** 681.3.

US/1044-4750
**CLARION TECH JOURNAL, THE.** [Clar. tech j.]. Vol. 1, No. 1 (July/Aug. 1989)-. Periodical. English. Six times a year (Jan., Mar., May, July, Sept., Nov.). $60.00 US; $70.00 Canada & Mexico; $90.00 others. PC Information Group, PO Box 1301, 1126 East Broadway, Winona MN 55987. **Tel** (800)321-8285 or (507)452-2824, FAX (507)452-0037. **DD** 005. **Ad Acc.**

PH/0116-7847
**CMU JOURNAL OF SCIENCE.** [CMU j. sci.]. **Added/Corp** Central Mindanao University. **VFOAT** Journal of Science. **VAT** Central Mindano University Journal of Science. Vol. 1, No. 1 (July-Dec. 1988)-. Periodical. English. Twice a year. P60.00 Philippines; $4.00 other. Central Mindanao University / Library, University Town, Musuan, Bukidnon 8710 Philippines. **ED** Dr. Herminio M. Pava. **[CCC].** ***Continues** CMU Journal of Agriculture, Food and Nutrition, 0115-4931.*
**Desc:** A multidisciplinary science journal.
**Ind/Abst** Nutr. Abstr. Rev., Ser. B, Live Feeds and Feed.; Poult. Abstr.; World Agric. Econ.

BL
**CNPQ BOLETIM. Main/Corp** Conselho Nacional de Desenvolvimento Cientifico e Tecnologico. Bulletin. Portuguese. Praia do Flamengo 200, Rio de Janeiro Brazil. **LC** Q180.B7; C65A. **DD** 507/.2081.

US/0366-757X
**CODATA BULLETIN. *Ceased.*** [CODATA bull.]. **Main/Corp** CODATA. **Added/Corp** CODATA. Bulletin. **VAT** Committee on Data for Science and Technology Bulletin. (Oct. 1969) -Ceased with Vol. 24, No. 4, (1992). Academic Scholarly Publication. English. qt. Taylor & Francis Ltd., Rankine Road, Basingstoke Hampshire, RG24 8PR United Kingdom. **Tel** 011 44 256 840366, FAX 011 44 256 479438, telex 858540. **(Subscription address:** Taylor & Francis Inc., 1900 Frost Road, Suite 101, Bristol PA 19007-1598.**) ED** Edgar F Westrum (editor's address: University of Michigan, Department of Chemistry, Ann Arbor, MI 48109); Phyllis Glaeser (editor's address: CODATA Secretariat, 51 Boulevard de Montmorency, 75016 Paris France). **LC** Q183.9; .I54. **DD** 502/.8/54. **NLM** W1 C542X. **CODEN** CODBA4. **[CCC].** available on microfilm and microfiche from University Microfilms International (UMI). Documents available from CASDDS.
**Desc:** Covers properties and behavior of matter, characteristics of biological and geological systems, as well as related related experimental and observational data.
**Ind/Abst** AESIS Q.; Chem. Abstr. (1969-1984); Ei Page One; Energy Res. Abstr. (June 1975-19??); GeoRef; Int. Aerosp. Abstr.; Life Sci. Collect.; Soils Fert.

GW/0538-6918
**CODATA NEWSLETTER.** [CODATA newsl.]. **Main/Corp** CODATA. **Added/Corp** CODATA. Newsletter. **VAT** Committee on Data for Science and Technology Newsletter. Vol. 1 (Oct. 1968)-. Periodical. English. Four times a year. CODATA, 51 Boulevard de Montmorency, 75016 Paris France. **Tel** 011 31 1 45250496. **LC** Q10; .I639. **DD** 507/.2. **NLM** W1 C543.
**Ind/Abst** Energy Res. Abstr. (June 1975-); World Ceram. Abstr.

BL/0103-3247
**COLECAO CLE.** [Colec. CLE]. **VFOAT** Colecao Centro de Logica, Epistemologia e Historia da Ciencia. (1987)-. Monographic series. Portuguese. ir. Price varies per volume. **UDC** 16.
**Ind/Abst** Zentralbl. Math. Ihre Grenzgeb.

FR
**COLLECTION DE TRAVAUX DE L'ACADEMIE INTERNATIONALE D'HISTOIRE DES SCIENCES. Main/Corp** Academie Internationale d'Histoire des Sciences. **Added/Corp** Unesco. No. 1 (1948)-. Monographic series. French. Price varies per volume. E. J. Brill, Postbus 9000, 2300 PA Leiden Netherlands. **Tel** 011 31 71 312624, FAX 011 31 71 317532, telex 39296 BRILL NL.
**Ind/Abst** Math. Rev.

FR/0768-0341
**COLLECTION ENSEIGNEMENT DES SCIENCES.** [Collect. Enseign. sci.]. **VFOAT** Enseignement des Sciences. (19??)-. Monographic series. French. Price varies per volume. Hermann Editeurs Science Arts, 293 rue Lecourbe, 75015 Paris France. **Tel** 011 33 1 45574540. **CODEN** ENSSBA. Documents available from BIOSIS Document Express. ***Continues** Enseignement des Sciences.*
**Ind/Abst** Biol. Abstr. (?-1985); Zentralbl. Math. Ihre Grenzgeb.

US/0740-462X
**COLLEGE OF SCIENCE ALUMNI DIRECTORY, THE PENNSYLVANIA STATE UNIVERSITY. See** College and School Publications-Alumni.

●US/1061-933X
**COLLOID JOURNAL OF THE RUSSIAN ACADEMY OF SCIENCES.** (COLLOID JOURNAL OF THE RUSSIAN ACADEMY OF SCIENCES: KOLLOIDNYI ZHURNAL.). [Colloid j. Russ. Acad. Sci.]. **Added/Corp** Consultants Bureau. **VFOAT** Kolloidnyi Zhurnal. (1992)-. Academic Scholarly Publication. English (translations available in Russian). bm. $1245.00 US; $1455.00 other. MAIK Nauka / Interperiodica, Ulitsa Profsoyuznaya 90, Moscow 117864 Russia. **DD** 541. **CODEN** CJRSEQ. **[CCC].** Documents available from Article Express International, The Genuine Article, Ask*IEEE, CASDDS. ***Continues** Colloid Journal of the USSR, 0010-1303.*
**Ind/Abst** AGRICOLA; Chem. Abstr. (1992-); Curr. Contents Phys. Chem. Earth Sci.; Ei Page One (1992-); Eng. Index Annu.; INSPEC (1992-); MINPROC (1992-); Nucl. Sci. Abstr. (1992-); Res. Alert [Full Cov.]; World Surf. Coat. Abstr. (1992-).

CK/0120-4335
**COLOMBIA, CIENCIA Y TECNOLOGIA. Added/Corp** Fondo Colombiano de Investigaciones Cientificas y Proyectos Especiales Francisco Jose de Caldas. **VFOAT** Ciencia y Tecnologia. (198?)-. Periodical. Spanish. qt. Colciencias, Transversal 9A/#133-28, Bogota Colombia. **Tel** 2179800, telex 44305. **ED** Marta Angulo De Solarte. **LC** Q33; .C54. **DD** 509/.861. ***Continues** Ciencia y Tecnologia (Bogota, Colombia).*

PO/0870-7650
**COLOQUIO/CIENCIAS. Added/Corp** Fundacao Calouste Gulbenkian. **VFOAT** Coloquio Ciencias. No. 1 (Feb. 1988)-. Periodical. Portuguese. Three times a year (May, July, Nov.). 1300$00. Fundacao Calouste Gulbenkian, Av de Berna 56 5th, 1093 Lisbon Codex Portugal. **LC** Q65; .C63. **DD** 505. **Bk Rev. Ad Acc.**

US/0361-2317
**COLOR RESEARCH AND APPLICATION.** [Color res. appl.]. Vol. 1 (Spring 1976)-. Academic Scholarly Publication. English. bm. $330.00 US; $390.00 Canada and Mexico; $412.50 other. John Wiley & Sons, Inc., 605 Third Avenue, New York NY 10158-0012. **Tel** (212)850-6000, (212)850-6645, FAX (212)850-6088, telex 12-7063. **(Subscription address:** John Wiley & Sons / England, Baffins Lane, Chichester, West Sussex PO19 1UD England.**) ED** Ellen C. Carter. **LC** QC494; .C63. **DD** 535.6/05. **CODEN** CREADU. **[CCC]. Ad Acc. Pr Rev. Circ:** 1,700. available on microfilm and microfiche from University Microfilms International (UMI). Documents available from Article Express International, The Genuine Article, Ask*IEEE, CASDDS.
**Desc:** An international journal reporting on the science, technology and application of color in business, art, design, education, and industry.
**Ind/Abst** Abstr. Bull. Inst. Pap. Sci. Tech.; Abstr. Graphic Arts Tech. Found. (1984); Art Archaeol. Tech. Abstr.; Bioeng. Abstr.; Chem. Abstr.; Curr. Contents Eng. Tech. Appl. Sci.; Ei Page One; Eng. Index Annu. [Select. Cov.]; Ergon. Abstr.; Graph. Arts Bull. Inst. Pap. Sci. Technol. (Jan. 1989-Feb.1989, May 1989-June 1989, Nov. 1989); INSPEC (Spring 1980-); Print. Abstr.; Res. Alert [Full Cov.]; Sci. Cit. Index; SCISEARCH; Soc. Sci. Cit. Index [Select. Cov.]; Text. Technol. Dig.; World Ceram. Abstr.; World Surf. Coat. Abstr.

US/0883-8208
**COLORADO HIGH TECHNOLOGY DIRECTORY. Added/Corp** Leading Edge Communications. **VFOAT** Colorado High Technology Directory Update. (1985)-. Directory. English. an. $94.00. Leading Edge Communications, 1121 Old Siskiyou Highway, Ashland OR 97520. **Tel** (503)482-4990. **ED** Charles J Koelsch. **LC** HC107.C73; H533. **DD** 338.7/62/00025788. Index available. **Circ:** 500. available on an online database.
**Desc:** A comprehensive reference tool for those interested in high tech research and development and high tech manufacturing firms in Colorado.

UK/0069-6277
**COLSTON PAPERS. See** Education-Higher Education.

CN
**COMMENT CA MARCHE.** V. 1-. Periodical. French. wk. $1.00 per issue. Comment Ca Marche, CP 305 Succursale Bourassa, Montreal Quebec H2C 3G2 Canada. **DD** 603.

CN/0317-8803
**COMMUNIQUE - CONSEIL DE LA JEUNESSE SCIENTIFIQUE. Main/Corp** Conseil de la Jeunesse Scientifique. **VFOAT** C J S-Communique. No. 1- Nov. 1973-. French. mo. Conseil De La Jeunesse Scientifique, Bureau 14, 230 Est Boul., Henri-Bourassa, Montreal Quebec H3L 1B8 Canada. **DD** 506/.2/714.

US
**COMPACT CAMBRIDGE LIFE SCIENCES COLLECTION [COMPUTER FILE]. Added/Corp** Cambridge Scientific Abstracts, Inc. **VFOAT** Cambridge Life Sciences Collection; Life Sciences Collection. (1984/85)-. English. qt. $2495.00 (disc plus two year backfile), $3495.00 (1985-present), $4995.00 (1982-present) US and Canada; $2575.00 (disc plus two year backfile), $3575.00 (1985-present), $5075.00 (1982-present) other (except UK; Asia; Australia). Cambridge Scientific Abstracts, 7200 Wisconsin Avenue, #601, Bethesda MD 20814-4823. **Tel** (301)961-6750, (800)843-7751, FAX (301)961-6720.
**Desc:** Designed specifically for life science professionals who seek interdisciplinary coverage. The Life Sciences Collection contains abstracts from more than 5,000 journals, books, monographs, conference papers, US patents, and other sources-covering 20 different fields across the scope of the life sciences.

US/0743-7692
**COMPARISON OF COMPENSATION PAID SCIENTISTS AND ENGINEERS IN RESEARCH AND DEVELOPMENT. See** Economics-Labor.

US
**COMPETITIVE ADVANCES. MATERIALS AND PROCESSES.** English. an. $45.00. SAMPE, PO Box 2459, Covina CA 91722. **ED** Stuart Lee. Index available. **Bk Rev. Ad Acc. Pr Rev. Circ:** 16,000 (ctrl).
**Desc:** Carries technical information on materials, processes, applications, news of society, symposiums, conferences, programs, book reviews and advancing the technology of new materials and their processing.

US/0736-1769
**COMPILATION OF ABSTRACTS OF THESES SUBMITTED BY CANDIDATES FOR DEGREES.** English. Naval Postgraduate School, Monterey CA 93940. **LC** T1; .U455A. **DD** 355/.005. ***Continues*** *Compilation of Abstracts of Dissertations, Theses, and Research Papers Submitted by Candidates for Degrees, 0363-7875.*

UK/0268-4055
**COMPLEMENTARY MEDICAL RESEARCH.** ***Title Change.*** **Added/Corp** Research Council for Complementary Medicine (England). Vol. 1, No. 1 (Feb. 1986)-(19??). Periodical. English. Three times a year. **NLM** W1; CO451W. ***Continued by*** *Complementary Therapies in Medicine.*
**Ind/Abst** EMBASE.

UK/0964-1816
**COMPLEXITY: AN INTERNATIONAL JOURNAL OF COMPLEX AND ADAPTIVE SYSTEMS.** ***Ceased.*** **VFOAT** Complexity. (1992)-(199?). English. Four times a year. Pergamon Press, An Imprint of Elsevier Science Ltd., The Boulevard, Langford Lane, Kidlington, Oxford OX5 1GB United Kingdom. **Tel** 011 44 865 843000, 011 44 865 843699, FAX 011 44 865 843010.

BE/0254-5128
**COMPTES-RENDUS DE L' ASSEMBLEE GENERALE DE LA COMMISSION INTERNATIONALE TECHNIQUE DE SUCRERIE.** [C.r. Assem. gen. Comm. int. tech. sucr.]. **Main/Corp** Commission Internationale Technique de Sucrerie. (19??)-. Monographic series. French (English, French and German). ir. Price varies per volume. CITS, Aandorenstraat 1, B-3300 Tienen Belgium. **Tel** 011 32 16 801211. **CODEN** CRISAX. Documents available from CASDDS.
**Ind/Abst** Chem. Abstr.

FR/0762-0969
**COMPTES RENDUS DE L'ACADEMIE DES SCIENCES.** (COMPTES RENDUS DE L'ACADEMIE DES SCIENCES. LA VIE DES SCIENCES.). [Vie sci.]. **Added/Corp** Academie des Sciences (France). **VFOAT** Vie des Sciences. Vol. 1 No. 1 (Jan. 1984)-. Periodical. French. qt (plus 1 supplement). 495.00F (institutions), 300.00F (individuals) France; 530.00F (institutions), 340.00F (individuals) other. Dunod Gauthier Villars, 15 rue Gossin, 92543 Montrouge cedex France. **Tel** 011 33 1 46 56 52 66, FAX 011 33 1 46 57 40 69. **(Subscription address:** Centrale des Revues, 11 rue Gossin, 92543 Montrouge Cedex France.**)** **LC** Q46; .C72. **DD** 505. **NLM** W1; CO454R. **[CCC].** Documents available from Ask*IEEE, CASDDS. ***Continues in part*** *Comptes Rendus des Seances de l'Academie des Sciences. Vie Academique, 0249-6321.*
**Ind/Abst** Chem. Abstr.; GeoRef; INSPEC (Feb./Mar. 1984-); Int. Aerosp. Abstr. (1991-); Meteorol. Geoastrophys. Abstr.

FR/0764-4450
**COMPTES RENDUS DE L'ACADEMIE DES SCIENCES. SERIE II, MECANIQUE, PHYSIQUE, CHIMIE, SCIENCES DE L'UNIVERS, SCIENCES DE LA TERRE.** ***Title Change.*** [C. r. Acad. sci., Ser. 2, Mec. phys. chim. sci. univers sci. terre]. **Added/Corp** Academie des Sciences (France). **VFOAT** Mecanique, Physique, Chimie, Sciences de l'Univers, Sciences de la Terre. (Jan. 7, 1984)-(1993). Academic Scholarly Publication. French (summaries and/or abstracts in English). Twenty-six times a year. Gauthier-Villars, 15 rue Gossin, 92543 Montrouge Cedex France. **Tel** 33 1 40 92 65 00, FAX 33 1 40 92 65 97. **(Subscription address:** Centrale des Revues, 11 rue Gossin, 92543 Montrouge Cedex France.**)** **LC** QD1; .A26. **DD** 505. **CODEN** CRAMED. **[CCC].** **Pr Rev.** Documents available from The Genuine Article, BIOSIS Document Express, Ask*IEEE, CASDDS. ***Continues*** *Comptes Rendus des Seances de l'Academie des Sciences. Serie II, Mecanique, Physique, Chimie, Sciences de l'Univers, Sciences de la Terre, 0249-6305.* ***Split into*** *Comptes Rendus de l'Academie des Sciences. Serie II, Mecanique, Physique, Chimie, Astronomie; Comptes Rendus de l'Academie des Sciences. Serie II, Sciences de la Terre et des Planetes.*
**Ind/Abst** Alum. Ind. Abstr. (?-?); Biol. Abstr. (?-?); Chem. Abstr. (1984-); Coal Abstr. (?-?); Curr. Chem. React. (?-?); Curr. Contents Phys. Chem. Earth Sci. (?-?); Ecol. Abstr. (?-?); Ei Page One (?-?); Fluid Abstr., Civil Eng. (?-?); Fluid Abstr. Proc. Eng. (?-?); FLUIDEX (?-?); Geogr. Abstr. Phys. Geogr. (?-?); Geogr. Abstr. Human Geogr. (?-?); Geol. Abstr. (?-?); GeoRef (?-?); Index Chem. (?-?); INSPEC (Jan. 1990-); Int. Aerosp. Abstr. (19??-19??); Met. Abstr. (?-?); Meteorol. Geoastrophys. Abstr. (?-?); PESTDOC (?-?); Res. Alert (?-?); Sci. Cit. Index (19??-19??); SCISEARCH (?-?); Zentra bl. Math. Ihre Grenzgeb. (?-?).

FR/0764-4469
**COMPTES RENDUS DE L'ACADEMIE DES SCIENCES. SERIE III, SCIENCES DE LA VIE.** [C. r. Acad. sci., Ser. 3, Sci. vie]. **Added/Corp** Academie des Sciences (France). **VFOAT** Sciences de la Vie. Vol. 298 No. 1 (Jan. 7, 1984)-. Academic Scholarly Publication. French (summaries and/or abstracts in English). mo. 2730.00 France; 3860.00F other. Gauthier-Villars, 15 rue Gossin, 92543 Montrouge Cedex France. **Tel** 33 1 40 92 65 00, FAX 33 1 40 92 65 97. **(Subscription address:** Centrale des Revues, 11 rue Gossin, 92543 Montrouge Cedex France.**)** **LC** Q2; .A26. **DD** 574/.05. **NLM** W1; CO454T; 8503078. **CODEN** CRASEV. **[CCC].** **Pr Rev.** Documents available from The Genuine Article, CASDDS. ***Continues*** *Comptes Rendus des Seances de l'Academie des Sciences. Serie III, Sciences de la Vie, 0249-6313.*
**Ind/Abst** AgBiotech News Inf.; Anim. Breed. Abstr.; Biocont. News Inf. (19??-19??); Biodeter. Abstr.; Chem. Abstr. (1984-); Crop Physiol. Abstr.; Curr. Aware. Biol. Sci., CABS; Curr. Contents, Agric. Biol. Environ. Sci.; Curr. Contents Life Sci.; Curr. Ref. Fish Res.; Dairy Sci. Abstr.; Ecol. Abstr.; EMBASE; Field Crop Abstr.; Geogr. Abstr. Phys. Geogr.; Geol. Abstr.; Grasslands For. Abstr.; Health Plan. Adminis.; Helminthol. Abstr. (19??-19??); Index Med. (1984-); Index Vet.; Maize Abstr.; Nematol. Abstr.; Nutr. Abstr. Rev., Ser. B, Live Feeds and Feed.; Ornamental Hort. (19??-19??); Life Sci. Collect.; PESTDOC; Pig News Inf.; Plant Breed. Abstr.; Plant Genet. Resour. Abstr.; Plant Grow. Reg. Abstr.; Potato Abstr.; Poult. Abstr.; Protozoolog. Abstr.; Res. Alert; Rev. Med. Vet. Entomol.; Rev. Med. Vet. Mycology; Rev. Plant Pathol.; Rice Abstr.; Sci. Cit. Index; SCISEARCH; Sorghum Mill. Abstr.; Soyabean Abstr.; Vet. Bull.; Wildl. Rev.; Zentralbl. Math. Ihre Grenzgeb.

US/0742-5686
**COMPUT-A-CAL.** ***Ceased.*** **See** Science and Technology-Abstracting, Bibliographies and Statistics.

UK/0308-4221
**COMPUTER APPLICATIONS.** [Comput. appl.]. V. 1- 1973-. Periodical. English. qt. £4.00. University of Nottingham Publications Secretary, Nottingham NG7 2RD United Kingdom. **CODEN** CPUABQ. Documents available from Ask*IEEE. ***Supersedes*** *Computer Applications in the Natural and Social Sciences, 0069-8105.*
**Ind/Abst** Comput. Rev.; INSPEC (1973-).

US
**COMPUTER LETTER.** Newsletter. English. Forty times a year. $595.00. Technological Partners, 419 Park Avenue South, Suite 500, New York NY 10016. **Tel** (212)696-9330. **ED** Richard A. Shaffer. Index available. cum. index. ctrl circ.
**Desc:** Provides business details to subscribers by analyzing trends developments and strategies in technology and finance.

US/0010-4876
**COMPUTING REPORT IN SCIENCE AND ENGINEERING.** V. 5, No. 2- 1969-. Periodical. English. Data Processing Division, International Business Machine, 1133 Westchester Avenue, White Plains NY 10604. **LC** TA345. **DD** 502/.8/54. ***Continues*** *Computing Report for the Scientist and Engineer.*

US
**CONFERENCE BRIEFS - UNITED STATES. NATIONAL BUREAU OF STANDARDS.** **Main/Corp** United States. National Bureau of Standards. Periodical. English. qt. Office of Information Activities, National Bureau of Standards, 14th Street & Constitution Avenue NW, Washington DC 20230. **Tel** (202)377-0703, (202)377-2000.

US/0194-0546
**CONFERENCE PAPERS ANNUAL INDEX.** (1978)-. English. an (Dec.). $475.00 US; $595.00 other. Cambridge Scientific Abstracts, 7200 Wisconsin Avenue, #601, Bethesda MD 20814-4823. **Tel** (301)961-6750, (800)843-7751, FAX (301)961-6720. **LC** Z7403; .A44; Q101. **DD** 016.5. available on magnetic tape; available on an online database; available via Internet (to the current year's abstracts and five-year backfiles) from Cambridge Scientific Abstracts. ***Continues*** *Annual Index to Current Programs.*

US/0162-704X
**CONFERENCE PAPERS INDEX.** [Conf. pap. index]. Vol. 6 (Jan. 1978)-. English. bm (plus annual index). $985.00 US; $995.00 other (includes annual index). Cambridge Scientific Abstracts, 7200 Wisconsin Avenue, #601, Bethesda MD 20814-4823. **Tel** (301)961-6750, (800)843-7751, FAX (301)961-6720. **ED** Sharmila Tarpara. **LC** Z7403; .C84; Q158.5. **DD** 016.5. **NLM** W 3.5 C976. Index Available Published separately--free--upon request. cum. index. available on magnetic tape; available on an online database; available via Internet (to the current year's abstracts and five-year backfiles) from Cambridge Scientific Abstracts. ***Continues*** *Current Programs, 0091-0139.*
**Desc:** Cites research papers presented at scientific and technical conferences throughout the world. Coverage includes all branches of engineering, robotics, animal and plant science, biology, physics and astronomy, mathematics and computer science, artificial intelligence, biochemistry, medicine, and pharmacology.
**Ind/Abst** Energy Res. Abstr. (June 1982-).

US/0731-308X
**CONFERENCE PROCEEDINGS / LOS ALAMOS SCIENTIFIC LABORATORY.** [Conf. proc.- Los Alamos Sci. Lab.]. Proceedings. English. Los Alamos Scientific Laboratory, PO Box 1663, Los Alamos NM 87645.
**Ind/Abst** GeoRef.

UK/0260-8316
**CONFERENCES & EXHIBITIONS INTERNATIONAL.** [Conf. exhib. int.]. **VFOAT** Conferences and Exhibitions International. Periodical. English. mo. Conferences & Exhibitions Publications Ltd, Wardrobe Chambers, 146A Queen Victoria Street, London EC4V 4DQ England. **LC** T391; .C77. **DD** 382.1. ***Continues*** *Conferences + Exhibitions, 0306-9397.*

●US/1063-1801
**CONFIGURATIONS (BALTIMORE, MD.).** (CONFIGURATIONS.). [Configurations]. **Added/Corp** Society for Literature and Science. (1993)-. Periodical. English. Three times a year. $53.00 US; $60.00 Canada and Mexico; $58.00 other. Johns Hopkins University Press, 2715 North Charles Street, Baltimore MD 21218-4319. **Tel** (410)516-6987, FAX (410)516-6968. **ED** Wilda Anderson, James Bono, and Kenneth Knoespel. **LC** IN PROCESS; PN55; .C66. **DD** 805. **NLM** W1; CO524. **[CCC].**
**Desc:** Devoted to the study of discourse pertaining to the theories and practices of science, technology, and medicine. Combining the insights of cultural criticism and the new historicism with recent advances in science studies.

US/1046-9672
**CONNECTICUT TECHNOLOGY DIRECTORY.** [Conn. technol. dir.]. **Added/Corp** Connecticut Innovations, Inc. Greater Hartford Chamber of Commerce. Technology Council. (1990)-. Directory. English. an. $65.00. Corporate Technology Information Services Inc, 12 Alfred Street, Suite 200, Woburn MA 01801-9998. **Tel** (617)932-3939, (800)333-8036, FAX (617)932-6335, telex 497-2961 CRPTECH. **ED** Steven W. Parker. **LC** HC107.C8; C595. **DD** 338.7/6200025746. Index available. cum. index. **Bk Rev. Ad Acc. Circ:** 1,000. available on diskette. ***Continues*** *Connecticut Directory of Technology Companies.*
**Desc:** Directory of over 1,350 manufacturers and developers of high-tech products in the state of Connecticut.

US/1055-7342
**CONNECTICUT TECHNOLOGY RESOURCE GUIDE.** ***Title Change.*** (CONNECTICUT TECHNOLOGY RESOURCE GUIDE/ SPONSORED BY CONNECTICUT INNOVATIONS, INC.). [Conn. technol. resour. guide]. **Added/Corp** Connecticut. Dept. of Economic Development. Connecticut Innovations, Inc. Corporate Technology Information Services. **VFOAT** Technology Resource Guide; Connecticut Technology Resource Gguide and Services Yellow Pages. (1992)-(1992). English. Corporate Technology Information Services Inc, 12 Alfred Street, Suite 200, Woburn MA 01801-9998. **Tel** (617)932-3939, (800)333-8036, FAX (617)932-6335, telex 497-2961 CRPTECH. **LC** T22.C8; C66. **DD** 338.7/62/00025746. ***Continued by*** *Technology Resource Guides.*

US/8756-4076
**CONNECTION TECHNOLOGY.** ***Title Change.*** [Connect. technol.]. (Mar./Apr. 1985)-(1992). Periodical. English. mo. IHS Publishing Group, 17730 West Peterson Road, Libertyville IL 60048. **Tel** (708)362-8711, FAX (708)362-3484. **ED** Jennifer Rose. **DD** 621. **CODEN** CNTEEM. **[CCC].** **Bk Rev. Ad Acc. Circ:** 35,000 (ctrl). Documents available from Article Express International, Ask*IEEE. ***Continued by*** *InterConnection Technology, 1065-0415.*
**Desc:** Serves manufacturers of electronic/electrical products and other products involving electronic/electrical operation, power, or control.
**Ind/Abst** Eng. Index Annu.; INSPEC (1987-).

FR/1156-4903
**CONSEIL INFORMATIQUE A LA DIRECTION GENERALE, LE.** ***Title Change.*** (198?)-(19??). Periodical. French. Six times a year. Bouhot & Le Gendre Publishers, 75 Bis Rue de Bellevue, F 92100 Boulogne France. **Tel** 011 33 1 46040708. **UDC** 658(443.611). ***Continued by*** *Informatique Strategie d'Enterprise.*

UK
**CONSERVATION MICRO NEWS.** **VFOAT** Micro News. Periodical. English. qt. Micro News Publications Circulation Department, c/o Nicholson Harris Associates, 25 Queen Anne's Gate, London SW1H 9BU England. **LC** QA75.5; .M49. **DD** 004.16/05. ***Continues*** *Micro News (Haywards Heath, England), 0267-6265.*

CN
**CONTACT.** **Added/Corp** National Research Council Canada. Natural Sciences and Engineering Research Council Canada. Vol. 1 (Sept. 1976)-. Periodical. English (French). qt. Free on request. Natural Sciences & Engineering Research Council, 200 Kent Street, Ottawa Ontario K1A 1H5 Canada. **Tel** (613)995-5992. **ED** Marilyn

Taylor. **DD** 354.710085/5. **Bk Rev. Circ:** 15,000 (ctrl). **Desc:** Newsletter providing information about research grants and scholarships available, results of competitions, program and policy changes, committee membership and highlights of research projects supported.

CN/1182-9028
**CONTACT / PLENTY CANADA.** [Contact - Plenty Can.]. **Added/Corp** Plenty Canada (Organization). Vol. 1, No. 1 (Summer 1990)-. Periodical. English. qt. Limited free distribution. Plenty Canada, Rural Route 3, Lanark, Ontario K0G 1K0 Canada. **DD** 338.9/17101724. ***Continues*** *Plenty Canada Update., 0848-1687.*

UK/1043-3996
**CONTEMPORARY TOPICS IN PURE AND APPLIED CONDENSED MATTER SCIENCE.** [Contemp. topics pure appl. condens. matter sci.]. Periodical. English. sa. Gordon & Breach Science Publishers, PO Box 90, Reading RG1 8JL England. **Tel** 011 44 734 560080, FAX 011 44 734 568211. **(Subscription address:** International Publishers Distributor at one of the following addresses: 820 Town Center Drive, Langhorne, PA 19047; or PO Box 90, Reading Berkshire RG1 8JL UK; or Kent Ridge PO Box 1180, Singapore 9111, Republic of Singapore**)** **DD** 541.

EC/0480-8029
**CONTRIBUCION - INSTITUTO ECUATORIANO DE CIENCIAS NATURALES.** (CONTRIBUCION - QUITO. INSTITUTO ECUATORIANO DE CIENCIAS NATURALES.). [Contrib. - Inst. Ecuat. Cienc. Nat.]. **Main/Corp** Instituto Ecuatoriano de Ciencias Naturales. No. 1-. Spanish. ir. Instituto Ecuatoriano de Ciencias Naturales, Quito Ecuador. **DD** 500. **CODEN** IECCAW. Documents available from BIOSIS Document Express. **Ind/Abst** Biol. Abstr. (-1978); GeoRef.

AG
**CONTRIBUCIONES CIENTIFICAS DEL INSTITUTO ANTARTICO ARGENTINO.** **Main/Corp** Instituto Antartico Argentino. Vol. 1 (1978)-. Academic Scholarly Publication. Spanish. ir. Direccion Nacional del Antartico, Instituto Antartico Argentina, Cerrito 1248, 1010 Buenos Aires Argentina. **Tel** 812 0071 72, FAX 54 1 812 2039. **LC** G877; .B83a. **DD** 919.8/9. **Circ:** 350 (ctrl).
**Desc:** Deals with results of scientific research carried out in Antarctica in the different fields of biological, earth and upper atmosphere sciences.

CH
**CONTRIBUCIONES CIENTIFICAS Y TECNOLOGICAS / UNIVERSIDAD TECNICA DEL ESTADO.** **Added/Corp** Universidad Tecnica del Estado (Chile). Comite de Investigaciones Cientificas y Tecnologicas. (1970)-. Periodical. Spanish. bm (6 issues). $30.00. Universidad de Santiago de Chile, Avd Ecuador 3469, Department Investments, Correo 2 Santiago Chile. **Tel** 761011. **CODEN** CCTEDC. Documents available from CASDDS. **Ind/Abst** Chem. Abstr.

CN/0589-5820
**CONTRIBUTIONS A L'ETUDE DES SCIENCES DE L'HOMME.** **Added/Corp** Centre de Recherches en Relations Humaines. (1952)-. Periodical. French (English and French). ir. Centre de Recherches en Relations Humaine, 2715 Cote St Catherine, Montreal Quebec H3T 1B6 Canada. **DD** 572.

UK
**CONTROL THEORY AND APPLICATIONS STUDIES SERIES.** Vol. 1 (1981)-. Monographic series. English. ir. Price varies per volume. John Wiley & Sons Ltd., Baffins Lane, Chichester West Sussex PO19 1UD England. **Tel** 0243 779777, FAX 0243 776128 BTG:JWP001, telex 86290 WIBOOKG. **(Subscription address:** North, South and Central America/ John Wiley & Sons, Inc., Subscription Department, 605 Third Avenue, New York, NY 10158-0012, USA; telephone: (212)850-6645; FAX: (212)850-6021**)**

US/0882-3561
**COOKSTOVE NEWS.** ***Ceased.*** **Added/Corp** Aprovecho Institute (Cottage Grove, Or.). (198-)-?. Periodical. English. qt (Feb., May, Aug., Nov.). Cookstove News, Aprovecho Institute, 80574 Hazleton Road. **Tel** (503)942-9434. **ED** Stephen Mallery. **DD** 683. Index available. cum. index. **Bk Rev. Circ:** 500.
**Desc:** News, features, designs and cooperation in permaculture and appropriate technology. Special emphasis on fuel-saving cookstoves for the Third World.

US
**COOPERATION SOUTH / UNITED NATIONS DEVELOPMENT PROGRAMME.** **Added/Corp** United Nations Development Programme. No. 1 (1985)-. Periodical. English (French and Spanish). qt. United Nations Development Programme / New York, 1900 One United Nations Plaza, New York NY 10017. **Tel** (212)906-5000, FAX (212)826-2057. **LC** IN PROCESS. ***Continues*** *TCDC News.*

US/1062-5399
**COOPERATIVE TECHNOLOGY RD&D REPORT.** (COOPERATIVE TECHNOLOGY RD&D REPORT : THE BUSINESS OF TECHNOLOGY COMMERCIALIZATION AT FEDERAL LABORATORIES AND UNIVERSITIES.). [Coop. technol. RD&D rep.]. (1991)-. Periodical. English. mo. $640.00. Technology Publishing Group, PO Box 5692, Washington DC 20016. **Tel** (202)966-9610, FAX (202)363-6929. **ED** Grant Stockdale. **DD** 338. **Bk Rev**, (Qty: 2). **Circ:** 1,000.
**Desc:** Dedicated to news, policy and case studies of government/industry technology and R&D partnerships.

US
**COPY TECHNOLOGY REVIEW.** **VFOAT** CTR. Periodical. English. mo. Copy Technology Consulting Company, 3871 Narcissus Way, Denver CO 80237.

CN/1187-4546
**CORPORATE PLAN SUMMARY, CAPITAL BUDGET SUMMARY, OPERATING BUDGET SUMMARY.** [Corp. plan summ. cap. budg. summ. oper. budg. summ.]. **Main/Corp** National Museum of Science and Technology (Canada). **VFOAT** Capital Budget Summary; Operating Budget Summary. (1991)-. English. **DD** 507/.4/71.

BL
**CORREIO DA UNESCO, O.** **See** The Arts.

US
**COUNCIL FOR AGRICULTURAL SCIENCE AND TECHNOLOGY PUBLICATIONS SUBSCRIPTION.** English. ir. $35.00 US; $50.00 other. Council for Agricultural Science and Technology, 4420 West Lincoln Way, Ames IA 50010. **Tel** (515)292-2125, FAX (515)292-4512. **ED** Kayleen A Niyo. **Circ:** 5,000.
**Desc:** Subscription includes task force reports, comments from CAST, special publications, NewsCAST, and Science of Food and Agriculture.

FR/1161-8043
**COURRIER DE LA PLANETE PARIS.** (COURRIER DE LA PLANETE.). **VFOAT** Solidarites Agricoles et Alimentaires Mensuel (Paris); SOLAGRAL Mensuel (Paris). (1991)-. Periodical. French. mo (10 issues). 195.89F France; 200.00F EEC; 250.00F other. SOLAGRAL, 11 Passage Penel, 75018 Paris France. **Tel** 011 33 1 42510600, 42511100. **UDC** 364(1-772)(44). ***Continues*** *La Lettre de SOLAGRAL (Paris), 0293-3055.* **Ind/Abst** Int. Labour Doc.

FR/0153-985X
**COURRIER DU CNRS, LE.** [Courrier CNRS]. **Added/Corp** Centre National de la Recherche Scientifique (France). **VAT** Courrier du Centre National de la Recherche Scientifique. (1971)-. Periodical. French. an (June). 65.00F. Editions du CNRS, 22 rue Saint Armand, F 75015 Paris France. **Tel** 011 33 1 45075050. **(Subscription address:** CNRS Editions, 20-22 rue Saint Amand, c/o Mme. Bodet, 75015 Paris France.**)** **ED** G. Delacote. **LC** Q180.F7; F7a. **DD** 505. ***Continues*** *Centre National de la Recherche Scientifique (France). Courrier.*
**Desc:** Journal of general interest to scientists.
**Ind/Abst** Energy Res. Abstr. (April 1982-); GeoRef; Life Sci. Collect.

US
**CPST OCCASSIONAL PAPERS.** (19??)-. English. Four times a year. $67.50 (members of Commission on Professionals in Science and Technology); $82.50 (non-member). Commission on Professionals in Science and Technology, 1500 Massachusetts Avenue Northwest, Suite 831, Washington DC 20005. **Tel** (202)223-6995. **ED** Betty Vetter. **Circ:** 100.

AT/0819-1530
**CREATION EX NIHILO.** **See** Religion and Theology.

US/0092-9166
**CREATION RESEARCH QUARTERLY.** **Main/Corp** Creation Research Society. (19??)-. Periodical. English. Four times a year (Mar., June, Sept., Dec.). comes with membership. Creation Research Society, PO Box 969, Ashland OH 44805-0969. **Tel** (419)281-5301. **(Subscription address:** P.O. Box 14016, Terre Haute, IN 47803**)** **ED** Eugene Chaffin. **LC** BS651; .C7a. **DD** 213/.05. Index available (bound in next issue, in September). **Bk Rev**, (Qty: 12-20). **Pr Rev. Circ:** 1,700. available on microfilm and microfiche from University Microfilms International (UMI).
**Desc:** Articles from a scientific viewpoint that support the creation model of science.
**Ind/Abst** Christ. Period. Index.

CN/0229-253X
**CREATION SCIENCE DIALOGUE.** [Creat. sci. dialogue]. **Added/Corp** Creation Science Association. (Winter 1980)-. Periodical. English. qt. 2.00Can$. Creation Science Association, 194 3803 Calgary Trail South 1136, Edmonton Alberta T6J 5M8 Canada. **Tel** (905)454-0933. **ED** Brad Dye and Margaret Helder. **DD** 213. **Bk Rev. Circ:** 12,000. ***Continues*** *Creation Dialogue., 0702-7176.*

**Desc:** General science articles of interest to professionals and laymen which have specific relation to the subject of origins.

FR/0293-0196
**CREATIONS CANNES LA BOCCA.** [Creations Cannes a Bocca]. (1981)-. Periodical. French. qt. 247.00F. PEMF Publ de l Ecole Moderne Francaise, 06376 Mouans Sartoux CX France. **Tel** 011 33 92 921757. **UDC** 37.013. ***Continues*** *Art Enfantin et Creations, 0339-929X.*

●US/1065-2388
**CRITICAL REVIEWS IN MULTIPHASE SCIENCE AND TECHNOLOGY.** (1993)-. Periodical. English. bm. $99.95 (individual); $270.00 (institution). Begell House Inc., PO Box 1109, Pearl River NY 10965. **Tel** (212)725-1999. **ED** G. F. Hewitt. ***Continues*** *Multiphase Science and Technology, 0267-1459.*
**Desc:** Provides in-depth and authoritative overviews of vital subject areas related to multiphase systems.

US/0501-5782
**CRREL REPORT.** [CRREL rep.]. **Main/Corp** U.S. Army Cold Regions Research and Engineering Laboratory. **Added/Corp** U.S. Army Cold Regions Research and Engineering Laboratory. Report. **VAT** Cold Regions Research and Engineering Laboratory Report. (1976)-. Monographic series. English. US Army Cold Regions Research, 72 Lyne Road, Hanover NH 03755. **Tel** (603)646-4100. **CODEN** XCRPAP. ***Formed by the union of*** *Technical Report - Corps of Engineers, U.S. Army, Cold Regions Research and Engineering Laboratory, 0149-3833* ***and*** *Research Report - Corps of Engineers, U.S. Army, Cold Regions Research and Engineering Laboratory, 0501-5812.*
**Ind/Abst** ASTIS Curr. Aware. Bull. (1978-); Aquat. Sci. Fish. Abstr. (Computer File); ASTIS Bibliogr. (1978-); Bioeng. Abstr.; GeoRef; Ocean. Abstr.

CN/0381-8047
**CRUCIBLE (TORONTO).** (THE CRUCIBLE.). [Crucible]. **Added/Corp** Science Teachers' Association of Ontario. (1964)-. Periodical. English. Six times a year. 50.00Can$ Canada; 55.00Can$ other. Science Teachers Association of Ontario, 10 Grasmere Crescent, London ONT N6G 4P2 Canada. **Tel** (519)432-8280. **ED** Gary Forsyth. **DD** 507. **Bk Rev. Ad Acc. Circ:** 1,600 (ctrl).
**Desc:** Science teaching for all levels.
**Ind/Abst** Alum. Ind. Abstr.; Met. Abstr.

II/0304-9841
**CSIO COMMUNICATIONS.** [CSIO commun.]. **Added/Corp** Central Scientific Instruments Organisation. (1974)-. Periodical. English. qt. $30.00. Central Scientific Instruments Organization, Chandigarh, India. **(Subscription address:** Prints India, 11 Darya Ganj, New Delhi 110002 India.**)** **CODEN** CSIOBT.

SA
**CSIR ANNUAL REPORT.** **Main/Corp** South African Council for Scientific and Industrial Research. 17th- 1961-. English. South African Council for Scientific and Industrial Research, PO Box 395, Pretoria 0001 South Africa. **Tel** 27 12 86-9211. **LC** Q85.S46; A18. **DD** 507/.2068. ***Supersedes in part*** *Jaarverslag.*

II
**CSIR HANDBOOK.** **Main/Corp** Council of Scientific & Industrial Research (India). **VFOAT** C.S.I.R. Handbook. (197?)-. English. Council of Scientific & Industrial Research, Publications & Information Director, Hillside Road, New Delhi 110012 India. **Tel** FAX 011 91 11 5731353. **LC** Q73; .A3. **DD** 507/.2054. ***Continues*** *Council of Scientific & Industrial Research (India). Handbook.*

AT/0007-912X
**CSIRO ABSTRACTS.** ***Ceased.*** (1952)-(199?). English. CSIRO Publications, PO Box 89, 314 Albert Street, East Melborne Victoria 3002 Australia. **Tel** 011 61 3 4187333, 4187217, FAX 011 61 3 4190459, telex AA 30236.
**Ind/Abst** Plant Breed. Abstr.; Protozoolog. Abstr.

AT
**CSIRO DIRECTORY.** **Main/Corp** Commonwealth Scientific and Industrial Research Organization (Australia). (1972)-. English. an. 12.00Aus$. CSIRO Publications, PO Box 89, 314 Albert Street, East Melborne Victoria 3002 Australia. **Tel** 011 61 3 4187333, 4187217, FAX 011 61 3 4190459, telex AA 30236. **DD** 507/.2094. **NLM** Q 180.A8 D618. ***Continues*** *Commonwealth Scientific and Industrial Research Organization (Australia). Divisions and Sections.*
**Ind/Abst** AESIS Q.

AT/0311-5836
**CSIRO INDEX.** ***Ceased.*** (CSIRO INDEX. MICROFORM.). [CSIRO index]. **Added/Corp** Commonwealth Scientific and Industrial Research Organization (Australia). Vol. 5, No. 1 (1979)-Vol. 13 (1989). Periodical. English. bm. CSIRO Publications, PO Box 89, 314 Albert Street, East Melborne Victoria 3002 Australia. **Tel** 011 61 3 4187333, 4187217, FAX 011 61 3 4190459, telex AA 30236. ***Continues*** *CSIRO Index.*

AT
**CST TECHNOLOGY TRANSACTIONS.** English. sm (Published Jan.-Dec.). 290.00Aus$; 355.00Aus$ UK and Europe; $480.00Aus$ other. Systems User & Management P L, 6 Alanna Street, Terrigal 2260, Australia. **Tel** 011 61 43 851188, FAX 011 61 43 852121. **ED** Norman F. Kemp.
**Desc:** Review of Australian Commonwealth, State, and Territory information and purchases. Also, official newsleter of the Government Technology Users Association.

UK
**CTI PLUS [COMPUTER FILE]. See** Science and Technology-Abstracting, Bibliographies and Statistics.

US/0889-8243
**CTNS BULLETIN.** [CTNS bull.]. **Added/Corp** Center for Theology and the Natural Sciences. **VAT** Center for Theology and the Natural Sciences Bulletin. (198?)-. Bulletin. English. Four times a year (Mar., June, Sept., Dec.). $25.00 one year; $50.00 two years. Center for Theology and Natural Sciences, 2400 Ridge Road, Berkeley CA 94709. **Tel** (510)848-8152, FAX (510)848-2535. **ED** W. Mark Richardson. **DD** 261. Index available. cum. index. **Bk Rev**, (Qty: 25-30). **Pr Rev. Circ:** 650. ***Continues** CTNS Newsletter.*
**Desc:** Promotes the interaction between science and religion through teaching, research and public forums.
**Ind/Abst** Index Book Rev. Relig.; Relig. Index One Period.

FR/0223-4386
**CULTURE TECHNIQUE. Added/Corp** Centre de Recherche sur la Culture Technique (France). **VFOAT** Machines au Foyer; Automation, Emploi; Philosophie, Histoire; Creation, Travail, Industrie. No. 2/3 (April/June 1980)-. Periodical. French. ir (two to three issues per year). 450.00F. CRCT, 69 Bis rue Charles Laffitte, 92200 Neuilly Sur-Seine France. **Tel** 33 1 47479527, FAX 33 1 47477399. **ED** Joce Lyn de Notolet.
**Ind/Abst** BHA : Biblio. Hist. Art.

UK/0376-4842
**CURRENT AWARENESS IN PARTICLE TECHNOLOGY / PUBLISHED AND COMPILED BY: PARTICLE SCIENCE AND TECHNOLOGY INFORMATION SERVICE, UNIVERSITY OF TECHNOLOGY, LOUGHBOROUGH, GREAT BRITAIN. Added/Corp** Loughborough University of Technology. Particle Science and Technology Information Service. Vol. 9, No. 1 (Jan. 1976)-. Periodical. English. mo. £215.00. University of Technology PSTIS Subscriptions, c/o R. W. Newbold, Department of Chemical Engineering, Loughborough LE11 3TU England. **Tel** 011 44 509 222528, telex 34319. **ED** Richard W. Newbold. cum. index. **Bk Rev. Circ:** 300. ***Continues** Particulate Information.*
**Desc:** Interdisciplinary listing of current literature in particle and powder science, technology and the application to applied science and technology.

US/0095-7917
**CURRENT CONTENTS. ENGINEERING, TECHNOLOGY & APPLIED SCIENCES. See** Engineering-Abstracting, Bibliographies and Statistics.

US/0011-3409
**CURRENT CONTENTS. LIFE SCIENCES. See** Science and Technology-Abstracting, Bibliographies and Statistics.

●US/1073-1229
**CURRENT CONTENTS. LIFE SCIENCES (CD-ROM VERSION). See** Science and Technology-Abstracting, Bibliographies and Statistics.

US/1062-3132
**CURRENT CONTENTS ON DISKETTE. ENGINEERING, TECHNOLOGY & APPLIED SCIENCES. See** Engineering.

US/1062-3078
**CURRENT CONTENTS ON DISKETTE. LIFE SCIENCES. J600. See** Science and Technology-Abstracting, Bibliographies and Statistics.

US/1062-3027
**CURRENT CONTENTS ON DISKETTE. LIFE SCIENCES. J1200. See** Science and Technology-Abstracting, Bibliographies and Statistics.

US/1062-3108
**CURRENT CONTENTS ON DISKETTE WITH ABSTRACTS. LIFE SCIENCES. See** Science and Technology-Abstracting, Bibliographies and Statistics.

II
**CURRENT LITERATURE ON SCIENCE OF SCIENCE. See** Science and Technology-Abstracting, Bibliographies and Statistics.

US/0590-4102
**CURRENT PRIMATE REFERENCES. See** Science and Technology-Abstracting, Bibliographies and Statistics.

NE
**CURRENT RESEARCH IN THE NETHERLANDS : MATHEMATICS, PHYSICS, GEOLOGY, ASTRONOMY.** English. Netherlands Organization for Scientific Research, Laan van Nieuw Oost Jndie 131, PO Box 93138, 2509 AC The Netherlands. **LC** Q180.N35; C87. **DD** 507/.20492.

NE
**CURRENT RESEARCH IN THE NETHERLANDS : TECHNOLOGICAL SCIENCES.** 1979/1980-. English. Netherlands Organization for Scientific Research, Laan van Nieuw Oost Jndie 131, PO Box 93138, 2509 AC The Netherlands.

II/0011-3891
**CURRENT SCIENCE.** [Curr. sci.]. **Added/Corp** Current Science Association. Indian Institute of Science, Bangalore. Vol. 1 (July 1932)-. Periodical. English. Twenty-four times a year. $175.00. Indian Academy of Sciences Circulation, PO Box 8005, Department of Sadashivanagar, Bangalore 560 080 India. **Tel** 011 91 812 342546, 342310, telex 0845-2178 ACAD IN. **(Subscription address:** Prints India, 11 Darya Ganj, New Delhi, 110002 India, (Phone: 011 91 11 3268645)) **ED** M R A Rao. **LC** Q1; .C78. **NLM** W1 CU81. **CODEN** CUSCAM. Index available. **Pr Rev. Circ:** 1,600. available on microfilm and microfiche from University Microfilms International (UMI). Documents available from The Genuine Article, BIOSIS Document Express, Ask*IEEE, CASDDS.
**Desc:** Provides a forum for views on major scientific issues. Its main features are editorials, special articles, short research communications and notes, as well as book reviews and information of general interest to the scientific community.
**Ind/Abst** AgBiotech News Inf.; Agrofor. Abstr. (19??-19??); Anim. Breed. Abstr.; Art Archaeol. Tech. Abstr.; Biocont. News Inf. (19??-19??); Biodeter. Abstr. (19??-19??); Biol. Abstr.; Ceram. Abstr.; Chem. Abstr.; CSA Neuro. Abstr. (?-?); Curr. Biotechnol.; Curr. Contents, Agric. Biol. Environ. Sci.; Curr. Lit. Sci. Sci.; Dairy Sci. Abstr.; EMBASE; Field Crop Abstr.; Food Sci. Technol. Abstr.; For. Prod. Abstr. (19??-19??); For. Abstr.; Geol. Abstr.; GeoRef; Grasslands For. Abstr.; Hortic. Abstr.; Immunol. Abstr.; Index Vet.; Indian Geosci. Abstr.; INSPEC (1968-); Int. Aerosp. Abstr.; Irr. Drain. Abstr.; Maize Abstr.; Meteorol. Geoastrophys. Abstr. (19??-); Microbiol. Abstr. Sect. B (19??-19??); Microbiol. Abstr. Sect. A; Microbiol. Abstr. Sect. C; Nematol. Abstr.; Numis. Lit.; Ornamental Hort. (1991-); Life Sci. Collect.; PESTDOC; Plant Breed. Abstr.; Plant Genet. Resour. Abstr.; Plant Grow. Reg. Abstr.; Potato Abstr.; Poult. Abstr.; Protozoolog. Abstr.; Res. Alert [Full Cov.]; Rev. Med. Vet. Entomol.; Rev. Med. Vet. Mycology; Rev. Plant Pathol.; Rice Abstr.; Rural Dev. Abstr.; Sci. Cit. Index; SCISEARCH; Seed Abstr.; Soc. Sci. Cit. Index [Select. Cov.]; Soils Fert.; Sorghum Mill. Abstr.; Soyabean Abstr.; Stat. Theory Method Abstr. (1959-1963); Surf. Treat. Technol. Abstr.; Vet. Bull.; Virol. AIDS Abstr.; Weed Abstr.; World Agric. Econ.

US/0011-3905
**CURRENT SCIENCE (MIDDLETOWN).** (CURRENT SCIENCE.). [Curr. sci.]. (19??)-. Periodical. English. Eighteen times a year (published bi-weekly Sept.-May). $29.95. Weekly Reader Corporation, 3001 Cindel Drive, Delran NJ 08370. **Tel** (609)786-1000, (800)446-3355, FAX (609)786-3360. **ED** Vincent J. Marteka. **Circ:** 350,000. available with illustrations; available in braille; available on microfilm and microfiche from University Microfilms International (UMI). Documents available from UMI Article Clearinghouse, Documents on Demand.
**Desc:** Covers stories in all areas of science and health curriculums.
**Ind/Abst** Acad. Search (July 1989-); Arts Humanit. Citation Index [Select. Cov.]; Child. Mag. Guide (1981-); Curr. Titles Electrochem.; Energy Inf. Abstr.; Environ. Abstr.; Gen. Sci. Source (Jul. 1989-); INFO-SOUTH Abstr.; Leadscan; Mag. Artic. Summar. Elite (July 1989-); Mag. Artic. Summar. Select; Mag. Artic. Summar. CD-ROM (July 1989-); Mag. Search; Mid. Search (Jul. 1989-); Newsp. Period. Abstr. (1989-); Nutr. Abstr. Rev., Ser. B, Live Feeds and Feed.; Nutr. Abstr. Rev., Ser. A, Hum. Exp.; Prim. Search (Jul. 1989-).

UK/0260-6593
**CURRENT TECHNOLOGY INDEX : CTI. See** Science and Technology-Abstracting, Bibliographies and Statistics.

UK/0742-2725
**CURRENT THEMES IN TROPICAL SCIENCE.** [Curr. themes trop. sci.]. (1982)-. English. Pergamon Press, An Imprint of Elsevier Science Ltd., The Boulevard, Langford Lane, Kidlington, Oxford OX5 1GB United Kingdom. **Tel** 011 44 865 843000, 011 44 865 843699, FAX 011 44 865 843010. **CODEN** CTTSE4. Documents available from CASDDS.
**Ind/Abst** Chem. Abstr.

US/0275-9098
**CURRENT TOPICS OF CONTEMPORARY THOUGHT.** [Curr. top. contemp. thought]. Began publication in 1969. Monographic series. English. ir. Price varies per volume. Gordon & Breach Science Publishers, Inc., PO Box 786, Cooper Station, New York NY 10276. **Tel** (212)206-8900, FAX (212)645-2459. **(Subscription address:** International Publishers Distributor at one of the following addresses: 820 Town Center Drive, Langhorne, PA 19047; or PO Box 90, Reading Berkshire RG1 8JL UK; or Kent Ridge PO Box 1180, Singapore 9111, Republic of Singapore**)**

US
**CURRENTS IN SCIENCE, TECHNOLOGY AND SOCIETY.** English. qt. $15.00. Access Research Network, PO Box 38069, Colorado Springs CO 80937. **Tel** (719)633-1772. **ED** Mark Hartwig.
**Desc:** Dedicated to providing accessible information on science, technology, and society.

LB
**CUTTINGTON RESEARCH JOURNAL. See** Literary and Political Reviews.

US/0011-4294
**CYCLES (PITTSBURGH).** (CYCLES.). [Cycles]. **Added/Corp** Foundation for the Study of Cycles (U.S.). **VFOAT** Cycles Magazine. Vol. 1 (June 1950)-. Periodical. English. bm (6 issues). Membership: $125.00 (corporations), $75.00 (individuals), $45.00 (students, instructors and libraries) US; $105.00 other. Foundation for the Study of Cycles Inc., 900 West Valley Road, Suite 502, Wayne PA 19087-1821. **Tel** (610)995-2120, FAX (610)995-2130. **ED** Diane Epperson. **LC** Q176; .F597. **DD** 501. **Bk Rev. Circ:** 2,500.
**Desc:** Articles on fluctuations (cycles) in all disciplines, including natural science, human behavior, with history and extrapolations. Also on methodology and computer techniques.
**Ind/Abst** Coal Abstr.; PAIS Int. Print (1991-).

●XR
**CZECHOSLOVAK INDUSTRY.** (1992)-. Periodical. English. **LC** T4; .C95. **DD** 609.437. ***Continues** Czechoslovak Heavy Industry, 0011-4618.*

NZ/0110-5221
**D. S. I. R. DISCUSSION PAPER.** [DSIR discuss. pap.]. **VFOAT** DSIR Discussion Paper; Discussion Paper. **VAT** Department of Scientific and Industrial Research Discussion Paper. No. 1 (1978)-. Monographic series. English. Price varies per volume. **CODEN** DDPAEX. **Circ:** 2,000. Documents available from BIOSIS Document Express, Ask*IEEE.
**Desc:** Analyzes problems and opportunities for New Zealand research within areas of concerns and gives recommendations on preferred options.
**Ind/Abst** Biol. Abstr. (1985-); INSPEC.

BG/0259-7365
**DACCA UNIVERSITY STUDIES. PART B, THE. *Title Change.*** (THE DHAKA UNIVERSITY STUDIES. PART B.). [Dhaka Univ. stud., Part B]. **Added/Corp** University of Dhaka. (1982)-Vol. 41, No. 2 (July 1993). Periodical. English. sa. University of Dhaka / Department of Chemistry, Dhaka 1000 Bangladesh. **LC** AS472.D3; A372. **DD** 505. **CODEN** DUBSDX. Documents available from BIOSIS Document Express, CASDDS. ***Continues** University of Dacca Dacca University Studies: Part B, 0253-5467.* ***Continued by** Dhaka University Journal of Science, 1022-2502.*
**Ind/Abst** Biol. Abstr. (19??-19??); Chem. Abstr. (19??-19??).

US/0011-5266
**DAEDALUS (CAMBRIDGE).** (DAEDALUS : PROCEEDINGS OF THE AMERICAN ACADEMY OF ARTS AND SCIENCES.). [Daedalus]. **Added/Corp** American Academy of Arts and Sciences. Vol. 86, No. 1 (May 1955)-. Proceedings. English. qt. $45.00 (institution), $30.00 (individual) $25.00 (student) US; $52.00 (institution), $37.00 (individual) other. Daedalus, 136 Irving Street, Suite 100, Cambridge MA 02138. **Tel** (617)491-2600, FAX (617)576-5088. **LC** Q11; .B7. **DD** 505. **NLM** W1 DA229. **CODEN** DAEDAU. **[CCC]. Pr Rev.** available on microfilm and microfiche from University Microfilms International (UMI). Documents available from The Genuine Article, BIOSIS Document Express, Ask*IEEE, UMI Article Clearinghouse, CASDDS, Magazine Collection. ***Continues** American Academy of Arts and Sciences. Proceedings of the American Academy of Arts and Sciences, 0199-9818.*
**Ind/Abst** ABC POL SCI; Abstr. Anthropol.; Acad. Abstr. Full Text Elite (July 1990-); Acad. Abstr. (July 1990-); Acad. Ind. [Computer File] (1984-); Acad. Search (July 1990-); Am. Hist. Life (1963-); Am. Hist. Life Part B (1963-); Am. Bibliogr. Slavic East Europ. Stud.; Annu. Bibliogr. Engl. Lang. Lit.; ARTbibliogr. Mod.; Arts Humanit. Citation Index [Full Cov.]; BHA : Biblio. Hist. Art; Biol. Abstr.; Book Rev. Index; Br. Archaeol. Bibliogr.; Chem. Abstr.; Child. Lit. Abstr. (19??-); Curr. Contents Arts Humanit.; Curr. Contents Soc. Behav. Sci.; Curr. Geogr. Publ. (199?-); Expand. Acad. Index (1984-); Gen. Period. Index (1985-); Geogr. Abstr. Human Geogr. (?-?); Guide Soc. Sci. Relig.; Health Devices Alerts; Health

Plan. Adminis.; High. Educ. Abstr. (1965-19??); Hospit. Health Admin. Index (Winter 1975-Summer 1989); Hum. Rights Intern. Rep.; Humanit. Index; Humanit. Source (Jul. 1990-); Index Period. Artic. Relat. Law; INFO-SOUTH Abstr.; INIS Atomindex [Micro.]; INSPEC (1968-Winter 1980); Int. Bibliogr. Sociol.; Int. Dev. Abstr. (?-?); Int. Polit. Sci. Abstr.; J. Plan. Lit.; Linguist. Lang. Behav. Abstr.; Mag. Index Plus (1989-); Mag. Search; Middle East Abstr. Index; MLA Int. Bibl. Books Artic. Mod. Lang. Lit.; Newsp. Period. Abstr. (1988-); PAIS Int. Print (1991-); Peace Res. Abstr. J. (1961-1963, 1972); Psychol. Abstr.; PsycINFO; PsycLit; Read. Guide Period. Lit.; Res. Alert [Full Cov.]; Res. High. Educ. Abstr.; Soc. Plann. Policy Dev. Abstr.; Soc. Sci. Cit. Index [Full Cov.]; Soc. Work Abstr. (?-?); Sociol. Abstr.; Mag. Index (1977-); U.S. Polit. Sci. Doc.; West. Hist. Q.

SU
**DALIL AL-MAARID WA-AL-ASWAQ AL-DAWLIYAH / IDAD DAIRAT AL-ILAM, AL-GHURFAH AL-TIJARIYAH AL-SINAIYAH, AL-RIYAD AL-MAMLAKAH AL-ARABIYAH AL-SAUDIYAH.** Arabic. Al-Ghurfah Al-Tijariyah Al-Sinaiyah Al-Riyad Al-Mamlakah Al-Arabiyah Al-Saudiyah, Shari Abd Al-Aziz IBN Abd Allah IBN Turki, Al-Riyad Saudi Arabia. **LC** T391; .D34.

US/1054-5468
**DATA CAPTURE CASE STUDIES AND TECHNOLOGY.** ***Title Change.*** Vol. 91.1 (1991)-(19??). Periodical. English. bm. Data Capture Press, PO Box 1625, Duxbury MA 02331. **DD** 004. ***Merged into*** *Automatic ID News.*

US
**DATA IN SCIENCE AND TECHNOLOGY.** (19??)-. Monographic series. English. ir. Price varies per volume. Springer-Verlag New York Inc., 175 5th Avenue, New York NY 10010. **Tel** (212)460-1500, telex 232 235 SPB UR. **(Subscription address:** Springer Verlag New York Inc. / for North America, 44 Hartz Way, Secaucus NJ 07096.) **ED** R. Poerschke.

UK
**DEALING WITH TECHNOLOGY.** English. sm. $895.00 US. Waters Information Services, PO Box 2248, Binghamton NY 13902-2248. **Tel** (607)770-8535, FAX (607)798-1692. available on an online database (files 16,636/Full-Text) from DIALOG.
**Ind/Abst** PROMT [Full Txt.]; PTS Newsl. Database [Full Txt.].

FR/1148-4675
**DECISION MICRO PARIS.** (DECISION MICRO.). (1990)-. Periodical. French. ir (43 per year). 548.48F France; 920.00F other. Groupe Tests, 26 Rue d'Oradour sur Glane, 75504 Paris Cedex 15 France. **Tel** 011 33 1 44253131. **UDC** 681.3.002.52. ***Continues*** *Decision Informatique (Paris), 0293-3896.*

XR/0300-4414
**DEJINY VED A TECHNIKY.** (DVT, DEJINY VED A TECHNIKY.). [Dejiny ved tech.]. **Added/Corp** Spolecnost pro Dejiny ved a Techniky. Ceskoslovenska Spolecnost pro Dejiny ved a Techniky. **VFOAT** Dejiny ved a Techniky. Vol. 1 (1968)-. Periodical. Czech (Slovak, French, English, German and Russian; summaries and/or abstracts in French and German). qt. DM124.00. Academia, Publishing House of the Czechoslovak Academy of Sciences, Czech AC SCI, Vodickova 40, PO Box 896, 112 29 Prague 1, Czech Republic. **Tel** 011 42 2 245117. **(Subscription address:** Kubon & Sagner, ABT Zeitschriftenimport, D 80328 Munich Germany.) **ED** Lubos Novy. **CODEN** DVTDAE. Index available. **Bk Rev.** available in microform. ***Continued in part by*** *Acta Historiae Rerum Naturalium Necnon Technicarum. Special Issue, 0231-6005.*
**Desc:** Deals with the history of the natural sciences, medicine, and technology as well as with the history of scientific institutions and their activities.
**Ind/Abst** Math. Rev.; Zentralbl. Math. Ihre Grenzgeb.

NE
**DELFT INTEGRAAL.** (1984)-. Dutch. Six times a year. Free. T U Delft, Tav DHR PH Broos, Stevinweg 1, 2628 CN Delft Netherlands. **Tel** 011 31 015 785860, FAX 011 31 015 781855. **ED** Philip Broos (editor's address: P. O. Box 5, 2600 AA Delft, The Netherlands). **Circ:** 23,500 (ctrl).

US
**DEMAND-SIDE TECHNOLOGY REPORT.** (1993)-. English. Twelve times a year. $527.00 US, Canada, & Mexico; $587.00 other. Cutter Information Corporation, 37 Broadway, Arlington MA 02174-5539. **Tel** (617)648-8700, (800)964-5118, FAX (617)648-8707, (617)648-1950, telex 650 100 9891.

SZ
**DENKSCHRIFTEN DER SCHWEIZERISCHEN ADAKEMIE DER NATURWISSENSCHAFTEN DSANW.** (19??)-. Monographic series. German. ir. Price varies per volume. Birkhaeuser Verlag Ag, Klosterberg 23, PO Box 133, CH-4010 Basel Switzerland. **Tel** 011 41 61 2717400, FAX 011 41 0 61 2717666, telex 963475 birk ch. ***Continues*** *Denkschriften der Schweizerischen Naturforschenden Gesellschaft DNSG.*

SZ/0366-970X
**DENKSCHRIFTEN DER SCHWEIZERISCHEN NATURFORSCHENDEN GESELLSCHAFT.** ***Title Change.*** [Denkschr. Schweiz. Naturforsch. Ges.]. **Main/Corp** Schweizerische Naturforschende Gesellschaft. **Added/Corp** Schweizerische Naturforschende Gesellschaft. **VFOAT** Memoires de la Societe Helvetique des Sciences Naturelles. (1920)-(19??). Monographic series. German. ir. Birkhaeuser Verlag Ag, Klosterberg 23, PO Box 133, CH-4010 Basel Switzerland. **Tel** 011 41 61 2717400, FAX 011 41 0 61 2717666, telex 963475 birk ch. **(Subscription address:** Switzerland/ PO Box 133, Elisabethenstr 19, CH-4010 Basel) **LC** Q67; .S42. **CODEN** DSNGA6. Documents available from BIOSIS Document Express. ***Continues*** *Neue Denkschriften der Schweizerischen Naturforschenden Gesellschaft.* ***Continued by*** *Denkschriften der Schweizerischen Akademie der Naturwissenschaften DSANW.*
**Ind/Abst** Biol. Abstr.; GeoRef; Life Sci. Collect.

RU/0135-0617
**DEPONIROVANNYE RUKOPISI / GOSUDARSTVENNYI KOMITET SSSR PO NAUKE I TEKHNIKE, AKADEMIIA NAUK SSSR, VSESOIUZNYI INSTITUT NAUCHNOI I TEKHNICHESKOI INFORMATSII, SEKTOR TEORII I METODIKI DEPONIROVANIIA NAUCHNYKH RABOT.** **Added/Corp** Vsesoiuznyi Institut Nauchnoi i Tekhnicheskoi Informatsii (Soviet Union). Sektor Teorii Metodiki Deponirovaniia Nauchnykh Rabot. (19??)-. Russian. mo. 6.24rub. **LC** Z7409; .D46; Q158.5.

NE
**DERMATO SELECTIEF.** Reed Healthcare Communications, Postbus 182, Reaal 2F, 2353 TL, Leiderdorp Netherlands. **Tel** (71)415151.

US/0279-2958
**DESARROLLO NACIONAL.** (19??)-. Periodical. Spanish. Five times a year. $50.00 North America; $60.00 other. Intercontinental Media, PO Box 3410, Milford CT 06460. **Tel** (203)226-7463. **ED** Dan Wasserman and Julio de la Torre. **Bk Rev. Ad Acc.** ctrl circ. ***Continues*** *Servicios Publicos, Desarrollo Nacional, 0099-1694.*
**Desc:** Infrastructure projects and technologies in the Third World.

UK/0958-3017
**DESIGN & TECHNOLOGY TEACHING.** [Des. technol. teach.]. **VFOAT** Design and Technology Teaching; Design Technology Teaching. (1990)-. Periodical. English. tq (Jan., May & Sept.). £18.00 UK; £21.00 other. Trentham Books Ltd, Westview House, 734 London Road, Oakhill, Stoke-on-Trent, Staffordshire ST4 5NP England. **Tel** 011 44 782 745567, FAX 011 44 782 745553. **DD** 607. ***Continues*** *Studies in Design Education Craft & Technology, 0142-4807.*
**Ind/Abst** Br. Educ. Index.

GW/0012-0278
**DEUTSCHE HEBE- UND FORDERTECHNIK.** ***Title Change.*** (DEUTSCHE HEBE- UND FORDERTECHNIK, IM DIENSTE DER TRANSPORTRATIONALISIERUNG DER AUTOMATION UND DER HYDRAULIK). [Dtsch. hebe-fordertech.]. (19??)-(19??). German (summaries and/or abstracts in English and French). AGT Verlag Thum GmbH, Postfach 109, Teinacherstr 34, D 71601 714 Ludwigsburg 10 Germany. **Tel** 011 49 7141 223156. **Bk Rev. Ad Acc. Circ:** 11,250 (ctrl). ***Continued by*** *DHF.*
**Ind/Abst** Coal Abstr.; Fluid Abstr., Civil Eng.; Fluid Abstr. Proc. Eng.; FLUIDEX.

GW/0722-0839
**DEUTSCHER FORSCHUNGSDIENST. GERMAN RESEARCH SERVICE.** (DEUTSCHER FORSCHUNGSDIENST : DF / GERMAN RESEARCH SERVICE.). [Dtsch. Forsch.dienst, Ger. res. serv.]. **Added/Corp** Deutsche Forschungsgemeinschaft. **VFOAT** DF; D.F.; German Research Service. Vol. 1 No. 1 (April 1962)-. Academic Scholarly Publication. English. Twelve times a year. DM80.00. Forschungsdienst GmbH, Ahrstrasse 45, D 53175 Bonn Germany. **Tel** 011 49 228 302206.
**Ind/Abst** EMBASE; GeoRef.

GW/0933-7814
**DEUTSCHER FORSCHUNGSDIENST. GERMAN RESEARCH SERVICE. SPECIAL SCIENCE REPORTS.** [Dtsch. Forsch.dienst, Ger. res. serv., Spec. sci. rep.]. **VFOAT** Deutscher Forschungsdienst. The German Research Service. Special Science reports; German Research Service. Special Science Reports; Df. Deutscher Forschungsdienst. German Research Service. Special Science Reports. (1985)-. Periodical. English. mo. German Science Service, Forschungsdienst Gmbh, Ahrstrasse 45 (Wissenschaftszentrum), Postfach 20 50 06, D-5300 Bonn 2 Germany. **UDC** 001.891.
**Ind/Abst** GeoRef; Meteorol. Geoastrophys. Abstr. (19??-).

UK/1053-7465
**DEVELOPMENTS IN NANOTECHNOLOGY.** (1991)-. Periodical. English. Gordon & Breach Science Publishers, PO Box 90, Reading RG1 8JL England. **Tel** 011 44 734 560080, FAX 011 44 734 568211. **(Subscription address:** International Publishers Distributor at one of the following addresses: 820 Town Center Drive, Langhorne, PA 19047; or PO Box 90, Reading Berkshire RG1 8JL UK; or Kent Ridge PO Box 1180, Singapore 9111, Republic of Singapore)

●BG/1022-2502
**DHAKA UNIVERSITY JOURNAL OF SCIENCE, THE.** **Added/Corp** University of Dhaka. **VFOAT** Journal of Science. Vol. 42, No. 1 (Jan. 1994)-. Periodical. English. sa. University of Dhaka / Department of Chemistry, Dhaka 1000 Bangladesh. **LC** AS472.D3; A372. ***Continues*** *Dhaka University Studies. Part B, 0259-7365.*

JA/0385-7360
**DIAMOND INDUSTRIA.** **VFOAT** Japan's Economic Journal; Daiyamondo Indasutoria; Industria. Vol. 16, No. 1 (Jan. 1986)-. Periodical. English. mo. $90.00. Diamond Lead Company, Ltd., 4-2 Kasumigaseki 1-Chome, Chiyoda-ku Tokyo 100 Japan. **Tel** 011 81 3 3504-6791, FAX 011 81 3 3504-6798, telex J-26145 DLED. **ED** Mr. Natsuki Mori. **LC** HC461; .I46. **DD** 338.0952. ***Continues*** *Industria (Tokyo, Japan), 0385-7360.*
**Desc:** This publication on Japanese business and the economy is intended for business people and investors. It is primarily devoted to articles on companies and their activities, industry trends and newly developed products.

CC/1001-1579
**DIANCHI.** (1981)-. Periodical. Chinese. bm. $60.00. Human Light Industry Research Institute, Changsha Hunan 410007 China. **Tel** 011 86 731 551901. **DD** 621.31242. Documents available from CASDDS.
**Ind/Abst** Chem. Abstr.

IT
**DIDATTICA SCIENTIFICA, LA.** Vol. 1 (Feb. 1971)-. Periodical. Italian. Three times a year. Instituto Italiano Edizioni, Via Crescenzi 88, 24100 Bergamo Italy. **LC** Q4; .D53.

US/1064-3125
**DIGEST - ANTENNAS AND PROPAGATION SOCIETY SYMPOSIUM.** (DIGEST / ANTENNAS AND PROPAGATION SOCIETY SYMPOSIUM ; SPONSORED BY ANTENNAS AND PROPAGATION SOCIETY OF THE INSTITUTE OF ELECTRICAL AND ELECTRONICS ENGINEERS ; ORGANIZED BY NATIONAL RESEARCH COUNCIL CANADA AND THE UNIVERSITY OF WESTERN ONTARIO.). [Dig. - Antennas Propag. Soc. Symp.]. **Main/Conf** S International Symposium. **Added/Corp** IEEE Antennas and Propagation Society. Institute of Electrical and Electronics Engineers. **VFOAT** IEEE Antennas and Propagation International Symposium. (1991)-. English. ir. IEEE, Institution of Electrical and Electronics Engineers, Inc., 345 East 47th Street, New York NY 10017-2394. **Tel** (908)981-1393, FAX (908)981-9667. **LC** TK7871.6; G2a. **DD** 621. ***Continues*** *AP-S International Symposium. International Symposium Digest, Antennas and Propagation.*
**Desc:** Information on antennas, electronic waves and radio wave propagation.

JA
**DIGEST OF JAPANESE INDUSTRY & TECHNOLOGY : DJIT.** **VFOAT** Digest of Japanese Industry and Technology; DJIT. (19??)-. Periodical. English. Seven times a year. $200.00. Tsusan Seisaku Kohosha, (Japan Trade & Industry Publicity Inc.), Toranomon Kotohira Kaikan, 2-8, Toranomon 1 chome, Minatoku, Tokyoto 105 Japan. **(Subscription address:** Maruzen Company Ltd., PO Box 5050, Import & Export Department, Tokyo 100 31 Japan.) **CODEN** DJITDS. Documents available from Ask*IEEE.
**Ind/Abst** Energy Inf. Abstr.; INSPEC (1985-).

YU/0419-1439
**DIJALEKTIKA.** **VFOAT** Dialectics; Dialektika; Dialectique. V. 1- 1966-. Periodical. Serbo-Croatian (Cyrillic) (summaries and/or abstracts in Russian and French). Univerzitet u Beogradu, Pravni Fakultet, Belgrade Stud TRG1 Yugoslavia. **LC** Q175.

GW/0722-9313
**DIN-KATALOG FUER TECHNISCHE REGELN.** [DIN-Kat. tech. Regeln]. **VFOAT** Deutsches Institut fuer Normung Katalog fuer Technische Regeln; DIN Catalogue of Technical Rules; Deutsches Institut fuer Normung : DIN-Katalog fuer Technische Regeln / 01; Deutsches Institut fuer Normung : DIN-Katalog fuer Technische Regeln / 02. (1982)-. Multiple languages. an. DM400.00. Beuth Verlag GmbH, Burggrafenstrasse 6, D-10787 Berlin Germany. **Tel** 011 49 30 260112573. **UDC** 006(430).

# Science and Technology

JO
**DIRASAT. SERIES B, PURE AND APPLIED SCIENCES. Added/Corp** Jamiah Al-Urduniyah. Imadat Al-Bahth Al-Ilmi. **VFOAT** Pure and Applied Sciences; Ulum Al-Bahtah Wa-Al-Tatbiqiyah; Dirasat. Silsilah B, Ulum Al-Bahtah Wa-Al-Tatbiqiyah. Vol. 17B, No. 1 (Jan. 1990)-. Periodical. English (Arabic). qt. **LC** Q4; .D57. **CODEN** DJSSE8. Documents available from BIOSIS Document Express, CASDDS. **Continues in part** Dirasat (Amman, Jordan), 0255-8033.
**Ind/Abst** Biol. Abstr. (1991-); Chem. Abstr.

●US
**DIRECTORY. Main/Corp** Early American Industries Association. (1991/1992)-. Directory. English. Early American Industries Association / Delaware, 495 Dogwood Drive, Hockessin DE 19707. **LC** T21; .E23a. **Continues** Membership Directory, 0424-0316.

US
**DIRECTORY / AMERICAN COUNCIL OF INDEPENDENT LABORATORIES, INC. Main/Corp** American Council of Independent Laboratories. Directory. English. be. Free (shipped book rate), $5.00 (shipped UPS). American Council of Independent Laboratories, 1725 K Street NW, Washington DC 20006. **Tel** (202)887-5872, **FAX** (202)887-0021. **LC** TA416; .A54. **Bk Rev. Continues** Directory / American Society of Commercial Laboratories.
**Desc:** Describes services of each member laboratory of ACIL. Includes detailed index of services and geographical index.

US
**DIRECTORY / BROOKHAVEN NATIONAL LABORATORY. Main/Corp** Brookhaven National Laboratory. (19??)-. English. an. Brookhaven National Laboratory, Associated Universities Inc., Upton NY 11973. **Tel** (212)620-8000.

US
**DIRECTORY OF AAAS FELLOWS. Main/Corp** American Association for the Advancement of Science. (1979)-. Directory. English. ir. Price varies per volume. American Association for the Advancement of Science, 1333 H Street Northwest, Washington DC 20005. **Tel** (202)326-6400, (203)326-6417, (202)326-6430, **FAX** (202)842-1065.

US/1044-4734
**DIRECTORY OF ASIAN HIGH TECH COMPANIES IN THE UNITED STATES.** [Dir. Asian high tech co. U. S.]. (Nov. 1990)-. Directory. English. $295.00. Mead Ventures Inc, PO Box 44952, Phoenix AZ 85064. **Tel** (602)234-0044, **FAX** (602)234-0076. **DD** 338. Index available.
**Desc:** This directory contains descriptions of the products and services of more than 350 Asian high tech companies with offices in the United States. Includes company's names, addresses, phone and fax numbers, key company contacts, and general information on the company's activities.

US
**DIRECTORY OF COMPUTER SOFTWARE APPLICATIONS. ATMOSPHERIC SCIENCES, A. See** Computers.

US/0070-5330
**DIRECTORY OF COMPUTERIZED INFORMATION IN SCIENCE AND TECHNOLOGY.** 1968-. Directory. English. ir. Science Associates International Inc., 465 West End Avenue, New York NY 10024. **Tel** (212)873-0656, **FAX** (212)873-5587.

AT/0727-6753
**DIRECTORY OF CSIRO RESEARCH PROGRAMS / COMPILED BY THE SCIENCE COMMUNICATION UNIT, BUREAU OF SCIENTIFIC SERVICES. Main/Corp** Commonwealth Scientific and Industrial Research Organization (Australia). Science Communication Unit. **VFOAT** Directory of C.S.I.R.O. Research Programs. (19??)-. English. an. CSIRO Publications, PO Box 89, 314 Albert Street, East Melborne Victoria 3002 Australia. **Tel** 011 61 3 4187333, 4187217, **FAX** 011 61 3 4190459, telex AA 30236. **LC** Q180.A8; C65b. **DD** 001.4/025/94. **Continues** Commonwealth Scientific and Industrial Research Organization (Australia). CSIRO Research Program.
**Ind/Abst** AESIS Q.

SI
**DIRECTORY OF CURRENT RESEARCH / NATIONAL UNIVERSITY OF SINGAPORE. Main/Corp** National University of Singapore. (1983)-. Directory. English. an. $20.00 (1 year), $35.00 (2 year). University of Singapore / Faculty of Business Administration, 10 Kent Ridge, Singapore 0511 Singapore. **Tel** 011 65 7723101, **FAX** 011 65 7792621 3571, telex 33943. **LC** Q180.S5; N37a. **DD** 001.4/09595/7.

US/0892-1660
**DIRECTORY OF EXPERTS AND CONSULTANTS IN SCIENCE AND ENGINEERING.** [Dir. experts consult. sci. eng.]. **VFOAT** Experts and Consultants in Science and Engineering. 2nd Ed. (1987)-. Monographic series. English. ir. Price varies per volume. Gale Research Inc., 835 Penobscot Building, Detroit MI 48226. **Tel** (800)877-GALE, (313)961-2242, **FAX** (313)961-6083, telex TWX 810-221-7086. **LC** TA12; .D4885. **DD** 620/.0025/7. **Formed by the union of** Leading Consultants in Technology, 0749-9000 **and** Directory of Expert Witnesses in Technology, 0749-9965.

CN/0829-6030
**DIRECTORY OF FEDERAL GOVERNMENT SCIENTIFIC & TECHNOLOGICAL ESTABLISHMENTS.** (DIRECTORY OF FEDERAL GOVERNMENT SCIENTIFIC & TECHNOLOGICAL ESTABLISHMENTS / STATISTICS CANADA, SCIENCE, TECHNOLOGY AND CAPTIAL STOCK DIVISION.). [Dir. fed. gov. sci. technol. establ.]. **Added/Corp** Statistics Canada. Science, Technology and Capital Stock Division. **VFOAT** Directory of Federal Government Scientific and Technological Establishments. (1985)-. English. an. 25.00Can$ Canada; $26.00 other. Statistics Canada, Publications Sales & Services, Main Building Room 1710, Ottawa Ontario K1A 0T6 Canada. **Tel** (613)951-5078, (800)267-6677, **FAX** (613)951-1584, telex 053-3585. **LC** Q180.6.C2; D57. **DD** 507/.2071.
**Desc:** A listing of federal establishments engaged in science and technology activities in the natural sciences and engineering, containing information on activities performed, specialized equipment, the number of scientists and engineers, as well as identifying institutional name and the name, address and phone number of a contact person.

US/0891-8333
**DIRECTORY OF FEDERAL LABORATORY & TECHNOLOGY RESOURCES.** (DIRECTORY OF FEDERAL LABORATORY & TECHNOLOGY RESOURCES : A GUIDE TO SERVICES, FACILITIES, AND EXPERTISE.). [Dir. fed. lab. technol. resour.]. **Added/Corp** Center for the Utilization of Federal Technology (U.S.) United States. National Technical Information Service. **VFOAT** Directory of Federal Laboratory and Technology Resources; Federal Laboratory & Technology Resources; Federal Laboratory and Technology Resources. (198?)-. Directory. English. be. $73.00 US, Canada and Mexico; $139.00 other. National Technical Information Service - NTIS, Room 2027S, 5285 Port Royal Road, Springfield VA 22161. **Tel** (703)487-4630, (703)487-4660, (703)487-4650, **FAX** (703)321-8547, telex 89-9405. **LC** T21; .D57. **DD** 602.5/73. **NLM** T 21; D598. **Continues** Directory of Federal Technology Resources, 0747-7880.

HU
**DIRECTORY OF HUNGARIAN RESEARCH INSTITUTIONS.** Directory. English. Hungarian Central Technical Library and Documentation Centre, POB 12, H-1428 Budapest Hungary. **LC** Q180.H8; D57. **DD** 001.4/3/025439.

IS
**DIRECTORY OF INDUSTRIAL LABORATORIES IN ISRAEL. Added/Corp** Merkaz ha-Leumi le-Medatekhnologi u-Madai (Israel). **VFOAT** Madrikh le-Maabadot Taasiyatiyot be-Yisrael. 4th ed. (1984)-. Directory. English (Hebrew). National Centre of Scientific Technology Information, PO Box 20125, Tel Aviv 61200 Israel. **Continues in part** Directory of Research Institutes & Industrial Laboratories in Israel, 0334-3197.

US
**DIRECTORY OF JAPANESE TECHNICAL RESOURCES IN THE UNITED STATES. Added/Corp** United States. National Technical Information Service. Office of International Affairs. **VFOAT** Japanese Technical Resources in the United States; NTIS Directory of Japanese Technical Resources in the United States. **VAT** National Technical Information Service Directory of Japanese Technical Resources in the United States. (1988)-. English. sa (2 issues). $50.00 North America. National Technical Information Service - NTIS, Room 2027S, 5285 Port Royal Road, Springfield VA 22161. **Tel** (703)487-4630, (703)487-4660, (703)487-4650, **FAX** (703)321-8547, telex 89-9405. **LC** T10.63.A1; N37. **DD** 609/.52. **Continues** Directory of Japanese Technical Resources.

US/0419-3350
**DIRECTORY OF PUBLISHED PROCEEDINGS. SERIES SEMT, SCIENCE/ENGINEERING/MEDICINE/TECHNOLOGY. ANNUAL CUMULATIVE VOLUME / INTERDOK. VFOAT** Interdok Directory of Published Proceedings. Series SEMT, Science/Medicine/Engineering/Technology. Annual Cumulative Volume. (Sept. l967 through June 1968)-. Directory. English. Ten times a year. $325.00 (with subscription to Directory of Published Proceedings Series); $425.00 other. InterDok Corporation, PO Box 326, Harrison NY 10528. **Tel** (914)835-3506, **FAX** (914)835-6757. **LC** Z7409; .D56. **DD** 016.5. **NLM** W 3.5 D598. **CODEN** ITDKB. **Continues** Directory of Published Proceedings. Annual Cumulative Volume, 0364-6025.

US
**DIRECTORY OF PUBLISHED PROCEEDINGS. SERIES SEMT SCIENCE/ENGINEERING/MEDICINE/TECHNOLOGY. CUMULATED INDEX SUPPLEMENT. Added/Corp** Inter-Dok Corporation. No. 1 (1970)-. Directory. English. Three times a year. $160.00. InterDok Corporation, PO Box 326, Harrison NY 10528. **Tel** (914)835-3506, **FAX** (914)835-6757.

IS
**DIRECTORY OF RESEARCH INSTITUTES IN ISRAEL. Added/Corp** Merkaz Ha-Leumi Le-meda Tekhnologi U-Madai (Israel). **VFOAT** Madrikh Li-Mekhone Mehkar Be-Yisrael. (1982)-. Directory. English (Hebrew). The Stockton Record, 530 East Market, Stockton CA 95202. **Tel** (209)948-1702 ext 322. **LC** Q180.I78; D56. **DD** 001.4/025/5694. **Continues in part** Directory of Research Institutes & Industrial Laboratories in Israel, 0334-3197.

TH
**DIRECTORY OF RESEARCH INSTITUTIONS IN THAILAND.** Directory. English. National Research Council of Thailand, 196 Phahon Yothin Road, Bangkok Thailand. **LC** Q180.T5; D57. **DD** 300.7/20593.

IS/0334-2824
**DIRECTORY OF SCIENTIFIC & TECHNICAL ASSOCIATIONS IN ISRAEL.** 3rd Ed.; 1978-. Directory. English (Hebrew). ir. $25.00 (plus airmail postage) US. National Center for Scientific and Technological Information, PO Box 20125, Tel Aviv 61201 Israel. **Tel** 03-5612676, **FAX** 03-5614619, telex 03-2332 IL. Index available. cum. index. **Bk Rev. Continues in part** Madrikh La-Agudot Veli-Mekhonim Madaiyim Ve-Tekhniyim Be-Yisrael.

CE
**DIRECTORY OF SCIENTIFIC AND TECHNICAL PERSONNEL OF SRI LANKA.** Directory. English. National Science Council of Ceylon, 47/5 Maitland Place, Colombo 7 Ceylon Sri Lanka. **LC** Q149.S75; D57. **DD** 502.5/549/3.

SA
**DIRECTORY OF SCIENTIFIC AND TECHNICAL SOCIETIES IN SOUTH AFRICA. VFOAT** Gids van Wetenskaplike en Tegniese Verenigings in Suid-Afrika. (1971)-. Directory. English (Afrikaans). be. South African Council for Scientific and Industrial Research, PO Box 395, Pretoria 0001 South Africa. **Tel** 27 12 86-9211. **ED** Marian de Wind. **LC** Q85; .D53. **DD** 506/.268. **NLM** Q 91 D598. **Circ:** 800. **Continues** Scientific and Technical Societies in South Africa.
**Desc:** Comprehensive listing of societies in South Africa active in the field of science or technology, stating office bearers, objectives, conditions for membership, publications, etc.

II/0419-3482
**DIRECTORY OF SCIENTIFIC RESEARCH INSTITUTIONS IN INDIA, THE.** 1969-. Directory. English. Rs1200 India; $600.00 other. INSDOC, 14 Satsang Vihar Marg, New Delhi 110067 India. **Tel** 011 91 11 6863617, **FAX** 665837, telex 031-73099. **LC** Q183.43.I5; D5. **DD** 507/.2/0954. Index available. cum. index. available on diskette; available on an online database.
**Desc:** Presents a comprehensive list of institutions in India engaged in fundamental and applied research in science and technology. Provides complete postal address, telephone, telex and provides details on areas of research important achievements, special facilities, and publications.

US/0417-6480
**DIRECTORY OF SCIENTIFIC RESOURCES IN GEORGIA.** [Dir. scient. resour. Ga.]. (1963)-. Directory. English. ir. Georgia Institute of Technology, 225 North Avenue SW, Atlanta GA 30322. **LC** T176; .D49. **DD** 607/.2/758.

PK
**DIRECTORY OF THE RESEARCH ESTABLISHMENTS IN PAKISTAN.** Directory. English. 20.00. National Science Council, Republic of China, Math Res Promotion Center NTU, Taipei Taiwan. **Tel** 011 886 2 3633860. **LC** Q180.P25; D54. **DD** 507/20549/1.

US/1071-8966
**DIRECTORY, PROCEEDINGS, AND HANDBOOK.** [Dir. proc. handb.]. **Main/Corp** National Association of Academies of Science (U.S.). **VFOAT** NAAS Directory, Proceedings, and Handbook. (199?)-. Directory. English. an (Oct.). $15.00. Northeast Missouri State University, Division of Fine Arts, Kirksville MO 63501. **Tel** (816)785-4442. **(Subscription address:** Northeast Missouri State University, Department of Biology, c/o Dr. Shaddy, Kirksville MO 63501.**)** **LC** Q11; .N28755a. **DD** 506/.073. ***Continues*** *National Association of Academies of Science (U.S.). Proceedings, Directory and Handbook of the National Association of Academies of Science, 0739-361X.*

US/0274-7529
**DISCOVER (CHICAGO, ILL.).** (DISCOVER.). [Discover]. Vol. 1, (Oct. 1980)-. Periodical. English. mo. $29.95. Walt Disney Publishing Inc., 500 South Buena Vista Street, Burbank CA 91521. **Tel** (818)567-5661. **(Subscription address:** Palm Coast Data, PO Box 420235, Agency Department, Palm Coast FL 32142.**)** **LC** Q1; .D57. **DD** 505. available on an online database from DIALOG; available on microfilm and microfiche from University Microfilms International (UMI). Documents available from UMI Article Clearinghouse, Documents on Demand.
**Desc:** The magazine of science and technology, their wonders, their uses, their impact on our lives.
**Ind/Abst** Abr. Read. Guide Period. Lit.; Acad. Abstr. Full Text Elite (Feb. 1984-); Acad. Abstr. (Feb. 1984-); Acad. Ind. [Computer File] (1985-); Acad. Search (Feb. 1984-); AGRICOLA [Select. Cov.]; Biol. Dig.; Can. Index (?-?); Can. Period. Index (19??-); Comput. Lit. Index; Environ. Abstr.; Expand. Acad. Index (1985-); F&S Index Plus Text, Int. [Select. Cov.]; Foods Adlibra; Gen. Period. Index (1985-); Gen. Sci. Index; Gen. Sci. Source (Jan. 1988-); GeoRef; Health Ref. Cent. (1987-) [Select. Cov.]; INFO-SOUTH Abstr.; Key Word Index Wildl. Res.; Mag. Artic. Summar. Elite (Feb. 1984-); Mag. Artic. Summar. Select (Feb. 1984-); Mag. Artic. Summar. CD-ROM (Feb. 1984-); Mag. Index Plus (1989-); Mag. Index. Sel. (1986-); Mag. Search; Mid. Search (Feb. 1984-); Newsp. Period. Abstr. (1986-); NEXIS (1980-); Prim. Search (Feb. 1984-); PROMT; Read. Guide Abstr. Select Ed.; Read. Guide Period. Lit.; Resource/One Ondisc (1986-); Mag. Index (1985-); TOM Gen. Index (1985-) [Full Txt.]; Vocat. Search (Feb. 1984-).

KE/1015-079X
**DISCOVERY AND INNOVATION.** [Discov. innov.]. **Added/Corp** African Academy of Sciences. Third World Academy of Sciences. Vol. 1, No. 1 (Mar. 1989)-. Periodical. English. Four times a year (Mar., June, Sept., Dec.). $60.00 (individuals), $70.00 (institutions) Africa; $70.00 (individuals), $90.00 (institutions) others. Academy Science Publishers, PO Box 14798, Nairobi Kenya. **Tel** 011 254 2 884401, 02, 03, 04, 05, FAX 011 254 2 884406, telex 25446 AFACS. **ED** Dr. Samson Kwaje and Professor T. T. Isoun. **LC** Q85.2; .D57. **DD** 509.6. **CODEN** DIINE4. Index available. cum. index. **Bk Rev. Ad Acc.** Full Page (B&W) $60.00 (individuals) & $70.00 (institutions). Half Page (B&W) $70.00 (individuals), $90.00 (institutions). **Circ:** 500 (ctrl). Documents available from The Genuine Article, BIOSIS Document Express, CASDDS.
**Ind/Abst** Agric. Eng. Abstr. (1991-); Anim. Breed. Abstr.; Biol. Abstr. (1989-); Chem. Abstr.; Curr. Contents, Agric. Biol. Environ. Sci.; Field Crop Abstr.; For. Abstr.; Helminthol. Abstr.; Hortic. Abstr.; Index Vet.; Maize Abstr.; Nutr. Abstr. Rev., Ser. B, Live Feeds and Feed.; Nutr. Abstr. Rev., Ser. A, Hum. Exp.; Plant Genet. Resour. Abstr.; Postharvest News Inf.; Poult. Abstr.; Protozoolog. Abstr.; Res. Alert [Select. Cov.]; Rev. Med. Vet. Entomol.; Rev. Plant Pathol.; Soc. Sci. Cit. Index [Select. Cov.]; Soils Fert.; Trop. Dis. Bull.; Weed Abstr.

US
**DISSERTATION ABSTRACTS INTERNATIONAL. A, THE HUMANITIES AND SOCIAL SCIENCES. B, THE SCIENCES AND ENGINEERING. CUMULATED AUTHOR INDEX (MICROFORM).** **See** Social Sciences-Abstracting, Bibliographies and Statistics.

AU/0419-4225
**DISSERTATIONEN DER UNIVERSITAT WIEN.** (19??)-. Periodical. German. ir. Verband der Wissenschaftlichen Gesellschaften Osterreichs, Lindengasse 37, A-1070 Vienna Austria. **Tel** 011 43 1 932166, 011 43 1 934756, telex 847/134981. **DD** 060. **Circ:** 200.
**Desc:** Each volume is a single doctoral dissertation. The subjects cover many sciences and humanities.
**Ind/Abst** MLA Int. Bibl. Books Artic. Mod. Lang. Lit.; Soils Fert.; Zentralbl. Math. Ihre Grenzgeb.

JA/0303-5514
**DNIAS ANNUAL REPORT + 1. Main/Corp** Kankyo to Kogyo O Musubu Kai. **VAT** DNIAS Annual Report Plus One. Multiple languages (Japanese). Kankyo to Kogyo O Musubu Kai, 7-22-1 Roppongi Minato-ku, Tokyo Japan. **LC** T4; .K3514.

BL
**DOCUMENTACAO AMAZONICA : CATALOGO COLETIVO.** V. 1- Jan./April 1974-. Portuguese. Superintendencia do Desenvolvimento da Amazonia, Coordenacao de Informatica, Divisao de Documentacao, Travessa Antonio Baena 1113, Marco 66.000 Belem Brazil. **LC** Z7165.B7; D6; HC188.A5. **DD** 016.33/0981/1.

II
**DOCUMENTATION BULLETIN (VAIKUNTHBHAI MEHTA SMARAK TRUST, DOCUMENTATION CENTRE-CUM-REFERENCE LIBRARY).** (DOCUMENTATION BULLETIN / CENTRE FOR STUDIES IN DECENTRALISED INDUSTRIES.). **Added/Corp** Centre for Studies in Decentralised Industries (Bombay, India) Vaikunthbhai Mehta Smarak Trust. (19??)-. English. qt. NKM International House, 5th Floor, 178 Backbay Reclamation Madam Cama Road, Bombay 400 020 India.

FR/0046-0478
**DOCUMENTATION PAR L'IMAGE, LA.** [Doc. image]. (1947)-. Periodical. French. Nine times a year (published monthly Sept.-May). 229.00F (1 year), 450.00F (2 year) France and French overseas departments and territories; 254.00F (1 year), 500.00F (2 year) other. Nathan Abonnements, 75640 Paris Cedex 13 France. **Tel** 011 33 1 44085000, 011 33 1 44085070, FAX 011 33 1 43375300. **ED** Catherine Denavarre. **UDC** 77.03. **[CCC].**

US
**DOE/ET. Main/Corp** United States. Dept. of Energy. Office of Energy Technology. **VAT** Department of Energy/Energy Technology. (19??)-. Monographic series. English. Price varies per volume. National Technical Information Service - NTIS, Room 2027S, 5285 Port Royal Road, Springfield VA 22161. **Tel** (703)487-4630, (703)487-4660, (703)487-4650, FAX (703)321-8547, telex 89-9405. **CODEN** USECD3. available on microfiche. Documents available from Article Express International.
**Ind/Abst** Bioeng. Abstr.; Ei Page One; Eng. Index Annu.

TA
**DOKLADHOI AKADEMIIAI ILMHOI JUMHURII TOJIKISTON / DOKLADY AKADEMII NAUK RESPUBLIKI TADZHIKISTAN. Added/Corp** Akademiiai Ilmhoi Jumhurii Tojikiston. **VFOAT** Doklady Akademii Nauk Respubliki Tadzhikistan. (199?)-. Periodical. Russian. mo. **CODEN** DTAREJ. ***Continues*** *Doklady Akademii Nauk TadzhikskoÊi SSR, 0002-3469.*
**Ind/Abst** Alum. Ind. Abstr.; Chem. Abstr.; Coal Abstr.; GeoRef; Int. Nurs. Index; Math. Rev.; Met. Abstr.

BU
**DOKLADI NA BULGARSKATA AKADEMIIA NA NAUKITE. Added/Corp** Bulgarska Akademiia na Naukite. **VFOAT** Comptes Rendus de l'Academie Bulgare des Sciences. (1991)-. English (Russian). mo. DM252.00. Scientific Information Centre, Bulgarian Academy of Sciences, 7 Noemvri St, 1040 Sofia Bulgaria. **Tel** FAX 87 77 3489 25 44. **(Subscription address:** Kubon & Sagner, ABT Zeitschriftenimport, D 80328 Munich Germany.**)** ***Continues*** *Comptes Rendus de l'Academie Bulgare des Sciences, 0366-8681.*
**Ind/Abst** Field Crop Abstr.; Index Vet.; Plant Grow. Reg. Abstr.; Rev. Agric. Entomol.; Rev. Plant Pathol.; Soyabean Abstr.; Weed Abstr.; Wheat Barley Trit. Abstr.

●BW
**DOKLADY AKADEMII NAUK BELARUSI. Added/Corp** Akademiia Nauk Belarusi. **VFOAT** Doklady of the Academy of Sciences of Belarus; Doklady AN Belarusi. (Jan. 1992)-. Academic Scholarly Publication. Russian (summaries and/or abstracts in English). Six times a year. $129.95. **(Subscription address:** East View Publications Inc., 3020 Harbor Lane North, Suite 110, Minneapolis MN 55447.**)** **LC** Q60; .A7497. **CODEN** DABSEU. Documents available from CASDDS. ***Continues*** *Doklady Akademii Nauk BSSR, 0002-354X.*
**Ind/Abst** Alum. Ind. Abstr.; Art Archaeol. Tech. Abstr.; Chem. Abstr. (1992-); Coal Abstr.; GeoRef; Int. Aerosp. Abstr.; Math. Rev.; Met. Abstr.; Sci. Cit. Index.

●RU/0869-5652
**DOKLADY AKADEMII NAUK / ROSSIISKAIA AKADEMIIA NAUK. Added/Corp** Rossiiskaia Akademiia Nauk. Vol. 322, No. 4 (1992)-. Periodical. Russian (table of contents in English). tm. $499.95 US and Canada; $524.95 other. **(Subscription address:** Victor Kamkin, 4956 Boiling Brook Parkway, Rockville MD 20852.**)** **LC** AS262; .S3663. **NLM** W1; DO637. **CODEN** DAKNEQ. ***Continues*** *Doklady Akademii nauk SSSR, 0002-3264.*
**Ind/Abst** Sci. Cit. Index.

UN/0201-8454
**DOKLADY AKADEMII NAUK UKRAINSKOI SSR. SERIIA B, GEOLOGICHESKIE, KHIMICHESKIE I BIOLOGICHESKIE NAUKI.** ***Title Change.*** [Dokl. Akad. nauk Ukr. SSR, Ser. B, Geol. him. biol. nauki]. **Added/Corp** Akademiia nauk Ukrainskoi RSR. **VFOAT** Geologicheskie, Khimicheskie I Biologicheskie Nauki. No. 1 (1975)-(19??). Periodical. Russian (summaries and/or abstracts in English; table of contents in English). mo. **(Subscription address:** Victor Kamkin, 4956 Boiling Brook Parkway, Rockville MD 20852.**)** **CODEN** DNNADO. **[CCC].** Documents available from BIOSIS Document Express, CASDDS. ***Merged with*** *Doklady Akademii nauk Ukrainskoi SSR. Matematika, Estestvoznanie, Tekhnicheskie Nauki, 0868-8044* ***to form*** *Doklady Akademii nauk Ukrainskoi SSR. Seriia A, Fiziko-Matematicheskie i Tekhnicheskie Nauki.*
**Ind/Abst** Biodeter. Abstr.; Biol. Abstr. (?-1990); Chem. Abstr. (?-?); Energy Res. Abstr. (Aug 1982-?); GeoRef; Potato Abstr. (?-?); Seed Abstr.

AJ
**DOKLADY / AKADEMIIA NAUK AZERBAIDZHANA. Added/Corp** Azarbaijan Elmlar Akademiiasy. **VFOAT** Maruzalar; Doklady Akademii Nauk Azerbaidzhana. (1990)-. Periodical. Russian (Azerbaijani; summaries and/or abstracts in English). mo. **(Subscription address:** Victor Kamkin, 4956 Boiling Brook Parkway, Rockville MD 20852.**)** ***Continues*** *Doklady (Azarbaijan SSR Elmlar Akademiiasy).*
**Ind/Abst** NAPRALERT.

AJ/0002-3078
**DOKLADY / AKADEMIIA NAUK AZERBAIDZHANSKOI SSR.** ***Title Change.*** **Main/Corp** Azarbaijan SSR Elmlar Akademiiasy. **Added/Corp** Azarbaijan SSR Elmlar Akademiiasy. **VFOAT** Maruzalar; Doklady Akademii Nauk Azerbaidzhanskoi SSR. Vol. 1 (1945)-(199?). Academic Scholarly Publication. Russian (Azerbaijani; summaries and/or abstracts in English; table of contents in Azerbaijani). mo. **(Subscription address:** Victor Kamkin, 4956 Boiling Brook Parkway, Rockville MD 20852.**)** **NLM** W1 DO64AB. **CODEN** DAZRA7. **[CCC].** Documents available from CASDDS. ***Continued by*** *Doklady (Azarbaijan Elmlar Akademiiasy).*
**Ind/Abst** AGRICOLA; Alum. Ind. Abstr.; Chem. Abstr. (?-?); GeoRef; Int. Aerosp. Abstr.; Math. Rev.; Met. Abstr.

SW/0366-8746
**DOKTORSAVHANDLINGAR VID CHALMERS TEKNISKA HOGSKOLA.** [Doktorsavh. Chalmers tek. hogsk.]. **Added/Corp** Chalmers Tekniska Hogskola. (1942)-. Monographic series. English (German and Swedish). Chalmers Tekniska Hogskola, S-41296 Goteberg S, Gothenburg Sweden. **Tel** 031/81 01 00, telex 2369 CHALBIB S. **LC** UNC. **CODEN** DCTHAT. Documents available from Article Express International.
**Ind/Abst** Bioeng. Abstr.; Ei Page One; Eng. Index Annu.

FR/0989-8107
**DOMOTIQUE NEWS PARIS.** (DOMOTIQUE NEWS). (1988)-. Periodical. French. mo (July/Aug. combined issue). 2090.00F France; 2360.00F other. Domopresse, CNIT BP 530, 92053 Paris La Defense, France. **Tel** 011 33 1 46921830. **ED** Bruno De Latour. **UDC** 333.

CC/0253-4258
**DONGBEI GONGXUEYUAN XUEBAO.** ***Title Change.*** (TUNG-PEI KUNG HSUEH YUAN HSUEH PAO.). [Dongbei gongxueyuan xuebao]. **Added/Corp** Tung-pei Kung Hsueh Yuan. **VFOAT** Journal of Northeast Institute of Technology; Journal of Northeast University of Technology; Dongbei Gongxueyuan Xuebao. (1955)-(1993). Academic Scholarly Publication. Chinese (English; summaries and/or abstracts in English; table of contents in English). qt. Science Press, 16 Donghuangchenggen North Street, Beijing 100707, People's Republic of China. **Tel** 011 86 1 4019821, 011 86 1 4010642, FAX 011 86 1 4012180, 011 86 1 4019810, telex 210147. **LC** T4; .T86. **DD** 605. **CODEN** THYPDK. Documents available from CASDDS. ***Continued by*** *Tung-pei ta Hsueh Hsueh Pao. Tzu Jan ko Hsueh Pan.*
**Ind/Abst** Chem. Abstr.; Math. Rev.

CC/1001-0505
**DONGNAN DAXUE XUEBAO. VFOAT** Journal of Southeast University. (1989)-. Academic Scholarly Publication. Chinese. bm. $120.00. Southeast University / Dongnan Daxue, Sibai Lou, Nanjing, Jiangsu 210018, People's Republic of China. **Tel** 025 6631700, FAX 025 712719. **ED** C. Shunsheng. **DD** 620. Documents available from CASDDS, CASDDS. ***Continues*** *Nanjing Gongxueyuan Xuebao, 0254-4180.*
**Desc:** Contains information on different aspects and engineering and science.
**Ind/Abst** Chem. Abstr.

●US/1071-7560
**DOODY'S HEALTH SCIENCES BOOK REVIEW JOURNAL. VFOAT** Doody's Journal. (1993)-. Periodical. English. Six times a year. $195.00 US

& Canada; $215.00 other. Doody Publishing Inc, 1145 Westgate, Suite 200, Oak Park IL 60301. **Tel** (708)386-9500, (800)219-9500, FAX (708)386-9500. **NLM** Z 1035.A1; D691.
**Desc:** For the librarian managing a health sciences collection, this publication provides timely and independent reviews of newly published books in a wide variety of health science specialties.

JA/0036-8172
**DOSHISHA DAIGAKU RIKOGAKU KENKYU HOKOKU.** (THE SCIENCE AND ENGINEERING REVIEW OF DOSHISHA UNIVERSITY.). [Doshisha Daigaku Rikogaku Kenkyu Hokoku]. **Main/Corp** Doshisha Daigaku. Vol. 1 (March 1960)-. Periodical. English (Japanese; summaries and/or abstracts in English). qt. $45.50. Doshisha Daigaku Rikogaku Kenkyujo, (Science & Engineering Research Inst., Doshisha University), Karasuma Higashi Iru, Imadegawa Doori, Kamigyoku, Kyotoshi, Kyotofu 602, Japan. **(Subscription address:** Japan Publications Trading Company, Ltd., PO Box 5030, Tokyo International, Tokyo 100-31 Japan.**) CODEN** DDRKAZ. Documents available from Ask*IEEE, CASDDS. ***Supersedes*** *Doshisha Kogaku Kaishi.*
**Ind/Abst** Alum. Ind. Abstr.; Chem. Abstr.; Fluid Abstr., Civil Eng.; Fluid Abstr. Proc. Eng.; FLUIDEX (1973-1990); GeoRef; INSPEC (1968-); Met. Abstr.

US/0012-6179
**DREXEL TECHNICAL JOURNAL.** [Drexel tech. j.]. V. 1- 1938-. Periodical. English. qt. $2.00. Drexel University, c/o Circulation Manager, 32nd and Chestnut Streets, Philadelphia PA 19104. **LC** T1; .D73. **CODEN** DTJODK. Documents available from CASDDS.
**Ind/Abst** Chem. Abstr. (1938-1978).

GW/0723-7537
**DRUCKLUFTTECHNIK (MAINZ).** (DRUCKLUFTTECHNIK.). [Drucklufttechnik]. (Nov. 1982)-. Periodical. German. bm. DM112.00. Vereinigte Fachverlage, Postfach 4068, D 55030 Mainz Germany. **Tel** 011 49 6131 992150. **[CCC].**
**Ind/Abst** Fluid Abstr., Civil Eng.; Fluid Abstr. Proc. Eng.; FLUIDEX (1982-).

NZ/0077-961X
**DSIR BULLETIN.** ***Ceased.*** (DSIR BULLETIN / NEW ZEALAND DEPARTMENT OF SCIENTIFIC AND INDUSTRIAL RESEARCH.). [DSIR bull.]. **Added/Corp** New Zealand. Dept. of Scientific and Industrial Research. **VFOAT** D.S.I.R. Bulletin. **VAT** Department of Scientific and Industrial Research Bulletin. (197?)-(19??). Bulletin. English. ir. Science Information Publishing Center, Box 9741, Wellington New Zealand. **Tel** 011 64 4 858939, FAX 011 64 4 850631, telex NZ 32076 RESERCH. **LC** S381; .A35. **CODEN** NEZSAC. ctrl circ. Documents available from BIOSIS Document Express, Ask*IEEE. ***Continues*** *Bulletin (New Zealand. Dept. of Scientific and Industrial Research), 0077-961X.*
**Desc:** Monograph series covering various physical, chemical and biological sciences.
**Ind/Abst** Biol. Abstr. (?-?); Geogr. Abstr. Phys. Geogr. (?-?); GeoRef; INSPEC (?-?); Life Sci. Collect. (?-?); Rev. Med. Vet. Entomol. (?-?).

NZ/0077-9636
**DSIR INFORMATION SERIES.** [DSIR inf. ser.]. **VAT** Department of Scientific and Industrial Research Information Series. Began with: No. 127, published in 1977. Academic Scholarly Publication. English. ir. Price varies per volume. Science Information Publishing Center, Box 9741, Wellington New Zealand. **Tel** 011 64 4 858939, FAX 011 64 4 850631, telex NZ 32076 RESERCH. **CODEN** NZIBAN. Documents available from CASDDS. ***Continues*** *Information Series (New Zealand. Dept. of Scientific and Industrial Research).*
**Desc:** Informative books for general reader or student on a wide range of science topics. Well illustrated.
**Ind/Abst** Chem. Abstr.; GeoRef; Life Sci. Collect.; Rev. Med. Vet. Mycology; Rev. Plant Pathol.; Soils Fert.

US
**EAST EUROPE REPORT. SCIENTIFIC AFFAIRS.** **VFOAT** Scientific Affairs. No. 635- July 2, 1979-. Periodical. English. Foreign Broadcast Information Service, Joint Publications Research Service, 5285 Port Royal Road, Springfield VA 22161. ***Continues*** *Translations on Eastern Europe. Scientific Affairs.*

US/0145-1421
**EAST/WEST TECHNOLOGY DIGEST.** ***Ceased.*** [East-West technol. dig.]. (197?)-Vol. 20 (1994). Periodical. English. mo. Welt Publishing Company, 1413 K Street NW, Suite 1400, Washington DC 20005. **Tel** (202)371-0555, FAX (202)408-9369, telex 281409 TAOA UR. **ED** Jerry Orvedahl and Larry Holland. **CODEN** EWTDDZ. **Circ:** 525. Documents available from CASDDS. ***Continues*** *Soviet Technology Digest.*
**Desc:** Newsletter reporting recently developed products and processes from USSR and East Block countries that are available for licensing and purchase in the West.
**Ind/Abst** Chem. Abstr.; Chem. Bus. Bull.; Chem. Bus. NewsBase (1986-); Chem. Bus. Update; Chem. Ind. Notes.

US/1040-0559
**EASTERN GREAT LAKES SALES GUIDE TO HIGH-TECH COMPANIES.** [East. Great Lakes sales guide to high tech co.]. **VFOAT** Eastern Great Lakes Region; Sales Guide to High Tech Companies. Eastern Great Lakes Region. English. qt. $145.00. Corporate Technology Information Services Inc, 12 Alfred Street, Suite 200, Woburn MA 01801-9998. **Tel** (617)932-3939, (800)333-8036, FAX (617)932-6335, telex 497-2961 CRPTECH. **ED** Steven W Parker. **LC** HC110.H53; E28. **DD** 338.7/62/0002577. Index available. cum. index. **Bk Rev. Ad Acc. Circ:** 3,000. available on diskette.
**Desc:** Regional directory of over 3,000 technology manufacturers and developers.

FR
**ECHAPPEMENT.** (19??)-. French. mo. 244.86F France; 295.00F other. Soc Francaise d Edition Presse, 48 50 Boulevard Senard, 92210 St Cloud France. **Tel** 011 33 1 47112000.

SZ/1043-8599
**ECONOMICS OF INNOVATION AND NEW TECHNOLOGY.** [Econ. innov. new technol.]. Vol. 1, No. 1/2 (1990)-. Periodical. English. qt. $226.00 (academic institutions), $352.00 (corporate institutions). Harwood Academic Publishers, PO Box 90, Reading RG1 8JL England. **Tel** 011 44 734 560080. **LC** HC79.T4; E255. **DD** 338/.064/05. **CODEN** EINTEO. **[CCC].**
**Ind/Abst** Econ. Lit. Index.

UK/0960-4634
**EDI IN FINANCE.** ***Title Change.*** [EDI finance]. (1990)-(199?). Academic Scholarly Publication. English. mo. Elsevier Science Publishers Ltd, Crown House, Linton Road, Barking Essex IG11 8JU England. **Tel** 011 44 81 5947272, FAX 081-594-5942, telex 896950. **DD** 332.028546. **[CCC].** available on an online database from DIALOG. ***Absorbed by*** *Incorporated into Financial Technology Insight, 0961-5342.*
**Ind/Abst** PTS Newsl. Database [Full Txt.].

UK
**EDINBURGH INFORMATION TECHNOLOGY SERIES.** **Added/Corp** University of Edinburgh. (1986)-. Monographic series. English. Price varies per volume.

US/1069-4749
**EDUCATION AND TECHNOLOGY.** **See** Education.

UK/0013-1377
**EDUCATION IN SCIENCE.** (EDUCATION IN SCIENCE : THE BULLETIN OF THE ASSOCIATION FOR SCIENCE EDUCATION.). [Educ. sci.]. **VFOAT** Bulletin of the Association for Science Education. (1962)-. Bulletin. English. Five times a year (Jan., Apr., June, Sept., Nov.). £26.00. Association for Science Education, College Lane, Hatfield Herts AL10 9AA England. **Tel** 011 44 707 267411, FAX 011 44 707 266532. **ED** B. G. Atwood. **Ad Acc. Circ:** 23,000 (ctrl). available on microfilm and microfiche from University Microfilms International (UMI). Documents available from Documents on Demand.
**Desc:** Official means of communication with members of the ASE - science education bulletin.
**Ind/Abst** Br. Educ. Index; Curr. Index J. Educ.; Educ. Technol. Abstr.; Environ. Abstr.; Tech. Educ. Train. Abstr.

US/0424-5997
**EDUCATIONAL RESOURCES & TECHNIQUES.** **VAT** Educational Resources and Techniques. V. 1- 1964-. Periodical. English. Three times a year. $15.00 US; $25.00 other. Education Resources Techniques, PO Box 5155, Denton TX 76203. **Tel** (917)565-3790. **ED** Ron Johnson. **Bk Rev. Ad Acc. Pr Rev. Circ:** 300 (ctrl). available on microfilm and microfiche from University Microfilms International (UMI).
**Desc:** Articles, editorials on the use of technology and related software in instructional settings.

US/0070-9425
**EDUCATORS GUIDE TO FREE SCIENCE MATERIALS / COMPILED AND EDITED BY MARY H. SATERSTROM.** **See** Education-Teaching and Curriculum.

US/0731-0633
**EFOC, FIBER OPTICS & COMMUNICATIONS PROCEEDINGS.** (EFOC ... FIBER OPTICS & COMMUNICATIONS PROCEEDINGS : PAPERS PRESENTED AT THE ... EUROPEAN FIBER OPTICS & COMMUNICATIONS EXPOSITION.). [EFOC, fiber optics commun. proc.]. **Main/Conf** European Fiber Optics & Communications Exposition. **VFOAT** EFOC; EFOC ... Fiber Optics & Communications; E.F.O.C. ... Fiber Optics and Communications Proceedings; Fiber Optics & Communications; Fiber Optics and Communications; Papers Presented at the ... European Fiber Optics and Communications Exposition. (19??)-. Academic Scholarly Publication. English. an. $125.00. Information Gatekeepers Inc., 214 Harvard Avenue, Boston MA 02134. **Tel** (617)232-3111, (800)323-1088, FAX (617)734-8562. **ED** Polishuk, Kennelly and Fasano. **CODEN** PREFDI. Documents available from CASDDS.
**Desc:** Papers presented at the European fiber optics and local area networks trade shows and conferences.
**Ind/Abst** Chem. Abstr.

TU/0254-5527
**EGE UNIVERSITESI FEN FAKULTESI DERGISI. SERI A.** (FEN FAKULTESI DERGISI. SERI A.). [Ege Univ. Fen Fak. derg., Seri A]. **Added/Corp** Ege Universitesi. Fen Fakultesi. **VFOAT** Journal of the Faculty of Science. Series A; Ege Universitesi Fen Fakultesi Dergisi. Seri A; E.U. Fen Fakultesi Dergisi. Seri A; FFD. (197?)-. Periodical. Turkish (English; summaries and/or abstracts in French and German). qt. **LC** Q80.T8; F46. **CODEN** FFDAD8. Documents available from CASDDS.
**Ind/Abst** Chem. Abstr.

JA
**EHIME DAIGAKU KYOIKU GAKUBU KIYO. DAI 3-BU, SHIZEN KAGAKU.** **VFOAT** Memoirs of the Faculty of Education, Ehime University. Series III, Natural Science. V. 1-. English (Japanese). Ehime Daigaku Kyoiku Gakubu, 3-ban Bunkyo-cho, Matsuyama-shi 790 Japan. **LC** Q4; .E36.

MY/0128-1828
**ELAEIS.** [Elaeis]. **Added/Corp** Institiut Penyelidikan Minyak Kelapa Sawit Malaysia. Vol. 1, No. 1 (June 1989)-. Academic Scholarly Publication. English. sa. $30.00. PORIM, PO Box 10620, Kuala Lumpur Malaysia. **Tel** 011 3 335155, telex MA31604. **ED** Dr. Yusof Basiron. **CODEN** ELAEE3. **Bk Rev,** (Qty: 2). **Ad Acc. Pr Rev. Circ:** 2,000 (ctrl). Documents available from CASDDS.
**Desc:** Full length original research on various aspects of oil palm and palm oil including process and technological developments.
**Ind/Abst** AGRICOLA [Full Cov.]; Chem. Abstr.; Dairy Sci. Abstr.; Food Sci. Technol. Abstr.; Hortic. Abstr.; Nutr. Abstr. Rev., Ser. B, Live Feeds and Feed.; Nutr. Abstr. Rev., Ser. A, Hum. Exp.; Plant Breed. Abstr.

US/0740-1922
**ELECTRON (WILLOUGHBY, OHIO), THE.** **See** Newspapers.

●UK/0965-2035
**ELECTRONIC DOCUMENTS.** [Electron. doc.]. Vol. 1, No. 1 (Jan. 1992)-. Periodical. English. mo. £95.00. Learned Information Ltd., Woodside Hinksey Hill, Oxford OX1 5AU England. **Tel** 44 865 730275, FAX 44 865 736354, telex 23667. **(Subscription address:** Learned Information, Inc. / North America Subscriptions, 143 Old Marlton Pike, Medford NJ 08055-8750.**) LC** TK5105; .E42. **DD** 651.5/0285. **CODEN** ELDOEE. Documents available from Ask*IEEE.
**Desc:** Publication about storing and exchanging information without paper. Reviews a particular technology used to store and disseminate information electronically - from image filing, to hypertext, to fax on demand.
**Ind/Abst** INSPEC (1992-).

US
**EMERGING TECHNOLOGY.** Periodical. English. Donaldson Lufkin & Jenrette Securities Corporation, 140 Broadway, New York NY 10005. **LC** HG4001; .E45. **DD** 338.7/4/0973.

●US/1075-0495
**EMERGING TECHNOLOGY (AMERICAN SOCIETY OF CIVIL ENGINEERS).** **See** Engineering-Civil Engineering.

US/0273-5717
**ENCOUNTERS (ST. PAUL, MINN.).** ***Ceased.*** (ENCOUNTERS/ THE SCIENCE MUSEUM OF MINNESOTA.). [Encounters]. Vol. 1, No. 1 (Mar. 1978)-(1993). Periodical. English. bm. Science Museum of Minnesota, 30 East 10th Street, St Paul MN 55101. **Tel** (612)222-6303. **ED** Susan Wichmann. **DD** 500. **Bk Rev. Ad Acc. Circ:** 24,000 (ctrl).
**Desc:** Membership magazine of the Science Museum of Minnesota. Articles include coverage of anthropology, biology, archaeology, paleontology, and technology.

US/0196-9110
**ENCYCLIA.** [Encyclia]. **Added/Corp** Utah Academy of Sciences, Arts, and Letters. Vol. 54 (1977)-. Academic Scholarly Publication. English. an. $12.00 (individual), $13.00 (joint, husband and wife), $150.00 (life), $165.00 (life, husband and wife) Comes with Utah Academy of Sciences, Arts & Letters membership. Brigham Young University / 990 SWKT, Joyce Penrod, Provo UT 84602. **Tel** (801)378-2083, FAX (801)378-5978. **ED** Linda Hunter Adams (phone: (801)378-3448). **LC** Q11; .U85. **DD** 081. **CODEN** ENCYDI. cum. index. **Circ:** 1,000 (ctrl). Documents available from CASDDS. ***Continues*** *Proceedings of the Utah Academy of Sciences, Arts, and Letters, 0083-4823.*
**Desc:** Scholarly papers on miscellaneous subjects in sciences, social sciences, letters, arts, business, and engineering.
**Ind/Abst** Chem. Abstr. (1977-1981); Curr. Geogr. Publ. (-19??); Field Crop Abstr.; Fish Rev.; GeoRef; Grasslands For. Abstr.; Hortic. Abstr.; Math. Rev.; MLA

Int. Bibl. Books Artic. Mod. Lang. Lit.; Life Sci. Collect.; Rev. Med. Vet. Mycology; Rev. Plant Pathol.; Soc. Plann. Policy Dev. Abstr.; Sociol. Abstr.; Wildl. Rev.

US/0898-9842
**ENCYCLOPEDIA OF PHYSICAL SCIENCE AND TECHNOLOGY. YEARBOOK.** ***Ceased.*** [Encycl. phys. sci. technol. yearb.]. **VFOAT** Physical Science and Technology. (1989)-Ceased with 1991 Edition. Academic Scholarly Publication. English. an. Academic Press, Inc., 6277 Sea Harbor Drive, Orlando FL 32887. **Tel** (800)543-9534, (407)345-4100, FAX (407)363-9661. **ED** Robert A Meyers. **LC** Q123; .E4973. **DD** 503.
**Desc:** A comprehensive encyclopedia covering the physical sciences, mathematics, and engineering.

UK/0160-9327
**ENDEAVOUR (NEW SERIES).** (ENDEAVOUR.). [Endeavour]. **Added/Corp** Imperial Chemical Industries, Ltd. Vol. 1-35, No. 1-126 (1942)-. Periodical. English. qt. $145.00 The Americas; £97.00 other. Pergamon Press, An Imprint of Elsevier Science Ltd., The Boulevard, Langford Lane, Kidlington, Oxford OX5 1GB United Kingdom. **Tel** 011 44 865 843000, 011 44 865 843699, FAX 011 44 865 843010. **(Subscription address:** Elsevier Science Ltd. Oxford Fulfillment Centre, PO Box 800, Kidlington, Oxford OX5 1DX United Kingdom.**)** **ED** Trevor Williams. **LC** Q1; .E5. **DD** 505. **NLM** W1 EN358. **CODEN** ENDEAS. **[CCC]**. cum. index. **Pr Rev.** available on microfilm and microfiche from University Microfilms International (UMI); available on microfiche from the publisher. Documents available from Article Express International, The Genuine Article, BIOSIS Document Express, UMI Article Clearinghouse, Ask*IEEE, CASDDS.
**Desc:** Founded by Imperial Chemical Industries (ICI), this journal continues to record the progress of science and technology in the service of mankind, in terms understandable not only to the practising scientists and engineer but for the interested general reader.
**Ind/Abst** Acad. Search (July 1993-); AgBiotech News Inf.; AGRICOLA; Alum. Ind. Abstr.; Art Archaeol. Tech. Abstr.; BHA : Biblio. Hist. Art; Biodeter. Abstr.; Biol. Abstr.; Br. Archaeol. Bibliogr.; Chem. Abstr.; Coal Abstr.; Curr. Aware. Biol. Sci., CABS; Curr. Biotechnol.; Curr. Contents, Agric. Biol. Environ. Sci.; Curr. Contents Eng. Tech. Appl. Sci.; Curr. Contents Life Sci. (1968-); Curr. Contents Phys. Chem. Earth Sci. (1968-); Curr. Ref. Fish Res.; Curr. Technol. Index; Ecol. Abstr.; Ei Page One; EMBASE; Energy Inf. Abstr.; Energy Res. Abstr.; Eng. Mater. Abstr.; Eng. Index Annu. [Select. Cov.]; Expand. Acad. Index (1989-); Field Crop Abstr.; Fish Rev.; Gen. Sci. Index; Gen. Sci. Source (Jul. 1993-); Geogr. Abstr. Phys. Geogr.; Geogr. Abstr. Human Geogr.; GeoRef; Grasslands For. Abstr.; Health Plan. Adminis.; Highw. Res. Abstr.; Hortic. Abstr.; Index Med.; INFO-SOUTH Abstr.; INSPEC (1977-); Int. Aerosp. Abstr. (1984-); Leadscan; Mag. Search; Met. Abstr.; Meteorol. Geoastrophys. Abstr.; Newsp. Period. Abstr. (1991-); Peace Res. Abstr. J. (1967-1980); Plant Breed. Abstr.; Protozoolog. Abstr.; Res. Alert [Full Cov.]; Rev. Med. Vet. Entomol.; Saf. Health Work; Sci. Cit. Index; SCISEARCH; Soils Fert.; Wildl. Rev.

IT/0391-5360
**ENERGIE ALTERNATIVE HTE.** (ENERGIE ALTERNATIVE, HABITAT, TERRITORIO, ENERGIA.). [Energ. altern. HTE]. **Added/Corp** International Solar Energy Society. Sezione Italiana. **VFOAT** HTE; Energie Alternative HTE. (1979)-. Periodical. Italian (summaries and/or abstracts in English, French and German). bm. L55000. Editoriale Peg SPa, Via Fratelli Bressan 2, 20126 Milan Italy. **Tel** 011 39 2 257-9841, FAX 02/2552779, telex 323088 PEGMOS I. **ED** Paolo Sonino. **LC** TJ163.13; .E5. **DD** 333.79. **CODEN** EHTEDZ. Index available. **Bk Rev. Ad Acc. Circ:** 5,100 (ctrl). Documents available from Article Express International.
**Desc:** High-level technical articles on research, existing plants in the field of alternative energies and energy saving.
**Ind/Abst** Bioeng. Abstr.; Coal Abstr.; Ei Page One; Energy Res. Abstr. (Nov. 1980-); Eng. Index Annu.; Int. Build. Serv. Abstr.

NE
**ENERGIE & MILIEUTECHNOLOGIE.** Dutch. qt. Stam Tijdschriften BV, Postbus 235, 2280 AE Rijswijk Netherlands. **Tel** +31 70 3988100, FAX +31 70 3988276, telex 33702 STAM NL. ***Continues*** *PT : Energie en Afvalbeheer.*

US/0745-984X
**ENERGY MANAGEMENT TECHNOLOGY.** ***Ceased.*** [Energy manage. technol.]. Vol. 7, No. 3 (Apr. 1983)-(19??). Periodical. English. bm. Intertec Publishing Corporation, 9800 Metcalf, Overland Park KS 66212. **Tel** (913)341-1300. **ED** Frank McGill. **LC** TJ163.5.F3; P57. **DD** 621.042/05. **Bk Rev. Ad Acc.** ctrl circ. available on microfilm and microfiche from University Microfilms International (UMI). ***Continues*** *Plant Energy Management, 0192-1118.*
**Desc:** Energy management products and services.
**Ind/Abst** Ei Page One; Energy Res. Abstr. (April 1983-); SportSearch.

BL/0100-0608
**ENGENHARIA NA INDUSTRIA (SAO PAULO).** (ENGENHARIA NA INDUSTRIA.). [Eng. ind.]. Academic Scholarly Publication. Portuguese. $100.00. Engetec, rua Nestor Pestana 125 50 Andar, Sao Paulo Brazil. **LC** T4; .E46. **CODEN** ENINDF. Documents available from CASDDS. ***Supersedes in part*** *Engenharia.*
**Ind/Abst** Chem. Abstr.

US/0013-7812
**ENGINEERING & SCIENCE.** **See** Engineering.

US/0092-2994
**ENGINEERING AND TECHNOLOGY GRADUATES.** (ENGINEERING AND TECHNOLOGY GRADUATES, A REPORT.). [Eng. technol. grad.]. **Main/Corp** Engineers Joint Council. Engineering Manpower Commission. English. $15.00. Engineers Joint Council, 345 East 47th Street, New York NY 10017. **Tel** (212)644-7840. **LC** TA157; .E67A. **DD** 331.7/62/000973.

IT/0392-176X
**ENOTECNICO, L'.** [Enotecnico]. (1890)-. Periodical. Italian. ir. L55000.00 Italy; L80000.00 other. Associaz Enotecnici Italiana, Viale Murillo 17, I 20149 Milan Italy. **Tel** 011 39 2 40072460. **UDC** 663.2.
**Ind/Abst** Plant Genet. Resour. Abstr.

SP/0212-4521
**ENSENANZA DE LAS CIENCIAS.** (1983)-. Periodical. Spanish. tq. ICE de la Universidad Autonoma, Edifici Rectorat, Barcelona, Spain. **UDC** 37:5.
**Ind/Abst** PsycINFO (1985-).

US/1042-5209
**ENVIRONMENTAL LAB.** [Environ. lab]. Vol. 1, No. 1 (March 1989)-. Periodical. English. mo. $57.00. Leo Douglas Publications, 9609 Gayton Road, Suite 100, Richmond VA 23233. **Tel** (804)741-6704. **ED** Mary Schaefer Benke. **DD** 620. Index available. **Ad Acc. Circ:** 20,000 (ctrl).
**Desc:** Serves environmental testing professionals through its coverage of scientific techniques, instrumentation focus, regulatory compliance, certification and accreditation, business management and development. Also addresses the environmental on-site analytical process as well as in-lab methodologies.
**Ind/Abst** Ind. Hyg. Dig. (19??-19??).

UK/0966-4904
**ENVIRONMENTAL PROTECTION TECHNOLOGY.** **See** Environmental Issues.

FR/0986-2943
**ENVIRONNEMENT & TECHNIQUE.** **See** Environmental Issues.

NE
**EOS.** (19??)-. mo (11 issues). Fl80.00 (latest issue). Telegraaf Tijdschriften Groep, Postbus 125, 1000 AC Amsterdam Netherlands. **Tel** 011 31 20 585333.

IT
**EPISTEMOLOGIA.** (Jan./June 1978)-. Periodical. English (Italian). Twice a year. $62.50. Tilgher Genova SAS, Via Assarotti 52, 16122 Genova Italy. **Tel** 011 39 10 870653, 8391140. **ED** Evandro Agazzi. **LC** Q174; .E64. **DD** 501. Index available in last issue of volume--attached. **Bk Rev. Ad Acc. Circ:** 1,000.
**Desc:** A journal for the philosophy of science which pays due attention to the analytic research on methods and contents of the sciences.
**Ind/Abst** Philos. Index.

SP
**EQUIPH.** Spanish. Ediciones Doyma SA, Travesera de Gracia 17 21, 08021 Barcelona Spain. **Tel** 011 34 3 2000711, 011 34 3 4145706, FAX 011 34 3 2091136, telex 51964 INK E.

US/0098-5376
**EQUIPMENT & TECHNOLOGY INTERNATIONAL.** **VAT** Equipment and Technology International. V. 1- 1975-. English. Intercontinental Publications, PO Box 5017, Westport CT 06880. **Tel** (203)226-7463, FAX (203)222-8793. **LC** T1; .E69. **DD** 605.

US/1057-7262
**EQUIPMENT WORLD.** [Equip. world]. Vol. 1, No. 1 (1989)-. Periodical. English. Twelve times a year. Free to US trade/construction companies; $98.00 US; $158.00 Canada & Mexico; $230.00 others. Randall Publishing, 3200 Rice Mine Road, Tuscaloosa AL 35403. **Tel** (800)777-3748, (205)349-2990. **LC** IN PROCESS. **DD** 624. ***Absorbed*** *Contractors Market Center, 0884-3376.*

GW/0342-0671
**ERZIEHUNG UND WISSENSCHAFT.** **See** Education.

US/0197-8543
**ESL-TR (UNITED STATES. AIR FORCE. AIR FORCE ENGINEERING AND SERVICES CENTER. ENGINEERING AND SERVICES LABORATORY).** (ESL-TR.). [ESL-TR]. **Main/Corp** Engineering Services Laboratory (U.S.). (197?)-. English. **CODEN** AFEED4. Documents available from CASDDS.
**Ind/Abst** Chem. Abstr.

UK
**ESN INFORMATION BULLETIN.** **Added/Corp** United States. Office of Naval Research. Branch Office, London. United States. Office of Naval Research. European Office. **VFOAT** European Science Notes Information Bulletin; ESNIB. (1987)-. Bulletin. English. mo. US Office of Naval Research, Branch Office/Department of Navy/FPO, New York NY 09510. **LC** Q1; .E68. **DD** 505. ***Continues*** *European Science Notes.*

FR
**ESPACE INFORMATION.** French. Cimm Informatique, 7 Bis Allee des Soupirs, 31000 Toulouse France.

IT
**ESSECOME.** Edis SRL, Via E Ponente 20 / 4, 40133 Bologna Italy. **Tel** 011 39 51 382606 or 312205, FAX 011 39 51 380605.

CN
**ESTIMATES. PART III, NATIONAL RESEARCH COUNCIL CANADA.** **See** Public Administration.

CN
**ESTIMATES. PART III, NATURAL SCIENCES AND ENGINEERING RESEARCH COUNCIL OF CANADA.** **Main/Corp** Canada. **VFOAT** Budget des Depenses. Partie III, Conseil de Recherches en Sciences Naturelles et en Genie. (19??)-. English (French). $6.00 Canada; $7.20 other. Canada Communication Group Publishers, Order Processing, Ottawa Ontario K1A 0S9 Canada. **Tel** (819)956-4800, (819)956-4802. **LC** Q127.C2; C32b. **DD** 354.710085.5.

CN
**ESTIMATES. PART III, SCIENCE COUNCIL OF CANADA.** **Main/Corp** Canada. **VFOAT** Budget des Depenses. Partie III, Conseil des Sciences du Canada. (19??)-. English (French). $3.00 Canada; $3.60 other. Canada Communication Group Publishers, Order Processing, Ottawa Ontario K1A 0S9 Canada. **Tel** (819)956-4800, (819)956-4802. **LC** Q127.C2; C32c. **DD** 354.710085/5.

AG
**ESTUDIOS INTERDISCIPLINARIOS.** Yearly V. 1- August 1973-. Periodical. Spanish. Argentina CEP, San Nicolas 66, Cordoba Argentina. **LC** AS78.A1; E78.

PO/0870-001X
**ESTUDOS, ENSAIOS E DOCUMENTOS (PORTUGAL. JUNTA DE INVESTIGACOES CIENTIFICAS DO ULTRAMAR).** (ESTUDOS, ENSAIOS E DOCUMENTOS.). [Estud., ensaios doc. - Junta Invest. Cient. Ultramar]. (1974)-. Academic Scholarly Publication. Portuguese (English and French). ir. Price varies per volume. Instituto de Investigacao Cientifica Tropical, Centro de Documentacao e Informacao, rua Jau 47, 1 300 Lisbon Portugal. **Tel** 645321. **CODEN** EEDUDG. Index available. **Circ:** 1,000 (ctrl). Documents available from CASDDS.
**Desc:** Publishes research from the field of scientific activities sponsored by the Institute for Scientific Tropical Research.
**Ind/Abst** Chem. Abstr.; GeoRef.

FR/1151-5422
**ETHIQUE.** **See** Ethics.

US/0270-188X
**ETTORE MAJORANA INTERNATIONAL SCIENCE SERIES : PHYSICAL SCIENCE.** [Ettore Majorana int. sci. ser., Phys. sci.]. (1979)-. Academic Scholarly Publication. English. ir. Price varies per volume. Plenum Press, 233 Spring Street, New York NY 10013-1578. **Tel** (212)620-8000, (800)221-9369, FAX (212)463-0742, (212)807-1047, telex 23/421139. **LC** UNC. **CODEN** EISSDB. Documents available from Ask*IEEE, CASDDS.
**Ind/Abst** Chem. Abstr.; INSPEC.

NE/0165-0394
**EUCLIDES (GRONINGEN, NETHERLANDS).** **See** Mathematics.

BE/1022-7059
**EUREKA NEWS.** (19??)-. English (French, German, Italian and Spanish). qt. Free on request. Eureka Secretariat, 19H Avenue des Arts, B 1040 Brussels Belgium. **Tel** 011 32 2 2292240, FAX 011 32 2 2187906. **ED** Kim Ruberg.
**Desc:** News on furthering Europe-wide cooperation in advanced technology projects with civilian ends.

GW
**EUROPAISCHE GEMEINSCHAFT, FORSCHUNGSPOLITIK UND FORSCHUNGSPRAXIS / BUNDESSTELLE FUR AUSSENHANDELSINFORMATION.** See Economics-Industry and Production.

UK/0957-767X
**EUROPEAN JOURNAL OF NON-DESTRUCTIVE TESTING, THE.** [Eur. j. non-destruct. test.]. (1991)-. Periodical. English. qt. £65.00 UK; £85.00 other. British Institute of Non-Destructive Testing, 1 Spencer Parade, Northampton NN1 5AA England. **Tel** 0604 30124, FAX 0604 231489. **ED** RS Sharpe. **DD** 620.112705. **Ad Acc.** available on microfilm and microfiche from University Microfilms International (UMI). Documents available from Article Express International.
**Desc:** A journal dealing with research in non-destructive testing and evaluation in Europe.
**Ind/Abst** Ei Page One; Eng. Index Annu.

NE/0377-2217
**EUROPEAN JOURNAL OF OPERATIONAL RESEARCH.** [Eur. j. oper. res.]. **Added/Corp** Association of European Operational Research Societies. Vol. 1 (1977)-. Academic Scholarly Publication. English. Twenty-four times a year (8 volumes). FI4680.00. Elsevier Science Publishers BV, PO Box 211, 1000 AE Amsterdam Netherlands. **Tel** 011 31 20 5803642, FAX 011 31 20 5862696, telex 15682. **ED** A Mercer, C B Tilanus, and H J Zimmermann. **LC** T57.6; .E92. **DD** 001.4/24. **CODEN** EJORDT. **[CCC]. Pr Rev.** available on microfilm and microfiche from University Microfilms International (UMI). Documents available from Article Express International, The Genuine Article, Ask*IEEE, UMI Article Clearinghouse.
**Desc:** Publishes papers for an international authorship, which contribute to the practice of decision making within and beyond Europe.
**Ind/Abst** ABI/INFORM Glob. Ed.; ABI Inform Ondisc (Jan. 1978-); BioBusiness (1986-); Bioeng. Abstr.; Biostatistica; Bus. Index (Jan. 1985-Dec. 1985); Coal Abstr.; Compumath Citation Index [Full Cov.]; Comput. Inf. Syst. Abstr. J. [Full Cov.]; Comput. Rev. (Jan. 1978-); Contents Pages Manage.; Curr. Contents Soc. Behav. Sci.; Ei Page One; Elect. Comm. Abstr.; EMBASE; Energy Res. Abstr. (Feb. 1979-); Eng. Index Annu.; Environ. Eng. Abstr.; Gen. BusinessFile (Jan. 1985-Dec. 1985); GeoRef; Inf. Sci. Abstr. (?-?); INSPEC (Jan. 1978-); Int. Abstr. Oper. Res. [Full Cov.]; Int. Bibliogr. Sociol.; Manuf. Process Eng. Abstr.; Math. Rev. (-199?); Mech. Eng. Abstr.; Oper. Res./Manag. Sci. (1977-); Pollut. Abstr. Indexes; Qual. Control Appl. Stat. (1986-); Res. Alert [Full Cov.]; Risk Abstr.; Selec. Coop. Index Manage. Period; Soc. Sci. Cit. Index [Full Cov.]; Solid State Supercond. Abstr.; Zentralbl. Math. Ihre Grenzgeb.

UK
**EUROPEAN RESEARCH CENTRES.** 5th ed.-. English. $545.00/set. Gale Research Inc., 835 Penobscot Building, Detroit MI 48226. **Tel** (800)877-GALE, (313)961-2242, FAX (313)961-6083, telex TWX 810-221-7086. **LC** Q180.E9; E88. ***Formed by the union of*** *European Research Index, 0071-304X* ***and*** *East European Research Index.*
**Desc:** Covers 31 major countries of eastern and western Europe and profiles more than 17,000 scientific, technological, agricultural, and medical laboratories and departments.

UK/0960-6130
**EUROPEAN RESEARCH IN REGIONAL SCIENCE.** (19??)-. English. Pion Ltd., 207 Brondesbury Park, London NW2 5JN England. **Tel** 011 44 81 459 0066, FAX 011 44 81 451 6454, telex 94016265 PION G.

UK
**EUROPEAN SOURCES OF SCIENTIFIC AND TECHNICAL INFORMATION.** 5th Ed. (1981)-. English. $300.00. Longman Group Ltd., Fourth Avenue, Longman House, Harlow Essex CM19 5SR England. **Tel** 011 44 279 429655, FAX 011 44 279 431059, telex 81259. **(Subscription address:** US and Canada: Gale Research Co., 835 Penobscot Building, Detroit, MI 48226**)** ***Continues*** *Guide to European Sources of Technical Information, 0072-8349.*
**Desc:** Includes information on patents and standards offices, national offices of information and scientific and technical organizations all arranged by country under 22 science subjects.

BE/0775-2903
**EUROTECH FORUM JOURNAL.** [Eurotech forum j.]. (1985)-. Periodical. English. mo (11 issues per year). 12600F. Xcoms Internationsl, 54 rue D'Angoussart, 1301 Bierges Belgium. **Tel** 011 32 10411172. **UDC** 62.

UK/0959-7735
**EUROTECHNOLOGY.** (19??)-. Periodical. English. Twelve times a year. £255.00. Longman Cartermill Ltd., Technology Center/St Andrews, Fife KY16 9EA Scotland. **Tel** 011 44 334 77660, FAX 011 44 334 77180. **ED** John Boyle (editor's address: Oxford Computer Consultants, 1 Kings Meadow, Oxford, UK; phone:011 44 865 793077). Index available. **Circ:** 200.
**Desc:** Journal of collaborative technology.

II/0531-495X
**EVERYMAN'S SCIENCE.** (1966)-. Periodical. English. bm. $6.00. Indian Science Congress Association, 14 Dr Biresh Guha Street, Calcutta 700017 India. **Tel** 44-4530. **UDC** 5.
**Ind/Abst** Indian Geosci. Abstr.

GW/0340-0220
**EXAKT.** (1974)-. Periodical. German. 42.00. DVA Deutsche Verlagsanstalt, Neckarstrasse 121, D-70190 Stuttgart Germany. **Tel** 011 49 711 26310. **LC** Q3; .I2. ***Continues*** *Ideen des Exakten Wissens, 0019-1426.*

US
**EXCITEMENT & FASCINATION OF SCIENCE, THE.** (19??)-. English. ir. $90.00 US; $95.00 other. Annual Reviews Inc., 4139 El Camino Way, PO Box 10139, Palo Alto CA 94303-0139. **Tel** (415)493-4400, (800)523-8635, FAX (415)855-9815.

US/0192-7469
**EXHAUST NEWS.** [Exhaust news]. (197?)-. Periodical. English. mo. $20.00. Exhaust News/Cruse L, PO Box 120937, Arlington TX 76012. **Tel** (817)860-2375. **ED** Lee Cruse. **Ad Acc. Circ:** 16,000 (ctrl).

SZ/0014-4754
**EXPERIENTIA.** [Experientia]. Vol. 1, No. 1 (April 15, 1945)-. Academic Scholarly Publication. French (English, German and Italian). mo. 944.70F Switzerland; 974.80F other. Birkhaeuser Verlag Ag, Klosterberg 23, PO Box 133, CH-4010 Basel Switzerland. **Tel** 011 41 61 2717400, FAX 011 41 0 61 2717666, telex 963475 birk ch. **(Subscription address:** Birkhauser Verlag AG, PO Box 151, CH 4106 Therwil Switzerland; Phone: 011 41 61 7217740**) ED** H. P. von Hahn. **LC** Q1.A1; E9. **DD** 505. **NLM** W1; EX223. **CODEN** EXPEAM. **[CCC]. Pr Rev.** available on microfilm and microfiche from University Microfilms International (UMI). Documents available from The Genuine Article, BIOSIS Document Express, CASDDS.
**Desc:** An interdisciplinary journal publishing single- and multi-author reviews, mini-reviews, full papers and short communications on all experimental and theoretical aspects of the life sciences.
**Ind/Abst** AgBiotech News Inf.; AGRICOLA [Select. Cov.]; Anal. Abstr.; Anim. Behav. Abstr.; Anim. Breed. Abstr.; Biocont. News Inf. (1991-); Biodeter. Abstr. (19??-19??); Biol. Abstr.; Chem Inform; Chem. Abstr.; Chem. Hazards Ind.; Chem. Titles; Chemorecept. Abstr.; Coal Abstr.; Crop Physiol. Abstr.; CSA Neuro. Abstr.; Curr. Aware. Biol. Sci., CABS; Curr. Biotechnol.; Curr. Chem. React.; Curr. Contents Life Sci.; Curr. Ref. Fish Res.; Dairy Sci. Abstr.; Ecol. Abstr. (?-?); Ecology Abstr.; EMBASE; Energy Res. Abstr.; Entomol. Abstr.; Field Crop Abstr.; For. Prod. Abstr.; For. Abstr.; Genet. Abstr.; GeoRef; Grasslands For. Abstr.; Health Saf. Sci. Abstr.; Health Plan. Adminis.; Helminthol. Abstr. (19??-19??); Hortic. Abstr.; Immunol. Abstr.; Index Chem.; Index Med.; Index Vet.; Lab. Hazards Bull.; Maize Abstr.; Mass Spect. Bull.; Microbiol. Abstr. Sect. B; Microbiol. Abstr. Sect. C; NAPRALERT; Nat. Prod. Updates; Nematol. Abstr.; Nutr. Abstr. Rev., Ser. B, Live Feeds and Feed.; Nutr. Abstr. Rev., Ser. A, Hum. Exp.; Nutr. Res. Newsl.; Ornamental Hort.; Life Sci. Collect.; PESTDOC; Plant Breed. Abstr.; Plant Grow. Reg. Abstr.; Poult. Abstr.; Protozoolog. Abstr.; Ref. Upd. Basic Ed.; Ref. Upd. Deluxe Ed.; Res. Alert [Full Cov.]; Rev. Agric. Entomol.; Rev. Med. Vet. Entomol.; Rev. Med. Vet. Mycology; Rev. Plant Pathol.; Rice Abstr.; Sci. Cit. Index; SCISEARCH; Small Anim. Abstr. Bibliogr.; Soc. Sci. Cit. Index [Select. Cov.]; Soils Fert.; Soyabean Abstr.; SportSearch; Stat. Theory Method Abstr. (1961-1963); Surf. Treat. Technol. Abstr.; Vet. Bull.; Vitis Vitic. Enol. Abstr.; Weed Abstr.; Wildl. Rev.

US
**EXPLORATIONS (ORONO, ME.).** ***Ceased.*** (EXPLORATIONS : A JOURNAL OF RESEARCH AT THE UNIVERSITY OF MAINE AT ORONO.). Vol. 1, No. 1 (Oct. 1984)-June (1992). Periodical. English. Carole J Bombard, Office of Research/Alumni Hall, University of Maine, Orono ME 04469. **Tel** (207)581-1506. **ED** Carole J Bombard. **Circ:** 7,000.
**Desc:** Articles by faculty and occasionally students in all areas of research at the University of Maine. Some teaching and public service included.
**Ind/Abst** Geogr. Abstr. Human Geogr. (?-?).

US/0014-5025
**EXPLORERS JOURNAL.** [Explor. j.]. **Added/Corp** Explorers Club. Vol. 1 (Nov. 1921)-. Periodical. English. qt. $20.00 (one year), $35.00 (two year), $48.00 (three year). The Explorers Club, 46 East 70th Street, New York NY 10021. **Tel** (212)628-8383. **ED** Tim O. Rockwell. **LC** G1; .E93. **DD** 910/.5. **CODEN** EXJOAM. cum. index. **Bk Rev. Ad Acc. Circ:** 3,500. available on microfilm. Documents available from BIOSIS Document Express.
**Desc:** Presents exploration reports on anthropology, zoology, archaeology and the earth sciences, with coverage of physics, navigation, aviation and field research.
**Ind/Abst** ASTIS Curr. Aware. Bull. (1978-); ASTIS Bibliogr. (1978-); Biol. Abstr.; GeoRef; Middle East Abstr. Index; Wildl. Rev.

SZ
**EXS.** (1989)-. Monographic series. German. ir. price varies per volume. Birkhaeuser Verlag Ag, Klosterberg 23, PO Box 133, CH-4010 Basel Switzerland. **Tel** 011 41 61 2717400, FAX 011 41 0 61 2717666, telex 963475 birk ch. **(Subscription address:** Birkhaueuser Boston Inc., PO Box 19429, Newark NJ 07195.**) NLM** W1; E65. **CODEN** EXSEE7. ***Continues*** *Experientia. Supplementum, 0071-335X.*
**Desc:** Covers a wide range of topics in all experimental and theoretical aspects of the life sciences.

JA
**EXTENDED ABSTRACTS OF THE CONFERENCE ON SOLID STATE DEVICES AND MATERIALS.** See Chemistry.

US/0092-9824
**F.A.S. PUBLIC INTEREST REPORT.** **Main/Corp** Federation of American Scientists. **VAT** Federation of American Scientists Public Interest Report. Vol. 26, No. 8 (Oct. 1973)-. Periodical. English. bm. comes with membership. Federation of American Scientists, 307 Massachusetts Avenue Northeast, Washington DC 20002. **Tel** (202)546-3300. **ED** Jeremy J. Stone. **LC** Q11; .F422. **DD** 509/.73. **NLM** W1 F201A. **Bk Rev. Circ:** 5,000 (ctrl). ***Continues*** *F.A.S. Newsletter, 0014-5653.*
**Desc:** Contains articles on arms control, compliance, international security, US-USSR relations, energy and environment, and other topics of science and society.
**Ind/Abst** Hum. Rights Intern. Rep.

GW
**F & M / ORGAN DER VDI/VDE-GESELLSCHAFT MIKRO- UND FEINWERKTECHNIK.** **Added/Corp** VDI/VDE-Gesellschaft Mikro- und Feinwerktechnik. **VFOAT** F und M. (199?)-. Periodical. German (summaries and/or abstracts in English). Eight times a year. DM168.00. Carl Hanser Verlag, Postfach 860420, D 81631 Munich Germany. **Tel** 011 49 89 998300, FAX 011 49 89 984809. **LC** Q184; .F18. **DD** 681/.05. **CODEN** FFMMEM. Documents available from Ask*IEEE. ***Continues*** *Feinwerktechnik & Messtechnik, 0340-1952.*
**Ind/Abst** INSPEC (1992-).

GW
**FABRIK.** ***Ceased.*** (1992)-(199?). Periodical. German. ir (10 issues). Verlag Technik GmbH Berlin, AM Friedrichshain 22, D 10407 Berlin Germany. **Tel** 011 49 30 428700. **LC** T3; .K343. ***Continues*** *Fertigungstechnik und Betrieb, 0015-024X.*
**Desc:** Scientific-technical practice-aligned journal on problems of typical machine building.

GW
**FACHBLATT FUR SELBSTBEDIENUNG.** 1.- Yearly volume; 1957-. Periodical. German. mo. Fachverlag Zellmer, Hugelstrasse 74, W-6000 Frankfurt Germany.

US/0429-9809
**FACSIMILE REPRINTS IN THE HISTORY OF SCIENCE.** 1 (1959)-. English. University of Illinois History of Science Society, Urbana IL 61802. **DD** 500.

CN/0710-6092
**FACTS & FEATURES / ONTARIO RESEARCH FOUNDATION.** [Facts features - Ont. Res. Found.]. **VAT** Facts and Features - Ontario Research Foundation. Vol. 1, No. 1 (Mar. 1980)-. Periodical. English. bm. Ontario Research Foundation, Sheridan Park Research Committee, Mississauga Ontario L5K 1B3 Canada. **Tel** (416)822-4111, FAX (416)823-1446, telex 06-982311. **DD** 001.4/09713/541.

UZ
**FAN VA TURMUSH.** **Added/Corp** Uzbekiston SSR Fanlar Akademiiasi. (1939)-. Periodical. Uzbek. mo. **(Subscription address:** Victor Kamkin, 4956 Boiling Brook Parkway, Rockville MD 20852.**)**

US/0198-8700
**FEDERAL FUNDS FOR RESEARCH AND DEVELOPMENT.** [Fed. funds res. dev.]. Began with V. 27, Fiscal Years 1977, 1978, and 1979. English. an. National Science Foundation, 1800 G Street Northwest, Washington DC 20550. **Tel** (202)357-9859, (202)357-9498. **LC** Q180.U5; F36. **DD** 338.973. **NLM** W2 A N37FE. available on microfiche (Vols. for (1983-) distributed to depository libraries). ***Continues*** *Federal Funds for Research, Development, and other Scientific Activities, 0083-2359.*
**Ind/Abst** F&S Index Plus Text, Int. [Select. Cov.]; Predicasts Forecasts.

●US/1065-6375
**FEDERAL LABORATORY CONSORTIUM HANDBOOK SERIES.** **Added/Corp** Federal Laboratory Consortium (U.S.). (1992)-. English. Federal Laboratory Consortium Administrator, PO Box 545, Sequim WA 98382-0545.

CN/0824-0310
**FEDERAL SCIENTIFIC ACTIVITIES. See** Science and Technology-Abstracting, Bibliographies and Statistics.

US/0145-2282
**FEDERAL SCIENTIFIC AND TECHNICAL COMMUNICATION ACTIVITIES : PROGRESS REPORT.** **Main/Corp** United States. National Science Foundation. Division of Science Information. English. an. US National Science Foundation, Division of Science Resources Studies, 1800 G Street NW, Washington DC 20550. **Tel** (202)357-9859. **LC** T10.63.A1; U54A. **DD** 507. **NLM** Z 699 F295. ***Continues*** *Federal Scientific and Technical Communication Activities, Progress Report, 0145-2282.*

US
**FEDERAL TECHNOLOGY TRANSFER.** ***Ceased.*** **Added/Corp** National Technology Transfer Institute. Vol. 5, No. 6 (Nov./Dec. 1985)-(Dec. 1993). Periodical. English. bm. Federal Technology Transfer, 7206 Ben Franklin Building, 1200 Pennsylvania Avenue, Washington DC 20044. **Tel** (703)931-0511. ***Continues*** *Technology Utilization.*

UK/0309-6688
**FEN. FINITE ELEMENT NEWS.** (FINITE ELEMENT NEWS : FEN.). [FEN, Finite elem. news]. **Added/Corp** Robinson and Associates. **VFOAT** FEN. (Jan. 1976)-. Periodical. English. bm. £38.00 UK & Europe; $78.00 US, Canada, Japan & Far East; Fl120.00 Netherlands; £43.00 other. Finite Element News, Great Bidlake Manor Bridestowe, Devon EX20 4NT England. **Tel** 44 83 786220. **ED** John Robinson. **Bk Rev. Ad Acc. Circ:** 1,500 (ctrl). Documents available from Ask*IEEE.
**Desc:** Finite element methods and related topics.
**Ind/Abst** Fluid Abstr., Civil Eng.; Fluid Abstr. Proc. Eng.; FLUIDEX (1974-); INSPEC (Feb. 1986-).

US/0742-650X
**FERNBANK QUARTERLY. Added/Corp** Fernbank Science Center (Atlanta, Ga.). (Spring 1975)-. Periodical. English. qt (4 issues). Comes with membership. Fernbank Museum of Natural History, 767 Clifton Road Northeast, Atlanta GA 30307. **Tel** (404)378-0127. **ED** Patsy Fenters O'Connor. **Bk Rev. Circ:** 5,000 (ctrl).
**Desc:** A science magazine covering a variety of disciplines oriented towards the person with an interest in science.

US/0071-4682
**FIBER SCIENCE SERIES.** [Fiber sci. ser.]. Vol. 1 (1970)-. Monographic series. English. ir. Price varies per volume. Marcel Dekker Inc., 270 Madison Avenue, New York NY 10016. **Tel** (212)696-9000, (800)228-1160, FAX (212)685-4540, telex 421419. **(Subscription address:** Marcel Dekker Inc, PO Box 5017, Monticello NY 12701.**) ED** Rebenfield. **CODEN** FSCSDC. Documents available from CASDDS.
**Desc:** Covers all aspects of fiber science, from fiber chemistry to textiles and more.
**Ind/Abst** Chem. Abstr. (1970-1979).

PH
**FILIPINAS JOURNAL OF SCIENCE AND CULTURE, THE.** Vol. 1-. Periodical. English. sa. Filipinas Foundation Inc, Makati Stock Exchange Building, 303 Ayala Avenue/Room 303, Makati Metro Manila Philippines. **LC** Q76; .F55. **DD** 505.

AT/0310-6020
**FILTER PERTH. *Ceased.* See** Education-Teaching and Curriculum.

UK/0265-1661
**FINANCIAL TECHNOLOGY INTERNATIONAL BULLETIN.** [Financ. technol. int. bull.]. **VFOAT** Financial Technology Bulletin. (1983)-. Newsletter. English. mo. £247.00 UK; £494.00 other. IBC Publishing, 57-61 Mortimer St., London W1N 7TD England. **Tel** 011 44 71 637 4383, FAX 011 44 71 636 6314. **ED** Paul Penrose. **DD** 332.1. **Bk Rev**, (Qty: 10-20). **Circ:** 1,000 (ctrl). available on an online database. Documents available from BLDSC.
**Ind/Abst** Infomat Int. Bus.

FI/0356-2654
**FINNISH FOUNDATION FOR ALCOHOL STUDIES (SERIES).** (THE FINNISH FOUNDATION FOR ALCOHOL STUDIES.). [Finn. Found. Alcohol Stud.]. **VFOAT** Alkoholitutkimussaation Julkaisuja. Vol. 16 (1969)-. Academic Scholarly Publication. English (Finnish). ir. Price varies per volume. Center of Alcohol Studies, Rutgers University, National Institute of Alcohol Abuse, Publishing Division, New Brunswick NJ 08903. **Tel** (201)932-2011. **CODEN** VTJUAT. Documents available from BIOSIS Document Express, CASDDS. ***Continues*** *Vakijuomakysymyksen Tutkimussaation Julkaisuja.*
**Ind/Abst** Biol. Abstr. (-1976); Chem. Abstr.

IT/0391-9757
**FISICA E TECNOLOGIA. *Title Change.*** [Fis. tecnol.]. **Added/Corp** Societa Ttaliana di Fisica. Vol. 1 (Jan./Mar. 1978)-(19??). Academic Scholarly Publication. Italian. qt. Editrice Compositori SRL, Viale Stalingrado 97 2, 40128 Bologna Italy. **Tel** 011 39 51 327811. **CODEN** FITEDJ. **Bk Rev. Ad Acc. Circ:** 1,000 (ctrl). Documents available from Ask*IEEE, CASDDS. ***Merged with*** *Nuovo Saggiatore Bolletino Della Societa Italiana Di Fisica.*
**Desc:** Addressed to industries and technological research, as it deals with specific subjects concerning the industrial and manufacturing appliances of physical process.
**Ind/Abst** Chem. Abstr.; INSPEC (Jan./March 1978-).

UN/0367-1631
**FIZIKA AERODISPERSNYH SISTEM (KIEV). See** Earth Sciences-Meteorology.

●CI/1330-0016
**FIZIKA B : A JOURNAL OF EXPERIMENTAL AND THEORETICAL PHYSICS. See** Physics.

FR/0769-1432
**FLASH ... SUR LA RECHERCHE SCIENTIFIQUE ET MEDICALE A L'UNIVERSITE PIERRE ET MARIE CURIE. See** Medical Science and Technology.

CC
**FLORA REPUBLICAE POPULARIS SINICAE.** Monographic series. Chinese. ir. Price varies per volume. Koeltz Scientific Books, PO Box 1360, D 61453 Koenigstein Germany. **Tel** 011 49 6174 4492, 3189, FAX 011 49 6174 1634.

US
**FLORIDA SCIENCE NEWSLETTER.** Newsletter. English.
**Ind/Abst** Pollut. Abstr. Indexes.

US/0098-4590
**FLORIDA SCIENTIST.** [Fla. sci.]. **Added/Corp** Florida Academy of Sciences. Vol. 36, (Winter 1973)-. Periodical. English. qt. $28.00 (individuals), $45.00 (libraries), $100.00 (institutions) US; $30.00 (individuals), $47.00 (libraries), $100.00 (institutions) other. Florida Academy of Sciences, PO Box 033012, Indialantic FL 32903. **Tel** (407)723-6835. **ED** Dean F Martin and Barbara B Martin. **LC** Q11; .F65. **DD** 509/.759. **CODEN** FLSCAQ. Index available. **Bk Rev. Pr Rev. Circ:** 1,050 (ctrl). available on microfilm and microfiche; available in microform from University Microfilms International (UMI). Documents available from BIOSIS Document Express, CASDDS. ***Continues*** *Quarterly Journal of the Florida Academy of Sciences, 0015-3850.*
**Desc:** A scientific and educational journal covering many categories of science for a highly diversified professional, non-professional, student and concerned citizen membership.
**Ind/Abst** AGRICOLA [Select. Cov.]; Biol. Abstr.; Chem. Abstr.; Ecol. Abstr.; Ecology Abstr.; EMBASE; Fish Rev.; GeoRef; Key Word Index Wildl. Res.; Life Sci. Collect.; Sel. Water Resour. Abstr.; Wildl. Rev.

IT
**FLUID AIP.** Italian. Ten times a year. L86000.00 Italy; L136000.00 other. Etas SRL, Via Mecenate 89, 20138 Milan Italy. **Tel** 011 39 2 580841.

NE/0169-5983
**FLUID DYNAMICS RESEARCH.** [Fluid dyn. res.]. **Added/Corp** Nihon Ryutai Rikigakkai. Vol. 1 No. 1 (Aug. 1986)-. Academic Scholarly Publication. English. Twelve times a year (2 volumes). Fl936.00. Elsevier Science Publishers BV, PO Box 211, 1000 AE Amsterdam Netherlands. **Tel** 011 31 20 5803642, FAX 011 31 20 5862696, telex 15682. **ED** T. Kambe. **CODEN** FDRSEH. **[CCC]. Pr Rev.** available on microfilm and microfiche from University Microfilms International (UMI). Documents available from Article Express International, The Genuine Article, Ask*IEEE.
**Desc:** Aims at publication of original and creative works in all fields of fluid dynamics, which are inspired by the advent of high speed computers and the development of new experimental techniques.
**Ind/Abst** Appl. Mech. Rev.; Curr. Contents Eng. Tech. Appl. Sci.; Ei Page One; Eng. Index Annu.; Fluid Abstr., Civil Eng.; Fluid Abstr. Proc. Eng.; FLUIDEX (199?-); GeoRef; INSPEC (1986-); Int. Aerosp. Abstr.; Res. Alert [Select. Cov.]; SCISEARCH; Soc. Sci. Cit. Index [Select. Cov.].

NE/0015-4997
**FOCUS (AMERSFOORT).** (FOCUS.). [Focus (Amersfoort)]. (1914)-. Academic Scholarly Publication. Dutch. Eleven times a year. Price varies. Uitgeverij Focus, Utrechtestraat 131, PB 15435, 1017 VM Amsterdam Netherlands. **Tel** 011 31 20 6264353. **CODEN** FOCUAL. Documents available from CASDDS.
**Ind/Abst** Chem. Abstr.

SA
**FOCUS ON RESEARCH.** Periodical. English (Afrikaans). Research and Publication Committee, University of Zululand, Private Bag, KWA-Dlangezwa 3886, Empangeni South Africa. **LC** Q127.S693; F6. **DD** 001.4/09684/91.

XR/0323-0139
**FOLIA FACULTATIS SCIENTIARUM NATURALIUM UNIVERSITATIS PURKYNIANAE BRUNENSIS. GEOLOGIA.** [Folia Fac. Sci. Nat. Univ. Purkynianae Brunensis, Geol.]. **VFOAT** Geologia. 1-. Monographic series. Czech (summaries and/or abstracts in Russian, English and German). Price varies per volume. Univ J E Purkyne V Brne, Janackovo Nam 2A, Brno Czech Republic. **LC** Q1. **DD** 550.

NO/0368-6302
**FORHANDLINGER - DET KONGELIGE NORSKE VIDENSKABERS SELSKAB.** [Forh. - K. Nor. Vidensk. Selsk.]. **Main/Corp** Kongelige Norske Videnskabers Selskab. V. 1- 1926/28-. Norwegian. an. Kongelige Worske Videnskabers, Erling Skakkes GT 47, Tronoheim 7000 Norway. **LC** AS283; .T82. **DD** 506.2481. **CODEN** KNSFA2. Documents available from Ask*IEEE. ***Continues in part*** *Norske Videnskabs Selskab. Arsberetning.*
**Ind/Abst** Anthropol. Index; GeoRef; INSPEC; Math. Rev.; Stat. Theory Method Abstr. (1966).

FR
**FORMATIONS DE RECHERCHE, LES. Main/Corp** Centre National de la Recherche Scientifique (France). French. Centre National de la Recherche Scientifique, Informascience, 26 rue Boyer, 75971 Paris France. **Tel** 61.41.11.05, telex CNRSDOC 220880 F. **LC** Q180.F7; F7B. **DD** 001.4/3/0944.

GW
**FORSCHUNG AN DER TECHNISCHEN UNIVERSITAT BERLIN. Main/Corp** Berlin. Technische Universitat. Kommission fur Forschung und Wissenschaftlichen Nachwuchs. German. Strasse des 17 Juni 135, 1 Berlin 12 Germany. **LC** T173; .B519335.

GW/0172-1518
**FORSCHUNG (BOPPARD).** (FORSCHUNG : MITTEILUNGEN DER DFG / DEUTSCHE FORSCHUNGSGEMEINSCHAFT.). [Forschung]. **Added/Corp** Deutsche Forschungsgemeinschaft. **VAT** Forschung Mitteilungen der Deutsche Forschungsgemeinschaft. (1979)-. Periodical. German. qt. $45.00. VCH Gesellschaft GmbH, Postfach 101161, D 69451 Weinheim Germany. **Tel** 011 49 6201 606459, FAX 011 49 6201 606184. **(Subscription address:** VCH Publishers Inc., 303 Northwest 12th Avenue, Journals Department, Deerfield FL 33442.**) LC** Q180.G4; D417. **DD** 505. **[CCC]. Circ:** 55,000. ***Continues*** *Mitteilungen (Deutsche Forschungsgemeinschaft).*
**Ind/Abst** Energy Res. Abstr. (1982-); GeoRef; Soc. Plann. Policy Dev. Abstr.; Sociol. Abstr.

GW/0340-7608
**FORSCHUNGSBERICHT - BUNDESMINISTERIUM FUER FORSCHUNG UND TECHNOLOGIE. T, TECHNOLOGISCHE FORSCHUNG UND ENTWICKLUNG. VFOAT** BMFT-FB-T. (1973)-. Periodical. German. ir. Fachinformationszentrum Karlsruhe, Physics & Math, D 76344 Eggenstein Germany. **Tel** 011 49 7247 808149. **UDC** 62. Documents available from CASDDS.
**Ind/Abst** Chem. Abstr.

GW
**FORSCHUNGSBERICHT - UNIVERSITAT ULM. Main/Corp** Ulm. Universitat. German. Universitat Ulm, Oberer Eselsberg Postfach 4066, W-79 Ulm Germany. **LC** Q49; .U47A.

GW/0343-5520
**FORSCHUNGSBERICHTE AUS TECHNIK UND NATURWISSENSCHAFTEN. Added/Corp** Universitatsbibliothek und TIB (Hannover, Germany) Fachinformationszentrum Energie, Physik, Mathematik. **VFOAT** Reports in the Fields of Science and Technology. (19??)-. Periodical. English (German). qt. $550.00. VCH Gesellschaft GmbH, Postfach 101161, D 69451 Weinheim Germany. **Tel** 011 49 6201 606459, FAX 011 49 6201 606184. **(Subscription address:** VCH Publishers Inc., 303 Northwest 12th Avenue, Journals Department, Deerfield FL 33442.**) ED** Technische Informationsbibliothek, Welfengarten 1B D-3000 Hannover; telephone (0511)7622268, telex 922168 tibhn d, FAX (0511)715936. **LC** Z7403; .F59; Q158.5. **DD** 016.5. **[CCC].**

GW/0367-2492
**FORSCHUNGSBERICHTE DES LANDES NORDRHEIN-WESTFALEN.** [Forschungsber. Landes Nordrh.-Westfal.]. **Main/Corp** North Rhine-Westphalia (Germany). Ministerium fuer Wirtschaft, Mittelstand und Verkehr. (1960)-. Academic Scholarly Publication. German. Price varies per volume. Westdeutscher Verlag GmbH, Postfach 5829, D 65048 Wiesbaden Germany. **Tel** 011 49 611 160220. **CODEN** FLNWAR. Documents available from Article Express International, BIOSIS Document Express, Ask*IEEE, CASDDS. ***Continues*** *North Rhine-Westphalia. Ministerium fuer Wirtschaft und Verkehr.*

*Forschungsberichte.*
**Ind/Abst** Alum. Ind. Abstr.; Bioeng. Abstr.; Biol. Abstr.; Ceram. Abstr. (19??-); Chem. Abstr.; Ei Page One; Energy Res. Abstr.; Eng. Index Annu.; GeoRef (1968-); INSPEC; Math. Rev. (1968-); Met. Abstr.

AU
**FORSCHUNGSFORDERUNGEN UND FORSCHUNGSAUFTRAGE.** **Main/Corp** Austria. Bundesministerium fur Wissenschaft und Forschung. (1975)-. German. an. Free. Bundesministerium for Wissenschaft und Forschung, Minoritenplatz 5, Vienna Austria. **Tel** (0222)66 20-0. **LC** Q180.A85; A87a. **Bk Rev**. **Ad Acc**. **Circ:** 1,000.
**Desc:** Research funds and contracts contracted by federal ministry to institutions or experts outside the government.

SZ
**FORSCHUNGSPOLITISCHE ZIELVORSTELLUNGEN.** 1980-. German. Schweizerischer Wissenschaftsrat Wildhainweg, 9 Postfach 2732, 3001 Bern Switzerland. **Tel** (031)619666. **LC** Q180.S9; F65. **DD** 338.9494. **Circ:** 4,000 (ctrl).
**Desc:** Swiss research policy: means and ends.

SA/0015-8054
**FORT HARE PAPERS.** [Fort Hare pap.]. **Added/Corp** South African Native College, Fort Hare. Vol. 1 (June 1945)-. English (Afrikaans). ir. R5.00. Fort Hare University Press, Private Bag X1314,, Alice, Republic of Ciskei,, South Africa. **Tel** FAX 0404-32011, telex 250863. **ED** N.J. Prins. **LC** AS611; .F6. **CODEN** FHPADE. available on microfilm from University Microfilms International (UMI). Documents available from BIOSIS Document Express.
**Desc:** Includes information on the arts, humanities, and economics in South Africa.
**Ind/Abst** Annu. Bibliogr. Engl. Lang. Lit.; Anthropol. Index; Biol. Abstr. (-1987); MLA Int. Bibl. Books Artic. Mod. Lang. Lit.

UK/0046-4686
**FORTHCOMING INTERNATIONAL SCIENTIFIC AND TECHNICAL CONFERENCES.** [Forthcom. Int. Sci. Tech. Conf.]. **Added/Corp** Great Britain. Dept. of Education and Science. Aslib. (1971)-. Periodical. English. qt. £68.00 (member), £85.00 (non-member) Europe; £74.00 (member), £93.00 (non-member). ASLIB, Information House, 20-24 Old Street, London EC1V 9AP England. **Tel** 011 44 71 253 4488, FAX 011 44 71 430 0514, telex 23667 AJLIB G. **(Subscription address:** North America/ 143 Old Marlton Pike, Medford, NJ 08055-8707**) NLM** T 6; F7392.
**Desc:** This publication offers details on upcoming British and international conferences in all fields of science and technology - medicine, statistics, law, social science, and librarianship and information management, as well as the pure and applied sciences.
**Ind/Abst** Fluid Abstr., Civil Eng.; Fluid Abstr. Proc. Eng.; FLUIDEX (1973-); J. Ferrocement.

FI/0533-070X
**FORUM FOR EKONOMI OCH TEKNIK.** [Forum ekon. tek.]. Vol. 1 (Jan. 26, 1968)-. Periodical. Swedish. Twenty times a year. Fmk280.00. Forum for Ekonomi Och Tecknik, Mannerheimvaegen 18, 00100 Helsinki Finland. **Tel** (0)643445. **ED** Ragnhild Artimo. **Bk Rev**. **Ad Acc**. **Circ:** 12,841 (ctrl). ***Supersedes*** *Tekniskt Forum.*
**Ind/Abst** Energy Res. Abstr.

IO
**FORUM PENDIDIKAN SCIENCE DAN MATEMATIKA.** Periodical. Indonesian. IKIP Jogjakarta, Kampus IKIP Karangmalang, Jogjakarta Indonesia. **LC** Q183.4.I53; K413.

US/0306-4964
**FOUNDATION.** **See** Literature.

FR/1157-3724
**FRANCIS BULLETIN SIGNALETIQUE. 522, HISTOIRE DES SCIENCES ET DES TECHNIQUES.** **Added/Corp** Institut de l'Information Scientifique et Technique (France). **VFOAT** Histoire des Sciences et des Techniques; History of Science and Technology. Vol. 45, No. 1 (1991)-. Bulletin. French. qt (4 issues). 465.00F France; 490.00F other. CNRS / Institut d'Information Scientifique et Technique, (Centre National de la Recherche Scientifique), 15 Quai Anatole France, Paris 75700 France. **Tel** 011 33 1 47531515, telex 299 356 F. **(Subscription address:** Institut d'Information Scientifique et Technique Diffusion, 2 Allee du Parc de Brabois, 54514 Vandoeuvre Nancy France.**) LC** Z7405.H6; B795. Index available (free). available on CD-ROM. ***Continues*** *Bulletin Signaletique. 522, Histoire des Sciences et des Techniques, 0007-5574.*

GW
**FRANKREICH, FORSCHUNGSPOLITIK UND FORSCHUNGSPRAXIS / BUNDESSTELLE FUR AUSSENHANDELSINFORMATION.** **Added/Corp** Bundesstelle fur Aussenhandelsinformation (Germany). (19??)-. German. Bundesstelle fuer Aussenhandelsinformation, Agrippastr 87 93, D 50676 Cologne Germany. **Tel** 011 49 221 2057316, FAX 011 49 221 2057212. **LC** Q180.55.G3; F7. **DD** 001.4/0943.

FR/0532-6826
**FRENCH SCIENCE NEWS.** Began in 1957. Periodical. English. Association pour la Diffusion de la Pensee Francaise, 11 rue Georges Pitard, 75 Paris 1SE France. **DD** 500.

US/1062-4767
**FRONTIER PERSPECTIVES.** [Front. perspect.]. **Added/Corp** Temple University. Center for Frontier Sciences. (199?)-. Periodical. English. sa. $25.00. Center for Frontier Sciences, Temple University, Ritter Hall 003-00, Philadelphia PA 19122. **LC** Q11; .F73. **DD** 505.
**Ind/Abst** Except. Hum. Exp.

FR/0985-2220
**FTS FRENCH TECHNOLOGY SURVEY.** ***Ceased.*** (FRENCH TECHNOLOGY SURVEY.). (1987?)-(19??). English. bm. ADITECH, 96 Blvd Auguste Blanqui, 75013 Paris France. **Tel** 011 33 1 47071441. **CODEN** FTSUE4.
**Ind/Abst** BioBusiness; F&S Index Plus Text, Int. [Select. Cov.]; Infomat Int. Bus.; PROMT.

CH/1016-1538
**FU JEN STUDIES : NATURAL SCIENCES.** ***Title Change.*** [Fu jen stud., Nat. sci.]. **Added/Corp** Fu Jen ta Hsueh (Hsin-Chuang Shih, Taiwan) Fu Jen ta Hsueh (Hsin-Chuang Shih, Taiwan). Li Hsueh Yuan. No. 6 (1973)-(19??). Academic Scholarly Publication. English (Chinese). an. College of Science and Engineering, Fu Jen Catholic University, 24205 Hsinchuang Taipei Taiwan. **Tel** (02)903-1111, FAX 886 2 901 4749. **ED** Frank E. Budenholzer. **LC** Q72.5; .F8. **CODEN** FJSTEX. **Circ:** 300. Documents available from BIOSIS Document Express. ***Supersedes in part*** *Fu Jen Studies. Natural Sciences & Foreign Language, 1018-7251.* ***Continued by*** *Fu Jen Studies. Science and Engineering.*
**Desc:** Contains reports of original research in basic and applied sciences. Written primarily by the faculty of the College of Science and Engineering, Fu Jen Catholic University.
**Ind/Abst** Biol. Abstr. (1985-199?).

CH
**FU JEN STUDIES. SCIENCE AND ENGINEERING.** **Added/Corp** Fu Jen ta Hsueh (Hsin-Chuang Shih, Taiwan). Li Kung Hsueh Yuan. **VFOAT** Science and Engineering; Fu Jen Hsueh Chih. (19??)-. Periodical. English (summaries and/or abstracts in Chinese). Fu Jen Studies, Fu Jen University, Hsin Chuang 242 Taiwan. **LC** Q72.5; .F8. **DD** 505. **Circ:** 300. ***Continues*** *Fu Jen Studies. Natural Sciences.*
**Ind/Abst** Biol. Abstr.

CC/0427-7104
**FU TAN HSUEH PAO. TZU JAN KO HSUEH PAN.** [Fu-tan hsueh pao, Tzu jan k'o hsueh]. **Added/Corp** Fu Tan Ta Hsueh (Shanghai, China). **VFOAT** Tzu Jan Ko Hsueh Pan; Natural Science; Journal of Fudan University. Natural Science. (1955)-. Periodical. Chinese (summaries and/or abstracts in English). bm. $4.00 (per issue). Shanghai Kexue Jishu Chubanshe / Shanghai Science and Technical Publishers, 450 Ruijin Road, Shanghai 200020 People's Republic of China. **Tel** 5484906. **(Subscription address:** China International Book Trading Corporation, PO Box 399, Library Service Department, Beijing 100044 People's Republic of China.**) ED** Z. Xiuling. **LC** Q4; .F82. **DD** 505. **CODEN** FHPTAY. Documents available from CASDDS, BLDSC.
**Ind/Abst** Math. Rev.; NAPRALERT.

CC/1000-5277
**FUJIAN SHIFAN DAXUE XUEBAO (ZIRAN KEXUE BAN).** (FU-CHIEN SHIH FAN TA HSUEH HSUEH PAO. TZU JAN KO HSUEH PAN.). [Fujian shifan daxue xuebao]. **Added/Corp** Fu-Chien Shih Fan Ta Hsueh. **VFOAT** Journal of Fujian Teachers University. Natural Science. (19??)-. Periodical. Chinese (summaries and/or abstracts in English). qt. **LC** Q4; .F8. **DD** 505. **CODEN** FSDKES. Documents available from CASDDS.
**Ind/Abst** Chem. Abstr.

JA
**FUKUI DAIGAKU KOGAKUBU SENI KINOSEI ZAIRYO KENKYU SHISETSU HOKOKU.** **VFOAT** Bulletin of the Research Institute for Material Science and Engineering, Faculty of Engineering, Fukui University, Fukui, Japan; Bulletin of the Institute for Material Science and Engineering Faculty of Engineering, Fukui University, Fukui, Japan. Periodical. Japanese (summaries and/or abstracts in English). an. Free. Fukui Daigaku Kogakubu Seni Kinosei Zairyo Kenkyu Shisetsu, 9-1 Bunkyo 3-chome, Fukui-shi 910 Japan. **Tel** 0776-23-0500 ext. 866. ***Continues*** *Seni Kinasei Zairyo Kenkyu Shisetsu Hokoku.*

JA
**FUKUOKA DAIGAKU KENKYUSHO HO : SHIZEN KAGAKU HEN.** **Main/Corp** Fukuoka Daigaku. Kenkyujo. **VFOAT** Bulletin of the Institute for Advanced Research of Fukuoka University: Natural Sciences. No. 1- ; 1977-. Japanese (English). ir (two or three issues per year). Fukuoka Daigaku Kenkyusho, 8-19-1 Nanakuma Jonan-ku, Fukuoka 814-01 Japan. **LC** Q4; .F874C. **Circ:** 700.

JA
**FUKUOKA DAIGAKU KOGAKU SHUHO.** **Main/Corp** Fukuoka Daigaku. Kenkyujo. **VFOAT** Fukuoka University Review of Technological Sciences. Academic Scholarly Publication. Japanese (summaries and/or abstracts in English). sa. Fukuoka Daigaku Kenkyusho, 8-19-1 Nanakuma Jonan-ku, Fukuoka 814-01 Japan. **LC** T4; .F84A. **CODEN** FDKSDF. **Circ:** 700. Documents available from CASDDS.
**Ind/Abst** Chem. Abstr.; Coal Abstr.

JA/0386-118X
**FUKUOKA DAIGAKU RIGAKU SHUHO.** [Fukuoka Daigaku rigaku shuho]. **Main/Corp** Fukuoka Daigaku. Kenkyujo. **Added/Corp** Fukuoka Daigaku. Fukuoka Daigaku. Fukuoka University Science Reports. Fukuoka Daigaku. Kenkyujo. Fukuoka University Science Reports. **VFOAT** Fukuoka University Science Reports. (1978)-. English (Japanese). Fukuoka Daigaku Sogo Kenkyujo, (Central Research Inst., Fukuoka University), 19-1, Nanakuma 8 Chome, Jonanku,, Fukuokashi, Fukuokaken 814-01 Japan. **LC** Q4; .F874b. **DD** 505. **CODEN** FDRSDG. Documents available from CASDDS.
**Ind/Abst** Chem. Abstr.

JA
**FUKUOKA KYOIKU DAIGAKU KIYO. DAI 3-BUNSATSU, SUGAKU, RIKA, GIJUTSUKA HEN.** **Added/Corp** Fukuoka Kyoiku Daigaku. **VFOAT** Sugaku, Rika, Gijutsuka Hen; Mathematics, Natural Sciences, and Technology; Bulletin of Fukuoka University of Education. Part III, Mathematics, Natural Sciences, and Technology. (1984)-. Periodical. English (Japanese). an. Fukuoka Kyoiku Daigaku, (Fukuoka University of Education), Akama, Munakatashi, Fukuokaken 811-41 Japan. **LC** Q4; .F875. **CODEN** FKDNEF. Documents available from BIOSIS Document Express, CASDDS. ***Continues*** *Fukuoka Kyoiku Daigaku Kiyo. Dai 3-Bunsatsu. Rika Hen, 0532-811X.*
**Ind/Abst** Biol. Abstr.; Chem. Abstr.

●US/1064-122X
**FULLERENE SCIENCE AND TECHNOLOGY.** Vol. 1, No. 1 (Feb. 1993)-. Periodical. English. Six times a year. $395.00 US; $416.00 other. Marcel Dekker Inc., 270 Madison Avenue, New York NY 10016. **Tel** (212)696-9000, (800)228-1160, FAX (212)685-4540, telex 421419. **(Subscription address:** Marcel Dekker Inc, PO Box 5017, Monticello NY 12701.**) LC** IN PROCESS. **DD** 546. **CODEN** FTECEG. **Pr Rev.**
**Desc:** Publishes original papers from all fields of scientific inquiry related to fullerene compounds. Provides a worldwide forum for investigators interested in fundamental and applied fullerene science issues. Discussing theoretical, experimental and applicatory aspects of fullerenes, it covers various topics.

JA/0386-6157
**FUNTAI KOGAKKAISHI.** (FUNTAI KOGAKU KAISHI.). [Funtai Kogakkaishi]. **Added/Corp** Funtai Kogakkai (Japan). **VFOAT** Journal of the Society of Powder Technology, Japan. Vol. 15 (1978)-. Academic Scholarly Publication. Japanese. mo. $590.00. Shibunkaku Kaikan, 33 2 17 Tanaka Sekiden Sakyoku, Kyotoshi Kyotofu 606 Japan. **(Subscription address:** Kyowa Book Company Inc., 1-38 Kanda Jinbo-Cho, Chiyoda-Ku Tokyo 101, Japan**) CODEN** FKKADA. cum. index. Documents available from CASDDS. ***Continues*** *Funtai Kogaku Kenkyukaishi.*
**Ind/Abst** Ceram. Abstr. (19??-); Chem. Abstr.; Coal Abstr.

●SZ
**FUTURA : ERGEBNISSE DER FORSCHUNGSPOLITISCHEN FRUEHERKENNUNG (FER) DES SCHWEIZERISCHEN WISSENSCHAFTSRATES / RESULTATS DE LA DETECTION AVANCEE EN POLITIQUE DE LA RECHERCHE DU CONSEIL SUISSE DE LA SCIENCE / FINDINGS OF THE EARLY WARNING SYSTEM IN SCIENCE POLICY OF THE SWISS SCIENCE COUNCIL.** **Added/Corp** Forschungspolitische Frueherkennung (FER) Schweizerischer Wissenschaftsrat. (1993)-. Periodical. German (English, French and Italian). qt. Schweizerischer Wissenschaftsrat Wildhainweg, 9 Postfach 2732, 3001 Bern Switzerland. **Tel** (031)619666. **LC** Q127.S9; F88. **DD** 338.949406. ***Continues*** *FUTURA FER.*

SZ
**FUTURA FER : ERGEBNISSE DER FORSCHUNGSPOLITISCHEN FRUEHERKENNUNG (FER) DES SCHWEIZERISCHEN WISSENSCHAFTSRATES / RESULTATS DE LA DETECTION AVANCEE EN POLITIQUE DE LA RECHERCHE DU CONSEIL SUISSE DE LA SCIENCE / FINDINGS OF THE EARLY WARNING SYSTEM IN SCIENCE POLICY OF THE SWISS SCIENCE COUNCIL.** ***Title Change.*** **Added/Corp** Forschungspolitische Frueherkennung (FER) Schweizerischer Wissenschaftsrat. **VFOAT** Ergebnisse der Forschungspolitischen Fruherkennung (FER) des Schweizerischen Wissenschaftsrates; Resultats de la Detection Avancee en Politique de la Recherche du Conseil Suisse de la Science; Findings of the Early Warning System in Science Policy of the Swiss Science Council. (1989)-(1992). English (French and German). qt. Schweizerischer Wissenschaftsrat Wildhainweg, 9 Postfach 2732, 3001 Bern Switzerland. **Tel** (031)619666. **LC** Q127.S9; F88. **DD** 338.949406. ***Continued by*** *Futura (Bern, Switzerland).*
**Ind/Abst** PAIS Int. Print.

US/0273-0138
**FUTURE SURVEY ANNUAL.** [Future surv. annu.]. **Added/Corp** World Future Society. (1979)-. English. an. $35.00. World Future Society, 7910 Woodmont Avenue, Suite 450, Bethesda MD 20814. **Tel** (301)656-8274, FAX (301)951-0394. **ED** Michael Marien. **LC** Z5990; .F88; CB161. **DD** 016.3034. Index available. **Bk Rev. Circ:** 2,500 (ctrl).
**Desc:** Abstracts of literature in futures-related fields, assembled from the monthly Future Survey.

US/8755-3317
**FUTURES RESEARCH QUARTERLY.** [Futures res. q.]. **Added/Corp** World Future Society. Vol. 1, No. 1 (Spring 1985)-. Periodical. English. qt (Jan., Apr., Jul., Oct.). $70.00 (individuals); $90.00 (institutions). World Future Society, 7910 Woodmont Avenue, Suite 450, Bethesda MD 20814. **Tel** (301)656-8274, FAX (301)951-0394. **ED** Kenneth W. Hunter and Audrey Clayton. **LC** CB158; .F85. **DD** 303.4/9/05. **Bk Rev. Circ:** 1,500. available on microfilm and microfiche from University Microfilms International (UMI). ***Continues*** *World Future Society Bulletin, 0049-8092.*
**Desc:** A professional journal on strategic planning, policy analysis, technical forecasting, issues on management, and other futures-related areas.
**Ind/Abst** Curr. Index J. Educ.; Fut. Surv.

US
**FUTURETECH'S STRATEGIC MARKETS.** English. mo. $1500.00 US; $1560.00 other. Technical Insights Inc., PO Box 1304, Fort Lee NJ 07024-9967. **Tel** (201)568-4744, FAX (201)568-8247, telex 425900 SWIFT UI. **ED** Karen Dean. Index available. cum. index.
**Desc:** Focuses on strategic technologies that have been judged capable of making an impact on broad industrial fronts, giving a forecast of when the uncovered technology will result in marketable products/processes.

DK
**FUTURIBLERNE.** Periodical. Danish. Four times a year. kr225.00. Society for Futures Studies, Trommesalen 7, DK-1614 Copenhagen V Denmark. **Tel** 01 31 40 49. **LC** T174; .F87. Index available. **Circ:** 400 (ctrl).
**Desc:** Addresses a selected issue on a interdisciplinary base.

US/0164-1220
**FUTURICS.** [Futurics]. **Added/Corp** Minnesota Futurists. (19??)-. Periodical. English. Four times a year (Feb., May, Aug., Nov.). $50.00 US & Canada; $67.00 other. Minnesota Futurists, 365 Summit Avenue, St Paul MN 55102. **Tel** (612)290-2846. **ED** Earl C. Joseph. **LC** CB161; .F793. **DD** 303.4. **Bk Rev**, (Qty: 2-10). **Ad Acc. Pr Rev. Circ:** 500. available on microfilm and microfiche from University Microfilms International (UMI).
**Desc:** Deals with alternative futures from multiple views-technological, societal, educational, political, economic, international, scientific, forecasts, trends, and forces of change.
**Ind/Abst** Foods Adlibra; Soc. Plann. Policy Dev. Abstr.; Sociol. Abstr.

US/0016-3317
**FUTURIST, THE.** [Futurist]. **Added/Corp** World Future Society. Vol. 1 (Feb. 1967)-. Periodical. English. bm (Feb., Apr., June, Aug., Oct., Dec.). $42.00 (one year), $80.00 (two year), $118.00 (three year). World Future Society, 7910 Woodmont Avenue, Suite 450, Bethesda MD 20814. **Tel** (301)656-8274, FAX (301)951-0394. **ED** Edward Cornish. **LC** CB158; .F88. **DD** 905. **CODEN** FUTUAC. **[CCC].** Index available. cum. index. **Bk Rev. Ad Acc. Pr Rev. Circ:** 25,000 (ctrl). available on microfilm and microfiche from University Microfilms International (UMI). Documents available from The Genuine Article, Ask*IEEE, UMI Article Clearinghouse, Documents on Demand, Magazine Collection.
**Desc:** Features include articles by a wide variety of experts, editorials, interviews, pictorials, and shorter items covering latest developments in studies of the future.
**Ind/Abst** ABI/INFORM Glob. Ed.; ABI Inform Ondisc (April 1973-); Acad. Abstr. Full Text Elite (July 1986-); Acad. Abstr. (July 1986-); Acad. Ind. [Computer File] (1984-); Acad. Search (July 1986-); AGRICOLA; Arts Humanit. Citation Index [Select. Cov.]; Book Rev. Index; Bus. Index (1979-?); Comput. Bus. (19??-19??); Curr. Contents Soc. Behav. Sci.; Curr. Index J. Educ.; Curr. Lit. Fam. Plan. (19??-199?); Energy Inf. Abstr.; Energy Res. Abstr. (Aug. 1978-); Environ. Abstr.; Expand. Acad. Index (1984-); Foods Adlibra; Gen. Period. Index (1985-); INFO-SOUTH Abstr.; INIS Atomindex [Micro.]; INSPEC (Aug. 1983-Nov./Dec. 1989); Int. Labour Doc.; J. Plan. Lit.; LABORDOC; Mag. Artic. Summar. Elite (July 1986-); Mag. Artic. Summar. Select (Jan. 1986-); Mag. Artic. Summar. CD-ROM (July 1986-); Mag. ASAP Plus [Full Txt.]; Mag. ASAP Sel. [Full Txt.]; Mag. Express (1988-) [Full Txt.]; Mag. Index Plus (1989-); Mag. Index. Sel. (1986-); Mag. Search; Newsp. Period. Abstr. (1988-); Peace Res. Abstr. J. (1967-1975, 1985); Read. Guide Abstr. Select Ed.; Read. Guide Period. Lit.; Res. Alert [Full Cov.]; Resource/One Ondisc; Soc. Plann. Policy Dev. Abstr.; Soc. Sci. Source (Jan. 1986-); Soc. Sci. Cit. Index [Full Cov.]; Soc. Sci. Index; Soc. Sci. Index Fulltext (Nov. 1988-) [Full Txt.]; Sociol. Abstr.; Mag. Index (1977-); Trade Ind. ASAP [Full Txt.]; Trade Ind. Index [Full Txt.]; UMI ABI/Inform--Bus. Period. Ondisc (Jan. 1988-) [Full Txt.]; Urban Aff. Abstr.; Vocat. Search (July 1986-).

US/0016-3317
**FUTURIST. [MICROFILM], THE.** **Added/Corp** World Future Society. Vol. 1 Feb. (1967)-. Periodical. English. bm. World Future Society, 7910 Woodmont Avenue, Suite 450, Bethesda MD 20814. **Tel** (301)656-8274, FAX (301)951-0394. **ED** Edward Cornish. **LC** CB158; .F88. **[CCC].**
**Desc:** Features include articles by a wide variety of experts, editorials, interviews, pictorials, and shorter items covering latest developments in studies of the future.

US
**FUTUTETECH.** English. mo. $1,500.00 North America; $1,560.00 other. Technical Insights Inc., PO Box 1304, Fort Lee NJ 07024-9967. **Tel** (201)568-4744, FAX (201)568-8247, telex 425900 SWIFT UI.

JA
**GAKKAI SENTA NEWS.** (19??)-. Periodical. Japanese. mo. ¥1000. Gakkaishi Kanko Senta, (Center for Academic Publications, Japan), 4-16, Yayoi 2 Chome, Bunkyoku, Tokyoto 113, Japan. **ED** Tadahiro Ohmi. **LC** AS541; .G34. **Bk Rev. Ad Acc. Circ:** 3,000.
**Desc:** Gives academic (scientific) meeting information and related topics mainly domestic societies and associations of Japan.

JA
**GAKUJUTSU KIYO / KOCHI KOGYO KOTO SENMON GAKKO.** [Kochi Kogyo Koto Senmon Gakko gakujutsu kiyo]. **Added/Corp** Kochi Kogyo Koto Senmon Gakko. **VFOAT** Bulletin of Kochi Technical College. (1965)-. Japanese (summaries and/or abstracts in English). an. **CODEN** KKOCAK. Documents available from CASDDS.
**Ind/Abst** Chem. Abstr.

YU/0350-123X
**GALAKSIJA.** Periodical. Serbo-Croatian (Roman). Twelve times a year. $20.00. BIGZ, Vojvode Misica 17, 11000 Belgrad Yugoslavia. **Tel** 650-161, 12-819, 651-841. **ED** Aleksandar Petrovic. **LC** Q4; .G28. cum. index. **Bk Rev. Ad Acc. Circ:** 50,000 (ctrl).

HU/0133-2430
**GALAKTIKA.** [Galaktika]. (1972)-. Periodical. Hungarian. Twelve times a year. $41.00. **(Subscription address:** Kultura, PO Box 149, H 1389 Budapest 62 Hungary, (phone: 011 36 1 359370)) **UDC** 82-3.

LY/0253-634X
**GARYOUNIS SCIENTIFIC BULLETIN.** [Garyounis sci. bull.]. Vol. 1, No. 1 (Feb. 1979)-. Academic Scholarly Publication. English. Director of Research Center, Garyounis University, PO Box 9521, Benghazi Libya. **CODEN** GSBUDO. Documents available from CASDDS.
**Ind/Abst** Chem. Abstr. (1979-1980); Math. Rev.

GW/0723-2225
**GATE ESCHBORN.** [Gate Eschborn]. **VFOAT** German Appropriate Technology Exchange (Eschborn); Gate Questions, Answers, Information. (1982)-. Periodical. English. qt. **UDC** 339.96(100.77).
**Ind/Abst** Abstr. AIT Rep. Publ. Energy.

IT
**GE RI CO NEWS : BOLLETINO DI INFORMAZIONE E INNOVAZIONE RICERCA TECNOLOGICA.** Italian (English). sm. free. Consorzio Genova Ricerche, Via Acciaio 139, 16151 Genoa Italy. **Tel** 39 10 6514000, FAX 39 10 603801. **Bk Rev. Circ:** 1,200 (ctrl).
**Desc:** Information and communication technology, technology transfer, and EEC research projects.

AT/1032-2302
**GEMS WODEN.** **See** Mathematics.

US
**GENERAL CATALOG OF INFORMATION SERVICES / NATIONAL TECHNICAL INFORMATION SERVICE.** **Main/Corp** United States. National Technical Information Service. Catalog. English. an. National Technical Information Service - NTIS, Room 2027S, 5285 Port Royal Road, Springfield VA 22161. **Tel** (703)487-4630, (703)487-4660, (703)487-4650, FAX (703)321-8547, telex 89-9405. ***Continues*** *NTIS Information Services General Catalog for North America.*

FR/0379-2218
**GENERAL INFORMATION PROGRAMME. UNISIST NEWSLETTER.** (GENERAL INFORMATION PROGRAMME - UNISIST NEWSLETTER.). [Gen. inf. programme, UNISIST newsl.]. **Main/Corp** UNESCO. General Information Programme. **VFOAT** Unisist Newsletter. (1979)-. Periodical. English (French, Spanish, Arabic and Russian). qt. Free. UNESCO / France, 31 rue Francois Bonvin, 75732 Paris Cedex 15 France. **Tel** 011 33 1 45684564, 011 33 1 45684565, FAX 011 33 1 42733007, telex 204461 Paris. **LC** Q223; .U46b. **DD** 025/.04. **NLM** Z 1007 G326. Index available. cum. index. **Circ:** 10,000. ***Formed by the union of*** *Bibliography, Documentation, Terminology, 0523-2821* ***and*** *UNISIST Newsletter.*
**Desc:** Provides current information on activities in the fields of scientific and technological information, documentation, libraries and archives.
**Ind/Abst** Inf. Sci. Abstr.

US/0162-1963
**GENERAL SCIENCE INDEX.** **See** Science and Technology-Abstracting, Bibliographies and Statistics.

US/0162-1963
**GENERAL SCIENCE INDEX. CD-ROM.** English. mo. $1,295.00. H W Wilson Company, 950 University Avenue, Bronx NY 10452. **Tel** (800)367-6770, (718)588-8400, FAX (718)590-1617, telex 4990003 HWILSON. **ED** James Kochones. Index available. cum. index. ctrl circ. available on magnetic tape from WILSONTAPE; available in print; available on an online database from WILSONLINE; available on diskette from WILSONSEARCH.
**Desc:** Contains citations to articles and book reviews from English language periodicals in the general sciences. Covers astronomy, atmospheric science, biology, botany, chemistry, conservation and environment, earth sciences, food and nutrition, genetics, health & medicine, mathematics, microbiology, oceanography, physics, physiology and zoology.

●US/1073-1954
**GENERAL SCIENCE SOURCE.** **See** Science and Technology-Abstracting, Bibliographies and Statistics.

US
**GENERAL TECHNICAL REPORT FPL-IMP-GTR.** (1991)-. Periodical. English.

US/0272-9032
**GENETIC TECHNOLOGY NEWS.** [Genet. technol. news]. Vol. 1, No. 1 (Feb. 1981)-. Periodical. English. mo. $585.00, North America; $645.00, other. Technical Insights Inc., PO Box 1304, Fort Lee NJ 07024-9967. **Tel** (201)568-4744, FAX (201)568-8247, telex 425900 SWIFT UI. **ED** Albert S. Hester, Laurel A. Vanderkleed and Richard Consolas. **NLM** W1; GE285. **CODEN** GTNEEA. **[CCC].** available on an online database (files 16,636/Full-Text) from DIALOG. Documents available from CASDDS.
**Desc:** Focuses on genetic engineering and its uses in the chemical, pharmaceutical, food processing, and energy industries as well as in agriculture, animal breeding and medicine.
**Ind/Abst** Abstr. BioCommer.; AGRICOLA [Select. Cov.]; BioBusiness (1984-); Chem. Abstr.; Chem. Ind. Notes; NEXIS (1982-); PROMT [Full Txt.]; PTS Newsl. Database [Full Txt.].

US/0147-9369
**GEORGIA JOURNAL OF SCIENCE.** [Ga. j. sci.]. **Added/Corp** Georgia Academy of Science. Vol. 35, No. 1 (1977)-. Academic Scholarly Publication. English. qt. $30.00 institutions; $20.00 individuals. Georgia Academy of Science, Georgia South Western College, Americus GA 31709. **Tel** (912)928-1606. **ED** Dr. Norris L O'Dell. **LC** Q11; .G42. **DD** 505. **CODEN** GJSCDQ. **Bk Rev**, (Qty: 4/yr). **Pr Rev. Circ:** 800. available on microfilm and microfiche from University Microfilms International (UMI). Documents available from BIOSIS Document Express, CASDDS. ***Continues*** *Bulletin of the Georgia Academy of Science, 0016-8114.*
**Desc:** Results of studies and investigations.
**Ind/Abst** AGRICOLA; Biol. Abstr.; Chem. Abstr. (1977-1983); Coal Abstr.; Ecol. Abstr. (?-?); Energy Res. Abstr. (June 1977-); Fish Rev.; GeoRef; Wildl. Rev.

GW/0172-1526
**GERMAN RESEARCH : REPORTS OF THE DFG.** **Added/Corp** Deutsche Forschungsgemeinschaft. **VFOAT** Reports of the DFG German Research. (Vol. 1, 1979)-. Periodical. English. Three times a year. $45.00. VCH Gesellschaft GmbH,

## Science and Technology

Postfach 101161, D 69451 Weinheim Germany. **Tel** 011 49 6201 606459, FAX 011 49 6201 606184. **(Subscription address:** VCH Publishers Inc., 303 Northwest 12th Avenue, Journals Department, Deerfield FL 33442.) **[CCC]. Circ:** 8,500.
**Desc:** Illustrated articles in a journalistic mode, describing research projects.

GW
**GESAMTAUSGABE NICOLAUS COPERNICUS.** (19??)-. German. VCH Gesellschaft GmbH, Postfach 101161, D 69451 Weinheim Germany. **Tel** 011 49 6201 606459, FAX 011 49 6201 606184. **(Subscription address:** VCH Publishers Inc., 303 Northwest 12th Avenue, Journals Department, Deerfield FL 33442.)

●NE
**GEWINA. Added/Corp** Genootschap voor Geschiedenis der Geneeskunde, Wiskunde, Natuurwetenschappen en Techniek. (1992)-. Periodical. Dutch. qt. **Continues** Tijdschrift voor de Geschiedenis der Geneeskunde, Natuurwetenschappen, Wiskunde en Techniek, 0167-2088.
**Desc:** Investigates medicine, mathematics, science, and technology.

GH/0016-9544
**GHANA JOURNAL OF SCIENCE.** [Ghana j. sci.]. Vol. 1; Oct. 1961-. Periodical. English. sa. $5.90. Ghana Science Association, University of Ghana, Legon Ghana. **LC** Q1. **NLM** W1 GH373. **CODEN** GHJSAC. available on microfilm from University Microfilms International (UMI). Documents available from BIOSIS Document Express, CASDDS.
**Ind/Abst** AGRICOLA; Biol. Abstr. (-1980); Chem. Abstr.; GeoRef; Life Sci. Collect.; Soc. Plann. Policy Dev. Abstr.; Sociol. Abstr. (?-?); Zentralbl. Math. Ihre Grenzgeb.

NE
**GIDS VOOR HET AANVRAGEN VAN Z. W.O.-STEUN / NEDERLANDSE ORGANISATIE VOOR ZURIVER-WETENSCHAPPELIJK ONDERZOEK. VFOAT** Gids voor het Aanvragen van Zwo-Steun. Dutch. Free. Nederlandse Organisatie voor Zuiver-Wetenschappelijk Onderzoek, Juliana van Stolberglaan 148, Postbus 93138, S-Gravenhage 250GAC Netherlands. **Tel** (070)4966 49. **LC** Q57; .G53. **DD** 001.4/025/492. **Circ:** 9,500 (ctrl).
**Desc:** Directory for applicants to Zuiver Wetenschappelijk Onderzoek, subsidies, fellowships, and scholarships.

JA
**GIJUTSU JOHO.** (19??)-. Japanese. $73.00. 60 Ogura 649-62, Wakayama Japan. **LC** T4 .G573.

JA
**GIJUTSU KENKYU HONBU GIHO. VFOAT** Technical Report; Technical Report of Technical Research and Development Institute. Japanese (summaries and/or abstracts in English). Boeicho Gijutsu Kenkyu Honbu Gijutsubu Chosaka, 2-24 Ikejiri 1, Setagaya-ku Tokyo-to 154 Japan. **LC** PAR. **Continues** Giho (Boeicho Gijutsu Kenkyu Hongu (Japan)).

JA
**GIJUTSU TO NINGEN.** No. 1- Spring 1972-. Japanese. mo. $124.00. Gijutsu To Ningen, 6-12, Kagurazaka 3 Chome, Shinjukuku, Tokyoto 162 Japan. **LC** T4; .G58.

IT
**GIORNALE DELLE PROVE NON DISTRUTTIVE.** Assn IT Prove Non Distruttive, Via A Foresti 5, 25126 Brescia Italy.

IT
**GIORNALE DI SCIENZE AMBIENTALI.** **Suspended.** (19??)-Suspended (199?). Italian. bm. Editrice Sant Andrea, Via Montalbino 9/6, 20159 Milan, Italy. **Tel** 011 39 2 95740844.

RU
**GIPOTEZY, PROGNOZY. Title Change.** (1988)-(199?). Russian. an. Izdatelstvo Znanie, Novaya Pl., 3-4,, 101835 Moscow Russia. **LC** Q4; B8. **Continues** Budushchee Nauki, 0524-918X. **Continued by** Fantastika i Nauka.

YU/0081-3974
**GLAS - SRPSKA ADADEMIJA NAUKA I UMETNOSTI. ODELJENJE TEHNICKIH NAUKA.** [Glas - Srp. akad. nauka umet., Od. teh. nauka]. (19??)-. Serbo-Croatian (Cyrillic). ir. Documents available from Ask*IEEE.
**Ind/Abst** INSPEC; Int. Aerosp. Abstr.

US/0743-9008
**GMRMLN UPDATE. See** Library and Information Sciences.

US/0199-5464
**GNSI NEWSLETTER. Main/Corp** Guild of Natural Science Illustrators (U.S.). **Added/Corp** Guild of Natural Science Illustrators (U.S.). Newsletter. **VAT** Guild of Natural Science Illustrators Newsletter. (19??)-. Periodical. English. Ten times a year (monthly except June & Aug.). $40.00. Guild of Natural Science Illustrators Inc, PO Box 652, Ben Franklin Station, Washington DC 20044. **Tel** (301)238-3165, FAX (301)762-0189. **ED** Norman Frisch. Index available. cum. index. **Bk Rev**. **Circ:** 1,100.
**Desc:** Devoted to providing information about and encouraging high standards of competence in the field of natural science.

IT
**GOLEM NEWSLETTER. Ceased.** (19??)-(1994). Newsletter. Italian (English). Twelve times a year (English edition published quarterly). Edizioni Dedalo Spa, Casella Postale 362, Bari 70100 Italy. **Tel** 011 39 080 5311400, FAX 011 39 080 5311414. cum. index. **Ad Acc.** ctrl circ.
**Desc:** The newsletter relates the use and development of technological advances with the research and practice in education.

US/0161-1127
**GOVERNMENT R & D REPORT. VAT** Government Research and Development Report. Vol. 1 (Feb. 1, 1974)-. Periodical. English. sm. $80.00. MIT Station, PO Box 284, Cambridge MA 02139. **LC** Q180.U5; G59. **DD** 353.008/1.

US/0145-532X
**GOVERNMENT REPORTS ANNUAL INDEX. Added/Corp** United States. National Technical Information Service. Vol. 75 (1975)-. English. an. $630.00 US; $785.00 other. National Technical Information Service - NTIS, Room 2027S, 5285 Port Royal Road, Springfield VA 22161. **Tel** (703)487-4630, (703)487-4660, (703)487-4650, FAX (703)321-8547, telex 89-9405. **LC** Z7405.R4; G64; G158.5. **DD** 016.5. **NLM** ZQ 1 G72. **Continues** Government Reports Index, 0097-9015.
**Desc:** Six volume hard bound set of government reports announced by NTIS and indexed by keyword, personal author, corporate author, contract grant number and order/report number.

US/0882-3766
**GOVERNMENT RESEARCH DIRECTORY.** [Gov. res. dir.]. **Added/Corp** Gale Research Company. 3rd Ed. (1985)-. Directory. English. ir. Price varies per volume. Gale Research Inc., 835 Penobscot Building, Detroit MI 48226. **Tel** (800)877-GALE, (313)961-2242, FAX (313)961-6083, telex TWX 810-221-7086. **ED** Annette Piccirelli. **LC** Q179.98; .G68. **DD** 001.4/025/73. **NLM** Q 179.98; G721. **Continues** Government Research Centers Directory, 0270-4811.
**Desc:** Describes over 3,700 research facilities operated by the United States government, including research centers, bureaus, and institutes; R & D installations; testing and experiment stations, and major research-supporting service units.

XV
**GOZDARSKI VESTNIK. Added/Corp** Zveza Inzenirjev in Tehnikov Gozdarstva in Lesne Industrije SRS. (19??)-. Periodical. Slovenian. ir.
**Ind/Abst** Grasslands For. Abstr.; Plant Genet. Resour. Abstr.

US/0094-7881
**GRADUATE SCIENCE EDUCATION STUDENT SUPPORT AND POSTDOCTORALS. Main/Corp** National Science Foundation (U.S.). (1972)-. English. an. National Science Foundation, 1800 G Street Northwest, Washington DC 20550. **Tel** (202)357-9859, (202)357-9498. **LC** Q183.3.A1; U55A. **DD** 507/.1/73. **Continues** Graduate Student Support and Manpower Resources in Graduate Science Education, 0092-6604.

US
**GRANTS FOR SCIENCE AND TECHNOLOGY PROGRAMS. See** Philanthropy.

●US/1060-1600
**GREATER SILICON VALLEY TECHNOLOGY RESOURCE GUIDE.** [Gt. Silicon Val. technol. resour. guide]. **Added/Corp** Corporate Technology Information Services. San Jose (Calif.). Office of Economic Development. **VFOAT** Greater Silicon Valley Technology Resource Guide and Services Yellow Pages. (1992/93 Ed.)-. English. $45.00. **DD** 338.

GW
**GRENZGEBIETE DER WISSENSCHAFT.** Vol. 16 (1967)-. German. qt. Resch Verlag, Maximilianstr 8, Postfach 8, A-6010 Innsbruck Austria. **ED** Andreas Resch. **Continues** Verborgene Welt.
**Ind/Abst** Except. Hum. Exp.

JA/0385-7204
**GS NEWS TECHNICAL REPORT.** [GS news tech. rep.]. **Added/Corp** Nihon Denchi Kabushiki Kaisha. **VFOAT** G.S. News Technical Report. (1927)-. Periodical. Japanese (summaries and/or abstracts in English). sa. Nihon Denchi Kabushiki Kaisha, Kyoto Japan. **CODEN** GSNTAA. Documents available from CASDDS.
**Ind/Abst** Chem. Abstr.

AG/0301-7567
**GUIA DE REUNIONES CIENTIFICAS Y TECNICAS EN ARGENTINA.** [Guia reun. cient. tec. Argent.]. Spanish. **LC** Q101; .G85.

BL
**GUIA INDUSTRIAL ABRIL.** 1973-. Portuguese. 100.00. Editora Abril SA, Rua do Curtume 769 Lapa, 05066 900 Sao Paulo SP Brazil. **Tel** 011 55 11 8239222, 011 55 11 2623322, FAX 011 55 11 8643796. **LC** T12.5.B7; G8.

ZA
**GUIDE BOOK FOR FIRST YEAR STUDENTS IN THE SCHOOL OF NATURAL SCIENCES. Main/Corp** University of Zambia. School of Natural Sciences. English. University of Zambia, PO Box 32379, Lusaka Zambia. **Tel** 213221, telex ZA 44370. **LC** Q183.4.Z33; U53A. **DD** 507/.11/6894.

CN/0849-195X
**GUIDE METHODOLOGIQUE, L'EDUCATION AU MILIEU NATUREL.** [Guide methodol. educ. milieu nat.]. **Added/Corp** Quebec (Province). Direction du Plein Air et des Parcs. **VFOAT** L'Education au Milieu Naturel; Education au Milieu Naturel, Guide Methodologique; Preparation et Realisation d'une Activite d'Interpretation Dynamique. (1990)-. Periodical. French. **DD** 508/.07/0714.

UK
**GUIDE TO INFORMATION TECHNOLOGY.** (19??)-. Periodical. English. £160.40. Croner Publ Ltd, Croner House, London Road, Kingston upon Thames, Surrey KT2 6SR England. **Tel** 011 44 81 5473333, FAX 081 547-2637.

US
**GUIDE TO PROGRAMS / NATIONAL SCIENCE FOUNDATION. Main/Corp** National Science Foundation (U.S.). (19??)-. Government Publication. English. an. $15.50. Superintendent of Documents, US Government Printing Office, Washington DC 20402. **Tel** (202)275-3328, FAX (202)786-2377. **LC** Q180.U5; A549. **DD** 507/.2073. **NLM** Q 181.A1 N279G.

US/0738-2324
**GUIDE TO THE HIGH TECHNOLOGY INDUSTRIES.** [Guide high technol. ind.]. 1st Ed.-. English. an. Ballinger Publishing Company, 10 E 53rd Street, New York NY 10022-5244.

UK
**GULF COMMS GUIDE.** English. an. £10.00. Information Technology Publishing Company, Angus House, 13 Tilehouse Street HITC, Hertfordshire SG5 2DU England. **Tel** 011 44 462 420785, FAX 011 44 462 420786.

JA/0017-5668
**GUNMA DAIGAKU KYOIKU GAKUBU KIYO : SHIZEN KAGAKU HEN. Main/Corp** Gunma Daigaku. Kyoiku Gakubu. **VFOAT** Science Reports of the Faculty of Education, Gumma University. V. 15- ; 1966-. Academic Scholarly Publication. English (Esperanto and Japanese). an. Gumma Daigaku Kyoiku Gakubu, 1375-Banchi Aramaki-cho, Maebashi-shi 371 Japan. **LC** Q4; .G84A. **CODEN** GDSHAU. Documents available from CASDDS. **Continues** Gumma Daigaku Kyoiku Kiyo: Shizen Kagaku Hen.
**Ind/Abst** Chem. Abstr.; Sorghum Mill. Abstr.

JA
**GYOMU NEMPO - OSAKA FURITSU KOGYO GIJUTSU KENKYUJO. Main/Corp** Osaka Furitsu Kogyo Gijutsu Kenkyujo. **VFOAT** Osaka Furitsu Kogyo Gijutsu Kenjyujo Gyomu Nempo. (19??)-. Periodical. Japanese. Osaka Furitsu Kogyo Gijutsu Kenkyujo, 1-53 Enokojima 2-chome, Nishi-ku, Osaka Japan. **LC** T178.O73; O82a.

CC/1000-5897
**HA'ERBIN KEXUE JISHU DAXUE XUEBAO. VFOAT** Journal of Harbin University of Science and Technology. (1979)-. Academic Scholarly Publication. Chinese. qt. Harbin Kexue Jishu Daxue, Xuebao Bianjibu, 22 Xuefo Lu, Nangang-qu, Harbin, Heilongjiang 150080, People's Republic of China. **Tel** 61081. **ED** R. Shanzhi. **DD** 605. Documents available from CASDDS.
**Ind/Abst** Chem. Abstr.

JA
**HAKODATE KOGYO KOTO SEMMON GAKKO KIYO.** [Hakodate Kogyo Koto Senmon Gakko kiyo]. **Main/Corp** Hakodate Kogyo Koto Semmon Gakko. **VFOAT** Research Reports, Hakodate Technical College. No. 1 (1967)-. Academic Scholarly Publication. Japanese (summaries and/or abstracts in English). No 226 Tokuracho Hakodate, Hokkaido Japan. **LC** T4;

# Science and Technology

.H28A. **CODEN** HKSKDY. Documents available from CASDDS.
**Ind/Abst** Chem. Abstr.

KO/0440-1123
**HAKSURWON NONMUNJIP. CHAYON KWAHAK PYON.** (HAKSURWON NONMUNJIP. CHAYON KWAHAKPYON.). [Haksurwon nonmunjip. Chayon kwahakpyon]. **Added/Corp** Taehan Minguk Haksurwon. **VFOAT** Journal of the National Academy of Sciences, Republic of Korea. Natural Sciences. (1961)-. Periodical. Korean (English and Korean). an. Taehan Minguk Haksurwon, Seoul Korea. **LC** Q4; .H347. **CODEN** HNCKA6. Documents available from CASDDS.
*Continues in part* Haksurwon Nonmunjip.
**Ind/Abst** Chem. Abstr.

JA
**HAKUSHI GAKUI ROMBUN NO GAIYO OYOBI SHINSA NO YOSHI. Main/Corp** Tokai Daigaku. Rigakubu. (19??)-. Periodical. Japanese. Tokai Daigaku Rigakubu, Kaname Hiratsuke, Hiratsuka Japan. **LC** Q4; .T58a.

ZA
**HANDBOOK AND ANNUAL REVIEW. Main/Corp** University of Zambia. Technology Development and Advisory Unit. 1st- 1975/76-. English. University of Zambia, PO Box 32379, Lusaka Zambia. **Tel** 213221, telex ZA 44370. **LC** T173.L977; A36. **DD** 338.96894.

AT/1031-6892
**HANDBOOK - AUSTRALIAN ACADEMY OF TECHNOLOGICAL SCIENCES AND ENGINEERING.** [Handb. - Aust. Acad. Technol. Sci. Eng.]. **Added/Corp** Australian Academy of Technological Sciences and Engineering. (1988)-. English. ir. **DD** 606.094. *Continues* Handbook - Australian Academy of Technological Sciences, 0158-5029.
**Ind/Abst** AESIS Q.

UG
**HANDBOOK - MAKERERE UNIVERSITY. SCIENCE FACULTY. Main/Corp** Makerere University. Science Faculty. English. Makerere University, PO Box 7062, Kampala Uganda. **Tel** 554582. **LC** Q183.4.U35; M34A. **DD** 507/.11676/1.

NE/0167-3785
**HANDBOOK OF POWDER TECHNOLOGY.** Vol. 1-. Monographic series. English. Price varies per volume. Elsevier Science Publishers BV, PO Box 211, 1000 AE Amsterdam Netherlands. **Tel** 011 31 20 5803642, FAX 011 31 20 5862696, telex 15682. **ED** J C Williams and T Allen.
**Desc:** A major reference work and a continuous source of up-to-date information on all specialised areas in the field of powder technology.

NE
**HANDBOOKS IN OPERATIONS RESEARCH AND MANAGEMENT SCIENCE.** Vol. 1 (1989)-. Monographic series. English.
**Ind/Abst** Zentralbl. Math. Ihre Grenzgeb.

GW/0174-5026
**HANDBUCH DER GROSSFORSCHUNG / ARBEITSGEMEINSCHAFT DER GROSSFORSCHUNGSEINRICHTUNGEN (AGR). Main/Corp** Arbeitsgemeinschaft der Grossforschungseinrichtungen (Germany). (1985/86)-. German. Arbeitsgemeinschaft der Grossforschungseinrichtungen, Ahr-Strasse 45 Wissenschaftszentrum, W-5300 Bonn-Bad Godesberg Germany. **LC** Q180.3; .A72A. **DD** 506/.043.

KO
**HANGUK KISUL. Added/Corp** Hanguk Kisul Yongyok Hyophoe. (19??)-. Periodical. English (French, Korean and Spanish). Not for sale. Hanguk Kisul Yongyok Hyophoe, San 76-561 Yoksam-dong, Kangnam-ku Seoul Korea. **LC** T174.3; .H35.

KO
**HANGUK KISUL YONGUSO CHONGNAM.** 1985-. Korean (English). be. W45000. Korea Industrial Research Institutes, 35-3 Yoido-dong Youngdeungpo-ku, Seoul 150-010 South Korea. **Tel** 02-780-7601, FAX 02-785-5771. **ED** Chang-Hyon Paek. **LC** T177.K6; H36. Index available. **Ad Acc. Circ:** 7,000 (ctrl).
**Desc:** Includes the overall picture of technology development in industrial labs and public research institutes.

KO
**HANGUK OR HAKHOE CHI. VFOAT** Hanguk O.R. Hakhoe Chi; Journal of the Korean Operations Research Society. Periodical. English (Korean). **LC** T57.6.A1; H36.
**Ind/Abst** Int. Abstr. Oper. Res. [Full Cov.].

CC/0253-3618
**HANGZHOU DAXUE XUEBAO. ZIRAN KEXUE BAN.** (HANG-CHOU TA HSUEH HSUEH PAO. TZU ZAN KO HSUEH PAN.). [Hangzhou daxue xuebao. Ziran kexue ban]. **VFOAT** Journal of Hangzhou University. Natural Science Edition. (19??)-. Academic Scholarly Publication. Chinese. bm. $6.00. China National Publishing Company, 380 Bei Su Zhou Lu, Shanghai, People's Republic of China. **LC** Q4; .H35. **DD** 505. **CODEN** HHHPD7. **Ad Acc. Circ:** 3,000. Documents available from CASDDS.
**Desc:** Endeavors to establish significant research articles of the faculty of Hangzhou University in natural sciences including mathematics, physics, chemistry, biology, and geography.
**Ind/Abst** Chem. Abstr.; Math. Rev.; NAPRALERT; Zentralbl. Math. Ihre Grenzgeb.

US
**HARVARD CASE HISTORIES IN EXPERIMENTAL SCIENCE.** English. ir. Harvard University Press, 79 Garden Street, Cambridge MA 02138. **Tel** (617)496-1344, (800)448-2242.

US/0897-3393
**HARVARD JOURNAL OF LAW & TECHNOLOGY.** *See* Law.

US
**HARVARD MONOGRAPHS IN THE HISTORY OF SCIENCE.** Monographic series. English. ir. Price varies per volume. Harvard University Press, 79 Garden Street, Cambridge MA 02138. **Tel** (617)496-1344, (800)448-2242.

● US/1062-7022
**HARVARD SCIENCE REVIEW (1992).** (HARVARD SCIENCE REVIEW.). [Harv. sci. rev.]. Vol. 5, No. 1 (Winter 1992)-. Periodical. English. Harvard Science Review, Box 139, Divinity Avenue, Cambridge MA 02138. **DD** 500. *Continues* Harvard Radcliffe Science Review, 1051-7170.

US
**HARVARD STUDIES IN TECHNOLOGY AND SOCIETY.** Periodical. English. ir. Harvard University Press, 79 Garden Street, Cambridge MA 02138. **Tel** (617)496-1344, (800)448-2242.

US
**HEAD-MEDIA TECHNOLOGY NEWSLETTER.** Newsletter. English. qt (July, Oct., Jan. April). $295.00. Peripheral Research Corporation, 351 South Hitchcock Way #B-200, Santa Barbara CA 93105. **Tel** (805)963-8081, FAX (805)569-2512.

UK/0967-6813
**HEADS OF SCIENCE.** (1992)-. Periodical. English. bm. £91.70. Croner Publ Ltd, Croner House, London Road, Kingston upon Thames, Surrey KT2 6SR England. **Tel** 011 44 81 5473333, FAX 081 547-2637.

CN/0711-3463
**HEBDO SCIENCE.** (HEBDO-SCIENCE.). [Hebdo-sci.]. (1978)-. Periodical. French. wk (52 issues). 95.00 Can$ institutions; 300.00Can$ corporations. Agence Science Press, 3995 Saint Catherine East, Montreal Quebec H1W 2G7 Canada. **Tel** (514)522-1304. **DD** 505.

CC/1000-5358
**HEBEI GONGXUEYUAN XUEBAO. VFOAT** Journal of Hebei Institute of Technology. (1973)-. Periodical. Chinese. qt. Tianjin Gai Kan Bian-Wei-Hui, People's Republic of China. **DD** 620. Documents available from CASDDS.
**Ind/Abst** Chem. Abstr.

CC/1001-9383
**HEBEI SHENG KEXUEYUAN XUEBAO.** (HO-PEI SHENG KO HSUEH YUAN HSUEH PAO.). [Hebei sheng kexueyuan xuebao]. **Added/Corp** Ho-Pei Sheng Ko Hsueh Yuan. **VFOAT** Journal of the Hebei Academy of Sciences. (1984)-. Periodical. Chinese (summaries and/or abstracts in English). Ho-Pei Sheng Ko Hsueh Yuan Hsueh Pao Pien Wei Hui, People's Republic of China. **LC** Q111; .H6. **DD** 505. **CODEN** HKXUEM. Documents available from CASDDS.
**Ind/Abst** Chem. Abstr.

CC/1000-5854
**HEBEI SHIFAN DAXUE XUEBAO ZIRAN KEXUE BAN.** (HEBEI SHIFAN DAXUE XUEBAO.). **VFOAT** Journal of Hebei Normal University (Natural Science Ed.) (1963)-. Academic Scholarly Publication. Chinese. qt. Hebei Shifan Daxue, Hebei Normal University, Yuhua Lu, Shijiazhuang, Hebei 050016 People's Republic of China. **Tel** 49941. **ED** Jin Shixun. **DD** 505. Documents available from CASDDS.
**Ind/Abst** Chem. Abstr.

US/0073-1595
**HEIDELBERG SCIENCE LIBRARY.** Vol. 1 (1967)-. Monographic series. English. ir. Price varies per volume. Springer-Verlag New York Inc., 175 5th Avenue, New York NY 10010. **Tel** (212)460-1500, telex 232 235 SPB UR. (**Subscription address:** Springer Verlag New York Inc. / for North America, 44 Hartz Way, Secaucus NJ 07096.) **CODEN** HSCLAA. Documents available from BIOSIS Document Express.
**Desc:** Studies on molecular and genetic counseling.
**Ind/Abst** Biol. Abstr.

GW/0073-1641
**HEIDELBERGER JAHRBUCHER.** [Heidelb. Jahrb.]. **Added/Corp** Universitats-Gesellschaft Heidelberg. Vol. 1 (1957)-. Monographic series. German. ir. Price varies per volume. Springer-Verlag GmbH & Company KG, Heidelberg Platz 3, D 14197 Berlin Germany. **Tel** 011 49 30 8207223, FAX 011 49 30 8214091, telex 183 319 SPBLN D. (**Subscription address:** Springer Verlag New York Inc. / for North America, 44 Hartz Way, Secaucus NJ 07096.) **LC** AS181; .H4. **CODEN** HDJBAC. **[CCC]**. Documents available from BIOSIS Document Express.
**Ind/Abst** Am. Hist. Life (1954-); BHA : Biblio. Hist. Art; Biol. Abstr.

AT/0017-9973
**HELICTITE.** [Helictite]. **Added/Corp** Speleological Research Council Limited. (1962)-. Periodical. English. Twice a year (July, Nov.). 20.00Aus$. Helictite, PO Box 183, Broadway NSW 2007 Australia. **ED** J. James and G. Cox. **CODEN** HELIBH. Index available. cum. index. **Bk Rev. Ad Acc. Pr Rev. Circ:** 200 (ctrl).
**Desc:** Scientific aspects of speleology, biology, chemistry, geography, geomorphology, history, hydrology, meteorology, photography, and caving techniques.
**Ind/Abst** AESIS Q.; GeoRef.

US/1047-5230
**HELLER REPORT ON EDUCATIONAL TECHNOLOGY AND TELECOMMUNICATIONS MARKETS, THE.** [Heller rep. educ. technol. telecommun. mark.]. **VFOAT** Heller Report. (1989)-. Periodical. English. mo. $395.00. Nelson B Heller and Association, 1910 First Street, Suite 303, Highland Park IL 60035. **Tel** (708)441-2920, FAX (708)926-0202. **ED** Anne Wujick (phone:703)548-1037). **DD** 384. **[CCC]**.

● RU/1019-3316
**HERALD OF THE RUSSIAN ACADEMY OF SCIENCES.** [Her. Russ. Acad. Sci.]. **Added/Corp** Rossiiskaia Akademiia Nauk. Vol. 62, No. 3 (Mar. 1992)-. Periodical. English (translations available in Russian). bm (6 issues). $356.00 US and Canada; $445.00 other. MAIK Nauka / Interperiodica, Ulitsa Profsoyuznaya 90, Moscow 117864 Russia. (**Subscription address:** Interperiodica Publishing, Subscription Office, PO Box 1831, Birmingham AL 35201-1831.) **LC** Q60; .V453. **DD** 505. *Continues* Vestnik Akademii Nauk SSSR. English. Herald of the USSR Academy of Sciences, 1057-509X.
**Desc:** Publishes the major work presented to the Russian Academy each month. The contents cover many subjects in the natural, technical, and social sciences.

GW/0018-0637
**HERCYNIA.** Ceased. [Hercynia]. Vol. 1 (1963)-Ceased (Aug. 1991). Academic Scholarly Publication. German. qt. Deutscher Judo Verband, Redaktion Ippon Segewaldweg 40, D 12557 Berlin Germany. **Tel** 011 49 711 210770, telex 051 678. **CODEN** HERCAS. Index Available, published separately, free-automatically sent. Documents available from BIOSIS Document Express, CASDDS. *Continues* Hercynia.
**Ind/Abst** Biol. Abstr.; Chem. Abstr.; Coal Abstr.; Crop Physiol. Abstr.; Ecol. Abstr.; EMBASE; For. Abstr.; Geogr. Abstr. Phys. Geogr.; Geogr. Abstr. Human Geogr. (?-?); Geol. Abstr.; GeoRef; Hortic. Abstr.; Key Word Index Wildl. Res.; Maize Abstr.; Nematol. Abstr.; Ornamental Hort. (1991-); Postharvest News Inf.; Rev. Med. Vet. Entomol.; Soils Fert.; Weed Abstr.

JA/0367-5866
**HI-HAKAI KENSA.** (HIHAKAI KENSA : NDI / NIHON HIHAKAI KENSA KYOKAI.). [Hi-hakai kensa]. **Added/Corp** Nihon Hihakai Kensa Kyokai. **VFOAT** Journal of N.D.I.; N.D.I.; NDI. **VAT** Journal of Non-Destructive Inspection. (1952)-. Academic Scholarly Publication. Japanese. mo. $270.00. Nihon Hihakai Kensa Kyokai, (Japanese Soc. for Non-Destructive Inspection), Hashimoto Biru, 4-5, Asakusabashi 5 Chome, Taitoku, Tokyoto 111 Japan. (**Subscription address:** Kyowa Book Company Inc., 1-38 Kanda Jinbo-Cho, Chiyoda-Ku Tokyo 101, Japan) **CODEN** HIHKAU. **Circ:** 5,000 (ctrl). Documents available from CASDDS.
**Desc:** Report of technical studies about nondestructive inspection, data, and explanations.
**Ind/Abst** Chem. Abstr.

IT
**HI TECH.** Edinvest SRL, Via Delle Quattro Fontane # 15, 00184 Rome Italy.

GW/0176-3474
**HIGH TECH DEUTSCHE AUSG. Title Change.** [High tech.Dtsch. Ausg.]. (19??)-(Jan. 1992). Periodical. German. bm. MP Management Presse Verlag,

Baierbrunner Str 33, Postfach 701349, W 8000 Munich 70 Germany. **Tel** 011 49 89 787280. **UDC** 62:65.01. ***Merged into*** *Wirtschaftswoche.*

FR
**HIGH TECH DIGEST.** ***Ceased.*** (19??)-(19??). French. Reproduire, 40 rue St Anne, 75002 Paris France. **Tel** 011 33 1 40150261, FAX 011 33 1 42963708.

US/0885-2715
**HIGH TECHNOLOGY LAW JOURNAL.** **See** Law.

US
**HIGH TECHNOLOGY MARKET PLACE DIRECTORY.** ***Ceased.*** **VFOAT** High Technology Marketplace Directory. 1st Ed. (1985)-(19??). Directory. English. Princeton Hightech Group Inc, PO Box 5204, Middlebush NJ 08873. **Tel** (908)545-8795. **LC** HC110.H53; H53. **DD** 338.7/4/02573.

JA
**HIMEJI KOGYO DAIGAKU KOGAKUBU KENKYU HOKOKU.** **Added/Corp** Himeji Kogyo Daigaku. Kogakubu. **VFOAT** Reports of the Faculty of Engineering, Himeji Institute of Technology. No. 43 (1990)-. Periodical. Japanese (English). an. **LC** IN PROCESS. Documents available from CASDDS. ***Continues*** *Himeji Kogyo Daigaku Kenkyu Hokoku. A, 0439-1535.*
**Ind/Abst** Chem. Abstr.

JA/0018-1951
**HINSHITSU KANRI.** **See** Engineering.

BE/0773-1922
**HINTERLAND ENGLISH ED.** [HinterlandEngl. ed.]. (1976)-. Periodical. English. qt. **UDC** 659. ***Continues*** *Hinterland (Ed. Quadrilingue), 0018-1978.*
**Ind/Abst** Fluid Abstr., Civil Eng.; Fluid Abstr. Proc. Eng.; FLUIDEX (199?-).

JA
**HIROSHIMA DAIGAKU SOGO KAGAKUBU KIYO. 3, JOHO KODO KAGAKU KENKYU.** **VFOAT** Joho Kodo Kagaku Kenkyu; Memoirs of the Faculty of Integrated Arts and Sciences, Hiroshima University. 3, Studies in Information and Behavior Sciences. Periodical. English (Japanese). an. Hiroshima Daigaku Sogo Kagakubu, (Faculty of Integrated Arts and Sciences, Hiroshima University), 1-89 Higashisendacho 1-chome, Nakaku Hiroshimashi, Hiroshimaken 730 Japan. **LC** Q4; .H58.

JA/0915-194X
**HIROSHIMA KENRITSU SEIBU KOGYO GIJUTSU SENTA KENKYU HOKOKU.** **VFOAT** Bulletin of the Industrial Research Institute, Hiroshima Prefecture, West (1988). (1988)-. Periodical. Multiple languages. an. **DD** 620. Documents available from CASDDS. ***Continues*** *Hiroshima Kenritsu Seibu Kogyo Gijutsu Senta Hokoku, 0910-4429.*
**Ind/Abst** Chem. Abstr.

JA/0285-4821
**HISTORIA SCIENTIARUM.** (HISTORIA SCIENTIARUM : INTERNATIONAL JOURNAL OF THE HISTORY OF SCIENCE SOCIETY OF JAPAN.). [Hist. sci.]. No. 19 (Sept. 1980)-. English (French and German). Three times a year. Price varies. Nihon Kagakushi Gakkai, (History of Science Soc. of Japan), 16-3-91, Nihonbashi 2 Chome, Chuoku, Tokyoto 103 Japan. **(Subscription address:** Japan Publications Trading Company, Ltd., PO Box 5030, Tokyo International, Tokyo 100-31 Japan.**)** **LC** Q124.6. **DD** 509. **NLM** W1 HI79M. ***Continues*** *Japanese Studies in the History of Science, 0090-0176.*
**Ind/Abst** Am. Hist. Life (1971-); Math. Rev.; Zentralbl. Math. Ihre Grenzgeb.

AT/0727-3061
**HISTORICAL RECORDS OF AUSTRALIAN SCIENCE.** **Added/Corp** Australian Academy of Science. Vol. 5, No. 1 (Nov. 1980)-. Monographic series. English. ir. $32.95Aus$. Australian Academy of Science, GPO Box 783, Canberra ACT 2601 Australia. **Tel** 011 61 6 2475777, FAX 011 61 6 2574620, telex ACSI AA 62406. **LC** Q93; .A879. **DD** 509.94. **Circ:** 1,000. ***Continues*** *Records of the Australian Academy of Science, 0067-155X.*
**Desc:** Publishes original papers and reviews of books on the history of science, pure and applied, in Australia and the South-West Pacific, together with biographical memoirs commissioned by the Council of the Academy of Deceased Fellows of the Australian Academy of Science.
**Ind/Abst** AESIS Q.; Am. Hist. Life (1982-); APAIS, Aust. Public Aff. Inf. Ser.

SZ/0734-1512
**HISTORY AND TECHNOLOGY.** [Hist. technol.]. Vol. 1, No. 1 (Oct. 1983)-. Periodical. English (French). qt. $255.00 (academic institutions), $397.00 (corporate institutions). Harwood Academic Publishers, PO Box 90, Reading RG1 8JL England. **Tel** 011 44 734 560080. **(Subscription address:** International Publishers Distributor at one of the following addresses: 820 Town Center Drive, Langhorne, PA 19047; or PO Box 90, Reading Berkshire RG1 8JL UK; or Kent Ridge PO Box 1180, Singapore 9111, Republic of Singapore**)** **ED** P. Redondi. **LC** T14.7; .H56. **DD** 609. **CODEN** HITEE8. **[CCC]. Bk Rev. Ad Acc.**
**Ind/Abst** Am. Hist. Life (1985-); Int. Bibliogr. Sociol.; Math. Rev.

UK/0073-2753
**HISTORY OF SCIENCE.** [Hist. sci.]. Vol. 1 (1962)-. Periodical. English. qt. $132.00. Science History Publications Ltd., 16 Rutherford Road, Cambridge CB2 2HH England. **Tel** 011 44 223 565532. **ED** R S Porter. **LC** Q125; .H63. **NLM** W1 HI88. **CODEN** HISCAR. **[CCC].** Index available. cum. index. **Bk Rev. Ad Acc. Pr Rev. Circ:** 750. Documents available from The Genuine Article.
**Desc:** Discussion articles on the history of science.
**Ind/Abst** Acad. Search (July 1993-); Am. Hist. Life (1967-); Arts Humanit. Citation Index [Full Cov.]; Curr. Contents Arts Humanit.; Curr. Contents Soc. Behav. Sci.; Gen. Sci. Source (Jul. 1993-); GeoRef; Hist. Source (July 1993-); INFO-SOUTH Abstr.; Mag. Search; Math. Rev.; Res. Alert [Full Cov.]; Soc. Sci. Cit. Index [Full Cov.].

●US/1062-5445
**HISTORY OF SCIENCE AND TECHNOLOGY.** (1992)-. Periodical. English. Harwood Academic Publishers / New York, PO Box 786, Cooper Station, New York NY 10276. **Tel** (212)206-8900, (201)643-7500. **(Subscription address:** International Publishers Distributor at one of the following addresses: 820 Town Center Drive, Langhorne, PA 19047; or PO Box 90, Reading Berkshire RG1 8JL UK; or Kent Ridge PO Box 1180, Singapore 9111, Republic of Singapore**)**

UK/0307-5451
**HISTORY OF TECHNOLOGY.** [Hist. technol.]. (1976)-. English. an. Price varies. Mansell Publishing Ltd., Stanley House, 3 Fleets Lane, Poole Dorset BH15 3AJ England. **Tel** 011 44 71 8394900, telex 9413701 CASPUB G. **(Subscription address:** Cassell PC's Dataprocessing, 360 West 31st Street, New York NY 10001.**)** **ED** Norman Smith. **LC** T14.7; .H57. **DD** 609. **Circ:** 750.
**Desc:** A collection of essays on the technical problems of different periods and societies and the measures taken to solve them.
**Ind/Abst** Acad. Search (Jan. 1993-); Am. Hist. Life (1976-); Gen. Sci. Source (Jul. 1993-); Hist. Source (July 1993-); INFO-SOUTH Abstr.; Mag. Search.

CN/0316-1269
**HISTORY, TECHNOLOGY, AND ART MONOGRAPH.** No. 1-. Monographic series. English. ir. Price varies per volume. Royal Ontario Museum Publications Service, 100 Queens Park, Toronto Ontario M5S 2C6 Canada. **Tel** (416)586-5581. **UDC** 908. ***Continues*** *Royal Ontario Museum. Division of Art and Archaeology. Occasional Paper, 0082-5077.*

JA/0018-277X
**HITACHI REVIEW.** [Hitachi rev.]. **Added/Corp** Hitachi Seisakujo. Vol. 1 (Jan. 1952)-. Academic Scholarly Publication. English. bm. $114.00. Hitachi Seisakujo Sendenbu, (Hitachi Ltd.), 4-6, Kanda Surugadai, Chiyodaku, Tokyoto 101 Japan. **(Subscription address:** Kyowa Book Company Inc., 1 38 Kanda Jinbocho Chiyoda-ku, Tokyo 101 Japan.**)** **LC** T1; .H55. **CODEN** HITAAQ. Documents available from Article Express International, Ask*IEEE, CASDDS.
**Ind/Abst** Alum. Ind. Abstr.; Bioeng. Abstr.; Chem. Abstr.; Civ. Struct. Eng. Abstr.; Comput. Inf. Syst. Abstr. J. [Full Cov.]; Comput. Rev.; Ei Page One; Elect. Comm. Abstr.; EMBASE; Eng. Mater. Abstr.; Eng. Index Annu.; Fluid Abstr., Civil Eng.; Fluid Abstr. Proc. Eng.; FLUIDEX (1973-); INSPEC (1968-); Leadscan; Manuf. Process Eng. Abstr.; Mech. Eng. Abstr.; Met. Abstr.; Solid State Supercond. Abstr.; World Publ. Monit.

JA/0018-277X
**HITACHI TECHNOLOGY.** English. an. Hitachi Ltd, Advertising Department, 6 Kanda Surugadai 4-chome, Chiyoda-ku Tokyo 101 Japan. **Tel** 03-258-1111, J22432 HITACHY, FAX 03-258-5498, telex J22395. **LC** T1; .H56. **DD** 605. **Circ:** 30,000 (ctrl).

JA/0018-2788
**HITACHI ZOSEN GIHO.** [Hitachi Zosen giho]. **Added/Corp** Hitachi Zosen Kabushiki Kaisha. Gijutsu Kenkyujo. **VFOAT** Hitachi Zosen Technical Review. (1937)-. Periodical. Japanese (English). qt. Hitachi Zosen Kabushiki Kaisha Gijutsu Kenkyujo, Osaka Japan. **CODEN** HZOGA2. Documents available from Ask*IEEE, CASDDS.
**Ind/Abst** Chem. Abstr.; INSPEC (March 1979-).

JA/0073-2788
**HITOTSUBASHI JOURNAL OF ARTS & SCIENCES.** **See** The Arts.

GW/0018-3822
**HOB. DIE HOLZBEARBEITUNG.** [HOB, Holzbearb.]. **VFOAT** Holzbearbeitung (1973). (1973)-. Periodical. German. Ten times a year (Plus 1 special issue). DM231.10. A G T Verlag Thum GMBH, Postfach 109, D 71601 Ludwigsburg Germany. **Tel** 011 49 7141 223156. **UDC** 674.02. ***Continues*** *Die Holzbearbeitung (1954), 0179-9576.*

JA
**HOKKAI GAKUEN DAIGAKU KOGAKUBU KENKYU HOKOKU.** **Main/Corp** Hokkai Gakuen Daigaku. Kogakubu. No. 1- ; 1972-. Japanese. Hokkai Gakuen Daigaku Kogakubu, (Faculty of Engineering, Hokkai Gakuen University), Nishi 11 Chome, Minami 26 JO,, Chuoku, Sapporoshi,, Hokkaido 064 Japan. **LC** T4; .H59.
**Ind/Abst** Coal Abstr.; Eng. Mater. Abstr.

JA/0385-0862
**HOKKAIDO KOGYO DAIGAKU KENKYU KIYO.** (KENKYU KIYO / HOKKAIDO DOGYO DAIGAKU.). [Hokkaido Kogyo Daigaku kenkyu kiyo]. **VFOAT** Memoirs of the Hokkaido Institute of Technology. Began in 1970. Academic Scholarly Publication. Japanese (English). an. Hokkaido Kogyo Daigaku, 419-2 Teine Maeda Nishi-ku, Sapporo-shi 061-24 Japan. **LC** T4; .K45. **CODEN** HODKDL. Documents available from Ask*IEEE, CASDDS.
**Ind/Abst** Chem. Abstr.; INSPEC (1981-).

JA/0441-0734
**HOKKAIDO KOGYO KAIHATSU SHIKENJO HOKOKU.** [Hokkaido Kogyo Kaihatsu Shikenjo hokoku]. **Main/Corp** Hokkaido Kogyo Kaihatsu Shikenjo. **Added/Corp** Hokkaido Kogyo Kaihatsu Shikenjo. Reports of the Government Industrial Development Laboratory, Hokkaido. **VFOAT** Reports of the Government Industrial Development Laboratory, Hokkaido. (1966)-. Japanese (summaries and/or abstracts in English). Sapporo, 41-2 Higashi-Tsukisamu, Toyohira-Ku Japan. **LC** T177.J3; H6a. **CODEN** HKKHAG. Documents available from CASDDS.
**Ind/Abst** Chem. Abstr.

JA
**HOKKAIDO KOGYO KAIHATSU SHIKENJO NEMPO.** **Main/Corp** Hokkaido Kogyo Kaihatsu Shikenjo. Japanese. Hokkaido Kogyo Kaihatsu Shikenjo, (Government Industrial Development Laboratory), 41-2 Higashi Tsukisamu, Toyohira-ku Sapporo 061-01, Hokkaido Japan. **LC** T178.H64; H64A.

JA/0367-5939
**HOKKAIDO KYOIKU DAIGAKU KIYO. A SUGAKU-, BUTSURIGAKU-, KAGAKU-, KOGAKU-HEN. DAI 2-BU.** [Hokkaido Kyoiku Daigaku kiyo. Dai 2-bu, A Sugaku, butsurigaku, kagaku, kogaku-hen]. **Main/Corp** Hokkaido Kyoiku Daigaku. **Added/Corp** Hokkaido Kyoiku Daigaku. Journal of Hokkaido University of Education. Section II A. **VFOAT** Journal of Hokkaido University of Education. Section II A. (1967)-. Japanese (English). Hokkaido Kyoiku Daigaku, Nishi 13-chome Minami 24-jo Chuo-ku, Sapporo 064 Japan. **LC** Q77; .H64b. **DD** 505. **CODEN** HKDSAE.
**Ind/Abst** GeoRef; Math. Rev.

JA
**HOKKAIDO KYOIKU DAIGAKU KIYO. DAI 2-BU; C KATEI-, TAIIKU-HEN.** **Main/Corp** Hokkaido Kyoiku Daigaku. **VFOAT** Journal of Hokkaido University of Education. Multiple languages (English and Japanese). Hokkaido Kyoiku Daigaku, Nishi 13-chome Minami 24-jo Chuo-ku, Sapporo 064 Japan. **LC** Q77; .H64A. **DD** 505.

UN/0453-8307
**HOLODILNAJA TEHNIKA I TEHNOLOGIJA.** (KHOLODILNAIA TEKHNIKA I TEKHNOLOGIIA / MINISTERSTVO VYSSHEGO I SREDNEGO SPETSIALNOGO OBRAZOVANIIA USSR.). [Holod. teh. tehnol.]. **Added/Corp** Ukraine. Ministerstvo Vyshchoi i Serednoi Spetsialnoi Osvity. (1965)-. Periodical. Russian. **CODEN** KHTTA7. Documents available from CASDDS.
**Ind/Abst** Chem. Abstr.

US
**HOWARD UNIVERSITY JOURNAL OF SCIENCE, THE.** **Main/Corp** Howard University. Washington, DC. Physics Department. V. 1, No. 4- Winter 1973-. English. Howard University Journal of Science, PO Box 1098, Howard University, Washington DC 20059. ***Continues*** *Howard University Reviews of Science, 0093-6057.*

US/0093-6057
**HOWARD UNIVERSITY REVIEWS OF SCIENCE, THE.** **Main/Corp** Howard University, Washington, DC. Physics Department. Vol. 1, No. 3 (Nov. 1972)-. English. Howard University Physics Department, Washington DC 20001. **LC** Q1; .H6. **DD** 505. ***Continues*** *Howard University Reviews of Science.*

CC/0438-0479
**HSIA-MEN TA HSUEH HSUEH PAO. TZU JAN KO HSUEH PAN.** (HSIA-MEN TA HSUEH HSUEH PAO. TZU JAN KO HSUEH PAN.). [Hsia-men ta hsueh hsueh pao. Tzu jan ko hsueh pan]. **Added/Corp** Hsia-men ta Hsueh. **VFOAT** Journal of Xiamen University. Natural Science; Acta Scientiarum Naturalium, Universitatis Amoiensis. (19??)-. Academic Scholarly Publication. Chinese (summaries and/or abstracts in English). qt. $1.50 (per issue). Xiamen Daxue / Xiamen University, c/o Xiamen Daxue Tushuguan, Xiamne,

Fujian 361005, People's Republic of China. **Tel** 592-2086255. **(Subscription address:** China International Book Trading Corporation, PO Box 399, Library Service Department, Beijing 100044 People's Republic of China.**) LC** Q4; .H73. **DD** 605. Documents available from CASDDS, BLDSC, Ask*IEEE.
**Ind/Abst** INSPEC (May 1984-); Math. Rev.; NAPRALERT.

CH
**HSING CHENG YUAN KUO CHIA KO HSUEH WEI YUAN HUI NIEN PAO.**
**Added/Corp** Kuo Chia ko Hsueh wei Yuan hui. (1977)-. Chinese (English). an. Free. Hsing Cheng Yuan Kuo Chia Ko Hsueh Wei Yuan Hui, #2 Kuang-chou Street, Taipei Taiwan. **Tel** (02)3614681. **LC** Q72; .H74. **DD** 354.51/24900855. **Circ:** 2,000. ***Continues*** *Kuo Chia ko Hsueh wei Yuan Hui. Kuo Chia ko Hsueh wei Yuan Hui Nien Pao.*
**Desc:** Summarizes all activities, research projects and results of the NSC over the past fiscal year.

CC
**HSUEH PAO. TZU JAN KO HSUEH PAN.**
**Added/Corp** Hu-nan Ta Hsueh. **VFOAT** Journal of Hunan University; Hu-nan Ta Hsueh Hsueh Pao. Tzu Jan Ko Hsueh Pan. (19??)-. Academic Scholarly Publication. Chinese (English). qt. RMBY1.20. **LC** Q4; .H775. **DD** 505. **CODEN** HDKEEU. Documents available from CASDDS.
**Ind/Abst** Chem. Abstr. (-1988); Math. Rev. (1985-); Zentralbl. Math. Ihre Grenzgeb.

CC
**HSUEH PAO (WU-HAN KUNG HSUEH YUAN).** (HSUEH PAO.). **Added/Corp** Wu-han Kung Hsueh Yuan. **VFOAT** Wuhan Gongxueyuan Xuebao; Wu-Han Kung Hsueh Yuan Hsueh Pao; Journal of Wuhan Institute of Technology. (19??)-. Periodical. Chinese. qt. $24.00 US. Wuhan Institute of Technology, Matanghan Wuhan, People's Republic of China. **Tel** 871939. **ED** Gao Shixtu, Yang Xiaohuan, Li Daowen and Xu Xianglong. **LC** T4; .H79. **DD** 605. Index available. **Bk Rev. Circ:** 1,500.
**Desc:** A comprehensive publication; each issue mainly covers research achievements related to the design and manufacture of machine forging and casting, material protection, enterprise management, automobiles, tribology, electrical automation, etc.
**Ind/Abst** Math. Rev. (1988-).

GW/0341-101X
**HTM. HARTEREI-TECHNISCHE MITTEILUNGEN.** [HTM, Harterei-tech. Mitt.]. **VFOAT** Harterei-Technische Mitteilungen. (1976)-. Periodical. German. Six times a year. DM405.00. Carl Hanser Verlag, Postfach 860420, D 81631 Munich Germany. **Tel** 011 49 89 998300, FAX 011 49 89 984809. **UDC** 621.785.5/.7. Documents available from CASDDS. ***Continues*** *Harterei-Technische Mitteilungen, 0017-6583.*
**Ind/Abst** Chem. Abstr.

CH
**HUA-KANG LI KO HSUEH PAO. VFOAT** Hwa Kang Journal of Sciences. V. 1, (June 1981)-. Periodical. Chinese (English). an. College of Sciences, Chinese Culture University, Hwa Kang Yang Ming Shan Taipei Taiwan. **LC** Q4; .H88. **DD** 505.

CC/1000-565X
**HUANAN LIGONG DAXUE XUEBAO ZIRAN KEXUE BAN.** (HUANAN LIGONG DAXUE XUEBAO.). **VFOAT** Journal of South China University of Technology (Natural Sciences). (1988)-. Academic Scholarly Publication. Chinese. qt. Huanan Ligong Daxue / Xuebao Bianjibu, Wushan, Guangzhou, Guangdong 510641, People's Republic of China. **Tel** 511311. **ED** Xu Bingzheng. **DD** 505. Documents available from CASDDS. ***Continues*** *Huanan Gongxueyuan Xuebao (Ziran Kexue Ban), 0438-119X.*
**Ind/Abst** Chem. Abstr.

US/0073-3776
**HUDSON INSTITUTE REPORT TO THE MEMBERS, THE. Main/Corp** Hudson Institute. (19??)-. English. an. Watt Publishing Company, 122 South Wesley Avenue, Mount Morris IL 61054. **Tel** (815)734-4171, FAX (815)734-7021, telex TWX 910-642-2891. **LC** Q180.U5; H83a. **DD** 001.4/3.

US/1045-2729
**HUMAN ECOLOGY & ENERGY BALANCING SCIENTIST, THE.** **See** Public Health and Safety.

NE/0167-2533
**HUMAN SYSTEMS MANAGEMENT.** [Hum. syst. manage.]. **VFOAT** HSM; H.S.M. Vol. 1, No. 1 (Feb. 1980)-. Periodical. English. qt. Fl406.00. IOS Press, Van Diemenstraat 94, 1013 CN Amsterdam Netherlands. **Tel** 011 31 20 6382189, FAX 011 31 20 620 3419. **ED** Manfred Kochen. **CODEN** HSMADU. **Bk Rev. Ad Acc.** available on microfilm and microfiche from University Microfilms International (UMI). Documents available from Ask*IEEE, UMI Article Clearinghouse.
**Desc:** Addresses a new and increasingly urgent need: to comprehend, analyze, and manage the organizational and managerial impacts of high technology.
**Ind/Abst** ABI/INFORM Glob. Ed.; ABI Inform Ondisc (April 1981-); Appl. Soc. Sci. Index Abstr.; Contents Pages Manage.; Hum. Resour. Abstr. (?-?); INSPEC (Feb. 1980-); Int. Polit. Sci. Abstr.; Person. Manage. Abstr.; Selec. Coop. Index Manage. Period; Soc. Plann. Policy Dev. Abstr.; Sociol. Abstr.; Tech. Educ. Train. Abstr.; Urban Aff. Abstr.; Work Relat. Abstr.

US
**HUMAN/TECHNOLOGY INTERACTION IN COMPLEX SYSTEMS.** English. $78.75. JAI Press Inc., 55 Old Post Road, Suite 2, PO Box 1678, Greenwich CT 06836-1678. **Tel** (203)661-7602, FAX (203)661-0792. **ED** William B. Rouse.
**Desc:** Reports on advances in theory and applicants associated with understanding and improving the relationships and performance of humans and technology in complex sociotechnical systems where computer, communications, and related technologies are central elements. Reports of multidisciplinary efforts in complex domains are of particular interest.

CC/1000-2537
**HUNAN SHIFAN DAXUE XUEBAO (ZIRAN KEXUE BAN).** (HU-NAN SHIH FAN TA HSUEH TZU JAN KO HSUEH HSUEH PAO.). [Hunan shifan daxue xuebao]. **Added/Corp** Hu-Nan Shih Fan Ta Hsueh. **VFOAT** Acta Scientiarum Naturalium Universitatis Normalensis Hunanensis; Journal of Hunan Normal University; Natural Science Journal of Hunan Normal University; Natural Sciences Journal of Hunan Normal University. (198?)-. Periodical. Chinese (summaries and/or abstracts in English). qt. Hunan Shifan Daxue, Xuebao Bianjibu, Yuelushan, Changsha, Hunan 410081 People's Republic of China. **Tel** 883131. **(Subscription address:** China International Book Trading Corporation, PO Box 399, Library Service Department, Beijing 100044 People's Republic of China.**) ED** G. Weizhong. **CODEN** HSXKEE. Documents available from BIOSIS Document Express, BLDSC, Article Express International, CASDDS. ***Continues*** *Hu-Nan Shih Yuan Hsueh Pao. Tzu Jan Ko Hsueh Pan, 1001-9472.*
**Ind/Abst** Biol. Abstr.; Chem. Abstr.

US/0747-1599
**HYBRID CIRCUIT TECHNOLOGY.** ***Title Change.*** [Hybrid circuit technol.]. Vol. 1, No. 1 (Jan. 1984)-Feb.(1992). Periodical. English. mo. IHS Publishing Group, 17730 West Peterson Road, Libertyville IL 60048. **Tel** (708)362-8711, FAX (708)362-3484. **ED** Diane Pirocanac. **DD** 621. **CODEN** HCTEEY. **[CCC]. Bk Rev. Ad Acc. Circ:** 22,000 (ctrl). Documents available from Article Express International, Ask*IEEE. ***Continued by*** *Advanced Packaging, 1065-0555.*
**Desc:** Serves the fields of custom and captive electronic hybrid circuit fabrication, assembly, production, testing, packaging, etc.
**Ind/Abst** Ceram. Abstr. (19??-19??); Ei Page One; Eng. Index Annu.; INSPEC (Jan. 1988-Feb. 1992).

UK/0954-917X
**I T L G.** [I T L G]. **VFOAT** Information Technology for Local Government. (1988)-. Government Publication. English. Six times a year. £35.00 UK; £43.00 other. Government Computing / England, Southbank House, Black Prince Road, London FE1 7SJ England. **Tel** 011 44 71 5829191.

JA
**IBARAKI DAIGAKU KYOIKUGAKUBU KIYO : SHIZEN KAGAKU. Main/Corp** Ibaraki Daigaku. Kyoikugakubu. **VFOAT** Bulletin of the Faculty of Education, Ibaraki University : Natural Science. No. 1-1978-. Japanese (summaries and/or abstracts in English). Ibaraki Daigaku, 1-1 Bunkyo, Mito 310 Japan. **LC** Q4; .I23A. ***Supersedes in part*** *Ibaraki Daigaku Kyoikugakubu Kiyo.*

SP/0211-0776
**IBERICA. ACTUALIDAD CIENTIFICA.** (196?)-. Periodical. Spanish. mo (Except Aug.). 3750ptas. Iberica, Apartado 23095, 08080 Barcelona Spain. **Tel** 011 34 3 2403241, 011 34 3 2434349. **LC** T4; .I22. ***Continues*** *Revista Iberica de Endocrinologia.*

FI/1018-4635
**ICLAS NEWS. Added/Corp** International Council for Laboratory Animal Science. Vol. 1, No. 1 (Spring 1991)-. Periodical. English. Twice a year. Free on request. ICLAS - International Council for Laboratory Animal Science, PO Box 6, SF 702, Dept. of Physiology, 11 Kuopio, Finland. **Tel** 011 358 9 71163080, 011 358 9 71163110, FAX 011 358 9 71163410, 011 358 9 71163112, telex 4221KUYSF. **ED** Prof. Osmo Hanninen. **NLM** W1; IC408. **Bk Rev**, (Qty: 10). **Ad Acc. Circ:** 300 (ctrl). ***Continues*** *ICLAS Bulletin, 0333-2241.*
**Desc:** Deals with laboratory animal science.

CN/1189-6078
**ICO. INTELLIGENCE ARTIFICIELLE ET SCIENCES COGNITIVES AU QUEBEC.** (ICO.). [ICO, Intell. artif. sci. cogn. Que.]. **VFOAT** Intelligence Artificielle et Sciences Cognitives au Quebec; ICO Quebec. (19??)-. Periodical. French. tq (Feb., May, Oct.). 116.00 Can$ Canada; 126.00Can$ US; 140.00Can$ other (libraries); 100.00Can$ Canada; 110.00Can$ US; 140.00Can$ other. GIRICO, 276 rue St Jacques, Bureau 912, Montreal Quebec, H3B 3G1 Canada. **Tel** (514)985-5459, FAX (514)985-2720. **ED** Ghislain Levesque. **DD** 006.3. **Bk Rev**, (Qty: 3). **Ad Acc. Circ:** 1,000.
**Desc:** Research and development review in the domain of cognitive and computer science.
**Ind/Abst** Point Repere (1991-).

US/0892-676X
**ID SYSTEMS.** [ID syst.]. **Added/Corp** North American Technology (Firm). Vol. 7, No. 1 (Jan./Feb. 1987)-. Periodical. English. Ten times a year. $55.00. Helmers Publishing Inc., 174 Concord Street, PO Box 874, Peterborough NH 03458-0874. **Tel** (603)924-9631, FAX (603)924-7408. **ED** Deborah Navas. **LC** HF5416; .B363. **DD** 006.4/2. **[CCC].** Index available. **Bk Rev. Ad Acc. Circ:** 50,000 (ctrl). ***Continues*** *Bar Code News, 8750-8702.*
**Desc:** Journal of automated data collection, provides information to users of bar code equipment and other types of automatic identification equipment, such as optical character recognition, voice recognition and radio frequency identification.
**Ind/Abst** Abstr. Bull. Inst. Pap. Sci. Tech.; Ei Page One; Graph. Arts Bull. Inst. Pap. Sci. Technol. (April, July, Nov. 1989); Int. Packag. Abstr.

UK/0268-6171
**IEE MANAGEMENT OF TECHNOLOGY SERIES.** (IEE MANAGEMENT OF TECHNOLOGY SERIES.). [IEE manage. technol. ser.]. **VFOAT** Institution of Electrical Engineers Management of Technology Series. (1984)-. Monographic series. English. ir. Price varies per volume. Institution of Electrical Engineers / IEE, Michael Faraday House, Six Hills Way, Stevenage Herts SG1 2AY UK. **Tel** 011 44 438 313311, FAX 011 44 438 742840, telex 825578 IEESTV G. **(Subscription address:** IEE / UK, Publications Sales Department, PO Box 96, Stevenage, Herts, SG1 2SD England.**)** Documents available from Article Express International, Ask*IEEE.
**Ind/Abst** Ei Page One; Eng. Index Annu.; INSPEC.

US/0278-0097
**IEEE TECHNOLOGY & SOCIETY MAGAZINE.** [IEEE technol. soc. mag.]. **Added/Corp** IEEE Society on Social Implications of Technology. **VFOAT** I.E.E.E. Technology and Society Magazine; I.E.E.E. Technology & Society Magazine; Technology and Society Magazine; Technology & Society Magazine; IEEE Technology and Society Magazine. Vol. 1, No. 1 (Mar. 1982)-. Periodical. English. qt. $105.00. IEEE, Institution of Electrical and Electronics Engineers, Inc., 345 East 47th Street, New York NY 10017-2394. **Tel** (908)981-1393, FAX (908)981-9667. **(Subscription address:** IEEE / Institute of Electrical and Electronics Engineers, 445 Hoes Lane, PO Box 1331, Piscataway NJ 08855-1331.**) LC** T14.5; .I35. **DD** 306/46/05. **[CCC].** available on microfiche. Documents available from Article Express International, Ask*IEEE. ***Continues*** *Technology and Society, 0194-3359.*
**Desc:** The impact of technology (as embodied by the fields of interest in IEEE) on society, the impact of society on the engineering profession, the history of the societal aspects of electrotechnology and professional, social, and economic responsibility in the practice of engineering and its related technology.
**Ind/Abst** Appl. Sci. Technol. Index (1991-); Ei Page One; Eng. Index Annu.; Expand. Acad. Index (1992-); Index IEEE Publ.; Inf. Sci. Abstr.; INSPEC (Sep. 1983-); J. Plan. Lit.; Peace Res. Abstr. J. (1982-); Pollut. Abstr. Indexes.

●JA/0916-8532
**IEICE TRANSACTIONS ON INFORMATION AND SYSTEMS.**
**Added/Corp** Denshi Joho Tsushin Gakkai (Japan). **VFOAT** IEICE Transactions; Institute of Electronics, Information and Communication Engineers Transactions on Information and systems; Transactions on Information and Systems. (1992)-. Periodical. English. mo. $100.00. Institute of Electronics / Tokyo, Information and Communication Engineers, Tokyo Japan. **(Subscription address:** Maruzen Company Ltd., PO Box 5050, Import & Export Department, Tokyo 100 31 Japan.**)** Documents available from The Genuine Article, Ask*IEEE. ***Continues in part*** *IEICE Transactions on Communications, Electronics, Information, and Systems, 0917-1673.*
**Ind/Abst** Curr. Contents Eng. Tech. Appl. Sci. (19??-); INSPEC (Jan. 1992-); Res. Alert (19??-) [Select. Cov.]; SCISEARCH (19??-).

GW
**IGW-REPORT UBER WISSENCHAFT UND TECHNOLOGIE. Added/Corp** Institut fuer Gesellschaft und Wissenschaft. **VFOAT** IGW-Report Uber Wissenschaft und Technologie in der DDR und Anderen RGW-Landern. No. 1 (Nov. 1987)-. German. Institut fur Gesellschaft und Wissenschaft, Aussere Brucker Str 33, Postfach 1409, 8520 Erlangen-Nurnberg Germany. ***Continues*** *Wissenschaften in der DDR.*
**Ind/Abst** PAIS Int. Print.

KO
**IHAK NONJIP. Added/Corp** Koryo Taehakkyo. Ikwa Taehak. **VFOAT** Journal of Natural Sciences. (19??)-. Periodical. Korean (English; summaries and/or abstracts in English). Koryo Taehakkyo Ikwa Taehak, Seoul Korea. **LC** Q4; .I435. Documents available from CASDDS.
**Ind/Abst** Chem. Abstr.

SP
**ILERDA CIENCIES: ANUARI DE L'INSTITUT D'ESTUDIS ILERDENCS.**
**Added/Corp** Institut d'Estudis Ilerdencs. **VFOAT** Ciencies. Num. 48 (1990)-. Periodical. Catalan (Spanish; summaries and/or abstracts in English). Instituto de

Estudios Ilerdenses, Diputacion Provincial de Lerida, 25071 Lerida Spain. **LC** Q65; .I43. ***Continues in part*** *Ilerda, 0212-565X.*

●US/1065-7770
**ILLINOIS TECHNOLOGY RESOURCE GUIDE.** **Added/Corp** Corporate Technology Information Services. (1992)-. English. $90.00. Corporate Technology Information Services Inc, 12 Alfred Street, Suite 200, Woburn MA 01801-9998. **Tel** (617)932-3939, (800)333-8036, FAX (617)932-6335, telex 497-2961 CRPTECH.

US/0886-8042
**IMAGE PROCESSING TECHNOLOGY.** [Image process. technol.]. (Jan. 1986)-. Periodical. English. mo. $125.00 US; $175.00 other. Robert Griffiths Associates, 110 Brainerd Road/Suite A, Allston MA 02134. **DD** 006.

IT/0019-2708
**IMBALLAGGIO : ORGANO UFFICIALE DELL'ISTITUTO ITALIANO IMBALLAGGIO.** **Added/Corp** Istituto Italiano Imballaggio. (1951)-. Periodical. Italian (English). mo. L100000.00 Italy; L155000.00 other. Etas SRL, Via Mecenate 89, 20138 Milan Italy. **Tel** 011 39 2 580841. **Ad Acc.**
**Desc:** Provides a forum for discussion and analysis of all aspects of packaging such as materials, production processes and technology, quality control and innovations.
**Ind/Abst** Dairy Sci. Abstr.; Food Sci. Technol. Abstr.; Int. Packag. Abstr.

UK/0019-2872
**IMPACT OF SCIENCE ON SOCIETY.** ***Ceased.*** [Impact sci. soc.]. **Added/Corp** Unesco. Vol. 1, No. 1 (Apr./June 1950)-Vol. 42, No. 4 (1992). Periodical. English (French, Spanish, Russian, Arabic, Chinese and Korean). qt. Taylor & Francis Ltd., Rankine Road, Basingstoke Hampshire, RG24 8PR United Kingdom. **Tel** 011 44 256 840366, FAX 011 44 256 479438, telex 858540. **(Subscription address:** Taylor & Francis Inc., 1900 Frost Road, Suite 101, Bristol PA 19007-1598.**) ED** H J Moore. **LC** Q1; .I4. **DD** 505. **NLM** W1 IM595. **CODEN** ISSOA8. Index available. **Pr Rev. Circ:** 25,000. available on microfilm and microfiche from University Microfilms International (UMI). Documents available from The Genuine Article, BIOSIS Document Express, UMI Article Clearinghouse, CASDDS, Documents on Demand.
**Desc:** The aim is to stimulate wide public debate on timely issues concerning the interaction between science/technology and society. When scientific and technological breakthrough is accompanied by complex and often unpredictable social consequences, the journal helps interpret cause and effect.
**Ind/Abst** Acad. Abstr. Full Text Elite (Jan. 1992-Sept. 1992); Acad. Abstr. (Jan. 1992-Sept. 1992); Acad. Ind. [Computer File] (1992-); Acad. Search (Jan. 1992-Sept. 1992); AgBiotech News Inf.; Agrofor. Abstr.; Anim. Breed. Abstr.; Appl. Soc. Sci. Index Abstr.; Biol. Abstr.; Chem. Abstr.; Coal Abstr.; Curr. Geogr. Publ. (199?-); Curr. Index J. Educ.; Curr. Lit. Sci. Sci.; Ecol. Abstr.; Energy Inf. Abstr.; Environ. Abstr.; Environ. Period. Bibliogr.; Ergon. Abstr.; Expand. Acad. Index (1989-); Gen. Sci. Index (1992-); Gen. Sci. Source (Jan. 1992-Sept. 1992) [Full Txt.]; Geogr. Abstr. Human Geogr.; GeoRef; Health Plan. Adminis.; Index Vet.; INFO-SOUTH Abstr.; Int. Aerosp. Abstr.; Int. Bibliogr. Sociol.; Int. Labour Doc.; Leis. Recreat. Tour. Abstr.; Mag. Artic. Summar. Elite (Jan. 1992-Dec. 1992); Mag. Artic. Summar. CD-ROM (Jan. 1992-Sept. 1992); Mag. Search; Middle East Abstr. Index; Newsp. Period. Abstr. (1991-); Nucl. Sci. Abstr.; PAIS Int. Print (1991-); Peace Res. Abstr. J. (1964-1972; 1978-1982); Plant Breed. Abstr.; Protozoolog. Abstr.; Public Aff. Inf. Serv. Bull.; Res. Alert [Full Cov.]; Rev. Agric. Entomol.; Rev. Med. Vet. Entomol.; Rice Abstr.; Rural Dev. Abstr.; Soc. Plann. Policy Dev. Abstr.; Soc. Sci. Source (Jan. 1992-); Soc. Sci. Cit. Index [Full Cov.]; Soc. Sci. Index; Soc. Sci. Index Fulltext (1988-) [Full Txt.]; Soc. Welf. Soc. Plan./Policy Soc. Dev.; Sociol. Abstr.; Soils Fert.; SportSearch; Vocat. Search (Jan. 1992-Sept. 1992); World Agric. Econ.

KO
**IMPACT OF SCIENCE ON SOCIETY.** (KWAHAK KWA SAHOE / IMPACT OF SCIENCE ON SOCIETY.). **Added/Corp** Yunesuko Hanguk Wiwonhoe. **VFOAT** Impact of Science on Society. Vol. 1 (1984)-. Periodical. Korean (translations available in English). qt. W6.000. Yunesuko Hanguk Wiwonhoe, 50-16 Myong-dong Chung-ku, Seoul Korea. **LC** Q175.4; .I543a.

UA
**IMPACT OF SCIENCE ON SOCIETY.** (AL-ILM WA-AL-MUJTAMA.). Periodical. Arabic. qt. £E0.25 single issue. Markaz Matbuat Al-Yunisku, 1 Shari Talat Harb Midan Al-Tahrir, Al-Qahirah Egypt. **LC** Q1; .I42.

FR/0304-2944
**IMPACT, SCIENCE ET SOCIETE.** ***Ceased.*** [Impact, sci. soc.]. (1950)-(19??). Periodical. French. qt. UNESCO / France, 31 rue Francois Bonvin, 75732 Paris Cedex 15 France. **Tel** 011 33 1 45684564, 011 33 1 45684565, FAX 011 33 1 42733007, telex 204461 Paris. **LC** Q124.6; .I46. **DD** 301.24/3.
**Ind/Abst** Energy Res. Abstr. (Feb. 1983-); GeoRef; Int. Polit. Sci. Abstr.; Point Repere (1983-).

CN/0826-0648
**IN TOUCH (OTTAWA).** ***Ceased.*** (IN TOUCH.). [In touch]. **Main/Corp** Science Council of Canada. **VFOAT** Resonances. Vol. 1, No. 1 (Oct./Nov. 1983)-(199?). Periodical. English (French). bm. Science Council of Canada, 100 Metcalfe Street, Ottawa Ontario K1P 5M1 Canada. **Tel** (819)997-2560. **DD** 509/.71. **Circ:** 20,000.
**Desc:** Newsletter, describes the activities and areas of research conducted by the Science Council of Canada.

US
**INDEX OF PUBLICATIONS / TECHNICAL AIDS BRANCH, OFFICE OF INDUSTRIAL RESOURCES, INTERNATIONAL COOPERATION ADMINISTRATION.** **Main/Corp** United States. International Cooperation Administration. Technical Aids Branch. 1957-. English. US Army Publications Center, 2800 Eastern Boulevard, Baltimore MD 21220.

US/0149-8088
**INDEX TO SCIENTIFIC & TECHNICAL PROCEEDINGS.** [Index sci. tech. proc.]. **Added/Corp** Institute for Scientific Information. **VFOAT** Scientific & Technical Proceedings; ISTP. **VAT** Index to Scientific and Technical Proceedings. (Jan. 1978)-. Academic Scholarly Publication. English. mo. $1695.00 print; $1790.00 CD-ROM, $2340.00 (combination print and CD-ROM). Institute for Scientific Information, 3501 Market Street, Philadelphia PA 19104. **Tel** (215)386-0100, (800)523-1850, FAX (215)386-6362, telex 84-5305. **(Subscription address:** Institute for Scientific Information, PO Box 71416, Chicago IL 60694.**)** **LC** Z7403; .I4; Q158.5. **DD** 016.5. **NLM** W 3.5 I39.
**Desc:** Provides access to proceedings papers' titles from nearly 100 disciplines.
**Ind/Abst** Energy Res. Abstr. (Feb. 1983-).

US/0884-8440
**INDEX TO SCIENTIFIC BOOK CONTENTS.** (INDEX TO SCIENTIFIC BOOK CONTENTS : ISBC.). [Index sci. book contents]. **Added/Corp** Institute for Scientific Information. **VFOAT** ISBC. (1985)-. Academic Scholarly Publication. English. qt. $1475.00. Institute for Scientific Information, 3501 Market Street, Philadelphia PA 19104. **Tel** (215)386-0100, (800)523-1850, FAX (215)386-6362, telex 84-5305. **(Subscription address:** Institute for Scientific Information, PO Box 71416, Chicago IL 60694.**)** **LC** Z7401; .I37; Q158.5. **DD** 501/.6. **NLM** Z 7401; I38.

US/0360-0661
**INDEX TO SCIENTIFIC REVIEWS. See** Science and Technology-Abstracting, Bibliographies and Statistics.

US
**INDEX TO STANDARD INTEREST PROFILES IN SCIENCE AND TECHNOLOGY, AN.** (1979)-. English. an. $25.00. Indiana University / Chemical Information Center, 814 East 3rd Street, Bloomington IN 47405. **Tel** (812)337-0441. **Circ:** 25. available on diskette. ***Continues*** *Index to Computer-Produced Standard Interest Profilesin Chemistry, Applied Chemistry, Chemical Engineering, and Metallurgy.*
**Desc:** An index to standard interest profiles, macro profiles, and package alerting services produced by ISI, Chemical Abstracts Service, Biosis, and others.

II
**INDIAN BOTANICAL CONTACTOR : IBC.** **Added/Corp** Avichal Science Foundation (India). **VFOAT** IBC. (198?)-. Periodical. English. qt. Indian Botanical Contractor, Sardar Patel University, Department of Biosciences, Vallabh Vidyanagar 388 120 India. **CODEN** IBCOEH. Documents available from BIOSIS Document Express, CASDDS.
**Ind/Abst** Biol. Abstr.; Chem. Abstr.

II/0019-5235
**INDIAN JOURNAL OF HISTORY OF SCIENCE.** [Indian j. hist. sci.]. **Added/Corp** National Commission for the Compilation of History of Sciences in India. Indian National Science Academy. National Institute of Sciences of India. **VFOAT** I.J.H.S.; IJHS. Vol. 1, No. 1 (May 1966)-. Periodical. English. qt. $120.00. Indian National Science Academy, 1 Bahadur Shah Zafar Marg, New Delhi 110 002 India. **(Subscription address:** Prints India, 11 Darya Ganj, New Delhi, 110002 India, (Phone: 011 91 11 3268645)**)** **LC** Q125; .I45. **DD** 509. **NLM** W1 IN209C. **CODEN** IJHSA4. Documents available from CASDDS.
**Ind/Abst** Am. Hist. Life (1987-); Art Archaeol. Tech. Abstr.; Chem. Abstr.; GeoRef; Math. Rev.; Zentralbl. Math. Ihre Grenzgeb.

II/0970-0811
**INDIAN JOURNAL OF PHYSICAL & NATURAL SCIENCES. SECTION A.** (INDIAN JOURNAL OF PHYSICAL & NATURAL SCIENCES. SEC. A : IJPNS). [Indian j. phys. nat. sci., Sect. A]. **VFOAT** Indian Journal of Physical and Natural Sciences. Sec. A; IJPNS. (1982)-. Periodical. English. sa. $50.00. **(Subscription address:** Prints India, 11 Darya Ganj, New Delhi 110002 India.**) CODEN** IJNAEI. Documents available from BIOSIS Document Express, CASDDS. ***Continues in part*** *Indian Journal of Physical and Natural Sciences, 0254-2943.*
**Ind/Abst** Biol. Abstr.; Chem. Abstr.

II/0019-5480
**INDIAN JOURNAL OF PHYSICS AND PROCEEDINGS OF THE INDIAN ASSOCIATION FOR THE CULTIVATION OF SCIENCE.** (INDIAN JOURNAL OF PHYSICS A & B INCLUDES PROCEEDINGS OF THE INDIAN ASSOCIATION FOR THE CULTIVATION OF SCIENCE.). **Added/Corp** Indian Association for the Cultivation of Science. Vol. 1 (1916)-. Academic Scholarly Publication. English. Twelve times a year. Rs800.00. Indian Association of Cultivation of Science, 2-3 Raja Subadh Mullick Road, Jadavpur, Calcutta 700032 India. **Tel** 46-9371-5, FAX 91 33 4732805, telex 021-5501 IACS IN. **(Subscription address:** Prints India, 11 Darya Ganj, New Delhi 110002 India.**) ED** S.P. Sen Gupta. **LC** Q73; .C3. **CODEN** IJPYAS. Index available. **Bk Rev**, (Qty: 550). **Ad Acc. Acid Free. Circ:** 600 (ctrl). Documents available from CASDDS.
**Ind/Abst** Chem. Abstr.; Leadscan.

II/0019-5669
**INDIAN JOURNAL OF TECHNOLOGY.** ***Title Change.*** [Indian j. technol.]. **Added/Corp** Council of Scientific & Industrial Research (India) Indian National Science Academy. Vol. 1, No. 1 (Jan. 1963)-Vol. 31, No. 12 (Dec. 1993). Academic Scholarly Publication. English. mo. Council of Scientific & Industrial Research, Publications & Information Director, Hillside Road, New Delhi 110012 India. **Tel** FAX 011 91 11 5731353. **ED** Subbiah Arunachalam. **LC** T1; .I165. **DD** 605. **CODEN** IJOTA8. **Bk Rev. Ad Acc. Pr Rev. Circ:** 1,000. available on microfilm and microfiche from University Microfilms International (UMI). Documents available from Article Express International, The Genuine Article, BIOSIS Document Express, Ask*IEEE, CASDDS, Documents on Demand. ***Continues*** *Journal of Scientific and Industrial Research. Section D: Technology, 0368-4237.* ***Split into*** *Indian Journal of Chemical Technology, 0971-457X* ***and*** *Indian Journal of Engineering & Materials Sciences, 0971-4588.*
**Desc:** Original research papers and occasional review articles in mechanical, chemical engineering, metallurgy, applied chemistry, applied mathematics, etc.
**Ind/Abst** AGRICOLA; Alum. Ind. Abstr.; Anal. Abstr.; Bioeng. Abstr.; Biol. Abstr.; Ceram. Abstr.; Chem. Abstr.; Coal Abstr.; Curr. Biotechnol.; Curr. Contents Eng. Tech. Appl. Sci.; Curr. Titles Electrochem.; Dairy Sci. Abstr.; Ei Page One; EMBASE; Energy Inf. Abstr.; Eng. Mater. Abstr.; Eng. Index Annu.; Environ. Abstr.; Fluid Abstr. Civil Eng.; Fluid Abstr. Proc. Eng.; FLUIDEX (1973-); Food Sci. Technol. Abstr.; Gas Abstr.; Geol. Abstr.; INSPEC (1968-); Int. Aerosp. Abstr.; Leadscan; Met. Abstr.; MINPROC; Nutr. Abstr. Rev., Ser. B, Live Feeds and Feed.; Nutr. Abstr. Rev., Ser. A, Hum. Exp.; Old Testam. Abstr.; Life Sci. Collect.; Proc. Chem. Eng.; Res. Alert [Select. Cov.]; SCISEARCH; Sug. Indus. Abstr.; Theoret. Chem. Eng.; World Text. Abstr.; Zentralbl. Math. Ihre Grenzgeb.

II/0019-6339
**INDIAN SCIENCE ABSTRACTS. See** Science and Technology-Abstracting, Bibliographies and Statistics.

II
**INDIAN SCIENCE INDEX.** (1975)-. English (Bengali, Sanskrit, Hindi and German). an. Rs80.00 India; Rs300.00 other. Centre for Asian Dokumentation, K 15 / CIT Building, Christopher Road, Calcutta 700014 India. **(Subscription address:** Central Ne Ws Agency Ltd., 23/90 Connaught Circus, New Delhi 110 001 India**) ED** S Chaudhuri. **LC** Q1; .I545. **DD** 016.5. **Bk Rev. Ad Acc.** ctrl circ.
**Desc:** Records writings on pre-modern period and folk science. Contributions are included from the scientists of South Asia.

CN/0843-753X
**INDICATORS OF SCIENCE AND TECHNOLOGY (OTTAWA).** (INDICATORS OF SCIENCE AND TECHNOLOGY / STATISTICS CANADA, SCIENCE, TECHNOLOGY AND CAPITAL STOCK DIVISION.). [Indic. sci. technol.]. **Added/Corp** Statistics Canada. Science, Technology and Capital Stock Division. **VFOAT** Indicateurs de l'Activite Scientifique et Technologique. Vol. 1, No. 1 (July 1989)-. English (French). qt. 18.00Can$ Canada; $21.50 US; $25.25 other. Statistics Canada, Publications Sales & Services, Main Building Room 1710, Ottawa Ontario K1A 0T6 Canada. **Tel** (613)951-5078, (800)267-6677, FAX (613)951-1584, telex 053-3585. **LC** Q172.5.S34; I53. **DD** 338.97106. ***Continues*** *Science and Technology Indicators, 0825-5717.*

SP/0210-9409
**INDICE ESPANOL DE CIENCIA Y TECNOLOGIA.** [Indice esp. cienc. tecnol.]. **Added/Corp** Instituto de Informacion y Documentacion en Ciencia y Tecnologia (Spain). Nos. 1 & 2; (1981)-.

# Science and Technology

Abstracting/Indexing Service. Spanish. sa. 5000ptas. Instituto de Informacion y Documentacion, Cientifica (CINDOC), Joaquin Costa, 22, 28002 Madrid Spain. **Tel** 011 34 1 563-5482 87, **FAX** (91)564 26 44, telex 22628 CIDMD E. **ED** Concepcion Ortega Fernandez. **LC** Z7401; .I42; Q158.5. **DD** 016.5. Index available. **Pr Rev. Circ:** 1,200 (ctrl). available on CD-ROM.
**Desc:** Belongs to the Spanish Council of Scientific Research. Fulfills three activities: research (terminology, automatic translation, bibliometry and statistical documentation), professional information (specific courses) and public services (online information retrieval and dissemination, photodocumentation and translation).

II
**INDUSTRIAL HERALD.** Vol. 22, No. 31 (Aug. 8 to 21, 1987)-. Periodical. English. bw. Rs5.00. The Industrial Herald Weekly, 710 Mount Road, Madras 600 006 India. **Continues** Industrial Herald Weekly.

SI
**INDUSTRIAL NEWS AND RESEARCH.** Periodical. English. Singapore Institute of Standards and Industrial Research, 1 Science Park Drive, Singapore Science Park, Singapore 0511 Singapore. **Tel** 011 65 778-7777, **FAX** 011 65 778-0086, telex RS 28499 SISIR. **LC** T1; .I242. **DD** 605.

CN/0824-8133
**INDUSTRIAL RESEARCH AND DEVELOPMENT STATISTICS ... WITH ... FORECASTS.** See Science and Technology-Abstracting, Bibliographies and Statistics.

UK/0265-3214
**INDUSTRIAL RESEARCH IN THE UNITED KINGDOM.** (1980)-. English. ir. $323.00. Longman Group Ltd., Fourth Avenue, Longman House, Harlow Essex CM19 5SR England. **Tel** 011 44 279 429655, **FAX** 011 44 279 431059, telex 81259. **(Subscription address:** US and Canada: Gale Research Co., 835 Penobscot Building, Detroit, MI 48226) **LC** T177.G7; I5. **DD** 607/.2/.41. **Continues** Industrial Research in Britain.
**Desc:** Contains information about a wide range of organizations, firms, and agencies engaged in industrial research in the United Kingdom.

AT
**INDUSTRIAL RESEARCH NEWS / CSIRO.** VFOAT IRN; I.R.N. (19??)-. Periodical. English. bm. Free. CSIRO Publications, PO Box 89, 314 Albert Street, East Melborne Victoria 3002 Australia. **Tel** 011 63 4187333, 4187217, **FAX** 011 63 4190459, telex AA 30236. **LC** Discard.
**Ind/Abst** AESIS Q.; Coal Abstr.

IT
**INF INN : INFORMAZIONE INNOVATIVA.** Italian. Twenty-two times a year. L600000. Centro Studi L' Uomo Ambiente, Via Delle Palme 113, 35137 Padoua Italy. **Tel** 11 39 49 8759622, **FAX** 11 39 49 657264. **Ad Acc. Circ:** 3,000 (ctrl).
**Desc:** Biotechnology, science technology, scientific, technological and legislative news, legislation and environmental matter.

GW/0170-4664
**INFOBRIEF RESEARCH AND TECHNOLOGY.** [Infobrief res. technol.]. VFOAT Technologie-Beratung-Siegfried-Neumann-GmbH-und-Co.-KG (Wachtberg):Infobrief / Technologie-Beratung-Siegfried-Neumann-GmbH-und-Co.-KG; Research and Technology. (1977)-. Periodical. English. sm (24 issues per year). 10500F Europe; 12400F other. InfoBrief Sarl, PO Box 206, 2012 Luxembourg, Belgium. **Tel** 011 352 330833. **UDC** 6 : :001.89 :338.246.027. Index Available Published separately--free--upon request. **Continues** INFODOC Research and Technology, 0170-4672.

AT/1031-953X
**INFONET.** English. qt. (Comes with Victorian Information Technology Teachers Association membership). VIITA, PO Box 261, Abotsford VIC 3067 Australia. **Tel** (03)419 9622.
**Ind/Abst** Aust. Educ. Index.

MX/0185-0261
**INFORMACION CIENTIFICA Y TECNOLOGICA.** (INFORMACION CIENTIFICA Y TECNOLOGICA : ICYT.). [Inf. cient. tecnol.]. **Added/Corp** Consejo Nacional de Ciencia y Tecnologia (Mexico). VFOAT ICyT. Vol. 1 No. 1 (July 15, 1979)-. Periodical. Spanish. Twelve times a year. $46.00 Americas; $57.00 Europe; $70.00 Africa; $77.00 Asia. Consejo Nacional Ciencia y Tecno, Av Constituyentes 1046 Lomas A, CP 11950 Mexico DF Mexico. **Tel** 011 52 5 3277400. **LC** Q23; .I55. **DD** 505. **CODEN** ICTEEB. Documents available from Ask*IEEE.
**Ind/Abst** INSPEC (1986).

SZ/0019-9915
**INFORMATIK.** *Suspended.* [Informatik]. Vol. 16 (1969)-Suspended (Jan. 1992). Periodical. German. bm. $28.01. Deutscher Judo Verband, Redaktion Ippon Segegwaldweg 40, D 12557 Berlin Germany. **Tel** 011 49 711 210770, telex 051 678. **LC** Q224.3.G3; I53.

Documents available from Ask*IEEE. **Continues** Ziid Zeitschrift.
**Ind/Abst** BMT Abstr. (-1990); Energy Res. Abstr. (March 1982-); INSPEC (1972-); Libr. Inf. Sci. Abstr.; Math. Rev.

IT
**INFORMATION & TECHNOLOGY.** ESTE, Via North Battaglia, 22, 20127 Milan Italy. **Tel** 011 39 2 55018039.

IT
**INFORMATION AND TECHNOLOGY.** Italian. mo. L80000.00 Italy; L130000.00 other. ESTE, Via North Battaglia, 22, 20127 Milan Italy. **Tel** 011 39 2 55018039. **Continues** EDP Telematica Notizie.
**Ind/Abst** Infomat Int. Bus.

US/0888-1723
**INFORMATION BULLETIN / ERIC CLEARINGHOUSE FOR SCIENCE, MATHEMATICS AND ENVIRONMENTAL EDUCATION.** [Inf. bull. - ERIC Clgh. Sci. Math. Environ. Educ.]. **Added/Corp** ERIC Clearinghouse for Science, Mathematics, and Environmental Education. (Spring 1979)-. Bulletin. English. qt. $3.00. ERIC Clearinghouse for Science, Mathematics, and Environmental Education, 1200 Chambers OSU, Columbus OH 43212. **Tel** (614)292-6717. **ED** Patricia Blosser. **DD** 507. **Circ:** 3,500.
**Desc:** Presents three topical issues and one general issue each year. Topical issues focus on: science, mathematics, and environmental education.

US/0030-8889
**INFORMATION BULLETIN - PACIFIC SCIENCE ASSOCIATION.** [Inf. bull. - Pac. Sci. Assoc.]. **Main/Corp** Pacific Science Association. **Added/Corp** Bernice Pauahi Bishop Museum. (July 1949)-. Bulletin. English. Four times a year (includes supplements of "Pacific Research Titles"). $25.00 (individuals), $50.00 (institutions) membership. Pacific Science Association, PO Box 17801, Honolulu HI 96817. **Tel** (808)847-3511, **FAX** (808)841-8968. **ED** L. G. Eldredge (editor's telephone: (808)848-4139). **Circ:** 800.

●UK
**INFORMATION MANAGEMENT & TECHNOLOGY.** See Library and Information Sciences-Abstracting, Bibliographies and Statistics.

US
**INFORMATION RESEARCH AND RESOURCE REPORTS.** Vol. 1-. Monographic series. English. Price varies per volume. Elsevier Science Publishing Company Inc, Madison Square Station, PO Box 882, New York NY 10159-0882. **Tel** (212)633-3950, **FAX** (212)633-3990. Documents available from Ask*IEEE.
**Ind/Abst** INSPEC.

FR
**INFORMATION TECHNOLOGIES.** (19??)-. Periodical. French. Twenty-three times a year. 2550.00F France; 2800.00F other. Bouhot & Le Gendre Publishers, 75 Bis Rue de Bellevue, F 92100 Boulogne France. **Tel** 011 33 1 46040708. **(Subscription address:** Centrale des Revues, 11 rue Gossin, 92543 Montrouge Cedex France.) **Continues** Informatique US en Direct, 0243-4695.

AT/1322-3526
**INFORMATION TECHNOLOGY MANAGEMENT.** English. an. 285.00Aus$ Australia; 295.00Aus$ New Zealand; 300.00Aus$ Asia; 305.00Aus$ US and Europe. Paul Budde Communication Pty Ltd, 2643 George Downes Drive, Bucketty NSW 2250 Australia. **Tel** 61 (0)49 988 144, **FAX** 61 (0)49 988 247. **ED** Paul Budde. Index available. **Ad Acc. Pr Rev. Circ:** 8,100 (ctrl).
**Desc:** Describes, in a non-technical way, new technologies that form the basis of telecommunications applications. Aimed at senior management and marketing/sales management.

●FR
**INFORMATION TECHNOLOGY OUTLOOK: LES PERSPECTIVES DES TECHNOLOGIES DE L'INFORMATION.** **Added/Corp** Organisation for Economic Co-operation and Development. Committee for Information, Computer, and Communications Policy. VFOAT Perspectives des Technologies de l'Information. (1992)-. English (French). OECD Publications and Information Center, 2 rue Andre-Pascal, 75775 Paris Cedex 16 France. **Tel** 011 33 1 45248167, US;(202)785-6323, **FAX** 011 33 1 45248500 OR 45248176, telex 620 160 OCDE.

●US/1060-3344
**INFORMATION TECHNOLOGY SERVICES MEMBER DIRECTORY.** **Added/Corp** Information Technology Association of America. Information Technology Services Division. (1992)-. Directory. English. Information Technology Association of America, 1616 North Fort Myer Drive, Suite 1300, Arlington VA 22209-3106.

GW
**INFORMATIONEN - UNIVERSITAT BIELEFELD.** **Main/Corp** Universitat Bielefeld. German. Universitat Bielefeld, Postfach 8640, 48 Bielefeld Germany. **LC** Q180.G4; B54.

FR
**INFORMATIONS ET DOCUMENTS - BCEOM.** **Main/Corp** France. Bureau Central d'Etude pour les Equipements d'Outre-Mer. Periodical. French (summaries and/or abstracts in English and Spanish). qt. Bureau Central d'Etudes pour les Equipements d'Outre-Mer, 15 Square Max-Hymans, Paris 15E France. **LC** T2; .B87A.

GW
**INFORMATIONSBLATT FUR DEUTSCHE WISSENSCHAFTLER IM AUSLAND.** German. ir. Bouvier GMBH & Company KG ABT Verlag, Am HOF 28, D53113 Bonn Germany. **Tel** 011 49 228 7290141. **LC** Q49; .I54. **DD** 509/.43.

AU
**INFORMATIONSTAG FUR SPRENGTECHNIK INTERNATIONAL : PROCEEDINGS / MEDIENENHABER UND HERSTELLER, WIRTSCHAFTSFORDERUNGSTNSTITUT DER KAMMER DER GEWERPLICHEN WIRTSCHAFT FUR GEROSTEREICH.** Proceedings. German (English). an. Wirtschaftsforderungsinstitut der Kammer der Gewerblichen Wirtschaft fur Oberosterreich, Wiener Strasse 150, 4024 Linz Austria. **LC** TA748; .I54A. **DD** 622/.2.

FR
**INFORMATIQUE ET STRATEGIE D'ENTREPRISE.** (19??)-. Periodical. French. Six times a year. 3300.00F France; 3400.00 other. Bouhot & Le Gendre Publishers, 75 Bis Rue de Bellevue, F 92100 Boulogne France. **Tel** 011 33 1 46040708. **(Subscription address:** Centrale des Revues, 11 rue Gossin, 92543 Montrouge Cedex France.) **Continues** Le Conseil Informatique a la Direction Generale, 1156-4903.

FR/0243-4695
**INFORMATIQUE U.S. EN DIRECT, L'.** *Title Change.* [Inform. U.S. direct]. VFOAT Informatique United States en direct. (19??)-(19??). Periodical. French. Twenty-three times a year. Bouhot & Le Gendre Publishers, 75 Bis Rue de Bellevue, F 92100 Boulogne France. **Tel** 011 33 1 46040708. **(Subscription address:** Centrale des Revues, 11 rue Gossin, 92543 Montrouge Cedex France.) **UDC** A681.3. **Continued by** L'Informatique aux Etats-Unis, 0754-0426.

BL/0019-0233
**INFORMATIVO DO INT.** [Inf. INT]. **Added/Corp** Instituto Nacional de Tecnologia (Brazil). VFOAT Informativo do I.N.T. **VAT** Informativo do Instituto Nacional de Tecnologia. (1973)-. Periodical. Portuguese. qt. **CODEN** ININDP. Documents available from CASDDS. **Continues** Instituto Nacional de Tecnologia (Brazil) Boletim do INT.
**Ind/Abst** Chem. Abstr.

CK/0302-4830
**INFORMATIVO - SNI.** **Main/Corp** Sistema Nacional de Informacion. **VAT** Informativo - Sistema Nacional de Informacion. V. 1- May 1972-. Spanish. Colciencias, Transversal 9A/#133-28, Bogota Colombia. **Tel** 2179800, telex 44305. **LC** Q224.3.C7; S56A.

UN
**INFORMATSIONNYI UKAZATEL BIBLIOGRAFICHESKIKH RABOT, VYPOLNENNYKH BIBLIOTEKAMI I NAUCHNYMI UCHREZHDENIIAMI SISTEMY AN USSR V ... GODU / AKADEMIIA NAUK UKRAINSKOI SSR, TSENTRALNAIA BIBLIOTEKA.** Began with Vol. for 1971. Russian (Ukrainian). an. **LC** Z7403; .I603; Q158. **DD** 016.5.

UY/0378-8601
**INFORME DE INVESTIGACION - CENTRO DE INVESTIGACIONES TECHNOGICAS.** (INFORME DE INVESTIGACION / ANCAP, CENTRO DE INVESTIGACIONES TECNOLOGICAS.). [Inf. invest. - Cent. invest. tecnol.]. **Added/Corp** Uruguay. Administracion Nacional de Combustibles, Alcohol y Portland. Centro de Investigaciones Technologicas. (19??)-. Monographic series. Spanish. **CODEN** IICUDF. Documents available from CASDDS.
**Ind/Abst** Chem. Abstr.

VE/0378-1836
**INFORME - UNIVERSIDAD CENTRAL DE VENEZUELA, FACULTAD DE INGENIERIA, ESCUELA DE GEOLOGIA Y MINAS, LABORATORIO DE PETROGRAFIA Y GEOQUIMICA.** [Inf., Univ. Cent. Venez., Esc. Geol. Minas, Lab. Petrogr. Geoquim.].

**Main/Corp** Venezuela. Universidad Central, Caracas. Escuela de Geologia y Minas. Academic Scholarly Publication. Multiple languages. Price varies per volume. Universidad Central Caracas / Venezuela, Apartado 50926, Caracas 105 Venezuela. **CODEN** IUCGDN. Documents available from CASDDS.
**Ind/Abst** Chem. Abstr. (1976); GeoRef.

●CN/1197-4532
**INITIATIVE (ST. JOHN).** (INITIATIVE / JUNIOR HIGH TECHNOLOGY.). [Initiative]. **Added/Corp** New Brunswick Teachers' Association. Junior High Technology Council. Vol. 19, No. 1 (Fall 1992)-. Periodical. English. Three times a year. New Brunswick Teachers' Association, PO Box 752, Fredericton New Brunswick E3B 5R6 Canada. **Tel** (506)452-8921. **DD** 607. ***Continues*** *Industrial Arts Initiative., 0710-1945.*

IS/0334-3847
**INNOVATION.** ***Ceased.*** [Innovation]. (Dec. 1975)-(19??). Periodical. English. Ten times a year (monthly with June/July and Nov./Dec. issues combined). A G Publications Ltd, PO Box 7422, 31070 Haifa Israel. **Tel** 972 4 255104, FAX 972 4 255104. **ED** A Greenfield. **LC** T173.8; .I55. **DD** 338/.064/09569405. Index available. **Circ:** 1,000. ***Absorbed*** *Technical Progress in Israel.*
**Desc:** A report on industrial research and development and science based industry in Israel.
**Ind/Abst** PROMT [Full Txt.]; PTS Newsl. Database [Full Txt.].

LU/0255-0806
**INNOVATION AND TECHNOLOGY TRANSFER/ DG XIII.** **Added/Corp** Commission of the European Communities. Directorate-General XIII. Vol. 9/3 (July 1988)-. Newsletter. English (French, German, Italian and Spanish). ir (5-6 issues per year). Free on request. Office for Official Publications of the European Communities, 2 Rue Mercier, 2985 Luxembourg Luxembourg. **Tel** 011 352 499281, FAX 011 352 488573. **ED** A. Von Witzleben. **CODEN** ITETEW. **Bk Rev. Circ:** 48,000. ***Continues in part*** *Newsletter, New Technologies and Innovation Policy.*
**Desc:** Contains information on technology transfer.
**Ind/Abst** Chem. Bus. Bull.; Chem. Bus. NewsBase (1990-); Chem. Bus. Update.

AT/0156-0069
**INNOVATION IN AUSTRALIAN TECHNOLOGY / AUSTRALIAN ACADEMY OF TECHNOLOGICAL SCIENCES.** ***Ceased.*** **Added/Corp** Australian Academy of Technological Sciences. Vol. (1970/1975)-(199?). English. be. Australian Academy of Technological Sciences, Ian McLennan House, 197 Royal Parade, Parkville, Victoria Australia 3052. **Tel** 61 3 3470622, FAX 61 3 3478237. **LC** T173.8; .I566. **DD** 609.94.
**Ind/Abst** AESIS Q.

UK/0264-9861
**INNOVATION ST. ANDREWS.** **See** Engineering.

●US/1059-2091
**INNOVATIONS & IDEAS.** **VFOAT** Innovations and Ideas; American Innovations. (1992)-. English. $29.99. Publishing & Business Consultants, PO Box 75392, Los Angeles CA 90075. **Tel** (213)732-3477, FAX (213)732-9123. **ED** Andeson Napoleon Atia. **Ad Acc.** Full Page (B&W) $5750.00. Half Page (B&W) $3575.00. Full Page (Color) $8750.00 (2 color). Half Page (Color) $5500.00 (2 color). **Circ:** 166,000 total.
**Desc:** Focused on the curious minded individual fascinated with the practical applications of science at home, office or in the environment. Features articles on new products, devices and services with direct relevance to the consumer.

US/0890-300X
**INNOVATOR'S DIGEST.** (198?)-. English. bw. $269.00 US; $309.00 Canada; $389.00 other. Infoteam Inc., PO Box 15640, Plantation FL 33318. **Tel** (305)473-9560. **DD** 338. **[CCC].** available on an online database (files 16,636/Full-Text) from DIALOG. ***Continues*** *Information for Innovators.*
**Ind/Abst** PROMT [Full Txt.]; PTS Newsl. Database [Full Txt.].

IT
**INNOVAZIONE : IMPIANTI E PRODUZIONE.** ***Ceased.*** (19??)-(Dec. 1993). Franco Angeli Riviste SRL, Viale Monza 106, 20127 Milan Italy. **Tel** 011 39 2 2827651, 011 39 2 289562.

●US/1067-909X
**INOCULUM (ITHACA, N.Y.).** (INOCULUM : NEWSLETTER OF THE MYCOLOGICAL SOCIETY OF AMERICA.). [Inoculum]. **Main/Corp** Mycological Society of America. **VFOAT** MSA Newsletter; Newsletter. Vol. 43, Nos. 1/2/3 (June 1992)-. Newsletter. English. qt. **DD** 589. ***Continues*** *Mycological Society of America. Newsletter, 0541-4938.*

US
**INQUIRY : SCIENCE AND TECHNOLOGY AT THE AMES LABORATORY.** **Added/Corp** Ames Laboratory. Vol. 1, No. 1 (Winter 1991)-. Periodical. English. qt. Ames Laboratory, 201 Spedding Hall, Ames IA 50011-3020.

CN/0836-3218
**INRS NOUVELLES.** (INRS NOUVELLES : BULLETIN D'INFORMATION DE L'INSTITUT NATIONAL DE LA RECHERCHE SCIENTIFIQUE.). [INRS nouv.]. **VFOAT** Bulletin de l'Institut National de la Recherche Scientifique. **VAT** Institut National de la Recherche Scientifique Nouvelles. Vol. 1, No. 1 (May 1985)-. Bulletin. French. qt. Free. Institut National de la Recherche Scientifique / Canada, CP 7500, Sainte-Foy Quebec G1V 4C7 Canada. **DD** 507/.20714. ctrl circ. ***Continues*** *Intercom, 0380-4755.*

●US/1061-2629
**INSIDE BT.** **See** Communication-Telecommunications.

IT
**INSTALLATORE TECNICO.** (19??)-. Italian. mo (11 issues). L70000 Italy; L140000 other. Cida Editrice Srl, Viale Certosa 238, 20156 Milan Italy. **Tel** 011 39 2 3085141.

US
**INSTRUMENT REPORT.** English. mo. $195.00 US; $275.00 other. Applied Technology Associates, 839 West Belden Ave, Chicago IL 60614. **Tel** (312)929-5507. **ED** Robert DeCresce. Index available. cum. index.
**Desc:** Publications about new instruments and products in the clinical laboratory. It's focus is on the cost effectiveness and operational advantages of new technologies.

GW/0340-8655
**INSTRUMENT UND FORSCHUNG.** Began in 1974. Academic Scholarly Publication. German. ir. Colors Messtchnik GmbH, Barbarossastrasse 3, Postfach 12 40, W-7073 Lorch/Wurtt Germany. **LC** Q184; .I59. **CODEN** INFODD. Documents available from CASDDS.
**Ind/Abst** Chem. Abstr.

US
**INSTUMENT REPORT.** English (French). mo. $225.00. Applied Technology Associates, 839 West Belden Ave, Chicago IL 60614. **Tel** (312)929-5507.

CL
**INTEC.** **Main/Corp** Comite de Investigaciones Tecnologicas de Chile. (19??)-. Spanish. be. INTEC, Avda Santa Matria 6500, Casilla 667, Santiago Chile. **Tel** 2282083. **LC** T4; .C62a.

●US/1065-2469
**INTEGRAL TRANSFORMS AND SPECIAL FUNCTIONS.** (1993)-. Periodical. English. qt. $330.00. Gordon & Breach Science Publishers, PO Box 90, Reading RG1 8JL England. **Tel** 011 44 734 560080, FAX 011 44 734 568211. **(Subscription address:** Gordon & Breach Science Publishers / England, PO Box 90, Reading RG1 8JL England.**)**

US/0731-2911
**INTER-SOCIETY COLOR COUNCIL NEWS.** [Inter-Soc. Color Counc. news]. **Added/Corp** Inter-Society Color Council. **VFOAT** News. (19??)-. English. bm. $60.00 library; $45.00 other. Inter-Society Color Council Inc, 11491 Sunset Hills Road, Reston VA 22090. **Tel** (301)589-4747. **ED** Mary Ellen Zuyus. **LC** QC495; .I58. **DD** 535.6/05. **Bk Rev. Circ:** 1,000 (ctrl). ***Continues*** *Newsletter, 0300-7588.*
**Desc:** Reports and developments relating to the science of color from the standpoint of the artist, educator, scientist, colorist and designer.

VE/0378-1844
**INTERCIENCIA.** [Interciencia]. **Added/Corp** Asociacion Interciencia. Vol. 1 (May/June 1976)-. Academic Scholarly Publication. Multiple languages (English, Portuguese and Spanish). bm. $60.00 US and Canada; $63.00 Europe, China, USSR and Israel; $45.00 Latin America and Africa; $65.00 other. Interciencia, Apartado de Correo 51842, Caracas 1050A Venezuela. **Tel** 011 58 2 923224. **ED** Marcel Roche. **LC** Q4; .I617. **DD** 505. **NLM** W1 IN671. **CODEN** ITRCDB. **[CCC].** Index available. cum. index. **Pr Rev. Circ:** 2,500. Documents available from The Genuine Article, BIOSIS Document Express, CASDDS, Documents on Demand.
**Desc:** A multidisciplinary journal with its principal object being the cooperation among the scientific community in Latin America, the areas of the Amazons, environment, and education. Original articles and research accepted.
**Ind/Abst** Biol. Abstr.; Chem. Abstr. (1976-1983); Coal Abstr.; Curr. Contents, Agric. Biol. Environ. Sci.; Energy Inf. Abstr.; Energy Res. Abstr. (Feb. 1977-); Environ. Abstr.; GeoRef; HAPI Hisp. Am. Period. Index; Int. Aerosp. Abstr.; Life Sci. Collect.; Pollut. Abstr. Indexes; Protozoolog. Abstr.; Res. Alert [Full Cov.]; Rural Dev. Abstr.; Sci. Cit. Index (1976-); SCISEARCH; Soc. Sci. Cit. Index [Select. Cov.]; Soils Fert.; Wildl. Rev.; World Agric. Econ.

UK/0308-0188
**INTERDISCIPLINARY SCIENCE REVIEWS : ISR.** [ISR, Interdiscip. sci. rev.]. **VFOAT** ISR. Vol. 1, No. 1 (March 1976)-. Academic Scholarly Publication. English. Four times a year (Mar., June, Sept., Dec.). £165.00 EEC Countries; £189.75 others. The Institute of Materials, 1 Carlton House Terrace, London SW1Y 5DB England. **Tel** 011 44 71 839 4071, FAX (071)839 2078. **ED** A. R. Michaelis. **LC** Q1; .I577. **DD** 505. **NLM** W1; IN678. **CODEN** ISCRD8. **[CCC]. Bk Rev. Ad Acc. Pr Rev. Circ:** 800 (ctrl). available on microfilm and microfiche from University Microfilms International (UMI). Documents available from The Genuine Article, Ask*IEEE, CASDDS.
**Desc:** Publishes reviews by international experts in the physical, biological, engineering and social sciences. The primary concerns are the interaction between two or more natural sciences or technologies, the effects of science and technology on society, and the furthering of cultural and scientific links between science, the arts and humanities. Provides a medium through which specialists and students of all scientific disciplines can learn and communicate with each other to their mutual benefit.
**Ind/Abst** Arts Humanit. Citation Index [Select. Cov.]; Chem. Abstr.; CSA Neuro. Abstr. (?-?); Curr. Biotechnol.; Curr. Contents Phys. Chem. Earth Sci.; EMBASE; Energy Res. Abstr. (Oct. 1978-); GeoRef; INSPEC (March 1976-); Int. Aerosp. Abstr.; Math. Rev.; Life Sci. Collect.; Res. Alert [Full Cov.]; SCISEARCH; Soc. Sci. Cit. Index [Full Cov.].

CN/0826-4864
**INTERFACE (MONTREAL. 1984).** (INTERFACE : LA REVUE DE L'ACFAS.). [Interface]. **Added/Corp** Association Canadienne-Francaise pour l'Avancement des Sciences. (1984)-. Periodical. French. Six times a year (Jan., Mar., May, July, Sept., Nov.). 36.00Can$ (individuals); 78.00Can$ (institutions). Association for Canadian Francaise Advancement Sciences, 425 de la Gauchetiere Est., Montreal Quebec H2L 2M7 Canada. **Tel** (514)849-0045, FAX (514)849-5558. **ED** Sophie Malavoy. **DD** 507/.20714. Index available. cum. index. **Bk Rev**, (Qty: 5). **Ad Acc, Adv Mgr:** Pierette LeFrancois, **Tel** (514)466-3095. **Circ:** 8,000 (ctrl). ***Continues*** *Association Canadienne-Francaise pour l'Avancement des Sciences. Bulletin de l'A C F A S., 0066-8850.*
**Desc:** A magazine for French speaking scientists. Covers all fields: humanities, natural sciences, engineering, and biology.
**Ind/Abst** Can. Period. Index (Jan. 1991-); Point Repere (1988-).

NE
**INTERMEDIAIR.** VNU Business Publications BV, Postbus 9479, 1006 AC Amsterdam Netherlands. **Tel** 011 31 20 5102911, 011 31 20 5102879, FAX 011 31 20 6170291.

UK/0020-580X
**INTERNATIONAL ABSTRACTS IN OPERATIONS RESEARCH.** **See** Science and Technology-Abstracting, Bibliographies and Statistics.

US/0749-0682
**INTERNATIONAL ANNUAL JOURNAL OF ARTS, SCIENCES, ENGINEERING, AGRICULTURE, AND TECHNOLOGY.** (1991)-. Periodical. English. an. $200.00. Siveast Consultants, PO Box 271, 410 South State Street, Dover DE 19901. **ED** C V Ramasastry. **Bk Rev. Circ:** 200 (ctrl).
**Desc:** Aims to provide link between research and practice between researchers, university professors, consultants from various specializations. Aims to bring together new ideas and research findings.

GW
**INTERNATIONAL BIBLIOGRAPHY ON OPERATIONS RESEARCH, CONTROL THEORY, SYSTEM SCIENCE.** **VFOAT** IBOR. V. 2-. Bibliography. English. ir. $79.13. Kontohows I & D Service, August Metz WEG 9D, 6100 Darmstadt Germany. **LC** Z7672; .I57; T57.6. **DD** 016.0014/24. ***Continues*** *Internationale Grosse Operations Research Bibliographie.*

US/0364-3670
**INTERNATIONAL CODEN DIRECTORY.** (INTERNATIONAL CODEN DIRECTORY [MICROFORM].). [Int. CODEN dir.]. **Added/Corp** American Chemical Society. (197?)-. Directory. English. ir (directory published every five years, supplements published annually). $1600.00 (includes supplements). Chemical Abstracts Service, (Subsidiary of The American Chemical Society), 2540 Olentangy River Road, PO Box 3012, Columbus OH 43210-0012. **Tel** (614)447-3731, (800)753-4227, FAX (614)447-3751. **(Subscription address:** Chemical Abstracts Service, Customer Service Department, PO Box 3012, Columbus OH 43210.**) LC** Microfiche 84/92,042 (Z). **DD** 505. **CODEN** ICDIDA. ***Continues*** *CODEN for Periodical Titles.*

FR
**INTERNATIONAL DEFENCE ET TECHNOLOGY.** French (English). qt. 705.19F France; 720.00F Europe; 850.00F other. Connection

International, 87 Rue de l'Amiral Roussin, 75015 Paris France. **Tel** 011 33 1 45302228, FAX 011 33 1 45302269. **Ad Acc.**

FR/1148-3555
**INTERNATIONAL DOMOTIQUE NEWS PARIS.** (INTERNATIONAL DOMOTIQUE NEWS). (1989)-. Periodical. English. mo (10 issues per year). 1800.00F France; 2000.00F other. Domopresse, CNIT BP 530, 92053 Paris La Defense, France. **Tel** 011 33 1 46921830. **ED** Bruno De Latour. **UDC** 681.3. **Bk Rev. Ad Acc.**
**Desc:** Newsletter on home automation and the intelligent building industry.

US/0742-3985
**INTERNATIONAL GUIDE TO PERIODICALS & REFERENCE WORKS.** [Int. guide period. ref. works]. **Main/Corp** Maxwell Scientific International. **VFOAT** International Guide to Periodicals and Reference Works. 1984/85-. English. be. Free. Maxwell Scientific International, Fairview Park, Elmsford NJ 10523. ***Continues*** *Maxwell Scientific International. Guide to Collections of International Periodicals, 0197-6605.*

US/0882-3553
**INTERNATIONAL HIGH TECHNOLOGY REPORT.** ***Ceased.*** [Int. high technol. rep.]. **VFOAT** IHTR. Ceased (April 1986). Periodical. English. mo. Amersham Associates, 733 15th Street NW, Suite 1036, Washington DC 20005. **Tel** (202)328-8709. **ED** David S Harvey. **DD** 621. **Circ:** 150.
**Desc:** A report on key trends in overseas high technology development from a business viewpoint.

UK
**INTERNATIONAL JOURNAL FOR DEVELOPMENT TECHNOLOGY.**
***Suspended.*** English. qt. $25.00. International Center Technical Research, 11/12 Pall Mall, London SW1Y 5LU England. **Tel** 930-682516. **ED** B Nath. **CODEN** IJDTDO. **Bk Rev. Circ:** 1,400.
**Desc:** Provides a forum for the discussion of technologies relevant to the less developed countries and the way they can be identified, developed, and applied.
**Ind/Abst** Agrofor. Abstr.

UK/0020-7179
**INTERNATIONAL JOURNAL OF CONTROL.** [Int. j. control]. Vol. 1 (Jan. 1965)-. Periodical. English. mo. £845.00 UK; $1395.00 other. Taylor & Francis Ltd., Rankine Road, Basingstoke Hampshire, RG24 8PR United Kingdom. **Tel** 011 44 256 840366, FAX 011 44 256 479438, telex 858540. **(Subscription address:** Taylor & Francis Inc., 1900 Frost Road, Suite 101, Bristol PA 19007-1598.**) ED** John O'Reilly (editor's address: Department of Electronics and Electrical Engineering, University of Glasgow, Glasgow, G12 8QQ Scotland). **LC** TJ212; .I55. **CODEN** IJCOAZ. **[CCC]. Pr Rev.** available on microfilm and microfiche from University Microfilms International (UMI). Documents available from Article Express International, The Genuine Article, Ask*IEEE, CASDDS, Documents on Demand. ***Continues in part*** *Journal of Electronics and Control.*
**Desc:** Devoted to control systems in its widest sense, publishing high quality papers in diverse areas of control theory and control applications. Publishes important papers on multivariable control, adaptive control, non-linear systems and computer-aided design. Aims to promote the increasingly important topics of intelligent control, robotics, automation, controller implementation, etc.
**Ind/Abst** Bioeng. Abstr.; Chem. Abstr.; Compumath Citation Index [Full Cov.]; Curr. Contents Eng. Tech. Appl. Sci.; Curr. Technol. Index; Ei Page One; Electron. Commun. Abstr. J.; Energy Inf. Abstr.; Eng. Index Annu.; Environ. Abstr.; INSPEC (1968-); Int. Aerosp. Abstr.; ISMEC Bull.; Math. Rev.; Nucl. Sci. Abstr.; Ornamental Hort.; Pollut. Abstr. Indexes; Res. Alert [Full Cov.]; Saf. Sci. Abstr. J.; Sci. Cit. Index; SCISEARCH; Stat. Theory Method Abstr. (1970-1981); Zentralbl. Math. Ihre Grenzgeb.

US/0020-7233
**INTERNATIONAL JOURNAL OF ENVIRONMENTAL STUDIES, THE.** **See** Environmental Issues.

US/0899-9457
**INTERNATIONAL JOURNAL OF IMAGING SYSTEMS AND TECHNOLOGY.** [Int. j. imaging syst. technol.]. **VFOAT** Imaging Systems and Technology. Vol. 1, No. 1 Summer (1989)-. Periodical. English. Four times a year. $260.00 (US); $300.00 (Canada and Mexico); $315.00 (other). John Wiley & Sons, Inc., 605 Third Avenue, New York NY 10158-0012. **Tel** (212)850-6000, (212)850-6645, FAX (212)850-6088, telex 12-7063. **(Subscription address:** John Wiley & Sons / England, Baffins Lane, Chichester, West Sussex PO19 1UD England.**) ED** Glen Wade, Hua Lee, and Enders A. Robinson. **LC** TK8315; .I59. **DD** 621.36/7. **CODEN** IJITEG. **[CCC].** available on microfilm and microfiche from University Microfilms International (UMI). Documents available from Article Express International, Ask*IEEE.
**Desc:** Offers comprehensive coverage of the theory and applications of areas such as electrical engineering, mechanical engineering, chemistry, radiology, geology, geography, astronomy, computer science, mathematics, material science and oceanography.
**Ind/Abst** Ei Page One; Eng. Index Annu.; GeoRef; INSPEC (1989-); Int. Aerosp. Abstr.

●US/1055-7490
**INTERNATIONAL JOURNAL OF MATHEMATICAL AND STATISTICAL SCIENCES.** (1992)-. Statistical Publication. English. sa. $100.00 (institutions). Berkley Cambridge Press, PO Box 947, Carmichael CA 95609-0947.

NE/1037-0544
**INTERNATIONAL JOURNAL OF SALT LAKE RESEARCH.** (1992)-. English. qt. $288.00. Kluwer Academic Publishers, Postbus 322, 3300 AH Dordrecht, The Netherlands. **Tel** 011 (31) 78 524400, FAX 011 31 78 183273, telex 20083. **ED** W.D. Williams.
**Desc:** Aims to encourage and support publication of articles about inland saline waters and other non-marine saline environments, and provide a better focus for such publication. Accepts papers or reviews on any topic of chemical, physical, biological, geological, geochemical and hydrological interest.

US/0891-5083
**INTERNATIONAL JOURNAL OF SCIENCE AND TECHNOLOGY.** (INTERNATIONAL JOURNAL OF SCIENCE AND TECHNOLOGY : IJST.). [Int. j. sci. technol.]. **Added/Corp** Foundation for International Development. **VFOAT** IJST. Vol. 1, No. 1 (Spring 1988)-. Academic Scholarly Publication. English. Twice a year (Spring & Fall). $50.00. Association of Muslim Scientists Engineers, PO Box 38, Plainfield IN 46168. **Tel** (317)839-8157, FAX (317)839-1840, telex (650)225-4110. **ED** Dr. Iqbal J. Unus. **LC** Q1; .I584. **DD** 505. **CODEN** IJSTEW. ($45.00). cum. index. **Bk Rev**, (Qty: 1). **Ad Acc, Adv Mgr:** Dina Soliman, **Tel** (317)839-8157. **Pr Rev. Circ:** 800 (ctrl).
**Desc:** Concerned with the collection, distribution and dissemination of science and engineering information within an Islamic framework through well-written scholarly articles.
**Ind/Abst** Peace Res. Abstr. J. (1962-1965).

UK/0950-0693
**INTERNATIONAL JOURNAL OF SCIENCE EDUCATION.** [Int. j. sci. educ.]. Vol. 9, No. 1 (Jan./March 1987)-. Academic Scholarly Publication. English (French and German). bm. £188.00 UK; $310.00 other. Taylor & Francis Ltd., Rankine Road, Basingstoke Hampshire, RG24 8PR United Kingdom. **Tel** 011 44 256 840366, FAX 011 44 256 479438, telex 858540. **(Subscription address:** Taylor & Francis Inc., 1900 Frost Road, Suite 101, Bristol PA 19007-1598.**) ED** John K. Gilbert, Kate Johnston, Beverley Bell and Gaalen Erikson. **LC** Q181.A1; E9. **DD** 507/.1. **CODEN** ISEDEB. **[CCC]. Bk Rev. Pr Rev.** available on microfilm and microfiche from University Microfilms International (UMI). Documents available from The Genuine Article, BIOSIS Document Express, Ask*IEEE. ***Continues*** *European Journal of Science Education, 0140-5284.*
**Desc:** Bridges the gap between research and practice, providing information, ideas and opinion, serving as a medium for the publication of definitive research findings, and setting these in the context of the classroom. The journal is comprised of general articles, papers on innovations and developments, research reports and book reviews.
**Ind/Abst** Biol. Abstr. (1987-); Br. Educ. Index; Curr. Contents Soc. Behav. Sci.; Curr. Index J. Educ. (1987-); Educ. Index (1992-); EMBASE (1987-); INSPEC (1987-); Res. Alert [Full Cov.]; Res. High. Educ. Abstr.; Soc. Sci. Cit. Index [Full Cov.]; Sociol. Educ. Abstr.; Stud. Women Abstr.; Tech. Educ. Train. Abstr.

NE/1381-2416
**INTERNATIONAL JOURNAL OF SPEECH TECHNOLOGY.** (19??)-. English. sa. $239.00. Kluwer Academic Publishers, Postbus 322, 3300 AH Dordrecht, The Netherlands. **Tel** 011 (31) 78 524400, FAX 011 31 78 183273, telex 20083.

NE/0957-7572
**INTERNATIONAL JOURNAL OF TECHNOLOGY AND DESIGN EDUCATION.** [Int. j. technol. des. educ.]. (1990)-. Periodical. English. tq. $226.00. Kluwer Academic Publishers, Postbus 322, 3300 AH Dordrecht, The Netherlands. **Tel** 011 (31) 78 524400, FAX 011 31 78 183273, telex 20083. **ED** Edgar Jenkins. **DD** 607. **Pr Rev. Acid Free.**
**Desc:** Seeks to encourage research and scholarly writing about any aspect of technology and design education. Critical, review, and comparative studies are particularly prominent.
**Ind/Abst** Br. Educ. Index.

SZ/0267-5730
**INTERNATIONAL JOURNAL OF TECHNOLOGY MANAGEMENT.** [Int. j. technol. manag.]. **Added/Corp** Unesco. **VFOAT** Journal International de la Gestion Technologique. Vol. 1, No. 1/2 (1986)-. Periodical. English (summaries and/or abstracts in French, German and Japanese). Eight times a year. £210.00 UK; $315.00 North America; DM530.00 other. Inderscience Enterprises Ltd, World Trade Center Building, 110 Avenue Louis Casai, Case Postale 306, CH-1215 Geneva-Aeroport Switzerland. **Tel** 011 41 22 7383437, FAX 011 41 22 7910885, telex 28 99 50. **ED** M. A. Dorgham. **LC** T1; .I59. **DD** 606.8. **CODEN** IJTMEG. Index available. cum. index. **Bk Rev. Ad Acc. Pr Rev. Circ:** 20,000. Documents available from UMI Article Clearinghouse, Ask*IEEE.
**Desc:** A vehicle to provide a refereed and authoritative source of information in the field of management and technology. Aims to establish channels of communication between government departments, technology executives in industry, commerce and related business, and academic experts in the field.
**Ind/Abst** ABI/INFORM Glob. Ed.; ABI Inform Ondisc (1986-); Acad. Search (July 1993-); Bus. Period. Index; Bus. Source (Jul. 1993-); Ei Page One; Gen. BusinessFile (1992-); INFO-SOUTH Abstr.; INSPEC (1986-); Manage. Market. Abstr.; Wilson Bus. Abstr.

US/0896-2294
**INTERNATIONAL JOURNAL ON THE UNITY OF THE SCIENCES.** ***Suspended.*** [Int. j. unity sci.]. **Added/Corp** International Cultural Foundation. **VFOAT** IJUS. Vol. 1, No. 1 (Spring 1988)-Vol. 5, No. 4 (Jan. 1993). Periodical. English. qt. $30.00. International Journal on the Unity of the Sciences, 481 Eighth Avenue, New York NY 10001. **Tel** (212)947-1756, FAX (212)244-6739. **(Subscription address:** PO Box 1311, New York, NY 10116**) ED** Marcelo Almso. **LC** BD255; .I674. **DD** 001. **NLM** W1; IN796I. **CODEN** IJUSE5. Index available. cum. index. **Bk Rev. Ad Acc. Circ:** 500.
**Desc:** Interdisciplinary studies of knowledge and values.
**Ind/Abst** Int. Polit. Sci. Abstr.; Soc. Plann. Policy Dev. Abstr.

US/1046-7211
**INTERNATIONAL NEW PRODUCT NEWSLETTER.** [Int. new prod. newsl.]. **Added/Corp** Transcommunications International Inc. (1971)-. Newsletter. English. mo. $175.00 North America; $250.00 other. International New Product Newsletter, PO Box 1146, Marblehead MA 01945. **Tel** (508)741-0224, FAX (508)741-0224. **ED** Pamela Michaelson. **LC** HF5415.153; .I57. **DD** 338. **CODEN** INPNAN. cum. index. available on an online database from AOL. ***Continues*** *New Product Newsletter.*

UK
**INTERNATIONAL PROJECT MANAGEMENT YEARBOOK.** ***Ceased.*** **VFOAT** Project Management Yearbook. (1985)-Ceased (1988). English. an. Butterworth Heinemann Publishers, Linacre House, Jordan Hill, Oxford OX2 8DP England. **Tel** 011 44 865 310366. **LC** T56.8; .I54. **DD** 658.4/04/05.

US/0278-2731
**INTERNATIONAL RESEARCH CENTERS DIRECTORY.** [Int. res. cent. dir.]. **VFOAT** IRCD. 1st Ed., Issue No. 1 (Jan. 1982)-. Directory. English. ir. $410.00. Gale Research Inc., 835 Penobscot Building, Detroit MI 48226. **Tel** (800)877-GALE, (313)961-2242, FAX (313)961-6083, telex TWX 810-221-7086. **ED** Thomas Cichonski. **LC** Q179.98; .I58. **DD** 001.4/025. **NLM** Q 179.98 I61. available on magnetic tape; available on diskette; available on an online database (File 115) from DIALOG.
**Desc:** Over 7,600 entries provide details on research facilities of all types, including government, university, and private research firms in 150 countries worldwide.

US
**INTERNATIONAL SCIENCE AND TECHNOLOGY INSIGHT.** **Added/Corp** National Science Foundation (U.S.). Division of International Programs. **VFOAT** Insight; INT Insight; INT/Insight. (1990)-. Periodical. English. qt. **LC** Q124.6; .I68. **DD** 338.9/26./05. ***Continues*** *International S&T Insight.*
**Ind/Abst** Int. Aerosp. Abstr.

US/0074-7866
**INTERNATIONAL SCIENCE REVIEW SERIES.** [Int. sci. rev. ser.]. **VFOAT** ISRS. V. 1-. Monographic series. English. ir. Price varies per volume. Gordon & Breach Science Publishers, Inc., PO Box 786, Cooper Station, New York NY 10276. **Tel** (212)206-8900, FAX (212)645-2459. **(Subscription address:** International Publishers Distributor at one of the following addresses: 820 Town Center Drive, Langhorne, PA 19047; or PO Box 90, Reading Berkshire RG1 8JL UK; or Kent Ridge PO Box 1180, Singapore 9111, Republic of Singapore**)**

UK/0146-5589
**INTERNATIONAL SERIES IN THE SCIENCE OF THE SOLID STATE.** [Int. ser. sci. solid state]. Academic Scholarly Publication. English. ir. Price varies per volume. Pergamon Press, An Imprint of Elsevier Science Ltd., The Boulevard, Langford Lane, Kidlington, Oxford OX5 1GB United Kingdom. **Tel** 011 44 865 843000, 011 44 865 843699, FAX 011 44 865 843010. **(Subscription address:** US/ 395 Saw Mill River Road, Elmsford, NY 10523; Can/ 150 Consumers Road/Suite 104, Willowdale Ontario M2J 1P9; Aus-NZ/ POB 544, Potts Point NSW 2011**) CODEN** ISSTDQ. Documents available from Ask*IEEE, CASDDS.

*Continues International Series of Monographs in the Science of the Solid State, 0146-5570.*
**Ind/Abst** Chem. Abstr.; INSPEC.

UK/0269-8595
**INTERNATIONAL STUDIES IN THE PHILOSOPHY OF SCIENCE : I.S.P.S.**
**VFOAT** I.S.P.S.; ISPS. Vol. 1, No. 1 (Sept. 1986)-. Periodical. English. Three times a year (Mar., July, Oct.). £120.00. Carfax Publishing Company, PO Box 25 Abingdon, Oxfordshire OX14 3UE England. **Tel** 011 44 235 555335, FAX (0279)31067, telex 817484. **(Subscription address:** US and Canada/ PO Box 2025, Dunnellon, FL 34430-2025; telephone:(904)489-6996) **ED** W. H. Newton-Smith, K. V. Wilkes & R. Viale. **[CCC].** Index available. available on microfiche.
**Desc:** An interdisciplinary journal that publishes articles from philosophers, historians and sociologists of science.
**Ind/Abst** Int. Bibliogr. Sociol.; Philos. Index.

UK/0965-528X
**INTERNATIONAL YEARBOOK OF LAW, COMPUTERS AND TECHNOLOGY.**
English. an (April). £92.00. Carfax Publishing Company, PO Box 25 Abingdon, Oxfordshire OX14 3UE England. **Tel** 011 44 235 555335, FAX (0279)31067, telex 817484. **(Subscription address:** US and Canada/ PO Box 2025, Dunnellon, FL 34430-2025; telephone:(904)489-6996) **[CCC].**

GW/0374-3365
**INTERNATIONALES WISSENSCHAFTLICHES KOLLOQUIUM. Main/Conf** Internationales Wissenschaftliches Kolloquium (Technische Hochschule Ilmenau. (1956)-. Academic Scholarly Publication. English (German and Russian). an. Price varies per volume. Technische Hochschule, Karl-Marx-Stadt, Leninstrasse 16, O-701 Leipzig Germany. **LC** Q101; .I694A. **DD** 505. **CODEN** IWKLAL. Documents available from CASDDS.
**Ind/Abst** Chem. Abstr.

RM
**INVATAMINTUL LICEAL SI TEHNIC PROFESIONAL. Added/Corp** Romania. Ministerul Educatiei si Invatamintului. **VFOAT** Revista Invatamintul Liceal Si Tehnic Profesional. (197?)-. Periodical. Romanian. Ten times a year. Ministerul Educatiei si Invatamintului, Str. Spiru Haret Nr. 12, Bucharest Romania. **(Subscription address:** Ilexim Press Department, PO Box 1, 136-1-137, Bucharest, Romania.) **LC** T61; .I75. available with illustrations. ***Continues** Invatamintul Profesional Si Tehnic.*
**Desc:** Publication of methodological guidance and exchange of experiments for teachers.

US/0883-9859
**INVENTORS' DIGEST (COLORADO SPRINGS, COLO.).** (INVESTORS' DIGEST.). [Invent. dig.]. **Added/Corp** Affiliated Inventors Foundation (Colorado Springs, Colo.). Vol. 1, No. 1 (Spring 1985)-. Periodical. English. Six times a year. $22.00 (one year), $37.50 (two years) US; $27.00 (one year), $47.50 (two years) Canada; $40.00 (one year), $73.50 (two years) other. JMH Publishing Co., 2132 East Bijou Street, Colorado Springs CO 80909. **Tel** (719)635-1916, (800)838-8808, FAX (719)635-1578. **ED** Joanne Hayes. **DD** 608. **Bk Rev**, (Qty: 6-12). **Ad Acc. Circ:** 3,500.
**Desc:** For both novice and professional inventors. Articles cover all phases of invention developement.

US/0748-7851
**INVENTORS' VOICE.** (INVENTORS' VOICE / AFFILIATED INVENTORS FOUNDATION, INC.). Vol. 1, No. 1 (May-June 1983)-. Periodical. English. bm. $15.00. JMH Publishing Co., 2132 East Bijou Street, Colorado Springs CO 80909. **Tel** (719)635-1916, (800)838-8808, FAX (719)635-1578. **ED** Joanne H Mordus. **LC** T201; .I67. **DD** 608.773/05. **Bk Rev. Ad Acc. Circ:** 18,000 (ctrl).
**Desc:** Contains articles about the invention and patenting process geared to the inventor. Success and war stories about experienced inventors.

NZ/0113-051X
**INVERMAY TECHNICAL REPORT.**
[Invermay tech. rep.]. (1987)-. Monographic series. English. ir. **DD** 630.993. ***Continues** Technical Report - Invermay Research Centre, 0110-649X.*
**Ind/Abst** Agric. Eng. Abstr.

SP/0210-136X
**INVESTIGACION Y CIENCIA.** (1976)-. Spanish. Twelve times a year. 8631.25ptas others (airmail); 7700ptas Spain (surface mail). Prensa Cientifica SA, Muntaner 339 Pral 1A, 08021 Barcelona Spain. **Tel** 011 34 3 4143344, FAX 011 34 93 4145413.

AT/0815-9602
**INVESTIGATING.** (INVESTIGATING AUSTRALIAN PRIMARY SCIENCE JOURNAL.). [Investigating]. **Added/Corp** Australian Science Teachers Association. (1985)-. Periodical. English. Four times a year (Mar., May, Aug., Nov.). 27.00Aus$ (individuals), 32.00Aus$ (institutions) Australia; 37.00Aus$ (individuals), 42.00Aus$ (institutions) others. Australian Science Teachers Association, PO Box 2682, Canberra ACT 2601 Australia. **Tel** 011 61 6 258 9250, FAX 011 61 6 258 9565. **ED** Mark Mackling, (phone: 09 370 6339). **DD** 372.35044. **Bk Rev. Ad Acc, Adv Mgr:** Ian Pattie, **Tel** (003)314048. **Circ:** 3,000.

US
**INVESTIGATIONS IN SCIENCE EDUCATION.** ***Suspended.*** Vol. 1, Autumn 1974-Suspended with Vol. 14, No. 4. Periodical. English. qt. $8.00. SMEAC Information Reference Center, 1200 Chambers Road/Room 310, Columbus OH 43212. **Tel** (614)292-6717. **ED** Patricia Blosser. **Circ:** 800 (ctrl).
**Desc:** Contains critical reviews and abstracts to research in science education, k-college.

US/0021-0676
**IOWA SCIENCE TEACHERS' JOURNAL.**
**Added/Corp** Iowa Science Teachers' Association. Vol. 1 (Oct. 1963)-. Periodical. English. Three times a year. $9.00 US; $10.00 other. Iowa Academy of Science, University of Northern Iowa, Cedar Falls IA 50614. **Tel** (319)273-2021. **ED** Carl Bollwinkel. **Bk Rev. Ad Acc. Pr Rev.**
**Desc:** A refereed scientific journal with articles appropriate for K-12 science teachers. Articles are devoted to classroom activities and teaching strategies. Calendar of Iowa Science Education events.

UK/0958-5222
**IPMS BULLETIN.** [IPMS bull.]. **VFOAT** Bulletin - Institution of Professionals, Managers and Specialists. (1989)-. Periodical. English. Twelve times a year. £24.00 UK; £31.00 others. TG Scott Subscriber Services, 6 Bourne Enterprise Center, Wrotham Road, Borough Green, Kent TN15 8DG England. **Tel** 011 44 01 732 884023, FAX 011 44 01 732 884034. ***Continues** IPCS Bulletin, 0265-0975.*
**Desc:** News and views on employment issues affecting scientists and technologists in the public and private sector.

IQ/0067-2904
**IRAQI JOURNAL OF SCIENCE.** (IRAQI JOURNAL OF SCIENCE. AL-MAJALLAH AL-IRAQIYAH LIL-ULUM.). [Iraqi j. sci.]. **Added/Corp** Jamiat Baghdad. Kulliyat Al-Ulum. **VFOAT** Majallah Al-Iraqiyah Lil-Ulum. Vol. 18, No. 2 (1977)-. Periodical. English (summaries and/or abstracts in Arabic). University of Baghdad, College of Science, Bahgdad Iraq. **LC** Q80.I68; B33a. **DD** 505. **CODEN** IRJSD5. Documents available from BIOSIS Document Express, Ask*IEEE, CASDDS. ***Continues** Bulletin of the College of Science.*
**Ind/Abst** Biol. Abstr.; Chem. Abstr.; INSPEC (1980-); Math. Rev.; Zentralbl. Math. Ihre Grenzgeb.

US/0019-0578
**ISA TRANSACTIONS.** (ISA TRANSACTIONS : A PUBLICATION OF INSTRUMENT SOCIETY OF AMERICA.). [ISA trans.]. **Main/Corp** Instrument Society of America. **Added/Corp** Instrument Society of America. Vol. 1 (Jan. 1962)-. Academic Scholarly Publication. English. qt (1 volume). Fl320.00. Elsevier Science Publishers BV, PO Box 211, 1000 AE Amsterdam Netherlands. **Tel** 011 31 20 5803642, FAX 011 31 20 5862696, telex 15682. **ED** G E Dreifke and W S Bloor. **LC** TA165; .A143. **NLM** W1 I27. **CODEN** ISATAZ. **[CCC]. Bk Rev. Ad Acc. Pr Rev. Circ:** 1,000 (ctrl). available on microfilm and microfiche from University Microfilms International (UMI). Documents available from Article Express International, The Genuine Article, BIOSIS Document Express, Ask*IEEE, CASDDS, Documents on Demand.
**Desc:** Devoted exclusively to the publication of significant contributions to the fields of instrumentation and measurement in process control engineering. It includes papers presented at recent ISA conferences, symposia, and technical meetings, as well as other important developments in instrumentation.
**Ind/Abst** Alum. Ind. Abstr.; Appl. Sci. Technol. Index; Bioeng. Abstr.; Biol. Abstr.; Chem. Abstr.; Civ. Struct. Eng. Abstr.; Coal Abstr.; Comput. Abstr.; Comput. Inf. Syst. Abstr. J. [Full Cov.]; Curr. Contents Eng. Tech. Appl. Sci.; Ei Page One; Elect. Comm. Abstr.; EMBASE; Energy Inf. Abstr.; Energy Res. Abstr.; Eng. Mater. Abstr.; Eng. Index Annu.; Environ. Abstr.; Fluid Abstr., Civil Eng.; Fluid Abstr. Proc. Eng.; FLUIDEX (1973-); Index Med.; INSPEC (1968-); Int. Aerosp. Abstr.; Manuf. Process Eng. Abstr.; Met. Abstr.; Res. Alert [Select. Cov.]; SCISEARCH; Shock Vibr. Dig.; Solid State Supercond. Abstr.

US
**ISI ALERT. Main/Corp** Institute for Scientific Information. **VFOAT** Alert. Vol. 1, No. 1 (May 1977)-. Academic Scholarly Publication. English. Institute for Scientific Information, 3501 Market Street, Philadelphia PA 19104. **Tel** (215)386-0100, (800)523-1850, FAX (215)386-6362, telex 84-5305.

US/0021-1753
**ISIS.** [Isis]. Vol. 1, No. 1 (1913)-. Academic Scholarly Publication. English. qt (4 issues). $125.00 institution; $49.00 individual (subscriptions are concurrent with membership in the History of Science Society). University of Chicago Press / Journals Division, PO Box 37005, 5720 South Woodlawn, Chicago IL 60637. **Tel** (312)753-3347, FAX (312)753-0811. **(Subscription telephone:** (312)753-8083) **ED** Ronald L. Numbers. **LC** Q1. **DD** 509. **NLM** W1 IS409. **CODEN** ISISA4. Index available. cum. index. **Bk Rev. Ad Acc. Pr Rev. Acid Free. Circ:** 4,500. available on microfilm and microfiche from University Microfilms International (UMI). Documents available from Article Express International, The Genuine Article, BIOSIS Document Express, UMI Article Clearinghouse, Ask*IEEE, CASDDS.
**Desc:** Features scholarly articles, research notes, and commentary on the history of science, medicine, and technology, and their cultural influences.
**Ind/Abst** Acad. Abstr. Full Text Elite (July 1990-); Acad. Abstr. (July 1990-); Acad. Ind. [Computer File] (1987-); Acad. Search (July 1990-); Am. Hist. Life (1954-); Am. Bibliogr. Slavic East Europ. Stud.; Arts Humanit. Citation Index [Full Cov.]; Biol. Abstr.; Book Rev. Index; Chem. Abstr.; Curr. Contents Arts Humanit.; Curr. Contents Soc. Behav. Sci.; Ei Page One; Eng. Index Annu.; Expand. Acad. Index (1987-); Gen. Sci. Index; Gen. Sci. Source (Jul. 1990-); GeoRef; Humanit. Index; Humanit. Source (Jul. 1990-); Index Med.; Index Book Rev. Relig.; INFO-SOUTH Abstr.; INSPEC (1968-Sep. 1980, Dec. 1990-); Mag. Search; Math. Rev.; Middle East Abstr. Index; Newsp. Period. Abstr. (1991-); Res. Alert [Full Cov.]; Soc. Sci. Cit. Index [Full Cov.]; West. Hist. Q.; Zentralbl. Math. Ihre Grenzgeb.

US
**ISIS GUIDE TO THE HISTORY OF SCIENCE.** ***Ceased.*** **Added/Corp** History of Science Society. 1st Ed.; (19??)-No. 8. English. ir (every four years). University of Chicago Press / Book Department, 11030 South Langley Avenue, Chicago IL 60628. **Tel** (800)621-2736, (312)568-1550, FAX (312)753-0811, telex 23933. **ED** Arnold Thackray. **Ad Acc. Circ:** 4,500.
**Desc:** Official guide to the history of science. A listing with descriptions of the discipline's societies, organizations, publications, scholars, graduate and research programs.

PK
**ISLAMIC THOUGHT AND SCIENTIFIC CREATIVITY : A QUARTERLY JOURNAL OF THE COMSTECH. Added/Corp** Organisation of Islamic Conference. Standing Committee on Scientific and Technological Cooperation. Vol. 1, No. 1 (Jan./Mar. 1990)-. Periodical. English. qt. COMSTECH, 3 Constitution Avenue, Sector G-5, Islamabad, Pakistan. **LC** BP190.5.S3; I86. **DD** 297/.1975.
**Ind/Abst** Middle East J.

US
**ISOTECH JOURNAL OF THERMOMETRY. Added/Corp** Isothermal Technology Ltd. Vol. 1, No. 1 (1st Quarter 1990)-. Periodical. English. sa. $25.00. Isothermal Technology Ltd, 2307 Whitley Drive, Durham NC 27707. **Tel** (919)490-1897, FAX (919)493-7717. **(Subscription address:** Europe/ Pine Grove, Southport PR9 9AG Merseyside England) **ED** Henry E Sostman and John P Tavener. **LC** QC270; .I86. **DD** 536/.5/0287. **Bk Rev. Pr Rev. Circ:** 500.
**Desc:** Articles and information regarding the measurement of temperature in science and industry.

US
**ISRAEL HIGH TECH REPORT.** English. mo. $195.00 (US & Israel); $215.00 (other). Israel Publications, 47 Byron Place, Scarsdale NY 10583. **Tel** (914) 723-8321, telex 33511. available on an online database (files 16,636/Full-Text) from DIALOG.
**Ind/Abst** PTS Newsl. Database [Full Txt.].

●UK/1350-7583
**ISSUES IN ENVIRONMENTAL SCIENCE AND TECHNOLOGY.** (1994)-. English. Twice a year. £25.00 EC; $47.00 US; £27.00 other. Royal Society of Chemistry, Thomas Graham House, Science Park, Cambridge CB4 4WF England. **Tel** 011 44 223 420066, FAX 011 44 223 423429, telex 818293 ROYAL. **(Subscription address:** Turpin Distribution Services Limited, Blackhorse Road, Letchworth, Hertfordshire SG6 1HN, United Kingdom.)
**Desc:** Publishes review articles on topics of global concern, written by world experts in the specialized fields. Presents a multi-disciplinary approach to pollution and environmental science, as well as focusing on issues such as economic, legal, and political concerns.

US/0748-5492
**ISSUES IN SCIENCE AND TECHNOLOGY.** [Issues sci. technol.]. **Added/Corp** National Academy of Sciences (U.S.) National Academy of Engineering. **VFOAT** Issues. Vol. 1, No. 1 (Fall 1984)-. Periodical. English. Four times a year. $69.00 (institutions), $36.00 (individuals) US; $75.00 other. National Academy Press, 2101 Constitution Avenue NW, Lockbox 285, Washington DC 20055. **Tel** (800)624-6242, (202)334-3313, FAX (202)334-2451. **(Subscription address:** Issues in Science and Technology, The University of Texas at Dallas, PO Box 830688, Mail Station AD13, Richardson TX 75083-0688.) **ED** Steven J. Marcus. **LC** Q124.6; .I85. **DD** 338.9/26. **NLM** W1; IS669H. Index available. **Bk Rev. Ad Acc. Pr Rev. Circ:** 15,000. available on microfilm and microfiche from University Microfilms International (UMI). Documents available from The Genuine Article, UMI Article Clearinghouse.
**Desc:** Provides a nonpartisan forum for the exchange of

ideas on policy issues involving science, technology and health.
**Ind/Abst** Abr. Read. Guide Period. Lit.; Abstr. Bull. Inst. Pap. Sci. Tech.; Acad. Abstr. Full Text Elite (July 1990-); Acad. Abstr. (July 1990-); Acad. Ind. [Computer File] (1987-); Acad. Search (July 1990-); Access (1985-?); AGRICOLA [Select. Cov.]; Curr. Contents Eng. Tech. Appl. Sci.; Curr. Contents Soc. Behav. Sci.; Curr. Index J. Educ.; Ei Page One; Energy Inf. Abstr.; Expand. Acad. Index (1987-); Fut. Surv.; Gen. Period. Index (1987-); Gen. Sci. Index; Gen. Sci. Source (Jul. 1990-); Health Plan. Adminis.; Hospit. Manage. Rev.; Index Period. Artic. Relat. Law; INFO-SOUTH Abstr.; INIS Atomindex [Micro.]; Int. Aerosp. Abstr.; J. Plan. Lit.; Mag. Index Plus (1992-); Mag. Search; Newsp. Period. Abstr. (1990-); PAIS Int. Print (1991-); Pollut. Abstr. Indexes; Read. Guide Abstr. Select Ed.; Read. Guide Period. Lit.; Res. Alert [Full Cov.]; Sci. Cit. Index; SCISEARCH; Soc. Sci. Cit. Index [Full Cov.].

CN/1187-2950
**ISTC NEW BRUNSWICK/PRINCE EDWARD ISLAND.** (ISTC NOUVEAU-BRUNSWICK/ILE-DU-PRINCE-EDOUARD : UNE PUBLICATION D'INDUSTRIE, SCIENCES ET TECHNOLOGIE CANADA.). [ISTC N.B./P.E.I.]. **Added/Corp** Canada. Industrie, Sciences et Technologie Canada. **VFOAT** ISTC New Brunswick/Prince Edward Island. **VAT** Industry, Science and Technology Canada New Brunswick/Prince Edward Island. Vol. 3, No 1 (Sept. 1991)-. Periodical. French (English). ir. **DD** 354.7150082. ***Continues*** *ISTC Nouveau-Brunswick., 1180-9353.*

US
**ISTP SEARCH.** English. Magnetic Tape: $14155.00 (academic), $17695.00 (corporate). Institute for Scientific Information, 3501 Market Street, Philadelphia PA 19104. **Tel** (215)386-0100, (800)523-1850, FAX (215)386-6362, telex 84-5305. **(Subscription address:** Institute for Scientific Information, PO Box 71416, Chicago, IL 60694) available on magnetic tape.
**Desc:** The online format of the Index to Scientific & Technical Proceedings. Provides the same coverage as the ISTP.

GW/0937-3764
**IT. IBEROAMERICANA DE TECHNOLOGIAS.** [IT, Iberoam. tecnol.]. **VFOAT** Iberoamericana de Tecnologias. (1989)-. Periodical. German. mo (9 issues per year). DM88.00 Germany; DM128.00 other. Iberoamericana Verlags GmbH, Celsiusstrasse 112, W-5300 Bonn 1 Germany. **Tel** 011 49 228 252033. **UDC** 62 :355/359.

US
**IT SPECTRUM.** ***Ceased.*** (19??)-(Fall 1993). English. bm. Codd and Date Inc., 1772A Technology Drive, San Jose CA 95110. **Tel** (408)441-6400, FAX (408)437-8936. ***Continues*** *Relational Journal.*

RU/0202-8158
**ITOGI NAUKI I TEKHNIKI. SERIIA EKONOMIKA, ORGANIZATSIIA, TEKHNOLOGIIA I OBORUDOVANIE POLIGRAFICHESKOGO PROIZVODSTVA / VSESOIUZNYI INSTITUT NAUCHNOI I TEKHNICHESKOI INFORMATSII.** **Added/Corp** Vsesoiuznyi Institut Nauchnoi I Tekhnicheskoi Informatsii (Soviet Union). **VFOAT** Seriia Ekonomika, Organizatsiia, Tekhnologiia I Oborudovanie Poligraficheskogo Proizvodstva; Itogi Nauki I Tekhniki. Ekonomika, Organizatsiia, Tekhnologiia I I Oborudovanie Poligraficheskogo Proizvodstva; Ekonomika, Organizatsiia, Tekhnologiia I Oborudovanie Poligraficheskogo Proizvodstva. (1979)-. Periodical. Russian. be. 1.50rub. VINITI - Vsesoyuznyi Institut Nauchno-Tekhnicheskoi Informatsii, All-Union Scientific and Technical Information Institute, Baltiiskaia Ulitsa 14, 125219 Moscow Russia. **Tel** 238-46-00, FAX 9430060, telex 411164. **LC** Z244.5; .I86. ***Continues*** *Itogi Nauki i Tekhniki. Ekonomika, Organizatsiia I Tekhnologiia Poligraficheskogo Proizvodstva.*

UZ/0516-2629
**IZVESTIA AKADEMII NAUK UZBEKSKIJ SSR. SERIA TEHNICESKIH NAUK.** ***Title Change.*** **See** Engineering.

BU/0068-371X
**IZVESTIIA.** **Main/Corp** Bulgarska Akademiia Na Naukite, Sofia. Tsentralna Khelmintologichna Laboratoriia. **VFOAT** Bulletin. (1955)-. Academic Scholarly Publication. Bulgarian (summaries and/or abstracts in Russian, German, French and English). Bulgarska Akademiia na Naukite, 7 Noemvri 1, Sofia Bulgaria. **DD** 616.

KZ/0002-3191
**IZVESTIIA AKADEMII NAUK KAZAKHSKOI SSR. SERIIA FIZIKO-MATEMATICHESKAIA.** ***Title Change.*** [Izv. Akad. nauk Kaz. SSR, Ser. fiz.-mat.]. **Added/Corp** Qazaq SSR Ghylym Akademiiasy. **VFOAT** Seriia Fiziko-Matematicheskaia. No. 2 (1966)-(199?). Periodical. Russian (summaries and/or abstracts in English and Kazakh). bm. **LC** Q4; .A277. **CODEN** IAKFBK. Documents available from CASDDS. ***Continues*** *Qazaq SSR Ghylym Akademiiasy. Izvestiia. Seriia Fiziko-Matematicheskikh Nauk.* ***Continued by*** *Izvestiia Akademii Nauk Respubliki Kazakhstan. Seriiia Fiziko-Matematicheskaia.*
**Ind/Abst** Chem. Abstr. (?-?).

KZ
**IZVESTIIA AKADEMII NAUK RESPUBLIKI KAZAKHSTAN. SERIIA FIZIKO-MATEMATICHESKAIA.** **Added/Corp** Qazaq SSR Ghylym Akademiiasy. **VFOAT** Seriia Fiziko-Matematicheskaia. (199?)-. Periodical. Russian (summaries and/or abstracts in English and Kazakh). bm. **LC** Q4; .A277. ***Continues*** *Izvestiia Akademii Nauk Kazakhskoi SSR. Seriia Fiziko-Matematicheskaia.*

●RU
**IZVESTIIA AKADEMII NAUK. TEKHNICHESKAIA KIBERNETIKA / ROSSIISKAIA AKADEMIIA NAUK.** **Added/Corp** Rossiiskaia Akademiia Nauk. **VFOAT** Tekhnicheskaia Kibernetika; Izvestiia Rossiiskoi Akademii Nauk. Tekhnicheskaia Kibernetika. (1992)-. Academic Scholarly Publication. Russian. Six times a year. $202.00. Izdatelstvo Nauka / Akademiia Nauk, Publishing House of the Russian Academy of Sciences, Leninskii Porspekt 14, 117901 Moscow Russia. **Tel** 011 95 954-21-53, FAX 011 95 938-21-44, telex 411964. **(Subscription address:** East View Publications Inc., 3020 Harbor Lane North, Suite 110, Minneapolis MN 55447.) ***Continues*** *Izvestiia Akademii Nauk SSSR. Tekhnicheskaia Kibernetika.*

UZ
**IZVESTIIA AKADEMII NAUK UZSSR. TEKHNICHESKIE NAUKI.** **See** Engineering.

RU
**IZVESTIIA SIBIRSKOGO OTDELENIIA AN SSSR. SIBIRSKII FIZIKO-TEKHNICHESKII ZHURNAL.** **VFOAT** Izvestiia Sibirskogo Otdeleniia Akademii Nauk SSSR. Sibirskii Fiziko-Tekhnicheskii Zhurnal; Sibirskii Fiziko-Tekhnicheskii Zhurnal. Vol. 1 (Jan./Feb. 1991)-. Periodical. Russian. bm. ***Continues*** *Izvestiia Sibirskogo Otdeleniia Akademii Nauk SSSR. Seriia Tekhnicheskikh Nauk, 0002-3434.*
**Ind/Abst** Math. Rev.

RU/0321-2653
**IZVESTIJA SEVERO-KAVKAZSKOGO NAUCNOGO CENTRA VYSSEJ SKOLY. TEHNICESKIE NAUKI.** (IZVESTIIA SEVERO-KAVKAZSKOGO NAUCHNOGO TSENTRA VYSSHEI SHKOLY. TEKHNICHESKIE NAUKI.). [Izv. Ser.-Kavk. naucn. centra vyss. sk., Teh. nauk]. **Added/Corp** Severo-Kavkazskii Nauchnyi Tsentr Vysshei Shkoly. Rostovskii Gosudarstvennyi Universitet. Soviet Union. Ministerstvo Vysshego i Srednego Spetsialnogo Obrazovaniia. Russian S.F.S.R. Ministerstvo Vysshego i Srednego Spetsialnogo Obrazovaniia. **VFOAT** Tekhnicheskie Nauki. (1973)-. Academic Scholarly Publication. Russian. Four times a year. $159.95. **(Subscription address:** East View Publications Inc., 3020 Harbor Lane North, Suite 110, Minneapolis MN 55447.) **LC** T4; .I97. **CODEN** ISSND8. Documents available from CASDDS.
**Ind/Abst** Chem. Abstr.; Energy Res. Abstr. (Oct. 1982-); Int. Aerosp. Abstr.; Math. Rev.; Zentralbl. Math. Ihre Grenzgeb.

NE/0920-7724
**JAARBOEK VOOR DE GESCHIEDENIS VAN BEDRIJF EN TECHNIEK.** **Added/Corp** Stichting JbGBT. **VFOAT** JbGBT. (1984)-. Dutch. an.
**Ind/Abst** Am. Hist. Life (1988-).

SZ
**JAHRBUCH.** **Main/Corp** Schweizerische Akademie der Naturwissenschaften. **VFOAT** Annuaire. (1989)-. German (French). Schweizerische Akademie der Naturwissenschaften, Hirschengraben 11, 3001 Bern Switzerland. **LC** QH5; .J33. ***Continues*** *Jahrbuch. Administrativer Teil.*

GW/0341-2865
**JAHRBUCH DER HEIDELBERGER AKADEMIE DER WISSENSCHAFTEN.** [Jahrb. Heidelb. Akad. Wiss.]. **Main/Corp** Heidelberger Akademie der Wissenschaften. Began in 1962/63. German. an. Universitatsverlag Carl Winter, POB 106140, D 69051 Heidelberg Germany. **Tel** 011 49 6221 770260. **LC** AS182; .H37. **DD** 053/.1. ***Continues*** *Sitzungsberichte der Heidelberger Akademie der Wissenschaften. Jahresheft.*
**Ind/Abst** GeoRef; Math. Rev.

GW/0341-0218
**JAHRBUCH - MAX-PLANCK-GESELLSCHAFT.** (JAHRBUCH ... DER MAX-PLANCK-GESELLSCHAFT ZUR FORDERUNG DER WISSENSCHAFTEN.). [Jahrb. - Max-Planck-Ges.]. **Main/Corp** Max-Planck-Gesellschaft. **Added/Corp** Max-Planck-Gesellschaft zur Forderung der Wissenschaften. (1951)-. Academic Scholarly Publication. German. an. DM98.00. Vandenhoeck & Ruprecht, Robert Bosch Breite 6, D-37079 Goettingen Germany. **Tel** 011 49 551 695911, FAX 011 49 551 695917, telex 965226 VAN d. **LC** Q3; .K32. **CODEN** MPJADF. **Ad Acc.** Documents available from BIOSIS Document Express, CASDDS. ***Continues*** *Jahrbuch ... der Kaiser-Wilhelm-Gesellschaft zur Forderung der Wissenschaften.*
**Ind/Abst** Biol. Abstr.; Chem. Abstr.

GW
**JAHRBUCH SCHWEISSTECHNIK / HERAUSGEBER, DEUTSCHER VERBAND FUER SCHWEISSTECHNIK E.V. (DVS).** (1987)-. German. an. DM30.00. Deutscher Verlag fur Schweisstechnik GmbH, Aachener Strasse 172, Postfach 2725, W-4000 Dusseldorf 1 Germany. **Tel** 211/157590, FAX 211/1575950, telex 8582583. **LC** TS227.A1; J33. **Ad Acc. Circ:** 10,000.

GW
**JAHRESBERICHT (HAMBURGER SYNCHROTRONSTRAHLUNGSLABOR HASYLAB).** (JAHRESBERICHT / HAMBURGER SYNCHROTRONSTRAHLUNGSLABOR HASYLAB AM DEUTSCHEN ELEKTRONEN-SYNCHROTRON DESY.). **Added/Corp** Hamburger Synchrotronstrahlungslabor HASYLAB. German. **LC** QC793.5.E627; J34. **DD** 539.7/35/0943515.

KO/0253-6277
**JANYEN GWAHAG DAIHAG NONMUNJIB.** (CHAYON KWAHAK TAEHAK NONMUNJIP.). [Janyen gwahag daihag nonmunjib]. **VFOAT** Proceedings of the College of Natural Sciences. Academic Scholarly Publication. Korean (English). College of Natural Sciences, Seoul National University, 56 Shinlim-dong, Kwanak-ku 151, Seoul South Korea. **LC** Q4; .C397. **CODEN** CKTNDR. Documents available from CASDDS. ***Absorbed*** *Proceedings of the College of Natural Sciences. Section I, Mathematics.*
**Ind/Abst** Chem. Abstr.; Math. Rev.

JA
**JAPAN BIOTECH LETTER.** ***Ceased.*** (19??)-(March 1993). sm. Egis KK, 22-1 Ichibancho Chiyoda-ku, Tokyo 102 Japan. **Tel** 011 81 3 3264 1060.

UK
**JAPAN HIGH TECH REPORT.** English. mo. £299.00 UK; $525.00 US. World Business Publications Ltd., 960 High Road, Britannia 4th Floor, London N12 9RY England. **Tel** 11 44 81 446 5141, FAX 11 44 81 446 3659, telex 9419208.

US/1055-8004
**JAPAN TECHNOLOGY MONITOR.** [Jpn. technol. monit.]. **VFOAT** JTM. (1990)-. English. bw. Coda International, 3528 Torrance Boulevard, Suite 213, Torrance CA 90503. **LC** IN PROCESS. **DD** 338.

JA
**JAPANESE JOURNAL OF ADVANCED AUTOMATION TECHNOLOGY.** English. bm (6 issues). ¥72000.00. **(Subscription address:** Maruzen Company Ltd., PO Box 5050, Import & Export Department, Tokyo 100 31 Japan.)

●US/1058-7314
**JAPANESE TECHNOLOGY REVIEWS. SECTION C, NEW MATERIALS.** **VFOAT** New Materials. (1992)-. Periodical. English. Twice a year (1 volume). $218.00 (academic institutions), $304.00 (corporate institutions). Gordon & Breach Science Publishers, Inc., PO Box 786, Cooper Station, New York NY 10276. **Tel** (212)206-8900, FAX (212)645-2459. **(Subscription address:** Gordon & Breach Science Publishers / US, 820 Town Center Drive, Langhorne PA 19047.) **[CCC].** ***Continues in part*** *Japanese Technology Reviews, 0898-5693.*

US
**JAYNE LECTURES.** **Added/Corp** American Philosophical Society. (1961)-. Monographic series. English. ir. Price varies per volume. American Philosophical Society, PO Box 40098, Philadelphia PA 19106. **Tel** (215)440-3427, FAX (215)440-3436. **LC** Q11; .P612 subser. **DD** 081. ***Supersedes*** *Jayne Memorial Lecture.*

CN/0714-4067
**JE ME PETITDERBROUILLE.** (JE ME PETITDEBROUILLE : JOURNAL DU CLUB DES PETITS DEBROUILLARDS.). [Je petitdebrouille]. **Added/Corp** Club des Petits Debrouillards. No. 1 (Jan. 1982)-. Periodical. French (English). mo. $15.00. Club des Debrouillards, 4545 Pierre-de-Coubertin, Case postale 1000 Succursale M, Montreal Quebec H1V 3R2 Canada. **Tel** (514)252-3027. **DD** 500. **Ad Acc. Circ:** 16,000.
**Desc:** From earth to the stars, from animal and plant life to the human body, any scientific subject that may interest children.
**Ind/Abst** Point Repere (1992-).

JA
**JETI.** **VFOAT** Japan Energy and Technology Intelligence; Japan Energy & Technology Intelligence : JETI; J.E.T.I. V. 32, No. 1 (1984)-. Academic Scholarly Publication. Japanese. mo. $172.00 (add $50.00 postage). Sekiyu Bunkasha, 4-9, Nihonbashi Honcho 1 Chome, Chuoku, Tokyoto 103 Japan. **LC** PAR. **CODEN** JETIEE. Documents available from CASDDS. ***Formed by the union of*** *Sekiyu Bunka* ***and*** *Sekiyu to Sekiyu Kagaku.*
**Ind/Abst** Chem. Abstr. (1984-); Coal Abstr.

JA/0385-8502
**JITCHUKEN ZENRINSHO KENKYUHO.** **See** Pharmacy and Pharmacology.

II
**JNANABHA.** **Added/Corp** Dayanand Vedic Postgraduate College. Lijnana Parishad. (19??)-. Periodical. English. Twelve times a year. Vijnana Parishad, Dayanand Vedic Post-Graduate, Orai, India. **(Subscription address:** Prints India, 11 Darya Ganj, New Delhi 110002 India.**)** **LC** Q1; .J58. **DD** 505.
**Ind/Abst** Math. Rev.; Zentralbl. Math. Ihre Grenzgeb.

●US
**JOB CHOICES ... IN SCIENCE & ENGINEERING.** **See** Occupations and Careers.

US
**JOHNS HOPKINS STUDIES IN THE HISTORY OF TECHNOLOGY.** No. 1 (1978)-. Monographic series. English. ir. Price varies per volume. Johns Hopkins University Press, 2715 North Charles Street, Baltimore MD 21218-4319. **Tel** (410)516-6987, FAX (410)516-6968.

JA
**JOHO NO KAGAKU TO GIJUTSU.** Japanese. mo. Y20802. Information Sci & Tec Association/Japan, Sasaki Building 5-7 Koisikawa 2, Bunkyoku Tokyo 112 Japan. **Tel** 011 81 3 38133791.

BL/0100-7319
**JORNAL SUL-AMERICANO DE BIOCIENCIAS.** [J. sul-am. biocienc.]. **VFOAT** South American Journal of Bio-Sciences; JSAB. Began with: 2 (2-4), published 1980. Academic Scholarly Publication. Portuguese (summaries and/or abstracts in English). $20.00. **NLM** W1; JO982R. **CODEN** JLBSD2. Documents available from BIOSIS Document Express. ***Continues*** *Jornal Sul-Americano de Medicina.*
**Ind/Abst** Biol. Abstr. (-1982); EMBASE.

AT/0035-9173
**JOURNAL AND PROCEEDINGS OF THE ROYAL SOCIETY OF NEW SOUTH WALES.** [J. proc. R. Soc. New South Wales]. **Main/Corp** Royal Society of New South Wales, Sydney. **Added/Corp** Royal Society of New South Wales, Sydney. Transactions of the Royal Society of New South Wales. Royal Society of New South Wales, Sydney. Transactions and Proceedings of the Royal Society of New South Wales. Vol. 1 (1867)-. Proceedings. English. sa (May & Dec.). 48.00Aus$. Royal Society of New South Wales, PO Box 1525, Macquarie Centre, New South Wales 2113 Australia. **Tel** 011 61 2 887-4448. **ED** M Krysko von Tryst. **CODEN** JPRSA5. **[CCC].** Index available (Included in Dec. issue). cum. index. **Circ:** 900. Documents available from Ask*IEEE, CASDDS.
**Desc:** Research papers on all branches of science, earth sciences, biology, astronomy, chemistry, physics, mathematics and agriculture, as well as papers on art, literature, and philosophy.
**Ind/Abst** AESIS Q.; AGRICOLA; Ceram. Abstr.; Chem. Abstr.; Geogr. Abstr. Phys. Geogr. (?-?); Geol. Abstr.; GeoRef; INSPEC (1968-); Zentralbl. Math. Ihre Grenzgeb.

II
**JOURNAL - ANDHRA PRADESH AKADEMI OF SCIENCES.** **Main/Corp** Andhra Pradesh Akademi of Sciences. English. Andhra Pradesh Akademi of Sciences, c/o Osmania University Campus, Hyderabad-7 India. **LC** Q1; .A55A. **DD** 505.

NE/0925-4560
**JOURNAL FOR GENERAL PHILOSOPHY OF SCIENCE.** **See** Philosophy.

SY/0379-2927
**JOURNAL FOR THE HISTORY OF ARABIC SCIENCE.** **Added/Corp** Jamiat Halab. Mahad al-Turath al-Ilmi al-Arabi. **VFOAT** Majallat Tarikh Al-Ulum Al-Arabiyah. Vol. 1 (May 1977)-. Periodical. English (Arabic, French and German). an. $30.00. Syrian Society of History of Science, Institute for the History of Arabic Science, Aleppo University, Aleppo Syria. **Tel** 011 236130, telex 331018 ALUNIV SY. **ED** Ahmad Y Al-Hassan, Khaled Maghout and Roshdi Rashed. **LC** Q127.A5; J68. **DD** 509/.17/671. **NLM** W1 JO399P. Index available. cum. index. **Bk Rev**. **Ad Acc. Circ:** 1,000 (ctrl).
**Desc:** An international review devoted exclusively to the history of Arabic-Islamic science: exact sciences, technology, applied sciences and medical sciences.
**Ind/Abst** Math. Rev.

JA/0915-5651
**JOURNAL OF ADVANCED SCIENCE / SOCIETY OF ADVANCED SCIENCE.** **Added/Corp** Society of Advanced Science (Japan). **VFOAT** JAS. Vol. 1, No. 1 (1989)-. Periodical. Japanese (summaries and/or abstracts in English). qt. **LC** Q77; .J68. **CODEN** JAVSEQ. Documents available from CASDDS.
**Ind/Abst** Chem. Abstr.

US/0092-2447
**JOURNAL OF APPLIED MEASUREMENTS.** [J. appl. meas.]. **Added/Corp** Precision Measurments Association. Precision Measurments Association. Newsnotes. National Conference of Standards Laboratories. Vol. 1 (July/Aug. 1977)-. Periodical. English. bm. Precision Measurements Association, 745 N Hollywood Way, Burbank CA 91505. **LC** T50; .J68. **DD** 620/.004/4.
**Desc:** Vols. for 1973- includes: Newsnotes, issued by: Precision Measurements Association ... .

II/0379-5470
**JOURNAL OF ARMAMENT STUDIES.** **See** Military and Defense.

BG/0378-8121
**JOURNAL OF BANGLADESH ACADEMY OF SCIENCES.** [J. Bangladesh Acad. Sci.]. **Main/Corp** Bangladesh Academy of Sciences. V. 1-. Academic Scholarly Publication. English. sa. TK150.00 Bangladesh; £15.00, $30.00 other. Bangladesh Academy of Sciences, Dhaka University, Department of Chemistry, Dacca 2 Bangladesh. **Tel** 91 506360. **ED** S Z Haider. **LC** Q80.B3; B36A. **DD** 505. **CODEN** JBACDF. Index available. cum. index. **Circ:** 500 (ctrl). Documents available from BIOSIS Document Express, Ask*IEEE, CASDDS.
**Desc:** Covers chemistry, biochemistry, biological sciences, mathematics, electronics, physics, botany, earth sciences, engineering, medical sciences and energy.
**Ind/Abst** Biol. Abstr.; Chem. Abstr.; INSPEC (1982-); Soils Fert.

UK/0733-5210
**JOURNAL OF CEREAL SCIENCE.** **See** Agriculture-Crop Production and Soil.

US/0047-231X
**JOURNAL OF COLLEGE SCIENCE TEACHING.** [J. coll. sci. teach.]. **Added/Corp** National Science Teachers Association. **VFOAT** College Science Teaching; JCST. Vol. 1 (Oct. 1971)-. Periodical. English. Six times a year. $52.00. National Science Teachers Association, 1840 Wilson Boulevard, Arlington VA 22201-3000. **Tel** (703)243-7100, FAX (703)243-7177, (703)522-5413. **ED** Lester G. Paldy. **LC** Q183.U6; J68. **DD** 507/.11/73. **CODEN** JSCTBN. Index available. cum. index. **Bk Rev**. **Ad Acc**. **Pr Rev. Circ:** 4,800 (ctrl). available on microfilm and microfiche from University Microfilms International (UMI). Documents available from BIOSIS Document Express, Ask*IEEE, UMI Article Clearinghouse, CASDDS.
**Desc:** Devoted to college science teaching at the undergraduate level. Considers all areas of science, including interdisciplinary efforts. Provides a forum for ideas, reports and innovative college science teaching techniques. Columns offer reviews, demonstrations, problem-solving techniques, legislative updates and new products.
**Ind/Abst** Acad. Search (July 1993-); Biol. Abstr.; Chem. Abstr.; Contents Pages Educ.; Curr. Index J. Educ.; Educ. Index; Expand. Acad. Index (1992-); INFO-SOUTH Abstr.; INSPEC (1986-); Med. Rev. Dig.; Newsp. Period. Abstr. (1991-).

US/0095-8956
**JOURNAL OF COMBINATORIAL THEORY. SERIES B.** **See** Mathematics.

US
**JOURNAL OF ELEMENTARY SCIENCE EDUCATION.** **See** Education-Teaching and Curriculum.

US/0887-9532
**JOURNAL OF EPSILON PI TAU, THE.** **See** Education.

●US/1069-5869
**JOURNAL OF FOURIER ANALYSIS AND APPLICATIONS, THE.** **See** Mathematics.

UK/0954-027X
**JOURNAL OF HARD MATERIALS.** [J. hard mater.]. **VFOAT** Hard Materials. Vol. 1, No. 1 (1990)-. Periodical. English. qt (Mar., Jun., Sept., Dec.). $210.00. Institute of Physics, Techno House, Redcliffe Way, Bristol BS1 6NX England. **Tel** 011 44 272 297481, FAX 011 44 272 294318, telex 449149 INSTP G. **(Subscription address:** American Institute of Physics, Publishing Sales, 500 Sunnyside Blvd., Woodbury NY 11797.**)** **ED** C.A. Brookes, University of Hull. **CODEN** JOHME2. **[CCC].** Index available (bound in Dec. issue). **Ad Acc, Adv Mgr:** Sarah Alder, **Tel** 0272 297481. **Circ:** 120. available on microfiche. Documents available from Ask*IEEE, CASDDS.
**Desc:** Original research on properties of hard materials in bulk form and as coatings. Hardness in excess of 1000HV30 are covered.
**Ind/Abst** Chem. Abstr.; INSPEC (1990-).

●US/1062-3701
**JOURNAL OF IMAGING SCIENCE AND TECHNOLOGY, THE.** (THE JOURNAL OF IMAGING SCIENCE AND TECHNOLOGY/ IS&T, SOCIETY FOR IMAGING SCIENCE AND TECHNOLOGY.). [J. imaging sci. technol.]. **Added/Corp** IS&T: The Society for Imaging Science and Technology. **VFOAT** Imaging Science and Technology. Vol. 36, No. 1 (Jan./Feb. 1992)-. Academic Scholarly Publication. English. bm. $120.00 US; $135.00 other. Society for Imaging Science and Technology, 7003 Kilworth Lane, Springfield VA 22151. **Tel** (703)642-9090, FAX (703)642-9094. **DD** 770. **NLM** W1; JO676BV. **CODEN** JIMTE6. **Ad Acc. Acid Free.** Documents available from Article Express International, The Genuine Article, Ask*IEEE, CASDDS. ***Formed by the union of*** *Journal of Imaging Technology, 0747-3583* ***and*** *Journal of Imaging Science, 8750-9237.*
**Desc:** Provide the imaging community documentation of a broad range of research, development, and applications in imaging.
**Ind/Abst** Chem. Abstr.; Curr. Contents Eng. Tech. Appl. Sci.; Ei Page One; Eng. Index Annu.; INSPEC; Res. Alert [Full Cov.]; Sci. Cit. Index; SCISEARCH.

US/0882-6404
**JOURNAL OF INDUSTRIAL TECHNOLOGY / THE NATIONAL ASSOCIATION OF INDUSTRIAL TECHNOLOGY.** [J. ind. technol.]. **Added/Corp** National Association of Industrial Technology. **VFOAT** Industrial Technology. (1984)-. Periodical. English. qt. Free (members); $20.00 US, $30.00 Canada, $40.00 other (non-members). National Association of Industrial Technology, 3157 Packard Road Suite A, Ann Arbor MI 48108. **Tel** (313)677-0720, FAX (313)677-2407. **ED** Kelly L. Patton. **DD** 607. **Bk Rev**, (Qty: 2). **Ad Acc. Pr Rev. Circ:** 3,500 (ctrl).
**Desc:** A national technical journal featuring reviewed and non-reviewed articles and items of interest to persons involved in industrial technology and industrial technology education.

●US/1064-1246
**JOURNAL OF INTELLIGENT & FUZZY SYSTEMS.** [J. intell. fuzzy syst.]. **VFOAT** Journal of Intelligent and Fuzzy Systems. Vol. 1, No. 1 (1993)-. Periodical. English. qt. $295.00 US; $335.00 Canada and Mexico; $350.00 other. John Wiley & Sons, Inc., 605 Third Avenue, New York NY 10158-0012. **Tel** (212)850-6000, (212)850-6645, FAX (212)850-6088, telex 12-7063. **(Subscription address:** John Wiley & Sons / England, Baffins Lane, Chichester, West Sussex PO19 1UD England.**)** **ED** Mohammad Jamshidi and Timothy J. Ross. **LC** TJ217.5.; J68. **DD** 602/.8563. **CODEN** JIFSE2.
**Desc:** Fosters the exchange and dissemination of applications and case studies in the areas of fuzzy logic and intelligent systems among working professionals and professionals in education and research.

US/1045-389X
**JOURNAL OF INTELLIGENT MATERIAL SYSTEMS AND STRUCTURES.** [J. intell. mater. syst. struct.]. Vol. 1 No. 1 (Jan. 1990)-. Periodical. English. bm. $425.00 (one year), $840.00 (two year), $1,255.00 (three year). Technomic Publishing Company, Inc., 851 New Holland Avenue, Box 3535, Lancaster PA 17604. **Tel** (717)291-5609, (800)233-9936, FAX (717)295-4538. **LC** TA418.9.S62; J68. **DD** 620.1/1. **CODEN** JMSSER. **[CCC].** available on microfilm and microfiche from University Microfilms International (UMI). Documents available from Article Express International, Ask*IEEE.
**Desc:** Publishes original papers describing experimental or theoretical work on all aspects of intelligent materials systems and structure research.
**Ind/Abst** Ceram. Abstr. (199?-); Civ. Struct. Eng. Abstr.; Comput. Inf. Syst. Abstr. J. [Full Cov.]; Ei Page One; Elect. Comm. Abstr.; Eng. Index Annu.; Environ. Eng. Abstr.; INSPEC (Jan. 1990-); Int. Aerosp. Abstr.; Mater. Sci. Eng. Abstr.; Mech. Eng. Abstr.; Solid State Supercond. Abstr.

US/0022-2038
**JOURNAL OF IRREPRODUCIBLE RESULTS, THE.** [J. irreprod. results]. Academic Scholarly Publication. English. bm. $40.00 US; $46.00 Canada and Mexico; $62.00 other (institutions), $16.50 US; $22.00 Canada and Mexico; $38.50 other (individuals). Blackwell Scientific Publishers, 238 Main Street, Cambridge MA 02142. **Tel** (617)547-7110, (800)835-6770, FAX (617)547-0789. **(Subscription address:** UK/ Marston Book Services, PO Box 87, Oxford UK; Aus/ 54 University Street, Carlton Victoria 3053 Australia; Germany/ Meinekestrasse 4, D-1000 Berlin 15 Germany; France/ Arnette, 2 rue Casimir Delavigne, 75006 Paris France; Austria/ Blackwell MZV, Medizinische Zeitschriftenverlags Gesellschaft, Feldgasse 13, A-1238 Vienna Austria**)** **ED** George H Scherr. **LC** Q167; .J68. **NLM** W1 JO732. **[CCC].** cum.

index. **Bk Rev**. **Ad Acc**. **Circ:** 50,000. available on microfilm and microfiche from University Microfilms International (UMI).
**Desc:** Humorous satire.

SU
**JOURNAL OF KING SAUD UNIVERSITY. SCIENCE.** **Added/Corp** Jamiat Al-Malik Saud. Imadat Shuun Al-Maktabat. **VFOAT** Science; Ulum; Majallat Jamiat Al-Malik Saud. Ulum. Vol. 1, No. 1/2 (1989)-. Periodical. English (Arabic). sa. King Saud University, University Libraries, PO Box 22480, 11495 Riyadh Saudi Arabia. **LC** Q80.S2; J68. **DD** 505. **CODEN** JKSSED. Documents available from CASDDS. ***Formed by the union of*** *Journal of the College of Science, King Saud University, 0735-9799; Journal of Engineering Sciences, 0377-9254* ***and*** *Journal of the College of Agriculture, University of Riyadh.*
**Ind/Abst** Chem. Abstr.

US/1005-0302
**JOURNAL OF MATERIALS SCIENCE & TECHNOLOGY.** (199?)-. English. bm. $375.00. Allerton Press, Inc., 150 Fifth Avenue, New York NY 10011. **Tel** (212)924-3950, FAX (212)463-9684, telex 427441 ALPRES. ***Continues*** *Chinese Journal of Metal Science & Technology, 1000-3029.*

NE/0376-7388
**JOURNAL OF MEMBRANE SCIENCE.** [J. membr. sci.]. Vol. 1 (March 1976)-. Academic Scholarly Publication. English. Thirty-nine times a year (13 volumes). FI5746.00. Elsevier Science Publishers BV, PO Box 211, 1000 AE Amsterdam Netherlands. **Tel** 011 31 20 5803642, FAX 011 31 20 5862696, telex 15682. **ED** W.J. Koros. **LC** TP159.M4; J68. **DD** 660.2/8424. **NLM** W1 JO76I. **CODEN** JMESDO. **[CCC]**. **Bk Rev**. **Ad Acc**. **Pr Rev**. available on microfilm and microfiche from University Microfilms International (UMI). Documents available from Article Express International, The Genuine Article, BIOSIS Document Express, Ask*IEEE, CASDDS, Documents on Demand.
**Desc:** Provides a focal point for membranologists and a vehicle for the dissemination of information dealing with the science and technology of membrane processes and phenomena.
**Ind/Abst** Bioeng. Abstr.; Biol. Abstr.; Chem. Abstr.; Chem. Titles; Curr. Biotechnol.; Curr. Contents Eng. Tech. Appl. Sci.; Curr. Contents Phys. Chem. Earth Sci.; Dairy Sci. Abstr.; Ei Page One; EMBASE; Energy Inf. Abstr.; Eng. Index Annu.; Environ. Abstr.; Fluid Abstr., Civil Eng.; Fluid Abstr. Proc. Eng.; FLUIDEX (19??-); Food Sci. Technol. Abstr.; HTFS Dig.; INSPEC (March 1977-); Life Sci. Collect.; Pollut. Abstr. Indexes; Polymer Contents; Proc. Chem. Eng.; Res. Alert [Full Cov.]; Sci. Cit. Index; SCISEARCH; Theoret. Chem. Eng.

JA
**JOURNAL OF NATURAL DISASTER SCIENCE.** ***Ceased.*** Vol. 7, No. 2 (1985)-(1988). Periodical. English. sa. Kyoto Daigaku Kenkyujo, (Disaster Prevention Research Inst., Kyoto University), Gokasho, Ujishi, Kyotofu 611 Japan. **(Subscription address:** Maruzen Company Ltd., PO Box 5050, Import & Export Department, Tokyo 100 31 Japan.**)** Documents available from Article Express International. ***Continues*** *Natural Disaster Science, 0388-4090.*
**Ind/Abst** Abstr. J. Earthq. Eng.; Bioeng. Abstr.; Ei Page One; Eng. Index Annu.; GeoRef.

PK/0022-2941
**JOURNAL OF NATURAL SCIENCES AND MATHEMATICS.** [J. nat. sci. math.]. **Added/Corp** Government College (Lahore, Pakistan). Research Council. (19??)-. Periodical. English. sa. $20.00. Government College Lahore, Physics Department, PO Box 1750, Lahore 54000 Pakistan. **Tel** (042)53668. **ED** M. Zakria Butt. **LC** Q1; .J75. **DD** 505. **CODEN** JNSMAC. **Circ:** 250. Documents available from CASDDS.
**Ind/Abst** Chem. Abstr.; Math. Rev.; Zentralbl. Math. Ihre Grenzgeb.

US/1043-609X
**JOURNAL OF NIH RESEARCH, THE.** **See** Biology.

US/0938-8974
**JOURNAL OF NONLINEAR SCIENCE.** [J. nonlinear sci.]. Vol. 1, No. 1 (1991)-. Periodical. English. Six times a year. $317.00. Springer-Verlag New York Inc., 175 5th Avenue, New York NY 10010. **Tel** (212)460-1500, telex 232 235 SPB UR. **(Subscription address:** Springer Verlag New York Inc. / for North America, 44 Hartz Way, Secaucus NJ 07096.**) ED** E A Kuznetsov and S R Wiggins. **LC** QC20.7.N6; J68. **DD** 003/.75. **CODEN** JNSCEK. **[CCC]**. available on microfilm and microfiche from University Microfilms International (UMI). Documents available from The Genuine Article.
**Desc:** Publishes innovative, high-quality research papers that augment the fundamental ways we analyze, describe and predict aspects of our nonlinear world.
**Ind/Abst** Compumath Citation Index [Full Cov.]; Curr. Contents Phys. Chem. Earth Sci.; Math. Rev.; Res. Alert [Full Cov.]; Sci. Cit. Index.

US/0022-3239
**JOURNAL OF OPTIMIZATION THEORY AND APPLICATIONS.** **See** Mathematics.

JA/0914-9244
**JOURNAL OF PHOTOPOLYMER SCIENCE AND TECHNOLOGY.** [J. photopolym. sci. tech.]. **VFOAT** Fotoporima Konwakaishi. (1988)-. Periodical. English (Japanese). qt. $170.00. **(Subscription address:** Maruzen Company Ltd., PO Box 5050, Import & Export Department, Tokyo 100 31 Japan.**) DD** 660.

PL
**JOURNAL OF POLISH SCIENCE.** ***Ceased.*** (19??)-(19??). English. **(Subscription address:** ARS Polona, PO Box 1001, 00068 Warsaw Poland.**)**

NE/1380-2224
**JOURNAL OF POROUS MATERIALS.** (19??)-. English. qt. $446.00. Kluwer Academic Publishers, Postbus 322, 3300 AH Dordrecht, The Netherlands. **Tel** 011 (31) 78 524400, FAX 011 31 78 183273, telex 20083.

US/8755-1985
**JOURNAL OF PROTECTIVE COATINGS & LININGS.** [J. prot. coat. linings]. **Added/Corp** Steel Structures Painting Council. **VFOAT** Journal of Protective Coatings and Linings. Vol. 1, No. 1 (June 1984)-. Periodical. English. mo. £70.00. Journal of Protective Coatings & Linings, 24 South 18th Street, Pittsburgh PA 15203. **Tel** (412)431-8300, FAX (412)431-5428. **(Subscription address:** TG Scott Subscriber Services, 6 Bourne Enterprise Centre, Kent TN15 8DG United Kingdom.**) ED** Harold E Hower. **LC** TP934; .J68. **DD** 667/.9/05. Index available. **Bk Rev**. **Ad Acc**. **Circ:** 13,000 (ctrl). available on microfilm. Documents available from Article Express International.
**Desc:** Describes new technology and practices for cleaning surfaces, and selecting and applying paints and coatings for industrial structures such as bridges, ships, and storage tanks.
**Ind/Abst** Abstr. Bull. Inst. Pap. Sci. Tech.; Constr. Index; Corros. Abstr.; Ei Page One; Eng. Mater. Abstr.; Eng. Index Annu.; World Surf. Coat. Abstr.

TU/0022-4057
**JOURNAL OF PURE AND APPLIED SCIENCES (ANKARA).** (JOURNAL OF PURE AND APPLIED SCIENCES. TEMEL VE UYGULAMALI BILIMLER DERGISI.). [J. pure appl. sci.]. **Added/Corp** Orta Dogu Teknik Universitesi (Ankara, Turkey). **VFOAT** Temel ve Uygulamali Bilimler Dergisi. (Apr. 1968)-. Academic Scholarly Publication. English (Turkish; summaries and/or abstracts in Turkish). Three times a year. Middle East Technical University, Faculty of Economic and Administrative Sciences, Ankara 06531 Turkey. **Tel** 011 91 41 2101000 ext. 2006. **ED** Mustafa Erdik. **LC** Q80.T8; J68. **DD** 505. **CODEN** JPASBN. **Bk Rev**. **Circ:** 400. Documents available from CASDDS.
**Desc:** Middle East Technical University journal of pure and applied sciences publishes original papers, review papers and book reviews in the fields of engineering and science.
**Ind/Abst** Chem. Abstr. (1982-); GeoRef; Int. Aerosp. Abstr.; Math. Rev.; Zentralbl. Math. Ihre Grenzgeb.

PK/0255-3643
**JOURNAL OF PURE AND APPLIED SCIENCES BAHAWALPUR.** [J. pure applied sci. Bahawalpur]. (1982)-. Periodical. English. sa.
**Ind/Abst** Zentralbl. Math. Ihre Grenzgeb.

US/0022-4065
**JOURNAL OF QUALITY TECHNOLOGY.** [J. qual. technol.]. **Added/Corp** American Society for Quality Control. Vol. 1 (Jan. 1969)-. Periodical. English. qt. $30.00 (nonmembers), $20.00 (members). American Society for Quality Control, 611 East Wisconsin Avenue, PO Box 3005, Milwaukee WI 53201. **Tel** (414)272-8575, (800)248-1946, FAX (414)272-1734, telex 316567. **LC** TS156.Q3; J65. **DD** 620/.0045/08. **CODEN** JQUTAU. **[CCC]**. **Pr Rev**. available on microfilm and microfiche from University Microfilms International (UMI). Documents available from The Genuine Article, UMI Article Clearinghouse, Ask*IEEE. ***Continues in part*** *Industrial Quality Control.*
**Desc:** Contains articles covering the technical aspects of quality control, reliability, and related disciplines that comprise the field of quality technology.
**Ind/Abst** ABI/INFORM Glob. Ed.; ABI Inform Ondisc (Jan. 1989-); Appl. Sci. Technol. Index; Biostatistica; Comput. Rev.; Curr. Contents Eng. Tech. Appl. Sci.; Curr. Index Stat.; Ei Page One; Energy Res. Abstr. (April 1978-); Eng. Mater. Abstr.; Food Sci. Technol. Abstr.; INSPEC (Oct. 1973-); Int. Aerosp. Abstr. (19??-19??); Oper. Res./Manag. Sci.; Qual. Control Appl. Stat.; Res. Alert [Full Cov.]; Sci. Cit. Index; SCISEARCH; Stat. Theory Method Abstr. (1971-1981).

II/0970-1990
**JOURNAL OF RECENT ADVANCES IN APPLIED SCIENCES.** **See** Biology.

US/0022-4308
**JOURNAL OF RESEARCH IN SCIENCE TEACHING.** [J. res. sci. teach.]. **Added/Corp** National Association for Research in Science Teaching. Association for the Education of Teachers in Science. Vol. 1 (Mar. 1963)-. Periodical. English. Ten times a year. $350.00 US; $450.00 Canada and Mexico; $487.50 other. John Wiley & Sons, Inc., 605 Third Avenue, New York NY 10158-0012. **Tel** (212)850-6000, (212)850-6645, FAX (212)850-6088, telex 12-7063. **(Subscription address:** John Wiley & Sons / England, Baffins Lane, Chichester, West Sussex PO19 1UD England.**) ED** Ronald G. Good. **LC** Q181.A1; J6. **DD** 507. **CODEN** JRSTAR. **[CCC]**. **Ad Acc**. **Pr Rev**. **Circ:** 2,000. available on microfilm and microfiche from University Microfilms International (UMI). Documents available from The Genuine Article, CASDDS.
**Desc:** Publishes articles related to the philosophy, historical perspective, teaching strategies, curriculum development and other topics relevant to science education.
**Ind/Abst** Acad. Search (July 1993-); Chem. Abstr.; Child Dev. Abstr. Bibliogr.; Contents Pages Educ.; Curr. Contents Soc. Behav. Sci.; Curr. Index J. Educ.; Educ. Index; Educ. Technol. Abstr.; Gen. Sci. Source (Jul. 1993-); INFO-SOUTH Abstr.; Mag. Search; Middle East Abstr. Index; Multicult. Educ. Abstr.; Psychol. Abstr. (1981-); PsycINFO; PsycLit; Res. Alert [Full Cov.]; Res. High. Educ. Abstr.; Soc. Sci. Cit. Index [Full Cov.]; Sociol. Educ. Abstr.; Stud. Women Abstr.; Tech. Educ. Train. Abstr.

●US/1065-7304
**JOURNAL OF RUSSIAN TECHNOLOGY.** (JOURNAL OF RUSSIAN TECHNOLOGY / SUPPORTED BY THE RUSSIAN ACADEMY OF SCIENCES ; COORDINATED BY FORUM, INTERNATIONAL NON-GOVERNMENTAL ORGANIZATION, THE WORLD FORUM OF SCIENTISTS AND EXPERTS.). [J. Russ. technol.]. **Added/Corp** Rossiiskaia Akademiia Nauk. Forum (Organization). (1993)-. Periodical. English. qt. $310.00. International Venture Publishing Ltd., c/o Sanford J Durst, 29-28 41st Avenue, Long Island City NY 11101. **Tel** (718)706-0303, FAX (718)706-0891. **DD** 600.
**Desc:** Covers on-going technological research in the former Soviet and Union.

MY/0126-7663
**JOURNAL OF SCIENCE AND MATHEMATICS EDUCATION IN SOUTHEAST ASIA.** **See** Education.

PK/0250-5339
**JOURNAL OF SCIENCE AND TECHNOLOGY.** [J. sci. technol.]. V. 1- Jan. 1977-. Academic Scholarly Publication. English. sa. $10.00. University of Peshawar, Peshawar Pakistan. **LC** Q80.P3; J68. **DD** 505. **CODEN** JSTPDU. Documents available from BIOSIS Document Express, CASDDS.
**Ind/Abst** Biol. Abstr.; Chem. Abstr. (1977-1979).

●US/1059-0145
**JOURNAL OF SCIENCE EDUCATION AND TECHNOLOGY.** [J. sci. educ. technol.]. Vol. 1, No. 1 (Mar. 1992)-. Periodical. English. Four times a year. $150.00 institutions, $52.00 individuals US; $175.00 institutions, $61.00 individuals other. Plenum Press, 233 Spring Street, New York NY 10013-1578. **Tel** (212)620-8000, (800)221-9369, FAX (212)463-0742, (212)807-1047, telex 23/421139. **LC** Q183.3.A1; J68. **DD** 507.1/073. **CODEN** JSEEEP. **[CCC]**.
**Ind/Abst** Curr. Index J. Educ.

US/1046-560X
**JOURNAL OF SCIENCE TEACHER EDUCATION.** **See** Education-Teaching and Curriculum.

IR/1016-1104
**JOURNAL OF SCIENCES, ISLAMIC REPUBLIC OF IRAN.** **Added/Corp** National Center for Scientific Research (Iran). Vol. 1, No. 1 (Fall 1989)-. Periodical. English. qt. $30.00 (individual), $40.00 (institutional). National Center for Scientific Research, 1188 Enghelab Ave, Tehran 13158 Iran. **LC** Q80.I67; J68. **DD** 505. **CODEN** JSIIEN. Documents available from CASDDS.
**Ind/Abst** Chem. Abstr.; Zentralbl. Math. Ihre Grenzgeb.

II
**JOURNAL OF SCIENTIFIC & INDUSTRIAL RESEARCH.** **Added/Corp** Council of Scientific & Industrial Research (India). **VFOAT** Journal of Scientific and Industrial Research. Vol. 22, No. 1 (Jan. 1963)-. Academic Scholarly Publication. English. Twelve times a year. $160.00. Council of Scientific & Industrial Research, Publications & Information Director, Hillside Road, New Delhi 110012 India. **Tel** FAX 011 91 11 5731353. **(Subscription address:** Prints India, 11 Darya Ganj, New Delhi 110002 India.**)** Documents available from Ask*IEEE, CASDDS, Documents on Demand. ***Continues*** *Journal of Scientific & Industrial Research. A, General, 0368-4202.*
**Ind/Abst** AgBiotech News Inf.; Agric. Eng. Abstr. (1991-); Anal. Abstr.; Biodeter. Abstr.; Biol. Abstr.; Ceram. Abstr.

(19??-19??); Chem. Abstr.; Crop Physiol. Abstr.; Curr. Biotechnol.; Curr. Titles Electrochem.; EMBASE; Environ. Abstr.; Food Sci. Technol. Abstr.; For. Prod. Abstr. (19??-19??); GeoRef; Helminthol. Abstr. (19??-19??); Index Vet.; Indian Geosci. Abstr.; INSPEC (1968-); Int. Aerosp. Abstr.; Leadscan; Methods Organ. Synth.; MINPROC; Plant Grow. Reg. Abstr.; Proc. Chem. Eng.; Protozoolog. Abstr.; Res. Alert [Full Cov.]; Rev. Med. Vet. Entomol.; Sci. Cit. Index; SCISEARCH; SEA Abstr.; Soc. Sci. Cit. Index [Select. Cov.]; Theoret. Chem. Eng.; Weed Abstr.; Wheat Barley Trit. Abstr.; World Text. Abstr.

US/0885-7474
**JOURNAL OF SCIENTIFIC COMPUTING.** [J. sci. comput.]. Vol. 1, No. 1 (1986)-. Periodical. English. Four times a year. $235.00 institutions, $57.00 individuals US; $275.00 institutions, $67.00 individuals other. Plenum Press, 233 Spring Street, New York NY 10013-1578. **Tel** (212)620-8000, (800)221-9369, FAX (212)463-0742, (212)807-1047, telex 23/421139. **ED** Stephen A. Orzag. **LC** Q183.9; .J68. **DD** 502.8/5. **CODEN** JSCOEB. **[CCC].** available on microfilm and microfiche from University Microfilms International (UMI). Documents available from Article Express International, Ask*IEEE.
**Ind/Abst** ACM Guide Comput. Lit.; Comput. Rev.; Ei Page One; Eng. Index Annu.; Inf. Sci. Abstr.; INSPEC (1986-); Int. Aerosp. Abstr.; Math. Rev. (1987-); Zentralbl. Math. Ihre Grenzgeb.

US/0892-3310
**JOURNAL OF SCIENTIFIC EXPLORATION.** (JOURNAL OF SCIENTIFIC EXPLORATION : A PUBLICATION OF THE SOCIETY FOR SCIENTIFIC EXPLORATION.). [J. sci. explor.]. **Added/Corp** Society for Scientific Exploration. Vol. 1, No. 1, (1987)-. Periodical. English. Four times a year (Mar., June, Sept., Dec.). $45.00 (individuals), $100.00 (institutions). Journal of Scientific Exploration, Stanford University, ERL 306, Stanford CA 94305. **Tel** (415)593-8581, FAX (415)595-4466. **ED** Marsha Sims. **LC** Q180.55.M4; J68. **DD** 001.4/2. **[CCC]. Pr Rev. Acid Free. Circ:** 1,000.
**Desc:** Devoted to the study of anomalous phenomena including phenomena outside the current paradigms of the sciences and phenomena within scientific paradigms but at variance with current scientific knowledge.
**Ind/Abst** Ei Page One; Except. Hum. Exp.

II/0253-7230
**JOURNAL OF SCIENTIFIC RESEARCH (BHOPAL).** (JOURNAL OF SCIENTIFIC RESEARCH.). [J. sci. res.]. Vol. 1 (Dec. 1978)-. Periodical. English. $60.00. Scientific Publisher of India, Bhopal India. **NLM** W1 JO875TR. **CODEN** JSREDL. Documents available from BIOSIS Document Express, CASDDS.
**Ind/Abst** Biol. Abstr.; Chem. Abstr.; Math. Rev.

II/0250-5347
**JOURNAL OF SHIVAJI UNIVERSITY. SCIENCE.** [J. Shivaji Univ., Sci.]. **Added/Corp** Shivaji University. **VFOAT** Science Journal of Shivaji University. (1976)-. Academic Scholarly Publication. English. an. **CODEN** JSUSDA. Documents available from CASDDS. ***Continues in part** Shivaji University. Journal, 0368-4199.*
**Ind/Abst** Chem. Abstr.; Math. Rev.

US/0928-0707
**JOURNAL OF SOL-GEL SCIENCE AND TECHNOLOGY.** bm. $694.00. Kluwer Academic Publishers / Massachusetts, PO Box 358, Accord Station, Hingham MA 02018. **Tel** (617)871-6600.

CC
**JOURNAL OF SOUTHEAST UNIVERSITY. Added/Corp** Tung Nan Ta Hsueh. **VFOAT** Tung Nan Ta Hsueh Hsueh Pao; Dongnan Daxue Xuebao. (198?)-. Academic Scholarly Publication. English. sa. Dongbei Nongye Daxue, Xuebao Bianjibu, Xiangfang-qu, Harbin, Heilongjiang 150030, People's Republic of China. **Tel** 5665886, FAX 5663336. **LC** T1; .J84. **DD** 605. **CODEN** DDXUEV. Documents available from CASDDS. ***Continues** Hsueh Pao (Nan-ching Kung Hsueh Yuan).*
**Ind/Abst** Chem. Abstr.; Math. Rev.; Zentralbl. Math. Ihre Grenzgeb.

II/0970-1893
**JOURNAL OF SURFACE SCIENCE AND TECHNOLOGY.** [J. surf. sci. technol.]. **Added/Corp** Indian Society for Surface Science & Technology. **VFOAT** JSST. Vol. 1, No. 1 (Jan. 1985)-. Academic Scholarly Publication. English. sa. $100.00. Indian Society for Surface Science & Technology, Calcutta, India. **(Subscription address:** Prints India, 11 Darya Ganj, New Delhi, 110002 India, (Phone: 011 91 11 3268645)) **CODEN** JSSTE4. Documents available from CASDDS.
**Ind/Abst** Chem. Abstr. (1985-); Food Sci. Technol. Abstr.

II/0047-2824
**JOURNAL OF TECHNOLOGY.** [J. technol.]. **Added/Corp** Bengal Engineering College, Howrah, India. Vol. 1 (June 1956)-. English. Twice a year. Bengal Engineering College, Howrah 711103, West Bengal India. **CODEN** JTBEAD. Documents available from Ask*IEEE.
**Ind/Abst** INSPEC (1968-); Int. Aerosp. Abstr.; Math. Rev.; Zentralbl. Math. Ihre Grenzgeb.

●US/1059-7069
**JOURNAL OF TECHNOLOGY AND TEACHER EDUCATION.** **See** Education.

US/1045-1064
**JOURNAL OF TECHNOLOGY EDUCATION.** [J. technol. educ.]. **Added/Corp** Virginia Polytechnic Institute and State University. Technology Education Program. International Technology Education Association. Council on Technology Teacher Education (U.S.). **VFOAT** JTE. Vol. 1, No. 1 (Fall 1989)-. Periodical. English. sa (Spring & Fall). $8.00 US; $12.00 other. Journal of Technology Education, Virginia Polytechnic University, Vocational & Technical Education, Blacksburg VA 24061. **Tel** (703)231-6480. **ED** Mark Sanders. **LC** T61; .J69. **DD** 607.1. **Bk Rev. Pr Rev. Circ:** 700 (ctrl).
**Desc:** Provides a forum for scholarly discussion on topics relating to technology education. Conceptual as well as research based manuscripts are within the scope of the journal. In addition, the journal publishes scholarly book reviews, editorials, guest articles, and reactions.

US/0892-9912
**JOURNAL OF TECHNOLOGY TRANSFER, THE.** [J. technol. transf.]. **Added/Corp** Technology Transfer Society. **VFOAT** Technology Transfer. Vol. 1 (Fall 1976)-. Periodical. English. qt (4 issues). $90.00 US; $120.00 other (also comes with Technology Transfer Society membership). Technology Transfer Society, 611 North Capitol Avenue, Indianapolis IN 46204. **Tel** (317)262-5022. **ED** James Jolly. **LC** T174.3; .J68. **DD** 338.9/26. Index available (free). **Bk Rev**, (Qty: 4). **Circ:** 800. available on CD-ROM.
**Desc:** Original papers on technology transfer, assessment, forecasting and utilization, theory and practice in business, universities and medical laboratories.
**Ind/Abst** AGRICOLA [Select. Cov.].

US/0002-4112
**JOURNAL OF THE ALABAMA ACADEMY OF SCIENCE, THE.** [J. Ala. Acad. Sci.]. **Added/Corp** Alabama Academy of Science. Vol. 1 (1926)-. Periodical. English. qt (Jan., April, July, Oct.). $20.00. University of Alabama Birmingham / Biology, Biology Department, c/o R Watson, Birmingham AL 35294. **Tel** (205)934-2031. **ED** R Watson. **NLM** W1 JO907H. **CODEN** JAASAJ. Index available. cum. index. **Bk Rev. Pr Rev. Circ:** 1,000. available on microfilm and microfiche from University Microfilms International (UMI). Documents available from BIOSIS Document Express, CASDDS.
**Desc:** Original research and review articles published in areas including biology, chemistry, mathematics, physics, social science, engineering and economics.
**Ind/Abst** AGRICOLA [Select. Cov.]; Am. Hist. Life (1964-1973); Biol. Abstr.; Chem. Abstr.; Fish Rev.; GeoRef; Int. Aerosp. Abstr.; Wildl. Rev. (1964-1973).

II/0970-4183
**JOURNAL OF THE ANDAMAN SCIENCE ASSOCIATION.** (1985)-. Periodical. English. sa. **UDC** 5.
**Ind/Abst** Agrofor. Abstr.; Anim. Breed. Abstr.; Field Crop Abstr.; For. Prod. Abstr. (1991-); For. Abstr.; Helminthol. Abstr.; Hortic. Abstr.; Index Vet.; Irr. Drain. Abstr.; Maize Abstr.; Nematol. Abstr.; Plant Breed. Abstr.; Plant Genet. Resour. Abstr.; Poult. Abstr.; Rev. Agric. Entomol.; Rev. Med. Vet. Entomol.; Rev. Plant Pathol.; Rice Abstr.; Soils Fert.; Soyabean Abstr.

II/0587-1921
**JOURNAL OF THE ASSAM SCIENCE SOCIETY.** (JOURNAL.). [J. Assam Science Society]. **Main/Corp** Assam Science Society. **VFOAT** Journal of the Assam Science Society. (1955)-. Periodical. English. Four times a year. **(Subscription address:** Prints India, 11 Darya Ganj, New Delhi, 110002 India, telephone: 011 91 11 3268645) **LC** Q73; .A86. **CODEN** JASYBQ.
**Ind/Abst** Plant Breed. Abstr.; Wheat Barley Trit. Abstr.

CC
**JOURNAL OF THE DALIAN INSTITUTE OF TECHNOLOGY.** (19??)-. Chinese (English). Chung-Kuo Kuo Chi Shu Tien, PO Box 2820, Beijing, China.
**Ind/Abst** Concr. Abstr.

US/0013-6220
**JOURNAL OF THE ELISHA MITCHELL SCIENTIFIC SOCIETY.** [J. Elisha Mitchell Sci. Soc.]. **Main/Corp** Elisha Mitchell Scientific Society, Chapel Hill, N.C. **Added/Corp** North Carolina Academy of Science. University of North Carolina (1793-1962). Vol. 1 (1884)-. Periodical. English. qt (March, June, Sep., Dec.). $20.00 (members), $50.00 other. North Carolina Academy of Science Inc., 1219 Broad Street, Durham NC 27705. **Tel** (919)286-3366 Ext. 681, FAX (919)286-5960. **ED** Robert R. Bryden Ph.D, Journal of the Elisha Mitchell Scientific Society, PO Box 1676 Morehead City, NC 28557; editor's phone: (919)726-2035. **LC** Q11; .E4. **CODEN** JEMSA5. Index available. cum. index. **Pr Rev. Acid Free. Circ:** 800. available on microfilm and microfiche from University Microfilms International (UMI). Documents available from BIOSIS Document Express, CASDDS.
**Desc:** Publishes papers in all scientific disciplines - biology, chemistry, physics, geology, psychology, mathematics, science education and history of science particularly as related to North Carolina and the Southeast. Also publishes papers on public policy as related to environmental concerns. Authors need not be members of the North Carolina Academy of Science.
**Ind/Abst** AGRICOLA; Anim. Breed. Abstr.; Biol. Abstr.; Chem. Abstr.; Curr. Geogr. Publ. (199?-); For. Abstr.; GeoRef; Grasslands For. Abstr.; Helminthol. Abstr. (1991-); Math. Rev.; Life Sci. Collect.; Rev. Med. Vet. Entomol.; Rev. Med. Vet. Mycology; Soils Fert.; Vitis Vitic. Enol. Abstr.; Zentralbl. Math. Ihre Grenzgeb.

JA/0371-7712
**JOURNAL OF THE FACULTY OF SCIENCE, UNIVERSITY OF TOKYO. SECTION III : BOTANY. Main/Corp** Tokyo Daigaku. Rigakubu. Vol. 1, (1925)-. Periodical. English. $124.00. **LC** QK1. **UDC** 58. ***Supersedes** Journal of the College of Science.*
**Ind/Abst** AGRICOLA.

US/0016-0032
**JOURNAL OF THE FRANKLIN INSTITUTE.** [J. Franklin Inst.]. **Added/Corp** Franklin Institute (Philadelphia, Pa.). Vol. 5 (1828)-. Periodical. English. Six times a year. $753.00 The Americas; £505.00 other. Pergamon Press, An Imprint of Elsevier Science Ltd., The Boulevard, Langford Lane, Kidlington, Oxford OX5 1GB United Kingdom. **Tel** 011 44 865 843000, 011 44 865 843699, FAX 011 44 865 843010. **(Subscription address:** Elsevier Science Ltd. Oxford Fulfillment Centre, PO Box 800, Kidlington, Oxford OX5 1DX United Kingdom.) **ED** Martin Pomerantz. **NLM** W1 J0923. **CODEN** JFINAB. **[CCC].** cum. index. **Pr Rev.** available on microfilm and microfiche from University Microfilms International (UMI); available on microfiche from the publisher. Documents available from Article Express International, The Genuine Article, Ask*IEEE, Petroleum Abstracts Document Delivery Service, CASDDS. ***Continues** Franklin Journal and American Mechanics' Magazine, 0093-7029.*
**Ind/Abst** Acoust. Abstr.; Appl. Mech. Rev.; Bioeng. Abstr.; Ceram. Abstr.; Chem. Abstr. (1829-1983); Comput. Abstr.; Comput. Rev.; Curr. Contents Eng. Tech. Appl. Sci.; Ei Page One; Eng. Index Annu. [Select. Cov.]; GeoRef; INSPEC (1968-); Int. Aerosp. Abstr.; Math. Rev.; Pet. Abstr.; Plant Breed. Abstr.; Pollut. Abstr. Indexes; Proc. Chem. Eng.; Res. Alert [Full Cov.]; Sci. Cit. Index; SCISEARCH; Shock Vibr. Dig.; Surf. Treat. Technol. Abstr.; Theoret. Chem. Eng.; World Surf. Coat. Abstr.; Zentralbl. Math. Ihre Grenzgeb.

US/0536-3012
**JOURNAL OF THE IDAHO ACADEMY OF SCIENCE.** [J. Idaho Acad. Sci.]. **Main/Corp** Idaho Academy of Science. **Added/Corp** Idaho Academy of Science. (1960)-. Periodical. English. Twice a year. $15.00. Idaho Academy of Science, Boise State University, Boise ID 83725. **Tel** (208)385-3975. **ED** Duane Letourneau. **DD** 051. **Bk Rev. Pr Rev. Circ:** 400.
**Desc:** Articles on research in all scientific fields, particularly as pertaining to Idaho.
**Ind/Abst** Fish Rev.; Wildl. Rev.

II/0019-4964
**JOURNAL OF THE INDIAN INSTITUTE OF SCIENCE.** [J. Indian inst. sci.]. **Main/Corp** Indian Institute of Science, Bangalore. Vol. 1 (Feb. 1914)-. Periodical. English. bm. $40.00. Indian Institute of Science, c/o IISC Library, Bangalore 560012 India. **Tel** 344411-2256, FAX 91-812-341683, telex 0845-8349 IISCIN. **(Subscription address:** Prints India, 11 Darya Ganj, New Delhi 110002 India.) **ED** M Vijayan, R Narayana, N M Malwad. **LC** Q1; .I5. **CODEN** JIISAD. Index available. cum. index. **Bk Rev. Ad Acc. Pr Rev. Circ:** 500. available on microfiche (from University Microfilms Int.). Documents available from BIOSIS Document Express, Ask*IEEE, CASDDS.
**Desc:** Publishes original and review papers in many branches of science and engineering.
**Ind/Abst** AGRICOLA; Alum. Ind. Abstr.; Biol. Abstr. (1986-); Ceram. Abstr.; Chem. Abstr.; Eng. Mater. Abstr.; INSPEC (1968-); Math. Rev.; Met. Abstr.; Life Sci. Collect.; PESTDOC; Rev. Med. Vet. Entomol.; SEA Abstr.; Zentralbl. Math. Ihre Grenzgeb.

II/0970-4140
**JOURNAL OF THE INDIAN INSTITUTE OF SCIENCE 1960.** (1960)-. Periodical. English. qt. Indian Institute of Science, c/o IISC Library, Bangalore 560012 India. **Tel** 344411-2256, FAX 91-812-341683, telex 0845-8349 IISCIN. **UDC** 5.
**Ind/Abst** Ei Page One; Int. Aerosp. Abstr.

II
**JOURNAL OF THE INDIAN INSTITUTE OF SCIENCE. SECTION A: ENGINEERING AND TECHNOLOGY. Main/Corp** Indian Institute of Science, Bangalore. Vol. 59, No. 1 (Jan. 1977)-. Periodical. English. bm. Indian

Institute of Science, c/o IISC Library, Bangalore 560012 India. **Tel** 344411-2256, FAX 91-812-341683, telex 0845-8349 IISCIN. ***Continues in part*** *Indian Institute of Science, Bangalore. Journal of the Indian Institute of Science.*
**Ind/Abst** Ceram. Abstr. (19??-).

II
**JOURNAL OF THE INDIAN INSTITUTE OF SCIENCE. SECTION B: PHYSICAL AND CHEMICAL SCIENCES.** **Main/Corp** Indian Institute of Science, Bangalore. Vol. 59, No. 2 (Feb. 1977)-. Periodical. English. Three times a year. Indian Institute of Science, c/o IISC Library, Bangalore 560012 India. **Tel** 344411-2256, FAX 91-812-341683, telex 0845-8349 IISCIN. ***Continues in part*** *Indian Institute of Science, Bangalore. Journal of the Indian Institute of Science.*
**Ind/Abst** Ceram. Abstr. (19??-).

II/0368-2684
**JOURNAL OF THE INDIAN INSTITUTE OF SCIENCE. SECTION C: BIOLOGICAL SCIENCES.** **Main/Corp** Indian Institute of Science, Bangalore. Vol. 59, No. 4 (Apr. 1977)-. Periodical. English. Six times a year. **(Subscription address:** Prints India, 11 Darya Ganj, New Delhi, 110002 India, telephone: 011 91 11 3268645**)** **CODEN** JISCAF. Documents available from BIOSIS Document Express. ***Continues in part*** *Indian Institute of Science, Bangalore. Journal of the Indian Institute of Science.*
**Ind/Abst** Biol. Abstr.; NAPRALERT.

US/0896-8381
**JOURNAL OF THE IOWA ACADEMY OF SCIENCE, THE.** (THE JOURNAL OF THE IOWA ACADEMY OF SCIENCE : JIAS.). [J. Iowa Acad. Sci.]. **Added/Corp** Iowa Academy of Science. **VFOAT** JIAS. Vol. 95, No. 1 (Mar. 1988)-. Academic Scholarly Publication. English. qt. $20.00 US; $22.00 other. Iowa Academy of Science, University of Northern Iowa, Cedar Falls IA 50614. **Tel** (319)273-2021. **ED** Roger and Marilyn Bachmann. **LC** Q11; .I5. **DD** 505. **CODEN** JIASEB. **Bk Rev**. **Ad Acc**. **Pr Rev. Circ:** 2,000. available on microfilm and microfiche from University Microfilms International (UMI). Documents available from BIOSIS Document Express, Ask*IEEE, CASDDS. ***Continues*** *Iowa Academy of Science. Proceedings of the Iowa Academy of Science, 0085-2236.*
**Desc:** A refereed scientific journal publishing articles in all areas of biological and physical science.
**Ind/Abst** AgBiotech News Inf.; AGRICOLA [Select. Cov.]; Biol. Abstr.; Chem. Abstr.; Coal Abstr. (1988-); EMBASE (1988-); Field Crop Abstr.; Fish Rev.; GeoRef (1988-); Grasslands For. Abstr.; INSPEC (March 1988-); Maize Abstr.; Math. Rev.; Nematol. Abstr.; Life Sci. Collect. (1988-); Plant Breed. Abstr.; Plant Genet. Resour. Abstr.; Rev. Agric. Entomol.; Rev. Plant Pathol.; Seed Abstr.; Soils Fert.; Soyabean Abstr.; Wildl. Rev.

II/0075-5168
**JOURNAL OF THE KARNATAK UNIVERSITY. SCIENCE.** [J. Karnatak Univ., Sci.]. **Main/Corp** Karnatak University, Dharwar, India. V. 4- 1959-. Academic Scholarly Publication. English. an. Karnatak University, Dhawar 580003, Karnatak India. **LC** Q1; .K25. **DD** 505. **CODEN** KUJSAB. Documents available from CASDDS. ***Continues in part*** *Karnatak University, Dharwar, India. Journal.*
**Ind/Abst** Chem. Abstr.; GeoRef; Math. Rev.; Stat. Theory Method Abstr. (1969-1971).

US/0026-539X
**JOURNAL OF THE MINNESOTA ACADEMY OF SCIENCE.** [J. Minn. Acad. Sci.]. **Added/Corp** Minnesota Academy of Science (1932)-. Vol. 32, No. 1 (1964)-. Periodical. English. Twice a year (Fall/Winter, Spring). $20.00 US; $22.00 Canada; $26.00 other. Minnesota Academy of Science, 350 Robert Street North 583, St Paul MN 55101. **Tel** (613)227-6361. **ED** Alan Olness. **LC** Q11; .M615. **NLM** W1 JO94K. **CODEN** JMNAAC. **Bk Rev. Circ:** 600. available on microfilm and microfiche from University Microfilms International (UMI). Documents available from BIOSIS Document Express, CASDDS. ***Formed by the union of*** *Minnesota Journal of Science, 0544-3598; Minnesota Academy of Science (1932- ). Meeting. Proceedings of the Minnesota Academy of Science, 0096-9397.*
**Ind/Abst** AGRICOLA [Select. Cov.]; Biol. Abstr.; Chem. Abstr.; Dairy Sci. Abstr.; EMBASE; Field Crop Abstr.; Fish Rev.; GeoRef; Grasslands For. Abstr.; Soils Fert.; Wildl. Rev.

US/0076-9436
**JOURNAL OF THE MISSISSIPPI ACADEMY OF SCIENCES.** [J. Miss. Acad. Sci.]. **Main/Corp** Mississippi Academy of Sciences. Vol. 1 (1939)-. Periodical. English. Four times a year. $25.00. Mississippi Academy of Science, 405 Briarwood Drive, Suite 107E, Jackson MD 39206-3029. **Tel** (601)353-6527. **ED** John Tiftickjian. **LC** Q11; .M66. **DD** 505. **CODEN** JMSSAN. Index available. cum. index. **Ad Acc. Pr Rev. Circ:** 1200. Documents available from BIOSIS Document Express, CASDDS.
**Ind/Abst** AGRICOLA [Select. Cov.]; Biodeter. Abstr. (1991-); Biol. Abstr.; Chem. Abstr.; Fish Rev.; GeoRef; Plant Grow. Reg. Abstr.; Rev. Agric. Entomol.; Rev. Plant Pathol.; Soyabean Abstr.; Weed Abstr.; Wildl. Rev.

TH/0028-0011
**JOURNAL OF THE NATIONAL RESEARCH COUNCIL OF THAILAND.** (WARASAN SAMNAKNGAN KHANA KAMMAKAN WICHAI HNG CHAT.). [J. natl. res. coun. Thail.]. **Added/Corp** Thailand. Samnakngan Khana Kammakan Wichai Hng Chat. **VFOAT** Journal of the National Research Council of Thailand. Vol. 6, Nos. 1-4 (Mar.-Dec. 1974)-. Periodical. Thai (English). qt. 60.00B Thailand; $7.00 US. National Research Council / Thailand, 196 Phahonyothin Road, Bangkok Thailand. **Tel** 5792285, telex 82213 NARECOU TH. **ED** Choompol Swasdiyakorn. **CODEN** JRCTAF. **Circ:** 1,000 (ctrl). Documents available from Ask*IEEE, CASDDS. ***Continues*** *Warasan Sapha Wichai Hng Chat.*
**Ind/Abst** AGRICOLA; Chem. Abstr. (-1987); EMBASE; GeoRef; INSPEC (1968-); Plant Breed. Abstr.; Plant Grow. Reg. Abstr.; SEA Abstr.; Trop. Dis. Bull.

CE/0300-9254
**JOURNAL OF THE NATIONAL SCIENCE COUNCIL OF SRI LANKA.** [J. Natl. Sci. Counc. Sri Lanka]. **Main/Corp** National Science Council of Sri Lanka. Vol. 1 (Aug. 1973)-. Periodical. English (Sinhalese and Tamil). Twice a year. $5.75 Sri Lanka; $27.00 other. Natural Resources Energy and Science Authority of Sri Lanka, 47 Maitland Place, Colombo 7 Sri Lanka. **Tel** 596771, 596772, 596773. **ED** B.A. Abeywickrama. **LC** Q4; .N145a. **DD** 505. **NLM** W1 JO941PK. **CODEN** JNSCBH. **[CCC]**. Index available. **Pr Rev. Circ:** 300 (ctrl). Documents available from BIOSIS Document Express, CASDDS.
**Desc:** Includes research and review papers and short communications in all fields of science and technology mainly by Sri Lankan scientists.
**Ind/Abst** AGRICOLA; Biodeter. Abstr.; Biol. Abstr.; Chem. Abstr.; Crop Physiol. Abstr.; Dairy Sci. Abstr.; Field Crop Abstr.; Food Sci. Technol. Abstr.; GeoRef; Grasslands For. Abstr.; Irr. Drain. Abstr.; NAPRALERT; Pig News Inf.; Plant Breed. Abstr.; Rice Abstr.; SEA Abstr.; Soils Fert.; Soyabean Abstr.; Zentralbl. Math. Ihre Grenzgeb.

US/0271-776X
**JOURNAL OF THE NATIONAL TECHNICAL ASSOCIATION.** [J. Natl. Tech. Assoc.]. **Main/Corp** National Technical Association. **VFOAT** NTA Journal. (19??)-. Academic Scholarly Publication. English. qt. $30.00 US; $40.00 Canada; $50.00 other; Also included with membership. Black Collegiate Services Inc., 1240 South Broad Street, New Orleans LA 70125. **Tel** (504)821-5694, FAX (504)821-5713. **CODEN** JNTADI. available on microfilm from University Microfilms International (UMI). Documents available from CASDDS.
**Ind/Abst** Chem. Abstr. (1926-1985); Coal Abstr.; Energy Res. Abstr. (Dec. 1980-).

UK/0160-5682
**JOURNAL OF THE OPERATIONAL RESEARCH SOCIETY, THE.** **See** Mathematics.

JA/0453-4514
**JOURNAL OF THE OPERATIONS RESEARCH SOCIETY OF JAPAN.** [J. Oper. Res. Soc. Jpn.]. **Main/Corp** Keiei Kagaku Kyokai. **Added/Corp** Nihon Opereshonzu Risachi Gakkai. **VFOAT** Nihon Opereshonzu Risachi Gakkai Ronbunshi. Vol. 1, No. 1 (Oct. 1957)-. Periodical. English (Japanese). Four times a year (Mar., June, Sept., Dec.). ¥13200.00. Operations Research Society of Japan, 2-4-16 Yayoi Gakkai Center Building, Bunkyo-KU Tokyo 113 Japan. **LC** T57.6.A1; K44a. **CODEN** JORJA5. cum. index. **Pr Rev.** Documents available from The Genuine Article, Ask*IEEE.
**Ind/Abst** Compumath Citation Index [Full Cov.]; INSPEC (March 1971-); Int. Abstr. Oper. Res. [Full Cov.]; Int. Aerosp. Abstr.; Math. Rev.; Life Sci. Collect.; Res. Alert [Full Cov.]; SCISEARCH; Soc. Sci. Cit. Index [Select. Cov.]; Stat. Theory Method Abstr. (1982-1984, 1986-1987); Zentralbl. Math. Ihre Grenzgeb.

US/1044-6753
**JOURNAL OF THE PENNSYLVANIA ACADEMY OF SCIENCE.** [J. Pa. Acad. Sci.]. Vol. 62, No. 1 (Sept. 1988)-. Academic Scholarly Publication. English. Four times a year (Jan., Mar., July, Nov.). $35.00 US & Canada; $44.00 Europe; $43.00 Pan America; $46.00 Japan; $47.00 others. Pennsylvania Academy of Science, PO Box 392, Gettysburg College, Gettysburg PA 17325-1486. **Tel** (717)337-6158, FAX (717)337-6666. **ED** Shyamal K. Majumdar. **DD** 506. **NLM** W1; JO946CV. **CODEN** JPSCEY. cum. index. **Ad Acc. Pr Rev. Circ:** 800 (ctrl). Documents available from BIOSIS Document Express, CASDDS. ***Continues*** *Proceedings of the Pennsylvania Academy of Science, 0096-9222.*
**Desc:** General science journal open to all branches of science. The subject matter is not limited geographically to Pennsylvania.
**Ind/Abst** Biol. Abstr.; Chem. Abstr. (1988-); Fish Rev. (Jan. 1989-July 1992); GeoRef; Wildl. Rev. (Jan. 1989-July 1992).

NZ/0303-6758
**JOURNAL OF THE ROYAL SOCIETY OF NEW ZEALAND.** [J. R. Soc. N. Z.]. **Added/Corp** Royal Society of New Zealand. Vol. 1, No. 1 (May 1971)-. Academic Scholarly Publication. English. qt (Mar., June, Sep., Dec.). NZ$170.00 New Zealand/Australia; $140.00 other (institution). SIR Publishing, PO Box 399, Wellington, New Zealand. **Tel** 011 64 4 472 7421, FAX 011 64 4 473 1841. **ED** C. M. King. **LC** Q1; .R7. **DD** 505. **CODEN** JRNZAK. **[CCC]. Bk Rev. Ad Acc. Pr Rev. Circ:** 800 (ctrl). Documents available from The Genuine Article, BIOSIS Document Express, CASDDS, Petroleum Abstracts Document Delivery Service, Documents on Demand. ***Formed by the union of*** *Transactions of the Royal Society of New Zealand. Earth Sciences; Transactions of the Royal Society of New Zealand. General* ***and*** *Transactions of the Royal Society of New Zealand. Biological Sciences, 0557-417X.*
**Desc:** Original and review papers on the natural sciences in New Zealand.
**Ind/Abst** AGRICOLA; Biol. Abstr.; Chem. Abstr.; Curr. Aware. Biol. Sci., CABS; Curr. Contents, Agric. Biol. Environ. Sci.; Curr. Ref. Fish Res.; Ecol. Abstr.; Ecology Abstr.; Environ. Abstr.; Geogr. Abstr. Phys. Geogr. (?-?); Geol. Abstr.; GeoRef; Life Sci. Collect.; Pet. Abstr.; Res. Alert [Full Cov.]; Sci. Cit. Index; SCISEARCH; Soils Fert.

TH/0303-8122
**JOURNAL OF THE SCIENCE SOCIETY OF THAILAND.** [J. Sci. Soc. Thail.]. (Mar. 1975)-. Academic Scholarly Publication. English (Thai). Four times a year. $20.00. Science Society of Thailand, Chulalongkorn University, Faculty of Science, Bangkok 5 Thailand. **LC** Q80.T5. **DD** 505. **NLM** W1 JO954FS. **CODEN** VKSTDB. **Pr Rev.** Documents available from The Genuine Article, Ask*IEEE, CASDDS.
**Ind/Abst** Abstr. AIT Rep. Publ. Energy; AgBiotech News Inf.; Anim. Breed. Abstr.; Biocont. News Inf. (1991-); Chem. Abstr.; Coal Abstr.; Curr. Biotechnol.; Curr. Contents, Agric. Biol. Environ. Sci.; Curr. Ref. Fish Res.; Helminthol. Abstr. (19??-19??); INSPEC (Sept. 1975-); J. Ferrocement; Plant Breed. Abstr.; Res. Alert [Full Cov.]; Rev. Med. Vet. Entomol.; Sci. Cit. Index; SCISEARCH.

SI/0129-3729
**JOURNAL OF THE SINGAPORE NATIONAL ACADEMY OF SCIENCE.** [J. Singap. Natl. Acad. Sci.]. **Main/Corp** Singapore National Academy of Science. V. 1- 1969-. Periodical. English. $20.00. 11 Napier Road, Singapore 10 Singapore. **LC** Q80.S5; S47A. **DD** 505. **CODEN** JSNABL. Documents available from Ask*IEEE, CASDDS.
**Ind/Abst** Chem. Abstr.; INSPEC (1969-); Math. Rev.; Zentralbl. Math. Ihre Grenzgeb.

US/0040-313X
**JOURNAL OF THE TENNESSEE ACADEMY OF SCIENCE.** [J. Tenn. Acad. Sci.]. **Main/Corp** Tennessee Academy of Science. Vol. 1 (1926)-. Academic Scholarly Publication. English. Four times a year (Jan., Apr., July, Oct.). $30.00. Tennessee Technological University / Biology Department, c/o John Harris, PO Box 5063, Cookeville TN 38505. **Tel** (615)372-3143. **ED** Dr. Phyllis Kennedy, (phone: (901)678-2597). **LC** Q11; .T32. **DD** 505. **NLM** W1 TE415P. **CODEN** JTASAG. **Pr Rev. Circ:** 900 (ctrl). available on microfilm. Documents available from BIOSIS Document Express, CASDDS. ***Continues*** *Tennessee Academy of Science. Transactions of the Tennessee Academy of Science.*
**Desc:** Scientific research from all areas of science with more articles in biology.
**Ind/Abst** AGRICOLA [Select. Cov.]; Agrofor. Abstr. (1991-); Biol. Abstr.; Chem. Abstr.; Coal Abstr.; CSA Neuro. Abstr. (?-?); Ecology Abstr.; EMBASE; Energy Res. Abstr.; Fish Rev.; For. Prod. Abstr. (1991-); For. Abstr.; GeoRef; Key Word Index Wildl. Res.; Life Sci. Collect.; Rev. Plant Pathol.; Soils Fert.; Wildl. Rev.; Zentralbl. Math. Ihre Grenzgeb.

II/0368-4644
**JOURNAL OF THE UNIVERSITY OF BOMBAY, SCIENCE: PHYSICAL SCIENCES, MATHEMATICS, BIOLOGICAL SCIENCES AND MEDICINE.** **See** Mathematics.

KU/0376-4818
**JOURNAL OF THE UNIVERSITY OF KUWAIT, SCIENCE, THE.** [J. Univ. Kuwait, Sci.]. **Main/Corp** Jamiat Al-Kuwayt. Kulliyat Al-Ulum. **VFOAT** Majallat Jamiat Al-Kuwayt, Al-Ulum. V. 1- 1974-. Academic Scholarly Publication. English (summaries and/or abstracts in Arabic). an. Free. University of Kuwait, Fac of Science, PO Box 5969, AL Kuwait. **Tel** 0095 846725. **LC** Q80.K9; J35A. **DD** 505. **CODEN** JUKSD8. **Pr Rev.** Documents available from The Genuine Article, BIOSIS Document Express, Ask*IEEE, Petroleum Abstracts Document Delivery Service, CASDDS.
**Ind/Abst** Anal. Abstr.; Biocont. News Inf.; Biol. Abstr.; Chem. Abstr.; Crop Physiol. Abstr.; Curr. Contents Phys. Chem. Earth Sci.; EMBASE; Energy Res. Abstr. (Aug. 1976-); Field Crop Abstr.; For. Abstr.; INSPEC (1974-); Irr. Drain. Abstr.; Math. Rev.; Microbiol. Abstr. Sect. C; Life Sci. Collect.; Pet. Abstr.; Plant Breed. Abstr.; Plant Grow. Reg. Abstr.; Res. Alert [Full Cov.]; Rev. Med. Vet.

# Science and Technology

Entomol.; Rev. Plant Pathol.; Sci. Cit. Index; SCISEARCH; Seed Abstr.; Soc. Sci. Cit. Index [Select. Cov.]; Wheat Barley Trit. Abstr.; Zentralbl. Math. Ihre Grenzgeb.

II/0551-4932
**JOURNAL OF THE UNIVERSITY OF POONA, SCIENCE AND TECHNOLOGY.** (JOURNAL OF THE UNIVERSITY OF POONA. PUNEM VIDYAPITHA PATRIKA.). [J. Univ. Poona, Sci. Technol.]. **Main/Corp** University of Poona. **Added/Corp** University of Poona. Punem Vidyapitha Patrika. **VFOAT** Punem Vidyapitha Patrika. No. 1 (1952)-. Academic Scholarly Publication. English (Marathi). an. **LC** AS472.P6; A3. **CODEN** JUPOAİ. Documents available from BIOSIS Document Express, CASDDS.
**Ind/Abst** Biol. Abstr.; Chem. Abstr.; GeoRef; Math. Rev.; Zentralbl. Math. Ihre Grenzgeb.

US/0043-0439
**JOURNAL OF THE WASHINGTON ACADEMY OF SCIENCES.** [J. Wash. Acad. Sci.]. **Main/Corp** Washington Academy of Sciences, Washington, D.C. Vol. 1 (July 19, 1911)-. Academic Scholarly Publication. English. qt. $25.00 US; $30.00 (surface mail) other. Washington Academy of Sciences, 6 Tegner Court, Rockville MD 20850. **Tel** (301)424-3126. **ED** John O'Hare. **LC** Q11. **DD** 506/.2753. **NLM** W1 WA57. **CODEN** JWASA3. **Bk Rev. Circ:** 850. available on microfilm and microfiche from University Microfilms International (UMI). Documents available from BIOSIS Document Express, CASDDS. **Supersedes** Proceedings of the Washington Academy of Sciences, 0363-1095.
**Desc:** Original scientific research, critical reviews, historical articles, proceedings of scholarly meetings of its fifty affiliated societies, and reports of the academy.
**Ind/Abst** AGRICOLA; Biol. Abstr.; Biol. Dig.; Chem. Abstr.; Ei Page One; Fish Rev.; HILITES; Life Sci. Collect.; Surf. Treat. Technol. Abstr.; Wildl. Rev.

II
**JOURNAL : SCIENCE. Main/Corp** Nagpur University. Vol. 1 (1970)-. English. an. Rs10.00. Nagpur University, Nagpur-1 India. **LC** Q1; .N15a. **DD** 505.

II/0970-4116
**JOURNAL : SCIENCE, TECHNOLOGY & MEDICINE.** [J. Jiwaji Univ., Sci. technol. med.]. **Main/Corp** Jiwaju University. Vol. 1 (Jan. 1973)-. English. 16.00Can$ (individuals), 18.00Can$ (institutions) Canada; 18.00Can$ (individuals), 20.00Can$ (institutions) other. **LC** Q73; .J58A. **DD** 505.
**Ind/Abst** Math. Rev.

●US
**JPRS REPORT. SCIENCE & TECHNOLOGY. CENTRAL EURASIA. CHEMISTRY [MICROFORM] / FOREIGN BROADCAST INFORMATION SERVICE.** See Chemistry.

●US
**JPRS REPORT. SCIENCE & TECHNOLOGY. CENTRAL EURASIA. ENGINEERING & EQUIPMENT [MICROFORM] / FOREIGN BROADCAST INFORMATION SERVICE.** See Engineering.

US
**JPRS REPORT. SCIENCE & TECHNOLOGY. CHINA. Added/Corp** United States. Joint Publications Research Service. United States. Foreign Broadcast Information System. **VFOAT** Science & Technology. China; Science and Technology. China; China. (1987)-. Periodical. English (translations available in Chinese). **NLM** Z 7407.C5; J89. available on microfiche. **Continues in part** China Report. Science and Technology, 0271-0099.

US
**JPRS REPORT. SCIENCE & TECHNOLOGY. EUROPE. Title Change. Added/Corp** United States. Joint Publications Research Service. United States. Foreign Broadcast Information Service. **VFOAT** J.P.R.S. Report. Europe; Science & Technology; Europe. **VAT** Joint Publications Research Service Report. Science and Technology. Europe. JPRS-EST-88-001 (May 10, 1988)-(1993). Periodical. English (translations available in Multiple languages). Joint Publications Research Services, PO Box 12507, Arlington VA 22209. **Continues** JPRS Report. Science & Technology. Europe & Latin America. **Continued by** JPRS Report. Science & Technology. Europe/International.

●US
**JPRS REPORT. SCIENCE & TECHNOLOGY. EUROPE/INTERNATIONAL. Added/Corp** United States. Joint Publications Research Service.

United States. Foreign Broadcast Information Service. **VFOAT** JPRS Report. Europe/International; Science & Technology. Europe/International; Science and Technology. Europe/International; Europe/International; Europe International. **VAT** Joint Publications Research Service report. Science & technology. Europe/international. (1993)-. Periodical. English (translations available in Multiple languages). ir. Joint Publications Research Services, PO Box 12507, Arlington VA 22209. **Continues** JPRS Report. Science & Technology. Europe.

US
**JPRS REPORT. SCIENCE & TECHNOLOGY. JAPAN. MICROFORM. VFOAT** Science & Technology. Japan. **VAT** Joint Publications Research Service Report. Science and Technology. Japan. (June 1987)-. English. ir. Joint Publications Research Services, PO Box 12507, Arlington VA 22209. available on microfiche (Vols. for 1987 distributed to depository libraries). **Continues** Japan Report (Arlington, VA.). Science and Technology.

US
**JPRS REPORT. SCIENCE & TECHNOLOGY. USSR, EARTH SCIENCES. VFOAT** Science & Technology. Earth Sciences; Science and Technology. USSR, Earth Sciences; USSR, Earth Sciences. **VAT** Joint Publications Research Service Report. Science and Technology. Union of Soviet Socialist Republics, Earth Sciences. JPRS-UES-87-005 (July 9, 1987). Periodical. English. Joint Publications Research Services, PO Box 12507, Arlington VA 22209. **Continues** USSR Report. Earth Sciences.

US/0898-3690
**JPRS REPORT. SCIENCE & TECHNOLOGY. USSR, LIFE SCIENCES. Title Change.** [JPRS rep., Sci. technol., USSR, life sci.]. **Added/Corp** United States. Joint Publications Research Service. United States. Foreign Broadcast Information Service. **VFOAT** Science & Technology. USSR, Life Sciences; USSR, Life Sciences. **VAT** Joint Publications Research Service Report. Science & Technology. Union of Soviet Socialist Republics, Life Sciences. (June 23, 1987)-(1992). English (translations available in Russian). ir. Joint Publications Research Services, PO Box 12507, Arlington VA 22209. **DD** 570. **NLM** ZW 1; J89. available on microfiche (Vols. for 1987 distributed to depository libraries). **Continues** USSR Report. Life Sciences. Biomedical and Behavioral Sciences (Public Ed.), 0740-1264. **Continued by** JPRS Report. Science & Technology. Central Eurasia. Life Sciences.
**Ind/Abst** Life Sci. Collect. (1987-).

US/0897-1277
**JURIMETRICS (CHICAGO, ILL.).** See Law.

MY/0126-9569
**JURNAL SAINS - INSTITUT PENYELIDIKAN GETAH MALAYSIA.** (JURNAL SAINS INSTITUT PENYELIDIKAN GETAH MALAYSIA.). [J. sains - Inst. Penyelidikan Getah Malays.]. **Added/Corp** Rubber Research Institute of Malaysia. **VFOAT** Jurnal Sains IPGM. (1979)-. Academic Scholarly Publication. English. sa. Institut Penyelidikan Getah Malaysia, 260 Jl Ampang, Peti Surat 150, Kuala Lumpur 01-02 Malaysia. **LC** PAR. **CODEN** JSIMDY. Documents available from CASDDS. **Continues** Jurnal Sains Pusat Penyelidikan Getah Malaysia, 0126-6136.
**Ind/Abst** Chem. Abstr. (1979-1981).

CU/0449-4555
**JUVENTUD TECNICA.** Periodical. Spanish. Ediciones Cubanas, Obispo 527, Altos ESQ Bernaza, CP 10100 Havana Cuba. **Tel** 011 632980, 631942, FAX 011 631011, telex 512337, 6540. **LC** T4; .J87. **DD** 605.

JA
**KAGAKU GIJUTSU KENKYU CHOSA HOKOKU / HENSHU SORIFU TOKEIKYOKU. VFOAT** Report on the Survey of Research and Development in Japan; Statistical Survey of Researches. Began in 1960. Japanese (English). an. Somucho Tokeikyoku, (Statistics Bureau, Management & Coordination Agency), 19-1, Wakamatsucho, Shinjukuku, Tokyoto 162 Japan. **LC** Q180.J3; A3. **DD** 001.4/0952. **Continues** Kenkyu Kikan Kihan Tokei Chosa Kekka Hokoku.

JA
**KAGAKU GIJUTSU ROPPO / HENSHU KAGAKU GIJUTSUCHO. Main/Corp** Japan. Japanese. ¥4800. Taisei Shuppansha, 1-7-11 Hanegi 1, Setagaya-ku, Tokyo-to Japan. **LC** LAW.

JA
**KAGAKU: SCIENCE.** Japanese. mo. $159.00. (**Subscription address:** Kyowa Book Company Inc., 1-38 Kanda Jinbo-Cho, Chiyoda-Ku, Tokyo 101, Japan (Phone: 03-3293-0727))

JA
**KAGAKU SHINBUN. VFOAT** Science News. Periodical. Japanese. ¥5000. Kagaku Shinbunsha, 8-1 Hamamatsu-cho 1 Minato-ku, Tokyo-to Japan. **LC** Q4; .K126.

JA/0022-7692
**KAGAKUSHI KENKYU. Added/Corp** Nippom Kagakushi Gakkai. **VFOAT** Kagakusi Kenkyu. Journal of History of Science, Japan; Journal of History of Science, Japan. (1??)-. Periodical. Japanese (table of contents in English). qt. $88.00. Kagakushi Gakkai, (Japanese Soc. for the History of Chemistry), Chiba Kogyo Daigaku, 2-17, Tsudanuma 2 Chome, Narashinoshi, Chibaken 275 Japan. (**Subscription address:** Kyowa Book Company Inc., 1 38 Kanda Jinbocho Chiyoda-ku, Tokyo 101 Japan.) **NLM** W1 KA369. Documents available from CASDDS.
**Ind/Abst** Am. Hist. Life (1988-); Chem. Abstr.

JA/0916-3905
**KAGOSHIMA-KEN KOGYO GIJUTSU SENTA KENKYU HOKOKU. VFOAT** Reports of Kagoshima Prefectural Institute of Industrial Technology. (1987)-. Periodical. Japanese. an. **DD** 620. Documents available from CASDDS.
**Ind/Abst** Chem. Abstr.

JA
**KAIHO - KANTO GAKUIN DAIGAKU KOGAKUBU KOGAKKAI. Main/Corp** Kanto Gakuin Daigaku Kogaku Kogakkai. (19??)-. Japanese. 4834 Mutsuuracho Kanazawa-ku, Yokohama 236 Japan. **LC** T4; .K37a.

JA/0287-2951
**KAIJO HOAN DAIGAKKO KENKYU HOKOKU. RIKOGAKU-KEI. VFOAT** Report of Japan Maritime Safety Academy. Part 2. Science and Engineering Section; Kenkyu Hokoku - Kaijo Hoan Daigakko. Dai 2-bu. Rikogaku-Kei. (1955)-. Periodical. Multiple languages. sa. Kaijo Hoancho Kaijo Hoan Daigakko, Japan Maritime Safety Academy, Maritime Safety Agency), 5-1, Wakabacho, Kureshi, Hiroshimaken 737 Japan. **DD** 623.88. Documents available from CASDDS.
**Ind/Abst** Chem. Abstr.

CN/0848-0893
**KALEIDOSCOPE REGINA.** (KALEIDOSCOPE). (1989)-. Periodical. English. bm. 11.00Can$. Saskatchewan Science Center, PO Box 5071, Regina SASK S4P 3M3 Canada. **Tel** (306)791-7900, FAX (306)525-0194. **ED** Edward Willett. **Circ:** 2,000.
**Desc:** Newsletter of the Saskatchewan Science Centre.

JA/0387-0324
**KANAGAWA DAIGAKU KOGAKU KOGAKU KENKYUJO SHOHO.** (KOGAKU KENKYUJO SHOHO / KANAGAWA DAIGAKU.). [Kanagawa Daigaku Kogaku Kogaku Kenkyujo Shoho]. **Added/Corp** Kanagawa Daigaku. Kogaku Kenkyujo. **VFOAT** Science Reports of Research Institute for Engineering Kanagawa University. (1978)-. Japanese. an. **CODEN** KSKDDS. Documents available from CASDDS.
**Ind/Abst** Chem. Abstr.; Math. Rev.; Zentralbl. Math. Ihre Grenzgeb.

JA/0387-0995
**KANAZAWA DAIGAKU KYOIKUGAKUBU KIYO : SHIZEN KAGAKU HEN.** See Education-Higher Education.

II
**KANPUR UNIVERSITY RESEARCH JOURNAL (SCIENCE). Added/Corp** Kanpur University. Vol. 1 (Dec. 1980)-. English. an. **LC** Q1; .K14. **DD** 505.
**Ind/Abst** Seed Abstr.

JA/0286-1933
**KANZEI CHUO BUNSEKISHOHO.** [Kanzei Chuo Bunsekishoho]. **VFOAT** Reports of the Central Customs Laboratory. (1965)-. Periodical. Multiple languages. sa. Okurasho Kanzei Chuo Bunsekijo, (Central Customs Lab., Ministry of Finance), 531, Iwase, Matsudoshi, Chibaken 271 Japan. **DD** 540. Documents available from CASDDS.
**Ind/Abst** Chem. Abstr.

PK/0250-5363
**KARACHI UNIVERSITY JOURNAL OF SCIENCE.** [Karachi Univ. j. sci.]. **Main/Corp** University of Karachi. **Added/Corp** University of Karachi. Journal of Science. Vol. 5 (1977)-. Periodical. English. sa. **LC** Q80.P3; K37a. **DD** 505. **CODEN** KUJSDE. Documents available from Ask*IEEE, CASDDS.

*Continues* *Journal of Science.*
**Ind/Abst** Chem. Abstr.; INSPEC (Dec. 1981-); Math. Rev.; Zentralbl. Math. Ihre Grenzgeb.

JA/0912-7305
**KASOKUKI KAGAKU TOKYO.** [Kasokuki kagakuTokyo]. **VFOAT** Journal of Accelerator Science and Technology. (1984)-. Periodical. Multiple languages. Aionikusu K.K., (Ionics Publishing Co., Ltd.), 3-4, Koishikawa 2 Chome, Bunkyoku, Tokyoto 112 Japan. **DD** 539.73. Documents available from CASDDS.
**Ind/Abst** Chem. Abstr.

BU
**KATALOG NA SUVETSKITE REFERATIVNI I INFORMATSIONNI SPISANIIA ZA ... GODINA.** **Added/Corp** Bulgaria. Ministerstvo na Suobshteniiata. (19??)-. Russian (Bulgarian). Ministerstvo na Suobshteniiata TS, Sofia Bulgaria. **LC** Z7409; .K25; Q158.5.

JA
**KEIRYO KENKYUJO NEMPO.** **Main/Corp** Kogyo Gijutsuin Keiryo Kenkyujo (Japan). Japanese. Kogyo Gijutsuin Keiryo Kenkyujo, (National Research Lab. of Metrology, Agency of Industrial Science & Technology), 1-4, Umezono 1 Chome, Tsukubashi, Ibarakiken 305 Japan. **LC** T50; .K425A.

JA
**KENKYU HOKOKU / BULLETIN OF THE INDUSTRIAL RESEARCH CENTER OF EHIME PREFECTURE. EHIME-KEN KOGYO GIJUTSU SENTA.** [Ehime-ken Kogyo Gijutsu kenkyu hokoku]. **Added/Corp** Ehime-Ken Kogyo Gijutsu Senta. **VFOAT** Bulletin of the Industrial Research Center of Ehime Prefecture; Ehime-Ken Kogyo Gijutsu Kenkyu Hokoku. (1964)-. Bulletin. Japanese. an. **CODEN** EKSHDQ. Documents available from CASDDS.
**Ind/Abst** Chem. Abstr.

JA
**KENKYU KIYO - AKASHI KOGYO KOTO SEMMON GAKKO.** **Main/Corp** Akashi Kogyo Koto Semmon Gakko. **VFOAT** Memoirs of the Akashi Technological College. English (Japanese). Akashi Kogyo Koto Semmon Gakko Nishioka Uozumicho, Akashi 67 Japan. **LC** AS552.A57; A27.

JA/0285-5364
**KENKYU KIYO - AKITA KOGYO KOTO SENMON GAKKO.** (AKITA KOGYO KOTO SENMON GAKKO KENKYU KIYO.). [Kenkyu kiyo - Akita Kogyo Koto Senmon Gakko]. **Added/Corp** Akita Kogyo Koto Senmon Gakko. **VFOAT** Kenkyu Kiyo; Research Reports of Akita Technical College; Research Reports of Akita National College of Technology. (1966)-. Periodical. Japanese (English). an. Akita Kogyo Koto Senmon Gakko, (Akita National College of Technology), 1-1 Iijima, Bunkyocho, Akitashi, Akitaken 011 Japan. **LC** IN PROCESS. **CODEN** AKKIDD. Documents available from CASDDS.
**Ind/Abst** Chem. Abstr.

JA/0570-006X
**KENKYU KIYO / RESEARCH REPORTS OF THE ANAN TECHNICAL COLLEGE. ANAN KOGYO KOTO SENMON GAKKO.** [Kenkyu kiyo - Anan Kogyo Koto Senmon Gakko]. **Added/Corp** Anan Kogyo Koto Senmon Gakko. **VFOAT** Research Reports of the Anan Technical College. (1965)-. Japanese (summaries and/or abstracts in English). an. **CODEN** KAKGDD. Documents available from CASDDS.
**Ind/Abst** Chem. Abstr.

JA
**KENKYU KIYO. SHIZEN KAGAKU HEN / NATURAL SCIENCE. BULLETIN OF THE FACULTY OF EDUCATION, KAGOSHIMA UNIVERSITY. KAGOSHIMA DAIGAKU KYOIKUGAKUBU.** [Kenkyu kiyo, Shizen kagaku-hen]. **Added/Corp** Kagoshima Daigaku. Kyoikugakubu. **VFOAT** Bulletin of the Faculty of Education, Kagoshima University. Natural Science; Kagoshima Daigaku Kyoikugakubu Kenkyu Kiyo. Shizen Kagaku Hen. (19??)-. Bulletin. Japanese. an. Kagoshima Daigaku Kyoikugakubu, Korimoto 1-Chome 20-6, Kagoshima-shi 890 Japan. **CODEN** KDSHA6. Documents available from CASDDS. *Continues Kagoshima Daigaku Kyoikugakubu Kyoiku Kenkyujo Kenkyu Kiyo.*
**Ind/Abst** Chem. Abstr.; Math. Rev.

JA/0388-4821
**KENKYU NENPO / NIHON DAIGAKU BUNRI GAKUBU (MISHIMA).** **Added/Corp** Nihon Daigaku. Bunri Gakubu (Mishima). **VFOAT** Annual Report of the Researches. (1959)-. Academic Scholarly Publication. Japanese (English). an. Nihon Daigaku Mishima Gakuen, Bunkyo-cho 2-chome, Mishima-shi, Shizuoka-ken 411, Tokyo Japan. **LC** PAR. Documents available from CASDDS. *Continues Nihon Daigaku Mishima Kyoyobu Kenkyu Nenpo.*
**Ind/Abst** Chem. Abstr.

US/1045-3415
**KENTUCKY ADVANCED TECHNOLOGY DIRECTORY, THE.** 1989-. Directory. English. an. $25.00. Corporate Technology Information Services Inc, 12 Alfred Street, Suite 200, Woburn MA 01801-9998. **Tel** (617)932-3939, (800)333-8036, FAX (617)932-6335, telex 497-2961 CRPTECH. **ED** Steven W Parker and Dodie Stein. **LC** T12.3.K4; K44. **DD** 338.7/62/00025769. Index available. cum. index. **Circ:** 1,000. available on diskette.
**Desc:** Directory of 650+ manufacturers and developers of advanced technology products in the state of Kentucky.

KE/0250-8265
**KENYA JOURNAL OF SCIENCE AND TECHNOLOGY. SERIES A, PHYSICAL AND CHEMICAL SCIENCES.** [Kenya j. sci. technol., Ser. A, Phys. chem. sci.]. **VFOAT** Physical and Chemical Sciences. Vol. 1, No. 1-. Academic Scholarly Publication. English. sa. Free. Kenya National Academy, PO Box 47288, Nairobi Kenya. **Tel** 721138. **ED** J K A Mati. **CODEN** KJSSDG. **Bk Rev. Ad Acc. Circ:** 4,000. Documents available from CASDDS.
**Desc:** For promotion of science and technology.
**Ind/Abst** Chem. Abstr.

GW
**KEPLER JOHANNES GESAMMELTE WERKE.** Monographic series. German. ir. Price varies per volume. CH Beck Verlagsbuchhandlung, D 80791 Munich Germany. **Tel** 011 49 89 381891.

CH/0250-1651
**KEXUE FAZHAN.** (KO HSUEH FA CHAN.). [Kexue fazhan]. **Added/Corp** Kuo Chia Ko Hsueh Wei Yuan Hui. **VFOAT** National Science Council Monthly. (Jan. 1973)-. Periodical. Chinese. mo. NT$60.00. National Science Council / Taiwan, Fl.17 No. 106, Sec. 2, Ho-Ping East Road, 10636 Taipei, Taiwan. **LC** Q4; .K569. **CODEN** KHFKDF. Documents available from BIOSIS Document Express, CASDDS.
**Ind/Abst** Biol. Abstr.; Chem. Abstr.; Nutr. Abstr. Rev., Ser. B, Live Feeds and Feed.; Plant Breed. Abstr.; Plant Grow. Reg. Abstr.; Soyabean Abstr.

US/0097-7411
**KEXUE TONGBAO (SCIENTIA).** [Kexue tongbao, Sci.]. July 1974-. Periodical. English (Chinese). mo. $90.00 (six issues). Plenum / China Program, 227 West 17th Street, New York NY 10011. **LC** Q1. **DD** 505. **NLM** W1 KE765. **CODEN** KETOD8. Documents available from Ask*IEEE, CASDDS.
**Ind/Abst** Art Archaeol. Tech. Abstr.; Chem. Abstr.; Coal Abstr.; Ei Page One; Field Crop Abstr.; INSPEC (July 1973); Meteorol. Geoastrophys. Abstr. (-199?); Methods Organ. Synth.; Nat. Prod. Updates; Plant Breed. Abstr.; SEA Abstr.; Soils Fert.; Weed Abstr.; Zentralbl. Math. Ihre Grenzgeb.

YU
**KIBERNETIKA, AUTOMATIZACIJA POSLOVANJA : MESECNI CASOPIS ZAVODA ZA EKONOMSKI EKSPERTIZE.** V. 21, No. 10 (Oct. 1980)-. Periodical. Serbo-Croatian (Roman). mo. Zavod za Ekonomske Ekspertize, 11071 Novi Belgrad Palmira, Toljatija 3, Postanski Fah 104, Belgrad Yugoslavia. **LC** T57.5; .A86. *Continues Automatizacija Poslovanja.*

KO
**KICHO KWAHAK YONGU.** **VFOAT** Journal of Natural Sciences. V. 1-. Periodical. English (Korean). Yongham Taehakkyo Pusol, Kicho Kwahak Yonguso 241-1, Tae-dong Kyongsan-up Kyongbuk 632 Korea. **LC** Q4; .K48.
**Ind/Abst** Energy Res. Abstr. (Aug. 1982-).

KO
**KICHO KWAHAK YONGUSO NONMUNJIP.** **Added/Corp** Inha Taehakkyo. Kicho Kwahak Yonguso. **VFOAT** Bulletin of the Institute for Basic Science; Inha Taehakkyo Kicho Kwahak Yonguso Nonmunjip. (197?)-. Periodical. Korean (English). **LC** Q111; .K4. Documents available from CASDDS.
**Ind/Abst** Chem. Abstr.

JA/0388-4252
**KIKAI GIJUTSU KENKYUJO SHOHO.** (KIKAI GIJUTSU KENKYUJO SHOHO / JOURNAL OF MECHANICAL ENGINEERING LABORATORY.). [Kikai Gijutsu Kenkyujo shoho]. **Added/Corp** Kikai Gijutsu Kenkyujo. **VFOAT** Journal of Mechanical Engineering Laboratory. Vol. 25, No. 3 (May 1971)-. Academic Scholarly Publication. Japanese (summaries and/or abstracts in English). Six times a year. Free. Mechanical Engineering Laboratory, 12 1 4 Chome Suginami ku, Tokyo Japan. **Tel** 0298-54-2501. **ED** Kenichi Matsuno. **CODEN** KGKSBL. **Pr Rev. Circ:** 700 (ctrl). Documents available from Article Express International, Ask*IEEE, CASDDS. *Continues Kikai Shikenjo Shoho.*
**Desc:** The final and progress reports of researches of mechanical engineering made by the researchers of Mechanical Engineering Laboratory.
**Ind/Abst** Alum. Ind. Abstr.; Bioeng. Abstr.; Chem. Abstr.; Ei Page One; Eng. Index Annu.; Fluid Abstr., Civil Eng.; Fluid Abstr. Proc. Eng.; FLUIDEX (1973-1990); INSPEC (May 1971-); Met. Abstr.; SCISEARCH.

TU/0368-7163
**KIMYA VE SANAYI.** **See** Chemistry.

JA/0386-4928
**KINKI DAIGAKU RIKOGAKUBU KENKYU HOKOKU.** [Kinki Daigaku Rikogakubu kenkyu hokoku]. **VFOAT** Journal of the Faculty of Science and Technology, Kinki University. Began in 1966. Academic Scholarly Publication. Japanese (summaries and/or abstracts in English). an. Free. Kinki Daigaku Rikogakubu, 3-4-1 Kowakae, Higashi Osaka-shi Osaka-fu Japan. **Tel** (06)721-2332. **ED** Yoshihide Honda. **LC** Q77; .K46. **CODEN** KDRKBB. **Circ:** 1,000 (ctrl). Documents available from CASDDS.
**Desc:** Our journal contains the contributions from over eleven departments in the Faculty of Science and Technology, Kinki University.
**Ind/Abst** Chem. Abstr.; Math. Rev.

KO
**KISUL SIDAE.** V. 1-. Periodical. Korean. bm. Hanguk Chigop Hullyon Kwalli Kongdan, 370-4 Kongdok-dong Mapo-ku, Seoul Korea. **LC** T163.K6; K57.

JA/0285-5283
**KITAKYUSHU KOGYO KOTO SENMON GAKKO KENKYU HOKOKU.** [Kitakyushu Kogyo Koto Senmon Gakko kenkyu hokoku]. **Added/Corp** Kitakyushu Kogyo Koto Senmon Gakko. **VFOAT** Research Report of Kitakyushu Technical College. (1968)-. Japanese. an. Kitakyushu Kogyo Koto Senmon Gakko, (Kitakyushu College of Technology), 140, Shii, Kokuraminamiku, Kitakyushushi, Fukuokaken 803, Japan. **CODEN** KKKHDI. Documents available from CASDDS.
**Ind/Abst** Chem. Abstr.

GW/0941-2131
**KLINISCHES LABOR.** **VFOAT** Clinical Laboratory. (Aug 10 1991)-. Periodical. German (English). Ten times a year. DM190.00 Germany; DM195.00 other. Verlag Klinisches Labor GmbH, Im Breitspiel 15, D 69126 Heidelberg Germany. **Tel** 011 49 6221 343233, FAX 011 49 6221 343210. **ED** H. Schmidt-Gayk (editor's phone: 011 49 6221 343215). Index available (available on diskette). **Bk Rev**, (Qty: approx. 30/year). **Ad Acc, Adv Mgr:** E. Buck. **Pr Rev. Circ:** 5,000. *Continues Arztliche Laboratorium.*
**Ind/Abst** Curr. Aware. Biol. Sci., CABS; EMBASE.

XR/0231-5394
**KNIZNICE ODBORNYCH A VEDECKYCH SPISU VYSOKEHO UCENI TECHNICKEHO V BRNE. SVAZEK A.** [Kniz. odb. ved. sp. Vys. uc. tech. Brne, Sv. A]. **Added/Corp** Vysoke Uceni Technicke v Brne. **VFOAT** Sobranie Spetsialnykh i Nauchniykh Sochinenii Politekhnicheskogo Instituta v g. Brno. [A]; Publications of Technical and Scientific Papers of the Technical University in Brno. [A]. (1962)-. Academic Scholarly Publication. Czech. **CODEN** KOVADC. Documents available from CASDDS.
**Ind/Abst** Chem. Abstr. (-1987); Math. Rev.; Zentralbl. Math. Ihre Grenzgeb.

US/0897-1986
**KNOWLEDGE AND POLICY.** **See** Communication.

CC
**KO HSUEH HSUEH YU KO HSUEH CHI SHU KUAN LI.** **VFOAT** Scientology and Management of S. & T. Began in 1980. Periodical. Chinese. 0.39. Post Office, Tien-Chin Shih, People's Republic of China. **LC** Q179.9.K6. **DD** 507/.2.

CC
**KO HSUEH HUA PAO.** **VFOAT** Science Pictorial; Popular Science; Kexue Huabao. Began with Jan. 1937 issue. Periodical. Chinese. RMBY0.26. Science Press, 16 Donghuangchenggen North Street, Beijing 100707, People's Republic of China. **Tel** 011 86 1 4019821, 011 86 1 4010642, FAX 011 86 1 4012180, 011 86 1 4019810, telex 210147. **LC** Q4; .K572 . **DD** 505.

CH
**KO HSUEH SHIH TAI.** **VFOAT** The Age of Science; Age of Science. Periodical. Chinese. NT$0.38. Science Press, 16 Donghuangchenggen North Street, Beijing 100707, People's Republic of China. **Tel** 011 86 1 4019821, 011 86 1 4010642, FAX 011 86 1 4012180, 011 86 1 4019810, telex 210147. **LC** Q4; .K592. **DD** 505.

CC
**KO HSUEH TAN SO.** **VFOAT** Science Exploration; Ko Hsueh Tan So Tsung Kan. (1981)-. Periodical. Chinese (summaries and/or abstracts in English). qt. **LC** Q4; .K5938. **DD** 505.
**Ind/Abst** Zentralbl. Math. Ihre Grenzgeb.

JA/0913-4794
**KOBELCO TECHNOLOGY REVIEW.** **Added/Corp** Kobe Seikojo. **VFOAT** Technology Review. No. 1 (Feb. 1987)-. Periodical. English. sa. Kobe Steel Ltd, 3-18 Wakinohamacho, 1-Chome Chuoku, Kobe 651 Hyogo Japan. **LC** T1; .K63. **DD** 605. **CODEN** KTREE6.

# Science and Technology

Documents available from Article Express International, CASDDS.
**Ind/Abst** Chem. Abstr.; Ei Page One; Eng. Index Annu.

JA/0389-0244
**KOCHI DAIGAKU GAKUJUTSU KENKYU HOKOKU. SHIZEN KAGAKU.** [Kochi Daigaku gakujutsu kenkyu hokoku, Shizen kagaku]. **Added/Corp** Kochi Daigaku. **VFOAT** Research Reports of the Kochi University. Natural Science. Vol. 1 (1951)-. Periodical. Japanese (English). an. Kochi Daigaku, (Kochi University), 5-1, Akebonocho 2 Chome, Kochishi, Kochiken 780, Japan. **CODEN** KDGAAR. Documents available from CASDDS. *Continues* Kochi Daigaku Gakujutsu Kenkyu Hokoku. Shizen Kagaku 1.
**Ind/Abst** Chem. Abstr.

JA/0389-0449
**KOCHI DAIGAKU KYOIKU GAKUBU KENKYU HOKOKU. DAI 3-BU.** [Kochi Daigaku Kyoiku Gakubu kenkyu hokoku. Dai 3-bu]. **VFOAT** Bulletin of the Faculty of Education, Kochi University. Series 3. Began with No. 19, published in 1967. Academic Scholarly Publication. English (Japanese). an. Kochi Daigaku Kyoiku Gakubu, 5-ban 1-go Akebono-cho 2-chome, Kochi-shi-Japan. **LC** Q77; .K52. **CODEN** KDKDDP. Documents available from CASDDS. *Continues in part* Kochi Daigaku Kyoiku Gakubu Kenkyu Hokoku.
**Ind/Abst** Chem. Abstr. (1967-1983).

JA
**KOGAI SHIGEN KENKYUJO IHO.** *Title Change.* **Main/Corp** Kogai Shigen Kenkyujo. **Added/Corp** Kogai Shigen Kenkyujo. Bulletin of the National Research Institute for Pollution and Resources. **VFOAT** Bulletin of the National Research Institute for Pollution. Vol. 1 (Dec. 1971)-(19??). Academic Scholarly Publication. Multiple languages (Japanese and English). qt. Kogyo Gijutsuin Kogai Shigen Kenkyujo, (National Research Inst. for Pollution & Resources, Agency of Industrial Science & Technology), 16-3, Onogawa, Tsukubashi, Ibarakiken 305 Japan. **LC** Q4; .K63a. **NLM** W1 KO289G. **CODEN** KSKID9. Documents available from CASDDS. *Continued by* Shigen to Kankyo / Journal of Nire.
**Ind/Abst** Chem. Abstr. (?-?); Coal Abstr. (?-?).

JA
**KOGIKEN NYUSU. Main/Corp** Kansai Daigaku, Osaka Kogyo Gijutsu Kenkyujo. Vol. 4, No. 4 (1978)-. Bulletin. Japanese. an. Kansai Gaidai University, IRI 16 1 Kitakatahoko Cho, Hirakata City Osaka 573 Japan. **Tel** 011 81 720 555552. **LC** T178.K28; K36a.

JA
**KOGYO GIJUTSU.** V. 1- ; 1960-. Periodical. Japanese. mo. ¥4488. Kogyo Gijutsuin, (Agency of Industrial Science & Technology), 8-10, Kudan Kita 1 Chome, Chiyodaku, Tokyoto 102, Japan. **LC** T4; .K64.
**Ind/Abst** Coal Abstr.; Eng. Mater. Abstr.

JA
**KOGYO GIJUTSU ZASSHI NENKAN.**
**Added/Corp** Nihon Kagaku Gijutsu Shinko Zaidan. (1973)-. Periodical. Japanese. Nihon Kagaku Gijutsu Shinko Zaidan, 14-7 Hongo 2-chome Bunkyo-ku, Tokyo 113 Japan. **LC** Z7913; K28.

JA
**KOGYO GIJUTSUIN SHIKEN KENKYUJO KENKYU KEIKAKU.**
**Added/Corp** Kogyo Gijutsuin (Japan). (19??)-. Periodical. Japanese. an. ¥2800. Nihon Sangyo Gijutsu Shinko Kyokai, (Japan Industrial Technology Association), 7-4 Nishishinbashi 2 chome, Minatoku, Tokyoto 105 Japan. **LC** T177.J3; K65.

JA
**KOGYO GIJUTSUIN SHOKAI. Main/Corp** Japan. Kogyo Gijutsuin. (19??)-. Periodical. Japanese. Kogyo Gijutsuin, (Agency of Industrial Science and Technology), 3-1 Kasumigaseki 1 chome, Chiyodaku Tokyoto 100 Japan. **LC** T177.J3; J36d.

JA/0286-6943
**KOGYO TOSO.** *See* Chemistry.

JA
**KOKURITSU KAGAKU HAKUBUTSUKAN NYUSU. Main/Corp** Kokuritsu Kagaku Hakubutsukan (Japan). Periodical. Japanese. mo. ¥30 single issue. 7-20 Ueno Koen Taito-ku, Tokyo 100 Japan. **LC** Q4; .K64A.

JA
**KOKURITSU KYOKUCHI KENKYUJO YORAN. Main/Corp** Kokuritsu Kyokuchi Kenkyujo. Japanese. 9-10 Kaga, 1 Itabasko-ku, Tokyo Japan. **LC** Q77; .K5613.

JA
**KOKYO SHIKEN KENKYU KIKAN ANNAI : RIKOGAKU TEMA HEN.** Japanese. Nihon Kagaku Gijutsu Joho Senta, (Japan Information Center of Science & Technology), 5-2, Nagatacho 2 Chome, Chiyodaku, Tokyoto 100 Japan. **LC** Z7403; .K634; Q158.5.

RU
**KONFERENTSII, SOVESHCHANIIA, SIMPOZIUMY I VYSTAVKI, PROVODIMYE V STRANAKH-CHLENAKH TSENTRA.**
**Main/Corp** Mezhdunarodnyi Tsentr Nauchnoi I Tekhnicheskoi Infromatsii. (19??)-. Multiple languages (Russian, Multiple languages and Undetermined). Liubertsy, Oktiabrskii Prospekt 403, Moscow Russia. **LC** T6; .M47a.

KO
**KONGHAK NONJIP.** *See* Engineering.

SW
**KONGLIGA SVENSKA VETENSKAPS-AKADEMIENS HANDLINGAR. Main/Corp** Kunglinga Svenska Vetenskapsakademien. **VFOAT** Handlingar. (1???)-. Swedish. mo. Scandinavian University Press, PO Box 2959 Toeyen, N 0608 Oslo 6 Norway. **Tel** 011 47 2 2575400, FAX 011 47 2 2575353, telex 71896 UROR N. (**Subscription address:** Scandinavian University Press, 200 Meacham Ave., Elmont NY 11003.)

KO
**KONGOP KISUL. VFOAT** Industrial Technology for Machinery & Shipbuilding; Industrial Technology for Machinery and Shipbuilding. Periodical. Korean (Korean). mo. Hanguk Kigye Yonguso, 66 Sangnam-dong Changwon-si, Kyongnam Korea. **LC** T4; .K666.

KO
**KONGOP KISUL YONGU. VFOAT** Journal of Industrial Technology. V. 1- No. 1- 1981-. Periodical. English (Korean). Hansa Taehak Kongop Kisul, Yonguso 2881 Taemyong, 3-don-Nam-ku, Taegu Korea. **LC** T4; .K668.
**Ind/Abst** Energy Res. Abstr. (Oct. 1981-).

KO/0023-4052
**KOREAN SCIENTIFIC ABSTRACTS.**
[Korean sci. abstr.]. **Added/Corp** Hanguk Kwahak Kisul Chongbo Sento. Vol. 1 (March 1969)-. English. bm. Korean Scientific and Technological Information Center, CPO Box 1229, Seoul S Korea. **LC** Q1; .K6.
**Ind/Abst** AESIS Q.; BMT Abstr.; Fish Rev.; Math. Rev.; World Ceram. Abstr.

IT
**KOS : RIVISTA DI CULTURA E STORIA DELLE SCIENZE MEDICHE, NATURALI E UMANE DIRETTA DA MASSIMO PIATTELLI PALMARINI. Added/Corp** Franco Maria Ricci (Firm). Vol. 1, No. 1 (Feb. 1984)-. Periodical. Italian. mo (11 issues). L70000 Italy; L100000 other. Europa Scienze Umane Editrice, Via Olgettina 60, 20132 Milan Italy. **Tel** 011 39 2 26410150.

JA
**KOSETSU SHIKENJO GIJUTSU SHIDO JIREI RISUTO.** Japanese. an. Chusho Kigyo Joho Senta, Sankaido Building, 9-13 Akasaka 1-chome, Minato-ku 107 Tokyo Japan. **LC** Z7914.R5; K67; T177.J3.

JA
**KOSETSU SHIKENJO KENKYU BUNKEN SHOROKUSHU.** *Title Change.* **Added/Corp** Chusho Kigyo Joho Senta. (19??)-?. Japanese. an. Chusho Kigyo Joho Senta, Sankaido Building, 9-13 Akasaka 1-chome, Minato-ku 107 Tokyo Japan. **LC** Z7914.R5; K69; T177.J3. *Continued by* Kosetsu Shikenjo Kenkyu Seika Shorokushu.

JA
**KOSETSU SHIKENJO KENKYU SEIKA SHOROKUSHU.** Japanese. Chusho Kigyo Joho Senta, Sankaido Building, 9-13 Akasaka 1-chome, Minato-ku 107 Tokyo Japan. **LC** Z7914.R5; K69 ; T 177.J3. *Continues* Koestsu Shikenjo Kenkyu Bunken Horokushu.

SW/0368-6213
**KOSMOS (STOCKHOLM).** (KOSMOS; FYSISKA UPPSATSER.). [Kosmos]. **Added/Corp** Svenska Fysikersamfundet. (1921)-. Swedish. an. Scandinavian University Press, PO Box 2959 Toeyen, N 0608 Oslo 6 Norway. **Tel** 011 47 2 2575400, FAX 011 47 2 2575353, telex 71896 UROR N. (**Subscription address:** Scandinavian University Press, 200 Meacham Ave., Elmont NY 11003.) **LC** Q4; .K64. **CODEN** KMOSAE.
**Ind/Abst** Energy Res. Abstr. (Aug. 1973-).

GW/0023-4230
**KOSMOS (STUTTGART).** (KOSMOS.). [Kosmos]. **Added/Corp** Kosmos, Gesellschaft der Naturfreunde (Stuttgart, Germany). Vol. 1 (Jan. 1904)-. Academic Scholarly Publication. German. Twelve times a year. DM99.60 Germany; DM104.40 others. DVA Deutsche Verlagsanstalt, Postfach 800649, Neckarstrasse 121, D-70190 Stuttgart Germany. **Tel** 011 49 711 26310. (**Subscription address:** Zenit Pressvertrieb GmbH, Postfach 810640, D 70525 Stuttgart Germany.) **LC** Q3; .K8. **CODEN** KSMSAC. [CCC]. cum. index. **Bk Rev. Ad Acc. Circ:** 100,000 (ctrl) **Absorbed** Orion; Tier & Naturfotografie.

**Desc:** Popular magazine about natural history, and science.
**Ind/Abst** EMBASE; Energy Res. Abstr. (April 1978-); GeoRef; Key Word Index Wildl. Res.; Peace Res. Abstr. J. (1963-1964).

JA/0385-132X
**KUMAMOTO KOGYO DAIGAKU KENKYU HOKOKU.** (KENKYU HOKOKU / KUMAMOTO KOGYO DAIGAKU). [Kumamoto Kogyo Daigaku kenkyu hokoku]. **Added/Corp** Kumamoto Kogyo Daigaku. **VFOAT** Bulletin of the Kumamoto Institute of Technology. (1976)-. Academic Scholarly Publication. Japanese (Japanese). sa. Kumamoto Kogyo Daigaku, 22-ban 1-go Ikeda 4-chome, Kumamoto-shi 860 Japan. **LC** T4; .K44. **CODEN** KHKDDJ. Documents available from CASDDS.
**Ind/Abst** Chem. Abstr.

CH
**KUNG CHU CHI SHU. VFOAT** Gongju Jishu. Periodical. Chinese. bm. NT$0.35. SSU-Chuan Sheng Cheng-tu Shih Yu Chu, China. **LC** TJ1180; .K77.

HK
**KUNG YEH YUEH KAN.** First published in Aug. 1975-. Chinese. $3.00 single issue. Industry Magazine, Rooms 302/Tak Cheong Commercial Building, 215 Portland Street, Mongkok Kowloon, Chiu-Lung Hong Kong. **LC** T4; .K78.

JA
**KUNI NO SHIKEN KENKYU GYOMU KEIKAKU. Added/Corp** Japan. Kagaku Gijutsucho. Kenkyu Choseikyoku. (19??)-. Periodical. Japanese. an. ¥10000. Kagaku Gijutsucho Kenkyu Gijutsu Seisakukyoku, (Science and Technology Policy Bureau,, Science and Technology Agency), 2-1 Kasumigaseki 2 chome, Chiyodaku Tokyoto 100 Japan. **LC** Q180.J3; K85.

CC
**KUO LI CHUNG HSING TA HSUEH LI KUNG HSUEH PAO / KUO LI CHUNG HSING TA HSUEH LI KUNG HSUEH PAO PIEN CHI WEI YUAN HUI. Added/Corp** Tai-wan Sheng li Chung Hsing ta Hsueh. li Kung Hsueh Yuan. **VFOAT** Journal of the College of Science & Engineering, National Chung Hsing University. (19??)-. Periodical. Chinese (English). **CODEN** KLCPEA. Documents available from CASDDS. *Continues* Li Kung Hsueh pao, 0459-1887.
**Ind/Abst** Chem. Abstr.; Seed Abstr.

HU/0866-5192
**KUTATASSZERVEZESI TAJEKOZTATO. Added/Corp** Magyar Tudomanyos Akademia. Konyvtar. **VFOAT** Bulletin of Research Management. Vol. 1 (1991)-. Periodical. Hungarian (summaries and/or abstracts in English; table of contents in English). qt. *Continues* Kutatas-Fejlesztes.

KO
**KWAGIWON SOSIK.** Periodical. Korean. qt. Hanguk Hwahak Kisurwon, 207-43 Chongnyangni-dong Tong Daemun-ku, Seoul Korea. **LC** T178.H344; K88.

KO
**KWAHAK SEDAE / KWAHAK SEDAE YOKKUM. Added/Corp** Kwahak Sedae (Journal). Vol 1. (1991)-. Periodical. Korean. Toso Chulpan Tongnyok, 118-20 Nokpon-Dong Unpyong-Ku, Seoul Korea. **LC** T4; .K88.

PL/0023-589X
**KWARTALNIK HISTORII NAUKI I TECHNIKI.** [Kwart. hist. nauki tech.]. **Added/Corp** Instytut Historii Nauki, Oswiaty i Techniki (Polska Akademia Nauk). **VFOAT** Kvartalnyi Zhurnal Istorii Nauki i Tekhniki Quarterly Journal of the History of Science and Technology. (1956)-. Periodical. Polish (summaries and/or abstracts in English and Russian). $62.00. (**Subscription address:** ARS Polona, PO Box 1001, 00068 Warsaw Poland.) **LC** Q4; .K8. **NLM** W1 KW177. **CODEN** KNITAB. cum. index. *Continues* Studia i Materialy, do Dziejow Nauki Polskiej.
**Ind/Abst** Am. Hist. Life (1964-1969, 1979-); Math. Rev.

JA/0533-9529
**KYOIKUGAKUBU KENKYU HOKOKU. SHIZEN KAGAKU (GIFU).** (GIFU DAIGAKU KYOIKUGAKUBU KENKYU HOKOKU. SHIZEN KAGAKU.). [Kyoikugakubu kenkyu hokoku. Shizen kagaku]. **VFOAT** Science Report of the Faculty of Education, Gifu University. Natural Science. V. 3, No. 5, (1966)-. Academic Scholarly Publication. English (Japanese). an. Gifu Daigaku Kyoikugakubu, (Faculty of Education, Gifu University), 1-1, Yanagido, Gifushi, Gifuken 501-11 Japan. **LC** Q4; .G47. **CODEN** GDGKAD. Documents available from CASDDS. *Continues* Gifu Daigaku Gakugei Gakubu Kenkyu Hokoku. Shizen Kagaku, 0434-0078.
**Ind/Abst** Chem. Abstr.; Math. Rev.

JA
**KYOKAN KENKYU GYOSEKI ICHIRAN.** **VFOAT** Tokyo Kogyo Daigaku Kyokan Kenkyu Gyoseki

Ichiran. 1973/75-. Multiple languages (English and Japanese). 12-1 Ookayama 1, Meguro-ku, Tokyo Japan. **LC** Z7913; .K95; T45.

JA
**KYOKAN KENKYU YOROKU. Main/Corp** Boei Daigakko (Japan). **VFOAT** Digest of Researches by Faculty Members, National Defense Academy. Began with 1956 issue. Japanese (Japanese). an. Boli Daigakko, 10-20 Hashirimizu, 1-chome, Yokosuka 239 Japan. **LC** T4; .B58A.

JA
**KYOKUCHIKEN NYUSU. Main/Corp** Kokuritsu Kyokuchi Kenkyujo. **VAT** Kokuritsu Kyokuchi Kenkyujo Nyusu. 1 (August 1974)-. Periodical. Japanese. bm. Kokuritsu Kyokuchi Kenkyujo, (National Inst. of Polar Research), 9-10, Kaga 1 Chome, Itabashiku, Tokyoto 173, Japan. **LC** Q77; .K55a.

JA/0914-2177
**KYOTO PASTEUR KENKYUJO KENKYU HOKOKU.** [Kyoto Pasteur Kenkyujo kenkyu hokoku]. **VFOAT** Bulletin de l'Institut Pasteur de Kyoto. (1987)-. Periodical. Multiple languages. an. **DD** 616.9. Documents available from CASDDS.
**Ind/Abst** Chem. Abstr.

JA/0368-6264
**KYUSHU DAIGAKU NOGAKUBU GAKUGEI ZASSHI.** (SCIENCE BULLETIN OF THE FACULTY OF AGRICULTURE, KYUSHU UNIVERSITY.). [Kyushu Daigaku Nogakubu gakugei zasshi]. **Added/Corp** Kyushu Daigaku. Nogakubu. Vol 1 (Dec 1924)-. Bulletin. Japanese (English). qt. Kyushu Daigaku Nogakubu, (Faculty of Agriculture, Kyushu University), 10-1, Hakozaki 6 Chome, Higashiku, Fukuokashi, Fukuokaken 812 Japan.
**Ind/Abst** AgBiotech News Inf.; Field Crop Abstr.; Grasslands For. Abstr.; Plant Breed. Abstr.; Rev. Agric. Entomol.; Rice Abstr.; Soils Fert.; Vet. Bull.; World Agric. Econ.

JA/0453-0357
**KYUSHU KOGYO DAIGAKU KENKYU HOKOKU, KOGAKU.** (KYUSHU KOGYO DAIGAKU KENKYU HOKOKU (KOGAKU). BULLETIN OF THE KYUSHU INSTITUTE OF TECHNOLOGY (SCIENCE AND TECHNOLOGY).). [Kyushu Kogyo Daigaku kenkyu hokoku, kogaku]. **Main/Corp** Kyushu Kogyo Daigaku. **Added/Corp** Kyushu Kogyo Daigaku. Bulletin (Science and Technology). **VFOAT** Bulletin of the Kyushu Institute of Technology (Science and Technology). (1955)-. Bulletin. Multiple languages (Japanese and English). sa. Free on request. Kyushu Institute of Technology, 1 Sensuicho, Tobata Kitakyushu 804 Japan. **LC** T4; .K93a. **CODEN** KKDKAN. ***Continues*** *Kyushu Kogyo Daigaku. Kyushu Kogyo Daigaku Kenkyu Hokoku.*

JA/0286-2018
**KYUSHU KOGYO GIJUTSU SHIKENJO HOKOKU. TOKUSHUGO.** [Kyushu Kogyo Gijutsu Shikenjo hokoku, Tokushugo]. **VFOAT** Reports of the Government Industrial Research Institute, Kyushu. March 1980-. Periodical. English (Japanese). Kyushu Kogyo Gijutsu Shikenjo Shukumachi, Tosu-shi, Saga-ken 841 Japan. **LC** T4; .K953.
**Ind/Abst** Coal Abstr.

SP/0213-7275
**LAB 2000.** [LAB 2000]. **VFOAT** LAB Dos Mil. (1985)-. Periodical. Spanish. bm. 9400.00ptas. Ediciones Mayo SA, Muntaner 374 4TA Planta, 08006 Barcelona Spain. **Tel** 011 34 3 209 0255, FAX 34-3-202 0643. **ED** Jose Mayoral and Josep Ferrando. **UDC** 615. **Ad Acc.** ctrl circ.
**Desc:** Articles about analytical medicine, nuclear medicine, and biology for people working in analysis laboratories.

AT/0159-2033
**LAB TALK.** English. bm. 50.00Aus$. Science Teachers Assn of Victoria, PO Box 190, Richmond VIC 3121 Australia. **Tel** 011 61 3 4282633, FAX (03)347 1905.
**Ind/Abst** Aust. Educ. Index.

II/0368-7430
**LABDEV. PART A, PHYSICAL SCIENCES.** [Labdev. Part A]. **VFOAT** Physical Sciences. Vol. 6-A, No. 1 (Jan. 1968)-. Periodical. English. ir. **CODEN** LAPSBF. ***Continues in part*** *Labdev.*
**Ind/Abst** Math. Rev.

FR
**LABORATOIRES ET CENTRES DE RECHERCHE : RAPPORT D'ACTIVITE / ECOLE POLYTECHNIQUE. Main/Corp** Ecole Polytechnique (France). French. Ecole Polytechniques, Laboratories at Centres de Recherche, Rte Saclay, 91128 Palaiseau Cedex France. **LC** T178.E324; E26A. **DD** 607/.44.

NE
**LABORATORY AUTOMATION AND INFORMATION MANAGEMENT.** (19??)-. Academic Scholarly Publication. English. Three times a year (1 volume). Fl520.00. Elsevier Science Publishers BV, PO Box 211, 1000 AE Amsterdam Netherlands. **Tel** 011 31 20 5803642, FAX 011 31 20 5862696, telex 15682. ***Continues*** *Chemometrics and Intelligent Laboratory Systems : Laboratory Information Management.*

CN/0381-6729
**LABORATORY BUYERS GUIDE.** (1975/1976)-. Consumer Publication. English. an. 70.00Can$. Southam Information and Technology Group Inc., 1450 Don Mills Road, Don Mills Ontario M3B 2X7 Canada. **Tel** (416)445-6641, (800)668-2374, FAX (416)442-2261. **ED** Rita Tate. **DD** 338.4/7/5028. **Ad Acc. Circ:** 20,000 (ctrl). ***Supersedes*** *Laboratory Guide, 0381-6737.*
**Desc:** Comprehensive directory of instruments, equipment, materials and chemicals for every type of laboratory. All products are linked to their manufacturers and/or distributors.

US/0023-6810
**LABORATORY EQUIPMENT. See** Business-Purchasing.

●UK/0967-389X
**LABORATORY EQUIPMENT BUYERS GUIDE. VFOAT** Laboratory Equipment. (1993)-. Consumer Publication. English. an. £70.00. Benn Business Information Service Ltd, Riverbank House, Angel Lane, Tonbridge Kent TN9 1SE England. **Tel** 011 44 732 362666, FAX 011 44 732 770483, telex 95454 BBIS. **LC** Q183.A1; L3. **DD** 681/.75/02541. ***Continues*** *Laboratory Equipment Directory, 0141-8963.*

UK/0023-6829
**LABORATORY EQUIPMENT DIGEST.** [Lab. equip. dig.]. (Feb. 1963)-. Academic Scholarly Publication. English. mo. £65.00 UK and Northern Ireland; $170.00 Europe; $180.00 other. Morgan Grampian, 40 Beresford Street Woolwich, London SE18 6BQ England. **Tel** 011 44 81 855 7777, FAX 011 44 81 855 5548, telex 896238. **ED** M Spear. **LC** Q185; .L35. **DD** 681/.75/05. **CODEN** LEQDA2. **Bk Rev. Ad Acc. Circ:** 15,548 (ctrl). available on microfilm and microfiche from University Microfilms International (UMI). Documents available from Ask*IEEE, CASDDS.
**Desc:** Laboratory products and applied technology covering industrial, medical, research, educational and governmental sectors.
**Ind/Abst** Abstr. BioCommer.; Chem. Abstr.; EMBASE; INSPEC (Dec. 1969-); Life Sci. Collect.; Saf. Health Work; World Surf. Coat. Abstr.; World Text. Abstr.

UK/0141-8963
**LABORATORY EQUIPMENT DIRECTORY.** ***Title Change.*** [Lab. equip. dir.]. (1975)-(199?). English. an. Morgan Grampian, 40 Beresford Street Woolwich, London SE18 6BQ England. **Tel** 011 44 81 855 7777, FAX 011 44 81 855 5548, telex 896238. **(Subscription address:** Benn Business Information Services, Riverbank House Angel Lane, Tonbridge Kent TN9 1SE England.**) ED** P. Brown. **LC** Q183.A1; L3. **DD** 681/.75/02541. **Ad Acc. Circ:** 2,000. ***Continues*** *Laboratory Equipment Directory & Buyers Guide.* ***Continued by*** *Laboratory Equipment Buyers Guide, 0967-389X.*

UK
**LABORATORY EQUIPMENT DIRECTORY & BUYERS GUIDE.** Directory. English. an. £6.00. Gerard Mann Ltd, 1 - 3 Astoria Parade, London SW16 1PF England. **LC** Q183.A1; L3. **DD** 338.4/7/5028.

UK/0023-6853
**LABORATORY PRACTICE.** ***Title Change.*** [Lab. pract.]. Vol. 1-41 No. 12 (Apr. 1952)-(Dec. 1992). Academic Scholarly Publication. English. mo. United Trade Press Ltd, 33/35 Bowling Green Lane, London EC1R 0DA England. **Tel** (01)837-1212. **LC** Q183; .L3. **NLM** W1 LA231. **CODEN** LABPA3. cum. index. Documents available from BIOSIS Document Express, Ask*IEEE, CASDDS. ***Absorbed by*** *Laboratory News, 0266-7169.*
**Ind/Abst** Abstr. BioCommer.; AGRICOLA; Alum. Ind. Abstr.; Anal. Abstr.; Biol. Abstr.; Ceram. Abstr.; Chem. Abstr.; Chem. Hazards Ind.; Curr. Biotechnol.; Curr. Technol. Index; Dairy Sci. Abstr.; EMBASE; Eng. Mater. Abstr.; Fluid Abstr., Civil Eng.; Fluid Abstr. Proc. Eng.; FLUIDEX (1973-); Food Sci. Technol. Abstr.; Index Med.; INSPEC (1968-); Int. Aerosp. Abstr.; Lab. Hazards Bull.; Mass Spect. Bull.; Met. Abstr.; Nutr. Abstr. Rev., Ser. A, Hum. Exp.; Life Sci. Collect.; Rev. Agric. Entomol.; Soils Fert.; Trop. Dis. Bull.; World Ceram. Abstr.; World Surf. Coat. Abstr.

CN/0047-3855
**LABORATORY PRODUCT NEWS.** Vol. 1 (Mar. 1971)-. Periodical. English. bm. 26.00Can$ (one year), 34.00Can$ (two year), 42.00Can$ (three year) Canada; 49.00Can$ (one year), 65.00Can$ (two year) US; 80.00Can$ other. Southam Information and Technology Group Inc., 1450 Don Mills Road, Don Mills Ontario M3B 2X7 Canada. **Tel** (416)445-6641, (800)668-2374, FAX (416)442-2261. **ED** Rita Tate. **Bk Rev. Ad Acc. Circ:** 19,100 (ctrl). ***Continues*** *Laboratory Guide, 0075-7500.*
**Desc:** Instruments, equipment, chemicals and materials for every type of research, clinical testing and industrial quality control, laboratory.

UK
**LABORATORY PRODUCTS TECHNOLOGY.** mo. Free to qualified readers; £56.00 other. International Scientific Communications Ltd, 5 Whittle Parkway, Progress Business Center, Slough SL1 6DQ England. **Tel** 011 44 628 668881.
**Ind/Abst** Abstr. BioCommer. (-199?).

US/0272-3778
**LABORATORY REGULATION MANUAL. See** Law.

US/1048-0706
**LABORATORY REGULATION NEWS.** ***Title Change.*** (LABORATORY REGULATION NEWS / BNA.). [Lab. regul. news]. **Added/Corp** Bureau of National Affairs (Washington, D.C.). Vol. 1, No. 1 (Jan. 23, 1990)-(1993). Periodical. English. bw. Buraff Publications Inc., 714 Church Street, Alexandria VA 22314. **Tel** (800)333-1291, (703)739-8500. **DD** 351. **NLM** W1; LA231HG. **CODEN** LRENEX. **[CCC].** ***Continued by*** *Environmental Laboratory Washington Report, 1070-2504.*

CC/0455-2059
**LANZHOU DAXUE XUEBAO. ZIRAN KEXUE BAN.** (LAN-CHOU TA HSUEH HSUEN PAO. TZU JAN KO HSUEH PAN.). [Lanzhou daxue xuebao. Ziran kexue ban]. **Added/Corp** Lan-chou ta Hsueh. **VFOAT** Journal of Lanzhou University. Natural Sciences. (1957)-. Academic Scholarly Publication. Chinese (summaries and/or abstracts in English). qt. RMBY0.60. **LC** Q4; .L35. **DD** 505. **CODEN** LCTHAF. Documents available from CASDDS.
**Ind/Abst** Chem. Abstr.; Math. Rev.; NAPRALERT; Zentralbl. Math. Ihre Grenzgeb.

IT
**LASER: APPLICAZIONI INDUSTRIALI TECHNOLOGIE MERCATO.** ***Title Change.*** (19??)-(19??). Italian. ir. Gruppo Editoriale Jackson Spa, Via Gorki 69, 20092 Cinisello Balsamo Italy. **Tel** 011 39 2 66034401. ***Merged into*** *Meccanica Oggi.*

UK/0267-9671
**LASER DISC REVIEW.** [Laser disc rev.]. (1985)-. Periodical. English. bm. £9.00 UK; £12.50 other. Laser Disc Review, PO Box 526, London SW10 9AB England. **Tel** 011 41 071 3514535. **DD** 621.388332. ***Continues*** *New Flats.*

LV/0868-6556
**LATVIJAS ZINATNU AKADEMIJAS VESTIS.** (LATVIJAS ZINATNU AKADEMIJAS VESTIS : AV IZVESTIIA LATVIISKOI AKADEMII NAUK.). [Latv. ZinÂat. akad. vÂestis]. **Added/Corp** Latvijas Zinatnu Akademija. **VFOAT** AV; Izvestiia Latviiskoi Akademii Nauk; Proceedings of the Latvian Academy of Sciences. **VAT** Akademijas Vestis. (1990)-. Academic Scholarly Publication. Latvian (Russian; summaries and/or abstracts in English and German). mo. Zinatne / Science Publishing House, Turgeneva Iela 19, Riga Latvia 1530. **Tel** 3712 212 797. **(Subscription address:** Victor Kamkin, 4956 Boiling Brook Parkway, Rockville MD 20852.**) LC** AS262; .R6. **CODEN** LZAVEP. Documents available from BIOSIS Document Express, Ask*IEEE, CASDDS. ***Continues*** *Latvijas PSR Zinatnu Akademijas Vestis, 0132-6422.*
**Ind/Abst** Am. Hist. Life; Biol. Abstr. (1990-); Chem. Abstr.; INSPEC (1990-); Math. Rev.

US/0278-3916
**LAW/TECHNOLOGY.** (LAW/TECHNOLOGY / WORLD PEACE THROUGH LAW CENTER.). [Law/technol.]. **Added/Corp** World Peace Through Law Center. World Association of Lawyers. World Peace Through Law Center. Section on Law/Technology. **VFOAT** Law Technology. Vol. 13, No. 3 (1980)-. Periodical. English (Spanish). qt. $85.00. World Peace Through Law Center, 1000 Connecticut Avenue NW, Suite 202, Washington DC 20036. **Tel** (202)466-5428, FAX (202)452-8540, telex 440456. **LC** K87; .L38. **DD** 344/.095; 342.495. **CODEN** LATEDT. available on microfilm and microfiche from University Microfilms International (UMI). Documents available from Ask*IEEE. ***Continues*** *Law and Computer Technology, 0023-9178.*
**Ind/Abst** Comput. Lit. Index; Comput. Rev.; Curr. Law Index (1980-); INSPEC (1980-); Law Office Inf. Serv.; Leg. Resour. Index (1980-); LegalTrac (1980-); PAIS Int. Print (1991-?).

US/1071-9121
**LAW TECHNOLOGY PRODUCT NEWS. See** Law.

UK/0964-1645
**LC-MS UPDATE.** [LC/MS update]. (1991)-. English. Six times a year (Jan., Mar., May, July, Sept., Nov.). $310.00. HD Science Limited, 4A Bessell Lane Stapleford, Nottingham NG9 7BX England. **Tel** 011 44 602 491704, FAX 011 44 602 491703. **ED** Steve Down. **DD** 016.5430894. Index available (published separately). cum. index. **Bk Rev**, (Qty: 25/year). **Ad Acc.** ctrl circ. available on diskette (DOS program).

# Science and Technology

US/0090-5232
**LC SCIENCE TRACER BULLET.** See Science and Technology-Abstracting, Bibliographies and Statistics.

SZ
**LEITUNG UND PLANUNG VON WISSENSCHAFT UND TECHNIK.** Periodical. Multiple languages (German and Russian). mo. Deutscher Judo Verband, Redaktion Ippon Segewaldweg 40, D 12557 Berlin Germany. **Tel** 011 49 711 210770, telex 051 678. **LC** Z7403; .L535; Q158.5.

●US/1071-4391
**LEONARDO ELECTRONIC ALMANAC.** See The Arts.

GW
**LEOPOLDINA.** [Leopoldina]. Year 1- 1955-. Periodical. German. 15.00M. **LC** Q49; .H1652. **DD** 505. **CODEN** LEOPAS. *Supersedes* Leopoldina.
**Ind/Abst** AGRICOLA; GeoRef.

RU/0132-8743
**LESOVEDEIE I LESNOE KHOZIAISTVO.** **Added/Corp** Belaruski Tekhnalahichny Instytut Imia S.M. Kirava. (1972)-. Periodical. Russian. an.
**Ind/Abst** Agrofor. Abstr.; For. Prod. Abstr. (1991-); For. Abstr.; Rev. Plant Pathol.; Soils Fert.

FR/0765-0094
**LETTRE EUROPEENNE DU PROGRES TECHNIQUE, LA.** [Lett. eur. prog. tech.]. (1984)-. Periodical. French. Ten times a year. 2526.93F EEC; 2700.00F other. Association National de la Recherche Technique, 101 Av Raymond Poincare, F-75116 Paris France. **Tel** 011 33 1 45017227, FAX 011 33 1 47018529, telex 642632. **ED** Francoise Girault. **UDC** 65.012.1.

FR
**LIBRE MONDIAL DES INVENTIONS, LE.** French. 168.00F. Compagnie 12, 210 rue du Faubourg St Etoile, 75012 Paris France. **Tel** 011 33 1 43709900.

LY/0368-7481
**LIBYAN JOURNAL OF SCIENCE, THE.** [Libyan. ji. sci.]. **Added/Corp** Jamiah al-Libiyah. Kulliyat al-Ulum. Vol. 1 (May 1971)-. Academic Scholarly Publication. English (summaries and/or abstracts in Arabic). an. Al Fateh University, Faculty of Science, PO Box 13258, Tripoli Libya. **LC** Q1; .L48. **CODEN** LBJSAP. Documents available from BIOSIS Document Express, CASDDS.
**Ind/Abst** Biol. Abstr. (-1984); Chem. Abstr.; GeoRef; Math. Rev.; Life Sci. Collect.; Stat. Theory Method Abstr. (1979, 1984).

US/1056-2672
**LIFE SCIENCE BOOK REVIEW.** (1991)-. Periodical. English. bm. $24.00. Life Science Book Review, PO Box 24906, Winston-Salem NC 27114.

US
**LIFE SCIENCES.** **Added/Corp** ICN Pharmaceuticals. Life Sciences Group. **VFOAT** ICN Life Sciences. Issue 1 (1974)-. Periodical. English. ICN Pharmaceuticals, Cleveland OH. Documents available from The Genuine Article.
**Ind/Abst** Calcium Calcif. Tissue Abstr.; Curr. Chem. React.; Curr. Contents Life Sci.; Res. Alert [Full Cov.].

UK/0268-7429
**LIGHTING + SOUND INTERNATIONAL.** English. mo. £45.00 UK; £60.00 (surface), £85.00 (air) other. Professional Lighting & Sound Association, 7 Highlight House, St Leonards Road, Eastbourne BN21 3UN England. **Tel** 011 44 323 642639, FAX 0323 646905. **ED** John Offord. **Bk Rev. Ad Acc. Circ:** 7,800 (ctrl).
**Desc:** Editorial content covering the developement and use of both lighting, sound and related equipment and services in the entertainment and leisure industries.

GW
**LINA : LITERATURINDEX NATURWISSENSCHAFTEN.** (19??)-. $53.00. Georg Thieme Verlag Stuttgart, Postfach 301120, D 70451 Stuttgart Germany. **Tel** 011 49 711 89310, FAX 011 49 711 8931298, telex 7 252 275 GTVD.
(**Subscription address:** Thieme Medical Publishers Inc., 381 Park Avenue South, New York NY 10016.)

US/0896-4130
**LINCOLN LABORATORY JOURNAL, THE.** [Linc. Lab. j.]. **Added/Corp** Lincoln Laboratory. Vol. 1, No. 1 (Spring 1988)-. Periodical. English. sa. Free (qualified professionals). Massachusetts Institute of Technology (MIT) / Lincoln Laboratory, PO Box 73, MacDonald Room A163, Lexington MA 02173. **Tel** (617)981-5500. **LC** T1; .L53. **DD** 601. Documents available from Ask*IEEE.
**Ind/Abst** ACM Guide Comput. Lit.; Comput. Rev.; INSPEC (1988-); Int. Aerosp. Abstr.

FR/0981-4183
**LINEAIRES.** (1986)-. Periodical. French. Eleven times a year. 264.65F France. Editions du Boisbaudry, BP 6359, 35036 Rennes Cedex France. **Tel** 011 33 99 322121. **UDC** 658:664.

IS/0792-9765
**LINK.** See Business.

CH/1001-9499
**LINYE KE-JI.** See Forestry.

BE
**LISTE DES BENEFICIAIRES D'UNE SUBVENTION DU FONDS NATIONAL DE LA RECHERCHE SCIENTIFIQUE OU D'UN DES TROIS FONDS ASSOCIES AVEC INDICATION DES RECHERCHES POURSUIVIES ET DE L'INSTITUTION D'ACCUEIL.** **Main/Corp** Fonds National de la Recherche Scientifique (Belgium). **VFOAT** Lijst der Kredietgenieters van het Nationaal Fonds von Wetenschappelijk Onderzoek en van de Geassocieerde Fondsen, Met Opgave van Hun Programma en Onthaalinstelling. Multiple languages (English, Dutch and French). Rue d'Egmont 5, 1050 Bruxelles Belgium. **LC** Q180.B4; F62.

US/0146-6968
**LISTING OF PEER REVIEWERS USED BY NSF DIVISIONS.** **Main/Corp** United States. National Science Foundation. **VAT** Listing of Peer Reviewers Used by National Science Foundation Divisions. 1975/76-. English. an. $8.60. National Science Foundation, 1800 G Street Northwest, Washington DC 20550. **Tel** (202)357-9859, (202)357-9498. **LC** Q149.U5; U54A. **DD** 502.5/73.

GW/0932-7754
**LITERATUR-SCHNELLDIENST KUNSTSTOFFE, KAUTSCHUK, FASERN.** (1973)-. German. Twelve times a year. DM2095.00 Germany, DM 2215.00 others (surface mail); DM2405.00 (airmail). Deutsches Kinststoff Institut, Schlossgartenstrasse 6, D-64289 Darmstadt Germany. **Tel** 011 49 6151 162106, FAX 011 49 6151 292855. **UDC** 678(01).

IT
**LITO NEWSLETTER. Ceased.** (19??)-(19??). Newsletter. Ist Sulle Produzioni Avanzate, Viale Papiniano 59, 20123 Milan Italy.

SP/0210-8615
**LLULL: BOLETIN DE LA SOCIEDAD ESPANOLA DE HISTORIA DE LAS CIENCIAS.** **Added/Corp** Sociedad Espanola de Historia de las Ciencias. Sociedad Espanola de Historia de las Ciencias y de las Tecnicas. (19??)-. Periodical. Spanish (summaries and/or abstracts in English). an. $75.00. Secretariado de Publicaciones, Ciudad Universitaria, S/N Edificio Geologica, 50009 Zaragoza Spain. **Tel** 011 34 76 555493. **LC** Q124.6; .L57. **DD** 509.
**Ind/Abst** Am. Hist. Life (1987-).

IT
**LOGISTICA.** mo. L9000 (single issue); L80000 (one year), L140000 (two year) Italy; L145000 Europe; L200000 other. Tecniche Nuove SPA, Via Ciro Menotti 14, 20129 Milan Italy. **Tel** 011 39 2 75701, FAX 011 39 2 7610351, telex 334647 TECHS I. *Continues* Magazzini & Trasportilogistica.

US/0024-5852
**LOGISTICS SPECTRUM.** [Logist. spectr.]. **Added/Corp** Society of Logistics Engineers. Vol. 1, (Sept. 1967)-. Periodical. English. qt (Mar., June, Sept., Dec.). $50.00 (US); $60.00 (other) includes postage. Society of Logistics Engineers, 8100 Professional Pl, Suite 211, Hyattsville MD 20785. **Tel** (301)459-8446, FAX (301)459-1522. **ED** James R. Stock. **LC** U168; .L63. **DD** 355.4/1/05. [CCC]. Index available. **Bk Rev. Ad Acc. Circ:** 9,500 (ctrl).
**Desc:** Journal for individuals working, studying or expressing interest in a career in logistics technology, management, engineering, education, products support and physical distribution.
**Ind/Abst** Air Univ. Libr. Index Mil. Period.; Int. Aerosp. Abstr.

US/0748-2116
**LOGOS (ARGONNE, ILL.).** (LOGOS.). [Logos]. Periodical. English. Four times a year. Free. Argonne National Laboratory, 9700 South Cass Aveue, Argonne IL 60439. **Tel** (708)972-2000, FAX (708)972-5510. **ED** Evelyn Brown. **LC** QC789.2.U62; A755. **DD** 605. **Circ:** 10,000 (ctrl).
**Desc:** Updated reports on selected programs at Argonne National Laboratory.
**Ind/Abst** Eng. Mater. Abstr.

US/0273-7116
**LOS ALAMOS SCIENCE.** (LOS ALAMOS SCIENCE / LOS ALAMOS SCIENTIFIC LABORATORY.). [Los Alamos sci.]. Vol. 1, No. 1 (Summer 1980)-V. 3, No. 3 (Fall 1982)-. Academic Scholarly Publication. English. qt. Free. Los Alamos Scientific Laboratory, PO Box 1663, Los Alamos NM 87645. **LC** Q11; .L5. **DD** 505. **CODEN** LASCDI. Documents available from CASDDS.
**Ind/Abst** Chem. Abstr.; GeoRef; Math. Rev.

SW/0076-1648
**LYCHNOS.** [Lychnos]. **Added/Corp** Lardomshistoriska Samfundet. (1936)-. Swedish (English, French and German). an. available on microfilm and microfiche from University Microfilms International (UMI).
**Ind/Abst** Am. Hist. Life (1962-1974,1979-).

SW
**LYCHNOS ARSBOK.** (19??)-. Swedish. ir. Kr174.00. Almqvist & Wiksell International, PO Box 4627, S-11691 Stockholm Sweden. **Tel** 011-46-8-6408800.

SW/0076-1648
**LYCHNOS: LARDOMSHISTORISKA SAMFUNDETS ARSBOK.** **Added/Corp** Lardomshistoriska Samfundet. **VFOAT** Annual of the Swedish History of Science Society; Annuaire de la Societe Suedoise d'Histoire des Sciences; Jahrbuch der Schwedischen Gesellschaft fur Geschichte der Wissenschaften. (1936)-. Multiple languages (Swedish, English, French and German; summaries and/or abstracts in French and German). an. Kr272.00. Almqvist & Wiksell International, PO Box 4627, S-11691 Stockholm Sweden. **Tel** 011-46-8-6408800. **ED** Gunnar Eriksson. **LC** Q64; .L96. **NLM** W1 LY51E. **Bk Rev. Ad Acc. Circ:** 2,000 (ctrl).
**Desc:** Yearbook devoted to history of science; ideas and general culture.

US
**M. I. T. EAST ASIAN SCIENCE SERIES.** **Main/Corp** Massachusetts Institute of Technology. **VFOAT** MIT East Asian Science Series; East Asian Science Series. Vol. 1 (1973)-. Monographic series. English. ir. Price varies per volume. Massachusetts Institute of Technology (MIT) Press, 55 Hayward Street, Cambridge MA 02142-1399. **Tel** (617)253-2889, (617)625-8481, FAX (617)258-6779.

UK
**M T P INTERNATIONAL REVIEW OF SCIENCE.** (1974)-. Monographic series. English. ir. Price varies per volume. University Park Press, PO Box 4034, New York NY 10163.

US/1060-278X
**MACROMOLECULAR REPORTS.** See Chemistry.

UA/1012-5965
**MAGALLAT AL-DILTA LI-L-ULUM.** (DELTA JOURNAL OF SCIENCE.). [Magallat al-Dilta li-l-ulum]. **Added/Corp** Jamiat Tanta. Kulliyat al-Ulum. **VFOAT** Delta J. Sci.; Majallat al-Dilta Lil-Ulum. Vol. 1 (1977)-. Periodical. English. sa. **LC** Q1; .D45. **DD** 505. **CODEN** DJSCES. Documents available from CASDDS.
**Ind/Abst** Chem. Abstr.; Ecol. Abstr.; Math. Rev.

CN
**MAGAZINE INFO TECH.** (19??)-. English. Ten times a year. 27.32Can$ Canada. Publications Transcontinental Inc, 1100 Rene-Levesque, 24Fl Boulevard West, Montreal Quebec H3B 4X9 Canada. **Tel** (514)392-9000, FAX (514)392-4724. *Continues* Info Tech.

HU/0025-0325
**MAGYAR TUDOMANY.** (MAGYAR TUDOMANY : A MAGYAR TUDOMANYOS AKADEMIA ERTESITOJE.). [M. tud.]. **Added/Corp** Magyar Tudomanyos Akademia. Vol. 62 (1956)-. Academic Scholarly Publication. Hungarian. mo. $54.00. Akademiai Kiado, Publishing House of the Hungarian Academy of Sciences, Prielle Kornelia u. 19-35, H-1117 Budapest Hungary. **Tel** 011 36 1 1811991, FAX 011 36 1 1811991, telex 22-6228 AKNYO H. **ED** F. B. Straub. **NLM** W1 MA431. **Bk Rev. Ad Acc. Circ:** 3,400. *Continues* Akademiai Ertesito.
**Desc:** Science management and sociology of science.
**Ind/Abst** Am. Hist. Life (1971-); BHA : Biblio. Hist. Art; World Agric. Econ.

FR/1011-792X
**MAIN SCIENCE AND TECHNOLOGY INDICATORS.** **Added/Corp** Organisation for Economic Co-Operation and Development. **VFOAT** Principaux Indicateurs de la Science et de la Technologie. (1987)-. English (French). sa. $42.00. OECD Publications and Information Center, 2 rue Andre-Pascal, 75775 Paris Cedex 16 France. **Tel** 011 33 1 45248167, US:(202)785-6323, FAX 011 33 1 45248500 OR 45248176, telex 620 160 OCDE. (**Subscription address:** OECD Publications Center, 2001 L Street, Suite 700, Washington DC 20036.) **LC** Q172.5.S34; M35. **DD** 338.9. **CODEN** MSTIE9. available on diskette.
**Desc:** Contains data on the scientific and technological performance of the OECD member countries. Includes final and provisional results and forecasts for governments, includes data on such topics as the resources devoted to research and development, patents, the technological balance of payments, and international trade in high-technology products.

# Science and Technology

US
**MAINE SCIENCE & TECHNOLOGY REPORT : A PUBLICATION OF THE MAINE SCIENCE AND TECHNOLOGY COMMISSION.** **Added/Corp** Maine Science and Technology Commission. **VFOAT** Maine Science and Technology Report. (1990)-. Periodical. English. qt. **LC** WMLC L 83/9249.

IO
**MAJALAH BPPT / BADAN PENKAJIAN DAN PENERAPAN TEKNOLOGI.** **VFOAT** Majalah B.P.P.T. No. 1 (1982)-. Periodical. Indonesian. Badan Pengkajian Dan Penerapan Teknologi, JL M H Thamrin No 8, Jakarta Pusat Indonesia. **LC** T4; .M34.

MW
**MALAWI JOURNAL OF SCIENCE.** V. 1- 1972-. English. Association for the Advancement of Science of Malawi, Chancellor College, PO Box 280, Zomba Malawi. **LC** Q91.M3; A835. **DD** 505.

MW/1019-7079
**MALAWI JOURNAL OF SCIENCE & TECHNOLOGY.** [Malawi j. sci. technol.]. **VFOAT** Malawi Journal of Science and Technology. (1992)-. Periodical. English. University of Malawi / Science, Chancellor College, Faculty of Science, PO Box 280, Zomba Malawi. **Tel** 522222 (ZOMBA), FAX 522108, telex 44742. **UDC** 62.

MY/0126-7906
**MALAYSIAN JOURNAL OF SCIENCE.** [Malays. j. sci.]. **Added/Corp** University of Malaya (1962-1966). Faculty of Science. **VFOAT** Jernel Sains Malaysia. Vol. 1 (1972)-. English. an. $10.00. University of Malaysia / Faculty of Science, 59100 Kuala Lumpur Malaysia. **Tel** 603 7555466. **LC** Q1; .M24. **DD** 505. **NLM** W1 MA5247K. **CODEN** MLJSA4. Documents available from CASDDS.
**Ind/Abst** Chem. Abstr.; GeoRef.

US/1047-7926
**MANAGE IT.** [Manage IT]. **Added/Corp** CAUSE (Association). **VAT** Manage Information Technology. Vol. 1, No. 1 (Feb. 1990)-. Periodical. English. Four times a year. Free on request. CAUSE, 4840 Pearl East Circle, Suite 302E, Boulder CO 80301. **Tel** (303)449-4430, FAX (303)440-0461. **DD** 378.

US/0736-5225
**MANAGEMENT TECHNOLOGY (NEW YORK, N.Y. : 1983).** (MANAGEMENT TECHNOLOGY.). [Manage. technol.]. Vol. 1, No. 1 (May 1983)-. Periodical. English. mo. $36.00 US; $48.00 Canada. International Thomson Organization, 345 Park Avenue/6th Floor, New York NY 10010-1706. **Tel** (212)686-7744. **LC** T58.6; .M3565. **DD** 658.4/038/05.

CN/0843-7823
**MANITOBA JOURNAL OF TECHNOLOGY EDUCATION.** [Manit. j. technol. educ.]. **Added/Corp** Manitoba Industrial Arts Association. Vol. 1, No. 1 (Feb. 1991)-. Periodical. English. qt. Free to members (membership: $10.00 per year). Manitoba Industrial Arts Association, c/o Dennis Mogg, 220-21 Clayton Drive, Winnipeg Manitoba R2M 1G2 Canada. **DD** 607/.127127. **Continues** Manitoba Industrial Arts Association (Newsmagazine)., 0834-9681.

CN/0315-9159
**MANITOBA SCIENCE TEACHER.** (THE MANITOBA SCIENCE TEACHER.). [Manit. sci. teach.]. **Added/Corp** Science Teachers' Association of Manitoba. (Nov. 1959)-. Periodical. English. ir. Science Teachers Association of Manitoba, SE Lipton & Portage, Winnipeg Manitoba 10 Canada.

US/1060-2712
**MANUFACTURING AUTOMATION.** See Manufacturing.

SP/0025-2646
**MANUTENCION Y ALMACENAJE.** [Manut. almac.]. (1965)-. Periodical. Spanish. Ten times a year. 13709ptas Spain and Portugal; 16449ptas other Europe; 22449ptas other. CETISA Boixareu Editores SA, C Concepcion Arenal 5 7, 08027 Barcelona Spain. **Tel** 011 34 3 3527061. **ED** Laura Tremosa. **UDC** 664. **Bk Rev. Ad Acc. Circ:** 6,500 (ctrl). **Continues** Manejo de Materiales, 0211-3821.
**Desc:** Logistics, material handling, warehousing, packaging, and transport.

IT
**MANUTENZIONE : TECNICA E MANAGEMENT.** (19??)-. Italian. bm (6 issues). L60000. Trieste Consult Srl, Piazza Scorcola 1, 34134 Trieste Italy. **Tel** 011 39 40 364580.

US/0891-7973
**MAPICS THE MAGAZINE.** See Business-General Management.

UK
**MARKETS YEAR BOOK.** (1???)-. Periodical. English. ir. Worlds Fair Ltd, PO Box 57 / Daltry Street, Oldham OL1 4BB England. **Tel** 011 44 61 624-3687, FAX 011 44 61 665-1260, 011 44 61 628-6921, telex 667352.

US/1047-6423
**MARYLAND HIGH-TECH DIRECTORY.** [Md. high-tech dir.]. **Added/Corp** Maryland. Dept. of Economic and Employment Development. **VFOAT** High Tech Directory; High-Tech Directory. **VAT** Maryland High Tech Directory. (1989)-. Directory. English. $25.00. Maryland Department of Economic and Community Development, 45 Calvert Street, Annapolis MD 21401. **Tel** (312)337-1084. **LC** HC107.M33; H535. **DD** 338.7/62/00025752. **Continues** High-Tech Directory.

US/1056-4055
**MARYLAND TECHNOLOGY RESOURCE GUIDE.** (1991)-. Periodical. English. $45.00. Corptech TRG Sales, Department SMD, 12 Alfred Street, #200, Woburn MA 01801.

KE
**MASENO JOURNAL OF EDUCATION, ARTS AND SCIENCE.** See Education.

US/8750-2100
**MASS HIGH TECH.** [Mass high tech]. **Added/Corp** Tech Times, Inc. Mass Tech Times, Inc. **VAT** Massachusetts High Technology. Vol. 1, No. 1 (Oct. 25, 1982)-. Periodical. English. Twenty-five times a year. $28.00. Mass High Tech, 500 West Cummings Park, Suite 3500, Woburn MA 01801. **Tel** (617)935-1100. **ED** Patrick Porter. **DD** 621. Index available. cum. index. **Bk Rev. Ad Acc. Circ:** 25,000 (ctrl). available on microfilm from University Microfilms International (UMI); available on an online database (file 635/Full-Text) from DIALOG. Documents available from UMI Article Clearinghouse.
**Desc:** News of a general nature for technical professionals in the high technology industry in New England. Includes electronics, communications, computers and defense.
**Ind/Abst** Bus. Dateline; PROMT.

●US/1060-1554
**MASSACHUSETTS TECHNOLOGY RESOURCE GUIDE.** (MASSACHUSETTS TECHNOLOGY RESOURCE GUIDE / SPONSORED BY [THE] CENTER FOR TECHNOLOGY COMMERCIALIZATION, INC.). [Mass. technol. resour. guide]. **Added/Corp** Center for Technology Commercialization. Corporate Technology Information Services. **VFOAT** Massachusetts Technology Resource Guide and Services Yellow Pages. (1992/93 ed.)-. English. $45.00. Corporate Technology Information Services Inc, 12 Alfred Street, Suite 200, Woburn MA 01801-9998. **Tel** (617)932-3939, (800)333-8036, FAX (617)932-6335, telex 497-2961 CRPTECH. **DD** 621.

US/0736-7910
**MASTERS THESES IN THE PURE AND APPLIED SCIENCES ACCEPTED BY COLLEGES AND UNIVERSITIES OF THE UNITED STATES AND CANADA.** [Masters theses pure appl. sci. accept. coll. univ. U. S. Can.]. **Added/Corp** Purdue University. Center for Information and Numerical Data Analysis and Synthesis. **VFOAT** Masters Theses in the Pure and Applied Sciences. Vol. 18 (1974)-. Monographic series. English. ir. Price varies per volume. Plenum Press, 233 Spring Street, New York NY 10013-1578. **Tel** (212)620-8000, (800)221-9369, FAX (212)463-0742, (212)807-1047, telex 23/421139. **ED** Wade H. Shafer. **DD** 016.5. **NLM** Z 7401 M423. **Continues** Masters Theses in the Pure and Applied Sciences Accepted by Colleges and Universities of the United States.
**Desc:** Covers academic dissertations in science and engineering.

GW/0170-589X
**MATERIALKUNDLICH-TECHNISCHE REIHE.** [Materialkd. tech. Reihe]. (1976)-. Academic Scholarly Publication. German. ir. Price varies per volume. Gebruder Borntraeger Verlagsbuchhandlung, Johannesstrasse 3-A, D-70176 Stuttgart Germany. **Tel** 0711/62 50 01, FAX (0711)625005, telex 723363 SCHB D. **ED** G. Petzow. **CODEN** MTREDR. Documents available from CASDDS.
**Ind/Abst** Chem. Abstr. (1976-1980).

●US/1062-5496
**MATERIALS SCIENCE CITATION INDEX.** (MATERIALS SCIENCE CITATION INDEX [COMPUTER FILE] : A CD-ROM DATABASE WITH ABSTRACTS.). **Added/Corp** Institute for Scientific Information. **VFOAT** Materials Science. (1992)-. English. bm. $994.00. Institute for Scientific Information, 3501 Market Street, Philadelphia PA 19104. **Tel** (215)386-0100, (800)523-1850, FAX (215)386-6362, telex 84-5305. **(Subscription address:** Institute for Scientific Information, PO Box 71416, Chicago IL 60694.)

US/0076-5201
**MATERIALS SCIENCE RESEARCH.** [Mater. sci. res.]. Vol. 1 (1963)-. Monographic series. English. ir. Price varies per volume. Plenum Press, 233 Spring Street, New York NY 10013-1578. **Tel** (212)620-8000, (800)221-9369, FAX (212)463-0742, (212)807-1047, telex 23/421139. **LC** UNC. **CODEN** MTSRAY. **[CCC].** Documents available from Article Express International, Ask*IEEE, CASDDS.
**Ind/Abst** Bioeng. Abstr.; Chem. Abstr.; Ei Page One; Eng. Index Annu.; INSPEC.

RU/0301-1933
**MATERIALY NAUCNOJ STUDENCESKOJ KONFERENCII.** (MATERIALY NAUCHNOI STUDENCHESKOI KONFERENTSII.). **Main/Corp** Smolenskii Gosudarstvennyi Meditsinskii Institut. Nauchnoe Studencheskoe Obschestvo. **VFOAT** Teziszy Dokladov. Vol. 1 (1949)-. Russian.

SI/0218-2025
**MATHEMATICAL MODELS & METHODS IN APPLIED SCIENCES : MP3SAS.** See Mathematics.

CN/0848-7499
**MATHEMATICS AND SCIENCES BULLETIN.** See Mathematics.

US/0076-5392
**MATHEMATICS IN SCIENCE AND ENGINEERING.** See Mathematics.

US
**MCGRAW-HILL DICTIONARY OF SCIENTIFIC AND TECHNICAL TERMS.** See Encyclopedias and General Reference Books.

US
**MCGRAW-HILL ENCYCLOPEDIA OF SCIENCE & TECHNOLOGY.** See Encyclopedias and General Reference Books.

US/0076-2016
**MCGRAW-HILL YEARBOOK OF SCIENCE AND TECHNOLOGY.** [McGraw-Hill yearb. sci. technol.]. **VFOAT** Yearbook of Science and Technology. (1962)-. English. an. $105.00. McGraw Hill Publishing Company, Inc., 1221 Avenue of the Americas, New York NY 10020. **Tel** (212)512-6410, (800)525-5003, FAX (212)512-6111. **(Subscription address:** McGraw Hill Inc., PO Box 40, Blue Ridge Summit, PA 17294; telephone: (800)233-1128) **LC** Q121; .M312. **DD** 505. **NLM** Q 121 M1471. cum. index.
**Ind/Abst** AGRICOLA.

US/0148-0057
**MEASUREMENTS & CONTROL.** (M & C, MEASUREMENTS & CONTROL.). [Meas. control]. **Added/Corp** Measurements & Data Corporation. Measurements & Control Society. Southern California Meter Association. Journal of the Southern California Meter Association. **VFOAT** Measurements & control. **VAT** Measurements and Control. Vol.11 (Jan./Feb. 1977)-. Periodical. English. bm. $22.00 (one year), $35.00 (two year) US; $35.00 other. Measurement & Data Corporation, 2994 West Liberty Avenue, Pittsburgh PA 15216. **Tel** (412)343-9666, FAX (412)343-9685. **ED** Milton Aronson and Harish Saluja. **LC** T50; .M2. **DD** 389/.1/05. **Bk Rev. Ad Acc. Circ:** 101,000 (ctrl). available on microfilm and microfiche from University Microfilms International (UMI). **Continues** M & D, Measurements & Data, 0025-6323.

US/0047-6382
**MECHELECIV.** [Mecheleciv]. V. 1- July 1942-. Periodical. English. bm. $2.00. Mecheleciv, Davis-Hodgkins House, The George Washington University, 2142 G Street NW, Washington DC 20052. **Tel** (202)676-3998. **ED** Daniel L Briller. **Ad Acc. Circ:** 10,000.
**Desc:** A student published, student written, student operated technical magazine. Cooperatively published with the Engineer Alumni Association at George Washington University, Washington DC.

NO/0373-5605
**MEDDELELSER / NORSK PALARINSTITUTT.** [Medd. - Nor. polarinst.]. **Main/Corp** Norsk Polarinstitutt. No. 68-. Monographic series. Norwegian (English and German). ir. Price varies per volume. Norsk Polarinstitutt, PO Box 158, N-1330 Oslo Lufthavn Norway. **Tel** 011 47 02 123650, FAX 011 47 02 123854, telex 74745 POLAR N. **(Subscription address:** Norwegian University Press, Publications Expediting Inc., 200 Meacham Avenue, Elmont, NY 11003) **ED** Thor Larsen and Annemor Brekke. **CODEN** NPMEAG. **Circ:** 800. **Continues** Norges Svalbard- Og Ishavs-underskelser. Meddelelser.
**Desc:** Popular science publication treating subjects concerning the polar regions.
**Ind/Abst** GeoRef.

DK/0106-1054
**MEDDELELSER OM GRNLAND. BIOSCIENCE.** See Biology.

BE/0001-4176
**MEDEDELINGEN DER ZITTINGEN - KONINKLIJKE ACADEMIE VOOR OVERZEESE WETTENSCHAPEN.** (BULLETIN DES SEANCES / ACADEMIE ROYALE DES SCIENCES D'OUTRE-MER.). [Meded. zitt. - K. Acad. Overz. Wett.]. **Main/Corp** Academie Royale des Sciences d'Outre-Mer. **Added/Corp** Academie Royale des Sciences d'Outre-Mer. Annuaire. Academie Royale des Sciences d'Outre-Mer. Jaarboek. **VFOAT** Mededelingen der Zittingen. New. Ser. 5/6 (1959)-. Periodical. French (Dutch, English and French). Four times a year. 2500F. Acad Royale de Belgique, rue Decale 1, B1000 Brussels Belgium. **Tel** 011 32 2 5380211. **(Subscription address:** Librarie Transatlantique, 126 Chaussee de Wavre, 1050 Brussels Belgium.**)** **NLM** W1 BU597. **CODEN** AOBSAN. Index available in last issue of volume--attached. ***Continues*** *Academie Royale des Sciences Coloniales (Belgium). Bulletin des Seances.*
**Ind/Abst** Anthropol. Index; GeoRef; Rev. Med. Vet. Mycology; Rev. Plant Pathol.; Trop. Dis. Bull.

IT/1120-1932
**MEDIAPLUSNEWS.** **See** Business.

JA/0389-1887
**MEDICAL TECHNOLOGY (TOKYO. 1973).** **See** Medical Science and Technology.

JA
**MEIJI DAIGAKU RIKO GAKUBU KENKYU HOKOKU.** **Added/Corp** Meiji Daigaku. Riko Gakubu. **VFOAT** Kenkyu Hokoku; Research Reports. No. 1 (1990)-. Periodical. Japanese (summaries and/or abstracts in English). Meiji Daigaku Kogakubu, 5158 Ikuta Tama-ku (214), Kawasaki Japan. **LC** Q179.9; .M45. ***Continues*** *Research Reports of the Faculty of Engineering, Meiji University, 0465-6075.*

JA
**MEIJI SEIKA KENKYU NENPO.** [Meiji Seika kenkyu nempo]. **Added/Corp** Meiji Seika Kabushiki Kaisha. Chuo Kenkyujo. **VFOAT** Scientific Reports of Meiji Seika Kaisha. (1959)-. Periodical. Japanese (summaries and/or abstracts in English). Meiji Seika K.K. Chuo Kenkyujo, (Research Lab., Meiji Seika Kaisha, Ltd.), 760, Morookacho, Kohokuku, Yokohamashi, Kanagawaken 222, Japan. **CODEN** MSKNA9. Documents available from CASDDS.
**Ind/Abst** Chem. Abstr.

JA/0386-4952
**MEIJO DAIGAKU RIKO GAKUBU KENKYU HOKOKU.** [Meijo Daigaku Rikogakubu kenkyu hokoku]. **Added/Corp** Meijo Daigaku. Riko Gakubu. **VFOAT** Research Reports of the Faculty of Science and Technology, Meijyo University. (1957)-. Japanese (summaries and/or abstracts in English). **CODEN** MDRKAW. Documents available from CASDDS.
**Ind/Abst** Chem. Abstr.; Zentralbl. Math. Ihre Grenzgeb.

JA/0388-130X
**MEISEI DAIGAKU KENKYU KIYO. RIKO GAKUBU.** (RESEARCH BULLETIN OF MEISEI UNIVERSITY. PHYSICAL SCIENCES AND ENGINEERING.). [Meisei Daigaku kenkyu kiyo, Riko Gakubu]. **Added/Corp** Meisei Daigaku. **VFOAT** Kenkyu Kiyo. Riko Gakubu. (1965)-. Bulletin. English (French and Japanese). an. Meisei Daigaku, (Meisei University), 337, Hodokubo, Hinoshi, Tokyoto 191 Japan. **CODEN** MDKRDL. Documents available from CASDDS.
**Ind/Abst** Chem. Abstr.; Zentralbl. Math. Ihre Grenzgeb.

NE
**MEMBRANE SCIENCE AND DESALINATION.** (1975)-. Academic Scholarly Publication. English. Forty-two times a year. Fl4,515 (includes the Journal of Membrane Science and Desalination). Elsevier Science Publishers BV, PO Box 211, 1000 AE Amsterdam Netherlands. **Tel** 011 31 20 5803642, FAX 011 31 20 5862696, telex 15682. available on microfilm from University Microfilms International (UMI).

FR
**MEMBRES DE L'ASSOCIATION NATIONALE DE LA RECHERCHE TECHNIQUE ET LEURS TRAVAUX, LES.** **Main/Corp** Association Nationale de la Recherche Technique. French. be. Association National de la Recherche Technique, 101 Av Raymond Poincare, F-75116 Paris France. **Tel** 011 33 1 45017227, FAX 011 33 1 47018529, telex 642632. **LC** WMLC L 83/2526.

SZ/0037-9611
**MEMOIRES DE LA SOCIETE VAUDOISE DES SCIENCES NATURELLES.** [Mem. Soc. vaudoise sci. nat.]. **Main/Corp** Societe Vaudoise des Sciences Naturelles, Lausanne. Vol. 1, No. 1 (April 29, 1922)-. Monographic series. English (French and German). ir. Price varies per volume. SUSN, Palais de Rumine, 1005 Lausanne Switzerland. **LC** Q67; .L33. **DD** 505. **CODEN** MSVNAU. Documents available from BIOSIS Document Express, CASDDS.
**Ind/Abst** Biol. Abstr.; Chem. Abstr.; Ecol. Abstr.; Geogr. Abstr. Human Geogr.; GeoRef; Life Sci. Collect.

JA/0911-0305
**MEMOIRS OF THE FACULTY OF ENGINEERING AND DESIGN, KYOTO INSTITUTE OF TECHNOLOGY. SERIES OF SCIENCE AND TECHNOLOGY.** [Mem. Fac. Eng. Des. Kyoto Inst. Technol., Ser. sci. technol.]. **Added/Corp** Kyoto Kogei Seni Daigaku. Kogeigakubu. **VFOAT** Series of Science and Technology. Vol. 33 (1984)-. Periodical. English. Kyoto Kogei Seni Daigaku Kogeigakubu, (Faculty of Engineering & Design, Kyoto Inst. of Tecnology), Matsugasaki Goshokaidocho, Sakyoku,, Kyotoshi, Kyotofu 606 Japan. **LC** IN PROCESS. **CODEN** MFETEC. Documents available from Ask*IEEE, CASDDS. ***Continues*** *Kyoto Kogei Seni Daigaku. Kogeigakubu. Memoirs of the Faculty of Industrial Arts, Kyoto Technical University: Science and Technology, 0014-6773.*
**Ind/Abst** Chem. Abstr.; Energy Inf. Abstr.; INSPEC (1985-); Math. Rev.

JA/0078-6659
**MEMOIRS OF THE FACULTY OF ENGINEERING, OSAKA CITY UNIVERSITY.** **See** Engineering.

JA
**MEMOIRS OF THE FACULTY OF TECHNOLOGY, KANAZAWA UNIVERSITY.** English. Kanazawa University, 2-40-20 Kodatsuno, 2-chome, Kanazawa, Japan.
**Ind/Abst** Abstr. J. Earthq. Eng.

JA/0369-0369
**MEMOIRS OF THE INSTITUTE OF SCIENTIFIC AND INDUSTRIAL RESEARCH, OSAKA UNIVERSITY.** **Main/Corp** Osaka Daigaku (Japan). Sangyo Kagaku Kenkyujo. Vol. 6 (1948)-. Academic Scholarly Publication. English. an. Osaka Daigaku Sangyo Kagaku Kenkyujo, (Institute of Scientific and Industrial Research), Osaka University, 8-1 Mihogaoka Ibarakishi, Osakafu 567 Japan. **Tel** 06-877-5111, telex 5286213 ISIROU. **LC** Q180.J3; O712. **DD** 505. **CODEN** MISIAW. **Circ:** 550. Documents available from CASDDS.
**Desc:** Review papers and abstracts of the papers published in journals, etc.
**Ind/Abst** Chem. Abstr.; Energy Inf. Abstr.

JA/0452-4160
**MEMOIRS OF THE KONAN UNIVERSITY. SCIENCE SERIES.** [Mem. KÂonan Univ., Sci. ser.]. **Main/Corp** Konan Daigaku. (1955)-. Periodical. English. Konan Daigaku, (Konan University), 9-1, Okamoto 8 Chome, Higashinadaku, Kobeshi, Hyogoken 658 Japan. **LC** Q1; .K56a. **CODEN** MKOUAS. Documents available from BIOSIS Document Express, CASDDS.
**Ind/Abst** Biol. Abstr.; Chem. Abstr.; Zentralbl. Math. Ihre Grenzgeb.

US/0097-2622
**MEMOIRS OF THE SOUTHERN CALIFORNIA ACADEMY OF SCIENCES.** [Mem. South. Calif. Acad. Sci.]. **Main/Corp** Southern California Academy of Sciences, Los Angeles. Vol. 1 (1938)-. Monographic series. English. ir. Price varies per volume. Southern California Academy of Sciences, 900 West Exposition Boulevard, Los Angeles CA 90007. **Tel** (310)744-3384. **CODEN** MSCAAW. Index available. **Pr Rev.**
**Ind/Abst** GeoRef.

SP
**MEMORIA - CONSEJO SUPERIOR DE INVESTIGACIONES CIENTIFICAS.** **Main/Corp** Consejo Superior de Investigaciones Cientificas (Spain). (1940/41)-. Spanish. ir. Consejo Superior Investigacion Cientificas (CSIC), Vitruvio 8, 28006 Madrid Spain. **Tel** 011 34 1 5612833, FAX 011 34 1 4113077, telex 42182. **LC** AS302; .M7153. **DD** 066.

VE
**MEMORIA - SOCIEDAD DE CIENCIAS NATURALES LA SALLE.** **Main/Corp** Sociedad de Ciencias Naturales la Salle, Caracas. **VFOAT** Memoria de la S. C. N.-La Salle. No. 1- July 1941-. Spanish. ir. Sociedad de Ciencias Naturales la Salle, Apartado 1930, Caracas 1010-A Venezuela. **CODEN** SCNSAR.

PO/0870-0036
**MEMORIAS DO INSTITUTO DE INVESTIGACAO CIENTIFICA TROPICAL.** Portuguese. ir. Instituto de Investigacao Cientifica Tropical, Centro de Documentacao e Informacao, rua Jau 47, 1 300 Lisbon Portugal. **Tel** 645321. **Circ:** 1,000 (ctrl).

IT
**MEMORIE / CLASSE DI SCIENZE FISICHE, MATEMATICHE E NATURALI.** **Main/Corp** Accademia Nazionale dei Lincei. Classe di Scienze Fisiche, Matematiche e Naturali. Ser. 8, V. 1-. Monographic series. Italian (English, French, German and Spanish). ir. Price varies per volume. Accademia Nazionale dei Lincei, Via Lungara 10 Uff Diff Pubbl., 00165 Rome Italy. **Tel** 011 39 6 6838831. **Circ:** 850. ***Continues*** *Memorie Della Classe di Scienze Fisiche, Matematiche e Naturali.*
**Desc:** Publishes only contributions of fellows of the Academy of Lincei or scholars presented by a fellow; requires a 200-word abstract.

IT
**MEMORIE E RENDICONTI / ACCADEMIA DI SCIENZE, LETTERE E BELLE ARTI DEGLI ZELANTI E DEI DAFNICI.** **Added/Corp** Accademia di Scienze, Lettere e belle Arti degli Zelantea e dei Dafnici. (19??)-. Italian. an. ***Continues*** *Memorie e Rendiconti (Accademia di Scienze, Lettere e belle Arte di Acireale).*
**Ind/Abst** BHA : Biblio. Hist. Art.

RM/0254-8607
**MEMORIILE SECTIILOR STIINTIFICE / ACADEMIA REPUBLICII SOCIALISTE ROMANIA.** [Mem. sect. stint. - Acad. Repub. soc. Rom.]. **Added/Corp** Academia Republicii Socialiste Romania. **VFOAT** Memoirs of the Scientific Sections of the Academy of the Socialist Republic of Romania. (19??)-. Academic Scholarly Publication. English (French, German and Romanian). lei23.50. Editura Academia Republicii Socialiste Romania, Calea Victoriei Nr 125, R-79717 Bucuresti Romania. **Tel** telex 10376 PRSFI R. **LC** Q1.A1; M45. **DD** 505. **CODEN** MSARD8. Documents available from CASDDS.
**Ind/Abst** Chem. Abstr.; Math. Rev.; Zentralbl. Math. Ihre Grenzgeb.

NE
**MENS EN WETENSCHAP.** (19??)-. Periodical. Dutch. Eight times a year. Fl1200. Stichting Educatief Centrum, Postbus 386, 1270 AJ Huizen Netherlands. **(Subscription address:** Soumillion, Avenue Massenet 28, 1190 Brussels Belgium.**)**

AT/0815-0796
**METASCIENCE.** **Added/Corp** Australasian Association for the History, Philosophy, and Social Studies of Science. **VFOAT** Meta Science. Vol. 1/2 (1984)-. Periodical. English. Twice a year. 50.00Aus$ institutions; 40.00Aus$ individuals. AAHPSSS / Australasian Association for the History, Philosophy and Social Studies of Science, PO Box 1 / University of New South Wales, Dr. D. Miller, Kensington 2033 Australia. **Tel** 011 61 2 6972359 Ext. 5062, FAX 011 61 2 3137984. **ED** Michael Shortland (editor's address: Unit for History and Philosophy of Science, University of Sydney, Sydney NSW 2006 Australia; phone: 011 61 2 6924801). **Bk Rev**, (Qty: 70/year). **Ad Acc. Circ:** 180 (ctrl).
**Desc:** Covers the history, philosophy, and social studies of science.

NE/0377-9025
**METHODS AND PHENOMENA.** [Methods phenom.]. (1975)-. Monographic series. English. ir. Elsevier Science Publishers BV, PO Box 211, 1000 AE Amsterdam Netherlands. **Tel** 011 31 20 5803642, FAX 011 31 20 5862696, telex 15682. **CODEN** MPTTDK. Documents available from CASDDS.
**Ind/Abst** Chem. Abstr.

RU
**MEZHVUZOVSKII SBORNIK NAUCHNYKH TRUDOV / PERMSKII POLITEKHNICHESKII INSTITUT.** **Main/Corp** Permskii Politekhnicheskii Institut. **Added/Corp** Permskii Politekhnicheskii Institut. Permskii Gosudarstvennyi Universitet Imeni A.M. Gorkogo. (197?)-. Monographic series. Russian. Price varies per volume. **LC** T4; .P36. ***Continues*** *Sbornik Nauchnykh Trudov (Permskii Politekhnicheskii Institut).*

UK
**MICIS NEWS.** qt. Free. Microbial Culture Information Service, Laboratory of the Government Chemist, Queens Road, Teddington Middx TW11 0LY United Kingdom.
**Ind/Abst** Abstr. BioCommer. (-199?).

US/1065-9900
**MICROQUEST REPORT.** [Microquest rep.]. (1989)-. Periodical. English. mo. $495.00 US; $550.00 other. Microquest, 454 Las Gallinas Avenue, Suite 250, San Rafael CA 94903. **Tel** (415)479-4723, FAX (415)479-8636. **ED** Mark Ross. **DD** _a004.

FR
**MICROSCOPIE ELECTRONIQUE ET DIFFRACTION ELECTRONIQUE. E30.** French. 1041.42F France; 1080.00F other. Institut de l'Information Scientique et Technique (INIST), 2 Allee du Parc de Brabois, 54514 Vandoeuvre Nancy Cedex France. **Tel** 011 33 83 504600, FAX 011 33 83 504650. ***Continues*** *Pascal Explore. E30: Microscopie et Diffraction Electronique.*

US/1040-0575
**MID-ATLANTIC SALES GUIDE TO HIGH-TECH COMPANIES.** [Mid-Atl. sales guide high tech co.]. **VFOAT** Sales Guide to High Tech Companies. Mid-Atlantic Region. (1988)-. English. qt.

$145.00. Corporate Technology Information Services Inc, 12 Alfred Street, Suite 200, Woburn MA 01801-9998. **Tel** (617)932-3939, (800)333-8036, FAX (617)932-6335, telex 497-2961 CRPTECH. **ED** Steven W Parker. **LC** HC110.H53; M53. **DD** 338.7/62/0002574. Index available. cum. index. **Bk Rev. Ad Acc. Circ:** 3,000. available on diskette.
**Desc:** Regional directory of over 3,000 technology manufacturers and developers.

GW/0938-880X
**MID FRANKFURT. VFOAT**
Medien-Informations-Dienst. (1990)-. Periodical. German. ir. Verlag Bleuel und Debes, Monstrasse 125, W-6000 Frankfurt 60 Germany. **UDC** 02.

UK/0026-4695
**MINERVA (LONDON).** (MINERVA.). [Minerva]. **Added/Corp** International Association for Cultural Freedom. Committee on Science and Freedom. Vol. 1 (Autumn 1962)-. Academic Scholarly Publication. English. Four times a year (seasonally). $52.00 (individuals), $135.00 (institutions) North America; £27.00 (individuals), £75.00 (institutions) UK; £30.00 (individuals), £78.00 (institutions) other. Minerva Quarterly Review Ltd, 19 Nottingham Road, London SW17 7EA England. **Tel** 011 44 81 6821782, FAX 011 44 81 7676161. **ED** Professor Edward Shils. **LC** AS121; .M5. **DD** 052. **NLM** W1 MI629. Index available (bound 4th iss.). cum. index (1962-1992 - $34.00). **Bk Rev**, (Qty: 12). **Ad Acc, Adv Mgr:** G. Anderson, **Tel** (081)682-1782. **Pr Rev. Circ:** 750. Documents available from The Genuine Article.
**Desc:** Presents scholarly analysis of higher-educational and scientific institutions. It deals with these institutions and their traditions historically and in their interactions with political, economic, moral and administrative problems.
**Ind/Abst** Am. Hist. Life (1979-); BHA : Biblio. Hist. Art; Br. Educ. Index; Contents Pages Manage.; Curr. Contents Soc. Behav. Sci.; Int. Bibliogr. Sociol.; Int. Polit. Sci. Abstr.; Middle East Abstr. Index; PAIS Int. Print (1991-); Public Aff. Inf. Serv. Bul.; Res. Alert [Full Cov.]; Res. High. Educ. Abstr.; Soc. Plann. Policy Dev. Abstr.; Soc. Sci. Cit. Index [Full Cov.]; Sociol. Abstr. (?-?).

US/0076-9258
**MINNESOTA STUDIES IN THE PHILOSOPHY OF SCIENCE. Added/Corp** Minnesota Center for Philosophy of Science. Vol. 1 (1956)-. Monographic series. English. ir. Price varies per volume. University of Minnesota Press, 2037 University Avenue Southeast, Minneapolis MN 55414. **Tel** (612)642-2516, (612)624-0005. **LC** Q175; .M64. **DD** 501. **[CCC].** Documents available from The Genuine Article.
**Ind/Abst** Math. Rev.; Res. Alert [Full Cov.].

US/1060-8281
**MINNESOTA TECHNOLOGY.** [Minn. technol.]. **Added/Corp** Greater Minnesota Corporation. Vol. 1, No. 1 (Spring 1991)-. Periodical. English. qt. Free in Minnesota; $14.00 other. Minnesota Technology, Inc., 111 3rd Avenue South, Suite 400, Minneapolis MN 55401. **Tel** (612)338-7722. **DD** 600.

US/0744-2505
**MIT REPORT (CAMBRIDGE, MASS. : 1981), THE.** ***Ceased.*** (THE MIT REPORT / MASSACHUSETTS INSTITUTE OF TECHNOLOGY, INDUSTRIAL LIAISON PROGRAM.). **VFOAT** M.I.T. Report. **VAT** Massachusetts Institute of Technology Report. (1981)-(19??). Periodical. English. ir. Massachusetts Institute of Technology (MIT) Press, 55 Hayward Street, Cambridge MA 02142-1399. **Tel** (617)253-2889, (617)625-8481, FAX (617)258-6779. ***Formed by the union of*** *Monthly List of Publications* ***and*** *Reports on Research.*
**Ind/Abst** Coal Abstr. (?-?).

US/0364-3972
**MITRE TECHNICAL REPORT.** [Mitre tech. rep.]. **Main/Corp** Mitre Corporation. Academic Scholarly Publication. English. Price varies per volume. Mitre Corporation, McLean VA 22101. **CODEN** MITRDX. Documents available from CASDDS.
**Ind/Abst** Chem. Abstr.

JA/0388-3396
**MITSUBISHI GENSHIRYOKU GIHO.** [Mitsubishi genshiryoku giho]. **Added/Corp** Mitsubishi Jukogyo Kabushiki Kaisha. (19??)-. Academic Scholarly Publication. Japanese. qt. Mitsubishi Jukogyo Kabushiki Kaishi, Maru-no-Uchi 2-5-1, Chiyoda-ku, Tokyo-to 100 Japan. **CODEN** MGGIDT. Documents available from CASDDS.
**Ind/Abst** Chem. Abstr.

JA/0387-2432
**MITSUBISHI JUKO GIHO.** [Mitsubishi juko giho]. **Added/Corp** Mitsubishi Jukogyo Kabushiki Kaisha. (1964)-. Academic Scholarly Publication. English (Japanese and English). bm. $62.00. Mitsubishi Jukogyo K.K., (Mitsubishi Heavy Industries, Ltd.), 5-1, Marunouchi 2 Chome, Chiyodaku, Tokyoto 100, Japan. **(Subscription address:** Kyowa Book Company Inc., 1-38 Kanda Jinbo-Cho, Chiyoda-Ku Tokyo 101, Japan**) CODEN** MIJGAF. Documents available from CASDDS.
**Ind/Abst** Acoust. Abstr.; BMT Abstr.; Chem. Abstr.

GW
**MITTEILUNGEN DES AMTES FUR STANDARDISIERUNG, MESSWESEN UND WARENPRUFUNG. Main/Corp** Germany (East). Amt fur Standardisierung, Messwesen und Warenprufung. Periodical. German. sm. Amt fur Standardisierung Mebwesen und Warenprufung, Furstenwalder Damm 388, Berlin O-1162 Germany. **Tel** 6441457, telex 011-2630. **LC** T59.2.G32; G43A.

AU/0369-1055
**MITTEILUNGEN DES NATURWISSENSCHAFTLICHEN VEREINES FUER STEIERMARK.** [Mitt. Naturwiss. Ver. Steiermark]. **Main/Corp** Naturwissenschaftlicher Verein fur Steiermark, Graz. No. 1 (1863)-. German. an. **LC** Q44; .S8. **DD** 505. **CODEN** MNVSAAMNMAAD. Documents available from CASDDS.
**Ind/Abst** Chem. Abstr.; GeoRef.

AU
**MITTEILUNGEN / OSTERREICHISCHES GETRANKE INSTITUT. Added/Corp** Osterreichisches Getranke Institut. Verband der Brauereien (Austria) Verband de Hefeindustrie (Austria) Verband der Spiritusindustrie (Austria). **VFOAT** Mitteilungen des Osterreichischen Getranke Instituts. (Jan./Feb. 1991)-. Periodical. German. bm (6 issues). S270.00 Austria; S650.00 other. Oesterreichisches Getraenke Institut, Michaelerstr 25, A 1182 Vienna Austria. **Tel** 011 43 1 4796924, FAX 011 43 1 692477. **LC** WMLC 91/4395. **CODEN** MOINE9. ***Continues*** *Mitteilungen der Versuchsstation fuer das Garungsgewerbe Sowie des Instituts fuer Angewandte Mikrobiologie und der Dozentur fuer Lagertechnik und Vorratsschutz der Hochschule fuer Bodenkultur in Wien, 0369-271X.*
**Ind/Abst** Food Sci. Technol. Abstr.

GW/0030-834X
**MITTEILUNGEN - PTB.** (PTB MITTEILUNGEN : AMTS- UND MITTEILUNGSBLATT DER PHYSIKALISCH - TECHNISCHEN BUNDESANSTALT BRAUNSCHWEIG-BERLIN.). [Mitt. - PTB]. **Added/Corp** Physikalisch-Technische Bundesanstalt (Germany). **VFOAT** Mitteilungen. (19??)-. Academic Scholarly Publication. German (summaries and/or abstracts in English). Six times a year. DM222.00. Vieweg Publishing, PO Box 5829, D 65048 Wiesbaden Germany. **Tel** 011 49 611 160230, FAX 011 49 611 160229. **ED** W. Hauser and E. Seiler. **CODEN** PTBMAZ. **[CCC].** Index available. **Bk Rev. Ad Acc. Pr Rev.** Documents available from Article Express International, The Genuine Article, CASDDS. ***Continues*** *Amtsblatt der Physikalisch-Technischen Bundesanstalt.*
**Ind/Abst** Chem. Abstr.; Curr. Contents Eng. Tech. Appl. Sci.; Eng. Index Annu. [Select. Cov.]; Res. Alert [Select. Cov.].

JA/0286-3707
**MIYAGI KOGYO KOTO SENMON GAKKO KENKYU KIYO.** (KENKYU KIYO.). [Miyagi Kogyo Koto Senmon Gakko kenkyu kiyo]. **Added/Corp** Miyagi Kogyo Koto Senmon Gakko. **VFOAT** Research Reports, Miyagi Technical College. (1964)-. Japanese (summaries and/or abstracts in English). an. **CODEN** KKMGDP. Documents available from CASDDS.
**Ind/Abst** Chem. Abstr.

CC/0254-6140
**MO FENLI KEXUE YU JISHU.** (MO FEN LI KO HSUEH YU CHI SHU. SCIENCE AND TECHNOLOGY.). [Mo fenli kexue yu jishu]. **VFOAT** Mo Fen li; Membrane Separation Science and Technology; Membrane Separation; Science and Technology of Membrane Separation. (1981)-. Academic Scholarly Publication. Chinese (summaries and/or abstracts in English). qt. **CODEN** MFKJDB. Documents available from CASDDS.
**Ind/Abst** Chem. Abstr.

US/0742-7107
**MODELTEC.** [Modeltec]. **Added/Corp** Steam Automobile Club of America. **VFOAT** Modeltec Magazine. Vol. 1, No. 1 (May 1984)-. Periodical. English. mo. $31.00 US; $38.00 other. Modeltec, PO Box 1226, St Cloud MN 56302. **Tel** (612)654-0815. **(Subscription address:** Box 286, Cadillac MI 49601**) ED** George Broad. **LC** WMLC L 83/7272. **DD** 625. Index available. **Bk Rev. Ad Acc. Circ:** 3,200. ***Absorbed*** *Steam Automobile, 0561-9726.*
**Desc:** Plans, instructions for building live steam large-scale operating models of locomotives, stationary engines, boats, gasoline hit-and-miss engines, meets, suppliers' advertising, machining techniques.

PL/0462-9760
**MODY TECHNIK.** [Mody Tech.]. (1950)-. Periodical. Polish. mo. $69.00. **(Subscription address:** ARS Polona, PO Box 1001, 00068 Warsaw Poland.**) UDC** 37.031. ***Continues*** *Mody Zawodowiec.*

LI
**MOKSLAS IR GYVENIMAS. Added/Corp** Lietuvos TSR "Zinijos" Draugija. (1972)-. Periodical. Lithuanian. mo. $19.00. **(Subscription address:** Victor Kamkin, 4956 Boiling Brook Parkway, Rockville MD 20852.**) LC** Q4; .M63. ***Continues*** *MG, Mokslas Ir Gyvenimas.*

FR/0221-0436
**MONDES ET CULTURES : COMPTES RENDUS TRIMESTRIELS DES SEANCES DE L'ACADEMIE DES SCIENCES D'OUTRE-MER.** [Mondes cult.]. **Added/Corp** Academie des Sciences d'Outre-mer. Vol. 38, No. 1 (1978)-. Periodical. French. qt. 300.00F. Academie des Sciences d'Outre Mer, 15 rue La Perouse, F-75116 Paris France. **Tel** 011 33 1 47208793. **ED** M. Gilbert Mangin. **LC** JV1802; .A314. Index available. cum. index. **Bk Rev. Circ:** 1,000 (ctrl). ***Continues*** *Comptes Rendus Trimestriels des Seances de l'Academie des Science d'Outre-Mer.*
**Ind/Abst** Am. Hist. Life (1986-).

US
**MONKEYSHINES ON HEALTH AND SCIENCE.** Periodical. English. Twice a year (fall and spring). $18.00. North Carolina Learning Institute for Fitness & Education, PO Box 10245, Greensboro NC 27404. **Tel** (919)292-6999.
**Desc:** Covers earth, health, and life sciences.

US
**MONOCLONAL ANTIBODIES BIBLIOGRAPHY.** Vol. 1; 1984-. Bibliography. English. Scientific Newsletters Inc, PO Box 3205, Mission Viejo CA 92690. **Tel** (714)497-3522. **NLM** ZQW 575; M751.

PL/0860-097X
**MONOGRAFIA - POLITECHNIKA KRAKOWSKA IM. TADEUSZA KOSCIUSZKI.** (MONOGRAFIA.). [Monogr. - Politech. Krak. im. Tadeusza Kosciuszki]. (1984)-. Academic Scholarly Publication. Multiple languages. ir. Price varies per volume. **UDC** 62. Documents available from CASDDS.
**Ind/Abst** Chem. Abstr.; Math. Rev.

AG/0327-5426
**MONOGRAFIAS DE LA ACADEMIA NACIONAL DE CIENCIAS EXACTAS, FISICAS Y NATURALES.** [Monogr. Acad. nac. cienc. exactas fis. nat.]. (1983)-. Academic Scholarly Publication. Spanish. ir. Price varies per volume. **UDC** 5. Documents available from CASDDS.
**Ind/Abst** Chem. Abstr.

BL/0102-1958
**MONOGRAFIAS (INSTITUTO DE PESQUISAS TECNOLOGICAS).** (MONOGRAFIAS / INSTITUTO DE PESQUISAS TECHNOLOGICAS DO ESTADO DE SAO PAULO.). [Monogr. - Inst. Pesqui. Tecnol. Estado Sao Paulo]. 1-. Monographic series. Portuguese. ir. Price varies per volume.
**Ind/Abst** GeoRef.

US
**MONOGRAM REPORTS.** (MR REPORTS / RAND CORPORATION.). (19??)-. Monographic series. English. ir. Price varies per volume. Rand Corporation, 1700 Main Street, PO Box 2138, Santa Monica CA 90407-2138. **Tel** (310)393-0411. ***Continues in part*** *R : Report / Rand Corporation.*
**Desc:** Research on a variety of given subjects.

US
**MONOGRAPH - INDIANA ACADEMY OF SCIENCE. Main/Corp** Indiana Academy of Science. No. 1 (1969)-. Monographic series. English. ir. Price varies per volume. Indiana Academy of Sciences, Indiana State Library, 140 North Senate Avenue, Indianapolis IN 46204. **Tel** (317)232-3686. **ED** William R. Eberly. ctrl circ.

US
**MONOGRAPHS AND TEXTBOOKS IN PHYSICAL SCIENCE.** Humanities Press, 165 1st Avenue, Atlantic Highlands NJ 07716. **Tel** (908)872-1441, (800)221-3845, FAX (908)872-0717, telex 752233.

NE/0929-9629
**MONTE CARLO METHODS AND APPLICATIONS.** (199?)-. English. qt. DM330.00. VSP International Science Publishers, Godfried van Seystlaan 47, 3703 BR Zeist Netherlands. **Tel** 011 31 3404 25790, FAX 011 31 3404 32081, telex 40217 USP NL. **(Subscription address:** VSP International Science Publishers, PO Box 346, 3700 AH Zeist Netherlands.**)**

US/0027-1284
**MOSAIC (WASHINGTON).** ***Ceased.*** (MOSAIC.). [Mosaic]. Vol. 1, No. 1 (Winter 1970)-Ceased with Fall Iss. (1992). Periodical. English. qt. National Science Foundation, 1800 G Street Northwest, Washington DC 20550. **Tel** (202)357-9859, (202)357-9498. **LC** Q11. **NLM** W1 MO917F. **CODEN** MOSAAG. available on microfilm from University Microfilms International (UMI). Documents available from UMI Article Clearinghouse.
**Ind/Abst** Acad. Abstr. Full Text Elite (Jan. 1992-Sept. 1992); Acad. Search (Jan. 1992-Sept. 1992); Access (?-?); AGRICOLA (?-?) [Select. Cov.]; Alum. Ind. Abstr. (?-?); Biol. Dig. (?-?); Eng. Mater. Abstr. (?-?); Environ.

Period. Bibliogr. (?-?); Expand. Acad. Index (1989-19??); Gen. Sci. Index (?-?); Gen. Sci. Source (Jan. 1992-Sept. 1992); GeoRef (?-?); INFO-SOUTH Abstr.; Mag. Search; Met. Abstr. (?-?); Middle East Abstr. Index (?-?); Newsp. Period. Abstr. (1991-); Soc. Plann. Policy Dev. Abstr.; Sociol. Abstr. (?-?); Vocat. Search (Jan. 1992-Sept. 1992).

II/0970-6704
**MOVING TECHNOLOGY.** [Mov. Technol.]. (1986)-. Periodical. English. bm. **UDC** 63 :338.
**Ind/Abst** Agric. Eng. Abstr.; Soils Fert.

GW/0341-7727
**MPG SPIEGEL.** [MPG Spiegel]. **Added/Corp** Max-Planck-Gesellschaft zur Forderung der Wissenschaften. **VFOAT** M.P.G. Spiegel. (1973)-. Periodical. German. Six times a year. Max-Planck-Gesellschaft zur Forderung der Wissenschaften, Hofgarteustr. 2, D 80535 Munich Germany. **Tel** 089 2108 1275, FAX 089 2108 1111, telex 522203 MPGDMUD. **ED** Michael Globig, Horst Meermann, Hintsches, W Frese. **LC** Q49; .M3514. **DD** 505. **Bk Rev. Circ:** 21,000.
**Ind/Abst** Energy Res. Abstr. (Sept. 1976-); GeoRef.

AT
**MRL TECHNICAL NOTE. Added/Corp** Materials Research Laboratory (Australia). **VFOAT** MRL-TN. (1989)-. Monographic series. English. DSTO Materials Research Laboratory, Maribyrnong Victoria Australia. Documents available from CASDDS. ***Continues*** *Technical Note (Materials Research Laboratory (Australia)). Technical Note.*
**Ind/Abst** Chem. Abstr.

IO
**MUHIBBAH. Added/Corp** Universitas Islam Indonesia. Dewan Mahasiswa. Universitas Islam Indonesia. Lembaga Pers Mahasiswa. (19??)-. Periodical. Multiple languages (Indonesian and English). mo. 150 each issue. Universitas Islam Indonesia, Jl Cik Di Tiro, Yogyakarta Indonesia. **LC** Q183.4.I5; M82.

US/0276-1459
**MULTIPHASE SCIENCE AND TECHNOLOGY.** ***Title Change.*** [Multiph. sci. technol.]. Vol. 1 (1982)-(19??). Academic Scholarly Publication. English. ir. Taylor & Francis Ltd., Rankine Road, Basingstoke Hampshire, RG24 8PR United Kingdom. **Tel** 011 44 256 840366, FAX 011 44 256 479438, telex 858540. **(Subscription address:** Taylor & Francis Inc., 1900 Frost Road, Suite 101, Bristol PA 19007-1598.) **LC** TP156.E65; M842. **DD** 660/.0414/05. **CODEN** MSTEDU. **[CCC].** Documents available from CASDDS. ***Continued by*** *Critical Reviews in Multiphase Science & Technology, 1065-2388.*
**Ind/Abst** Chem. Abstr.

SP/0211-3058
**MUNDO CIENTIFICO.** (1981)-. Spanish. Eleven times a year. 651.00ptas Spain; $64.00 others (surface mail); $92.00 Europe; $109.00 others (airmail). Editorial Fontalba SA, Valencia 359 6TO 1, 08009 Barcelona Spain. **Tel** 011 34 3 4585508.

GW/0065-5295
**NACHRICHTEN DER AKADEMIE DER WISSENSCHAFTEN IN GOTTINGEN. II, MATHEMATISCH-PHYSIKALISCHE KLASSE.** [Nachr. Akad. Wiss. Gott., 2]. **Added/Corp** Akademie der Wissenschaften in Gottingen. Mathematisch-Physikalische Klasse. No. 9 (1958)-. Monographic series. German. ir. Price varies per volume. Vandenhoeck & Ruprecht, Robert Bosch Breite 6, D-37079 Goettingen Germany. **Tel** 011 49 551 695911, FAX 011 49 551 695917, telex 965226 VAN d. **LC** AS182; .G8225. **CODEN** NAAKA5. Index Available, published separately, free-automatically sent. ***Formed by the union of*** *Nachrichten der Akademie der Wissenschaften in Gottingen. Mathematisch-Physikalische Klasse. IIa, Mathematisch-Physikalisch-Chemische Abteilung* ***and*** *Nachrichten der Akademie der Wissenschaften in Gottingen. Mathematisch-Physikalische Klasse. IIb, Biologisch-Physiologisch-Chemische Abteilung.*
**Ind/Abst** GeoRef; Math. Rev.; Zentralbl. Math. Ihre Grenzgeb.

JA/0388-5631
**NAGAOKA GIJUTSU KAGAKU DAIGAKU KENKYU HOKOKU. VFOAT** Technical Report of the Technological University of Nagaoka. Academic Scholarly Publication. Japanese (English). Nagaoka Gijutsu Kagaku Daigaku Kami-tomiokamachi, Nagaoka-shi 949-54 Japan. **LC** T4; .N178. **CODEN** NKHUD7. Documents available from CASDDS.
**Ind/Abst** Chem. Abstr.

JA/0027-7568
**NAGAOKA KOGYO KOTO SENMON GAKKO KENKYU KIYO.** [Nagaoka Kogyo Koto Semmon Gakko kenkyu kiyo]. **Added/Corp** Nagaoka Kogyo Koto Senmon Gakko. **VFOAT** Research Reports of the Nagaoka Technical College. (1966)-. Academic Scholarly Publication. Japanese (English). qt. Nagaoka Technical College, Nishi Katakai Machi Nagaok Shi, Niigataken Japan. **CODEN** NKSKBU. Documents available from CASDDS. ***Continues*** *Nagaoka Kogyo Tanki Daigaku Koto Senmon Gakko Kenkyu Kiyo.*
**Ind/Abst** Chem. Abstr.

JA/0369-3171
**NAGOYA KOGYO DAIGAKU GAKUHO.** [Nagoya Kogyo Daigaku gakuho]. **Added/Corp** Nagoya Kogyo Daigaku. **VFOAT** Bulletin of Nagoya Institute of Technology. (1949)-. Academic Scholarly Publication. Japanese (English). Nagoya Kogyo Daigaku, (Nagoya Inst. of Technology), Gokisocho, Showaku, Nagoyashi, Aichiken 466, Japan. **CODEN** NADGA8. Documents available from CASDDS.
**Ind/Abst** Chem. Abstr.

JA
**NAGOYA KOGYO GIJUTSU SHIKENJO NEMPO. Main/Corp** Nagoya Kogyo Gijutsu Shikenjo. Japanese. Kohyo Gijutsuin Nagoya, Kogyo Gijutsu Shienjo Hiratecho 1-chome Kita-ku, Nagoya 462 Japan. **Tel** 052-911-2111, FAX 052-916-2802. **LC** T178.N3; N34B. Index available. **Circ:** 650 (ctrl).

CC/0469-5097
**NANJING DAXUE XUEBAO. ZIRAN KEXUE.** (NAN-CHING TA HSUEH HSUEH PAO. TZU JAN KO HSUEH.). [Nanjing daxue xuebao. Ziran kexue]. **Added/Corp** Nan-ching ta Hsueh. **VFOAT** Nanjing Daxue Xuebao; Nanking Univesity Journal. Natural Sciences Edition; Journal of Nanjing University. Natural Sciences. (19??)-. Academic Scholarly Publication. Chinese. qt. Nanjing University Press / Nanjing Daxue Chubanshe, Nanjing, Jiangsu 210008, People's Republic of China. **Tel** 637651. **ED** Q. Qinyue. **LC** Q111; .N26. **DD** 505. **CODEN** NCHPAZ. Documents available from CASDDS, BLDSC, CASDDS.
**Ind/Abst** Art Archaeol. Tech. Abstr.; Chem. Abstr.; For. Abstr.; GeoRef; Math. Rev.; Protozoolog. Abstr.; Zentralbl. Math. Ihre Grenzgeb.

JA/0387-1150
**NARA KOGYO KOTO SENMON GAKKO KENKYU KIYO.** (KENKYU KIYO.). [Nara Kogyo Koto Senmon Gakko kenkyu kiyo]. **Added/Corp** Nara Kogyo Koto Senmon Gakko. **VFOAT** Research Reports of Nara Technical College. (1965)-. Japanese (English). an. **CODEN** NKKOB2. Documents available from CASDDS.
**Ind/Abst** Chem. Abstr.

JA/0547-2407
**NARA KYOIKU DAIGAKU KIYO. SHIZEN KAGAKU.** [Nara Kyoiku Daigaku kiyo, Shizen kagaku]. **Added/Corp** Nara Kyoiku Daigaku. **VFOAT** Bulletin of Nara University of Education. Natural Science. (1967)-. Japanese (English; summaries and/or abstracts in English). an. Nara Kyoiku Daigaku, (Nara University of Education), Takabatakecho, Narashi, Naraken 630 Japan. **CODEN** NKDSAC. ***Continues*** *Nara Gakugei Daigaku Kiyo. Shizen Kagaku.*
**Ind/Abst** Seed Abstr.; Weed Abstr.

US/0145-319X
**NASA TECH BRIEFS (WASHINGTON, D.C. 1976).** (NASA TECH BRIEFS.). [NASA tech briefs]. **Added/Corp** United States. National Aeronautics and Space Administration. **VFOAT** Tech Briefs. **VAT** National Aeronautics and Space Administration Tech Briefs. Vol. 1, No. 1 (Spring 1976)-. Periodical. English. mo. $75.00 US; $160.00 other. NASA Tech Briefs, 41 East 42nd Street, Suite 921, New York NY 10017. **Tel** (212)490-3999, FAX (212)986-7864. **ED** Bill Schnirring. **LC** TL521.3.T4; A28. **DD** 629.4/05. **[CCC].** Index available. **Bk Rev. Ad Acc. Circ:** 150,000 (ctrl). Documents available from Ask*IEEE. ***Continues*** *NASA Tech Brief, 0096-7491.*
**Desc:** Advanced technology utilizing research and developments to create new products, improve existing products, create or improve processing methods and/or procedures for more efficient production.
**Ind/Abst** Abstr. Bull. Inst. Pap. Sci. Tech.; Alum. Ind. Abstr.; Ceram. Abstr.; Energy Res. Abstr. (Oct. 1976-); Eng. Mater. Abstr.; INSPEC (Spring 1979-1981); Int. Aerosp. Abstr.; Met. Abstr.

US
**NATIONAL ACADEMY OF SCIENCES PUBLICATION. Added/Corp** National Academy of Sciences (U.S.). (19??)-. Monographic series. English. Price varies per volume. National Academy of Sciences, 2101 Constitution Avenue NW, Washington DC 20418. **Tel** (202)334-2525, FAX (202)334-2926.

II/0250-541X
**NATIONAL ACADEMY SCIENCE LETTERS.** [Natl. Acad. Sci. lett.]. **Main/Corp** National Academy of Sciences, India. **Added/Corp** National Academy of Sciences, India. Science Letters. Vol. 1 (Jan. 1978)-. Academic Scholarly Publication. English. Twelve times a year. $50.00. National Academy of Sciences India, 5 Lajpatrai Road, Allahabad 211002 India. **Tel** 55224. **LC** Q73; .N2517. **DD** 505. **CODEN** NASLDX. **Bk Rev. Pr Rev. Circ:** 200. Documents available from The Genuine Article, BIOSIS Document Express, Ask*IEEE, CASDDS.
**Desc:** This journal publishes short original research papers breaking fresh ground in all branches of science, medicine and engineering.
**Ind/Abst** Anim. Breed. Abstr.; Biocont. News Inf.; Biodeter. Abstr.; Biol. Abstr.; Chem. Abstr.; Cot. Trop. Fibr. Abstr. Bibliogr.; Crop Physiol. Abstr.; Curr. Contents, Agric. Biol. Environ. Sci.; Curr. Ref. Fish Res.; Ecol. Abstr. (?-?); Field Crop Abstr.; For. Abstr.; Hortic. Abstr.; INSPEC (April 1978-); Maize Abstr.; Math. Rev.; Nematol. Abstr.; Nutr. Abstr. Rev., Ser. B, Live Feeds and Feed.; Ornamental Hort. (1991-); Life Sci. Collect.; Plant Breed. Abstr.; Plant Grow. Reg. Abstr.; Potato Abstr.; Res. Alert [Select. Cov.]; Rev. Agric. Entomol.; Rev. Med. Vet. Entomol.; Rev. Med. Vet. Mycology; Rev. Plant Pathol.; Rice Abstr.; SCISEARCH; Seed Abstr.; Soils Fert.; Sorghum Mill. Abstr.; Soyabean Abstr.; Weed Abstr.; Wheat Barley Trit. Abstr.; Zentralbl. Math. Ihre Grenzgeb.

US
**NATIONAL AEROSPACE STANDARDS. Main/Corp** National Aerospace Standards Committee (U.S.). Vol. 5 (19??)-. Periodical. English. ir. $825.00. Global Engineering Documents Services, 15 Inverness Way East, Englewood CO 80112. **Tel** (800)624-3974. **ED** Kitty Stover. ***Continues*** *National Aircraft Standards.*
**Desc:** Contains over 2,500 primarily procurement documents for parts and components of high technology systems.

US
**NATIONAL INSTITUTES OF HEALTH INTERNATIONAL AWARDS FOR BIOMEDICAL RESEARCH AND RESEARCH TRAINING. Main/Corp** John E. Fogarty International Center for Advanced Study in the Health Sciences. International Cooperation and Geographic Studies Branch. English. an. John E Fogarty International Center for Advanced Study in the Health Sciences, 9000 Rockville Pike, Bethesda MD 20205. **LC** R852; .J64. **DD** 610/.7/9. **NLM** WA 22 AA1 N36. ***Continues*** *International Awards for Biomedical Research and Research Training.*

US
**NATIONAL PATTERNS OF R&D RESOURCES. VFOAT** National Patterns of R and D Resources. (1989)-. English. an. National Science Foundation, 1800 G Street Northwest, Washington DC 20550. **Tel** (202)357-9859, (202)357-9498. ***Continues*** *National Patterns of Science and Technology Resources.*
**Ind/Abst** F&S Index Plus Text, Int. [Select. Cov.]; Predicasts Forecasts.

SI
**NATIONAL SURVEY OF SCIENTIFIC MANPOWER. See** Economics-Labor.

JA/0028-0291
**NATIONAL TECHNICAL REPORT.** [Natl. tech. rep.]. **Added/Corp** Matsushita Denki Sangyo. (1955)-. Academic Scholarly Publication. Japanese. bm. Matsushita Tekuno Risachi, (Matsushita Technoresearch Co., Inc.), 3-15, Yagumonakamachi, Moriguchishi, Osakafu 570, Japan. **CODEN** NTROAV. Documents available from Article Express International, Ask*IEEE, CASDDS.
**Ind/Abst** Bioeng. Abstr.; Chem. Abstr.; Ei Page One; Energy Res. Abstr.; Eng. Index Annu.; INSPEC (Oct. 1968-).

US/0168-132X
**NATO ASI SERIES. SERIES E, APPLIED SCIENCE.** [NATO ASI ser., Ser. E Appl. sci.]. **Added/Corp** North Atlantic Treaty Organization. Scientific Affairs Division. **VFOAT** N.A.T.O. A.S.I. Series. Series E, Applied Science. **VAT** North Atlantic Treaty Organization Advanced Science Institutes Series. Series E, Applied Science. (19??)-. Monographic series. English. ir. Price varies per volume. **(Subscription address:** Kluwer Academic Publishers / US Subscriptions, PO Box 253, Accord Station, Hingham MA 02018.) **CODEN** NAESDI. **[CCC].** Documents available from BIOSIS Document Express, Ask*IEEE, CASDDS.
**Ind/Abst** Agric. Eng. Abstr. (1991-); Biol. Abstr. (1985-); Ceram. Abstr. (19??-); Chem. Abstr.; INSPEC; Irr. Drain. Abstr.; Maize Abstr.; Plant Grow. Reg. Abstr.; Soyabean Abstr.; Zentralbl. Math. Ihre Grenzgeb.

US/0197-5145
**NATO CONFERENCE SERIES : VI, MATERIALS SCIENCE.** [NATO conf. ser., VI, Mater. sci.]. Vol. 1 (1979)-. Academic Scholarly Publication. English. ir. Price varies per volume. North Atlantic Treaty Organization / NATO Scientific Affairs Division, B 1110 Brussels Belgium. **CODEN** NCSSDY. Documents available from Article Express International, Ask*IEEE, CASDDS.
**Ind/Abst** Bioeng. Abstr.; Chem. Abstr.; Ei Page One; Eng. Index Annu.; INSPEC.

BE
**NATO SCIENCE AND SOCIETY NEWSLETTER.** Newsletter. English. North Atlantic Treaty Organization / NATO Scientific Affairs Division, B 1110 Brussels Belgium.
**Ind/Abst** Energy Inf. Abstr.

PH/0028-0682
**NATURAL AND APPLIED SCIENCE BULLETIN.** [Nat. appl. sci. bull.]. **Added/Corp** University of the Philippines. College of Liberal Arts. University of the Philippines. College of Arts and Sciences. Vol. 1 (Oct. 1930)-. Academic Scholarly Publication. English. qt (Jan., Apr., July, Oct.). $15.00. Natural & Applied Science Bulletin, University of the Philippines, Institute of Biology, Diliman Quezon City 3004 Philippines. **Tel** 97 60 61 ext. 536. **CODEN** NASBAY. cum. index. Documents available from BIOSIS Document Express, CASDDS.
**Ind/Abst** AGRICOLA; Biol. Abstr. (-1970); Chem. Abstr.; GeoRef; Index Philip. Period.; Philip. Sci. Technol. Abstr.

US
**NATURAL SCIENCE CENTERS: DIRECTORY.** **Added/Corp** Natural Science for Youth Foundation. (1975/76)-. English. ir. $53.45. Natural Science for Youth Foundation, 130 Azalea Drive, Roswell GA 30075. **Tel** 800 992-6793. ***Continues** Natural Science Centers for Youth.*

JA/0029-8190
**NATURAL SCIENCE REPORT OF THE OCHANOMIZU UNIVERSITY.** (OCHANOMIZU JOSHI DAIGAKU SHIZEN KAGAKU HOKOKU.). [Nat. sci. rep. Ochanomizu Univ.]. **Added/Corp** Ochanomizu Joshi Daigaku. **VFOAT** Natural Science Report of the Ochanomizu University. (1951)-. Periodical. English (French, German and Japanese). ir. Eiichi Ishiguro, 36 Ootsuk Machip O, Koishikawa, Tokyo Japan. **LC** Q77; .02. **CODEN** NASOA5.
**Ind/Abst** GeoRef; Math. Rev.; Zentralbl. Math. Ihre Grenzgeb.

PK/0253-830X
**NATURAL SCIENCES.** [Nat. sci.]. V. 1- Apr. 1979-. Academic Scholarly Publication. English. $35.00. **NLM** W1 NA805T. **CODEN** NASIDO. Documents available from CASDDS.
**Ind/Abst** Chem. Abstr.

US/0277-609X
**NATURALISTS' DIRECTORY AND ALMANAC, INTERNATIONAL, THE.** [Nat. dir. alm. int.]. 43rd (1979/1980)-. Directory. English. an. $35.00 (46th edition). Sandhill Crane Press Inc., PO Box 147050, Gainesville FL 32614. **Tel** (904)371-9858, FAX (904)371-9969. ***Continues** Naturalists' Directory, International, 0193-1148.*

UK/0028-0836
**NATURE (LONDON).** (NATURE.). [Nature]. Vol. 1 (Nov. 4, 1869)-. Academic Scholarly Publication. English (Chinese). wk. £200.00 UK; £210.00 Europe; £280.00 other. MacMillan Journals Ltd., 4 Little Essex Street, London WC2R 3LF England. **Tel** 011 44 71 836 6633. **(Subscription address:** Nature Order Department, Macmillan Magazines, Ltd., Brunel Road, Basingstoke, Hants RG21 2XS England.**) ED** John Maddox. **LC** Q1; .N2. **DD** 505. **NLM** W1 NA81. **CODEN** NATUAS. **[CCC].** Index available. cum. index. **Bk Rev. Ad Acc. Pr Rev. Circ:** 40,000. available on microfilm and microfiche from University Microfilms International (UMI). Documents available from Article Express International, The Genuine Article, BIOSIS Document Express, Ask*IEEE, UMI Article Clearinghouse, Petroleum Abstracts Document Delivery Service, CASDDS, Documents on Demand.
**Desc:** Includes the fields of cell and molecular biology, biochemistry, microbiology, biology, biotechnology, genetics, medicine, pharmacology, astronomy, atmospheric science, chemistry, earth science, engineering and mathematics, oceanography, physics, and behavioral science for manufacturers, governments, research institutes, universities, colleges and other professional institutes, libraries, and technical centers.
**Ind/Abst** Abstr. Bull. Inst. Pap. Sci. Tech.; Abstr. BioCommer.; Acad. Abstr. Full Text Elite (Feb. 1989-); Acad. Abstr. (Feb. 1989-); Acad. Ind. [Computer File] (1987-); Acad. Search (Feb. 1989-); AESIS Q.; AgBiotech News Inf.; AGRICOLA [Select. Cov.]; Alum. Ind. Abstr.; Anal. Abstr.; Anim. Behav. Abstr.; Anthropol. Index; Aquat. Sci. Fish. Abstr. (Computer File); Art Archaeol. Tech. Abstr.; Arts Humanit. Citation Index [Select. Cov.]; BioBusiness; Biocont. News Inf.; Biodeter. Abstr. (19??-19??); Biol. Abstr.; Biol. Dig.; Biostatistica (19??-); Book Rev. Index; Br. Archaeol. Bibliogr.; Calcium Calcif. Tissue Abstr.; Ceram. Abstr. (19??-); Chem. Abstr.; Chem. Hazards Ind.; Chem. Titles; Chemorecept. Abstr.; Coal Abstr.; Comput. Rev.; Crop Physiol. Abstr.; CSA Neuro. Abstr.; Curr. Aware. Biol. Sci., CABS; Curr. Biotechnol.; Curr. Chem. React.; Curr. Index J. Educ.; Curr. Ref. Fish Res.; Curr. Technol. Index; Dairy Sci. Abstr.; Dev. Med. Child Neurol.; Ecol. Abstr.; Ecology Abstr.; Ei Page One; Elect. Comm. Abstr.; EMBASE; Eng. Mater. Abstr.; Eng. Index Annu. [Select. Cov.]; Entomol. Abstr.; Environ. Abstr.; Expand. Acad. Index (1987-); Field Crop Abstr.; Fish Rev.; Fluid Abstr., Civil Eng.; Fluid Abstr. Proc. Eng.; FLUIDEX; Food Sci. Technol. Abstr.; Foods Adlibra; For. Abstr.; Gen. Sci. Index; Gen. Sci. Source (Jan. 1989-); Genet. Abstr.; Geogr. Abstr. Phys. Geogr.; Geogr. Abstr. Human Geogr.; GeoRef; Health Saf. Sci. Abstr.; Health Index (1989-); Health Ref. Cent. (Jan. 1989-) [Full Cov.]; Helminthol. Abstr. (19??-19??); Hum. Genome Abstr.; Immunol. Abstr.; Index Chem.; Index Med.; Index Vet.; Indian Geosci. Abstr.; INFO-SOUTH Abstr.; INSPEC (1968-); Int. Aerosp. Abstr.; Int. Dev. Abstr.; Int. Pharm. Abstr.; J. Watch; Lab. Hazards Bull.; Leadscan; Mag. Artic. Summar. Elite (Jan. 1989-); Mag. Artic. Summar. Select (Jan. 1989-); Mag. Artic. Summar. CD-ROM (Feb. 1989-); Mag. Search; Maize Abstr.; Mass Spect. Bull.; Mater. Sci. Eng. Abstr.; Met. Abstr.; Meteorol. Geoastrophys. Abstr. (19??-199?); Microbiol. Abstr. Sect. B; Microbiol. Abstr. Sect. A; Microbiol. Abstr. Sect. C; Middle East Abstr. Index; NAPRALERT; Nat. Prod. Updates; Nematol. Abstr.; Newsp. Period. Abstr. (1987-); Nucl. Acids Abstr.; Nutr. Abstr. Rev., Ser. B, Live Feeds and Feed.; Nutr. Abstr. Rev., Ser. A, Hum. Exp.; Nutr. Res. Newsl.; Ocean. Abstr.; Oncog. Growth Factors Abstr.; Peace Res. Abstr. J. (1963-); PESTDOC; Pet. Abstr.; Pig News Inf.; Plant Breed. Abstr.; Plant Genet. Resour. Abstr.; Plant Grow. Reg. Abstr.; Pollut. Abstr. Indexes; Poult. Abstr.; Protozoolog. Abstr.; Psychol. Abstr. (1928-); PsycLit; Ref. Upd. Basic Ed.; Ref. Upd. Deluxe Ed.; Res. Alert [Full Cov.]; Res. High. Educ. Abstr.; Rev. Agric. Entomol.; Rev. Med. Vet. Entomol.; Rev. Med. Vet. Mycology; Rev. Plant Pathol.; Rice Abstr.; Risk Abstr.; Sci. Cit. Index; SCISEARCH; Soc. Sci. Cit. Index [Select. Cov.]; Soils Fert.; Solid State Supercond. Abstr.; Soyabean Abstr.; Stat. Theory Method Abstr. (1959-1963, 1968-1972, 1976, 1978); Vet. Bull.; Trop. Dis. Bull.; Virol. AIDS Abstr.; Vitis Vitic. Enol. Abstr.; Vocat. Search (Feb. 1989-); Weed Abstr.; Wheat Barley Trit. Abstr.; Wildl. Rev.; World Agric. Econ.; World Ceram. Abstr.

NO/0028-0887
**NATUREN.** (NATUREN; ILLUSTRERET MAANDSKRIFT FOR POPULAER NATURVIDENSKAB.). [Naturen]. Vol. 1 (1877)-. Periodical. Norwegian. bm. Kr265.00, $48.00. Scandinavian University Press, PO Box 2959 Toeyen, N 0608 Oslo 6 Norway. **Tel** 011 47 2 2575400, FAX 011 47 2 2575353, telex 71896 UROR N. **(Subscription address:** Scandinavian University Press, 200 Meacham Ave., Elmont NY 11003.**) ED** Eyvind Alver. **CODEN** NTUNA9. Index available. **Bk Rev. Ad Acc. Circ:** 2,300. Documents available from CASDDS.
**Desc:** Popular scientific journal of natural science.
**Ind/Abst** Chem. Abstr.; Energy Res. Abstr. (May 1974-); GeoRef.

NO
**NATUREN.** Vol. 1, (1877)-. Periodical. Norwegian. bm. Kr265.00, $48.00. Scandinavian University Press, PO Box 2959 Toeyen, N 0608 Oslo 6 Norway. **Tel** 011 47 2 2575400, FAX 011 47 2 2575353, telex 71896 UROR N. **(Subscription address:** Scandinavian University Press, 200 Meacham Ave., Elmont NY 11003.**) ED** Eyvind Alver. **LC** Q4; .N15. **Bk Rev. Ad Acc. Circ:** 2,200.
**Desc:** Popular journal on natural science.

DK/0028-0895
**NATURENS VERDEN.** [Nat. verden]. (1917)-. Periodical. Danish. Ten times a year. Rhodos, 36 Strandgade, 1401 Copenhagen K Denmark. **Tel** 011 45 31543020, FAX 011 45 954742, telex 31 502. **ED** Niels Blaedel. **LC** Q4; .N185. Index available. cum. index. **Bk Rev. Circ:** 8,000 (ctrl). Documents available from BIOSIS Document Express, CASDDS.
**Ind/Abst** Biol. Abstr.; Chem. Abstr.; Energy Res. Abstr. (Aug. 1976-); Zool. Rec.

FR/1240-1307
**NATURES-SCIENCES-SOCIETES.** (19??)-. Periodical. English. Four times a year. 570.00F (institutions), 400.00F (individuals), 330.00F (students) France; 700.00F (institutions), 490.00F (individuals), 400.00F (students) other. Dunod Gauthier Villars, 15 rue Gossin, 92543 Montrouge cedex France. **Tel** 011 33 1 46 56 52 66, FAX 011 33 1 46 57 40 69. **(Subscription address:** Centrale des Revues, 11 rue Gossin, 92543 Montrouge Cedex France.**)**

SW
**NATURVETENSKAPLIGA FORSKNINGSRADETS ARSBOK.** **Added/Corp** Naturvetenskapliga Forskningsradet (Sweden). (1977)-. Periodical. Swedish. an. Kr150.00 Sweden; Kr120.00 other. Swedish Science Press, PO Box 118, S 751 04 Uppsala Sweden. **Tel** 011 46 18 365566, FAX 011 48 18 365277. **ED** Britt Aniansson. **LC** Q180.S8; A32. **DD** 001.4/09485. ***Continues** Svensk Naturvetenskap.*
**Desc:** Summarizes the activities of the Swedish National Science Research Council for the past year. It reports on budget, foreign exchange programs, education and publications in the field. Included are biology, radiation and oceanographic research.

GW/0028-1042
**NATURWISSENSCHAFTEN, DIE.** [Naturwissenschaften]. **Added/Corp** Kaiser Wilhelm-Gesellschaft zur Forderung der Wissenschaften. Max-Planck-Gesellschaft zur Forderung der Wissenschaften. Gesellschaft Deutscher Naturforscher und Arzte. Vol. 1 (Jan. 1913)-. Academic Scholarly Publication. German (English). Twelve times a year. DM364.00. Springer-Verlag GmbH & Company KG, Heidelberger Platz 3, D 14197 Berlin Germany. **Tel** 011 49 30 8207223, FAX 011 49 30 8214091, telex 183 319 SPBLN D. **(Subscription address:** Springer Verlag New York Inc. / for North America, 44 Hartz Way, Secaucus NJ 07096.**) ED** H Autrum. **LC** Q3; .N7. **DD** 574/.05. **NLM** W1 NA924. **CODEN** NATWAY. **[CCC].** cum. index. **Bk Rev. Pr Rev.** available on microfilm and microfiche from University Microfilms International (UMI). Documents available from The Genuine Article, BIOSIS Document Express, Ask*IEEE, CASDDS, ADONIS. ***Supersedes** Naturwissenschaftliche Rundschau (Braunschweig, Germany), 0178-1049.*
**Desc:** Objective of this journal is to inform students and researchers in the natural sciences of developments in fields outside their own through survey articles, research reports and updates from academia.
**Ind/Abst** ADONIS; AgBiotech News Inf.; AGRICOLA; Anim. Behav. Abstr.; Aquat. Sci. Fish. Abstr. (Computer File); Art Archaeol. Tech. Abstr.; Biocont. News Inf.; Biodeter. Abstr.; Biol. Abstr.; Chem Inform; Chem. Abstr.; Chem. Titles; Coal Abstr.; Crop Physiol. Abstr.; CSA Neuro. Abstr.; Curr. Aware. Biol. Sci., CABS; Curr. Biotechnol.; Curr. Chem. React.; Curr. Contents Life Sci.; Curr. Contents Phys. Chem. Earth Sci.; Curr. Ref. Fish Res.; Ecology Abstr.; EMBASE; Energy Res. Abstr.; Entomol. Abstr.; For. Abstr.; GeoRef; Helminthol. Abstr. (19??-19??); Index Chem.; Index Med.; INSPEC (1968-); Int. Aerosp. Abstr.; Irr. Drain. Abstr.; Maize Abstr.; Microbiol. Abstr. Sect. C; NAPRALERT; Nematol. Abstr.; Nutr. Abstr. Rev., Ser. A, Hum. Exp.; Oncog. Growth Factors Abstr.; Life Sci. Collect.; PESTDOC; Plant Breed. Abstr.; Plant Genet. Resour. Abstr.; Plant Grow. Reg. Abstr.; Pollut. Abstr. Indexes; Postharvest News Inf.; Potato Abstr.; Ref. Upd. Deluxe Ed.; Res. Alert [Full Cov.]; Rev. Agric. Entomol.; Rev. Med. Vet. Entomol.; Rev. Plant Pathol.; Sci. Cit. Index; SCISEARCH; Soc. Sci. Cit. Index [Select. Cov.]; Soils Fert.; Stat. Theory Method Abstr. (1961-1963, 1967); Surf. Treat. Technol. Abstr.; Vitis Vitic. Enol. Abstr.; Weed Abstr.; Wildl. Rev.

GW/0028-1050
**NATURWISSENSCHAFTLICHE RUNDSCHAU.** [Naturwiss. Rundsch.]. Vol. 1 (July 1948)-. Academic Scholarly Publication. German. mo. DM153.00. Wissenschaftliche Verlagsgesellschaft mbH, Postfach 101061, D 70009 Stuttgart Germany. **Tel** 011 49 711 258200, FAX 011 49 711 2582290, telex 723636 DAZ D. **ED** Hans Rotta and Roswitha Schmid. **LC** Q3; .N823. **DD** 505. **NLM** W1 NA939. **CODEN** NARSAC. **[CCC].** Documents available from BIOSIS Document Express, CASDDS.
**Ind/Abst** AGRICOLA; Art Archaeol. Tech. Abstr.; Biol. Abstr.; Chem. Abstr.; Coal Abstr.; EMBASE; Energy Res. Abstr.; Geol. Abstr.; GeoRef; Int. Aerosp. Abstr.; Key Word Index Wildl. Res.; Meteorol. Geoastrophys. Abstr. (-199?); Nucl. Sci. Abstr.; Life Sci. Collect.; PESTDOC; Vitis Vitic. Enol. Abstr.

NE/0028-1093
**NATUUR EN TECHNIEK.** [Nat. tech.]. (1931)-. Academic Scholarly Publication. Dutch. mo. Fl130.00. Natuur en Techniek, Postbus 415, 6200 AK Maastricht Netherlands. **Tel** 011 31 43 254044, FAX (0)43-216124, telex 56642 NATU NL. **ED** J.M. Martens and G.M.N. Verschuuren. **LC** Q4; .N22. Index available. **Bk Rev. Ad Acc. Circ:** 45,000 (ctrl). Documents available from CASDDS.
**Desc:** Publishes articles in the field of biology, archeology, medicine, astronomy, chemistry, physics and technology, on the results of research written by scientists.
**Ind/Abst** Chem. Abstr.; EMBASE; Saf. Health Work.

RU
**NAUCHNYE TRUDY / GRUZINSKII POLITEKHNICHESKII INSTITUT IM. V.I. LENINA.** [Naucn. tr. - Gruz. politeh. inst. im. V.I. Lenina]. **Added/Corp** Gruzinskii Politekhnicheskii Institut im. V.I. Lenina. (1972)-. Academic Scholarly Publication. Russian. Price varies per volume. **CODEN** NTGLD4. Documents available from CASDDS.
**Ind/Abst** Chem. Abstr.

YU
**NAUCNI I STRUCNI SKUPOVI U JUGOSLAVIJI I U INOSTRANSTVU.** **VFOAT** Scientific and Professional Meetings in Yugoslavia and Foreign Countries. Began in 1975. Serbo-Croatian (Roman). 800.00. Jugoslovenski Centar za Tehnicku I Naucnu Dokumentaciju, Slobodana Penezica Krcuna, 29-31 Postfach 724, Belgrad Yugoslavia. **LC** Q101; .N32.

UN
**NAUKA-FANTASTYKA.** **Added/Corp** Leninska Kommunistychna Spilka Molodi Ukrainy. TSentralnyi Komitet. **VFOAT** Nauka Fantastyka; NF. (1991)-. Periodical. Ukrainian. mo. **LC** Q4; .Z7. ***Continues** Znannia ta Pratsia.*

RU/0548-0345
**NAUKA I CHELOVECHESTVO.** (1962)-. Academic Scholarly Publication. Russian. Izdatelstvo Znanie, Novaya Pl., 3-4,, 101835 Moscow Russia. **CODEN** NCHEA2. Documents available from CASDDS.
**Ind/Abst** Chem. Abstr.

LV/0236-2767
**NAUKA I MY.** **Added/Corp** Latvijas Komunistiska Partija. Centrala Komiteja. Vol. 1 (1990)-. Periodical. Russian. mo. **(Subscription address:** Victor Kamkin, 4956 Boiling Brook Parkway, Rockville MD 20852.**) LC** T4; .N2715. **CODEN** NAMYE9. ***Continues** Nauka i Tekhnika, 0201-7857.*

RU/0028-1263
**NAUKA I ZIZN.** (NAUKA I ZHIZN.). [Nauka zizn]. **Added/Corp** Vsesoiuznoe Obshchestvo "Znanie.". Vol. 1 (Oct. 1934)-. Periodical. Russian. mo. $149.95. Izdatelstvo Pressa, Myasnitskaia 24, 101877 Moscow Russia. **Tel** 011 95 923 2122, FAX 011 95 200 2259. **(Subscription address:** East View Publications Inc., 3020 Harbor Lane North, Suite 110, Minneapolis MN 55447.) **LC** Q4; .N43. **DD** 505. **NLM** W1 NA985. available on microfilm from University Microfilms International (UMI).
**Ind/Abst** Int. Aerosp. Abstr.

PL/0028-1271
**NAUKA POLSKA.** [Nauka pol.]. **Added/Corp** Polska Akademia Nauk. Vol. 1, No. 1 (1953)-. Periodical. Polish (summaries and/or abstracts in English and Russian; table of contents in English and Russian). bm. $123.00. **(Subscription address:** ARS Polona, PO Box 1001, 00068 Warsaw Poland.) **LC** AS261; .N3. **NLM** W1 NA9857. ***Absorbed*** *Sprawozdania z Czynnosci i Prac.*
**Ind/Abst** AGRICOLA; Am. Hist. Life (1954-1974, 1976-1977, 1979-); Coal Abstr.

RU
**NAUKA SEGODNIA.** (1973)-. Russian. an. 0.59rub (single issue). Izdatelstvo Znanie, Novaya Pl., 3-4,, 101835 Moscow Russia. **LC** Q9; .N33.

YU/0350-1388
**NAUKA U PRAKSI BEOGRAD.** (1971)-. Periodical. Multiple languages. qt. **UDC** 63.
**Ind/Abst** Maize Abstr.; Nutr. Abstr. Rev., Ser. B, Live Feeds and Feed.; Soils Fert.; Soyabean Abstr.

ZA
**NCSR/TR / NATIONAL COUNCIL FOR SCIENTIFIC RESEARCH, ZAMBIA.** No. 1-. Monographic series. English. Price varies per volume. National Council for Scientific Research, PO Box CH 158 Chelston, Lusaka Zambia. **LC** Q91.Z33; Z316. **DD** 508/.1.

AA/1010-4003
**NDERTUESI.** [Ndertuesi]. **Added/Corp** Albania. Ministria e Ndertimit. (19??)-. Academic Scholarly Publication. Albanian. qt. $7.27. Book Distribution Enterprise, Rruga Kavajes, Tirana, Albania. **Tel** 011 355 42 27246. **LC** T4; .N28.
**Ind/Abst** EMBASE.

●US/1063-3588
**NDT UPDATE. See** Military and Defense.

JA/0285-4139
**NEC GIHO.** [NEC giho]. **Added/Corp** Nihon Denki Kabushiki Kaisha. **VFOAT** NEC Technical Journal. (1981)-. Periodical. Japanese (summaries and/or abstracts in English). mo. Free on request. NEC Cultural Center Ltd., c/o Nippon Denki Bekkan, 31-ban 25-go Shiba 2-chome, Minato-ku 105 Tokyo-to Japan. **LC** TK7800; .N42. Documents available from Ask*IEEE.
**Ind/Abst** INSPEC (1984-); Int. Aerosp. Abstr.; Math. Rev.

NE/0028-209X
**NEDERLANDS MELK- EN ZUIVELTIJSCHRIFT.** (NETHERLANDS MILK AND DAIRY JOURNAL.). [Ned. Melk-Zzuiveltijschr.]. **Added/Corp** Genootschap ter Bevordering Van Melkkunde. Centrum Vvoor Landbouwpublikaties en Landbouwdocumentatie (Netherlands). **VFOAT** Nederlands Melk- en Zuiveltijschrift. (1969)-. Academic Scholarly Publication. English. Four times a year (Mar., May., Oct., Dec.). F80.00 Netherlands; F90.00 other. Netherlands Milk & Dairy, PO Box 8129, 6700 EV Wageningen Netherlands. **Tel** 011 31 8370 82289, FAX 011 31 8370 83669. **ED** A. Noomen. **CODEN** NMDJAX. Index available (4th issue). **Pr Rev. Circ:** 700. Documents available from The Genuine Article, BIOSIS Document Express, CASDDS. ***Continues*** *Nederlands Melk- en Zuiveltijschrift, 0028-209X.*
**Desc:** Contains original papers and abstracts on key issues and developments in all areas of dairy management, production and trade.
**Ind/Abst** Biodeter. Abstr.; Biol. Abstr.; Chem. Abstr.; Curr. Aware. Biol. Sci., CABS; Curr. Contents, Agric. Biol. Environ. Sci.; Dairy Sci. Abstr.; EMBASE; Food Sci. Technol. Abstr.; Foods Adlibra; Index Vet.; Nutr. Abstr. Rev., Ser. B, Live Feeds and Feed.; Nutr. Abstr. Rev., Ser. A, Hum. Exp.; Life Sci. Collect.; Res. Alert [Full Cov.]; Sci. Cit. Index; SCISEARCH; Soyabean Abstr.; Vet. Bull.

NE/0926-4264
**NEDERLANDS TIJDSCHRIFT VOOR NATUURKUNDE (AMSTERDAM. 1991).** (NEDERLANDS TIJDSCHRIFT VOOR NATUURKUNDE.). [Ned. tijdschr. natuurkd.]. **Added/Corp** Nederlandse Natuurkundige Vereniging. (Jan 15 1991)-. Academic Scholarly Publication. Dutch. Twenty-two times a year. Fl130.00. Nederlandse Natuurkundige Vereniging, Postbus 302, 1170 AH Badhoeuedorp Netherland. **Tel** 011 31 20 6580228, FAX 011 31 20 6592477. **CODEN** NTINEL. Index available. **Bk Rev. Ad Acc, Adv Mgr:** M Bruning, **Tel** FAX - 0175-41847. ctrl circ. Documents available from Ask*IEEE, CASDDS. ***Formed by the union of*** *Nederlands Tijdschrift voor Natuurkunde. A, 0378-6374* ***and*** *Nederlands Tijdschrift voor Natuurkunde. B, 0166-5987.*
**Ind/Abst** Chem. Abstr.; INSPEC (1968-).

CC/1000-1638
**NEIMENGGU DAXUE XUEBAO (ZIRAN KEXUE BAN).** (NEI MENG-KUO TA HSUEH HSUEH PAO. TZU JAN KO HSUEH.). [Neimenggu daxue xuebao]. **Added/Corp** Nei Meng-gu ta Hsueh. **VFOAT** Neimenggu Daxue Xuebao. Ziran Kexue; Acta Scientarum Naturalium Universitatis Intramongolicae. (19??)-. Academic Scholarly Publication. Chinese. qt. $20.00 (per issue). Nei Menggu Daxue, Inner Mongolian University, No. 1 West University Road, Huhhot, Nei Menggu 010021, People's Republic of China. **Tel** 0471 43156, FAX 04741 611761. **(Subscription address:** China International Book Trading Corporation, PO Box 399, Library Service Department, Beijing 100044 People's Republic of China.) **ED** F. Tianqi. **CODEN** NDZKEJ. Documents available from CASDDS.
**Ind/Abst** Math. Rev.; Potato Abstr.; Rev. Plant Pathol.

RU/0301-5386
**NEKOTORYE FILOSOFSKIE VOPROSY SOVREMENNOGO ESTESTVOZNANIJA. See** Philosophy.

JA
**NEMPO. Main/Corp** Kagoshima-Ken Kogyo Shikenjo. (19??)-. Japanese. an. Free. Kagoshima-ken Kogyo Shikenjo, 7-6 Take 1-chome, Kagoshima-shi 890 Japan. **Tel** 0992-54-9158. **ED** Kagoshima-Ken Kogyo Shikenjo. **LC** T178.K24; K33a. **CODEN** KKPODU. **Circ:** 350 (ctrl). Documents available from CASDDS.
**Ind/Abst** Chem. Abstr. (19??-1985).

JA
**NEMPO.** [Nenpo - Fukui-ken Kogyo Shikenjo]. **Main/Corp** Fukui-ken Kogyo Shikenjo. Academic Scholarly Publication. Japanese. an. Fukui-ken Kogyo Shikenjo, 920 Wakaecho, Fukui-shi 910 Japan. **LC** T178.F84; F84A. **CODEN** FKSNDL. Documents available from CASDDS.
**Ind/Abst** Chem. Abstr. (1969-1980).

US/1056-5744
**NEO-TECH REPORT, THE.** [Neo-tech rep.]. (1990)-. Periodical. English. mo. I & O Publishing Co., 850 South Boulder Highway, Henderson NV 89015. **DD** 051.

US/0028-3045
**NETWORKS (NEW YORK).** (NETWORKS.). [Networks]. Vol. 1 (1971)-. Periodical. English. Eight times a year. $640.00 US; $720.00 Canada and Mexico; $750.00 other. John Wiley & Sons, Inc., 605 Third Avenue, New York NY 10158-0012. **Tel** (212)850-6000, (212)850-6645, FAX (212)850-6088, telex 12-7063. **(Subscription address:** John Wiley & Sons / England, Baffins Lane, Chichester, West Sussex PO19 1UD England.) **ED** Frank T. Boesch, I. T. Frisch, and D. J. Kleitman. **DD** 003/.05. **CODEN** NTWKAA. **[CCC]. Pr Rev.** available on microfilm and microfiche from University Microfilms International (UMI). Documents available from Article Express International, The Genuine Article, Ask*IEEE.
**Desc:** Focuses on both applications and theory for innovations in design and use of computer networks, telecommunications, transportation systems, power grids, distribution systems and other networks.
**Ind/Abst** Commun. Abstr. (?-?); Compumath Citation Index [Full Cov.]; Comput. Rev.; Curr. Contents Eng. Tech. Appl. Sci.; Ei Page One; Eng. Index Annu.; Inf. Sci. Abstr.; INSPEC (1971-); Int. Abstr. Oper. Res. [Select. Cov.]; Math. Rev.; Res. Alert [Full Cov.]; Sci. Cit. Index; SCISEARCH; Soc. Sci. Cit. Index [Select. Cov.]; Zentralbl. Math. Ihre Grenzgeb.

SZ/0028-3398
**NEUE TECHNIK.** [Neue Tech.]. **Added/Corp** Schweizerische Gesellschaft fuer Automatik. Schweizerische Gesellschaft von Fachleuten der Kerntechnik. **VFOAT** Nouvelles Techniques; New Techniques. (1959)-. Periodical. German (French and English). mo (11 issues). 75.00F Switzerland; 95.00F other Europe; 109.00F other. Diagonal Verlags AG, Industriestrasse 21, CH 5507 Mellingen Switzerland. **Tel** 011 41 56 910291. **ED** O. Boldinger. **LC** TJ212; .N4. **CODEN** NETEA8. **Bk Rev. Ad Acc.** Documents available from Ask*IEEE.
**Desc:** Industrial electronics.
**Ind/Abst** Energy Res. Abstr.; INSPEC (1968-); Saf. Health Work.

SZ
**NEUJAHRSBLATT (ZURICH).** (NEUJAHRSBLATT, HRSG. VON DER NATURFORSCHENDEN GESELLSCHAFT IN ZURICH.). **Main/Corp** Naturforschende Gesellschaft in Zurich. **Added/Corp** Naturforschende Gesellschaft in Zurich. Zuricherische Jugend. Naturforschende Gesellschaft in Zurich. An die Zurcherische Jugend von der Naturforschenden Gesellschaft. **VFOAT** Zurcherische Jugend. Vol. 1 (1799)-. Monographic series. German. Price varies per volume. **LC** Q67; .Z96. cum. index.

US/0882-6382
**NEW & EMERGING TECHNOLOGY.** ***Ceased.*** [New emerg. technol.]. **VFOAT** New and Emerging Technology. (1985)-?. Periodical. English. mo. Midwest Technology Information Center, PO Box 1188, Bay City MI 48706. **Tel** (517)895-8184. **ED** D Lawrence Rogers. **DD** 600. Index available. **Bk Rev. Circ:** 1,340. ***Continues*** *Midwest Technology.*
**Desc:** Reports on new technological products and new technology-based companies; especially automation, biotechnology, medical technology and socio-technical developments affecting industry, the stock market and the global economy.

CN
**NEW BIOTECH BUSINESS.** ***Title Change.*** mo. Winter House Scientific Publications Inc, PO Box 7131 Station J, Ottowa Ontario K2A 4C5 Canada. ***Continued by*** *Canadian Biotech News.*
**Ind/Abst** Abstr. BioCommer. (-19??).

US/1040-0591
**NEW ENGLAND SALES GUIDE TO HIGH-TECH COMPANIES. Added/Corp** Corporate Technology Information Services. **VFOAT** New England Region; Sales Guide to High Tech Companies. New England Region. (1988)-. Directory. English. an. $185.00. Corporate Technology Information Services Inc, 12 Alfred Street, Suite 200, Woburn MA 01801-9998. **Tel** (617)932-3939, (800)333-8036, FAX (617)932-6335, telex 497-2961 CRPTECH. **ED** Steven W. Parker. **LC** HC107.A11; N349. **DD** 338.7/62/0002574. Index available. cum. index. **Bk Rev. Ad Acc. Circ:** 3,000. available on diskette.
**Desc:** Regional directory with over 3,000 technology manufacturers and developers.

US/0740-3569
**NEW FROM EUROPE.** ***Ceased.*** [New Eur.]. (Feb. 1980)-(May 1993). Periodical. English. mo. Prestwick Publications Inc, 390 North Federal Highway, Suite 401A, Deerfield Beach FL 33441-2209. **Tel** (407)427-2924. **ED** Roy H. Roecker. **Bk Rev.**
**Desc:** Covers new products and new technologies.

UK/0955-4777
**NEW MATERIALS WORLD.** ***Title Change.*** [New mater. world]. (1988)-(19??). Periodical. English. an. World Business Publs Ltd, 960 High Road, Britannia 4th Floor, London N12 9RY England. **Tel** 011 44 81 446 5141. **DD** 620.11. ***Continued by*** *Performance Materials Technology.*
**Desc:** Covers the full advanced materials spectrum, metals, ceramics, polymers, composites, fibres, glass and advances in materials processing.

US/0270-3017
**NEW MEXICO JOURNAL OF SCIENCE.** [N.M. j. sci.]. **Added/Corp** New Mexico Academy of Science. **VFOAT** Journal of science. Began with: Vol. 18, No. 2 (Dec. 1978). Academic Scholarly Publication. English. ir (publishes 1 or 2 issues per volume). $30.00. New Mexico Academy of Science, 2517 Cutler NE, Albuquerque NM 87106. **Tel** (505) 265-1620. **ED** John Shunny. **LC** Q11; .N43. **DD** 505. **CODEN** NMJSDP. **Bk Rev. Circ:** 400 (ctrl). Documents available from BIOSIS Document Express, CASDDS. ***Continues*** *Bulletin - New Mexico Academy of Science, 0028-6133.*
**Desc:** Publishes papers in all branches of science, emphasizing New Mexico and the southwestern United States.
**Ind/Abst** Biol. Abstr. (-1984); Chem. Abstr. (1978-1981); GeoRef; Rev. Med. Vet. Entomol.

US/0028-6591
**NEW RESEARCH CENTERS. Added/Corp** Gale Research Company. 2nd Ed. Issue No. 1 (May 1965)-. English. $300.00. Gale Research Inc., 835 Penobscot Building, Detroit MI 48226. **Tel** (800)877-GALE, (313)961-2242, FAX (313)961-6083, telex TWX 810-221-7086. **ED** M. Watkins. **LC** AS25; .D52. **DD** 006. **NLM** Q 180.U5 D598N. cum. index.
**Desc:** Periodical supplements to Research Centers Directory.

SW/1100-956X
**NEW SCANDINAVIAN TECHNOLOGY.** [New Scand. technol.]. (1989)-. Periodical. Swedish. qt. Bjare Information AB, Box 5173, S 10244 Stockholm Sweden. **UDC** 62.
**Ind/Abst** Abstr. Bull. Inst. Pap. Sci. Tech.

●US/1065-917X
**NEW SCIENCE CENTERS SUPPORT PROGRAM INFORMATION SERVICE BULLETIN. Added/Corp** Association of Science-Technology Centers. New Science Centers Support Program. **VFOAT** Information Service Bulletin. (1992)-. Bulletin. English. mo. Association of Science-Technology Centers, 1025 Vermont Avenue NW, Suite 500, Washington DC 20005-3516.

UK/0262-4079
**NEW SCIENTIST (1971).** (NEW SCIENTIST.). [New scientist]. Vol. 52, No. 772, (Dec. 2, 1971)-. Academic Scholarly Publication. English. wk. $140.00. IPC Magazines Ltd., Perrymount Road, Haywards Heath, West Sussex RH16 3DH England. **Tel** 011 44 444 440421. **LC** Q1; .N52. **DD** 505. **NLM** W1 NE494. **CODEN** NWSCAL. **[CCC]. Pr Rev.** available on microfilm and microfiche from University Microfilms International (UMI).

Documents available from Ask*IEEE, UMI Article Clearinghouse, CASDDS, Documents on Demand. ***Continues*** *New Scientist and Science Journal, 0369-5808.*
**Ind/Abst** Abstr. Bull. Inst. Paper Chem.; Abstr. Bull. Inst. Pap. Sci. Tech.; Abstr. BioCommer.; Abstr. Hum. Comput. Interact.; Acad. Abstr. Full Text Elite (July 1990-); Acad. Abstr. (July 1990-); Acad. Ind. [Computer File] (1987-); Acad. Search (July 1990-); AESIS Q.; AgBiotech News Inf.; AGRICOLA; Alum. Ind. Abstr.; Appl. Sci. Technol. Index; Art Archaeol. Tech. Abstr.; Arts Humanit. Citation Index [Select. Cov.]; BioBusiness (1990-); Biocont. News Inf. (19??-19??); Biodeter. Abstr. (19??-19??); Biol. Dig.; Book Rev. Digest (July 1990-); Book Rev. Index; Br. Archaeol. Bibliogr.; Br. Humanit. Index; Chem. Abstr.; CIS Abstr.; Coal Abstr.; Comput. Rev.; Cot. Trop. Fibr. Abstr. Bibliogr.; Curr. Ref. Fish Res.; Curr. Technol. Index; Dairy Sci. Abstr.; Electron. Pub. Abstr.; EMBASE; Energy Inf. Abstr.; Eng. Mater. Abstr.; Environ. Abstr.; Expand. Acad. Index (1987-); F&S Index Plus Text, Int. [Select. Cov.]; Fish Rev.; Fluid Abstr., Civil Eng.; Fluid Abstr. Proc. Eng.; FLUIDEX (1973-); Foods Adlibra; For. Abstr.; Gen. Sci. Index; Gen. Sci. Source (Jul. 1990-); Geol. Abstr.; GeoRef; Health Index (1989-); Health Source (Jul. 1990-); Helminthol. Abstr. (19??-19??); HILITES; HTFS Dig.; Index Vet.; INFO-SOUTH Abstr.; Infomat Int. Bus.; INSPEC (Dec. 1971-); Int. Aerosp. Abstr. (19??-19??); Int. Labour Doc.; Int. Packag. Abstr.; Mag. Artic. Summar. Elite (July 1990-); Mag. Artic. Summar. Select (July 1990-); Mag. Artic. Summar. CD-ROM (July 1990-); Mag. Search; Mass Spect. Bull. (?-?); Med. Abstr. Newsl.; Met. Abstr.; Middle East Abstr. Index; Nematol. Abstr.; Newsp. Period. Abstr. (1990-); Nonwovens Abstr.; Nutr. Res. Newsl.; Pap. Board Abstr.; Peace Res. Abstr. J. (1964-1967, 1976-1985, 1988-); Pollut. Abstr. Indexes; Predicasts; Print. Abstr.; Proc. Chem. Eng.; PROMT; Protozoolog. Abstr.; Rev. Med. Vet. Mycology; Risk Abstr.; Saf. Health Work; Sci. Fict. Fantasy Book Rev. Index; Soc. Sci. Cit. Index [Select. Cov.]; SPORT Discus; SportSearch; Theoret. Chem. Eng.; Wildl. Rev.; World Publ. Monit.

GW/0935-2694
**NEW TECH NEWS MUNICH.** (1988)-. Periodical. Multiple languages. qt. **UDC** 621.38.
**Ind/Abst** Int. Aerosp. Abstr.

JA
**NEW TECHNOLOGY JAPAN. Added/Corp** Nihon Boeki Shinkokai. Kikai Gijutsubu. Vol. 14, No. 2 (May 1986)-. Periodical. English. mo. $268.00. **(Subscription address:** Maruzen Company Ltd., PO Box 5050, Import & Export Department, Tokyo 100 31 Japan.**) LC** T1; .J36. **DD** 609/.51. ***Continues*** *Japan Industrial & Technological Bulletin, 0385-6542.*
**Desc:** Authoritative magazine covering Japanese technological developments and the companies behind them.
**Ind/Abst** F&S Index Plus Text, Int. [Select. Cov.]; PROMT.

US/0894-0789
**NEW TECHNOLOGY WEEK.** [New technol. week]. Vol. 1, No. 1 (June 4, 1987)-. Periodical. English. wk (50 issues). $799.00. King Publishing Group, 627 National Press Building, Washington DC 20045. **Tel** (202)638-4260, FAX (202)662-9744. **ED** Richard A. McCormack. **LC** T1; .N457. **DD** 600. **[CCC].** Index available. **Bk Rev.** available on an online database (files 16,636/Full-Text) from DIALOG; NEWSNET; and Predicasts, Inc.
**Desc:** Covers superconductivity, HDTV, semiconductors, national labs, policy, etc.
**Ind/Abst** Comput. Lit. Index; PROMT [Full Txt.]; PTS Newsl. Database [Full Txt.].

FR
**NEW TRENDS IN INTEGRATED SCIENCE TEACHING. Added/Corp** Unesco. **VFOAT** Tendances Nouvelles de l'Integration des Enseignements Scientifiques. Vol. 1 (1969/70)-. Periodical. English (French). ir. Price varies per volume. UNESCO / France, 31 rue Francois Bonvin, 75732 Paris Cedex 15 France. **Tel** 011 33 1 45684564, 011 33 1 45684565, FAX 011 33 1 42733007, telex 204461 Paris. **LC** Q181.A1; N48. **DD** 507/.1.

US/1040-0583
**NEW YORK METRO SALES GUIDE TO HIGH-TECH COMPANIES.** [N. Y. Metro sales guide to high tech co.]. **VFOAT** New York Metro Region; Sales Guide to High Tech Companies. New York Metro Region. (1988)-. English. qt. $145.00. Corporate Technology Information Services Inc, 12 Alfred Street, Suite 200, Woburn MA 01801-9998. **Tel** (617)932-3939, (800)333-8036, FAX (617)932-6335, telex 497-2961 CRPTECH. **ED** Steven W Parker. **LC** HC108.N69; N48. **DD** 338.7/62/000257471. Index available. cum. index. **Bk Rev. Ad Acc. Circ:** 3,000. available on diskette.
**Desc:** Regional directory of over 3,000 technology manufacturers and developers.

●US/1065-8041
**NEW YORK TECHNOLOGY RESOURCE GUIDE. Added/Corp** Corporate Technology Information Services. (1992)-. English. $90.00. Corporate Technology Information Services Inc, 12 Alfred Street, Suite 200, Woburn MA 01801-9998. **Tel** (617)932-3939, (800)333-8036, FAX (617)932-6335, telex 497-2961 CRPTECH.

NZ/0110-5124
**NEW ZEALAND ANTARCTIC RECORD.**
**See** Geography.

NZ/0028-8667
**NEW ZEALAND SCIENCE REVIEW.**
**Added/Corp** New Zealand Association of Scientists. (Dec. 1942)-. Periodical. English. ir (2-3 times per year). 45.00NZ$. New Zealand Association of Scientists, PO Box 1874, Wellington New Zealand. **ED** F.B. Shorland. **[CCC].** Index available in last issue of volume--attached. cum. index. **Bk Rev. Ad Acc. Circ:** 400 (ctrl).
**Desc:** Concerns science policy and ethics.

UK
**NEWCOMEN BULLETIN / NEWCOMEN SOCIETY FOR THE STUDY OF THE HISTORY OF ENGINEERING AND TECHNOLOGY, THE. Main/Corp** Newcomen Society for the Study of the History of Engineering and Technology (London, England). No. 30 (1953)-. Academic Scholarly Publication. English. tq (3 issues). £33.00 (Comes with Newcomen Society membership.). Newcomen Society Science Museum, South Kensington, London SW7 2DD England. **Tel** 011 44 71 5891793. **Bk Rev.** ***Continues*** *NQB, The Newcomen Quarterly Bulletin.*

IT
**NEWS 3X-400 (ITALIAN EDITION).** (NEWS 3X-400.). (19??)-. Periodical. Italian. mo (July/Aug. combined). L150000 Italy; L210000 other. Duke Italia, Viale Lunigiana 42, 20125 Milan Italy. **Tel** 011 39 2 67711222. **Bk Rev. Ad Acc. Circ:** 16000.

US/0146-4647
**NEWS DIGEST - ITA.** ***Ceased.*** (ITA NEWS DIGEST.). **Main/Corp** International Tape Association. **VAT** International Tape Association News Digest. Ceased Vol. 14, No. 26 (July 1986). Periodical. English. bm. International Tape Association 10018. **Tel** (212)956-7110. **ED** Charles Van Horn. **LC** TK7881.6; .I57A. **DD** 384. **Circ:** 2,500.
**Desc:** Articles by industry experts: how technology affects the quality of sound, video, and data recording, and the best strategies to market and distribute the results.

US
**NEWS / NATIONAL SCIENCE FOUNDATION. Added/Corp** National Science Foundation (U.S.). (19??)-. Periodical. English. Ten times a year. Free on request. National Science Foundation, 1800 G Street Northwest, Washington DC 20550. **Tel** (202)357-9859, (202)357-9498.

US/0027-8432
**NEWS REPORT (NATIONAL RESEARCH COUNCIL (US)).** (NEWS REPORT / NATIONAL ACADEMY OF SCIENCES, NATIONAL RESEARCH COUNCIL OF THE UNITED STATES OF AMERICA.). [News rep. - Natl. Res. Counc. (U. S.)]. **Added/Corp** National Research Council (U.S.) National Academy of Sciences (U.S.) National Academy of Engineering. Institute of Medicine (U.S.). **VFOAT** NewsReport. Vol. 1, No. 1 (Jan.-Feb. 1951)-. Periodical. English. Four times a year. $10.00 US; $12.00 other. National Academy Press, 2101 Constitution Avenue NW, Lockbox 285, Washington DC 20055. **Tel** (800)624-6242, (202)334-3313, FAX (202)334-2451. **(Subscription address:** NewsReport, PO Box 665, Holmes PA 19043.**) LC** Q11; .N2928. **DD** 505. **NLM** W2 A N14N. Documents available from Documents on Demand.
**Ind/Abst** AGRICOLA [Select. Cov.]; Biocont. News Inf. (1991-); Energy Inf. Abstr.; Environ. Abstr.; GeoRef; Helminthol. Abstr. (1991-); Ind. Hyg. Dig. (19??-).

US/0899-1235
**NEWSFACES IN HIGH TECHNOLOGY.** [Newsfaces high technol.]. **VFOAT** News Faces in High Technology. 1989-. Periodical. English. an. $495.00. Newsfaces, 15951 Los Gatos Boulevard/#15, Los Gatos CA 95032. **LC** Z475; .N48. **DD** 605.

CN/0834-1788
**NEWSLETTER / APPLIED SCIENCE TECHNOLOGISTS AND TECHNICIANS OF BRITISH COLUMBIA.** [Newsl. - Appl. Sci. Technol. Tech. B.C.]. **Added/Corp** Applied Science Technologists and Technicians of British Columbia. No. 24 (Sept. 1985)-. Periodical. English. bm. $38.00. Applied Science Technologists and Technicians of British Columbia - ASTTBC, 10767-148th Street, Surrey British Columbia V3R OS4 Canada. **Tel** (604)585-2788, FAX (604)585-2790. **ED** Ted Noowell. **DD** 606/.0711. **Ad Acc, Adv Mgr:** Ted Noowell. **Circ:** 7,500 (ctrl). ***Continues*** *SETBC Info., 0824-7129.*

AT
**NEWSLETTER / AUSTRALIA-JAPAN RESEARCH CENTRE. Main/Corp** Australia-Japan Research Centre. **Added/Corp** Australian National University. Australian National University. Research School of Pacific Studies. (Feb. 1987)-. Newsletter. English.

UK/0951-4635
**NEWSLETTER - BRITISH LIBRARY. SCIENCE REFERENCE AND INFORMATION SERVICE.** (NEWSLETTER.). [Newsl. - Br. Libr. Sci. Ref. Inf. Serv.]. **VFOAT** Newsletter - British Library. Science Technology & Industry. Science Reference and Information Service. (1987)-. Newsletter. English. qt. Free on request. British Library Science Reference Information Service, 25 Southampton Building, London WC21 1AW England. **Tel** 011 44 1 6361544. **DD** 026.5. ***Continues*** *British Library Science Technology & Industry Science Reference and Information Service SRIS News.*
**Ind/Abst** HILITES.

US/0270-2401
**NEWSLETTER FOR INVENTORS, A.**
**Added/Corp** United Inventors and Scientists. (19??)-. Newsletter. English. $21.00. United Inventors and Scientists, 9017 Reseda Boulevard, Northridge CA 91324.

DK/0106-1372
**NEWSLETTER FROM THE COMMISSION FOR SCIENTIFIC RESEARCH IN GREENLAND.** No. 1- Apr. 1979-. Newsletter. English. ir. Free. Commission for Scientific Research, Oster Voldgade 10, DK-1350 Copenhagen K Denmark. **Tel** 451113666, FAX 01 936815, telex 27125. **ED** Gregers E Andersen. Index available. **Bk Rev. Ad Acc. Circ:** 2,000 (ctrl).
**Desc:** Forthcoming scientific research activities in Greenland, abstracts of Meddelelser Om Gronland Publications, general information about arctic scientific research.

US/0739-4934
**NEWSLETTER / HISTORY OF SCIENCE SOCIETY.** [Hist. Sci. Soc. newsl.]. **Added/Corp** History of Science Society. (1972)-. Newsletter. English. qt (Jan., Apr., July, Oct.). $25.00. Isis Business Office, PO Box 529, Canton MA 02021. **Tel** (617)828-8450.

US/0300-7588
**NEWSLETTER - INTER-SOCIETY COLOR COUNCIL.** ***Title Change.*** (NEWSLETTER.). [Newsl. - Inter-Soc. Color Counc.]. **Main/Corp** Inter-Society Color Council. **Added/Corp** Inter-Society Color Council. Report of the Annual Meeting. **VFOAT** ISCC Newsletter. **VAT** Inter-Society Color Council Newsletter. No. 1 Oct. 16, (1933)-(19??). Newsletter. English. ir. **LC** QC495; .I58. **DD** 535/.6/05. ***Continued by*** *Inter-Society Color Council News, 0731-2911.*

US/0276-2471
**NEWSLETTER - NATIONAL TECHNICAL ASSOCIATION.** [Newsl. - Natl. Tech. Assoc.]. **Main/Corp** National Technical Association. Newsletter. English. mo. National Technical Association, Suite 715, Southern Building, 1425 H Street NW, Washington DC 20005.

US/0160-4228
**NEWSLETTER - PENNSYLVANIA ACADEMY OF SCIENCE.** [Newsl., Pa. Acad. Sci.]. **Main/Corp** Pennsylvania Academy of Science. **VFOAT** Pennsylvania Science News-Letter; PAS Newsletter. Vol. 1 (Feb. 1943)-. Newsletter. English. Five times a year. Pennsylvania Academy of Science, PO Box 392, Gettysburg College, Gettysburg PA 17325-1486. **Tel** (717)337-6158, FAX (717)337-6666. **CODEN** NPASDZ. **Ad Acc. Circ:** 800 (ctrl).
**Ind/Abst** GeoRef.

US
**NEWSLETTER - VERMONT INSTITUTE OF NATURAL SCIENCE. Main/Corp** Vermont Institute of Natural Science. Newsletter. English. mo. Vermont Institute of Natural Science, Church Hill Road, Woodstock VT 05091. **Tel** (802)457-2779.

US/1045-3350
**NEWSLINE (SPRINGFIELD, VA.).** (NEWSLINE / NATIONAL TECHNICAL INFORMATION SERVICE.). [NewsLine]. **Added/Corp** United States. National Technical Information Service. **VFOAT** NTIS Newsline. No. 1 (Spring 1980)-. Periodical. English. qt. Free on request. National Technical Information Service - NTIS, Room 2027S, 5285 Port Royal Road, Springfield VA 22161. **Tel** (703)487-4630, (703)487-4660, (703)487-4650, FAX (703)321-8547, telex 89-9405. **ED** Tiffany M. Rushton. **DD** 605.
**Desc:** Published as an outreach activity of the National Technical Information Service to provide customers with current information about NTIS and its products and services. The mission of NTIS is to help stimulate America's progress through nationwide dissemination of scientific, technical, and engineering information.

JA/0027-657X
**NHK LABORATORIES NOTE.** [NHK Lab. Note]. (1???)-. Periodical. English. Ten times a year. Free

on request. Information Services & Patents Division, NHK Science & Technical Research Kimuta, Tokyo 157 Japan. **Tel** 011 81 3 3615 5111. **CODEN** NHKLA5. Documents available from Ask*IEEE.
**Ind/Abst** Ei Page One; INSPEC (1968-); Int. Aerosp. Abstr.

NR/0029-0114
**NIGERIAN JOURNAL OF SCIENCE.** [Niger. j. sci.]. **Added/Corp** Science Association of Nigeria. Vol. 1 (March 1966)-. Periodical. English (French and German). sa. $8.60. Science Association of Nigeria Ibadan, Box 4039 University of Ibadan, Ibadan Nigeria. **LC** Q1; .N585. **CODEN** NJSCAW. ***Supersedes*** *Proceedings of the Science Association of Nigeria.*
**Ind/Abst** Math. Rev.; Life Sci. Collect.; Soyabean Abstr.; Zentralbl. Math. Ihre Grenzgeb.

JA/0389-2514
**NIHON KOGYO DAIGAKU KENKYU HOKOKU.** [Nihon Kogyo Daigaku kenkyu hokoku]. **Added/Corp** Nihon Kogyo Daigaku. **VFOAT** Report of Researches Nippon Institute of Technology. (1971)-. Academic Scholarly Publication. Japanese. **CODEN** NKDHDG. Documents available from CASDDS.
**Ind/Abst** Chem. Abstr.

JA
**NIHON KYOIKU KOGAKU ZASSHI. VFOAT** Japan Journal of Educational Technology. Periodical. Japanese (summaries and/or abstracts in English). qt. Nihon Gakkai Jimu Senta Jigyobu 20-6 Mukogaoka 1, Bunkyo-ku Tokyo-to 113 Japan. **LC** LB1028.35; .N53.

JA
**NIHON NO KAGAKUSHA / NIHON KAGAKUSHA KAIGI HENSHU. VFOAT** Journal of Japanese Scientists. Began in 1966. Periodical. Japanese. mo. Nihon Kagakusha Kaigi, 9-16 Yushima-1 Bunkyo-ku, Tokyo-to 113 Japan. **LC** Q4; .N54.

JA
**NIHON SUTENRESU GIHO.** [Nihon Sutenresu giho]. **Added/Corp** Nihon Sutenresu Kabushiki Kaisha. Gijutsubu. **VFOAT** Nippon Stainless Technical Report. (1960)-. Academic Scholarly Publication. Japanese. **CODEN** NSUGBG. Documents available from CASDDS.
**Ind/Abst** Alum. Ind. Abstr.; Chem. Abstr.; Met. Abstr.

JA
**NIIGATA DAIGAKU KYOIKUGAKUBU KIYO: SHIZEN KAGAKU HEN. Main/Corp** Niigata Daigaku. Kyoiku Gakubu. **Added/Corp** Niigata Daigaku. Kyoiku Gakubu. Memoirs. **VFOAT** Memoirs of the Faculty of Education. (19??)-. Academic Scholarly Publication. Multiple languages (Japanese and English). Niigata Daigaku Kyoikugakubu, (Faculty of Education, Niigata University), 8050, Igarashi Ninocho, Niigatashi, Niigataken 950-11, Japan. **LC** Q4; .N55a. **CODEN** NDSKBF. Documents available from CASDDS. ***Continues in part*** *Niigata Daigaku. Kyoikugakubu. Niigata Daigaku Kyoikugakubu Kiyo.*
**Ind/Abst** Chem. Abstr.

JA/0286-2743
**NIIHAMA KOGYO KOTO SENMON GAKKO KIYO. RIKOGAKU HEN.** [Niihama Kogyo Koto Senmon Gakko kiyo, Rikogaku-hen]. **Added/Corp** Niihama Kogyo Koto Senmon Gakko. **VFOAT** Rikogaku Hen; Science and Engineering; Memoirs of the Niihama Technical College. Science and Engineering. (1969)-. Academic Scholarly Publication. Japanese (summaries and/or abstracts in English). Niihama Kogyo Koto Senmon Gakko, (Niihama National College of Technology), 7-1, Yakumocho, Niihamashi, Ehimeken 792 Japan. **LC** Q4; .N56. **CODEN** NKHEDR. Documents available from CASDDS. ***Continues in part*** *Niihama Kogyo Senmon Gakko kiyo.*
**Ind/Abst** Chem. Abstr.

JA
**NIKKEI MICRODEVICES.** Japanese. mo. $339.20. **(Subscription address:** Overseas Courier Services of America Inc., 5 East 44th Street, New York, NY 10017)

II/0970-0188
**NISSAT NEWSLETTER. VFOAT** National Information System in Science and Technology Newsletter. (1979)-. Newsletter. English. qt.
**Ind/Abst** Indian Libr. Sci. Abstr.

JA/0285-5275
**NISSEKI REBYU.** [Nisseki rebyu]. **Added/Corp** Nisseki Sekiyu Kabushiki Kaisha. **VFOAT** Nisseki Technical Review; NTR; N.T.R. (1959)-. Academic Scholarly Publication. Japanese. bm. Nippon Sekiyu K.K. Gijutsu Shohinbu, (Nippon Oil Co., Ltd.), 3-12, Nishishinbashi 1 Chome, Minatoku, Tokyoto 105, Japan. **CODEN** NREBBG. Documents available from CASDDS.
**Ind/Abst** Chem. Abstr.

PH
**NIST JOURNAL. VAT** National Institute of Science and Technology Journal. Vol. 1, No. 1 (Oct./Dec. 1984)-. Periodical. English. qt. National Institute of Science Technology, PO Box 774, Manila Philippines. **LC** T1; .N57. **DD** 605.
**Ind/Abst** Philip. Sci. Technol. Abstr.

JA/0915-0544
**NKK TECHNICAL REVIEW.** [NKK tech. rev.]. **VFOAT** Nippon Kokan Technical Review. (1988)-. Periodical. English. Three times a year. Free on request. NK Techno Service Co. Ltd., 1 1 Minamiwatarida Kawasaki ku, Kawasaki 210 Japan. **Tel** 011 81 044 322-6615. **DD** 671. Documents available from Article Express International, Ask*IEEE. ***Continues*** *Nippon Kokan Technical Report Overseas, 0546-1731.*
**Ind/Abst** Ei Page One; Eng. Index Annu.; INSPEC (1988-); Int. Aerosp. Abstr.

SW/0346-8313
**NOBEL SYMPOSIA.** [Nobel symp.]. Vol. 1 (1965)-. Academic Scholarly Publication. English. ir. Price varies per volume. Nobelstiftelsen, Sturegatan 14, 114 36 Stockholm 60 Sweden. **Tel** 011 46 8 6630920. **NLM** W3 NO369. **CODEN** NOSYBW. Documents available from BIOSIS Document Express, CASDDS.
**Ind/Abst** Biol. Abstr.; Chem. Abstr.

RM
**NOESIS (BUCHAREST, ROMANIA).** (NOESIS : TRAVAUX DU COMITE ROUMAIN D'HISTOIRE ET DE PHILOSOPHIE DES SCIENCES.). **Added/Corp** Academia Republicii Socialiste Romania. Comite Roumain d'Histoire et de Philosophie des Sciences. **VFOAT** Travaux du Comite Roumain d'Histoire et de Philosophie des Sciences. (1972)-. Periodical. English (French, German and Russian). Editura Academia Republicii Socialiste Romania, Calea Victoriei Nr 125, R-79717 Bucuresti Romania. **Tel** telex 10376 PRSFI R. **LC** Q127.R6; N635. **DD** 509.498.

KO
**NONGCHON SAENGHWAL KWAHAK. Added/Corp** Nongchon Yongyang Kaeson Yonsuwon (Korea). **VFOAT** Rural Life Science. (1990)-. Periodical. Korean. qt. Nongchon Yongyang Kaeson Yonsuwon, 88-2 Sodun-dong, Suwoni-si Korea 170. ***Continues*** *Sikpum kwa Yongyang.*

CC
**NONGCUN KEXUE. VFOAT** Science in the Countryside. Chinese. mo. $21.60. China National Publ Industry Trade, PO Box 782, Beijing, People's Republic of China. **Tel** 011 86 1 4215031.

US/0938-9008
**NONLINEAR SCIENCE TODAY.** [Nonlinear sci. today]. Vol. 1, No. 1 (1991)-. Periodical. English. Four times a year. $27.00. Springer-Verlag New York Inc., 175 5th Avenue, New York NY 10010. **Tel** (212)460-1500, telex 232 235 SPB UR. **(Subscription address:** Springer Verlag New York Inc. / for North America, 44 Hartz Way, Secaucus NJ 07096.) **LC** QA427; .N665. **DD** 501/.175. **CODEN** NSTOE4. **[CCC]**. Documents available from The Genuine Article.
**Desc:** Published in conjunction with the "Journal of Nonlinear Science"; provides a forum of communication for researchers in many disciplines. Features articles addressing the topics covered in the "Journal" in a less technical manner; provides a forum for debate and the dissemination of professional news.
**Ind/Abst** Compumath Citation Index [Full Cov.]; Curr. Contents Phys. Chem. Earth Sci.; Math. Rev.; Res. Alert [Full Cov.]; Sci. Cit. Index; SCISEARCH.

US/0029-1625
**NORELCO REPORTER.** [Norelco report.]. **Added/Corp** North American Philips Co. Philips Electronics, Inc. Philips Electronic Instruments, Inc. **VFOAT** Philips Reporter. Vol. 1, No. 1 (Sept. 1953)-. Periodical. English. ir. Free. Philips Electronic Instruments, 750 South Fulton Street, Mount Vernon NY 10550. **LC** Q184; .N58. **DD** 507.8. **CODEN** NORRA5. Documents available from BIOSIS Document Express, Ask*IEEE, CASDDS.
**Ind/Abst** Alum. Ind. Abstr. (-1986); Biol. Abstr. (-1986); Ceram. Abstr. (19??-); Chem. Abstr. (-1986); GeoRef (-1986); INSPEC (July 1968-1986); Int. Aerosp. Abstr. (-1986); Met. Abstr. (-1986).

IT
**NORMATIVA TECNICA.** Italian. ir. L1230000. Schedario Tecnico Editore Spa, Via Cavour 100, 12011 Borgo S Dalmazzo Italy. **Tel** 011 39 171 262296, FAX 011 39 171 262357. cum. index. **Ad Acc. Circ:** 15,000 (ctrl). available on CD-ROM.
**Desc:** Law, decrees, and technical norms regarding the law.

FR
**NORMELEC.** French. an. 2550.00F France; 2700.00F other. Editions Tests, 4 Place du Colonel Fabien, 75491 Paris Cedex 10 France. **Tel** 011 33 1 42402201.

US/1040-0540
**NORTH CENTRAL SALES GUIDE TO HIGH-TECH COMPANIES.** [North Cent. sales guide to high tech co.]. **VFOAT** North Central Region; Sales Guide to High Tech Companies. North Central Region. English. qt. $145.00. Corporate Technology Information Services Inc, 12 Alfred Street, Suite 200, Woburn MA 01801-9998. **Tel** (617)932-3939, (800)333-8036, FAX (617)932-6335, telex 497-2961 CRPTECH. **ED** Steven W Parker. **LC** HC110.H53; N67. **DD** 338.7/62/0002577. Index available. cum. index. **Bk Rev. Ad Acc. Circ:** 3,000. available on diskette.
**Desc:** Regional directory of over 3,000 technology manufacturers and developers.

US/0885-5110
**NORTH HOLLAND SERIES IN SYSTEM SCIENCE AND ENGINEERING.** [North-Holl. ser. syst. sci. eng.]. **VFOAT** North-Holland Series in System Science and Engineering. (1978)-. Monographic series. English. Elsevier Science Publishing Company Inc, Madison Square Station, PO Box 882, New York NY 10159-0882. **Tel** (212)633-3950, FAX (212)633-3990. **DD** 620.
**Ind/Abst** Math. Rev.; Zentralbl. Math. Ihre Grenzgeb.

CN/0380-0881
**NORTHPOINT. Added/Corp** Association of Certified Survey Technicians and Technologists of Ontario. Association of Survey Technicians of Ontario. Vol. 1 (July 1964)-. Periodical. English. qt. 20.00Can$. Association Certified Survey Technicians, 10 Four Seasons Pl/Suite 404, Islington Ontario M9B 6H7 Canada. **Tel** (416)620-1885. **ED** R. Fowler (Telephone: (613)226-5442) and R.C. Cooper. Index available. **Ad Acc. Circ:** 1,000 (ctrl).
**Desc:** Articles for the education and technical advancement of the survey technician both field and office.

US/1040-0516
**NORTHWEST SALES GUIDE TO HIGH-TECH COMPANIES.** [Northwest sales guide high tech co.]. **VFOAT** Northwest Region; Sales Guide to High Tech Companies. Northwest Region. English. qt. $145.00. Corporate Technology Information Services Inc, 12 Alfred Street, Suite 200, Woburn MA 01801-9998. **Tel** (617)932-3939, (800)333-8036, FAX (617)932-6335, telex 497-2961 CRPTECH. **ED** Steven W Parker. **LC** HC110.H53; N68. **DD** 338.7/62/00025795. Index available. cum. index. **Bk Rev. Ad Acc. Circ:** 3,000. available on diskette.
**Desc:** Regional directory of over 3,000 technology manufacturers and developers.

US/0029-344X
**NORTHWEST SCIENCE.** [Northwest sci.]. **Added/Corp** Northwest Scientific Association. Vol. 1 (March 1927)-. Academic Scholarly Publication. English. qt (plus 1 abstracts issue). comes with membership. Washington State University Press, Cooper Publications, Room 40, Pullman WA 99164. **Tel** (509)335-3518. **ED** Fred Bohm. **LC** Q1; .N6. **CODEN** NOSCAX. Index available. **Bk Rev. Ad Acc. Pr Rev. Circ:** 1,200 (ctrl). available on microfilm and microfiche from University Microfilms International (UMI). Documents available from The Genuine Article, BIOSIS Document Express, CASDDS.
**Desc:** Publishes articles in the basic, applied and social sciences that deal with the Pacific Northwest.
**Ind/Abst** Abstr. Anthropol.; AGRICOLA [Select. Cov.]; Biol. Abstr.; Chem. Abstr.; Curr. Aware. Biol. Sci., CABS; Curr. Contents, Agric. Biol. Environ. Sci.; Curr. Ref. Fish Res.; Ecol. Abstr.; Ecology Abstr.; EMBASE; Fish Rev.; For. Prod. Abstr. (1991-); For. Abstr.; Geogr. Abstr. Phys. Geogr.; Geogr. Abstr. Human Geogr.; Geol. Abstr.; GeoRef; Grasslands For. Abstr.; Int. Aerosp. Abstr.; Key Word Index Wildl. Res.; Life Sci. Collect.; Res. Alert [Select. Cov.]; Rev. Plant Pathol.; SCISEARCH; Soils Fert.; Weed Abstr.; Wildl. Rev.

UK/0035-9149
**NOTES AND RECORDS OF THE ROYAL SOCIETY OF LONDON.** [Notes rec. R. Soc. Lond.]. **Main/Corp** Royal Society (Great Britain). (April 1938)-. Periodical. English. sa (Jan. and July). £31.00 UK & Europe; $56.00 US; £34.00 other. Royal Society, 6 Carlton House Terrace, London SW1Y 5AG England. **Tel** 011 44 71 839 5561, FAX 071-976 1837, telex 917876 ROYAL G. **ED** D. G. King-Hele. **LC** Q41; .L835. **DD** 506.242. **NLM** W1 NO739D. **CODEN** NOREAY. Index available. cum. index. **Pr Rev. Circ:** 1,400. Documents available from The Genuine Article. ***Supersedes*** *Occasional Notices of the Royal Society of London.*
**Desc:** Definitive papers on the history of science, medicine and technology.
**Ind/Abst** Am. Hist. Life (1964-); Arts Humanit. Citation Index [Full Cov.]; Curr. Contents Arts Humanit.; Int. Bibliogr. Sociol.; Math. Rev.; Res. Alert [Full Cov.]; Romant. Move.; Zentralbl. Math. Ihre Grenzgeb.

IT
**NOTIZIE AIRI.** Italian. bm. L60.000. Airi, Via Aiaccio 20, 00198 Rome Italy. **Tel** 39 6 8848831, FAX 39 6 552949. **ED** Alessandra Spitz. **Bk Rev. Ad Acc.** available on audiocassette.
**Desc:** Strategies and policies in research and development in Italy and around Europe. R and D activities of Italian firms.

US/0029-4543
**NOTRE DAME TECHNICAL REVIEW, THE.** [Notre Dame tech. rev.]. V. 1- Nov. 1949-. Periodical. English. qt. University of Notre Dame Box 91, Notre Dame IN 46556. **Tel** (219)239-6346, FAX (219)239-8148.

US/0029-4608
**NOTULAE NATURAE OF THE ACADEMY NATURAL SCIENCES OF PHILADELPHIA.** [Not. nat. Acad. Nat. Sci. Philadelphia]. **Main/Corp** Academy of Natural Sciences of Philadelphia. **VFOAT** Notulae Naturae. No. 1 (1939)-. Monographic series. English. ir. Price varies per volume. Academy of Natural Sciences, 1900 Benjamin Franklin Parkway, Philadelphia PA 19103. **Tel** (215)299-1130, FAX (215)299-1028. **ED** William F. Smith-Vaniz. **LC** Q111; .N63. **CODEN** NONAA2. **Pr Rev. Circ:** 300 (ctrl).
**Desc:** Original research in systematics, evolution, ecology, taxonomy and biogeography. Most articles contain analyses of new data, but succinct reviews and speculative or theoretical works that make major contributions may also appear.
**Ind/Abst** AGRICOLA; GeoRef; Life Sci. Collect.

BE/0771-7369
**NOUVELLES DE LA SCIENCE ET DES TECHNOLOGIES.** (1983)-. Periodical. French. Four times a year (within the seasons of the year). 2000F Belgium; 2800F other. Gordes, Ave Jeanne 44, B-1050 Brussels Belgium. **Tel** 32 2 6503444, FAX 32 2 6419274. **LC** IN PROCESS. **Ad Acc. Circ:** 5,000.
**Desc:** New technologies in various fields in medicine, agriculture, laboratories, pharmacies, space, communications.

FR/0246-1226
**NOUVELLES DE L'ACADEMIE / ACADEMIE DES SCIENCES, LES.** [Nouv. Acad.]. **Main/Corp** Academie des Sciences (France). Jan. 1984-. Periodical. French. mo. Academie des Sciences, 23 Quai de Conti, 75006 Paris France. **Tel** 33 1 43 26 66 21, telex 206521F. **Bk Rev. Ad Acc. Circ:** 750 (ctrl). ***Continues in part*** *Comptes Rendus des Seances de l'Academie des Sciences. Vie Academique.*

GW/0369-5034
**NOVA ACTA LEOPOLDINA.** (NOVA ACTA LEOPOLDINA : ABHANDLUNGEN DER KAISERLICH LEOPOLDINISCH-CAROLINISCH DEUTSCHEN AKADEMIE DER NATURFORSCHER.). [Nova acta Leopold.]. New Series Vol. 1, No. 2 and 3. Academic Scholarly Publication. German. ir. Price varies per volume. Deutsche Akademie der Naturforscher Leopoldina, August Bebel Str. 50A, 4010 Halle, Germany. **Tel** 0345-24723, FAX 0345-21727. **ED** J H Scharf. **LC** Q49; .H162. **CODEN** NOALA4. Documents available from BIOSIS Document Express, CASDDS. ***Continues*** *Nova Acta.*
**Desc:** Composes all branches of natural sciences from pure mathematics to applied biology.
**Ind/Abst** AGRICOLA; Biol. Abstr.; Chem. Abstr.; Energy Res. Abstr. (March 1982-); GeoRef; Int. Aerosp. Abstr.; Math. Rev.; Life Sci. Collect.; Zentralbl. Math. Ihre Grenzgeb.

XV/0029-5051
**NOVA PROIZVODNJA. Added/Corp** Slovenia (Federated Republic, 1945- ). Uprava za Napredek Proizvodnji. (1950)-. Academic Scholarly Publication. Serbo-Croatian (Roman) (summaries and/or abstracts in English). bm. **LC** T4; .N824. **CODEN** NOVPAJ. Documents available from CASDDS.
**Ind/Abst** Chem. Abstr.

RU
**NOVAIA INOSTRANNAIA LITERATURA PO OBSHCHESTVENNYM NAUKAM: NAUKOVEDENIE. Added/Corp** Institut Nauchnoi Informatsii po Obshchestvennym Naukam (Akademiia Nauk SSSR). (1976)-. Multiple languages (Russian and Multiple languages). mo. 0.35rub (single issue). Izdatelstvo Nauka / Akademiia Nauk, Publishing House of the Russian Academy of Sciences, Leninskii Porspekt 14, 117901 Moscow Russia. **Tel** 011 95 954-21-53, FAX 011 95 938-21-44, telex 411964. **ED** N I Makeshin and E P Sokolova. **LC** Z7403; .N934; Q158.5. ***Continues*** *Novaia Literatura O Nauke I Nauchno-Issledovatelskoi Rabote za Rubezhom.*

RU/0134-2754
**NOVAIA OTECHESTVENNAIA LITERATURA PO OBSHCHESTVENNYM NAUKAM. NAUKOVEDENIE / ROSSIISKAIA AKADEMIIA NAUK, INSTITUT NAUCHNOI INFORMATSII PO OBSHCHESTVENNYM NAUKAM.** ***Title Change.*** **Added/Corp** Institut Nauchnoi Informatsii po Obshchestvennym Naukam (Rossiiskaia Akademiia Nauk). **VFOAT** Naukovedenie. (1992)-(1992). Periodical. Russian. mo. **(Subscription address:** East View Publications Inc., 3020 Harbor Lane North, Suite 110, Minneapolis MN 55447.) **LC** Z5055.R78; N6; Q4. ***Continues*** *Novaia Sovetskaia Literatura po Obshchestvennym Naukam. Naukovedenie.* ***Continued by*** *Novaia Literatura po Sotsialnym i Gumanitarnym Naukam. Naukovedenie.*

RU
**NOVYE KNIGI ZA RUBEZHOM: SERIIA A. MATEMATIKA, MEKHANIKA, ASTRONOMIIA, FIZIKA, GEOFIZIKA, KHIMIIA, GEOLOGIIA.** Vol. 10 (Jan. 1957)-. Periodical. Russian. mo. $145.00. **(Subscription address:** Victor Kamkin, 4956 Boiling Brook Parkway, Rockville MD 20852.) **LC** Z7403; .N953. ***Supersedes in part*** *Novye Knigi za Rubezhom.*

RU
**NOVYE KNIGI ZA RUBEZHOM: SERIIA B. TEKHNIKA.** (1957)-. Periodical. Russian. mo. $145.00. **(Subscription address:** Victor Kamkin, 4956 Boiling Brook Parkway, Rockville MD 20852.) **LC** Z7911; .N6. ***Supersedes in part*** *Novye Knigi za Rubezhom.*

PH/0116-6107
**NRCP DIRECTORY.** [NRCP dir.]. **VFOAT** N.R.C.P. Directory. 1981-. Directory. English. NRCP General Santos Avenue, Bicutan Tagig, Metro Manila Philippines. **LC** Q141. **DD** 502/.5/599. **NLM** Q 145; N961.

PH
**NRCP RESEARCH BULLETIN. Main/Corp** National Research Council of the Philippines. **VAT** National Research Council of the Philippines Research Bulletin. Academic Scholarly Publication. English. **LC** Q180.P45; N32A. **DD** 505. Documents available from CASDDS.
**Ind/Abst** Chem. Abstr.; Index Philip. Period.; Philip. Sci. Technol. Abstr.

PP
**NRI SPECIAL PUBLICATION. Added/Corp** National Research Institute (Papua New Guinea). **VFOAT** Special Publication. No. 13 (1989)-. Monographic series. English. ir. Price varies per volume. National Research Institute, PO Box 5854 Boroko, Boroko Papua New Guinea. **LC** IN PROCESS. ***Continues*** *IASER Special Publication.*

PH
**NSDB-UP RESEARCH HIGHLIGHTS. Added/Corp** University of the Philippines. Office of Research Coordination. NSDB Assisted-UPS Research Integrated Program. Vol. 1, No. 2 (April/June 1979)-. Periodical. English. NSDB-UP Integrated Research Program, Office of Research Coordination, University of the Philippines, Quezon City Philippines. ***Continues*** *Research Linkage.*
**Ind/Abst** Philip. Sci. Technol. Abstr.

US
**NSF GRANT POLICY MANUAL. Main/Corp** National Science Foundation (U.S.). **VFOAT** Grant Policy Manual. (Oct. 1977)-. Government Publication. English. ir. $21.00 domestic; $26.25 other. Superintendent of Documents, US Government Printing Office, Washington DC 20402. **Tel** (202)275-3328, FAX (202)786-2377. **CODEN** NGPMDT. ***Continues*** *NSF Grant Administration Manual.*
**Desc:** Compendium of basic NSF grant policies and procedures for use by the grantee community and by NSF staff.

CN/0712-6298
**NSIAA NEWS.** ***Title Change.*** [NSIAA news]. **Added/Corp** Nova Scotia Industrial Arts Association. Nova Scotia Teachers Union. **VFOAT** NSIAA Newsletter. **VAT** Nova Scotia Industrial Arts Association News. Vol. 1, No. 1 (June 1982)-(199?). Periodical. English. NSIAA News, c/o Nova Scotia Teachers Union, PO Box 1060, Armdale Nova Scotia B3L 4L7 Canada. **DD** 607/.716. ***Continued by*** *NSTEA News.*

US
**NSTA REPORT / NATIONAL SCIENCE TEACHERS ASSOCIATION.** **See** Education-Teaching and Curriculum.

FR/0992-3020
**NTI. NOUVELLES TECHNOLOGIES DE L'INFORMATION.** (NTI.). **VFOAT** Nouvelles Technologies de l'Information. (1988)-. Periodical. French. Twenty times a year. 783.55F France; 900.00F other. A Jour, 11 rue du Marche St Honore, 75001 Paris France. **Tel** 011 33 1 44553849. **UDC** 654 : 681.3.

US
**NTIS ALERT. FOREIGN TECHNOLOGY.** ***Ceased.*** (1992)-(199?). English. sm. National Technical Information Service - NTIS, Room 2027S, 5285 Port Royal Road, Springfield VA 22161. **Tel** (703)487-4630, (703)487-4660, (703)487-4650, FAX (703)321-8547, telex 89-9405. available on an online database (file 636/Full-Text) from DIALOG. ***Continues*** *Foreign Technology / NTIS, 0884-7541.*
**Ind/Abst** PTS Newsl. Database (19??-19??) [Full Txt.].

US/1064-0479
**NTIS BIBLIOGRAPHIC DATABASE.** **See** Science and Technology-Abstracting, Bibliographies and Statistics.

US/0731-3004
**NTIS TITLE INDEX ON MICROFICHE.** (NTIS TITLE INDEX. MICROFORM.). [NTIS title index microfiche]. **Main/Corp** United States. National Technical Information Service. **VFOAT** N.T.I.S. Title Index on Microfiche. July 1964-Dec. 1978-. Periodical. English. qt. National Technical Information Service - NTIS, Room 2027S, 5285 Port Royal Road, Springfield VA 22161. **Tel** (703)487-4630, (703)487-4660, (703)487-4650, FAX (703)321-8547, telex 89-9405. **NLM** ZQ 1 N15.

SZ/0036-6978
**NTM.** [NTM]. **VAT** Naturwissenschaften, Technik und Medizin. (1960)-. Academic Scholarly Publication. German (English and French). Four times a year. 101.20F Switzerland; 108.50F other. Birkhaeuser Verlag Ag, Klosterberg 23, PO Box 133, CH-4010 Basel Switzerland. **Tel** 011 41 61 2717400, FAX 011 41 0 61 2717666, telex 963475 birk ch. **(Subscription address:** Birkhauser Verlag AG, PO Box 151, CH 4106 Therwil Switzerland; Phone: 011 41 61 7217740) **ED** D. von Engelhardt, H. Wussing, P. Zimmermann. **LC** Q125; .N2. **NLM** W1 N69. Documents available from BIOSIS Document Express, CASDDS.
**Desc:** Committed to examining a multitude of historical topics in the natural sciences, technology and medicine, always with reference to the history of ideas and social history.
**Ind/Abst** Biol. Abstr.; Chem. Abstr.; Energy Res. Abstr. (Mar. 1982-); Math. Rev.; Zentralbl. Math. Ihre Grenzgeb.

JA/0286-2794
**NUMAZU KOGYO KOTO SENMON GAKKO KENKYU HOKOKU.** [Numazu Kogyo Koto Senmon Gakko kenkyu hokoku]. **Added/Corp** Numazu Kogyo Koto Senmon Gakko. **VFOAT** Research Reports of Numazu Technical College. (1964)-. Academic Scholarly Publication. Japanese. Numazu Kogyo Koto Senmon Gakko, (Numazu College of Technology), 3600, Ooka, Numazushi, Shizuokaken 410 Japan. **CODEN** NKKHDH. Documents available from CASDDS.
**Ind/Abst** Chem. Abstr.

IT
**NUNCIUS.** Vol. 1, No. 1 (1986)-. Periodical. Italian (summaries and/or abstracts in English and Italian). sa. L53000 Italy; L68000 other. Istituto e Museo di Storia della Scienza di Firenze, Plazza dei Giudici 1, Firenze Italy. **Tel** (055)293493. **LC** Q127.I8. **DD** 505. **NLM** W1; NU218. Index available. cum. index. **Bk Rev.** ***Continues*** *Annali dell'Istituto e Museo di Storia della Scienza di Firenze, 0391-3341.*
**Ind/Abst** Am. Hist. Life (1986-).

IT
**NUOVA SCIENZA.** Nuova Scienza, Lungo Tevere Dei San Gallo 1, 00186 Rome Italy.

GW
**NURNBERGER FORSCHUNGSBERICHTE. Added/Corp** Nurnberger Forschungsvereinigung. Monographic series. German. Price varies per volume.

KO/0250-3395
**NYENGU BOGO - NYENNAM DAIHAGGYO GONNEB GISUR NYENGUSO.** (YONGU POGO.). [Nyengu bogo - Nyennam Daihaggyo Gonneb Gisur Nyenguso]. **VFOAT** Report. Began in 1973. Academic Scholarly Publication. English (Korean). an. Yongnam Taehakkyo Chulpanbu, 214-1 Tae-dong Kyongsan-up, Kyongbuk Korea. **LC** T4; .Y65. **CODEN** YNTPDO. Documents available from CASDDS.
**Ind/Abst** Chem. Abstr.

JA/0389-3693
**OBAYASHI REPOTO.** [Obayashi repoto]. (1978)-. Periodical. Japanese. Obayashi Corporation, 75, 3-chome, Kyobashi, Higashi-ku, Osaka, Japan. **DD** 720.
**Ind/Abst** Abstr. J. Earthq. Eng.

RU
**OBSHCHESTVENNYE NAUKI ZA RUBEZHOM. SERIIA 8: NAUKOVEDENIE.** ***Title Change.*** **Added/Corp** Institut Nauchnoi Informatsii po Obshchestvennym Naukam (Akademiia Nauk SSSR). **VFOAT** Naukovedenie. **VAT** Obshchestvennye Nauki za Rubezhom. Seriia Vosem : Naukovedenie. (1973)-(1992). Academic Scholarly Publication. Russian. qt. Izdatelstvo Nauka / Akademiia Nauk, Publishing House of the Russian Academy of Sciences, Leninskii Porspekt 14, 117901 Moscow Russia. **Tel** 011 95 954-21-53, FAX 011 95 938-21-44, telex 411964. **LC** Q4; .O17. ***Continued by*** *Sotsialnye i Gumanitarnye Nauki. Seriia 8, Naukovedenie, 0202-2141.*

US/0148-0944
**OCCASIONAL PAPER - MISSOURI ACADEMY OF SCIENCE.** [Occas. pap., Mo. Acad. Sci.]. **Main/Corp** Missouri Academy of Science. No. 3-. Academic Scholarly Publication. English. ir. $4.50. Missouri Academy of Science, c/o NMSU, PO Box 828, Kirksville MO 63501. **Tel** (816)785-4635. **ED** Harry Sauer. **CODEN** OPMSD4. **Pr Rev. Circ:** 1,000 (ctrl). Documents available from CASDDS. ***Continues*** *Bulletin of the Missouri Academy of Science. Supplement, 0093-853X.*

**Desc:** Refereed publications containing archival material; complete work on a specific subject published as needed.
**Ind/Abst** Chem. Abstr.

US/0069-6145
## OCCASIONAL PAPER (UNIVERSITY OF COLORADO, BOULDER. INSTITUTE OF ARCTIC AND ALPINE RESEARCH).
(OCCASIONAL PAPER / INSTITUTE OF ARCTIC AND ALPINE RESEARCH.). [Occas. pap. - Inst. Arct. Alp. Res. Univ. Colo.]. Began publication in 1974. Monographic series. English. ir. Price varies per volume. University of Colorado / Boulder, Colorado, Campus Box 450, Boulder CO 80309. **Tel** (303)492-3765, FAX (303)492-6388. **ED** Kathleen A Salzberg. **CODEN** CAAOA. **Circ:** 150. available on microfiche (from National Technical Information Service Springfield, VA). Documents available from BIOSIS Document Express. ***Continues*** *Occasional Paper (University of Colorado (Boulder Campus). Institute of Arctic and Alpine Research).*
**Desc:** Monographs of work by Institute personnel.
**Ind/Abst** ASTIS Curr. Aware. Bull. (1978-); ASTIS Bibliogr. (1978-); Biol. Abstr.; Ecol. Abstr. (?-?); GeoRef; Life Sci. Collect.

US/0068-5461
## OCCASIONAL PAPERS OF THE CALIFORNIA ACADEMY OF SCIENCES.
[Occas. pap. Calif. Acad. Sci.]. **Added/Corp** California Academy of Sciences. (1890)-. Monographic series. English. ir. Price varies per volume. CAS Scientific Publications, Golden Gate Park, San Francisco CA 94118. **Tel** (415)750-7243. **LC** Q11; .C18. **DD** 505. **CODEN** OPCAAX.

PL/0137-3714
## OCHRONA POWIETRZA.
(1967)-. Periodical. Polish. bm. $36.00. **(Subscription address:** ARS Polona, PO Box 1001, 00068 Warsaw Poland.) **UDC** 628.5.
**Ind/Abst** Ceram. Abstr. (19??-).

SZ
## OEIL, L'.
(1993)-. French. Ten times a year. 136.00F Switzerland; 163.00F Europe; 186.00F other. L'Oeil, Chemin du Closel 5, CP 350, 1020 Renens Switzerland. **Tel** 011 41 21 6350427, FAX 011 41 21 6359646.
**Ind/Abst** Archit. Period. Index (Oct. 1975-Mar. 1978); Avery Index Archit. Period. Suppl. Colum. Univ. (Jan.-April, July-Dec. 1990-); BHA : Biblio. Hist. Art.

US
## OFFICE OF HEALTH TECHNOLOGY ASSESSMENT REPORTS / NATIONAL CENTER FOR HEALTH SERVICES RESEARCH AND HEALTH CARE TECHNOLOGY ASSESSMENT.
**Added/Corp** National Center for Health Services Research and Health Care Technology Assessment (U.S.). Office of Health Technology Assessment. United States. Agency for Health Care Policy and Research. Office of Health Technology Assessment. **VFOAT** Health Technology Assessment Series, Office of Health Technology Assessment Reports. (1985)-. English. an. Free. Agency for Health Care Policy and Research, PO Box 8547, Silver Springs MD 20907. **Tel** (800)358-9295. **LC** R854.U5; H43. **DD** 610/.28. **NLM** W1; OF455M. Index available. cum. index. available on microfiche. ***Continues*** *Health Technology Assessment Reports (Annual), 8755-9765.*
**Desc:** Assesses the saftey and clinical effectiveness of new or unestablished diagnostic and treatment technologies proposed for coverage of the request of medical and other federal health programs.
**Ind/Abst** Abstr. Clin. Care Guidel.

US/0747-0649
## OFFICE OF INSTRUCTIONAL TECHNOLOGY NEWSLETTER.
***Title Change.*** (OFFICE OF INSTRUCTIONAL TECHNOLOGY NEWSLETTER : AN INFORMAL PUBLICATION OF THE STATE DEPARTMENT OF EDUCATION'S OFFICE OF INSTRUCTIONAL TECHNOLOGY.). [Off. Instruct. Technol. newsl.]. **Added/Corp** South Carolina. Office of Instructional Technology. Vol. 1, No. 1 (Feb. 1984)-(19??). Newsletter. English. qt. Office of Instructional Technology Newsletter, Drawer L, Columbia SC 29250. **DD** 371. ***Continues*** *South Carolina Scene/ITV-Radio Newsletter, 0745-2861.* ***Continued by*** *Instructional Technology/News, 1065-9803.*

US/0030-0950
## OHIO JOURNAL OF SCIENCE, THE.
[Ohio j. sci.]. **Added/Corp** Ohio State University. Scientific Society. Ohio Academy of Science. Vol. 16 (Nov. 1915)-. Academic Scholarly Publication. English. Five times a year. $40.00 US; $45.00 other. Ohio Academy of Science, 1500 W Third Avenue, Suite 223, Columbus OH 43212-2817. **Tel** (614)488-2228, FAX (614)488-2228. **ED** Lee Meserve, Bowling Green State University, Department of Biological Sciences, Bowling Green, OH 43403. **NLM** W1 OH333. **CODEN** OJSCA9. **[CCC].** Index available in last issue of volume--attached. cum. index. **Bk Rev**, (Qty: 20). **Ad Acc, Adv Mgr:** L. Elfner. **Pr Rev. Circ:** 2,500 (ctrl). Documents available from The Genuine Article, BIOSIS Document Express, CASDDS, Documents on Demand. ***Continues*** *Ohio Naturalist and Journal of Science.*
**Desc:** Original peer reviewed papers in all science fields.
**Ind/Abst** AGRICOLA [Select. Cov.]; Anim. Breed. Abstr.; Art Archaeol. Tech. Abstr.; Biodeter. Abstr. (1991-); Biol. Abstr.; Chem. Abstr.; Coal Abstr.; Curr. Biotechnol.; Curr. Contents, Agric. Biol. Environ. Sci.; Curr. Ref. Fish Res.; Ecol. Abstr.; EMBASE; Energy Inf. Abstr.; Environ. Abstr.; Field Crop Abstr.; Fish Rev.; For. Abstr.; Geogr. Abstr. Phys. Geogr.; Geogr. Abstr. Human Geogr.; GeoRef; Int. Aerosp. Abstr.; Irr. Drain. Abstr.; Key Word Index Wildl. Res.; Maize Abstr.; Nematol. Abstr.; Life Sci. Collect.; Plant Breed. Abstr.; Poult. Abstr.; Res. Alert [Full Cov.]; Rev. Agric. Entomol.; Sci. Cit. Index; SCISEARCH; Seed Abstr.; Soc. Sci. Cit. Index [Select. Cov.]; Soils Fert.; Soyabean Abstr.; SportSearch; Weed Abstr.; Wildl. Rev.

JA/0285-7685
## OKAYAMA RIKA DAIGAKU KIYO. A, SHIZEN KAGAKU.
[Okayama Rika Daigaku kiyo, A, Shizen kagaku]. **VFOAT** Bulletin of the Okayama University of Science. A, Natural Science. No. 17 (1981)-. Periodical. Japanese (English). an. Okayama Rika Daigaku 1, Ridaicho Okayama-shi 700 Japan. **CODEN** ORDKDH. Documents available from Ask*IEEE. ***Continues in part*** *Oakyama Rika Daigaku Kiyo.*
**Ind/Abst** INSPEC (1983-).

JA/0912-5566
## OKI TECHNICAL REVIEW.
[Oki tech. rev.]. (1987)-. Periodical. English. qt (4 issues). Free on request. Oki Electric Industry Ltd., 7-12-1 Chome Toranomon, Minato ku Tokyo 105 Japan. **Tel** 011 81 3 3501 3111. **DD** 621.3.

IT/0391-8645
## OLEODINAMICA PNEUMATICA LUBRIFICAZIONE.
[Oleodin. Pneum. Lubrif.]. (1974)-. Periodical. Italian. mo. L85000.00 Italy; L150000.00 other Europe; L210000.00 other. Tecniche Nuove SPA, Via Ciro Menotti 14, 20129 Milan Italy. **Tel** 011 39 2 75701, FAX 011 39 2 7610351, telex 334647 TECHS I. **UDC** 621.4. ***Continues*** *Oleodinamica Pneumatica, 0030-2104; Lubrificazione Industriale e per Autoveicoli, 0024-7162.*

CN/0380-1969
## ONTARIO TECHNOLOGIST, THE.
[Ont. technol.]. **Added/Corp** Ontario Association of Certified Engineering Technicians and Technologists. Vol. 5, No. 8 (Dec. 1962)-. Periodical. English. Six times a year. 35.00Can$ Canada; $45.00 other. Ontario Association of Certified Engineering Technicians and Technologists, 10 Four Seasons Place/Suite 404, Islington Ontario M9B 6H7 Canada. **Tel** (416)621-9621. **ED** Ruth M. Klein. **Bk Rev. Ad Acc. Circ:** 16,000 (ctrl).
**Desc:** Primarily engineering and applied science technology reports on current professional issues including manpower and careers.
**Ind/Abst** Energy Res. Abstr. (July 1979-).

NE/0167-6377
## OPERATIONS RESEARCH LETTERS.
(OPERATIONS RESEARCH LETTERS : A JOURNAL OF THE OPERATIONS RESEARCH SOCIETY OF AMERICA ...). [Oper. res. lett.]. **Added/Corp** Operations Research Society of America. Vol. 1, No. 1 (Oct. 1981)-. Academic Scholarly Publication. English. Eight times a year (2 volumes). Fl828.00. Elsevier Science Publishers BV, PO Box 211, 1000 AE Amsterdam Netherlands. **Tel** 011 31 20 5803642, FAX 011 31 20 5862696, telex 15682. **ED** G L Nemhauser. **LC** T57.6.A1; O62. **DD** 658.4/03/4. **CODEN** ORLED5. **[CCC]. Pr Rev.** available on microfilm and microfiche from University Microfilms International (UMI). Documents available from Article Express International, The Genuine Article, Ask*IEEE.
**Desc:** A publication for literature in operations research and the management and decision sciences.
**Ind/Abst** Bioeng. Abstr.; Biostatistica; Compumath Citation Index [Full Cov.]; Comput. Abstr.; Contents Pages Manage.; Curr. Contents Eng. Tech. Appl. Sci.; Ei Page One; Eng. Index Annu. [Select. Cov.]; INSPEC (Oct. 1981-); Int. Abstr. Oper. Res. [Full Cov.]; Math. Rev.; Oper. Res./Manag. Sci.; Res. Alert [Full Cov.]; Sci. Cit. Index; SCISEARCH; Soc. Sci. Cit. Index [Select. Cov.]; Zentralbl. Math. Ihre Grenzgeb.

UK
## OPPORTUNITIES IN AGRICULTURE, DEVELOPMENT & BIOLOGICALLY RELATED ARTS & SCIENCES.
**See** Agriculture.

US
## OR/MS TODAY.
**VFOAT** OR MS Today; Operations Research/Management Science Today; Operations Research Management Science Today. Vol. 1 (Jan. 1974)-. English. Six times a year. $20.00 US; $40.00 other. Operations Research Society of America, 1314 Guilford Avenue, Baltimore MD 21202. **Tel** (410)850-0300, (800)850-0300. **ED** John Llwewllyn. **Ad Acc. Circ:** 12,000.
**Desc:** Contains news of Society and Institute affairs, items of professional interest, and extensive advertising announcing jobs and services available to members.

GW/0171-6468
## OR-SPEKTRUM.
(OR SPEKTRUM : ORGAN DER DEUTSCHEN GESELLSCHAFT FUER OPERATIONS RESEARCH.). [OR-Spektrum]. **Added/Corp** Deutsche Gesellschaft fuer Operations Research. **VFOAT** O.R. Spektrum; Operations Research-Spektrum. Vol. 1, No. 1 (1979)-. Academic Scholarly Publication. English (German). Four times a year. DM298.00. Springer-Verlag GmbH & Company KG, Heidelberger Platz 3, D 14197 Berlin Germany. **Tel** 011 49 30 8207223, FAX 011 49 30 8214091, telex 183 319 SPBLN D. **(Subscription address:** Springer Verlag New York Inc. / for North America, 44 Hartz Way, Secaucus NJ 07096.) **ED** U Derigs. **LC** T57.6.A1; O7. **DD** 658.4/03/4. **CODEN** ORSPD5. **[CCC]. Pr Rev.** available on microfilm from University Microfilms International (UMI). Documents available from The Genuine Article, Ask*IEEE.
**Desc:** Of interest to those in technical school, economics, and management who deal with questions of operations research as results-oriented, scientific and technical tools of problem solving. Includes original articles, case studies and software reports.
**Ind/Abst** Compumath Citation Index [Full Cov.]; EMBASE; INSPEC (1979-); Int. Abstr. Oper. Res. [Full Cov.]; Math. Rev. (1984-); Oper. Res./Manag. Sci.; Qual. Control Appl. Stat.; Res. Alert [Full Cov.]; SCISEARCH; Soc. Sci. Cit. Index [Select. Cov.]; Stat. Theory Method Abstr. (1984); Zentralbl. Math. Ihre Grenzgeb.

SZ
## ORGAMATIK.
bm. 98.00F. Orgamatik, Loewenstr 16, CH-8021 Zuerich Switzerland.

PL/0078-6500
## ORGANON.
[Organon]. No. 1- 1964-. Multiple languages (French and English). ir. $6.25. **(Subscription address:** ARS Polona, PO Box 1001, 00068 Warsaw Poland.) **LC** Q9; .O7. **NLM** W1 OR663S. ***Supersedes*** *Organon, International Review.*
**Ind/Abst** Am. Hist. Life (1969-1972); Math. Rev.; Philos. Index.

US/0093-7495
## ORIGINS (LOMA LINDA).
(ORIGINS.). [Orig.]. **Added/Corp** Geoscience Research Institute, Loma Linda, Calif. Vol. 1, (1974)-. Periodical. English. Twice a year. $8.00. Geoscience Research Institute, Loma Linda University, Loma Linda CA 92350. **Tel** (909)824-4548, FAX (909)824-4314. **ED** Ariel A. Roth. **LC** BS651; .O7. **DD** 213/.05. **CODEN** ORIGD. Index available. **Bk Rev**, (Qty: 4). **Pr Rev. Circ:** 2100.
**Desc:** Publishes articles dealing with the broad question of origins, especially interpretations of science and the Bible.
**Ind/Abst** GeoRef.

FR/0758-833X
## ORSTOM ACTUALITES.
**Added/Corp** O.R.S.T.O.M. (Agency : France). No. 1 (Mar./Apr. 1984)-. French (summaries and/or abstracts in English and Spanish). ir. ORSTOM, 213, rue da la Fayette, 75010 Paris, France. **Tel** 011 48 03 7777, FAX DIST: 011 40 34 6913. **ED** Catherin Fontaine. **LC** WMLC 93/425; Q180.F7; O7. Index available. **Bk Rev**, (Qty: 20). **Circ:** 9,000 (ctrl). available on diskette.
**Ind/Abst** AgBiotech News Inf.; Biodeter. Abstr.; Plant Breed. Abstr.

JA/0386-4987
## OSAKA DENKI TSUSHIN DAIGAKU KENKYU RONSHU. SHIZEN KAGAKU HEN.
**VFOAT** Reports of Osaka Electro-Communication University. Natural Science. No. 1 (1965)-. Periodical. English (Japanese). Osaka Denki Tsushin Daigaku, 18-ban 8-go Hatsu-cho, Neyagawa-shi 572 Japan. **LC** Q4; .O79.

JA/0472-142X
## OSAKA KOGYO GIJUTSU SHIKENJO, KIHO.
(OSAKA KOGYO GIJUTSU SHIKENJO, KIHO. BULLETIN OF THE GOVERNMENT INDUSTRIAL RESEARCH INSTITUTE, OSAKA.). [Osaka Kogyo Gijutsu Shikenjo, kiho]. **Main/Corp** Osaka Kogyo Gijutsu Shikenjo. **Added/Corp** Osaka Kogyo Gijutsu Shikenjo. Bulletin of the Government Industrial Research Institute, Osaka. Osaka Kogyo Gijutsu Shikenjo. Bulletin of the Osaka Industrial Research Institute. **VFOAT** Bulletin of the Government Industrial Research Institute, Osaka. No. 4 (1953)-. Academic Scholarly Publication. Japanese (English). qt. $270.00. Kogyo Gijutsuin Osaka Kogyo Gijutsu Shikenjo, (Government Industrial Research Inst., Osaka, Agency of Industrial Science and Technology), 8-31, Midorigaoka 1 Chome, Ikedashi, Osakafu 563, Japan. **(Subscription address:** Maruzen Company Ltd., PO Box 5050, Import & Export Department, Tokyo 100 31 Japan.) **LC** TA4; .O86b. **DD** 605. **CODEN** OKGKAE. ctrl circ. Documents available from Ask*IEEE, CASDDS. ***Continues*** *Osaka Kogyo Gijutsu Shikenjo. Osaka Kogyo Shikenjo Kiho.*
**Desc:** Bulletin of the Government Industrial Research Institute of Osaka.
**Ind/Abst** Chem. Abstr.; Fluid Abstr., Civil Eng.; Fluid Abstr. Proc. Eng.; FLUIDEX (1973-); INSPEC (198?-).

PL
## OSIAGNIECIA NAUKOWO-BADAWCZE POLITECHNIKI GDANSKIEJ W ... ROKU / POLITECHNIKA GDANSKA.
Periodical. Polish. 40.00. **LC** T173.G37; O84. **DD** 670/.28.

US/0369-7827
**OSIRIS (BRUGES).** (OSIRIS.). [Osiris]. **Added/Corp** History of Science Society. Vol. 1 (Jan. 1936)-Vol. 15 (1968); 2nd Ser., Vol. 1 (1985)-. English (French). an. $39.00 (cloth), $25.00 (paperback). University of Chicago Press / Book Department, 11030 South Langley Avenue, Chicago IL 60628. **Tel** (800)621-2736, (312)568-1550, FAX (312)753-0811, telex 23933. **LC** Q1; .O7. **DD** 505. **NLM** W1 OS304. **CODEN** OSIRE3. Documents available from The Genuine Article, BIOSIS Document Express.
**Desc:** Presents major themes and research in the history of science and its cultural influences, including guest edited volumes on topics of wide interest to the history of science community and authoritative monographs by major scholars.
**Ind/Abst** Arts Humanit. Citation Index [Full Cov.]; Biol. Abstr. (1986-); Curr. Contents Arts Humanit.; Curr. Contents Soc. Behav. Sci.; Math. Rev. (1985-); Res. Alert [Full Cov.]; Soc. Sci. Cit. Index [Full Cov.].

IT
**OSSERVATORIO ISFOL. VFOAT** Osservatorio. **VAT** Osservatorio Istituto per lo Sviluppo della Formazione Professionaledei Lavoratori. Periodical. Italian. bm. ISFOL, Via Bartolomeo Eustachio 8, 00161 Rome Italy. **LC** T129; .O83. **DD** 745.2/071045. ***Continues*** *Osservatorio sul Mercato del Lavoro e delle Professioni, 0391-3775.*

US/0279-0025
**OSU QUEST. See** Education-Higher Education.

CN/0380-6251
**OTTAWA R & D REPORT. Added/Corp** Capital Communications Limited. (May 1970)-. Periodical. English. Twelve times a year. 125.00Can$. E L Littlejohn and Assoc. Ltd., Minto Pl Pstl Outlet, Box 56067, Ottawa Ontario K1R 7Z1 Canada. **Tel** (613)235-9183, FAX (613)594-3857. **ED** B. Wrangham. **CODEN** ODREE6. **Circ:** 150.
**Desc:** Canadian research and development news. Federal provincial governments, industry and university.

UK/0165-0262
**OUTLOOK ON SCIENCE POLICY. VFOAT** Outlook: Science Policy. Vol. 1 (June 1978)-. Periodical. English. mo (11 issues per year). £106.00. Beech Tree Publishing, 10 Waterford Close, Guildford Surrey GU1 2EP England. **Tel** +44 483 67497, FAX +44 0483 67497. **(Subscription address:** World-Wide Subscription Services, Unit 4, Gibbs Reed Farm Pashley Road, Ticehurst TN5 7HE England.**) NLM** W1 OU553H. Index available. **Circ:** 350.
**Desc:** News on science and technology policies, and reports internationally.

US/0030-8641
**PACIFIC DISCOVERY.** [Pac. discovery]. **Added/Corp** California Academy of Sciences. Vol. 1 (Jan./Feb. 1948)-. Periodical. English. qt. $12.95 US; $22.00 other. California Academy of Sciences, Golden Gate Park, San Francisco CA 94118. **Tel** (415)750-7344. **ED** Keith K Howell (editor's phone: (415)750-7117). **LC** Q1; .P15. **DD** 505. **CODEN** PADIAZ. Index available. **Bk Rev**, (Qty: 8-10). **Ad Acc, Adv Mgr:** Doug Corwin, **Tel** (415)750-7116. **Circ:** 35,000. available on microfilm from University Microfilms International (UMI). Documents available from BIOSIS Document Express.
**Desc:** Discoveries and new understandings in natural history and science research, mainly in the Pacific region.
**Ind/Abst** AGRICOLA; Aquat. Sci. Fish. Abstr. (Computer File); Biol. Abstr.; Calif. Period. Index (19??-); Ecol. Abstr. (?-?); Ocean. Abstr.; Life Sci. Collect.; Wildl. Rev.

US/0030-8870
**PACIFIC SCIENCE.** [Pac. sci.]. **Added/Corp** University of Hawaii (Honolulu). Vol. 1 (Jan. 1947)-. Periodical. English. qt (January, April, July and October). $50.00 (one year), $90.00 (two year) institution, $33.00 (one year), $59.00 (two year) individual, $13.00 (single issue), US; $55.00 (one year), $99.00 (two year) institution, $39.00 (one year), $70.00 (two year) individual, $14.00 (single issue) other. University of Hawaii Press, 2840 Kolowalu Street, Honolulu HI 96822. **Tel** (808)956-8833, (808)948-8697, FAX (808)988-6052. **ED** E. Alison Kay. **LC** QH1; .P2. **DD** 574.05. **CODEN** PASCAP. **Ad Acc. Circ:** 780. available on microfilm and microfiche from University Microfilms International (UMI). Documents available from BIOSIS Document Express, CASDDS.
**Desc:** Multidisciplinary journal devoted to reporting research in biological and physical sciences, with a focus in the Pacific basin. Features review articles providing a synthesis of current knowledge.
**Ind/Abst** AGRICOLA; Biocont. News Inf.; Biodeter. Abstr.; Biol. Abstr.; Chem. Abstr.; Ecol. Abstr.; Ecology Abstr.; Environ. Period. Bibliogr.; Fish Rev.; Geogr. Abstr. Phys. Geogr.; Geol. Abstr.; GeoRef; Int. Aerosp. Abstr.; Nematol. Abstr.; Ocean. Abstr.; Life Sci. Collect.; Rev. Med. Vet. Entomol.; Soils Fert.; Wildl. Rev.

PK/0030-9877
**PAKISTAN JOURNAL OF SCIENCE.** [Pak. j. sci.]. Vol. 1, (Jan. 1949)-. Periodical. English. qt. Rs40.00 Pakistan; $25.00 US. Pakistan Association for Advancement of Science, 273-N, Model Town, Lahore Pakistan. **Tel** 835712. **ED** Ghulam Rasool Chaudhry. **LC** Q73; .P26. **DD** 506.254. **NLM** W1 PA357. **CODEN** PAJSAS. Index available. **Ad Acc. Circ:** 1,000. Documents available from BIOSIS Document Express, Ask*IEEE, CASDDS. ***Continued in part by*** *Pakistan Journal of Scientific Research, 0552-9050.*
**Desc:** A research journal devoted to general scientific articles and dissemination of scientific information.
**Ind/Abst** AGRICOLA; Biol. Abstr.; Chem. Abstr.; Food Sci. Technol. Abstr.; GeoRef; INSPEC (1968-); Meteorol. Geoastrophys. Abstr. (-199?); Life Sci. Collect.; Surf. Treat. Technol. Abstr.

PK/0030-9885
**PAKISTAN JOURNAL OF SCIENTIFIC AND INDUSTRIAL RESEARCH.** [Pak. j. sci. ind. res.]. **Added/Corp** Pakistan Council of Scientific and Industrial Research. Vol. 1 (Jan. 1958)-. Academic Scholarly Publication. English. Twelve times a year. $168.00. PCSIR Scientific Information Directorate, 39 Garden Road Saddar, Karachi 74400 Pakistan. **Tel** 011 92 21 7725943, 011 92 21 7762033, FAX 011 92 21 2636704, telex 27425. **ED** Dr. J.N. Usmani. **LC** Q180.A1; P33. **DD** 507.2. **NLM** W1 PA357R. **CODEN** PSIRAA. **Bk Rev. Ad Acc, Adv Mgr:** Dr. J. N. Usmani, **Tel** 7725943. **Pr Rev. Circ:** 500. available on microfilm from University Microfilms International (UMI); available on microfiche from University Microfilms International (UMI). Documents available from BIOSIS Document Express, Ask*IEEE, CASDDS.
**Ind/Abst** AgBiotech News Inf.; AGRICOLA; Agric. Eng. Abstr. (1991-); Agrofor. Abstr. (1991-); BioBusiness (-1990); Biodeter. Abstr. (19??-19??); Biol. Abstr.; Ceram. Abstr.; Chem. Abstr.; Chemorecept. Abstr.; Cot. Trop. Fibr. Abstr. Bibliogr.; Crop Physiol. Abstr.; Curr. Biotechnol.; Dairy Sci. Abstr.; Ecol. Abstr.; EMBASE; Field Crop Abstr.; Fish Rev.; Food Sci. Technol. Abstr.; For. Prod. Abstr. (1991-); For. Abstr.; Geogr. Abstr. Phys. Geogr.; Geogr. Abstr. Human Geogr.; Geol. Abstr.; GeoRef; Hortic. Abstr.; INSPEC (1968-); Int. Dev. Abstr.; Irr. Drain. Abstr.; Maize Abstr.; Microbiol. Abstr. Sect. B (19??-19??); Microbiol. Abstr. Sect. A; Microbiol. Abstr. Sect. C; Nematol. Abstr.; Nutr. Abstr. Rev., Ser. B, Live Feeds and Feed.; Life Sci. Collect.; Plant Breed. Abstr.; Plant Grow. Reg. Abstr.; Postharvest News Inf.; Poult. Abstr.; Rev. Agric. Entomol.; Rev. Med. Vet. Entomol.; Rev. Med. Vet. Mycology; Rev. Plant Pathol.; Rice Abstr.; SEA Abstr.; Seed Abstr.; Soils Fert.; Sorghum Mill. Abstr.; Soyabean Abstr.; Sug. Indus. Abstr.; Wildl. Rev.

PK/0552-9050
**PAKISTAN JOURNAL OF SCIENTIFIC RESEARCH.** [Pak. j. sci. res.]. Vol. 1, (Jan. 1949)-. Periodical. English. qt. $25.00. Pakistan Association for the Advancement of Science, 273-N, Model Town, Lahore Pakistan. **Tel** 835712. **ED** Dr. Ghulam Rasool Chaudhry. **LC** Q180.P25; P2. **DD** 505. **NLM** W1 PA358. **CODEN** PJSRAV. Index available. cum. index. **Bk Rev. Ad Acc. Pr Rev. Circ:** 1000 (ctrl). Documents available from Ask*IEEE, CASDDS. ***Continues in part*** *Pakistan Journal of Science.*
**Ind/Abst** Ceram. Abstr. (19??-); Chem. Abstr.; Food Sci. Technol. Abstr.; INSPEC (1968-); Life Sci. Collect.; Poult. Abstr.

II/0377-9386
**PANTNAGAR JOURNAL OF RESEARCH.** [Pantnagar j. res.]. V. 1- Jan. 1976-. Academic Scholarly Publication. English. 10. Business Manager of the University Book Depot, Govind Ballabh Pant, University of Agriculture and Technology, Pantnagar 263145 District Naini Tal Uttar Pradesh India. **CODEN** PJREDO. Documents available from CASDDS.
**Ind/Abst** Chem. Abstr. (1976-1979).

AT/0080-4703
**PAPERS AND PROCEEDINGS OF THE ROYAL SOCIETY OF TASMANIA.** [Pap. proc. R. Soc. Tasmania]. **Main/Corp** Royal Society of Tasmania. Vol. 1 (1863)-. English. an (Nov.). 30.00Aus$. Royal Society of Tasmania, GPO Box 1166M, Hobart Tasmania 7001 Australia. **Tel** 002 350777, FAX 002 347139. **ED** M. R. Banks. **LC** Q93; .T2. **CODEN** PPRTA6. **Circ:** 700 (ctrl). Documents available from BIOSIS Document Express. ***Supersedes*** *Papers and Proceedings of The Royal Society of Van Diemen's Land.*
**Desc:** Scientific publication.
**Ind/Abst** AESIS Q.; Art Archaeol. Tech. Abstr.; Biol. Abstr.; Ecol. Abstr. (?-?); Geogr. Abstr. Phys. Geogr. (?-?); Geogr. Abstr. Human Geogr. (?-?); Geol. Abstr.; GeoRef; Math. Rev.; Life Sci. Collect.; Vitis Vitic. Enol. Abstr.

US
**PARTIALLY ORDERED SYSTEMS.** (1991)-. English. Three times a year. $69.00. Springer-Verlag New York Inc., 175 5th Avenue, New York NY 10010. **Tel** (212)460-1500, telex 232 235 SPB UR. **(Subscription address:** Springer Verlag New York Inc. / for North America, 44 Hartz Way, Secaucus NJ 07096.**)**
**Desc:** The study of partially ordered systems tends to cut across the conventional boundaries of separating physics, chemistry, and biology, and is by its nature interdisciplinary.

CN/1185-1953
**PARTNERS (KANATA).** (PARTNERS.). [Partners]. **Added/Corp** Ottawa-Carleton Learning Foundation. Ottawa Carleton Research Institute. Vol. 1, No. 1 (Mar. 1990)-. Periodical. English. qt. Ottawa-Carleton Learning Foundation, Suite 401, 340 March Road, Kanata, Ontario K2K 2E4 Canada. **DD** 607/.71383/05.
**Ind/Abst** Trop. Dis. Bull.

US
**PB - U.S. CLEARINGHOUSE FOR FEDERAL SCIENTIFIC AND TECHNICAL INFORMATION.** ***Title Change.*** **Main/Corp** Clearinghouse for Federal Scientific and Technical Information (U.S.). No. 164496-190196(?). Periodical. English. ***Continues*** *U.S. Office of Technical Service. PB.* ***Continued by*** *PB.*

●US/1059-1990
**PBC SCIENCE BRIEFS. VFOAT** Science Briefs. **VAT** Publishing and Business Consultants Science Briefs. (1993)-. English. qt. Publishing & Business Consultants, PO Box 75392, Los Angeles CA 90075. **Tel** (213)732-3477, FAX (213)732-9123.

IT
**PCB MAGAZINE.** Italian. L99000 Italy; L200000 other. Gruppo Editoriale JCE SRL, Via Ferri 6, 20092 Cinisello B Milan Italy. **Tel** 011 39 2 660251, FAX 011 39 2 66025343.

US/1065-0261
**PENNSYLVANIA BUSINESS AND TECHNOLOGY.** [Pa. bus. technol.]. **Added/Corp** Pittsburgh High Technology Council (Pa.) Pennsylvania Technology Council. **VFOAT** Business and Technology. Vol. 2, No. 4 (4th Quarter 1991)-. Periodical. English. qt. $19.95. Pittsburgh High Technology Council, 4516 Henry Street, Pittsburgh PA 15213. **Tel** (412)687-2700. **DD** 338. Documents available from UMI Article Clearinghouse. ***Continues*** *Pennsylvania Technology.*
**Ind/Abst** Bus. Dateline (Jan. 1992-) [Full Txt.].

●US
**PENNSYLVANIA TECHNOLOGY DIRECTORY. Added/Corp** Pennsylvania Technology Council. Corporate Technology Information Services. (1992)-. Directory. English. Pittsburgh High Technology Council, 4516 Henry Street, Pittsburgh PA 15213. **Tel** (412)687-2700. **LC** HC107.P43; H536. **DD** 338.7/62/00025748. ***Continues*** *Pennsylvania High-Tech Directory.*

US/0098-776X
**PENSEE (PORTLAND).** (PENSEE.). [Pensee]. Began with Feb. 1971 issue. Periodical. English. qt. $10.00. Student Academic Freedom Forum, Po Box 414, Portland OR 97207. **LC** Q1; .P4. **DD** 505. **CODEN** PNSEAK. Documents available from The Genuine Article.
**Ind/Abst** Am. Hist. Life (1954-1974,1977-1978,1986-); Arts Humanit. Citation Index [Full Cov.]; Curr. Contents Arts Humanit.; GeoRef; Int. Aerosp. Abstr.; Res. Alert [Full Cov.]; Soc. Sci. Cit. Index [Select. Cov.].

MX/0185-1004
**PERIODICA. See** Science and Technology-Abstracting, Bibliographies and Statistics.

US/0891-3889
**PERIODICALS SCANNED AND ABSTRACTED. LIFE SCIENCES COLLECTION. See** Science and Technology-Abstracting, Bibliographies and Statistics.

FR/0298-9018
**PERISCOPE. SPHERES.** (PERISCOPE.). [Perisc., Spheres]. (1983)-. Monographic series. French. Ten times a year. 280.12F EEC Countries; 277.18F France; 358.94F French Overseas Dept.; 333.90F French Overseas Territories; 271.00F others. PEMF Publ de l Ecole Moderne Francaise, 06376 Mouans Sartoux CX France. **Tel** 011 33 92 921757. **UDC** 5 (03).

UK/0309-2690
**PERKIN-ELMER ANALYTICAL NEWS.** [Perkin-Elmer anal. news]. **VFOAT** Analytical News. (1970)-. Academic Scholarly Publication. English. **CODEN** PKANA4. Documents available from CASDDS.
**Ind/Abst** Anal. Abstr.; Chem. Abstr.

●US/1063-6145
**PERSPECTIVES ON SCIENCE.** (PERSPECTIVES ON SCIENCE: HISTORICAL, PHILOSOPHICAL, SOCIAL.). [Perspect. sci.]. **VFOAT** Perspectives on Science, Historical, Philosophical, Social. Vol. 1, No. 1 (Spring 1993)-. Periodical. English. qt (4 issues). $77.00 (institutions), $37.00 (individuals), $26.00 (students). University of Chicago Press / Journals Division, PO Box 37005, 5720 South Woodlawn, Chicago IL 60637. **Tel** (312)753-3347, FAX (312)753-0811. **(Subscription telephone:** (312)753-8083**) ED** Joseph C. Pitt. **LC** IN PROCESS; Q124.6; .P37. **DD** 500. **Ad Acc. Acid Free.**
**Desc:** Devoted to studies of the sciences that integrated historical, philosophical, and sociological perspectives. Its interdisciplinary approach is intended to foster a more comprehensive understanding of the sciences and the contexts in which they develop.

US/0892-2675
**PERSPECTIVES ON SCIENCE AND CHRISTIAN FAITH.** **See** Religion and Theology.

GW/0933-1271
**PERSPEKTIVEN DER FORSCHUNG UND IHRER FORDERUNG / DFG, DEUTSCHE FORSCHUNGSGEMEINSCHAFT.**
**Added/Corp** Deutsche Forschungsgemeinschaft. **VFOAT** Aufgaben und Finanzierung. 1990-. Periodical. German. VCH Gesellschaft GmbH, Postfach 101161, D 69451 Weinheim Germany. **Tel** 011 49 6201 606459, FAX 011 49 6201 606184. **(Subscription address:** VCH Publishers Inc., 303 Northwest 12th Avenue, Journals Department, Deerfield FL 33442.**)** ***Continues*** *Aufgaben und Finanzierung, 0418-8403.*

BL/0101-7438
**PESQUISA OPERACIONAL.** Periodical. Portuguese.
**Ind/Abst** Int. Abstr. Oper. Res. [Select. Cov.].

PH/0031-7683
**PHILIPPINE JOURNAL OF SCIENCE, THE.** [Philipp. j. sci.]. Vol. 1 (Jan. 1906)-. Periodical. English. Four times a year. $80.00. Science and Technology Information Institute, PO Box 2131, Manila Philippines. **Tel** 011 63 2 822 0961. **LC** Q75; .P51. **DD** 505. **NLM** W1 PH575. **CODEN** PJSCAK. Index available in last issue of volume--attached. cum. index. **Bk Rev. Circ:** 1,000. Documents available from BIOSIS Document Express, CASDDS. ***Supersedes*** *Publications / Philippines. Bureau of Government Laboratories.*
**Desc:** A publication designed for both technical and general audiences.
**Ind/Abst** AGRICOLA; Biocont. News Inf.; Biodeter. Abstr.; Biol. Abstr.; Ceram. Abstr.; Chem. Abstr.; EMBASE; Fish Rev.; Food Sci. Technol. Abstr.; GeoRef; Index Philip. Period. (-199?); Philip. Sci. Technol. Abstr.; Plant Grow. Reg. Abstr.; Rev. Med. Vet. Entomol.; Rev. Plant Pathol.; Rice Abstr.; Wildl. Rev.

PH/0115-8724
**PHILIPPINE SCIENCE & TECHNOLOGY ABSTRACTS.** **See** Science and Technology-Abstracting, Bibliographies and Statistics.

PH
**PHILIPPINE TECHNICAL INFORMATION SHEETS.** English. Science and Technology Information Institute, PO Box 2131, Manila Philippines. **Tel** 011 63 2 822 0961.
**Desc:** Compiled articles that lend to the state-of-the-art information, on selected Philippine science and technology.

PH/0116-7294
**PHILIPPINE TECHNOLOGY JOURNAL.** Vol. 12, No. 1 (Jan./March 1987)-. Periodical. English. qt. P160.00 Philippines; $28.00 (surface mail), $32.00 (airmail) other. Science and Technology Information Institute, PO Box 2131, Manila Philippines. **Tel** 011 63 2 822 0961. **CODEN** PTEJEB. **Bk Rev. Ad Acc. Circ:** 2,000. ***Continues*** *NSTA Technology Journal, 0115-9275.*
**Desc:** Devoted to a range of interdisciplinary fields, particularly those exemplifying various relevant technologies. Serves as a major medium for applied and technology researches.

NE/0165-5817
**PHILIPS JOURNAL OF RESEARCH.** **See** Engineering-Electricity, Electrical Engineering, Electronics.

NE
**PHILIPS TECHNISCH TIJDSCHRIFT.** ***Ceased.*** ( )-Vol. 44 (?). Periodical. Dutch. Twelve times a year. Philips Research Laboratories, PO Box 80000, 5600 JA Eindhoven The Netherlands. **Tel** 081-594-7272, FAX 081-594-5942, telex 896950. **LC** T4; .P5. Index available. cum. index. **Circ:** 1,900 (ctrl).
**Desc:** General, technical and scientific journal; Dutch edition of Philips Technical Review.

RU
**PHILOSOPHICAL AND SOCIAL ASPECTS OF SCIENCE AND TECHNOLOGY SERIES / USSR ACADEMY OF SCIENCES, THE SCIENTIFIC COUNCIL FOR PHILOSOPHICAL AND SOCIAL ASPECTS OF SCIENCE AND TECHNOLOGY.** **Added/Corp** Nauchnyi Sovet po Filosofskim i Sotsialnym Problemam Nauki i Tekhniki (Akademiia Nauk SSSR). **VFOAT** Philosophical and Social Aspects of Science and Technology. (1987)-. Monographic series. English. Price varies per volume. Social Sciences Today Editorial Board, Academy of Sciences, 33/12 Arbat, Moscow 121002 Russia. **Tel** 241-09-06.

US/0277-2434
**PHILOSOPHY IN SCIENCE.** [Philos. sci.]. **Added/Corp** Specola Vaticana. Center for Interdisciplinary Studies. Papieska Akademia Teologiczna (Krakow, Poland). (1983)-. Periodical. English. ir. $48.00. Pachart Publishing House, Pachart Foundation, 1130 San Lucas Circle, PO Box 35549, Tucson AZ 85740. **Tel** (602)297-4797, FAX (602)297-4797. **ED** M. Heller, W. R. Stoeger, S. J. Zycinski, and J. M. Zycinski. **LC** Q174; .P565. **DD** 501. **Bk Rev.**
**Desc:** Aims to foster the development and understanding of philosophical questions as they are encountered within the sciences and seeks to promote mutually enriching dialogue at the professional level among scientists, philosophers and philosophers of science.
**Ind/Abst** Philos. Index.

US/0163-0881
**PHILOSOPHY OF SCIENCE ASSOCIATION NEWSLETTER.** ***Ceased.***
**Main/Corp** Philosophy of Science Association. **VFOAT** Newsletter. (197?)-(1992). Newsletter. English. qt. Michigan State University Philosophy Department, East Lansing MI 48823. **Tel** (517)353-9392. **ED** Paul Tang. **Circ:** 850 (ctrl).
**Desc:** Provides a channel for communication of such information as grants, conferences, new periodicals and bibliographic notes.

US/0031-8248
**PHILOSOPHY OF SCIENCE (EAST LANSING).** (PHILOSOPHY OF SCIENCE.). [Philos. sci.]. Vol. 1 (Jan. 1934)-. Periodical. English. qt. $60.00 US; $65.00 other. Philosophy of Science Association, 18 Morrill Hall, Department of Philosophy, East Lansing MI 48824. **Tel** (517)353-9392. **ED** Robert E Butts. **LC** Q1. **DD** 505. **NLM** W1 PH619. **CODEN** PHSCA6. **[CCC].** Index available. **Bk Rev. Ad Acc. Pr Rev. Circ:** 2,200 (ctrl). available on microfilm and microfiche from University Microfilms International (UMI). Documents available from The Genuine Article, BIOSIS Document Express, Ask*IEEE, UMI Article Clearinghouse.
**Desc:** Carries essays, discussion articles, and book reviews in the general area of philosophy of science.
**Ind/Abst** Acad. Search (July 1993-); Arts Humanit. Citation Index [Full Cov.]; Biol. Abstr.; Curr. Contents Arts Humanit.; Curr. Contents Soc. Behav. Sci.; Curr. Lit. Sci. Sci.; Expand. Acad. Index (1989-); Gen. Sci. Source (Jul. 1993-); Humanit. Index; Humanit. Source (Jul. 1993-); INFO-SOUTH Abstr.; INSPEC (June 1972-); Mag. Search; Math. Rev.; Newsp. Period. Abstr. (1991-); Philos. Index; Res. Alert [Full Cov.]; Soc. Plann. Policy Dev. Abstr.; Soc. Sci. Cit. Index [Full Cov.]; Sociol. Abstr.

GR
**PHONE TES PROODOU.** Periodical. Greek, Modern. 5.00. D Kounousos, Kratinou 7, Athens Greece. **LC** Q4; .P49.

US
**PHYSICAL SCIENCES ON FILE.** (19??)-. English. $155.00. Facts on File Publications, 460 Park Avenue South, New York NY 10016. **Tel** (212)683-2244, (800)322-8755, FAX (212)683-3633, telex 238 552 FACTS UR. available with illustrations.
**Desc:** Provides instructive information on units of measurements, force and energy, waves, sound and light, electricity, electronics, structure of matter, chemistry of carbon, changes in matter, patterns matter: nonmetals, patters in matter: metals and chemical reactions.

IT/0031-9414
**PHYSIS (FIRENZE).** (PHYSIS.). [Physis]. Vol. 1 (1959)-. Periodical. Italian. tq. L90000 (Italy); L115000 (other). Casa Editrice Leo S. Olschki, Viuzzo del Pozzetto, Casella Postale 66, 50126 Florence Italy. **Tel** 011 39 55 6530684, FAX 011 39 55 6530214. **LC** Q54; .P53. **NLM** W1 PH986H. **CODEN** PYSSA3.
**Ind/Abst** Am. Hist. Life (1964-); Math. Rev.

US
**PITTSBURGH SERIES IN PHILOSOPHY AND HISTORY OF SCIENCE.** (19??)-. Monographic series. English. ir. price varies per volume. University of California Press, 2120 Berkeley Way, Berkeley CA 94720. **Tel** (510)642-4191, (510)642-3907, FAX (510)642-9917.

US/1049-8052
**PIXEL (WATSONVILLE, CALIF.).** ***Suspended.*** **See** Computers-Computer Graphics and Design.

US/1051-9998
**PLASMA DEVICES AND OPERATIONS.** [Plasma devices oper.]. Vol. 1, No. 1 (Dec. 1990)-. Periodical. English. ir (4 issues per volume). $444.00 (university and hospital libraries), $693.00 other. Gordon & Breach Science Publishers, Inc., PO Box 786, Cooper Station, New York NY 10276. **Tel** (212)206-8900, FAX (212)645-2459. **(Subscription address:** Gordon & Breach Science Publishers / England, PO Box 90, Reading RG1 8JL England.**)** **LC** TA2001; .P58. **DD** 621.48/5. **CODEN** PDOPEZ. **[CCC].**

UK
**PLI KNOW HOW.** No. 106- Feb. 1973-. Periodical. English. mo. £10.50. **LC** TS1; .I5162. **DD** 608/.7. ***Continues*** *Product Licensing Index.*

XR/0032-2423
**POKROKY MATEMATIKY, FYSIKY A ASTRONOMIE.** [Pokr. mat., fys. astron.].
**Added/Corp** Jednota Ceskoslovenskych Matematiku a Fysiku v Praze. Vol. 1 (1956)-. Academic Scholarly Publication. Czech (Slovak). bm. DM152.00. Academia, Publishing House of the Czechoslovak Academy of Sciences, Czech AC SCI, Vodickova 40, PO Box 896, 112 29 Prague 1, Czech Republic. **Tel** 011 42 2 245117. **(Subscription address:** Kubon & Sagner, ABT Zeitschriftenimport, D 80328 Munich Germany.**)** **ED** O. Kowalski, M. Rozsival. **LC** Q44.J3; A25. **CODEN** PMFAA4. Index available. **Bk Rev. Circ:** 7,500 (ctrl). Documents available from CASDDS.
**Desc:** Publishes articles on advances in the above named scientific fields; modern trends in the teaching of mathematics and physics; and the history and philosophy of science.
**Ind/Abst** Chem. Abstr. (1956-1983); Int. Aerosp. Abstr.; Math. Rev.; Zentralbl. Math. Ihre Grenzgeb.

UK/0032-2474
**POLAR RECORD, THE.** [Polar rec.].
**Added/Corp** Scott Polar Research Institute. Vol. 1, No. 1 (Jan. 1931)-. Academic Scholarly Publication. English. qt. $120.00 US, Canada and Mexico; £66.00 other. Cambridge University Press, The Edinburgh Building, Shaftesbury Road, Cambridge CB2 2RU United Kingdom. **Tel** 011 44 223 312393, FAX 011 44 223 325959. **(Subscription address:** Cambridge University Press / North America, 110 Midland Avenue, Port Chester NY 10573.**)** **ED** Bernard Stonehouse. **LC** G575; .P6. **DD** 919.8. **CODEN** POLRAV. Index available. cum. index. **Bk Rev. Ad Acc. Pr Rev. Circ:** 1,200 (ctrl). available on microfilm and microfiche from University Microfilms International (UMI). Documents available from BIOSIS Document Express, CASDDS, Documents on Demand.
**Desc:** Covers both polar regions and caters to a wide range of interests from anthropology through archaeology, art, botany, history, geography, geology, glaciology, law, medicine, oceanography, politics, psychology and sociology to zoology. Articles and notes are authoritative but non-technical. Some provide historical perspective, others up-to-date views on current polar affairs and happenings, or reports on recent exploration and research.
**Ind/Abst** ASTIS Curr. Aware. Bull. (1978-); Am. Hist. Life (1964-); AQUAREF; Aquat. Sci. Fish. Abstr. (Computer File); ASTIS Bibliogr. (1978-); Biol. Abstr. (1991-); Chem. Abstr.; Curr. Aware. Biol. Sci., CABS; Curr. Geogr. Publ. (199?-); Ecol. Abstr.; Ecology Abstr.; Energy Inf. Abstr.; Environ. Abstr.; Environ. Period. Bibliogr.; Geogr. Abstr. Phys. Geogr.; Geogr. Abstr. Human Geogr.; Geol. Abstr.; GeoRef; Int. Aerosp. Abstr.; Int. Polit. Sci. Abstr.; Meteorol. Geoastrophys. Abstr.; Ocean. Abstr.; Life Sci. Collect.

GW/0032-2490
**POLARFORSCHUNG.** [Polarforschung].
**Added/Corp** Deutsche Gesellschaft fuer Polarforschung. Archiv fuer Polarforschung in Kiel. Deutsche Archiv fuer Polarforschung. Vereinigung zur Foerderung des Archivs fuer Polarforschung, Kiel. Vol. 1 (1931)-. Periodical. German (English). Three times a year. DM120.00. Duetsche ges Polarforschung EV / Alfred Wegener Institut, Kolumbusst, D 27580 Bremerhaven Germany. **Tel** 471-4831169. **ED** D. Futterer and E. Treude. **LC** G600; .P6. **DD** 998/.005; 919.8. **CODEN** POLFAT. Index available. **Bk Rev. Circ:** 800 (ctrl).
**Desc:** Covers all aspects of polar research.
**Ind/Abst** ASTIS Curr. Aware. Bull. (1978-); AQUAREF (19??-19??); ASTIS Bibliogr. (1978-); Ecology Abstr.; Geogr. Abstr. Phys. Geogr. (?-?); GeoRef; Key Word Index Wildl. Res.; Ocean. Abstr.

PL/0138-0338
**POLISH POLAR RESEARCH.** (POLISH POLAR RESEARCH / POLISH ACADEMY OF SCIENCES / POLSKIE BADANIA POLARNE / POLSKA AKADEMIA NAUK.). [Pol. polar res.]. **Added/Corp** Polska Akademia Nauk. Komitet Badan Polarnych. **VFOAT** Polskie Badania Polarne. Vol. 1, No. 1 (1980)-. Periodical. English (summaries and/or abstracts in Polish and Russian). Four times a year. $60.00. Polish Academy of Sciences, Institute of Philosophy and Sociology, Nowy Swiat, Warsaw Poland. **(Subscription address:** ARS Polona, PO Box 1001, 00068 Warsaw Poland.**)** **LC** G575; .P66. **DD** 919.8/005. **Bk Rev. Ad Acc. Circ:** 650 (ctrl).
**Desc:** Theory, practice, collection, elaboration, and finding classification of scientific information, library science, librarianship, and languages of information.
**Ind/Abst** Ecol. Abstr.; Ecology Abstr.; Geogr. Abstr. Phys. Geogr.; Geol. Abstr.; Ocean. Abstr.; Life Sci. Collect.

PL/0032-3004
**POLISH TECHNICAL AND ECONOMIC ABSTRACTS.** **See** Economics.

PL/0032-3012
**POLISH TECHNICAL REVIEW.** [Pol. tech. rev.]. (1964)-. Academic Scholarly Publication. English. bm. $90.00. Ruch, Wronia 33, Warsaw Poland. **LC** T26.P5; P6. **CODEN** PTRWA9. Documents available from Ask*IEEE, CASDDS.
**Ind/Abst** Alum. Ind. Abstr.; Chem. Abstr.; Coal Abstr.; EMBASE; Eng. Mater. Abstr.; INSPEC (1971-); Met. Abstr.; Surf. Treat. Technol. Abstr.

SZ
**POLITIQUE DE LA SCIENCE.** (1972)-. Periodical. French. Office Federal Education Science, PO Box 2732, Wildhainweg 9, CH-3001 Berne Switzerland.

NE
**POLYTECHNISCHE TIJDSCHRIFT.** H. Stam Tydshriften N.V., Postbus 375, Caregielpein 5, The Hague Netherlands.
**Ind/Abst** Concr. Abstr.

US/0032-4558
**POPULAR MECHANICS (NEW YORK. 1959).** (POPULAR MECHANICS.). [Pop. mech.]. Vol. 112, No. 2 (Aug. 1959)-. Periodical. English. mo. $15.94. The Hearst Corporation, 250 West 55th Street, New York NY 10019. **Tel** (212)649-4014. **(Subscription address:** CDS Agency Hard Copy, PO Box 4966, Des Moines IA 50340.**) LC** T1; .P77. **DD** 605. **Ad Acc.** available on microfilm and microfiche from University Microfilms International (UMI); available on an online database (file 647/Full-Text) from DIALOG. Documents available from UMI Article Clearinghouse, Magazine Collection. ***Continues*** *Popular Mechanics Magazine, 0736-993X.*
**Ind/Abst** Abr. Read. Guide Period. Lit.; Acad. Abstr. Full Text Elite (Jan. 1984-); Acad. Abstr. (Jan. 1984-); Acad. Ind. [Computer File] (1984-1988); Acad. Search (Jan. 1984-); Can. Index (?-?); Can. Period. Index (19??-); Coal Abstr.; Consum. Index Prod. Eval. Inf. Source; Energy Res. Abstr. (July 1976-); Expand. Acad. Index (1984-); Gen. Period. Index (1985-); Highw. Res. Abstr.; Index Inf.; INFO-SOUTH Abstr.; Mag. Artic. Summar. Elite (Feb. 1984-); Mag. Artic. Summar. Select (Feb. 1984-); Mag. Artic. Summar. CD-ROM (Jan. 1984-); Mag. Express (1986-) [Full Txt.]; Mag. Index Plus (1989-); Mag. Index Sel. Microfiche (1986-) [Full Txt.]; Mag. Index. Sel. (1986-); Mag. Search; Mid. Search (Jan. 1984-); Newsp. Period. Abstr. (1986-); Read. Guide Abstr. Select Ed.; Read. Guide Period. Lit.; Resource/One Ondisc; Mag. Index (1977-); TOM Gen. Index (1985-) [Full Txt.]; Vocat. Search (Jan. 1984-).

US/0161-7370
**POPULAR SCIENCE (NEW YORK, N.Y.).** (POPULAR SCIENCE.). [Pop. sci.]. **VFOAT** Popular Science Monthly. Vol. 157, No. 1 (July 1950)-. Periodical. English. mo. $13.94 (one year), $24.97 (two year), $36.97 (three year). Times Mirror Magazines, Two Park Avenue, New York NY 10016. **Tel** (212)779-5000. **(Subscription address:** CDS Agency Hard Copy, PO Box 4966, Des Moines IA 50340.**) ED** Ken Gilmore. **LC** AP2; .P8. **DD** 505. **CODEN** PSCIEP. **[CCC]. Ad Acc.** available on microfilm and microfiche from University Microfilms International (UMI); available on an online database (file 647/Full-Text) from DIALOG. Documents available from UMI Article Clearinghouse, Magazine Collection. ***Continues*** *Popular Science Monthly (New York, N.Y. : 1900).*
**Desc:** The "what's new" magazine of science and technology. Covers energy, new products for the home, work, and leisure. Provides easy-to-follow blueprints for projects you can build yourself, and test reports on new cars, electronics, cameras, and more.
**Ind/Abst** Abr. Read. Guide Period. Lit.; Acad. Abstr. Full Text Elite (Jan. 1984-) [Full Txt.]; Acad. Abstr. (Jan. 1984-); Acad. Ind. [Computer File] (1984-1988); Acad. Search (Jan. 1984-); Can. Index (?-?); Can. Period. Index (19??-); Coal Abstr.; Consum. Index Prod. Eval. Inf. Source; Energy Inf. Abstr.; Energy Res. Abstr. (Aug. 1976-); Expand. Acad. Index (1984-1988); Gen. Period. Index (1985-); Gen. Sci. Index; Gen. Sci. Source (Jan. 1988-) [Full Txt.]; Health Source (Jan. 1984-); Index Inf.; INFO-SOUTH Abstr.; Mag. Artic. Summar. Elite (Jan. 1984-) [Full Txt.]; Mag. Artic. Summar. Select (Jan. 1984-) [Full Txt.]; Mag. Artic. Summar. CD-ROM (Jan. 1984-); Mag. Express (1986-) [Full Txt.]; Mag. Index Plus (1989-); Mag. Index Sel. Microfiche (1986-) [Full Txt.]; Mag. Index. Sel. (1986-); Mag. Search; Mid. Search (Jan. 1984-); Newsp. Period. Abstr. (1986-); Prim. Search (Jan. 1984-); Read. Guide Abstr. Select Ed.; Read. Guide Period. Lit.; Resource/One Ondisc; Mag. Index (1977-); TOM Gen. Index (1985-) [Full Txt.]; Vocat. Search (Jan. 1984-) [Full Txt.].

US/0360-0297
**POPULAR SCIENCE SERIES.** [Pop. sci. ser.]. Vol. 1. Monographic series. English. ir. Price varies per volume. Illinois State Museum, Spring and Edwards Street, Springfield IL 62706. **Tel** (217)782-7386, FAX (217)782-1254. **DD** 500.
**Desc:** Nontechnical books on natural history with special emphasis on Illinois, for general reading and field study.
**Ind/Abst** GeoRef.

JA
**POPYURA SAIENSU.** **VFOAT** Popular Science. Periodical. Japanese (Japanese). mo. ¥710 each issue. Daiyamondo Sha, (Diamond Inc.), 4-2 1-chome Kasumigaseki, Chiyoda-ku Tokyoto 100 Japan. **LC** Q4; .P62.

GW
**PORTUGAL, FORSCHUNGSPOLITIK UND FORSCHUNGSPRAXIS / BUNDESSTELLE FUER AUSSENHANDELSINFORMATION.** German. DM3.00. Bundesstelle fuer Aussenhandelsinformation, Agrippastr 87 93, D 50676 Cologne Germany. **Tel** 011 49 221 2057316, FAX 011 49 221 2057212. **LC** Q180.P6; P67. **DD** 507/.20469.

KE/0253-5963
**POST, KENYA.** [POST, Kenya]. **VAT** Promotion of Science and Technology Kenya. Vol. 1 (Jan. 1973)-. Academic Scholarly Publication. English. Free. Kenya National Academy, PO Box 47288, Nairobi Kenya. **Tel** 721138. **ED** J K G Mati. **LC** Q225; .P67. **DD** 509/.676/2. **CODEN** POKEDO. **Bk Rev. Ad Acc. Circ:** 4,000. Documents available from CASDDS.
**Desc:** A magazine for promoting science and technology through young people by inculcating scientific attitudes.
**Ind/Abst** Chem. Abstr.

FR/0153-4092
**POUR LA SCIENCE.** [Science]. (Nov. 1977)-. Periodical. French. mo. 325.00F. Pour la Science, 8 rue Ferou, 75006 Paris France. **ED** P. Boulanger. **Bk Rev. Ad Acc. Circ:** 60,000.
**Desc:** The French translation of Scientific American.
**Ind/Abst** Alum. Ind. Abstr.; Coal Abstr.; Energy Res. Abstr. (July 1979-); GeoRef; Int. Labour Doc.; Met. Abstr.; Point Repere (1983-).

UK
**POWTECH; PROCEEDINGS OF THE INTERNATIONAL POWDER TECHNOLOGY AND BULK SOLIDS CONFERENCE.** **Main/Conf** International Powder Technology and Bulk Solids Conference. **Added/Corp** Powder Advisory Centre. (1971)-. Monographic series. English. ir. Price varies per volume. Heyden & Son Ltd, Spectrum House, Hillview Gardens, London NW4 2JQ England. **Tel** (215)382-6673.

PL/0208-9092
**PRACE OSRODKA BADAWCZO-ROZWOJOWEGO PRZETWORNIKOW OBRAZU.** [Pr. Osr. Bad.-Rozw. Przetwor. Obrazu]. No. 1-. Academic Scholarly Publication. Polish. ir. Osrodek Badawczo-Rozwojowy Elektroniki Prozniowej, Ul Dluga 44/50, 00-241 Warszawa Poland. **CODEN** PBRODW. Documents available from Ask*IEEE, CASDDS.
**Ind/Abst** Chem. Abstr.; INSPEC (1981-).

II
**PRAKRUTI.** Periodical. English. sa. $2.00. Utkal University, Vani Vihar, Bhubaneswar Orissa 75104 India. **LC** Q73; .P7. **DD** 505.

FR/0556-137X
**PREPARONS L'AVENIR.** ***Ceased.*** [Prep. avenir]. (1967)-(1993). Periodical. French. Five times a year. Editions Magnard, 122 Blvd St Germain, Paris 6 France. **UDC** 37.

RU
**PREPRINT (INSTITUT ANALITICHESKOGO PRIBOROSTROENIIA (AKADEMIIA NAUK SSSR).** (PREPRINT / AKADEMIIA NAUK SSSR, NAUCHNO-TEKNICHESKOE OBEDINENIE, INSTITUT ANALITICHESKOGO PRIBOROSTROENIIA.). **Added/Corp** Institut Analiticheskogo Priborostroeniia (Akademiia Nauk SSSR). (19??)-. Monographic series. Russian. ir. Price varies per volume.

US
**PREPRINTS IN PARTICLES AND FIELDS.** ***Ceased.*** **Added/Corp** Stanford University. Stanford Linear Accelerator Center. Library. (19??)-(Sept. 1993). Periodical. English. wk. SLAC-PPF, Attn Accounting Department, PO Box 4349, Stanford CA 94305. **Tel** (415)854-3300.

AT/0314-9935
**PRESIDENTIAL ADDRESS OF THE AUSTRALIAN ACADEMY OF TECHNOLOGICAL SCIENCES.** ***Ceased.*** [Pres. address Aust. Acad. Technol. Sci.]. (1976)-(199?). Periodical. English. an. Australian Academy of Technological Sciences, Ian McLennan House, 197 Royal Parade, Parkville, Victoria Australia 3052. **Tel** 61 3 3470622, FAX 61 3 3478237. **DD** 609.94.
**Ind/Abst** AESIS Q.

RU/0032-8162
**PRIBORY I TEHNIKA EKSPERIMENTA.** (PTE. PRIBORY I TEKHNIKA EKSPERIMENTA.). [Prib. teh. eksp.]. **Added/Corp** Akademiia Nauk SSSR. **VFOAT** PTE. (July 1956)-. Academic Scholarly Publication. Russian. bm. $224.00. Izdatelstvo Nauka / Akademiia Nauk, Publishing House of the Russian Academy of Sciences, Leninskii Porspekt 14, 117901 Moscow Russia. **Tel** 011 95 954-21-53, FAX 011 95 938-21-44, telex 411964. **(Subscription address:** East View Publications Inc., 3020 Harbor Lane North, Suite 110, Minneapolis MN 55447.**) LC** QC53; .P2. **CODEN** PRTEAJ. **[CCC].** Index available. Documents available from Article Express International, Ask*IEEE, CASDDS.
**Ind/Abst** Chem. Abstr.; Eng. Index Annu.; INSPEC (1968-); Int. Aerosp. Abstr.

AT/0155-4395
**PRIMARY SCIENCE BULLETIN CANBERRA.** **See** Education-Teaching and Curriculum.

UK/0269-2465
**PRIMARY SCIENCE REVIEW.** [Prim. sci. rev.]. (1986)-. Periodical. English. Five times a year (Feb., Apr., June, Oct., Dec.). £36.00. Association for Science Education, College Lane, Hatfield Herts AL10 9AA England. **Tel** 011 44 707 267411, FAX 011 44 707 266532. **DD** 372.350941. ***Absorbed*** *Teaching Science, 0028-0763.*
**Ind/Abst** Br. Educ. Index.

NE/0929-9637
**PRIMARY SENSORY NEURON.** (19??)-. English. qt. DM270.00. VSP International Science Publishers, Godfried van Seystlaan 47, 3703 BR Zeist Netherlands. **Tel** 011 31 3404 25790, FAX 011 31 3404 32081, telex 40217 USP NL. **(Subscription address:** VSP International Science Publishers, PO Box 346, 3700 AH Zeist Netherlands.**)**

BU/0032-8731
**PRIORDA.** (PRIRODA.). [Priorda]. **Added/Corp** Bulgarska Akademiia na Naukite. Vol. 1 (Jan./Feb. 1952)-. Academic Scholarly Publication. Bulgarian. bm (6 issues). DM114.00. **(Subscription address:** Kubon & Sagner, ABT Zeitschriftenimport, D 80328 Munich Germany.**) CODEN** PRIRB4. Documents available from CASDDS.
**Ind/Abst** AGRICOLA; Chem. Abstr.; Curr. Biotechnol.; Curr. Dig. Post Sov. Press.

RU/0032-874X
**PRIRODA.** [Priroda]. **Added/Corp** Akademiia Nauk SSSR. (1912)-. Periodical. Russian (table of contents in English). mo. $99.95. Izdatelstvo Nauka / Akademiia Nauk, Publishing House of the Russian Academy of Sciences, Leninskii Porspekt 14, 117901 Moscow Russia. **Tel** 011 95 954-21-53, FAX 011 95 938-21-44, telex 411964. **(Subscription address:** East View Publications Inc., 3020 Harbor Lane North, Suite 110, Minneapolis MN 55447.**) LC** Q4; .P8. **NLM** W1 PR525E. **CODEN** PRIRA3. **[CCC].** Index available. **Bk Rev. Circ:** 62,000. available on microfilm from University Microfilms International (UMI). Documents available from Ask*IEEE, CASDDS.
**Ind/Abst** AGRICOLA; Anim. Breed. Abstr.; Art Archaeol. Tech. Abstr.; Chem. Abstr.; Curr. Biotechnol.; GeoRef; INSPEC (1975-); Int. Aerosp. Abstr.; Math. Rev. (1988-); Plant Breed. Abstr.; Soils Fert.

XR/0139-6544
**PRIRODNI VEDY.** 1971-. Academic Scholarly Publication. Czech (German). Statni Pedagogicke Nakladatelstvi, Ostrovni 30, 113 01 Prague 1 Czech Republic. **Tel** (2)203787, FAX (2)293883. **LC** Q4; .P8138. **CODEN** SPOEBE. Documents available from CASDDS. ***Continued in part by*** *Prirodni Vedy a Matematika.*
**Ind/Abst** Chem. Abstr. (1971-1981).

US
**PROBABLE LEVELS OF R&D EXPENDITURES IN ... .** **Added/Corp** Battelle Memorial Institute. Columbus Laboratories. **VFOAT** Probable Levels of R & D Expenditures in ...; Probable Levels of R and D Expenditures in ... . (19??)-(1993). English. an. Battelle Memorial Institute, 505 King Avenue, Columbus OH 43201-2693. **Tel** (614)424-7818, FAX (614)424-3889. **ED** Jules Duga. ***Continued by*** *Trends in U.S. R & D Funding for ... .*
**Desc:** Projects volume of R&D spending and performance in the U.S.
**Ind/Abst** F&S Index Plus Text, Int. (?-?) [Select. Cov.]; Predicasts Forecasts (?-?).

US/1062-4155
**PROBE.** (1991)-. English. mo. $53.00 US; $68.00 other. Probe, Box 1321, New York NY 10025. **Tel** (212)545-0088. **ED** David R Zimmerman. **Bk Rev.**
**Desc:** A journalistic, investigative and analytic newsletter. It explores science, media, policy and personal health from a rational, science-based, critical perspective in the tradition of I.F. Stone.

CU
**PROBLEMAS DE ORGANIZACION DE LA CIENCIA.** **Main/Corp** Instituto de Documentacion e Informacion Cientifica y Tecnica (Academia de Ciencias de Cuba). Spanish. Ediciones Cubanas, Obispo 527, Altos ESQ Bernaza, CP 10100 Havana Cuba. **Tel** 011 632980, 631942, FAX 011 631011, telex 512337, 6540. **LC** Q29; .A2413.

IT/0369-8408
**PROBLEMI ATTUALI DI SCIENZA E DI CULTURA.** [Probl. attuali sci. cult.]. **Added/Corp** Accademia Nazionale dei Lincei. (1947)-. Monographic series. Italian. ir. Price varies per volume. Accademia Nazionale dei Lincei, Via Lungara 10 Uff Diff Pubbl., 00165 Rome Italy. **Tel** 011 39 6 6838831. **(Subscription address:** Bardi Editore, Salita de Crescenzi 16, 00186 Rome Italy; telephone: 011 39 6 68801490**) LC** AS222; .R53. **DD** 055/.1.
**Ind/Abst** GeoRef.

PL
**PROBLEMS OF THE SCIENCE OF SCIENCE.** 1st- 1970-. Periodical. Multiple languages (English and French). ir. **(Subscription address:** ARS Polona, PO Box 1001, 00068 Warsaw Poland.**)**
**Ind/Abst** Soc. Plann. Policy Dev. Abstr.; Sociol. Abstr. (?-?).

PL/0032-9487
**PROBLEMY.** [Problemy]. (1945)-. Periodical. Polish. mo. $36.00. **(Subscription address:** ARS Polona, PO Box 1001, 00068 Warsaw Poland.**) UDC** 001.

RU/0555-2923
**PROBLEMY PEREDACI INFORMACII.** (PROBLEMY PEREDACHI INFORMATSII.). [Probl. pereda. inf.]. **Added/Corp** Akademiia Nauk SSSR. (1965)-. Academic Scholarly Publication. Russian. Six times a year. $80.00. Izdatelstvo Nauka / Akademiia Nauk, Publishing House of the Russian Academy of Sciences, Leninskii Porspekt 14, 117901 Moscow Russia. **Tel** 011 95 954-21-53, FAX 011 95 938-21-44, telex 411964. **(Subscription address:** East View Publications Inc., 3020 Harbor Lane North, Suite 110, Minneapolis MN 55447.**) LC** Q350; .P72. **CODEN** PPDIA5. cum. index. Documents available from Article Express International, Ask*IEEE. ***Supersedes*** *Problemy Peredachi Informatsii.*
**Ind/Abst** Eng. Index Annu.; INSPEC (1968-); Math. Rev.; Zentralbl. Math. Ihre Grenzgeb.

US/0361-2007
**PROCEEDINGS, ANNUAL TECHNICAL MEETING - INSTITUTE OF ENVIRONMENTAL SCIENCES.** [Proc. annu. tech. meet. Inst. Environ. Sci.]. **Main/Corp** Institute of Environmental Sciences. 1960. Academic Scholarly Publication. English. an. $100.00 (members), $125.00 (non-members). Institute of Environmental Sciences, 940 East Northwest Highway, Mount Prospect IL 60056. **Tel** (312)255-1561, FAX (312)255-1699. **ED** Janet Ehmann. **CODEN** IESPAF. Index available. **Bk Rev. Circ:** 2,000. Documents available from Article Express International, BIOSIS Document Express, CASDDS.
**Desc:** Contains papers presented at meetings dealing with contamination, control, energy, waste, disposal, product reliability, reliability growth and stress screening.
**Ind/Abst** AGRICOLA; Bioeng. Abstr.; Biol. Abstr.; Chem. Abstr.; Ei Page One; Eng. Index Annu.; GeoRef.

US/0739-361X
**PROCEEDINGS, DIRECTORY AND HANDBOOK OF THE NATIONAL ASSOCIATION OF ACADEMIES OF SCIENCE, THE.** ***Title Change.*** [Proc. dir. handb. Natl. Assoc. Acad. Sci.]. **Main/Corp** National Association of Academies of Science (U.S.). **VFOAT** Proceedings, Directory and Handbook. (198?)-(19??). English. an. Northeast Missouri State University, Division of Fine Arts, Kirksville MO 63501. **Tel** (816)785-4442. **(Subscription address:** Northeast Missouri State University, Department of Biology, c/o Dr. Shaddy, Kirksville MO 63501.**) ED** Claire Oswald (editor's address: Nebraska Academy of Science 1901 South 72nd Street Omaha NE 68124; editor's telephone number: (402)399-2609). **LC** Q11; .N28755a. **DD** 506/.073. ***Continues*** *National Association of Academies of Science (U.S.). Directory and Handbook of the National Association of Academies of Science.* ***Continued by*** *National Association of Academies of Science (U.S.). Directory, Proceedings, and Handbook, 1071-8966.*
**Desc:** Comprehensive information on activities of state science academies. United States of America. Includes members of the National Association of Academies of Science. Contains summary of annual symposium held during meeting of American Association for the Advancement of Science.

IO/0522-2133
**PROCEEDINGS - INSTITUT TEKNOLOGI BANDUNG.** [Proc. - Inst. Teknol. Bandung]. **Main/Corp** Institut Teknologi Bandung. V. 4- 1967-. Proceedings. English (Indonesian). Jl Surapati 1, Bandung Indonesia. **LC** Q75. **CODEN** PITBBG. ***Continues*** *Madjalah - Institut Teknologi Bandung; Proceedings - Institut Teknologi Bandung.*
**Ind/Abst** GeoRef.

US/0277-8211
**PROCEEDINGS / INTERNATIONAL CEMENT SEMINAR.** [Proc. - Int. Cem. Semin.]. **Main/Conf** International Cement Seminar. **VFOAT** I.C.S. Proceedings; Proceedings of the International Cement Seminar. Academic Scholarly Publication. English. an. $40.00. 300 West Adams Street, Chicago IL 60606. **LC** TP881; .I5A. **DD** 666/.94/05. **CODEN** PCESDK. Documents available from CASDDS.
**Ind/Abst** Chem. Abstr.

BG
**PROCEEDINGS OF THE ... ANNUAL BANGLADESH SCIENCE CONFERENCE.** **Main/Conf** Bangladesh Science Conference. Proceedings. English. an. **LC** Q101; .B36A. **DD** 505.

US/0730-7845
**PROCEEDINGS OF THE ARAB SCHOOL ON SCIENCE AND TECHNOLOGY.** ***Ceased.*** [Proc. Arab Sch. Sci. Technol.]. **Main/Conf** Arab School on Science and Technology. (1982)-(19??). Monographic series. English. ir. Taylor & Francis Ltd., Rankine Road, Basingstoke Hampshire, RG24 8PR United Kingdom. **Tel** 011 44 256 840366, FAX 011 44 256 479438, telex 858540. **(Subscription address:** Taylor & Francis Inc., 1900 Frost Road, Suite 101, Bristol PA 19007-1598.**)**
**Ind/Abst** Math. Rev. (19??)-(19??).

US/0097-4374
**PROCEEDINGS OF THE ARKANSAS ACADEMY OF SCIENCE.** [Proc. Arkansas Acad. Sci.]. **Main/Corp** Arkansas Academy of Science. Vol. 1 (1941)-. Proceedings. English. an. $25.00 US; $26.50 other. Arkansas Academy of Science, c/o Dr Robert W Wiley, Department of Natural Sciences, University of Arkansas at Monticello, Monticello AR 71655. **Tel** (212)850-6645, FAX (212)850-6088, telex 12-7063. **ED** Harvey Barton. **LC** AS36; .A78. **DD** 061.67. **CODEN** AKASAO. cum. index. **Pr Rev. Circ:** 450 (ctrl). Documents available from BIOSIS Document Express, CASDDS.
**Desc:** A publication of the papers presented at the annual meeting of the Arkansas Academy of Science covering all fields of science.
**Ind/Abst** AGRICOLA; Biol. Abstr.; Chem. Abstr.; EMBASE; Fish Rev. (Jan. 1989-July 1992); For. Abstr.; GeoRef; Key Word Index Wildl. Res.; Rev. Agric. Entomol.; Rice Abstr.; Wildl. Rev. (Jan. 1989-July 1992).

IE/0332-3226
**PROCEEDINGS OF THE BAIL ... CONFERENCE.** (1980)-. Monographic series. English. ir. Price varies per volume. Boole Press Ltd, 26 Temple Lane, Temple Bar Dublin 2 Ireland. **Tel** 011 353 1 6797655, telex 30547 SHCN E1.

US/0068-547X
**PROCEEDINGS OF THE CALIFORNIA ACADEMY OF SCIENCES, 4TH SERIES.** [Proc. Calif. Acad. Sci.]. **Main/Corp** California Academy of Sciences, San Francisco. Vol. 1 (1907)-. Proceedings. English. Price varies per volume. California Academy of Sciences, Golden State Park, San Francisco CA 94181-9961. **Tel** (415)221-5100. **LC** Q11; .C253. **CODEN** PCASAV. available on microfilm from University Microfilms International (UMI). Documents available from BIOSIS Document Express, CASDDS. ***Formed by the union of*** *Proceedings of the California Academy of Sciences. 3D Ser. : Botany; Proceedings of the California Academy of Sciences. 3D Ser. : Geology; Proceedings of the California Academy of Sciences. 3D Ser. : Mathematics-Physics* ***and*** *Proceedings of the California Academy of Sciences. 3D Ser. : Zoology.*
**Desc:** Vol. 25 is composed entirely of the Alice Eastwood semi-centennial publications, No. 1-18, of the California Academy of Sciences.
**Ind/Abst** AGRICOLA [Select. Cov.]; Biol. Abstr.; Chem. Abstr.; Fish Rev. (Jan. 1989-July 1992); GeoRef; Life Sci. Collect.; Wildl. Rev. (Jan. 1989-July 1992).

US/0069-8644
**PROCEEDINGS OF THE CONFERENCE ON REMOTE SYSTEMS TECHNOLOGY.** [Proc. Conf. Remote Syst. Technol.]. **Main/Conf** Conference on Remote Systems Technology. **Added/Corp** American Nuclear Society. Remote Systems Technology Division. (1964)-. Academic Scholarly Publication. English. an. $50.00 North America; $55.00 other. American Nuclear Society, PO Box 97781, Chicago IL 60678-7781. **Tel** (708)352-6611, FAX (708)579-8314. **ED** Lorretta Palagi. **LC** TK9151.6; .C66a. **DD** 621.48. **CODEN** CRSTBJ. **Circ:** 300. Documents available from Article Express International, Ask*IEEE, CASDDS. ***Continues*** *Proceedings of the Conference on Hot Laboratories and Equipment, 0097-1480.*
**Desc:** Papers from remote system technology presentations at ANS national meetings. Coverage includes: hostile environments, manipulators, robots and hot cells.
**Ind/Abst** Bioeng. Abstr.; Chem. Abstr.; Ei Page One; Eng. Index Annu.; INSPEC.

JA/0563-6795
**PROCEEDINGS OF THE FACULTY OF SCIENCE OF TOKAI UNIVERSITY.** ***Title Change.*** [Proc. Fac. Sci. Tokai Univ.]. **Main/Corp** Tokai Daigaku. Rigakubu. Vol. 1 (1966)-(1992). Academic Scholarly Publication. English. Tokai University, Faculty of Science, Tokyo Japan. **LC** Q77; .T5816. **DD** 505. **CODEN** TUFPBE. Documents available from CASDDS. ***Continued by*** *Proceedings of the School of Science of Tokai University.*
**Ind/Abst** Chem. Abstr. (?-?); Math. Rev. (?-?); Zentralbl. Math. Ihre Grenzgeb. (?-?).

FR/0303-1136
**PROCEEDINGS OF THE FULL BOARD MEETING - ISCU AB.** (PROCEEDINGS OF THE FULL BOARD MEETING.). **Added/Corp** International Council of Scientific Unions. Abstracting Board. **VFOAT** Proceedings of the General Assembly Meeting. (1970)-. Proceedings. English. ICSU AB, 17 rue Mirabeau, 75016 Paris France. **NLM** W1; PR582NF.

II/0370-0046
**PROCEEDINGS OF THE INDIAN NATIONAL SCIENCE ACADEMY. PART A, PHYSICAL SCIENCES.** [Proc. Indian Natl. Sci. Acad., Part A]. **Main/Corp** Indian National Science Academy. **VFOAT** Physical Sciences. Vol. 36, No. 1 (Jan. 1970)-. Proceedings. English. qt. $50.00. Indian National Science Academy, 1 Bahadur Shah Zafar Marg, New Delhi 110 002 India. **(Subscription address:** Prints India, 11 Darya Ganj, New Delhi, 110002 India, (Phone: 011 91 11 3268645)**) LC** Q73; .I774a. **DD** 500.2/05. **NLM** W1 PR585W. **CODEN** PIPSBD. Documents available from Ask*IEEE, CASDDS. ***Continues*** *Proceedings of the National Institute of Sciences of India. Part A, Physical Sciences.*
**Ind/Abst** Alum. Ind. Abstr.; Ceram. Abstr.; Chem. Abstr.; GeoRef; Indian Geosci. Abstr.; INSPEC (Jan. 1970-); Int. Aerosp. Abstr.; Math. Rev.; Met. Abstr.; NAPRALERT; Soils Fert.; Zentralbl. Math. Ihre Grenzgeb.

II/0373-0786
**PROCEEDINGS OF THE INDIAN SCIENCE CONGRESS.** [Proc. Indian Sci. Congr.]. **Main/Conf** Indian Science Congress Association. **Added/Corp** Indian Science Congress. Proceedings. Asiatic Society (Calcutta, India). (1914)-. Proceedings. English. qt. $40.00. Indian Books and Periodicals, 2429 Tilak Street, Pahar Ganj, New Delhi 110005 India. **(Subscription address:** Prints India, 11 Darya Ganj, New Delhi 110002 India.**) CODEN** PISCAD. Documents available from BIOSIS Document Express, CASDDS.
**Ind/Abst** Biol. Abstr.; Chem. Abstr. (1914-1982); GeoRef; Stat. Theory Method Abstr. (1959-1963).

US/0073-6767
**PROCEEDINGS OF THE INDIANA ACADEMY OF SCIENCE.** [Proc. Indiana Acad. Sci.]. **Main/Corp** Indiana Academy of Science. Vol. 1; 1891-. Proceedings. English. an. $12.00. Indiana Academy of Science, Indiana State Library, 140 North Senate Avenue, Indianapolis IN 46204-2296. **Tel** (317)232-3686. **ED** Donald R Winslow. **LC** Q11; .I38. **DD** 500. **NLM** W1 PR585Y. **CODEN** PIACAP. Index available. cum. index. ctrl circ. Documents available from BIOSIS Document Express, CASDDS. ***Continues*** *Indiana Academy of Science. Proceedings of the Annual Meeting.*
**Desc:** Series of scientific papers presented at the annual fall meeting of the Academy.
**Ind/Abst** Biol. Abstr.; Chem. Abstr.; Fish Rev.; GeoRef; Life Sci. Collect.; Surf. Treat. Technol. Abstr.

US/0190-4132
**PROCEEDINGS OF THE INTERNATIONAL CONFERENCE ON LASERS.** [Proc. Int. Conf. Lasers]. **Main/Conf** International Conference on Lasers. **Added/Corp** Society for Optical & Quantum Electronics. **VFOAT** Lasers. (1978)-. Academic Scholarly Publication. English. an (June). $155.00. STS Press / Virginia, PO Box 245, McLean VA 22101. **Tel** (703)642-5835, FAX (703)642-5838. **ED** V. J. Corcoran and Terri Goldman (editor's address: 5645 East General Washington Drive, Alexandria, VA 22312, phone: (703)642-5835). **LC** TA1673; .I5578a. **DD** 621.36/6. **CODEN** PICLDV. **[CCC]. Bk Rev**, (Qty: 2). **Circ:** 300 (ctrl). Documents available from Ask*IEEE, CASDDS.
**Desc:** Scientific and research papers presented at the conference.
**Ind/Abst** Chem. Abstr.; INSPEC (1986-).

US/0732-0175
**PROCEEDINGS OF THE INTERNATIONAL SYMPOSIUM ON COMPUTER AIDED SEISMIC ANALYSIS AND DISCRIMINATION.** [Proc. Int. Symp. Comput. Aides Seism. Anal. Discrim.]. **Main/Conf** International Symposium on Computer Aided Seismic Analysis and Discrimination. **VFOAT** IEEE Computer-Aided Seismic Analysis & Discrimination. 1st (1977)-. Proceedings. English. IEEE, Institution of Electrical and Electronics Engineers, Inc., 345 East 47th Street, New York NY 10017-2394. **Tel** (908)981-1393, FAX (908)981-9667. **(Subscription address:** IEEE Service Center, 445 Hoes Lane, Piscataway, NJ 08854; telephone: (201)981-1393**)**
**Ind/Abst** GeoRef; Index IEEE Publ.

NE/0924-8323
**PROCEEDINGS OF THE KONINKLIJKE NEDERLANDSE AKADEMIE VAN WETENSCHAPPEN (1990).** (PROCEEDINGS OF THE KONINKLIJKE NEDERLANDSE AKADEMIE VAN WETENSCHAPPEN. BIOLOGICAL, CHEMICAL, GEOLOGICAL, PHYSICAL, AND MEDICAL SCIENCES.). [Proc. K. Ned. Akad. Wet.]. **Added/Corp** Koninklijke Nederlandse Akademie van Wetenschappen. **VFOAT** Biological, Chemical, Geological, Physical and Medical Sciences; Proceedings of the Royal Netherlands Academy of Arts and Sciences. Vol. 93 No. 1 (Mar. 26, 1990)-. Academic Scholarly Publication. English (French

and German). qt. Fl283.00. Elsevier Science Publishers BV, PO Box 211, 1000 AE Amsterdam Netherlands. **Tel** 011 31 20 5803642, FAX 011 31 20 5862696, telex 15682. **LC** Q57; .P762. **CODEN** PKNSEK. Documents available from The Genuine Article, BIOSIS Document Express, Ask*IEEE, CASDDS. ***Formed by the union of*** *Proceedings of the Koninklijke Nederlandse Akademie van Wetenschappen. Series B, Palaeontology, Geology, Physics, Chemistry, Anthropology, 0920-2250* ***and*** *Proceedings of the Koninklijke Nederlandse Akademie van Wetenschappen. Series C, Biological and Medical Sciences, 0023-3374.*
**Ind/Abst** Biol. Abstr. (1991-); Chem. Abstr.; Curr. Contents, Agric. Biol. Environ. Sci.; Curr. Contents Phys. Chem. Earth Sci.; GeoRef; INSPEC (1990-); Leadscan; Math. Rev.; Res. Alert [Full Cov.]; Sci. Cit. Index; SCISEARCH.

US/0096-9192
**PROCEEDINGS OF THE LOUISIANA ACADEMY OF SCIENCES, THE.** [Proc. La. Acad. Sci.]. **Main/Corp** Louisiana Academy of Sciences. Vol.1 (1932). Proceedings. English. an. $20.00. Centenary College Department of Biology, Shreveport LA 71104. **Tel** (318)868-5209, (318)868-2572. **LC** Q11; .L54. **DD** 505. **CODEN** PLAAA6. Index available. Documents available from BIOSIS Document Express, CASDDS.
**Ind/Abst** AGRICOLA [Select. Cov.]; Biol. Abstr.; Chem. Abstr.; Energy Res. Abstr.; Fish Rev.; Life Sci. Collect.; Wildl. Rev.

US/0096-9206
**PROCEEDINGS OF THE MONTANA ACADEMY OF SCIENCES.** [Proc. Mont. Acad. Sci.]. **Main/Corp** Montana Academy of Sciences. Vol. 1 (1940)-. Proceedings. English. an. $12.00. Montana Academy of Sciences, Montana Tech/Dr Joanne Cortese, Butte MT 59701. **Tel** (406)496-4460, FAX (406)496-4133. **ED** Joan Cook, MSU, Bozeman, MT 59717; Telephone: (406)994-6280. **LC** Q11; .M75. **DD** 506.2786. **CODEN** PMASAX. **Circ:** 500. Documents available from BIOSIS Document Express, CASDDS.
**Desc:** Papers and abstracts of papers presented at the annual meeting of the Montana Academy of Sciences, plus a few additional selected scientific papers.
**Ind/Abst** AGRICOLA [Select. Cov.]; Biol. Abstr. (-1985); Chem. Abstr. (1940/1941-1983); Fish Rev.; GeoRef; Key Word Index Wildl. Res.; Wildl. Rev.

US/0027-8424
**PROCEEDINGS OF THE NATIONAL ACADEMY OF SCIENCE OF THE UNITED STATES OF AMERICA.** [Proc. Natl. Acad. Sci. U. S. A.]. **Main/Corp** National Academy of Sciences (U.S.). Vol. 1 (Jan. 1915)-. Academic Scholarly Publication. English. Twenty-four times a year. $530.00 (institutions), $250.00 (individuals) US; $625.00 (institutions), $345.00 (individuals) other. National Academy Press, 2101 Constitution Avenue NW, Lockbox 285, Washington DC 20055. **Tel** (800)624-6242, (202)334-3313, FAX (202)334-2451. **(Subscription address:** National Academy of Sciences, Box 285, Washington DC 20055.**) ED** Maxine F. Singer. **LC** Q11; .N26. **DD** 505. **NLM** W1 PR586A. **CODEN** PNASA6. **[CCC].** cum. index. **Acid Free. Circ:** 9,500 (ctrl). available on microfilm and microfiche from University Microfilms International (UMI). Documents available from The Genuine Article, BIOSIS Document Express, Ask*IEEE, UMI Article Clearinghouse, CASDDS, Documents on Demand.
**Desc:** Reports that describe the results of original theoretical or experimental research of exceptional importance and broad interest to diverse groups of scientists.
**Ind/Abst** AgBiotech News Inf.; AGRICOLA [Select. Cov.]; Anal. Abstr.; Aquat. Sci. Fish. Abstr. (Computer File); Art Archaeol. Tech. Abstr.; Biodeter. Abstr.; Biol. Agric. Index; Biol. Abstr.; Biotechnol. Res. Abstr.; Calcium Calcif. Tissue Abstr.; Chem. Abstr.; Chem. Titles; Chemorecept. Abstr.; Crop Physiol. Abstr.; CSA Neuro. Abstr.; Curr. Aware. Biol. Sci., CABS; Curr. Biotechnol.; Curr. Contents Life Sci.; Curr. Ref. Fish Res.; Dairy Sci. Abstr.; Ecol. Abstr.; Ecology Abstr.; EMBASE; Energy Inf. Abstr.; Energy Res. Abstr.; Entomol. Abstr.; Environ. Abstr.; Field Crop Abstr.; Fish Rev.; Food Sci. Technol. Abstr.; Foods Adlibra; For. Abstr.; Gen. Sci. Index; Genet. Abstr.; GeoRef; Helminthol. Abstr.; Hum. Genome Abstr.; Immunol. Abstr.; Index Med.; Index Vet.; INSPEC (1968-); Int. Aerosp. Abstr.; Maize Abstr.; Mass Spect. Bull.; Math. Rev.; Microbiol. Abstr. Sect. B; Microbiol. Abstr. Sect. A; Microbiol. Abstr. Sect. C; Nematol. Abstr.; Newsp. Period. Abstr. (1992-); Nucl. Acids Abstr.; Nutr. Abstr. Rev., Ser. A, Hum. Exp.; Nutr. Res. Newsl.; Ocean. Abstr.; Oncog. Growth Factors Abstr.; Life Sci. Collect.; PESTDOC; Pig News Inf.; Plant Breed. Abstr.; Plant Genet. Resour. Abstr.; Plant Grow. Reg. Abstr.; Pollut. Abstr. Indexes; Potato Abstr.; Poult. Abstr.; Protozoolog. Abstr.; Ref. Upd. Basic Ed.; Ref. Upd. Deluxe Ed.; Res. Alert [Full Cov.]; Rev. Med. Vet. Entomol.; Rev. Med. Vet. Mycology; Rev. Plant Pathol.; Rice Abstr.; Sci. Cit. Index; SCISEARCH; Seed Abstr.; Small Anim. Abstr. Bibliogr.; Soc. Sci. Cit. Index [Select. Cov.]; Soils Fert.; Sorghum Mill. Abstr.; Stat. Theory Method Abstr. (1959-1963); Surf. Treat. Technol. Abstr.; Vet. Bull.; Trop. Dis. Bull.; Virol. AIDS Abstr.; Weed Abstr.; Wildl. Rev.; Zentralbl. Math. Ihre Grenzgeb.

II/0369-8211
**PROCEEDINGS OF THE NATIONAL ACADEMY OF SCIENCES, INDIA. SECTION B : BIOLOGICAL SCIENCES.** (PROCEEDINGS OF THE NATIONAL ACADEMY OF SCIENCES, INDIA. SECTION B.). [Proc. Natl. Acad. Sci., India, Sect. B]. **Added/Corp** National Academy of Sciences, India. **VFOAT** Section B. Vol. 12, Pt. 4 (Nov. 1942)-. Academic Scholarly Publication. English. Four times a year. $50.00 (surface mail); Rs90.00 (members); Rs120.00 (non-members). National Academy of Sciences India, 5 Lajpatrai Road, Allahabad 211002 India. **Tel** 55224. **LC** Q73; .P76. **CODEN** PAIBA6. Documents available from BIOSIS Document Express, CASDDS. ***Continues in part*** *Proceedings of the National Academy of Sciences, India, 0369-3236.*
**Ind/Abst** Biol. Abstr.; Chem. Abstr.

CH/0255-6588
**PROCEEDINGS OF THE NATIONAL SCIENCE COUNCIL, REPUBLIC OF CHINA. PART A, PHYSICAL SCIENCE AND ENGINEERING.** [Proc. Natl. Sci. Counc. Repub. China, Part A, Phys. sci. eng.]. **Added/Corp** Kuo Chia Ko Hsueh Wei Yuan Hui. **VFOAT** Physical Science and Engineering; Yen Chiu Hui Kan. Tzu Jan Ko Hsueh Yu Kung Cheng; Tzu Jan Ko Hseuh Yu Kung Cheng. Vol. 8, No. 1 (Jan. 1984)-. Academic Scholarly Publication. English (Multiple languages; summaries and/or abstracts in Chinese). Six times a year. $24.00. National Science Council ROC, 106 Ho-ping East Road SRC 2, Taipei Taiwan 10636. **Tel** 011 886 2 737764, FAX 011 886 2 7377248. **LC** QH301; .P743. **DD** 505. **CODEN** PNAEE2. **Pr Rev. Circ:** 2,400. available on microfiche from National Information Service Corporation (NISC). Documents available from BIOSIS Document Express, Ask*IEEE, CASDDS. ***Continues*** *Proceedings of the National Science Council, Republic of China. Part A, Applied Sciences, 0253-8415.*
**Ind/Abst** AGRICOLA; Biol. Abstr. (1984-); Chem. Abstr. (1984-); For. Prod. Abstr.; GeoRef; INSPEC (1992-); Int. Aerosp. Abstr. (1984-); Rice Abstr.; SEA Abstr.

US/0096-9214
**PROCEEDINGS OF THE NORTH DAKOTA ACADEMY OF SCIENCE.** [Proc. N. D. Acad. Sci.]. **Main/Corp** North Dakota Academy of Science. **Added/Corp** Minnesota Academy of Science (1932)- University of North Dakota. North Dakota State University. Minot State College. Vol. 1 (1947)-. Proceedings. English. an (Published in April). $7.50 US; $10.00 other. North Dakota Academy of Science, PO Box 5567, University Station, Fargo ND 58105. **Tel** (701)777-2742. **ED** Roy Garvey. **LC** Q11; .N86. **DD** 506.2784. **NLM** W1 PR586EN. **CODEN** PNDAAZ. Index available. **Pr Rev. Circ:** 750. Documents available from BIOSIS Document Express.
**Desc:** Proceedings and papers from symposia, professional and collegiate sessions of annual meeting of interest to North Dakota scientists.
**Ind/Abst** AGRICOLA [Select. Cov.]; Biol. Abstr.; Crop Physiol. Abstr.; Fish Rev.; GeoRef; Wildl. Rev.

CN/0078-2521
**PROCEEDINGS OF THE NOVA SCOTIAN INSTITUTE OF SCIENCE.** [Proceed. N.S. Inst. Sci.]. **Main/Corp** Nova Scotian Institute of Science. Vol. 18, Pt. 1 (1931)-. Periodical. English (French). qt. 15.00Can$. Nova Scotian Institute of Science, c/o Dalhousie University, Killam Library, Halifax Nova Scotia B3H 4H8 Canada. **Tel** (902)494-2331. **ED** Dr. Alan Taylor. **LC** Q21; .N9. **CODEN** PNSIAW. **[CCC].** Index available. **Circ:** 450. Documents available from CASDDS. ***Continues*** *The Proceedings and Transactions of the Nova Scotian Institute of Science, 0370-2235.*
**Desc:** Proceedings of the Nova Scotian Institute of Science; regional original articles and review articles in the physical and natural sciences.
**Ind/Abst** AGRICOLA [Select. Cov.]; Chem. Abstr. (1930-1982); Fish Rev.; GeoRef; Plant Grow. Reg. Abstr.; Rev. Plant Pathol.; Rice Abstr.; Soils Fert.; Sorghum Mill. Abstr.; Weed Abstr.; Wildl. Rev.

US/0078-4303
**PROCEEDINGS OF THE OKLAHOMA ACADEMY OF SCIENCE.** [Proc. Okla. Acad. Sci.]. **Main/Corp** Oklahoma Academy of Science. **Added/Corp** University of Oklahoma. Oklahoma Junior Academy of Science. Transactions. Vol. 1 (1920)-. Academic Scholarly Publication. English. an (Dec.). $25.00 (individual), $27.00 (library). Oklahoma Academy of Science, PO Box 4424, Tulsa OK 74159. **ED** Franklin R. Leach. **LC** Q11; .O4. **DD** 505. **NLM** W1 PR586M. **CODEN** POASAD. cum. index. **Pr Rev. Circ:** 600 (ctrl). Documents available from BIOSIS Document Express, CASDDS.
**Desc:** Vols. 1-49 are Proceedings of the 1st-57th annual meetings.
**Ind/Abst** AGRICOLA [Select. Cov.]; Biol. Abstr.; Chem. Abstr.; EMBASE; Fish Rev. (Jan. 1989-July 1992); For. Abstr.; GeoRef; Index Vet.; Int. Aerosp. Abstr.; Weed Abstr.; Wildl. Rev. (Jan. 1989-July 1992).

US/0370-1093
**PROCEEDINGS OF THE OREGON ACADEMY OF SCIENCE.** [Proc. Or. Acad. Sci.]. **Main/Corp** Oregon Academy of Science. Vol. 1 (1943/1947)-. Proceedings. English. an. $8.00. Science Technology Division Library, Oregon State University, Corvalis OR 97331. **Tel** (503)754-4594. **ED** Claude Curran. **LC** Q11; .O576. **DD** 506.2795. **CODEN** PORSAU. **Circ:** 150. Documents available from BIOSIS Document Express.
**Desc:** Consists of abstracts of papers given at the annual meetings of the academy. Selected papers are published in full.
**Ind/Abst** Biol. Abstr.; GeoRef.

PK/0377-2969
**PROCEEDINGS OF THE PAKISTAN ACADEMY OF SCIENCES.** (PROCEEDINGS.). [Proc. Pak. Acad. Sci.]. **Main/Corp** Pakistan Academy of Sciences. Proceedings. English. sa. Pakistan Academy of Sciences, PO Box 1090, Islamabad Pakistan. **LC** Q1; .P24A. **DD** 505. **CODEN** PKSPAW. Documents available from BIOSIS Document Express, Ask*IEEE, CASDDS.
**Ind/Abst** Biol. Abstr.; Chem. Abstr.; INSPEC (1982-); Math. Rev.

US/0096-4166
**PROCEEDINGS OF THE ROCHESTER ACADEMY OF SCIENCE.** [Proc. Rochester Acad. Sci.]. **Main/Corp** Rochester Academy of Science, Rochester, N.Y. Vol. 1 (Jan. 1889)-. Proceedings. English. ir. University of Rochester / Rochester Academy of Science, Rochester NY 14627. **Tel** (716)275-4485. **LC** Q11; .R8. **DD** 505. **NLM** W1 PR586ST. **CODEN** PROSA2. Documents available from BIOSIS Document Express.
**Desc:** History and work of the Rochester Academy of Science.
**Ind/Abst** Biol. Abstr.; GeoRef.

UK/0035-8959
**PROCEEDINGS OF THE ROYAL INSTITUTION OF GREAT BRITAIN.** [Proc. R. Inst. G.B.]. **Added/Corp** Royal Institution of Great Britain. **VFOAT** Speaking of Science. Vol. 26 (1929-1931)-. Academic Scholarly Publication. English. an. $79.00. Science Reviews Ltd, 18 Oaklands Gate, Northwood Middlesex, HA6 3AA England. **Tel** 011 44 923 823586. **ED** J M Thomas, Richard Catlow, S T Nash. **LC** Q41; .R8. **CODEN** PIGBAI. **Circ:** 1500. available on microfilm from University Microfilms International (UMI). Documents available from Ask*IEEE, CASDDS. ***Continues*** *Notices of the Proceedings at the Meetings of the Members.*
**Desc:** Discourses given at the Royal Institution.
**Ind/Abst** Am. Hist. Life (1956-); Chem. Abstr.; INSPEC (1969-).

IE/0035-8975
**PROCEEDINGS OF THE ROYAL IRISH ACADEMY. SECTION A. MATHEMATICAL AND PHYSICAL SCIENCES.** **See** Mathematics.

NE/0924-8328
**PROCEEDINGS OF THE ROYAL NETHERLANDS ACADEMY OF ARTS AND SCIENCES: BIOLOGICAL, CHEMICAL, GEOLOGICAL, PHYSICAL AND MEDICAL SCIENCES.** Proceedings. English. Four times a year (1 volume). Fl355.00. Elsevier Science Publishers BV, PO Box 211, 1000 AE Amsterdam Netherlands. **Tel** 011 31 20 5803642, FAX 011 31 20 5862696, telex 15682.

NZ/0557-4161
**PROCEEDINGS OF THE ROYAL SOCIETY OF NEW ZEALAND.** ***Suspended.*** [Proc. R. Soc. N. Z.]. **Main/Corp** Royal Society of New Zealand. Vol. 85 (May 1957)-Vol. 119/120 (1994). Proceedings. English. an (June). 38.00NZ$. Royal Society of New Zealand, PO Box 598, Wellington New Zealand. **Tel** 011 64 4 727421, FAX 011 64 4 731841. **ED** B. E. Harford. **CODEN** PSNZAP. Each issue contains an index to its own contents (no volume index)--loose. **Bk Rev. Ad Acc. Circ:** 770 (ctrl).
**Desc:** The report of the Royal Society of New Zealand, the concerns and activities of its staff and fellows.
**Ind/Abst** Ceram. Abstr.; GeoRef; Stat. Theory Method Abstr. (1959-1963).

AT/0080-469X
**PROCEEDINGS OF THE ROYAL SOCIETY OF QUEENSLAND.** [Proc. R. Soc. Queensl.]. **Main/Corp** Royal Society of Queensland. Vol. 1 (1885)-. Proceedings. English. an. 25.00Aus$. Royal Society of Queensland, PO Box 21, St Lucia Queensland 4067 Australia. **Tel** 011 44 07 840 7684. **ED** E.D. McKenzie. **LC** Q93; .Q3. **CODEN** PRSQAG. cum. index. **Pr Rev. Circ:** 800. Documents available from BIOSIS Document Express, CASDDS. ***Supersedes*** *Philosophical Society of Queensland. Transactions.*
**Desc:** Scientific papers in any specialized area of science pertaining to Queensland and adjacent areas and some important review lectures.
**Ind/Abst** AESIS Q.; Anim. Breed. Abstr.; Biol. Abstr.; Chem. Abstr.; Fish Rev. (Jan. 1989-July 1992); GeoRef; Index Med.; Life Sci. Collect.; Plant Genet. Resour. Abstr.; Protozoolog. Abstr.; Rev. Med. Vet. Entomol.; Wildl. Rev. (Jan. 1989-July 1992).

AT/0035-9211
**PROCEEDINGS OF THE ROYAL SOCIETY OF VICTORIA.** [Proc. R. Soc. Vic.]. **Main/Corp** Royal Society of Victoria (Melbourne, Vic.). Vol. 1; June 1989-. Proceedings. English. sa. 65.00Aus$. Royal Society of Victoria, 9 Victoria Street, Melbourne 3000 Australia. **Tel** (03)663 5259. **ED** D Holloway. **LC** Q93; .V6. **NLM** W1 PR5861G. **CODEN** PRSVAV. **[CCC].** cum. index. **Circ:** 1,000. Documents available from BIOSIS Document Express, Ask*IEEE. ***Continues in part*** *Transactions and Proceedings of the Royal Society of Victoria.*
**Desc:** Papers on scientific research, projects on geology, zoology, biology, botany, agriculture, meteorology, paleontology and social sciences.
**Ind/Abst** AESIS Q.; Agrofor. Abstr.; Biol. Abstr.; Ecol. Abstr.; Geogr. Abstr. Phys. Geogr.; Geol. Abstr.; INSPEC (1968-); Life Sci. Collect.

●JA/0563-6759
**PROCEEDINGS OF THE SCHOOL OF SCIENCE OF TOKAI UNIVERSITY. VFOAT** Tokai Daigaku Kiyo. Rigakubu . (1993)-. English (Japanese). an. Tokai University, Faculty of Science, Tokyo Japan. ***Continues*** *Tokai Daigaku Kiyo. Rigakubu. Proceedings of the Faculty of Science of Tokai University, 0563-6795.*
**Ind/Abst** Chem. Abstr.; Math. Rev.; Zentralbl. Math. Ihre Grenzgeb.

US/0096-378X
**PROCEEDINGS OF THE SOUTH DAKOTA ACADEMY OF SCIENCE.** [Proc. S. Dak. Acad. Sci.]. **Main/Corp** South Dakota Academy of Science. Vol. 1 (1916)-. Proceedings. English. an. $13.75. South Dakota Academy of Science, Department of Math, Augustana College, Sioux Falls SD 57107. **Tel** (605)336-4825. **ED** Carroll Hanten. **LC** Q11; .S82. **NLM** W1 PR5868. **CODEN** PSDAA2. **Bk Rev. Ad Acc. Circ:** 350 (ctrl). Documents available from BIOSIS Document Express, CASDDS.
**Desc:** Research by South Dakota scientists in all areas of biological, physical, and mathematical sciences.
**Ind/Abst** Biol. Abstr.; Chem. Abstr. (-1985); Fish Rev. (Jan. 1989-July 1992); GeoRef; Plant Grow. Reg. Abstr.; Wildl. Rev. (Jan. 1989-July 1992).

CN
**PROCEEDINGS OF THE SPECIAL COMMITTEE OF THE SENATE ON SCIENCE POLICY. Main/Corp** Canada. Parliament. Senate. Special Committee on Science Policy. **VFOAT** Deliberations du Comite Special du Senat sur la Politique Scientifique. Proceedings. Multiple languages (English and French). Deliberations du Comite, Ottawa Ontario K1A 0S9 Canada. **LC** Q180.C2; C38C. **DD** 338.971.

US/0096-4263
**PROCEEDINGS OF THE WEST VIRGINIA ACADEMY OF SCIENCE.** [Proc. W. Va. Acad. Sci.]. **Main/Corp** West Virginia Academy of Science. (1924)-. Proceedings. English. qt. West Virginia Academy of Science, Box 129, West Virginia Wesleyan College, Buckhannon WV 26201. **LC** Q11; .W597. **DD** 506. **CODEN** PWVAAI. cum. index. Documents available from BIOSIS Document Express, CASDDS.
**Desc:** List of members in vol. 2.
**Ind/Abst** Biol. Abstr.; Chem. Abstr.; Coal Abstr.; Fish Rev. (Jan. 1989-July 1992); GeoRef; Int. Aerosp. Abstr.; Math. Rev.; Plant Grow. Reg. Abstr.; Wildl. Rev. (Jan. 1989-July 1992); Zentralbl. Math. Ihre Grenzgeb.

US/0093-450X
**PROCEEDINGS - PHILIP MORRIS SCIENCE SYMPOSIUM.** (PROCEEDINGS.). (1973)-. Academic Scholarly Publication. English. **NLM** W3 PH51. **CODEN** PPMSDF. Documents available from CASDDS.
**Ind/Abst** Chem. Abstr.

US
**PROCEEDINGS / STC, SOCIETY FOR TECHNICAL COMMUNICATION ANNUAL CONFERENCE. Main/Corp** Society for Technical Communication. Conference. (May 10-13, 1992)-. English. an. Univelt Inc., PO Box 28130, San Diego CA 92128. **Tel** (619)746-4005. **LC** T10.5; .I57. **DD** 601.4. **CODEN** PCNCEI. ***Continues*** *International Technical Communications Conference. Proceedings.*

KO
**PROCEEDINGS, THE ... INTERNATIONAL SYMPOSIA. Main/Corp** Taehan Minguk Haksurwon. 9th (1981)-. Proceedings. English. an. **LC** Q1; .T33A. **DD** 505. ***Continues*** *Taehan Minguk Haksurwon. Proceedings, The ... International Symposium.*

US
**PROCESS TECHNOLOGY CONFERENCE PROCEEDINGS / SPONSORED BY THE PROCESS TECHNOLOGY DIVISION OF THE IRON AND STEEL SOCIETY, INC. Added/Corp** Iron and Steel Society. Process Technology Division. (1988)-. English. an. Iron and Steel Society of AIME, 410 Commonwealth Drive, Warrendale PA 15086. **Tel** (412)776-9460, FAX (412)776-0430, telex 6503113507. **LC** TN701.5; .P75a. **DD** 669/.141. ***Continues*** *Process Technology Conference. Proceedings of the ... Process Technology Conference.*

UK/0960-3158
**PROCESSING OF ADVANCED MATERIALS.** [Process. adv. mater.]. (1991)-. Periodical. English. qt. $245.00 US and Canada; £145.00 Europe; £160.00 other. Chapman & Hall, 2-6 Boundary Row, London SE1 8HN England. **Tel** 011 44 71 865 0066, FAX 011 44 71 522 9623, telex 290164 Chapmag. **(Subscription address:** Chapman & Hall, Cheriton House, North Way, Andover, Hampshire, SP10 5BE England.**)** **DD** 620.112. **Pr Rev.** Documents available from The Genuine Article.
**Desc:** Covers all aspects of processing including recently developed methods for forming, joining, machining and surface modification when these techniques are applied to the treatment of advanced materials (composites, ceramics, plastics, electronic materials and new alloys). Deals with the fundamentals of processing methods, analytical and numerical models, development of experimental techniques and new industrial practices employed in the manufacturing of advanced materials into usable products.
**Ind/Abst** Res. Alert [Full Cov.].

US/1058-546X
**PRODUCT & PROCESS INNOVATION.**
**See** Engineering-Industrial Engineering and Design.

US/1050-7043
**PRODUCT DATA INTERNATIONAL.** [Prod. data int.]. **VFOAT** PDI. (Sept. 1990)-. Periodical. English. Six times a year (Jan., Mar., May, July, Sept., Nov.). $375.00 US & Canada; $395.00 other. Warthen Technical Information Services, N5303 Broughton Road, Albany WI 53502-9725. **Tel** (608)862-1702, FAX (608)862-1702. **ED** Barbara D. Warthen. **DD** 004. Index available (published separately). **Bk Rev**, (Qty: varies). **Ad Acc.** available on an online database.
**Desc:** Report on 16ES, PDES, STEP (data exchange/integration standards) and related activities for computer integrated manufacturing and construction.

IT/0032-9991
**PRODUTTIVITA.** [Produttivita]. Yearly V. 1- Oct. 1950-. Periodical. Italian. **LC** T4; .P823.
**Ind/Abst** Saf. Health Work.

NE/0552-2668
**PROFESSOR DR. F. DE VRIES LECTURES.** V. 1- 1955-. Monographic series. English. ir. Price varies per volume. Elsevier Science Publishing Company Inc, Madison Square Station, PO Box 882, New York NY 10159-0882. **Tel** (212)633-3950, FAX (212)633-3990.

IE/0332-3218
**PROFILES OF GENIUS SERIES.** Vol. 1 (1983)-. Monographic series. English. Price varies per volume. Boole Press Ltd, 26 Temple Lane, Temple Bar Dublin 2 Ireland. **Tel** 011 353 1 6797655, telex 30547 SHCN E1.
**Ind/Abst** Zentralbl. Math. Ihre Grenzgeb.

IT
**PROGETTARE.** Italian. L103000.00 Italy; L158000.00 other. Etas SRL, Via Mecenate 89, 20138 Milan Italy. **Tel** 011 39 2 580841.

IT
**PROGETTISTA, IL.** Italian. mo. Ediesse Milan, V S Gregario 48, 20124 Milan Italy. **Tel** 011 39 2 66988170.

IT/0392-4823
**PROGETTISTA INDUSTRIALE, IL.** [Prog. ind.]. (1981)-. Periodical. Italian. mo (10 issues). L75000 Italy; L140000 Europe; L185000 other. Tecniche Nuove SPA, Via Ciro Menotti 14, 20129 Milan Italy. **Tel** 011 39 2 75701, FAX 011 39 2 7610351, telex 334647 TECHS I. **UDC** 65.015.

US/0195-6132
**PROGRAM REPORT (NATIONAL SCIENCE FOUNDATION (US)).** (PROGRAM REPORT - NATIONAL SCIENCE FOUNDATION.). [Program rep. - Natl. Sci. Found.]. Began with March 1977. Monographic series. English. Price varies per volume. National Science Foundation, 1800 G Street Northwest, Washington DC 20550. **Tel** (202)357-9859, (202)357-9498. **LC** Q180.U5; U54L. **DD** 505. **NLM** W2 A N37P.
**Desc:** Each issue covers a different subject.
**Ind/Abst** GeoRef.

US/0149-6034
**PROGRAMS AND PLANS / ENVIRONMENTAL RESEARCH LABORATORIES. Main/Corp** Environmental Research Laboratories (U.S.). **VFOAT** Programs & Plans. English. an. Environmental Research Laboratories, Programs Office, 325 Broadway, Boulder CO 80303. **LC** Q180.U5; E58A. **DD** 353.008/55. available on microfiche (Vols. for (1982/1983-) distributed to depository libraries).

FR/0397-8060
**PROGRES TECHNIQUE, LE.** [Prog. tech.]. **Added/Corp** Association Nationale de la Recherche Technique. (1976)-. Academic Scholarly Publication. French. Five times a year. 250.00F (members), 450.00F (non-members) France; 300.00F (members), 500.00F (non-members) others. Association National de la Recherche Technique, 101 Av Raymond Poincare, F-75116 Paris France. **Tel** 011 33 1 45017227, FAX 011 33 1 47018529, telex 642632. **ED** Beinadette Ragot. **LC** T175; .P74. **DD** 338.9. **CODEN** PRTCDG. **Ad Acc, Adv Mgr:** M. Pagezy. ctrl circ. Documents available from CASDDS.
**Ind/Abst** Alum. Ind. Abstr.; Chem. Abstr. (1976-1982); Energy Res. Abstr. (April 1982-); Eng. Mater. Abstr.; Met. Abstr.

CC/1002-0071
**PROGRESS IN NATURAL SCIENCE : COMMUNICATION OF STATE KEY LABORATORIES OF CHINA. Added/Corp** National Natural Science Foundation of China. Vol. 1, No. 1 (Feb. 1991)-. Periodical. English. bm (6 issues). £108.00 UK; $179.00 other. Taylor & Francis Ltd., Rankine Road, Basingstoke Hampshire, RG24 8PR United Kingdom. **Tel** 011 44 256 840366, FAX 011 44 256 479438, telex 858540. **(Subscription address:** Taylor & Francis Inc., 1900 Frost Road, Suite 101, Bristol PA 19007-1598.**)** **LC** IN PROCESS.

US/0583-936X
**PROGRESS IN TECHNOLOGY. Main/Corp** Society of Automotive Engineers. **VFOAT** Technical Progress Series. (1961)-. Monographic series. English. ir. Price varies per volume. Society of Automotive Engineers, 400 Commonwealth Drive, Warrendale PA 15096. **Tel** (412)776-4841, (412)772-7106, FAX (412)776-5760.

IE
**PROGRESS REPORT. Main/Corp** National Science Council (Ireland). (19??)-. English. Government Publications, 4 5 Harcourt Road, Dublin 2 Ireland. **Tel** 011 353 1 6613111 Ext.4005. **LC** Q127.I73; N37a. **DD** 354/.415/0085505.

KE
**PROGRESS REPORT - COAST INSTITUTE OF TECHNOLOGY. Main/Corp** Coast Institute of Technology. English. Progress Report - Coast Institute of Technology, Mombosa 90424 Kenya. **LC** T173.M645; A23. **DD** 607/.11/67623.

US/0748-2701
**PROJECT SUMMARIES - NATIONAL SCIENCE FOUNDATION (U.S.). DIVISION OF SCIENCE RESOURCES STUDIES.** (PROJECT SUMMARIES / DIVISION OF SCIENCE RESOURCES STUDIES, NATIONAL SCIENCE FOUNDATION.). [Proj. summ. - Natl. Sci. Found. (U.S.), Div. Sci. Resour. Stud.]. **Main/Corp** National Science Foundation (U.S.). Division of Science Resources Studies. 1980/81-. English. an. National Science Foundation, 1800 G Street Northwest, Washington DC 20550. **Tel** (202)357-9859, (202)357-9498. **LC** Q11; .U8217. **DD** 338.97306.

CN/1188-0368
**PROVING GROUND : ENVIRONMENTAL RESEARCH & TECHNOLOGY DEVELOPMENT, THE.** [Proving ground]. **Added/Corp** Ontario. Ministry of the Environment. Research and Technology Branch. (Oct. 1991)-. Periodical. English. **DD** 363.7/009713/05.

FR
**PROVISIONAL VERBATIM RECORD, PLENARY MEETING. Main/Corp** United Nations Educational, Scientific and Cultural Organization. General Conference. **VFOAT** VR. (19??)-. Government Publication. English. ir. United Nations Publications, 2 United Nations Plaza, Room DC2 0853, Department 007C, New York NY 10017. **Tel** (212)963-8303, (800)253-9646.

PL
**PRZEGLAD INFORMACJI O NAUKOZNAWSTWIE. Added/Corp** Polska Akademia Nauk. Osrodek Dokumentacji i Informacji Naukowej. (19??)-. Periodical. Polish. qt. **(Subscription address:** ARS Polona, PO Box 1001, 00068 Warsaw Poland.**)** **LC** Q4; .P82.

PL/0033-2364
**PRZEGLAD SPAWALNICTWA. Added/Corp** Stowarzyszenia Inzynierow I Technikow Mechanikow Polskich. **VFOAT** PS. (1949)-. Academic Scholarly Publication. Polish (summaries and/or abstracts in English and Russian). mo. $96.00. Wydawnictwa Czasopism Tech, Czackiego 3/5, Warsaw Poland. **Tel** 27-25-42. **Bk Rev. Ad Acc. Circ:** 1,000. Documents available from CASDDS.
**Desc:** New techniques and technology in industry. Latest invented patents or other interesting research and developing results. Modern robots with computers and welding equipment.

**Ind/Abst** Alum. Ind. Abstr.; Chem. Abstr.; Eng. Mater. Abstr.; Met. Abstr.; Saf. Health Work; Surf. Treat. Technol. Abstr.

PL/0033-2380
**PRZEGLAD TECHNICZNY.** [Prz. tech.]. **VFOAT** Innowacje. 1866-. Periodical. Polish. wk. **Ind/Abst** Saf. Health Work.

US/0270-8647
**PSA (EAST LANSING, MICH.).** (PSA; PROCEEDINGS OF THE BIENNIAL MEETING OF THE PHILOSOPHY OF SCIENCE ASSOCIATION.). [PSA]. **Main/Corp** Philosophy of Science Association. **Added/Corp** Philosophy of Science Association. Proceedings of the Biennial Meeting of the Philosophy of Science Association. **VAT** Philosophy of Science Association. (1970)-. Proceedings. English. be. Philosophy of Science Association, 18 Morrill Hall, Department of Philosophy, East Lansing MI 48824. **Tel** (517)353-9392. **LC** Q174; .P58a; Q174; .B67. **DD** 501. **NLM** W1 PH619E.

NE/0032-4094
**PT. PROCESTECHNIEK. See** Engineering.

GW/0933-4807
**PTERIDINES.** ***Ceased.*** [Pteridines]. Vol. 1, No. 1 (Jan. 1989)-(19??). Academic Scholarly Publication. English. qt. Walter de Gruyter Inc., PO Box 303421, D 10728 Berlin Germany. **Tel** 011 49 30 260050, FAX 011 49 30 26005251. **(Subscription address:** US and Canada/ 200 Saw Mill River Road, Hawthorne, NY 10532**) ED** Joseph R Bertino, John A Blair, Frank M Huennekens, Wolfgang Pfleiderer, and Helmut Wachter. **NLM** W1; PT73. **CODEN** PTRDEO. **[CCC]. Bk Rev. Ad Acc. Circ:** 500. Documents available from BIOSIS Document Express, CASDDS.
**Desc:** A new international journal covering all areas of science relating to pteridines and related materials. The aim of the journal is to provide a comprehensive coverage of this field within one journal and thus stimulate interdisciplinary cooperation, research and advances in medical science.
**Ind/Abst** Biol. Abstr.; Chem. Abstr.; EMBASE.

US/0091-1720
**PUBLIC SCIENCE NEWSLETTER.** ***Ceased.*** **Added/Corp** Massachusetts Institute of Technology. Dept. of Political Science. Science and Public Policy Program. Vol. 4 (Jan. 1973)-(19??). Newsletter. English. mo. Massachusetts Institute of Technology (MIT) Press, 55 Hayward Street, Cambridge MA 02142-1399. **Tel** (617)253-2889, (617)625-8481, FAX (617)258-6779. **LC** Q127.U6; S314a. **NLM** W1 PU638. ***Continues*** *SPPSG Newsletter.*

US/0882-1445
**PUBLIC TECHNOLOGY.** [Public technol.]. Periodical. English. mo. $35.00 US; $45.00 other. Public Technology Inc, 1301 Pennsylvania Avenue NW, Washington DC 20004. **Tel** (202)626-2400, FAX (202)626-2498. **ED** Lydia Manchester. **DD** 303. Index available. **Bk Rev. Circ:** 4,000 (ctrl). ***Continues*** *Public Technology News, 0194-1623.*
**Desc:** Illustrated articles on cost-effective technologies for local governments and how they are being implemented. Also reports on new research and technological trends.
**Ind/Abst** Urban Aff. Abstr.

●UK/0963-6625
**PUBLIC UNDERSTANDING OF SCIENCE.** **Added/Corp** Institute of Physics (Great Britain) Science Museum (Great Britain). Vol. 1 (1992)-. Periodical. English (summaries and/or abstracts in French and Spanish). qt. $112.00. Institute of Physics, Techno House, Redcliffe Way, Bristol BS1 6NX England. **Tel** 011 44 272 297481, FAX 011 44 272 294318, telex 449149 INSTP G. **(Subscription address:** American Institute of Physics, Publishing Sales, 500 Sunnyside Blvd., Woodbury NY 11797.**) ED** John Durant. **LC** Q225; .P8. **DD** 501.4. **NLM** W1; PU639. **CODEN** PUNSEM. Index available in last issue of volume--attached. **Bk Rev.** available on microfiche.
**Desc:** Provides a forum for the emerging interdisciplinary field of public understanding of science. It encourages open debate of contrasting and even conflicting viewpoints on all aspects of the interrelationships between science and the public.

BL/0100-7092
**PUBLICACAO ACIESP.** (PUBLICACAO ACIESP / ACADEMIA DE CIENCIAS DO ESTADO DE SAO PAULO EM CONVENIO COM SECRETARIA DA CULTURA, CIENCIA E TECNOLOGIA.). [Publ. ACIESP]. **Added/Corp** Academia de Ciencias do Estado de Sao Paulo. Sao Paulo (Brazil : State). Secretaria de Cultura, Ciencia e Tecnologia. **VAT** Publicacao Academia de Ciencias do Estado de Sao Paulo. (19??)-. Academic Scholarly Publication. Portuguese. **LC** UNC. **CODEN** PUACDA. Documents available from CASDDS.
**Ind/Abst** Chem. Abstr.

US/0071-7754
**PUBLICATION - FORT BURGWIN RESEARCH CENTER.** **Main/Corp** Fort Burgwin Research Center. Vol. 1 (1961)-. Monographic series. English. Price varies per volume. Fort Burgwin Research Center Inc, Southern Methodist University, Dallas TX 75275. **CODEN** PFBCDC.
**Ind/Abst** GeoRef.

CN/0077-5584
**PUBLICATIONS OF THE NATIONAL RESEARCH COUNCIL OF CANADA.** [Publ. Natl. Res. Counc. Can.]. **VFOAT** Publications du Conseil National de Recherches du Canada. 1918/38-. Academic Scholarly Publication. English. Canada Institute for Scientific and Technical Information, National Research Council of Canada, Ottawa Ontario K1A 0S2 Canada. **Tel** (613)993-3736, telex 053-3115. **NLM** Z 7401 P975. **CODEN** NTCPAR.
**Ind/Abst** EMBASE; GeoRef.

FI/0358-5069
**PUBLICATIONS / TECHNICAL RESEARCH CENTRE OF FINLAND.** [Publ. - Tech. Res. Cent. Finl.]. **Added/Corp** Valtion Teknillinen Tutkimuskeskus. (1981)-. Academic Scholarly Publication. English. ir. Price varies per volume. Valtion Teknillinen Tutkimuskeskus, Technical Research Centre of Finland, Vuorimiehentie 5, PO Box 45, FIN 02044 VTT Finland. **Tel** 011 358 0 4561, FAX 011 358 0455 4374, telex 125175 VTTIN SF. **CODEN** PTRFDT. Index available. cum. index. **Pr Rev. Circ:** 400. Documents available from Ask*IEEE, CASDDS. ***Formed by the union of*** *Valtion Teknillinen Tutkimuskeskus. Materiaali - Ja Prosessitekniikan Tutimusosasto. Publication - Technical Research Centre of Finland. Materials and Processing Technology, 0355-3388; Valtion Teknillinen Tutkimuskeskus. Rakennus - Ja Yladyskuntatekniikan Tutkimusosasto. Publication - Technical Research Centre of Finland, Building Technology and Community Development; Valtion Teknillinen Tutkimuskeskus. Yleinen Osasto Publication - Technical Research Centre of Finland, General Division* ***and*** *Valtion Teknillinen Tutkimuskeskus. Electrical and Nuclear Technology. Publication - Technical Research Centre of Finland. Electrical and Nuclear Technology, 0355-3396.*
**Desc:** Consists of technical and scientific research results.
**Ind/Abst** Biodeter. Abstr. (19??-19??); Chem. Abstr. (1981-1983); Food Sci. Technol. Abstr.; Geogr. Abstr. Human Geogr. (?-?); INSPEC; Life Sci. Collect.

SZ
**PUBLIKATIONEN (EIDGENOSSISCHE TECHNISCHE HOCHSCHULE ZURICH. INSTITUT FUR ORTS-, REGIONAL- UND LANDESPLANUNG).** (PUBLIKATIONEN : KURZFASSUNGEN.). German. Verlag der Fachvereine Austieferung, Postfach 566, CH-6314 Unteraegeri Switzerland. **LC** WMLC L 83/1407.

GW/0073-8433
**PUBLIKATIONEN ZU WISSENSCHAFTLICHEN FILMEN, SEKTION TECHNISCHE WISSENSCHAFTEN, NATURWISSENSCHAFTEN.** [Publ. wiss. Filmen, Sekt. tech. Wiss., Naturwiss.]. German (summaries and/or abstracts in English and French). ir. Institut fur den Wissenschaftlichen Film, Nonnenstieg 72 Y, W-3400 Gottingen Germany. **Tel** 0551-2020, FAX 0551-202200, telex 96691. **ED** H K Galle. **LC** T65.5.M6; P82.
**Ind/Abst** Energy Res. Abstr. (March 1982-).

US
**PUBLISHED SEARCH MASTER CATALOG / U.S. DEPARTMENT OF COMMERCE, NATIONAL TECHNICAL INFORMATION SERVICE. See** Communication-Abstracting, Bibliographies and Statistics.

US/0033-4685
**PURSUIT (COLUMBIA).** ***Suspended.*** **See** Parapsychology and Occultism.

KO
**PUSAN SUSAN TAEHAK YON'GU POGO.** **VFOAT** Chayon Kwahakpyon; Bulletin of Pusan Fisheries College. Part, Natural Sciences. V. 1-Dec. 1956-. Academic Scholarly Publication. Korean (summaries and/or abstracts in English). $30.00. Hanguk Susan Hakhoe, National Fisheries University of Pusan, Pusan 608 Korea. **LC** Q4; .P87A. **DD** 505. **CODEN** PSCKAR. ctrl circ. Documents available from BIOSIS Document Express, CASDDS. ***Continues in part*** *Pusan Susan Taehak Yongu Pogo (1964).*
**Ind/Abst** Biol. Abstr.; Chem. Abstr.; Energy Res. Abstr. (Nov. 1982-).

QA/0255-6677
**QATAR UNIVERSITY SCIENCE BULLETIN.** [Qatar Univ. sci. bull.]. **Added/Corp** Jamiat Qatar. **VFOAT** Science Bulletin. Vol. 1, No. 1 (1981)-. Academic Scholarly Publication. English. **CODEN** QUSBD6. Documents available from BIOSIS Document Express, CASDDS.
**Ind/Abst** Biol. Abstr. (1986-); Chem. Abstr.; Math. Rev. (1988-).

IT
**QUADERNI CERIS.** (19??)-. Italian. qt. Free on request. Ceris Cnr, Via Avogadro 8, 10121 Turin Italy. **Tel** 011 39 11 515953. ***Continues*** *Bollettino Ceris.*

IT
**QUADERNI INTERNAZIONALI DI STORIA DELLA MEDICINA E DELLA SANITA.** (199?)-. Periodical. Italian (summaries and/or abstracts in English). sa. L36000 Italy; L42000 other. CISO Toscano, Instituto di Patalogia Speciale Medica, Ospedale South, Maria della Scala, Piazzo Duomo 2, 53100 Siena Italy. **Tel** 011 39 577 299264. **NLM** W1; QU149M.

US/1052-9411
**QUALITY ASSURANCE (SAN DIEGO, CALIF.).** (QUALITY ASSURANCE : QA.). [Qual. assur.]. **VFOAT** QA. Vol. 1, No. 1 (Oct. 1991)-. Academic Scholarly Publication. English. qt. $192.00 US and Canada. Academic Press, Inc., 6277 Sea Harbor Drive, Orlando FL 32887. **Tel** (800)543-9534, (407)345-4100, FAX (407)363-9661. **ED** Frederick Coulston, Gary L. Yingling and Travis Griffin. **LC** TS156.6; .Q33. **DD** 658.5/62. **NLM** W1; QU158KD. **CODEN** QUASE2. **[CCC].** Documents available from CASDDS.
**Desc:** Devoted to examining issues of quality assurance and quality control as they relate to biological, physical and engineering science, and technology.
**Ind/Abst** Chem. Abstr.

US/0033-5207
**QUALITY CONTROL AND APPLIED STATISTICS. See** Science and Technology-Abstracting, Bibliographies and Statistics.

UK/0266-3104
**QUALITY TECHNOLOGY HANDBOOK.** (QUALITY TECHNOLOGY HANDBOOK / PRODUCED BY THE HARWELL NONDESTRUCTIVE TESTING CENTRE.). [Qual. technol. handb.]. **Added/Corp** Harwell Nondestructive Testing Centre (Oxfordshire). **VFOAT** Quality Technology Hand Book. (1975)-. English. ir. Butterworth & Co. Ltd. / Kent, England, Borough Green, Sevenoaks Kent TN15 8PH England. **Tel** 011 44 732-884567, FAX 011 44 732-885996. **LC** TA417.2; .Q82. **DD** 620.1/127/025. ***Continues*** *Quality Technology.*
**Desc:** Covers quality control and non-destructive testing.

UK/0264-2344
**QUALITY TODAY.** [Qual. today]. (Feb. 1983)-. Periodical. English. ir (10 issues). £71.00 UK; £88.00 other. Nexus Business Communications, Warwick House, Azalea Drive, c/o Dr. Swanle, Kent BR8 8HY England. **Tel** 011 44 322 660070. **CODEN** QUTODG. Documents available from Ask*IEEE. ***Continues*** *Measurement and Inspection Technology;* ***Absorbed*** *Quality Testing Today.*
**Ind/Abst** Alum. Ind. Abstr.; Curr. Technol. Index (1983-); Energy Res. Abstr. (Feb. 1983-); Eng. Mater. Abstr.; Fluid Abstr., Civil Eng.; Fluid Abstr. Proc. Eng.; FLUIDEX (1983-1990); INSPEC (1983-1991); Met. Abstr.; World Ceram. Abstr.

GW
**QUANTITATIVE AUSWERTUNG VON DUNNSCHICHT CHROMATOGRAMMEN.** ***Ceased.*** (19??)-Vol. 12. German. Git Verlag GmbH, Postfach 110564, D 64220 Darmstadt Germany. **Tel** 011 49 6151 80900.

US/0273-1355
**QUARTERLY REPORT - MIT SEA GRANT PROGRAM.** [Q. rep. - MIT Sea Grant Prog.]. **Main/Corp** Massachusetts Institute of Technology. Sea Grant Program. **VAT** Quarterly Report - Massachusetts Institute of Technology Sea Grant Program. (19??)-. Periodical. English. qt. Free. Massachusetts Institute of Technology (MIT) / Sea Grant College Program, Building E38/Room 360, Cambridge MA 02139. **Tel** (617)253-3461. **ED** Karen Hartley and Carolyn Levi. **Circ:** 2,000. Documents available from Documents on Demand.
**Ind/Abst** Environ. Abstr.; Ocean. Abstr.

US
**QUARTERLY SUPPLEMENT, DIRECTORY OF PUBLIC HIGH-TECH CORPORATIONS.** **Added/Corp** American Investor Information Services. **VFOAT** Directory of Public High-Tech Corporations. Vol. 3, No. 3 (1985)-. Directory. English. qt. American Investor Information Services Inc, 311 Bainbridge Street, Philadelphia PA 19147. **Tel** (215)925-2761. ***Continues*** *New Issues in High Technology.*

CN/0021-6127
**QUEBEC SCIENCE.** [Que. sci.]. **Added/Corp** Universite du Quebec. **VFOAT** Magazine Quebec; Le Magazine Quebec Science. Vol. 8, No. 3 (Jan. 1970)-. Periodical. French. Ten times a year. 30.00Can$ Canada; 43.00Can$ other. Les Presses de L'Universite de Quebec, 2875 Boulevard Laurier, St. Foy Quebec G1V 2M3 Canada. **Tel** (418)657-4390 Ext. 2860. **ED** J. Dallaire. **DD** 505. Index available. **Bk Rev. Ad Acc. Circ:** 28,000. available on microfilm and microfiche from University Microfilms International (UMI). ***Continues*** *Jeune Scientifique, 0317-400X.*

**Desc:** Science news magazine that gives priority to research conducted in Quebec, while taking into account significant scientific developments in Canada and the rest of the world.
**Ind/Abst** AQUAREF (1971-1990); Can. Period. Index (19??-); Environ.; Point Repere (1983-).

CN/0711-5288
**QUEBEC TECHNOLOGIE.** [Que. technol.]. Dec./Jan. 1980-. Periodical. French. bm. Free. Quebec Technologie, c/o La Corporation Professionnelle des Technologues des Sciences Appliquees du Quebec, 4152 rue St-Denis, Montreal Quebec H2W 2M5 Canada. **DD** 606/.0714. ctrl circ. ***Continues** Technicien (Corporation des Techniciens Professionnels du Quebec).*

AT
**QUEENSLAND SCIENCE TEACHER. See** Education-Teaching and Curriculum.

US/0149-6670
**QUEST (REDONDO BEACH).** (QUEST.). [Quest]. **Added/Corp** TRW Defense and Space Systems Group. **VFOAT** TRW/DSSG/Quest. Vol. 1 (Winter 1976/1977)-. Periodical. English. sa. Free on request. TRW Defense and Space Systems Group, One Space Park, E2 9080, Redondo Beach CA 90278. **Tel** (213)812-4724. **LC** T1; .Q48. **DD** 620/.005.
**Ind/Abst** Int. Aerosp. Abstr.

UK/0954-920X
**QUESTIONS (BIRMINGHAM). See** Education-Teaching and Curriculum.

MX/0185-5093
**QUIPU. Added/Corp** Sociedad Latinoamericana de Historia de las Ciencias y la Tecnologia. Consejo Nacional de Ciencia y Tecnologia (Mexico). **VFOAT** Revista Latinoamericana de Historia de las Ciencias y la Tecnologia. Vol. 1, No. 1 (1984)-. Periodical. Spanish (English, Spanish and Portuguese). Three times a year (Jan., May, Sept.). $25.00 (individuals); $100.00 (institutions). Society Latinoamericana Historia, Apartado Postal 21-873, 04000 Mexico DF Mexico. **Tel** 011 52 5 5344651, FAX 011 52 5 5344651. **ED** Dr. Juan Jose Saldana (phone: 622-18-64). **NLM** W1; QU964W. Index available. cum. index. **Bk Rev. Ad Acc.** ctrl circ.
**Desc:** The history and studies of science and technology in Latin America.
**Ind/Abst** Am. Hist. Life (1984-).

US/0565-8284
**R & D ACTIVITIES IN STATE GOVERNMENT AGENCIES. Added/Corp** National Science Foundation (U.S.) United States. Bureau of the Census. (1964/65)-. Periodical. English. be. National Science Foundation, 1800 G Street Northwest, Washington DC 20550. **Tel** (202)357-9859, (202)357-9498. **LC** Q180.U5; A3436. **DD** 600; 500.

US
**R & D CONTRACTS, GRANTS FOR TRAINING, CONSTRUCTION, AND MEDICAL LIBRARIES. Added/Corp** National Institutes of Health (U.S.). Division of Research Grants. Information Systems Branch. Statistical Analysis Unit. **VFOAT** R and D Contracts, Grants for Training, Construction, and Medical Libraries. (Fiscal year 1989 funds)-. English. US Department of Health and Human Services, 200 Independence Avenue Southwest, Washington DC 20201. ***Formed by the union of** Research and Development Contracts, 0363-583X **and** Grants for Training, Construction, Medical Libraries (Bethesda, Md. : 1983), 8756-551X.*

US/0033-6793
**R & D CONTRACTS MONTHLY.** [R D contracts mon.]. **Added/Corp** Government Data Publications (Firm). **VAT** Research and Development Contracts Monthly. (19??)-. Periodical. English. mo. $76.00. Government Data Publications / New York, GDP Building, 1661 McDonald Avenue, Brooklyn NY 11230. **Tel** (718)627-0819. **ED** Siegfried Lobel. **DD** 650.
**Desc:** Each issue lists research and development, design, research engineering and prototype production contracts and is divided into three pre-sorted sections of immediately usable, 100 percent current data.

UK/0033-6807
**R & D MANAGEMENT.** [R & D manage.]. **VFOAT** R and D Management; R&D Management. Vol. 1 (Oct. 1970)-. Academic Scholarly Publication. English. Four times a year. £157.00 UK and Europe; $299.00 North America; £193.00 other. Basil Blackwell Publishers Ltd, 108 Cowley Road, Oxford 0X4 1JF England. **Tel** 011 44 865 791100, FAX 011 44 865 791347, telex 837022 OXBOOK G. **(Subscription address:** Blackwell Publishers / UK, Marston Book Services, PO Box 87, Oxford OX2 0DT England.**) ED** Sidney Epton and Alan Pearson. **LC** T175.5; .R15. **DD** 658.5/7/05. **CODEN** RDMAAW. **[CCC]. Bk Rev. Ad Acc. Pr Rev. Circ:** 1,000. available on microfilm and microfiche from University Microfilms International (UMI). Documents available from The Genuine Article, UMI Article Clearinghouse, Ask*IEEE.
**Desc:** Promotes a better understanding of the problems of managing research and development wherever they occur throughout the world.

**Ind/Abst** ABI/INFORM Glob. Ed.; ABI Inform Ondisc (Feb. 1979-); Anbar Account. Finan. Abstr. [Full Txt.]; Anbar Mark. Distr. Abstr. [Full Txt.]; Anbar Top Manage. Abstr. [Full Txt.]; Bus. ASAP (1992-) [Full Txt.]; Bus. Index (1985-); Contents Pages Manage.; Curr. Contents Soc. Behav. Sci.; Gen. BusinessFile (1985-); Gen. Period. Index (1985-); INSPEC (June 1972-); Int. Abstr. Oper. Res. [Select. Cov.]; Int. Aerosp. Abstr.; Int. Bibliogr. Sociol.; Manage. Market. Abstr.; Manage. Bibliogr. Rev.; Oper. Prod. Manage. Abstr. [Full Txt.]; Oper. Res./Manag. Sci.; PAIS Int. Print (1991-); Person. Train. Abstr. [Full Txt.]; Res. Alert [Full Cov.]; Selec. Coop. Index Manage. Period; Soc. Sci. Cit. Index [Full Cov.]; Tech. Educ. Train. Abstr.; Trade Ind. ASAP [Full Txt.]; Trade Ind. Index [Full Txt.]; UMI ABI/Inform--Bus. Period. Ondisc (Jan. 1990-) [Full Txt.]; Women Manage. Rev. [Full Txt.]; World Ceram. Abstr.; World Publ. Monit.; World Text. Abstr.

US/0192-3692
**R - RAND CORPORATION.** (R : REPORT / RAND CORPORATION.). [R - Rand Corp.]. **Main/Corp** Rand Corporation. **Added/Corp** Rand Corporation. **VFOAT** Report; Rand Report. (1948)-. Monographic series. English. ir. Price varies per volume. Rand Corporation, 1700 Main Street, PO Box 2138, Santa Monica CA 90407-2138. **Tel** (310)393-0411. **LC** T1; .R185. **CODEN** RCRRD2. Documents available from Ask*IEEE, CASDDS. ***Continues** Rand Corporation. Reports - Rand. **Continued in part by** MR Reports.*
**Ind/Abst** Chem. Abstr.; Ei Page One; INSPEC.

UK/0963-0678
**RADIO TECHNOLOGY INTERNATIONAL. See** Communication-Broadcasting.

JA/0033-8303
**RADIOISOTOPES.** [Radioisotopes]. **Added/Corp** Nihon Hoshasei Doi Genso Kyokai. Nihon Aisotopu Kyokai. Vol. 1, No. 5 (1952)-. Periodical. Japanese (English). mo. $170.00. Japan Radioisotopes Association, 28-45 Honkomagome 2 chome, Bunkyo-ku Tokyo 113-91 Japan. **Tel** 03-946-7110, FAX 03-946-2640. **(Subscription address:** Kyowa Book Company Inc., 1 38 Kanda Jinbocho Chiyoda-ku, Tokyo 101 Japan.**) ED** Hisao Yamashita. **LC** R895.A1; R28. **NLM** W1 RA265. **CODEN** RAISAB. Index available. **Ad Acc. Circ:** 4,000 (ctrl). Documents available from BIOSIS Document Express, Ask*IEEE, CASDDS.
**Desc:** Presents papers in the fields of physics, biochemistry, medical science, pharmacology and engineering by using radioisotopes.
**Ind/Abst** Biol. Abstr.; Chem. Abstr.; Curr. Biotechnol.; EMBASE; Energy Res. Abstr.; Food Sci. Technol. Abstr.; Index Med.; INSPEC (Dec. 1979-).

FR/0399-0559
**RAIRO : RECHERCHE OPERATIONNELLE.** [R.A.I.R.O. Rech. oper.]. **Added/Corp** Association Francaise Pour la Cybernetique Economique et Technique. **VFOAT** Recherche Operationnelle; Operations Research; RAIRO: Operations Research; RAIRO, Revue Francaise d'Automatique, d'Informatique et de Recherche Operationnelle. **VAT** Revue Francaise d'Automatique, d'Informatique et de Recherche Operationnelle: Recherche Operationnelle. Vol. 11 (Feb. 1977)-. Periodical. English (French). Four times a year. 790.00F France; 1060.00F other. Dunod Gauthier Villars, 15 rue Gossin, 92543 Montrouge cedex France. **Tel** 011 33 1 46 56 52 66, FAX 011 33 1 46 57 40 69. **(Subscription address:** Centrale des Revues, 11 rue Gossin, 92543 Montrouge Cedex France.**) LC** T57.6; .R46. **DD** 658.4/034. **CODEN** RSROD3. **[CCC]. Pr Rev.** Documents available from The Genuine Article, Ask*IEEE. ***Continues** Revue Francaise d'Automatique, Informatique, Recherche Operationnelle: Recherche Operationnelle, 0397-9350.*
**Ind/Abst** Compumath Citation Index; Curr. Contents Eng. Tech. Appl. Sci.; Energy Res. Abstr. (1983-); INSPEC (Feb. 1979-); Int. Abstr. Oper. Res.; Math. Rev.; Res. Alert; Soc. Sci. Cit. Index [Select. Cov.]; Stat. Theory Method Abstr. (1978, 1982-1983, 1986-1987); Zentralbl. Math. Ihre Grenzgeb.

US/0092-2803
**RAND PAPER SERIES.** (THE RAND PAPER SERIES.). [Rand pap. ser.]. **Added/Corp** Rand Corporation. (1947)-. Monographic series. English. ir. Price varies per volume. Rand Corporation, 1700 Main Street, PO Box 2138, Santa Monica CA 90407-2138. **Tel** (310)393-0411. **LC** AS36; .R28. **DD** 081. **CODEN** RCOPAC. ***Continues** Rand Corporation. Paper.*
**Ind/Abst** Popul. Index (?-?); Stat. Theory Method Abstr. (1977).

CN/0830-1093
**R&D - ALBERTA RESEARCH COUNCIL.** (R&D.). [R D - Alta. Res. Counc.]. **Added/Corp** Alberta Research Council. **VFOAT** Research and Development - Alberta Research Council; R and D - Alberta Research Council; R&D Newsletter. (1982)-. Periodical. English. bm (6 issues). AOSTRA Provincial Treasurer, 500 Highfield Place, 10010-106 Street, Edmonton Alberta T5J 3L8 Canada. **Tel** (403)427-7623, FAX (403)427-3198, telex 037-3519. **DD** 354.712300855.

●US/1061-1894
**R&D INNOVATOR.** [R&D innov.]. **VFOAT** R & D Innovator; R and D Innovator. Vol. 1, No. 1 (Aug. 1992)-. Periodical. English. mo. $144.00 US, Canada and Mexico; $168.00 other. Winston J. Brill & Associates, 4134 Cherokee Drive, Madison WI 53711. **Tel** (608)231-6766, FAX (608)231-6794. **ED** Winston J. Brill, Ph.D. **DD** 658. Index available (published separately). cum. index. **Bk Rev**, (Qty: 6-12). **Circ:** 1,000 (ctrl).
**Desc:** Serves as a resource for productivity and creativity in research and development. Articles by Nobel Prize winners, industrial research leaders, historians of science and technology, management experts, and psychologists. Each issue contains a feature article, an article about creativity, an article on a specific discovery, and an article providing practical solutions to common laboratory problems.

PH/0115-9984
**R&D PHILIPPINES.** English. P150.00 Philippines; $30.00 (airmail) other. Science and Technology Information Institute, PO Box 2131, Manila Philippines. **Tel** 011 63 2 822 0961. Index available. cum. index. **Circ:** 250.
**Desc:** Cumulation of completed, on going and pipeline R&D's with complete bibliographical information.

US/0735-0872
**R&D REVIEW (JACKSON, MISS.).** (R & D REVIEW / MISSISSIPPI RESEARCH & DEVELOPMENT CENTER.). [RD rev.]. **Main/Corp** Mississippi Research and Development Center. **VFOAT** R and D Review. English. Mississippi Research and Development Center, PO Drawer 2470, 3825 Ridgewood Road, Jackson MS 39205. **LC** Q180.U5; M545A. **DD** 353.97620082.

US/0190-5511
**RANGE SCIENCE SERIES (DENVER).** (RANGE SCIENCE SERIES.). [Range sci. ser.]. **Added/Corp** Society for Range Management. No. 1 (Oct. 1972)-. Monographic series. English. ir. Price varies per volume. Society for Range Management, 1839 York Street, Denver CO 80206. **Tel** (303)355-7070, (303)571-0174. **LC** UNC. **CODEN** SRMTBT.
**Ind/Abst** GeoRef.

CN/0837-645X
**RAPPORT ANNUEL / FONDS FCAR, FONDS POUR LA FORMATION DE CHERCHEURS ET L'AIDE A LA RECHERCHE.** [Rapp. annu. - Fonds FCAR]. **Main/Corp** Fonds FCAR (Quebec). 1984/85-. French. an. Fonds FCAR, Fonds pour la Formation de Chercheurs et L'Aide a la Recherche, 3700 rue du Campanile, Bureau 102, Sainte-Foy Quebec G1X 4G6 Canada. **LC** Q180.C2; Q417A. **DD** 001.4/4/09714. ***Continues** Rapport Annuel / Fonds F.C.A.C. pour l'Aide et le Soutien a la recherche, 0711-5237.*

RW
**RAPPORT ANNUEL / INSTITUT NATIONAL DE RECHERCHE SCIENTIFIQUE (I.N.R.S.). Main/Corp** Institut National de Recherche Scientifique. (1986)-. French. an. Institut National de Recherche Scientifique, Lome Togo. **LC** Q91; .I59. ***Continues** Rapport - Institut National de Recherche Scientifique.*

CN/1187-3736
**RAPPORT ANNUEL - MUSEE NATIONAL DES SCIENCES ET DE LA TECHNOLOGIE (OTTAWA).** (RAPPORT ANNUEL.). [Rapp. annu. - Mus. natl. sci. technol.]. **Main/Corp** Musee National des Sciences et de la Technologie (Canada). (1991)-. French. **DD** 507/.4/71. ***Continues in part** Musees Nationaux du Canada. Rapport Annuel - les Musees Nationaux du Canada., 0704-1616.*

BE/0069-1968
**RAPPORT D'ACTIVITE - CENTRE NATIONAL DE DOCUMENTATION SCIENTIFIQUE ET TECHNIQUE.** [Rapp. act. - Cent. natl. doc. sci. tech.]. **Main/Corp** Belgium. Centre National de Documentation Scientifique et Technique. (19??)-. French. Bibliotheque Royal Albert, Boulevard de l'Empereur 4, B-1000 Brussels Belgium. **Tel** 011 32 2 5195551. **LC** T10.65.B4; B44a. **DD** 607/.2/4933. **NLM** Z 699.A1 C397R. **CODEN** CDORBV.
**Ind/Abst** GeoRef.

GO
**RAPPORT D'ACTIVITE - INSTITUT DE RECHERCHES TECHNOLOGIQUES. Main/Corp** Institut de Recherches Technologiques (Libreville, Gabon). 1976/77-. French. Centre National de la Recherche Scientifique et Technologique Institut de Recherches Technologiques, B P 14 070 Akebe, Libreville Republique Gabonaise. **LC** T177.G23; I57A. **DD** 607/.2/6721.

FR
**RAPPORT D'ACTIVITES SUR LES RECHERCHES A L'ENSTA. Main/Corp** Ecole Nationale Superieure de Techniques Avancees. French. Ecole Nationale Superieure de Techniques Avancees, 32

Blvd Victor, Paris 75015 France. **LC** T178.E32; E26A. **DD** 620/.007/2044361. ***Continues** Activities Recherche - Ecole Nationale Superieure de Techniques Avancees, 0376-6268.*

FR
**RAPPORT NATIONAL DE CONJONCTURE SCIENTIFIQUE : RAPPORT DE SYNTHESE.** **Main/Corp** France. Centre National de la Recherche Scientifique. Comite National de la Recherche Scientifique. French. CNRS / Institut d'Information Scientifique et Technique, (Centre National de la Recherche Scientifique), 15 Quai Anatole France, Paris 75700 France. **Tel** 011 33 1 47531515, telex 299 356 F. **LC** Q46; .F7216. **DD** 505.

CN
**RAPPORT TECHNIQUE (UNIVERSITE LAVAL. DEPARTEMENT D'INFORMATIQUE).** (RAPPORT TECHNIQUE / DEPARTEMENT D'INFORMATIQUE, FACULTE DES SCIENCES ET DE GENIE, UNIVERSITE LAVAL.). RT/7501-. Monographic series. English (French). Price varies per volume. Dep d'Informatique Faculte des Sciences et de Genie, Universite Laval, Quebec Quebec G1K 7P4 Canada. **DD** 000.

UK/0307-8531
**RARE EARTH BULLETIN.** [Rare earth bull.]. (1973)-. Periodical. English. bm. £151.00 UK and Europe; £163.00 (add £15.00 airmail) other. Multi Science Publishing Company Ltd., 107 High Street, Brentwood, Essex CM14 4RX England. **Tel** 011 44 277 224632, FAX 011 44 277 223453, telex 89-8452. **ED** J.M.H. Wilson. **LC** QD172.R2; R26. **DD** 505. **[CCC].**
**Desc:** Searches the world's journals for reported work on the lanthanides, and yttrium and scandium, translates it where necessary, summarizes and classifies it.
**Ind/Abst** GeoRef.

FR/0222-0776
**RBM. REVUE EUROPEENNE DE BIOTECHNOLOGIE MEDICALE.** [RBM Rev. eur. biotechnol. med.]. **VFOAT** RBM. Revue Europeenne de Technologie Biomedicale; Revue Europeenne de Technologie Biomedicale; European Revue of Biomedical Technology; Revue Europeenne de Biotechnologie Medicale. (1979)-. Academic Scholarly Publication. French. Eight times a year. 595.00F France; 665.00F other. Editions Scientifique Elsevier, 141 rue de Javel, 75747 Paris Cedex 15 France. **Tel** 011 33 1 47 07 11 22, FAX 011 33 1 43 36 80 93. **(Subscription address:** Editions Scientifiques Elsevier / for North America, PO Box 7247-7576, Philadelphia PA 19170-7576.**)** **UDC** 61. **[CCC].**

US/0273-2211
**RCUH ANNUAL REPORT.** ***Title Change.*** [RCUH annu. rep.]. **Main/Corp** Research Corporation of the University of Hawaii. **VAT** Research Corporation of the University of Hawaii Annual Report. (19??)-(19??). English. an. Research Corporation of the University of Hawaii, Honolulu HI 96822. **LC** Q180.U5; R386a. **DD** 574/.0720969. ***Continued by** Research Corporation of the University of Hawaii Annual Report.*

FR/0484-0305
**READAPTATION PARIS.** [Readaptation Paris]. (1953)-. Periodical. French. Ten times a year. 285.00F France; 274.50F Other. ONISEP Diffusion, 46 52 rue Albert, 75635 Paris Cedex 13 France. **Tel** 011 33 1 40776000, FAX 45 86 60 85, telex 202962 F ONISEP N. **UDC** 376.
**Ind/Abst** Point Repere (1979-1988).

FR
**RECAPITULATIF MENSUEL DES SIGNALEMENTS D'ORIGINE CEDOCAR.** **Main/Corp** Centre de Documentation de l'Armement. **VFOAT** Nouveautes Scientifiques et Techniques. **VAT** Recapitulatif Mensuel des Signalements d'Origine Centre de Documentation de l'Armement. No. 1- Jan. 1976-. Multiple languages (English, French, German, Italian and Russian). 85. 2 Bd Victor, 75996 Paris France. **LC** Z7403; .C45; Q158.5. **DD** 016.623. ***Supersedes** Bulletin Signaletique.*

CN/1187-1768
**RECHERCHE DEVELOPPEMENT AU QUEBEC, LA.** [Rech. dev. Que.]. **Added/Corp** Bureau de la Statistique du Quebec. (1991)-. French. be. Statistique Quebec, 117 rue Saint Andre, Quebec Quebec G1K 3Y3 Canada. **Tel** (514)283-2642. **DD** 607.

FR/0767-0273
**RECHERCHE ET INDUSTRIE.** (1985)-. Periodical. French. mo. 3558.00F. Lexeme, 1 rue Tupin, 69002 Lyon France. **Tel** 78929893, FAX (16)78421798, telex 350625F. **UDC** 167 : 338.45 (44-12). **Bk Rev. Ad Acc.**
**Desc:** Relations between science and business.

FR/0029-5671
**RECHERCHE (PARIS. 1970).** (LA RECHERCHE.). [Recherche]. **Added/Corp** Societe d'Editions Scientifiques (Paris, France). No. 1 (May 1970)-. Academic Scholarly Publication. French. mo (11 issues). 333.00F France; 410.00F other. Societe D'Editions Scientifiques, 5 Rue Jacques Callot, 75006 Paris France. **Tel** 011 33 1 43548395. **ED** Paul Tolila. **LC** Q2; .A782. **NLM** W1 RE107N. **CODEN** RCCHBV. **[CCC].** Index available. **Bk Rev. Ad Acc. Pr Rev. Circ:** 94,847 (ctrl). Documents available from The Genuine Article, Ask*IEEE, CASDDS. ***Supersedes** Atomes; **Absorbed** Nucleus; Science Progres d'Ecouverte.*
**Desc:** A multi-disciplinary magazine for readers with a scientific background, which covers all modern scientific and technical developments. The articles are written by French and other writers.
**Ind/Abst** Alum. Ind. Abstr.; Chem. Abstr.; Coal Abstr.; EMBASE; Energy Res. Abstr. (Jan. 1971-); For. Abstr.; GeoRef; INSPEC (July-Aug. 1972-); Int. Aerosp. Abstr.; Environ.; Met. Abstr.; Nutr. Abstr. Rev., Ser. A, Hum. Exp.; Life Sci. Collect.; Point Repere (1983-); Res. Alert [Full Cov.]; Sci. Cit. Index; SCISEARCH; Soc. Plann. Policy Dev. Abstr.; Soc. Sci. Cit. Index [Select. Cov.]; Sociol. Abstr.; Soils Fert.; World Agric. Econ.

NZ/0067-0464
**RECORDS OF THE AUCKLAND INSTITUTE AND MUSEUM.** [Rec. Auckl. Inst. Mus.]. **Main/Corp** Auckland Institute and Museum. (1930)-. English. an. Auckland Institute & Museum, N Gardner, 6 Tuj Glen Road, Birkenhead Auckland 10 New Zealand. **LC** Q93; .A82. **DD** 505. **CODEN** RAUIA7. Documents available from BIOSIS Document Express.
**Ind/Abst** Anthropol. Lit.; Biol. Abstr.; GeoRef.

MY/0377-3450
**RECSAM ANNUAL REPORT.** **Main/Corp** RECSAM (Organization). **VAT** Regional Centre for Education in Science and Mathematics Annual Report. (19??)-. English. an. 5.00Mal$ Malaysia; $2.50 US. Regional Centre for Education in Science and Mathematics, Seameo-Recsam, Glugor Penang Malaysia. **Tel** 04-883266/7 CABLE: RECSAM, PENANG. **LC** Q183.4.A7; R43b. **DD** 507/.1059. **Circ:** 70 (ctrl).
**Desc:** Presents successfully initiated programmes as well as completed ones.

US/0146-2172
**REFERENCE DATA REPORT.** (REFERENCE DATA REPORT : AN INFORMAL COMMUNICATION OF THE NATIONAL STANDARD REFERENCE DATA SYSTEM.). [Ref. data rep.]. **VFOAT** N.S.R.D.S. Reference Data Report; NSRDS Reference Data Report. **VAT** National Standard Reference Data System Reference Data Report. Began with V. 1 (Jan./Feb. 1977). Periodical. English. bm. National Bureau of Standards Office of Standard Reference Data, Washington DC 20234. **Tel** (301)975-3058. ***Continues** NSRDS News, 0146-2180.*

US
**REGULATORY FOCUS.** ***Ceased.*** V. 1, No. 1 (1981)-Ceased (1984). Periodical. English. bm. HLW Technical Regulatory Services, 287 Childs Road, Bashing Redge NJ 07920. **Tel** (201)953-2000.

IS
**REHOVOT.** V. 5, No. 1- Summer 1968-. English. an. Free. Weizmann Institute of Science, Public Affairs Office, PO Box 26, 76100 Rehovot Israel. **LC** Q1; .R34. **DD** 505. **NLM** W1 RE177K. **Circ:** 19,000 (ctrl). ***Continues** Rehovoth.*

GW/0931-9190
**REINRAUMTECHNIK.** ***Ceased.*** (1987)-(Dec. 1992). Periodical. German. Six times a year. Vieweg Publishing, PO Box 5829, D 65048 Wiesbaden Germany. **Tel** 011 49 611 160230, FAX 011 49 611 160229. **ED** Manfred Heyde. **UDC** 628.5.052. **Bk Rev. Ad Acc. Circ:** 6,000.
**Desc:** Deals with all subjects of clean-rooms technology.

BL
**RELATORIO.** ***Title Change.*** **Main/Corp** Instituto Nacional da Propriedade Industrial. (1986)-(198?). Portuguese. Instituto Nacional da Propriedade Industrial, rua Mariz E Barros, No 13, CEP 20270, Rio de Janeiro Brazil. **LC** T241.A2; I57a. **DD** 607.2081. ***Continues** Relatorio de Atividades - Instituto Nacional da Propriedade Industrial. **Continued by** Instituto Nacional da Propriedade Industrial. Relatorio Anual.*

BL
**RELATORIO DE ATIVIDADES - SECRETARIA DE TECNOLOGIA INDUSTRIAL.** **Main/Corp** Brazil. Secretaria de Tecnologia Industrial. (19??)-. Portuguese. an. free. Superintendencia da Borracha, Av Almirante Baroso 81, 4 Andar Rio de Janeiro Brazil. **LC** T25.B8; B73a.

AO/0003-343X
**RELATORIOS E COMUNICOES - INSTITUTO DE INVESTIGACAO CIENTIFICA DE ANGOLA.** (RELATORIOS E COMUNICOES.). [Relat. comun. - Inst. invest. cient. Angola]. **Main/Corp** Instituto de Investigacao Cientificia de Angola. (1962)-. Monographic series. Portuguese. ir. Price varies per volume. Instituto de Investigacao Cientifica de Angola, Departamento de Documentacao e Informacao, Box 3244, Luanda Angola. **LC** Q180.A58; A26. **DD** 508/.1. **CODEN** RCIAA5.
**Ind/Abst** GeoRef.

US/1050-9186
**REMITTANCE AND DOCUMENT PROCESSING TODAY.** [Remit. doc. process. today]. **Added/Corp** Recognition Technologies Users Association. **VFOAT** Today. (198?)-. Periodical. English. qt. $130.00 US; $150.00 other. Association for Work Process Improvement, 10 High Street, Suite 630, Boston MA 02110. **Tel** (617)426-1167, FAX (617)426-8911. **ED** Franklin Cooper. **LC** HF5548.125; .R46. **DD** 651.8/05. Index available. cum. index. **Ad Acc.** ctrl circ. Documents available from Ask*IEEE. ***Continues** Recognition Technologies Today, 0883-5594.*
**Desc:** For data processing managers and professionals concerned with management and productivity of the automated information processing environment, specifically OCR image, and MICR technology applications in remittance and document processing.
**Ind/Abst** INSPEC (1987-).

CN
**REMOTE SENSING IN CANADA.** **Added/Corp** Canada Centre for Remote Sensing. **VFOAT** Teledetection au Canada. No. 1, (July 1972)-. Periodical. English (French). Three times a year. Free. Canada Centre for Remote Sensing, 588 Booth Street, Ottawa ONT K1A OY7 Canada. **Tel** (613)947-1315, FAX (613)943-8828. **ED** Christine Langham. **CODEN** RSCADM. **Bk Rev. Circ:** 3,000 (ctrl). available on an online database.
**Desc:** Newsletter designed to keep users abreast of research and applications of remotely sensed data, chiefly images obtained by satellite or aerial photography.
**Ind/Abst** GeoRef.

IT/0370-727X
**RENDICONTI DEL SEMINARIO DELLA FACOLTA DI SCIENZE DELL'UNIVERSITA DE CAGLIARI.** [Rend. Semin. fac. sci. Univ. Cagliari]. **Added/Corp** Universita di Cagliari. Facolta di Scienze. Seminario. (Jan. 1931)-. Academic Scholarly Publication. Italian. qt. **LC** Q54; .C34. **NLM** W1 CA132. **CODEN** RSFSAK. Documents available from CASDDS.
**Ind/Abst** Chem. Abstr.; GeoRef; Int. Aerosp. Abstr.; Math. Rev.

US/0034-4508
**RENSSELAER ENGINEER.** **See** Engineering.

IT
**REPERTORIO DEL FILM INDUSTRIALE.** Italian. 3,000. F Angeli, Casella Postale 4294, Milan Italy. **LC** T65.5.M6; R45.

UK/0521-1573
**REPORT - BRITISH SCHOOLS EXPLORING SOCIETY.** **Main/Corp** British Schools Exploring Society. **VFOAT** BSES Report. English. an. £75.00. British Schools Exploring Society, 175 Temple Chamber, Temple Avenue, EC 44 London. **LC** Q41.B927; A16. **DD** 508.3/05. ***Continues** Annual Report - British Schools Exploring Society, 0306-3399.*

AT
**REPORT - DEPARTMENT OF SCIENCE, ANTARCTIC DIVISION.** **Main/Corp** Australia. Dept. of Science. Antarctic Division. English. $0.50. Government Printer / Australia, PO Box 84, Canberra, Australian Capital Territory, 2600 Australia. **LC** J905; .L3 subser; Q180.A6. **DD** 328.94/01 S; 507/.2/0989.

NZ/0110-9561
**REPORT IPD.TS - INDUSTRIAL PROCESSING DIVISION, DEPARTMENT OF SCIENTIFIC AND INDUSTRIAL RESEARCH.** (REPORT IPD.TS.). [Rep. IPD.TS - Ind. Process. Div., Dep. Sci. Ind. Res.]. **Added/Corp** New Zealand. Industrial Processing Division. **VFOAT** Technical Series IPD.TS; Report I.P.D. T.S.; Technical Series I.P.D. T.S. (1978)-. Academic Scholarly Publication. English. **CODEN** RNZDD9. Documents available from CASDDS.
**Ind/Abst** Chem. Abstr.

CN
**REPORT - NATIONAL RESEARCH COUNCIL OF CANADA.** **Main/Corp** National Research Council of Canada. 1918-. Academic Scholarly Publication. English. Price varies per volume. **LC** Q180.C2. Documents available from CASDDS.
**Ind/Abst** Chem. Abstr.

UK/0261-7005
**REPORT OF THE COUNCIL FOR THE YEAR ... / SCIENCE AND ENGINEERING RESEARCH COUNCIL.** **Main/Corp** Science and Engineering Research Council (Great Britain). **VFOAT** Report of the Science and Engineering Research Council for the Year ... . 1980-1981-. English. an. £6.00. Science & Engineering Research Council, Central Office, North Star Avenue, Swindon SN2 1ET England. **Tel** +44 793 411000, FAX +44 793 411400, telex 449466 GTN 1434. **LC** Q180.G7; S38A. **DD** 507/.2041. ***Continues** Science Research Council (Great Britain). Report of the Council for the Year ... .*

NZ
**REPORT OF THE DEPARTMENT OF SCIENTIFIC AND INDUSTRIAL RESEARCH.** **Main/Corp** New Zealand. Dept. of Scientific and Industrial Research. (1958)-. English. an (June). 1.65NZ$. Science Information Publishing Center, Box 9741, Wellington New Zealand. **Tel** 011 64 4 858939, FAX 011 64 4 850631, telex NZ 32076 RESERCH. **(Subscription address:** DSIR Publishing Company / Mt. Albert, Private Bag 120, Mt. Albert Road, Auckland New Zealand.**)** **Circ:** 1,600 (ctrl). ***Continues*** *New Zealand. Dept. of Scientific and Industrial Research. Annual Report of the Department of Scientific and Industrial Research, 0077-9601.*
**Desc:** A report to the New Zealand Parliament of activities of Department of Scientific and Industrial Research.

JA/0040-9006
**REPORT OF THE INSTITUTE OF INDUSTRIAL SCIENCE, UNIVERSITY OF TOKYO.** [Rep. Inst. Ind. Sci., Univ. Tokyo]. **Added/Corp** Tokyo Daigaku. Seisan Gijutsu Kenkyujo. **VFOAT** Tokyo Daigaku Seisan Gijutsu Kenkyujo Hokoku; Seisan Gijutsu Kenkyujo Hokoku, Tokyo Daigaku. Vol. 1 (1950)-. Monographic series. English (Japanese). Price varies per volume. Institute of Industrial Science, University of Tokyo, 22-1 Roppongi, 7-chome, Minato-ku, Tokyo 106, Japan. **CODEN** RIISAX. Documents available from Ask*IEEE.
**Ind/Abst** Abstr. J. Earthq. Eng.; INSPEC (Oct. 1972-).

US
**REPORT OF THE NATIONAL CRITICAL TECHNOLOGIES PANEL.** **Added/Corp** United States. Office of Science and Technology Policy. National Critical Technologies Panel (U.S.). (Mar 1991)-. Periodical. English. be. $25.50 US, Canada & Mexico; $44.00 other. National Critical Technologies Panel, 1101 Wilson Boulevard, Suite 1500, Arlington VA 22209. **(Subscription address:** National Technical Information Service, 5285 Port Royal Road, Springfield, VA 22161**)** **LC** T174.5; .R47. **DD** 338.97306.

US
**REPORT OF THE TREASURER FOR THE FISCAL YEAR ENDED JUNE 30 ... / NATIONAL ACADEMY OF SCIENCES, INCLUDING NATIONAL ACADEMY OF ENGINEERING, NATIONAL RESEARCH COUNCIL AND INSTITUTE OF MEDICINE.** **Main/Corp** National Academy of Sciences (U.S.). English. an. National Academy of Sciences, 2101 Constitution Avenue NW, Washington DC 20418. **Tel** (202)334-2525, FAX (202)334-2926. **LC** Q11; .N2812. **DD** 506/.073. **NLM** W1; NA218C.

US/0896-2472
**REPORT (OHIO STATE UNIVERSITY. BYRD POLAR RESEARCH CENTER).** (REPORT / BYRD POLAR RESEARCH CENTER, THE OHIO STATE UNIVERSITY.). [Rep. - Byrd Polar Res. Cent.]. No. 1 (1987)-. English. ir. Byrd Polar Research Center, Ohio State University, 125 South Oval Mall, Columbus OH 43210. **Tel** (614)292-6531, FAX (614)292-4697, telex 4945696 OSUPOLAR. **ED** Peter J Anderson. **DD** 919. **Circ:** 500. ***Continues*** *Report (Ohio State University. Institute of Polar Studies), 0078-415X.*
**Desc:** Reports on scientific investigations which are too lengthy for regular journal articles, also preliminary results of research.
**Ind/Abst** ASTIS Curr. Aware. Bull. (1987-); ASTIS Bibliogr. (1987-); GeoRef (1987-).

US/1064-2358
**REPORTS - NATIONAL CENTER FOR SCIENCE EDUCATION (U.S.).** **See** Education.

JA/0583-0923
**REPORTS OF FACULTY OF SCIENCE, SHIZUOKA UNIVERSITY.** [Rep. Fac. Sci., Shizuoka Univ.]. **Added/Corp** Shizuoka Daigaku. Rigakubu. **VFOAT** Shizuoka Daigaku Rigakubu Kenkyu Hokoku. Vol. 1, No. 1 (1965)-. Periodical. English. an. Shizuoka Daigaku Rigakubu, (Faculty of Science, Shizuoka University), 836, Oya, Shizuokashi, Shizuokaken 422 Japan. **LC** Q77; .S53a. **DD** 505. **CODEN** RFSSBT. Documents available from BIOSIS Document Express, CASDDS. ***Continues*** *Shizuoka Daigaku. Bunrigakubu. Reports of Liberal Arts and Science Faculty, Shizuoka University. Section Natural Science.*
**Ind/Abst** Biol. Abstr.; Chem. Abstr.; Math. Rev.; Zentralbl. Math. Ihre Grenzgeb.

US/0885-8373
**REPORTS OF INVESTIGATIONS - SOUTHERN METHODIST UNIVERSITY. INSTITUTE FOR THE STUDY OF EARTH AND MAN.** (REPORTS OF INVESTIGATIONS.). [Rep. invest. - South. Methodist Univ., Inst. Study Earth Man]. **Main/Corp** Southern Methodist University. Institute for the Study of Earth and Man. N. No. 1- 1975-. English. Botanical Research Institute of Texas, 509 Pecan Street, Fort Worth TX 76102. **Tel** (817)332-4441, FAX (817)332-4112. **DD** 550. **CODEN** RISMDY.
**Ind/Abst** GeoRef.

GW
**REPORTS ON SCIENCE AND TECHNOLOGY / LINDE.** **Added/Corp** Linde Aktiengesellschaft. (1991)-. Periodical. English (translations available in German). Linde AG, Lincolnstrasse 21, Wiesbaden Germany. **Tel** 011 49 6112200. **LC** T1; .L55. ***Continues*** *Linde Reports on Science and Technology, 0024-3736.*

US/0731-4981
**RESEARCH & CREATIVE ACTIVITY.** [Res. creat. act.]. **VAT** Research and Creative Activity. Began with Nov. 1977 issue. Periodical. English. qt. Free. Office of Research and Graduate Development, Indiana University, Bryan 104, Bloomington IN 47405. **Tel** (812)335-8913, (812)335-4152. **ED** Albert Wertheim and Steve Sanders. **LC** Q180.U5; R37. **DD** 001.4/09772. Index available. **Circ:** 4,200 (ctrl).
**Desc:** In-depth articles describing the research/creative activities of faculty members from all disciplines on the Indiana University-Bloomington campus.

US/0746-9179
**RESEARCH & DEVELOPMENT (BARRINGTON, ILL.).** (RESEARCH & DEVELOPMENT.). [Res. dev.]. **VFOAT** Research and Development; R&D; R&D Magazine. Vol. 26, No. 1 (Jan. 1984)-. Academic Scholarly Publication. English. mo (13 issues). $75.00 US; $112.00 Canada; $105.00 Mexico; $135.00 (surface mail) other. Cahners Publishing Company, 249 West 17th Street, New York NY 10011. **Tel** (212)645-0067, FAX (212)242-6987. **(Subscription address:** Cahners Publishing Company / Colorado, Paid Subscription Service Center, PO Box 7610, Highlands Ranch CO 80126-7610.**)** **LC** T175; .I494. **DD** 607/.2. **CODEN** REDEEA. **[CCC]**. ctrl circ. available on microfilm and microfiche from University Microfilms International (UMI). Documents available from Article Express International, UMI Article Clearinghouse, CASDDS. ***Continues*** *Industrial Research & Development, 0160-4074.*
**Desc:** The high technology journal of applied research and development. Articles contain sound scientific data from all R&D fronts, written in a smooth, flowing style that makes concepts easy to absorb and apply to the reader's own professional environment.
**Ind/Abst** ABI/INFORM Glob. Ed.; ABI Inform Ondisc; Acad. Search (July 1993-); AGRICOLA [Select. Cov.]; Bioeng. Abstr.; Bus. Index (1985-1989); Bus. Period. Index; Bus. Source (Jul. 1993-); Ceram. Abstr. (19??-); Chem. Abstr. (1984-); Coal Abstr.; Ei Page One; Eng. Index Annu.; F&S Index Plus Text, Int. [Select. Cov.]; Fluid Abstr., Civil Eng.; Fluid Abstr. Proc. Eng.; FLUIDEX (1984-); Foods Adlibra; Gen. BusinessFile (1985-1989); Gen. Period. Index (1985-1989); INFO-SOUTH Abstr.; Leadscan; Mag. Search; Newsp. Period. Abstr. (1988-); PROMT; Sci. Cit. Index; Soc. Sci. Cit. Index [Select. Cov.]; Stat. Ref. Index; Mag. Index (Jan. 1984-); Wilson Bus. Abstr.; World Ceram. Abstr.

II/0257-3245
**RESEARCH AND DEVELOPMENT REPORTER.** (1985)-. Periodical. English. sa. $30.00. Research and Development Reporter, 18/9 Trikuta Nagar Jammu-Tawi, Jammu and Kashmir 180004 India. **(Subscription address:** Prints India, 11 Darya Ganj, New Delhi, 110002 India, (Phone: 011 91 11 3268645)**)** **ED** R. S. Sharma. **UDC** 5.
**Ind/Abst** Agrofor. Abstr.; Crop Physiol. Abstr.; Field Crop Abstr.; For. Abstr.; Hortic. Abstr.; Irr. Drain. Abstr.; Maize Abstr.; Plant Breed. Abstr.; Plant Genet. Resour. Abstr.; Plant Grow. Reg. Abstr.; Postharvest News Inf.; Rev. Agric. Entomol.; Rev. Plant Pathol.; Rice Abstr.; Seed Abstr.; Soils Fert.; Sorghum Mill. Abstr.

US
**RESEARCH & DEVELOPMENT. TELEPHONE DIRECTORY.** **See** Encyclopedias and General Reference Books.

II/0034-513X
**RESEARCH AND INDUSTRY.** [Res. ind.]. **Added/Corp** Council of Scientific and Industrial Research (India). Vol. 1 (Jan. 1956)-. Periodical. English. qt. $100.00. Council of Scientific & Industrial Research, Publications & Information Director, Hillside Road, New Delhi 110012 India. **Tel** FAX 011 91 11 5731353. **(Subscription address:** Prints India, 11 Darya Ganj, New Delhi, 110002 India, (Phone: 011 91 11 3268645)**)** **LC** T1; .R42. **DD** 607.254. **CODEN** RSIDAO. **Pr Rev.** Documents available from Article Express International, The Genuine Article, CASDDS, Documents on Demand.
**Ind/Abst** AGRICOLA; Agric. Eng. Abstr. (1991-); Anal. Abstr.; Bibliogr. Mission. (1988-); BioBusiness; Biodeter. Abstr. (1991-); Bioeng. Abstr.; Ceram. Abstr. (19??-); Chem. Abstr.; Curr. Biotechnol.; Curr. Contents Eng. Tech. Appl. Sci.; Ei Page One; Energy Res. Abstr.; Eng. Index Annu.; Environ. Abstr.; Food Sci. Technol. Abstr.; Indian Geosci. Abstr.; Leadscan; Res. Alert [Select. Cov.]; Rice Abstr.; SEA Abstr.; Surf. Treat. Technol. Abstr.

US/0276-0401
**RESEARCH AND INVENTION.** [Res. invent.]. V. 1- 1972-. Periodical. English. Three times a year. Research Corporation, 44 South Bayles Avenue 200, Port WA NY 11050-3709.

US/0277-7290
**RESEARCH AND TECHNOLOGY ANNUAL REPORT.** [Res. tech. annu. rep.]. **Main/Corp** Earth Resources Laboratory (U.S.). (19??)-. English. an. Pat Conner, Earth Resources Laboratory, National Space Technology Laboratories, NSTL Station MS 39529. **LC** G70.4; .E24A. **DD** 621.36/78.

II
**RESEARCH BULLETIN - INDIAN INSTITUTE OF TECHNOLOGY, BOMBAY.** **Main/Corp** Indian Institute of Technology, Bombay. V. 1- 1976-. Bulletin. English. an. Indian Institute of Technology, Powai 400076 India. **LC** T1; .I392A. **DD** 605.

II/0555-7631
**RESEARCH BULLETIN OF THE PANJAB UNIVERSITY. SCIENCE.** [Res. bull. Panjab Univ., Sci.]. **Added/Corp** Panjab University. (March 1959)-. Academic Scholarly Publication. English. qt. $25.00. Research Bulletin of the Panjab University, Chandigarh 160014 India. **CODEN** RBJUAT. Documents available from BIOSIS Document Express, CASDDS. ***Continues*** *Research Bulletin of the Panjab University.*
**Ind/Abst** Biocont. News Inf. (1991-); Biol. Abstr.; Chem. Abstr.; Crop Physiol. Abstr.; Field Crop Abstr.; Fish Rev. (Jan. 1989-July 1992); GeoRef; Hortic. Abstr.; Indian Geosci. Abstr.; Math. Rev.; Life Sci. Collect.; Poult. Abstr.; Protozoolog. Abstr.; Rev. Agric. Entomol.; Rev. Med. Vet. Entomol.; Rev. Med. Vet. Mycology; Seed Abstr.; Soils Fert.; Wildl. Rev. (Jan. 1989-July 1992); Zentralbl. Math. Ihre Grenzgeb.

II
**RESEARCH BULLETIN. SCIENCE SECTION.** **Main/Corp** Panjab University. **Added/Corp** Panjab University Research Bulletin. Vol. 1-9 No. 1-156, (1950)-(1958); New Ser., Vol. 10 (Mar. 1959)-. Bulletin. English. qt. Research Bulletin (Science), Panjab University, Chandigarh 160014 India. **LC** Q180.I5; P85.
**Ind/Abst** Postharvest News Inf.

US
**RESEARCH CORPORATION OF THE UNIVERSITY OF HAWAII ANNUAL REPORT, THE.** ***Title Change.*** **Main/Corp** Research Corporation of the University of Hawaii. (1979)-(19??). English. Research Corporation of the University of Hawaii, Honolulu HI 96822. **LC** Q180.U5; R386a. **DD** 574/.0720969. ***Continues*** *Research Corporation of the University of Hawaii.; RCUH Annual Report, 0273-2211.* ***Continued by*** *Research Corporation of the University of Hawaii.; Annual Report.*

UK/0374-4353
**RESEARCH DISCLOSURE.** [Res. discl.]. (1972)-. Academic Scholarly Publication. English (French, German and Swedish). Twelve times a year. $145.00 US & Canada; £95.00 UK; £105.00 other. Kenneth Mason Publications Ltd, 12A North Street Emsworth, Hampshire P010 7DD England. **Tel** 011 44 243 377977. **ED** J. Jeffree. **CODEN** RSDSBB. **[CCC]**. Index available. Documents available from Ask*IEEE, CASDDS. ***Continues in part*** *Product Licensing Index, 0032-9770.*
**Desc:** Disclosure as a supplement or alternative to patenting while maintaining freedom for own use of such technology.
**Ind/Abst** Abstr. Bull. Inst. Paper Chem.; Abstr. Bull. Inst. Pap. Sci. Tech.; Chem. Abstr.; Electron. Pub. Abstr.; Food Sci. Technol. Abstr.; INSPEC (Sept. 1972-); Int. Packag. Abstr.; Nonwovens Abstr.; Pap. Board Abstr.; Print. Abstr.; Text. Technol. Dig.; World Publ. Monit.; World Text. Abstr.

UK/0958-2029
**RESEARCH EVALUATION.** Vol. 1, No. 1 (Apr. 1991)-. Academic Scholarly Publication. English. Three times a year. £68.00. Beech Tree Publishing, 10 Waterford Close, Guildford Surrey GU1 2EP England. **Tel** +44 483 67497, FAX +44 0483 67497. **(Subscription address:** World-Wide Subscription Services, Unit 4, Gibbs Reed Farm Pashley Road, Ticehurst TN5 7HE England.**)** **ED** A. J. Van Rann and Carlos Kruytbosch. **CODEN** REEVEW. Index available. **Bk Rev. Ad Acc. Pr Rev. Acid Free.** Documents available from The UnCover Company, FAXON Xpress, BLDSC, The Genuine Article.
**Desc:** Coverage starts with level of individuals programs and goes right through to international comparison of national science and technology input/output.

US/0732-5606
**RESEARCH FRONTS IN ISI/BIOMED.** [Res. fronts ISI/BIOMED]. **Added/Corp** Institute for Scientific Information. (19??)-. Academic Scholarly Publication. English. an. Institute for Scientific Information, 3501 Market Street, Philadelphia PA 19104.

Tel (215)386-0100, (800)523-1850, FAX (215)386-6362, telex 84-5305. **(Subscription address:** Institute for Scientific Information, PO Box 71416, Chicago, IL 60694**)**

US/0161-7249
**RESEARCH IN PHILOSOPHY & TECHNOLOGY.** [Res. philos. technol.]. **Added/Corp** Society for Philosophy & Technology (U.S.). **VAT** Research in Philosophy and Technology. Vol. 1 (1978)-. English. ir. $73.25. JAI Press Inc., 55 Old Post Road, Suite 2, PO Box 1678, Greenwich CT 06836-1678. **Tel** (203)661-7602, FAX (203)661-0792. **ED** Frederick Ferre. **LC** T14; .R43. **DD** 601.

US/8756-9299
**RESEARCH IN PHILOSOPHY & TECHNOLOGY. SUPPLEMENT.** [Res. philos. technol., Suppl.]. **Added/Corp** Society for Philosophy & Technology (U.S.). **VFOAT** Research in Philosophy and Technology; Research in Philosophy and Technology. Supplement. Vol. 1 (1984)-. Monographic series. English. ir. JAI Press Inc., 55 Old Post Road, Suite 2, PO Box 1678, Greenwich CT 06836-1678. **Tel** (203)661-7602, FAX (203)661-0792. **ED** Paul Durbin. **LC** UNC.

US
**RESEARCH IN PROGRESS. PHYSICS, CHEMISTRY, BIOLOGICAL SCIENCES, MATHEMATICS, ENGINEERING SCIENCES, METALLURGY AND MATERIALS SCIENCE, GEOSCIENCES, ELECTRONICS, EUROPEAN RESEARCH PROGRAM / U.S. ARMY RESEARCH OFFICE.** **VFOAT** Physics, Chemistry, Biological Sciences, Mathematics, Engineering Sciences, Metallurgy and Materials Science, Geosciences, Electronics, European Research Program; Research in Progress Between ... and ... . 1982-. English. an. US Army Research Office, PO Box 12211, Research Triangle Park NC 27709. ***Formed by the union of*** *Research in Progress. Chemistry, Biological Sciences, Engineering Sciences, Metallurgy and Materials Science, European Research Program* ***and*** *Research in Progress. Physics, Electronics, Mathematics, Geosciences, European Research Program.*

UK/0263-5143
**RESEARCH IN SCIENCE & TECHNOLOGICAL EDUCATION.** [Res. sci. technol. educ.]. **VFOAT** Research in Science and Technological Education. Vol. 1, No. 1 (1983)-. Periodical. English. sa (May and November). £147.00. Carfax Publishing Company, PO Box 25 Abingdon, Oxfordshire OX14 3UE England. **Tel** 011 44 235 555335, FAX (0279)31067, telex 817484. **(Subscription address:** US and Canada/ PO Box 2025, Dunnellon, FL 34430-2025; telephone:(904)489-6996**)** **ED** Chris R. Brown. **DD** 507. **[CCC].** Index available. available on microfiche.
**Ind/Abst** Br. Educ. Index; Curr. Index J. Educ. (March 1990); Psychol. Abstr. (1983-); PsycINFO (1990-); PsycLit.

II/0253-9306
**RESEARCH JOURNAL. SCIENCE / UNIVERSITY OF INDORE.** [Res. j. - Univ. Indore. Sci.]. **Added/Corp** University of Indore. **VFOAT** Sodha Patrika. Vijnana. (197?)-. Periodical. English (Hindi). University of Indore, University House, Indore 452-001 India. **CODEN** UIRJAG. Documents available from CASDDS.
**Ind/Abst** Chem. Abstr.

TH
**RESEARCH MONOGRAPH.** **Added/Corp** Asian Institute of Technology. Division of Human Settlements Development. (19??)-. Monographic series. English. Asian Institute of Technology / Regional Energy Resources Information Center / RERIC, PO Box 2754, 10501 Bangkok, Thailand. **Tel** 011 66 2 516-0110-29, 011 66 2 516-0130-44, FAX 011 66 2 516-2126. **LC** UNC.
**Ind/Abst** Irr. Drain. Abstr.; Maize Abstr.; Rice Abstr.; Soils Fert.; Soyabean Abstr.

US/0093-7991
**RESEARCH NEWS - DIVISION OF RESEARCH DEVELOPMENT AND ADMINISTRATION.** [Res. news, Div. Res. Dev. Adm.]. **Main/Corp** University of Michigan. Division of Research Development and Administration. Vol. 24 (July/Aug. 1973)-. Periodical. English. Four times a year (Spring, Summer, Fall and Winter). Free on request US; $6.00 Canada & Mexico; $15.00 other. University of Michigan / Room 1032, 3003 South State, Room 1032, Ann Arbor MI 48109-1248. **Tel** (313)763-5587, FAX (313)763-4053, telex 4320815. **ED** Lee Kattermun (phone: (313)763-5587). **LC** Q1; .M48a. **DD** 505. **CODEN** RNWSD5RSNWA4. **Circ:** 10,000. available on microfilm from University Microfilms International (UMI). Documents available from BIOSIS Document Express. ***Continues*** *University of Michigan. Office of Research and Administration. Research News.*
**Desc:** Reports on the research and scholarship at the University of Michigan. These reports can be put in a language that non-specialists can understand.
**Ind/Abst** Biol. Abstr.; Index Free Period.

JA
**RESEARCH NOTES AND MEMORANDA OF APPLIED GEOMETRY FOR PREVENIENT NATURAL PHILOSOPHY.** **Added/Corp** Research Association of Applied Geometry (Japan). (19??)-. Monographic series. English (summaries and/or abstracts in Japanese). Price varies per volume. Post-RAAG Library, c/o Mr. Kazuo Kondo, 1570, Yotsukaido, Yotsukaidoshi, Chibaken 284, Japan. **LC** Q1; .R45. **DD** 505.
**Ind/Abst** Zentralbl. Math. Ihre Grenzgeb.

US/0737-1071
**RESEARCH ON TECHNOLOGICAL INNOVATION MANAGEMENT AND POLICY.** **See** Business-General Management.

NE/0048-7333
**RESEARCH POLICY.** [Res. policy]. (Nov. 1971)-. Academic Scholarly Publication. English (summaries and/or abstracts in French and German). Six times a year (1 volume). Fl1090.00. Elsevier Science Publishers BV, PO Box 211, 1000 AE Amsterdam Netherlands. **Tel** 011 31 20 5803642, FAX 011 31 20 5862696, telex 15682. **ED** A S Bean, M Y Bernard, R Coenen, C Freeman, H Krauch, K L R Pavitt, D Roessner and J M Utterback. **DD** 658.5/7/05. **NLM** W1; RE233B. **CODEN** REPYBP. **[CCC].** Each issue contains an index to its own contents (no volume index)--loose. **Pr Rev.** available on microfilm and microfiche from University Microfilms International (UMI). Documents available from The Genuine Article, UMI Article Clearinghouse, Documents on Demand.
**Desc:** Devoted to the exploration of the policy problems posed by these research and development activities, and in particular their interaction with economic, social and political processes.
**Ind/Abst** ABI/INFORM Glob. Ed.; ABI Inform Ondisc (Jan. 1981-); Curr. Contents Soc. Behav. Sci.; Curr. Lit. Sci. Sci.; Ei Page One; Energy Inf. Abstr.; Environ. Abstr.; Gen. BusinessFile (1992-); Int. Polit. Sci. Abstr.; Manage. Market. Abstr.; Res. Alert [Full Cov.]; Soc. Sci. Cit. Index [Full Cov.].

UK
**RESEARCH REGISTER / UNIVERSITY OF STRATHCLYDE.** **Main/Corp** University of Strathclyde. English. an. Free. University of Strathclyde / Glasgow, Glasgow G1 1XQ Scotland. **Tel** 041-552 4400, FAX 041-552 0775, telex 77472 UNSUBG. **ED** Katharine M E Liston. **LC** Q41; .U54A. **DD** 001.4/09414/43. **Circ:** 500 (ctrl).
**Desc:** A brief record of research in progress, publications, and theses approved for higher degrees of the University in the year shown.

FI/0783-8069
**RESEARCH REPORT - LAPPEENRANTA UNIVERSITY OF TECHNOLOGY. DEPARTMENT OF INFORMATION TECHNOLOGY.** [Res. rep. - Lap.ran. Univ. Technol., Dep. Inf. Technol]. **VFOAT** Research Report - Lappeenrannan Teknillinen Korkeakoulu. Tietotekniikan Osasto. (1987)-. Multiple languages. ir. **UDC** 62. ***Continues*** *Research Report - Lappeenranta University of Technology. Department of Physics and Mathematics, 0357-5950.*
**Ind/Abst** Zentralbl. Math. Ihre Grenzgeb.

AT/0810-9966
**RESEARCH REPORT - SUPERVISING SCIENTIST FOR THE ALLIGATOR RIVERS REGION.** [Res. rep. - Superv. Sci. Alligator Rivers Reg.]. (1982)-. English. ir. Australian Bureau of Statistics, PO Box 10, Belconnen Australian Capital Territory, 2616 Australia. **Tel** 011 61 6 2527911, FAX 011 61 6 2516009. **DD** 333.72099429.
**Ind/Abst** AESIS Q.

AU/0378-9004
**RESEARCH REPORTS - INTERNATIONAL INSTITUTE FOR APPLIED SYSTEMS ANALYSIS.** (RESEARCH REPORTS.). [Res. rep. - Int. Inst. Appl. Syst. Anal.]. **Added/Corp** International Institute for Applied Systems Analysis. **VFOAT** Research Reports. (19??)-. Academic Scholarly Publication. English. ir. Price varies per volume. International Institute for Applied Systems Analysis, Publications Department, A-2361 Laxenburg Austria. **Tel** 2236-71521 302, FAX 2236-71313, telex 079137 IIASAA. **LC** UNC. **CODEN** IIARDU. Index available. cum. index. Documents available from Ask*IEEE, CASDDS.
**Ind/Abst** Chem. Abstr.; INSPEC; Popul. Index (?-?); Soils Fert.; Zentralbl. Math. Ihre Grenzgeb.

US/0364-0175
**RESEARCH REPORTS / SMITHSONIAN INSTITUTION.** [Res. rep., Smithson. Inst.]. **Added/Corp** Smithsonian Institution. Office of Public Affairs. **VFOAT** Smithsonian Research Reports. (Spring 1972)-. Periodical. English. qt. Smithsonian Institution, 1100 Jefferson Drive SW, Washington DC 20560. **Tel** (202)357-2605. **LC** Q179.9; .R42. **CODEN** SIRRDL. Documents available from Documents on Demand.
**Ind/Abst** Biol. Dig.; Environ. Abstr.

US/0278-1743
**RESEARCH SERVICES DIRECTORY.** 1st. Ed. (1981)-. Directory. English. ir (every three years). $315.00. Gale Research Inc., 835 Penobscot Building, Detroit MI 48226. **Tel** (800)877-GALE, (313)961-2242, FAX (313)961-6083, telex TWX 810-221-7086. **ED** Annette Piccirelli. **LC** Q179.98; .R47. **DD** 001.4/025/73. **NLM** Q 179.98 R431.
**Desc:** Details the services, facilities, and expertise offered by more than 4,000 research and development companies in the United States. Covers high technology research firms as well as those in management and marketing.

US
**RESEARCH SUMMARY / DIVISION OF BIOLOGICAL AND MEDICAL RESEARCH, ARGONNE NATIONAL LABORATORY.** **Main/Corp** Argonne National Laboratory. Division of Biological and Medical Research. (1985)-. English. an. National Technical Information Service - NTIS, Room 2027S, 5285 Port Royal Road, Springfield VA 22161. **Tel** (703)487-4630, (703)487-4660, (703)487-4650, FAX (703)321-8547, telex 89-9405. Each issue contains an index to its own contents (no volume index)--loose. ***Continues*** *Annual Research Summary / Argonne National Laboratory. Division of Biological and Medical Research.*

US/0895-6308
**RESEARCH TECHNOLOGY MANAGEMENT.** [Res. technol. manag.]. **VAT** Research Technology Management. Vol. 31, No. 1 (Jan./Feb. 1988)-. Periodical. English. bm. $50.00 (individual), $90.00 (institution). Sheridan Press, PO Box 465, Hanover PA 17331. **Tel** (800)352-2210, (717)632-3535, FAX (717)633-8900. **LC** T175.5. **DD** 607/.2. **CODEN** RTMAEC. **[CCC].** **Pr Rev.** available on microfilm and microfiche from University Microfilms International (UMI); available on an online database (file 15/Full-Text) from DIALOG. Documents available from The Genuine Article. ***Continues*** *Research Management, 0034-5334.*
**Ind/Abst** Abstr. Bull. Inst. Pap. Sci. Tech.; Acad. Search (July 1993-); BioBusiness; Bus. Index (1988-); Bus. Period. Index; Bus. Source (Jul. 1993-); Contents Pages Manage.; Curr. Contents Eng. Tech. Appl. Sci.; Curr. Contents Soc. Behav. Sci.; Ei Page One; Energy Inf. Abstr.; Gen. BusinessFile (1988-); Gen. Period. Index (1988-); INFO-SOUTH Abstr.; Mag. Search; Manage. Market. Abstr.; PAIS Int. Print; Res. Alert [Full Cov.]; Selec. Coop. Index Manage. Period; Soc. Sci. Cit. Index [Full Cov.]; Trade Ind. Index; UMI ABI/Inform--Bus. Period. Ondisc (Jan. 1988-) [Full Txt.]; Wilson Bus. Abstr.; Work Relat. Abstr.

CN/0700-6004
**RESEAU.** **Added/Corp** Universite du Quebec. Vol. 1, 15/29 Oct. (1969)-. French. ir (9 issues). Free. Universite du Quebec, 2875 Boulevard Laurier, Ste Foy Quebec G1V 2M3 Canada. **Tel** (418)657-4218 ext. 2289.

US/0034-6748
**REVIEW OF SCIENTIFIC INSTRUMENTS.** [Rev. sci. instrum.]. **Added/Corp** Optical Society of America. American Institute of Physics. Vol. 1 (Jan. 1930)-. Periodical. English. mo. $900.00 US; $925.00 Canada, Mexico, Central & South America, and the Caribbean; $960.00 other. American Institute of Physics, 500 Sunnyside Boulevard, Woodbury NY 11797-2999. **Tel** (516)576-2200, FAX (516)349-7669, telex 960983. **LC** Q184; .R5. **NLM** W1 RE255. **CODEN** RSINAK. **[CCC].** Index available (bound in last issue). **Pr Rev.** available on microfilm and microfiche. Documents available from Article Express International, The Genuine Article, BIOSIS Document Express, Ask*IEEE, CASDDS. ***Continues in part*** *Journal of the Optical Society of America and Review of Scientific Instruments, 0093-4119.*
**Ind/Abst** Abstr. Bull. Inst. Pap. Sci. Tech.; Alum. Ind. Abstr.; Appl. Sci. Technol. Index; Biol. Abstr.; Ceram. Abstr. (19??-); Chem. Abstr.; Coal Abstr.; Curr. Contents Eng. Tech. Appl. Sci.; Curr. Contents Phys. Chem. Earth Sci.; Curr. Phys. Index; Ei Page One; Energy Res. Abstr.; Eng. Index Annu. [Select. Cov.]; Fluid Abstr., Civil Eng.; Fluid Abstr. Proc. Eng.; FLUIDEX; Gas Abstr.; GeoRef; HTFS Dig.; Index Med.; INSPEC (1968-); Int. Aerosp. Abstr.; Mass Spect. Bull.; Met. Abstr.; Res. Alert [Full Cov.]; Sci. Cit. Index; SCISEARCH; SPIN (1970-); World Ceram. Abstr.

AT
**REVIEWS IN RURAL SCIENCE.** (1974)-. Academic Scholarly Publication. English. ir. $18.45. Reviews in Rural Science, University of New England, Publishing Unit, Armidale New South Wales 2351 Australia. **Tel** (067)73-2898. Documents available from CASDDS.
**Ind/Abst** Chem. Abstr.

BL/0100-6711
**REVISTA BRASILEIRA DE TECNOLOGIA.** [Rev. Bras. Tecnol.]. Began in 1970. Periodical. Portuguese (English). bm. $1.29. CNPQ/Coordenacao Editorial, Avenue West, 3N Quadra 511 Bloca A 1A, 70750 Brasilia DF Brazil. **CODEN** RBTNAO. Documents available from CASDDS.
**Ind/Abst** Chem. Abstr. (1970-1982).

PO
**REVISTA DA FACULDADE DE CIENCIAS.** **Main/Corp** Coimbra. Universidade. Faculdade de Ciencias. V.1- 1931-. Portuguese. Universidad de Lisbon, Faculdade de Ciencias, Lisbon 2 Portugal. **LC** Q4. **DD** 505. cum. index.
**Ind/Abst** Stat. Theory Method Abstr. (1968).

CU
**REVISTA DE INFORMACION CIENTIFICA Y TECNICA CUBANA.** Spanish. Ediciones Cubanas, Obispo 527, Altos ESQ Bernaza, CP 10100 Havana Cuba. **Tel** 011 632980, 631942, FAX 011 631011, telex 512337, 6540. **LC** Q4; .R365. ***Continues*** *Boletin de Informacion Cientifica y Tecnica Cubana.*

SP/1130-4723
**REVISTA DE LA ACADEMIA CANARIA DE CIENCIAS.** [Rev. Acad. Canar. Cienc.]. **Added/Corp** Academia Canaria de Ciencias. **VFOAT** Folia Canariensis Academiae Scientiarum. (1990)-. Periodical. Multiple languages. an. **UDC** 5.
**Ind/Abst** Zentralbl. Math. Ihre Grenzgeb.

SP/0370-3207
**REVISTA DE LA ACADEMIA DE CIENCIAS EXACTAS, FISICO-QUIMICAS Y NATURALES DE ZARAGOZA.** [Rev. Acad. cienc. exactas, fis.-quim. nat. Zaragoza]. **Main/Corp** Academia de Ciencias Exactas, Fisico-Quimicas y Naturales de Zaragoza. **VFOAT** Revista de la Academia de Ciencias. Vol. 1 (1916)-; New Ser., Vol. 1 (1946)-. Periodical. Spanish (summaries and/or abstracts in English). **LC** Q65; .A3. **CODEN** RACZA2. Documents available from CASDDS.
**Ind/Abst** Chem. Abstr.

SP/0034-0596
**REVISTA DE LA REAL ACADEMIA DE CIENCIAS EXACTAS, FISICAS Y NATURALES DE MADRID.** [Rev. R. Acad. Cienc. Exactas, Fis. Nat. Madr.]. **Main/Corp** Real Academia de Ciencias Exactas, Fisicas y Naturales de Madrid. (Apr. 1904)-. Periodical. Spanish (summaries and/or abstracts in English). Four times a year. 6000ptas. Real Academia de Ciencias Exactas, Calle Valverde 22, 28004 Madrid Spain. **Tel** 011 34 1 531 3529. **LC** Q65; .M183. **CODEN** RCFNAT. Documents available from BIOSIS Document Express, CASDDS.
**Ind/Abst** Biol. Abstr.; Chem. Abstr.; Math. Rev.; Zentralbl. Math. Ihre Grenzgeb.

PY/0379-9123
**REVISTA DE LA SOCIEDAD CIENTIFICA DEL PARAGUAY.** [Rev. Soc. Cient. Parag.]. **Main/Corp** Sociedad Cientifica del Paraguay. Began in June 1921. Periodical. Spanish. **LC** Q33; .P2513. **DD** 506.289. **CODEN** SCPGB2. Documents available from BIOSIS Document Express.
**Ind/Abst** Biol. Abstr.; Energy Res. Abstr.; GeoRef.

PR
**REVISTA DE LA UNIVERSIDAD POLITECNICA DE PUERTO RICO.** **Added/Corp** Universidad Politecnica de Puerto Rico. Vol. 1, No. 1 (June 1991)-. Periodical. Spanish (English). sa. **LC** T4; .R383. **DD** 605.

CU/0029-5736
**REVISTA TECNOLOGICA.** Periodical. Spanish. bm. Ediciones Cubanas, Obispo 527, Altos ESQ Bernaza, CP 10100 Havana Cuba. **Tel** 011 632980, 631942, FAX 011 631011, telex 512337, 6540. **CODEN** RTECA8. cum. index. ***Continues*** *Nuestra Industria, Revista Tecnologica.*
**Ind/Abst** GeoRef.

BE/0378-4606
**REVUE DE L'UNIVERSITE DE BRUXELLES.** [Rev. Univ. Brux.]. **Main/Corp** Universite Libre de Bruxelles. **Added/Corp** Universite Libre de Bruxelles. 1st Year, No 1-2 (Dec./Jan. 1895-1896)-45th Year, No. 1-2 (Oct./Nov./Dec. 1939-Jan. 1940)-. Monographic series. French. qt. 1300F Belgium; 1600F other. Editions University de Bruxelles, Avenue Paul Heger 26, B-1050 Bruxelles Belgium. **Tel** 32 2 642 3789, 3799, FAX 32 2 642 3794, telex 23069 UNILIB. **ED** Jacques Sojcher. **LC** AS242; .B53. **Circ:** 1,200 (ctrl). available in microform.
**Desc:** This review contributes to the spreading of research and reflections of the University in all fields. Review about human sciences.
**Ind/Abst** Am. Hist. Life (1972-); ARTbibliogr. Mod. (1984-); BHA : Biblio. Hist. Art; Romant. Move.

CG
**REVUE DE L'UNIVERSITE NATIONALE DU ZAIRE, CAMPUS DE LUBUMBASHI. SERIE B : SCIENCES.** **Main/Corp** Universite Nationale du Zaire, Campus de Lubumbashi. French. Universite Nationale du Zaire / Lubumbashi, Campus de Lubumbashi, Service des Publications et des Echanges, BP 2896, Lubumbashi Zaire. **LC** Q91.C6; U54A. **DD** 505.

FR/0296-5321
**REVUE DES LABORATOIRES D'ESSAIS, LA.** [Rev. lab. essai]. (1984)-. Periodical. French. qt. 260.00F France; 345.00F other. ASTE, 8 rue Roquepine, 75008 Paris France. **Tel** 33 1 42665829, FAX 33 1 42661206. **ED** H Jeau Delatte. **UDC** 620. **Ad Acc, Adv Mgr:** Johane Cagna, **Tel** 33 1 45085009. **Circ:** 4,0000 (ctrl). ***Continues*** *Revue de l'Association pour le Developpement des Sciences et Techniques de l'Environnement, 0249-6658.*

BE/0035-2160
**REVUE DES QUESTIONS SCIENTIFIQUES.** [Rev. quest. sci.]. **Added/Corp** Societe Scientifique de Bruxelles. Union Catholique des Scientifiques Francais. Vol. 1 (Jan. 1877)-. Periodical. French. qt. 1700.00F Belgium; 1650.00F France; 1900.00F other. Societe Scientifique Bruxelles, 61 rue de Bruxelles, 5000 Namur Belique. **Tel** 011 32 81 724464, FAX 011 32 81 724502, telex 59222. **ED** C. Courtoy. **LC** Q2; .R45. **DD** 505. **CODEN** RQSCAN. Index available. **Bk Rev. Ad Acc. Circ:** 800. Documents available from CASDDS.
**Desc:** Information on sciences with emphasis on critical reflexion and history.
**Ind/Abst** Chem. Abstr. (-1987); EMBASE; Geol. Abstr.; GeoRef; Math. Rev.; Point Repere (1979); Zentralbl. Math. Ihre Grenzgeb.

FR/0151-4105
**REVUE D'HISTOIRE DES SCIENCES.** [Rev. hist. sci.]. **Added/Corp** Centre International de Synthese. Section d'Histoire des Sciences. Centre National de la Recherche Scientifique (France). Vol. 24 (1971)-. Periodical. French (summaries and/or abstracts in English). qt. 430.00F France; 510.00F other. Presses Universitaires de France, Department des Revues, 14 Avenue du Bois de l'Epine, BP 90, 91003 Evry Cedex France. **Tel** (1)60 77 82 05, FAX (1) 60 79 20 45, telex PUF 600 474 F. **NLM** W1 RE831E. **Bk Rev.** ***Continues*** *Revue d'Histoire des Sciences et de Leurs Applications.*
**Desc:** For those interested in the development of scientific ideas and techniques. Includes original work on scientists of the past.
**Ind/Abst** Am. Hist. Life (1990-); Math. Rev. (1987-); Point Repere (1979); Romant. Move.; Zentralbl. Math. Ihre Grenzgeb.

FR/0339-7521
**REVUE DU PALAIS DE LA DECOUVERTE.** (REVUE.). [Rev. Palais decouv.]. **Main/Corp** Palais de la Decouverie (Paris, France). (1972)-. Periodical. French. Ten times a year (monthly except Aug. & Sep.). 160.00F France; 190.00F other. Le Palais de la Decouverte, Avenue Franklin Roosevelt, 75008 Paris France. **Tel** 33 1 40748091, FAX 33 1 40748094. **ED** Michel Demazure. **LC** Q46; .P27a. **DD** 505. Index available (in July, Aug. & Sep. issues). cum. index. **Bk Rev,** (Qty: 6). **Ad Acc, Adv Mgr:** same as editor. **Circ:** 5,500 (ctrl).
**Ind/Abst** Energy Res. Abstr. (July 1979-); Int. Aerosp. Abstr.; Math. Rev.

FR/0297-4592
**REVUE FRANCAISE DE LOGISTIQUE.** (1985)-. Periodical. French. qt. 380.00F France; 490.00F other European Community; 530.00F other. Septel, 22 Avenue Gustave Flauber, 92500 Rueil Malmaison France. **Tel** 011 33 1 47660366, FAX 011 33 1 47168013. **UDC** 658.

SZ/0374-4256
**REVUE POLYTECHNIQUE.** [Rev. Polytech.]. (1969)-. French. Thirteen times a year. 70.00F Switzerland; 80.00F other Europe; 160.00F other. Editions Marcel Meichtry, 26 Chemin de la Caroline, CH1213 Petit Lancy Switzerland. **Tel** 011 41 22 7911027, FAX 011 41 22 7928834. **CODEN** RVPTBR. Index available. cum. index. **Bk Rev. Ad Acc. Pr Rev.** ctrl circ.
**Desc:** Technical and scientific features pertaining to data processing electronics, telecoms, machinery and mechanical construction, civil engineering and biotechnology.

FR
**REVUE RECHERCHES.** French. Four times a year. Revue Recherches, 20 Bis Rue Hippolyte Maindron, 75014 Paris France.

FR/1148-2893
**REVUE TECHNIQUE - GEC ALSTHOM.** **See** Engineering-Electricity, Electrical Engineering, Electronics.

LU/0035-4260
**REVUE TECHNIQUE LUXEMBOURGEOISE.** [Rev. tech. luxemb.]. (1909)-. Academic Scholarly Publication. English. qt. 306.40F. Dawson France SA, BP 40, 91121 Palaiseau Cedex France. **Tel** 011 33 1 69104700, telex 220064F. **CODEN** RTLXA4. Documents available from Article Express International, CASDDS.
**Ind/Abst** Alum. Ind. Abstr.; Chem. Abstr.; Coal Abstr.; Ei Page One; Eng. Index Annu.; Met. Abstr.

IT
**RICERCA E INNOVAZIONE.** (19??)-. Italian. Six times a year. L30000 Italy; L60000 other. Selcom Editore Srl, C So Vittorio Emanuele II 92, 10121 Turin Italy. **Tel** (011-39-11)562-7457, 562-8729, FAX (011-39-11)562-9943. **Bk Rev. Ad Acc. Circ:** 12,000 (ctrl).

MY
**RINTISAINS.** Malay. $0.80 single issue. Yayasan Persuratan Ilmu, Tingkat Tiga,Wisma Mirama, 50460 Kuala Lumpur Malaysia. **Tel** 03-2481011. **LC** Q4; .R56.

SY
**RISALAT MAHAD AL-TURATH AL-ILMI AL-ARABI.** **Main/Corp** Jamiat Halab. Mahad Al-Turath Al-Ilmi Al-Arabi. **VFOAT** Institute for the History of Arabic Science Newsletter; I.H.A.S. News Letter. Periodical. Arabic (English). qt. Free. Syrian Society of History of Science, Institute for the History of Arabic Science, Aleppo University, Aleppo Syria. **Tel** 011 236130, telex 331018 ALUNIV SY. **LC** Q127.A5; J35A. **Ad Acc. Circ:** 1,000 (ctrl).
**Desc:** Provides up-to-date news of Institute for the History of Arabic Science activities and other institutes' activities concerning the study of Arabic-Islamic science and civilization.

US/0272-4332
**RISK ANALYSIS.** **See** Public Health and Safety.

US/1073-8673
**RISK (CONCORD, N.H.).** (RISK : HEALTH, SAFETY & ENVIRONMENT.). [Risk]. **Added/Corp** Franklin Pierce Law Center. Vol. 5, No. 1 (winter 1994)-. Periodical. English. qt. $30.00. Franklin Pierce Law Center, 2 White Street, Concord NH 03301. **Tel** (603)228-1541, FAX (603)224-3342, (603)228-0388. **ED** Thomas G. Field, Jr. **DD** 344. **NLM** W1; RI285CM. ***Continues*** *Risk, Issues in Health & Safety, 1047-0484.*
**Desc:** Explores basic issues affecting public and private efforts to manage science and technology for net reduction the probability, sverity and aversive quality of health, safety and environmental impacts.
**Ind/Abst** Index Leg. Period. (1994-).

IT
**RIVISTA DELLA STAZIONE SPERIMENTALE DEL VETRO.** **Added/Corp** Stazione Sperimentale del Vetro. Vol. 1, No. 1 (Jan./Feb. 1971)-. Periodical. Italian (French and English). bm (6 issues). L50000 Italy; L100000 other. Faenza Editrice, Via P de Crescenzi 44, 48018 Faenza Italy. **Tel** 011 39 546 663488, FAX 011 39 546 660440, telex 550387. **ED** G. Bonetti. Index available (Free). cum. index. **Bk Rev. Ad Acc. Circ:** 2,000 (ctrl). Documents available from CASDDS.
**Desc:** Science and technology of silicates, properties, measurement and control, raw materials, glass furnaces and refractories, and manufacturing processes.
**Ind/Abst** Ceram. Abstr.; Chem. Abstr.; Eng. Mater. Abstr.

US/0883-8046
**ROCKY MOUNTAIN HIGH TECHNOLOGY DIRECTORY.** [Rocky Mt. high technol. dir.]. (1986)-. English. an (Jan.). $155.00. Leading Edge Communications, 1121 Old Siskiyou Highway, Ashland OR 97520. **Tel** (503)482-4990. **ED** Charles J. Koelsch. **LC** T12.3.W47; R63. **DD** 381/.45/02578. **Ad Acc. Circ:** 5,000. available on an online database.
**Desc:** A comprehensive reference tool for those interested in high tech research and development and high tech manufacturing firms in the Rocky Mountain Region.

NE
**ROESTVAST STAAL.** (19??)-. Periodical. Dutch. mo (except Jan. and July). Fl149.06. Technologie Commun Market BV, Postbus 101, 2300 AC Leiden Netherlands. **Tel** 011 31 71 144044.

KO/0253-6315
**RONMUNJIB - CUNNAM DAIHAGGYO GONNEB GYONYUG NYENGUSO.** (NONMUNJIP.). [Ronmunjib - Cunnam daihaggyo gonneb gyonyug nyenguso]. **Added/Corp** Chungnam Taehakkyo. Kongop Kyoyuk Yonguso. **VFOAT** Report of the Industrial Education Research Center, Chungnam National University; Chungnam Taehakkyo Kongop Kyoyuk Yonguso Nonmunjip. (1978)-. Academic Scholarly Publication. English (Korean). sa. **LC** T4; .N7. **CODEN** NTKYDT. Documents available from CASDDS. ***Continues*** *Chungnam Taehakkyo. Kongop Kisul Kaebal*

# Science and Technology

Yonguso. Nonmunjip - Chungnam Taehakkyo. Kongop Kisul Kaebal Yonguso, 0253-388X. **Ind/Abst** Chem. Abstr.

XR
**ROZPRAVY CESKOSLOVENSKE AKADEMIE VED. RADA MATEMATICKYCH A PRIRODNICH VED.** See Mathematics.

XR/0069-228X
**ROZPRAVY. RADA MATEMATICKYCH A PRIRODNICH VED. Main/Corp** Ceskoslovenska Akademie Ved. Vol. 63- 1953-. Periodical. Czech (English and German). ir. kcs35.00. Academia, Publishing House of the Czechoslovak Academy of Sciences, Czech AC SCI, Vodickova 40, PO Box 896, 112 29 Prague 1, Czech Republic. **Tel** 011 42 2 245117. **ED** Eduard Hala. **LC** Q44. **Circ:** 1,500. *Supersedes in part Ceska Akademie Ved a Umeni, Prague. Trida 2. Rozpravy.*
**Desc:** Pertains to mathematics, chemistry, biology and physics.
**Ind/Abst** GeoRef; Zentralbl. Math. Ihre Grenzgeb.

XR
**ROZPRAVY. RADA TECHNICKYCH VED. Main/Corp** Ceskoslovenska Akademie Ved. Vol. 64 (1954)-. Academic Scholarly Publication. Multiple languages (Czech). **(Subscription address:** Artia Pegas Press Ltd., Palac Metro Narodni Trida 25, 11210 Prague 1 Czech Republic.) **LC** T4.
**Desc:** Prints original scholarly studies, supplying most recent scholarly information to not only professionals and scholars but also for public both at home and abroad for technical sciences.

UK
**RSA JOURNAL. Main/Corp** Royal Society of Arts (Great Britain). **VFOAT** RSA, The Royal Society for the Encouragement of Arts, Manufactures, and Commerce Journal. **VAT** Royal Society of Arts Journal. Vol. 136, No. 5377 (Dec. 1987 1987)-. Periodical. English. mo. £60.00 UK; £65.00 other. RSA Journal, 8 John Adam Street, London WC2N 6EZ England. **Tel** 071-930-5115, FAX 071-839-5805. **ED** Sarah Curtis. **LC** T1; .S64. **DD** 050. Index available. **Bk Rev. Ad Acc. Circ:** 15,400. *Continues Journal of the Royal Society of Arts.*
**Desc:** Active in five main areas: the arts, manufactures and commerce, design, education and the environment.
**Ind/Abst** Archit. Period. Index; Avery Index Archit. Period. Suppl. Colum. Univ. (Mar. 1990-); BHA : Biblio. Hist. Art; Br. Humanit. Index; Geogr. Abstr. Human Geogr.; World Ceram. Abstr.

US/0485-8255
**RSRI DISCUSSION PAPER SERIES.** [RSRI discuss. pap. ser.]. **Main/Corp** Regional Science Research Institute. **Added/Corp** Regional Science Research Institute. Discussion Paper Series. **VAT** Regional Science Research Institute Discussion Paper Series. (1963)-. Monographic series. English. ir. Price varies per volume. Regional Science Research Institute, PO Box 329, Hightstown NJ 08520. **Tel** (609)448-6966. **ED** Benjamin Stevens. **LC** UNC. **Circ:** 300.
**Desc:** Various topics in the field of regional science. Most recent papers on input-output techniques and empirical location analysis.
**Ind/Abst** GeoRef.

UK/0263-8355
**RUTHERFORD APPLETON LABORATORY.** [Rutherford Appleton lab.]. (1982)-. English. an. Documents available from CASDDS. *Continues Rutherford and Appleton Laboratories.*
**Ind/Abst** Chem. Abstr.

JA/0289-0917
**RYUKOKU KIYO.** See Humanities.

KO
**SAENGSAN KISUL YONGU. VFOAT** Production Technology Research. Periodical. Korean (summaries and/or abstracts in English). Choson Taehakkyo Saengsan Kisul Yonguso, 17 Pullo-dong, Tong-ku Kwangju-si Korea. **LC** T4; .S144.

MY/0126-6039
**SAINS MALAYSIANA.** [Sains Malays.]. Vol. 1- July 1972-. Periodical. Multiple languages (English and Malayalam). an. 60.00Mal$. Perpustkaan, PO Box 1124, Kuala Lumpur Malaysia. **LC** Q1; .C0DEN SAMADP. Documents available from CASDDS.
**Ind/Abst** Chem. Abstr.; Energy Res. Abstr. (April 1977-); GeoRef.

KO
**SAIONSU. VFOAT** The Newsmagazine of Science; News Magazine of Science; Newsmagazine of Science. V. 1- (1982/5)-. Periodical. Korean (Korean). mo. W29,000. Saionsu SA 79-1 Pangsan-Dong, Chung-ku Seoul Korea. **LC** Q4; .S225.

US
**SAMS TRANSISTOR RADIO. Main/Corp** Howard W. Sams & Co. **VFOAT** Transistor Radio. English. mo. $3.50 (single issue). Howard Sams & Company, Inc., 2647 Waterfront Parkway E Drive, Indianapolis IN 46214. **Tel** (800)428-7267, (317)298-5400. **LC** TK6564.T7; S3. **DD** 621.3841/87. **Bk Rev. Ad Acc.** *Continues Sams Photofact Transistor Radio Series.*
**Desc:** Full service documentation for repair of popular transistor radios.

US/0276-3672
**SANDIA SCIENCE NEWS.** [Sandia sci. news]. **Added/Corp** Sandia Laboratories. (19??)-. Periodical. English. Twelve times a year. Free. Sandia Laboratories, Public Information Division 3161, Box 5800, Albuquerque NM 87185. **Tel** (505)844-7767. available on an online database (file 648/Full-Text) from DIALOG.
**Ind/Abst** F&S Index Plus Text, Int. [Select. Cov.]; PROMT.

US/0734-5879
**SANDIA TECHNOLOGY.** [Sandia technol.]. **Main/Corp** Sandia Laboratories. **Added/Corp** English. National Technical Information Service - NTIS, Room 2027S, 5285 Port Royal Road, Springfield VA 22161. **Tel** (703)487-4630, (703)487-4660, (703)487-4650, FAX (703)321-8547, telex 89-9405.
**Ind/Abst** GeoRef.

JA/0914-854X
**SANGYO GIJUTSU SOGO KENKYUJO HOKOKU. Added/Corp** Osaka Furitsu Sangyo Gijutsu Sogo Kenkyujo. **VFOAT** Reports of Industrial Technology Research Institute. (1988)-. Periodical. Japanese (summaries and/or abstracts in English). Osaka Furitsu Sangyo Gijutsu Sogo Kenkyujo (Research Inst.), 1-53, Enokijima 2 Chome, Nishiku, Osakashi, Osakafu 550 Japan. **LC** T178.O74; S26. Documents available from CASDDS.
**Ind/Abst** Chem. Abstr.

IT
**SANITA SCIENZA E STORIA.** *Ceased.* (19??)-(Dec. 1993). Italian. sa. Franco Angeli Riviste SRL, Viale Monza 106, 20127 Milan Italy. **Tel** 011 39 2 2827651, 011 39 2 289562.

JA/0285-9815
**SANKEN GIHO.** [Sanken giho]. **VFOAT** Sanken Technical Report. (1966)-. Periodical. Japanese. Sanken Denki K.K., (Sanken Electric Co., Ltd.), 6-3, Kitano 3 Chome, Niizashi, Saitamaken 352, Japan. **CODEN** STEQDU. Documents available from CASDDS.
**Ind/Abst** Chem. Abstr.

JA/0080-6064
**SANKYO KENKYUJO NENPO.** [Sankyo Kenkyusho nempo]. **Added/Corp** Sankyo Kabushiki Kaisha Kenkyujo. **VFOAT** Annual Report of Sankyo Research Laboratories. (1963)-. Japanese (English). an. Sankyo K.K. Sogo Kenkyujo, (Research Inst., Sankyo Co., Ltd.), 2-58, Hiromachi 1 Chome, Shinagawaku, Tokyoto 140, Japan. **NLM** W1 SA781J. **CODEN** SKKNAJ. Documents available from CASDDS. *Continues Takamine Kenkyujo Nenpo.*
**Ind/Abst** Chem. Abstr.

KO
**SANOP KISUL. Main/Corp** Han'Guk Sanop Unhaeng. **VFOAT** Industry & Technology. Periodical. Korean (Korean). 120 single issue. **LC** T4; .H35A.

KO
**SANOP, KISUL TONGHYANG. VFOAT** Survey of Industrial & Technological Development; Survey of Industrial and Technological Development; Wolgan Sanop, Kisul Tonghyang. Periodical. Korean (Korean). mo. W48,000. Hanguk Sanop Kyongje Kisul Yonguwon, 206-9 Chongnyangni-dong Tongdaemun-ku, Seoul Korea. **LC** T4; .S146.

KO
**SANOP KWAHAK KISUL YONGUSO NONMUNJIP. Added/Corp** Inha Taehakkyo. Sanop Kwahak Kisul Yonguso. **VFOAT** Bulletin of the Institute for Science and Technology. (19??)-. Academic Scholarly Publication. Korean (English). **LC** T4; .S1465. Documents available from CASDDS.
**Ind/Abst** Chem. Abstr.

US
**SANTA FE INSTITUTE STUDIES IN THE SCIENCES OF COMPLEXITY. LECTURES. Added/Corp** Santa Fe Institute (Santa Fe, N.M.). **VFOAT** Lectures; Studies in the Sciences of Complexity. Lectures; Lectures Volume in the Santa Fe Institue Studies in Sciences of Complexity. Vol. 1 (1989)-. Monographic series. English. Price varies per volume. Addison Wesley Publishing Company, 350 Bridge Parkway, Suite 208, Redwood City CA 94065. **Tel** (415)594-4423, (800)447-2226.
**Ind/Abst** Zentralbl. Math. Ihre Grenzgeb.

IT/0036-4681
**SAPERE.** [Sapere]. (1935)-. Periodical. Italian. Twelve times a year. L60000 Italy; L90000 other. Edizioni Dedalo Spa, Casella Postale 362, Bari 70100 Italy. **Tel** 011 39 080 5311400, FAX 011 39 080 5311414. **UDC** 5. **CODEN** SAPE-A. Index available in last issue of volume--attached. **Bk Rev.** (Qty: 60/year). **Ad Acc, Adv Mgr:** R. Coga. ctrl circ.
**Desc:** A review of scientific divulgation. It deals with energy, armaments, nourishments, medicine didactics, environment, etc.

IO/0216-4167
**SARI KARANGAN INDONESIA.** V. 1, No. 1 (March 1982)-. Indonesian. ir. $6.00 (includes shipping). Biro Publikasi, Ilmiah-Lipi Widya Grana, Jl Jen Gatot Subroto, Jakarta Indonesia. **LC** Q1; .S235. *Continues Indonesian Abstracts, 0019-7319.*

JA/0386-4391
**SASEBO KOGYO KOTO SENMON GAKKO KENKYU HOKOKU.** (KENKYU HOKOKU / SASEBO KOGYO KOTO SENMON GAKKO.). [Sasebo Kogyo Koto Senmon Gakko kenkyu hokoku]. **Added/Corp** Sasebo Kogyo Koto Senmon Gakko. **VFOAT** Saseboo Kogyo Koto Senmon Gakko Kenkyu Hokoku; Research Reports of Sasebo Technical College. (1967)-. Japanese. an. **CODEN** SKHODA. Documents available from CASDDS. *Continues Sasebo Kogyo Koto Senmon Gakko Kenkyu Kiyo.*
**Ind/Abst** Chem. Abstr.

RU/0131-1638
**SBORNIK ANNOTACIJ NAUCNO-ISSLEDOVATELSKIH RABOT - TOMSKIJ POLITEHNICESKIJ INSTITUT IM. S.M. KIROVA.** (SBORNIK ANNOTATSII NAUCHO-ISSLEDOVATELSKIKH RABOT TOMSKII POLITEKHNICHESKII INSTITUT IM. S.M. KIROVA.). **Main/Corp** Tomskii Politekhnicheskii Institut Im. S.M. Kirova. (19??)-. Academic Scholarly Publication. Russian. Izdatelstvo Tomskogo Universiteta / Tomsk State University, Prospekt Lenina 36, 634050 Tomsk Russia. **Tel** 23-44-65, FAX 22-24-66, telex 128258. **CODEN** SANIDK. Documents available from CASDDS.
**Ind/Abst** Chem. Abstr. (?-1975).

RU/0301-1909
**SBORNIK NAUCHNYKH TRUDOV MONIIAG. Main/Corp** Moskovskii Oblastnoi Nauchno-Issledovatelskii Institut Akusherstva i Ginekologii. Vol. 6 (1971)-. Monographic series. Russian. Price varies per volume. *Continues Trudy MONIIAG, 0301-1763.*

II/0036-679X
**SCHOOL SCIENCE. Added/Corp** National Council for Educational Research and Training. Vol. 1 (1962)-. Periodical. English. qt. $20.00. National Council of Educational Research, Sri Aurobindo Marg/Publishing Unit, New Delhi 16 India. **Tel** 654524, telex 31-62814. **(Subscription address:** Prints India, 11 Darya Ganj, New Delhi, 110002 India, (Phone: 011 91 11 3268645)) **ED** R Singh. **Bk Rev. Circ:** 1,000.
**Desc:** Serves as an open forum for discussion of various aspects of science education, its problems and prospects, and individual experiences of teachers and students.

US/0036-6803
**SCHOOL SCIENCE AND MATHEMATICS.** [Sch. sci. math.]. **Added/Corp** School Science and Mathematics Association (U.S.) Central Association of Science and Mathematics Teachers (U.S.). Vol. 5, No 1 (Jan. 1905)-. Academic Scholarly Publication. English. Eight times a year (Oct.-May). $38.00 US; $46.00 (surface mail), $96.00 (air mail) other. School Science & Math Association, Bloomsburg University, Curriculum & Foundation, Bloomsburg PA 17815. **Tel** (717)389-4915, FAX (717)389-3894. **ED** Larry Enochs. **LC** Q1; .S28. **CODEN** SSMAAC. Index available. **Bk Rev. Ad Acc. Circ:** 3,900 (ctrl). available on microfilm and microfiche from University Microfilms International (UMI). Documents available from UMI Article Clearinghouse, CASDDS. *Continues School Science.*
**Desc:** Journal for teachers of science or mathematics in grades kindergarten to 12. Articles with practical ideas for classroom use.
**Ind/Abst** Acad. Ind. [Computer File] (1987-); Acad. Search (July 1993-); Chem. Abstr.; Contents Pages Educ.; Curr. Index J. Educ.; Educ. Index; Expand. Acad. Index (1987-); Gen. Sci. Source (Jul. 1993-); INFO-SOUTH Abstr.; Mag. Search; Newsp. Period. Abstr. (1989-).

UK/0036-6811
**SCHOOL SCIENCE REVIEW.** (THE SCHOOL SCIENCE REVIEW.). [Sch. sci. rev.]. **Added/Corp** Association for Science Education. Science Masters' Association. Association of Women Science Teachers. Vol. 1 (1919)-. Academic Scholarly Publication. English. qt. £54.00. Association for Science Education, College Lane, Hatfield Herts AL10 9AA England. **Tel** 011 44 707 267411, FAX 011 44 707 266532. **ED** A. A. Bishop. **LC**

Q1; .S29. **DD** 507/.1. **CODEN** SSCRAD. cum. index. **Bk Rev. Ad Acc. Circ:** 19,500 (ctrl). available on microfilm and microfiche from University Microfilms International (UMI). Documents available from Ask*IEEE, CASDDS, Documents on Demand.
**Desc:** General articles of interest to science teachers; experimental notes for teachers; book, apparatus, visual aid and software reviews; and correspondence.
**Ind/Abst** Br. Educ. Index; Chem. Abstr.; Chem. Hazards Ind.; Curr. Index J. Educ.; Educ. Technol. Abstr.; EMBASE; Environ. Abstr.; INSPEC (1968-June 1974); Lab. Hazards Bull.; Stud. Women Abstr.; Tech. Educ. Train. Abstr.

GW
**SCHRIFTEN ZUR NATURWISSENSCHAFTS- UND TEHNIKGESCHICHTE.** (1979)-. Monographic series. German. ir. Price varies per volume. Verlag Georg DW Callwey GmbH, Postfach 800409, D 81604 Munich Germany. **Tel** 011 49 89 43600533.

GW/0170-6322
**SCHRIFTENREIHE DES DEUTSCHEN WOLLFORSCHUNGS INSTITUTES AN DER TECHNISCHEN HOCHSCHULE AACHEN.** (SCHRIFTENREIHE DES DEUTSCHEN WOLLFORSCHUNGSINSTITUTES / DEUTSCHES WOLLFORSCHUNGSINSTITUT AN DER TECHNISCHEN HOCHSCHULE AACHEN.). [Schriftr. Dtsch. Wollforsch. inst Tech. Hochsch. Aachen]. **Added/Corp** Deutsches Wollforschungsinstitut an der Technischen Hochschule Aachen. (1963)-. German (summaries and/or abstracts in English). **CODEN** DWTSDZ. Documents available from CASDDS.
**Ind/Abst** Chem. Abstr.

GW
**SCHRIFTENREIHE FUER GESCHICHTE DER NATURWISSENSCHAFTEN.** German. ir. Akademie-Verlag GmbH, Muehlenstrasse 33 34, D 13162 Berlin Germany. **Tel** 011 49 30 47889300, FAX 011 49 30 47889357. **(Subscription address:** VCH Publishers Inc., 303 Northwest 12th Avenue, Journals Department, Deerfield FL 33442.**)**

SZ/0040-151X
**SCHWEIZERISCHE TECHNISCHE ZEITSCHRIFT.** [Schweiz. tech. Z.]. **Added/Corp** Schweizerischer Techniker-Verband. **VFOAT** Revue Technique Suisse; Rivista Tecnica Svizzera; STZ. Schweiz. Technische Zeitschrift. (1926)-. Academic Scholarly Publication. German. mo. 125.00F. Schweiz Technische Zeitschrift, Weinbergstrasse 41, CH 8023 Zurich Switzerland. **Tel** 011 41 1 473794, FAX 011 41 1 2514802. **LC** T3; .S46. **DD** 605. **CODEN** STZTA5. Documents available from Ask*IEEE. ***Formed by the union of*** *Schweizerische Techniker-Zeitung* ***and*** *Technik und Betrieb.*
**Ind/Abst** Alum. Ind. Abstr.; EMBASE; INSPEC (Nov. 1976-); Int. Aerosp. Abstr.; Met. Abstr.; Saf. Health Work.

US
**SCI JCR [MICROFORM]. Added/Corp** Institute for Scientific Information. **VFOAT** SCI Journal Citation Reports; Science Citation Index Journal Citation Reports; Journal Citation Reports; JCR. (1989)-. English. an. $330.00. Institute for Scientific Information, 3501 Market Street, Philadelphia PA 19104. **Tel** (215)386-0100, (800)523-1850, FAX (215)386-6362, telex 84-5305. **(Subscription address:** Institute for Scientific Information, PO Box 71416, Chicago IL 60694.**) LC** Microfiche (o) 93/6009. **DD** 016.5. ***Continues*** *SCI Journal Citation Reports, 0161-3170.*

US
**SCI NEWS.** ***Ceased.*** **VAT** Science Citation Index News. Vol. 1 (1978)-(1981). Academic Scholarly Publication. English. qt. Institute for Scientific Information, 3501 Market Street, Philadelphia PA 19104. **Tel** (215)386-0100, (800)523-1850, FAX (215)386-6362, telex 84-5305. **(Subscription address:** Institute for Scientific Information, PO Box 71416, Chicago, IL 60694**)**

HU/0133-1027
**SCIENCAJ KOMUNIKAJOJ - BUDAPESTA TERITORIA KOMITATO DE HUNGARA ESPERANTO-ASOCIO.**
**VFOAT** Etudes Scientifiques - Budapesta Teritoria Komitato de Hungara Esperanto-Asocio; Naucnye Coobsenia - Budapesta Teritoria Komitato de Hungara Esperanto-Asocio; Scientific Papers - Budapesta Teritoria Komitato de Hungara Esperanto-Asocio; Trabajos Cientificos - Budapesta Teritoria Komitato de Hungara Esperanto-Asocio; Tudomanyos Kozlemenyek - Budapesta Teritoria Komitato de Hungara Esperanto-Asocio; Wissenschaftliche Mitteilungen - Budapesta Teritoria Komitato de Hungara Esperanto-Asocio. (?976)-. Multiple languages. ir. **UDC** 001.92. Documents available from CASDDS.
**Ind/Abst** Chem. Abstr.

US/0036-8121
**SCIENCE ACTIVITIES.** [Sci. act.]. Vol. 1 (June 1969)-. Periodical. English. qt. $32.00 (individuals), $58.00 (institutional), add $12.00 (foreign postage). Heldref Publications, 1319 Eighteenth Street Northwest, Washington DC 20036-1802. **Tel** (202)296-6267, (800)365-9753, FAX (202)296-5149. **ED** Joseph D Exline, Rosanne W Fortner, and Warren E Yasso. **LC** Q181.A1; S29. **DD** 507. **[CCC]. Bk Rev. Ad Acc. Circ:** 1,500. available on microfilm and microfiche from University Microfilms International (UMI).
**Desc:** Contains up-to-date, creative science projects for the K-12 classroom teacher. A one-step source of experiments, explorations, and projects in the biological, physical and behavioral sciences, its ideas have been teacher-tested, providing actual classroom experiences. Regular departments feature news notes, computer news and new products for the classroom.
**Ind/Abst** Acad. Abstr. Full Text Elite (July 1993-) [Full Txt.]; Acad. Abstr. (July 1993-); Acad. Search (July 1993-); Curr. Index J. Educ.; Educ. Index; Gen. Sci. Source (Jul. 1993-) [Full Txt.]; INFO-SOUTH Abstr.; Mag. Artic. Summar. Elite (July 1993-) [Full Txt.]; Mag. Artic. Summar. CD-ROM (July 1993-); Mag. Search; Med. Rev. Dig.; Mid. Search (Aug. 1993-) [Full Txt.]; Prim. Search (July 1993-) [Full Txt.].

UK
**SCIENCE & BUSINESS. VFOAT** Science and Business. Sept./Oct. 1988-. Periodical. English. **LC** HC260.T4; S28. **DD** 338/.06. ***Continues*** *Science & Business Link-Up, 0267-8837.*

US/0036-8148
**SCIENCE AND CHILDREN. See** Education-Teaching and Curriculum.

UK/0954-4194
**SCIENCE & CHRISTIAN BELIEF. See** Religion and Theology.

UK
**SCIENCE AND CIVILISATION IN CHINA.** Academic Scholarly Publication. English. Cambridge University Press, The Edinburgh Building, Shaftesbury Road, Cambridge CB2 2RU United Kingdom. **Tel** 011 44 223 312393, FAX 011 44 223 325959. **LC** Q127.C5. **DD** 509.51.

II/0036-8156
**SCIENCE & CULTURE.** [Sci. & cult.]. **Added/Corp** Indian Science News Association. **VAT** Science and Culture. Vol. 1 (June 1935)-. Academic Scholarly Publication. English. mo. $30.00. Indian Science News Association, 92 Acharya Prafulla, Chandra Road, Calcutta 9 India. **(Subscription address:** Prints India, 11 Darya Ganj, New Delhi, 110002 India, (Phone: 011 91 11 3268645)**) LC** QH1; .S35. **DD** 506. **CODEN** SCINAL. **Bk Rev. Ad Acc. Circ:** 2,000. Documents available from Ask*IEEE, CASDDS.
**Ind/Abst** Abstr. Anthropol.; AGRICOLA; Art Archaeol. Tech. Abstr.; Chem. Abstr.; EMBASE; Food Sci. Technol. Abstr.; Hortic. Abstr.; Indian Geosci. Abstr.; INSPEC (1968-); Microbiol. Abstr. Sect. A; Microbiol. Abstr. Sect. C; NAPRALERT; Nematol. Abstr.; Peace Res. Abstr. J. (1965-1966); Life Sci. Collect.; Rev. Agric. Entomol.; Soils Fert.

II/0036-8164
**SCIENCE & ENGINEERING.** [Sci. eng.]. **Added/Corp** India Society of Engineers. **VAT** Science and Engineering. Vol. 1 (July 1948)-. Periodical. English. Twelve times a year. $10.00. India Society of Engineers, 12B Netaji Subhas Road, Calcutta 1 India. **LC** T1; .I162. **DD** 605. ***Supersedes*** *India Society of Engineers. Journal, 0368-2609.*
**Ind/Abst** Alum. Ind. Abstr.; Eng. Mater. Abstr.; Met. Abstr.; Surf. Treat. Technol. Abstr.

US/1048-6313
**SCIENCE & ENGINEERING INDICATORS. See** Engineering.

US/0278-9620
**SCIENCE AND ENGINEERING PERSONNEL.** [Sci. eng. pers.]. 1980-. English. be. National Science Foundation, 1800 G Street Northwest, Washington DC 20550. **Tel** (202)357-9859, (202)357-9498. **LC** Q149.U5; S3115. **DD** 331.12/915/0973.

II/0970-5139
**SCIENCE AND ENVIRONMENT.** [Sci. environ.]. (1979)-. Academic Scholarly Publication. English. sa. $50.00. **(Subscription address:** Prints India, 11 Darya Ganj, New Delhi, 110002 India, (Phone: 011 91 11 3268645)**) LC** Q1; .S362. **DD** 505. **CODEN** SCENE5. Documents available from BIOSIS Document Express, CASDDS.
**Ind/Abst** Biol. Abstr. (1986-); Chem. Abstr.; Nematol. Abstr.; Pollut. Abstr. Indexes.

US/0048-9581
**SCIENCE & GOVERNMENT REPORT.** [Sci. gov. rep.]. **VAT** Science and Government Report. Vol. 1 (Feb. 1, 1971)-. Periodical. English. sm (except only one issue in Jan., Jul., Aug., and Sep.). $455.00 (1 year), $780.00 (2 year), $1050.00 (3 year) US; $480.00 (1 year), $810.00 (2 year), $1,095.00 (3 year) surface mail, other. Science & Government Report, PO Box 6226, Northwest Station, Washington DC 20015. **Tel** (202)244-4135, (800)522-1970, (800)522-1970. **ED** Daniel S. Greenberg. **LC** Q127.U6; S312. **DD** 353.008/55/05. **NLM** W1 SC668M. **[CCC]. Bk Rev. Circ:** 1,600. available on microfilm and microfiche from University Microfilms International (UMI).
**Desc:** Reporting, analysis, and grant-contract information regarding science politics at the federal and international levels.

NE/0925-5842
**SCIENCE AND INDUSTRY.** [Sci. ind.]. **VFOAT** Philips: Science and Industry; Science and Industry, Philips. New Series 3- 1975-. Periodical. English. ir. Ned Philips Bedr BV, I&E Library, HKF-17, 5600 MD Eindhoven Netherlands. **Tel** 040-(7)-84306. **Bk Rev. Ad Acc.** ctrl circ. Documents available from Ask*IEEE. ***Continues*** *Serving Science and Industry.*
**Ind/Abst** Alum. Ind. Abstr.; Art Archaeol. Tech. Abstr.; Eng. Mater. Abstr.; INSPEC (1976-1980); Met. Abstr.; Pap. Board Abstr.

US/0272-4510
**SCIENCE & LIVING TOMORROW.** [Sci. living tomorrow]. **VAT** Science and Living Tomorrow. V. 1- June 1980-. Periodical. English. mo. $18.00 US; $24.00 other. Four R's Publications Corporation, Box 1604, Grand Central Station, New York NY 10017. **LC** Q1; .S3643. **DD** 505.

UK/0302-3427
**SCIENCE & PUBLIC POLICY. See** Public Administration.

US/1048-8642
**SCIENCE & RELIGION NEWS. See** Religion and Theology.

US
**SCIENCE AND TECHNOLOGY : A REPORT TO THE CONGRESS. Main/Corp** United States. Office of Science and Technology Policy. (1990)-. English. **LC** Q180.U5; U54k. ***Continues*** *United States. Office of Science and Technology Policy. Science and Technology Report and Outlook.*
**Desc:** Congressional report concerning federal aid to research in industrial science and state technology.

US/0895-2000
**SCIENCE AND TECHNOLOGY DATA BOOK.** ***Title Change.*** (SCIENCE AND TECHNOLOGY DATA BOOK / DIVISION OF SCIENCE RESOURCES STUDIES, NATIONAL SCIENCE FOUNDATION.). [Sci. technol. data book]. **Added/Corp** National Science Foundation (U.S.). Division of Science Resources Studies. (1983)-(199?). English. National Science Foundation, 1800 G Street Northwest, Washington DC 20550. **Tel** (202)357-9859, (202)357-9498. **DD** 500. **NLM** W2; A N3704s. ***Continued by*** *Science and Technology Pocket Data Book.*
**Ind/Abst** Predicasts Forecasts.

JA/0286-0406
**SCIENCE & TECHNOLOGY IN JAPAN (TOKYO. 1982).** (SCIENCE & TECHNOLOGY IN JAPAN.). [Sci. technol. Jpn.]. **Added/Corp** Japan. Kagaku Gijutsucho. **VFOAT** Science and Technology in Japan. Vol. 1, No. 1 (Jan. 1982)-. Periodical. English. qt. $66.00. Three I Publications Ltd, Yamaguchi Building, 2-8-5 Uchikanda Chiyoda-ku 101, Tokyo 101 Japan. **Tel** (03)291-3761, FAX (03)291-3764. **(Subscription address:** Maruzen Company Ltd., PO Box 5050, Import & Export Department, Tokyo 100 31 Japan.**) ED** Tatsuya Arakawa. **LC** Q127.J3; S35. **DD** 609.52. **CODEN** STJAE8. **Ad Acc. Circ:** 20,000.
**Desc:** Provides a complete overview of the latest trends in science and technology in a wide range of fields.
**Ind/Abst** BioBusiness; Ei Page One; Energy Inf. Abstr.

US/0194-262X
**SCIENCE & TECHNOLOGY LIBRARIES (NEW YORK, N.Y.). See** Library and Information Sciences.

US
**SCIENCE AND TECHNOLOGY MICROFORM / NEWSBANK, INC.**
**Added/Corp** NewsBank, Inc. Vol. 21, SCI 1 (Jan. 1990)-. Periodical. English. mo. Newsbank Inc, 58 Pine Street, New Canaan CT 06840. **Tel** (800)243-7694, (800)762-8182, FAX (203)966-6254. **LC** Q1.A1; S34.

●US/1062-967X
**SCIENCE AND TECHNOLOGY OF BUILDING SEALS, SEALANTS, GLAZING AND WATERPROOFING.**
**Added/Corp** American Society for Testing and Materials. (1992)-. Periodical. English. be. ASTM - American Society fo Testing and Materials, 1916 Race Street, Philadelphia PA 19103. **Tel** (215)299-5585.

NZ
**SCIENCE AND TECHNOLOGY PLAN.**
**Added/Corp** New Zealand. National Research Advisory Council. (1984)-. English. an. National Research Advisory Council, Box 12240, Wellington New Zealand. **LC** Q127.N2; S3. **DD** 338.4/75/09931.

US
**SCIENCE AND TECHNOLOGY POCKET DATA BOOK / DIVISION OF SCIENCE RESOURCES STUDIES, NATIONAL SCIENCE FOUNDATION. Added/Corp** National Science Foundation (U.S.). Division of Science

Resources Studies. (199?)-. English. National Science Foundation, 1800 G Street Northwest, Washington DC 20550. **Tel** (202)357-9859, (202)357-9498. ***Continues*** *Science and Technology Data Book, 0895-2000.*

FR
**SCIENCE AND TECHNOLOGY POLICY.** **Added/Corp** Organisation for Economic Co-Operation and Development. (1991)-. English. be. 250.00F. OECD Publications and Information Center, 2 rue Andre-Pascal, 75775 Paris Cedex 16 France. **Tel** 011 33 1 45248167, US:(202)785-6323, FAX 011 33 1 45248500 OR 45248176, telex 620 160 OCDE. **LC** Q124.6; .S35. **DD** 338.926. ***Continues*** *Science and Technology Policy Outlook.*

UK/0952-9616
**SCIENCE AND TECHNOLOGY POLICY.** **Added/Corp** British Library. Science, Technology, and Industry. No. 1 (March 1988)-. Periodical. English. Six times a year. £100.00 UK; £110.00 other. British Library / Publications Sale Unit, Boston Spa, Wetherby, West Yorkshire LS23 7BQ England. **Tel** 011 44 937 546546 546543, FAX 011 44 937 546333, telex 557381. **(Subscription address:** Turpin Distribution Services Limited, Blackhorse Road, Letchworth, Hertfordshire SG6 1HN, United Kingdom.**)** ***Continues*** *New Technology (Letchworth, England).*

SI
**SCIENCE & TECHNOLOGY QUARTERLY.** ***Ceased.*** **VFOAT** Science and Technology Quarterly. Vol. 1, No. 1 (July 1980)-Vol. 6, No. 2 (1987). Periodical. English. qt. Science Council of Singapore, 63 Blk 1, Science Park Drive, Singapore 0511 Republic of Singapore.

US
**SCIENCE AND TECHNOLOGY REPORT AND OUTLOOK.** ***Title Change.*** **Main/Corp** United States. Office of Science and Technology Policy. **Added/Corp** National Science Foundation (U.S.). (1985/88)-(198?). English. ***Continues*** *Biennial Science and Technology Report to the Congress.* ***Continued by*** *United States. Office of Science and Technology Policy. Science and Technology.*

BE/0377-7901
**SCIENCE AND TECHNOLOGY YEARBOOK.** [Sci. technol. yearb.]. English. an. Services de Programmation de la Politique Scientifique, rue de la Science 8, 1040 Bruxelles Belgium. **LC** Q127.B4; S35. **DD** 509/.493.

FR/0992-5899
**SCIENCE & VIE JUNIOR.** **VFOAT** Science et Vie Junior. (1989)-. Periodical. French. Eleven times a year. 53.00Can$. Excelsior Publications, 1 rue du Colonel Pierre Avia, 75503 Paris Cedex 15 France. **Tel** 011 33 1 46484848, FAX 011 33 1 46484793. **(Subscription address:** Periodica Inc., PO Box 444, 1155 Ducharme, Outrement Quebec H2V 4R6 Canada.**)**
**Ind/Abst** Point Repere (1991-).

FR/0760-6516
**SCIENCE & VIE. MICRO.** [Sci. vie, Micro]. **VFOAT** Science et Vie. Micro; S.V.M. Science et Vie Micro. (1983)-. Periodical. French. Eleven times a year. 220.00F France; 389.00F other. Excelsior Publications, 1 rue du Colonel Pierre Avia, 75503 Paris Cedex 15 France. **Tel** 011 33 1 46484848, FAX 011 33 1 46484793.
**Ind/Abst** Point Repere (1983-).

UK/0950-5431
**SCIENCE AS CULTURE.** Vol. 1 (1987)-. Periodical. English. qt. $65.00 (institutions) US; $80.00 (institutions) Canada & Mexico. Free Association Books, 26 Freegrove Road, London N7 9RQ England. **Tel** 011 44 71 6095646. **(Subscription address:** Guilford Publications, Inc., 72 Spring Street, New York NY 10012.**)** **ED** Robert Young. **[CCC]. Bk Rev. Ad Acc. Circ:** 2,500. ***Continues*** *Radical Science Series.*
**Desc:** Explores all the ways in which science, technology and medicine are involved in shaping the values which contend for influence in the wider society.
**Ind/Abst** Altern. Press Index (199?-); Int. Bibliogr. Sociol.; Left Index; Soc. Plann. Policy Dev. Abstr.

US/0098-342X
**SCIENCE BOOKS & FILMS.** [Sci. books films]. **Added/Corp** American Association for the Advancement of Science. **VFOAT** AAAS Science Books & Films; Science Books and Films. **VAT** AAAS Science Books & Films; Science Books and Films. Vol. 11 (May 1975)-. Periodical. English. ir (9 issues). $40.00. American Association for the Advancement of Science, 1333 H Street Northwest, Washington DC 20005. **Tel** (202)326-6400, (203)326-6417, (202)326-6430, FAX (202)842-1065. **(Subscription address:** Science Books and Films, Subscription Service, PO Box 3000, Dept. SB & F, Denville NJ 07834.**)** **ED** Maria Sosa and Nancy C. Van Gorden. **LC** Z7403; .S33; Q158.5. **DD** 016.5. **NLM** Z 7401 A11. **Bk Rev. Ad Acc. Circ:** 4,500. available on microfilm and microfiche from University Microfilms International (UMI). ***Continues*** *AAAS Science Books, 0036-8253.*
**Desc:** Professional review journal for teachers and librarians. Each issue evaluates 300 books, films, videocassettes, and filmstrips for general audiences, educators, and students (kindergarten through second year in college); covers all scientific disciplines.
**Ind/Abst** Book Rev. Digest; Book Rev. Index; Child. Lit. Abstr. (19??-); Med. Rev. Dig.

IE/0332-1126
**SCIENCE BUDGET.** **Added/Corp** Ireland. National Board for Science and Technology. (1980)-. English. an. National Board for Science and Technology, Shelbourne House Shelbourne Road, Dublin 4 Ireland. **Tel** (01)683311, telex 30327 NBSTE I. **ED** Anne Fitzgerald. **LC** Q127.I73; S34. **DD** 354.4170085/5/06. **Bk Rev. Ad Acc. Circ:** 1,000.
**Desc:** Inventory of publicly funded science and technology in Ireland, program descriptions and commentary on national policy for statistics and technology.

US/1044-6052
**SCIENCE CITATION INDEX (COMPACT DISC ED.).** **See** Science and Technology-Abstracting, Bibliographies and Statistics.

US/0036-827X
**SCIENCE CITATION INDEX. GUIDE AND LISTS OF SOURCE PUBLICATIONS.** **Added/Corp** Institute for Scientific Information. (1977)-. Academic Scholarly Publication. English. bm. $12450.00. Institute for Scientific Information, 3501 Market Street, Philadelphia PA 19104. **Tel** (215)386-0100, (800)523-1850, FAX (215)386-6362, telex 84-5305. **(Subscription address:** Institute for Scientific Information, PO Box 71416, Chicago IL 60694.**)** ***Continues*** *Science Citation Index. Guide and Journal Lists.*

US/0036-827X
**SCIENCE CITATION INDEX (PRINT ED.).** **See** Science and Technology-Abstracting, Bibliographies and Statistics.

●US/1061-1290
**SCIENCE CITATION INDEX WITH ABSTRACTS.** **See** Science and Technology-Abstracting, Bibliographies and Statistics.

●US/1075-5470
**SCIENCE COMMUNICATION.** (1994)-. Periodical. English. qt (Mar., June, Sept., Dec.). $154.00. SAGE Periodical Press, 2455 Teller Road, Thousand Oaks CA 91320. **Tel** (805)499-0721, FAX (805)499-0871, telex 100799. ***Continues*** *Knowledge (Beverly Hills, Calif.), 0164-0259.*

CN/0820-9219
**SCIENCE COUNCIL OF CANADA REPORT (1979).** (SCIENCE COUNCIL OF CANADA REPORT.). [Sci. Counc. Can. rep.]. **Added/Corp** Science Council of Canada. (1979)-. Monographic series. English. ir. Price varies per volume. Science Council of Canada, 100 Metcalfe Street, Ottawa Ontario K1P 5M1 Canada. **Tel** (819)997-2560. **DD** 509/.71. Index available. **Circ:** 6,000. Documents available from BLDSC. ***Continues*** *Science Council of Canada. Report., 0080-7486.*

PH/0115-7809
**SCIENCE DILIMAN.** [Sci. Diliman]. **Added/Corp** University of the Philippines. Vol. 1 (1980)-. Academic Scholarly Publication. English. sa. University of the Philippines / Editor Science Diliman, Room 01/ Virata Hall, Diliman Quezon City 3004 Philippines. **NLM** W1; SC692N. **CODEN** SCDIEJ. Documents available from CASDDS.
**Ind/Abst** Chem. Abstr.; Index Philip. Period. (-199?); Philip. Sci. Technol. Abstr.

UK
**SCIENCE EDUCATION IN THE REGION.** **See** Education-Higher Education.

US/1022-6117
**SCIENCE EDUCATION INTERNATIONAL.** **See** Education.

AT
**SCIENCE EDUCATION NEWS.** English. qt. 35.00Aus$. Science Teachers Association of New South Wales, Box 187, Rozelle NSW 2039 Australia. **Tel** (02)939 6107. **ED** Catherine Odlum.
**Ind/Abst** Aust. Educ. Index.

US/0036-8326
**SCIENCE EDUCATION (SALEM, MASS.).** (SCIENCE EDUCATION.). [Sci. educ.]. **Added/Corp** National Association for Research in Science Teaching. National Council of Supervisors of Elementary Science (U.S.) National Council on Elementary Science (U.S.) National Council for Elementary Science (U.S.) Council of Elementary Science International. Council for Elementary Science International. Science Association of the Middle States (U.S.) Association for the Education of Teachers in Science. Association for the Education of Teachers in Science. Science Teacher Education Section. Vol. 13, No. 4 (May 1929)-. Periodical. English. Six times a year. $282.00 (US); $342.00 (Canada and Mexico); $364.50 (other). John Wiley & Sons, Inc., 605 Third Avenue, New York NY 10158-0012. **Tel** (212)850-6000, (212)850-6645, FAX (212)850-6088, telex 12-7063. **(Subscription address:** John Wiley & Sons / England, Baffins Lane, Chichester, West Sussex PO19 1UD England.**)** **ED** Leopold E. Klopfer. **DD** 507. **NLM** W1 SC693. **CODEN** SEDUAV. **[CCC]. Ad Acc. Pr Rev. Circ:** 2,000. available on microfilm and microfiche from University Microfilms International (UMI). Documents available from The Genuine Article, UMI Article Clearinghouse. ***Continues*** *General Science Quarterly, 0097-0352;* ***Absorbed*** *Summary of Research in Science Education, 0360-2907.*
**Desc:** Contains practices, issues and trends occurring both in America and abroad in science instruction, learning and preparation of science teachers.
**Ind/Abst** Acad. Search (July 1993-); Contents Pages Educ.; Curr. Contents Soc. Behav. Sci.; Curr. Index J. Educ.; Educ. Index; Expand. Acad. Index (1992-); Gen. Sci. Source (Jul. 1993-); INFO-SOUTH Abstr.; Mag. Search; Newsp. Period. Abstr. (1992-); Psychoanal. Abstr.; Psychol. Abstr. (1989-); PsycINFO; PsycLit; PsycScan: Appl. Exp. Eng. Psych.; PsycScan: LD/MR; PsycScan: Neuropsych.; Res. Alert [Full Cov.]; Res. High. Educ. Abstr.; SEA Abstr.; Soc. Sci. Cit. Index [Full Cov.]; Stud. Women Abstr.; Tech. Educ. Train. Abstr.

CN/0825-9879
**SCIENCE ET FRANCOPHONIE.** [Sci. francoph.]. **Added/Corp** Lingue Internationale des Scientifiques pour l'Usage de la Langue Francaise. (1982)-. Periodical. French. ir. Science et Francophonie Lisulf, 1200 rue Latour, Saint-Laurent Quebec H4L 4S4 Canada. **Tel** (514)747-2308. **DD** 501/.41.

FR/0243-7694
**SCIENCE ET RECHERCHE.** [Echos groupe CEA]. Began in 1980. Academic Scholarly Publication. French. an. CEA Department des Relations Publiques et de la Communication, 31-33 rue de la Federation, 75752 Paris Cedex 15 France. **CODEN** SCRHDH. Documents available from CASDDS.
**Ind/Abst** Chem. Abstr. (1980-1982).

●CN/1188-4290
**SCIENCE ET TECHNOLOGIE AU QUEBEC.** (REPERTOIRE DESCRIPTIF. SCIENCE ET TECHNOLOGIE AU QUEBEC.). [Sci. technol. Qu,e.]. **Added/Corp** Quebec dans le Monde (Association). **VFOAT** Science et Technologie au Quebec. (1993/1994)-. French. an. $34.95. Quebec Dans Le Monde, CP 8503, Sainte-Foy Quebec G1V 4N5 Canada. **Tel** (418)659-5540, FAX (418)659-4143. **(Subscription address:** Schoenhorfs Foreign Books Inc., 76A Mount Auburn Street, Cambridge MA 02138.**)** **DD** 502/.5/714. ***Continues*** *Repertoire Descriptif. Le Monde de la Science et de la Technologie au Quebec., 0847-4966.*

FR/0036-8369
**SCIENCE ET VIE.** [Sci. vie]. **VFOAT** Science et la Vie; Science & Vie. (April 1913)-. Periodical. French. mo. 242.00F France; 48.00Can$. Excelsior Publications, 1 rue du Colonel Pierre Avia, 75503 Paris Cedex 15 France. **Tel** 011 33 1 46484848, FAX 011 33 1 46484793. **ED** M. Jacques Dupuy, Melle Yvuene Dupuy, M. Paul Dupuy. Index available. **Bk Rev. Ad Acc. Circ:** 356,687 (ctrl).
**Ind/Abst** Coal Abstr.; Point Repere; SportSearch.

US/0036-8369
**SCIENCE ET VIE. MICROFORM.** ***Ceased.*** **VFOAT** Science & Vie; Science et la Vie. Vol. 63, No. 306 (1943)-?. French. Excelsior Publicatons, 1 rue du Colonel Pierre Avia, 75015 Paris France. **Tel** 33 1 46484848, FAX 33 1 46484793. **LC** MICROFILM 07638. ***Continues*** *Science et la Vie.*

FR/0151-0282
**SCIENCE ET VIE. NUMERO HORS SERIE.** [Sci. vie, Numero hors ser.]. **VFOAT** Science & Vie. Numero Hors Serie. (1945)-. Periodical. French. qt.
**Ind/Abst** Point Repere (1979-).

FR
**SCIENCE FILM.** Periodical. Multiple languages (English and French). International Scientific Film Association, 38 Avenue des Ternes 17, Paris France. **LC** Q192; .S3182. **DD** 502/.8.

UK/0144-8447
**SCIENCE FOR PEOPLE (LONDON).** ***Suspended.*** (SCIENCE FOR PEOPLE.). [Sci. people]. (1972)-Vol. 70 (1989). Periodical. English. qt. £5.00 individuals, £12.00 institutions. British Society for Social Responsibility in Science, 25 Horsell Road, London N5 1XL England. **Tel** 01-607 9615. **Bk Rev. Ad Acc.** ***Continues*** *BSSRS News Sheet.*
**Desc:** A radical science magazine.
**Ind/Abst** Altern. Press Index (-1989).

UK/1048-7042
**SCIENCE GLOBAL SECURITY MONOGRAPH SERIES.** (1990)-. Periodical. English. ir. Gordon & Breach Science Publishers, PO Box 90, Reading RG1 8JL England. **Tel** 011 44 734 560080, FAX 011 44 734 568211. **(Subscription address:** International Publishers Distributor at one of the following addresses: 820 Town Center Drive, Langhorne, PA 19047; or PO Box 90, Reading Berkshire RG1 8JL UK; or Kent Ridge PO Box 1180, Singapore 9111, Republic of Singapore**)**

US/0890-7110
**SCIENCE/HEALTH ABSTRACTS.** [Sci./health abstr.]. **Added/Corp** Yuchi Pines Institute. **VFOAT** Science Health Abstracts. (198?)-. Periodical. English. bm. $6.00. Yuchi Pines Institute, Box 319, Fort Mitchell AL 36856. **ED** Phylis Austin. **DD** 613. Index available. **Bk Rev. Circ:** 1,000.

FR/0999-7342
**SCIENCE ILLUSTREE BAGNOLET.** (SCIENCE ILLUSTREE.). (1989)-. Periodical. French. mo. 305.58F. Editions Fogtdal, 77 rue des Rigondes, 93178 Bagnolet Cedex France. **Tel** 011 33 1 48978888. **UDC** 082.

CC/1001-6511
**SCIENCE IN CHINA. SERIES A, MATHEMATICS, PHYSICS, ASTRONOMY & TECHNOLOGICAL SCIENCES.** [Sci. China, Ser. A Math. phys. astron. technol. sci.]. **Added/Corp** Hung-Kuo ko Hsueh Yuan. **VFOAT** Mathematics, Physics, Astronomy & Technological Sciences; Mathematics, Physics, Astronomy and Technological Sciences; Scientia Sinica. Vol. 32, No. 1 (Jan. 1989)-. Periodical. English. mo. $619.00 (regular subscription), $932.00 (combination subscription with Series B) The Americas; £415.00 (regular subscription), £625.00 (combination subscription with Series B) other. Pergamon Press, An Imprint of Elsevier Science Ltd., The Boulevard, Langford Lane, Kidlington, Oxford OX5 1GB United Kingdom. **Tel** 011 44 865 843000, 011 44 865 843699, FAX 011 44 865 843010. **(Subscription address:** Elsevier Science Ltd. Oxford Fulfillment Centre, PO Box 800, Kidlington, Oxford OX5 1DX United Kingdom.**) ED** Yan Dongsheng. **LC** QA1; .S348. **DD** 500.2/05. **CODEN** SCASEY. **Pr Rev.** available on microfilm and microfiche from University Microfilms International (UMI). Documents available from The Genuine Article, Ask*IEEE, CASDDS. ***Continues*** *Scientia Sinica. Series A, Mathematical, Physical, Astronomical & Technical Sciences, 0253-5831.*
**Desc:** Provides regular and rapid reviews of current important developments in scientific research in China for scientific workers in both China and other countries. Contains academic papers on the latest achievements in pure and applied sciences in mathematics, physics, astronomy and technological sciences.
**Ind/Abst** Ceram. Abstr. (19??-); Chem. Abstr.; Curr. Contents Phys. Chem. Earth Sci.; INSPEC (Jan. 1989-); Int. Aerosp. Abstr.; Leadscan; Meteorol. Geoastrophys. Abstr. (199?-); Res. Alert [Full Cov.]; Sci. Cit. Index; SCISEARCH; SEA Abstr.; Soc. Sci. Cit. Index [Select. Cov.]; Zentralbl. Math. Ihre Grenzgeb.

CC/1001-652X
**SCIENCE IN CHINA. SERIES B, CHEMISTRY, LIFE SCIENCES & EARTH SCIENCES.** [Sci. China, Ser. B Chem. life sci. earth sci.]. **Added/Corp** Chung-Kuo ko Hsueh Yuan. **VFOAT** Chemistry, Life Sciences & Earth Sciences; Chemistry, Life Sciences and Earth Sciences. Vol. 32, No. 1 (Jan. 1989)-. Periodical. English. mo. $619.00 (regular subscription), $932.00 (combination subscription with Series A) The Americas; £415.00 (regular subscription), £625.00 (combination subscription with Series A) other. Pergamon Press, An Imprint of Elsevier Science Ltd., The Boulevard, Langford Lane, Kidlington, Oxford OX5 1GB United Kingdom. **Tel** 011 44 865 843000, 011 44 865 843699, FAX 011 44 865 843010. **(Subscription address:** Elsevier Science Ltd. Oxford Fulfillment Centre, PO Box 800, Kidlington, Oxford OX5 1DX United Kingdom.**) ED** Yan Dongsheng. **LC** QD1; .S26. **DD** 540. **NLM** W1; SC72P. **CODEN** SCBSE5. available on microfilm and microfiche from University Microfilms International (UMI). Documents available from The Genuine Article, BIOSIS Document Express, CASDDS. ***Continues*** *Scientia Sinica. Series B, Chemical, Biological, Agricultural, Medical & Earth Sciences, 0253-5823.*
**Desc:** Provides regular and rapid reviews of current important developments in scientific research in China for scientific workers in both China and other countries. Includes academic papers in chemistry, life sciences and earth sciences.
**Ind/Abst** AgBiotech News Inf.; Biol. Abstr.; Chem. Abstr.; Curr. Contents Life Sci.; Ecol. Abstr.; Geogr. Abstr. Phys. Geogr.; GeoRef; Helminthol. Abstr. (1991-); Index Med. (Jan. 1989-); Leadscan; Meteorol. Geoastrophys. Abstr. (199?-); Plant Grow. Reg. Abstr.; Protozoolog. Abstr.; Res. Alert [Full Cov.]; Sci. Cit. Index; SCISEARCH; SEA Abstr.; Soc. Sci. Cit. Index [Select. Cov.]; Soils Fert.; Soyabean Abstr.; Weed Abstr.

UK/0269-8897
**SCIENCE IN CONTEXT. VFOAT** SIC, Science in Context. Vol. 1, No. 1 (March 1987)-. Academic Scholarly Publication. English. qt. $104.00 US, Canada & Mexico; £56.00 other. Cambridge University Press, The Edinburgh Building, Shaftesbury Road, Cambridge CB2 2RU United Kingdom. **Tel** 011 44 223 312393, FAX 011 44 223 325959. **(Subscription address:** Cambridge University Press / North America, 110 Midland Avenue, Port Chester NY 10573.**) ED** Gideon Freudenthal. **LC** Q175.4; .S343. **DD** 500. **NLM** W1; SC72L. **CODEN** SCCOEW. **[CCC].** available on microfilm and microfiche from University Microfilms International (UMI).
**Desc:** Devoted to the study of the sciences from the points of view of comparative epistemology and historical sociology of scientific knowledge. Committed to an inter-disciplinary approach to the study of science and its cultural development, it does not segregate considerations drawn from history, philosophy and sociology. Controversies within scientific knowledge and debates about methodology are presented in their contexts.
**Ind/Abst** Am. Hist. Life (1987-).

PP/0310-4303
**SCIENCE IN NEW GUINEA.** [Sci. New Guinea]. **Added/Corp** University of Papua New Guinea. Vol. 1, No. 1 (Nov. 1972)-. Periodical. English. Three times a year. k.30.00 (institutions), k.20.00 (individuals and schools) Papua New Guinea; k.35.00 Australia and New Zealand; k.36.50 Asia and the Pacific; k.42.50 Europe, Africa and America. University of Papua New Guinea, PO Box 320, Moresby Papua New Guinea. **Tel** 011 675 245201, FAX 011 675 267187, telex 22366. **ED** J.I. Menzies (editor's phone: 011 675 267396). **LC** WMLC 93/196. Index available in last issue of volume--attached. **Bk Rev**, (Qty: varies). **Ad Acc. Pr Rev. Circ:** 200.
**Desc:** Material in agriculture, botany, chemistry, conservation, fisheries, forestry, geology, geophysics, physical geography, mathematics, physics, science teaching, zoology, archaeology.
**Ind/Abst** AGRICOLA; Ecol. Abstr.; Field Crop Abstr.; Fish Rev. (19??-199?); Food Sci. Technol. Abstr.; For. Prod. Abstr.; For. Abstr.; Geogr. Abstr. Phys. Geogr.; GeoRef; Helminthol. Abstr. (1991-); Int. Dev. Abstr.; Wildl. Rev. (19??-199?).

UK/0263-6271
**SCIENCE IN PARLIAMENT.** English. Five times a year (Feb., Apr., June, Oct., Dec.). £72.50. Westminster Publishing Ltd, 28 Ponsonby Terrace, London SW1P 4QA England. **Tel** 011 44 71 821 6772, FAX 011 44 71 834 6694. **ED** Dr. Maurice Goldsmith (phone: (041)821-6772). **[CCC]. Bk Rev**, (Qty: 5). **Ad Acc.**
**Desc:** A scientific forum in a special position as an influential link between academia and industry, the Houses of Parliament, the European community and the European Parliament.
**Ind/Abst** Leadscan.

●RU
**SCIENCE IN RUSSIA / RUSSIAN ACADEMY OF SCIENCES. Added/Corp** Rossiiskaia Akademiia Nauk. No. 2-3 (Mar./Jun 1992)-. Academic Scholarly Publication. English. bm. Izdatelstvo Nauka / Akademiia Nauk, Publishing House of the Russian Academy of Sciences, Leninskii Porspekt 14, 117901 Moscow Russia. **Tel** 011 95 954-21-53, FAX 011 95 938-21-44, telex 411964. **LC** Q127.S696; S33. **DD** 505. ***Continues*** *Nauka v SSSR. English. Science in USSR, 0203-4638.*
**Ind/Abst** GeoRef.

RU/0203-4638
**SCIENCE IN USSR.** ***Title Change.*** [Sci. USSR]. **Added/Corp** Akademiia Nauk SSSR. **VFOAT** Science in U.S.S.R.; Science in the USSR. (1981) No. 1-(1992) No. 1. Periodical. English (German, Spanish and Russian). bm. **LC** Q127.S696; S33. **DD** 505. ***Continued by*** *Nauka v Rossii (Moscow, Russia). English. Science in Russia.*
**Desc:** Acquaints the reader with major achievements of Soviet scientists, science life in the USSR, the history of Soviet science and outstanding Soviet scientists.
**Ind/Abst** GeoRef.

PK/1013-5316
**SCIENCE INTERNATIONAL LAHORE.** [Sci. int.Lahore]. (1988)-. Periodical. English. qt. Lahore Publications International, Lahore Pakistan. Documents available from CASDDS.
**Ind/Abst** Chem. Abstr.

US/1064-7015
**SCIENCE IS ELEMENTARY.** (SCIENCE IS ELEMENTARY : A SCIENCE TEACHING RESOURCE PUBLICATION.). [Sci. elem.]. **Added/Corp** Museum Institute for Teaching Science. (1987)- Vol. 5 (Oct. 1992)-Vol. 6 (Oct. 1993)-. Periodical. English. Four times a year (Mar., May, Oct., Dec.). $22.00. Museum Institute for Teachers Science (MITS), Inc., 79 Milk Street, Suite 210, Boston MA 02109-3903. **Tel** (617)695-9771, FAX (617)695-9845. **ED** Beverly Maffel, (617)695-9771. **LC** Q181.A1; S364. **DD** 372.3/5/05. **Bk Rev. Circ:** 400.
**Desc:** Science activities for K-6 Students.

US/0036-8423
**SCIENCE NEWS (WASHINGTON).** (SCIENCE NEWS.). [Sci. news]. **Added/Corp** Science Service. Vol. 89, No. 11 (Mar. 12, 1966)-. Academic Scholarly Publication. English. wk (published on Saturday). $44.50 (one year), $78.00 (two year) US; $50.50 (one year), $90.00 (two year) other. Science News, 1719 N Street Northwest, Washington DC 20036. **Tel** (202)785-2255, FAX (202)785-3751. **(Subscription address:** 205 West Center Street, Subscription Department, Marion, OH 43302; telephone: (800)347-6969 or (614)383-5231**) ED** Patrick Young. **LC** Q1; .S76. **DD** 505. **NLM** W1 SC75. **CODEN** SCNEBK. Index available. **Bk Rev. Ad Acc. Circ:** 196,073 (ctrl). available on microfilm and microfiche from University Microfilms International (UMI). Documents available from UMI Article Clearinghouse, CASDDS, Documents on Demand. ***Continues*** *Science News Letter, 0096-4018.*
**Desc:** Provides facts and commentary on developments in the world of science.
**Ind/Abst** Abr. Read. Guide Period. Lit.; Abstr. Bull. Inst. Pap. Sci. Tech.; Acad. Abstr. Full Text Elite (Jan. 1984-) [Full Txt.]; Acad. Abstr. (Jan. 1984-); Acad. Ind. [Computer File] (1984-); Acad. Search (Jan. 1984-); AGRICOLA [Select. Cov.]; Biol. Dig.; Can. Period. Index (19??-); Chem. Abstr.; Curr. Index J. Educ.; Environ. Abstr.; Expand. Acad. Index (1984-); F&S Index Plus Text, Int. [Select. Cov.]; Foods Adlibra; Garden Lit. (1992-); Gen. Period. Index (1985-); Gen. Sci. Index; Gen. Sci. Source (Jan. 1988-) [Full Txt.]; GeoRef; Health Ref. Cent. (1987-) [Select. Cov.]; Health Source (Jan. 1984-); INFO-SOUTH Abstr.; Mag. Artic. Summar. Elite (Jan. 1984-) [Full Txt.]; Mag. Artic. Summar. Select (Jan. 1984-) [Full Txt.]; Mag. Artic. Summar. CD-ROM (Jan. 1984-); Mag. ASAP Plus [Full Txt.]; Mag. ASAP Sel. [Full Txt.]; Mag. Express (1986-) [Full Txt.]; Mag. Index Plus (1989-); Mag. Index. Sel. (1986-); Mag. Search; Mid. Search (Jan. 1984-) [Full Txt.]; Newsp. Period. Abstr. (1986-); Nutr. Res. Newsl.; PROMT; Read. Guide Abstr. Select Ed.; Read. Guide Period. Lit.; Resource/One Ondisc; Mag. Index (1977-); TOM Gen. Index (1985-) [Full Txt.]; Vocat. Search (Jan. 1984-) [Full Txt.].

US
**SCIENCE NOTES.** English. New Jersey State Museum, PO Box 1868, Trenton NJ 08607. **LC** Q11; .S2685. **DD** 505.

SA
**SCIENCE POLICY DIGEST.** (1988)-. Newsletter. English. qt. Directorate S & T Policy, Foundation for Research Development, PO Box 2600, Pretoria 0001 South Africa. **Tel** 012 841-4273, FAX 012 804-2679, telex 3-21356 FRD SA. ctrl circ.

NE/0811-4536
**SCIENCE POLICY IN THE NETHERLANDS. Added/Corp** Netherlands. Ministerie van Onderwijs en Wetenschappen. **VFOAT** Science Policy. (1979)-. Periodical. English. Five times a year. Free on request. Ministry of Education & Science Netherlands, PO Box 25000, 2700 LZ Zoetermeer Netherlands. **Tel** 317 953 2825. **LC** Q127.N2; S33. **DD** 338.949206.

FR
**SCIENCE POLICY STUDIES AND DOCUMENTS. Added/Corp** Unesco. No. 1 (1965)-. Monographic series. English (French and English). ir. Price varies per volume. UNESCO / France, 31 rue Francois Bonvin, 75732 Paris Cedex 15 France. **Tel** 011 33 1 45684564, 011 33 1 45684565, FAX 011 33 1 42733007, telex 204461 Paris. **(Subscription address:** UNIPUB, 4611 F Assembly Drive, Lanham MD 20706.**)**

US/1049-7730
**SCIENCE PROBE!.** ***Ceased.*** [Sci. probe]. Vol. 1, No. 1 (Nov. 1990)-Vol. 2, No. 4 (Nov. 1992). Periodical. English. qt. Science Probe!, 500-B Bi-County Boulevard, Farmingdale NY 11735. **Tel** (516)293-0467. **LC** Q162; .S415. **DD** 505.
**Desc:** Devoted entirely to amateur scientists and encourages them to perform serious research. In each issue, the reader joins a community of amateur scientists who seek scientific knowledge.
**Ind/Abst** Access (1992); Curr. Index J. Educ.

UK/0036-8504
**SCIENCE PROGRESS (1916).** (SCIENCE PROGRESS.). [Sci. prog.]. Vol. 11 No. 41 (July 1916)-. Academic Scholarly Publication. English. qt. $168.00. Science Reviews Ltd, 18 Oaklands Gate, Northwood Middlesex, HA6 3AA England. **Tel** 011 44 923 823586. **LC** Q1; .S79. **NLM** W1 SC756. **CODEN** SCPRAY. **[CCC].** Index available. **Ad Acc. Pr Rev.** available on microfilm from University Microfilms International (UMI). Documents available from The Genuine Article, BIOSIS Document Express, Ask*IEEE, CASDDS. ***Continues*** *Science Progress in the Twentieth Century, 0302-1785.*
**Desc:** Reviews of a particular region of research.
**Ind/Abst** AGRICOLA; Biodeter. Abstr.; Biol. Abstr.; Ceram. Abstr. (19??-); Chem. Abstr.; Curr. Aware. Biol. Sci., CABS; Curr. Technol. Index; Ecol. Abstr.; EMBASE; Geogr. Abstr. Phys. Geogr.; Geogr. Abstr. Human Geogr. (?-?); Geol. Abstr.; GeoRef; Helminthol. Abstr.; Index

Med.; Index Sci. Rev. [Full Cov.]; INSPEC (1968-); Int. Aerosp. Abstr.; Int. Dev. Abstr.; Life Sci. Collect.; Protozoolog. Abstr.; Res. Alert [Full Cov.]; Rev. Med. Vet. Entomol.; Rev. Plant Pathol.; Sci. Cit. Index (19??-19??); SCISEARCH; Soils Fert.

US/0090-9378
**SCIENCE QUEST.** V. 1- Jan. 1973-. Periodical. English. bm. $4.50. Science Quest, 5513 Pershing Avenue, Downers Grove IL 60515. **LC** Q175.4; .S35. **DD** 301.24/3/05.

AT
**SCIENCE REPORT / HERMAN RESEARCH LABORATORY.** (19??)-. English. sa. State Electricity Commission of Queensland, Herman Research Laboratory, Howard Street, Richmond Victoria 3121 Australia. **LC** Discard.

JA
**SCIENCE REPORT OF THE FACULTY OF EDUCATION, GIFU UNIVERSITY (NATURAL SCIENCE).** **Main/Corp** Gifu, Japan. University. Faculty of Education. Vol. 3, No. 5 (1966)-. English (Japanese). **Continues** *Gifu, Japan. University. Faculty of Liberal Arts and Education. Science Report of the Faculty of Liberal Arts and Education, Gifu University (Natural Science).*
**Ind/Abst** Zentralbl. Math. Ihre Grenzgeb.

II/0036-8512
**SCIENCE REPORTER.** **Added/Corp** Council of Scientific & Industrial Research (India). Vol. 1 (Jan. 1964)-. Academic Scholarly Publication. English. mo. $15.00. Council of Scientific & Industrial Research, Publications & Information Director, Hillside Road, New Delhi 110012 India. **Tel** FAX 011 91 11 5731353. **(Subscription address:** Prints India, 11 Darya Ganj, New Delhi 110002 India.**)** **ED** Biman Basu, C.B. Sharma, Dilip M. Salwi. **LC** Q1; .S797. **DD** 505. **CODEN** SCRPA4. **Bk Rev**, (Qty: 48). **Ad Acc. Circ:** 50,000. Documents available from CASDDS.
**Ind/Abst** Chem. Abstr. (1964-1978).

JA/0367-6439
**SCIENCE REPORTS OF THE HIROSAKI UNIVERSITY.** (HIROSAKI DAIGAKU RIKA HOKOKU.). [Sci. rep. Hirosaki Univ.]. **Added/Corp** Hirosaki Daigaku. Rigakubu. **VFOAT** Science Reports of the Hirosaki University. (1965)-. Academic Scholarly Publication. Japanese (English). sa. Hirosaki Daigaku Rigakubu, (Faculty of Science, Hirosaki University), 3 Bunkyocho, Hirosakishi Aomoriken 036 Japan. **LC** Q4; .H56. **CODEN** HUSRAK. Documents available from CASDDS. **Continues** *Science Reports of the Faculty of Literature and Science, Hirosaki University.*
**Ind/Abst** Chem. Abstr.; Math. Rev.; Life Sci. Collect.; Zentralbl. Math. Ihre Grenzgeb.

JA/0022-8338
**SCIENCE REPORTS OF THE KANAZAWA UNIVERSITY, THE.** [Sci. rep. Kanazawa Univ.]. **Added/Corp** Kanazawa Daigaku. Rigakubu. **VFOAT** Kanazawa Daigaku Rika Hokoku. (Mar. 1951)-. Academic Scholarly Publication. English. sa. Kanazawa Daigaku Rigakubu, (Faculty of Science, Kanazawa University), 1-1, Marunouchi, Kanazawashi, Ishikawaken 920 Japan. **LC** Q4; .K14. **CODEN** SRKAAT. Documents available from CASDDS.
**Ind/Abst** Chem. Abstr. (1951-1982); Math. Rev.; Zentralbl. Math. Ihre Grenzgeb.

JA/0040-8808
**SCIENCE REPORTS OF THE RESEARCH INSTITUTES. SERIES A, PHYSICS, CHEMISTRY, AND METALLURGY.** [Sci. rep. Res. Inst., Tohoku Univ., Ser. A]. **Added/Corp** Tohoku Daigaku. Tohoku Daigaku Kenkyujo Hokoku. Butsurigaku, Kagaku, Yakingaku. **VFOAT** Tohoku Daigaku Kenkyujo Hokoku. Butsurigaku, Kagaku, Yakingaku. Vol. 1 (May 1949)-. Periodical. English. ir. Tohoku Daigaku Kenkyujo Rengokai, (Research Institutes, Tohoku University), c/o Tohoku Daigaku Kinzoku, Zairyo Kenkyujo, 1-1, Katahira, 2 Chome, Sendaishi, Miyagiken 980 Japan. **(Subscription address:** Japan Publications Trading Company, Ltd., PO Box 5030, Tokyo International, Tokyo 100-31 Japan.**)** **LC** Q77.T55; A32. **DD** 530.72. **CODEN** SRTAA6. Documents available from Article Express International, The Genuine Article, Ask*IEEE, CASDDS.
**Ind/Abst** Alum. Ind. Abstr.; Bioeng. Abstr. (1968-); Chem. Abstr.; Coal Abstr.; Ei Page One (1968-); Eng. Index Annu.; INSPEC; Leadscan; Met. Abstr.; Res. Alert [Full Cov.]; Sci. Cit. Index; SCISEARCH.

JA
**SCIENCE REPORTS OF THE YOKOHAMA NATIONAL UNIVERSITY. SECTION I : MATHEMATICS, PHYSICS, CHEMISTRY.** **Main/Corp** Yokohama Kokuritsu Daigaku. Kyoikugakubu. **VFOAT** Yokohama Kokuritsu Daigaku Rika Kiyo. Dai 1-Rui: Sugaku, Butsurigaku, Kagaku. No. 4- 1955-. English (English). Yokohama National University, 41 Shimizugaoka Minami-ku, Yokohama Japan. **LC** Q77; .Y6. **DD** 500.2/05. Documents available from Ask*IEEE. **Continues** *Science Reports of the Yokohama National University. Section I. Mathematics, Physics.*
**Ind/Abst** INSPEC (1968-); Zentralbl. Math. Ihre Grenzgeb.

JA/0386-4006
**SCIENCE REPORTS OF TOKYO WOMAN'S CHRISTIAN UNIVERSITY.** [Tokyo Joshi Daigaku kiyo ronshu, Kagaku bumon hokoku]. **VFOAT** Tokyo Joshi Daigaku Kiyo Ronshu. Kagaku Bumon Hokoku; Kagaku Bumon Hokoku. Academic Scholarly Publication. English (Japanese). an. Tokyo Woman's Christian University, Zempukuji Suginami, Tokyo Japan. **CODEN** SRTUDZ. Documents available from CASDDS. **Continues** *Science Reports of Tokyo Woman's Christian College.*
**Ind/Abst** Chem. Abstr. (1982); Math. Rev.; Zentralbl. Math. Ihre Grenzgeb.

JA/0474-781X
**SCIENCE REPORTS - OSAKA UNIVERSITY. COLLEGE OF GENERAL EDUCATION.** **See** Education-Physical Education and Training.

US
**SCIENCE RESEARCH ANNUAL.** 1980-. English. an. Illinois Legislative Council, 222 S College/3rd Floor, Springfield IL 62704.

US/0566-9995
**SCIENCE RESOURCES STUDIES HIGHLIGHTS.** ***Ceased.*** Periodical. English. National Science Foundation, 1800 G Street Northwest, Washington DC 20550. **Tel** (202)357-9859, (202)357-9498. **LC** Q180.U5; U54D. **DD** 509.73.

II/0253-6684
**SCIENCE REVIEW (CALCUTTA).** (SCIENCE REVIEW.). [Sci. rev.]. Vol. 1-. Academic Scholarly Publication. English. Indian Science News Association, 92 Acharya Prafulla, Chandra Road, Calcutta 9 India. **CODEN** SCRVDP. Documents available from CASDDS.
**Ind/Abst** Chem. Abstr. (1980).

US/0887-2376
**SCIENCE SCOPE (WASHINGTON, D.C.).** (SCIENCE SCOPE / NATIONAL SCIENCE TEACHERS ASSOCIATION.). [Sci. scope]. **Added/Corp** National Science Teachers Association. (19??)-. Periodical. English. Eight times a year. $52.00. National Science Teachers Association, 1840 Wilson Boulevard, Arlington VA 22201-3000. **Tel** (703)243-7100, FAX (703)243-7177, (703)522-5413. **ED** Steven Rakow and Crystal Lal. **LC** LB1585.3; .M52. **DD** 507. Index available. **Bk Rev. Ad Acc. Pr Rev. Circ:** 12,000 (ctrl). available on microfilm and microfiche from University Microfilms International (UMI). **Continues** *Middle Jr. High Science Bulletin, 0160-306X.*
**Desc:** Devoted specifically to middle school and junior high science teaching. Includes classroom activities, posters, teaching tips and reviews, along with educational theory on the ways adolescents learn. Particularly helpful to the new middle/junior high science teacher.
**Ind/Abst** Curr. Index J. Educ.; Educ. Index (1992-); Gen. Sci. Source (Jan. 1994-); Mid. Search (Jan. 1994-).

CN/0706-0793
**SCIENCE STATISTICS.** **See** Science and Technology-Abstracting, Bibliographies and Statistics.

US/0036-8555
**SCIENCE TEACHER (WASHINGTON, D.C.), THE.** (THE SCIENCE TEACHER.). [Sci. teach.]. **Added/Corp** American Science Teachers Association. Illinois Association of Chemistry Teachers. American Council of Science Teachers. National Science Teachers Association. (1936)-. Periodical. English. Nine times a year. $52.00. National Science Teachers Association, 1840 Wilson Boulevard, Arlington VA 22201-3000. **Tel** (703)243-7100, FAX (703)243-7177, (703)522-5413. **ED** Juliana Texley. **LC** Q181; .S38. **DD** 507. cum. index. **Bk Rev. Ad Acc. Circ:** 27,000 (ctrl). available on microfilm and microfiche from University Microfilms International (UMI). Documents available from UMI Article Clearinghouse. **Continues** *Illinois Chemistry Teacher.*
**Desc:** Professional journal for junior and senior high school science teachers. Offers articles on a wide range of scientific topics, innovative teaching ideas and experiments, current research, news on free or inexpensive materials, reviews, posters and more.
**Ind/Abst** Acad. Abstr. Full Text Elite (Jan. 1992-); Acad. Abstr. (Jan. 1992-); Acad. Ind. [Computer File] (1987-); Acad. Search (Jan. 1992-); Biol. Dig.; Contents Pages Educ.; Curr. Index J. Educ.; Educ. Index; Expand. Acad. Index (1987-); Gen. Sci. Source (Jan. 1992-); GeoRef; Health Source (Jan. 1992-); INFO-SOUTH Abstr.; Int. Aerosp. Abstr.; Mag. Artic. Summar. Elite (Jan. 1992-); Mag. Artic. Summar. Select (Jan. 1992-); Mag. Artic. Summar. CD-ROM (Jan. 1992-); Mag. Search; Med. Rev. Dig.; Mid. Search (Jan. 1992-); Newsp. Period. Abstr. (1989-); Prim. Search (Jan. 1992-).

UK/0950-0707
**SCIENCE, TECHNOLOGY & DEVELOPMENT.** **Added/Corp** Third World Scientific & Technological Development Forum. Third World Science, Technology & Development Forum. **VFOAT** Science, Technology and Development. (1986)-. Periodical. English. Three times a year. $115.00. Frank Cass & Company Ltd, Newbury House, 890-900 Eastern Avenue, Newbury Park, Ilford, Essex IG2 7HH United Kingdom. **Tel** 011 44 81 599 8866, FAX 011 44 81 599 0984, telex 897719. **ED** Ahmed Shibli, UK. **LC** Q127.2; .S35. **Ad Acc, Adv Mgr:** Anne Kidson. **Continues** *Epoch (Glasgow, Scotland).*
**Desc:** Provides a platform for the discussion of issues related to science, technology and development in the countries of the Third World and thus invites articles, comments and other material on these issues. One of the more important issues addressed is the appropriateness and choice of technology for development.
**Ind/Abst** Agric. Eng. Abstr.; For. Prod. Abstr. (1991-); Geogr. Abstr. Human Geogr.; Int. Bibliogr. Sociol.; Int. Labour Doc.; Irr. Drain. Abstr.; LABORDOC; Rural Dev. Abstr.; World Agric. Econ.

US/0162-2439
**SCIENCE, TECHNOLOGY & HUMAN VALUES.** [Sci. technol. human values]. **Added/Corp** Harvard University. Program on Science, Technology, and Public Policy. Massachusetts Institute of Technology. Program in Science, Technology and Society. John F. Kennedy School of Government. Society for Social Studies of Science. **VFOAT** Science, Technology and Human Values. No. 25 (Fall 1978)-. Periodical. English. qt (Jan., Apr., July, Oct.). $144.00. SAGE Periodical Press, 2455 Teller Road, Thousand Oaks CA 91320. **Tel** (805)499-0721, FAX (805)499-0871, telex 100799. **ED** Olga Amsterdamska (University of Amsterdam). **LC** Q175.4; .S365. **DD** 303.4/83. **[CCC]. Ad Acc. Pr Rev. Acid Free. Circ:** 1,200. available on microfilm and microfiche from University Microfilms International (UMI). Documents available from The Genuine Article, UMI Article Clearinghouse. **Continues** *Newsletter on Science, Technology, & Human Values, 0738-2618;* **Absorbed** *Science & Technology Studies, 0886-3040.*
**Desc:** Contains research and commentary on the development and dynamics of science and technology, including their involvement in politics, society and culture.
**Ind/Abst** Curr. Contents Soc. Behav. Sci.; Curr. Index J. Educ.; Curr. Lit. Sci. Sci.; Expand. Acad. Index (1992-); Index Period. Artic. Relat. Law; Int. Polit. Sci. Abstr.; Newsp. Period. Abstr. (1992-); PAIS Int. Print; Philos. Index; Res. Alert [Full Cov.]; Sage Public Adm. Abstr.; Soc. Plann. Policy Dev. Abstr.; Soc. Sci. Cit. Index [Full Cov.]; Sociol. Abstr.

US/0275-8075
**SCIENCE, TECHNOLOGY & SOCIETY.** (SCIENCE, TECHNOLOGY & SOCIETY : CURRICULUM NEWSLETTER OF THE LEHIGH UNIVERSITY STS PROGRAM.). [Sci., techno. soc.]. **Added/Corp** Lehigh University. **VAT** Science, Technology and Society. (1977)-. Newsletter. English. Four times a year. $8.00. Lehigh University, STS Program, 9 West Packer Avenue, Maginnes Hall, Bethlehem PA 18015. **Tel** (215)758-3350, FAX (215)758-3079. **ED** Dr. Stephen H. Cutcliffe. **Bk Rev**, (Qty: 75-100). **Circ:** 650 (ctrl).
**Desc:** Publishes short articles on the theoretical and speculative aspects of curriculum development, in-depth program and course descriptions, reviews of texts and annotated bibliography of current books and articles. Announcements regarding STS activities, questions, comments and/or forthcoming meetings.

UK
**SCIENCE TODAY.** English. mo. $121.00. Bennett Coleman & Co Ltd, PO Box 57, Gloucester GL2 6DS England. **Tel** 011 44 452 306654. **Bk Rev. Ad Acc. Circ:** 48,000 (ctrl).
**Desc:** Science and technology in India and internationally.

SW/0036-8598
**SCIENCE TOOLS.** (SCIENCE TOOLS. THE L.K.B. INSTRUMENT JOURNAL.). [Sci. tools]. **VFOAT** L.K.B. Instrument Journal. Vol. 1 (April 1954)-. Periodical. English. qt. **NLM** W1 SC781E. **CODEN** SCTOAB. Documents available from Ask*IEEE, CASDDS.
**Ind/Abst** Anal. Abstr.; Chem. Abstr. (-1983); INSPEC (1968-).

US/0043-0749
**SCIENCE TRENDS.** [Sci. trends]. Vol. 31, No. 11 (Dec. 1973)-. Periodical. English. sm (published monthly in July and August). $650.00 (one year), $1,150.00 (two year). Trends Publishing Inc., 1079 National Press Building, Washington DC 20045. **Tel** (202)393-0031, FAX (202)393-1732. **ED** A Kranish. **Bk Rev.** ctrl circ. available on microfilm and microfiche from University Microfilms International (UMI). **Continues** *Washington Science Trends, 0511-3342.*

**Desc:** Gives late developments in R&D and general science topics. Lists meetings of interest and book reviews.

US/0163-4720
**SCIENCE UPDATE.** English. an. Gaylord Brothers Inc, Box 4901, Syracuse NY 13221. **Tel** (315)457-5070. **ED** T G Aylesworth and S Klein. **LC** Q1; .S8145. **DD** 505.

CN/0848-6832
**SCIENCE UPDATE (YELLOWKNIFE).** (SCIENCE UPDATE / SCIENCE INSTITUTE OF THE NORTHWEST TERRITORIES.). [Sci. update]. **Added/Corp** Science Institute of the Northwest Territories. **VFOAT** N.W.T. Science Update. No. 1 (1990)-. Periodical. English. **DD** 509.7192.

US/0036-8075
**SCIENCE (WASHINGTON, D.C.).** (SCIENCE.). [Science]. **Added/Corp** American Association for the Advancement of Science. Vol. 1, No. 1 (Feb. 9, 1883)-. Academic Scholarly Publication. English. wk. $228.00 (institution) US; $281.00 (institution) Canada, Mexico and Caribbean. American Association for the Advancement of Science, 1333 H Street Northwest, Washington DC 20005. **Tel** (202)326-6400, (203)326-6417, (202)326-6430, FAX (202)842-1065. **(Subscription address:** Fulfillment Corporation of America, PO Box 1962, Marion OH 43305.) **ED** Daniel E. Koshland, Jr. **LC** Q1; .S35. **DD** 505. **NLM** W1 SC653. **CODEN** SCIEAS. **[CCC].** Index available (bound in last issue). **Bk Rev. Ad Acc. Pr Rev. Circ:** 154,000. available on microfilm and microfiche from University Microfilms International (UMI). Documents available from Article Express International, The Genuine Article, BIOSIS Document Express, Ask*IEEE, UMI Article Clearinghouse, CASDDS. ***Continues*** *Science, 0036-8075;* ***Absorbed*** *Scientific Monthly, 0096-3771.*
**Desc:** Published for scientists, engineers and others interested in science; contains articles, original research reports, news sections, editorials, and letters. Special issues devoted to science-related topics such as biotechnology.
**Ind/Abst** Abstr. Bull. Inst. Pap. Sci. Tech.; Abstr. J. Earthq. Eng.; Abstr. Graphic Arts Tech. Found. (1984-); Abstr. BioCommer.; Acad. Abstr. Full Text Elite (Jan. 1984-); Acad. Abstr. (Jan. 1984-); Acad. Ind. [Computer File] (1984-); Acad. Search (Jan. 1984-); AESIS Q.; AGRICOLA [Select. Cov.]; Alum. Ind. Abstr.; Appl. Sci. Technol. Index; Aquat. Sci. Fish. Abstr. (Computer File); Art Archaeol. Tech. Abstr.; Arts Humanit. Citation Index [Select. Cov.]; BioBusiness (1988-); Biol. Abstr.; Biol. Dig.; Biotechnol. Res. Abstr.; Br. Archaeol. Bibliogr.; Calcium Calcif. Tissue Abstr.; Ceram. Abstr.; Chem Inform; Chem. Abstr.; Chem. Hazards Ind.; Chem. Titles; Chemorecept. Abstr.; Civ. Struct. Eng. Abstr.; Coal Abstr.; Comput. Rev.; Crim. Justice Abstr.; Crop Physiol. Abstr.; CSA Neuro. Abstr.; Curr. Biotechnol.; Curr. Chem. React.; Curr. Index J. Educ.; Curr. Lit. Fam. Plan.; Curr. Ref. Fish Res.; Curr. Titl. Dent.; Dairy Sci. Abstr.; Dev. Med. Child Neurol.; Ecol. Abstr.; Ecology Abstr.; Elect. Comm. Abstr.; EMBASE; Energy Res. Abstr. (Oct. 1975-); Eng. Index Annu. [Select. Cov.]; Entomol. Abstr.; Environ. Period. Bibliogr. (?-?); Expand. Acad. Index (1984-); Field Crop Abstr.; Food Sci. Technol. Abstr.; Foods Adlibra; For. Prod. Abstr. (1991-); For. Abstr.; Gas Abstr.; Gen. Period. Index (Jan. 1985-Dec. 1985, Jan. 1986-July 1986); Gen. Sci. Index; Genet. Abstr.; Geogr. Abstr. Phys. Geogr.; Geogr. Abstr. Human Geogr.; Geol. Abstr.; GeoRef; Health Saf. Sci. Abstr.; Health Index (1989-); Health Ref. Cent. (Jan. 1989-) [Full Cov.]; Helminthol. Abstr. (1991-); Hum. Genome Abstr.; Immunol. Abstr.; Index Chem.; Index Med.; Index Period. Artic. Relat. Law; Index Vet.; Infobank (Jan. 1969-); INSPEC (1968-); Int. Aerosp. Abstr.; Int. Dev. Abstr.; J. Watch (199?-); Lab. Hazards Bull.; Lit. Pat. Abstr., Oilfield Chem. (1972-); Lit. Abstr., Catal. Catal.; Lit. Abstr., Health Environ.; Lit. Abstr., Pet. Refin. Petrochem.; Lit. Abstr., Pet. Substit.; Lit. Abstr., Transp. Storage; Mag. Artic. Summar. Elite (Jan. 1984-); Mag. Artic. Summar. Select (Jan. 1984-); Mag. Artic. Summar. CD-ROM (Jan. 1984-); Mag. Express (1986-) [Full Txt.]; Mag. Index Plus (1989-); Mag. Index. Sel. (1986-); Maize Abstr.; Mass Spect. Bull.; Mater. Sci. Eng. Abstr.; Mech. Eng. Abstr.; Met. Abstr.; Meteorol. Geoastrophys. Abstr.; Microbiol. Abstr. Sect. B; Microbiol. Abstr. Sect. A; Microbiol. Abstr. Sect. C; Middle East Abstr. Index; Nematol. Abstr.; Newsp. Period. Abstr. (1986-); Nucl. Acids Abstr.; Nutr. Res. Newsl.; Ocean. Abstr.; Oncog. Growth Factors Abstr.; Ornamental Hort. (19??-19??); Peace Res. Abstr. J. (1945-1987); Physic. Medline Plus; Pig News Inf.; Plant Breed. Abstr.; Plant Genet. Resour. Abstr.; Plant Grow. Reg. Abstr.; Pollut. Abstr. Indexes; Popul. Index; Potato Abstr.; Poult. Abstr.; Protozoolog. Abstr.; Psychol. Abstr. (1925-); PsycINFO; PsycLit; Read. Guide Abstr. Select Ed.; Read. Guide Period. Lit.; Ref. Upd. Basic Ed.; Ref. Upd. Deluxe Ed.; Res. Alert [Full Cov.]; Resource/One Ondisc; Rev. Plant Pathol.; Risk Abstr.; Sci. Cit. Index; SCISEARCH; Small Anim. Abstr. Bibliogr.; Soc. Plann. Policy Dev. Abstr.; Soc. Sci. Cit. Index [Select. Cov.]; Solid State Supercond. Abstr.; Text. Technol. Dig.; Mag. Index (1977-); TOM Gen. Index (1985-); Trop. Dis. Bull.; Virol. AIDS Abstr.; Vitis Vitic. Enol. Abstr.

US/1047-8043
**SCIENCE WATCH.** [Sci. watch]. **Added/Corp** Institute for Scientific Information. Institute for Scientific Information. Research Dept. Vol. 1, No. 1 (Jan. 1990)-. Academic Scholarly Publication. English. Ten times a year. $365.00. Institute for Scientific Information, 3501 Market Street, Philadelphia PA 19104. **Tel** (215)386-0100, (800)523-1850, FAX (215)386-6362, telex 84-5305. **(Subscription address:** Institute for Scientific Information, PO Box 71416, Chicago IL 60694.) **DD** 500. **NLM** W1; SC784. **CODEN** SCWAEM.
**Desc:** Provides current reports on biotechnology, physics, chemistry, and medicine. Also gives information on performances of universities, research labs, and countries.

US/0036-8601
**SCIENCE WORLD.** (19??)-. Periodical. English. Fourteen times a year. $25.00. Scholastic Inc., 2931 East McCarty Street, PO Box 3710, Jefferson City MO 65102-9957. **Tel** (314)636-5271, (800)631-1586. available on microfilm from University Microfilms International (UMI).
**Ind/Abst** Acad. Abstr. Full Text Elite (Dec. 1991-); Acad. Abstr. (Dec. 1991-); Biol. Dig.; Child. Mag. Guide; Gen. Sci. Source (Jan. 1992-); Health Source (Jan. 1992-); Mid. Search (Jan. 1992-).

US
**SCIENCE WORLD.** English.

US/1041-1410
**SCIENCE WORLD (1987).** (SCIENCE WORLD.). [Sci. world]. **VFOAT** Scholastic Science World. Vol. 44, No. 4 (Oct. 16, 1987)-. Periodical. English. bw. $25.00. Scholastic Inc., 2931 East McCarty Street, PO Box 3710, Jefferson City MO 65102-9957. **Tel** (314)636-5271, (800)631-1586. **LC** Q1; .S8147. **DD** 505. available on microfilm and microfiche from University Microfilms International (UMI). Documents available from UMI Article Clearinghouse, Magazine Collection. ***Continues*** *Scholastic Science World, 0162-8399.*
**Ind/Abst** Acad. Search (Dec. 1991-); Gen. Period. Index (1991-); Mag. Index Plus (1991-); Mag. Index Sel. Microfiche (1991-) [Full Txt.]; Mag. Index. Sel. (1991-); Mag. Search; Newsp. Period. Abstr. (1988-); Prim. Search (Dec. 1991-); Mag. Index (Jan. 1991-); TOM Gen. Index (1991-) [Full Txt.].

US/0080-7621
**SCIENCE YEAR.** (SCIENCE YEAR / THE WORLD BOOK SCIENCE ANNUAL.). [Sci. year]. **Added/Corp** Field Enterprises Educational Corporation. Childcraft International Inc. **VFOAT** World Book Science Annual. (1965)-. English. an. $25.40. World Book Encyclopedia Inc., 2515 East 43rd Street, Chattanooga TN 37422. **Tel** (800)874-0520, (615)867-9081. **LC** Q9; .S33. Index available.
**Desc:** Subject specialists have composed the 'Special Reports' in each volume, and science, technical, and health writers have contributed to the 'file' or encyclopedia-type articles.

US/0147-3654
**SCIENCELAND.** (19??)-. Periodical. English. Eight times a year (monthly Sept. through May excluding Dec.). $19.95 US, $25.00 other (student edition); $15.00 (teacher's manual). Scienceland Inc., 501 Fifth Avenue/Suite 2108, New York NY 10017-6165. **Tel** (212)490-2180, FAX (212)490-2187. **ED** A. H. Matano. Index available. cum. index. **Circ:** 20,000. available on microfilm and microfiche from University Microfilms International (UMI).
**Desc:** Encourages children from preschool to K-3 to get excited about reading and scientific understanding with its photo features and illustrated stories.
**Ind/Abst** Child. Mag. Guide (1981-); Gen. Sci. Source (Jul. 1993-); Mag. Search; Mid. Search (Jul. 1993-); Prim. Search (Jul. 1993-).

FR/1142-4877
**SCIENCES & AVENIR. HORS SERIE.** **VFOAT** Sciences et Avenir. Numero Special; Sciences & Avenir. Numero Special; Sciences et Avenir. Hors Serie. (19??)-. Periodical. French. ir.
**Ind/Abst** Point Repere (1982-).

FR
**SCIENCES & TECHNOLOGIES.** **VFOAT** Sciences et Technologies; Science & Technologie; Science et Technologie. No. 1 (Jan. 1988)-. Periodical. French. mo. 330.00F France; 412.50F other (one year), 616.00F France; 776.00F other (two year). 14 rue de Savoie, 75006 Paris France. **Tel** 011 33 1 46340300. **LC** T2; .S32. **DD** 505.

FR/0154-0319
**SCIENCES DE LA VIE. LEXIQUE.** French (English). 1,100.00F (per volume), 1,840.00F (two volumes). Centre National de la Recherche Scientifique, Informascience, 26 rue Boyer, 75971 Paris France. **Tel** 61.41.11.05, telex CNRSDOC 220880 F. **LC** Z695.1.L55; S34. **DD** 025.4/957.

FR/0154-0351
**SCIENCES DE L'INGENIEUR. LEXIQUE.** French. Informascience, Centre de Documentation Scientifique et Technique Service des Abonnements, 26 rue Boyer, 75971 Paris Cedex 20 France. **LC** Z695.1.S3; S35. **DD** 025.4/96.

FR/0036-8636
**SCIENCES ET AVENIR.** [Sci. avenir]. **VFOAT** Sciences & Avenir. No. 1 (May 19, 1947)-. Academic Scholarly Publication. French. Twelve times a year. 235.00F France; 289.00F other. Sciences et Avenir, 23 Rue de Turbigo, 75002 Paris France. **Tel** 011 33 1 40263100. **ED** G. Lefevrve. **LC** Q2; .S475. **[CCC].** ***Absorbed*** *Terre, Air, Mer; Avenir.*
**Ind/Abst** Coal Abstr.; EMBASE; Energy Res. Abstr.; GeoRef; Point Repere.

FR/0987-0717
**SCIENCES ET NATURE.** **VFOAT** Sciences & Nature. (1987)-. Periodical. French. Eleven times a year. 279.00F France; 369.00F other. Winning International Europe, 22 rue de la Concorde, 1050 Brussels Belgium. **Tel** 011 32 2 5139510. **UDC** 5-053.7. ***Continues*** *L'Argonaute.*

FR/0294-0264
**SCIENCES ET TECHNIQUES EN PERSPECTIVE.** **Added/Corp** Universite de Nantes. Equipe de Recherche: Sciences, Techniques, et Societes. Vol. 1 (Year 1981-1982)-. Periodical. English (French). Four times a year. 250.00F. Universite de Nantes / Institut de Mathematiques, 2 Chemin de la Houssiniere, 44072 Nantes Cedex France. **Tel** 011 33 40 373037, 373004. **ED** J. Dhombres. **LC** Q46; .S23. **DD** 505. Index available. cum. index. **Bk Rev. Ad Acc. Circ:** 500.
**Desc:** A series about science and its surroundings in the 18th and 19th centuries with an emphasis on mathematization of the sciences.
**Ind/Abst** Am. Hist. Life (1984-); Math. Rev.

US/0036-861X
**SCIENCES (NEW YORK), THE.** (THE SCIENCES.). [Sciences]. **Added/Corp** New York Academy of Sciences. Vol. 1 (June 1961)-. Periodical. English. Six times a year. $18.00 US; $25.00 other. New York Academy of Sciences, 2 East 63rd Street, New York NY 10021. **Tel** (212)838-0230, (800)843-6927, FAX (212)888-2894. **(Subscription address:** Usaco Corporation / for Japan, 13-12 Shimbashi 1-Chome, Minato-ku, Tokyo 105 Japan.) **ED** Peter Brown. **LC** Q1; .S8147. **DD** 505. **NLM** W1 SC787. **CODEN** SCNCAD. Index available. **Bk Rev. Ad Acc. Pr Rev. Circ:** 75,000 (ctrl). available on microfilm and microfiche from University Microfilms International (UMI). Documents available from The Genuine Article, BIOSIS Document Express, UMI Article Clearinghouse, Documents on Demand.
**Desc:** A non-technical magazine reporting on physical and life sciences and the impact of science and technology on the world today.
**Ind/Abst** Abr. Read. Guide Period. Lit.; Acad. Abstr. Full Text Elite (Jan. 1992-); Acad. Abstr. (Jan. 1992-); Acad. Search (Jan. 1992-); Access (1976-?); AGRICOLA; Biol. Abstr.; EMBASE; Energy Inf. Abstr.; Environ. Abstr.; Expand. Acad. Index (1989-); Garden Lit. (1992-); Gen. Sci. Index; Gen. Sci. Source (Jan. 1992-); GeoRef; INFO-SOUTH Abstr.; Int. Aerosp. Abstr.; Mag. Artic. Summar. Elite (Jan. 1992-); Mag. Artic. Summar. Select (Jan. 1992-); Mag. Artic. Summar. CD-ROM (Jan. 1992-); Mag. Search; Newsp. Period. Abstr. (1991-); Life Sci. Collect.; Plant Breed. Abstr.; Read. Guide Period. Lit.; Res. Alert [Full Cov.]; Sci. Cit. Index; SCISEARCH; Soc. Plann. Policy Dev. Abstr.; Soc. Sci. Cit. Index [Select. Cov.]; Sociol. Abstr.; Soils Fert.

CG/0377-5135
**SCIENCES, TECHNIQUES, INFORMATIONS CRIAC.** [Sci., tech., inf. CRIAC]. **Main/Corp** Centre de Recherches Industrielles en Afrique Centrale. **VAT** Sciences, Techniques, Informations Centre de Recherches Industrielles en Afrique Centrale. No. 1- 1974-. Academic Scholarly Publication. French. Centre de Recherches Industrielles en Afrique Centrale, BP 54, Av du President Ileo, Lubumbashi Congo Zaire. **LC** T175; .C44B. **CODEN** STICD8. Documents available from CASDDS. ***Supersedes*** *Bulletin d'Information - Centre de Recherches Industrielles en Afrique Centrale.*
**Ind/Abst** Chem. Abstr.

II
**SCIENCETECH BULLETIN.** **Added/Corp** India. National Committee on Science and Technology. India. Dept. of Science and Technology. (19??)-. Periodical. English. mo. Technology Bhawan, New Mehrauli Road, New Delhi 110029 India. **LC** T27.I4; S38. **DD** 609/.54.

CN/0829-2507
**SCIENTIA CANADENSIS.** [Sci. can.]. **VFOAT** Journal of the History of Canadian Science, Technology and Medicine; Revue d'Histoire des Sciences, des Techniques et de la Medecine au Canada. Vol. 8, No. 1 (June 1984)-. Periodical. English (French). Twice a year. $25.00. Becker Associates, 36 Bessemer Court, Unit 3, Concord Ontario L4K 3C9 Canada. **Tel** (416)669-5373, FAX (416)669-1927. **ED** Richard A. Jarrell. **DD** 509/.71. Index available. cum. index. **Bk Rev. Ad Acc.** ***Continues*** *HSTC Bulletin, 0228-0086.*
**Desc:** History of Canadian science, technology and medicine.

IO
**SCIENTIAE.** Periodical. Indonesian (Indonesian). 350. PO Box 82, Bandung Indonesia. **LC** T4; .S27.
**Ind/Abst** Eng. Mater. Abstr.; Stat. Theory Method Abstr. (1959-1963).

CN
**SCIENTIFIC ACTIVITIES : FEDERAL GOVERNMENT COSTS AND EXPENDITURES.** **Main/Corp** Canada. Ministry of State, Science and Technology. **VFOAT** Activites Scientifiques: Couts et Depenses Supportes par le Gouvernement Federal. Multiple languages (English and French). an. Information Canada, 171 Slater Street, Ottawa Ontario K1A 0S9 Canada. **Tel** (819)997-1095. **LC** Q180.C2; C36A. **DD** 354/.71/008.

PL/0079-323X
**SCIENTIFIC ACTIVITIES OF THE POLISH ACADEMY OF SCIENCES, INSTITUTE OF FUNDAMENTAL TECHNOLOGICAL RESEARCH.** [Sci. act. Pol. Acad. Sci., Inst. Fundam. Technol. Res.]. **Main/Corp** Instytut Podstawowych Problemow Techniki (Polska Akademia Nauk). Polish (English and Russian). an. Panstwowe Wydawn Naukowe, Miodowa 10, PO Box 391, 00251 Warsaw Poland. **LC** T4; .P652. **DD** 607/.2/438.

US/0036-8733
**SCIENTIFIC AMERICAN.** [Sci. Am.]. Vol. 1 (Aug. 28, 1845)-Vol. 14 (June 25, 1859); New Series Vol. 1 (July 2, 1859)-. Academic Scholarly Publication. English (Italian, French, German, Spanish, Hungarian, Japanese, Chinese, Russian and Arabic). mo. $39.95 (institution), $36.00 (individual) US and possessions; $47.62 (institution), $43.93 (individual) GST included, Canada; $50.95 (institution), $47.00 (individual) other. Scientific American Medicine, 415 Madison Avenue, New York NY 10017. **Tel** (212)754-0550, (800)333-1199. **(Subscription address:** CDS Agency Hard Copy, PO Box 4966, Des Moines IA 50340.**) ED** Jonathan Piel. **LC** T1; .S5. **DD** 505. **NLM** W1 SC833. **CODEN** SCAMAC. **[CCC]**. Index available (bound in issue). cum. index. **Bk Rev. Pr Rev. Circ:** 659,222. available on microfilm and microfiche from University Microfilms International (UMI); available on an online database (files 647,748/Full-Text) from DIALOG. Documents available from ADONIS, The Genuine Article, BIOSIS Document Express, Ask*IEEE, UMI Article Clearinghouse, Petroleum Abstracts Document Delivery Service, CASDDS, Documents on Demand, Magazine Collection. ***Absorbed** People's Journal; Scientific American Monthly, 0740-6495.*
**Desc:** Authoritative articles on all sciences by scientists who do the research reported. Edited for the interested layman. Features science and the citizen, computer reactions, the amateur scientists, reviews of current books in science, and bibliographies. Back issues are available.
**Ind/Abst** Abr. Read. Guide Period. Lit.; Abstr. Bull. Inst. Pap. Sci. Tech.; Abstr. Graphic Arts Tech. Found. (1984-); Abstr. Anthropol.; Abstr. BioCommer.; Acad. Abstr. Full Text Elite (Jan. 1984-); Acad. Abstr. (Jan. 1984-); Acad. Ind. [Computer File] (1984-); Acad. Search (Jan. 1984-); Acoust. Abstr.; AESIS Q.; AgBiotech News Inf.; AGRICOLA [Select. Cov.]; Alum. Ind. Abstr.; Anim. Breed. Abstr.; Appl. Sci. Technol. Index; Art Archaeol. Tech. Abstr.; Arts Humanit. Citation Index [Select. Cov.]; Aviat. Tradescan [Select. Cov.]; Biogr. Index; Biol. Abstr. (1986-); Biol. Dig.; Biostatistica; Book Rev. Digest; Book Rev. Index (1965-); Br. Archaeol. Bibliogr.; Can. Period. Index (19??-); Ceram. Abstr.; Chem. Abstr.; Coal Abstr.; Comput. Lit. Index; Comput. Rev.; Cumul. Index Nurs. Allied Health Lit.; Curr. Aware. Biol. Sci., CABS; Curr. Biotechnol.; Curr. Contents, Agric. Biol. Environ. Sci.; Curr. Contents Eng. Tech. Appl. Sci.; Curr. Contents Life Sci.; Curr. Contents Phys. Chem. Earth Sci.; Curr. Geogr. Publ. (199?-); Curr. Index J. Educ.; Curr. Lit. Fam. Plan.; Curr. Ref. Fish Res.; Data Process. Dig.; Dent. Abstr.; EMBASE; Energy Inf. Abstr.; Eng. Mater. Abstr.; Eng. Index Annu. [Select. Cov.]; Environ. Abstr.; Expand. Acad. Index (1984-); F&S Index Plus Text, Int. [Select. Cov.]; Fish Rev. (Jan. 1989-July 1992); Fluid Abstr., Civil Eng.; Fluid Abstr. Proc. Eng.; FLUIDEX; Food Sci. Technol. Abstr.; Foods Adlibra; Garden Lit. (1992-); Gas Abstr.; Gen. Period. Index (1985-); Gen. Sci. Index; Gen. Sci. Source (Jan. 1988-); Geogr. Abstr. Human Geogr. (?-?); Geol. Abstr.; GeoRef; Health Ref. Cent. (1987-) [Select. Cov.]; Health Source (Jan. 1984-); HILITES; Index Med.; Index Inf.; Index Period. Artic. Relat. Law; INFO-SOUTH Abstr.; INSPEC (June 1991-); Int. Aerosp. Abstr.; Int. Bibliogr. Sociol.; Int. Packag. Abstr.; J. Ferrocement; Leadscan; Mag. Artic. Summar. Elite (Jan. 1984-); Mag. Artic. Summar. Select (Jan. 1984-); Mag. Artic. Summar. CD-ROM (Jan. 1984-); Mag. Index Plus (1989-); Mag. Index Sel. Microfiche (1986-) [Full Txt.]; Mag. Index. Sel. (1986-); Mag. Search; Math. Rev.; Met. Abstr.; Middle East Abstr. Index; Newsp. Period. Abstr. (1986-); Numis. Lit.; Nutr. Res. Newsl.; Ocean. Abstr.; Oncog. Growth Factors Abstr.; Peace Res. Abstr. J. (1958-1966, 1970-1979, 1983-); Pet. Abstr.; Physic. Medline Plus; Pollut. Abstr. Indexes; Popul. Index; Print. Abstr.; Psychol. Abstr. (1929-); PsycINFO (?-?); PsycLit; Read. Guide Abstr. Select Ed.; Read. Guide Period. Lit.; Ref. Upd. Basic Ed.; Ref. Upd. Deluxe Ed.; Res. Alert [Full Cov.]; Resource/One Ondisc (1986-); Rev. Med. Vet. Entomol.; Sage Fam. Stud. Abstr. (?-?); Sage Urban Stud. Abstr (?-?); Sci. Cit. Index; SCISEARCH; Shock Vibr. Dig.; Soc. Plann. Policy Dev. Abstr.; Soc. Sci. Cit. Index [Select. Cov.]; Sociol. Abstr. (?-?); Text. Technol. Dig.; Mag. Index (1977-); TOM Gen. Index (1985-) [Full Txt.]; Trop. Dis. Bull.; Virol. AIDS Abstr.; Vocat. Search (Jan. 1984-); Weed Abstr.; Wildl. Rev. (Jan. 1989-July 1992); World Agric. Econ.; World Publ. Monit.

US/1040-3213
**SCIENTIFIC AMERICAN LIBRARY SERIES.** [Sci. Am. Libr. ser.]. (19??)-. Monographic series. English. bm. Price varies per volume. Scientific American Library, PO Box 646, Holmes PA 19043. **Tel** (215)237-1163. **DD** 500.

US/1048-0943
**SCIENTIFIC AMERICAN. SPECIAL ISSUE.** [Sci. Am., Spec. issue]. **Added/Corp** Scientific American, Inc. **VFOAT** Special Issue. Vol. 1 (1988)-. Periodical. English. ir. $4.95 (each issue). Scientific American Medicine, 415 Madison Avenue, New York NY 10017. **Tel** (212)754-0550, (800)333-1199. **(Subscription address:** W. H. Freeman & Company, 4419 West 1980 South, Salt Lake City UT 84104.**) ED** Jonathon Piel. **LC** T1; .S563. **DD** 600. **Ad Acc.**
**Desc:** Each issue covers a particular topic and presents articles on that subject from the pages of Scientific American with updates from the original authors.

US/0889-1729
**SCIENTIFIC AND TECHNICAL ORGANIZATIONS AND AGENCIES DIRECTORY.** [Sci. tech. organ. agencies dir.]. **Added/Corp** Gale Research Company. **VFOAT** STOAD. 1st Ed. (1985)-. Directory. English. $195.00. Gale Research Inc., 835 Penobscot Building, Detroit MI 48226. **Tel** (800)877-GALE, (313)961-2242, FAX (313)961-6083, telex TWX 810-221-7086. **ED** Peter Dresser. **LC** Q145; .S35. **DD** 506/.073. **NLM** Q 145; S4155.
**Desc:** Presents more than 20,000 entries covering scientific and technical organizations located in the United States and throughout the world.

US/0882-2034
**SCIENTIFIC AWAKENING IN THE RESTORATION.** No. 1-. Periodical. English. AMS Press Inc., 56 East 13th Street, New York NY 10003. **Tel** (212)777-4700, FAX (212)995-5413, telex 710 581 2302. **DD** 190.

US/0277-7355
**SCIENTIFIC, ENGINEERING, AND MEDICAL SOCIETIES PUBLICATIONS IN PRINT.** ***Ceased.*** [Sci., eng., med. soc. publ. print]. (1977)-(1981). English. be. R R Bowker, A Reed Reference Publishing Company, Part of Reed International PLC, PO Box 31, 121 Chanlon Drive, New Providence NJ 07974. **Tel** (908)464-6800, (800)521-8110, FAX (908)665-6688, telex 138-755. **LC** Z7911; .S396; T45. **DD** 016.5. **NLM** Z 7911 S416. ***Continues** Scientific, Technical, and Engineering Societies Publications in Print, 0730-1820.*

US/0036-8768
**SCIENTIFIC, ENGINEERING, TECHNICAL MANPOWER COMMENTS.** [Sci. eng. tec. manpow. comments]. **Added/Corp** Scientific Manpower Commission. Engineers Joint Council. Engineering Manpower Commission. Commission on Professionals in Science and Technology. **VFOAT** Manpower Comments; SET Manpower Comments. Vol. 1 (Nov. 1964)-. Periodical. English. Nine times a year. $90.00 (one year); $170.00 (two years), $250.00 (three years); $70.00 (one year), $130.00 (two years), $190.00 (three years) membership. Commission on Professionals in Science and Technology, 1500 Massachusetts Avenue Northwest, Suite 831, Washington DC 20005. **Tel** (202)223-6995. **ED** Betty M. Vetter and Eleanor L. Babco. **LC** TA157; .S4. **NLM** W1 SC842. **[CCC]**. cum. index. **Circ:** 1,200. available in microform from University Microfilms International (UMI).
**Desc:** Human resources in science and engineering.
**Ind/Abst** Abstr. Bull. Inst. Pap. Sci. Tech.

FR
**SCIENTIFIC ET TECHNICAL RES.** (19??)-. French. Twenty-two times a year. 497.00F Far East; 283.00F Middle East; 240.00F Europe; 397.00F other. L'Expansion, 31 cours des Juilliottes, 94703 Maisons Alfort France.

US/0196-8440
**SCIENTIFIC HONEYWELLER.** [Sci. Honeyweller]. **Added/Corp** Honeywell, Inc. Vol. 1, No. 1 (Mar. 1980)-. Periodical. English. an. Free on request. Honeywell Inc., 1000 Boone Avenue North, Golden Valley MN 55427. **Tel** (612)541-6752. **ED** Diana Lutz. **LC** T1; .S6153. **DD** 605. **Circ:** 18,000 (ctrl). available on microfiche.
**Desc:** Tutorial descriptions of Honeywell research and technology.

US/1048-5678
**SCIENTIFIC INFORMATION BULLETIN.** ***Ceased.*** (SCIENTIFIC INFORMATION BULLETIN / DEPARTMENT OF THE NAVY, OFFICE OF NAVAL RESEARCH, FAR EAST [AND] DEPARTMENT OF THE AIR FORCE, OFFICE OF SCIENTIFIC RESEARCH, FAR EAST [AND] UNITED STATES, ARMY RESEARCH OFFICE, FAR EAST.). [Sci. inf. bull.]. **Added/Corp** United States. Office of Naval Research. Liaison Office, Far East. United States. Air Force. Office of Scientific Research. Far East. United States. Army Research Office. Far East. United States. Office of Naval Research. Asian Office. **VFOAT** Office of Naval Research, Far East Sci Bul; ONRFE Sci Bul. Vol. 13, No. 1 (Jan./March 1988)-(199?). Government Publication. English. qt. Superintendent of Documents, US Government Printing Office, Washington DC 20402. **Tel** (202)275-3328, FAX (202)786-2377. **LC** Q1; .S8149. **DD** 505. **CODEN** SINBEM. Index available. **Circ:** 7,000 (ctrl). ***Continues** Scientific Bulletin (San Francisco, Calif.), 0271-7077.*
**Desc:** Presents articles on recent scientific research in Far Eastern countries.
**Ind/Abst** Ceram. Abstr. (19??-); GeoRef.

US/0565-8306
**SCIENTIFIC MANPOWER.** **Main/Corp** National Science Foundation (U.S.). 1956-. English. an. US Government Printing Office / National Science Foundation, 1800 G Street NW, Washington DC 20550. **Tel** (202)357-9859. **LC** Q147; .U527. **DD** 506.9. ***Continues** Papers of the Conference on Scientific Manpower.*
**Desc:** Includes the papers of the 5th 1956- conference on Scientific Manpower held at the 123rd- annual meeting of the American Association for the Advancement of Science.

US/0487-8965
**SCIENTIFIC MEETINGS.** [Sci. meet.]. Vol. 21, (Jan. 1977)-. Periodical. English. Four times a year (Jan., Apr., July, Oct.). $70.00 (surface mail); $ 90.00 (airmail). Scientific Meetings Publishing, PO Box 81662, San Diego CA 92138. **Tel** (619)270-2910, FAX (619)270-2910. **LC** Q101; .S63. **DD** 506. **NLM** W 3.5 S426. Index available. **Circ:** 1,500. available on microfilm and microfiche from University Microfilms International (UMI). ***Continues** Scientific Meetings.*
**Desc:** The leading source of information on forthcoming events of all important scientific, technical, medical, health, engineering and management meetings held throughout the world.

JA/0289-7520
**SCIENTIFIC PAPERS OF THE COLLEGE OF ARTS AND SCIENCES, THE UNIVERSITY OF TOKYO.** [Sci. pap. Coll. Arts Sci., Univ. Tokyo]. **Added/Corp** Tokyo Daigaku. Kyoyo Gakubu. **VFOAT** Tokyo Daigaku Kyoyobu Shizen Kagaku Kiyo. Vol. 33, No. 1 (June 1983)-. Academic Scholarly Publication. English. Twice a year. University of Tokyo / College of Arts and Sciences, Daigaku Kyoyogakubu, 8-1 Komaba 3-Chome, Meguro-ku, Tokyo 153 Japam. **LC** Q1; .T6. **DD** 505. **CODEN** SPCTDZ. ctrl circ. Documents available from BIOSIS Document Express, Ask*IEEE, CASDDS. ***Continues** Tokyo Daigaku. Kyoyo Gakubu. Scientific Papers of the College of General Education, 0040-8964.*
**Ind/Abst** Biol. Abstr. (1985-); Chem. Abstr. (1983-); GeoRef; INSPEC (1983-); Math. Rev.; Zentralbl. Math. Ihre Grenzgeb.

●US/1058-9244
**SCIENTIFIC PROGRAMMING.** [Sci. program.]. (1992)-. Periodical. English. Four times a year. $180.00 (US); $220.00 (Canada & Mexico); $235.00 (other). John Wiley & Sons, Inc., 605 Third Avenue, New York NY 10158-0012. **Tel** (212)850-6000, (212)850-6645, FAX (212)850-6088, telex 12-7063. **(Subscription address:** John Wiley & Sons / England, Baffins Lane, Chichester, West Sussex PO19 1UD England.**) ED** Robert G. Babb and Ronald H. Perrott. **LC** QA76.6; .S428. **DD** 502/.8551. **CODEN** SCIPEV.
**Desc:** Provides a meeting ground for research in and practical experience with software engineering environments, tools, languages and models of computation aimed specifically at supporting scientific and engineering computing.

US/0161-4452
**SCIENTIFIC PUBLICATIONS OF THE SCIENCE MUSEUM OF MINNESOTA.** [Sci. publ. Sci. Mus. Minn.]. **Main/Corp** Science Museum of Minnesota. New Series V. 2-. Monographic series. English. ir. Price varies per volume. Science Museum of Minnesota, 30 East 10th Street, St Paul MN 55101. **Tel** (612)222-6303. **LC** Q11; .S2683. **DD** 500. **CODEN** SCSPBA. ***Continues** Scientific Publications of the Science Museum.*
**Ind/Abst** GeoRef.

US
**SCIENTIFIC SALARIES' SURVEY / PREPARED BY D. DIETRICH ASSOCIATES, INC.** **Added/Corp** D. Dietrich Associates. (1990)-. English. an (June). $170.00. Dietrich Associates Inc, Box 511, Phoenixville PA 19460. **Tel** (215)935-1563. **LC** Q149.U5; S93. **DD** 331.2/815/0973. ***Continues** Survey of Scientific Salaries, 0276-4261.*

CN
**SCIENTIFIC SERIES / ENVIRONMENT CANADA.** (1991)-. Periodical. English. Environment Canada / Emergencies Science Division, Ottawa Ontario K1A 0H3 Canada. **Tel** (819)998-9622.
**Ind/Abst** Ecol. Abstr.; Geogr. Abstr. Phys. Geogr.; Geogr. Abstr. Human Geogr.

US/1043-4224
**SCIENTIFIC SLEUTHING REVIEW.** **Added/Corp** George Washington University. Forensic Sciences Dept. Vol. 13, No. 1 (Winter 1989)-. Periodical. English. qt. $24.00 US; $29.00 other. Scientific Sleuthing Inc, c/o Prof James E Starrs, George Washington University, National Law Center, Washington DC 20052. **Tel** (202)994-6770, FAX (202)994-9446. **ED** James E. Starrs. **LC** KF9214; .S35. **DD** 345.73/005; 347.30505. Index available. cum. index. **Bk Rev**. **Ad Acc. Circ:** 800. ***Continues** Scientific Sleuthing Newsletter, 0749-1395.*
**Desc:** Contains science in law enforcement, decisions, articles and commentaries.

UK/0036-8857
**SCIENTIFIC WORLD.** ***Ceased.*** **Added/Corp** World Federation of Scientific Workers. Vol. 1, (1957)-Vol. 37 (1994). Periodical. English. Four times a year (Mar., June, Sept., Dec.). World Federation of Scientific Workers, 6 Endsleigh Street, London WC1H ODX England. **Tel** 011 44 903 816141, FAX 011 44 903 816411. **(Subscription address:** C. Russell, 38 Market Field, West Sussex BN44 3SU England, Tel. 44 903 816141) **LC** Q1; .S8415. **DD** 505. **NLM** W1 SC87F. **Bk Rev**. **Ad Acc**. ctrl circ.
**Ind/Abst** Biol. Dig.; Int. Labour Doc.

II
**SCIENTIST OF PHYSICAL SCIENCES.** **VFOAT** SPS; Scientist Phyl. Sciences. Vol. 1, No. 1 (Nov. 1989)-. Periodical. English. sa. $50.00 (institution), $15.00 (individual). A H Ansari, PO Box 93, Bhopal 462 001 India. Documents available from CASDDS.
**Ind/Abst** Chem. Abstr.

US/0890-3670
**SCIENTIST (PHILADELPHIA, PA.), THE.** (THE SCIENTIST.). [Scientist]. **Added/Corp** Institute for Scientific Information. Vol. 1, No. 1 Oct. 20, (1986)-. Academic Scholarly Publication. English. Twenty-four times a year. $58.00 (except non tax exempt New Jersey Residents) US; $62.06 (non tax exempt New Jersey Residents includes 7% sales tax); $82.00 (Canada & Mexico); $79.00 (other) surface mail; $133.00 (1 year); $244.00 (2 year) airmail;. Institute for Scientific Information, 3501 Market Street, Philadelphia PA 19104. **Tel** (215)386-0100, (800)523-1850, FAX (215)386-6362, telex 84-5305. **(Subscription address:** Institute for Scientific Information, PO Box 71416, Chicago, IL 60694**)** **ED** Tom Ewing, telephone: (215)386-0100 Ext.1604. **LC** Q1; .S8422. **DD** 505; 502. **NLM** W1; SC87R. **[CCC]**. cum. index. **Ad Acc**, **Adv Mgr:** Pat LaValley, **Tel** (215)386-0100, Ext. 1544. **Pr Rev. Circ:** 50,000 (ctrl). available on microfilm and microfiche from University Microfilms International (UMI). Documents available from The Genuine Article.
**Desc:** An informative, international newspaper written for science professionals. It reports the business of science, as well as politics, trends, and controversies.
**Ind/Abst** Abstr. Bull. Inst. Pap. Sci. Tech.; Abstr. BioCommer.; AGRICOLA [Select. Cov.]; Curr. Contents, Agric. Biol. Environ. Sci.; Curr. Contents Clin. Med.; Curr. Contents Eng. Tech. Appl. Sci.; Curr. Contents Life Sci.; Curr. Contents Phys. Chem. Earth Sci.; Curr. Contents Soc. Behav. Sci.; Res. Alert [Full Cov.]; Sci. Cit. Index; SCISEARCH; Soc. Sci. Cit. Index [Select. Cov.].

NE/0138-9130
**SCIENTOMETRICS.** [Scientometrics]. Vol. 1 (Sept. 1978)-. Academic Scholarly Publication. English. Nine times a year (3 vols.). Fl1080.00. Elsevier Science Publishers BV, PO Box 211, 1000 AE Amsterdam Netherlands. **Tel** 011 31 20 5803642, FAX 011 31 20 5862696, telex 15682. **ED** Tibor Braun (editor's address: Institute of Inorganic and Analytical Chemistry, L Eotvos University, PO Box 123, H-1443 Budapest Hungary), M T Beck, G M Dobrov, E Garfield, and Michael J Moravcsik (editor's address: Institute of Theoretical Science, University of Oregon, Eugene OR 97403). **LC** Q1; .S8424. **DD** 505. **NLM** W1 SC8705. **CODEN** SCNTDX. **[CCC]. Bk Rev**. **Ad Acc**. **Pr Rev**. available on microfilm and microfiche from University Microfilms International (UMI). Documents available from The Genuine Article, BIOSIS Document Express, Ask*IEEE, CASDDS.
**Desc:** Provides a forum for the publication of original studies, short communications, preliminary reports, review papers, letters to the editor and book reviews on scientometrics. Emphasis is placed on investigations in which the development and mechanism of science are studied by means of mathematical (statistical) methods.
**Ind/Abst** Biol. Abstr.; Chem. Abstr.; Compumath Citation Index [Full Cov.]; Curr. Contents Soc. Behav. Sci.; Curr. Lit. Sci. Sci.; Inf. Sci. Abstr. [Full Cov.]; INSPEC (Sept. 1978-); Libr. Inf. Sci. Abstr.; Life Sci. Collect. (Sept. 1978-); Res. Alert [Full Cov.]; Soc. Plann. Policy Dev. Abstr.; Soc. Sci. Cit. Index [Full Cov.]; Sociol. Abstr.; Soc. Res. Methodol. Abstr. (1990-); World Publ. Monit. (Sept. 1978-).

IT/0392-7946
**SCIENZASOCIETA.** [Scienzasocieta]. Vol. 1, No. 1 (Feb./March 1983)-. Periodical. Italian. Three times a year. L30000 Italy; L60000 other. La Ribalta Coop Arl, Via Cerrate Casale 31C, 73100 Lecce Italy. **LC** WMLC 93/4785.

IT
**SCIENZE QUADERNI, LE.** (19??)-. Italian. bm (6 issues). L52500. Le Scienze, Piazza della Repubblica 8, 20121 Milan Italy. **Tel** 011 39 2 6554265.

AT/0157-6488
**SCIOS.** (19??)-. English. Science Teachers Association of Western Australia, Unit 9, 25 Walters Drive, Osborne Park WA 6017 Australia.
**Ind/Abst** Aust. Educ. Index.

US/1071-4103
**SCIPHERS (COLLEGE STATION, TEX.).** **See** Journalism.

US/0036-8288
**SCIS NEWSLETTER.** **Main/Corp** Science Curriculum Improvement Study. **VAT** Science Curriculum Improvement Study Newsletter. Newsletter. English. Science Curriculum Improvement Study, Lawrence Hall of Science, University of California, Berkeley CA 94720.

US
**SCISEARCH [ONLINE DATABASE].** **See** Science and Technology-Abstracting, Bibliographies and Statistics.

US/0196-6006
**SCITECH BOOK NEWS.** **VAT** Sci Tech Book News. (1977)-. Periodical. English. mo (except combined July/Aug. and Sept./Oct.). $65.00 institutional, $45.00 individual US and Canada; $80.00 institutional, $60.00 individual other. Book News Inc, 5600 NE Hassalo Street, Portland OR 97213. **Tel** (503)281-9230. **ED** Jane Erskine. **Bk Rev**. **Ad Acc. Circ:** 5,400 (ctrl).
**Desc:** Speedy compact reviews of very high-level books in science, technology, medicine, agriculture, engineering and the bibliography of all.
**Ind/Abst** Book Rev. Index (1984-); Int. Aerosp. Abstr.

US/1063-8717
**SCITECH REFERENCE PLUS.** **See** Science and Technology-Abstracting, Bibliographies and Statistics.

AT/1030-4649
**SCITECH TECHNOLOGY DIRECTORY.** [Scitech technol. dir.]. (1988)-. English. an. $145.00. Scitech Publications, PO Box 1915, Canberra ACT 2601 Australia. **Tel** 011 61 62 477220, FAX 011 61 6 249-6648. **DD** 606.02594. ***Continues** Technology Directory, 0817-9905.*

UK/0271-972X
**SCOPE (CHICHESTER).** **See** Environmental Issues-Ecology.

IT
**SCUOLAOFFICINA.** **Added/Corp** Museo-Laboratorio Aldini-Valeriani (Bologna, Italy). (19??)-. Periodical. Italian (summaries and/or abstracts in English). Twice a year. L15000. Museo Aldini Scuolaofficina, V Bassanelli 9 11, 40129 Bologna Italy. **Tel** 011 39 51 370367, FAX (051)353500. **ED** Roberto Curti. Index available. **Ad Acc**. available on diskette.
**Desc:** History of Technology, conservation of industrial heritage, museography (museums of science and technology), and problems of innovation.

PH
**SEA ABSTRACTS.** **See** Science and Technology-Abstracting, Bibliographies and Statistics.

US/0360-8476
**SEARCH AT THE STATE UNIVERSITY OF NEW YORK.** (SEARCH.). V. 1- Fall 1975-. Periodical. English. qt. State University of New York, State University Plaza, Albany NY 12246. **LC** Q11; .S4. **DD** 051.

AT/0004-9549
**SEARCH (SYDNEY).** (SEARCH.). [Search]. **Added/Corp** ANZAAS. Vol. 1 (July 1970)-. Academic Scholarly Publication. English. Ten times a year. 180.00Aus$ (institutions), 54.00Aus$ (individuals) Australia and New Zealand; $165.00 (institutions), $55.00 (individuals) other. Control Publications Pty Limited, 14 Acheron Street, Doncaster, Victoria 3108 Australia. **Tel** 011 61 3 8489041, FAX 011 61 3 8482626. **(Subscription address:** Marston Book Services Ltd., PO Box 87, Oxford OX2 0DT England.**)** **ED** S. Garnett. **LC** Q1; .A772. **DD** 505. **NLM** W1 SE162. **CODEN** SRCHAA. **[CCC]**. Index available. **Bk Rev**. **Ad Acc**. **Pr Rev. Circ:** 3,000. available on microfilm and microfiche from University Microfilms International (UMI). Documents available from The Genuine Article, BIOSIS Document Express, CASDDS. ***Continues** Australian Journal of Science.*
**Desc:** Multidisciplinary science and technology journal published by the Australian and New Zealand Association for the Advancement of Science.
**Ind/Abst** AGRICOLA; Aust. Educ. Index; Biol. Abstr.; Chem. Abstr.; Comput. Rev.; Curr. Contents, Agric. Biol. Environ. Sci.; EMBASE; Fish Rev.; For. Abstr.; Geogr. Abstr. Phys. Geogr.; GeoRef; Index Vet.; Meteorol. Geoastrophys. Abstr. (-199?); Res. Alert [Full Cov.]; Rice Abstr.; Sci. Cit. Index; SCISEARCH; Soc. Sci. Cit. Index [Select. Cov.]; Wildl. Rev.

ET
**SEDOC NEWSLETTER.** **VFOAT** S.E.D.O.C. Newsletter. No. 1 (June/July 1981)-. Newsletter. English. bm. SEDOC Ethiopia, POB 5788, Addis Ababa Ethiopia. **LC** T1; .S618.
**Ind/Abst** Bibliogr. Mission.

US
**SEI SUBSCRIBER PROGRAM.** English (French). an. $100.00. Carnegie Mellon University / Software Engineering Institute, Pittsburgh PA 15213. **Tel** (412)268-7700, FAX (412)268-5758.
**Desc:** Informs individuals about SEI events, work in progress, and new initiatives.

JA/0386-7536
**SEIKATSU KAGAKU KENKYUJO KENKYU HOKOKU.** [Seikatsu Kagaku Kenkyujo kenkyu hokoku]. **Added/Corp** Miyagi Gakuin Joshi Daigaku. Seikatsu Kagaku Kenkyujo. **VFOAT** Annual Report of the Institute of Living Sciences. (1966)-. Japanese (English). an. Miyagi Gakuin Joshi Daigaku Seikatsu Kagaku Kenkyujo, (Inst. of Living Science, Miyagi Gakuin Women's College), 1-1, Sakuragaoka 9 Chome, Sendaishi, Miyagiken 980, Japan. **CODEN** MJHOD5. Documents available from CASDDS.
**Ind/Abst** Chem. Abstr.

JA/0582-4184
**SEIKEI DAIGAKU KOGAKUBU KOGAKU HOKOKU.** (SEIKEI DAIGAKU KOGAKUBU KOGAKU HOKOKU / SEIKEI DAIGAKU KOGAKUBU.). [Seikei Daigaku Kogakubu kogaku hokoku]. **Added/Corp** Seikei Daigaku. Kogakubu. **VFOAT** Seikei Daigaku Kogaku Hokoku; Technology Reports of the Seikei University. (1964)-. Periodical. Japanese (English). sa. Seikei Daigaku Kogakubu, (College of Engineering, Seikei University), 3-1, Kitamachi 3 Chome, Kichijoji, Musashinoshi, Tokyoto 180 Japan. **CODEN** SKKGAW. Documents available from CASDDS.
**Ind/Abst** Chem. Abstr.

JA/0285-3299
**SEIRIGAKU GIJUTSU KENKYUKAI HOKOKU.** [Seirigaku Gijutsu Kenkyukai hokoku]. **Added/Corp** Seirigaku Kenkyujo (Japan) Gijutsuka. (1979)-(19??). Japanese. Okazaki Kokuritsu Kyodo Kenkyu Kiko Seirigaku Kenkyujo, (National Inst. for Physiological Sciences, Okazaki National Research Institutes), 38, Saigo Naka Myodaiji, Okazakishi, Aichiken 444, Japan. **CODEN** SGKHEB. Documents available from CASDDS. ***Continued in part by** Seirigaku Kenkyujo Gijutsuka Hokoku, 0913-0322.*
**Ind/Abst** Chem. Abstr.

JA/0913-0322
**SEIRIGAKU KENKYUJO GIJUTSUKA HOKOKU.** [Seirigaku Kenkyujo Gijutsuka hokoku]. **VFOAT** Annual report of the Technical Division of National Institute for Physiological Sciences. (1986)-. Periodical. Japanese. an. Okazaki Kokuritsu Kyodo Kenkyu Kiko Seirigaku Kenkyujo, (National Inst. for Physiological Sciences, Okazaki National Research Institutes), 38, Saigo Naka Myodaiji, Okazakishi, Aichiken 444, Japan. **DD** 574. Documents available from CASDDS. ***Continues in part** Seirigaku Gijutsu Kenkyukai Hokoku, 0285-3299.*
**Ind/Abst** Chem. Abstr.

JA/0037-105X
**SEISAN KENKYU.** [Seisan kenkyÂu]. **Added/Corp** Tokyo Daigaku. Seisen Gijutsu Kenkyujo. **VFOAT** Monthly Journal of the Institute of Industrial Science, University of Tokyo; Seisan-Kenkyu. (1949)-. Periodical. Japanese. mo. Institute of Industrial Science, University of Tokyo, 22-1 Roppongi, 7-chome, Minato-ku, Tokyo 106, Japan. **CODEN** SEKEAI. Documents available from CASDDS.
**Ind/Abst** Abstr. J. Earthq. Eng.; Chem. Abstr.

NE/0926-4183
**SELECTIEF DEN HAAG. 1991.** (SELECTIEF.). [Selectief Den Haag, 1991]. **Added/Corp** viesraad voor het Wetenschaps- en Technologiebeleid. Informatiebank. (1991)-. Periodical. Dutch (English, German and French). bw. Fl70.00 UK; Fl320.00 other. AWT Informatiebank, PO Box 18524 Javastraat 42, 2502EM Sgravenhage Netherlands. **Tel** 011 31 70 639922. **UDC** 001 :351.854. **Bk Rev**. ***Continues** Tweekbericht ('s-Gravenhage), 0921-7606.*

FR/0395-8930
**SEMENCES ET PROGRES.** [Semences prog.]. (1974)-. Periodical. French. qt. 117.00F France; 300.00F (surface), 350.00F (air) other. Semences et Progres, 44 rue du Louvre, 75001 Paris France. **Tel** 011 33 1 42363960. **UDC** 631.52. Index available. **Bk Rev**. **Ad Acc. Circ:** 11,500.

US
**SEMI MEMBERSHIP DIRECTORY.** **Main/Corp** Semiconductor Equipment and Materials Institute. **VAT** Semiconductor Equipment and Materials Institute Membership Directory. Directory. English. Semiconductor Equipment, 805 East Middlefield, Mountain View CA 94043-4080. **Tel** (415)964-5111, FAX (415)967-5375, telex 856-777 SEMI-MNTV. **LC** TK7805; .S44a. ***Continues** SEMI Directory, 0146-4264.*

# Science and Technology

II/0037-1947
**SEMINAR.** No. 1 (Sept. 1959)-. Periodical. English. mo. $30.00. **(Subscription address:** Prints India, 11 Darya Ganj, New Delhi, 110002 India, (Phone: 011 91 11 3268645))

II
**SEMINAR REPORTEUR.** (1971)-. Periodical. English. mo. $30.00. Seminar Reporteur, Delhi, India. **(Subscription address:** Prints India, 11 Darya Ganj, New Delhi, 110002 India, (Phone: 011 91 11 3268645)) **LC** HC431; .S45. **DD** 338.0954.

GW
**SENSOR MAGAZINE.** German. Four times a year. DM88.00. Magazin Verlag H Krauel, Jaegerweg 14, W-3052 Bad Nenndorf Germany. **Tel** 011 49 5723 5534.

UK/0260-2288
**SENSOR REVIEW.** [Sens. rev.]. Vol. 1, No. 1 (Jan. 1981)-. Academic Scholarly Publication. English. qt. $719.00. MCB University Press, 60 62 Toller Lane, Bradford West Yorkshire BD8 9BX England. **Tel** 011 44 274 499821, **FAX** 011 44 274 547143, telex 51317 MCBUNI G. **(Subscription address:** MCB University Press / US and Canada Subscriptions, PO Box 10812, Birmingham AL 35201-0812.) **ED** Clive Loughlin. **LC** TA165; .S4568. **DD** 681/.2. **CODEN** SNRVDY. **[CCC].** **Bk Rev. Circ:** 3,000. available on an online database (file 636/Full-Text) from DIALOG. Documents available from Article Express International, Ask*IEEE, CASDDS. **Desc:** Coverage of international technical development and radio growth in new types of sensors and new areas of application as well as business development. **Ind/Abst** Abstr. Hum. Comput. Interact.; Bioeng. Abstr.; Chem. Abstr. (1981-1983); Ei Page One; Eng. Index Annu.; Fluid Abstr., Civil Eng.; Fluid Abstr. Proc. Eng.; FLUIDEX (19??-); HTFS Dig.; INSPEC (Jan. 1981-); Pollut. Abstr. Indexes; Robotics Abstr.

JA
**SENTAN GIJUTSU KAIHATSU SORAN.** Japanese. ¥18000. Jukagaku Kogyo Tsushinsha, (Heavy and Chemical Industry News Agency), 2-15 Kanda Jinbo-cho Chiyoda-ku, Tokyo 101 Japan. **LC** T177.J3; S46.

CN/0316-8395
**SERIAL TITLES IN THE PURE AND APPLIED SCIENCES (WINDSOR).** (SERIAL TITLES IN THE PURE AND APPLIED SCIENCES; A HOLDINGS LIST.). **Main/Corp** University of Windsor. Library. 6th Ed. (1969)-. Periodical. English. an. Free. Library / Winsdor, University of Windsor, Windsor Ontario N9B 3P4 Canada. **DD** 016.505. *Continues* University of Windsor. Library. Periodical and Serial Titles in the Pure and Applied Sciences., 0316-8387.

CL
**SERIE "INFORMACION Y DOCUMENTACION".** **Main/Corp** Comision Nacional de Investigacion Cientifica y Tecnologica. **Added/Corp** Comision Nacional de Investigacion Cientifica y Tecnologica. Informacion y Documentacion. (19??)-. Monographic series. Spanish. ir. Price varies per volume. Comision Nacional de Investigacion Cientifica y Tecnologica, Casilla 297, Santiago Chile. **Tel** 2744537, telex 340191 CNCT CK CHILE. **Circ:** 300.

CK/0120-5099
**SERIE MEMORIAS DE EVENTOS CIENTIFICOS COLOMBIANOS.** See Biology-Botany.

US/0276-9662
**SERIES IN THERMAL AND TRANSPORT SCIENCES.** [Ser. therm. transp. sci.]. Monographic series. English. ir. Price varies per volume. John Wiley & Sons, Inc., 605 Third Avenue, New York NY 10158-0012. **Tel** (212)850-6000, (212)850-6645, **FAX** (212)850-6088, telex 12-7063. **(Subscription address:** John Wiley & Sons / England, Baffins Lane, Chichester, West Sussex PO19 1UD England.)

UK/0953-9212
**SERVICE MANAGEMENT.** [Serv. manag.]. (1986)-. Periodical. English. mo. £66.00. Findlay Publications Ltd, Franks Hall, Horton Kirby, Kent DA4 9LL England. **Tel** 011 44 (0322)222222, **FAX** 011 44 (0322)289577. **DD** 004. **Desc:** Information on high-technology service.

XR
**SEZNAM PLATNYCH CESKOSLOVENSKYCH STATNICH A OBOROVYCH NOREM.** **Main/Corp** Czechoslovakia. Urad Pro Normalizaci a Mereni. Czech. Urad Pro Normalizaci A Meveni, Vinohradska Trida 32, Prague Czech Republic. **LC** T59.2.C95; C93A. *Continues* Seznam Platnych Ceskoslovenskych Statnich Norem.

CC
**SHAN-TUNG TA HSUEH HSUEH PAO. TZU JAN KO HSUEH PAN / ZIRAN KEXUE BAN. SHANDONG DAXUE XUEBAO.** **Added/Corp** Shan-Tung Ta Hsueh. **VFOAT** Shandong Daxue Xuebao. Ziran Kexue Ban. (19??)-. Periodical. Chinese. Shan-tung ta Hsueh Hsueh pao, Pien chi wei Yuan hui,, Chi-nan China. **CODEN** SDXKEU. Documents available from CASDDS. **Ind/Abst** Chem. Abstr.

CC
**SHANG-HAI SHIH CHUNG HSIAO HSUEH CHIAO YU KUNG TSO CHING YEN HSUAN PIEN. CHUNG HSUEH LI KO FEN TSE / SHANG-HAI SHIH CHIAO YU HU PIEN.** **Added/Corp** Shanghai (China). Chiao yu Chu. (1982)-. Periodical. Chinese. an. RMB¥0.32. Hsin Hua Shu Tien / Shang-Hai Fa Hsing So, Shanghai, People's Republic of China. **LC** Q183.4.C52; S537.

CC/0253-9942
**SHANGHAI JIAOTONG DAXUE XUEBAO.** (SHANG-HAI CHIAO-TUNG TA HSUEH HSUEH PAO). [Shanghai jiaotong daxue xuebao]. **Added/Corp** Shang-Hai Chiao Tung Ta Hsueh. **VFOAT** Journal of Shanghai Jiaotong University; Shanghai Jiaotong Daxue Xuebao; Journal of Shanghai Chiaotung University. (19??)-. Academic Scholarly Publication. Chinese (summaries and/or abstracts in English). Six times a year. $20.34. Science Press, 16 Donghuangchenggen North Street, Beijing 100707, People's Republic of China. **Tel** 011 86 1 4019821, 011 86 1 4010642, **FAX** 011 86 1 4012180, 011 86 1 4019810, telex 210147. **(Subscription address:** China International Book Trading Corporation, PO Box 399, Library Service Department, Beijing 100044 People's Republic of China.) **LC** Q4; .S488. **DD** 505. **CODEN** SCTPDH. **Circ:** 3,500. Documents available from Ask*IEEE, CASDDS. **Desc:** Carries distinguished theses and reviews contributed by staff and students of Shanghai Jiao Tong University. **Ind/Abst** Chem. Abstr.; INSPEC; Math. Rev.; Zentralbl. Math. Ihre Grenzgeb.

CC/0258-7041
**SHANGHAI KEJI DAXUE XUEBAO.** (SHANG-HAI KO CHI TA HSUEH HSUEH PAO.). [Shanghai keji daxue xuebao]. **Added/Corp** Shang-Hai Ko Hsueh Chi Shu Ta Hsueh Hsueh Pao; Journal of Shanghai University of Science and Technology. **VAT** Hsueh Pao - Shang-Hai Ko Chi Ta Hsueh Pao. (19??)-. Periodical. Chinese (summaries and/or abstracts in English). **LC** Q111; .S46. **CODEN** SKDXDH. Documents available from CASDDS. **Ind/Abst** Chem. Abstr.

CC/0253-2395
**SHANXI DAXUE XUEBAO. ZIRAN KEXUE BAN.** (SHAN-HSI TA HSUEH HSUEH PAO. TZU JAN KO HSUEH PAN.). [Shanxi daxue xuebao. Ziran kexue ban]. **Added/Corp** Shan-Hsi Ta Hsueh. **VFOAT** Shanxi University Journal; Journal of Shanxi University. Natural Science Edition. (1979)-. Academic Scholarly Publication. Chinese (English). Four times a year. $4.20. China National Publishing Company, 380 Bei Su Zhou Lu, Shanghai, People's Republic of China. **LC** Q4; .S4877. **DD** 505. **CODEN** SDXKDT. Documents available from CASDDS. **Ind/Abst** Chem. Abstr.; Math. Rev.; Zentralbl. Math. Ihre Grenzgeb.

CH
**SHAO NIEN KO CHI.** **VFOAT** Shao Nian Ke Ji. 1- April 1977-. Periodical. Chinese. $0.19 per copy. **LC** Q163; .S484.

CC
**SHAO NIEN KO HSUEH.** **VFOAT** Shaonian Kexue. (1977)-. Periodical. Chinese. Twelve times a year. $15.37. Science Press, 16 Donghuangchenggen North Street, Beijing 100707, People's Republic of China. **Tel** 011 86 1 4019821, 011 86 1 4010642, **FAX** 011 86 1 4012180, 011 86 1 4019810, telex 210147. **(Subscription address:** China International Book Trading Corporation, PO Box 399, Library Service Department, Beijing 100044 People's Republic of China.) **LC** Q163; .S4842. **DD** 505.

CH
**SHAO NIEN TAN SO CHE / KUANG-TUNG SHENG KO PU CHUANG TSO HSIEH HUI.** Periodical. Chinese. NT$0.22. Kuang-Tung Sheng Hsin Hua Shu Tien, Canton, People's Republic of China. **LC** Q163; .S4847. **DD** 500.

JA/0285-0362
**SHARP GIHO.** (SHAPU GIHO.). **VFOAT** Sharp Technical Journal. [Sharp giho]. Periodical. English (Japanese). Shapu K.K. Gijutsu Honbu, (Technical Headquarter, Sharp Co., Ltd.), 2613-1, Ichinomotocho,, Tenrishi, Naraken 632, Japan. **CODEN** STEJD9. Documents available from The Genuine Article, Ask*IEEE, CASDDS. **Ind/Abst** Chem. Abstr.; INSPEC (1984-); Res. Alert; Soc. Sci. Cit. Index [Select. Cov.].

UK
**SHD.** See Computers.

CH
**SHEN PIEN TI KO HSUEH.** **VFOAT** Shenbian de Kexue. Periodical. Chinese. qt. NT$0.28. Nei Meng-ku Hsin Hua Shu Tien, People's Republic of China. **LC** Q4; .S489. **DD** 505.

JA/0385-1109
**SHIMA MARINRANDO KENKYU HOKOKU.** **Main/Corp** Shima Marinrando. **VFOAT** Science Report of Shima Marineland. Began publication with No. 1; July 1972. Periodical. Japanese (English). Shima Marineland Kashikojima, Ago-cho Shima-gun, Mie Prefecture 517-05 Japan.

JA/0387-9925
**SHIMANE DAIGAKU RIGAKUBU KIYO.** (MEMOIRS OF THE FACULTY OF SCIENCE, SHIMANE UNIVERSITY.). [Shimane Daigaku Rigakubu kiyo]. Began in 1978. Academic Scholarly Publication. Japanese (English). Shimane Daigaku Rigakubu, Nishikawazu-cho, Matsue-shi Japan. **LC** Q1; .S847. **DD** 505. **CODEN** SDRKDX. Documents available from CASDDS. *Continues* Memoirs. Natural Sciences. **Ind/Abst** Chem. Abstr.; Math. Rev.; Zentralbl. Math. Ihre Grenzgeb.

JA/0371-005X
**SHIMAZU HYORON.** [Shimadzu hyÂoron]. **Added/Corp** Shimadzu Seisakusho. **VFOAT** Shimadzu Review. (1940)-. Academic Scholarly Publication. Japanese. qt. Shimadzu Seisakusho Ltd., 1 Nishinokyo Kuwabaracho, Nakagyo ku Kyoto 604 Japan. **CODEN** SHHYAG. Documents available from CASDDS. **Ind/Abst** Chem. Abstr.

JA
**SHIMIZU TECHNICAL RESEARCH BULLETIN.** **Added/Corp** Shimizu Kensetsu Kabushiki Kaisha. Research Institute. No. 1 (Mar. 1982)-. Bulletin. English. Research Institute of Shimizu Construction Company, Information Service Section, 4-17 Etchujima 3-chome, Koto-ku, Tokyo Japan. **Ind/Abst** Abstr. J. Earthq. Eng.

JA
**SHINKU TANKU NEMPO.** Japanese. an. ¥18000 Japan. Zenkoku Kampo Hambai Kyodo Kumiai, 2-4 Toranomon 2 Minato-ku, Tokyo 105 Japan. **Tel** (03)459-8881, **FAX** (03)294-4673. **LC** AZ188.J3; S5. Index available. **Circ:** 1,500.

JA/0559-8680
**SHIONOGI KENKYUSHO NENPO.** [Shionogi kenkyusho nenpo]. **VFOAT** Annual Report of Shionogi Research Laboratory. (1951)-. English. an. Shionogi Seiyaku KK Kenkyujo, 12-4 Sagisu 5-chome, Fukushima-ku 553, Osakashi, Osakafu Japan. **CODEN** SKNEA7SRLAB. **Ind/Abst** EMBASE.

JA
**SHIZEN KAGAKU RONSO.** No. 1- (March 1969)-. Periodical. Japanese. Kyoto Joshi Daigaku Shizen Kagaku Hoken Taiiku Kenkyushitsu, 35 Imagumano Kitahiyoshi-cho Higashi yama-ku, Kyoto-shi 605 Japan. **LC** Q4; .S5223.

JA/0916-6572
**SHIZUOKA-KEN SHIZUOKA KOGYO GIJUTSU SENTA KENKYU HOKOKU.** **VFOAT** Reports of the Shizuoka Industrial Technology Center. (1990)-. Periodical. Multiple languages. an. **DD** 620. *Continues* Shizuoka-ken Kogyo Gijutsu Senta Kenkyu Hokoku, 0910-9323. **Ind/Abst** Biodeter. Abstr.; For. Prod. Abstr. (1991-).

AA
**SHKENCA DHE JETA.** **Added/Corp** BRPSH Organization. KQ. (19??)-. Periodical. Albanian. bm. $9.00. Book Distribution Enterprise, Rruga Kavajes, Tirana, Albania. **Tel** 011 355 42 27246. **LC** Q4; .S523.

US/0738-6524
**SHROUD SPECTRUM INTERNATIONAL.** Vol. 1, No. 1 (1981)-. Periodical. English. Four times a year (Mar., June, Sept., Dec.). $18.00. Indiana Center for Shroud Studies, Route 3 Box 557, Nashville IN 47448-9550. **Tel** (812)988-4870. **ED** Dorothy Crispino. Index available. **Bk Rev. Pr Rev.** **Desc:** The only journal in the world that is peer-reviewed and entirely devoted to sindonology; presents authoritative articles by European and American scholars/scientists, plus ancient and medieval texts.

KO
**SIMENTU KAGONGOP.** **VFOAT** Cement Processing Industry. Periodical. Korean (Korean). qt. **LC** TP880.K6; S574.

KO
**SIN CHEPUM, SIN KISUL.** **VFOAT** Industrial Technology. Periodical. Korean (Korean). bm. W3,000. Hanguk Kwahak Kisul Chongbo Sento, 206-9 Chongyangni-dong, Tongdaemun-ku, Seoul South Korea. **LC** T4; .S3148.

# Science and Technology

PH/0115-8864
**SINAG-AGHAM. Added/Corp** UP-NSTA Integrated Research Program "A.". **VFOAT** Sinagagham. (19??)-. Periodical. English. qt. P12.00 (per copy). University of the Philippines UP - NSTA Integrated Research Program, PNB Building, UP Campus, Diliman Quezon City Philippines. **LC** Q127.P46; S56. **DD** 505. **Ind/Abst** Index Philip. Period. (-199?); Philip. Sci. Technol. Abstr.

PK/0080-9624
**SIND UNIVERSITY RESEARCH JOURNAL. SCIENCE SERIES.** [Sind Univ. res. j., Sci. ser.]. **Added/Corp** University of Sind. Faculty of Science. **VFOAT** Sind University Science Research Journal. Vol. 1 (Nov. 1965)-. English. sa. **LC** Q1.A1; S5. **CODEN** SURJAA. Documents available from BIOSIS Document Express.
**Ind/Abst** Biol. Abstr. (1965-1987); Life Sci. Collect.

SI/0217-1880
**SINGAPORE SCIENTIST.** [Singap. sci.]. (1981)-. Periodical. English. Three times a year. 20.00Sing$. Science Centre Board, Off Jurong Town Hall Road, Singapore 2260 Singapore. **Tel** 011 69 5603316. **DD** 505. **Continues** Science Centre Bulletin, 0129-5381.

US/1071-1910
**SINGER REPORT ON MANAGED CARE SYSTEMS AND TECHNOLOGY, THE.** [Singer rep. manag. care syst. technol.]. **Added/Corp** Charles J. Singer & Co. (19??)-. Periodical. English. Nine times a year (every 6 weeks). $395.00. Charles J. Singer & Co, 401 Edgewater Place, Suite 580Building 1 Unit 18, Wakefield MA 01880. **Tel** (617)246-7585 ext.228, FAX (617)246-7737. **ED** Rich Luhr. **DD** 005. Index available. cum. index. ctrl circ.

US/0737-0350
**SIPISCOPE.** (SIPISCOPE). [SIPISCOPE]. **Added/Corp** Scientists' Institute for Public Information. **VAT** Scientists' Institute for Public Information Scope. (19??)-. Periodical. English. Four times a year. Free on request (for journalists only). SIPI - Scientists' Institute for Public Information, 355 Lexington Avenue, 16th Floor, New York NY 10017. **Tel** (212)661-9110.
**Ind/Abst** Hum. Rights Intern. Rep.

IT/0393-9472
**SISTEMARICERCA. VFOAT** Sistema Ricerca. No. 1 (Jan./March 1986)-. Periodical. Italian. qt. L50000 (institutions), L35000 (individuals) Italy; L70000 other. Ediesse / Rome, Via dei Frentani 4A, 00185 Rome Italy. **Tel** 011 39 6 44870286, 44870288, FAX 011 39 6 4481260.

AU/0723-791X
**SITZUNGSBERICHTE. ABT. 1, BIOLOGISCHE WISSENSCHAFTEN UND ERDWISSENSCHAFTEN. Added/Corp** Osterreichische Akademie der Wissenschaften. Mathematisch-Naturwissenschaftliche Klasse. Vol. 191 (1982)-. Monographic series. German. ir. Price varies per volume. Springer-Verlag Wien, Sachsenplatz 4 6, PO Box 89, A-1201 Vienna Austria. **Tel** 011 43 1 3302415. **(Subscription address:** Springer Verlag New York Inc. / for North America, 44 Hartz Way, Secaucus NJ 07096.**) CODEN** OAWBAV. Documents available from BIOSIS Document Express. **Continues** Sitzungsberichte. Abt. 1, Biologie, Mineralogie, Erdkunde und Verwandte Wissenschaften, 0029-8808.
**Ind/Abst** Biol. Abstr.; GeoRef; Life Sci. Collect.

GW/0371-0165
**SITZUNGSBERICHTE DER HEIDELBERGER AKADEMIE DER WISSENSCHAFTEN, MATHEMATISCH-NATURWISSENSCHAFTLICHE KLASSE.** [Sitzungsber. Heidelb. Akad. Wiss., Math.-Naturwiss. Kl.]. **Main/Corp** Heidelberger Akademie der Wissenschaften. **Added/Corp** Heidelberger Akademie der Wissenschaften. Mathematisch-Naturwissenschaftliche Klasse. No. 1 (1909)-. Monographic series. German. ir. Price varies per volume. Springer-Verlag GmbH & Company KG, Heidelberger Platz 3, D 14197 Berlin Germany. **Tel** 011 49 30 8207223, FAX 011 49 30 8214091, telex 183 319 SPBLN D. **(Subscription address:** Springer Verlag New York Inc. / for North America, 44 Hartz Way, Secaucus NJ 07096.**) LC** AS182; .H4. **CODEN** SHWMAL.
**Ind/Abst** GeoRef; Int. Aerosp. Abstr.; Math. Rev.; Zentralbl. Math. Ihre Grenzgeb.

GW/0371-327X
**SITZUNGSBERICHTE DER SACHSISCHEN AKADEMIE DER WISSENSCHAFTEN ZU LEIPZIG. MATHEMATISCH-NATURWISSENSCHAFTLICHE KLASSE. See** Mathematics.

PL
**SKAD OSOBOWY W ROKU AKADEMICKIM ... / POLITECHNIKA ODZKA. Main/Corp** Politechnika Odzka. Polish. an. Redakcja Wydawnictw Naukowych Politechniki Odzkiej, 93-005 Odz UI, Wolczanska 219 Poland. **LC** T173.L8; A33.

SW/0284-3757
**SKB TECHNICAL REPORT.** [SKB tech. rep.]. **Added/Corp** Svensk Karnbranslehantering AB. (1985)-. Monographic series. English. Svensk Karnbranslehantering, Box 5864, S-102 48 Stockholm Sweden. **CODEN** STRPEP. **Continues** SKBF KBS Teknisk Rapport, 0348-7504.

●US/1063-9330
**SKEPTIC (ALTADENA, CALIF.).** (SKEPTIC). [Skeptic]. **Added/Corp** Skeptics Society. Vol. 1, No. 1 (Spring 1992)-. Periodical. English. Four times a year (Feb., May, Aug., Nov.). $35.00 US; $40.00 Canada & Mexico. Skeptics Society, 2761 North Marengo, Altadena CA 91001. **Tel** (818)794-3119, FAX (818)794-1301. **ED** Michael Shermer. **LC** IN PROCESS. **DD** 149. Index available. cum. index. **Bk Rev**, (Qty: 30-40). **Ad Acc. Acid Free. Circ:** 6,000 paid.
**Desc:** Strives to investigate and promote scientific methods, and disseminate information on science, magic, superstition, and skepticism and the history of these traditions.
**Ind/Abst** Mag. Index.

NO/0368-6310
**SKRIFTER (KONGELIGE NORSKE VIDENSKABERS SELSKAB).** (SKRIFTER / DET KONGELIGE NORSKE VIDENSKABERS SELSKAB). [Skr. - K. Nor. vidensk. selsk.]. **Added/Corp** Kongelige Norske Videnskabers Selskab. (1970)-. Monographic series. Norwegian. ir. Price varies per volume. Royal Norwegian Society of Sciences, Erling Skakkes gt., 47 b, N-7013 Trondheim Norway. **Tel** 011 47 73 59 21 57, FAX 011 47 73 59 58 95. **(Subscription address:** Publications Expediting Inc., 200 Meacham Avenue, Elmont NY 11003.**) ED** Nils Soevik. **CODEN** KNSSA7. available with illustrations; available with charts. Documents available from BIOSIS Document Express, Ask*IEEE. **Continues** KGL. Norske Videnskabers Selskabs Skrifter.
**Ind/Abst** Biol. Abstr.; Energy Res. Abstr.; GeoRef; INSPEC (1968-); Math. Rev.; Zentralbl. Math. Ihre Grenzgeb.

NO/0369-5417
**SKRIFTER - NORSK POLARINSTITUTT.** [Skr., Nor. polarinst.]. **Main/Corp** Norsk Polarinstitutt. **Added/Corp** Norsk Polarinstitutt. Norway. Kongelige Industri-, Handverk- og Skipsfartsdepartement. Norway. Kongelige Departement for Industri og Handverk. (1948)-. Monographic series. English (French and German). ir. Price varies per volume. Norsk Polarinstitutt, PO Box 158, N-1330 Oslo Lufthavn Norway. **Tel** 011 47 02 123650, FAX 011 47 02 123854, telex 74745 POLAR N. **ED** Thor Larsen and Annemor Brekke. **LC** Q115; .N896. **DD** 508.98. **CODEN** NPOSAY. **Circ:** 800. Documents available from BIOSIS Document Express, Ask*IEEE. **Continues** Skrifter - Norges Svalbard- og Ishavs-Undersekelser.
**Desc:** Monographs on subjects within the field of polar research.
**Ind/Abst** ASTIS Curr. Aware. Bull. (1978-); ASTIS Bibliogr. (1978-); Biol. Abstr.; GeoRef; INSPEC (1985-); Life Sci. Collect.

XR/0037-668X
**SLABOPROUDY OBZOR.** (SLABOPROUDY OBZOR : CASOPIS FEDERALNIHO MINISTERSTVA ELEKTROTECHNICKEHO PRUMYSLU.). [Slaboproudy obz.]. **Added/Corp** Czechoslovakia. Federalni Ministerstvo Elektrotechnickeho Prumyslu. (1936)-. Academic Scholarly Publication. Czech. Twelve times a year. $107.80. **(Subscription address:** Artia Pegas Press Ltd., Palac Metro Narodni Trida 25, 11210 Prague 1 Czech Republic.**) CODEN** SLOZAE. Documents available from Ask*IEEE, CASDDS.
**Ind/Abst** Chem. Abstr.; Energy Res. Abstr.; INSPEC (1968-); Saf. Health Work.

US/0037-7333
**SMITHSONIAN. See** Natural History.

US/0081-0258
**SMITHSONIAN STUDIES IN HISTORY AND TECHNOLOGY. See** History(General).

US/0273-4982
**SMITHSONIAN YEAR (1980). Ceased.** (SMITHSONIAN YEAR : ANNUAL REPORT OF THE SMITHSONIAN INSTITUTION.). [Smithson. year]. **Main/Corp** Smithsonian Institution. **Added/Corp** Smithsonian Institution. Press. (1979)-(19??). English. an. Superintendent of Documents, US Government Printing Office, Washington DC 20402. **Tel** (202)275-3328, FAX (202)786-2377. **LC** Q11; .S79b. **DD** 353.0085/3. ctrl circ. available on microfilm and microfiche from University Microfilms International (UMI). **Continues** Smithsonian. Programs and Activities - Smithsonian Institution, 0190-714X.
**Desc:** A report on the Smithsonian Institution.
**Ind/Abst** Life Sci. Collect.

US/0890-7900
**SMT TRENDS. See** Engineering-Electricity, Electrical Engineering, Electronics.

CN/0710-2216
**SNIPS (FREDERICTON, N.B.).** (SNIPS.). [Snips]. Periodical. English. Three times a year. Free. New Brunswick Teachers' Association, PO Box 752, Fredericton New Brunswick E3B 5R6 Canada. **Tel** (506)452-8921. **DD** 607/.12715. ctrl circ. **Continues** Industrial Teacher, 0710-2208.

NE/0167-2320
**SOCIOLOGY OF THE SCIENCES.** Vol. 1 (1977)-. Monographic series. English. an. Price varies per volume. Kluwer Academic Publishers, Postbus 322, 3300 AH Dordrecht, The Netherlands. **Tel** 011 (31) 78 524400, FAX 011 31 78 183273, telex 20083. **(Subscription address:** Kluwer Academic Publishers / US Subscriptions, PO Box 253, Accord Station, Hingham MA 02018.**) LC** UNC. **NLM** W1 SO879NM.
**Ind/Abst** Int. Bibliogr. Sociol.

CN/0710-779X
**SOLUTIONS (FREDERICTON).** (SOLUTIONS : THE NEWSLETTER OF THE SCIENCE COUNCIL OF THE NEW BRUNSWICK TEACHERS' ASSOCIATION.). [Solutions]. Newsletter. English. Three times a year. Free. New Brunswick Teachers' Association, PO Box 752, Fredericton New Brunswick E3B 5R6 Canada. **Tel** (506)452-8921. **DD** 507/.12715. ctrl circ.

GW
**SONDERREIHE, OFFENTLICHE VORTRAGE / UNIVERSITAT DES SAARLANDES. Added/Corp** Universitat des Saarlandes. **VFOAT** Offentliche Vortrage. 1988-. Periodical. German (French). Universitat des Saarlandes, St Johanner Stadtwald, 6600 Saarbrucken Germany. **Tel** (0681)302-2089, telex 4428 851.

GS
**SOOBSHCHENIIA AKADEMII NAUK GRUZII. Added/Corp** Sakartvelos Mecnierebata Akademia. **VFOAT** Sakartvelos SSR Mecnierebata Akademiis Moambe; Bulletin of the Academy of Sciences of Georgia. (1990)-. Periodical. Russian (English and Georgian). mo. **LC** Q4; .S66. **Continues** Soobshcheniia Akademii nauk Gruzinskoi SSR.
**Ind/Abst** Ornamental Hort. (1991-).

JA/0286-9713
**SOSHIKI KAGAKU / ORGANIZATION SCIENCE / HENSHU, SOSHIKI GAKKAI. Added/Corp** Soshiki Gakkai (Japan). **VFOAT** Organization Science. (19??)-. Periodical. Japanese (Japanese; summaries and/or abstracts in English). Four times a year. $62.00. **(Subscription address:** Kyowa Book Company Inc., 1 38 Kanda Jinbocho Chiyoda-ku, Tokyo 101 Japan.**) LC** HD28; .S628.

●RU/0202-2141
**SOTSIALNYE I GUMANITARNYE NAUKI. SERIIA 8, NAUKOVEDENIE : OTECHESTVENNAIA I ZARUBEZHNAIA LITERATURA / ROSSIISKAIA AKADEMIIA NAUK, INSTITUT NAUCHNOI INFORMATSII PO OBSHCHESTVENNYM NAUKAM. Added/Corp** Institut Nauchnoi Informatsii po Obshchestvennym Naukam (Rossiiskaia Akademiia Nauk). **VFOAT** Naukovedenie; Otechestvennaia i Zarubezhnaia Literatura. **VAT** Sotsialnyi i Gumanitarnye Nauki. Seriia Vosem, Naukovedenie. (1993)-. Periodical. Russian. qt. **LC** Q4; .017. **Continues** Obshchestvennye Nauki za Rubezhom. Seriia 8, Naukovedenie.

US/1060-0973
**SOURCEBOOK FOR SCIENCE, MATHEMATICS, AND TECHNOLOGY EDUCATION.** [Sourceb. sci. math. technol. educ.]. **Added/Corp** American Association for the Advancement of Science. Directorate for Education and Human Resources Programs. (1991)-. English. an. $16.95. American Association for the Advancement of Science, 1333 H Street Northwest, Washington DC 20005. **Tel** (202)326-6400, (203)326-6417, (202)326-6430, FAX (202)842-1065. **LC** Q181.A1; A68 subser.; Q183.3.A1. **DD** 500 S; 507/.1/073. **Continues** AAAS Science Education Directory.

GW/0172-6315
**SOURCES IN THE HISTORY OF MATHEMATICS AND PHYSICAL SCIENCES. See** Mathematics.

SA/0038-2353
**SOUTH AFRICAN JOURNAL OF SCIENCE.** [S. Afr. j. sci.]. **Added/Corp** South African Association for the Advancement of Science. **VFOAT** Suid-Afrikaanse Joernaal van Wetenskap; Suid-Afrikaanse Tydskrif vir Wetenskap; Report of the Annual Meeting of the South African Association for the Advancements of Sciences. Vol. 6 (Aug. 1909)-. Academic Scholarly Publication. English (Afrikaans). Eleven times a year (Nov./Dec. issued combined). R270.00 (institutions), R173.00 (individuals) South Africa; R272.00 (institutions), R186.00 (individuals) other. Foundation for Education Science & Technology, PO Box 1758, Pretoria 0001 South Africa. **Tel** 011 27 12 3226404, FAX 011 27 12 3207803. **ED** Graham Baker. **LC** Q85; .S5. **DD** 506.268. **NLM** W1 SO905T. **CODEN** SAJSAR. Index available. cum. index. **Bk Rev. Ad Acc. Pr Rev. Circ:** 2,000. available on microfilm and microfiche from University Microfilms International (UMI). Documents available from The Genuine Article, BIOSIS Document Express, CASDDS. ***Continues** Report of the South African Association for the Advancement of Science;* ***Absorbed** South African Science.*
**Ind/Abst** Abstr. Anthropol. (19??-); AgBiotech News Inf.; AGRICOLA; Agrofor. Abstr.; Alum. Ind. Abstr.; Anim. Breed. Abstr.; Anthropol. Index; Art Archaeol. Tech. Abstr.; Biocont. News Inf.; Biol. Abstr.; Chem. Abstr.; Crop Physiol. Abstr.; CSA Neuro. Abstr. (?-?); Curr. Aware. Biol. Sci., CABS; Curr. Contents, Agric. Biol. Environ. Sci.; Curr. Contents Life Sci.; Curr. Ref. Fish Res.; Dairy Sci. Abstr.; Ecol. Abstr.; Ecology Abstr.; EMBASE; Eng. Mater. Abstr.; Entomol. Abstr.; Field Crop Abstr.; For. Prod. Abstr. (19??-19??); For. Abstr.; Geogr. Abstr. Phys. Geogr.; Geogr. Abstr. Human Geogr.; Geol. Abstr.; GeoRef; Grasslands For. Abstr.; Hortic. Abstr.; Index Vet.; Int. Aerosp. Abstr.; Int. Dev. Abstr.; Key Word Index Wildl. Res.; Maize Abstr.; Met. Abstr.; Meteorol. Geoastrophys. Abstr. (-199?); NAPRALERT; Nematol. Abstr.; Ocean. Abstr.; Ornamental Hort.; Life Sci. Collect.; Pig News Inf.; Plant Breed. Abstr.; Plant Grow. Reg. Abstr.; Potato Abstr.; Poult. Abstr.; Ref. Upd. Deluxe Ed.; Res. Alert [Full Cov.]; Res. High. Educ. Abstr.; Rev. Med. Vet. Entomol.; Rev. Plant Pathol.; Risk Abstr.; Sci. Cit. Index; SCISEARCH; Seed Abstr.; Soc. Sci. Cit. Index [Select. Cov.]; Soils Fert.; Vet. Bull.; Weed Abstr.

US/1040-0532
**SOUTH CENTRAL SALES GUIDE TO HIGH-TECH COMPANIES.** [South Cent. sales guide high tech co.]. **VFOAT** South Central Region; Sales Guide to High Tech Companies. South Central Region. English. qt. $145.00. Corporate Technology Information Services Inc, 12 Alfred Street, Suite 200, Woburn MA 01801-9998. **Tel** (617)932-3939, (800)333-8036, FAX (617)932-6335, telex 497-2961 CRPTECH. **ED** Steven W Parker. **LC** HC110.H53; S68. **DD** 338.7/62/0002576. Index available. cum. index. **Bk Rev. Ad Acc. Circ:** 3,000. available on diskette.
**Desc:** Regional directory of over 3,000 technology manufacturers and developers.

FJ/1011-5145
**SOUTH PACIFIC RESEARCH REGISTER. Added/Corp** University of the South Pacific. Pacific Information Centre. (1982)-. Directory. English. an. 13.00Fij$ Fiji; $10.00 US. University of the South Pacific Library, Pacific Information Centre, PO Box 1168, Suva Fiji. **Tel** 313900, FAX 300830, telex 2276 USP FJ. **ED** Jayshree Manitora. **LC** Q180.O3; S65. **DD** 016.99. Index available. **Circ:** 250. Documents available from FAXON Xpress.
**Desc:** A register of names of researchers and the title of their research relating to the South Pacific.

US/1040-0567
**SOUTHEAST SALES GUIDE TO HIGH-TECH COMPANIES.** [Southeast sales guide high-tech co.]. **VFOAT** Southeast Region; Sales Guide to High Tech Companies. Southeast Region. English. qt. $145.00. Corporate Technology Information Services Inc, 12 Alfred Street, Suite 200, Woburn MA 01801-9998. **Tel** (617)932-3939, (800)333-8036, FAX (617)932-6335, telex 497-2961 CRPTECH. **ED** Steven W Parker. **LC** HC110.I53; S65. **DD** 338.7/62/0002575. Index available. cum. index. **Bk Rev. Ad Acc. Circ:** 3,000. available on diskette.
**Desc:** Regional directory of over 3,000 technology manufacturers and developers.

US/1040-0524
**SOUTHWEST SALES GUIDE TO HIGH-TECH COMPANIES.** [Southwest sales guide high tech co.]. **VFOAT** Southwest Region; Sales Guide to High Tech Companies. Southwest Region. English. qt. $145.00. Corporate Technology Information Services Inc, 12 Alfred Street, Suite 200, Woburn MA 01801-9998. **Tel** (617)932-3939, (800)333-8036, FAX (617)932-6335, telex 497-2961 CRPTECH. **ED** Steven W Parker. **LC** HC110.H53; S686. **DD** 338.7/62/0002579. Index available. cum. index. **Bk Rev. Ad Acc. Circ:** 3,000. available on diskette.
**Desc:** Regional directory of over 3,000 technology manufacturers and developers.

US/1049-5940
**SOVIET AEROSPACE & TECHNOLOGY.** ***Title Change.*** [Sov. aerosp. technol.]. **VFOAT** Soviet Aerospace and Technology. Vol. 54, No. 6 (Mar. 26, 1990)-Vol. 56, No. 5 (Mar. 9, 1992). Periodical. English. bw. Grune & Stratton Inc., 6277 Sea Harbor Drive, Orlando FL 32887. **Tel** (800)782-4479, (407)345-2567. **LC** TL789.8.R9; S66. **DD** 629.4/0947. available on an online database (files 636,648/Full-Text) from DIALOG. ***Continues** Soviet Aerospace, 0092-105X.* ***Continued by** Russian Aerospace & Technology.*
**Ind/Abst** F&S Index Plus Text, Int. [Select. Cov.]; PTS Newsl. Database [Full Txt.].

SZ/0734-9351
**SOVIET SCIENTIFIC REVIEWS. SECTION D, PHYSICOCHEMICAL BIOLOGY REVIEWS.** ***Ceased.*** [Sov. sci. rev., D, Physicochem. biol. rev.]. **VFOAT** Physicochemical Biology Reviews. Vol. 4 (1984)-Vol. 12. English (translations available in Russian). an. Harwood Academic Publishers, PO Box 90, Reading RG1 8JL England. **Tel** 011 44 734 560080. **(Subscription address:** International Publishers Distributor at one of the following addresses: 820 Town Center Drive, Langhorne, PA 19047; or PO Box 90, Reading Berkshire RG1 8JL UK; or Kent Ridge PO Box 1180, Singapore 9111, Republic of Singapore) **ED** V. P. Skulachev. **LC** QH301; .S783. **DD** 574/.05. **NLM** W1; SO996WE. **CODEN** SRDREF. **[CCC].** Documents available from BIOSIS Document Express. ***Continues** Soviet Scientific Reviews. Section D, Biology Reviews, 0143-0424.*
**Ind/Abst** Biol. Abstr. (-1984).

UK/0953-4016
**SOVIET TECHNOLOGY ALERT.** ***Title Change.*** [Sov. technol. alert]. (1988)-(1993). Periodical. English. mo. Newmedia International Japan, AV Infanta Carlota 123 5 A, 08029 Barcelona Spain. **Tel** 011 34 3 4195690, FAX 414 42 13. **DD** 609.47. **[CCC].** available on an online database (files 16,636/Full-Text) from DIALOG. ***Continued by** Advanced Russian Technologies.*
**Ind/Abst** PROMT [Full Txt.]; PTS Newsl. Database [Full Txt.].

UK
**SOVIET TECHNOLOGY DIGEST.** ***Title Change.*** **Added/Corp** Pergamon Institute. (Dec. 1960)-(19??). Periodical. English. mo. ***Continues** Digest of Soviet Technology.* ***Continued by** East-West Technology Digest, 0145-1421.*

●US/1061-5350
**SPACE STATION FREEDOM NEWS.** **See** Aeronautics, Astronautics.

US/0889-6054
**SPACE TODAY.** ***Suspended.*** **See** Astronomy.

US/1071-6092
**SPECIAL TECHNOLOGIES.** ***Title Change.*** [Spec. technol.]. **Added/Corp** American Pioneer Technologies, Inc. Vol. 1, No. 1 (Sept. 15, 1993)-(June 1994). Periodical. English. bw (25 issues). Phillips Business Information, Inc., 1201 Seven Locks Road, Potomac MD 20854. **Tel** (301)424-3338, (800)777-5006, FAX (301)309-3847. **DD** 363. ***Merged into** Tactical Technology, 1059-0552.*

UK/0155-7785
**SPECULATIONS IN SCIENCE AND TECHNOLOGY.** [Speculations sci. technol.]. Vol. 1 (April 1978)-. Academic Scholarly Publication. English. qt. £121.00 (institution), £68.00 (individual) UK; $242.00 (institution), $136.00 (individual) US. Chapman & Hall, 2-6 Boundary Row, London SE1 8HN England. **Tel** 011 44 71 865 0066, FAX 011 44 71 522 9623, telex 290164 Chapmag. **(Subscription address:** International Thomson Publishing Svcs. Ltd., Subscription Department North Way Andover, Hampshire SP10 5BE England.) **ED** Alan L. Mackay. **LC** Q1; .S87. **DD** 505. **NLM** W1 SP325I. **CODEN** SPSTDD. **[CCC]. Bk Rev. Ad Acc. Circ:** 800. Documents available from Article Express International, BIOSIS Document Express, Ask*IEEE, CASDDS.
**Desc:** Logically argued contributions which go beyond the realm of conventional journals of science and technology to serve the international scientific community as the focus of intellectual debate.
**Ind/Abst** Alum. Ind. Abstr.; Bioeng. Abstr.; Biol. Abstr.; Chem. Abstr.; Comput. Abstr.; CSA Neuro. Abstr. (?-?); Ei Page One; EMBASE; Eng. Mater. Abstr.; Eng. Index Annu.; GeoRef; INSPEC (April 1979-); Int. Aerosp. Abstr.; Mech. Eng. Abstr.; Met. Abstr.; Life Sci. Collect.; Soc. Plann. Policy Dev. Abstr.; Sociol. Abstr. (?-?).

GW/0170-2971
**SPEKTRUM DER WISSENSCHAFT.** [Spektrum Wiss.]. (1978)-. Periodical. German. mo. 111.60M. Spektrum der Wissenschaft, Boschstr 12, D-69469 Weinnheim Germany. **Tel** 011 49 6201 606150, FAX 011 49 6201 606184. **ED** Albrecht Kunkel. **UDC** 5. Index available.

NE/0168-468X
**SPEUR- EN ONTWIKKELINGSWERK IN NEDERLAND / CENTRAAL BUREAU VOOR DE STATISTIEK, HOOFDAFDELING STATISTIEKEN VAN ONDERWIJS EN WETENSCHAPPEN. VFOAT** Research and Development in the Netherlands. Began in 1959. Dutch. an. Fl25.00. Centraal Bureau voor de Statistiek, AFD ALG Zaken, Postbus 959, 2270 AZ Voorburg Netherlands. **Tel** 011 31 70 3373800, FAX 011 31 038 7429, telex 32692 CBS NL. **LC** Q180.N35; S66. **DD** 001.4/09492.

FI/0783-5892
**SPHINX (HELSINKI, FINLAND).** (SPHINX / FINSKA VETENSKAPS-SOCIETETEN.). **Added/Corp** Suomen Tiedeseura. (1984)-. Swedish (Finnish). an. Finnish Society of Sciences & Letters, Mariankatu 5, FIN-00170 Helsinki Finland. **Tel** 633005, FAX 661065. **ED** Johan Chydenius. **LC** Q60.2; .S67. **CODEN** SASUEE. **Circ:** 500. Documents available from BIOSIS Document Express. ***Continues in part** Suomen Tiedeseura. Arsbok - Societas Scientiarum Fennica, 0371-2885.*
**Desc:** Papers read at the meetings of the Finnish Society of Sciences and letters.
**Ind/Abst** Biol. Abstr. (1988-).

US/0148-2203
**SPINOFF.** (SPINOFF / NATIONAL AERONAUTICS & SPACE ADMINISTRATION, TECHNOLOGY UTILIZATION OFFICE.). [Spinoff]. **Added/Corp** United States. National Aeronautics and Space Administration. Technology Utilization Office. United States. National Aeronautics and Space Administration. Technology Utilization Division. United States. Office of Space and Terrestrial Applications. Technology Transfer Division. United States. National Aeronautics and Space Administration. Technology Utilization and Industry Affairs Division. United States. Ional Aeronautics and Space Administration. Commercial Development and Technology Transfer Division. (1976)-. Government Publication. English. an. $14.00 (one year), $25.00 (two year). Superintendent of Documents, US Government Printing Office, Washington DC 20402. **Tel** (202)275-3328, FAX (202)786-2377. **LC** T1; .U39a. **DD** 605. ***Continues** Technology Utilization Program Report, 0098-0749.*
**Ind/Abst** Index Inf.

BU/0007-3989
**SPISANIE NA BULGARSKATA AKADEMIIA NA NAUKITE.** [Spis. Blg. akad. nauk.]. **Main/Corp** Bulgarska Akademiia na Naukite. Vol. 1 (1953)-. Periodical. Bulgarian. bm (6 issues). DM255.00. **(Subscription address:** Kubon & Sagner, ABT Zeitschriftenimport, D 80328 Munich Germany.) **LC** AS343; .S6113. ***Continues** Bulgarska Akademiia na Naukite. Spisanie na Bulgarska Akademiia na Naukite, 0007-3989.*
**Ind/Abst** AGRICOLA; Alum. Ind. Abstr.; Int. Aerosp. Abstr.; Met. Abstr.

●US/1056-6724
**SPORT SCIENCE REVIEW (CHAMPAIGN, ILL.).** **See** Recreation, Leisure-Sports.

GW/0172-7389
**SPRINGER SERIES IN SYNERGETICS.** (1978)-. Academic Scholarly Publication. English. ir. Price varies per volume. Springer-Verlag GmbH & Company KG, Heidelberger Platz 3, D 14197 Berlin Germany. **Tel** 011 49 30 8207223, FAX 011 49 30 8214091, telex 183 319 SPBLN D. **(Subscription address:** Springer Verlag New York Inc. / for North America, 44 Hartz Way, Secaucus NJ 07096.) **LC** UNC. **CODEN** SSSYDF. Documents available from Ask*IEEE, CASDDS.
**Ind/Abst** Chem. Abstr.; INSPEC; Zentralbl. Math. Ihre Grenzgeb.

RU
**SPUTNIK MOLODOGO RABOCHEGO.** (19??)-. Russian. 0.36rub. Izdatelstvo Molodaia Gvardiia, Novodmitrovskaya Ul., 5A, 125015 Moscow Russia. **Tel** 095-285-0830. **LC** HC340.T4; S67.

US/1062-8142
**SRA JOURNAL.** [SRA j.]. **Added/Corp** Society of Research Administrators. **VAT** Society of Research Administrators Journal. Vol. 23, No. 1 (Summer 1991)-. Periodical. English. qt. $25.00. SRA Executive Office, 500 North Michigan Avenue, Suite 1400, Chicago IL 60611. **LC** Q180.55.M3; S6a. **DD** 001. Documents available from The Genuine Article, UMI Article Clearinghouse. ***Continues** Journal of the Society of Research Administrators, 0038-0024.*
**Ind/Abst** ABI/INFORM Glob. Ed.; ABI Inform Ondisc (Fall 1987-); Acad. Search (July 1993-199?); Bus. Index (1991-); Curr. Index J. Educ.; Gen. BusinessFile (1991-); Gen. Period. Index (1991-); INFO-SOUTH Abstr.; Mag. Search; Res. Alert [Full Cov.]; Soc. Sci. Cit. Index [Full Cov.]; Trade Ind. Index [Full Txt.]; UMI ABI/Inform--Bus. Period. Ondisc (Fall 1987-) [Full Txt.].

YU/0374-0803
**SRPSKA AKADEMIJA NAUKA I UMETNOSTI. GLAS. ODELJENJE TEHNICKIH NAUKA.** (ODELJENJE TEHNICKIH NAUKA / SRPSKA AKADEMIJA NAUKA I UMETNOSTI.). [Srp. akad. nauka umet., Glas, Od. teh. nauka]. **Added/Corp** Srpska Akademija Nauka i Umetnosti. Odeljenje Tehnickih Nauka. **VFOAT** Classe des Sciences Techniques. (19??)-. Periodical. Serbo-Croatian (Cyrillic) (summaries and/or abstracts in English and French). **LC**

T4; .S715a. **CODEN** GSANDW. Documents available from CASDDS.
**Ind/Abst** Chem. Abstr.

US/0036-1917
**SSRS NEWSLETTER.** ***Ceased.*** [SSRS newsl.]. **Main/Corp** Society for Social Responsibility in Science. **VAT** Society for Social Responsibility in Science Newsletter. Newsletter. English. mo. Hayward, 875 5th Avenue, New York NY 10021. **LC** Q175.4; .S63A. **DD** 174/.95/0973.

CC/0490-6756
**SSU-CHUAN TA HSUEH HSUEH PAO. TZU JAN KO HSUEH PAN. See** Natural History.

JA
**STA TODAY / SCIENCE AND TECHNOLOGY AGENCY, JAPAN.** **Added/Corp** Japan. Kagaku Gijutsucho. Kagaku Gijutsu Koho Zaidan (Japan). **VFOAT** Science and Technology Agency Ttoday. (198?)-. Periodical. English. mo. **LC** Q77; .S73. **DD** 509.51. **CODEN** STTOEW. Documents available from CASDDS.
**Ind/Abst** Chem. Abstr. (1990-); Int. Aerosp. Abstr.

NE
**STANDBY.** Hofstad Vakpersbv, Postbus 119, 2700 AC Zoetermeer Netherlands.

●US/1065-6928
**STAR TREK FEDERATION SCIENCE (EXHIBIT GUIDE).** (STAR TREK FEDERATION SCIENCE.). **VFOAT** Exhibit Guide Star Trek Federation Science. (1992)-. Periodical. English. qt. $5.95. Science Network, 8696 JFK Station, Boston MA 02114-0036.

●US/1065-691X
**STAR TREK FEDERATION SCIENCE (TEACHER'S GUIDE).** (STAR TREK FEDERATION SCIENCE.). **VFOAT** Teacher's Guide Star Trek Federation Science. (1992)-. Periodical. English. qt. $5.95. Science Network, 8696 JFK Station, Boston MA 02114-0036.

US
**STATE AWARD SUMMARY, FISCAL YEAR / NATIONAL SCIENCE FOUNDATION.** **Main/Corp** National Science Foundation (U.S.). (1991)-. English. **LC** Q180.U5; A343. ***Continues*** *National Science Foundation (U.S.). Fiscal Year ... Awards (By State and NSF Directorate).*

UK/0276-8267
**STATE OF THE ART REPORT.** ***Ceased.*** [State art rep.]. Ser. 10, No. 1-Ceased Vol. 15, 1987. Monographic series. English. ir. Pergamon Press, An Imprint of Elsevier Science Ltd., The Boulevard, Langford Lane, Kidlington, Oxford OX5 1GB United Kingdom. **Tel** 011 44 865 843000, 011 44 865 843699, FAX 011 44 865 843010. **(Subscription address:** US/ 395 Saw Mill River Road, Elmsford, NY 10523; Can/ 150 Consumers Road/Suite 104, Willowdale Ontario M2J 1P9; Aus-NZ/ POB 544, Potts Point NSW 2011) **[CCC].** available on microfilm and microfiche from University Microfilms International (UMI). ***Continues*** *Infotech State of the Art Report, 0734-8487.*
**Desc:** Eight reports are published annually, each addressing major technical and managerial issues in computing, including previously unpublished papers from the world's leading authorities. In each report selected papers are analysed and discussed, and coordinated into an integrated framework by editors who know their subject from every angle. Contains a fully annotated bibliography and keyword index.

CN/0715-7908
**STATISTIQUES SUR LA RECHERCHE ET LE DEVELOPPEMENT INDUSTRIELS AU QUEBEC.** [Stat. rech. dev. ind. Que.]. **Added/Corp** Bureau de la Statistique du Quebec. Service des Statistiques Generales. (1979)-. French. an. 36.00Can$. Statistique Quebec, 117 rue Saint Andre, Quebec Quebec G1K 3Y3 Canada. **Tel** (514)283-2642. **(Subscription address:** Research Publications Quebec, 200 Rene Leves, Montreal Quebec H2O 1X4 Canada.) **DD** 607/.2/714.

US/0737-013X
**STATUS OF SCIENCE REVIEWS.** [Status sci. rev.]. English. an. National Science Foundation, 1800 G Street Northwest, Washington DC 20550. **Tel** (202)357-9859, (202)357-9498. **LC** Q127.U6; S73. **DD** 509/.73.

RU
**STEKLO, SITALLY I SILIKATY / MINISTERSTVO VYSSHEGO I SREDNOGO SPETSIALNOGO OBRAZOVANIIA BSSR, BELORUSSKII TEKHOLOGICHESKII INSTITUT IM. S.M. KIROVA.** **Added/Corp** Belorusskii Tekhnologicheskii Institut im. S.M. Kirova. (1977)-. Academic Scholarly Publication. English. **CODEN** SSISDF. Documents available from CASDDS.
**Ind/Abst** Ceram. Abstr. (19??-); Chem. Abstr.

INT/1010-5239
**STI REVUE.** [STI rev. Ed. fr.]. **VFOAT** Science Technologie Industrie Revue; STI Revue de la Science, de la Technologie et de l'Industrie. (1986)-. Periodical. French. sa. $44.00. OECD Publications and Information Center, 2 rue Andre-Pascal, 75775 Paris Cedex 16 France. **Tel** 011 33 1 45248167, US:(202)785-6323, FAX 011 33 1 45248500 OR 45248176, telex 620 160 OCDE. **(Subscription address:** OECD Publications Center, 2001 L Street, Suite 700, Washington DC 20036.)
**Desc:** French edition of the OECD's journal presenting articles on governmental science and technology policy.

XV/0039-2480
**STROJNISKI VESTNIK.** Slovak (English, German and Serbo-Croatian (Roman)). qt. 100.00 Din Yugoslavia; $98.00 US. Assn Mech Eng & Tech Slovenia, Murnikova 2, POB 197/IV, Ljubljana Slovenia. **Tel** (061)223-133, FAX 061-218-567, telex 32240 FAKSTR YU. **ED** Joze Puhar. Index available. **Bk Rev. Ad Acc. Circ:** 2,500 (ctrl). Documents available from Article Express International.
**Desc:** Covers mechanical engineering and machinery, technology, metals and metallurgy.
**Ind/Abst** Alum. Ind. Abstr.; Comput. Inf. Syst. Abstr. J. [Full Cov.]; Ei Page One; Eng. Index Annu.; Environ. Eng. Abstr.; Int. Aerosp. Abstr.; Mech. Eng. Abstr.; Met. Abstr.

IT
**STUDI & NOTIZIE.** **Added/Corp** Centro per la Storia della Tecnica. **VFOAT** Studi e Notizie. **VAT** Studi e Notizie. No. 1 (April 1977)-. Italian. Four times a year. L50000. Elres, Piazza Matteotti 5, 16123 Genova Italy. **Tel** 011 39 10 280751, 290410.

IT/0585-5616
**STUDI TRENTINI DI SCIENZE NATURALI. SEZIONE B. BIOLOGICA.** [Studi Trentini sci. nat., Sez. B]. **Added/Corp** Museo Tridentino di Scienze Naturale. Academic Scholarly Publication. Italian (English and German). an. L50000.00 Italy; L70000.00 other. Museo Tridentino di Scienze Naturali Trento, Via Calepina 14, CP 393, 38100 Trento Italy. **Tel** 011 39 461 239760. **CODEN** SSNBBL. Index available. cum. index. **Circ:** 1,000 (ctrl). Documents available from CASDDS.
**Desc:** Covers geology, quaternary, applied geology, palaeontology, petrography, hydrology, physical geography, sedimentology, mine, zoology, entomology, arachnology, mammals, ornithology, limnology, sociobiology.
**Ind/Abst** Chem. Abstr.; GeoRef.

PL/0208-421X
**STUDIA I MATERIAY OCEANOLOGICZNE.** (STUDIA I MATERIAY OCEANOLOGICZNE / POLSKA AKADEMIA NAUK, KOMITET BADAN MORZA.). [Stud. mater. oceanol.]. **Added/Corp** Polska Akademia Nauk. Komitet Badan Morza. (19??)-. Academic Scholarly Publication. Polish (summaries and/or abstracts in English). bm. **CODEN** SMOCDN. Documents available from CASDDS.
**Ind/Abst** Chem. Abstr.

PL/0081-6590
**STUDIA I MATERIAY Z DZIEJOW NAUKI POLSKIEJ. SERIA C : HISTORIA NAUK MATEMATYCZNYCH, FIZYKO-CHEMICZNYCH I GEOLOGICZNO-GEOGRAFICZNYCH.** **VFOAT** Historia Nauk Matematycznych, Fizyko-Chemicznych i Geologiczno-Geograficznych. Vol. 1- 1957-. Polish (summaries and/or abstracts in Russian and English). ***Supersedes in part*** *Studia I Materiay Z Dziejow Nauki Polskiej.*

SW
**STUDIEHANDBOK.** **Main/Corp** Kungl. Tekniska Hogskolan Hogskolan. Swedish. an. Tekniska Hogskolan, 100 44 Stockholm 70 Sweden. **LC** T173.S889; S78A.

GW
**STUDIEN ZUR GESCHICHTE DER AKADEMIE DER WISSENSCHAFTEN DER DDR.** Vol. 1 (1975)-. Monographic series. German. Price varies per volume. Akademie-Verlag GmbH, Muehlenstrasse 33 34, D 13162 Berlin Germany. **Tel** 011 49 30 47889300, FAX 011 49 30 47889357. **(Subscription address:** VCH Publishers Inc., 303 Northwest 12th Avenue, Journals Department, Deerfield FL 33442.)

UK/0039-3681
**STUDIES IN HISTORY AND PHILOSOPHY OF SCIENCE.** [Stud. hist. philos. sci.]. Vol. 1 (May 1970)-. Periodical. English. Seven times a year. $373.00 The Americas; £250.00 other. Pergamon Press, An Imprint of Elsevier Science Ltd., The Boulevard, Langford Lane, Kidlington, Oxford OX5 1GB United Kingdom. **Tel** 011 44 865 843000, 011 44 865 843699, FAX 011 44 865 843010. **(Subscription address:** Elsevier Science Ltd. Oxford Fulfillment Centre, PO Box 800, Kidlington, Oxford OX5 1DX United Kingdom.) **ED** Nicholas Jardine. **LC** Q125; .S94. **DD** 509. **NLM** W1 ST92L. **CODEN** SHPSB5. **[CCC]. Pr Rev.** available on microfilm and microfiche from University Microfilms International (UMI). Documents available from The Genuine Article, BIOSIS Document Express, Ask*IEEE, UMI Article Clearinghouse.
**Ind/Abst** Acad. Search (July 1993-); Am. Hist. Life (1977-); Appl. Soc. Sci. Index Abstr.; Arts Humanit. Citation Index [Full Cov.]; Biol. Abstr.; Br. Humanit. Index; Curr. Contents Arts Humanit.; Curr. Contents Soc. Behav. Sci.; Curr. Lit. Sci. Sci.; Expand. Acad. Index (1989-); Gen. Sci. Source (Jul. 1993-); GeoRef; Hist. Source (July 1993-); Humanit. Index; INFO-SOUTH Abstr.; INSPEC (March 1978-); Int. Bibliogr. Sociol.; Mag. Search; Math. Rev.; Newsp. Period. Abstr. (1991-); Life Sci. Collect.; Philos. Index; Res. Alert [Full Cov.]; Romant. Move.; Soc. Plann. Policy Dev. Abstr.; Soc. Sci. Cit. Index [Full Cov.]; Sociol. Abstr.; Zentralbl. Math. Ihre Grenzgeb.

II
**STUDIES IN HISTORY OF MEDICINE AND SCIENCE. See** Medical Science and Technology.

UK/0305-7267
**STUDIES IN SCIENCE EDUCATION.** [Stud. sci. educ.]. V. 1- 1974-. Periodical. English. an. $36.00. Nafferton Books, Lloyds Bank Chambers, Market Place, Driffield East Yorkshire YO25 0JL England. **Tel** 011 44 377 256861. **ED** Edgar Jenkins. **Bk Rev. Ad Acc. Circ:** 800. available on microfilm and microfiche from University Microfilms International (UMI).
**Desc:** All aspects of science education.
**Ind/Abst** Br. Educ. Index; Curr. Index J. Educ.; School Organ. Manage. Abstr.; Tech. Educ. Train. Abstr.

US/0896-1905
**STUDIES IN TECHNOLOGY AND SOCIAL CHANGE SERIES.** [Stud. technol. soc. change ser.]. No. 1; 1988-. Monographic series. English. ir. Price varies per volume. Iowa State University Technology & Social Change Program, Ames IA 50011. **DD** 604.
**Ind/Abst** World Agric. Econ.

NE/0169-5533
**STUDIES IN THE HISTORY OF MODERN SCIENCE.** ***Ceased.*** [Stud. hist. mod. sci.]. Vol. 1-?. Periodical. English. ir. Reidel Publishing, 101 Philip Drive, Norwell MA 02061-1677. **Tel** (617)871-6600, telex 200190. **ED** Robert S Cohen, Erwin N Hiebert, and Everett I Mendelsohn.
**Ind/Abst** Math. Rev.

NE/0378-3766
**STUDIES IN THE MANAGEMENT SCIENCES.** [TIMS stud. manage. sci.]. **VFOAT** Studies in the Management Sciences; North-Holland TIMS Studies in the Management Sciences. Vol. 1 (19??)-. Monographic series. English. ir. Price varies per volume. Elsevier Science Publishers BV, PO Box 211, 1000 AE Amsterdam Netherlands. **Tel** 011 31 20 5803642, FAX 011 31 20 5862696, telex 15682. **[CCC].** Documents available from Ask*IEEE.
**Ind/Abst** INSPEC; Zentralbl. Math. Ihre Grenzgeb.

US/0578-3461
**STUDY - CITIZENS' RESEARCH FOUNDATION.** **Main/Corp** Citizens' Research Foundation. Vol. 1 1960-. Monographic series. English. Price varies per volume. Citizens Research Foundation, 245 Nassau Street, Princeton NJ 08540.

SA/0254-3486
**SUID-AFRIKAANSE TYDSKRIF VIR NATUURWETENSKAP EN TEGNOLOGIE.** [S.-Afr. tydskr. natuurwet. tegnol.]. **VFOAT** Natuurwetenskap en Tegnologie. Academic Scholarly Publication. Afrikaans (summaries and/or abstracts in English). qt (March, June, Sept., Dec.). R38.00. Suid-Afrikaanse Akademie vir Wetenskap en Kuns, Posbus 538, Pretoria 0001 South Africa. **Tel** (012)285082, FAX (012)285091. **ED** A Strasheim. **CODEN** SATTDF. **Bk Rev. Ad Acc. Circ:** 1,500. Documents available from Ask*IEEE, CASDDS. ***Continues*** *Tydskrif vir Natuurwetenskappe.*
**Desc:** Contributions from any field of the natural sciences and technology are published, and must be written in Afrikaans.
**Ind/Abst** Chem. Abstr.; Energy Res. Abstr. (Sept. 1982-); INSPEC (1973-); Math. Rev.; Life Sci. Collect.; Zentralbl. Math. Ihre Grenzgeb.

JA/0387-1304
**SUMITOMO JUKIKAI GIHO.** [Sumitomo jukikai giho]. **VFOAT** Technical Review. (1970)-. Academic Scholarly Publication. Japanese (Japanese). Three times a year. Sumitomo Jukikai Kogyo K K, Shin-Otemachi Biru, Otemachi 2-2-1, Chiyoda-ku, Tokyo-to 100 Japan. **CODEN** SJGHA8. Documents available from CASDDS. ***Continues*** *Sumitomo Kikai Giho.*
**Ind/Abst** BMT Abstr.; Chem. Abstr.; Coal Abstr.

US/0161-4169
**SUMMARIES OF PROJECTS COMPLETED.** (SUMMARIES OF PROJECTS COMPLETED IN FISCAL YEAR ... / NATIONAL

# Science and Technology

SCIENCE FOUNDATION.). Began with 1976/77. English. an. National Science Foundation, 1800 G Street Northwest, Washington DC 20550. **Tel** (202)357-9859, (202)357-9498. **LC** Q180.U5; U54J. **DD** 505. available on microfiche (Vols. for (1980-) distributed to depository libraries).

CN/0848-6840
## SUNATUINNARNIK QAUJISAQTULIRINIRMUT TUSAGAKSAIT. (SUNATUINNARNIK QAUJISAQTULIRINIRMUT TUSAGAKSAIT / NUNATSIARMI SUNATUINNARNIK QAUJISAQTIIT.).
**Added/Corp** Science Institute of the Northwest Territories. **VFOAT** Nunatsiarmi Sunatuinnarnik Qaujisaqtulirinirmut Tusagaksait. No. 1 (1990)-. Periodical. Eskimo. **DD** 509.7192.

US/0739-3350
## SUPERCONDUCTIVE TECHNOLOGY IN REVIEW. *Suspended.* [Supercond. technol. rev.].
**VFOAT** STIR; S.T.I.R. Issue No. 1 (July 1982)-?. English. qt. $55.00. Educational Technology Center, Illinois Institute of Technology, Chicago IL 60616. *Continues Superconducting Devices and Materials, 0039-5714.*

US/1042-4105
## SUPERCONDUCTOR INDUSTRY.
[Supercond. ind.]. **VFOAT** Superconductor. (Fall 1988)-. Periodical. English. mo. $17.00 (one year), $32.00 (two years) US; $19.00 (one year), $35.00 (two years) Canada and Mexico; $21.00 other; $48.00 airmail. Rodman Publications Corporation, 17 S Franklin Turnpike, PO Box 555, Ramsey NJ 07446. **Tel** (201)825-2552, FAX (201)825-0553. **ED** Lee Carson. **DD** 621. **[CCC]**. Index available. **Bk Rev**. **Ad Acc**. **Circ**: 6,500 (ctrl). Documents available from Ask*IEEE.
**Desc**: Edited for those in industry academia and government who are involved in both high and low temperature superconductor research and production.
**Ind/Abst** Energy Inf. Abstr.; F&S Index Plus Text, Int. [Select. Cov.]; INSPEC (Fall 1988-); PROMT.

UK/0749-6036
## SUPERLATTICES AND MICROSTRUCTURES. [Superlattices microstruct.]. Vol. 1, No. 1 (1985)-. Academic Scholarly Publication. English. Eight times a year. $305.00. Academic Press Ltd., A Division of Harcourt Brace & Company Ltd., 24-28 Oval Road, London NW1 7DX England. **Tel** 071 267 4466, FAX 071 482 2293, 071 485 4752, telex 25775 ACPRES G. **(Subscription address:** Harcourt Brace & Company, Ltd., Foots Cray, High Street, Sidcup Kent DA14 5HP England.**) ED** J. D. Dow. **LC** QC611.8.S86; S86. **DD** 530.4/1. **CODEN** SUMIEK. **[CCC]**. **Pr Rev**. Documents available from Article Express International, The Genuine Article, Ask*IEEE, CASDDS.
**Desc**: Devoted to the physics, chemistry, materials science, and electrical engineering aspects of submicron structures and the materials from which such structures will be fabricated. The journal deals with not only semiconductors but also with materials possessing metallic, insulating, and superconducting properties.
**Ind/Abst** Chem. Abstr. (1985-); Curr. Contents Eng. Tech. Appl. Sci.; Curr. Contents Phys. Chem. Earth Sci.; Ei Page One; Eng. Index Annu.; INSPEC (1985-); Res. Alert [Full Cov.]; Sci. Cit. Index; SCISEARCH.

NE/0167-2584
## SURFACE SCIENCE LETTERS. (Jan. 1980)-.
Academic Scholarly Publication. English. Eighteen times a year. Elsevier Science Publishers BV, PO Box 211, 1000 AE Amsterdam Netherlands. **Tel** 011 31 20 5803642, FAX 011 31 20 5862696, telex 15682. **[CCC]**. available on microfilm and microfiche from University Microfilms International (UMI).

RU
## SVODNYI KATALOG BIBLIOGRAFICHESKIKH RABOT, VYPOLNENNYKH V SOVETSKOM SOIUZE: ESTESTVENNYE I FIZIKO-MATEMATICHESKIE NAUKI. *Title Change.* See Science and Technology-Abstracting, Bibliographies and Statistics.

CN/0704-576X
## SYLLOGEUS - NATIONAL MUSEUM OF NATURAL SCIENCES. *See* Museums and Galleries.

US
## SYSTEM DYNAMICS NEWSLETTER.
Newsletter. English. an. $7.25. Massachusetts Institute of Technology (MIT) / Systems Dynamic Group, Building E40-294, Cambridge MA 02139. **Tel** (617)253-1550.

FR/0988-5730
## SYSTEMES EXPERTS PARIS. (SYSTEMES EXPERTS.). (1987)-. Periodical. French. Twenty-two times a year. 2742.00F France; 2800.00F other. A Jour, 11 rue du Marche St Honore, 75001 Paris France. **Tel** 011 33 1 44553849. **ED** Ph Collier. **UDC** 681.3.

FR
## SYSTEMS EXPERTS : APPLICATIONS TECHNOLOGIES ACTEURS. French. mo (July/Aug. issue combined). 1650.00F. A Jour, 11 rue du Marche St Honore, 75001 Paris France. **Tel** 011 33 1 44553849.

CC/0253-0031
## TA-LIEN KUNG HSUEH YUAN HSUEH PAO. *Title Change.* [Dalian gongxueyuan xuebao].
**Added/Corp** Ta-Lien Kung Hsueh Yuan. **VFOAT** Journal of Dalian Engineering Institute; Journal of Dalian Institute of Technology. (19??)-(198?). Academic Scholarly Publication. Chinese (summaries and/or abstracts in English). qt. Science Press, 16 Donghuangchenggen North Street, Beijing 100707, People's Republic of China. **Tel** 011 86 1 4019821, 011 86 1 4010642, FAX 011 86 1 4012180, 011 86 1 4019810, telex 210147. **LC** T4; .T159. **DD** 605. **CODEN** TKHPDO. Documents available from Ask*IEEE, CASDDS. *Continued by Ta-Lien li Kung ta Hsueh Hsueh pao, 1000-8608.*
**Ind/Abst** Chem. Abstr.; INSPEC (1978-); Math. Rev.; Zentralbl. Math. Ihre Grenzgeb.

CH
## TA TZU JAN TAN SO. **VFOAT** Exploration of Nature. V. 1, 1982. Periodical. Chinese. qt. NT$1.20. **LC** Q4; .T23. **DD** 505.
**Ind/Abst** Math. Rev.

AU/1017-1592
## TAATIGKEITSBERICHT DER OESTERREICHISCHEN AKADEMIE DER WISSENSCHAFTEN. [Taatigk.ber. Oesterr. Akad. Wiss.]. **Main/Corp** Oesterreichische Akademie der Wissenschaften. (1978/1979)-. German. ir. Oesterreichischen Akademie Wissenschaften, Dr. Ignaz Seipel Platz 2, A-1010 Vienna Austria. **Tel** 011 43 1 51581. **LC** AS142; .V356. **DD** 505. Price: 2,000. *Continues in part Oesterreichische Akademie der Wissenschaften Almanach, 0378-8644.*
**Desc**: Informs about the activities of the different institutes of the Austrian Academy of Sciences; gives a survey of the variety of problems and duties of the Academy.
**Ind/Abst** GeoRef.

FR
## TABLE PAR DENOMINATIONS DE MARQUES DE FABRIQUE, DE COMMERCE OU DE SERVICE. French. an.
Departement de Diffusion de l'Imprimerie Nationale, BP 514, 59505 Douai Cedex France. **Tel** (1)42 94 52 52, telex 290 368 INPI PARIS. **LC** T271.V1; F7B. **DD** 602/.75. *Continues Bulletin Officiel de la Propriete Industrielle. Table par Denominations de Marques de Fabrique, de Commerce ou de Service.*
**Desc**: Alphabetical indexes to marks and registrants respectively.

JA/0286-7117
## TACHIKAWA TANDAI KIYO. [Tachikawa Tandai kiyo]. **Added/Corp** Tokyo Toritsu Tachikawa Tanki Daigaku. **VFOAT** Journal of the Tachikawa College of Tokyo. (1958)-. Academic Scholarly Publication. Japanese. **CODEN** TTAKD3. Documents available from CASDDS.
**Ind/Abst** Chem. Abstr.

US/1059-0552
## TACTICAL TECHNOLOGY. (1991)-.
Periodical. English. bw (25 issues). $545.00 US; $580.00 other. Phillips Business Information, Inc., 1201 Seven Locks Road, Potomac MD 20854. **Tel** (301)424-3338, (800)777-5006, FAX (301)309-3847. **[CCC]**. available on an online database (file 636/Full-Text) from DIALOG. *Absorbed Special Technologies, 1071-6092.*
**Ind/Abst** PTS Newsl. Database [Full Txt.].

UA
## TADRIS AL-ULUM WA-AL-RIYADIYAT.
**Main/Corp** Al-Munazzamah Al-Arabiyah Lil-Tarbiyah Wa-Al-Thaqafah Wa-Al-Ulum. **VFOAT** Science and Mathematics Education. Vol. 1-. Periodical. Multiple languages (Arabic and English). 109 Tahreer Street, Al-Qahirah United Arab Republic Egypt. **LC** Q183.4.A65; M85A.

GW/0232-5683
## TAGUNGSBAND - KAMMER DER TECHNIK SUHL. (TAGUNGSBAND / KDT, HERAUSGEBER, KAMMER TECHNIK SUHL.). [Tagungsband - Kammer Tech. Suhl]. **Main/Corp** Kammer der Technik. Bezirksverband Suhl. (19??)-. Academic Scholarly Publication. German. **CODEN** TKSUDQ. Documents available from CASDDS.
**Ind/Abst** Chem. Abstr. (1979-1989).

CH/0371-845X
## TAI-WAN KO HSUEH. **Added/Corp** Tai-Wan Sheng ko Hsueh Chen Hsing Hui. **VFOAT** Formosan Science. (1947)-. Academic Scholarly Publication. English (Chinese). qt. Taiwan Sheng K'o Hsue Chen Hsing Hui, (The Formosan Association for the Advancement of Science), No. 57, 67 Lane, Lin Sun Road North, Taipei, Taiwan. **LC** Q4; .T27. **DD** 505. **CODEN** TKHSAU. Documents available from BIOSIS Document Express, CASDDS.
**Ind/Abst** Biol. Abstr. (?-1987); Chem. Abstr.; Math. Rev.; Zentralbl. Math. Ihre Grenzgeb.

JA/0285-0028
## TAIKABUTSU OVERSEAS. [Taikabutsu overseas]. **Added/Corp** Taikabutsu Gijutsu Kyokai (Japan). Vol. 1, No. 1 (Apr. 1981)-. Academic Scholarly Publication. English. qt. $500.00. Technical Association of Refractories, 3-13 Ginza 7-chome Chuo-ku, Tokyo 104 Japan. **Tel** 03-508-0051. **(Subscription address:** Maruzen Company Ltd., PO Box 5050, Import & Export Department, Tokyo 100 31 Japan.**) ED** Ichiro Isshibashi. **LC** TN677.5; .T35. **CODEN** TAOVD7. **Ad Acc**. **Circ**: 300. Documents available from CASDDS.
**Desc**: Discusses Japan's refractory industry and the growth of technology.
**Ind/Abst** Alum. Ind. Abstr.; Ceram. Abstr.; Chem. Abstr.; Coal Abstr.; Eng. Mater. Abstr.; Met. Abstr.

JA/0387-2254
## TAISEI KENSETSU GIJUTSU KENKYUJOHO. (TAISEI KENSETSU GIJUTSU KENKYUJO HO.). [Taisei Kensetsu Gijutsu Kenkyujoho]. **Added/Corp** Taisei Kensetsu Kabushiki Kaisha. Gijutsu Kenkyujo. **VFOAT** Reports of the Technical Research Institute, Taisei Corporation. (1968)-. Academic Scholarly Publication. Japanese (summaries and/or abstracts in English). Taisei Kensetsu K.K. Gijutsu Kenkyujo, (Technical Research Inst., Taisei Corp.), 344-1, Nasecho, Totsukaku, Yokohamashi, Kanagawaken 245, Japan. **CODEN** TKGJAW. Documents available from CASDDS.
**Ind/Abst** Chem. Abstr.

JA
## TAISEI TECHNICAL RESEARCH REPORT. Tohoku University, Sendai 980 Japan. **Tel** 0222-27-6200.
**Ind/Abst** Abstr. J. Earthq. Eng.

CC/1000-1611
## TAIYUAN GONGYE DAXUE XUEBAO. (TAI-YUAN KUNG YEH TA HSUEH HSUEH PAO.). [Taiyuan gongye daxue xuebao]. **Added/Corp** Tai-Yuan Kung Yeh ta Hsueh. **VFOAT** Journal of Taiyuan University of Technology. (19??)-. Academic Scholarly Publication. Chinese. qt. Taiyuan Gongye Daxue, Taiyuan Industrial University, 11 Yingze Dajie, Taiyuan, Shanxi 030024 People's Republic of China. **Tel** 665528. **ED** Lu Wenxiong. **CODEN** TGDXEZ. Documents available from CASDDS. *Continues Tai-Yuan Kung Hsueh Yuan Hsueh Pao, 0253-2387.*
**Ind/Abst** Chem. Abstr.

JA/0371-5167
## TAKEDA KENKYUJO HO. [Takeda Kenkyusho ho]. **VFOAT** Journal of the Takeda Research Laboratories. Began in 1970. Academic Scholarly Publication. Japanese. qt. Takeda Yakuhin Kogyo Kabushiki Kaisha, 17-85 Jusohonmanchi 2-chome, Yodogawa-ku Osaka 532 Japan. **CODEN** TAKHAA. Documents available from BIOSIS Document Express, CASDDS.
**Ind/Abst** AGRICOLA; Biol. Abstr.; Chem. Abstr.; EMBASE [Select. Cov.].

JA
## TAKENAKA TECHNICAL RESEARCH REPORT. Takenaka Technical Research Laboratory, 5-14 2-Chome Minamisuna, Tokyo, Japan.
**Ind/Abst** Concr. Abstr.

VM/0255-2876
## TAP CHI KHOA HOC KY THUAT. Periodical. Vietnamese. Vien Khoa Hoc Vietnam, 70 Tran Hung Dao, Ha-Noi Vietnam. **LC** T4; .K47. *Continues Khoa Hoc Ky Thuat.*

US/0167-9406
## TASKS FOR VEGETATION SCIENCE.
[Tasks veg. sci.]. **VFOAT** Tasks for Vegetation Sciences; T:VS. (198?)-. Academic Scholarly Publication. English. ir. Price varies per volume. Kluwer Academic Publishers / Massachusetts, PO Box 358, Accord Station, Hingham MA 02018. **Tel** (617)871-6600. **(Subscription address:** Kluwer Academic Publishers / Netherlands, PO Box 322, 3300 AH Dordrecht Netherlands.**) CODEN** TUSCD8. Documents available from BIOSIS Document Express, CASDDS.
**Ind/Abst** AGRICOLA [Full Cov.]; Biol. Abstr.; Chem. Abstr.

UK/0028-0763
## TEACHING SCIENCE. *Title Change.* Vol. 1, No. 1 (Spring 1983)-. Periodical. English. Three times a year. Association for Science Education, College Lane, Hatfield Herts AL10 9AA England. **Tel** 011 44 707 267411, FAX 011 44 707 266532. Index available. cum. index. **Bk Rev**. **Ad Acc**. **Circ**: 900 (ctrl). available in microform. *Continues Natural Science in Schools. Absorbed by*

*Primary Science Review, 0269-2465.*
**Desc:** Articles on science and technology teaching and conservation to children up to about 13 years. Teaching aids, background information, news, research reports and book reviews.
**Ind/Abst** Br. Educ. Index.

US/0889-6461
**TECH STREET JOURNAL.** ***Ceased.*** [Tech str. j.]. Vol. 1, No. 1, Jan. (1983)-?. Periodical. English. mo. Tech Street Journal, 238 Littleton Road, Westford MA 01886. **Tel** (508)692-2290, FAX (508)692-4760. **ED** John Gantz. **DD** 338. available on CD-ROM; available on an online database (file 675/Full-Text) from DIALOG.
**Ind/Abst** Comput. ASAP [Full Txt.]; Comput. Database [Full Txt.]; Comput. Lit. Index.

US
**TECH TALK (CAMBRIDGE, MASS.).** (TECH TALK / MASSACHUSETTS INSTITUTE OF TECHNOLOGY?). Periodical. English. ir. $15.00. Tech Talk, c/o Business Manager, Massachusetts Institute of Technology/Room 5-113, Cambridge MA 02139.

PH
**TECH TIPS.** Vol. 1, No. 1 (Sept. 1986)-. English. bm. $45.00. Science and Technology Information Institute, PO Box 2131, Manila Philippines. **Tel** 011 63 2 822 0961.
**Desc:** Profile of current technological breakthroughs.

AT
**TECHNICAL AND FURTHER EDUCATION. APPLIED SCIENCES : TAFE.** **Main/Corp** Western Australia. Technical Education Division. **VFOAT** Applied Sciences. (19??)-. English. Nelson Wadsworth, PO Box 4725, Melbourne Victoria, 3001 Australia. **Tel** 03 329-5199. **LC** WMLC L 83/980.

US
**TECHNICAL BOOKS & MONOGRAPHS.** **Main/Corp** United States. Dept. of Energy. 1978-. English. $3.75. National Technical Information Service - NTIS, Room 2027S, 5285 Port Royal Road, Springfield VA 22161. **Tel** (703)487-4630, (703)487-4660, (703)487-4650, FAX (703)321-8547, telex 89-9405. **LC** Z5853.P83; U544C; TJ163.2. **DD** 016.6. ***Continues*** *Technical Books & Monographs, 0501-6398.*

UK/0263-5178
**TECHNICAL BULLETIN (EGGS AUTHORITY).** (TECHNICAL BULLETIN / THE EGGS AUTHORITY.). Began in 1977. Bulletin. English.

US/0049-3155
**TECHNICAL COMMUNICATION (WASHINGTON).** (TECHNICAL COMMUNICATION.). [Tech. commun.]. **Added/Corp** Society for Technical Communication. Vol. 18, No. 4, 3rd Quarter (1971)-. Periodical. English. qt. $55.00 (1 year), $100.00 (2 year), $135.00 (3 year) US; $85.00 (1 year), $130.00 (2 year), $165.00 (3 year) other. Society for Technical Communication, 901 Stuart Street, Suite 904, Arlington VA 22203. **Tel** (703)522-4114. **(Subscription address:** Fulco, 30 Broad Street, Denville NJ 07834.**) DD** 808/.066/602105. **CODEN** TLCMBT. **[CCC].** available on microfilm and microfiche from University Microfilms International (UMI). Documents available from Article Express International, UMI Article Clearinghouse. ***Continues*** *Technical Communications, 0049-3155.*
**Desc:** Provides information for professionals in all media of technical communication.
**Ind/Abst** Acad. Search (July 1993-); Bioeng. Abstr.; Bus. Index (1985-); Bus. Period. Index; Bus. Source (Jul. 1993-); Educ. Technol. Abstr.; Ei Page One; Eng. Index Annu.; Gen. BusinessFile (1985-); Gen. Period. Index (1985-); Health Devices Alerts; INFO-SOUTH Abstr.; Int. Aerosp. Abstr.; Libr. Inf. Sci. Abstr.; Mag. Index Plus (1989-); Mag. Search; Newsp. Period. Abstr. (1988-); Print. Abstr.; Mag. Index (1985-); Wilson Bus. Abstr.

AT/0810-9532
**TECHNICAL MEMORANDUM - SUPERVISING SCIENTIST FOR THE ALLIGATOR RIVERS REGION.** [Tech. memo. - Superv. Sci. Alligator Rivers Reg.]. (1981)-. Monographic series. English. ir. Price varies per volume. Australian Bureau of Statistics, PO Box 10, Belconnen Australian Capital Territory, 2616 Australia. **Tel** 011 61 6 2527911, FAX 011 61 6 2516009. **DD** 333.72099429.
**Ind/Abst** AESIS Q.

US/0736-6965
**TECHNICAL NEWS - PERKIN-ELMER CORPORATION.** (TECHNICAL NEWS.). [Tech. news - Perkin-Elmer Corp.]. Academic Scholarly Publication. English. qt. Editorial Office Optical Group CT 06810. **CODEN** TNPEDI. Documents available from Ask*IEEE, CASDDS.
**Ind/Abst** Alum. Ind. Abstr.; Chem. Abstr.; INSPEC (June 1982-); Met. Abstr.

US/0362-2886
**TECHNICAL REPORT - MARINE SCIENCES RESEARCH CENTER, STATE UNIVERSITY OF NEW YORK.** [Tech. rep. Mar. Sci. Res. Cent. State Univ. N.Y.]. **Main/Corp** State University of New York at Stony Brook. Marine Sciences Research Center. **VFOAT** Technical Report Series. Monographic series. English. Price varies per volume. Marine Sciences Research Center, State University of New York, Stony Brook NY 11794. **Tel** (516)632-8700. **CODEN** NYTRAH. ctrl circ. Documents available from BIOSIS Document Express.
**Ind/Abst** Biol. Abstr.; GeoRef.

US/0077-796X
**TECHNICAL REPORT SERIES P. PHYSICAL SCIENCES PUBLICATION.** **Added/Corp** University of Nevada. Desert Research Institute. United States. Bureau of Reclaimation. **VFOAT** Physical Sciences Publication. No. 1 (1966)-. Monographic series. English. Price varies per volume. University of Nevada Desert Research Institute, Human Systems, 3700 Stead Campus, University of Nevada, Reno NV 89507. **DD** 500. ***Continues*** *Technical Report - Desert Research Institute.*

JA
**TECHNICAL RESEARCH REPORT OF HAZAMA-GUMI.** Hazama-Gumi Ltd., Technical Research Institute, 17-23 Honmachi-Nishi, 4 chome Yono-shi, Saitama, Japan.
**Ind/Abst** Abstr. J. Earthq. Eng.

FR/0994-7590
**TECHNICAL REVIEW / GEC ALSTHOM.**
**See** Engineering-Electricity, Electrical Engineering, Electronics.

UK/0267-5307
**TECHNICAL REVIEW MIDDLE EAST.** [Tech. rev. Middle East ed.]. (1984)-. Periodical. English (Arabic). Six times a year. $76.00. Alain Charles Publishing Ltd., 27 Wilfred Street, London SW1E 6PR England. **Tel** 011 44 71 834 7676, FAX 011 44 71 973 0076, telex 297166/7. **ED** Valerie Hart. **Ad Acc, Adv Mgr:** Patricia Fairfield. **Circ:** 18,879 (ctrl). Documents available from FAXON Xpress.
**Desc:** Contains practical information and ideas serving the special requirements of managers in the Middle East region. Covers telecommunications, banking, aviation, petrochemicals, transportation, power, construction, insurance, irrigation, business travel and packaging; also new products and developments in the Middle East.
**Ind/Abst** Int. Labour Doc.

UK/0497-0489
**TECHNICAL TRANSLATION BULLETIN.** ***Ceased.*** [Techn. transl. bull.]. V. 7- 1960 or 1961-Ceased April (1988). Bulletin. English. Three times a year. Learned Information Ltd., Woodside Hinksey Hill, Oxford OX1 5AU England. **Tel** 44 865 730275, FAX 44 865 736354, telex 23667. **(Subscription address:** North America/ 143 Old Marlton Pike, Medford, NJ 08055-8707**)** ***Continues*** *Engineering Translator's Bulletin.*
**Ind/Abst** Lang. Teach.

XR/0322-8533
**TECHNICKE ZPRAVY (CKD PRAHA (FIRM) : 1978).** (TECHNICKE ZPRAVY : TZ.). **VFOAT** TZ; T.Z. 1-. Czech (summaries and/or abstracts in English, French, German and Russian). ir. CKD Praha, U Kolbenky 159, Prague 8 Czech Republic. **LC** T4; .T143. ***Continues*** *Technicke Zpravy (Ckd Praha (Firm) : 1964).*
**Ind/Abst** Alum. Ind. Abstr.; Met. Abstr.

NE/0169-622X
**TECHNIEK IN DE GGEZONDHEIDSZORG : BEHEER EN TOEPASSING.** **VFOAT** TG. Techniek in de Gezondheidszorg : Beheer en Toepassing. (1984)-. Periodical. Dutch. mo. Fl105.00. Keesing Noordervliet Bv, De Molen 82-86, 3995 Ax Houten Netherlands. **Tel** 011 31 3403 58585, FAX 011 31 3403 58500. **(Subscription address:** Keesing Noordervliet BV, Postbus 1118, 1000 BC Amsterdam Netherlands.**) UDC** 613. **CODEN** 62.

GW/0040-1099
**TECHNIK, DIE.** [Technik]. Vol. 1 (July 1946)-. Periodical. German. mo. Deutscher Judo Verband, Redaktion Ippon Segewaldweg 40, D 12557 Berlin Germany. **Tel** 011 49 711 210770, telex 051 678. **LC** T3; .T16. **DD** 605. ***Continued in part by*** *Schweisstechnik.*
**Ind/Abst** EMBASE; Energy Res. Abstr. (Oct. 1976-); Saf. Health Work; Surf. Treat. Technol. Abstr.

AU
**TECHNIK REPORT.** (Sept. 1974)-. Periodical. German. Twelve times a year. S540.00 Austria; S750.00 others. Verlag Technik Report GmbH / Austria, Markgraf Fudiger Strasse 8, A1150 Wien Austria. **Tel** 011 43 1 98170. **LC** T3; .T24. **DD** 605.

GW/0723-0664
**TECHNIK UND GESELLSCHAFT (FRANKFURT AM MAIN, GERMANY).** (TECHNIK UND GESELLSCHAFT.). German. ir. $25.00 US. Campus Verlag, Heelstrasse 149, D-60488 Frankfurt Germany. **Tel** 011 49 69 96751606, FAX 011 49 69 7682046. **LC** T14.5; .T398. **Bk Rev. Ad Acc. Circ:** 800.

HU
**TECHNIKA.** **Added/Corp** Orszagos Muszaki Konyvtar es Dokumentacios Kozpont (Hungary). (1957)-. Periodical. Hungarian. $30.50. **(Subscription address:** Kultura, PO Box 149, H 1389 Budapest 62 Hungary**) LC** Microfilm 03112 T; T4.

GW/0040-117X
**TECHNIKGESCHICHTE.** (TECHNIK GESCHICHTE : BEITRAEGE ZUR GESCHICHTE DER TECHNIK UND INDUSTRIE.). [Technikgeschichte]. **Added/Corp** Verein Deutscher Ingenieure. **VFOAT** Technikgeschichte. Vol. 22 (1933)-. Academic Scholarly Publication. German. Four times a year (Mar., May, July, Nov.). $151.00 (add $16.00 for postage). Kiepert KG, Hardenbergstrasse 4 5, D 10623 Berlin Germany. **Tel** 011 49 30 31100922. **CODEN** TECHDZ. **[CCC].** ***Continues*** *Beitrage zur Geschichte der Technik und Industrie.*
**Desc:** Deals with the historical development of technology in its scientific, social, economic and political relationships.
**Ind/Abst** EMBASE; Math. Rev.

IS/0040-1188
**TECHNION.** [Technion]. **Added/Corp** Tekhniyon, Makhon Tekhnologi le-Yisrael. Vol. 1 (June 1965)-. Periodical. English. bm. Israel Institute of Technology, Haifa, Technion City, Israel. **LC** T173; .H1335. **CODEN** TCNNAN. Documents available from Ask*IEEE.
**Ind/Abst** INSPEC (Feb. 1969-); PROMT [Full Txt.].

FR/0040-1250
**TECHNIQUE MODERNE, LA.** [Tech. mod.]. Vol. 1 (Dec. 1908)-. Academic Scholarly Publication. French. bm. 810.00F (France); 1100.00F (other). Sirpe, 76 Rue de Rivoli, 75004 Paris France. **Tel** 011 33 1 42785220. **ED** Roger Drouhin. **LC** T2; .T25. **CODEN** TEMDA2. **[CCC].** Index available. cum. index. **Bk Rev. Ad Acc. Circ:** 3,000 (ctrl). available on microfilm from University Microfilms International (UMI). Documents available from Ask*IEEE, CASDDS.
**Desc:** Technical progresses for industry.
**Ind/Abst** Alum. Ind. Abstr.; Chem. Abstr.; Coal Abstr.; EMBASE; Energy Res. Abstr.; INSPEC (1968-); Int. Aerosp. Abstr.; Met. Abstr.; Point Repere (1979-1980); Surf. Treat. Technol. Abstr.

FR/0248-6016
**TECHNIQUES & CULTURE.** **VFOAT** Techniques et Culture. (1978)-. French. sa. 125.00F (individuals), 170.00F (institutions). MSH Techniques et Culture CNRS, 27 rue Paul Bert, 94204 Ivry Cedex France. **Tel** 011 33 1 49604036. **Bk Rev.**
**Ind/Abst** Anthropol. Lit.

FR
**TECHNIQUES ET MANAGEMENT DES PROJETS INFORMATIQUES.** (19??)-. French. Ten times a year. 1950.00F France; 2150.00F other. Bouhot & Le Gendre Publishers, 75 Bis Rue de Bellevue, F 92100 Boulogne France. **Tel** 011 33 1 46040708. **(Subscription address:** Centrale des Revues, 11 rue Gossin, 92543 Montrouge Cedex France.**)** ***Continues*** *L'Encyclopedie du Chef de Projet Informatique.*

GW/0371-5264
**TECHNISCH-WISSENSFHAFTLICHE ABHANDLUNGEN DER OSRAM-GESELLSCHAFT.** [Tech.-wiss. Abh. Osram-Ges.]. **Added/Corp** Osram G. m. b. H., Kommanditgesellschaft. (1930)-. Periodical. German. ir. Springer-Verlag New York Inc., 175 5th Avenue, New York NY 10010. **Tel** (212)460-1500, telex 232 235 SPB UR. **(Subscription address:** Springer Verlag New York Inc. / for North America, 44 Hartz Way, Secaucus NJ 07096.**) [CCC].** ***Continues*** *Technisch-Wissenschaftliche Abhandlungen.*
**Ind/Abst** Ceram. Abstr.; Energy Res. Abstr. (Sept. 1975-).

GW
**TECHNISCHE GEMEINSCHAFT.** Began with Oct. 1953 issue. Periodical. German. mo. **LC** T3; .T515.
**Ind/Abst** Coal Abstr.

SZ/0040-1471
**TECHNISCHE MITTEILUNGEN DER SCHWEIZERISCHEN TELEGRAPHEN- UND TELEPHON-VERWALTUNG.** ***Title Change.*** (TECHNISCHE MITTEILUNGEN.). [Tech. Mitt. Schweiz. Telegr. Teleph.-Verwalt.]. **Main/Corp** Switzerland. Generaldirektion der Post-, Telegraphen und Telephon-Verwaltung. **Added/Corp** Switzerland. Generaldirektion der Post-, Telegraphen und Telephonverwaltung. Bulletin Technique. Switzerland. Generaldirektion der Post-, Telegraphen und Telephonverwaltung. Bollettino Tecnico. **VFOAT** Bulletin Technique; Bollettino Tecnico. Vol. 1 (Feb. 1923)-(19??). German. bm. Vulkan-Verlag, Dr. W. Classen, Postfach 103962, D 45039 Essen 1 Germany. **Tel** 011 49 201 8200214, telex 8579008. **ED** Ing E Steinmetz. **LC** TK4; .S9. **CODEN** TMPTAJ. Index available. **Bk Rev. Ad Acc. Circ:** 2,800. Documents available from Ask*IEEE. ***Continued by*** *Technische Mitteilungen (Schweizerische Post-, Telephon- und Telegraphenbetriebe).*
**Desc:** Actual information from industry, economy and science.

**Ind/Abst** Alum. Ind. Abstr. (1968-); Coal Abstr.; Ei Page One; Eng. Mater. Abstr. (1968-); INSPEC (1968-); Met. Abstr. (1968-).

SZ/0040-148X
**TECHNISCHE RUNDSCHAU.** ***Title Change.*** [Tech. Rundsch.]. **VFOAT** TR; TR Technische Rundschau. (May 1949)-Vol. 85 No. 43 (Oct. 1993). Periodical. English. Fifty-two times a year. Hallwag AG, Nordring 4, CH-3001 Bern Switzerland. **Tel** 011 41 31 3323131, FAX 031/414133, telex 912661 HAWA CH. ***Continues*** *Technische Rundschau und Allgemeine Industrie- und Handelszeitung.* ***Continued by*** *TR Transfer.*
**Ind/Abst** Alum. Ind. Abstr.; Met. Abstr.; Saf. Health Work.

GW
**TECHNISCHER JAHRESBERICHT.** **Main/Corp** Berufsgenossenschaft der Feinmechanik und Elektrotechnik. German. Oberlander Ufer 130, 5 Koln 1 Germany. **LC** T55.A1; B39A.

JA/0911-5544
**TECHNO JAPAN.** [Techno Jpn.]. **Added/Corp** Fuji Gaikoku Shijo Chosa Kabushiki Kaisha. Vol. 18, No. 10 (Oct. 1985)-. Periodical. English. mo. $330.00. Fuji Marketing Research Company, 7F Daini Bunsei Building, 11-7 Toranomon 1-Chome, Minato-Ku, Tokyo 105 Japan. **(Subscription address:** Maruzen Company Ltd., PO Box 5050, Import & Export Department, Tokyo 100 31 Japan.**)** **LC** T1; .T257. **DD** 605. ***Continues*** *Technocrat, 0040-1609.*
**Ind/Abst** Abstr. J. Earthq. Eng.; HTFS Dig.

IT
**TECHNOAMBIENTE.** (19??)-. Italian. Four times a year. L50000. Ctro Sicurezza Applicata Organ, C So M D Azeglio 42, 10125 Turin Italy. **Tel** 011 39 11 6508737.

US/0040-1625
**TECHNOLOGICAL FORECASTING AND SOCIAL CHANGE.** [Technol. forecast. soc. change]. **VFOAT** Technological Forecasting & Social Change. (Aug. 1970)-. Academic Scholarly Publication. English. Nine times a year (3 volumes). $397.00 US; $444.00 other. Elsevier Science Publishing Company Inc, Madison Square Station, PO Box 882, New York NY 10159-0882. **Tel** (212)633-3950, FAX (212)633-3990. **ED** Harold A Linstone. **LC** T174; .T38. **DD** 658.4/01. **CODEN** TFSCB3. **[CCC]**. **Pr Rev.** available on microfilm and microfiche from University Microfilms International (UMI). Documents available from Article Express International, The Genuine Article, Ask*IEEE, Documents on Demand. ***Continues*** *Technological Forecasting, 0099-3964.*
**Desc:** A major forum for those who wish to deal directly with methodology and practice of technological forecasting and future studies as planning tools as they interrelate social, environmental and technological factors.
**Ind/Abst** Acad. Search (July 1993-); Bioeng. Abstr.; Bus. Index (1985-); Bus. Period. Index; Coal Abstr.; Commun. Abstr.; Contents Pages Manage.; Curr. Contents Soc. Behav. Sci.; Curr. Lit. Sci. Sci.; Ei Page One; EMBASE; Energy Inf. Abstr.; Energy Res. Abstr. (March 1978-); Eng. Index Annu.; Environ. Abstr.; Gen. BusinessFile (1985-); Gen. Period. Index (1985-); Geogr. Abstr. Phys. Geogr.; Geogr. Abstr. Human Geogr.; Highw. Res. Abstr.; INFO-SOUTH Abstr.; INSPEC (1970-); Int. Abstr. Oper. Res. [Select. Cov.]; Int. Aerosp. Abstr.; Int. Dev. Abstr.; Int. Polit. Sci. Abstr.; J. Plan. Lit.; Mag. Search; Manage. Market. Abstr.; Oper. Res./Manag. Sci.; Life Sci. Collect.; Qual. Control Appl. Stat.; Res. Alert [Full Cov.]; Selec. Coop. Index Manage. Period; Soc. Plann. Policy Dev. Abstr.; Soc. Sci. Cit. Index [Full Cov.]; Sociol. Abstr.; Wilson Bus. Abstr.

FR
**TECHNOLOGIE SCIENCES & TECHNIQUES INDUSTRIELLES.** (19??)-. French. Nine times a year. 230.00F France; 275.00F other. Centre National Documentation Pedagogique, 21 Square St. Charles, BP 7, 75012 Paris, France. **Tel** 011 33 1 40020333, 011 33 1 46349425. **(Subscription address:** CNDP Abonnements, B 750, 60732 Genevieve Cedex 9 France.**)** ***Continues*** *Techniques Industrielles.*

CN/0840-4836
**TECHNOLOGIES DE L'INFORMATION ET SOCIETE.** (TECHNOLOGIES DE L'INFORMATION ET SOCIETE : [REVUE].). [Technol. inf. soc.]. **Added/Corp** Presses de l'Universite du Quebec. Societe Quebecoise de Communication et de Recherche en Informatique. Technologies de l'Information et Societe. **VFOAT** TIS. Vol. 1, No 1 (1988)-. Periodical. French (summaries and/or abstracts in English and Spanish). Four times a year. 530.00F (institutions), 300.00F (individuals), 200.00F (students). Dunod Gauthier Villars, 15 rue Gossin, 92543 Montrouge cedex France. **Tel** 011 33 1 46 56 52 66, FAX 011 33 1 46 57 40 69. **(Subscription address:** Centrale des Revues, 11 rue Gossin, 92543 Montrouge Cedex France.**)** **LC** PAR. **CODEN** TINSEG. Documents available from Ask*IEEE.
**Ind/Abst** INSPEC (1988-); Point Repere (1988-); Soc. Plann. Policy Dev. Abstr.

FR/0992-1788
**TECHNOLOGIES PARIS. 1988.** (TECHNOLOGIES.). (1988)-. Periodical. French. mo. Cepit Groupe Usine Nouvelle, 6 Rue Marius Aufan BTMT D 1 ET, F 92300 Levallois Perr France. **Tel** 011 33 1 47582020. **UDC** 65. ***Continues*** *L'Usine Nouvelle. Edition Mensuelle, 0150-682X.*
**Ind/Abst** Int. Labour Doc.

CN/0825-5172
**TECHNOLOGUE.** (LE TECHNOLOGUE / ORDRE DES TECHNOLOGUES DES SCIENCES APPLIQUEES DU QUEBEC.). [Technologue]. **Added/Corp** Ordre des Technologues des Sciences Appliquees du Quebec. (April 1984)-. Periodical. French (English). Six times a year. 30.00Can$ Canada; 35.00Can$ other. Corporation Professionnelle des Technologues des Sciences Appliquees du Quebec, 1265 Berri Bureau 720, Montreal Quebec H2L 4X4 Canada. **Tel** (514)845-3247, FAX (514)845-3643. **ED** Michel Douville. **DD** 606/.0714. **Ad Acc. Circ:** 15,000. ***Continues*** *Bulletin d'Information (Corporation Professionnelle des Technologues des Sciences Appliquees du Quebec), 0711-530X.*
**Desc:** Technology in general - new products, information, etc., as well as professional law issues in Quebec.

US/1050-043X
**TECHNOLOGY ACCESS REPORT.** [Technol. access rep.]. **Added/Corp** University R&D Opportunities, Inc. Vol. 2, No. 2 (Apr. 10, 1989)-. Periodical. English. mo. $497.00 US, Canada, and Mexico; $572.00 other. Univ. R&D Opportunities Inc., 16 Digital Drive, Suite 250, Novato CA 94949. **Tel** (415)883-7600. **DD** 605. **[CCC]**. available on an online database (files 16,636/Full-Text) from DIALOG. ***Continues*** *Technology Access.*
**Ind/Abst** PROMT [Full Txt.]; PTS Newsl. Database [Full Txt.].

US/1054-4267
**TECHNOLOGY ALERT (PLANTATION, FLA.).** (TECHNOLOGY ALERT.). [Technol. alert]. **VFOAT** MAA Technology Alert. (Jan. 1987)-. Periodical. English. bm. $109.00 US; $129.00 Canada; $159.00 (surface), $179.00 (air) other. Merton Allen Associates, PO Box 15640, Plantation FL 33318-5640. **DD** 605. available on an online database (file 636/Full-Text) from DIALOG.

UK/0953-7325
**TECHNOLOGY ANALYSIS & STRATEGIC MANAGEMENT.** **VFOAT** Technology Analysis and Strategic Management. (1989)-. Periodical. English. qt. £148.00. Carfax Publishing Company, PO Box 25 Abingdon, Oxfordshire OX14 3UE England. **Tel** 011 44 235 555335, FAX (0279)31067, telex 817484. **(Subscription address:** US and Canada/ PO Box 2025, Dunnellon, FL 34430-2025; telephone:(904)489-6996**)** **ED** harry Rothman. **LC** HD45; .T3957. **DD** 658.4/012/05. **[CCC]**. Index available. available on microfiche. Documents available from UMI Article Clearinghouse.
**Ind/Abst** ABI/INFORM Glob. Ed.; Geogr. Abstr. Human Geogr.; Int. Dev. Abstr.

US/0040-165X
**TECHNOLOGY AND CULTURE.** [Technol. cult.]. **Added/Corp** Society for the History of Technology. Vol. 1 (Winter 1959)-. Periodical. English. qt (4 issues). $71.00 institution, $32.00 individual (all individual subscribers are enrolled as members of the Society for the History of Technology), $26.00 emeritus, $20.00 student. University of Chicago Press / Journals Division, PO Box 37005, 5720 South Woodlawn, Chicago IL 60637. **Tel** (312)753-3347, FAX (312)753-0811. **(Subscription telephone:** (312)753-8083**)** **ED** Robert C. Post. **LC** T1; .T27. **NLM** W1 TE211. **[CCC]**. **Pr Rev. Acid Free.** available on microfilm and microfiche from University Microfilms International (UMI). Documents available from The Genuine Article, UMI Article Clearinghouse.
**Desc:** Investigates the interaction of technology with its social and cultural environment; it transcends cultural and geographical boundaries to provide a scope of research extending from examinations of specific devices to analyses of the complex relationship between technology and society.
**Ind/Abst** Acad. Abstr. Full Text Elite (July 1990-); Acad. Abstr. (July 1990-); Acad. Ind. [Computer File] (1987-); Acad. Search (July 1990-); Am. Hist. Life (1960-); Am. Bibliogr. Slavic East Europ. Stud.; Appl. Sci. Technol. Index; Appl. Soc. Sci. Index Abstr.; Art Archaeol. Tech. Abstr.; Arts Humanit. Citation Index [Full Cov.]; BHA : Biblio. Hist. Art; Book Rev. Index; Br. Archaeol. Bibliogr.; Curr. Contents Arts Humanit.; Curr. Contents Soc. Behav. Sci.; EMBASE; Expand. Acad. Index (1987-); Gen. Period. Index (1987-); INFO-SOUTH Abstr.; Int. Aerosp. Abstr.; Int. Bibliogr. Sociol.; Int. Civil Eng. Abstr.; Mag. Search; Middle East Abstr. Index; Newsp. Period. Abstr. (1991-); Res. Alert [Full Cov.]; Soc. Plann. Policy Dev. Abstr.; Soc. Sci. Source (Jul. 1990-); Soc. Sci. Cit. Index [Full Cov.]; Soc. Sci. Index; Soc. Sci. Index Fulltext (Oct. 1988-) [Full Txt.]; Sociol. Abstr.; Soft. Abstr. Eng.; West. Hist. Q.

US/0890-7889
**TECHNOLOGY AND LEARNING.** ***Ceased.*** [Technol. learn.]. Vol. 1, No. 1 (1987)-Ceased with Vol. 3. Periodical. English. bm. Lawrence Erlbaum Associates, 365 Broadway, Suite 102, Hillsdale NJ 07642. **Tel** (201)666-4110, (800)926-6579, FAX (201)666-2394.
**Ind/Abst** Abstr. Hum. Comput. Interact. (?-?).

US/0364-9105
**TECHNOLOGY ASSESSMENT & FORECAST.** **Added/Corp** United States. Patent and Trademark Office. Office of Technology Assessment and Forecast. **VAT** Technology Assessment and Forecast. (Aug. 1975)-. Government Publication. English. ir. Superintendent of Documents, US Government Printing Office, Washington DC 20402. **Tel** (202)275-3328, FAX (202)786-2377. **LC** T223.J4; U54a. **DD** 608/.7/73. ***Continues*** *Technology Assessment and Forecast, 0364-9105.*

US/0882-8660
**TECHNOLOGY ASSESSMENT (COMPUTER/ELECTRONICS ED.).** (TECHNOLOGY ASSESSMENT.). [Technol. assess.]. Began in 1984?. Periodical. English. mo. $225.00. American Institute of Technology Assessment, Box 730, Concord MA 01742. **LC** T1; .T276. **DD** 605.

US/0092-2234
**TECHNOLOGY ASSESSMENT (NEW YORK, N.Y.).** (TECHNOLOGY ASSESSMENT.). [Technol. assess.]. V. 1- 1972-. Periodical. English. Gordon & Breach Science Publishers, Inc., PO Box 786, Cooper Station, New York NY 10276. **Tel** (212)206-8900, FAX (212)645-2459. **(Subscription address:** International Publishers Distributor at one of the following addresses: 820 Town Center Drive, Langhorne, PA 19047; or PO Box 90, Reading Berkshire RG1 8JL UK; or Kent Ridge PO Box 1180, Singapore 9111, Republic of Singapore**)** **LC** T174.5; .T4. **DD** 301.24/3.

US/0273-2580
**TECHNOLOGY (BOCA RATON).** (TECHNOLOGY.). [Technology]. **Added/Corp** Social Issues Resources Series, Inc. Vol. 1, Article 1 (1978)-. English. Social Issues Resources Series Inc, PO Box 2348, Boca Raton FL 33427. **Tel** (800)327-0513, (407)994-0079. **ED** E. C. Goldstein. **LC** T14.5; .T4413. **DD** 303.4/83.
**Desc:** Interdisciplinary resource material consisting of reprinted articles from popular and professional journals, newspapers, magazines and government documents.

US/0091-7885
**TECHNOLOGY BOOK GUIDE.** 1974-. English. an. GK Hall & Co, 100 Front Street, Riverside NJ 08075. **Tel** (800)257-5755 ext. 2223. **LC** Z7913; .T466; T45. **DD** 016.6.

US/0895-903X
**TECHNOLOGY BUSINESS.** [Technol. bus.]. **Added/Corp** Southern California Technology Executives' Network. **VFOAT** Financing & Developing Technology Business; Financing and Developing Technology Business. (1987)-. Periodical. English. qt. $39.00 US and Canada. Technology Business, 4667 MacArthur Building Suite 200, Newport Beach CA 92660. **Tel** (714)852-9115. **DD** 650. ***Continues*** *Southern California Technology Business, 0888-9821.*
**Desc:** For technology executives; contains features written by, for and about technology company entrepreneurs seeking to finance and expand their companies.

UK/0965-0326
**TECHNOLOGY COMMERCIALISATION (EUROPE ED.).** (TECHNOLOGY COMMERCIALISATION.). [Technol. commer.]. (1991)-. Periodical. English. mo. Technology Commercialisation, Ltd. / England, Premier House 8, 10 Portland Terrace, Southampton SO1 0EG England. **Tel** 011 44 703 211600.

US/1059-292X
**TECHNOLOGY COMMERCIALIZATION (NORTH AMERICAN ED.).** (TECHNOLOGY COMMERCIALIZATION.). [Technol. commer.]. (1991)-. Periodical. English. mo. $175.00. Technology Commercialisation, Ltd. / Virginia, PO Box 10060, Arlington VA 22210. **DD** 338.

US/0163-2698
**TECHNOLOGY EXCHANGE BULLETIN.** [Tech. exch. bull.]. V. 1- Oct. 1978-. Bulletin. English. mo. $24.00 US; $30.00 other. Institute for Invention and Innovation, PO Box 436, Arlington MA 02174.

US/0886-0890
**TECHNOLOGY FORECASTS AND TECHNOLOGY SURVEYS.** [Technol. forecasts technol. surv.]. (1968)-. Periodical. English. mo. $160.00 US; $164.00 Canada and Mexico; $172.00 other. Technology Forecasts, 205 South Beverly Drive, Suite 208, Beverly Hills CA 90212. **Tel** (310)273-3486. **ED** Irwin Stambler and Willard Wilks. **DD** 600. **Bk Rev.**
**Desc:** Presents information on major advances and forecasts of future trends in many areas of science and technology. Articles on forecasting methodology also may be presented.

US/0896-744X
**TECHNOLOGY FUTURES NEWSLETTER.** ***Title Change.*** [Technol. futures newsl.]. **VFOAT** Technology Futures. (198?)-(19??). Periodical. English. Twelve times a year. Burrus Research Associates Inc., PO Box 26413, Milwaukee WI

53226. **Tel** (414)774-7790, (800)827-6770, FAX (414)774-8330. **ED** Patti A. Thomsen (phone: (414)786-7232). **DD** 605. cum. index. ***Continued by*** *Technotrends Newsletter.*
**Desc:** News and information on the futures of our technology in different aspects such as diseases, brain research, biodegradable fish nets and lines, cancer, batteries and other related fields.

US/0160-791X
**TECHNOLOGY IN SOCIETY.** [Technol. soc.]. Vol. 1 (Spring 1979)-. Academic Scholarly Publication. English. qt. $455.00 The Americas; £305.00 other. Pergamon Press, An Imprint of Elsevier Science Ltd., The Boulevard, Langford Lane, Kidlington, Oxford OX5 1GB United Kingdom. **Tel** 011 44 865 843000, 011 44 865 843699, FAX 011 44 865 843010. **(Subscription address:** Elsevier Science Ltd. Oxford Fulfillment Centre, PO Box 800, Kidlington, Oxford OX5 1DX United Kingdom.**) ED** George Bugliarello and George Schillinger. **LC** T14.5; .T443. **DD** 303.4/83/05. **[CCC]. Pr Rev.** available on microfilm and microfiche from University Microfilms International (UMI). Documents available from The Genuine Article, Documents on Demand.
**Desc:** Provides a focus for a wide range of interdisciplinary fields most simply identified by these terms: technology assessment; science, technology and society; economics of technology; technology transfer; appropriate technology and economic development; ethical and value implications of science and technology; and technology forecasting.
**Ind/Abst** Biostatistica; Commun. Abstr. (?-?); Curr. Contents Soc. Behav. Sci.; Ei Page One; EMBASE; Energy Inf. Abstr.; Energy Res. Abstr. (Jan. 1982-); Environ. Abstr.; Ergon. Abstr.; Index Period. Artic. Relat. Law; Inf. Sci. Abstr.; Int. Aerosp. Abstr.; Oper. Res./Manag. Sci.; Qual. Control Appl. Stat.; Res. Alert [Full Cov.]; Soc. Plann. Policy Dev. Abstr.; Soc. Sci. Cit. Index [Full Cov.]; Sociol. Abstr.

IE/0040-1676
**TECHNOLOGY IRELAND.** [Technol. Irel.]. **Added/Corp** Institute for Industrial Research and Standards (Ireland). Technical Information Division. Institute for Industrial Research and Standards (Ireland) Institute for Industrial Research and Standards (Ireland). Technical Information Dept. Vol. 1 (Apr. 1969)-. Academic Scholarly Publication. English. Ten times a year (monthly with July/Aug. and Nov./Dec. issues combined). 25.00p Ireland; 28.50p UK & Northern Ireland; 32.00p Europe; 45.50p other. Forbairt, Glasnevin, Dublin 9 Ireland. **Tel** 011 353 1 8370101, FAX 011 353 1 8367122, telex 32501. **ED** Tom Kennedy and Mary Mulvihill. **LC** T1; .T278. **DD** 605. **CODEN** TEIRDR. Index available. cum. index. **Bk Rev. Ad Acc, Adv Mgr:** D. Black. **Circ:** 5,500 (ctrl).
**Desc:** Materials Ireland is an industrially oriented R+D organsiation which brings together 5 major research institutions and many of Ireland's leading experts in Materials Technology. Industrialists can now access directly a unique range of capabilities and in-depth expertise.
**Ind/Abst** BioBusiness (1989-); Coal Abstr.; EMBASE; Food Sci. Technol. Abstr.; Int. Civil Eng. Abstr.; Int. Packag. Abstr.; Nonwovens Abstr.; Pap. Board Abstr.; Print. Abstr.; Soft. Abstr. Eng.; World Publ. Monit.

US/0886-103X
**TECHNOLOGY MANAGEMENT ACTION.** [Techol. manage. action]. (19??)-. Periodical. English. mo. $145.00 (one year), $250.00 (two year), $301.00 (three year) US; $165.00 (one year), $285.00 (two year), $344.00 (three year) Canada and Mexico; $195.00 (one year), $336.00 (two year), $407.00 (three year) other. Technology News Center, A Division of Lynn-Western Newswires, 6810 Butler Valley Road, Korbel CA 95550. **Tel** (707)668-4027, FAX (707)668-4055. **ED** Norman Lynn. **DD** 658. Index available. cum. index. **Bk Rev. Circ:** 3,500. available on an online database from Lynn-Western Newswires Bulletin Board System.
**Desc:** Edited for professionals engaged in technology, policy, planning, marketing, financing, technology transfer, worldwide.

CN/0824-0353
**TECHNOLOGY NOTEBOOK (TECHNICAL UNIVERSITY OF NOVA SCOTIA).** ***Ceased.*** (TECHNOLOGY NOTEBOOK.). [Technol. noteb.]. Vol. 1, No. 1, Oct. (1982)-?. Periodical. English. wk. Technical University of Nova Scotia, PO Box 1000, Halifax Nova Scotia B3J 2X4 Canada. **DD** 609/.71.

US/1058-2282
**TECHNOLOGY NY REPORT.** [Technol. NY rep.]. **Added/Corp** Anderson Research & Communications (Firm : Troy, N.Y.). **VFOAT** Technology Report. **VAT** Technology New York Report. Vol. 6, No. 1 Jan. (1988)-. Periodical. English. Eleven times a year. $150.00 US and Canada; $170.00 other. Technology New York, 1223 Peoples Avenue, Troy NY 12180. **Tel** (518)276-8769, FAX (518)276-6380. **ED** Olga K. Anderson. **DD** 605. **Circ:** 1,000.
**Desc:** Covers high technology developments in business, the public sector and academia, focusing principally on New York State.

JA/0030-6177
**TECHNOLOGY REPORTS OF THE OSAKA UNIVERSITY.** **See** Engineering.

JA
**TECHNOLOGY REPORTS OF THE TOHOKU UNIVERSITY. LIST OF OTHER PUBLICATIONS, THE.** **VFOAT** Tohoku Daigaku Kogaku Hokoku; Kokogaku Hokoku. List of other Publications. No. 1 (1976-1980)-. English (Japanese). Tohoku Daigaku Kogakubu Aza Aoba, Aramaki, Sendai-shi 980 Japan. **LC** Z7911; .T43; T1. **DD** 016.6.

JA/0386-3433
**TECHNOLOGY REPORTS OF THE YAMAGUCHI UNIVERSITY.** [Technol. rep. Yamaguchi Univ.]. **Main/Corp** Yamaguchi Daigaku. Vol. 1 (Dec 1972)-. Academic Scholarly Publication. English. Yamaguchi Daigaku Kogakubu / Engineering, (Faculty of Engineering, Yamaguchi University), Tokiwadai, Ubesei, Yamaguchiken 755, Japan. **LC** T1; .Y34a. **DD** 605. **CODEN** TRYUAY. Documents available from Ask*IEEE, CASDDS.
**Ind/Abst** Chem. Abstr.; GeoRef; INSPEC (Dec. 1983-); Int. Aerosp. Abstr.

US
**TECHNOLOGY RESOURCE GUIDES.** (1993)-. English. an. $495.00. Corporate Technology Information Services Inc, 12 Alfred Street, Suite 200, Woburn MA 01801-9998. **Tel** (617)932-3939, (800)333-8036, FAX (617)932-6335, telex 497-2961 CRPTECH. Index available. **Bk Rev. Circ:** 5,000 (ctrl). available on an online database from ORBIT.
**Desc:** The series of regional Technology Resource Guides profile thousands of local technology manufacturers - firms involved in such high growth, high-tech activities as lasers, computers, advanced materials and biotechnology. Detailed corporate profiles are listed alphabetically and cross indexed by city and 250+ product categories.

US/0040-1692
**TECHNOLOGY REVIEW.** [Technol. rev.]. **Added/Corp** Massachusetts Institute of Technology. Alumni Association. Massachusetts Institute of Technology. Association of Class Secretaries. Vol. 1 (Jan. 1899)-. Academic Scholarly Publication. English. Eight times a year. $30.00. Massachusetts Institute of Technology (MIT), Building W 59, Cambridge MA 02139. **Tel** (617)253-8291. **(Subscription address:** Kable Publishers Aide, 308 East Hitt Street, Subscription Department, Mt. Morris IL 61054-1473.**) ED** John I. Mattill. **LC** T171; .M47. **NLM** W1 TE211M. **CODEN** TEREAU. cum. index. **Bk Rev. Ad Acc. Pr Rev. Circ:** 75,000. available on microfilm and microfiche from University Microfilms International (UMI); available on an online database (files 15,647,648/Full-Text) from DIALOG. Documents available from Article Express International, The Genuine Article, UMI Article Clearinghouse, CASDDS, Documents on Demand.
**Desc:** Looks at the potential and problems of today's technological advancements.
**Ind/Abst** ABI/INFORM Glob. Ed.; ABI Inform Ondisc (March 1973-); Abstr. Bull. Inst. Pap. Sci. Tech.; Acad. Abstr. Full Text Elite (Feb. 1984-) [Full Txt.]; Acad. Abstr. (Feb. 1984-); Acad. Ind. [Computer File] (1984-); Acad. Search (Feb. 1984-); ACM Guide Comput. Lit.; AGRICOLA [Select. Cov.]; Am. Bibliogr. Slavic East Europ. Stud.; Appl. Sci. Technol. Index; Aviat. Tradescan [Select. Cov.]; BioBusiness; Bioeng. Abstr.; Biol. Dig.; Book Rev. Index; Bus. ASAP (1990-) [Full Txt.]; Bus. Index (1985-); Bus. Period. Index; Chem. Abstr.; Coal Abstr.; Commun. Abstr. (?-?); Comput. Bus. (19??-19??); Comput. Lit. Index; Comput. Rev.; Curr. Contents Eng. Tech. Appl. Sci.; Ei Page One; EMBASE; Energy Inf. Abstr.; Energy Res. Abstr.; Eng. Mater. Abstr.; Eng. Index Annu. [Select. Cov.]; Environ. Abstr.; Environ. Period. Bibliogr.; Expand. Acad. Index (1984-); F&S Index Plus Text, Int. [Select. Cov.]; Fut. Surv.; Gen. BusinessFile (1985-); Geogr. Abstr. Phys. Geogr. (?-?); Geogr. Abstr. Human Geogr.; Geol. Abstr.; GeoRef; Guide Soc. Sci. Relig.; Health Devices Alerts; Hospit. Health Admin. Index; INFO-SOUTH Abstr.; Int. Aerosp. Abstr.; Int. Dev. Abstr.; J. Ferrocement; J. Plan. Lit.; Mag. Artic. Summar. Elite (Feb. 1984-) [Full Txt.]; Mag. Artic. Summar. Select (Feb. 1984-) [Full Txt.]; Mag. Artic. Summar. CD-ROM (Feb. 1984-); Mag. ASAP Plus [Full Txt.]; Mag. ASAP Sel. [Full Txt.]; Mag. Express (1986-) [Full Txt.]; Mag. Index Plus (1989-); Mag. Index. Sel. (1986-); Mag. Search; Newsp. Period. Abstr. (1986-); PAIS Int. Print; PROMT; Read. Guide Abstr. Select Ed.; Read. Guide Period. Lit.; Res. Alert [Full Cov.]; Resource/One Ondisc; Robotics Abstr.; Sage Public Adm. Abstr. (?-?); Sci. Cit. Index; SCISEARCH; Soc. Sci. Cit. Index [Select. Cov.]; Surf. Treat. Technol. Abstr.; Mag. Index (1985-); UMI ABI/Inform--Bus. Period. Ondisc (Nov. 1987-) [Full Txt.]; Vocat. Search (Feb. 1984-) [Full Txt.]; Wilson Bus. Abstr.

GW
**TECHNOLOGY SOURCES.** English. Twice a year. $78.00 (add $5.90 postage). Walter de Gruyter Inc., PO Box 303421, D 10728 Berlin Germany. **Tel** 011 49 30 260050, FAX 011 49 30 26005251.

US/1059-0609
**TECHNOLOGY SPECIAL INTEREST SECTION NEWSLETTER.** **Added/Corp** American Occupational Therapy Association. Technology Special Interest Section. (1991)-. Newsletter. English. qt. $20.00. American Occupational Therapy Association, 1383 Piccard Drive, PO Box 1725, Rockville MD 20849. **Tel** (301)948-9626, FAX (301)948-5512. **ED** Jennifer Angelo. **NLM** W1; TE211NL. **Circ:** 2000 (ctrl).
**Desc:** Contains articles highlighting technical advances and applications in the field of occupational therapy.

UK/0258-0551
**TECHNOLOGY STRATEGIES.** [Technol. strateg.]. (1985)-. Periodical. English. mo. $959.00. MCB University Press, 60 62 Toller Lane, Bradford West Yorkshire BD8 9BX England. **Tel** 011 44 274 499821, FAX 011 44 274 547143, telex 51317 MCBUNI G. **(Subscription address:** MCB University Press / US and Canada Subscriptions, PO Box 10812, Birmingham AL 35201-0812.**) UDC** 65. **Circ:** 1,000.
**Desc:** Covers global technology strategies.

GW/0940-9467
**TECHNOLOGY STUDIES.** (199?)-. English. Twice a year. $84.20. Walter de Gruyter Inc., PO Box 303421, D 10728 Berlin Germany. **Tel** 011 49 30 260050, FAX 011 49 30 26005251.

US/0746-3537
**TECHNOLOGY TEACHER, THE.** [Technol. teach.]. **Added/Corp** American Industrial Arts Association. International Technology Education Association. Vol. 43, No. 1 (Sept./Oct. 1983)-. Periodical. English. mo (Eight times a year). $55.00 US; $70.00 other. International Technology Education Association, 1914 Association Drive, Reston VA 22091. **Tel** (703)860-2100, FAX (703)860-0353. **ED** Judy Miller. **LC** T61; .M28. **DD** 607/.73. Index available. cum. index. **Bk Rev. Ad Acc. Pr Rev. Circ:** 7,000. available on microfilm and microfiche from University Microfilms International (UMI). ***Continues*** *Man/Society/Technology, 0022-1813.*
**Desc:** Covering the theory, practice and application of technology education and its role in achieving a technologically literate society.
**Ind/Abst** Acad. Search (July 1993-); Curr. Index J. Educ. (March 1990); Educ. Index; INFO-SOUTH Abstr.; Mag. Search.

US
**TECHNOLOGY TODAY.** **Added/Corp** Southwest Research Institute. Vol. 1 (Sept. 1978)-. Periodical. English. Three times a year. Free on request. Southwest Research Institute / Technology Today, 6220 Culbra Road, San Antonio TX 78238. **Tel** (210)684-5111. ***Continues*** *Tomorrow Through Research.*

CN/0712-9467
**TECHNOLOGY TODAY (MISSISSAUGA).** (TECHNOLOGY TODAY / ONTARIO RESEARCH FOUNDATION.). [Technol. today]. **Added/Corp** Ontario Research Foundation. ORTECH International. (1978)-. Periodical. English. qt. Free. Ortech International, 2395 Speakman Drive, Mississauga Ontario, L5K 1B3 Canada. **Tel** (416)822-4111, FAX (416)823-1446. **ED** T Kingry. **DD** 609/.713. **CODEN** TETOE6. **Circ:** 10,000 (ctrl). ***Continues*** *Ontario Research Newsletter.*

US
**TECHNOLOGY TRACKING.** English. ir. £496.00. PRS Consulting Group Inc, 2301 West Big Beaver/Suite 620, Troy MI 48084. **Tel** (313)649-7110.

US/0889-0250
**TECHNOLOGY TRANSFER ABSTRACTS.** (TECHNOLOGY TRANSFER ABSTRACTS : TTA.). [Technol. transf. abstr.]. **VFOAT** TTA. (Oct. 1986)-. Periodical. English. qt. $100.00 US; $150.00 other. Berardino Publishing, Technology Transfer Abstracts, PO Box 9802/#831, Austin TX 78766. **DD** 605.

●US
**TECHNOLOGY TRANSFER WEEK.** **See** Military and Defense.

US/0732-5533
**TECHNOLOGY UPDATE.** ***Ceased.*** (TECHNOLOGY UPDATE / PREDICASTS.). [Technol. update]. **Added/Corp** Predicasts, Inc. Vol. 38, No. 21 (May 29, 1982)-(19??). Periodical. English. wk. Predicasts Inc., A Ziff Communications Company, 11001 Cedar Avenue, Cleveland OH 44106. **Tel** (800)321-6388, (216)795-3000, FAX (216)229-9944, telex 985 604. **(Subscription address:** Information Access Company, PO Box 61000, Department 1851, San Francisco, CA 94161; Phone: (800)321-6388**) LC** T1; .G3. **DD** 605. **NLM** ZQ 1 T24. **[CCC]. *Continues*** *Technical Survey (Newark, N.J.), 0040-1005.*

AT/0158-2755
**TECHNOTE DARWIN.** [Technote Darwin]. (1979)-. Monographic series. English. tw. Free. Department of Primary Industry & Fisheries, GPO Box 990, Darwin Northern Territory 5794 Australia. **Tel** 895511, telex 1410825. **DD** 338.099429. **Circ:** 100.
**Ind/Abst** Soils Fert.

FR
**TECHNOTES. REPORTS.** (19??)-. Periodical. English (French). ir. $500.00 (per Report). Innovation 128, 24 rue du Quatre Septembre, 75002 Paris France. **Tel** 011 33 1 42680971.

US
**TECHNOTRENDS NEWSLETTER.** (19??)-. English. Twelve times a year. $49.95 (one year), $70.00 (two years). Burrus Research Associates Inc., PO Box 26413, Milwaukee WI 53226. **Tel** (414)774-7790, (800)827-6770, FAX (414)774-8330. **ED** Patti A. Thomsen. Index available. cum. index. ***Continues*** *Technology Futures Newsletter.*

US/1054-979X
**TECHSCAN (NEW YORK, N.Y.).** (TECHSCAN : THE MANAGER'S GUIDE TO TECHNOLOGY.). [TechScan]. **Added/Corp** Richmond Research. **VFOAT** Tech Scan. Mar. (1991)-. Periodical. English. mo. $87.50. Richmond Research, PO Box 537, Village Station, New York NY 10014-0537. **DD** 658.

FR
**TECHTRENDS.** **VFOAT** Techtendances. (19??)-. Monographic series. English (French). ir. Price varies per volume. Innovation 128, 24 rue du Quatre Septembre, 75002 Paris France. **Tel** 011 33 1 42680971.

US/0891-267X
**TECHTRENDS INTERNATIONAL.** [TechTrends int.]. **VFOAT** Tech Trends International; TechTrends; Tech Trends; International TechTrends; International Tech Trends. Vol. 1, No. 1 (Feb. 3, 1986)-. Periodical. English. wk. $800.00 (cover), $395.00 (charter member), $295.00 (institutions). Technology Trends Inc, 2425 Wilson Boulevard/Suite 307, Arlington VA 22201-3385. **DD** 605.

IT
**TECNEWS.** ***Ceased.*** (19??)-(Dec. 1992). Italian. mo. Tecmen Srl, P de Ferrari 4/63, 16121 Genoa Italy. **Tel** 011 39 10 291968.

SP
**TECNICA DEL PUNTO.** Spanish. mo. 6980ptas Spain; 6900ptas other. Prensa Tecnica, Caspe 118, 120 Piso 6-1A, 08013 Barcelona Spain. **Tel** 011 34 3 2455190, 011 34 3 2455198, 011 34 3 2455199.

CU/0138-8800
**TECNICA POPULAR.** Periodical. Spanish. bm. Ediciones Cubanas, Obispo 527, Altos ESQ Bernaza, CP 10100 Havana Cuba. **Tel** 011 632980, 631942, FAX 011 631011, telex 512337, 6540. **LC** T4; .T226. **DD** 605.

CK/0367-8210
**TECNOLOGIA.** [Tecnolog,ia]. **Added/Corp** Instituto de Investigaciones Tecnologicas (Bogota, Colombia). **VFOAT** IIT Tecnologia; Revista del Instituto de Investigaciones Tecnologicas. **VAT** Instituto de Investigaciones Tecnologicas Tecnologia. No. 21 (Jan./Feb. 1963)-. Periodical. Spanish. bm. ***Continues*** *Revista del Instituto de Investigaciones Technologicas.*
**Ind/Abst** Sorghum Mill. Abstr.

IT
**TECNOLOGIA DELLA DEFORMAZIONE.** (19??)-(19??). Italian. bm. L45000. Morgan Edizioni Ecniche, Piazzale Archinto 9, 20159 Milan Italy. **Tel** (039)02-48010095, FAX 48010011.

CR/0379-3982
**TECNOLOGIA EN MARCHA / INSTITUTO TECNOLOGICO--COSTA RICA.** **Added/Corp** Instituto Tecnologico (Costa Rica). (19??)-. Periodical. Spanish. qt. Instituto Tecnologico de Costa Rica, Apartado 159-7050, Cartago Costa Rica. **LC** T4; .T22735. **DD** 605. ***Continues*** *Revista Tecnologia en Marcha.*
**Ind/Abst** Agrofor. Abstr. (1991-); Biodeter. Abstr. (1991-); For. Prod. Abstr. (1991-); For. Abstr.; Hortic. Abstr.; Plant Grow. Reg. Abstr.; Postharvest News Inf.; Rev. Med. Vet. Mycology; Seed Abstr.

SP/0214-4662
**TECNOLOGIA Y ARQUITECTURA.** Spanish. qt. 6000.00ptas. Ignacio Saez de Ibarra, Samaniego 6, 01008 Vitoria-Gasteiz Spain. **Tel** 011 34 1 45248100.

AG
**TECNOLOGIA Y GESTION.** **Added/Corp** Instituto Argentino de Racionalizacion de Materiales. **VFOAT** IRAM, Tecnologia y Gestion. (19??)-. Periodical. Spanish. qt. Instituto Argentino de Racionalizacion de Materiales Chile, 1192 Buenos Aires Argentina. **LC** TA401; .I42. ***Continues*** *Instituto Argentino de Racionalizacion de Materiales. IRAM, Tecnologia y Gestion.*

IT
**TECNOLOGIE PER LA SANITA.** Edisan, Via Paitone 9, 25122 Brescia Italy.

YU/0040-2176
**TEHNIKA (BEOGRAD).** (TEHNIKA.). [Tehnika]. Began 1946. Periodical. Serbo-Croatian (Roman) (summaries and/or abstracts in English, French, German and Russian). mo. **(Subscription address:** Jugoslovenska Knjiga, PO Box 36, YU 11001 Belgrade Yugoslovia.**) CODEN** TEHBA5. Documents available from Ask*IEEE, CASDDS.
**Ind/Abst** Alum. Ind. Abstr.; Chem. Abstr.; Coal Abstr.; Energy Res. Abstr.; INSPEC (1967-); Met. Abstr.

FI/0040-2303
**TEKNIIKKA.** [Tekniikka]. (1970)-. Periodical. Finnish (summaries and/or abstracts in English, German and Swedish). mo. **LC** T4; .T245. ***Supersedes*** *Teknillinen Aikakauslehti; Insinoorilehti.*
**Ind/Abst** Energy Res. Abstr. (Jan. 1971-); Selec. Coop. Index Manage. Period.

SW
**TEKNISK TIDSKRIFT-NY TEKNIK.** **VFOAT** NY Teknik-Teknisk Tidskrift. Began with issue for Feb. 22, 1979. Periodical. Swedish. ir. Kr200.00. Ingenjorsforlaget AB, Box 27315, 102 54 Stockholm Sweden. **Tel** (08)651750. **LC** T4; .T285. ctrl circ. ***Formed by the union of*** *NY Teknik* ***and*** *Teknisk Tidskrift.*
**Ind/Abst** Energy Res. Abstr. (Feb. 1979-); Eng. Mater. Abstr.; Int. Packag. Abstr.

NO/0800-532X
**TEKNISK UKEBLAD.** **Added/Corp** Norske Sivilingenirers Forening. Polytekniske Forening (Norway). Norges Ingenirorganisasjon -- NITO. **VFOAT** Technology Review Weekly; Teknisk Ukeblad, Teknikk; TU; Teknisk Ukeblad/Teknikk. (1977)-. Periodical. Norwegian. Forty-eight times a year. $120.00. Ingeniorforlaget A S, Kronprinsens Gate 17, 0202 Oslo 2 Norway. ***Continues*** *Teknisk Ukeblad Teknikk.*
**Ind/Abst** Saf. Health Work; Selec. Coop. Index Manage. Period.

MY
**TEKNOLOGI.** **Added/Corp** Universiti Teknologi Malaysia. Fakulti Kejuruteraan Letrik. (April 1977)-. Periodical. English (Malay). Twice a year. $10.00. Universiti Teknologi Malaysia, Gurney Road, 54100 Kuala Lumpur Malaysia. **Tel** FAX 07 572555, telex UTM MA 60205. **ED** Mohd Zali B. Shaari. **LC** T1; .T34. **Circ:** 500.

IT
**TEKNOS.** Italian. bm. L75.000. Iniziativa 2000, Via Santa Maria Valle 1, 20123 Milan Italy. **Tel** (6)3295207. **ED** G Raiola and F Bulgarelli. **Bk Rev. Ad Acc. Pr Rev. Circ:** 10,000.
**Desc:** Papers and pieces of information by researchers, statesmen, and managers on technological innovation. Each issue reports a historical survey evidencing the advances of science and technology in the past.

TU
**TEKSTIL & TEKNIK.** (19??)-. Turkish. Twelve times a year. $100.00. Tekstil & Teknik, Catalcesme SK, 17 2 Cagaloglu, Istanbul Turkey 34410. **Tel** 010 9011 526 180000.

PL
**TEMAT.** Periodical. Polish. RSW Prasa-Kriazka-Ruch, Centrala Kolportazu Prasy i Wydawnictw, Towarowa 28, 00-958 Warsaw Poland. **LC** T212; .R32. ***Continues*** *Wynalazczosc I Racjonalizacja.*

XR
**TEORIE VEDY.** **Added/Corp** Ustav Teorie a Historie Vedy CSAV. Vysoka Skola Ekonomicka v Praze. **VFOAT** TV; Theory of Science. (1990)-. Periodical. Czech. qt. Ustav Teorie a Degin Vedy CSAV, Ed 0 SMrcek, Jilska 1 110 00 Prague 1 Czech Republic. **Tel** 296451. **LC** Q44; .T26. ***Continues*** *Teorie Rozvoje Vedy, 0139-987X.*

HU/0040-3717
**TERMESZET VILAGA.** **Added/Corp** Tudomanyos Ismeretterjeszto Tarsulat. Vol. 12, No. 1, Jan. (1968)-. Periodical. Hungarian (table of contents in English, German and Russian). mo. **LC** Q44; .B93. **CODEN** TEVIAS. Documents available from CASDDS. ***Continues*** *Termeszettudomanyi Kozlony.*
**Ind/Abst** Chem. Abstr.

US
**TESSERACT. EARLY SCIENTIFIC INSTRUMENTS.** (19??)-. English. Four times a year (Mar., June, Sept., Nov.). $18.00. Tesseract, PO Box 151, Hastings-on-Hudson NY 10706. **Tel** (914)478-2594, FAX (914)478-5473.
**Desc:** Catalog of early scientific and medical instruments for sale.

US/0896-9779
**TEXAS HIGH TECHNOLOGY DIRECTORY.** [Tex. high technol. dir.]. 1988/89-. Directory. English. an. $110.00. Leading Edge Communications, 1121 Old Siskiyou Highway, Ashland OR 97520. **Tel** (503)482-4990. **ED** Charles J Koelsch. **DD** 338. **Circ:** 1,000.
**Desc:** A comprehensive reference tool for those interested in high tech research and development and high tech manufacturing firms in Texas.

US/0040-4403
**TEXAS JOURNAL OF SCIENCE, THE.** [Tex. j. sci.]. Vol. 1 (March 1949)-. Academic Scholarly Publication. English. qt. $50.00. Texas Academy of Science, PO Box 10986, ASU Station, San Angelo TX 76909. **Tel** (915)942-2184. **ED** Dr J Knox Jones, Jr. **LC** Q1. **DD** 505. **NLM** W1 TE774. **CODEN** TJSCAU. **Pr Rev. Circ:** 1000. Documents available from The Genuine Article, BIOSIS Document Express, Ask*IEEE, CASDDS.
**Ind/Abst** AGRICOLA [Select. Cov.]; Biol. Abstr.; Chem. Abstr.; Curr. Aware. Biol. Sci., CABS; Curr. Contents, Agric. Biol. Environ. Sci.; EMBASE; Fish Rev. (Jan. 1989-July 1992); For. Abstr.; GeoRef; Grasslands For. Abstr.; Helminthol. Abstr. (1991-); Hortic. Abstr.; INSPEC (Feb. 1972-); Int. Aerosp. Abstr.; Math. Rev.; Ornamental Hort. (1991-); Life Sci. Collect.; Protozoolog. Abstr.; Res. Alert [Select. Cov.]; Rev. Med. Vet. Entomol.; Soils Fert.; Wildl. Rev. (Jan. 1989-July 1992).

TH
**THAI ABSTRACTS. SERIES A: SCIENCE AND TECHNOLOGY.** **Added/Corp** Sun Borikan Ekkasan Kanwichai Hng Prathet Thai. No. 1 (Jan. 1974)-. English. Thai National Documentation Center, 196 Phahonyothin Road, 9 Bangkok Thailand. **LC** Q1; .T44. **DD** 508/.1.

SP/0495-4548
**THEORIA.** **See** Philosophy.

II/0970-860X
**THIRD WORLD SCIENCE & ENVIRONMENT PERSPECTIVES.** [Third world sci. environ. perspect.]. **Added/Corp** Centre for Science, Technology, and Environmental Policy Studies (New Delhi, India). **VFOAT** Third World Science and Environment Perspectives; STEPS Quarterly. (1989)-. Periodical. English. qt. $25.00. Centre for Science Technology & Environmental Policy Studies, New Delhi, India. **(Subscription address:** Prints India, 11 Darya Ganj, New Delhi, 110002 India, (Phone: 011 91 11 3268645)**) LC** Q180.D44; T45. **DD** 338.926/09172/4.

SA
**TI, TECHNICAL INFORMATION FOR INDUSTRY.** **Main/Corp** South African Council for Scientific and Industrial Research. Vol. 1 (Jan. 1963)-. Periodical. English. ir. CSIR Publishing Division, PO Box 395, Pretoria 0001 South Africa. **Tel** 011 27 12 8412911 ext. 3765. **ED** E. L. Burger. ctrl circ.
**Desc:** Informs industry and interested persons about research and developments at the CSIR and services available.
**Ind/Abst** Energy Res. Abstr. (July 1977-).

CC/0493-2137
**TIANJIN DAXUE XUEBAO.** (TIEN-CHIN TA HSUEH HSUEH PAO.). [Tianjin daxue xuebao]. **Added/Corp** Tien-Chin ta Hsueh. **VFOAT** Journal of Tianjin University. (19??)-. Academic Scholarly Publication. Chinese (summaries and/or abstracts in English). bm. $4.14. Tianjin Daxue / Tianjin University, Qilitai, Nankai qu, Tianjin 300072, People's Republic of China. **Tel** 3358116. **(Subscription address:** China International Book Trading Corporation, PO Box 399, Library Service Department, Beijing 100044 People's Republic of China.**) ED** W. Yongshi. **LC** Q4; .T43. **DD** 505. **CODEN** TCHHA9. **Circ:** 3,700. Documents available from Article Express International, CASDDS.
**Desc:** An advanced academic publication which carries papers on recent achievements in scientific research, mainly on technology and engineering.
**Ind/Abst** Bioeng. Abstr.; Chem. Abstr.; Ei Page One; Eng. Index Annu.; Math. Rev.

CH
**TIEN HSIN CHI SHU / TELECOMS TECHNICAL QUARTERLY.** **Added/Corp** China (Republic : 1949-). Tien Hsin Tsung Chu. **VFOAT** Telecoms Technical Quarterly. (1981)-. Periodical. Chinese (summaries and/or abstracts in English). qt. Directorate General of Telecommunications, 31 Aikuo East Road, Taipei 106 Taiwan. **LC** TK5101.A1; T53. **DD** 621.38/05.

US/1041-6587
**TIES (PHILADELPHIA, PA.).** (TIES : TECHNOLOGY, INNOVATION & ENTREPRENEURSHIP FOR STUDENTS.). [TIES]. **Added/Corp** Drexel University. **VFOAT** Technology, Innovation & Entrepreneurship for Students; TIES Magazine. (Jan./Feb. 1989)-. Periodical. English. bm (6 issues). Free (technology teachers), $25.00 (other). Trenton State College, Department of Technology Studies, Armstrong Hall, Trenton NJ 08650. **Tel** (609)771-3333. **DD** 605. **Circ:** 54,000.
**Desc:** Explores inventive minds and new technology including the regular feature Design Briefs, which hopes to challenge students' problem-solving abilities.

NE/0166-591X
**TIJDSCHRIFT VOOR ONDERWIJSRESEARCH.** [Tijdschr. onderwijsres.]. **Added/Corp** Stichting Onderwijsresearch (Netherlands). Volume 1 (Nov. 1975)-. Periodical. Dutch (summaries and/or abstracts in English). qt. Fl192.50 (Institutions). Swets & Zeitlinger BV, Heereweg 347B PO Box 825, 2160 SZ Lisse Holland. **Tel** 011 31 2521 35111, FAX 02521-15888, telex 41325. **(Subscription address:** Swets Publishing Service, PO Box 825, 2160 SZ Lisse The Netherlands**) ED** B M P Creemers. **LC** Q4; .T44. **Bk Rev. Ad Acc. Circ:** 800.
**Desc:** Contains the results of educational research in

Holland and Belgium with contributions on research methodology, techniques, statistical analysis and educational research policy.
**Ind/Abst** Psychol. Abstr. (1975-); PsycINFO (1975-); PsycLit; Soc. Res. Methodol. Abstr. (1986-).

US/0145-0123
**TJS SPEC. PUBL.** **VAT** Texas Journal of Science Special Publication. No. 1 (1976)-. Academic Scholarly Publication. English. qt. Price varies per volume. Texas Academy of Science, PO Box 10986, ASU Station, San Angelo TX 76909. **Tel** (915)942-2184. **ED** J Knox Jomes Jr. **CODEN** TJSPD4. Index available. cum. index. **Pr Rev. Circ:** 1,000. available on microfilm. Documents available from CASDDS.
**Desc:** Scholarly manuscripts in any field of science, technology, or science education will be considered. Instructions to authors are published one or more times per year.
**Ind/Abst** Chem. Abstr.

FI/0355-4287
**TM. TEKNIIKAN MAAILMA.** (TM.). [TM, Tek. maailma]. **VFOAT** World of Technology. (1974)-. Periodical. Finnish. ir. Tilaajapalvetu Sub Svc, Puutarhakatu 16, 33210 Tampere 21 Finland. **Tel** 011 358 31 156665. **UDC** 62.

AT/1033-6893
**TODAY'S LIFE SCIENCE.** **VFOAT** Life Science. Vol. 1, No. 1 (July 1989)-. Periodical. English. mo. 83.00Aus$ Australia; 107.00Aus$ New Zealand, Papua New Guinea; 111.00Aus$ Malaysia, Indonesia, Fiji; 112.00Aus$ Japan, India, Hong Kong; 125.00Aus$ US, Canada, Lebanon; 135.00Aus$ Europe, Africa, former USSR. Thomson Publications / Australia, 47 Chippen Street, Chippendale New South Wales, 2008 Australia. **Tel** 011 61 2 6992411, FAX 011 61 2 698 3920, telex 122226. **(Subscription address:** Thomson Publications Australia, PO Box 815, Strawberry Hills, New South Wales, 2012 Australia.**)** **NLM** W1; TO172G. **CODEN** TOLSEE. **Ad Acc. Circ:** 7,000 (ctrl).
**Desc:** Easy to read topical reviews in molecular medicine, microbiology, hematology, immunology biochemistry, biology, etc.
**Ind/Abst** EMBASE [Select. Cov.].

●US/1059-9274
**TODAY'S SCIENCE ON FILE.** [Today's sci. file]. (1992)-. Periodical. English. mo. $190.00. Facts on File Publications, 460 Park Avenue South, New York NY 10016. **Tel** (212)683-2244, (800)322-8755, FAX (212)683-3633, telex 238 552 FACTS UR. **DD** 505.

JA
**TOHOKU KOGYO GIJUTSU SHIKENJO HOKOKU.** **Main/Corp** Tohoku Kogyo Gijutsu Shikenjo. **VFOAT** Reports of the Government Industrial Research Institute, Tohoku. No. 1- ; 1972-. Japanese (English). Government Industrial Research Institute Tohoku, Agency of Industrial Science and Technology, Ministry of International Trade and Industry, 2-1 4-chome Nigatake Sendai 983 Japan. **LC** T177.J3; T63A. **CODEN** TGSHDR. Documents available from CASDDS.
**Ind/Abst** Chem. Abstr.

JA
**TOKAI DAIGAKU KIYO : KOGAKUBU.** **VFOAT** Proceedings of the Faculty of Engineering of Tokai University. 1958-. Periodical. Japanese (English; summaries and/or abstracts in Japanese and English). ir. Tokai Building, 27-4 Shinjuku 3, Shinjuku-ku 160 Tokyo Japan. **LC** T4; .T574B.
**Ind/Abst** Eng. Mater. Abstr.

JA/0563-6981
**TOKUSHIMA DAIGAKU KYOYOBU KIYO. SHIZEN KAGAKU.** [Tokushima Daigaku Kyoyobu kiyo, Shizen kagaku]. **Added/Corp** Tokushima Daigaku. Kyoyobu. **VFOAT** Journal of Science, College of General Education, University of Tokushima; Journal of Science. (1966)-. Periodical. Japanese (English). an. Tokushima University, School of Medicine, 18-15 Kuramoto-cho 3-chome, Tokushima-shi, Tokushima-ken 770 Japan. **Tel** 0886-31-3111, FAX 0886-33-0771. **CODEN** TDKSBV. Documents available from CASDDS.
**Ind/Abst** Chem. Abstr.

JA
**TOKYO KODAI KURONIKURU GAKUJUTSU SOKUHO.** **Main/Corp** Tokyo Kogyo Daigaku. **Added/Corp** Tokyo Kogyo Daigaku. Gakujutsu Sokuho. No. 1 (Oct. 1970)-. Periodical. Japanese. Tokyo Kogyo Daigahn Kohoshitsu, Tokyo Japan. **LC** Z7913; .T65a.

JA
**TOKYO-TO SHIKEN KENKYU KIKAN NO KENKYU KEIKAKU.** Japanese. Tokyo-To Somukyoku, 5-1 Marunouchi 3, Chiyoda-ku, Tokyo Japan. **LC** Q180.J3; T65.

JA
**TOKYO TORITSU KOGYO GIJUTSU SENTA KENKYU HOKOKU.** **VFOAT** Report of the Tokyo Metropolitan Industrial Technic Institute. Academic Scholarly Publication. Japanese (summaries and/or abstracts in English). Tokyo Toritsu Kogyo Gijutsu Senta, 13-10 Nishigaoka 3 Kita-ku, Tokyo 115 Japan. **LC** PAR. **CODEN** TKGHDT. Documents available from CASDDS.
**Ind/Abst** Chem. Abstr.

US/0745-9297
**TOLEDO TECHNICAL TOPICS.** (TOLEDO TECHNICAL TOPICS : OFFICIAL PUBLICATION OF TOLEDO TECHNICAL COUNCIL.). [Toledo tech. top.]. Vol. 20, No. 8 (July-August 1966)-. Periodical. English. qt. Toledo Technical Topics, 2801 West Bancroft, Toledo OH 43606. ***Continues*** *Toledo Technical Journal.*

US
**TOP BID.** Periodical. English. sa (includes monthly updates). $348.00. Randall Publishing, 3200 Rice Mine Road, Tuscaloosa AL 35403. **Tel** (800)777-3748, (205)349-2990.

JA/0916-1465
**TOSHIBA'S SELECTED PAPERS ON SCIENCE & TECHNOLOGY.** [Toshiba's sel. pap. sci. technol.]. (1989)-. Periodical. English. sa. **DD** 621.3.
**Ind/Abst** Int. Aerosp. Abstr.

JA
**TOTTORI-KEN KOGYO SHIKENJO KENKYU HOKOKU.** No. 1 (1979)-. Japanese. Tottori-Ken Kogyo Shikenjo 390. **LC** T178.T67; T68.

US
**TOUCHSTONE / UNIVERSITY OF WISCONSIN-MADISON, UNIVERSITY-INDUSTRY RESEARCH PROGRAM.** **Added/Corp** University of Wisconsin--Madison. University-Industry Research Program. Vol. 17, No. 1 (Jan./Feb. 1983)-. Periodical. English. qt. University of Wisconsin-Madison University-Industry Research Program, 1215 WARF Bldg, 610 Walnut Street, Madison WI 53705. ***Continues*** *Research (University of Wisconsin--Madison. University-Industry Research Program).*
**Ind/Abst** Abstr. Bull. Inst. Pap. Sci. Tech.

JA/0285-9610
**TOYAMA DAIGAKU KYOIKU GAKUBU KIYO. B, RIKAKEI.** [Toyama Daigaku Kyoiku Gakubu kiyo, B, Rika-kei]. **VFOAT** Memoirs of the Faculty of Education, Toyama University. Began in 1978. Academic Scholarly Publication. Japanese (English). an. Toyama Daigaku Kyoiku Gakubu, 3190 Gofuku, Toyama-shi 930 Japan. **Tel** 0764-41-1271. **ED** Tsutomu Anayama. **LC** Q4; .T66. **CODEN** TDKBDG. Index available. cum. index (partly). **Circ:** 600 (ctrl). Documents available from CASDDS.
**Ind/Abst** Chem. Abstr.

JA/0389-9330
**TOYAMA KENRITSU GIJUTSU TANKI DAIGAKU KENKYU HOKOKU.** (KENKYU HOKOKU / TOYAMA KENRITSU GIJUTSU TANKI DAIGAKU.). [Toyama Kenritsu Gijutsu Tanki Daigaku kenkyu hokoku]. **Added/Corp** Toyama Kenritsu Gijutsu Tanki Daigaku. **VFOAT** Bulletin of Research, Toyama College of Technology; Toyama Kenritsu Gijutsu Tanki Daigaku Kenkyu Hokoku. (1968)-. Japanese. an. **CODEN** TGTHDW. Documents available from CASDDS.
**Ind/Abst** Chem. Abstr.

●SZ
**TR TRANSFER : TECHNISCHE RUNDSCHAU TRANSFER.** **VFOAT** Technische Rundschau Transfer; TR-Transfer. Vol. 85 No. 44 (Nov. 5, 1993)-. Periodical. German. Fifty-two times a year. 126.00F. Hallwag AG, Nordring 4, CH-3001 Bern Switzerland. **Tel** 011 41 31 3323131, FAX 031/414133, telex 912661 HAWA CH. ***Continues*** *Technische Rundschau (Bern, Switzerland).*

NE/0924-0829
**TRACTRIX.** **Added/Corp** Genootschap voor Geschiedenis der Geneeskunde, Wiskunde, Natuurwetenschappen en Techniek. Vol. 1 (1989)-. English (French, German and Dutch). an (Dec.). F67.00. Editions Rodopi BV, Keizersgracht 302-304, 1016 Ex Amsterdam Netherlands. **Tel** 011 31 20 6227507, FAX 011 31 20 380948. **ED** H. F. Cohen, S. B. Engelsman, C. Hakfoort, D. van Lente, H. Marland and and L. C. Palm. **LC** Q127.N4; T7. **NLM** W1; TR1092. **Bk Rev.** **Ad Acc. Circ:** 700.
**Ind/Abst** Am. Hist. Life (1989-).

UK/0372-0187
**TRANSACTIONS - NEWCOMEN SOCIETY FOR THE STUDY OF THE HISTORY OF ENGINEERING AND TECHNOLOGY.** [Trans. - Newcomen Soc. Study Hist. Eng. Technol.]. **Main/Corp** Newcomen Society for the Study of the History of Engineering and Technology, London. V. 1- 1920/21-. English. ir. Black Bear Press Ltd, King's Hedges Road, Cambridge CB4 2PQ England. **Tel** 011 44 223 424571. **LC** T1; .N47. **DD** 620/.009.

US/0093-6456
**TRANSACTIONS OF THE DELAWARE ACADEMY OF SCIENCE.** (TRANSACTIONS.). **Main/Corp** Delaware Academy of Science. V. 1/2- 1970/71-. English. an. $4.00 US; $5.00 other. Delaware Academy of Science, 1355 Old Baltimore Pike Road, Newark DE 19702. **Tel** (302)368-5703. **ED** Yvonne Blades (editor's address: 636 Woodville Drive, Hockenssen DE 19707). **LC** Q11; .D4216. **DD** 505. **Ad Acc.**
**Desc:** Consists of papers given at the spring and fall meetings of the Delaware Academy of Science, usually centered around a theme of Delaware science.

US/0019-2252
**TRANSACTIONS OF THE ILLINOIS STATE ACADEMY OF SCIENCE.** [Trans. Ill. State Acad. Sci.]. **Main/Corp** Illinois State Academy of Science. **VFOAT** Transactions of the Illinois Academy of Science. Vol. 1 (1908)-. English. qt. $25.00. Illinois State Museum, Spring and Edwards Street, Springfield IL 62706. **Tel** (217)782-7386, FAX (217)782-1254. **ED** Teresa L. North. **LC** Q11; .I32. **DD** 505. **CODEN** TISAAH. **Ad Acc. Circ:** 1,100 (ctrl). available on microfilm and microfiche from University Microfilms International (UMI). Documents available from BIOSIS Document Express, CASDDS.
**Ind/Abst** AGRICOLA [Select. Cov.]; Anim. Breed. Abstr.; Biol. Abstr.; Chem. Abstr.; Ecol. Abstr. (?-?); EMBASE; Fish Rev.; For. Abstr.; GeoRef; Helminthol. Abstr. (19??-19??); Index Vet.; Key Word Index Wildl. Res.; Maize Abstr.; Math. Rev.; Nutr. Abstr. Rev., Ser. B, Live Feeds and Feed.; Postharvest News Inf.; Rev. Med. Vet. Entomol.; Rev. Med. Vet. Mycology; Soils Fert.; Soyabean Abstr.; Weed Abstr.; Wildl. Rev.; Zentralbl. Math. Ihre Grenzgeb.

US/0022-8443
**TRANSACTIONS OF THE KANSAS ACADEMY OF SCIENCE (1903).** (TRANSACTIONS OF THE KANSAS ACADEMY OF SCIENCE.). [Trans. Kans. Acad. Sci.]. **Added/Corp** Kansas Academy of Science. **VFOAT** Transactions. Vol. 18 (1903)-. Periodical. English. sa. $30.00. Kansas Geological Survey, 1930 Constant Avenue, University of Kansas, Lawrence KS 66046. **Tel** (913)864-3965. **ED** J. Robert Berg. **LC** Q11; .K2. **DD** 505. **NLM** W1 TR226G. **CODEN** TSASAH. Index available. cum. index. **Pr Rev. Circ:** 500 (ctrl). Documents available from BIOSIS Document Express, CASDDS. ***Continues*** *Transactions of the ... Annual Meetings of the Kansas Academy of Science.*
**Desc:** Papers describing the results of research in the natural and behavioral sciences.
**Ind/Abst** Biol. Abstr.; Chem. Abstr.; Crop Physiol. Abstr.; Ecol. Abstr.; Energy Res. Abstr.; Field Crop Abstr.; Fish Rev.; Geogr. Abstr. Phys. Geogr.; GeoRef; Index Med.; Key Word Index Wildl. Res.; Life Sci. Collect.; Rev. Plant Pathol.; Seed Abstr.; Soils Fert.; Sorghum Mill. Abstr.; Wildl. Rev.

US/0023-0081
**TRANSACTIONS OF THE KENTUCKY ACADEMY OF SCIENCE.** [Trans. Ky. Acad. Sci.]. **Main/Corp** Kentucky Academy of Science. Vol. 1, (1923)-. Academic Scholarly Publication. English. Twice a year (Mar., Sept.). $50.00 US; $60.00 other. Kentucky Academy of Science, PO Box 4484, Lexington KY 40544. **Tel** (606)257-4902, FAX (606)323-1120. **ED** Bradley Branson. **LC** Q11; .K42. **CODEN** TKASAT. Index available. **Pr Rev. Circ:** 15,000 (ctrl). Documents available from BIOSIS Document Express, CASDDS.
**Desc:** The official publication of the academy. Publishes original papers based on research in any field of science.
**Ind/Abst** AGRICOLA [Select. Cov.]; Biol. Abstr.; Chem. Abstr.; EMBASE; Fish Rev.; GeoRef; Sci. Cit. Index (19??-19??); Sel. Water Resour. Abstr.; Wildl. Rev.

US/0544-540X
**TRANSACTIONS OF THE MISSOURI ACADEMY OF SCIENCE.** [Trans. Mo. Acad. Sci.]. **Main/Corp** Missouri Academy of Science. Vol. 1 (1967)-. English. an (Dec.). $13.00. Missouri Academy of Science, c/o NMSU, PO Box 828, Kirksville MO 63501. **Tel** (816)785-4635. **ED** Harry Sauer. **LC** Q11; .M68. **DD** 505. **CODEN** MISTBW. **Pr Rev. Circ:** 1,300 (ctrl). Documents available from BIOSIS Document Express, CASDDS.
**Desc:** The official technical publication of the Academy, containing refereed works in areas of scientific interest; 24 sections: Agriculture, atmospheric sciences, biology, bio-medical, chemistry, computer science, conservation, economics, engineering, entomology, environmental science, exercise, physiology, forensic science, geography, geology/geophysics, gerontology and herpetology.
**Ind/Abst** AGRICOLA [Select. Cov.]; Biol. Abstr.; Chem. Abstr. (1967-1980); EMBASE; Fish Rev. (Jan. 1989-July 1992); GeoRef; Int. Aerosp. Abstr.; Key Word Index Wildl. Res. (1967-1980); Soils Fert.; Wildl. Rev. (Jan. 1989-July 1992).

PH/0115-8848
**TRANSACTIONS OF THE NATIONAL ACADEMY OF SCIENCE AND TECHNOLOGY.** [Trans. Natl. Acad. Sci. Technol.]. Vol. 1 (1979)-. Academic Scholarly Publication. English.

an. **LC** Q80.P6; T7. **DD** 505. **CODEN** TNAPEB. Documents available from BIOSIS Document Express, CASDDS.
**Ind/Abst** Agrofor. Abstr.; Biol. Abstr. (1985-); Chem. Abstr. (1985-); Crop Physiol. Abstr.; Hortic. Abstr.; Seed Abstr.; Soils Fert.

US/0163-9013
**TRANSACTIONS OF THE NEBRASKA ACADEMY OF SCIENCES AND AFFILIATED SOCIETIES.** [Trans. Nebr. Acad. Sci. Affil. Soc.]. **Main/Corp** Nebraska Academy of Sciences. Vol. 4 (1977)-. Academic Scholarly Publication. English. an. $10.00-$15.00. Nebraska Academy of Sciences Inc, 302 Morrill Hall, 14th and U Streets, Lincoln NE 68588-0339. **Tel** (402)472-2662. **ED** Robert Kaul, C Bertrand Schultz, T Mylan Stout. **LC** Q1; .N38. **DD** 505. **CODEN** TNASDJ. Index available. cum. index. **Circ:** 1,800. Documents available from CASDDS. ***Continues*** *Transactions of the Nebraska Academy of Sciences, 0077-6351.*
**Ind/Abst** AGRICOLA [Select. Cov.]; Chem. Abstr. (1977-1981); Fish Rev. (Jan. 1989-July 1992); For. Prod. Abstr. (1991-); For. Abstr.; GeoRef; Wildl. Rev. (Jan. 1989-July 1992).

SA/0035-919X
**TRANSACTIONS OF THE ROYAL SOCIETY OF SOUTH AFRICA.** [Trans. R. Soc. S. Afr.]. **Main/Corp** Royal Society of South Africa. Vol. 1 (1910)-. Periodical. English. ir. Royal Society of South Africa, Hahn Building PO Box 594, Cape Town 8000 South Africa. **Tel** 27 21 6502543. **LC** Q85; .C22. **DD** 506.268. **CODEN** TRSAAC. cum. index. available on microfilm and microfiche from University Microfilms International (UMI). Documents available from The Genuine Article, BIOSIS Document Express, Documents on Demand. ***Supersedes*** *Royal Society of South Africa. Transactions of the South African Philosophical Society.*
**Ind/Abst** Biol. Abstr.; Curr. Aware. Biol. Sci., CABS; Curr. Contents, Agric. Biol. Environ. Sci.; EMBASE; Energy Inf. Abstr.; Environ. Abstr.; GeoRef; Math. Rev.; Life Sci. Collect.; Res. Alert [Full Cov.]; Sci. Cit. Index (19??-19??); SCISEARCH; Sel. Water Resour. Abstr.

AT/0372-1426
**TRANSACTIONS OF THE ROYAL SOCIETY OF SOUTH AUSTRALIA INCORPORATED.** (TRANSACTIONS OF THE ROYAL SOCIETY OF SOUTH AUSTRALIA.). [Trans. R. Soc. S. Aust.]. **Main/Corp** Royal Society of South Australia. (1937)-. Periodical. English. Twice a year (May, Nov.). 40.00Aus$. Royal Society of South Australia, South Aust Museum, North Terrace, Adelaide South Australia 5000 Australia. **Tel** 011 61 8 2235360. **ED** Dr. M Davies. **CODEN** TSAUAN. Index available (index published separately). cum. index. **Circ:** 850 (ctrl). Documents available from BIOSIS Document Express. ***Continues*** *Transactions and Proceedings of the Royal Society of South Australia, 0372-0888.*
**Desc:** Original papers in natural sciences: botany, zoology, earth sciences, and anthropology.
**Ind/Abst** Abstr. Anthropol.; AESIS Q.; AGRICOLA; Biol. Abstr.; For. Abstr.; GeoRef; Nematol. Abstr.; Life Sci. Collect.; Rev. Agric. Entomol.; Rev. Med. Vet. Entomol.

US/0084-0505
**TRANSACTIONS OF THE WISCONSIN ACADEMY OF SCIENCES, ARTS, AND LETTERS.** [Trans. Wis. Acad. Sci. Arts Lett.]. **Main/Corp** Wisconsin Academy of Sciences, Arts and Letters. **VFOAT** Transactions - Wisconsin Academy of Sciences, Arts, and Letters. Vol. 1 (1872)-. Periodical. English. an. comes with membership. Wisconsin Academy of Sciences, Arts & Letters, 1922 University Avenue, Madison WI 53705. **Tel** (608)263-1692, FAX (608)265-3039. **LC** AS36; .W7. **DD** 061/.75. **CODEN** TWASAB. Documents available from BIOSIS Document Express, CASDDS.
**Ind/Abst** AGRICOLA [Select. Cov.]; Biol. Abstr.; Chem. Abstr.; For. Abstr.; GeoRef; Math. Rev.; MLA Int. Bibl. Books Artic. Mod. Lang. Lit.; Soils Fert.

RH/0254-2765
**TRANSACTIONS OF THE ZIMBABWE SCIENTIFIC ASSOCIATION.** [Trans. Zimbabwe Sci. Assoc.]. Vol. 60, No. 1 (April 1980)-. Monographic series. English. Price varies per volume. **LC** Q180.55.M4; T7. **DD** 505. **CODEN** TZASDZ. Documents available from BIOSIS Document Express, Ask*IEEE. ***Continues*** *Transactions of the Rhodesia Scientific Association, 0379-9638.*
**Ind/Abst** Anthropol. Index; Biol. Abstr.; INSPEC (April 1980-); Rev. Med. Vet. Entomol.

UK/0143-7275
**TRANSDUCER TECHNOLOGY.** Periodical. English. Documents available from Ask*IEEE.
**Ind/Abst** Infomat Int. Bus.; INSPEC (March/April 1980-).

●US/1064-4156
**TRENCHLESS TECHNOLOGY.** Vol. 1, No. 1 (July/Aug. 1992)-. Periodical. English. Twelve times a year. $59.00. Trenchless Technology Inc., PO Box 190, Pennisula OH 44264. **Tel** (216)467-7588. **DD** 624.

XR
**TREND.** Began in 1969. Periodical. Czech (summaries and/or abstracts in English and Russian). Six times a year. kcs120.00. Narodni Informacni Stredisko, Havelkova 22, 130 00 Prague 3, Czech Republic. **Tel** PRAQUE 26 63 41, FAX (02)264775, telex 122214. **LC** T174; .T74. **Bk Rev. Circ:** 1,500 (ctrl).

PH
**TRENDS IN TECHNOLOGY.** Periodical. English. Economic Development Foundation, 6764 Ayala Avenue Makati Rizal, PO Box 1896, Manila Philippines. **LC** TR1; .T7. **DD** 605.

●US
**TRENDS IN U.S. R & D FUNDING FOR ... . Added/Corp** Battelle Memorial Institute. **VFOAT** Trends in US R & D Funding for ...; Trends in United States R & D Funding for ...; Battelle's R and D Forecast; Battelle's R & D Forecast. (1994)-. English. an. Battelle Memorial Institute, 505 King Avenue, Columbus OH 43201-2693. **Tel** (614)424-7818, FAX (614)424-3889. **LC** Q180.US; P8. ***Continues*** *Probable Levels of R&D Expenditures In ... .*

RU
**TRUDY SEVERO-VOSTOCHNOGO KOMPLEKSNOGO NAUCHNO-ISSLEDOVATELSKOGO INSTITUTA. Main/Corp** Severo-Vostochnyi Kompleksnyi Nauchno-Issledovatelskii Institut (Akademiia Nauk SSSR). (1962)-. Monographic series. Russian (summaries and/or abstracts in English). Price varies per volume. Izdatelstvo Nauka / Akademiia Nauk, Publishing House of the Russian Academy of Sciences, Leninskii Porspekt 14, 117901 Moscow Russia. **Tel** 011 95 954-21-53, FAX 011 95 938-21-44, telex 411964. **LC** Q60; .A644.

JA
**TSUSHO SANGYOSHO KOGYO GIJUTSUIN SHIKOKU KOGYO GIJUTSU SHIKENJO YORAN.** ***Ceased.*** **Main/Corp** Sikoku Kogyo Gizyutu Sikensyo. (19??)-?. Japanese. Shikoki Kogyo Gijutsu Shikenjo, 3-3 Hananomiyacho 2-chome (760), Takamatsu Japan. **LC** T178.S55; S53a.

●CC/1005-3026
**TUNG-PEI TA HSUEH HSUEH PAO. TZU JAN KO HSUEH PAN. Added/Corp** Tung-pei ta Hsueh (1993). **VFOAT** Journal of Northeastern University. Natural Science; Dongbei Daxue Xuebao. (1994)-. Periodical. Chinese (summaries and/or abstracts in English; table of contents in English). bm. **(Subscription address:** China International Book Trading Corporation, PO Box 399, Library Service Department, Beijing 100044 People's Republic of China.**)** **LC** T4; .T86. ***Continues*** *Tung-pei Kung Hsueh Yuan Hsueh Pao.*

FI/0784-1469
**TUTKIMAS JA TEKNIIKKA. See** Science and Technology-Abstracting, Bibliographies and Statistics.

FI/0358-5077
**TUTKIMUKSIA (VALTION TEKNILLINEN TUTKIMUSKESKUS).** (TUTKIMUKSIA.). [Tutk. - Valt. tek. tutk. k.]. **VFOAT** Forskningsrapporter - Statens Tekniska Forskningscentral; Research Reports / Technical Research Centre of Finland; Forskningsrapporter; Research Reports. Vol. 1, (1981)-. Academic Scholarly Publication. Finnish (English and Swedish). ir. Price varies per volume. Valtion Teknillinen Tutkimuskeskus, Technical Research Centre of Finland, Vuorimiehentie 5, PO Box 45, FIN 02044 VTT Finland. **Tel** 011 358 0 4561, FAX 011 358 0455 4374, telex 125175 VTTIN SF. **(Subscription address:** POB 42, SF-02151 Espoo Finland**)** **CODEN** TUTUDX. Index available. Documents available from BIOSIS Document Express, Ask*IEEE, CASDDS.
**Ind/Abst** Biol. Abstr.; Chem. Abstr.; INSPEC.

CH
**TZU JAN KO HSUEH NIEN CHIEN. VFOAT** Science Yearbook. Chinese. an. NT$3.85. Hsin Hua Shu Tien / Shang-Hai Fa Hsing So, Shanghai, People's Republic of China. **LC** Q127.C5; T97. **DD** 509/.51.

LB
**U. L. SCIENCE MAGAZINE. Main/Corp** Monrovia, Liberia. University of Liberia. Division of Science. V. 1- July 1972-. Periodical. English. $2.00. Kabingh Koroma, UL Science and Technology Magazine, College of Science and Technology, University of Liberia, Montrovia Liberia. **LC** Q1; .M76A. **DD** 505. ***Supersedes*** *Liberian Naturalist.*

US
**U.S. / R&D.** ***Title Change.*** **Added/Corp** Government Data Publications, Washington D.C. **VFOAT** GDP'S U.S. / R&D. (June 1975)-(19??). Periodical. English. mo. Government Data Publications / New York, GDP Building, 1661 McDonald Avenue, Brooklyn NY 11230. **Tel** (718)627-0819. **ED** Siegfried Lobel. **Bk Rev.** ***Continued by*** *Business Science Technology Developments & News.*
**Desc:** Contains articles on studies, contracts, trends, developments, special events, depth reports, analyses, political currents, new products and techniques, meetings and exclusives.
**Ind/Abst** Trade Ind. Index.

US
**U S S R REPORT: MATERIALS SCIENCE.** Joint Publications Research Services, PO Box 12507, Arlington VA 22209.

US/0163-2302
**U.S. SCIENTISTS AND ENGINEERS. Main/Corp** National Science Foundation (U.S.). **VFOAT** US Scientists and Engineers. **VAT** United States Scientists and Engineers. Began with 1974. English. be. National Science Foundation, 1800 G Street Northwest, Washington DC 20550. **Tel** (202)357-9859, (202)357-9498. **LC** Q149.U5; U54B. **DD** 331.1/1. **NLM** W2 A N37U. available on microfiche (Vols. for (1980-) distributed to depository libraries).

RU/0136-8109
**UCHENYE ZAPISKI LENINGRADSKOGO ORDENA LENINA GOSUDARSTVENNOGO UNIVERSITETA IMENI A.A. ZHDANOVA. SERIIA MATEMATICHESKIKH NAUK. Added/Corp** Leningradskii Gosudarstvennyi Universitet Imeni A.A. Zhdanova. **VFOAT** Scientific Papers of the Leningrad State University; Seriia Matematicheskikh Nauk; Uchenye Zapiski Leningradskogo Ordena Lenina Gosudarstvennogo; Versiteta Imeni A.A. Zhdanova. Matematicheskii Fakultet. IIA Matematicheskikh Nauk; Uchenye Zapiski Leningradskogo Ordena Lenina Gosudarstvennogo Versiteta Imeni A.A. Zhdanova. Matematiko-Mekhanicheskii Ultet. Seriia Matematicheskikh Nauk. Vol. 29 (1957)-. Monographic series. Russian (summaries and/or abstracts in English; table of contents in English). ir. Price varies per volume. St Petersburg State University / Izdatelstvo Leningradskogo Universiteta, Universitetskaia Nab 7/9, 199034 St Petersburg Russia. **Tel** 011 95 218-97-88, FAX 011 95 218-51-52, telex 121481. ***Continues*** *Uchenye Zapiski Leningradskogo Gosudarstvennogo Ordena Lenina Universiteta Imeni A.A. Zhdanova. Seriia Matematicheskikh Nauk.*
**Ind/Abst** Math. Rev.

IT/0394-8293
**UFFICIO TECNICO, L'.** (1979)-. Periodical. Italian. mo. L196000 (institutions), L110000 (individuals). Maggioli Editore, Casella Postale 290, 47037 Rimini, Italy. **Tel** 011 39 541 628666, FAX 011 39 541 742217. **UDC** 69.

UK
**UNDERCURRENTS.** Periodical. English. qt. $2.50. 34 Cholmley Gardens Aldred Road, London NW6 England. **LC** Q162; .U53. **DD** 505.

XR
**UNIGEO - SBORNIK PRACI.** Czech. sa. Free. Unigeo Ostrava, Mistecka ul 258, 720 02 Ostrava Czech Republic. **Tel** 69-3624, FAX 69-354 365, telex 052109. **Ad Acc. Circ:** 300 (ctrl).

US/0080-1461
**UNIQUE 3-IN-1 RESEARCH & DEVELOPMENT DIRECTORY.** [Unique 3-in-1 res. dev. dir.]. **Added/Corp** Government Data Publications (Firm). **VFOAT** Unique Three-in-One Research and Development Directory; Unique 3-in-1 Research and Development Directory; Research & Development Directory; Research and Development Directory. **VAT** Unique Three-in-One Research and Development Directory. (1963)-. Directory. English. an. $15.00. Government Data Publications / New York, GDP Building, 1661 McDonald Avenue, Brooklyn NY 11230. **Tel** (718)627-0819. **ED** Siegfried Lobel. **LC** Q180.U5; R38. **DD** 507/.2/073.
**Desc:** This 3-part directory contains research and development contracts awarded over the previous 12-month period. Each listing contains awardee, address, agency, description of work, and dollar amount of contract.

US
**UNITED STATES CONVENTIONS AND TRADE SHOWS. Added/Corp** United States Travel Service. (19??)-. English. US Department of Commerce / United States Travel Service, Springfield VA 22161. **LC** T391; .U54. **DD** 607/.34/73.

US
**UNITED TECHNOLOGIES MAGAZINE. Added/Corp** United Technologies Corporation. Vol. 1 (1980)-. Periodical. English. ir. United Technologies Corporation, PO Box 981, South Windsor CT 06074. **Tel** (203)282-4200. ***Supersedes*** *United Technologies Bee Hive.*

GW/0341-0102
**UNIVERSITAS. See** The Arts-Art.

US/0022-8850
**UNIVERSITY OF KANSAS SCIENCE BULLETIN, THE.** [Univ. Kans. sci. bull.]. **VFOAT** Science Bulletin. (1902)-. Academic Scholarly

Publication. English. ir. $30.00 (per volume). University of Kansas Libraries, Exchange and Gifts Department, Library Sales Office, Lawrence KS 66045. **Tel** (913)864-4610. **(Subscription telephone:** (913)864-3425) **ED** C D Michener. **LC** Q1; .K17. **DD** 508. **CODEN** UKSBAB. **Pr Rev. Circ:** 1,000. Documents available from BIOSIS Document Express, CASDDS. ***Supersedes*** *Kansas University Quarterly, 0885-4068.*
**Desc:** Intended for long papers, especially in fields such as systematics, ecology, and behavior.
**Ind/Abst** AGRICOLA [Select. Cov.]; Biol. Abstr.; Chem. Abstr.; Fish Rev.; GeoRef; Zool. Rec.; Wildl. Rev.

FI/0786-8413
**UNIVERSITY OF OULU. DEPARTMENT OF INFORMATION PROCESSING SCIENCE. SERIES A, RESEARCH PAPERS.** [Univ. Oulu, Dep. Inf. Process. Sci., A]. (1991)-. Monographic series. English. ir. **UDC** 681.3. ***Continues*** *Research Papers - University of Oulu. Institute of Information Processing Science. Series A, 0784-638X.*
**Ind/Abst** Zentralbl. Math. Ihre Grenzgeb.

UK
**UNIVERSITY OF WALES REVIEW / SCIENCE & TECHNOLOGY.** ***Ceased.*** (19??)-(1993). English. Welsh Development Agency, Pearl House, Greyfriars Road, Cardiff CF1 3XX Wales.

FR
**UNIXSYSTEM.** ***Ceased.*** (19??)-(19??). French. bm. Societe Parisienne d'Edition, 9 Passage des Marais 9, 75010 Paris France. **Tel** 011 33 1 42089582.

RU/0207-6756
**UPRAVLENIE I NAUCHNO-TEKHNICHESKII PROGRESS.** **Added/Corp** International Centre for Scientific and Technical Information. Akademiia Nauk SSSR. Komitet po Sistemnomu Analizu. (19??)-. Russian (Russian; summaries and/or abstracts in English). Tsentr Nauchnoi i Tekhnicheskoi Informatsii, Ulitsa Kuusinena, 21B Mezhdunarodnyi, 125252 Moscow Russia. **LC** T4; .D67 subser.; TS155.8.

US/0049-5700
**URETHANE PLASTICS AND PRODUCTS.** [Urethane plast. prod.]. (Jan. 1970)-. Periodical. English. mo. $195.00 (one year), $380.00 (two year), $565.00 (three year). Technomic Publishing Company, Inc., 851 New Holland Avenue, Box 3535, Lancaster PA 17604. **Tel** (717)291-5609, (800)233-9936, FAX (717)295-4538. **LC** TP1180.P8; U76. **DD** 668.4/23. **[CCC]. Circ:** 250. available on microfilm from University Microfilms International (UMI).
**Desc:** News and information on the urethane industry. New developments in urethane chemicals, market trends, regulatory/legal actions and technology.

US/1055-3436
**US2U AMERICAN TECHNOLOGY REPORTER.** [US2U Am. technol. report.]. **VFOAT** US2U; American Technology Reporter. Vol. 1, No. 1 (Jan.-Feb. 1991)-. Periodical. English. bm. $194.00. Militron News, Inc., 24-25 243rd Street, Douglaston NY 11363. **DD** 338.

US
**USSR AND EASTERN EUROPE SCIENTIFIC ABSTRACTS. BIOMEDICAL AND BEHAVIORAL SCIENCES.** **VFOAT** Biomedical and Behavioral Sciences. No. 1- Mar. 13, 1973-. Periodical. English. National Technical Information Service - NTIS, Room 2027S, 5285 Port Royal Road, Springfield VA 22161. **Tel** (703)487-4630, (703)487-4660, (703)487-4650, FAX (703)321-8547, telex 89-9405. ***Continues*** *USSR and Eastern Europe Scientific Abstracts. Biomedical Sciences.*

US/0892-497X
**USSR TECHNOLOGY UPDATE.** ***Ceased.*** [USSR technol. update]. **VAT** Union of Soviet Socialist Republics Technology Update. (1986)-Ceased Vol. 19 (1991). Periodical. English. bw. USSR Technology Update, 7700 Leesburg Pike/Suite 250, Falls Church VA 22043. **Tel** (703)556-0278. **ED** H Randall Morgan. **DD** 337. **[CCC].**
**Desc:** Coverage of current, technical and economic literature of the Soviet Union and Eastern Europe.

●UZ/0134-4307
**UZBEKISTON RESPUBLIKASI FANLAR AKADEMIIASINING MABRUZALARI.** **Added/Corp** Uzbekiston Respublikasi Fanlar Akademiiasi. **VFOAT** Doklady Akademii Nauk Respubiki Uzbekistan. (1992)-. Periodical. Russian (table of contents in English and Uzbek). mo. ***Continues*** *Doklady Akademii Nauk UzSSR, 0134-4307.*
**Ind/Abst** Abstr. Bull. Inst. Pap. Sci. Tech.; GeoRef; Int. Aerosp. Abstr.

II
**VAIJNANIKA.** Hindi (Hindi). 1.00 single issue. **LC** Q4; .V3.

US
**VAN NOSTRAND'S SCIENTIFIC ENCYCLOPEDIA.** ***Ceased.*** **See** Encyclopedias and General Reference Books.

GW/0042-1758
**VDI NACHRICHTEN.** [VDI Nachr.]. **Added/Corp** Verein Deutscher Ingenieure. Deutscher Verband Technisch-Wissenschaftlicher Vereine. **VFOAT** VDI-Nachrichten. (1947)-. Periodical. German. wk. DM159.00 Germany; DM206.00 other. VDI Verlag GmbH, Postfach 101054, D 40001 Dusseldorf Germany. **Tel** 011 49 211 6188313, FAX 011 49 211 6188133. **CODEN** VDNAAD. **[CCC].** ***Continues*** *VDI-Nachrichten aus Naturwissenschaft, Technik, Industrie.*
**Ind/Abst** Alum. Ind. Abstr.; Coal Abstr.; Energy Res. Abstr.; Fluid Abstr., Civil Eng.; Fluid Abstr. Proc. Eng.; FLUIDEX (1973-1990); Infomat Int. Bus.; Met. Abstr.

XR
**VEDA A ZIVOT.** (1935)-. Periodical. Czech. mo. $47.00. **(Subscription address:** Artia Pegas Press Ltd., Palac Metro Narodni Trida 25, 11210 Prague 1 Czech Republic.**)**

XR/0231-6900
**VEDECKE PRACE OVOCNARSKE.** [Ved. pr. ovoc. - Vyzk. slechtit. ust. ovoc. v Holovousich]. **VFOAT** Scientific Studies on Pomology. 1960-. Academic Scholarly Publication. Czech (summaries and/or abstracts in English, German and Russian). ir. Obarovy Podnik Sempra, Prague Czech Republic. **CODEN** VPOVAT. Documents available from CASDDS.
**Ind/Abst** Chem. Abstr. (1960-1981); Nematol. Abstr.; Plant Breed. Abstr.; Plant Grow. Reg. Abstr.; Soils Fert.

XO/0375-5010
**VEDECKE PRACE VYSKUMNEHO USTAVU ZIVOCISNEJ VYROBY V NITRE.** [Ved. pr. Vysk. ustavu zivocisnej vyroby Nitre]. **Added/Corp** Vyskumny Ustav Zivocisnej Vyroby v Nitre. **VFOAT** Nauchnye Trudy Nauchno-Issedlovatelskogo Instituta Zhivotnovodstva v Gorode Nitra; Scientific Works of the Research Institute of Animal Production at Nitra. (196?)-. Academic Scholarly Publication. Slovak (summaries and/or abstracts in English, Russian and Slovak). **CODEN** VPVZB9. Documents available from CASDDS.
**Ind/Abst** Chem. Abstr.

VE
**VENEZUELA AHORA: CIENCIA.** **Added/Corp** Venezuela. Ministerio de Informacion y Turismo. (1977)-. Periodical. Spanish. mo. Ministerio de Informacion Y Turismo, Apartado de Correos 192, Caracas Venezuela.

US/0738-7199
**VENTURE PRODUCT NEWS.** ***Title Change.*** **VFOAT** Venture/Product News. (1983)-?. Periodical. English. mo. Genium Publishing Corporation, One Genium Plaza, Schenectady NY 12304. **Tel** (518)377-8854, FAX (518)377-1891. **ED** Robert A Roy. **Bk Rev.** ***Merged with*** *Selected Business Ventures. Electronic, Electric and Electromechanical, 0161-0171; Selected Business Ventures. Measuring, Testing and Controls, 0161-018X; Selected Business Ventures. Chemicals, Chemical Processes and Plastics, 0161-021X; Selected Business Ventures. Materials, Forming and Production Methods, 0161-0201* ***and*** *Selected Business Ventures. Mechanical Fabrications, 0161-0163* ***to form*** *Selected Business Fabrications. Consumer Products, 0161-0198.*
**Desc:** Newsletter lists approximately 80 products and processes available to others via licensing from US and foreign industry, universities, research and development labs, government agencies, individuals and other sources.

US/0092-556X
**VENTURES IN RESEARCH.** **Added/Corp** C.W. Post Center. Ser. 1 (1972)-. English. an. $4.95. Long Island University, CWPost Kansas, Brookville NY 11548. **Tel** (516)299-2395. **ED** Donald K. Frank. **LC** AS36.P864; A37. **DD** 081. **Bk Rev.** ctrl circ.
**Desc:** Lectures by the faculty of C. W. Post Campus of Long Island University.

NE/0373-4668
**VERHANDELINGEN DER KONINKLIJKE NEDERLANDSE AKADEMIE VAN WETENSCHAPPEN, AFDELING NATUURKUNDE. EERSTE SECTIE.** (VERHANDELINGEN DER KONINKLIJKE NEDERLANDSE AKADEMIE VAN WETERSCHAPPEN, AFD. NATUURKUNDE. EERSTE REEKS.). [Verh. Kon. Ned. Akad. Wet., Afd. Natuurkd., Eerste sect.]. **Added/Corp** Koninklijke Nederlandse Akademie van Wetenschappen. Afdeling Natuurkunde. Vol. 20, No. 1 (1951)-. Monographic series. Dutch (English, French and German). ir. Price varies per volume. **LC** Q57; .A532. **DD** 505. **CODEN** VNANAN. Index Available, published separately, free-automatically sent. ***Continues*** *Verhandelingen (Koninklijke Nederlandse Akademie van Wetenschappen. Afdeling Natuurkunde).*
**Ind/Abst** GeoRef.

BE/0372-6916
**VERHANDELINGEN VAN DE KONINKLIJKE ACADEMIE VOOR WETENSCHAPPEN, LETTEREN EN SCHONE KUNSTEN VAN BELGIE, KLASSE DER WETENSCHAPPEN.** [Verh. K. Acad. Wet., Lett. Schone Kunsten Belg., Kl. Wet.]. **Main/Corp** Academie voor Wetenschappen, Letteren en Schone Kunsten Van Belgie. Klasse der Wetenschappen. (1972)-. Monographic series. Dutch (English). ir. Price varies per volume. Koninklijke Academie voor Wetenschappen, Letteren en Schone Kunsten Van Belgie, Hertogsstraat 1, B-1000 Brussels Belgium. **Tel** 011 32 2 5112623, FAX 011 32 2 5110143. **ED** G. Verbeke. **LC** Q56; .V45. **CODEN** VKKWAB. Index available. cum. index. **Circ:** 600. Documents available from BIOSIS Document Express. ***Continues*** *Koninklijke Vlaamse Academie voor Wetenschappen, Letteren en Schone Kunsten van Belgie. Klasse der Wetenschappen. Verhandelingen.*
**Ind/Abst** Biol. Abstr.; Math. Rev.; Zentralbl. Math. Ihre Grenzgeb.

SZ/0077-6122
**VERHANDLUNGEN DER NATURFORSCHENDEN GESELLSCHAFT IN BASEL.** [Verh. Naturforsch. Ges. Basel]. **Added/Corp** Naturforschende Gesellschaft in Basel. Vol. 1 (1854/1857)-. German (French; summaries and/or abstracts in English). an. Price varies per volume. Birkhaeuser Verlag Ag, Klosterberg 23, PO Box 133, CH-4010 Basel Switzerland. **Tel** 011 41 61 2717400, FAX 011 41 0 61 2717666, telex 963475 birk ch. **ED** Raffael Winker. **NLM** W1 VE483Z. **CODEN** VNGBAH. Index Available, published separately, free-automatically sent. cum. index. available on microfilm and microfiche from University Microfilms International (UMI). Documents available from BIOSIS Document Express. ***Supersedes*** *Bericht Uber die Verhandlungen der Naturforschenden Gesellschaft in Basel.*
**Desc:** Publishes original scientific papers, with emphasis on zoology, paleontology, geology, botany, mathematics, astronomy, and ethnology. Contributions describing museum holdings in Basel are also accepted.
**Ind/Abst** Anthropol. Index; Biol. Abstr.; GeoRef; Key Word Index Wildl. Res.; Life Sci. Collect.

SW
**VERKSAMHETSBERATTELSE.** **Main/Corp** Naturvetenskapliga Forskningsradet (Sweden). Swedish. Naturvetenskapliga Forskningsradet, Swedish Natural Science Research Council, Wenner Gren Center, Box 6711, S-113 85 Stockholm Sweden. **Tel** (0)18 365566. **LC** Q180.S8; N38D.

KZ
**VESTNIK AKADEMII NAUK RESPUBLIKI KAZAKHSTAN / QAZAQSTAN RESPUBLIKASY GHYLYM AKADEMIIASYNYNG KHABARSHYSY.** ***Title Change.*** **Added/Corp** Qazaqstan Respublikasy Ghylym Akademiiasy. **VFOAT** Qazaqstan Respublikasy Ghylym Akademiiasynyng Khabarshysy. (1992)-(1992). Academic Scholarly Publication. Russian (Kazakh). mo. Izdatelstvo Gylym / Science Publishing House, Ulitsa Pushkina 111-113, 480100 Alma-Ata Kazakhstan. **Tel** 3272 61 18 77. **LC** AS262; .A5913. **CODEN** VANKEQ. Documents available from CASDDS. ***Continues*** *Vestnik Akademii Nauk Kazakhskoi SSR, 0002-3213.* ***Continued by*** *Vestnik Natsionalnoi Akademii Nauk Respubliki Kazakhstan.*
**Ind/Abst** Chem. Abstr.

RU/0002-3442
**VESTNIK AKADEMII NAUK SSSR.** ***Title Change.*** [Vestn. Akad. nauk SSSR]. **Main/Corp** Akademiia Nauk SSSR. (1931)-(1992). Academic Scholarly Publication. Russian. mo. **(Subscription address:** Victor Kamkin, 4956 Boiling Brook Parkway, Rockville MD 20852.**) LC** AS262; .A627. **NLM** W1; VE818. **CODEN** VANSAC. **[CCC]. Pr Rev.** available on microfilm from University Microfilms International (UMI). Documents available from CASDDS. ***Continued by*** *Vestnik Rossiiskoi Akademii Nauk.*
**Ind/Abst** Am. Hist. Life (1955); Chem. Abstr.; Curr. Biotechnol.; Energy Res. Abstr.; GeoRef; Int. Aerosp. Abstr. (19??-1992); Math. Rev.; Sci. Cit. Index (19??-19??); SCISEARCH; Soc. Plann. Policy Dev. Abstr.; Sociol. Abstr. (1955).

KZ
**VESTNIK NATSIONALNOI AKADEMII NAUK RESPUBLIKI KAZAKHSTAN / QAZAQSTAN RESPUBLIKASY ULTTYQ GHYLYM AKADEMIIASYNYNG KHABARSHYSY.** **Added/Corp** Qazaqstan Respublikasy Ulttyq Ghylym Akademiiasy. **VFOAT** Qazaqstan Respublikasy Ulttyq Ghylym Akademiiasynyng Khabarshysy. (1993)-. Periodical. Russian (Kazakh). bm (6 issues). Izdatelstvo Gylym / Science Publishing House, Ulitsa Pushkina 111-113, 480100 Alma-Ata Kazakhstan. **Tel** 3272 61 18 77. **LC** AS262; .A5913. **CODEN** VNRKEZ. Documents available

from CASDDS. **Continues** *Vestnik Akademii Nauk Respubliki Kazakhstan.*
**Ind/Abst** Chem. Abstr.

●RU
**VESTNIK ROSSIISKOI AKADEMII NAUK.**
**Added/Corp** Rossiiskaia Akademiia Nauk. (1992)-. Academic Scholarly Publication. Russian. mo. $173.00. Izdatelstvo Nauka / Akademiia Nauk, Publishing House of the Russian Academy of Sciences, Leninskii Porspekt 14, 117901 Moscow Russia. **Tel** 011 95 954-21-53, FAX 011 95 938-21-44, telex 411964. **(Subscription address:** East View Publications Inc., 3020 Harbor Lane North, Suite 110, Minneapolis MN 55447.) **LC** AS262; .A627. **NLM** W1; VE844R. **CODEN** VRANEL. Documents available from The Genuine Article, CASDDS. **Continues** *Akademiia nauk SSSR. Vestnik Akademii nauk SSSR, 0002-3442.*
**Ind/Abst** Arts Humanit. Citation Index [Select. Cov.]; Chem. Abstr.; Curr. Contents Eng. Tech. Appl. Sci.; Res. Alert [Full Cov.]; Sci. Cit. Index; Soc. Sci. Cit. Index [Select. Cov.].

SW
**VETENSKAPSAKADEMIEN. Main/Corp** Kungliga Svenska Vetenskapsakademien. Swedish. Vetenskapsakademien, 104 05 Stockholm Sweden. **LC** Q64; .S9225.

II/0377-8487
**VIGNANA BHARATHI.** [Vignana bharathi]. **Added/Corp** Bangalore, India (City). University. Dept. of Publications and Extension Lectures. Vol. 1 (1975)-. Academic Scholarly Publication. English. sa. **LC** Q73; .V5. **CODEN** VBHAD6. Documents available from CASDDS.
**Ind/Abst** Chem. Abstr.; GeoRef; Math. Rev.; Zentralbl. Math. Ihre Grenzgeb.

US
**VINES OBSERVER.** (19??)-. English. bm. $279.00 US; $299.00 other. Wellesley Information Services, 108 Arnold Road, Newton MA 02159. **Tel** (617)969-6666, FAX (617)969-9998. **ED** Bonnie Penzias. Index available. cum. index. **Circ:** 700-1,200.

CE
**VINGNANAM. Added/Corp** University of Jaffna. Science Faculty. **VFOAT** Journal of Science. Vol. 1, No. 1 (Dec. 1986)-. Periodical. English (Tamil). sa. **LC** Q80.C4; V55.
**Ind/Abst** Postharvest News Inf.; Rev. Plant Pathol.

US/0042-658X
**VIRGINIA JOURNAL OF SCIENCE.** [Va. j. sci.]. **Added/Corp** Virginia Academy of Science. (Jan. 1940)-. Periodical. English. qt (Mar., Jun., Sep., Dec.). $27.50 US; $35.00 other. J. S. Reynolds Community College, Department of Biology, J. H. Martin, PO Box 85622, Richmond VA 23285-5622. **Tel** (804)371-3064. **ED** James H. Martin. **LC** Q1; .V5. **DD** 505. **NLM** W1 VI799. **CODEN** VJSCAI. Index available (Bound in all issues). **Pr Rev. Circ:** 1,500. available on microfilm and microfiche from University Microfilms International (UMI). Documents available from BIOSIS Document Express, CASDDS. **Supersedes** *Claytonia.*
**Desc:** Original articles in science and engineering dealing with advancements in science and technology and the impact on man and society.
**Ind/Abst** AgBiotech News Inf. (19??-); AGRICOLA (19??-); Biol. Abstr. (19??-); Chem. Abstr. (1940-1983); Ecology Abstr. (19??-); EMBASE (19??-); Fish Rev. (19??-); For. Abstr. (19??-); GeoRef (19??-); Grasslands For. Abstr. (19??-); Index Vet. (19??-); Int. Aerosp. Abstr. (19??-); Key Word Index Wildl. Res. (19??-); Math. Rev. (19??-); Life Sci. Collect. (19??-); Plant Breed. Abstr. (19??-); Protozoolog. Abstr. (19??-); Rev. Med. Vet. Entomol. (19??-); Rev. Med. Vet. Mycology (19??-); Soils Fert. (19??-); Stat. Theory Method Abstr. (1968-); Wildl. Rev. (19??-).

UN
**VISNYK AKADEMII NAUK UKRAINY : NAUKOVYI TA HROMADSKO-POLITYCHNYI ZHURNAL PREZYDII AKADEMII NAUK UKRAINY.**
**Added/Corp** Akademiia Nauk Ukrainy. Prezydium. **VFOAT** Visnyk; Vestnik Akademii Nauk Ukrainy. (1991)-. Periodical. Ukrainian. mo. **LC** AS262; .A72. **CODEN** VANUEM. **Continues** *Visnyk Akademii Nauk Ukrainskoi Radianskoi Sotsialistychnoi Respubliky, 0372-6436.*

US/1045-1498
**VOICE TECHNOLOGY NEWS. See** Engineering-Mechanical Engineering and Machinery.

RU/0507-3367
**VOPROSY ISTORII ESTESTVOZNANIJA I TEKHNIKI.** (VOPROSY ISTORII ESTESTVOZNANIIA I TEKHNIKI / AKADEMIIA NAUK SSSR, INSTITUT ISTORII ESTESTVOZNANIIA I TEKHNIKI.). [Vopr. istor. estestvozn. teh.]. **Added/Corp** Institut Istorii Estestvoznaniia i Tekhniki (Akademiia Nauk SSSR). Vol. 1 (1980)-. Academic Scholarly Publication. Russian (summaries and/or abstracts in English). Four times a year. $151.00. Izdatelstvo Nauka / Akademiia Nauk, Publishing House of the Russian Academy of Sciences, Leninskii Porspekt 14, 117901 Moscow Russia. **Tel** 011 95 954-21-53, FAX 011 95 938-21-44, telex 411964. **(Subscription address:** East View Publications Inc., 3020 Harbor Lane North, Suite 110, Minneapolis MN 55447.) **LC** Q124.6; .V66. **Continues** *Voprosy Istorii Estestvoznaniia i Tekhniki.*
**Ind/Abst** Am. Hist. Life (1981-); Math. Rev.; Zentralbl. Math. Ihre Grenzgeb.

GW/0066-5754
**VORTRAGE - RHEINISCH-WESTFALISCHE AKADEMIE DER WISSENSCHAFTEN, N, NATUR-, INGENIEUR- UND WIRTSCHAFTSWISSENSCHAFTEN.** (NATUR-, INGENIEUR- UND WIRTSCHAFTSWISSENSCHAFTEN.). [Vortr. - Rhein.-Westfal. Akad. Wiss., N]. **Main/Corp** Rheinisch-Westfalische Akademie der Wissenschaften. No. 204- 1970-. Academic Scholarly Publication. German. ir. Price varies per volume. Westdeutscher Verlag GmbH, Postfach 5829, D 65048 Wiesbaden Germany. **Tel** 011 49 611 160220. **LC** Q49.C95; A8. **DD** 508/.1. **CODEN** RWAVAW. Documents available from BIOSIS Document Express, CASDDS. **Continues** *Natur-, Ingenieur- und Gesellschaftswissenschaften.*
**Ind/Abst** Biol. Abstr.; Chem. Abstr.; GeoRef; Life Sci. Collect.; Zentralbl. Math. Ihre Grenzgeb.

FI/1235-0613
**VTT JULKAISUJA.** (1992)-. Monographic series. Multiple languages. ir. Price varies per volume. Valtion Teknillinen Tutkimuskeskus, Technical Research Centre of Finland, Vuorimiehentie 5, PO Box 45, FIN 02044 VTT Finland. **Tel** 011 358 0 4561, FAX 011 358 0455 4374, telex 125175 VTTIN SF. **UDC** 62. **CODEN** 681.3. Index available. cum. index. **Pr Rev. Circ:** 250.
**Desc:** Consists of technical and scientific research results. Intended for Scandinavian researchers.

FI/0357-9387
**VTT SYMPOSIUM.** [VTT symp.]. **Added/Corp** Valtion Teknillinen Tutkimuskeskus. (1974)-. Academic Scholarly Publication. English (Swedish and English). ir. Price varies per volume. Valtion Teknillinen Tutkimuskeskus, Technical Research Centre of Finland, Vuorimiehentie 5, PO Box 45, FIN 02044 VTT Finland. **Tel** 011 358 0 4561, FAX 011 358 0455 4374, telex 125175 VTTIN SF. **CODEN** VTTSE9. Index available. cum. index. **Circ:** 350. Documents available from Ask*IEEE, CASDDS.
**Desc:** Collected papers of international and selected domestic conferences which the Technical Research Centre of Finland (VTT) has wholly or partly arranged.
**Ind/Abst** Chem. Abstr.; INSPEC.

FI/1235-0605
**VTT TIEDOTTEITA. VFOAT** Research Notes. (1992)-. Monographic series. Multiple languages (English and Swedish). ir. Price varies per volume. Valtion Teknillinen Tutkimuskeskus, Technical Research Centre of Finland, Vuorimiehentie 5, PO Box 45, FIN 02044 VTT Finland. **Tel** 011 358 0 4561, FAX 011 358 0455 4374, telex 125175 VTTIN SF. **UDC** 62. **CODEN** 681.3. Index available. cum. index. **Circ:** 200.
**Desc:** Includes guidance for practice, summaries of research, literature reviews, testing and research methods, and reviews.

JA
**WAKAYAMA KOGYO KOTO SENMON GAKKO KENKYU KIYO. Added/Corp** Wakayama Kogyo Koto Senmon Gakko. **VFOAT** Kenku Kiyo; Memoirs of Wakayama National College of Technology. (19??)-. Periodical. Japanese (English). Wakayama Kogyo Shikenjo, (Wakayama National College of Technology), 77, Noshima, Nadacho, Goboshi, Wakayamaken 644, Japan. Documents available from CASDDS.
**Ind/Abst** Chem. Abstr.

JA/0286-1275
**WASEDA JINBUN SHIZEN KAGAKU KENKYU. VFOAT** Waseda Journal of General Sciences. Began in 1967. Periodical. Japanese. Waseda Daigaku Shakai Kagakubu Gakkai, c/o Waseda Daigaku Shakai, Kagakubu 6-1, Nishi Waseda 1, Shinjuku-ku Tokyo-to Japan. **LC** AS552.W37; A46.

US/0740-0535
**WASHINGTON FEDERAL SCIENCE NEWSLETTER.** (WASHINGTON FEDERAL SCIENCE NEWSLETTER : WFSN.). [Wash. fed. sci. newsl.]. **VFOAT** WFSN; FSN; W.F.S.N.; F.S.N. (1990)-. Newsletter. English. Twenty-two times a year (twice a month, except for January and August). $310.00 North America; $400.00 other. Washington Federal Science, 1057-B National Press Building, Washington DC 20045. **Tel** (202)393-3640. **ED** Dr Murray Felsher. **DD** 505. **Bk Rev**, (Qty: 50+). available on an online database from NEWSNET.
**Desc:** Monitors, tracks and reports on all federal science/technology through the Halls of Congress and the Corridors of Civilian and military Federal agencies.

US/0164-7369
**WASHINGTON SCIENCE TEACHERS' JOURNAL. Main/Corp** Washington Science Teachers' Association. (19??-). Periodical. English. qt. $5.50. Washington Science Teachers, 16221 45th Avenue South, Seattle WA 98188. **Tel** (206)825-3365.

●US
**WASHINGTON STATE ADVANCED TECHNOLOGY : THE ANNUAL SURVEY OF THE STATE'S TECHNOLOGY COMPANIES. VFOAT** Advanced Technology Washington State. (1993)-. English. **LC** T12.3.W2; A38. **DD** 338.7/616/025797. **Continues** *Advanced Technology in Washington State, 0749-4874.*

US/1058-9163
**WASHINGTON TECHNOLOGY.** [Wash. technol.]. (1986)-. Periodical. English. sm. $49.00. Technews Inc, 1953 Gallows Road/Suite 130, Vienna VA 22182. **Tel** (703)848-2800. **DD** 330.
**Ind/Abst** Abstr. BioCommer. (-199?); PROMT (19??-).

IT/1121-208X
**WATT MILANO.** [Watt Milano]. (1988)-. Periodical. Italian. Nineteen times a year. L93100 Italy; L186200 other. Gruppo Editoriale Jackson Spa, Via Gorki 69, 20092 Cinisello Balsamo Italy. **Tel** 011 39 2 66034401. **UDC** 537.

US/0083-7989
**WENNER-GREN CENTER INTERNATIONAL SYMPOSIUM SERIES.** Vol. 1 (1963)-. Academic Scholarly Publication. English. ir. Price varies per volume. Stockton Press, 49 West 24th Street, New York NY 10010. **Tel** (800)221-2123, (212)673-4400, FAX (212)673-9842. **NLM** W3 WE429. **CODEN** WGCSAA. Documents available from BIOSIS Document Express, CASDDS.
**Ind/Abst** Biol. Abstr. (-1979); Chem. Abstr.

AT/0049-7347
**WESTERN AUSTRALIAN INSTITUTE OF TECHNOLOGY GAZETTE.** (19??)-. English. Western Australian Institute of Technology, Hayman Road, South Bentley WA 6102 Australia.
**Ind/Abst** Aust. Educ. Index (1978-1981).

AT/1033-3738
**WHAT RESEARCH SAYS TO THE SCIENCE AND MATHEMATICS TEACHER. See** Education-Teaching and Curriculum.

AT/0812-423X
**WHIRRAKEE.** (1980)-. Periodical. English. Eleven times a year. 25.00Aus$. Bendigo Field Naturalist Club, PO Box 396, Bendigo Victoria 3550 Australia. **Tel** 61 54 431091.

●US/1063-5599
**WHO'S WHO IN SCIENCE AND ENGINEERING.** [Who's who sci. eng.]. (1993)-. English. Marquis Who's Who, A Reed Reference Publishing Company, Part of Reed International PLC, 121 Chanlon Road, New Providence NJ 07974. **Tel** (908)464-6800, (800)521-8110, FAX (908)665-6688, telex 138 755. **LC** Q141; .W576. **DD** 509.2/2. available on magnetic tape and CD-ROM.

●UK/0966-9094
**WINDOW ON DRUG MONITORING.** (1993)-. English. mo. £50.00 EC; $90.00 US; £50.00 other. Royal Society of Chemistry, Thomas Graham House, Science Park, Cambridge CB4 4WF England. **Tel** 011 44 223 420066, FAX 011 44 223 423429, telex 818293 ROYAL. **(Subscription address:** Turpin Distribution Services Limited, Blackhorse Road, Letchworth, Hertfordshire SG6 1HN, United Kingdom.)
**Desc:** Designed for the busy worker to keep up-to-date with new developments in the analysis of therapeutic drugs and drugs of abuse in biological tissues and fluids.

US/0745-0729
**WINDOWS (COLLEGE STATION, TEX.).** (WINDOWS.). [Windows]. **Added/Corp** Texas Engineering Experiment Station. Vol. 1, No. 1 (Spring 1982)-. Periodical. English. qt. Free. Texas Engineering Experiment Station, 332 Wisenbaker, Engineering Resource Center, College Station TX 77843. **Tel** (409)845-5510. **ED** Laura Colunga. **DD** 605. **Circ:** 5,000 (ctrl).
**Desc:** Science and technology research performed at Texas universities and non-profit research institutions.

US/0888-8612
**WINDS OF CHANGE (BOULDER, COLO.).** (WINDS OF CHANGE : A MAGAZINE FOR AMERICAN INDIANS IN SCIENCE AND TECHNOLOGY.). [Winds change]. **Added/Corp** American Indian Science and Engineering Society. University of Colorado, Boulder. School of Education. Vol. 1, No. 1 (Feb. 1986)-. Periodical. English. Four times a year (Jan., Apr., July, Oct.). $24.00 (one year); $42.00 (two years). Aises Publishing, 1630 30th Street, Suite 301, Boulder CO 80301. **Tel** (303)444-9099. **ED** James R. Weidlein, (editor's address: 4730 Walnut, Suite 212,

Boulder, CO 80301). **DD** 605. **Bk Rev**, (Qty: 4-8). **Ad Acc, Adv Mgr:** B. Wakshul, **Tel** (303)443-2270. **Circ:** 75,000. available on videocassette.
**Desc:** The primary goal is to nurture building of community by bridging science technology with traditional native values.
**Ind/Abst** Curr. Index J. Educ. (March 1990).

AT/0815-0753
**WISENET. See** Women's Interests.

GW/0510-6966
**WISSENSCHAFT UND FORTSCHRITT.** [Wiss. fortschr.]. (May 1951)-. Periodical. German. mo. DM36.00. Deutscher Judo Verband, Redaktion Ippon Segewaldweg 40, D 12557 Berlin Germany. **Tel** 011 49 711 210770, telex 051 678. **LC** Q3; .W5. **CODEN** WIFOAR. Documents available from CASDDS.
**Ind/Abst** AGRICOLA; Chem. Abstr.; Coal Abstr.

GW
**WISSENSCHAFT UND GEGENWART. GEISTESWISSENCHAFTLICHE REIHE.** No. 45- 1969-. Periodical. German. ir. Vittorio Klostermann, Frauenlobstrasse 22, D 60487 Frankfurt Germany. **Tel** 011 49 69 9708160. ***Continues in part*** *Wissenschaft und Gegenwart.*

GW
**WISSENSCHAFTEN IN DER DDR. *Title Change.*** 1975-. German. an. Institut fur Gesellschaft und Wissenschaft, Aussere Brucker Str 33, Postfach 1409, 8520 Erlangen-Nurnberg Germany. **LC** H5; .A14 subser; Q127; .G35. ***Continues*** *Jahresbericht zur Wissenschaftsentwicklung und Wissenschaftspolitik in der DDR.* ***Continued by*** *IGW-Report uber Wissenschaftsentwicklung und Technologie.*

GW/0863-5544
**WISSENSCHAFTLICHE TAGUNGEN DER TECHNISCHEN UNIVERSITAT KARL-MARX-STADT.** (1987)-. Academic Scholarly Publication. German. ir. Technische Hochschule Karl-Marx-Stadt / Leipzig, Leninstrasse 16, O-701 Leipzig Germany. **Tel** 668536. **UDC** 37. Documents available from CASDDS.
**Ind/Abst** Chem. Abstr.

GW/0863-0631
**WISSENSCHAFTLICHE ZEITSCHRIFT DER HUMBOLDT-UNIVERSITAT ZU BERLIN. REIHE MATHEMATIK/NATURWISSENSCHAFTEN.** Vol. 37, No. 1 (1988)-. Periodical. German (English). qt. Deutscher Judo Verband, Redaktion Ippon Segewaldweg 40, D 12557 Berlin Germany. **Tel** 011 49 711 210770, telex 051 678. **CODEN** WZHNEL. Documents available from BIOSIS Document Express. ***Continues*** *Wissenschaftliche Zeitschrift der Humboldt-Universitat zu Berlin.*
**Ind/Abst** Biol. Abstr.; Index Vet.; Potato Abstr.

GW/0138-290X
**WISSENSCHAFTLICHE ZEITSCHRIFT DER PADAGOGISCHEN HOCHSCHULE "KARL LIEBKNECHT" POTSDAM.** (WISSENSCHAFTLICHE ZEITSCHRIFT / PADAGOGISCHE HOCHSCHULE KARL LIEBKNECHT POTSDAM.). [Wiss. Z. Padagog. Hochsch. "Karl Liebknecht" Potsdam]. **Added/Corp** Padagogische Hochschule "Karl Liebknecht" Potsdam. Brandenburgische Landeshochschule. **VFOAT** Wissenschaftliche Zeitschrift der Padagogischen Hochschule "Karl Liebknecht" Potsdam; Wissenschaftliche Zeitschrift der Brandenburgischen Landeshochschule. Vol. 16, No. 1 (1972)-. Academic Scholarly Publication. German (summaries and/or abstracts in English and Russian; table of contents in English and Russian). qt. **LC** Q3; .P66a. **CODEN** WPKLAO. Documents available from CASDDS. ***Continues*** *Padagogische Hochschule Potsdam. Wissenschaftliche Zeitschrift der Padagogischen Hochschule Potsdam.*
**Ind/Abst** Chem. Abstr. (?-1990)(19??-); Math. Rev.; MLA Int. Bibl. Books Artic. Mod. Lang. Lit.; Soc. Plann. Policy Dev. Abstr.; Sociol. Abstr.

GW/0323-6129
**WISSENSCHAFTLICHE ZEITSCHRIFT DER TECHNISCHE HOCHSCHULE LEIPZIG.** (WISSENSCHAFTLICHE ZEITSCHRIFT.). [Wiss. Z. Tech. Hochsch. Leipz.]. **Added/Corp** Technische Hochschule Leipzig. (1977)-. Academic Scholarly Publication. German. ir. LKG Leipziger Kommissions & Grossbuchhandel, Leninstrasse 16, Postfach 520, D 04005 Leipzig, Germany. **Tel** 011 49 341 71370. **LC** T3; .W67. **CODEN** WZTLD6. Documents available from CASDDS.
**Ind/Abst** Chem. Abstr.; Zentralbl. Math. Ihre Grenzgeb.

GW/0043-6925
**WISSENSCHAFTLICHE ZEITSCHRIFT DER TECHNISCHEN UNIVERSITAT DRESDEN.** [Wissenschaftl. Z. Tech. Univ. Dresd.]. **Main/Corp** Technische Universitat Dresden. Vol. 10 No. 5 (1961)-. Academic Scholarly Publication. English. ir. Technische Universitaet Dresden, Wissenschaftliche Publikationen, Mommsenstr. 13, 8027 Dresden, Germany. **Tel** 0351-4632773, FAX 0351-4637165. **DD** 600. **CODEN** WZTUAU. Documents available from Ask*IEEE, CASDDS. ***Continues*** *Dresden. Technische Universitat. Wissenschaftliche Zeitschrift.*
**Ind/Abst** Bibliogr. Carto.; Chem. Abstr.; Coal Abstr.; Comput. Rev.; Curr. Biotechnol.; Ecol. Abstr.; EMBASE; Energy Res. Abstr.; Fluid Abstr., Civil Eng.; Fluid Abstr. Proc. Eng.; FLUIDEX (1973-); For. Prod. Abstr. (1991-); For. Abstr.; Geogr. Abstr. Phys. Geogr.; Geogr. Abstr. Human Geogr.; GeoRef; INSPEC (1968-); Int. Aerosp. Abstr.; Int. Dev. Abstr. (?-?); Leis. Recreat. Tour. Abstr.; Math. Rev.; Plant Breed. Abstr.; Rev. Agric. Entomol.; Zentralbl. Math. Ihre Grenzgeb.

GW/0863-1204
**WISSENSCHAFTLICHE ZEITSCHRIFT DER UNIVERSITAT ROSTOCK. NATURWISSENSCHAFTLICHE REIHE.** [Wiss. Z. Wilhelm-Pieck-Univ. Rostock, Nat.wiss. Reihe]. **VFOAT** WZ Rostock; W. Z. Rostock; Wissenschaftliche Zeitschrift Rostock. Vol. 31, No. 1-. Academic Scholarly Publication. German (summaries and/or abstracts in English and Russian). ir (ten issues per year). DM244.00. Universitat Rostock, Abt Wissenschaftspublizistik, Vogelsang 13/14, Rostock O-2500 Germany. **Tel** 37 81/369 577. **ED** S C Gerhard Maess. **LC** Q3; .R6. **DD** 505. **CODEN** WWNRD7. Index available. **Ad Acc. Circ:** 1,250 (ctrl). available on microfiche; available on microfilm. Documents available from BIOSIS Document Express, CASDDS. ***Continues*** *Wissenschaftliche Zeitschrift der Wilhelm-Pieck-Universitat Rostock. Mathematisch- Naturwissenschaftliche Reihe, 0323-4681.*
**Desc:** Covers agriculture, biology, chemistry, engineering, fish culture and fisheries, medicine, physics, and zoology.
**Ind/Abst** Agric. Eng. Abstr.; Biol. Abstr.; Chem. Abstr.; EMBASE (1982-); Helminthol. Abstr. (1991-); Maize Abstr.; Nutr. Abstr. Rev., Ser. B, Live Feeds and Feed.; Plant Grow. Reg. Abstr.; Postharvest News Inf.; Potato Abstr.; Protozoolog. Abstr.; Zentralbl. Math. Ihre Grenzgeb.

GW/0138-1504
**WISSENSCHAFTLICHE ZEITSCHRIFT - MARTIN-LUTHER-UNIV. HALLE-WITTENBERG. MATHEMATISCH-NATURWISSENSCHAFTLICHE REIHE.** (WISSENSCHAFTLICHE ZEITSCHRIFT. MATHEMATISCH-NATURWISSENSCHAFTLICHE REIHE. / MARTIN-LUTHER-UNIVERSITAT HALLE-WITTENBERG.). [Wiss. Z. - Martin-Luther-Univ. Halle-Wittenb., Math.-nat.wiss. Reihe]. **Added/Corp** Martin-Luther-Universitat Halle-Wittenberg. (1966)-. Academic Scholarly Publication. German. bm. LKG Leipziger Kommissions & Grossbuchhandel, Leninstrasse 16, Postfach 520, D 04005 Leipzig, Germany. **Tel** 011 49 341 71370. **LC** Q49; .H35. **DD** 505. **NLM** W1 WI984H. **CODEN** WMHMAP. Documents available from BIOSIS Document Express, CASDDS. ***Continues*** *Wissenschaftliche Zeitschrift der Martin-Luther-Universitat Halle-Wittenberg. Mathematisch-Naturwissenschaftliche Reihe, 0138-1504.*
**Ind/Abst** Am. Hist. Life; Biol. Abstr.; Chem. Abstr.; GeoRef; Math. Rev.; Plant Grow. Reg. Abstr.; Rev. Med. Vet. Entomol.; Soc. Plann. Policy Dev. Abstr.; Sociol. Abstr.

CC
**WO MEN AI KO HSUEH. VFOAT** Women Ai Kexue. Vol. 17 (March 1978). Periodical. Chinese. mo. $5.13. Science Press, 16 Donghuangchenggen North Street, Beijing 100707, People's Republic of China. **Tel** 011 86 1 4019821, 011 86 1 4010642, FAX 011 86 1 4012180, 011 86 1 4019810, telex 210147. **LC** Q163; .S484. **DD** 505. ***Continues*** *Shao Nien Ko Chi.*

CH
**WOLGAN KWAHAK. VFOAT** Newton Graphic Science Magazine; Kwahak. (1985)-. Periodical. Chinese. Twelve times a year. $158.00 Hong Kong & Macu; $170.00 Asia; $181.00 others. Newton Publishing Co. Ltd., 9th Floor #233-2 Pao Chian Road, Hsin Ten Taipei Taiwan. **Tel** 011 886 2 9159500, FAX 011 886 2 9159486. **ED** Mr. Liu Chun Tsu. **LC** Q4; .W64. cum. index. **Bk Rev. Ad Acc, Adv Mgr:** Mr. Lee Wen Lung. **Circ:** 30,000 (ctrl).
**Desc:** This magazine uses full color illustrations and exciting photography to make science interesting and easy to understand. It covers a variety of different topics, so that every issue is like a encyclopedia.

US/0739-666X
**WOMEN AND MINORITIES IN SCIENCE AND ENGINEERING.** [Women minor. sci. eng.]. **Added/Corp** National Science Foundation (U.S.). (Jan. 1982)-. English. an. Free on request. National Science Foundation, 1800 G Street Northwest, Washington DC 20550. **Tel** (202)357-9859, (202)357-9498. **LC** Q130; .W648. **DD** 331.4/815/0973. **NLM** Q 130; W872.

US
**WONDERSCIENCE : FUN PHYSICAL SCIENCE ACTIVITIES FOR CHILDREN AND ADULTS TO DO TOGETHER.** (1988)-. English. Eight times a year. $5.00 (add $2.50 for postage) North America; $10.00 (add $2.50 for postage) other. PO Box 57136 West End Station, Washington DC 20037. **Tel** (202)872-6179, FAX (202)872-6336. **ED** James Kessler and Gayle Ater. Index available. **Circ:** 15,000.
**Desc:** Show how adults and children can work as partners exploring science with common materials and having fun at the same time.

US/0897-926X
**WORCESTER POLYTECHNIC INSTITUTE STUDIES IN SCIENCE, TECHNOLOGY, AND CULTURE.** [Worcest. Polytech. Inst. stud. sci. technol. cult.]. **VFOAT** Studies in Science, Technology and Culture. 1989-. Monographic series. English. ir. Price varies per volume. Peter Lang Publishing, 62 West 45th Street, 4th Floor, New York NY 10036. **Tel** (212)764-1471, (800)770-5264, telex 6973364 PLNY. **ED** Lance Schachterle and Francis C Lutz. **DD** 306. **Pr Rev.**
**Desc:** Contains monographs and collected essays which investigate the relationships between science and technology and culture.

●US/1059-1931
**WORLD & SCIENCE, THE. VFOAT** World and Science; World of Science. (1992)-. Periodical. English. qt. $29.99. Publishing & Business Consultants, PO Box 75392, Los Angeles CA 90075. **Tel** (213)732-3477, FAX (213)732-9123. **ED** Andeson Napoleon Atia. **Ad Acc.** Full Page (B&W) $5750.00. Half Page (B&W) $3575.00. Full Page (Color) $8750.00 (2 color). Half Page (Color) $5500.00 (2 color). **Circ:** 164,000 total.
**Desc:** Of interest to those fascinated with science as a universal discipline. Features articles in biology, zoology, anthropology, astronomy, physics and chemistry.

US/0253-7494
**WORLD BANK TECHNICAL PAPER.** [World Bank tech. pap.]. (1982)-. Monographic series. English. ir. Price varies per volume. World Bank Publications, 1818 H Street Northwest, Washington DC 20433. **Tel** (202)473-1155, (202)473-1155, FAX (202)522-3224, telex WUI 64145 WORLDBANK. Documents available from BIOSIS Document Express.
**Ind/Abst** AgBiotech News Inf.; Agrofor. Abstr. (1991-); Biol. Abstr.; Dairy Sci. Abstr.; Ecol. Abstr.; For. Prod. Abstr.; For. Abstr.; Geogr. Abstr. Phys. Geogr.; Geogr. Abstr. Human Geogr.; GeoRef; Int. Dev. Abstr.; Leis. Recreat. Tour. Abstr.; Plant Genet. Resour. Abstr.; Rural Dev. Abstr.; Soils Fert.; Wheat Barley Trit. Abstr.; World Agric. Econ.

US
**WORLD EMPLOYMENT PROGRAMME RESEARCH WORKING PAPER. WEP-2-22. VFOAT** Working Paper; Working Papers; WEP 2-22. (1974)-. Monographic series. English. Price varies per volume. ILO Publications, 1828 L Street Northwest, Suite 801, Washington DC 20036. **Tel** (202)653-7652, FAX (202)653-7687. **(Subscription address:** ILO Publications, International Labour Office, CII-1211 Geneva 22 Switzerland)
**Ind/Abst** Rice Abstr.; Rural Dev. Abstr.; Sug. Indus. Abstr.

US/0043-8677
**WORLD MEETINGS OUTSIDE UNITED STATES AND CANADA.** [World meet. outs. U. S. Can.]. **Added/Corp** World Meetings Information Center. Vol. 2, No. 3 (July 1969)-. Periodical. English. qt. $185.00 US; $200.00 other. Macmillan Publishing Company, 100 Front Street, Box 500, Riverside NJ 08075-7500. **Tel** (800)257-5755, (609)461-6500, FAX (609)461-7070. **ED** Clark Hansen. **DD** 060. **NLM** W 3.5 W922. **CODEN** WMUCBR. **Circ:** 1,000. ***Continues*** *World Meetings Outside U.S.A. and Canada, 0043-8677.*
**Desc:** Registry of future medical, scientific, and technical meetings to be held outside the United States and Canada.

US/0043-8693
**WORLD MEETINGS: UNITED STATES AND CANADA.** [World meet. U. S. Can.]. **Added/Corp** World Meetings Information Center. Technical Meetings Information Service. Vol. 5, No. 2 (April 1967)-. Periodical. English. qt. $185.00 US and Canada; $200.00 other. Macmillan Publishing Company, 100 Front Street, Box 500, Riverside NJ 08075-7500. **Tel** (800)257-5755, (609)461-6500, FAX (609)461-7070. **LC** Q11; .T2. **DD** 506/.2/7. **NLM** W 3.5 W927. **CODEN** WMUCAQ. ***Continues*** *TMIS Technical Meetings Index.*
**Ind/Abst** FLUIDEX (1973-).

●US/1071-0973
**WORLD OF INVENTION.** (1993)-. English. ir. $69.95. Gale Research Inc., 835 Penobscot Building, Detroit MI 48226. **Tel** (800)877-GALE, (313)961-2242, FAX (313)961-6083, telex TWX 810-221-7086. **ED** Bridget Travers.
**Desc:** Identifies over 1,200 inventors and inventions.

Designed to answer the most frequently asked questions in science, technology, medicine and transportation, as well as everyday life.

●US/1071-0981
**WORLD OF SCIENTIFIC DISCOVERY.** (1993)-. English. ir. $69.95. Gale Research Inc., 835 Penobscot Building, Detroit MI 48226. **Tel** (800)877-GALE, (313)961-2242, FAX (313)961-6083, telex TWX 810-221-7086. **ED** Bridget Travers.
**Desc:** Focuses on scientific discoveries throughout history, with an emphasis on processes rather than complex concepts. Uses plain language to answer all the basic questions.

NE/0259-8264
**WORLD TRANSLATIONS INDEX : A JOINT PUBLICATION OF INTERNATIONAL TRANSLATIONS CENTRE [AND] CENTRE NATIONAL DE LA RECHERCHE SCIENTIFIQUE IN CO-OPERATION WITH THE NATIONAL TRANSLATIONS CENTER AT THE JOHN CRERAR LIBRARY OF THE UNIVERSITY OF CHICAGO.** **Added/Corp** International Translations Centre. Centre National de la Recherche Scientifique (France) National Translations Center (U.S.). Vol. 1, No. 1 (May 1987)-. English (French and German). Ten times a year. Fl1450.00 Netherlands, Belgium, Germany, UK, France, Portugal, Spain and Sweden; Fl1575.00 other. International Translations Centre, Schuttersveld 2, 2611 WE Delft Netherlands. **Tel** 011 31 15 142242, 011 31 15 142243, FAX 011 31 15 158535, telex 38104. **LC** Z7403; .W95; Q158.5. **DD** 016.5. **NLM** ZQ 1; W2977. Index available. cum. index. **Ad Acc. Circ:** 600. ***Formed by the union of*** *World Transindex, 0378-6803* ***and*** *Translations Register-Index, 0041-1256.*
**Desc:** Some 30,000 references of translations in all fields of science and technology are announced. Ten issues with source and author indexes.

●II
**WORLD'S LATEST TECHNOLOGIES AND NEW PRODUCTS.** (1991)-. Periodical. English. Twenty-six times a year. $250.00. Bajaj Capital Investment Centre, New Delhi, India. **(Subscription address:** Prints India, 11 Darya Ganj, New Delhi, 110002 India, (Phone: 011 91 11 3268645))

US/0148-6128
**WPI JOURNAL.** **Main/Corp** Worcester Polytechnic Institute, Worcester, Mass. **VAT** Worcester Polytechnic Institute Journal. (1869)-. Periodical. English. qt. free. Worcester Polytechnic Institute, Alumni Association, Worcester MA 01609. **Tel** (508)831-5000. **ED** Kenneth L. McDonnell. **LC** TA1; .W9. **DD** 607/.11/7443. **Circ:** 22,000 (ctrl). ***Continues*** *Journal of the Worcester Polytechnic Institute.*
**Desc:** Alumni magazine, stories on issues in education, engineering, science. People and technology oriented.

●US/1062-0168
**WRITING AND EDITING FOR SCIENCE AND TECHNOLOGY.** [Writ. ed. sci. technol.]. (May-June 1992)-. English. $75.00. Ariadne Press, 10607 Springvale Court, Great Falls VA 22066. **DD** 808.

CC
**WU-HAN TA HSUEH HSUEH PAO. TZU JAN KO HSUEH PAN.** **VFOAT** Journal of Wuhan University. Natural Sciences Edition. (19??)-. Periodical. Chinese (summaries and/or abstracts in English). qt. Science Press, 16 Donghuangchenggen North Street, Beijing 100707, People's Republic of China. **Tel** 011 86 1 4019821, 011 86 1 4010642, FAX 011 86 1 4012180, 011 86 1 4019810, telex 210147. **LC** Q4; .W8. **DD** 505. **UDC** 501.
**Ind/Abst** Math. Rev.

CH/0253-9888
**WUHAN DAXUE XUEBAO. ZIRAN. KEXUE.** (WU-HAN TA HSUEH HSUEH PAO: TZU JAN K'O HSUEH PAN.). [Wuhan daxue xuebao. Ziran. kexue]. **Added/Corp** Wu-Han ta Hsueh. **VFOAT** Wuhandaxue Xuebao. (19??)-. Academic Scholarly Publication. Chinese. qt. ¥24. Wuhandaxue, Xuebao Bianjibu, Luo Jia Shan, Wuchang-qu, Muhan, Hubei 430072, People's Republic of China. **(Subscription address:** China International Book Trading Corporation, PO Box 399, Library Service Department, Beijing 100044 People's Republic of China.**)** **ED** Li Weihua and Yang Yugao. **CODEN** WTHPDI. Documents available from CASDDS. ***Supersedes*** *Wu-Han ta Hsueh Tzu Jan K'o Hsueh Hsueh Pao.*
**Ind/Abst** Chem. Abstr.; Math. Rev.

CC/1000-2405
**WUHAN GONGYE DAXUE XUEBAO.** **VFOAT** Journal of Wuhan University of Technology. (1986)-. Academic Scholarly Publication. Chinese. qt. Wuhan Institute of Technology, Matanghan Wuhan, People's Republic of China. **Tel** 871939. **DD** 605. Documents available from CASDDS.
**Ind/Abst** Chem. Abstr.

CC/1000-5900
**XIANGTAN DAXUE ZIRAN KEXUE XUEBAO.** (HSIANG-TAN TA HSUEH TZU JAN KO HSUEH HSUEH PAO.). [Xiangtan daxue ziran kexue xuebao]. **Added/Corp** Hsiang-Tan ta Hsueh. **VFOAT** Natural Science Journal of Xiangtan University. (19??)-. Academic Scholarly Publication. Chinese. sa. **CODEN** XDZXEW. Documents available from CASDDS.
**Ind/Abst** Chem. Abstr. (1985-).

CC/1000-2758
**XIBEI GONGYE DAXUE XUEBAO.** **VFOAT** Journal of Northwestern Polytechnical University. (1957)-. Periodical. Chinese. qt. **DD** 620. Documents available from Article Express International.
**Ind/Abst** Ei Page One; Eng. Index Annu.; Int. Aerosp. Abstr.

CC/1000-5811
**XIBEI QINGGONGYE XUEYUAN XUEBAO.** **VFOAT** Journal of Northwest Institute of Light Industry. (1982)-. Periodical. Chinese. qt. **DD** 670. Documents available from CASDDS.
**Ind/Abst** Chem. Abstr.

CH/0254-6167
**XIBEI SHIFAN XUEYUAN XUEBAO. ZIRAN KEXUE BAN.** (HSI PEI SHIH FAN HSUEH YUAN HSUEH PAO. TZU JAN KO HSUEH PAN.). [Xibei shifan xueyuan xuebao. Ziran kexue ban]. **VFOAT** Journal of the Northwestern Teachers College. Natural Science; Xibeishifan Xueyuanxuebao. Academic Scholarly Publication. Chinese (Chinese). qt. NT$0.50. Post Office, Lan-Chou Shih, People's Republic of China. **Tel** 26492. **LC** Q4; .H7. **DD** 505. **CODEN** XSXKDJ. Documents available from CASDDS.
**Ind/Abst** Chem. Abstr.

SI/0303-089X
**XIN GINGNIAN KEXUE.** (HSIN CHING NIEN KO HSUEH.). First published in May 1972-. Chinese. $0.30 single issue. 111-E Jalan Satu, Singapore 14 Singapore. **LC** Q111; .H7.

CC/0376-656X
**XINY IYAOXUE ZAZHI.** (HSIN I YAO HSUEH TSA CHIH.). [Xinyiyaoxue zazhi]. **VFOAT** Xinyiyaoxue Zazhi. (197?)-. Periodical. Chinese. mo. **CODEN** HIYCDQ.
**Ind/Abst** NAPRALERT.

US/0091-0287
**YALE SCIENTIFIC.** [Yale sci.]. Vol. 33 (Oct. 1958)-. Periodical. English. qt. $8.00 (one year); $15.00 (two year). Yale Scientific Magazine, 305 Crown Street, New Haven CT 06511. **Tel** (203)432-2374. **ED** Gautam Prakash. **NLM** W1 YA459. Index available. cum. index. **Bk Rev. Ad Acc. Circ:** 7,000 (ctrl). available on microfilm and microfiche from University Microfilms International (UMI). ***Continues*** *Yale Scientific Magazine, 0044-0140.*
**Desc:** Features in-depth reports on new and exciting research going on at Yale, with general interest topics in science. Targeted at the layman.
**Ind/Abst** Biol. Dig.; Int. Aerosp. Abstr.

JA
**YAMAGATA DAIGAKU KIYO : KYOIKU DAGAKU.** **Main/Corp** Yamagata Daigaku. **Added/Corp** Yamagata Daigaku. Bulletin of the Yamagata University: Educational Science. **VFOAT** Bulletin of the Yamagata University: Educational Science. Vol. 1- 1927 March 1952-. Japanese (summaries and/or abstracts in English). Yamagata Daigaku, (Yamagata University), Kojirakawamachi, Yamagatashi, Yamagataken 990 Japan. **LC** L67; .Y35A. **DD** 370/.952.

JA/0513-4692
**YAMAGATA DAIGAKU KIYO: SHIZEN KAGAKU.** [Yamagata Daigaku Kiyo, shizen kagaku]. **Main/Corp** Yamagata Daigaku. **VFOAT** Bulletin of the Yamagata University: Natural Science. Vol. 1- 1925- March 1950-. Academic Scholarly Publication. Japanese (English). Yamagata Daigaku, (Yamagata University), Kojirakawamachi, Yamagatashi, Yamagataken 990 Japan. **LC** Q4; .Y32A. **CODEN** YDKSAH. Documents available from Ask*IEEE, CASDDS.
**Ind/Abst** Chem. Abstr.; INSPEC (March 1974-); Math. Rev.

JA/0385-8766
**YAMANASHI DAIGAKU KYOIKU GAKUBU KENKYU HOKOKU. DAI 2 BUNSATSU, SHIZEN KAGAKU KEI.** **Added/Corp** Yamanashi Daigaku. Kyoiku Gakubu. **VFOAT** Memoirs of the Faculty of Liberal Arts & Education. Part 2, Mathematics & Natural Sciences. (1967)-. Periodical. Japanese (English). an. Yamanashi Daigaku Kyoikugakubu, (Faculty of Liberal Arts & Education, Yamanashi University), 4-37, Takeda 4 Chome, Kofushi, Yamanashiken 400, Japan. **LC** Q4; .Y35. Documents available from CASDDS. ***Continues in part*** *Yamanashi Daigaku Gakugei Gakubu Kenkyu Hokoku.*
**Ind/Abst** Chem. Abstr.

JA/0914-711X
**YAMANASHI-KEN KOGYO GIJUTSU SENTA KENKYU HOKOKU.** **Added/Corp** Yamanashi-Ken Kogyo Gijutsu Senta. **VFOAT** Report of the Yamanashi Industrial Technology Center. (1986)-. Periodical. Japanese. **LC** IN PROCESS. **CODEN** YKGHEH. Documents available from CASDDS.
**Ind/Abst** Chem. Abstr.

II
**YEAR BOOK - ANDHRA PRADESH AKADEMI OF SCIENCES.** **Main/Corp** Andhra Pradesh Akademi of Sciences. English. an. Andhra Pradesh Akademi of Sciences, c/o Osmania University Campus, Hyderabad-7 India. **LC** Q73; .A718. **DD** 506/.254/84.

AT/0067-1584
**YEAR BOOK / AUSTRALIAN ACADEMY OF SCIENCE.** **Main/Corp** Australian Academy of Science. (1984/85)-. Periodical. English. an. $30.00Aus$. Australian Academy of Science, GPO Box 783, Canberra ACT 2601 Australia. **Tel** 011 61 6 2475777, FAX 011 61 6 2574620, telex ACSI AA 62406. **LC** IN PROCESS. ***Continues*** *Australian Academy of Science. Handbook.*

US/0069-066X
**YEAR BOOK - CARNEGIE INSTITUTION OF WASHINGTON.** [Year b. - Carnegie Inst. Wash.]. **Main/Corp** Carnegie Institution of Washington. No. 1 (1902)-. English. an. $8.00. Carnegie Institution of Washington, 1530 P Street NW, Washington DC 20005. **Tel** (202)387-6411. **ED** Ray Bowers. **LC** AS32. **DD** 505. **NLM** W1 YE102P. **CODEN** CIWYAO. **Circ:** 600. Documents available from BIOSIS Document Express.
**Desc:** Describes for the nonspecialist reader the year's work by the institution's scientists in biology, astronomy, and the earth sciences. Includes opening commentary by the President.
**Ind/Abst** AGRICOLA; Biol. Abstr.; GeoRef.

II/0073-6619
**YEAR BOOK OF THE INDIAN NATIONAL SCIENCE ACADEMY, THE.** **Main/Corp** Indian National Science Academy. (19??)-. English. an. Indian National Science Academy, 1 Bahadur Shah Zafar Marg, New Delhi 110 002 India. **(Subscription address:** Prints India, 11 Darya Ganj, New Delhi 110002 India.**)** **LC** Q73; .N33. **DD** 506/.254. **NLM** W1; IN256NJ. ***Continues*** *Year Book of the National Institute of Sciences of India, 0375-5193.*

US/1060-5037
**YEAR IN REVIEW - CRANBROOK INSTITUTE OF SCIENCE.** **See** Museums and Galleries.

AT
**YEARBOOK - AUSTRALIAN ACADEMY OF SCIENCE.** **Main/Corp** Australian Academy of Science. (1956)-. English. an. 18.00Aus$ Australia; 28.00Aus$ others. Australian Academy of Science, GPO Box 783, Canberra ACT 2601 Australia. **Tel** 011 61 6 2475777, FAX 011 61 6 2574620, telex ACSI AA 62406.

US/0096-3291
**YEARBOOK OF SCIENCE AND THE FUTURE.** (1975)-. English. an (Published in June). $36.95. Encyclopedia Britannica Inc, Britannica Centre, 310 South Michigan Avenue, Chicago IL 60604. **Tel** (312)347-7453, FAX (312)347-7914, (312)289-2178. **ED** David Calhoun. **LC** Q9; .B78. **DD** 505. Index available (In each volume). cum. index (Three-year). ***Continues*** *Britannica Yearbook of Science and the Future.*
**Desc:** Contains articles on scientific and technological disciplines that describe the major developments in those fields during the previous twelve months. All the mathematical, physical, and biological disciplines are included, and the social sciences are touched upon.
**Ind/Abst** AGRICOLA.

CC/1001-3725
**YIBIAO CAILIAO.** **VFOAT** Journal of Instrument Materials. (1970)-. Periodical. Chinese. bm. Chongqing Gai Kan Bianjibu, People's Republic of China. **DD** 681.7. Documents available from CASDDS.
**Ind/Abst** Chem. Abstr.

CC/0255-8297
**YINGYONG KEXUE XUEBAO.** (YING YUNG KO HSUEH HSUEH PAO.). [Yingyong kexue xuebao]. **VFOAT** Journal of Applied Sciences. (1983)-. Periodical. Chinese (summaries and/or abstracts in English). qt. $60.00. Shanghai Scientific and Technical Publishers, Journal Department, 450 Ruijin 2 lu, Shanghai 200020, People's Republic of China. **Tel** 4310310. **ED** H. Hongjia. **LC** T4; .Y56. **DD** 605. **CODEN** YKXUD4. Documents available from BLDSC, CASDDS.
**Ind/Abst** Chem. Abstr.

CC/0254-3087
**YIQI YIBIAO XUEBAO.** (I CHI I PIAO HSUEH PAO.). [Yiqi yibiao xuebao]. **Added/Corp** Chung-kuo I Chi I Piao Hsueh Hui. **VFOAT** Chinese Journal of Scientific Instrument. (1980)-. Periodical. Chinese (summaries and/or abstracts in English). qt. **(Subscription address:** China International Book

# Science and Technology

Trading Corporation, PO Box 399, Library Service Department, Beijing 100044 People's Republic of China.) **LC** IN PROCESS. **CODEN** YYXUDY. Documents available from Ask*IEEE, CASDDS.
**Ind/Abst** Chem. Abstr.; INSPEC (Feb. 1981-).

KO
**YONBO. Main/Corp** Soul Taehakkyo. Kongkwa Taehak. **VFOAT** Soul Taehakkyo Kongkwa Taehak Yonbo. V. 1- (1981-82)-. Korean. an. Soul Taehakkyo Kongkwa Taehak / Sillim-dong, San 56-1 Sillim-dong Kwanak-ku, Seoul Korea. **LC** T173.S4588; A45.

KO
**YONGU NONMUNJIP (HANGUK ENOJI YONGUSO).** (YONGU NONMUNJIP.). Periodical. English (Korean). Hanguk Enoji Yonguso, 170-2 Kongnung-dong, Tobong-ku Seoul South Korea. **LC** T9001; .Y65. **Continues** Yongu Nonmunjip (Hanguk Wonjaryok Yonguso).

KO
**YONGU NONMUNJIP (ULSAN KONGKWA TAEHAK. PYONGSOL KONGOP CHONMUN TAEHAK).** (YONGU NONMUNJIP.). **VFOAT** U.J.C.T. Report; UJCT Report. Periodical. English (Korean). **LC** T4; .Y64.
**Ind/Abst** Energy Res. Abstr. (Oct. 1981-).

KO
**YON'GU POGO - KUNGNIP K ONGOP PYOJUN SIHOMSO. Main/Corp** Kungnip Kongop Pyojun Sihomso. Report. **Added/Corp** Kungnip Kongop Pyojun Sihomso. Report. **VFOAT** Report of National Industrial Standards Research Institute. (19??)-. Periodical. Korean (summaries and/or abstracts in English). **LC** T4; .K79a. Documents available from CASDDS.
**Ind/Abst** Chem. Abstr.

JA
**YORAN - HOKKAIDO KOGYO KAIHATSU. Main/Corp** Hokkaido Kogyo Kaihatsu Shikenjo. (19??)-. Periodical. Japanese. Hokkaido Kogyo Kaihatsu Shikenjo, (Government Industrial Development Laboratory), 41-2 Higashi Tsukisamu, Toyohira-ku Sapporo 061-01, Hokkaido Japan. **LC** T178.H64; H64b.

JA
**YORAN- [TOHOKU KOGYO GIJUTSU SHIKENJO]. Main/Corp** Tohoku Kogyo Gijutsu Shikenjo. (19??)-. Japanese. Tohoku Kogyo Gijutsu Shikenjo, Haramachi-Nigatake Miyagi-ken, Sendai 983 Japan. **LC** T178.T63; T63a.

PL/0044-1619
**ZAGADNIENIA NAUKOZNAWSTWA. Added/Corp** Polska Akademia Nauk. Komisja Naukoznawstwa. Vol. 1, No. 1 (1965)-. Periodical. Polish (summaries and/or abstracts in Russian and English). qt. $60.00. **(Subscription address:** ARS Polona, PO Box 1001, 00068 Warsaw Poland.) **LC** Q4; .Z33.

GW
**ZAHLENSPIEGEL.** 1976-. German. an. Technische Universitat Hannover, Welfengarten 1B, 3000 Hannover 1 Germany. **LC** T173; .H2437.

JA/0916-4456
**ZAIKEN HOKOKU. Added/Corp** Waseda Daigaku. Kagami Kinen Zairyo Gijutsu Kenkyujo. **VFOAT** Transactions of Laboratory for Materials Science and Technology, Waseda University. (1989)-. Periodical. Japanese (summaries and/or abstracts in English). **LC** IN PROCESS. **CODEN** ZAHOEI. Documents available from CASDDS. **Continues** Waseda Daigaku. Imono Kenkyujo. Chuken Hokoku, 0289-4181.
**Ind/Abst** Chem. Abstr.

JA/0388-3930
**ZAIRYO KAGAKU.** [Zairyo kagaku]. **Added/Corp** Nihon Zairyo Kagakkai. (1964)-. Periodical. Japanese. Six times a year. Nihon Zairyo Kagakkai, (Materials Science Soc. of Japan), Tokyo Kogyo Daigaku, 4259, Nagatsutacho, Midoriku, Yokohamashi, Kanagawaken 227, Japan. **(Subscription address:** Kyowa Book Company Inc., 1 38 Kanda Jinbocho Chiyoda-ku, Tokyo 101 Japan.) **CODEN** ZAKGA5. Documents available from CASDDS.
**Ind/Abst** Chem. Abstr.

ZA/0378-8857
**ZAMBIA JOURNAL OF SCIENCE AND TECHNOLOGY.** [Zambia j. sci. technol.]. V. 1- Jan. 1976-. Academic Scholarly Publication. English. qt. K15.00. National Council for Scientific Research, PO Box CH 158 Chelston, Lusaka Zambia. **LC** Q91.Z33; Z317. **DD** 505. **NLM** W1 ZA756. **CODEN** ZJSTDE. Documents available from BIOSIS Document Express, CASDDS.
**Ind/Abst** Biol. Abstr.; Chem. Abstr.; Food Sci. Technol. Abstr.; GeoRef.

IQ
**ZANCO : THE SCIENTIFIC JOURNAL OF SALAHADDIN UNIVERSITY. Added/Corp** Jamiat Salah al-Din. **VFOAT** Zanku. Vol. 1, No. 1 (1988)-. Periodical. English (Arabic). qt. **CODEN** ZANCEC.
**Ind/Abst** Food Sci. Technol. Abstr.; Hortic. Abstr.; Plant Breed. Abstr.; Plant Grow. Reg. Abstr.; Postharvest News Inf.; Rev. Agric. Entomol.; Soils Fert.; Wheat Barley Trit. Abstr.

XN/0352-4906
**ZBORNIK MATICE SRPSKE ZA PRIRODNE NAUKE.** [Zb. Matice srp. prir. nauke]. (1984)-. Serbo-Croatian (Cyrillic). sa. **UDC** 5. Documents available from CASDDS. **Continues** Zbornik za Prirodne Nauke, 0461-4461.
**Ind/Abst** Chem. Abstr.

XO/0371-4616
**ZBORNIK VEDECKYCH PRAC VYSOKEJ SKOLY TECHNICKEJ V KOSICIACH.** [Zb. ved. pr. Vys. sk. tech. Kosiciach]. 1968-. Periodical. English (German, Russian and Slovak; summaries and/or abstracts in German, Russian and Slovak). ir. Alfa / Slovakia, Hurbanovo Nam 3, 815 89 Bratislava Slovakia. **Tel** 7 331-441, **FAX** 7 594-43. **LC** TA4; .K6. **DD** 605. **CODEN** SVVSAU. Documents available from CASDDS. **Continues** Sbornik Vedeckych Prac Vysokej Skoly Technickej v Kosiciach.
**Ind/Abst** Alum. Ind. Abstr.; Chem. Abstr.; Eng. Mater. Abstr.; Met. Abstr.

GW/0170-6241
**ZEITSCHRIFT FUER SEMIOTIK.** Vol. 1 (1979)-. Periodical. German (summaries and/or abstracts in English). qt. DM105.60 Germany; DM110.40 other. Stauffenberg Verlag, Postfach 2567, West 7400 Tuebingen 5 Germany. **Tel** 011 49 7071 78091, 011 49 7071 78092. **ED** Roland Posner. **LC** P99; .Z43. **DD** 401/.41/05. **CODEN** ZESEE3. **Bk Rev**. **Ad Acc**. **Circ:** 1,200. Documents available from The Genuine Article.
**Desc:** Covers theoretical and historical bases of semiotics, semiotic bases of sciences, semiotics of everyday life and aesthetic experience and problems of application.
**Ind/Abst** Arts Humanit. Citation Index [Full Cov.]; Curr. Contents Arts Humanit.; Res. Alert [Full Cov.]; Soc. Sci. Cit. Index [Select. Cov.].

AU/0514-2946
**ZEMENT UND BETON. Added/Corp** Verein der Osterreichischen Zementfabrikanten. Osterreichischer Betonverein. (19??)-. Academic Scholarly Publication. German. mo. **LC** TA680; .Z34. **CODEN** ZMBEA4. Documents available from CASDDS.
**Ind/Abst** Chem. Abstr.; Int. Civil Eng. Abstr.

UK/0084-5442
**ZENITH.** V. 1- 1963-. Periodical. English. an. £10.00. Oxford University Scientific Society, University Museum, Oxford England.

PL/0208-6360
**ZESZYTY NAUKOWE - AKADEMIA TECHNICZNO-ROLNICZA IM. JANA I JEDRZEJA SNIADECKICH W BYDGOSZCZY. CHEMIA I TECHNOLOGIA CHEMICZNA. See** Chemistry.

PL/0372-9400
**ZESZYTY NAUKOWE AKADEMII GORNICZO-HUTNICZEJ IM. STANISAWA STASZICA. GORNICTWO. See** Earth Sciences-Mineralogy.

PL/0044-4405
**ZESZYTY NAUKOWE KATOLICKIEGO UNIWERSYTETU LUBELSKIEGO. Added/Corp** Katolicki Uniwersytet Lubelski. Vol. 1, No. 1 (1958)-. Periodical. Polish (summaries and/or abstracts in English and French). qt. Price on Request. **(Subscription address:** ARS Polona, PO Box 1001, 00068 Warsaw Poland.) **LC** AS262.L84; A14. cum. index.

PL/0372-9524
**ZESZYTY NAUKOWE POLITECHNIKI CZESTOCHOWSKIEJ. NAUKI TECHNICZNE. HUTNICTWO.** (NAUKI TECHNICZNE. HUTNICTWO.). [Zesz. nauk. Politech. CzOest., Nauki tech., Hut.]. **Added/Corp** Politechniki Czestochowskiej. **VFOAT** Hutnictwo. (1969)-. Academic Scholarly Publication. Polish (summaries and/or abstracts in English and Russian). **CODEN** ZNTHA8. Documents available from CASDDS.
**Ind/Abst** Alum. Ind. Abstr.; Chem. Abstr.; Met. Abstr.

PL/0416-7341
**ZESZYTY NAUKOWE POLITECHNIKI GDANSKIEJ. CHEMIA.** [Zesz. nauk. Politech. Gdan., Chem.]. **Added/Corp** Politechnika Gdanska. **VFOAT** Chemia. (1955)-. Academic Scholarly Publication. Polish (summaries and/or abstracts in English, German and Russian). Panstwowe Wydawn Naukowe, Miodowa 10, PO Box 391, 00251 Warsaw Poland. **CODEN** ZNGCAU. Documents available from CASDDS.
**Ind/Abst** Chem. Abstr. (1955-1980)(19??-); Energy Res. Abstr. (July 1982-).

CC/0253-9748
**ZHENKONG KEXUE YU JISHU.** (CHEN KUNG KO HSUEH YU CHI SHU.). [Zhenkong kexue yu jishu]. **Added/Corp** Chung-Kuo Chen Kung Hsueh Hui. **VFOAT** Vacuum Science and Technology; Zhenkong Kexue Yu Jishu. (1981)-. Academic Scholarly Publication. Chinese (summaries and/or abstracts in English). bm. $28.02. **(Subscription address:** China International Book Trading Corporation, PO Box 399, Library Service Department, Beijing 100044 People's Republic of China.) **LC** TJ940; .C485. **DD** 621.5/5/05. **CODEN** CKKSDV. Documents available from CASDDS.
**Ind/Abst** Chem. Abstr.

CC/0254-5896
**ZHONGGUO KEXUE. A, SHUXUE, WULIXUE, TIANWENXUE, JISHUKEXUE.** (CHUNG-KUO KO HSUEH. A CHI. SHU HSUEH, WU LI HSUEH, TIEN WEN HSUEH, CHI SHU KO HSUEH / CHUNG-KUO KO HSUEH YUAN, CHU PAN.). [Zhongguo kexue. A, Shuxue, wulixue, tianwenxue, jishukexue]. **Added/Corp** Chung-kuo ko Hsueh Yuan. **VFOAT** Scientia Sinica. (1982)-. Periodical. Chinese. mo. $82.30. **(Subscription address:** China International Book Trading Corporation, PO Box 399, Library Service Department, Beijing 100044 People's Republic of China.) **Continues in part** Chung-kuo ko Hsueh, 0301-9632.

CC/0254-590X
**ZHONGGUO KEXUE. B, HUAXUE, SHENGWUXUE, NONGXUE, YIXUE, DIXUE.** (CHUNG-KUO KO HSUEH. B CHI. HUA HSUEH, SHENG WU HSUEH, NUNG HSUEH, I HSUEH, TI HSUEH / CHUNG-KUO KO HSUEH YUAN, CHU PAN.). [Zhongguo kexue. B, Huaxue, shengwuxue, nongxue, yixue, dixue]. **Added/Corp** Chung-kuo ko Hsueh Yuan. **VFOAT** Scientia Sinica. (1982)-. Periodical. Chinese. mo. $96.36. **(Subscription address:** China International Book Trading Corporation, PO Box 399, Library Service Department, Beijing 100044 People's Republic of China.) **Continues in part** Chung-kuo ko Hsueh, 0301-9632.

CC/0253-2778
**ZHONGGUO KEXUE JISHU DAXUE XUEBAO.** (CHUNG-KUO KO HSUEH CHI SHU TA HSUEH HSUEH PAO.). [Zhongguo kexue jishu daxue xuebao]. **Added/Corp** Chung-kuo ko Hsueh Chi Shu ta Hsueh. **VFOAT** Journal of the China University of Science and Technology. (1965)-. Academic Scholarly Publication. Chinese (summaries and/or abstracts in English). bm. $6.66. Tianjin Daxue / Tianjin University, Qilitai, Nankai qu, Tianjin 300072, People's Republic of China. **Tel** 3358116. **(Subscription address:** China International Book Trading Corporation, PO Box 399, Library Service Department, Beijing 100044 People's Republic of China.) **ED** W. Yongshi. **LC** Q4; .C4226. **DD** 505. **CODEN** CKHPD7. **Circ:** 2,000. Documents available from CASDDS, Article Express International, CASDDS.
**Ind/Abst** Chem. Abstr.; Int. Aerosp. Abstr.; Math. Rev.; Zentralbl. Math. Ihre Grenzgeb.

CC/1000-758X
**ZHONGGUO KONGJIAN KEXUE JISHU. See** Aeronautics, Astronautics.

CC/0253-973X
**ZHONGHUA YIXUE JIANYAN ZAZHI.** (CHUNG-HUA I HSUEH CHIEN YEN TSA CHIH.). [Zhonghua Yixue Jianyan Zazhi]. **Added/Corp** Chung-hua i Hsueh hui (China : 1949- ). **VFOAT** Zhonghua Yixue Jianyan Zazhi; Chinese Journal of Medical Laboratory Technology. (1978)-. Academic Scholarly Publication. Chinese (table of contents in English). qt. **NLM** W1 CH982AB. **CODEN** CHCCDO. Documents available from CASDDS.
**Ind/Abst** Chem. Abstr.; NAPRALERT.

RH/1016-1503
**ZIMBABWE SCIENCE NEWS, THE.** [Zimb. sci. news]. **Added/Corp** Zimbabwe Scientific Association. Vol. 14 No. 4 (Apr./May 1980)-. Periodical. English. Four times a year. $10.00. University of Zimbabwe / Physics Department, PO Box MP 167, Harare Zimbabwe. **Tel** 011 263 4 303211 ext. 1497. **ED** Pete Morgan. **CODEN** ZSNED7. cum. index. **Bk Rev**. **Circ:** 1,650 (ctrl). Documents available from BIOSIS Document Express. **Continues** Zimbabwe Rhodesia Science News, 0253-049X.
**Ind/Abst** Anthropol. (19??-); Biol. Abstr.; Crop Physiol. Abstr.; Life Sci. Collect.

CC/0253-9608
**ZIRAN ZAZHI.** (TZU JAN TSA CHIH. ZIRAN ZAZHI.). [Ziran zazhi]. **VFOAT** Ziran Zazhi; Nature Journal. (1978)-. Academic Scholarly Publication. Chinese. mo. $2.30. Ziran Zashi, PO Box 040-056, Shanghai, 200040 People's Republic of China. **Tel** 4336850. **ED** H. Zongying. **LC** Q4; .T95. **CODEN** TJTCD4. Documents available from CASDDS.
**Ind/Abst** Chem. Abstr.; Math. Rev.; NAPRALERT.

YU/0351-0999
**ZITO HLEB.** [Zito hleb]. **Added/Corp** Savez Drustava za Unapreenje Ishrane Naroda Jugoslavije. OOUR Jugoslovenski Institut Prehrambenog Inzenjerstva za Tehnologiju Secera, Zita i Brasna, Skroba i

Konditorskih Proizvoda. Tehnoloski Fakultet. Zavod za Tehnologiju Zita i Brasna (Novi Sad, Serbia). (1974)-. Academic Scholarly Publication. Serbo-Croatian (Roman) (summaries and/or abstracts in German). bm. **CODEN** ZIHLDU. Documents available from CASDDS.
**Ind/Abst** Chem. Abstr.

RU/0130-1640
**ZNANIE--SILA. Added/Corp** Vsesoiuznyi Leninskii Kommunisticheskii Soiuz Molodezhi. Tentralnyi Komitet. Russian S.F.S.R. Narodnyi Komissariat Prosveshcheniia. Soviet Union. Glavnoe Upravlenie Trudovykh Rezervov. Soviet Union. Ministerstvo Trudovykh Rezervov. Glavnoe Upravlenie Professionalnogo Obrazovaniia Ministerstva Kultury SSSR. Gosudarstvennyi Komitet Soveta Ministrov SSSR po Professionalno-Tekhnicheskomu Obrazovaniiu. Soviet Union. Gosudarstvennyi Komitet po Professionalno-Tekhnicheskomu Obrazovaniiu. Vsesoiuznoe Obshchestvo "Znanie.". (1926)-. Periodical. Russian. mo. $89.95. **(Subscription address:** East View Publications Inc., 3020 Harbor Lane North, Suite 110, Minneapolis MN 55447.) **LC** T4; .Z5.

CI
**ZNANSTVENOISTRAZIVACKE I RAZVOJNE ORGANIZACIJE. Main/Corp** Republicki Zavod Za Statistiku Sr Hrvatske. Serbo-Croatian (Roman). an. 7,000Din Yugoslavia. Republicki Zavod Za Statistiku SRH, Ilica 3, Zagreb Croatia. **Tel** (041)424-422. **LC** Q180.Y8; C76A. **Circ:** 400.

GW/0340-9422
**ZOR. ZEITSCHRIFT FUER OPERATIONS-RESEARCH.** (ZEITSCHRIFT FUER OPERATIONS RESEARCH.). [ZOR. Z. Oper.-Res.arch]. **Added/Corp** Deutsche Gesellschaft fuer Operations Research. **VFOAT** ZOR. Vol. 16 (1972)-. Periodical. English (German). Six times a year. DM388.50. Springer-Verlag GmbH & Company KG, Heidelberger Platz 3, D 14197 Berlin Germany. **Tel** 011 49 30 8207223, FAX 011 49 30 8214091, telex 183 319 SPBLN D. **(Subscription address:** Springer Verlag New York Inc. / for North America, 44 Hartz Way, Secaucus NJ 07096.) **ED** U Rieder. **LC** T57.6.A1; Z44. **[CCC]. Bk Rev. Ad Acc. Circ:** 400. Documents available from Article Express International, Ask*IEEE. ***Continues*** *Unternehmensforschung, 0042-0573.*
**Desc:** Publishes quality papers in operations research and related optimization theory, including works on mathematical programming, dynamic programming and control, stochastic programming, discrete optimization, graphs and networks, game theory, stochastic decision processes, inventory, queueing and reliability.
**Ind/Abst** Bioeng. Abstr.; Ei Page One; Energy Res. Abstr. (March 1982-); Eng. Index Annu.; INSPEC (1972-1987); Int. Abstr. Oper. Res. [Full Cov.]; Math. Rev.; Zentralbl. Math. Ihre Grenzgeb.

XR
**ZPRAVODAJ - FEDERALNI MINISTERSTVO PRO TECHNICKY A INVESTICNI ROZVOJ, MINISTERSTVO VYSTAVBY A TECHNIKY CSR, MINISTERSTVO VYSTAVBY A TECHNIKY SSR. Main/Corp** Czechoslovakia. Federalni Ministerstvo Pro Technicky a Investicni Rozvoj. Vol. 3 (1971)-. Czech. ir (8 numbers a year). kcs8.00. Federalni Ministerstvo Pro Technicky A Investicni, Rozvoj Slezska 9, Prague 2 Czech Republic. **LC** T26.C9; C93A. ***Continues*** *Zpravodaj - Federalni Vybor pro Technicky a Investicni Rozvoj, Ministerstvo Vystavby a Techniky CSR a SSR.*

XR/0044-5355
**ZPRAVODAJ VZLU.** (ZPRAVODAJ VYZKUMNEHO A ZKHUSEBNIHO LETECKHO USTAVU.). [Zpr. VZLU]. **VFOAT** Zpravodaj Vyzkumneho a Zkhusebniho Leteckeho Ustavu. (1962)-. Periodical. Multiple languages. bm. SNTL - Nakladatelstvi Technicke Literatury, Technical Literature, Spalena 51, 113 02 Prague 1 Czech Republic. **Tel** (2)297670. **UDC** 629.13.
**Ind/Abst** Int. Aerosp. Abstr.

JA/0387-5512
**ZUGAKU KENKYU. VFOAT** Journal of Graphic Science of Japan. Periodical. Japanese (summaries and/or abstracts in English). Nihon Zugakkai, c/o Tokyo Daigaku Kyoyo Gakubu Zugaku Kyoshitsu, 8-1 Komaba Meguro-ku Tokyo-to 153 Japan.

AI/0033-1163
**ZVARTNOTS. Added/Corp** Armenian S.S.R. Goskomekonomika. (1991)-. Periodical. Russian. mo. **CODEN** ZVARE3. ***Continues*** *Promyshlennost, Stroitelstvo i Arkhitektura Armenii, 0033-1163.*

NE
**ZWO : PLAATS EN PERSPECTIEF. Main/Corp** Netherlands (Kingdom, 1815- ). Nederlandse Organisatie voor Zuiver-Wetenschappelijk Onderzoek. Dutch. Netherlands Organization for Scientific Research, Laan van Nieuw Oost Jndie 131, PO Box 93138, 2509 AC The Netherlands. **LC** Q180.N35; N47A. **Circ:** 8,000.
**Desc:** Indications for science policy principles of ZWO in the 1980's.

## ABSTRACTING, BIBLIOGRAPHIES AND STATISTICS

JA/0912-2311
**ABSTRACTS OF SCIENCE AND TECHNOLOGY IN JAPAN: ENERGY TECHNOLOGY. *Ceased.*** [Abstr. sci. technol. Jpn., Energy technol.]. (1986)-Vol. 13 (1993). Periodical. English. ir. Nihon Kagaku Gijutsu Joho Senta, (Japan Information Center of Science & Technology), 5-2, Nagatacho 2 Chome, Chiyodaku, Tokyoto 100 Japan. **(Subscription address:** Japan Publications Trading Company, Ltd., PO Box 5030, Tokyo International, Tokyo 100-31 Japan.) **DD** 016.621. ***Continues*** *Abstracts of Science and Technology in Japan. Renewable Energy, 0287-5012.*

US/0000-1287
**AMERICAN MEN & WOMEN OF SCIENCE.** [Am. men women sci.]. **Added/Corp** R.R. Bowker Company. Database Publishing Group. **VFOAT** American Men and Women of Science. 17th Ed. (1990)-. English. ir. $850.00 (8 volume set). R R Bowker, A Reed Reference Publishing Company, Part of Reed International PLC, PO Box 31, 121 Chanlon Drive, New Providence NJ 07974. **Tel** (908)464-6800, (800)521-8110, FAX (908)665-6688, telex 138-755. **LC** Q141; .A474. **DD** 509.2/2; B. available on magnetic tape, an online database, and CD-ROM. ***Continues*** *American Men and Women of Science. Physical and Biological Sciences, 0192-8570.*
**Desc:** Resource for information on over 125,000 leading US and Canadian scientists and engineers.

US/0146-0048
**AMERICAN MEN AND WOMEN OF SCIENCE: BIOLOGY.** (19??)-. Periodical. English. ir. $850.00 (8 volume set). R R Bowker, A Reed Reference Publishing Company, Part of Reed International PLC, PO Box 31, 121 Chanlon Drive, New Providence NJ 07974. **Tel** (908)464-6800, (800)521-8110, FAX (908)665-6688, telex 138-755. **LC** QH26; .A45. **DD** 574/.02/2; B. available on magnetic tape, an online database, and CD-ROM.

US/0146-0056
**AMERICAN MEN AND WOMEN OF SCIENCE: CHEMISTRY.** (19??)-. English. ir. $850.00 (8 volume set). R R Bowker, A Reed Reference Publishing Company, Part of Reed International PLC, PO Box 31, 121 Chanlon Drive, New Providence NJ 07974. **Tel** (908)464-6800, (800)521-8110, FAX (908)665-6688, telex 138-755. **LC** QD21; .A45. **DD** 540/.92/2; B. available on magnetic tape, an online database, and CD-ROM.

US/0146-0064
**AMERICAN MEN AND WOMEN OF SCIENCE: CONSULTANTS.** (1977)-. English. ir. $850.00 (8 volume set). R R Bowker, A Reed Reference Publishing Company, Part of Reed International PLC, PO Box 31, 121 Chanlon Drive, New Providence NJ 07974. **Tel** (908)464-6800, (800)521-8110, FAX (908)665-6688, telex 138-755. **LC** Q141; .A465. **DD** 509/.2/2. available on magnetic tape, an online database, and CD-ROM.

US/0094-5315
**AMERICAN MEN AND WOMEN OF SCIENCE: ECONOMICS. Added/Corp** Jaques Cattell Press. (1974)-. English. ir. $850.00 (8 volume set). R R Bowker, A Reed Reference Publishing Company, Part of Reed International PLC, PO Box 31, 121 Chanlon Drive, New Providence NJ 07974. **Tel** (908)464-6800, (800)521-8110, FAX (908)665-6688, telex 138-755. **LC** HB119.A3; A43. **DD** 330/.092/2; B. available on magnetic tape, an online database, and CD-ROM.

US/0145-9996
**AMERICAN MEN AND WOMEN OF SCIENCE: MEDICAL AND HEALTH SCIENCES.** (19??)-. English. ir. $850.00 (8 volume set). R R Bowker, A Reed Reference Publishing Company, Part of Reed International PLC, PO Box 31, 121 Chanlon Drive, New Providence NJ 07974. **Tel** (908)464-6800, (800)521-8110, FAX (908)665-6688, telex 138-755. **LC** R153; .A538. **DD** 610/.92/2; B. **NLM** W 22 AA1 A53. available on magnetic tape, an online database, and CD-ROM.

US/0146-003X
**AMERICAN MEN AND WOMEN OF SCIENCE: PHYSICS, ASTRONOMY, MATHEMATICS, STATISTICS, AND COMPUTER SCIENCE.** (19??)-. English. ir. $850.00 (8 volume set). R R Bowker, A Reed Reference Publishing Company, Part of Reed International PLC, PO Box 31, 121 Chanlon Drive, New Providence NJ 07974. **Tel** (908)464-6800, (800)521-8110, FAX (908)665-6688, telex 138-755. **LC** Q141; .A467. **DD** 509/.2/2; B. available on magnetic tape, an online database, and CD-ROM.

US/0003-6986
**APPLIED SCIENCE & TECHNOLOGY INDEX.** [Appl. sci. technol. index]. **Added/Corp** H.W. Wilson Company. **VAT** Applied Science and Technology Index. Vol. 46 (1958)-. Abstracting/Indexing Service. English. mo (except July, with quarterly cumulations). Print edition priced on the service basis. H W Wilson Company, 950 University Avenue, Bronx NY 10452. **Tel** (800)367-6770, (718)588-8400, FAX (718)590-1617, telex 4990003 HWILSON. **ED** Joyce Howard. **LC** Z7913; .I7. **NLM** ZT 15 I421. **Circ:** 4,000. available on CD-ROM from WILSONDISC; available on magnetic tape from WILSONTAPE; available on diskette from WILSONSEARCH; available on an online database from WILSONLINE. ***Continues in part*** *Industrial Arts Index, 0275-1682.*
**Desc:** Covers areas such as acoustical imaging, industrial robotics, computer languages and waste disposal. Puts the latest reports and methodology in science and technology at your fingertips.
**Ind/Abst** Abstr. Bull. Inst. Pap. Sci. Tech.; MINPROC; Mintec, Min. Technol. Abstr.

US/1063-8695
**APPLIED SCIENCE & TECHNOLOGY INDEX (CD-ROM ED.).** (APPLIED SCIENCE & TECHNOLOGY INDEX [COMPUTER FILE].). [Appl. sci. technol. index]. **Added/Corp** H.W. Wilson Company. **VFOAT** Applied Science and Technology Index; WILSONDISC Applied Science & Technology Index; WILSONDISC Applied Science and Technology Index. (198?)-. English. mo. $1495.00. H W Wilson Company, 950 University Avenue, Bronx NY 10452. **Tel** (800)367-6770, (718)588-8400, FAX (718)590-1617, telex 4990003 HWILSON. **LC** Z7913. **DD** 605. available in print; available on magnetic tape from WILSONTAPE; available on diskette from WILSONSEARCH; available on an online database from WILSONLINE.
**Desc:** Covers areas such as aeronautics and space science, artificial intelligence and machine learning, chemistry, computer technology, construction, engineering, engineering materials, environmental engineering and waste management, food, geology, marine technology and oceanography, mathematics, metallurgy, meteorology, mineralogy, neural networks and optical computing, petroleum and gas, physics, plastics, robotics, solid state technology, telecommunications, textiles, and transportation.

CN/0226-1685
**ASTIS BIBLIOGRAPHY.** (A S T I S BIBLIOGRAPHY [MICROFORM].). [ASTIS bibliogr.]. **Main/Corp** Arctic Science and Technology Information System. **Added/Corp** Arctic Institute of North America. (1979)-. Abstracting/Indexing Service. English (French). an (Mar.). 105.00Can$ Canada; $110.00 other. Arctic Institute of North America, University of Calgary, 2500 University Drive Northwest, Calgary Alberta T2N 1N4 Canada. **Tel** (403)220-7515, FAX (403)282-4609. **ED** Ross Goodwin. **LC** Microfiche (o) 90/6868. **DD** 016.9719. Index available. cum. index. **Circ:** 100. available on CD-ROM (on Arctic & Antarctic Regions A NISC DISC CD-ROM Publication) from National Information Service Corporation (NISC).
**Desc:** A multi-disciplinary arctic abstracting and indexing service.

BL
**BIBLIOGRAFIA BRASILEIRA DE POLITICA CIENTIFICA E TECNOLOGICA.** Vol. 1 (1983)-. Portuguese. an. **LC** Z7405.P8; B52; Q127.B8. **DD** 016.33898102.

SZ/0067-6829
**BIBLIOGRAPHIA SCIENTIAE NATURALIS HELVETICA.** [Bibl. sci. nat. Helv.]. **Added/Corp** Schweizerische Landesbibliothek. Vol. 24 (1948)-. Periodical. German (French). an. 30.00F. Schweizerische Landesbibliothe, Hallwylstrasse 15, 3000 Berne Switzerland. **Tel** 011 41 31 618911. **ED** A Caflisch. Index available. **Circ:** 800. ***Continues*** *Bibliographie der Schweizerischen Naturwissenschaftlichen und Geographischen Literatur;* ***Absorbed*** *Bibliographie der Forstlichen Literatur der Schweiz.*
**Desc:** Bibliography of books and articles on serials dealing with science, geography, agriculture, forestry, and engineering.
**Ind/Abst** GeoRef; Math. Rev.

US/0360-2761
**BIBLIOGRAPHIC GUIDE TO TECHNOLOGY. Main/Corp** New York Public Library. Research Libraries. **Added/Corp** Engineering Societies Library. Classed Subject Catalog. (1975)-. English. an. $345.00. GK Hall & Co, 100 Front Street, Riverside NJ 08075. **Tel** (800)257-5755 ext. 2223. **LC** Z5854; .N48a Suppl. 2; TA145. **DD** 016.6. ***Continues*** *Technology Book Guide, 0091-7885.*

SZ/0253-8296
**BULLETIN BIBLIOGRAPHIQUE SPELEOLOGIQUE.** [Speleol. abstr.]. **VFOAT** Speleological Abstracts. Bulletin. English (French). an. 26.50F Switzerland; 29.00F Europe; 31.50F other. Bulletin Bibliographique Speleologique, Speleological Abstracts, Strassburgerallee 116, CH-4055 Basel Switzerland. **Tel** 061 43 77 55. **(Subscription address:**

Bibliotheque SSS, Case Postale 77, CH-5300 Turgi Switzerland) **LC** Z6033.C3; B84; GB601.A1. **DD** 016.5514/4. Index available. **Bk Rev. Circ:** 1,000.
**Desc:** Offers annual digest of several thousand texts concerning speleology world-wide. Geographic and author index. Arranged by subject.
**Ind/Abst** GeoRef.

US/1049-1317
**C2C ABSTRACTS JAPAN. MATERIALS SCIENCES.** [C2C abstr. Jap., Mat. sci.]. **VFOAT** Materials Sciences. Vol. 1, No. 1 (Feb. 1990)-. English. mo. $200.00. SCAN C2C Inc, Attn Carol G Heffernan Marketing Director, 500 E Street Southwest, Suite 800, 8th Floor, Washington DC 20024. **Tel** (202)863-3850, (800)525-3865, FAX (202)863-3855. **DD** 620. Index available. cum. index. available on CD-ROM from DIALOG; available on an online database from ORBIT; DATA-STAR; and DIALOG.
**Desc:** English abstracts of over 500 Japanese science, technical and business journals in the field of Materials sciences.

TR/1011-4866
**CARINDEX, SCIENCE & TECHNOLOGY.** [Carindex sci. technol.]. Periodical. English. Twice a year. $45.00. Carindex, University of the West Indies Library, St. Augustine Trinidad. **Tel** (809)663-1359. **(Subscription address:** The Press - University of the West Indies, 1A Aqueduct Flats, Mona Campus, Kingston 7, Jamaica**) ED** Lutishoor Salisbury, Hannah Francis. **UDC** 62.
**Desc:** Print version of a bibliographic database of the literature of science, technology and agriculture. Includes indexing terms and abstracts of articles indexed.

●US
**CATALOGUE OF OTA PUBLICATIONS.** **Main/Corp** United States. Congress. Office of Technology Assessment. (Jan. 1993)-. English. Congressional and Public Affairs Office, Office of Technology Assessment, US Congress, Washington DC 20510-8025. ***Continues*** *United States. Congress. Office of Technology Assessment. Catalog of Publications.*

UK
**CATCHWORD AND TRADE NAME INDEX : CATNI.** **VFOAT** CATNI. Vol. 1, No. 1 (March 1981)-. Abstracting/Indexing Service. English. Three times a year. £165.00 EEC; £175.00 other. Bowker Saur Ltd., A Reed Reference Publishing Company, Part of Reed International PLC, 59-60 Grosvenor Street, London WIX 9DA England. **Tel** 011 44 71 4935841, FAX 011 44 71 4991590. **(Subscription address:** World-Wide Subscription Services, Unit 4, Gibbs Reed Farm Pashley Road, Ticehurst TN5 7HE England.**)** available on CD-ROM (with Current Technology Index as CTI Plus).
**Desc:** Features coverage of the industry leading journals covered in Current Technology Index, manufacturer's names, product names, organization names, geographical names, motor vehicle companies, aircraft companies, technical jargon/catchwords, buildings and structures, legislative acts and bills, and names of disasters.

US/0734-6468
**CHARACTERISTICS OF DOCTORAL SCIENTISTS AND ENGINEERS IN THE UNITED STATES. DETAILED STATISTICAL TABLES.** [Charact. dr. sci. eng. U. S., Detail. stat. tables]. 1979-. Statistical Publication. English. be. National Science Foundation, 1800 G Street Northwest, Washington DC 20550. **Tel** (202)357-9859, (202)357-9498. **LC** Q149.U5. **DD** 331.12/915/0973. **NLM** W2 A N37C. available on microfiche (Vols. for (1981-) distributed to depository libraries). ***Continues*** *Characteristics of Doctoral Scientists and Engineers in the United States. Technical Notes and Detailed Statistical Tables.*

US/0742-5686
**COMPUT-A-CAL.** ***Ceased.*** [Comput-a-cal]. **VFOAT** Comput A Cal. (Nov./Dec. 1983)-Ceased Jan. 1988. Abstracting/Indexing Service. English. bm. Topicator / Oregon, PO Box 1009, Clackamas OR 97015-1009. **Tel** (303)689-2037. **ED** Wendell Wolles. Index available. cum. index. ctrl circ.
**Desc:** Reference guide to articles published in computer-related periodical press.

UK
**CTI PLUS [COMPUTER FILE].** Abstracting/Indexing Service. English. qt. £850.00. Bowker Saur Ltd., A Reed Reference Publishing Company, Part of Reed International PLC, 59-60 Grosvenor Street, London WIX 9DA England. **Tel** 011 44 71 4935841, FAX 011 44 71 4991590. available in print (as Current Technology Index / Catchword and Trade Name Index).
**Desc:** Provides access to current technology initiatives and innovation from around the world. Made up of Current Technology Index and Catchword and Trade Name Index.

US/0011-3409
**CURRENT CONTENTS. LIFE SCIENCES.** [Curr. contents. Life sci.]. **Added/Corp** Institute for Scientific Information. Vol. 10 (1967)-. Abstracting/Indexing Service. English. wk. $488.00. Institute for Scientific Information, 3501 Market Street, Philadelphia PA 19104. **Tel** (215)386-0100, (800)523-1850, FAX (215)386-6362, telex 84-5305. **(Subscription address:** Institute for Scientific Information, PO Box 71416, Chicago IL 60694.**) LC** Z5321; .C87; QH301. **DD** 016.574. **NLM** ZW 1 C959. **Ad Acc. Circ:** 340,000. available on diskette; available on magnetic tape and an online database (as Current Contents Search); available on CD-ROM. Documents available from The Genuine Article. ***Continues*** *Current Contents. Your Weekly Guide to the Chemical, Pharmaco-Medical & Life Sciences, 0272-1503.*
**Desc:** Listing of tables of contents from over 1,200 journals in the life sciences.
**Ind/Abst** Abstr. Bull. Inst. Pap. Sci. Tech.; Curr. Contents Life Sci.; Res. Alert [Full Cov.]; Sci. Cit. Index; SCISEARCH; Soc. Sci. Cit. Index [Full Cov.]; Trop. Dis. Bull.

●US/1073-1229
**CURRENT CONTENTS. LIFE SCIENCES (CD-ROM VERSION).** (CURRENT CONTENTS. LIFE SCIENCES [COMPUTER FILE].). **Added/Corp** Institute for Scientific Information. **VFOAT** Life Sciences. (1994)-. English. wk. $2,495.00. Institute for Scientific Information, 3501 Market Street, Philadelphia PA 19104. **Tel** (215)386-0100, (800)523-1850, FAX (215)386-6362, telex 84-5305. **(Subscription address:** Institute for Scientific Information, PO Box 71416, Chicago, IL 60694**)** available in print; available on diskette; available on magnetic tape and an online database.

US/1062-3078
**CURRENT CONTENTS ON DISKETTE. LIFE SCIENCES. J600.** (CURRENT CONTENTS ON DISKETTE. LIFE SCIENCES. J600 [COMPUTER FILE].). [Curr. contents diskette, Life sci., J600]. **VFOAT** Life Sciences; J600. Vol. 32, Issue 5 (Jan. 30, 1989)-. Periodical. English. wk. $525.00 print; $769.00 combined with diskette. Institute for Scientific Information, 3501 Market Street, Philadelphia PA 19104. **Tel** (215)386-0100, (800)523-1850, FAX (215)386-6362, telex 84-5305. **(Subscription address:** Institute for Scientific Information, PO Box 71416, Chicago IL 60694.**) DD** 016. available in print; available on magnetic tape and an online database; available on CD-ROM. ***Continues in part*** *Current Contents on Diskette. Life Sciences.*

US/1062-3027
**CURRENT CONTENTS ON DISKETTE. LIFE SCIENCES. J1200.** (CURRENT CONTENTS ON DISKETTE. LIFE SCIENCES. J1200 [COMPUTER FILE].). [Curr. contents diskette, Life sci., J1200]. **VFOAT** Life Sciences; J1200. Vol. 32, Issue 5 (Jan. 30, 1989)-. Periodical. English. wk. $695.00 print; $949.00 other. Institute for Scientific Information, 3501 Market Street, Philadelphia PA 19104. **Tel** (215)386-0100, (800)523-1850, FAX (215)386-6362, telex 84-5305. **(Subscription address:** Institute for Scientific Information, PO Box 71416, Chicago IL 60694.**) DD** 016. available in print; available on magnetic tape and an online database; available on CD-ROM. ***Continues in part*** *Current Contents on Diskette. Life Sciences.*

US/1062-3108
**CURRENT CONTENTS ON DISKETTE WITH ABSTRACTS. LIFE SCIENCES.** (CURRENT CONTENTS ON DISKETTE WITH ABSTRACTS. LIFE SCIENCES [COMPUTER FILE].). [Curr. contents diskette abstr., Life. sci.]. **VFOAT** Life Sciences. Vol. 34, Issue 18 (May 6, 1991)-. Abstracting/Indexing Service. English. wk. $4132.00 (1-10) workstations. Institute for Scientific Information, 3501 Market Street, Philadelphia PA 19104. **Tel** (215)386-0100, (800)523-1850, FAX (215)386-6362, telex 84-5305. **(Subscription address:** Institute for Scientific Information, PO Box 71416, Chicago, IL 60694**) DD** 016. available in print; available on magnetic tape and an online database; available on CD-ROM.

II
**CURRENT LITERATURE ON SCIENCE OF SCIENCE.** **Added/Corp** Council of Scientific & Industrial Research (India). Vol. 1 (Jan. 1972)-. Abstracting/Indexing Service. English. mo. $90.00. Prints India, 11 Darya Ganj, New Delhi 11002 India. **Tel** 011 91 11 3268645. **(Subscription address:** World-Wide Subscription Services, Unit 4, Gibbs Reed Farm Pashley Road, Ticehurst TN5 7HE England.**) LC** Z7405.R4; C88. **DD** 016.30124/8. **Circ:** 500. ***Supersedes*** *Index to Literature on Science of Science.*
**Desc:** Keeps abreast of the latest developments in science and technology.

US/0590-4102
**CURRENT PRIMATE REFERENCES.** [Curr. primate ref.]. **Added/Corp** University of Washington. Primate Information Center. (Sept. 30, 1966)-. Abstracting/Indexing Service. English. mo. $60.00 US; $80.00 other. Primate Information Center, University of Washington SJ-50, Seattle WA 98195. **Tel** (206)543-4376, FAX (206)685-0305. **ED** Jackie Pritchard. **NLM** Z 7996.P85 C976. Index available. cum. index. **Ad Acc. Circ:** 500 (ctrl). ***Supersedes*** *Unverified Primate References.*
**Desc:** Citations of natural and life sciences publication on nonhuman primates, sorted to subject headings with author's addresses, primate species and author's index.

UK/0260-6593
**CURRENT TECHNOLOGY INDEX : CTI.** [CTI. Curr.technol. index]. **Added/Corp** Library Association. **VFOAT** CTI. Vol. 1, No. 1 (Jan. 1981)-. Abstracting/Indexing Service. English. bm. £635.00 EEC, £685.00 other (issue & A/V). Bowker Saur Ltd., A Reed Reference Publishing Company, Part of Reed International PLC, 59-60 Grosvenor Street, London WIX 9DA England. **Tel** 011 44 71 4935841, FAX 011 44 71 4991590. **(Subscription address:** World-Wide Subscription Services, Unit 4, Gibbs Reed Farm Pashley Road, Ticehurst TN5 7HE England.**) LC** Z7913; .B7; T45. **DD** 016.6. **NLM** ZQ 1 C975. ctrl circ. available on microfilm; available on magnetic tape; available on an online database from DIALOG; available on CD-ROM (CTI PLus). ***Continues*** *British Technology Index, 0007-1889.*
**Desc:** Lists and abstracts the substantial articles which have appeared in technical journals in the preceding two months; often an article appears in the index within weeks of its original publication and many of the journals included, are neither abstracted nor indexed elsewhere.

US/0886-0076
**DIRECTORY OF AMERICAN RESEARCH AND TECHNOLOGY.** (DIRECTORY OF AMERICAN RESEARCH AND TECHNOLOGY / EDITED BY JAQUES CATTELL PRESS.). [Dir. Am. res. technol.]. **Added/Corp** Jaques Cattell Press. R.R. Bowker Company. Directories/New Products Group. R.R. Bowker Company. Publications Systems Dept. R.R. Bowker Company. Database Publishing Group. 20th Ed. (1986)-. Directory. English. an. $329.95. R R Bowker, A Reed Reference Publishing Company, Part of Reed International PLC, PO Box 31, 121 Chanlon Drive, New Providence NJ 07974. **Tel** (908)464-6800, (800)521-8110, FAX (908)665-6688, telex 138-755. **LC** T176; .I65. **DD** 607/.2/73. **NLM** T 176; I42. **CODEN** DARTEB. **[CCC]**. available on magnetic tape and CD-ROM. ***Continues*** *Industrial Research Laboratories of the United States, Including Consulting Research Laboratories, 0073-7623.*
**Desc:** Profiles more than 11,000 US and Canadian corporate facilities active in commercially- applicable basic or applied research in hundreds of areas.

II/0419-2745
**DIRECTORY OF INDIAN SCIENTIFIC PERIODICALS.** 1st- Ed., 1964-. Directory. English. ir. INSDOC, 14 Satsang Vihar Marg, New Delhi 110067 India. **Tel** 011 91 11 6863617, FAX 665837, telex 031-73099. **LC** Z7403. **DD** 016.5/05.

JA/0916-1198
**DIRECTORY OF JAPANESE SCIENTIFIC PERIODICALS.** **Added/Corp** Japan. MonbushÂo. Kokuritsu Kokkai Toshokan (Japan). **VFOAT** Nihon Kagaku Gijutsu Kankei Chikuji Kankobutsu Mokuroku. (1962)-. Directory. English (Japanese). ir. **(Subscription address:** Maruzen Company Ltd., PO Box 5050, Import & Export Department, Tokyo 100 31 Japan.**) DD** 050. **NLM** ZQ 1 N691. ***Continues*** *Directory of Japanese Learned Periodicals, 0419-280X.*

US
**DIRECTORY OF PUBLISHED PROCEEDINGS. SERIES - SCIENCE/ENGINEERING/MEDICINE/ TECHNOLOGY.** [Dir. publ. proc., Ser. SEMT-Sci.-eng.-med.-technol.]. Vol. 3 (Sept. 1967)-. Directory. English. Ten times a year. $545.00. InterDok Corporation, PO Box 326, Harrison NY 10528. **Tel** (914)835-3506, FAX (914)835-6757. Index available. cum. index. ctrl circ. ***Continues*** *Directory of Published Proceedings.* ***Continued in part by*** *Directory of Published Proceedings. Series MLS, Medical/Life Sciences., 1060-1759.*
**Desc:** Complete worldwide coverage of the national and international conference proceedings literature, including data on sponsors, date and location of meeting, secondary proceedings titles, editors, report and/or special identification numbers.
**Ind/Abst** MINPROC; Mintec, Min. Technol. Abstr.

CN/0824-0310
**FEDERAL SCIENTIFIC ACTIVITIES.** (FEDERAL SCIENTIFIC ACTIVITIES / STATISTICS CANADA, SERVICES, SCIENCE AND TECHNOLOY DIVISION.). [Fed. sci. act.]. **Added/Corp** Statistics Canada. Science and Technology Statistics Division. Statistics Canada. Science, Technology and Capital Stock Division. Statistics Canada. Science and Technology Section. **VFOAT** Activites Scientifiques Federales. (1985)-. English (French). an. 48.00Can$, Canada; $58.00 US; $68.00 other. Statistics Canada, Publications Sales & Services, Main Building Room 1710, Ottawa Ontario K1A 0T6 Canada. **Tel** (613)951-5078, (800)267-6677, FAX (613)951-1584, telex 053-3585. **LC** Q180.C2; F396. **DD** 609/.71. **Circ:** 350. ***Continues*** *Canada. Ministry of State, Science and Technology. Federal Science Activities, 0706-2206;* ***Absorbed*** *Activites Scientifiques Federales (Statistique Canada. Division de la Statistique, 0714-1173.*
**Desc:** Provides statistical information on the federal

government's activities in science and technology. Expenditure and person-year data are provided for the latest five years by type of science, by performing sector and by federal department or agency. Distribution of expenditures by province are provided for government laboratories and for payments to industries and universities.

JA
**GAKUJUTSU ZASSHI SOGO MOKUROKU. OBUN HEN. HOIBAN.** **VFOAT** Union List of Scientific Periodicals in European Languages. 1982-. English. 10000. **(Subscription address:** Kinokuniya Company Ltd., 38-1 Sakuragaoka 5, chome Setagaya-ku, Tokyo 156 Japan.) ***Continues*** *Gakujutsu Zasshi Sogo Mokuroku. Shizen Kagaku Obun Hen.*

US/0162-1963
**GENERAL SCIENCE INDEX. Added/Corp** H.W. Wilson Company. Vol. 1 (1979)-. Abstracting/Indexing Service. English. mo (except June and December). Sold on the service basis. H W Wilson Company, 950 University Avenue, Bronx NY 10452. **Tel** (800)367-6770, (718)588-8400, FAX (718)590-1617, telex 4990003 HWILSON. **ED** James Kochones. **LC** Z7401; .G46. **DD** 016.5. Index available. cum. index. ctrl circ. available on an online database from WILSONLINE; available on CD-ROM from WILSONDISC; available on magnetic tape from WILSONTAPE; available on diskette from WILSONSEARCH.
**Desc:** Contains approximately 218,000 citations to articles and book reviews in 140 English language periodicals in the general sciences. Covers astronomy, atmospheric science, biology, botany, chemistry, conservation and environment, earth sciences, food and nutrition, genetics, health and medicine, mathematics, microbiology, oceanography, physics, physiology, and zoology.

●US/1073-1954
**GENERAL SCIENCE SOURCE.** (GENERAL SCIENCE SOURCE [COMPUTER FILE] EBSCO CD-ROM.). **Added/Corp** EBSCO Publishing (Firm). **VFOAT** EBSCO CD-ROM. (1993)-. Abstracting/Indexing Service. English. mo. $1495.00. EBSCO Publishing / Boston, 83 Pine Street, Peabody MA 01960. **Tel** (800)653-2726 North America, (508)535-8500, FAX (508)535-8545. **ED** Melissa Kummerer.
**Desc:** Provides access to abstracts and indexing coverage of nearly 195 journals covering biology, physics, chemistry, botany, environmental science and earth science. Full text titles include Science News, Popular Science, Environment, Astronomy, Bulletin of the Atomic Scientists and many more.

US/0097-9007
**GOVERNMENT REPORTS ANNOUNCEMENTS & INDEX.** [Gov. rep. announce. index]. **Added/Corp** United States. National Technical Information Service. **VFOAT** Government Reports Announcements and Index. Vol. 75, No. 7 (April 4, 1975)-. English. Twenty-four times a year. $535.00 US; $725.00 other. National Technical Information Service - NTIS, Room 2027S, 5285 Port Royal Road, Springfield VA 22161. **Tel** (703)487-4630, (703)487-4660, (703)487-4650, FAX (703)321-8547, telex 89-9405. **LC** Z7916; .G78; T45. **DD** 016.6. **NLM** ZQ 1 G719. available on microfilm and microfiche from University Microfilms International (UMI). Documents available from CASDDS. ***Formed by the union of*** *Government Reports Index (Semimonthly)* ***and*** *Government Reports Announcements, 0096-0799.*
**Desc:** Summarizes titles that were entered into the NTIS collection since the previous edition. Covers virtually every information item NTIS adds.
**Ind/Abst** Chem. Abstr.; Eng. Mater. Abstr.; Ergon. Abstr.; Fluid Abstr., Civil Eng.; Fluid Abstr. Proc. Eng.; FLUIDEX (1975-); Int. Aerosp. Abstr.; Int. Packag. Abstr.; Manage. Market. Abstr.; Pap. Board Abstr.; Print. Abstr.; Shock Vibr. Dig.; Weed Abstr.

US/0360-0661
**INDEX TO SCIENTIFIC REVIEWS.** (INDEX TO SCIENTIFIC REVIEWS : AN INTERNATIONAL INTERDISCIPLINARY INDEX TO THE REVIEW LITERATURE OF SCIENCE, MEDICINE, AGRICULTURE, TECHNOLOGY, AND THE BEHAVIORAL SCIENCES.). [Index sci. rev.]. **Added/Corp** Institute for Scientific Information. **VFOAT** ISR; I.S.R. (1974)-. Abstracting/Indexing Service. English. sa. $1060.00. Institute for Scientific Information, 3501 Market Street, Philadelphia PA 19104. **Tel** (215)386-0100, (800)523-1850, FAX (215)386-6362, telex 84-5305. **(Subscription address:** Institute for Scientific Information, PO Box 71416, Chicago IL 60694.) **LC** Z7403; .I42; Q1. **DD** 501/.6. **NLM** ZQ 1 I345.
**Desc:** Presents complete bibliographic data on published reviews and review-type articles. Covers all the disciplines of the sciences.

II/0019-6339
**INDIAN SCIENCE ABSTRACTS.** [Indian sci. abstr.]. **Added/Corp** Indian National Scientific Documentation Centre. **VFOAT** ISA. Vol. 1, No. 1 (Jan. 1965)-. Abstracting/Indexing Service. English. bw. $600.00. INSDOC, 14 Satsang Vihar Marg, New Delhi 110067 India. **Tel** 011 91 11 6863617, FAX 665837, telex 031-73099. **(Subscription address:** Prints India, 11 Darya Ganj, New Delhi 110002 India.) **ED** O N Chaddha. **LC** Q1; .I54. **NLM** ZQ 1 I39. **CODEN** IDSAAV. Index available. **Circ:** 500. ***Continues*** *Bibliography of Scientific Publications of South and South East Asia, 0409-4166.*
**Desc:** An abstracting periodical reporting work published in India, and also work done in India but published abroad.
**Ind/Abst** Abstr. Bull. Inst. Pap. Sci. Tech.; Anim. Breed. Abstr.; Field Crop Abstr.; Grasslands For. Abstr.; Hortic. Abstr.; Math. Rev.; Nutr. Abstr. Rev., Ser. B, Live Feeds and Feed.; Nutr. Abstr. Rev., Ser. A, Hum. Exp.; Plant Breed. Abstr.; World Surf. Coat. Abstr.

CN/0824-8133
**INDUSTRIAL RESEARCH AND DEVELOPMENT STATISTICS ... WITH ... FORECASTS.** (INDUSTRIAL RESEARCH AND DEVELOPMENT STATISTICS ... (WITH ... FORECASTS) / STATISTICS CANADA, SCIENCE AND TECHNOLOGY STATISTICS DIVISION.). [Ind. res. dev. stat. forecasts]. **Added/Corp** Statistics Canada. Science and Technology Statistics Division. **VFOAT** Statistiques sur la Recherche et le Developpement Industriels .. (Avec des Previsions pour ...). 1st Issue (1982)-. English (French). 48.00Can$, Canada; $58.00 US; $68.00 other. Statistics Canada, Publications Sales & Services, Main Building Room 1710, Ottawa Ontario K1A 0T6 Canada. **Tel** (613)951-5078, (800)267-6677, FAX (613)951-1584, telex 053-3585. **DD** 338.4/75/0971.
**Desc:** Presents statistics on research and development (R&D) activities performed and funded by the Canadian business enterprises. It covers current and capital expenditures on R&D, R&D as a percentage of sales, by provinces and employment and size.

UK/0959-2350
**INFORMATION MANAGEMENT & TECHNOLOGY / ANBAR ABSTRACTS.** **Added/Corp** Anbar Abstracts (Firm). **VFOAT** Information Management and Technology; Information Management and Technology Abstracts; Anbar Information Management and Technology Abstracts; Information Management & Technology Abstracts; Anbar Information Management & Technology Abstracts. Vol. 1, No. 1 (Feb. 1990)-. Periodical. English. qt. $2999.00. MCB University Press, 60 62 Toller Lane, Bradford West Yorkshire BD8 9BX England. **Tel** 011 44 274 499821, FAX 011 44 274 547143, telex 51317 MCBUNI G. **(Subscription address:** MCB University Press / US and Canada Subscriptions, PO Box 10812, Birmingham AL 35201-0812.) **LC** T58.64; .I515. **DD** 658.4/038. available on diskette (from Anbar).
**Desc:** Contains abstracts of articles on the use, management and flow of information in organizations, already identified as a topic of major importance.

UK/0020-580X
**INTERNATIONAL ABSTRACTS IN OPERATIONS RESEARCH.** [Int. abstr. oper. res.]. **Added/Corp** International Federation of Operational Research Societies. Operations Research Society of America. **VFOAT** O.R. International Abstracts in Operations Research; IAOR. Vol. 1 (Nov. 1961)-. Abstracting/Indexing Service. English. bm. £225.00 UK and EEC countries; £225.00 (surface mail), £270.00 (airmail) other. Macmillan Magazines Ltd., Houndmills, Basingstoke, Hampshire RG21 2XS England. **Tel** 011 44 256 29242, FAX 011 44 256 812358, telex 858493. **ED** Graham K. Rand. **LC** Q500; .I5. **DD** 658.4/03/4. **NLM** Z 7405.07 I61. **[CCC]. Circ:** 8,000. available on microfilm and microfiche from University Microfilms International (UMI).
**Desc:** Provides a continuous flow of information to researchers and practitioners in the field of operations research, mathematicians, and econometricians.
**Ind/Abst** Oper. Res./Manag. Sci.

US
**JOURNAL OF THE COLORADO-WYOMING ACADEMY OF SCIENCE, THE. Main/Corp** Colorado-Wyoming Academy of Science. Vol. 1, No. 1 (Apr. 1929)-. Academic Scholarly Publication. English. an (Apr.). $3.00. University of Northern Colorado Department of Biology, c/o Ronald Plakke, Greeley CO 80639. **Tel** (303)351-2329. **ED** David L. Pringle (editor's address: Chemistry Department, University of Northern Colorado, Greeley, CO 80639). **Circ:** 400. Documents available from BIOSIS Document Express, CASDDS.
**Desc:** Abstracts presented on the annual meeting of the science.
**Ind/Abst** Biol. Abstr.; Chem. Abstr.; Fish Rev.; GeoRef; Wildl. Rev.

US/0090-5232
**LC SCIENCE TRACER BULLET.** [LC sci. tracer bullet]. **VAT** Library of Congress Science Tracer Bullet. (1972)-. Monographic series. English. ir. Free. Library of Congress / Science & Technology Division, Washington DC 20540. **Tel** (202)287-6171. **ED** Constance Carter. **LC** Z7401; .L14; Q158.5. **DD** 016.5.
**Desc:** Informal series of reference guides targeted to the literature of a given topic (acid rain, AIDS, optical disk technology, anorexia nervosa, and science fair projects).

US/0739-5914
**MIND, THE MEETINGS INDEX. SERIES SEMT, SCIENCE, ENGINEERING, MEDICINE, TECHNOLOGY.** [MInd, meet. index, Ser. SEMT, sci., eng., med., technol.]. **VFOAT** MInd; M.I.N.D., The Meetings Index; Meetings Index; Series S.E.M.T., Science, Engineering, Medicine, Technology; Series SEMT, Science, Engineering, Medicine, Technology; Science, Engineering, Medicine, Technology. Vol. 1, No. 1 (Feb. 1984)-. English. bm. $460.00 US, Canada & Mexico; $485.00 other. InterDok Corporation, PO Box 326, Harrison NY 10528. **Tel** (914)835-3506, FAX (914)835-6757. **ED** Yvette Roper. **LC** Z7403; .M635; Q158.5. **DD** 016.5. **NLM** W 3.5; M663. **Bk Rev.** ctrl circ.
**Desc:** Source to the total national and international future meetings data.

US/1064-0479
**NTIS BIBLIOGRAPHIC DATABASE.** (NTIS BIBLIOGRAPHIC DATABASE [COMPUTER FILE] / NATIONAL TECHNICAL INFORMATION SERVICE, U.S. DEPARTMENT OF COMMERCE.). [NTIS bibliogr. database]. **Added/Corp** United States. National Technical Information Service. SilverPlatter Information, Inc. **VFOAT** NTIS. (1983)-. English. sm. Price varies. National Technical Information Service - NTIS, Room 2027S, 5285 Port Royal Road, Springfield VA 22161. **Tel** (703)487-4630, (703)487-4660, (703)487-4650, FAX (703)321-8547, telex 89-9405. **LC** Z7401. **DD** 505. available in print (As: Government Reports Announcements & Guide); available on an online database from STN International; ORBIT; ESA-IRS; DIALOG; DATA-STAR; CISTI; and BRS; available on CD-ROM from SilverPlatter (US); OCLC; and DIALOG.
**Desc:** Contains summaries of scientific, technical, engineering, and business information products acquired by NTIS.

GW/0722-3218
**PACKAGING SCIENCE AND TECHNOLOGY ABSTRACTS.** (PACKAGING SCIENCE AND TECHNOLOGY ABSTRACTS. PSTA.). [Packag. sci. technol. abstr.]. **VFOAT** Referatedienst Verpackung; PSTA. Packaging Science and Technology Abstracts. (1982)-. German (English). Five times a year (Feb., Apr., June, Aug/Oct., Dec.). DM600.00 Germany; DM625.00 other. Fraunhofer Institute Lebensmittel-Technologie, Schragenhofstr 35, D-80992 Munich, Germany. **Tel** 011 49 89 14900956, FAX 011 49 89 1400980. **ED** Julia Elze. **UDC** 621.798 (01). Index available. cum. index. **Ad Acc, Adv Mgr:** J. Elze. **Circ:** 150. available on an online database from CISTI; DATA-STAR; ORBIT; Fiz-Technik; DIMDI; and DIALOG.
**Desc:** Summarises as an abstract each item of the world's literature relevant to packaging science and technology.

MX/0185-1004
**PERIODICA. Added/Corp** Universidad Nacional Autonoma de Mexico. Centro de Informacion Cientifica y Humanistica. Vol. 1, No. 1-2 (Jan-June 1978)-. Spanish (English and Portuguese). Four times a year. $192.00 US and Canada; $180.00 Mexico; $193.00 other. Centro de Informacion Cientifica y Humanistica, Apartado 70 392, Mexico 20 DF Mexico. **Tel** 011 52 5 5480208, 011 52 5 6223964. **LC** Z7403; .P47; Q158.5. **DD** 016.5. Index available. cum. index. **Circ:** 300. available on CD-ROM.
**Desc:** Classifies per specialism the information of primary Latin American journals in the field of general science and technology. Publishes an index of subjects in Spanish and English, and an index of authors.
**Ind/Abst** Bibliogr. Mission.

US/0891-3889
**PERIODICALS SCANNED AND ABSTRACTED. LIFE SCIENCES COLLECTION.** [Period. scanned abstr., Life sci. collect.]. **Added/Corp** Cambridge Scientific Abstracts, Inc. **VFOAT** Life Sciences Collection. (1981)-. Abstracting/Indexing Service. English. qt. Cambridge Scientific Abstracts, 7200 Wisconsin Avenue, #601, Bethesda MD 20814-4823. **Tel** (301)961-6750, (800)843-7751, FAX (301)961-6720. **ED** Angela Hitti. **DD** 570. **NLM** ZW 1; P455. available on magnetic tape; available on CD-ROM; available on an online database; available via Internet (to the current year's abstracts and five-year backfiles) from Cambridge Scientific Abstracts.

PH/0115-8724
**PHILIPPINE SCIENCE & TECHNOLOGY ABSTRACTS. Added/Corp** Science Promotion Institute (Philippines). Scientific Clearinghouse and Documentation Services Division. Philippines. National Science and Technology Authority. **VFOAT** Philippine Science and Technology Abstracts. Vol. 1, Nos. 4-6 (Aug. 1983)-. Abstracting/Indexing Service. English. qt. P48.00 Philippines; $24.00 (airmail) other. Science and Technology Information Institute, PO Box 2131, Manila Philippines. **Tel** 011 63 2 822 0961. **Circ:** 500. ***Continues*** *Philippine Science and Technology Abstract Bibliography, 0115-8724.*
**Desc:** The most recent Philippine publication dealing with scientific and technological studies.
**Ind/Abst** J. Ferrocement.

US/0277-2434
**PHILOSOPHY IN SCIENCE. See** Science and Technology.

US
**PUBLISHED SEARCH CATALOG.**
**Added/Corp** United States. National Technical Information Service. (1986)-. Catalog. English. an. Free on request. National Technical Information Service - NTIS, Room 2027S, 5285 Port Royal Road, Springfield VA 22161. **Tel** (703)487-4630, (703)487-4660, (703)487-4650, FAX (703)321-8547, telex 89-9405. ***Continues*** *Published Searches, 0743-6955.*
**Desc:** Exclusively prepared bibliographies providing the most current data available on a specific topic from an individual database source. Contains from 50 to 250 citations of reports and studies with full abstracts.

US/0033-5207
**QUALITY CONTROL AND APPLIED STATISTICS.** [Qual. control appl. stat.]. **Added/Corp** Executive Sciences Institute. **VFOAT** QCAS. Vol. 1 (1956)-. Abstracting/Indexing Service. English. bm (6 issues). $151.00 US; $180.00 other. Executive Sciences Institute, 1005 Mississippi Avenue, PO Box 4318, Davenport IA 52808-4318. **Tel** (319)324-4463, FAX (319)322-3725. **(Subscription address:** Executive Sciences Institute, PO Box 4318, Davenport, IA 52808**) ED** Bruce Brocka. **LC** TS156.A1; Q335. **DD** 658.5/62/015195. Index available (annual). cum. index. **Bk Rev. Pr Rev. Circ:** 500.
**Desc:** Quality control, applied statistics, reliability, experimental design, data analysis, quality management, software quality, practical applications.

US/1044-6052
**SCIENCE CITATION INDEX (COMPACT DISC ED.).** (SCIENCE CITATION INDEX [COMPUTER FILE].). [Sci. cit. index]. **Added/Corp** Institute for Scientific Information. **VFOAT** SCI CDE; SCI. (198?)-. Abstracting/Indexing Service. English. qt. $13425.00 (CD-ROM); $15950.00 (combination print & CD-ROM). Institute for Scientific Information, 3501 Market Street, Philadelphia PA 19104. **Tel** (215)386-0100, (800)523-1850, FAX (215)386-6362, telex 84-5305. **(Subscription address:** Institute for Scientific Information, PO Box 71416, Chicago IL 60694.**) LC** Z7401. **DD** 505. available in print (Science Citation Index) from Institute for Scientific Information; available on magnetic tape and an online database (as SciSearch) from Institute for Scientific Information.
**Desc:** Provides electronic access to full bibliographic data and cited references on items contained in scientific and technical journals.

US/0036-827X
**SCIENCE CITATION INDEX (PRINT ED.).** (SCIENCE CITATION INDEX.). [Sci. cit. index]. **Added/Corp** Institute for Scientific Information. (1961)-. Abstracting/Indexing Service. English. bm. $11,730.00. Institute for Scientific Information, 3501 Market Street, Philadelphia PA 19104. **Tel** (215)386-0100, (800)523-1850, FAX (215)386-6362, telex 84-5305. **(Subscription address:** Institute for Scientific Information, PO Box 71416, Chicago IL 60694.**) LC** Z7401; .S365. **DD** 016.5. **NLM** ZQ 1 S411.

●US/1061-1290
**SCIENCE CITATION INDEX WITH ABSTRACTS.** (SCIENCE CITATION INDEX WITH ABSTRACTS [COMPUTER FILE].). [Sci. cit. index abstr.]. **Added/Corp** Institute for Scientific Information. (Jan-Mar 1992)-. Abstracting/Indexing Service. English. qt. $17080.00; $20380.00 (print & CD with abstracts). Institute for Scientific Information, 3501 Market Street, Philadelphia PA 19104. **Tel** (215)386-0100, (800)523-1850, FAX (215)386-6362, telex 84-5305. **(Subscription address:** Institute for Scientific Information, PO Box 71416, Chicago IL 60694.**) DD** 016. available in print (as Science Citation Index); available on magnetic tape and an online database (as SciSearch).
**Desc:** Provides instant electronic access to full bibliographic data and cited references, plus complete, English-language author abstracts, on the items contained in over 3,100 of the world's leading scientific and technical journals.

CN/0706-0793
**SCIENCE STATISTICS.** (SCIENCE STATISTICS / EDUCATION, SCIENCE AND CULTURE DIVISION.). [Sci. stat.]. **Added/Corp** Statistique Canada. Division de l'Education, des Sciences et de la Culture. Statistique Canada. Division de la Statistique des Sciences et de la Technologie. Statistique Canada. Division des Sciences, de la Technologie et du Stock de Capital. Statistique Canada. Division des Services, des Sciences et de la Technologie. **VFOAT** Statistique des Sciences. Vol. 1, (Aug. 1977)-. Periodical. French (English). mo. 76.00Can$ Canada; $92.00 US; $107.00 other. Statistics Canada, Publications Sales & Services, Main Building Room 1710, Ottawa Ontario K1A 0T6 Canada. **Tel** (613)951-5078, (800)267-6677, FAX (613)951-1584, telex 053-3585. **DD** 609/.71. ***Continues in part*** *Service Bulletin (Statistique Canada. Division de l'Education, des Sciences et de la Culture), 0317-5391.*
**Desc:** Statistics of science and technology prepared by the Science Statistics Centre. Contains summary statistics from recently completed surveys and studies, descriptions of current surveys and notices of available statistical tabulations.

US/0000-054X
**SCIENTIFIC AND TECHNICAL BOOKS AND SERIALS IN PRINT. Added/Corp** R.R. Bowker Company. **VFOAT** Sci-Tech Books and Serials in Print. (1978)-. English. an. $299.95. R R Bowker, A Reed Reference Publishing Company, Part of Reed International PLC, PO Box 31, 121 Chanlon Drive, New Providence NJ 07974. **Tel** (908)464-6800, (800)521-8110, FAX (908)665-6688, telex 138-755. **LC** Z7401; .S573; Q158.5. **DD** 016.5. **NLM** Z 7401 S414. **[CCC].** available on magnetic tape and CD-ROM. ***Continues*** *Scientific and Technical Books in Print, 0000-0248.*
**Desc:** Contains complete listings for more than 140,000 books and 25,000 periodicals published worldwide, including serials in translation from the former Soviet Union.

US
**SCIENTIFIC DIRECTORY AND ANNUAL BIBLIOGRAPHY.** (SCIENTIFIC DIRECTORY ... ANNUAL BIBLIOGRAPHY ... / NATIONAL INSTITUTES OF HEALTH.). **Main/Corp** National Institutes of Health (U.S.). Directory. English. an. National Institutes of Health, 9000 Rockville Pike, Bethesda MD 20014. **Tel** (301)496-6975. **NLM** ZWA 4 N277S. ***Continues*** *Scientific Directory and Annual Bibliography, 0083-2197.*

US
**SCISEARCH [ONLINE DATABASE].**
Abstracting/Indexing Service. English. wk (frequency of updates). Magnetic Tape: $29495.00 (academic), $36880.00 (corporate). Institute for Scientific Information, 3501 Market Street, Philadelphia PA 19104. **Tel** (215)386-0100, (800)523-1850, FAX (215)386-6362, telex 84-5305. **(Subscription address:** Institute for Scientific Information, PO Box 71416, Chicago, IL 60694**)** available on magnetic tape.
**Desc:** The online database for Science Citation Index.

US/1063-8717
**SCITECH REFERENCE PLUS.** (SCITECH REFERENCE PLUS [COMPUTER FILE].). [SciTech ref. plus]. **Added/Corp** Bowker Electonic Publishing. (1989)-. English. an. $995.00. R R Bowker Electronic Publishing, A Reed Reference Publishing Company, Part of Reed International PLC, 121 Chanlon Drive, New Providence NJ 07974. **Tel** (800)323-3288. **LC** Z403. **DD** 505.
**Desc:** Available in DOS format, this complete bibliographic collection consists of Scitech books and serials, biographical data on science professionals and corporate profiles of research and business facilities.

PH
**SEA ABSTRACTS.** Vol. 1 No. 1 (1984)-. Abstracting/Indexing Service. English. qt. P48.00 Philippines; $24.00 (airmail) other. Science and Technology Information Institute, PO Box 2131, Manila Philippines. **Tel** 011 63 2 822 0961.
**Desc:** Compilation of abstract/summaries of the latest scientific and technical studies in Asia excluding the Philippines.

RU
**SVODNYI KATALOG BIBLIOGRAFICHESKIKH RABOT, VYPOLNENNYKH V SOVETSKOM SOIUZE: ESTESTVENNYE I FIZIKO-MATEMATICHESKIE NAUKI. *Title Change.* Added/Corp** Akademiia Nauk SSSR. Biblioteka. (1962)-(1992). Periodical. Russian. qt. Ban, 199164 Birzhevaia 1 D 1, St. Petersburg Russia. **LC** Z7409; .S75; Q158.5. ***Continued by*** *Svodnyi Katalog Bibliograficheskikh Rabot. Estestvennye i Fiziko-Matematicheskie Nauki.*

IE/0040-1676
**TECHNOLOGY IRELAND. See** Science and Technology.

US/0040-1706
**TECHNOMETRICS.** [Technometrics]. **Added/Corp** American Society for Quality Control. American Statistical Association. Vol. 1 (Feb. 1959)-. Periodical. English. qt. $32.00 (individual), $55.00 (library). American Statistical Association, 1429 Duke Street, Alexandria VA 22314. **Tel** (703)684-1221, (202)393-3253, FAX (703)684-2037 (orders). **ED** Vijayan N. Nair. **LC** QA276; .T4. **DD** 310.5. **NLM** W1 TE211P. **CODEN** TCMTA2. **[CCC].** Index available (bound in Nov. issue). cum. index. **Bk Rev. Pr Rev. Circ:** 6,000 (ctrl). available on microfilm and microfiche from University Microfilms International (UMI). Documents available from Article Express International, The Genuine Article, Ask*IEEE.
**Desc:** Publishes papers describing new statistical techniques and illustrating innovative application of known statistical methods; expository papers on particular statistical methods; papers on philosophy and problems of applying statistical methods. Co-published by American Society for Quality Control.
**Ind/Abst** Abstr. Bull. Inst. Pap. Sci. Tech.; ACM Guide Comput. Lit.; Appl. Sci. Technol. Index; Bioeng. Abstr.; Biostatistica; Compumath Citation Index [Full Cov.]; Comput. Rev.; Curr. Contents Phys. Chem. Earth Sci.; Curr. Index Stat.; Ei Page One; Eng. Index Annu. [Select. Cov.]; GeoRef; INSPEC (Aug. 1987-); Int. Aerosp. Abstr.; Math. Rev.; Oper. Res./Manag. Sci.; Qual. Control Appl. Stat.; Res. Alert [Full Cov.]; Sci. Cit. Index; SCISEARCH; Stat. Theory Method Abstr. (1959-1963, 1966-1984, 1986-1987); World Text. Abstr.; Zentralbl. Math. Ihre Grenzgeb.

II
**TENOLAI.** Ital 1- Culai 1974-. Periodical. Tamil (English). qt. Rs8.00. Kodumudi Shanmukam, 11-B Second Avenue, Indira Nagar, Madras 600020 India. **Tel** 416639 MADRAS INDIA. **ED** Kodumudi Shanmugam Bragadham. **LC** Z6605.T3; T4. Index available. **Bk Rev. Ad Acc. Circ:** 2,000 (ctrl).
**Desc:** Epigraphy, archaeology, tamilology, history, science engineering, etc. Special attempt to publish source material for history and literature from palm leaves, research papers.

FI/0784-1469
**TUTKIMAS JA TEKNIIKKA.** [Tutkimus ja tekniikka]. **VFOAT** Forskning och Teknik. (1977)-. Multiple languages. ir. Teknillisten Tieteiden Akatemia, Helsinki Finland. **UDC** 001.89. ***Continues*** *TTA. Tutkimus ja Tekniikka, 0355-2578.*
**Ind/Abst** Selec. Coop. Index Manage. Period.

CN/0082-7657
**UNION LIST OF SCIENTIFIC SERIALS IN CANADIAN LIBRARIES.** (UNION LIST OF SCIENTIFIC SERIALS IN CANADIAN LIBRARIES / COMPILED AND EDITED IN THE LIBRARY OF THE NATIONAL RESEARCH COUNCIL.). **Added/Corp** Canada Institute for Scientific and Technical Information. National Research Council of Canada. Library. National Science Library (Canada). **VFOAT** Catalogue Collectif des Publications Scientifiques dans les Bibliotheques Canadiennes. 1st Ed. (1957)-. English (French). be. 350.00Can$. National Research Council of Canada, Receiver General for Canada, Ottawa Ontario K1A 0R6 Canada. **Tel** (613)993-0362, FAX (613)952-7656. **ED** M. Kaiserman. **LC** Z7403; .U3425; Q158.5. **DD** 016.5/05. **Circ:** 2,000. available on microfiche.
**Desc:** Union list of 75,000 scientific, technical and medical serials in Canadian libraries.

US
**WORLD GUIDE TO SCIENTIFIC ASSOCIATIONS AND LEARNED SOCIETIES. VFOAT** Verbande und Gesellschaften der Wissenschaft; Ein Internationales Verzeichnis. 2nd Ed. (1978)-. Periodical. English (German). ir. $245.00. K.G. Saur Verlag KG, A Reed Reference Publishing Company, Part of Reed International PLC, Ortlerstrasse 8, D 81373 Munich Germany. **Tel** 011 49 89 769020, FAX 011 49 89 76902150, telex 5212067-SAUR-D. **ED** Michael Sachs. ***Continues*** *World Guide to Scientific Associations.*
**Desc:** This reference includes 18,000 associations-international, national, and regional, from 150 countries in all areas of science, culture and technology; over 12,000 associations periodicals and bulletins; a special index of official association abbreviations; and a subject index of activities organized by country.

JA
**ZASSHI KIJI SAKUIN. KAGAKU GIJUTSU HEN. VFOAT** Japanese Periodicals Index. Vol. 1, No. 1 (1950)-. Multiple languages (Japanese and English). mo. The National Diet Library, 10-1-1 Chome Nagatacho, Chiyoda ku Tokyo 100 Japan. **LC** Z7403; Q158. **NLM** ZQ 1; Z37.

## SECURITY SYSTEMS AND ALARMS

IT/0391-6227
**ANTIFURTO.** [Antifurto]. (1974)-. Periodical. Italian. mo. L140000.00 Italy; L165000.00 Europe; L195000.00 other. EPC Spa, Via dell'Acqua Traversa 187/189, 00135 Rome Italy. **Tel** 011 39 6 3313000, FAX 011 39 6 3313212. **ED** Livio Colasanti. **UDC** 364. **Bk Rev. Ad Acc, Adv Mgr:** Roberto Recalcati. **Circ:** 8,000.
**Desc:** Presents news on antitheft protection for businesses.

CN/0709-3403
**CANADIAN SECURITY.** Vol. 1 (Sept./Oct. 1979)-. Periodical. English. Seven times a year. $40.00 US. Security Publishing Ltd., PO Box 430 Station O, Toronto Ontario M4A 2P1 Canada. **Tel** (416)755-4343, FAX (416)755-7487. **ED** Bob Robinson. **DD** 658.4/7. **Bk Rev**, (Qty: varies). **Ad Acc, Adv Mgr:** Jack Percival. **Circ:** 11,182 (ctrl). ***Supersedes*** *Resources Protection, 0315-3231.*
**Desc:** Dedicated to the protection of persons, property and information including all security concerns: essential communications, alarms, CCTV, law enforcement, locksmithing, fire safety and emergency services.

US/1040-4201
**CORPORATE SECURITY (NEW YORK, N.Y.).** (CORPORATE SECURITY.). [Corp. secur.]. (Feb. 1981)-. Newsletter. English. bw. $295.00. Business Research Publications, 1333 H Street Northwest, 2nd Floor West, Washington DC 20005. **Tel** (202)842-3022, (800)822-6338, FAX (202)842-3023. **ED** Gail Hayden. **DD** 658. ***Continues*** *Protection Management.*
**Desc:** Examines timely security issues such as employee theft, access control, computer security industrial espionage, employee substance abuse, arson, wiretapping, and disaster planning.
**Ind/Abst** Crim. Justice Period. Index.

UK
**FIRE & SECURITY PROTECTION.** ***Ceased.*** **VFOAT** Fire and Security Protection. (1986)- Ceased with Vol. 52, No. 6 (199?). Periodical. English. qt. A E Morgan Publications Ltd, Stanley House, 9 West Street, Epsom Surrey KT18 7RL England. **Tel** 011 44 3727 41411, FAX 0372 744493, telex 291561 VIA SOS G. **(Subscription address:** Unit 4, Durham Road, Borehamwood Herts WD6 1LW England**) ED** Mike Connolly. **Bk Rev. Ad Acc. Circ:** 1,250 (ctrl). ***Continues*** *Fire Protection.*
**Desc:** Covers all facets of fire and security protection industry.
**Ind/Abst** Int. Build. Serv. Abstr.

CN/0823-0382
**FORUM / CANADIAN SOCIETY FOR INDUSTRIAL SECURITY.** [Forum - Can. Soc. Ind. Secur.]. **Added/Corp** Canadian Society for Industrial Security. **VFOAT** CSIS "Forum". **VAT** Forum - Societe Canadienne de la Surete Industrielle. (Jan. 1983)-. Periodical. English (French; summaries and/or abstracts in French). Four times a year. 30.00Can$ Canada; 36.60Can$ North America; 73.20Can$ other. Canadian Society for Industrial Security, 3 Unity Road, Toronto Ontario M4J 5A3 Canada. **Tel** (416)461-4109. **DD** 363.2/89. ***Continues*** *Canadian Society for Industrial Security. CSIS Forum, 0229-3226.*

UK
**HANDBOOK OF SECURITY.** (19??)-. English. tq. £154.75. Croner Publ Ltd, Croner House, London Road, Kingston upon Thames, Surrey KT2 6SR England. **Tel** 011 44 81 5473333, FAX 081 547-2637. **ED** Nicholas O'Connor. Index available (bound in each issue). cum. index. **Pr Rev. Acid Free. Circ:** 1,000 (ctrl).
**Desc:** A double-volume, looseleaf book which covers all aspects of industrial and commercial security from protection of assets to staff safety and from fire safety to equipment analysis.

UK
**PRACTICAL PREMISES SECURITY.** (19??)-. Periodical. English. £101.40. Croner Publ Ltd, Croner House, London Road, Kingston upon Thames, Surrey KT2 6SR England. **Tel** 011 44 81 5473333, FAX 081 547-2637.

US
**SDM FIELD GUIDE.** (199?)-. English. qt (4 issues). $29.00 US; $38.00 Canada; $35.00 Mexico; $50.00 (surface mail) other. Cahners Publishing Company, 249 West 17th Street, New York NY 10011. **Tel** (212)645-0067, FAX (212)242-6987. **(Subscription address:** Cahners Publishing Company / Colorado, Paid Subscription Service Center, PO Box 7610, Highlands Ranch CO 80126-7610.**)**
**Desc:** Gives readers practical advice on security system installation and service.

CN/0826-1083
**SECURITY & PROTECTION.** [Secur. prot.]. **VAT** Security and Protection (Calgary). Vol. 1, No. 1-. Periodical. English. mo. $24.00. Security & Protection, 3105 1212-31st Avenue NE, Calgary Alberta T2E 7S8 Canada. **DD** 381/.4568176.
**Ind/Abst** Int. Build. Serv. Abstr.

US/0747-6205
**SECURITY, ANTI-TERRORISM AND LOSS PREVENTION EQUIPMENT AND DEVICES BUYERS GUIDE.** ***Ceased.*** [Bill Daniels' illus. trade ref., Secur. anti-terror. loss prev. equip. de

vices buy. guide]. **Added/Corp** Bill Daniels Co. **VFOAT** Security, Anti-Terrorism and Loss Prevention Equipment and Devices Buyers Guide. (1986/87)-(19??). Consumer Publication. English. ir. Bill Daniels Company, PO Box 2056, Shawnee Mission KS 66201. **Tel** (913)492-9900. **LC** TH9730; .I43. **DD** 621.389/2. ***Continues*** *Illustrated Security and Closed Circuit TV Equipment Reference Catalog, 0740-6622.*

AT
**SECURITY AUSTRALIA.** English. mo (11 issues). 69.00Aus$ Australia; 99.00Aus$ Papua New Guinea, New Zealand, and Southeast Asia; 119.00Aus$ other. Reed Business Publishing Pty Ltd. / Australia, 1 5 Railway Street, Level 12 North Tower, Chatswood W 2067 NSW Australia. **Tel** 011 61 2 3725222, FAX 011 61 2 4197533. ***Absorbed*** *Security and Law Enforcement News.*

AT
**SECURITY AUSTRALIA DIRECTORY.** Directory. English. an. 25.00Aus$ Australia; 35.00Aus$ Papua New Guinea and New Zealand; 45.00Aus$ other. Reed Business Publishing Pty Ltd. / Australia, 1 5 Railway Street, Level 12 North Tower, Chatswood W 2067 NSW Australia. **Tel** 011 61 2 3725222, FAX 011 61 2 4197533.

US/0164-3320
**SECURITY DEALER.** (SECURITY DEALER : THE PROFESSIONAL MAGAZINE FOR RETAIL DEALERS & INSTALLERS & DISTRIBUTORS OF SECURITY PRODUCTS & SERVICES.). [Secur. deal.]. Vol. 1 (Jan. 1979)-. Periodical. English. Twelve times a year. $40.00 US; $65.00 other. PTN Publishing Company, 445 Broad Hollow Road, Melville NY 11747. **Tel** (516)845-2700, FAX (516)845-7109. **LC** HD9999.S45; S43. **DD** 621.389/28/0688. **CODEN** SEDEEL.

US/0049-0016
**SECURITY DISTRIBUTING & MARKETING.** (SECURITY DISTRIBUTING & MARKETING : SDM.). [Secur. distrib. mark.]. **Added/Corp** National Burglar and Fire Alarm Association (U.S.) Security Equipment Industry Association. **VFOAT** SDM; Security Distributing and Marketing. Vol. 1, No. 1 (Jan. 1971)-. Periodical. English. mo (13 issues). $70.00 US; $128.00 Canada; $120.00 Mexico; $150.00 (surface mail) other. Cahners Publishing Company, 249 West 17th Street, New York NY 10011. **Tel** (212)645-0067, FAX (212)242-6987. **(Subscription address:** Cahners Publishing Company / Colorado, Paid Subscription Service Center, PO Box 7610, Highlands Ranch CO 80126-7610.**) LC** HD9999.S453; U563. **DD** 381/.456213892. **[CCC].** available on microfilm and microfiche from University Microfilms International (UMI).
**Desc:** Magazine for the security professional concerned with sales, installation, service and distribution of security and/or technology and management.
**Ind/Abst** Crim. Justice Period. Index; Stat. Ref. Index.

●US
**SECURITY FOR BUYERS OF PRODUCTS, SYSTEMS AND SERVICES.** **VFOAT** Security Magazine; Security. Vol. 29, No. 1 (Jan. 1992)-. Periodical. English. mo. $70.00 US; $102.00 Canada; $95.00 Mexico; $130.00 (surface mail) other. Cahners Publishing Company, 249 West 17th Street, New York NY 10011. **Tel** (212)645-0067, FAX (212)242-6987. **(Subscription address:** Cahners Publishing Company / Colorado, Paid Subscription Service Center, PO Box 7610, Highlands Ranch CO 80126-7610.**)** ***Continues*** *Security (Newton, Mass.), 0890-8826.*
**Desc:** Intended for executives concerned with corporate and international security. Covers methods and equipment used to protect lives, property and assets from all types of risk, including internal theft, business interruption, fire, burglary, robbery, fraud, shoplifting, industrial espionage, computer crime and terrorism.

UK/0049-0024
**SECURITY GAZETTE.** [Secur. gaz.]. (1958)-. Periodical. English. mo. £30.00 UK; £40.00 Europe; £50.00 other. EMAP Business & Computer Publishing Ltd., 1 Lincoln Court 1 Lincoln Road, Peterborough PE1 2RP England. **Tel** 011/44/733/68900, FAX 011/44/733/349290. **(Subscription address:** EMAP Business Publishing, Ferrari House Audit House, Field End, Ruislip Middlesex HA4 9UY England.**) [CCC].**
**Ind/Abst** Infomat Int. Bus.

US
**SECURITY INDUSTRY BUYERS GUIDE.** **Added/Corp** Bell Atlantic Corporation. American Society for Industrial Security. (1987/1988)-. Consumer Publication. English. an. $169.00. Phillips Business Information, Inc., 1201 Seven Locks Road, Potomac MD 20854. **Tel** (301)424-3338, (800)777-5006, FAX (301)309-3847.
**Desc:** Contains facts and figures, names and numbers for suppliers of security products, systems and services.

US/0736-0401
**SECURITY LETTER SOURCE BOOK.** [Secur. lett. source book]. **Added/Corp** Security Letter, Inc. **VFOAT** Security Letter Sourcebook; Source Book. Vol. 1 (1983)-. English. be (every two years). $75.00. Butterworth Heinemann / Woburn, MA, 225 Wildwood Avenue, Unit B, Woburn MA 01801. **Tel** (800)366-2665, FAX (617)928-2620, telex 880052. **LC** HD9999.S453; U565. **DD** 363.2.

US/1062-1628
**SECURITY MANAGEMENT BULLETIN.** **See** Business-General Management.

US/1045-831X
**SECURITY SALES.** [Secur. sales]. **VFOAT** Security Sales Magazine. Vol. 11, No. 7 (July 1989)-. Periodical. English. Thirteen times a year. $35.00 US; $42.00 Canada; $53.00 other. Bobit Publishing, 2512 Artesia Boulevard, Redondo Beach CA 90278. **Tel** (310)376-8788, (800)334-8152, FAX (213)376-9043. **LC** TH9739; .A45. **DD** 384. ***Continues*** *Alarm Installer & Dealer (Agoura Hills, Calif.).*

UK
**SECURITY SPECIFIER.** (19??)-. English. Six times a year (Jan., Mar., May, July, Sept., Nov.). £15.00 UK; £18.00 Europe; £25.00 others. Portland Communications Ltd, 32 Portland Street, Cheltenham Gloschester, GL52 2PB England. **Tel** 011 44 242 236336, FAX 011 44 242 222331. **ED** Andrew Ritson. **Ad Acc, Adv Mgr:** Chris Musk, **Tel** 0242 236336.
**Desc:** News and information on CCTV, access controls, ID systems, gates & barriers, cameras, suppliers, emergency door devices, and security lights.

US/0745-6751
**SECURITY SYSTEMS ADMINISTRATION.** ***Ceased.*** [Secur. syst. adm.]. Vol. 11, No. 10 (Oct. 1982)-(1987). Periodical. English. mo. PTN Publishing Company, 445 Broad Hollow Road, Melville NY 11747. **Tel** (516)845-2700, FAX (516)845-7109. ***Continues*** *Security Industry & Product News, 0745-3329.*

●US/1068-8374
**SECURITY TECHNOLOGY NEWS.** **See** Computers-Computer Crimes and Security.

GW
**SICHERHEITSTECHNIK.** **See** Law-Law Enforcement and Criminology.

US/1062-3450
**UNCLASSIFIED (WASHINGTON, D.C.).** (UNCLASSIFIED / ASSOCIATION OF NATIONAL SECURITY ALUMNI.). [Unclassified]. **Added/Corp** Association of National Security Alumni (U.S.). Vol. 1, No. 1 (May 1989)-. Periodical. English. Six times a year (Feb., Apr., June, Aug., Oct., Dec.). $20.00 North America; $25.00 Europe; $30.00 (others. Association National Security Alumni, 921 Pleasant Street, Des Moines IA 50309. **ED** Verne Lyon, (phone: (515)283-2115). **LC** JK468.I6; U53. **DD** 327. Index available. cum. index. **Bk Rev,** (Qty: 8-10). **Ad Acc. Pr Rev. Circ:** 700. ***Absorbed*** *Campus Watch.*

GW/0935-5758
**WIK. ZEITSCHRIFT FUER WIRTSCHAFT, KRIMINALITAT UND SICHERHEIT.** [WIK, Z. Wirtsch. Krim. Sicherh.]. **VFOAT** Zeitschrift fuer Wirtschaft, Kriminalitat und Sicherheit. (1987)-. Periodical. German. bm. DM157.01 Germany; DM194.00 other. Secumedia Verlags GmbH, Postfach 1234, D 55205 Ingelheim Germany. **Tel** 011 49 6725 5995, FAX 011 49 6725 5994. **UDC** 343.53. ***Continues*** *WIK. Wirtschafts-Kriminalitat, 0177-5251.*
**Desc:** International magazine for security in business and administration. It contains news and analyzes product information, specially chosen for the users of security techniques.

## SENIOR CITIZENS

CN/0840-5395
**50 PLUS (DURHAM, ONT.).** (50 PLUS.). [50 plus]. **VAT** Fifty Plus (Durham). Vol. 1, No. 1 (Dec./Jan. 1989)-. Periodical. English. mo. $24.00. 50 Plus, PO Box 130, Durham Ontario N0G 1R0 Canada. **Tel** (519)369-5155, FAX (519)369-5096. **ED** John Elvidge, Lise Mollow, Leslie Grove. **DD** 305.2/6/09713. **Bk Rev. Ad Acc. Circ:** 35,000 monthly (ctrl).
**Desc:** A news magazine for adults 50 and over.

US
**A.I.M.** **Added/Corp** Michigan. Office of Services to the Aging. **VFOAT** A.I.M. (Aging In Michigan). Vol. 4, No. 10, June (1978)-. Periodical. English. bm. Free. Office Services to the Aging, PO Box 30026, Lansing MI 48909. **Tel** (517)373-8230. **ED** Linda Kimball. **Circ:** 11,000. ***Continues*** *A.I.M., Aging in Michigan.*
**Desc:** Contains news and information on programs, services and legislation of interest to Michigan senior citizens.

US/1044-1123
**AARP BULLETIN.** (AARP BULLETIN : A PUBLICATION OF THE AMERICAN ASSOCIATION OF RETIRED PERSONS.). [AARP bull.]. **Added/Corp** American Association of Retired Persons. **VAT** American Association of Retired Persons Bulletin. (198?)-. Bulletin. English. Eleven times a year (July/Aug. issues combined). Comes with American Association of Retired Persons membership. AARP - American Association of Retired Persons, PO Box 199, Long Beach CA 90801. **Tel** (310)496-2277. **DD** 646. ***Continues*** *AARP News Bulletin, 0001-0200.*

CN/0826-497X
**ACA NEWS (EDMONTON).** (ACA NEWS.). [ACA news]. **Added/Corp** Alberta Council on Aging. Vol. 16, No. 1 (Jan. 1984)-. Periodical. English. Ten times a year. Free. Alberta Council on Aging, 10506 Jasper Avenue / Room 501, Edmonton Alberta T5J 2W9 Canada. **Tel** (403)423-7781. **ED** Jean Holt. **DD**

305.2/6/097123. **Bk Rev**. **Ad Acc**. **Circ:** 6,000 (ctrl). ***Continues*** *Alberta Council on Aging. News, 0383-7998.* **Ind/Abst** Account. Tax Datab. (Nov. 1991-) [Full Txt.].

AT/1032-9005
**ACTION NETWORK.** [Action netw.]. **Added/Corp** Australian Pensioner's Federation. (1989)-. Periodical. English. Five times a year (Mar., May, July, Sept., Nov.). 10.00Aus$. Australian Pensioners Superannuants Federation, 8-24 Kippax Street, Suite 62, Surry Hills New South Wales, 2010 Australia. **Tel** 011 61 02 281 4566, FAX 011 61 02 281 5951. **ED** Paul Newton. **DD** 362.60994. **Bk Rev**. **Ad Acc**. **Circ:** 50,000. ***Continues*** *APF News Information, 1030-1860.*

US/0192-4788
**ACTIVITIES, ADAPTATION & AGING. See** Medical Science and Technology-Geriatrics.

US
**ACTIVITY DIRECTOR'S GUIDE.** (19??)-. Periodical. English. Twenty-four times a year. $25.00. Eymann Publications, PO Box 3577, Reno NV 89505. **Tel** (702)333-6651.

US
**ADVOCACY FOR SENIOR CITIZENS PRACTICE MANUAL.** English. ir. $99.95. Center for Public Representation, 121 South Pinckney Street, Madison WI 53703. **Tel** (608)251-4008, (800)369-0388, FAX (608)251-1263.

US/0161-1151
**AGED CARE & SERVICES REVIEW.** ***Title Change.*** **See** Sociology-Social Services and Welfare.

US/0002-0966
**AGING.** ***Ceased.*** **See** Medical Science and Technology-Geriatrics.

US/0892-5372
**AGING ALERT.** [Aging alert]. **Added/Corp** Area Agencies on Aging Association of Michigan. (19??)-. Periodical. English. Ten times a year (September - June). $20.00 (institutions); $10.00 (individuals). Michigan Center Aging Policy, 115 West Allegan, Suite 610, Lansing MI 48933. **Tel** (517)482-4871. **ED** Mary Ablan. **DD** 362. **Circ:** 1,000.
**Desc:** A newsletter informing senior citizens of relevant issues.

US/0273-2467
**AGING (BOCA RATON).** (AGING.). [Aging]. Vol. 1, Article 1-. English. an. Social Issues Resources Series Inc, PO Box 2348, Boca Raton FL 33427. **Tel** (800)327-0513, (407)994-0079. **ED** Eleanor C Goldstein. **LC** HQ1064.U5; A63334. **DD** 305.2/6/05.
**Desc:** Interdisciplinary resource material consisting of reprinted articles from popular and professional journals, newspapers, magazines and government documents.

US/0742-3438
**AGING NETWORK NEWS. VFOAT** ANN. (19??)-. Periodical. English. mo. $55.00 (1 year), $90.00 (2 year) US; $65.00 (1 year), $105.00 (2 year) other. Hansan & Group Inc, PO Box 1223, McLean VA 22101. **Tel** (703)734-3266, (800)659-8708, FAX (703)847-0573. **ED** John E Hansan. **Bk Rev**. **Ad Acc**. **Circ:** 1,200. ***Continues*** *Aging Program Letter, 0742-3438.*
**Desc:** The resource for an aging society. It is written by and for persons who work with and for older people in any setting anywhere in the United States. It is directed at individuals and organizations serving older persons. Each month the magazine features articles, news items, resources, book reviews, and columns focused on issues and programs pertinent to the field of aging, e.g. mental health, rural issues, long-term care, housing, physical well-being, etc.

●US
**AGING NEWS ALERT : THE SENIOR SERVICES & FUNDING REPORT.** No. 92-7/13 (July 15, 1992)-. Periodical. English. sm. $218.00. CD Publications, 8204 Fenton Street, Silver Spring MD 20910. **Tel** (800)666-6380, (301)588-6380, FAX (301)588-6385. Index available (free). ***Continues*** *Aging Action Alert, 1050-3188;* ***Absorbed*** *Senior Care Professional, 1051-6913* ***and*** *Senior Law Report, 1050-3250.*

CN/0704-4488
**ALBERTA FACT SHEET.** (FACT SHEET.). [Alta. fact sheet]. (1974)-. English. bm. Seniors Advisory Council for Alberta, 10109 106 Street, Energy Square Building, Edmonton Alberta T5J 4L7 Canada. **Circ:** 3,000 (ctrl).
**Desc:** Information of interest to those working with older people. Newsletter regarding conferences, publications, new ideas and new programs relating to aging.

NO/0801-9991
**ALDRING OG ELDRE.** [Aldring eldre]. **VFOAT** Aldring & Eldre. Vol. 1 (1988)-. Periodical. Norwegian. qt. Kr385.00, $68.00. Scandinavian University Press, PO Box 2959 Toeyen, N 0608 Oslo 6 Norway. **Tel** 011 47 2 2575400, FAX 011 47 2 2575353, telex 71896 UROR N. **(Subscription address:** Scandinavian University Press, 200 Meacham Ave., Elmont NY 11003.) **ED** Svein Olav Daatland. **DD** 362.6. **[CCC]**. **Bk Rev**. **Ad Acc**. **Circ:** 2,200. ***Continues*** *Gerontologisk Magasin, 0800-2509.*
**Desc:** A journal for those who work or have an interest in the care of senior citizens and their position in society.

US/1059-3799
**ALL-UNIVERSITY GERONTOLOGY CENTER PUBLIC POLICY SERIES.** **Added/Corp** Maxwell Graduate School of Citizenship and Public Affairs. All-University Gerontology Center. (1991)-. Monographic series. English. Maxwell School of Citizenship and Public Affairs, Syracuse University, 313 Maxwell Hall, Syracuse NY 13244-1090.

●US/1055-8306
**AMERICAN SENIOR, THE.** (1993)-. Periodical. English. qt. $29.99. Publishing & Business Consultants, PO Box 75392, Los Angeles CA 90075. **Tel** (213)732-3477, FAX (213)732-9123. **ED** Andeson Napoleon Atia. **Ad Acc**. Full Page (B&W) $5750.00. Half Page (B&W) $3575.00. Full Page (Color) $8750.00 (2 color). Half Page (Color) $5500.00 (2 color). **Circ:** 169,000 total.
**Desc:** Of interest to seniors and those with seniors in the family. Features articles on health and productive living, travel and investments.

UK
**ANNUAL REPORT - CENTRE FOR POLICY ON AGING (LONDON, ENGLAND).** **Main/Corp** Centre for Policy on Aging (London, England). English. an. Free. Centre for Policy on Aging, 25-31 Ironmonger Row, London EC1R 3QP England. **Tel** 011 44 712531787. **ED** Deidre Winne-Harley. **LC** HV1481.G7; N33. **DD** 362.6/06/041. **Circ:** 3,000 (ctrl). ***Continues*** *Centre for Policy on Aging (London, England). Annual Report for the Year Ended 30th September ... .*
**Desc:** Summary of the year's activities.

CN/0704-2663
**ANNUAL REPORT - ONTARIO ADVISORY COUNCIL ON SENIOR CITIZENS.** **Main/Corp** Ontario Advisory Council on Senior Citizens. **VFOAT** Rapport Annuel. 1974/75-. English. an. Ontario Advisory Council on Senior Citizens, 700 Bay Street/Suite 203, Toronto Ontario H5G 1Z6 Canada. **LC** HV1475.O5; O54A. **DD** 354/.713/00846.

SW
**ARBETSKARFTSUNDERSOKNINGEN. BEFOLKNINGEN I ALDERN 65-74 AR : AKU.** **Added/Corp** Sweden. Statistiska Centralbyran. Avdelningen for Arbetsmarknadsstatistik. **VFOAT** Befolkningen i Aldern 65-74 ar; Aku. (1986)-. Swedish. SCB Statistiska Centralbyran, 11581 Stockholm Sweden. **LC** HD6283.S8; A74.

US/0270-0425
**ARIZONA SENIOR WORLD, THE. See** Newspapers.

US/0147-8117
**AUDIT REPORT, COMMISSION ON AGING.** [Audit rep. - Comm. Aging]. **Main/Corp** Tennessee. Division of State Audit. English. Tennessee Comptroller of the Treasury, Nashville TN 37219. **LC** HV1468.T2; T43A.

CN/0835-8702
**BEL AGE, LE.** [Bel age]. Vol. 1, No. 1 (Oct. 1987)-. Periodical. French. Ten times a year. 9.95Can$ Canada; 20.00Can$ other. Publications Transcontinental Inc, 1100 Rene-Levesque, 24Fl Boulevard West, Montreal Quebec H3B 4X9 Canada. **Tel** (514)392-9000, FAX (514)392-4724. **ED** Francine Tremblay and Jean-Louis Gauthier. **DD** 305.2/6/05. **Ad Acc**.
**Desc:** For readers over 50; provides articles, columns, and practical advice adapted to their lifestyle. Covers money management, careers, psychology, family relations, health, leisure, and travel.
**Ind/Abst** Can. Period. Index (19??-); Point Repere.

US/0888-1537
**BIFOCAL. See** Law-Legal Aid.

CN/0835-8710
**BREF DE L'ACAQ, EN.** ***Title Change.*** [En bref ACAQ]. **Added/Corp** Association des Centres d'Accueil du Quebec. **VFOAT** En Bref de l'Association des Centres d'Accueil du Quebec. Vol. 4, No. 13 (July 1990)-Vol. 7, No. 11 (1993). Periodical. French. sm. Association des Centres d'Accueil du Quebec, Bureau 110, 65 Est Rue Sherbrooke, Montreal, Quebec H2X 1C4 Canada. **DD** 362.6/1/060714. ***Continues*** *L'ACAQ en Bref., 1184-6380.* ***Continued by*** *En Bref (Confederation Quebecoise des Centres d'Hebergement et de Readaptation), 1197-6233.*

CN/0229-866X
**BULLETIN DE L'AGE D'OR, LE.** [Bull. age or]. Vol. 1, No. 1-. Bulletin. French. qt. Free. **DD** 305.2/6/09714. ctrl circ.

CN
**CANADIAN SENIORITY.** (19??)-. English. Six times a year. 20.00Can$. Foresight Publications Inc., 12140 Horse Shoe Way, Suite 100, Richmond BC V7A 4V5 Canada. **Tel** (604)272-4772, FAX (604)275-7859. ***Continues*** *Foresight.*

US
**CAPSULE.** Newsletter. English. Six times a year (Feb., Apr., June, Aug., Oct., Dec.). $15.00 (individuals); $25.00 (institutions) US; $20.00 (individuals), $30.00 (institutions) other. Children of Aging Parents, 1609 Woodbourne Road, Suite 302A, Levittown PA 19057. **Tel** (215)945-6900, FAX (215)945-8720. **ED** Louise Fradkin. **Bk Rev**, (Qty: 6).
**Desc:** Focuses on the children and care-givers of elderly citizens.

UK/0968-8838
**CARERS WORLD. See** Physically Impaired.

UK
**CARING : FOR THE DISABLED CARERS AND THE ELDERLY.** ***Title Change.*** **See** Physically Impaired.

●CN/1193-8544
**CARP. CANADIAN ASSOCIATION OF RETIRED PERSONS.** (CARP : CANADA'S NATIONAL NEWSPAPER FOR FIFTY-PLUS LIFESTYLES.). [CARP, Can. Assoc. Retired Pers.]. **Added/Corp** Canadian Association of Retired Persons. Vol. 8, No. 4 (Oct. 1992)-. Periodical. English. bm. 10.00Can$ (one year), 25.00Can$ (three year) Canada; 20.00Can$ (one year), 50.00Can$ other (comes with membership). Canadian Association of Retired Persons, 27 Queen Street East, Suite 1304, Toronto ONT M5C 2M6 Canada. **Tel** (416)363-8748, FAX (416)363-8747. **ED** David Judge. **DD** 305.26/0971/05. Index available. **Bk Rev**. **Ad Acc**, **Adv Mgr:** Keith Gardner, **Tel** (416)363-5562 ext.301. **Circ:** 90,000 (ctrl). ***Continues*** *C.A.R.P. News (Canadian Association of Retired Persons)., 0838-990X.*

CN/0826-4694
**CENTRE ON AGING NEWS.** [Cent. Aging news]. Vol. 1, No. 1 (Summer 82)-. Periodical. English. ir. Free. University of Manitoba Centre on Aging, 338 Isbister Building, Winnipeg Manitoba R3T 2N2 Canada. **Tel** (204)474-8754. **DD** 612/.67/06071274. **Circ:** 1,500.

US/0731-7115
**CLINICAL GERONTOLOGIST. See** Medical Science and Technology-Geriatrics.

US
**CONTEMPORARY SENIORHEALTH.** **VFOAT** Contemporary Senior Health. Vol. 1, No. 1 (Summer 1989)-. English. qt. $19.00 US and Canada. Medical Publishing Enterprises, 15 22 Fair Lawn Avenue, Fair Lawn NJ 07410. **Tel** (201)796-6500.
**Desc:** Guide to cost-effective managed care.

US
**CORBEL FORMS MANUAL.** English. $350.00 (first time), $160.00 (renew). Corbel & Company, 1660 Prudential Drive, Jacksonville FL 32207. **Tel** (904)399-5888, FAX (904)399-5551. **ED** Corbel & Company. available on an online database.
**Desc:** Manual used in creation of various qualified retirement plans.

US/0748-1195
**DECEMBER ROSE.** ***Suspended.*** Vol. 1, No. 1, (Dec. 1984)-?. Periodical. English. qt. $10.00. December Rose Association, 255 South Hill Street, Los Angeles CA 90012. **Tel** (310)617-7002. **ED** Don Jarman. **Bk Rev**. **Ad Acc**. **Circ:** 80,000 (ctrl).
**Desc:** Seeks to be a showcase for the creativity of older people. It publishes material written by or about seniors.

US/0734-3213
**DEVELOPMENT IN AGING.** (DEVELOPMENTS IN AGING : A REPORT OF THE SPECIAL COMMITTEE ON AGING, UNITED STATES SENATE.). **Main/Corp** United States. Congress. Senate. Special Committee on Aging. (19??)-. English. ir. Price varies per volume. Bernan Associates, 4611-F Assembly Drive, Lanham MD 20706-4391. **Tel** (301)459-7666, (800)274-4447 US, (800)233-0504 CANADA, FAX (301)459-0056, telex 7108260418. **LC** HQ1064.U5; U53a. **DD** 305.2/6/0973. **NLM** W2 A C84D. available on microfiche (Vols. for (1981-) distributed to some depository libraries).

US
**DIRECT LOAN PROGRAM FOR THE ELDERLY OR HANDICAPPED. See** Sociology-Social Services and Welfare.

US
**DIRECTORY OF MEMBERS / AMERICAN ASSOCIATION OF HOMES FOR THE AGING. See** Sociology-Social Services and Welfare.

US/0888-7624
**DIRECTORY OF NURSING HOMES (PHOENIX, ARIZ.). See** Medical Science and Technology-Hospital Administration and Medical Centers.

CN/0824-5398
**DIRECTORY OF RESOURCES FOR SENIOR CITIZENS OF OTTAWA-CARLETON.** **See** Sociology-Social Services and Welfare.

●US/1053-6825
**DIRECTORY OF RETIREMENT FACILITIES, THE.** **Added/Corp** Health Care Investment Analysts, Inc. (1993)-. Directory. English. an. $199.00 (all except CT, IL, MD, MI, OH, SC, & WA); $210.94 (CT), $211.44 (IL), $208.95 (MD & SC), $206.96 (MI), $214.72 (WA) includes applicable sales tax. HCIA, 300 East Lombard Street, Baltimore MD 21202. **Tel** (410)576-9600, (800)568-3282. **LC** HV1454.2.U6; N38. **NLM** WT 22; AA1 N25. ***Continues** National Directory of Retirement Facilities, 1053-6825.*

US/0098-2709
**DIRECTORY OF SENIOR CENTERS AND CLUBS.** Directory. English. National Council on the Aging, Department 5087, Washington DC 20061. **Tel** (202)479-1200. **LC** HQ1060; .D56. **DD** 362.6/3/02573. ***Continues** National Directory of Senior Centers.*

US
**DISTRICT OF COLUMBIA PLAN ON AGING.** **Main/Corp** District of Columbia. Office on Aging. FY 1982-1984-. English. **LC** HQ1064.U6; W252A. **DD** 352.94/4/09753. ***Continues** District of Columbia Plan on Aging for Fiscal Years ... .*

JA/0288-3619
**EIJINGU.** **VFOAT** Aging. V. 1, No. 1 (1983)-. Periodical. Japanese (Japanese). bm. ¥4440. Chuo Hoki Shuppan Kabushiki Kaisha 27-4, Yoyogi 2 Shibuya-ku, Tokyo-to 151 Japan. **LC** HQ1060; .K54. ***Continues** Kikan Rojin Mondai.*

CN/0013-4074
**ELDER STATESMAN, THE.** ***Title Change.*** [Elder statesman]. **VFOAT** Elder Statesman Publication. (1967)-(1992)-. Periodical. English. mo. **DD** 305.26/09711. ***Continues** Senior Citizens' Association News, The Pensioner, 0553-6251 **and** Elder Statesman Handbook, 0834-244X. **Continued by** Today's Times (Vancouver, B.C.), 1193-171X.*

US/1060-4545
**ELDER UPDATE.** (ELDER UPDATE / STATE OF FLORIDA, DEPT. OF ELDER AFFAIRS.). [Elder update]. **Added/Corp** Florida. Dept. of Elder Affairs. (Dec. 1991)-. Periodical. English. mo. Free. Elder Update, Department of Elder Affairs, 1317 Winewood Boulevard, Building 1, Room 317, Tallahassee FL 32399-0700. ***Continues** Senior Consumer.*

US/1047-7055
**ELDERLAW REPORT, THE.** **See** Law.

US
**ELDERSONG.** **See** Music.

CN/0705-9418
**ESPECIALLY FOR SENIORS.** ***Ceased.*** [Espec. sr.]. **Added/Corp** Ontario Advisory Council on Senior Citizens. (June 1975)-(Jan. 1992). Periodical. English (French). qt. Ontario Advisory Council on Senior Citizens, 700 Bay Street/Suite 203, Toronto Ontario H5G 1Z6 Canada.

US/1054-3473
**EXPERIENCE : THE MAGAZINE OF THE SENIOR LAWYERS DIVISION, AMERICAN BAR ASSOCIATION.** **See** Law.

CN/0848-6778
**FACT SHEET / SENIORS ADVISORY COUNCIL FOR ALBERTA.** [Fact sheet - Sr. Advis. Counc. Alta.]. **Added/Corp** Seniors Advisory Council for Alberta. Issue No. 1 (1990)-. Periodical. English. **DD** 362.6/097123. ***Continues** Fact Sheet (Provincial Senior Citizens Advisory Council (Alta.)), 0846-720X.*

CN/1183-0484
**FAST (COMMUNITY LEADERS' ED.).** (FAST.). [FAST]. **Added/Corp** Toronto (Ont.). Mayor's Committee on Aging. **VFOAT** Fact Affecting Seniors in Toronto. Vol. 1, Ed. 1 (1990)-. Periodical. English. sa. Limited free distribution. Toronto Mayor's Committee on Aging, Department of the City Clerk, City Hall, Toronto, Ontario M5H 2N2 Canada. **DD** 305.26/09713/54105.

CN/0840-4496
**FIFTY-FIVE PLUS (BATTERSEA).** (FIFTY-FIVE PLUS.). [Fifty-five plus]. **VFOAT** 55 Plus. Vol. 1, Issue 1 (Oct./Nov. 1988)-. Periodical. English. bm (6 issues). 16.05Can$ Canada; 32.10Can$ other. Limestone City Publications, Box 47, Battersea Ontario K0H 1H0 Canada. **Tel** (613)353-2060. **ED** Sharon Freeman. **DD** 305.2/6/09713. **Bk Rev**, (Qty: 12-18). **Ad Acc, Adv Mgr:** J. Walsh. **Circ:** 35,000.
**Desc:** Readership enjoys a combination of creative efforts and expert advice. Helps to dispel the traditional image of older Canadians prevalent in most Canadian publications. Seeks lively editorials that are inspiring and that provide our readers with choices in the areas of health, finance, housing, relationships, travel and more.

AT
**FIFTY SOMETHING.** English. bm. 15.00Aus$ single membership; 20.00Aus$ joint membership. National Seniors Association, 168 Edward Street, GPO Box 1450, Brisbane, 4000 Australia. **Tel** 011 61 7 2212977, FAX 011 61 7 0356. **ED** M. Shanely. **Bk Rev**. **Ad Acc, Adv Mgr:** K. Osgood. **Circ:** 40,000 (ctrl).

US/0160-5739
**FLORIDA RETIREMENT LIVING.** **Added/Corp** Florida Retirement Advisory Board. (19??)-. Periodical. English. Ten times a year. $12.00. Gidder House Publishing Inc, PO Box 161848, Altamonte Springs FL 32716. **Tel** (407)774-8668. **ED** Dyeann Dummer, (phone: (407)774-1095). **Bk Rev**, (Qty: 6). **Ad Acc, Adv Mgr:** R. Dummer. **Circ:** 35,000 (ctrl).
**Desc:** Housing and lifestyles for active retirees including finances, fitness, travel and attitudes.

US
**FLORIDA RETIREMENT SYSTEM ANNUAL REPORT / PREPARED BY THE DIVISION OF RETIREMENT'S STATE RETIREMENT ACTUARY, RESEARCH, EDUCATION, & POLICY SECTION, BUREAU OF ACCOUNTING AND DIVISION AUDIT STAFF.** **See** Economics-Labor.

US/0740-4956
**FOCUS, LIBRARY SERVICE TO OLDER ADULTS, PEOPLE WITH DISABILITIES.** **See** Library and Information Sciences.

CN/0711-3927
**FORESIGHT (EDMONTON).** ***Title Change.*** (FORESIGHT : THE MAGAZINE FOR RETIREMENT PLANNING.). [Foresight]. **Added/Corp** Alberta Council on Aging. **VAT** Foresight Magazine. Vol. 1, No. 1 (Sept. 1981)-(19??). Periodical. English. bm (Jan., Mar., May, July, Sept., Nov.). Foresight Publications Inc., 12140 Horse Shoe Way, Suite 100, Richmond BC V7A 4V5 Canada. **Tel** (604)272-4772, FAX (604)275-7859. **ED** David Todd. **DD** 646.7/9/05. **Bk Rev**, (Qty: 10). **Ad Acc, Adv Mgr:** Eric, **Tel** (604)275-7971. **Circ:** 50,000 (ctrl). ***Continued by** Canadian Seniority, 1198-7294.*
**Ind/Abst** Can. Period. Index.

US/1056-3423
**FOURTH SEASON.** (FOURTH SEASON : A JOURNAL FOR INVOLVED RETIREMENT.). [Fourth seas.]. (1990)-. Periodical. English. mo. Free. Fourth Season, 611 South Federal Highway, Suite M-3, Stuart FL 34994-2934. **DD** 306.

US/0738-7806
**GENERATIONS (SAN FRANCISCO, CALIF.).** (GENERATIONS.). [Generations]. **Added/Corp** Western Gerontological Society. American Society on Aging. (1976)-. Periodical. English. qt. $40.00 US; $50.00 Canada; $65.00 other. American Society on Aging, 833 Market Street/Suite 512, San Francisco CA 94103. **Tel** (415)882-2910, FAX (415)882-4280. **ED** Mary Johnson. **CODEN** GENREC. **Bk Rev**. **Ad Acc**. **Pr Rev**. **Circ:** 12,000 (ctrl).
**Desc:** One of the most widely read publications on aging, each issue is devoted to a single topic that is covered from a diversity of in-depth perspectives. Written in a lively easy-to-read style, it is read by teachers and students, researchers and practitioners, policy makers, administrators and business people.
**Ind/Abst** Abstr. Anthropol.; Abstr. Soc. Gerontol.; Acad. Abstr. Full Text Elite (Jan. 1992-); Acad. Abstr. (Jan. 1992-); Acad. Search (Jan. 1992-); AGRICOLA; Book Rev. Index; Cumul. Index Nurs. Allied Health Lit.; Curr. Index J. Educ.; Health Period. Database [Full Txt.]; Health Ref. Cent. (Jan. 1989-) [Full Txt.] [Full Cov.]; Health Source (Jan. 1992-); Index Period. Lit. Aging; INFO-SOUTH Abstr.; Mag. Search; PAIS Int. Print; Psychol. Abstr. (1985-); PsycINFO; Soc. Plann. Policy Dev. Abstr.; Sociol. Abstr. (1988-).

CN/0225-4271
**GERONTOPHILE (SAINTE-FOY).** (LE GERONTOPHILE : BULLETIN DE L'ASSOCIATION QUEBECOISE DE GERONTOLOGIE.). [Gerontophile]. **Added/Corp** Association Quebecoise de Gerontologie. **VAT** Gerontophile (Montreal. 1979). Vol. 1 No. 1 (Mar. 1979)-. Bulletin. French. ir. 50.00Can$ (institutions), 30.00Can$ (individuals) Canada; 62.00Can$ (institutions), 42.00Can$ (individuals) other. Le Gerontophile Chambre, 2467 Pavillon de Koninck, Laval Quebec G1K 7P4 Canada. **DD** 305.2/6/05.
**Ind/Abst** Point Repere (1991-).

US
**GOLDEN YEARS MAGAZINE.** (1983)-. English. bm. $6.95. Golden Years Magazine, PO Box 537, 233 East New Haven Avenue, Melbourne FL 32902. **Tel** (407)725-4888. Index available. **Bk Rev**. **Ad Acc**.

CN/0847-1126
**GOOD TIMES (TORONTO).** (GOOD TIMES.). [Good times]. Vol. 1, No. 1 (Nov./Dec. 1989)-. Periodical. English. Ten times a year. 21.54Can$ Quebec; 19.95Can$ Canada; 29.95Can$ other. Publications Transcontinental Inc, 1100 Rene-Levesque, 24Fl Boulevard West, Montreal Quebec H3B 4X9 Canada. **Tel** (514)392-9000, FAX (514)392-4724. **DD** 646.7/9/0971. ***Continues** Discovery (Toronto, Ont.), 0710-0957.*
**Ind/Abst** Can. Period. Index (19??-).

●US/1068-1345
**GRAND TIMES.** [Grand times]. (1992)-. Periodical. English. bm (Feb., Apr., June, Aug., Oct., Dec.). $19.97 (one year), $35.95 (two year). Grand Times, PO Box 9493, Deptartment ME3, Berkeley CA 94709. **Tel** (510)848-0456. **DD** 051. **Bk Rev**, (Qty: 18). **Ad Acc**. **Circ:** 20,000.

US
**GROWING OLDER.** No. 1 1976-. Periodical. English. an. Rational Island Publishers, 719 2nd Avenue North, Seattle WA 98109.

CN/0846-0671
**GUIDE DU PASSAGE A LA RETRAITE.** [Guide pass. retraite]. **Added/Corp** Quebec (Province). Office de la Protection du Consommateur. (1990)-. French. 9.95Can$. Publications Senior, Inc., 5148 Boulevard Saint-Laurent, Montreal, Quebec H2T 1R8 Canada. **DD** 646.7/9/0971405.

US/0889-051X
**GUIDE TO FLORIDA RETIREMENT LIVING.** [Guide Fla. retire. living]. English. an. $2.00. Gidder House Publishing Inc, PO Box 161848, Altamonte Springs FL 32716. **Tel** (407)774-8668. **ED** Joe Hoeddinghaus. **DD** 910. **Bk Rev**. **Ad Acc**. **Circ:** 50,000 (ctrl).
**Desc:** Takes a good look at manufactured housing, retirement communities and lifestyles in the Sunshine State.

US/1050-3234
**HOUSING THE ELDERLY REPORT.** [Hous. elder. rep.]. (1982)-. Periodical. English. mo. $167.00. CD Publications, 8204 Fenton Street, Silver Spring MD 20910. **Tel** (800)666-6380, (301)588-6380, FAX (301)588-6385. **LC** HD7287.92.U5; H68. **DD** 362. ***Absorbed** Retirement Housing Business Report.*

CN/0847-5288
**INDEPENDENT SENIOR, THE.** [Indep. sr.]. Vol. 1, No. 1 Jan. (1990)-. Periodical. English. Ten times a year. 15.00Can$ Canada; 22.00Can$ other. KW Publishing Ltd, 1268 West Pender Street, Vancouver British Columbia V6E 2Z8 Canada. **Tel** (604)688-2271, FAX (604)688-2038. **ED** Adrian Leonard. **DD** 305.26/09711. **Bk Rev**, (Qty: 6). **Ad Acc, Adv Mgr:** Phil Vachon. **Circ:** 42,500 (ctrl). ***Continues** Seniors' Advocate (Vancouver, B.C.), 0843-4905.*
**Desc:** News and information for those 55 years of age and over.

US
**INFORMATION STATEMENT FOR APPLICANTS AND GRANTEES MODEL PROJECTS ON AGING.** **Main/Corp** United States. Administration on Aging. English. Administration on Aging, 330 Independence Avenue SW, Washington DC 20201. **LC** HV1465; .U54A.

NE
**INSTELLINGEN.** **See** Public Health and Safety.

US/1059-2431
**INSTITUTE ON AGING NEWSLETTER.** [Inst. Aging newsl.]. **Added/Corp** University of Pennsylvania. Institute on Aging. Vol. 1, No. 1 (Spring 1991)-. Newsletter. English. Three times a year. Free. University of Pennsylvania / Institute on Aging, 3615 Chestnut Street, Philadelphia PA 19104-6006. **DD** 305. ***Continues** Center for the Study of Aging Newsletter.*

CN/0704-7029
**JOURNAL DE L'AGE D'OR, LE.** **See** Sociology-Social Services and Welfare.

US/0895-9420
**JOURNAL OF AGING & SOCIAL POLICY.** [J. aging soc. policy]. **VFOAT** Journal of Aging and Social Policy. Vol. 1, No. 1/2 (1989)-. Periodical. English. qt. $115.00 US; $161.00 other. The Haworth Press Inc, 10 Alice Street, Binghamton NY 13904-1580. **Tel** (607)722-5857, (800)3-HAWORTH, FAX (607)722-1424. **ED** Scott Bass (editor's address: Gerontology Institute, University of Massachusetts, Boston, MA 02125). **LC** HV1457; .J68. **DD** 362.6/0973/05. **NLM** W1; JO534BK. **CODEN** JSPOE8. **Bk Rev**. **Ad Acc**. **Pr Rev**. **Acid Free**. **Circ:** 336. available on microfilm and microfiche from University Microfilms International (UMI). Documents available from Haworth Document Delivery Service.
**Desc:** A forum for the analysis, argument, research and advocacy of social policy as it effects the aging population, making it an invaluable resource for all professionals engaged in policy and program development for the elderly.

**Ind/Abst** Abstr. Soc. Gerontol.; Biol. Dig.; Geogr. Abstr. Human Geogr.; Hum. Resour. Abstr.; Index Period. Artic. Relat. Law; Index Period. Lit. Aging (19??-19??); PAIS Int. Print (1991-); Psychol. Abstr.; Soc. Plann. Policy Dev. Abstr.; Soc. Work Abstr. [Select. Cov.]; Sociol. Abstr.

US/0890-4065
**JOURNAL OF AGING STUDIES. See** Sociology.

US/0894-6566
**JOURNAL OF ELDER ABUSE & NEGLECT. See** Sociology-Social Services and Welfare.

US/0163-4372
**JOURNAL OF GERONTOLOGICAL SOCIAL WORK. See** Sociology-Social Services and Welfare.

US/0276-3893
**JOURNAL OF HOUSING FOR THE ELDERLY. See** Housing and Urban Development.

US/0742-6291
**JOURNAL OF MINORITY AGING, THE.** V. 3, No. 6- Aug. 1978-. Periodical. English. sa. $30.00. Black Aging, PO Box 8813, Durham NC 27707. **Tel** (919)489-2563. **ED** Jacquelyne J Jackson. **LC** HQ1064.U5. **DD** 362.6/0973. **Bk Rev**. **Ad Acc. Circ:** 750 (ctrl). ***Continues*** *Black Aging.*
**Desc:** Research about aging of older minorities in the United States. Emphasizing public policies, services, and age changes.

US/0163-9366
**JOURNAL OF NUTRITION FOR THE ELDERLY. See** Nutrition and Dietetics.

US/1050-2289
**JOURNAL OF RELIGIOUS GERONTOLOGY. See** Medical Science and Technology-Geriatrics.

US/0895-2841
**JOURNAL OF WOMEN & AGING. See** Women's Interests.

US/0744-0677
**LIFE LINES (LINCOLN, NEB.).** (LIFE LINES.). V. 1- Oct. 1974- (No. 1- ). Periodical. English. bm. Lincoln Area Agency on Aging, Life Lines Magazine, 129 North 10th Street/Room 241, Lincoln NE 68508-3846. **Ad Acc. Circ:** 32,000 (ctrl).
**Desc:** The publication's purpose is to educate and inform persons on topics, programs, issues and activities that are of concern to the mature population.

CN/0824-1503
**MAIN DE L'AGE D'OR, LA.** [Main age or]. Vol. 1, No. 1 (Winter 1984)-. Periodical. French. qt. Free. La Main de l'Age d'Or, CP 421, Drummondville Quebec J2B 6W3 Canada. **DD** 305.2/6/05. ctrl circ.

US/0162-427X
**MATURE LIVING (NASHVILLE).** (MATURE LIVING.). **Added/Corp** Southern Baptist Convention. Sunday School Board. (19??)-. Periodical. English. mo. $14.80. Southern Baptist Convention, 901 Commerce, Suite 750, Nashville TN 37203. **Tel** (615)244-2355, FAX (615)742-8919. **(Subscription address:** Sunday School Board - Customer Service, 127 Ninth Avenue North, Nashville, TN 37234 USA; telephone: (800)458-2772**) ED** Jack Gulledge. **Bk Rev**. **Ad Acc. Circ:** 306,000 (ctrl).
**Desc:** A leisure-reading magazine in large print for older adults, sixty plus with a Christian-orientation.
**Ind/Abst** South. Baptist Period. Index.

US/0742-0935
**MATURE OUTLOOK.** [Mature outlook]. **Added/Corp** Mature Outlook (Organization). Vol. 1, No. 1 (Winter 1984)-. Periodical. English. bm. $6.00. Mature Outlook, 6001 North Clark Street, Chicago IL 60660. **Tel** (800)336-6330, (312)764-8210. **DD** 646. **Ad Acc. Circ:** 900,000 (ctrl).
**Desc:** A lifestyle publication edited for people age 50 and over. It features personalities, travel information, money management and other topics of interest to this age group.

US/0748-4003
**MATURE OUTLOOK NEWSLETTER.** **Added/Corp** Mature Outlook (Organization). (1984)-. Newsletter. English. bm. $6.00. Mature Outlook, 6001 North Clark Street, Chicago IL 60660. **Tel** (800)336-6330, (312)764-8210. **ED** Ann Meyer. **DD** 646. **Ad Acc. Circ:** 900,000 (ctrl).
**Desc:** A guide to money management, healthcare and fitness, and travel. Designed to appeal to the special interests and concerns of people age 50 and older.

US/0025-6021
**MATURE YEARS. See** Religion and Theology.

●US/1062-9556
**MEMORIES PLUS.** (1992)-. Periodical. English. mo. $5.00. Memories Plus, PO Box 1339, Albany OR 97321. **Tel** (503)928-4798. **ED** Margaret L Ingram. **Ad Acc. Circ:** 750-1000.

US/0026-8046
**MODERN MATURITY.** [Mod. matur.]. **Added/Corp** American Association of Retired Persons. Vol. 1 (Oct./Nov. 1958)-. Periodical. English. bm (6 issues). Comes with AARP membership. AARP - American Association of Retired Persons, PO Box 199, Long Beach CA 90801. **Tel** (310)496-2277. **LC** HQ1060; .M6. **DD** 646. available on an online database (file 647/Full-Text) from DIALOG. ***Absorbed*** *We; Journal of Lifetime Living* ***and*** *Dynamic Years, 0148-799X.*

US/0747-6302
**MODERN MATURITY (NRTA ED.).** (MODERN MATURITY : PUBLICATION OF THE AMERICAN ASSOCIATION OF RETIRED PERSONS.). [Mod. matur.]. **Added/Corp** American Association of Retired Persons. National Retired Teachers Association. Vol. 25, No. 1 (Feb.-March 1982)-. Periodical. English. bm (6 issues). Comes with American Association of Retired Persons membership. AARP - American Association of Retired Persons, PO Box 199, Long Beach CA 90801. **Tel** (310)496-2277. **ED** Henry Fenwick and Ian Ledgerwood. **DD** 646. **Bk Rev**. **Ad Acc. Circ:** 22,400,000 (ctrl). available on microfilm and microfiche from University Microfilms International (UMI). Documents available from UMI Article Clearinghouse. ***Continues*** *NRTA Journal, 0027-6979.*
**Ind/Abst** Abr. Read. Guide Period. Lit.; Acad. Abstr. Full Text Elite (Jan. 1984-); Acad. Abstr. (Jan. 1984-); Acad. Search (Jan. 1984-); Consum. Health Nutr. Index (Jan. 1990); Foods Adlibra; Gen. Period. Index (1985-); Health Ref. Cent. (1987-) [Full Txt.] [Select. Cov.]; Health Source (Jan. 1984-); Mag. Artic. Summar. Elite (Jan. 1984-); Mag. Artic. Summar. Select (Jan. 1984-); Mag. Artic. Summar. CD-ROM (Jan. 1984-); Mag. ASAP Plus [Full Txt.]; Mag. ASAP Sel. [Full Txt.]; Mag. Index Plus (1989-); Mag. Index. Sel. (1986-); Mag. Search; Newsp. Period. Abstr. (1988-); Read. Guide Abstr. Select Ed.; Read. Guide Period. Lit.; Mag. Index (1977-); Vocat. Search (Jan. 1984-).

US/0889-4744
**MONTHLY MINI-LESSONS IN CARE OF THE AGING.** [Mon. mini-lessons care aging]. **VFOAT** Monthly Mini Lessons in Care of the Aging. (1986)-. Periodical. English. mo. $25.00. Eymann Publications, PO Box 3577, Reno NV 89505. **Tel** (702)333-6651. **DD** 362.

CN/0831-3040
**MSOS JOURNAL.** [MSOS j.]. **Added/Corp** Manitoba Society of Seniors. **VAT** Manitoba Society of Seniors journal. (1985)-. Periodical. English. mo. 12.00Can$, Canada--except Manitoba; 14.00Can$, Manitoba; 17.00Can$ other. MSOS Journal, 803 294 Portage Ave., Winnipeg Man R3C 0B9 Canada. **Tel** (204)942-3147. **ED** Irvin J. Krocker. **DD** 362.6/097127. **Bk Rev**, (Qty: 15). **Ad Acc**, **Adv Mgr:** Ray Gislason. **Circ:** 30,000 (ctrl). ***Continues*** *Manitoba Seniors Journal., 0826-5704.*
**Desc:** News and information of interest to Manitoba Seniors.

US/1053-6825
**NATIONAL DIRECTORY OF RETIREMENT FACILITIES.** ***Title Change.*** [Natl. dir. retire. facil.]. (1986)-(19??). Directory. English. Oryx Press, 4041 North Central Avenue, #700, Phoenix AZ 85012-3397. **Tel** (800)279-ORYX, (602)265-2651, FAX (602)265-6250, (800)279-4663, (800)279-6799. **LC** HV1454.2.U6; N38. **DD** 362.6/1/02573. **NLM** WT 22; AA1 N25. ***Continued by*** *Directory of Retirement Facilities.*
**Desc:** Covers more than 18,000 personal and boarding care, congregate and semi-independent living, independent living, and life care facilities.

CN/0849-2115
**NATIONAL NEWS - NATIONAL PENSIONERS AND SENIOR CITIZENS FEDERATION.** (NATIONAL NEWS.). [Natl. news - Natl. Pension. Sr. Citiz. Fed.]. **Added/Corp** National Pensioners and Senior Citizens Federation. Vol. 22, No. 3 (May/June 1990)-. Periodical. English. qt. 10.00Can$. National Pensioners & Senior Citizens Federation, 3033 Lakeshore Boulevard West, Toronto Ontario M8V 1K5 Canada. **Tel** (416)251-7042, FAX (416)251-7042. **ED** Edith M. Johnston. **DD** 305.26/0971/05. **Bk Rev**. **Ad Acc. Circ:** 2,000. ***Continues*** *Nat'l Pensioners, Senior Citizens News., 0380-0989.*

US/1045-9073
**NCOA NETWORKS.** [NCOA netw.]. **Added/Corp** National Council on the Aging. **VAT** National Council on the Aging Networks. Vol. 1, No. 1 (Oct. 15, 1989)-. Periodical. English. Six times a year. $175.00 organzations (membership), $90.00 individuals (membership). National Council on the Aging, Department 5087, Washington DC 20061. **Tel** (202)479-1200. **(Subscription address:** National Council on the Aging Membership, 409 3rd Street SW / 2nd Floor, Washington DC 20024.**) ED** Dianna M. Porter. **DD** 362. **Ad Acc. Circ:** 7,000 (ctrl).

JA
**NENKIN FUKUSHI JIGYODAN NEMPO. See** Sociology-Social Services and Welfare.

JA
**NENKIN KENKYU NENPO. See** Sociology-Social Services and Welfare.

US/1041-6277
**NEW CHOICES FOR THE BEST YEARS.** ***Title Change.*** [New choices best years]. **VFOAT** New Choices. Vol. 28, No. 12 (Dec. 1988)-. Periodical. English. mo. R D Publications, 28 West 23rd Street, New York NY 10010. **Tel** (800)365-5005, (212)366-8630. **ED** Kate Greer. **LC** HQ1060; .H36. **DD** 301. Index available. cum. index. **Bk Rev**. **Ad Acc. Circ:** 591,133. available on microfilm and microfiche from University Microfilms International (UMI). Documents available from UMI Article Clearinghouse, Magazine Collection. ***Continues*** *50 Plus, 0163-2027.* ***Continued by*** *New Choices for Retirement Living, 1061-2157.*
**Desc:** Published for men and women in their middle years, 45 to 65. Focuses on and puts into perspective the interests and topics germane adults in this lifestage: travel, health, nutrition, fitness, and personal finance to home, garden, food, pets, cars, sports and intergenerational family relationships.
**Ind/Abst** Gen. Period. Index (1988-1992); Health Ref. Cent. (1987-) [Select. Cov.]; INFO-SOUTH Abstr.; Mag. Artic. Summar. Select; Mag. Artic. Summar. CD-ROM (Jan. 1989); Mag. Index Plus (1989-1991); Mag. Index. Sel. (1989-1992); Mag. Search; Read. Guide Abstr. Select Ed.; Read. Guide Period. Lit.; Resource/One Ondisc (1988-1992); Mag. Index.

US/0163-2248
**NEW ENGLAND SENIOR CITIZEN.** ***Ceased.*** (1970)-?. Periodical. English. mo. R A de Vito, 470 Boston Post Road, Weston MA 02193. **Tel** (617)899-2702, FAX (617)899-4361. **ED** Shirley Copithorne. **Bk Rev**. **Ad Acc. Circ:** 50,000 (ctrl).
**Desc:** Upbeat tabloid newspaper. Covers entertainment and travel for those over 50.

UK/0140-2447
**NEW LITERATURE ON OLD AGE.** **Added/Corp** Centre for Policy on Ageing (London, England). (19??)-. Periodical. English. bm. £18.00 UK; £20.00 other. World Wide Subscription Services, Unit 4, Gibbs Reed Farm, East Sussex TN5 7HE England. **Tel** (0580)200657, FAX (0580)200616. **ED** Gillian Crosby. **Circ:** 600 (ctrl).
**Desc:** An information service giving details of new books, literature, conferences and courses on aging in Britain, Europe and US.

CN/0710-958X
**NEWS FOR SENIORS.** [News srs.]. Periodical. English. mo. 5.00Can$ Canada. Society for the Retired and Semi-Retired, 10004-105th Street, Edmonton Alberta P5J 1C3 Canada. **Tel** (403)423-5510. **DD** 362.6/097123/3. **Bk Rev**. **Ad Acc. Circ:** 20,000.
**Desc:** Provides articles on topics of interest to older readers including information on special programs and services available through the society for the retired and semi-retired.

CN/0712-676X
**NEWSLETTER - CANADIAN ASSOCIATION ON GERONTOLOGY.** (NEWSLETTER.). [Newsl. - Can. Assoc. Gerontol.]. **Main/Corp** Canadian Association on Gerontology. **VFOAT** Bulletin d'Information. Newsletter. English (French). qt. 19.80Can$ (individuals), 30.00Can$ (institutions). Canadian Association on Gerontology, 1080-167 Lombard Avenue, Winnipeg Manitoba R3B 0V3 Canada. **Tel** (204)944-9158, FAX (204)943-8468. **ED** Dana Mohr. **DD** 305.2/6/0971. **Bk Rev**. **Ad Acc. Circ:** 1,500 (ctrl).
**Desc:** The CAG/Acg newsletter includes feature articles on many aspects of aging, news and reports from the CAG/Acg divisions and each province, a calendar of events, and a Running Canadian Bibliography.

US/1044-1107
**NRTA BULLETIN.** (NRTA BULLETIN : A PUBLICATION OF THE NATIONAL RETIRED TEACHERS ASSOCIATION DIVISION OF AARP.). [NRTA bull.]. **Added/Corp** American Association of Retired Persons. National Retired Teachers Association Division. **VAT** National Retired Teachers Association Bulletin. Vol. 30, No. 6 (June 1989)-. Periodical. English. mo. Comes with American Association of Retired Persons membership. AARP - American Association of Retired Persons, PO Box 199, Long Beach CA 90801. **Tel** (310)496-2277. **DD** 646. ***Continues*** *NRTA News Bulletin, 0027-6987.*

US/0277-7460
**NSCLC WASHINGTON WEEKLY. See** Law.

US/1061-4753
**NURSING HOMES (1991). See** Medical Science and Technology-Hospital Administration and Medical Centers.

●US/1072-477X
**OLDER AMERICANS INFORMATION DIRECTORY.** (1993)-. Directory. English. $79.00. Gale Research Inc., 835 Penobscot Building, Detroit MI 48226. **Tel** (800)877-GALE, (313)961-2242, FAX (313)961-6083, telex TWX 810-221-7086. **ED** John Krol. available on magnetic tape; available on diskette.
**Desc:** Offers complete descriptions and contact information for 5,000 organizations and agencies in the nonprofit, private, public, education and government sections. Targeted towards senior citizens.

US
**OLDER NEBRASKAN'S VOICE, THE.** **VFOAT** Voice. Vol. 6 (Jan. 1975)-. Periodical. English. qt. free. The Nebraska Department of Aging, PO Box 95044, Centennial Mall South, Lincoln NE 68509. **Tel** (402)471-2306. **ED** Monica Frank Pribil. **Circ:** 15,000. available on audiocassette. ***Continues*** *Older Nebraskan.*
**Desc:** Designed to provide a variety of information to older adults and service providers on topics of interest to them.

CN/0319-0196
**PEEL SENIORS REGIONAL NEWS.** No. 1 (May 1974)-. Periodical. English. ir. Peel Seniors Regional News, c/o Mrs. M. Thrower, 2515 Shepard Avenue, Mississauga Ontario L5A 2H7. **DD** 362.6/3/09713535.

CN/0824-5479
**PRIME TIME MAGAZINE.** [Prime time mag.]. Vol. 1, No. 1 (Aug. 1983)-. Periodical. English. mo. $1.00 Each Number. Lifestyle Publications, 975 Alston Street, Victoria BC V9A 3S5. **DD** 051.

US/0194-2611
**PRIME TIME (NEW YORK).** (PRIME TIME.). (Jan. 1980)-. Periodical. English. bm. 18.00Aus$ (Australia); 36.00Aus$ (other). Diverse Publishing Company Pty Limited, PO Box 370, North Melbourne Vic, 3051 Australia. **Tel** 11 61 3 3296040. **ED** Russ Gleeson. **LC** WMLC L 83/132. **Bk Rev. Ad Acc.**
**Desc:** Generally deals with retired persons and their needs when retired.

US/0195-5934
**PRIME TIMES (MADISON).** (PRIME TIMES.). [Prime times]. **Added/Corp** National Association for Retired Credit Union People. (Spring 1979)-. Periodical. English. Four times a year. $15.00. National Association for Retired Credit Union People, PO Box 391, Madison WI 53701. **Tel** (608)238-4286. **ED** Mark S. Cooper. **DD** 051. **Bk Rev. Ad Acc. Circ:** 70,000 (ctrl).
**Desc:** Consumer information, investigative reporting, personal profiles, humor and fiction; aims to help people redefine retirement and help them take a fresh, active approach to growing older.

US/1055-3037
**PUBLIC POLICY AND AGING REPORT, THE.** [Public policy aging rep.]. **Added/Corp** Policy Research Associates. (198?)-. Periodical. English. bm. $30.00 US; $35.00 Canada; $40.00 other. University of Chicago Center on Aging, Health and Society, 1155 East 60th Street, Chicago IL 60637. **Tel** (312)702-9284, FAX (312)702-0926. **ED** Elizabeth Lawlor and Edward F Lawlor. **DD** 362. **NLM** W1; PU634F. Index available (bound in first issue). cum. index. **Bk Rev**, (Qty: 6). **Circ:** 1,200.
**Desc:** Provides timely and accesible policy analysis in the field of aging. Contents include original in-depth analyses of important issues in aging and policy,, critical reviews of recent books, summaries of national legislation, presentations of court decisions, regulations and new policy initiatives, statistics, and synopses of journal articles.

US
**REMEMBERING YESTERDAY.** English. mo (12 issues). $15.00. Eymann Publications, PO Box 3577, Reno NV 89505. **Tel** (702)333-6651.

CN/1186-2246
**RESPITE CARE SERVICES FOR SENIORS IN METROPOLITAN TORONTO.** [Respite care serv. sr. Metrop. Tor.]. **Added/Corp** Senior People's Resources in North Toronto (Association) Metropolitan Toronto Respite Care Coordination Committee. **VFOAT** Directory. (1989/1990)-. English. Senior People's Resources in North Toronto, 641 Eglinton Avenue West, Toronto, Ontario M5W 1C5 Canada. **DD** 362.6/025/713541.

US
**RETIREE NEWSLETTER.** (19??)-. Newsletter. English. mo. US Department of Transportation / US Coast Guard, 2100 Second Street Southwest, Washington DC 20953-0001. **Tel** (202)267-2229.
**Desc:** Contains news of general interest, suggestions, and information to keep Coast Guard retirees and their dependents abreast of developments as well as other events of significance.

CN/1184-0765
**RETIREMENT GUIDE.** ***Ceased.*** [Retire. guide]. (1990)-(199?). English. Retirement Guide, 301-1201 West Pender Street, Vancouver, British Columbia V6E 2V2 Canada. **DD** 646.7/9.

AT
**RETIREMENT INDUSTRY JOURNAL, THE.** (19??)-. English. Six times a year. 90.00Aus$ Australia; 150.00Aus$ other. Retirement Industry Journal, PO Box 513, Mudgeeraba Queensland 4213 Australia. **Tel** 011 61 75 302888, FAX 011 61 75 303944. **ED** Karen A. Linnell. **Ad Acc. Pr Rev. Circ:** 6,500 (ctrl).
**Desc:** Filled with news, information, features and comments on health, housing, travel, lifestyle, investment and wealth areas.

US/0093-5352
**RETIREMENT LETTER.** [Retire. lett.]. (1973)-. Periodical. English. Sixteen times a year. $49.95. Phillips Business Information, Inc., 1201 Seven Locks Road, Potomac MD 20854. **Tel** (301)424-3338, (800)777-5006, FAX (301)309-3847. **[CCC].** ***Absorbed*** *Communique; Bottom Line; Retirement Money.*

CN/0844-5982
**RETIREMENT LIFESTYLE.** [Retire. lifestyle]. (Jan. 1989)-. Periodical. English. Six times a year (Jan., Mar., May, July, Sept., Nov.). 21.40Can$ Canada; 29.40Can$ US. Foresight Publications Inc., 12140 Horse Shoe Way, Suite 100, Richmond BC V7A 4V5 Canada. **Tel** (604)272-4772, FAX (604)275-7859. **ED** Rick Delaney, (phone: (604)272-4772). **DD** 305.2/6/0971233. **Bk Rev**, (Qty: 6-10). **Ad Acc, Adv Mgr:** Eric, **Tel** (604)275-7971. **Circ:** 50,000 (ctrl). ***Continues*** *Well Off Mature People., 0844-5974.*

US/0278-3304
**RETIREMENT PROCEEDINGS.** **Main/Conf** MFOA Conference on Public Finance. 1973-. Proceedings. English. an. Municipal Finance Officers Association, 180 North Michigan Avenue/Suite 800, Chicago IL 60601. ***Continues*** *Municipal Finance Officers Association of the United States and Canada. Retirement Papers.*

JA
**ROJIN IRYO JIGYO NENPO.** Japanese. an. Free. Toyko-To Rojin Sogo Kenkyujo, 35-2 Sakaecho, Itabashi-ku 173 Tokyo Japan. **Tel** (03)964-1131, FAX (03)964-1982. **ED** Yasuo Toyokura. **LC** RA564.8; .R64. **Circ:** 1,000 (ctrl).
**Desc:** The report of Tokyo-To Geriatric Hospital which is conducting the result of activities of the hospital in clinical activities and clinical researches including administrative organization, personnels and badget.

JA/0286-8539
**ROJIN MONDAI KENKYU.** **VFOAT** Journal for the Study of Gerontology. Vol. 1 (1981)-. Periodical. Japanese (Japanese). Osaka Furitsu Rojin Sogo Senta Suita-shi, 565 Japan. **LC** HQ1064.J3; R625.

US/0276-0800
**SANTA BARBARA SENIOR WORLD, THE.** **VFOAT** Senior World/Santa Barbara. (1980)-. Newspaper. English. Twelve times a year. Senior World Publications, 1000 Pioneer Way, PO Box 1565, El Cajon CA 92022. **Tel** (619)593-2910. **ED** Laura Impastato, Sandy Pasqua, Ronald Miller and Gerald Goodrum. **Ad Acc. Circ:** 45,000 (ctrl). available on microfilm.
**Desc:** News of legislation, finance, health, travel, housing, and features for the active senior adults.

GW
**SECHZIG -NA UND .** (19??)-. German. DM28.00 Germany; DM38.00 other. Sisu Steinschulte Verlag, Bismarckstr 10, W-5300 Bonn 2 Germany. **Tel** 0228/361063, FAX 0228/351130, telex 885 540. **ED** Sisu Steinschulte, Peter Borg, Dr Kulteiner, Ruth Keller, Dr Lehmann, Ria Lorbach, Erich Weber. Index available. **Bk Rev. Ad Acc. Pr Rev. Circ:** 55,000 (ctrl).
**Desc:** A senior magazine for active, healthy and wealthy people. Colorful and many sided for those who are young at heart.

US/1055-2820
**SEN TEX.** (SEN TEX : LITERATURE ON AGING--SUMMARIES.). [SEN TEX]. **Added/Corp** Long Island University. Southampton Campus. Graduate Gerontology Program. Vol. 1, No. 1 (Spring 1991)-. Periodical. English. qt. Free. Long Island University, Southampton Campus, Graduate Gerontology Program, Southampton NY 11968. **DD** 362.

US/0740-7122
**SENIOR ADVOCATE (SACRAMENTO, CALIF.), THE.** ***Ceased.*** (THE SENIOR ADVOCATE : MONTHLY NEWSLETTER OF THE CALIFORNIA COMMISSION ON AGING.). [Sr. advocate]. **Added/Corp** California Commission on Aging. (198?)-(19??). Newsletter. English. mo. California Commission on Aging, 1020 9th Street, Number 260, Sacramento CA 95814. **Tel** (916)322-5630. **DD** 362. ***Continues*** *Newsletter (California Commission on Aging).*

US/1051-6913
**SENIOR CARE PROFESSIONAL.** ***Title Change.*** (SENIOR CARE PROFESSIONAL : THE MONTHLY REPORT INCORPORATING FAMILIES OF THE AGED.). [Sr. care prof.]. (1990)-(1993). Periodical. English. mo. CD Publications, 8204 Fenton Street, Silver Spring MD 20910. **Tel** (800)666-6380, (301)588-6380, FAX (301)588-6385. **DD** 362. **NLM** W1; SE495L. ***Continues*** *Families of the Aged, 1050-3455.* ***Merged into*** *Aging News Alert.*

US/0882-9403
**SENIOR CITIZENS ADVOCATE AND ASPECTS OF AGING.** **VFOAT** Senior Citizens Advocate; Senior Citizens Advocate, Aspects of Aging; Senior Citizens Advocate / Aspects of Aging. Periodical. English. qt. Senior Citizens Advocate, 40 West 68th Street, New York NY 10023. **Tel** (212)724-3200. **ED** Candice Cohen. **Circ:** 56,000 (ctrl).
**Desc:** An action newspaper and information clearinghouse of programs and services of interest to older adults and those that work for and with them.

CN/0714-5756
**SENIOR CITIZENS' CONSULTANTS OF ST. CATHARINES INC.** (SENIOR CITIZENS' CONSULTANTS OF ST. CATHARINES : [NEWSLETTER] / SENIOR CITIZENS' CONSULTANTS OF ST. CATHARINES.). [Sr. Citiz. Consult. St. Catharines Inc.]. **Added/Corp** Senior Citizens Consultants of St. Catharines. Vol. 4, No. 1 (Jan. 1982)-. Newsletter. English. mo. 7.00Can$. Senior Citizens Consultants Newsletter, 366 St Paul Street 3N2 Canada. **Tel** (416)682-1955 OR (416)682-6335. **DD** 362.6/09713/51. **Ad Acc. Circ:** 2,600 (ctrl). ***Continues*** *Senior Citizens' Advisory Council (Newsletter), 0229-2785.*

US/0559-4677
**SENIOR CITIZENS NEWS (WASHINGTON, D.C.).** (SENIOR CITIZENS NEWS.). [Sr. citiz. news]. **Added/Corp** National Council of Senior Citizens. (19??)-. Periodical. English. mo. $12.00. National Council of Senior Citizens Law Center, 1331 F Street Northwest, Washington DC 20004. **Tel** (202)347-8800. **DD** 362.

US/0049-0199
**SENIOR CITIZENS TODAY.** (19??)-. Periodical. English. Six times a year. $10.00. Senior Citizens Today, PO Box 163270, Sacramento CA 95816. **Tel** (916)455-0723. **ED** Charles W. Skoien Jr. **Ad Acc, Adv Mgr:** Marty. **Circ:** 7,000 - 10,000 (ctrl).
**Desc:** State and national news and information regarding seniors citizens.

US/0883-1939
**SENIOR CITIZENS WORLD.** (197?)-. Periodical. English. ir (8 issues per year). $10.00. Hoflin Publishing Ltd, 4401 Zephyr Street, Wheat Ridge CO 80033-3299. **Tel** (303)934-5656.

US
**SENIOR DIGEST.** English. mo. $4.00 over 60, Baltimore Co. resident; $6.00 other. Baltimore County Agency on Aging, 611 Central Avenue, Towson MD 21204. **Tel** (410)887-3050. **ED** Diane Caplan and Nancy Katz. **Bk Rev**, (Qty: 100). **Ad Acc, Adv Mgr:** Carolyn Giordana. **Circ:** 11,800.
**Desc:** News and information of interest to senior citizens.

US/0730-577X
**SENIOR GUARDIAN, THE.** [Sr. guard.]. **Added/Corp** National Alliance of Senior Citizens (U.S.). (1975)-. Periodical. English. bm (6 issues). $15.00. National Alliance Senior Citizens, 1700 18th Street Northwest, Suite 401, Arlington VA 20009. **Tel** (202)986-0117. **ED** C. C. Clinkscales III. **Circ:** 34,000.
**Desc:** Senior citizen issue periodical dealing with state and federal legislation from a moderate and conservative point-of-view.

US/1044-548X
**SENIOR HEALTH CARE.** ***Ceased.*** **See** Public Health and Safety.

US/1044-209X
**SENIOR HEALTH DIGEST.** **See** Public Health and Safety.

US/1050-3250
**SENIOR LAW REPORT.** ***Title Change.*** **See** Law.

US/0160-4783
**SENIOR LIFE.** V. 1- June/July 1978-. Periodical. English. bm. $9.00 Continental US; $15.00 Alaska, Hawaii, Puerto Rico, Virgin Islands, and Canada. Giles Corporation, 500 Newport Center Drive, Suite 500, Newport CA 92660. available on microfilm from University Microfilms International (UMI).

SA/0037-2234
**SENIOR NEWS.** [Senior News]. **VFOAT** Senior News. (1968)- Vol. 26 (Mar. 1993)-. Periodical. Multiple languages (English). Three times a year (Jan., Mar., Sept.). R8.80 South Africa; Free on request, other. South Africa Council for the Aged, PO Box 2335, 8000 Cape Town south Africa. **Tel** 011 27 21 246270, FAX 011 27 21

## Senior Citizens

232168. **ED** Mrs. Pinky Vilakazi, P. O. Box 591070 Kengray 2100, Johannesburg, South Africa, 011 6229494. **DD** _a301.435. **Bk Rev.** (Qty: 2). **Ad Acc. Circ:** 5000 (ctrl).
 **Desc:** a newsletter of the South Africa Council for the aged.

CN/0714-5624
**SENIOR SCENE.** (THE SENIOR SCENE.). [Sr. scene]. **Added/Corp** Protestant School Board of Greater Montreal. Services Educatifs d'Aide Personnelle et d'Animation Culturelle. Senior Scene Group, Inc. (1977)-. Periodical. English. Four times a year. 1.00Can$ donation. The Senior Scene Newspaper Inc., 1200 Atwater Avenue/Main Floor, Montreal Quebec H3Z 1X4 Canada. **Tel** (514)933-2048. **DD** 305.2/6/09714281.
 **Desc:** A newspaper for senior citizens by senior citizens. All workers and writers are volunteers.

AT
**SENIOR SCENE.** Periodical. English. qt. 20.00Aus$ Australia; 24.00Aus$ other. Senior Scene, PO Box 304, Chelsea VIC 3196 Australia. **Tel** 011 63 3 7760477. **ED** Ken Weaver. Index available. cum. index. **Bk Rev. Ad Acc. Circ:** 32,000 (ctrl).

CN
**SENIOR SENTINEL.** Periodical. English. mo. $10.00Can$. Senior Citizens Council of Ottawa, Room 508 294 Albert Street, Ottawa, Ontario K1P6E6 Canada. **Tel** (613)234-8044.

US
**SENIOR SPECTRUM.** English. wk. $17.00 California; $22.00 other. Senior Spectrum Newspapers, PO Box 1030, Rancho Cordova CA 95741. **Tel** (916)852-6222, **FAX** (916)852-6397. **ED** Bob Carney. Index available. **Ad Acc, Adv Mgr:** J.Walacek.

US/0149-7413
**SENIOR TRIBUNE, THE.** Periodical. English. mo. $3.00. Senior Tribune Subscriptions, PO Box 28285, Atlanta GA 30328.

US/0146-2539
**SENIOR WORLD.** Title Change. Vol. 1 (Nov. 1973)-(19??). Periodical. English. mo. Senior World Publications, 1000 Pioneer Way, PO Box 1565, El Cajon CA 92022. **Tel** (619)593-2910. Continued by Senior World of San Diego.
 **Ind/Abst** Calif. Period. Index (-19??).

US
**SENIOR WORLD NEWSMAGAZINE.** (19??)-. English. mo. $30.00. Senior World, PO Drawer 1565, El Cajon CA 92022. **Tel** (619)593-2910. **ED** Laura Impastato and Sandra Pasqua. **Ad Acc. Circ:** 550,000 (ctrl). available on microfilm.
 **Desc:** Tabloid for older adults, 55 plus, covering travel, finance, health, housing, and legislation.

CN/0714-8798
**SENIOR WORLD QUARTERLY.** Suspended. [Sr. world q.]. Vol. 1, No. 1 (Spring 1981)-?. Periodical. English. qt. 7.00Can$ U.S. Senior World / Canada, PO Box 128 Station A, St John New Brunswick E2L 3X8 Canada. **Tel** (506)657-8671. **ED** Louise Adler. **DD** 362.6/0971. **Bk Rev. Ad Acc. Circ:** 30,000 (ctrl).
 **Desc:** Among topics included are maintaining health, financial security, and full living. Intended for Canadians of 55 years or older.

CN/0715-4046
**SENIORS TODAY.** [Sr. today]. Vol. 1, No. 1 (Feb. 24, 1982)-. Periodical. English. Twenty-four times a year (1st and 15th of the month). 18.77Can$. McCaine-Davies Commun Limited, 232 Henderson Highway, Winnipeg MANI R2L 1L9 Canada. **Tel** (204)982-4002, FAX (204)982-4001. **ED** Heather McCaine-Davies. **DD** 362.6/097127/4. **Bk Rev.** (Qty: 2-10). **Ad Acc. Circ:** 20,000 (ctrl).
 **Desc:** Manitoba's newspaper for people of age 50 and better.

US
**SENIORVIEW.** (19??)-. Periodical. English. mo. $4.00. SeniorView, 2200 Drake Ave., Huntsville AL 35801. **Tel** (205)880-0607. **ED** Anne Parris.

JA
**SHAKAI-RONENGAKU. VFOAT** Social Gerontology. No. 1- 1974-Nen 3-Gatsu. Periodical. Multiple languages (Japanese and English). Tokyo-to Rojin Sogo Kenkujo, 35-2 Sakaecho, Itabasko-ku 173 Tokyo Japan. **LC** HQ1060; .S5. **NLM** W1; SH247D.

US/1056-1218
**SHEPARD'S ELDER CARE/LAW NEWSLETTER.** See Law-Estate Planning.

US
**SOUTHERN CALIFORNIA SENIOR LIFE.** English. mo (12 issues per year). $20.00. Southern California Senior Life, 9075 West Pico Blvd, Suite 203, Los Angeles CA 90035. **Tel** (213)276-1870. **ED** Jerry Beigel. **Bk Rev. Ad Acc. Circ:** 160,000 (ctrl).

US/1053-4911
**SOUTHWESTERN (DENTON, TEX.), THE.** Title Change. (THE SOUTHWESTERN : THE JOURNAL OF AGING FOR THE SOUTHWEST.). [Southwestern]. **Added/Corp** Southwest Society on Aging. (1987)-(1992). Periodical. English. sa. Southwest Society on Aging, PO Box 13346, University of North Texas, Denton TX 76203. **Tel** (817)565-2823. **LC** WMLC 90/0823. **DD** 362. Continued by Southwest Journal on Aging, 1070-6127.
 **Ind/Abst** Abstr. Soc. Gerontol.; Sage Fam. Stud. Abstr.

CN/0700-5229
**SPOKESMAN (EDMONTON).** Suspended. See Physically Impaired.

US
**SR. TEXAS.** English. mo $14.95. Sr. Texas, 11551 Forest Central Dr./ #305, Dallas TX 75243. **Tel** (214)341-9429, FAX (214)341-9779. **ED** Frank Kelly. **Ad Acc, Adv Mgr:** S. Schwaller, **Tel** (214)341-9429. **Circ:** 50,000.
 **Desc:** Consumer publication with legislature, health, travel, financial, and lifestyle consumer information to adults fifty and older.

US/8755-321X
**SUCCESSFUL MARKETING TO SENIOR CITIZENS.** Ceased. See Business-Marketing.

●US/1063-5742
**SUCCESSFUL RETIREMENT.** [Success. retire.]. Vol. 1, Issue 1 (Jan./Feb. 1993)-. Periodical. English. bm (6 issues) $24.00. Hochman Associates, 950 Third Avenue, 16th Floor, New York NY 10022. **Tel** (212)371-4932. (Subscription address: CDS Agency Hard Copy, PO Box 4966, Des Moines IA 50340.) **DD** 306.
 **Desc:** Aimed at people who are contemplating retirement and those who are already retired. Magazine to demonstrate the good, carefree and exciting parts of retirement life.

CN/0708-7632
**TEMPS DE VIVRE (MONTREAL).** Title Change. (LE TEMPS DE VIVRE.). [Temps vivre]. Vol. 1 (Feb./March 1979)-(19??). Periodical. French. mo. Supermagazine, 8050 Boulevard Metropolitan East, Montreal Quebec H1K 1A1 Canada. **Tel** (514)353-7660. **ED** Daniele Moisan-Dubois. **DD** 301.43/5/09714. **Bk Rev. Ad Acc. Circ:** 40,000 (ctrl). Absorbed by Le Bel Age, 0835-8702.
 **Desc:** A magazine regarding the needs and informatives for senior citizens.

CN/0827-6854
**TODAY'S SENIORS.** [Today's sr.]. Issue 3 (Oct. 23, 1985)-. Periodical. English. mo. 17.95Can$. Today's Seniors, 1091 Brevik Place, Mississauga Ontario L4W 3R7 Canada. **Tel** (905)238-0555. **ED** Don Atanasoff. **DD** 305.2/6/09713541. **Ad Acc. Circ:** 270,000 (ctrl). available in microform. Continues The Senior-Watch Review, 0827-6862.
 **Desc:** Information related to senior citizens.

CN/1187-5887
**TODAY'S SENIORS HOUSING CHOICES GUIDE.** See Housing and Urban Development.

●CN/1193-171X
**TODAY'S TIMES.** [Today's times]. (1992)-. Periodical. English. Six times a year. $20.00 (one year) Canada; $26.00 (one year) others. Today's Times Publications, 301 1201 West Pender Street, Vancouver BC V6E 2V2 Canada. **Tel** (604)683-1344. **DD** 305.2609711. Continues Elder Statesman, 0013-4074.

CN/0229-2602
**TOP GENERATION NEWSLETTER.** (TOP GENERATION NEWSLETTER : A NEWSLETTER FOR SENIOR CITIZENS.). [Top gener. newsl.]. Newsletter. English (French). ir. $2.00 members, $2.50 nonmembers. C Dean, 1984 Connaught Avenue, Halifax Nova Scotia B3N 1S6 Canada. **DD** 305.2/6/09716.

US/0161-8288
**TRAINING AND MANPOWER DEVELOPMENT ACTIVITIES.** See Sociology-Social Services and Welfare.

US
**UNITED RETIREMENT BULLETIN.** Ceased. **Added/Corp** United Business Service Company. Vol. 3, No. 7 (July 1977)-(July 1994). Periodical. English. mo. Babson - United Investment Advisors Inc., 101 Prescott Street, Wellesley Hills MA 02181. **Tel** (617)235-0900. **ED** Edith Tucker. Index available. **Bk Rev. Circ:** 10,000. Continues United Retirement Newsletter.
 **Desc:** Provides helpful information on retirement planning and living.

US/1043-9250
**UNITED SENIORS HEALTH REPORT.** [United Sr. health rep.]. **Added/Corp** United Seniors Health Cooperative (U.S.). (1986)-. Periodical. English. Five times a year. $15.00. United Seniors Health Cooperative, 1331 H Street NW Suite 500, Washington DC 20005. **Tel** (202)393-6222, FAX (202)783-0588. **ED** Monique Rothschild (editor's phone: (202)234-0097). **DD** 362. **Bk Rev.**

CN/1181-8328
**VIE CONTINUE, LA.** Ceased. [Vie contin.]. **Added/Corp** Universite du Quebec. Direction du Perfectionnement. Vol. 1, No 1 (1990)-(1992). Periodical. French. Tele-Universite / Perfectionnement, 2635 Blvd Hochelaga, 7th Floor, Sainte Foy Quebec G1V 5C4 Canada. **Tel** (800)463-4722, (418)657-2262. **DD** 305.24/4.

CN/0228-2623
**VIEIL ART, LE.** [Vieil art]. V. 1- Sept./Oct. 1977-. Periodical. French. bm. $2.00. Ateliers Vieil Art, 1014 Rue Jogues, Drummondville-Sud, Quebec J2B 4X6 Canada. **DD** 305.2/6/05.

US/1056-4020
**VITAL TIMES.** [Vital times]. **VFOAT** Vital Times for the Fifty-Plus Lifestyle. Vol. 1, No. 1 (June 1991)-. Periodical. English. mo. $10.00. Chicagoland Senior Communications Corp., 1500 Skokie Boulevard, Suite 330, Northbrook IL 60062. **DD** 051.

CN/0228-5517
**VIVRE +.** [Vivre +]. V. 1, No. 1 (April 1973)- V. 4, No. 2, (Dec. 1976). Periodical. French. bm. Des 65 Du Diocese D' Ottawa, 233, Av. Murray, Ottawa Ontario K1N 5M9. **DD** 305.2/6/09713.

CN/0382-0068
**VOICE OF UNITED SENIOR CITIENS OF ONTARIO, INC.** (VOICE CANADA.). [Voice United Sr. Citiz. Ont.]. **Main/Corp** United Senior Citizens of Ontario. **VAT** Voice (Toronto). Vol. 1 (Sept. 1969)-. Periodical. English. Ten times a year (Except July & Aug.). 10.00Can$. United Senior Citizens Ontario, 3033 Lakeshore Boulevard West, Toronto ONT M8V 1K5 Canada. **Tel** (416)252-2021, FAX (416)251-7042. **ED** Edith M. Johnston, (phone: (416)252-2021). **Bk Rev. Ad Acc. Circ:** 2,000. Supersedes United Senior Citizens of Ontario. Bulletin, 0049-5441.

US
**VOLUNTEER & VISITOR'S GUIDE.** See Medical Science and Technology-Geriatrics.

CN/1184-7832
**WESTCOAST REFLECTIONS.** [Westcoast reflect.]. Vol. 1, No. 5 (Jan. 1991)-. Periodical. English. mo. $27.00 per year. **DD** 305.26. Continues Victoria's Westcoast Reflections, 1182-994X.

●US/1060-0094
**WHERE TO RETIRE.** [Where retire]. Vol. 1, No. 1 (Spring 1992)-. Periodical. English. qt. $11.80. Vacation Publications Inc, 1502 Augusta Drive, Suite 415, Houston TX 77057. **Tel** (713)974-6903, FAX (713)974-0445. **DD** 646.

US/0731-6526
**WOODALL'S ... RETIREMENT DIRECTORY.** Ceased. (1982)-?. Directory. English. an. Woodall Publishing Company, 28167 North Keith Drive, Lake Forest IL 60015. **Tel** (708)362-6700. **LC** HQ1063; .W664. **DD** 646.7/9. **Ad Acc.** Continues Woodall's ... Sunbelt Retirement Directory, 0731-5635.
 **Desc:** A complete, illustrated directory featuring all leisure living opportunities for those people contemplating active retirement.

AT/1031-6620
**YOUR RETIREMENT CHIPPENDALE.** [Your retire. Chippendale]. (1989)-. English. an. 9.95Aus$. Rutland Cowling-Smith & Associates, 67-69 Regent Street, Chippendale NSW 2008 Australia. **Tel** 011 61 2 3604922, FAX 011 61 2 3694859. **DD** 646.790994.

IS
**ZIKNA.** V. 1- Fall 1972-. English. sa. POB 11243, Tel Aviv Israel. **LC** HQ1060; .Z54.

## SEWING AND NEEDLEWORK

US/0278-7504
**100'S OF NEEDLEWORK & CRAFT IDEAS. VFOAT** Hundreds of Needlework and Craft Ideas; 100's of Needlework and Craft Ideas. (19??)-. Periodical. English. sa. $2.25. Meredith Corporation, Locust at 17th, Des Moines IA 50309. **Tel** (515)284-3000. **LC** TT740; .A17. **DD** 746.4/05.

US/8756-6591
**AMERICAN QUILTER. Added/Corp** American Quilter's Society. Vol. 1, No. 1 (Summer 1985)-. Periodical. English. Four times a year. $15.00 (one year), $27.00 (two years), $40.00 (three years) Comes with American Quilters Society membership. American Quilter's Society, PO Box 3290, Paducah KY 42002-3290. **Tel** (205)898-7903. **ED** Marty Bowne and Mary Lou Schwinn. **LC** TT835; .A48. **DD** 746.46/0973.

**Bk Rev. Ad Acc. Circ:** 75,000 (ctrl).
**Desc:** Informative, entertaining information on making quilts, quilters personalities, quilting techniques and quilt exhibits.

●US/1064-1718
**AMERICA'S BEST QUILTING PROJECTS.** (1993)-. Periodical. English. Rodale Press Inc., 400 South 10th Street, Emmaus PA 18098. **Tel** (215)967-5171, (800)666-2503.

US/0745-6360
**ANNIE'S CROCHET NEWSLETTER.** **VFOAT** Crochet Newsletter. (198?)-. Periodical. English. bm (6 issues). $14.95. Annie's Attic, Dept CA01, Route 2, Box 212B, Big Sandy TX 75755. **Tel** (903)636-4303. **(Subscription address:** Neodata / Colorado, PO Box 2606, Boulder Boulder CO 80322.**)** Index available. **Ad Acc.**

AT
**AUSTRALIAN HAND WEAVER AND SPINNER / HAND WEAVERS AND SPINNERS GUILD OF NEW SOUTH WALES, THE.** **Added/Corp** Hand Weavers and Spinners Guild of New South Wales. **VFOAT** Hand Weaver and Spinner. (19??)-. Periodical. English. Twice a year (June & Nov.). 30.00Aus$. Handweaver Spinners Guild of New South Wales, PO Box 653, Burwood 2134, Australia. **Tel** 011 61 2 8718452. **Bk Rev**, (Qty: 2). **Ad Acc. Pr Rev. Circ:** 600 (ctrl).
**Desc:** Contains articles by members, tutors and outside specialists in the field of weaving, spinning, dyeing, felting, ect.

NE/0927-1368
**BABY & PEUTER.** **See** Women's Interests.

US/0273-0197
**BULLETIN OF THE NEEDLE AND BOBBIN CLUB, THE.** ***Suspended.*** [Bull. Needle Bobbin Club]. **Main/Corp** Needle and Bobbin Club, New York. Vol. 1 (1916)-(1994). Periodical. English. an. Needle & Bobbin Club, 955 5th Avenue, New York NY 10021. **Tel** (212)876-8372. **ED** Ann Hecht and Jean Mailey. **LC** NK9100; .N4. **DD** 746/.05. **Bk Rev. Ad Acc. Ind/Abst** ARTbibliogr. Mod.

US/0895-6871
**BUTTERICK HOME CATALOG (1985).** (BUTTERICK HOME CATALOG.). [Butterick home cat.]. **VFOAT** Butterick. Vol. 17, No. 2 (Summer 1985)-. Catalog. English. qt. $8.95 US; $16.15 other. Butterick Company Inc., 2900 Beale Avenue, Altoona PA 16603. **Tel** (814)943-5281, (800)766-3619. **(Subscription address:** Butterick Home Catalog, PO Box 569, Altoona, PA 16603**) ED** Deborah Osis. **DD** 646. **Ad Acc. Circ:** 200,000 (ctrl). ***Continues*** *Butterick Sewing World.*
**Desc:** Contains information concerning fashions, fabrics, notions, home sewing and accessories.

US/0882-2697
**CALIFORNIA ASSOCIATION OF MACHINE EMBROIDERY.** Issue 1 (Jan. 1985)-. Periodical. English. bm. $30.00 Membership. Gloria Waterman, 7207 Pomelo Drive, Canoga Park CA 91307.

CN/0381-7369
**CANADA QUILTS.** (Dec. 1973)-. Periodical. English. Five times a year. $22.00. Canada Quilts, PO Box 39, Station A, Hamilton Ontario L8N 3A2 Canada. **Tel** (905)523-5828. **ED** Marilynn Holowachuk. **DD** 746.4/6/0971. **Bk Rev. Ad Acc. Circ:** 3,500 (ctrl).
**Desc:** Canada's quilting magazine with 24 pages full of news, ideas, patterns, instruction and color photographs relating to quilting. For all types of quilters: the cottage craft person, quilt guilds, teachers, fibre artists, the individual quilter and related businesses.

CN/0824-1856
**CANADIAN LACEMAKER GAZETTE.** Vol. 1 (Spring)-. Periodical. English. qt. 16.00Can$. Canadian Lacemaker Gazette, c/o K Russell, R R 3/Site 388/C 22, Courtenay British Columbia V9N 5M8 Canada. **ED** Jeannie M Martin. **DD** 746.2/2/0971. **Bk Rev. Ad Acc. Circ:** 300.
**Desc:** Bobbin lacemaking lessons patterns, hints and news. Regular honiton and pointground columns as well as tatting and some needlelace. Related advertising.

CN/0831-2907
**CARRIAGE TRADE (SARNIA, ONT.).** **See** Textiles.

US
**CAST ON.** (19??)-. English. Five times a year. $23.00. The Knitting Guild of America, PO Box 1606, Knoxville TN 37901. **Tel** (615)524-2401.
**Desc:** Provides education and communication to those wishing to advance the quality of workmanship and creativity in their knitting endeavors.

US/1045-3814
**CELEBRATIONS TO CROSS STITCH AND CRAFT.** ***Title Change.*** [Celebr. cross stitch craft]. **VFOAT** Celebrations to Cross-Stitch and Craft; Celebrations; Leisure Arts. (1989)-(19??). Periodical. English. qt. Leisure Arts, PO Box 5595, Little Rock AR 72215. **Tel** (501)868-8800 ext. 338. ***Continued by*** *Make Everyday Special, 1076-9999.*

US/1047-0328
**CHRISTMAS (BIRMINGHAM, ALA.).** **See** The Arts-Crafts and Decorative Arts.

US/0164-3460
**COUNTED THREAD.** **Added/Corp** Counted Thread Society of America. Vol. 6 (March 1979)-. Periodical. English. qt. $11.00. Counted Thread Society of America, 1285 South Jason Street, Denver CO 80223. **Tel** (303)733-0196. **ED** Joan McBride. Index available. cum. index. **Bk Rev. Ad Acc. Circ:** 6,000 (ctrl).
**Desc:** Publishes articles and charts on counted cross stitch, blackwork, pulled thread, ethnic counted embroideries, and other information about counted thread embroidery.

US/0887-9818
**CRAFT & NEEDLEWORK AGE.** [Craft needlework age]. **VFOAT** Craft and Needlework Age. Vol. 38, No. 469 (Jan. 1984)-. Periodical. English. Thirteen times a year. $20.00 US; $60.00 other. Hobby Publishing Inc, Box 420, Englishtown NJ 07726. **Tel** (201)446-4900, FAX (201)446-5488. **ED** Karen Ancona. **LC** TT159; .C7. **DD** 688. **Bk Rev. Ad Acc. Circ:** 32,000 (ctrl). ***Continues*** *Craft & Needlework Age/World of Miniatures, 0744-2319.*
**Desc:** Trade publication serving the craft and needlework industry with quarterly features on quilting, yarns and notions at all levels.

US
**CRAFTRENDS SEW BUSINESS.** English. mo. $26.00 US and Canada; $34.00 other. Century Communications Inc, 6201 Howard Street, Niles IL 60714-3435. **Tel** (708)647-1200, FAX (708)647-7055. ***Absorbed*** *Sew Business Magazine;* ***Continues*** *Craftrends.*

US/0092-4180
**CRAFTS & SEWING.** ***Ceased.*** **See** The Arts-Crafts and Decorative Arts.

US/0887-2384
**CREATIVE NEEDLE.** (198?)-. Periodical. English. bm. $22.00. Creative Needle Magazine, 1 Apollo Road, Lookout Mountain GA 30750. **Tel** (706)820-2600, FAX (706)820-2164.

US/0887-3690
**CREATIVE QUILTING.** [Creat. quilt.]. Vol. 1, Issue 1 (Summer 1986)-. Periodical. English. bm (6 issues). $24.00. Hochman Associates, 950 Third Avenue, 16th Floor, New York NY 10022. **Tel** (212)371-4932. **(Subscription address:** CDS Agency Hard Copy, PO Box 4966, Des Moines IA 50340.**) LC** WMLC 90/0751. **DD** 746.
**Desc:** A digest-size encyclopedia of quilt making that will teach you to create treasured heirlooms that will delight family and friends for years to come.

●US/1074-1798
**CROCHET DIGEST.** (1993)-. Periodical. English. qt. $9.95. House of White Birches, 306 East Parr Road, Berne IN 46711. **Tel** (219)589-8741, FAX (219)589-8093. **(Subscription address:** Palm Coast Data, PO Box 420235, Agency Department, Palm Coast FL 32142.**) ED** Laura Scott. **Circ:** 35,430. ***Continues*** *Women's Circle Crochet, 0279-1978.*
**Desc:** Includes patterns for afghans, doilies, toys, clothing, holiday decorations, and bazaar items.

US/8750-8877
**CROCHET FANTASY.** (198?)-. Periodical. English. bm (6 issues). $16.97. All American Crafts Inc., 243 Newton Sparta Road, Newton NJ 07860. **Tel** (201)383-8080, telex 844380. **(Subscription address:** Kable Publishers Aide, 308 East Hitt Street, Subscription Department, Mt. Morris IL 61054-1473.**)**

US/0894-5659
**CROCHET PATTERNS BY HERRSCHNERS.** ***Title Change.*** [Crochet patterns Herrschners]. **Added/Corp** Herrschners, Inc. **VFOAT** Crochet Patterns. (1987-1992). Periodical. English. bm. Herrschners, 999 Plaza Drive/Suite 660, Schaumburg IL 60195. **DD** 746. ***Continued by*** *McCall's Crochet Patterns, 1065-0288.*

US/0164-7962
**CROCHET WORLD.** Vol. 1 (Mar./Apr. 1978)-. Periodical. English. bm. $12.97 US; 19.95Can$ Canada; $21.02 other. House of White Birches, 306 East Parr Road, Berne IN 46711. **Tel** (219)589-8741, FAX (219)589-8093. **(Subscription address:** Palm Coast Data, PO Box 420235, Agency Department, Palm Coast FL 32142.**) ED** Susan Hankins. Index available. **Ad Acc. Circ:** 78,769.
**Desc:** Each issue includes 25-35 crochet patterns, including toys, afghans, dolls, doilies, clothing and household accessories. Also features crochet contests, a question-and-answer column, and crochet tips and techniques.

US/1057-7076
**CROCHET WORLD SPECIAL.** [Crochet world spec.]. **VFOAT** Crochet World. (19??)-. Periodical. English. qt. $9.95 US; 17.95Can$ Canada. House of White Birches, 306 East Parr Road, Berne IN 46711. **Tel** (219)589-8741, FAX (219)589-8093. **(Subscription address:** Palm Coast Data, PO Box 420235, Agency Department, Palm Coast FL 32142.**) ED** Susan Hankins. **LC** WMLC 91/3327. **DD** 746. **Circ:** 46,199. ***Continues*** *Crochet Today Fashions, 1041-0759.*
**Desc:** Focuses on crochet patterns for the seasons and holidays, with a creative section of projects for home, family and gift-giving.

US/1063-9950
**CROSS COUNTRY STITCHING.** [Cross ctry. stitch.]. Vol. 1, No. 1 (March/April 1989)-. English. bm (Jan., Mar., May, July, Sept., Nov.). $14.95 (one year), $27.95 (two year), $39.95 (three year). Jeremiah Junction Incorporated, PO Box 710, Manchester CT 06040. **Tel** (203)646-0665, FAX (203)643-1880. **ED** Linda Coleman. **LC** WMLC L 83/6931. **DD** 746.
**Desc:** Counted cross stitch projects, for home decor and wearables.

AT/1037-339X
**CROSS STITCH.** (19??)-. English. bm. £24.00. Jill Oxton Publications, PO Box 283 Park Holme, SA 5043 Australia. **Tel** 011 61 8 2762722, FAX 011 61 8 2762722. **(Subscription address:** World-Wide Subscription Services, Unit 4, Gibbs Reed Farm Pashley Road, Ticehurst TN5 7HE England.**)**

US/0886-6600
**CROSS STITCH & COUNTRY CRAFTS.** **VFOAT** Cross Stitch and Country Crafts; Cross Stitch. Vol. 1, No. 1, (1985)-. Periodical. English. bm (6 issues). $19.97. Meredith Corporation, Locust at 17th, Des Moines IA 50309. **Tel** (515)284-3000. **(Subscription address:** Neodata / Colorado, PO Box 2606, Boulder Boulder CO 80322.**) ED** Joan Cravens. **LC** WMLC L 83/2291. **DD** 746. Index available. **Circ:** 1,800 (ctrl).
**Desc:** Contains cross stitch designs, patterns and projects, step-by-step photo guide and over 26 colorful projects in each issue for introductory and advanced levels.

AT
**CROSS STITCH AUSTRALIA.** English. Four times a year. 56.70Aus$. Jill Oxton Publications, PO Box 283 Park Holme, SA 5043 Australia. **Tel** 011 61 8 2762722, FAX 011 61 8 2762722. **ED** Jill Oxton. **Ad Acc.**

US/1054-3430
**CROSS-STITCH PLUS.** [Cross-stitch plus]. **VFOAT** Cross Stitch Plus. (1991)-. Periodical. English. bm. $12.97 US; 19.95Can$ Canada. House of White Birches, 306 East Parr Road, Berne IN 46711. **Tel** (219)589-8741, FAX (219)589-8093. **(Subscription address:** Palm Coast Data, PO Box 420235, Agency Department, Palm Coast FL 32142.**) ED** Lana Schurb. **DD** 746. **Circ:** 65,400. ***Continues*** *Counted Cross-Stitch Plus, 1054-2612.*
**Desc:** Includes cross-stitch designs for samplers, quick gifts, household and apparel accents, and seasonal items.

US/1055-2871
**CROSS STITCHER, THE.** [Cross stitcher]. (1984)-. Periodical. English. bm. $14.97 US; $27.97 other. Clapper Communications, 701 Lee Street, Suite 1000, Des Plaines IL 60016. **Tel** (800)272-3871 or (708)297-7400. **(Subscription address:** Clapper Communications, 2400 Devon, Suite 375, Des Plaines IL 60018.**) ED** B. J. McDonald. **LC** WMLC 91/735. **DD** 746. Index available. **Ad Acc.**
**Desc:** A cross stitch magazine, with at least 20 designs in each issue. Includes floss conversion charts so that stitchers can use their favorites, and specially enlarged, easy-to-read-charts.

US/1054-1551
**CROSSSTITCH SAMPLER.** [CrossStitch sampl.]. **VFOAT** Cross Sstitch Sampler. Vol. 9, No. 1 (Spring 1991)-. Periodical. English. qt. $13.98 (one year), $21.98 (two years). Sampler Publications Inc, 707 Kautz Road, St Charles IL 60174. **Tel** (708)377-8000 ext.270. **DD** 746. **Bk Rev. Ad Acc.** ***Continues*** *Needlewords, 0890-5312.*

DK/0416-6817
**DANISH HANDCRAFT GUILD.** (1961)-. Periodical. English. Four times a year (Feb., May, Aug., Nov.). $46.00 membership. Danish Handcraft Guild, Kildebakken 20, DK 2860 Soborg Denmark. **Tel** 011 45 3966 3028, FAX 011 45 3167 1544. **DD** 745.

US/1072-6381
**DOLL COLLECTOR'S PRICE GUIDE.** (1991)-. English. qt. $12.97. House of White Birches, 306 East Parr Road, Berne IN 46711. **Tel** (219)589-8741, FAX (219)589-8093. **(Subscription address:** Palm Coast Data, PO Box 420235, Agency Department, Palm Coast FL 32142.**) ED** Cary Raesner. **Circ:** 43,985.
**Desc:** Includes sections in identifying and pricing dolls of all media, as well as auction and show reports and informative articles of interest ot collectors.

AT/1033-4513
**DOWN UNDER QUILTS.** [Down under quilts]. (1988)-. Periodical. English. Four times a year (Mar., June, Sept., Dec.). 24.00Aus$ Australia; 40.00Aus$ other. Down Under Quilts, PO Box 619, Beenliegh QLD, 4207 Australia. **Tel** 011 61 7 2875549, FAX 011 61 7 2875549. **ED** Yvonne Rein (phone: (07)287-5549). **DD** 746.97. **Bk Rev**, (Qty: 45). **Ad Acc. Circ:** 11,000 (ctrl).
**Desc:** Information on patchwork and quilting.

UK/0013-6611
**EMBROIDERY.** [Embroidery]. **Added/Corp** Embroiderers' Guild. Vol. 1, (1932)- Vol. 7 (1939); New Series Vol. 1, (1950)-. Periodical. English. Four times a year (Mar., June, Sept., Dec.). £12.40 UK; £16.50 other. E. G. Enterprises Ltd., PO Box 42B, East Molesey Surrey KT8 9BB England. **Tel** 011 44 81 9431229. **ED** Valerie Campbell-Harding. Index available. cum. index. **Bk Rev. Ad Acc. Circ:** 13,700.
**Desc:** A magazine for the professional, amateur, teacher and the historian. All aspects of the craft are regularly covered.
**Ind/Abst** ARTbibliogr. Mod.

US/8750-8869
**FASHION KNITTING.** [Fash. knitting]. (198?)-. Periodical. English. Six times a year. $16.97. All American Crafts Inc., 243 Newton Sparta Road, Newton NJ 07860. **Tel** (201)383-8080, telex 844380. **(Subscription address:** Kable Publishers Aide, 308 East Hitt Street, Subscription Department, Mt. Morris IL 61054-1473.)

US/0164-324X
**FIBERARTS.** [Fiberarts]. Vol. 3, (Jan./Feb. 1976)-. Periodical. English. Five times a year. $22.00 US; $27.00 other. Altamont Press Inc, 50 College Street, Asheville NC 28801. **Tel** (704)253-0467, FAX (704)253-7952. **ED** Ann Batchelder. **LC** TT697; .F52. **DD** 746/.05. **Circ:** 2,200. **Continues** *Fibercraft Newsletter.*
**Desc:** The magazine of textiles. Articles on weaving, wearables, dyeing, needlework, sewing. Artists, techniques and design.
**Ind/Abst** Art Archaeol. Tech. Abstr.; Art Index; Ethnoarts Index; Index Inf. (1990-); Text. Technol. Dig.

US/0198-8387
**FIBERSCOPE.** **See** Textiles.

US/0270-2959
**FLYING NEEDLE, THE.** (THE FLYING NEEDLE / NATIONAL STANDARDS COUNCIL OF AMERICAN EMBROIDERERS COUNCIL OF AMERICAN EMBROIDERERS.). (19??)-. Periodical. English. qt. $20.00 US; $25.00 Canada. Flying Needle, 10020 Dechaux Road, East, Puyallup WA 98371. **LC** TT740; .F58. **DD** 746.44/05. Index available. **Bk Rev. Ad Acc. Circ:** 2,500 (ctrl).
**Desc:** Embroidery, historic and contemporary news of the Council of American Embroideries.

US/1040-3965
**FOR THE LOVE OF CROSS STITCH.** [For love cross stitch]. **VFOAT** Cross Stitch. Vol. 1, No. 1 (1988)-. Periodical. English. bm (6 issues). $16.00. Leisure Arts, PO Box 5595, Little Rock AR 72215. **Tel** (501)868-8800 ext. 338. **(Subscription address:** Palm Coast Data, PO Box 420235, Agency Department, Palm Coast FL 32142.) **ED** Anne Van Wagnor Young. **DD** 646. **Ad Acc.**
**Desc:** Full Color craft publication.

US/0436-1539
**GOOD HOUSEKEEPING NEEDLECRAFT.** (1968)-. Periodical. English. Available on newsstand only. The Hearst Corporation, 250 West 55th Street, New York NY 10019. **Tel** (212)649-4014.
**Ind/Abst** Index Inf.

US/0275-9640
**HANDMADE (ASHEVILLE, N.C.).** (HANDMADE.). [Handmade]. Vol. 1, No. 1 (Apr.-June 1981)-. Periodical. English. bm. $26.97. Lark Communications, 50 College Street, Asheville NC 28801. **Tel** (704)253-0468. **ED** Rob Pulleyn. **LC** WMLC L 83/33. **Bk Rev. Ad Acc. Circ:** 100,000.
**Desc:** Sewing, knitting, needlework, weaving and crafts, lively, exciting and challenging projects and articles.
**Ind/Abst** Index Inf. (1981-1986).

US/0198-8212
**HANDWOVEN.** **See** Textiles.

US/0747-0940
**HAPPY HANDS NEEDLECRAFT NEWS.** **VFOAT** Needlecraft News. Periodical. English. bm. $6.00 US; $8.50 other. Happy Hands Needlecraft News, Subscriber Service Center, PO Box 10713, Des Moines IA 50340.

US
**HOLIDAY CRAFTS & GRANNY SQUARES.** **VFOAT** Holiday Crafts and Granny Squares. (Sept. 1990)-. English. $2.95 (per issue). Diamandis Communications, Inc., 1633 Broadway, New York NY 10019. **LC** WMLC 91/2268. **DD** 745.594/12.

US/0893-1879
**HOOKED ON CROCHET!.** No. 1 (Jan./Feb. 1987)-. Periodical. English. bm (Jan., Mar., May, July, Sept., Nov.). $14.95 (one year), $25.95 (two year). Needlecraft Shop, 23 Old Pecan Road, Big Sandy TX 75755. **Tel** (903)636-4011 ext 211, FAX (903)636-2288. **DD** 746.

US/0883-0797
**JUST CROSSSTITCH.** **VFOAT** Just Cross Stitch. Vol. 1, No. 1 (May/June 1983)-. Periodical. English. Six times a year. $16.98 US; $22.98 other. PJS Publications Inc., News Plaza, PO Box 1790, Peoria IL 61656. **Tel** (309)682-6626, FAX (309)682-7394. **(Subscription address:** CDS / SIFD Agency Control, 1901 Bell Avenue, Des Moines IA 50315.) **ED** Lorna Reeves. **LC** TT778.C76; J87. **DD** 746.44. Index available. **Ad Acc, Adv Mgr:** Mike Nish, **Tel** (309)682-6626. **Circ:** 199,000.
**Desc:** Articles on cross stitch shops, graphs for cross-stitching, instructions for cross-stitching, pictures of each finished product for which graphs are included.

NE
**KNIP.** Medianet BV, Postbus 6298, 2001 LN Haarlem Netherlands. **Tel** 011 31 23 173311.

CN/0711-639X
**KNIT & CHAT.** [Knit chat]. Vol. 1, No. 1 (1981)-. Periodical. English. ir. $18.58. Knit and Chat, PO Box 363, Lancaster Ontario K0C 1N0 Canada. **Tel** (514)626-9478. **ED** May MacLean. **DD** 746.4. **Bk Rev. Ad Acc. Circ:** 20,000 (ctrl).
**Desc:** Concerns the homecrafts and crafts using yarn/thread and needle(s) as a medium. Includes knitting, sewing, needlepoint, crochet, talting, quilting, etc. Also includes book reviews, historical features, etc.

KO
**KNIT SANOP / KNITTING INDUSTRY.** **Added/Corp** Taehan Meriyasu Kongop Hyoptong Chohap Yonhaphoe. **VFOAT** Knitting Industry. (19??)-. Periodical. Korean (Korean). qt. Taehan Meriyasu Kongop Hyoptong Chohap Yonhaphoe, 48 1-Ka Sinmunno Chongno-ku, Seoul Korea. **LC** HD9969.K5; K57.

US
**KNITKING MAGAZINE.** (1965)-. Periodical. English. Four times a year. $24.00 (one year), $46.00 (two years), $66.00 (three years) US; add $5.00 postage other. Knitking, 1128 Crenshaw Boulevard, Los Angeles CA 90019-9979. **Tel** (213)938-2077.
**Desc:** A pattern magazine for home machine knitting; each issue features 20 original designs.

US/0747-9026
**KNITTERS.** [Knitters]. (1984)-. Periodical. English. qt (Feb., May., Aug., Nov.). $16.00 (one year), $30.00 (two year). Golden Fleece Publications, PO Box 1525, Sioux Falls SD 57101. **Tel** (605)338-2450, FAX (605)338-2994. **DD** 746. **Ad Acc, Adv Mgr:** Karen Bright.

US/0090-8215
**KNITTER'S JOURNAL.** [Knit. j.]. V. 1- May/June 1973-. Periodical. English. bm. $7.00. Handweaver and Craftsman Inc, 220 Fifth Avenue, New York NY 10001. **LC** TT820; .K6946. **DD** 746.4/3.

US/1072-7167
**KNITTING DIGEST.** (19??)-. English. mo. $14.95. House of White Birches, 306 East Parr Road, Berne IN 46711. **Tel** (219)589-8741, FAX (219)589-8093. **(Subscription address:** Palm Coast Data, PO Box 420235, Agency Department, Palm Coast FL 32142.) **ED** Laure Scott. **Circ:** 30,166. ***Continues*** *Knitting World.*
**Desc:** Features 15-25 projects per issue including afghans, clothing, holiday items, dolls and toys.

US/8750-9768
**KNITTING ELEGANCE.** ***Ceased.*** ( )-Issue 33 (1988). Periodical. English (French, Dutch, Italian and German). bm. All American Crafts Inc., 243 Newton Sparta Road, Newton NJ 07860. **Tel** (201)383-8080, telex 844380. **ED** Frederik Plynaar and Wendie R Blanchard. **Circ:** 79,000.
**Desc:** Features today's most fashionable sweaters using high-quality yarns. Each issues in beautifully photographed and includes complete knitting instructions.

GW/0177-4875
**KNITTING TECHNIQUE.** Vol. 7, No. 1 (Jan. 1985)-. Periodical. English. bm (Jan., Mar., May, July, Sep., Nov.). DM114.00. Meisenbach GmbH, Postfach 2069, D 96011 Bamberg Germany. **Tel** 011 49 951 861135. **[CCC].** ***Continues*** *WST Knitting Technic, 0173-4415.*
**Desc:** Technical journal for knitting and knitwear finishing industries including fashion trends.
**Ind/Abst** Text. Technol. Dig.

US/0023-2300
**KNITTING TIMES.** [Knitt. times]. **Added/Corp** National Knitwear and Sportswear Association (U.S.) National Knitted Outerwear Association. Knitted Textile Association. Knitted Fabric Group. **VFOAT** Knitting Times Newsweekly; Knitting Times. Vol. 39, No. 33 (Aug. 10, 1970)-. Periodical. English. Fourteen times a year (Monthly with two special issues). $35.00 (1 year), $60.00 (2 year), $80.00 (3 year) US; $56.00 (1 year), $100.00 (2 year), $130.00 (3 year) (surface mail) other; $131.00 (1 year), $250.00 (2 year), $355.00 (3 year) (air mail). Knitting Times, 386 Park Avenue South, New York NY 10016. **Tel** (212)683-7520, FAX (212)532-0766, telex 239801. **ED** David Gross. **LC** TT679; .K75. **DD** 677/.661/05. Index available. cum. index. **Bk Rev. Ad Acc. Circ:** 8,000. available on microfilm and microfiche from University Microfilms International (UMI). ***Continues*** *Knitted Outerwear Times;* ***Absorbed*** *Apparel World, 0277-9609.* ***Continued in part by*** *Apparel World, 0277-9609.*
**Desc:** Trade publication covering yarns, machinery and apparel for the knit wear industry.
**Ind/Abst** Text. Technol. Dig.; World Text. Abstr.

US/0194-8083
**KNITTING WORLD (SEABROOK, N.H.).** ***Title Change.*** (KNITTING WORLD.). [Knitt. world]. (197?)-(19??). Periodical. English. bm. House of White Birches, 306 East Parr Road, Berne IN 46711. **Tel** (219)589-8741, FAX (219)589-8093. **ED** Anne Jefferson. Index available. **Ad Acc. Circ:** 8,000. ***Continued by*** *Knitting Digest.*
**Desc:** A knitting lover's dream come true; 25-30 knitting patterns per issue, and loads of other information. Only pennies per pattern.

US
**LACE COLLECTOR, THE.** ***Ceased.*** Vol. 1, No. 1 (Winter 1991)-(April 1994). Periodical. English. qt. The Lace Merchant, PO Box 222, Plainwell MI 49080.

US/0732-9504
**LADY'S CIRCLE KNITTING & CROCHET CREATIVE IDEAS.** **VFOAT** Lady's Circle Knitting and Crochet Creative Ideas; Knitting and Crochet Creative Ideas; Knitting & Crochet Creative Ideas. Periodical. English. qt. $9.00 US; $11.00 other. Lopez Publications Inc., 152 Madison Avenue, Suite 905 & 906, New York NY 10016. **Tel** (212)689-3933. ***Continues*** *Lady's Circle Knitting & Crochet Guide, 0731-9975.*

US/0731-9916
**LADY'S CIRCLE PATCHWORK QUILTS.** **VFOAT** Patchwork Quilts. (19??)-. Periodical. English. mo (10 issues). $19.95 US; $27.95 other. Lopez Publications Inc., 152 Madison Avenue, Suite 905 & 906, New York NY 10016. **Tel** (212)689-3933. **(Subscription address:** Kable Publishers Aide, 308 East Hitt Street, Subscription Department, Mt. Morris IL 61054-1473.) **ED** Carter Houck. **Bk Rev. Ad Acc. Circ:** 70,000.
**Desc:** Shows all aspects of quilting techniques along with ready-to-use patterns for piecing and applique, and brilliant color photos.

US/1057-7971
**LADY'S CIRCLE PATCHWORK QUILTS PRESENTS QUILT CRAFT.** [Lady's circ. patchw. quilts presents quilt craft]. **VFOAT** Quilt Craft. Vol. 1, No. 16 (1991)-. Periodical. English. bm. $3.95 (single issue, U.S./Can.). Lopez Publications, Inc., 111 East 35th Street, New York NY 10016. **LC** WMLC 91/1292. **DD** 646.

US/0738-2936
**LAPEL PIN POTPOURRI.** No. 1 (Fall 1982)-. Periodical. English. sa. $5.50. Lapel Pin Potpourri, Rural Route 1 Box 28, Charlotte Hall MD 20622. **Tel** (301)884-4823. **ED** Roberta J Kieliger. **Circ:** 500.
**Desc:** For crochet lapel pin enthusiasts to share their ideas, containing designs with monthly themes, birthday ideas, and accompanying verses for nursing home residents, hospital patients and meals-on-wheels recipients.

US/0161-6218
**LIST OF ART NEEDLEWORK, YARN KNITTING STORES.** **VFOAT** Art Needlework, Yarn Knitting Shops; Art Needlework, Yarn & Knitting Shops. English. Leads-Prospects, Inc., 234 Fifth Avenue, New York NY 10001. **LC** TT751; .L55. **DD** 338.4/7/746402573.

UK/0269-9761
**MACHINE KNITTING MONTHLY.** [Mach. knitt. mon.]. (1986)-. Periodical. English. mo. £18.00 UK; £27.00 other. Machine Knitting Monthly Ltd, 3 Bridge Avenue, Maidenhead Berks SL6 1RR England. **Tel** 011 44 628 770289. **ED** Sheila Berriff. **DD** 746.43. **Bk Rev. Ad Acc.**
**Desc:** Latest patterns, features, news and letters from UK's leading experts in crafts as contributors.

US/0886-1188
**MACKNIT.** ***Ceased.*** [Macknit]. (Fall/Winter 1985)-Ceased Vol. 5 (1987). Periodical. English. sa. Knitting Machine Studio Inc, PO Box 8145, Englewood NJ 07631. **Tel** (201)568-3369. **ED** John Cuniberti and Marlene Cuniberti. **DD** 746. **Bk Rev. Ad Acc. Circ:** 25,000 (ctrl).
**Desc:** A full color magazine for the home knitting machine craft: techniques, traditions, events and people. Featuring top designer patterns.

US/0246-5957
**MAGIC CROCHET.** Periodical. English. bm. Real Time Publishing, RR 1 Box 423 C, Cold Spring NY 10516.

●US/1075-9999
**MAKE EVERYDAY SPECIAL.** [Make everyday spec.]. **VFOAT** Make Every Day Special. (1994)-. Periodical. English. bm. $15.00 US; $18.00 Canada; $31.00 other. Leisure Arts, PO Box 5595, Little Rock AR 72215. **Tel** (501)868-8800 ext. 338. **(Subscription address:** Palm Coast Data, PO Box 420235, Agency Department, Palm Coast FL 32142.**)** **DD** 680. ***Continues*** *Celebrations to Cross Stitch and Craft, 1045-3814.*

US/0276-6671
**MCCALL'S CHRISTMAS KNIT & CROCHET.** **VFOAT** Mccall's Christmas Knit and Crochet. English. $2.95. ABC Leisure Magazine Inc, 825 7th Avenue, New York NY 10019. **Tel** (212)265-8360. **LC** TT820; .M485. **DD** 746.43041.

US/1065-0288
**MCCALL'S CROCHET PATTERNS.** ***Title Change.*** [McCall's crochet patterns]. **VFOAT** Crochet Patterns. Vol. 6, No. 4 (Aug. 1992)-(199?). Periodical. English. Six times a year. PJS Publications Inc., News Plaza, PO Box 1790, Peoria IL 61656. **Tel** (309)682-6626, FAX (309)682-7394. **(Subscription address:** CDS / SIFD Agency Control, 1901 Bell Avenue, Des Moines IA 50315.**)** **LC** WMLC 91/5301. **DD** 746. ***Continues*** *Crochet Patterns by Herrschners, 0894-5659.* ***Continued by*** *McCall's Crochet, 1074-1852.*

US/1069-2894
**MCCALL'S NEEDLEWORK.** [McCall's needlework]. (199?)-. Periodical. English. Six times a year. $15.98 US; $21.98 other. PJS Publications Inc., News Plaza, PO Box 1790, Peoria IL 61656. **Tel** (309)682-6626, FAX (309)682-7394. **(Subscription address:** CDS Agency Hard Copy, PO Box 4966, Des Moines IA 50340.**)** **DD** 746. ***Continues*** *McCall's Needlework Crafts, 0024-8924.*
**Ind/Abst** Mag. Artic. Summar. Elite (June 1993-); Mag. Artic. Summar. CD-ROM (June 1993-).

US/0024-8924
**MCCALL'S NEEDLEWORK & CRAFTS.** ***Title Change.*** [McCall's needlework crafts]. **VAT** McCall's Needlework and Crafts. (19??)-(199?). Periodical. English. bm. PJS Publications Inc., News Plaza, PO Box 1790, Peoria IL 61656. **Tel** (309)682-6626, FAX (309)682-7394. **DD** 746. available on microfilm and microfiche from University Microfilms International (UMI). Documents available from UMI Article Clearinghouse. ***Continued by*** *McCall's Needlework, 1069-2894.*
**Desc:** Designed for the active woman who wants to create beautiful things to wear and to decorate her home. Each issue emphasizes leisure-time activities: fashions to knit and crochet, decorating ideas, bazaar items, gift ideas, and creative cooking.
**Ind/Abst** Index Inf. (1978-); Mag. Artic. Summar. Elite (July 1989-May 1993); Mag. Artic. Summar. Select (July 1989-); Mag. Artic. Summar. CD-ROM (July 1989-May 1993); Mag. Search; Newsp. Period. Abstr. (1992-).

US/0198-2478
**MCCALL'S (PATTERN BOOK).** (MCCALL'S.). [McCall's]. (19??)-. English. mo. McCalls Pattern Company, PO Box 3325, Manhattan KS 66502. **Tel** (800)255-2762, (913)776-4041. **LC** TT500; .M144. **DD** 646.4/07.

US/0198-6457
**MCCALL'S PATTERNS.** [McCall's patterns]. (19??)-. Periodical. English. qt. McCall Publishing Company, 110 5th Avenue, New York NY 10011. **Tel** (212)463-1000. **LC** TT500; .M223. **DD** 646.4/304.

●US/1072-8295
**MCCALL'S QUILTING.** **VFOAT** Quilting. (1993)-. Periodical. English. Six times a year. $19.98 US; $21.98 other. PJS Publications Inc., News Plaza, PO Box 1790, Peoria IL 61656. **Tel** (309)682-6626, FAX (309)682-7394.

US/0364-8192
**MCCALL'S STITCHERY: APPLIQUE.** Vol. 2 (19??)-. English. $1.35. McCall Publishing Company, 110 5th Avenue, New York NY 10011. **Tel** (212)463-1000. **LC** TT779; .M33. **DD** 746.4/4.

KO
**MERIYASU KONGOP YONBO.** **See** Textiles.

US/1065-0245
**MINIATURE QUILTS.** [Miniat. quilts]. (Spring 1991)-. Periodical. English. bm. $15.95 (one year), $29.95 (two year). Chitra Publications, 2 Public Avenue, Montrose PA 18801. **Tel** (717)278-1984, FAX (717)278-2223. **ED** Patti Bachelor and Nancy Roberts. **LC** WMLC 91/4775. **DD** 746. **Bk Rev**, (Qty: 6). **Ad Acc**, **Adv Mgr:** Carol Newman. **Circ:** 70,000.

US
**NEEDLE ARTS.** **Added/Corp** Embroiderers' Guild of America. (1970)-. Periodical. English. qt. comes with membership. Embroiders Guild of America, 335 West Broadway/Suite 100, Louisville KY 40202. **Tel** (502)589-6956, FAX (502)589-3242. Index available. cum. index. **Bk Rev**. **Ad Acc**. **Circ:** 22,000 (ctrl).
**Ind/Abst** Art Archaeol. Tech. Abstr.; Text. Technol. Dig.

US/1040-5518
**NEEDLEPOINT PLUS.** ***Ceased.*** Vol. 15, No. 5 (Jan./Feb. 1989)-(19??). Periodical. English. bm (6 issues). EGW Publishing Company, 1041 Shary Circle, Concord CA 94518. **Tel** (510)671-9852, (800)777-1164, FAX (510)671-0692. **(Subscription address:** Neodata, PO Box 2606, Boulder, CO 80322**)** **ED** Gerri Zeggers. **DD** 746. **Bk Rev**. **Ad Acc**. ***Continues*** *Needlepoint News, 0145-8256.*
**Ind/Abst** Index Inf.

●US/1067-2249
**PIECEWORK (LOVELAND, COLO.).** **See** The Arts-Crafts and Decorative Arts.

●US/1065-5867
**PINK BOOK (MOUNTAIN VIEW, CALIF.), THE.** (THE PINK BOOK : THE BAY AREA DIRECTORY OF FABRIC, YARN AND NEEDLECRAFT.). (1992)-. Directory. English. $4.95. Mishken Publications, PO Box 51991, Palo Alto CA 94303.

US/1072-6373
**PLASTIC CANVAS WORLD.** (1991)-. English. bm. $12.97. House of White Birches, 306 East Parr Road, Berne IN 46711. **Tel** (219)589-8741, FAX (219)589-8093. **(Subscription address:** Palm Coast Data, PO Box 420235, Agency Department, Palm Coast FL 32142.**)** **ED** Marjorie Pearl. **Circ:** 69,649.
**Desc:** Provides plastic canvas projects from top designers for home, holidays, family and friends with full-color photos and easy-to-follow patterns.

CN/0823-7697
**POINTS A POINTS.** [Points points]. No. 1-. Periodical. French. ir. $2,95 le no. Points A Point, 1309 Est, Rue Beaubien, Montreal Quebec, H2G 1K7. **DD** 746.43/2041/05.

US/0891-5237
**PROFESSIONAL QUILTER MAGAZINE, THE.** [Prof. quilt. mag.]. **VFOAT** Professional Quilter. (19??)-. Periodical. English. Four times a year. $20.00. Oliver Press, 104 Bramblewood Lane, Lewisberry PA 17339. **ED** Jeannie Spears. **DD** 746. **Bk Rev**. **Ad Acc**. **Circ:** 2,000. available with illustrations.

UK
**PROFITABLE MACHINE KNITTING : THE PRACTICAL AND SENSIBLE GUIDE TO EARNING MONEY WITH YOUR KNITTING MACHINE.** English. mo. £20.40 UK; £25.00 other. Litharne Ltd, PO Box 9, Stratford-upon-Avon, Warwickshire CV37 8RS England. **Tel** 011 44 789 7206040, FAX 011 44 789 720888.

US/1048-3659
**QUICK & EASY CRAFTS.** [Quick easy crafts]. **VFOAT** Quick and Easy Crafts; Women's Circle Quick & Easy Crafts; Women's Circle Quick and Easy Crafts. Vol. 23, No. 1 (Feb. 1990)-. Periodical. English. bm. $12.97. House of White Birches, 306 East Parr Road, Berne IN 46711. **Tel** (219)589-8741, FAX (219)589-8093. **(Subscription address:** Palm Coast Data, PO Box 420235, Agency Department, Palm Coast FL 32142.**)** **ED** Beth Schwartz Wheeler. **LC** TT740; .Q53. **DD** 746/.05. **Circ:** 338,500. ***Continues*** *Women's Circle Country Needlecraft, 0892-8223.*
**Desc:** Covers high-quality handcrafts that take minimal time and effort.

US/0885-0631
**QUICK & EASY CROCHET.** [Quick easy crochet]. **VFOAT** Quick and Easy Crochet. Vol. I, No. 1 (Winter 1986)-. Periodical. English. bm (6 issues). $24.00. Hochman Associates, 950 Third Avenue, 16th Floor, New York NY 10022. **Tel** (212)371-4932. **(Subscription address:** CDS Agency Hard Copy, PO Box 4966, Des Moines IA 50340.**)** **LC** WMLC 93/1612. **DD** 746.
**Desc:** Contains ideas, patterns and hints for anyone who loves crocheting or who wants to learn.

US/1045-5965
**QUICK & EASY QUILTING.** [Quick easy quilt.]. **VFOAT** Quick and Easy Quilting. Vol. 11, No. 3 (Fall 1989)-. Periodical. English. bm. $14.95. House of White Birches, 306 East Parr Road, Berne IN 46711. **Tel** (219)589-8741, FAX (219)589-8093. **(Subscription address:** Palm Coast Data, PO Box 420235, Agency Department, Palm Coast FL 32142.**)** **ED** Sandra Hatch. **LC** TT835; .Q535. **DD** 746.46/05. **Circ:** 88,700. ***Continues*** *Quilt World Omnibook, 0199-0985.*
**Desc:** Focuses on time-saving quilting techniques which help to complete top-quality quilted projects in a short time/. Projects include place mats, wall hangings, vests, totes and toys.

US/0740-4093
**QUILT DIGEST, THE.** ***Ceased.*** [Quilt dig.]. 1st Ed. (1983)-?. English. an. The Quilt Digest Press, 955 14th Street, San Francisco CA 94114. **Tel** (415)431-1222. **ED** Michael M Kile. **LC** WMLC L 83/142.
**Desc:** The leading series on antique and contemporary quilts. Profuse color illustrations. Leading authorities on a wide variety of quilt and quilt-related subjects.

US/0149-8045
**QUILT WORLD.** [Quilt world]. Vol. 1 Mar./Apr. (1976)-. Periodical. English. bm. $12.97. House of White Birches, 306 East Parr Road, Berne IN 46711. **Tel** (219)589-8741, FAX (219)589-8093. **(Subscription address:** Palm Coast Data, PO Box 420235, Agency Department, Palm Coast FL 32142.**)** **ED** Sandra Hatch. **LC** TT835; . Q53. **DD** 746.9/7. Index available. **Ad Acc**. **Circ:** 71,668.
**Desc:** Featuring: quilt designs, quilt features, quilt talk, quilt pictures, quilt news, quilt exchanges, quilt letters, quilt columnists, etc.

US/0274-712X
**QUILTER'S NEWSLETTER MAGAZINE.** [Quilt. newsl. mag.]. **VFOAT** QN. (19??)-. Periodical. English. Ten times a year. $19.95 US; $29.95 other. Leman Publications, Box 394, 6700 West 44th Avenue, Wheatridge CO 80033. **Tel** (303)420-4272. **(Subscription address:** Neodata / Colorado, PO Box 2606, Boulder Boulder CO 80322.**)** **ED** Bonnie Leman. **LC** TT835; .Q536. **DD** 746.46/05. **Bk Rev**. **Ad Acc**. **Circ:** 134,000.
**Desc:** Articles on design, technique, history, new and old quilt patterns, trends, museum quilts, and current events in quilting. Exhibitions, quilt shows, quiltmaking lessons, and quilt competitions.
**Ind/Abst** Index Inf.

US/1072-9259
**QUILTER'S TREASURY.** (199?)-. English. bm. $12.97. House of White Birches, 306 East Parr Road, Berne IN 46711. **Tel** (219)589-8741, FAX (219)589-8093. **(Subscription address:** Palm Coast Data, PO Box 420235, Agency Department, Palm Coast FL 32142.**)** ***Continues*** *Stitch 'n Sew Quilts.*

●US/1064-7325
**QUILTESSENCE (THIEF RIVER FALLS, MINN.).** (QUILTESSENCE : THE NEWSLETTER FOR QUILTERS, BY QUILTERS.). [Quiltessence]. **VFOAT** Quilt Essence. (1992)-. Newsletter. English. bm. $14.00. Fine Publications, RR2, Box 121, Thief River Falls MN 56701. **DD** 746.

US/0190-0935
**QUILTING AND RELATED NEEDLEWORK.** V. 1- (Issue 1- ); Feb. 1979-. Periodical. English. qt. $5.00. Ruth Briggs Quilts, PO Box 403, Rancho Santa Fe CA 92067.

US/1040-4457
**QUILTING TODAY.** [Quilt. today]. Vol. 1, No. 1 (Mar. 1987)-. Periodical. English. bm. $15.95 (one year), $29.95 (two year). Chitra Publications, 2 Public Avenue, Montrose PA 18801. **Tel** (717)278-1984, FAX (717)278-2223. **(Subscription address:** Chitra Publications, PO Box 1737, Riverton NJ 08077.**)** **LC** TT835; .Q547. **DD** 746.46/05.

US/1047-1634
**QUILTMAKER (WHEATRIDGE, COLO.).** (QUILTMAKER.). [Quiltmaker]. (19??)-. Periodical. English. bm (6 issues). $19.95 US; $25.95 other. Leman Publications, Box 394, 6700 West 44th Avenue, Wheatridge CO 80033. **Tel** (303)420-4272. **(Subscription address:** Neodata / Colorado, PO Box 2606, Boulder Boulder CO 80322.**)** **DD** 746.
**Ind/Abst** Index Inf.

US/1076-058X
**ROUND BOBBIN.** (19??)-. Trade Publication. English. mo. $35.00 US; $45.00 Canada; $60.00 other. Independent Sewing Machine Dealers Association, 1100 H Brandywine Boulevard, Zanesville OH 43702. **Tel** (614)452-4541, FAX (614)452-2552. **ED** Duane R. Meyers. **Bk Rev**. **Ad Acc**. **Circ:** 4,000 (ctrl).
**Desc:** International trade magazine for the retail sewing industry. Contains information on sewing machines, sewing notions, and business management columns.

US/0745-6905
**RUG HOOKER NEWS & VIEWS, THE.** ***Ceased.*** **VFOAT** Rug Hooker News and Views. ( )-(1989). Periodical. English. bm. Leith Publications Inc, Kennebunkport ME 04046.

GW
**SANDRA : TOLLE STRICKMODE.** Dutch (English, French and Italian). Twelve times a year. $36.00. Gruner und Jahr Ag & Co, Abonnenten Service, D 20080 Hamburg Germany. **Tel** 011 49 40 37030. **Ad Acc**. **Circ:** 560,000 (ctrl).
**Desc:** Fashion for knitting.

US
**SANTA CLAUS.** **See** The Arts-Crafts and Decorative Arts.

US/0899-8302
**SERGER UPDATE, THE.** [Serger update]. (Nov. 1987)-. Newsletter. English. Twelve times a year. $48.00. PJS Publications Inc., News Plaza, PO Box 1790, Peoria IL 61656. **Tel** (309)682-6626, FAX (309)682-7394. **(Subscription address:** CDS / SIFD Agency Control, 1901 Bell Avenue, Des Moines IA 50315.**)** **DD** 646. ***Continues*** *Palmer/Pletsch Serger Update.*

US/1063-9160
**SEW BEAUTIFUL.** [Sew beautiful]. Vol. 1, No. 1 (Fall 1987)-. Periodical. English. ir (6 issues). $25.95 US; $39.00 Canada and Mexico; $63.00 other. Sew Beautiful, 518 Madison Street, Huntsville AL 35801. **Tel** (205)533-9586. **ED** Amelia Johnson. **LC** WMLC 91/6101. **DD** 646. Index available (published separately). **Ad Acc, Adv Mgr:** Kathy McMakin, **Tel** same as publisher. **Circ:** 50,000.
**Desc:** A magazine of heirloom sewing and smocking.

US/0029-4292
**SEW BUSINESS.** ***Title Change.*** [Sew bus.]. Vol. 110, No. 5 (May 1971)-(1992). Periodical. English. mo. Miller Freeman Inc., 600 Harrison Street, San Francisco CA 94107. **Tel** (415)905-2337, FAX (415)905-2240, telex 278273. **DD** 746. ***Continues*** *Notions & Home Sewing.* ***Absorbed by*** *Craftrends Sew Business.*

CN/0821-4247
**SEW IT BEGINS.** ***Ceased.*** [Sew it begins]. Issue No. 1 (June 1983)-?. Periodical. English. ir. F Wershler, Box 263 Station A, Winnipeg Manitoba R3K 2A1 Canada. **Tel** 832-0123. **ED** Frances A Wershler. **DD** 646.2/05. **Bk Rev. Circ:** 300.
**Desc:** Canadian sewing newsletter for people who sew crafts, clothing and home decorating items. Discusses sewing techniques, notions and equipment with ideas and patterns for projects.

US/0888-577X
**SEW IT SEAMS.** [Sew it seams]. (1986)-. Periodical. English. Four times a year. Sew it Seams, PO Box 2698, Kirkland WA 98083-2698. **Tel** (206)822-6700. **ED** Christopher T. Lewis. **DD** 646. **Bk Rev. Ad Acc. Circ:** 15,000 (ctrl).
**Desc:** Sewing education with clear, concise, technical articles. Articles range from beginner to advanced sewing.

US/0273-8120
**SEW NEWS.** [Sew news]. No. 1 (Nov./Dec. 1980)-. Periodical. English. Twelve times a year. $23.98 US; $33.98 other. PJS Publications Inc., News Plaza, PO Box 1790, Peoria IL 61656. **Tel** (309)682-6626, FAX (309)682-7394. **(Subscription address:** CDS / SIFD Agency Control, 1901 Bell Avenue, Des Moines IA 50315.**)** **DD** 646.
**Ind/Abst** Mag. Search; Vocat. Search (Jan. 1993-).

US
**SEWING DECOR.** (19??)-. Periodical. English. Six times a year. $19.98 US; $29.98 other. PJS Publications Inc., News Plaza, PO Box 1790, Peoria IL 61656. **Tel** (309)682-6626, FAX (309)682-7394. **(Subscription address:** CDS / SIFD Agency Control, 1901 Bell Avenue, Des Moines IA 50315.**)**

US/0899-8310
**SEWING UPDATE, THE.** [Sewing update]. (Nov. 1987)-. Newsletter. English. Six times a year. $24.00. PJS Publications Inc., News Plaza, PO Box 1790, Peoria IL 61656. **Tel** (309)682-6626, FAX (309)682-7394. **(Subscription address:** CDS / SIFD Agency Control, 1901 Bell Avenue, Des Moines IA 50315.**)** **DD** 646. ***Continues*** *Plamer/Pletsch Sewing Update.*

US/0091-1879
**SIMPLICITY FASHIONS. Added/Corp** Simplicity Pattern Co. (19??)-. English. Three times a year. $2.00. Simplicity Pattern Company / New York, 200 Madison Avenue, New York NY 10016. **Tel** (212)576-0500. **LC** TT500; .S486. **DD** 646.4/3/005. ***Continues*** *Simplicity (New York, N.Y. : 1951).*

US/0488-8812
**SIMPLICITY SCHOOL CATALOG. Main/Corp** Simplicity Pattern Co. (19??)-. Catalog. English (Spanish and French). Four times a year (published in March, June, Oct., and Dec.). $48.00. Simplicity Pattern Company / Michigan, 901 Wayne Street, Niles MI 49121. **Tel** (616)683-4100, ext 355. Index available.

●US/1061-3234
**SIMPLY CROSS STITCH.** No. 1 (Sept./Oct. 1991)-. Periodical. English. Six times a year. $14.95. Needlecraft Shop, 23 Old Pecan Road, Big Sandy TX 75755. **Tel** (903)636-4011 Ext. 211. **DD** 746.

US/0883-3710
**SOMETHING SPECIAL PATTERN CLUB.** [Something spec. pattern club]. **VFOAT** Something Special Pattern Club Newsletter. (198?)-. Periodical. English. bm. $10.00. National Information Center for Children and Youth with Disabilities, PO Box 1492, Washington DC 20013. **Tel** (703)893-6061. **ED** June Blanchard. **Ad Acc. Circ:** 1,500 (ctrl).
**Desc:** A 32 page full color needlecraft pattern booklet on sewing, crochet, needlepoint etc. Full size pattern sheet. Articles, contests and more.

US/0198-8239
**SPIN-OFF (LOVELAND, COLO.). See** Textiles.

US/0744-1649
**STITCH 'N SEW QUILTS.** ***Title Change.*** **VFOAT** Stitch and Sew Quilts. Vol. 1, No. 1 (Jan./Feb. 1982)-(19??). Periodical. English. bm. House of White Birches, 306 East Parr Road, Berne IN 46711. **Tel** (219)589-8741, FAX (219)589-8093. **ED** Sandra Hatch. Index available. **Bk Rev. Ad Acc. Circ:** 63,000. ***Continued by*** *Quilter's Treasury.*

DK
**STOF & SAKS. VAT** Stof Og Saks. Periodical. Danish. Dansk Beklaedings - OG, Textilarbejderforbund, Postbox 16, 4550 Asnaes Denmark.

US/1070-0560
**SUNBONNET CRAFTS.** ***Ceased.*** [Sunbonnet crafts]. (199?)-(Fall 1994). Periodical. English. qt. House of White Birches, 306 East Parr Road, Berne IN 46711. **Tel** (219)589-8741, FAX (219)589-8093. **ED** Laura Scott. **LC** WMLC 93/945. **DD** 745. **Circ:** 50,072.
**Desc:** Contains crafts featuring Sunbonnet Sue and friends. Projects include cross-stitch, quilting, applique, duplicate stitch, plastic canvas, painting and more.

US/0278-7466
**SWEATERS AND AFGHANS.** ***Ceased.*** (19??)-(19??). Periodical. English. an. Meredith Publications / Special Interest Section, 1716 Locust Street, Des Moines IA 50309. **Tel** (515)284-3000. **LC** TT825; .S93. **DD** 746.9/2.

FR
**TOUTE LA BRODERIE.** French. mo. $17.00 (one year), $33.00 (two year). Snege Editions, BP 7085, 23 rue Chalopin, 69341 Lyon Cedex 07 France. **Tel** 011 33 78 720688.

AT
**TOWN & COUNTRY NEEDLECRAFT.** (19??)-. Periodical. English. Six times a year. 26.70Aus$ Australia; 44.70Aus$ New Zealand & Papua New Guinea; 57.00Aus$ US & Canada; 60.00Aus$ Europe & Africa; 47.00Aus$ Singapore, Malaysia, Indonesia; 52.00Aus$ Hong Kong, China, Japan, India. Federal Publishing Co Pty Ltd, PO Box 199, 180 Bourke Road, Alexandria New South Wales, 2015 Australia. **Tel** 011 61 2 693 6666, FAX 011 61 2 693 9935. **(Subscription address:** Federal Publishing Co. Pty Ltd., PO Box 199, Alexandria NSW 2015 Australia.**)**

US/1050-4435
**TRADITIONAL QUILTWORKS.** [Tradit. quiltw.]. No. 1 (Oct. 1988)-. Periodical. English. bm. $15.95 (one year), $29.95 (two year). Chitra Publications, 2 Public Avenue, Montrose PA 18801. **Tel** (717)278-1984, FAX (717)278-2223. **(Subscription address:** Chitra Publications, PO Box 1737, Riverton NJ 08077.**)** **ED** Patti Bachelor and Nancy Roberts. **LC** WMLC 91/3388. **DD** 746. **Ad Acc, Adv Mgr:** Carol Newman. **Circ:** 94,000.
**Desc:** Contains how-to-information, workshops, supports lessons in design and drafting and includes colorful diagrams. Each issue features a notable quilting teacher.

US/0277-0628
**UNCOVERINGS.** (UNCOVERINGS : THE ... RESEARCH PAPERS OF THE AMERICAN QUILT STUDY GROUP.). [Uncoverings]. **Added/Corp** American Quilt Study Group. (1980)-. Academic Scholarly Publication. English. an (Oct.). $20.00 US & Canada; $22.00 other. American Quilt Study Group, 660 Mission Street, Suite #400, San Francisco CA 94105. **Tel** (415)495-0163, FAX (415)495-3516. **ED** Virginia Gunn (editor's address: 819 Qinby Avenue, Wooster, OH. 44691. **LC** TT835; .U52. **DD** 746.9/7/0973. **Bk Rev.**
**Desc:** Scholarly papers on the history of quilts, quiltmaking and quiltmakers.
**Ind/Abst** BHA : Biblio. Hist. Art.

US/0890-9237
**VOGUE KNITTING INTERNATIONAL.** [Vogue knitt. int.]. **VFOAT** Knitting International; Vogue Knitting. (198?)-. English. Three times a year. $11.95 US; $18.70 other. Butterick Company Inc., 2900 Beale Avenue, Altoona PA 16603. **Tel** (814)943-5281, (800)766-3619. **(Subscription address:** Vogue Knitting Magazine, PO Box 1072, Altoona, PA 16603**)** **LC** TT820; .V625. **DD** 746.9/2. **Ad Acc.** ***Continues*** *Vogue Knitting.*
**Desc:** Provides knitting instructions and fashions.

US/0095-2788
**VOGUE PATTERNS.** Vol. 46, No. 6 (June/July 1972)-. Periodical. English. bm. $12.95 US; $26.15 other. Butterick Company Inc., 2900 Beale Avenue, Altoona PA 16603. **Tel** (814)943-5281, (800)766-3619. **(Subscription address:** Vogue Patterns Magazine, PO Box 751, Altoona, PA 16603**)** **LC** TT500; .V717. **DD** 646.4/04/05. ***Continues*** *International Vogue Pattern Book.*

UK/0142-338X
**VOGUE PATTERNS (BRITISH EDITION).** (VOGUE PATTERNS.). (19??)-. Periodical. English. bm. £13.50 UK; £18.00. Butterick Company Inc., 2900 Beale Avenue, Altoona PA 16603. **Tel** (814)943-5281, (800)766-3619. **(Subscription address:** Butterick Company Ltd., New Lane Havant, Hants PO92nd England**)** **ED** Wendy Rawlins. **Ad Acc. Circ:** 49,659 (ctrl).
**Desc:** International designer fashion, very easy and very vogue designs for all occasions. Also provides tips and articles on dressmaking skills.

US/1073-0680
**WEARABLE CRAFTS.** (199?)-. English. bm. $14.95. House of White Birches, 306 East Parr Road, Berne IN 46711. **Tel** (219)589-8741, FAX (219)589-8093. **(Subscription address:** Palm Coast Data, PO Box 420235, Agency Department, Palm Coast FL 32142.**)** **ED** Beth Schwartz Wheeler. **Circ:** 81,345. ***Continues*** *Wearable Wonders, 1057-7556.*
**Desc:** Contains designer artwear projects in a variety of clothing, jewelry, and accessories.

US/0509-089X
**WOMEN'S CIRCLE.** (19??)-. Periodical. English. Six times a year (Jan., Mar., May, July, Sept., Nov.). $9.95. House of White Birches, 306 East Parr Road, Berne IN 46711. **Tel** (219)589-8741, FAX (219)589-8093. **(Subscription address:** Palm Coast Data, PO Box 420235, Agency Department, Palm Coast FL 32142.**)** **ED** Marjorie Pearl. **Ad Acc. Circ:** 49,749.
**Desc:** Features women who have turned hobbies and skills into successful home businesses. Readers share interests, from fund-raising ideas to favorite recipes and crafts.

US/0279-1978
**WOMENS CIRCLE CROCHET.** ***Title Change.*** **VFOAT** Crochet. Vol. 1, No. 1 (Fall 1981)-(19??). Periodical. English. qt. House of White Birches, 306 East Parr Road, Berne IN 46711. **Tel** (219)589-8741, FAX (219)589-8093. **ED** Anne Jefferson. **Ad Acc. Circ:** 80,000. ***Continued by*** *Crochet Digest.*
**Desc:** At least 15 to 20 wonderful exciting crochet patterns. Patterns come to just pennies in cost when you subscribe.

US/0745-0575
**WOMEN'S HOUSEHOLD CROCHET.** Vol. 1, No. 4 (Winter 1982)-. Periodical. English. qt. $9.95. House of White Birches, 306 East Parr Road, Berne IN 46711. **Tel** (219)589-8741, FAX (219)589-8093. **(Subscription address:** Palm Coast Data, PO Box 420235, Agency Department, Palm Coast FL 32142.**)** **ED** Susan Hankins. **Ad Acc. Circ:** 34,500. ***Continues*** *Crochet for Women Only, 0744-1665.*
**Desc:** Showcases crochet patterns especially for the home including doilies, afghans, kitchen and bath accents, and holiday patterns.

US/0730-7640
**YARNCRAFT. VFOAT** Yarn Craft. No. 1-. Periodical. English. bm. $11.70. Honkey-Tonk Publishing, PO Box 238, West Hempstead NY 11552.

## SEXUAL LIFE

US/0742-4701
**ADVOCATE MEN.** [Advocate men]. **VFOAT** Men. Vol. 1, No. 1 (June 1984)-. Periodical. English. Twelve times a year. $54.00. Liberation Publications, 6922 Holywood Boulevard, 10th Floor, Los Angeles CA 90028. **Tel** (213)871-1225. **(Subscription address:** Advocate / Illinois, PO Box 589, Mt. Morris IL 61054.**)** **DD** 051. ***Continued in part by*** *Men of Advocate Men, 0882-9713.*

CN/0843-4611
**ANNALS OF SEX RESEARCH.** ***Title Change.*** [Ann. sex res.]. Vol. 1, No. 1 (1988)-(1994). Periodical. English. qt. Juniper Press, 1310 Shorewood Drive, La Crosse WI 54601. **Tel** (608)788-0096. **DD** 306.7/05. **NLM** W1; AN625D. ***Continued by*** *Sexual Abuse : A Journal of Research and Treatment.*
**Ind/Abst** Am. Humanit. Index (199?-); Psychol. Abstr. (1988-); PsycINFO; PsycLit.

US/1053-2528
**ANNUAL REVIEW OF SEX RESEARCH.** [Annu. rev. sex res.]. **Added/Corp** Society for the Scientific Study of Sex (U.S.). Vol. 1 (1990)-. English. $26.00 US; $31.00 other (paper bound for individual readers only); $48.00 US; $55.0 other (cloth bound for multi-reader subscribers only). Society for the Scientific Study of Sex, PO Box 208, Mount Vernon IA 52314. **Tel** (319)895-8407. **LC** HQ60; .A48. **DD** 306.7/05. **NLM** W1; AN77976L.

US/0004-0002
**ARCHIVES OF SEXUAL BEHAVIOR.** [Arch. sex. behav.]. Vol. 1 (1971)-. Academic Scholarly Publication. English. Six times a year. $395.00 institutions, $83.00 individuals US; $460.00 institutions, $97.00 individuals other. Plenum Press, 233 Spring Street, New York NY 10013-1578. **Tel** (212)620-8000, (800)221-9369, FAX (212)463-0742, (212)807-1047, telex 23/421139. **ED** Richard K. Green. **LC** HQ1; .A7. **DD** 301.41/05. **NLM** W1 AR488K. **CODEN** ASXBA8. **[CCC].** Index available. **Pr Rev.** available on microfilm and microfiche from University Microfilms International (UMI). Documents available from The Genuine Article, BIOSIS Document Express, UMI Article Clearinghouse, CASDDS.
**Desc:** Dedicated to the publication of information which will enhance understanding of human sexual behavior.
**Ind/Abst** Abstr. Anthropol.; Acad. Search (July 1993-); Annals Behav. Med.; Biol. Abstr.; Chem. Abstr.

(1971-1983); Crim. Justice Abstr.; Curr. Contents Soc. Behav. Sci.; EMBASE; Expand. Acad. Index (1989-); Health Plan. Adminis.; High. Educ. Abstr. (1976-); Index Med.; INFO-SOUTH Abstr.; Linguist. Lang. Behav. Abstr.; Med. Abstr. Newsl.; Middle East Abstr. Index; Mod. Med.; Multicult. Educ. Abstr. (1971-); Newsp. Period. Abstr. (1991-); Life Sci. Collect.; Psychol. Abstr. (1971-); PsycINFO; PsycLit; Res. Alert [Full Cov.]; Soc. Plann. Policy Dev. Abstr.; Soc. Sci. Source (Jul. 1993-); Soc. Sci. Cit. Index [Full Cov.]; Soc. Sci. Index (1971-1983); Soc. Sci. Index Fulltext (Oct. 1988-) [Full Txt.]; Sociol. Abstr.; Stud. Women Abstr.; Women Stud. Abstr.

AT
**AUSTRALASIAN GAY AND LESBIAN LAW JOURNAL.** English. sa. 44.00Aus$ Australia; 50.00Aus$ other. Federation Press Pty Ltd, PO Box 45, Annandale New South Wales 2038 Australia. **Tel** 011 61 02 5522200. ***Continues*** *Australian Gay and Lesbian Law Journal.*

US/0193-7782
**BILL-DALE MARCINKO'S AFTA. See** Literary and Political Reviews.

●US
**BIZARRE SEX AND OTHER CRIMES OF PASSION.** (1992)-. English. an. $9.50. T A L Publications, PO Box 1837, Leesburg VA 22075. **Tel** (703)777-6324, FAX (703)771-8413. **Circ:** 2,000.
**Desc:** Features horror literature of an erotic nature.

US
**BOB DAMRON'S ADDRESS BOOK.** English. ir. Best Guide, 66 N Z Voorburgwal Amsterdam The Netherlands. **Tel** (020)699 1583, FAX (020)6950907. **Ad Acc.**

UK/0301-5572
**BRITISH JOURNAL OF SEXUAL MEDICINE.** ***Ceased.*** **See** Medical Science and Technology.

FR/0336-5913
**CAHIERS DE SEXOLOGIE CLINIQUE.** [Cah. sexol. clin.]. (1975)-. Periodical. French. bm. 391.77F France; 500.00F other. Docteur Tordjman, 72 Quai Louis Bleriot, 75016 Paris France. **Tel** 011 33 1 40503899. **UDC** 61.

●CN/1188-4517
**CANADIAN JOURNAL OF HUMAN SEXUALITY, THE.** [Can. j. hum. sex.]. **Added/Corp** Sieccan. Vol. 1, No. 1 (1992)-. Periodical. English (French). Four times a year (Mar., June, Sept., Dec.). 35.00Can$ (individuals), 50.00Can$ (institutions) Canada; 45.00Can$ (individuals), 60.00Can$ (institutions) others. SIECCAN, 850 Coxwell Avenue, East York Ontario M4C 5R1 Canada. **Tel** (416)466-5304, FAX (416)778-0785. **ED** Michael Barrett, Ph.D. **DD** 616.6/906/05. **CODEN** CJHSEA. Index available. cum. index. **Bk Rev. Pr Rev. Circ:** 1,000. ***Continues*** *Sieccan Journal., 0844-3718.*
**Desc:** This journal publishes manuscripts from a variety of disciplines related to the study of human sexuality.

US/0747-0819
**CLUB INTERNATIONAL (NEWTOWN, CONN.). See** Men's Interests.

CN/0712-6042
**COEUR ATOUT.** [Coeur atout]. **VFOAT** Coeur A Tout. Vol. 1, No. 1-. Periodical. French. $1.00 per no. Coeur Atout, a/s Publications Domaine Ltee, 4270 Avenue Papineau, Montreal Quebec H2H 1S9 Canada. **DD** 306.7/05.

CN/0317-3607
**CONFIDENCES (MONTREAL. 1972).** (CONFIDENCES.). Issue 1 (197?)-. French. Edi Monde, 23 25 rue de Berri, 75388 Paris Cedex 08 France. **Tel** 011 33 1 45624455. **DD** 301.41/7/05. ***Continues*** *Le Nouveau Confidences, 0316-7453.*

CN/0701-0818
**CONTACT (MONTREAL. 1976).** (CONTACT.). Vol. 1, (Dec. 15, 1976)-. Periodical. French. Eleven times a year. $21.35 (individuals), $30.00 (institutions). Science Teachers Assn of Victoria, PO Box 190, Richmond VIC 3121 Australia. **Tel** 011 61 3 4282633, FAX (03)347 1905. **DD** 301.41/7/05.

US/0748-0679
**CURRENT RESEARCH UPDATES IN HUMAN SEXUALITY.** [Curr. res. updates human sex.]. (Jan. 1984)-. Periodical. English. mo. $70.00 (libraries), $48.00 (regular) US; $90.00 (libraries), $63.00 (regular) other. Current Research Updates Publishing, PO Box 2831, Bellingham WA 98227. **Tel** (206)647-1568. **ED** E.R. Mahoney. **DD** 306. Index available. cum. index. **Circ:** 500.
**Desc:** Published papers from more than 800 professional journals covering 25 major subject areas in sexuality.

US/0147-1139
**DIGNITY.** V. 1- Feb. 1970-. Periodical. English. mo. $15.00 with membership. Dignity, Inc., 755 Boylston Street, Room 413, Boston MA 02116.

US/1072-5644
**FRIGHTEN THE HORSES.** [Fright. horses]. (1990)-. Periodical. English. qt (Jan., Apr., June, Oct.). $18.00 US; $25.00 Canada; $30.00 other. Heat Seeking Publishing, 41 Sutter Street #1108, San Francisco CA 94104. **ED** Mark Pritchard and Cris Gutierrez (Editors' Telephone: (415)824-0282). **DD** 051. **Bk Rev**, (Qty: 5-10). **Ad Acc, Adv Mgr:** Nishauga Bliss, **Tel** (510)704-9736. **Circ:** 5000.
**Desc:** Fiction, news, and opinion about sex, feminism, politics and freedom of expression.

UK/0954-0253
**GENDER AND EDUCATION.** Vol. 1, No. 1 (1989)-. Periodical. English. Three times a year (Mar., June, Oct.). £137.00. Carfax Publishing Company, PO Box 25 Abingdon, Oxfordshire OX14 3UE England. **Tel** 011 44 235 555335, FAX (0279)31067, telex 817484. **(Subscription address:** US and Canada/ PO Box 2025, Dunnellon, FL 34430-2025; telephone:(904)489-6996) **CODEN** GEEDER. **[CCC].** Index available. available on microfiche.
**Ind/Abst** Br. Educ. Index; Soc. Plann. Policy Dev. Abstr.; Spec. Educ. Needs Abstr.

UK/0265-8143
**GLAD RAG : JOURNAL OF THE TRANSVESTITE/TRANSSEXUAL SOCIAL GROUP (UK), THE. Added/Corp** Transvestite/Transsexual Social Group (UK). (19??)-. Periodical. English. TV/TS Group, Central Office, 274 Upper Street, Islington, London N1 2UA England. **LC** HQ77.9; .G55. **DD** 306.7/7.

US
**HUMAN SEXUALITY.** 5th ed. (1980/81)-. Periodical. English. an. $12.95. Dushkin Publishing Group Inc., Sluice Dock, Guilford CT 06437. **Tel** (203)453-4351, (800)243-6532, FAX (203)453-6000. **ED** Ollie Pocs. **LC** HQ21; .F687. **DD** 306.7/0973/05. ***Continues*** *Readings in Human Sexuality (Guilford, Conn.), 0163-836X.*
**Desc:** Collection of public press articles covering current issues in human sexuality.

US/0163-8262
**IMPACT (SYRACUSE).** (IMPACT.). Vol. 1 (Oct. 1978)-. Periodical. English. an. Syracuse University / Institute for Family Research and Education, Syracuse NY 13244. **LC** HQ57; .I45. **DD** 306.7/05.

UK
**INFORMATION BULLETIN : SPOD. See** Physically Impaired.

CN/0712-8339
**INTERDIT.** [Interdit]. Periodical. French. mo. $1.25 per no. Distributeurs Associes Du Quebec, 3600 Boul Du Tricentenaire, Montreal Quebec H1B 5M8. **DD** 306.7/05.

US/8756-1379
**JOCK.** Vol. 1, No. 1 (Jan. 1985)-. Periodical. English. mo. $35.00. Jock Publishing Company Inc, 7715 Sunset Boulevard/Suite 210, Los Angeles CA 90046.

US/0898-7386
**JOURNAL OF CLINICAL PRACTICE IN SEXUALITY, THE.** [J. clin. pract. sex.]. **VFOAT** Clinical Practice in Sexuality. Vol. 1, No. 1 (Oct. 1985)-. Periodical. English. Twelve times a year. Gordon L Deal Inc., 3 Bunker Hill Run, East Brunswick NJ 08816. **DD** 616. **NLM** W1; JO5899IM.

US/0091-8369
**JOURNAL OF HOMOSEXUALITY. See** Homosexuality.

US/0890-7064
**JOURNAL OF PSYCHOLOGY & HUMAN SEXUALITY. See** Psychology.

US/0092-623X
**JOURNAL OF SEX & MARITAL THERAPY.** [J. sex marital ther.]. **VAT** Journal of Sex and Marital Therapy. Vol. 1, Fall (1974)-. Academic Scholarly Publication. English. qt. $80.00 (institution), $38.00 (individuals). Brunner Mazel, 19 Union Square West, New York NY 10003. **Tel** (212)924-3344, (800)825-3089. **ED** Helen Kaplan, Clifford Sager. **LC** RC556; .J67. **DD** 616.8/583/005. **NLM** W1 JO876F. **CODEN** JSMTB. **Bk Rev. Ad Acc. Pr Rev. Circ:** 2,000. available on microfilm and microfiche from University Microfilms International (UMI). Documents available from The Genuine Article.
**Desc:** Provides a forum for new clinical techniques and conceptualizations emerging from the practice of sex and marital therapy.
**Ind/Abst** AGRICOLA; Annals Behav. Med.; Crim. Justice Abstr.; Curr. Contents Soc. Behav. Sci.; EMBASE; High. Educ. Abstr.; Index Med.; Middle East Abstr. Index; Psychol. Abstr. (1974-); PsycINFO; PsycLit; Res. Alert [Full Cov.]; Sage Fam. Stud. Abstr.; Soc. Plann. Policy Dev. Abstr.; Soc. Sci. Cit. Index [Full Cov.]; Sociol. Abstr.; Stud. Women Abstr.

US/0161-4576
**JOURNAL OF SEX EDUCATION AND THERAPY. Added/Corp** American Association of Sex Educators and Counselors. **VFOAT** Journal of Sex Education & Therapy; Sex Education and Therapy. Vol. 1 (Spring/Summer 1975)-. Periodical. English. Four times a year. $77.00 (institutions); $92.00 others. Guilford Publications Inc., 72 Spring Street, New York NY 10012. **Tel** (212)431-9800, (800)365-7006, FAX (212)966-6708. **ED** R. Taylor Segraves. **LC** HQ1; .J49. **DD** 306.7/05. **NLM** W1 JO876P. **CODEN** JSETE2. **[CCC]. Bk Rev. Ad Acc. Circ:** 4,500. available on microfilm and microfiche from University Microfilms International (UMI).
**Desc:** A non-profit education association dedicated to the highest standard of education training research ethics and patient care in the field of human sexuality.
**Ind/Abst** Abstr. Anthropol. (19??-); Contents Pages Educ.; Curr. Lit. Fam. Plan.; High. Educ. Abstr. (1979-); Middle East Abstr. Index; Psychol. Abstr. (1985-); PsycINFO; PsycLit; Soc. Plann. Policy Dev. Abstr.; Soc. Work Abstr. [Select. Cov.].

US/0022-4499
**JOURNAL OF SEX RESEARCH, THE. Added/Corp** Society for the Scientific Study of Sex. (Mar. 1965)-. Periodical. English. ir. University Microfilms International, 300 North Zeeb Road, Ann Arbor MI 48106-1346. **Tel** (313)761-4700, (800)521-0600 Exts. 2490, 2491, FAX (313)973-1540. **LC** HQ5; .J6. ***Supersedes*** *Advances in Sex Research.*

US/0022-4499
**JOURNAL OF SEX RESEARCH, THE.** [J. sex res.]. **Added/Corp** Society for the Scientific Study of Sex (U.S.). Vol. 1 (Mar. 1965)-. Academic Scholarly Publication. English. Four times a year. $55.00 (individuals), $87.00 (institutions) surface mail; $71.00 (individuals), $101.00 (institutions) airmail. Society for Scientific Study of Sex, PO Box 208, Mount Vernon IA 52314. **Tel** (319)895-8407, FAX (319)895-6203. **ED** Elizabeth Rice Allgeier. **LC** HQ5; .J6. **DD** 612.6/0072. **NLM** W1 JO876R. **CODEN** JSXRAJ. **Bk Rev. Ad Acc. Pr Rev. Circ:** 2,500. available on microfilm and microfiche from University Microfilms International (UMI). Documents available from The Genuine Article, UMI Article Clearinghouse. ***Continues*** *Advances in Sex Research.*
**Desc:** Published by the society for the scientific study of sex, the journal serves as a forum for the interdisciplinary exchange of knowledge among professionals concerned with sexuality. Articles reporting original empirical research are emphasized. Includes contributions of nurses, physicians, biologists, psychologists, educators, therapists, and others.
**Ind/Abst** Abstr. Anthropol. (19??-); Acad. Search (Jan. 1994-); Annals Behav. Med.; Appl. Soc. Sci. Index Abstr.; Crim. Justice Abstr.; Curr. Contents Soc. Behav. Sci.; Curr. Lit. Fam. Plan.; EMBASE; Expand. Acad. Index (1989-); INFO-SOUTH Abstr.; Mag. Search; Middle East Abstr. Index; Multicult. Educ. Abstr.; Newsp. Period. Abstr. (1991-); Psychol. Abstr. (1967-); PsycINFO; PsycLit; Res. Alert [Full Cov.]; Sage Fam. Stud. Abstr.; Soc. Plann. Policy Dev. Abstr.; Soc. Sci. Source (Jul. 1993-); Soc. Sci. Cit. Index [Full Cov.]; Soc. Sci. Index Fulltext (1988-) [Full Txt.]; Sociol. Abstr.; Stud. Women Abstr. (1967-).

UK/0963-6757
**JOURNAL OF SEXUAL HEALTH.** (THE JOURNAL OF SEXUAL HEALTH.). [J. sex. health]. Periodical. English. bm (Jan., Mar., May, July, Sept., Nov.). £45.00 UK; £75.00 other. Galen Publishing Ltd, Old Stables / Sabadene / Church Road, Catsield Sussex TN33 9DP England. **Tel** 011 44 424 892988, FAX 011 44 424 892087. **ED** Dr. Alan J. Riley. **DD** 612.6. Index available. cum. index. **Bk Rev**, (Qty: 6 - 10). **Ad Acc, Adv Mgr:** P. Bradbury. **Circ:** 10,000 (ctrl).
**Desc:** Topical reviews of sexual and reproductive health issues concerning diagnosis, treatment, councelling etc.

US/0276-3850
**JOURNAL OF SOCIAL WORK & HUMAN SEXUALITY.** ***Title Change.*** **See** Sociology-Social Services and Welfare.

US/1043-4070
**JOURNAL OF THE HISTORY OF SEXUALITY.** [J. hist. sex.]. **VFOAT** JHS. Vol. 1, No. 1 (July 1990)-. Periodical. English. qt. $82.00 institution, $35.00 individual, $24.00. University of Chicago Press / Journals Division, PO Box 37005, 5720 South Woodlawn, Chicago IL 60637. **Tel** (312)753-3347, FAX (312)753-0811. **(Subscription telephone:** (312)753-8083) **ED** John C. Fout. **LC** HQ12; .J66. **DD** 306.7/09. **CODEN** JHSEEI. **[CCC]. Ad Acc. Acid Free.** available on microfilm. Documents available from The Genuine Article.
**Desc:** A scholarly journal illuminating the history of human sexuality in all its expressions, recognizing various differences of class, culture, gender, race, and sexual preference. Provides a forum for historical, critical, and theoretical research in this emerging field.
**Ind/Abst** Arts Humanit. Citation Index [Select. Cov.]; BHA : Biblio. Hist. Art; Curr. Contents Soc. Behav. Sci.; Int. Bibliogr. Sociol.; Res. Alert [Full Cov.]; Soc. Plann. Policy Dev. Abstr.; Soc. Sci. Cit. Index [Full Cov.].

# Sexual Life

US/0145-2398
**KALOS.** See Homosexuality.

US/0899-8272
**LIBIDO (CHICAGO, ILL.).** See Literature.

US/0271-0846
**LUZ (NEW YORK).** (LUZ.). [Luz] (1953)-. Periodical. Spanish. mo. $15.00. Luz Magazine, 313 West 53rd Street, New York NY 10019. **Tel** (305)592-1760. **DD** 613.
 **Desc:** Sex education.

US/0025-7001
**MEDICAL ASPECTS OF HUMAN SEXUALITY.** Ceased. [Med. asp. hum. sex.]. **VFOAT** Human Sexuality. Vol. 1 (Sept. 1967)-Vol. 26 (1992). Periodical. English. mo. Cahners Publishing Company, 249 West 17th Street, New York NY 10011. **Tel** (212)645-0067, FAX (212)242-6987. **(Subscription address:** PO Box 173306, Denver, CO 80217-3306) **ED** Charlotte Isler. **DD** 613. **NLM** W1 ME21. **CODEN** MAHSA. **[CCC].** **Ad Acc. Circ:** 131,000 (ctrl).
 **Desc:** Articles on sexual marital and family aspects that require counseling in the physician's office practice.
 **Ind/Abst** Curr. Lit. Fam. Plan. (19??-1992); EMBASE; Energy Res. Abstr. (Aug. 1982-); Med. Abstr. Newsl.; NAPRALERT; PsycINFO; PsycLit.

FR/0985-9861
**MES CONFIDENCES EROTIQUES.** **VFOAT** Collection Mes Confidences Erotiques. (1987)-. Monographic series. French. ir. Prices varies per volume. Edimonde Loisirs, 90 rue de Flandre, 75947 Paris Cedex 19 France. **Tel** 011 33 1 44894489. **UDC** 392.

CN/0383-6185
**MON SEXE.** (MON SEXE...ET CELUI DES AUTRES.). First issued in 1976?. Periodical. French. wk. Messageries Dynamiques Inc, 775 Boulevard Lebeau, Saint-Laurent Quebec H4N 1S5 Canada. **Tel** (800)463-4645, (514)332-0680. **DD** 301.41/05.

US
**MONOGRAPH (ASSOCIATION OF SEXOLOGISTS).** (MONOGRAPH.). **Added/Corp** Association of Sexologists. (1981)-. Monographic series. English. Price varies per volume. The Association of Sexologists, 1523 Franklin Street, San Francisco CA 94109.

US/0090-2039
**MOVIE X.** See Motion Picture.

CN/0710-1988
**MYSTIQUE (TORONTO).** (MYSTIQUE.). [Mystique]. (1972)-. Periodical. English. qt. 24.00Can$. Mystique, PO Box 561 Station Q Canada. **Tel** (416)690-5910. **ED** Ron Michaels, Wendy Michaels. **DD** 306.7/3. **Bk Rev. Ad Acc. Circ:** 25,000.
 **Desc:** Articles on alternative lifestyles mostly focusing on swinging couples.

DK/0108-271X
**NORDISK SEXOLOGI.** See Psychology.

CN/0226-5958
**NOUVELLES DES SWINGERS.** **VFOAT** Swingers. V. 1- Aug. 1969-. Periodical. French. mo. Les Publications Joyesues, CP 145 Succursale H, Montreal Quebec H3G 2K5 Canada. **DD** 306.7/05.

AT/1036-8124
**ON THE LEVEL ASHFIELD.** See Health and Personal Fitness.

US
**ORALRAMA!.** English. Leisure Plus Publications Inc, 462 Broadway, Suite 4000, New York NY 10013.

CN/0712-6018
**ORGASME.** [Orgasme]. Vol. 1, No. 1 (1981)-. Periodical. French. mo. Domaine Ltee, CP 368 Succursale NDG, Montreal Quebec H4A 3P7 Canada. **DD** 306.7/05.

US/0278-5811
**OUT HEALTH.** See Public Health and Safety.

NE/0167-5907
**PAIDIKA.** See Homosexuality.

US/0896-2898
**PAN-EROTIC REVIEW.** **VFOAT** Pan Erotic Review. (1990)-. English. an. $30.00. Red Alder Books, PO Box 2992, Santa Cruz CA 95063. **Tel** (408)426-7082. **ED** David Steinberg. **Bk Rev**.

US
**PARTNERS TASK FORCE FOR GAY AND LESBIAN COUPLES.** English. Partners, Box 9685, Seattle WA 98109-0685. **Tel** (206)784-1519.
 **Desc:** Provides information, support, and advocacy for same-sex couples and those who serve them. Now offers special editions and back issues.

US
**PLEASURE QUEST.** (1989)-. English. $12.00. Pleasure Quest, 462 Gilbert Road, Mesa AZ 85204. **ED** Phillip Fry.
 **Desc:** Success guide to sensual adventures and romance.

IT
**PROBLEMI DI SESSUALITA E FECONDITA UMANA.** IST Ricerca Sessualita Fecondi, Via Volta 9, 27100 Pavia Italy.

IT/0391-9935
**QUADERNI DI CONTRACCEZIONE, FERTILITA, SESSUALITA.** (CONTRACCEZIONE, FERTILITA, SESSUALITA. QUADERNI.). (1975)-. Periodical. Italian. Six times a year. L40000. Contraccezione Fertilita Sessualita, Piazzale Ungheria 73, 90141 Palermo Italy. **Tel** 011 39 91 321922. **NLM** W1 CO778CK.

CN/1184-020X
**REPERTOIRE DES RESSOURCES EN SEXUALITE, LE.** [Repert. ressour. sex.]. **Added/Corp** Association des Sexologues du Quebec. Quebec (Province). Ministere du Loisir, de la Chasse et de la Peche. **VFOAT** Repertoire des Ressources en Sexualite, Montreal-Quebec. (1990/1991)-. French. be. 20.00Can$ per volume. L'Index, Productions en Sexologie, CP 57, Succursale R, Montreal Quebec H2S 3K6. **DD** 362.82/86. **Continues** Repertoire des Resources en Sexualite du Grand Montreal.

CN/0707-9516
**REVUE QUEBECOISE DE SEXOLOGIE.** Suspended. [Rev. que. sexol.]. Vol. 1 (July/Aug./Sept. 1979)-?. Periodical. French. qt. $12.00, $3.50 (per issue) Canada; $15.00 other. Collectif d'Informations Sexuelles et Sexologique, 6109 Av Durocher, Outremont Quebec H2V 3Y7 Canada. **DD** 301.41/05.
 **Ind/Abst** Point Repere (1982).

IT/0392-1670
**RIVISTA DI SESSUOLOGIA ROMA.** [Riv. sessuol. Roma]. (1977)-. Periodical. Italian. qt. L55000 Italy; L80000 other. Clueb Coop Libraria Univ Edi, Bologna Via Marsala 24, 40126 Bologna Italy. **Tel** 011 39 51 220736, 224780, FAX 011 39 51 237758. **UDC** 61.

CN/0712-6026
**SCANDALE (MONTREAL).** (SCANDALE.). [Scandale]. Periodical. French. $1.25 per no. Domaine Ltee, CP 368 Succursale NDG, Montreal Quebec H4A 3P7 Canada. **DD** 306.7/05.

US
**SEX NEWS.** Periodical. English.
 **Ind/Abst** Curr. Lit. Fam. Plan.

US/0740-3593
**SEX OVER FORTY.** **VFOAT** Sex Over 40. Vol. 1, (June 1982)-. Periodical. English. Twelve times a year. $36.00 one year; $64.00 two years. Sex Over Forty, PO Box 1600, Chapel Hill NC 27515. **Tel** (919)929-2143, FAX (919)942-0792. **Circ:** 40,000.

CN/0712-6034
**SEXE PLUS.** [Sexe plus]. (1980)-. Periodical. French. $1.25 per no. Domaine Ltee, CP 368 Succursale NDG, Montreal Quebec H4A 3P7 Canada. **DD** 306.7/05.

●US
**SEXUAL ABUSE : A JOURNAL OF RESEARCH AND TREATMENT.** See Psychology.

UK/0267-4653
**SEXUAL AND MARITAL THERAPY.** See Family and Marriage.

US/0739-7321
**SEXUAL BEHAVIOR (NEW YORK, N.Y. : 1982).** (SEXUAL BEHAVIOR.). [Sex. behav.]. (1982)-. Monographic series. English. Price varies per volume. Marcel Dekker Inc., 270 Madison Avenue, New York NY 10016. **Tel** (212)696-9000, (800)228-1160, FAX (212)685-4540, telex 421419. **(Subscription address:** Marcel Dekker Inc, PO Box 5017, Monticello NY 12701.) **ED** Richard C. Friedman. **NLM** W1 SE99E.

US/0884-4372
**SEXUAL COERCION & ASSAULT.** See Sociology.

US
**SEXUAL FREEDOM.** **Added/Corp** Sexual Freedom League. (1969)-. English. ir. San Francisco Sexual Freedom League, PO Box 14034, San Francisco CA 94114. **LC** HQ1; .S43. **DD** 301.41/7/05.

US/0148-7914
**SEXUAL HEALTH AND RELATIONSHIPS.** **VFOAT** SHAR. V. 1- Jan. 1978-. Periodical. English. mo. $9.50. SHAR, PO Box 627, Northampton MA 01060.

JA/0917-7507
**SEXUAL SCIENCE.** [Sex. sci.]. **VFOAT** Gekkan Sekusharu Saiensu. (1991)-. Periodical. Japanese. mo. Nihon Akuseru Shupuringa Shuppan K.K., Japan Publishing Inc., Axel Springer, 2-1 Niban-cho, Chiyoda-ku, Tokyo 102 Japan.

CN/1191-1131
**SEXUALITE NOUVELLE.** [Sex. nouv.]. No 1 (1991)-. Periodical. French. qt. 2.80Can$ per issue. Artistes et Vedettes 2000, 2348 Est Rue Ontario, Montreal Quebec. **DD** 306.7.

US/0146-1044
**SEXUALITY AND DISABILITY.** See Physically Impaired.

US/0273-2564
**SEXUALITY (BOCA RATON).** (SEXUALITY.). [Sexuality]. V. 1, Article 1-. Periodical. English. an (approximately 20 articles each year.). Social Issues Resources Series Inc, PO Box 2348, Boca Raton FL 33427. **Tel** (800)327-0513, (407)994-0079. **ED** Eleanor C Goldstein. **LC** HQ18.U5; S513. **DD** 306.7/0973.
 **Desc:** Interdisciplinary resource materials consisting of reprinted articles from popular and professional journals, newspapers, magazines and government documents.

GW/0944-7105
**SEXUOLOGIE.** German. Four times a year. DM136.00 Germany; DM144.00 other. Gustav Fischer Verlag Stuttgart, Postfach 720143, Wollgrasweg 49, D 70577 Stuttgart Germany. **Tel** 011 49 711 458030, FAX 0711-4580334, telex 2627-7111488. **(Subscription address:** VCH Publishers Inc., 303 Northwest 12th Avenue, Journals Department, Deerfield FL 33442.)

US/0091-3995
**SIECUS REPORT.** [SIECUS rep.]. **Main/Corp** Sex Information and Education Council of the U.S. **VAT** Sex Information and Education Council of the United States Report. Vol. 1 (Sept. 1972)-. Periodical. English. bm. Comes with Sex Information & Education Council Membership. Sex Information & Education Council of the U.S., 130 West 42nd Street/Suite 2500, New York NY 10036. **Tel** (212)819-9770, FAX (212)819-9776. **ED** Janet Jamar. **LC** HQ1; .S37. **DD** 301.41/7/05. **NLM** W1 S355N. Index available. **Bk Rev. Ad Acc. Circ:** 3,500. available on microfilm and microfiche from University Microfilms International (UMI). Documents available from UMI Article Clearinghouse. **Continues** SIECUS Newsletter, 0036-150X.
 **Desc:** Covers all aspects of human sexuality.
 **Ind/Abst** Curr. Lit. Fam. Plan.; Educ. Index; Expand. Acad. Index (1992-); Med. Rev. Dig.; Newsp. Period. Abstr. (1992-).

CN/0712-5984
**SUPER SEXE.** [Super sexe]. (1981)-. Periodical. French. $1.25 each number. Super Sexe, a/s Publications Domaine Ltee, 4270 Av Papineau Canada. **DD** 306.7/05.

CN/0727-6836
**SWINGTIME NEWS.** [Swingtime news]. **VFOAT** Confidentially Yours, Swingtime News. (1969)-. Periodical. English. Swingtime News, PO Box 2410, New Westminster British Columbia V3L 5B6 Canada. **DD** 306.7/3.

NE
**TIJDSCHRIFT VOOR KREATIEVE THERAPIE.** Dutch. qt. NVKT, Kastanjelaan 36, 1214 LJ Hilversum Netherlands. **Tel** 011 31 35 283808.

NE/0167-5915
**TIJDSCHRIFT VOOR SEKSUOLOGIE.** Dutch. qt. Fl63.00 Netherlands; 1200F Belgium. Stichting Tijdschrift Voor Seksuologie, Debussylaan 3, 5242 HH Rosmalen Netherlands. **Tel** 010-4087587, FAX 010-4366832. **ED** A K Slob (editor's address: M F Erasmus Universiteit, Postbus 1738, 3000 DR Rotterdam Netherlands). Index available. cum. index. **Bk Rev. Ad Acc. Pr Rev. Circ:** 750 (ctrl).

US/0148-7388
**TURNABOUT.** No. 1- June 1963-. Periodical. English. qt. $3.00 each issue. Abbe De Choisy Press, PO Box 4053, Grand Central Station, New York NY 10017. **LC** HQ77; .T8. **DD** 362.1/9.

●US/1061-6977
**X, THE FUTURE OF SEX.** **VFOAT** X. (1992)-. Periodical. English. qt. $4.95 (single issue). Kundalini Publishing, 1095 Market Street, Suite 812, San Francisco CA 94103.

GW/0932-8114
**ZEITSCHRIFT FUER SEXUALFORSCHUNG.** Vol. 1, No. 1 (March 1988)-. Periodical. German (summaries and/or abstracts in English). qt. $71.00. Ferdinand Enke Verlag, Ruedigerstrasse 14, D-70469 Stuttgart Germany. **Tel** 011 49 711 8931124, 011 49 711 893123. **(Subscription address:** Thieme Medical Publishers Inc., 381 Park Avenue South, New York NY 10016.) **LC** HQ21; .Z38. **DD** 306.7/072. **NLM** W1; ZE593G.
 **Ind/Abst** Int. Bibliogr. Sociol.; PsycINFO (1988-); PsycLit; Soc. Plann. Policy Dev. Abstr.

# SOCIAL SCIENCES

SP/0213-6252
**ABACO.** No. 1 (1986)-. Periodical. Spanish. sa. Fundacion Fondo para la Investigacion Economica y Social, Juan Hurtado de Mendoza 14, 28036 Madrid Spain. **Tel** 011 34 1 3504400, FAX 011 34 1 3508040.

RU
**ABC OF SOCIAL AND POLITICAL KNOWLEDGE. VFOAT** ABC Sotsial No-Politicheskikh Znanii. 1-. Monographic series. English. Price varies per volume.

GW
**ABG.** ***Ceased.*** **Added/Corp** Institut fur Gesellschaft und Wissenschaft. **VFOAT** Analysen und Berichte aus Gesellschaft und Wissenschaft. (19??)-(1992). German. Institut fur Gesellschaft und Wissenschaft, Aussere Brucker Str 33, Postfach 1409, 8520 Erlangen-Nurnberg Germany. **LC** H5; .A14. **DD** 300/.5; 943/.1/0072. ***Continues*** *Analysen und Berichte aus Gesellschaftswissenschaften, 0572-3287.*

GW/0002-2977
**ABHANDLUNGEN DER GEISTES- UND SOZIALWISSENSCHAFTLICHEN KLASSE / AKADEMIE DER WISSENSCHAFTEN UND DER LITERATUR.** [Abh. Geistes- Soz.wiss. Kl. - Akad. Wiss. Lit.]. **Added/Corp** Akademie der Wissenschaften und der Literatur (Germany). Geistes- und Sozialwissenschaftliche Klasse. (1950)-. Monographic series. German (English and French). ir. Price varies per volume. Franz Steiner Verlag GmbH, Postfach 101061, D 70009 Stuttgart Germany. **Tel** 011 49 0711 2582372, FAX 011 49 0711 2582290, telex 723636 daz d. **LC** AS182; .M232. **NLM** W1 AK323.

GE
**ABHANDLUNGEN ZUR HANDELS-UND SOZIALGESCHICHTE. Added/Corp** Hansischer Geschichtsverein (Weimar, Germany). Vol. 1 (1958)-. Periodical. German. ir. DM48.00 (latest volume). Verlag Hermann Boehlaus Nachfolger, Postfach 260, D 99403 Weimar Germany. **Tel** 011 49 3643 2071, . **(Subscription address:** Verlag H. Boehlaus Nachfolger, Postfach 546, D 72488 Sigmaringen Germany.**)**

MR
**ABHATH.** Periodical. Arabic. qt. 170.00MD. Majallat Abhath, SB 1377, Al-Rabat Morocco. **LC** H8.A7; A23. **Bk Rev. Ad Acc. Circ:** 6,500 (ctrl).
**Desc:** Publishes studies and book reviews about economy, sociology, law, history, anthropology, and political sciences on Morocco or Maghreb countries, Arab countries, and Islam.

US
**ABSTRACTS OF ARI RESEARCH PUBLICATIONS. Main/Corp** U.S. Army Research Institute for the Behavioral and Social Sciences. **VFOAT** Abstracts of A.R.I. Research Publications. English. an. US Army Research Institute for the Behavioral and Social Sciences, c/o Peri-Pot, 5001 Eisenhower Avenue, Alexandria VA 22333. available on microfiche (Vols. for (FY 1974-1975-) distributed to depository libraries).

NE/0169-605X
**ABSTRACTS ON RURAL DEVELOPMENT IN THE TROPICS.** ***Ceased.*** **VFOAT** Rural. Vol. 1, No. 1 (Jan./March 1986)-(Jan. 1995). Periodical. English. Six times a year (Feb., Apr., June, Aug., Oct., Dec.). Royal Tropical Institute, Information & Documentation, Mauritskade 63, 1092 AD Amsterdam Netherlands. **Tel** 11 31 20 5688330, FAX 11 31 20 6654423, telex 15080 KIT NL. **ED** C. J. Pesch and R. A. Stunt. **LC** HN981.C6; A27. **DD** 307.1/4/091724. Index available. cum. index (provided at the end of the volume). **Ad Acc. Circ:** 500 (ctrl). available on CD-ROM (KIT Abstracts) from KIT Institute; available on diskette.
**Desc:** Abstracting journal for which up to 1,500 new items per year of practical interest to rural development and extension workers in tropical and subtropical areas are selected from worldwide literature.

PY
**ACCION. VFOAT** Revista Paraguaya de Educacion y del Hogar; Revista Paraguaya de Reflexion y Dialogo. 2. Ser., No. 1- Apr. 1964-. Periodical. Spanish. bm. $10.00, $15.00 (airmail) US. Accion Revista de Reflexion y Dialogo, Colon 1301 C Correo 1072, Asuncion Paraguay. **Tel** 33962. **ED** Angel Camina. **Bk Rev. Ad Acc. Circ:** 1,000 (ctrl).
**Desc:** Reflections on Paraguay and Latin America in its various aspects: political, social, religious, human rights, art, and literature; also includes documents.
**Ind/Abst** Leis. Recreat. Tour. Abstr.; Rural Dev. Abstr.; World Agric. Econ.

CN/0226-2568
**ACQUISITIONS / METROPOLITAN TORONTO LIBRARY, SOCIAL SCIENCES DEPARTMENT.** [Acquis. - Metrop. Toronto Libr., Soc. Sci. Dep.]. **Main/Corp** Metropolitan Toronto Library. Social Sciences Dept. **Added/Corp** Metropolitan Toronto Library Board. Vol. 1, No. 1 (March 1980)-. Periodical. English. Metropolitan Toronto Library Board, 789 Yonge Street, Toronto Ontario M4W 2G8 Canada. **Tel** (416)393-7134, telex 06-22232. **DD** 016.3. ***Continues*** *Metropolitan Toronto Library. Social Sciences Dept. Selected List of New Titles, 0226-0328.*

XR/0232-0487
**ACTA MUSEI REGINAEHRADECENSIS. SERIE B, SCIENTIAE SOCIALES. Added/Corp** Muzeum v Hradci Kralove. **VFOAT** Prace Muzea v Hradci Kralove. (1981)-. Periodical. Czech. Charles University / Univerzita Karlova, Ovocnytrh 5, 116 36 Prague 1 Czech Republic. **Tel** 228441. **LC** H8.C9; A36. ***Continues*** *Prace Muzea v Hradci Kralove. Serie B, Vedy Spolecenske.*
**Ind/Abst** BHA : Biblio. Hist. Art.

FR/0335-5322
**ACTES DE LA RECHERCHE EN SCIENCES SOCIALES.** [Actes rech. sci. soc.]. **Added/Corp** Maison des Sciences de l'Homme (Paris, France) Ecole des Hautes Etudes en Sciences Sociales. (1975)-. Periodical. French (summaries and/or abstracts in English and German). Four times a year. 220.56F France; 300.00F other. Editions du Seuil, 27 rue Jacob, 75261 Paris Cedex 06 France. **Tel** 011 33 1 69092409 or, 40465050. **(Subscription address:** Centrale des Revues, 11 rue Gossin, Gauthier Villars, 92543, Montrouge Cedex France**) ED** Pierre Bourdieu. **LC** H3; .A28. **DD** 300/.944. **Pr Rev. Circ:** 2,500. Documents available from The Genuine Article.
**Desc:** Publishes results of leading research in sociology, ethnology, social psychology, psychology, social history, sociolinguistics and the economics of consumption.
**Ind/Abst** Am. Hist. Life (1983-); ARTbibliogr. Mod. (1984-); Arts Humanit. Citation Index [Select. Cov.]; Int. Polit. Sci. Abstr.; Linguist. Lang. Behav. Abstr.; Multicult. Educ. Abstr.; Res. Alert [Full Cov.]; Soc. Plann. Policy Dev. Abstr.; Soc. Sci. Cit. Index [Full Cov.]; Sociol. Abstr. [Full Cov.]; Sociol. Educ. Abstr.

US/0001-8449
**ADOLESCENCE. See** Children and Youth Interests.

UK/0192-4346
**ADVANCES IN EXPERIENTIAL SOCIAL PROCESSES.** ***Ceased.*** (1978)-Vol. 2. English. John Wiley & Sons Ltd., Baffins Lane, Chichester West Sussex PO19 1UD England. **Tel** 0243 779777, FAX 0243 776128 BTG:JWP001, telex 86290 WIBOOKG. **(Subscription address:** North, South and Central America/ John Wiley & Sons, Inc., Subscription Department, 605 Third Avenue, New York, NY 10158-0012, USA; telephone: (212)850-6645; FAX: (212)850-6021**) ED** C L Cooper and C P Alderfer.

US/1047-2010
**ADVANCES IN SOCIAL SCIENCE AND COMPUTERS.** [Adv. soc. sci. comput.]. Vol. 1 (1989)-. English. an. $73.25. JAI Press Inc., 55 Old Post Road, Suite 2, PO Box 1678, Greenwich CT 06836-1678. **Tel** (203)661-7602, FAX (203)661-0792. **ED** David Garson and Stuart Nagel. **LC** H61.3; .A38. **DD** 300/.285.

IT/0390-1181
**AFFARI SOCIALI INTERNAZIONALI.** [Aff. soc. int.]. Vol. 1 (Mar. 1973)-. Periodical. Italian. Three times a year. L104000 Italy; L1500000 other. Franco Angeli Riviste SRL, Viale Monza 106, 20127 Milan Italy. **Tel** 011 39 2 2827651, 011 39 2 289562. **ED** Pier Marcello Masotti. **LC** H7; .A36.
**Ind/Abst** Int. Labour Doc.; LABORDOC; Leis. Recreat. Tour. Abstr.; PAIS Int. Print; World Agric. Econ.

SA/0256-2804
**AFRICA INSIGHT.** [Afr. insight]. **Added/Corp** Africa Institute of South Africa. Vol 10, No. 1 (1980)-. Periodical. English. Four times a year. R40.00. Africa Institute of South Africa, PO Box 630, Pretoria 0001 South Africa. **Tel** 011 27 12 328-6970, FAX 011 27 12 323-8153. **ED** Richard Cornwell. **LC** HC501; .S64. **DD** 960/.05. Index available. cum. index. **Circ:** 4,000 (ctrl). available on microfilm and microfiche from University Microfilms International (UMI). ***Continues*** *South African Journal of African Affairs.*
**Desc:** Presents illustrated articles and statistics on political, socio-economic and cultural issues in Africa, especially Southern Africa.
**Ind/Abst** Abstr. Anthropol. (19??-); Geogr. Abstr. Human Geogr. (?-?); Int. Bibliogr. Sociol.; Int. Dev. Abstr. (?-?); Leis. Recreat. Tour. Abstr.; Rural Dev. Abstr.; World Agric. Econ.

TZ/0002-0117
**AFRICAN REVIEW (DAR ES SALAAM, TANZANIA).** (THE AFRICAN REVIEW.). [Afr. rev.]. **Added/Corp** Chuo Kikuu Cha Dar Es Salaam. Dept. of Political Science. Chuo Kikuu Cha Dar Es Salaam. Dept. of Political Science and Public Administration. Vol. 1, No. 1 (March 1971)-. Periodical. English. sa (June, Dec.). $35.00 institutions; $25.00 individuals. University of Dar es Salaam Department of Political Science, PO Box 35042, Dar es Salaam Tanzania. **Tel** 011 255 51 43130, FAX 011 255 051 48457, 011 255 051 43395, telex 41327 UNISCIE, 41561 UNIVIP. **ED** Prof. Rwekaza Mukandala. **LC** DT31; .A66. **DD** 320.9/6/03. **Bk Rev. Ad Acc. Circ:** 500 (ctrl).
**Desc:** Deals with African politics, development and international affairs; it also deals with publication of academic research findings especially in social sciences, policy making, and administration.
**Ind/Abst** ABC POL SCI; Am. Hist. Life (1971-); Int. Dev. Abstr. (?-?); Int. Labour Doc.; Int. Polit. Sci. Abstr.; Leis. Recreat. Tour. Abstr.; Public Aff. Inf. Serv. Bull.; Rural Dev. Abstr.; World Agric. Econ.

ZA/0002-0168
**AFRICAN SOCIAL RESEARCH.** ***Suspended.*** [Afr. soc. res.]. **Added/Corp** University of Zambia. Institute for African Studies. University of Zambia. Institute for Social Research. No. 1 (June 1966)-Suspended. Periodical. English. sa. K14.00 Zambia; $18.00 US. University of Zambia, PO Box 32379, Lusaka Zambia. **Tel** 213221, telex ZA 44370. **LC** HN771; .A35. **DD** 309.1/6. **NLM** W1 AF56. **CODEN** ASREDO. cum. index. **Circ:** 1,000. ***Continues*** *Rhodes-Livingstone Journal.*
**Ind/Abst** Am. Hist. Life (1956-); Anthropol. Index; Appl. Soc. Sci. Index Abstr.; Int. Dev. Abstr. (1968-?); Leis. Recreat. Tour. Abstr. (1966-); Psychol. Abstr. (1968-); Rural Dev. Abstr. (1966-); Soc. Plann. Policy Dev. Abstr.; Sociol. Abstr. (?-?); World Agric. Econ. (1966-).

KE
**AFRICAN SOCIAL STUDIES FORUM. VFOAT** ASSF. (March 1986)-. Periodical. English. sa. Sh60.00 Kenya; $40.00 US. African Social Studies Programme, PO Box 44777, Nairobi Kenya. **Tel** 747960. **ED** Martin Yiga Matovu, Evaret Standa, and Peter Muyanda-Mutebi. **LC** H62.5.A34; A37. **DD** 300/.7/106. **Bk Rev. Ad Acc. Circ:** 1,000.
**Desc:** All articles are critically reviewed by a competent board of social studies educators before they are selected for publication.

●UK/1352-2175
**AFRICAN STUDIES ABSTRACTS : THE ABSTRACTS JOURNAL OF THE AFRICAN STUDIES CENTRE, LEIDEN. See** Social Sciences-Abstracting, Bibliographies and Statistics.

SL/0259-9651
**AFRICANA RESEARCH BULLETIN.** [Afr. res. bull.]. **Added/Corp** Fourah Bay College. Institute of African Studies. Vol. 1 (Oct. 1970)-. Bulletin. English. Twice a year. $15.00 (latest volume). University of Sierra Leone / Institute of African Studies, Fourah Bay, Freetown Sierra Leone Africa. **Tel** 011 232 22 24092. **ED** C. Magbaily Fyle. **LC** DT470; .A64. **DD** 916.6/03/05. **Bk Rev. Ad Acc. Circ:** 250.
**Desc:** Articles on the humanities and social sciences, particularly in Sierra Leone, and more in West Africa.
**Ind/Abst** Int. Bibliogr. Sociol.; MLA Int. Bibl. Books Artic. Mod. Lang. Lit.

GW
**AFRIKA JAHRBUCH. See** Political Science.

GW/0002-0397
**AFRIKASPECTRUM.** (AFRIKA SPECTRUM.). [Afrikaspectrum]. **Added/Corp** Deutsches Institut fuer Afrika-Forschung. (1966)-. Periodical. German (English and French; summaries and/or abstracts in French and English). Three times a year (Spring, Autumn, & Winter). DM70.00 Germany; DM80.00 Europe; DM90.00 others. Institut fuer Afrika-Kunde, Neuer Jungfernstieg 21, D 20354 Hamburg Germany. **Tel** 011 49 40 3562523, 011 49 40 3562524. **ED** Harald Voss. **LC** DT1; .A285. **DD** 960/.05. Index available. **Bk Rev. Ad Acc. Circ:** 500 (ctrl).
**Desc:** Concerned with various aspects of politics, economics and related topics in contemporary Africa.
**Ind/Abst** Int. Bibliogr. Sociol.; Int. Labour Doc.; LABORDOC; PAIS Int. Print; World Agric. Econ.

US/0894-0762
**AFRO SCHOLAR NEWSLETTER.** (AFRO SCHOLAR NEWSLETTER / AFRO-AMERICAN STUDIES AND RESEARCH PROGRAM.). [Afro sch. newsl.]. **Added/Corp** University of Illinois at Urbana-Champaign. Afro-American Studies and Research Program. No. 1 (Oct. 1980)-. Periodical. English. Four times a year. $25.00. Afro Scholar Newsletter, PO Box 803351, Chicago IL 60680. **Tel** (312)538-2188. **ED** Abdul Alkalimat. **DD** 305. **Bk Rev. Ad Acc. Circ:** 5,000 (ctrl).

IT/0002-094X
**AGGIORNAMENTI SOCIALI. See** Religion and Theology.

JA/0002-2942
**AJIA KEIZAI. See** Economics.

SJ
**AL-BUHUTH.** Periodical. Arabic. PO Box 2402, Al-Khartum Sudan. **LC** Q180.S73; B83.

UK/0950-3110
**AL-MASAQ.** **Added/Corp** University of Leeds. Dept. of Modern Arabic Studies. **VFOAT** Studia Arabo-Islamica Mediterranea. Vol. 1 (1988)-. English (French). an. $16.00. University of Leeds / IMP School of History, Leeds LS2 9JT England. **Tel** 011 44 532 333423. **LC** DS36.85; .M38.
**Ind/Abst** Middle East J.

KU
**ALAM AL-FIKR.** (1970)-. Periodical. Arabic. qt. **LC** AP95.A6; A49.
**Ind/Abst** Annu. Bibliogr. Engl. Lang. Lit.; Middle East J. (?-?).

CN/0843-9931
**ALBERTA (EDMONTON).** ***Ceased.*** **See** The Arts.

MY/0127-5127
**ALIRAN MONTHLY.** [Aliran mon.]. **Added/Corp** Aliran (Association). Vol. 4, No. 1 (Jan. 1984)-. Periodical. English (Malay). Twelve times a year. 46.00Mal$. Aliran Kesedaran Negara, PO Box 1049, Pulan Penang, Malaysia. **Tel** 011 60 4 871608, FAX 011 60 4 863990. **ED** P. Ramakrishnan. **LC** IN PROCESS. **Bk Rev. Circ:** 12,000. ***Continues*** *Aliran, 0127-5127.*
**Ind/Abst** Hum. Rights Intern. Rep.

UY
**AMERICA MERIDIONAL : REVISTA DE LA SOCIEDAD REGIONAL DE CIENCIAS HUMANAS.** 1-. Periodical. Spanish. sa. Manuel Errazquin, 2351 Punta Carretas, Montevideo Republica Oriental del Uruguay. **LC** F2201; .A5. **DD** 980/.005.

US/0002-7642
**AMERICAN BEHAVIORAL SCIENTIST (BEVERLY HILLS).** (THE AMERICAN BEHAVIORAL SCIENTIST.). [Am. behav. sci.]. **VFOAT** ABS. Vol. 4, No. 1 (Sept. 1960)-. Periodical. English. Eight times a year. $220.00. SAGE Periodical Press, 2455 Teller Road, Thousand Oaks CA 91320. **Tel** (805)499-0721, FAX (805)499-0871, telex 100799. **LC** H1; .A472. **DD** 302. **NLM** W1 AM281L. **[CCC]. Pr Rev. Acid Free.** available on microfilm and microfiche from University Microfilms International (UMI). Documents available from The Genuine Article, UMI Article Clearinghouse. ***Continues*** *Political Research, Organization and Design.*
**Desc:** Focuses on theme-organized issues prepared under guest editors on emerging cross-disciplinary interests, research, and problems in the social sciences.
**Ind/Abst** ABC POL SCI; Acad. Abstr. Full Text Elite (July 1990-); Acad. Abstr. (July 1990-); Acad. Ind. [Computer File] (1987-); Acad. Search (July 1990-); Am. Hist. Life (1970-); Annu. Bibliogr. Engl. Lang. Lit.; Appl. Soc. Sci. Index Abstr.; Commun. Abstr.; Contents Pages Manage.; Crim. Justice Abstr.; Curr. Contents Soc. Behav. Sci.; Curr. Index J. Educ.; Educ. Adm. Abstr. (?-?); Expand. Acad. Index (1987-); Health Plan. Adminis.; High. Educ. Abstr. (1965-19??); Hum. Resour. Abstr. (?-?); Index Period. Artic. Relat. Law (19??-19??); INFO-SOUTH Abstr.; Int. Bibliogr. Sociol.; Int. Polit. Sci. Abstr.; Mag. Search; Middle East Abstr. Index; Newsp. Period. Abstr. (1991-); PAIS Int. Print (1991-); Psychol. Abstr. (1962-); PsycINFO; PsycLit; Res. Alert [Full Cov.]; Sage Public Adm. Abstr. (?-?); Soc. Plann. Policy Dev. Abstr.; Soc. Sci. Source (Jul. 1990-); Soc. Sci. Cit. Index [Full Cov.]; Soc. Sci. Index; Soc. Sci. Index Fulltext (Sept. 1988-) [Full Txt.]; Sociol. Abstr. (?-?); Sociol. Educ. Abstr.; SportSearch; U.S. Polit. Sci. Doc.; Urban Aff. Abstr.; Women Stud. Abstr.; Work Relat. Abstr.

US/0192-5903
**AMERICAN COMMUNITIES TOMORROW.** Vol. 1 (1978)-. Periodical. English. Twice a year (Spring & Fall). $25.00. Social Science Services & Resources, PO Box 241, Aurora IL 60507.

US/1051-8967
**AMERICAN JOURNAL OF CASE MANAGEMENT, THE.** (JOURNAL OF CASE MANAGEMENT.). **Added/Corp** Case Management Institute. (1991)-. Periodical. English. qt. $39.00 (1 year, individuals), $69.00 (2 year, individuals), $78.00 (1 year, institutions), $129.00 (2 year, institutions) US; $44.00 (1 year, individuals), $79.00 (2 year, individuals), $87.00 (1 year, institutions), $149.00 (2 year, institutions) other. Springer Publishing Company, 536 Broadway, New York NY 10012-3955. **Tel** (212)431-4370, FAX (212)941-7842. **ED** Joan Quinn,RN,MS,FAAN. Index available. cum. index. **Bk Rev. Ad Acc. Pr Rev.**
**Desc:** A comprehensive resource offering the latest thinking on contemporary case management, philosophy and practice.

US/0002-9246
**AMERICAN JOURNAL OF ECONOMICS AND SOCIOLOGY, THE.** [Am. j. econ. sociol.]. **Added/Corp** Robert Schalkenbach Foundation. Vol. 1 (Oct. 1941)-. Periodical. English (summaries and/or abstracts in French, Russian and Chinese). qt (Jan., Apr., July, Oct.). $40.00 (one year), $80.00 (two year). American Journal of Economics & Sociology, 41 East 72nd Street, New York NY 10021. **Tel** (212)988-1680. **ED** Frank C. Genovese. **LC** H1; .A48. **DD** 305. **NLM** W1 AM45V. **CODEN** AJESA3. **[CCC].** Index available (bound in Oct. issue). **Pr Rev. Acid Free. Circ:** 2,500. available on microfilm and microfiche from University Microfilms International (UMI). Documents available from The Genuine Article, UMI Article Clearinghouse.
**Desc:** A scientific journal which seeks to report and encourage interdisciplinary cooperation, research, and synthesis in the social sciences and philosophy as a means of ameliorating economic, social and political problems.
**Ind/Abst** ABC POL SCI; ABI/INFORM Glob. Ed.; ABI Inform Ondisc (Jan. 1975-); Acad. Abstr. Full Text Elite (Jan. 1991-); Acad. Abstr. (Jan. 1991-); Acad. Ind. [Computer File] (1987-); Acad. Search (Jan. 1991-); Am. Hist. Life (1963-); Arts Humanit. Citation Index [Select. Cov.]; BioBusiness (1986-); Contents Recent Econ. J.; Contents Pages Manage.; Crim. Justice Abstr.; Curr. Contents Soc. Behav. Sci.; Econ. Lit. Index (19??-); Educ. Adm. Abstr.; Energy Res. Abstr. (Apr. 1976-); Expand. Acad. Index (1987-); Geogr. Abstr. Human Geogr. (?-?); Health Plan. Adminis.; Hum. Resour. Abstr.; Index Period. Artic. Relat. Law (19??-19??); INFO-SOUTH Abstr.; Int. Aerosp. Abstr.; Int. Bibliogr. Sociol.; Int. Labour Doc.; Int. Polit. Sci. Abstr.; J. Econ. Lit.; J. Plan. Lit.; LABORDOC; Leis. Recreat. Tour. Abstr.; Linguist. Lang. Behav. Abstr.; Mag. Search; Middle East Abstr. Index; Multicult. Educ. Abstr.; Newsp. Period. Abstr. (1991-); PAIS Int. Print (1991-); Peace Res. Abstr. J. (1965-1981); Res. Alert [Full Cov.]; Rural Dev. Abstr.; Sage Public Adm. Abstr.; Sage Race Relat. Abstr.; Soc. Plann. Policy Dev. Abstr.; Soc. Sci. Source (Jul. 1990-); Soc. Sci. Cit. Index [Full Cov.]; Soc. Sci. Index; Soc. Sci. Index Fulltext (Oct. 1988-) [Full Txt.]; Soc. Work Abstr. [Select. Cov.]; Sociol. Abstr. [Full Cov.]; Sociol. Educ. Abstr.; SportSearch; Stud. Women Abstr.; U.S. Polit. Sci. Doc. (199?-); Urban Aff. Abstr.; West. Hist. Q.; Women Stud. Abstr.; Work Relat. Abstr.; World Agric. Econ.

US/0887-7653
**AMERICAN JOURNAL OF ISLAMIC SOCIAL SCIENCES, THE.** [Am. j. Islam. soc. sci.]. **Added/Corp** Association of Muslim Social Scientists. International Institute of Islamic Thought. **VFOAT** Islamic Social Sciences; AJISS. Vol. 2, No. 1 (July 1985)-. Academic Scholarly Publication. English. Four times a year (Mar., June, Sept., Dec.). $30.00 (individuals); $45.00 (institutions). American Islamic Journal of Social Sciences, PO Box 669, Herndon VA 22070. **Tel** (703)471-1133, FAX (703)471-3922. **LC** BP1; .A56. **DD** 3909/.0917671. Index available. **Bk Rev. Ad Acc. Circ:** 2,000. available on microfilm and microfiche from University Microfilms International (UMI). ***Continues*** *American Journal of Islamic Studies, 0742-6763.*
**Desc:** Committed to serious research and scholarship, the journal wishes to serve as a bridge between muslim intellectuals and scholars all over the world to effect the development of a scholarly approach in the field of Islamic social sciences and human studies.
**Ind/Abst** Am. Hist. Life (1985-); Index Islam. Lit.; Index Book Rev. Relig.; Int. Bibliogr. Sociol.; Int. Polit. Sci. Abstr.; Linguist. Lang. Behav. Abstr.; PAIS Int. Print; Relig. Index One Period.; Soc. Plann. Policy Dev. Abstr.; Sociol. Abstr.; Middle East J.

US/0569-7344
**AMERICAN REVIEW OF ART AND SCIENCE.** ***Suspended.*** **See** The Arts-Art.

GW/0178-1987
**AMERICAN STUDIES (MUNICH, GERMANY).** (AMERICAN STUDIES.). [Am. stud. (Munch., Schr.reihe)]. (1983)-. Monographic series. English (German). Price varies per volume. Wilhelm Fink Verlag, Ohmstrasse 5, D 80802 Munich Germany. **Tel** 011 49 89 348017, 348018. ***Continues*** *Amerikastudien.*
**Ind/Abst** Abstr. Engl. Stud.; MLA Int. Bibl. Books Artic. Mod. Lang. Lit.

US/0275-8407
**AMS STUDIES IN MODERN SOCIETY.** [AMS stud. mod. soc.]. **VFOAT** A.M.S. Studies in Modern Society. No. 15 (1982)-. Monographic series. English. ir. Price varies per volume. AMS Press Inc., 56 East 13th Street, New York NY 10003. **Tel** (212)777-4700, FAX (212)995-5413, telex 710 581 2302.
**Desc:** Presents volumes on issues that affect society today. Topics have included the women's movement, housing, public policy, racial conflict, and capital punishment.

RM/1015-9606
**ANALELE UNIVERSITATII DIN GALATI. FASCICULA I, STIINTE SOCIALE SI UMANISTE.** [An. Univ. Galati, Fasc. I St. soc. um.]. Bulletin. Romanian (French and German). an. Price varies. Redactia Analelor, 6200 Galati, Str Domneasca Nr. 47 Romania. **Tel** 40 93 413602, FAX 40 93 412328. **ED** Mihai Jascanu. **UDC** 3. **Bk Rev. Ad Acc. Pr Rev. Circ:** 250 (ctrl). Documents available.
**Ind/Abst** Annu. Bibliogr. Engl. Lang. Lit.

RM
**ANALELE UNIVERSITATII DIN TIMISOARA. STIINTE SOCIALE SI ECONOMICE.** **Added/Corp** Universitatea din Timisoara. **VFOAT** Stiinte Sociale Si Economice. Vol. 1 (1982)-. Periodical. English (French, German and Romanian). an. DM164.00. Universitatea Din Timisoara Facultatea de Stiinte Economice Bul Vasile Parvan, NR 4, 1900 Timisoara Romania. **Tel** 961/12805. **(Subscription address:** Kubon & Sagner, ABT Zeitschriftenimport, D 80328 Munich Germany.) **LC** H8.R65; A53. **DD** 300/.5. Index available. cum. index. **Bk Rev.** ***Separated from*** *Analele Universitatii Din Timisoara. Stiinte Economice* ***and*** *Analele Universitatii Din Timisoara. Stiinte Sociale.*

AG
**ANALES - ACADEMIA NACIONAL DE CIENCIAS MORALES Y POLITICAS.** **Main/Corp** Academia Nacional de Ciencias Morales y Politicas. (1972)-. Spanish. Academia Nacional de Ciencias Morales Y Politicas, Avda Corrientes, Buenos Aires 1723 Argentina. **LC** H19; .A53a.

CL/0716-6478
**ANALES DEL INSTITUTO DE LA PATAGONIA. SERIE CIENCIAS SOCIALES.** [An. Inst. Patagon., Ser. Cienc. soc.]. **Added/Corp** Universidad de Magallanes. Instituto de la Patagonia. **VFOAT** Serie Ciencias Sociales; Anales del Instituto de la Patagonia, Universidad de Magallanes. Vol. 15 (1984)-. Periodical. Spanish. an. 2.500Chil$ Chile; $10.00 other. Universidad de Magallanes, Punta Arenas, Ave Presidente Bulnes Km 4, Casilla Correo 113-D, Punta Arenas Chile. **Tel** FAX (061)223039, telex 380004 UMAE - CK. **ED** Sr B Mateo Martinic. **LC** F3186; .A57. **DD** 983/.644/005. **CODEN** APSOE5. Index available. cum. index. **Bk Rev. Circ:** 1,000 (ctrl). Documents available from BIOSIS Document Express. ***Continues in part*** *Anales del Instituto de la Patagonia, 0085-1922.*
**Desc:** Original research articles on social and natural sciences referring to Patagonia, Tierra del Fuego, Antarctica, and adjacent islands in the Pacific Ocean.
**Ind/Abst** Biol. Abstr. (1991-).

PE
**ANALISIS.** No. 1- Jan./March 1977-. Periodical. Spanish. Apartado 11093, Correo Santa Beatriz, Lima Peru. **LC** H8; .A53.

GW/0171-5860
**ANALYSE & KRITIK.** **VFOAT** Analyse und Kritik. (19??)-. Periodical. German (English). sa. DM72.80 Germany; DM80.40 other. Westdeutscher Verlag GmbH, Postfach 5829, D 65048 Wiesbaden Germany. **Tel** 011 49 611 160220. **(Subscription address:** VVA Bertelsmann Dist GmbH, Postfach 7600, D 33310 Guetersloh Germany) **LC** H1; .A12. **DD** 300/.5. **[CCC]. Ad Acc. Circ:** 800.

GW
**ANGEWANDTE SOZIALFORSCHUNG.** (19??)-. German. ir (4 issues). DM60.00. Henrik Kreutz, Kneippstrasse 1, W 8500 Nuernberg FR Germany.
**Ind/Abst** Linguist. Lang. Behav. Abstr.; Soc. Plann. Policy Dev. Abstr.; Sociol. Abstr. [Full Cov.]; Soc. Res. Methodol. Abstr. (1992-).

FR/0563-9727
**ANNALES DE L'UNIVERSITE DES SCIENCES SOCIALES DE TOULOUSE.** [Ann. Univ. sci. soc. Toulouse]. (1971)-. Periodical. French. an. 140.00F. Universite Toulouse I Science Sociales, Place Anatole France, 31042 Toulouse Cedex France. **Tel** 61 23 11 45. **UDC** 3:001. ***Continues*** *Annales de la Faculte de Droit et des Sciences Economiques de Toulouse, 0986-1254.*

FR
**ANNALES; ECONOMIES, SOCIETES, CIVILISATIONS.** (19??)-. French. bm. $108.00. Librairie Armand Colin, BP 22, 41354 Vineuil Cedex France. **Tel** 011 33 54 438994. Documents available from The Genuine Article.
**Ind/Abst** Am. Hist. Life (1954-); Res. Alert [Full Cov.]; Soc. Sci. Cit. Index [Full Cov.].

IT/0531-9870
**ANNALI DELLA FONDAZIONE LUIGI EINAUDI.** [Ann. Fond. Luigi Einaudi]. **Main/Corp** Fondazione Luigi Einaudi. Vol. 1 (1967)-. Italian. an. L50.000. Fondazione Luigi Einaudi, Via Principe Amedeo 34, 10123 Turin Italy. **LC** H17; .F65. Index available. cum. index. **Bk Rev. Ad Acc.**
**Ind/Abst** Am. Hist. Life (1967-); Int. Bibliogr. Sociol.

IT
**ANNALI DELL'ISTITUTO "ALCIDE CERVI".** **Added/Corp** Istituto "Alcide Cervi". **VFOAT** Annali. (1979)-. Periodical. Italian. an. price varies per volume. Edizioni Dedalo Spa, Casella Postale 362, Bari 70100 Italy. **Tel** 011 39 080 5311400, FAX 011 39 080 5311414. **LC** HD1536.I8; A64. **DD** 305.5/63.

US/0002-7162
**ANNALS OF THE AMERICAN ACADEMY OF POLITICAL AND SOCIAL SCIENCE.** [Ann. Am. Acad. Polit. Soc. Sci.]. **Added/Corp** American Academy of Political and Social Science. Vol. 1 (1890)-. English. bm (Jan., Mar., May, July, Sept., Nov.). $168.00 (paper edition); $196.00 (cloth edition). SAGE Periodical Press, 2455 Teller Road, Thousand Oaks CA 91320. **Tel** (805)499-0721, FAX (805)499-0871, telex 100799. **ED** Richard D. Lambert and Alan W. Heston (associate

editor). **LC** H1; .A4. **DD** 300. **NLM** W1 AN626K. **CODEN** AAYPA. Index available. cum. index. **Pr Rev. Acid Free.** available on microfilm and microfiche from University Microfilms International (UMI). Documents available from The Genuine Article, UMI Article Clearinghouse, Magazine Collection.
**Desc:** Forum for the interdisciplinary discussion of single problems and policy issues affecting America and the world community.
**Ind/Abst** ABC POL SCI; Abstr. Anthropol.; Acad. Abstr. Full Text Elite (July 1990-); Acad. Abstr. (July 1990-); Acad. Ind. [Computer File] (1984-); Acad. Search (July 1990-); Am. Hist. Life (1954-); Am. Bibliogr. Slavic East Europ. Stud.; Annu. Bibliogr. Engl. Lang. Lit.; Book Rev. Digest; Book Rev. Index; Br. Archaeol. Bibliogr.; Commun. Abstr.; Crim. Justice Abstr.; Curr. Contents Soc. Behav. Sci.; Curr. Geogr. Publ. (199?-); Educ. Adm. Abstr. (?-?); EMBASE; Expand. Acad. Index (1985-); Gen. Period. Index (1985-); Health Plan. Adminis.; High. Educ. Abstr. (1965-19??); Hospit. Health Admin. Index; Hum. Resour. Abstr. (?-?); Index Period. Artic. Relat. Law (19??-19??); Int. Bibliogr. Sociol.; Int. Dev. Abstr. (?-?); Int. Labour Doc.; Int. Polit. Sci. Abstr.; J. Econ. Lit.; LABORDOC; Linguist. Lang. Behav. Abstr.; Mag. Index Plus (1989-); Mag. Search; Middle East Abstr. Index; Newsp. Period. Abstr. (1990-); PAIS Int. Print (1991-); Peace Res. Abstr. J. (1966-1971, 1976-1977, 1979-1983, 1988-); Read. Guide Period. Lit.; Res. Alert [Full Cov.]; Sage Public Adm. Abstr.; Sage Urban Stud. Abstr (?-?); Soc. Plann. Policy Dev. Abstr.; Soc. Sci. Cit. Index [Full Cov.]; Soc. Sci. Index; Soc. Sci. Index Fulltext (Nov. 1986-) [Full Txt.]; Soc. Work Abstr. (Spring, Summer 1987-) [Select. Cov.]; Sociol. Abstr.; SportSearch; Mag. Index (1977-); U.S. Polit. Sci. Doc.; Urban Aff. Abstr.; Women Stud. Abstr.; Work Relat. Abstr.

JA/0563-8054
**ANNALS OF THE INSTITUTE OF SOCIAL SCIENCE.** **Added/Corp** Tokyo Daigaku. Shakai Kagaku Kenkyujo. No. 7 (1966)-. Periodical. English. an. Institute of Social Sciences, University of Tokyo, 7-3-1 Hongo, Bunkyo ku Tokyo 113 Japan. ***Continues*** *Social Science Abstracts.*
**Desc:** Includes a list of its publications and the table of contents of Shakai Kagaku Kenkyu (Journal of Social Science).
**Ind/Abst** Int. Bibliogr. Sociol.; PAIS Int. Print (1991-?).

US/0160-7383
**ANNALS OF TOURISM RESEARCH.** [Ann. tour. res.]. **Added/Corp** University of Wisconsin--Stout. Dept. of Habitational Resources, Tourism. Society for the Advancement of the Tourism Industry. **VFOAT** ATR, Annals of Tourism Research. Vol. 1, (Nov. 1973)-. Periodical. English (summaries and/or abstracts in French). Four times a year. $291.00 The Americas; £195.00 other. Pergamon Press, An Imprint of Elsevier Science Ltd., The Boulevard, Langford Lane, Kidlington, Oxford OX5 1GB United Kingdom. **Tel** 011 44 865 843000, 011 44 865 843699, FAX 011 44 865 843010. **(Subscription address:** Elsevier Science Ltd. Oxford Fulfillment Centre, PO Box 800, Kidlington, Oxford OX5 1DX United Kingdom.**) ED** Jafar Jafari (editor' address: Department of Habitational Resources, University of Wisconsin-Stout, Menomonie WI 54571). **LC** G155.A1; A58. **DD** 338.4/7/9105. **[CCC].** Index available. cum. index. **Bk Rev. Ad Acc. Pr Rev. Circ:** 1,700. available on microfilm and microfiche from University Microfilms International (UMI). Documents available from The Genuine Article.
**Desc:** A social sciences journal focusing upon the academic perspectives on tourism. A multidisciplinary intercultural journal, dedicated to developing theoretical constructs.
**Ind/Abst** Abstr. Anthropol.; Am. Bibliogr. Slavic East Europ. Stud.; Anthropol. Lit. (-Vol. 11, 1989); Curr. Contents Soc. Behav. Sci.; Geogr. Abstr. Human Geogr.; Int. Dev. Abstr.; LABORDOC; Leis. Recreat. Tour. Abstr.; Linguist. Lang. Behav. Abstr.; PAIS Int. Print (1991-); Res. Alert [Full Cov.]; Rural Dev. Abstr.; Soc. Plann. Policy Dev. Abstr.; Soc. Sci. Cit. Index [Full Cov.]; Sociol. Abstr.; SPORT Discus; SportSearch; World Agric. Econ.

BE/0066-2380
**ANNEE SOCIALE / INSTITUT DE SOCIOLOGIE, UNIVERSITE LIBRE DE BRUXELLES, L'.** 1960-. French. sa. 1500F. Cendis/Ris, Ave Jeanne 44, Center Soc Econ Reg, 1050 Brussels Belgium. **Tel** 011 32 2 6423350. **LC** HN501; .A56. Index available. **Ad Acc. Circ:** 1,000 (ctrl).
**Desc:** A synthesis of Belgian social life.
**Ind/Abst** Int. Bibliogr. Sociol.; PAIS Int. Print (1991-).

US/0731-339X
**ANNUAL GUIDE TO PUBLIC POLICY EXPERTS, THE.** 1982-. English. an. $4.00. The Heritage Foundation, 214 Massachusetts Avenue NE, Washington DC 20002. **Tel** (202)546-4400. **LC** H50; .A55. **DD** 361.6/1/02573.

VI/0069-0503
**ANNUAL REPORT.** **Main/Corp** Caribbean Research Institute. (1965)-. English. an. Free. College of Virgin Island, Caribbean Research Institute, St Thomas VI West Indies. **LC** H67.C28; A34.

US
**ANNUAL REPORT - ECONOMIC AND SOCIAL COMMISSION FOR ASIA AND THE PACIFIC.** **Main/Corp** United Nations. Economic and Social Commission for Asia and the Pacific. (19??)-. Government Publication. English. an. United Nations Publications, 2 United Nations Plaza, Room DC2 0853, Department 007C, New York NY 10017. **Tel** (212)963-8303, (800)253-9646. **LC** JX1977; .A2 subser; HC411. **DD** 300/.8 S; 341.7/59. ***Continues*** *United Nations. Economic Commission for Asia and the Far East. Report.*

UK
**ANNUAL REPORT - INSTITUTE OF DEVELOPMENT STUDIES AT THE UNIVERSITY OF SUSSEX.** **Main/Corp** University of Sussex Institute of Development Studies. 3rd (1968/1969)-. Periodical. English. an. Free on request. Institute of Development Studies, University of Sussex, Brighton BN1 9RE England. **Tel** 011 44 1273 606261, FAX 011 44 1273 678420, telex 877997 IDSBTN G. **ED** Zoe Mars. **Circ:** 7,500. available on videocassette.
**Desc:** An account of research, teaching, and consultancy at the IDS - a post-doctoral research institute working on Third World problems from an interdisciplinary social science perspective.

US/0093-5085
**ANNUAL REPORT - NORTH CAROLINA HUMAN RELATIONS COMMISSION.** (ANNUAL REPORT.). **Main/Corp** North Carolina. Human Relations Commission. English. an. North Carolina Human Relations Commission, PO Box 12525, Raleigh NC 27605. **LC** F251; .N835A. **DD** 353.9/756/0084.

JA
**ANNUAL REPORT OF THE INSTITUTE OF SOCIAL SCIENCES, MEIJI UNIVERSITY.** **Main/Corp** Meiji Daigaku, Tokyo. Shakai Kagaku Kenkyujo. **VFOAT** Meiji Daigaku Shakai Kagaku Kenkyujo Nempo. No. 1 (1959)-. Japanese. Meiji University, 1-1 Higashi-Mita, Tama-Ku, 1-chome, Kawasaki-Shi, Kanagawa-Ken 214 Japan. **LC** H8; .M375B.

US/0361-462X
**ANNUAL REPORT - SOCIAL SCIENCE RESEARCH COUNCIL (NEW YORK).** (ANNUAL REPORT - SOCIAL SCIENCE RESEARCH COUNCIL.). **Main/Corp** Social Science Research Council (U.S.). (1927)-. English. an. Free. Social Science Research Council / New York, 605 3rd Avenue, New York NY 10158. **Tel** (212)661-0280, FAX (212)370-7896. **ED** David L. Sills. **LC** H11; .S6. **DD** 300/.6/273. **NLM** W1 SO128. **Circ:** 7,500. ***Continues*** *Annual Report of the Chairman - Social Science Research Council, 0740-655X.*

US
**ANNUAL REPORT / THE BROOKINGS INSTITUTION.** **See** Economics.

US/0092-7481
**ANNUAL REPORT / THE URBAN INSTITUTE.** [Annu. rep. - Urban Inst.]. **Main/Corp** Urban Institute. English. an. The Urban Institute, 2100 Main Street Northwest, Washington DC 20037. **Tel** (202)833-7200. **ED** Susan Brown. **LC** HT167; .U72A. **DD** 361. **Circ:** 10,000. ***Continues*** *Report / Urban Institute Report, 1042-7783.*

ZA
**ANNUAL REPORT - UNIVERSITY OF ZAMBIA. SCHOOL OF HUMANITIES & SOCIAL SCIENCES.** **See** Humanities.

UK
**ANNUAL REVIEW - TAVISTOCK INSTITUTE OF HUMAN RELATIONS, LONDON.** **Main/Corp** Tavistock Institute of Human Relations, London. (19??)-. Corporate Report. English. an. Free. Tavistock Institute, 120 Belsize Lane, London NW3 5BA England. **Tel** 011 44 71 435 7111, FAX 011 44 71 794 4661. **LC** HM47.G72; L67a. **DD** 362/.9421.
**Desc:** Review of the previous year's activities of the Tavistock Institute of Human Relations.

US/0275-312X
**ANTARA KITA.** ***Suspended.*** [Antara kita]. No. 1 (Dec. 1976)-Suspended. Periodical. English. Antara Kita Randal Baier, 110 Olin Library Cornell University, Ithaca NY 14853. **Tel** (607)255-4247. **DD** 959. ***Continues*** *Kabar Angin.*

GR/0302-1122
**ANTHROPINES SHESEIS.** (ANTHROPINES SCHESEIS.). [Anthrop. sheseis]. V. 1- 1972-. Greek, Modern. $10.00. Voukourestiou 4, Athens Greece. **LC** H8; .A57.

CK/0066-5045
**ANUARIO COLOMBIANO DE HISTORIA SOCIAL Y DE LA CULTURA.** V. 1- (No. 1- ); 1963-. Spanish. an. Universidad de Antioquia / Departamento de Publicaciones, Apartado 1226, Medellin Colombia. **Tel** 11 57 4 2631311, 011 57 4 2630011, FAX 11 57 4 2638282.
**Ind/Abst** Am. Hist. Life (1964-1965, 1969-); HAPI Hisp. Am. Period. Index.

CR/0377-7316
**ANUARIO DE ESTUDIOS CENTROAMERICANOS.** [Anu. estud. centroam.]. 1- 1974-. Academic Scholarly Publication. Spanish (English). Twice a year (July and December). C360.00 Costa Rica; $18.00 other. Universidad de Costa Rica / Publicaciones, Apartado 75, 2060 Ciudad Univeridad, San Jose Costa Rica. **Tel** 011 506 2247051, 011 506 2253133, FAX 011 506 342723, telex 2544 UNICORI. **ED** Hector Perez Brignoli. **LC** F1421; .A56. **UDC** 972.8(058); 908.728(058). **Circ:** 750.
**Desc:** Contains scholarly articles and essays on the history, sociology and learning of Central America. Includes perspectives and reinterpretations, with statistical documentation.
**Ind/Abst** Am. Hist. Life (1974-); HAPI Hisp. Am. Period. Index; Int. Bibliogr. Sociol.; PAIS Int. Print (1991-).

JA
**AOYAMA SHAKAI KAGAKU KIYO.** **Added/Corp** Aoyama Gakuin Daigaku, Tokyo. Daigakuin. **VFOAT** Aoyama Journal of Social Sciences. No. 1 (March 1973)-. Periodical. Japanese (English). Aoyama Gakuin Daigoku Daigakuin, 4-4-25 Shibuya Shibuya-ku, Tokyo 150 Japan. **Tel** 03 4098111. **LC** H8; A.58. **Circ:** 1,100 (ctrl).

US
**APPLIED SOCIAL RESEARCH METHODS SERIES.** **See** Sociology.

PE/0252-1865
**APUNTES.** **Added/Corp** Universidad del Pacifico. Centro de Investigacion. Vol. 1 (1973)-. Spanish. sa. price varies per volume. Universidad del Pacifico Centro de Investigacion, Avenida Salaverry 2020 Jesus Maria, Lima 100 Peru. **Tel** 011 51 14 712277, telex 08787. **LC** H8; .A65. **DD** 300/.5. **Circ:** 800.
**Ind/Abst** HAPI Hisp. Am. Period. Index; Int. Bibliogr. Sociol.

CE
**AQUINAS JOURNAL.** **Added/Corp** Aquinas College (Colombo, Sri Lanka). Vol. 1, No. 1 (June 1984)-. Academic Scholarly Publication. English. be. $10.00. Aquinas Journal / Aquinas College of Higher Studies, Colombo 8, Sri Lanka. **Tel** 694014/694709. **ED** Rev. Fr. Chrispin Leo. **LC** AS475.A1; A67. **DD** 052. Index available (not with every issue). cum. index. **Bk Rev. Pr Rev. Acid Free. Circ:** 250.
**Desc:** Interdisciplinary learned journal.
**Ind/Abst** Bibliogr. Mission.

UK/0269-2325
**ARAB JOURNAL OF THE SOCIAL SCIENCES, THE.** ***Suspended.*** (1986)-(19??). Periodical. English. sa. Kegan Paul International Ltd, PO Box 256, 118 Bedford Avenue, London WC1B35W England. **Tel** 011 44 71 580 5511.
**Ind/Abst** Am. Hist. Life.

GW/0066-6505
**ARCHIV FUER SOZIALGESCHICHTE.** **See** History(General)-History of Europe.

GW/0004-1157
**ARGUMENT, DAS.** **See** Philosophy.

CN/1191-1115
**ARGUS ETHNIQUE.** [Arg. ethn.]. **VFOAT** Ethnique. Vol. 1, No. 1 (1989)-. French. an (Spring). 39.00Can$ Canada; 44.00Can$ US; 49.00Can$ others. Argus Communications Inc, 1161 Lac Cache, CP 26, St Alexis, Quebec, J0K 1V0 Canada. **Tel** (819)265-2072, FAX (819)265-3135. **DD** 305.8/0025/714.

US/0747-9921
**ARIS FUNDING REPORT. SOCIAL AND NATURAL SCIENCES REPORT.** **Added/Corp** Academic Research Information System. **VFOAT** Social and Natural Sciences Report; Funding Reports. **VAT** Academic Research Information System. Social and Natural Sciences Report. (198?)-. Periodical. English. ir. $225.00. Academic Research Information System, 2940 16th Street, Suite 314, San Francisco CA 94103. **Tel** (415)558-8133, FAX (415)558-8135.

US/0196-8122
**ARKANSAS SOCIAL STUDIES TEACHER, THE.** [Ark. soc. stud. teach.]. V. 1- 1975-. Periodical. English. an. $2.00. Kent Collector, SUNY Plattsburgh Art Museum, Plattsburgh NY 12901. **LC** H62; .A664. **DD** 300/.7/1073.

DK/0106-2778
**ARSBERETNING / ROSKILDE UNIVERSITETSCENTER, INSTITUT FOR GEOGRAFI, SAMFUNDSANALYSE OG DATALOGI.** **Main/Corp** Roskilde Universitetscenter. Institut For Geografi, Samfundsanalyse Og Datalogi.

# Social Sciences

Danish. an. Roskilde Universitetscenter Institut for Geografi Samfundsanalyse Og Datalogi, Postbox 260, 4000 Roskilde Denmark. **LC** H67.R744; R67A.

AT/0812-7158
**ARTISAN MELBOURNE.** See Education-Teaching and Curriculum.

TH
**ASIAN ACTION : NEWSLETTER OF THE ASIAN CULTURAL FORUM ON DEVELOPMENT. Added/Corp** Asian Cultural Forum on Development. No. 1-5 (1976)-. Newsletter. English. **LC** HN655.2.C6; A75. **DD** 307.1/4/095. cum. index.
**Ind/Abst** Hum. Rights Intern. Rep.

II
**ASIAN JOURNAL OF ECONOMICS AND SOCIAL STUDIES.** See Economics.

HK/0304-8675
**ASIAN PROFILE.** [Asian profile]. (1973)-. English. bm. $80.00 (1 year), $160.00 (2 year). Asian Research Service, Sub Department, GPO Box 2232, Hong Kong Hong Kong. **Tel** 011 852 5 707227, telex 63899 CONPA HX. **ED** Nelson Leung. **LC** DS1; .A4746. **DD** 950/.05. **Bk Rev**, (Qty: 10). **Ad Acc**; **Adv Mgr:** Winnie Leing. **Circ:** 2,000. available on microfilm and microfiche from University Microfilms International (UMI).
**Desc:** Devoted to multi-disciplinary study of Asian affairs. Provides a forum for the exchange of ideas among scholars.
**Ind/Abst** Am. Hist. Life (1973-?)(1979-?); Asia.-Pac. Econ. Lit.; Hum. Rights Intern. Rep.; Index Islam. Lit.; Int. Bibliogr. Sociol.; Int. Polit. Sci. Abstr.; Leis. Recreat. Tour. Abstr.; Middle East Abstr. Index; PAIS Int. Print (1991-); Rice Abstr.; Rural Dev. Abstr.; Soils Fert.; World Agric. Econ.

US/0004-4687
**ASIAN SURVEY.** [Asian surv.]. **Added/Corp** University of California, Berkeley. Institute of International Studies. Vol. 1 (Mar. 1961)-. Periodical. English. mo. $49.00 (individuals), $98.00 (institutions), $27.00 (students). University of California Press, 2120 Berkeley Way, Berkeley CA 94720. **Tel** (510)642-4191, (510)642-3907, FAX (510)642-9917. **ED** Robert A. Scalapino, Leo E. Rose, and Joyce K. Kallgren. **LC** DS1; .A492. **DD** 330.9/5/042. **[CCC]**. **Bk Rev**. **Ad Acc**. **Pr Rev. Circ:** 3,100. available on microfilm and microfiche from University Microfilms International (UMI). Documents available from The Genuine Article, UMI Article Clearinghouse. **Supersedes** Far Eastern Survey, 0362-8949.
**Desc:** Study of political, economic and social trends in contemporary Asia.
**Ind/Abst** ABC POL SCI; Abstr. Anthropol.; Acad. Abstr. Full Text Elite (Jan. 1992-); Acad. Abstr. (Jan. 1992-); Acad. Ind. [Computer File] (1987-); Acad. Search (Jan. 1992-); Am. Hist. Life (1968-); Am. Bibliogr. Slavic East Europ. Stud.; Asia.-Pac. Econ. Lit.; Crim. Justice Abstr.; Curr. Contents Soc. Behav. Sci.; Curr. Geogr. Publ. (199?-); Expand. Acad. Index (1989-); Geogr. Abstr. Human Geogr.; Index Islam. Lit.; INFO-SOUTH Abstr.; Int. Bibliogr. Sociol.; Int. Dev. Abstr.; Int. Labour Doc.; Int. Polit. Sci. Abstr.; LABORDOC; Leis. Recreat. Tour. Abstr.; Mag. Search; Middle East Abstr. Index; Newsp. Period. Abstr. (1989-); Res. Alert [Full Cov.]; Rural Dev. Abstr.; Sage Public Adm. Abstr. (?-?); Soc. Sci. Source (Jan. 1992-); Soc. Sci. Cit. Index [Full Cov.]; Soc. Sci. Index; Soc. Sci. Index Fulltext (Sept. 1988-) [Full Txt.]; U.S. Polit. Sci. Doc.; World Agric. Econ.

US/1045-5930
**ASPEN INSTITUTE QUARTERLY (QUEENSTOWN, MD.), THE. Ceased.** (THE ASPEN INSTITUTE QUARTERLY : AQ : ISSUES AND ARGUMENTS FOR LEADERS.). [Aspen Inst. q.]. **Added/Corp** Aspen Institute. **VFOAT** AQ. Vol. 1, No. 1 (Autumn 1989)-Vol. 7, No. 1 (1995) 1#. Academic Scholarly Publication. English. qt. Aspen Institute, PO Box 444, Carmichael Road, Queenstown MD 21658. **Tel** (401)267-7168, (303)925-7010. **(Subscription address:** AQ, PO Box 16975, North Hollywood CA 91615.) **LC** AS30; .A87.

CN/1189-3532
**ASSESSMENT HIGHLIGHTS. GRADE 9 SOCIAL STUDIES ACHIEVEMENT TESTING PROGRAM.** See Education.

UK/0950-2238
**ASSIA. APPLIED SOCIAL SCIENCES INDEX & ABSTRACTS.** See Social Sciences-Abstracting, Bibliographies and Statistics.

UK
**ASSIA PLUS [COMPUTER FILE].** See Social Sciences-Abstracting, Bibliographies and Statistics.

UK/0265-2587
**ASSIGNATION.** [ASSIGnation]. **VFOAT** Aslib Social Sciences Information Group Nation. (1983)-. Periodical. English. qt. £15.00. Aslib Social Sciences Information, 5 Tavistock Place Hogan, London WC1 9SS England. **DD** 026.36194105.

FR
**ASSURANCES SOCIALES.** French. qt. 358.29F. Les Editions ESF, 17 rue Viete, 75854 Paris Cedex 17 France. **Tel** 011 33 1 44156200.

FR/0220-1186
**ASTRAPI PARIS. 1978.** [Astrapi Paris, 1978]. (1978)-. Periodical. French. sm (24 issues). 102.51Can$; 682.64F France; 799.00F other. Bayard Presse, Svc Client, 3 rue Bayard/Dept 2, 75393 Paris Cedex 08 France. **Tel** 011 33 1 44356060, 011 33 1 44356262. **(Subscription address:** Bayard Presse Notre Temps, BP2, 99505 Paris Enterprises France.) **UDC** 08.

VE
**ATLANTIDA.** Spanish. Universidad Simon Bolivar, Valle de Sartenejas, Caracas Venezuela. **LC** H8; .A86.
**Ind/Abst** Am. Hist. Life (1963-1972); Indice Hist. Esp.

FR
**ATLAS DE LA REVOLUTION FRANCAISE.** (19??)-. Monographic series. French. ir. Price varies per volume. Editions de l'Ecole des Hautes Etudes en Sciences Sociales, 131 BD Saint Michel, 75005 Paris France. **Tel** 011 33 1 43 54 47 15, FAX 011 33 1 43 54 80 73. **ED** Serge Bonin and Claude Langlois. **Circ:** 2,000.

US/1043-5972
**ATMOSPHERE CRISIS, THE.** [Atmos. crisis]. Vol. 1, Articles 1-100 (1981/1989)-. English. an. $80.00. Social Issues Resources Series Inc, PO Box 2348, Boca Raton FL 33427. **Tel** (800)327-0513, (407)994-0079. **LC** QC912.3; .A85. **DD** 363.73/92.
**Desc:** Contains more than 100 reprints, most from 1988 and 1989, that cover the scientific, sociological, political and medical aspects of the greenhouse effect and ozone depletion.

IT
**ATTI. Main/Corp** Accademia delle Scienze di Torino. Classe di Scienze Morali, Storiche e Filologiche. Vol. 42 (1907)-. Periodical. Italian. ir. Bottega d'Erasmo, Via Gaud Ferrari 9, 10124 Turin Italy. **Supersedes in part** Accademia delle Scienze di Torino. Atti.
**Ind/Abst** BHA : Biblio. Hist. Art.

AT/0818-8149
**AUSTRALIAN SLAVONIC AND EAST EUROPEAN STUDIES : JOURNAL OF THE AUSTRALIAN AND NEW ZEALAND SLAVISTS' ASSOCIATION AND OF THE AUSTRALASIAN ASSOCIATION FOR STUDY OF THE SOCIALIST COUNTRIES.** See Linguistics.

FR
**AUTREMENT. SERIE MONDE. VFOAT** Serie Monde; Monde. No. 35 (January 1989)-. Periodical. French. Fourteen times a year. Editions Autrement, 4 rue d'Enghien, 75010 Paris France. **Tel** 011 33 1 47701250. **LC** IN PROCESS. **Ad Acc**. **Circ:** 20,000. **Continues** Autrement. Hors Serie, 0763-6504.

II
**AVADH JOURNAL OF SOCIAL SCIENCES : AJOSS, THE. Added/Corp** Avadh Society of Social Scientists. **VFOAT** AJOSS. Vol. 1 (Winter 1984)-. Periodical. English. Rs30.00, $8.00 US per issue. Avadh Society of Social Scientists, C/2 Sector G, Aliganj Lucknow-226020 India. **LC** H62.5.I5; A9. **DD** 300/.959.
**Ind/Abst** Soc. Plann. Policy Dev. Abstr.

●US
**BALTIC STUDIES NEWSLETTER. Added/Corp** Association for the Advancement of Baltic Studies. Vol. 17, No. 1 (Mar. 1993)-. Newsletter. English (German). Four times a year. $25.00. Association for the Advancement of Baltic Studies, 111 Knob Hill Road, Hackettstown NJ 07840. **Tel** (908)852-5258. **Continues** Association for the Advancement of Baltic Studies. AABS Newsletter.

US/1052-0996
**BALTIMORE/ANNAPOLIS.** See Business.

AI
**BANBER EREVANI HAMALSARANI. HASARAKAKAN GITUTYUNNER / EREVANI PETAKAN HAMALSARAN. Added/Corp** Erevani Petakan Hamalsaran. **VFOAT** Hasarakakan Gitutyunner; Obshchestvennye Nauki; Vestnik Erevanskogo Universiteta. Obshchestvennye Nauki; Herald. (1967)-. Periodical. Armenian (Russian; table of contents in English). tq. **LC** AS588.E7; A23.
**Formed by the union of** Seriia Iuridicheskikh Nauk; Seriia Istoriko-Filosofskikh Nauk; Seriia Filologicheskikh Nauk **and** Seriia Ekonomicheskikh Nauk.
**Ind/Abst** Numis. Lit.

BL
**BC. VFOAT** BC Politico, Economico E Financiero. (19??)-. Periodical. English. $360. **LC** H8; .B17.

US/0094-3673
**BEHAVIOR SCIENCE RESEARCH. Title Change.** [Behav. sci. res.]. **Added/Corp** Human Relations Area Files, Inc. Vol. 9 (1974)-(1993). Periodical. English. an. Human Relations Area Files, PO Box 703A, Yale Station, New Haven CT 06520. **Tel** (203)624-8619, FAX (203)777-2337. **ED** Melvin Ember and Judith G Camera. **LC** H1; .B45. **DD** 300/.5. **NLM** W1; BE128B. available on microfilm and microfiche from University Microfilms International (UMI). **Continues** Behavior Science Notes, 0005-7886. **Continued by** Cross-Cultural Research, 1069-3971.
**Ind/Abst** Abstr. Res. Pastor. Care Couns. (19??-); Anthropol. Index; Anthropol. Lit.; Appl. Soc. Sci. Index Abstr.; Int. Bibliogr. Sociol.; Int. Polit. Sci. Abstr.; Peace Res. Abstr. J. (1967-1977); Psychol. Abstr. (1974-); PsycINFO; PsycLit; U.S. Polit. Sci. Doc.

US/0163-9269
**BEHAVIORAL & SOCIAL SCIENCES LIBRARIAN.** See Library and Information Sciences.

CC/1000-3541
**BEIFANG LUNCONG.** (PEI FANG LUN TSUNG / [HA-ERH-PIN SHIH FAN TA HSUEH].). [Beifang luncong]. **Added/Corp** Ha-Erh-Pin Shih Fan Ta Hsueh. **VFOAT** Beifang Luncong. (1979)-. Periodical. Chinese. bm. $15.90. **(Subscription address:** China International Book Trading Corporation, PO Box 399, Library Service Department, Beijing 100044 People's Republic of China.) **LC** AS452.H3194; A24. **Continues** Ha-Erh-Pin Shih Yuan Hsueh Pao.
**Desc:** Contains information on the social sciences.

GW/0863-4564
**BERLINER DEBATTE INITIAL : ZEITSCHRIFT FUER SOCIALWISSENSCHAFTLICHEN DISKURS. Added/Corp** Berliner Debatte Initial E.V. **VFOAT** Initial. (1991)-. Periodical. German. Six times a year. DM70.00. Ges Sozialwissen Forschung & Oderberger, Str 44, D 10435 Berlin Germany. **Tel** 011 49 30 4482681. **LC** HM33; .B43. **DD** 300/.5. **Continues** Initial (Berlin, Germany).

US/0882-4355
**BETWEEN OUR SELVES.** [Between our selves]. Vol. 1, No. 1 (Winter 1985)-. Periodical. English. qt. $15.00. B O S, PO Box 1939, Washington DC 20013. **DD** 305.

●BE
**BIBLIO 12. Added/Corp** Commission of the European Communities. Library (Brussels, Belgium). **VFOAT** Biblio Twelve; Biblio Douze. No. 1 (1993)-. Periodical. English (French, German and Italian). **LC** HC241.2; .B52. **Continues** Biblio 1992.

BE
**BIBLIO 1992. Title Change. Added/Corp** Commission of the European Communities. Library (Brussels, Belgium). **VFOAT** Biblio Nineteen Ninety-Two; Biblio Dix-Neuf Cent Quatre-Vingt Douze; Biblio Mille Neuf Cent Quatre-Vingt Douze. No. 1 (1989)-No. 33 (1992). English (French, German and Italian). bm. **LC** IN PROCESS; HC241.2; .B52. **Continued by** Biblio 12.

NE/0922-6842
**BIBLIOGRAFIE VAN NEDERLANDS NATIONAAL EN INTERNATIONAAL ONDERZOEK OP SOCIAAL-WETENSCHAPPELIJK TERREIN.** See Social Sciences-Abstracting, Bibliographies and Statistics.

NE
**BIBLIOGRAFIE VAN REGIONALE ONDERZOEKINGEN OP SOCIAAL-WETENSCHAPPELIJK TERREIN / CENTRAAL BUREAU VOOR DE STATISTIEK, AFDELING BIBLIOTHEEK EN DOCUMENTATIE.** See Social Sciences-Abstracting, Bibliographies and Statistics.

US/0097-7020
**BIBLIOGRAPHIE COURANTE D'ARTICLES DE PERIODIQUES POSTERIEURS A 1944 SUR LES PROBLEMES POLITIQUES, ECONOMIQUES, ET SOCIAUX. SUPPLEMENT. VFOAT** Index to Post-1944 Periodical Articles on Political, Economic, and Social Problems Supplement. Began in 1968. French. an. GK Hall & Co, 100 Front Street, Riverside NJ 08075. **Tel** (800)257-5755 ext. 2223. **LC** AI7; .F6 SUPPL. **DD** 016.05.

BE
**BIBLIOGRAPHIE DE L'AFRIQUE SUD-SAHARIENNE, SCIENCES HUMAINES ET SOCIALES. Added/Corp** Musee Royal de l'Afrique Centrale. (1978)-. French

(Multiple languages). an. 12.00F. Musee Royal de l'Afrique Centrale, Stenweg OP Leuven 13, 1980 Tervuren Belgium. **Tel** 011 32 2 7675401. **ED** Mercel d'Hertefelt. **LC** Z5113; .T33; DT351. **DD** 016.967. **Circ:** 500 (ctrl). ***Continues*** *Bibliographie Ethnographique de l'Afrique Sud-Saharienne.*
**Desc:** Bibliography on social sciences and humanities in Africa, South of Sahara.
**Ind/Abst** Anthropol. Index; Bibliogr. Mission.

FR
**BIBLIOGRAPHIE DES TRAVAUX EN LANGUE FRANCAISE SUR L'AFRIQUE AU SUD DU SAHARA, SCIENCES HUMAINES ET SOCIALES.** **See** Social Sciences-Abstracting, Bibliographies and Statistics.

UK
**BIOSOCIAL SOCIETY SERIES.** **See** Biology.

PL
**BIULETYN IGS / SZKOA GOWNA HANDLOWA, INSTYTUT GOSPODARSTWA SPOECZNEGO.**
**Added/Corp** Szkoa Gowna Handlowa w Warszawie. Instytut Gospodarstwa Spoecznego. (19??)-. Periodical. Polish (summaries and/or abstracts in English and Russian). qt. **(Subscription address:** ARS Polona, PO Box 1001, 00068 Warsaw Poland.**)** **LC** H19.W4; A38. ***Continues*** *Szkoa Gowna Planowania i Statystyki (Warsaw, Poland). Instytut Gospodarstwa Spoecznego. Biuletyn.*
**Ind/Abst** Popul. Index.

RU
**BIULLETEN REGISTRATSII NIR. OBSHCHESTVENNYE NAUKI. SERIIA 1 / VSESOIUZNYI NAUCHNO-TEKHNICHESKII INFORMATSIONNYI TSENTR.** **Added/Corp** Vsesoiuznyi Nauchno-Tekhnicheskii Informatsionnyi Tsentr. (19??)-. Russian. qt. VINITI - Vsesoyuznyi Institut Nauchno-Tekhnicheskoi Informatsii, All-Union Scientific and Technical Information Institute, Baltiiskaia Ulitsa 14, 125219 Moscow Russia. **Tel** 238-46-00, FAX 9430060, telex 411160. **LC** H62.A1; B57. ***Continues*** *Biulleten Registratsii. Obshchestvennye Nauki. Seriia 1, Marksizm-Leninizm, Filosofiia, Sotsiologiia, Psikhologiia.*

US/0006-4696
**BLESSINGS OF LIBERTY, THE.**
**Added/Corp** Foundation for Religious Action in the Social and Civil Order. Vol. 1 (July 1956)-. Periodical. English. qt. $3.00. Charles W Lowry, PO Box 1829, Pinehurst NC 28374. **Tel** (919)692-6726. **ED** Charles W Lowry. **LC** HN39.U6; B57. **Circ:** 1,100.
**Desc:** Features articles dealing with national and world affairs against an historical background and from a theological perspective.

US/0895-5786
**BLUEPRINT FOR SOCIAL JUSTICE.**
[Bluepr. soc. justice]. **Added/Corp** Loyola University (New Orleans, La.). Institute of Human Relations. **VFOAT** Blueprint. Vol. 33 (May 1980)-. Periodical. English. Ten times a year (Except July and August). Free. Blue Print for Social Justice / Loyola University, Twomey Center, New Orleans LA 70118. **Tel** (504)861-5830, FAX (504)861-5853. **ED** Richard McCarthy. **DD** 261. Index available. **Circ:** 3,000 (ctrl). ***Continues*** *Blueprint for the Christian Reshaping of Society.*
**Desc:** Explores current issues of social concern and reaches a diverse audience. Provide information to Father Twomey's fellow Jesuits who did not have easy access to comtemporary social issues, the Blueprint has since become a teaching tool, a resource for speakers and study groups, and curiously, a debating tool in U. S. Congress.

TU
**BOGAZICI UNIVERSITESI DERGISI. SOSYAL BILIMLER.** **VFOAT** Bogazici University Journal. Social Sciences; Sosyal Bilimler. V. 1- 1973-. Periodical. Multiple languages. an. Bogazici University, Public Relations Office, Harbiye-Istanbul Turkey.

BL
**BOLETIM DE CIENCIAS SOCIAIS.** Bulletin. Portuguese (English). bm. Universidade Federal de Santa Catarina, Departamento de Ciencias Sociais, Centro de Ciencias Humanas, Caixa Postal 476, CEP 88000, Florianopolis Brazil. **Tel** (0482)339253. **ED** Paulo J Krischke, Ilka Bosventura Lette. **LC** HC186; .B58. **DD** 981/.005. Index available. **Bk Rev. Circ:** 500 (ctrl).
**Desc:** Primarily designed for academic circulation of papers produced by faculty and graduate students of this university's division of graduate studies in the social sciences.

PO/0871-3643
**BOLETIM DO CENTRO DE DOCUMENTACAO 25 DE ABRIL.**
**Added/Corp** Centro de Documentacao 25 de Abril (Universidade de Coimbra). **VFOAT** Boletim. No. 1 (Feb. 1989)-. Bulletin. Portuguese. tq. 3$500 (institutions), 2$500 (indiviudals) Portugal; 6$000 (institutions), 5$000 (individuals) other. Universidade de Coimbra, 3049 Coimbra Codex Portugal. **LC** H8.P8; B645. **DD** 016.3. **Bk Rev.**

BL
**BOLETIM TECHNICO INFORMATIVO.**
**Main/Corp** Universidade do Amazonas. Centro de Pesquisas Socio-Economicas. (19??)-. Bulletin. Portuguese. Divisuo de Documentacao, rua Jose Paranagua 200, Caixa Postal 378, Manaus Brazil. **LC** H67.U55; A25.

BL
**BOLETIM / UNIVERSIDADE ESTADUAL DE LONDRINA, CCH, CENTRO DE LETRAS E CIENCIAS HUMANAS.**
**Added/Corp** Universidade Estadual de Londrina. Centro de Letras e Ciencias Humanas. (19??)-. Bulletin. Portuguese. sa. Universidade Estadual de Londrina, Centro de Letras e Ciencias Humanas, Campus Universitario, Caixa Postal 6001, CEP 86051-970, Londrina Parana Brazil. **ED** Joaquim Carvalho da Silva. **LC** H8.P8; B64. **DD** 300/.5. **Bk Rev.**
**Desc:** Publishes the studies and research of professors at the University of Londrina in Brazil in the fields of letters and humanities. Articles on these same subjects are also accepted from outside scholars. Includes articles on religion and philosophy.
**Ind/Abst** Linguist. Lang. Behav. Abstr.; Soc. Plann. Policy Dev. Abstr.; Sociol. Abstr.

PE/0253-0015
**BOLETIN DE LIMA.** [Bol. Lima]. No. 1 (July 1979)-. Periodical. German (Spanish; summaries and/or abstracts in English). bm (6 issues). $100.00 Peru; $150.00 other. Editorial los Pinos Eirl, Casilla 18-1027, Lima 18 Peru. **Tel** 011 51 14 460031, FAX 011 51 14 464007. **ED** F Uilliger. **LC** F3401; .B59. **DD** 985/.005. **CODEN** BLIMEY. **[CCC].** Index available. **Bk Rev. Ad Acc. Circ:** 1,000.
**Desc:** The only Peruvian publication that covers areas such as archeology, biology, ecology, folklore, geography, history, etc.
**Ind/Abst** Math. Rev.

SP
**BOLETIN DE SUMARIOS.** (19??)-. Bulletin. Spanish. Six times a year. Ministerio Asuntos Sociales, Publicaciones Alonso Cano 20, 28003 Madrid, Spain. **Tel** 011 34 1 3477353, 011 34 1 3477351.

CN/0703-8968
**BRIAR PATCH.** [Briar patch]. **Added/Corp** Briar Patch Society. Briarpatch Inc. (1973)-. Periodical. English. Ten times a year (Dec./Jan. and July/Aug. issues combined). 43.00Can$ (institutions); 33.00Can$ (individuals). Briarpatch, Huston House, 2138 McIntyre Street, Regina Saskatchewan S4P 2R7 Canada. **Tel** (306)525-2949, FAX (306)565-3430, telex RYB4069. **ED** George Martin Manz. **DD** 330.9/7124. **Bk Rev**, (Qty: 20). **Ad Acc, Adv Mgr:** George Manz. **Circ:** 2,000 (ctrl). available on microfiche from Micromedia Limited; available on microfilm.
**Desc:** Provides an alternative political view for those interested in politics, the environment, Aboriginal and women's rights and international affairs. We bring you articles the mainstream media won't touch.
**Ind/Abst** Altern. Press Index; Can. Index; Can. Period. Index (19??-).

US/1060-2941
**BRIEFING (SHAWNEE MISSION, KAN.).**
***Ceased.*** (BRIEFING : THE COMPREHENSIVE SOURCE FOR INTERNATIONAL SECURITY INTELLIGENCE.). [Briefing]. Vol. 4, No. 1 (Jan. 1992)-(1992). Periodical. English. mo. Varro Press, 7130 Village Dr., PO Box 8413, Shawnee Mission KS 66208. **Tel** (913)432-5856. **DD** 303. ***Continues*** *Briefing--Terrorism and Low Intensity Conflict, 1041-0244.*

UK/0951-6204
**BRITISH REVIEW OF NEW ZEALAND STUDIES : BRONZS.** **VFOAT** BRONZS. No. 1 (July 1988)-. English. an.
**Ind/Abst** Int. Bibliogr. Sociol.

US/0745-1253
**BROOKINGS REVIEW, THE.** [Brookings rev.].
**Added/Corp** Brookings Institution. Vol. 1, No. 1 (Fall 1982)-. Periodical. English. qt (4 issues). $17.95 (1 year), $32.95 (2 year). Brookings Institution, 1775 Massachusetts Avenue NW, Washington DC 20036. **Tel** (202)797-6112. **LC** H1; .B76. **DD** 300/.5. **[CCC].** available on microfilm and microfiche from University Microfilms International (UMI); available on an online database (file 15/Full-Text) from DIALOG. Documents available from UMI Article Clearinghouse. ***Continues*** *Brookings Bulletin (Washington, D.C. : 1962), 0007-229X.*
**Desc:** The public policy magazine of the Brookings Institution with articles on economics, foreign policy and government.
**Ind/Abst** ABI/INFORM Glob. Ed.; ABI Inform Ondisc (Spring 1983-); Acad. Abstr. Full Text Elite (July 1990-); Acad. Abstr. (July 1990-); Acad. Ind. [Computer File] (1984-); Acad. Search (July 1990-); Am. Bibliogr. Slavic East Europ. Stud.; Bus. ASAP (1992-) [Full Txt.]; Bus. Index (1985-); Energy Res. Abstr. (Oct. 1982-); Expand. Acad. Index (1984-); Gen. BusinessFile (1985-); Gen. Period. Index (1985); Health Plan. Adminis.; Hospit. Health Admin. Index; INFO-SOUTH Abstr.; J. Plan. Lit.; Middle East Abstr. Index; Newsp. Period. Abstr. (1988-); PAIS Int. Print (1991-); Read. Guide Period. Lit.; UMI ABI/Inform--Bus. Period. Ondisc (Spring 1988-) [Full Txt.].

US/1053-7368
**BROWN'S DIRECTORY OF INSTRUCTIONAL PROGRAMS (K-8). SOCIAL STUDIES.** **See** Education-Teaching and Curriculum.

FR/0767-9866
**BSP BAREME SOCIAL PERIODIQUE.**
[BSP Bareme liaisons soc. period.]. (1969)-. Periodical. French. qt. 246.82F. Liaisons Sociales, 1 Avenue E Belin, F 92856 Rueil Mal France. **Tel** 011 33 1 41299872. **UDC** 338.

YU/0561-7359
**BULLETIN - ACADEMIE SERBE DES SCIENCES ET DES ARTS. CLASSE DES SCIENCES SOCIALES.** **Main/Corp** Srpska Akademija Nauka i Umetnosti. **Added/Corp** Srpska Akademija Nauka i Umenosti, Belgrad. Bulletin. Section des Sciences Sociales. No. 1 (1952)-. Bulletin. Multiple languages (French, English and German).
**Ind/Abst** Am. Hist. Life (1952-); BHA : Biblio. Hist. Art.

FR/0007-4071
**BULLETIN ANALYTIQUE DE DOCUMENTATION POLITIQUE, ECONOMIQUE ET SOCIALE CONTEMPORAINE / FONDATION NATIONAL DES SCIENCES POLITIQUES.** [Bull. anal. doc. polit., econ. soc. contemp.]. **Added/Corp** Fondation Nationale des Sciences Politiques. Vol. 1 (May 1946)-. Bulletin. French. mo. 845.00F (institutions), 405.00F (individuals) France; 695.00F (institutions), 485.00F (individuals) other. Presses de la Fondation, Nationale des Sciences Politiques, 44 Rue du Four, 75006 Paris France. **Tel** 011 33 1 44393960, FAX 011 33 1 45480441. **ED** Nicole Richard. **LC** Z7163; .F7. **DD** 016.3. **[CCC].** Index available. **Ad Acc.**
**Desc:** Brief annotations of articles in social science periodicals on current issues and developments; worldwide coverage.
**Ind/Abst** Popul. Index.

CN/0008-4557
**BULLETIN - CANADIAN COMMISSION FOR UNESCO.** **Main/Corp** Canadian Commission for UNESCO. **VFOAT** Bulletin - Commission Canadienne pour l'UNESCO. Vol. 11, No. 2 (Dec. 1968)-. Bulletin. English (French). Four times a year. Free. Canadian Commission for UNESCO Bulletin, PO Box 1047, 99 Metcalfe Street, Ottawa Ontario K1P 5V8 Canada. **Tel** (613)237-3400, telex 053-4573 CANCONARTS OTT. **ED** Olga Jurgens and Carmelia Quinn. **LC** AS4.U825; C22. **Bk Rev. Circ:** 5,000 (ctrl). ***Continues*** *Canadian National Commission for UNESCO. Bulletin, 0317-574X.*
**Desc:** Covers activities of the Canadian Commission for UNESCO and UNESCO news of particular interest to Canadians.

SA
**BULLETIN / CSD.** ***Title Change.*** **Added/Corp** Centre for Science Development (Human Sciences Research Council). **VFOAT** CSD/SWO Bulletin. Vol. 3 No. 1 (Jan./Feb. 1991)- Vol. 6 (Jan. 1993). Bulletin. Afrikaans (English). Ten times a year (Jan/Feb. and Nov/Dec. issues combined). Center for Science & Development, PO box 270, 0001 Pretoria South Africa. **Tel** 011 27 12 2022724, FAX 011 27 12 3265362. **ED** Marilyn Farouharson. **LC** Q127.S693; B85. **DD** 338.96806. **Bk Rev. Ad Acc. Circ:** 3,700. available on an online database. ***Continues*** *Bulletin (Institute for Research Development (Human Sciences Research Council)), 1017-6136.* ***Continued by*** *CSD Bulletin.*

FR/0037-8895
**BULLETIN DE LA SOCIETE ARCHEOLOGIQUE, HISTORIQUE, LITTERAIRE & SCIENTIFIQUE DU GERS.** **Main/Corp** Societe Archeologique, Historique, Litteraire et Scientifique du Gers. (1900)-. Monographic series. French. qt. Price varies per volume. Societe Archeologique, Historique Litteraire & Scientifique du Gers, 13 Place Saluste du Bartas, 32000 Auch France. **Tel** 011 33 62 630837. **LC** DC611.G35; S65a. **DD** 944/.771/005.

US
**BULLETIN DE LIAISON: INVENTAIRE DESCRIPTIF DES UNITES DE RECHERCHE ET DE FORMATION EN SCIENCES SOCIALES, AMERIQUE LATINE. LIAISON BULLETIN: DIRECTORY OF SOCIAL SCIENCE RESEARCH AND TRAINING UNITS, LATIN AMERICA.** **Added/Corp** Organisation for Economic Co-operation and Development. Development Centre. **VFOAT** Liaison Bulletin : Directory of Social

Science Research and Training Units, Latin America; Inventaire Descriptif des Unites de Recherche et de Formation en Sciences Sociales, Amerique Latine; Directory of Social Science Research and Training Units, Latin America. (19??)-. Multiple languages (English and French). ir. $6.50. OECD Publications and Information Center, 2 rue Andre-Pascal, 75775 Paris Cedex 16 France. **Tel** 011 33 1 45248167, US:(202)785-6323, FAX 011 33 1 45248500 OR 45248176, telex 620 160 OCDE. **(Subscription address:** OECD Publications Center, 2001 L Street, Suite 700, Washington DC 20036.**)**

FR/0220-2018
**BULLETIN DU CENTRE DE RECHERCHES D'HISTOIRE DES MOUVEMENTS SOCIAUX ET DU SYNDICALISME.** ***Title Change.*** [Bull. Cent. rech. hist. mouv. soc. synd.]. **Main/Corp** Universite de Paris I: Pantheonsorbonne. Centre de Recherches d'Histoire des Mouvements Sociaux et du Syndicalisme. No. 2 (1977/78)-(19??). Bulletin. French. an. 9 rue Malher, 75004 Paris France. **Tel** 42 78 33 22. ***Supersedes*** *Bulletin du Centre d'Histoire du Syndicalisme.* ***Continued by*** *Bulletin (Universite de Paris I: Pantheon-Sorbonne. Centre de Recherches d'Histoire des Mouvements Sociaux et du Syndicalisme).*
**Ind/Abst** Am. Hist. Life.

CN/0229-4001
**BULLETIN (MONTREAL CITIZENSHIP COUNCIL).** (BULLETIN / CONSEIL DU CIVISME DE MONTREAL.). [Bull. - Cons. civisme Montr.]. No. 1 (March 1978)-. Bulletin. English (French). Free. Montreal Citizenship Council, 10025 Boulevard de l'Acadie, Montreal Quebec H4N 1L6 Canada. **DD** 305.8/00971.

US/0077-4049
**BULLETIN / NATIONAL COUNCIL FOR THE SOCIAL STUDIES.** **Added/Corp** National Council for the Social Studies. No. 6 (1936)-. Bulletin. English. ir. Comes with comprehensive membership, Social Education, and The Social Studies Professional: $75.00 US; $80.00 overseas. National Council for the Social Studies, 3501 Newark Street Northwest, Washington DC 20016-3167. **Tel** (202)966-7840, FAX (202)966-2061. **LC** H62; .N31b. ***Continues*** *Publications of the National Council for the Social Studies.*

BE
**BULLETIN OF INFORMATION ON CURRENT RESEARCH ON HUMAN SCIENCES CONCERNING AFRICA. BULLETIN D'INFORMATION SUR LES RECHERCHES DANS LES SCIENCES HUMAINES CONCERNANT L'AFRIQUE.** **Main/Corp** International Centre for African Economic and Social Documentation. **VFOAT** Bulletin d'Information sur les Recherches dans les Sciences Humaines Concernant l'Afrique. (196?)-. Bulletin. English (French). sa. CIDESA, Place Royale 7, 1000 Brussels Belgium. **DD** 960; 016. ***Continues*** *Bulletin d'Information sur les Theses et les Etudes en Cours ou en Projet; Bulletin of Information on Theses and Studies in Progress or Proposed.*

II/0541-7562
**BULLETIN OF THE INSTITUTE OF TRADITIONAL CULTURES.** **Main/Corp** Institute of Traditional Cultures. **Added/Corp** University of Madras. (1957)-. Bulletin. English (Tamil). Twice a year. Rs20.00. University of Madras Registrar, University Building Chepauk, Madras 600 005 India. **LC** AS472.M13; A15. **Ad Acc. Circ:** 250.
**Desc:** Covers anthropology, dance, education (general), folklore, literature music, religion, sociology and history (general).

FR
**BULLETIN OFFICIEL DES AFFAIRES SOCIALES.** Bulletin. French. wk. Direction des Journaux Officiels, 26 rue Desaix, 75727 Paris Cedex 15 France. **Tel** 011 33 1 40587500.

JA
**BUNKAGAKU NENPO (KOBE DAIGAKU. BUNKAGAKU KENKYUKA).** **See** Humanities.

UV
**C.E.S.A.O. AUJOURD'HUI, LE.** **Main/Corp** Centre d'Etudes Economiques et Sociales d'Afrique Occidentale. French. Centre d'Etudes Economiques et Sociales d'Afrique Occidentale, Upper Volta. **LC** H62.5.A343; C45A. **DD** 309.2/232/66.

BL
**CADERNOS DE CIENCIAS SOCIAIS.** **Added/Corp** Pontificia Universidade Catolica de Minas Gerais (Brazil). Departamento de Sociologia. Vol. 1, No. 1 (Aug 1991)-. Periodical. Portuguese. sa.

FR/0755-9208
**CAHIERS D'ECONOMIE ET SOCIOLOGIE RURALES.** **Added/Corp** Institut National de la Recherche Agronomique (France). No. 1 (June 1984)-. Periodical. French. qt. 360.00F France & CEE; 430.00 other. Institut National de la Recherche Agronomique, Route de Staint Cyr, 78026 Versailles Cedex France. **Tel** 011 33 1 30833406, FAX 011 33 1 30833449, telex INRAPUB 699 368 F. **ED** Y. Leon. **LC** HN49.C6; C34. **DD** 307.1/412/05.
**Desc:** Deals with agriculture and related activities in terms of their economics, their social characteristics and their relations with the national and international economy or with society as a whole. Intended for readers interested in research trends, methods and results - specialist civil servants, decision makers and specialists in the food and agriculture sectors of the economy, as well as teachers and instructors.
**Ind/Abst** Dairy Sci. Abstr.; Maize Abstr.; PAIS Int. Print; Pig News Inf.; Poult. Abstr.; Soyabean Abstr.; World Agric. Econ.

FR/0008-0039
**CAHIERS DES NATURALISTES.** (CAHIERS DES NATURALISTES : BULLETIN DES NATURALISTES PARISIENS.). [Cah. nat.]. **Added/Corp** Naturalistes Parisiens (Society). New Series Vol. 8, No. 1/2 (Jan./Feb. 1983)-. Periodical. French. Four times a year. 260.00F. Cahiers des Naturalistes, 45 rue Buffon, 75005 Paris France. **ED** Claude Dupuis. **CODEN** CNBNAN. Index available. **Bk Rev**, (Qty: 4/yr). **Circ:** 600. Documents available from BIOSIS Document Express. ***Continues*** *Feuille des Naturalistes, 0245-9043.*
**Ind/Abst** Biol. Abstr.; For. Abstr.; GeoRef; Rev. Med. Vet. Entomol.

FR/0768-9829
**CAHIERS DES SCIENCES HUMAINES.** [Cah. sci. hum.]. **Added/Corp** O.R.S.T.O.M. (Agency : France). Vol. 22, No. 1 (1986)-. Periodical. French. Four times a year. 315.00F. Editions de l'ORSTOM, 72 Route d'Aulnay, 93143 Bondy Cedex France. **Tel** 011 33 1 48025500. **LC** DT521; .C3. **DD** 909/.09301/05. ***Continues*** *Cahiers O.R.S.T.O.M. Serie Sciences Humaines.*
**Ind/Abst** Geogr. Abstr. Human Geogr.; Int. Bibliogr. Sociol.; Int. Dev. Abstr.; Int. Labour Doc.; LABORDOC; Popul. Index; Rural Dev. Abstr.; Soils Fert.; Soyabean Abstr.; World Agric. Econ.

BE/0250-1619
**CAHIERS DU CEDAF, LES.** [Cah. CEDAF.]. **Main/Corp** Centre d'Etude et de Documentation Africaines. **Added/Corp** Centre d'Etude et de Documentation Africaines. No. 1, (1971)-. Monographic series. French (English and Dutch). Six times a year. 2000F Belgium; 2300F other. CEDAF, 7 rue Belliard 65, 1040 Brussels Belgium. **Tel** 011 2 2307362, FAX 011 2 2307605. **ED** Verhaegen Benoit and Reyntjens Filip. **LC** DT1; .C45. available on diskette.
**Desc:** Central and North African social and political sciences, economics, education and history.
**Ind/Abst** Int. Bibliogr. Sociol.; Int. Labour Doc.

BD
**CAHIERS DU CURDES.** **See** Economics.

SZ/0008-0497
**CAHIERS VILFREDO PARETO.** Vol. 1 (1963)-. Periodical. French. ir. 75.00F. Librairie Droz SA, 11 rue Massot BP 389, CH 1211 Geneva 12 Switzerland. **Tel** 011 41 22 3466666, FAX 011 41 22 472391. **ED** G Busino. **[CCC]. Circ:** 600.
**Desc:** Social sciences.
**Ind/Abst** Int. Bibliogr. Sociol.; Soc. Plann. Policy Dev. Abstr.; Sociol. Abstr. (?-?).

UA
**CAIRO PAPERS IN SOCIAL SCIENCE.** **Added/Corp** American University in Cairo. **VFOAT** Buhuth al-Qahirah fi al-Ulum al-Ijtimaiyah; Cairo Papers. (1977)-. Periodical. English. qt. $35.00 (institutions), $25.00 (individuals). Trustees - American University of Cairo, 113 Sharia Kasr el Aini, Cairo Egypt. **Tel** 20 2 354 2964. **ED** Nicholas S. Hopkins. **LC** HN786; .A43. **DD** 306/.0962/05. **Bk Rev**. **Ad Acc. Circ:** 44. available on diskette.
**Desc:** Publishes results of indigenous research on social, economic, and political developments in the Middle East.

CN/0043-8170
**CANADA & THE WORLD.** ***Ceased.*** [Can. world]. **VFOAT** Canada and the World. Vol. 36, No. 1, (Sept. 1970)-(May 1994). Periodical. English. Nine times a year. RL Taylor, Box 22099 Westmont Postal Outlet, Waterloo Ontario N2L 6J7 Canada. **Tel** (519)746-5796. **ED** Robert Taylor. **LC** D839; .W53. **Ad Acc. Circ:** 27,000. available on microfilm and microfiche from University Microfilms International (UMI). Documents available from UMI Article Clearinghouse. ***Continues*** *World Affairs, 0317-6800.*
**Desc:** Designed for use as a teaching aid in high school social science and current events classes.
**Ind/Abst** Acad. Abstr. Full Text Elite (Jan. 1990-) [Full Txt.]; Acad. Abstr. (Jan. 1990-); Acad. Search (Jan. 1990-); Can. Index; Can. Period. Index; Mag. Artic. Summar. Elite (Jan. 1990-May 1994) [Full Txt.]; Mag. Artic. Summar. Select (Jan. 1990-) [Full Txt.]; Mag. Artic. Summar. CD-ROM (Jan. 1990-); Mag. Search; Mid. Search (Jan. 1990-) [Full Txt.]; Newsp. Period. Abstr. (1988-); Prim. Search (Jan. 1990-) [Full Txt.]; Read. Guide Period. Lit.; Vocat. Search (Jan. 1990-) [Full Txt.].

CN
**CANADA & THE WORLD BACKGROUNDER.** (199?)-. English. ir (6 issues). 39.00Can$ Canada; 45.00Can$ other (basic service). RL Taylor, Box 22099 Westmont Postal Outlet, Waterloo Ontario N2L 6J7 Canada. **Tel** (519)746-5796.
**Ind/Abst** Mag. Artic. Summar. Elite (June 1994-) [Full Txt.].

CN/0008-400X
**CANADIAN JOURNAL OF BEHAVIOURAL SCIENCE.** **See** Psychology.

CN/0829-1888
**CANADIAN MEDIA DIRECTORS COUNCIL MEDIA DIGEST.** (MEDIA DIGEST / THE CANADIAN MEDIA DIRECTORS COUNCIL.). [Can. Med. Dir. Counc. media dig.]. **VFOAT** CMDC Media Digest. **VAT** Media Digest - Canadian Media Directors Council. (1972)-. English. an. 5.00Can$. Maclean Hunter Canada / Montreal, 1001 bvd. de Maisonneuve W., Montreal, Quebec H3A 3E1 Canada. **Tel** 514-845-5141, FAX 514-845-4302, telex 055-60604. **DD** 302.2/34/0971.

CN
**CANADIAN PLAINS STUDIES.** **See** History(General)-History of North, South, and Central America.

CN/0317-7904
**CANADIAN REVIEW OF STUDIES IN NATIONALISM.** **See** History(General)-Abstracting, Bibliographies and Statistics.

CN
**CANADIAN SOCIAL SCIENCE DATA CATALOG.** **Added/Corp** York University (Toronto, Ont.). Institute for Behavioural Research. York University,(Toronto, Ont.). Institute for Behavioural Research. Data Bank/Information Systems. (1974)-. Catalog. English. ir. 10.00Can$. York University / Ontario, Canada, 212 Founders College, 4700 Keele Street, North York Ontario M3J 1P3 Canada. **Tel** (416)736-5356.

SP
**CARABO, EL.** No. 1 (1976)-. Periodical. Spanish. bm. 1,000 ptas. Secisa, Apartado 1315, Madrid Spain. **LC** H8; .C37.

TR
**CARINDEX, SOCIAL SCIENCES AND HUMANITIES.** **Added/Corp** Association of Caribbean University and Research Libraries. Indexing Committee. Vol. 6, No. 1/2 (Mar. 1982)-Vol. 7, No. 1/2 (1983); New Ser. Vol. 1, No. 1 (1985)-. English. sa. $45.00. Carindex, University of the West Indies Library, St. Augustine Trinidad. **Tel** (809)663-1359. **(Subscription address:** The Press - University of the West Indies, 1A Aqueduct Flats, Mona Campus, Kingston 7, Jamaica**)** **ED** Annette Knight. **LC** Z7163; .C27; H53.C37. **DD** 016.3/009729. ***Continues*** *Carindex, Social Sciences.*
**Desc:** Abstracting journal covering the Caribbean region. Includes journal articles, conference proceedings, theses on all social sciences and humanities subjects.

AG
**CARTA DE CLACSO.** **Added/Corp** Consejo Latinoamericano de Ciencias Sociales. **VAT** Carta de Consejo Latinoamericano de Ciencias Sociales. (197?)-. Newsletter. Spanish. bm. $30.00. CLACSO, Callao 875 3ER, 1023 Buenos Aires Argentina. **Tel** 54 1 811 6588, FAX 54 1 812 8954. Index available. **Bk Rev. Ad Acc, Adv Mgr:** Jorge Fraga. Full Page (B&W) $300.00. Half Page (B&W) $175.00. **Acid Free. Circ:** 2,000 (ctrl).
**Desc:** Provides information on programs and activities of over 100 research institutes in the social sciences throughout Latin America and the Caribbean.

XR/0323-0570
**CASOPIS MORAVSKEHO MUZEA. VEDY SPOLECENSKE.** (CASOPIS MORAVSKEHO MUSEA V BRNE. VEDY SPOLECENSKE.). [Cas. Morav. muz., Vedy spol.]. **VFOAT** Casopis Moravskeho Muzea v Brne; Vedy Spolecenske; Acta Musei Moraviae Scientiae Sociales; Scientiae Sociales. No. 37 (1952)-. Czech (English and German). an. $29.40. **(Subscription address:** Artia Pegas Press Ltd., Palac Metro Narodni Trida 25, 11210 Prague 1 Czech Republic.**)** ***Continues*** *Casopis Moravskeho Musea v Brne. 2, Vedy Historicke.*
**Ind/Abst** BHA : Biblio. Hist. Art; GeoRef.

XR
**CASOPIS NARODNIHO MUZEA V PRAZE. RADA HISTORICKA.** **Added/Corp** Narodni Muzeum v Praze. **VFOAT** Rada Historicka. Vol. 146, No. 1/2 (1977)-. Periodical. Czech. qt. **(Subscription address:** Artia Pegas Press Ltd., Palac Metro Narodni Trida 25, 11210 Prague 1 Czech Republic.**)** **LC** H8; .P73. ***Continues*** *Casopis Narodniho Muzea. Historicke Muzeum.*

US
**CATALOG OF TRAINING ACTIVITIES / U.S. DEPARTMENT OF COMMERCE, BUREAU OF THE CENSUS.** **Main/Corp** United States. Bureau of the Census. Data User Services Division. **VFOAT** Data User Training. (1979)-. Government Publication. English. US Department of Commerce / Bureau of the Census, Data User Services Division, Customer Services, Washington DC 20233-0800. **Tel** (301)763-4100. **(Subscription address:** Superintendent of Documents, US Government Printing Office, Washington DC 20402.**)** ***Continues*** *United States. Bureau of the Census. Data User Services Division. Data User Education & Training Activities.*

US/0273-3072
**CATO JOURNAL, THE.** [Cato j.]. **Added/Corp** Cato Institute. Vol. 1, No. 1 (Spring 1981)-. Periodical. English. Three times a year. $50.00 (institutions), $24.00 (individuals). Cato Institute, 1000 Massachusetts Avenue NW, Washington DC 20001. **Tel** (202)842-0200, (800)767-1241, FAX (202)842-3490. **ED** James A. Dorn. **LC** H1; .C34. **DD** 361.6/1/05. **Pr Rev.** available on microfilm and microfiche from University Microfilms International (UMI). Documents available from The Genuine Article, UMI Article Clearinghouse, Documents on Demand.
**Desc:** An interdisciplinary journal of public policy analysis written for scholars and intelligent lay-people alike.
**Ind/Abst** ABC POL SCI; ABI/INFORM Glob. Ed.; ABI Inform Ondisc (Fall 1983-); Am. Hist. Life (1981-); Curr. Contents Soc. Behav. Sci.; Econ. Lit. Index; Energy Res. Abstr. (July 1982-); Environ. Abstr.; Expand. Acad. Index (1992-); Index Period. Artic. Relat. Law (19??-19??); INIS Atomindex [Micro.]; Int. Polit. Sci. Abstr.; J. Econ. Lit.; J. Plan. Lit.; Newsp. Period. Abstr. (1991-); PAIS Int. Print (1991-); Res. Alert [Full Cov.]; Soc. Sci. Cit. Index [Full Cov.].

US/0734-5119
**CBASSE NEWSLETTER.** [CBASSE newsl.]. **Main/Corp** Commission on Behavioral and Social Sciences and Education (National Research Council). **VFOAT** C.B.A.S.S.E. Newsletter. Newsletter. English. ir. Commission on Behavioral and Social Sciences and Education, 2101 Constitution Avenue NW, Washington DC 20418. **Tel** (202)334-2300. **Circ:** 2,500 (ctrl). ***Continues*** *ABASS Newsletter, 0361-9222.*
**Desc:** Provides information about behavioral and social sciences, education, and public policy of interest to social and behavioral scientists and policy makers. Describes activities of Commission on Behavioral and Social Sciences and Education, National Research Council.

US
**CCSSA NEWSLETTER.** **Main/Corp** Community College Social Science Association (U.S.). **VAT** Community College Social Science Association Newsletter. Vol. 1 (1976)-. Periodical. English. Six times a year. $25.00. Community College Educators, PO Box 191303, San Diego CA 92119. **Tel** (619)448-4709. **LC** Discard.

DK
**CDR IN.** **See** Economics.

DK/0108-6596
**CDR RESEARCH REPORT.** **Added/Corp** Centret for Udviklingsforskning (Denmark). No. 1 (1982)-. Monographic series. English. ir. Price varies per volume. Centre for Development Research, NY Kongensgade 9, DK-1472 Copenhagen K Denmark. **Tel** 45 114 5700, FAX 45 33 140125. **Circ:** 500 (ctrl).
**Desc:** Presents the results of the centre's social science research projects on development issues in Third World countries.
**Ind/Abst** Geogr. Abstr. Human Geogr.; Int. Dev. Abstr.

US/0731-809X
**CENTER FOR POLICY RESEARCH MONOGRAPH SERIES.** [Cent. Pol. Res. monogr. ser.]. Vol. 1 (1980)-. Monographic series. English. ir. Price varies per volume. Human Sciences Press, PO Box 735, 233 Spring Street, New York NY 10013. **Tel** (212)620-8000, FAX (212)807-1047, telex 23421139.

US/0098-924X
**CENTERPOINT.** ***Ceased.*** [Centerpoint]. Vol. 1 (Spring 1974)-Ceased Vol. 4, No. 3. Periodical. English. qt. University of New York, 33 W 42nd Street, New York NY 10036. **Tel** (212)790-4448. **LC** AP2; .C373. **DD** 051.
**Ind/Abst** Am. Hist. Life (1974-1980); MLA Int. Bibl. Books Artic. Mod. Lang. Lit.; Music Index (-19??); Psychol. Abstr. (1974-); Soc. Plann. Policy Dev. Abstr.; Sociol. Abstr. (?-?).

CR
**CENTROAMERICA INTERNACIONAL.** **Added/Corp** Facultad Latinoamericana de Ciencias Sociales. Secretaria General. No. 1 (Sept./Oct. 1989)-. Periodical. Spanish. bm. $5.00 Costa Rica; $10.00 Central America; $20.00 North America; $30.00 other. Flacso, Apartado Postal 11747 1000, San Jose, Costa Rica. **Tel** 011 506 2248059. **LC** F1439.5; .C473. **DD** 327.728.
**Ind/Abst** PAIS Int. Print.

KO
**CHAYU AKADEMI YON'GU NONCHONG.** **Main/Corp** Chayu Akademi. **Added/Corp** Chayu Akademi. Journal. **VFOAT** Journal of Freedom Academy. Vol. 1 (1977)-. Periodical. Korean. ir. Not for sale. Chayu Akademi, San 1 Sokkwan-dong Songbuk-ku, Seoul Korea. **LC** H8; .C47a.

CC
**CHE-CHIANG HSUEH KAN. ZHEJIANGXUEKAN CHE-CHIANG SHENG SHE HUI KO HSUEH YEN CHIU SO.** **Added/Corp** Che-Chiang Sheng she hui ko Hsueh yen Chiu so. **VFOAT** Zhejiangxuekan. (19??)-. Periodical. Chinese. bm. NT$4.80. **ED** Xie Bao-sen. **LC** AS451; .C35. **DD** 089/.951. **Bk Rev. Ad Acc. Circ:** 3,000.
**Desc:** A comprehensive academic and theoretical magazine directed by the Provincial Academy of Social Sciences of Zhejiang.

CC/1000-579X
**CHIANG-HSI SHIH FAN TA HSUEH HSUEH PAO. CHE HSUEH SHE HUI KO HSUEH PAN.** **Added/Corp** Chiang-Hsi Shih Fan Ta Hsueh. **VFOAT** Jiangxi Shifandaxue Xuebao; Journal of Jiangxi Normal University. Philosophy and Social Sciences edition; Journal of Jiangxi Teachers University. Philosophy and Social Sciences Edition. (1984)-. Academic Scholarly Publication. Chinese. qt. $20.00. Jiangxi Shifan Daxue / Xuebao Bianjibu, Jiangxi Normal University, Journal Editorial Department, Beijing Xilu, Nanchang, Jiangxi 330027 People's Republic of China. **Tel** 333993. **ED** C. Dingru. **LC** AS452.N352; A17. **DD** 089/.951. ***Continues*** *Chiang-Hsi Shih Yuan Hsueh Pao. Che Hsueh She Hui Ko Hsueh Pan.*

US/0149-7006
**CHICOREL INDEX TO ABSTRACTING AND INDEXING SERVICES : PERIODICALS IN HUMANITIES AND THE SOCIAL SCIENCES.** **See** Humanities.

UK/0956-3113
**CHILDREN AND WAR.** [Child. war]. (1988)-. Periodical. English. qt. £7.00 UK; £10.00 other. Peach Pledge Union, 6 Endsleigh Street, London WCIH 0DX England. **Tel** (071)387 5501. **ED** Jan Melichan. **DD** 305.23. **Bk Rev. Ad Acc. Circ:** 1,500.

US/0191-3166
**CHINA AND US.** **Added/Corp** U.S.-China Peoples' Friendship Association. (19??)-. English. bm. China Friendship Association, 41 Union Square West/Room 1228, New York NY 10003. **Tel** (212)255-4727. **LC** E183.8.C5; C464. **DD** 301.29/73/051.

US/0272-0086
**CHINA EXCHANGE NEWS.** [China exch. news]. **Added/Corp** Committee on Scholarly Communication with the People's Republic of China (U.S.). Vol. 8, No. 1 (Feb. 1980)-. Periodical. English. Four times a year. Free on request. National Academy Press, 2101 Constitution Avenue NW, Lockbox 285, Washington DC 20055. **Tel** (800)624-6242, (202)334-3313, FAX (202)334-2451. **(Subscription address:** Committee on Scholarly Communication with China, 1055 Thomas Jefferson Street NW, Suite 2013, Washington DC 20007.**) ED** Kathlin Smith. **LC** E183.8.C5; C47. **DD** 303.4/82. Index available. **Bk Rev. Circ:** 5,000. ***Continues*** *China Exchange Newsletter, 0145-6318.*
**Desc:** A review of education, science and academic relations with the PRC.
**Ind/Abst** GeoRef; Int. Labour Doc.

II
**CHOICE INDIA.** **VAT** Choice. Vol. 1, No. 1 (Aug. 1984)-. Periodical. English. Twelve times a year. $27.00. Manager of Circulation Choice India, F 10/14 Model Town, Delhi 110009 India. **Tel** 7111976. **(Subscription address:** Prints India, 11 Darya Ganj, New Delhi 110002 India.**) ED** Rama Jha. **Bk Rev. Ad Acc. Circ:** 10,000.
**Desc:** Socio-cultural issues facing contemporary India in areas like cultural policy, book industry, interviews with politicians, artists, economists, industrialists; includes commentaries on arts.

CN/0713-4002
**CHO'N-TRO'I.** [Cho'n-tro'i]. **VFOAT** L'Horizon; Horizon; Horizon-Cho-N-Tro'I; Chon Troi. **VAT** Horizon (Sherbrooke). April 4, 1982-. Periodical. French (Vietnamese). $0.50 per number. Chon-Tro'I, 4345 rue Brunalt, Sherbrooke Quebec J1L 1S7 Canada. **DD** 305.8/9592/071.

KO
**CHON'GUK TAEHAKSAENG HAKSUL YON'GU PALPYO NONMUNJIP : SAHOE KWAHAK PUNYA.** Korean. Songagungwan Taehakkyo Hakto Hoguktan, 53-3-ka Myongyun-dong, Chongno-ku Seoul South Korea. **Tel** 434-0983. **ED** Sim O Mamm. **LC** H8; .C524. ctrl circ.

●FR
**CHRONIQUES DE LA S.E.D.E.I.S.** **See** Economics.

JA/0910-4348
**CHUGOKU KENKYU GEPPO.** **Added/Corp** Chugoku Kenkyujo (Tokyo, Japan). (May 1960)-. Periodical. Japanese. mo. $202.00. **(Subscription address:** Maruzen Company Ltd., PO Box 5050, Import & Export Department, Tokyo 100 31 Japan.**) LC** DS701; .C734. ctrl circ. ***Continues*** *Chugoku Shiryo Geppo.*
**Desc:** Presents a study of China.

CC
**CHUNG-KUO SHE HUI HSUEH NIEN CHIEN.** **VFOAT** China Social Science Yearbook. Chinese. China National Publishing Import & Export Corporation, 16 Gongti E Rd., Chaoyang Dist., Beijing 100704, People's Republic of China. **Tel** 011 8601 50630169, 5066688, FAX 011 8601 5063101, 5063010, telex 22313.

CC
**CHUNG-KUO SHE HUI KO HSUEH.** **VFOAT** Zhongguo Shehui Kexue; Social Sciences in China. (19??)-. Periodical. Chinese (English). Six times a year. $22.30. Science Press, 16 Donghuangchenggen North Street, Beijing 100707, People's Republic of China. **Tel** 011 86 1 4019821, 011 86 1 4010642, FAX 011 86 1 4012180, 011 86 1 4019810, telex 210147. **(Subscription address:** China International Book Trading Corporation, PO Box 399, Library Service Department, Beijing 100044 People's Republic of China.**) LC** H8.C47; C48. **DD** 300/.5.

CC/0412-443X
**CHUNG-SHAN TA HSUEH HSUEH PAO. CHE HSUEH SHE HUI KO HSUEH PAN.** **Main/Corp** Chung-Shan ta Hsueh (Canton, China). **VFOAT** Che Hsueh She Hui Ko Hsueh Pan; Journal of Sun Yatsen University. Social Science Edition. (19??)-. Academic Scholarly Publication. Chinese (table of contents in English). qt. Zhongshan Daxue, Xuebao Bianjibu, 135 Xingang Xilu, Guangzhou, Guangdong 210275 People's Republic of China. **Tel** 020-446300. **(Subscription address:** China International Book Trading Corporation, PO Box 399, Library Service Department, Beijing 100044 People's Republic of China.**) LC** AS451; .C48a. Index available. **Bk Rev. Circ:** 6,000. Documents available from CASDDS.
**Ind/Abst** Chem. Abstr.

JA/0529-6838
**CHUOKORON.** (19??)-. Periodical. Japanese. mo. $156.00. **(Subscription address:** Kyowa Book Company Inc., 1 38 Kanda Jinbocho Chiyoda-ku, Tokyo 101 Japan.**) DD** 895.

BL
**CIENCIAS HUMANAS.** V. 1- April/July 1977-. Periodical. Portuguese. qt. $8.00. Universidade Gama Filho, rua Manoel Vitorino, 625 Piedade Brazil. **LC** AP66; .C43.

MX/0185-0903
**CITAS LATINOAMERICANAS EN CIENCIAS SOCIALES Y HUMANIDADES : CLASE.** **Added/Corp** Universidad Nacional Autonoma de Mexico. Coordinacion de la Investigacion Cientifica. **VFOAT** CLASE; Latinoamericanas en Ciencias Sociales, Humanidades. Vol. 12, No. 1 (1987)-. Spanish (English and Portuguese). qt (4 issues). $192.00 US and Canada; $180.00 Mexico $193.00 others. Centro de Informacion Cientifica y Humanistica, Apartado 70 392, Mexico 20 DF Mexico. **Tel** 011 52 5 5480208, 011 52 5 6223964. **LC** Z7163; .C58; H8.S7. **DD** 016.3. available on CD-ROM. ***Continues*** *Citas Latinoamericanas en Sociologia, Economia y Humanidades, 0185-0903.*
**Desc:** Citations of Latin-American articles of over 750 serials in sociology, economics, and humanities.

US
**CLIPS / CONGRESSIONAL INSTITUTE FOR THE FUTURE.** (19??)-. English. qt (Mar., June, Sept., Dec.). $45.00 libraries & individuals; $195.00 institutions. Congressional Institute for the Future, 409 Third Street Southwest, Suite 204, Washington DC 20024. **Tel** (202)863-1700. **ED** Elaine Wicker. **Circ:** 450.

SG/0850-8712
**CODESRIA BULLETIN.** **Added/Corp** Codesria. (1987)-. Bulletin. English. qt. Free, Africa; $10.00 other. CODESRIA, BP 3304, Dakar Senegal Africa. **Tel** 011 221 230211, 239374, telex 61339. **LC** H62.5.A34; A38. **DD** 300/.72/06. Index available. **Bk Rev**, (Qty: 4). **Ad Acc.** ctrl circ. ***Continues*** *Africana (Dakar, Senegal : 1980).*
**Ind/Abst** Hum. Rights Intern. Rep.; Int. Labour Doc.

VE/0505-172X
**COLECCION CIENCIAS SOCIALES.** **Main/Corp** Universidad Central de Venezuela. Vol. 1 (1961)-. Spanish. ir. Ediciones de la Biblioteca, Universidad Central de Venezuela, Caracas Venzuela. **DD** 300.

UK/0076-0773
**COLLECTED SEMINAR PAPERS / UNIVERSITY OF LONDON, INSTITUTE OF COMMONWEALTH STUDIES.** **Added/Corp** University of London. Institute of Commonwealth Studies. **VFOAT** Collected Seminar

# Social Sciences

Papers on ... . (Apr./May 1966)-. Monographic series. English. ir. Price varies per volume. University of London Institute of Commonwealth Studies, 27-28 Russell, London WC1B 5DS England. **Tel** 01 580 5876, FAX 01 255 2160. **LC** UNC. **Circ:** 300.
 **Desc:** Research papers presented at the Institute's seminars.

FR/0588-2478
**COLLECTION "SCIENCES SOCIALES DU TRAVAIL.".** **Added/Corp** Universite Paris - Sud. Centre de Recherches en Sciences Sociales du Travail. Universite Paris - Sud. Centre de Recherches en Sciences Sociales du Travail. Paris. Universite. Institut des Sciences Sociales du Travail. **VFOAT** Sciences Sociales du Travail. (1966)-. Monographic series. French. ir. Price varies per volume. Librairie Armand Colin, BP 22, 41354 Vineuil Cedex France. **Tel** 011 33 54 438994. **DD** 330.

US/0010-1702
**COLORADO PROSPECTOR.** See History(General)-History of North, South, and Central America.

US/0010-1923
**COLUMBIA JOURNAL OF LAW AND SOCIAL PROBLEMS.** See Law.

US/0010-1966
**COLUMBIA LIBRARY COLUMNS.** See Humanities.

FI/0355-256X
**COMMENTATIONES SCIENTIARUM SOCIALIUM.** (1971)-. Monographic series. English. ir. Price varies per volume. Societas Scientiarum Fennica, (Finnish Society of Sciences and Letters), Marieg 5,, SF 000170 Helsinki 17 Finland. **Tel** 011 358 633005.
 **Ind/Abst** Selec. Coop. Index Manage. Period.

US
**COMMON CONCERN.** (19??)-. English. Four times a year. $5.00. National Board YMCA of the USA, 726 Broadway, New York NY 10003. **Tel** (212)614-2700.
 **Ind/Abst** Hum. Rights Intern. Rep.

US/0747-6086
**COMMUNITY SERVICE BUSINESS.** [Community serv. bus.]. **VFOAT** CSB. Vol. 5, No. 1 (July 1984)-. Periodical. English. mo. $10.00. MLP Enterprises, 236 East Durham Street, Philadelphia PA 19119. **ED** M L Peebles. **DD** 361. **Bk Rev. Ad Acc. Circ:** 150 (ctrl).
 Continues *CBO Management Report, 0272-6300.*
 **Desc:** National business newsletter for community organizations and other local nonprofit groups. Features financial news, technology, etc.

US/0733-4540
**COMPARATIVE CIVILIZATIONS REVIEW.** [Comp. civiliz. rev.]. (1979)-. Periodical. English. Twice a year. $20.00 (individuals and institutions), $5.00 (students and retirees) US and Canada; add $4.00 postage other. International Society for the Comparative Study of Civilizations, 2070 Foreign Languages Building, 707 South Mathews Avenue, Urbana IL 61801. **Tel** (217)333-4987, FAX (217)244-2223. **ED** Prof. Wayne M. Bledsoe. **LC** CB3; .C58. **DD** 901. **Bk Rev. Pr Rev. Circ:** 500.
 **Desc:** Studies concerned with the comparison of whole civilizations, theories and methods useful in the comparative study of civilizations, issues in humanities and social sciences viewed from comparative civilizational perspective.
 **Ind/Abst** Abstr. Engl. Stud.; Linguist. Lang. Behav. Abstr.; MLA Int. Bibl. Books Artic. Mod. Lang. Lit.; Soc. Plann. Policy Dev. Abstr.; Sociol. Abstr.

UK/0010-4175
**COMPARATIVE STUDIES IN SOCIETY AND HISTORY.** [Comp. stud. soc. hist.]. **Added/Corp** Society for the Comparative Study of Society and History (U.S.). Vol. 1, No. 1 (Oct. 1958)-. Academic Scholarly Publication. English. qt (January, April, July, October). $82.00 US, Canada & Mexico; £59.00 other. Cambridge University Press, The Edinburgh Building, Shaftesbury Road, Cambridge CB2 2RU United Kingdom. **Tel** 011 44 223 312393, FAX 011 44 223 325959. **(Subscription address:** Cambridge University Press / North America, 110 Midland Avenue, Port Chester NY 10573.) **ED** Raymond Grew. **LC** H1; .C73. **DD** 305. **[CCC].** cum. index. **Bk Rev. Pr Rev.** available on microfilm and microfiche from University Microfilms International (UMI). Documents available from The Genuine Article, UMI Article Clearinghouse.
 **Desc:** An international forum for presentation and discussion of new research into problems of change and stability that recur in human societies through time or in the contemporary world. Sets up a working alliance between specialists in all branches of the social sciences and humanities. Debate and review articles bring the general reader in touch with current findings and issues. In each part, articles on a particular question are grouped together to stimulate comparison of diverse cases.
 **Ind/Abst** ABC POL SCI; Acad. Abstr. Full Text Elite (July 1990-); Acad. Abstr. (July 1990-); Acad. Ind. [Computer File] (1987-); Acad. Search (July 1990-); Am. Hist. Life (1958-); Anthropol. Index; Anthropol. Lit.; Appl. Soc. Sci. Index Abstr. (1958-); Arts Humanit. Citation Index [Full Cov.]; Curr. Contents Arts Humanit.; Curr. Contents Soc. Behav. Sci.; Expand. Acad. Index (1987-); Geogr. Abstr. Human Geogr.; Hist. Source (July 1990-); Humanit. Index; INFO-SOUTH Abstr.; Int. Bibliogr. Sociol.; Int. Dev. Abstr.; Int. Polit. Sci. Abstr.; Leis. Recreat. Tour. Abstr.; Linguist. Lang. Behav. Abstr.; Mag. Search; Middle East Abstr. Index; Newsp. Period. Abstr. (1991-); Res. Alert [Full Cov.]; Rural Dev. Abstr.; Soc. Plann. Policy Dev. Abstr.; Soc. Sci. Source (Jul. 1990-); Soc. Sci. Cit. Index [Full Cov.]; Sociol. Abstr.; U.S. Polit. Sci. Doc.; West. Hist. Q.; World Agric. Econ. (1958-).

US/0892-5569
**COMPARATIVE URBAN AND COMMUNITY RESEARCH.** [Comp. urban community res.]. Vol. 1 (1988)-. English. an. $19.95. Transaction Publishers / Rutgers State University, New Brunswick NJ 08903. **Tel** (908)932-2280 Ext. 105, FAX (908)932-3138. **ED** Michael Smith. **LC** HT110; .C65. **DD** 307.76/05. **CODEN** CUCEEK. **Circ:** 1,000. available on microfilm and microfiche from University Microfilms International (UMI). Continues *Comparative Urban Research, 0090-3892.*
 **Desc:** An interdisciplinary review of theoretical, empirical and applied research on the processes of urbanization and community change throughout the world.
 **Ind/Abst** ABC POL SCI; Int. Polit. Sci. Abstr.

US/0095-2737
**COMPUTERS & SOCIETY.** See Computers.

PO/0871-1771
**COMUNICACOES DO INSTITUTO DE INVESTIGACAO CIENTIFICA TROPICAL, SERIE DE CIENCIAS HISTORICAS, ECONOMICAS E SOCIOLOGICAS.** See Economics.

II/0970-6437
**CONCEPT NEWS.** [Concept News]. (1976)-. Periodical. English. mo. Rs12.00. Concept Publishing Company, A/15-16 Commercial Block, Mohan Garden, New Delhi A/110 059 India. **Tel** (11)5554042. **ED** Naurang Rai. **UDC** 016(048.1). **Bk Rev. Ad Acc. Circ:** 6,000.

US
**CONCERNED : THE OFFICIAL PUBLICATION OF THE CONTEMPORARY SOCIAL PROBLEMS SPECIAL INTEREST SECTION, AMERICAN ASSOCIATION OF LAW LIBRARIES.** **Added/Corp** American Association of Law Libraries. Contemporary Social Problems Special Interest Section. Vol. 1, No. 1 (Nov. 1983)-. Periodical. English. ir. Free to members of the American Association of Law Libraries Special Interest Section. American Association of Law Libraries, 53 West Jackson Boulevard, Suite 940, Chicago IL 60604. **Tel** (312)939-4764, FAX (312)431-1097, telex ABA7603. Continues *American Association of Law Libraries. Contemporary Social Problems Special Interest Section Contemporary Social Problems.*

US/0888-6091
**CONFLUENCIA (GREELEY, COLO.).** (CONFLUENCIA.). **Added/Corp** University of Northern Colorado. Dept. of Hispanic Studies. Vol. 1, No. 1 (Fall 1985)-. Periodical. English (Spanish). sa. $16.00 (individuals) $20.00 (institutions) US & Canada; $20.00 (individuals), $25.00 (institutions) other. Confluencia, Revista Hispanica, University of Northern Colorado, Hispanic Studies Department, Greeley CO 80639. **Tel** (303)351-2811. **DD** 946. **CODEN** CONFE2. available on microfilm and microfiche from University Microfilms International (UMI). Documents available from The Genuine Article.
 **Ind/Abst** Arts Humanit. Citation Index (19??-19??) [Full Cov.]; Curr. Contents Arts Humanit.; HAPI Hisp. Am. Period. Index; Res. Alert [Full Cov.]; Soc. Sci. Cit. Index [Select. Cov.].

US/0363-9460
**CONFRONTATION/CHANGE LITERARY REVIEW.** **VFOAT** Confrontation/Change Review; Confrontation/Change. V. 1- Fall/Winter 1976-. Periodical. English. qt $10.00. Confrontation/Change Review, 1107 Lexington Avenue, Dayton OH 45407-1608. **Tel** (513)275-6879. **ED** F M Finney. **Bk Rev. Ad Acc. Circ:** 2,000.
 **Desc:** A journal of social and applied economics, political science fiction and book reviews. Focus on blacks and Third World international affairs.

UK/0573-777X
**CONTACT.** See Religion and Theology.

US
**CONTEMPORARY SOCIAL PROBLEMS.** Title Change. **Main/Corp** American Association of Law Libraries. Contemporary Social Problems Special Interest Section. (19??)-(19??). Periodical. English. American Association of Law Libraries, 53 West Jackson Boulevard, Suite 940, Chicago IL 60604. **Tel** (312)939-4764, FAX (312)431-1097, telex ABA7603. Continued by *Concerned.*
 **Ind/Abst** Leg. Inf. Manage. Index (19??-).

II
**CONTEMPORARY SOCIAL SCIENCES.** V. 1- Jan./March 1972-. Periodical. English. A-14 Green Park Extension, New Delhi 16 India. **LC** H8; .C668. **DD** 300.

US/1041-3030
**CONTEMPORARY SSOCIAL PSYCHOLOGY.** See Psychology.

UK/0951-4937
**CONTEMPORARY WALES : AN ANNUAL REVIEW OF ECONOMIC AND SOCIAL RESEARCH.** See Economics.

US/1056-1072
**CONTENTION (BLOOMINGTON, IND.).** (CONTENTION : DEBATES IN SOCIETY, CULTURE, AND SCIENCE.). [Contention]. Vol. 1, No. 1 (Fall 1991)-. Periodical. English. Three times a year. $45.00. Indiana University Press, 601 North Morton Street, Bloomington IN 47404. **Tel** (812)855-3830, (800)842-6796. **LC** H1; .C84. **DD** 300/.5. **CODEN** CDSSEN.
 **Ind/Abst** Linguist. Lang. Behav. Abstr.; Soc. Plann. Policy Dev. Abstr.; Sociol. Abstr.

BL
**CONTRAPONTO.** **Added/Corp** Centro de Estudos Noel Nutels. Vol. 1, (Nov. 1976)-. Portuguese. **LC** H8; .C68. **DD** 300/.5.

US/0196-9099
**CONTRIBUTIONS IN BLACK STUDIES.** See Humanities.

US/1050-2955
**CORNELL EAST ASIA SERIES.** See General Interest-General Interest-Asia.

US/0749-4394
**COSSA WASHINGTON UPDATE.** [C0SSA Wash. Update]. **Added/Corp** Consortium of Social Science Associations. **VFOAT** C.O.S.S.A. Washington Update. **VAT** Consortium of Social Science Associations Washington Update. (19??)-. Periodical. English. Twenty-two times a year (Bi-weekly except Aug., Dec.). $120.00. Consortium of Social Science Associations, 1522 K Street NW Suite 836, Washington DC 20005. **Tel** (202) 842-3525, FAX (202) 842-2788. **DD** 300.

US/0887-6398
**COUNTER-TERRORISM.** Title Change. **VFOAT** Counter Terrorism. (1986)-?. English. bw. Interests Ltd, 8512 Cedar Street, Silver Spring MD 20910-4347. **Tel** (301)588-7916, FAX (301)588-2085, telex 6501701421. **ED** Frank G McGuire. **LC** HV6432; .C67. **DD** 363.3/2/05. **[CCC]. Bk Rev.** available in microform from University Microfilms International (UMI). Continued by *Counter-terrorism and Security Intelligence, 1053-1939.*

BE/0577-148X
**COURRIER HEBDOMADAIRE DU C.R.I.S.P.** **Added/Corp** Centre de Recherche et d'Information Socio-Politiques. **VFOAT** Courrier Hebdomadaire du CRISP; CH. (19??)-. Periodical. French. Forty times a year. 9500F. Centre Rech Info Socio Politiq, rue du Congres 35, B-1000 Brussels Belgium. **Tel** 011 32 2 2183226. **LC** JN6101; .C68.

CN/0827-4045
**COURRIER ROUMAIN (MONTREAL).** (LE COURRIER ROUMAIN / FEDERATION DES ASSOCIATIONS ROUMAINES DU CANADA.). [Courr. roum.]. Periodical. French (Romanian). mo. $10.00. Federation des Associations Roumaines du Canada, 3500 rue Fullum, Montreal Quebec H2K 3P6 Canada. **Tel** (514)521-1777. **ED** Jean Taranu. **DD** 305.8/59/071. **Ad Acc. Circ:** 250 (ctrl).
 **Desc:** Covers ethics, multicultural, and cultural-national tradition.

US/0740-3399
**CREATION SOCIAL SCIENCE AND HUMANITIES QUARTERLY.** Ceased. [Creat. Soc. Sci. Humanit. q.]. **Added/Corp** Creation Social Science and Humanities Society. **VFOAT** C.S.S.H. Quarterly; CSSH Quarterly. Vol. 1, No. 1 (Fall 1978)-Vol. 16. Periodical. English. qt. Creation Social Science and Humanities Society, 1429 North Holyoke, Humanities Society, Wichita KS 67208. **Tel** (316)683-3610. **ED** Paul D Ackerman, 4726 E 25th N, Wichita, KS 37220, (316)686-0988. Index available. cum. index. **Bk Rev** (Qty: 6-8 per year). **Circ:** 800.
 **Desc:** Publishes articles, book reviews, poetry, announcements, letters relating to social sciences and humanities and biblical creation perspectives. The journal is directed to readers with a college background or equivalent.
 **Ind/Abst** Christ. Period. Index (19??-).

US/1040-0419
**CREATIVITY RESEARCH JOURNAL.** (THE CREATIVITY RESEARCH JOURNAL.). [Creat. res. j.]. **VFOAT** Journal of Creativity Research. Vol. 1 (Dec. 1988)-. Periodical. English. qt. $110.00 US & Canada; $135.00 other. Lawrence Erlbaum Associates, 365 Broadway, Suite 102, Hillsdale NJ 07642. **Tel** (201)666-4110, (800)926-6579, FAX (201)666-2394. **LC** WMLC 93/1373. **DD** 153. Index available. cum. index. **Bk Rev. Ad Acc. Circ:** 400.
**Desc:** Covers creative abilities.
**Ind/Abst** Except. Child Educ. Resour.; Psychol. Abstr. (1988-); PsycINFO; PsycLit.

US/0363-6283
**CRITICAL ISSUES (WASHINGTON DC).** (CRITICAL ISSUES.). **Main/Corp** Heritage Foundation, Washington, D.C. Began in 1976. Monographic series. English. ir. Price varies per volume. Heritage Foundation, 214 Massachusetts Avenue Northeast, Washington DC 20002. **Tel** (202)546-4400.
**Desc:** Deals with a range of subjects including education, social security, enterprise zones, the environment, reformation of the military, and Soviet strategy of terror. Gives a more in-depth look at some of today's issues.

AT
**CRITICAL PEDAGOGY NETWORK. See** Education.

US/0730-2304
**CRITICAL TEXTS.** ***Suspended.*** **See** Literary and Political Reviews.

●US/1069-3971
**CROSS-CULTURAL RESEARCH.** (CROSS-CULTURAL RESEARCH : OFFICIAL JOURNAL OF THE SOCIETY FOR CROSS-CULTURAL RESEARCH / SPONSORED BY THE HUMAN RELATIONS AREA FILES, INC.). [Cross-cult. res.]. **Added/Corp** Society for Cross-Cultural Research. Human Relations Area Files, Inc. **VFOAT** Cross Cultural Research. Vol. 27, No. 1 & 2 (Feb./May 1993)-. Periodical. English. qt. $97.00. SAGE Periodical Press, 2455 Teller Road, Thousand Oaks CA 91320. **Tel** (805)499-0721, FAX (805)499-0871, telex 100799. **ED** Melvin Ember. **LC** H1; .B45. **DD** 300/.5. **NLM** W1; CR329. **Pr Rev. Acid Free.** ***Continues*** *Behavior Science Research, 0094-3673.*
**Desc:** Published studies pertaining to cross-cultural or comparative issues in the social and behavioral sciences.

US/0271-9177
**CROSS-CULTURAL RESEARCH AND METHODOLOGY SERIES.** [Cross-cult. res. methodol. ser.]. (19??)-. Monographic series. English. ir. Price varies per volume. Sage Publications Ltd., 6 Bonhill Street, London EC2A 4PU, UK. **Tel** 071 374 0645, FAX 071 374 8741, telex 296207 SAGE G. **Acid Free.**

●SA
**CSD BULLETIN. Added/Corp** Centre for Science Development (Human Sciences Research Council). **VFOAT** CSD/SWO Bulletin. (1994)-. Bulletin. Afrikaans (English). Ten times a year (Jan/Feb. and Nov/Dec. issues combined). R25.00. Center for Science & Development, PO box 270, 0001 Pretoria South Africa. **Tel** 011 27 12 2022724, FAX 011 27 12 3265362. **ED** Marilyn Farouharson. **LC** Q127.S693; B85. **DD** 338.96806. **Bk Rev. Ad Acc. Circ:** 3,700. available on an online database. ***Continues*** *Bulletin / CSD, 1017-6136.*

BE
**CSKW MEDEDELINGEN.** Dutch. qt. 250.00F. Centrum Voor Soc Kultur Werk, Groeneweg 151, 3030 Heverlee Belgium.

II
**CSSSC MONOGRAPH. VFOAT** C.S.S.S.C. Monograph. 1-. Monographic series. English. Price varies per volume. Registrar / Calcutta, Centre for Studies in Social Sciences Calcutta, 10 Lake Terrace, Calcutta 700 029 India.

SP/0213-5612
**CUADERNOS DE ACCION SOCIAL.** ***Ceased.*** (19??)-(19??). Spanish. mo. Subsecretaria, Subdireccion General de Documentacion y Publicaciones, Jose Abascal 39, 28003 Madrid Spain. **Tel** 011 34 1 3477353.

VE/0798-0841
**CUADERNOS DE ACTUALIDAD INTERNACIONAL.** [Cuad. actual. int.]. (1989)-. Periodical. Spanish. sa. Bs500 Venezuela; $32.00 US; $40.00 other. CENDES, Apartado Postal 6622, Caracas 1010-A Venezuela. **Tel** 7523266, FAX 7522691. **(Subscription address:** CENDES, Poba International #151, PO Box 02-5255, Miami FL 33102-5255 USA**) DD** 505. **Ad Acc. Pr Rev. Circ:** 1,000 (ctrl).
**Desc:** A selection of articles to Documentattion Francaise.

CU
**CUADERNOS DE NUESTRA AMERICA. See** Political Science.

UY
**CUADERNOS DEL CLAEH. Added/Corp** Centro Latinoamericano de Economia Humana. **VFOAT** Cuadernos del Centro Latinoamericano de Economia Humana. (1985)-. Periodical. Spanish. qt. $55.00 US, Canada & Europe; $45.00 The Americas; $60.00 other. Centro Latinoamericano de Economia Humana, Zelmar Michelini 1220, Montevideo Uruguay. **Tel** 011 598 2 907194, 011 598 2 910433. **LC** HC121; .P83. Index available. cum. index. **Ad Acc.** ***Continues*** *Publicacion del Centro Latinoamericano de Economia Humana.*
**Ind/Abst** Am. Hist. Life (1986-); LABORDOC; PAIS Int. Print (1991-).

MX
**CUADERNOS POLITICOS.** ***Suspended.*** No. 1 (July/Sept. 1974)-Suspended with No. 60. Periodical. Spanish. qt. $18.00. Ediciones Era, Apartado Postal 74-092, Avena 102, 09810 Mexico DF Mexico. **Tel** 581-77-44. **LC** F1414.2; .C75. **Ad Acc. Circ:** 3,000.
**Desc:** Journal for political and social analyses especially for the Latin American countries.
**Ind/Abst** HAPI Hisp. Am. Period. Index; Leis. Recreat. Tour. Abstr.; Rural Dev. Abstr.; World Agric. Econ.

US/0894-2714
**CUBAN HERITAGE.** ***Suspended.*** [Cuban herit.]. Vol. 1, No. 1 (Summer 1987)-?. Periodical. English. qt. $12.00. Cuban Heritage, Florida International University Foundation, University Park Campus/PC 111, Miami FL 33199. **LC** F1751; .C978. **DD** 972.91/005.

US/0882-3049
**CULTURA LUDENS.** Monographic series. English. Price varies per volume. John Benjamins, 821 Bethlehem Pike, Philadelphia PA 19118. **Tel** (215)836-1200, (020)73 81 56, FAX (215)836-1204, (020)73 97 73. **(Subscription address:** Netherlands/ Amsteldijk 44, PO Box 52519, NL-1007 HA Amsterdam**) ED** Mihai Spariosu. **DD** 306. **Bk Rev.**
**Desc:** Focuses on interrelationship of play and initiation in western culture, treating them as broad cultural phenomena and key concepts in the direction of our civilization.
**Ind/Abst** MLA Int. Bibl. Books Artic. Mod. Lang. Lit.

US/0882-4371
**CULTURAL CRITIQUE.** [Cult. crit.]. **Added/Corp** Society for Cultural Critique. No. 1 (Fall 1985)-. Periodical. English. tq (3 issues). $52.00 institutions, $28.00 individuals US; $63.00 institutions, $39.00 individuals other. Oxford University Press / New York, 200 Madison Avenue, New York NY 10016. **Tel** (212)679-7300, (919)677-0977, (800)451-7556, (800)445-9714, FAX (919)677-1303. **(Subscription address:** Oxford University Press / USA, Journals Marketing Department, Oxford University Press, 2001 Evans Road, Cary NC 27513.**) LC** AC5; .C84. **DD** 306. **[CCC]. Ad Acc. Circ:** 2,000 (ctrl). available on microfilm and microfiche from University Microfilms International (UMI). Documents available from The Genuine Article.
**Desc:** International journal of cultural studies.
**Ind/Abst** Altern. Press Index (-199?); Am. Hist. Life (1989); Arts Humanit. Citation Index [Full Cov.]; Curr. Contents Arts Humanit.; Film Lit. Index (19??-); Left Index; Linguist. Lang. Behav. Abstr.; Res. Alert [Full Cov.]; Romant. Move.; Soc. Plann. Policy Dev. Abstr.; Soc. Sci. Cit. Index [Select. Cov.]; Sociol. Abstr.

UK/0950-2386
**CULTURAL STUDIES (LONDON, ENGLAND).** (CULTURAL STUDIES.). Vol. 1, No. 1 (Jan. 1987)-. Periodical. English. Three times a year. $65.00 (US & Canada); £66.00 (UK); £72.00 (other). Routledge, 11 New Fetter Lane, London EC4P 4EE England. **Tel** 071 583 9855, FAX 071 842 2298. **(Subscription address:** Kinokuniya Company Ltd., 38-1 Sakuragaoka 5, chome Setagaya-ku, Tokyo 156 Japan.**) CODEN** CUSTE9. **[CCC].** ***Continues*** *Australian Journal of Cultural Studies, 0810-9648.*
**Ind/Abst** APAIS, Aust. Public Aff. Inf. Ser.; Appl. Soc. Sci. Index Abstr.; Arts Humanit. Citation Index [Full Cov.]; Commun. Abstr.; Int. Bibliogr. Sociol.; Linguist. Lang. Behav. Abstr.; Soc. Plann. Policy Dev. Abstr.; Soc. Sci. Cit. Index [Full Cov.]; Sociol. Abstr.

US/0888-8779
**CULTURE, ETHNICITY, AND NATION.** [Cult. eth. nation]. Vol. 1, (1989)-. Monographic series. English. ir. Price varies per volume. Peter Lang Publishing, 62 West 45th Street, 4th Floor, New York NY 10036. **Tel** (212)764-1471, (800)770-5264, telex 6973364 PLNY. **LC** UNC. **DD** 300.

JA/0386-7293
**CURRENT CONTENTS OF ACADEMIC JOURNALS IN JAPAN. THE HUMANITIES AND SOCIAL SCIENCES. See** Humanities.

US/1062-3140
**CURRENT CONTENTS ON DISKETTE. SOCIAL & BEHAVIORAL SCIENCES.** (CURRENT CONTENTS ON DISKETTE. SOCIAL & BEHAVIORAL SCIENCES [COMPUTER FILE].). [Curr. contents diskette, Soc. behav. sci.]. **VFOAT** Social & Behavioral Sciences; Social and Behavioral Sciences. Vol. 22, Issue 32 (Aug. 6, 1990)-. Periodical. English. wk. $525.00. Institute for Scientific Information, 3501 Market Street, Philadelphia PA 19104. **Tel** (215)386-0100, (800)523-1850, FAX (215)386-6362, telex 84-5305. **(Subscription address:** Institute for Scientific Information, PO Box 71416, Chicago IL 60694.**) DD** 016.

US/0092-6361
**CURRENT CONTENTS. SOCIAL & BEHAVIORAL SCIENCES. See** Social Sciences-Abstracting, Bibliographies and Statistics.

PH
**CURRENT EVENTS DIGEST. See** Education.

UK/0267-1964
**CURRENT RESEARCH IN BRITAIN. SOCIAL SCIENCES.** [Curr. res. Br., Soc. sci.]. **VFOAT** CRB. Social Sciences. 1st. Ed.- 1985-. English. an. £50.00 UK; £54.00 other. British Library / Lending Division, Boston Spa, Wetherby West Yorkshire LS 237BQ England. **Tel** 0937 546060, FAX 0937 546333, telex 557381. **LC** H62.5.G7. **DD** 300/.5. **NLM** H 62.5.G7; C976. ***Continues in part*** *Research in British Universities, Polytechnics and Colleges.*

SW
**CURRENT RESEARCH PROJECTS.** ***Title Change.*** **Main/Corp** Industriens Utredningsinstitut (Sweden). English. Industriens Utredningsinstitut, Grevgatan 34, Box 5037, S102 41 Stockholm Sweden. **LC** H62.5.S8; I53A. **DD** 330/.07/20485. ***Continued by*** *Verksamheten (Industriens Utredningsinstitut (Sweden). English. IUI Research Program.*

US/0192-6802
**CURRENT WORLD LEADERS. See** Political Science-International Relations.

US/0011-4294
**CYCLES (PITTSBURGH). See** Science and Technology.

CY
**CYPRUS REVIEW, THE. Added/Corp** Intercollege (Nicosia, Cyprus). Vol. 1, No. 1 (Spring 1989)-. Periodical. English. sa. $40.00 institutions; $25.00 individuals. Intercollege, PO Box 4005, Nicosia, Cyprus. **Tel** 011-357-2-456892, 011-357-2-456813, 456208, FAX 011-357-2-456704, telex 4969 INTERCOL CY. **ED** Iacovos Ioannou, Andreas Theophanous. **LC** DS54.A2; C963. **DD** 956.45/005. **CODEN** CYREEL. **Bk Rev. Ad Acc.**
**Desc:** Original scholarly thesis and dissertation summaries, review papers, "think pieces", journal reviews and subject bibliographies of social, economic, and political issues.
**Ind/Abst** Econ. Lit. Index; PAIS Int. Print; Soc. Plann. Policy Dev. Abstr.; Middle East J.

BG/1013-543X
**DACCA UNIVERSITY STUDIES. PART A, THE. See** The Arts.

BL/0011-5258
**DADOS (RIO DE JANEIRO).** (DADOS.). [Dados]. **Added/Corp** Instituto Universitario de Pesquisas do Rio de Janeiro. Sociedade Brasileira de Instrucao. Vol. 1 (1966)-. Periodical. Portuguese (summaries and/or abstracts in English and French). tq (3 issues). $61.00 (institutions); $29.00 (individuals) surface mail. SBI/IUPERJ, Rua da Matriz 82, Botafogo 22260 Rio de Janeiro Brazil. **Tel** 011 55 21 2860996. **ED** Charles Pessanha. Documents available from The Genuine Article.
**Ind/Abst** Arts Humanit. Citation Index [Select. Cov.]; Curr. Contents Soc. Behav. Sci.; HAPI Hisp. Am. Period. Index; Int. Polit. Sci. Abstr.; Linguist. Lang. Behav. Abstr. (?-?); Res. Alert [Full Cov.]; Soc. Plann. Policy Dev. Abstr. (?-?); Soc. Sci. Cit. Index [Full Cov.]; Sociol. Abstr. (?-?).

US/0011-5266
**DAEDALUS (CAMBRIDGE). See** Science and Technology.

US/0747-4857
**DATA BOOK OF SOCIAL STUDIES MATERIALS AND RESOURCES.** ***Ceased.*** [Data book soc. stud. mater. resour.]. **Added/Corp** ERIC Clearinghouse for Social Studies/Social Science Education. Social Science Education Consortium. National Institute of Education (U.S.). Vol. 5 (1980)-?. English. an. Social Science Education Consortium, 855 Broadway, Boulder CO 80302. **Tel** (303)492-8154. **ED** Ann M Williams. **LC** HG1; .D48. **DD** 300/.7. **Circ:** 400. available on microfiche (Vols. (8-) distributed to depository libraries). ***Continues*** *Social Studies Materials and Resources Data Book.*
**Desc:** Analyses of elementary and secondary social studies, social science textbooks, teacher resources, supplementary materials, non-print materials and ERIC documents.

GW
**DBJR. VAT** Deutscher Bundesjugendring. English. an. Deutscher Bundesjugendring, Haager Weg 44, 5300 Bonn 1 Germany. **LC** HQ799.8.G4; D48A. **DD** 305.2/35/0943. ***Continues*** *Jahresbericht (Deutscher Bundesjugendring).*

BL
**DEBATE & [I.E. E] CRITICA.** No. 1 (July/Dec. 1973)-. Portuguese. sa. Editora de Humanismo Ciencia e Technologia, rue Conde de Sarzedas 38, Sao Paulo Brazil. **LC** H8; .D38. **DD** 300/.5.

AG/0046-001X
**DESARROLLO ECONOMICO (BUENOS AIRES).** (DESARROLLO ECONOMICO.). [Desarro. econ. (B. Aires)]. Vol. 1 (No. 1 April/June (1961)-. Periodical. Spanish (English). Four times a year. $68.00 Argentina & bordering countries; $74.00 other countries of America; $76.00 Europe; $80.00 other. Instituto de Desarrollo Economico y Social, Araoz 2836, 1425 Buenos Aires Argentina. **Tel** 54 1 8044949, FAX 54 1 8045856. **ED** Juan Carols Torre. **LC** HD85.S7; D48. Index available. cum. index. **Ad Acc**, **Adv Mgr:** Getulio E. Steinbach. **Pr Rev. Circ:** 2,000 (ctrl). available in microform. Documents available from The Genuine Article.
**Desc:** Analysis and study of Argentine and Latin American problems in the fields of economics, sociology, history, political science and culture.
**Ind/Abst** Am. Hist. Life (1978-); Econ. Lit. Index; HAPI Hisp. Am. Period. Index; Int. Bibliogr. Sociol.; Int. Labour Doc.; J. Econ. Lit.; LABORDOC; Leis. Recreat. Tour. Abstr.; Linguist. Lang. Behav. Abstr.; PAIS Int. Print (1991-); Res. Alert [Full Cov.]; Rural Dev. Abstr.; Soc. Plann. Policy Dev. Abstr.; Soc. Sci. Cit. Index [Full Cov.]; Sociol. Abstr.; World Agric. Econ.

JA/0012-1533
**DEVELOPING ECONOMIES, THE.** [Dev. econ.]. **Added/Corp** Ajia Keizai Kenkyujo (Japan). (Jan. 1963)-. Periodical. English. qt. $94.00. **(Subscription address:** Maruzen Company Ltd., PO Box 5050, Import & Export Department, Tokyo 100 31 Japan.**)** **LC** HC59.7; .D4. **DD** 330.9172/4. cum. index. **Pr Rev.** ctrl circ. Documents available from The Genuine Article.
**Desc:** An international and interdisciplinary forum for social science studies of developing countries, stimulating theoretical, empirical and comparative studies of the problems confronted by them.
**Ind/Abst** AGRICOLA; Asia.-Pac. Econ. Lit.; Contents Recent Econ. J.; Curr. Contents Soc. Behav. Sci.; Econ. Lit. Index; Geogr. Abstr. Human Geogr.; Int. Bibliogr. Sociol.; Int. Dev. Abstr.; Int. Labour Doc.; J. Econ. Lit.; LABORDOC; Leis. Recreat. Tour. Abstr.; Middle East Abstr. Index; Res. Alert [Full Cov.]; Rice Abstr.; Rural Dev. Abstr.; Soc. Plann. Policy Dev. Abstr.; Soc. Sci. Cit. Index [Full Cov.]; Sociol. Abstr. (?-?); West. Hist. Q.; World Agric. Econ.

UK/0012-155X
**DEVELOPMENT AND CHANGE.** [Dev. change]. **Added/Corp** Institute of Social Studies (Netherlands). Vol. 1, No. 1 (1969)-. Academic Scholarly Publication. English. Four times a year (Jan., Apr., July, Oct.). $169.00 North America; £110.00 others. Basil Blackwell Publishers Ltd, 108 Cowley Road, Oxford 0X4 1JF England. **Tel** 011 44 865 791100, FAX 011 44 865 791347, telex 837022 OXBOOK G. **(Subscription address:** Blackwell Publishers / UK, Marston Book Services, PO Box 87, Oxford OX2 0DT England.**)** **ED** Martin Doornbos, Henk Van Roosmalen and Ashwani Saith. **LC** HD82; .D387. **DD** 309.2/05. **[CCC]. Pr Rev.** Documents available from The Genuine Article.
**Desc:** Devoted to the critical analysis and discussion of current issues of development. Publishes articles from all the social sciences and intellectual persuasions which contribute to an understanding of Third World problems.
**Ind/Abst** ABC POL SCI; AGRICOLA; Am. Hist. Life (1975-); Appl. Soc. Sci. Index Abstr.; Arts Humanit. Citation Index [Select. Cov.]; Curr. Contents Soc. Behav. Sci.; Dairy Sci. Abstr.; Econ. Lit. Index (199?-); Geogr. Abstr. Human Geogr.; Hum. Rights Intern. Rep.; Int. Bibliogr. Sociol.; Int. Dev. Abstr.; Int. Labour Doc.; Int. Polit. Sci. Abstr.; J. Econ. Lit.; J. Plan. Lit.; LABORDOC; Linguist. Lang. Behav. Abstr.; Middle East Abstr. Index; Nutr. Abstr. Rev., Ser. A, Hum. Exp.; Res. Alert [Full Cov.]; Rice Abstr.; Rural Dev. Abstr.; Soc. Plann. Policy Dev. Abstr.; Soc. Sci. Cit. Index [Full Cov.]; Sociol. Abstr.; World Agric. Econ.

MY
**DEWAN MASYARAKAT.** **Added/Corp** Dewan Bahasa dan Pustaka. (1963)-. Malay. Twelve times a year. 21.00Mal$. Dewan Bahasa Dan Pustaka, Peti Surat 803, 50926 Kuala Lumpur Malaysia. **Tel** 001 60 3 2484211. **ED** Jalil A. Rahman. **LC** HN700.6; .A44. **Bk Rev. Ad Acc. Circ:** 70,000. ***Continues** Dewan Masharakat.*
**Desc:** A social-political magazine meant for the general public.

US/1044-2057
**DIASPORA (NEW YORK, N.Y.).** (DIASPORA : A JOURNAL OF TRANSNATIONAL STUDIES.). [Diaspora]. **Added/Corp** Zoryan Institute for Contemporary Armenian Research and Documentation. Vol. 1, No. 1 (Spring 1991)-. Periodical. English. tq (3 issues). $51.00 institutions, $25.50 individuals US; $61.00 institutions, $35.50 individuals other. Oxford University Press / New York, 200 Madison Avenue, New York NY 10016. **Tel** (212)679-7300, (919)677-0977, (800)451-7556, (800)445-9714, FAX (919)677-1303. **(Subscription address:** Oxford University Press / USA, Journals Marketing Department, Oxford University Press, 2001 Evans Road, Cary NC 27513.**)** **LC** JV6001.A1; D53. **DD** 304.8. **[CCC].** available on microfilm and microfiche from University Microfilms International (UMI).

SP
**DIEZ MINUTOS.** Spanish. Editorial Graficas Espejo, Calle Santa Engracia 23, 28010 Madrid Spain. **Tel** 011 34 1 5938462.

PH/0012-2858
**DILIMAN REVIEW, THE.** [Diliman rev.]. **Added/Corp** University of the Philippines. College of Liberal Arts. University of the Philippines. College of Arts and Sciences. Vol. 1, No. 1 (Jan. 1953)-. Periodical. English (Tagalog). qt (4 issues). P30.00. University of Philippines College of Law, Room 208 210, Second Floor Palma Hall, Diliman Quezon City, Philippines. **Tel** 011 63 2 982471 ext. 6901, FAX 6 32 97 67 85. **ED** Francisco Nemenzo. **LC** AP8; .D54. **DD** 378.91. cum. index. **Bk Rev. Ad Acc. Circ:** 4,000 (ctrl).
**Desc:** Documents and analysis of Philippine contemporary history; uses interdisciplinary approach to serve as a forum for ideas; serves to popularize specialized and technical studies in the sciences, social sciences and the arts.
**Ind/Abst** Abstr. Engl. Stud.; Index Philip. Period.; MLA Int. Bibl. Books Artic. Mod. Lang. Lit.

US/0093-6251
**DIRECTORY OF CROSS-CULTURAL RESEARCH AND RESEARCHERS.** **Added/Corp** Western Washington State College. Center for Cross-Cultural Research. (19??)-. Directory. English. Western Washington State College, Center for Cross-Cultural Research, Bellingham WA 98225. **LC** H62; .D56. **DD** 300/.7/2.

US/0091-7672
**DIRECTORY OF STATE - USDA RURAL DEVELOPMENT COMMITTEES.** Directory. English. US Department of Agriculture, 14th Street and Independence Avenue SW, Washington DC 20250. **Tel** (202)720-5457. **LC** HN90.C6; D57. **DD** 309.2/63/02573.

US/1048-2350
**DIRECTORY OF TAIWAN SCHOLARS.** [Dir. Taiwan sch.]. **Added/Corp** Michigan State University. Asian Studies Center. Association for Asian Studies. Committee on Taiwan Studies. Taiwan Studies Group. (1988)-. Directory. English. an. $10.00 (one year); $18.00 (two years) Comes with Taiwan Studies Newsletter. Michigan State University / Department of English, 201 Morrill Hall, East Lansing MI 48824-1035. **Tel** (517)355-9571, (517)355-7570. **LC** CT3990.A2; D55. **DD** 951. ***Separated from** Taiwan Studies Newsletter, 1048-2342.*

CN/0820-0890
**DIRES.** (DIRES : LA REVUE DU CEGEP DE SAINT-LAURENT.). [Dires]. **Added/Corp** College d'Enseignement General et Professionnel de Saint-Laurent. Vol. 1, No. 1 (Mar. 1983)-. French. Twice a year (Apr. & Oct.). 15.00Can$ one year. Cegep De Saint-Laurent, Service De L'Information, 625, Boulevard Sainte Croix, Sainte-Laurent Quebec H4L 3X7 Canada. **Tel** (514)747-6521. **ED** Rachele Trehblay. **DD** 054/.1. **Ad Acc. Circ:** 500 (ctrl).
**Ind/Abst** MLA Int. Bibl. Books Artic. Mod. Lang. Lit.

UK/0957-9265
**DISCOURSE & SOCIETY.** **VFOAT** Discourse and Society. Vol. 1, No. 1 (July 1990)-. Periodical. English. qt. £85.00 (one year), £170.00 (two year). Sage Publications Ltd., 6 Bonhill Street, London EC2A 4PU, UK. **Tel** 071 374 0645, FAX 071 374 8741, telex 296207 SAGE G. **ED** Teun A. Van Dijk. **LC** P302; .D5476. **DD** 401/.41/05. **CODEN** DISOEN. **Acid Free.**
**Desc:** Explores the relevance of discourse analysis to the social sciences. Stimulates a problem-oriented and critical approach and pays particular attention to the political implications of discourse and communication.
**Ind/Abst** Commun. Abstr.; Linguist. Lang. Behav. Abstr.; Sage Fam. Stud. Abstr.; Soc. Plann. Policy Dev. Abstr.; Sociol. Abstr.

US/0419-4209
**DISSERTATION ABSTRACTS INTERNATIONAL. A, THE HUMANITIES AND SOCIAL SCIENCES.** **See** Humanities.

UK/0262-8015
**DITCHLEY NEWSLETTER, THE.** **Added/Corp** Ditchley Foundation. No. 1 (Spring 1981)-. Newsletter. English. Three times a year. $15.00 US; $19.00 other. American Ditchley Foundation, 477 Madison Avenue, New York NY 10022. **Tel** (212)752-6515, FAX (212)752-6518. ***Continues** Ditchley Journal, 0305-4322.*
**Desc:** Contains synopses of reports on Ditchley conferences and information about the Foundation's programs and other activities.

SP
**DOCUMENTACION SOCIAL.** **Added/Corp** Centro de Estudios de Sociologia Aplicada de Caritas Nacional. (1???)-. Periodical. Spanish. Four times a year (Feb., May, Sept., Dec.). $68.00 Spain; $90.00 others. Caritas Espanola, San Bernardo 99 Bis/7A Planta, 28015 Madrid 8 Spain. **Tel** 011 34 1 445 5300.
**Ind/Abst** Selec. Coop. Index Manage. Period.

CL
**DOCUMENTACION SOCIAL CATOLICA LATINOAMERICANA : DOCLA / INSTITUTO LATINOAMERICANO DE DOCTRINA Y ESTUDIOS SOCIALES.** **VFOAT** DOCLA. Periodical. Spanish. bm. $14.00. Ilades, Casilla 14.446 Correo 21, Santiago Chile. **Tel** 717499. **LC** HN110.5; .D63. **DD** 261.8/3/098.

NE
**DOCUMENTATIEBLAD / LEIDEN AFRIKA-STUDIECENTRUM.** ***Title Change.*** **See** Social Sciences-Abstracting, Bibliographies and Statistics.

II/0376-8651
**DOCUMENTATION SERVICE BULLETIN.** **Added/Corp** India. Dept. of Social Welfare. (19??)-. Bulletin. English. an. Government of India / Department of Social Welfare, Shastri Bhavan, New Delhi India. **LC** Z7163; .D64. **DD** 016.3091/54/04.

AG/0325-8483
**DOCUMENTO DE TRABAJO / INSTITUTO TORCUATO DI TELLA, CENTRO DE INVESTIGACIONES SOCIALES.** **See** Economics-Labor.

GW/0342-037X
**DOKUMENTATIONSDIENST LATEINAMERIKA. AUSGEWAHLTE NEUERE LITERATUR.** (DOKUMENTATIONSDIENST LATEINAMERIKA. AUSGEWAEHLTE NEUERE LITERATUR / DOCUMENTACION LATINOAMERICANA. BOLETIN BIBLIOGRAFICO / INSTITUT FUER IBEROAMERIKA-KUNDE, DOKUMENTATIONS-LEITSTELLE LATEINAMERIKA, IM VERBUND DER STIFTUNG DEUTSCHES UEBERSEE-INSTITUT.). [Dokumentationsd. Lateinam., Ausgew. neuere Lit.]. **Added/Corp** Institut fuer Iberoamerika-Kunde. Dokumentations-Leitstelle. Deutsches Uebersee-Institut. Deutsches Uebersee-Institut. Referat Lateinamerika. **VFOAT** Boletin de Documentacion Latinoamericana; Documentacion Latinoamericana. (1973)-. Periodical. German (Spanish). Twice a year. DM15.00. Deutsches Uebersee Institut, Neuer Jungfernstieg 21, D 20354 Hamburg Germany. **Tel** 011 49 40 3562581. **LC** Z7165.L3; D64. **Bk Rev. Circ:** 500 (ctrl). ***Continues** Dokumentationsdienst Lateinamerika, 0300-4899.*
**Desc:** Documentation of social sciences literature on Latin America.

GW/0012-5172
**DOKUMENTE (KOLN).** (DOKUMENTE; ZEITSCHRIFT FUER UBERNATIONALE ZUSAMMENARBEIT.). [Dokumente]. Vol. 1- ; Sept. 1945-. Periodical. German. qt. **LC** H5; .D65. available on an online database.
**Ind/Abst** Am. Hist. Life (1963-1969).

GW/0012-6063
**DREI (STUTTGART, GERMANY : 1948).** **See** Humanities.

CN/0384-6008
**DROIT POPULAIRE, LE.** V. 1- July 1972-. Periodical. French. mo. Free. Association Pour La Defense Des Droits Sociaux, Du Montreal Metropolitain, 1850 Est, Rue Ontario, Montreal Quebec H2K 1T7. **DD** 309.1/714/281.

ES/0014-1445
**ECA.** (ESTUDIOS CENTRO AMERICANOS : ECA.). [ECA]. **Added/Corp** Universidad Centroamericana Jose Simeon Canas. **VFOAT** E.C.A.; ECA. **VAT** Estudios Centroamericanos. Vol. 1, No. 1 (Jan./Feb. 1946)-. Periodical. Spanish. Eight times a year. $70.00 North and South America; $40.00 Central America; $60.00 Europe; $70.00 other. University of Centroamericanos, Apartado 01 575 Cl Cantabri 11, San Salvador El Salvador. **Tel** 011 503 240744. **LC** AP63; .E15. **CODEN** ESCEES.
**Ind/Abst** Am. Hist. Life (1955-); HAPI Hisp. Am. Period. Index (1955-199?).

US/0896-1360
**ECCSSA JOURNAL, THE.** [ECCSSA j.]. **Added/Corp** Eastern Community College Social Science Association. **VAT** Eastern Community College Social Science Association Journal. Vol. 1, No. 1 (Winter 1986)-. Periodical. English. an (Mar.). $7.50. ECCSSA, 300 Jay Street, N704 New York City Technical College, Brooklyn NY 11201. **Tel** (718)260-5783. **DD** 300.

PO/0390-5330
**ECONOMIA E SOCIOLOGIA.** (ECONOMIA E SOCIOLOGIA / INSTITUTO DE ESTUDOS SUPERIORES DE EVORA.). [Econ. sociol.]. **Added/Corp** Instituto de Estudos Superiores de Evora. Instituto Superior Economico e Social (Evora, Portugal) Instituto Superior Economico e Social (Evora, Portugal). Gabinete de Investigacao e Accao Social. No. 4 (1968)-.

Periodical. Portuguese. sa. $20.00. Revista Economia e Sociologia, Rua Vasco da Gama 15, 7000 Evora Portugal. **Tel** 011 351 23 23327. **LC** HC391; .E264. **DD** 306/.09469. ***Continues*** *Estudos Eborenses.*
**Ind/Abst** PAIS Int. Print.

VE/0012-9895
**ECONOMIA Y CIENCIAS SOCIALES.** [Econ. cienc. soc.]. **Added/Corp** Universidad Central de Venezuela. Facultad de Ciencias Economicas y Sociales. Universidad Central de Venezuela. Facultad de Economia. Universidad Central de Venezuela. Instituto de Investigaciones Economicas y Sociales. (Sept. 1958)-. Periodical. Spanish. ir. University Central de Venezuela, Faculty Economia Institute de Inves, Caracas Venezuela. **LC** H8.S7; E25. **DD** 300/.5.
**Ind/Abst** Am. Hist. Life (1968); HAPI Hisp. Am. Period. Index (19??-); Int. Polit. Sci. Abstr. (1968); Stat. Theory Method Abstr. (1970).

IE/0012-9984
**ECONOMIC AND SOCIAL REVIEW, THE.** [Econ. soc. rev.]. Vol. 1, (Oct. 1969)-. Periodical. English. qt (Jan., Apr., July, Oct.). 35.00p (Europe), 55.00p. Economic & Social Research Institute / Dublin, 4 Burlington Road, Dublin 4 Ireland. **Tel** 011 353 1 6760115 Ext. 427. **ED** P. Clancy and M. Moore. **LC** HC257.I6; E26. **DD** 309.1/415. Index Bound in First Issue (of each volume). **Pr Rev. Circ:** 450 (ctrl). Documents available from The Genuine Article.
**Desc:** A journal of the social sciences with topics including economics, sociology, demography, politics, social geography, statistics and psychology.
**Ind/Abst** Am. Hist. Life (1978-); Appl. Soc. Sci. Index Abstr.; Arts Humanit. Citation Index [Select. Cov.]; Contents Recent Econ. J.; Contents Pages Manage. (1974-); Curr. Contents Soc. Behav. Sci.; Econ. Lit. Index; Geogr. Abstr. Human Geogr. (1978-); Int. Bibliogr. Sociol.; Int. Polit. Sci. Abstr. (1978-); J. Econ. Lit.; Leis. Recreat. Tour. Abstr.; Middle East Abstr. Index; PAIS Int. Print (1991-); Res. Alert [Full Cov.]; Rural Dev. Abstr.; Soc. Sci. Cit. Index [Full Cov.]; Stat. Theory Method Abstr. (1979, 1986); World Agric. Econ.

UK
**ECONOMIC AND SOCIAL STUDIES.** **See** Economics.

TH
**ECONOMIC AND SOCIAL SURVEY OF ASIA AND THE PACIFIC.** **Main/Corp** United Nations. Economic and Social Commission for Asia and the Pacific. (1974)-. Government Publication. English. an. price varies per volume. United Nations Publications, 2 United Nations Plaza, Room DC2 0853, Department 007C, New York NY 10017. **Tel** (212)963-8303, (800)253-9646. **LC** JX1977; .A2 subser; HC411. **DD** 300 S; 330.95/042. ***Continues*** *Economic Survey of Asia and the Far East.*
**Desc:** Presents a collection of articles on topics such as; developmentsl developments, energy supply, trade between developing countries and East European countries, economics and sociology of alternative energy sources, and individual country reports on economic performances and prospects.
**Ind/Abst** Int. Labour Doc.; Middle East Abstr. Index.

US/0070-8534
**ECONOMIC EDUCATION EXPERIENCES OF ENTERPRISING TEACHERS.** **Main/Corp** Joint Council on Economic Education. Vol. 1, (1962)-. English. an (May). $7.95. National Council on Economic Education, 432 Park Ave South, New York NY 10016. **Tel** (212)685-5499, (800)338-1192, FAX (212)213-2872. **ED** J. W. Clark and P. L. Guyton. **LC** H62; .J5843.

UK/0308-5147
**ECONOMY AND SOCIETY.** [Econ. soc.]. Vol. 1 (Feb. 1972)-. Periodical. English. Four times a year. $115.00 (US & Canada); £68.00 (UK); £74.00 (other). Routledge, 11 New Fetter Lane, London EC4P 4EE England. **Tel** 071 583 9855, FAX 071 842 2298. **(Subscription address:** Kinokuniya Company Ltd., 38-1 Sakuragaoka 5, chome Setagaya-ku, Tokyo 156 Japan.**) ED** H M Gane. **DD** 300/.5. **[CCC]. Bk Rev. Ad Acc. Pr Rev. Circ:** 1,000. available on microfilm and microfiche from University Microfilms International (UMI). Documents available from The Genuine Article.
**Desc:** A journal for Marxist scholarships and analysis of the social sciences, with particular emphasis on philosophical and political debate.
**Ind/Abst** Am. Hist. Life (1987-1990); Appl. Soc. Sci. Index Abstr.; Arts Humanit. Citation Index [Select. Cov.]; Curr. Contents Soc. Behav. Sci.; Geogr. Abstr. Human Geogr.; Int. Bibliogr. Sociol.; Int. Dev. Abstr.; Int. Polit. Sci. Abstr.; Middle East Abstr. Index; Res. Alert [Full Cov.]; Soc. Plann. Policy Dev. Abstr.; Soc. Sci. Cit. Index [Full Cov.]; Sociol. Abstr. [Full Cov.].

UK/0424-5318
**EDUCATION & SOCIAL SCIENCE.** **See** Education.

ER
**EESTI TEADUSTE AKADEEMIA TOIMETISED. UHISKONNATEADUSED.** **Added/Corp** Eesti Teaduste Akadeemia. **VFOAT** Uhiskonnateadused; Obshchestvennye Nauki; Social Sciences; Izvestiia Akademii nauk Estonii. Obshchestvennye Nauki; Proceedings of the Estonian Academy of Sciences. Social Sciences; Eesti TA Akadeemia Toimetised. Uhiskonnateadused; Izvestiia AN Estonii. Obshchestvennye Nauki. (1990)-. Periodical. Estonian (English, French, German and Russian). qt. $139.95. Kirjastus Perioodika, Pk 107, Parnu Mnt 8, Tallinn EE0090 Estonia. **Tel** 0142 441 262, FAX 0142 442 484. **(Subscription address:** East View Publications Inc., 3020 Harbor Lane North, Suite 110, Minneapolis MN 55447.**) LC** AS262.E3; A2. ***Continues*** *Eesti NSV Teaduste Akadeemia Toimetised. Uhiskonnateaduste Seeria, 0373-6431.*
**Ind/Abst** Am. Hist. Life; Soc. Plann. Policy Dev. Abstr.

BE
**EF-AVISEN.** **See** Ethnic Interests.

GW/0424-6985
**EINHEIT DER GESELLSCHAFTSWISSENSCHAFTEN, DIE.** (DIE EINHEIT DER GESELLSCHAFTSWISSENSCHAFTEN; STUDIEN IN DEN GRENZBEREICHEN DER WIRTSCHAFTS- UND SOZIALWISSENSCHAFTEN.). Vol. 1 (1964)-. Monographic series. German. ir. Price varies per volume. JCB Mohr / Paul Siebeck, Postfach 2040, D 72010 Tuebingen Germany. **Tel** 011 49 7071 9230, FAX 011 49 7071 51104, telex 7/262872 mohr d. **ED** Erik Boettcher. **DD** 300.
**Desc:** Covers all fields of social science through monographs on such topics as the rise and fall of nations, criteria for scientific theories, individualism and work theory.
**Ind/Abst** Math. Rev.

SP
**ELEKTOR.** Spanish. mo. 8700ptas. Ingelek, Benito Castro No 12 Bis, 28028 Madrid Spain. **Tel** 011 34 1 2556228.

US/0196-9110
**ENCYCLIA.** **See** Science and Technology.

CN/0705-0631
**ENTRE NOUS (TROIS-RIVIERES).** (ENTRE NOUS.). First issue in 1975?. Periodical. French. ir. Free. CRD-04, 1617 rue Royale, Trois-Rivieres G9A 4K2 Canada. **DD** 309.2/5/0971445.

US/0883-9719
**ENVIRON (FORT COLLINS, COLO.).** (ENVIRON.). No. 1 (Summer 1985)-. Periodical. English. Four times a year. $30.00 (institutions); $25.00 (health professionals); $18.00 others. Environ/Wary Canary Press, PO Box 8820, Fort Collins CO 80525. **Tel** (303)223-8816. **DD** 304. Documents available from Documents on Demand.
**Desc:** Ecologic living and health for environmentally aware general readership. Alternatives in food, agriculture, building design, and public policy.
**Ind/Abst** Environ. Abstr.

UK/0263-7758
**ENVIRONMENT AND PLANNING. D, SOCIETY & SPACE.** [Environ. plann., D]. **VFOAT** Society & Space; Society and Space. Vol. 1, No. 1 (Mar. 1983)-. Periodical. English. bm. £137.00 UK $235.00 US. Pion Ltd., 207 Brondesbury Park, London NW2 5JN England. **Tel** 011 44 81 459 0066, FAX 011 44 81 451 6454, telex 94016265 PION G. **ED** M. Dear. **LC** H1; .E58. **DD** 300/.5. Index available. **Bk Rev. Ad Acc. Pr Rev.** Documents available from The Genuine Article.
**Desc:** Development of social theory in the explanation of time-space relationships. Covers topics such as the state, de-industrialization, uneven development, labor markets, social welfare, housing and planning.
**Ind/Abst** Acad. Search (Jan. 1993-); Arts Humanit. Citation Index [Select. Cov.]; Avery Index Archit. Period. Suppl. Colum. Univ. (June 1989-); Curr. Contents Soc. Behav. Sci.; Gen. Sci. Source (Jan. 1993-); Geogr. Abstr. Human Geogr.; Int. Bibliogr. Sociol.; Int. Dev. Abstr.; J. Plan. Lit.; PAIS Int. Print (1991-); Res. Alert [Full Cov.]; Sage Urban Stud. Abstr; Soc. Sci. Cit. Index [Full Cov.].

GR
**EPISTEMONIKE SKEPSE.** Periodical. Greek, Modern (table of contents in English). bm. Skepsi Inc, Averok 26, Athens 104 33 Greece.

GR
**EPITHEORESE TON EUROPAIKON KOINOTETON.** **VFOAT** Revue des Communautes Europeennes. Periodical. Greek, Modern (summaries and/or abstracts in French). qt. $75.00. Europublishing Ltd, 6 rue Kriezotou, Athens 134 Greece. **LC** H8.G74; E64.

GR/0013-9696
**EPITHEORESIS KOINONIKON EREUNON.** [Epitheor. koin. ereun.]. **Added/Corp** Ethnikon Kentron Koinonikon Ereunon (Greece). **VFOAT** Epitheorese Koinonikon Ereunon; Greek Review of Social Research. (Sept. 1969)-. Periodical. Greek, Modern (English and German). qt. $30.00. National Center of Social Research, 1 Sophocleous Street, Athens 122 Greece. **Tel** 011 30 1 3212611. **LC** H8; .E64.
**Ind/Abst** Soc. Plann. Policy Dev. Abstr.; Sociol. Abstr.

GW
**ERGEBNISSE UND METHODEN MODERNER SPRACHWISSENSCHAFT.** (1977)-. Monographic series. German. ir. Price varies per volume. Gunter Naar Verlag, Dischingerwet 5, Postfach 2567, D7400 Tuebingen 5 Germany. **Tel** 070711 9797 0, telex 75288.

BO
**ESTADO & SOCIEDAD.** **VFOAT** Estado y Sociedad. Vol. 1, No. 1 (1985)-. Periodical. Spanish.
**Ind/Abst** HAPI Hisp. Am. Period. Index; PAIS Int. Print.

CN
**ESTIMATES. PART III, SOCIAL SCIENCES AND HUMANITIES RESEARCH COUNCIL.** **Main/Corp** Canada. **VFOAT** Budget des Depenses. Partie III, Conseil de Recherches en Sciences Humaines. (19??)-. English (French). $6.00 Canada; $7.20 other. Canada Communication Group Publishers, Order Processing, Ottawa Ontario K1A 0S9 Canada. **Tel** (819)956-4800, (819)956-4802. **LC** AZ188.C2; C36a. **DD** 001.3.

INT/1013-4069
**ESTUDIOS DEL DESARROLLO.** **VFOAT** Development Studies Journal. (1991)-. Periodical. Spanish (English). an. Bs800 Venezuela; $20.00 North America; $25.00 other. CENDES, Apartado Postal 6622, Caracas 1010-A Venezuela. **Tel** 7523266, FAX 7522691. **(Subscription address:** Poba International, No. 151, Box 02-5255, Miami FL 33102-5255.**) ED** Nelson Prato Barbosa. **UDC** 658. **Bk Rev. Ad Acc. Pr Rev. Circ:** 1,000 (ctrl).
**Desc:** Covers areas of contemporary social science.

MX
**ESTUDIOS SOCIALES.** **Added/Corp** Centro de Investigacion en Alimentacion y Desarrollo (Hermosillo, Mexico) Colegio de Sonora. Universidad de Sonora. Centro de Investigaciones Economicas y Sociales. Vol. 1, No. 1 (Jan./June 1990)-. Periodical. Spanish. sa. **LC** H53.M6; E88.

AG/0327-4934
**ESTUDIOS SOCIALES SANTA FE.** (ESTUDIOS SOCIALES). [Estud. soc.St.Fe]. (1991)-. Periodical. Spanish. sa. Universidad Nacional del Litoral, Bulevar Pellegrimi 2750, 3000 Santo Fe Argentina. **ED** Dario Macor. **UDC** 3.

CL/0716-0321
**ESTUDIOS SOCIALES (SANTIAGO, CHILE).** (ESTUDIOS SOCIALES / CPU.). **Added/Corp** Corporacion de Promocion Universitaria. **VFOAT** Revista Estudios Sociales. (Mar. 1973)-. Periodical. Spanish (summaries and/or abstracts in English). qt. $60.00 US and Canada; $50.00 South America; $88.00 other. Corporacion de Promocion Universitaria, Casilla 1056 Correo 22, Santiago Chile. **Tel** 011 56 2 2043418, , FAX 011 56 2 2741828. **ED** Patricio Dooner. **LC** HC191; .E89. **Bk Rev**, (Qty: 4). **Ad Acc. Circ:** 1,000 (ctrl).
**Ind/Abst** HAPI Hisp. Am. Period. Index; Int. Labour Doc.; LABORDOC; PAIS Int. Print (1991-).

DR/1017-0596
**ESTUDIOS SOCIALES (SANTO DOMINGO).** (ESTUDIOS SOCIALES.). [Estud. soc.]. **Added/Corp** Jesuits. Centro de Investigacion y Accion Social. (1968)-. Periodical. Spanish. Four times a year (Jan., Apr., July, Oct.). $25.00. Centro de Investigacion y Accion Social de la Compania de Jesus, A Llluberes SJ Apdo 1004, Santo Domingo Dominican Republic. **ED** Jesus M. Zaglul. **LC** HN216; .E78. **DD** 306/.097293. **Ad Acc, Adv Mgr:** Manuel Maza. **Pr Rev. Circ:** 1,000.
**Desc:** Journal of research of information about social sciences inparticular. The analysis of the Caribbean and Dominican reality.
**Ind/Abst** Am. Hist. Life (1974-); HAPI Hisp. Am. Period. Index; Soc. Plann. Policy Dev. Abstr.; Soc. Welf. Soc. Plan./Policy Soc. Dev.; Sociol. Abstr. (?-?) [Full Cov.].

BL
**ESTUDOS HISTORICOS.** **See** History(General)-History of North, South, and Central America.

GW/0937-938X
**ETHIK UND SOZIALWISSENSCHAFTEN.** **See** Ethics.

AT
**ETHOS.** **See** Education.

AT/1034-4128
**ETHOS PAPERS.** **See** Education-Teaching and Curriculum.

IT
**EUI WORKING PAPER. SPS / DEPARTMENT OF POLITICAL AND SOCIAL SCIENCES, EUROPEAN UNIVERSITY INSTITUTE.** **Added/Corp** European University Institute. Dept. of Political and Social Sciences. **VFOAT** SPS; EUI Working Papers in Political

and Social Sciences. (1990)-. Monographic series. English. Price varies per volume. **LC** IN PROCESS. ***Continues in part*** *EUI Working Paper.*

US/0893-6862
**EUROPAISCHE STADTKULTUR.** [Cult. Eur. cities]. **VFOAT** Culture of European Cities; Culture de la Ville Europeenne. Monographic series. English (French and German). an. Price varies per volume. Peter Lang Publishing, 62 West 45th Street, 4th Floor, New York NY 10036. **Tel** (212)764-1471, (800)770-5264, telex 6973364 PLNY. **DD** 307.

UK
**EUROPEAN GAY REVIEW, THE.** Vol. 1- 1986-. Periodical. English. qt.

US/0886-1633
**EVALUATION PRACTICE.** [Eval. pract.]. **Added/Corp** American Evaluation Association. Vol. 7, No. 1 (Feb. 1986)-. Periodical. English. Three times a year. $150.00 (institutions), $60.00 (individuals) US; $165.00 (institutions), $75.00 (individuals) (surface mail), $180.00 (institutions), $90.00 (individuals) (air mail), other. JAI Press Inc., 55 Old Post Road, Suite 2, PO Box 1678, Greenwich CT 06836-1678. **Tel** (203)661-7602, FAX (203)661-0792. **ED** MF "Midge" Smith. **LC** H1; .E76. **DD** 658.4/013/05. **[CCC].** available on microfilm from University Microfilms International (UMI). ***Continues*** *Evaluation News (Beverly Hills, Calif.), 0191-8036.*
**Desc:** Assists evaluators to improve the practice of their profession, to develop their skills, encourage dialogue, and to improve their knowledge base.
**Ind/Abst** Curr. Index J. Educ. (March 1990); Curr. Lit. Fam. Plan. (19??-199?); Educ. Adm. Abstr. (?-?); Hum. Resour. Abstr. (?-?); Sage Public Adm. Abstr. (?-?); Soc. Plann. Policy Dev. Abstr.

US/0893-5017
**EXCEL (SAN FRANCISCO, CALIF.).** (EXCEL : QUARTERLY JOURNAL FOR BLACK PROFESSIONALS.). [Excel]. (198?)-. Periodical. English. Four times a year (Publishes quarterly with one special issue). $9.95. Excel / The Quarterly Journal, PO Box 12100, San Francisco CA 94112. **Tel** (415)957-3628, (415)267-3056. **ED** Herb Boyd and Don Brown. **DD** 305. **Bk Rev. Ad Acc. Circ:** 130,000 (ctrl).
**Desc:** A lifestyle magazine.

●CK/0121-6279
**EXTERNADISTA : REVISTA DE LA UNIVERSIDAD EXTERNADO DE COLOMBIA.** **See** Law.

US/0741-577X
**F.A.R.O.G. FORUM JOURNAL BILINGUE.** [F.A.R.O.G. forum]. **Added/Corp** University of Maine at Orono. Franco-American Office. University of Maine at Orono. Franco-American Resource Opportunity Group. **VFOAT** FAROG Forum. **VAT** Franco-American Resource Opportunity Group forum. (19??)-. Periodical. French (English). Four times a year. $35.00 institutions; $10.00 individuals US; $15.00 other. University of Maine l'Office Franco Americain, Orono ME 04469. **Tel** (207)581-3764, FAX (207)581-1455. **ED** Rhea Robbins. **Bk Rev**, (Qty: 5 or 6). **Ad Acc.**
**Desc:** A socio-cultural journal dealing with Franco-American populations; community and academic in focus.

FR/0014-6269
**FACE AU RISQUE.** [Face risque]. (1958)-. Periodical. French. mo (11 issues). 990.00F France; 1300.00F other. Centre National de Prevention et de Protection, Rte de la Chappelle, Reanville St. Just, BP 2265, F-27950 St. Marcel France. **Tel** 011 33 32 536432. **ED** Marc Bohy. **UDC** 36.07. Index available. **Bk Rev.** ctrl circ.

US/0747-0126
**FARO (NEW WILMINGTON, PA.), IL.** ***Ceased.*** (IL FARO.). Periodical. Italian. mo. Il Faro, PO Box 226, New Wilmington PA 16142.

●US/1070-549X
**FEMINISM AND THE SOCIAL SCIENCES.** (1994)-. English. Peter Lang Publishing, 62 West 45th Street, 4th Floor, New York NY 10036. **Tel** (212)764-1471, (800)770-5264, telex 6973364 PLNY.

IT
**FILOSOFIA E SOCIETA.** Vol. 1 (March 1972)-. Periodical. Italian. qt. L30000 Italy; L40000 other. Bibliotheca Gabrielle Chiusano, LGO Olgiata 15 106 2C9, 00123 Rome Italy. **Tel** 011 39 6 3788350. **ED** Lido Chiusano. **Ad Acc.**

CE
**FOCUS.** Vol. 1 (June 1977)-. Periodical. English. mo. 36.00. Collective, 26 Clifford Avenue, Colombo Sri Lanka Ceylon. **LC** H1; .F62. **DD** 300/.5.

CN/0710-7692
**FOCUS (NEW BRUNSWICK TEACHERS' ASSOCIATION. SOCIAL STUDIES COUNCIL).** (FOCUS.). [Focus]. Vol. 7, No. 2 (Jan. 1977)-. Periodical. English. Three times a year. Free. New Brunswick Teachers' Association, PO Box 752, Fredericton New Brunswick E3B 5R6 Canada. **Tel** (506)452-8921. **DD** 300/.7/0715. ctrl circ. ***Continues*** *Social Studies News, 0710-7684.*

CN/0822-3637
**FOCUS ON AGING.** (FOCUS ON AGING / PROGRAMME IN GERONTOLOGY, UNIVERSITY OF TORONTO.). [Focus aging]. **Added/Corp** University of Toronto. Programme in Gerontology. University of Toronto. Centre for Studies of Aging. Vol. 1, No. 1 (Feb. 1980)-. Periodical. English. tq. 9.35Can$. Centre in Gerontology, University of Toronto, 455 Spadina Avenue, Toronto Ontario M5S 2G8 Canada. **Tel** (416)978-4706. **ED** Anne Craik. **DD** 362.6/042/0720713. **Circ:** 900 (ctrl).

DK/0105-712X
**FOLK OG FORSKNING / UDG. AF UNIVERSTETSFORENINGEN FOR DET SYDLIGE OG VESTLIGE JYLLAND.** **See** Humanities.

SW/0349-6279
**FOLKETS HISTORIA.** **See** History(General).

IT
**FORME E LA STORIA, LE.** **See** Literature.

AU
**FORSCHUNGSPOLITISCHE DOKUMENTATION.** **Added/Corp** Austria. Bundesministerium fuer Wissenschaft und Forschung. Sektion Forschung. (1968/71)-. German. ir. Bundesministerium for Wissenschaft und Forschung, Minoritenplatz 5, Vienna Austria. **Tel** (0222)66 20-0. **LC** Z7164.S68; F67.

IO/0376-5687
**FORUM (SEMARANG).** (FORUM.). Indonesian. Universitas Diponegoro Fakultas Sosial & Politik, Jl Imam Barjo S H, Semarang Indonesia. **LC** H8; .F65.

GW/0532-6028
**FRANKFURTER WIRTSCHAFTS- UND SOZIALWISSENSCHAFTLICHE STUDIEN.** **Added/Corp** Frankfurt am Main. Universitat. Wirtschafts- und Sozialwissenschaftliche Fakultat. Issue 1 (1957)-. Monographic series. German. ir. Price varies per volume. Duncker und Humblot Verlag, Postfach 410329, D-12113 Berlin Germany. **Tel** 011 49 30 79000612, 011 49 30 79000613.

US/0533-0130
**FRANKLIN LECTURES IN THE SCIENCES AND HUMANITIES, THE.** **Added/Corp** Auburn University. 1st Series (1970)-. Monographic series. English. ir. Price varies per volume. University of Alabama / School of Law, PO Box 870380, Tuscaloosa AL 35487-0380. **Tel** (205)348-1175. **Pr Rev.**

TU
**FRAT UNIVERSITESI DERGISI. SOSYAL BILIMLER.** **Added/Corp** Frat Universitesi. Sosyal Bilimler Enstitusu. **VFOAT** Sosyal Bilimler. (1987)-. Periodical. Turkish. sa. **LC** H8.T87; F57.

MX/0187-7372
**FRONTERA NORTE.** **Added/Corp** Colegio de la Frontera Norte (Tijuana, Baja California Norte, Mexico). Vol. 1, No. 1 (Jun. 1989)-. Periodical. Spanish (English). Twice a year. $20.00 Mexico; $25.00 other. El Colegio de la Frontera Norte, Boulevard Abelardo, Rodriguez 21, Tijuana Baja CA 22320. **Tel** 011 52 661 33535. **LC** E183.8.M6; F76. **DD** 303.48/272073.
**Ind/Abst** HAPI Hisp. Am. Period. Index (1989-).

CN/1180-3479
**FRONTIERES (MONTREAL).** (FRONTIERES.). [Frontieres]. **Added/Corp** Universite du Quebec a Montreal. **VFOAT** Revue Frontieres. Vol. 1 No 1 (Spring 1988)-. Periodical. French. tq. 35.00Can$ (institution), 22.00Can$ (individual) US; 31.00Can$ (institution), 20.00Can$ (individual) Canada; 40.00Can$ (institution), 26.00Can$ (other). Frontieres UQAM Universitie du Quebec a Montreal, A 4535 CP 8888 Succ, Montreal Quebec, H3C 3P8 Canada. **Tel** (514) 987-6177. **DD** 306.9/05.
**Ind/Abst** Point Repere (1991-).

CN/0821-4808
**FUTURE PLANNER.** [Future plann.]. Vol. 1, No. 1 (March 1983)-. Periodical. English. qt. $15.00. Future Planner, 118 Thomas Street, Oakville Ontario L6J 3A8 Canada. **Tel** (416)845-7244. **DD** 307/.12.

CN/0834-3241
**FUTURES CANADA (1984).** (FUTURES CANADA.). [Futur. Can.]. Vol. 6, No. 2 (1984)-. Periodical. French (English). Association Canadienne des Etudes Prospectives, 3764 Cote-des-Neiges, Montreal Quebec H3H 1V6 Canada. **DD** 909.82/05. ***Continues*** *Futures (Association Canadienne des Etudes Prospectives), 0829-402X.*

SZ
**GDI IMPULS.** **Added/Corp** Gottlieb Duttweiler-Institut. Vol. 1, No. 4, (Oct. 1982)-. Periodical. German. qt (Mar., June., Sept., Dec.). 120.00F. Gottlieb Duttweiler-Institut, CH-8803 Ruschlikon Switzerland. **Tel** 011 41 1 7246111, FAX 011 41 1 7246262, telex 826 510. **ED** Karin Frick. **LC** H5; .G38. **DD** 300/.5. cum. index. ctrl circ. available on an online database.
**Desc:** A publication with future oriented contributions from researchers and consultants for top management. Regularly features are well-known authorities describing and analysing developments and trends in society, technology, economics and management.

GW/0016-5875
**GEGENWARTSKUNDE.** (195?)-. Periodical. German. Four times a year. DM42.00 Germany; DM43.00 others. Leske Verlag & Budrich GmbH, Postfach 300551, Gerhart Hauptmann Strasse 27, W-5090 Leverkusen 3 Opladen Germany. **Tel** 011 49 21712079. **ED** Walter Gagel, Bernhard Schafers, Hans-Hermann Hartwich, and Gottrik Wewer. **[CCC].** Index available. cum. index. **Bk Rev. Ad Acc. Pr Rev. Circ:** 4,000 (ctrl).
**Desc:** Publishes the results of economic, political science sociological research for the use of teachers of social sciences in secondary schools.
**Ind/Abst** Am. Hist. Life (1973); Int. Polit. Sci. Abstr.; Soc. Sci. Cit. Index [Full Cov.].

JA
**GENDAI TO SHISO.** No. 1 (Oct. 1970)-. Periodical. Japanese. qt. ¥2400. Aoki Shoten, 1-60 Jimbocho Kanda, Chiyodaku Tokyo 101 Japan. **Tel** 03 2920481, FAX 03 2920475. **LC** H8; .G44.
**Ind/Abst** Am. Hist. Life (1975-1978).

US/0891-2432
**GENDER & SOCIETY.** (GENDER & SOCIETY : OFFICIAL PUBLICATION OF SOCIOLOGISTS FOR WOMEN IN SOCIETY.). [Gend. soc.]. **Added/Corp** Sociologists for Women in Society (U.S.). **VFOAT** Gender and Society. Vol. 1, No. 1 (March 1987)-. Periodical. English. bm. $148.00. SAGE Periodical Press, 2455 Teller Road, Thousand Oaks CA 91320. **Tel** (805)499-0721, FAX (805)499-0871, telex 100799. **ED** Margaret Andersen (University of Delaware). **LC** HQ1075; .G457. **DD** 305.3. **[CCC].** Index available. cum. index. **Bk Rev. Ad Acc. Acid Free. Circ:** 1,873. available on microfilm and microfiche from University Microfilms International (UMI). Documents available from The Genuine Article, UMI Article Clearinghouse.
**Desc:** Focuses on the social and structural study of gender as a basic principle of the social order and as a primary social category. Emphasizing theory and research, this publication aims to advance both the study of gender and feminist scholarship.
**Ind/Abst** Acad. Ind. [Computer File] (1992-); Am. Hist. Life (1988-); Chicano Index; Curr. Contents Soc. Behav. Sci.; Expand. Acad. Index (1992-); Int. Bibliogr. Sociol.; Newsp. Period. Abstr. (1992-); Psychol. Abstr. (1987-); PsycINFO (1990-); PsycLit; Res. Alert [Full Cov.]; Sage Fam. Stud. Abstr.; Soc. Plann. Policy Dev. Abstr.; Soc. Sci. Cit. Index [Full Cov.]; Spec. Educ. Needs Abstr.; Women Stud. Abstr.; Work Relat. Abstr.

US
**GENERAL SERIES REPRINT.** **Main/Corp** Brookings Institution. **VFOAT** Brookings General Series Reprint. (1973)-. English. mo. $20.00. Brookings Institution, 1775 Massachusetts Avenue NW, Washington DC 20036. **Tel** (202)797-6112. ***Continues*** *Brookings Institution, Washington, D.C. Reprint.*

US/0072-0798
**GENERAL SYSTEMS.** (GENERAL SYSTEMS : YEARBOOK OF THE SOCIETY FOR THE ADVANCEMENT OF GENERAL SYSTEMS THEORY.). [Gen. syst.]. **Added/Corp** Society for the Advancement of General Systems Theory. Society for General Systems Research. International Society for the Systems Sciences. Vol. 1 (1956)-. English. an. $35.00. International Society Systems Sciences, PO Box 6808, Louisville KY 40206. **Tel** (502)899-3332. **ED** William J. Reckmeyer. **LC** H9; .G4. **DD** 006.
**Ind/Abst** Int. Polit. Sci. Abstr.

FR/1155-3219
**GENESES.** (Sept. 1990)-. Periodical. French. Four times a year. 274.12F France, 280.00F European Union, 340.00F others (individuals); 313.28F France, 320.00F European Union, 380.00F others (institutions). Editions Belin, 8 rue Ferou, 75278 Paris Cedex 06 France. **Tel** 011 46 1 46342142. **LC** H3; .G46. **DD** 300/.5.
**Ind/Abst** Int. Bibliogr. Sociol.

US/0016-8408
**GEORGIA SOCIAL SCIENCE JOURNAL.** ***Ceased.*** [Ga. soc. sci. j.]. **Added/Corp** Georgia Council for the Social Sciences. Vol. 2, No. 3 (Spring 1970)-(Oct. 1994). Periodical. English. Three times a year (Fall, Winter and Spring). Georgia Council Social Science, 411 Tucker Hall / University of Georgia, Athens GA 30602-7014. **Tel** (404)542-7265, FAX (706)542-6506. **ED** Elmer Williams. **DD** 300. **Circ:** 1,300. available on microfilm and microfiche from University Microfilms International (UMI). ***Continues*** *Georgia Reporter.*
**Ind/Abst** Curr. Index J. Educ.

US/1045-0300
**GERMAN POLITICS AND SOCIETY.** (GERMAN POLITICS AND SOCIETY / THE CENTER FOR EUROPEAN STUDIES, HARVARD UNIVERSITY.). [Ger. polit. soc.]. **Added/Corp** Harvard University. Center for European Studies. University of California, Berkeley.

Center for German and European Studies. Georgetown University. Center for German and European Studies. Minda de Gunzburg Center for European Studies (Harvard University). **VFOAT** GP and S; GP&S; German Politics & Society. No. 9 (Oct. 1986)-. Periodical. English. Three times a year. $30.00 (institutions), $21.00 (individuals). German Politics & Society, 2223 Fulton Street, University of California, Berkeley CA 94720. **Tel** (510)642-4065. **ED** Diane Forman Kent. **LC** DD1; .G3817. **DD** 943/.005. **Bk Rev**, (Qty: 30-35/ yr). **Ad Acc. Circ:** 500. ***Continues*** *German Studies Newsletter, 0882-7079.*
**Desc:** A journal which considers contemporary political, economic and social issues in Germany.

GW/0340-613X
**GESCHICHTE UND GESELLSCHAFT (GOTTINGEN).** (GESCHICHTE UND GESELLSCHAFT.). [Gesch. Ges.]. Vol. 1- ; 1975-. Periodical. German. qt. DM78.00. Vandenhoeck & Ruprecht, Robert Bosch Breite 6, D-37079 Goettingen Germany. **Tel** 011 49 551 695911, FAX 011 49 551 695917, telex 965226 VAN d. **LC** H5; .G42. **[CCC]. Pr Rev.** Documents available from The Genuine Article.
**Ind/Abst** Am. Hist. Life (1983-); Arts Humanit. Citation Index [Full Cov.]; Curr. Contents Arts Humanit.; Curr. Contents Soc. Behav. Sci.; Energy Res. Abstr. (Dec. 1979-); Int. Bibliogr. Sociol.; Res. Alert [Full Cov.]; Soc. Sci. Cit. Index [Full Cov.].

AU/0016-9099
**GESELLSCHAFT UND POLITIK.** **Added/Corp** Institut fuer Sozialpolitik und Sozialreform (Vienna, Austria). (1965)-. Periodical. German. qt. S180.00. Ebendorferstrasse 6/14, Vienna 1010 Austria. **Tel** 0043 222 22674. **LC** HN401; .G47. **DD** 361.6/1/09436. **Bk Rev. Ad Acc. Circ:** 1,000 (ctrl). ***Continues*** *Schriftenreihe des Institutes fuer Sozialpolitik und Sozialreform.*

FR
**GESTION SOCIALE.** French. 4250.00F. Liaisons Sociales, 1 Avenue E Belin, F 92856 Rueil Mal France. **Tel** 011 33 1 41299872.

GH/0046-5925
**GHANA SOCIAL SCIENCE JOURNAL.** [Ghana soc. sci. j.]. **Added/Corp** Ghana. University, Legon. Faculty of Social Studies. Vol. 1 (May 1971)-. Periodical. English. Twice a year. $9.80 UK; $6.80 Ghana; $11.70 others. Ghana Social Science Journal, c/o Faculty of Social Science, PO Box 72, Legon Accra Ghana. **LC** H1; .G47. **DD** 300/.5.

US
**GLOBAL ISSUES (GUILFORD, CONN.).** (GLOBAL ISSUES.). **VFOAT** Annual Editions. 85/86-. English. an. $10.95. Dushkin Publishing Group Inc., Sluice Dock, Guilford CT 06437. **Tel** (203)453-4351, (800)243-6532, FAX (203)453-6000. **ED** Robert M Jackson. **LC** HN1; .G56.
**Desc:** Presents a wide range of thoughtful, timely articles from an international perspective analyzing major global concerns and the complex interrelationships of factors that produce issue areas.

FR
**GLOBE.** French. Globe, 3 rue des Pyramides, F-75001 Paris France.

US
**GRANT$ FOR SOCIAL AND POLITICAL SCIENCE PROGRAMS.** See Philanthropy.

US
**GRANT LIST / DIVISION OF SOCIAL AND ECONOMIC SCIENCE.** Fiscal year 1979-. English. an. National Science Foundation, 1800 G Street Northwest, Washington DC 20550. **Tel** (202)357-9859, (202)357-9498. **LC** H62.5.U5; G73. **DD** 338.4/33/0072073. ***Continues*** *Division of Social Sciences Grant List.*

US/1052-5165
**GREAT PLAINS RESEARCH.** See Natural History.

GR
**GREEK REVIEW OF SOCIAL RESEARCH.** **VFOAT** Epitheoresis Koinonikon Ereunon. Periodical. Greek, Modern (summaries and/or abstracts in English). Four times a year. $25.00. Greek Review of Social Research, Sophokleous 1, 10559 Athens Greece. **Tel** 01-3212611. **Bk Rev. Circ:** 1,500.

●US/0926-2644
**GROUP DECISION AND NEGOTIATION.** **Added/Corp** Institute of Management Sciences. Institute of Management Sciences. College on Group Decision and Negotiation. Vol. 1, No. 1 (Apr. 1992)-. Periodical. English. bm. $539.00. Kluwer Academic Publishers, Postbus 322, 3300 AH Dordrecht, The Netherlands. **Tel** 011 (31) 78 524400, FAX 011 31 78 183273, telex 20083. **ED** Melvin Shakun. **Pr Rev. Acid Free.** available on microfilm and microfiche from University Microfilms International (UMI).
**Desc:** Examines evolving, unifying approaches to group decision and negotiation processes. Approaches include: (1) computer group decision and decision and negotiation support systems (GDNSS), (2) artificial intelligence and management science, (3) applied game theory, experiment and social choice, and (4) cognitive/behavioral sciences in group decision and negotiation. A number of research studies combine two or more of these fields.
**Ind/Abst** Int. Bibliogr. Sociol.

US/0890-0280
**GUANGARA LIBERTARIA.** See History(General).

US
**GUIDE TO GIFTS AND BEQUESTS. NEW YORK/FLORIDA, THE.** (1990)-. Periodical. English. te. Institutions Press Inc, PO Box 505, Murray Hill Station, New York NY 10156. **LC** AS29.5; .G84. **DD** 300/.25/73. ***Continues*** *Guide to Gifts and Bequests.*

US/1054-0946
**GUIDE TO SOCIAL SCIENCE AND RELIGION.** See Religion and Theology-Abstracting, Bibliographies and Statistics.

●US/1058-4862
**GUIDES TO MAJOR SOCIAL SCIENCE DATA BASES.** [Guides major soc. sci. data bases]. (1992)-. Monographic series. English. Three times a year. Price varies per volume. SAGE Periodical Press, 2455 Teller Road, Thousand Oaks CA 91320. **Tel** (805)499-0721, FAX (805)499-0871, telex 100799. **DD** 301. **Acid Free.**

US/1068-0853
**HEALTHCARE SYSTEM REFORM ALERT.** [Healthc. syst. reform alert]. Vol. 1, No. 1 (July 1991)-. Periodical. English. Twelve times a year. $227.00 (one year), $404.00 (two years), $579.00 (three years), $197.00 (intriductory subscription). Health Resources Publishing, 3100 Highway 138, Wall Township NJ 07719-1442. **Tel** (908)681-1133, FAX (908)681-0490. **DD** 344. Index available. ***Continues*** *Hospital Capital Formation Management Letter.*
**Desc:** Provides up-to-the-minute information regarding healthcare reform, covering such issues as legislative proposals, cost containment features of reform proposals, strategies that could control costs and a multitude of other critical news to keep company CEOs and top management leadership informed on what the likely outcomes are for healthcare reform.

CC/1000-1565
**HEBEI DAXUE XUEBAO ZIRAN KEXUE BAN.** (HEBEI DAXUE XUEBAO.). **VFOAT** Journal of Hebei University. (1952)-. Academic Scholarly Publication. Chinese. qt. $12.00 US. Hebei Daxue, Hebei University, Baoding, Hebei 071002, People's Republic of China. **Tel** 0312-222929. **DD** 505. Documents available from CASDDS.
**Ind/Abst** Chem. Abstr.

FR
**HISTOIRE, ECONOMIE ET SOCIETE.** See Economics-Economic History, Conditions.

CN/0018-2257
**HISTOIRE SOCIALE.** (HISTOIRE SOCIALE. SOCIAL HISTORY.). [Hist. soc.]. **Added/Corp** University of Ottawa. Carleton University. **VFOAT** Social History. Vol. 1 (April 1968)-. Periodical. English (French). Twice a year. $37.50. University of Toronto Press, 5201 Dufferin Street, Downsview Ontario M3H 5T8 Canada. **Tel** (416)667-7781, (416)667-7782, FAX (416)667-7803. **LC** HN1; .H57. Index available (bound in Nov. issue). cum. index. **Bk Rev**, (Qty: 65). **Ad Acc. Pr Rev. Circ:** 700 (ctrl). Documents available from The Genuine Article.
**Desc:** Although particularly oriented to Canadian social history, it publishes studies of all types of social phenomena without methodological, temporal or geographical restriction.
**Ind/Abst** Am. Hist. Life (1972-); Am. Bibliogr. Slavic East Europ. Stud.; Arts Humanit. Citation Index (19??-19??) [Full Cov.]; Middle East Abstr. Index; Point Repere (1983-); Res. Alert [Full Cov.]; Soc. Sci. Cit. Index [Full Cov.]; Sociol. Educ. Abstr.; Stud. Women Abstr.

SP/0214-2570
**HISTORIA SOCIAL (VALENCIA, SPAIN).** (HISTORIA SOCIAL.). No. 1 (1988)-. Periodical. Spanish. Three times a year. Centro de la UNED, c/o Casa de la Misericordia 34, 46014 Valencia Spain.

US/0161-5440
**HISTORICAL METHODS.** [Hist. methods]. Vol. 11 (Winter 1978)-. Academic Scholarly Publication. English. qt. $83.00 (institution), $39.00 (individual). Heldref Publications, 1319 Eighteenth Street Northwest, Washington DC 20036-1802. **Tel** (202)296-6267, (800)365-9753, FAX (202)296-5149. **ED** Myron P Gutmann. **LC** H1; .H525. **DD** 300/.5. **[CCC]. Bk Rev. Ad Acc. Circ:** 700. available on microfilm and microfiche from University Microfilms International (UMI). Documents available from The Genuine Article. ***Continues*** *Historical Methods Newsletter, 0018-2494.*
**Desc:** Contains information on new data resources, theoretical and practical discussions of data collection, sampling procedures, statistical analyses, computer programs, and related subjects. Frequent features include review essays and reports on research in progress.
**Ind/Abst** Acad. Search (Jan. 1994-); Am. Hist. Life (1967-); Arts Humanit. Citation Index [Full Cov.]; Curr. Contents Arts Humanit.; Curr. Index J. Educ. (March 1990); EMBASE; Geogr. Abstr. Human Geogr.; Hist. Source (July 1993-); Humanit. Source (Jul. 1993-); INFO-SOUTH Abstr.; Mag. Search; Popul. Index; Res. Alert [Full Cov.]; Romant. Move.; Soc. Sci. Cit. Index [Select. Cov.]; Soc. Res. Methodol. Abstr. (1982-).

GW/0172-6404
**HISTORICAL SOCIAL RESEARCH (QUANTUM (ASSOCIATION) : 1979).** (HISTORICAL SOCIAL RESEARCH. SUPPLEMENT : OFFICIAL JOURNAL OF QUANTUM AND INTERQUANT.). **Added/Corp** Zentrum fuer Historische Sozialforschung (Cologne, Germany) QUANTUM (Association) INTERQUANT (Association). **VFOAT** Historische Sozialforschung; HSR. Supplement; HSR. Beiheft. No. 1 (1988)-. Academic Scholarly Publication. German (English). Four times a year. DM60.00. Quantum, Liliencronstrasse 6, D 50931 Koln Germany. **Tel** 011 49 221 4769434, FAX 011 49 221 4769455. **ED** Dr. Wilhelm H. Schroder. **LC** HM1; .H565. Index available. cum. index. **Circ:** 1,500 (ctrl).
**Desc:** The application of formal methods in history. The most prominent are: quantitative research, computational linguistics and computer science technologies.

GW/0173-2145
**HISTORISCHE SOZIALFORSCHUNG.** [Hist. Soz.forsch.]. **Added/Corp** Zentrum fur Historische Sozialforschung (Cologne, Germany) Informationszentrum Sozialwissenschaften (Bonn, Germany). **VFOAT** Historical Social Research. (1979)-. German. an. Klett-Cotta Verlagsgemeinschft, PO Box 106016, D 70049 Stuttgart Germany. **Tel** 011 49 711 66720. **LC** H62.5.G4; Q36. **DD** 300/.72043. ***Continues*** *Quantum Dokumentation.*
**Ind/Abst** Am. Hist. Life.

UK/0952-6951
**HISTORY OF THE HUMAN SCIENCES.** [Hist. human sci.]. Vol. 1, No. 1 (May 1988)-. Periodical. English. qt. £105.00. Sage Publications Ltd., 6 Bonhill Street, London EC2A 4PU, UK. **Tel** 071 374 0645, FAX 071 374 8741, telex 296207 SAGE G. **LC** H1; .H527. **DD** 300/.9. **[CCC]. Acid Free.** Documents available from The Genuine Article.
**Ind/Abst** Am. Hist. Life (1988-); Arts Humanit. Citation Index [Select. Cov.]; Br. Humanit. Index; Curr. Contents Soc. Behav. Sci.; Int. Bibliogr. Sociol.; Res. Alert [Full Cov.]; Soc. Plann. Policy Dev. Abstr.; Soc. Sci. Cit. Index [Full Cov.].

JA/0559-7102
**HITOTSUBASHI DAIGAKU KENKYU NENPO. SHAKAIGAKU KENKYU.** **Added/Corp** Hitotsubashi Daigaku. Hitotsubashi Gakkai. Hitotsubashi Daigaku Hitotsubashi Gakkai Kenkyu Nenpo Henshu Iinkai. Hitotsubashi Daigaku Kenkyu Nenpo Henshu Iinkai. **VFOAT** Shakaigaku Kenkyu. (1956)-. Periodical. Japanese. an. Hitotsubashi Daigaku, (Hitotsubashi University), 2-1, Naka, Kunitachishi, Tokyoto 186 Japan. **LC** H8.J3; H58.
**Ind/Abst** Am. Hist. Life (1956-1970).

JA/0073-280X
**HITOTSUBASHI JOURNAL OF SOCIAL STUDIES.** **Added/Corp** Hitotsubashi Daigaku. Hitotsubashi Gakkai. (Aug. 1960)-. Periodical. English (French, German and Russian). an. $20.00. **(Subscription address:** Kyowa Book Company Inc., 1 38 Kanda Jinbocho Chiyoda-ku, Tokyo 101 Japan.**) LC** H1; .H54. **DD** 300/.5. ***Continues in part*** *Annals of the Hitotsubashi Academy, 0439-2841.*
**Ind/Abst** Int. Bibliogr. Sociol.; PAIS Int. Print (1991-).

JA/0018-2818
**HITOTSUBASHI RONSO.** **Added/Corp** Tokyo Shoka Daigaku. Hitotsubashi Ronso Henshujo. Tokyo Sangyo Daigaku. Hitotsubashi Ronso Henshujo. Hitotsubashi Gakkai. **VFOAT** Ikkyo Ronso. (Jan. 1938)-. Periodical. Japanese. mo. ¥10000 Japan; ¥11000 North America. Nihon Hyoronsha, 3-10-10 Minami-Ootsuka, Toshima-ku, Tokyo-to 170 Japan. **Tel** 03-987-8611, FAX 03-987-8590. **ED** Taketoshi Yamamoto. **LC** H1; .H55. Index available. cum. index. **Bk Rev. Ad Acc. Circ:** 3,000.
**Ind/Abst** Am. Hist. Life (1954-).

PR/0252-8908
**HOMINES.** [Homines]. **Added/Corp** Inter American University of Puerto Rico. San Juan Campus. Departamento de Ciencias Sociales. Inter American University of Puerto Rico. Metropolitan Campus. Departamento de Ciencias Sociales. Inter American University of Puerto Rico. Metropolitan Campus. Division de Ciencias y Profesiones de la Conducta. Vol. 1, No. 1 (May 1977)-. Periodical. Spanish (English). Twice a year. $22.00 US, Caribbean & Central America; $15.00 Puerto Rico $25.00 other. Revista Homines, University Interamericana, Apdo 191293, San Juan PR 00919. **Tel** (809)250-1912 exts. 2194 or 2280. **ED** Dr. Aline Frambes-Buxeda. **LC** H8.S7; H65. **DD** 300/.5. **CODEN** HOMIER. Index available ($20.00). cum. index ((1977-1992)). **Bk Rev. Ad Acc. Circ:** 7,000 (ctrl).

**Desc:** General and current world topics and news.
**Ind/Abst** HAPI Hisp. Am. Period. Index; Int. Bibliogr. Sociol.; Soc. Plann. Policy Dev. Abstr.

CN/0823-6119
**HORS D'ORDRE.** [Hors ordre]. Vol. 1, No. 1 (Jan./Feb. 1983)-. Periodical. French. bm. $5.00 per year. Initiative D'un Mouvement D'Animation Jeunesse, 85, CP 106, Montreal Quebec H2E 2Z7 Canada. **DD** 305.2/35/09714.

US/0195-3869
**HRAF NEWSLETTER.** [HRAF newsl.]. **Main/Corp** Human Relations Area Files, Inc. **VAT** Human Relations Area Files Newsletter. Vol. 1 (Nov. 1975)-. Periodical. English. Four times a year (Mar., June, Sept., Dec.). Free. Human Relations Area Files, PO Box 703A, Yale Station, New Haven CT 06520. **Tel** (203)624-8619, FAX (203)777-2337. **DD** 302.

CC
**HSI PEI SHIH TA HSUEH PAO. SHE HUI KO HSUEH PAN.** **Added/Corp** Hsi Pei Shih Fan Ta Hsueh (China). **VFOAT** Xibei Shida Xuebao; Journal of the Northwestern Teachers University. Social Sciences. (1989)-. Periodical. Chinese (table of contents in English). bm. **LC** AS451; .H74. ***Continues*** *Hsi Pei Shih Yuan Hsueh Pao.*

CC
**HSIA-MEN TA HSUEH HSUEH PAO. CHE HSUEH SHE HUI KO HSUEH PAN.** **See** Philosophy.

CC
**HSUEH LI LUN.** **VFOAT** Xuelilun. Periodical. Chinese. mo. RMBY0.20. Post Office, Ha-Erh-Pin Shih, People's Republic of China. **LC** AP95.C4; H8185. **DD** 300/.951.

CC
**HSUEH PAO. CHE HSUEH SHE HUI KO HSUEH PAN.** **VFOAT** Xinan Shifan Xueyuan Xuebao; Journal of Southwest Teachers College. Philosophy and Social Sciences Edition; Hsi Nan Shih Fan Hsueh Yuan Hsueh Pao. Che Hsueh She Hui Ko Hsueh Pan. Periodical. Chinese. qt. RMBY2000. Post Office, Chung-Ching Shih, People's Republic of China. **Tel** 3578. **ED** Ji Ping. **LC** AS452.C5914; A14. **Bk Rev. Circ:** 4,000.
**Desc:** A comprehensive academic theoretical magazine, publishing the latest achievements in the research and study of literature, history, philosophy, economics and education.

CC
**HSUEH PAO (SSU-CHUAN TA HSUEH).** (HSUEH PAO). **Added/Corp** Ssu-Chuan ta Hsueh. **VFOAT** Ssu-Chuan Ta Hsueh Hsueh Pao. Che Hsueh She Hui Ko Hsueh Pan; Journal of Sichuan University. Social Science Edition. (19??)-. Periodical. Chinese. qt. RMBY0.40. SSU-Chuan Jen Min Chu Pan She, Post Office, Cheng-Tu Shih, People's Republic of China. **LC** AS452.C462; A2. **DD** 089/.951.

CC
**HSUEH SHU CHI KAN.** **Added/Corp** Shang-hai She Hui Ko Hsueh Yuan. **VFOAT** Xueshu Jikan; Quarterly Journal of the Shanghai Academy of Social Sciences; Shang-hai She Hui Ko Hsueh Yuan Hsueh Shu Chi Kan. (1985)-. Periodical. Chinese. qt. RMBY1.30. Chung-Kuo Kuo Chi Tu Shu Mao I Tsung Kung SSU, PO Box 2820, Beijing, People's Republic of China. **Tel** 23724. **LC** AS452.S48; A28. **DD** 089/.951.
**Ind/Abst** Am. Hist. Life (1991-).

CH
**HUA-KANG SHE HUI KO HSUEH PAO.** **VFOAT** Hwa Kang Journal of Social Sciences. V. 1 (June 1981)-. Periodical. Chinese (English). Chung-Kuo Wen Hua Ta Hsueh She Hui Ko Hsueh Yuan, Hua-Kang Ta Cheng Kuan Yang-Ming-Shan, Taipei Taiwan. **LC** H8.C47; .H87. **DD** 300/.5.

CN/0714-4873
**HUMAN AFFAIRS.** [Hum. aff.]. Vol. 1, No. 1 (Fall 1981)-. Periodical. English. sa. $10.00 per year. Human Affairs, PO Box 32 Station A, Kingston Ontario K7M 6P9 Canada. **DD** 300/.5.

US/8755-7878
**HUMAN ECOLOGIST, THE.** [Hum. ecol.]. **Added/Corp** Human Ecology Action League. (19??)-. Periodical. English. qt (Mar., June, Sept., Dec.). $20.00. Human Ecology Action League, PO Box 49126, Atlanta GA 30359. **Tel** (404)248-1898, FAX (404)248-0162. **ED** Diane Thomas. **DD** 304. Index available. cum. index. **Bk Rev. Ad Acc, Adv Mgr:** L. Jones.
**Desc:** Journal of environmental illness, a complex syndrome. Featuring related health issues such as the effect on humans of the indiscriminate use of pesticides and sensitizing chemicals.

NE/0167-9457
**HUMAN MOVEMENT SCIENCE.** [Hum. mov. sci.]. Vol. 1, No. 1 (May 1982)-. Academic Scholarly Publication. English. bm (1 volume). Fl694.00. Elsevier Science Publishers BV, PO Box 211, 1000 AE Amsterdam Netherlands. **Tel** 011 31 20 5803642, FAX 011 31 20 5862696, telex 15682. **ED** H T A Whiting. **LC** QP303; .H851. **NLM** W1 HU448M. **CODEN** HMSCDO. **[CCC]. Pr Rev.** available on microfilm and microfiche from University Microfilms International (UMI). Documents available from The Genuine Article, BIOSIS Document Express, Ask*IEEE.
**Desc:** Provides a medium for publication of research and review articles of a mono-, multi- or interdisciplinary nature.
**Ind/Abst** Abstr. Hum. Comput. Interact. (?-?); Biol. Abstr.; Curr. Contents Soc. Behav. Sci.; EMBASE; Ergon. Abstr.; Index Med.; INSPEC (Feb. 1991-); Phys. Educ. Index; Psychoanal. Abstr.; Psychol. Abstr. (1990-); PsycINFO; PsycLit; PsycScan: Appl. Exp. Eng. Psych.; PsycScan: LD/MR; PsycScan: Neuropsych.; Res. Alert [Full Cov.]; Soc. Plann. Policy Dev. Abstr.; Soc. Sci. Cit. Index [Full Cov.]; Sociol. Abstr.; SPORT Discus; SportSearch.

US/0018-7267
**HUMAN RELATIONS (NEW YORK).** (HUMAN RELATIONS.). [Hum. relat.]. **Added/Corp** Tavistock Institute of Human Relations. University of Michigan. Research Center for Group Dynamics. Vol. 1 (June 1947)-. Periodical. English. Twelve times a year. $395.00 institutions, $125.00 individuals US; $460.00 institutions, $125.00 individuals other. Plenum Press, 233 Spring Street, New York NY 10013-1578. **Tel** (212)620-8000, (800)221-9369, FAX (212)463-0742, (212)807-1047, telex 23/421139. **ED** Ray Loveridge. **LC** H1; .H8. **DD** 305. **NLM** W1 HU461. **CODEN** HUREAA. **[CCC].** Index available. **Pr Rev.** available on microfilm and microfiche from University Microfilms International (UMI). Documents available from The Genuine Article, UMI Article Clearinghouse.
**Desc:** Founded on the belief that social scientists in all fields should work toward integration in their attempts to understand the complexities of human problems.
**Ind/Abst** ABI/INFORM Glob. Ed.; ABI Inform Ondisc (July 1972-); Abstr. Anthropol.; Acad. Search (July 1993-); Appl. Soc. Sci. Index Abstr.; Bus. ASAP (1992-) [Full Txt.]; Bus. Index (1985-); Commun. Abstr.; Contents Pages Manage.; Crim. Justice Abstr.; Crim. Penol. Police Sci. Abstr.; Cumul. Index Nurs. Allied Health Lit.; Curr. Contents Soc. Behav. Sci.; Ergon. Abstr.; Expand. Acad. Index (1984-); Gen. BusinessFile (1985-); Gen. Period. Index (1985-); High. Educ. Abstr. (1972-); Hum. Resour. Abstr. (?-?); INFO-SOUTH Abstr.; Int. Bibliogr. Sociol.; Int. Labour Doc.; Mag. Search; Manage. Contents; Middle East Abstr. Index; Multicult. Educ. Abstr.; Newsp. Period. Abstr. (1989-); Peace Res. Abstr. J. (1967-1985); Psychol. Abstr. (1949-); PsycINFO; PsycLit; PsycScan: Appl. Psych.; Res. Alert [Full Cov.]; School Organ. Manage. Abstr.; Selec. Coop. Index Manage. Period; Soc. Plann. Policy Dev. Abstr.; Soc. Sci. Source (Jul. 1993-); Soc. Sci. Cit. Index [Full Cov.]; Soc. Sci. Index; Soc. Sci. Index Fulltext (Oct. 1988-) [Full Txt.]; Soc. Work Abstr. (Summer 1987-?) [Select. Cov.]; Sociol. Abstr.; Sociol. Educ. Abstr.; Stud. Women Abstr.; Women Stud. Abstr.; Work Relat. Abstr.

US/0160-4341
**HUMBOLDT JOURNAL OF SOCIAL RELATIONS.** [Humboldt j. soc. relat.]. **Added/Corp** Humboldt State University. California State University, Humboldt. Dept. of Sociology, Anthropology and Social Welfare. Vol. 1 (Fall 1973)-. Periodical. English. sa. $16.00 (individuals), $26.00 (institutions) US; $20.00 (individuals), $30.00 (institutions) other. Humboldt State University, CBSS, Gist Hall 208, Arcata CA 95521. **Tel** (707)826-5445. **ED** Sing C. Cheu. **LC** HN65; .H854. **DD** 300/.5. **CODEN** HJSRAB. **Bk Rev**, (Qty: 12). **Circ:** 500.
**Desc:** An interdisciplinary social science journal which publishes original research critical essays, and book reviews in the areas of sociology, anthropology, social welfare, geography, political science, and economics.
**Ind/Abst** Am. Hist. Life (1991-); Middle East Abstr. Index; Psychol. Abstr. (1973-); PsycINFO; PsycLit; Soc. Plann. Policy Dev. Abstr.; Soc. Welf. Soc. Plan./Policy Soc. Dev.; Sociol. Abstr. [Full Cov.].

II/0970-9061
**IASSI QUARTERLY.** **Added/Corp** Indian Association of Social Science Institutions. **VAT** Indian Association of Social Science Institutions Quarterly. (198?)-. Periodical. English. Four times a year. $30.00. Indian Association of Social Science Institution, IASSI Indraprastha Estate, New Delhi, 110002 India. **Tel** 011 91 11 3315284. **LC** H62.5.I5; I27. **DD** 300/.954/05. ***Continues*** *IASSI Quarterly Bulletin.*

US/0739-1137
**IASSIST QUARTERLY.** **See** Library and Information Sciences-Abstracting, Bibliographies and Statistics.

SW/0046-8444
**IBERO-AMERICANA.** (IBERO-AMERICANA : NORDIC JOURNAL OF LATIN AMERICAN STUDIES.). **Added/Corp** Nordiska Samarbetskommitten for Latinamerika-Forskning. Latinamerika-Institutet i Stockholm. Nordiska Samfundet for Latinamerika-Forskning. (1971)-. Periodical. English (Spanish and Swedish). Twice a year. $20.00. NOSALF / Stockholm University, Stockholm University, 106 91 Stockholm Sweden. **Tel** 011 46 8 162884. **DD** 016.918. ***Continues*** *Ibero-Americana (Stockholm, Sweden : 1960).* ***Continued in part by*** *Latinoamericana (Stockholm, Sweden).*
**Ind/Abst** Am. Hist. Life (1991-); HAPI Hisp. Am. Period. Index.

GR
**ICHNEUTES.** Greek, Modern. mo. Ichneutes, Apellou 5, Athens 105 51 Greece.

SZ
**ICMC NEWSLETTER.** ***Title Change.*** **Main/Corp** International Catholic Migration Commission. **Added/Corp** International Catholic Migration Commission. **VAT** International Catholic Migration Commission Newsletter. Vol. 1 (1977)-(19??). Newsletter. English (French and Spanish). qt. International Catholic Migration Commission, 37-39 rue de Vermont, CP 96, 1211 Geneva 20 CIC Switzerland. **Tel** (022)33 41 50, telex 28 100 ICMC CH. **ED** Dennis Clagett. **Circ:** 6,700 (ctrl). ***Continued by*** *ICMC Today.*
**Desc:** Features new reports, analysis and operational documents related to the activities of ICMC and affiliated member agencies throughout the world.

US/0198-6848
**ICPSR BULLETIN.** [ICPSR bull.]. **Main/Corp** Inter-University Consortium for Political and Social Research. **VFOAT** I.C.P.S.R. Bulletin. **VAT** Inter-University Consortium for Political and Social Research bulletin. (July 1981)-. Bulletin. English. Four times a year. Free. ICPSR Inter University Consortium for Political and Social Research, University of Michigan, PO Box 1248, Ann Arbor MI 48106. **Tel** (313)764-2570.

II
**ICSSR JOURNAL OF ABSTRACTS AND REVIEWS. SOCIOLOGY AND SOCIAL ANTHROPOLOGY / INDIAN COUNCIL OF SOCIAL SCIENCE RESEARCH.** **Added/Corp** Indian Council of Social Science Research. **VFOAT** I.C.S.S.R. Journal of Abstracts and Reviews; Sociology and Social Anthropology. **VAT** Indian Council of Social Science Research Journal of Abstracts and Reviews. Vol. 4, No. 1 (Jan./June 1975)-. Periodical. English. sa. Rs12.00 (individuals and institutions) Vols. 1-6; Rs16.00 (individuals), Rs20.00 (institutions) Vols. 7-13; Rs30.00 (individuals), Rs50.00 (institutions) Vol. 14 onwards. Indian Council of Social Science Research, 35 Ferozshah Road, New Delhi 110 001 India. **Tel** 011 91 11 38959, 011 91 11 381571. **(Subscription address:** Prints India, 11 Darya Ganj, New Delhi, 110002 India, (Phone: 011 91 11 3268645)) **ED** A R Saiyed. **LC** H35; .I52a. **DD** 300/.72. **Bk Rev. Ad Acc. Circ:** 550. ***Continues*** *ICSSR Journal of Abstracts and Reviews.*
**Desc:** Publishes selected reviews of publications in the broad fields indicated in the journal's title, as well as abstracts of research works.

II/0018-9049
**ICSSR NEWSLETTER.** **Main/Corp** Indian Council of Social Science Research. (Nov. 1969)-. Newsletter. English. qt. Indian Council of Social Science Research, 35 Ferozshah Road, New Delhi 110 001 India. **Tel** 011 91 11 38959, 011 91 11 381571. **ED** S. Saraswathi. **LC** H62.5.I5; I53. **DD** 300/.5. **Bk Rev. Circ:** 5,500.
**Desc:** Contains news of general interest to the social science community on the multi-faceted activities of ICSSR, its regional centres and research institutes supported by the council. It lists research projects and fellowships and other activities supported by ICSSR. Also covers abstracts of selected research reports with policy implication to government, policy makers and social scientists.
**Ind/Abst** Anthropol. Index; Int. Bibliogr. Sociol.; Soc. Work Abstr. (?-?).

II
**ICSSR RESEARCH ABSTRACTS QUARTERLY.** **Main/Corp** Indian Council of Social Science Research. Vol. 1 (Oct. 1971)-. English. qt (4 issues). $8.00. Indian Council of Social Science Research, 35 Ferozshah Road, New Delhi 110 001 India. **Tel** 011 91 11 38959, 011 91 11 381571. **ED** S. Saraswathi. **LC** H35; .I5. **Ad Acc. Circ:** 550. ***Continues*** *Indian Council of Social Science Research. Research Abstracts.*
**Desc:** Covers abstracts of reports of researches supported by ICSSR stating out the objectives, the methodology, and the major findings of the researches.

US/0897-5027
**ID MAGAZINE.** [iD mag.]. **VFOAT** ID. **VAT** Independent Magazine. Vol. 1, No. 1 (1988)-. Periodical. English. qt. $10.00. Independent Publishing, PO Box 3042, Springfield IL 62708-3042. **DD** 306.

AG/0326-386X
**IDEAS EN CIENCIAS SOCIALES / UNIVERSIDAD DE BELGRANO.** **Added/Corp** Universidad de Belgrano. Vol. 1, No. 1 (Jan./March 1984)-. Academic Scholarly Publication. Spanish. ir (8 per year). $54.00. Fundacion de la Universidad de Belgrano, Teodoro Garcia 2090 1er Piso, 1426 Buenos Aires Argentina. **Tel** 011 54 1 7742133, 011 54 1 7734767. **ED** Avelino Porto. **LC** H8.S7; I33. **DD** 300/.5. **Bk Rev. Ad Acc. Circ:** 1,000.
**Desc:** Reflects the works done in the Universidad de

Belgrano (Buenos Aires) in the fields of social sciences (sociology, political science, education) with special interest in Argentine and Latin American research.

GR
**IDEES.** (19??)-. Periodical. Greek, Modern. mo. Voulis 24, Athens Greece. **LC** H8; .I3.

IT
**IDOC INTERNAZIONALE. See** Religion and Theology.

MY
**ILMU MASYARAKAT : TERBITAN PERSATUAN SAINS SOSIAL MALAYSIA. Added/Corp** Persatuan Sains Sosial Malaysia. **VFOAT** Malaysian Social Science Association Publication. Vol. 1 (Jan/Mar 1983)-. Periodical. English (Malay). qt. $25.00 US; $30.00 other. ILMU Masyarakat d/a Jabatan Antropologi and Sosiologi, Universiti Malaya, Kuala Lumpur Malaysia. **Tel** 03-7555266. **ED** Syed Husin Ali. **LC** H1; .A143. **DD** 300/.9595. **Bk Rev. Ad Acc. Circ:** 1,200.
**Desc:** Covers various aspects of social sciences, especially sociology, anthropology and economics in Southeast Asian countries, particularly Malaysia.

AT
**IMPACT. Added/Corp** Central Methodist Mission, Sydney. (1959)-. Periodical. English. Eleven times a year (Except Jan.). 35.00Aus$ (institutions), 31.50Aus$ (individuals) Australia; 55.00Aus$ (institutions), 51.50Aus$ (individuals) others. Australian Council of Social Service, 8-24 Kippax Street, Surry Hills 2010, New South Wales Australia. **Tel** 011 61 2 2123277. **ED** Cornelius G. Breed. ctrl circ.
**Desc:** Asian magazine for human transformation.

PH/0300-4155
**IMPACT (MANILA).** (IMPACT.). [Impact]. **Added/Corp** Social Impact Foundation. (April 1966)-. Periodical. English. mo. $30.00 (1 year), $80.00 (3 year) North America and Europe; $20.00 (1 year), $55.00 (3 year) Africa and Latin America; $25.00 (1 year), $70.00 (3 year) Australia and New Zealand; $9.00 (1 year), $25.00 (3 year) other. Human Development, PO Box 2950, Manila Philippines. **Tel** 011 63 2 827 6581. **ED** C.G. Breed. **LC** DS1; .I43. **DD** 950/.42/05. Index available. cum. index. **Bk Rev**, (Qty: 15). **Ad Acc. Circ:** 2,000. available on microfilm from University Microfilms International (UMI).
**Ind/Abst** Hum. Rights Intern. Rep.; Soc. Plann. Policy Dev. Abstr.; Sociol. Abstr.

CN/0228-2518
**IN SUMMARY.** [summary]. **Added/Corp** University of Alberta. Population Research Laboratory. Vol. 1 (Oct. 1979)-. Periodical. English. Three times a year. Free. Population Research Laboratory / Department of Social Science, University of Alberta 1 62, Edmonton Alberta T6G 2H4 Canada. **Tel** (403)492-4659. **DD** 300/.7/20712. **Circ:** 600 (ctrl).

US/0160-5992
**IN THESE TIMES.** [In these times]. **Added/Corp** Institute for Policy Studies. Institute for Public Affairs (Chicago, Ill.). Vol. 1, (Nov. 15-21 1976)-. Periodical. English. Twenty-six times a year. $35.95 (individuals), $59.00 (institutions) US; $61.95 (individuals), $86.00 (institutions) Canada; $75.95 (individuals), $100.00 (institutitons) others. Institute for Public Affairs, 2040 North Milwaukee Avenue, Chicago IL 60647-4002. **Tel** (312)772-0100, (800)435-0715, FAX (312)772-4180. **(Subscription address:** Kable Publishers Aide, 308 East Hitt Street, Subscription Department, Mt. Morris IL 61054-1473.**) ED** James Weinstein. **LC** AP2; .I526. **DD** 051. Index available. **Bk Rev. Ad Acc, Adv Mgr:** Bruce Embry. **Pr Rev. Circ:** 42,000. available on microfilm and microfiche from University Microfilms International (UMI); available on audiocassette.
**Desc:** A commitment to provide readers with in-depth, responsible analysis of the news. Our purpose is to make sense of the disjointed facts and sound bites Americans now receive from TV and daily newspapers, so that our readers can participate more intelligently as citizens in a democratic society.
**Ind/Abst** Altern. Press Index; Chicano Index; Left Index.

SG
**INDEX OF AFRICAN SOCIAL SCIENCE PERIODICAL ARTICLES / COUNCIL FOR THE DEVELOPMENT OF ECONOMIC AND SOCIAL RESEARCH IN AFRICA. Added/Corp** Codesria. **VFOAT** Index des Articles de Periodiques Africains de Sciences Sociales. Vol. 1 (1989)-. English (French). **LC** H53.A34; I53. **DD** 016.3/0096.
**Ind/Abst** Int. Labour Doc.

US/0191-0574
**INDEX TO SOCIAL SCIENCES & HUMANITIES PROCEEDINGS.** [Index soc. sci. humanit. proc.]. **Added/Corp** Institute for Scientific Information. **VAT** Index to Social Sciences and Humanities Proceedings. (Jan./March 1979)-. Academic Scholarly Publication. English. qt. $1100.00 print; $1175.00 CD-ROM; $1520.00 combination print and CD-ROM. Institute for Scientific Information, 3501 Market Street, Philadelphia PA 19104. **Tel** (215)386-0100, (800)523-1850, FAX (215)386-6362, telex 84-5305. **(Subscription address:** Institute for Scientific Information, PO Box 71416, Chicago IL 60694.**) LC** Z7163; .I5; H61. **DD** 016.3. **NLM** ZW 3.5 I38.
**Desc:** Provides access to proceedings papers from nearly 100 disciplines.

US/1040-628X
**INDIA TIMES (LOS GATOS, CALIF.).** (INDIA TIMES.). [India times]. (May 1987)-. Periodical. English. mo (12 issues). $15.00. Mahan Hind Corporation, 5130 Colorado Street, Long Beach CA 90814. **Tel** (213)498-5850. **DD** 305.

II/0018-8727
**INDIAN BEHAVIOURAL SCIENCES ABSTRACTS.** ***Suspended.*** **Added/Corp** Behavioural Sciences Centre. **VFOAT** IBSA; Indian Behavioural Sciences Abstracts. Vol. 1 (Jan. 1970)-Vol. 5 (1974). Periodical. English. qt. Indian Council of Social Science Research, 35 Ferozshah Road, New Delhi 110 001 India. **Tel** 011 91 11 38959, 011 91 11 381571. **LC** H62.5.I5; I5.

II
**INDIAN DISSERTATION ABSTRACTS. Added/Corp** Indian Council of Social Science Research. Association of Indian Universities. Vol. 1 (Jan./Mar. 1973)-. Periodical. English. qt. $25.00. Indian Council of Social Science Research, 35 Ferozshah Road, New Delhi 110 001 India. **Tel** 011 91 11 38959, 011 91 11 381571. **(Subscription address:** Prints India, 11 Darya Ganj, New Delhi 110002 India.**) ED** Dinesh C Sharma. cum. index. **Ad Acc. Circ:** 550.
**Desc:** Publishes abstracts of doctoral dissertations in social sciences awarded in Indian universities; highlighting the problem studied, the methodology followed, and major finding.

US/0971-52155
**INDIAN JOURNAL OF GENDER STUDIES.** English. sa (Mar. and Sept.). $78.00. SAGE Periodical Press, 2455 Teller Road, Thousand Oaks CA 91320. **Tel** (805)499-0721, FAX (805)499-0871, telex 100799.

II/0019-5626
**INDIAN JOURNAL OF SOCIAL RESEARCH.** [Indian j. soc. res.]. **Added/Corp** Baraut, India. Jat Vedic College. Dept. of Sociology. **VFOAT** IJSR. Vol. 2 (July 1961)-. Periodical. English. Four times a year (Mar., June, Sept., Dec.). $160.00. Academic & Law Serials, F-22 B/3 Laxmi Nagar, Delhi 110092 India. **Tel** 11 91 11 2413394, 011 91 11 2420827, FAX 11 91 11 2223543. **(Subscription address:** Prints India, 11 Darya Ganj, New Delhi 110002 India.**) LC** H62.A1; I5. **Bk Rev. Ad Acc, Adv Mgr:** Vivek Pori, **Tel** 11 91 11 2420827. ***Continues*** *Journal of Social Research.*
**Ind/Abst** Am. Hist. Life (1962-1967); Appl. Soc. Sci. Index Abstr.; Soc. Plann. Policy Dev. Abstr.; Sociol. Abstr.

II/0971-0817.
**INDIAN JOURNAL OF SOCIAL SCIENCE. Added/Corp** Indian Council of Social Science Research. Vol. 1, No. 1 (Jan./March 1988)-. Periodical. English. qt (Mar., June, Sept., Dec.). $80.00. SAGE Periodical Press, 2455 Teller Road, Thousand Oaks CA 91320. **Tel** (805)499-0721, FAX (805)499-0871, telex 100799. **ED** Sukhomoy Chakravarty. **LC** H1; .I38. **DD** 300/.954/05. **CODEN** INJSEC. Index available (fourth issue). **Ad Acc.** available on microfilm and microfiche from University Microfilms International (UMI).
**Desc:** Promotes scientific discussion on the diverse concerns of social science research. The problems of development and social change, the interface between science, society, culture and technology, and a comprehension of future patterns of development as they relate to the developing countries are discusssed.
**Ind/Abst** Geogr. Abstr. Human Geogr.; Int. Bibliogr. Sociol.; Int. Dev. Abstr.; Soc. Plann. Policy Dev. Abstr.

II/0376-9879
**INDIAN JOURNAL OF SOCIAL SCIENCES. Added/Corp** Society for the Study of Social Sciences. Vol. 1 (Sept. 1971)-. Periodical. English. tq. $5.00. Society for the Study of Social Sciences, Department of Sociology, Osmania University, Hyderabad 500007 India. **LC** H1; .I39. **DD** 300/.954.

BL
**INDICADORES SOCIAIS DE SERGIPE / GOVERNO DO ESTADO DE SERGIPE, SECRETARIA DO PLANEJAMENTO, COORDENACAO DE PLANEJAMENTO E ESTATISTICA, CPE.** No. 1 (1979)-. Portuguese. an. Secretaria do Planejamento do Estado de Sergipe, Coordenacao de Planejamento e Estatistica, Praca Fausto Cardoso, s/No Ed Walter Franco, 5 O Andar, 49 000 Aracaju Sergipe. **LC** HN284; .I524. **DD** 306/.0981/41.

BL
**INDICADORES SOCIAIS RS. Main/Corp** Rio Grande do sul, Brazil (State). Secretaria de Coordenacao e Planejamento. Superintendencia de Planejamento Global. No. 1- Nov. 1973-. Portuguese. Fundacao de Economia e Estatistica, Rua Duque de Caixias 1691, 90010 Porto Alegre, Rio Grande do Sul, Brazil. **Tel** 0512-259455, FAX 0512-25006, telex 0515042. **LC** HN290.R48; R57A. **DD** 309.1/81/6.

SP/0213-019X
**INDICE ESPANOL DE CIENCIAS SOCIALES. SERIE A, PSICOLOGIA Y CIENCIAS DE LA EDUCACION. Added/Corp** Instituto de Informacion y Documentacion en Ciencias Sociales y Humanidades (Spain). **VFOAT** Psicologia y Ciencias de la Educacion. Vol. 5 (1981)-. Spanish. ir. 5500.00ptas. Consejo Superior Investigacion Cientificas (CSIC), Vitruvio 8, 28006 Madrid Spain. **Tel** 011 34 1 5612833, FAX 011 34 1 4113077, telex 42182. available on CD-ROM. ***Continues in part*** *Indice Espanol de Ciencias Sociales, 0211-1373.*

CU
**INDICE GENERAL DE PUBLICACIONES PERIODICAS CUBANAS.** No. 1- Jan./June 1970-. Spanish. an. $24.00 US. Ediciones Cubanas, Obispo 527, Altos ESQ Bernaza, CP 10100 Havana Cuba. **Tel** 011 632980, 631942, FAX 011 631011, telex 512337, 6540. **LC** AI17; .I5. **Bk Rev. Ad Acc. Circ:** 20,000.
**Desc:** Contains analytical writings of the most outstanding articles published in Cuban magazines on general matters and the social sciences during the preceding year.

CK/0120-6478
**INDICE HISPANOAMERICANO DE CIENCIAS SOCIALES.** Vol. 1, No. 1 (Jan./Feb. 1985)-. Periodical. Spanish (Portuguese and English). qt. 14,000Col$ Colombia; 60.00Col$ US. Indizar Ltda, Apartado Aereo 10058 Centrl, Bogota Colombia. **Tel** 2821407. cum. index. **Ad Acc. Circ:** 150.
**Desc:** A professional company specialized in information sources and services.

US/0161-4177
**INDIVIDUAL AND THE FUTURE OF ORGANIZATIONS, THE. Main/Corp** Franklin Foundation. V. 7- 1976/77-. English. an. University Plaza, Atlanta GA 30303. **LC** H1; .F63A. **DD** 300/.5. ***Continues*** *Man and the Future of Organizations, 0097-6261.*

AT/0813-4820
**INDONESIAN STUDIES.** (INDONESIAN STUDIES : BULLETIN OF THE INDONESIAN CULTURAL AND EDUCATIONAL INSTITUTE.). [Indones. stud.]. Vol. 1, No. 1 (1984)-. Bulletin. English (Indonesian). sa. 40.00Aus$ (institutions), 30.00Aus$ (individuals), 15.00Aus$ (students & pensioners). Indonesian Cultural and Educational Institute, PO Box 73, Clayton Victoria 3168 Australia. **Tel** 61 3 3448791, FAX 61 3 3448612.

GW/0537-5762
**INDUSTRIELLE WELT. Added/Corp** Arbeitskreis fuer Moderne Sozialgeschichte. Vol. 1 (1962)-. German. ir. Bouvier GMBH & Company KG ABT Verlag, Am HOF 28, D53113 Bonn Germany. **Tel** 011 49 228 7290141. **LC** HN5; .I5.

SZ
**INFORMATION LETTER (LUTHERAN WORLD FEDERATION. DEPT. OF STUDIES).** (INFORMATION LETTER - LUTHERAN WORLD FEDERATION.). No. 1 (Sept. 1972)-. Periodical. English. ir. Free. Lutheran World Federation, 150 Route de Ferney, CP 2100, Geneva 20 Switzerland. **Tel** 011 41 22 7916111.

BL/0524-2932
**INFORMATIVO. Main/Corp** Brazil. Departamento Nacional de Portos e Vias Navegaveis. (1966)-. Periodical. Portuguese. mo. Fun Dacao Getulio Verga, Caxia Postfach 9052, 188 ZC02 Rio de Janeiro Brazil. **Tel** 5510698. **ED** Benedicto Silva. **DD** 387. **Bk Rev.** ctrl circ.
**Desc:** Includes areas of administration documentation, teaching and research besides sections on literature, social sciences and international relations.

CK
**INFORME DE LABORES DE LA SECRETARIA EJECTIVA DEL CONVENIO ANDRES BELLO. Main/Corp** Secretaria Ejecutiva Permanente del Convenio Andres Bello. Spanish. Carrera 21, No 33 A-64, AP Aereo, Bogota Colombia. **LC** H19; .S415.

UK/1012-8050
**INNOVATION IN SOCIAL SCIENCE RESEARCH. Added/Corp** Interdisciplinary Centre for Comparative Research in the Social Sciences. **VFOAT** Innovation. (19??)-. English. qt. £142.00. Carfax Publishing Company, PO Box 25 Abingdon, Oxfordshire OX14 3UE England. **Tel** 011 44 235 555335, FAX (0279)31067, telex 817484. **(Subscription address:** US and Canada/ PO Box 2025, Dunnellon, FL 34430-2025; telephone:(904)489-6996**) ED** Ronald J. Pohoryles. **LC** H1; .I566. Index available. available on microfiche.
**Ind/Abst** Soc. Plann. Policy Dev. Abstr.

FR/0988-3266
**INRA SCIENCES SOCIALES.** **VFOAT** Institut National de la Recherche Agronomique Sciences Sociales. (1988)-. Periodical. French. bm (6 issues). 130.00F France and CEE; 160.00F other. Institut National de la Recherche Agronomique, Route de Staint Cyr, 78026 Versailles Cedex France. **Tel** 011 33 1 30833406, FAX 011 33 1 30833449, telex INRAPUB 699 368 F. **ED** Ch. Grignon. **UDC** 631.
**Desc:** Newsletter of the INRA Rural Economy and Sociology Department. Directed to professionals in farming, the agro-food industries, teaching, research and technical journalism.
**Ind/Abst** Plant Genet. Resour. Abstr.; World Agric. Econ.

●CN/1188-746X
**INROADS (OTTAWA).** (INROADS : A JOURNAL OF OPINION.). [Inroads]. (Fall 1992)-. Periodical. English. sa. 46.50Can$ (individuals, 2 year) Canada; 55.80Can$ (2 year) other. Inroads Inc., P.O.Box 77042, Ottawa ONT K1S 5N2 Canada. **Tel** (613)730-5835, FAX (613)730-5835. **ED** Vincent Chetcuti. **DD** 051. **Ad Acc. Circ:** 500.
**Desc:** Discusses contemporary Canadian issues such as the Constitution and the economy from different viewpoints.

US/0095-2184
**INTEGRITY FORUM.** Vol. 3, No. 8 (June-July 1977)-. Periodical. English. bm. 11250 Roger Bacon Drive, Suite 19, Reston VA 22090. ***Continues*** *Integrity (Fort Valley, Ga.), 0095-2184.*

US/1055-0542
**INTELLIGENT SYSTEMS : THE NEWSLETTER OF THE FOUNDATION FOR INTELLIGENT SYSTEMS IN THE SOCIAL SCIENCES, ARTS & HUMANITIES.** [Intell. syst.]. **Added/Corp** Foundation for Intelligent Systems in the Social Sciences, Arts & Humanities. Vol. 1, No. 1 (Spring 1991)-. Newsletter. English. qt. $25.00. Foundation for Intelligent Systems in the Social Sciences, Arts & Humanities, 2637 Asilomar Drive, Antioch CA 94509. **DD** 003.

US/1055-2804
**INTERCULTURAL STUDIES.** [Intercult. stud.]. Vol. 1 (1991)-. Monographic series. English. Peter Lang Publishing, 62 West 45th Street, 4th Floor, New York NY 10036. **Tel** (212)764-1471, (800)770-5264, telex 6973364 PLNY. **DD** 306.

US/0882-7966
**INTERNATIONAL BAROMETER.** [Int. barom.]. Vol. 1, No. 1 (June 1985)-. Periodical. English. mo. $147.00 US and Canada; $175.00 other. Issue Action Publications Inc, 207 Loudoun Street Southeast, Leesburg VA 22075-3076. **Tel** (703)777-8450. **ED** Teresa Yancey Crane. **DD** 303. Index available. cum. index.
**Desc:** A newsletter reporting on activist organizations and their initiatives on public policy issues affecting business.

II/0020-613X
**INTERNATIONAL BEHAVIOURAL SCIENTIST.** [Int. behav. sci.]. V. 1- March 1969-. Periodical. English. qt. Sadhna Prakashan, Rastogi St Subhash Bazar, Meerut India. **LC** H1; .I64. **DD** 300/.5. available on microfilm from University Microfilms International (UMI).
**Ind/Abst** Int. Polit. Sci. Abstr.; Soc. Plann. Policy Dev. Abstr.; Sociol. Abstr. (?-?).

US/0094-4084
**INTERNATIONAL DIRECTORY OF BEHAVIOR AND DESIGN RESEARCH.** 1974-. Directory. English. sa. $12.00. PO Box 57, Orangeburg NY 10962. **LC** H57; .I57. **DD** 300/.25.

HK
**INTERNATIONAL DIRECTORY OF CENTERS FOR ASIAN STUDIES.** ***Suspended.*** **Added/Corp** Asian Research Service. (19??)-Suspended with 6th Edition. English. an. Asian Research Service, Sub Department, GPO Box 2232, Hong Kong Hong Kong. **Tel** 011 852 5 707227, telex 63899 CONPA HX. **ED** Nelson Leung. **LC** DS32.8; .I5. **DD** 950/.07/2. **Circ:** 2,000.
**Desc:** Provides important information about major research centers and institutions concerned with Asian studies in various countries of the world.

SW
**INTERNATIONAL DIRECTORY OF SOCIAL SCIENCE ORGANIZATIONS / COMPILED AND EDITED BY INTERNATIONAL FEDERATION OF SOCIAL SCIENCE ORGANIZATIONS, IFSSO.** **Added/Corp** International Federation of Social Science Organizations. **VFOAT** Social Science Organizations. (1982)-. English. ir. Scandinavian University Press, PO Box 2959 Toeyen, N 0608 Oslo 6 Norway. **Tel** 011 47 2 2575400, FAX 011 47 2 2575353, telex 71896 UROR N. **(Subscription address:** Scandinavian University Press, 200 Meacham Ave., Elmont NY 11003.) **LC** H62.A1; C58a. **DD** 300/.25. ***Continues*** *International Directory of Social Science Research Councils, 0193-337X.*

UK/0268-4012
**INTERNATIONAL JOURNAL OF INFORMATION MANAGEMENT.** **See** Library and Information Sciences.

UK/0267-9655
**INTERNATIONAL JOURNAL OF MORAL AND SOCIAL STUDIES.** ***Ceased.*** **See** Ethics.

US/0891-4486
**INTERNATIONAL JOURNAL OF POLITICS, CULTURE, AND SOCIETY.** **See** Sociology.

UK/0306-8293
**INTERNATIONAL JOURNAL OF SOCIAL ECONOMICS.** **See** Economics.

US/0889-0293
**INTERNATIONAL JOURNAL OF SOCIAL EDUCATION, THE.** (THE INTERNATIONAL JOURNAL OF SOCIAL EDUCATION : OFFICIAL JOURNAL OF THE INDIANA COUNCIL FOR THE SOCIAL STUDIES.). [Int. j. soc. educ.]. **Added/Corp** Indiana Council for the Social Studies. **VFOAT** IJSE. Vol. 1, No. 1 (Spring 1986)-. Periodical. English. Three times a year. $10.00. Ball State University / Department of History, Muncie IN 47306. **Tel** (317)285-8700. **ED** John E. Weakland. **LC** H1; .I644. **DD** 300/.7/1. **Ad Acc. Pr Rev. Circ:** 1,090. available on microfilm and microfiche from University Microfilms International (UMI). ***Continues*** *Indiana Social Studies Quarterly, 0019-6746.*
**Desc:** Each issue is thematic and includes articles and issues on content (anthropology, history, geography, economics, sociology, political science, and psychology), and social studies methodology, including the use of computers.
**Ind/Abst** Am. Hist. Life (1986-); Curr. Index J. Educ.; Educ. Index (1992-).

US/0251-1266
**INTERNATIONAL JOURNAL ON POLICY AND INFORMATION.** ***Title Change.*** [Int. j. policy inf.]. **Added/Corp** Tan-Chiang Wen li Hsueh Yuan. Graduate School of Information Engineering. Knowledge Systems Institute. **VFOAT** Policy and Information. (1977)-(19??). Periodical. English. sa. Knowledge Systems Institute, 1153 Oak Street, PO Box 576, Winnetka IL 60093-0576. **Tel** (312)835-1426. **ED** Chang Shi-Kuo. **LC** H1; .I646. **DD** 361.6/1/05. **CODEN** IJPIDH. **Bk Rev. Ad Acc. Circ:** 800 (ctrl). Documents available from Article Express International, Ask*IEEE. ***Continues in part*** *Policy Analysis and Information Systems.* ***Merged with*** *Tamkang Journal of Management Sciences, 0255-6863* ***to form*** *International Journal of Information and Management Sciences, 1017-1819.*
**Desc:** The application of information science theory and technology to decision making and policy analysis in management, business, economics, regional planning and social sciences.
**Ind/Abst** Bioeng. Abstr.; Ei Page One; Eng. Index Annu.; INSPEC (June 1980-).

US/0734-4791
**INTERNATIONAL POPULAR CULTURE.** ***Ceased.*** [Int. pop. cult.]. **VFOAT** Pop. Vol. 1 (Fall 1979)-?. Periodical. English. sa. College of Staten Island, 130 Stuyvesant Place, Staten Island NY 10301. **Tel** (212)390-7988.

YU/0543-3665
**INTERNATIONAL PROBLEMS (BEOGRAD).** (INTERNATIONAL PROBLEMS.). [Int. probl.]. **Added/Corp** Institut za Meunarodnu Politiku i Privredu (Belgrade, Serbia). (1961)-. Periodical. English (translations available in Serbo-Croatian (Roman)). an. **LC** H1; .M35. **DD** 300/.5. ***Continues*** *Meunarodni Problemi.; English Ed., 0352-5554.*
**Ind/Abst** Am. Hist. Life (1970-1977).

CN/0825-0456
**INTERNATIONAL SEMIOTIC SPECTRUM.** **See** Humanities.

FR
**INTERNATIONAL SOCIAL SCIENCE COUNCIL : [DIRECTORY].** **Main/Corp** International Social Science Council. (19??)-. English. ir. UNESCO / France, 31 rue Francois Bonvin, 75732 Paris Cedex 15 France. **Tel** 011 33 1 45684564, 011 33 1 45684565, FAX 011 33 1 42733007, telex 204461 Paris. **LC** H10; .I57a.

FR/0020-8701
**INTERNATIONAL SOCIAL SCIENCE JOURNAL.** [Int. soc. sci. j.]. **Added/Corp** Unesco. **VFOAT** ISSJ. Vol. 11, No. 1 (1959)-. Academic Scholarly Publication. English (French). Four times a year (Feb., May, Aug., Nov.). £51.50 UK & Europe; $102.00 North America; £65.50 other. Basil Blackwell Publishers Ltd, 108 Cowley Road, Oxford 0X4 1JF England. **Tel** 011 44 865 791100, FAX 011 44 865 791347, telex 837022 OXBOOK G. **(Subscription address:** Blackwell Publishers / UK, Marston Book Services, PO Box 87, Oxford OX2 0DT England.) **ED** Ali Kazancigil. **LC** H1; .A2. **DD** 305. **NLM** W1 IN841N. **Ad Acc. Pr Rev. Circ:** 4,000 (ctrl). available on microfilm and microfiche from University Microfilms International (UMI). Documents available from The Genuine Article, UMI Article Clearinghouse. ***Continues*** *International Social Science Bulletin, 1012-9537.*
**Desc:** International and multidisciplinary with thematic issues on all social science disciplines and study areas.
**Ind/Abst** ABC POL SCI; Abstr. Anthropol.; Acad. Search (July 1993-); Am. Hist. Life (1955-1974, 1977-); Anthropol. Index; Appl. Soc. Sci. Index Abstr.; Arts Humanit. Citation Index [Select. Cov.]; Contents Pages Manage.; Curr. Contents Soc. Behav. Sci.; Curr. Index J. Educ.; Expand. Acad. Index (1989-); Geogr. Abstr. Human Geogr.; GeoRef; INFO-SOUTH Abstr.; Int. Bibliogr. Sociol.; Int. Dev. Abstr.; Int. Labour Doc.; Int. Polit. Sci. Abstr.; J. Econ. Lit.; LABORDOC; Leis. Recreat. Tour. Abstr.; Middle East Abstr. Index; MLA Int. Bibl. Books Artic. Mod. Lang. Lit.; Multicult. Educ. Abstr.; Newsp. Period. Abstr. (1991-); PAIS Int. Print (1991-); Peace Res. Abstr. J. (1954-1976); Res. Alert [Full Cov.]; Rural Dev. Abstr.; Sage Urban Stud. Abstr (?-?); School Organ. Manage. Abstr.; Soc. Plann. Policy Dev. Abstr.; Soc. Sci. Source (Jul. 1993-); Soc. Sci. Cit. Index [Full Cov.]; Soc. Sci. Index; Soc. Sci. Index Fulltext (Nov. 1988-) [Full Txt.]; Soc. Work Abstr. (?-?); Sociol. Abstr. [Full Cov.]; Sociol. Educ. Abstr.; Soc. Res. Methodol. Abstr. (1975-); West. Hist. Q.; Women Stud. Abstr.; World Agric. Econ.

US/0278-2308
**INTERNATIONAL SOCIAL SCIENCE REVIEW.** [Int. soc. sci. rev.]. **Added/Corp** Pi Gamma Mu. Vol. 57, No. 1 (Winter 1982)-. Academic Scholarly Publication. English. qt. $10.00 (one year), $18.00 (two year) US. Pi Gamma Mu, 1001 Millington, Suite B, Winfield KS 67156. **Tel** (316)221-3128. **ED** Panos D. Bardis. **LC** H1; .S55. **DD** 300/.5. **[CCC].** Index available. **Bk Rev. Circ:** 4,400 (ctrl). ***Continues*** *Social Science (Winfield, Kan.), 0037-7848.*
**Desc:** Scholarly articles from single social science disciplines (economics, history, international relations, political science, sociology/anthropology) or interdisciplinary treatments of social science subjects.
**Ind/Abst** Acad. Search (July 1993-); Am. Hist. Life (1963-); Am. Bibliogr. Slavic East Europ. Stud.; Appl. Soc. Sci. Index Abstr.; INFO-SOUTH Abstr.; Int. Polit. Sci. Abstr.; Middle East Abstr. Index; Multicult. Educ. Abstr.; PAIS Int. Print (1991-); Peace Res. Abstr. J. (1982-); Soc. Plann. Policy Dev. Abstr.; Soc. Sci. Source (Jul. 1993-); Soc. Work Abstr. (Summer 1987-?) [Select. Cov.]; Sociol. Abstr.; Sociol. Educ. Abstr.; Stud. Women Abstr.; Tech. Educ. Train. Abstr.

GW/0020-9449
**INTERNATIONALES ASIEN FORUM.** [Int. Asienforum]. **VFOAT** International Quarterly for Asian Studies. Vol. 1 (Jan. 1970)-. Periodical. German (English). qt. DM112.50. Weltforum Verlagsgesellschaft, Marienburger Strasse 22, D 50968 Cologne Germany. **Tel** 011 49 221 376950. **ED** Detlef Kantowsky and Alois Graf von Waldburg-Zeil. **Bk Rev.** ctrl circ.
**Desc:** Reports on current political, economic, social, scientific and cultural problems. Strategies and experiences in the Asiatic countries. Domestic and foreign policies, internal structure and foreign economic relations are covered through reports, analyses and documentation.
**Ind/Abst** Am. Hist. Life (1979-); Int. Polit. Sci. Abstr.; Middle East Abstr. Index; World Agric. Econ.

US/0198-8875
**IREX OCCASIONAL PAPERS.** [IREX occas. pap.]. **Main/Corp** International Research and Exchanges Board. **VAT** International Research and Exchanges Board Occasional Papers. Vol. 1, No. 1-. Monographic series. English. ir (four to five issues per year). Price varies per volume. International Research and Exchanges Board, 126 Alexander Street, Princeton NJ 08540-7102. **Tel** (609)683-9500, telex 233508 IRE UR. **ED** J Bradley Ivie. **LC** H31; .I68A; HF1411. **DD** 300.
**Desc:** Occasional papers address timely policy and academic issues on Soviet and Eastern European studies and US-Soviet and US-Eastern European relations.

US/0896-1301
**IRIS (CHARLOTTESVILLE, VA.).** (IRIS.). [Iris]. Began Spring 1978. Periodical. English. sa. $9.00 (institutions), $35.00 other. Iris, Box 323 HSC / University of Virginia, Charlottesville VA 22908. **Tel** (804)824-4500. **ED** Rebecca Hyman. **DD** 305. **Bk Rev. Ad Acc. Circ:** 2,500 (ctrl).
**Desc:** Contains articles of general interest, news, the arts, fiction, poetry, book reviews of interest to women.

US/0899-7977
**ISI ATLAS OF SCIENCE. SOCIAL SCIENCES.** **VFOAT** Social Sciences. **VAT** Institute for Scientific Information Atlas of Science. Social Sciences. 1989-. Academic Scholarly Publication. English. qt. $295.00 institutions. Institute for Scientific Information, 3501 Market Street, Philadelphia PA 19104. **Tel** (215)386-0100, (800)523-1850, FAX (215)386-6362, telex 84-5305. **(Subscription address:** Institute for Scientific Information, PO Box 71416, Chicago, IL 60694)

PO
**ISLENHA.** **Added/Corp** Madeira Islands. Direccao Regional dos Assuntos Culturais. **VFOAT** Revista Islenha. No. 1 (July-Dec. 1987)-. Periodical. Portuguese (English and French). Twice a year (June & Dec.). 2,275$00 Portugal & Spain; 3,110$00 others. Direccao Regional dos Assuntos Culturais, rua dos Ferreiros 165, 9000 Funchal Portugal. **Tel** 011 351 2 33164, FAX 011 351 2 32151. **LC** DP702.M18; I84. **Circ:** 1,000.

US/0020-2622
**ISR NEWSLETTER.** [ISR newsl.]. **Main/Corp** University of Michigan. Institute for Social Research. **Added/Corp** University of Michigan. Institute for Social Research. Newsletter. **VAT** Institute for Social Research Newsletter. (Winter 1969)-. Periodical. English. Three times a year. Free. Institute for Social Research / University of Michigan, PO Box 1248, Ann Arbor MI 48106-1248. **Tel** (313)764-8363. **ED** Linda J. Stafford and Sonya R. Kennedy. **Circ:** 13,000. available on microfilm and microfiche from University Microfilms International (UMI).
**Desc:** Describes research findings from ISR's three centers (Survey Research Center, Center for Political Studies, Research Center for Group Dynamics). Written for a general audience.
**Ind/Abst** Index Period. Artic. Relat. Law.

IS
**ISRAEL SOCIAL SCIENCE RESEARCH.** **Added/Corp** Hubert H. Humphrey Center for Social Ecology. Vol. 1, No. 1 (1983)-. Periodical. English. Twice a year (Two single issues or one double issue per year). $15.00 (individual); $25.00 (institution). Humphrey Institute Social Ecology, Ben-Gurion University, PO Box 653, Beer-Sheva 84105 Israel. **Tel** 011 972 57 461429, FAX 011 972 5771536. **ED** Stephen Sharot and Eliezer Ben-Rafael. **LC** WMLC 93/1788. **Bk Rev**, (Qty: 4-10). **Pr Rev. Circ:** 550-650 (ctrl).
**Desc:** A multidisciplinary journal of the social science research about Israel and other issues relating to the social behavior in Israeli society. Articles may be from sociology, psychology, anthropology, economics, political science, history, education, and linguistics.
**Ind/Abst** Psychol. Abstr. (1983-); PsycINFO; PsycLit; Soc. Plann. Policy Dev. Abstr.; Sociol. Abstr. (1983-) [Full Cov.]; Middle East J.

US/0049-0903
**ITEMS - SOCIAL SCIENCE RESEARCH COUNCIL (U.S.).** (ITEMS - SOCIAL SCIENCE RESEARCH COUNCIL.). [Items - Soc. Sci. Res. Counc.]. **Main/Corp** Social Science Research Council (U.S.). Vol. 1 (Mar. 1947)-. Periodical. English. ir. Social Science Research Council / New York, 605 3rd Avenue, New York NY 10158. **Tel** (212)661-0280, FAX (212)370-7896. **ED** Gloria Kirchheimer. **LC** H62; .S7243. **DD** 307.2. **NLM** W1 IT57K. **Bk Rev. Circ:** 7,500. available on microfilm and microfiche from University Microfilms International (UMI).
**Ind/Abst** Am. Hist. Life (1966-); Am. Bibliogr. Slavic East Europ. Stud.; Anthropol. Index; Index Free Period.; Middle East Abstr. Index; Soc. Res. Methodol. Abstr. (1984-); Trop. Dis. Bull.

DK/0105-6387
**IWGIA NEWSLETTER.** (BOLETIN DEL GRUPO INTERNACIONAL DE TRABAJO SOBRE ASUNTOS INDIGENAS (IWGIA).). **VFOAT** Boletin IWGIA. Vol. 1, No. 1 (March 1981)-. Periodical. Spanish. qt. $18.00 (individuals), $32.00 (institutions). International Work Group for Indigenous Affairs, Fiolstraede 10, DK-1171 Copenhagen K Denmark. **Tel** 011 45 1 33124724. **LC** GN380; .I94.

MX
**IZTAPALAPA.** V. 1- (No. 1- ). Periodical. Spanish. sa. $100.00. Uam Unidad Iztapalapa, Division de Ciencias, Sociales y Humanidades Michoacan y Michoacan y la Purisima, Iztapalapa DF Mexico. **LC** H8.S7; I96. **DD** 300/.5.

GW/0075-2770
**JAHRBUCH FUER SOZIALWISSENSCHAFT.** [Jahrb. Sozialwiss.]. Vol.1, No. 1 (1950)-. Periodical. German. Three times a year. DM169.00. Vandenhoeck & Ruprecht, Robert Bosch Breite 6, D-37079 Goettingen Germany. **Tel** 011 49 551 695911, FAX 011 49 551 695917, telex 965226 VAN d. **ED** Harold Jurgensen. **LC** H9; .J18. **NLM** W1 JA196P. **[CCC].** Index available. **Pr Rev.** Documents available from The Genuine Article.
**Ind/Abst** Curr. Contents Soc. Behav. Sci.; Int. Polit. Sci. Abstr.; PAIS Int. Print; Res. Alert [Full Cov.]; Soc. Sci. Cit. Index [Full Cov.]; World Agric. Econ.

GW
**JAHRESBERICHT (GERMANY (WEST). BUNDESMINISTERIUM FUR INNERDEUTSCHE BEZIEHUNGEN).** (JAHRESBERICHT / BUNDESMINISTER FUR INNERDEUTSCHE BEZIEHUNGEN.). German. an. Free. Bundesministerium fur Innerdeutsche Beziehungen, Postfach 16 40, 5300 Bonn 1 Germany. **Tel** 0228/207-235, telex 886 776 BGAD. **LC** DD259.4; .J326. **DD** 303.4/8243/0431. **Circ:** 25,000.
**Desc:** Description of the work of the Federal Ministry for Intra German Relations.

GW
**JAHRESBERICHT - OSTEUROPA-INSTITUT.** **Main/Corp** Osteuropa-Institut Munchen. (19??)-. Academic Scholarly Publication. German (English, Russian and Ukrainian). an. Free on request. Osteuropa-Institut, Scheinerstrasse 11, 8000 Munchen 80 Germany. **Tel** 011 49 89 983821, FAX 011 49 89 9810110. **LC** H62.5.G4; M86a. **Circ:** 300.

GW
**JAHRESBERICHT - RHEINLAND PFALZ, MINISTERIUM FUER SOZIALES, GESUNDHEIT UND SPORT.** **Main/Corp** Rhineland-Palatinate. (Germany). Ministerium fur Soziales, Gesundheit und Sport. German. an. Ministerium fur Soziales Gesundheit und Sport, Bauhofstrasse 4 65, Mainz Germany. **LC** HN458.R53; R47A.

JA/0021-4450
**JAPAN INTERPRETER.** **Added/Corp** Nihon Shakai Shiso Kenkyusho, Tokyo. Vol. 6 (Spring 1970)-. Periodical. English. sa. $10.00. Ctr Japan Social and Political Studies, 9 29 12 Seijo, Setagaya-ku Tokyo 157 Japan. **LC** H1; .J56. **DD** 300/.5. ***Continues** Journal of Social and Political Ideas in Japan, 0388-0478.*
**Ind/Abst** Am. Hist. Life (1963-1980); MLA Int. Bibl. Books Artic. Mod. Lang. Lit.

US/0882-9411
**JASA SHARE.** **VFOAT** Jasa-Share; Share. 1-. Periodical. English (Russian). Jasa-Share, 40 West 68th Street, New York NY 10023. **DD** 305.

US/0021-6704
**JEWISH SOCIAL STUDIES.** **See** Religion and Theology-Judaism.

JA
**JIMBUNGAKU RONSHU.** **VFOAT** Journal of Humanistic Studies. Japanese. Bukkyo Daigaku Bungakubu Gakkai, 9-6 Murasakino Kita Hananobo-cho, Kita-ku Kyoto Japan. **LC** AS552.B84; A24.

US/0075-3904
**JOHNS HOPKINS UNIVERSITY STUDIES IN HISTORICAL AND POLITICAL SCIENCE, THE.** **Added/Corp** Johns Hopkins University. **VFOAT** Studies in Historical and Political Science. Ser. 1 (1882/83)-. Monographic series. English. ir. Price varies per volume. Johns Hopkins University Press, 2715 North Charles Street, Baltimore MD 21218-4319. **Tel** (410)516-6987, FAX (410)516-6968. **DD** 300/.5. **[CCC].** available on microfilm and microfiche from University Microfilms International (UMI).

MX
**JORNADAS.** **Main/Corp** Colegio de Mexico. No. 58 (1966)-. Monographic series. Spanish. ir. Price varies per volume. Colegio de Mexico AC, Camino Al Ajusco No 20, 10740 Mexico DF Mexico. **Tel** 011 52 5 6455955 Ext. 3133, telex 1777585 COLME. Index available. cum. index. **Pr Rev. Circ:** 1,000. ***Continues** Mexico (City). Colegio de Mexico. Centro de Estudios Sociales. Jornadas.*
**Desc:** Different issues on economics, sociology, history of Mexico and education.

FR/0300-953X
**JOURNAL DE LA SOCIETE DES OCEANISTES MICROFILM.** **See** Archaeology.

SA
**JOURNAL FOR CONTEMPORARY HISTORY / JOERNAAL VIR EIETYDSE GESKIEDENIS.** **See** Political Science-International Relations.

AU
**JOURNAL FUR SOZIALFORSCHUNG (VIENNA, AUSTRIA : 1987).** (JOURNAL FUER SOZIALFORSCHUNG.). Vol. 27, No. 1 (1987)-. German. qt. Campus Verlag, Heelstrasse 149, D-60488 Frankfurt Germany. **Tel** 011 49 69 96751606, FAX 011 49 69 7682046.

US/0739-8069
**JOURNAL - MIDDLE STATES COUNCIL FOR THE SOCIAL STUDIES (U.S.).** (JOURNAL / MIDDLE STATES COUNCIL FOR THE SOCIAL STUDIES.). [J. - Middle States Counc. Soc. Stud. (U.S.)]. **Added/Corp** Middle States Council for the Social Studies (U.S.). **VFOAT** MSCSS Journal; Journal of the Middle States Council for the Social Studies. Vol. 1 (Fall 1978)-. English. ir. $5.00 (regular member); $7.50 (contributing member); $2.00 (building member). Rider College, PO Box 6400, Lawrenceville NJ 08648. **Tel** (609)896-5176. **LC** H62.5.U5; J59. **DD** 300/.7/1. Index available (bound in 4th issue). ***Continues** Middle States Council for the Social Studies (U.S.) Annual Proceedings and Bulletin of the Middle States Council for the Social Studies.*
**Ind/Abst** Curr. Index J. Educ.

US/0021-8863
**JOURNAL OF APPLIED BEHAVIORAL SCIENCE, THE.** [J. appl. behav. sci.]. **Added/Corp** NTL Institute for Applied Behavioral Science. National Training Laboratories (National Education Association of the United States). Vol. 1 (Jan./March 1965)-. Periodical. English. qt (Mar., June, Sept., Dec.). $136.00. SAGE Periodical Press, 2455 Teller Road, Thousand Oaks CA 91320. **Tel** (805)499-0721, FAX (805)499-0871, telex 100799. **ED** Clayton P. Alderfer (Rutgers University). **LC** H1; .J53. **DD** 305. **NLM** W1 JO539S. **CODEN** JABHAP. **[CCC].** Index available. **Ad Acc. Pr Rev. Acid Free. Circ:** 3,000. available on microfilm and microfiche from University Microfilms International (UMI). Documents available from The Genuine Article, UMI Article Clearinghouse.
**Desc:** Reports the latest research on behavioral science and its applications to organizations, social policy and community activity.
**Ind/Abst** ABC POL SCI; ABI/INFORM Glob. Ed.; ABI Inform Ondisc (July 1971-); Acad. Ind. [Computer File] (1992-); Acad. Search (July 1993-); Appl. Soc. Sci. Index Abstr.; Bus. Index (1985-); Chicano Index; Contents Pages Manage.; Cumul. Index Nurs. Allied Health Lit.; Curr. Contents Soc. Behav. Sci.; Educ. Adm. Abstr. (?-?); Expand. Acad. Index (1984-); Gen. BusinessFile (1985-); Gen. Period. Index (1985-); High. Educ. Abstr. (1965-19??); Hospit. Health Admin. Index; Hum. Resour. Abstr. (?-?); Index Period. Artic. Relat. Law (19??-19??); INFO-SOUTH Abstr.; Int. Polit. Sci. Abstr.; Manage. Contents; Middle East Abstr. Index; Multicult. Educ. Abstr.; Newsp. Period. Abstr. (1991-); Peace Res. Abstr. J. (1965-1969); Person. Manage. Abstr.; Psychol. Abstr. (1965-); PsycINFO; PsycLit; PsycScan: Appl. Psych.; Res. Alert [Full Cov.]; Sage Public Adm. Abstr. (?-?); Selec. Coop. Index Manage. Period; Soc. Plann. Policy Dev. Abstr.; Soc. Sci. Source (Jul. 1993-); Soc. Sci. Index; Soc. Sci. Index Fulltext (1988-) [Full Txt.]; Soc. Work Abstr. (Summer 1987-?) [Select. Cov.]; Sociol. Abstr.; Soc. Res. Methodol. Abstr. (1979-); Stud. Women Abstr.; Tech. Educ. Train. Abstr.; Work Relat. Abstr.

●UK
**JOURNAL OF AREA STUDIES.** **Added/Corp** Loughborough University of Technology. Dept. of European Studies. Portsmouth Polytechnic. No. 1 (1992)-. Periodical. English. sa (2 issues). £30.00 institutions; £20.00 individuals. Loughborough University / Department of European Studies, Loughborough Leicestershire, LE11 3TU England. **Tel** 011 44 509 222981, 011 44 509 222991, FAX 011 44 509 269395. **LC** D839; .J681. ***Continues** Journal of Area Studies, 0261-3530.*
**Desc:** Theory and methodology of area studies. Comparative and cross-area research mainly in social science. Oriented towards current public issues.
**Ind/Abst** ABC POL SCI; Am. Hist. Life.

UK/0021-9320
**JOURNAL OF BIOSOCIAL SCIENCE.** [J. biosoc. sci.]. **Added/Corp** Galton Foundation (Great Britain). **VFOAT** Biosocial Science. Vol. 1 (Jan. 1969)-. Academic Scholarly Publication. English. qt. $126.00 US; £66.00 UK. Portland Press Ltd., PO Box 32 Commerce Way, Colchester CO2 8HP Essex England. **Tel** 011 44 206 796351, FAX 011 44 206 799331, telex 987275 BIOSOC G. **ED** D. F. Roberts. **LC** HQ750.A1; J68. **NLM** W1 JO568. **CODEN** JBSLAR. Index available. cum. index. **Bk Rev. Ad Acc. Pr Rev. Circ:** 570 (ctrl). Documents available from The Genuine Article, CASDDS. ***Continues** Eugenics Review.*
**Desc:** Contains original papers, lectures and reviews on social aspects of human biology and biosocial aspects of demography. Interdisciplinary material preferred.
**Ind/Abst** Abstr. Anthropol.; AGRICOLA; Anthropol. Index; Anthropol. Lit.; Chem. Abstr.; Curr. Contents Soc. Behav. Sci.; Curr. Lit. Fam. Plan.; EMBASE; Index Med.; Int. Bibliogr. Sociol.; Leis. Recreat. Tour. Abstr.; Med. Abstr. Newsl.; Middle East Abstr. Index; Nutr. Abstr. Rev., Ser. B, Live Feeds and Feed.; Nutr. Abstr. Rev., Ser. A, Hum. Exp.; Popul. Index; Psychol. Abstr. (1976-); PsycINFO; PsycLit; Res. Alert [Full Cov.]; Rural Dev. Abstr.; Sci. Cit. Index; SCISEARCH; Soc. Plann. Policy Dev. Abstr.; Soc. Sci. Cit. Index [Full Cov.]; Sociol. Abstr.; Sociol. Educ. Abstr.; SportSearch; Stud. Women Abstr.; Trop. Dis. Bull.; Women Stud. Abstr.; World Agric. Econ.

UK/0300-9645
**JOURNAL OF BIOSOCIAL SCIENCE. SUPPLEMENT.** [J. biosoc. sci., Suppl.]. **Added/Corp** Galton Foundation (Great Britain). (July 1969)-. Academic Scholarly Publication. English. qt. $126.00 US; £66.00 UK (Comes with Journal of Biosocial Science). Portland Press Ltd., PO Box 32 Commerce Way, Colchester CO2 8HP Essex England. **Tel** 011 44 206 796351, FAX 011 44 206 799331, telex 987275 BIOSOC G. **LC** UNC. **NLM** W1 JO568A. **CODEN** JBSCBZ. Documents available from BIOSIS Document Express, CASDDS.
**Ind/Abst** Biol. Abstr. (1986-); Chem. Abstr.; Index Med.

US/1044-0755
**JOURNAL OF COMPUTING & SOCIETY.** ***Ceased.*** [J. comput. soc.]. (1990)-(1990). Periodical. English. qt. Ablex Publishing Corporation, 355 Chestnut Street, Norwood NJ 07648. **Tel** (201)767-8450, (201)767-8455 (Customer Service), FAX (201)767-6717.

**ED** Gary Chapman. **LC** QA76.9.C66; J683. **DD** 303.48/34. Index available. cum. index. **Bk Rev. Ad Acc. Circ:** 500.

SA/0258-9001
**JOURNAL OF CONTEMPORARY AFRICAN STUDIES : JCAS. See** Humanities.

UK/0047-2336
**JOURNAL OF CONTEMPORARY ASIA. See** History(General)-History of Asia.

●US/1071-5568
**JOURNAL OF CULTURAL DIVERSITY.** [J. cult. divers.]. **VFOAT** JCD. Vol. 1, No. 1 (Winter 1994)-. Periodical. English. Four times a year (Jan., Apr., July, Oct.). $50.00 (individuals), $100.00 (institutions) US; $100.00 Canada; $50.00 others. Tucker Publications Inc., PO Box 580, Lisle IL 60532. **Tel** (708)969-3809, FAX (708)969-3895. **ED** Dr. Ruth W. Johnson (editor's address: 444 Garden Avenue, Mt. Vernon, NY 10553). **DD** 305. Index available. cum. index. **Bk Rev**, (Qty: 1-2). **Ad Acc, Adv Mgr:** Monique, **Tel** (708)969-3809. **Pr Rev. Circ:** 500.

●UK
**JOURNAL OF ECONOMIC AND SOCIAL INTELLIGENCE.** (1993)-. Periodical. English. Three times a year. £60.00. Taylor Graham Publishing, 500 Chesham House, 150 Regent Street, London W1R 5FA United Kingdom. **Bk Rev. Ad Acc. Pr Rev.** ***Continues*** *Social Intelligence, 0961-2882.*

US/0747-9662
**JOURNAL OF ECONOMIC AND SOCIAL MEASUREMENT.** [J. econ. soc. meas.]. Vol. 13, No. 1 (Apr. 1985)-. Periodical. English. qt. Fl376.00. IOS Press, Van Diemenstraat 94, 1013 CN Amsterdam Netherlands. **Tel** 011 31 20 6382189, FAX 011 31 20 620 3419. **ED** Charles Renfro. **LC** H62.A1; R47. **DD** 300/.72073. **CODEN** JEMEEZ. **[CCC].** Documents available from UMI Article Clearinghouse. ***Continues*** *Review of Public Data Use, 0092-2846.*
**Desc:** A unique guide to the production, distribution and use of publicly available statistical data. It publishes original articles and information on quantitative research and methodology using publicly available data bases.
**Ind/Abst** Appl. Soc. Sci. Index Abstr.; Curr. Contents Soc. Behav. Sci.; Econ. Lit. Index (-1986); Expand. Acad. Index (1992-); Health Plan. Adminis.; Hospit. Health Admin. Index (1985-); Hum. Resour. Abstr. (?-?); Int. Bibliogr. Sociol.; J. Econ. Lit. (1985-); Newsp. Period. Abstr. (1992-); PAIS Int. Print (1991-); Life Sci. Collect.; Popul. Index (1985-); Soc. Plann. Policy Dev. Abstr.; Sociol. Abstr. (1985-); Urban Aff. Abstr.; Women Stud. Abstr. (1985-).

UK/0958-9287
**JOURNAL OF EUROPEAN SOCIAL POLICY. See** General Interest-General Interest-Europe.

US/0895-7258
**JOURNAL OF INDO-EUROPEAN STUDIES : MONOGRAPH SERIES.** [J. Indo-Eur. stud. monogr. ser.]. **Added/Corp** Institute for the Study of Man (Washington, D.C.). **VFOAT** Journal of Indo-European Studies Monograph Series. No. 1 (1975)-. Monographic series. English. ir. Price varies per volume. Institute for the Study of Man, 1133 13th Street Northwest, Suite C2, Washington DC 20005. **Tel** (202)371-2700. **ED** Roger Pearson. **DD** 910. **Pr Rev. Circ:** 400.
**Desc:** Linguistic monographs relating to Indo-European studies.
**Ind/Abst** Soc. Plann. Policy Dev. Abstr.

GW/0932-4569
**JOURNAL OF INSTITUTIONAL AND THEORETICAL ECONOMICS : JITE. VFOAT** JITE; Zeitschrift Fuer Die Gesamte Staatswissenschaft. Vol. 142 No. 1, March (1986)-. Periodical. English. qt. DM312.00. JCB Mohr / Paul Siebeck, Postfach 2040, D 72010 Tuebingen Germany. **Tel** 011 49 7071 9230, FAX 011 49 7071 51104, telex 7/262872 mohr d. **ED** Rudolf Richter and Ekkehart Schlicht. **LC** H5; .Z4. **[CCC]. Bk Rev. Ad Acc. Circ:** 850. Documents available from The Genuine Article. ***Continues*** *Zeitschrift Fuer Die Gesamte Staatswissenschaft, 0044-2550.*
**Desc:** One of the oldest reviews in the field of political economy, deals traditionally with problems of economics, social policy, and their legal framework.
**Ind/Abst** Arts Humanit. Citation Index [Select. Cov.]; Econ. Lit. Index (19??-); Int. Polit. Sci. Abstr.; J. Econ. Lit.; Res. Alert [Full Cov.]; Soc. Sci. Cit. Index [Full Cov.]; World Agric. Econ.

US/0363-2873
**JOURNAL OF LIBERTARIAN STUDIES, THE.** [J. libert. stud.]. V. 1-. Periodical. English. an. $32.00 (institutions), $24.00 (individuals) surface mail, $34.00 (one year), $26.00 (two year) Canada and Mexico; $38.00 (one year), $30.00 (two year) other. Center for Libertarian Studies, PO Box 4091, Burlingame CA 94011. **Tel** (415)342-6569. **ED** Murray N Rothbard. **LC** JC571; .J64. **DD** 301.5/92/05. **[CCC]. Bk Rev. Ad Acc. Circ:** 1,000 (ctrl). available on microfilm and microfiche from University Microfilms International (UMI).
**Desc:** Academic journal studying libertarian theory and principles in economics, history, philosophy, education, political science, law and public policy.
**Ind/Abst** Am. Hist. Life (1977-); Int. Bibliogr. Sociol.; Int. Polit. Sci. Abstr.; Philos. Index.

PH/0115-2408
**JOURNAL OF NORTHERN LUZON. See** Education.

US/0888-6601
**JOURNAL OF PAN AFRICAN STUDIES, THE.** [J. Pan Afr. stud.]. **Added/Corp** California Institute of Pan African Studies. Vol. 1, No. 1 (1987)-. Periodical. English. qt. $20.00 US; $25.00 other. California Institute of Pan-African Studies, PO Box 13063, Fresno CA 93794-3063. **Tel** (209)266-2550. **ED** Itibari M. Zulu. **DD** 305. Index available. **Bk Rev. Ad Acc. Pr Rev. Circ:** 1,500 (ctrl).
**Desc:** International afrocentric review of African culture and consciousness.
**Ind/Abst** Ethnoarts Index.

US/0161-8938
**JOURNAL OF POLICY MODELING.** [J. policy model.]. **Added/Corp** Society for Policy Modeling. Vol. 1 (Jan. 1979)-. Academic Scholarly Publication. English. Six times a year (1 volume). $235.00 US; $271.00 other. Elsevier Science Publishing Company Inc, Madison Square Station, PO Box 882, New York NY 10159-0882. **Tel** (212)633-3950, FAX (212)633-3990. **ED** Antonio Maria Costa. **LC** H1; .J553. **DD** 300/.1/51. **CODEN** JPMOD5. **[CCC]. Ad Acc. Pr Rev.** available on microfilm and microfiche from University Microfilms International (UMI). Documents available from The Genuine Article, UMI Article Clearinghouse.
**Desc:** Provides a forum for analysis and debate concerning international policy issues. The journal addresses questions of critical import to the world community as a whole, and it focuses upon the economic, social, and political interdependencies between national and regional systems.
**Ind/Abst** ABI/INFORM Glob. Ed.; ABI Inform Ondisc (Jan. 1980-); Acad. Search (July 1993-); Appl. Soc. Sci. Index Abstr.; Bus. Index (1985-); Contents Recent Econ. J.; Curr. Contents Soc. Behav. Sci.; Econ. Lit. Index; Energy Res. Abstr. (Sept. 1979-); Gen. BusinessFile (1985-); Gen. Period. Index (1985-); INFO-SOUTH Abstr.; Int. Labour Doc.; Int. Polit. Sci. Abstr.; J. Econ. Lit. (1983-); J. Plan. Lit.; LABORDOC; Mag. Search; Middle East Abstr. Index; Res. Alert [Full Cov.]; Soc. Plann. Policy Dev. Abstr.; Soc. Sci. Source (Jul. 1993-); Soc. Sci. Cit. Index [Full Cov.]; Sociol. Abstr.; U.S. Polit. Sci. Doc.; Wheat Barley Trit. Abstr.; World Agric. Econ.

US/1049-6343
**JOURNAL OF PREVENTIVE PSYCHIATRY AND ALLIED DISCIPLINES.** ***Ceased.*** **See** Medical Science and Technology-Psychiatry.

US/0195-6000
**JOURNAL OF PUBLIC AND INTERNATIONAL AFFAIRS.** ***Ceased.*** [J. pub. int. aff.]. Vol. 1 (1979)-Vol. 5 (1985). English. sa. Graduate School of Public and International Affairs, University of Pittsburgh, Editorial Office, Pittsburgh PA 15260. **LC** H1; .J554. **DD** 300/.5.
**Ind/Abst** Middle East Abstr. Index.

II/0970-3357
**JOURNAL OF RURAL DEVELOPMENT (HYDERABAD, INDIA).** (JOURNAL OF RURAL DEVELOPMENT.). **Added/Corp** National Institute of Rural Development (India). Vol. 1, No. 1 (Jan. 1982)-. Periodical. English. Six times a year (Jan., Mar., May, July, Sept., Nov.). $50.00. National Institute of Rural Development, Rajendranagar, Hyderabad 500 030 India. **Tel** 48001-4, telex 425-6510. **(Subscription address:** Prints India, 11 Darya Ganj, New Delhi 110002 India.**) ED** R. P. Kapoor. **LC** HN690.Z9; C65565. **DD** 307/.14/0954. Index available. **Bk Rev. Circ:** 1,000. ***Formed by the union of*** *Behavioural Sciences and Rural Development,* *0379-797X* ***and*** *Rural Development Digest.*
**Desc:** Deals with behavioral aspects of rural development, poverty-alleviation programs, effect of socio-economic structures on development, agricultural productivity and related aspects, people's participation in development.
**Ind/Abst** Agrofor. Abstr.; For. Prod. Abstr. (1991-); For. Abstr.; Geogr. Abstr. Human Geogr.; Poult. Abstr.; Rural Dev. Abstr.; World Agric. Econ.

US
**JOURNAL OF SOCIAL AND BEHAVIORAL SCIENCES. Added/Corp** Association of Social and Behavioral Scientists. (19??)-. Periodical. English. qt. $25.00. Association of Social and Behavioral Scientists, Grambling State University, Box 710, Grambling LA 71245. **Tel** (318)274-7287. **LC** H1; .J73. **DD** 300/.5. ***Continues*** *Journal of Social Science Teachers.*
**Ind/Abst** Middle East Abstr. Index.

II/0377-0508
**JOURNAL OF SOCIAL AND ECONOMIC STUDIES (NEW DELHI, INDIA).** (JOURNAL OF SOCIAL AND ECONOMIC STUDIES.). [J. soc. econ. stud.]. Vol. 1, No. 1 (Jan./March 1984)-. Periodical. English. an. $50.00. Sage Publications Ltd., 6 Bonhill Street, London EC2A 4PU, UK. **Tel** 071 374 0645, FAX 071 374 8741, telex 296207 SAGE G. **Acid Free.** ***Continues*** *Journal of Social and Economic Studies, 0377-0508.*
**Ind/Abst** Soc. Plann. Policy Dev. Abstr.

RH
**JOURNAL OF SOCIAL DEVELOPMENT IN AFRICA. Added/Corp** School of Social Work (Harare, Zimbabwe). Vol. 1 No. 1 (1986)-. Periodical. English. Twice a year (Feb., & July). $10.00 (individuals), $20.00 (institutions) Third World countries; $15.00 (individuals), $30.00 (institutions) others. School of Social Work / Zimbabwe, P Bag 66022, Kopje Harare Zimbabwe. **Tel** 011 263 14 707414 15 16. **ED** N. Hall. **LC** HN780.Z9; C657. **DD** 307.1/4/096. Index available (bound in issue). cum. index. **Bk Rev**, (Qty: 16). **Ad Acc. Pr Rev. Circ:** 150.
**Desc:** Multi-disciplinary journal specializing in social development in Africa. Particular areas of concern include analysis of issues affecting development, poverty and popular participation.
**Ind/Abst** Agrofor. Abstr. (1991-); Appl. Soc. Sci. Index Abstr.; Educ. Adm. Abstr. (?-?); Geogr. Abstr. Human Geogr.; Hum. Resour. Abstr.; Int. Bibliogr. Sociol.; Int. Dev. Abstr.; Int. Labour Doc.; LABORDOC; Rural Dev. Abstr.; Soc. Work Abstr. [Select. Cov.]; World Agric. Econ.

US/0022-4529
**JOURNAL OF SOCIAL HISTORY.** [J. soc. hist.]. Vol. 1 (Fall 1967)-. Periodical. English. qt. $28.00 (individuals), $60.00 (institutions). Carnegie Mellon University / Journal of Social History, H&SS Dean's Office, 5000 Forbes Avenue, Pittsburgh PA 15213-3890. **Tel** (412)268-2884. **LC** HN1; .J6. **DD** 309.1. **[CCC]. Pr Rev.** available on microfilm and microfiche from University Microfilms International (UMI). Documents available from The Genuine Article, UMI Article Clearinghouse.
**Ind/Abst** Acad. Abstr. Full Text Elite (Jan. 1992-); Acad. Abstr. (Jan. 1992-); Acad. Search (Jan. 1992-); Am. Hist. Life (1967-); Am. Bibliogr. Slavic East Europ. Stud.; Arts Humanit. Citation Index [Full Cov.]; Book Rev. Index (1984-); Crim. Justice Abstr.; Curr. Contents Arts Humanit.; Curr. Contents Soc. Behav. Sci.; Expand. Acad. Index (1989-); Hist. Source (Jan. 1992-); Humanit. Index; Humanit. Source (Jan. 1992-); INFO-SOUTH Abstr.; Int. Bibliogr. Sociol.; Mag. Search; Middle East Abstr. Index; Newsp. Period. Abstr. (1991-); Res. Alert [Full Cov.]; Soc. Plann. Policy Dev. Abstr.; Soc. Sci. Source (Jan. 1992-); Soc. Sci. Cit. Index [Full Cov.]; Soc. Sci. Index; Soc. Sci. Index Fulltext (Winter 1988-) [Full Txt.]; Soc. Work Abstr. (?-?); Sociol. Abstr.; SportSearch; U.S. Polit. Sci. Doc.; West. Hist. Q.; Women Stud. Abstr.

US/0022-4537
**JOURNAL OF SOCIAL ISSUES, THE.** [J. soc. issues]. **Added/Corp** Society for the Psychological Study of Social Issues. Vol. 1 (Feb. 1945)-. Periodical. English. Four times a year. $225.00 institutions, $48.00 individuals US; $265.00 institutions, $56.00 individuals other. Plenum Press, 233 Spring Street, New York NY 10013-1578. **Tel** (212)620-8000, (800)221-9369, FAX (212)463-0742, (212)807-1047, telex 23/421139. **ED** Stuart Oskamp. **LC** HN51; .J6. **DD** 305. **NLM** W1 JO888I. **CODEN** JSISAF. **[CCC]. Pr Rev.** available on microfilm and microfiche from University Microfilms International (UMI). Documents available from The Genuine Article, UMI Article Clearinghouse.
**Desc:** Sponsored by the SPSSI with concern for research on the psychological aspects of important social issues. Seeks to bring theory and practice into focus on human problems.
**Ind/Abst** ABC POL SCI; Abstr. Anthropol.; Acad. Abstr. Full Text Elite (July 1990-); Acad. Abstr. (July 1990-); Acad. Ind. [Computer File] (1987-); Acad. Search (July 1990-); AGRICOLA; Am. Hist. Life (1971-); Appl. Soc. Sci. Index Abstr.; Arts Humanit. Citation Index [Select. Cov.]; Commun. Abstr.; Crim. Justice Abstr.; Crim. Penol. Police Sci. Abstr.; Curr. Contents Soc. Behav. Sci.; Curr. Index J. Educ.; Expand. Acad. Index (1987-); Geogr. Abstr. Human Geogr.; High. Educ. Abstr. (1965-); Hum. Resour. Abstr. (?-?); Humanit. Source (Jul. 1990-); Index Period. Artic. Relat. Law (19??-19??); INFO-SOUTH Abstr.; Int. Bibliogr. Sociol.; Int. Dev. Abstr.; Int. Polit. Sci. Abstr.; J. Plan. Lit.; Mag. Search; Middle East Abstr. Index; Multicult. Educ. Abstr.; Newsp. Period. Abstr. (1989-); PAIS Int. Print (1991-); Peace Res. Abstr. J. (1962, 1977), (1983, 1984);; Psychol. Abstr. (1945-); PsycINFO; PsycLit; PsycScan: Appl. Psych.; Res. Alert [Full Cov.]; Sage Fam. Stud. Abstr.; Sage Race Relat. Abstr.; Soc. Plann. Policy Dev. Abstr.; Soc. Sci. Source (Jul. 1990-); Soc. Sci. Cit. Index [Full Cov.]; Soc. Sci. Index; Soc. Sci. Index Fulltext (Fall 1988-) [Full Txt.]; Soc. Work Abstr. (Summer 1987-) [Select. Cov.]; Sociol. Abstr.; Sociol. Educ. Abstr.; Spec. Educ. Needs Abstr.; Stud. Women Abstr.; U.S. Polit. Sci. Doc.; West. Hist. Q.; Women Stud. Abstr.

US/0047-2786
**JOURNAL OF SOCIAL PHILOSOPHY.** [J. soc. philos.]. (19??)-. Periodical. English. Three times a year. $25.00 (individuals), $75.00 (institutions) US;

$30.00 (individuals), $80.00 (institutions) other. Trinity University, Department of Philosophy, San Antonio TX 78212. **Tel** (210)736-7488, FAX (210)736-7305. **ED** Peter A. French. **LC** H1; .J565. **DD** 300/.5. **Ad Acc**, **Adv Mgr:** K.Eicher. **Circ:** 600. available on microfilm and microfiche from University Microfilms International (UMI).
**Desc:** The journal covers an area of social philosophy which seeks to wrestle with the interfacing of academic interests and the operation of social institutions that apply the insights and techniques of many disciplines.
**Ind/Abst** Philos. Index; Relig. Index One Period. (1980-).

US/0278-839X
**JOURNAL OF SOCIAL, POLITICAL AND ECONOMIC STUDIES, THE.** [J. soc. polit. econ. stud.]. **Added/Corp** Council for Social and Economic Studies (U.S.) George Mason University. Contemporary Economics and Business Association. Vol. 6, No. 1 (Spring 1981)-. Periodical. English. Four times a year (Mar., June, Sept., Dec.). $32.50 (individuals); $70.00 (insitutions). Council on Social and Economic Studies, PO Box 34070, Washington DC 20043. **Tel** (202)371-2700. **ED** Roger Pearson. **LC** H1; .J563. **DD** 300/.5. Index available. **Bk Rev. Ad Acc. Pr Rev. Circ:** 1,250. available on microfilm and microfiche from University Microfilms International (UMI). Documents available from The Genuine Article, UMI Article Clearinghouse. ***Continues*** *Journal of Social and Political Studies, 0193-5941.*
**Desc:** Contemporary policy issues of international, social, political, and economic significance.
**Ind/Abst** ABC POL SCI; Acad. Abstr. Full Text Elite (Jan. 1992-); Acad. Abstr. (Jan. 1992-); Acad. Search (Jan. 1992-); Am. Hist. Life (1977-); Am. Bibliogr. Slavic East Europ. Stud.; Appl. Soc. Sci. Index Abstr.; Arts Humanit. Citation Index [Select. Cov.]; Curr. Contents Soc. Behav. Sci.; Expand. Acad. Index (1989-); Index Period. Artic. Relat. Law (-19??); INFO-SOUTH Abstr.; Int. Polit. Sci. Abstr.; Mag. Search; Middle East Abstr. Index; Newsp. Period. Abstr. (1991-); PAIS Int. Print (1991-); Res. Alert [Full Cov.]; Soc. Sci. Source (Jan. 1992-); Soc. Sci. Cit. Index [Full Cov.]; Soc. Sci. Index; Soc. Sci. Index Fulltext (Spring 1988-) [Full Txt.]; U.S. Polit. Sci. Doc. (-199?).

US/0196-2000
**JOURNAL OF SOCIAL RECONSTRUCTION.** ***Suspended.*** [J. soc. reconstr.]. Vol. 1 (Jan./Mar. 1980)-Suspended with Vol. 1, No. 2. Periodical. English. qt. $39.50. Earl M Coleman, White Gates, West Mount Airy Road, Croton-on-Hudson NY 10510. **LC** HN51; .J63. **DD** 361.6/1/0973. **[CCC].**

MW
**JOURNAL OF SOCIAL SCIENCE.** **Added/Corp** University of Malawi. Vol. 1 (1972)-. English. an. K4.00 Malawi; $7.00 North America; £2.50 US. Journal of Social Science of Malawi, PO Box 280, Zomba Malawi. **Tel** 522 222, telex 4742 MI. **ED** Kings M Phiri. **LC** H1; .J59. **DD** 300/.5. **Bk Rev. Ad Acc. Circ:** 500.
**Desc:** A descriptive and analytical periodical in the Africanist field that addresses social science issues about Africa generally and Malawi in particular.
**Ind/Abst** Am. Hist. Life (1985-); Int. Bibliogr. Sociol.; Int. Polit. Sci. Abstr.

PK
**JOURNAL OF SOCIAL SCIENCES & HUMANITIES.** **Added/Corp** University of Karachi. **VFOAT** Journal of Social Sciences and Humanities. 1 & 2 (1984)-. Periodical. English. sa. $10.00. Panstwowe Wydawn Naukowe, Miodowa 10, PO Box 391, 00251 Warsaw Poland. **LC** AS569.A1; J68. **DD** 300/.5.
**Ind/Abst** Psychol. Abstr. (1984-); PsycLit.

BG
**JOURNAL OF SOCIAL STUDIES, THE.** Vol. 1 (Jan. 1978)-. English. qt. $48.00 institutions; $40.00 individuals. Centre for Social Studies, Dhaka University, Room 1107/Arts Building, Dhaka-1000 Bangladesh. **Tel** 011 880 500800, telex 011 880 2 865583. **ED** B K Jahangir. **LC** H1; .J62. **DD** 300/.5. Index available. **Bk Rev**, (Qty: 3-4). **Ad Acc. Circ:** 500 (ctrl).
**Ind/Abst** Geogr. Abstr. Human Geogr.; Int. Bibliogr. Sociol.; Int. Dev. Abstr.; Rice Abstr.; World Agric. Econ.

US/0885-985X
**JOURNAL OF SOCIAL STUDIES RESEARCH.** [J. soc. stud. res.]. V. 1- Winter 1977-. Periodical. English. sa. $10.00 US; $12.00 other. Journal of Social Studies, The University of Georgia, 215 Tucker Hall, Athens GA 30602. **Tel** (404)542-7265. **ED** Michael Hawkins. **LC** H1; .J68. **DD** 300. **Bk Rev. Circ:** 400. available on microfilm and microfiche from University Microfilms International (UMI).
**Desc:** Publishes article length manuscripts, brief reports, and special monographs on research, evaluation, and developmental activities.
**Ind/Abst** Curr. Index J. Educ.

US/0022-5061
**JOURNAL OF THE HISTORY OF THE BEHAVIORAL SCIENCES.** **See** Psychology.

US/0361-5154
**JOURNAL OF THE HUMANITIES AND SOCIAL SCIENCES.** **See** Humanities.

II
**JOURNAL OF THE NORTH-EAST INDIA COUNCIL FOR SOCIAL SCIENCE RESEARCH, THE.** **Main/Corp** North-East India Council for Social Science Research. Periodical. English. sa. Rs40.00 India; $18.00 US; £6.00 other. North-East India Council for Social Science Research, B T Hostel, Shillong 793003 Meghalaya India. **Tel** SHILLONG 24501. **ED** B Pakem, J B Bhattacharjee, D N Majumdar, S Sen, and B Dattaray. **LC** HN681; .N67A. **Bk Rev. Ad Acc. Circ:** 1,000 (ctrl).
**Desc:** Our focus is on North-East India. Economic, social and political aspects.

PK/0034-5431
**JOURNAL OF THE RESEARCH SOCIETY OF PAKISTAN.** **Main/Corp** Research Society of Pakistan. V. 1- 1964-. Periodical. English (Urdu). qt. Rs40.00 Pakistan; $8.00 other. Punjab University Library, Old Campus, University of the Punjab, Lahore Pakistan. **Tel** 65907. **ED** A Shakoor Ahsan. **LC** DS376. **DD** 954.9/005. **Bk Rev. Ad Acc. Circ:** 500 (ctrl).
**Desc:** Historical, cultural, political, literary, linguistic and topographical features of Pakistan, and work connected with Muslim heritage in the South Asian subcontinent.
**Ind/Abst** Am. Hist. Life (1989-); Index Islam. Lit.; Int. Bibliogr. Sociol.

SI
**JOURNAL OF THE SOUTH SEAS SOCIETY.** **See** History(General)-History of Asia.

US/0743-0019
**JOURNAL OF TURKISH STUDIES.** [J. Turk. stud.]. **Added/Corp** Harvard University. Center for Middle Eastern Studies. **VFOAT** Turkluk Bilgisi Arastrmalar; TUBA. Vol. 1 (1977)-. English (French, German and Turkish). an. price varies per volume. Tekin / Journal of Turkish Studies, PO Box 1447, Duxbury MA 02331. **Tel** (617)585-8796. **LC** DR438.94; .J68. **DD** 956.1/005.
**Ind/Abst** Am. Hist. Life (1989-); Index Islam. Lit.; Numis. Lit.

CN/0228-1635
**JOURNAL OF UKRAINIAN STUDIES.** **See** Humanities.

US/0047-2891
**JOURNAL OF YOUTH AND ADOLESCENCE.** [J. youth adolesc.]. Vol. 1 (March 1972)-. Periodical. English. Six times a year. $345.00 institutions, $62.00 individuals US; $405.00 institutions, $73.00 individuals other. Plenum Press, 233 Spring Street, New York NY 10013-1578. **Tel** (212)620-8000, (800)221-9369, FAX (212)463-0742, (212)807-1047, telex 23/421139. **ED** Daniel Offer. **LC** HQ796; .J625. **DD** 301.43/1/05. **NLM** W1 JO974G. **CODEN** JYADA. **[CCC].** Index available. **Pr Rev.** available on microfilm and microfiche from University Microfilms International (UMI). Documents available from The Genuine Article, BIOSIS Document Express, UMI Article Clearinghouse.
**Desc:** Provides a single high-level medium of communication for psychiatrists, psychologists, biologists, sociologists, educators and professionals who address themselves to the subject of youth and adolescence.
**Ind/Abst** Acad. Search (July 1993-); AGRICOLA [Select. Cov.]; Appl. Soc. Sci. Index Abstr.; Biol. Abstr.; Commun. Abstr. (?-?); Crim. Justice Abstr.; Curr. Contents Soc. Behav. Sci.; Curr. Index J. Educ.; Curr. Lit. Fam. Plan.; Educ. Index (-1992); Educ. Adm. Abstr.; EMBASE; Except. Child Educ. Resour. (19??-19??); Expand. Acad. Index (1989-); High. Educ. Abstr. (1973-); INFO-SOUTH Abstr.; Mag. Search; Middle East Abstr. Index; Multicult. Educ. Abstr.; Newsp. Period. Abstr. (1991-); Psychol. Abstr. (1972-); PsycINFO; PsycLit; Res. Alert [Full Cov.]; Risk Abstr.; Sage Fam. Stud. Abstr.; Sage Urban Stud. Abstr (?-?); Soc. Plann. Policy Dev. Abstr.; Soc. Sci. Source (Jul. 1993-); Soc. Sci. Cit. Index [Full Cov.]; Soc. Sci. Index; Soc. Sci. Index Fulltext (Oct. 1988-) [Full Txt.]; Sociol. Abstr.; Sociol. Educ. Abstr.; Spec. Educ. Needs Abstr.; Stud. Women Abstr.; Women Stud. Abstr.

US/1051-7103
**JOURNAL / PHILADELPHIA SOCIAL STUDIES COUNCIL, THE.** (1991)-. English. $6.00 (single issue). Philadelphia Social Studies Council, c/o Dr. Alfonz Lengyel, 1522 Schoolhouse Road, Ambler PA 19002.

IO
**JPS, JURNAL PENELITIAN SOSIAL.** **VFOAT** Jurnal Penelitian Sosial. Vol. 1- Jan. 1976-. Periodical. Indonesian. 1500. Fakultas Ilmu-Ilmu Sosial, Universitas Indonesia, Perpustaan Kampus U I, Jl Pemuda Rawamangun, Jakarta Indonesia. **LC** H62.A1; J26.

YU/0022-6114
**JUGOSLOVENSKI PREGLED; INFORMATIVNO DOKUMENTARNI PRIRUCNIK O JUGOSLAVIJI.** **Added/Corp** Publicisticko-Izdavacki Zavod "Jugoslavija" (Belgrade, Serbia). Vol. 1 (1957)-. Periodical. Serbo-Croatian (Roman) (English). Twelve times a year. $50.00. Jugoslovenki Pregled, Mose Pijade 8, POB 677, 11001 Belgrade Yugoslavia. **LC** DR301; .J89. cum. index. ctrl circ.
**Desc:** Systematic, factual information on political, economic, social and cultural developments in Yugoslavia, based on official sources; compiled, written and edited by prominent specialists.

MY/0127-4082
**KAJIAN MALAYSIA : JOURNAL OF MALAYSIAN STUDIES.** **See** History(General)-History of Asia.

US/0890-1422
**KEEPING UP.** (KEEPING UP : NEWS BULLETIN OF THE CLEARINGHOUSE FOR SOCIAL STUDIES/SOCIAL SCIENCE EDUCATION / ERIC.). [Keep. up]. **VFOAT** ERIC Keeping Up. Bulletin. English. an. Free. Social Studies Development Center, Indiana University, 2805 East 10th Street/Suite 120, Bloomington IN 47408. **Tel** (812)855-3838. **DD** 300. Index available. **Bk Rev. Circ:** 5,000 (ctrl).
**Desc:** Showcases past and upcoming activities of the ERIC Clearinghouse; includes items of interest of social science/social studies educators.

IO
**KEGIATAN L.S.D. SELURUH INDONESIA.** **Main/Corp** Indonesia. Direktorat Jenderal Pembangunan Masyarakat Desa. **VAT** Kegiatan Lembaga Sosial Desa Seluruh Indonesia. Vol. 1 (1974)-. Indonesian. ir. Departemen Dalam Negeri, JL Pasar Minggu Pejatan, Jakarta Selatan Indonesia. **LC** HN710.Z9; C617b.

JA/0289-0747
**KENKYU NENPO (TAKUSHOKU DAIGAKU. KENKYUJO).** (KENKYU NENPO.). **Added/Corp** Takushoku Daigaku. Kenkyujo. **VFOAT** Annals of Takushoku University. (1981)-. Periodical. Japanese (table of contents in English). sa. Takushoku Daigau Kenkyujo, 4-14 Kohinata 3 Bunkyo-ku, Tokyo-to Japan. **LC** H8.J3; K46.

US/0743-8478
**KETTERING REPORT.** **Main/Corp** Charles F Kettering Foundation. 1981/1982-. English. sa. The Charles F.Kettering Foundation, 200 Commons Road, Dayton OH 45459-2799. **Tel** (513)434-7300, (800)221-3657, FAX (513)439-9804. **ED** Robert E Daley. **LC** AS911.C46; A25. **DD** 300/.5. **Circ:** 10,000 (ctrl). ***Continues*** *Annual Report - Charles F. Kettering Foundation.*
**Desc:** A report of a research foundation concerned with basic problems in education, government, and science.

JA
**KITAKYUSHU DAIGAKU SHOKEI RONSHU.** **VFOAT** Kitakyushu-Daigaku Sho-Kei-Ronshu; Journal of Economics and Business Administration. Japanese (Japanese). Kitakyushu Daigaku Shokei, Gakkai Kitagata Kokura Minami-ku, Kitakyushu Japan. **LC** H8; .K52.

RU/0235-5043
**KLUB (MOSCOW, R.S.F.S.R. : 1989).** (KLUB.). **Added/Corp** Soviet Union. Ministerstvo Kultury. Vsesoiuznyi Tsentralnyi Sovet Professionalnykh Soiuzov. (1989)-. Periodical. Russian. mo. $99.95. Klub, Starokaluzhskoe Shosse 1, 117630 Moscow Russia. **(Subscription address:** East View Publications Inc., 3020 Harbor Lane North, Suite 110, Minneapolis MN 55447.) **LC** PAR. ***Continues*** *Klub i Khudozhestvennaia Samodeiatelnost, 0023-219X.*

US/0164-0259
**KNOWLEDGE (BEVERLY HILLS, CALIF.).** (KNOWLEDGE.). [Knowledge]. Vol. 1 (Sept. 1979)-. Periodical. English. qt (4 issues). $141.00 institution, $51.00 individual. SAGE Periodical Press, 2455 Teller Road, Thousand Oaks CA 91320. **Tel** (805)499-0721, FAX (805)499-0871, telex 100799. **ED** Marcel C. LaFollette (George Washington University). **LC** H62; .K626. **DD** 300/.7/2. **NLM** W1 KN735M. **[CCC]. Pr Rev. Acid Free.** available on microfilm and microfiche from University Microfilms International (UMI). Documents available from The Genuine Article.
**Desc:** An international, interdisciplinary social science journal that examines the nature of expertise and the translation of knowledge into practice and policy.
**Ind/Abst** Curr. Index J. Educ.; Educ. Adm. Abstr.; Res. Alert [Full Cov.]; Sage Public Adm. Abstr.; Soc. Plann. Policy Dev. Abstr.; Soc. Sci. Cit. Index [Full Cov.].

JA/0023-2793
**KOKKA GAKKAI ZASSHI.** **See** Political Science.

KO
**KOREAN SOCIAL SCIENCE JOURNAL.** **Added/Corp** Yunesuko Hanguk Wiwonhoe. Hanguk Sahoe Kwahak Yongu Hyobuihoe. Vol. 10 (1983)-. English. an (Mar.). $10.00. Korean National Commission, PO Box Central 64, Seoul Korea. **Tel** 011 82 2 7762805, FAX 011 82 2 7743956, telex 23231 2 Ext. 6364. cum. index. **Ad Acc. Circ:** 1,000. ***Continues*** *Social Science Journal.*
**Desc:** Representative articles on social sciences of Korea.
**Ind/Abst** Int. Bibliogr. Sociol.; Int. Polit. Sci. Abstr.

# Social Sciences

**NE**
**KOSMOS + OEKUMENE.** See Religion and Theology.

**CC**
**KUEI-CHOU SHE HUI KO HSUEH.** VFOAT Guizhou Shehui Kexue; Social Sciences in Guizhou. Periodical. Chinese. bm. $4.86. Science Press, 16 Donghuangchenggen North Street, Beijing 100707, People's Republic of China. **Tel** 011 86 1 4019821, 011 86 1 4010642, FAX 011 86 1 4012180, 011 86 1 4019810, telex 210147. **LC** H53.C55; K84. **DD** 300/.95134.

SZ/0023-5962
**KYKLOS.** (KYKLOS; INTERNATIONALE ZEITSCHRIFT FUER SOZIALWISSENSCHAFTEN.). [Kyklos]. VFOAT International Review for Social Sciences. (1947)-. Academic Scholarly Publication. English (French and German). qt. $169.00 North America; £107.00 UK & Europe; £109.00 other. Basil Blackwell Publishers Ltd, 108 Cowley Road, Oxford 0X4 1JF England. **Tel** 011 44 865 791100, FAX 011 44 865 791347, telex 837022 OXBOOK G. (Subscription address: Blackwell Publishers / UK, Marston Book Services, PO Box 87, Oxford OX2 0DT England.) **ED** R. L. Frey and B. S. Frey. **LC** H1; .A15. **[CCC]**. **Bk Rev**. **Ad Acc**. **Pr Rev**. **Circ**: 2,500. available on microfilm and microfiche from University Microfilms International (UMI) Documents available from The Genuine Article, UMI Article Clearinghouse.
**Ind/Abst** Acad. Search (July 1993-); AGRICOLA; Am. Hist. Life (1954-1959, 1966-); Contents Recent Econ. J.; Curr. Contents Soc. Behav. Sci.; Econ. Lit. Index; Geogr. Abstr. Human Geogr.; INFO-SOUTH Abstr.; Int. Bibliogr. Sociol.; Int. Dev. Abstr.; Int. Labour Doc.; Int. Polit. Sci. Abstr.; J. Econ. Lit.; LABORDOC; Mag. Search; Middle East Abstr. Index; Newsp. Period. Abstr. (1991-); PAIS Int. Print (1991-); Res. Alert [Full Cov.]; Soc. Sci. Source (Jul. 1993-); Soc. Sci. Cit. Index [Full Cov.]; Soc. Sci. Index; Soc. Sci. Index Fulltext (1988-) [Full Txt.].

**JA**
**KYODO KENKYU KATSUDO HOKOKUSHO.** **Main/Corp** Momoyama Gakuin Daigaku. Sogo Kenkyujo. VFOAT Momoyama Gakuin Daigaku Kyodo Kenkyu Katsudo Hokokusho; Activity Reports of Collaborative Research. Vol. 1, (1980)-. Japanese. Momoyama Gakuin Daigaku Sogo Kenkyujo, 237-1 Nishino Sakai-shi, Osaka-fu 588 Japan. **Tel** 0722-36-1181. **LC** AZ188.J3; M65a. **Circ**: 550.
**Desc**: Activity reports of collaborative research in the Research Institute including their lists of members and publications.

CC/1000-2804
**LAN-CHOU TA HSUEH HSUEH PAO. SHE HUI KO HSUEH PAN.** **Added/Corp** Lan-chou Ta Hsueh. VFOAT Lanzhoudaxue Xuebao; Journal of Lanzhou University. Social Sciences. (19??)-. Periodical. Chinese. qt. $16.14. (Subscription address: China International Book Trading Corporation, PO Box 399, Library Service Department, Beijing 100044 People's Republic of China.) **LC** H8.C47; L35. **DD** 300/.5.

**IO**
**LAPORAN TAHUNAN - PROYEK PENGEMBANGAN PUSAT DOKUMENTASI DAN INFORMASI BIDANG ILMU-ILMU SOSIAL DAN KEMANUSIAAN.** **Main/Corp** Proyek Pengembangan Pusat Dokumentasi dan Informasi Bidang Ilmu-Ilmu Sosial dan Kemanusiaan. Began with 1974/75 Vol. Indonesian. Pusat Dokumentasi Ilmiah Nasional, J1 Jenderal Gatot Subroto, PO Box 3065 JKT, Jakarta Indonesia. **LC** H62.5.I6; P76A.

US/0890-7218
**LASA FORUM / LATIN AMERICAN STUDIES ASSOCIATION.** See History(General)-History of North, South, and Central America.

US/0023-9216
**LAW & SOCIETY REVIEW.** See Law.

●CN/1192-1927
**LEFT HISTORY.** See Political Science.

US/0149-0400
**LEISURE SCIENCES.** [Leis. sci.]. Vol. 1 (1977)-. Periodical. English. qt. $75.00 UK; $124.00 other. Taylor & Francis Ltd., Rankine Road, Basingstoke Hampshire, RG24 8PR United Kingdom. **Tel** 011 44 256 840366, FAX 011 44 256 479438, telex 858540. (Subscription address: Taylor & Francis Inc., 1900 Frost Road, Suite 101, Bristol PA 19007-1598.) **ED** Thomas L. Goodale. **LC** GV1; .L37. **DD** 301.5/7. **CODEN** LESCDC. **[CCC]**. **Bk Rev**. **Ad Acc**. **Circ**: 600. available on microfilm and microfiche from University Microfilms International (UMI) Documents available from The Genuine Article.
**Desc**: Articles cover leisure behavior with emphasis on developing and testing theory. Contents relate to planning and design of leisure environments, forest and coastal recreation, travel and tourism development, and urban leisure systems. Also published are methodological notes and philosophical and policy treatises, calendar of research meetings and conferences, announcements and book reviews.
**Ind/Abst** Commun. Abstr. (?-?); Curr. Contents Soc. Behav. Sci.; Environ. Period. Bibliogr.; Geogr. Abstr. Human Geogr.; Int. Dev. Abstr. (?-?); J. Plan. Lit.; Leis. Recreat. Tour. Abstr.; Psychol. Abstr. (1980-); PsycINFO; PsycLit; Public Aff. Inf. Serv. Bull. (1985-); Res. Alert [Full Cov.]; Sage Fam. Stud. Abstr. (?-?); Sage Urban Stud. Abstr (?-?); Soc. Sci. Cit. Index [Full Cov.]; SPORT Discus; SportSearch.

US/0092-718X
**LETTERS & PAPERS ON THE SOCIAL SCIENCES.** Ceased. (LETTERS & PAPERS ON THE SOCIAL SCIENCES; AN UNDERGRADUATE REVIEW.). Vol. 1 (Fall 1973)-Ceased ?. Periodical. English. sa. Johns Hopkins University / Population Information Program, 111 Market Place, Suite 310, Baltimore MD 21202. **Tel** (410)659-6300, FAX (410)659-6311. **LC** H1; .L45. **DD** 300/.5.

GW/0340-0425
**LEVIATHAN (DUSSELDORF).** (LEVIATHAN.). [Leviathan]. (1973)-. Periodical. German. qt. DM87.00 Germany; DM102.60 other. Westdeutscher Verlag GmbH, Postfach 5829, D 65048 Wiesbaden Germany. **Tel** 011 49 611 160220. (Subscription address: VVA Bertelsmann Dist GmbH, Postfach 7600, D 33310 Guetersloh Germany) **LC** H5; .L47. **DD** 300/.5. **[CCC]**. **Bk Rev**. **Ad Acc**. **Circ**: 2,000.
**Ind/Abst** Energy Res. Abstr. (1981-).

**FR**
**LIAISONS SOCIALES.** French. ir. 1815.00F. Liaisons Sociales, 1 Avenue E Belin, F 92856 Rueil Mal France. **Tel** 011 33 1 41299872.
**Ind/Abst** LABORDOC.

FR/0294-8168
**LIAISONS SOCIALES. BREF SOCIAL.** (1961)-. Periodical. French. da. Liaisons Sociales, 1 Avenue E Belin, F 92856 Rueil Mal France. **Tel** 011 33 1 41299872. **UDC** 36.
**Ind/Abst** LABORDOC.

FR/0417-870X
**LIAISONS SOCIALES. DOCUMENTS.** (1964)-. Periodical. French. Liaisons Sociales, 1 Avenue E Belin, F 92856 Rueil Mal France. **Tel** 011 33 1 41299872. **UDC** 36.
**Ind/Abst** LABORDOC.

**FR**
**LIBRE POLITIQUE, ANTHROPOLOGIE, PHILOSOPHIE.** 1-. French. sa. Editions Payot, 106 BD Saint Germain, Paris 75006 France. **LC** H3; .L52.

US/1045-6368
**LIE GROUPS. HISTORY, FRONTIERS, AND APPLICATIONS.** [Lie groups, Hist. front. appl.]. VFOAT Lie Groups. Series A, History, Frontiers, and Applications. (1975)-(1983). Monographic series. English. **DD** 512. **Continued in part by** Lie Froups. Series B, Systems Information and Control.
**Ind/Abst** Zentralbl. Math. Ihre Grenzgeb.

**GW**
**LITERATURWISSENSCHAFT, GESELLSCHAFTSWISSENSCHAFT.** VFOAT LGW. (19??)-. Periodical. German. ir. Price varies per volume. Bouvier GMBH & Company KG ABT Verlag, AM HOF 28, D53113 Bonn Germany. **Tel** 011 49 228 7290141.

●UK/0966-8349
**LOCATION SCIENCE.** Vol. 1, No. 1 (May 1993)-. Periodical. English. qt. $224.00 The Americas; £150.00 other. Pergamon Press, An Imprint of Elsevier Science Ltd., The Boulevard, Langford Lane, Kidlington, Oxford OX5 1GB United Kingdom. **Tel** 011 44 865 843000, 011 44 865 843699, FAX 011 44 865 843010. (Subscription address: Elsevier Science Ltd. Journal Fulfillment Centre, PO Box 800, Kidlington, Oxford OX5 1DX United Kingdom.) **ED** Richard Church, John Current, and H. Eiselt. **[CCC]**.

US/1040-2748
**LOUISIANA SOCIAL STUDIES JOURNAL.** (LOUISIANA SOCIAL STUDIES JOURNAL / LOUISIANA COUNCIL FOR THE SOCIAL STUDIES.). [La. soc. stud. j.]. **Added/Corp** Louisiana Council for the Social Studies. Vol. 13, No. 1 (Fall 1986)-. Periodical. English. an. $5.00. Louisiana Council for the Social Studies, PO Box 94064, Baton Rouge LA 70804. **Tel** (504)342-1136. **LC** H62.A1; L36. **DD** 300/.71/0763. **Continues** LCSS Journal.
**Ind/Abst** Curr. Index J. Educ.

AI/0320-8117
**LRABER HASARAKAKAN GITUTYUNNERI.** (LRABER HASARAKAKAN GITUTYUNNERI / HAYKAKAN SSH GITUTYUNNERI AKADEMIA.). [Lrab. hasar. gitut.]. **Added/Corp** Haykakan SSH Gitutyunneri Akademia. VFOAT Vestnik Obshchestvennykh Nauk. (1966)-. Periodical. Armenian (Russian; table of contents in English). Twice a year. $79.95. **LC** H19; .L73. **Continues** Teghekagir. Hasarakakan Gitutyunner.
**Ind/Abst** BHA : Biblio. Hist. Art.

**BL**
**LUA NOVA.** See Philosophy.

US/0885-4378
**LUCHA STRUGGLE.** [Lucha struggle]. Vol. 4, No. 3 (June 1980)-. Periodical. English. bm. $20.00 (library), $10.00 (individuals) US, (add $5.00 for postage) other. New York Circus Inc, PO Box 37, Times Square Station, New York NY 10108. **Tel** (212)928-7600, FAX (212)928-2757. **ED** Rigoberto Avila and David J Kalke. **DD** 322. Index available. **Bk Rev**. **Ad Acc**. ctrl circ. **Continues** New York Circus.
**Desc**: Journal of Christian reflection on struggles for liberation. Focus on social change and the popular church in Latin America.
**Ind/Abst** Altern. Press Index; Hum. Rights Intern. Rep.

SW/1101-9948
**LUND MONOGRAPHS IN SOCIAL ANTHROPOLOGY.** See Anthropology.

**JA**
**MACHIKANEYAMA RONSO: SHIGAKUHEN.** See Humanities.

CN/0226-2428
**MAIEUTICS.** Ceased. [Maieutics]. Vol. 1, No. 1 (Spring 1980)-Ceased ?. Periodical. English. sa. Centre for Theory in the Humanities and Social Sciences University, 4700 Keele Street, Downsview Ontario M3J 1P3 Canada. **DD** 300/.1.

**IO**
**MAJALAH ILMIAH FAKULTAS ILMU SOSIAL UNIVERSITAS AIRLANGGA.** Vol. 1 No. 1 (Apr.-June 1981)-. Periodical. Indonesian. qt. Dampus Fakultas Ilmu Sosial Unair, Jl Airlangga, Surabaya Indonesia. **LC** H8.I5; M34.

KU/0253-1097
**MAJALLAT AL-ULUM AL-IJTIMAIYAH.** (JOURNAL OF THE SOCIAL SCIENCES.). [J. soc. sci.]. VFOAT JSS. (19??)-. Periodical. English. $40.00. University of Kuwait, Fac of Science, PO Box 5969, AL Kuwait. **Tel** 0095 846725. **LC** H1; .M3. **DD** 300/.5.
**Ind/Abst** Soc. Plann. Policy Dev. Abstr.; Sociol. Abstr.; Middle East J. (?-?).

UK/0025-2034
**MANCHESTER SCHOOL OF ECONOMIC AND SOCIAL STUDIES, THE.** See Economics.

CN/0316-6473
**MANITOBA SOCIAL SCIENCE TEACHER, THE.** [Mait. soc. sci. teach.]. **Added/Corp** Manitoba Social Science Teachers' Association. (1974)-. Periodical. English. Four times a year. 10.00Can$. Manitoba Teachers Society, 191 Harcourt Street, Winnipeg Manitoba R3J 3H2 Canada. **Tel** (204)888-7961 ext.254, FAX (204)831-0877. **DD** 372.8/3/05. **Supersedes** Manitoba Geography Teachers, 0316-6457.

**US**
**MANNERING REPORT, THE.** (19??)-. English. Six times a year (Jan., Mar., May, July, Sept., Nov.). $30.00 US. Options Unlimited Inc., 617 Sunrise Lane, Green Bay WI 54301. **Tel** (414)339-0011, FAX (414)339-0012. **ED** Wendy Mannering. **Bk Rev**, (Qty: 6). **Circ**: 100 (ctrl). **Continues** The Rising Sun.

●BL/0103-8915
**MARGEM.** **Added/Corp** Pontificia Universidade Catolica de Sao Paulo. Faculdade de Ciencias Sociais. Pontificia Universidade Catolica de Sao Paulo. Programa de Estudos Pos-Graduados em Ciencias Sociais. Pontificia Universidade Catolica de Sao Paulo. Programa de Estudos Pos-Graduados em Historia. (1992)-. Periodical. Portuguese. sa. Pontificia Universidade Catolica de Sao Paulo, Faculdade de Ciencias Sociais, Rua Monte Alegre 984, Sala S-21, 05014 Sao Paulo SP Brazil. **Tel** 263-0211 Ext. 337. **ED** Jose Mario Ortiz Ramos. **LC** H8.P8; M37. **DD** 300/.5.

US/1066-9795
**MASTER'S THESES DIRECTORIES. THE ARTS AND SOCIAL SCIENCES.** Title Change. See The Arts.

**IO**
**MASYARAKAT INDONESIA.** Vol. 1, Aug. (1974)-. Periodical. English (Indonesian). sa. Rp800. Lembaga Ilmu Pengetahuan Indonesia, Biro Publikasi Ilmiah Lipi, Medan Merdeka Selatan No 11, Jakarta Indonesia. **LC** H8; .M36.
**Ind/Abst** Agrofor. Abstr.; Rice Abstr.; Rural Dev. Abstr.

**IO**
**MASYARAKAT KITA.** Vol. 1- Oct. 1976-. Periodical. English (Indonesian). Pusat Pengkajian Ilmu-Ilmu Sosial, Jalan Merbau No 38A, Medan Indonesia. **LC** H35; .M343.

NE/0165-4896
**MATHEMATICAL SOCIAL SCIENCES.** [Math. soc. sci.]. Vol. 1, No. 1 (Sept. 1980)-. Academic Scholarly Publication. English. Six times a year (2 vols.). Fl840.00. Elsevier Science Publishers BV, PO Box 211, 1000 AE Amsterdam Netherlands. **Tel** 011 31 20 5803642, FAX 011 31 20 5862696, telex 15682. **ED** Ki Hang Kim. **CODEN** MSOSDD. **[CCC]**. **Pr Rev.** available on microfilm and microfiche from University Microfilms International (UMI). Documents available from The Genuine Article, Ask*IEEE.
**Desc:** Publishes original research, as well as survey papers, short notes, news items, calendar of meetings and book reviews, which are of broad interest in the mathematical social sciences.
**Ind/Abst** Compumath Citation Index [Full Cov.]; Curr. Contents Soc. Behav. Sci.; Econ. Lit. Index; Educ. Adm. Abstr. (?-?); Hum. Resour. Abstr.; INSPEC (Sept. 1980-); Int. Bibliogr. Sociol.; J. Econ. Lit.; Math. Rev.; Res. Alert [Full Cov.]; Sage Urban Stud. Abstr (?-?); Soc. Plann. Policy Dev. Abstr.; Soc. Sci. Cit. Index [Full Cov.]; Sociol. Abstr.; Soc. Res. Methodol. Abstr. (1982-); Zentralbl. Math. Ihre Grenzgeb.

JA/0461-4593
**MATSUYAMA DAIGAKU RONSHU.** **Added/Corp** Matsuyama Daigaku. Matsuyama Daigaku. Gakujutsu Kenkyukai. **VFOAT** Matsuyama University Review. (1989)-. Periodical. Japanese (English). bm. **LC** H8.J3; M38. ***Continues*** *Matsuyama Shodai Ronshu, 0461-4593.*
**Ind/Abst** Am. Hist. Life (1955-1977,1979-1988).

US
**MATTER OF FACT : STATEMENTS CONTAINING STATISTICS ON CURRENT SOCIAL, ECONOMIC AND POLITICAL ISSUES.** (19??)-. English. sa. $84.50. Pierian Press, PO Box 1808, Ann Arbor MI 48106. **Tel** (313)434-5530, (800)678-2435, FAX (313)434-6409. ***Continues*** *Matter of Fact : Digest of Current Facts with Citations to Sources, 0897-3954.*
**Desc:** Contains abstracts of articles from more than 300 newspapers and periodicals, the Congressional Record, and Congressional hearings. Abstracts contain statistical data on a wide range of contemporary issues relating to public policy and governmental decision making.

US/0025-6110
**MAXWELL REVIEW.** [Maxwell rev.]. V. 1- 1965-. Periodical. English. sa. $1.50 students, $4.00 others. Maxwell Review, 502 Maxwell Hall, Syracuse University, Syracuse NY 13210. **LC** H1; .M33. **DD** 300/.5. available on microfilm from University Microfilms International (UMI).

SP/1130-6157
**MAYAB (MADRID).** (MAYAB.). [Mayab]. **Added/Corp** Sociedad Espanola de Estudios Mayas. Instituto de Cooperacion Iberoamericana (Madrid, Spain). No. 1 (1985)-. Spanish. an. Sociedad Espanola de Estudios Mayas, Departamento de Antropologia y Etnologia de America, Facultad de Geografia e Historia, Universidad Complutense, E-28040 Madrid Spain.
**Ind/Abst** Anthropol. Lit.

GW/0025-8350
**MEDIUM (FRANKFURT).** **See** Communication.

IS/0025-8679
**MEGAMOT / MOSAD SOLD LEMAAN HA-YELED VEHA-NOAR.** **Added/Corp** Mosad Sold Lemaan ha-Yeled Veha-Noar. Mekhon Henriyetah Sold. (1949)-. Periodical. Hebrew (summaries and/or abstracts in English). Four times a year. Hennrietta Szold Institute, 9 Columbia Street, Kiryat Menachem, Jerusalem 96583 Israel. **Tel** 02-419191, FAX 02-437698. **ED** Kalman Benyanini and Nurit Ranel. **NLM** W1 ME879. Index available. cum. index. **Ad Acc.** **Pr Rev. Circ:** 1,000.
**Ind/Abst** Int. Bibliogr. Sociol.; PsycINFO; PsycLit.

JA
**MEIJI DAIGAKU SHAKAI KAGAKU KENKYUJO KIYO.** **Main/Corp** Meiji Daigaku, Tokyo. Shakai Kagaku Kenkyujo. **VFOAT** Memoirs of the Institute of Social Sciences, Meiji University. No. 1 (1963)-. Japanese (summaries and/or abstracts in English). Meiji Daigaku, 1 Kanda Surugadai 1 Chiyoda-ku, Tokyo Japan. **LC** H8; .M375A.

PE
**MEMORIA - DESCO.** **Main/Corp** Desco. Spanish. Desco Publications, Leon de la Fuente 110, Lima 17 Peru. **Tel** 011 51 14 627193. **LC** H62.5.P45; D47A.

SP/0368-8283
**MEMORIAS.** [Mem. R. Acad. Cienc. Artes Barc.]. **Main/Corp** Real Academia de Ciencias y Artes de Barcelona. Ser. 3, Vol. 1 (1892)-. Academic Scholarly Publication. Spanish (Catalan and English; summaries and/or abstracts in French). ir (six to eight issues per year). 15000ptas Spain; $140.00 other. Real Academia Ciencias y Artes, Rambla de los Estudios 115, E-08002 Barcelona Spain. **Tel** 07-34-3-317 05 36. **CODEN** MACBAB. cum. index. **Circ:** 460 (ctrl). Documents available from CASDDS. ***Continues*** *Memorias de la Real Academia de Ciencias Naturales y Actes de Barcelona, 0210-7783.*
**Desc:** Accounts of researchers carried out by Academicians and/or co-workers.
**Ind/Abst** Chem. Abstr. (1892-1983); GeoRef.

MZ/0076-1184
**MEMORIAS DO INSTITUTO DE INVESTIGACAO CIENTIFICA DE MOCAMBIQUE. SERIES C, CIENCIAS HUMANAS.** **VFOAT** Ciencias Humanas. Vol. 7 (1965)-. Portuguese. **NLM** W1 ME903QC. ***Continues in part*** *Memorias do Instituto de Investigacao Cientifica de Mocambique.*

NE/0025-9454
**MENS EN MAATSCHAPPIJ.** **See** Sociology.

IT/0394-4115
**MERIDIANA.** **Added/Corp** Istituto Meridionale di Storia e Scienze Sociali. (Sept. 1987)-. Periodical. Italian. tq. L90000 Italy; L130000 other. Donzelli Editore, Via Mentana 2, 00185 Rome Italy. **Tel** 011 39 6 440610.

GW/0932-6510
**METHODIKA.** ***Ceased.*** Vol. 1, Issue 1 (1987)-(1994). Periodical. English. sa. Hogrefe & Huber Publishers, 12 Bruce Park Avenue, Toronto Ontario M4P 2S3 Canada. **Tel** (416)482-6339, FAX (416)484-4200. **LC** H61; .M4919. **DD** 300/.1.
**Desc:** International forum for all researchers involved in developing formal procedures and models in psychology, education, sociology, and other social and behavioral sciences.
**Ind/Abst** Psychol. Abstr. (1987-); PsycINFO (1990-); PsycLit; Soc. Plann. Policy Dev. Abstr.; Soc. Res. Methodol. Abstr. (1987-).

NE/0543-6095
**METHODOLOGY AND SCIENCE.** [Methodol. sci.]. **Added/Corp** Methodology and Science Foundation (Netherlands). (Jan. 1968)-. Periodical. English (French). Four times a year (Mar., June, Sept., Dec.). Methodology & Science Foundation, Beelslaan 20, 2012 PK Haarlem Netherlands. **Tel** 011 31 23 280290. **(Subscription address:** Dr P. H. Esser, Beelslaan 20, 2012 PK Haarlem The Netherlands) **ED** Piet H. Esser. **Bk Rev.** **Ad Acc.** **Pr Rev. Circ:** 250 (ctrl).
**Desc:** Empirical study of the foundations of sciences and their methodology, psycho-linguistics and mutual understanding significants.
**Ind/Abst** Philos. Index.

GW/0076-6828
**METHODS AND MODELS IN THE SOCIAL SCIENCES.** (1971)-. Monographic series. English. ir. Price varies per volume. Walter de Gruyter Inc., PO Box 303421, D 10728 Berlin Germany. **Tel** 011 49 30 260050, FAX 011 49 30 26005251. **(Subscription address:** Walter de Gruyter Inc., 200 Saw Mill River Road, Hawthorne NY 10532.**)**

US/0277-0806
**MICHIGAN SOCIAL STUDIES TEXTBOOK STUDY.** **See** Education.

DK/0901-0025
**MICRO PUBLICATIONS, SOCIAL SCIENCE SERIES.** [Micro publ. soc. sci. ser.]. **VFOAT** Social Science Series. (1984)-. Monographic series. English. ir. **DD** 301. **CODEN** 30.1.
**Ind/Abst** Soc. Plann. Policy Dev. Abstr.

US/0026-5497
**MINNESOTA HISTORY.** **See** History(General)-History of North, South, and Central America.

IT
**MINORANZE.** **Added/Corp** Centre Internacional Escarre sobre les Minories Etniques i Nacionals. (Apr. 1976)-. Periodical. Italian. qt. Minoranze, Virale Bligny 22, 20136 Milan Italy.

US/0026-637X
**MISSISSIPPI QUARTERLY, THE.** **See** Humanities.

UK/0963-9489
**MODERN & CONTEMPORARY FRANCE.** [Mod. contemp. Fr.]. **Added/Corp** Association for the Study of Modern and Contemporary France (Great Britain). **VFOAT** Modern and Contemporary France; Review. (Nov. 1984)-. Periodical. English (French). qt (Jan., Mar., Jul., Aug.). £60.00 Europe; £64.00 Other (Institution). Longman Group Ltd., Fourth Avenue, Longman House, Harlow Essex CM19 5SR England. **Tel** 011 44 279 429655, FAX 011 44 279 431059, telex 81259. **ED** Eric Cahan, Tony Chafer, Brian Jenkins. **Bk Rev.** ctrl circ. ***Continues*** *Review (Association for the Study of Modern and Contemporary France (Great Britain)).*
**Desc:** Review of the Association for the Study of Modern and Contemporary France.
**Ind/Abst** Am. Hist. Life (1989-).

US/0097-7004
**MODERN CHINA.** **See** History(General)-History of Asia.

US/0147-0779
**MODERN GREEK SOCIETY.** **Added/Corp** Modern Greek Studies Association. (Oct. 1973)-. English. sa (May, December). $20.00 (one year), $50.00 (three year). Modern Greek Society Newsletter, PO Box 9411, Providence RI 02940. **Tel** (401)274-2397, FAX (401)456-8379. **ED** Peter S. Allen and P. Nikiforos Diamandouros. **LC** DF755.82.U6; M6. **DD** 949.5/005. **Bk Rev. Circ:** 600.
**Desc:** Bibliography and general information about social science research on Modern Greece and Cyprus.
**Ind/Abst** Am. Bibliogr. Slavic East Europ. Stud. (19??-19??).

CN/0318-8280
**MONDES NOUVEAUX.** ***Title Change.*** **Added/Corp** Canadian Catholic Organization for Development and Peace. Vol. 1 (Feb. 1975)-?. Periodical. French. qt. Organisation Catholique Canadienne pour le Developpment et la Paix, 2111 rue Centre, Montreal Quebec H3K 1J5 Canada. **DD** 309.1/172/4. ***Merged with*** *Solidarites, 0383-6711* ***to form*** *Developpement et Paix; Information, 0318-8299.*

US/0190-9185
**MONITORING THE FUTURE.** **Added/Corp** University of Michigan. Survey Research Center. (1975)-. English. an. $40.00. University of Michigan Survey Research Center, PO Box 1248, Ann Arbor MI 48106. **Tel** (313)936-0099. **ED** Lloyd D. Johnston, Jerald G. Bachman and Patrick M. O'Malley. **LC** HQ796; .M5756. **DD** 305.2/3/0973.

US/0739-439X
**MONOGRAPH AND RESEARCH SERIES (UNIVERSITY OF CALIFORNIA, LOS ANGELES. INSTITUTE OF INDUSTRIAL RELATIONS).** (MONOGRAPH AND RESEARCH SERIES.). [Monogr. Res. Ser. - Univ. Calif., Los Angeles, Inst. Ind. Relat.]. **Added/Corp** University of California, Los Angeles. Institute of Industrial Relations. No. 28 (1981)-. Monographic series. English. ir. Price varies per volume. Regents of University of California, Institute of Industrial Relations, Los Angeles CA 90024-1478. **Tel** (310)825-9191, FAX (213)825-3731. **ED** Jane Wildhorn. Index available. cum. index. **Ad Acc. Circ:** 350. ***Continues*** *Monograph Series (University of California, Los Angeles. Institute of Industrial Relations).*
**Desc:** The series covers a wide range of topics of interest to academics and practitioners in all areas of industrial relations.

PP
**MONOGRAPH / INSTITUTE OF APPLIED SOCIAL AND ECONOMIC RESEARCH.** **Added/Corp** Institute of Applied Social and Economic Research. (1976)-. Monographic series. English. ir. Price varies per volume. The National Research Institute, PO Box 5854, Boroko Papua New Guinea. **Tel** (675)260300, FAX (675)260213. **ED** Wari Iamo. **Pr Rev. Circ:** 200.
**Desc:** Scholarly writings based on research on the social, economic and political problems of Papua, New Guinea with practical applications for government planning and policy making.
**Ind/Abst** Geogr. Abstr. Human Geogr.; Int. Dev. Abstr.

US
**MONOGRAPHS. SOCIAL SCIENCES - UNIVERSITY OF FLORIDA.** **Main/Corp** University of Florida. No. 1 (1959)-. Monographic series. English. ir. Price varies per volume. University of Florida Press, 15 Northwest 15th Street, Gainesville FL 32611. **Tel** (904)392-5717, (800)226-3822. **ED** George Pozzetta. Index available (bound in all issues). **Pr Rev. Circ:** 1,000.
**Desc:** Various topics in the social sciences. Each volume is by a single author on a single topic.

US/0093-5778
**MONTCLAIR JOURNAL OF SOCIAL SCIENCES AND HUMANITIES, THE.** ***Suspended.*** [Montclair j. soc. sci. humanit.]. Periodical. English. sa. $3.00. Montclair State College, School of Social Science and Humanities, Upper Montclair NJ 07043. **LC** H1; .M64. **DD** 300/.5.
**Ind/Abst** Am. Hist. Life (1972-1974).

SP/0210-0581
**MORALIA.** Vol. 1 (1979)-. Periodical. Spanish. qt. 3.900ptas Spain; $45.00 Latin America; $55.00 other. Moralia, Felix Boix 13, 28036 Madrid Spain. **Tel** 34 1 3453600, FAX 34 1 3453600. Index available. **Circ:** 1,000 (ctrl). ***Continues*** *Pentecostes.*
**Desc:** Covers ethics, morals, Bible, christianity, practical theology, social sciences, anthropology, psychology, and philosophy.

FR/0027-2671
**MOUVEMENT SOCIAL, LE.** **See** History(General).

BE/0024-8320
**MRAX INFORMATION.** (19??)-. Newspaper. French. qt. 500.00F Belgium; 600.00F other. Mrax Information, 37 rue de la Poste, 1210 Brussels Belgium. **Tel** 011 32 2 217 5694, 011 32 2 218 2371, FAX 011 32 2

219 6959. **ED** Jean-Marie Faux. **Bk Rev**, (Qty: 5-6). **Ad Acc, Adv Mgr:** Myriam Mottard. **Pr Rev. Circ:** 1000 (ctrl). available on diskette.
**Desc:** Covers subjects such as racism, immigration, asylum seekers, human rights at a national and international level, and cultural news about films, music exhibitions and books.

NG
**MU KARA SANI NOUVELLE FORMULE : BULLETIN D'INFORMATION ET DE LIAISON DE L'INSTITUT DE RECHERCHES EN SCIENCES HUMAINES L'UNIVERSITE DE NIAMEY.** V. 1, No. 1 (Year 1982)-. Bulletin. French. sa. 25.00CFAF Niger; $10.00 US. Institut de Recherches en Sciences Humaines, BP 318, Niamey Niger. **Tel** (227)735141. **LC** DT515.A2; M8. **Ad Acc.** ***Continues*** *MU Kaara Sani.*

VE/0379-6922
**MUNDO NUEVO. See** Political Science-International Relations.

US/0148-0995
**MUSLIM SCIENTIST.** [Muslim sci.]. Academic Scholarly Publication. English. qt. $35.00 US and Canada, $40.00 other. Association of Muslim Scientists Engineers, PO Box 38, Plainfield IN 46168. **Tel** (317)839-8157, FAX (317)839-1840, telex (650)225-4110. **ED** Sulayman Nyang. **CODEN** MUSCDX. **Bk Rev. Ad Acc. Circ:** 1,500 (ctrl). Documents available from CASDDS.
**Desc:** To facilitate the collection, distribution and dissemination of social sciences information within an Islamic framework through well written scholarly articles.
**Ind/Abst** Chem. Abstr.

SP
**MUY INTERESANTE.** (19??)-. Spanish. mo. 10180ptas. G & J Espana SA, Marques de Villamagna 4, 28001 Madrid Spain. **Tel** 011 34 1 4316631, FAX 011 34 1 2767881, telex 43419 ORBSA E.

JA
**NANZAN REVIEW OF AMERICAN STUDIES : A JOURNAL OF CENTER FOR AMERICAN STUDIES, NANZAN UNIVERSITY. Added/Corp** Nanzan Daigaku. Amerika Kenkyu Senta. Vol. 1 (1979)-. Periodical. English. an. free. Center for American Studies at Nanzan University, 18 Yamazato-cho Showo-ku, Nagoya 466 Japan. **Tel** 011 81 52 832311. **LC** E169.1; .N315. **DD** 973/.05. **Bk Rev. Circ:** 500 (ctrl).
**Desc:** Monographs in American studies in the field of social sciences such as history, sociology, economics, and political science, etc. US-Japan relationship is also emphasized.

AG
**NAO REVISTA DE LA CULTURA DEL MEDITERRANEO.** Spanish. Three times a year. $10.00 (individuals), $30.00 (institutions) Latin America; $15.00 (individuals), $40.00 (institutions) other.
**Ind/Abst** Philos. Index.

US/0162-1831
**NATIONAL FORUM (ANN ARBOR). See** Education-Higher Education.

US/0164-7415
**NATIONAL RIGHT TO LIFE NEWS. See** Birth Control.

AT
**NATIONAL SOCIAL SCIENCE SURVEY REPORT.** English. bm. 350.00Aus$. Anutech Pty Limited, GPO Box 4, Canberra Act, 2601 Australia. **Tel** 011 61 6 2492479, FAX 011 61 6 2575088. **(Subscription address:** Bibliotech, GPO Box 4, Canberra ACT 2601 Australia)

AT/1031-4067
**NATIONAL SOCIAL SCIENCE SURVEY REPORT / RESEARCH SCHOOL OF SOCIAL SCIENCES, AUSTRALIAN NATIONAL UNIVERSITY. Added/Corp** Australian National University. Research School of Social Sciences. Vol. 1, No. 1 (Aug. 1988)-. Periodical. English. bm. 350.00Aus$. Anutech Pty Limited, GPO Box 4, Canberra Act, 2601 Australia. **Tel** 011 61 6 2492479, FAX 011 61 6 2575088. **LC** WMLC 93/1912.

US/0890-6130
**NATURE, SOCIETY, AND THOUGHT.** (NATURE, SOCIETY, AND THOUGHT : NST.). [Nature soc. thought]. **VFOAT** NST. Vol. 1 No. 1 (Fall 1987)-. Academic Scholarly Publication. English. qt. $28.00 (institutions), $15.00 (individuals). University of Minnesota Nature Society, 116 Church Street SE, Minneapolis MN 55455. **Tel** (612)922-7993, FAX (612)624-4578. **ED** Erwin Marquit. **LC** B809.8; .N354. **DD** 146/.32/05. **[CCC].** Index available (bound in fourth issue). **Bk Rev**, (Qty: 10). **Ad Acc. Pr Rev. Circ:** 750.
**Desc:** Interdisciplinary scholarly journal of dialectical and historical materialism, and literature.
**Ind/Abst** Altern. Press Index (199?-); Left Index; Soc. Plann. Policy Dev. Abstr.

RU
**NAUCHNYE TRUDY ISEP AN SSSR / AKADEMIIA NAUK SSSR, LENINGRADSKII NAUCHNYI TSENTR, INSTITUT SOTSIALNO EKONOMICHESKIKH PROBLEM. Added/Corp** Institut Sotsialno-Ekonomicheskikh Problem (Akademiia Nauk SSSR). (19??)-. Russian. ir. **LC** Z7165.S65; N38; HC331.

SP
**NEGACIONES.** No. 1 (Oct. 1976)-. Periodical. Spanish. tq. 8000ptas. Editorial Ayuso, San Bernardo 34, Madrid Spain. **LC** H8; .N45.

MY/0127-0095
**NEGARA.** [Negara]. **Added/Corp** Lembaga Perpaduan Negara. Vol. 1, No. 1 (Dec. 1974)-. Periodical. English (Malay). sa. **LC** HN700.6; .A54. **DD** 306/.09595.
**Ind/Abst** Hum. Rights Intern. Rep.

CC
**NEI MENG-KU FU NU.** (19??)-. Periodical. Chinese. NT$0.20. Post Office, Hu-Ho-Hao-T E Shih, People's Republic of China. **LC** HQ1769.I56; N44. **DD** 305.4/0951/77.

NP
**NEPAL DOCUMENTATION.** No. 1- 1972-. Multiple languages (English and Nepali). Centre for Economic Development and Administration Assistant Editor, Publications and Information Services Division, Ceda Post Box No 797, Kirtipur Kathmandu Nepal. **LC** Z7165.N37; N36. **DD** 309.1/549/6.

NE
**NETHERLANDS' JOURNAL OF SOCIAL SCIENCES : A PUBLICATION OF THE NETHERLANDS' SOCIOLOGICAL AND ANTHROPOLOGICAL SOCIETY, THE. Added/Corp** Nederlandse Sociologische en Antropologische Vereniging. **VFOAT** Sociologia Neerlandica; Netherlands' Journal of Sociology. Vol. 25, No. 1 (April 1989)-. Periodical. English (translations available in Dutch). sa. Fl95.00 Netherlands; Fl125.00 other. Van Gorcum & Company BV, PO Box 43, NL 9400 AA Assen Netherlands. **Tel** 011 31 5920 46846, FAX 011 31 5920 72064. **NLM** W1; NE229L. **CODEN** NJSCE2. Documents available from The Genuine Article. ***Continues*** *Netherlands Journal of Sociology, 0038-0172.*
**Ind/Abst** Curr. Contents Soc. Behav. Sci.; Res. Alert [Full Cov.]; Soc. Sci. Cit. Index [Full Cov.].

GW/0177-6738
**NEUE GESELLSCHAFT, FRANKFURTER HEFTE, DIE. Added/Corp** Friedrich-Ebert-Stiftung. **VFOAT** NG/FH. Vol. 32, No. 1 (Jan. 1985)-. Periodical. German. mo. DM99.00. Verlag JHW Dietz Nachf GmbH, In der Raste 2, D 53129 Bonn Germany. **Tel** 011 49 228 238083, FAX 011 49 228 234104. **LC** H5; .N36. **[CCC].** ***Formed by the union of*** *Neue Gesellschaft, 0028-3177* ***and*** *Frankfurter Hefte, 0015-9999.*
**Ind/Abst** Int. Bibliogr. Sociol.; MLA Int. Bibl. Books Artic. Mod. Lang. Lit.

GW/0028-3320
**NEUE POLITISCHE LITERATUR.** [Neue polit. lit.]. Vol. 1, (July 1956)-. Periodical. German. Three times a year. DM88.00. Verlag Peter Lang GmbH, Eschborner Landstrasse 42-50, D 60489 Frankfurt Germany. **Tel** 011 49 69 7807050. **(Subscription address:** Peter Lang AG, Jupiterstrasse 15, CH 3000 Bern 15 Switzerland.) **LC** H5; .N38. **DD** 300/.5. **[CCC]. Bk Rev. Ad Acc. Circ:** 1,000. available on an online database. ***Continues*** *Politische Literatur.*
**Desc:** Reviews in the fields of contemporary history and political science.
**Ind/Abst** Am. Hist. Life (1974, 1976-); Int. Bibliogr. Sociol.

SP/1130-0426
**NEUVA REVISTA DE POLITICA, CULTURA Y ARTE. VFOAT** Nueva Revista. No. 1 (Feb. 1990)-. Periodical. Spanish. mo. 7000ptas Europe; 11000ptas other. Cempro, Plaza Conde Valle Suchil 20, 28015 Madrid Spain. **Tel** 011 34 1 4462050, 011 34 1 4472700. **LC** DP1; .N83. **DD** 946/.005.

US
**NEW APPROACHES TO SOCIAL SCIENCE HISTORY.** Vol. 1-. Monographic series. English. Price varies per volume. SAGE Periodical Press, 2455 Teller Road, Thousand Oaks CA 91320. **Tel** (805)499-0721, FAX (805)499-0871, telex 100799. **Acid Free.**

CN/0824-1813
**NEW EDITION.** (THE NEW EDITION / NATIONAL COUNCIL OF JEWISH WOMEN IN CANADA.). [New ed.]. Vol. 1, No. 1 (June 1984)-. Periodical. English. ir. Free. National Council of Jewish Women of Canada, Suite 401, 1111 Finch Avenue, Downsview Ontario M3J 2E5. **DD** 305.4/88924/071. ctrl circ. ***Continues*** *Keeping You Posted, 0317-719X.*

US/0747-4970
**NEW ENGLAND JOURNAL OF BLACK STUDIES. See** Ethnic Interests.

US
**NEW ENGLAND JOURNAL OF HISTORY / NEW ENGLAND HISTORY TEACHERS ASSOCIATION, THE. Added/Corp** New England History Teachers' Association. Vol. 45, No. 1 (Spring 1988)-. Periodical. English. Three times a year (Mar., June, Oct.). $10.00. New England History Teachers Association, 127 Marked Tree Road, Needham MA 02192. **Tel** (617)444-3181. **ED** James Weland. **LC** H1; .N4. **DD** 974/.005. **Bk Rev.** ctrl circ. ***Continues*** *New England Social Studies Bulletin, 0028-4912.*
**Ind/Abst** Am. Hist. Life (1954-1978, 1986-); Curr. Index J. Educ. (March 1990).

TU/0896-6346
**NEW PERSPECTIVES ON TURKEY.** [New perspect. Turk.]. **Added/Corp** Bard College. Simon's Rock. Vol. 1, No. 1 (Fall 1987)-. Periodical. English. sa. $25.00 (institutions), $15.00 (individuals). Tarih Vakfi Yildiz Sarayi, Arabacilar Dairesi Barbaros, 80700 Besiktas Istanbul Turkey. **Tel** 011 90 212 2273733. **ED** Insan Tunali and Ahmet Tonak. **LC** DR401; .N39. **DD** 306. **Bk Rev. Ad Acc. Pr Rev. Circ:** 200 (ctrl).
**Desc:** Includes studies relating historical and contemporary issues in the culture and the socio-economic structure of Turkey . Comparative perspectives and theoretical contributions relevant to research targeting Turkey and the Ottoman Empire is also solicited.
**Ind/Abst** Am. Hist. Life (1987-); Int. Bibliogr. Sociol.; Middle East J.

US/0028-6613
**NEW SCHOLAR, THE.** [New sc.]. Vol. 1 (Apr. 1969)-. Periodical. English (Spanish). ir. $18.00 (individuals), $36.00 (institutions). New Scholar, South Hall 4607, University of California, Santa Barbara CA 93106. **Tel** (805)893-8473, FAX (805)961-8016. **ED** Vernon Kjonegaard and Ines Talamantez. **LC** H1; .N46. **DD** 300/.5. **CODEN** NESCDY. Index available. cum. index. **Bk Rev. Ad Acc. Pr Rev. Circ:** 1,100 (ctrl). available on microfilm from University Microfilms International (UMI). Documents available from The Genuine Article.
**Desc:** Provides a multidisciplinary forum for scholars seeking a fuller understanding of the unique human condition and experience in the Americas. Well-written essays on developments in the literature of the humanities and social sciences. A strong emphasis on creative methodology and interpretation.
**Ind/Abst** Altern. Press Index (-199?); Am. Hist. Life (1970-); Am. Humanit. Index (1970-199?); Arts Humanit. Citation Index (19??-19??) [Full Cov.]; Curr. Contents Arts Humanit.; HAPI Hisp. Am. Period. Index; Middle East Abstr. Index; MLA Int. Bibl. Books Artic. Mod. Lang. Lit.; Psychol. Abstr.; Res. Alert [Full Cov.]; Soc. Plann. Policy Dev. Abstr.; Sociol. Abstr.

UK/0954-2361
**NEW STATESMAN & SOCIETY.** (NEW STATESMAN SOCIETY.). [New statesman soc.]. **VFOAT** New Statesman and Society; New Statesman, New Society; New Statesman & Society. Vol. 1, No. 1 (June 1988)-. Periodical. English. wk (52 issues). £85.00 (institution), £70.00 (individual) UK; $165.00 (institution), $138.00 (individual) US. Statesman and Nation Publishing Company, 38 Kingsland Road, Foundation House, London E2 8DQ England. **Tel** 011 44 71 739 1737. **LC** AP4; .N6425. **CODEN** NESSEF. available on microfilm and microfiche from University Microfilms International (UMI); available on an online database (file 647/Full-Text) from DIALOG. Documents available from The Genuine Article, UMI Article Clearinghouse. ***Formed by the union of*** *New Statesman (London, England : 1957), 0028-6842* ***and*** *New Society, 0028-6729.*
**Ind/Abst** Acad. Abstr. Full Text Elite (Jan. 1991-); Acad. Abstr. (July 1990-); Acad. Ind. [Computer File] (1988-); Acad. Search (Jan. 1991-); Arts Humanit. Citation Index [Select. Cov.]; Book Rev. Digest; Book Rev. Index; Br. Educ. Index; Br. Humanit. Index; Child. Lit. Abstr. (19??-); Crim. Penol. Police Sci. Abstr.; Expand. Acad. Index (1988-); Gen. Period. Index (1988-); Highw. Res. Abstr.; INFO-SOUTH Abstr.; Mag. Index Plus (1989-); Mag. Search; Newsp. Period. Abstr. (1988-); Res. Alert [Full Cov.]; Romant. Move.; Soc. Plann. Policy Dev. Abstr.; Soc. Sci. Source (Jul. 1990-); Soc. Sci. Cit. Index [Full Cov.]; Soc. Sci. Index; Soc. Sci. Index Fulltext (Sept. 1988-) [Full Txt.]; Sociol. Educ. Abstr.; Stud. Women Abstr.; Mag. Index.

US/1059-7395
**NEW STUDIES ON THE LEFT.** [New stud. left]. **VFOAT** Studies on the Left. Vol. 14 No. 1 (Spring/Summer 1989)-. Periodical. English. qt. Saxifrage Publications, 1484 Wicklow, Boulder CO 80303. **Tel** (303)666-7068. **DD** 362. available on microfilm and microfiche from University Microfilms International (UMI). ***Continues*** *Issues in Radical Therapy (Springfield, Ill. : 1982), 0886-0629.*
**Ind/Abst** Altern. Press Index (199?-).

## Social Sciences

UK/0960-748X
**NEW TIMES : THE JOURNAL OF DEMOCRATIC LEFT.** Added/Corp Democratic Left. VFOAT Journal of Democratic Left. (1991)-. Periodical. English. Twenty-four times a year. £15.00 UK; £25.00 Europe; £35.00 others. Democratic Left, 6 Cynthia Street, London N1 9BR England. **Tel** 011 71 278 4443, FAX 011 71 278 4425. **ED** Mike Power. **Bk Rev. Ad Acc. Circ:** 5,000.
**Desc:** Deals with politics in the widest sense of a left viewpoint.

CN/0078-0332
**NEWFOUNDLAND SOCIAL AND ECONOMIC PAPERS.** Added/Corp Newfoundland. Memorial University, St. John's. Institute of Social and Economic Research. (1968)-. Monographic series. English. ir. Price varies per volume. Institute of Social and Economic Research / Canada, University of Newfoundland, St. John's Newfoundland A1C 5S7 Canada. **Tel** (709)737-8156, (709)737-2041. **ED** Robert Paine. **Bk Rev. Ad Acc.**
**Desc:** Topics include community studies, rural development and problems of modernization, the fisheries, and ethnicity and colonialism in the Canadian Arctic.

US/8756-3940
**NEWSCURRENTS (MADISON, WIS.).** (NEWSCURRENTS.). **Added/Corp** Knowledge Unlimited (Firm). **VFOAT** News Currents. (1984)-. Periodical. English. wk. $199.00 (filmstrips & teacher guide), $289.00 (indepth articles, filmstrips & teacher guide). Knowledge Unlimited, PO Box 52, Madison WI 53701. **Tel** (800)356-2303, (608)836-6660, , FAX (608)831-1570. **ED** Jon Burack. **Circ:** 8,000 schools (ctrl). **Continues** VEC News.
**Desc:** A weekly current events discussion program that uses a timely color filmstrip and teacher's discussion guide. Material is written on three distinct discussion levels and is appropriate for grades 3-12.

US/0162-976X
**NEWSLETTER - ASSOCIATION FOR THE ADVANCEMENT OF BALTIC STUDIES, INC.** Title Change. **Main/Corp** Association for the Advancement of Baltic Studies. **VFOAT** AABS Newsletter. (19??)-(1993). Newsletter. English (German). qt. Association for the Advancement of Baltic Studies, 111 Knob Hill Road, Hackettstown NJ 07840. **Tel** (908)852-5258. **Continued by** Newsletter of Baltic Studies.
**Ind/Abst** Am. Bibliogr. Slavic East Europ. Stud. (19??-).

CN/0843-0764
**NEWSLETTER / BRITISH COLUMBIA SOCIAL STUDIES TEACHERS' ASSOCIATION OF THE BRITISH COLUMBIA TEACHERS' FEDERATION.** Title Change. See Education-Teaching and Curriculum.

US
**NEWSLETTER OF THE NEW YORK STATE COUNCIL FOR THE SOCIAL STUDIES, THE.** Added/Corp New York State Council for the Social Studies. VFOAT Newsletter. (19??)-. Periodical. English. Twice a year. $20.00 Comes with New York State Council for the Social Studies membership. New York State Council Social Studies, PO Box 625, White Plains NY 10603-0625. **Tel** (914)761-7206. **ED** Dr. Wayne Ross. **Bk Rev. Ad Acc. Pr Rev. Circ:** 2,000.
**Desc:** Research and pedagogy of Social Studies Education.

CN/0714-6647
**NEWSLETTER - SOCIAL SCIENCE COMPUTING LABORATORY.** (NEWSLETTER / SOCIAL SCIENCE COMPUTING LABORATORY, THE UNIVERSITY OF WESTERN ONTARIO.). [Newsl. - Soc. Sci. Comput. Lab.]. **Main/Corp** University of Western Ontario. Social Science Computing Laboratory. **VFOAT** SSCL Newsletter. **VAT** Social Science Computing Laboratory Newsletter. Vol. 1, No. 1 (Sept. 1982)-. Newsletter. English. Free. Social Science Computing Laboratory, University of Western Ontario, London Ontario N6A 5C2 Canada. **DD** 025/.063/00971326.

CN/0834-1729
**NEWSLETTER (YORK UNIVERSITY (TORONTO, ONT.). INSTITUTE FOR SOCIAL RESEARCH).** (NEWSLETTER / INSTITUTE FOR SOCIAL RESEARCH, YORK UNIVERSITY.). [Newsl. - Inst. Soc. Res., York Univ.]. Vol. 2, No. 5 (Jan. 1985)-. Newsletter. English. qt. Free. Institute for Social Research / Ontario, York University, 4700 Keele Street, North York Ontario M3J 1P3 Canada. **Tel** (416)736-5061, FAX (416)736-5687. **ED** Freda Marsden. **DD** 300/.7/20713541. **Circ:** 1,000 (ctrl). **Continues** Newsletter (York University (Toronto, Ont.). Institute for Behavioural Research), 0834-1710.

BE
**NIEUWE MAAND, DE.** Dutch. mo (10 issues). 1400.00F Belgium; 1900.00F other. Kritak Tydschriften, Diestsestraat 2491, B-3000 Louvain Belgium. **Tel** 011 32 16 231264.

NE/0028-9930
**NIEUWE WEST-INDISCHE GIDS.** [Nieuwe West-Indische gids]. **VFOAT** New West Indian Guide. Vol. 40 (July 1960)-. Periodical. Dutch (English). Twice a year. Fl125.00 (includes annual reference book Caribbean Abstracts). Royal Institute of Linguistics and Anthropology, PO Box 9515, 2300 RA Leiden, The Netherlands. **Tel** 011 31 71 272372, FAX 011 31 71 272638. **ED** Gert Oostindie. Index available. cum. index. **Bk Rev. Ad Acc. Circ:** 350. **Continues** West-Indische Gids, 0372-7289; **Absorbed** Christoffel; Vox Guyane.
**Desc:** Publishes articles and book reviews relating to the Caribbean region in the social sciences and humanities.
**Ind/Abst** Am. Hist. Life (1987-); Int. Bibliogr. Sociol.

NR/0029-0092
**NIGERIAN JOURNAL OF ECONOMIC AND SOCIAL STUDIES, THE.** See Economics.

JA
**NIRA NEWS.** (19??)-. Japanese. mo. Free. National Institute for Research Advancement, Center for Policy Activities, Shinjuku Mitsui Bldg 37th Floor, 2-1-1 Nishi-Shinjuku, Shinjuku-ku Tokyo 163-04 Japan. **Tel** 011 81 3 3344-3371, FAX 011 81 3 3345-1449. **ED** Izumi Morishima. Acid Free. **Circ:** 14,000 (ctrl) **Continues** Gekkan NIRA.
**Desc:** Includes information of on-going research projects, symposiums conducted by NIRA, and NIRA publications.

JA
**NIRA SOGO KINKYU KAIHATSU KIKO ... NENJI HOKOKUSHO.** Main/Corp Sogo Kenkyu Kaihatsu Kiko. **VAT** National Institute for Research Advancement i.e. Sogo Kenkyu Kaihatsu Kiko. 1974-. Japanese (English). an. free. Shinjuku Mitsui Building, 37-kai 1-1 Nishi Shinjuku 2-chome, Shinjuku-ku 163 Tokyo Japan. **Tel** (03)3344-3371. LC H62.5.J3; S63A. **Circ:** 1,500.
**Desc:** NIRA's annual report.

US/0882-8075
**NODE, THE.** [Node]. Added/Corp Performing Arts Social Society (San Francisco, Calif.). Vol. 1, Issue 1 (May/June/July 1985)-. Periodical. English. Four times a year (Feb., May, Aug., Nov.). $36.00 (includes membership in The Utopian Philanthropists' Society of PASS). Performing Arts Social Society, 547 Fredrick Street, San Francisco CA 94117-2753. **Tel** FAX (415)759-2490. **DD** 303.

NO/0801-7220
**NORDISK ST-FORUM.** Added/Corp Nordic Committee for Soviet and East European Studies. **VFOAT** Nordisk St Forum. No. 1 (1987)-. Periodical. Danish (Norwegian and Danish). qt. Kr315.00, $55.00. Scandinavian University Press, PO Box 2959 Toeyen, N 0608 Oslo 6 Norway. **Tel** 011 47 2 2575400, FAX 011 47 2 2575353, telex 71896 UROR N. **(Subscription address:** Scandinavian University Press, 200 Meacham Ave., Elmont NY 11003.) **ED** Trond Oevstedal and Unni Kloevstad. **LC** DJK1; .N67. **Bk Rev. Ad Acc. Circ:** 800 (ctrl). **Formed by the union of** Forum St, 0800-4951; Bulletinen for Oststatsforskningen, 0349-3709 **and** St-Nyt (Arhus, Denmark), 0108-4380.
**Desc:** A Nordic journal on culture and society in the Soviet Union and Eastern Europe.
**Ind/Abst** Am. Hist. Life (1989-).

CN
**NORTHERN REVIEW (WHITEHORSE).** See The Arts.

US/0196-1063
**NORTHERN SOCIAL SCIENCE REVIEW.** [North. soc. sci. rev.]. Periodical. English. an. Free. Editor NSSR, Social Science Department of Northern State College, Aberdeen SD 57401. **Tel** (605)622-2601. **ED** Tracey Gladstone, Robert Stahl and Hillar Neumann. **LC** H1; .N67. **DD** 300/.5. **Circ:** 300 (ctrl).
**Desc:** An inter-disciplinary journal of the social sciences regularly publishing articles in the fields of history, sociology, political science, economics and psychology.

FR
**NOUVEAU DEHOVE, LE.** French. Editions Lamy SA, 187-189 Quai de Valmy, 75490 Paris Cedex 10 France. **Tel** 011 33 1 44721200, 011 33 1 44721212, FAX 011 33 1 44721395.

RU
**NOVAIA SOVETSKAIA I INOSTRANNAIA LITERATURA PO KULTURE I ISKUSSTVU: KULTURNO-PROSVETITELNAIA RABOTA I NARODNOE TVORCHESTVO.** Added/Corp Informtsentr po Problemam Kultury i Iskusstva (Soviet Union). **VFOAT** Novaia Sovetskaia i Inostrannaia Literatura po Kulturno-Prosvetitelnoi Rabote.

(1974)-. Multiple languages (Russian and Multiple languages). mo. $18.60. Gosudarstvennaia Biblioteka, Informatsionnyi Tsentr, Imeni V. I. Lenina, Prospekt Kalinina 3, 121019 Moscow Russia. **(Subscription address:** Victor Kamkin, 4956 Boiling Brook Parkway, Rockville MD 20852.) **LC** Z2517.C55; N68; AZ710. **Continues** Novaia Sovetskaia i Inostrannaia Literatura po Kulturno-Prosvetitelnci Rabote.

RU
**NOVAIA SOVETSKAIA LITERATURA PO OBSHCHESTVENNYM NAUKAM.** See Literature.

XR
**NOVINKY LITERATURY. POLITIKA.** Added/Corp Statni Knihovna CSR. **VFOAT** Politika. Vol. 1/2, (1971)-. Czech. S x times a year. kcs36.50. **(Subscription address:** Artia Pegas Press Ltd., Palac Metro Narodni Trida 25, 11210 Prague 1 Czech Republic.) **LC** Z7161.A15; N6. **Continues** Novinky Literatury. Spolecenske Vedy. Rada V, Politika.

PL/0029-5388
**NOWE DROGI.** Ceased. [Nowe drogi]. Vol. 1 No. 1 (1947)-?. Periodical. Polish. mo. **(Subscription address:** ARS Polona, PO Box 1001, 00068 Warsaw Poland.) **LC** H8; .N88. **DD** 300/.5.
**Ind/Abst** Am. Hist. Life (1955-1976, 1979-1983).

MY
**NUSANTARA.** Bilangan 1- Jan. 1972-. Periodical. Multiple languages (English and Malay). $6.50 single issue. Yayasan Persuratan Ilmu, Tingkat Tiga, Wisma Mirama, 50460 Kuala Lumpur Malaysia. **Tel** 03-2481011. **LC** H8; .N92.

SZ
**OBJECTIF AFRIQUE DU SUD.** Added/Corp Schweizerischer Evangelischer Kirchenbund. No. 1 (March 1986)-. Periodical. French. Three times a year.

RU
**OBSHCHESTVENNAIA MYSL ZA RUBEZHOM. KNIZHNOE OBOZRENTE.** **VFOAT** Knizhnoe Obozrenie. (1990)-. Periodical. Russian. Twelve times a year. $58.00. **(Subscription address:** East View Publications Inc., 3020 Harbor Lane North, Suite 110, Minneapolis MN 55447.) **Continues** Novye Knigi Za Rubezhom Po Obshchestvennym Naukam.

RU/0869-0499
**OBSHCHESTVENNYE NAUKI I SOVREMENNOST : ONS.** Added/Corp Koordinatsionnyi Sovet Po Obshchestvennym Nnaukam (Akademiia Nauk SSSR). **VFOAT** ONS. (1991)-. Academic Scholarly Publication. Russian. Six times a year. $89.95. Izdatelstvo Nauka / Akademiia Nauk, Publishing House of the Russian Academy of Sciences, Leninskii Porspekt 14, 117901 Moscow Russia. **Tel** 011 95 954-21-53, FAX 011 95 938-21-44, telex 411964. **(Subscription address:** East View Publications Inc., 3020 Harbor Lane North, Suite 110, Minneapolis MN 55447.) **LC** H8; .0237. **DD** 300/.5. **Continues** Obshchestvennye Nauki, 0132-3458.

RU/0202-2036
**OBSHCHESTVENNYE NAUKI V SSSR. SERIIA 1 : PROBLEMY NAUCHNOGO KOMMUNIZMA.** Ceased. **VFOAT** Problemy Nauchnogo Kommunizma. **VAT** Obshchestvennye Nauki V SSSR. Seriia Odin : Problemy Nauchnogo Kommunizma. Began in 1973-199?. Academic Scholarly Publication. Russian. bm. Izdatelstvo Nauka / Akademiia Nauk, Publishing House of the Russian Academy of Sciences, Leninskii Porspekt 14, 117901 Moscow Russia. **Tel** 011 95 954-21-53, FAX 011 95 938-21-44, telex 411964. **LC** H8; .024.

UK/0077-4928
**OCCASIONAL PAPERS / NATIONAL INSTITUTE OF ECONOMIC AND SOCIAL RESEARCH.** See Economics.

JA
**OKINAWA KOKUSAI DAIGAKU BUNGAKUBU KIYO : SHAKAIGAKKA-HEN.** Main/Corp Okinawa Kokusat Daigaku. Bungakubu. Shakaigakka. **VFOAT** Bulletin of the Department of Sociology, Okinawa Kokusai University. Japanese (table of contents in English). an. Free. 276-2 Ginowan, Ginowan City Okinawa Japan. **ED** Hitoshi Yamada. **LC** H8; .O35A. **Circ:** 800.
**Desc:** Consists mainly of works of faculty members of the Department of Sociology.

US/0095-5868
**OPT, THE MAGAZINE ON PEOPLE AND THINGS.** V. 6- May 1974-. Periodical. English. sm. $3.80. Xerox Education Center, 1250 Fairwood Avenue, Columbus OH 43216. **LC** LH1; .O66. **DD** 051.

GW/0170-8406
**ORGANIZATION STUDIES.** [Organ. stud.]. Issue 1 (1980)-. Periodical. English. Six times a year. $248.50. Walter de Gruyter Inc., PO Box 303421, D

10728 Berlin Germany. **Tel** 011 49 30 260050, FAX 011 49 30 26005251. **ED** David J. Hickson. **[CCC]. Bk Rev. Ad Acc. Pr Rev. Circ:** 1,000. available on microfilm and microfiche from University Microfilms International (UMI). Documents available from The Genuine Article, UMI Article Clearinghouse.
**Desc:** Aims to promote the understanding of organizations and the social relevance of that understanding.
**Ind/Abst** ABI/INFORM Glob. Ed.; ABI Inform Ondisc (Spring 1981-); Bus. ASAP (1992-) [Full Txt.]; Bus. Index (1985-); Contents Pages Manage.; Cumul. Index Nurs. Allied Health Lit.; Curr. Contents Soc. Behav. Sci.; Gen. BusinessFile (1985-); Gen. Period. Index (1985-); Int. Bibliogr. Sociol.; Int. Polit. Sci. Abstr.; Manage. Contents; Middle East Abstr. Index; Person. Manage. Abstr.; Pollut. Abstr. Indexes; Psychol. Abstr. (1982-); PsycINFO; PsycLit; Res. Alert [Full Cov.]; Selec. Coop. Index Manage. Period; Soc. Plann. Policy Dev. Abstr.; Soc. Sci. Cit. Index [Full Cov.]; Sociol. Abstr.; UMI ABI/Inform--Bus. Period. Ondisc (1987-) [Full Txt.].

●CN/0845-0382
**ORIENTATIONS TRIENNALES ET PLAN ANNUEL / GOUVERNEMENT DU QUEBEC, CONSEIL DU STATUT DE LA FEMME.** [Orientat. trienn. plan annu. Gouv. Que., Cons. statut femme]. **Main/Corp** Quebec (Province). Conseil du Statut de la Femme. (1992)-. French. **DD** 305.4/2/09714.

GW/0724-5246
**ORIENTIERUNGEN ZUR WIRTSCHAFTS- UND GESELLSCHAFTSPOLITIK. VFOAT** Orientierungen (Bonn). (1979)-. Periodical. German (English). qt. DM76.00 Germany; DM82.00 other. Gustav Fischer Verlag Stuttgart, Postfach 720143, Wollgrasweg 49, D 70577 Stuttgart Germany. **Tel** 011 49 711 458030, FAX 0711-4580334, telex 2627-7111488. **(Subscription address:** VCH Publishers Inc., 303 Northwest 12th Avenue, Journals Department, Deerfield FL 33442.**) UDC** 32.

AU
**OSTERREICHISCHE ZEITSCHRIFT FUER STATISTIK UND INFORMATIK. Added/Corp** Osterreichische Statistische Gesellschaft. **VFOAT** ZSI. (1985)-. Periodical. German. qt. Verlag Orac Gesellschaft, Graben 17, 1010 Vienna, Austria. **LC** HA1; .O38.
**Ind/Abst** Popul. Index.

UK
**OUTSIDES (LONDON, ENGLAND).** (OUTSIDER : NEWSLETTER OF THE MINORITY RIGHTS GROUP.). Newsletter. English. Minority Rights Group, 379 Brixton Road, London SW9 7DE England. **Tel** 044 071 978 9498, FAX 044 071 738 6265.

US/1065-5905
**OZONE NEWS.** (OZONE NEWS / INTERNATIONAL OZONE ASSOCIATION.). (197?)-. Periodical. English. bm. $100.00 US; $106.00 Canada; $119.00 other. International Ozone Association, 1331 Patuxent Drive, Ashton MD 20861. **Tel** (301)924-4224, FAX (301)774-4493, telex 822060. **ED** Dr. Rip G Rice. **DD** 363. **Bk Rev**, (Qty: 1-5). **Ad Acc, Adv Mgr:** same as editor. **Circ:** 1,400.
**Desc:** Contains news and some technical information regarding ozone and its many applications.

US
**PACIFIC RESEARCH TITLES.** English. ir. Free to members of the Pacific Science Association. Pacific Science Association, PO Box 17801, Honolulu HI 96817. **Tel** (808)847-3511, FAX (808)841-8968.
**Desc:** Created to stimulate multidisciplinary interests in the greater Pacific region. Publishes the tables of contents of journals and periodicals published in or about the region.

US/1064-4660
**PAIS INTERNATIONAL. See** Economics.

US/1051-4015
**PAIS INTERNATIONAL IN PRINT. See** Social Sciences-Abstracting, Bibliographies and Statistics.

US
**PAIS ON CD-ROM [COMPUTER FILE]. See** Social Sciences-Abstracting, Bibliographies and Statistics.

●US/1072-0103
**PAIS (PEABODY, MASS.). See** Social Sciences-Abstracting, Bibliographies and Statistics.

PK
**PAKISTAN JOURNAL OF SOCIAL SCIENCES.** Vol. 6, No. 2 (July/Dec. 1980)-. Periodical. English. sa. Quaid-I-Azam University Faculty of Social Sciences, Islamabad Pakistan. **LC** DS376; .S37. **DD** 954.9/005. ***Continues*** *Scrutiny.*

NR/8755-7436
**PAN-AFRICAN SOCIAL SCIENCE REVIEW.** [Pan Afr. soc. sci. rev.]. **Added/Corp** University of Port Harcourt. Dept. of Sociology. **VFOAT** Pan African Social Science Review (PASSR); PASSR. No. 1 (Oct. 1984)-. English. an. $10.00 individuals, $20.00 institutions. Victor Manfredi, Department of Anthropology, Harvard University, Cambridge MA 02138. **ED** Mark Anikpo. **DD** 300. **Bk Rev. Ad Acc. Circ:** 2,500.
**Desc:** Critical, interdisciplinary forum in the social sciences from a Pan-African perspective, based in the Department of Sociology, University of Port Harcourt, Nigeria.

FR
**PANORAMA (PARIS, FRANCE).** (PANORAMA / UNESCO.). **Added/Corp** Unesco. No. 1-2 (1984)-. Periodical. English. tq. Free. UNESCO / France, 31 rue Francois Bonvin, 75732 Paris Cedex 15 France. **Tel** 011 33 1 45684564, 011 33 1 45684565, FAX 011 33 1 42733007, telex 204461 Paris. **LC** CB3; .P33. **DD** 306/.4/05. ***Formed by the union of*** *World Cultural Heritage* ***and*** *Cultural Development, 0378-7621.*

US/0732-1082
**PAPERS IN THE SOCIAL SCIENCES.** (PAPERS IN THE SOCIAL SCIENCES : A JOURNAL OF THE COLLEGE OF LIBERAL AND FINE ARTS, UNIVERSITY OF THE DISTRICT OF COLUMBIA.). [Pap. soc. sci.]. Vol. 2 (1982)-. English. an. $5.00. Editor of Papers in the Social Sciences, University of the District of Columbia College of Liberal and Fine Arts, 4200 Connecticut Avenue NW, Washington DC 20008. **LC** H1; .P34. **DD** 300/.5. ***Continues*** *Working Papers in the Social Sciences.*
**Ind/Abst** Psychol. Abstr. (1982-); PsycINFO; PsycLit.

US/0149-1547
**PEASANT STUDIES.** ***Suspended.*** (Jan. 1976)-Vol. 19, Issue 4. Periodical. English. qt. $30.00 institutions; $25.00 individuals. University of Utah Department of History, 211 Carlson Hall, Salt Lake City UT 84112. **Tel** (801)581-6121. **ED** Anand A Yang. **LC** HD101; .P4. **DD** 305.5/63. **Bk Rev. Ad Acc. Pr Rev. Circ:** 500 (ctrl). ***Continues*** *Peasant Studies Newsletter, 0162-203X.*
**Desc:** Peasant societies worldwide; all chronological periods.
**Ind/Abst** Am. Hist. Life (1972-); Anthropol. Index; Anthropol. Lit.; Appl. Soc. Sci. Index Abstr.; Int. Dev. Abstr. (?-?); Middle East Abstr. Index; Rural Dev. Abstr.; Soc. Plann. Policy Dev. Abstr.; World Agric. Econ.

CC
**PEI-CHING SHIH FAN TA HSUEH HSUEH PAO : SHE HUI KO HSUEH PAN. BEIJING SHIFAN DAXUE XUEBAO. Added/Corp** Pei-Ching Shih Fan Ta Hsueh. **VFOAT** Beijing Shifan Daxue Xuebao; Journal of Beijing Normal University. Social Science Edition. Vol. 1, No. 1 (Sept 1956)-. Academic Scholarly Publication. Chinese. bm. RMBY17. Beijing Normal University, (Beijing Shifan Daxue), Beitaipingzhuang, Beijing 100875, People's Repubic of China. **Tel** 2012288. **(Subscription address:** China International Book Trading Corporation, PO Box 399, Library Service Department, Beijing 100044 People's Republic of China.**) ED** Bai Shouyi. **LC** AS452.P25; A2. **DD** 300/.5. Documents available from CASDDS. ***Continues*** *Pei-Ching Shih Ta Hsueh Pao: She Hui Ko Hsueh Pan.*
**Ind/Abst** Chem. Abstr.

CC
**PEI-CHING TA HSUEH HSUEH PAO: CHE HSUEH SHE HUI KO HSUEH PAN. Added/Corp** Pei-Ching Ta Hsueh. Ching Hua Ta Hsueh (Peking, China) Pei-Ching Ta Hsueh. Pei-Ching Ta Hsueh Hsueh Pao: Che Hsueh She Hui Ko Hsueh Pan. **VFOAT** Beijingdaxue Xuebao. (19??)-. Periodical. Chinese. bm. $19.92. **(Subscription address:** China International Book Trading Corporation, PO Box 399, Library Service Department, Beijing 100044 People's Republic of China.**) LC** AS451; .P4.

AT/0815-6816
**PELANGI TOOWOOMBA.** [Pelangi Toowoomba]. **VFOAT** Rainbow (Toowoomba). (1986)-. English (Indonesian); summaries and/or abstracts in English and Indonesian). ir. 18.00Aus$. USQ Press, University of Southern Queensland, PO Box 58, Darling Heights, Toowoomba QLD 4350 Australia. **DD** 499.22105. **[CCC].**
**Desc:** Articles on Indonesia with a concentration on the cultural aspects of the Indonesian language.

IO
**PENYELIDIK.** V. 1- Oct. 1972-. Malay. $2.50 single issue. Persatuan Pelajar-Pelajar Lupusan Sekolah Alam Shah, Jalan Cheras, Kuala Lumpur Malaysia. **LC** H62.A1; P45.

BL/0101-3459
**PERSPECTIVAS / UNIVERSIDADE ESTADUAL PAULISTA. Added/Corp** Universidade Estadual Paulista. Vol. 1, No. 1 (1976)-. Periodical. Portuguese (summaries and/or abstracts in English). an. Universidade Estadual Paulista, Coordenadoria Geral de Bibliotecas, Av. Vicente Ferreira 1 2 7 8, CP 603, CEP 17526-901 Marilia SP Brazil. **LC** AS80.A1; P47. **DD** 068/.81.
**Desc:** Articles and research in the social sciences.
**Ind/Abst** Soc. Plann. Policy Dev. Abstr.

US/0743-0388
**PERSPECTIVES (ARLINGTON, VA.). See** Public Administration.

CN/0316-3334
**PERSPECTIVES (SASKATOON).** (PERSPECTIVES.). [Perspectives]. **Added/Corp** Saskatchewan Council of Social Science Teachers. Vol. 8 (Fall 1972)-. Periodical. English. qt (4 issues). 20.00Can$ (institution); 15.00Can$ (individual). Saskatchewan Teachers Federation, PO Box 1108, Saskatoon Saskatchewan, S7K 3N3 Canada. **Tel** (306)373-1660. **ED** John Schaller. **Bk Rev. Ad Acc. Circ:** 200. ***Formed by the union of*** *Social Sciences for the Seventies, 0316-3644* ***and*** *Social Science Teachers Newsletter, 0316-3318.*
**Desc:** Deals with issues and ideas involved in teaching the social sciences to elementary and secondary students. Covers both subject matter and pedagogy.
**Ind/Abst** LegalTrac (1980-1984).

CN/0711-4931
**PERSPECTIVES / THE NIAGARA INSTITUTE.** [Perspectives - Niagara Inst.]. **Main/Corp** Niagara Institute. Vol. 1, No. 1 (Spring 1981)-. Periodical. English. Three times a year. Free. Niagara Institute, PO Box 1041, Niagara-on-the-Lake Ontario L0S 1J0 Canada. **DD** 303.3/4/06071351. ctrl circ.

US
**PHENOMENOLOGY & SOCIAL SCIENCE NEWSLETTER.** Newsletter. English. Three times a year. $25.00. Fielding Institute, 2112 Santa Barbara Rd, Santa Barbara CA 93105. **Tel** (805)687-1099 ext.2145. **ED** Valerie Malhatra Bentz, (editor's address: The Fielding Institute, 2112 Santa Barbara Street, Santa Barbara, CA 93105). **Bk Rev. Circ:** 500.

PH
**PHILIPPINE SOCIAL SCIENCES REVIEW. Added/Corp** University of the Philippines. College of Social Sciences and Philosophy. **VFOAT** Rebyu ng Agham-Panlipunan ng Pilipinas. Vol. 48, No. 1-4 (Jan.-Dec. 1984)-. Periodical. English. qt. ***Continues*** *Philippine Social Sciences and Humanities Review, 0031-7802.*

PH/0031-7837
**PHILIPPINE STUDIES. See** History(General).

US/0048-3915
**PHILOSOPHY & PUBLIC AFFAIRS.** [Philos. public aff.]. **VFOAT** Philosophy and Public Affairs. **VAT** Philosophy and Public Affairs. Vol. 1 (Fall 1971)-. Periodical. English. Four times a year. $60.00 US; $64.50 Canada and Mexico; $68.00 other. Princeton University Press, 41 William Street, Princeton NJ 08540. **Tel** (609)258-4900. **(Subscription address:** John Hopkins University Press, Journals Publishing Division, PO Box 19966, Baltimore MD 21211.**) ED** Frank Hunt. **LC** H1; .P54. **DD** 300/.5. **Bk Rev. Ad Acc. Pr Rev. Acid Free. Circ:** 3,000 (ctrl). available on microfilm and microfiche from University Microfilms International (UMI). Documents available from The Genuine Article, UMI Article Clearinghouse, Documents on Demand.
**Desc:** Discussions of public concern in law, political science, economics, sociology, and ethics.
**Ind/Abst** ABC POL SCI; ABI/INFORM Glob. Ed.; Acad. Abstr. Full Text Elite (Jan. 1992-); Acad. Abstr. (Jan. 1992-); Acad. Search (Jan. 1992-); Arts Humanit. Citation Index [Full Cov.]; Crim. Penol. Police Sci. Abstr.; Curr. Contents Arts Humanit.; Curr. Contents Soc. Behav. Sci.; Energy Inf. Abstr.; Environ. Abstr.; Expand. Acad. Index (1989-); Humanit. Index; Humanit. Source (Jan. 1992-); Index Period. Artic. Relat. Law; INFO-SOUTH Abstr.; Int. Bibliogr. Sociol.; Int. Polit. Sci. Abstr.; Mag. Search; Middle East Abstr. Index; Newsp. Period. Abstr. (1991-); Philos. Index; Res. Alert [Full Cov.]; Sage Public Adm. Abstr. (?-?); Soc. Plann. Policy Dev. Abstr.; Soc. Sci. Source (Jan. 1992-); Soc. Sci. Cit. Index [Full Cov.]; Sociol. Abstr.; U.S. Polit. Sci. Doc.; Women Stud. Abstr.

US/0048-3931
**PHILOSOPHY OF THE SOCIAL SCIENCES.** [Philos. soc. sci.]. **Added/Corp** York University (Toronto, Ont.). Dept. of Philosophy. **VFOAT** Philosophie des Sciences Sociales. Vol. 1 (Jan. 1971)-. Periodical. English. qt (Mar., June, Sept., Dec.). $126.00. SAGE Periodical Press, 2455 Teller Road, Thousand Oaks CA 91320. **Tel** (805)499-0721, FAX (805)499-0871, telex 100799. **ED** John O'Neill, I. C. Jarvie, J. N. Hattiangadi and J. O. Wisdom. **LC** H1; .P55. Index available. **Ad Acc. Pr Rev. Acid Free.** available on microfilm and microfiche from University Microfilms International (UMI). Documents available from The Genuine Article.
**Desc:** Publishes articles, discussions, symposia and literature surveys of interest both to philosophers concerned with the social sciences and to social scientists concerned with the philosophical foundations of their subject.
**Ind/Abst** Appl. Soc. Sci. Index Abstr.; Arts Humanit.

Citation Index [Full Cov.]; Can. Index (?-?); Can. Period. Index (19??-); Curr. Contents Arts Humanit.; Curr. Contents Soc. Behav. Sci.; Except. Hum. Exp.; Int. Bibliogr. Sociol.; Int. Polit. Sci. Abstr.; Middle East Abstr. Index; Philos. Index; Res. Alert [Full Cov.]; Soc. Plann. Policy Dev. Abstr.; Soc. Sci. Cit. Index [Full Cov.]; Sociol. Abstr.

US/0031-8906
**PHYLON (1960).** (PHYLON.). [Phylon]. (Spring 1960)-. Periodical. English. qt. $40.00 (institution), $35.00 (individual). Atlanta University, 223 James P Brawley Drive, Atlanta GA 30314. **Tel** (404)681-0251, FAX (404)681-0251. **ED** Wilbur Watson. **LC** E185.5; .P5. **DD** 909/.0496/005. **Bk Rev. Ad Acc. Circ:** 2,000 (ctrl). available on microfilm and microfiche from University Microfilms International (UMI). ***Continues** PHYLON Quarterly, 0885-6826.*
**Desc:** Examines issues of race and culture as they relate to social and political behaviors and literary analysis.
**Ind/Abst** Acad. Abstr. Full Text Elite (Jan. 1992-); Acad. Abstr. (Jan. 1992-); Acad. Ind. [Computer File] (1987-); Acad. Search (Jan. 1992-); Am. Hist. Life (1954-1987); Annu. Bibliogr. Engl. Lang. Lit.; Book Rev. Index; Commun. Abstr. (?-?); Curr. Index J. Educ.; Expand. Acad. Index (1987-); Guide Soc. Sci. Relig.; INFO-SOUTH Abstr.; Int. Polit. Sci. Abstr.; Mag. Search; Middle East Abstr. Index; MLA Int. Bibl. Books Artic. Mod. Lang. Lit.; Psychol. Abstr.; Sage Race Relat. Abstr.; Soc. Plann. Policy Dev. Abstr.; Soc. Sci. Source (Jul. 1990-); Soc. Sci. Index; Soc. Sci. Index Fulltext (Winter 1987-) [Full Txt.]; Sociol. Abstr.; Sociol. Educ. Abstr.; SportSearch; Women Stud. Abstr.

IS
**PI HA-ATON. MUSAF.** No. 1- 1971-. Hebrew. Mussaf, Student's Center, Yerushalayim Israel. **LC** HL7; .P5.

US/1060-2542
**PLAGUE WATCH.** No. 1 (1991)-. Periodical. English. bm. $23.50. Demigalt Media, PO Box 1287, Houston TX 77251-1287. **DD** 304.

US/1050-3536
**PLANET THREE.** (PLANET THREE : P3.). [Planet three]. **VFOAT** P3. No. 1 (March 1990)-. Periodical. English. mo. $18.00. P3 Foundation, PO Box 52, Montgomery VT 05470. **Tel** (802)326-4669. **ED** Jackie Kaufman. **DD** 304. **Circ:** 12,000.
**Desc:** Teaches children environmental awareness; included are cartoons, puzzles, posters, colorful graphics and profiles of adults working to protect the environment.

US/0894-4253
**PLAY & CULTURE.** ***Ceased.*** [Play cult.]. **Added/Corp** Association for the Study of Play. **VFOAT** Play and Culture. Vol. 1, No. 1 (Feb. 1988)-Ceased with Vol. 5, No. 4 (Nov. 1992). Periodical. English. qt. Human Kinetics Publishers Inc, 1607 North Market Street, PO Box 5076, Champaign IL 61825-5076. **Tel** (217)351-5076, FAX (217)351-2674. **ED** Margaret Carlisle Duncan. **DD** 306. **CODEN** PLCUEC. **[CCC]. Bk Rev. Ad Acc. Pr Rev.** Documents available from The Genuine Article.
**Desc:** Purpose is to stimulate and communicate research, critical thought, and theory in all areas related to the topic of play in humans and in animals, across various cultural, social and activity settings.
**Ind/Abst** Anthropol. Lit.; Child. Lit. Abstr. (19??-19??); Commun. Abstr.; Curr. Contents Soc. Behav. Sci.; Leis. Recreat. Tour. Abstr.; Phys. Educ. Index; Psychol. Abstr. (1988-); PsycINFO; PsycLit; Res. Alert [Full Cov.]; Soc. Plann. Policy Dev. Abstr.; SPORT Discus.

NE/0048-4482
**PLURAL SOCIETIES.** ***Ceased.*** [Plur. soc.]. **Added/Corp** Stichting Plurale Samenlevingen. Vol. 1, No. 1 (1970)-Vol. 22, No. 1 and 2 (Nov. 1992). Academic Scholarly Publication. English. qt. E. J. Brill, Postbus 9000, 2300 PA Leiden Netherlands. **Tel** 011 31 71 312624, FAX 011 31 71 317532, telex 39296 BRILL NL. **ED** W. A. Veenhoven. **LC** HM73; .P57. **DD** 301.1. **Bk Rev. Ad Acc. Circ:** 800 (ctrl).
**Desc:** An independent international forum for scholarly discussion on the interaction between coexisting human communities. Includes case studies.
**Ind/Abst** ABC POL SCI; Am. Hist. Life (1975-); Anthropol. Lit.; Int. Polit. Sci. Abstr.; Leis. Recreat. Tour. Abstr.; Middle East Abstr. Index; Soc. Plann. Policy Dev. Abstr.; Middle East J.

CR
**POLEMICA.** ***Ceased.*** **Added/Corp** Instituto Centroamericano de Documentacion e Investigacion Social. (19??)-(19??). Periodical. Spanish. Three times a year. Flacso, Apartado Postal 11747 1000, San Jose, Costa Rica. **Tel** 011 506 2248059.
**Ind/Abst** Hum. Rights Intern. Rep.; LABORDOC.

US/0741-8485
**POLICY AND RESEARCH REPORT.** (POLICY AND RESEARCH REPORT / THE URBAN INSTITUTE.). [Policy res. rep.]. **Added/Corp** Urban Institute. **VFOAT** Urban Institute Policy and Research Report. Vol. 9, No. 1 (Fall 1979)-. Periodical. English. qt. Free on request. The Urban Institute, 2100 Main Street Northwest, Washington DC 20037. **Tel** (202)833-7200. **Bk Rev. Circ:** 10,000. ***Continues** Search, 0582-3552.*
**Desc:** Social and economic problems that confront the nation and government policies and programs designed to alleviate such problems.
**Ind/Abst** J. Plan. Lit.

US/0272-0671
**POLICY PUBLISHERS AND ASSOCIATIONS DIRECTORY.** ***Ceased.*** [Policy publ. assoc. dir.]. (1980)-?. Directory. English. Policy Studies Organization, 361 Lincoln Hall, University of Illinois, Urbana IL 61801. **Tel** (217)359-8541. **LC** H61; .P58578. **DD** 070.5.

US/0146-5945
**POLICY REVIEW (WASHINGTON).** (POLICY REVIEW.). [Policy rev.]. **Added/Corp** Heritage Foundation (Washington, D.C.). (Summer 1977)-. Periodical. English. qt. $22.00. Heritage Foundation, 214 Massachusetts Avenue Northeast, Washington DC 20002. **Tel** (202)546-4400. **ED** Adam Meyerson. **LC** H1; .P69. **DD** 300/.5. Index available. cum. index. **Bk Rev. Ad Acc. Pr Rev. Circ:** 16,000. available on microfilm and microfiche from University Microfilms International (UMI). Documents available from The Genuine Article, UMI Article Clearinghouse, Documents on Demand.
**Desc:** A forum for conservative debate on the major political issues of our time.
**Ind/Abst** ABC POL SCI; Abr. Read. Guide Period. Lit.; Acad. Abstr. Full Text Elite (Jan. 1992-); Acad. Abstr. (Jan. 1992-); Acad. Search (Jan. 1992-); Am. Bibliogr. Slavic East Europ. Stud.; Book Rev. Index; Crim. Penol. Police Sci. Abstr.; Curr. Contents Soc. Behav. Sci.; Curr. Index J. Educ.; Environ. Abstr.; Expand. Acad. Index (1989-); Index Period. Artic. Relat. Law; INFO-SOUTH Abstr.; Int. Polit. Sci. Abstr.; J. Econ. Lit.; Mag. Search; Middle East Abstr. Index; Newsp. Period. Abstr. (1991-); PAIS Int. Print (1991-); Read. Guide Abstr. Select Ed.; Read. Guide Period. Lit.; Res. Alert [Full Cov.]; Soc. Plann. Policy Dev. Abstr.; Soc. Sci. Source (Jan. 1992-); Soc. Sci. Cit. Index [Full Cov.]; Soc. Sci. Index; Soc. Sci. Index Fulltext (Fall 1988-) [Full Txt.]; Sociol. Abstr.

US/0362-6016
**POLICY STUDIES DIRECTORY, THE.** ***Ceased.*** (1973)-?. Directory. English. Policy Studies Organization, 361 Lincoln Hall, University of Illinois, Urbana IL 61801. **Tel** (217)359-8541. **LC** H62.5.U5; P6. **DD** 309.2/12/071173.

US/0032-2970
**POLISH REVIEW (NEW YORK. 1956), THE.** (THE POLISH REVIEW.). [Pol. rev.]. **Added/Corp** Polish Institute of Arts and Sciences in America. V. 1- Winter (1956)-. Academic Scholarly Publication. English. qt (Mar., Jun., Sep., Dec.). $25.00 (individuals), $30.00 (institutions) US; $27.00 (individuals), $32.00 (institutions) other. The Polish Review, 208 East 30th Street, New York NY 10016. **Tel** (212)686-4164. **(Subscription address:** Paul J Best, 51 Pardee Place, New Haven, CT 06515**) ED** Joseph Wieczerzak. **LC** DK4010; .P64. **DD** 943.8. Index available. cum. index. **Bk Rev**, (Qty: 30). **Ad Acc, Adv Mgr:** Jane Kedron. **Pr Rev. Circ:** 1,500. available on microfilm and microfiche from University Microfilms International (UMI).
**Desc:** Scholarly journal devoted to Polish affairs (social sciences and humanities) in widest sense of the term.
**Ind/Abst** Acad. Search (Jan. 1994-); Am. Hist. Life (1956-); Am. Bibliogr. Slavic East Europ. Stud.; ARTbibliogr. Mod.; INFO-SOUTH Abstr.; Int. Polit. Sci. Abstr.; Mag. Search; Middle East Abstr. Index; MLA Int. Bibl. Books Artic. Mod. Lang. Lit.

SP/0210-7872
**POLITICA Y SOCIEDAD (MADRID, SPAIN).** (POLITICA Y SOCIEDAD : REVISTA DE LA UNIVERSIDAD COMPLUTENSE, FACULTAD DE CIENCIAS POLITICAS Y SOCIOLOGIA.). No. 1 (1988)-. Periodical. Spanish. qt. **LC** H8.S7; P65.
**Ind/Abst** Soc. Plann. Policy Dev. Abstr.

US/0032-3292
**POLITICS & SOCIETY.** [Polit. soc.]. **VFOAT** Politics and Society. Vol. 1, No. 1 (Nov. 1970)-. Periodical. English. qt (Mar., June., Sept., Dec.). $143.00. SAGE Periodical Press, 2455 Teller Road, Thousand Oaks CA 91320. **Tel** (805)499-0721, FAX (805)499-0871, telex 100799. **LC** H1; .P83. **DD** 300/.5. **CODEN** PSOCEX. Index available. **Bk Rev. Ad Acc. Pr Rev. Acid Free. Circ:** 1,000 (ctrl). available on microfilm and microfiche from University Microfilms International (UMI). Documents available from The Genuine Article, UMI Article Clearinghouse.
**Desc:** An alternative, critical voice of the social sciences that raises questions about the way the world is organized politically, economically and socially. Presents engaged as well as rational discourse and reconstructs social inquiry through scholarship addressed to fundamental questions of theory, policy and politics.
**Ind/Abst** ABC POL SCI; Acad. Abstr. Full Text Elite (Jan. 1992-); Acad. Abstr. (Jan. 1992-); Acad. Search (Jan. 1992-); Altern. Press Index (-199?); Am. Hist. Life (1970-); Am. Bibliogr. Slavic East Europ. Stud.; Appl. Soc. Sci. Index Abstr.; Arts Humanit. Citation Index [Select. Cov.]; Crim. Justice Abstr.; Curr. Contents Soc. Behav. Sci.; Expand. Acad. Index (1989-); INFO-SOUTH Abstr.; Int. Bibliogr. Sociol.; Int. Polit. Sci. Abstr.; Left Index; Mag. Search; Middle East Abstr. Index; Newsp. Period. Abstr. (1991-); Res. Alert [Full Cov.]; Soc. Sci. Source (Jan. 1992-); Soc. Sci. Cit. Index [Full Cov.]; Soc. Sci. Index; Soc. Sci. Index Fulltext (Dec. 1988-) [Full Txt.]; U.S. Polit. Sci. Doc.

GW/0032-3446
**POLITISCHE MEINUNG, DIE.** [Polit. Mein.]. Vol. 1 (June 1956)-. Periodical. German. bm. DM54.00. Verlag A Fromm GmbH, Postfach 1948, 49009 Osnabrueck Germany. **Tel** 011 49 541 310334, FAX 011 49 541 310440. **ED** Bernhard Vogel. **LC** H5; .P75. **DD** 300/.5; 327. Index available.
**Ind/Abst** Energy Res. Abstr. (Sept. 1982-).

US/0098-7921
**POPULATION AND DEVELOPMENT REVIEW.** **See** Population Studies.

CN/0703-7139
**POSSIBLES.** [Possibles]. Vol. 1 (Fall 1976)-. Periodical. French. Four times a year. $25.00 (individuals); $40.00 (institutions). Revue Possibles, BP 114 Succursale Cote-des-Neiges, Montreal Quebec H3C 2S4 Canada. **Tel** (514)731-1749. **DD** 971.4/005. **Bk Rev**, (Qty: 5-6). **Ad Acc. Circ:** 1,200.
**Ind/Abst** Point Repere (1983-); Soc. Plann. Policy Dev. Abstr.; Soc. Welf. Soc. Plan./Policy Soc. Dev.; Sociol. Abstr.

AT/0814-5105
**POVERTY LINES AUSTRALIA.** [Poverty lines, Aust.]. (1983)-. Periodical. English. qt. 12.00Aus$. Institute of Applied Economic and Social Research / Australia, University of Melbourne, Economics Building, Parkville Victoria 3052 Australia. **Tel** 011 61 3 3445330, FAX 011 61 3 3445630, telex 35185. **ED** Sarah Carne. **DD** 362.50994. **Circ:** 300 (ctrl).
**Desc:** Outlines and presents the updated poverty lines and pension rates as calculated by the ABS.

US/0743-9253
**POWER AND ELITES.** [Power elites]. Vol. 1, No. 1 (Fall 1984)-. Periodical. English. sa. $12.00 individuals, $14.00 institutions. Associated Faculty Press Inc, 90 South Bayles Avenue, Port Washington KY 11050. **DD** 305.

PL/0208-5437
**PRACE Z NAUK SPOECZNYCH.** **Main/Corp** Uniwersytet Slaski W Katowicach. 1- 1975-. Polish (summaries and/or abstracts in English and Russian). 13.00 single issue. Uniwersytet Slaski, Ul Bankowa 14, 40-007 Katowice Poland. **Tel** 59-69-15, FAX 48 32 599-506, telex 0315584 USKPL. **LC** H8; .U57A.

IT
**PRATICA SOCIALE.** ***Suspended.*** (19??)-(Dec. 1991). Italian. Asscom, Via A Sauli 36, 20127 Milan Italy. **Tel** 011 39 2 26827333.

US/0032-8456
**PRINCETON UNIVERSITY LIBRARY CHRONICLE, THE.** **See** Humanities.

IO
**PRISMA.** **See** Economics.

FR/0015-9743
**PROBLEMES POLITIQUES ET SOCIAUX.** **Added/Corp** France. Documentation Francaise. (19??)-. Periodical. French. Twenty-four times a year. Price varies. Documentation Francaise, 29 Quai Voltaire, 75344 Paris Cedex 7 France. **Tel** 011 33 1 40157000, FAX 011 33 1 40157230, telex 204 826 DOCFRAN. **(Subscription address:** Documentation Francaise, 124 rue Henri Barbusse, 93308 Aubervilliers Cedex France.**) LC** H3; .P73. ***Supersedes** Articles et Documents.*
**Ind/Abst** Int. Bibliogr. Sociol.; Int. Labour Doc.; LABORDOC; Point Repere.

IT
**PROBLEMI DI CIVILTA.** Yearly V. 1- 1978-. Periodical. Italian (summaries and/or abstracts in English, French, German and Spanish). L20.000. Societa Ed Napoletana, Corso Umberto I 34, 80138 Naples Italy. **LC** H1; .A164.

US/0885-2316
**PROCEEDINGS / ... ANNUAL THIRD WORLD CONFERENCE.** **See** Economics-International Economics.

US/0537-3247
**PROCEEDINGS / INDIANA ACADEMY OF THE SOCIAL SCIENCES.** **Main/Corp** Indiana Academy of the Social Sciences. (1958)-. English. ir. Indiana University Northwest, 3400 Broadway, Gary IN 46408. **Tel** (219)980-6698. **LC** HC107.I6; I47. **DD** 300/.5. **Circ:** 300. ***Continues** Indiana Academy of the Social Sciences. Meeting. Proceedings of the Annual Meeting.*

US/0737-5425
**PROGRAM ON ENVIRONMENT AND BEHAVIOR MONOGRAPH.** (PROGRAM ON ENVIRONMENT AND BEHAVIOR.). [Program Environ. Behav. monogr.]. Monograph #35-. Monographic series. English. ir. Price varies per volume. University of

Colorado / Campus Box 482, Campus Box 482, Boulder CO 80309. **Tel** (303)492-6818, FAX (303)492-2151. **ED** Dan Butler. Index available. cum. index. **Circ:** 80 (ctrl). ***Continues*** *Program on Technology, Environment, and Man, 0145-9961.*
**Desc:** Covers human response, research and government policy on natural hazards.
**Ind/Abst** GeoRef.

●CN/1191-7431
**PROGRAMMES DE SUBVENTIONS ET DE BOURSES DE CARRIERE DU CONSEIL QUEBECOIS DE LA RECHERCHE SOCIALE.** **Added/Corp** Conseil Quebecois de la Recherche Sociale. (1993/1994)-. French. an. **LC** H62.5.C22; S83. ***Continues*** *Subventions a la Recherche, Bourses d'Excellence et Subventions pour Etudes et Analyses, 0837-9971.*

FR
**PROJECT.** French. Dawson France SA, BP 40, 91121 Palaiseau Cedex France. **Tel** 011 33 1 69104700, telex 220064F.

IT
**PROMETEO (MILAN, ITALY).** (PROMETEO.). Year 1, No. 1 (Feb./Apr. 1983)-. Periodical. Italian. Four times a year. L30000 Italy; L47600 others. Arnoldo Mondadori Editore, UFF Cont Abbonamenti, 20090 Segrate MI Italy. **Tel** 011 39 2 75422015, telex 320457 MONDMI I. **ED** Andreina Vanni. **Bk Rev. Ad Acc. Circ:** 10,000.
**Desc:** A review concerning history, anthropology, biology semiology, philosophy, archaeology, ethnology, ethno history and new technologies.
**Ind/Abst** Romant. Move.

PH
**PSSC SOCIAL SCIENCE INFORMATION.** **Main/Corp** Philippine Social Science Council. **Added/Corp** Philippine Social Science Council. Social Science information. Vol. 1 (May 1973)-. Periodical. English. qt. $13.00. PSSC Central Subscription Service, PO Box 205 UP Diliman, Quezon City 1101 Philippines. **Tel** 011 63 2 9229621. **ED** Olivia Caoili. **LC** H62.5.P47; P48a. **DD** 300/.9599. **Bk Rev. Ad Acc. Circ:** 1,000.
**Desc:** Contains articles relative to the status and growth of political science in the Philippines.

US/0079-7294
**PSYCHOANALYTIC STUDY OF SOCIETY.** [Psychoanal. study soc.]. Vol. 1, (1960)-. English. ir. $36.00. Lawrence Erlbaum Associates, 365 Broadway, Suite 102, Hillsdale NJ 07642. **Tel** (201)666-4110, (800)926-6579, FAX (201)666-2394. **ED** L. B. Boyer and S. A. Grolnick. **LC** H9; .P75. **DD** 305.8. **NLM** W1 PS452. **[CCC].** ***Supersedes*** *Psychoanalysis and the Social Sciences, 1068-3410.*
**Ind/Abst** Anthropol. Lit.; Middle East Abstr. Index.

US/0033-3557
**PUBLIC INTEREST, THE.** [Public interest]. No. 1 (Fall 1965)-. Periodical. English. qt (published seasonally). $30.00 (institutions), $25.00 (individuals) US; $33.00 (institutions), $28.00 (individuals) other. Public Interest, 1112 16th Street Northwest, Suite 530, Washington DC 20036. **Tel** (202)785-8555, FAX (202)467-0006. **(Subscription address:** The Public Interest, Subscription Department, PO Box 3000, Dept. PI, Denville NJ 07834.**) ED** Irving Kristol and Nathan Glazer. **LC** H1; .P86. **DD** 300/.5. **CODEN** PUBIBV. **Bk Rev. Pr Rev. Circ:** 9,000. available on microfilm and microfiche from University Microfilms International (UMI). Documents available from The Genuine Article, UMI Article Clearinghouse.
**Desc:** Journal of domestic policy, covering topics from homelessness to racial politics, from the environment to drugs and crime.
**Ind/Abst** ABC POL SCI; ABI/INFORM Glob. Ed.; ABI Inform Ondisc (Summer 1976-); Acad. Abstr. Full Text Elite (July 1990-); Acad. Abstr. (July 1990-); Acad. Ind. [Computer File] (1987-); Acad. Search (July 1990-); AGRICOLA; Am. Hist. Life (1966-); Avery Index Archit. Period. Suppl. Colum. Univ. (1990-); Bus. Period. Index; Chicano Index; Crim. Justice Abstr.; Curr. Contents Soc. Behav. Sci.; Curr. Index J. Educ.; Expand. Acad. Index (1987-); Gen. Period. Index (1987-); Health Plan. Adminis.; Hospit. Health Admin. Index; Index Period. Artic. Relat. Law; INFO-SOUTH Abstr.; Int. Bibliogr. Sociol.; Int. Polit. Sci. Abstr.; J. Plan. Lit.; Mag. Search; Middle East Abstr. Index; Newsp. Period. Abstr. (1990-); PAIS Int. Print (1991-); Read. Guide Period. Lit.; Res. Alert [Full Cov.]; Soc. Plann. Policy Dev. Abstr.; Soc. Sci. Source (Jul. 1990-); Soc. Sci. Cit. Index [Full Cov.]; Soc. Sci. Index; Soc. Sci. Index Fulltext (Fall 1988-) [Full Txt.]; Soc. Work Abstr. (Spring 1987-) [Select. Cov.]; Sociol. Abstr.; Sociol. Educ. Abstr.; Tech. Educ. Train. Abstr.; UMI ABI/Inform--Bus. Period. Ondisc (Spring 1988-) [Full Txt.]; U.S. Polit. Sci. Doc.; Urban Aff. Abstr.; Wilson Bus. Abstr.

US
**PUBLIC POLICY STUDIES IN THE SOUTH.** 1975-. English. an. $5.00. Clark Atlanta University, JP Brawley Drive and Fair Street SW, Atlanta GA 30314. **Tel** (404)880-8524, 880-8525. **LC** H62.5.U5; P83. **DD** 300/.25/75.

US/1053-9751
**PUBLIC PULSE, THE.** (PUBLIC PULSE.). [Public pulse]. **Added/Corp** Roper Organization. (1986)-. Periodical. English. Twelve times a year. $247.00. Roper Organization Inc., 205 East 42nd Street, 7th Floor, New York NY 10017. **Tel** (212)599-0700. **DD** 303.

NE
**PUBLICATIONS OF THE INSTITUTE OF SOCIAL STUDIES. PAPERBACK SERIES.** **Main/Corp** Institute of Social Studies (Netherlands). (1970)-. Monographic series. English. ir. Price varies per volume. Walter de Gruyter Inc. / Hawthorne, 200 Saw Mill River Road, Hawthorne NY 10532. **Tel** (914)747-0110, GERMANY: 011/49/30/260050, FAX (914)747-1326, telex 646677.

BE
**PUISSANCE.** bm. 300.00F. Puissance, Rue Th Massart 13, 6518 La Hestre Belgium.

US/1040-8061
**PUNTOS.** [Puntos]. Vol. 1, No. 1 (Sept. 1987)-. Periodical. Multiple languages (English and Spanish). mo. $18.00. DER Media Group Inc, 7719 El Pensador Drive, Dallas TX 75248-4309. **DD** 305.
**Desc:** Directed to the Hispanic community with an editorial concept based on education, service, information, and orientation.

IT
**QUADERNI / FONDAZIONE GIANGIACOMO FELTRINELLI.** **Added/Corp** Fondazione Giangiacomo Feltrinelli. No. 1 (1977)-. Periodical. Italian. sa. L120000 Italy; L150000 other. Franco Angeli Riviste SRL, Viale Monza 106, 20127 Milan Italy. **Tel** 011 39 2 2827651, 011 39 2 289562. **LC** H7; .Q3.

SP/0210-7554
**QUADERNS D'ALLIBERAMENT.** **See** Political Science.

US/0888-5397
**QUALITATIVE RESEARCH METHODS.** [Qual. res. methods]. Vol. 1 (1986)-. Monographic series. English. ir. Price varies. SAGE Periodical Press, 2455 Teller Road, Thousand Oaks CA 91320. **Tel** (805)499-0721, FAX (805)499-0871, telex 100799. **DD** 001. **Acid Free.**
**Desc:** Contains information related to the social sciences.

US/0149-192X
**QUANTITATIVE APPLICATIONS IN THE SOCIAL SCIENCES.** (SAGE UNIVERSITY PAPERS SERIES. QUANTITATIVE APPLICATIONS IN THE SOCIAL SCIENCES.). [Quant. appl. soc. sci.]. **VFOAT** Quantitative Applications in the of Social Sciences; Sage University Paper Series. Quantitative Applications in the Social Sciences; Sage University Papers. Quantitative Applications in the Social Sciences; Sage University Paper. Quantitative Applications in the Social Sciences. (1976)-. Monographic series. English. ir. Price varies per volume. SAGE Periodical Press, 2455 Teller Road, Thousand Oaks CA 91320. **Tel** (805)499-0721, FAX (805)499-0871, telex 100799. **DD** 300. **Acid Free.**
**Desc:** Consists of concise, accessible papers on methodology in the social science fields. Designed to meet the demand for methodological works readily accessible to students and teachers with a limited knowledge of statistics and mathematics.
**Ind/Abst** Math. Rev. (1988-).

CN/0840-8785
**QUEBEC FRANCE.** [Que. Fr.]. Vol. 13, No. 3 (Autumn 1988)-. Periodical. French. qt. 2.50Can$ per no. Association Quebec-France, 9 Place Royale, Quebec Quebec G1X 4G2 Canada. **DD** 303.4/82714/044. ***Continues*** *Neuve-France, 0226-5362.*

CN/0033-6041
**QUEEN'S QUARTERLY.** [Queen's q.]. **Added/Corp** Queen's University (Kingston, Ont.). Vol. 1 (July 1893)-. Periodical. English. qt (4 issues). $40.00 (one year), $105.00 (three year). Queen's Quarterly, Queens University, Kingston Ontario K7L 3N6 Canada. **Tel** (613)545-2667, FAX (613)545-2667. **ED** Dr. Boris Castel (editor's address: 184 Union Street, Queens University, Kingston, Ontario K7L 3N6 Canada). **LC** AP5; .Q3. **[CCC].** Index available (bound in Dec. issue). **Bk Rev. Ad Acc. Circ:** 3,000. available on microfilm and microfiche from University Microfilms International (UMI). Documents available from The Genuine Article.
**Desc:** Review of politics, the humanities, science, arts and letters.
**Ind/Abst** Abstr. Engl. Stud.; Am. Hist. Life (1954-); Annu. Bibliogr. Engl. Lang. Lit.; Arts Humanit. Citation Index [Full Cov.]; Book Rev. Index; Can. Index; Can. Period. Index; Int. Polit. Sci. Abstr.; MLA Int. Bibl. Books Artic. Mod. Lang. Lit.; PAIS Int. Print (1991-); Res. Alert [Full Cov.]; Romant. Move.; Soc. Plann. Policy Dev. Abstr.; Soc. Sci. Cit. Index [Select. Cov.]; Sociol. Abstr.

BL
**QUESTAO SOCIAL NO BRASIL, A.** 1-. Monographic series. Portuguese. ir. Price varies per volume. Lech Livraria Editora Ciencias Humanas, rua 7 de Abril 264 Subsolo B Sala 5, CEP 01044 Sao Paulo Brazil.

IT
**QUESTE ISTITUZIONI.** **Added/Corp** Gruppo di Studio su Societa e Istituzioni (Rome, Italy). (19??)-. Periodical. Italian. Four times a year. L75000.00 Italy; L110000.00 other. Queste Istituzioni Richerche, V E Q Visconti 8 Scala Belli, 00193 Rome Italy. **Tel** 011 39 6 3215319, FAX 011 39 6 3215283. Index available. cum. index.

CN/0229-6829
**QUESTIONS DE CULTURE.** **Added/Corp** Institut Quebecois de Recherche sur la Culture. No. 1 (1981)-. Monographic series. French. ir. Price varies per volume. Institut Quebecois de Recherche sur la Culture, 14 rue Haldemand, Quebec Quebec G1R 4N4 Canada. **Tel** (418)643-4695. **Circ:** 1,000.

US/1054-6871
**RAMDIL SOCIAL SCIENCE RESOURCE GUIDES.** [RAMDIL soc. sci. resour. guides]. **VFOAT** Social Science Resource Guides. (1991)-. Monographic series. English. $9.95 (single issue). Ramdil, 1298 Lakemont Drive, Pittsburgh PA 15243. **DD** 300.

NO/0803-0030
**RAPPORT - CHR. MICHELSENS INSTITUTT, AVDELING FOR SAMFUNNSVITENSKAP OG UTVIKLING.** (RAPPORT.). [Rapp. - Chr. Michelsens inst. Avd. samf.vitensk. utvikl.]. **VFOAT** Report - Chr. Michelsen Institute, Department of Social Science and Development. (1990)-. Monographic series. Multiple languages. ir. Price varies per volume. **DD** 300. ***Continues in part*** *DERAP Publications, 0800-2053; Publications - Programme of Human Rights Studies, 0801-5856.*
**Ind/Abst** Int. Dev. Abstr.

CN/0824-3883
**RAPPORT SUR LES FEMMES.** [Rapp. femmes]. **Added/Corp** New Democratic Party of Ontario. (Sept. 1982)-. Periodical. French. Free. Parti Nouveau Democratique, Chambre des Communes, Ottawa Ontario K1A 0A6 Canada. **DD** 305.4/2/0971.

IT
**RASSEGNA DI CULTURA E VITA SCOLASTICA.** Vol. 1, No. 1 (Jan. 1947)-. Periodical. Italian. bm (5 issues). L20000. Rassegna de Cultura Vita Scolastica, Via G Borsi 3, 00197 Rome, Italy. **Tel** 011 39 6 3335429. Index available. cum. index. **Bk Rev**, (Qty: 35). **Circ:** 6,000 (ctrl).
**Desc:** Covers Italian culture including art, history, literature, philosophy and more.

US/1043-4631
**RATIONALITY AND SOCIETY.** [Ration. soc.]. (1989)-. Periodical. English. qt. $152.00. SAGE Periodical Press, 2455 Teller Road, Thousand Oaks CA 91320. **Tel** (805)499-0721, FAX (805)499-0871, telex 100799. **ED** James S. Coleman (University of Chicago). **LC** H62.A1; R37. **CODEN** RTSOEG. Index available (fourth issue). cum. index. **Ad Acc. Acid Free. Circ:** 162. available on microfilm and microfiche from University Microfilms International (UMI).
**Desc:** Focuses on the growing contributions of rational-choice based theory, and the questions and controversies surrounding this growth. Publishes work in social theory and social research based on the rational-action paradigm, as well as work challenging this paradigm.
**Ind/Abst** Curr. Contents Soc. Behav. Sci.; Sage Public Adm. Abstr.; Soc. Plann. Policy Dev. Abstr.; Soc. Sci. Cit. Index [Full Cov.]; Sociol. Abstr. (1989-) [Full Cov.].

US/1071-0043
**RAVEN (TRENTON, N.J.).** (RAVEN.). **Added/Corp** North American Vexillological Association. (1993)-. Periodical. English. an. $12.00 North America; $15.00 other. North American Vexillological Association, 1977 North Olden Avenue, Suite 225, Trenton NJ 08618. **Tel** (214)539-4653, FAX (214)423-8849. **ED** Dr. Scot M. Guenter (Editor's Address - San Jose State University, Humanities Department, One Washington Square, San Jose, CA 95192-0092; telephone 408-924-1366). **Ad Acc, Adv Mgr:** Jon T. Radel, **Tel** (703)960-5128. **Pr Rev. Circ:** 300.
**Desc:** Includes social science articles relates to current and historical flags and seals with particular interest on North America.

US/0048-6906
**REASON.** [Reason]. **Added/Corp** Reason Foundation. (Spring 1968)-. Periodical. English. Eleven times a year (Monthly with Aug./Sept. combined). $20.00 (1 year), $35.00 (2 year), $50.00 (3 year) US; $28.00 (1 year), $51.00 (2 year), $74.00 (3 year). Reason Foundation, 3415 South Sepulveda Blvd., Suite 400, Los Angeles CA 90034. **Tel** (310)391-2245, FAX (310)391-4395. **ED** Virginia Postrel. **LC** H1; .R35. **DD** 300/.5. **Bk Rev. Ad Acc, Adv Mgr:** Mike Griffin. **Circ:** 45,000. available on microfilm from University Microfilms International (UMI). Documents available from UMI Article Clearinghouse.

**Desc:** A "think" magazine designed for the individual. Articles include economic, environmental, political, and cultural topics. Magazine of "free minds and free markets." Bright ideas before they're news.
**Ind/Abst** Acad. Abstr. (Jan. 1994-); Acad. Search (Jan. 1994-); Am. Hist. Life (1977-1986); Book Rev. Index; Gen. Period. Index (1989-); Index Period. Artic. Relat. Law (19??-19??); Mag. Index Plus (1989-); Newsp. Period. Abstr. (1991-); PAIS Int. Print; Read. Guide Abstr. Select Ed.; Read. Guide Period. Lit. (1991-); Sage Fam. Stud. Abstr. (?-?); Sage Public Adm. Abstr. (?-?); Mag. Index (1989-).

US/0363-1893
**REASON PAPERS.** [Reason pap.]. Began with Fall 1974 issue. English. $4.00. Prof Tibor Machan, 2251 Harvard, Palo Alto CA 94306. **LC** H1; .R353. **DD** 300/.5.
**Ind/Abst** Philos. Index.

BE/0303-9625
**RECHERCHES SOCIOLOGIQUES.** [Rech. sociol.]. Vol. 1 (June 1970)-. Periodical. French (summaries and/or abstracts in English). Three times a year (April, July, and November). $67.00. Centre Recherches Sociologique, Place Montesquieu 1/10, 1348 Louvain la Neuve Belgium. **Tel** 011 32 10 474204, FAX 011 32 10 474603. **LC** HM3; .R37. **DD** 301/.05. Index available. cum. index. **Bk Rev**, (Qty: 30). **Circ:** 1,500.
**Desc:** Analyzing social movements, society's orientations and the evolution of society's structures.
**Ind/Abst** Am. Hist. Life (1979-1986)(1979-); Soc. Plann. Policy Dev. Abstr.; Sociol. Abstr. [Full Cov.].

BE
**RECUEILS DE LA SOCIETE JEAN BODIN POUR L'HISTOIRE COMPARATIVE DES INSTITUTIONS.** **Main/Corp** Societe Jean Bodin pour l'Histoire Comparative des Institutions. 1- 1936-. Monographic series. French. Price varies per volume. **LC** H13.

US/0730-3335
**REFERENCE SOURCES FOR THE SOCIAL SCIENCES AND HUMANITIES.** [Ref. sources soc. sci. humanit.]. No. 1 (1982)-. Monographic series. English. ir. Price varies per volume. Greenwood Press Inc., PO Box 5007, Westport CT 06881-5007. **Tel** (203)226-3571, FAX (203)222-1502. **ED** Raymond G. McInnis.

UK/0034-3404
**REGIONAL STUDIES.** [Reg. stud.]. **Added/Corp** Regional Studies Association (London, England). Vol. 1 (May 1967)-. Academic Scholarly Publication. English. Eight times a year. £170.00. Carfax Publishing Company, PO Box 25 Abingdon, Oxfordshire OX14 3UE England. **Tel** 011 44 235 555335, FAX (0279)31067, telex 817484. **(Subscription address:** US and Canada/ PO Box 2025, Dunnellon, FL 34430-2025; telephone:(904)489-6996) **ED** James Taylor. **LC** HT390; .R43. **CODEN** REGSAT. **[CCC]. Bk Rev. Pr Rev.** available on microfilm and microfiche from University Microfilms International (UMI). Documents available from The Genuine Article, UMI Article Clearinghouse.
**Desc:** Publishes the results of original research on such topics as industrial, retail and office location, labour markets, housing, migration, recreation, transport, communications and the evaluation of public policy, wherever any of these topics have a bearing on urban and regional development.
**Ind/Abst** Appl. Soc. Sci. Index Abstr.; Archit. Period. Index (1977-1981); Avery Index Archit. Period. Suppl. Colum. Univ. (1990-); Br. Humanit. Index; Contents Pages Manage.; Curr. Contents Soc. Behav. Sci.; Curr. Geogr. Publ. (199?-); Econ. Lit. Index; EMBASE; Expand. Acad. Index (1992-); Geogr. Abstr. Human Geogr.; Index Econ. Artic. J. Collect. Vol.; Int. Bibliogr. Sociol.; Int. Dev. Abstr.; Int. Labour Doc.; Int. Polit. Sci. Abstr.; J. Econ. Lit.; J. Plan. Lit.; Leis. Recreat. Tour. Abstr.; Middle East Abstr. Index; Newsp. Period. Abstr. (1992-); PAIS Int. Print; Popul. Index; Res. Alert [Full Cov.]; Sage Urban Stud. Abstr; SCISEARCH; Soc. Plann. Policy Dev. Abstr.; Soc. Sci. Cit. Index [Full Cov.]; Sociol. Abstr.; SportSearch.

FR
**REPERTOIRE DES THESES AFRICANISTES FRANCAISES / CENTRE D'ETUDES AFRICAINES - CARDAN, ECOLE DES HAUTES ETUDES EN SCIENCES SOCIALES.** ***Title Change.*** (1977)-?. French. an. Sec des Publ du Cea Cardan, 54 Bd Raspail, Paris 75006 France. **Tel** (1)5443979. **LC** Z3501; .R44; DT3. **DD** 016.96. ***Absorbed by*** *Inventaire de Theses Africanistes de Langue Francaise en Cours; Inventaire de Theses et Memoires Africanistes de Langue Francaise Soutenus.*
**Desc:** Publication examines doctoral theses written during the year in France dealing with social sciences, law, political science, economic science of continental Africa and its islands.

SP
**REPERTORIO LEGISLATIVO ACCION SOCIAL.** (19??)-. Periodical. Spanish. Four times a year. 4567ptas (with covers), 1000ptas (without covers). Ministerio Asuntos Sociales Publicaciones, Alonso Cano 20, 28003 Madrid Spain. **Tel** 011 34 1 3477353, 011 34 1 3477351.

PR
**REPORT.** **Main/Corp** Puerto Rico. University. Social Science Research Center. (1946/47)-. English. Universidad de Puerto Rico / Ciencias Sociales, Facultad de Ciencias Sociales, Rio Piedras 00931 Puerto Rico. **LC** HC157.P8; A1584. **DD** 307.2.

US/1051-6972
**REPORT FROM THE INSTITUTE FOR PHILOSOPHY & PUBLIC POLICY.** [Rep. Inst. Philos. Public Policy]. **Added/Corp** University of Maryland, College Park. Institute for Philosophy and Public Policy. **VFOAT** Philosophy & Public Policy; Philosophy and Public Policy. Vol. 10, No. 1 (Winter 1990)-. Periodical. English. qt (Jan., Apr., July, Oct.). Free. Institute for Philosophy and Public Policy, Room 0123/Woods Hall, Center for Philosophy, University of Maryland, College Park MD 20742. **Tel** (301)454-6573, FAX (301)314-9346. **ED** Arthur Evenchik. **LC** H1; .Q65. **DD** 361. **Ad Acc. Circ:** 9,500. ***Continues*** *QQ, 0735-8555.*
**Desc:** Features articles on the concepts and values that underline various policy issues such as equal opportunity, environmental protection, biotechnology, regulation of risk, the role of the media in a democrary, medical ethics and issues in legal ethics.

US/0363-1109
**REPORT - INSTITUTE FOR THE FUTURE.** (REPORT / INSTITUTE FOR THE FUTURE.). [Rep. - Inst. Future]. **Added/Corp** Institute for the Future. (19??)-. Monographic series. English. ir. Price varies per volume. Institute for the Future, 2740 Sand Hill Road, Menlo Park CA 94025. **LC** UNC. ***Continues*** *IFF Report.*

AG
**REPORT OF ACTIVITIES - CEDES.** **Main/Corp** Centro de Estudios de Estado y Sociedad. (19??)-. English. Centro de Estudios de Estado y Sociedad, Hipolito Yrigoyen 1156, 1086 Buenos Aires Argentina. **Tel** 961-2496/8072. **LC** H62.A1; C47a. **DD** 300/.7/2082.

US/0082-8203
**REPORT OF THE ECONOMIC AND SOCIAL COUNCIL FOR THE YEAR ... UNITED NATIONS.** (REPORT OF THE ECONOMIC AND SOCIAL COUNCIL / UNITED NATIONS.). [Rep. Econ. Soc. Counc. year - U. N.]. **Main/Corp** United Nations. Economic and Social Council. **Added/Corp** United Nations. **VFOAT** Report of the Economic and Social Council for the Year ... . (30 Aug. 1948/15 Aug. 1949)-. Government Publication. English. ir. $25.00. United Nations Publications, 2 United Nations Plaza, Room DC2 0853, Department 007C, New York NY 10017. **Tel** (212)963-8303, (800)253-9646. ***Continues*** *United Nations. Economic and Social Council. Report of the Economic and Social Council to the General Assembly.*

US/0094-7326
**REPORT OF THE NEW MEXICO VETERANS' SERVICE COMMISSION.** **See** Public Administration.

US/1043-3856
**REPORT ON GUATEMALA.** [Rep. Guatem.]. **Added/Corp** Guatemala News and Information Bureau. National Network in Solidarity with the People of Guatemala (U.S.). Vol. 8, Issue 1 (March/April 1987)-. Periodical. English (Spanish). Four times a year (Mar., June, Sept., Dec.). $12.00 (individual); $18.00 (institution); $18.00 other. Guatemala News & Information Bureau, PO Box 28594, Oakland CA 94604. **Tel** (415)835-0810, FAX (415)835-3017. **ED** David Loeb. **DD** 354. **Bk Rev**, (Qty: 1-2). **Circ:** 3,000. ***Formed by the union of*** *Guatemala, 0893-6196* ***and*** *Network News.*
**Desc:** Provides reports and analysis on current events in Guatemala, focusing on political, social, economic, and cultural development. Regular features also includes interviews with Guatemalan activists and listings of new resources.
**Ind/Abst** Hum. Rights Intern. Rep.

BG
**REPORT ON THE BACKGROUND, CURRENT PROGRAMMES AND PLANNED DEVELOPMENT OF THE BANGLADESH INSTITUTE OF DEVELOPMENT STUDIES, A.** ***Title Change.*** **Main/Corp** Bangladesh Institute of Development Studies. (1975)-?. English. Bangladesh Institute of Development Studies, E-17 Agargaon, PO Box 3854, Dhaka 7 Bangladesh. **Tel** FAX 880-2-813023. **ED** Omar Haider Choudhury. **LC** H62.5.B35; B35a. **DD** 338.9549/2. Index available. **Bk Rev. Ad Acc. Circ:** 5,000 (ctrl). ***Continued by*** *Bangladesh Institute of Development Studies. Report on the Background, Organization and Research Activities of the Institute.*

US/0080-1348
**REPORTS AND PAPERS IN THE SOCIAL SCIENCES.** **Main/Corp** United Nations Educational, Scientific and Cultural Organization. Social Science Clearing House. No. 1 (1955)-. English. ir. UNIPUB, 4611-F Assembly Drive, Lanham MD 20706-4391. **Tel** (800)274-4888, FAX (301)459-0056, telex 28787 GATT CH. **LC** AS4.U8.

UK/0414-0524
**REPORTS : SS.** **Main/Conf** Inter-African Conference. Social Sciences. **Added/Corp** Commission for Technical Co-operation in Africa South of the Sahara. **VFOAT** Reports: Social Sciences. 1 (1955)-. Periodical. English. Europa Publications Ltd, 18 Bedford Square, London WC1B 3JN England. **Tel** 011 44 71 5808236, telex 21540 EUROPA G. **DD** 338.9.

KE
**RESEARCH AND PUBLICATIONS.** **See** Economics.

US/1052-3707
**RESEARCH & SOCIETY.** [Res. soc.]. **Added/Corp** State University of New York at Buffalo. Graduate Group in Marxist Studies. **VFOAT** Research and Society. No. 1 (1988)-. Periodical. English. Research and Society, Suny at Buffalo, Buffalo NY 14261. **LC** H1; .R38. **DD** 300/.5. **CODEN** RSSOE9.
**Ind/Abst** Am. Hist. Life (1988-).

US/0732-1317
**RESEARCH IN PUBLIC POLICY ANALYSIS AND MANAGEMENT.** (RESEARCH IN PUBLIC POLICY ANALYSIS AND MANAGEMENT : OFFICIAL PUBLICATION OF THE ASSOCIATION FOR PUBLIC POLICY ANALYSIS AND MANAGEMENT.). [Res. public policy anal. manage.]. **Added/Corp** Association for Public Policy Analysis and Management (U.S.). Vol. 1 (1981)-. English. ir. $73.25. JAI Press Inc., 55 Old Post Road, Suite 2, PO Box 1678, Greenwich CT 06836-1678. **Tel** (203)661-7602, FAX (203)661-0792. **ED** Stuart Nagel. **LC** H97; .R47. **DD** 361.6/1/05. **NLM** W1 RE227KM. **[CCC].**

UK/0956-9014
**RESEARCH ON LATIN AMERICA IN THE HUMANITIES AND SOCIAL SCIENCES IN THE UNIVERSITIES AND POLYTECHNICS OF THE UNITED KINGDOM.** **See** Humanities.

UK/0264-519X
**RESEARCH, POLICY AND PLANNING : THE JOURNAL OF THE SOCIAL SERVICES RESEARCH GROUP.** Vol. 1, No. 1 (1983)-. Periodical. English. sa. £21.00. Research Policy & Planning, PO Box 536, Manchester Social Services, Manchester M60 2AF England. **Tel** 011 44 61 234 3880. **(Subscription address:** Brian McClay, Bradford SSB, Olicana House, Chapel Street, Bradford BD1 5BY England) **ED** Roger Lightup. **Bk Rev. Ad Acc. Circ:** 500.
**Desc:** Devoted to publishing social services research by practitioners working in local and central government, institutes of higher education.

SW/0080-6714
**RESEARCH REPORT.** **Main/Corp** Nordiska Afrikainstitutet. **Added/Corp** Nordiska Afrikainstitutet. Vol. 1 (1967)-. Monographic series. English. ir. Price varies per volume. Nordiska Afrikaainstitutet, Sturegatan 9 1 TR EPOS, S 753 14 Uppsala Sweden. **Tel** 011 46 18 1833325. **LC** DT1; .N64. **DD** 309.1/6.

US/0092-847X
**RESEARCH REPORT - INSTITUTE FOR RESEARCH ON POVERTY (MADISON).** (RESEARCH REPORT.). **Main/Corp** Wisconsin. University--Madison. Institute for Research on Poverty. English. sa. $3.50 (Discussion Papers), $2.00 (reprints). University of Wisconsin-Madison Institute for Research on Poverty, 1180 Observatory Drive, Madison WI 53706. **Tel** (608)262-6358. **ED** Charles F. Manski. **LC** HC110.P6; W57A. **DD** 301.44/1.

UK/0266-2159
**RESEARCH SUPPORTED BY THE ECONOMIC AND SOCIAL RESEARCH COUNCIL.** **Main/Corp** Economic and Social Research Council (Great Britain). (1984)-. English. an. £6.50. Economic and Social Research Council, Cherry Orchard East, Kembrey Park, Swindon SN2 6UQ England. **Tel** (01)637-1499, FAX 0793 487916. **ED** Bernard Reid. **LC** H62.5.G7; S64d. **DD** 300/.72041. **Circ:** 1,500 (ctrl). ***Continues*** *Research Supported by the Social Science Research Council.*
**Desc:** Lists research projects in the fields of economic affairs, education and human development, environment and planning, government and law, industry and employment and social affairs.

FR
**REUSSIR.** French. qt. 96.00F France; 140.00F other. Les Francas, 10/14 rue Tolain, 75020 Paris France. **Tel** 011 33 1 44642100, FAX 011 33 1 43672829, telex 680

086 F. **(Subscription address:** Editions Jeunes Annees/Reussir Service Abonnements, 4 rue Andre Boulle, 94942 Creteil Cedex 9 France**) ED** (editor's address: Les Francas, 10 rue Tolain, 75020 Paris France).

II/0258-1701
**REVIEW JOURNAL OF PHILOSOPHY & SOCIAL SCIENCE.** See Philosophy.

CN
**REVIEW OF ANTI-SEMITISM IN CANADA, THE. Added/Corp** League for Human Rights of B'nai B'rith. **VFOAT** Rapport Annuel sur l'Antisemitisme au Canada; Rapport sur l'Antisemitisme au Canada. (1983)-. Periodical. English (French). an. 7.00Can$. League for Human Rights, 15 Hove Street, Downsview ONT M3H 4Y8 Canada. **Tel** (905)633-6224. **DD** 305.8/924/071. ***Continues*** *Rapport Annuel sur l'Antisemitisme au Canada, 0828-6167.*

US/1050-2130
**REVIEW / OHIO COUNCIL FOR THE SOCIAL STUDIES, THE.** See Political Science.

PE
**REVISTA ANDINA. Added/Corp** Centro de Estudios Rurales Andinos Bartolome de las Casas. Vol. 1, No. 1 (Sept. 1983)-. Periodical. Spanish. sa. $50.00 (institutions), $40.00 (individuals) Latin America; $75.00 (institutions), $60.00 (individuals) other. Centro Bartolome de las Casas, Apartado Postal 14 0087, Lima Peru. **Tel** 51 84 14 223703, 51 84 14 429992, FAX 51 14 427894. **ED** Gabriela Rames. **LC** F2212; .R48. **DD** 980/.005. cum. index. **Bk Rev. Ad Acc, Adv Mgr:** same as editor. **Circ:** 1,000.
**Desc:** Articles on economic, political and sociological conditions in the Andean countries of South America, past and present. Publishes catalogs of archival and archaeological interest.
**Ind/Abst** Anthropol. Lit.

PO
**REVISTA CRITICA DE CIENCIAS SOCIAIS.** No. 1 (June 1978)-. Portuguese. Three times a year. $30.00 (individuals), $50.00 (institutions) (add $10.00 airmail postage) other. Revista Critica de Ciencias Sociais, Apartado 3087, 3000 Coimbra Portugal. **Tel** (039)26459. **LC** H8.P8; R47. Index available. **Bk Rev. Ad Acc. Circ:** 1,500 (ctrl).
**Ind/Abst** Am. Hist. Life (1986-); Int. Polit. Sci. Abstr.

BL
**REVISTA DE CIENCIAS HUMANAS. Added/Corp** Universidade Federal de Santa Catarina. Vol. 1, No. 1 (Jan. 1982)-. Periodical. Portuguese. sa. Cr$700.00. Editora da UFSC, Caixa Postal 476, 88000 Florianopolis SC Brazil. **Tel** (0482)339408. **(Subscription address:** Revista de Ciencias Humanas, Av Rio Branco 109-703, 20054 Rio de Janeiro Brazil.**) LC** H8.P8; R48. **DD** 300/.5.

BL/0303-9862
**REVISTA DE CIENCIAS SOCIAIS.** [Rev. cienc. soc.]. **Added/Corp** Ceara, Brazil (State). Universidade Federal. Departamento de Sociologia. Vol. 1-2, Semester (1970)-. Academic Scholarly Publication. Portuguese. Three times a year. Elsevier Science Publishers BV, PO Box 211, 1000 AE Amsterdam Netherlands. **Tel** 011 31 20 5803642, FAX 011 31 20 5862696, telex 15682. **ED** Amauray de Souza and Charles Pessanha. **LC** H8; .R5118.
**Desc:** Publishes original articles of academic quality and social relevance.
**Ind/Abst** HAPI Hisp. Am. Period. Index (19??-); Int. Bibliogr. Sociol.; Soc. Plann. Policy Dev. Abstr.; Sociol. Abstr. (?-?).

UY
**REVISTA DE CIENCIAS SOCIALES. Added/Corp** Instituto de Ciencias Sociales (Fundacion de Cultura Universitaria). (198?)-. Periodical. Spanish. Instituto de Ciencias Sociales, Fundacion de Cultura Universitaria, 25 de Mayo 568, Casilla de Correo 1155, Montevideo, Uruguay.
**Ind/Abst** PAIS Int. Print.

PR/0034-7817
**REVISTA DE CIENCIAS SOCIALES (RIO PIEDRAS, P.R.).** (REVISTA DE CIENCIAS SOCIALES.). [Rev. cienc. soc.]. **Added/Corp** University of Puerto Rico (Rio Piedras Campus). Social Science Research Center. (March 1957)-. Periodical. Spanish. Twice a year. $20.00. Universidad de Puerto Rico / Facultad de Ciencias Sociales, Apartado 23345, San Juan Puerto Rico 00931. **Tel** (809)764-0000 ext. 2250 or 2104, FAX (809)763-2943. **ED** Dr. Juan M. Cavrion. **DD** 305. **NLM** W1 RE38V. **Bk Rev**, (Qty: 3-6/year). **Circ:** 1,000.
**Ind/Abst** Am. Hist. Life; HAPI Hisp. Am. Period. Index; Int. Bibliogr. Sociol.; LABORDOC; Psychol. Abstr. (1973-); Soc. Plann. Policy Dev. Abstr.; Soc. Welf. Soc. Plan./Policy Soc. Dev.; Sociol. Abstr.

CR/0482-5276
**REVISTA DE CIENCIAS SOCIALES (SAN JOSE).** (REVISTA DE CIENCIAS SOCIALES.). [Rev. cienc. soc.]. **Added/Corp** Universidad de Costa Rica. No. 4 (1959)-. Periodical. Spanish. Four times a year (Mar., June, Sept., Dec.). $40.00. University de Costa Rica, Apartado 75 2060, Ciudad Universite, San Jose Costa Rica. **Tel** 011 506 2247051, 011 506 2253133, telex 2544. **ED** Daniel Camacho. **LC** K19; .D25. Index available (Free). **Bk Rev. Ad Acc. Pr Rev. Circ:** 1,500 (ctrl). ***Continues*** *Revista de Ciencias Juridico-Sociales.*
**Desc:** Covers anthropology, archaeology, economics, geography, history, political science, psychology, agricultural production and union workers.
**Ind/Abst** Am. Hist. Life (1986-); HAPI Hisp. Am. Period. Index; Int. Labour Doc.; Int. Polit. Sci. Abstr.

CL
**REVISTA DE CIENCIAS SOCIALES (UNIVERSIDAD DE VALPARAISO. FACULTAD DE CIENCIAS JURIDICAS, ECONOMICAS Y SOCIALES).** See Law.

SP/0213-7585
**REVISTA DE ESTUDIOS REGIONALES. Added/Corp** Universidad de Malaga. Facultad de Ciencias Economicas y Empresariales. No. 1 (Jan./June 1978)-. Periodical. Spanish. Three times a year. 2570ptas Spain; 4570ptas other. Universidad de Malaga / Economia, Department Estadistica Y Econometria, El Ejido Facultad Economia, Apartado 4, 29071 Malaga Spain. **Tel** 011 34 52131297, 2131210. **LC** H53.S7; R48. **DD** 300/.946/805. **Ad Acc. Circ:** 1,000 (ctrl).
**Ind/Abst** PAIS Int. Print.

SP/0015-6043
**REVISTA DE FOMENTO SOCIAL.** [Rev. fom. soc.]. **VFOAT** FS. Revista de Fomento Social. (1964)-. Periodical. Spanish. qt. $32.00 Latin America; $35.20 other. Centro Loyola, Pablo Aranda 3, 28006 Madrid Spain. **Tel** 011 34 1 565-4930, 562-6604, FAX 011 34 1 563-4073. **UDC** 304. **Bk Rev. Ad Acc. Pr Rev. Circ:** 4,000. ***Continues*** *Fomento Social, 0210-4113.*
**Desc:** Social, economic , political issues from the point of view of Christian ethics.
**Ind/Abst** Int. Bibliogr. Sociol.

AG/0325-9587
**REVISTA DE LA UNIVERSIDAD NACIONAL DE RIO CUARTO. Added/Corp** Universidad Nacional de Rio Cuarto. Vol. 1, No. 1 (1981)-. Periodical. Spanish (summaries and/or abstracts in English). sa. Enlace Rutas 8 Y 36 Km 603, 5800 Rio Cuarto Argentina. **Tel** 32265, telex 54572 CUMRC AR. **LC** Q33; .R55. **DD** 086/.1.
**Ind/Abst** Nematol. Abstr.

SP/0034-8724
**REVISTA DE POLITICA SOCIAL. Added/Corp** Instituto de Estudios Politicos (Spain). (1949)-. Periodical. Spanish. qt. cum. index. ***Continues*** *Revista de Estudios Politicos. Suplemento de Politica Social.*
**Ind/Abst** Am. Hist. Life (1955-1980).

SP
**REVISTA DE SERVICIOS SOCIALES Y POLITICA SOCIAL.** Spanish. qt. 2800.00ptas Spain; 3800.00ptas other. Consejo Gral Col Diplomado, Calle Campomanes 10, 28013 Madrid Spain. **Tel** 011 34 1 5415776.

SP
**REVISTA DESARROLLO.** Spanish. Three times a year. $25.00. Sociedad Internacional Para El Desarrollo, Santa Catalina 6, 28014 Madrid Spain. **Tel** 011 34 1 5377481.

BL/0020-3874
**REVISTA DO INSTITUTO DE ESTUDOS BRASILEIROS.** (REVISTA DO INSTITUTO DE ESTUDOS BRASILEIROS : PUBLICACAO DO INSTITUTO DE ESTUDOS BRASILEIROS DA UNIVERSIDADE DE SAO PAULO.). [Rev. Inst. Estud. Bras.]. **Added/Corp** Universidade de Sao Paulo. Instituto de Estudos Brasileiros. No. 1 (1966)-. Periodical. Portuguese. ir. Universidade de Sao Paulo / Estudos Brasil, Instituto de Estudos Brasil, CP 11154, Sao Paulo Brazil. **LC** F2501; .S275.
**Ind/Abst** Am. Hist. Life (1966-); HAPI Hisp. Am. Period. Index.

NE/0924-0608
**REVISTA EUROPEA DE ESTUDIOS LATINOAMERICANOS Y DEL CARIBE. EUROPEAN REVIEW OF LATIN AMERICAN AND CARIBBEAN STUDIES. Added/Corp** Centrum voor Studie en Documentatie van Latijns Amerika (Amsterdam, Netherlands) Koninklijk Instituut voor Taal-, Land- en Volkenkunde (Netherlands). **VFOAT** European Review of Latin American and Caribbean Studies. Vol. 47 (Dec. 1989)-. Periodical. English (Spanish). Twice a year (June and December). $55.00 (institutions), $30.00 (individuals). Center for Latin American Research and Documentation, Keizersgracht 395-397, 1016 EK Amsterdam, Paises Bajos, The Netherlands. **Tel** 011 31 20 5253498, FAX 011 31 20 6255127. **ED** Kathleen Willingham. **LC** F1401; .B67. **DD** 980/.005. **CODEN** RELCEA. Index available. **Bk Rev**, (Qty: 25). **Ad Acc. Pr Rev. Circ:** 1,000 (ctrl). ***Continues*** *Boletin de Estudios Latinoamericanos y del Caribe, 0304-2634.*
**Desc:** Articles relative to the zone of Latin American and the Caribbean in the fields of the social sciences which reflect substantial empirical research and/or to problems of historical interpretation.
**Ind/Abst** Am. Hist. Life; HAPI Hisp. Am. Period. Index (19??-); Int. Bibliogr. Sociol.; PAIS Int. Print.

BE
**REVISTA INTERNACIONAL DE CIENCIAS ADMINISTRATIVAS. Added/Corp** International Institute of Administrative Sciences. 1957-. Periodical. Spanish (French and English; summaries and/or abstracts in Spanish). qt. $48.00. International Institute of Administrative Sciences, 1 rue Defacqz Box 11, B-1050 Brussels Belgium. **Tel** 32 2 5389165, telex 65933 IISA B. ***Continues in part*** *Revue Internationale des Sciences Administratives (Brussels, Belgium : 1927), 0303-965X.*

SP/0379-0762
**REVISTA INTERNACIONAL DE CIENCIAS SOCIALES.** [Rev. int. cienc. soc.]. (1976)-. Periodical. Spanish (English and French). qt. $27.00 developing countries; $45.00 developed countries. Centre UNESCO de Catalunya, Mallorca 285, 08037 Barcelona Spain. **Tel** 011 34 3 2071716, FAX 257 58 51. **UDC** 30. Index available. cum. index. **Bk Rev.** ctrl circ.
**Desc:** Different articles in the field of Social Sciences.

PO
**REVISTA INTERNACIONAL DE ESTUDOS AFRICANOS. VFOAT** International Journal of African Studies. No. 1 (Jan./June 1984)-. Periodical. summaries and/or abstracts in English. sa. $15.00. Instituto de Investigacao Cientifica Tropical, Centro de Documentacao e Informacao, rua Jau 47, 1 300 Lisbon Portugal. **Tel** 645321. **LC** H62.5.A343; R48. **DD** 300/.96. Index available. ctrl circ.

SP/0034-9712
**REVISTA INTERNACIONAL DE SOCIOLOGIA.** (REVISTA INTERNACIONAL DE SOCIOLOGIA / CONSEJO SUPERIOR DE INVESTIGACIONES CIENTIFICAS, SECCION DE SOCIOLOGIA DEL INSTITUTO "SANCHO DE MONCADA".). [Rev. int. sociol.]. **Added/Corp** Instituto "Sancho de Moncada." Instituto "Balmes" de Sociologia. Instituto de Sociologia "Jaime Balmes." Instituto de Economia y Geografia Aplicadas (Spain) Instituto de Estudios Sociales Avanzados (Spain). Vol. 1, No. 1 (Jan./March 1943)-. Periodical. Spanish. qt. 4500ptas. Consejo Superior Investigacion Cientificas (CSIC), Vitruvio 8, 28006 Madrid Spain. **Tel** 011 34 1 5612833, FAX 011 34 1 4113077, telex 42182.
**Ind/Abst** Am. Hist. Life (1956-1960, 1965-1972); Soc. Plann. Policy Dev. Abstr.; Sociol. Abstr. [Full Cov.].

MX/0185-1918
**REVISTA MEXICANA DE CIENCIAS POLITICAS Y SOCIALES.** [Rev. mex. cienc. polit. soc.]. **Added/Corp** Universidad Nacional Autonoma de Mexico. Facultad de Ciencias Politicas y Sociales. New Series, Vol. 21 No. 81 (July/Sept. 1975)-. Periodical. Spanish. Four times a year. $90.00. Centro de Estudios Latinoamericanos, Area del Caribe, Facultad de Ciencias Politicas y Sociales, EDIF C Piso 2 Unam, 04510 Mexico 20 DF Mexico. **Tel** 011 52 5 6656211 ext. 7965. **LC** JA5; .R56. ***Continues*** *Revista Mexicana de Ciencia Politica, 0034-9976.*
**Ind/Abst** ABC POL SCI; Am. Hist. Life (1971-); HAPI Hisp. Am. Period. Index; Int. Polit. Sci. Abstr.; Soc. Plann. Policy Dev. Abstr.; Sociol. Abstr.

VE/0035-0230
**REVISTA NACIONAL DE CULTURA (CARACAS, VENEZUELA).** (REVISTA NACIONAL DE CULTURA.). [Rev. nac. cult.]. Vol. 1, No. 1 (Nov. 1938)-. Periodical. Spanish. bm. Instituto Nacional de Cultura y Bellas Artes, Apartado 6238, Caracus Venezuela. **LC** AS90.A1; R4. **DD** 056. cum. index.
**Ind/Abst** Abstr. Engl. Stud.; Am. Hist. Life (1955-1984); HAPI Hisp. Am. Period. Index.

PY/0035-0354
**REVISTA PARAGUAYA DE SOCIOLOGIA.** [Rev. parag. sociol.]. Year 1- (No. 1-) Sept./Dec. 1964-. Periodical. Spanish. Three times a year. $30.00. Centro Paraguayo Est Sociologi Correo 2157, Asuncion Paraguay. **Tel** 43-734. **ED** Grazziella Corvalan. **LC** HM7; .R55. cum. index. **Bk Rev.** available on microfilm and microfiche from University Microfilms International (UMI).
**Desc:** Deals with social sciences in general.
**Ind/Abst** HAPI Hisp. Am. Period. Index; Int. Bibliogr. Sociol.; Int. Labour Doc.; LABORDOC; Soc. Plann. Policy Dev. Abstr.; Sociol. Abstr. [Full Cov.].

PE/1011-0410
**REVISTA PERUANA DE CIENCIAS SOCIALES : RPCS. Added/Corp** Asociacion Peruana para el Fomento de las Ciencias Sociales. **VFOAT** RPCS. Vol. 1, No. 1 (1987)-. Periodical. Spanish. tq. **LC** H8.S7; R49.
**Ind/Abst** Soc. Plann. Policy Dev. Abstr.

PR/0360-7917
**REVISTA/REVIEW INTERAMERICANA.** [Rev./rev. interam.]. **Added/Corp** Inter American University of Puerto Rico. **VFOAT** Review Interamericana. **VAT** Revista Review Interamericana. Vol. 6 (Spring 1976)-. Academic Scholarly Publication. English (Spanish). sa. $18.00. Universidad Interamericana de Puerto Rico, Call Box 5100, San German, Puerto Rico 00753. **Tel** (809)264-1919 1095 1912 ext.373. **ED** Hector R. Felicono Ramos. **LC** AS74.A1; R46. **DD** 050. **[CCC]. Bk Rev. Ad Acc. Circ:** 800. ***Continues*** *Revista Interamericana.*
**Desc:** Multidisciplinary scholarly journal in the social sciences and humanities on topics concerning Puerto Rico, the Caribbean, Latin America.
**Ind/Abst** Abstr. Engl. Stud.; Am. Hist. Life (1971-); HAPI Hisp. Am. Period. Index; Index Am. Period. Verse; MLA Int. Bibl. Books Artic. Mod. Lang. Lit.

CU
**REVISTA UNIVERSIDAD DE LA HABANA.** Spanish. Three times a year. Ediciones Cubanas, Obispo 527, Altos ESQ Bernaza, CP 10100 Havana Cuba. **Tel** 011 632980, 631942, FAX 011 631011, telex 512337, 6540.

UY
**REVISTA URUGUAYA DE CIENCIAS SOCIALES.** V. 1- April/June 1972-. Periodical. Spanish. qt. $40.00 US; $40.00 other. Libreria Anticuaria Americana, Juan Carlos Gomez 1435, 11000 Montevideo Uruguay. **Tel** 90 71 94 OR 91 04 33. **ED** Juan I Risso. **LC** H8; .R56. Index available. cum. index. **Bk Rev. Circ:** 2,000 (ctrl).
**Desc:** Dedicated to sociology applied to the Uruguayan reality: political reality, health, social classes, education, social movements, cooperative system, work etc.

BE/0771-6796
**REVUE DE L'INSTITUT DE SOCIOLOGIE.** [Rev. Inst. sociol.]. **Main/Corp** Brussels. Universite Libre. Institut de Sociologie Sovay. **Added/Corp** Instituts Solvay. Institut de Sociologie. Institut de Sociologie Solvay. Universite Libre de Bruxelles. Institut de Sociologie. Fondation Universitaire de Belgique. Vol. 1, No. 1 (July 1920)-. Periodical. French. qt. 1300F (Belgium & Luxembourg); 1650F (other). Institut de Sociologie de l'Universite Libre de Bruxelles, Avenue Jeanne 44, 1050 Brussels Belgium. **Tel** 011 32 2 6503359, 011 32 2 6503457, FAX 011 32 2 6503521, telex UNILIB 23069 B. **LC** H13; .B728. **NLM** W1 RE79. **Bk Rev. Ad Acc. Circ:** 7,200. ***Continues*** *Bulletin (Instituts Solvay. Institut de Sociologie).*
**Desc:** The publication is devoted to the social sciences: political science, political economy, social economy, general sociology, and sociology of work.
**Ind/Abst** Am. Hist. Life (1969-1975, 1977-); Int. Bibliogr. Sociol.; Int. Labour Doc.; Soc. Plann. Policy Dev. Abstr.; Sociol. Abstr. [Full Cov.].

FR
**REVUE DES COMITES D'ENTREPRISE & EQUIVALENTS.** French. qt. 130.00F France; 215.00F other. Editions de la Vie Ouvriere, 33 rue Bouret, 75168 Paris Cedex 19 France. **Tel** 011 33 1 40403636, FAX 42 09 97 36, telex LAVEO 21114 GF.

FR/0336-1578
**REVUE DES SCIENCES SOCIALES DE LA FRANCE DE L'EST. Added/Corp** Universite des Sciences Humaines de Strasbourg. (1972)-. French. an. 120.00F. Universite des Sciences Humaines, 22 rue Descartes, 67084 Strasbourg Cedex France. **Tel** 011 33 88 417317. **ED** Freddy Raphael. **Ad Acc. Circ:** 900 (ctrl).
**Desc:** Devoted to cultural, economics, demographic and social problems of the eastern part of France.

BE
**REVUE DU TRAVAIL.** Vol. 1, No. 1 (Jan. 1896)-. Periodical. French. qt. Free. Ministere de l'Emploi Travail, 51 rue Belliard, B-1040 Bruxelles Belgium. **Tel** 32-2-233 44 42, FAX 32-2-233 4488. Index available. cum. index. **Ad Acc.**
**Ind/Abst** Int. Bibliogr. Sociol.; Int. Labour Doc.; LABORDOC; PAIS Int. Print; Saf. Health Work.

BE/0035-306X
**REVUE GENERALE. PERSPECTIVES EUROPEENES DES SCIENCES HUMAINES.** (Nov. 1945)-. Periodical. French. mo. Editions Duculot SA, Avenue de Lauzelle 65, B-1348 Louvain La Neuve Belgium. **Tel** 32 10 471911, FAX 32 10 471925. ***Formed by the union of*** *Revue Belge* ***and*** *Revue Generale.*

FR/0304-3037
**REVUE INTERNATIONALE DES SCIENCES SOCIALES.** [Rev. int. sci. soc.]. **VFOAT** International Journal of Social Sciences. (1949)-. Periodical. French. qt. 250.00F Third World countries; 390.00F other. Editions ERES, 11 rue des Alouettes 31520, Ramonville St. Agne France. **Tel** 011 33 61 751576. **UDC** 30. Index available (bound in last issue).
**Ind/Abst** LABORDOC.

FR/0035-385X
**REVUE POLITIQUE ET PARLEMENTAIRE.** (1894)-. Periodical. French. bm. 660.00F France; 740.00F other. Revue Politique et Parlementaire, 108 rue de Rivoli, 75001 Paris France. **Tel** 33 1 40390376, FAX 33 1 40390377. **ED** Editors: July 1894-Dec. 1901, Marcel Fournier; Jan. 1902- Fernand Foure. **LC** H3; .R4. cum. index.
**Ind/Abst** Am. Hist. Life (1954-1957,1965-1971); PAIS Int. Print.

RM/0035-4023
**REVUE ROUMAINE DES SCIENCES SOCIALES. SERIE DE SCIENCES JURIDIQUES.** [Rev. roum. sci. soc., Ser. sci. jurid.]. **Added/Corp** Academia Republicii Socialiste Rom„ania. Academia Republicii Populare Romine. Vol. 8 (1964)-. Periodical. French (English, German and Russian). sa. $95.00. Editura Academia Republicii Socialiste Romania, Calea Victoriei Nr 125, R-79717 Bucuresti Romania. **Tel** telex 10376 PRSFI R. **(Subscription address:** Orion Press SRL, SPL Independentei 202-A, Bucharest 6 Romania.) ***Supersedes in part*** *Revue des Sciences Sociales.*
**Desc:** Information and examination of the main problems of general theory and methodology in juridical sciences.
**Ind/Abst** Int. Bibliogr. Sociol.; Int. Polit. Sci. Abstr.

TI/0035-4333
**REVUE TUNISIENNE DE SCIENCES SOCIALES.** (REVUE TUNISIENNE DE SCIENCES SOCIALES : PUBLICATION DU CENTRE D'ETUDES ET DE RECHERCHES ECONOMIQUES ET SOCIALES.). [Rev. tunis. sci. soc.]. **Added/Corp** Jamiah Al-Tunisiyah. Markaz Al-Dirasat Wa-al-Abhath Al-Iqtisadiyah Wa-al-Ijtimaiyah. **VFOAT** Majallah Al-Tunisiyah Lil- Ulum Al-Ijtimaiyah. No. 1 (Sept. 1964)-. Periodical. French. ir. Price varies. CERES - Centre d'Etudes et de Recherches Economiques et Sociales, 23 rue d'Espagne, 1000 Tunis Tunisia. **Tel** 011 216 1 242994, 011 216 1 248053. **LC** H3; .R44. **NLM** W1 RE973S.
**Ind/Abst** MLA Int. Bibl. Books Artic. Mod. Lang. Lit.; Popul. Index.

JA
**RISSHO DAIGAKU JIMBUN KAGAKU KENKYUJO NEMPO. / ANNUAL REPORT OF THE INSTITUTE OF CULTURAL SCIENCES, RISSHO UNIVERSITY. Main/Corp** Rissho Daigaku. Jimbun Kagaku Kenkyujo. **Added/Corp** Rissho Daigaku. Jimbun Kagaku Kenkyujo. Annual Report of the Institute of Cultural Sciences, Rissho University. **VFOAT** Annual Report of the Institute of Cultural Sciences, Rissho University. (19??)-. Periodical. Japanese. an. Rissho Daigaku, 2 Osaki 4-chome Shinagawa-ku, Tokyo Japan. **LC** AS552.R56; A24.

IT/0393-3415
**RIVISTA DI STORIA ECONOMICA. See** Economics-Economic History, Conditions.

IT/0035-676X
**RIVISTA INTERNAZIONALE DI SCIENZE SOCIALI.** [Riv. int. sci. soc.]. **Added/Corp** Universita Cattolica del Sacro Cuore. Vol. 42 (1934)-. Periodical. Italian. Four times a year. L98000 Italy; $120.00 others. Vita e Pensiero, Pubblic University, Largo Gemelli 1, 20123 Milan Italy. **Tel** 011 39 2 72342310, 011 39 2 72342370. ***Continues*** *Rivista Internazionale di Scienze Sociali e Discipline Ausiliare.*
**Ind/Abst** Am. Hist. Life (1973-); Int. Bibliogr. Sociol.; Soc. Plann. Policy Dev. Abstr.; Sociol. Abstr. (?-?); Stat. Theory Method Abstr. (1959-1963).

IS/0334-4762
**RIV'ON LE-MEHKAR HEVRATI. Added/Corp** Universitat Hefah. Hug Le-Sotsyologyah. Universitat Hefah. Hug le-Madae Ha-Medinah. **VFOAT** Social Research Review. (1972)-. Periodical. Hebrew (English; summaries and/or abstracts in English). ir. $3.75. Zalman Aranne Workers College, 5 Nehardea Street, Tel Aviv Israel. **Tel** (03)5440888. **ED** Avraham Wolfensohn. **Bk Rev. Ad Acc. Circ:** 200.
**Desc:** Each issue gives a number of articles- surveys of researchers - in the social sciences(general). Anthropology and methodology of social sciences.

PL
**ROCZNIKI NAUK SPOECZNYCH. VFOAT** Annales des Sciences Sociales; Annals of Social Sciences. Multiple languages (French, German and Polish; summaries and/or abstracts in French, German and English). 70.00. **LC** H9; .R63.

XR/0069-2298
**ROZPRAVY CESKOSLOVENSKE AKADEMIE VED. RADA SPOLECENSKYCH VED. Main/Corp** Ceskoslovenska Akademie Ved. Vol. 63 (1953)-. Academic Scholarly Publication. Czech. **(Subscription address:** Artia Pegas Press Ltd., Palac Metro Narodni Trida 25, 11210 Prague 1 Czech Republic.) **LC** AS142. ***Supersedes*** *Rozpravy Ceske Akademie Ved a Umeni, Trida 1; Rozpravy Ceske Akademie Ved a Umeni, Trida 3.*
**Desc:** Prints original scholarly studies, supplying most recent scholarly information to not only professionals and scholars, but also for public both at home and abroad, regarding social sciences.
**Ind/Abst** Helminthol. Abstr. (1991-); Numis. Lit.

PL/0035-9629
**RUCH PRAWNICZY, EKONOMICZNY I SOCJOLOGICZNY. Added/Corp** Uniwersytet im. Adama Mickiewicza w Poznaniu. Akademia Ekonomiczna w Poznaniu. Vol. 24 (1962)-. Periodical. Polish (summaries and/or abstracts in English and French). qt. $56.00. **(Subscription address:** ARS Polona, PO Box 1001, 00068 Warsaw Poland.) ***Continues*** *Ruch Prawniczy I Ekonomiczny.*

●US/1066-0127
**RUSSIA AND HER NEIGHBORS.** [Russ. her neighb.]. **Added/Corp** Highgate Road Social Science Research Station (Berkeley, Calif.). (1992)-. Periodical. English. qt. $30.00 (institutions), $25.00 (individuals) US; $35.00 (institutions), $30.00 (individuals) other. Highgate Road Social Sciences Research Station, 32 Highgate Road, Berkeley CA 94707. **Tel** (510)525-3248, FAX (510)525-3313. **DD** 947. Index available. cum. index. **Bk Rev. Ad Acc. Circ:** 100-500. ***Continues*** *Station Relay.*
**Desc:** Research in and dissemination of information about Russian social sciences, particularly anthropology and sociology, including the study of Russian ethnic groups originating from the former Soviet Union.

●US/1061-1428
**RUSSIAN SOCIAL SCIENCE REVIEW.** (RUSSIAN SOCIAL SCIENCE REVIEW : A JOURNAL OF TRANSLATIONS.). [Russ. soc. sci. rev.]. Vol. 33, No. 2 (Mar./Apr. 1992)-. Periodical. English (translations available in Russian). bm. $118.00 US; $161.00 other. M. E. Sharpe Inc., 80 Business Park Drive, Armonk NY 10504. **Tel** (914)273-1800, (800)541-6563, FAX (914)273-2106. **LC** AS261; .S6. **DD** 057/.1. Documents available from UMI Article Clearinghouse. ***Continues*** *Soviet Review, 0038-5794.*
**Ind/Abst** Acad. Abstr. (Mar. 1992-); Acad. Search (Mar. 1992-); Mag. Search; Newsp. Period. Abstr. (1990-).

FR/0038-7282
**S.P.E.L.D - INFORMATION. See** Law.

US
**SAGE LIBRARY OF SOCIAL RESEARCH.** Vol. 1 (1973)-. Monographic series. English. ir. Price varies per volume. SAGE Periodical Press, 2455 Teller Road, Thousand Oaks CA 91320. **Tel** (805)499-0721, FAX (805)499-0871, telex 100799. **LC** UNC. Index available. **Acid Free.**

KO
**SAHOE KWAHAK NONCHONG. VFOAT** Journal of the Social Science. V. 1- Series-. Periodical. Korean. Kukche Taehak Sahoe Kwahak Yonguso, 2-2-2 Chungjong-no Sodaemun-ku, Seoul South Korea. **LC** H8.K6; S25.

KO
**SAHOE KWAHAK NONMUNJIP (MYONGJI TAEHAKKYO. SAHOE KWAHAK YONGUSO).** (SAHOE KWAHAK NONMUNJIP.). **VFOAT** Journal of Social Science. Periodical. English (Korean). Not for Sale. Myongji Taehak Chulpanbu, 50-3 Nam Kajwa-dong Sodaemun-ku, Seoul Korea. **LC** H8.K6; S256.

KO
**SAHOE KWAHAK (YONGNAM TAEHAKKYO. SAHOE KWAHAK YONGUSO).** (SAHOE KWAHAK.). **VFOAT** Social Science. Periodical. English (German and Korean). Yongnam Taehakkyo Sahoe Kwahak Yonguso, Taegu Korea. **LC** H8.K6; S23. **DD** 300/.5.
**Ind/Abst** Am. Hist. Life (1957-1958).

KO
**SAHOE KWAHAK YONGU (YONGNAM TAEHAKKYO. SAHOE KWAHAK YONGUSO).** (SAHOE KWAHAK YONGU.). **Added/Corp** Yongnam Taehakkyo. Sahoe Kwahak Yonguso. **VFOAT** Journal of Social Science. Vol. 1 No. 1.2 (Aug. 1981)-. Periodical. English (German and Korean). Not for sale. Institute of Social Science / South Korea, Yeungnam University, Gyongsan Korea. **LC** H8.K6; S26.

US/0160-7537
**SALT (KENNEBUNK). See** College and School Publications.

SW
**SAMHALLSVETENSKAPLIGA STUDIER.** (1946)-. Monographic series. Swedish. ir. Price varies per volume. Gleerup Bokforlag, Box 1205, 22105 Lund Sweden.

CN/0711-3021
**SASKATCHEWAN COUNCIL OF SOCIAL STUDIES TEACHER.** (SASKATCHEWAN COUNCIL OF SOCIAL STUDIES TEACHERS : NEWSLETTER.). [Sask. Counc. Soc. Stud. Teach.].

# Social Sciences

**Added/Corp** Saskatchewan Council of Social Studies Teachers. (Nov. 3, 1976)-. Newsletter. English. Saskatchewan Teachers Federation, PO Box 1108, Saskatoon Saskatchewan, S7K 3N3 Canada. **Tel** (306)373-1660. **DD** 300/.7/07124. **Continues** Social Studies Teachers Newsletter, 0711-3013.

US/0036-5637
**SCANDINAVIAN STUDIES: PUBLICATION OF THE SOCIETY FOR THE ADVANCEMENT OF SCANDINAVIAN STUDY.** See Literature.

GW/0723-4880
**SCHRIFTEN ZUR EUROPAISCHEN SOZIAL- UND VERFASSUNGSGESCHICHTE.** 1984-. Monographic series. German. Price varies per volume. Verlag Peter Lang AG, Jupiterstrasse 15, CH-3000 Bern 15 Switzerland. **Tel** 011 41 31 9411122, FAX 011 41 31 321131.

GW/0582-0588
**SCHRIFTEN ZUR WIRTSCHAFTS- UND SOZIALGESCHICHTE.** Vol. 1 (1966)-. Monographic series. German. ir (2 or 3 per year). Price varies per volume. Duncker und Humblot Verlag, Postfach 410329, D-12113 Berlin Germany. **Tel** 011 49 30 79000612, 011 49 30 79000613.

UK/0268-490X
**SCIENCE AND PUBLIC AFFAIRS (LONDON, ENGLAND).** (SCIENCE AND PUBLIC AFFAIRS). **Added/Corp** Royal Society (Great Britain). (1986)-. English. sa. £21.00 UK; US/Canada: £11.00 other. Royal Society, 6 Carlton House Terrace, London SW1Y 5AG England. **Tel** 011 44 71 839 5561, FAX 071-976 1837, telex 917876 ROYAL G. **ED** Walter Bodmer. **LC** Q175.4; .S29. **DD** 303.4/83/05. **Circ:** 628.
**Desc:** Covers policies in science and public affairs.
**Ind/Abst** Am. Hist. Life; Index Vet.; PAIS Int. Print; Rural Dev. Abstr.

US/0036-8237
**SCIENCE AND SOCIETY (NEW YORK. 1936).** (SCIENCE & SOCIETY.). [Sci. society]. **VFOAT** Science and Society. Vol. 1 (Fall 1936)-. Periodical. English. Four times a year. $75.00 (institutions); $90.00 others. Guilford Publications Inc., 72 Spring Street, New York NY 10012. **Tel** (212)431-9800, (800)365-7006, FAX (212)966-6708. **(Subscription address:** Turpin Distribution Services Limited, Blackhorse Road, Letchworth, Hertfordshire SG6 1HN, United Kingdom.**)** **ED** David Laibman. **LC** H1; .S25. **DD** 305. **NLM** W1 SC686. **[CCC].** Index available. cum. index. **Bk Rev. Ad Acc. Pr Rev.** available on microfilm and microfiche from University Microfilms International (UMI). Documents available from The Genuine Article, UMI Article Clearinghouse.
**Desc:** Oldest theoretical independent Marxist journal in the world. Subjects covered in history, humanities, economics and social sciences.
**Ind/Abst** ABC POL SCI; Acad. Abstr. Full Text Elite (July 1990-); Acad. Abstr. (July 1990-); Acad. Ind. [Computer File] (1987-); Acad. Search (July 1990-); Altern. Press Index; Am. Hist. Life (1963-); Am. Bibliogr. Slavic East Europ. Stud.; Appl. Soc. Sci. Index Abstr.; Arts Humanit. Citation Index [Select. Cov.]; Book Rev. Index; Curr. Contents Soc. Behav. Sci.; Econ. Lit. Index; Expand. Acad. Index (1987-); Gen. Sci. Source (Jul. 1990-); Health Source (Jul. 1990-); Index Period. Artic. Relat. Law; INFO-SOUTH Abstr.; Int. Bibliogr. Sociol.; Int. Labour Doc.; Int. Polit. Sci. Abstr.; J. Econ. Lit.; Left Index; Mag. Search; Middle East Abstr. Index; Newsp. Period. Abstr. (1990-); PAIS Int. Print (?-?); Res. Alert [Full Cov.]; Romant. Move.; Soc. Plann. Policy Dev. Abstr.; Soc. Sci. Source (Jul. 1990-); Soc. Sci. Cit. Index [Full Cov.]; Soc. Sci. Index; Soc. Sci. Index Fulltext (Fall 1988-) [Full Txt.]; Sociol. Abstr.; West. Hist. Q.; Women Stud. Abstr.; Work Relat. Abstr.

AE
**SCIENCES SOCIALES PANORAMA : REVUE TRIMESTRIELLE EDITEE SOUS L'EGIDE DU MINISTERE DE L'ENSEIGNEMENT SUPERIEUR ET DE LA RECHERCHE SCIENTIFIQUE, O.N.R.S. Added/Corp** Hayah al-Wataniyah lil-Bahth al-Ilmi (Algeria). **VFOAT** Ulum al-Ijtimaiyah; Revue des Sciences Sociales. No. 1 (Sept. 1979)-. Periodical. Arabic (French). ir. 150.00F. Sciences Sociales Panorama, 51 rue Didouche Mourad, Algiers Algeria. **LC** H1; .S26. **DD** 300/.5.

PE/0559-1414
**SCIENTIA ET PRAXIS.** [Sci. prax.]. **Added/Corp** Universidad Nacional Mayor de San Marcos. No. 1 (1964)-. Spanish (English). Grafica Panamericana, Av Javier Prado S/N Monterrico, Lima Peru. **LC** H8; .S34.
**Ind/Abst** Am. Hist. Life (1970-1971).

UK/0269-5030
**SCOTTISH ECONOMIC & SOCIAL HISTORY. Added/Corp** Economic and Social History Society of Scotland. University of Glasgow. Dept. of Economic History. **VFOAT** Scottish Economic and Social History. Vol. 1, No. 1 (1981)-. English. an. £15.00 UK; £10.00 other. Economic and Social History Society Scotland, University of Strathclyde History Department, Glasgow G1 1XQ Scotland. **Tel** 011 31 6671011 ext. 6354. **ED** Chris Watley. **LC** HC257.S4; S3276. **DD** 330.9411/005. **Ad Acc. Circ:** 600.
**Desc:** Articles, surveys, and reviews on all aspects of Scottish economic social history.
**Ind/Abst** Am. Hist. Life (1991-).

JA/0386-7536
**SEIKATSU KAGAKU KENKYUJO KENKYU HOKOKU.** See Science and Technology.

JA
**SEIKEI RONSO. Added/Corp** Meiji Daigaku. Seiji Keizai Kenkyujo. **VFOAT** Review of Economics and Political Science; Review of Economics & Political Science. (1926)-. Periodical. Japanese. bm. **LC** H8.J3; S45. cum. index.
**Ind/Abst** Am. Hist. Life (1954-1957).

US/0423-183X
**SELECTED PAPERS FROM THE ENGLISH INSTITUTE. Added/Corp** English Institute. No. 1 (1959)-. Monographic series. English. ir. price varies per volume. Johns Hopkins University Press, 2715 North Charles Street, Baltimore MD 21218-4319. **Tel** (410)516-6987, FAX (410)516-6968. **LC** UNC.
**Ind/Abst** MLA Int. Bibl. Books Artic. Mod. Lang. Lit.

US
**SELECTIONS FROM THE ANNALES, ECONOMIES, SOCIETES, CIVILISATIONS.** (19??)-. Monographic series. English. ir. Price varies per volume. Johns Hopkins University Press, 2715 North Charles Street, Baltimore MD 21218-4319. **Tel** (410)516-6987, FAX (410)516-6968. **ED** Robert Forster and Orest A. Ranum. Index available. **Bk Rev. Circ:** 4,000.
**Desc:** Covers social science and international historic research.
**Ind/Abst** Arts Humanit. Citation Index (19??-19??) [Full Cov.]; Geogr. Abstr. Human Geogr.

TU
**SEMINER.** (1982)-. Turkish. an. Ege Universitesi / Sosyal Bilimler, Sosyal Bilimler Fakültesi, Bornova Izmir Turkey. **LC** H62.5.T8; S45.

US/1054-8386
**SEMIOTICS AND THE HUMAN SCIENCES.** [Semiot. human sci.]. **VFOAT** Semiotics & the Human Sciences. Vol. 1 (1991)-. Monographic series. English. Peter Lang Publishing, 62 West 45th Street, 4th Floor, New York NY 10036. **Tel** (212)764-1471, (800)770-5264, telex 6973364 PLNY. **DD** 302.

CN/0316-8379
**SERIAL TITLES IN THE HUMANITIES AND SOCIAL SCIENCES (WINDSOR).** See Humanities.

PE
**SERIE COSTA CENTRAL / TALLER DE ESTUDIOS ANDINOS.** No. 1-. Monographic series. Spanish. Price varies per volume. Taller de Estudios Andinos, Department de Ciencias Humanas Apartado 456, la Molina Lima Peru.

FR
**SERIE U.R.S.S. VAT** Serie Union des Republiques Socialistes Sovietiques. French. 20.00F. Documentation Francaise, 29 Quai Voltaire, 75344 Paris Cedex 7 France. **Tel** 011 33 1 40157000, FAX 011 33 1 40157230, telex 204 826 DOCFRAN. **LC** H3; .P73 subser. **DD** 300/.8 S; 309.1/47.

RH
**SERIES IN SOCIAL STUDIES : OCCASIONAL PAPER. Added/Corp** University of Rhodesia. (1974)-. Monographic series. English. an. Price varies per volume. University of Zimbabwe / Department of Sociology, PO Box HP 45, Mount Pleasant Harare Rhodesia.
**Desc:** Covers sociology, population studies and anthropology.

UY
**SERVICIO DE DOCUMENTACION SOCIAL.** Periodical. Spanish. qt. Instituo de Estudios Socials Consejo Uruguays de Bienestar Social, Pza Independencia 838 P 5 Esc 19, Montevideo Uruguay. **LC** HV110.5; .S38. **Continues** Servicio de Documentacion (Montevideo, Uruguay).

US
**SEXUAL ABUSE.** See Public Health and Safety.

JA
**SHAKAI BUNKA KENKYU. Added/Corp** Hiroshima Daigaku. Sogo Kagakubu. **VFOAT** Studies in Social Sciences. Vol. 1 (1975)-. Periodical. Japanese. Hiroshima Daigaku Sogo Kagakubu, (Faculty of Integrated Arts and Sciences, Hiroshima University), 1-89 Higashisendacho 1-chome, Nakaku Hiroshimashi, Hiroshimaken 730 Japan. **LC** H8; .S39.

JA/0387-3307
**SHAKAI KAGAKU KENKYU (TOKYO. 1948).** (SHAKAI KAGAKU KENKYU.). [Shakai kagaku kenkyu]. **VFOAT** Journal of Social Science. V. 1 (1948)-. Periodical. English. bm.
**Ind/Abst** Am. Hist. Life (1954-).

JA
**SHAKAI KAGAKU RON SHU. Added/Corp** Kochi Tanki Daigaku Shakai Kagakukai. Kochi Tanki Daigaku. Kochi Tanki Daigaku Kenkyu Hokoku. Kochi Tanki Daigaku. Report of Studies, Kochi Junior College. **VFOAT** Shakaikagaku Ronshu, Report of Studies, Kochi Junior College; Shakaikagaku Ronshu. (19??)-. Periodical. Japanese. Kochi Tanki Daigaku Shakai Kagakukai, 5-ban 15-go Eikokujicho, Kochi Japan. **LC** H8; .S446.

JA
**SHAKAI KAGAKU TOKYU. VFOAT** Social Science Review; Waseda Bulletin of Social Sciences. V. 1- 1956-. Periodical. Multiple languages (English and Japanese). Waseda Daigaku Shakai Kagaku Kenkyujo, 1-6-7 Totsukamachi, Shinjuku-ku 160 Tokyo Japan. **LC** H8; .S4463.
**Ind/Abst** Am. Hist. Life (1956, 1962-).

JA
**SHAKAI SHISO SHI KENKYU. Added/Corp** Shakai Shiso Shigakkai. Shakai Shiso Shigakkai Nempo. Shakai Shiso Shigakkai. **VFOAT** Annals of the Society for the History of Social Thought. **VFOAT** Annals of the Society for the History of Social Thought. (1977)-. Periodical. Japanese. an. Hokuju Shuppan, 153 1-2-6 Nakameguro, Meguro-ku Tokyo-to Japan. **Tel** 03-715-1525. **LC** H8; .S4465. **Circ:** 2,000.

JA/0285-4015
**SHAKAIGAKU KENKYUJO KIYO. VFOAT** Bulletin of Sociological Studies. Japanese. Bukkyo Daigaku Shakaigaku Kenkyujo, 96 Murasakino Kita, Hananobo-ku Kita-ku, 603 Kyoto-shi Japan. **LC** H8.J3; S5.

JA
**SHAKAIKA KYOIKU KENKYU / NIHON SHAKAIKA KYOIKU GAKKAI HENSHU. VFOAT** The Journal of Social Studies; Journal of Social Studies. Began in 1953. Japanese (Japanese). Nihon Shakaika Kyoiku Gakkai, c/o Tokyo Gakugei Daigaku Shakaika Kyoiku Kenkyushitsu Nukui Kita-Machi 4-chome, Koganei-shi Tokyo-to 184 Japan. **LC** H62.5.J3; S478.

JA
**SHAKAIKA KYOIKU RONSO : NIHON SHAKAIKA KYOIKU KENKYUKAI NENPO. Added/Corp** Nihon Shakaika Kyoiku Kenkyukai. **VFOAT** Nihon Shakaika Kyoiku Kenkyukai Nenpo. (19??)-. Japanese. an. Nihon Shakaika Kyoiku Kenkyukai, c/o Hiroshima Daigaku Kyoiku Gakabu, Higashi Senda-cho, Naka-ku, Hiroshima-shi Japan. **LC** H62.5.J3; S483.

CC
**SHAN-HSI SHIH TA HSUEH PAO. CHE HSUEH SHE HUI KO HSUEH PAN. Added/Corp** Shan-hsi Shih fan ta Hsueh (Sian, China). **VFOAT** Shannxi Shida Xuebao; Shaanxi Teachers University Journal. Philosophy and Social Sciences. (19??)-. Periodical. Chinese. Four times a year. $12.08. Science Press, 16 Donghuangchenggen North Street, Beijing 100707, People's Republic of China. **Tel** 011 86 1 4019821, 011 86 1 4010642, FAX 011 86 1 4012180, 011 86 1 4019810, telex 210147. **(Subscription address:** China International Book Trading Corporation, PO Box 399, Library Service Department, Beijing 100044 People's Republic of China.**) ED** Yin Shiming, Xie Hengshan, Chen Jianzhong, Qu Jiayuan and Niu Xiao. **LC** H8.C47; S52. **DD** 059/.951. **Bk Rev. Ad Acc. Circ:** 10,000.
**Desc:** It is recognized as one of the major academic periodicals published in China. It has wide social influence both internally and abroad.

CC
**SHAN-HSI TA HSUEH HSUEH PAO. CHE HSUEH SHE HUI KO HSUEH PAN. Added/Corp** Shan-Hsi ta Hsueh. **VFOAT** Shanxi University Journal; Shanxi University Journal. Philosophy and Social Sciences. (19??)-. Periodical. Chinese. qt. Post Office / China, People's Republic of China. **LC** AS452.T38; A38. **DD** 300/.5.

CC
**SHE HUI KO HSUEH CHI KAN (LIAO-NING SHE HUI KO HSUEH YUAN).** (SHE HUI KO HSUEH CHI KAN.). **VFOAT**

Shehuikexuejikan. Periodical. Chinese. bm. RMBY0.60. Science Press, 16 Donghuangchenggen North Street, Beijing 100707, People's Republic of China. **Tel** 011 86 1 4019821, 011 86 1 4010642, FAX 011 86 1 4012180, 011 86 1 4019810, telex 210147. **LC** H8.C47; S53. **DD** 300/.5.

CH
**SHE HUI KO HSUEH (LAN-CHOU SHIH, CHINA).** (SHE HUI KO HSUEH / KAN-SU SHENG SHE HUI KO HSUEH YUAN CHU PAN.). **VFOAT** Social Science. Periodical. Chinese. bm. NT$0.30. Post Office Lan-Chou Shih, Lan-Chou Shih, People's Republic of China. **LC** AS452.L37; A3. **DD** 300/.5.

CC
**SHE HUI KO HSUEH / SHANG-HAI SHE HUI KO HSUEH YUAN, SHE HUI KO HSUEH PIEN WEI HUI.** **VFOAT** Shehui Kexue; She Hui Kexue; Social Sciences. Periodical. Chinese. mo. RMBY0.35. Science Press, 16 Donghuangchenggen North Street, Beijing 100707, People's Republic of China. **Tel** 011 86 1 4019821, 011 86 1 4010642, FAX 011 86 1 4012180, 011 86 1 4019810, telex 210147. **LC** AS451; .S48. **DD** 300/.5.

CH/0077-5835
**SHEHUI KEXUE LUNCONG.** (SHE HUI KO HSUEH LUN TSUNG.). [Shehui kexue luncong]. **Added/Corp** Kuo li Tai-wan ta Hsueh. Fa Hsueh Yuan. **VFOAT** Journal of Social Science. (1950)-. Periodical. Chinese (English). an. National Taiwan University / College of Law, Taipei, Taiwan. **Tel** FAX 02-3948914. **LC** H8.C47; S55. **DD** 300/.5.
**Ind/Abst** Am. Hist. Life (1966-).

CH/0258-8412
**SI YU YAN.** **See** Humanities.

US/0736-6906
**SIGCHI BULLETIN.** **See** Computers-Computer Systems.

MR
**SIGNES DU PRESENT.** ***Suspended.*** **VFOAT** Bulletin Economique et Social du Maroc. No. 1 (Feb./April 1988)-?. Periodical. French. qt. Societe d'Etudes Economiques, BP 535, Rabat-Chellah Morocco. ***Continues*** *Bulletin Economique et Social du Maroc.*

US/1046-8781
**SIMULATION & GAMING.** **See** Computers-Simulation.

BL/0103-4332
**SINTESE.** New No., V. 1- (No. 1- ); Jan./June 1974-. Portuguese. $25.00. Centro Joao XXIII RJ e Grupo de Reflexao, Belo Horizonte Brazil. **Tel** (031)4410233. **LC** H8; .S49. **Bk Rev.** **Ad Acc.** **Circ:** 500. ***Continues*** *Sintese Politicia, Economica, Social.*
**Ind/Abst** Int. Polit. Sci. Abstr.

AG
**SINTOMAS EN LA CIENCIA, LA CULTURA, Y LA TECNICA.** No. 1 (Nov. 1980)-. Periodical. Spanish. sa.

SP/0210-0223
**SISTEMA (MADRID).** (SISTEMA.). [Sistema]. **Added/Corp** Fundacion Fondo Social Universitario. Instituto de Tecnicas Sociales. No. 1 (Jan. 1973)-. Spanish. ir. 4500ptas Spain; 5500ptas other. Fundacion Sistema, Calle Fuencarrral 127, Piso 1, 28010 Madrid Spain. **Tel** 011 34 1 4487319 or, 4487339. **LC** H8; .S53. Index available. cum. index. **Bk Rev.** **Ad Acc.** **Circ:** 8,000.
**Ind/Abst** Am. Hist. Life (1973-1974); Int. Bibliogr. Sociol.; Int. Polit. Sci. Abstr.; PAIS Int. Print.

US/0037-7333
**SMITHSONIAN.** **See** Natural History.

US
**SMITHSONIAN FOLKLIFE STUDIES.** **VFOAT** Folklife Studies. No. 1-. Monographic series. English. Price varies per volume. Smithsonian Institute, 1000 Jefferson Drive SW, Washington DC 20560. **Tel** (202)357-1300. **DD** 306.

BE
**SOCIAAL.** ir. 1150.00F. Santvoortbeeklaan 21-23, B-2100 Deurne Belgium. **Tel** 011 32 3 3256880.

US/0272-765X
**SOCIAL ACTION & THE LAW.** ***Ceased.*** **See** Law.

AT/0155-977X
**SOCIAL ANALYSIS (ADELAIDE, S. AUST.).** (SOCIAL ANALYSIS.). [Soc. anal.]. **Added/Corp** University of Adelaide. Dept. of Anthropology. No. 1 (Feb. 1979)-. Periodical. English. Twice a year. 49.00Aus$ (institutions), 31.00Aus$ (individuals) Australia; 50.80Aus$ (institutions), 32.80Aus4 (individuals) other. University of Adelaide / Department of Anthropology, Adelaide SA 5005 Australia. **Tel** 011 61 8 3706806, FAX (08)22-20264, telex UNIVAD AA 89141. **ED** Kingsley Garbett. **LC** HM1; .S616. **DD** 301/.05. **Ad Acc.** **Pr Rev.** **Circ:** 300 (ctrl).
**Desc:** Publishes articles primarily in the fields of anthropology and sociology but includes articles from cognate disciplines where these contribute to deepening our understanding of human behavior.
**Ind/Abst** Anthropol. Lit.; APAIS, Aust. Public Aff. Inf. Ser. (1983-); Int. Bibliogr. Sociol.; Soc. Plann. Policy Dev. Abstr.

US
**SOCIAL AND BEHAVIORAL SCIENCES JOURNAL.** **Added/Corp** University of South Carolina at Aiken. College of Social Sciences and Professions. (198?)-. Periodical. English. an. University of South Carolina Social and Behavioral Sciences, Aiken SC 29801. **LC** H1; .S48. **DD** 300/.5. ***Continues*** *Social and Behavioral Sciences.*

JM/0037-7651
**SOCIAL AND ECONOMIC STUDIES.** [Soc. econ. stud.]. **Added/Corp** University of the West Indies (Mona, Jamaica). Institute of Social and Economic Research. University College of the West Indies (Mona, Jamaica). Institute of Social and Economic Research. Vol. 1, (Feb. 1953)-. Periodical. English (French and Spanish). qt. $40.00 (institution); $25.00 (individual). Institute of Social and Economic Research / Jamaica, University of the West Indies, Mona Kingston 7 Jamaica. **Tel** (809)927-1660 ext 2408, FAX (809)927-2409. **ED** J Edward Greene (809)927-1020. **LC** HN244; .S6. **DD** 972.9. Index available. cum. index. **Bk Rev.** **Ad Acc.** **Adv Mgr:** Ms. A Paul, **Tel** (809)927-1020. **Circ:** 730 (ctrl). available on microfilm and microfiche from University Microfilms International (UMI). Documents available from The Genuine Article.
**Desc:** Contains reports on the work undertaken by, or in association with, the Institute of Social & Economic Research. It welcomes contributions on the social, economic and political problems and policy issues of the Caribbean, Latin America and the Third World, as well as contributions of a general theoretical nature.
**Ind/Abst** Am. Hist. Life (1970-)(1957-); Anthropol. Index; Appl. Soc. Sci. Index Abstr.; Contents Recent Econ. J.; Econ. Lit. Index; HAPI Hisp. Am. Period. Index; Int. Bibliogr. Sociol.; Int. Dev. Abstr. (?-?); Int. Labour Doc.; J. Econ. Lit.; LABORDOC; Multicult. Educ. Abstr.; PAIS Int. Print (?-?); Peace Res. Abstr. J. (1961-1964); Popul. Index (?-?); Res. Alert [Full Cov.]; Soc. Plann. Policy Dev. Abstr.; Soc. Sci. Cit. Index [Full Cov.]; Soc. Sci. Index; Sociol. Abstr.; Sociol. Educ. Abstr.; Stud. Women Abstr.

UK/0037-7686
**SOCIAL COMPASS.** [Soc. compass]. **Added/Corp** Centre de Recherches Socio-Religieuses. Katholiek Sociaal-Kerkelijk Instituut. International Catholic Institute for Social Research. Roomsch-Katholieke Centraal Bureau voor Onderwijs en Opvoeding. International Federation of Catholic Institutes for Social Research. International Federation of Institutes for Social and Socio-Religious Research. Universite Catholique de Louvain (1970- ). **VFOAT** Sociaal Kompas. Vol. 1 (May/June 1953)-. Periodical. Dutch (English, French and German). qt. £88.00. Sage Publications Ltd., 6 Bonhill Street, London EC2A 4PU, UK. **Tel** 071 374 0645, FAX 071 374 8741, telex 296207 SAGE G. **ED** F. Houtart and A. Bastenier. **LC** BL60; .S6. **DD** 306/.6. cum. index. **Pr Rev.** **Acid Free.** Documents available from The Genuine Article.
**Desc:** Provides a uniqe forum for all scholars in sociology, anthropology, religious studies and theology concerned with the sociology of religion.
**Ind/Abst** Arts Humanit. Citation Index [Full Cov.]; Curr. Contents Arts Humanit.; Curr. Contents Soc. Behav. Sci.; Index Book Rev. Relig.; Int. Bibliogr. Sociol.; Int. Polit. Sci. Abstr.; Middle East Abstr. Index; Relig. Index One Period. (1971-); Relig. Theol. Abstr.; Res. Alert [Full Cov.]; Soc. Plann. Policy Dev. Abstr.; Soc. Sci. Cit. Index [Full Cov.]; Sociol. Abstr. [Full Cov.].

US/0737-7762
**SOCIAL CONCEPT.** ***Ceased.*** [Soc. concept]. Vol. 1, No. 1 (May 1983)-Vol. 7. Periodical. English. an. Social Concept, University of Notre Dame, 406 Decio Hall, Notre Dame IN 46556. **Tel** (219)631-8294, FAX (219)631-8609. **ED** Philip Mirowski. **LC** H1; .S523. **DD** 300/.5. Index available. **Bk Rev.** **Ad Acc.** **Pr Rev.** **Circ:** 500 (ctrl).
**Desc:** Investigation of nature of social life as a complex system: its inner logic, manifold contradictions, and laws of self-development. Treatment of economic and social history, and history of social sciences.
**Ind/Abst** Left Index.

US/0037-7724
**SOCIAL EDUCATION.** [Soc. educ.]. **Added/Corp** National Council for the Social Studies. American Historical Association. Vol. 1 (Jan. 1937)-. Periodical. English. Seven times a year. $55.00 (institutions) US; $60.00 overseas. National Council for the Social Studies, 3501 Newark Street Northwest, Washington DC 20016-3167. **Tel** (202)966-7840, FAX (202)966-2061. **ED** Salvatore J. Natoli. **LC** H62.A1; S6. **DD** 307. Index available in last issue of volume--attached. cum. index. **Bk Rev.** **Ad Acc.** available on microfilm and microfiche from University Microfilms International (UMI). Documents available from UMI Article Clearinghouse.
**Ind/Abst** Acad. Ind. [Computer File] (1987-); Am. Hist. Life (1963-); Am. Bibliogr. Slavic East Europ. Stud.; Appl. Soc. Sci. Index Abstr.; Book Rev. Index; Contents Pages Educ.; Curr. Geogr. Publ. (199?-); Curr. Index J. Educ.; Educ. Index; Educ. Adm. Abstr. (?-?); Expand. Acad. Index (1987-); Hum. Rights Intern. Rep.; Med. Rev. Dig.; Middle East Abstr. Index; Newsp. Period. Abstr. (1989-); Sociol. Educ. Abstr.; SportSearch; Stud. Women Abstr.; West. Hist. Q.; Women Stud. Abstr.

IT
**SOCIAL FORECASTING: DOCUMENTATION.** **Added/Corp** Istituto Ricerche Applicate Documentazione e Studi. (19??)-. English. **LC** CB158; .S6. **DD** 309/.025.

US/0885-6729
**SOCIAL INDICATORS NETWORK NEWS.** (SOCIAL INDICATORS NETWORK NEWS : SINET.). [Soc. indic. netw. news]. **VFOAT** SINET. (Fall 1984)-. Periodical. English. qt. $16.00 US and Canada; $18.00 other. SINET, Abbott L. Ferriss, PO Box 24064, Emory University, Atlanta GA 30322. **Tel** (404)373-4756. **ED** Abbott L Ferriss. **DD** 303. **Bk Rev.** **Ad Acc.** **Circ:** 400. ***Continues*** *Social Indicators Newsletter, 0363-3195.*
**Desc:** Reports on on-going and published social indicator and quality of life studies of interest to policymaking, evaluation, measurement of social change, etc.
**Ind/Abst** Protozoolog. Abstr.

NE/0303-8300
**SOCIAL INDICATORS RESEARCH.** [Soc. indic. res.]. Vol. 1 (May 1974)-. Periodical. English. ir (Nine issues per year). $912.00. Kluwer Academic Publishers, Postbus 322, 3300 AH Dordrecht, The Netherlands. **Tel** 011 (31) 78 524400, FAX 011 31 78 183273, telex 20083. **ED** Alex C Michalos. **LC** HN25; .S64. **DD** 309/.07/2. **NLM** W1 SO115. **[CCC].** **Bk Rev.** **Ad Acc.** **Pr Rev.** **Acid Free.** **Circ:** 800. available on microfilm and microfiche from University Microfilms International (UMI). Documents available from The Genuine Article, UMI Article Clearinghouse.
**Desc:** Health, population, shelter, transportation, natural environment, social customs and morality, mental health, law enforcement, politics, education, religion, the media and the arts, etc. are topics covered.
**Ind/Abst** Acad. Search (July 1993-); AGRICOLA; Appl. Soc. Sci. Index Abstr.; Curr. Contents Soc. Behav. Sci.; Educ. Adm. Abstr. (?-?); Expand. Acad. Index (1992-); Hum. Resour. Abstr. (?-?); Index Period. Artic. Relat. Law (19??-19??); INFO-SOUTH Abstr.; Int. Bibliogr. Sociol.; Leis. Recreat. Tour. Abstr.; Mag. Search; Middle East Abstr. Index; Newsp. Period. Abstr. (1992-); PAIS Int. Print; Philos. Index; Psychol. Abstr. (1987-); PsycINFO; PsycLit; Res. Alert [Full Cov.]; Rural Dev. Abstr.; Sage Fam. Stud. Abstr. (?-?); Sage Urban Stud. Abstr (?-?); Soc. Plann. Policy Dev. Abstr.; Soc. Sci. Cit. Index [Full Cov.]; Soc. Work Abstr. [Select. Cov.]; Sociol. Abstr.; World Agric. Econ.

US/0885-7466
**SOCIAL JUSTICE RESEARCH (NEW YORK, N.Y.).** (SOCIAL JUSTICE RESEARCH.). [Soc. justice res.]. Vol. 1, No. 1 (Mar. 1987)-. Periodical. English. Four times a year. $185.00 institutions, $42.00 individuals US; $215.00 institutions, $52.00 individuals other. Plenum Press, 233 Spring Street, New York NY 10013-1578. **Tel** (212)620-8000, (800)221-9369, FAX (212)463-0742, (212)807-1047, telex 23/421139. **ED** Melvin J. Lerner. **LC** JC578; .S56. **DD** 320/.01/1. **CODEN** SJREEO. **[CCC].** available on microfilm and microfiche from University Microfilms International (UMI).
**Ind/Abst** Appl. Soc. Sci. Index Abstr.; Crim. Justice Abstr.; Soc. Plann. Policy Dev. Abstr.

US/0882-3529
**SOCIAL MARKETING UPDATE.** (ACTUALIDADES SOBRE MERCADO SOCIAL.). Periodical. Spanish (translations available in English). qt. Free. The Futures Group, 1029 Vermont Avenue NW, Washington DC 20005. **DD** 363.

UK/0265-0525
**SOCIAL PHILOSOPHY & POLICY.** **Added/Corp** Bowling Green State University. Social Philosophy & Policy Center. **VFOAT** Social Philosophy and Policy. Vol. 1, Issue 1 (Autumn 1983)-. Academic Scholarly Publication. English. sa. $75.00 US, Canada & Mexico; £50.00 other. Cambridge University Press, The Edinburgh Building, Shaftesbury Road, Cambridge CB2 2RU United Kingdom. **Tel** 011 44 223 312393, FAX 011 44 223 325959. **(Subscription address:** Cambridge University Press / North America, 110 Midland Avenue, Port Chester NY 10573.**)** **ED** Ellen Frankel Paul, Fred D. Miller, Jr and Jeffrey Paul. **LC** H61; .S5898. **DD** 361.6/1/05. **[CCC].** **Pr Rev.** available on microfilm and microfiche from University Microfilms International (UMI). Documents available from The Genuine Article.
**Desc:** An interdisciplinary journal with an emphasis on the philosophical underpinnings of enduring social policy debates. The issues are thematic in format, examining a specific area of concern with contributions from scholars in philosophy, economics, political science and law. While not primarily a journal of policy prescriptions, articles typically connect theory with practice.
**Ind/Abst** Appl. Soc. Sci. Index Abstr.; Arts Humanit. Citation Index (19??-19??) [Full Cov.]; Curr. Contents Arts Humanit.; Curr. Contents Soc. Behav. Sci.; Index Period. Artic. Relat. Law (19??-19??); Int. Bibliogr. Sociol.; Int. Polit. Sci. Abstr.; Philos. Index; Res. Alert [Full Cov.]; Soc. Plann. Policy Dev. Abstr.; Soc. Sci. Cit. Index [Full Cov.].

UK/0276-9654
**SOCIAL POLICY RESEARCH MONOGRAPHS SERIES.** [Soc. policy res. monogr. ser.]. 1-. Monographic series. English. ir. Price varies per volume. John Wiley & Sons Ltd., Baffins Lane, Chichester West Sussex PO19 1UD England. **Tel** 0243 779777, FAX 0243 776128 BTG:JWP001, telex 86290 WIBOOKG. **(Subscription address:** North, South and Central America/ John Wiley & Sons, Inc., Subscription Department, 605 Third Avenue, New York, NY 10158-0012, USA; telephone: (212)850-6645; FAX: (212)850-6021**)**

US/0192-8686
**SOCIAL PRACTICE.** Fall 1978-. Periodical. English. qt. $6.00. Inter-University Consortium for Ethics and Aesthetics, PO Box 211, Winfield IL 60190. **LC** HN1; .S57. **DD** 300/.5.

US/0037-7791
**SOCIAL PROBLEMS.** [Soc. probl.]. **Added/Corp** Society for the Study of Social Problems. Vol. 1, (June 1953)-. Academic Scholarly Publication. English. qt (Feb., May, Aug., Nov.). $77.00. University of California Press, 2120 Berkeley Way, Berkeley CA 94720. **Tel** (510)642-4191, (510)642-3907, FAX (510)642-9917. **ED** Robert Perrucci. **LC** HN1; .S58. **DD** 301.153; 301.46*. **NLM** W1 SO123. **CODEN** SOPRAG. **[CCC].** cum. index. **Bk Rev. Ad Acc. Pr Rev. Circ:** 3,500 (ctrl). available on microfilm and microfiche from University Microfilms International (UMI). Documents available from The Genuine Article, UMI Article Clearinghouse.
**Desc:** Articles cover a broad range of social phenomena. Recent articles deal with health and illness, crime and deviance, corporate power, sexual and racial discrimination, migrant and immigrant workers.
**Ind/Abst** Acad. Abstr. Full Text Elite (July 1990-); Acad. Abstr. (July 1990-); Acad. Search (July 1990-); AGRICOLA; Am. Hist. Life (1974-); Appl. Soc. Sci. Index Abstr.; Commun. Abstr. (?-?); Curr. Contents Soc. Behav. Sci.; Curr. Index J. Educ.; EMBASE; Health Plan. Adminis.; High. Educ. Abstr. (1965-); Hum. Resour. Abstr.; Index Period. Artic. Relat. Law; INFO-SOUTH Abstr.; Int. Bibliogr. Sociol.; Int. Polit. Sci. Abstr.; J. Plan. Lit.; Mag. Search; Newsp. Period. Abstr. (1986-); PAIS Int. Print; Peace Res. Abstr. J. (1976-1982); Psychol. Abstr. (1954-); PsycINFO; PsycLit; Res. Alert [Full Cov.]; Res. High. Educ. Abstr.; Sage Fam. Stud. Abstr.; Soc. Plann. Policy Dev. Abstr.; Soc. Sci. Source (Jul. 1990-); Soc. Sci. Cit. Index [Full Cov.]; Soc. Sci. Index; Soc. Sci. Index Fulltext (Oct. 1988-) [Full Txt.]; Soc. Work Abstr. [Select. Cov.]; Sociol. Abstr. [Full Cov.]; Sociol. Educ. Abstr.; Stud. Women Abstr.; Women Stud. Abstr.; Work Relat. Abstr.

US/0737-6871
**SOCIAL PROCESS IN HAWAII (1979).** (SOCIAL PROCESS IN HAWAII.). [Soc. process Hawaii]. **Added/Corp** University of Hawaii at Manoa. Dept. of Sociology. Vol. 27 (1979)-. Periodical. English. an. $6.00. University of Hawaii Press, 2840 Kolowalu Street, Honolulu HI 96822. **Tel** (808)956-8833, (808)948-8697, FAX (808)988-6052. **ED** Kiyoshi Ikeda and Michael G Weinstein. **Ad Acc. Circ:** 100 (ctrl). ***Continues** Social Process.*
**Desc:** Current issues reflect both the traditional social science image of Hawaii as a social laboratory and the state's image as a microcosm of the modern world.

US/0037-783X
**SOCIAL RESEARCH.** [Soc. res.]. **Added/Corp** New School for Social Research. Graduate Faculty of Political and Social Science. Vol. 1 (Feb. 1934)-. Periodical. English. qt. $70.00 (institutions), $24.00 (individuals) US; $74.00 (institutions), $28.00 (individuals) other. New School for Social Research, 65 Fifth Avenue, Room 354, New York NY 10003. **Tel** (212)229-5659, FAX (212)229-5315. **ED** Arien Mack (editors telephone: (212) 229-5776). **LC** H1; .S53. **DD** 305. **NLM** W1 SO125. **Pr Rev. Circ:** 3,000. available in reprints (Kraus Reprint Co.); available on microfilm and microfiche from University Microfilms International (UMI). Documents available from The Genuine Article, UMI Article Clearinghouse.
**Desc:** An international quarterly of the social sciences.
**Ind/Abst** ABC POL SCI; Acad. Abstr. Full Text Elite (Jan. 1992-); Acad. Abstr. (Jan. 1992-); Acad. Search (Jan. 1992-); Am. Hist. Life (1970-); Am. Bibliogr. Slavic East Europ. Stud.; Appl. Soc. Sci. Index Abstr.; Arts Humanit. Citation Index [Select. Cov.]; Commun. Abstr. (?-?); Crim. Penol. Police Sci. Abstr.; Curr. Contents Soc. Behav. Sci.; Expand. Acad. Index (1989-); INFO-SOUTH Abstr.; Int. Bibliogr. Sociol.; Int. Labour Doc.; Int. Polit. Sci. Abstr.; J. Econ. Lit.; Mag. Search; Middle East Abstr. Index; Newsp. Period. Abstr. (1991-); PAIS Int. Print (1968-1984); Peace Res. Abstr. J. (1963-1986); Res. Alert [Full Cov.]; Soc. Plann. Policy Dev. Abstr.; Soc. Sci. Source (Jan. 1992-); Soc. Sci. Cit. Index [Full Cov.]; Soc. Sci. Index; Soc. Sci. Index Fulltext (Autumn 1988-) [Full Txt.]; Sociol. Abstr.; U.S. Polit. Sci. Doc.; West. Hist. Q.

NE/0167-8477
**SOCIAL RESEARCH METHODOLOGY ABSTRACTS.** **See** Social Sciences-Abstracting, Bibliographies and Statistics.

US/0277-9536
**SOCIAL SCIENCE & MEDICINE (1982).** (SOCIAL SCIENCE & MEDICINE.). [Soc. sci. med.]. **VFOAT** Social Science and Medicine. Vol. 16, No. 1 (1982)-. Periodical. English. Twenty-four times a year. $1796.00 The Americas; £1205.00 other. Pergamon Press, An Imprint of Elsevier Science Ltd., The Boulevard, Langford Lane, Kidlington, Oxford OX5 1GB United Kingdom. **Tel** 011 44 865 843000, 011 44 865 843699, FAX 011 44 865 843010. **(Subscription address:** Elsevier Science Ltd. Oxford Fulfillment Centre, PO Box 800, Kidlington, Oxford OX5 1DX United Kingdom.**)** **ED** Peter J. M. McEwan. **LC** RA418; .S644. **DD** 362.1/05. **NLM** W1 SO127G. **CODEN** SSMDEP. **[CCC]. Bk Rev. Ad Acc. Pr Rev.** available on microfilm and microfiche from University Microfilms International (UMI); available on microfiche from the publisher. Documents available from The Genuine Article, BIOSIS Document Express, UMI Article Clearinghouse. ***Formed by the union of** Social Science & Medicine. Part A, 0271-7123; Social Science & Medicine. Part B, 0160-7987; Social Science & Medicine. Part C, 0160-7995; Social Science & Medicine. Part D, 0160-8002; Social Science & Medicine. Part E, 0271-5384 **and** Social Science & Medicine. Part F, 0271-5392.*
**Desc:** Provides an international forum for the exchange of ideas and information among social scientists, medical researchers and practitioners, and health administrators and planners. Emphasis is placed on the practical application of research to solve current problems in preventive medicine, health care and the comparative analysis of health systems.
**Ind/Abst** Abstr. Res. Pastor. Care Couns. (19??-); Annals Behav. Med.; Appl. Soc. Sci. Index Abstr.; Arts Humanit. Citation Index [Select. Cov.]; Biol. Abstr.; Chicano Index; Cumul. Index Nurs. Allied Health Lit. (1984-); Curr. Aware. Biol. Sci., CABS; Curr. Contents Soc. Behav. Sci.; Dairy Sci. Abstr.; EMBASE; Expand. Acad. Index (1989-); Geogr. Abstr. Human Geogr.; Helminthol. Abstr. (1991-); High. Educ. Abstr. (1982-19??); Index Med.; Int. Bibliogr. Sociol.; Int. Dev. Abstr.; Int. Pharm. Abstr. (19??-19??); Leis. Recreat. Tour. Abstr.; Middle East Abstr. Index; Multicult. Educ. Abstr.; Newsp. Period. Abstr. (1989-); Nutr. Abstr. Rev., Ser. A, Hum. Exp.; PAIS Int. Print; Life Sci. Collect. (1985-); Popul. Index; Protozoolog. Abstr.; Psychol. Abstr. (1982-); PsycINFO (1969-); PsycLit; Res. Alert [Full Cov.]; Res. High. Educ. Abstr.; Rev. Med. Vet. Entomol.; Rice Abstr.; Risk Abstr.; Rural Dev. Abstr.; Soc. Plann. Policy Dev. Abstr.; Soc. Sci. Cit. Index [Full Cov.]; Soc. Sci. Index; Soc. Sci. Index Fulltext (1988-) [Full Txt.]; Sociol. Abstr.; Stud. Women Abstr. (1985-); Tech. Educ. Train. Abstr.; Trop. Dis. Bull.; World Agric. Econ.

US/0894-4393
**SOCIAL SCIENCE COMPUTER REVIEW.** **See** Computers-Microcomputers, Personal Computers.

US/0145-5532
**SOCIAL SCIENCE HISTORY.** [Soc. sci. hist.]. **Added/Corp** Social Science History Association. Vol. 1 (Fall 1976)-. Periodical. English. qt (4 issues). $65.00 (institutions), $30.00 (individuals) US; $77.00 (institutions), $42.00 (individuals) other; includes membership in the Social Science History Association. Duke University Press, PO Box 90660, Durham NC 27708-0660. **Tel** (919)687-3600, (919)688-5134 (orders), FAX (919)688-4574, telex 802829. **ED** Ron Aminzade, Mary Jo Maynes, Russell R. Menard and Steven Ruggles. **LC** H1; .S612. **DD** 300/.5. **[CCC]. Bk Rev. Ad Acc. Pr Rev. Circ:** 900. available on microfilm and microfiche from University Microfilms International (UMI). Documents available from The Genuine Article.
**Desc:** Presents innovative research by historians, sociologists, anthropologists, political scientists, and demographers, providing an interdisciplinary forum for longitudinal analysis and studies with consciously theoretical orientations.
**Ind/Abst** Abstr. Soc. Gerontol.; Am. Hist. Life (1976-); Appl. Soc. Sci. Index Abstr.; Arts Humanit. Citation Index [Full Cov.]; Crim. Justice Abstr.; Curr. Contents Arts Humanit.; Curr. Contents Soc. Behav. Sci.; Int. Bibliogr. Sociol.; Int. Polit. Sci. Abstr.; Res. Alert [Full Cov.]; Sage Urban Stud. Abstr; Soc. Plann. Policy Dev. Abstr.; Soc. Sci. Cit. Index [Full Cov.]; Soc. Work Abstr. (?-?); Sociol. Abstr.; Stud. Women Abstr.; U.S. Polit. Sci. Doc.; West. Hist. Q.

UK/0539-0184
**SOCIAL SCIENCE INFORMATION.** (SOCIAL SCIENCE INFORMATION / INTERNATIONAL SOCIAL SCIENCE COUNCIL.). [Soc. sci. inf.]. **Added/Corp** International Social Science Council. **VFOAT** Information sur les Sciences Sociales. Vol. 6, No. 1 (Feb. 1967)-. Periodical. English (French). qt. £125.00. Sage Publications Ltd., 6 Bonhill Street, London EC2A 4PU, UK. **Tel** 071 374 0645, FAX 071 374 8741, telex 296207 SAGE G. **ED** Elina Almasy and Anne Rocha-Perazzo. **LC** H1; .A1454. **NLM** W1 SO129. **CODEN** SSCIBL. **Pr Rev. Acid Free.** Documents available from The Genuine Article. ***Continues** Social Sciences Information, 0539-0184.*
**Desc:** Provides a forum for research in social anthropology, sociology of science, social psychology, sociological theory.
**Ind/Abst** ABC POL SCI; Am. Hist. Life (1982-); Appl. Soc. Sci. Index Abstr.; Arts Humanit. Citation Index [Select. Cov.]; Curr. Contents Soc. Behav. Sci.; Curr. Geogr. Publ. (199?-); Hum. Resour. Abstr. (?-?); Index Philip. Period.; Int. Bibliogr. Sociol.; Int. Polit. Sci. Abstr.; MLA Int. Bibl. Books Artic. Mod. Lang. Lit.; Psychol. Abstr. (1969-); PsycINFO (?-?); PsycLit; Res. Alert [Full Cov.]; Rural Dev. Abstr.; Sage Public Adm. Abstr. (?-?); Soc. Plann. Policy Dev. Abstr.; Soc. Sci. Cit. Index [Select. Cov.]; Sociol. Abstr.; Sociol. Educ. Abstr.; World Agric. Econ.

II/0970-1087
**SOCIAL SCIENCE INTERNATIONAL.** **Added/Corp** Centre for Good Living (Cuttack, India). (198?)-. Periodical. English. sa. Centre for Good Living, Jagannath Ballav, Cuttack 753 001 India. **LC** H1; .S6124. **DD** 300/.5.
**Ind/Abst** Psychol. Abstr. (1985-); PsycLit.

US/0362-3319
**SOCIAL SCIENCE JOURNAL (FORT COLLINS), THE.** (THE SOCIAL SCIENCE JOURNAL.). [Soc. sci. j.]. **Added/Corp** Western Social Science Association. Vol. 12, No. 3/Vol. 13, No. 1 (Oct. 1975/Jan. 1976)-. Periodical. English. qt. $150.00 (institutions), $60.00 (individuals) US; $170.00 (institutions), $80.00 (individuals) (surface mail), $190.00 (institutions), $100.00 (individuals) (air mail) other. JAI Press Inc., 55 Old Post Road, Suite 2, PO Box 1678, Greenwich CT 06836-1678. **Tel** (203)661-7602, FAX (203)661-0792. **ED** Michael Katovich, Ed McNertney, Don Jackson, and Fred Erisman. **LC** H1; .R6. **DD** 300/.5. **[CCC].** Index available. **Bk Rev. Ad Acc. Pr Rev.** available on microfilm and microfiche from University Microfilms International (UMI). Documents available from The Genuine Article, UMI Article Clearinghouse. ***Continues** Rocky Mountain Social Science Journal, 0035-7634.*
**Desc:** Seeks to publish articles that cut across disciplinary boundaries to bring original insights and conclusions.
**Ind/Abst** Acad. Abstr. Full Text Elite (Jan. 1992-); Acad. Abstr. (Jan. 1992-); Acad. Search (Jan. 1992-); Am. Hist. Life (1966-); Am. Bibliogr. Slavic East Europ. Stud.; Arts Humanit. Citation Index [Select. Cov.]; Commun. Abstr. (?-?); Crim. Justice Abstr.; Curr. Contents Soc. Behav. Sci.; Expand. Acad. Index (1989-); Hum. Resour. Abstr.; INFO-SOUTH Abstr.; Int. Polit. Sci. Abstr.; Mag. Search; Newsp. Period. Abstr. (1991-); PAIS Int. Print; Psychol. Abstr. (1984-); PsycINFO (1990-); PsycLit; Res. Alert [Full Cov.]; Risk Abstr.; Soc. Plann. Policy Dev. Abstr.; Soc. Sci. Source (Jan. 1992-); Soc. Sci. Cit. Index [Full Cov.]; Soc. Sci. Index; Soc. Sci. Index Fulltext (Nov. 1988-) [Full Txt.]; Sociol. Abstr.; SportSearch; West. Hist. Q.

US/0195-7791
**SOCIAL SCIENCE MONITOR.** **Added/Corp** Communication Research Associates. (197?)-Vol. 13, No. 5 (1991). Periodical. English. mo. £150.00 North America; $160.00 other. Communication Research Associates Inc., 10606 Mantz Road, Silver Spring MD 20903. **Tel** (301)445-3230. **ED** Ray E Hiebert, Sheila J Gibbons and Michael Naver. **[CCC].** Index available. **Bk Rev.** ***Absorbed** High-Tech Alert for the Professional Communicator, 0888-9511.*
**Desc:** Social science and analysis, TV, networks, cable, satellite and teleconferencing developments.

II
**SOCIAL SCIENCE PROBINGS.** Vol. 1, No. 1 (March 1984)-. Periodical. English. Four times a year. Rs10.00 India; Rs24.00 others. People's Publishing House Pvt Ltd, 5E Rani Jhansi Road, New Delhi 110055 India. **Tel** 011 91 11 523349. **LC** HN681; .S596. **DD** 306/.0954.

US/0038-4941
**SOCIAL SCIENCE QUARTERLY.** [Soc. sci. q.]. **Added/Corp** Southwestern Social Science Association. University of Texas at Austin. Vol. 49, (June 1968)-. Periodical. English. qt. $54.00 (institutions), $25.00 (individuals) US; add $10.00 postage other. University of Texas Press, PO Box 7819, Austin TX 78713. **Tel** (512)471-4531, FAX (512)320-0668, telex 776453 UTEXPRES AUS. **ED** Charles M. Bonjean. **LC** H1; .S65. **DD** 305. **[CCC]. Pr Rev.** available on microfilm and microfiche from University Microfilms International (UMI). Documents available from The Genuine Article, UMI Article Clearinghouse. ***Continues** Southwestern Social Science Quarterly, 0276-1742.*
**Desc:** The leading academic title in its field publishing current research on a broad range of topics, including political science, sociology, economics, history, geography and women's studies. The journal of the Southwestern Social Science Association.
**Ind/Abst** ABC POL SCI; Acad. Abstr. Full Text Elite (July 1990-); Acad. Abstr. (July 1990-); Acad. Search (July 1990-); Am. Hist. Life (1968-); Am. Bibliogr. Slavic East Europ. Stud.; Annu. Bibliogr. Engl. Lang. Lit.; Appl. Soc. Sci. Index Abstr.; Arts Humanit. Citation Index [Select. Cov.]; Book Rev. Index; Commun. Abstr. (?-?); Crim. Justice Abstr.; Curr. Contents Soc. Behav. Sci. 3; Curr. Index J. Educ.; Curr. Index Stat.; Econ. Lit. Index; Educ. Adm. Abstr. (?-?); Expand. Acad. Index (1989-); High. Educ. Abstr. (1969-); Hum. Resour. Abstr.; INFO-SOUTH Abstr.; Int. Bibliogr. Sociol.; Int. Polit. Sci. Abstr.; J. Econ. Lit.; J. Plan. Lit.; Mag. Search; Middle East Abstr. Index; Multicult. Educ. Abstr.; Newsp. Period. Abstr. (1989-); PAIS Int. Print; Popul. Index; Res. Alert [Full Cov.]; Res. High. Educ. Abstr.; Sage Fam. Stud. Abstr.; Sage Public Adm. Abstr. (?-?); Sage Race Relat. Abstr.; Sage Urban Stud. Abstr (?-?); Soc. Plann. Policy Dev. Abstr.; Soc. Sci. Source (Jul. 1990-); Soc. Sci. Cit. Index [Full Cov.]; Soc.

Sci. Index; Soc. Sci. Index Fulltext (Sept. 1988-) [Full Txt.]; Sociol. Abstr.; Sociol. Educ. Abstr.; SportSearch; Stud. Women Abstr.; U.S. Polit. Sci. Doc.; West. Hist. Q.; Women Stud. Abstr.; Work Relat. Abstr.

US/0037-7872
**SOCIAL SCIENCE RECORD.** [Soc. sci. rec.]. **Added/Corp** New York State Council for the Social Studies. Vol. 1 (Spring 1964)-. Periodical. English. sa (Spring & Fall). $20.00. New York State Council for the Social Sciences, PO Box 625, White Plains NY 10603-0625. **Tel** (914)761-7206. **ED** Stephanie & Stephen Schechter. **LC** H62.5.U5; S64. **DD** 300/.7/1273. **[CCC]. Bk Rev. Ad Acc. Pr Rev. Circ:** 1,500 (ctrl). available on microfilm and microfiche from University Microfilms International (UMI).
**Desc:** A journal of theoretical and practical articles dealing with social studies education.
**Ind/Abst** Curr. Index J. Educ.

US/0049-089X
**SOCIAL SCIENCE RESEARCH.** [Soc. sci. res.]. Vol. 1 (Apr. 1972)-. Academic Scholarly Publication. English. qt (4 issues). $189.00 US and Canada; $245.00 other. Academic Press, Inc., 6277 Sea Harbor Drive, Orlando FL 32887. **Tel** (800)543-9534, (407)345-4100, FAX (407)363-9661. **ED** Peter H. Rossi and James D. Wright. **LC** H1; .S613. **DD** 300/.7/2. **NLM** W1 SO127N. **CODEN** SSREBG. **[CCC]. Pr Rev.** Documents available from The Genuine Article, UMI Article Clearinghouse.
**Desc:** Publishes papers devoted to quantitative social science research and methodology. Features articles that illustrate the use of quantitative methods in the empirical solution of methods that cut across traditional disciplinary lines.
**Ind/Abst** ABC POL SCI; Acad. Search (Jan. 1994-); Am. Hist. Life (1983-); Appl. Soc. Sci. Index Abstr.; Chicano Index; Commun. Abstr. (?-?); Crim. Justice Abstr.; Crim. Penol. Police Sci. Abstr.; Curr. Contents Soc. Behav. Sci.; Expand. Acad. Index (1989-); Index Period. Artic. Relat. Law (19??-19??); INFO-SOUTH Abstr.; J. Plan. Lit.; Mag. Search; Middle East Abstr. Index; Multicult. Educ. Abstr.; Newsp. Period. Abstr. (1991-); Popul. Index; Psychol. Abstr. (1972-); PsycINFO; PsycLit; Res. Alert [Full Cov.]; Soc. Plann. Policy Dev. Abstr.; Soc. Sci. Source (Jul. 1993-); Soc. Sci. Cit. Index [Full Cov.]; Soc. Sci. Index; Soc. Sci. Index Fulltext (Dec. 1988-) [Full Txt.]; Sociol. Abstr.; Sociol. Educ. Abstr.; Spec. Educ. Needs Abstr.; Soc. Res. Methodol. Abstr. (1975-); U.S. Polit. Sci. Doc.

TH
**SOCIAL SCIENCE REVIEW. VFOAT** Review of Social Science; Review of Thai Social Science. V. 1-Mar. 1976-. Periodical. English. ir. Social Science Association Press, PO Box 5/84, Bangkok 5 Thailand. **LC** H1; .S6138. **DD** 300/.9593. ***Continues*** *Journal of Social Science Review.*

CE
**SOCIAL SCIENCE REVIEW (SOCIAL SCIENTISTS ASSOCIATION OF SRI LANKA).** (SOCIAL SCIENCE REVIEW : JOURNAL OF THE SOCIAL SCIENTISTS ASSOCIATION OF SRI LANKA.). No. 1 (Sept. 1979)-. Periodical. English. qt. $15.00. Editor Social Science Review, c/o SLAAS, 120/10 Wijerama Mawatha, Colombo Sri Lanka Ceylon.

●US/1063-9802
**SOCIAL SCIENCE SOURCE. See** Social Sciences-Abstracting, Bibliographies and Statistics.

US
**SOCIAL SCIENCE STUDIES. Main/Corp** University of Chicago. (1924)-. Periodical. English.

UK/0309-7544
**SOCIAL SCIENCE TEACHER. See** Education-Teaching and Curriculum.

AT/0312-1844
**SOCIAL SCIENCE TEACHER SYDNEY.** [Soc. sci. teach.Syd.]. (1971)-. Periodical. English. ir. **DD** 300.712944.
**Ind/Abst** Aust. Educ. Index.

RU/0134-5486
**SOCIAL SCIENCES.** [Soc. sci.]. **Added/Corp** Akademiia Nauk SSSR. Otdelenie Obshchestvennykh Nauk. Akademiia Nauk SSSR. Sectsiia Obshchestvennykh Nauk. Vol. 1, No. 1 (1970)-. Academic Scholarly Publication. English (French, German, Spanish and Portuguese). qt. $53.00. Izdatelstvo Nauka / Akademiia Nauk, Publishing House of the Russian Academy of Sciences, Leninskii Porspekt 14, 117901 Moscow Russia. **Tel** 011 95 954-21-53, FAX 011 95 938-21-44, telex 411964. **(Subscription address:** Victor Kamkin, 4956 Boiling Brook Parkway, Rockville MD 20852.**) LC** H1; .S615. **DD** 300/.5. **Bk Rev. Circ:** 5,400.
**Desc:** Deals with theoretical problems of social sciences, including world history, history of the Soviet Union, philosophy, economics and sociology; published by the USSR Academy of Sciences.
**Ind/Abst** Am. Hist. Life (1982-); Int. Aerosp. Abstr.; Int. Bibliogr. Sociol.; Int. Labour Doc.

RU
**SOCIAL SCIENCES AND HUMANITIES IN RUSSIA / RUSSIAN ACADEMY OF SCIENCES, INSTITUTE OF SCIENTIFIC INFORMATION ON SOCIAL SCIENCES.** **Added/Corp** Institut Nauchnoi Informatsii po Obshchestvennym Naukam (Rossiiskaia Akademiia Nauk). **VFOAT** Sotsialnye i Gumanitarnye Issledovaniia v Rossii. (1991)-. Academic Scholarly Publication. English. Izdatelstvo Nauka / Akademiia Nauk, Publishing House of the Russian Academy of Sciences, Leninskii Porspekt 14, 117901 Moscow Russia. **Tel** 011 95 954-21-53, FAX 011 95 938-21-44, telex 411964. **LC** Z7161; .S655; H62.A1. ***Continues*** *Social Sciences in the USSR.*

US/1044-6044
**SOCIAL SCIENCES CITATION INDEX (COMPACT DISC ED.).** (SOCIAL SCIENCES CITATION INDEX [COMPUTER FILE].). [Soc. sci. cit. index]. **Added/Corp** Institute for Scientific Information. **VFOAT** SSCI CDE; SSCI. (1986)-. English. qt. $5955.00 (CD-ROM); $7565.00 (combination print & CD-ROM). Institute for Scientific Information, 3501 Market Street, Philadelphia PA 19104. **Tel** (215)386-0100, (800)523-1850, FAX (215)386-6362, telex 84-5305. **(Subscription address:** Institute for Scientific Information, PO Box 71416, Chicago IL 60694.**) LC** Z7161. **DD** 305. available in print.

US/0091-3707
**SOCIAL SCIENCES CITATION INDEX (PRINT ED.). See** Social Sciences-Abstracting, Bibliographies and Statistics.

●US/1061-1282
**SOCIAL SCIENCES CITATION INDEX WITH ABSTRACTS.** (SOCIAL SCIENCES CITATION INDEX WITH ABSTRACTS [COMPUTER FILE].). [Soc. sci. cit. index abstr.]. **Added/Corp** Institute for Scientific Information. (Jan/Mar 1992)-. Abstracting/Indexing Service. English. qt. $7550.00; $9030.00 (print & CD with Abstracts). Institute for Scientific Information, 3501 Market Street, Philadelphia PA 19104. **Tel** (215)386-0100, (800)523-1850, FAX (215)386-6362, telex 84-5305. **(Subscription address:** Institute for Scientific Information, PO Box 71416, Chicago, IL 60694**) DD** 016.

CC/0252-9203
**SOCIAL SCIENCES IN CHINA.** [Soc. sci. China]. **Added/Corp** Chung-Kuo She Hui Ko Hsueh Yuan. **VFOAT** Chung-Kuo She Hui Ko Hsueh. Vol. 1 (March 1980)-. Periodical. English. qt. $39.10. **(Subscription address:** China International Book Trading Corporation, PO Box 399, Library Service Department, Beijing 100044 People's Republic of China.**) LC** HC426; .S58. **DD** 300/.951.
**Desc:** Introduces academic achievements in philosophy and the social sciences.
**Ind/Abst** Appl. Soc. Sci. Index Abstr.; Geogr. Abstr. Human Geogr. (?-?); Int. Bibliogr. Sociol.; Int. Dev. Abstr. (?-?); Int. Labour Doc.; LABORDOC; PAIS Int. Print; Rural Dev. Abstr.

●UK/1352-4127
**SOCIAL SCIENCES IN HEALTH.** (1995)-. English. qt. £60.00 (institution), £27.50 (individual) EC; $105.00 (institution), $49.00 (individual) US; £65.00 (institution), £29.50 (individual) other. Edward Arnold, 338 Euston Road, London NW1 3BH England. **Tel** 011 44 71 873 6000, FAX 011 44 071 873 6325. **(Subscription address:** Turpin Distribution Services Limited, Blackhorse Road, Letchworth, Hertfordshire SG6 1HN, United Kingdom.**) ED** Mary Fraser. **Bk Rev.**
**Desc:** Shows how the social sciences interact with the practice of health care while exploring current theories and models, topical issues and the role of the social sciences in the practice of health care, management and research.

US/0094-4920
**SOCIAL SCIENCES INDEX. See** Social Sciences-Abstracting, Bibliographies and Statistics.

US
**SOCIAL SCIENCES INDEX / FULLTEXT. See** Social Sciences-Abstracting, Bibliographies and Statistics.

II
**SOCIAL SCIENCES RESEARCH JOURNAL.** Began with issue for April/June 1976. Periodical. English. Three times a year. Rs30.00 India; $6.00 US. Panjan University Campus, Chief Editor, Social Sciences Research, Journal Arts Block No 3, Chandigarh 160014 India. **LC** H1; .S624. **DD** 300/.5.

UK
**SOCIAL SCIENCES (SWINDON, WILTSHIRE, ENGLAND).** (SOCIAL SCIENCES : NEWS FROM THE ESRC.). **Added/Corp** Economic and Social Research Council (Great Britain). (July 1989)-. Periodical. English. Six times a year (Feb., Apr., June, Aug., Oct. Dec.). Free. Economic & Social Research Council, Polaris House, North Star Avenue, Swindon SN2 1UJ England. **Tel** 011 44 793 413000, FAX 011 44 793 413001. **ED** Andrew Smith. **LC** H65; .S63. **DD** 300/.72. **Bk Rev. Circ:** 10,000. ***Continues*** *ESRC Newsletter, 0266-2639.*
**Desc:** Published in recognition of the need for ESRC to communicate more speedily and effectively with its constituency audiences.

II/0970-0293
**SOCIAL SCIENTIST (NEW DELHI).** (SOCIAL SCIENTIST.). [Soc. sci.]. **Added/Corp** Indian School of Social Sciences (New Delhi, India). Vol. 1 (Aug. 1972)-. Periodical. English. Twelve times a year. $60.00. Journal of Arts & Ideas / Social Scientists, R-271, Lower Ground Floor, Greater Kailash-I, New Delhi 110048 India. **(Subscription address:** Prints India, 11 Darya Ganj, New Delhi 110002 India.**) ED** Professor Prabhat Patnaik. **LC** HN681; .S597. **DD** 309.1/54. **UDC** 3. **Bk Rev. Ad Acc. Circ:** 2,000.
**Ind/Abst** Int. Bibliogr. Sociol.; Int. Labour Doc.; LABORDOC.

US
**SOCIAL SCISEARCH.** English. Magnetic Tape: $17695.00 (academic), $22130.00 (corporate) with references. Institute for Scientific Information, 3501 Market Street, Philadelphia PA 19104. **Tel** (215)386-0100, (800)523-1850, FAX (215)386-6362, telex 84-5305. **(Subscription address:** Institute for Scientific Information, PO Box 71416, Chicago, IL 60694**)** available on magnetic tape.
**Desc:** The online format of the Social Sciences Citation Index. Provides the same coverage as the other SSCI indexes.

US/0271-4086
**SOCIAL SERVICE DELIVERY SYSTEMS.** ***Ceased.*** [Soc. serv. deliv. syst.]. V. 1-?. Monographic series. English. an. SAGE Periodical Press, 2455 Teller Road, Thousand Oaks CA 91320. **Tel** (805)499-0721, FAX (805)499-0871, telex 100799. **ED** M I Teicher. **NLM** W1 SO1322.

UK
**SOCIAL SERVICES RESEARCH.** Periodical. English. qt. £45.00 UK; £55.00 North America. University of Birmingham / English, Department of English, Birmingham D15 2TT England. **Tel** 021-414-5733, FAX 021-414-3689. **(Subscription address:** University of Birmingham, Department of Social Policy and Social Work, Edgbaston, Birmingham B15 2TT England**) ED** N M Thomas. **LC** HV1; .S63. **DD** 361/.05. Index available. cum. index. **Bk Rev. Circ:** 400 (ctrl).
**Ind/Abst** Appl. Soc. Sci. Index Abstr.

CN/0848-7537
**SOCIAL STUDIES 30 BULLETIN.** [Soc. stud. 30 bull.]. **Added/Corp** Alberta. Student Evaluation Branch. **VAT** Social Studies Thirty Bulletin. (1989/1990)-. Bulletin. English. **DD** 300/.71/27123. ***Continues*** *Social Studies 30., 0848-7529.*

US/1056-0300
**SOCIAL STUDIES AND THE YOUNG LEARNER.** [Soc. stud. young learn.]. **Added/Corp** National Council for the Social Studies. Vol. 1, No. 1 (Sept./Oct. 1988)-. Periodical. English. Four times a year. $30.00 US; $35.00 overseas. National Council for the Social Studies, 3501 Newark Street Northwest, Washington DC 20016-3167. **Tel** (202)966-7840, FAX (202)966-2061. **LC** LB1584; .S6365. **DD** 372.83/044/0973. available on microfilm and microfiche from University Microfilms International (UMI).
**Desc:** For creative teaching in grades K-6; includes teaching strategies, methods, and activities.
**Ind/Abst** Curr. Index J. Educ.

US/0886-9286
**SOCIAL STUDIES JOURNAL (PENNSYLVANIA COUNCIL FOR THE SOCIAL STUDIES).** (THE SOCIAL STUDIES JOURNAL.). [Soc. stud. j. - Pa. Counc. Soc. Stud.]. **Added/Corp** Pennsylvania Council for the Social Studies. (19??)-. Periodical. English. an (Jan.). $10.00; Also comes with membership. Pennsylvania Council for Social Studies, PO Box 11191, c/o Edward Gallagher, Erie PA 16514. **Tel** (814)226-6584. **LC** LB1584; .S639. **DD** 300.
**Ind/Abst** Curr. Index J. Educ.

UK/0306-3127
**SOCIAL STUDIES OF SCIENCE.** [Soc. stud. sci.]. Vol. 5 (Feb. 1975)-. Periodical. English. qt. £125.00. Sage Publications Ltd., 6 Bonhill Street, London EC2A 4PU, UK. **Tel** 071 374 0645, FAX 071 374 8741, telex 296207 SAGE G. **ED** David Edge and Roy McLeod. **LC** Q1; .S812. **DD** 301.24/3/05. **NLM** W1 SO133K. **Ad Acc. Pr Rev. Acid Free.** Documents available from The Genuine Article. ***Continues*** *Science Studies, 0036-8539.*
**Desc:** Serves the growing community of historians, philosophers, sociologists, political scientists and economists who are contributing research on the study of science in its social dimension.
**Ind/Abst** ABC POL SCI; Am. Hist. Life (1975-); Appl. Soc. Sci. Index Abstr.; Arts Humanit. Citation Index [Full Cov.]; Curr. Contents Arts Humanit.; Curr. Contents Life Sci.; Curr. Contents Soc. Behav. Sci.; EMBASE; Energy Res. Abstr. (Oct. 1981-); Middle East Abstr. Index; Life Sci. Collect.; Protozoolog. Abstr.; Res. Alert [Full Cov.];

Res. High. Educ. Abstr.; Sci. Cit. Index; SCISEARCH; Soc. Plann. Policy Dev. Abstr.; Soc. Sci. Cit. Index [Full Cov.]; Sociol. Abstr. [Full Cov.]; Stud. Women Abstr.

US/0037-7996
**SOCIAL STUDIES (PHILADELPHIA, PA. : 1953).** (THE SOCIAL STUDIES.). [Soc. stud.]. Vol. 44, No. 6 (Oct. 1953)-. Periodical. English. bm. $33.00 (individuals), $55.00 (institutional), add $14.00 (foreign postage). Heldref Publications, 1319 Eighteenth Street Northwest, Washington DC 20036-1802. **Tel** (202)296-6267, (800)365-9753, FAX (202)296-5149. **ED** Rodney F Allen, Gloria Contreras, and Ron H Pahl. **LC** D16.3; .S65. **[CCC]. Bk Rev. Ad Acc. Circ:** 2,700. available on microfilm and microfiche from University Microfilms International (UMI). Documents available from UMI Article Clearinghouse. ***Continues** Social Studies for Teachers and Administrators, 0037-7996.*
**Desc:** Offers teachers an independent forum for publishing their ideas about the teaching of social studies at all levels. Presents teachers' practical methods and class-room-tested suggestions for teaching history, political science, economics, geography, and future studies. Periodic special issues provide teachers with extensive resource material in one convenient source.
**Ind/Abst** Acad. Abstr. Full Text Elite (July 1990-) [Full Txt.]; Acad. Abstr. (July 1990-); Acad. Ind. [Computer File] (1987-); Acad. Search (July 1990-); Am. Hist. Life (1963-); Book Rev. Index; Contents Pages Educ.; Curr. Index J. Educ. (March 1990); Educ. Index; Expand. Acad. Index (1987-); INFO-SOUTH Abstr.; Mag. Artic. Summar. Elite (July 1990-) [Full Txt.]; Mag. Artic. Summar. Select (July 1990-); Mag. Artic. Summar. CD-ROM (July 1990-); Mag. Search; Newsp. Period. Abstr. (1989-); Soc. Sci. Source (Jul. 1990-) [Full Txt.]; Spec. Educ. Needs Abstr.; West. Hist. Q.

US/0586-6235
**SOCIAL STUDIES PROFESSIONAL, THE.** (THE SOCIAL STUDIES PROFESSIONAL : A NEWSLETTER FROM THE NATIONAL COUNCIL FOR THE SOCIAL STUDIES.). [Soc. stud. prof.]. **Added/Corp** National Council for the Social Studies. No. 1 (1969)-. Newsletter. English. Five times a year. Comes with membership and Social Education: $60.00 US; $65.00 overseas. National Council for the Social Studies, 3501 Newark Street Northwest, Washington DC 20016-3167. **Tel** (202)966-7840, FAX (202)966-2061. available on microfilm and microfiche from University Microfilms International (UMI).
**Ind/Abst** Curr. Index J. Educ. (March 1990).

US/1056-6325
**SOCIAL STUDIES REVIEW (MILLBRAE, CALIF.).** (SOCIAL STUDIES REVIEW.). [Soc. stud. rev.]. **Added/Corp** California Council for the Social Studies. Vol. 13, (Fall 1973)-. Periodical. English. Three times a year (Feb., June, Oct.). $25.00. California Council for Social Studies, 1255 Vista Grande, Millbrae CA 94030. **Tel** (415)692-4830, FAX (415)692-4830. **ED** Dr. Bill Hanna (phone: (408)924-5541). **DD** 375. **Bk Rev. Ad Acc, Adv Mgr:** Mezzetta, Sabato. **Circ:** 2,500 (ctrl). available on microfilm from University Microfilms International (UMI). Documents available. ***Continues** California Council for the Social Studies. Review.*
**Desc:** Educational publication with various subjects relating to social studies and articles of interest to social studies educators.
**Ind/Abst** Br. Humanit. Index; Curr. Index J. Educ.

US/1047-7217
**SOCIAL STUDIES REVIEW (NEW YORK, N.Y.).** (SOCIAL STUDIES REVIEW : A PUBLICATION OF THE AMERICAN TEXTBOOK COUNCIL.). [Soc. stud. rev.]. **Added/Corp** American Textbook Council. No. 1 (Spring 1989)-. Periodical. English. Four times a year. $20.00 (individuals); $30.00 (institutions). American Textbook Council, 475 Riverside Drive, Room 518, New York NY 10115. **Tel** (212)870-2760, FAX (212)870-3112. **ED** Gilbert T. Sewall. **LC** H62.5.U5; S6498. **DD** 300/.71/073. **Bk Rev. Circ:** 5,000.

US/1056-4675
**SOCIAL STUDIES TEXAN, THE.** (THE SOCIAL STUDIES TEXAN : THE OFFICIAL PUBLICATION OF THE TEXAS COUNCIL FOR THE SOCIAL STUDIES.). [Soc. stud. Tex.]. **Added/Corp** Texas Council for the Social Studies. **VFOAT** Texan. (1985)-. Periodical. English. Three times a year. $20.00 (institution). The Social Studies Texan, 1849 Central Drive, Bedford TX 76022. **DD** 375.
**Ind/Abst** Curr. Index J. Educ.

US/0037-802X
**SOCIAL THEORY AND PRACTICE.** [Soc. theory pract.]. **Added/Corp** Florida State University. Dept. of Philosophy. Florida State University. Center for Social Philosophy. Vol. 1 (Spring 1970)-. Periodical. English. tq (May, Aug., Nov.). $12.00 (individuals), $33.00 (institutions). Florida State University / Department of Philosophy, Tallahassee FL 32306. **Tel** (904)644-0224, FAX (904)644-3832. **ED** Russel M. Dancy. **LC** H1; .S63. **DD** 300/.5. Index available. **Bk Rev**, (Qty: 3-6). **Ad Acc. Pr Rev. Circ:** 750. available on microfilm and microfiche from University Microfilms International (UMI). Documents available from UMI Article Clearinghouse.
**Desc:** Includes discussion of important and controversial issues in social, political, legal, economic, educational, and moral philosophy. Constructive criticism is welcome.
**Ind/Abst** ABC POL SCI; Acad. Abstr. Full Text Elite (Jan. 1992-); Acad. Abstr. (Jan. 1992-); Acad. Search (Jan. 1992-); Am. Hist. Life (1972-); Appl. Soc. Sci. Index Abstr.; Crim. Penol. Police Sci. Abstr. (?-?); Curr. Index J. Educ.; Expand. Acad. Index (1989-); INFO-SOUTH Abstr.; Int. Polit. Sci. Abstr.; Mag. Search; Middle East Abstr. Index; Newsp. Period. Abstr. (1991-); Philos. Index; Soc. Plann. Policy Dev. Abstr.; Soc. Sci. Source (Jan. 1992-); Soc. Sci. Index; Soc. Sci. Index Fulltext (Summer 1988-) [Full Txt.]; Sociol. Abstr.; Sociol. Educ. Abstr.

IT
**SOCIAL TRENDS.** (19??)-. Italian. Four times a year. Free on request. Social Trends, c/o Eurisko, Via Monterosa 15, 20149 Milan Italy. **Tel** 011 39 2 4987816. **Bk Rev. Circ:** 4,500.
**Desc:** Information and news about sociocultural evolution in Italy and Europe.

CN
**SOCIALIST STUDIES/ETUDES SOCIALIST: A CANADIAN ANNUAL.** (1992)-. English (French). Eleven times a year. 19.95Can$; $19.95 US; 19.95Can$ (add mailing cost) other. The University of Manitoba, University College, Winnepeg Manitoba R3T 2M8 Canada. **Tel** (204)474-9119, FAX (204)261-0021. **ED** Jesse Vorst. **Pr Rev. Circ:** 1000.
**Desc:** Collection of topical articles on themes of interest to Canadian activists and academics.

FR
**SOCIETE FRANCAISE.** (19??)-. Periodical. French. Four times a year. 244.86F France; 500.00F other. IRM / Institut de Recherches Marxistes, 64 Boulevard Auguste Blanqui, 75013 Paris France. **Tel** 011 33 1 43364534.

●UK/1063-1119
**SOCIETY & ANIMALS.** (SOCIETY AND ANIMALS: SOCIAL SCIENTIFIC STUDIES OF THE HUMAN EXPERIENCE OF OTHER ANIMALS.). [Soc. anim.]. **Added/Corp** Psychologists for the Ethical Treatment of Animals. **VFOAT** Society and Animals. (1993)-. Periodical. English. Twice a year. $55.00 (institutions), $30.00 (individuals). The White Horse Press, 10 High Street, Knapwell, Cambridge CB3 8NR England. **Tel** 011 44 9 547527. **LC** QL85; .S63. **NLM** W1; SO85K. **CODEN** SANIEL. **[CCC].**
**Ind/Abst** Arts Humanit. Citation Index [Select. Cov.]; Soc. Sci. Cit. Index [Select. Cov.].

IS
**SOCIETY AND WELFARE.** **Added/Corp** Israel. Misrad Ha-avodah Veha-revahah. (August 1978)-. Periodical. English. qt (Mar., June, Sept., Dec.). $35.00. Women's League of Israel, YAD Harutzim 10, Taliot, Jerusalem, 91012 Israel. ***Continues** SAAD.*

US/0147-2011
**SOCIETY (NEW BRUNSWICK).** (SOCIETY.). [Soc.]. (1972)-. Periodical. English. Six times a year. Fl153.50 (individual), Fl311.00 (institution). Transaction Publishers / Rutgers State University, New Brunswick NJ 08903. **Tel** (908)932-2280 Ext. 105, FAX (908)932-3138. **ED** Irving Louis Horowitz. **LC** H1; .T72. **DD** 309.1/73/092. **NLM** W1 SO85. **[CCC]. Bk Rev. Ad Acc. Pr Rev. Circ:** 10,000. available on microfilm and microfiche from University Microfilms International (UMI); Johnson Associates; and Bell & Howell; available on labels. Documents available from The Genuine Article, UMI Article Clearinghouse. ***Continues** Trans-Action, 0041-1035.*
**Desc:** Presents new ideas and research findings from all the social sciences for decision makers and others concerned with trends in modern society. Each issue features special symposia and policy-relevent research.
**Ind/Abst** ABC POL SCI; Abr. Read. Guide Period. Lit.; Acad. Abstr. Full Text Elite (Jan. 1984-); Acad. Abstr. (Jan. 1984-); Acad. Ind. [Computer File] (1984-); Acad. Search (Jan. 1984-); Am. Hist. Life (1972-); Am. Bibliogr. Slavic East Europ. Stud.; ARTbibliogr. Mod.; Arts Humanit. Citation Index [Select. Cov.]; Book Rev. Digest; Book Rev. Index; Crim. Penol. Police Sci. Abstr.; Curr. Index J. Educ.; EMBASE; Film Lit. Index; Gen. Period. Index (1985-); Guide Soc. Sci. Relig.; INFO-SOUTH Abstr.; Int. Bibliogr. Sociol.; Mag. Artic. Summar. Elite (Jan. 1984-); Mag. Artic. Summar. Select (Jan. 1984-); Mag. Artic. Summar. CD-ROM (Jan. 1984-); Mag. Index Plus (1989-); Mag. Index. Sel. (1986-); Mag. Search; Multicult. Educ. Abstr.; Newsp. Period. Abstr. (1988-); PAIS Int. Print; Peace Res. Abstr. J. (1965-1971, 1979-1981); Read. Guide Abstr. Select Ed.; Read. Guide Period. Lit.; Res. Alert [Full Cov.]; Soc. Plann. Policy Dev. Abstr.; Soc. Sci. Source (Jan. 1984-); Soc. Sci. Cit. Index [Full Cov.]; Soc. Work Abstr. [Select. Cov.]; Sociol. Abstr. (?-?); Mag. Index (1977-); U.S. Polit. Sci. Doc. (-199?); Urban Aff. Abstr.; Vocat. Search (Jan. 1984-).

SI/0217-9520
**SOJOURN (SINGAPORE, SINGAPORE).** (SOJOURN.). **Added/Corp** Institute of Southeast Asian Studies. Vol. 1, No. 1 (Feb. 1986)-. Periodical. English. sa. $16.00 (individuals), $21.00 (institutions) Southeast Asia, Japan, Australia & New Zealand; $19.00 (individuals), $25.00 (institutions) Europe & North America; 25.00Sin$ (individuals), 30.00Sing$ (institutions) Singapore, Malaysia & Brunei. Institute of Southeast Asian Studies / Singapore, Heng Mui Keng Terrace, Pasir Panjang Road, Singapore 0511 Republic of Singapore. **Tel** (11) 65 8702447, FAX 011 65 7781735, telex 37068. **ED** Subbiah Gunosekaran, Amanda Rojah, Sharon Liddigue. **LC** HN690.8; .A63. **DD** 306/.0959. **Pr Rev. Circ:** 600.
**Desc:** Review of significant developments and trends in the region, with particular emphasis on the Asian countries. Analysis made of major political, economic, social and strategic developments with Southeast Asia.
**Ind/Abst** Am. Hist. Life (1988-); Index Islam. Lit.; Int. Bibliogr. Sociol.; PAIS Int. Print; Soc. Plann. Policy Dev. Abstr.

US/1050-0219
**SOLUTIONS FOR BETTER HEALTH.** ***Suspended.*** [Solut. better health]. (May 1990)-Suspended (July/Aug. 1990). Periodical. English. mo. $14.95 US; $18.45 Canada. Haymarket Group Ltd, 45 West 34th Street, New York NY 10001. **Tel** (212)239-0855. **DD** 362. available on an online database (file 149/Full-Text) from DIALOG. ***Continues** Mature Health (New York, N.Y.), 1045-022X.*
**Ind/Abst** Health Index (May 1990-Aug. 1990); Health Period. Database [Full Txt.]; Health Ref. Cent. (Jan. 1989-) [Full Txt.] [Full Cov.].

NO
**SOSIALT UTSYN / SOCIAL SURVEY.** **Added/Corp** Norway. Statistisk Sentralbyraa. **VFOAT** Social Survey. (1974)-. Norwegian (English and Norwegian). Scandinavian University Press, PO Box 2959 Toeyen, N 0608 Oslo 6 Norway. **Tel** 011 47 2 2575400, FAX 011 47 2 2575353, telex 71896 UROR N. **(Subscription address:** Scandinavian University Press, 200 Meacham Ave., Elmont NY 11003.**)** **LC** HN561; .S62. **DD** 306/.09481.

NO
**SOSIOLOGISK TIDSSKRIFT.** Norwegian. Four times a year. Kr370.00, $66.00. Scandinavian University Press, PO Box 2959 Toeyen, N 0608 Oslo 6 Norway. **Tel** 011 47 2 2575400, FAX 011 47 2 2575353, telex 71896 UROR N. **(Subscription address:** Scandinavian University Press, 200 Meacham Ave., Elmont NY 11003.**)**

II
**SOUTH ASIA JOURNAL : QUARTERLY JOURNAL OF INDIAN COUNCIL FOR SOUTH ASIAN COOPERATION.** ***Ceased.*** Vol. 1, No. 1 (July-Sept. 1987)-(1992). Periodical. English. qt (July, Oct., Jan., April). SAGE Periodical Press, 2455 Teller Road, Thousand Oaks CA 91320. **Tel** (805)499-0721, FAX (805)499-0871, telex 100799. **ED** Bimal Prasad. **LC** DS331; .S653. **DD** 954/.005. Index available (fourth issue). **Ad Acc.** available on microfilm.
**Desc:** Provides analyses of regional and national political, economic, historical, and cultural issues among the nations of South Asia.
**Ind/Abst** Geogr. Abstr. Human Geogr.; Int. Dev. Abstr.; PAIS Int. Print.

UK/0262-7280
**SOUTH ASIA RESEARCH.** **See** Humanities.

SI
**SOUTHEAST ASIAN JOURNAL OF SOCIAL SCIENCE.** Vol. 1, (1973)-. Periodical. English. Twice a year (May, Oct.). $46.00. Chopmen Publishers Pty Ltd., 37 Jalan Peminpin, Singapore 2057 Republic of Singapore. **Tel** 011 65 3441495, FAX 011 65 3440180. **ED** Peter S. J. Chen. **LC** HN661; .S59. **DD** 301/.0959. **Bk Rev. Ad Acc. Circ:** 500. ***Formed by the union of** Southeast Asian Journal of Sociology **and** Southeast Asian Journal of Economic Development and Social Change; **Absorbed** Southeast Asia Ethnicity and Development Newsletter.*
**Desc:** Comprehensive analyses of the process of social change and development in Southeast Asian societies.
**Ind/Abst** Appl. Soc. Sci. Index Abstr.; Rural Dev. Abstr.

US/1047-7942
**SOUTHERN SOCIAL STUDIES JOURNAL.** [South soc. stud. j.]. **Added/Corp** Kentucky Council for the Social Studies. **VFOAT** SSSJ. Vol. 16, No. 1 (Fall 1990)-. Periodical. English. Twice a year (May, Nov.). $10.00. Southern Social Studies, UPO 738, Morehead KY 40351. **Tel** (606)783-2590, FAX (606)783-2678. **ED** Charles Holt and Kent Freeland. **LC** H62.A1; S68. **DD** 330. Index available ($5.00 extra). **Bk Rev. Ad Acc. Pr Rev. Circ:** 350. ***Continues** Southern Social Studies Quarterly, 0741-143X.*
**Desc:** Publishes articles for and by people interested in social studies.

US/0049-1683
**SOUTHWESTERN JOURNAL OF SOCIAL EDUCATION.** ***Ceased.*** [Southwest. j. soc. educ.]. V. 1- Fall (1970)-?. Periodical. English. sa. North Texas State University, PO Box 5427, Denton TX 76201. **Tel** (817)565-3442. **DD** 300. available on microfilm and microfiche from University Microfilms International (UMI).
**Ind/Abst** Curr. Index J. Educ.

RU
**SOVETSKAIA LITERATURA PO OBSHCHIM PROBLEMAM KULTURNO-PROSVETITELNOI RABOTY I KLUBOVEDENIIU.** **Added/Corp** Informtsentr po Problemam Kultury i Iskusstva (Soviet Union). (19??)-. Russian. 0.34rub. Gosudarstvennaia Biblioteka, Informatsionnyi Tsentr, Imeni V. I. Lenina, Prospekt Kalinina 3, 121019 Moscow Russia. **LC** Z7164.C84; S68; HN46.R9.

GW
**SOZIALE BEWEGUNGEN : ANALYSE UND DOKUMENTATION DES IMSF.** **See** Economics-Labor.

GW/0038-6073
**SOZIALE WELT.** [Soz. Welt]. **Added/Corp** Sozialforschungsstelle an der Universitat Munster. Arbeitsgemeinschaft Sozialwissenschaftlicher Institute (Germany). (Oct. 1949)-. Periodical. German (summaries and/or abstracts in English). qt (Mar., June, Oct., Dec.). DM80.00 Germany; $50.00 US. Verlag Otto Schwartz & Company, Annastrasse 7, D 37075 Goettingen Germany. **Tel** 011 49 551 31051, 011 49 551 31052, FAX 011 49 551 372812. **LC** H5; .S55. **DD** 300/.5. Index available. cum. index. **Ad Acc. Circ:** 1,500.
**Ind/Abst** Int. Bibliogr. Sociol.; Int. Polit. Sci. Abstr.; Philos. Index; Soc. Plann. Policy Dev. Abstr.; Sociol. Abstr. [Full Cov.].

GW/0038-609X
**SOZIALER FORTSCHRITT (BERLIN).** (SOZIALER FORTSCHRITT.). [Soz. fortschr.]. Vol. 1 (1952)-. Periodical. German. mo. DM76.00. Duncker und Humblot Verlag, Postfach 410329, D-12113 Berlin Germany. **Tel** 011 49 30 79000612, 011 49 30 79000613. **LC** HN441; .G423. **[CCC].**
**Ind/Abst** Int. Labour Doc.; LABORDOC.

GW/0584-5998
**SOZIALPOLITISCHE SCHRIFTEN.** (1956)-. Monographic series. German. ir. Price varies per volume. Duncker und Humblot Verlag, Postfach 410329, D-12113 Berlin Germany. **Tel** 011 49 30 79000612, 011 49 30 79000613.

GW
**SOZIALWISSENSCHAFTLICHE ABHANDLUNGEN DER GORRES-GESELLSCHAFT.** Vol. 1 (1978)-. Monographic series. German. Price varies per volume. Duncker und Humblot Verlag, Postfach 410329, D-12113 Berlin Germany. **Tel** 011 49 30 79000612, 011 49 30 79000613.

UA/1012-0319
**SPECIALISED NATIONAL COUNCILS' MAGAZINE, THE.** [Spec. Natl. Counc. mag.]. **Main/Corp** Egypt. Al-Majalis Al-Qawmiyah Al-Mutakhassisah. Al-Amanah Al-Ammah. 1 (June 1976)-. Periodical. English. qt. Arab Socialist Union Building, Nile Corniche, Cairo Egypt. **LC** HN786; .A46A. **DD** 309.1/62.

CN/0228-8982
**SPECTRUM (MONTREAL. 1981).** (SPECTRUM / THE COUNCIL OF QUEBEC MINORITIES.). [Spectrum]. Vol. 1, No. 1 (Jan. 1981)-. Periodical. English (French). ir. Free. Council of Quebec Minorities, Suite 2/3437 Peel Street, Montreal Quebec H3A 1W7 Canada. **DD** 305/.06/0714. ***Continues*** *Interaction (Montreal, Quebec).*

CE/0258-9710
**SRI LANKA JOURNAL OF SOCIAL SCIENCES.** [Sri Lanka j. soc. sci.]. V. 1- June 1978-. Periodical. English. sa. Rs25.00 Sri Lanka; $8.50 US. Natl Resources Energy & Science Authority, 47 Maitland Place, Colombo 7 Sri Lanka Ceylon. **Tel** 01-596771, 01-596772, 01-596773. **LC** H1; .S67. **DD** 300/.5. **UDC** 3. **[CCC].** Index available. cum. index. **Circ:** 500.
**Desc:** Incorporates research sponsored by the Natural Resources Energy and Science Authority on social sciences and those written by researchers working independently.
**Ind/Abst** Appl. Soc. Sci. Index Abstr.; Int. Bibliogr. Sociol.

US
**SSCI JCR [MICROFORM] / ISI.** **Added/Corp** Institute for Scientific Information. **VFOAT** SSCI Journal Citation Reports; Social Sciences Citation Index Journal Citation Reports; Journal Citation Reports; JCR. (1989)-. English. $330.00. Institute for Scientific Information, 3501 Market Street, Philadelphia PA 19104. **Tel** (215)386-0100, (800)523-1850, FAX (215)386-6362, telex 84-5305. **(Subscription address:** Institute for Scientific Information, PO Box 71416, Chicago IL 60694.**)** **LC** Z7161; .S652. ***Continues*** *SSCI Journal Citation Reports, 0161-3162.*

CN/0839-4377
**SSHRC NEWS.** [SSHRC news]. **Main/Corp** Social Sciences and Humanities Research Council of Canada. **VFOAT** Nouvelles du CRSH. **VAT** Social Sciences and Humanities Research Council of Canada News; Nouvelles du Conseil de Recherches en Sciences Humaines du Canada. Vol. 1, No. 1 (Spring 1988)-. Periodical. English (French). qt. Free. Social Sciences and Humanities Research Council of Canada, PO Box 1610, 255 Albert Street K1P 6G4 Canada. **Tel** (613)992-0691. **DD** 354.710085. ***Continues*** *Council Update, 0225-1787.*

UK
**SSRC STUDENTSHIP HANDBOOK. POSTGRADUATE STUDENTSHIPS IN THE SOCIAL SCIENCES.** **Main/Corp** Social Science Research Council (Great Britain). Postgraduate Training Division. English. **LC** H62.5.G7; S64A. **DD** 300/.7/1141. ***Continues*** *Postgraduate Studentships in the Social Sciences.*

US/0093-2582
**ST. CROIX REVIEW, THE.** **Added/Corp** Religion and Society, Inc. (Stillwater, Minn.). **VAT** Saint Croix Review. Vol. 7 (Feb. 1974)-. Periodical. English. bm. $25.00. Religion and Society Inc, PO Box 244, Stillwater NM 55082. **Tel** (612)439-7190. **ED** Angie McDonald. **LC** AS30; .S252. **DD** 081. **Bk Rev. Circ:** 1,400. available on microfiche from Xerox; and KTO Microform; available on microfilm and microfiche from University Microfilms International (UMI). ***Continues*** *Religion and Society, 0034-396X.*
**Desc:** Discussion of social issues and activism.

US/0890-6270
**STARMONT POPULAR CULTURE STUDIES.** [Starmont pop. cult. stud.]. (1989)-. Monographic series. English. bm. Price varies per volume. Starmont House, PO Box 851, Mercer Island WA 98040. **Tel** (206)232-848, FAX (206)232-9274. **(Subscription address:** Borgo Press PO Box 2845 San Bernardino, CA 92406 (909) 884-5813**)** ***Continues*** *Starmont Pulp and Dime Store Studies, 0885-0658.*
**Desc:** Monographs on popular culture, including story collections from pulp sources and critical works on genre writers.

US
**STATION RELAY, THE.** ***Title Change.*** [Stn. relay]. Vol. 1, No. 1 (Sept. 1985)-(199?). Academic Scholarly Publication. English. Five times a year (Sept., Nov., Jan., March, May). Social Science Research Station Inc, 32 Highgate Road, Berkeley CA 94707. **Tel** (510)525-3248. **ED** Eugenia Miller, Ethel Dunn, Stephen P Dunn. Index available. cum. index. **Bk Rev. Ad Acc. Circ:** 250. ***Continued by*** *Russia and Her Neighborhoods, 1066-0127.*
**Desc:** Abstracts and analysis of articles from the Soviet press and scholarly periodicals on topics ranging from agriculture to women. Travel notes by readers; letters; comments.

SA
**STRATEGIC REVIEW FOR SOUTHERN AFRICA.** **Added/Corp** University of Pretoria. Institute for Strategic Studies. **VFOAT** Strategiese Oorsig vir Suider-Afrika. (198?)-. Periodical. English (Afrikaans). sa. Comes with the Institute for Strategic Studies publications subscription - $45.00 (airmail). Institute of Strategic Studies, University of Pretoria, Pretoria 0002 South Africa. **Tel** 011 27 12 4202407, FAX 011 27 12 432185. **ED** M. Hough and Mrs. M. A. Van der Merve. **LC** UA10.5; .I85. Index available. cum. index. **Bk Rev. Ad Acc. Circ:** 2,000 (ctrl). ***Continues*** *ISSUP Strategic Review.*
**Desc:** Contains articles on current strategic matters.

IT/0303-4615
**STUDI NOVECENTESCHI.** [Studi novecent.]. **Added/Corp** Universit-a di Padova. Istituto di Filologia e Letteratura Italiana. No. 1 (March 1972)-. Periodical. Italian. sa (2 issues). L120000 Italy; L190000 other. Giardini Editori Stampatori, Via Santa Bibbiana 28, 56127 Pisa Italy. **Tel** 011 39 50 934242.
**Ind/Abst** MLA Int. Bibl. Books Artic. Mod. Lang. Lit.; Romant. Move.

PL/0860-102X
**STUDIA I MATERIAY Z DZIEJOW NAUKI POLSKIEJ. SERIA II, HISTORIA NAUK SCISYCH, PRZYRODNICZYCH I TECHNICZNYCH.** **VFOAT** Historia nauk Scisych, Przyrodniczych i Technicznych. (1988)-. Polish (summaries and/or abstracts in English; table of contents in English). ir. Panstwowe Wydawn Naukowe, Miodowa 10, PO Box 391, 00251 Warsaw Poland. **LC** Q127.P6; S7817.

PL/0039-3371
**STUDIA SOCJOLOGICZNE.** [Stud. socjol.]. **Added/Corp** Instytut Filozofii i Socjologii (Polska Akademia Nauk). Vol. 1, No. 1 (1961)-. Periodical. Polish (English and Russian; table of contents in Russian and English). qt. Price on Request. **(Subscription address:** ARS Polona, PO Box 1001, 00068 Warsaw Poland.**)** **CODEN** STSOCP.
**Ind/Abst** Peace Res. Abstr. J. (1958-1962, 1964); Psychol. Abstr. (1968-); Soc. Plann. Policy Dev. Abstr.; Sociol. Abstr. [Full Cov.].

US/0039-3606
**STUDIES IN COMPARATIVE INTERNATIONAL DEVELOPMENT.** [Stud. comp. int. dev.]. Vol. 1 (1965)-. Periodical. English. Four times a year. Fl186.00 (individual), Fl316.00 (institution). Transaction Publishers / Rutgers State University, New Brunswick NJ 08903. **Tel** (908)932-2280 Ext. 105, FAX (908)932-3138. **ED** John D Martz. **LC** H31; .S82. **DD** 300/.5. **[CCC]. Bk Rev. Ad Acc. Pr Rev. Circ:** 1,150. available on labels; available on microfilm and microfiche from University Microfilms International (UMI). Documents available from The Genuine Article, UMI Article Clearinghouse.
**Desc:** A interdisciplinary social science journal exploring current issues in development theory and practice. Open to all theorectical, methodological, and ideological approaches in examining the relationship between population, technology, and policy in a developmental context.
**Ind/Abst** ABC POL SCI; ABI/INFORM Glob. Ed.; Am. Hist. Life (1973-); Appl. Soc. Sci. Index Abstr.; Curr. Contents Soc. Behav. Sci.; Geogr. Abstr. Human Geogr.; HAPI Hisp. Am. Period. Index; Int. Bibliogr. Sociol.; Int. Dev. Abstr.; Int. Labour Doc.; Int. Polit. Sci. Abstr.; LABORDOC; Middle East Abstr. Index; Res. Alert [Full Cov.]; Soc. Plann. Policy Dev. Abstr.; Soc. Sci. Cit. Index [Full Cov.]; Sociol. Abstr.; U.S. Polit. Sci. Doc.

US/1043-5786
**STUDIES IN EUROPEAN THOUGHT.** [Stud. Eur. thought]. (1990)-. Monographic series. English. ir. Price varies per volume. Peter Lang Publishing, 62 West 45th Street, 4th Floor, New York NY 10036. **Tel** (212)764-1471, (800)770-5264, telex 6973364 PLNY. **DD** 080.

DK/0078-3307
**STUDIES IN HISTORY AND SOCIAL SCIENCES.** **See** History(General).

US/0730-9139
**STUDIES IN LATIN AMERICAN POPULAR CULTURE.** **See** The Arts.

US
**STUDIES IN MARXISM (MINNEAPOLIS, MINN.).** (STUDIES IN MARXISM.). Vol. 1 (1977)-. Monographic series. English. ir. Price varies per volume. Marxist Education Press, 116 Church Street Southeast, University of Minnesota, Minneapolis MN 55455. **Tel** (612)922-7993. **ED** Doris G. Marquit. cum. index. **Circ:** 1,300.
**Desc:** Monographs, textbooks, collections of papers dealing with application of Marxist methods to all fields.

US/1042-3192
**STUDIES IN QUALITATIVE METHODOLOGY.** [Stud. qual. methodol.]. Vol. 1 (1988)-. English. ir. $73.25. JAI Press Inc., 55 Old Post Road, Suite 2, PO Box 1678, Greenwich CT 06836-1678. **Tel** (203)661-7602, FAX (203)661-0792. **ED** Robert G. Burgess. **LC** H62.A1; S78. **DD** 300/.72.

NE/0081-8518
**STUDIES IN SOCIAL LIFE.** 1- 1953-. Monographic series. English. ir. Price varies per volume. Martinus Nijhoff Publishers, Subsidiary of Kluwer Academic Publishers, Koraalrood 50, 2718 SC Zoetermeer Netherlands. **Tel** 011 31 79 684400.

US
**STUDIES IN SOCIETY.** (1978)-. Monographic series. English. ir. Price varies per volume. Harper Collins Publishers, Keystone Industrial Park, Scranton PA 18512. **Tel** (800)242-7737, (800)233-4727, FAX (800)822-4090. **LC** UNC.

US/0081-8682
**STUDIES IN THE SOCIAL SCIENCES (CARROLLTON, GA.).** (STUDIES IN THE SOCIAL SCIENCES / WEST GEORGIA COLLEGE.). **Main/Corp** West Georgia College. **Added/Corp** West Georgia College. Vol. 1 (1962)-. English. an. $5.00. West Georgia College Sociology Department, Carrollton GA 30118-0001. **Tel** (404)834-4336. **ED** Pick Conner. **DD** 300. **Circ:** 500.
**Desc:** This work will interest sociologists, historians, psychologists, and all observers of social phenomena, past and present.
**Ind/Abst** Am. Hist. Life (1972-); Geogr. Abstr. Human Geogr. (?-?).

US/1056-9189
**STUDIES IN THIRD WORLD SOCIETIES.** [Stud. third world soc.]. **Added/Corp** College of William and Mary. Dept. of Anthropology. No. 1 (Nov. 1976)-. Monographic series. English. ir. Price varies per volume. College of William and Mary, Department of Anthropology, Williamsburg VA 23185. **Tel** (804)221-1055. **DD** 909.
**Ind/Abst** Anthropol. Lit.; Geogr. Abstr. Human Geogr.; Int. Dev. Abstr.; Soc. Plann. Policy Dev. Abstr.

CN/0837-9971
**SUBVENTIONS A LA RECHERCHE, BOURSES D'EXCELLENCE ET SUBVENTIONS POUR ETUDESET ANALYSES.** ***Title Change.*** [Subvent. rech. bourses excell. subvent. etud. anal.]. **Added/Corp** Conseil

Quebecois de la Recherche Sociale. (1985/86)-(1993). French. an. Conseil Quebecois de la Recherche Sociale, 1075 rue Raymond-Casgrain, ler etage, Quebec Quebec G1S 2E4 Canada. **Tel** (418)643-7582. **DD** 001.4/4. **Circ:** 7,000. ***Continues*** *Subventions a la Recherche et Bourses d'Excellence sur des Themes Proposes, 0837-9963.* ***Continued by*** *Programmes de Subventions et de Bourses de Carriere du Conseil Quebecois de la Recherche Sociale, 1191-7431.*
**Desc:** Description of grants and bursaries.

GW/0722-480X
**SUDOST EUROPA : [MONATSSCHRIFT DER ABTEILUNG GEGENWARTSFORSCHUNG DES SUDOST-INSTITUTS]. Added/Corp** Sudost-Institut Munchen. Abteilung Gegenwartsforschung. **VFOAT** Sudosteuropa. Vol. 31, No. 1 (Jan. 1982)-. Periodical. German (English). bm. DM94.00. R Oldenbourg Verlag, Postfach 801360, D 81613 Munich Germany. **Tel** 011 49 89 450190, FAX 011 49 89 45019305. **ED** F.L. Altmann, A.U. Gabanyi, W. Hoepken, J. Reuter, K. Sitzler Vondung, G. Seewann. **LC** H5; .W5. **DD** 947/.0005. **[CCC]**. Index available. cum. index. **Bk Rev. Ad Acc. Circ:** 700 (ctrl). ***Continues*** *Wissenschaftlicher Dienst Sudosteuropa.*
**Desc:** Studies, comments, and documentation on current political, economic, social, and cultural developments in South-Eastern Europe, mainly in the socialist countries.

US/0274-9181
**SUNBURST (ROSEVILLE).** (SUNBURST.). **Added/Corp** California Council for the Social Studies. (19??)-. Periodical. English. qt. $20.00. California Council of Social Studies, 1255 Vista Grande, Millbrae CA 94030. **Tel** (916)786-6056. **ED** John Hergsheimner. **Ad Acc. Circ:** 1,500 (ctrl).
**Desc:** This publication is a composite of all local council news in the State, as well as announcements of upcoming workshops, conferences and meetings.

CN/0714-0045
**SURVEY METHODOLOGY.** [Surv. methodol.]. **Added/Corp** Statistics Canada. Household Surveys Development Division. Statistics Canada. Statistical Services Field. Statistics Canada. Statistics Canada. Social Survey Methods Division. **VFOAT** Techniques d'Enquete. Vol. 1, No. 1 (June 1975)-. Periodical. English (French). sa. 45.00Can$ Canada; $54.00 US; $63.00 other. Statistics Canada, Publications Sales & Services, Main Building Room 1710, Ottawa Ontario K1A 0T6 Canada. **Tel** (613)951-5078, (800)267-6677, FAX (613)951-1584, telex 053-3585. **LC** HA31.2; .S87. **DD** 001.4/22/05.
**Desc:** Publishes articles dealing with various aspects of statistical developments, with emphasis on the development and evaluation of specific methodologies as applied to data collection or the data itself.
**Ind/Abst** Biostatistica (19??-); Curr. Index Stat.; Soc. Res. Methodol. Abstr. (1991-); Stat. Theory Method Abstr. (1986-1987).

RU
**SVODNYI BIULLETEN NOVYKH INOSTRANNYKH KNIG, POSTUPIVSHIKH V BIBLIOTEKI SSSR: OBSHCHESTVENNYE NAUKI. Added/Corp** Vsesoiuznaia Gosudarstvennaia Biblioteka Inostrannoi Literatury (Soviet Union). **VAT** Svodnyi Biulleten Novykh Inostrannykh Knig, Postupivshikh V Biblioteki Soiuza Sovetskikh Sotsialisticheskikh Respublik: Obshchestvennye Nauki. (1977)-. Multiple languages (Russian and Multiple languages). bm. $41.50. Izdatelstvo Kniga, 50 Gorky Ulitsa, 125047 Moscow Russia. **LC** Z7161; .S99; H62. ***Supersedes*** *Svodnyi Biulleten Novykh Inostrannykh Knig, Postupivshikh V Krupneishie Biblioteki SSSR. Seriia B. Obshchestvennye Nauki.*

SW
**SWEDISH BEHAVIORAL SCIENCE RESEARCH REPORTS. Main/Corp** Statens Psykologisk-Pedagogiska Bibliotek. **VFOAT** Beteendevetenskapliga Rapporter. English. National Library for Psychology and Education, Box 23099 S-104 35, 23 Stockholm Sweden. **LC** H62.5.S8; S7A. **DD** 300/.7/20485.

AU
**SWS RUNDSCHAU. Added/Corp** Sozialwissenschaftliche Studiengesellchaft (Vienna, Austria). (1987)-. Periodical. German. qt. S480.00 Austria; S520.00 other. Sozialwissenschaftliche Studiengesellschaft, Maria Theresien Strasse 9 8B, A-1090 Vienna Austria. **Tel** 011 43 1 343127. Index available. ***Continues*** *Journal fur Sozialforschung.*

NE/0166-6991
**SYNTHESE LIBRARY. See** Philosophy.

PL/0860-2212
**SZCZECINSKIE ROCZNIKI NAUKOWE. NAUKI SPOECZNE.** (NAUKI SPOECZNE / SZCZECINSKIE TOWARZYSTWO NAUKOWE.). [Szczec. rocz. nauk. Nauki spoecz.]. (1986)-. Polish (summaries and/or abstracts in English and Russian). ir.

PN/0494-7061
**TAREAS.** [Tareas]. (Oct. 1960)-. Spanish. Three times a year. $8.00 Panama; $12.00 Latin America and Caribbean; $15.00 other. Centro Estudios Latinoamericanos Cela, Apartado 87-1918, Panama 7 Rep. de Panama. **Tel** 011 507 23-0028, FAX 011 507 69-2032. **LC** F1561; .T36. Index available. **Pr Rev. Circ:** 1,500.
**Desc:** Publication of social sciences at the local and Latino-American level.

HU/0231-2522
**TARSADALOMKUTATAS. Added/Corp** Magyar Tudomanyos Akademia. Gazdasag- es Jogtudomanyok Osztalya. (1983)-. Academic Scholarly Publication. Hungarian. qt. $22.00. Akademiai Kiado, Publishing House of the Hungarian Academy of Sciences, Prielle Kornelia u. 19-35, H-1117 Budapest Hungary. **Tel** 011 36 1 1811991, FAX 011 36 1 1811991, telex 22-6228 AKNYO H. **LC** H8; .M32a. cum. index. ***Continues*** *Gazdasag es Jodtudomany, 050-4795.*
**Ind/Abst** Soc. Plann. Policy Dev. Abstr.

HU
**TARSADALOMTUDOMANYI KOZLEMENYEK. Added/Corp** Magyar Szocialista Munkaspart. Tarsadalomtudomanyi Intezet. (19??)-. Periodical. Hungarian (summaries and/or abstracts in English and Russian). qt. 40.00F. **(Subscription address:** Kultura, Hungarian Foreign Trading Company, PO Box 149, H-1389 Budapest Hungary**) LC** H8; .T32.

CN/0040-1587
**TECHNOCRACY DIGEST.** Periodical. English. qt. $5.00. The Northwest Technocrat, 7513 Greenwood Avenue, Seattle WA 98103. **Tel** (206) 784-2111. **ED** Ed McBurnie.
**Desc:** Science in the social field.

US/0090-6514
**TELOS (ST. LOUIS).** (TELOS.). [Telos]. No. 1 (Spring 1968)-. Academic Scholarly Publication. English. qt. $80.00 (institutions), $32.00 (individuals) US; $96.00 (institutions), $36.80 (individuals) other. Telos Press LTD, 431 East 12th Street, New York NY 10009. **Tel** (212)228-6479, FAX (212)228-6379. **ED** Paul Piccone. **LC** H1; .T44. **DD** 300/.5. cum. index. **Bk Rev. Ad Acc. Circ:** 2,500 (ctrl). available on microfilm and microfiche from University Microfilms International (UMI). Documents available from UMI Article Clearinghouse.
**Desc:** A scholarly journal of social and political theory. Each issue includes notes and commentary as well as a review section. Translations from foreign publications are also often included.
**Ind/Abst** Acad. Abstr. Full Text Elite (July 1990-); Acad. Abstr. (July 1990-); Acad. Search (July 1990-); Altern. Press Index; Am. Bibliogr. Slavic East Europ. Stud.; Hum. Rights Intern. Rep.; INFO-SOUTH Abstr.; Int. Bibliogr. Sociol.; Int. Polit. Sci. Abstr.; Left Index; Mag. Search; Middle East Abstr. Index; Newsp. Period. Abstr. (1986-); Philos. Index; Soc. Plann. Policy Dev. Abstr.; Soc. Sci. Source (Jul. 1990-); Sociol. Abstr.

AG/0327-3210
**TERRITORIO PARA LA PRODUCCION Y CRITICA EN GEOGRAFIA Y CIENCIAS SOCIALES. See** Geography.

CN
**THEORIA/PRAXIS: A GRADUATE JOURNAL OF THEORY AND CRITICISM. VFOAT** Theoria. (1992)-. English (French). $10.00 (individuals), $15.00 (institutions) North America and Canada. Centre for the Study of Theory and Criticism, University of Western Ontario, London Ontario N6C 1B1 Canada. **Tel** (519)661-3442, FAX (519)661-3640. **ED** Grant Stirling and Imre Szeman. **Bk Rev. Ad Acc. Pr Rev. Circ:** 300. available on diskette.
**Desc:** International interdisciplinary graduate student journal which deals with the examination and development of theoretical positions, including feminism, post-colonial discourse, semiotics, marxism, contemporary art criticism, critical theory, psychoanalysis, hermeneutics, poststructuralism, and others.

NE/0040-5833
**THEORY AND DECISION. See** Philosophy.

US/0093-3104
**THEORY AND RESEARCH IN SOCIAL EDUCATION.** [Theory res. soc. educ.]. **Added/Corp** National Council for the Social Studies. College and University Faculty Assembly. **VFOAT** TRSE. Vol. 1 (Oct. 1973)-. Academic Scholarly Publication. English. Four times a year (published seasonally). $35.00 US; $40.00 overseas. National Council for the Social Studies, 3501 Newark Street Northwest, Washington DC 20016-3167. **Tel** (202)966-7840, FAX (202)966-2061. **LC** H1; .T47. **DD** 300/.7. **Bk Rev. Ad Acc. Pr Rev. Circ:** 600. available on microfilm and microfiche from University Microfilms International (UMI).
**Desc:** A scholarly, refereed journal for social studies specialists.
**Ind/Abst** Contents Pages Educ.; Curr. Index J. Educ.; Educ. Index (1992-); Psychol. Abstr. (1973-); PsycINFO; PsycLit; Sociol. Educ. Abstr.; Stud. Women Abstr.

UK/0263-2764
**THEORY, CULTURE & SOCIETY.** (THEORY, CULTURE & SOCIETY.). [Theory cult. soc.]. **VFOAT** Theory, Culture and Society. Vol. 1, No. 1 (Spring 1982)-. Periodical. English. qt. £99.00. Sage Publications Ltd., 6 Bonhill Street, London EC2A 4PU, UK. **Tel** 071 374 0645, FAX 071 374 8741, telex 296207 SAGE G. **ED** Mike Featherstone. **Acid Free.** Documents available from The Genuine Article.
**Desc:** Caters for the resurgence of interest in culture within contemporary social science. Features papers by and about modern social and cultural theorists such as Foucault, Bourdieu, Baudrillard, Goffman, Bell, Parsons, Elias, Gadamer, Luhmann, Habermas and Giddens.
**Ind/Abst** Altern. Press Index; Arts Humanit. Citation Index [Select. Cov.]; Curr. Contents Soc. Behav. Sci.; Except. Hum. Exp.; Int. Bibliogr. Sociol.; Res. Alert [Full Cov.]; Soc. Plann. Policy Dev. Abstr.; Soc. Sci. Cit. Index [Full Cov.]; Sociol. Abstr. [Full Cov.]; Sociol. Educ. Abstr.

US/0885-2200
**THIRD WORLD IN PERSPECTIVE.** [Third world perspect.]. **Added/Corp** Third World Conference Foundation. Vol. 1, No. 1 (1991)-. Periodical. English. sa. $120.00. Third World Conference Foundation, PO Box 53110, Chicago IL 60653. **Tel** (312)241-6688. **LC** D880; .T49.

NO/0040-716X
**TIDSSKRIFT FOR SAMFUNNSFORSKNING.** [Tidsskr. samf.forsk.]. **Added/Corp** Institutt for Samfunnsforskning (Oslo, Norway). Vol. 1, (1960)-. Periodical. Norwegian (summaries and/or abstracts in English). qt. Kr525.00, $93.00. Scandinavian University Press, PO Box 2959 Toeyen, N 0608 Oslo 6 Norway. **Tel** 011 47 2 2575400, FAX 011 47 2 2575353, telex 71896 UROR N. **(Subscription address:** Scandinavian University Press, 200 Meacham Ave., Elmont NY 11003.**) ED** Tor Bjoerklund. cum. index. **Bk Rev. Ad Acc. Pr Rev. Circ:** 1,500. Documents available from The Genuine Article.
**Desc:** Social research including sociology, social anthropology, social psychology and political science.
**Ind/Abst** Am. Hist. Life (1969-); Commun. Abstr. (?-?); Curr. Contents Soc. Behav. Sci.; Res. Alert [Full Cov.]; Soc. Plann. Policy Dev. Abstr.; Soc. Sci. Cit. Index [Full Cov.]; Sociol. Abstr.; Sociol. Educ. Abstr.; Stud. Women Abstr.; Tech. Educ. Train. Abstr.

NE/0168-8626
**TIJDSCHRIFT VOOR AGOLOGIE. *Title Change.*** (1972)-(19??). Periodical. Dutch (summaries and/or abstracts in English). bm. Uitgeverij Boom, Postbus 400, 7940 AK Meppel Netherlands. **Tel** 011 31 20 5220 57012, FAX 011 31 20 5220 54452, telex 42829. ***Continued by*** *Sociaale Interventie.*
**Desc:** Covers social and organizational change.

BE/0040-7615
**TIJDSCHRIFT VOOR SOCIALE WETENSCHAPPEN.** [Tijdschr. soc. wet.]. **Added/Corp** Rijksuniversiteit te Gent. Studie en Onderzoekcentrum voor Sociale Wetenschappen. Rijksuniversiteit te Gent. Seminarie voor Sociologie. (1956)-. Periodical. Dutch (summaries and/or abstracts in English and French). Four times a year. Seminarie voor Algemene en Byzondere Sociologie, Universiteitstraat 4, Gent B-9000 Belgium. **Tel** 011 32 91 257651. **ED** M. Versichelen. **LC** H8; .T5. **DD** 330/.5. Index available. **Bk Rev. Circ:** 675.
**Desc:** Articles on sociology, social sciences, criminology, psychology and economy.
**Ind/Abst** Soc. Plann. Policy Dev. Abstr.; Sociol. Abstr. [Full Cov.]; Soc. Res. Methodol. Abstr. (1975-).

US/0730-479X
**TOCQUEVILLE REVIEW, THE.** (THE TOCQUEVILLE REVIEW. LA REVUE TOCQUEVILLE.). [Tocqueville rev.]. **Main/Corp** Tocqueville Society. **Added/Corp** Tocqueville Society. Revue Tocqueville. **VFOAT** Revue Tocqueville. Vol. 1 (Fall 1979)-. Periodical. English (French). sa. $35.00. University of Toronto Press, 5201 Dufferin Street, Downsview Ontario M3H 5T8 Canada. **Tel** (416)667-7781, (416)667-7782, FAX (416)667-7803. **ED** Henri Mendras. **LC** H1; .T62a. **DD** 300/.5. **Bk Rev. Ad Acc. Pr Rev. Circ:** 500 (ctrl).
**Desc:** Bilingual journal that provides continuous coverage of political and social trends in Europe and America.
**Ind/Abst** Am. Hist. Life (1983-); Int. Polit. Sci. Abstr.; Soc. Plann. Policy Dev. Abstr.

TU
**TOPLUM VE BILIM.** (1977)-. Periodical. Turkish. qt. **LC** H8.T87; T66.
**Ind/Abst** Am. Hist. Life (1989-).

CN/0228-6858
**TOWNSHIPS CROSSROADS. *Title Change.*** [Townsh. crossroads]. No. 1 (July 4, 1980)-. Periodical. English. qt. Townships Crossroads, c/o Townshippers Association, Room 310/31 King West, Sherbrooke Quebec J1H 1N5 Canada. **DD** 305.7/21/07146. ***Continued by*** *Crossroads (Sherbrooke, Quebec), 0834-907X.*

MX/0185-6286
**TRACE (MEXICO CITY, MEXICO).** (TRACE.). **Added/Corp** Centre d'Etudes Mexicaines et

# Social Sciences

Centramericaines (Mexico City, Mexico) Institut Francais d'Amerique Latine (Mexico). No. 7 (Oct. 1984)-. Monographic series. French (Spanish). Twice a year. Price varies per volume. Centre d'Etudes Mexicaines et Centramericaines, Sierra Leona 330, Mexico 11000 DF Mexico. **Tel** 011 52 5 5405921, 5405922. **ED** Joelle Gaillac. **Bk Rev. Ad Acc. Circ:** 1,000 (ctrl). *Continues Bulletin (Centre d'Etudes Mexicaines et Centramericaines (Mexico City, Mexico))*.
**Ind/Abst** Anthropol. Lit.; Int. Bibliogr. Sociol.

US/1050-2092
## TRADITIONAL DWELLINGS AND SETTLEMENTS REVIEW. (TRADITIONAL DWELLINGS AND SETTLEMENTS REVIEW : JOURNAL OF THE INTERNATIONAL ASSOCIATION FOR THE STUDY OF TRADITIONAL ENVIRONMENTS.). [Tradit. dwell. settl. rev.]. **Added/Corp** International Association for the Study of Traditional Environments. Vol. 1, No. 1 (Fall 1989)-. Periodical. English. Twice a year (Spring and Fall). $45.00 (individuals); $90.00 (institutions). IASTE / Center for Environmental Design Research, University of California Berkeley, 390 Wurster Hall, Berkeley CA 94720. **Tel** (510)642-2896, FAX (510)643-5571. **ED** Nezar Alsayyad. **LC** HT51; .T72. **DD** 307/.05. **Bk Rev,** (Qty: 6-8). **Pr Rev. Circ:** 500 (ctrl).
**Desc:** Of interest to those within the disciplines of architecture, anthropology, , geography, history, planning and folklore interested in the study of traditional dwellings and settlements.

US/1052-5017
## TRANSFORMATIONS (WAYNE, N.J.). (TRANSFORMATION : THE NEW JERSEY PROJECT JOURNAL.). [Transformations]. **Added/Corp** New Jersey Project. **VFOAT** New Jersey Project Journal. Vol. 1, No. 1 (Spring 1990)-. Periodical. English. Twice a year (Feb., Aug.). $15.00 (individuals); $25.00 (institutions). New Jersey Project, W. M. Patterson, Col White Hall 315, Wayne NJ 07470. **LC** LB2361.5; .T73. **DD** 370.

GY/1012-8263
## TRANSITION. **Added/Corp** University of Guyana. Faculty of Social Sciences. University of Guyana. Institute of Development Studies. Vol. 1 (1978)-. Periodical. English. Four times a year. $10.00. University of Guyana / Institute of Development Studies, PO Box 101110, Georgetown Guyana. **Tel** 011 592 2 54841. **LC** H1; .T74.

●BE
**TRANSITIONS. See** Political Science-International Relations.

IT
**TRANSIZIONE.** No. 1 (1985)-. Periodical. Italian. ir. Casa Editrice L Cappelli Spa, Via Marsili 9, 40124 Bologna Italy. **Tel** 330411. *Continues Problemi della Transizione.*

SZ/0378-5424
## TRAVAIL ET SOCIETE. **Ceased. See** Economics-Labor.

FR
**TRAVAUX.** French. Dawson France SA, BP 40, 91121 Palaiseau Cedex France. **Tel** 011 33 1 69104700, telex 220064F.

FR
## TRAVAUX ET MEMOIRES DE L'INSTITUT D'ETHNOLOGIE. **Main/Corp** Paris. Universite. Institut d'Ethnologie. 1 (1926)-. Monographic series. French (Spanish and Quechua). sa. Price varies per volume. Institut d'Ethnologie Musee de l'Homme, Palais de Chaillot, Place du Trocadero 75116 Paris France. **Tel** 45 53 82 15. Index available.
**Desc:** Volumes of ethnology, archaeology, linguistics, monographies, ethnohistoric studies, codex and oral literature, both urban and European.

UK/0082-660X
## TRIVIUM (CARDIFF, WALES). (TRIVIUM.). [Trivium]. **Added/Corp** St. David's College (Lampeter, Wales) St. David's University College (Lampeter, Wales). Vol. 1 (May 1966)-. English. ir. $7.50 (per copy). St. Davids University College, c/o The Editor, Lampeter SA48 7ED Wales England. **Tel** 0570 422351. **LC** AS122.S24; A3. Documents available from The Genuine Article.
**Ind/Abst** Arts Humanit. Citation Index (19??-19??) [Full Cov.]; MLA Int. Bibl. Books Artic. Mod. Lang. Lit.; Res. Alert [Full Cov.].

CH
## TUNG HAI SHE HUI KO HSUEH HSUEH PAO. **VFOAT** Tunghai Journal of Social Sciences. V. 1-. Periodical. Chinese (English). Tunghai University, Taichung 400 Taiwan. **LC** H8.C47; T85. **DD** 300/.5.

CC
## TUNG-PEI SHIH TA HSUEH PAO. CHE HSUEH SHE HUI KO HSUEH PAN. See Philosophy.

TK
## TURKMENISTAN YLYMLAR AKADEMIIASYNYNG KHABARLARY. GUMANITAR YLYMLARY. **Added/Corp** Turkmenistan Ylymlar Akademiiasy. **VFOAT** Gumanitar

Ylymlary; Izvestiia Akademii nauk Turkmenistana. Gumanitarnye Nauki; Proceedings of the Academy of Sciences of the Turkmenistan. Humanitarnye Sciences; Gumanitarnye Nauki. (1991)-. Periodical. Russian (Turkmen; summaries and/or abstracts in English). bm. **LC** H19.A59; A2. *Continues Turkmenistan SSR Ylymlar Akademiiasynyng Khabarlary. Gumanitar Ylymlary, 0205-9932.*

US
## UNIVERSITY OF ILLINOIS INSTITUTE OF GOVERNMENT AND PUBLIC AFFAIRS WORK PAPERS. English. ir. Free. University of Illinois / Government, Urbana-Champaign Campus, Institute of Government and Public Affairs, 1201 West Nevada Street, Urbana IL 61801. **Tel** (217)333-3340, FAX (217)244-4817. **ED** Peter F Nardulli. **Circ:** 150 (ctrl)

AT
**UNIYA.** (19??). Periodical. English. qt. 10.00Aus$. Uniya, 24 Roslyn Street, P.O.Box 522, Kings Cross, NSW 2011 Australia. **Tel** 011 61 02 356 3888, FAX 011 61 02 356 3021.

GW/0342-5258
## UNSERE JUGEND. **See** Education.

GW/0566-2761
## UNTERSUCHUNGEN ZUR GEGENWARTSKUNDE SUDOSTEUROPAS. **Added/Corp** Munich Sudost-Institut. Vol. 1 (1957)-. Monographic series. German. ir. Price varies per volume. R Oldenbourg Verlag, Postfach 801360, D 81613 Munich Germany. **Tel** 011 49 89 450190, FAX 011 49 89 45019305. **Circ:** 1,000 (ctrl).
**Desc:** Historical reports and comments on Albania, Bulgaria, Yugoslavia, Romania, Hungary and their political, economic, social and cultural developments.

SA/1011-5544
**UPDATE. Added/Corp** South African Institute of Race Relations. (Mar. 1989-July 1989)-. Periodical. English. tq. Auden House, Publications Department, 68 de Korte Street, 2001 Braamfontein, South Africa. **LC** HN801; .A55. **DD** 305.8/96/06805. *Continues Social and Economic Update, 1011-5544.*

CN/1187-3043
## UPDATE - SOCIAL SCIENCE FEDERATION OF CANADA. (BULLETIN / FEDERATION CANADIENNE DES SCIENCES SOCIALES.). [Update - Soc. Sci. Fed. Can.]. **Added/Corp** Federation Canadienne des Sciences Sociales. **VFOAT** Update. **VAT** Bulletin - Federation Canadienne des Sciences Sociales. Vol. 3, No 2 (April 1991)-. Bulletin. French (English). bm. Federation Canadienne des Sciences Sociales, #415, 151 Rue Slater, Ottawa Ontario K1P 5H3. **DD** 300/.971/05. *Continues SSFC Update., 0848-4910.*

CN/1187-3043
## UPDATE / SOCIAL SCIENCE FEDERATION OF CANADA. [Update - Soc. Sci. Fed. Can.]. **Added/Corp** Social Science Federation of Canada. **VFOAT** Bulletin. **VAT** Bulletin - Federation Canadienne des Sciences Sociales. Vol. 3, No. 2 (Apr. 1991)-. Periodical. English (French). ir. Free on request. Social Science Federation of Canada, 151 Slater Street/Suite 415, Ottawa Ontario K1P 5H3 Canada. **Tel** (613)238-6112. **DD** 300/.971/05. *Continues SSFC Update., 0848-4910.*

US/0272-3638
## URBAN GEOGRAPHY. **See** Geography.

KE
**UTAFITI.** V. 1 (1976)-. Periodical. English. sa. $5.20. PO Box 30022, Nairobi Kenya Africa. **LC** H1; .U82. **DD** 300/.5.
**Ind/Abst** Am. Hist. Life (1985-); Int. Bibliogr. Sociol.; Sage Public Adm. Abstr. (?-?).

US/0897-4357
**UTOPIA 2.** [Utop. 2]. **VFOAT** Utopia Two. Periodical. English. qt. Kerista Consciousness Church, 547 Frederick Street, San Francisco CA 94117. **DD** 307. *Continues Kerista, 0743-3301.*

HU/0865-3763
## VENGERSKII MERIDIAN. (1990)-. Periodical. Russian. qt. **LC** HM7; .V46.

CN/0317-8471
## VERS DEMAIN (EDITION FRANCAISE). (VERS DEMAIN.). **Added/Corp** Institut d'Action Politique. (Nov. 1939)-. Periodical. French. bm (6 issues). 5.00Can$ Canada; 7.00Can$ other. Louis Even Institute of Social Justice, 1101 Rue Principale, Rougemont Quebec J0L 1M0 Canada. **Tel** (514)469-2209. *Supersedes Cahiers du Credit Social, 0382-5752.*

GW/0083-5846
## VERSTANDLICHE WISSENSCHAFT. **See** History(General).

FR/0042-5605
**VIE SOCIALE. Added/Corp** Cedias. No. 1 (Jan. 1964)-. Periodical. French. bm. 260.00F France; 310.00F other. CEDIAS, 5 rue Las-Cases, 75007 Paris France. **Tel** 011 33 1 45516610, 011 33 1 47039246. **ED** Brigitte Bouquet. **LC** H3; .V5. **NLM** W1 VI227. **Bk Rev,** (Qty: 6). **Ad Acc. Circ:** 1,200 (ctrl). *Supersedes Cahiers du Musee Social.*

GW/0042-5699
## VIERTELJAHRSCHRIFT FUER SOZIAL- UND WIRTSCHAFTSGESCHICHTE. **See** Economics-Economic History, Conditions.

GW
## VIERTELJAHRSCHRIFT FUR SOZIAL- UND WIRTSCHAFTSGESCHICHTE BEIHEFTE. **VFOAT** VSWG. Beihefte. No. 38 (1954)-. Monographic series. German. ir. Price varies per volume. Franz Steiner Verlag GmbH, Postfach 101061, D 70009 Stuttgart Germany. **Tel** 011 49 0711 2582372, FAX 011 49 0711 2582290, telex 723636 daz d. **LC** H5; .V6 Suppl. *Continues Beiheft ... aur Vierteljahrschrift fur Sozial- und Wirtschaftsgeschichte.*

NP
**VILLAGE NEPAL.** Vol. 1, No. 1 (Nov. 1980)-. English. sa. $3.00. Village Nepal, 1/138 GA Pulchowk, Lalitpur Nepal. **LC** HN670.9.Z9; C683.

US/0507-1305
## VIRGINIA SOCIAL SCIENCE JOURNAL. [Va. soc. sci. j.]. **Added/Corp** Virginia Social Science Association. Virginia Commonwealth University. School of Business. **VFOAT** VSSJ. Vol. 1 (April 1966)-. Periodical. English. an (April). $15.00. James Madison University / Marketing, Marketing Department, Harrisonburg VA 22807. **Tel** (703)568-3241. **(Subscription address:** James Madison University, Marketing Department, c/o Dr. Bertsch, Harrisonburg VA 22807.) **ED** Thomas Bertsch and Gregory Weiss. **LC** H1; .V54. **DD** 301. cum. index. **Ad Acc. Pr Rev. Circ:** 200.
**Desc:** Contains original research articles in the various disciplines of social science, with cross-disciplinary papers on people and society. Advancements in science and technology and the impact of these on man and society.
**Ind/Abst** PAIS Int. Print.

●BL
**VOZES CULTURA. VFOAT** Cultura Vozes. (1992)-. Periodical. Persian. bm. $65.00. Editora Vozes Ltda, R Frei Luis, 100 CP 90023, 25689 Petropolis RJ Brazil. **Tel** 11 55 242 435112. **LC** AP66; .V68. Index available (Bound in Dec. issue). *Continues Revista de Cultura Vozes.*

JA/0286-1283
## WASEDA SHAKAI KAGAKU KENKYU. **VFOAT** Waseda Journal of Social Sciences. Began in 1967. Periodical. Japanese. Waseda Daigaku Shakai Kagakubu Gakkai, c/o Waseda Daigaku Shakai, Kagakubu 6-1, Nishi Waseda 1, Shinjuku-ku Tokyo-to Japan. **LC** H8.J3; .W37.

US/0083-7393
## WASHINGTON. **See** Business.

GW/0043-2636
## WELTWIRTSCHAFTLICHES ARCHIV. [Weltwirtsch. Arch.]. **Added/Corp** Universitat Kiel. Institut fuer Weltwirtschaft. (1913)-. Periodical. German. qt. DM158.00. JCB Mohr / Paul Siebeck, Postfach 2040, D 72010 Tuebingen Germany. **Tel** 011 49 7071 9230, FAX 011 49 7071 51104, telex 7/262872 mohr d. **ED** Horst Siebert. **LC** H5; .W4. **[CCC].** cum. index. **Pr Rev.** Documents available from The Genuine Article.
**Desc:** Review of world economics, founded in 1914. Publishes articles on international economics with strong emphasis on empirical research and policy relevance.
**Ind/Abst** Arts Humanit. Citation Index [Select. Cov.]; Contents Recent Econ. J.; Curr. Contents Soc. Behav. Sci.; Econ. Lit. Index; Int. Labour Doc.; J. Econ. Lit.; Mag. Search; PAIS Int. Print; Res. Alert [Full Cov.]; Selec. Coop. Index Manage. Period; Soc. Sci. Cit. Index [Full Cov.]; Stat. Theory Method Abstr. (1959-1963).

CC/0511-4772
**WENWU.** (WEN WU.). [Wenwu]. **VFOAT** Cultural Relics. (1959)-. Periodical. Chinese. mo. $43.90. **(Subscription address:** China International Book Trading Corporation, PO Box 399, Library Service Department, Beijing 100044 People's Republic of China.) *Continues Wen Wu Tsan Kao Tzu Liao.*
**Desc:** Contains information on cultural relics.
**Ind/Abst** Am. Hist. Life (1977-).

US/0735-0392
## WESTERN CIVILIZATION. **See** History(General).

US/0197-4327
## WESTERN JOURNAL OF BLACK STUDIES, THE. **See** Ethnic Interests.

GW
**WISSENSCHAFTLICHE ZEITSCHRIFT DER HUMBOLDT-UNIVERSITAT ZU BERLIN. GEISTES- UND SOZIALWISSENSCHAFTEN.** **Added/Corp** Humboldt-Universitat zu Berlin. **VFOAT** Geistes- und Sozialswissenschaften; Wiss. Zeitschrift der Humboldt-Universitat zu Berlin. Reihe Geistes- U. Sozialwiss.; Wiss. Zeitschrift der Humboldt-Univ. Zu Berlin, Geistes- und Sozialwiss. (1991)-. Periodical. German (English). **LC** AS182; .B68. ***Continues*** *Wissenschaftliche Zeitschrift der Humboldt-Universitat zu Berlin. Reihe Gesellschaftswissenschaften, 0863-0623.*
**Ind/Abst** Am. Hist. Life; BHA : Biblio. Hist. Art.

TH/0125-8370
**WITTHAYASAN KASETSAT. SAKHA SANGKHOMMASAT.** **Added/Corp** Mahawitthayalai Kasetsat. **VFOAT** Sakha Sangkhommasat; Social Sciences; Kasetsart Journal. Social Sciences. (1980)-. Periodical. Thai (English). sa. **LC** H8.T47; W57. **CODEN** KJSSEH.
**Ind/Abst** Agrofor. Abstr.; For. Abstr.

II
**WORKERS EDUCATION.** **See** Economics-Labor.

US/0732-7749
**WORKING PAPER SERIES - UNIVERSITY OF ARIZONA. MEXICAN AMERICAN STUDIES AND RESEARCH CENTER.** (WORKING PAPER SERIES / MASRC, MEXICAN AMERICAN STUDIES AND RESEARCH CENTER.). [Work. pap. ser. - Univ. Ariz., Mex. Am. Stud. Res. Cent.]. Monographic series. English (Spanish). ir (three to four times a year). Price varies per volume. University of Arizona / Mexican Studies, Mexican American Studies and Research Center, Modern Languages Room 209, Tucson AZ 85721. **Tel** (602)621-7551. **ED** John A Garcia. **DD** 305. **Bk Rev**. **Ad Acc. Circ:** 75.
**Desc:** Policy areas of economics, education, acculturation of Hispanics in the US and expressive culture.

US
**WORKING PAPERS INDEX.** ***Ceased.*** **Added/Corp** John F. Kennedy School of Government. Library. (Sept 1991)-(1992). English.

NE
**WORKING PAPERS SERIES / INSTITUTE OF SOCIAL STUDIES, NETHERLANDS.** **Added/Corp** Institute of Social Studies (Netherlands). **VFOAT** Working Paper General Series; Working Papers; ISS Working Paper, General Series; Working Paper. No. 1 (1982)-. Monographic series. English. Price varies per volume. Walter De Gruyter Inc, 200 Saw Mill River Road, Hawthorne NY 10532. **Tel** (914)747-0110. **(Subscription address:** Germany/ PO Box 110240, 1 Berlin 11**)**
**Ind/Abst** Dairy Sci. Abstr.

US/0193-7871
**WORLD EAGLE.** **See** Social Sciences-Abstracting, Bibliographies and Statistics.

FR/0251-4877
**WORLD LIST OF SOCIAL SCIENCE PERIODICALS.** (LISTE MONDIALE DES PERIODIQUES SPECIALISES DANS LES SCIENCES SOCIALES.). [World list soc. sci. period.]. **Added/Corp** Unesco. International Committee for Social Sciences Documentation. International Committee for Social Science Information and Documentation. Unesco. Social Science Documentation Centre. Unesco. Social and Human Sciences Documentation Centre. **VFOAT** World List of Social Science Periodicals. (1953)-. Monographic series. English (French and Spanish). ir. Price varies per volume. UNESCO / France, 31 rue Francois Bonvin, 75732 Paris Cedex 15 France. **Tel** 011 33 1 45684564, 011 33 1 45684565, FAX 011 33 1 42733007, telex 204461 Paris. **(Subscription address:** UNIPUB, 4611 F Assembly Drive, Lanham MD 20706.**)** **LC** Z7163; .L523; H1.

US/0194-6161
**WORLD MEETINGS. SOCIAL & BEHAVIORAL SCIENCES, HUMAN SERVICES & MANAGEMENT.** **Added/Corp** World Meetings Information Center. **VFOAT** Social & Behavioral Sciences, Human Services & Management; Social and Behavioral Sciences, Human Services and Management. Vol. 7, No. 2 (Apr. 1977)-. Periodical. English. qt. $170.00 US; $185.00 other. Macmillan Publishing Company, 100 Front Street, Box 500, Riverside NJ 08075-7500. **Tel** (800)257-5755, (609)461-6500, FAX (609)461-7070. **LC** AS8; .W75. **DD** 327/.17. **NLM** W 3.5 W926. **CODEN** WMSMPF. Index available (bound in all issues.). ***Continues*** *World Meetings. Social & Behavioral Sciences, Education & Management, 0043-8685.*
**Desc:** Registry of future meetings in the areas of social science, management, computer science, education, environment and energy as well as other subject areas.

US/0273-480X
**WORLD'S FAIR (CORTE MADERA, CALIF.).** (WORLD'S FAIR.). [World's fair]. Vol. 1, No. 1, (Feb. 1981)-. Periodical. English. Four times a year (Jan., Apr., July, Oct.). $45.00 one year; $75.00 two year; $105.00 three year. World's Fair, PO Box 339, Department ABE, Corte Madera CA 94925. **Tel** (415)924-6035, FAX (415)924-5053. **ED** Alfred Heller. **LC** T391; .W67. Index available (once a year in January). **Bk Rev**, (Qty: 0-3). **Ad Acc. Circ:** 5,000 (ctrl).
**Desc:** The people, pageantry and politics of world fairs and world-quality events on the past, present and future. A journal of fact and commentary with fine illustrations.

PP
**YAGL-AMBU; PAPUA NEW GUINEA JOURNAL OF THE SOCIAL SCIENCES AND HUMANITIES.** **Added/Corp** University of Papua New Guinea. **VFOAT** Papua New Guinea Journal of the Social Sciences and Humanities. Vol. 1 (Mar. 1974)-. Periodical. English. Three times a year. $30.00. University Bookshop of Papua New Guinea, PO Box 4820, Papua New Guinea. **Tel** 011 675 260900. **ED** Desh Gupta. **Bk Rev. Circ:** 300 (ctrl).
**Desc:** Examines issues concerned with Papua New Guinea's social and economic developments.
**Ind/Abst** Int. Bibliogr. Sociol.

US/0044-0124
**YALE REVIEW, THE.** [Yale rev.]. **Added/Corp** Yale University. Vol. 1 (May 1892)-Vol. 19 (Feb. 1911); New Series, Vol. 1 , (Oct. 1911)-. Periodical. English. qt. $50.00 North America; $56.00 other. Blackwell Publishers, 238 Main Street, Cambridge MA 02142. **Tel** (617)547-7110, (800)835-6770, FAX (617)547-0789. **ED** Kai Erikson. **LC** AP2; .Y2. **DD** 051. **[CCC].** Index available. cum. index. **Bk Rev**. **Ad Acc. Circ:** 6,000. available on microfilm and microfiche from University Microfilms International (UMI). Documents available from UMI Article Clearinghouse. ***Supersedes*** *New Englander and Yale Review.*
**Ind/Abst** Abstr. Engl. Stud.; Acad. Ind. [Computer File] (1984-); Am. Hist. Life (1954-1958); Am. Bibliogr. Slavic East Europ. Stud.; Annu. Bibliogr. Engl. Lang. Lit.; BHA : Biblio. Hist. Art; Book Rev. Digest; Book Rev. Index (?-1991); Expand. Acad. Index (1984-); Film Lit. Index (1973-1990); Gen. Period. Index (1985-); Humanit. Index; Index Am. Period. Verse; Int. Polit. Sci. Abstr.; Lit. Crit. Regist. (1954-1958); Mag. Index Plus (1989-); Middle East Abstr. Index; MLA Int. Bibl. Books Artic. Mod. Lang. Lit.; Newsp. Period. Abstr. (1989-); Read. Guide Period. Lit.; Romant. Move. (1977-); Mag. Index (1977-?); West. Hist. Q.

CH
**YENCHING JOURNAL OF SOCIAL STUDIES, THE.** **Added/Corp** Yenching University, Peking. Vol. 1 (June, 1938)-. Periodical. English. sa. Yenching University, Beijing, People's Republic of China. **LC** H1; .Y4. **DD** 305.

KO
**YONGS NONCHONG.** **VFOAT** Yonsei Nonchong. Vol. 1, Ser. 1 (1962)-. Periodical. Korean (English and French). an. Yonse Taehakkyo Teahagwon, 134 Sinchon-dong Sodaemun-ku, South Korea. **LC** AS559.A1; Y66. **DD** 059/.957.

CR
**YPSILON : REVISTA CENTROAMERICA DE PLANIFICACION.** **Added/Corp** Universidad Nacional (Costa Rica). Escuela de Planificacion Y Promocion Social. No. 1 (Jan./Jun. 1991)-. Periodical. Spanish. sa.

RH/0379-0622
**ZAMBEZIA.** [Zambezia]. **Added/Corp** University College of Rhodesia. University of Rhodesia. University of Zimbabwe. Began with Vol. 1, No. 1 (Jan. 1969)-. Academic Scholarly Publication. English. sa (June and Dec.). $15.00. University of Zimbabwe / Publications Department, PO Box MP 45, Mount Pleasant Harare Zimbabwe. **Tel** 011 263 303211 ext. 236, FAX 011 263 732828, telex 26580 UNIVZ ZW. **ED** R. S. Roberts. **LC** H1; .Z35. **DD** 300/.967. **Bk Rev. Ad Acc. Circ:** 400.
**Desc:** Main focus is on South Central Africa. Includes academic articles covering all disciplines of the university. Monograph supplements also published.
**Ind/Abst** Am. Hist. Life (1969-); Int. Bibliogr. Sociol.; MLA Int. Bibl. Books Artic. Mod. Lang. Lit.

YU
**ZBORNIK MATICE SRPSKE ZA DRUSTVENE NAUKE.** **Added/Corp** Matica Srpska (Novi Sad, Serbia). Odeljenje za Drustvene Nauke. **VFOAT** Proceedings for Social Sciences. (1984)-. Periodical. Serbo-Croatian (Cyrillic) (summaries and/or abstracts in English). sa. **LC** AS346; .N62. ***Continues*** *Zbornik za Drustvene Nauke, 0044-1937.*
**Ind/Abst** Am. Hist. Life.

SZ
**ZEITSCHRIFT FUER KULTUR, POLITIK, KIRCHE.** **VFOAT** Zeitschrift Kultur, Politik, Kirche. Vol. 39, No. 1 (Feb. 1990)-. German. bm. Laenggass Druck AG Bern, Laenggassstrasse 65, Postfach 1289, CH 3001 Bern Switzerland. **Tel** 011 41 31 242431. Index available.

AU
**ZEITSCHRIFT FUR GANZHEITSFORSCHUNG.** **See** Philosophy.

PL/0208-7669
**ZESZYTY NAUKOWE NAUK SPOECZNYCH I EKONOMICZNYCH.** **VFOAT** Seria Nauk Spoecznych i Ekonomicznych. Periodical. Polish (summaries and/or abstracts in English and Russian). **LC** H8.P6; Z47.
**Ind/Abst** Potato Abstr.

SP/0210-2692
**ZONA ABIERTA.** (Oct. 1974)-. Periodical. Spanish. Four times a year. 3200.00ptas Spain; 4000.00ptas Europe; 6200.00ptas the Americas. Fundacion Pablo Iglesias, Monte Esquinza, 30-2nd D. Madrid Spain. **Tel** 11 34 1 3104313, 5344573, FAX 11 34 1 3194585. **LC** H8; .Z65. **Ad Acc**, **Adv Mgr:** Mercedes Garcia Lenberg. **Circ:** 3,000.

## ABSTRACTING, BIBLIOGRAPHIES AND STATISTICS

●UK/1352-2175
**AFRICAN STUDIES ABSTRACTS : THE ABSTRACTS JOURNAL OF THE AFRICAN STUDIES CENTRE, LEIDEN.** **Added/Corp** Rijksuniversiteit te Leiden. Afrika-Studiecentrum. Vol. 25, No. 1 (1994)-. Periodical. English (French, German, Dutch and Afrikaans). qt. £80.00 (Institutions), £40.00 (Individuals). Bowker Saur Ltd., A Reed Reference Publishing Company, Part of Reed International PLC, 59-60 Grosvenor Street, London WIX 9DA England. **Tel** 011 44 71 4935841, FAX 011 44 71 4991590. **(Subscription address:** World-Wide Subscription Services, Unit 4, Gibbs Reed Farm Pashley Road, Ticehurst TN5 7HE England.**)** **LC** Z3501; .L37; DT1. ***Continues*** *Documentatieblad, 0166-2694.*

JA/0563-8054
**ANNALS OF THE INSTITUTE OF SOCIAL SCIENCE.** **See** Social Sciences.

II/0066-8478
**ASIAN SOCIAL SCIENCE BIBLIOGRAPHY WITH ANNOTATIONS AND ABSTRACTS.** **Added/Corp** Institute of Economic Growth (India). (1966)-. Bibliography. English. an. Institute of Economic Growth, University Enclave, Delhi 110007 India. **LC** Z7165.A74; A83; HC411. **DD** 016.3/0095. ***Continues*** *Southern Asia Social Science Bibliography.*

UK/0950-2238
**ASSIA. APPLIED SOCIAL SCIENCES INDEX & ABSTRACTS.** (APPLIED SOCIAL SCIENCES INDEX & ABSTRACTS.). [ASSIA, Appl. soc. sci. index & abstr.]. **Added/Corp** Library Association. **VFOAT** ASSIA. Vol. 1, No. 1 (1987)-. Abstracting/Indexing Service. English. bm. £700.00 EEC; £7650.00 other (issue & index). Bowker Saur Ltd., A Reed Reference Publishing Company, Part of Reed International PLC, 59-60 Grosvenor Street, London WIX 9DA England. **Tel** 011 44 71 4935841, FAX 011 44 71 4991590. **(Subscription address:** World-Wide Subscription Services, Unit 4, Gibbs Reed Farm Pashley Road, Ticehurst TN5 7HE England.**)** **ED** Peter Broxis. **LC** Z7163; .A66; H1. **DD** 016.3. **NLM** Z 7161; A652. Index available. **Circ:** 400. available on an online database (file ASSI) from DATA-STAR; available on CD-ROM (as ASSIA Plus).
**Desc:** Reference tool for the legal and medical professions, social workers, prison and probation officers, planners, psychologists, sociologists, educationalists and social anthropologists. Also covers the requirements of students studying social sciences, nursing, teaching, public administration, sociology, law, psychology, and youth community.

UK
**ASSIA PLUS [COMPUTER FILE].** Abstracting/Indexing Service. English. qt. £1150.00. Bowker Saur Ltd., A Reed Reference Publishing Company, Part of Reed International PLC, 59-60 Grosvenor Street, London WIX 9DA England. **Tel** 011 44 71 4935841, FAX 011 44 71 4991590. **ED** P. F. Broxis. available in print (as Applied Social Sciences Index and Abstracts); available on an online database (as ASSIA Online) from DATA-STAR.
**Desc:** Includes the complete Applied Social Science Index and Abstracts backfile (1987 to date). Provides access to over 100,000 records.

NE/0922-6842
**BIBLIOGRAFIE VAN NEDERLANDS NATIONAAL EN INTERNATIONAAL ONDERZOEK OP SOCIAAL-WETENSCHAPPELIJK TERREIN.** **Added/Corp** Sociaal-Wetenschappelijk Informatie- en Documentatiecentrum (Koninklijke

Nederlandse Akademie van Wetenschappen). Afdeling Documentaire Informatie. **VFOAT** BNI; Bibliography of Dutch National and International Studies in the Social Sciences. (1987/1988)-. Dutch. an. Fl30.00. SWIDOC, Herengracht 410-412/1017 BS, NL 1000 Amsterdam Netherlands. **Tel** 011 31 20 6225061. **LC** Z7161.A2; B516; H62.5.N4.

NE
**BIBLIOGRAFIE VAN REGIONALE ONDERZOEKINGEN OP SOCIAAL-WETENSCHAPPELIJK TERREIN / CENTRAAL BUREAU VOOR DE STATISTIEK, AFDELING BIBLIOTHEEK EN DOCUMENTATIE.** **Added/Corp** Netherlands. Centraal Bureau voor de Statistiek. Afdeling Bibliotheek en Documentatie. **VFOAT** Bibliography of Regional Studies in the Social Sciences. (1979)-. Dutch. an. Fl33.00. SWIDOC, Herengracht 410-412/1017 BS, NL 1000 Amsterdam Netherlands. **Tel** 011 31 20 6225061. **LC** Z7165.N4; B5; HN517. ***Continues*** *Bibliografie van Regionale Onderzoekingen Op Sociaal-Wetenschappelijk Terrein. Supplement.*

FR
**BIBLIOGRAPHIE DES TRAVAUX EN LANGUE FRANCAISE SUR L'AFRIQUE AU SUD DU SAHARA, SCIENCES HUMAINES ET SOCIALES.** **Added/Corp** Ecole des Hautes Etudes en Sciences Sociales. Centre d'Etudes Africaines. **VFOAT** Bibliographie Francaise sur l'Afrique au sud du Sahara. (1977)-. French. an. 145.00F (latest edition). Sec des Publ du Cea Cardan, 54 Bd Raspail, Paris 75006 France. **Tel** (1)5443979. **LC** Z3501; .B527; DT351. **DD** 016.967. **NLM** Z 3501; B582. ***Formed by the union of*** *Bibliographie Francaise sur l'Afrique au Sud du Sahara* ***and*** *Fiches d'Ouvrages: Sciences Humaines Africanistes.*
**Desc:** Bibliography of works in the French language concerning Africa south of the Sahara desert. Directed at researchers-librarians who want to find publication references, books and articles.

US/0572-807X
**BIBLIOGRAPHY : PUBLICATIONS RESULTING FROM COUNCIL SUPPORT.** **Main/Corp** Columbia University. Council for Research in the Social Sciences. 1- 1925/56?-. Bibliography. English. University of Columbia, 526 West 113th Street, New York NY 10025.

AT
**BULLETIN / WESTERN SYDNEY CLEARINGHOUSE.** **Added/Corp** Western Sydney's Regional Information and Research Service. Western Sydney Clearinghouse. No. 1 (1985)-. Bulletin. English. Three times a year. $10.00. Western Sydney Regional Information and Research Service, PO Box 457, Blacktown New South Wales 2148 Australia. **Circ:** 350 (ctrl).
**Desc:** Statistical information, analyses, and commentary on social and urban issues in Sydney.

NE/0925-0885
**CARIBBEAN ABSTRACTS / EDITED AND PUBLISHED BY THE DEPARTMENT OF CARIBBEAN STUDIES OF THE ROYAL INSTITUTE OF LINGUISTICS AND ANTHROPOLOGY.** **Main/Corp** Koninklijk Instituut voor Taal-, Land- en Volkenkunde (Netherlands). Caraibische Afdeling. No. 1 (1990)-. English (Dutch, French and Spanish). an. Fl40.00. Royal Institute of Linguistics and Anthropology, PO Box 9515, 2300 RA Leiden, The Netherlands. **Tel** 011 31 71 272372, FAX 011 31 71 272638. **ED** Jo Derkx, Rosemarijn Hofte and Irene Rolfes. **LC** Z1595; .K66a; F21559. **DD** 016.9729. Index available. ***Continues*** *Koninklijk Instituut voor Taal-, Land- en Volkenkunde (Netherlands). Cen. Cat. Caraibiana.*
**Desc:** Contains abstracts of selected books and articles in the humanities and social sciences acquired by the Department of Caribbean Studies of the Royal Institute of Linguistics and Anthropology.

US/0887-3569
**CONTEMPORARY SOCIAL ISSUES (SANTA CRUZ, CALIF.).** (CONTEMPORARY SOCIAL ISSUES.). [Contemp. soc. issues]. No. 1 (1986)-. Monographic series. English. qt. $50.00. Reference and Research Services, 511 Lincoln Street, Santa Cruz CA 95060. **Tel** (408)426-4479. **ED** Joan Nordquist. **DD** 300.
**Desc:** A series of bibliographies containing current materials on critical social and political issues. Represents various viewpoints and includes the authoritative work on the subject.

US/0092-6361
**CURRENT CONTENTS. SOCIAL & BEHAVIORAL SCIENCES.** [Curr. contents, Soc. behav. sci.]. **Added/Corp** Institute for Scientific Information. **VFOAT** Current Contents. Social and Behavioral Sciences; Social & Behavioral Sciences; Social and Behavioral Sciences. **VAT** Current Contents. Social and Behavioral Sciences. Vol. 6, No. 2, (Jan. 2, 1974)-. Abstracting/Indexing Service. English. wk (51 issues). $488.00 print; $779.00 combined with diskette. Institute for Scientific Information, 3501 Market Street, Philadelphia PA 19104. **Tel** (215)386-0100, (800)523-1850, FAX (215)386-6362, telex 84-5305. **(Subscription address:** Institute for Scientific Information, PO Box 71416, Chicago IL 60694.**)** **DD** 300. **NLM** Z 7161 C976. available on diskette; available on magnetic tape and an online database (as Current Contents Search). Documents available from The Genuine Article. ***Continues*** *Current Contents. Behavioral, Social & Educational Sciences, 0011-3387.*
**Desc:** Presents the tables of contents from social and behavioral sciences journals.
**Ind/Abst** Curr. Contents Soc. Behav. Sci.; Popul. Index; Res. Alert [Full Cov.]; Sci. Cit. Index; SCISEARCH; Soc. Sci. Cit. Index [Full Cov.]; Soc. Res. Methodol. Abstr. (1975-).

FR
**DIMENSIONS ECONOMIQUES DE LA BOURGOGNE.** **Added/Corp** Institut National de la Statistique et des Etudes Economiques (France). (May 1971)-. Periodical. French. bm. 130.00F France; 162.00F other. INSEE Bourgogne SVC Abonnement, 2 rue Hoche, 21035 Dijon France. **Tel** 011 33 80 406749. **LC** HA1228.B8; A32. **Bk Rev. Circ:** 1,500 (ctrl). ***Supersedes in part*** *Bulletin de Statistique: Bourgogne (Cote-Dor, Nievre, Saone-et-Loire, Yonne), Franche-Comte (Doubs, Jura, Haute-Saone, Territoire de Belfort).*
**Desc:** Publishes socio-economic information on the Dijon region of France with statistical analysis.

US/0012-3307
**DIRECTORY OF PUBLISHED PROCEEDINGS. SERIES SSH: SOCIAL SCIENCES/HUMANITIES.** [Dir. publ. proc., Ser. S.S.H. Soc. sci.-humanit.]. Vol. 1/4 (1968/1971)-. Directory. English. qt. $365.00. InterDok Corporation, PO Box 326, Harrison NY 10528. **Tel** (914)835-3506, FAX (914)835-6757. **LC** Z7161; .D56. **DD** 300/.25. **NLM** W 3.5 D599. ***Supersedes in part*** *Directory of Published Proceedings.*
**Desc:** Offers complete coverage of the conference proceedings literature in all phases of the social sciences and humanities. Included is the published proceedings literature in education, economics, business administration, law, management, religion, psychology, social welfare, and other areas of research in the social sciences.

US
**DISSERTATION ABSTRACTS INTERNATIONAL. A, THE HUMANITIES AND SOCIAL SCIENCES. B, THE SCIENCES AND ENGINEERING. CUMULATED AUTHOR INDEX (MICROFORM).** **Added/Corp** Xerox University Microfilms. University Microfilms International. **VFOAT** Dissertation Abstracts International. Cumulated Author Index; Cumulated Author Index. Vol. 34 (1973-1974)-. Periodical. English. mo. $575.00 US and Canada; $695.00 other. University Microfilms International, 300 North Zeeb Road, Ann Arbor MI 48106-1346. **Tel** (313)761-4700, (800)521-0600 Exts. 2490, 2491, FAX (313)973-1540. Index available. cum. index. ctrl circ. available on CD-ROM (Dissertation Abstracts Ondisc) from University Microfilms International (UMI).
**Desc:** Publication of abstracts of dissertations available on microfilm or as zerographic reproductions.
**Ind/Abst** Abstr. Res. Pastor. Care Couns.; Leis. Recreat. Tour. Abstr.; Rural Dev. Abstr.; World Agric. Econ.

NE
**DOCUMENTATIEBLAD / LEIDEN AFRIKA-STUDIECENTRUM.** ***Title Change.*** **Added/Corp** Rijksuniversiteit te Leiden. Afrika-Studiecentrum. (1968)-(1994). Periodical. Dutch (Afrikaans, English, French, German and Italian). qt. Afrika Studiecentrum, PO Box 9555, 2300 RB Leiden Netherlands. **Tel** 011 31 71 273372, 273354. **LC** Z3501; .L37; DT3. ***Continued by*** *African Studies Abstracts.*

NE/0046-0885
**EXCERPTA INDONESICA.** **Added/Corp** Koninklijk Instituut voor Taal-, Land- en Volkenkunde (Netherlands). Afdeling Documentatie Modern Indonesie. **VFOAT** EI. No. 1 (Jan. 1970)-. Periodical. English. Twice a year. Fl36.00. Royal Institute of Linguistics and Anthropology, PO Box 9515, 2300 RA Leiden, The Netherlands. **Tel** 011 31 71 272372, FAX 011 31 71 272638. **ED** R.S. Karni. **LC** Z3273; .E83. Index available (index of keywords included in each issue). **Ad Acc. Circ:** 1,000. available in microform. ***Continued in part by*** *Current Indonesian Studies in the Netherlands.*
**Desc:** Abstracts of periodical articles and books on Indonesia in the social sciences and humanities.

FR/1142-2513
**HORIZON. SCIENCES ECONOMIQUES ET SOCIALES.** **See** Economics-Abstracting, Bibliographies and Statistics.

HU/0133-5839
**KULFOLDI TARSADALOMTUDOMANYI KEZIKONYVEK.** Began in 1975. Hungarian (Multiple languages). sa. Orszagos Szechenyi Konyvtar, Budavari Palota F Epulet, 1827 Budapest Hungary. **Tel** 757-533/475, FAX (361)156-8731, telex 224226. **LC** Z7161; .K953; H85.

TA
**OBSHCHESTVENNYE NAUKI V TADZHIKISTANE; UKAZATEL LITERATURY.** Multiple languages. qt. **LC** Z7165.T27; O27; H62.

US/1051-4015
**PAIS INTERNATIONAL IN PRINT.** [PAIS int. print]. **Added/Corp** Public Affairs Information Service. **VAT** Public Affairs Information Service International in Print. Vol. 1, No. 1 (Jan. 1991)-. Abstracting/Indexing Service. English (French, Spanish, German, Italian and Portuguese). mo. $540.00 (full subscription). Public Affairs Information Service Inc., 521 West 43rd Street, Fifth Floor, New York NY 10036. **Tel** (212)736-6629, (800)288-7247, FAX (212)643-2848. **ED** Barbera Preschel. **LC** Z7164.E2; P34; HB1.A1. **NLM** Z 7163; P9761. Index available. cum. index. **Circ:** 3,000. available on CD-ROM from EBSCO Publishing - Peabody; and SilverPlatter (US); available on an online database from OCLC EPIC; DATA-STAR; DIALOG; and PAIS. ***Formed by the union of*** *PAIS Bulletin, 0898-2201* ***and*** *PAIS Foreign Language Index, 0896-792X.*
**Desc:** Publishes bibliographic indexes to the public policy literature of business, economics, finance, law, international relations, government, political science, and other social sciences. Covers journal articles, books, and government documents published world-wide in English, French, German, Italian, Portuguese and Spanish.
**Ind/Abst** Popul. Index.

US
**PAIS ON CD-ROM [COMPUTER FILE].** **Added/Corp** Public Affairs Information Service. **VFOAT** PAIS. **VAT** Public Affairs Information Service on CD-ROM. (1972)-. English (French, German, Italian, Portuguese and Spanish). qt. $1600.00 non-subscribers; $1405.00 subscribers to PAIS. Public Affairs Information Service Inc., 521 West 43rd Street, Fifth Floor, New York NY 10036. **Tel** (212)736-6629, (800)288-7247, FAX (212)643-2848. **ED** Gwen Sloan. **LC** Z7163; .P352. Index available. cum. index. available in print from PAIS Intl.; available on an online database from BRS; DIALOG; Epic (OCLC); and DATA-STAR.
**Desc:** Bibliographic index with citations to books, journal articles, government documents and reports of public and private agencies dealing with public policy aspects of contemporary social, economic, and political issues. Contains combined machine-readable records (1972-) from all three printed publications with additional subject headings and editorially supplied abstract-like notes.

●US/1072-0103
**PAIS (PEABODY, MASS.).** (PAIS [COMPUTER FILE] : EBSCO CD-ROM.). [PAIS]. **Added/Corp** Public Affairs Information Service. (1993)-. Periodical. English. qt. $1995.00. EBSCO Publishing / Boston, 83 Pine Street, Peabody MA 01960. **Tel** (800)653-2726 North America, (508)535-8500, FAX (508)535-8545. **DD** 016.

NE/0033-5177
**QUALITY & QUANTITY.** **See** Mathematics.

YU
**SAMOUPRAVNE INTERESNE ZAJEDNICE.** **Main/Corp** Savezni Zavod Za Statistiku (Yugoslavia). 1973-. Serbo-Croatian (Roman). 10.00. Savezni Zavod za Statistiku, Kneza Milosa 20, Belgrad Yugoslavia. **LC** HA1631; .A33 subser; HS71.Y8.

NE/0167-8477
**SOCIAL RESEARCH METHODOLOGY ABSTRACTS.** (SRM ABSTRACTS.). [Soc. res. methodol. abstr.]. **Added/Corp** Erasmus Universiteit Rotterdam. SRM-Documentation Centre. **VFOAT** S.R.M. Abstracts; Social Research Methodology Abstracts. Vol. 1 (Summer 1979)-. Abstracting/Indexing Service. English. Five times a year. $225.00. Erasmus University / SRM-Documentation Centre, Postbus 1738 Kamer BT 13, 3000 DR Rotterdam, The Netherlands. **Tel** 010 4081198, FAX 010 4529510. **LC** H62.A1; S67. **DD** 016.3. cum. index. available on CD-ROM (as SRM/SIByl CD-ROM); available on an online database (as SRM Online Database). ***Continues in part*** *SRM Abstract Bulletin.*
**Desc:** SRM is of interest to social and behavioral scientists, lecturers and students and all those interested in the field of social research methodology. It is also of interest to social science researchers. The SRM-Database aids social science researchers in designing a research project and in their choice of methods and analysis techniques.

●US/1063-9802
**SOCIAL SCIENCE SOURCE.** (SOCIAL SCIENCE SOURCE [COMPUTER FILE] / DATA PREPARED AND COMPILED BY EBSCO PUBLISHING.). [Soc. sci. source]. **Added/Corp** EBSCO Publishing (Firm). (Oct. 1992)-. Abstracting/Indexing

Service. English. mo. $1495.00. EBSCO Publishing / Boston, 83 Pine Street, Peabody MA 01960. **Tel** (800)653-2726 North America, (508)535-8500, FAX (508)535-8545. **ED** Melissa Kummerer. **DD** 300. **Pr Rev.**
**Desc:** Provides keyword access to abstract and index coverage of over 400 journals in the areas of political science, economics, public policy, international relations, sociology and psychology. Full text of important journals is accompanied by tables, charts and selected graphic images on a single disc.

US/0091-3707
**SOCIAL SCIENCES CITATION INDEX (PRINT ED.).** (SOCIAL SCIENCES CITATION INDEX.). [Soc. sci. cit. index]. **Added/Corp** Institute for Scientific Information. (19??)-. Abstracting/Indexing Service. English. Seven times a year. $5680.00 print; $7565.00 (combination print & CD-ROM). Institute for Scientific Information, 3501 Market Street, Philadelphia PA 19104. **Tel** (215)386-0100, (800)523-1850, FAX (215)386-6362, telex 84-5305. **(Subscription address:** Institute for Scientific Information, PO Box 71416, Chicago IL 60694.**) LC** Z7161; .S65. **DD** 016.3. **NLM** Z 7161 S678. cum. index (5 and 10 cumulative year indexes). available on CD-ROM (as Social Sciences Citation Index Compact Disc Edition with Abstracts); and (as Social Sciences Citation Index Compact Disc Edition); available on magnetic tape and an online database (as Social SciSearch).
**Desc:** Complete bibliographic data and cited references on items contained in over 1,400 social sciences journals. Includes individual selected items from over 3,100 scientific and technical journals.

US/0094-4920
**SOCIAL SCIENCES INDEX.** [Soc. sci. index]. Vol. 1 (1975)-. Abstracting/Indexing Service. English. qt (with an annual cumulation). Print edition sold on the service basis. H W Wilson Company, 950 University Avenue, Bronx NY 10452. **Tel** (800)367-6770, (718)588-8400, FAX (718)590-1617, telex 4990003 HWILSON. **ED** Cheryl Ehrens. **LC** AI3; .S62. **DD** 016.3. **NLM** ZAI 3 S679. Index available. cum. index. **Bk Rev.** ctrl circ. available on an online database from WILSONLINE; available on CD-ROM from WILSONDISC; available on diskette from WILSONSEARCH; available on magnetic tape from WILSONTAPE. ***Supersedes in part*** *Social Sciences & Humanities Index, 0037-7899.*
**Desc:** An author and subject index to periodicals in the fields of anthropology, community health and medicine, economics, international relations, law, criminology and police science, political science, psychology and psychiatry, public administration, sociology, social work and related subjects.

US/1063-3308
**SOCIAL SCIENCES INDEX (CD-ROM ED.).** (SOCIAL SCIENCES INDEX [COMPUTER FILE].). [Soc. sci. index]. **Added/Corp** H.W. Wilson Company. **VFOAT** Wilsondisc Social Sciences Index; SSI. (198?)-. English. mo. $1295.00. H W Wilson Company, 950 University Avenue, Bronx NY 10452. **Tel** (800)367-6770, (718)588-8400, FAX (718)590-1617, telex 4990003 HWILSON. **LC** AI3. **DD** 300.
**Desc:** Contains full articles from the indexed journals in the Social Sciences Index, covering such subject areas as anthropology, community health and medical care, economics, ethnic studies, psychology, psychiatry, social work, sociology, and urban studies.

US
**SOCIAL SCIENCES INDEX / FULLTEXT.** Abstracting/Indexing Service. English. mo. $17,500.00 (annual base subscription). University Microfilms International, 300 North Zeeb Road, Ann Arbor MI 48106-1346. **Tel** (313)761-4700, (800)521-0600 Exts. 2490, 2491, FAX (313)973-1540. available on microfilm; available in print.
**Desc:** Provides access to complete material from journals indexed in The H.W. Wilson Company's Social Sciences Index. Contains cover-to-cover article images from nearly 350 titles.

US/0887-3577
**SOCIAL THEORY.** [Soc. theory]. No. 1 (1986)-. Monographic series. English. qt. $50.00 US. Reference and Research Services, 511 Lincoln Street, Santa Cruz CA 95060. **Tel** (408)426-4479. **ED** Joan Nordquist. **LC** UNC. **DD** 301.
**Desc:** A series of bibliographies on the work of contemporary social theorists.

NE/0168-8456
**SUPPLEMENT BIJ DE SOCIAAL-ECONOMISCHE MAANDSTATISTIEK / CENTRAL BUREAU VOOR DE STATISTIEK. VFOAT** Sociaal-Economische Maandstatistiek. Vol. 1984, No. 1-. Periodical. Dutch. Fl47.50. Centraal Bureau voor de Statistiek, AFD ALG Zaken, Postbus 959, 2270 AZ Voorburg Netherlands. **Tel** 011 31 70 3373800, FAX 011 31 038 7429, telex 32692 CBS NL. **LC** HC321; .S87.

CN/0227-3187
**UNION LIST OF SERIALS IN THE SOCIAL SCIENCES AND HUMANITIES HELD BY CANADIAN LIBRARIES.** (UNION LIST OF SERIALS IN THE SOCIAL SCIENCES AND HUMANITIES HELD BY CANADIAN LIBRARIES [MICROFORM].). [Union list ser. soc. sci. humanit. Can. libr.]. **Added/Corp** National Library of Canada. **VFOAT** Liste Collective des Publications en Serie dans le Domaine des Sciences Sociales et Humaines dans les Bibliotheques Canadiennes. 2nd Ed. (June 1981)-. Bibliography. English (French). an. 72.00Can$ Canada; 86.40Can$ other. National Library of Canada, 395 Wellington Street, Ottawa Ontario K1A 0N4 Canada. **Tel** (613)995-7969, (613)995-7969, (819)994-6881, FAX (613)991-9871. **LC** Microfiche (o) 93/6012. **DD** 016.3/005. available on audiocassette; available in braille; available in large print. ***Continues*** *Union List of Serials in the Social Sciences and Humanities in Canadian Libraries Microform, 0227-3187.*
**Desc:** Lists approximately 180,000 social sciences and humanities serial titles held by 400-plus Canadian libraries which contribute to the National Library's Union Catalogue.

US/0193-7871
**WORLD EAGLE.** (1977)-. Periodical. English. Ten times a year (not published in July and August). $49.95 US; $55.45 other. World Eagle, 111 Kings Street, Littleton MA 01460. **Tel** (508)486-9180, (800)634-3805, FAX (508)486-9652. **ED** Martine Crandall-Hollick. Each issue contains an index to its own contents (no volume index)--loose. cum. index. ctrl circ.
**Desc:** Social studies resource of comparative current data, including maps and graphs, both national and global. Covers developing countries, employment, voting, economy, taxes, military expenditures, energy, trade, population, etc.

# SOCIETIES AND CLUBS

US/0279-7097
**ADVOCATE (MUNCIE, IND.), THE.** (THE ADVOCATE / UNITED SOCIETY OF FRIENDS WOMEN.). [Advocate]. **Added/Corp** United Society of Friends Women (Muncie, Ind.). Vol. 93, No. 1 (Jan. 1977)-. Periodical. English. Six times a year. $7.00. The Advocate, 146 Cottage Street, Apartment 1, New Bedford MA 02740. **ED** Lynn Peery Mills, (editor's address: 7323 South Mooresville Road, Indianapolis, IN 46221, phone: (317)856-7081). **Bk Rev**, (Qty: varies). ctrl circ. ***Continues*** *Friends Missionary Advocate.*
**Desc:** Articles pertaining to activities and missionary projects.

SU
**AL-JAMIAH / TUSDIRUHA JAMIAT AL-MALIK FAYSAL BI-AL-MINTAQAH AL-SHARQIYAH. Main/Corp** Jamiah (Damman, Saudi Arabic). Periodical. Arabic (English). an. SB 1982, Damman Saudi Arabia. **LC** AS587.D35; A25.

JO
**AL-MAJALLAH AL-THAQAFIYAH / TASDURU AN AL-JAMIAH AL-URDUNIYAH.** No. 1, (April 1983)-. Arabic. qt. Al-Jamiah Al-Urduniyah, Amman Al-Urdun Jordan. **LC** AS593.A934; A35.

US/0002-6387
**ALPHA DELTA KAPPAN. Added/Corp** Alpha Delta Kappa. **VFOAT** Kappan. (1933)-. Periodical. English. Twice a year (May & Dec.). $3.00 US; $9.00 other. Honorary Society for Women Educators / Alpha Delta Kappan, 1615 West 92nd Street, Kansas City MO 64114-3296. **Tel** (816)363-5525. **ED** Jan Estell. **Circ:** 58,000 (ctrl).
**Desc:** Deals with educational developments and classroom projects, professional accomplishments of members.

US
**ALUMNAE DIRECTORY / ALPHA GAMMA DELTA. Main/Corp** Alpha Gamma Delta. **VFOAT** Alpha Gamma Delta Fraternity Alumnae Directory. (19??)-. Directory. English. Bernard C. Harris Publishing Company, 3 Barker Avenue, White Plains NY 10601. **Tel** (914)946-7500. **LC** LJ145.A59295; A4a. **DD** 378/.198/56.
**Desc:** The alumnae directory of Alpha Gamma Delta Fraternity.

US/0738-5218
**AMERICAN MENSA REGISTER. Main/Corp** American Mensa Limited. English. tw. American Mensa Committee, 2626 East 14th Street, Brooklyn NY 11235. **Tel** (718)934-3700, FAX (718)332-1183. **ED** Donna Porter. **LC** BF431; .A566B. **DD** 367. **Circ:** 55,000 (ctrl).

US/0003-0376
**AMERICAN PEN, THE.** **See** Literature.

UK/0309-8710
**ANNALS OF THE ISRAEL PHYSICAL SOCIETY.** [Ann. Isr. Phys. Soc.]. V. 1-. Academic Scholarly Publication. English. ir. Price varies per volume. Institute of Physics, Techno House, Redcliffe Way, Bristol BS1 6NX England. **Tel** 011 44 272 297481, FAX 011 44 272 294318, telex 449149 INSTP G. **(Subscription address:** American Institute of Physics, Publishing Sales, 500 Sunnyside Blvd., Woodbury NY 11797.**) CODEN** AIPSDK. **[CCC].** Documents available from Ask*IEEE, CASDDS.
**Ind/Abst** Chem. Abstr.; INSPEC (1980-); Math. Rev.

US
**ANNUAL 4-H YOUTH DEVELOPMENT ENROLLMENT REPORT. VAT** Annual Four-H Youth Development Enrollment Report; Annual Four H Youth Development Enrollment Report. (1980)-. Government Publication. English. an. US Department of Agriculture, 14th Street and Independence Avenue SW, Washington DC 20250. **Tel** (202)720-5457. ***Continues*** *Summary Annual 4-H Youth Development Enrollment Report, 0147-2801.*

UK
**ANNUAL GENERAL MEETING / DEVON AND CORNWALL RECORD SOCIETY. Main/Corp** Devon and Cornwall Record Society. (19??)-. English. an. £12.00 Comes with Devon and Cornwall Record Society membership. Devon Cornwall Record Society, 7 The Close, Exeter Devon EX1 1EZ England. **Tel** Exeter 74727. **Bk Rev. Circ:** 1,000. ***Continues*** *Devon and Cornwall Record Society. Annual Report.*

US/0884-1381
**ANNUAL REPORT - CAMP FIRE, INC.** (ANNUAL REPORT / CAMP FIRE.). [Annu. rep. - Camp Fire inc.]. **Main/Corp** Camp Fire, Inc. English. an. Camp Fire Inc, 4601 Madison Avenue, Kansas City MO 64112. **Tel** (816)756-1950. **ED** William Kitchen. **LC** HS3260.U54; C3513. **DD** 369.47/05.

US/0363-3047
**ANNUAL REPORT - TWENTIETH CENTURY FUND. Main/Corp** Twentieth Century Fund. (19??)-. Periodical. English. qt. Free on request. Twentieth Century Fund, 41 East 70th Street, New York NY 10021. **Tel** (212)535-4441. **ED** Beverly Goldberg. **LC** AS25; .T8.

UK/0959-3640
**ANNUAL REPORT - YORK GEORGIAN SOCIETY.** (YORK GEORGIAN SOCIETY ANNUAL REPORT.). [Annu. rep. - York Georgian Soc.]. **Main/Corp** York Georgian Society. **Added/Corp** York Georgian Society. Annual Report. **VFOAT** Annual Report - York Georgian Society. (1945)-. English. an. £10.00. York Georgian Society, Kings Manor, York Y01 2EW England. **ED** Helen Kirk. **LC** NA12; .Y6718. **DD** 720/.6/242843. Index available. cum. index. **Bk Rev**, (Qty: 1-2). **Circ:** 500. Documents available from BLDSC.
**Desc:** Reports on year's events plus articles on architecture and decorative arts and many more.
**Ind/Abst** Avery Index Archit. Period. Suppl. Colum. Univ. (19??-199?).

MX
**ANUARIO VERITAS / UNIVERSIDAD REGIOMONTANA. VFOAT** Veritas. 1 (1982)-. Spanish (English). an. Universidad Regiomontana, Department de Publicaciones, Monterrey NL Mexico. **LC** AS63.M64; A14. **DD** 056/.1.

JA
**ASAHI GURAFU BESSATSU.** (19??)-. Japanese. qt. ¥980. Asshi Shinbunsha, 3-2 Tsukiji 5 Chuo-ku, Tokyo-to 104 Japan. **LC** AS551; .A8.

US
**ASIA (NEW YORK, N.Y. : 1984).** (ASIA : NEWSLETTER OF THE ASIA SOCIETY.). Newsletter. English. bm. The Asia Society Archives, 725 Park Avenue, Department of Gallery, New York NY 10021. **Tel** (212)288-6400 Ext.231, FAX (212)517-8315, telex 224953 ASIA UR. **LC** DS1; .A47123. ***Continues*** *Asia.*
**Ind/Abst** Middle East Abstr. Index.

CN/1186-9798
**ASSOCIATIONS CANADA.** (ASSOCIATIONS CANADA : AN ENCYCLOPEDIC DIRECTORY, UN REPERTOIRE ENCYCLOPEDIQUE.). [Assoc. Can.]. (1991)-. Directory. French (English). an. 197.50Can$. Canadian Almanac and Directory Publishing Co., 2775 Matheson Boulevard East, Mississauga Ontario L4W 9Z9 Canada. **Tel** (905)238-6074. **(Subscription address:** Copp Clark Pitman, 2775 Matheson Boulevard East, Mississauga Ontario L4W 9Z9 Canada**) LC** AS40; .A86. **DD** 061.1/025.

CN/1186-9798
**ASSOCIATIONS CANADA.** (ASSOCIATIONS CANADA : AN ENCYCLOPEDIC DIRECTORY). [Assoc. Can.]. (1991)-. Directory. English (French). an. 197.50Can$. Canadian Almanac and Directory Publishing Co., 2775 Matheson Boulevard East, Mississauga Ontario L4W 9Z9 Canada. **Tel** (905)238-6074. **(Subscription address:** Copp Clark Pitman, 2775 Matheson Boulevard East, Mississauga Ontario L4W 9Z9 Canada**) DD** 061.1/025.

US/0161-0023
**ASSOCIATIONS OF DELAWARE VALLEY.** English. an. Greater Philadelphia Chamber of Commerce, 1346 Chestnut Street/Suite 800, Philadelphia PA 19107. **Tel** (215)545-1234. **LC** HS61.D3; A78A. **DD** 366/.0025/749. Index available. ctrl circ.
**Desc:** Lists the names, addresses and officers of over 600 associations and related types of associations located in eleven-county Delaware Valley area. Major classifications are: civic association, professional association, service organization, and trade associations.

●CN/1188-4274
**ASSOCIATIONS QUEBEC.** (ASSOCIATIONS QUEBEC, REPERTOIRE.). [Assoc. Que.]. **Added/Corp** Quebec dans le Monde (Association). Ed. (1992/1993)-. French. 69.95Can$ per volume. Quebec Dans Le Monde, CP 8503, Sainte-Foy Quebec G1V 4N5 Canada. **Tel** (418)659-5540, FAX (418)659-4143. **DD** 061/.14.

US/0196-6316
**AWARDS, HONORS, AND PRIZES.** [Awards honors prizes]. **Added/Corp** Gale Research Company. 1st Ed. (1969)-. English. ir. $391.00/set. Gale Research Inc., 835 Penobscot Building, Detroit MI 48226. **Tel** (800)877-GALE, (313)961-2242, FAX (313)961-6083, telex TWX 810-221-7086. **ED** Gita Siegman. **LC** AS8; .A93. **DD** 001.4/4. **NLM** AS 8 A96469.
**Desc:** Alphabetical directory of organizations in the United States and Canada that sponsor awards in virtually every field of human endeavor, from academic awards to prizes in sports.

US/0279-7933
**BANTHA TRACKS.** (BANTHA TRACKS : NEWSLETTER OF THE OFFICIAL STAR WARS FAN CLUB.). **Added/Corp** Official Star Wars Fan Club. (19??)-. Newsletter. English. qt. Lucasfilm Ltd., Universal City CA.

CN/0381-6982
**BARDY, LE.** 1st Yearly V.- Jan. 1966-. Periodical. English. mo. $15.48. Soc St Jean Baptiste de Quebec, 2601 Avenue de Vitre, Quebec Que G1J 4 B9 Canada. **Tel** (418)522-4624. ***Supersedes*** *Chez-Nous, Chez-Nous.*

GW
**BERICHT - STIFTUNG VOLKSWAGENWERK.** ***Title Change.*** **Main/Corp** Stiftung Volkswagenwerk. German. an. Vandenhoeck & Ruprecht, Robert Bosch Breite 6, D-37079 Goettingen Germany. **Tel** 011 49 551 695911, FAX 011 49 551 695917, telex 965226 VAN d. **LC** AS182.S79; A18. **Circ:** 13,500. ***Continues*** *Jahresbericht. Stiftung Volkswagenwerk.* ***Continued by*** *Bericht. Volkswagenstiftung., 0585-9012.*
**Desc:** General information on funding facilities, special research projects, financial statistics, etc.

CN/0714-7546
**BIC (MONTREAL, QUEBEC : 1981).** (BIC : BULLETIN D'INFORMATION AUX CADRES.). [BIC, Bull. inf. cadres]. **Added/Corp** Federation Quebecoise du Guidisme et du Scoutisme. **VAT** Bulletin d'Information aux Cadres. No. 1 (Oct. 1981)-. Bulletin. French. ir. Free. Federation Quebecoise du Guidisme et du Scoutisme, 1415 Est rue Jarry, Montreal Quebec H2E 2Z7 Canada. **DD** 369.43/06/0714. ***Continues*** *Guide-Express, Mini-Scoutbec, 0713-5505.*

UK
**BIENNIAL REPORT / WORLD ASSOCIATION OF GIRL GUIDES AND GIRL SCOUTS.** Vol. 1 (1931)-. English. be.

CN/0228-4448
**BIVOUAC.** (BIVOUAC : MAGAZINE DES SCOUTS DU QUEBEC / FEDERATION DES SCOUTS DU QUEBEC.). [Bivouac]. Periodical. French. $2,00. Federation des Scouts du Quebec, 1415 Est rue Jarry, Montreal Quebec H2E 2Z7 Canada. **DD** 369.43/09714.

BL
**BOLETIM - CONSELHO FEDERAL DE CULTURA.** **Main/Corp** Conselho Federal de Cultura (Brazil). Yearly V. 1 (Jan./March 1971)-. Bulletin. Portuguese. qt. Conselho Federal de Cultura, rua de Imprensa 16-70 Andar, Rio de Janeiro Brazil. **LC** AS80.C65; A2.

UK
**BOOK OF THE OLD EDINBURGH CLUB, THE.** ***Ceased.*** **Main/Corp** Old Edinburgh Club. Vol. 1 (1908)-(19??). English. ir. Old Edinburgh, 25 Regent Terrace, Edinburgh EH75BS Scotland United Kingdom. **Tel** 031-557-4111. **ED** Ian Gauld. **LC** DA7890.E2; O32. Index available. cum. index. **Circ:** 500 (ctrl).
**Desc:** Publication of articles and documents relating to the history, culture and development of Edinburgh.

US/0006-8535
**BOXWOOD BULLETIN, THE.** **Added/Corp** American Boxwood Society. Vol. 1 (Oct. 1961)-. Periodical. English. Four times a year (Jan., Apr., July, Oct.). $15.00 (regular), $30.00 (contributing), $50.00 (sustaining), $250.00 (life), $500.00 (patron) Comes with American Boxwood Society membership. American Boxwood Society, PO Box 85, Boyce VA 22620. **Tel** (703)665-5879. **ED** Mrs. Robert L. Frackelton, (editor's address: 1714 Greenway Drive, Fredericksburg, VA 22401, phone: (703)373-7975). cum. index.

CN/0006-9264
**BRATSTVO (TORONTO).** (BRATSTVO.). **VFOAT** Fraternity. Vol. 1 (1954)-. Periodical. Serbo-Croatian (Roman). mo. 35.00Can$. Bratstvo, 1 Secroft Cres, North York, Ontario, M3N 1R5 Canada. **Tel** (416)769-7181, FAX (416)850-4401. **ED** William DuRovic. **Bk Rev.** **Ad Acc.** **Circ:** 2,200.

UK
**BRITISH ACADEMY DIRECTORY, THE.** **Main/Corp** British Academy. (197?)-. Directory. English. an. Free. British Academy, 20-21 Cornwall Terrace, London NW1 4QP United Kingdom. **Tel** 011 44 71 487 5966, FAX 011 44 71 224 3807, telex 263194. **Circ:** 1,260. ***Continues*** *British Academy. Yearbook of the British Academy.*

AT/0300-4678
**BROTHERHOOD ACTION.** **Added/Corp** Brotherhood of St. Laurence. (19??)-. Periodical. English. Four times a year. $2.00. Brotherhood of St Laurence, 67 Brunswick Street, Fitzroy Victoria 3065 Australia. **Tel** 011 61 3 4197055, FAX 011 61 3 4172691. **ED** Caroline Taylor-Steele. **Bk Rev.** **Ad Acc.** **Circ:** 7,000 (ctrl).
**Desc:** News and information about the supporters of the brotherhood of St. Laurence. Also includes articles about its work in social action for the disadvantaged.

SZ
**BUENDERWALD.** ir. Swiss Book Center / Schweizer Buchzentrum, Postfach 522, CH 4600 Olten 1 Switzerland. **Tel** 011 41 62 476161.

FR
**BULLETIN.** **Main/Corp** Societe J.-K. Huysmans. **VFOAT** Cahiers J.-K. Huysmans. (March 1928)-. Bulletin. French. ir (1 or 2 per year). 150.00F. Societe Joris-Karl Huysmans, 22 rue Guynemer, 75006 Paris France. **ED** M. Rancoeur. **Bk Rev.** **Pr Rev.** **Circ:** 200.

SZ
**BULLETIN ARPEA.** Bulletin. French. bm. $35.00. ARPEA Administration, Chemin Marniere 34, CH-2068 Hauterive Switzerland. **Tel** 011 41 21 38334012.

US/0742-8995
**BULLETIN - COSMOS CLUB (WASHINGTON, D.C.).** (BULLETIN - COSMOS CLUB.). **Main/Corp** Cosmos Club (Washington, D.C.). **VFOAT** Cosmos Club Bulletin. V. 1- Nov. 1947-. Bulletin. English. mo. Cosmos Club, 2121 Massachusetts Avenue Northwest, Washington DC 20008. **Tel** (202)387-7783. **LC** HS2725.W3; C714.

FR/1167-3648
**BULLETIN DE LA BIBLIOTHEQUE FORNEY ET DE SES AMIS.** **Added/Corp** Bibliotheque Forney. Societe des Amis. (19??)-. Bulletin. French. Three times a year. 100.00F. Societe Amis Bibliotheque Forney, 1 rue du Figuier, 75004 Paris France. **Tel** 011 33 1 42781460, FAX 011 33 1 42782259. **LC** Z927; .P175a. **DD** 027.4/44/36. Index available. ***Continues*** *Bulletin de la Societe des Amis de la Bibliotheque Forney.*

FR
**BULLETIN DE LA SOCIETE DES AMIS DE MONTAIGNE.** **Added/Corp** Societe des Amis de Montaigne. (19??)-. Bulletin. French. qt. 80.00F. Dawson France SA, BP 40, 91121 Palaiseau Cedex France. **Tel** 011 33 1 69104700, telex 220064F. ***Continues*** *Bulletin des Amis de Montaigne.*
**Ind/Abst** MLA Int. Bibl. Books Artic. Mod. Lang. Lit.; Romant. Move.

CN/0228-1503
**BULLETIN DE L'ANIMATEUR, LE.** [Bull. anim.]. No. 25- Jan. 1980-. Bulletin. French. bm. $4.00. Federation des Scouts du Quebec, 1415 Est rue Jarry, Montreal Quebec H2E 2Z7 Canada. **DD** 369.43/05. ***Continues*** *Fiches de l'Animateur, 0228-149X.*

US/0192-6993
**BULLETIN - EARLY SITES RESEARCH SOCIETY.** **Main/Corp** Early Sites Research Society. V. 1- Summer 1973-. Bulletin. English. qt. $10.00 individuals (includes membership), $4.00 institutions (includes membership). Early Sites Research Society, Long Hill, Rowley MA 01969. **Tel** (617)948-2410.

US/8755-5670
**BULLETIN OF TAU BETA PI, THE.** [Bull. Tau Beta Pi]. Vol. 58, No. 2 (Dec. 1984)-. Bulletin. English. Three times a year. Tau Beta Pi Association, PO Box 8840, University Station, Knoxville TN 37996-4800. **Tel** (615)546-4578. **ED** James D Froula. **DD** 620. **Circ:** 12,000 (ctrl). ***Continues*** *Council Bulletin of Tau Beta Pi, 0161-8814.*
**Desc:** A newsletter to active collegiate members. Items of interest in running a chapter and help in career.

UK
**BULLETIN - ORIENTAL BIRD CLUB.** **VFOAT** Bulletin of the Oriental Bird Club. No. 1 (Spring 1985)-. Bulletin. English. sm. Oriental Bird Club, The Lodge, Sandy Bedford SG19 2DL England. **Tel** 011 44 509 231655.
**Ind/Abst** Fish Rev.; Wildl. Rev.

JA
**BUMMEI JIHYO.** **Added/Corp** Nihon Bunka Rengokai. (19??)-. Periodical. Japanese. ¥200. Nihon Bunka Rengokai, 1312-255 Uchikoshicho 192, Hachioji Japan. **Tel** 0426-35-8451. **ED** Noboru Komiyama. **LC** AS551; .B78. **Bk Rev.** **Circ:** 2,000.
**Desc:** Promotion of Japanese cultural development thru academic association, giving the meaning of arts and sciences to the world.

JA
**BUNKA.** **VFOAT** Culture. March 1974 Edition-. Japanese (Japanese). Komazawa Daigaku Bungakubu Bunkagaku Kyoshitsu, 23 Komazawa 1-chome, Setagaya-ku, Tokyo Japan. **LC** AS552.K67; A2.

US
**CAMELLIA REVIEW, THE.** **Added/Corp** Southern California Camellia Society. Vol. 12 (Oct. 1950)-. Periodical. English. qt (4 issues). Comes with Southern California Camellia Society membership. Southern California Camellia Society, 7475 Brydon Road, La Verne CA 91750. **Tel** (818)447-7598. ***Continues*** *Southern California Camellia Society. Southern California Camellia Society Bulletin.*

US/0092-1289
**CAMP FIRE LEADERSHIP.** ***Ceased.*** **Added/Corp** Camp Fire Girls. ( )-Vol. 66, No. 3 (Sept. 1987). Periodical. English. Three times a year. Camp Fire Inc, 4601 Madison Avenue, Kansas City MO 64112. **Tel** (816)756-1950. **ED** William Ketchen and Gwen Belment. **LC** HS3353.C3; A19. **DD** 369.47/05. **Circ:** 45,000 (ctrl). ***Continues*** *Camp Fire Girl, 0008-2287.*
**Desc:** Articles appropriate to adults who work with Camp Fire youth members, including project descriptions, activity ideas and social issues that involve youth.

CN/0715-3775
**CANADIAN IRIS SOCIETY NEWSLETTER.** [Can. Iris Soc. newsl.]. Newsletter. English. qt. Free to members. Canadian Iris Society News, c/o Royal Botanical Gardens, Box 399 Station A, Hamilton Ontario L8N 3H8 Canada. **Tel** (519)863-6508. **ED** Alan Laing (editor's address: 3 Browning Court, Aurora, Ontario L4G 2J5). **DD** 635.9/3424/05. **Circ:** 470 (ctrl).

UK/0262-995X
**CANTERBURY AND YORK SOCIETY (SERIES).** (CANTERBURY AND YORK SOCIETY.). **Added/Corp** Canterbury and York Society. Vol. 54 (1957)-. Monographic series. English (Latin). ir. Price varies per volume. Canterbury and York Society, 15 Cusack Close, Twickenham TW1 4TB England. **(Subscription address:** Boydell & Brewer, PO Box 41026, Rochester NY 14604.) **ED** A. K. McHardy. **LC** BX5013.C3; A5. **DD** 283/.41. **Circ:** 400 (ctrl). ***Continues*** *Canterbury and York Series.*

US
**CAPITAL COGS.** **Main/Corp** Rotary Club of Albany. V. 1- 1921-. Periodical. English. wk. Rotary Club of Albany, Best Western Thurway House, 1375 Washington Avenue, Albany NY 12206.

US
**CARNATION.** Periodical. English. qt (Jan., April, July, Oct.). $10.00, $3.00 (single copy). Delta Sigma Phi Fraternity, 1331 N. Delaware St., Indianapolis IN 46202. **Tel** (317) 634-1899, FAX (317)634-1410. **ED** Tim Jensen. **Circ:** 59,000 (ctrl).
**Desc:** The official exoteric publication of Delta Sigma Phi fraternity. Contains articles on alumni and news of general interest to those alumni.

HK
**CHENG MING (NAN-CHANG SHIH, CHINA).** (CHENG MING.). **Added/Corp** Chiang-Hsi Sheng Che Hsueh She Hui Ko Hsueh Hsueh Hui Lien Ho Hui. **VFOAT** Zheng Ming; Zhengming. (19??)-. Periodical. Chinese. mo. $61.00. Pak KA Publisher, PO Box 20370, Hennessy Road, Hong Kong Hong Kong. **Tel** 011 852 5 740664. **(Subscription address:** Evergreen Publ & Stationery, 136 South Atlantic Boulevard, Monterey Park CA 91754.) **LC** AS451; .C38. **DD** 089/.951.

JA
**CHI NO KOKOGAKU.** (April/May 1975)-. Periodical. Japanese. bm. ¥2880. Shakai Shiso Sha, 1-25-21 Hongo, Bunkyoku Tokyo 113 Japan. **LC** AS551; .C47.

CC/0253-3626
**CHONGQING DAXUE XUEBAO.** (CHUNG-CHING TA HSUEH HSUEH PAO.). [Chongqing daxue xuebao]. **VFOAT** Journal of Chongqing University. Academic Scholarly Publication. Chinese. qt. $5.76. Science Press, 16 Donghuangchenggen North Street, Beijing 100707, People's Republic of China. **Tel** 011 86 1 4019821, 011 86 1 4010642, FAX 011 86 1 4012180, 011 86 1 4019810, telex 210147. **LC** AS451; .C475. **DD**

089/.951. **CODEN** CPAOD4. Documents available from CASDDS.
**Ind/Abst** Chem. Abstr.

US
**CHRONICLE, THE.** **Added/Corp** Quapaw Quarter Association. Vol. 17, No. 5 (Oct./Nov. 1990)-. Newspaper. English. bm. $10.00. Quapaw Quarterly Association, PO Box 165023, Little Rock AR 72216. **Tel** (501)371-0075, FAX (501)374-8142. **ED** Chuck Heinbockel. **Bk Rev**, (Qty: 6). **Photos**. **Ad Acc**, **Adv Mgr:** Ralph Mann. Full Page (B&W) $690.00. Half Page (B&W) $660.00. ***Continues*** *Quapaw Quarter Chronicle.*

CH
**CHUNG-CHOU HSUEH KAN.** **VFOAT** Zhongzhouxuekan. Periodical. Chinese. bm. NT$0.45. Post Office Cheng-chou Shih, Cheng-chou Shih, People's Republic of China. **LC** AS452.C4614; A15. **DD** 089/.951.

UK
**CINEMA ORGAN SOCIETY : NEWSLETTER.** **Main/Corp** Cinema Organ Society. Newsletter. English. mo. Cinema Organ Society, 3 Dorthy Farm Road, Raleigh Essex SS6 8RE England. **LC** PAR. ***Continues*** *Newsletter - Cinema Organ Society.*

US/0194-5785
**CIVITAN MAGAZINE, THE.** [Civitan mag.]. Periodical. English. bm. $6.00. Civitan Magazine, PO Box 130744, Birmingham AL 35213-0744. **Tel** (205)591-8910, FAX (205)592-6307. **ED** Dorothy Wellborn. **DD** 369. **Ad Acc. Circ:** 38,000 (ctrl). ***Continues*** *Civitan, 0300-7413.*

US/0009-9589
**CLUB MANAGEMENT.** [Club manage.]. **Added/Corp** Club Managers Association of America. (193?)-. Periodical. English. Twelve times a year. $21.95 US; $45.00 other. Finan Publishing Company, 8730 Big Bend Boulevard, St Louis MO 63119. **Tel** (314)961-6644. **DD** 647. available on microfilm and microfiche from University Microfilms International (UMI); available on an online database (file 485/Full-Text) from DIALOG. ***Continues*** *Modern Club Management.*
**Ind/Abst** Account. Tax Datab. (1974-) [Full Txt.].

AT/0045-7205
**CLUB MANAGEMENT IN AUSTRALIA.** (1961)-. Periodical. English. Eleven times a year (Dec/Jan. issue combined). $40.00. Club Management Association Australia, 2A Lord Street, Botany New South Wales 2019 Australia. **Tel** 02 2646691, telex 21887. **ED** Andrew Dettre. **Ad Acc.** ctrl circ.

US/0747-0827
**CLUB (NEWTOWN, CONN.).** (CLUB.). (19??)-. Periodical. English. Thirteen times a year. $49.00. Paragon Publishing Inc., PO Box 200, Sandy Hook CT 06482. **Tel** (203)426-6533.
**Desc:** News, information and pictures of today's most beautiful women.

US/0438-6256
**CLUBS IN TOWN AND COUNTRY.** Began in 1953. English. an. Free. PKF Publishing, 1728 Banks, Houston TX 77098. **Tel** (713)942-0414. **ED** Gary L Carr. **LC** HS2507; .C58. **DD** 367/.973/05. **Circ:** 16,000.
**Desc:** Statistical review of financial data on private clubs for both city and country clubs. Designed as a reference and management or operational aid for clubs and club managers.

CN
**COLOMBIEN, LE.** ***Ceased.*** **Added/Corp** Knights of Columbus. (1???)-(1???). Periodical. French. mo. Chevaliers du Columb du Quebec, 3565 Berri, Montreal Quebec H2L 4G5 Canada. **Tel** (203)772-2130.

US/0746-3979
**COMMUNICATOR OF PHI DELTA CHI FRATERNITY, THE.** **Main/Corp** Phi Delta Chi Fraternity. **VFOAT** Who's Who in Phi Delta Chi; Communicator of Phi Delta Chi Pharmacy Fraternity; Communicator of Phi Delta Chi. (1909)-. Periodical. English. qt. $8.00. Phi Delta Chi Executive Director, 2300 Ninth Street South/Suite 209, Arlington VA 22204. **Tel** (703)920-3700, FAX (703)892-2084. **ED** John D Grabenstein. **LC** LJ105.P615; P47a. **Ad Acc. Circ:** 4,500. ***Continues*** *Communicator.*
**Desc:** News, information and articles on professional topics of interest to the brothers and friends of this professional pharmacy fraternity.

US/1044-7202
**COMMUNICO.** (COMMUNICO : THE NATIONAL MAGAZINE FOR MEMBERS OF UNICO.). [CommUnico]. Periodical. English. bm. $10.00. Communico Magazine, 72 Burroughs Place, Bloomfield NJ 07033. **DD** 369. ***Continues*** *UNICO, 0194-553X.*

IT
**COMUNE, LA.** Vol. 1- May 1971-. Periodical. Italian. 1000 single issue. Laboratorio Teatrale, Via Lago di Varano 67, 58100 Grosseto Italy. **LC** AS221; .C65.

US
**COOTIE COURIER.** (1972)-. English. PO Box 627, 125 West North Street, Fostoria OH 44830.

US/1058-2029
**COSMOS (WASHINGTON, D.C.).** (COSMOS.). [Cosmos]. **Added/Corp** Cosmos Club (Washington, D.C.). Vol. 1, No. 1 (1991)-. Periodical. English. an. $9.00. Cosmos Club, 2121 Massachusetts Avenue Northwest, Washington DC 20008. **Tel** (202)387-7783. **LC** AP2; .C845. **DD** 051.

US/0195-9050
**CSA JOURNAL, THE.** (CSA JOURNAL : OFFICIAL PUBLICATION OF CSA FRATERNAL LIFE.). **Main/Corp** CSA Fraternal Life (Society). English (Czech). mo. $12.00. CSA Journal, CSA Plaza, 2701 South Harlem Avenue, Berwyn IL 60402. **ED** Marie V Jensen. **LC** E184.B67. ctrl circ. ***Continues*** *CSA Journal, 0195-9050.*

US
**DEAN BURGON NEWS, THE.** **Added/Corp** Dean Burgon Society. Vol. 1, No. 1 (Jan. 1979)-. Periodical. English. ir. Dean Burgon Society, PO Box 359, Collingswood NJ 08108. **Tel** (609)854-4452. **ED** D.A. Waite. **Bk Rev.**

US/0745-0958
**DELTA EPSILON SIGMA JOURNAL.** **VFOAT** Journal. Vol. 27, No. 2 (May 1982)-. Periodical. English. qt. Delta Sigma Epsilon Journal, Union-Hoermann Press, 2175 Kerper Boulevard, PO Box 916, Dubuque IA 52001. **ED** George Herndl (editor's address: Belmont Abbey College, Belmont NC 28012). **LC** LJ75; .D2. **Circ:** 12,000 (ctrl). ***Continues*** *Delta Epsilon Sigma Bulletin, 0011-8028.*
**Desc:** Contains articles of fiction, poetry, and essays.

US/0011-8052
**DELTA PI EPSILON JOURNAL.** **See** Business.

US/1058-7985
**DIRECTORY. ASSOCIATIONS. EAST NORTH CENTRAL REGION, THE.** [Dir., Assoc., East North Cent. reg.]. **Added/Corp** American Business Directories, Inc. **VFOAT** Associations. East North Central Region; East North Central Region; Directory of Associations. East North Central Region. (1991)-. Directory. English. $325.00. American Business Directory, 5711 South 86th Circle, Omaha NE 68127. **Tel** (402)593-4600, FAX (402)331-5481. **LC** AS29.5; .D56. **DD** 338.7/025/77. ***Continues in part*** *Directory. Associations.*

US/1058-8027
**DIRECTORY. ASSOCIATIONS. MOUNTAIN REGION, THE.** [Dir., Assoc., Mt. reg.]. **Added/Corp** American Business Directories, Inc. **VFOAT** Associations. Mountain Region; Mountain Region; Directory of Associations. Mountain Region. (1991)-. Directory. English. $110.00. American Business Directory, 5711 South 86th Circle, Omaha NE 68127. **Tel** (402)593-4600, FAX (402)331-5481. **LC** AS29.5; .D565. **DD** 338.7/025/78. ***Continues in part*** *Directory. Associations.*

US/1058-8000
**DIRECTORY. ASSOCIATIONS. SOUTH ATLANTIC REGION, THE.** [Dir., Assoc., South Alt. reg.]. **Added/Corp** American Business Directories, Inc. **VFOAT** Associations. South Atlantic Region; South Atlantic Region; Directory of Associations. South Atlantic Region. (1991)-. Directory. English. $345.00. American Business Directory, 5711 South 86th Circle, Omaha NE 68127. **Tel** (402)593-4600, FAX (402)331-5481. **LC** AS29.5; .D568. **DD** 338.7/025/75. ***Continues in part*** *Directory. Associations.*

US/1058-8019
**DIRECTORY. ASSOCIATIONS. SOUTH CENTRAL REGION, THE.** [Dir., Assoc., South Cent. reg.]. **Added/Corp** American Business Directories, Inc. **VFOAT** Associations. South Central Region; South Central Region; Directory of Associations. South Central Region. (1991)-. Directory. English. $160.00. American Business Directory, 5711 South 86th Circle, Omaha NE 68127. **Tel** (402)593-4600, FAX (402)331-5481. **LC** AS29.5; .D569. **DD** 338.7/025/75. ***Continues in part*** *Directory. Associations.*

US/1058-7993
**DIRECTORY. ASSOCIATIONS. WEST NORTH CENTRAL REGION, THE.** [Dir., Assoc., West North Cent. reg.]. **Added/Corp** American Business Directories, Inc. **VFOAT** Associations. West North Central Region; West North Central Region; Directory of Associations. West North Central Region. (1991)-. Directory. English. $125.00. American Business Directory, 5711 South 86th Circle, Omaha NE 68127. **Tel** (402)593-4600, FAX (402)331-5481. **LC** AS29.5; .D5694. **DD** 338.7/025/77. ***Continues in part*** *Directory. Associations.*

CN/0316-0734
**DIRECTORY OF ASSOCIATIONS IN CANADA.** **VFOAT** Repertoire des Associations du Canada. (1973)-. Directory. English (French). an. $2,165 (complete file). Micromedia Limited, 20 Victoria Street, Toronto Ontario M5C 2N8 Canada. **Tel** (416)362-5211, (800)387-2689, FAX (416)362-6161, telex 06524668. **ED** Brian Land and Diane Gallagher. **LC** AS40; .D49. **DD** 061/.1. **Bk Rev. Ad Acc. Circ:** 2,000 (ctrl). available on an online database (thru CAN/OLE).
**Desc:** Listing of associations in Canada. Guide to business, government, researchers, librarians, the tourism industry and the media.

NZ
**DIRECTORY OF AUSTRALIAN ASSOCIATIONS.** (1978/79)-. Directory. English. Three times a year. 320.00Aus$ Australia; 345.25Aus$ US and Israel. Information Australia Group Pty. Ltd., 45 Flinders Lane, Melbourne Victoria 3000 Australia. **Tel** 11 61 3 6542800. **LC** AS718; .D57. **DD** 068/.94. **NLM** HD 2429.A8 D598. Index available.

UK/0309-5487
**DIRECTORY OF BRITISH ASSOCIATIONS & ASSOCIATIONS IN IRELAND.** [Dir. Br. assoc. assoc. Irel.]. **VFOAT** Directory of British Associations and Associations in Ireland; Directory of British Associations. Ed. 4 (1974/1975)-. Directory. English. be. $180.00. CBD Research Ltd, 15 Wickham Road, Beckenham Kent BR3 2JS England. **Tel** 011 44 81 6507745, FAX 011 44 81 6500768. **(Subscription address:** ca94) **ED** G. .P Henderson and S. P. A. Henderson. **NLM** AS 118; D598. **CODEN** DBAIE2. ***Continues*** *Directory of British Associations.*
**Desc:** Gives information needed to contact more than 7,000 national organizations based in England, Wales, Scotland, and Ireland. Includes local and regional organizations of national significance.

UK
**DIRECTORY OF EUROPEAN PROFESSIONAL & LEARNED SOCIETIES.** **VFOAT** Directory of European Professional and Learned Societies; Repertoire des Societes Professionnelles et Savantes en Europe; Handbuch der Beruflichen Gelehrten Gesellschaften Europas. (1989)-. Directory. English (French and German). ir. £85.00. CBD Research Ltd, 15 Wickham Road, Beckenham Kent BR3 2JS England. **Tel** 011 44 81 6507745, FAX 011 44 81 6500768. **LC** HD6497.E85; D57. **DD** 068/.4. **NLM** AS 98; D598. ***Continues in part*** *Directory of European Associations. Part 2. National Learned, Scientific and Technical Societies.*
**Desc:** Provides coverage of European-based professional and learned associations, together with scientific and technical societies. Contains information on associations and societies.

UK
**DIRECTORY OF MEMBER ARCHIVES.** **See** Sound Recordings and Systems.

SA
**DIRECTORY OF SOUTH AFRICAN ASSOCIATIONS.** **Added/Corp** South African Council for Scientific and Industrial Research. Division of Information Services. **VFOAT** Gids van Suid-Afrikaanse Verenigings. (1991)-. Directory. English. **LC** AS611.A7; D5.

US/0098-5368
**DIRECTORY OF STATE, REGIONAL AND COMMERCIAL ORGANIZATIONS.** **See** Business-Commerce.

IT
**DOC ITALIA / ISTITUTO NAZIONAL DELL'INFORMAZIONE.** Began with 1978 Vol. Italian. be. L175000 Italy; L300000 other. Editoriale Italiana, Via Vigliena 10, 00192 Rome Italy. **Tel** 011 39 6 3212653, FAX 011 39 6 3211359, telex 3230177. **ED** Giordano Treveri Gennari. **LC** AS218; .D6. **DD** 065. Index available. cum. index. **Ad Acc. Circ:** 5,000. ***Continues*** *Doc.*
**Desc:** Reference book with managers' names and addresses; information about projects and activities of scientific, cultural, data-collecting institutions in Italy.

UK
**ECONOMETRIC SOCIETY PUBLICATION.** No. 1-. Monographic series. English. Price varies per volume. Cambridge University Press, The Edinburgh Building, Shaftesbury Road, Cambridge CB2 2RU United Kingdom. **Tel** 011 44 223 312393, FAX 011 44 223 325959. **(Subscription address:** US/ 110 Midland Avenue, Port Chester, NY 10573**)**

UK
**ELGAR SOCIETY JOURNAL, THE.** **Main/Corp** Elgar Society. Vol. 1 (Jan. 1979)-. Academic Scholarly Publication. English. Three times a year. £10.00 UK; £20.00 US. Elgar Society, 115 Monkhams Avenue, Woodford Green, Essex 1G8 0ER United Kingdom. **Tel** 081-506-0912. **ED** Geoffrey Hodgkins. **LC** ML410.E41; E35. **DD** 780/.92/4; B. **Bk Rev. Ad Acc. Circ:** 1,300 (ctrl). ***Supersedes*** *Newsletter - Elgar Society.*
**Desc:** Articles, news and reviews of books and records on the music and life of the composer Sir Edward Elgar and his times.

US
**ELIZABETHAN CLUB SERIES, THE.** (19??)-. Monographic series. English. ir. Price varies per volume. Yale University Press, PO Box 209040, New Haven CT 06520. **Tel** (203)432-0940, (800)987-7323, FAX (203)432-0948.

US/0013-6263
**ELKS MAGAZINE, THE.** [Elks mag.]. **Added/Corp** Elks (Fraternal Order) Elks (Fraternal Order). Vol. 1 (June 1922)-. Periodical. English. mo (with July / Aug. and Dec. / Jan. issues combined). $5.00. Elks Magazine, 425 West Diversey Parkway, Chicago IL 60614. **Tel** (312)956-4500. **ED** Fred D. Oakes and Judith L. Keogh. **LC** HS1510.E4; A137. **DD** 366. **Bk Rev. Ad Acc. Circ:** 1,500,000 (ctrl).
**Desc:** Fraternal news of the Benevolent and Protective Order of Elks plus articles of timely general interest; regular columns on business, health, travel and retirement.

US/0013-6794
**EMPIRE STATE MASON.** V. 1- Oct. 1952-. Periodical. English. qt. Grand Lodge FTAM State of New York, 71 West 23rd Street, New York NY 10010. **Tel** (212)741-4500. **Bk Rev. Ad Acc. Circ:** 150,000 (ctrl).
**Desc:** The official publication of the Grand Lodge of Free and Accepted Masons of the state of New York. Edited for members of the Masonic fraternity and their families.

US/0894-2846
**ENCYCLOPEDIA OF ASSOCIATIONS. REGIONAL, STATE, AND LOCAL ORGANIZATIONS.** [Encycl. assoc., Reg. state local organ.]. **Added/Corp** Gale Research Company. **VFOAT** Regional, State, and Local Organizations. 1st Ed. (1989)-. English. be. $469.00. Gale Research Inc., 835 Penobscot Building, Detroit MI 48226. **Tel** (800)877-GALE, (313)961-2242, FAX (313)961-6083, telex TWX 810-221-7086. **ED** Grant Eldridge. **LC** AS22; .E53. **DD** 061/.3.
**Desc:** A guide to more than 50,000 US non-profit membership organizations with interstate, state, intrastate, city, or local scope and interest. Includes trade and professional associations, social welfare and public affair organizations, and religious, sports, and hobby groups with voluntary members. Especially helpful to businesses that market products on a regional or local level, to advertisers looking for locally published periodicals, to sales people developing a new client list, and to students, researchers, or general readers interested in obtaining information from local groups and associations.

JA
**EPISUTEME. EPISTEME. VFOAT** Episteme. (Oct. 1975)-. Periodical. Japanese. mo. ¥9600. Asahi Shuppansha, 7-9 Iidabashi 2 Chiyoda-ku, Tokyo Japan. **LC** AS551; .E65.

●BE
**EURO WHO'S WHO: WHO'S WHO IN THE EUROPEAN COMMUNITIES AND IN THE OTHER EUROPEAN ORGANIZATIONS.** **See** Biographies.

CH
**EVENSONGS, THE. VFOAT** Yeh Ko. Periodical. Multiple languages (Chinese and English). The Evensongs Association of English Department, Evening School/TamKang College, No 5 Lane 199 Kinghua Street, Taipei Taiwan. **LC** AS455.A1; E83. **DD** 052.

US/0014-4487
**EXCHANGITE, THE. Added/Corp** National Exchange Club. Vol. 1 (Dec. 1921)-. Periodical. English. Eight times a year. $4.00. National Exchange Club, 3050 Central Avenue, Toledo OH 43606. **Tel** (419)535-3232. **ED** Philip A. Flis. **Circ:** 44,000 (ctrl).
**Desc:** News and features relative to the functioning and fund raising, motivation, and service programs of exchange clubs and the education of its members.

US
**FAN CLUB DIRECTORY, THE.** Issue 9 (1985)-. Directory. English. an. $7.00. The Fan Club Directory, 2987 S Wentworth Avenue, Milwaukee WI 53207. **Tel** (414)483-8204. **ED** J H Spearo. **LC** HS2507; .F36. **DD** 790/.025. **Ad Acc. Circ:** 1,000. ***Continues*** *International Fan Club Directory.*
**Desc:** A listing of fan clubs world-wide.

CN/1180-3444
**FIL DE LIAISON.** (LE FIL DE LIAISON / CERCLE DE FERMIERES D'EVAIN.). [Fil liaison]. **Added/Corp** Cercle de Fermieres d'Evain. (1990/1991)-. Periodical. French. 6.00Can$ per volume. Cercle de Fermieres D'Evian, CP 84, Evain, Quebec J0Z 1Y0 Canada. **DD** 061/.1413/025.

UK/0430-876X
**FOLK DIRECTORY, THE. Added/Corp** English Folk Dance and Song Society, London. (1965)-. Directory. English. an. English Folk Dance and Song Society, Cecil Sharp House, 2 Regents Park Road, London NW1 7AY England. **Tel** 011 44 71 485 2206. **ED** David Purves. **DD** 780. **Bk Rev. Ad Acc. Circ:** 3,000 (ctrl).
**Desc:** Listings of folk dance, song, music clubs, groups, performers, services and suppliers.

CN/0715-5301
**FORUM - CANADIAN COUNCIL ON 4-H CLUBS.** (FORUM.). [Forum - Can. Counc. 4-H Clubs]. **VAT** Forum - Canadian 4-H Foundation; Forum - Conseil Canadien des Cercles 4-H; Forum - Fondation des 4-H du Canada; Forum - National 4-H Office. Periodical. English (French). qt. Canadian Council on 4-H Clubs, 323 Chapel Street, Ottawa Ontario K1N 7Z2. **DD** 630/.6/071.

US/0006-9256
**FRATERNAL HERALD.** V. 60- Jan. 1957-. Periodical. English (Czech). mo. $3.00. Fraternal Herald, 1900 1st Avenue NE, Cedar Rapids IA 52402. **Tel** (319)363-2653. **ED** Diane S Nolan. **Bk Rev. Circ:** 24,000 (ctrl). ***Continues*** *Bratrsky Vestnik.*
**Desc:** Official organ of Czech fraternal benefit society describing/reporting lodge activities, insurance products and Czech activities and history.

US
**FRATERNITY-SORORITY DIRECTORY... LELAND'S ANNUAL.** Directory. English.

MX/0185-3716
**GACETA (MEXICO CITY, MEXICO : 1954).** (LA GACETA : PUBLICACION DEL FONDO DE CULTURA ECONOMICA.). **Added/Corp** Fondo de Cultura Economica (Mexico). **VFOAT** Gaceta del Fondo de Cultura Economica. Vol. 1, No. 1 (Sept. 1954)-. Periodical. Spanish. Twelve times a year. $30.00. Fondo de Cultura Economica, Av Picacho Ajusco 227 / Pedregal, 14200 Mexico DF Mexico. **Tel** 011 52 5 2274670 71, FAX 011 52 5 2274683, telex 01775866. **ED** Jaime Garcia Terres, Adolfo Castanon, Jaime Moreno Villarreal, Alejandro Katz, Jose Luis Rivas, and Rafael Vargas. **LC** AS63.F6; A3. **DD** 300/.5. **Circ:** 10,000 (ctrl).

JA/0418-0038
**GAKUJUTSU KENKYU NEMPO / DOSHISHA JOSHI DAIGAKU. VFOAT** Annual Reports of Studies. Began in 1950. Academic Scholarly Publication. English (Japanese). an. 500. Doshisha Joshi Daigaku, 602 Gembucho, Imadegawadori Teramachi Nishi Iru, Kamigyo-ku 602, Kyoto-shi Japan. **LC** AS552.D64; A2. **DD** 050. **CODEN** DOJDAH. Documents available from CASDDS.
**Ind/Abst** Chem. Abstr.; MLA Int. Bibl. Books Artic. Mod. Lang. Lit.

US/1065-5050
**GALE GLOBAL ACCESS. ASSOCIATIONS.** ***Title Change.*** (GALE GLOBAL ACCESS. ASSOCIATIONS [COMPUTER FILE].). [Gale glob. access, Assoc.]. **Added/Corp** Gale Research Inc. SilverPlatter Information, Inc. **VFOAT** Associations; Global Access. Associations. (19??)-(199?). English. sa. Silverplatter Information Inc., 100 River Ridge Drive, Norwood MA 02062. **Tel** (800)343-0064, (617)769-2599, FAX (617)235-1715. **LC** AS2. **DD** 060. ***Continued by*** *Encyclopedia of Associations CD-ROM, 1070-2318.*
**Desc:** Contains descriptions of national organizations of the United States, international organizations, regional, state and local organizations and supplements. Coverage includes trade and professional associations, national organizations of the United States and other countries, social welfare and public affairs organizations, religious, and sports and hobby groups.

US/0746-7079
**GARNET AND WHITE, THE.** V. 1- 1900-. Periodical. English. qt. Alpha Chi Rho, 109 Oxford Way, Neptune NJ 07753.

US/0433-2091
**GATOR GREEK, THE. Added/Corp** Florida. University, Gainesville. Interfraternity Council. Vol. 1 (Nov. 11, 1960)-. Periodical. English. bm. University of Florida Interfraternity Council, Gainesville FL 32601. **DD** 371.8.

US/0017-0577
**GIRL SCOUT LEADER. Added/Corp** Girl Scouts of the United States of America. (Dec. 1923)-. Periodical. English. qt. $5.00. Girl Scouts of the USA, 420 Fifth Avenue, New York NY 10018-2702. **Tel** (212)852-8000, FAX (212)852-6511. **ED** Carolyn Caggine. **Circ:** 800,000 (ctrl). ***Continues*** *Field News.*
**Desc:** Designed to provide current information on activities and ideas of interest to adults in Girl Scouting. Includes program ideas, and trends which affects the interest of girls and women.

US/0747-508X
**GIRL SCOUTS AROUND NEW YORK.** Periodical. English. bm. Girl Scout Council of Greater New York, 335 East 46th Street, New York NY 10017.

US/1062-466X
**GLOBAL NOMAD, THE.** [Glob. nomad]. **Added/Corp** Global Nomads Washington Area. (1991)-. Periodical. English. bm. $15.00 (includes membership). The Global Nomad, PO Box 30524, Bethesda MD 20824. **DD** 367. ***Continues*** *Global Nomads DC.*

CN/0315-0151
**GO INFO. Main/Corp** Gais de l'Outaouais. **Added/Corp** Gays d'Ottawa. Vol. 1 (July 1972)-. Periodical. French (English). mo. 17.50Can$ Canada; 18.00Can$ other. Association of Lesbians & Gays of Ottawa, PO Box 2919 Station D, Ottawa Ontario K1P 5W9 Canada. **Tel** (613)233-0152.

YU
**GODISNJAK ZA ... / VOJVOANSKA AKADEMIJA NAUKA I UMETNOSTI. Main/Corp** Vojvoanska Akademija Nauka i Umetnosti. 1 (1980/1981)-. Serbo-Croatian (Roman). an. Vojvoanska Akademija Nauka i Umetnosti, Svetozara Markovica 6, Novi Sad Yugoslavia. **LC** AS346.N67; A37.

US
**GOLD STAR MOTHER (WASHINGTON, D.C. : 1985).** (THE GOLD STAR MOTHER.). Vol. No. 1 (Sept./Oct. 1985)-. Periodical. English. bm. American Gold Star Mothers, 2128 Leroy Avenue NW, Washington DC 20008. **Tel** (202)265-0991. **ED** Ruth Watts. **LC** D570.A15; A616. ***Continues*** *Gold Star Mother.*

UK/0141-5085
**GRAINGER SOCIETY JOURNAL, THE.** **See** Music.

US/0434-5797
**GREAT MASTERS OF THE PAST.** Vol. 1 (1955)-. English. **DD** 709.

US/0277-108X
**GROUP HQ DIRECTORY. VFOAT** Group Headquarters Directory; Group H.Q. Directory. 1982-. Directory. English. an. $95.00. Group HQ Directory, 633 Third Avenue, New York NY 10017. **LC** AS29.5; .G76. **DD** 061/.3.

MW
**GUIDE TO PROFESSIONAL BODIES IN MALAWI.** (19??)-. English. Centraf Associates Ltd, PO Box 30462, Chichiri Blantyre 3 Malawi. **LC** AS621.A1; G85. **DD** 068.6897.

CN/0826-0095
**HALIFAX AND DARTMOUTH CLUBS AND ORGANIZATIONS (1983).** (HALIFAX AND DARTMOUTH CLUBS AND ORGANIZATIONS.). [Halifax Dartmouth clubs organ.]. 1982/83-. English. an. Dartmouth Regional Library, 100 Wyse Road, Dartmouth Nova Scotia B3A 1M1 Canada. **DD** 061/.1622. ***Continues*** *Clubs and Organizations, 0383-1744.*

UK
**HEATHER SOCIETY BULLETIN, THE. Added/Corp** Heather Society. Vol. 2, No. 16 (Spring 1979)-. Periodical. English. ir. £6.00 (single), £7.00 (family) Comes with Heather Society membership. Heather Society, All Saints Road, Creeting, St. Mary 1P6 8PJ England. **Tel** 0449 711220. **ED** D. Everett. Index available. cum. index. **Bk Rev. Ad Acc.** ctrl circ. available on videocassette. ***Continues*** *Bulletin (Heather Society).*

JA
**HIBARINO : TOYOHASHI GIJUTSU KAGAKU DAIGAKU JIMBUN KAGAKUKEI KIYO. VFOAT** Lark Hill : Bulletin of the School of Humanities, Toyohashi University of Technology. No. 1- (1979)-. Periodical. Japanese (summaries and/or abstracts in English and German). an. Toyohashi Gijutsu Kagaku Daigaku, 1-1 Hibarigaoka Tempakucho, Toyohashi-shi 440 Japan. **LC** AS552.T724; A25. **DD** 080.

CC
**HO-PEI HSUEH KAN. Added/Corp** Ho-Pei Sheng She Hui ko Hsueh Yuan. Ho-Pei Sheng Che Hsueh She Hui ko Hsueh Hsueh Hui Lien Ho Hui. **VFOAT** Hebei Xuekan. (19??)-. Periodical. Chinese. qt. Post Office / China, People's Republic of China. **LC** AS451; .H6. **DD** 089/.951.

US/0738-2421
**HOLLY SOCIETY JOURNAL.** [Holly Soc. j.]. **Added/Corp** Holly Society of America. Vol. 1, No. 1 (Spring 1983)-. Periodical. English. qt (4 issues). Comes with Holly Society of America membership; $30.00 (institution membership), $15.00 (individual membership). Holly Society of America, 11318 West Murdock, Wichita KS 67212. **Tel** (316)721-5668. **ED** Ann R. Farnham (editor's address: 68 Lochatong Road, West Trenton, NJ 08628). **Ad Acc. Circ:** 750. ***Continues*** *Holly Letter, 0046-774X.*
**Desc:** Contains information about the genus Ilex for skilled growers as well as novices. A publication for holly enthusiasts.
**Ind/Abst** AGRICOLA [Select. Cov.]; For. Abstr.; Ornamental Hort.; Plant Breed. Abstr.; Rev. Agric. Entomol.

CC
**HSU-CHOU SHIH FAN HSUEH YUAN HSUEH PAO. CHE HSUEH SHE HUI KO HSUEH PAN. VFOAT** Xuzhou Shifan Xueyuan Xuebao. Periodical. Chinese. qt. 0.40. Post Office, Hsu-chou Shih, People's Republic of China. **LC** AS452.H87; A3. **DD** 059/.951.

# Societies and Clubs

BL/0102-9479
**HUMANIDADES (BRASILIA, BRAZIL).**
(HUMANIDADES.). Vol. 1, No. 1 (Oct./Dec. 1982 1982)-. Periodical. Portuguese (Portuguese). qt. Editora Universidade de Brasilia, Caixa Postal 153001, Campus Universitario, 7910 Brasilia DF Brazil. **LC** AS80.A1; H85. **DD** 056/.9.

JA
**IBARAKI DAIGAKU IZURA BIJUTSU BUNKA KENKYUJO HO. Main/Corp** Ibaraki Daigaku. Izura Bijutsu Bunka Kenkyujo. Japanese. Ibaraki Daigaku Izura Bijutsu Bunka Kenkyujo, Ho 2-1-1 Bunkyo, Mito Japan. **LC** AS552.I215; A25.

VE
**IDEAS CONCRETAS. VFOAT** IC. June/July 1972-. Periodical. Spanish. Avenida Libertador-Esquina las Acacias-Edificio las Vegas, 58 Piso-oficina 5-B, Caracas Venezuela. **LC** AS90.A1; I3.

US/0019-6622
**INDIANA FREEMASON, THE. Added/Corp** Freemasons. Indiana. Grand Lodge. (1923)-. Periodical. English. mo. $8.00. Indiana Freemason Printing, Box 38, Franklin IN 46131-0038. **Tel** (317)736-5741. **ED** C. C. Falkner Jr. **Ad Acc. Circ:** 7,500.
**Desc:** Fraternal history and lodge news.

XR/0231-5386
**INFORMACNI PRIRUCKA / CESKOSLOVENSKA AKADEMIE VED.**
[Inform. priruc. - Cs. Akad. Ved.]. **Main/Corp** Ceskoslovenska Akademie Ved. **Added/Corp** Slovenska Akademie Vied. (19??)-. Czech (Slovak). ir. Ceskoslovenska Akademie Zemedelska / Institute of Scientific & Technical Information for Agriculture, Slezska 7, 120 56 Prague 2, Czech Republic. **LC** AS142; .C4. **NLM** AS 142.C4 C421.

BL
**INTER-ACAO.** V. 1- Nov. 1975-. Portuguese. Faculdade de Educacao da Universidade Federal de Goias, Praca Universitaria S/N, 70 000 Golaria Brazil. **LC** AS80.A1; I57.

US/0094-5838
**INTERFACE (ATLANTA).** (INTERFACE.). V. 1- Summer/Fall 1973-. English. University System of Georgia, Board of Regents, 244 Washington Street SW, Atlanta GA 30334. **LC** AS36.U6; A27. **DD** 051.

US
**J.C.I. NEWS.** (19??)-. Periodical. English. Junior Chamber International, 400 University Drive, PO Box 140577, Coral Gables FL 33134. **Tel** (305)446-7608. *Continues Leader, 0743-5754.*

NE
**JAARBOEK - MAATSCHAPPIJ DER NEDERLANDSE LETTERKUNDE TE LEIDEN. Main/Corp** Maatschappij der Nederlandse Letterkunde te Leiden. Dutch. an. Maatschappy der Ned Letterkunde, Rapenburg 70-74, Leiden Netherlands. **LC** AS244. cum. index.

GW
**JAHRBUCH / AKADEMIE FORUM MASONICUM. Added/Corp** Forum Masonicum. Akademie. (1988)-. German. an.

GW/0304-2154
**JAHRBUCH DER AKADEMIE DER WISSENSCHAFTEN DER DDR. Main/Corp** Akademie der Wissenschaften der DDR. (19??)-. Monographic series. German. ir. Price varies per volume. Akademie-Verlag GmbH, Muehlenstrasse 33 34, D 13162 Berlin Germany. **Tel** 011 49 30 47889300, FAX 011 49 30 47889357. **(Subscription address:** VCH Verlagsges Export Books, Postfach 101161, D 69451 Weinheim Germany.) **LC** AS182; .B345. **DD** 063. *Continues Akademie der Wissenschaften, Berlin. Jahrbuch.*
**Desc:** Gives an up-to-date survey on scientific activities of the departments of the Academy of sciences and informs on bodies, personalia and honours awarded.

GW
**JAHRESBERICHT. BD. 2, PROGRAMME UND PROJEKTE. Main/Corp** Deutsche Forschungsgemeinschaft. **VFOAT** Programme und Projekte. (1991)-. German. Kennedyalle 40, Postfach 2050004, W-5300 Bonn 2 Godesberg Germany. **Tel** 0228-885-1, FAX 0228-885-2221, telex (17)22 83 12 DFG. *Continues Deutsche Forschungsgemeinschaft. Programme und Projekte.*

CN/0383-672X
**JALONS (REPENTIGNY). Title Change.**
(JALONS.). V. 1- Dec. 15, 1973-. Periodical. French. ir. Federation des Eclaireurs du Quebec, Secretariat National, 217 de l'Etoile, Laval Quebec H7N 4T4 Canada. **DD** 369.43/09714. *Continued by Maitrise, 0383-8595.*

US/0893-0031
**JAYCEES MAGAZINE (GREENSBORO, N.C.).** (JAYCEES MAGAZINE.). [Jaycees mag.]. **Added/Corp** United States Jaycees. Vol. 1, No. 1 (Feb./March 1987)-. Periodical. English. qt (Feb., May, Aug., Nov.). $10.00 US, Canada & Mexico; $15.00 other. United States Junior Chamber of Commerce, PO Box 7/Publications Dept, Tulsa OK 74121-0007. **Tel** (918)584-2481, FAX (918)584-4422. **ED** Bob Hardy. **DD** 369. available on microfilm and microfiche from University Microfilms International (UMI). *Continues Future, 0016-3260.*

US/0364-6572
**JOHN & MARY'S JOURNAL. VAT** John and Mary's Journal. No. 2- Spring 1976-. Academic Scholarly Publication. English. an. $5.00. Dickinson College Friends of the Library, Carlisle PA 17013. **Tel** (717)245-1399. **ED** Beverly Eddy. **LC** AS36.D53; A27. **DD** 051. Index available. cum. index. **Circ:** 500.
**Desc:** Publishes scholarly articles based on archival research and sources, usually in history of education, humanities, history of science.

US/0744-3943
**JONQUIL. VFOAT** ESA Jonquil for Women; Jonquil for ESA Women. Periodical. English. Four times a year. $9.50. Epsilon Sigma Alpha International, 363 W Drake Road, Fort Collins CO 80526. **Tel** (303)223-2824, FAX (303)223-4456. **ED** Ginifer Maceau. **Ad Acc. Circ:** 18,000 (ctrl). *Continues Jonquil for ESA Women, 0164-9477.*
**Desc:** Member information, programs, and materials.

US
**JOURNAL OF SCOUTING HISTORY.**
English. sa. $5.00 (US); $7.50 (Canada & Mexico); $10.00 (other). Journal of Scouting History, 3700 First City Tower, Houston TX 77002. **Tel** (713)658-8881, (713)754-6205. **ED** Nelson R. Block. **Bk Rev**, (Qty: 2/yr). **Ad Acc. Circ:** 300.
**Desc:** Articles on the history of the Boy Scout movement.

US/0197-3789
**JOURNAL OF THE AMERICAN BAMBOO SOCIETY. Ceased. Main/Corp** American Bamboo Soc.]. **Main/Corp** American Bamboo Society. **Added/Corp** American Bamboo Society. Vol. 1 (Feb. 1980)-(19??). Periodical. English. ir. American Bamboo Society, PO Box 640, Springville CA 93265. **Tel** (209)539-2145. **Circ:** 800.
**Ind/Abst** AGRICOLA.

BG/0377-0540
**JOURNAL OF THE ASIATIC SOCIETY OF BANGLADESH. Main/Corp** Asiatic Society of Bangladesh. V. 16 (Dec. 1971)-. English. Three times a year. $10.00. Asiatic Society of Bangladesh, Dacca Museum Building, Dacca Bangladesh. **LC** AS599.A8; A3. **DD** 052. *Continues Journal of the Asiatic Society of Pakistan, 0571-317X.*
**Ind/Abst** Am. Hist. Life (1964,1969-).

II/0004-9709
**JOURNAL OF THE ASIATIC SOCIETY OF BOMBAY. Main/Corp** Asiatic Society of Bombay. Vol. 1 (July 1841)-. English. ir. $40.00. Hindustan Book Agency, 17 UB Jawahar Nagar, Delhi 7 India. **(Subscription address:** Prints India, 11 Darya Ganj, New Delhi 110002 India.) **LC** AS472; .B7.
**Ind/Abst** Anthropol. Index; MLA Int. Bibl. Books Artic. Mod. Lang. Lit.

CH/0578-154X
**JOURNAL OF THE CHINA SOCIETY.**
**Main/Corp** Chung-Kuo Hsuen Hui, T'ai-Pei. V. 1- 1961-. Periodical. English. Journal of the China Society, PO Box 1321, Taipei Taiwan.

HK/0085-5774
**JOURNAL OF THE HONG KONG BRANCH OF THE ROYAL ASIATIC SOCIETY.** [J. Hong Kong Branch R. Asiat. Soc.]. Vol. 1, (1960-61)-. English. an. HK$110.00 (Volume 25). Royal Asiatic Society, Hong Kong Branch, PO Box 3864, Hong Kong. **ED** Patrick Hase. **LC** DS1; .R57. Index available. cum. index. **Bk Rev. Circ:** 1,000 (ctrl).
**Desc:** Journal covers history and culture of Hong Kong, China and Asia.
**Ind/Abst** Am. Hist. Life (1960-1977, 1979-); Anthropol. Index.

IE
**JOURNAL OF THE OLD DROGHEDA SOCIETY. Added/Corp** Old Drogheda Society (Drogheda, Ireland). No. 1 (1976)-. Periodical. English. an. 6.00p. Journal of the Old Drogheda, 26 Maple Drive Greenhills, County Louth Ireland.

UK/0374-3519
**JOURNAL OF THE ROYAL SIGNALS INSTITUTION.** [J. R. Signals Inst.]. (1954)-. Periodical. English. Three times a year. £7.56 UK; £10.14 EEC countries; £9.90 other. RHQ Royal Signals, 16 Regency Street, London SW1P 4AD England. **Tel** 011 44 71 414 8432. **CODEN** JRSIBT. Documents available from Ask*IEEE.
**Ind/Abst** INSPEC (Winter 1971-).

CN/1182-2589
**JOURNAL PLUS, LE.** [J. plus]. **Added/Corp** Federation Quebecoise du Guidisme et du Scoutisme. (Sept. 1989)-. Periodical. French. Quipo, c/o Federation Quebecoise du Guidisme et du Scoutisme, 1415 East rue Jarry, Montreal Quebec H2E 2Z7 Canada. **DD** 369.43/09714/05. *Continues Quipo, 0713-6080.*

UK/0308-4949
**JOURNAL - ROYAL BRITISH LEGION.**
(JOURNAL.). **Main/Corp** Royal British Legion. Periodical. English. mo. £5.00 per copy. National Executive Council, Royal British Legion, Pall Mall, London SW1Y 5JY England. **LC** D546.A11; A2. **DD** 369/.242. *Continues British Legion Journal.*

JA
**KAGAKU/NINGEN.** Japanese. Kanto Gakuin Daigaku Kegakubu Kyoyo Gakkai, 4834 Rokuuramachi, Kanazawa-ku, Yokohama-shi Japan. **LC** AS552.K33; A32.

JA
**KANAZAWA DAIGAKU BUNGAKUBU RONSHU. KODO KAGAKUKA HEN.**
**VFOAT** Studies and Essays. Behavioral Sciences and Philosophy; Studies and Essays. Behavioral Sciences sic and Philosophy. 1980-. Periodical. Japanese. Kanazawa Daigaku Bungakubu, 1-1 Marunouchi, Kanazawa-shi 920 Japan. **LC** AS552.K26; A275.

US
**KANSAS JOURNAL. Added/Corp** Kansas 4-H Foundation. **VFOAT** Kansas 4-H Journal. (Feb 1955)-. Periodical. English. mo. Kansas 4-H Foundation, Umberger Hall, Kansas State University, Manhattan KS 66506.

US/0888-8868
**KAPPA ALPHA JOURNAL, THE.** [Kappa Alpha j.]. **Main/Corp** Kappa Alpha (Southern Order). Periodical. English. qt. Kappa Alpha Order/National Administration Office, PO Box 1865, Lexington VA 24450. **Tel** (703)463-1865, FAX (703)463-2140. **ED** William E Garner. **LC** LJ75; .K2. **DD** 371. **Ad Acc. Circ:** 65,500 (ctrl).

JA
**KEGON.** (19??)-. Periodical. Japanese. mo. ¥6000. Kokon Hyoronsa, 22-2 Hommachi 6, Shibuya-ku, Tokyo Japan. **LC** AS551; .K43.

JA
**KENKYU KIYO - RISSHO JOSHI DAIGAKU TANKI DAIGAKUBU. Main/Corp** Rissho Joshi Daigaku. Tanki Daigakubu. **Added/Corp** Rissho Joshi Daigaku. Tanki Daigakubu. Annual Reports of Studies. **VFOAT** Annual Reports of Studies. (19??)-. Periodical. Multiple languages (English and Japanese). Rissho Joshi Daigaku Tanki Daigakubu, 2-17 Hatanodai 3 Shinagawa-ku, Tokyo Japan. **LC** AS552.R57; A28.

US/0740-6185
**KENTUCKY CLUBWOMAN, THE.** (THE KENTUCKY CLUBWOMAN: [OFFICIAL PUBLICATION OF G.F.W.C./KENTUCKY FEDERATION OF WOMEN'S CLUBS] / KFWC, KENTUCKY FEDERATION OF WOMEN'S CLUBS.). **Added/Corp** Kentucky Federation of Women's Clubs. **VFOAT** Kentucky Club Woman. (19??)-. Periodical. English. qt (Jan., March, June, Aug.). $1.50. Kentucky Federation Woman's Clubs, 1228 Cherokee Road, Louisville KY 40204. **Tel** (502)451-8435. **ED** Fay Trusty. **Ad Acc. Circ:** 6,000 (ctrl).
**Desc:** News and feature articles pertaining to club work.

JA
**KISARAZU KOGYO KOTO SEMMON GAKKO KIYO. Main/Corp** Kisarazu Kogyo Koto Semmon Gakko. **VFOAT** Bulletin of Kisarazu Technical College. Academic Scholarly Publication. Japanese (summaries and/or abstracts in English). Kisarazu Kogyo Koto Semmon Gakko, 834 Gion 292, Kisarazu Japan. **LC** AS552.K42; A3. **CODEN** KKSKDX. Documents available from CASDDS.
**Ind/Abst** Chem. Abstr.

US/0162-5276
**KIWANIS.** (KIWANIS: A MAGAZINE FOR COMMUNITY LEADERS.). [Kiwanis]. **Added/Corp** Kiwanis International. Vol. 61, No. 9 (Oct. 1976)-. Periodical. English. Ten times a year. $6.50 members; $7.50 nonmembers. Kiwanis International, 3636 Woodview Trace, Indianapolis IN 46268. **Tel** (317)875-8755, FAX (317)879-0204. **LC** HF5001; .K43. **Circ:** 543,000. available on microfilm. *Continues Kiwanis Magazine, 0023-1975.*
**Desc:** Magazine for the members of Kiwanis clubs throughout the U.S.

JA
**KIYO - CHUO DAIGAKU BUNGAKUBU.**
**Main/Corp** Chuo Daigaku, Tokyo Bungakubu. **VFOAT** Journal of the Faculty of Literature. Began with Dec. 1954 issue. Periodical. Japanese. Chuo Daigaku Bugakubu, 9 Kanda Surugadai 3 Chiyoda-ku, Tokyo Japan. **LC** AS552.C5; A23.

JA
**KIYO - HIROSAKI DAIGAKU IRYO GIJUTSU TANKI DAIGAKUBU. Main/Corp** Hirosaki Daigaku. Iryo Gijutsu Tanki Daigakubu. **VFOAT** Hirosaki Daigaku Iryo Gijutsu Tanki Daigakubu Kiyo;

## Societies and Clubs

JA
**Hirosaki Daigaku Tanki Daigakubu Kiyo.** No. 1 (1976)-. Bulletin. Japanese. an. Hiroski Daigaku Tanki Daigakubu Iryo Gijitsu Tanki Daigakubu, (School of Allied Medical Sciences,, Hirosaki University), 66-1 Honcho Hirosakishi, Aomoriken 036 Japan. **LC** AS552.H53; A3.

JA
**KOGAKKAN DAIGAKU KIYO. Main/Corp** Kogakkan Daigaku. **VFOAT** Bulletin of Kogakkan University. (1963)-. Japanese (Japanese). Kogakkan Daigaku, Kuratayama 516, Ise Japan. **LC** AS552.K53; A24.

JA
**KOKUSAI JIJO. Added/Corp** Nagasaki Gaikokugo Tanki Daigaku. Kokusai Jijo Kenkyujo. No. 1 (1970)-. Periodical. Japanese. Nagasaki Gaikokugo Tanki Diagaku Kobusai Jijo Kenjujo, 243 Izumimachi, Nagasaki Japan. **LC** AS551; .K65.

CC
**KUEI-YANG SHIH YUAN HSUEH PAO. SHE HUI KO HSUEH PAN. VFOAT** Guiyang Shiyuan Xuebao. Periodical. Chinese. qt. RMBY1.20. Post Office Kuei-Yang, Kuei-Yang, People's Republic of China. **LC** AS452.K78; A27.

KO
**KUKCHE HAKSUL KANGYONHOE NONMUNJIP. Title Change.** Periodical. Korean. Haksurwon, 1 Sejongno Chongno-ku, Seoul South Korea. **LC** AS559.A1; K84. **Continued by** Kukche Haksul Taehoe Nonmunjip.

KO
**KUKCHE HAKSUL TAEHOE NONMUNJIP. Added/Corp** Taehan Minguk Haksurwon. **VFOAT** Proceedings ... International Symposia. (1985)-. Periodical. Korean (English). Haksurwon, 1 Sejongno Chongno-ku, Seoul South Korea. **LC** AS559.A1; K84. **Continues** Kukche Haksul Kangyonhoe Nonmunjip.

KO
**KYOYUK NONCHONG (TONGGUK TAEHAKKYO. KYOYUK TAEHAGWON).** (KYOYUK NONCHONG.). V. 1-. Periodical. Korean. Tongguk Taehakkyo Kyoyuk Taehagwon, 26 3-ka Pil-dong, Chung-ku, Seoul South Korea. **LC** AS559.S62; A24.

CC
**LAN-CHOU HSUEH KAN. VFOAT** Lan Zhou Xue Kan. Periodical. Chinese. qt. RMBY0.30. Post Office, Lan-Chou Shih, People's Republic of China. **Tel** 26492. **LC** AS451; .L35. **DD** 089/.951. **Ad Acc. Circ:** 3,500. **Desc:** Economic theory, study of the change in socio-economics, philosophy, sociology, history of north-west Lan-chou province.

CN/0704-0318
**LIMOI.** Mar. 1975-. Periodical. French. ir. Guides Catholiques du Canada, Diocese d'Ottawa, 353 rue Friel, Ottawa Ontario K1N 7W7 Canada. **DD** 369.463/09713/8.

UK/0161-6366
**LINNEAN SOCIETY SYMPOSIUM SERIES.** [Linn. Soc. symp. ser.]. No. 1-. Academic Scholarly Publication. English. Price varies per volume. Academic Press Ltd., A Division of Harcourt Brace & Company Ltd., 24-28 Oval Road, London NW1 7DX England. **Tel** 071 267 4466, **FAX** 071 482 2293, 071 485 4752, telex 25775 ACPRES G. **(Subscription address:** Harcourt Brace Jovanovich Limited, Footscray High Street, Sidcup, Kent DA14 5HP UK, (Phone: 081-300-3322)) **CODEN** LSSSDM. Documents available from BIOSIS Document Express, CASDDS. **Ind/Abst** Biol. Abstr.; Chem. Abstr.; GeoRef.

US/0024-4163
**LION (UNITED STATES ED.), THE.** (THE LION.). [Lion]. **Added/Corp** Lions International. (1918)-. Periodical. English. mo. $6.00 US; $12.00 other. Lions International, 300 22nd Street, Oak Brook IL 60521. **Tel** (708)571-5466. **ED** Robert Kleinfelder. **LC** HS2705.L5; L5. **Ad Acc, Adv Mgr:** Mary Kay Rietz, **Tel** (708)571-5466. **Circ:** 640,000 (ctrl). **Desc:** The official publication of lions clubs international. Content deals primarily with activities of lions clubs and articles of interest to service-oriented individuals.

BL
**LOGOS. Added/Corp** Faculdade de Filosofia, Ciencias e Letras de Divinopolis. Vol. 1 No. 1 (April 1974)-. Portuguese (Portuguese). Faculdade de Filosofia / Divinopolis, Ciencias e Letras de Divinopolis, Av 21 de Abril 645 35 500, Divinopolis Brazil. **LC** AS80.F32; L63. **Supersedes** Dialogo.

UK
**LUTE : THE JOURNAL OF THE LUTE SOCIETY, THE.** Vol. 22 (1982)-. Periodical. English. sa. Francesca McManus, 71 Priory Road, Kew Gardens, Richmond Surrey England. **LC** ML5; .L89. **DD** 787.8/3/05. **Formed by the union of** Lute Society (Great Britain) Journal **and** Lute Society (Great Britain) Newsletter.

JA
**MACHIKANEYAMA RONSO: SHINRIGAKU, SHAKAIGAKU, KYOIKUGAKU HEN. VFOAT** Machikaneyama Ronso: Psychology, Sociology, Education. No. 6- 1973-. Japanese (English). Osaka Daigaku Bungakubu, 1-1 Machikaneyamacho, Toyonaka Osaka Japan. **Tel** (06)844-1151. **LC** AS551; .M33. **Continues** Machikaneyama Ronso: Kyoikugakuhen.

US/0738-3053
**MAGNOLIA (HAMMOND, LA.).** (MAGNOLIA.). [Magnolia]. **Added/Corp** American Magnolia Society. Magnolia Society. Vol. 16, No. 1 (Spring/Summer 1980)-. Periodical. English. sa. $18.00. Magnolia Society, 907 South Chesnut, Hammond LA 70404. **Tel** (504)542-9477. **ED** Larry W Langford (editor's address: PO Box 99, Gibson TN 38338; editor's phone: (901)787-6873). **LC** SB413.M34; M34. **DD** 635.9/33114. Index available. **Bk Rev,** (Qty: Occasionally). **Ad Acc. Circ:** 550 (ctrl). **Continues** Newsletter of the American Magnolia Society, 0730-5737.

US/0161-584X
**MAINE LEGIONNAIRE, THE.** Periodical. English. bm. $6.00, free to members. The Maine Legionnaire, PO Box 900, Waterville ME 04901-0900. **Tel** (207)873-0107. **ED** Charles H Michaud and Michelle L McRae. Index available. cum. index. **Ad Acc. Circ:** 27,000 (ctrl). **Desc:** Current veterans issues.

MR
**MAJALLAT KULLIYAT AL-ADAB WA-AL-ULUM AL-INSANIYAH BI-AL-RABAT. Main/Corp** Jamiat Muhammad V. Kulliyat Al-Adab. **VFOAT** Majallat Kulliyat Al Adab; Majallat Kulliat Al Adab. (1977)-. Periodical. Arabic. 3 rue Ibn Battouta, Al-Rabat Morocco. **LC** AS697; .A37a.

SU
**MAJALLAT MARKAZ AL-BUHUTH. VFOAT** Journal of the Research Centre. No. 1, (1982)-. Periodical. Arabic (English). an. S B 18011, Al-Riyad Saudi Arabia. **LC** AS587.R595; A33.

US/0883-5616
**MAKING WAVES (PASADENA, CALIF.).** (MAKING WAVES : SURFRIDER FOUNDATION NEWSLETTER.). **VFOAT** Surfrider Foundation Newsletter. Spring 1985-. Newsletter. English. $25.00 membership. Surfrider Foundation, PO Box 60582, Pasadena CA 91106.

SU
**MANAR (JIDDAH, SAUDI ARABIA).** (AL-MANAR.). **Added/Corp** Jamiat al-Malik Abd al-Aziz. Lajnah al-Thaqafiyah. (19??)-. Periodical. Arabic. mo. Jamiat Al-Malik ABD Al-Aziz S B 1540, Jiddah Majallat, Al-Manar Al-Lajnah Al-Thaqafiyah Al-Ammah Saudi Arabia. **LC** AS587.J524; A26.

US
**MANUAL - UNITED NATIONS EDUCATIONAL, SCIENTIFIC AND CULTURAL ORGANIZATION. GENERAL CONFERENCE. Main/Corp** United Nations Educational, Scientific and Cultural Organization. General Conference. **Added/Corp** United Nations Educational, Scientific and Cultural Organization. General Conference. Final Act, Constitution, Rules of Procedure. United Nations Educational, Scientific and Cultural Organization. General Conference. Conference manual. (1950)-. English. UNIPUB, 4611-F Assembly Drive, Lanham MD 20706-4391. **Tel** (800)274-4888, **FAX** (301)459-0056, telex 892798 GATT CH. **LC** AS4.U82; G37. **DD** 060.

US/0746-8725
**MASSACHUSETTS AUXILIARE, THE.** Periodical. English. qt. $2.00. Massachusetts Auxiliare, 30 Seneca Street, Lawrence MA 01844.

US/0275-6226
**MAZAMA.** [Mazama]. Began publication May 1, 1896. Periodical. English. mo. $3.50. Mazamas Club, 909 NW 19th Avenue, Portland OR 97209. **Ind/Abst** GeoRef.

CN/0820-4217
**MC. MENSA CANADA COMMUNICATIONS.** (MC I.E. SQUARED : MENSA CANADA COMMUNICATIONS.). [MC@. Mensa Can. commun.]. **VFOAT** MC; MENSA Journal. VAT MENSA Canada Communications (1981). Vol. 14, No. 7 (Sept. 1981)-. Periodical. English. mo. Free to MENSA Canada members. MENSA Canada Communication, 361 Yonge Street, Toronto Ontario M5B 1S1 Canada. **DD** 153.9/8/06071. **Continues** MENSA Canada Communications, 0229-5342.

US/0196-2078
**MCCONNAUGHEY BULLETIN (MCCONNAUGHEY AND VARIANTS) OF THE MCCONNAUGHEY SOCIETY OF AMERICA, INC, THE. Main/Corp** McConnaughey Society of America. **VFOAT** Annual Bulletin - McConnaughey Society of America; McConnaughey Bulletin. No. 1- 1963-. Bulletin. English. an. $17.50, $12.00 (retired). The McConnaughey Society of America Inc, PO Box 47051, Indianapolis IN 46247-0051. **Tel** WEEKDAYS: (317)786-4363, OTHER TIMES: (317)786-8380, **FAX** (317)782-1821. **ED** Pat McConnaughay Gregory. Index available. **Circ:** 150-200 (ctrl). **Desc:** Information of, for, by and about McConnaugheys, including the variant spellings.

CN/0226-7500
**MEETINGS CANADA.** [Meet. Can.]. Apr. 1980-. Periodical. English. ir. $22.50 Canada; $30.00 US; $45.00 other. Sovereign Publications / Canada, 110 Church Street, Toronto Ontario M6B 1J8 Canada. **DD** 061/.1/05.

US
**MEMBERSHIP DIRECTORY / AMERICAN MEDICAL WRITERS ASSOCIATION. Main/Corp** American Medical Writers Association. Began with 1949 issue?. Directory. English. an. $35.00. American Medical Writers Association, 9650 Rockville Pike, Bethesda MD 20814-3928. **Tel** (301)986-9119. **LC** WMLC L 83/1208. **NLM** WZ 22; AA1 A5m. **Circ:** 3,500. **Continues** Membership Directory / Mississippi Valley Medical Editors' Association.

US/0363-3616
**MEMBERSHIP LIST - AMERICAN MENSA LIMITED. Main/Corp** American Mensa Limited. (1966)-. English. an. American Mensa Committee, 2626 East 14th Street, Brooklyn NY 11235. **Tel** (718)934-3700, **FAX** (718)332-1183. **LC** BF431; .A566a. **DD** 367/.973. **Ad Acc, Adv Mgr:** Shoshana Shafran, **Pr Rev. Circ:** 50,000 (ctrl). **Desc:** General information articles, classifieds, and personal ads for the local group's members.

BE
**MEMOIRES DE L'ACADEMIE ROYALE DES SCIENCES, DES LETTRES ET DES BEAUX-ARTS DE BELGIQUE. Added/Corp** Academie Royale des Sciences, des Lettres et des Beaux-Arts de Belgique. Vol. 20. (18??)-. French. ir. Librarie Alain Ferration, Chausse de Charleroi 162, B 1060 Brussels, Belgium. **Tel** 011 32 2 5386917. **LC** AS242; .B321. **DD** 068.493. **Continues** Nouveaux Memoires de l'Academie Royale des Sciences, et Belles-Lettres de Belgique.

PO/0378-116X
**MEMORIAS DA ACADEMIA DAS CIENCIAS DE LISBOA. CLASSE DE LETRAS.** [Mem. Acad. Cienc. Lisboa, Cl. Let.]. **Main/Corp** Academia das Ciencias de Lisboa. Classe de Letras. Vol. 1 (1936)-. Portuguese. ir. Academia das Ciencias de Lisboa, R Academia das Ciencia 19 1200, Lisbon Portugal. **LC** AS304; .L414. **DD** 066.9. **Continues** Historia e Memorias. Nova Serie. **Ind/Abst** MLA Int. Bibl. Books Artic. Mod. Lang. Lit.

US/0025-9543
**MENSA BULLETIN.** [Mensa bull.]. **Added/Corp** American Mensa Limited. 105 (Nov. 1967)-. Bulletin. English. Ten times a year. $12.00. American Mensa Committee, 2626 East 14th Street, Brooklyn NY 11235. **Tel** (718)934-3700, **FAX** (718)332-1183. **LC** AS36.A4868; A3. **DD** 051. **Bk Rev. Ad Acc. Circ:** 55,000 (ctrl). **Continues** Intelligence. **Desc:** Basically a house organ for the members of Mensa, the high I.Q. society. Articles on intelligence, education of the gifted, humor, puzzles and letters, and classifieds.

US/1049-0175
**MICHIGAN 4-H TODAY.** [Mich. 4-H today]. **Added/Corp** Michigan 4-H Youth Programs. **VFOAT** Michigan 4 H Today; Michigan Four H Today. Vol. 1, No. 1 (Mar. 1990)-. Periodical. English. sa. Michigan 4-H Youth Programs, 6H Berkey Hall, Michigan State University, East Lansing MI 48824-1111. **DD** 366. **Ind/Abst** AGRICOLA [Full Cov.].

US
**MISC. Added/Corp** University of Pittsburgh. Pitt Program Council. **VFOAT** Miscellaneous. (1991)-. English. **LC** LD6016; .M57.

US
**MISSISSIPPI 4-H NEWS. Title Change.** Periodical. English. bm. **Continued by** 4-H Review, 0886-5892.

US/0026-6299
**MISSISSIPPI LEGION'AIRE. Added/Corp** American Legion. Dept. of Mississippi. **VFOAT** Mississippi Legionaire. (19??)-. Periodical. English. Six times a year. $3.00. Mississippi Legion'aire, PO Box 688, Jackson MS 39205. **Tel** (601)352-4986. **DD** 369. **Ad Acc.** ctrl circ. **Desc:** A newspaper dedicated to furnishing news and items of interest to the American Legion Veterans of the State of Mississippi.

BL/0532-8381
**MONOGRAFIA - FUNDACAO GETULIO VARGAS.** **Main/Corp** Fundacao Getulio Vargas. Vol. 1 (1964)-. Portuguese. Caixa Postal 9052, Rio de Janeiro GB Brazil. **DD** 060.

US/0435-4419
**MONOGRAPH.** **Main/Corp** George Eastman House. Vol. 1 (1960)-. English. George Eastman House, 900 East Avenue, Rochester NY 14607. **Tel** (716)271-3361. **ED** Barbara Hall. **DD** 770. ctrl circ.
**Desc:** Covers exhibit information fundraising, special programs-films, receptions, trips; annual report-finance, and goals.

CN/0710-0159
**MONTAGE (TORONTO. 1981).** (MONTAGE.). [Montage]. Vol. 5, No. 6 (June 1981)-. Periodical. English. $5.00 Canada; $8.00 other. Montage, 496 Dufferin Avenue, Toronto Ontario M5A 2J9 Canada. **DD** 367/.9713. ***Continues*** *Tan, 0227-3314.*

CH
**NAN-CHING SHIH YUAN HSUEH PAO. CHE HSUEH SHE HUI KO HSUEH PAN.** Periodical. Chinese. qt. NT$0.35. Post Office, Nan-Ching, People's Republic of China. **LC** AS452.N385; A3. **DD** 089/.951.

AG
**NAO.** **Added/Corp** Fundacion "Los Cedros" (Buenos Aires, Argentina). Vol. 1, No. 1 (1980)-. Periodical. Spanish. Fundacion Los Cedros, AV Las Heras 1965, 1ER Piso, Depto B, Buenos Aires Argentina. **LC** AS78.A1; N36. **DD** 056/.1.

US/1062-4244
**NATIONAL NEWS - AMERICAN LEGION AUXILIARY.** **Main/Corp** American Legion. Auxiliary. Periodical. English. bm. $5.00. American Legion Auxiliary, 777 North Meridian Street, Indianapolis IN 46204. **Tel** (317)635-6291. **ED** Mary L Hardin and Judi Wesner. **Ad Acc.** ctrl circ.
**Desc:** Material of interest to the membership of the American Legion Auxiliary. A group whose median age is 35 to 70, middle class, married and homeowners. A group whose interests are home, community, and country.

US/0734-354X
**NATIONAL TRADE AND PROFESSIONAL ASSOCIATIONS OF THE UNITED STATES (WASHINGTON, D.C. : 1982).** (NATIONAL TRADE AND PROFESSIONAL ASSOCIATIONS OF THE UNITED STATES.). [Natl. trade prof. assoc. U. S.]. **VFOAT** NTPA; N.T.P.A.; National Trade & Professional Associations of the United States. 17th Ed. (1982)-. English. an. $75.00 D.C., $79.50 other. Columbia Books Inc, 1212 New York Avenue NW/Suite 330, Washington DC 20005. **Tel** (202)898-0662, FAX (202)898-0775. **ED** John J Russell. **LC** HD2425; .D53. **DD** 061/.3. **NLM** HD 2425 N277. Index available. **Circ:** 8,500. ***Continues*** *National Trade and Professional Associations of the United States and Canada and Labor Unions, 0094-8284.*
**Desc:** Contains more than 6,000 trade associations, professional societies and labor unions. Each entry consists of the address, date established, the principal executive, number of members, size of staff, telephone, annual budget, publications, annual meetings and historical data.

DK/0084-9308
**NATIONALMUSEETS ARBEJDSMARK.** [Natl.mus. arb.mark]. **Added/Corp** Nationalmuseet (Denmark). (1958)-. Danish. an. **LC** AS281.A2; C6. ***Continues*** *Fra Nationalmuseets Arbejdsmark.*
**Ind/Abst** Anthropol. Lit.; Art Archaeol. Tech. Abstr.; Avery Index Archit. Period. Suppl. Colum. Univ. (19??-199?); BHA : Biblio. Hist. Art; Numis. Lit.

CN/0228-2585
**NEUVE EGLISE.** [Neuve eglise]. V. 1- Mar. 1979-. Periodical. French. ir. Association des Scouts du Canada, 9907 rue Parthenais, Montreal Quebec H2B 2L3 Canada. **DD** 248.8/32/05.

CN/0382-8417
**NEWS FROM CANADA-JAPAN SOCIETY OF VANCOUVER.** **Main/Corp** Canada-Japan Society of Vancouver. Began publication in 1971?. English. ir. Canada-Japan Society of Vancouver, 207 West Hastings Street, Vancouver BC V6B 1H7. **DD** 301.29/71/052.

US/0271-7522
**NEWS-LETTER - NATIONAL SOCIETY OF UNITED STATES DAUGHTERS OF 1812.** **Main/Corp** National Society of United States Daughters of 1812. **VAT** News-Letter - National Society of United States Daughters of Eighteen Hundred Twelve. (19??)-. Periodical. English. Three times a year (July, Nov. and Feb.). National Society of United States, Daughters of 1812, Rt 1, Box 358, c/o Mrs R J Moore, Worton MD 21678. **Tel** (703)751-0539. **LC** E351.6; .A2.
**Desc:** Includes proceedings of the Associate Council and the annual directory of the Society.

CN/0822-2401
**NEWS LETTER OF THE ST. ANDREW'S SOCIETY OF TORONTO.** [News lett. St. Andrew's Soc. Tor.]. **Main/Corp** St. Andrew's Society of Toronto. No. 2 (Oct. 1983)-. Periodical. English. qt. Free. St Andrew's Society of Toronto, Toronto Ontario M5R 1Y2 Canada. **DD** 369/.2713541. ctrl circ. ***Continues*** *St. Andrew's Society of Toronto Quarterly Newsletter, 0822-8337.*

CN/0703-783X
**NEWS - ONTARIO COUNCIL OF RABBIT CLUBS.** **Main/Corp** Ontario Council of Rabbit Clubs. Jan. 1977-. Periodical. English. mo. $3 per year $1.50 per year to youth under 18. Ontario Council of Rabbit Clubs, B Schmidt Secretary, Searchmont Ontario P0S 1J0 Canada. **DD** 636/.93/2209713.

US/1041-5963
**NEWSLETTER - AMERICAN COUNCIL OF LEARNED SOCIETIES.** (NEWSLETTER / ACLS.). [Newsl. - Am. Counc. Learn. Soc.]. **Added/Corp** American Council of Learned Societies. **VFOAT** ACLS Newsletter. 2nd Series, Vol. 1 No. 1 (Summer 1987)-. Newsletter. English. Four times a year. Free. American Council of Learned Societies, 228 East 45th Street, 16th Floor/ACLS, New York NY 10017. **Tel** (212)697-1505. **LC** AS36; .A48556. **DD** 061. available on microfilm from University Microfilms International (UMI). ***Continues*** *American Council of Learned Societies. ACLS Newsletter.*
**Ind/Abst** Annu. Bibliogr. Engl. Lang. Lit.; Comput. Rev.; Soc. Plann. Policy Dev. Abstr.; Sociol. Abstr. (?-?).

UK/0260-3780
**NEWSLETTER - BEATRIX POTTER SOCIETY.** **See** Literature.

US/0196-8998
**NEWSLETTER - BYRON SOCIETY.** [Newsl. - Byron Soc.]. **Main/Corp** Byron Society. American Committee. **VFOAT** Byron Society Newsletter. Vol. 1 (1973)-. Newsletter. English. an. comes with membership. Byron Society Journal Ltd., 259 New Jersey Avenue, Collingswood NJ 08108. **Tel** (212)854-4632.

CN/0822-8353
**NEWSLETTER / SCARBOROUGH HISTORICAL SOCIETY.** [Newsl. - Scarb. Hist. Soc.]. **Added/Corp** Scarborough Historical Society. (1974)-. Newsletter. English. bm (6 issues). Comes with Scarborough Historical Society membership, 10.00Can$ (membership). Scarborough Historical Society, PO Box 593, Station A, Scarborough Ontario M1K 5C4 Canada. **Tel** (905)282-2710. **ED** Richard Schofield. **DD** 971.3/541. Index available (published separately). cum. index. **Circ:** 350 (ctrl).

UK
**NEWSLETTER - THE DONIZETTI SOCIETY.** **Main/Corp** Donizetti Society. Began publication in 1973. Newsletter. English. qt. Donizetti Society, 56 Harbut Road, London SW11 2RB England.

CN/0705-1611
**NEWSLETTER - THE JOHN MACMURRAY SOCIETY.** **Main/Corp** John MacMurray Society. V. 1- Spring 1976-. Newsletter. English. Free. John MacMurray Society, 265 Scott Road, Toronto Ontario M6M 3V3 Canada. **DD** 192.

VM
**NGUYET SAN MINH DUC.** Vol. 1/2- No. 6/7, 1972-. Vietnamese. Truong Dai-Hoc Nhan-Van Va Nghe-Thuat, 245/5 Pham-Hong-Thai, Saigon Vietnam. **LC** AS496.V53; A34.

JA/0387-1533
**NIHON REOROJI GAKKAI SHI.** [Nihon Reoroji Gakkaishi]. **VFOAT** Journal of the Society of Rheology, Japan; Nihon Reoroji Gakkai Shi. No. 1-. Academic Scholarly Publication. Japanese (summaries and/or abstracts in English). qt. Nihon Reoroji Gakkai, 1-Banchi No 101 Yoshida Izumiden-cho Sakyo-ku, Kyoto-shi 606 Japan. **Tel** 075-761-5323, FAX 075-761-5325. **ED** T Masuda. **LC** QC189; .N54. **CODEN** NRGADP. Documents available from CASDDS.
**Ind/Abst** Chem. Abstr.; Polymer Contents.

CH
**NING-HSIA SHE HUI KO HSUEH.** Periodical. Chinese. qt. NT$0.40. Ning-Hsia ta Hsueh Hsueh Pao, Post Office, Yin-Chuan Shih, People's Republic of China. **LC** AS452.Y55; A24. **DD** 089/.951.

US
**NORTH CAROLINA COUNCIL OF WOMEN'S ORGANIZATIONS ANNUAL DIRECTORY.** **Main/Corp** North Carolina Council of Women's Organizations. 23rd Ed. (1979)-. Directory. English. an. $24.00 (add $1.50 for postage) libraries and non-profit organizations; $30.00 (add $1.50 for postage) others. North Carolina Council of Women's Organizations, PO Box 17712, Raleigh NC 27619. **Tel** (919)832-0618. **ED** Betty Cook. **LC** HS61; .D5. **DD** 366/.0088042. Index available. **Ad Acc. Circ:** 1,000 (ctrl). ***Continues*** *Annual Directory of North Carolina Organizations.*
**Desc:** Directory of North Carolina Organizations, listing their officers and boards of directors, and principal meeting dates. Includes description of organizations purposes and program interests.

SA/0039-4807
**NUUSBRIEF.** **Main/Corp** Suid-Afrikaanse Akademie Vir Wetenskap en Kuns. Vol. 1, (19??)-. Periodical. Afrikaans. Four times a year (Mar., June, Sept., Dec.). R12.00. Suid Afrikakao Wetenskap Kuns, Box 538, Pretoria 0001 South Africa. **Tel** 011 27 12 3285082. **ED** D. J. C. Geldenhuys. **Ad Acc. Circ:** 2,000.
**Desc:** General news regarding the activities of the SA Akademie vir Wetenskap en Kuns and its members.

UK
**OCCASIONAL PAPERS - DUGDALE SOCIETY.** **Main/Corp** Dugdale Society. No. 1 (1924)-. Monographic series. English. ir. Price varies per volume. The Dugdale Society, The Shakespeare Centre, Stratford Avon CV37 6QW England. **Tel** 011 44 0789 204016.

US
**ODYSSEY. A JOURNAL OF THE CENTRAL CALIFORNIA COUNCIL OF DIVING CLUBS.** English. Four times a year (Jan./Feb. & Nov./Dec. issues combined). $15.00 Includes Central California Diving Council Non-Club Affilated membership. Cen Cal, PO Box 779, Daly City CA 94017. **Tel** (415)583-8492, FAX (408)294-3496.

US/0362-8019
**OFFICERS, COMMITTEES, CONSTITUTION AND BY-LAWS, MEMBERS / GROLIER CLUB.** [Off. comm. const. by-laws memb. - Grolier Club]. **Main/Corp** Grolier Club. English. an. Grolier Club, 47th East 60th Street, New York NY 10022. **LC** Z1008.G886; A19. **DD** 070.5. ctrl circ. ***Continues*** *Grolier Club. Officers, Committee, Members (1931).*

US/0362-8019
**OFFICERS, COMMITTEES, CONSTITUTION AND BY-LAWS, MEMBERS, REPORTS OF OFFICERS AND COMMITTEES.** **Main/Corp** Grolier Club. 1884-. English. an. Grolier Club, 47th East 60th Street, New York NY 10022. **LC** Z1008; .G873.
**Desc:** List of publications of the club from 1884 are contained in 1899 and, with list of exhibition catalogues (previously issued 1900) in 1906-and from 1917-1927.

US/0747-5055
**OFFICIAL PRICE GUIDE TO SCOUTING COLLECTIBLES, THE.** **VFOAT** Scouting Collectibles; Scouting. 1st Ed. (1983)-. English. ir. $7.85. Random House Inc., 400 Hahn Road, Westminster MD 21157. **Tel** (800)726-0600, (800)733-3000, FAX (800)659-2436. **LC** HS3313.A4; O38. **DD** 369.43/0973/075.

●CN/1192-7445
**OFFICIAL STAR TREK FAN CLUB OF CANADA.** (THE OFFICIAL STAR TREK FAN CLUB OF CANADA : [MAGAZINE].). [Off. Star Trek Fan Club Can.]. **Added/Corp** Star Trek Fan Club of Canada. **VFOAT** Star Trek Magazine. Vol. 1, No. 1 (Winter 1993)-. Periodical. English. qt. 23.95Can$. Marquee Publications, 77 Mowat Avenue, Suite 621, Toronto Ontario, M6K 3E3 Canada. **Tel** (416)538-1000, FAX (416)538-0201. **ED** Ron Base. **DD** 791.45/72. **Bk Rev. Circ:** 25,000.

JA
**ONKO SOSHI.** No. 1-. Periodical. Japanese. Onko Gakkai, 9-1 Higashi 2 Shibuya-ku, Tokyo 150 Japan. **LC** AS552.T7152; A25.

US/0744-9755
**OPTIMIST HOTLINE.** ***Title Change.*** [Optim. hotline]. **Main/Corp** Optimist International. **VFOAT** Hotline. (19??)-(19??). Periodical. English (French). qt. Optimist International, 4494 Lindell Boulevard, St Louis MO 63108. **Tel** (314)371-6000, FAX (314)371-6006. **DD** 369. ctrl circ. ***Continued by*** *Optimist Leadership Hotline, 1067-3709.*
**Desc:** Newsletter for Optimist Club Leaders.

US/0744-4672
**OPTIMIST MAGAZINE, THE.** **Added/Corp** Optimist International. (19??)-. Periodical. English (French). Eight times a year. $4.50 (members), $5.00 (non-members). Optimist International, 4494 Lindell Boulevard, St Louis MO 63108. **Tel** (314)371-6000, FAX (314)371-6006. **ED** Patricia A. Gamma. **LC** HS2501; .O6. **DD** 367/.05. **Ad Acc. Circ:** 166,000 (ctrl). ***Continues*** *Optimist International.*
**Desc:** Features news of interest to Optimist Club members in the US, Canada and Caribbean.

US/0882-5769
**ORGANIZATION TRENDS.** **See** Philanthropy.

# Societies and Clubs

US/0700-4176
**OUTLOOK (VANCOUVER).** (THE OUTLOOK.).
Dec. 1973-. English.
**Ind/Abst** Bibliogr. Mission.; Missionalia.

US/0746-5130
**P. E. O. RECORD.** Began with issue for Jan. 1889. Periodical. English. mo. $5.00 US. P E O Record, 3700 Grand Avenue, Des Moines IA 50712. **Tel** (515)255-3153. **ED** Anne Johnson. **LC** HQ1903.P2; A3. **DD** 371.856. Index available. ctrl circ.
**Desc:** Fraternal news; general news.

US/0744-8392
**PA. JAYCEES FUTURE.** (PA. JAYCEES FUTURE : OFFICIAL PUBLICATION OF THE PENNSYLVANIA JAYCEES.). **Added/Corp** Pennsylvania Jaycees. **VFOAT** Pennsylvania Jaycees Future. (19??)-. Periodical. English. qt. Pennsylvania Jaycees, 200 Richardson Drive, Lancaster PA 17603.

US/0199-0861
**PALMETTO STAR NEWS.** Periodical. English. mo. $3.00. Grand Chapter of South Carolina, Order of the Eastern Star, PO Box 228, Swansea SC 29160.

US
**PANHELLENICALLY SPEAKING ... THE RUSHEE'S HANDBOOK. Main/Corp** Florida. University, Gainesville. Panhellenic Association. **VFOAT** A Key to the Greeks. English.

US
**PAPERS READ AT THE MEETING OF GRAND DRAGONS, KNIGHTS OF THE KU KLUX KLAN. Main/Corp** Ku Klux Klan (1915- ). 1st - 1923-. English. Arno Press, 3 Park Avenue, New York NY 10016. **Tel** (212)725-2050. **LC** HS2330.K6; A32. **DD** 322.4/2/0973.

US/1051-3450
**PENNSYLVANIA MINUTEMAN, THE.** [Pa. minuteman]. **Added/Corp** Sons of the American Revolution. Pennsylvania Society. (19??)-. Periodical. English. qt. $4.00. Pennsylvania Minuteman, R D # 1, Box 422NUE, Monongahela PA 15063. **Tel** (215)536-2239. **DD** 369.

US/0745-3027
**PERSPECTIVE (COLUMBUS, OHIO).** (PERSPECTIVE/ JOURNAL OF THE ASSOCIATION OF PROFESSIONAL DIRECTORS OF YMCA'S. PROFESSIONAL DIRECTORS OF YMCA'S.). **Added/Corp** Association of Professional Directors of YMCAs (U.S.). Vol. 1, (Feb. 1975)-. Periodical. English. Eight times a year. $20.00. Association of Professional Directors of YMCA's, 8200 Humboldt Avenue, Suite 1110, Bloomington MN 55431. **Tel** (612)885-0273. **LC** BV1000; .P44. **DD** 267/.33/05. **Continues** Forum; Absorbed Journal of Physical Education and Program, 0735-0139.

US/0093-5328
**PHI KAPPA PHI NEWSLETTER. Main/Corp** Phi Kappa Phi. No. 15 (Aug. 1973)-. Newsletter. English. qt. National Forum / Phi Kappa Phi, 129 Quad Center, Auburn University, Auburn AL 36849-5306. **Tel** (205)844-5200, FAX (205)844-5994. **Circ:** 120,000. **Continues in part** Phi Kappa Phi. Journal.
**Desc:** Contains information about the actions of the board of directors, national committees and local chapters. Also includes columns listing members publications and achievements.

US/0885-4947
**PILGRIM JOURNAL, THE.** (THE PILGRIM JOURNAL / PILGRIM SOCIETY). [Pilgrim j.]. **Added/Corp** Pilgrim Society (Plymouth, Mass.). Vol. 1, No. 1 (Dec. 1985)-. Periodical. English. ir. Pilgrim Society, 75 Court Street, Plymouth MA 02360. **Tel** (508)746-1620. **ED** Laurence R. Pizer and Hope A. Thurlby. **DD** 974. **Circ:** 2,000 (ctrl). **Continues** Pilgrim Society Notes, 0031-9813.

XR
**PIONYRSKA STAFETA. Added/Corp** Sdruzeni Pionyru CSSR. Vol. 1 (1969)-. Periodical. Czech. mo. **(Subscription address:** Artia Pegas Press Ltd., Palac Metro Narodni Trida 25, 11210 Prague 1 Czech Republic.) **LC** HS3325.C9; P56.

US
**PITTSBURGH CLUB DIRECTORY. Added/Corp** Typing Plus (Firm). (1990)-. Directory. English. Typing Plus, Chamber of Commerce Building, 411 Seventh Avenue, Suite 1203, Pittsburgh PA 15219. **LC** HS2513.P6; P58.

CN/0316-8158
**POLICY, ORGANIZATION AND RULES - GIRL GUIDES OF CANADA. Title Change. Main/Corp** Girl Guides of Canada. Periodical. English. be. Girl Guides of Canada, 50 Merton Street, Toronto Ontario, M4S 1A3 Canada. **Tel** (416)487-5281, FAX (416)487-5570. **DD** 369/463/0971. ctrl circ. **Continued by** Opportunities, Adult Leadership Programme, 0828-6426.

US/0363-5678
**PRANCING HORSE, THE.** [Pranc. horse]. Periodical. English. qt. $30.00 US; $45.00 other. Ferrari Club of America, c/o Tutt Association, 24154 Haggerty Road, Farmington Hills MI 48024. **DD** 629.

IT
**PRASSI E TEORIA.** Ceased. Periodical. Italian. qt. Franco Angeli Editore Riviste, Via le Monza 106, 20127 Milan Italy. **Tel** 011 39 2 2827651 or, 289562, FAX 011 39 2 258004, telex 051-511650. **LC** AS221; .P7.

CN/0317-0179
**PRESENTATION - SOCIETE ROYALE DU CANADA. Main/Corp** Royal Society of Canada. **Added/Corp** Societe Royale du Canada. Section Francaise. Societe Royale du Canada. Section des Lettres et Sciences Humaines. **VFOAT** Reception. No. 1 (1943/44)-. Periodical. French. an. 6.00Can$ Canada. Societe Royale du Canada, Box 9734, Ottawa Ontario K1G 5J4 Canada. **Tel** (613)991-6990, FAX (613)991-6996. **DD** 061/.1.

US
**PRESENTING THE SEASON.** English. qt. $10.00 (one year), $17.00 (two year). Presenting the Season, PO Box 420133, Atlanta GA 30342. **Tel** (404)565-1499. **ED** Gloria Lane. **Bk Rev**. **Ad Acc**. **Circ:** 65,000.
**Desc:** Social events in Atlanta and the Southeast.

US/0270-3467
**PRESIDENTS REPORT - COLONIAL WILLIAMSBURG FOUNDATION, THE.**
**Title Change. Main/Corp** Colonial Williamsburg Foundation. (1971)-?. English. an. Colonial Williamsburg Foundation, PO Box C, Williamsburg VA 23187. **Tel** (804)229-1000. **Continues** Annual Report - Colonial Williamsburg Foundation, 0270-3475. **Continued by** Annual Report (Colonial Williamsburg Foundation : 1984), 1049-3085.

US/0887-8420
**PRIVATE CLUBS.** [Priv. clubs]. Vol. 1, No. 1 (Mar. 1986)-. Periodical. English. mo. 2711 LBJ Freeway, Suite 800, Dallas TX 75234.

UK
**PROCEEDINGS (JAPAN SOCIETY (LONDON, ENGLAND)).** (PROCEEDINGS / THE JAPAN SOCIETY.). **VFOAT** Proceedings of the Japan Society. 105 (Dec. 1986)-. Proceedings. English. Japan Society of London, 162-168 Regent Street Square/Room 331, London W1R 5TB England. **Continues** Bulletin (Japan Society of London), 0021-4701.

UK/0024-0281
**PROCEEDINGS OF THE LEEDS PHILOSOPHICAL AND LITERARY SOCIETY, LITERARY AND HISTORICAL SECTION.** [Proc. Leeds Philos. Lit. Soc., Lit. Hist. Sect.]. **Main/Corp** Leeds Philosophical and Literary Society. **Added/Corp** Leeds Philosophical and Literary Society. Literary and Historical Section. (1925)-. Proceedings. English. ir (2-3 issues). Price varies per volume. Central Museum, Calverley Pt, Leeds LS1 3AA England. **Tel** 011 44 532 452894. **ED** I. S. Moxon. **LC** AS12; .L262. **DD** 080. **[CCC]**. **Pr Rev. Circ:** 600.
**Desc:** Scholarly works in any area of the humanities.
**Ind/Abst** Abstr. Engl. Stud.; Am. Hist. Life (1955-); MLA Int. Bibl. Books Artic. Mod. Lang. Lit.

CN
**PROCEEDINGS OF THE ROYAL SOCIETY OF CANADA. DELIBERATIONS DE LA SOCIETE ROYALE DU CANADA. Main/Corp** Royal Society of Canada. **Added/Corp** Royal Society of Canada. Deliberations de la Societe Royal du Canada. Royal Society of Canada. List of Officers and Members and Minutes of Proceedings. **VFOAT** Deliberations de la Societe Royale du Canada. Ser. 1 Vol. 1 (1882/1883)-Vol. 12, (1894); Series 2, Vol. 1 (1895)-Vol. 12 1906; Ser. 3, Vol. 1 (1907)-Vol. 56, (1961/1962); Ser. 4, Vol. 1 (1962/1963)-. Proceedings. English (French). an. $6.75. Royal Society of Canada, PO Box 9734, Ottawa Ontario K1G 5J4 Canada. **Tel** (613)991-6990. cum. index. **Ind/Abst** Can. Period. Index (19??)-.

UK/0083-629X
**PROCEEDINGS OF THE VIRGIL SOCIETY. Main/Corp** Virgil Society. **Added/Corp** Virgil Society. No. 1 (1962)-. Proceedings. English. ir. University College / Department of Latin, Gower Street, London WC1E England. **ED** M.M. Willcock. **Bk Rev**. **Circ:** 250 (ctrl).
**Desc:** Publication of lectures given to the Virgil Society. Also, articles and reviews.

CN/0384-7357
**PROCES-VERBAL DU CONGRES GENERAL ANNUEL - SOCIETE SAINT-JEAN-BAPTISTE DE QUEBEC. Main/Corp** Societe Saint-Jean-Baptiste de Quebec. First issue in 1936. Periodical. French. Free. Societe Saint-Jean-Baptiste De Quebec, 430 Chemin Sainte-Foy, Quebec, Quebec G1S 2J5. **DD** 369/.2/714471. ctrl circ.

UK/0309-0019
**PRS NEWS. VAT** Performing Right Society News. No. 26 (March 1988)-. Periodical. English. sa. Free. Performing Right Society, 29/33 Berners Street, London W1P 4AA England. **Tel** 011 44 876 3444, FAX 01 631 4138, telex 892678. **ED** Lesley Bray. **LC** ML5; .P243. **DD** 790.2/0941/05. **Bk Rev. Circ:** 25,000 (ctrl). **Continues** Performing Right News.

US/0033-2569
**PSI CHI NEWSLETTER.** See Psychology.

UK
**PUBLIC SERVICE ACTION.** English. bm. £8.00. Scat Publications, 1 Sidney Street, Sheffield S1 4RG England. **Tel** 011 44 742726683.

AG/0429-8829
**PUBLICACIONES - FUNDACION VITORIA Y SUAREZ. Main/Corp** Fundacion Vitoria y Suarez. Vol. 1 (1951)-. Spanish. **DD** 060.

UK/0305-8727
**PUBLICATIONS ... . Main/Corp** Bristol Record Society. Vol. 1 (1930)-. Monographic series. English. ir. Price varies per volume. Bristol Record Office, The Council House, College Green, Bristol BS1 5TR England. **Tel** 0272-303030. **ED** J. H. Bettey.

US
**PUBLICATIONS IN OPERATIONS RESEARCH. Main/Corp** Operations Research Society of America. English. ir. John Wiley & Sons, Inc., 605 Third Avenue, New York NY 10158-0012. **Tel** (212)850-6000, (212)850-6645, FAX (212)850-6088, telex 12-7063. **(Subscription address:** John Wiley & Sons / England, Baffins Lane, Chichester, West Sussex PO19 1UD England.)

US/0882-2336
**PUBLICATIONS OF THE GENERAL SOCIETY OF COLONIAL WARS.** [Publ. Gen. Soc. Colon. Wars]. **Added/Corp** General Society of Colonial Wars (U.S.). (18??)-. Monographic series. English. Price varies per volume. Society of Colonial Wars / Ohio, Office of the Secretary General, 840 Woodbine Avenue, Glendale OH 45246. **DD** 369.

UK
**PUBLICATIONS OF THE PIPE ROLL SOCIETY, THE. Added/Corp** Pipe Roll Society (Great Britain). Vol. 1 (1884)-. Monographic series. English (English). ir. Price varies per volume. Pipe Roll Society, Chancery Lane, London WC2 A1LR England. **Tel** 011 44 876 3444. **ED** D. Crook. **LC** DA170; .P82. cum. index. **Bk Rev. Circ:** 320 (ctrl). **Desc:** Publishes financial documents of Medieval England.

UK/0082-4232
**PUBLICATIONS OF THE THORESBY SOCIETY. Main/Corp** Thoresby Society. **Added/Corp** Thoresby Society. (1889)-. Monographic series. English. ir. Price varies per volume. Thoresby Society, 23 Clarendon Road, Leeds LS2 9NZ England. **LC** DA670.Y59; T4. **DD** 942.8/19. cum. index. **Ind/Abst** Br. Archaeol. Bibliogr.

US/0199-0144
**PYTHIAN INTERNATIONAL. Added/Corp** Knights of Pythias. Supreme Lodge. Periodical. English. qt. Supreme Lodge Knights of Pythias, 2785 East Desert Inn, Suite 150, Las Vegas NV 89121-3623. **LC** HS1201; .P67.

US/0741-9635
**QUARTERLY NEWS JOURNAL OF THE CROSBY ARBORETUM, A. Added/Corp** Crosby Arboretum. (Winter 1983)-. Periodical. English. Four times a year (Jan., Mar., June, Sept.). $50.00 (non-profit); $100.00 (corporate); $20.00 (individuals) Comes with Crosby Arboretum membership. The Crosby Arboretum, 3702 Hardy Street, PO Box 190, Hattiesburg MS 39466. **Tel** (601)799-2311. **ED** Mr. & Mrs. William Conery. ctrl circ.
**Desc:** A report on activities and events of the arboretum.

US
**QUILL OF ALPHA XI DELTA, THE.** English. qt. $1.50. Alpha Xi Delta, 8702 Founders Road, Indianapolis IN 46268. **ED** Alanna Williams.
**Desc:** The informational and educational quarterly of Alpha Xi Delta sorority.

PH
**RAMON MAGSAYSAY AWARDS, THE.**
1958-1962-. English. Ramon Magsaysay Award Foundation, Ramon Magsaysay Center, 1680 Roxas Boulevard, Manila Philippines. **LC** AS911.R39; A33. **DD** 001.4/4.

FR
**RECORDS OF THE GENERAL CONFERENCE OF THE UNITED NATIONS EDUCATIONAL, SCIENTIFIC AND CULTURAL ORGANIZATION.** **Main/Corp** UNESCO. General Conference. 1st Session; 1946-. English. UNIPUB, 4611-F Assembly Drive, Lanham MD 20706-4391. **Tel** (800)274-4888, FAX (301)459-0056, telex 28787 GATT CH. **LC** AS4.U8. **DD** 060.

US/0885-8144
**REFLECTIONS (INDIANAPOLIS, IND.).** **See** Medical Science and Technology-Nursing.

CN/0714-4261
**REGISTRE-ANNUAIRE - MENSA CANADA.** (REGISTRE-ANNUAIRE.). [Regist.-annu. - Mensa Can.]. **Main/Corp** Mensa Canada Society. 1975-. English (French). Mensa Canada Registre Annuaire, Montreal Quebec H2C 2V9 Canada. **DD** 367/.025/71. ***Continues*** *Mensa Canada Society. Directory, 0714-4253.*

US/0160-7057
**REPORT - CONFERENCE OF PRESIDENTS OF MAJOR AMERICAN JEWISH ORGANIZATIONS.** **Main/Conf** Conference of Presidents of Major American Jewish Organizations. (1968)-. English. an. Conference of Presidents of Major American Jewish Organizations, 515 Park Avenue, New York NY 10022. **LC** DS101; .C64a. **DD** 909/.04/924. ***Continues*** *Annual Report - Conference of Presidents of Major American Jewish Organizations, 0160-7049.*

FR
**REPORT OF THE DIRECTOR GENERAL ON THE ACTIVITIES OF THE ORGANIZATION IN ... .** **Main/Corp** UNESCO. **Added/Corp** Unesco. Executive Board. **VFOAT** Report by the Director General and the Executive Board on the Activities of the Organization During the Year ...; Supplementary Report by the Director-General on the Activities of the Organization from 1 Jan. to 30 June ... . (1947)-. English. an. Price varies. **(Subscription address:** UNIPUB, 4611 F Assembly Drive, Lanham MD 20706.) **LC** AS4.U8; A35. **DD** 060.

AT
**REPORT OF THE REGISTRAR OF FRIENDLY SOCIETIES FOR THE YEAR ENDED 30 JUNE.** **Main/Corp** Victoria. Office of the Registrar of Friendly Societies. **VFOAT** Annual Report. English. an. **LC** HG9245.A83; V594A. **DD** 334/.7/0994505. ***Continues in part*** *Report of the Government Statist on Friendly Societies and Benefit Associations for the Year Ended 30 June ... with Statistics for the Year Ended 30 June ... Together with the Report of the Registrar of Friendly Societies for the Year Ended 30 June ... .*

US/0149-8754
**REPORTER (GRANADA HILLS), THE.** (THE REPORTER.). **Added/Corp** Phi Alpha Delta Law Fraternity, International. (19??)-. Periodical. English. qt. Free. Phi Alpha Delta, 10722 White Oak Avenue, Grenade Hills CA 91344. **Tel** (703)860-0213. **LC** UNC.
**Desc:** Provides a forum for the exchange of information pertinent to the practice of law in the military as well as the civilian community. Each issue contains three to six articles on current topics of interest in the law and sections devoted to military justice, claims, and tort litigation and preventive law.

US/0736-217X
**REPORTING FROM THE RUSSELL SAGE FOUNDATION.** [Rep. Russell Sage Found.]. **Added/Corp** Russell Sage Foundation. **VFOAT** Reporting. No. 1 (Dec. 1982)-. Periodical. English. Twice a year (May & Nov.). Free. Russell Sage Foundation, 112 East 64th Street, c/o Diane Garba, New York NY 10021. **Tel** (212)750-6000.

US/0090-8010
**REPORTS OF OFFICERS AND PROCEEDINGS OF THE SUPREME LODGE OF THE ANCIENT ORDER OF UNITED WORKMEN.** (REPORT OF OFFICERS AND PROCEEDINGS.). **Main/Corp** Ancient Order of United Workmen. Supreme Lodge. Proceedings. English. Report of Officers and Proceedings, PO Box 98830, Seattle WA 98188. **LC** HS1510.A58; A4. **DD** 366.

US/0190-227X
**REPORTS OF THE PRESIDENT AND THE TREASURER - JOHN SIMON GUGGENHEIM MEMORIAL FOUNDATION.** **Main/Corp** John Simon Guggenheim Memorial Foundation. 1961/62-. English. an. John Simon Guggenheim Memorial Foundation, 90 Park Avenue, New York NY 10016. **LC** AS911; .J6. **DD** 061/.3. **NLM** AS 911 J6. ***Continues*** *John Simon Guggenheim Memorial Foundation. Reports of the Secretary General and of the Treasurer.*
**Desc:** Includes: Biographies of fellows appointed; reappointments; publications, musical compositions, academic appointments and index of fellows.

UK/0048-8267
**RICARDIAN.** (THE RICARDIAN : JOURNAL OF THE RICHARD III SOCIETY.). [Ricardian]. **Added/Corp** Richard III Society. (19??)-. Periodical. English. qt. Free to members, £7.50, £2.00 (per issues) nonmembers. Ricardian - Richard III Society, 17 Enfield Cloisters, Fanshaw Street, London N1 6LD England. **(Subscription address:** Membership Department, PO Box 320, Bromley Kent BR2 9QR England) **ED** A F Sutton. **LC** DA260; .R53. **DD** 941.04/6. Index available. cum. index. **Bk Rev. Ad Acc. Circ:** 4,400 (ctrl).
**Desc:** Journal of the Richard III Society. Articles, notes, and reviews on Fifteenth Century history related to the life and times of Richard III.
**Ind/Abst** Am. Hist. Life.

JA
**RISSHO DAIGAKU KYOYOBU RONSHU. LOTUS.** **Main/Corp** Rissho Daigaku, Tokyo. Kyoyobu. **VFOAT** Lotus. (19??)-. Japanese (Japanese). Rissho Daigaku Kyoyobu, 2-16 Osaki 4-chome, Shinagawa-ku, Tokyo Japan. **LC** AS552.R56; A27.

US/0035-838X
**ROTARIAN, THE.** (THE ROTARIAN / INTERNATIONAL ASSOCIATION OF ROTARY CLUBS.). [Rotarian]. **Added/Corp** International Association of Rotary Clubs. Rotary International. Vol. 3, No. 1 (Sept. 1912)-. Periodical. English. mo. $12.00. Rotary International, 1 Rotary Center, 1560 Sherman Avenue, Evanston IL 60201. **Tel** (708)866-3000, FAX (708)328-8554. **ED** Will White. **LC** HF5001; .R7. Index available. **Ad Acc**, **Adv Mgr Tel** (708)866-3195. available on microfilm and microfiche from University Microfilms International (UMI). ***Continues*** *National Rotarian.*
**Ind/Abst** Index Free Period.; Read. Guide Period. Lit.

US/0035-905X
**ROYAL NEIGHBOR, THE.** **Added/Corp** Royal Neighbors of America. (19??)-. Periodical. English. mo. The Royal Neighbor Magazine, 230 Sixteenth Street, Rock Island IL 61201. **Tel** (309)788-4561. **ED** Priscilla Ann Curtis. **LC** HS1510.R895; A16. **Circ:** 175,000.

CN/0381-5145
**S P K W KANADZIE.** V. 1- April 1962-. Periodical. Polish (English). qt. Polish Combatant's Association in Canada, 206 Beverly Street, Toronto Ontario M5T 1Z3 Canada.

JA
**SAITAMA DAIGAKU KIYO. SOGO HEN.** **VFOAT** Sogo Hen; Liberal Arts; Journal of Saitama University. Liberal Arts. V. 1-. Periodical. Japanese (Japanese). Saitama Daigaku, 255 Shimookubo, Urawa-shi Japan. **LC** AS552.U727; A35.
**Ind/Abst** Am. Hist. Life (1958-1964).

US/0196-8564
**SAN DIEGO SOURCE BOOK.** **VFOAT** Source Book. 1st. Ed. (1980)-. English. Four times a year (Feb., May, Aug., Nov.). $511.83 San Diego & Orange County; $619.56 others;. Bernardo Press, 16496 Bernardo Center Drive, Rancho Bernardo CA 92128. **Tel** (619)451-3790. **ED** Jack Mayo and Beverly Zirkle. **Circ:** 500 (ctrl).
**Desc:** Directory of business, trade and professional groups, civic, social and fraternal clubs, special interest groups, hobbies and athletic clubs of San Diego County.

US/0161-0511
**SAR MAGAZINE, THE.** **Main/Corp** Sons of the American Revolution. **Added/Corp** Sons of the American Revolution. Magazine. **VAT** The Sons of the American Revolution Magazine. (1967)-. Periodical. English. qt. $10.00. National Society of the Sons of the American Revolution, 1000 South Fourth Street, Louisville KY 40203. **Tel** (502)589-1776. **ED** Winston C Williams (414)782-9410. **LC** E202.3; .A5. **DD** 369/.13. **Bk Rev. Ad Acc. Circ:** 24,000. ***Continues*** *Sons of the American Revolution. Sons of the American Revolution Magazine.*
**Desc:** Patriotic, historical and educational publication.

US/0279-7011
**SCOTTISH RITE JOURNAL.** **Added/Corp** Scottish Rite (Masonic Order). Valley of St. Paul (Minn.). Vol. 1 June (1921)-. Periodical. English. qt. $4.00. Scottish Rite Journal, Southern Jurisdiction, 1733 16th Street Northwest, Washington DC 20009-3199. **Tel** (202)232-3579, FAX (202)387-1843. **ED** John Boettjer. Index available. **Bk Rev. Ad Acc. Circ:** 515,000.

CN/0318-3521
**SCOUTING NEWS.** Spring Issue 1975-. Periodical. English. PO Box 533, Charlottetown Prince Edward Island C1A 7L1 Canada. **DD** 369.43/05. ***Supersedes*** *Scouting in Prince Edward Island, 0318-3513.*

UK/0036-9500
**SCOUTING (NORTH BRUNSWICK).** (SCOUTING.). [Scout.]. **Added/Corp** Boy Scouts of America. Boy Scouts of America. Annual Report. Vol. 1 (April 15, 1913)-. Periodical. English. Twelve times a year. £13.20 UK; £20.00 others. Scout Association, Baden-Powell House, Queen's Gate, London SW7 5JS England. **Tel** 011 44 1 5847030, FAX 011 44 1 5819953. **LC** HS3313.B7; A715. **DD** 369.43/0973. available on microfilm and microfiche from University Microfilms International (UMI). ***Absorbed*** *Scoutmastership Notes; National Sea Scout.*
**Desc:** News and information of the boys scouts events and activities.
**Ind/Abst** Gen. Period. Index (Jan. 1985-Dec. 1985); Mag. Index (1977-Dec. 1985).

JA
**SEIJO BUNGEI.** **Added/Corp** Seijo Daigaku. Bungeigakubu. Kenkyushitsu. (19??)-. Periodical. Japanese. qt. Seijo Daigaku Bungeigakubu Kenkyushitsu, 1-20 Seijo 6, Setagaya-ku 157, Tokyo Japan. **LC** AS552.S44; A27.

JA
**SEINAN GAKUIN DAIGAKU BUNRI RON SHU.** **Main/Corp** Seinan Gakuin Daigaku. Gakujutsu Kenkyujo. **Added/Corp** Seinan Gakuin Daigaku. Bunri ron Shu. Seinan Gakuin Daigaku. Studies in Literature and Science. **VFOAT** Studies in Literature and Science of Seinan Gakuin University. (1960)-. Multiple languages (Japanese and English). ir. Seinan Gakuin Daigaku Gakujutsu Kenkyujo, 2-92 Nishijin 6-chome Nishi-ku 814, Fukuoka Japan. **LC** AS552.S444; A37.

CC
**SHE HUI KO HSUEH YEN CHIU (CHENG-TU, CHINA).** (SHE HUI KO HSUEH YEN CHIU). **Added/Corp** Ssu-Chuan Sheng She Hui Ko Hsueh Yuan. Ssu-Chuan Sheng Che Hsueh She Hui Ko Hsueh Hsueh Hui Lien Ho Hui. **VFOAT** Shehui Kexue Yanjiu. (1979)-. Periodical. Chinese. bm. RMBY0.50. Post Office, Cheng-Tu, People's Republic of China. **LC** AS452.C46165; A35. **DD** 059/.951.

CC
**SHEN-YANG SHIH FAN HSUEH YUAN HSUEH PAO. CHE HSUEH SHE HUI KO HSUEH PAN.** **VFOAT** Shenyangshifanxueyuanxuebao; Shenyangshifan Xueyuanxuebao. Periodical. Chinese. qt. RMBY0.35. Post Office, Shen-Yang Shih, People's Republic of China. **LC** AS452.S54; A35. **DD** 089/.951.

JA
**SHO TO KIROKU NO JIMMEI JITEN.** **Added/Corp** Jiyu Kokuminsha. (1973)-. Periodical. Japanese. ¥920. Jiyu Kokumin Sha, c/o Daiichi Seimei Bunkan, 8 Kyobashi-2 Chuo-ku, Tokyo Japan. **LC** AS548; .S47.

CN/0820-0424
**SIGNE DE PISTE.** [Signe piste]. **VAT** Amis du Signe de Piste (1980). No. 41 (Oct. 1980)-. Periodical. French. ir. $12.00. Signe De Piste, No 12 7154 rue Hamilton, Ville Eymard Montreal Quebec H4E 3E1 Canada. **DD** 369.43/05. ***Continues*** *Amis du Signe de Piste, 0709-5147.*

US/8750-5347
**SINFONIAN (1980), THE.** **See** Music.

AU
**SITZUNGBERICHTE.** **Main/Corp** Akademie der Wissenschaften, Vienna. Mathematisch-Naturwissenschaften Klasse. **Added/Corp** Kaiserliche Akademie der Wissenschaften, Vienna. Mathematisch-Naturwissenschaftliche Klasse. Sitzungsberichte. Vol. 1 (1848)-. Periodical. German. ir. cum. index. available on microfilm.

CN/0383-8587
**SOIS PRET.** V. 2, No 1- Dec. 1976/Jan. 1977-. Periodical. French. bm. $5.00, Free to members Canada; $8.00 other. Revue Sois Pret, 217 de Letoile, Laval Quebec H7H 4T4 Canada. **DD** 369.43/05. ***Continues*** *Scout du Quebec, 0319-1702.*

US
**SON OF THE STARS.** 1st- Ed. English. George Banta Publishing Company, 450 Ahnaip Street, Menasha WI 54952. **LC** LJ75.B54; S6. **DD** 371.855.
**Desc:** Includes "The songs of the fraternity."

US/0279-2451
**SOONER JAYCEE.** (SOONER JAYCEE : THE OFFICIAL PUBLICATION OF THE OKLAHOMA JAYCEES.). **Main/Corp** Oklahoma Jaycees. Vol. 1, No. 1 (Sept. issue 1982)-. Periodical. English. bm. Oklahoma Jaycees, State Headquarters, PO Box 348, 109 South Cleveland, Cushing OK 74023. ***Continues*** *Sooner Jaycee, 0279-2451.*

UK/0584-4029
**SOUTHAMPTON RECORDS SERIES.** 1 (1951)-. Monographic series. English. ir. Price varies per volume. University of Southampton / G. L. Felix, c/o G.L. Felix, Southampton SO9 5NH England. ***Supersedes*** *Publications of the Southampton Record Society.*

TU
**SPOR KULUPLERI.** **VFOAT** Sport Clubs. (1982)-. English (Turkish). **LC** HA1911; .A3 subser; GV661.

# Sociology

US/0038-9854
**STAR AND LAMP OF PI KAPPA PHI, THE.** *Title Change.* See College and School Publications.

JA/0389-9268
**TAKAMATSU KOGYO KOTO SENMON GAKKO KENKYU KIYO.** (KENKYU KIYO.). [Takamatsu Kogyo Koto Senmon Gakko kenkyu kiyo]. **Main/Corp** Takamatsu Kogyo Koto Senmon Gakko. **VFOAT** Takamatsu Kogyo Koto Semmon Gakko Kenkyu Kiyo; Annual Reports of Takamatsu Technical College. No. 1- 1965-. Academic Scholarly Publication. Japanese (summaries and/or abstracts in English). an. No 355 Chokushicho, Takamatsu Japan. **Tel** 0878-67-0276, FAX 0878-67-0281. **ED** Takamatsu Kosen. **LC** AS552; .T315. **CODEN** TAKYDU. **Circ:** 350 (ctrl). Documents available from CASDDS.
**Ind/Abst** Chem. Abstr. (1965-1982); Int. Bibliogr. Sociol.

BL
**TEMAS EM FOCO.** No. 1- 1970-. Periodical. Portuguese. Rua Monsenhor Coutinho 224, Manaus Brazil. **LC** AS80.U53; T4.

US/0274-6697
**TENNES-SIERRAN, THE.** Periodical. English. mo. Sierra Club Tennessee Chapter, 3524 Pinellas Lane, Chattanooga TN 37412.

NE/0165-5094
**TIRADE.** [Tirade]. (1957)-. Periodical. Dutch. bm. Fl74.00. GA Van Oorschots Um BV, Herengracht 613, 1017 CE Amsterdam The Netherlands. **Tel** 011 31 20 231484. **LC** AS243; .T5.
**Ind/Abst** MLA Int. Bibl. Books Artic. Mod. Lang. Lit.

US/8755-3600
**TORCH (INDIANAPOLIS, IND.).** (TORCH / SIGMA DELTA TAU.). Fall 1983-. Periodical. English. sa. Sigma Delta Tau National Office, 9202 North Meridian Street/Suite 305, Indianapolis IN 46260. **LC** LJ145.S52; T67. **DD** 378/.19856/05. *Continues* Torch of Sigma Delta Tau, 0495-8837.

US/0363-3152
**TRANSACTIONS OF THE HUGUENOT SOCIETY OF SOUTH CAROLINA.** [Trans. Huguenot Soc. S. C.]. **Main/Corp** Huguenot Society of South Carolina. No. 1 (1889)-. English. an (Fall). $12.00. Huguenot Society of South Carolina, 138 Logan Street, Charleston SC 29401. **Tel** (803)723-3235. **LC** F280.H8; H8. Index available. cum. index. **Bk Rev**, (Qty: 1-5). **Circ:** 4,000 (ctrl).
**Ind/Abst** Genealogical Period. Annu. Index.

CN/0380-1667
**TUMBLEWEED.** **Added/Corp** Girl Guides of Canada. Alberta Council. (Sept. 1975)-. Periodical. English. mo. Girl Guides of Canada Alberta Council, 10169-104th Street, Room 202, Edmonton Alberta T5J 1A5 Canada. **DD** 369.463/05. *Supersedes* Girls Guides of Canada. Alberta Council. Newsletter, 0380-1675.

CH/0379-7309
**TUNG HSUEH PAO, TA.** **Added/Corp** Ta Tung Kung Hsueh Yuan. **VFOAT** Tatung Journal. (19??)-. Academic Scholarly Publication. Multiple languages (Chinese and English). Ta Tung Kung Hsueh Yuan, Taipei Taiwan. **LC** AS455.T25; A17. **CODEN** TTHPCI. Documents available from CASDDS.
**Ind/Abst** Chem. Abstr.

US/0016-6618
**UMBRA.** Vol. 1, No. 1-2, Winter 1963-Dec. 1963; No. 3- 1967/68-. Periodical. English. ir. Society of Umbra, Box 4338, Sather Gate, Berkeley CA 94704.

FR
**UNESCO FEATURES.** **Added/Corp** Unesco. (July 15, 1949)-. Periodical. English. bm. UNESCO / France, 31 rue Francois Bonvin, 75732 Paris Cedex 15 France. **Tel** 011 33 1 45684564, 011 33 1 45684565, FAX 011 33 1 42733007, telex 204461 Paris. **LC** AS4.U8; A55. **DD** 060. *Continues in part* UNESCO Newsletter.

CN/0524-5613
**VARSITY OUTDOOR CLUB JOURNAL, THE.** See Recreation, Leisure-Outdoor Life.

US/0886-3865
**VICTORIANS INSTITUTE JOURNAL.** **Main/Corp** Victorians Institute. **Added/Corp** Victorians Institute. Old Dominion University. East Carolina University. **VFOAT** Victorians Institute Journal. VIJ. Vol. 1 (July 1972)-. English. an. $14.00 US/ $17.00 other (institutions); $10.00 US; $13.00 other (individuals). Victorians Institute Journal, East Carolina University, English Department, Greenville NC 27834. **Tel** (919)757-6041. **ED** Donald Lawler. **LC** AS36; .V45. **DD** 051. Index available (Free on request). **Bk Rev**. **Ad Acc**.
**Ind/Abst** Am. Humanit. Index (-199?); Annu. Bibliogr. Engl. Lang. Lit. (19??-); Lit. Crit. Regist. (19??-); MLA Int. Bibl. Books Artic. Mod. Lang. Lit. (19??-).

US/0739-9324
**VOICE OF THE TURTLE (SAN DIEGO, CALIF.).** (VOICE OF THE TURTLE : THE MONTHLY NEWSLETTER OF THE SAN DIEGO TURTLE AND TORTOISE SOCIETY.). **Added/Corp** San Diego Turtle and Tortoise Society. (19??)-. Periodical. English. Twelve times a year. $10.00. San Diego Turtle & Tortoise Society, 13963 Lyons Valley Road, Jamul CA 91935. **Tel** (619)669-0078. **ED** Judy Taylor. **Bk Rev**. **Ad Acc**. **Circ:** 1,000 (ctrl).
**Desc:** Articles and turtles and tortoise care, medication and general information.

US/0042-9384
**VYTIS.** Periodical. English (Lithuanian). mo (ten no. a year). Knights of Lithuania, 2524 West 45th Street, Chicago IL 60632. **LC** HS2008.L49; A15.

IO
**WARTA UNIVERSITAS RIAU.** **Main/Corp** Universitas Riau. Periodical. Indonesian. Hupenmas Universitas Riau, Jalan Ronggowarsito, Pekanbaru Indonesia. **LC** AS522.U54; A36.

US/1060-393X
**WASHINGTON MASONIC TRIBUNE : THE OFFICIAL MAGAZINE OF THE MASONIC GRAND LODGE OF WASHINGTON.** **Added/Corp** Freemasons. Grand Lodge of Washington. (1991)-. Periodical. English. mo. Washington Masonic Tribune, 47 St Helens Avenue, Tacoma WA 98402. *Continues* Masonic Tribune, 0025-4673.

NE
**WERKEN UITGEGEVEN DOOR DE LINSCHOTEN-VEREENIGING.** **Added/Corp** Linschoten-Vereeniging, The Hague. (1909)-. Monographic series. Dutch. ir. Price varies per volume. Martinus Nijhoff Publishers, Distribution Center Kluwer Academic Publishers, Koraalrood 50, 2718 SC Zoetermeer Netherlands. **Tel** 011 31 79 684400. cum. index.

US/0092-4164
**WHERE THE TRAILS CROSS.** See Genealogy and Heraldry.

US/0164-5145
**WHITE TRIANGLE NEWS.** **Added/Corp** Hudson-Essex-Terraplane Club. (19??)-. Periodical. English. bm. $20.00. White Triangle News, Box 715, Milford IN 46542. **Tel** (313)482-5200. ctrl circ.

UK
**WIRE : OFFICIAL ORGAN OF THE ROYAL SIGNALS ASSOCIATION, THE.** (19??)-. Periodical. English. bm. £10.38 UK; £12.72 Europe; £15.60 other. RHQ Royal Signals, 56 Regency Street, London SW1P 4AD England. **Tel** 011 44 71 414 8432.

US
**WISCONSIN DIALOGUE : A FACULTY JOURNAL FOR THE UNIVERSITY OF WISCONSIN-EAU CLAIRE.** No. 1 (Fall 1980)-. Periodical. English. an. University of Wisconsin - Eau Claire, Eau Claire WI 54702-4004. **Tel** (715)826-2639. **LC** AS30; .W56. **DD** 051.

UK/0141-4577
**WORCESTERSHIRE HISTORICAL SOCIETY (PUBLICATIONS).** (PUBLICATIONS.). **Main/Corp** Worcestershire Historical Society. New Series 1- 1928-. Monographic series. English. Price varies per volume. Worcestershire Historical Society, 7 Prestwich Avenue, Red Hill Brown, Worcester WR5 1QA England.

US
**WORK REPORTS - EARLY SITES RESEARCH SOCIETY.** **Main/Corp** Early Sites Research Society. (1976)-. Periodical. English. ir. Early Sites Research Society, Long Hill, Rowley MA 01969. **Tel** (617)948-2410.

UK
**WORKS ISSUED BY THE HAKLUYT SOCIETY. EXTRA SERIES.** **Main/Corp** Hakluyt Society. Monographic series. English. Price varies per volume. British Library, Great Russell Street, London WC1B 3DG England.

US/0732-7676
**WORLD FUTURE SOCIETY.** (WORLD FUTURE SOCIETY : NEWSLETTER / WASHINGTON D.C. CHAPTER.). **Main/Corp** World Future Society. Washington D.C. Chapter. (19??)-. Newsletter. English. mo. World Future Society, 7910 Woodmont Avenue, Suite 450, Bethesda MD 20814. **Tel** (301)656-8274, FAX (301)951-0394. ctrl circ.

SZ/0043-8995
**WORLD SCOUTING.** **VFOAT** Scoutisme Mondial. Vol. 1 (Jan./Feb. 1965)-. Periodical. English (French). qt. World Souting Bureau, Box 241, 1211 Geneva 4 Switzerland. **LC** HS3312; .W59. *Supersedes* World Scouting Bulletin, 0510-9426.

UK/0080-4576
**YEAR BOOK OF THE ROYAL SOCIETY OF EDINBURGH.** [Year book R. Soc. Edinb.]. **Main/Corp** Royal Society of Edinburgh. (1941)-. English. an (Oct.). £10.00. Royal Society of Edinburgh, 22 24 George Street, Edinburgh EH2 2PQ Scotland. **Tel** 011 44 031-225-6057, FAX 011 44 031-220-6889. **ED** T. G. Dart. **LC** Q41; .E23. **DD** 068.41. **NLM** W1 YE374E. **CODEN** RSEYAX. **Circ:** 1,500.
**Desc:** Presents proceedings of meetings, obituaries, list of fellows, prizes, awards, laws of the society, and an annual report.
**Ind/Abst** GeoRef.

UK/0080-4673
**YEAR-BOOK OF THE ROYAL SOCIETY OF LONDON.** **Main/Corp** Royal Society (Great Britain). **VFOAT** Year-Book of the Royal Society. **VAT** Year Book of the Royal Society of London. (1896/1897)-. English. sa. £12.50 UK; $31.00 US/Canada; £18.50 other. Royal Society, 6 Carlton House Terrace, London SW1Y 5AG England. **Tel** 011 44 71 839 5561, FAX 071-976 1837, telex 917876 ROYAL G. **ED** King-Hele. **NLM** W1 YE34R. **[CCC]**. **Circ:** 247.
**Desc:** A Journal for the History of Science.

UK/0440-5757
**YEARBOOK OF THE HEATHER SOCIETY.** (1963)-. English. an. £6.00 (single), £7.00 (family). Heather Society, All Saints Road, Creeting, St. Mary 1P6 8PJ England. **Tel** 0449 711220. **ED** Dr. E.C. Nelson. Index available. cum. index. **Ad Acc**, **Adv Mgr:** Arnold Stow, **Tel** (0494)449397. **Circ:** 900 (ctrl).

TU
**YENI UFUKLAR.** Turkish. 100.00. Can Yaknlar, PK 1034 Karakoy, Istanbul Turkey. **LC** AS348.A1; Y45.

KO
**YON'GU NONJIP - IHWA YOJA TAEHAKKYO, TAEHAGWON.** **Main/Corp** Ihwa Yoja Taehakkyo, Seoul, Korea. Taehagwon. Periodical. Korean. 11-1 Taehyon-dong, Sodaemun-ku, Seoul Korea. **LC** AS559.A1; I38A. **DD** 059/.957. ctrl circ.

KO
**YON'GU NONMUNJIP - TAEPYONGYANG CHANGHAK MUNHWA CHAEDAN.** **Main/Corp** Taepyongyang Changhak Munhwa Chaedan. Vol.1 (1977)-. Periodical. English (Korean). 181 2-ka Hangangno Yongsan-ku, Seoul Korea. **LC** AS559.A1; T33a. ctrl circ.

# SOCIOLOGY

FR
**200 GROUPES FRANCAIS D'AFRIQUE NOIRE : A28.** French. an. 1190.00F. IC Publications Ediafric, 10 rue Vineuse, 75116 Paris France. **Tel** 011 33 1 44308100.

DK/0001-6993
**ACTA SOCIOLOGICA.** [Acta sociol.]. **Added/Corp** Scandinavian Sociological Association. Vol. 1 (1955)-. Periodical. English (Danish, French, German, Norwegian and Swedish). qt. Kr650.00, $108.00. Scandinavian University Press, PO Box 2959 Toeyen, N 0608 Oslo 6 Norway. **Tel** 011 47 2 2575400, FAX 011 47 2 2575353, telex 71896 UROR N. **(Subscription address:** Scandinavian University Press, 200 Meacham Ave., Elmont NY 11003.) **ED** Peter Hedstroem. **LC** HM1.A1; A3. **DD** 301. **NLM** W1 AC949JM. **[CCC]**. cum. index. **Bk Rev**. **Ad Acc**. **Pr Rev. Circ:** 3,000. available on microfilm and microfiche from University Microfilms International (UMI). Documents available from The Genuine Article, UMI Article Clearinghouse.
**Desc:** Journal of the Scandinavian Sociological Association presenting high-quality articles in sociology - both full-length original papers and review essays - carefully selected for the interests of an international forum. This international sociological journal is often quoted, and its articles are frequently reprinted.
**Ind/Abst** ABC POL SCI; Acad. Abstr. Full Text Elite (Jan. 1992-); Acad. Abstr. (Jan. 1992-); Acad. Search (Jan. 1992-); Am. Hist. Life (1978-); Appl. Soc. Sci. Index Abstr.; Arts Humanit. Citation Index [Select. Cov.]; Curr. Contents Soc. Behav. Sci.; Expand. Acad. Index (1989-); Hum. Resour. Abstr. (?-?); INFO-SOUTH Abstr.; Int. Bibliogr. Sociol.; Int. Polit. Sci. Abstr.; Linguist. Lang. Behav. Abstr.; Mag. Search; Middle East Abstr. Index; Multicult. Educ. Abstr.; Newsp. Period. Abstr. (1991-); PAIS Int. Print; Res. Alert [Full Cov.]; Sage Fam. Stud. Abstr. (?-?); Sage Public Adm. Abstr. (?-?); Sage Urban Stud. Abstr; Soc. Plann. Policy Dev. Abstr.; Soc. Source (Jan. 1992-); Soc. Sci. Cit. Index [Full Cov.]; Soc. Sci. Index; Soc. Sci. Index Fulltext (1988-) [Full Txt.];

Sociol. Abstr. [Full Cov.]; Sociol. Educ. Abstr.; Spec. Educ. Needs Abstr.; SPORT Discus; Stud. Women Abstr.; Tech. Educ. Train. Abstr.

PL/0208-600X
**ACTA UNIVERSITATIS LODZIENSIS. FOLIA SOCIOLOGICA.** **VFOAT** Folia Sociologica. 1-. Polish (English). **LC** HM7; .A28. ***Continues in part*** *Acta Universitatis Lodziensis. Zeszyty Naukowe Uniwersytetu Odzkiego. Seria 3: Nauki Ekonomiczne i Socjologiczne.*
**Ind/Abst** Int. Bibliogr. Sociol.; Zentralbl. Math. Ihre Grenzgeb.

FR
**ACTES ET COMMUNICATIONS / INSTITUT NATIONAL DE LA RECHERCHE AGRONOMIQUE, DEPARTEMENT D'ECONOMIE ET SOCIOLOGIE RURALES.** **See** Agriculture.

FR
**ACTIVITE SCIENTIFIQUE DU CENTRE DE SOCIOLOGIE URBAINE, L'.** **Main/Corp** Centre de Sociologie Urbaine (France). 1978-1981-. French. 118 rue de la Tombe Issoire, 75014 Paris France. **LC** HT135; .C43A. **DD** 307.7/6/06044361.

US/0883-3656
**ADVANCES IN APPLIED SOCIAL PSYCHOLOGY.** **See** Psychology.

US/0065-2601
**ADVANCES IN EXPERIMENTAL SOCIAL PSYCHOLOGY.** **See** Psychology.

US/0882-6145
**ADVANCES IN GROUP PROCESSES.** [Adv. group process.]. Vol. 1 (1984)-. English. an. $73.25. JAI Press Inc., 55 Old Post Road, Suite 2, PO Box 1678, Greenwich CT 06836-1678. **Tel** (203)661-7602, FAX (203)661-0792. **ED** Edward J. Lawler, Barry Markovsky, Cecilia Ridgeway, and Henry A. Walker. **LC** HM131; .A314. **DD** 302.3. **[CCC].**

●US/1069-0573
**ADVANCES IN HUMAN ECOLOGY.** [Adv. hum. ecol.]. **Added/Corp** Society for Human Ecology. Vol. 1 (1992)-. English. ir. $73.25. JAI Press Inc., 55 Old Post Road, Suite 2, PO Box 1678, Greenwich CT 06836-1678. **Tel** (203)661-7602, FAX (203)661-0792. **ED** Lee Freese. **LC** GF1; .A38. **DD** 304.2/05.
**Desc:** Publishes review papers on scientific human ecology, interpreted to include structural and functional changes in human social organization and sociocultural systems. Goal is to promote the growth of human ecology as an interdisciplinary problem-solving paradigm.

US/0275-5742
**ADVANCES IN MEDICAL SOCIAL SCIENCE.** [Adv. med. soc. sci.]. Vol. 1 (1983)-. Monographic series. English. an. Price varies per volume. Gordon & Breach Science Publishers, Inc., PO Box 786, Cooper Station, New York NY 10276. **Tel** (212)206-8900, FAX (212)645-2459. **(Subscription address:** Gordon & Breach Science Publishers / US, 820 Town Center Drive, Langhorne PA 19047.**)** **DD** 362. **NLM** W1; AD679P.

US/1057-6290
**ADVANCES IN MEDICAL SOCIOLOGY.** [Adv. med. sociol.]. Vol. 1 (1990)-. English. ir. $73.25. JAI Press Inc., 55 Old Post Road, Suite 2, PO Box 1678, Greenwich CT 06836-1678. **Tel** (203)661-7602, FAX (203)661-0792. **ED** Gary Albrecht. **LC** RA418; .A517. **DD** 362.1/05. **NLM** W1; AD679PL. **CODEN** AMSOEI.
**Ind/Abst** Linguist. Lang. Behav. Abstr.; Soc. Plann. Policy Dev. Abstr.; Sociol. Abstr. [Full Cov.].

US/0898-2007
**ADVANCES IN SOCIAL COGNITION.** [Adv. soc. cogn.]. Vol. 1 (1988)-. Periodical. English. an. Lawrence Erlbaum Associates, 365 Broadway, Suite 102, Hillsdale NJ 07642. **Tel** (201)666-4110, (800)926-6579, FAX (201)666-2394. **LC** HM291; .A345. **DD** 302/.12. **NLM** W1; AD858L.
**Desc:** Covers social perception and cognition.

US/1047-2002
**ADVANCES IN SOCIAL SCIENCE METHODOLOGY.** [Adv. soc. sci. methodol.]. Vol. 1 (1989)-. English. an. $73.25. JAI Press Inc., 55 Old Post Road, Suite 2, PO Box 1678, Greenwich CT 06836-1678. **Tel** (203)661-7602, FAX (203)661-0792. **ED** Bruce Thompson. **LC** H61; .A394. **DD** 300/.72.

●UK/0001-9844
**AFRICA RESEARCH BULLETIN. POLITICAL, SOCIAL, AND CULTURAL SERIES.** **VFOAT** Political, Social, and Cultural Series. Vol. 29, No. 1 (Jan. 1st-31st 1992)-. Academic Scholarly Publication. English. mo. £230.00 UK and Europe; $401.00 North America; £259.00 other. Basil Blackwell Publishers Ltd, 108 Cowley Road, Oxford 0X4 1JF England. **Tel** 011 44 865 791100, FAX 011 44 865 791347, telex 837022 OXBOOK G. **(Subscription address:** Blackwell Publishers / UK, Marston Book Services, PO Box 87, Oxford OX2 0DT England.**)** **LC** DT1; .A2283. **[CCC].** ***Continues*** *Africa Research Bulletin. Political Series.*

US/0001-9887
**AFRICA TODAY.** **See** Political Science.

KE/1010-4127
**AFRICAN JOURNAL OF SOCIOLOGY.** [Afr. j. sociol.]. V. 1, No. 1 and 2 (May 1981)-. Periodical. English (French). sa. $15.00 Africa; $20.00 other. African Journal of Sociology, Department of Sociology, University of Nairobi, PO Box 30197, Nairobi Kenya. **ED** P O Chitere. **LC** HM22.A4; A34. **DD** 301/.096. **Bk Rev. Ad Acc.**
**Ind/Abst** Leis. Recreat. Tour. Abstr.; Rural Dev. Abstr.; Soc. Plann. Policy Dev. Abstr.; Sociol. Abstr. (?-?); World Agric. Econ.

FR/0336-2086
**AGECOP LIAISON.** **Main/Corp** Agence de Cooperation Culturelle et Technique. **VAT** Agence de Cooperation Culturelle et Technique Liaison. Periodical. French. mo (except Aug.). ACCT, 19 Avenue de Messine, Paris 75008 France. **LC** DT14; .A43A. **DD** 301.29/6.
**Ind/Abst** Leis. Recreat. Tour. Abstr.; Rural Dev. Abstr.; World Agric. Econ.

US/0275-6692
**AID BULLETIN (KENT, OHIO).** ***Ceased.*** (AID BULLETIN.). **VAT** Addiction Intervention with the Disabled Bulletin (Kent, Ohio). Vol. 1, No. 1 (Fall 1980)-(19??). Bulletin. English. qt. $6.00. Aid Bulletin, Kent State University, Department of Sociology, Kent OH 44242. **Tel** (216)672-2562.

US
**AIM : AMERICAS INTERCULTURAL MAGAZINE.** (19??)-. English. Four times a year. $10.00. AIM, PO Box 20554, Chicago IL 60620. **Tel** (312)874-6184. ***Continues*** *AIM : Racial Harmony & Peace.*

US/0194-2069
**AIM FOR RACIAL HARMONY & PEACE.** ***Title Change.*** **VFOAT** Racial Harmony & Peace; Aim 4 Racial Harmony & Peace; Aim Four Racial Harmony and Peace; AIM. **VAT** Aim, Racial Harmony and Peace. Vol. 3, No. 1 (Jan./Feb. 1976)-(19??). Periodical. English. qt. AIM, PO Box 20554, Chicago IL 60620. **Tel** (312)874-6184. **ED** Ruth Apilado. **LC** E184.A1; A4. **DD** 301.45/0973. **Bk Rev. Ad Acc. Circ:** 10,000. ***Continues*** *Aim for Racial Harmony, 0194-2077.* ***Continued by*** *AIM : Americas Intercultural Magazine.*
**Desc:** Articles, short stories promoting racial harmony and peace. We strive to eliminate racism from the human bloodstream. Want to be vehicle for promising new writers.

SY
**AL-THAQAFAH AL-USBUIYAH.** Began in 1960. Periodical. Arabic. wk. Shari Al-Arjantin, PO Box 2570, Dimashq Syria. **LC** DS36.8; .T45.

AU
**ALLENSBACHER JAHRBUCH DER DEMOSKOPIE.** 6.- Vol.; 1974/76-. German. an. $32.38. Verlag Fritz Molden GmbH, Stievestrasse 9, W-8000 Munich 19 Germany. **LC** HN460.P8; J34. ***Continues*** *Jahrbuch der Offentlichen Meinung, 0075-2347.*

CN/0702-8865
**ALTERNATE ROUTES.** [Altern. routes]. Vol. 1 (1977)-. English (French). an. Price varies. Alternate Routes, Department of Sociology and Anthropology, Carleton University, Ottawa Ontario K1S 5B6 Canada. **Tel** (613)788-2623. **DD** 301/.05. **Bk Rev. Ad Acc. Circ:** 350 (ctrl).
**Desc:** A multi-disciplinary journal of the social sciences, with editorial emphasis on critical, provocative analysis of theoretical and substantive issues which clearly have relevance for progressive political intervention.
**Ind/Abst** Left Index; Linguist. Lang. Behav. Abstr.; Soc. Plann. Policy Dev. Abstr.; Sociol. Abstr. [Full Cov.].

US/0149-337X
**AMERICAN CITY & COUNTY, THE.** [Am. city cty.]. **VFOAT** American City and County; American City. Vol. 90, No. 9 (Sept. 1975)-. Periodical. English. mo. $58.00. Argus Business, 6151 Powers Ferry Road, Atlanta GA 30339. **Tel** (404)995-2500, (800)233-3359. **ED** Ken Anderberg. **LC** HT101; .A5. **DD** 301.36/0973. **CODEN** ACCOD3. **[CCC].** available in microform from Xerox; available on microfilm and microfiche from University Microfilms International (UMI); available on an online database (files 15,647,648/Full-Text) from DIALOG. Documents available from Article Express International, UMI Article Clearinghouse, Magazine Collection. ***Continues*** *American City, 0002-7936;* ***Formed by the union of*** *Municipal Index, 0077-2151.*
**Ind/Abst** ABI/INFORM Glob. Ed.; ABI Inform Ondisc (Sept. 1991-); Appl. Sci. Technol. Index; Bioeng. Abstr.; Book Rev. Index (?-July 1989); Bus. ASAP (1990-) [Full Txt.]; Bus. Index (1985-); Ei Page One; EMBASE (June, Aug., Dec. 1989, Jan 1990-); Eng. Index Annu.; Gen. BusinessFile (1985-); Gen. Period. Index (1985-); Health Saf. Sci. Abstr.; Highw. Res. Abstr.; J. Plan. Lit.; Mag. ASAP Plus [Full Txt.]; Mag. Index Plus (1989-); Mag. Search; Newsp. Period. Abstr. (1986-); PAIS Int. Print (1991-); Pollut. Abstr. Indexes; Read. Guide Period. Lit.; Mag. Index (1977-); Trade Ind. ASAP [Full Txt.]; Trade Ind. Index (1981-) [Full Txt.]; Urban Aff. Abstr.

US/0091-0562
**AMERICAN JOURNAL OF COMMUNITY PSYCHOLOGY.** **See** Psychology.

US/0002-9602
**AMERICAN JOURNAL OF SOCIOLOGY.** (THE AMERICAN JOURNAL OF SOCIOLOGY.). [Am. j. sociol.]. **Added/Corp** University of Chicago. **VFOAT** AJS. Vol. 1 (July 1895)-. Periodical. English. bm. $96.00 (institution), $41.00 (individual), $36.00 (ASA and BSA individual member), $28.00 (student). University of Chicago Press / Journals Division, PO Box 37005, 5720 South Woodlawn, Chicago IL 60637. **Tel** (312)753-3347, FAX (312)753-0811. **(Subscription telephone:** (312)753-8083**)** **ED** Marta Tienda. **LC** HM1; .A7. **DD** 301. **[CCC].** cum. index. **Pr Rev. Acid Free.** available on microfilm and microfiche from University Microfilms International (UMI). Documents available from The Genuine Article, UMI Article Clearinghouse.
**Desc:** A voice for analysis and research in the social sciences, presenting work on the theory, methods, practice, and history of sociology. The journal also seeks the applications of perspectives from other social sciences, and publishes papers by psychologists, anthropologists, statisticians, economists, educators, historians, and political scientists.
**Ind/Abst** ABC POL SCI; Abstr. Anthropol.; Acad. Abstr. Full Text Elite (July 1990-); Acad. Abstr. (July 1990-); Acad. Ind. [Computer File] (1987-); Acad. Search (July 1990-); Am. Hist. Life (1969-); Am. Bibliogr. Slavic East Europ. Stud.; Annu. Bibliogr. Engl. Lang. Lit.; Anthropol. Index; Appl. Soc. Sci. Index Abstr.; Arts Humanit. Citation Index [Select. Cov.]; Book Rev. Digest; Book Rev. Index; Chicano Index; Commun. Abstr.; Contents Pages Manage.; Crim. Justice Abstr.; Curr. Contents Soc. Behav. Sci.; Curr. Index J. Educ.; Educ. Index; Expand. Acad. Index (1987-); Geogr. Abstr. Human Geogr.; Guide Soc. Sci. Relig.; Health Plan. Adminis.; Hum. Resour. Abstr.; Index Book Rev. Relig.; Index Period. Artic. Relat. Law; INFO-SOUTH Abstr.; Int. Labour Doc.; Int. Polit. Sci. Abstr.; J. Plan. Lit.; LABORDOC; Leis. Recreat. Tour. Abstr.; Linguist. Lang. Behav. Abstr.; Mag. Artic. Summar. Elite (July 1990-); Mag. Artic. Summar. Select (July 1990-); Mag. Artic. Summar. CD-ROM (July 1990-); Mag. Search; Middle East Abstr. Index; Multicult. Educ. Abstr.; Newsp. Period. Abstr. (1988-); PAIS Int. Print (1991-); Peace Res. Abstr. J. (1963-1972); Popul. Index; Psychol. Abstr. (1950-); PsycINFO; PsycLit; Res. Alert [Full Cov.]; Res. High. Educ. Abstr.; Romant. Move.; Rural Dev. Abstr.; Sage Fam. Stud. Abstr.; Sage Race Relat. Abstr.; Sage Urban Stud. Abstr; School Organ. Manage. Abstr.; Selec. Coop. Index Manage. Period; Soc. Plann. Policy Dev. Abstr.; Soc. Sci. Source (Jul. 1990-); Soc. Sci. Cit. Index [Full Cov.]; Soc. Sci. Index; Soc. Sci. Index Fulltext (Jan. 1989-) [Full Txt.]; Soc. Work Abstr. [Select. Cov.]; Sociol. Abstr. [Full Cov.]; Sociol. Educ. Abstr.; Soc. Res. Methodol. Abstr. (1975-); Stat. Theory Method Abstr. (1959-1963); Stud. Women Abstr.; U.S. Polit. Sci. Doc.; West. Hist. Q.; Women Stud. Abstr.; Work Relat. Abstr.; World Agric. Econ.

US/0885-6893
**AMERICAN PUBLIC OPINION DATA.** (AMERICAN PUBLIC OPINION DATA. [MICROFORM].). [Am. public opin. data]. **Added/Corp** Opinion Research Service (U.S.). (1981)-. English. an. $299.00. Opinion Research Service, 4948 St. Elmo Avenue, Suite 207, Bethesda MD 20814. **LC** Microfiche (o) 87/200. **DD** 303. Index available. cum. index. available on microfiche.
**Desc:** Provides answers to most of the questions listed in the American Public Opinion index.

US/0740-8978
**AMERICAN PUBLIC OPINION INDEX.** [Am. public opin. index]. **Added/Corp** Opinion Research Service (U.S.). (1981)-. English. an. $299.00 (latest edition). Opinion Research Service, 4948 St. Elmo Avenue, Suite 207, Bethesda MD 20814. **LC** HM261; .A463. **DD** 016.3033/8/0973. Index available. cum. index. available on microfiche.
**Desc:** National, state and local public opinion polls gives quick access to precisely the opinion information that is needed.

US/0003-1224
**AMERICAN SOCIOLOGICAL REVIEW.** [Am. sociol. rev.]. **Added/Corp** American Sociological Association. American Sociological Society. **VFOAT** ASR. Vol. 1 (Feb. 1936)-. Periodical. English. bm (6 issues). $105.00 (institutions), $50.00 (individuals) US; $113.00 (insitutions), $58.00 (individuals) other. American Sociological Association, 1722 North Street Northwest, Washington DC 20036-2981. **Tel** (202)833-3410, FAX (202)785-0146. **ED** Sheldon Stryker. **LC** HM1; .A75. **DD** 305. **NLM** W1 AM808. **CODEN** ASRRB. cum. index. **Bk Rev. Pr Rev. Circ:** 15,000. available on microfilm and microfiche from University Microfilms International (UMI). Documents available from The Genuine Article, UMI Article Clearinghouse. ***Supersedes in part*** *Directory / American Sociological Association.*
**Ind/Abst** ABC POL SCI; ABI/INFORM Glob. Ed.; Abstr. Anthropol.; Acad. Abstr. Full Text Elite (July 1990-); Acad. Abstr. (July 1990-); Acad. Ind. [Computer File] (1987-); Acad. Search (July 1990-); Am. Hist. Life (1963-); Am.

Bibliogr. Slavic East Europ. Stud.; Annu. Bibliogr. Engl. Lang. Lit.; Appl. Soc. Sci. Index Abstr.; Chicano Index; Contents Pages Manage.; Crim. Justice Abstr.; Curr. Contents Soc. Behav. Sci.; Curr. Index J. Educ.; Expand. Acad. Index (1987-); Geogr. Abstr. Human Geogr.; Guide Soc. Sci. Relig.; Health Plan. Adminis.; Index Period. Artic. Relat. Law; INFO-SOUTH Abstr.; Int. Bibliogr. Sociol.; Int. Dev. Abstr.; Int. Labour Doc.; Int. Polit. Sci. Abstr.; J. Plan. Lit.; Leis. Recreat. Tour. Abstr.; Linguist. Lang. Behav. Abstr.; Mag. Search; Middle East Abstr. Index; Multicult. Educ. Abstr.; Newsp. Period. Abstr. (1986-); PAIS Int. Print (1991-); Peace Res. Abstr. J. (1966-1971); Popul. Index; Psychol. Abstr. (1936-); PsycINFO; PsycLit; Res. Alert [Full Cov.]; Rural Dev. Abstr.; Sage Race Relat. Abstr.; School Organ. Manage. Abstr.; Selec. Coop. Index Manage. Period; Soc. Plann. Policy Dev. Abstr.; Soc. Sci. Source (Jul. 1990-); Soc. Sci. Cit. Index [Full Cov.]; Soc. Sci. Index; Soc. Sci. Index Fulltext (Dec. 1988-) [Full Txt.]; Soc. Work Abstr. [Select. Cov.]; Sociol. Abstr. [Full Cov.]; Sociol. Educ. Abstr.; Soc. Res. Methodol. Abstr. (1975-); Stud. Women Abstr.; U.S. Polit. Sci. Doc.; Women Stud. Abstr.; Work Relat. Abstr.; World Agric. Econ.

US/0003-1232
**AMERICAN SOCIOLOGIST, THE.** [Am. sociol.]. Vol. 1 (Nov. 1965)-. Periodical. English. Four times a year. Fl158.00 (individual), Fl297.50 (institution). Transaction Publishers / Rutgers State University, New Brunswick NJ 08903. **Tel** (908)932-2280 Ext. 105, FAX (908)932-3138. **ED** Richard H. Hall. **LC** HM9; .A713. **DD** 301. **NLM** W1 AM808K. **[CCC]. Circ:** 600. available on labels; available on microfilm and microfiche from University Microfilms International (UMI).
**Desc:** Examines the history, current status, and future prospects of sociology as a profession and discipline. The journal emphasizes new trends in the profession and focuses on how sociologists have shaped or influenced social policy and the intellectual issues of the age. It also publishes professional opinions, special features, interviews, and review essays. It has a new emphasis on the global context of the sociological disciplines.
**Ind/Abst** Curr. Index J. Educ. (March 1990); Educ. Adm. Abstr.; Hum. Resour. Abstr. (?-?); Int. Bibliogr. Sociol.; Int. Polit. Sci. Abstr.; J. Plan. Lit.; Linguist. Lang. Behav. Abstr.; PAIS Int. Print (1991-?); Res. High. Educ. Abstr.; Sage Fam. Stud. Abstr. (?-?); Sage Public Adm. Abstr. (?-?); Soc. Plann. Policy Dev. Abstr.; Soc. Sci. Index; Sociol. Abstr. [Full Cov.]; U.S. Polit. Sci. Doc.

US/1061-8198
**AMERICANS TALK ISSUES.** [Am. talk issues]. **Added/Corp** Americans Talk Issues Foundation. Survey #15 (Mar. 19-24, 1991)-. Periodical. English. Americans Talk Issues Foundation, Alan F Kay, 907 6th Street SW, Number 602 C, Washington DC 20024. **DD** 320. ***Continues*** *Americans Talk Security, 1060-8508.*

NE/0921-4933
**AMSTERDAMS SOCIOLOGISCH TIJDSCHRIFT 1988.** (AMSTERDAMS SOCIOLOGISCH TIJDSCHRIFT.). [Amst. sociol. tijdschr.1988]. (1988)-. Periodical. Dutch. qt. **UDC** 303.2. ***Continues*** *Sociologisch Tijdschrift, 0168-731X.*
**Ind/Abst** Linguist. Lang. Behav. Abstr.; Soc. Plann. Policy Dev. Abstr.; Sociol. Abstr. (1987-) [Full Cov.].

RM/0068-3302
**ANALELE UNIVERSITATII BUCURESTI: SOCIOLOGIE.** [An. Univ. Bucur., Sociol.]. **Main/Corp** Universitatea Din Bucuresti. (19??)-. Romanian (summaries and/or abstracts in English and Russian). an. DM143.00. Universitetea din Bucaresti, B-Dul Gh Gheorghiu-Dej Nr 64, Bucuresti Romania. **(Subscription address:** Kubon & Sagner, ABT Zeitschriftenimport, D 80328 Munich Germany.**) LC** HN15; .B79a.
**Ind/Abst** Am. Hist. Life (1959-1971).

PO/0003-2573
**ANALISE SOCIAL.** [Anal. soc.]. **Added/Corp** Gabinete de Investigacoes Sociais (Portugal) Universidade de Lisboa. Instituto de Ciencias Sociais. (Jan. 1963)-. Periodical. Portuguese (summaries and/or abstracts in English and French). Five times a year. $65.00. Instituto de Ciencias Sociais, Universite of Lisbon, Av das Forcas Armadas, Edificio ISCTE Ala Sul 1, 1600 Lisbon Portugal. **Tel** 011 351 1 7932272. **LC** HM7; .A5. **Bk Rev. Circ:** 3,000.
**Ind/Abst** Am. Hist. Life; Int. Bibliogr. Sociol.; Int. Labour Doc.; Int. Polit. Sci. Abstr.; Linguist. Lang. Behav. Abstr.; Soc. Plann. Policy Dev. Abstr.; Sociol. Abstr.

IT
**ANDES (ROME, ITALY).** ***Suspended.*** **See** Political Science.

FR/0180-930X
**ANNALES DE LA RECHERCHE URBAINE, LES. Added/Corp** Centre de recherche d'urbanisme. No. 1 (Oct. 1978)-. Periodical. French (summaries and/or abstracts in English and Spanish). qt. 500.00F (institutions), 340.00F (individuals) France; 600.00F (institutions), 375.00F (individuals) other. Min Equipment Logement and Transport, Arche Sud, 92065 Paris la Defense France. **Tel** 011 33 1 40812121. **(Subscription address:** Centrale des Revues, 11 rue Gossin, 92543 Montrouge Cedex France.**) ED** Anne Querrien. **[CCC]. Bk Rev. Ad Acc. Circ:** 1,150. ***Continues*** *Annales - Centre de Recherche d'Urbanisme, 0338-6880.*
**Desc:** Results of research in urban problems theory and practice, social movements, town planning, land management, and social practices in cities; improvement of the environment.
**Ind/Abst** Am. Hist. Life (1978-); Avery Index Archit. Period. Suppl. Colum. Univ. (Mar./Apr., June-Spet., Dec. 1989, Oct. 1990-); GeoRef; PAIS Int. Print (1991-).

HU/0524-9023
**ANNALES UNIVERSITATIS SCIENTIARUM BUDAPESTINENSIS DE ROLANDO EOTVOS NOMINATAE. SECTIO PHILOSOPHICA ET SOCIOLOGICA. See** Philosophy.

IT/0066-2275
**ANNALI DI SOCIOLOGIA.** [Ann. sociol.]. **Added/Corp** Centro di Studi Sociologici, Milan. Vol. 1 (1964)-. Italian. Twice a year. L90000. Association Italo Tedesca Sociologia, Via Verdi 26, 38100 Trento Italy. **Tel** 011 39 461 881344. **LC** WMLC L 83/5833.
**Ind/Abst** Linguist. Lang. Behav. Abstr.; Soc. Plann. Policy Dev. Abstr.; Sociol. Abstr. [Full Cov.].

FR/0066-2399
**ANNEE SOCIOLOGIQUE (1940/48).** (L'ANNEE SOCIOLOGIQUE.). [Annee sociol.]. 3rd Ser., (1940/1948)-. French. an. 370.00F France; 420.00F other. Presses Universitaires de France, Department des Revues, 14 Avenue du Bois de l'Epine, BP 90, 91003 Evry Cedex France. **Tel** (1)60 77 82 05, FAX (1) 60 79 20 45, telex PUF 600 474 F. **[CCC]. Bk Rev.** ***Formed by the union of*** *Annales Sociologiques. Serie A, Sociologie Generale; Annales Sociologiques. Serie B, Sociologie Religieuse; Annales Sociologiques. Serie C, Sociologie Juridique et Morale; Annales Sociologiques. Serie D, Sociologie Economique* ***and*** *Annales Sociologiques. Serie E, Morphologie Sociale, Langage, Technologie, Esthetique.*
**Desc:** A collection of reports on important sociological studies and on sociological research in progress during the year.
**Ind/Abst** Int. Bibliogr. Sociol.; Int. Polit. Sci. Abstr.; Linguist. Lang. Behav. Abstr.; Soc. Plann. Policy Dev. Abstr.; Sociol. Abstr.

FR/0245-9930
**ANNUAIRE CNRS SCIENCES DE L'HOMME ET DE LA SOCIETE. Added/Corp** Centre National de la Recherche Scientifique (France). **VFOAT** Sciences de l'Homme et de la Societe. **VAT** Annuaire Centre National de la Recherche Scientifique Sciences de l'Homme et de la Societe. French. Institut de l'Information Scientifique et Technique, 54 Boulevard Raspail, BP 140, 75260 Paris Cedex 06 France. ***Continues*** *Annuaire CNRS Sciences de l'Homme.*

CN/0703-2153
**ANNUAIRE TELEPHONIQUE - CENTRE DE CULTURE DIALOGUE ORIENTAL. Main/Corp** Centre de Culture Dialogue Oriental. **VFOAT** Directory Book - Centre de Culture Dialogue Oriental. Began with 1972/73 issue?. English (French). an. Centre De Culture Dialogue Oriental, Suite 5, 5336 Queen Mary Road, Montreal Quebec H3K 1T8. **DD** 301.45/11/920714281. ***Continues*** *L S C A.*

US
**ANNUAL PROCEEDINGS - AMERICAN SOCIOLOGICAL ASSOCIATION. Main/Corp** American Sociological Association. **Added/Corp** American Sociological Association. Proceedings. **VFOAT** Proceedings - American Sociological Association. (19??)-. Proceedings. English. an. $6.00. American Sociological Association, 1722 North Street Northwest, Washington DC 20036-2981. **Tel** (202)833-3410, FAX (202)785-0146. **(Subscription address:** American Sociological Association, 49 Sheridan Avenue, Albany, NY 12210; telephone: (800)877-2693**) Circ:** 3,500.
**Desc:** Abstracts of papers presented at the Annual Meeting of the American Sociological Association. Distributed at the meeting and by request.

CN
**ANNUAL REPORT - CANADIAN COUNCIL ON SOCIAL DEVELOPMENT. Main/Corp** Canadian Council on Social Development. 51st (1970/71)-. English (French). an. Free on request. Canadian Council on Social Development, 55 Parkdale Avenue, Ottawa Ontario K1Y 4G1 Canada. **Tel** (613)728-1865, FAX (613)728-9387. **DD** 362. **Circ:** 5,000. ***Continues*** *Canadian Welfare Council. Annual Report.*
**Desc:** Report of projects and activities undertaken by the Canadian Council on Social Development during the year, and projected projects for future.

US/0743-5118
**ANNUAL REPORT - FIELD FOUNDATION OF ILLINOIS.** (ANNUAL REPORT FOR THE YEAR ENDED APRIL 30 ... / THE FIELD FOUNDATION OF ILLINOIS, INC.). [Annu. rep. - Field Found. Ill.]. **Main/Corp** Field Foundation of Illinois. English. an. Field Foundation of Illinois Inc, 135 South LaSalle Street, Chicago IL 60603. **LC** AS36.C425; A3. **DD** 361.7/632.

CN/0711-7000
**ANNUAL REPORT - TASKFORCE ON THE CHURCHES AND CORPORATE RESPONSIBILITY.** (?975)-. English. an (Nov.). 5.00Can$ US & Canada; 6.00Can$ others. Taskforce Church & Corporate Responsibility, 129 St. Clair Avenue West, Toronto Ontario M4V 1N5 Canada. **Tel** (416)923-1758, FAX (416)927-7554. **Circ:** 800.
**Desc:** A useful reference source on corporate social responsibility issues relating to the environment, aborginal concerns, human rights, corporate governance, banking and military industries.

US/0163-5557
**ANNUAL REPORT / THE JAPAN-UNITED STATES FRIENDSHIP COMMISSION.** ***Title Change.*** **Main/Corp** Japan-United States Friendship Commission. (1977)-?. English. an. Japan-United States Friendship Commission, 1200 Pennsylvania Avenue NW/3407, Washington DC 20004-2483. **LC** E183.8.J3; J335A. **DD** 301.29/73/052. ***Continued by*** *Biennial Report (Japan-United States Friendship Commission).*

US
**ANNUAL REPORT / THE NETHERLANDS-AMERICA COMMUNITY ASSOCIATION, INC. Main/Corp** Netherlands-America Community Association. English. an. Netherlands-America Community Association Inc, One Rockefeller Plaza, New York NY 10020. **LC** E184.D9; N45A. **DD** 361.7/7.

US/0739-7127
**ANNUAL REPORT - TUSKEGEE INSTITUTE. HUMAN RESOURCES DEVELOPMENT CENTER.** (ANNUAL REPORT / HUMAN RESOURCES DEVELOPMENT CENTER, CARVER RESEARCH FOUNDATION, TUSKEGEE INSTITUTE, ALABAMA.). **Main/Corp** Tuskegee Institute. Human Resources Development Center. English. an. Tuskegee Institute, Human Resources Development Center, Carver Research Foundation, Tuskegee AL. **LC** HN79.A43; C67A. **DD** 307/.14/09761.

US/0899-5370
**ANNUAL REVIEW OF NICARAGUAN SOCIOLOGY.** ***Ceased.*** [Annu. rev. Nicar. sociol.]. **Added/Corp** Loyola University (New Orleans, La.) Institute of Human Relations. Universidad Centroamericana (Nicaragua). Vol. 1 (1988)-(19??). Periodical. English. an. Institute of Human Relations, Box 12, Loyola University, New Orleans LA 70118. **Tel** (504)865-2011. **DD** 301.
**Ind/Abst** Soc. Plann. Policy Dev. Abstr.; Sociol. Abstr. (1988-) [Full Cov.].

US/0360-0572
**ANNUAL REVIEW OF SOCIOLOGY.** [Annu. rev. sociology]. Vol. 1 (1975)-. English. an (August). $52.00 US; $57.00 other. Annual Reviews Inc., 4139 El Camino Way, PO Box 10139, Palo Alto CA 94303-0139. **Tel** (415)493-4400, (800)523-8635, FAX (415)855-9815. **ED** Judith Blake. **LC** HM1; .A763. **DD** 301/.05. **NLM** W1 AN7798. **CODEN** ARVSDB. **[CCC].** Index available. cum. index. **Pr Rev.** ctrl circ. available on microfilm and microfiche from University Microfilms International (UMI). Documents available from The Genuine Article, BIOSIS Document Express, UMI Article Clearinghouse.
**Desc:** Comprehensive, thorough articles that review the coverage of latest advances in sociology, written by acknowledged experts in the field. Extensive literature citations included.
**Ind/Abst** Acad. Abstr. Full Text Elite (July 1990-); Acad. Abstr. (July 1990-); Acad. Search (July 1990-); Biol. Abstr.; Curr. Contents Soc. Behav. Sci.; Expand. Acad. Index (1989-); INFO-SOUTH Abstr.; Int. Bibliogr. Sociol.; Int. Polit. Sci. Abstr.; LABORDOC; Linguist. Lang. Behav. Abstr.; Mag. Search; Newsp. Period. Abstr. (1990-); Popul. Index; Psychol. Abstr. (1975-); PsycINFO (1990-); PsycLit; Res. Alert [Full Cov.]; Risk Abstr. (19??-19??); Rural Dev. Abstr.; Sage Race Relat. Abstr.; Soc. Plann. Policy Dev. Abstr.; Soc. Sci. Source (Jul. 1990-); Soc. Sci. Cit. Index [Full Cov.]; Soc. Sci. Index; Soc. Sci. Index Fulltext (1989-) [Full Txt.]; Sociol. Abstr. [Full Cov.]; Soc. Res. Methodol. Abstr. (1981-); World Agric. Econ.

●US/1068-8595
**APPLIED BEHAVIORAL SCIENCE REVIEW. See** Psychology.

US
**APPLIED SOCIAL PSYCHOLOGY. See** Psychology.

US
**APPLIED SOCIAL RESEARCH METHODS SERIES. VFOAT** Applied Social Research Methods. Vol. 1 (1984)-. Monographic series. English. Price varies per volume. SAGE Periodical Press, 2455 Teller Road, Thousand Oaks CA 91320. **Tel** (805)499-0721, FAX (805)499-0871, telex 100799. **Acid Free.**

FR/0335-5985
**ARCHIVES DE SCIENCES SOCIALES DES RELIGIONS.** See Religion and Theology.

FR/0003-9756
**ARCHIVES EUROPEENNES DE SOCIOLOGIE.** [Arch. eur. sociol.]. **VFOAT** European Journal of Sociology; Europaisches Archiv fur Soziologie. Vol. 1 (1960)-. Academic Scholarly Publication. French (English, French and German). sa (May and November). $115.00 US, Canada & Mexico; £66.00 other. Cambridge University Press, The Edinburgh Building, Shaftesbury Road, Cambridge CB2 2RU United Kingdom. **Tel** 011 44 223 312393, FAX 011 44 223 325959. **(Subscription address:** Cambridge University Press / North America, 110 Midland Avenue, Port Chester NY 10573.**) ED** Eric De Dampierre, Jon Elster, Jacques Lautman, Steven Lukes and Claus Offe. **LC** HM1.A1; A7. **DD** 301/.05. **NLM** W1 AR38K. **Pr Rev.** available on microfilm and microfiche from University Microfilms International (UMI). Documents available from The Genuine Article.
**Desc:** Strives to reflect and respond to the new agenda set for social scientists by the recent profound changes in the world's political and economic climate. The journal will continue to publish original articles of broad interdisciplinary scope. The journal's review articles explore key topics with reference to the most important relevant publications.
**Ind/Abst** Am. Hist. Life (1973-); Appl. Soc. Sci. Index Abstr.; Arts Humanit. Citation Index [Select. Cov.]; Crim. Penol. Police Sci. Abstr.; Curr. Contents Soc. Behav. Sci.; Int. Bibliogr. Sociol.; Int. Polit. Sci. Abstr.; Linguist. Lang. Behav. Abstr.; Res. Alert [Full Cov.]; Soc. Plann. Policy Dev. Abstr.; Soc. Sci. Cit. Index [Full Cov.]; Sociol. Abstr. [Full Cov.].

GW/0341-3039
**ARGUMENT-SONDERBANDE. VFOAT** Argument-Sonderband; AS. (1974)-. Monographic series. German. ir. Price varies per volume. Argument Verlag GmbH, Rentzelstr 1, D 21046 Hamburg Germany. **Tel** 011 49 40 453680, 011 49 40 456018. cum. index.

US/0095-327X
**ARMED FORCES AND SOCIETY.** See Military and Defense.

US
**ASA MONOGRAPHS.** See Anthropology.

IT/0394-6479
**ASPE. AGENZIA DI STAMPA SUI PROBLEMI DELL' EMARGINAZIONE.** [ASPE, Agenzia Stampa Probl. Emarginazione]. **VFOAT** Agenzia di Stampa sui Problemi dell'Emarginazione. (1982)-. Periodical. Italian. Twenty-four times a year. L60000 (institutions) Italy; L80000 (institutions) public; L110000 others. Associazione Gruppo Abele, Via Giolitti 21, 10123 Turin Italy. **Tel** 011 39 11 8142745, FAX 011 39 8395577. **UDC** 316.34. **Ad Acc, Adv Mgr:** Lulena Ortalda, **Tel** 011 8142748.

AT/0004-8690
**AUSTRALIAN AND NEW ZEALAND JOURNAL OF SOCIOLOGY, THE.** [Aust. N.Z. j. sociol.]. **Added/Corp** Sociological Association of Australia and New Zealand. **VFOAT** Journal of Sociology; ANZJS. Vol. 1 (April 1965)-. Periodical. English. Three times a year (Mar., July, Nov.). 45.00Aus$ (individuals), 66.00Aus$ (institutions) Australia; 53.00Aus$ (individuals), 72.00Aus$ (institutions) surface mail; 59.00Aus$ (individuals), 79.00Aus$ (institutions) airmail. LaTrobe University Press, LaTrobe University C A Day, Bundoora Victoria 3083 Australia. **Tel** 011 61 3 4791460, FAX (03)470 2011, telex AA 33143. **(Subscription address:** P. O. Box 3083, Bundora VIC 3083 Australia, telephone: 011 61 3 004634**) ED** Yoshio Sugimoto (editor's address: Sociology Department, LaTrobe University, Bundoora Victoria Australia 3083). **LC** HM1; .A78. **DD** 301/.05. **NLM** W1 AU498K. **Bk Rev. Ad Acc. Pr Rev. Circ:** 1,100 (ctrl). available on microfilm from Xerox; available on microfilm and microfiche from University Microfilms International (UMI). Documents available from The Genuine Article.
**Desc:** News and information of oriented sociology.
**Ind/Abst** Am. Hist. Life (1965-); APAIS, Aust. Public Aff. Inf. Ser. (1966-); Appl. Soc. Sci. Index Abstr.; Arts Humanit. Citation Index [Select. Cov.]; Aust. Educ. Index (1978-); Crim. Justice Abstr.; Curr. Contents Soc. Behav. Sci.; Int. Bibliogr. Sociol.; Linguist. Lang. Behav. Abstr.; Middle East Abstr. Index; Multicult. Educ. Abstr.; Psychol. Abstr. (1982-); PsycINFO; PsycLit; Res. Alert [Full Cov.]; Risk Abstr. (19??-19??); Soc. Plann. Policy Dev. Abstr.; Soc. Sci. Cit. Index [Full Cov.]; Sociol. Abstr. [Full Cov.]; Sociol. Educ. Abstr.; SportSearch; Stud. Women Abstr.

US/0145-0034
**BEHAVIOR & SOCIETY.** ***Ceased.*** **VAT** Behavior and Society. (19??)-(Jan. 1992). English. wk (with annual subject index). National Technical Information Service - NTIS, Room 2027S, 5285 Port Royal Road, Springfield VA 22161. **Tel** (703)487-4630, (703)487-4660, (703)487-4650, FAX (703)321-8547, telex 89-9405.

GW
**BEITRAGE ZUR GESCHICHTE DER FDJ.** No. 1-. Periodical. German. an. DM8.00 Germany; DM16.00 US. Wilhelm-Pieck-Universitat Rostock, Abt Wissenschaftspublizistik, Vogelsang 13/14, Rostock O-2500 Germany. **Tel** GDR 81/369 577. **ED** Rektor D Widhelm. **LC** HQ799.G5; B385. **DD** 301.43/15/06243. **Ad Acc. Circ:** 350 (ctrl).
**Desc:** History of German workers youth-movement.

GW
**BEITRAGE ZUR WISENSSOZIOLOGIE, BEITRAGE ZUR RELIGIONS-SOZIOLOGIE. VFOAT** Beitrage zur Religions-Soziologie; Contributions to the Sociology of Knowledge; Contributions to the Sociology of Religion. English (French and German; summaries and/or abstracts in French, English and German). Westdeutscher Verlag GmbH, Postfach 5829, D 65048 Wiesbaden Germany. **Tel** 011 49 611 160220. **LC** BD175; .B385. **DD** 301.2/1.

NE
**BELEID & MAATSCHAPPIJ. JAARBOEK. VFOAT** Beleid en Maatschappij. Jaarboek. (1986)-. Periodical. Dutch. bm (6 issues). Fl173.00 (institutions), Fl102.00 (individuals) Netherlands; Fl183.50 (institutions), Fl134.50 (individuals) other. Uitgeverij Boom, Postbus 400, 7940 AK Meppel Netherlands. **Tel** 011 31 20 5220 57012, FAX 011 31 20 5220 54452, telex 42829. **LC** HN1; .B44.
**Ind/Abst** Soc. Res. Methodol. Abstr. (1990-).

US/0067-5830
**BERKELEY JOURNAL OF SOCIOLOGY.** [Berkeley j. sociol.]. Vol. 5, No. 1, (Fall 1959)-. English. an. $15.00 (institutions), $8.00 (individuals) US; $20.50 (institutions) other. University of California Department of Sociology, 410 Barrows Hall, Berkeley CA 94720. **Tel** (510)642-2771, FAX (510)642-0659. **LC** HM1; .B4. **DD** 301. **Bk Rev. Ad Acc. Pr Rev. Circ:** 1,000. ***Continues*** *Berkeley Publications in Society and Institutions.*
**Desc:** Critical review of mainstream sociology and other forms of social control.
**Ind/Abst** Altern. Press Index; Am. Bibliogr. Slavic East Europ. Stud.; Int. Bibliogr. Sociol.; Linguist. Lang. Behav. Abstr.; Middle East Abstr. Index; Soc. Plann. Policy Dev. Abstr.; Sociol. Abstr. [Full Cov.]; Stud. Women Abstr.

GW
**BERLINER JOURNAL FUER SOZIOLOGIE. VFOAT** Berlin Journal of Sociology. German (English). qt. $115.00. Akademie-Verlag GmbH, Muehlenstrasse 33 34, D 13162 Berlin Germany. **Tel** 011 49 30 47889300, FAX 011 49 30 47889357. **(Subscription address:** VCH Publishers Inc., 303 Northwest 12th Avenue, Journals Department, Deerfield FL 33442.**) ED** Frank Ettrich (Editor's Address: Fachbereich Sozialwissenschaften der Humboldt, Universitat zu Berlin, Erieseering 42, o-1136 Berlin, Germany). Index available. **Bk Rev**, (Qty: 12). **Ad Acc, Adv Mgr:** Axel Mischke, **Tel** (030)2236 377. **Circ:** 400.
**Desc:** Professional publication which is open to theoretical debates and the presentation of well-founded empirical results.
**Ind/Abst** Ethnoarts Index; Int. Bibliogr. Sociol.; Linguist. Lang. Behav. Abstr.; Soc. Plann. Policy Dev. Abstr.; Sociol. Abstr. (1991-) [Full Cov.].

NE/0923-4284
**BEYOND APARTHEID.** ***Ceased.*** **See** Economics.

CK/0121-5183
**BEYOND LAW / MAS ALLA DEL DERECHO.** See Law.

II/0304-9116
**BHARATA VARSHA.** (AHE BHARATA VARSHA). **Added/Corp** Indian Institute for National Integration. Vol. 1 (April 1973)-. Periodical. English. qt. $4.00. Mr Ramahari Mishra Honorary Executive Director, Indian Institute for National Integration, Cuttack India. **LC** HN681; .B53. **DD** 309.1/54/04.

NE/0167-8272
**BIBLIOGRAFIE NEDERLANDSE SOCIOLOGIE. Added/Corp** Rijksuniversiteit te Utrecht. Sociologisch Instituut. Afdeling Bibliotheek en Documentatie. Rijksuniversiteit te Utrecht. Bibliotheek. Bureau BNS. **VFOAT** BNS. (1970)-. Dutch. an. F95.00 (1990 edition). Bur Bibliografie Nederlandse Sociologie, Postbus 80140, 3508 TC Utrecht Netherlands. **Tel** 011 31 30 531890. **LC** Z7164.S68; B52; HM22.N4. Index available. **Circ:** 200 (ctrl).
**Ind/Abst** Soc. Res. Methodol. Abstr. (1980-).

FR/0982-3417
**BIBLIOGRAPHIE - INSTITUT NATIONAL DE LA RECHERCHE AGRONOMIQUE, DEPARTEMENT D'ECONOMIE ET DE LA SOCIOLOGIE RURALES.** See Agriculture-Abstracting, Bibliographies and Statistics.

US/0742-6895
**BIBLIOGRAPHIES AND INDEXES IN SOCIOLOGY.** See Sociology-Abstracting, Bibliographies and Statistics.

US/0740-2163
**BLACK MALE/FEMALE RELATIONSHIPS.** [Black male/female relatsh.]. **VAT** Black Male Female Relationships. V. 1, No. 1 (June/July 1979)-. Periodical. English. ir. $6.00. Black Think Tank, Inc., 1801 Bush Street, Suite 118, San Francisco CA 94109. **ED** Nathan Hare. **Bk Rev. Ad Acc. Circ:** 3,000. available on microfilm and microfiche from University Microfilms International (UMI).
**Desc:** Studies in black male/female relationships and how these are shaped by and interface with social, political and situational factors.

NE/0927-2720
**BLIKOPENER DEN BOSCH.** (BLIKOPENER.). [Blikopener Den Bosch]. (1990)-. Periodical. Dutch. ir (7 issues per year). Fl24.80. Malmberg BV, PO Box 233 Leeghwaterlaan 16, 5223 BA Den Bosch Netherlands. **Tel** 011 31 73 288711, telex 50058. **UDC** 304 + 930. ***Continues*** *Keesings Blikopener, 0165-3512.*

●US
**BLUE BOOK OF THE ASSOCIATION FOR PUBLIC OPINION RESEARCH, WORLD ASSOCIATION FOR PUBLIC OPINION RESEARCH : AGENCIES & ORGANIZATIONS REPRESENTED IN AAPOR/WAPOR MEMBERSHIP, THE. Added/Corp** American Association for Public Opinion Research. **VFOAT** Agencies & Organizations; Agencies and Organizations. (1991/1992)-. English. ***Continues*** *Agencies & Organizations Represented in AAPOR Membership.*

FR/0759-1063
**BMS. BULLETIN DE METHODOLOGIE SOCIOLOGIQUE.** [BMS. Bull. methodol. sociol.]. **VFOAT** Bulletin de Methodologie Sociologique (Paris). (1983)-. Periodical. French. sa. **UDC** 30.08.
**Ind/Abst** Linguist. Lang. Behav. Abstr.; Soc. Plann. Policy Dev. Abstr.; Sociol. Abstr. (1983-).

MX
**BOLETIN / COMITE CRISTIANO DE SOLIDARIDAD MONSENOR ROMERO.** **See** Religion and Theology.

MX
**BOLETIN INFORMATIVO - CENTRO DE INVESTIGACION PARA LA INTEGRACION SOCIAL. Main/Corp** Centro de Investigacion Para la Integracion Social. No. 1- ; Oct. 1977/Oct. 1978-. Spanish. Centro de Investigacion Para la Integracion Social, Plaza del Carmen No 7, San Angel Mexico 20 DF Mexico.

IT
**BOLLETTINO DELLA DOXA. Main/Corp** Doxa, Istituto per le Ricerche Statistiche e l'Analisi dell'Opinione Pubblica, Milan. Vol. 1 (1946)-. Periodical. Italian. sm (with occasional double issues). L100000. Doxa, Via B Panizza 7, 20144 Milan Italy. **Tel** 011 39 2 48193320, FAX 011 39 2 48193286, telex 321 101. cum. index. **Bk Rev. Ad Acc. Circ:** 2,000 (ctrl).
**Desc:** Results of public opinion surveys in Italy and other countries.

GW/0068-0044
**BONNER BEITRAEGE ZUR SOZIOLOGIE / INSTITUT FUER SOZIOLOGIE DER UNIVERSITAT BONN. Added/Corp** Universitat Bonn. Institut fur Soziologie. No. 1, (1964)-. Monographic series. German. ir. Price varies per volume. Ferdinand Enke Verlag, Ruedigerstrasse 14, D-70469 Stuttgart Germany. **Tel** 011 49 711 8931124, 011 49 711 893123. **(Subscription address:** Georg Thieme Verlag Stuttgart, Postfach 301120, D 70451 Stuttgart Germany**) ED** G. Eisermann. **LC** HM15; .B58.

UK/0007-1315
**BRITISH JOURNAL OF SOCIOLOGY, THE.** [Br. j. sociol.]. **Added/Corp** London School of Economics and Political Science. Vol. 1 (March 1950)-. Periodical. English. Three times a year. $120.00 (US & Canada); £78.00 (UK); £84.00 (other). Routledge, 11 New Fetter Lane, London EC4P 4EE England. **Tel** 071 583 9855, FAX 071 842 2298. **(Subscription address:** Kinokuniya Company Ltd., 38-1 Sakuragaoka 5, chome Setagaya-ku, Tokyo 156 Japan.**) ED** Cohen (Rencys). **LC** HM1; .B75. **DD** 301/.05. **NLM** W1 BR637D. **[CCC]**. cum. index. **Bk Rev. Ad Acc. Pr Rev. Circ:** 2,600. available on microfilm. Documents available from The Genuine Article, UMI Article Clearinghouse.
**Desc:** The leading British journal in its field, providing a medium for the publication of original papers in sociology and related subjects.
**Ind/Abst** ABI/INFORM Glob. Ed.; Abstr. Anthropol.; Acad. Abstr. Full Text Elite (Jan. 1992-); Acad. Abstr. (Jan. 1992-); Acad. Search (Jan. 1992-); Am. Hist. Life (1955-1976, 1979-); Anthropol. Index; Appl. Soc. Sci.

Index Abstr.; Contents Pages Manage.; Crim. Justice Abstr.; Crim. Penol. Police Sci. Abstr.; Expand. Acad. Index (1989-); Geogr. Abstr. Human Geogr.; Health Plan. Adminis.; Index Med.; Index Book Rev. Relig.; INFO-SOUTH Abstr.; Int. Bibliogr. Sociol.; Int. Labour Doc.; Int. Polit. Sci. Abstr.; Linguist. Lang. Behav. Abstr.; Middle East Abstr. Index; Newsp. Period. Abstr. (1991-); Peace Res. Abstr. J. (1950-1980); Psychol. Abstr. (1950-); PsycINFO; PsycLit; Res. Alert [Full Cov.]; Res. High. Educ. Abstr.; School Organ. Manage. Abstr.; Selec. Coop. Index Manage. Period; Soc. Plann. Policy Dev. Abstr.; Soc. Sci. Source (Jan. 1992-); Soc. Sci. Cit. Index [Full Cov.]; Soc. Sci. Index; Soc. Sci. Index Fulltext (Dec. 1988-) [Full Txt.]; Soc. Work Abstr. (Spring, Summer 1987-?) [Select. Cov.]; Sociol. Abstr.; Sociol. Educ. Abstr.; Spec. Educ. Needs Abstr.; Stat. Theory Method Abstr. (1959-1963); Women Stud. Abstr.; Work Relat. Abstr.

UK/0142-5692
**BRITISH JOURNAL OF SOCIOLOGY OF EDUCATION.** [Br. j. sociol. educ.]. Vol. 1, No. 1 (March 1980)-. Periodical. English. qt (Mar., Jun., Sep., Dec.). £168.00. Carfax Publishing Company, PO Box 25 Abingdon, Oxfordshire OX14 3UE England. **Tel** 011 44 235 555335, FAX (0279)31067, telex 817484. **(Subscription address:** US and Canada/ PO Box 2025, Dunnellon, FL 34430-2025; telephone:(904)489-6996**)** **ED** Len Barton. **LC** LC191.8.G7; B74. **DD** 370.19/05. **[CCC].** Index available. **Bk Rev. Ad Acc. Pr Rev.** available on microfiche. Documents available from The Genuine Article.
**Desc:** The empirical research in the sociology of education.
**Ind/Abst** Appl. Soc. Sci. Index Abstr.; Br. Educ. Index; Curr. Contents Soc. Behav. Sci.; Curr. Index J. Educ.; Educ. Technol. Abstr.; Linguist. Lang. Behav. Abstr.; Multicult. Educ. Abstr.; Res. Alert [Full Cov.]; Res. High. Educ. Abstr.; School Organ. Manage. Abstr.; Soc. Plann. Policy Dev. Abstr.; Soc. Sci. Cit. Index [Full Cov.]; Sociol. Abstr. [Full Cov.]; Sociol. Educ. Abstr.; Spec. Educ. Needs Abstr.; Stud. Women Abstr.; Work Relat. Abstr. (-19??).

UK/0144-1329
**BRITISH PUBLIC OPINION. VFOAT** British Public Opinion Newsletter. (19??)-. Periodical. English. Ten times a year. £75.00. British Public Opinion, 32 Old Queen Street, London SW1 9HP England. **Tel** 011 44 71 2220232, FAX 011 44 71 2221653, telex 295230. **ED** Robert M. Worcester. Index available. **Circ:** 400.
**Desc:** Resume of published British public opinion poll findings.
**Ind/Abst** Energy Res. Abstr. (Aug. 1980-).

MV
**BULETINUL ACADEMIEI DE STIINTE A REPUBLICII MOLDOVA. ECONOMIE SI SOCIOLOGIE. See** Economics.

NE
**BULLETIN SOCIALE GEOGRAFIE ONTWIKKELINGSLANDEN; SERIE 2 (UTRECHT). Main/Corp** Utrecht. Rijksuniversiteit. Geografisch Instituut. No. 1- March 1971-. Bulletin. Dutch. Heidelberglaan 2, Utrecht Netherlands. **LC** HN980; .U85. **DD** 309.1/172/4.

JA
**BUNKAGAKU NENPO. Added/Corp** Doshisha Daigaku Bunkagakkai. **VFOAT** Annual Report of Cultural Studies. (1950)-. Periodical. French (Japanese). ¥500. Doshisha Kaigaku Bunkagakkai, c/o Doshisha Daigaku Bungakubu Bunka Gakka Kenkyushitsu, Karasumaru Imadegawa, Kyoto Japan. **LC** AS552.D58; B85.

BL/0102-9711
**CADERNOS DO CEAS.** [Cad. CEAS]. **Added/Corp** Centro de Estudos e Acao Social (Salvador, Brazil). **VAT** Cadernos do Centro de Estudos e Acao Social. (1969)-. Periodical. Portuguese. bm. $35.00. Centro de Estudos e Acao Social, Rua Aristides Novis 101, Salvador Bahia Brazil. **Tel** 011 55 71 2471232. **LC** HN281; .C33.
**Ind/Abst** Hum. Rights Intern. Rep.

BL/0103-5673
**CADERNOS DO CEDI.** [Cad. CEDI]. **VFOAT** Cadernos do Centro Ecumenico de Documentacao e Informacao. (1979)-. Periodical. Portuguese. ir. Centro Ecumenico de Documentacao e Informacao, Caixa Postal 16.082, 22241 Rio de Janeiro RJ Brazil. **UDC** 30.
**Ind/Abst** Hum. Rights Intern. Rep.

BE/0575-0598
**CAHIERS DE CLIO.** [Cah. Clio]. **VFOAT** Clio, Cahiers; Clio, Cahiers; Clio. (1965)-. Periodical. French. qt. Maggy Hodeige, Rue Saint-Gilles 343 - Bte 054, B4000 Liege Belgium. **LC** AS241; .C3. **DD** 301/.05.
**Ind/Abst** Am. Hist. Life (1980-).

BE/0771-6680
**CAHIERS DE LA WALLONIE ET DE BRUXELLES / GROUPE DE SOCIOLOGIE WALLONNE, LES.** ***Ceased.*** Yearly V. 8, No. 37, (Oct. 1982)-(1993). Periodical. French. qt. Groupe de Sociologie Wallonne, Universite Catholique de Louvain, 1 Place Montesquieu, 1348 Louvain-la-Neuve Belgium. **LC** HN510.W34; C34. ***Continues*** *Cahiers de la Wallonie.*

FR
**CAHIERS DE L'OBSERVATION DU CHANGEMENT SOCIAL / ATP OBSERVATION CONTINUE DU CHANGEMENT SOCIAL ET CULTURAL.** Vol. 1-. French. 31.00F. Editions du CNRS, 22 rue Saint Armand, F 75015 Paris France. **Tel** 011 33 1 45075050. **LC** HN421; .C33. **DD** 303.4/0944.
**Desc:** Demographic and socio-economic news of France by region, focusing on agricultural vs metropolitan milieux, ecology, juvenile life and educational systems.

CN/0831-1048
**CAHIERS DE RECHERCHE SOCIOLOGIQUE.** [Cah. rech. sociol.]. **Added/Corp** Universite du Quebec a Montreal. Departement de Sociologie. **VAT** Cahiers de Recherches Sociologiques. Vol. 1 (Sept. 1983)-. Periodical. French. sa. 28.00Can$ (1 year), 50.00Can$ (2 year) institutions; 20.00Can$ (1 year), 38.00Can$ (2 year) individuals, Canada; 24.00Can$ (1 year), 45.00Can$ (2 year) individuals, other. University Quebec at Montreal, PO Box 8888/Succursale Point A, Montreal Quebec H3C 3P8 Canada. **Tel** (514)987-7747, (514)987-4851, FAX (514)987-3251. **DD** 301/.05. **CODEN** CARSEV.
**Ind/Abst** Linguist. Lang. Behav. Abstr.; PAIS Foreign Lang. Index (1988-); PAIS Int. Print (1991-?); Point Repere; Soc. Plann. Policy Dev. Abstr.; Sociol. Abstr. (1983-) [Full Cov.].

FR/0761-9871
**CAHIERS DE SOCIOLOGIE ECONOMIQUE ET CULTURELLE, ETHNOPSYCHOLOGIE. Added/Corp** Institut Havrais de Sociologie Economique et de Psychologie des Peuples. No. 1 (June 1984)-. Periodical. French (summaries and/or abstracts in English). Twice a year (June, Dec.). 140.00F France; 160.00F other. INHSEPP, 56 rue Anatole France, 76600 le Harve France. **Tel** 011 33 35 424755 or 466955. **LC** GN502; .E73. **DD** 306/.05. Index available. cum. index. **Bk Rev. Ad Acc. Pr Rev. Circ:** 50 (ctrl). ***Continues*** *Ethnopsychologie, Cahiers de Sociologie Economique.*
**Ind/Abst** Linguist. Lang. Behav. Abstr.; Soc. Plann. Policy Dev. Abstr.; Sociol. Abstr. (1984-) [Full Cov.].

FR
**CAHIERS DES ETUDES RURALES.** Periodical. French. ir. Walter de Gruyter Inc. / Hawthorne, 200 Saw Mill River Road, Hawthorne NY 10532. **Tel** (914)747-0110, GERMANY: 011/49/30/260050, FAX (914)747-1326, telex 646677. **(Subscription address:** Germany/ PO Box 110240, 1 Berlin 11**)**

FR
**CAHIERS D'ETUDE DE SOCIOLOGIE CULTURELLE.** 1- 1971-. Periodical. French. INHSEPP, 56 rue Anatole France, 76600 le Harve France. **Tel** 011 33 35 424755 or 466955.

FR/0008-0276
**CAHIERS INTERNATIONAUX DE SOCIOLOGIE.** [Cah. int. sociol.]. Vol. 1 (1946)-. Periodical. French. sa. 260.00F France; 330.00F other. Presses Universitaires de France, Department des Revues, 14 Avenue du Bois de l'Epine, BP 90, 91003 Evry Cedex France. **Tel** (1)60 77 82 05, FAX (1) 60 79 20 45, telex PUF 600 474 F. **ED** Georges Balandier. **LC** HM3; .C3. **DD** 301/.05. **NLM** W1 CA145. **[CCC]. Pr Rev.** Documents available from The Genuine Article.
**Desc:** Applies a contemporary sociological orientation to various analyses of reality, including psychology, demography and ethnological studies. Also of interest to historians and geographers.
**Ind/Abst** Arts Humanit. Citation Index [Select. Cov.]; Int. Bibliogr. Sociol.; Int. Polit. Sci. Abstr.; Leis. Recreat. Tour. Abstr.; Linguist. Lang. Behav. Abstr.; Point Repere (1983-); Res. Alert [Full Cov.]; Rural Dev. Abstr.; Soc. Plann. Policy Dev. Abstr.; Soc. Sci. Cit. Index [Full Cov.]; Sociol. Abstr. [Full Cov.]; SportSearch; World Agric. Econ.

FR
**CAHIERS POUR L'ANALYSE CONCRETE.** 1-. French. ir. 70.00F France; 90.00F North America. Centre de Sociologie Historique, BP 112, 45202 Montargis Cedex France. **Tel** (16)38938690. **Circ:** 400.
**Ind/Abst** Am. Hist. Life (1985-).

US/0739-9189
**CALC REPORT. See** Religion and Theology.

US/0271-1095
**CALIFORNIA OPINION INDEX.** [Calif. opin. index]. **Added/Corp** Field Institute. (19??)-. English. ir. Field Institute, 550 Kearny Street, San Francisco CA 94108. **Tel** (415)392-5763.

US/0162-8712
**CALIFORNIA SOCIOLOGIST.** [Calif. sociol.]. **Added/Corp** California State University, Los Angeles. Vol. 1 (Winter 1978)-. Periodical. English. Twice a year. $8.00 (individual); $12.00 (institutions); $15.00 (others). California State University at Los Angeles / Department of Sociology, 5151 State University Drive, Los Angeles CA 90032. **Tel** (213)343-2200, FAX (213)343-5155. **ED** Terry Kandal. **LC** HM1; .C34. **DD** 301/.05. **Bk Rev. Ad Acc. Pr Rev. Circ:** 200.
**Desc:** A journal for sociologist and social workers. It publishes original research and theoretical articles.
**Ind/Abst** Linguist. Lang. Behav. Abstr.; Soc. Plann. Policy Dev. Abstr.; Soc. Work Abstr. [Select. Cov.]; Sociol. Abstr. [Full Cov.].

UK
**CAMBRIDGE STUDIES IN ORAL AND LITERATE CULTURE. VFOAT** Studies in Oral and Literate Culture. No. 1 (1981)-. Monographic series. English. ir. Price varies per volume. Cambridge University Press / New York, 40 West 20th Street, New York NY 10011-4211. **Tel** (212)924-3900, (800)221-4512. **(Subscription address:** Cambridge University Press / Outside of North America, Journal Fulfillment Department, The Edinburgh Building, Cambridge CB2 2RU United Kingdom.**)**

UK
**CAMBRIDGE STUDIES IN SOCIOLOGY.** Vol. 1 (1968)-. Academic Scholarly Publication. English. ir. Price varies per volume. Cambridge University Press, The Edinburgh Building, Shaftesbury Road, Cambridge CB2 2RU United Kingdom. **Tel** 011 44 223 312393, FAX 011 44 223 325959. **(Subscription address:** North America/ Cambridge University Press, 40 West 20th Street, New York, NY 10011-4211; telephone: (212)924-3900**)**

CN/0318-6431
**CANADIAN JOURNAL OF SOCIOLOGY.** [Can. j. sociol.]. **Added/Corp** University of Alberta. **VFOAT** Cahiers Canadiens de Sociologie. (Spring 1975)-. Periodical. English (French; summaries and/or abstracts in French). Four times a year (Mar., June, Sept., Dec.). 46.73 (individuals), 79.44Can$ (institutions) Canada; $50.00 (individuals), $85.00 (institutions) others. Canadian Journal of Sociology, Department of Sociology, University of Alberta, Edmonton Alberta T6G 2H4 Canada. **Tel** (403)492-5941. **ED** Richard Ericson and Nico Stehr. **LC** HM1; .C35. **DD** 301/.05. Index available. cum. index. **Bk Rev. Ad Acc. Pr Rev. Circ:** 1,000. available on microfiche from Micromedia Limited. Documents available from The Genuine Article.
**Desc:** General information on sociology devoted to focus on family or criminology interest.
**Ind/Abst** Appl. Soc. Sci. Index Abstr.; Arts Humanit. Citation Index [Select. Cov.]; Can. Index; Can. Period. Index (19??-); Crim. Justice Abstr.; Curr. Contents Soc. Behav. Sci.; Hum. Resour. Abstr. (?-?); Index Period. Artic. Relat. Law (19??-19??); Int. Bibliogr. Sociol.; Linguist. Lang. Behav. Abstr.; Res. Alert [Full Cov.]; Sage Fam. Stud. Abstr. (?-?); Sage Race Relat. Abstr.; Soc. Plann. Policy Dev. Abstr.; Soc. Sci. Cit. Index [Full Cov.]; Sociol. Abstr. [Full Cov.]; Sociol. Educ. Abstr.; Stud. Women Abstr.

CN/0008-4948
**CANADIAN REVIEW OF SOCIOLOGY AND ANTHROPOLOGY, THE. See** Anthropology.

CN/0831-5698
**CANADIAN SOCIAL TRENDS.** [Can. soc. trends]. **Added/Corp** Statistics Canada. (Summer 1986)-. Periodical. English. qt. 34.00Can$ Canada; $41.00 US; $48.00 other. Statistics Canada, Publications Sales & Services, Main Building Room 1710, Ottawa Ontario K1A 0T6 Canada. **Tel** (613)951-5078, (800)267-6677, FAX (613)951-1584, telex 053-3585. **LC** HN101; .C37. **DD** 306/.0971/05. Documents available from UMI Article Clearinghouse.
**Desc:** This publication discusses the social, economic and demographic changes affecting the lives of Canadians.
**Ind/Abst** Am. Hist. Life (1987-); Can. Index; Can. Period. Index (1987-); Expand. Acad. Index (1992-); Newsp. Period. Abstr. (1992-); PAIS Int. Print; Popul. Index.

US/0149-6948
**CASE ANALYSIS IN SOCIAL SCIENCE IN SOCIAL THERAPY.** ***Ceased.*** [Case anal. soc. sci. soc. therapy]. **VFOAT** Case Analysis. Vol. 1 (Fall/Winter 1978)-Vol. 3, No. 2 (Summer 1993). Periodical. English. ir (1 per year). Progressive Publisher, 401 East 32 1002, Chicago IL 60618. **Tel** (312)225-9181. **ED** Kenneth Ives. **LC** HM1; .C357. **DD** 301/.07/2. **Bk Rev. Circ:** 100.
**Desc:** Case studies from various fields, thoroughly analyzed. Factors and frameworks for case comparisons, inductive methods for developing theory from data.
**Ind/Abst** Linguist. Lang. Behav. Abstr.; Psychol. Abstr. (1977-); PsycLit; Soc. Plann. Policy Dev. Abstr.; Soc. Work Abstr. [Select. Cov.]; Sociol. Abstr. (?-?).

CN/0008-7661
**CATALYST (PETERBOROUGH).** ***Ceased.*** (CATALYST.). [Catalyst]. **Added/Corp** Trent University. New York. State University, Buffalo. Sociology Club. No. 1 (Summer 1965)-(19??). Periodical. English. Catalyst / SUNY, State University of New York, Department of Sociology, Buffalo NY 14261. **Tel** (716)645-2417. available on microfilm and microfiche from University Microfilms International (UMI). Documents available.

**Ind/Abst** Am. Hist. Life (1969-1985); Int. Bibliogr. Sociol.; Linguist. Lang. Behav. Abstr.; Soc. Plann. Policy Dev. Abstr.; Sociol. Abstr. [Full Cov.]; Sociol. Educ. Abstr.

US/0886-8190
**CATHOLIC SINGLES.** ***Ceased.*** [Cathol. singles]. Periodical. English (Spanish and Korean). sa. PO Box 1920, Evanston IL 60204. **Tel** (312)731-8769. **ED** Fred C Wilson. **DD** 305. Index available. cum. index. **Bk Rev. Ad Acc. Circ:** 20,000 (ctrl).
**Desc:** Purpose is to establish solid Christian marriages, minister to the lonely and to promote racial harmony on an international basis.

CN/0316-5175
**CDS. CONSEIL DE DEVELOPPEMENT SOCIAL DU MONTREAL METROPOLITAIN.** (LE CDS.). **Main/Corp** Conseil de Developpement Social du Montreal Metropolitain. V. 1-April 1974-. Periodical. French. bm. $3.00. Le Conseil De Developpement Social Du Montreal Metropolitain, 445, Rue St-Francois-Xavier, Montreal Quebec H2Y 2T1 Canada. **DD** 309.1/714/281.

●US/1065-7150
**CHANTEH (ARLINGTON, VA.).** (CHANTEH : IRANIAN CROSS-CULTURAL QUARTERLY.). [Chanteh]. **Added/Corp** Bunyadi Farhangii Par (Washington, D.C.). Vol. 1, No. 1 (Fall 1992)-. Periodical. English. Four times a year. $35.00. PAR Cultural Foundation, PO Box 703, Falls Church VA 22040. **Tel** (703)533-1727. **LC** WMLC 93/946. **DD** 305.

US/1070-8146
**CHAOS NETWORK, THE.** [Chaos netw.]. (19??)-. Periodical. English. qt (Feb., May, Aug., Nov.). $79.00 US; $95.00 other. People Technologies, PO Box 4100, Urbana IL 61801. **Tel** (217)328-0032, FAX (217)328-0032. **ED** Mark Michaels. **DD** 302. **Bk Rev. Circ:** 600 (ctrl).
**Desc:** Covers organization, social systems, and chaotic behavior in systems.

SA/0258-8927
**CHILD CARE WORKER, THE. VFOAT** Kinderversorger. (1983)-. Periodical. English. Eleven times a year (monthly except Dec.). R46.64 (institutions), R36.27 (individuals). National Association Child Care Workers, PO Box 28323, 4055 Malvern South Africa. **Tel** 31 4631033, 31 4631099, FAX 31 441106. **ED** Mr. Brian Gannon (editor's address: Box 23199 Claremont 7735 South Africa; editor's phone: 31 21 7883610). **UDC** 362.7. cum. index. **Bk Rev. Ad Acc.** ctrl circ.

II/0009-4455
**CHINA REPORT (NEW DELHI).** (CHINA REPORT.). [China rep.]. **Added/Corp** Centre for the Study of Developing Societies. Vol. 9, No. 2 (March-April 1973)-. Periodical. English. qt (Feb., May, Aug., Nov.). $82.00. SAGE Periodical Press, 2455 Teller Road, Thousand Oaks CA 91320. **Tel** (805)499-0721, FAX (805)499-0871, telex 100799. **ED** C. R. M. Rao. Index available. cum. index. **Ad Acc.** available on microfilm and microfiche from University Microfilms International (UMI). ***Continues*** *China Report (China Study Centre (India)), 0009-4455.*
**Desc:** Encourages the increased understanding of contemporary China and its East Asian neighbors, their cultures and ways of development, and their impact on India and other South Asian countries.
**Ind/Abst** Am. Hist. Life (1970-?, 1973-); Int. Bibliogr. Sociol.; Int. Dev. Abstr.; Rural Dev. Abstr.

US/0009-4625
**CHINESE SOCIOLOGY AND ANTHROPOLOGY.** [Chin. sociol. anthropol.]. **Added/Corp** M.E. Sharpe, Inc. International Arts and Sciences Press. Vol. 1 (Fall 1968)-. Periodical. English (Chinese). qt. $381.00 US; $421.00 other. M. E. Sharpe Inc., 80 Business Park Drive, Armonk NY 10504. **Tel** (914)273-1800, (800)541-6563, FAX (914)273-2106. **LC** HM1; .C45. **Pr Rev.** available on microfilm from University Microfilms International (UMI). Documents available from The Genuine Article.
**Desc:** Covers complex social issues that receive particular attention in the Chinese periodicals and journals whose articles are translated in 'Chinese Sociology and Anthropology'.
**Ind/Abst** Abstr. Anthropol.; Am. Hist. Life (1988-); Arts Humanit. Citation Index [Select. Cov.]; Res. Alert [Full Cov.]; Soc. Plann. Policy Dev. Abstr.; Soc. Sci. Cit. Index [Full Cov.]; Sociol. Abstr. (?-?); Sociol. Educ. Abstr.

KO
**CHONGHWA.** Periodical. Korean. mo. Sahoe Chonghwa Wiwonhoe, 32-3 3-ka Namsan-dong, Chung-ku, Seoul South Korea. **LC** HN730.5.Z9; M627.

US/0733-6470
**CHRONOS (WALTHAM, MASS.).** (CHRONOS.). [Chronos]. No. 1 (Fall 1981)-. English. an. $3.00. Brandeis University History Department, Waltham MA 02254. **LC** HN1; .C47. **DD** 301/.09.

CH
**CHUNG-HUA MIN KUO MIN I TSE YEN HUI PIEN. Main/Corp** Chung-Hua Min Kuo Min I Tse Yen Hsieh Hui. **VFOAT** Public Opinion in China. Chinese. **LC** HM261; .C55A.

IT/0009-7152
**CINEMA SOCIETA. See** Motion Picture.

US
**CITY WATCH : A RESEARCH BULLETIN OF THE INSTITUTE OF GLOBAL URBAN STUDIES.** (19??)-. Bulletin. English. bm (6 issues). $8.00. Institute of Global Urban Studies, Cities for Christ, PO Box 300340, Escondido CA 92030. **Tel** (619)489-1811.

US/1047-2169
**CIVIC ARTS REVIEW, THE.** [Civ. arts rev.]. Vol. 1, No. 1 (Summer 1988)-. Periodical. English. qt. Arneson Institute, Ohio Wesleyan University, Delaware OH 43015. **LC** H62.A1; A68. **DD** 300/.5. ***Continues*** *Antaeus Report.*

BE/0009-8140
**CIVILISATIONS.** [Civilisations]. **Added/Corp** International Institute of Differing Civilizations. Vol. 1 (Jan. 1951)-. Periodical. English (French). sa. 1300F Belgium; 1400F other. Institut de Sociologie de l'Universite Libre de Bruxelles, Avenue Jeanne 44, 1050 Brussels Belgium. **Tel** 011 32 2 6503359, 011 32 2 6503457, FAX 011 32 2 6503521, telex UNILIB 23069 B. **LC** AP1; .C55. **DD** 054. **Bk Rev. Ad Acc.**
**Desc:** Non-western civilizations. Covers anthropology, ethnology, sociology, political science, economic problems.
**Ind/Abst** ABC POL SCI; Am. Hist. Life (1955-1961, 1964-); Anthropol. Index; Int. Bibliogr. Sociol.; Int. Dev. Abstr. (?-?); Int. Polit. Sci. Abstr.; Leis. Recreat. Tour. Abstr.; Middle East Abstr. Index; PAIS Int. Print; Rural Dev. Abstr.; World Agric. Econ.

US/0730-840X
**CLINICAL SOCIOLOGY REVIEW.** ***Ceased.*** [Clin. sociol. rev.]. **Added/Corp** Clinical Sociology Association. Sociological Practice Association. Vol. 1 (1982)-(1992). Periodical. English. an. Michigan State University Press, 1405 South Harrison Road, Manly Miles 25, East Lansing MI 48823-5202. **Tel** (517)355-9543, FAX (800)678-2120, (517)336-2611. **ED** David J Kallen. **LC** HM1; .C54. **DD** 616.89/14. **CODEN** CSRUDT. **Bk Rev. Circ:** 750. Documents available from BIOSIS Document Express.
**Desc:** Publishes articles, essays, and research reports concerned with clinical uses of sociological theory, findings or methods, which demonstrate how clinical practice contributes to the development of theory, or how theory may be used to bring about change.
**Ind/Abst** Biol. Abstr. (1985-); Chicano Index; Linguist. Lang. Behav. Abstr.; Psychol. Abstr. (1982-); PsycINFO; Soc. Plann. Policy Dev. Abstr.; Soc. Work Abstr. [Select. Cov.]; Sociol. Abstr. [Full Cov.].

SP
**COMENTARIO SOCIOLOGICO. Main/Corp** Confederacion Espanola de Cajas de Ahorros. Direccion de Estudios Sociales. **Added/Corp** Confederacion Espanola de Cajas de Ahorros. Direccion de Estudios Sociales. Estructura Social de Espana. **VFOAT** Estructura Social de Espana. (197?)-. Spanish. Direccion de Estudios Sociales de la Confederation Espanola de Cajas de Ahorros, Alcala 27, Madrid 14 Spain. **LC** HN581; .C66a. **DD** 946.083/05. ***Continues*** *Confederacion Espanola de Cajas de Ahorros. Servicio de Estudios Sociologicos. Comentario Sociologico.*

US/0739-1250
**COMMUNAL SOCIETIES.** [Communal soc.]. **Added/Corp** Murray State University. National Historic Communal Societies Association (U.S.). Vol. 1 (Autumn 1981)-. Periodical. English. an. $15.00. Communal Studies Association, 8600 University Boulevard, University of South Indiana, Evansville IN 47712. **Tel** (812)464-1719. **ED** Mario S. DePillis. **LC** HX653; .C65. **DD** 335/.973. **Bk Rev. Circ:** 1,000 (ctrl).
**Desc:** Interdisciplinary monographs and book reviews concerning historic and current communal societies worldwide.
**Ind/Abst** Am. Hist. Life (1986-); Index Book Rev. Relig.

CN/0315-5900
**COMMUNIQUE - INTERMET. Main/Corp** Intermet. V. 1- Jan. 1970-. Periodical. English. ir. $12.00. Intermet, Suite 1200/130 Bloor Street West, Toronto Ontario M4W 1A2 Canada. **DD** 301.36/4/072. ***Absorbed*** *Internet. Communique. Ed. Francaise, 0315-5919.*

UK/0010-3802
**COMMUNITY DEVELOPMENT JOURNAL.** [Community dev. j.]. Vol. 1 (Jan. 1966)-. Periodical. English. qt. £46.00 UK and Europe; $85.00 other. Oxford University Press, Walton Street, Oxford OX2 6DP England. **Tel** 011 44 865 56767, FAX 011 44 865 267773, telex 837330 OXPRES G. **(Subscription address:** Oxford University Press / USA, Journals Marketing Department, Oxford University Press, 2001 Evans Road, Cary NC 27513.**) ED** Gary Craig. **LC** HN1; .C612. **[CCC].** Index available. **Bk Rev. Ad Acc. Pr Rev. Circ:** 1,500 (ctrl). available on microfilm and microfiche from University Microfilms International (UMI). Documents available from The Genuine Article. ***Continues*** *Community Development Bulletin.*
**Desc:** Community work and development in developed and developing countries. Subjects include: community studies which throw light on community problems; community power, politics and government; village, town and regional planning; community development and related programmes; community work programmes; and education, health, recreation and welfare in the community content.
**Ind/Abst** Appl. Soc. Sci. Index Abstr.; Curr. Contents Soc. Behav. Sci.; Curr. Index J. Educ.; Geogr. Abstr. Human Geogr.; Int. Bibliogr. Sociol.; Int. Dev. Abstr.; Int. Labour Doc.; Int. Polit. Sci. Abstr.; J. Ferrocement; Linguist. Lang. Behav. Abstr.; Middle East Abstr. Index; Multicult. Educ. Abstr.; PAIS Int. Print (1991-); Res. Alert [Full Cov.]; Rural Dev. Abstr.; Soc. Plann. Policy Dev. Abstr.; Soc. Sci. Cit. Index [Full Cov.]; Soc. Work Abstr. [Select. Cov.]; Sociol. Abstr.; World Agric. Econ.

FR
**COMPAGNONNAGE: ORGANE DES COMPAGNONS DU DEVOIR.** Compagnonnage, 82 rue de l'Hotel de Ville, 75004 Paris France.

US/0195-6310
**COMPARATIVE SOCIAL RESEARCH.** [Comp. soc. res.]. Vol. 2 (1979)-. English. ir. $73.25. JAI Press Inc., 55 Old Post Road, Suite 2, PO Box 1678, Greenwich CT 06836-1678. **Tel** (203)661-7602, FAX (203)661-0792. **ED** Craig Calhoun. **LC** HM1; .C64. **DD** 301/.05. **NLM** W1; CO437H. **[CCC].** ***Continues*** *Comparative Studies in Sociology, 0164-1247.*
**Ind/Abst** Am. Hist. Life (1986-); Int. Bibliogr. Sociol.; Linguist. Lang. Behav. Abstr.; Soc. Plann. Policy Dev. Abstr.; Sociol. Abstr.

US/1059-5422
**COMPETITIVENESS REVIEW.** (COMPETITIVENESS REVIEW : CR.). [Compet. rev.]. **Added/Corp** American Society for Competitiveness. **VFOAT** CR. Vol. 1, No. 1 & 2 (1991)-. Periodical. English. qt. $20.00 (institutions). Competitiveness Review, PO Box 1658, Indiana PA 15705. **DD** 301.

IT/0010-4418
**COMPRENDRE. Added/Corp** Societe Europeenne de Culture. No. 1 (1950)-. Periodical. French (English). ir. L55000 Italy; L65000 other. Societe Europeenne de Culture, Dordosuro 909, 30123 Venice Italy. **Tel** 011 39 41 5230210. **ED** Giuseppe Galasso. **LC** AY832; .S6. Index available. cum. index. **Circ:** 2,000 (ctrl).
**Desc:** Theoretical and practical organ of politics of culture.

VE
**COMUNICACION.** 1-. Periodical. Spanish. qt. $19.00. Centro de Comunicacion Social Jesus Maria Pellin, Apartado 20133, Caracas Venezuela. **Tel** 563-50-96. **ED** Fundacion Centro Gumilla. **LC** HM258; .C5894. **DD** 301.14. **Ad Acc.** ctrl circ.
**Desc:** Information pertaining to communications, press, and broadcasting.

US/0899-9910
**CONFLICT AND CONSCIOUSNESS.** [Confl. conscious.]. English. an. Peter Lang Publishing, 62 West 45th Street, 4th Floor, New York NY 10036. **Tel** (212)764-1471, (800)770-5264, telex 6973364 PLNY. **DD** 303.

CN/0838-8881
**CONJONCTURES (MONTREAL).** (CONJONCTURES.). [Conjonctures]. No. 9 (Spring 1988)-. Periodical. French. sa. 30.00Can$. Conjonctures, 4076 rue Saint-Hubert, Montreal Quebec, H2L 4A8 Canada. **Tel** (514)527-2700. **DD** 320/.05. ***Continues*** *Conjonctures et Politique., 0827-5548.*
**Ind/Abst** Point Repere (1985-).

CN/0226-1766
**CONNECTIONS (TORONTO).** (CONNECTIONS : BULLETIN OF THE INTERNATIONAL NETWORK FOR SOCIAL NETWORK ANALYSIS.). [Connections]. **Added/Corp** International Network for Social Network Analysis. Vol. 1, No. 1 (Summer 1977)-. Periodical. English (French). Three times a year. $30.00 (institutions), $18.00 (individuals). Center for Applied Anthropology, INSNA, University of South Florida, Tampa FL 33620. **ED** Susan Greenbaum. **LC** HM131; .C7455. **DD** 302/.072. Index available. **Bk Rev. Ad Acc. Circ:** 300. available on diskette (IBM PC).
**Desc:** News, abstracts, book summaries, features about social network analysis of interest to social science academics, clinicians and practitioners.
**Ind/Abst** Soc. Plann. Policy Dev. Abstr.; Sociol. Abstr.

CN/0845-874X
**CONNEXIONS DIGEST, THE.** [Connex. dig.]. **Added/Corp** Connexions Information Sharing Services. **VFOAT** Connexions Annual. Vol. 12, No. 1 (1989)-. Periodical. English. qt. 15.50Can$ Canada; 18.50Can$ US; 20.50Can$ other. Connexions / Canada, Station D, PO Box 158, Toronto Ontario M6T 3J8 Canada. **Tel** (416)537-3949. **DD** 361.2/05. ***Continues*** *Connexions., 0708-9422.*

CN/0319-2385
**CONSTRUCTIVE CITIZEN PARTICIPATION.** Vol. 1, (June 1973)-. Newsletter. English. Four times a year (Mar., June, Sept., Dec.). $9.00 (individuals), $25.00 (institutions) Canada; $11.00 (individuals), $27.00 (institution), other. Connor Development Services, 5096 Catalina Terrace, Victoria British Columbia, V8Y 2A5 Canada. **Tel** (604)658-1323, FAX (604)658-8110. **ED** Desmond M. Connor. Index Available, published separately, free-automatically sent (Free). cum. index. **Bk Rev**, (Qty: 100). **Circ:** 300.
**Desc:** New developments in the field of resolving public courtesy. Articles on rising issues, practical techniques, and publication reviews.

US
**CONTEMPORARY ETHNOGRAPHIC STUDIES.** English. $73.25. JAI Press Inc., 55 Old Post Road, Suite 2, PO Box 1678, Greenwich CT 06836-1678. **Tel** (203)661-7602, FAX (203)661-0792. **ED** Jaber Gubrium.

US/0094-3061
**CONTEMPORARY SOCIOLOGY (WASHINGTON).** (CONTEMPORARY SOCIOLOGY.). [Contemp. sociol.]. **Added/Corp** American Sociological Association. Vol. 1, No. 1 (Jan. 1972)-. Periodical. English. bm (6 issues). $105.00 (institutions), $50.00 (individuals) US; $113.00 (institutions), $58.00 (individuals) other. American Sociological Association, 1722 North Street Northwest, Washington DC 20036-2981. **Tel** (202)833-3410, FAX (202)785-0146. **ED** Ida Harper Simpson. **LC** HM1; .C65. **DD** 30L/.05; 301. **NLM** Z 7164.S68 C761. Index available. cum. index. **Bk Rev. Ad Acc. Circ:** 8,000. Documents available from The Genuine Article, UMI Article Clearinghouse.
**Desc:** Publishes reviews and critical discussions of recent works in sociology and related disciplines which merit the attention of sociologists.
**Ind/Abst** Acad. Abstr. Full Text Elite (July 1990-); Acad. Abstr. (July 1990-); Acad. Ind. [Computer File] (1987-); Acad. Search (July 1990-); Am. Bibliogr. Slavic East Europ. Stud.; Arts Humanit. Citation Index [Select. Cov.]; Book Rev. Digest; Book Rev. Index; Curr. Contents Soc. Behav. Sci.; Expand. Acad. Index (1987-); Index Book Rev. Relig.; INFO-SOUTH Abstr.; Linguist. Lang. Behav. Abstr.; Mag. Search; Middle East Abstr. Index; Newsp. Period. Abstr. (1992-); Res. Alert [Full Cov.]; Sage Race Relat. Abstr.; Soc. Plann. Policy Dev. Abstr.; Soc. Sci. Source (Jul. 1990-); Soc. Sci. Cit. Index [Full Cov.]; Sociol. Abstr. [Full Cov.]; Soc. Res. Methodol. Abstr. (1975-); Women Stud. Abstr.

US
**CONTEMPORARY STUDIES IN SOCIOLOGY.** Vol. 1 (1983)-. Monographic series. English. ir. $73.25. JAI Press Inc., 55 Old Post Road, Suite 2, PO Box 1678, Greenwich CT 06836-1678. **Tel** (203)661-7602, FAX (203)661-0792. **ED** Gerald M. Platt and Chad Gordon.

UK/0268-4160
**CONTINUITY AND CHANGE. Added/Corp** Tulane Law School. Cambridge Group for the History of Population and Social Structure. Vol. 1, Pt. 1 (May 1986)-. Academic Scholarly Publication. English. Three times a year (May, Aug., and Dec.). $94.00 US, Canada & Mexico; £59.00 other. Cambridge University Press, The Edinburgh Building, Shaftesbury Road, Cambridge CB2 2RU United Kingdom. **Tel** 011 44 223 312393, FAX 011 44 223 325959. **(Subscription address:** Cambridge University Press / North America, 110 Midland Avenue, Port Chester NY 10573.) **ED** Lloyd Bonfield and Richard Wall. **LC** HM104; .C66. **DD** 301/.09. **[CCC].** available on microfilm from University Microfilms International (UMI). Documents available.
**Desc:** Aims to define a field of historical sociology concerned with long-term continuities and discontinuities in the structures of past societies. Emphasis is upon studies whose agenda or methodology combines elements from traditional fields such as history, sociology, law, demography, economics or anthropology, or ranges freely between them. There is a strong commitment to comparative studies over a broad range of cultures and time spans.
**Ind/Abst** Am. Hist. Life (1986-); Br. Humanit. Index; Geogr. Abstr. Human Geogr.; Int. Bibliogr. Sociol.; Linguist. Lang. Behav. Abstr.; Popul. Index; Soc. Plann. Policy Dev. Abstr.; Sociol. Abstr.

US/0084-9278
**CONTRIBUTIONS IN SOCIOLOGY.** (1970)-. Monographic series. English. Seven times a year. Price varies per volume. Greenwood Press Inc., PO Box 5007, Westport CT 06881-5007. **Tel** (203)226-3571, FAX (203)222-1502. **ED** Don Martindale.

US/0069-9667
**CONTRIBUTIONS TO INDIAN SOCIOLOGY. NEW SERIES. Added/Corp** Institute of Economic Growth, Delhi. Research Centre on Social and Economic Development in Asia. No. 1 (Dec. 1967)-. Periodical. English. sa (May and November). $83.00. SAGE Periodical Press, 2455 Teller Road, Thousand Oaks CA 91320. **Tel** (805)499-0721, FAX (805)499-0871, telex 100799. **ED** T. N. Madan. **LC** HN681; .C62. **DD** 309.1/54; 301. **Pr Rev. *Continues*** *Contributions to Indian Sociology.*
**Desc:** A distinguished international forum for research on Indian and South Asian societies.
**Ind/Abst** Anthropol. Index; Arts Humanit. Citation Index [Select. Cov.]; Int. Bibliogr. Sociol.; Linguist. Lang. Behav. Abstr.; Soc. Plann. Policy Dev. Abstr.; Sociol. Abstr. (1985-) [Full Cov.].

US/0198-9871
**CONTRIBUTIONS TO THE STUDY OF POPULAR CULTURE.** [Contr. study pop. culture]. No. 1 (1981)-. Monographic series. English. ir. Price varies per volume. Greenwood Press Inc., PO Box 5007, Westport CT 06881-5007. **Tel** (203)226-3571, FAX (203)222-1502.
**Desc:** An interdisciplinary series which examines popular culture topics and theory throughout the world.

DK/0903-2703
**COPENHAGEN PAPERS IN EAST AND SOUTHEAST ASIAN STUDIES. Added/Corp** Kbenhavns Universitet. Center For East and Southeast Asian Studies. **VFOAT** Copenhagen Papers. (1987)-. Monographic series. English. an. Museum Tusculanum Press, University of Copenhagen, Njalsgade 94, DK-2300 Copenhagen D Denmark. **Tel** 011 45 31542211. **ED** Kjeld Erik Brodsgaard. **Bk Rev. Ad Acc.**
**Desc:** Includes articles on aspects of the political, economic, social or cultural development of east and southeast asian countries.

CN/1183-479X
**CRCS NEWSLETTER / CENTRE FOR RESEARCH ON CULTURE AND SOCIETY, CARLETON UNIVERSITY.** [CRCS newsl.]. **Added/Corp** Carleton University. Centre for Research on Culture and Society. **VFOAT** Centre for Research on Culture and Society Newsletter. Issue 1 (Winter 1991)-. Newsletter. English. Three times a year. Centre for Research on Culture and Society, Carleton University, Room A929, Loeb Building, Ottawa Ontario K1S 5B6 Canada. **DD** 306.4/0971/072.

NE/0925-4994
**CRIME, LAW, AND SOCIAL CHANGE. See** Law-Law Enforcement and Criminology.

US/8755-3325
**CRITICA (LA JOLLA, CALIF.).** (CRITICA : A JOURNAL OF CRITICAL ESSAYS / CHICANO STUDIES, UNIVERSITY OF CALIFORNIA, SAN DIEGO.). [Critica]. **Added/Corp** University of California, San Diego. Chicano Studies Program. Vol. 1, No. 1 (Spring 1984)-. Periodical. English (Spanish). Three times a year. $6.00 (individuals), $8.00 (institutions). University of California San Diego / Critica, c/o Barbara Reyes, La Jolla CA 92093. **Tel** (619)534-3276. **ED** Rosaura Sanchez (editor's address: 9500 Gilman Drive, 0414, LaJolla, CA 92093). **DD** 305. **Bk Rev. Ad Acc. Pr Rev. Circ:** 2,500.
**Desc:** An interdisciplinary refereed bilingual journal that serves as a forum for critical analysis of Chicano and Latino theoretical, ideological and historical issues.

IT/0011-1546
**CRITICA SOCIOLOGICA, LA.** [Crit. sociol.]. **Added/Corp** Universita Internazionale Degli Studi Sociale (Rome, Italy). Istituto di Sociologia. (Spring 1967)-. Periodical. Italian (English). qt. L60.000 Italy; L110.00 Europe; L130.000 other. SIARES, Corso Vittorio Emanuele 24, 00186 Rome Italy. **Tel** 011 39 6 6786760. **ED** Franco Ferrarotti. **LC** HM7; .C74. **DD** 301/.05. cum. index. **Bk Rev. Circ:** 2,000 (ctrl). Documents available.
**Ind/Abst** Int. Bibliogr. Sociol.; Int. Polit. Sci. Abstr.; Linguist. Lang. Behav. Abstr.; Soc. Plann. Policy Dev. Abstr.; Sociol. Abstr.

US/0896-9205
**CRITICAL SOCIOLOGY.** [Crit. sociol.]. **Added/Corp** University of Oregon. Dept. of Sociology. Vol. 15, No. 1 (Spring 1988)-. Periodical. English. Three times a year. $30.00 (institutions), $15.00 (individuals). University of Oregon Department of Sociology, Eugene OR 97403. **Tel** (503)346-5039. **LC** HM1; .I525. **DD** 301/.05. Index available. cum. index. **Bk Rev. Ad Acc. Pr Rev. Circ:** 800 (ctrl). available on microfilm and microfiche from University Microfilms International (UMI). Documents available from UMI Article Clearinghouse. ***Continues*** *Insurgent Sociologist, 0047-0384.*
**Ind/Abst** Altern. Press Index; Int. Bibliogr. Sociol.; Left Index; Linguist. Lang. Behav. Abstr.; Soc. Plann. Policy Dev. Abstr.; Sociol. Abstr. [Full Cov.]; Work Relat. Abstr.

BE/0770-0075
**CRITIQUE REGIONALE.** [Crit. reg.]. **Added/Corp** Universite Libre de Bruxelles. Institut de Sociologie. Comite pour l'Etude des Problemes de l'Emploi et du Chomage (Belgium) Universite Llibre de Bruxelles. Centre de Sociologie et d'Economie Regionales. **VFOAT** Cahiers de Sociologie et d'Economie Regionales. No. 1 (Nov. 1979)-. Periodical. French. qt. 1100.00F Belgium; 1300.00F other. Institut de Sociologie de l'Universite Libre de Bruxelles, Avenue Jeanne 44, 1050 Brussels Belgium. **Tel** 011 32 2 6503359, 011 32 2 6503457, FAX 011 32 2 6503521, telex UNILIB 23069 B.

CL/0716-0046
**CUADERNOS DE ECONOMIA (SANTIAGO). See** Economics.

US/0748-6499
**CULTIC STUDIES JOURNAL.** [Cultic stud. j.]. Vol. 1, No. 1 (May 1984)-. Academic Scholarly Publication. English. sa. $15.00 US; $18.00 Canada; $22.00 other. American Family Foundation, PO Box 2265, Bonita Springs FL 33959. **Tel** (813)495-3136. **ED** Michael D Langone. **LC** BP600; .C84. **DD** 291. **Bk Rev. Circ:** 350 (ctrl). ***Continues*** *Cultic Studies Newsletter.*
**Desc:** Offers readers an opportunity to deepen their understanding of social influence by learning about its most extreme manifestations and their effects on individuals and society. The only scholarly journal devoted exclusively to this vital, emerging field.
**Ind/Abst** Index Book Rev. Relig.; Psychol. Abstr. (1985-); PsycINFO; PsycLit; Relig. Index One Period.

IT
**CULTURA E NATURA.** Italian (Spanish). bm. L30.000 Italy; $50.00 other. Cultura Natura, Via Cassia 1791 Vill B, 00123 Italy Rome PT91. **Tel** 0039 6 3792366, FAX 0039 6 8085944. **ED** Michele Trimarehi. Index available. cum. index. **Ad Acc. Pr Rev. Circ:** 5,000 (ctrl).
**Desc:** A pluridisciplinary, integrated magazine dealing with present major issues to help people face and solve personal, professional, societal, and environmental conflicts.

NE/0921-3740
**CULTURAL DYNAMICS. *Ceased.*** Vol. 1, No. 1 (1988)-(1992). Periodical. English. Three times a year. E. J. Brill, Postbus 9000, 2300 PA Leiden Netherlands. **Tel** 011 31 71 312624, FAX 011 31 71 317532, telex 39296 BRILL NL. **ED** R. Pinxten. **CODEN** CUDYEH. **[CCC]. Circ:** 448.
**Desc:** A journal in philosophy and socio-cultural studies. It aims to be a forum for both theoretical and empirical studies that focus on dynamic aspects of socio-cultural phenomena and on dynamic models and theories. It includes special issues and invites papers on processes, changes, evolutions and histories of knowledge, social and cultural phenomena.
**Ind/Abst** Anthropol. Lit.; Linguist. Lang. Behav. Abstr.; Soc. Plann. Policy Dev. Abstr.; Sociol. Abstr.

US
**CULTURAL SURVIVAL REPORT. Added/Corp** Cultural Survival Inc. Cornell University. Latin American Studies Program. (198?)-. Monographic series. English. Price varies per volume. Cultural Survival Inc, 11 Divinity Avenue, Cambridge MA 02138. ***Continues*** *Occasional Paper (Cultural Survival Inc.), 0892-8843.*
**Ind/Abst** Hum. Rights Intern. Rep.

US/1048-4876
**CULTURE & AGRICULTURE. See** Agriculture.

●US/1063-634X
**CULTUREFRONT (NEW YORK, N.Y.). See** Humanities.

CN/0710-8559
**CULTURES CANADA : NEWSLETTER OF THE CANADIAN CONSULTATIVE COUNCIL ON MULTICULTURALISM. *Title Change.* Added/Corp** Canada. Multiculturalism Directorate. Canadian Consultative Council on Multiculturalism. **VFOAT** Canada Multiculturel. Vol. 1, No. 1 (Jan. 1980)-(19??). Periodical. English (French). ir. Multiculturalism & Citizenship, Canada Communications Branch, Ottawa Ontario K1A 0M5 Canada. **Tel** (819)994-0055. **Circ:** 18,000. ***Continued by*** *Together.*

CN/1185-9938
**CULTURES INTERNATIONAL.** (CULTURES INTERNATIONAL : THE QUARTERLY NEWSLETTER OF INTERNATIONAL CULTURAL RELATIONS.). [Cult. int.]. **Added/Corp** Canada. International Cultural Relations. **VFOAT** Cultures et le Monde : Trimestriel des Relations Culturelles Internationales. **VAT** Cultures et le Monde. Vol. 1, No. 1 (Winter 1991)-. Newsletter. English (French). qt. **DD** 303.48/271/005.

CN/1185-9938
**CULTURES INTERNATIONAL.** (CULTURES ET LE MONDE : TRIMESTRIEL DES RELATIONS CULTURELLES INTERNATIONALES.). [Cult. int.]. **Added/Corp** Canada. Relations Culturelles Internationales. **VFOAT** Cultures International : The Quarterly Newsletter of International Cultural Relations. **VAT** Cultures et le Monde. Vol. 1, No 1 (Winter 1991)-. Periodical. French (English). qt. **DD** 303.48/271/005.

BE
**CULTUUR EN MIGRATIE.** sm. 450F. Cultuur en Migratie VZW, Emile Delvastraat 35, 1020 Brussels Belgium.

SP/1017-4559
**CURRENT LEGAL SOCIOLOGY.** (1990)-. Periodical. English. sa. 6200ptas. Onati International Institute, Apartado Postal 28, 20560 Onati Guipuzcoa Spain. **Tel** 011 34 43 783064. **UDC** 301 :34. Index available. **Circ:** 500.

# Sociology

**Desc:** Bibliographic references to articles contained within serial publications analyzed by the Documentation Centre.

US/0090-824X
**CURRENT OPINION.** V. 1- Aug. 1972-. Periodical. English. mo. Roper Public Opinion Research Center, Williams College, PO Box 676, Williamstown MA 01267. **LC** HM261; .C86. **DD** 301.15/42/05.

US/0278-1204
**CURRENT PERSPECTIVES IN SOCIAL THEORY.** [Curr. perspect. soc. theory]. Vol. 1 (1980)-. English. ir. $73.25. JAI Press Inc., 55 Old Post Road, Suite 2, PO Box 1678, Greenwich CT 06836-1678. **Tel** (203)661-7602, FAX (203)661-0792. **ED** Ben Agger. **LC** HM1; .C87. **DD** 301/.01/8. **[CCC].** cum. index. Documents available from The Genuine Article.
**Ind/Abst** Linguist. Lang. Behav. Abstr.; Res. Alert [Full Cov.]; Soc. Plann. Policy Dev. Abstr.; Sociol. Abstr. [Full Cov.].

UK/0011-3921
**CURRENT SOCIOLOGY (PARIS, FRANCE).** (CURRENT SOCIOLOGY.). [Curr. sociol.]. **Added/Corp** Unesco. International Sociological Association. **VFOAT** Sociologie Contemporaine. Vol. 1 (1952)-. Periodical. English (French). tq. £92.00 (one year), £184.00 (two year). Sage Publications Ltd., 6 Bonhill Street, London EC2A 4PU, UK. **Tel** 071 374 0645, FAX 071 374 8741, telex 296207 SAGE G. **ED** William Outhwaite. **LC** Z7161; .C8. **NLM** W1 CU81N. **Bk Rev**. **Ad Acc**. Acid Free. Documents available from The Genuine Article, UMI Article Clearinghouse. *Continued in part by International Bibliography of Sociology*.
**Desc:** Focuses upon the theory, research and methodology of contemporary international sociology. Each issue is devoted to a substantial Trend Report on a particular sociological topic.
**Ind/Abst** ABC POL SCI (19??-19??); Acad. Abstr. Full Text Elite (Jan. 1992-); Acad. Abstr. (Jan. 1992-); Acad. Search (Jan. 1992-); Appl. Soc. Sci. Index Abstr.; Curr. Contents Soc. Behav. Sci.; Expand. Acad. Index (1989-); INFO-SOUTH Abstr.; Int. Bibliogr. Sociol.; Int. Labour Doc.; J. Plan. Lit.; LABORDOC; Linguist. Lang. Behav. Abstr.; Mag. Search; Middle East Abstr. Index; Newsp. Period. Abstr. (1991-); Res. Alert [Full Cov.]; Soc. Plann. Policy Dev. Abstr.; Soc. Sci. Source (Jan. 1992-); Soc. Sci. Index; Soc. Sci. Index Fulltext (Winter 1988-) [Full Txt.]; Sociol. Abstr. [Full Cov.].

CN/0715-7045
**CURRENTS (TORONTO).** (CURRENTS.). [Currents]. **Added/Corp** Urban Alliance on Race Relations. **VFOAT** Courants. Vol. 1, No. 1 (Winter 1983)-. Periodical. English (French). Four times a year. 32.71Can$ (institutions), 23.36Can$ (individuals) Canada; 40.00Can$ other. Urban Alliance for Race Relations, 675 King Street West, Suite 202, Toronto Ontario M5V 1M9 Canada. **Tel** (416)363-2607. **DD** 305.8/00971. **Bk Rev**. **Circ:** 1,000.
**Desc:** Contains readings in race relations. Analyses of research, initiatives, and ideas in race relations of particular interest to public, academic, and voluntary sectors.
**Ind/Abst** Hum. Rights Intern. Rep.

CN/0316-6791
**CUSSNEWS.** **Main/Corp** Canadian Institute of International Affairs. Advisory Committee on Canada-United States Studies. V. 1- Feb. 1974-. English. Three times a year. $4.25. Canadian Institute of International Affairs, 31 Wellesley Street East, Toronto Ontario M4Y 1G9 Canada. **Tel** (416)979-1851. **DD** 301.29/71/073.

DK/0905-5908
**DANSK SOCIOLOGI.** **Added/Corp** Dansk Sociologforening. (1990)-. Periodical. Danish. qt. kr484.00 Scandinavia; kr504.00 Europe; kr584.00 other. Frydenlund Grafisk Kommunika, Vesterbrokade 20, DK 1782 Copenhagen Denmark. **Tel** 011 45 31 242438. **LC** HN541; .D36. **CODEN** DSOCE3.

CN/0705-7032
**DAVANTAGE (POINTE-CLAIRE).** (DAVANTAGE.). V. 1- May 1978-. Periodical. French. mo. 0.60Can$ per no. Club STEP International, 400 Route 2-20, Point-Claire Quebec H9S 3X7 Canada. **DD** 301.43/15/09714.

PE
**DEBATES EN SOCIOLOGIA.** **Added/Corp** Pontificia Universidad Catolica del Peru. Departamento de Ciencias Sociales. Vol. 1 (Feb. 1977)-. Periodical. Spanish. ir. price varies per volume. Pontificia Universidad Catolica del Peru, Fondo Editorial, Apartado 1761, Lima 100 Peru. **Tel** 011 51 14 622540 or, 622220 ext. 220. **ED** Gonzalo Portocarrero. Index available. cum. index. **Bk Rev**. **Ad Acc**. **Pr Rev**. ctrl circ.

SP/0214-6908
**DELINCUENCIA VALENCIA.** [Delincuencia Valencia]. **VFOAT** Delinquency (Valencia). (1989)-. Periodical. Multiple languages. tq. Universidad de Valencia / Psicologia, Facultad de Psicologia, Avenida Blasco Ibanez 21, 46010 Valencia Spain. **Tel** 011 34 6 3864823. **UDC** 343.9.
**Ind/Abst** PsycINFO (1989-); PsycLit.

CN/0822-6733
**DEPARTMENTAL WORKING PAPER - CARLETON UNIVERSITY. DEPARTMENT OF SOCIOLOGY AND ANTHROPOLOGY.** See Anthropology.

UK/0956-9359
**DEVELOPMENTS IN SOCIOLOGY.** [Dev. sociol.]. (1986)-. English. an. £30.00. Causeway Press Ltd., PO Box 13, 129 New Court Way, Lancashire L39 5HP England. **Tel** 011 44 695 76048 or 77360. **DD** 301.

US/0163-9625
**DEVIANT BEHAVIOR.** See Psychology.

PN/0046-0206
**DIALOGO SOCIAL.** *Suspended*. See History(General).

CN/0703-2145
**DIALOGUE ORIENTAL GAZETTE.** **Added/Corp** Centre de Culture Dialogue Oriental. **VAT** Dialogue Oriental. Vol. 1 (Apr. 1974)-. Periodical. English (French). ir. Centre De Culture Dialogue Oriental, Suite 5, 5336 Queen Mary Road, Montreal Quebec H3K 1T8. **DD** 301.45/11/920714281.

FR/0242-8962
**DIALOGUE PARIS. 196?.** (DIALOGUE RECHERCHES CLINIQUES ET SOCIOLOGIQUES SUR LE COUPLE ET LA FAMILLE.). [Dialogue Paris, 196?]. **Added/Corp** Association Francaise des Centres de Consultation Conjugale. (196?)-. Periodical. French. qt (Mar., June, Oct., Dec.). 274.24F France; 380.00F other. Association Francaise Centers Consultation Conjugale, Revue Dialogue 44 rue Danton, 94270 L Kremlin Bicetre France. **Tel** 011 33 1 46708844, FAX 011 33 1 46712460. **UDC** 362.17.

US
**DIRASAT THAQAFIYAH.** **VFOAT** Cultural Studies Quarterly. Vol. 1 No. 1 (1991)-. Periodical. Arabic. qt. World Information Services, Inc., 2020 Pennsylvania Avenue NW, Suite 404, Washington DC 20006.

US/0362-4366
**DIRECTORY : COMMUNITY DEVELOPMENT EDUCATION AND TRAINING PROGRAMS THROUGHOUT THE WORLD.** **VFOAT** Community Development Education and Training Programs Throughout the World. Directory. English. $3.50 North America; $4.50 other. Community Development Society / Columbia, c/o Kenneth E Pigg, 209 Sociology, University of Missouri, Columbia MO 65211. **Tel** (314)882-4350. **ED** Gene Robertson. **LC** HN49.C6; D56. **DD** 301.35/07/11.

●US
**DIRECTORY OF MEMBERS / THE AMERICAN SOCIOLOGICAL ASSOCIATION.** **Main/Corp** American Sociological Association. (1992). Directory. English. be. **NLM** HM 51; A512d. *Continues American Sociological Association. Biographical Directory of Members, 1052-7184.*
**Desc:** Includes information on sociologists and sociology.

US/1055-6133
**DISCLOSURE (LEXINGTON, KY.).** (DISCLOSURE.). [DisClosure]. **Added/Corp** University of Kentucky. Committee on Social Theory. No. 1 (Fall 1991)-. Periodical. English. sa. $25.00 (institutions). University of Kentucky Committee on Social Theory, 1415 Patterson Office Tower, Lexington KY 40506-0027. **DD** 305.

●US/1064-7430
**DIVERSITY & DIVISION.** (DIVERSITY & DIVISION : A CRITICAL JOURNAL OF RACE AND CULTURE.). [Divers. div.]. **Added/Corp** Madison Center for Educational Affairs. **VFOAT** Diversity and Division. Vol. 2, No. 1 (Fall 1992)-. Periodical. English. qt. $13.00 US; $20.00 other. Madison Center for Educational Affairs, 1155 15th Street, Washington DC 20005. **Tel** (800)225-2862, (202)838-1801. **ED** David S Bernstein. **LC** E184.A1; D55. **DD** 305.8/00973. Index available. cum. index. **Bk Rev**, (Qty: 12). **Ad Acc**, **Adv Mgr:** Jeff Muir, **Tel** (202)833-1801. **Circ:** 10,000. available on an online database from Internet. *Continues Diversity (Washington, D.C.), 1061-7981.*

AT/0812-0102
**DIVERSITY EAST MELBOURNE.** [Diversity East Melb.]. (1983)-. Periodical. English. sa. 15.00Aus$. Catholic Education Office, PO Box 146, East Melbourne VIC 3002 Australia. **Tel** 03 665-0333, FAX 03 665-4417. **ED** Maria G. Puddu. **DD** 370.19'342'09945. **Circ:** 1,000.
**Desc:** Publishes issues of language and culture.

GW/0342-040X
**DOKUMENTATIONSDIENST AFRIKA. AUSGEWAHLTE NEUERE LITERATUR.** See General Interest-Abstracting, Bibliographies and Statistics.

IT
**DOLENTIUM HOMINUM : JOURNAL OF THE PONTIFICAL COUNCIL FOR PASTORAL ASSISTANCE TO HEALTH CARE WORKERS.** Italian (English; summaries and/or abstracts in Spanish, French and German). Three times a year. L40.000. Pont Con Pastor Operat Sanita, Via Conciliazione 3, 00193 Rome Italy.

FR/0758-6531
**DONNEES SOCIALES.** **Main/Corp** Institut National de la Statistique et des -Etudes -Economiques (France). (1973)-. French. ir. price varie per volume. CNGP Insee, BP 2718, 1 rue V Auriol, F 80027 Amiens, Cedex 1 France. **Tel** 011 33 22 927322. **LC** HN421; .F73a; HC271; .A218 subser.

US/1053-0797
**DREAMING (NEW YORK, N.Y.).** See Biology-Physiology.

US
**DURKHEIM STUDIES.** (19??)-. Periodical. English. an. $10.00 (one year), $18.00 (two year), $26.00 (three year), individual, $20.00 (one year), $36.00 (two year), $52.00 (three year), institution. University of Illinois / Department of Sociology, 326 Lincoln Hall, 702 South Wright Street, Urbana IL 61808. **Tel** (217)333-1950, FAX (217)333-5225. **ED** Bob Jones. **CODEN** DUSTEK.
**Ind/Abst** Soc. Plann. Policy Dev. Abstr.

US/0741-0263
**DYNAMIC (NEW YORK, N.Y.).** See Political Science.

AT/0310-222x
**EARTH GARDEN.** (Feb. 1976)-. Periodical. English. Four times a year (Mar., June, Sept., Dec.). 19.00Aus$ Australia; 29.00Aus$ other. Earth Garden Magazine, RMB 427, Trentham Vic 3458 Australia. **Tel** FAX 011 61 54 241743. **ED** Allan Thomas Gray. **Bk Rev**, (Qty: 20). **Ad Acc**, **Adv Mgr:** Judith Gray, **Tel** (054)241399. **Circ:** 18,000 (ctrl).
**Desc:** The Australian journal of self-sufficiency, with articles on growing food organically, building with natural materials (mudbricks, stone, timber) and renewable sources of energy. We are settling a vast, arid continent with 20th century new age people.

SZ
**ECHOES.** See Religion and Theology.

US/0013-0079
**ECONOMIC DEVELOPMENT AND CULTURAL CHANGE.** See Economics.

FR/0013-0567
**ECONOMIES ET SOCIETES.** See Economics.

BL
**EDUCACAO & [I.E. E] SOCIEDADE.** See Education.

AT/0726-2655
**EDUCATION AND SOCIETY (MELBOURNE).** See Education.

UA/0752-4412
**EGYPTE/MONDE ARABE.** See Political Science.

US/0882-3316
**EMERGING PATTERNS OF WORK AND COMMUNICATIONS IN AN INFORMATION AGE.** [Emerg. patterns work commun. inf. age]. No. 1-. Monographic series. English. Price varies per volume. Greenwood Press Inc., PO Box 5007, Westport CT 06881-5007. **Tel** (203)226-3571, FAX (203)222-1502. **DD** 658.

US/0194-3642
**EMPLOYMENT BULLETIN (AMERICAN SOCIOLOGICAL ASSOCIATION : 1976).** See Occupations and Careers.

US/0013-9165
**ENVIRONMENT AND BEHAVIOR.** See Environmental Issues-Ecology.

UK/0301-0643
**EPOCH (CROYDON).** (EPOCH.). [Epoch]. **Added/Corp** Howey Foundation. Vol. 1 (Autumn 1972)-. Periodical. English. qt. $3.07. Howey Foundation, 2 A Lebanon Road, Croydon Surrey CR0 6UR England. **LC** GF1; .E66. **DD** 301.31/05. **NLM** W1 EP465.

FR/0999-7822
**ESPACE SOCIAL EUROPEEN PARIS.** (ESPACE SOCIAL EUROPEEN.). (1989)-. Periodical. French. Forty-eight times a year. 1224.29F institutions; 617.04F institutions. OEPS, 24 rue du Sentier, F 75002 Paris France. **Tel** 011 33 1 40416843. **UDC** 36. *Continues Espace Social (Paris), 0994-1975.*

SP
**ESPANA, PANORAMICA SOCIAL.** **Main/Corp** Spain. Instituto Nacional de Estadistica.

(1974)-. Spanish. ir. Instituto Nacional de Estadistica, Avda Generalisimo 91, Madrid 91 Spain. **LC** HN584; .S65a. **DD** 309.1/46/082.

UK/0959-4779
**ESSAYS IN COGNITIVE PSYCHOLOGY.** [Essays cong. psychol.]. (1988)-. Monographic series. English. ir. Price varies per volume. Lawrence Erlbaum Associates, 365 Broadway, Suite 102, Hillsdale NJ 07642. **Tel** (201)666-4110, (800)926-6579, FAX (201)666-2394. **ED** David C. Plaut.

US/1047-5257
**ESSAYS IN PUBLIC WORKS HISTORY.** [Essays public works hist.]. **Added/Corp** Public Works Historical Society. **VFOAT** Public Works History. No. 1 (June 1976)-. Monographic series. English. an. $5.00. Public Works Historical Society, 1313 East 60th Street, Chicago IL 60637. **Tel** (312) 667-2200. **DD** 363.
**Ind/Abst** Am. Hist. Life (1985-).

CR/0303-9676
**ESTUDIOS SOCIALES CENTROAMERICANOS.** ***Suspended.*** [Estud. soc. centroam.]. **Added/Corp** Programa Centroamericano de Desarrollo de las Ciencias Sociales. Vol. 1 (Jan./Apr. 1972)-No. 56 (1991). Periodical. Spanish. Three times a year. $23.00. Confederacion Universitaria Centroamericana, Apartado 37 2060 Facio, San Jose Costa Rica. **Tel** 011 506 252744. **Pr Rev.**
**Ind/Abst** Am. Hist. Life (1979-?); HAPI Hisp. Am. Period. Index; Int. Labour Doc.; LABORDOC.

MX/0185-4186
**ESTUDIOS SOCIOLOGICOS.** [Estud. sociol.]. (1982)-. Periodical. Spanish. qt. $55.00 (institutions), $38.00 (individuals) US & Canada; $64.00 (institutions), $30.00 (individuals) Latin America; $64.00 (institutions), $46.00 (individuals) other. Colegio de Mexico AC, Camino Al Ajusco No 20, 10740 Mexico DF Mexico. **Tel** 011 52 5 6455955 Ext. 3133, telex 1777585 COLME. **DD** 301.
**Ind/Abst** Soc. Plann. Policy Dev. Abstr.; Sociol. Abstr. (1988-).

US/0425-4090
**ET AL.** Vol. 1 (Fall 1967)-. Periodical. English. Three times a year. **LC** HM1; .E7.

FR/0014-2182
**ETUDES RURALES.** **Added/Corp** Ecole des Hautes Etudes en Sciences Sociales. No. 57 (Jan./Mar. 1975)-. French. Four times a year. 380.00F (institutions), 255.00F (individuals) France; 440.00F (institutions), 255.00 (individuals) other. Dunod Gauthier Villars, 15 rue Gossin, 92543 Montrouge cedex France. **Tel** 011 33 1 46 56 52 66, FAX 011 33 1 46 57 40 69. **(Subscription address:** Centrale des Revues, 11 rue Gossin, 92543 Montrouge Cedex France.**)** ***Continues*** *Paris. Ecoles Pratique des Hautes Etudes. Section des Sciences Economiques et Sociales. Etudes Rurales.*
**Ind/Abst** Agrofor. Abstr. (1991-); Am. Hist. Life (1961-); Field Crop Abstr.; Geogr. Abstr. Human Geogr.; Grasslands For. Abstr.; Hortic. Abstr.; Int. Bibliogr. Sociol.; Int. Dev. Abstr.; Int. Labour Doc.; LABORDOC; Point Repere (1979-1980); Rice Abstr.; Rural Dev. Abstr.; Soc. Plann. Policy Dev. Abstr.; Sociol. Abstr.; Soils Fert.; SportSearch; World Agric. Econ.

FR/0249-6356
**ETUDES SOCIOCRITIQUES. CO-TEXTES.** [Etud. sociocrit., Co-textes]. **VFOAT** Co-Textes (Montpellier). (1980)-. Monographic series. French. sa. 100.00F (1 year), 170.00F (2 year) France; 120.00F (1 year), 205.00F (2 year) other. Centre d'Etudes Sociocritiques, Univ Paul Vallery, BP 5043, 34032 Montpellier Cedex France. **Tel** 011 33 67 142326. **UDC** 8.
**Ind/Abst** MLA Int. Bibl. Books Artic. Mod. Lang. Lit.

UK/0952-391X
**EUROPEAN JOURNAL OF INTERCULTURAL STUDIES.** **See** Ethnic Interests.

UK/0046-2772
**EUROPEAN JOURNAL OF SOCIAL PSYCHOLOGY.** [Eur. j. soc. psychol.]. Vol. 1 (1971)-. Periodical. English (summaries and/or abstracts in French and German). bm (Feb., Apr., June, Aug., Oct., Dec.). $425.00. John Wiley & Sons Ltd., Baffins Lane, Chichester West Sussex PO19 1UD England. **Tel** 0243 779777, FAX 0243 776128 BTG:JWP001, telex 86290 WIBOOKG. **(Subscription address:** John Wiley / Philadelphia, PO Box 7247, Philadelphia PA 19170.**) ED** Nick Emler. **LC** HM251; .E8. **DD** 301.1/05. **NLM** W1 EU72EK. **CODEN** EJSPA6. **[CCC]. Pr Rev. Circ:** 900. available on microfilm and microfiche from University Microfilms International (UMI). Documents available from The Genuine Article.
**Desc:** Promotes communication between social psychology researchers in Europe and provides a bridge between European and other research traditions. Articles typically fundamental in nature, both in the theoretical and empirical domain. The multitude of approaches stimulates progress toward a better understanding of the material discussed.
**Ind/Abst** Appl. Soc. Sci. Index Abstr.; Commun. Abstr. (?-?); Curr. Contents Soc. Behav. Sci.; Int. Bibliogr. Sociol.; Middle East Abstr. Index; Multicult. Educ. Abstr.; Psychol. Abstr. (1971-); PsycINFO; PsycLit; Res. Alert [Full Cov.]; Soc. Plann. Policy Dev. Abstr.; Soc. Sci. Cit. Index [Full Cov.]; Sociol. Abstr.; Sociol. Educ. Abstr.; Spec. Educ. Needs Abstr.; Stud. Women Abstr.

UK/1046-3283
**EUROPEAN REVIEW OF SOCIAL PSYCHOLOGY.** [Eur. rev. soc. psychol.]. (1990)-. English. an (March). $90.00. John Wiley & Sons Ltd., Baffins Lane, Chichester West Sussex PO19 1UD England. **Tel** 0243 779777, FAX 0243 776128 BTG:JWP001, telex 86290 WIBOOKG. **(Subscription address:** John Wiley / Philadelphia, PO Box 7247, Philadelphia PA 19170.**) ED** Wolfgang Stroebe and Miles Hewstone. **LC** HM251; .E82. **CODEN** ERSPEW. **[CCC].** available on microfilm and microfiche from University Microfilms International (UMI).
**Desc:** Reflects the dynamism of social psychology in Europe and the attention now paid to European ideas and research. A major purpose is to further the international exchange of ideas by providing an English language source for substantial accounts of theoretical and empirical work that have not been previously published in English.

UK/0266-7215
**EUROPEAN SOCIOLOGICAL REVIEW.** **VFOAT** ESR. Vol. 1, No. 1 (May 1985)-. Periodical. English. Three times a year. £62.00 UK and Europe; $115.00 other. Oxford University Press, Walton Street, Oxford OX2 6DP England. **Tel** 011 44 865 56767, FAX 011 44 865 267773, telex 837330 OXPRES G. **(Subscription address:** Oxford University Press / USA, Journals Marketing Department, Oxford University Press, 2001 Evans Road, Cary NC 27513.**) ED** Karl Ulrich Mayer, John H. Goldthorpe, Hannu Uusitalo. **LC** HM1; .E78. **DD** 301/.05. **[CCC]. Bk Rev. Ad Acc.** available on microfilm and microfiche from University Microfilms International (UMI).
**Desc:** All fields of sociology, aiming primarily to present papers in which research expertise is combined with substantive and theoretical significance.
**Ind/Abst** Appl. Soc. Sci. Index Abstr.; Crim. Justice Abstr.; Int. Bibliogr. Sociol.; Int. Polit. Sci. Abstr.; Soc. Plann. Policy Dev. Abstr.; Soc. Sci. Cit. Index [Full Cov.]; Sociol. Abstr. (1985-) [Full Cov.].

IT
**EUROPEAN YEARBOOK IN THE SOCIOLOGY OF LAW.** **Added/Corp** Universita di Macerata. Facolta di Giurisprudenza. Institute of Sociology of Law for Europe. **VFOAT** European Year Book in the Sociology of Law; EYSL. (1988)-. English. an. L58000. Guiffre Editore Spa, Via Busto Arsizio 40, 20151 Milan Italy. **Tel** 011 39 2 38089200. **LC** K5; .U8. **DD** 340/.115/05. ***Continues*** *European Yearbook in Law and Sociology.*

US/0575-4577
**EVALUATION COMMENT.** **See** Education.

US/0193-841X
**EVALUATION REVIEW.** [Eval. rev.]. Vol. 4 (Feb. 1980)-. Periodical. English. bm (Feb., Apr., June, Aug., Oct., Dec.). $204.00. SAGE Periodical Press, 2455 Teller Road, Thousand Oaks CA 91320. **Tel** (805)499-0721, FAX (805)499-0871, telex 100799. **ED** Richard A. Berk (University of California, Los Angeles). **LC** HM1; .E8. **DD** 300/.72. **NLM** W1 EV131HC. **[CCC]. Pr Rev. Acid Free.** available on microfilm and microfiche from University Microfilms International (UMI). Documents available from The Genuine Article. ***Continues*** *Evaluation Quarterly, 0145-4692.*
**Desc:** A forum for researchers, planners and policymakers engaged in the development, implementation and utilization of evaluation studies. Reflects a wide range of methodological and conceptual approaches to evaluation and its many applications.
**Ind/Abst** Commun. Abstr.; Crim. Justice Abstr.; Cumul. Index Nurs. Allied Health Lit.; Curr. Contents Soc. Behav. Sci.; Curr. Index J. Educ.; Curr. Law Index (1980-); Educ. Adm. Abstr.; Highw. Res. Abstr.; Hum. Resour. Abstr.; Int. Bibliogr. Sociol.; Leg. Resour. Index (1980-); LegalTrac (1980-); Middle East Abstr. Index; PAIS Int. Print (1991-); Psychol. Abstr. (1980-); PsycINFO; PsycLit; Res. Alert [Full Cov.]; Risk Abstr. (19??-19??); Sage Public Adm. Abstr.; Sage Urban Stud. Abstr; Soc. Plann. Policy Dev. Abstr.; Soc. Sci. Cit. Index [Full Cov.]; Soc. Work Abstr. [Select. Cov.]; Sociol. Abstr.; Sociol. Educ. Abstr.; Soc. Res. Methodol. Abstr. (1980-); Urban Aff. Abstr.

GW/0014-4045
**EXCERPTA BOTANICA. SECTIO B. SOCIOLOGICA.** **Added/Corp** International Association for Plant Taxonomy. **VFOAT** Sociologica. Vol. 1 (1959)-. Periodical. Multiple languages (English, French and German). Four times a year. DM464.00 Germany; DM480.00 other. Gustav Fischer Verlag Stuttgart, Postfach 720143, Wollgrasweg 49, D 70577 Stuttgart Germany. **Tel** 011 49 711 458030, FAX 0711-4580334, telex 2627-7111488. **(Subscription address:** VCH Publishers Inc., 303 Northwest 12th Avenue, Journals Department, Deerfield FL 33442.**) LC** Z5354.P7; E96; QK911. **DD** 016.5815/247. **[CCC].**
**Ind/Abst** Life Sci. Collect. (1985-).

GW
**EXILFORSCHUNG.** V. 1 (1983)-. German. an. Professor Dr Claus-Dieter Krohn, Weidenstieg 9, W-2000 Hamburg 20 Germany. **Tel** 089/432929. **LC** HV640; .E97. **Ad Acc.**

UK/0954-3082
**EXPLORATIONS IN SOCIOLOGY.** [Explor. soc.]. (1970)-. Monographic series. English. ir. Price varies per volume. Gower Publishing Co. Ltd., Gower House, Croft Road, Aldershot, Hampshire GU11 3HR England. **Tel** 011 44 252 331551, FAX 011 44 252 344405, telex 858001. **DD** 301.

US
**FACTS ABOUT TVA OPERATIONS.** **Main/Corp** Tennessee Valley Authority. **Added/Corp** Tennessee Valley Authority. **VAT** Facts About Tennessee Valley Authority Operations. (19??)-. Periodical. English. an. US Tennessee Valley Authority, W12D140 C K, 400 Commerce Avenue, Knoxville TN 37902. **LC** HN79.A135; A3. **DD** 627.1.

•US/0195-4520
**FIELD POLL, THE.** **Added/Corp** Field Institute. (1992)-. English. $150.00 (library); $250.00 (other). The Field Institute, 550 Kearny Street, San Francisco CA 94108-2527. **Tel** (415)392-5763, FAX (415)434-2541. **ED** Mark DiCamillo & Merrfield. **LC** HN90.P8; C35. **Circ:** 300 (ctrl). ***Continues*** *California Poll.*
**Desc:** A unique, statewide public opinion news feature service covering a wide range of political and social topics.

LI/0235-7186
**FILOSOFIJA, SOCIOLOGIJA / LIETUVOS MOKSLU AKADEMIJA.** **See** Philosophy.

CN/0824-197X
**FIRST READING.** [First read.]. **Added/Corp** Edmonton Social Planning Council. Vol. 1, No. 1 (Oct. 1982)-. Periodical. English. bm. comes with membership. Edmonton Social Planning Council, 9912 106th Street, Suite 41, Edmonton Alberta T5K 1C5 Canada. **Tel** (403)423-2031. **ED** Joseph Miller. **DD** 361.6/1/097123. **Bk Rev. Circ:** 1,000 (ctrl).
**Desc:** Analysis and discussion of social policy issues.

US/0740-0195
**FOCUS - JOINT CENTER FOR POLITICAL STUDIES.** **See** Ethnic Interests.

SZ/0740-9710
**FOOD & FOODWAYS.** [Food foodways]. **VFOAT** Food and Foodways. Vol. 1, No. 1 (1985)-. Periodical. English (French). Four times a year. $348.00 (academic institutions), $521.00 (corporate institutions). Harwood Academic Publishers, PO Box 90, Reading RG1 8JL England. **Tel** 011 44 734 560080. **(Subscription address:** Harwood Academic Publishers, PO Box 786, Cooper Station, New York NY 10276.**) LC** TX341; .F695. **DD** 306.3. **NLM** W1; FO426. **CODEN** FOFWEC. **[CCC].**
**Desc:** Explores the powerful but often subtle ways in which food has shaped and continues to shape our lives socially, economically, politically, mentally, and morally.
**Ind/Abst** AGRICOLA; Int. Bibliogr. Sociol.; Rice Abstr.

US/0749-6931
**FOOTNOTES (WASHINGTON, D.C.).** (FOOTNOTES.). [Footnotes]. **Added/Corp** American Sociological Association. **VFOAT** Foot Notes. (1973)-. Periodical. English. ir (9 issues). $25.00 US; $33.00 other. American Sociological Association, 1722 North Street Northwest, Washington DC 20036-2981. **Tel** (202)833-3410, FAX (202)785-0146. **ED** William V. d'Antonio. **LC** HM1; .F66. **DD** 301/.05. **Ad Acc. Circ:** 13,000.
**Desc:** This newsletter contains departmental news, activities of the association, the Washington office, news of the profession, plus the association's office reports and proceedings.
**Ind/Abst** Soc. Plann. Policy Dev. Abstr.; Sociol. Abstr. (?-?).

GW
**FORSCHUNGSPROJEKTE SOZIALISATION UND SOZIALPAEDAGOGIK.** **See** Education-Special Education and Rehabilitation.

SW/0284-351X
**FORSKNINGSRAPPORT (STOCKHOLMS UNIVERSITET. SOCIOLOGISKA INSTITUTIONEN).** (FORSKNINGSRAPPORT / SOCIOLOGISKA INSTITUTIONEN.). (1987)-. Monographic series. Swedish (English). Price varies per volume. Stockholm Universitet, Sociologiska Institutionen, Stockholm Sweden.

FR/1157-3716
**FRANCIS BULLETIN SIGNALETIQUE. 521, SOCIOLOGIE.** **Added/Corp** Institut de l'Information Scientifique et Technique (France). Sciences Humaines et Sociales. **VFOAT** Sociologie; Bulletin Signaletique. Sociologie. Vol. 45, No. 1 (1991)-. Bulletin.

French. qt (4 issues). 470.00F France; 495.00F other. CNRS / Institut d'Information Scientifique et Technique, (Centre National de la Recherche Scientifique), 15 Quai Anatole France, Paris 75700 France. **Tel** 011 33 1 47531515, telex 299 356 F. **(Subscription address:** Institut de l'Information Scientifique et Technique Diffusion, 2 Allee du Parc de Brabois, 54514 Vandoeuvre, Nancy France) **LC** H1; .A122. Index available (free). available on CD-ROM. ***Continues*** *Bulletin Signaletique. 521, Sociologie, 0765-1465.*

US/0736-9182
**FREE INQUIRY IN CREATIVE SOCIOLOGY.** [Free inq. creat. sociol.]. **Added/Corp** Sociology Consortium of Oklahoma. Oklahoma Sociology Association. Vol. 7 (May 1979)-. Periodical. English. Twice a year. $20.00 US & Canada; $23.00 other. University of Central Oklahoma Department of Sociology, 100 North University Drive, Edmond OK 73034-0182. **Tel** (405)341-2980 ext. 5626, FAX (405)341-4964. **ED** Dr. Joan Luxenburg. **LC** HM1; .F7. **DD** 301/.05. Index available (bound in second issue). **Ad Acc. Pr Rev. Circ:** 300. available on microfilm from University Microfilms International (UMI). ***Continues*** *Free Inquiry, 0886-1749.*
**Desc:** Articles from all areas of sociology. Cross cultural studies and studies of timely and controversial social issues are welcome. A variety of viewpoints of interest to the lay reader included.
**Ind/Abst** Middle East Abstr. Index; Soc. Plann. Policy Dev. Abstr.; Sociol. Abstr. [Full Cov.].

US/0882-1267
**FRENCH POLITICS AND SOCIETY. See** Political Science.

CC
**FU NU SHENG HUO (CHENG-CHOU SHIH, CHINA).** (FU NU SHENG HUO.). **VFOAT** Funu Sheng Huo. Periodical. Chinese. RMBY0.25. Post Office, Cheng-Chou, People's Republic of China. **LC** AP95.C4; F79. **DD** 305.4/0951.

II/0252-1873
**FUTURE (NEW DELHI, INDIA). See** Family and Marriage.

FR/0337-307X
**FUTURIBLES (PARIS).** (FUTURIBLES.). [Futuribles]. No. 40 (Jan. 1981)-. Periodical. French. Eleven times a year. 630.00F (France); 680.00F (other). Association Internationale Futuribles, 55 rue de Varenne, 75007 Paris France. **Tel** 11 33 1 42226310, FAX 42 22 65 54, telex 201220F. **ED** Futuribles Sarl. **LC** H3; .F88. **[CCC]**. Index available. cum. index. **Bk Rev. Ad Acc. Circ:** 3,000 (ctrl). ***Continues*** *Futuribles 2000 i.e. Deux Mille, 0337-307X.*
**Desc:** Journal of analysis, forecasting and future studies, including in-depth studies and information on opinions, facts and trends for the future.
**Ind/Abst** ABC POL SCI; Int. Labour Doc.; Int. Polit. Sci. Abstr.; LABORDOC; Leis. Recreat. Tour. Abstr.; PAIS Int. Print (1991-); Rural Dev. Abstr.; Selec. Coop. Index Manage. Period; Soc. Plann. Policy Dev. Abstr.; Sociol. Abstr.; World Agric. Econ.

US/0195-962X
**GALLUP POLL, THE.** (1971)-. English. an. $60.00. Scholarly Resources Inc., 104 Greenhill Avenue, Wilmington DE 19805. **Tel** (800)772-8937, (302)654-7713, FAX (302)654-3871. **ED** George H. Gallup. **LC** HN90.P8; G35. **DD** 303.3/8072/0973. Index available in last issue of volume--attached. **Circ:** 1,000.
**Desc:** Public opinion polls conducted by the Gallup Organization.

●CN/1197-4303
**GALLUP POLL (TORONTO. 1993).** (THE GALLUP POLL.). [Gallup poll]. **Added/Corp** Gallup Canada, Inc. (Aug. 19, 1993)-. Statistical Publication. English. Twice a week (Mon. & Thurs.). 550.00Can$. Gallup Canada Inc, 180 Bloor Street West, Toronto Ontario M5S 2V6 Canada. **Tel** (416)961-2811, FAX (416)961-3662, telex 0622361. **DD** 303.3/8711. ***Continues*** *Gallup Report (Toronto, Ont. : 1990), 1184-891X.*

US
**GALLUP REPORT, THE.** No. 184 (Jan. 1981)-. Periodical. English. mo. $45.00. Gallup Poll, PO Box 628, Princeton NJ 08542. **Tel** (609)924-9600. ***Continues*** *Gallup Opinion Index.*
**Ind/Abst** Expand. Acad. Index (1992-).

CN/1184-891X
**GALLUP REPORT (TORONTO. 1990).** ***Title Change.*** (THE GALLUP REPORT / GALLUP.). [Gallup rep.]. **Added/Corp** Gallup Canada, Inc. (Mar. 19, 1990)-(1993). Periodical. English. Twice a week (Mon. & Thurs.). Gallup Canada Inc, 180 Bloor Street West, Toronto Ontario M5S 2V6 Canada. **Tel** (416)961-2811, FAX (416)961-3662, telex 0622361. **DD** 303.3/8711. ***Continues*** *Gallup, 0834-9061.* ***Continued by*** *Gallup Poll (Toronto, Ont. : 1993), 1197-4303.*

●US/1061-5326
**GANG JOURNAL, THE. See** Law-Law Enforcement and Criminology.

US/0745-6468
**GARTH ANALYSIS, THE.** [Garth anal.]. Vol. 1, No. 1 (June 1982)-. Periodical. English. bm. $295.00. The Garth Analysis, 1501 3rd Avenue, New York NY 10028. **LC** HN90.P8; G38. **DD** 303.3/8/0973.

US/1047-4463
**GAUNTLET.** (GAUNTLET : EXPLORING THE LIMITS OF FREE EXPRESSION.). [Gauntlet]. (1990)-. Periodical. English. Twice a year. $12.95. Gauntlet, 309 Powell Road, Springfield PA 19064. **Tel** (215)328-5476. **DD** 363.
**Ind/Abst** Hum. Rights Intern. Rep.

UK/0968-6673
**GENDER, WORK AND ORGANISATION.** (19??)-. Academic Scholarly Publication. English. qt. $145.00 North America; £105.00 other. Basil Blackwell Publishers Ltd, 108 Cowley Road, Oxford 0X4 1JF England. **Tel** 011 44 865 791100, FAX 011 44 865 791347, telex 837022 OXBOOK G. **(Subscription address:** Blackwell Publishers / UK, Marston Book Services, PO Box 87, Oxford OX2 0DT England.**)**

US/0898-5928
**GENERATIONAL JOURNAL, THE.** ***Suspended.*** Vol. 1, No. 1 (April 15, 1988)-Suspended. Periodical. English. qt. $39.00 individuals, $29.00 government, $19.00 libraries. Americans Generational Equity, 608 Massachusetts Avenue NE, Washington DC 20002. **LC** HV85; .G45. **DD** 361/.973. ctrl circ.

SZ/0016-6774
**GENEVE-AFRIQUE.** ***Ceased.*** [Geneve-Afr.]. **VFOAT** Geneva-Africa; Acta Africana; Geneve Afrique. Vol. 1 (1962)-Ceased with Vol. 30, No. 2 (Jan. 1993). Periodical. French (English and French). sa. Institut Universite d'Etudes du Developpement, 24 rue Rothschild, Casa Postale 136, CH-1211 Geneva 21 Switzerland. **Tel** 011 41 22 7315940, FAX 011 41 22 7384416, telex 22810 IUED-CH, . **ED** Laurent Monnier. **LC** DT1; .G44. Index available. **Bk Rev. Ad Acc. Circ:** 1,500.
**Desc:** Aims to promote dialogue and scientific exchanges between Africa and Switzerland on an interdisciplinary basis.
**Ind/Abst** ABC POL SCI; Am. Hist. Life (1970-199?); Anthropol. Index; Geogr. Abstr. Phys. Geogr. (?-?); Hum. Rights Intern. Rep.; Int. Bibliogr. Sociol.; Int. Dev. Abstr.; Int. Labour Doc.; Int. Polit. Sci. Abstr.; MLA Int. Bibl. Books Artic. Mod. Lang. Lit.; Sage Public Adm. Abstr. (?-?).

GH/0435-9380
**GHANA JOURNAL OF SOCIOLOGY.** **Added/Corp** Ghana Sociological Association. Vol. 1 (1965)-. Periodical. English. Twice a year (Jan. & Sept.). University of Ghana / Department of Sociology, Legon Ghana West Africa. **DD** 301.
**Ind/Abst** Soc. Plann. Policy Dev. Abstr.; Sociol. Abstr. (?-?).

GW/0072-4874
**GOTTINGER ABHANDLUNGEN ZUR SOZIOLOGIE.** Vol. 1 (1957)-. Monographic series. German. ir. Price varies per volume. Ferdinand Enke Verlag, Ruedigerstrasse 14, D-70469 Stuttgart Germany. **Tel** 011 49 711 8931124, 011 49 711 893123. **(Subscription address:** Georg Thieme Verlag Stuttgart, Postfach 301120, D 70451 Stuttgart Germany.**) DD** 301.

CN/0383-6738
**GOUT DE VIVRE, LE.** (1972)-. Periodical. French. mo. 10.00Can$. Centre d'Activities Francaises, Place La Fontaine, C. P. 58, Penetary Onatario, L0K 1P0 Canada. **Tel** (705)549-6719. **ED** Patsy Lalonde. **DD** 054/.1. **Ad Acc. Circ:** 1,000.
**Desc:** Newspaper representing the Franco-Ontarian community in all of its aspects, a minority group interested in cultural, social, traditional and education as well as political events.

IT
**GRANDE PROMESSA.** Casa Reclusione Porto Azzuro, Via San Giovanni 1, 57036 Porto Azzuro Italy.

US/0896-0054
**GREAT PLAINS SOCIOLOGIST, THE.** [Great Plains sociol.]. **Added/Corp** University of South Dakota. Social Behavior Dept. Great Plains Sociological Association. Vol. 1, No. 1 (1988)-. English. an. $10.00. Great Plains Sociologist, 408-B Minard Hall, North Dakota State University, Fargo ND 58105. **Tel** (701)237-7637, FAX (701)298-1047. **ED** Gary A. Gorehom. **DD** 301. cum. index. **Bk Rev**, (Qty: 10). **Ad Acc. Pr Rev. Circ:** 300 (ctrl).
**Desc:** A general sociology journal with some preface given to research on or about The Great Plains.

US/0091-7052
**GUIDE TO GRADUATE DEPARTMENTS OF SOCIOLOGY. Added/Corp** American Sociological Association. **VFOAT** Graduate Departments of Sociology; Guide to Graduate Departments. (19??)-. English. an (March). $11.00. American Sociological Association, 1722 North Street Northwest, Washington DC 20036-2981. **Tel** (202)833-3410, FAX (202)785-0146. **ED** Karen Gray Edwards. **LC** HM47.U6; G84. **DD** 301/.07/1173. **Circ:** 2,200.
**Desc:** The listing of 250 graduate departments of sociology. Includes information on programs specialties, faculty, financial aid, tuition, enrollment and degrees offered and awarded.

II/0970-0242
**GURU NANAK JOURNAL OF SOCIOLOGY.** [Guru Nanak j. sociol.]. **Added/Corp** Guru Nanak Dev University. Sociology Dept. Vol. 1, No. 1-2 (April/Oct. 1980)-. Periodical. English. Twice a year. $10.00. Registrar Guru Nanak University, Department of Sociology, Amritsar 143005 India. **Tel** 62801/43. **ED** R. S. Sandhu. **LC** HN681; .G87. **UDC** 301. Index available. cum. index. **Bk Rev. Ad Acc. Circ:** 500.
**Desc:** Publishes articles on a broad range of topics in sociology.
**Ind/Abst** Soc. Plann. Policy Dev. Abstr.; Sociol. Abstr. [Full Cov.].

GY
**GUYANA JOURNAL OF SOCIOLOGY : OFFICIAL JOURNAL OF THE GUYANA SOCIOLOGICAL SOCIETY. Added/Corp** Guyana Sociological Society. University of Guyana. Dept. of Sociology. Vol. 1, No. 1 (Oct. 1975)-. Periodical. English. $5.00. **LC** HM1; .G89. **DD** 301/.05.

KO
**HANGUK SAHOE YONGU.** 1 (1983, 6)-. Periodical. Korean. W4,000. Hangilsa, 101-21 5-ka Anam-dong Songbuk-ku, Seoul 132 Korea. **LC** HN730.5; .A5.

CN/0822-126X
**HANSARD, OFFICIAL REPORT OF DEBATES / LEGISLATIVE ASSEMBLY OF ONTARIO, STANDING COMMITTEE ON SOCIAL DEVELOPMENT. See** Public Administration.

CN/0821-3186
**HAQQ (ST-LEONARD).** (AL-HAQQ.). [Hagg]. **VFOAT** La Verite; Verite; Truth. **VAT** Truth (St-Leonard); Verite (St-Leonard). Ad. (Jan. 1983)-. Periodical. French (English and Arabic). mo. $15.00. Maison d'Edition la Verite, CP 395 Jean-Talon, Saint-Leonard Quebec H1S 2Z3 Canada. **DD** 305.8/932/0714281.

US/0895-7983
**HARRIS POLL, THE.** [Harris poll]. Vol. 1 (Jan. 4, 1988)-. Periodical. English. Fifty-two times a year. $800.00 (profit); $195.00 (not for profit). Louis Harris and Associates, 630 5th Avenue, New York NY 10111. **Tel** (212)698-9600. **DD** 303. Index available. **Circ:** 200. ***Continues*** *Harris Survey, 0273-1037.*
**Desc:** Surveys of American public on current events, politics, and foreign policy.

US/0085-1442
**HARRIS SURVEY YEARBOOK OF PUBLIC OPINION, THE.** [Harris surv. yearb. public opin.]. **Added/Corp** Louis Harris and Associates. (1970)-. English. an. Louis Harris and Associates, 630 5th Avenue, New York NY 10111. **Tel** (212)698-9600. **LC** HN90.P8; H35. **DD** 306/.0973.

US/0146-5414
**HARVEST QUARTERLY.** No. 1- Mar. 1976-. Periodical. English. qt. $5.00. Harvest Publications, 907 Santa Barbara Street, Santa Barbara CA 93101. **LC** HN1; .H37. **DD** 301.24/05.

US/0891-7795
**HEALTH, SOCIETY, AND CULTURE.** [Health soc. cult.]. Vol. 1 (1987)-. Monographic series. English. ir. Price varies per volume. Gordon & Breach Science Publishers, Inc., PO Box 786, Cooper Station, New York NY 10276. **Tel** (212)206-8900, FAX (212)645-2459. **(Subscription address:** International Publishers Distributor at one of the following addresses: 820 Town Center Drive, Langhorne, PA 19047; or PO Box 90, Reading Berkshire RG1 8JL UK; or Kent Ridge PO Box 1180, Singapore 9111, Republic of Singapore**) DD** 306. **NLM** W1; HE578H.

US/0898-6495
**HIGH/SCOPE EARLY CHILDHOOD POLICY PAPERS.** [High/Scope early child. policy pap.]. **VFOAT** High Scope Early Childhood Policy Papers. No. 1 (1985)-. Monographic series. English. ir. Price varies per volume. High/Scope Press, 600 North River Street, Ypsilanti MI 48198. **ED** Lawrence J Schweinhart and David P Weikart. **DD** 362.

CN
**HISTOIRE ET SOCIOLOGIE DE LA CULTURE.** ***Ceased.*** Vol. 1 (1971)-Ceased Vol. 12. Monographic series. French. ir. Universite Laval Faculte des Sciences Sociales, Bureau des Communications, 3448 de Koninck, Quebec G1K 7P4 Canada. **Tel** (418)656-2131.

GW/0172-6404
**HISTORICAL SOCIAL RESEARCH (KOLN).** (HISTORICAL SOCIAL RESEARCH.). [Hist. soc. res.]. **Added/Corp** QUANTUM (Association) Zentrum fuer Historische Sozialforschung (Cologne,

Germany). **VFOAT** Historische Sozialforschung. No. 12 (Oct. 1979)-. Periodical. English (German). ir. Price varies. Scripta Mercaturae Verlag, c/o Harold Winkel, AM Rotenberg 5 9, D 55595 St Katharinen Germany. **Tel** 011 49 6706 8800. **ED** Heinrich Best, Wolfgang Bick, Paul J. Mueller, Herbert Reinke and Wilhelm H. Schroeder. **LC** HM1; .H57. **DD** 301/.07. Index available. cum. index. **Bk Rev**. **Ad Acc**. **Circ:** 850. ***Continues*** *QUANTUM Information.*
**Desc:** Devoted to the promotion of quantitative and computer-assisted historical social research.
**Ind/Abst** Am. Hist. Life (1979-); Int. Bibliogr. Sociol.; Int. Polit. Sci. Abstr.; Soc. Plann. Policy Dev. Abstr.; Sociol. Abstr.; Soc. Res. Methodol. Abstr. (1981-).

FR/0018-4306
**HOMME ET LA SOCIETE, L'.** No. 1 (July/Sept. 1966)-. Periodical. French. qt. 290.00F (France); 330.00F (other). L' Harmattan, 7 rue de l'Ecole Polytechnique, 75005 Paris France. **Tel** 11 33 1 43547910, 43257651. **LC** HM3; .H6. available on microfilm and microfiche from University Microfilms International (UMI).
**Ind/Abst** Int. Bibliogr. Sociol.; Point Repere (1979).

FR
**HOMME ET L'HUMANITE, L'.** **Added/Corp** Federation pour le Respect de L'Homme et de L'Humanite. (19??)-. Periodical. French. bm. 40.00F. F R H, 16250 N Banque Jordaan, 3 rue Saint-Georges, 75009 Paris France. **LC** CB197; .H65. **DD** 309/.05. ***Continues*** *Centre de Reflexion sur le Monde non Occidental. Bulletin.*

FR/0563-9743
**HOMO (TOULOUSE).** (HOMO.). [Homo]. **Added/Corp** Universite de Toulouse. Faculte des Lettres. Universite de Toulouse. Faculte des Lettres et Sciences Humaines. Universite de Toulouse-Le Mirail. (1953)-. Periodical. French (summaries and/or abstracts in English). an. 68.56F. Universite de Toulouse--Le Mirail, 56 Rue du Taur, 31000 Toulouse France. **Tel** 011 33 61 225831, FAX 011 33 61 218420. **LC** HM3; .H62. **DD** 301/.05. Documents available from The Genuine Article.
**Ind/Abst** Curr. Contents Soc. Behav. Sci.; MLA Int. Bibl. Books Artic. Mod. Lang. Lit.; Res. Alert [Full Cov.].

US/1055-2049
**HORIZONTN FUN KULTUR UN LEBN / WORKMEN'S CIRCLE.** **Added/Corp** Workmen's Circle (U.S.). **VFOAT** Horizons of Culture and Life. Winter (1991)-. Periodical. English (Yiddish). qt. $15.00. Workmen's Circle, 45 East 33rd Street, New York NY 10016. **Tel** (212)889-6800. ***Continues*** *Kultur un Lebn, 0023-513X.*

II
**HOW.** Periodical. English. $25.00. **LC** HN690.Z9; C6529. **DD** 307.7/2/0954.
**Ind/Abst** Index Inf. (1990-).

US/0148-8686
**HUMAN BEHAVIOR AND ENVIRONMENT.** (HUMAN BEHAVIOR AND ENVIRONMENT. ADVANCES IN THEORY AND RESEARCH.). [Hum. behav. environ.]. (1976)-. Monographic series. English. ir. Price varies per volume. Plenum Press, 233 Spring Street, New York NY 10013-1578. **Tel** (212)620-8000, (800)221-9369, FAX (212)463-0742, (212)807-1047, telex 23/421139. **ED** Irwin Altman and Joachim F. Wohlwill. **NLM** W1 HU444Q.
**Ind/Abst** Psychol. Abstr. (1981-); PsycINFO (1990-); PsycLit.

US/0018-7240
**HUMAN MOSAIC.** [Hum. mosaic]. **Added/Corp** Tulane University of Louisiana. Dept. of Anthropology. Tulane University of Louisiana. Dept. of Sociology. (1967)-. Periodical. English. Twice a year. $9.00. Tulane University / Department of Anthropology, New Orleans LA 70118. **Tel** (504)865-5336, FAX (504)865-5338. **ED** Kathryn Sampeck. **LC** GN1; .H82. **DD** 300/.5. **Bk Rev**, (Qty: 8). **Circ:** 250. available on microfilm from University Microfilms International (UMI). ***Continues*** *Mosaic.*
**Desc:** Social science-related articles of original research, contributed by undergraduates, graduate students, and other academically-oriented scholars.
**Ind/Abst** Abstr. Anthropol.; Middle East Abstr. Index; Soc. Plann. Policy Dev. Abstr.; Soc. Welf. Soc. Plan./Policy Soc. Dev.; Sociol. Abstr.

US/0160-5976
**HUMANITY & SOCIETY.** [Humanity soc.]. **Added/Corp** Association for Humanist Sociology (U.S.). **VFOAT** Humanity and Society. **VAT** Humanity and Society. Vol. 1 (Summer 1977)-. Periodical. English. qt (4 issues). $45.00 (institution), $35.00 (individual) US; $50.00 (institution), $40.00 (individual) other. Association for Humanist Sociology, John Jay College of Criminal Justice, 899 10th Avenue, New York NY 10019. **Tel** (212)237-8461, FAX (212)237-8901. **ED** Dragan Milovanovic (editor's telephone: (312)794-2629). **LC** HM1; .H86. **DD** 301/.05. **Bk Rev**, (Qty: 4 per year). **Pr Rev**. **Circ:** 500.
**Desc:** Publishes articles on a wide variety of topics: studies of inequality; war, peace, and international relations; aging and gerontology; family sex roles and sexuality; urban and environmental studies; political sociology and political economy; health and mental health; social theory; sociology of knowledge and science; social change, humanism and human rights; crime and deviance; and ethnic and intergroup relations.
**Ind/Abst** Soc. Plann. Policy Dev. Abstr.; Sociol. Abstr. [Full Cov.].

CN/0383-8501
**I S A BULLETIN (1975).** (I S A BULLETIN.). **Main/Corp** International Sociological Association. (Autumn 1975)-. Bulletin. English (French). International Sociological Association, PO Box 719, Station A, Montreal Quebec H3C 2V2 Canada. **DD** 301.06/21. ***Continues*** *I S A Newsletter, 0318-7292.*

JA
**IKEN TO ISHIKI NO HYAKKA JITEN.** **Added/Corp** Sankei. Sankei Shimbun Sha. Seron Chosashitsu. (1972)-. Periodical. Japanese. ¥2500. Sankei Publishing Ltd., Sankei-Honsha Building, 1-7-2 Otemachi 1 Chiyodaku 100 Japan. **Tel** 03 2317111, FAX 03 2424540. **LC** HN730.Z9; P853.

IT
**IMMAGINE RIFLESSA, L'.** **See** Literature.

CN/0700-3854
**IN REVIEW (TORONTO. 1975).** (IN REVIEW.). [In rev.]. **VFOAT** B M R in Review. Spring 1975-. Periodical. English. qt. Bureau of Municipal, 73 Richmond Street West/Suite 404 Canada. **Tel** (416)363-9265. **DD** 301.36/07/10713.
**Ind/Abst** Libr. Inf. Sci. Abstr.

IT
**INCHIESTA.** (19??)-. Periodical. Italian. Four times a year. L35000 Italy; L52500 other. Edizioni Dedalo Spa, Casella Postale 362, Bari 70100 Italy. **Tel** 011 39 080 5311400, FAX 011 39 080 5311414. **ED** Juri Kazepov (editor's address: c/o Fond. Bignaschi, Via Olmetti 3 Milan Italy; phone: 011 39 080 2879106). cum. index. **Bk Rev**, (Qty: 10/year). **Ad Acc**, **Adv Mgr:** R. Coga. ctrl circ. available on microfilm and microfiche from University Microfilms International (UMI).
**Desc:** Covers employment problems, the status of women, changes in the social structure, and educational questions. A tool for students, researchers, social, and political workers.
**Ind/Abst** Soc. Plann. Policy Dev. Abstr.

US/1056-3504
**INCITE INFORMATION.** (INCITE INFORMATION : NEWS ANALYSIS AND COMMENTARY.). (1991)-. Periodical. English. Six times a year. $10.00. Incite Information, PO Box 326, Arlington VA 22210. **DD** 301. ***Continues*** *Big Forehead Express, 1049-958X.*

US/0193-905X
**INDEX TO INTERNATIONAL PUBLIC OPINION.** [Index int. public opin.]. (1979)-. English. an. $199.50. Greenwood Press Inc., PO Box 5007, Westport CT 06881-5007. **Tel** (203)226-3571, FAX (203)222-1502. **LC** HM261; .I552. **DD** 016.3033/8.
**Desc:** Contains data from surveys of over 150 countries and arranged by major topic categories.

II
**INDIAN JOURNAL OF COMPARATIVE SOCIOLOGY.** V. 1- Aug. 1974-. Periodical. English. 20.00. Forum for Sociologists, L S Ainapur Secretary, Dhanvantri Building, T C Road, Dharwar India. **LC** HM1; .I45. **DD** 301/.05.

II/0970-7972
**INDIAN SOCIO-LEGAL JOURNAL.** **See** Law.

II
**INDO-KOREAN FRIENDSHIP.** Periodical. English. Rs0.60 single issue. All India Indo-Korean Friendship Association, Delhi-6 India. **LC** DS450.K7; I53. **DD** 301.29/519/3054.

AT/1033-6273
**INFORMATION AND SOCIETY.** English. Twice a year. $95.00 North America; $110.00 other. James Nicholas Publishers, PO Box 244, Albert Park 3206 Australia. **Tel** 011/61/3/6965545, FAX 011/61/3/6992040. **ED** Rea Zajda. cum. index. **Bk Rev**. **Ad Acc**. **Pr Rev**.
**Desc:** The journal is concerned with major and current issues in information research by focusing on current problems pertaining to information technology, communication theory, post-industrialism, and globalisation of technology.

FR/0046-9459
**INFORMATIONS SOCIALES.** [Inf. soc.]. **Added/Corp** Caisse Nationale des Allocations Familiales. Union Nationale des Caisses d'Allocations Familiales. (1947)-. French. Eight times a year. 200.00F one year; 360.00F two year. Caisse National Allocation Familia, 23 rue Daviel, 75634 Paris Cedex 13 France. **Tel** 011 33 1 45655244, FAX 011 33 1 45655377. **LC** HN421; .I5.
**Desc:** Covers the areas of social techniques and supplements social information.
**Ind/Abst** Int. Labour Doc.; PAIS Int. Print (1991-).

YU
**INFORMATIVE BULLETIN (SAVEZNI ZAVOD ZA MEUNARODNU NAUCNU, PROSVJETNO-KULTURNU I TEHNICKU SARADNJU (YUGOSLAVIA)).** (INFORMATIVE BULLETIN / FEDERAL ADMINISTRATION FOR INTERNATIONAL SCIENTIFIC, EDUCATIONAL, CULTURAL, AND TECHNICAL COOPERATION.). Bulletin. English. Federal Administration for International Scientific Educational Cultural and Technical Cooperation, Belgrade Yugoslavia. **LC** DR1303; .I54. **DD** 303.4/82497.

AU/0537-7250
**INNSBRUCKER BEITRAEGE ZUR KULTURWISSENSCHAFT.** Vol. 1- 1953-. Monographic series. German (English and French). ir. Price varies per volume. Institute fur Sprachwissenschaft, Universitat Innsbruck, Innsbruck Innrain 52 Austria. **Tel** 05222-724-3573. **Circ:** 400-500.
**Desc:** Publications in linguistics, philology, and history.
**Ind/Abst** MLA Int. Bibl. Books Artic. Mod. Lang. Lit.; Soc. Plann. Policy Dev. Abstr.; Sociol. Abstr. (?-?).

MX/0188-5340
**INSEH INFORMA.** (INSEH INFORMA : BOLETIN MENSUAL DE NOTICIAS.). [INSEH inf.]. **VFOAT** Instituto de Investigaciones Socioeconomicas de Honduras Informa. (1984)-. Periodical. Spanish. mo. **DD** 320.
**Ind/Abst** Hum. Rights Intern. Rep.

US/1059-2768
**INTER-VIEWS (PHILADELPHIA, PA.).** (INTER-VIEWS : CENTER FOR TRANSNATIONAL CULTURAL STUDIES, UNIVERSITY OF PENNSYLVANIA.). **Added/Corp** Center for Transnational Cultural Studies. (1991)-. Periodical. English. sa. Free. University of Pennsylvania / Center for Transnational and Cultural Studies, 33rd and Spruce, Philadelphia PA 19104.

US/1057-7769
**INTERCULTURAL COMMUNICATION STUDIES.** [Intercult. commun. stud.]. **Added/Corp** Institute for Cross-Cultural Research (U.S.). Vol. 1, No. 1 (Spring 1991)-. Periodical. English. sa. $88.00 (institutions). Institute for Cross-Cultural Research, Box 418, Trinity University, 715 Stadium Drive, San Antonio TX 78212. **DD** 302.

CN/0827-1550
**INTERCULTURAL HORIZONS.** ***Ceased.*** [Intercult. horiz.]. No. 1 (Aug. 1985)-Issue 29. Periodical. English (French). qt. Monchanin Crosscultural Centre, 4917 rue St Urbain, Montreal Quebec H2T 2W1 Canada. **Tel** (514)288-7229. **ED** Maryse Bouchard. **DD** 306/.06/0714281. **Bk Rev**. **Circ:** 1,000 (ctrl). ***Continues*** *Nouvelles Monchanin. English, 0822-5583.*
**Desc:** Articles on cross-cultural questions, intercultural exchanges, debates and conferences, community profiles, activities within Canada's ethnic communities, and articles and books useful in cultural research, intercultural education, etc.

CN/0712-1571
**INTERCULTURE (MONTREAL. ED. FRANCAISE).** **See** Religion and Theology.

UK/0085-2066
**INTERNATIONAL BIBLIOGRAPHY OF SOCIOLOGY.** **See** Sociology-Abstracting, Bibliographies and Statistics.

UK/0960-1546
**INTERNATIONAL CURRENT AWARENESS SERVICES : SOCIOLOGY AND RELATED DISCIPLINES.** ***Ceased.*** **Added/Corp** British Library of Political and Economic Science. **VFOAT** Sociology and Related Disciplines; Sociology. Vol. 1, No. 1 (Nov. 1990)-(March 1994). Periodical. English. Twelve times a year. Routledge, 11 New Fetter Lane, London EC4P 4EE England. **Tel** 071 583 9855, FAX 071 842 2298. **(Subscription address:** Kinokuniya Company Ltd., 38-1 Sakuragaoka 5, chome Setagaya-ku, Tokyo 156 Japan.) **[CCC].**

US/0091-4150
**INTERNATIONAL JOURNAL OF AGING & HUMAN DEVELOPMENT, THE.** [Int. j. aging hum. dev.]. **VFOAT** International Journal of Aging and Human Development. **VAT** International Journal of Aging and Human Development. Vol. 4 (Winter 1973)-. Academic Scholarly Publication. English. Eight times a year (two volumes, eight issues per year). $165.00. Baywood Publishing Company Inc., 26 Austin Avenue, PO Box 337, Amityville NY 11701. **Tel** (516)691-1270, (800)638-7819, FAX (516)691-1770. **ED** Robert J Kastenbaum and Jon Hendricks. **LC** HQ1060; .A33. **DD** 301.43/5/05. **NLM** W1 IN7652V. **CODEN** IJADDT. cum. index. **Bk Rev**. **Pr Rev**. Documents available from The Genuine Article, BIOSIS Document Express, UMI Article

Clearinghouse. ***Continues*** *Aging & Human Development, 0002-0974.*
**Desc:** Emphasizes psychological and social studies of aging and the aged; also, research that introduces observations from other fields that illuminate the "human" side of gerontology, or utilizes gerontological observations to illuminate problems in other fields.
**Ind/Abst** Abstr. Anthropol. (19??-); Abstr. Soc. Gerontol.; Abstr. Res. Pastor. Care Couns. (19??-); Acad. Search (July 1993-); Appl. Soc. Sci. Index Abstr.; Arts Humanit. Citation Index [Select. Cov.]; Biol. Abstr.; Book Rev. Index (1984-); Chicano Index; Cumul. Index Nurs. Allied Health Lit.; Curr. Contents Soc. Behav. Sci.; Curr. Index J. Educ.; EMBASE; Energy Res. Abstr. (Aug. 1982-); Expand. Acad. Index (1989-); Health Period. Database; Index Med.; Index Period. Lit. Aging; INFO-SOUTH Abstr.; Middle East Abstr. Index; Newsp. Period. Abstr. (1989-); Nutr. Res. Newsl.; Psychol. Abstr. (1973-); PsycINFO; PsycLit; Res. Alert [Full Cov.]; Sage Fam. Stud. Abstr.; Soc. Plann. Policy Dev. Abstr.; Soc. Sci. Source (Jul. 1993-); Soc. Sci. Cit. Index [Full Cov.]; Soc. Sci. Index Fulltext (1988-) [Full Txt.]; Soc. Work Abstr. [Select. Cov.]; Sociol. Abstr.; SPORT Discus; SportSearch (1984-).

US/1044-811X
**INTERNATIONAL JOURNAL OF BIOSOCIAL AND MEDICAL RESEARCH.** [Int. j. biosoc. med. res.]. **Added/Corp** Foundation for Biosocial Research. Vol. 11, No. 1 (1989)-. Periodical. English. Twice a year (July, & Nov.). $40.00 (institutions), $25.00 (individuals) US; $35.00 (individuals), $50.00 (institutions) others. Society for Biosocial Research, PO Box 1174, Tacoma WA 98401. **Tel** (206)922-0442. **ED** Alexander G. Schauss. **LC** BF1; .I44. **DD** 610/.5. **NLM** W1; IN76559. **CODEN** IJMREU. **[CCC].** Index available. cum. index. **Bk Rev. Pr Rev. Circ:** 1,000 (ctrl). ***Continues*** *International Journal for Biosocial Research, 0731-9169.*
**Desc:** Current research on nutrition and behavior toxic substances and behavior, color/light research and behavior, biomedical research, and human behavior.
**Ind/Abst** PsycINFO (1990-); PsycLit; Soc. Plann. Policy Dev. Abstr.

NE/0020-7152
**INTERNATIONAL JOURNAL OF COMPARATIVE SOCIOLOGY.** [Int. j. comp. sociol.]. **Added/Corp** Karnatak University. Dept. of Social Anthropology. Vol. 1 (March 1960)-. Periodical. English. sa (2 double issues). Fl150.00 (institutions) Netherlands; $85.75 other. E. J. Brill, Postbus 9000, 2300 PA Leiden Netherlands. **Tel** 011 31 71 312624, FAX 011 31 71 317532, telex 39296 BRILL NL. **ED** K. Ishwaran. **LC** HM1; .I54. **NLM** W1 IN766E. **[CCC]. Circ:** 292. Documents available from The Genuine Article, UMI Article Clearinghouse.
**Desc:** Focuses on problems of sociological documentation analysed specifically in a comparative perspective. Scholars agree that such a perspective is vital for the development of concepts, theories, models and methodologies that are truly cross-societal and cross-cultural.
**Ind/Abst** ABC POL SCI; Acad. Search (July 1993-); Am. Hist. Life (1966-1976); Curr. Contents Soc. Behav. Sci.; Expand. Acad. Index (1989-); Geogr. Abstr. Human Geogr.; Int. Dev. Abstr.; Int. Polit. Sci. Abstr.; Middle East Abstr. Index; Newsp. Period. Abstr. (1991-); Res. Alert [Full Cov.]; Soc. Plann. Policy Dev. Abstr.; Soc. Sci. Cit. Index [Full Cov.]; Soc. Sci. Index; Soc. Sci. Index Fulltext (Sept. 1987-) [Full Txt.]; Sociol. Abstr. [Full Cov.]; SportSearch; Stud. Women Abstr.; West. Hist. Q.

FI/0019-6398
**INTERNATIONAL JOURNAL OF CONTEMPORARY SOCIOLOGY.**
**Added/Corp** Auburn University. Dept. of Sociology and Anthropology. Vol. 8 (1971)-. Periodical. English. Twice a year (Apr., & Oct.). $40.00. International Journal of Contemporary Sociology, PO Box 111, University of Joensuu, SF 80101 Joensuu Finland. available on microfilm from University Microfilms International (UMI). ***Continues*** *Indian Sociological Bulletin, 0537-2550.*
**Ind/Abst** Am. Hist. Life (1965-); Appl. Soc. Sci. Index Abstr.; Int. Polit. Sci. Abstr.; Middle East Abstr. Index; Soc. Plann. Policy Dev. Abstr.; Sociol. Abstr. [Full Cov.].

US/0047-0732
**INTERNATIONAL JOURNAL OF GROUP TENSIONS.** [Int. j. group tens.]. **Added/Corp** International Organization for the Study of Group Tensions. Vol. 1 (Jan./March 1971)-. Periodical. English. qt. $195.00 US; $230.00 other. Human Sciences Press, PO Box 735, 233 Spring Street, New York NY 10013. **Tel** (212)620-8000, FAX (212)807-1047, telex 23421139. **(Subscription address:** Eurospan Ltd., Journals and Serials Division, 3 Henrietta Street, Covent Garden, London WC2E 8LU England.**)** **ED** Benjamin Wolman and Joseph Gittler. **LC** HN1; .I518. **DD** 301.6/3/05. **NLM** W1 IN766R. **CODEN** IJGTB3. available on microfilm and microfiche from University Microfilms International (UMI).
**Desc:** Devoted to the study of conflict in human group relations, this interdisciplinary journal draws together research and theoretical approaches from the psychological, social and philosophical disciplines. As a vehicle of communication for understanding group tensions among racial, ethnic, religious, political, national and international groups. The journal publishes findings and theoretical analyses pertaining to bias, prejudice, discrimination, hostility, and violence - and methods preventing and resolving them.
**Ind/Abst** Int. Polit. Sci. Abstr. (1971-); Middle East Abstr. Index; Peace Res. Abstr. J. (1973-1975); Psychol. Abstr. (1971-); Soc. Plann. Policy Dev. Abstr.

US/0148-1169
**INTERNATIONAL JOURNAL OF HUMAN RELATIONS, THE.** Vol. 1; 1976-. Periodical. English. an. Human Relations Association, PO Box 2039, Norman OK. **LC** HM1; .I55. **DD** 301.1/05.

US/0147-1767
**INTERNATIONAL JOURNAL OF INTERCULTURAL RELATIONS.** (INTERNATIONAL JOURNAL OF INTERCULTURAL RELATIONS : IJIR.). [Int. j. intercult. relat.]. **Added/Corp** Society for Intercultural Education, Training, and Research. **VFOAT** IJIR. Vol. 1, No. 1 (Spring 1977)-. Periodical. English. qt. $284.00 The Americas; £190.00 other. Pergamon Press, An Imprint of Elsevier Science Ltd., The Boulevard, Langford Lane, Kidlington, Oxford OX5 1GB United Kingdom. **Tel** 011 44 865 843000, 011 44 865 843699, FAX 011 44 865 843010. **(Subscription address:** Elsevier Science Ltd. Oxford Fulfillment Centre, PO Box 800, Kidlington, Oxford OX5 1DX United Kingdom.**)** **ED** Dan Landis. **LC** GN496; .I15. **DD** 301.2. **[CCC]. Pr Rev.** available on microfilm and microfiche from University Microfilms International (UMI). Documents available from The Genuine Article, UMI Article Clearinghouse.
**Ind/Abst** ABI/INFORM Glob. Ed.; Appl. Soc. Sci. Index Abstr.; Arts Humanit. Citation Index [Select. Cov.]; Curr. Contents Soc. Behav. Sci.; Psychol. Abstr. (1981-)(1977-1980); PsycINFO; PsycLit; Res. Alert [Full Cov.]; Sage Race Relat. Abstr.; Soc. Plann. Policy Dev. Abstr.; Soc. Sci. Cit. Index [Full Cov.]; Sociol. Abstr.; U.S. Polit. Sci. Doc.

US/0891-4486
**INTERNATIONAL JOURNAL OF POLITICS, CULTURE, AND SOCIETY.** [Int. j. polit. cult. soc.]. **Added/Corp** Florida Atlantic University. Moorhead State University. **VFOAT** Politics, Culture, and Society. Vol. 1, No. 1 (Fall 1987)-. Periodical. English. qt. £38.00 (individuals), £155.00 (institutions) UK; $205.00 US; $240.00 other. Human Sciences Press, PO Box 735, 233 Spring Street, New York NY 10013. **Tel** (212)620-8000, FAX (212)807-1047, telex 23421139. **(Subscription address:** Eurospan Ltd., Journals and Serials Division, 3 Henrietta Street, Covent Garden, London WC2E 8LU England.**)** **ED** Arthur J. Vidich, Stanford M. Lyman, Michael W. Hughey, Robert Jackall, and Guy Oakes. **LC** JA76; .I66. **DD** 306. **CODEN** ICSOE2. **[CCC].** Index available. cum. index. **Bk Rev. Ad Acc. Circ:** 165. available on microfilm and microfiche from University Microfilms International (UMI). ***Continues*** *State, Culture and Society, 0743-9245.*
**Desc:** Provides a forum for discussion, dialogue, and debate on points of tension between state and civil society, between nations and global institutions. Focus is the changing order of public and private spheres of life and the dialectic between national organizations and the emotional needs of human beings.
**Ind/Abst** Am. Hist. Life (1987-); Book Rev. Index (1987-?); Index Period. Lit. Aging (19??-19??); Int. Bibliogr. Sociol.; Int. Polit. Sci. Abstr.; PAIS Int. Print (1991-); Sage Public Adm. Abstr.; Soc. Plann. Policy Dev. Abstr.; Soc. Sci. Index (1987-); Soc. Work Abstr. (?-?); Sociol. Abstr. (1987-) [Full Cov.]; Sociol. Educ. Abstr.

UK/0954-2892
**INTERNATIONAL JOURNAL OF PUBLIC OPINION RESEARCH.** [Int. j. public opin. res.]. **Added/Corp** World Association for Public Opinion Research. **VFOAT** Public Opinion Research. Vol. 1, No. 1 (Spring 1989)-. Periodical. English. qt. £65.00 UK and Europe; $116.00 other. Oxford University Press, Walton Street, Oxford OX2 6DP England. **Tel** 011 44 865 56767, FAX 011 44 865 267773, telex 837330 OXPRES G. **(Subscription address:** Oxford University Press / USA, Journals Marketing Department, Oxford University Press, 2001 Evans Road, Cary NC 27513.**)** **LC** HM261; .I68. **DD** 303.3/8/05. **CODEN** IJPOE2. **[CCC].** available on microfilm and microfiche from University Microfilms International (UMI). Documents available from The Genuine Article, UMI Article Clearinghouse.
**Ind/Abst** Commun. Abstr.; Curr. Contents Soc. Behav. Sci.; Expand. Acad. Index (1992-); Newsp. Period. Abstr. (1992-); PAIS Int. Print (1991-); Res. Alert [Full Cov.]; Soc. Plann. Policy Dev. Abstr.; Soc. Sci. Cit. Index [Full Cov.]; Sociol. Abstr. (1989-) [Full Cov.].

US/0020-7659
**INTERNATIONAL JOURNAL OF SOCIOLOGY.** [Int. j. sociol.]. Vol. 1 (Spring 1971)-. Periodical. English. qt. $450.00 US; $495.00 other. M. E. Sharpe Inc., 80 Business Park Drive, Armonk NY 10504. **Tel** (914)273-1800, (800)541-6563, FAX (914)273-2106. **ED** Patricia A. Kolb. **LC** HM1; .I56. **DD** 301/.05. **NLM** W1 IN7889. **Bk Rev. Ad Acc. Circ:** 350 (ctrl). available on microfilm from University Microfilms International (UMI). ***Supersedes*** *Eastern European Studies in Sociology and Anthropology.*
**Desc:** Translations of major studies in all areas of sociology from sources throughout the world.
**Ind/Abst** Appl. Soc. Sci. Index Abstr.; Int. Polit. Sci. Abstr.; Middle East Abstr. Index; PAIS Int. Print (1991-); Soc. Plann. Policy Dev. Abstr.; Sociol. Abstr. (?-?); Sociol. Educ. Abstr.; Stud. Women Abstr.

UK/0144-333X
**INTERNATIONAL JOURNAL OF SOCIOLOGY & SOCIAL POLICY, THE.** [Int. j. sociol. soc. policy]. Vol. 1, No. 1- (1981)-. Periodical. English. Eight times a year. $1129.00. MCB University Press, 60 62 Toller Lane, Bradford West Yorkshire BD8 9BX England. **Tel** 011 44 274 499821, FAX 011 44 274 547143, telex 51317 MCBUNI G. **(Subscription address:** MCB University Press / US and Canada Subscriptions, PO Box 10812, Birmingham AL 35201-0812.**)** **ED** Barrie O Pettman. **LC** HM1; .I57. **DD** 301/.05. **Bk Rev.** available on an online database (file 15/Full-Text) from DIALOG. Documents available from UMI Article Clearinghouse. ***Continues*** *Scottish Journal of Sociology, 0309-4006.*
**Desc:** Publishes a wide variety of articles outlining the latest developments internationally within the fields of sociology and social policy.
**Ind/Abst** ABI/INFORM Glob. Ed.; ABI Inform Ondisc (1986-); Appl. Soc. Sci. Index Abstr.; Crim. Justice Abstr.; Geogr. Abstr. Human Geogr. (?-?); Int. Labour Doc.; Middle East Abstr. Index; PAIS Int. Print (1991-); Sage Race Relat. Abstr.; Soc. Plann. Policy Dev. Abstr.; Sociol. Abstr. [Full Cov.]; Sociol. Educ. Abstr.; Stud. Women Abstr.

UK/0194-6595
**INTERNATIONAL JOURNAL OF THE SOCIOLOGY OF LAW.** **See** Law.

II/0970-4841
**INTERNATIONAL REVIEW OF MODERN SOCIOLOGY.** [Int. rev. mod. sociol.]. Vol. 2 (March 1972)-. Periodical. English. sa. $70.00. Indian Books and Periodicals, 2429 Tilak Street, Pahar Ganj, New Delhi 110005 India. **(Subscription address:** Prints India, 11 Darya Ganj, New Delhi 110002 India.**)** **ED** Mansingh Dass. **LC** HM1; .I58. **DD** 301/.05. available on microfilm and microfiche from University Microfilms International (UMI). ***Continues*** *International Review of Sociology.*
**Ind/Abst** Appl. Soc. Sci. Index Abstr.; Soc. Plann. Policy Dev. Abstr.; Sociol. Abstr. [Full Cov.].

NE/0020-8590
**INTERNATIONAL REVIEW OF SOCIAL HISTORY.** (INTERNATIONAL REVIEW OF SOCIAL HISTORY / INTERNATIONAL INSTITUUT VOOR SOCIALE GESCHIEDENIS, AMSTERDAM.). [Int. rev. soc. hist.]. **Added/Corp** International Institute for Social History. Vol. 1, Pt. 1 (1956)-. Academic Scholarly Publication. English (French and German). Four times a year. $94.00 US, Canada & Mexico; £55.00 other. Cambridge University Press, The Edinburgh Building, Shaftesbury Road, Cambridge CB2 2RU United Kingdom. **Tel** 011 44 223 312393, FAX 011 44 223 325959. **(Subscription address:** Cambridge University Press / North America, 110 Midland Avenue, Port Chester NY 10573.**)** **ED** Van Woerden. **LC** HN1; .I53. **DD** 309. Index available. **Bk Rev. Ad Acc. Pr Rev. Circ:** 1,400 (ctrl). available on microfilm and microfiche from University Microfilms International (UMI). Documents available from The Genuine Article. ***Continues*** *Bulletin of the International Institute for Social History, Amsterdam, 0921-254X.*
**Desc:** A journal which functions as a forum for exchanges of views and which contributes to the further development of social history.
**Ind/Abst** Am. Hist. Life (1956-); Arts Humanit. Citation Index [Full Cov.]; Curr. Contents Arts Humanit.; Curr. Contents Soc. Behav. Sci.; Int. Bibliogr. Sociol.; Int. Polit. Sci. Abstr.; Middle East Abstr. Index; Res. Alert [Full Cov.]; Soc. Sci. Cit. Index [Full Cov.]; Soc. Sci. Index; Soc. Work Abstr. (?-?); Work Relat. Abstr.

AT/0726-4178
**INTERNATIONAL REVIEW OF SOCIOLOGY OF EDUCATION.** English. 60.00Aus$ Australia; $90.00 other. James Nicholas Publishers, PO Box 244, Albert Park 3206 Australia. **Tel** 011/61/3/6965545, FAX 011/61/3/6992040. **ED** Dr Joseph Zajda. Index available. cum. index. **Bk Rev. Ad Acc.** ctrl circ.
**Desc:** Focuses on major areas in sociology of education throughout the world.

CI/0351-5796
**INTERNATIONAL REVIEW OF THE AESTHETICS AND SOCIOLOGY OF MUSIC.** **See** Music.

US/1043-1365
**INTERNATIONAL SOCIAL MOVEMENT RESEARCH.** [Int. soc. mov. res.]. Vol. 1 (1988)-. English. an. $73.25. JAI Press Inc., 55 Old Post Road, Suite 2, PO Box 1678, Greenwich CT 06836-1678. **Tel** (203)661-7602, FAX (203)661-0792. **ED** Bert Klandermans. **LC** HN1; .I538. **DD** 303.4/84/05.
**Ind/Abst** Soc. Plann. Policy Dev. Abstr.

UK/0268-5809
**INTERNATIONAL SOCIOLOGY.** (INTERNATIONAL SOCIOLOGY : JOURNAL OF THE INTERNATIONAL SOCIOLOGICAL ASSOCIATION.).

[Int. sociol.]. Vol. 1, No. 1 (March 1986)-. Periodical. English. Four times a year (Mar., June, Sept., Dec.). £90.00. Sage Publications Ltd., 6 Bonhill Street, London EC2A 4PU, UK. **Tel** 071 374 0645, FAX 071 374 8741, telex 296207 SAGE G. **ED** Martin Albrow. **LC** HM1; .I583. **DD** 301/.05. **Pr Rev. Acid Free. Circ:** 2,380. Documents available from The Genuine Article.
**Desc:** The work of cross-cultural relevance from the international community of sociologists. Focuses on the fundamental issues of theory and method and on new direction in empirical research.
**Ind/Abst** Curr. Contents Soc. Behav. Sci.; Geogr. Abstr. Human Geogr. (?-?); Int. Bibliogr. Sociol.; Int. Dev. Abstr. (?-?); Int. Polit. Sci. Abstr.; PAIS Int. Print (1991-); Res. Alert [Full Cov.]; Soc. Plann. Policy Dev. Abstr.; Soc. Sci. Cit. Index [Full Cov.]; Sociol. Abstr. (1986-) [Full Cov.]; Soc. Res. Methodol. Abstr. (1992-).

US/1055-7180
**INTERNATIONAL STUDIES IN SOCIAL CHANGE.** (1991)-. Periodical. English. Gordon & Breach Science Publishers, Inc., PO Box 786, Cooper Station, New York NY 10276. **Tel** (212)206-8900, FAX (212)645-2459. **(Subscription address:** International Publishers Distributor at one of the following addresses: 820 Town Center Drive, Langhorne, PA 19047; or PO Box 90, Reading Berkshire RG1 8JL UK; or Kent Ridge PO Box 1180, Singapore 9111, Republic of Singapore**)**

NE/0074-8684
**INTERNATIONAL STUDIES IN SOCIOLOGY AND SOCIAL ANTHROPOLOGY.** Vol. 1 (1963)-. Monographic series. English. Price varies per volume. E. J. Brill, Postbus 9000, 2300 PA Leiden Netherlands. **Tel** 011 31 71 312624, FAX 011 31 71 317532, telex 39296 BRILL NL. **ED** K. Ishwaran.

UK/0962-0214
**INTERNATIONAL STUDIES IN SOCIOLOGY OF EDUCATION. See** Education.

US/1059-1036
**INTERNATIONAL TRAN SCRIPT. VFOAT** International TranScript. Vol. 1, No. 1 (Oct. 1991)-. Periodical. English. bm. $40.00 US, $44.00 Canada. Creative Designs Services, PO Box 61263, King of Prussia PA 19406-1263. **DD** 306.

US/0095-6945
**INTERSECTIONS.** 1974. English. an. $3.00. Center Urban and Environmental Studies, Rensselaer Polytechnic Institute, Troy NY 12181. **Tel** (518)270-6565. **ED** Peg Olsen. **LC** HC79.E5; I63. **DD** 301.31/05. **Bk Rev. Circ:** 500.
**Desc:** Subjects related to any facet of urban or environmental related research, public policy, or historical analysis.

MX/0021-261X
**ISTMO.** No. 1 (Jan./Feb. 1959)-. Periodical. Spanish. bm. $52.00. Centros Culturales de Mexico AC, Goya 73-303, Col Mixcoac, 03920 Mexico DF Mexico. **Tel** 011 52 5632557, 011 52 5631963. **ED** Patricia Montelongo. **LC** AP63; .I78. Index available. cum. index. **Bk Rev. Ad Acc. Circ:** 11,000.
**Desc:** Journal for cultural information. Fundamentally structured by subject: philosophy, education, heads of companies complemented with studies and commentaries on sociology, art and religion.

GW/0587-5277
**JAHRBUCH DES ARCHIVS DER DEUTSCHEN JUGENDBEWEGUNG. Main/Corp** Archiv der Deutschen Jugendbewegung. (1969)-. German. ir. Jahrbuch der Archivs der Burg Ludwigstein, c/o Dr. W. Fogge, D-37214 Witzenhausen Germany. **ED** Winfried Mogge. **LC** HN19; .A74a. **DD** 305.2/3/0943. **Bk Rev. Circ:** 2,000.
**Desc:** Contains history of the youth movement in the Third Reich from beginning to present, youth and national socialism, alternate lifestyles among the young, and bibliographies.

GW
**JAHRESBERICHT (INSTITUT FUR EMPIRISCHE SOZIOLOGIE FORSCHUNG)).** (JAHRESBERICHT / INSTITUT FUR EMPIRISCHE SOZIOLOGIE.). German. an. Institut fur Empirische Soziologie, Marienstrasse 2/IV, 8500 Nuernberg 1 Germany. **LC** HM5; .J35. **DD** 301/.01.

JA/0385-2318
**JAPAN FOUNDATION NEWSLETTER, THE.** [Jpn. Found. newsl.]. **Added/Corp** Kokusai Koryu Kikin. (Aug. 1973)-. Newsletter. English. bm. Free on request. Japan Foundation, Park Building, Kioicho-3-6, Chiyoda-ku, Tokyo 102 Japan. **Tel** 11 81 3 3263 4505, telex J-23424. **ED** Haruo Washi, Michiko Usui. **LC** DS821; .J3385. Index available. cum. index. **Bk Rev**, (Qty: 20). **Circ:** 8,000 (ctrl).
**Desc:** For individuals and organizations interested in Japanese Studies and international cultural exchange.
**Ind/Abst** Index Free Period.

UK/0021-6534
**JEWISH JOURNAL OF SOCIOLOGY, THE.** [Jew. j. sociol.]. **Added/Corp** World Jewish Congress. Vol. 1 (Apr. 1959)-. Periodical. English. Twice a year (June, Dec.). $23.00 (individuals), $30.00 (institutions). Jewish Journal of Sociology, 187 Glouchester Place, London NW1 6BU England. **Tel** 011 44 71 262-8939. **ED** Judith Freedman. **LC** DS101; .J4657. Index available. **Bk Rev. Ad Acc.** Documents available from The Genuine Article.
**Desc:** Articles on Jewish social affairs, reviews of books on Judaism and sociology, research notes and a chronicle.
**Ind/Abst** Anthropol. Index; Appl. Soc. Sci. Index Abstr.; Curr. Contents Soc. Behav. Sci.; Index Jew. Period. (19??-199?); Int. Bibliogr. Sociol.; Int. Polit. Sci. Abstr.; Middle East Abstr. Index; Res. Alert [Full Cov.]; Soc. Plann. Policy Dev. Abstr.; Soc. Sci. Cit. Index [Full Cov.]; Sociol. Abstr. [Full Cov.]; Middle East J.

BE
**JOURNAL DE REFLEXION SUR L'INFORMATIQUE. See** Computers.

AT/1035-4425
**JOURNAL FOR SOCIAL JUSTICE STUDIES.** [J. soc. justice stud.]. (1990)-. Monographic series. English. ir. Price varies per volume. Charles Sturt University, Mitchell Center for Studies & Justice, Bathurst NSW 2705 Australia. **Tel** 011 61 063 332778. **DD** 303.372994. ***Continues*** *Journal of Studies in Justice.*
**Ind/Abst** APAIS, Aust. Public Aff. Inf. Ser. (1990-).

AU/0253-3995
**JOURNAL FUER SOZIALFORSCHUNG. Added/Corp** Sozialwissenschaftliche Studiengesellschaft (Vienna, Austria) Internationale Studiengesellschaft fuer InterdisziplinÈare Sozialwissenschaft. (1981)-. Periodical. German. qt. **LC** HM261; .J68. **DD** 303.3/8/05. ***Continues*** *Journal fuer Angewandte Sozialforschung.*
**Ind/Abst** Soc. Plann. Policy Dev. Abstr.

US/0890-4065
**JOURNAL OF AGING STUDIES.** [J. aging stud.]. **VFOAT** Aging Studies. Vol. 1, No. 1 (Spring 1987)-. Academic Scholarly Publication. English. qt. $150.00 (institutions), $60.00 (individuals), US; $170.00 (institutions), $80.00 (individuals) (surface mail), $190.00 (institutions), $100.00 (individuals) (air mail) other. JAI Press Inc., 55 Old Post Road, Suite 2, PO Box 1678, Greenwich CT 06836-1678. **Tel** (203)661-7602, FAX (203)661-0792. **ED** Jaber F. Gubrium. **LC** HQ1060; .J59. **DD** 305.2/6/05. **NLM** W1; JO534BM. **[CCC]. Pr Rev.** Documents available from The Genuine Article.
**Desc:** Aims to feature scholarly papers offering new interpretations and challenging existing theory and empirical work.
**Ind/Abst** Abstr. Anthropol.; Abstr. Soc. Gerontol.; Curr. Contents Soc. Behav. Sci.; Psychoanal. Abstr.; PsycScan: Appl. Exp. Eng. Psych.; PsycScan: LD/MR; PsycScan: Neuropsych.; Res. Alert [Full Cov.]; Soc. Plann. Policy Dev. Abstr.; Soc. Sci. Cit. Index [Full Cov.].

US/0749-0232
**JOURNAL OF APPLIED SOCIOLOGY - SOCIETY FOR APPLIED SOCIOLOGY (U.S.).** (JOURNAL OF APPLIED SOCIOLOGY.). [J. appl. sociol. - Soc. Appl. Sociol. (U.S.)]. **Added/Corp** Society for Applied Sociology (U.S.). **VFOAT** JAS; J.A.S. (1984)-. English. Twice a year. $25.00. Management Support Services, 1117 E Spring Street, New Albany IN 47150. **Tel** (812)944-1826. **ED** M.D. Buffalo and J.D. Robson. **LC** HM1; .J6. **DD** 361. **Bk Rev. Ad Acc. Pr Rev. Circ:** 500.
**Desc:** Articles on the application of sociological knowledge and methods, practice-oriented articles, and works in progress.
**Ind/Abst** Soc. Plann. Policy Dev. Abstr.; Sociol. Abstr. [Full Cov.].

UK/0957-6851
**JOURNAL OF ASIAN PACIFIC COMMUNICATION. See** Communication.

UK/1052-9284
**JOURNAL OF COMMUNITY AND APPLIED SOCIAL PSYCHOLOGY.** [Community Appl. Soc. Psychol.]. **VFOAT** Journal of Community and Applied Social Psychology; Community & Applied Social Psychology. (1991)-. Periodical. English. Five times a year (includes special issue). $195.00. John Wiley & Sons Ltd., Baffins Lane, Chichester West Sussex PO19 1UD England. **Tel** 0243 779777, FAX 0243 776128 BTG:JWP001, telex 86290 WIBOOKG. **(Subscription address:** John Wiley / Philadelphia, PO Box 7247, Philadelphia PA 19170.**) ED** Geoffrey M. Stephenson and Jim Orford. **LC** HM251; .J525. **DD** 302/.05. **NLM** W1; JO593NG. **CODEN** JLCPEX. available on microfilm and microfiche from University Microfilms International (UMI). Documents available from The Genuine Article. ***Continues*** *Social Behaviour, 0885-6249.*
**Desc:** Aims to foster international communication among those concerned with the social psychological analysis and critical understanding of community issues and problems and to develop this understanding in the context of proposals for interventions and social policy.

**Ind/Abst** Curr. Contents Soc. Behav. Sci.; Int. Bibliogr. Sociol.; Psychol. Abstr. (1987-); PsycINFO; Res. Alert [Full Cov.]; Soc. Plann. Policy Dev. Abstr.; Soc. Sci. Cit. Index [Full Cov.]; Spec. Educ. Needs Abstr.

US/0194-2158
**JOURNAL OF COMMUNITY COMMUNICATION, THE. See** Communication.

US/0363-6666
**JOURNAL OF COMPARATIVE CULTURES, THE.** ***Ceased.*** Vol. 1 (1972)-( ). Periodical. English. qt. NABE - National Association for Bilingual Education, 1220 L Street Northwest, Suite 605, Washington DC 20005-4018. **Tel** (202)898-1829, FAX (202)789-2866.

US/0891-2416
**JOURNAL OF CONTEMPORARY ETHNOGRAPHY.** [J. contemp. ethnogr.]. **VFOAT** Contemporary Ethnography; JCE. Vol. 16, No. 1 (April 1987)-. Periodical. English. qt (Jan., Apr., July, Oct.). $170.00. SAGE Periodical Press, 2455 Teller Road, Thousand Oaks CA 91320. **Tel** (805)499-0721, FAX (805)499-0871, telex 100799. **ED** Patricia A. Adler and Peter Adler. **LC** HT101; .U677. **DD** 307.7/6/05. **NLM** W1; JO595S. **[CCC]. Pr Rev. Acid Free.** available on microfilm and microfiche from University Microfilms International (UMI). Documents available from The Genuine Article, UMI Article Clearinghouse. ***Continues*** *Urban Life, 0098-3039.*
**Desc:** Interdisciplinary journal of ethnography and qualitative research. Advances sociological knowledge through intensive, in-depth studies of human behavior in natural settings.
**Ind/Abst** Abstr. Anthropol.; Acad. Search (July 1993-); Anthropol. Index; Appl. Soc. Sci. Index Abstr.; Crim. Justice Abstr.; Curr. Contents Soc. Behav. Sci.; Curr. Index J. Educ.; Educ. Adm. Abstr.; Expand. Acad. Index (1989-); Hum. Resour. Abstr. (?-?); INFO-SOUTH Abstr.; Mag. Search; Newsp. Period. Abstr. (1991-); Psychol. Abstr.; Res. Alert [Full Cov.]; Sage Fam. Stud. Abstr. (?-?); Sage Urban Stud. Abstr (?-?); Soc. Plann. Policy Dev. Abstr.; Soc. Sci. Source (Jul. 1993-); Soc. Sci. Cit. Index [Full Cov.]; Soc. Sci. Index; Soc. Sci. Index Fulltext (Oct. 1988-) [Full Txt.]; Sociol. Abstr.; Soc. Res. Methodol. Abstr. (1992-).

US/0022-1031
**JOURNAL OF EXPERIMENTAL SOCIAL PSYCHOLOGY. See** Psychology.

US
**JOURNAL OF FAMILY AND CULTURE, THE.** Vol. 1, No. 1 (Spring 1985)-. Periodical. English. qt. $10.00. Free Congress Research and Education Foundation, 717 Second Street NE, Washington DC 20002. **Tel** (202)546-3000, (800)525-4992, FAX (202)546-7689. **NLM** W1; JO6443D.

UK/0277-6693
**JOURNAL OF FORECASTING.** [J. forecast.]. **VFOAT** Forecasting. Vol. 1, No. 1 (Jan./March 1982)-. Periodical. English. Seven times a year. $355.00. John Wiley & Sons Ltd., Baffins Lane, Chichester West Sussex PO19 1UD England. **Tel** 0243 779777, FAX 0243 776128 BTG:JWP001, telex 86290 WIBOOKG. **(Subscription address:** John Wiley / Philadelphia, PO Box 7247, Philadelphia PA 19170.**) ED** Derek W. Bunn (Editor's address: London Business School, Sussex Place, Regent's Park, London NW1 4SA United Kingdom). **LC** H61.4; .J68. **DD** 003/.2/05. **CODEN** JOFODV. **[CCC].** Index available (Bound in last issue). cum. index. **Pr Rev.** available on microfilm and microfiche from University Microfilms International (UMI). Documents available from The Genuine Article, UMI Article Clearinghouse.
**Desc:** Publishes referred papers on forecasting. It is a multidisciplinary, welcoming papers dealing with any aspect of forecasting: theoretical, practical, computational and methodological. This interdisciplinary journal is designed to provide a centralized focus on recent developments in the art and science of forecasting. It contains articles dealing with the development, maintenance and implementation of forecasting systems and the impact of uncertainty on the future of the organization.
**Ind/Abst** ABI/INFORM Glob. Ed.; ABI Inform Ondisc (Jan. 1983-); Acad. Search (July 1993-); Alum. Ind. Abstr.; Bus. Index (1986-); Contents Pages Manage.; Curr. Contents Soc. Behav. Sci.; Curr. Index Stat.; Gen. BusinessFile (1986-); Gen. Period. Index (1985-); INFO-SOUTH Abstr.; Int. Abstr. Oper. Res. [Select. Cov.]; Leis. Recreat. Tour. Abstr.; Mag. Search; Met. Abstr.; Res. Alert [Full Cov.]; Risk Abstr.; Selec. Coop. Index Manage. Period; Soc. Plann. Policy Dev. Abstr.; Soc. Sci. Cit. Index [Full Cov.]; Sociol. Abstr.; Stat. Theory Method Abstr.; UMI ABI/Inform--Bus. Period. Ondisc (Jan. 1988-) [Full Txt.].

UK/0952-1909
**JOURNAL OF HISTORICAL SOCIOLOGY.** [J. hist. sociol.]. Vol. 1, No. 1 (March 1988)-. Academic Scholarly Publication. English. Four times a year. £89.50 UK and Europe; $166.00 North America; £107.00 other. Basil Blackwell Publishers Ltd, 108 Cowley Road, Oxford 0X4 1JF England. **Tel** 011 44 865 791100, FAX 011 44 865 791347, telex 837022 OXBOOK G. **(Subscription address:** Blackwell

Publishers / UK, Marston Book Services, PO Box 87, Oxford OX2 0DT England.) **ED** Philip Lorrigan, Derek Sayer, Gavin Williams. **LC** HM104; .J68. **DD** 301. **[CCC].** Index available. **Bk Rev. Ad Acc. Circ:** 400. available on microfilm and microfiche from University Microfilms International (UMI).
**Desc:** Aims to further the rapprochement of history and the social sciences.
**Ind/Abst** Am. Hist. Life (1988-); Int. Bibliogr. Sociol.; Soc. Plann. Policy Dev. Abstr.; Sociol. Abstr. (1981-) [Full Cov.].

US/0047-2492
**JOURNAL OF INTERGROUP RELATIONS.** [J. intergroup relat.]. V. 1- Fall 1970-. Periodical. English. qt. $15.00 (one year), $27.50 (two year), $40.00 (three year) individuals, $17.50 (one year), $32.50 (two year), $47.50 (three year) institutions US; $19.00 (one year), $35.50 (two year), $52.00 (three year) individuals, $21.50 (one year), $40.50 (two year), $59.50 (three year) institutions other. National Association of Human Rights Workers, 115 South Andrews Avenue, Room 116, Ft Lauderdale FL 33301. **Tel** (305)357-6047. **ED** Fred Cloud. **DD** 305. **NLM** W1 JO716MA. **Bk Rev. Ad Acc. Circ:** 650 (ctrl). available on microfilm and microfiche from University Microfilms International (UMI). ***Supersedes*** *Journal of Intergroup Relations, 0047-2492.*
**Desc:** A quarterly publication of the National Association of Human Rights Workers. The only journal that chronicles the history of human rights in America. The premier journal for researchers interested in up-to-date trends in the field of human rights.
**Ind/Abst** Am. Hist. Life (1970-); Curr. Index J. Educ.

UK/0263-323X
**JOURNAL OF LAW AND SOCIETY. See** Law.

US/0022-250X
**JOURNAL OF MATHEMATICAL SOCIOLOGY, THE.** [J. math. sociol.]. Vol. 1 (Jan. 1971)-. Periodical. English. qt. $644.00 (academic institutions), $1004.00 (corporate institutions). Gordon & Breach Science Publishers, Inc., PO Box 786, Cooper Station, New York NY 10276. **Tel** (212)206-8900, FAX (212)645-2459. **(Subscription address:** International Publishers Distributor at one of the following addresses: 820 Town Center Drive, Langhorne, PA 19047; or PO Box 90, Reading Berkshire RG1 8JL UK; or Kent Ridge PO Box 1180, Singapore 9111, Republic of Singapore) **ED** Patrick Doreian. **LC** HM1; .J66. **DD** 301/.01/51. **CODEN** JMTSBX. **[CCC]. Bk Rev. Ad Acc. Pr Rev.** Documents available from The Genuine Article, Ask*IEEE.
**Ind/Abst** Compumath Citation Index [Full Cov.]; Curr. Contents Soc. Behav. Sci.; INSPEC (Jan. 1972-); Int. Bibliogr. Sociol.; Math. Rev.; Psychol. Abstr. (1971-); PsycINFO; PsycLit; Res. Alert [Full Cov.]; Soc. Plann. Policy Dev. Abstr.; Soc. Sci. Cit. Index [Full Cov.]; Sociol. Abstr. [Full Cov.]; Soc. Res. Methodol. Abstr. (1976-); Zentralbl. Math. Ihre Grenzgeb.

●US/1060-8265
**JOURNAL OF MEN'S STUDIES, THE. See** Men's Interests.

UK/0306-6150
**JOURNAL OF PEASANT STUDIES, THE.** [J. peasant stud.]. Vol. 1 (Oct. 1973)-. Periodical. English. qt. $185.00. Frank Cass & Company Ltd, Newbury House, 890-900 Eastern Avenue, Newbury Park, Ilford, Essex IG2 7HH United Kingdom. **Tel** 011 44 81 599 8866, FAX 011 44 81 599 0984, telex 897719. **ED** T.J. Byres and Henry Bernstein. **LC** HD1513.A3; J68. **DD** 301.44/43/05. **Bk Rev. Ad Acc, Adv Mgr:** Anne Kidson. **Pr Rev. Circ:** 927. available on microfilm and microfiche from University Microfilms International (UMI). Documents available from The Genuine Article.
**Desc:** A multi-disciplinary journal which provides a forum for peasant studies, based on the premise that studies of the peasantries within the broader systems and historical situations is the only way to achieve a true understanding of the role of peasants.
**Ind/Abst** AgBiotech News Inf.; Am. Hist. Life (1973-); Anthropol. Index; Anthropol. Lit.; Appl. Soc. Sci. Index Abstr.; Br. Humanit. Index; Curr. Contents Soc. Behav. Sci.; Geogr. Abstr. Human Geogr.; Int. Bibliogr. Sociol.; Int. Dev. Abstr.; Int. Labour Doc.; Int. Polit. Sci. Abstr.; LABORDOC; Middle East Abstr. Index; Multicult. Educ. Abstr.; PAIS Int. Print (1991-); Res. Alert [Full Cov.]; Rice Abstr.; Rural Dev. Abstr.; Soc. Plann. Policy Dev. Abstr.; Soc. Sci. Cit. Index [Full Cov.]; Sociol. Abstr.; Stud. Women Abstr.; Work Relat. Abstr.; World Agric. Econ.

UK/0743-0167
**JOURNAL OF RURAL STUDIES.** [J. rural stud.]. Vol. 1, No. 1 (1985)-. Periodical. English. qt. $306.00 The Americas; £205.00 other. Pergamon Press, An Imprint of Elsevier Science Ltd., The Boulevard, Langford Lane, Kidlington, Oxford OX5 1GB United Kingdom. **Tel** 011 44 865 843000, 011 44 865 843699, FAX 011 44 865 843010. **(Subscription address:** Elsevier Science Ltd. Oxford Fulfillment Centre, PO Box 800, Kidlington, Oxford OX5 1DX United Kingdom.) **ED** Paul Cloke. **LC** HT401; .J68. **DD** 307.7/2/05. **[CCC]. Pr Rev.** available on microfilm and microfiche from University Microfilms International (UMI). Documents available from The Genuine Article, Documents on Demand.
**Desc:** Focuses on the areas encompassing extensive land-use, with small-scale diffuse settlement patterns and communities linked into the surrounding landscape and milieux. Publishes up-to-date research from a wide range of multidisciplinary interests, including geography, economics, sociology, demography, agriculture, and planning.
**Ind/Abst** Abstr. Soc. Gerontol.; AGRICOLA [Full Cov.]; Curr. Aware. Biol. Sci., CABS; Curr. Contents Soc. Behav. Sci.; Curr. Index J. Educ. (March 1990); Dairy Sci. Abstr.; Environ. Abstr.; Environ. Period. Bibliogr.; Geogr. Abstr. Phys. Geogr.; Geogr. Abstr. Human Geogr.; Int. Bibliogr. Sociol.; Int. Dev. Abstr.; Maize Abstr.; PAIS Int. Print (1991-); Res. Alert [Full Cov.]; Rural Dev. Abstr.; Soc. Sci. Cit. Index [Full Cov.]; Wheat Barley Trit. Abstr.; World Agric. Econ.

●US/1061-7361
**JOURNAL OF SOCIAL AND EVOLUTIONARY SYSTEMS.** [J. soc. evol. syst.]. Vol. 15, No. 1 (1992)-. Periodical. English. qt. $225.00 (institutions), $90.00 (individuals) US; $245.00 (institutions), $110.00 (individuals) (surface mail), $265.00 (institutions), $130.00 (individuals) (air mail) other. JAI Press Inc., 55 Old Post Road, Suite 2, PO Box 1678, Greenwich CT 06836-1678. **Tel** (203)661-7602, FAX (203)661-0792. **ED** Paul Levinson. **LC** GN365.9; .J68. **DD** 304.5. **NLM** W1; JO877KE. **CODEN** JSESEX. Documents available from The Genuine Article. ***Continues*** *Journal of Social and Biological Structures, 0140-1750.*
**Desc:** Concerned with the unity, analogy, and relationships, theoretical and practical, between biological dynamics and mechanisms such as evolution, natural selection, and individual development, and social activities including technology, economics, politics, ideologies, literature, art, customs, and culture.
**Ind/Abst** Arts Humanit. Citation Index [Select. Cov.]; Curr. Contents Soc. Behav. Sci.; Res. Alert [Full Cov.]; Soc. Sci. Cit. Index [Full Cov.].

UK/0265-4075
**JOURNAL OF SOCIAL AND PERSONAL RELATIONSHIPS. See** Psychology.

●US/1053-0789
**JOURNAL OF SOCIAL DISTRESS AND THE HOMELESS. See** Sociology-Social Services and Welfare.

II
**JOURNAL OF SOCIAL TRANSFORMATION, THE.** V. 1- June 1977-. Periodical. English. qt. Rs8.00. Sanjivayya Institute of Socio-Economic Studies, Bapu Bhawan Sat Nagar Karol Bagh, New Delhi 110005 India. **LC** HN681; .J7. **DD** 309.1/54/05.

II
**JOURNAL OF SOCIOLOGICAL STUDIES, THE.** Vol. 1, No. 1 (Jan. 1982)-. Periodical. English. an. Rs50.00 India; $25.00 US. Kirti Khanna, Department of Sociology, University of Jodhpur, Jodhpur Rajasthan India. **Tel** 22306. **ED** Sheo Kumarlal. **LC** HN681; .J73. **DD** 301/.05. Index available. **Bk Rev. Ad Acc. Circ:** 100.
**Desc:** Eminent social scientists.
**Ind/Abst** Soc. Plann. Policy Dev. Abstr.; Sociol. Abstr. [Full Cov.].

CH
**JOURNAL OF SOCIOLOGY.** English (Chinese). an. $12.00. National Cheng Chi University, Department of Sociology, 64 Section 2 Chih Nan Wen Shan 116, Taipei Taiwan. **Tel** 011 866 2 9393091 ext 246. ***Continues*** *Journal of Ethnology & Sociology.*

US/0069-0864
**JOURNAL OF SOCIOLOGY (CLEVELAND).** (JOURNAL OF SOCIOLOGY.). **Main/Corp** Case Western Reserve University. (1967)-. Periodical. English. ir. Case Western Reserve University / School of Law, 11075 East Boulevard, Cleveland OH 44106. **Tel** (216)368-3304, FAX (216)368-6144. **LC** HM1; .C36a. **DD** 301/.05.

US/0193-7235
**JOURNAL OF SPORT AND SOCIAL ISSUES.** [J. sport soc. issues]. **Added/Corp** ARENA: Institute for Sport and Social Analysis. Vol. 1 (1976)-. Academic Scholarly Publication. English. qt (Feb., May, Aug., Nov.). $103.00. SAGE Periodical Press, 2455 Teller Road, Thousand Oaks CA 91320. **Tel** (805)499-0721, FAX (805)499-0871, telex 100799. **ED** Lawrence Wenner (Sport and Fitness Management Program, University of San Francisco). **LC** GV561; .J67. **DD** 796/.05. **Bk Rev. Ad Acc. Pr Rev. Acid Free. Circ:** 575 (ctrl).
**Desc:** Scholarly articles on all aspects of modern sports: emphasis on social problems and issues, such as racism, sexism, amateurism, academics, and youth sports.
**Ind/Abst** Altern. Press Index (199?-); Am. Bibliogr. Slavic East Europ. Stud. (19??-19??); Leis. Recreat. Tour. Abstr.; Phys. Educ. Index; Soc. Plann. Policy Dev. Abstr.; Sociol. Abstr. [Full Cov.]; SPORT Discus; SportSearch.

AT/1031-8313
**JOURNAL OF STUDIES IN JUSTICE.** ***Title Change.*** (1???)-(19??). English. sa (May & Nov.). Charles Sturt University, Mitchell Center for Studies & Justice, Bathurst NSW 2705 Australia. **Tel** 011 61 063 332778. ***Continued by*** *Journal for Social Justice Studies, 1035-4425.*
**Ind/Abst** APAIS, Aust. Public Aff. Inf. Ser. (1989-19??).

US/0010-3829
**JOURNAL OF THE COMMUNITY DEVELOPMENT SOCIETY.** [J. Community Dev. Soc.]. **Added/Corp** Community Development Society. Vol. 1 No. 1 (Spring 1970)-. Periodical. English. sa (May, Oct.). $55.00 US; $65.00 other. Community Development Society / Wisconsin, 1123 North Water Street, % Mikki Soltis, Milwaukee WI 53202. **Tel** (414) 276-8788, FAX (414) 276-7704. **ED** Jerry Hembd (editor's address: University of WI-Superior, Center for Economic Development, Superior, WI 54880; editor's telephone number: (715)394-8208). **LC** HN1; .C63. **DD** 301.3/4/05; 309.1. Index available. cum. index. **Bk Rev. Ad Acc. Pr Rev. Circ:** 1,000 (ctrl). available on microfilm and microfiche from University Microfilms International (UMI).
**Desc:** The official journal of the Community Development Society concerning the full range of social and economic issues for persons working and interested in community development.
**Ind/Abst** AGRICOLA [Full Cov.]; Crim. Justice Abstr.; Curr. Index J. Educ.; J. Plan. Lit.; PAIS Int. Print (1991-?); Soc. Plann. Policy Dev. Abstr.; Soc. Work Abstr. [Select. Cov.]; Sociol. Abstr.

US/0743-8532
**JOURNAL OF THE INSTITUTE FOR THE NEW MAN.** [J. Inst. New Man]. Vol. 1, No. 1-. Periodical. English. Institute for the New Man, PO Box 2919, Littleton CO 80161. **DD** 303.

US/1054-1802
**JOURNAL OF URBAN AND CULTURAL STUDIES. See** Education.

US/0047-2697
**JPMS; JOURNAL OF POLITICAL & MILITARY SOCIOLOGY.** [J. polit. mil. soc.]. **VFOAT** Journal of Political & Military Sociology). Vol. 1 (Spring 1973)-. Periodical. English. sa. $37.00 (institutions) US; $53.00 (airmail) Asia, Africa, former Soviet Republics; $52.00 (airmail) South America and Canada; $38.00 other. Social Science Research Institute, Department of Sociology, Northern Illinois University, DeKalb IL 60115. **Tel** (815)753-0352, (815)758-4088. **ED** George A Kourvetaris and Betty A Dobratz. **LC** HM1; .J22. **DD** 301.5/9/05. cum. index. **Bk Rev. Ad Acc. Pr Rev. Circ:** 1,000. available on microfilm from Xerox; available on microfilm and microfiche from University Microfilms International (UMI). Documents available from The Genuine Article.
**Desc:** Publishes articles which deal with the relationship of politics and the military, formal government and informal government, structures, empirical research papers, essays, theoretical pieces, and methodological papers.
**Ind/Abst** ABC POL SCI; Air Univ. Libr. Index Mil. Period.; Am. Hist. Life (1973-); Am. Bibliogr. Slavic East Europ. Stud.; Curr. Contents Soc. Behav. Sci.; Int. Polit. Sci. Abstr.; Middle East Abstr. Index; PAIS Int. Print (1991-); Res. Alert [Full Cov.]; Soc. Plann. Policy Dev. Abstr.; Soc. Sci. Cit. Index [Full Cov.]; Sociol. Abstr.; U.S. Polit. Sci. Doc.

MY/0126-5016
**JURNAL ANTROPOLOGI DAN SOSIOLOGI. See** Anthropology.

JA
**KAIHO NO HI O MOYASE. Main/Conf** Buraku Kaiho Shogakusei Zenkoku Shukai. **Added/Corp** Buraku Kaiho Domei. Chuo Hombu. (19??)-. Periodical. Japanese. ¥650. Buraku Kaiho Domei Chus Shuppankyoku, 1247 Kuboyoshicho Naniwa-ku, Osaka Japan. **LC** HT725.J3; B774a.

IO
**KATALOG BINA DESA.** Indonesian (English). ir. Sekretariat Pembinaan Sumber Daya Manusiawi Pedesaan, Jl Gunung Sahari III/7, Jakarta Pusat Indonesia. **Tel** (021) 8290435, telex YBS IA. **ED** Iman Suparyanto. **LC** HN710.Z9; C628. **Circ:** 1,000.
**Desc:** Inventory of Indonesian non-government organization working in the broad spectrum of community development activities throughout Indonesia.

JA
**KENKYUSHITSU IHO. Main/Corp** Hokkaido Daigaku (Japan). Shakaigaku Kenkyushitsu. No. 1- ; 1975-. Japanese. Hokkaido Daigaku Bungakubu Shakaigaku Kenkyushitsu, Kita 10-Jo, Nishi 7-Chome, Kita-ku 060, Sapporo Japan. **LC** HM7; .H64A.

II
**KERALA SOCIOLOGIST.** V. 1- 1973-. Periodical. English. sa. Rs50.00 India; $10.00 US. Kerala Sociological Society, c/o Department of Sociology, University of Kerala, Karyavattom Trivandrum 695581 India. **Tel** 8425. **ED** Jacob John Kattakkayam. **LC** HM1; .K47. **DD** 301/.05. Index available. **Bk Rev. Ad Acc. Circ:** 1,000 (ctrl).

# Sociology

EC
**KIPU.** (July 1983)-. Periodical. Spanish. sa. S/250.00 Ecuador; $20.00 other. Ediciones Abya-Yala, Casilla 8513, Quito Ecuador. **ED** Jose Juncosa. **LC** F3722; .K54. **DD** 986.6/00498. **Bk Rev. Ad Acc.** ctrl circ.
**Desc:** Information about the lives and problems of the poor.

US/0278-1557
**KNOWLEDGE AND SOCIETY, STUDIES IN THE SOCIOLOGY OF CULTURE PAST AND PRESENT.** [Knowl. soc., stud. sociol. cult. past present]. Vol. 3 (1981)-. English. ir. $73.25. JAI Press Inc., 55 Old Post Road, Suite 2, PO Box 1678, Greenwich CT 06836-1678. **Tel** (203)661-7602, **FAX** (203)661-0792. **ED** David Hess and Linda Layne. **LC** BD175; .R44. **DD** 306/.4. **CODEN** KSCPDO. **[CCC].** Continues Research in Sociology of Knowledge, Sciences and Art, 0163-0180.
**Ind/Abst** Soc. Plann. Policy Dev. Abstr.; Sociol. Abstr. [Full Cov.].

JA
**KOKUSAI KRYU.** Added/Corp Kokusai Koryu Kikin. (1974)-. Academic Scholarly Publication. Japanese. qt. ¥1200 Japan; ¥4000 US. Kokusai Koryu Kikin, c/o Park Building 3-6 Kioicho, Chiyoda-ku, Tokyo 102 Japan. **Tel** 03 2634504, telex J-23424 KIKINTYO. **ED** Yasuda Fonio. **LC** DS845; .K57. Index available. Circ: 8,000 (ctrl). **Desc:** Articles and interviews (Daniel Boorstin, Felix Guattari) on Japanese culture: language, film, performing arts, etc.

GW/0023-2653
**KOLNER ZEITSCHRIFT FUER SOZIOLOGIE UND SOZIALPSYCHOLOGIE.** (KOLNER ZEITSCHRIFT FUER SOZIOLOGIE UND SOZIALPSYCHOLOGIE / HERAUSGEGEBEN IM AUFTRAGE DES FORSCHUNGSINSTITUTS FUER SOZIAL UND VERWALTUNGSWISSENSCHAFTEN IN KOLN.). [Koln. Z. Soziol. Sozialpsychol.]. Added/Corp Universitat zu Koln. Forschungsinstitut fuer Sozial- und Verwaltungswissenschaften. Vol. 7, No. 1 (1955)-. Periodical. German. qt (Mar., June, Sep., Dec.). DM150.60 Germany; DM165.60 other. Westdeutscher Verlag GmbH, Postfach 5829, D 65048 Wiesbaden Germany. **Tel** 011 49 611 160220. (Subscription address: VVA Bertelsmann Dist GmbH, Postfach 7600, D 33310 Guetersloh Germany) **ED** Rene Konig. **NLM** W1 KO282N. **[CCC].** cum. index. **Bk Rev. Ad Acc. Pr Rev.** Circ: 3,200. Documents available from The Genuine Article. Continues Kolner Zeitschrift fur Soziologie.
**Ind/Abst** Crim. Penol. Police Sci. Abstr.; Curr. Contents Soc. Behav. Sci.; Int. Bibliogr. Sociol.; Int. Polit. Sci. Abstr.; Philos. Index; Psychol. Abstr. (1955-); PsycINFO (1990-); PsycLit; Res. Alert [Full Cov.]; Soc. Plann. Policy Dev. Abstr.; Soc. Sci. Cit. Index [Full Cov.]; Sociol. Abstr. [Full Cov.]; SportSearch; Soc. Res. Methodol. Abstr. (1978-).

RU
**KOMMERSANT : ORGAN SOIUZA OBEDINENNYKH KOOPERATIVOV SSSR.** Added/Corp Soiuz Obedinennykh Kooperativov SSSR. (19??)-. Newspaper. Russian. wk. $243.00. (Subscription address: East View Publications Inc., 3020 Harbor Lane North, Suite 110, Minneapolis MN 55447.)
**Desc:** Information on cooperative societies.

KO
**KOREA JOURNAL OF POPULATION AND DEVELOPMENT.** Added/Corp Soul Taehakkyo. Ingu mit Palchon Munje Yonguso. Vol. 19, No. 1 (July 1990)-. Periodical. English. sa. **LC** HN730.5; .A67a. **DD** 301/.0720519. **CODEN** KJPDEP. Continues Bulletin of the Population and Development Studies Center.
**Ind/Abst** Popul. Index.

UZ/0206-314X
**KPSS XXVI SEZDI QARORLARINI HAETGA TATBIQ ETISHDA UZBEKISTON MATBUOTI.** VFOAT KPSS 26 Sezdi Qarorlarini Haetga Tatbiq Etishda Uzbekiston Matbuoti. 1982-. Uzbek (Russian). an. **LC** Z7165.S652; U934; HN530.U9.

AU
**KRIMINALSOZIOLOGISCHE BIBLIOGRAPHIE.** See Law-Law Enforcement and Criminology.

GW/0454-6032
**KULTURPFLANZE : BEIHEFT. BERICHTE UND MITTEILUNGEN AUS DEM INSTITUT FUER KULTURPFLANZENFORSCHUNG DER DEUTSCHEN AKADEMIE DER WISSENSCHAFTEN ZU BERLIN IN GATERSLEBEN KRS. ASCHERSLEBEN, DIE.** Added/Corp Deutsche Akademie der Wissenschaften zu Berlin. Institut fur Kulturpflanzenforschung. (1956)-. Monographic series. German (English). ir. Price varies per volume.

Akademie-Verlag GmbH, Muehlenstrasse 33 34, D 13162 Berlin Germany. **Tel** 011 49 30 47889300, **FAX** 011 49 30 47889357. (Subscription address: VCH Publishers Inc., 303 Northwest 12th Avenue, Journals Department, Deerfield FL 33442.) **DD** 580.
**Ind/Abst** Rice Abstr.

BE/0023-5288
**KULTUURLEVEN.** (KULTUURLEVEN MAANDBLAD VOOR KULTUUR EN SAMENLEVING). (1934)-. Periodical. Dutch. Eight times a year. 1450.00F Belgium; 1945.00F Europe; 2245.00F other. Kultuurleven, Ravenstraat 112, 3000 Leuven Belgium. **Tel** 011 32 16 240196, 011 32 16 221801, **FAX** 011 32 16 222532. **UDC** 22/28. Index available (Bound in 8th iss.). **Bk Rev.** (Qty: 8). **Ad Acc, Adv Mgr:** M. Verminh.

KO
**KUNGMIN SAENGHWAL SIGAN CHOSA.** 1981-. Korean. W48.000. Hanguk Pansong Kongsa, 1 Youido-dong Yongdungpo-ku, Seoul 15 Korea. **LC** HN730.5.Z9; T54.

II/0023-5660
**KURUKSHETRA.** Added/Corp India (Republic). Community Projects Administration. India (Republic). Ministry of Community Development. India (Republic). Ministry of Community Development and Cooperation. India (Republic). Ministry of Food, Agriculture, Community Development and Cooperation. Vol. 1 (Aug. 1952)-. Periodical. English. Twenty-six times a year. $35.00. Ministry of Information and Broadcasting, Government of India, Patiala House, New Delhi 110 001 India. **Tel** 387983. (Subscription address: Prints India, 11 Darya Ganj, New Delhi 110002 India.) **LC** HN681; .K8. Continues Panchayati Raj.
**Ind/Abst** Dairy Sci. Abstr.; Soc. Plann. Policy Dev. Abstr.; Sociol. Abstr. (?-?).

JA/0387-3145
**KYOIKU SHAKAIGAKU KENKYU.** See Education.

IO
**LAPORAN KEGIATAN DEPARTEMEN SOSIAL.** Main/Corp Indonesia. Departemen Sosial. Indonesian. Departemen Sosial R I, Jln Ir H Juanda No 36, Jakarta Indonesia. **LC** HN702.5; .D46B.

US/0147-7307
**LAW AND HUMAN BEHAVIOR.** See Law.

US/0897-6546
**LAW & SOCIAL INQUIRY.** See Law.

CN/0701-1334
**LEISURE NEWSLETTER.** Title Change. (1973)-?. Newsletter. English (French). G Pronovost, University of Quebec at Trois-Rivieres, PO Box 500, Trois-Rivieres Quebec G9A 5H7 Canada. **DD** 301.5/7/072. Continued by Loisir Information, 0701-1342.

BE/0777-3455
**LEJOTIEK BRUSSEL.** [Lejotiek Bruss.]. (1987)-. Periodical. Dutch. mo. Lejo Vormingsdienst V, Leejong Simon Stevinstraat 14, B-1040 Brussels Belgium. **UDC** 37.

SW
**LEVNADSFORHALLANDEN ARSBOK.** VFOAT Living Conditions Yearbook. 1975-. Swedish. Ten times a year. Allmanna Forlaget Kundtjanst, S-162 89 Stockholm Sweden. **Tel** 8-7399630. **LC** HN572.5; .S7A.

US/1040-3760
**LIBERATOR (1988), THE.** (THE LIBERATOR : OFFICIAL NEWSLETTER OF THE MEN'S ORGANIZATIONS SUPPORT NETWORK.). [Liberator]. Added/Corp Men's Rights Assoc. Men's Organizations Support Network. Vol. 14, No. 7 (July 1988)-. Periodical. English. Twelve times a year. $24.00. Men's Rights Association, 17854 Lyons Street, Forest Lake MN 55025. **Tel** (612)464-7663. **ED** R. F. Doyle. **DD** 305. **Bk Rev. Ad Acc. Pr Rev. Circ:** 2,000. Continues Legal Beagle.
**Desc:** Covers gender issues from a male perspective.

RU
**LOGOS / LENINGRADSKII GOSUDARSTVENNYI UNIVERSITET.** Added/Corp Leningradskii Gosudarstvennyi Universitet. (1991)-. Russian. St Petersburg State University / Izdatelstvo Leningradskogo Universiteta, Universitetskaia Nab 7/9, 199034 St Petersburg Russia. **Tel** 011 95 218-97-88, **FAX** 011 95 218-51-52, telex 121481.

UK
**LONDON RISING TIDE, THE.** VFOAT Rising Tide. English. £4.50. **LC** HN30. **DD** 261.8/3/0441.

US/8756-4610
**LOSS, GRIEF & CARE.** See Psychology.

●SW/1102-4712
**LUND DISSERTATIONS IN SOCIOLOGY.** [Lund diss. sociol.]. (1992)-. Monographic series. English. ir. Price varies per volume.

Lund University Press, Box 141, S-22100 Lund Sweden. **Tel** 011 46 46 312000, **FAX** 011 46 46 305338, telex 33345 EDUCATE S. **ED** R. Persson. **UDC** 316.

GW
**MA BERICHTSBAND.** Main/Corp Arbeitsgemeinschaft Media-Analyse (Germany). VAT Media Analyse Berichtsband. 1972-. German. **LC** HN460.M3; A73A. Continues Berichtsband - Arbeitsgemeinschaft Leseranalyse.

IO/0541-721X
**MAJALAH ILMU-ILMU SASTRA INDONESIA.** VFOAT Indian Journal of Cultural Studies. V. 1- April 1963-. Indonesian (English). ir. $15.00. Mrs Haryati Soebadio, JL Kyai Maja 2A/Kebayoran Baru, Jakarta Selatan Indonesia.

US/0025-1550
**MAN-ENVIRONMENT SYSTEMS.** See Architecture.

CN/0825-3498
**MAN TO MAN (OTTAWA).** (MAN TO MAN : NEWSLETTER OF THE OTTAWA-HULL MEN'S FORUM.). [Man man]. V. 1, No. 1 (Summer 1984)-. Newsletter. English. Three times a year. Free. Ottawa-Hull Men's Forum, PO Box 177 Station B, Ottawa Ontario Canada. **DD** 305.3/2. ctrl circ.

II/0025-1615
**MANAB MON.** See Psychology.

GW
**MANNHEIMER SOZIALWISSENSCHAFTLICHE STUDIEN.** (1970)-. Monographic series. German. ir. Price varies per volume. Verlag Anton Hain Athenaeum, Wormer Strasse 99, D 55294 Bodenheim Germany. **Tel** 011 49 6135 3057. **Ad Acc.** Circ: 600.
**Desc:** Studies in sociology.

●BL/0103-8915
**MARGEM.** See Social Sciences.

IT
**MARGINALITA E SOCIETA.** Added/Corp Milan (Italy : Province). Assessorato ai Servizi Sociali e Cultura. Vol. 1 (1987)-. Periodical. Italian. Three times a year. L45000 Italy; L65000 other. Franco Angeli Riviste SRL, Viale Monza 106, 20127 Milan Italy. **Tel** 011 39 2 2827651, 011 39 2 289562. Continues Devianza Ed Emarginazione.

●US/1052-181X
**MARTIN LUTHER KING, JR. MEMORIAL STUDIES IN RELIGION, CULTURE, AND SOCIAL DEVELOPMENT.** VFOAT Studies in Religion, Culture, and Social Development. (1992)-. Monographic series. English. Price varies per volume. Peter Lang Publishing, 62 West 45th Street, 4th Floor, New York NY 10036. **Tel** (212)764-1471, (800)770-5264, telex 6973364 PLNY.

UK/0025-4118
**MARXISM TODAY.** Ceased. See General Interest-General Interest-Europe.

US/0743-7528
**MATERIAL CULTURE DIRECTORIES.** [Mater. cult. dir.]. 1988-. English. ir. Greenwood Press Inc., PO Box 5007, Westport CT 06881-5007. **Tel** (203)226-3571, **FAX** (203)222-1502. **DD** 305.

US/0149-6980
**MEDIA & VALUES.** See Communication.

UK/0163-4437
**MEDIA, CULTURE & SOCIETY.** [Media cult. soc.]. VFOAT Media, Culture, and Society. Vol. 1, No. 1 (Jan. 1979)-. Periodical. English. qt. £99.00. Sage Publications Ltd., 6 Bonhill Street, London EC2A 4PU, UK. **Tel** 071 374 0645, **FAX** 071 374 8741, telex 296207 SAGE G. **ED** Richard Collins and James Curran. **LC** HM258; .M373. **DD** 302.2/34/05. **Bk Rev. Ad Acc. Pr Rev. Acid Free.** Documents available from The Genuine Article, UMI Article Clearinghouse.
**Desc:** Focuses on the mass media within their political, cultural and historical contexts.
**Ind/Abst** Acad. Index. Full Text Elite (Jan. 1992-); Acad. Abstr. (Jan. 1992-); Acad. Search (Jan. 1992-); Arts Humanit. Citation Index [Select. Cov.]; Commun. Abstr.; Curr. Contents Soc. Behav. Sci.; Expand. Acad. Index (1989-); Humanit. Source (Jan. 1992-); INFO-SOUTH Abstr.; Int. Bibliogr. Sociol.; Int. Polit. Sci. Abstr.; Mag. Search; Middle East Abstr. Index; Newsp. Period. Abstr. (1991-); Res. Alert [Full Cov.]; Sage Fam. Stud. Abstr.; Soc. Plann. Policy Dev. Abstr.; Soc. Sci. Source (Jan. 1992-); Soc. Sci. Cit. Index [Full Cov.]; Soc. Sci. Index Fulltext (Oct. 1988-) [Full Txt.]; Sociol. Educ. Abstr.; Spec. Educ. Needs Abstr.; Stud. Women Abstr.

CN/0228-1554
**MEDIA WEST.** [Media west]. Vol. 1 (Mar. 1 1980)-. Periodical. English. bw. Pacific Rim Publications Ltd., 601

510 W Hastings Street, Vancouver British Columbia V6B 1L8 Canada. **Tel** (604)689-2021. **DD** 302.2/3/09712. **Ind/Abst** Can. Period. Index (Jan 1990-).

US/1051-7731
**MEDIAQUEST (BOSTON, MASS.).** (MEDIAQUEST.). [MediaQuest]. **VFOAT** Media Quest. (199?)-. Periodical. English. ir. $295.00. MediaQuest Publishing, PO Box 9222, Boston MA 02114. **Tel** (617)720-5751. **DD** 302.

GW
**MELANCHITHON-SCHRIFTEN DER STADT BRETTEN.** 1988-. Monographic series. German. Price varies per volume. Jan Thorbecke Verlag GmbH and Company, Karlstrasse 10, Postfach 546, D 72482 Sigmaringen Germany. **Tel** 011 49 7571 728100, FAX 011 07571-728-280, telex 732534.

CN/0708-0735
**MEMO FROM PROBE. Added/Corp** Pollution Probe (Ottawa, Ont.). (1976)-. Periodical. English. qt. Free. Pollution Probe-Ottawa, 53 Queen Street, Ottawa Ontario K1P 5C5 Canada. **DD** 301.31/06/271384. ctrl circ. ***Continues** Prober-O, 0319-2105.*

NE/0025-9454
**MENS EN MAATSCHAPPIJ.** [Mens maatsch.]. (1947)-. Periodical. Dutch. Four times a year. Fl117.92 (individuals), Fl216.98 (institutions) Netherlands; Fl125.00 (individuals), Fl230.00 (institutions) Belguim; Fl139.40 (individuals), Fl241.20 (institutions) others. Bohn Stafleu Van Loghum BV, Postbus 246, 3990 GA Houten Netherlands. **Tel** 011 31 3403 95782. **(Subscription address:** Intermedia BV, Postbus 4, 2400 MA Alphen Rijn Netherlands.) ***Continues** Mensch en Maatschappij.*
**Ind/Abst** Anthropol. Index; Anthropol. Lit.; Int. Bibliogr. Sociol.; Soc. Plann. Policy Dev. Abstr.; Sociol. Abstr. [Full Cov.]; Soc. Res. Methodol. Abstr. (1976-).

CL/0025-956X
**MENSAJE (SANTIAGO, CHILE). See** Religion and Theology.

US/0742-9797
**MEXICAN STUDIES. See** Economics.

JA
**MICHI; A JOURNAL FOR CULTURAL EXCHANGE.** V. 1- Spring 1978-. Periodical. English (Japanese). ¥1800. Yamaguchi Shoten, 72 Ichijoji Tsukidacho, Sakyo-ku 606, Kyoto Japan. **LC** HM258; .M52.

US
**MICHIGAN SOCIOLOGICAL REVIEW. Added/Corp** Michigan Sociological Association. Iss. 5 (Fall 1978); New Ser., No. 1 (Fall 1985)-. English. an. **CODEN** MSOREB. ***Supersedes** Peninsular Papers.*
**Ind/Abst** Soc. Plann. Policy Dev. Abstr.; Sociol. Abstr. (1985-) [Full Cov.].

US/0732-913X
**MID-AMERICAN REVIEW OF SOCIOLOGY.** [Mid-Am. rev. sociol.]. **Added/Corp** University of Kansas. Dept. of Sociology. **VFOAT** MARS. Vol. 1, No. 1 (Spring 1976)-. Periodical. English. sa. $20.00 institution; $8.00 individual. University of Kansas Department of Sociology, Lawrence KS 66045. **Tel** (913)864-4111. **ED** Mary E Kelly. **LC** HM1; .M5. **DD** 301/.05. **Bk Rev. Ad Acc. Pr Rev. Circ:** 400. available on microfilm and microfiche from University Microfilms International (UMI). ***Continues** Kansas Journal of Sociology, 0022-8648.*
**Desc:** Publishes articles on historical and contemporary issues in a wide range of subdisciplines within sociology.
**Ind/Abst** Index Period. Artic. Relat. Law (19??-19??); Soc. Plann. Policy Dev. Abstr.; Sociol. Abstr. [Full Cov.].

GW
**MILITAR UND SOZIALWISSENSCHAFTEN.** Vol. 1 (1988)-. Periodical. German. Nomos Verlagsgesellschaft, Postfach 610, D-76484 Baden Baden Germany. **Tel** 011 49 7221 21040.

CH
**MIN I TSA CHIH. VFOAT** Public Opinion Review. Periodical. Chinese (Chinese). **LC** HM261; .M53.

CH/0001-3935
**MINZUXUE YANJIUSUO JIKAN, ZHONGYANG YANJIUYUAN. See** Anthropology.

CN/0838-8083
**MOMENT (TORONTO).** (THE MOMENT.). [Moment]. **Added/Corp** Jesuit Centre for Social Faith and Justice. Vol. 1, No. 1 (Winter 1987)-. Periodical. English. Three times a year. 14.50Can$ (one year), 25.00Can$ (two years) institutions; 10.00Can$ (one year), 18.00Can$ (two years) individuals. Jesuit Centre, 947 Queen Street East, Toronto Ontario M4m 1J9 Canada. **Tel** (416)469-1123, FAX (416)469-3579. **ED** Christine Armeida. **DD** 971/.005.

CN/0701-2586
**MULTICULTURALISM.** [Multiculturalism]. **Added/Corp** University of Toronto. Guidance Centre. Ontario. Multicultural Development Branch. Vol. 1 (1977)-. Periodical. English. Three times a year. 25.00Can$ (institutions), 20.00Can$ (individuals) Canada; 30.00Can$ (institutions), 25.00Can$ (individuals) other. CCMIE, 316 Dalhousie Street, Suite 204, Ottawa Ontario K1N 7E7 Canada. **Tel** (613)241-4499. **DD** 301.45/1/0971.

AG
**MUTANTIA : ZONA DE LUCIDEZ IMPLACABLE.** (197?)-. Periodical. Spanish. bm. $40.00. Mutantia, c/o Miguel Grinberg, CC 260 Suc 12, 1412 Capital Argentina. **Tel** (541)30-4377. **ED** Federico Grinberg. **Bk Rev. Ad Acc. Circ:** 10,000.
**Desc:** Research and documentation of transformational processes within the individual and the social fabric, from the scope of a fourth world country.

US/0892-4287
**NATIONAL JOURNAL OF SOCIOLOGY.** (NATIONAL JOURNAL OF SOCIOLOGY : NJS.). [Natl. j. sociol.]. **Added/Corp** University of Texas at Austin. **VFOAT** NJS. Vol. 1, No. 1 (Spring 1987)-. Periodical. English. Twice a year. $15.00 institutions; $8.00 individuals. University of Texas at Austin National Journal of Sociology, Main Building 2300, Austin TX 78712. **Tel** (512)471-1122. **ED** John Sibley Butler (editor's phone: (512)471-1017). **LC** WMLC 93/1682; HM1; .N38. **DD** 301. Index available ($8.00). cum. index (first 5 vols. only). **Bk Rev**, (Qty: approx. 4). **Ad Acc. Circ:** 250.
**Ind/Abst** Soc. Plann. Policy Dev. Abstr.; Sociol. Abstr. (1987-) [Full Cov.].

US/1060-4960
**NATIONAL LONGITUDINAL SURVEY OF YOUTH, THE.** (THE NATIONAL LONGITUDINAL SURVEY OF YOUTH [COMPUTER FILE] : NLSY : [DATA].). [Natl. Longit. Surv. Youth]. **Added/Corp** National Longitudinal Survey of Youth Labor Market Experience (U.S.) Ohio State University. Center for Human Resource Research. United States. Bureau of Labor Statistics. NORC (Organization). **VFOAT** NLSY; National Longitudinal Survey of Labor Market Experience of Youth. (198?)-. English. Ohio State University / Human Resource Research, Center for Human Resource Research, Columbus OH 43210. **LC** HQ796; .N34. **DD** 305. available on magnetic tape.
**Desc:** Longitudinal study of 12,686 young men and women age 14-21. Interviewed about their work experience, military experience, training, schooling, family background, marital status, income and assets, health, fertility, child care, drug and alcohol use.

US/0148-8449
**NATIONAL OPINION POLL.** V. 1- Jan. 1978-. Periodical. English. mo. $36.00. National Opinion Poll Corporation, 30 North San Pedro Road, San Rafael CA 94903. **LC** HN90.P8; N37. **DD** 301.15/4/0973.

AT/0158-6270
**NATIONAL OUTLOOK SYDNEY.** (NATIONAL OUTLOOK.). [Natl. outlook Syd.]. (1979)-. Periodical. English. sa. 15.00Aus$ Australia; 20.00Aus$ other. Outlook Media Group Ltd., GPO Box 2134, Sydney NSW 2001, Australia. **Tel** 011 61 2 2675122. **DD** 994.005. **Circ:** 3,000.
**Desc:** Journal concerned with social ethics, theological developments, economics and political science.
**Ind/Abst** Hum. Rights Intern. Rep.

US/0897-4012
**NATIONAL VANGUARD.** [Natl. vanguard]. **Added/Corp** National Alliance (U.S.). No. 59 (April 1978)-. Periodical. English. Twelve times a year. National Alliance, PO Box 3535, Washington DC 20007. **Tel** (703)979-1886. **ED** William Pierce. **DD** 305. **Bk Rev. Circ:** 4,000. available on microfilm from The State Historical Society of Wisconsin. ***Continues** Attack.*
**Desc:** History, culture and mores of the European peoples, from a racial viewpoint; analysis and extrapolation of current social/political trends; exposition of radical alternatives.

CN/0701-8002
**NATURAL LIFE (UNIONVILLE. 1991). See** Health and Personal Fitness.

UK/0047-9586
**NEW COMMUNITY. See** Ethnic Interests.

US/0095-5248
**NEW FRONTIERS (SEATTLE).** (NEW FRONTIERS.). Summer 1974-. Periodical. English. sa. $3.00 single issue. Council of Executive Directors WA 98122. **LC** E185.5; .N463. **DD** 301.45/19/6073.

US/0890-1619
**NEW OPTIONS. *Ceased.* See** Political Science-International Relations.

US/1062-0443
**NEW PARADIGM DIGEST.** [New paradigm dig.]. (Summer 1991)-. Periodical. English. qt. New Paridigm Digest, 1118 5th Street, #1, Santa Monica CA 90403. **DD** 303.

II/0258-0381
**NEW QUEST.** [New quest]. **Added/Corp** Indian Association for Cultural Freedom. No. 1 (May 1977)-. Periodical. English. bm. $17.00. New Quest, 850/8A Shivajinagar, Pune 411004 India. **Tel** 011 91 212 345246. **(Subscription address:** Prints India, 11 Darya Ganj, New Delhi 110002 India.) **ED** M P Rege, M V Namjoshi and M L Raina. **LC** AP8; .N395. **DD** 052. **Circ:** 700 (ctrl). ***Supersedes** Quest.*
**Desc:** A journal of ideas and critical inquiry into social and political institutions. Also deals with philosophy and moral issues in human context.
**Ind/Abst** Int. Bibliogr. Sociol.; MLA Int. Bibl. Books Artic. Mod. Lang. Lit.

UK
**NEW TECHNOLOGY IN THE HUMAN SERVICES.** Vol. 4, No. 1 (Summer 1988)-. Periodical. English. an. £30.00 UK institutions; £60.00 US institutions; £20.00 US individual. Computers in Teaching Initiative, Social Work Study, University Southhampton, Southhampton S09 5NH England. **Tel** 11 44 703 593536, FAX 11 44 703 593939. **Bk Rev. Ad Acc. Pr Rev. Circ:** 500. ***Continues** Computer Applications in Social Work and Allied Professions, 0267-1980.*
**Desc:** Academic and practical papers for use in social services and in social services education.
**Ind/Abst** Soc. Work Abstr. [Select. Cov.].

NZ/0112-921X
**NEW ZEALAND SOCIOLOGY.** [N.Z. sociol.]. Vol. 1, No. 1 (May 1986)-. Periodical. English. sa. 40.00NZ$. New Zealand Sociology Subscriptions, Sociology Department Massey University, Palmerston North New Zealand. **Tel** 11 64 6 3569099.
**Ind/Abst** Soc. Plann. Policy Dev. Abstr.

US
**NEWSLETTER FOR AMERICAN-GERMAN CULTURAL STUDIES IN THE SOUTHEAST.** No. 1 (Jan. 1983)-. Newsletter. English. an. Duke University Center for International Studies, 2122 Campus Drive, Durham NC 27706. **ED** L R Phelps.

US/0077-5266
**NEWSLETTER - NATIONAL OPINION RESEARCH CENTER. Main/Corp** National Opinion Research Center. **VFOAT** NORC Newsletter. **VAT** National Opinion Research Center Newsletter. Newsletter. English. National Opinion Research Center, 6030 South Ellis Avenue, Chicago IL 60637. **Tel** (312)702-3285.

CN/0700-9798
**NEWSLETTER OF THE C A F. Main/Corp** Canadian Arab Federation. 1976-. Newsletter. English. Canadian Arab Federation, PO Box 416 Station K, Toronto Ontario M4P 2G8 Canada. **DD** 301.45/1/927071005. ***Supersedes** Arab Dawn., 0383-087X.*

CN/0711-723X
**NEWSLETTER (UNIVERSITY OF TORONTO. FACULTY OF SOCIAL WORK. ALUMNI ASSOCIATION).** (NEWSLETTER / SOCIAL WORK ALUMNI ASSOCIATION, UNIVERSITY OF TORONTO.). [Newsl. - Soc. Work Alumni Assoc., Univ. Tor.]. Newsletter. English. ir. Free. Alumni House, University of Toronto, 47 Willcocks Street, Toronto Ontario M5S 1A1 Canada. **DD** 378.713/541. ctrl circ.

NQ
**NICARAUAC : REVISTA BIMESTRAL DEL MINISTERIO DE CULTURA. *Ceased.*** **VFOAT** Revista Cultural Nicarauac. Vol. 1, No. 1, (May/June 1980)-(1988). Periodical. Spanish. bm. Revista Nicarauac, Apartado 3269, Managua Nicaragua. **Tel** 005052/22750. **LC** F1526.3; .N524. **DD** 972.8505. **Bk Rev.**
**Desc:** Culture, literature, poetry, art, and music of the new Nicaragua, from time to time on specific topics such as Christians and revolution, Atlantic Coast and Latin American culture.

IT
**NOI DONNE. Added/Corp** Unione delle Donne Italiane. (1944)-. Periodical. Italian. mo. L40000 Italy; L87000 US. Cooperative Libera Stampa, Via Trinita dei Pellegrini 12, 00186 Rome Italy. **Tel** 011 39 6 6864562. **ED** Anna Maria Crispino, Francisca Colli, Patrizia Giovannetti, Roberta Tatafiore, Mariella Gramaglia, Leila Di Paolo. Index available. **Circ:** 70,000.
**Desc:** The world seen through social, political, sentimental, family problems, women's faces in Italy and in the world.

KO
**NONGOCHON KAEBAL. VFOAT** AFDC Review. Periodical. Korean (Korean). Nongochon Kaebal Kongsa, 13-8 Noryangjin-dong, Kwanak-ku, Seoul Korea. **LC** HN730.5; .A57.

US/0893-5998
**NORC REPORTER, THE.** [NORC report.]. **VAT** National Opinion Research Center Reporter. Vol. 1, No. 1

(Winter 1987)-. Periodical. English. Three times a year. Free. National Opinion Research Center, 6030 South Ellis Avenue, Chicago IL 60637. **Tel** (312)702-3285. **ED** Susan Campbell. **DD** 300. **Circ:** 2,500.
**Desc:** Substantive and descriptive articles and news about research and articles of NORC.

US/0882-1968
**NORTH AMERICAN CULTURE.** (NORTH AMERICAN CULTURE : PUBLICATION OF THE SOCIETY FOR THE NORTH AMERICAN CULTURAL SURVEY.). [North Am. cult.]. **Added/Corp** Society for the North American Cultural Survey. Vol. 1 (1984)-. English. sa. $70.00 US, Canada, and Mexico; $80.00 other. Society of North American Cultural Survey, Oklahoma State University, Department of Geography, Stillwater OK 74078. **Tel** (405)744-7599, FAX (405)744-5620. **ED** Joe Seig, Telephone: (405)744-5178. **LC** E20; .N67. **DD** 970.053. **Pr Rev. Circ:** 120.
**Desc:** Exchanging ideas and reporting on multidisciplinary and interdisciplinary issues of culture in North America.

JA
**NOTORU DAMU SEISHIN JOSHI DAIGAKU KIYO : BUNKAGAKU HEN.** **Main/Corp** Notoru Damu Seishin Joshi Daigaku. **VFOAT** Notre Damu Seishin University Kiyo: Cultural Studies. Vol. 1 (1977)-. Japanese (summaries and/or abstracts in English). Notoru Damu Seishin Joshi Daigaku, 16-9 Ifukucho 2, Okayama 700 Japan. **LC** AS552.N6; A37. **DD** 059/.956. ***Supersedes** Kiyo.*

FR
**NOUS.** French. qt (4 issues). 45.00F. Editions Garibaldi, 53 rue Riquet, F-75019 Paris France. **Tel** 011 33 1 44-89-86-80, FAX 011 33 1 40-35-29-52. **ED** Pascal Corpart. **Bk Rev**, (Qty: 4). **Ad Acc, Adv Mgr:** Rene Boue. **Circ:** 14,000 (ctrl).
**Desc:** Deals with problems of society and the family.

FR/0048-0967
**NOUVELLE ECOLE.** **Added/Corp** Groupes de Recherche et d'Etudes pour la Civilization Europeenne. (19??)-. Periodical. French. Four times a year. Editions du Labyrinthe, 41 rue Barrault, 75013 Paris France.

RU
**NOVAIA OTECHESTVENNAIA LITERATURA PO OBSHCHESTVENNYM NAUKAM. FILOSOFIIA I SOTSIOLOGIIA / ROSSIISKAIA AKADEMIIA NAUK, INSTITUT NAUCHNOI INFORMATSII PO OBSHCHESTVENNYM NAUKAM.** ***Title Change.*** **See** Philosophy.

US
**NSV REPORT.** **Added/Corp** National Socialist Vanguard (Salinas, Calif.). Vol. 1, No. 1 (Jan./Mar. 1983)-. Periodical. English. Four times a year (Jan., Apr., July, Oct.). $5.00 (non-members); Free (members). National Socialist Vanguard, PO Box 328, The Dalles OR 97058. **Tel** (509)773-3919. **ED** Rick Cooper. **Bk Rev**, (Qty: 5). **Circ:** 1,000.
**Desc:** News and information on the all-white nation.

SP/0212-1891
**NUCLEAR ESPANA.** (NUCLEAR ESPANA : REVISTA DE LA SOCIEDAD NUCLEAR ESPANOLA.). [Nucl. esp.]. **Added/Corp** Sociedad Nuclear Espanola. (1982)-. Periodical. Spanish. ir (11 issues per year). $173.00 (Europe except Spain); $215.00 (other). Senda Editorial, Isla de Saipan 49, 28035 Madrid Spain. **Tel** 34 1 723-4750. **CODEN** NUESEN. Documents available from CASDDS.
**Ind/Abst** Chem. Abstr.

SP/1133-9535
**NUEVO LUNES, EL.** **See** Economics.

FR
**ONZE MONDIAL.** French. mo. 204.00F France; 264.00F other. Edimonde Loisirs, 90 rue de Flandre, 75947 Paris Cedex 19 France. **Tel** 011 33 1 44894489. ***Continues** Onze.*

UK/0143-0955
**ORAL HISTORY (COLCHESTER).** **See** History(General).

II
**ORGANISER.** Vol. 1, (1947)-. Periodical. English. Fifty-two times a year. Rs5501.00. Organiser, 29 Rani Jhansi Marg, New Delhi 110055 India. **Tel** 529888. **ED** V. Bhalia. **Bk Rev. Circ:** 12,000.
**Desc:** Concerned with social and political issues.

US/0885-6036
**ORGANIZER (WASHINGTON, D.C.).** (THE ORGANIZER.). [Organizer]. **Added/Corp** Institute for Social Justice. Vol. 9, No. 1 (Summer 1981)-. Periodical. English. Four times a year (Mar., June, Sept., Dec.). $20.00 (institutions), $12.50 (individuals). Acorn Publications, 1024 Elysian Fields, New Orleans LA 70117. **Tel** (504)943-0044. **LC** HN51; .O7x. **DD** 302. ***Continues** Just Economics.*
**Ind/Abst** Altern. Press Index.

CN/0828-8690
**OTTAWA MOSAIC, THE.** Vol. 1, No. 1 (May/June 1984)-. Periodical. English. bm. Free to residents of the Ottawa area. 18 Louisa St, Ottawa Ontario K1R 6Y6 Canada. **DD** 305.8/009713/84.

AU/1011-0070
**OZS, OSTERREICHISCHE ZEITSCHRIFT FUER SOZIOLOGIE.** [OZS, Osterr. Z. Soziol.]. **Added/Corp** Osterreichische Gesellschaft fuer Soziologie. **VFOAT** Osterreichische Zeitschrift fuer Soziologie. (1976)-. Academic Scholarly Publication. German (English). Four times a year. S300.00. Osterreichische Gesellschaft fuer Soziologie, Brunner Str. 72, A-1210 Vienna Austria. **Tel** 0222 29128 541, FAX 0222 29128 544. **ED** F. Traxler, E. Groebl-Steinbach, B. Schmeikal, M. Prisching, A. Grausgruber, A. Kirschner, R. Fuchshofer and M. Vanek. **LC** HM5; .O16. Index available. **Bk Rev**, (Qty: approx. 20 per year). **Pr Rev. Circ:** 600 (ctrl).
**Desc:** The scientific journal of the Austrian Sociological Association.
**Ind/Abst** Soc. Plann. Policy Dev. Abstr.; Sociol. Abstr. [Full Cov.].

NZ/0030-8978
**PACIFIC VIEWPOINT.** **See** Economics-Economic History, Conditions.

SP
**PAPERS: REVISTA DE SOCIOLOGIA.** No. 2 (1974)-. Catalan (Spanish). ir. ***Continues** Papers; Trabajos de Sociologia.*
**Ind/Abst** BHA : Biblio. Hist. Art.

US
**PAX.** **VFOAT** Pax, A Journal for Peace Through Culture; Pax, International Journal of Art, Science & Philosophy. (1983)-. Periodical. English. Three times a year. 217 Pershing Avenue, San Antonio TX 78209.
**Ind/Abst** Index Am. Period. Verse.

SZ
**PCR INFORMATION : REPORTS AND BACKGROUND PAPERS.** ***Title Change.*** **Added/Corp** World Council of Churches. Programme to Combat Racism. **VFOAT** P.C.R. Information. **VAT** Programme to Combat Racism Information. No. 1 (1979)-(19??). Monographic series. English. ir. World Council of Churches, PO Box 2100, CH 1211 Geneva 2 Switzerland. **Tel** 011 41 22 7906076, FAX 011 41 22 7910361, telex 23 423 OIK CH. **LC** BT734.2; .P35. ***Merged into** Echoes.*

RH
**PEOPLE AND PROJECTS.** Periodical. English. sa. Ministry of Education, Private Bag 7724, Causeway, Harare Zimbabwe. **LC** HN800.R64; C65. **DD** 309.2/63/096891. ***Continues** Projects and People.*

NP
**PEOPLE OF NEPAL : A RESEARCH AND DIGESTIVE QUARTERLY JOURNAL OF NEPAL SOCIOLOGY.** **VFOAT** Research and Digestive Quarterly Journal of Nepal Sociology. Vol. 1, No. 1 (Oct. 1991)-. Periodical. English (Nepali). qt. Rs30.00 (single issue). Heritage Research, Nepal-Antiquary, PO Box 5140, Kathmandu Nepal.

SP
**PERSPECTIVA SOCIAL.** 1- 1973-. Periodical. Multiple languages (Catalan, French and Spanish). sa. 1500ptas Spain; 1900ptas other. Institut Catolic d'Estudis Socials de Barcelona, Enric Granados 2, 08007 Barcelona Spain. **Tel** 93-253-28-00, 253-28-09, 323-25-50. **LC** HN1; .P47. **DD** 309.1.

CN/0710-4669
**PERSPECTIVES CANADA (ENGLISH EDITION).** (PERSPECTIVES CANADA.). [Perspect. Can.]. 3-. English. $9.50 Canada, $11.95 other countries. Printing and Publishing, Supply and Services Canada, Ottawa Ontario K1A 0S9 Canada. **LC** HN104; .C35B. **DD** 301/.0723; 309.1/73. ***Continues** Perspective Canada, 0710-4650.*
**Desc:** Contains selected statistical series describing the quality of life experienced by Canadians and the major social trends affecting Canadian society.

US/0079-1040
**PERSPECTIVES IN SOCIAL WORK.** ***Ceased.*** **Added/Corp** Adelphi University, Garden City, N.Y. School of Social Work. (1966)-(199?). Monographic series. English. ir. Adelphi University, School of Social Work, Garden City NY 11530.

US/1047-0905
**PERSPECTIVES ON SOCIAL PROBLEMS.** [Perspect. soc. probl.]. Vol. 1 (1989)-. English. ir. $73.25. JAI Press Inc., 55 Old Post Road, Suite 2, PO Box 1678, Greenwich CT 06836-1678. **Tel** (203)661-7602, FAX (203)661-0792. **ED** James Holstein and Gale Miller. **LC** HN41; .P47. **DD** 361.1. **Pr Rev.**
**Desc:** Purpose is to foster debates by providing a forum where sociologists of social problems can present and argue opposed positions on epistemological, moral, and political issues.

VM
**PHAT-TRIEN XA-HOI.** So 1- April 9, 1971-. Periodical. Vietnamese. qt. $4.50. Hoi Khoa Hoc Xa Hoi Viet Nam, 33 Dng Vinh Vien Chln, Saigon Vietnam. **LC** HN700.V5; A6.

PH
**PHILIPPINE BRIEFINGS.** 1-. English. Department of Public Information / Philippines, Room 210/National Press Club Building, Magallanes Drive, Intramuros Philippines. **LC** HN711; . P45. **DD** 309.1/599/04.

PH/0115-0243
**PHILIPPINE QUARTERLY OF CULTURE AND SOCIETY.** [Philipp. q. cult. soc.]. **Added/Corp** University of San Carlos. **VFOAT** San Carlos Publications. Vol. 1 (Mar. 1973)-. Periodical. English. qt. $30.00 institutions; $28.00 individuals. University of San Carlos / San Carlos Publications, 6000 Cebu City Philippines. **Tel** 011 63 32 72419, 011 63 32 72410. **ED** Joseph Baumgartner. **LC** DS651; .P498. **DD** 959.9/005. Index available (bound in 4th issue). **Bk Rev. Ad Acc. Circ:** 300. ***Supersedes** San Carlos Publications. Series E: Miscellaneous Contributions in the Humanities.*
**Desc:** Subjects on Philippine culture and society, past and present.
**Ind/Abst** Agrofor. Abstr.; Anthropol. Index; Anthropol. Lit.; Index Islam. Lit.; Index Philip. Period.; Int. Bibliogr. Sociol.; MLA Int. Bibl. Books Artic. Mod. Lang. Lit.

PH/0031-7810
**PHILIPPINE SOCIOLOGICAL REVIEW.** [Philipp. sociol. rev.]. **Added/Corp** Philippine Sociological Society. (Aug. 1953)-. Periodical. English. Four times a year. $20.00 Philippines; $25.00 others. PSSC Central Subscription Service, PO Box 205 UP Diliman, Quezon City 1101 Philippines. **Tel** 011 63 2 9229621. **ED** Ricardo G. Abad. **LC** HM1; .P5. **Bk Rev. Ad Acc. Circ:** 1,000.
**Desc:** Publishes original studies and papers on sociology, anthropology, and demography.
**Ind/Abst** Anthropol. Index; Index Philip. Period. (-199?); MLA Int. Bibl. Books Artic. Mod. Lang. Lit.; Soc. Plann. Policy Dev. Abstr.; Sociol. Abstr. [Full Cov.].

II/0377-2772
**PHILOSOPHY AND SOCIAL ACTION.** [Philos. soc. action]. **Added/Corp** Committee of Concerned Indian Philosophers for Social Action. Vol. 1 (Jan. 1975)-. English. qt. $50.00. Institute of Socio-Political Dynamics, M-120 Greater Kailash 1, New Delhi 110048 India. **Tel** 641-5365. **(Subscription address:** Prints India, 11 Darya Ganj, New Delhi 110002 India.**) ED** Dhirendra Sharma. **LC** HN681; .P5. **DD** 309.1/54/05. **Bk Rev. Ad Acc. Pr Rev. Circ:** 1,000.
**Desc:** Covers development science policy, Third World issues, human rights, and world peace.
**Ind/Abst** Curr. Lit. Sci. Sci.; Hum. Rights Intern. Rep.; Philos. Index; Soc. Plann. Policy Dev. Abstr.; Sociol. Abstr.

KO
**PIPUL / PEOPLE.** ***Title Change.*** **Added/Corp** Soul Sinmunsa. **VFOAT** People. Vol. 1, No. 1 (1992)-(1992). Periodical. Korean. wk. Soul Sinmunsa, 31 1-ka Taepyong-no, Chung-ku, Seoul South Korea. **LC** AP95.K6; P57. ***Continued by** Nyusu Pipul.*

FR
**POINT ECONOMIQUE DE L'AUVERGNE, LE.** **Main/Corp** Institut National de la Statistique et des Etudes Economiques (France). (May 1971)-. Periodical. French. bm (6 issues). 96.00F US. CNGP INSEE - Institut National de la Statistique et des Estudes Economiques, BP 2718, 1 rue V Auriol, F 80027 Amiens Cedex 1 France. **Tel** 011 33 22 927322. **LC** HA1228.A9; A32. ***Continues** Bulletin de Statistique: Auvergne (Allier, Cantal, Haute-Loire, Puy-de-Dome).*
**Desc:** Publishes socio-economic information on the Clermontferrand region of France in an accessible format with concise analysis of statistics.

IT
**POLIS (BOLOGNA, ITALY).** (POLIS.). Vol. 1, No. 1 (April 1987)-. Periodical. Italian (summaries and/or abstracts in English). Three times a year. L62000.00 Italy; L110000.00 (surface mail), L140000.00 (airmail) other. Editrice Turistica SRL, Via Rasella 155, 00187 Rome Italy. **Tel** 011 39 6 4821539. **LC** HN471; .P64. **CODEN** POLBEL.

PL/0032-2997
**POLISH SOCIOLOGICAL BULLETIN, THE.** ***Title Change.*** [Pol. sociol. bull.]. **Added/Corp** Polskie Towarzystwo Socjologiczne. No. 1/2 (1961)-(19??). Bulletin. English. qt. **(Subscription address:** ARS Polona, PO Box 1001, 00068 Warsaw Poland.**) LC** HM1; .P6. **DD** 301/.05. ***Continued by** Polish Sociological Review.*
**Ind/Abst** Appl. Soc. Sci. Index Abstr.; Int. Labour Doc.; Int. Polit. Sci. Abstr.; Soc. Plann. Policy Dev. Abstr.; Sociol. Abstr. (1961-) [Full Cov.]; Sociol. Educ. Abstr.; Soc. Res. Methodol. Abstr. (1988-).

PL
**POLISH SOCIOLOGICAL REVIEW.** English. qt. Price on Request. **(Subscription address:** ARS Polona, PO Box 1001, 00068 Warsaw Poland.**)** ***Continues*** *The Polish Sociological Bulletin.*

PL
**POLISH SOCIOLOGY OF LAW NEWSLETTER, THE.** **See** Law.

US/0190-9320
**POLITICAL BEHAVIOR.** **See** Political Science.

US/0198-8719
**POLITICAL POWER AND SOCIAL THEORY.** **See** Political Science.

UK/0954-6030
**POLITICS AND SOCIETY IN GERMANY, AUSTRIA, AND SWITZERLAND.** **Added/Corp** University of Nottingham. Institute of German, Austrian, & Swiss Affairs. Association for the Study of German Politics. **VFOAT** PASGAS. Vol. 1, No. 1 (Summer 1988)-. Periodical. English. Three times a year. £12.00. Institute German Austrian Swiss AFF, University of Nottingham, Nottingham NG7 2RD England. **Tel** 011 44 602 484848. **ED** Professor H. Sielken. **Bk Rev**, (Qty: 2). **Circ:** 500.

US/0887-171X
**POLLING REPORT, THE.** [Poll. rep.]. (198?)-. Periodical. English. sm. $195.00. Polling Report Inc, 509 Capitol Court Northeast, Suite 100, Washington DC 20002. **Tel** (202)544-5455, FAX (202)544-1695. **ED** Thomas H Silver. **DD** 303. **Bk Rev**, (Qty: 20). **Circ:** 400.
**Desc:** A compendium of current national and statewide public opinion surveys on political, business and public policy issues. Plus analytical articles by the country's leading experts, and comprehensive coverage of election polling.

CN/0316-7232
**PONTE (WILLOWDALE).** (IL PONTE.). **VFOAT** Bridge. Vol. 1- Sept. 1973-. Multiple languages (Italian and English). Il Ponte, 650 East Avenue Sheppard, Willowdale Ontario M2X 1B7 Canada. **DD** 301.45/1/510713541.

PL
**PORTUGIESISCHE FORSCHUNGEN.** **Main/Corp** Gorres Gesellschaft zur Pflege der Wissenschaft im Katholischen Deutschland. German.
**Desc:** Covers Portuguese culture and history. Also, can help to promote cultural relations between Portugal or Brazil and the German-speaking countries.

FR/0245-9442
**POUR.** [Pour]. **Added/Corp** Groupe de Recherche pour l'Education Permanente. (1966)-. Periodical. French. qt. 310.00F France; 350.00F other. GREP, 13 15 rue des Petites Ecuries, 75010 Paris France. **Tel** 011 33 1 48245036, FAX 011 33 1 48240054. Index available. **Bk Rev**. **Pr Rev. Circ:** 1,500.

US/0097-7950
**POVERTY IN TEXAS.** **Main/Corp** Texas. Office of Economic Opportunity. 1972-. English. an. Free. Office of Economic Opportunity / Austin, 611 South Congress Avenue, PO Box 13166 Capitol Station, Austin TX 78711. **Tel** (512)834-6217. **ED** Deborah Amberson. **LC** HC107.T43; P633A. **DD** 301.44/1. **Circ:** 1,100 (ctrl).
**Desc:** Technical newsletter designed for nonprofits serving elderly, handicapped, and poor persons. Topic of main concern is poverty and related issues. Monitors state/federal regulations affecting the poor.

PL/0138-0311
**PRAXIOLOGY.** **Added/Corp** Zakad Prakseologii (Polska Akademia Nauk). No. 1 (1980)-. English. Four times a year. Transaction Publishers / Rutgers State University, New Brunswick NJ 08903. **Tel** (908)932-2280 Ext. 105, FAX (908)932-3138. **(Subscription address:** ARS Polona, PO Box 1001, 00068 Warsaw Poland.**)** **ED** W. W. Gasparski and M. K. Mlicki. **LC** BD450; .P6. **DD** 128/.4/05.
**Desc:** Examines fundamental issues in the theory of human action, the nature of economics, and theoretical issues in such praxiological disciplines as design, accounting, market mechanisms, management and planning.

US/0883-3095
**PRE- AND PERI-NATAL PSYCHOLOGY JOURNAL.** **See** Medical Science and Technology-Gynecology and Obstetrics.

BU/0204-8620
**PROBLEMS OF CULTURE / COMMITTEE FOR CULTURE, RESEARCH INSTITUTE FOR CULTURE AT THE COMMITTEE FOR CULTURE, AND THE BULGARIAN ACADEMY OF SCIENCES.** **Added/Corp** Natsionalen Nauchnoinformatsionen Tsentur (Bulgaria) Bulgarska Akademiia na Naukite. (1978)-. Periodical. English. 4.20lv. Problems of Culture, 1000 Sofia, 4 Sofiiska Komuna Str PR, 1000 Sofia Bulgaria. **Tel** 883322. **ED** Elite Nicholov. **LC** HM101; .P87. **DD** 306. **Bk Rev. Circ:** 5,000.
**Desc:** Covers cultural problems and history, aesthetic training, education, management and social developments, arts and the mass media, creative personality problems, etc.

US/0271-4558
**PROCEEDINGS OF THE CONFERENCE OF THE AMERICAN COUNTRY LIFE ASSOCIATION, INC.** **Main/Corp** American Country Life Association. Proceedings. English. an. American Country Life Association, 2118 South Summit Avenue, Sioux Falls SD 57105. **Tel** (605)336-5236. **LC** HT407; .A3. ***Continues*** *Proceedings of the American Country Life Conference.*

GR
**PROGRAMMA DRASTERIOTETOS.** **Main/Corp** Ethnikon Kentron Koinonikon Ereunon. **VFOAT** Program of Activities. summaries and/or abstracts in English. Sophokleous 1, Athens Greece. **LC** HM48; .E84A.

SA
**PROGRESS IN INTER-GROUP AND RACE RELATIONS.** **Main/Corp** South Africa. Dept. of Information. English. Department of Information / Pretoria, Private Bag X152, Pretoria South Africa. **LC** DT763; .S5742A. **DD** 305.8/00968.

CN/1186-2432
**PROPOS (QUEBEC), A.** (L'A PROPOS.). [A propos]. **Added/Corp** Institut Quebecois de Recherche sur la Culture. Editions du Septenrion. Vol. 1, No 1 (1991)-. Periodical. French. Four times a year. Free. Institut Quebecois de Recherche sur la Culture, 14 rue Haldemand, Quebec Quebec G1R 4N4 Canada. **Tel** (418)643-4695. **DD** 971.4/005.

PL/0033-2356
**PRZEGLAD SOCJOLOGICZNY.** [Prz. socjol.]. **VFOAT** Sociological Review. Began in 1930. Polish (summaries and/or abstracts in English). an (irregular). $9.50. Zakad Narodowy Im Ossolinskich We Wrocawiu, Krakowskie Przedmiescie 7, 00 068 Warsaw Poland. **LC** HM7; .P7. **DD** 301/.05.
**Ind/Abst** Am. Hist. Life (1957-1989); Int. Bibliogr. Sociol.; Soc. Plann. Policy Dev. Abstr.; Sociol. Abstr. [Full Cov.].

US/0277-2469
**PSYCHOLOGY & SOCIAL THEORY.** **See** Psychology.

US/0885-7423
**PSYCHOLOGY AND SOCIOLOGY OF SPORT.** **See** Psychology.

US/0887-932X
**PUBLIC COMMUNICATION AND BEHAVIOR.** **See** Communication.

US/0033-362X
**PUBLIC OPINION QUARTERLY.** [Public opin. q.]. **Added/Corp** American Association for Public Opinion Research. Princeton University. School of Public Affairs. Woodrow Wilson School of Public and International Affairs. Columbia University. Advisory Committee on Communication. Vol. 1 (Jan. 1937)-. Academic Scholarly Publication. English. qt. $50.00 institution, $23.00 individual, $20.00 student. University of Chicago Press / Journals Division, PO Box 37005, 5720 South Woodlawn, Chicago IL 60637. **Tel** (312)753-3347, FAX (312)753-0811. **(Subscription telephone:** (312)753-8083**)** **ED** D. C. Poole. **LC** HM261.A1; P8. **DD** 301.15. **NLM** W1 PU627. **CODEN** POPQAE. **[CCC].** cum. index. **Pr Rev. Acid Free.** available on microfilm and microfiche from University Microfilms International (UMI). Documents available from The Genuine Article, UMI Article Clearinghouse.
**Desc:** Since 1937, this journal has been the leading scholarly journal devoted to public opinion and communication research, propaganda, survey methods, and related subjects.
**Ind/Abst** ABC POL SCI; ABI/INFORM Glob. Ed.; ABI Inform Ondisc (Fall 1971-); Acad. Abstr. Full Text Elite (Jan. 1990-); Acad. Abstr. (Jan. 1990-); Acad. Ind. [Computer File] (1984-); Acad. Search (Jan. 1990-); Am. Hist. Life (1963-); Appl. Soc. Sci. Index Abstr.; Book Rev. Index; Commun. Abstr.; Crim. Justice Abstr.; Crim. Penol. Police Sci. Abstr.; Curr. Contents Soc. Behav. Sci.; Expand. Acad. Index (1984-); Gen. Period. Index (1985-); Health Plan. Adminis.; Hospit. Health Admin. Index; Index Period. Artic. Relat. Law; INFO-SOUTH Abstr.; Infobank (1979-); Int. Bibliogr. Sociol.; Int. Polit. Sci. Abstr.; J. Plan. Lit.; Mag. Index Plus (1989-); Mag. Search; Middle East Abstr. Index; Newsp. Period. Abstr. (1986-); Nutr. Res. Newsl.; PAIS Int. Print (1991-); Peace Res. Abstr. J. (1977-1982); Psychol. Abstr. (1937-); PsycINFO; PsycLit; Res. Alert [Full Cov.]; Res. High. Educ. Abstr.; Sage Public Adm. Abstr.; Soc. Plann. Policy Dev. Abstr.; Soc. Sci. Source (Jul. 1990-); Soc. Sci. Cit. Index [Full Cov.]; Soc. Sci. Index; Soc. Sci. Index Fulltext (Fall 1988-) [Full Txt.]; Sociol. Abstr. [Full Cov.]; Soc. Res. Methodol. Abstr. (1976-); Stat. Ref. Index; Stat. Theory Method Abstr. (1959-1963); Mag. Index (1977-); UMI ABI/Inform--Bus. Period. Ondisc (Spring 1987-) [Full Txt.]; U.S. Polit. Sci. Doc.

IT/0481-097X
**QUADERNI DI CULTURA FRANCESE.** Vol. 1 (1959)-. Monographic series. Italian. Price varies per volume. Edizioni di Storia e Letteratura, Via Lancellotti 18, Rome 00186 Italy. **Tel** 011 39 6 68806556. **ED** Ettore Paratore. **DD** 944. **Circ:** 700.

IT/0033-4952
**QUADERNI DI SOCIOLOGIA.** [Quad. sociol.]. Vol. 1, No. 1 (1951)-. Periodical. Italian. Three times a year. L75000 Europe; L115000 other. Rosenberg & Sellier, Via Andrea Doria 14, 10123 Turin Italy. **Tel** 011 39 11 8127808, telex 224202 ROSSELI. **LC** HM7; .Q3.
**Ind/Abst** Am. Hist. Life (1970-1978); Int. Bibliogr. Sociol.; Soc. Plann. Policy Dev. Abstr.; Sociol. Abstr. [Full Cov.].

US/0033-510X
**QUAKER SERVICE BULLETIN / AMERICAN FRIENDS SERVICE COMMITTEE.** **Added/Corp** American Friends Service Committee. **VFOAT** Quaker Service; AFSC Bulletin. No. 108 (Winter 1970)-. Bulletin. English. tq. available on microfilm from University Microfilms International (UMI). ***Continues*** *Quaker Service (Cambridge, Mass.).*
**Ind/Abst** Hum. Rights Intern. Rep.

US/0162-0436
**QUALITATIVE SOCIOLOGY.** [Qual. sociol.]. **Added/Corp** University of Baltimore. **VFOAT** QS. Vol. 1 (May 1978)-. Periodical. English. qt. $235.00 US; $275.00 other. Human Sciences Press, PO Box 735, 233 Spring Street, New York NY 10013. **Tel** (212)620-8000, FAX (212)807-1047, telex 23421139. **(Subscription address:** Eurospan Ltd., Journals and Serials Division, 3 Henrietta Street, Covent Garden, London WC2E 8LU England.**)** **ED** Rosanna Hertz and Jonathan Imber. **LC** HM1; .Q34. **DD** 301/.05. **[CCC].** available on microfilm and microfiche from University Microfilms International (UMI).
**Desc:** Devoted to the qualitative interpretation of social life. A broad spectrum of topics and research methods is featured, including theoretical essays, fieldwork studies, discussions of the philosophy of social science, photographic studies and qualitative interpretations of quantitative data.
**Ind/Abst** Crim. Justice Abstr.; Multicult. Educ. Abstr.; PsycINFO (?-?); PsycLit; Soc. Plann. Policy Dev. Abstr.; Soc. Work Abstr. [Select. Cov.]; Sociol. Abstr. [Full Cov.]; Sociol. Educ. Abstr.; Spec. Educ. Needs Abstr.; Soc. Res. Methodol. Abstr. (1982-); Stud. Women Abstr.

US/0738-9752
**QUARTERLY JOURNAL OF IDEOLOGY.** (QUARTERLY JOURNAL OF IDEOLOGY : QJI.). [Q. j. ideol.]. **Added/Corp** Auburn University at Montgomery. Center for Demographic and Cultural Research. Louisana State University in Shreveport. **VFOAT** Journal of Ideology; QJI; Q.J.I. Vol. 1, No. 1 (Fall 1976)-. Periodical. English. Twice a year. $35.00. Louisiana State University - Shreveport / Department of Social Science, Shreveport LA 71115. **Tel** (318)797-5242, FAX (318)797-5156. **ED** Norman A Dolch and Laura Morrow, Telephone:(318)797-5235. **LC** B823.3; .Q37. **DD** 306. **Bk Rev**, (Qty: 8-10). **Ad Acc. Pr Rev. Circ:** 100.
**Desc:** Dedicated to critiquing conventional wisdom in subject matter in sociology, political science, economics, and philosophy.
**Ind/Abst** Romant. Move.; Soc. Plann. Policy Dev. Abstr.; Sociol. Abstr. [Full Cov.].

SP/0212-7210
**R T S. REVISTA DE TREBALL SOCIAL.** [R T S, Rev. treb. soc.]. **VFOAT** Revista de Treball Social; RTS. Revista de Trabajo Social; RTS; Revista de Trabajo Social. (1969)-. Periodical. Spanish (Catalan). qt. 2400.00ptas. Colegio Ofic Asistentes Social Diplomados, Puertaferrisa 18-1A, 08002 Barcelona Spain. **Tel** 011 34 3 3185593, 011 34 3 3170040. **UDC** 361.

SA
**RACE RELATIONS NEWS.** **Added/Corp** South African Institute of Race Relations. **VFOAT** RR News. Vol. 51, No. 2 and 3 (July 1989)-. Periodical. English. qt. Free. South African Institute of Race Relations, PO Box 31044, Braamfontein 2017 South Africa. **Tel** 011 27 11 4033600, FAX 011 27 11 4033671. ***Continues*** *SAIRR News.*
**Ind/Abst** Hum. Rights Intern. Rep.

FR
**RAPPORT D'ACTIVITE - MINISTERE DE L'EQUIPEMENT.** **Main/Corp** France. Ministere de l'Equipement. (1969)-. French. Ministere de l'Equipement, 21 rue Mathuring-Regnier, 75732 Paris Cedex 15 France. **LC** HT395.F7; F75A.

FR
**RAPPORT NATIONAL DE CONJONCTURE SCIENTIFIQUE : SCIENCES DE L'HOMME.** **Main/Corp** France. Centre National de la Recherche Scientifique. Comite National de la Recherche Scientifique. French. CNRS / Institut d'Information Scientifique et Technique, (Centre National de la Recherche Scientifique), 15 Quai Anatole France, Paris 75700 France. **Tel** 011 33 1 47531515, telex 299 356 F. **LC** HM101; .F755A. **DD** 301.2.

IT
**RAPPORTO SULLA SITUAZIONE SOCIALE DEL PAESE.** **Main/Corp** Centro Studi Investimenti Sociali. (1967)-. Italian. an. Franco Angeli Editore Riviste, Via le Monza 106, 20127 Milan Italy. **Tel** 011 39 2 2827651 or, 289562, FAX 011 39 2 258004, telex 051-511650. **(Subscription address:** Gestioni & Partecipazioni SRL, Viale Monza 106, 20127 Milan Italy.**)** **LC** HN471; .C46a.

IT/0079-9734
**RASSEGNA ITALIANA DI SOCIOLOGIA.** Vol. 1 (Jan./Mar. 1960)-. Periodical. Italian. qt. L80000.00 Italy; L140000.00 (surface mail), L160000.00 (airmail) other. Societa Editrice il Mulino, Strada Maggiore 37, 40125 Bologna Italy. **Tel** 011 39 51 256011, FAX 011 39 51 256034.
**Ind/Abst** Am. Hist. Life (1974-); Int. Bibliogr. Sociol.; Psychol. Abstr.; Soc. Plann. Policy Dev. Abstr.; Sociol. Abstr. [Full Cov.].

CN/0824-0574
**REBEL YOUTH.** ***Ceased.*** [Rebel youth.]. No. 66 (Feb./March 1984)-?. Periodical. English. Rebel Youth, 24 Cecil Street, 3rd Floor, Toronto Ontario M5T 1N2 Canada. **DD** 305.2/35/0971. ***Continues*** *Horizons (Toronto, Ont. : 1983), 0822-9996.*

FR/0034-124X
**RECHERCHE SOCIALE.** [Rech. soc.]. No.1 (Sept./Oct. 1965)-. Periodical. French (summaries and/or abstracts in French and English). qt. 239.96F France; 275.00F other. Foundation pour Recherche Sociale, 28 rue Godefroy Cavaignac, 75011 Paris France. **Tel** 011 33 1 44091512. **ED** Roger Benjamin. **LC** HM3; .R43. **Circ:** 1,000. ***Continues*** *Centre de Recherches Economiques et Sociales, Paris. Etudes et Documents.*
**Desc:** Aimed at students and teachers in higher education. Offers analytical technique for problems linked to economic development.
**Ind/Abst** ABC POL SCI (19??-1984); Am. Hist. Life (1972-1981); PAIS Int. Print.

CN/0034-1282
**RECHERCHES SOCIOGRAPHIQUES.** [Rech. sociogr.]. **Added/Corp** Universite Laval. Departement de Sociologie. Universite Laval. Departement de Sociologie et d'Anthropologie. Vol. 1 (1960)-. Periodical. French. Three times a year. 52.00Can$ (institutions), 28.00Can$ (individuals). Universite Laval Faculte des Sciences Sociales, Bureau des Communications, 3448 de Koninck, Quebec G1K 7P4 Canada. **Tel** (418)656-2131. **ED** Simon Langlois. ctrl circ. available on microfilm and microfiche from University Microfilms International (UMI).
**Desc:** Includes research in sociology, articles on the society of Quebec - crossroads of human sciences, research, monographs, critical essays, and balances.
**Ind/Abst** Am. Hist. Life (1963-); Int. Bibliogr. Sociol.; Int. Labour Doc.; Int. Polit. Sci. Abstr.; Point Repere (1983-); Soc. Plann. Policy Dev. Abstr.; Sociol. Abstr. [Full Cov.].

NE/0927-2704
**REFLECTOR DEN BOSCH.** (REFLECTOR.). [Reflector Den Bosch]. (1990)-. Periodical. Dutch. Seven times a year. Fl45.15. Malmberg BV, PO Box 233 Leeghwaterlaan 16, 5223 BA Den Bosch Netherlands. **Tel** 011 31 73 288711, telex 50058. **UDC** 304 + 930. ***Continues*** *Keesings Reflector, 0167-3432.*

AT/0158-7102
**REGIONAL JOURNAL OF SOCIAL ISSUES.** [Reg. j. soc. issues]. **Added/Corp** Warrnambool Institute of Advanced Education. (19??)-. Periodical. English. an. 10.00Aus$. Deakin University / School of Social Science, PO Box 423, Warrnambook Victoria, 3280 Australia. **Tel** 11 61 55 618314, FAX 11 61 55 618531. **ED** N Burdess. **Bk Rev. Ad Acc. Pr Rev. Circ:** 250.
**Desc:** Social issues arising in Australian society. Focuses on regional questions from multidisciplinary perspectives.
**Ind/Abst** APAIS, Aust. Public Aff. Inf. Ser. (1982-).

US/0362-3718
**REGIONAL PROFILES.** **Main/Corp** Massachusetts. Dept. of Community Affairs. Bureau of Regional Planning. English. an. Economist, Diary Department, 25 St James Street, London SW1A 1HG England. **Tel** (44)4023 81555, FAX (44)4023 81211, telex 927809. **LC** HT393.M4; M38A. **DD** 309.2/5/09744.

US/0733-0251
**REGISTRY OF MEMBERS - CLINICAL SOCIOLOGY ASSOCIATION.** (REGISTRY OF MEMBERS : A BIENNIAL PUBLICATION OF THE CLINICAL SOCIOLOGY ASSOCIATION / CLINICAL SOCIOLOGY ASSOCIATION.). **Main/Corp** Clinical Sociology Association. **VFOAT** CSA Registry. 1st ed. (1981)-. English. be. $5.00. John Glass, 4242 Wilkinson Avenue, Studio City CA 91604. **Tel** (914)469-4187. **ED** Elizabeth T Clark. **LC** HM9.C54; A38. **DD** 301/.06/01. **Bk Rev. Ad Acc. Circ:** 600 (ctrl).
**Desc:** Directory of the National Clinical Sociology Association. Listing of 500 clinical sociologists by alphabetical, geographic area, specialty areas.

IO
**REKAMAN PERISTIWA ... .** '82-. Indonesian. an. Penerbit Sinar Harapan, JL Dewi Sartika 136D Cawang, Jakarta Timur Indonesia. **Tel** 803208. **ED** Umar Nur Zain and Apul D Maharaja. **LC** AP95.I5; R44. **Ad Acc. Circ:** 10,000 (ctrl).
**Desc:** Chronological notes and details on affairs during the year.

II
**REPORT ON COMMUNITY DEVELOPMENT WEEK.** **Main/Corp** India. Dept. of Community Development. (1970)-. English. Government of India Press, Minto Road, New Delhi 111054 India. **LC** HN690.Z9; C653a. **DD** 309.2/3/0954.

US/0082-8068
**REPORT ON THE WORLD SOCIAL SITUATION.** [Rep. world soc. situat.]. **Added/Corp** United Nations. Bureau of Social Affairs. International Labour Office. United Nations. Dept. of Economic and Social Affairs. United Nations. Dept. of International Economic and Social Affairs. (1957)-. Government Publication. English. te. $24.95. United Nations Publications, 2 United Nations Plaza, Room DC2 0853, Department 007C, New York NY 10017. **Tel** (212)963-8303, (800)253-9646. **LC** HN17.5; .U46a. **DD** 300/.8 S; 309.1/046.
**Desc:** Basic aim of the report is to explore the design and delivery of social services and to assess their capacity to enhance the quality of living

US/0034-4907
**REPRESENTATIVE RESEARCH IN SOCIAL PSYCHOLOGY.** **See** Psychology.

UK/0955-7970
**RESEARCH HIGHLIGHTS IN SOCIAL WORK.** [Res. highlights soc. work]. (1982)-. Monographic series. English. ir. Jessica Kingsley Publishers, 118 Pentonville Road, London N1 9JN England. **Tel** 011 44 71 833 2307, FAX 011 44 71 837 2917. **ED** Prof. Gerard Rockford. **Circ:** 1,000. ***Continues*** *Research Highlights (Edinburgh), 0261-5568.*
**Desc:** Examines areas currently of particular interest to those in social and community work and related fields.

US/1058-5028
**RESEARCH IN COMMUNITY SOCIOLOGY.** [Res. community sociol.]. Vol. 1 (1990)-. English. ir. $73.25. JAI Press Inc., 55 Old Post Road, Suite 2, PO Box 1678, Greenwich CT 06836-1678. **Tel** (203)661-7602, FAX (203)661-0792. **ED** Dan Chekki. **LC** HT51; .R47. **DD** 307/.05.

US/0191-1937
**RESEARCH IN CORPORATE SOCIAL PERFORMANCE AND POLICY.** [Res. corp. soc. perform. policy]. Vol. 1 (1978)-. English. ir. $73.25. JAI Press Inc., 55 Old Post Road, Suite 2, PO Box 1678, Greenwich CT 06836-1678. **Tel** (203)661-7602, FAX (203)661-0792. **ED** James Post. **LC** HD28; .R46. **DD** 301.18/32/05.
**Desc:** Includes major themes such as international studies, business ethics, and government regulation.

US/0191-3085
**RESEARCH IN ORGANIZATIONAL BEHAVIOR.** [Res. organ. behav.]. Vol. 1 (1979)-. Periodical. English. ir. $73.25. JAI Press Inc., 55 Old Post Road, Suite 2, PO Box 1678, Greenwich CT 06836-1678. **Tel** (203)661-7602, FAX (203)661-0792. **ED** Barry M. Staw and L.L. Cummings. **LC** HD28; .R47. **DD** 301.18/32/05. **[CCC]. Pr Rev.** Documents available from The Genuine Article.
**Ind/Abst** Int. Polit. Sci. Abstr.; J. Plan. Lit.; Psychol. Abstr. (1983-); PsycINFO (?-?); PsycLit; PsycScan: Appl. Psych.; Res. Alert [Full Cov.]; Soc. Sci. Cit. Index [Full Cov.].

US/0895-9935
**RESEARCH IN POLITICAL SOCIOLOGY.** [Res. polit. sociol.]. **Added/Corp** American Sociological Association. Section on Political Sociology. Vol. 1 (1985)-. English. be. $73.25. JAI Press Inc., 55 Old Post Road, Suite 2, PO Box 1678, Greenwich CT 06836-1678. **Tel** (203)661-7602, FAX (203)661-0792. **ED** Philo Wasburn. **LC** JA76; .R45. **DD** 306/.2/05.
**Ind/Abst** Am. Bibliogr. Slavic East Europ. Stud.; Soc. Plann. Policy Dev. Abstr.; Sociol. Abstr. (1988-) [Full Cov.].

US/0195-7449
**RESEARCH IN RACE AND ETHNIC RELATIONS.** **See** Ethnic Interests.

US/1057-1922
**RESEARCH IN RURAL SOCIOLOGY AND DEVELOPMENT.** [Res. rural sociol. dev.]. Vol. 1 (1984)-. Monographic series. English. ir. $73.25. JAI Press Inc., 55 Old Post Road, Suite 2, PO Box 1678, Greenwich CT 06836-1678. **Tel** (203)661-7602, FAX (203)661-0792. **LC** HT401; .R47. **DD** 307.7/2/05.
**Ind/Abst** AGRICOLA [Full Cov.]; Soc. Plann. Policy Dev. Abstr.; Sociol. Abstr. (1984-) [Full Cov.].

US/0163-786X
**RESEARCH IN SOCIAL MOVEMENTS, CONFLICTS AND CHANGE.** [Res. soc. mov. confl. change]. Vol. 1 (1978)-. English. ir. $73.25. JAI Press Inc., 55 Old Post Road, Suite 2, PO Box 1678, Greenwich CT 06836-1678. **Tel** (203)661-7602, FAX (203)661-0792. **ED** Louis Kreisberg. **LC** HN1; .R47. **DD** 301.24/2/05. **[CCC].**
**Ind/Abst** Am. Bibliogr. Slavic East Europ. Stud.; Int. Bibliogr. Sociol.; Soc. Plann. Policy Dev. Abstr.; Sociol. Abstr. [Full Cov.].

US/1048-1591
**RESEARCH IN SOCIAL POLICY.** (RESEARCH IN SOCIAL POLICY : HISTORICAL AND CONTEMPORARY PERSPECTIVES.). [Res. soc. policy]. Vol. 1 (1987)-. English. ir. $73.25. JAI Press Inc., 55 Old Post Road, Suite 2, PO Box 1678, Greenwich CT 06836-1678. **Tel** (203)661-7602, FAX (203)661-0792. **ED** John H. Stanfield II. **LC** HN1; .R48. **DD** 361.6/1.
**Ind/Abst** Am. Bibliogr. Slavic East Europ. Stud. (19??-19??).

US/0196-1152
**RESEARCH IN SOCIAL PROBLEMS AND PUBLIC POLICY.** [Res. soc. probl. public policy]. Vol. 1 (1979)-. English. ir. $73.25. JAI Press Inc., 55 Old Post Road, Suite 2, PO Box 1678, Greenwich CT 06836-1678. **Tel** (203)661-7602, FAX (203)661-0792. **ED** William R. Freudenburg and Ted I.K. Youn. **LC** HM1; .R47. **DD** 301/.07/2. **NLM** W1 RE227N.
**Ind/Abst** Psychol. Abstr. (1982-); PsycINFO (?-?); PsycLit; Soc. Plann. Policy Dev. Abstr.; Sociol. Abstr. [Full Cov.].

US/0276-5624
**RESEARCH IN SOCIAL STRATIFICATION AND MOBILITY.** [Res. soc. stratif. mobil.]. Vol. 1 (1981)-. English. an. $73.25. JAI Press Inc., 55 Old Post Road, Suite 2, PO Box 1678, Greenwich CT 06836-1678. **Tel** (203)661-7602, FAX (203)661-0792. **ED** Robert Althauser. **LC** HT601; .R48. **DD** 305.5/072. **[CCC].**
**Ind/Abst** Int. Bibliogr. Sociol.; Soc. Plann. Policy Dev. Abstr.; Sociol. Abstr. [Full Cov.].

US/0197-5080
**RESEARCH IN SOCIOLOGY OF EDUCATION AND SOCIALIZATION.** [Res. sociol. educ. social.]. Vol. 1 (1980)-. English. an. $73.25. JAI Press Inc., 55 Old Post Road, Suite 2, PO Box 1678, Greenwich CT 06836-1678. **Tel** (203)661-7602, FAX (203)661-0792. **ED** Aaron M. Pallas. **LC** LC189.8; .R47. **DD** 370.19/0973. **[CCC].**
**Ind/Abst** Soc. Plann. Policy Dev. Abstr.; Sociol. Abstr. [Full Cov.].

US/0275-4959
**RESEARCH IN THE SOCIOLOGY OF HEALTH CARE.** [Res. sociol. health care]. Vol. 1 (1980)-. English. an. $73.25. JAI Press Inc., 55 Old Post Road, Suite 2, PO Box 1678, Greenwich CT 06836-1678. **Tel** (203)661-7602, FAX (203)661-0792. **ED** Jeanne Jacobs Kronenfeld and Rose Weitz. **LC** RA418; .R47. **DD** 362.1/042. **NLM** W1 RE227Q. **[CCC].**
**Ind/Abst** Soc. Plann. Policy Dev. Abstr.; Sociol. Abstr. [Full Cov.].

US/0733-558X
**RESEARCH IN THE SOCIOLOGY OF ORGANIZATIONS.** [Res. sociol. organ.]. Vol. 1 (1982)-. English. ir. $73.25. JAI Press Inc., 55 Old Post Road, Suite 2, PO Box 1678, Greenwich CT 06836-1678. **Tel** (203)661-7602, FAX (203)661-0792. **ED** Samuel B. Bacharach. **LC** HM131; .R46. **DD** 302.3/5. **[CCC].**
**Ind/Abst** Soc. Plann. Policy Dev. Abstr.; Sociol. Abstr. [Full Cov.].

US/0277-2833
**RESEARCH IN THE SOCIOLOGY OF WORK.** [Res. sociol. work]. Vol. 1 (1981)-. English. ir. $73.25. JAI Press Inc., 55 Old Post Road, Suite 2, PO Box 1678, Greenwich CT 06836-1678. **Tel** (203)661-7602, FAX (203)661-0792. **ED** Ida Harper Simpson and Richard L. Simpson. **LC** HD6951; .R47. **DD** 306/.3.
**Ind/Abst** Soc. Plann. Policy Dev. Abstr.; Sociol. Abstr. [Full Cov.].

US/1047-0042
**RESEARCH IN URBAN SOCIOLOGY.** [Res. urban sociol.]. Vol. 1 (1989)-. English. an. $73.25. JAI Press Inc., 55 Old Post Road, Suite 2, PO Box 1678, Greenwich CT 06836-1678. **Tel** (203)661-7602, FAX (203)661-0792. **ED** Ray Hutchison. **LC** HT101; .R39. **DD** 307.76/05. **CODEN** RUSOEN.
**Ind/Abst** Soc. Plann. Policy Dev. Abstr.

US
**RESEARCH ON DEMOCRACY AND SOCIETY.** Vol. 1 (1993)-. English. $73.25. JAI Press Inc., 55 Old Post Road, Suite 2, PO Box 1678, Greenwich CT 06836-1678. **Tel** (203)661-7602, FAX (203)661-0792. **ED** Frederick Weil. **LC** JC423; .R42.

US
**RESEARCH ON THE SOVIET UNION AND EASTERN EUROPE.** **VFOAT** Soviet Union and Eastern Europe. Vol. 1 (1990)-. English. sa. $73.25. JAI Press Inc., 55 Old Post Road, Suite 2, PO Box 1678, Greenwich CT 06836-1678. **Tel** (203)661-7602, FAX (203)661-0792. **ED** T. Anthony Jones. **LC** DK285; .R47. **DD** 947.085/4.

NZ/0069-3774
**RESEARCH PROJECT.** **See** Psychology.

CN/0316-070X
**RESEARCH REPORT - YORK UNIVERSITY. SOCIAL PSYCHOLOGY RESEARCH PROGRAMME. INSTITUTE FOR BEHAVIOURAL RESEARCH.**
(RESEARCH REPORT - YORK UNIVERSITY, INSTITUTE FOR BEHAVIOURAL RESEARCH, SOCIAL PSYCHOLOGY RESEARCH PROGRAMME.). **Main/Corp** York University (Toronto, Ont.). Institute for Behavioural Research. Social Psychology Research Programme. Began publication 1969?. Monographic series. English. Price varies per volume. Institute for Behavioural Research, York University, 4700 Keele Street, Downsview Ontario M3J 1P3 Canada. **DD** 301.1. ***Supersedes*** *Research Report - York University, Institute for Behavioural Research, Psychosocial Research Programme, 0316-067X.*

US/1053-0754
**RESPONSIVE COMMUNITY, THE.** (THE RESPONSIVE COMMUNITY : RIGHTS AND RESPONSIBILITIES.). [Responsive community]. **Added/Corp** Center for Policy Research (U.S.). Vol. 1, Issue 1 (Winter 1991)-. Periodical. English. Four times a year (Jan., Apr., July, Oct.). $68.00 institution, $27.00 individual. The Responsive Community, 2020 Pennsylvania Avenue Northwest, Suite 282, c/o M. Wanka, Washington DC 20006. **Tel** (202)994-8142, (800)245-7460, FAX (202)994-1639. **ED** Dana Mitra. **LC** JC330.15; .R47. **DD** 320/.01/1. **CODEN** RECOEZ. Index available. cum. index (author/title). **Bk Rev**, (Qty: 6-8). **Ad Acc, Adv Mgr:** Jun Lee, **Tel** (202)994-7907. **Pr Rev.** ctrl circ.
**Desc:** This journal is dedicated to exploring the balance between individual rights and community responsibilities through relevant social, moral, political and legal issues.
**Ind/Abst** PAIS Int. Print; Soc. Plann. Policy Dev. Abstr.

US/0270-1987
**REVIEW OF PERSONALITY AND SOCIAL PSYCHOLOGY.** ***Ceased.*** **See** Psychology.

UK/0261-0272
**REVIEWING SOCIOLOGY : A REVIEW JOURNAL FROM THE SCHOOL OF SOCIOLOGICAL STUDIES.** Vol. 1, Issue 1 (Autumn 1979)-. Periodical. English. University of Reading Department of Sociology, Malcolm Hamilton, Whiteknights RG6 2AA England.
**Ind/Abst** Soc. Plann. Policy Dev. Abstr.; Sociol. Abstr. [Full Cov.].

CI/0350-154X
**REVIJA ZA SOCIOLOGIJU.** [Rev. sociol.]. **Added/Corp** Sociolosko Drustvo Hrvatske. **VFOAT** Sociological Review. (1970)-. Periodical. Serbo-Croatian (Roman) (summaries and/or abstracts in English). qt. **LC** HM7; .R36.
**Ind/Abst** Soc. Plann. Policy Dev. Abstr.; Sociol. Abstr. (1971-) [Full Cov.].

BL/0103-2402
**REVISTA BRASILEIRA DE SOCIOLOGIA.** [Rev. bras. sociol.]. (1975)-. Periodical. Portuguese. sa. **UDC** 30.
**Ind/Abst** Soc. Plann. Policy Dev. Abstr.; Sociol. Abstr. (1975-).

CK/0120-159X
**REVISTA COLOMBIANA DE SOCIOLOGIA / DEPARTAMENTO DE SOCIOLOGIA, UNIVERSIDAD NACIONAL.** V. 1, No. 1 (Dec. 1979)-. Periodical. Spanish. El Departamento, Apartado Aereo 058443, Bogota Colombia. **LC** HM7; .R365.

SP/0303-9889
**REVISTA DE ESTUDIOS SOCIALES (MADRID, SPAIN).** (REVISTA DE ESTUDIOS SOCIALES.). [Rev. estud. soc.]. **Added/Corp** Centro de Estudios Sociales del Valle de los Caidos. Fundacion de la Santa Cruz del Valle de los Caidos. Centro de Estudios Sociales. No. 1 (Jan./April 1971)-. Periodical. Spanish. Three times a year. **LC** H8; .R5234. ***Continues*** *Fundacion de la Santa Cruz del Valle de los Caidos. Centro de Estudios Sociales. Boletin.*
**Ind/Abst** Soc. Plann. Policy Dev. Abstr.; Sociol. Abstr.

SP/0210-5233
**REVISTA ESPANOLA DE INVESTIGACIONES SOCIOLOGICAS.** (REIS.). [Rev. esp. invest. sociol.]. **Added/Corp** Centro de Investigaciones Sociologicas. **VFOAT** Revista Espanola de Investigaciones Sociologicas. No. 1 (Jan./March 1978)-. Periodical. Spanish. Four times a year. $45.00. Centro Investiga Sociologicas, Calle Montalban 8, 28014 Madrid Spain. **Tel** 011 34 1 5807600. **LC** HM7; .R356. **DD** 301/.05.
**Ind/Abst** Am. Hist. Life (1979-); Int. Polit. Sci. Abstr.; Selec. Coop. Index Manage. Period; Soc. Plann. Policy Dev. Abstr.; Sociol. Abstr.

MX/0187-8468
**REVISTA INTERAMERICANA DE SOCIOLOGIA.** [Rev. interam. sociol.]. Vol. 1 (1966)-. Periodical. Spanish. Three times a year. Asociacion Mexicana Socio, Providencia 330 Col del Valle, Mexico 12 DF Mexico.

SP/0034-9712
**REVISTA INTERNACIONAL DE SOCIOLOGIA.** **See** Social Sciences.

CL
**REVISTA MENSAJE.** **See** Religion and Theology.

MX/0035-0087
**REVISTA MEXICANA DE SOCIOLOGIA.** [Rev. mex. sociol.]. Yearly V. 1- March/April 1939-. Periodical. Spanish. qt. 43.00. Torre de Humanidades, 8 Piso, Ciudad Universitaria, Mexico 29 DF Mexico. **Tel** 550-5214 (29-48). **ED** Marvan L Ignacio. **LC** H8; .R53. **DD** 300/.5. cum. index. **Ad Acc. Circ:** 3,000 (ctrl). available on microfilm and microfiche from University Microfilms International (UMI).
**Desc:** Works concerning social problems of Mexico and Latin America. Reflections of contemporary social theories and historical analyses.
**Ind/Abst** Am. Hist. Life (1955-1960); Anthropol. Lit. (-Vol. 12, 1990); Chicano Index; HAPI Hisp. Am. Period. Index; Int. Bibliogr. Sociol.; Int. Labour Doc.; Int. Polit. Sci. Abstr.; LABORDOC; Soc. Plann. Policy Dev. Abstr.; Sociol. Abstr. [Full Cov.]; World Agric. Econ.

CN/0837-5771
**REVUE DE LA PROTECTION CIVILE, LA.** [Emerg. prep. dig.]. **VFOAT** Emergency Preparedness Digest. Vol. 14, No. 1 (Jan./March 1987)-. Periodical. French (English). qt. Canada Protection Civile, 122 Rue Bank 2E Etage, Ottawa Ontario K1A 0W6 Canada. **DD** 363.3/47/0971. ***Continues*** *La Revue; Plans des Mesures d'Urgence, 0317-3518.*

FR/0035-2969
**REVUE FRANCAISE DE SOCIOLOGIE.** [Rev. fr. sociol.]. Vol. 1 No. 1 (Jan./March 1960)-. Periodical. French (summaries and/or abstracts in English, German, Russian and Spanish). Four times a year. 360.00FF. Editions OPHRYS, 6 avenue Jean Jaures, 05003 Gap France. **Tel** 011 33 1 925 38572, FAX 011 33 1 925 33560. **ED** J. Stoetzel. **LC** HM3; .R42. **DD** 301/.05. **NLM** W1 RE848. cum. index. **Bk Rev. Pr Rev.** Documents available from The Genuine Article.
**Desc:** Theoretical and methodological articles recording fundamental research: trends and developments, research notes, debates, critical notes and reviews.
**Ind/Abst** BHA : Biblio. Hist. Art; Curr. Contents Soc. Behav. Sci.; Int. Bibliogr. Sociol.; Int. Labour Doc.; Int. Polit. Sci. Abstr.; LABORDOC; PAIS Int. Print; Point Repere (1983-); Res. Alert; Risk Abstr.; Soc. Plann. Policy Dev. Abstr.; Soc. Sci. Cit. Index; Sociol. Abstr.; Women Stud. Abstr.

FR/0035-2985
**REVUE FRANCAISE DES AFFAIRES SOCIALES.** [Rev. fr. aff. soc.]. **Added/Corp** France. Ministere des Affaires Sociales. (1967)-. Periodical. French. qt. $111.00. Masson Editeur, Box Postale 22, 41353 Vineuil 16 France. **Tel** 011 33 54 438994. **LC** HD4807; .R45. **DD** 331.05. **NLM** W1 RE848R. ***Continues*** *Revue Francaise du Travail.*

FR/0390-6701
**REVUE INTERNATIONALE DE SOCIOLOGIE.** [Rev. int. sociol.]. **Added/Corp** Institut International de Sociologie. Universita degli Studi di Roma "La Sapienza". Faculty of Statistics. **VFOAT** International Review of Sociology. Vol. 1, No. 1 (Jan.-Feb. 1893)-Vol. 47, No. 2-12, (Oct.-Dec. 1939). Periodical. French (English, German, Italian and Spanish). Three times a year. $110.00 (institution); $90.00 (individual). Edizioni Borla, Via delle Fornaci 50, 00165 Rome, Italy. **Tel** 011 39 6 39376728. **CODEN** RISOD6. cum. index.
**Ind/Abst** Psychol. Abstr. (1969-); Soc. Plann. Policy Dev. Abstr.; Sociol. Abstr. (1954-).

IT
**RICERCA SOCIALE, LA.** **Added/Corp** Universita di Bologna. Centro Studi Sui Problemi Della Citta e del Territorio. (1972)-. Periodical. Multiple languages (English, French and Italian). tq. L80000 Italy; L100000 other. Franco Angeli Riviste SRL, Viale Monza 106, 20127 Milan Italy. **Tel** 011 39 2 2827651, 011 39 2 289562. **LC** HT101; .R52.

US/0892-6255
**RING OF FIRE.** ***Suspended.*** **See** Anthropology.

JA/0913-1442
**RIRON TO HOHO.** [Riron to hoho]. **VFOAT** Sociological Theory and Methods. (1986)-. Periodical. Japanese (English). Twice a year. ¥2800.00 (institutions), ¥4800.00 (individuals). Japanese Association for Mathematical Sociology, Chuo University, Department of Sociology, 742-1 Higashi-Nakano, Hachioji-shi, Tokyo 192-03 Japan. **Tel** 81 426 74 3731, FAX 81 426 74 3853. **ED** Kiyoshi Shida. **DD** 301. **Bk Rev**, (Qty: 12). **Ad Acc, Adv Mgr:** Fumiaki Ojima. **Pr Rev. Acid Free. Circ:** 800.
**Desc:** Official journal of The Japanese Association for Mathematical Sociology. Devoted to theoretical and methodological development in mathematical sociology, quantitative sociology, and related disciplines.
**Ind/Abst** Linguist. Lang. Behav. Abstr.; Soc. Plann. Policy Dev. Abstr.; Sociol. Abstr.

US/0196-3589
**ROPER REPORTS.** **Added/Corp** Roper Organization. (19??)-. Periodical. English. Ten times a year. $20,000.00. Roper Organization Inc., 205 East 42nd Street, 7th Floor, New York NY 10017. **Tel** (212)599-0700. **LC** HN90.P8; R65. **DD** 301.15/4/0973.

US/0892-1008
**RPCVOICE.** [RPCVoice]. **VFOAT** RPC Voice. Periodical. English. National Council of Returned Peace Corps Volunteers, PO Box 65294, Washington DC 20035. **DD** 361.

SP/0302-7724
**RS. CUADERNOS DE REALIDADES SOCIALES.** [RS. cuad. realid. soc.]. **Added/Corp** Instituto de Sociologia Aplicada de Madrid. **VFOAT** Cuadernos de Realidades Sociales. **VAT** Realidades Sociales. Cuadernos de Realidades Sociales. (1973)-. Periodical. Spanish. Twice a year. 2000ptas one year. Instituto de Sociologia Aplicada, Claudio Coello 141 #4, 28006 Madrid Spain. **Tel** 011 34 1 620239, 011 34 1 621325. **ED** L. Perin. **LC** HN1; .R24. Index available. cum. index. **Bk Rev. Pr Rev. Circ:** 1,500 (ctrl).
**Desc:** Theoretical and empirical work about the social science.
**Ind/Abst** Soc. Plann. Policy Dev. Abstr.; Sociol. Abstr. [Full Cov.].

US/0161-7273
**RURAL DEVELOPMENT PROGRESS.** **Main/Corp** United States. Dept. of Agriculture. Office of the Secretary. 4th- 1976-. Government Publication. English. an. US Department of Agriculture, 14th Street and Independence Avenue SW, Washington DC 20250. **Tel** (202)720-5457. **LC** HN56; .D46A. **DD** 309.2/63/0973. ***Continues*** *Rural Development Goals, 0145-4102.*

CC/1002-8889
**RURAL ECONOMY AND SOCIETY.** **See** Economics.

UK/0956-7933
**RURAL HISTORY.** (RURAL HISTORY : ECONOMY, SOCIETY, CULTURE.). [Rural hist.]. Vol. 1, No. 1 (April 1990)-. Academic Scholarly Publication. English. sa. $69.00 US, Canada & Mexico; £43.00 other. Cambridge University Press, The Edinburgh Building, Shaftesbury Road, Cambridge CB2 2RU United Kingdom. **Tel** 011 44 223 312393, FAX 011 44 223 325959. **(Subscription address:** Cambridge University Press / North America, 110 Midland Avenue, Port Chester NY 10573.) **ED** Elizabeth Bellamy, Keith D M Snell, and Tom Williamson. **LC** HN8; .R87. **DD** 307.72/05. **CODEN** RUHIEI. **Bk Rev. Ad Acc. Pr Rev. Circ:** 1,000. available on microfilm and microfiche from University Microfilms International (UMI).
**Desc:** Forum for interdisciplinary exchange. Its definition of rural history ignores traditional subject boundaries to foster the cross-fertilization which is essential for an understanding of rural society. While concentrating on the English speaking world and Europe, the journal is not limited in geographical coverage.
**Ind/Abst** BHA : Biblio. Hist. Art; Br. Humanit. Index; Geogr. Abstr. Human Geogr.; Int. Bibliogr. Sociol.; Soc. Plann. Policy Dev. Abstr.; World Agric. Econ.

II/0036-0058
**RURAL INDIA.** [Rural India]. Vol. 1 (Nov. 1938)-. Periodical. English (Hindi). mo. $31.00. Adarsh Seva Sangha, Ishwardas Mansions, Nana Chowk, Bombay, 400007 India. **Tel** 3875041. **(Subscription address:** Prints India, 11 Darya Ganj, New Delhi, 110002 India, (Phone: 011 91 11 3268645)) **ED** G K Puranik. **LC** HN681; .R8. **DD** 307.7/2/0954.
**Ind/Abst** AGRICOLA.

UK/0036-0074
**RURAL LIFE.** V.1- 1954-. Periodical. English. qt. Institute of Rural Life at Home and Overseas, 27 Northumberland Road, New Barnet Herts England. ***Continues*** *Rural Life Bulletin.*

AT
**RURAL SOCIETY.** English. qt. 25.00Aus$ institutions; 15.00Aus$ individuals. Charles Sturt University CRSR, PO Box 588, Wagga Wagga NSW 2650 Australia. **Tel** 011 61 69 222763, FAX 011 61 69 222764.

US/0279-5957
**RURAL SOCIOLOGIST, THE.** (THE RURAL SOCIOLOGIST : A PUBLICATION OF THE RURAL SOCIOLOGICAL SOCIETY.). [Rural sociol.]. **Added/Corp** Rural Sociological Society. Vol. 1, No. 1 (Jan. 1981)-. Periodical. English. Four times a year. $18.00. Montana State University / Rural Sociological Society, Department of Sociology, Wilson Hall, Bozeman MT 59717. **Tel** (406)994-5248. **ED** Rex R. Campbell. **LC** HT401; .R78. **DD** 307.7/2/0973. **Circ:** 1,000 (ctrl). ***Continues*** *Newsline, 0198-9316.*
**Desc:** Forum for exchange of views on matters of concern to the profession of rural sociology.
**Ind/Abst** AGRICOLA [Full Cov.]; Appl. Soc. Sci. Index Abstr.; Curr. Index J. Educ. (March 1990); Geogr. Abstr. Phys. Geogr.; Geogr. Abstr. Human Geogr.; Int. Dev. Abstr.; J. Plan. Lit.; Rural Dev. Abstr.; World Agric. Econ.

US/0036-0112
**RURAL SOCIOLOGY.** [Rural sociol.]. **Added/Corp** American Sociological Society. Rural Sociology Section. Rural Sociological Society. Vol. 1, No. 1 (Mar. 1936)-. Periodical. English. Four times a year (published seasonally). $82.00 US and Canada; $89.00 Mexico; $97.00 other. Montana State University / Rural Sociological Society, Department of Sociology, Wilson Hall, Bozeman MT 59717. **Tel** (406)994-5248. **(Subscription address:** University of Illinois / Rural Sociological Society, c/o Institute for Environmental Studies, 1101 West Peabody Drive, Urbana IL 61801-4723.**) ED** Steve H. Murdock. **LC** HT401; .R8. **NLM** W1 RU714. **CODEN** RUSCA. Index available. cum. index. **Bk Rev. Pr Rev. Acid Free. Circ:** 2,500 (ctrl). available on microfilm and microfiche from University Microfilms International (UMI). Documents available from The Genuine Article, UMI Article Clearinghouse.
**Desc:** The object of the Rural Sociological Society is to promote the development of rural sociology through research, teaching, and extension work.
**Ind/Abst** Abstr. Anthropol.; Acad. Abstr. Full Text Elite (Jan. 1992-); Acad. Abstr. (Jan. 1992-); Acad. Search (Jan. 1992-); AgBiotech News Inf.; AGRICOLA [Full Cov.]; Am. Hist. Life (1963-); Appl. Soc. Sci. Index Abstr.; Chicano Index; Crim. Justice Abstr.; Curr. Contents Soc. Behav. Sci.; Curr. Geogr. Publ. (199?-); Curr. Index J. Educ.; Dairy Sci. Abstr.; Expand. Acad. Index (1989-); For. Prod. Abstr.; For. Abstr.; Geogr. Abstr. Phys. Geogr. (?-?); Geogr. Abstr. Human Geogr.; Hum. Resour. Abstr.; Index Period. Artic. Relat. Law (19??-19??); INFO-SOUTH Abstr.; Int. Bibliogr. Sociol.; Int. Dev. Abstr.; Int. Labour Doc.; Int. Polit. Sci. Abstr.; Mag. Search; Maize Abstr.; Middle East Abstr. Index; Multicult. Educ. Abstr.; Newsp. Period. Abstr. (1991-); PAIS Int. Print; Pig News Inf.; Popul. Index; Psychol. Abstr. (1952-); PsycINFO (?-?); PsycLit; Res. Alert [Full Cov.]; Rev. Agric. Entomol.; Risk Abstr.; Rural Dev. Abstr.; Sage Fam. Stud. Abstr. (?-?); Sage Public Adm. Abstr. (?-?); Sage Urban Stud. Abstr (?-?); Soc. Plann. Policy Dev. Abstr.; Soc. Sci. Source (Jan. 1992-); Soc. Sci. Cit. Index [Full Cov.]; Soc. Sci. Index; Soc. Sci. Index Fulltext (Fall 1988-) [Full Txt.]; Soc. Work Abstr. [Select. Cov.]; Sociol. Abstr. [Full Cov.]; Stud. Women Abstr.; West. Hist. Q.; Women Stud. Abstr.; World Agric. Econ.

US
**RURAL SOCIOLOGY RESEARCH REPORT. Added/Corp** Louisiana Agricultural Experiment Station. Dept. of Rural Sociology. (1990)-. Monographic series. English. Department of Rural Sociology, Louisiana Agricultural Experiment Station, LSU Agricultural Center, Baton Rouge LA 70803-5466.
**Ind/Abst** World Agric. Econ.

KO
**SAE MAUL YONGU (CHONNAM TAEHAKKYO. SAE MAUL YONGUSO).** (SAE MAUL YONGU.). **VFOAT** Saemaul Review. Periodical. Korean (English). an. Chonnam Taehakkyo Sae Maul Yonguso Yongbong-dong, Puk-ku, Kwangju-si Korea. **LC** HN730.5.Z9; C66587. Index available. cum. index. **Circ:** 500 (ctrl).
**Desc:** The reports of the study of all researchers.

●US/1062-5828
**SAFETY BRIEFS. WESTERN REGION.** (SAFETY BRIEFS. WESTERN REGION : EXECUTIVE LETTER TO THE AGRI-INPUTS INDUSTRY.). [Saf. briefs. West. reg.]. (1992)-. Periodical. English. bm. $32.00. Simpson Bayne Communications, PO Box 20087, Spokane WA 99204. **DD** 363.

UK/0307-9201
**SAGE RACE RELATIONS ABSTRACTS.** **See** Sociology-Abstracting, Bibliographies and Statistics.

UK
**SAGE STUDIES IN INTERNATIONAL SOCIOLOGY.** No. 1 (1975)-. Monographic series. English. ir. Price varies per volume. SAGE Periodical Press, 2455 Teller Road, Thousand Oaks CA 91320. **Tel** (805)499-0721, FAX (805)499-0871, telex 100799. **Acid Free.**

SA
**SAIRR ANNUAL REPORT. Main/Corp** South African Institute of Race Relations. (1983/84)-. English. an. $366.00 (subscription package). South African Institute of Race Relations, PO Box 31044, Braamfontein 2017 South Africa. **Tel** 011 27 11 4033600, FAX 011 27 11 4033671. ***Continues*** *South African Institute of Race Relations. Annual Report.*
**Desc:** Auditors' and directors' reports, balance sheets, income statements, source and application of funds statements and notes to the financial statements of the South African Institute of Race Relations.

II
**SAKSHARATA SANDESA.** Periodical. Marwari (Hindi). mo. Rs12.00. Seva Mandir, Fatehpura Udaipur 313001 India. **Tel** 28951. **ED** Ramkrishna Sharma. **LC** HN690.R3; S25. **Ad Acc. Circ:** 2,000 (ctrl).
**Desc:** Contains an editorial article which generally discusses current social and educational problems and the new ideas, policies and techniques proposed to solve them.

FR
**SAUVAGE, LE. VFOAT** Nouvel Observateur/Ecologie. No. 1- April/May 1973-. Periodical. French. 53.00F. C.C.P. 3 143-54, Paris France. **LC** HC79.E5; S27. **DD** 301.31/05.

XR
**SBORNIK PRACI TEORIE KULTURY.** Vol. 1- 1984-. Periodical. Czech (summaries and/or abstracts in Russian and German). kcs16.00. **(Subscription address:** Artia Pegas Press Ltd., Palac Metro Narodni Trida 25, 11210 Prague 1 Czech Republic.**) LC** HM101; .S2815.

GW/0435-8287
**SCHRIFTEN - GESELLSCHAFT FUER SOZIALEN FORTSCHRITT. Main/Corp** Gesellschaft fuer Sozialen Fortschritt. (1951)-. Monographic series. German. ir. Price varies per volume. Duncker und Humblot Verlag, Postfach 410329, D-12113 Berlin Germany. **Tel** 011 49 30 79000612, 011 49 30 79000613. **ED** Dunckere Humblot. **LC** HN5; .G43.

GW
**SCHRIFTEN ZUR KULTURSOZIOLOGIE.** 1984-. Monographic series. German. Price varies per volume. Dietrich Reimer Verlag, Unter Den Eichen 57, D-12203 Berlin Germany. **Tel** 011 49 30 8314081, FAX 011 49 30 831623.

GW/0179-4485
**SCHRIFTENREIHE DER FORSCHUNGSGESELLSCHAFT FUER AGRARPOLITIK UND AGRARSOZIOLOGIE E.V. BONN.** (SCHRIFTENREIHE DER FORSCHUNGSGESELLSCHAFT FUER AGRARPOLITIK UND AGRARSOZIOLOGIE.). [Schr.reihe Forsch.ges. Agrarpolit. Agrarsoziol. e.V. Bonn]. **Added/Corp** Forschungsgesellschaft fur Agrarpolitik und Agrarsoziologie (Bonn, Germany). (1979)-. Monographic series. German. ***Continues*** *Forschungsgesellschaft fur Agrarpolitik und Agrarsoziologie : [Schriftenreihe], 0532-2359.*
**Ind/Abst** For. Abstr.; World Agric. Econ.

SZ/0379-3664
**SCHWEIZERISCHE ZEITSCHRIFT FUER SOZIOLOGIE.** (SCHWEIZERISCHE ZEITSCHRIFT FUER SOZIOLOGIE. REVUE SUISSE DE SOCIOLOGIE.). [Schweiz. Z. Soziol.]. **Added/Corp** Schweizerische Gesellschaft fuer Soziologie. **VFOAT** Revue Suisse de Sociologie. (19??)-. Periodical. French (German). Three times a year. Seismo Verlag, Raemistrasse 69, Postfach 313, CH-8028 Zurich Switzerland. **Tel** 01 2611094, FAX 01 2521054. **LC** HM5; .S35.
**Ind/Abst** Int. Polit. Sci. Abstr.; Soc. Plann. Policy Dev. Abstr.; Sociol. Abstr. [Full Cov.]; Sociol. Educ. Abstr.

UK/0262-4591
**SEARCHLIGHT (LONDON).** (SEARCHLIGHT.). [SearchlightLond.]. (1977)-. Periodical. English. mo. £35.00 US. Searchlight / London, 37 B New Cavendish Street, London W1M 8JR England. **Tel** 011 44 71 6072646. **ED** Gerry Gable (editor's telephone: 011 49 71 284-4040). **DD** 320.941. **Bk Rev** (Qty: 4-6). **Ad Acc, Adv Mgr:** S. Gable, **Tel** 011 49 71 284-4040. **Circ:** 8,000. ***Continues*** *Searchlight on the Struggle Against Racism and Fascism* ***and*** *CARF. Campaign Against Racism & Fascism, 0140-735X.* ***Continued in part by*** *CARF. Campaign Against Racism & Fascism (1991), 0966-1050.*
**Desc:** Research and commentary into racism and fascism (from and anti-racist viewpoint) in the UK, Europe and elsewhere.

JA
**SEIKATSU-GAKU. Added/Corp** Nihon Seikatsu Gakkai. No. 1 (1975)-. Periodical. Japanese. Domesu Shuppan, 35-2 Komagome 1-chome Toshima-ku, Tokyo Japan. **LC** HN721; .S44.

CN/1183-160X
**SEMA (TORONTO).** (SEMA / THE UNIVERSITY OF TORONTO SEMIOTIC FORUM.). [SEMA]. **Added/Corp** University of Toronto. Semiotic Forum. Vol. 1, No. 1/2 (1991)-. Periodical. English. sa. Limited free distribution. University of Toronto Program in Semiotics, Victoria College, Room NF-217, Toronto Ontario M5S 1K7 Canada. **DD** 302.2.

US/0093-9579
**SEMIOTEXTE (NEW YORK).** (SEMIOTEXTE.). [Semiotexte]. (Feb. 1974)-. Periodical. Multiple languages (English and French). ir (every 4-6 months). $36.00 institutions; $15.00 individuals. Semiotexte, PO Box 568, Brooklyn NY 11211. **Tel** (718)387-6471. **ED** Sylvere Lotringer and Jim Fleming. **LC** P99; .S38. **DD** 301.2/1. Index available. **Bk Rev. Ad Acc. Circ:** 3,000.
**Desc:** The journal of a group analyzing the mechanisms which produce and maintain the present divisions of knowledge.
**Ind/Abst** MLA Int. Bibl. Books Artic. Mod. Lang. Lit.

CN/0076-3934
**SERIES 2 : RESEARCH REPORTS - CENTER FOR SETTLEMENT STUDIES, UNIVERSITY OF MANITOBA. Main/Corp** University of Manitoba. Center for Settlement Studies. No. 1- 1969-. Monographic series. English. Price varies per volume. University of Manitoba / Box 35, PO Box 35, Winnipeg Manitoba R3T 2N2 Canada. **DD** 301.34/0971.

NE
**SERIES ON THE DEVELOPMENT OF SOCIETIES.** V. 1-. Monographic series. English. Price varies per volume. Martinus Nijhoff Publishers, Subsidiary of Kluwer Academic Publishers, Koraalrood 50, 2718 SC Zoetermeer Netherlands. **Tel** 011 31 79 684400.

JA
**SERON CHOSA NENKAN. ZENKOKU SERON CHOSA NO GENKYO. Main/Corp** Japan. Sorifu. Naikaku Sori Daijin Kambo. **Added/Corp** Japan. Sorifu. Naikaku Sori Daijin Kambo. Zenkoku Seron Chosa no Genkyo. **VFOAT** Zenkoku Seron Chosa No Genkyo. (1???)-. Japanese. an. $34.27. Sorifu, Prime Minister's Office, 1-1-1 Nagata-cho, Chiyoda-ku Tokyo 100 Japan. **LC** HM261; .J34.

XR
**SESITY / USTAV PRO FILOSOFII A SOCIOLOGII CSAV.** **See** Philosophy.

US/0360-0025
**SEX ROLES.** [Sex roles]. Vol. 1 (March 1975)-. Periodical. English. Twenty-four times a year. $525.00 institutions, $75.00 individuals US; $615.00 institutions, $88.00 individuals other. Plenum Press, 233 Spring Street, New York NY 10013-1578. **Tel** (212)620-8000, (800)221-9369, FAX (212)463-0742, (212)807-1047, telex 23/421139. **ED** Phyllis A. Katz. **LC** HQ768; .S4. **DD** 301.41/05. **NLM** W1 SE987. **CODEN** SROLDH. **[CCC].** Index available. **Pr Rev.** available on microfilm and microfiche from University Microfilms International (UMI). Documents available from The Genuine Article, UMI Article Clearinghouse.
**Desc:** A forum that publishes original research articles and theoretical manuscripts concerned with the basic processes underlying gender role socialization in children and its consequences.
**Ind/Abst** Acad. Search (July 1993-); Appl. Soc. Sci. Index Abstr.; Arts Humanit. Citation Index [Select. Cov.]; Commun. Abstr. (?-?); Crim. Justice Abstr.; Curr. Contents Soc. Behav. Sci.; Curr. Index J. Educ.; EMBASE; Expand. Acad. Index (1989-); High. Educ. Abstr. (1978-); INFO-SOUTH Abstr.; Middle East Abstr. Index; Multicult. Educ. Abstr.; Newsp. Period. Abstr. (1989-); Psychol. Abstr. (1978-); PsycINFO; PsycLit; Res. Alert [Full Cov.]; Res. High. Educ. Abstr.; Sage Fam. Stud. Abstr. (?-?); School Organ. Manage. Abstr.; Soc. Plann. Policy Dev. Abstr.; Soc. Sci. Source (Jul. 1993-); Soc. Sci. Cit. Index [Full Cov.]; Soc. Sci. Index; Soc. Sci. Index Fulltext (July 1988-) [Full Txt.]; Soc. Work Abstr. [Select. Cov.]; Sociol. Abstr.; Sociol. Educ. Abstr.; Spec. Educ. Needs Abstr.; SportSearch; Stud. Women Abstr.; Women Stud. Abstr.

US/0884-4372
**SEXUAL COERCION & ASSAULT. VFOAT** Sexual Coercion and Assault; SCA. Vol. 1, No. 1 (Jan. 1986)-. Periodical. English. Six times a year. Current Research Updates Publishing, PO Box 2831, Bellingham WA 98227. **Tel** (206)647-1568. **ED** Py Bateman. **DD** 362. **NLM** W1; SE99EH. Index available. cum. index. **Bk Rev. Ad Acc. Circ:** 500.
**Desc:** Original research, review, theory, discussion papers, abstracts of all published papers from 800 worldwide journals, news and events, announcements, film reviews.
**Ind/Abst** Crim. Justice Abstr.

JA
**SHAKAI SEIKATSU TOKEI SHIHYO.**
**Added/Corp** Japan. Sorifu. Tokeikyoku. Japan. Somucho. Tokeikyoku. **VFOAT** Shakai Jinko Tokei Taikei; Statistical Indicators on Social Life. (March 1983)-. English (Japanese). an. Government Publications Service Center, 2-1 Kasumigaseki 1-Chome, Chiyoda-Ku Tokyo 100 Japan. **Tel** 011 81 3 3504 3885. **LC** HN724; .S48 .

JA/0021-5414
**SHAKAIGAKU HYORON. Added/Corp** Nihon Shakaigakkai. **VFOAT** Japanese Sociological Review. (1950)-. Periodical. Japanese. Four times a year. $84.00. **(Subscription address:** Kyowa Book Company Inc., 1 38 Kanda Jinbocho Chiyoda-ku, Tokyo 101 Japan.**)** cum. index.
**Ind/Abst** Int. Bibliogr. Sociol.; Soc. Plann. Policy Dev. Abstr.; Sociol. Abstr. [Full Cov.].

JA
**SHAKAIGAKU NENSHI. Added/Corp** Waseda Daigaku Shakaigakkai. **VFOAT** Annuals of Sociology. (1956)-. Periodical. Japanese. Waseda Daigaku Shakaigakkai, c/o Waseda Daigaku Bungakubu, Tokyo Japan. **LC** HM7; .S46.
**Ind/Abst** Int. Bibliogr. Sociol.

JA
**SHAKAISHI KENKYU.** 1 (Oct. 1982)-. Periodical. Japanese. sa. ¥1800 single issue. Nihon Edita Sukuru Shuppanbu, 6 Ichigaya Tamachi 1, Shinjuku-ku Tokyo 162 Japan. **LC** HN1; .S52.

CH/0077-5851
**SHE HUI HSUEH KAN.** [Shehui xuekan]. **VFOAT** Kuo Li Taiwan Ta Hsueh She Hui Hsueh Kan; Journal of Sociology. No. 1 (Dec. 1963)-. Chinese (summaries and/or abstracts in English). an. Kuo Li Tai-Wan Shih Fan Ta Hsueh Wen Hsueh Yuan, Taipei Taiwan.
**Ind/Abst** Soc. Plann. Policy Dev. Abstr.; Sociol. Abstr.

JA
**SHIMPO.** (Sept. 1978)-. Periodical. Japanese. ¥500. Daini Watanabe Building, 17-1 Kamiyamacho, Shibuya-ku Tokyo 150 Japan. **LC** HN723.5; .S445.

IT
**SI-RIVISTA STUDI SOCIALI DEL VENETO.** Italian. qt. Free. CISES Srl, Via Flacco 10, 35128 Padua Italy. **Tel** 011 39 49 8074522.

US
**SIDEWINDER STUDIES IN HISTORY AND SOCIOLOGY. See** History(General).

GW/0939-2327
**SIMMEL NEWSLETTER / [PRESENTED BY THE GEORG SIMMEL-GESELLSCHAFT E V., BIELEFELD]. Added/Corp** Georg Simmel-Gesellschaft. Universitat Bielefeld. Fakultat fuer Soziologie. Vol. 1, No. 1 (Summer 1991)-. English. be. DM39.00 (institutions), DM27.00 (individuals) Germany; DM40.00 (institutions), DM28.00 (individuals) Europe; DM42.00 (institutions), DM30.00 (individuals) other. Simmel Newsletter, Treptower Str. 16 George S. Ges., D 33619 Bielefeld Germany. **Tel** 011 49 521 1064608. **LC** WMLC 91/2064. **CODEN** SNEWE7.
**Ind/Abst** Soc. Plann. Policy Dev. Abstr.; Sociol. Abstr. (1991-) [Full Cov.].

SI/0129-9387
**SINGA.** No. 1 (Dec. 1980)-. Periodical. English. sa. $4.00. Singa, Cultural Affairs Division Ministry of Culture 3rd Floor City Hall, Singapore 0617 Singapore. **LC** PL3515; .A48. **DD** 808.8/995957/05.

US/0091-8652
**SINGLE.** [Single]. V. 1- Aug. 1973-. Periodical. English. mo. $12.00. Association Qeubecoise d'Urbanisme, CP 1315, Place Bonaventure, Montreal Quebec H5A 1H1. **LC** HQ800; .S48. **DD** 301.4.

US/0747-3184
**SINGLE (TAMPA, FLA.).** (SINGLE.). **VFOAT** Single Magazine. Began in 1984. Periodical. English. mo. $14.00. Single Life Inc., 7821 North Dale Marby, Suite 204, Tampa FL 33614. ***Continues** Single Life, 0746-9667.*

XR/0037-6833
**SLEZSKY SBORNIK.** [Slezsky sb.]. **Added/Corp** Ceskoslovenska Akademie Ved. Slezsky Ustav v Opave. Matice Opavska. **VFOAT** Acta Silesiaca. Vol. 41, No. 1 (1936)-. Periodical. Czech (summaries and/or abstracts in Russian and German; table of contents in Russian and German). qt. DM133.00. Academia, Publishing House of the Czechoslovak Academy of Sciences, Czech AC SCI, Vodickova 40, PO Box 896, 112 29 Prague 1, Czech Republic. **Tel** 011 42 2 245117. **(Subscription address:** Kubon & Sagner, ABT Zeitschriftenimport, D 80328 Munich Germany.**) ED** Dan Gawrecki. cum. index. **Bk Rev. Circ:** 960. ***Continues** Vestnik Matice Opavske.*
**Desc:** Studies on the rise and development of the industrial regions in Bohemia and Central Europe.
**Ind/Abst** Am. Hist. Life (1954-); BHA : Biblio. Hist. Art.

US/1046-4964
**SMALL GROUP RESEARCH.** [Small group res.]. (1990)-. Periodical. English. qt (Feb., May, Aug., Nov.). $166.00. SAGE Periodical Press, 2455 Teller Road, Thousand Oaks CA 91320. **Tel** (805)499-0721, FAX (805)499-0871, telex 100799. **ED** Charles Garvin and Richard Brian Polley. **LC** HM133; .S645. **DD** 302.3/4/072. **NLM** W1; SM22. **CODEN** SGREE3. **Acid Free.** available on microfilm and microfiche from University Microfilms International (UMI). Documents available from The Genuine Article. ***Formed by the union of** Small Group Behavior, 0090-5526 **and** International Journal of Small Group Research.*
**Desc:** Presents research, theoretical advancements and empirically supported applications with respect to all types of small groups.
**Ind/Abst** Commun. Abstr.; Curr. Contents Soc. Behav. Sci.; Educ. Adm. Abstr.; Hum. Resour. Abstr.; Person. Manage. Abstr.; Psychol. Abstr. (1970-); PsycINFO (1990-); PsycLit; Res. Alert [Full Cov.]; Soc. Sci. Cit. Index [Full Cov.]; Soc. Work Abstr. [Select. Cov.].

NE
**SOCIAAL BESTEK. Added/Corp** Vereniging van Directeuren van Overheidsorganen voor Sociale Arbeid. Stichting voor Opleiding tot Sociale Arbeid (Netherlands) Sociaal-Pedagogische Opleidingen van de Katholieke Leergangen (Netherlands). Vol. 31 (Jan. 9, 1969)-. Periodical. Dutch. Twenty-three times a year. F96.50. Infolio BV, Postbus 16500, 2500 BM Den Haag Netherlands. **Tel** 011 31 70 3819900, FAX 011 31 70 3632338. **ED** E. Velthuizen. **LC** HV4; .S6. **Bk Rev. Ad Acc. Circ:** 3,000. ***Continues** Sociale Zorg.*
**Desc:** Official periodical for directors and staff of social work administration and finance.

NE
**SOCIAAL-CULTUREEL KWARTAALBERICHT.** No. 1 (1979)-. Dutch. qt. Fl42.00. Centraal Bureau voor de Statistiek, AFD ALG Zaken, Postbus 959, 2270 AZ Voorburg Netherlands. **Tel** 011 31 70 3373800, FAX 011 31 038 7429, telex 32692 CBS NL. **LC** HN514; .S65.

NE
**SOCIAAL EN CULTUREEL RAPPORT.**
**Main/Corp** Netherlands. Sociaal en Cultureel Planbureau. 1974-. Dutch. Sociaal en Cultureel Planbureau, J C Van Markelaan 3, Rijswijk Netherlands. **LC** HN511; .S74A.

II/0037-7627
**SOCIAL ACTION (NEW DELHI).** (SOCIAL ACTION.). [Soc. action]. **Added/Corp** Indian Social Institute. (1951)-. Periodical. English. Four times a year (15th of Jan., April, July and Oct.). $40.00. Social Action Trust, Indian Social Institute, 10 Institutional Area, Lodi Road, New Delhi 110003 India. **Tel** 011 92 11 622379. **(Subscription address:** Prints India, 11 Darya Ganj, New Delhi, 110002 India, (Phone: 011 91 11 3268645)**) ED** Walter Fernandes. **LC** HN681; .S58. **DD** 309.154. **CODEN** SOACE2. Index available. cum. index. **Bk Rev**, (Qty: 50). **Ad Acc. Circ:** 1,000 (ctrl). available on microfilm.
**Desc:** Deals with current problems in a professional way, while at the same time keeping the perspective of the activists in the field. Deals with a specific theme of current interest.
**Ind/Abst** Agrofor. Abstr.; Bibliogr. Mission.; Book Rev. Index (?-1988)(-1988); Dairy Sci. Abstr.; For. Abstr.; Index Book Rev. Relig.; Int. Bibliogr. Sociol.; Int. Dev. Abstr. (?-?); Irr. Drain. Abstr.; Middle East Abstr. Index; Multicult. Educ. Abstr.; Relig. Index One Period.; Res. High. Educ. Abstr.; Rural Dev. Abstr.; Soc. Plann. Policy Dev. Abstr.; Sociol. Educ. Abstr.; Stud. Women Abstr.; World Agric. Econ.

AT/0155-0306
**SOCIAL ALTERNATIVES.** [Soc. altern.]. (Spring 1977)-. Periodical. English. qt. 39.00Aus$ (1 year), 68.00Aus$ (2 year) (institutions), 26.00Aus$ (1 year), 45.00Aus$ (2 year) (individuals) surface mail; 54.00Aus$ (1 year), 98.00Aus$ (2 year) (institutions), 41.00Aus$ (1 year), 75.00Aus$ (2 year) (individuals) air mail. University of Queensland / Department of Government, St. Lucia Queensland 4072 Australia. **Tel** 011 61 7 3652324, telex 40315. **ED** Ralph Summy and Les Hoey. **LC** HN841; .S65. **DD** 306/.0994. **Ad Acc. Circ:** 3,500 (ctrl).
**Desc:** Provides a forum for the analysis of social, cultural and economic oppression and focuses on the development of alternative proposals to greater freedom and democracy.
**Ind/Abst** Acad. Search (Jan. 1994-); Altern. Press Index; APAIS, Aust. Public Aff. Inf. Ser. (1983-); Aust. Educ. Index (1981-); Energy Res. Abstr. (April 1980-); Hum. Rights Intern. Rep.; INFO-SOUTH Abstr.; Mag. Search; Soc. Plann. Policy Dev. Abstr.; Soc. Welf. Soc. Plan./Policy Soc. Dev.; Sociol. Abstr.; SportSearch.

NE
**SOCIAL AND CULTURAL REPORT.**
**Main/Corp** Netherlands. Sociaal en Cultureel Planbureau. (1974)-. English (Dutch). Twice a year. Social and Cultural Report, PO Box 37, 2280 AA Rijswijk Netherlands. **Tel** 011 31 70 94 93 30. **LC** HN511; .S74b. **DD** 309.1/492/07.

IE
**SOCIAL ATTITUDES IN NORTHERN IRELAND.** (1991)-. English. Blackstaff Press Ltd, 3 Galway Park, Dundonald Belfast BT16 0AN Northern Ireland.
**Ind/Abst** Int. Bibliogr. Sociol.

NZ/0301-2212
**SOCIAL BEHAVIOR AND PERSONALITY.** [Soc. behav. pers.]. **Added/Corp** Society for Personality Research. Vol. 1 (1973)-. Periodical. English. Four times a year. $130.00. Society for Personality Research Inc., PO Box 1539, Palmerston North 5301 New Zealand. **Tel** 011 64 6 3555736, FAX 011 64 6 3555736. **ED** Robert A. C. Stewart, Ph.D. **LC** HM1; .S62. **DD** 301.1/05. **NLM** W1 SO104I. **CODEN** SBHPAF. **[CCC]. Bk Rev. Ad Acc. Pr Rev.** available on microfiche (University Microfilms Int.); available on photocopies (Institute of Scientific Information); available on microfilm and microfiche from University Microfilms International (UMI). Documents available from The Genuine Article, BIOSIS Document Express. ***Absorbed** Psychology and Human Development, 1011-5021.*
**Desc:** Publishes research and theoretical papers on all aspects of social psychology and developmental psychology and personality. Over 2,500 researchers and professionals in the following disciplines: psychology of personality, educational, social and developmental psychology, clinical psychology, psychiatry, sociology, cultural anthropology and management science.
**Ind/Abst** Abstr. Res. Pastor. Care Couns. (19??-); Appl. Soc. Sci. Index Abstr.; Biol. Abstr.; Curr. Contents Soc. Behav. Sci.; Curr. Index J. Educ.; High. Educ. Abstr. (1975-); Psychol. Abstr. (1973-); PsycINFO; PsycLit; Res. Alert [Full Cov.]; Soc. Plann. Policy Dev. Abstr.; Soc. Sci. Cit. Index [Full Cov.]; Sociol. Abstr.; SportSearch.

UK/0143-5051
**SOCIAL BIOLOGY AND HUMAN AFFAIRS.** [Soc. biol. human aff.]. **Added/Corp** British Social Biology Council. Vol. 45, No. 1 (1980)-. Periodical. English. sa. £5.00 (member of Biosocial Society); £11.00 (non-member) UK; £13.00 (non-member) other. Biosocial Society, H.M. MacBeth, Anthropology Unit, Oxford Polytech, Oxford 0X3 0BP England. **Tel** 11 44 865 819757. **NLM** W1 SO104M. **CODEN** SBHAD7. Documents available from BIOSIS Document Express. ***Continues** Biology and Human Affairs, 0006-3355.*
**Ind/Abst** Biol. Abstr. (-1982).

US/0278-016X
**SOCIAL COGNITION.** [Social cogn.]. Vol. 1 No. 1 (1982)-. Periodical. English. Four times a year. $110.00 (institutions); $130.00 others. Guilford Publications Inc., 72 Spring Street, New York NY 10012. **Tel** (212)431-9800, (800)365-7006, FAX (212)966-6708. **(Subscription address:** Turpin Distribution Services Limited, Blackhorse Road, Letchworth, Hertfordshire SG6 1HN, United Kingdom.**) ED** Donald Carlston. **LC** BF311; .S64. **DD** 153. **NLM** W1 SO104M. **[CCC].** Index available. **Bk Rev. Ad Acc. Pr Rev. Circ:** 550. available on microfilm and microfiche from University Microfilms International (UMI). Documents available from The Genuine Article, UMI Article Clearinghouse.
**Desc:** Reports of original research, conceptual analyses, and critical reviews of the role of cognitive processes in the study of personality, development and social behavior.
**Ind/Abst** Commun. Abstr.; Curr. Contents Soc. Behav. Sci.; Expand. Acad. Index (1992-); Int. Bibliogr. Sociol.; Multicult. Educ. Abstr.; Newsp. Period. Abstr. (1992-); Psychol. Abstr. (1982-); PsycINFO; PsycLit; Res. Alert [Full Cov.]; Sage Fam. Stud. Abstr.; Soc. Plann. Policy Dev. Abstr.; Soc. Sci. Cit. Index [Full Cov.]; Sociol. Educ. Abstr.; Spec. Educ. Needs Abstr.

SA/0253-3952
**SOCIAL DYNAMICS.** [Soc. dyn.]. **Added/Corp** University of Cape Town. Faculty of Social Science. Vol. 1 (June 1975)-. Periodical. English. sa. R45.06 individuals, R85.00 institutions, South Africa; R100.00 individuals, R160.00 institutions, other. University of Cape Town Center for African Studies, 7700 Rondebosch South Africa. **Tel** 011 27 21 6502338, telex 521439 SA. **ED** M. Savage, B. Nasson. **LC** HM1; .S63. **DD** 301/.05. **Bk Rev. Ad Acc. Pr Rev. Circ:** 600. Documents available from The Genuine Article.
**Desc:** Publishes academic articles from all relevant social sciences.
**Ind/Abst** Annu. Bibliogr. Engl. Lang. Lit.; Arts Humanit. Citation Index [Select. Cov.]; Curr. Contents Soc. Behav. Sci.; Int. Bibliogr. Sociol.; Res. Alert [Full Cov.]; Soc. Plann. Policy Dev. Abstr.; Soc. Sci. Cit. Index [Full Cov.]; Sociol. Abstr. [Full Cov.].

UK/0269-1728
**SOCIAL EPISTEMOLOGY. See** Philosophy.

US/0037-7732
**SOCIAL FORCES.** [Soc. forces]. **Added/Corp** Southern Sociological Society (U.S.). Vol. 4, (Sept. 1925)-. Periodical. English. qt (Mar., June, Sept., Dec.). $30.00 (one year), $85.00 (three year), (individual), $52.00 (one year), $145.00 (three year), (institutions) US; $38.00 (one year), $110.00 (three year) (individuals), $60.00 (one year), $170.00 (three year), (institutions) other. University of North Carolina Press, 116 South Boundary Street, PO Box 2288, Chapel Hill NC

27515-2288. **Tel** (919)966-3561, FAX (919)966-3829. **ED** Richard L. Simpson. **LC** HN51; .S5. **DD** 301. **NLM** W1 SO104R. **CODEN** SOFOAP. Index available in last issue of volume--attached. cum. index. **Ad Acc. Pr Rev. Circ:** 5,000 (ctrl). available on microfilm and microfiche from University Microfilms International (UMI). Documents available from The Genuine Article, UMI Article Clearinghouse. ***Continues** Journal of Social Forces.*
**Desc:** Highlights sociological inquiry and explores realms shared with social psychology, anthropology, political science, history and economics.
**Ind/Abst** ABC POL SCI; Abstr. Anthropol.; Acad. Abstr. Full Text Elite (July 1990-); Acad. Abstr. (July 1990-); Acad. Ind. [Computer File] (1987-); Acad. Search (July 1990-); Am. Hist. Life (1963-); Am. Bibliogr. Slavic East Europ. Stud.; Appl. Soc. Sci. Index Abstr.; Arts Humanit. Citation Index [Select. Cov.]; Book Rev. Index; Commun. Abstr. (?-?); Crim. Justice Abstr.; Crim. Penol. Police Sci. Abstr.; Curr. Contents Soc. Behav. Sci.; Curr. Index J. Educ. (March 1990); Expand. Acad. Index (1987-); Geogr. Abstr. Human Geogr.; High. Educ. Abstr. (1965-); Hum. Resour. Abstr.; Index Period. Artic. Relat. Law (19??-19??); INFO-SOUTH Abstr.; Int. Bibliogr. Sociol.; Int. Dev. Abstr.; Int. Polit. Sci. Abstr.; J. Plan. Lit.; Mag. Search; Middle East Abstr. Index; Multicult. Educ. Abstr.; Newsp. Period. Abstr. (1986-); Peace Res. Abstr. J. (1949-1972); Popul. Index; Psychol. Abstr. (1928-); PsycINFO; PsycLit; Res. Alert [Full Cov.]; Sage Fam. Stud. Abstr.; Sage Public Adm. Abstr.; Sage Race Relat. Abstr.; Sage Urban Stud. Abstr; Soc. Plann. Policy Dev. Abstr.; Soc. Sci. Source (Jul. 1990-); Soc. Sci. Cit. Index [Full Cov.]; Soc. Sci. Index; Soc. Sci. Index Fulltext (Sept. 1988-) [Full Txt.]; Soc. Work Abstr. (Spring, Summer 1987-) [Select. Cov.]; Sociol. Abstr. [Full Cov.]; Sociol. Educ. Abstr.; SportSearch; Soc. Res. Methodol. Abstr. (1975-); Stud. Women Abstr.; U.S. Polit. Sci. Doc.; Women Stud. Abstr.

●UK/1350-4630
**SOCIAL IDENTITIES.** Vol. 1 (1995)-. English. Twice a year. £58.00. Carfax Publishing Company, PO Box 25 Abingdon, Oxfordshire OX14 3UE England. **Tel** 011 44 235 555335, FAX (0279)31067, telex 817484. **ED** Abebe Zegeye & David Theo Goldberg. Index available. **Bk Rev.**
**Desc:** Furnishes an interdisciplinary and international focal point for theorizing issues at the interface of social identities. Addresses these issues in the context of the transforming political economies and cultures of postmodern and postcolonial conditions.

US/0741-5761
**SOCIAL IMPACT ASSESSMENT.** [Soc. impact. assess.]. **Added/Corp** Social Impact Assessment Center (New York, N.Y.) International Association for Impact Assessment. (197?)-. Periodical. English. Four times a year. $30.00 institutions; $20.00 individuals. Social Impact Assessment, c/o C.P. Wolf, Box 2087 Canal Street Station, New York NY 10013. **Tel** (212)966-2708.

FJ
**SOCIAL INDICATORS FOR FIJI. Main/Corp** Fiji. Bureau of Statistics. (1976)-. Government Publication. English. ir. 7.00Fij$. Government Printer Fiji Islands, PO Box 2221, Suva Fiji. **Tel** 011 679 315144. **LC** HN936.A8; F54a. **DD** 309.1/96/1105. **Ad Acc. Circ:** 82.
**Desc:** Industrial health and safety, economics, education and statistics.

PK
**SOCIAL INDICATORS OF PAKISTAN.** (1985)-. English. an. NGM Communication, PO Box 2627, Karachi 75900 Pakistan. **Tel** 011 92 21 428625. **LC** HN690.5.A85; S63. **DD** 306/.095491/021.

UK/0954-206X
**SOCIAL INVENTIONS.** [Soc. invent.]. (1985)-. Periodical. English. an. £15.00 UK; £17.00 other. Institute for Social Inventions, 20 Heber Road, London NW2 6AA England. **Tel** 011 44 81 2082853, FAX 011 44 81 452634. **Bk Rev**, (Qty: 40). **Circ:** 800.

DK/0904-3535
**SOCIAL KRITIK. Added/Corp** Selskabet til Fremme af Social Debat. (1988)-. Periodical. Danish. ir. kr375.00. Social Kritik, Nansensgade 68 Kld, DK 1366, Copenhagen Denmark. **Tel** 011 45 33939963.

BG
**SOCIAL MIRROR, THE.** V. 1- Jan./Feb. 1977-. Periodical. English. 10.00. **LC** HN690.6; .A58. **DD** 309.1/549/205.

SZ/0378-8733
**SOCIAL NETWORKS.** [Soc. networks]. **Added/Corp** International Network for Social Network Analysis. Vol. 1 (Aug. 3, 1978)-. Academic Scholarly Publication. English. qt (1 volume). Fl400.00. Elsevier Science Publishers BV, PO Box 211, 1000 AE Amsterdam Netherlands. **Tel** 011 31 20 5803642, FAX 011 31 20 5862696, telex 15682. **ED** Linton C Freeman, Larissa Lomnitz, J Clyde Mitchell, Barry Wellman, Harrison White, and Rolf Ziegler. **LC** HM73; .S627. **DD** 305/.05. **NLM** W1 SO121. **[CCC]. Pr Rev.** available on microfilm and microfiche from University Microfilms International (UMI). Documents available from The Genuine Article.
**Desc:** Provides a common forum for representatives of anthropology, sociology, history, social psychology, political science, human geography, biology, economics, communications science and other disciplines who share an interest in the study of the structure of human relations and associations that may be expressed in network form.
**Ind/Abst** Anthropol. Lit.; Appl. Soc. Sci. Index Abstr.; Curr. Contents Soc. Behav. Sci.; Int. Bibliogr. Sociol.; Math. Rev.; Middle East Abstr. Index; Psychol. Abstr. (1982-); PsycINFO; PsycLit; Res. Alert [Full Cov.]; Sage Fam. Stud. Abstr.; Soc. Plann. Policy Dev. Abstr.; Soc. Sci. Cit. Index [Full Cov.]; Sociol. Abstr.; Soc. Res. Methodol. Abstr. (1980-).

US/0882-4398
**SOCIAL ONCOLOGY NETWORK ... NEWSLETTER.** [Soc. oncol. netw. newsl.]. **VFOAT** Social Oncology Network. Vol. 1, No. 1 (Jan. 1985)-. Newsletter. English. qt. Free. Social Oncology Network Newsletter, c/o Dr E Clark, Department of Health Professions, Montclair State College, Upper Montclair NJ 07043. **Tel** (201)893-5192. **ED** Elizabeth J Clark. **DD** 616. **Bk Rev. Ad Acc. Circ:** 150.
**Desc:** Focuses on social issues of cancer. Primarily for sociologists, contains information on grants, relevant articles and books, conferences and available resources.

US
**SOCIAL PERSPECTIVES ON EMOTION.** (19??)-. Periodical. English. an. $73.25. JAI Press Inc., 55 Old Post Road, Suite 2, PO Box 1678, Greenwich CT 06836-1678. **Tel** (203)661-7602, FAX (203)661-0792. **ED** David Franks.

US/0037-7783
**SOCIAL POLICY.** [Soc. policy]. (May/June 1970)-. Periodical. English. qt (Feb., May., Aug., Nov.). $50.00 (institution), $20.00 (individual) US; $53.00 (institution), $23.00 (individual) postage included, other. Union Institute, 25 West 43rd Street, Room 620, New York NY 10036. **Tel** (212)642-2929, FAX (212)719-2488. **ED** Frank Riessman and Alan Gartner. **LC** HN51; .S54. **DD** 309.1/73. **NLM** W1 SO122P. **Bk Rev. Ad Acc. Pr Rev. Circ:** 3,000. available on microfilm and microfiche from University Microfilms International (UMI); available on microfilm from Johnson Associates; and Bell & Howell; available on audiocassette. Documents available from The Genuine Article, UMI Article Clearinghouse.
**Desc:** Emphasizes human service policy issues: education, health, mental health, self help, consumerism, neighborhood organizing, employment for social action leaders, academics, social welfare practitioners, etc.
**Ind/Abst** ABC POL SCI; Acad. Abstr. Full Text Elite (July 1990-); Acad. Abstr. (July 1990-); Acad. Ind. [Computer File] (1987-); Acad. Search (July 1990-); Altern. Press Index; Am. Hist. Life (1974-); Appl. Soc. Sci. Index Abstr.; Arts Humanit. Citation Index [Select. Cov.]; Curr. Contents Soc. Behav. Sci.; Curr. Index J. Educ.; Curr. Lit. Fam. Plan. (19??-199?); Expand. Acad. Index (1987-); Film Lit. Index; High. Educ. Abstr. (1971-19??); Hospit. Health Admin. Index; INFO-SOUTH Abstr.; Int. Bibliogr. Sociol.; Int. Labour Doc.; Int. Polit. Sci. Abstr.; J. Plan. Lit.; Left Index; Mag. Search; Middle East Abstr. Index; Newsp. Period. Abstr. (1988-); PAIS Int. Print; Res. Alert [Full Cov.]; Soc. Plann. Policy Dev. Abstr.; Soc. Sci. Source (Jul. 1990-); Soc. Sci. Cit. Index [Full Cov.]; Soc. Sci. Index; Soc. Sci. Index Fulltext (Summer 1988-) [Full Txt.]; Soc. Work Abstr. (Spring 1987-) [Select. Cov.]; Sociol. Abstr.; Women Stud. Abstr.

●US/1072-4745
**SOCIAL POLITICS.** [Soc. polit.]. **Added/Corp** Statens rad for Samhallsforskning (Sweden). Vol. 1, No. 1 (Spring 1994)-. Periodical. English. Three times a year. $40.00 (one year), $72.00 (two year), institutions; $22.00 (one year), $39.60 (two year), individuals. University of Illinois Press, 1325 South Oak Street, Champaign IL 61820. **Tel** (217)333-0950, FAX (217)244-8082. **DD** 306.
**Desc:** Research in gender studies, social policy, citizenship, and the role of the state in organizing relations in the family, the workplace, and society.

FR
**SOCIAL PRATIQUE.** French. ir. 460.00F (includes supplements). Liaisons Sociales, 1 Avenue E Belin, F 92856 Rueil Mal France. **Tel** 011 33 1 41299872.

US/0272-4464
**SOCIAL PROBLEMS (GUILFORD).** (SOCIAL PROBLEMS.). [Soc. probl.]. **VFOAT** Annual Editions, Social Problems. (19??)-. English. an. $12.95. Dushkin Publishing Group Inc., Sluice Dock, Guilford CT 06437. **Tel** (203)453-4351, (800)243-6532, FAX (203)453-6000. **ED** Leroy W. Barnes. **LC** HN51; .A78. **DD** 362/.042/0973. ***Continues** Annual Editions. Readings in Social Problems, 0094-9183.*
**Desc:** Examines current problems within North American and world societies.
**Ind/Abst** Acad. Ind. [Computer File] (1987-); Crim. Justice Abstr.; Expand. Acad. Index (1987-).

US/0190-2725
**SOCIAL PSYCHOLOGY QUARTERLY.** [Soc. psychol. q.]. **Added/Corp** American Sociological Association. Vol. 42 (March 1979)-. Periodical. English. qt (4 issues). $80.00 (institutions), $40.00 (individuals) US; $88.00 (institutions), $48.00 (individuals) other. American Sociological Association, 1722 North Street Northwest, Washington DC 20036-2981. **Tel** (202)833-3410, FAX (202)785-0146. **ED** Peter Burke. **LC** HM1; .S8. **DD** 302/.05. **NLM** W1 SO123TQ. Index available. cum. index. **Ad Acc. Circ:** 5,000. available on microfilm and microfiche from University Microfilms International (UMI). Documents available from The Genuine Article, UMI Article Clearinghouse. ***Continues** Social Psychology (American Sociology Association), 0147-829X.*
**Desc:** Publishes papers pertaining to the processes and products of social interaction. Includes study of relations to individuals or groups as they influence or are influenced by social forces.
**Ind/Abst** Acad. Abstr. Full Text Elite (Jan. 1992-); Acad. Abstr. (Jan. 1992-); Acad. Search (Jan. 1992-); Appl. Soc. Sci. Index Abstr.; Commun. Abstr. (?-?); Crim. Justice Abstr.; Curr. Contents Soc. Behav. Sci.; Expand. Acad. Index (1989-); High. Educ. Abstr. (1981-); INFO-SOUTH Abstr.; Int. Polit. Sci. Abstr.; J. Plan. Lit.; Mag. Search; Middle East Abstr. Index; MLA Int. Bibl. Books Artic. Mod. Lang. Lit.; Multicult. Educ. Abstr.; Newsp. Period. Abstr. (1991-); Psychol. Abstr. (1979-); PsycINFO; PsycLit; Res. Alert [Full Cov.]; Soc. Plann. Policy Dev. Abstr.; Soc. Sci. Source (Jan. 1992-); Soc. Sci. Cit. Index [Full Cov.]; Soc. Sci. Index; Soc. Sci. Index Fulltext (Dec. 1988-) [Full Txt.]; Sociol. Abstr. [Full Cov.]; Sociol. Educ. Abstr.; Stud. Women Abstr.

UK/0267-0712
**SOCIAL STUDIES REVIEW. *Ceased.*** Vol. 1 (1985). Ceased Vol. 6, Issur 5 (April 1991). English. bm. Philip Allan Publishers Ltd, Market Place, Deddington Oxford, OX15 0SE England. **Tel** 011 44 869 38652, FAX 011 44 869 38803.

AT/0037-8011
**SOCIAL SURVEY. Added/Corp** Institute of Social Order (Australia). (1952)-. Periodical. English. Eleven times a year. 5.50Aus$ (Australia); 12.00Aus$ (other). Institute of Social Order, PO Box 66A, Melbourne Victoria, 3001 Australia. **Tel** 11 61 3 8173977. **ED** W G Smith. **LC** HN30; .S57. Index available. **Bk Rev. Circ:** 3,000.

US/0164-2472
**SOCIAL TEXT.** [Soc. text]. Vol. 1 (Winter 1979)-. Periodical. English. qt (4 issues). $60.00 (institutions), $24.00 (individuals) US; $72.00 (institutions), $36.00 (individuals) other. Duke University Press, PO Box 90660, Durham NC 27708-0660. **Tel** (919)687-3600, (919)688-5134 (orders), FAX (919)688-4574, telex 802829. **ED** Bruce Robbins and Andrew Ross. **LC** HN1; .S59. **DD** 303.4/84/05. **Bk Rev. Ad Acc. Circ:** 2,000.
**Desc:** A journal on theory, culture, and ideology with an emphasis on social movements.
**Ind/Abst** Altern. Press Index; Left Index; Middle East Abstr. Index; Soc. Plann. Policy Dev. Abstr.; Sociol. Abstr.

UK/0306-7742
**SOCIAL TRENDS. See** Sociology-Abstracting, Bibliographies and Statistics.

CN
**SOCIAL WORK PERSPECTIVES.** English. Five times a year. 25.00Can$ Canada; 30.00Can$ US; 35.00Can$ other. British Columbia Association of Social Workers, 8-865 West 10th Avenue, Vancouver, British Columbia, V5Z 1L7 Canada. **Tel** (604)876-9535, (800)665-4747, FAX (604)876-3263. **ED** Stuart Alcock, RSW. **Circ:** 2,000.

XO
**SOCIALNI POLITIKA.** 1977-. Periodical. Czech (Slovak). mo. kcs24.00. Vydavatelstvo Obzor, 593 34 Bratislava, Cs Armady 35, Bratislava Slovakia. **LC** HN420.3; .A53. ***Supersedes** Socialna Politika.*

BL/0102-6992
**SOCIEDADE E ESTADO : REVISTA SEMESTRAL DO DEPARTAMENTO DE SOCIOLOGIA DA UNB. Added/Corp** Universidade de Brasilia. Departamento de Sociologia. Vol. 1 (1986)-. Periodical. Portuguese. sa. **LC** HN281; .S65. **DD** 361.6/1/0981.
**Ind/Abst** Soc. Plann. Policy Dev. Abstr.; Sociol. Abstr. (1989-) [Full Cov.].

FR
**SOCIETES CONTEMPORAINES.** No. 1 (March 1990)-. Periodical. French (summaries and/or abstracts in English). Four times a year. 265.00F France; 320.00F other. L' Harmattan, 7 rue de l'Ecole Polytechnique, 75005 Paris France. **Tel** 11 33 1 43547910, 43257651. **CODEN** SOCCEC.
**Ind/Abst** Soc. Plann. Policy Dev. Abstr.

FR/0765-3697
**SOCIETIES (PARIS, FRANCE).** (SOCIETES.). [Societes]. (1984)-. Periodical. French. Four times a year. 480.00F (institutions), 320.00F (individuals) France; 570.00F (institutions), 400.00F (individuals). Dunod Gauthier Villars, 15 rue Gossin, 92543 Montrouge cedex France. **Tel** 011 33 1 46 56 52 66, FAX 011 33 1 46 57 40 69. **(Subscription address:** Centrale des Revues, 11 rue Gossin, 92543 Montrouge Cedex France.**) ED** M. Maffesoli. **[CCC].**

II/0037-9662
**SOCIETY AND CULTURE.** [Soc. cult.]. **Added/Corp** Institute of Social Studies (Calcutta, India). Vol. 1 (July 1970)-. Periodical. English. ir. **(Subscription**

address: Prints India, 11 Darya Ganj, New Delhi 110002 India.) **LC** HN681; .S63. **DD** 301.3/5/0954.
**Ind/Abst** Am. Hist. Life (1973-1976).

CN/0381-1794
**SOCIETY (MONTREAL).** (SOCIETY.). [Society]. **Added/Corp** Canadian Sociology and Anthropology Association. **VFOAT** Societe. **VAT** Societe (Montreal). (1977)-. Periodical. English (French). Three times a year (Jan., May, Oct.). 10.00Can$ Canada; $12.00Can$ other. Concordia University CSAA, 1455 de Maisonneuve Ouest/Room 317-1, Montreal Quebec H3G 1M8 Canada. **Tel** (514)848-8780, FAX (514)848-3494. **ED** Victor Ujimoto. **DD** 301/.06/271. **Ad Acc. Circ:** 1,300. ***Supersedes*** *Canadian Sociology and Anthropology Association. Bulletin, 0008-5049.*
**Desc:** This newsletter carries the proceedings of meetings of the Association's committees in addition to articles related to professional concerns and social policy and serves as a vehicle for internal communications.
**Ind/Abst** Soc. Plann. Policy Dev. Abstr.; Sociol. Abstr. (?-?) [Full Cov.].

US/0038-0121
**SOCIO-ECONOMIC PLANNING SCIENCES. See** Economics.

FR
**SOCIO-ECONOMIC STUDIES. See** Economics.

US/1041-9861
**SOCIOCRITICISM.** [Sociocriticism]. Vol. 1, No. 1 (July 1985)-. Periodical. English (French). sa. 160.00F, $25.00 France; 350.00F, $50.00 other. Universite Paul Valery, BP 5043 Route de Mende, 34032 Montpellier, Cedex 1 France. **Tel** 11 33 67 142000, FAX 011 33 67 142052. **ED** Edmond Cros. **DD** 302. **Bk Rev. Ad Acc.**

US/1043-5727
**SOCIOCRITICISM (NEW YORK, N.Y.).** (SOCIOCRITICISM.). [Sociocriticism]. Monographic series. English. ir. Price varies per volume. Peter Lang Publishing, 62 West 45th Street, 4th Floor, New York NY 10036. **Tel** (212)764-1471, (800)770-5264, telex 6973364 PLNY. **DD** 801.

US/0198-7399
**SOCIOECONOMIC ISSUES OF HEALTH. See** Public Health and Safety.

US
**SOCIOFILE DATABASE [COMPUTER FILE], THE. VFOAT** Sociofile. (198?)-. English. sa. $1950.00. Silverplatter Information Inc., 100 River Ridge Drive, Norwood MA 02062. **Tel** (800)343-0064, (617)769-2599, FAX (617)235-1715. **LC** HM1; .S626.
**Desc:** Provides an index to and abstracts of the literature of sociology from 1,800 journals published worldwide. It includes abstracts of journal articles published in sociological abstracts since 1974 and the enhanced bibliographic citations for relevant dissertations that have been added to the database since 1986. Also included is the Social Planning Policy and Development Abstracts (SOPODA) database with detailed journal article abstracts since 1980. SOPODA expands on the theoretical focus of the disc with the applied aspects of sociology.

GW/0933-1883
**SOCIOLINGUISTICA. See** Linguistics.

XO/0049-1225
**SOCIOLOGIA. Added/Corp** Slovenska Akademia Vied. Sociologicky Ustav. Vol. 1 (1969)-. Periodical. Czech (summaries and/or abstracts in English and Russian). bm. $22.00. Veda, Publishing House of the Slovak Academy of Sciences, Klemensova 19, 814 30 Bratislava Slovakia. **Tel** (7)583-15. **(Subscription address:** Kubon & Sagner, ABT Zeitschriftenimport, D 80328 Munich Germany.) **ED** Vlastislav Bauch. **LC** HM7; .S56. **Bk Rev. Ad Acc. Circ:** 1,200 (ctrl).
**Desc:** Analysis of sociological theories, sociological problems of our civilization and its perspectives. Theoretical and empirical results achieved in the various sections of sociological research.
**Ind/Abst** Soc. Plann. Policy Dev. Abstr.; Sociol. Abstr. (1989-) [Full Cov.].

IT/0038-0156
**SOCIOLOGIA. Added/Corp** Istituto Luigi Sturzo, Rome. Vol. 1 (1967)-. Periodical. Italian (English, Italian and French). Three times a year. L60000 Italy; L70000 others. Istituto Luigi Sturzo, Via delle Coppelle 35, 00186 Rome Italy. **Tel** 011 39 6 6875528.
**Ind/Abst** Int. Bibliogr. Sociol.; Soc. Plann. Policy Dev. Abstr.; Sociol. Abstr. [Full Cov.].

BL
**SOCIOLOGIA.** V. 1- March 1939-. Periodical. Portuguese. qt. **ED** Romano Barreto and Emilio Willems. **LC** HM7. **DD** 301.
**Ind/Abst** Bibliogr. Mission.

IT/0392-5048
**SOCIOLOGIA DEL LAVORO.** [Sociol. lav.]. **Added/Corp** Centro Internazionale di Documentazione e Studi Sociologici sui Problemi del Lavoro. Year 1, No. 1 (Mar. 1978)-. Periodical. Italian (summaries and/or abstracts in English and French). Three times a year. L116000 Italy; L150000 other. Franco Angeli Riviste SRL, Viale Monza 106, 20127 Milan Italy. **Tel** 011 39 2 2827651, 011 39 2 289562. **ED** Franco Angeli. **LC** HD6951; .S54. **DD** 306/.36/05. **Ad Acc. Circ:** 1,000.
**Ind/Abst** Int. Bibliogr. Sociol.; Int. Labour Doc.; LABORDOC; Soc. Plann. Policy Dev. Abstr.; Sociol. Abstr. [Full Cov.].

SP
**SOCIOLOGIA DEL TRABAJO (MADRID, SPAIN).** (SOCIOLOGIA DEL TRABAJO.). (1979)-. Periodical. Spanish. Three times a year. Siglo XXI Espana Ediciones, Plaza 5, 28043 Madrid Spain. **LC** HD6957.S7; S65. **DD** 306/.36/0946.

IT
**SOCIOLOGIA E RICERCA SOCIALE. VFOAT** SRS. Year 1, No. 1 (June 1980)-. Periodical. Italian (summaries and/or abstracts in English). qt. L84000 Italy; L110000 other. Franco Angeli Riviste SRL, Viale Monza 106, 20127 Milan Italy. **Tel** 011 39 2 2827651, 011 39 2 289562. **LC** HM7; .S562. **DD** 301/.05.
**Ind/Abst** Soc. Plann. Policy Dev. Abstr.; Sociol. Abstr. (1981-) [Full Cov.].

II
**SOCIOLOGIA INDICA.** V. 1- May 1977-. Periodical. English (English). Rs30.00. **LC** HN681; .S64. **DD** 301/.05.

GW/0038-0164
**SOCIOLOGIA INTERNATIONALIS.** [Sociol. int.]. (1963)-. Periodical. English (French, German and Spanish). Twice a year. DM131.90 Germany; DM132.40 others. Duncker und Humblot Verlag, Postfach 410329, D-12113 Berlin Germany. **Tel** 011 49 30 79000612, 011 49 30 79000613. **ED** H. Winkmann. **LC** HM1.A1; S6. **DD** 301/.05. **[CCC].** Index Available, published separately, free-automatically sent. **Bk Rev. Ad Acc. Circ:** 600.
**Desc:** International journal for sociology and social psychology.
**Ind/Abst** Int. Bibliogr. Sociol.; Int. Polit. Sci. Abstr.; Soc. Plann. Policy Dev. Abstr.; Sociol. Abstr. [Full Cov.].

NE/0038-0199
**SOCIOLOGIA RURALIS.** [Sociol. rural.]. **Added/Corp** European Society for Rural Sociology. Vol. 1 (Spring 1960)-. Periodical. English (French and German). qt. Fl112.50 Netherlands; Fl135.00 other. Van Gorcum & Company BV, PO Box 43, NL 9400 AA Assen Netherlands. **Tel** 011 31 5920 46846, FAX 011 31 5920 72064. **ED** Anton J Jansen. **LC** HT401; .S58. **NLM** W1 SO878S. **Bk Rev. Ad Acc. Pr Rev. Circ:** 1,000 (ctrl). Documents available from The Genuine Article.
**Desc:** The journal is mainly concerned with theoretical and empirical contributions from the social sciences to rural problems in Europe and the developing countries.
**Ind/Abst** AGRICOLA; Appl. Soc. Sci. Index Abstr.; Curr. Contents Soc. Behav. Sci.; Geogr. Abstr. Human Geogr.; Int. Bibliogr. Sociol.; Int. Dev. Abstr.; Int. Labour Doc.; Int. Polit. Sci. Abstr.; Middle East Abstr. Index; PAIS Int. Print; Res. Alert [Full Cov.]; Rural Dev. Abstr.; Soc. Plann. Policy Dev. Abstr.; Soc. Sci. Cit. Index [Full Cov.]; Sociol. Abstr. [Full Cov.]; Sociol. Educ. Abstr.; World Agric. Econ.

IT/0392-4939
**SOCIOLOGIA URBANA E RURALE (UNIVERSITA DI BOLOGNA. CENTRO STUDI SUI PROBLEMI DELLA CITTA E DEL TERRITORIO).** (SOCIOLOGIA URBANA E RURALE.). [Sociol. urbana rurale]. **Added/Corp** Universita di Bologna. Centro Studi sui Problemi Della Citta e del Territorio. Vol. 1, No. 1 (1979)-. Periodical. Italian. Three times a year. L81000 Italy; L110000 other. Franco Angeli Riviste SRL, Viale Monza 106, 20127 Milan Italy. **Tel** 011 39 2 2827651, 011 39 2 289562. **ED** Paolo Guidicini. **LC** HM7; .S575. **DD** 301/.05.
**Ind/Abst** Int. Bibliogr. Sociol.; PAIS Int. Print.

MX/0187-0173
**SOCIOLOGICA. Added/Corp** Universidad Autonma Metropolitana. Unidad Azcapotzalco. Departamento de Sociolog,a. (1986)-. Periodical. Spanish. tq.
**Ind/Abst** Soc. Plann. Policy Dev. Abstr.

US/0038-0202
**SOCIOLOGICAL ABSTRACTS. See** Sociology-Abstracting, Bibliographies and Statistics.

II/0038-0229
**SOCIOLOGICAL BULLETIN.** [Sociol. bull.]. **Added/Corp** Indian Sociological Society. (1952)-. Bulletin. English. sa. $35.00. Indian Sociological Society, B-7/18 Safdarjung Enclave, New Delhi 110 029 India. **Tel** 666887 651510, FAX (91)11 688 5343, telex 31-61698 ISI. **(Subscription address:** Prints India, 11 Darya Ganj, New Delhi 110002 India.) **ED** P C Joshi and T K Oommen Mukherji. **LC** HN681; .S65. **Bk Rev. Ad Acc. Circ:** 1,700 (ctrl).
**Desc:** Consists of articles by Indian and other authors on a wide range of sociological themes, book reviews, and news about sociology in India.
**Ind/Abst** Am. Hist. Life (1967-1975); Appl. Soc. Sci. Index Abstr.; Int. Bibliogr. Sociol.; Soc. Plann. Policy Dev. Abstr.; Sociol. Abstr. [Full Cov.].

BE
**SOCIOLOGICAL CONTRIBUTIONS FROM FLANDERS.** Periodical. English. Belgium Etc, Transtraat 5, 2900 Londerzeel Belgium. **LC** HM1; .S675.

US/0038-0237
**SOCIOLOGICAL FOCUS (KENT, OHIO).** (SOCIOLOGICAL FOCUS.). [Sociol. focus]. **Added/Corp** North Central Sociological Association. Ohio Valley Sociological Society. Ohio State University. Dept. of Sociology. Vol. 1 (Fall 1967)-. Periodical. English. qt (Feb., May, Aug., Oct.). $45.00 US; $50.00 other. Sociological Focus, Western Michigan University, Department of Sociology, Kalamazoo MI 49008. **Tel** (616)387-5280. **ED** Stanly Rob. **LC** HM1; .S676. **DD** 301. Index available. **Bk Rev. Ad Acc. Pr Rev. Circ:** 700. available on microfilm and microfiche from University Microfilms International (UMI). Documents available from The Genuine Article, Documents on Demand. ***Supersedes*** *Ohio Valley Sociologist.*
**Desc:** Regional journal of North Central Sociological Association for publication of research in the field of sociology and related areas.
**Ind/Abst** Appl. Soc. Sci. Index Abstr.; Crim. Justice Abstr.; Curr. Contents Soc. Behav. Sci.; Energy Inf. Abstr.; Environ. Abstr.; Index Period. Artic. Relat. Law (19??-19??); Middle East Abstr. Index; Multicult. Educ. Abstr.; Res. Alert [Full Cov.]; Soc. Plann. Policy Dev. Abstr.; Soc. Sci. Cit. Index [Full Cov.]; Sociol. Abstr. [Full Cov.]; Sociol. Educ. Abstr.; Spec. Educ. Needs Abstr.; SportSearch; Stud. Women Abstr.

US/0884-8971
**SOCIOLOGICAL FORUM (RANDOLPH, N.J.).** (SOCIOLOGICAL FORUM.). **Added/Corp** Eastern Sociological Society (U.S.). **VFOAT** SF. Vol. 1, No. 1 (Winter 1986)-. Periodical. English. Four times a year. $165.00 institutions, $50.00 individuals US; $195.00 institutions, $59.00 individuals other. Plenum Press, 233 Spring Street, New York NY 10013-1578. **Tel** (212)620-8000, (800)221-9369, FAX (212)463-0742, (212)807-1047, telex 23/421139. **ED** Robin M. Williams Jr. **LC** HM1; .S6767. **DD** 301/.05. **[CCC]. Pr Rev.** available on microfilm and microfiche from University Microfilms International (UMI). Documents available from The Genuine Article.
**Desc:** Integrative articles and reviews that link subfields of sociology or related sociological research to other disciplines.
**Ind/Abst** Arts Humanit. Citation Index [Select. Cov.]; Curr. Contents Soc. Behav. Sci.; Educ. Adm. Abstr.; Hum. Resour. Abstr.; Int. Bibliogr. Sociol.; J. Plan. Lit.; Popul. Index; Psychol. Abstr. (1986-); PsycINFO (1990-); PsycLit; Res. Alert [Full Cov.]; Sage Fam. Stud. Abstr. (?-?); Sage Public Adm. Abstr.; Soc. Plann. Policy Dev. Abstr.; Soc. Sci. Cit. Index [Full Cov.]; Sociol. Abstr. [Full Cov.].

●US/1077-5048
**SOCIOLOGICAL IMAGINATION.** [Sociol. imagin.]. **Added/Corp** Wisconsin Sociological Association. (1994)-. Academic Scholarly Publication. English. qt. $20.00. Wisconsin Sociological Association, Department of Sociology, University of Wisconsin-Whitewater, Whitewater WI 53190. **Tel** (414)472-1133. **ED** Ronald Berger, Bruce Wiegand. **LC** HM1; .W5. **DD** 301. **CODEN** SIMAEE. **Bk Rev**, (Qty: 1-4). **Ad Acc. Circ:** 600. ***Continues*** *Wisconsin Sociologist, 0043-6666.*
**Desc:** Accepts for consideration papers which deal with issues of pure research, applied or evaluation research, or sociological-clinical practice.
**Ind/Abst** Lang. Lang. Behav. Abstr.; Soc. Welf. Soc. Plan./Policy Soc. Dev.; Sociol. Abstr.

US/0038-0245
**SOCIOLOGICAL INQUIRY.** [Sociol. inq.]. **Added/Corp** Alpha Kappa Delta. Vol. 31 (1961)-. Periodical. English. qt. $43.00 (institutions), $21.00 (individuals). University of Texas Press, PO Box 7819, Austin TX 78713. **Tel** (512)471-4531, FAX (512)320-0668, telex 776453 UTEXPRES AUS. **ED** Dennis L. Peck. **LC** HM1; .S68. **DD** 301. **[CCC].** Index available. **Ad Acc. Pr Rev. Circ:** 2,500 (ctrl). available on microfilm and microfiche from University Microfilms International (UMI). Documents available from The Genuine Article, UMI Article Clearinghouse. ***Continues*** *Alpha Kappa Deltan.*
**Desc:** Publishes the work of many of researchers and theorists in sociology as special issues on current topics. The journal of Alpha Kappa Delta, the International Sociology Honor Society.
**Ind/Abst** ABC POL SCI; Acad. Abstr. Full Text Elite (Jan. 1992-); Acad. Abstr. (Jan. 1992-); Acad. Search (Jan. 1992-); Am. Hist. Life (1973-); Appl. Soc. Sci. Index Abstr.; Commun. Abstr. (?-?); Crim. Justice Abstr.; Curr. Contents Soc. Behav. Sci.; Expand. Acad. Index (1989-); Index Period. Artic. Relat. Law (19??-19??); INFO-SOUTH Abstr.; Int. Polit. Sci. Abstr.; Mag. Search; Middle East Abstr. Index; Multicult. Educ. Abstr.; Newsp. Period. Abstr. (1991-); Peace Res. Abstr. J. (1968-1987); Res. Alert [Full Cov.]; Soc. Plann. Policy Dev. Abstr.; Soc. Sci. Source (Jan. 1992-); Soc. Sci. Cit. Index [Full Cov.]; Soc. Sci. Index; Soc. Sci. Index Fulltext (Fall 1988-) [Full Txt.]; Sociol. Abstr. [Full Cov.]; Sociol. Educ. Abstr.; Spec. Educ. Needs Abstr.; Stud. Women Abstr.

US/0081-1750
**SOCIOLOGICAL METHODOLOGY.** [Sociol. method.]. **Added/Corp** American Sociological Association. (1969)-. English. an. $73.00 North America; $97.00 other. Blackwell Publishers, 238 Main Street, Cambridge MA 02142. **Tel** (617)547-7110, (800)835-6770, FAX (617)547-0789. **ED** Clifford D Clogg. **LC** HM24; .S55. **DD** 301/.01/8. **NLM** W1 SO878X. Index available. **Ad Acc. Circ:** 1,500. available on microfilm and microfiche from University Microfilms International (UMI). Documents available from The Genuine Article.
**Desc:** Articles cover important research tools relevant to contemporary statistics, psychometrics and econometrics as well as sociology.
**Ind/Abst** Int. Bibliogr. Sociol.; Int. Polit. Sci. Abstr.; Res. Alert [Full Cov.]; Soc. Plann. Policy Dev. Abstr.; Sociol. Abstr. (1978-) [Full Cov.]; Soc. Res. Methodol. Abstr. (1980-).

US/0049-1241
**SOCIOLOGICAL METHODS & RESEARCH.** [Sociol. methods res.]. **VFOAT** Sociological Methods and Research; SMR. **VAT** Sociological Methods and Research. Vol. 1, No. 1 (Aug. 1972)-. Periodical. English. qt (Feb., May, Aug., Nov.). $183.00. SAGE Periodical Press, 2455 Teller Road, Thousand Oaks CA 91320. **Tel** (805)499-0721, FAX (805)499-0871, telex 100799. **ED** J. Scott Long (Indiana University). **LC** HM1; .S687. **DD** 301/.07/2. **[CCC]. Pr Rev. Acid Free.** available on microfilm and microfiche from University Microfilms International (UMI). Documents available from The Genuine Article.
**Desc:** Covers quantitative research and methodology in the social sciences.
**Ind/Abst** Appl. Soc. Sci. Index Abstr.; Curr. Contents Soc. Behav. Sci.; Curr. Index Stat.; Int. Bibliogr. Sociol.; J. Plan. Lit.; Middle East Abstr. Index; Res. Alert [Full Cov.]; Sage Urban Stud. Abstr (?-?); Soc. Plann. Policy Dev. Abstr.; Soc. Sci. Cit. Index [Full Cov.]; Soc. Work Abstr. [Select. Cov.]; Sociol. Abstr. [Full Cov.]; Sociol. Educ. Abstr.; Soc. Res. Methodol. Abstr. (1975-).

US/0149-4872
**SOCIOLOGICAL OBSERVATIONS.** Vol. 1 (1977)-. Monographic series. English. ir. Price varies per volume. SAGE Periodical Press, 2455 Teller Road, Thousand Oaks CA 91320. **Tel** (805)499-0721, FAX (805)499-0871, telex 100799. **LC** UNC. **Acid Free.**

US/0731-1214
**SOCIOLOGICAL PERSPECTIVES.** (SOCIOLOGICAL PERSPECTIVES : SP : OFFICIAL PUBLICATION OF THE PACIFIC SOCIOLOGICAL ASSOCIATION.). [Sociol. perspect.]. **Added/Corp** Pacific Sociological Association. **VFOAT** SP. Vol. 26, No. 1 (Jan. 1983)-. Periodical. English. qt. $150.00 (institutions), $60.00 (individuals) US; $170.00 (institutions), $80.00 (individuals) (surface mail), $190.00 (institutions), $100.00 (individuals) (air mail) other. JAI Press Inc., 55 Old Post Road, Suite 2, PO Box 1678, Greenwich CT 06836-1678. **Tel** (203)661-7602, FAX (203)661-0792. **ED** John Pock and Alice Crawford. **LC** HM1; .P33. **DD** 301/.05. **NLM** W1 SO879BH. **Pr Rev.** available on microfilm from University Microfilms International (UMI). Documents available from The Genuine Article, UMI Article Clearinghouse. ***Continues** Pacific Sociological Review, 0030-8919.*
**Desc:** Articles published are selected from papers presented at the annual meetings of the Association and from submitted manuscripts and are general in scope from all areas of the discipline.
**Ind/Abst** ABC POL SCI; Acad. Search (July 1993-); Am. Hist. Life (1982-); Crim. Justice Abstr.; Crim. Penol. Police Sci. Abstr.; Curr. Contents Soc. Behav. Sci.; Curr. Geogr. Publ. (199?-); Expand. Acad. Index (1992-); High. Educ. Abstr. (1983-19??); Hum. Resour. Abstr. (?-?); Index Period. Artic. Relat. Law (19??-19??); Int. Bibliogr. Sociol.; Int. Polit. Sci. Abstr.; Mag. Search; Middle East Abstr. Index; Multicult. Educ. Abstr.; Newsp. Period. Abstr. (1992-); Psychol. Abstr. (1985-); PsycLit; Res. Alert [Full Cov.]; Sage Fam. Stud. Abstr. (?-?); Sage Race Relat. Abstr.; Sage Urban Stud. Abstr (?-?); Soc. Plann. Policy Dev. Abstr.; Soc. Sci. Cit. Index [Full Cov.]; Soc. Work Abstr.; Sociol. Abstr. (1958-) [Full Cov.]; Sociol. Educ. Abstr.; Stud. Women Abstr.; U.S. Polit. Sci. Doc.

US/0163-8505
**SOCIOLOGICAL PRACTICE.** ***Ceased.*** [Sociol. pract.]. Vol. 3 (Spring 1979)-Vol. 11 (1993). Periodical. English. an. Michigan State University Press, 1405 South Harrison Road, Manly Miles 25, East Lansing MI 48823-5202. **Tel** (517)355-9543, FAX (800)678-2120, (517)336-2611. **LC** HM1; .S26. **DD** 301/.05. **Bk Rev. Circ:** 200. available on microfilm and microfiche from University Microfilms International (UMI). ***Continues** SP, Sociological Practice, 0360-845X.*
**Desc:** Applied sociology in various fields-function, problems, training needed. Problems and examples of research for applied and policy uses.
**Ind/Abst** Curr. Contents Soc. Behav. Sci.; Soc. Plann. Policy Dev. Abstr.; Sociol. Abstr. [Full Cov.]; Soc. Res. Methodol. Abstr. (1992-).

US/1050-6306
**SOCIOLOGICAL PRACTICE REVIEW.** ***Ceased.*** (SOCIOLOGICAL PRACTICE REVIEW : SPR.). [Sociol. pract. rev.]. **Added/Corp** American Sociological Association. **VFOAT** SPR. (1990)-(1992). Periodical. English. sa. **LC** HM1; .S62. **DD** 361. **CODEN** SPRRE3. available on microfilm and microfiche from University Microfilms International (UMI).
**Ind/Abst** PAIS Int. Print; Soc. Plann. Policy Dev. Abstr.; Sociol. Abstr. (1990-) [Full Cov.].

US/0038-0253
**SOCIOLOGICAL QUARTERLY.** [Sociol. q.]. **Added/Corp** Midwest Sociological Society. **VFOAT** SQ. Vol. 1 (Jan. 1960)-. Periodical. English. qt. $60.00 (individuals), $135.00 (institutions). University of California Press, 2120 Berkeley Way, Berkeley CA 94720. **Tel** (510)642-4191, (510)642-3907, FAX (510)642-9917. **ED** George J. McCall, Harry H. Bash, Patrick G. Jackson, and Michal M. McCall. **LC** HM1; .S69. **DD** 300/.5. **NLM** W1 SO879C. **CODEN** SOLQAR. **[CCC]. Ad Acc. Pr Rev. Circ:** 2,800. available on microfilm and microfiche from University Microfilms International (UMI). Documents available from The Genuine Article, UMI Article Clearinghouse. ***Supersedes** Midwest Sociologist.*
**Desc:** Presents works of interest to sociologists and other social scientists representing the wide range of the sociological enterprise. Publishes papers of exceptional quality that contribute to general knowledge of basic social institutions and processes.
**Ind/Abst** ABC POL SCI; Abstr. Res. Pastor. Care Couns. (19??-); Acad. Search (July 1993-); Am. Hist. Life (1967-); Appl. Soc. Sci. Index Abstr.; Arts Humanit. Citation Index [Select. Cov.]; Chicano Index; Commun. Abstr. (?-?); Contents Pages Manage.; Crim. Justice Abstr.; Curr. Contents Soc. Behav. Sci.; Expand. Acad. Index (1989-); High. Educ. Abstr. (1965-19??); Index Period. Artic. Relat. Law (19??-19??); INFO-SOUTH Abstr.; Int. Bibliogr. Sociol.; Int. Polit. Sci. Abstr. (1967-); Mag. Search; Middle East Abstr. Index; Multicult. Educ. Abstr.; Newsp. Period. Abstr. (1991-); Peace Res. Abstr. J. (1976-1981); Psychoanal. Abstr.; Psychol. Abstr. (1972-); PsycScan: Appl. Exp. Eng. Psych.; PsycScan: LD/MR; PsycScan: Neuropsych.; Res. Alert [Full Cov.]; Sage Race Relat. Abstr.; Soc. Plann. Policy Dev. Abstr.; Soc. Sci. Source (Jul. 1993-); Soc. Sci. Cit. Index [Full Cov.]; Soc. Sci. Index; Soc. Sci. Index Fulltext (Winter 1988-) [Full Txt.]; Soc. Work Abstr. (?-?); Sociol. Abstr. [Full Cov.]; Sociol. Educ. Abstr.; Stud. Women Abstr.; U.S. Polit. Sci. Doc.; West. Hist. Q.; Women Stud. Abstr.

●US/1061-0154
**SOCIOLOGICAL RESEARCH.** [Sociol. res.]. Vol. 31, No. 1 (Jan.-Feb 1992)-. Periodical. English (translations available in Russian). bm. $506.00 US; $557.00 other. M. E. Sharpe Inc., 80 Business Park Drive, Armonk NY 10504. **Tel** (914)273-1800, (800)541-6563, FAX (914)273-2106. **LC** HX542; .S6. **DD** 301. ***Continues** Soviet Sociology, 0038-5824.*
**Ind/Abst** Popul. Index.

UK/0038-0261
**SOCIOLOGICAL REVIEW, THE.** [Sociol. rev.]. Vol. 1-44, Jan. (1908)-(1952); New Series, Vol. 1 (July 1953)-. Academic Scholarly Publication. English. Five times a year. £80.00 UK and Europe; $144.00 North America; £93.00 other. Basil Blackwell Publishers Ltd, 108 Cowley Road, Oxford 0X4 1JF England. **Tel** 011 44 865 791100, FAX 011 44 865 791347, telex 837022 OXBOOK G. **(Subscription address:** Blackwell Publishers / UK, Marston Book Services, PO Box 87, Oxford OX2 0DT England.**) ED** G Fyfe. **LC** HM1; .S7. **NLM** W1 SO879E. **[CCC].** Index available. **Bk Rev. Ad Acc. Pr Rev. Circ:** 1,400. available on microfilm and microfiche from University Microfilms International (UMI). Documents available from The Genuine Article, UMI Article Clearinghouse. ***Supersedes** Sociological Papers.*
**Desc:** One of the oldest sociological journals, it will continue its policy of publishing articles on a wide range of sociological topics, and critical comments on previous articles.
**Ind/Abst** Acad. Abstr. Full Text Elite (Jan. 1992-); Acad. Abstr. (Jan. 1992-); Acad. Search (Jan. 1992-); AGRICOLA; Am. Hist. Life (1954-); Anthropol. Index; Appl. Soc. Sci. Index Abstr.; Arts Humanit. Citation Index [Select. Cov.]; Book Rev. Index; Contents Pages Manage.; Curr. Contents Soc. Behav. Sci.; Expand. Acad. Index (1989-); INFO-SOUTH Abstr.; Int. Bibliogr. Sociol.; Int. Labour Doc.; Int. Polit. Sci. Abstr.; Mag. Search; Middle East Abstr. Index; Multicult. Educ. Abstr.; Newsp. Period. Abstr. (1991-); Peace Res. Abstr. J. (1963-1965, 1969-1974); Res. Alert [Full Cov.]; Res. High. Educ. Abstr.; Soc. Plann. Policy Dev. Abstr.; Soc. Sci. Source (Jan. 1992-); Soc. Sci. Cit. Index [Full Cov.]; Soc. Sci. Index; Soc. Sci. Index Fulltext (Nov. 1988-) [Full Txt.]; Sociol. Abstr. [Full Cov.]; Sociol. Educ. Abstr.; Spec. Educ. Needs Abstr.; SportSearch; Soc. Res. Methodol. Abstr. (1975-); Stud. Women Abstr.; Tech. Educ. Train. Abstr.; Work Relat. Abstr.

UK/0081-1769
**SOCIOLOGICAL REVIEW MONOGRAPH, THE.** [Sociol. rev. monogr.]. **Added/Corp** University of Keele. No. 1 (1958)-. Monographic series. English. ir. Price varies per volume. University of Keele, Keele Staffordshire ST5 5BG England. **Tel** (0782)621111. **ED** John Eggleston, Ronald Frankenberg, and Gordon Fyfe. **LC** HM15; .S545. **NLM** W1 S0879F. **[CCC]. Bk Rev. Ad Acc. Circ:** 170.
**Desc:** Usually six articles plus extended review plus reviews and list of books received.
**Ind/Abst** Index Med.; Soc. Plann. Policy Dev. Abstr.; Sociol. Abstr. [Full Cov.].

US/0273-2173
**SOCIOLOGICAL SPECTRUM.** (SOCIOLOGICAL SPECTRUM : THE OFFICIAL JOURNAL OF THE MID-SOUTH SOCIOLOGICAL ASSOCIATION.). [Sociol. spectr.]. **Added/Corp** Mid-South Sociological Association. Vol. 1, No. 1 (Jan./March 1981)-. Periodical. English. qt (4 issues). £80.00 UK; $132.00 other. Taylor & Francis Ltd., Rankine Road, Basingstoke Hampshire, RG24 8PR United Kingdom. **Tel** 011 44 256 840366, FAX 011 44 256 479438, telex 858540. **(Subscription address:** Taylor & Francis Inc., 1900 Frost Road, Suite 101, Bristol PA 19007-1598.**) ED** J. Gipson Wells and Frank M. Howell (editor's address: Department of Sociology and Anthropology, Mississippi State University, Mississippi State, MS 39762, USA). **LC** HM1; .S717. **DD** 301/.05. **CODEN** SOSPDS. **[CCC]. Bk Rev. Ad Acc. Pr Rev. Circ:** 880. available on microfilm and microfiche from University Microfilms International (UMI). Documents available from The Genuine Article. ***Formed by the union of** Sociological Symposium, 0038-027X **and** Sociological Forum, 0160-3469.*
**Desc:** Publishes papers on theoretical, methodological, quantitative and qualitative research, and applied research in areas of sociology, social psychology, anthropology, and political science.
**Ind/Abst** Arts Humanit. Citation Index [Select. Cov.]; Crim. Justice Abstr.; Curr. Contents Soc. Behav. Sci.; Middle East Abstr. Index; Res. Alert [Full Cov.]; Soc. Plann. Policy Dev. Abstr.; Soc. Sci. Cit. Index [Full Cov.]; Soc. Welf. Soc. Plan./Policy Soc. Dev.; Sociol. Abstr. [Full Cov.].

US
**SOCIOLOGICAL STUDIES.** No. 1- Jan./Mar. 1977-. Periodical. English. qt. National Technical Information Service - NTIS, Room 2027S, 5285 Port Royal Road, Springfield VA 22161. **Tel** (703)487-4630, (703)487-4660, (703)487-4650, FAX (703)321-8547, telex 89-9405.

US/1058-8930
**SOCIOLOGICAL STUDIES OF CHILD DEVELOPMENT.** [Sociol. stud. child dev.]. Vol. 1 (1986)-. Monographic series. English. ir. $73.25. JAI Press Inc., 55 Old Post Road, Suite 2, PO Box 1678, Greenwich CT 06836-1678. **Tel** (203)661-7602, FAX (203)661-0792. **ED** Patricia Adler. **LC** HQ767.8; .S65. **DD** 305.2/3.
**Ind/Abst** Soc. Plann. Policy Dev. Abstr.; Sociol. Abstr. (1986-) [Full Cov.].

US
**SOCIOLOGICAL STUDIES OF CHILDREN.** (19??)-. Periodical. English. $73.25. JAI Press Inc., 55 Old Post Road, Suite 2, PO Box 1678, Greenwich CT 06836-1678. **Tel** (203)661-7602, FAX (203)661-0792. **ED** Nancy Mandell.

UK/0735-2751
**SOCIOLOGICAL THEORY.** [Sociol. theory]. **Added/Corp** American Sociological Association. (1983)-. Periodical. English. Three times a year. $66.50 North America; $74.00 other. Blackwell Publishers, 238 Main Street, Cambridge MA 02142. **Tel** (617)547-7110, (800)835-6770, FAX (617)547-0789. **ED** Norbert Wiley. **LC** HM24; .S5572. **DD** 301/.01. Index available. **Ad Acc. Circ:** 1,500. available on microfilm and microfiche from University Microfilms International (UMI).
**Desc:** Carries papers on all areas of sociological theory, including metatheory and new substantive theories.
**Ind/Abst** Int. Bibliogr. Sociol.; Soc. Plann. Policy Dev. Abstr.; Sociol. Abstr. [Full Cov.]; Soc. Res. Methodol. Abstr. (1992-).

●US/1070-1192
**SOCIOLOGICAL THEORY ABSTRACTS.** [Sociol. theory abstr.]. **Added/Corp** Sociological Abstracts, Inc. **VFOAT** Sociological Abstracts. Vol. 1 (July 1993)-. English. an. $60.00. Sociological Abstracts, PO Box 22206, San Diego CA 92192-0206. **Tel** (619)695-8803, FAX (619)695-0416. **DD** 301.

US/1060-0876
**SOCIOLOGICAL VIEWPOINTS.** [Sociol. viewp.]. **Added/Corp** Pennsylvania Sociological Society. National Council of State Sociological Associations (U.S.). Vol. 1, No. 1 (1985)-. Periodical. English. an (Fall). $10.00. University of Scranton, Sociology Department, Dr M. Y. Rynn, Scranton PA 18510. **Tel** (717)941-6137, FAX (717)941-6369. **ED** Dr. Midori Yamanouchi Rynn, Ph.D. **DD** 301. **Bk Rev. Pr Rev. Circ:** 150.
**Desc:** Journal papers are based on empirical research as well as those which deal with significant methodological and or theoretical issues, and critiques of various social events.
**Ind/Abst** Soc. Plann. Policy Dev. Abstr.

XR/0038-0288
**SOCIOLOGICKY CASOPIS.** [Sociol. cas.]. **Added/Corp** Vedecke Kolegium Filosofie a Sociologie CSAV. Vol. 1 (1965)-. Periodical. Czech (summaries and/or abstracts in English). qt. DM136.00. Academia, Publishing House of the Czechoslovak Academy of Sciences, Czech AC SCI, Vodickova 40, PO Box 896, 112 29 Prague 1, Czech Republic. **Tel** 011 42 2 245117. **(Subscription address:** Artia Pegas Press Ltd., Palac Metro Narodni Trida 25, 11210 Prague 1 Czech

Republic.) LC HM7; .S614. CODEN SLCSB2. Documents available from The Genuine Article.
**Desc:** Studies in general sociology and the specialized sociological branches. Publishes information from the Czech Republic and from abroad in various social subjects and the methodology of analysis and interpretation.
**Ind/Abst** Psychol. Abstr. (1966-); Res. Alert [Full Cov.]; Soc. Plann. Policy Dev. Abstr.; Soc. Sci. Cit. Index [Full Cov.]; Sociol. Abstr. [Full Cov.]; SportSearch.

CN/0038-030X
**SOCIOLOGIE ET SOCIETES.** [Sociol. soc.]. Vol. 1 (May 1969)-. Periodical. French (English and Spanish; summaries and/or abstracts in French, English and Spanish). Twice a year. $27.00 (individuals), $50.00 (institutions) Canada; $30.00 others. Presses de l'Universite de Montreal, PO Box 6128 Station A, Montreal Quebec H3C 3J7 Canada. **Tel** (514)343-6933. **(Subscription address:** Periodica Inc., PO Box 444, 1155 Ducharme, Outrement Quebec H2V 4R6 Canada.) **ED** Louis Mahev. **LC** HM3; S58. **Bk Rev. Ad Acc. Circ:** 1,500 (ctrl).
**Desc:** A thematic periodical dealing with sociological research inside and outside Quebec; the fruit of collaboration between Quebec sociologists and those of the United States, Europe and Latin America.
**Ind/Abst** Geogr. Abstr. Human Geogr.; Int. Dev. Abstr.; Int. Labour Doc.; Int. Polit. Sci. Abstr.; Point Repere (1983-); Psychol. Abstr. (1978-); PsycINFO (?-?); PsycLit; Soc. Plann. Policy Dev. Abstr.; Sociol. Abstr. [Full Cov.].

RM
**SOCIOLOGIE ROMANEASCA. Added/Corp** Institutul Social Roman. Sectia Sociologica. Asociatia Sociologilor din Romania. Institutul de Sociologie (Academia Romana). Vol. 1, (1936)-. Periodical. Romanian (table of contents in English, French and Russian). bm (6 issues). DM188.00. Editura Academia Republicii Socialiste Romania, Calea Victoriei Nr 125, R-79717 Bucuresti Romania. **Tel** telex 10376 PRSFI R. **(Subscription address:** Kubon & Sagner, ABT Zeitschriftenimport, D 80328 Munich Germany.) **ED** Sorin Radulescu. **LC** HN641; .S63. **CODEN** SOROEL. **Bk Rev.**

YU/0038-0318
**SOCIOLOGIJA.** (SOCIOLOGIJA; CASOPIS ZA SOCIOLOGIJU, SOCIJALNY PSIHOLOGIJU I SOCIJALNU ANTROPOLOGIJU.). [Sociologija]. **Added/Corp** Jugoslovensko Udruzenje za Sociologiju. Vol. 1 (1959)-. Periodical. Serbo-Croatian (Roman). Four times a year. $59.00. **(Subscription address:** Jugoslovenska Knjiga, PO Box 36, YU 11001 Belgrade Yugoslovia.)
**Ind/Abst** Soc. Plann. Policy Dev. Abstr.; Sociol. Abstr. (?-?) [Full Cov.].

CI/0038-0326
**SOCIOLOGIJA SELA.** [Sociol. sela]. **Added/Corp** Agrarni Institut. Centar za Sociologiju Sela, Grada i Prostora. **VFOAT** Rural Sociology; Sotsiologiia Derevni. (July / Sept. 1963)-. Periodical. Serbo-Croatian (Roman) (summaries and/or abstracts in English and Russian). qt. $20.00. Institut za Drustvena Istrazivanja, Amruseval 8, 1000 Zagreb Croatia. **Tel** (041)430-675, (041)430-775, FAX (041)433-298. **ED** Maja Stambuk. **LC** HT401; .S6. cum. index. **Bk Rev**, (Qty: 10). **Pr Rev. Circ:** 800 (ctrl). available on diskette.
**Desc:** Covers rural sociology, agrarian sociology, rural economy, demography articles, history, migration's studies, social ecology, and other sciences related to problems of village and province.
**Ind/Abst** Geogr. Abstr. Human Geogr. (?-?); Int. Dev. Abstr. (?-?); Soc. Plann. Policy Dev. Abstr.; Sociol. Abstr. [Full Cov.]; World Agric. Econ.

BE/0038-0334
**SOCIOLOGISCHE GIDS.** (SOCIOLOGISCHE GIDS. TIJDSCHRIFT VOOR SOCIOLOGIE EN SOCIAAL ONDERZOEK.). [Sociol. gids]. (1953)-. Periodical. Dutch (summaries and/or abstracts in English). bm. F154.50. Uitgeverij Boom, Postbus 400, 7940 AK Meppel Netherlands. **Tel** 011 31 20 5220 57012, FAX 011 31 20 5220 54452, telex 42829. **ED** H M Huttner. Index available. cum. index. **Bk Rev. Ad Acc. Circ:** 1,000 (ctrl).
**Desc:** A journal for sociology and social research.
**Ind/Abst** Int. Bibliogr. Sociol.; Soc. Plann. Policy Dev. Abstr.; Sociol. Abstr. [Full Cov.]; Soc. Res. Methodol. Abstr. (1975-).

SW/0038-0342
**SOCIOLOGISK FORSKNING.** [Sociol. forsk.]. **Added/Corp** Sveriges Sociologforbund. No. 1 (1964)-. Periodical. Swedish (English). qt. Kr250.00. Progek Prospar, Box 31003, S 400-32 Goteborg Sweden. **Tel** 011 46 31 243425. **ED** Staffan Marklund. **Bk Rev. Ad Acc. Pr Rev. Circ:** 1,000. Documents available from The Genuine Article.
**Desc:** Deals primarily with Swedish social planning and development.
**Ind/Abst** Arts Humanit. Citation Index [Select. Cov.]; Res. Alert [Full Cov.]; Soc. Plann. Policy Dev. Abstr.; Soc. Sci. Cit. Index [Full Cov.]; Sociol. Abstr. [Full Cov.]; SportSearch.

DK/0038-0350
**SOCIOLOGISKE MEDDELELSER.** [Sociol. medd.]. Ser. 1-. Danish (English). sa. The Institute for Lougitudinal Studies, Peder Huitterdis Straede 10, DK 1173 Copenhagen K Denmark. **LC** HM7; .S64.
**Ind/Abst** Am. Hist. Life (1977-); Soc. Plann. Policy Dev. Abstr.; Sociol. Abstr. (?-?).

GW/0038-0377
**SOCIOLOGUS; ZEITSCHRIFT FUER EMPIRISCHE ETHNOSOZIOLOGIE UND ETHNOPSYCHOLOGIE. JOURNAL FOR EMPIRICAL ETHNO-SOCIOLOGY AND ETHNO-PSYCHOLOGY. VFOAT** Journal for Empirical Ethno-Sociology and Ethno-Psychology. (1925)-. Periodical. German (English). sa (2 issues). DM99.70 Germany; DM100.20 other. Duncker und Humblot Verlag, Postfach 410329, D-12113 Berlin Germany. **Tel** 011 49 30 79000612, 011 49 30 79000613. **ED** W. Rudolph. **LC** HM5; .S6. **[CCC]. Ad Acc. Circ:** 500. ***Continues*** *Archiv fuer Anthropologie Volkerforschung und Kolonialen Kulturwandel.*
**Desc:** Journal for empirical ethno-sociology and ethno-psychology.
**Ind/Abst** Anthropol. Index; Anthropol. Lit.; Int. Bibliogr. Sociol.; Int. Polit. Sci. Abstr.

UK/0960-1546
**SOCIOLOGY AND RELATED DISCIPLINES / INTERNATIONAL CURRENT AWARENESS SERVICES.** ***Ceased.*** **Added/Corp** International Current Awareness Services. British Library of Political and Economic Science. **VFOAT** Sociology. Vol. 1, No. 1 (Nov. 1990)-(Mar. 1994). Periodical. English. mo. Routledge, 11 New Fetter Lane, London EC4P 4EE England. **Tel** 071 583 9855, FAX 071 842 2298. **(Subscription address:** Kinokuniya Company Ltd., 38-1 Sakuragaoka 5, chome Setagaya-ku, Tokyo 156 Japan.) **[CCC].**

US/0038-0393
**SOCIOLOGY AND SOCIAL RESEARCH.** ***Ceased.*** [Sociol. soc. res.]. Vol. 12 (Sept./Oct. 1927)-Vol. 76 No. 4 (July 1992). Periodical. English. qt. Sociology and Social Research, University of Southern California, 3518 University Avenue, Los Angeles CA 90089-0032. **Tel** (310)743-2658, telex 6302. **ED** Marcus Felson. **NLM** W1 SO879K. **CODEN** SSORA5. cum. index. **Circ:** 2,800. available on microfilm and microfiche from University Microfilms International (UMI). Documents available from The Genuine Article, UMI Article Clearinghouse. ***Formed by the union of*** *Journal of Applied Sociology* ***and*** *Bulletin of Social Research.*
**Desc:** Covers sociology and the social sciences with a special interest in papers that contribute to the practical application of sociological research methods. Aims to disseminate good social science, especially articles with new and interesting information.
**Ind/Abst** Acad. Abstr. Full Text Elite (Jan. 1991-Aug. 1992); Acad. Abstr. (Jan. 1991-Aug. 1992); Acad. Ind. [Computer File] (1987-); Acad. Search (Jan. 1991-Aug. 1992); Am. Hist. Life (1966-); Am. Bibliogr. Slavic East Europ. Stud.; Appl. Soc. Sci. Index Abstr.; Commun. Abstr. (?-?); Crim. Justice Abstr.; Curr. Contents Soc. Behav. Sci.; Curr. Index J. Educ.; Expand. Acad. Index (1987-); High. Educ. Abstr. (1965-); Index Period. Artic. Relat. Law (19??-19??); INFO-SOUTH Abstr.; Int. Bibliogr. Sociol.; Int. Polit. Sci. Abstr.; Mag. Search; Middle East Abstr. Index; Newsp. Period. Abstr. (1991-1992); Popul. Index; Psychol. Abstr. (1928-); PsycINFO; PsycLit; Res. Alert [Full Cov.]; Soc. Plann. Policy Dev. Abstr.; Soc. Sci. Source (Jul. 1990-); Soc. Sci. Cit. Index [Full Cov.]; Soc. Sci. Index; Soc. Sci. Index Fulltext (Oct. 1988-July 1992) [Full Txt.]; Sociol. Abstr. [Full Cov.]; Stud. Women Abstr.; Women Stud. Abstr.; Work Relat. Abstr. (-19??).

ET
**SOCIOLOGY ETHNOLOGY BULLETIN.** **See** Anthropology.

US/0277-9315
**SOCIOLOGY (GUILFORD, CONN.).** (SOCIOLOGY.). [Sociology]. **VFOAT** Annual Editions. Sociology. English. an. $10.95. Dushkin Publishing Group Inc., Sluice Dock, Guilford CT 06437. **Tel** (203)453-4351, (800)243-6532, FAX (203)453-6000. **ED** Kurt Finsterbusch. **LC** HM1; .A76. **DD** 301/.05. ***Continues*** *Annual Editions. Readings in Sociology, 0090-4236.*
**Desc:** Emphasizing social change, institutional crises, and prospects for the future, the articles help the reader develop a sociological perspective and determine how the issues of the day relate to the way in which society is structured.
**Ind/Abst** Crim. Justice Abstr.

US/0038-0407
**SOCIOLOGY OF EDUCATION.** **See** Education.

UK/0141-9889
**SOCIOLOGY OF HEALTH & ILLNESS.** [Sociol. health illn.]. **VFOAT** Sociology of Health and Illness. Vol. 1, No. 1 (June 1979)-. Academic Scholarly Publication. English. bm. £118.00 UK and Europe; $246.00 North America; £159.00 other. Basil Blackwell Publishers Ltd, 108 Cowley Road, Oxford 0X4 1JF England. **Tel** 011 44 865 791100, FAX 011 44 865 791347, telex 837022 OXBOOK G. **(Subscription address:** Blackwell Publishers / UK, Marston Book Services, PO Box 87, Oxford OX2 0DT England.) **ED** Anne Murcott. **LC** RA418; .S6738. **DD** 306/.46. **NLM** W1 SO879NE. **[CCC]. Bk Rev. Ad Acc. Pr Rev. Circ:** 750 (ctrl). available on microfilm and microfiche from University Microfilms International (UMI). Documents available from The Genuine Article.
**Desc:** An international journal publishing sociological articles on all aspects of health, illness and medicine-both theoretical and practical.
**Ind/Abst** Abstr. Soc. Gerontol.; Appl. Soc. Sci. Index Abstr.; Arts Humanit. Citation Index [Select. Cov.]; Curr. Contents Soc. Behav. Sci.; EMBASE; Hospit. Health Admin. Index; Hum. Resour. Abstr.; Int. Bibliogr. Sociol.; Int. Pharm. Abstr.; Middle East Abstr. Index; Multicult. Educ. Abstr.; Psychol. Abstr. (1979-); PsycINFO (?-?); PsycLit; Res. Alert [Full Cov.]; Risk Abstr.; Soc. Plann. Policy Dev. Abstr.; Soc. Sci. Cit. Index [Full Cov.]; Sociol. Abstr. [Full Cov.]; Sociol. Educ. Abstr.; Stud. Women Abstr.; Tech. Educ. Train. Abstr.; Trop. Dis. Bull.

●US/1069-4404
**SOCIOLOGY OF RELIGION.** **See** Religion and Theology.

UK/0038-0385
**SOCIOLOGY (OXFORD).** (SOCIOLOGY.). [Sociology]. **Added/Corp** British Sociological Association. Vol. 1, (Jan. 1967)-. Periodical. English. Four times a year (Feb., May, Aug., Nov.). £25.00 (individual), £72.00 (institution) UK; £30.00 (individual), £79.00 (institution), other. British Sociological Association, 351 Station Road, Dorridge-Solihull, West Midlands B93 8EY England. **Tel** 011 44 564 7724021. **ED** Professor Joan Busfield and Professor Ted Benton, (editor's address: Department of Sociology, University of Essex, Wivenhyde Park, Collhester Essex CO4 3SQ, England, phone: 44 206 873333). **LC** HM1; .S73. **DD** 301/.05. **NLM** W1 SO879J. Index available (Bound in 4th issue publish in November.). cum. index. **Bk Rev**, (Qty: 200). **Ad Acc, Adv Mgr:** J. Ward, **Tel** 0564 772402. **Pr Rev. Circ:** 3,500. available on microfilm and microfiche from University Microfilms International (UMI); available on an online database; available on CD-ROM. Documents available from The Genuine Article, UMI Article Clearinghouse.
**Desc:** Represents the diversity of discipline interests while offering much relevance to the specialist in sociology. International in scope, it has initiated debates on social stratification gender, work organizations, language, and the sociology of knowledge and power that have become the center of the discipline.
**Ind/Abst** Acad. Search (July 1993-); Am. Hist. Life (1976-); Contents Pages Manage.; Crim. Penol. Police Sci. Abstr.; Int. Bibliogr. Sociol.; Int. Polit. Sci. Abstr.; Newsp. Period. Abstr. (1991-); Res. Alert [Full Cov.]; Res. High. Educ. Abstr.; Soc. Plann. Policy Dev. Abstr.; Soc. Sci. Cit. Index [Full Cov.]; Soc. Sci. Index; Soc. Sci. Index Fulltext (Nov. 1988-) [Full Txt.]; Sociol. Abstr. [Full Cov.]; Sociol. Educ. Abstr.; Spec. Educ. Needs Abstr.; Soc. Res. Methodol. Abstr. (1979-); Stud. Women Abstr.

UK/0959-8499
**SOCIOLOGY REVIEW.** [Sociol. rev.]. (1991)-. Periodical. English. Four times a year (Sept., Nov., Feb., Apr.). £16.95 UK; £23.00 Europe; £28.50 other. Philip Allan Publishers Ltd, Market Place, Deddington Oxford, OX15 0SE England. **Tel** 011 44 869 38652, FAX 011 44 869 38803. **DD** 301. ***Continues*** *Social Studies Review, 0267-0712.*

YU/0085-6320
**SOCIOLOSKI PREGLED.** [Sociol. pregl.]. **Added/Corp** Srpsko Sociolosko Drustvo (Belgrade, Serbia) Sociolosko Drustvo Srbije Instituta Drustvenih Nauka (1957- : Belgrade, Serbia). Centar za Socioloska Istrazivanja. (1961)-. Periodical. Serbo-Croatian (Roman) (summaries and/or abstracts in English). qt. **LC** HM7; .S682.
**Ind/Abst** Soc. Plann. Policy Dev. Abstr.; Sociol. Abstr. (1961-) [Full Cov.].

US
**SOCIOMETRY MONOGRAPHS.** **Added/Corp** American Sociological Association. No. 1 (1941)-. Monographic series. English. ir. Price varies per volume. Beacon House Inc, PO Box 311, Beacon NY 12508. **Tel** (914)831-2318.
**Ind/Abst** Peace Res. Abstr. J. (1963-1968, 1974).

CL
**SOLIDARIDAD.** **See** Religion and Theology.

JA/0584-1380
**SOSHIOROJI.** [Soshioroji]. (1952)-. Periodical. Multiple languages. tq. **DD** 301.
**Ind/Abst** Soc. Plann. Policy Dev. Abstr.; Sociol. Abstr. (1987-).

NO/0332-6330
**SOSIOLOGI I DAG.** (19??)-. Periodical. Norwegian. Four times a year (Mar., June, Sept., Dec.). $59.00 (institution); $36.00 (individual). Novus Press, PO Box 748 Sentrum, N-0106 Oslo Norway. **Tel** 011 47 22 717450, FAX 011 47 22 718107.

FI/0038-1640
**SOSIOLOGIA.** [Sosiologia]. **Added/Corp** Westermarck Society. (1964)-. Periodical. Finnish (summaries and/or abstracts in English). qt. **LC** HM7;

.S69.
**Ind/Abst** Soc. Plann. Policy Dev. Abstr.; Sociol. Abstr. (1965-) [Full Cov.].

BU/0038-1683
**SOTSIOLOGICHESKI PROBLEMI.** **Added/Corp** Bulgarska Akademiia na Naukite. Institut po Sotsiologiia. Vol. 1 (1969)-. Periodical. Bulgarian (summaries and/or abstracts in English and Russian). Four times a year. DM168.00. **(Subscription address:** Kubon & Sagner, ABT Zeitschriftenimport, D 80328 Munich Germany.**)** **LC** HM7; .S7.
**Ind/Abst** Soc. Plann. Policy Dev. Abstr.; Sociol. Abstr. (?-?).

RU/0132-1625
**SOTSIOLOGICHESKIE ISSLEDOVANIIA.** **Added/Corp** Institut Sotsiologicheskikh Issledovanii (Akademiia Nauk SSSR). (July/Sept. 1974)-. Academic Scholarly Publication. Russian. Twelve times a year. $192.00. Izdatelstvo Nauka / Akademiia Nauk, Publishing House of the Russian Academy of Sciences, Leninskii Porspekt 14, 117901 Moscow Russia. **Tel** 011 95 954-21-53, FAX 011 95 938-21-44, telex 411964. **(Subscription address:** East View Publications Inc., 3020 Harbor Lane North, Suite 110, Minneapolis MN 55447.**)** **LC** HM7; .S698. **[CCC].** **Pr Rev.** Documents available from The Genuine Article.
**Ind/Abst** Am. Hist. Life (1981-); Int. Bibliogr. Sociol.; Int. Labour Doc.; LABORDOC; Popul. Index; Res. Alert [Full Cov.]; Soc. Plann. Policy Dev. Abstr.; Soc. Sci. Cit. Index [Full Cov.]; Sociol. Abstr. [Full Cov.].

●US/1068-8218
**SOUTHERN CULTURES.** (1993)-. Periodical. English. qt (4 issues). $32.00 (institutions), $24.00 (individuals) US; $44.00 (institutions), $36.00 (individuals) other. Duke University Press, PO Box 90660, Durham NC 27708-0660. **Tel** (919)687-3600, (919)688-5134 (orders), FAX (919)688-4574, telex 802829. **ED** John Shelton Reed and Harry L. Watson.
**Desc:** Explores aspects of the American South ranging from history, anthropology, political science and sociology to folklore, literature, and art. Contains articles, reviews, and other features focusing on common themes as well as conflict among the folk, popular and high cultures of the South.

US/0885-3436
**SOUTHERN RURAL SOCIOLOGY.** (SOUTHERN RURAL SOCIOLOGY : THE JOURNAL OF THE RURAL SOCIOLOGY SECTION, SOUTHERN ASSOCIATION OF AGRICULTURAL SCIENTISTS.). [South. rural sociol.]. **Added/Corp** Southern Association of Agricultural Scientists. Rural Sociology Section. Southern Rural Sociological Association. **VFOAT** SRS. Vol. 1 (1983)-. Periodical. English. an. $25.00. Southern Rural Sociologic Association, North Carolina State University, PO Box 70/ Attn:Dr Maurice E Voland, Belhaven NC 27810. **Tel** (919)964-2338, FAX (919)964-2340. **ED** Dr Doug Bachtel (editor's address: University of Georgia, Athens GA 30602; ph# (404)452-8940). **LC** HD1405; .A7. **DD** 307.7/2/0975. **Pr Rev. Circ:** 175. ***Continues*** *Southern Association of Agricultural Scientists. Rural Sociology Section. Rural Sociology in the South, 8756-162X.*
**Desc:** Rural sociological research reports primarily on work done in the southern universities.
**Ind/Abst** AGRICOLA [Full Cov.]; Geogr. Abstr. Human Geogr.

US/0038-4577
**SOUTHERN SOCIOLOGIST / THE SOUTHERN SOCIOLOGICAL SOCIETY, THE.** [South. sociol.]. **Added/Corp** Southern Sociological Society (U.S.) Emory University. Dept. of Sociology. Vol. 1 (1968)-. Periodical. English. qt (4 issues). $20.00. Southern Sociological Society, PO Box 6245, Mississippi State MS 39762-6245. **Tel** (601)325-2495, FAX (601)325-4564. **LC** HM1; .S83. **DD** 301/.0975.
**Ind/Abst** Sociol. Abstr.

US/0199-8668
**SOUTHERN STRUGGLE.** **Added/Corp** Southern Conference Educational Fund. Vol. 35 (Jan. 1977)-. Periodical. English. ir. $5.00. Southern Struggle, PO Box 10797, Atlanta GA 30310. **LC** HN79.A2; S67. **DD** 309.1/75. available on microfilm and microfiche from University Microfilms International (UMI). ***Continues*** *Southern Patriot, 0038-4402.*

GW
**SOZIALPADAGOGIK.** 1.- Yearly volume; (Jan. 1959)-. Periodical. German. bm. DM42.60 (one year), DM39.60 (students), DM8.10 (single issue). Gutersloher Verlagshaus, Postfach 450, D 33311 Guetersloh Germany. **Tel** 011 49 5241 74050. **LC** HN30; .S6.

GW
**SOZIALWISSENSCHAFTLICHE INFORMATIONEN.** **VFOAT** SOWI. Vol. 15, No. 1 (March 1986)-. Periodical. German. qt. Erhard Friedrich Verlag, Postfach 100150, D 30917 Seelze Germany. **Tel** 011 49 511 4000452. ***Continues*** *Sozialwissenschaftliche Informationen fur Unterricht und Studium.*
**Ind/Abst** Am. Hist. Life (1988-).

GW/0938-6076
**SOZIALWISSENSCHAFTLICHER FACHINFORMATIONSDIENST. SOZIALPOLITIK / INFORMATIONSZENTRUM SOZIALWISSENSCHAFTEN.** **Added/Corp** Informationszentrum Sozialwissenschaften (Bonn, Germany). **VFOAT** Sozialpolitik; SoFid. Sozialpolitik. (1990)-. Periodical. German. sa. ***Continues in part*** *Sozialwissenschaftlicher Fachinformationsdienst. Sozialpolitik, Sozialwesen, allgemeine soziale Probleme, 0176-4527.*

GW/0172-4797
**SOZIOLOGENKORRESPONDENZ.** [Soziologenkorrespondenz]. (1970)-. German. ir. **UDC** 30.
**Ind/Abst** Soc. Plann. Policy Dev. Abstr.; Sociol. Abstr. (1970-).

GW/0340-918X
**SOZIOLOGIE.** ***Ceased.*** [Soziologie]. **Added/Corp** Deutsche Gesellschaft fur Soziologie. (1973)-(1992). Periodical. German. sa. **LC** HM5; .S66. **DD** 301/.072/043.
**Ind/Abst** Soc. Plann. Policy Dev. Abstr.; Sociol. Abstr. (1975-19??) [Full Cov.].

GW/0584-6048
**SOZIOLOGISCHE ABHANDLUNGEN.** **Added/Corp** Berlin. Freie Universitaet. Wirtschafts-und Sozialwissenschaftliche Fakultaet. No. 1 (1961)-. Monographic series. German. ir. Price varies per volume. Duncker und Humblot Verlag, Postfach 410329, D-12113 Berlin Germany. **Tel** 011 49 30 79000612, 011 49 30 79000613. **DD** 301.

GW/0343-4109
**SOZIOLOGISCHE REVUE.** Vol. 1 (Jan. 1978)-. Periodical. German. qt. DM148.00. R Oldenbourg Verlag, Postfach 801360, D 81613 Munich Germany. **Tel** 011 49 89 450190, FAX 011 49 89 45019305. **ED** Johannes Weiss, Heinz Hartmann, Joachin Matther and Claus Offe. **Bk Rev. Ad Acc. Circ:** 1,500 (ctrl).
**Desc:** Prints reviews of German language literature on sociology and its related fields, including methodology, affording the reader a complete critical and current overview of the field.
**Ind/Abst** Soc. Plann. Policy Dev. Abstr.; Sociol. Abstr. [Full Cov.]; Sociol. Educ. Abstr.; Soc. Res. Methodol. Abstr. (1978-); Tech. Educ. Train. Abstr.

US/1047-0123
**SPECIAL REPORT ON LIVING.** ***Title Change.*** [Spec. rep. living]. **VFOAT** Living; Special Report, Living; Special Report. (Nov. 1988/Jan. 1989)-(199?). Periodical. English. qt. Whittle Communications, 333 Main Avenue, Knoxville TN 37902. **Tel** (615)595-5000, FAX (615)595-5877. **LC** HQ2044.U6; S68. **DD** 305.4/05. ***Merged with*** *Special Report, Fiction, 1047-2886; Special Report on Family, 1047-2878; Special Report on Health, 1047-272X; Special Report on Personalities, 1047-286X* ***and*** *Special Report on Sports, 1047-2851* ***to form*** *Special Report (Whittle Communications), 1059-5201.*

SA
**SPOTLIGHT / SOUTH AFRICAN INSTITUTE OF RACE RELATIONS.** **Added/Corp** South African Institute of Race Relations. **VFOAT** South African Institute of Race Relations Spotlight. No. 1 (Mar. 1991)-. Monographic series. English. South African Institute of Race Relations, PO Box 31044, Braamfontein 2017 South Africa. **Tel** 011 27 11 4033600, FAX 011 27 11 4033671.

US/0271-1192
**SPRINGER SERIES ON DEATH AND SUICIDE, THE.** **See** Philosophy.

NE
**SRM BIBLIOGRAPHY.** **VFOAT** Social Research Methodology Bibliography. (Summer 1979)-. Bibliography. English. qt. Erasmus Univ Srm Doc Cntr, Postbus 1738, Kamer BT 13, 3000 DR Rotterdam Netherlands. **Tel** 011 31 010 4081198. ***Supersedes in part*** *SRM Abstract Bulletin.*

US/0279-1293
**SRPSKA BORBA.** **See** Ethnic Interests.

IT/0039-291X
**STUDI DI SOCIOLOGIA.** [Studi sociol.]. **Added/Corp** Universita Cattolica del Sacro Cuore. (Jan./March 1963)-. Periodical. Italian. Four times a year. $86.00. Vita e Pensiero, Pubblic University, Largo Gemelli 1, 20123 Milan Italy. **Tel** 011 39 2 72342310, 011 39 2 72342370. **LC** HM7; .S8. **DD** 301/.05. cum. index.
**Ind/Abst** Soc. Plann. Policy Dev. Abstr.; Sociol. Abstr. [Full Cov.].

PL/0039-3231
**STUDIA MEDIEWISTYCZNE.** **See** Philosophy.

●US/1057-610X
**STUDIES IN CONFLICT AND TERRORISM.** [Stud. confl. terror.]. **VFOAT** Studies in Conflict & Terrorism. Vol. 15, No. 1 (Jan./Mar. 1992)-. Periodical. English. qt (4 issues). £84.00 UK; $139.00 other. Taylor & Francis Ltd., Rankine Road, Basingstoke Hampshire, RG24 8PR United Kingdom. **Tel** 011 44 256 840366, FAX 011 44 256 479438, telex 858540. **(Subscription address:** Taylor & Francis Inc., 1900 Frost Road, Suite 101, Bristol PA 19007-1598.**)** **ED** George K. Tanham and Bruce Hoffman (associate editor). **LC** HM136; .S85. **DD** 303.6. **CODEN** SCTREO. **[CCC].** Documents available from UMI Article Clearinghouse. ***Formed by the union of*** *Terrorism, 0149-0389* ***and*** *Conflict, 0149-5941.*
**Desc:** The aim of the journal is to cast light on all of the conflicts, their motivations and their forms in different parts of the world. The journal will publish theoretical and empirical studies that contribute to a better understanding of the causes and conflicts; as well as the strategies and tactics of the groups conducting them in order to deal with them more effectively and promote peaceful, orderly socio-economic improvements and world peace.
**Ind/Abst** ABC POL SCI; Acad. Search (July 1993-); Air Univ. Libr. Index Mil. Period. (199?-); Am. Hist. Life; INFO-SOUTH Abstr.; Newsp. Period. Abstr. (1992-); PAIS Int. Print; Soc. Plann. Policy Dev. Abstr.; Sociol. Abstr.

NE/0920-6221
**STUDIES IN HUMAN SOCIETY.** Vol. 1 (1986)-. Monographic series. English. ir. Price varies per volume. E. J. Brill, Postbus 9000, 2300 PA Leiden Netherlands. **Tel** 011 31 71 312624, FAX 011 31 71 317532, telex 39296 BRILL NL.

US/1059-4337
**STUDIES IN LAW, POLITICS AND SOCIETY.** [Stud. law polit. soc.]. Vol. 10 (1990)-. English. ir. $73.25. JAI Press Inc., 55 Old Post Road, Suite 2, PO Box 1678, Greenwich CT 06836-1678. **Tel** (203)661-7602, FAX (203)661-0792. **ED** Susan Silbey and Austin Sarat. **LC** K18; .E837. **CODEN** SLPSE2. ***Continues*** *Research in Law, Deviance and Social Control, 0737-1136.*
**Ind/Abst** Int. Bibliogr. Sociol.; Leg. Resour. Index; LegalTrac (1990-); Soc. Plann. Policy Dev. Abstr.

UK
**STUDIES IN SOCIOLOGY (GEORGE ALLEN & UNWIN).** (STUDIES IN SOCIOLOGY.). Vol. 1- 1967-. Monographic series. English. Price varies per volume. Unwin Hyman Ltd., 15 17 Broadwick Street, London W1V 1FP England. **Tel** 011 44 71 439 3126.

●US/1058-5621
**STUDIES IN SOUTHERN ITALIAN AND ITALIAN AMERICAN CULTURE.** **See** Ethnic Interests.

US/0163-2396
**STUDIES IN SYMBOLIC INTERACTION.** [Stud. symb. interact.]. Vol. 1 (1978)-. English. ir. $73.25. JAI Press Inc., 55 Old Post Road, Suite 2, PO Box 1678, Greenwich CT 06836-1678. **Tel** (203)661-7602, FAX (203)661-0792. **ED** Norman Denzin. **LC** HM1; .S84. **DD** 301.1. **[CCC].**
**Desc:** Devoted to the empirical study of human behavior and social life. It examines the nature, forms, conditions, and consequences of communicative interaction within, between, and among such social actors as individuals, groups, organizations, institutions, communities and nations.
**Ind/Abst** Psychol. Abstr. (1980-); PsycINFO (?-?); PsycLit; Soc. Plann. Policy Dev. Abstr.; Sociol. Abstr. [Full Cov.].

US/0734-4937
**STUDIES OF ISRAELI SOCIETY.** [Stud. Isr. soc.]. Vol. 1 (1980)-. Monographic series. English. ir. Price varies per volume. Transaction Publishers / Rutgers State University, New Brunswick NJ 08903. **Tel** (908)932-2280 Ext. 105, FAX (908)932-3138. **ED** Ernest Krausz. **LC** HN660; .A57. **Pr Rev.** available on microfiche; available on microfilm.
**Desc:** Presents in a single forum social science investigation of Israeli society previously published in a variety of international journals.

UK
**STUDIES OF THE SOCIAL SECURITY SYSTEM.** No. 1- 1982-. Monographic series. English. Price varies per volume. Policy Studies Institute, 100 Park Village East, London NW1 3SR England. **Tel** 011 44 1 387 2171.

US/0039-4394
**SUBTERRANEAN SOCIOLOGY NEWSLETTER / SUBTERRANEAN SOCIOLOGICAL ASSOCIATION, THE.** Began with Vol. 1 (July 1967). Newsletter. English. ir. $3.00. Marcello Truzzi, Subterranean Sociology, Department of Sociology, Eastern Michigan University, Ypsilanti MI 48197. **Tel** (313)487-4246. **ED** Marcello Truzzi. **Circ:** 300.

SA/0258-0144
**SUID-AFRIKAANSE TYDSKRIF VIR SOSIOLOGIE, DIE.** (DIE SUID-AFRIKAANSE TYDSKRIF VIR SOSIOLOGIE. THE SOUTH AFRICAN JOURNAL OF SOCIOLOGY.). [S.-Afr. tydskr. sosiol.]. **VFOAT** The South African Journal of Sociology. No. 1

(Nov. 1970)-. Periodical. Afrikaans (English). sa. R87.00 South Africa; R90.00 other. Foundation for Education Science & Technology, PO Box 1758, Pretoria 0001 South Africa. **Tel** 011 27 12 3226404, FAX 011 27 12 3207803. **LC** HM1; .S9. **[CCC].**
**Ind/Abst** Int. Bibliogr. Sociol.; Soc. Plann. Policy Dev. Abstr.; Sociol. Abstr.; Spec. Educ. Needs Abstr.

US/0273-2017
**SURVIVAL TOMORROW.** Vol. 1, No. 1 (Mar. 1981)-. Periodical. English. mo. Kephart Communications Inc, 1300 North 17th Street/Suite 1660, Alexandria VA 22209. **Tel** (703)836-3313.

AT
**SYDNEY STUDIES IN SOCIETY AND CULTURE.** **Added/Corp** Sydney Association for Studies in Society and Culture. (1983)-. Monographic series. English. ir. Price varies per volume. University of Sydney / Dept. of English, c/o Dr D. Speed, Sydney New South Wales 2006 Australia. **Tel** 011 61 02 6922374, FAX 011 61 02 6924203.
**Ind/Abst** Annu. Bibliogr. Engl. Lang. Lit.

US/0195-6086
**SYMBOLIC INTERACTION.** [Symb. interact.]. **Added/Corp** Society for the Study of Symbolic Interaction. Vol. 1 (Fall 1977)-. Periodical. English. Four times a year. $150.00 (institutions), $60.00 (individuals) US; $170.00 (institutions), $80.00 (individuals) (surface mail), $190.00 (institutions), $100.00 (individuals) (air mail) other. JAI Press Inc., 55 Old Post Road, Suite 2, PO Box 1678, Greenwich CT 06836-1678. **Tel** (203)661-7602, FAX (203)661-0792. **ED** Gary Alan Fine, Andrea Fontana, Steven Gordon, and Sherryl Kleinmann. **LC** HM1; .S96. **DD** 302. **[CCC]. Pr Rev.** Documents available from The Genuine Article.
**Desc:** Devoted to the empirical study of human behavior and social life. It examines the nature, forms, conditions, and consequences of communicative interaction within, between, and among such social actors as individuals, groups, organizations, institutions, communities and nations.
**Ind/Abst** Curr. Contents Soc. Behav. Sci.; Middle East Abstr. Index; Psychol. Abstr. (1979-); PsycINFO (?-?); PsycLit; Res. Alert [Full Cov.]; Soc. Plann. Policy Dev. Abstr.; Soc. Sci. Cit. Index [Full Cov.]; Sociol. Abstr. [Full Cov.].

HU/0133-3461
**SZOCIOLOGIA (BUDAPEST. 1972).** (SZOCIOLOGIA.). [Szociologia]. **Added/Corp** Magyar Tudomanyos Akademia, Budapest. Szociologial Bizottsag. (1972)-. Periodical. Hungarian. qt. $28.00. Magyar Tudomanyos Akademia, Szociologiai Kutatointezet, Uri u. 49, 1014 Budapest, Hungary. **ED** L. Cseh-Szombathy. **LC** HM7; .S94. Index available. **Bk Rev.**
**Ind/Abst** Soc. Plann. Policy Dev. Abstr.; Sociol. Abstr. [Full Cov.].

KU
**TAAWUN (KUWAIT, KUWAIT).** (AL-TAAWUN / ITTIHAD AL-JAMIYAT AL-TAAWUNIYAH AL-ISTIHLAKIYAH.). Periodical. Arabic. mo. 2.5. Ittihad Al-Jamiyat Al-Taawuniyah Al-Istihlakiyah SB 1836, Al-Safah Kuwait. **LC** HN669; .A55.

US/0164-8535
**TALK (NEW YORK).** (TALK.). [Talk]. Periodical. English. mo. Donovan Communications, 100 Park Avenue, New York NY 10017. **LC** AP2; .T1596. **DD** 305.4/05.

US/0092-055X
**TEACHING SOCIOLOGY.** [Teach. sociol.]. **Added/Corp** American Sociological Association. Vol. 1 (Oct. 1973)-. Periodical. English. qt (4 issues). $80.00 (institutions), $40.00 (individuals) US; $88.00 (institutions), $48.00 (individuals) other. American Sociological Association, 1722 North Street Northwest, Washington DC 20036-2981. **Tel** (202)833-3410, FAX (202)785-0146. **ED** Theodore C. Wagenaar. **LC** HM1; .T43. **DD** 301/.07. Index available. cum. index. **Bk Rev. Ad Acc. Pr Rev. Circ:** 2,000. available on microfilm and microfiche from University Microfilms International (UMI). Documents available from The Genuine Article.
***Absorbed*** *Teaching Newsletter.*
**Desc:** Publishes research articles, teaching tips and reports on teaching sociology in particular. Includes the shorter reports of class projects and innovations previously published in the Teaching Newsletter.
**Ind/Abst** Acad. Search (July 1993-); Appl. Soc. Sci. Index Abstr.; Arts Humanit. Citation Index [Select. Cov.]; Contents Pages Educ.; Crim. Justice Abstr.; Curr. Contents Soc. Behav. Sci.; Curr. Index J. Educ.; Educ. Index; Educ. Technol. Abstr.; INFO-SOUTH Abstr.; Mag. Search; Middle East Abstr. Index; Res. Alert [Full Cov.]; Res. High. Educ. Abstr.; Soc. Plann. Policy Dev. Abstr.; Soc. Sci. Cit. Index [Full Cov.]; Sociol. Abstr. [Full Cov.]; Sociol. Educ. Abstr.; Stud. Women Abstr.

●US/1066-2847
**TEACHING TOLERANCE.** [Teach. toler.]. **Added/Corp** Southern Poverty Law Center. Vol 1, No. 1 (Spring 1992)-. English. sa. (free upon request). Southern Poverty Law Center, 400 Washington Avenue, Montgomery AL 36104. **Tel** (205)264-0286. **DD** 371.
**Ind/Abst** Curr. Index J. Educ.

BL/0103-2070
**TEMPO SOCIAL : REVISTA DE SOCIOLOGIA DA USP / UNIVERSIDADE DE SAO PAULO, FACULDADE DE FILOSOFIA, LETRAS E CIENCIAS HUMANAS, DEPARTAMENTO DE SOCIOLOGIA.** **Added/Corp** Universidade de Sao Paulo. Departamento de Sociologia. Vol. 1, No. 1 (1989)-. Periodical. Portuguese. Universidade de Sao Paulo / Filosofia, Faculdade de Filosofia, Ciencias e Letras, CP 8105, Sao Paulo Brazil. **Tel** 011 55 11 813-3222 Ext 2191. **LC** HM22.B8; T46. **DD** 301/.05.
**Ind/Abst** PAIS Int. Print.

CN/0831-5701
**TENDANCES SOCIALES CANADIENNES.** [Tend. soc. can.]. **Added/Corp** Statistique Canada. (1986)-. Periodical. French. qt. 34.00Can$ Canada; $41.00 US; $48.00 other. Statistics Canada, Publications Sales & Services, Main Building Room 1710, Ottawa Ontario K1A 0T6 Canada. **Tel** (613)951-5078, (800)267-6677, FAX (613)951-1584, telex 053-3585. **DD** 306/.0971.
**Ind/Abst** Can. Period. Index (No. 20, Spring 1991-); Point Repere (1991-).

IT
**TEORIA SOCIOLOGICA.** (19??)-. Italian. sa. L66000 Italy; L90000 other. Franco Angeli Riviste SRL, Viale Monza 106, 20127 Milan Italy. **Tel** 011 39 2 2827651, 011 39 2 289562.

IT/0040-392X
**TERZO MONDO.** **Added/Corp** Centro Studi Terzo Mondo. (July/Sept. 1968)-. Periodical. Italian (English, French and Spanish). qt. L60000 (institutions), L30000 (individuals) Italy; $60.00 (institutions), $30.00 (individuals) other. Centro Studi Terzo Mondo, Via G Morgagni 39, 20129 Milan Italy. **Tel** 39 2 29409041. **ED** Umberto Melotti. **LC** D848; .T47. **DD** 905. **Bk Rev**, (Qty: 100). **Ad Acc, Adv Mgr:** V Meletti. **Circ:** 2,500.
**Desc:** Presents studies, research and documentation on Asia, Africa and Latin America, covering international problems, economic and cultural cooperation, developmental problems and politics. Also treats anthropology and sociology.
**Ind/Abst** Bibliogr. Mission.; Soc. Plann. Policy Dev. Abstr.

US/0748-1799
**TEXAS POLL REPORT, THE.** [Tex. Poll rep.]. **Added/Corp** Harte-Hanks Communications. Vol. 1, No. 1 (Feb. 1984)-. Periodical. English. qt. $40.00 (one year), $75.00 (two year). Texas Poll Report, 815 Brazos Suite 800, Austin TX 78701. **Tel** (512)478-9646. **DD** 303.

US
**THEORIES OF CONTEMPORARY CULTURE.** Vol. 1 (1977)-. Monographic series. English. ir. Price varies per volume. Indiana University Press, 601 North Morton Street, Bloomington IN 47404. **Tel** (812)855-3830, (800)842-6796.

NE/0304-2421
**THEORY AND SOCIETY.** [Theory soc.]. Vol. 1 (1974)-. Periodical. English. bm. $457.00. Kluwer Academic Publishers, Postbus 322, 3300 AH Dordrecht, The Netherlands. **Tel** 011 (31) 78 524400, FAX 011 31 78 183273, telex 20083. **ED** Janet Walker Gouldner and Robert K Merton. **LC** HM1; .T5. **DD** 301/.05. **[CCC]. Pr Rev. Acid Free.** available on microfilm and microfiche from University Microfilms International (UMI). Documents available from The Genuine Article.
**Desc:** A forum for the international community of scholars that publishes theoretically informed analyses of social processes. Its subject matter ranges from prehistory to contemporary affairs, from treatments of single individuals and national societies to world culture, from discussions of theory to methodological critique, from First World to Third World - but always in the effort to bring together theory, criticism and concrete observation.
**Ind/Abst** Acad. Search (July 1993-); Appl. Soc. Sci. Index Abstr.; Arts Humanit. Citation Index [Select. Cov.]; Curr. Contents Soc. Behav. Sci.; Humanit. Source (Jul. 1993-); Int. Bibliogr. Sociol.; Int. Polit. Sci. Abstr.; Left Index; Mag. Search; PAIS Int. Print; Peace Res. Abstr. J. (1975-1976); Res. Alert [Full Cov.]; Soc. Plann. Policy Dev. Abstr.; Soc. Sci. Cit. Index [Full Cov.]; Sociol. Abstr. [Full Cov.]; Sociol. Educ. Abstr.

US/0725-5136
**THESIS ELEVEN.** [Thesis eleven]. **VFOAT** Thesis 11. No. 1 (1980)-. Periodical. English. Three times a year. $35.00 (individuals), $85.00 (institutions). Massachusetts Institute of Technology (MIT) Press, 55 Hayward Street, Cambridge MA 02142-1399. **Tel** (617)253-2889, (617)625-8481, FAX (617)258-6779. **ED** Johann Arnason, Peter Beilharz, Michael Crozier, Kevin McDonald, Peter Murphy, David Roberts, Gillian Robinson, Philipa Rothfield, John Rundell. **LC** H61; .T468. **[CCC]. Bk Rev. Ad Acc. Circ:** 1,500. available on microfilm and microfiche from University Microfilms International (UMI).
**Desc:** Focus on theories of society, culture and politics and the self-understanding of modernity. Directed to scholars working in the areas of philosophy, social theory, political science and cultural studies.

**Ind/Abst** Altern. Press Index; APAIS, Aust. Public Aff. Inf. Ser.; Left Index; Sage Public Adm. Abstr. (?-?); Soc. Plann. Policy Dev. Abstr.; Sociol. Abstr.

CL
**TIERRA NUEVA.** **See** Religion and Theology.

FI
**TIETOJA KAUPUNGEISTA, KAUPPALOISTA JA KAUPUNKILIITOSTA.** **Main/Corp** Suomen Kaupunkiliitto. **VFOAT** Uppgifter Om Staderna, Kopingarna Och Stadsforbundet. Multiple languages (Finnish and Swedish). Suomen Kaupunkiliitto, Riksdagsgatan 4, 00100 10 Helsinki Finland. **LC** HT145.F5; S9A.

BE
**TIJDSCHRIFT VOOR SOCIOLOGIE.** **Added/Corp** Vereniging voor Sociologie (Belgium). (1980)-. Periodical. Dutch. qt. 938F. Tijdschrift Voor Sociologie, E Van Evenstraat 2C, B 3000 Leuven, Belgium.
**Ind/Abst** Soc. Plann. Policy Dev. Abstr.; Sociol. Abstr. (1984-) [Full Cov.].

CN/1180-0852
**TOGETHER (OTTAWA).** (TOGETHER : A NEWSLETTER ABOUT MULTICULTURALISM TODAY.). [Together]. **Added/Corp** Canada. Multiculturalism and Citizenship Canada. **VFOAT** Ensemble. Vol. 1, No. 1 (Winter 1990)-. Periodical. English (French). qt. Multiculturalism & Citizenship, Canada Communications Branch, Ottawa Ontario K1A 0M5 Canada. **Tel** (819)994-0055. **DD** 306.4/0971. ***Continues*** *Cultures Canada, 0710-8559.*

FI/0357-1823
**TRANSACTIONS OF THE WESTERMARCK SOCIETY.** [Trans. Westermarck Soc.]. **Main/Corp** Westermarck Society. Vol. 1 (1947)-. English. an.
**Ind/Abst** Soc. Plann. Policy Dev. Abstr.; Sociol. Abstr. (1956-) [Full Cov.].

CN/0823-9274
**TRANSMARGE.** [Transmarge]. No. O (Fall 1984)-. Periodical. French. $8.00 each number. Galeries d'Idees Dialyse, CP 745 Succursale C, Montreal Quebec H2L 4L5 Canada. **DD** 306/.1.

SZ
**TRAVAUX DE DROIT, D'ECONOMIE, DE SOCIOLOGIE ET DE SCIENCES POLITIQUES.** **See** Economics.

CN/1187-0877
**TRENDS IN HAMILTON-WENTWORTH.** [Trends Hamilt.-Wentworth]. **Added/Corp** Social Planning and Research Council of Hamilton and District. Vol. 3, Issue 1 (Winter 1991)-. Periodical. English. Social Planning and Research Council of Hamilton and District, 153 1/2 King Street East, Hamilton Ontario L8N 1B1 Canada. **Tel** (416)522-1148. **DD** 304.6. ***Continues*** *Trends and Forecasts, Hamilton-Wentworth., 1186-2335.*

CH
**TUNG WU CHENG CHIH SHE HUI HSUEH PAO.** **See** Political Science.

●CH/1019-0449
**TUNG WU SHE HUI HSUEH PAO.** **Added/Corp** Tung Wu ta Hsueh (Taipei, Taiwan). **VFOAT** Soochow Journal of Sociology. (Mar. 1992)-. Periodical. Chinese (English). Soochow University, Shin Lin, Taipei 11102 Taiwan. **LC** HM7; .T86. ***Continues*** *Tung Wu Cheng Chih She Hui Hsueh Pao, 0259-3785.*

PP
**UMBEN.** (19??)-. Periodical. English. tq (March, June, Sept.). k3.50 Australia and New Zealand; k4.00 Asia and Pacific; k6.00 other. Melanesian Institute, PO Box 571, Goroka EHP, Papua New Guinea. **Tel** 675 72 1777, FAX 675 72 1214. **ED** Alphonse Aime. Index available. cum. index. **Bk Rev**, (Qty: 1,000). **Ad Acc.** ctrl circ.

SW
**UMEA STUDIES IN SOCIOLOGY / UNIVERSITY OF UMEA.** No. 95 (1988)-. Monographic series. Swedish. Price varies per volume. ***Continues*** *Research Reports from the Department of Sociology, University of UMEA, 0556-7518.*

US
**UMUM NEWSLETTER / BLACK HISTORY MUSEUM.** **Added/Corp** Black History Museum Committee. (197?)-. Newsletter. English. Black History Museum, PO Box 15057, Philadelphia PA 19130. ***Continues*** *Black History Museum Umum Newsletter.*

US/0042-0468
**UNSCHEDULED EVENTS.** [Unsched. events]. **Added/Corp** Ohio State University. Disaster Research Center. Vol. 1 (Spring 1967)-. Periodical. English. tq. $22.00. Disaster Research Center, University of Delware, K. Tierny, Newark DE 19716. **Tel** (302)451-6618, FAX (302)451-2828. **ED** Joanne M Nigg. **Bk Rev. Circ:** 300.

# Sociology

**Desc:** News in the field of disasters and mass emergencies (mainly for members of the Committee of Disaster Research).

US/0083-4688
**URBAN AFFAIRS ANNUAL REVIEWS.** [Urban aff. annu. rev.]. Vol. 1 (1967)-. Monographic series. English. an. $169.00. SAGE Periodical Press, 2455 Teller Road, Thousand Oaks CA 91320. **Tel** (805)499-0721, FAX (805)499-0871, telex 100799. **LC** HT108; .U7. **DD** 301.3; 711/.4. Index available (Free). **Acid Free.**
**Ind/Abst** Int. Bibliogr. Sociol. (19??-).

US/0735-2425
**URBAN SOCIETY.** (AE : URBAN SOCIETY.). [Urban soc.]. **VFOAT** Annual Editions. Urban Society. 2nd Edition (1982)-. English. an. $12.95. Dushkin Publishing Group Inc., Sluice Dock, Guilford CT 06437. **Tel** (203)453-4351, (800)243-6532, FAX (203)453-6000. **ED** Jeffrey Elliot. **LC** HT101; .F62. **DD** 307.7/6/0973. Index available. *Continues* Focus: Urban Society, 0160-9815.
**Desc:** Selections reflect a broad approach to the study of urban life. Articles are chosen for clarity and relevancy in addressing the issues surrounding urbanization, for usefulness in the teaching/learning process, and for their ability to stimulate interest in students to pursue the study of urban society.

SA/0256-7008
**VECTOR KLOOF.** *See* Homosexuality.

CN/1183-6822
**VECTOR PUBLIC OPINION REPORT.** [Vector public opin. rep.]. **Added/Corp** Vector Public Education. (Jan. 1991)-. Periodical. English. ir. $195.00 per year, plus GST as applicable. CNS Circulation Services, PO Box 10, Station F, Toronto Ontario M4Y 1L8 Canada. **DD** 971.3/541/005. *Continues* Torontopinion., 0840-6839.

US/8750-8478
**VEKER, DER.** (DER VEKER : TSVEY HADOSHIM SHRIFT FUN YIDISHN SOTSYALISTISHN FARBAND.). [Veker]. **VFOAT** Wecker. Began publication in 1921. Periodical. Yiddish. bm. $10.00. Der Wecker, 45 East 33rd Street, New York NY 10016. **Tel** (212)686-1536. **ED** Elias Sehulruan. **DD** 301. Bk Rev. Circ: 1,000.

US/0099-1384
**VIDEOSOCIOLOGY. Added/Corp** Boston University. Graduate School. Boston University. Sociology Dept. Vol. 1 (May 1972)-. English. $7.00. Boston University Graduate School, c/o Alexander D Blumenstiel, 96 Cummington St / Boston Univ., Boston MA 02215. **LC** H62.A1; V5. **DD** 301/.07.

VM
**VIETNAM YOUTH.** *See* Children and Youth Interests.

US/0891-5172
**VIOLENCE, AGGRESSION TERRORISM. VFOAT** VAT; Violence, Aggression, and Terrorism. Vol. 1, No. 1 (1987)-. Periodical. English. qt. $115.00 institutions, $65.00 individuals. Decisions Issues Alternatives / Atlanta, 864 Somerset Drive Northwest, Atlanta GA 30327. **LC** HM283; .V55. **DD** 303.6/2/05.
**Ind/Abst** Crim. Justice Abstr.

●US
**VIRGINIA REVIEW OF SOCIOLOGY. Added/Corp** University of Virginia. Dept. of Sociology. **VFOAT** Law and Conflict Management. Vol. 1 (1992)-. English. $73.25. JAI Press Inc., 55 Old Post Road, Suite 2, PO Box 1678, Greenwich CT 06836-1678. **Tel** (203)661-7602, FAX (203)661-0792. **ED** Donald Black. **LC** HM1; .V57. **DD** 301/.05. **CODEN** VRSOEC.

US/1067-1684
**VISUAL SOCIOLOGY.** [Vis. sociol.]. **Added/Corp** International Visual Sociology Association. (198?)-. Periodical. English. sa. (Comes with International Visual Sociology Association membership). International Visual Sociology Association, University of Louisville, Department of Sociology, Louisville KY 40292. **Tel** (502)852-6836. **DD** 301. *Continues* Visual Sociology Review.
**Ind/Abst** Film Lit. Index (19??-); Soc. Plann. Policy Dev. Abstr. (19??-); Sociol. Abstr. (1986-) [Full Cov.].

IT
**VIVEREOGGI.** Cogi, Via Ugo Foscolo 3, 20121 Milan Italy.

●GT
**VOCES DEL TIEMPO : REVISTA DE RELIGION Y SOCIEDAD.** *See* Religion and Theology.

NE/0923-4365
**WAGENINGSE SOCIOLOGISCHE STUDIES : WSS. Added/Corp** Landbouwuniversiteit Wageningen. **VFOAT** WSS; Wageningen Studies in Sociology. (1989)-. Monographic series. Dutch (English). *Continues* Mededelingen van de Vakgroepen Sociologie van de Landbouwhogeschool.
**Ind/Abst** Rice Abstr.; World Agric. Econ.

AT/0729-2473
**WAR & SOCIETY.** *See* History(General).

UK/0308-4450
**WEST AFRICAN JOURNAL OF SOCIOLOGY AND POLITICAL SCIENCE, THE.** [West Afr. j. sociol. polit. sci.]. **VFOAT** The West African Journal of Sociology & Political Science. Vol. 1, No. 1 (Oct. 1975)-. Periodical. English. qt. $30.00. University of Ibadan Sociology Department, c/o Dr. J. Labinjoh, Ibadan Nigeria. **LC** HN820; .A65.
**Ind/Abst** Soc. Plann. Policy Dev. Abstr.; Sociol. Abstr. (?-?).

US/0734-9033
**WHOLE AGAIN RESOURCE GUIDE, THE.** [Whole again resour. guide]. 1982-. English. an. $26.95. Sourcenet, POB 6767, Santa Barbara CA 93160. **Tel** (805)964-6066. **ED** Tim Ryan. **LC** HM206; .W5. **DD** 304.2/025. Index available. **Bk Rev. Ad Acc.**
**Desc:** Describes over 3,000 alternative press journals, newspapers, and directories. Providing full order information.

PL/0511-9375
**WIES WSPOCZESNA; PISMO RUCHU LUDOWEGO. Title Change.** Vol. 1 (1957)-(19??). Periodical. Polish (summaries and/or abstracts in English and Russian). mo. **(Subscription address:** ARS Polona, PO Box 1001, 00068 Warsaw Poland.) **LC** HN536; .W5. *Continued by* Wies i Panstwo.
**Ind/Abst** Agric. Eng. Abstr.; Potato Abstr.; Poult. Abstr.

US/0043-6666
**WISCONSIN SOCIOLOGIST, THE. Title Change.** [Wis. sociol.]. **Added/Corp** Wisconsin Sociological Association. University of Wisconsin--Milwaukee. University of Wisconsin--Eau Claire. **VFOAT** WS. Vol. 1, (Spring 1962)-(1993). Periodical. English. Three times a year. Wisconsin Sociological Association, Department of Sociology, University of Wisconsin-Whitewater, Whitewater WI 53190. **Tel** (414)472-1133. **ED** Ronald Berger, Bruce Wiegand. **LC** HM1; .W5. **DD** 301/.05. **CODEN** WSSCA. **Bk Rev,** (Qty: 1-4). **Ad Acc. Pr Rev. Circ:** 600. *Continued by* Sociological Imagination.
**Desc:** Accepts for consideration papers which deal with issues of pure research, applied or evaluation research, or sociological-clinical practice.
**Ind/Abst** Crim. Justice Abstr. (?-?); Soc. Plann. Policy Dev. Abstr. (?-?); Sociol. Abstr. (?-?).

US
**WORKING PAPER. Main/Corp** Wisconsin Research and Development Center for Cognitive Learning. (1966)-. Monographic series. English. ir. Price varies per volume. University of Wisconsin / Demographic Ecology, 4412 Social Science Building, 1180 Observatory Drive, Madison WI 53706. **Tel** (608)262-2182. **Circ:** 700.
**Desc:** Demographic research articles.

CN/0226-1774
**WORKING PAPER SERIES (UNIVERSITY OF TORONTO. STRUCTURAL ANALYSIS PROGRAMME).** (WORKING PAPER SERIES / STRUCTURAL ANALYSIS PROGRAMME, DEPARTMENT OF SOCIOLOGY, UNIVERSITY OF TORONTO.). [Work. pap. ser. – Struct. Anal. programme, Dep. Sociol., Univ. Tor.]. **VAT** Working Paper - Structural Analysis Programme. Department of Sociology. University of Toronto. No. 6 (Dec. 1979)-. Monographic series. English. Price varies per volume. Structural Analysis Programme, University of Toronto, Department of Sociology, 563 Spadina Avenue, Toronto Ontario M5S 1A1 Canada. **DD** 301. *Continues* Research Paper (University of Toronto. Structural Analysis Programme), 0825-3773.

UK/0049-7991
**WORKING PAPERS IN CULTURAL STUDIES.** [Work. pap. cult. stud.]. **Main/Corp** University of Birmingham. Centre for Contemporary Cultural Studies. **VFOAT** Cultural Studies. 1- Spring 1971-. English. sa. Hutchinson Publishers, 3 Fitzroy Square, London WIP 6JD England. **LC** AS122.B53; A3. **DD** 082. *Supersedes* University of Birmingham. Centre for Contemporary Cultural Studies. Occasional Papers.
**Ind/Abst** Soc. Plann. Policy Dev. Abstr.; Sociol. Abstr. (?-?).

US/0891-1649
**WORLDLETTER. Ceased.** [Worldletter]. **VFOAT** World Letter. Ceased (Dec. 1988). Periodical. English. bm. Worldletter, Editorial Director, Environmental and Ground Water Institute, 200 Felgar Street/Room 127, University of Oklahoma, Norman OK 73019. **DD** 304.

UK
**X-RAY. Added/Corp** Africa Bureau (London, England). (19??)-. Periodical. English. mo. Africa Bureau, 48 Grafton Way, London W1 England. **LC** DT737; .X17. **DD** 301/45/1/0968.

US/0044-118X
**YOUTH & SOCIETY.** [Youth soc.]. **VAT** Youth and society. Vol. 1 (Sept. 1969)-. Periodical. English. qt (Mar., June, Sept., Dec.). $160.00. SAGE Periodical Press, 2455 Teller Road, Thousand Oaks CA 91320. **Tel** (805)499-0721, FAX (805)499-0871, telex 100799. **ED** Kathryn G. Herr (Albuquerque Academy). **LC** HQ793; .Y6. **DD** 301.43/15/05. **NLM** W1 YO99N. **[CCC]. Pr Rev. Acid Free.** available on microfilm and microfiche from University Microfilms International (UMI). Documents available from The Genuine Article, UMI Article Clearinghouse.
**Desc:** A cross-disciplinary, cross-cultural journal focusing on youth in society.
**Ind/Abst** Acad. Abstr. Full Text Elite (Jan. 1992-); Acad. Abstr. (Jan. 1992-); Acad. Search (Jan. 1992-); AGRICOLA [Full Cov.]; Am. Hist. Life (1970-); Appl. Soc. Sci. Index Abstr.; Commun. Abstr. (?-?); Contents Pages Educ.; Crim. Justice Abstr.; Curr. Contents Soc. Behav. Sci.; Curr. Index J. Educ.; Educ. Adm. Abstr.; Expand. Acad. Index (1989-); High. Educ. Abstr. (1973-); INFO-SOUTH Abstr.; Mag. Search; Middle East Abstr. Index; Multicult. Educ. Abstr.; Newsp. Period. Abstr. (1991-); Psychoanal. Abstr.; Psychol. Abstr. (1990-); PsycINFO; PsycLit; PsycScan: Appl. Exp. Eng. Psych.; PsycScan: LD/MR; PsycScan: Neuropsych.; Res. Alert [Full Cov.]; Sage Fam. Stud. Abstr.; Soc. Plann. Policy Dev. Abstr.; Soc. Sci. Source (Jan. 1992-); Soc. Sci. Cit. Index [Full Cov.]; Soc. Sci. Index; Soc. Sci. Index Fulltext (Sept. 1988-) [Full Txt.]; Soc. Work Abstr. [Select. Cov.]; Sociol. Abstr.; Sociol. Educ. Abstr. [Full Cov.]; SportSearch; U.S. Polit. Sci. Doc.; Urban Aff. Abstr.

UK
**YOUTH ORGANISATIONS OF GREAT BRITAIN.** Began with 1st issue, 1944/45. English.

AU
**ZEITSCHRIFT FUER GANZHEITSFORSCHUNG.** *See* Philosophy.

GW/0174-0202
**ZEITSCHRIFT FUER RECHTSSOZIOLOGIE.** Vol. 1, No. 1 (Sept. 1980)-. Periodical. English. sa. DM72.80 Germany; DM80.40 other. Westdeutscher Verlag GmbH, Postfach 5829, D 65048 Wiesbaden Germany. **Tel** 011 49 611 160220. **(Subscription address:** VVA Bertelsmann Dist GmbH, Postfach 7600, D 33310 Guetersloh Germany) **[CCC].**
**Ind/Abst** Index Foreign Leg. Per.; Soc. Plann. Policy Dev. Abstr.; Sociol. Abstr. (1980-) [Full Cov.].

GW/0720-4361
**ZEITSCHRIFT FUER SOZIALISATIONSFORSCHUNG UND ERZIEHUNGSSOZIOLOGIE. VFOAT** ZSE. Zeitschrift fuer Sozialisationsforschung und Erziehungssoziologie. (1981)-. Periodical. Multiple languages. qt. DM86.00. Juventa Verlag GmbH, Ehretstrasse 3, D 69469 Weinheim Germany. **Tel** 011 49 6201 61035, FAX 011 49 6201 13135. **UDC** 37.015.4. **[CCC].**
**Ind/Abst** Soc. Plann. Policy Dev. Abstr.; Sociol. Abstr. (1983-).

SZ/0044-3514
**ZEITSCHRIFT FUER SOZIALPSYCHOLOGIE.** *See* Psychology.

GW/0340-1804
**ZEITSCHRIFT FUER SOZIOLOGIE.** [Z. Soziol.]. **Added/Corp** Universitat Bielefeld. Fakultat fuer Soziologie. Vol. 1 (Jan. 1972)-. Periodical. Multiple languages (English and German). Six times a year. $102.00. Ferdinand Enke Verlag, Ruedigerstrasse 14, D-70469 Stuttgart Germany. **Tel** 011 49 711 8931124, 011 49 711 893123. **(Subscription address:** Thieme Medical Publishers Inc., 381 Park Avenue South, New York NY 10016.) **LC** HM5; .Z4. **DD** 301/.05. **[CCC].** available on microfilm from University Microfilms International (UMI). Documents available from The Genuine Article.
**Ind/Abst** Curr. Contents Soc. Behav. Sci.; Int. Bibliogr. Sociol.; Res. Alert [Full Cov.]; Soc. Plann. Policy Dev. Abstr.; Soc. Sci. Cit. Index [Full Cov.]; Sociol. Abstr. (1986-) [Full Cov.]; Soc. Res. Methodol. Abstr. (1975-).

PL
**ZESZYTY NAUKOWE UNIWERSYTETU JAGIELLONSKIEGO. PRACE SOCJOLOGICZNE. VFOAT** Prace Socjologiczne. (1973)-. Monographic series. Polish (summaries and/or

# Sociology

abstracts in English and Russian). ir. Price varies per volume. Panstwowe Wydawn Naukowe, Miodowa 10, PO Box 391, 00251 Warsaw Poland.

CN/0707-3976
**ZYCIE OTTAWY.** V. 1- May 7, 1978-. Periodical. Polish (English). bw. $7.00. Zycie Ottawy, Box 203 Station A, Ottawa Ontario K1P 6C4 Canada. **DD** 301.45/19/185071384.

## ABSTRACTING, BIBLIOGRAPHIES AND STATISTICS

US/0093-6715
**ANNUAL STATISTICAL REPORT - DIVISION OF FAMILY SERVICES.** (ANNUAL STATISTICAL REPORT.). **Main/Corp** Florida. Division of Family Services. Statistical Publication. English. an. Division of Family Services / Florida, PO Box 2050, Jacksonville FL 32203. **LC** HV86; .F643. **DD** 362/.9759.

US/0146-2148
**ANNUAL STATISTICAL REPORT. MENTAL HEALTH SERVICES. MENTAL RETARDATION SERVICES. VETERANS' HOMES SERVICE (NEBRASKA).** [Annu. stat. rep., Ment. health serv., Ment. retard. serv., Veterans' homes serv.]. **Main/Corp** Nebraska. Dept. of Public Institutions. Research and Statistics Section. Statistical Publication. English. an. Department of Public Institutions, State of Nebraska, Lincoln NE 68509. **LC** RA790.65.N2; N4A. **DD** 362.2/09782.

US/0147-6467
**ANNUAL STATISTICAL REPORT - SOUTH DAKOTA DEPARTMENT OF SOCIAL SERVICES.** (ANNUAL STATISTICAL REPORT.). **Main/Corp** South Dakota. Dept. of Social Services. Statistical Publication. English. an. Free. Department of Social Services / South Dakota, State Office Building, 700 Governors Drive, Pierre SD 57501. **Tel** (605)773-4855. **LC** HV86; .S784. **DD** 353.9/783/0084. **NLM** W2 AS8 D4A. **Circ**: 315 (ctrl).

BL
**ANUARIO ESTATISTICO. Main/Corp** Servico Social do Comercio. **Added/Corp** Servico Social do Comercio. Secao de Estatistica. (19??)-. Statistical Publication. Portuguese. an. Servico Social do Comercio / Rio de Janeiro, Av General Justo 307, Rio de Janeiro Brazil. **LC** HV192; .S48a.

BL
**ANUARIO ESTATISTICO - SERVICO SOCIAL DO COMERCIO, ADMINISTRACAO REGIONAL EM MINAS GERAIS. Main/Corp** Servico Social do Comercio. Administracao Regional Emminas Gerais. Portuguese. an. Servico Social do Comercio / Belo Horizonte, Administracao Regional em Minas Gerais, Rua Tupinambas 956, Belo Horizonte Brazil. **LC** HV194.M54; S47B. **DD** 361.6/0981/51.

US
**ASSISTANCE PAYMENTS STATISTICS. Added/Corp** Michigan. Dept. of Social Services. Michigan. Dept. of Social Services. Data Reporting Section. **VFOAT** Monthly Assistance Payments Statistics. (19??)-. Statistical Publication. English. mo. Free on request. Michigan Data Reporting Section, Department of Social Services, Lansing MI 48909. **Continues** Social Services Statistics.

●US/1063-1461
**BELIZE DATA GUIDE. Added/Corp** Central American Institute of Prehistoric and Traditional Cultures at Belize. (1992)-. English. be. $6.50. Central American Institute of Prehistoric, and Traditional Cultures At Belize, 68-769 First Street, Suite 286, Cathedral City CA 92234-1244.

GW/0342-3964
**BIBLIOGRAPHIE SOZIALISATION UND SOZIALPAEDAGOGIK.** German. qt. DM48.00. Verlag Deutsches Jugendinstitut, Freibadstrasse 30, 8000 Munchen 90 Germany. **Tel** 089/62306-0. **LC** Z7164.Y8; B52; HQ793. **DD** 016.30143/15. Index available. cum. index. **Circ**: 700 (ctrl). **Supersedes** Dokumentation.
**Desc**: Documentation of mainly German literature on youth and related fields. Information includes titles, keywords and indices.

US/0742-6895
**BIBLIOGRAPHIES AND INDEXES IN SOCIOLOGY.** [Bibliogr. indexes sociol.]. (1985)-. Monographic series. English. ir. Price varies per volume.

Greenwood Press Inc., PO Box 5007, Westport CT 06881-5007. **Tel** (203)226-3571, FAX (203)222-1502. **LC** UNC. **DD** 016.

US/0190-1591
**CALIFORNIA CRIPPLED CHILDREN SERVICES STATISTICAL REPORT. VFOAT** Statistical Report - Crippled Children Services. 1971/75-. Statistical Publication. English. an. California Children Services Program, 714 P Street/Room 323, Sacramento CA 95814. **Tel** (916)322-2090. **ED** James N Creeger. **NLM** W2 AC2 B905C. **Circ**: 2,000. **Continues** California Public Health Statistical Report.
**Desc**: Program description and statistics for two fiscal years. Statistics are by diagnosis (summary) and by county and state for California.

US/0566-0009
**CASELOAD STATISTICS : STATE VOCATIONAL REHABILITATION AGENCIES. Main/Corp** United States. Rehabilitation Services Administration. Division of Program Data and Analysis. Office of Administrative Support. 1977/78-. English. an. Free. Department of Education / Office of Special Education and Rehabilitative Services, 330 C Street SW, Room 3006, Washington DC 20201. **Tel** (202)205-5465, FAX (202)205-9874. **ED** Lawrence I Mars. **LC** HD7256.U5; A365. **DD** 362.8/5. **Circ**: 200. **Continues** Caseload Statistics: State Vocational Rehabilitation Agencies, 0566-0009.
**Desc**: Describes the state-federal program of vocational rehabilitation. Designed to provide a variety of services to disabled individuals to enable them to work in terms of the number of persons served and rehabilitated and and the volumes of cases entering and leaving the caseloads of state vocational rehabilitation agencies.

US
**CHILD ABUSE AND NEGLECT STATISTICS. Added/Corp** Illinois. Dept. of Children and Family Services. (1981)-. English. an. Department of Children and Family Services, One North Old State Capitol Plaza, Springfield IL 62706. **LC** HV742.I3; C45. **DD** 362.7/044.

US/0276-0320
**FOOD STAMP PROGRAM : STATISTICAL SUMMARY OF OPERATIONS.** [Food Stamp Program, Stat. summ. oper.]. **Main/Corp** United States. Food and Nutrition Service. May 1973-. Statistical Publication. English. mo. United States Department of Agriculture Food & Nutrition Service, 3101 Park Center Drive, Room 803, Alexandria VA 22302. **Tel** (703)305-2062, FAX (703)305-2908.

SP
**GUIA BIBLIOGRAFICA (SERVICIO INTERNACIONAL DE INFORMACION SOBRE SUBNORMALES).** (GUIA BIBLIOGRAFICA.). Spanish. Three times a year. $22.00. **LC** Z6122; .G84; HV1568. **DD** 016.3624. **Continues** Guia Bibliografica del Servicio Internacional de Informacion Sobre Subnormales.

US/1054-0946
**GUIDE TO SOCIAL SCIENCE AND RELIGION.** See Religion and Theology-Abstracting, Bibliographies and Statistics.

UK/0307-0824
**HEALTH AND PERSONAL SOCIAL SERVICES STATISTICS FOR ENGLAND WITH SUMMARY TABLES FOR GREAT BRITAIN.** (HEALTH AND PERSONAL SOCIAL SERVICES STATISTICS FOR ENGLAND (WITH SUMMARY TABLES FOR GREAT BRITAIN) / DEPARTMENT OF HEALTH AND SOCIAL SECURITY.). **Main/Corp** Great Britain. Dept. of Health and Social Security. **Added/Corp** Great Britain. Dept. of Health and Social Security. Great Britain. Dept. of Health. Great Britain. Government Statistical Service. (1973)-. English. an. £11.50. Her Majesty's Stationery Office, 51 Nine Elms Lane, London SW8 5DR England. **Tel** 011 44 71 873 8459, 011 44 71 873 8499, FAX 011 44 71 873 8499, 011 44 71 873 8456, telex 297138. **(Subscription address:** Her Majesty's Stationery Office, PO Box 276, Publications Centre, London SW8 5DT England.) **LC** RA407.5.G7; G72a. **DD** 362.1/0942. **NLM** W2 FA1 D425H. **Continues in part** Great Britain. Dept. of Health and Social Security. Health and Personal Social Services Statistics for England and Wales (with Summary Tables for Great Britain), 0300-998X.

UK/0307-0840
**HEALTH AND PERSONAL SOCIAL SERVICES STATISTICS FOR WALES. Main/Corp** Great Britain. Welsh Office. **Added/Corp** Great Britain. Welsh Office. Ystadegau Iechyd a Gwasanaethau Cymdeithasol Personol: Cymru. **VFOAT** Ystadegau Iechyd a Gwasanaethau Cymdeithasol Personol Cymru. No. 1 (1974)-. English (English). an. £5.00. Welsh Office Publications Unit, Crown Building, Cathay's Park, Cardiff CF1 3NQ Wales. **Tel** 011 44 222 825111. **LC** HV249; .W13a. **DD** 362.1/1/09429. **NLM** W2 FA1 W27K. **Continues in part** Great Britain. Dept. of

Health and Social Security. Health and Personal Social Services Statistics for England and Wales (with Summary Tables for Great Britain), 0300-998X.

GW
**HORBUCHVERZEICHNIS. Main/Corp** Leipzig. Deutsche Zentralbucherei fur Blinde. German. bm (five issues per year). 6.00M. Deutsche Zentralbucherei fur Blinde, Gustav-Adolf-Strauss 7, 701 Leipzig Germany. **Tel** 70 976. **ED** S Tschirner. **LC** Z5347; .L44A; HV1743.6. **DD** 011. **Circ**: 3,000.
**Desc**: Index of literature by subject.

US
**INTERNATIONAL BIBLIOGRAPHY OF SOCIAL SCIENCES: SOCIOLOGY.** Bibliography. English. an. $150.00. Routledge Chapman & Hall Inc, 29 West 35th Street, New York NY 10001. **Tel** (212)244-3336, (212)244-6412.
**Desc**: Covers over 1,500 journals published throughout the world in 30 languages and stands as the long-term reference resource in the field of social sciences.

UK/0085-2066
**INTERNATIONAL BIBLIOGRAPHY OF SOCIOLOGY.** (INTERNATIONAL BIBLIOGRAPHY OF SOCIOLOGY / PREPARED BY THE INTERNATIONAL COMMITTEE FOR SOCIAL SCIENCES DOCUMENTATION IN CO-OPERATION WITH THE INTERNATIONAL SOCIOLOGICAL ASSOCIATION.). [Int. bibliogr. sociol.]. **Added/Corp** International Committee for Social Sciences Documentation. International Sociological Association. Unesco. International Committee for Social Science Information and Documentation. **VFOAT** Bibliographie Internationale de Sociologie. Vol. 5 (195?)-. Abstracting/Indexing Service. English (French). an. $230.00. Routledge Chapman & Hall Inc, 29 West 35th Street, New York NY 10001. **Tel** (212)244-3336, (212)244-6412. **LC** Z7161; .I594. **DD** 016.301. **NLM** Z 7164.S68 I61. **Continues in part** Current Sociology (Paris, France).
**Desc**: Indexes the contents of journals in the social sciences.

US
**MEDICARE PROGRAM STATISTICS. SELECTED STATE DATA / HEALTH CARE FINANCING ADMINISTRATION. Added/Corp** United States. Health Care Financing Administration. United States. Health Care Financing Administration. Bureau of Data Management and Strategy. **VFOAT** Selected State Data. (1982)-. Government Publication. English. ir. Price varies per volume. Superintendent of Documents, US Government Printing Office, Washington DC 20402. **Tel** (202)275-3328, FAX (202)786-2377.

US
**MONTHLY STATISTICAL REPORT - NEW YORK (CITY). HUMAN RESOURCES ADMINISTRATION. Main/Corp** New York (N.Y.) Human Resources Administration. Statistical Publication. English. mo. The City of New York, Department of Social Services, New York NY 10013. **LC** HV87.N5; A475. **DD** 361.6/3/097471. **Continues** Monthly Statistical Report.

UK
**PERSONAL SOCIAL SERVICES STATISTICS, ESTIMATES. Added/Corp** Chartered Institute of Public Finance and Accountancy. Statistical Information Service. (1979)-. Periodical. English. an. £60.00. Chartered Institute of Public Finance and Accountancy, 2 3 Robert Street, London WC2N 6BH England. **Tel** 011 44 1 895 8823. **LC** HV245; .C59a. **DD** 361.6/0941. **NLM** W1 PE846. **Continues** Social Services Statistics Estimates, 0307-045x.

US/0093-7835
**PROGRAM STATISTICS - MICHIGAN DEPARTMENT OF SOCIAL SERVICES.** (PROGRAM STATISTICS.). **Main/Corp** Michigan. Dept. of Social Services. English. Department of Social Services / Michigan, 300 South Capitol Avenue, Lansing MI 48026. **LC** HV86; .M536 subser. **DD** 361/.9774 S; 362/.9774.

UK/0307-9201
**SAGE RACE RELATIONS ABSTRACTS.** [Sage race relat. abstr.]. **Added/Corp** Institute of Race Relations. Vol. 1 (Nov. 1975)-. Abstracting/Indexing Service. English. qt. £150.00. Sage Publications Ltd., 6 Bonhill Street, London EC2A 4PU, UK. **Tel** 071 374 0645, FAX 071 374 8741, telex 296207 SAGE G. **ED** Louis Kushnick. **LC** HT1501; .S23. **DD** 305.8/005. **NLM** Z 7164.R12 R118. **Acid Free. Continues** Race Relations Abstracts, 0033-7307.
**Desc**: Provides a unique source of current information in the challenging area of race relations. Issues covered include discrimination, education, employment, health, politics, law and legislation.

US/1042-8380
**SOCIAL PLANNING, POLICY & DEVELOPMENT ABSTRACTS.** [Soc. plann. policy dev. abstr.]. **VFOAT** Social Planning, Policy and

Development Abstracts; Social Policy/Planning and Development Abstracts; Social Policy/Planning & Development Abstracts; SOPODA. Vol. 6, No. 1 (June 1984)-. Abstracting/Indexing Service. English. sa (Jun. and Dec.). $165.00. Sociological Abstracts, PO Box 22206, San Diego CA 92192-0206. **Tel** (619)695-8803, FAX (619)695-0416. **LC** HV1; .S575. **DD** 361.6/1/0973. Index available. **Ad Acc.** available on CD-ROM (Sociofile) from SilverPlatter (US); available on an online database (as part of the SOCA file) from DATA-STAR; (as part of SA63) DIMDI; (in concatenation with Sociological Abstracts as SOCZ) BRS; and (as a subfile of Sociological Abstracts, file 37) DIALOG. Documents available. ***Continues*** *Social Welfare, Social Planning/Policy & Social Development, 0195-7988.*
**Desc:** SOPODA offers practitioners, social problem researchers, administrators, and information professionals access to detailed abstracts of the worldwide journal literature that spans a broad spectrum of relevant subject matter. Among the topics addressed are: violence, abuse, neglect; problems of aging; health policy; energy and environmental policy; housing policy; educational policy; and women and development.

UK/0950-7515
**SOCIAL SECURITY STATISTICS.** [Soc. secur. stat.]. **Main/Corp** Great Britain. Dept. of Health and Social Security. **Added/Corp** Great Britain. Dept. of Health and Social Security. Great Britain. Dept. of Social Security. (1972)-. English. ir. £19.80. Her Majesty's Stationery Office, 51 Nine Elms Lane, London SW8 5DR England. **Tel** 011 44 71 873 8459, 011 44 71 873 8499, FAX 011 44 71 873 8499, 011 44 71 873 8456, telex 297138. **(Subscription address:** Her Majesty's Stationery Office, PO Box 276, Publications Centre, London SW8 5DT England.**) LC** HD7165; .A15a. **DD** 368.4/00942. **NLM** W2; FA1 D425s.

UK/0309-4693
**SOCIAL SERVICE ABSTRACTS (LONDON).** (SOCIAL SERVICE ABSTRACTS / PREPARED BY THE DEPARTMENT OF HEALTH AND SOCIAL SECURITY LIBRARY DURING ...). [Soc. serv. abstr.]. **Added/Corp** Great Britain. Dept. of Health and Social Security Library. (19??)-. English. mo. £42.00. Her Majesty's Stationery Office, 51 Nine Elms Lane, London SW8 5DR England. **Tel** 011 44 71 873 8459, 011 44 71 873 8499, FAX 011 44 71 873 8499, 011 44 71 873 8456, telex 297138. **(Subscription address:** Her Majestys Stationery Offic, PO Box 276 Public Centre, London SW8 5DT England**) ED** Michael Gill. **LC** HV1; .S583. **DD** 016.361. **NLM** Z 7164.C4; S678. **[CCC].**
**Desc:** Summarizes the contents of publications covering the whole range of the personal social services. Covers a wide range of international publications - journals, articles, reports, books and pamphlets.
**Ind/Abst** Int. Bibliogr. Sociol.

UK/0306-7742
**SOCIAL TRENDS.** (SOCIAL TRENDS : A PUBLICATION OF THE GOVERNMENT STATISTICAL SERVICE / CENTRAL STATISTICAL OFFICE.). [Soc. trends]. **Added/Corp** Great Britain. Central Statistical Office. Great Britain. Her Majesty's Stationery Office. (1970)-. Statistical Publication. English. an. £27.00. Her Majesty's Stationery Office, 51 Nine Elms Lane, London SW8 5DR England. **Tel** 011 44 71 873 8459, 011 44 71 873 8499, FAX 011 44 71 873 8499, 011 44 71 873 8456, telex 297138. **(Subscription address:** Her Majesty's Stationery Office, PO Box 276, Publications Centre, London SW8 5DT England.**) LC** HA1134; .S6. **DD** 314.2.
**Ind/Abst** Soc. Plann. Policy Dev. Abstr.; Sociol. Abstr. (?-?); Trop. Dis. Bull.

●US/1070-5317
**SOCIAL WORK ABSTRACTS.** [Soc. work abstr.]. **Added/Corp** National Association of Social Workers. Vol. 30, No. 1 (Mar. 1994)-. Abstracting/Indexing Service. English. qt. $45.00 (NASW members), $95.00 (institutions), $65.00 (individuals). National Association of Social Workers, 750 First Street Northeast, Suite 700, Washington DC 20002-4241. **Tel** (800)638-8799, (202)408-8600, FAX (301)587-1321. **(Subscription address:** NASW Press / National Association of Social Workers, PO Box 431, Annapolis JCT MD 20701.**) DD** 361. **NLM** Z 7164.C4; S6784. ***Continues in part*** *Social Work Research and Abstracts, 0148-0847.*

US/0148-0847
**SOCIAL WORK RESEARCH & ABSTRACTS.** ***Title Change.*** [Soc. work res. abstr.]. **Added/Corp** National Association of Social Workers. **VFOAT** Social work Research and Abstracts. **VAT** Social Work Research and Abstracts. Vol. 13, No. 2 (Summer 1977)-(1993). Abstracting/Indexing Service. English. qt. National Association of Social Workers, 750 First Street Northeast, Suite 700, Washington DC 20002-4241. **Tel** (800)638-8799, (202)408-8600, FAX (301)587-1321. **(Subscription address:** PO Box 431, Annapolis JCT, MD 20701, Phone: (800)227-3590**) ED** Shirley M. Buttrick. **LC** HV1; .A2. **DD** 361/.005. **NLM** W1 SO137LE. **[CCC].** Index available. **Bk Rev. Ad Acc. Pr Rev. Circ:** 4,500. available on an online database; available on microfilm and microfiche from University Microfilms International (UMI). Documents available from The Genuine Article. ***Continues*** *Abstracts for Social Workers, 0001-3412.* ***Split into*** *Social Work Abstracts, 1070-5317* ***and*** *Social Work Research, 1070-5309.*

**Desc:** Contains one section with abstracts of articles on social services and another with original research articles. The premier database in social work.
**Ind/Abst** Appl. Soc. Sci. Index Abstr.; Curr. Contents Soc. Behav. Sci.; Health Plan. Adminis.; Hospit. Health Admin. Index; Psychol. Abstr. (1981-); PsycINFO; PsycLit; Res. Alert [Full Cov.]; Soc. Plann. Policy Dev. Abstr.; Soc. Sci. Cit. Index [Full Cov.]; Soc. Work Abstr. (Spring 1987-) [Full Cov.]; Sociol. Abstr. (?-?).

US/0038-0202
**SOCIOLOGICAL ABSTRACTS.** [Sociol. abstr.]. Vol. 1 (Jan./Oct. 1953)-. Abstracting/Indexing Service. English. bm. $280.00 Mexico, Central America, South America (except Venezuela), Caribbean, Fiji, India, Sri Lanka, Bangladesh, Pakistan, and Africa (except South Africa); $395.00 other. Sociological Abstracts, PO Box 22206, San Diego CA 92192-0206. **Tel** (619)695-8803, FAX (619)695-0416. **ED** Leo P. Chall. **LC** HM1; .S67. **DD** 301. **NLM** Z 7164.S68 S678. **CODEN** SOABA. **[CCC].** Index available (annually). cum. index. **Bk Rev. Ad Acc. Circ:** 1,900. available on an online database (as file label SA^#) from DIMDI; Epic (OCLC); (as file label SOCA on After Dark) BRS; (as file label SOCA) BRS/Colleague; (as file label SOCA) BRS; (as file SOCS1 on Knowledge Index) DIALOG; (as file 37) DIALOG; and (as file label SOCA) DATA-STAR; available on CD-ROM (Sociofile) from SilverPlatter (US); available on microfilm and microfiche from University Microfilms International (UMI). Documents available.
**Desc:** The SA database consists of five distinct components: in depth, nonevaluative abstracts of journal articles, abstracts of conference papers presented at various cooperating sociological association meetings worldwide, relevant listings from Dissertation Abstracts International, enhanced bibliographic citations of book reviews from the journals SA abstracts, and detailed abstracts of selected sociology books and texts.
**Ind/Abst** Anthropol. Index; Popul. Index (?-?); Soc. Res. Methodol. Abstr. (1975-).

●US/1070-1192
**SOCIOLOGICAL THEORY ABSTRACTS.**
**See** Sociology.

UK
**STATISTICAL INFORMATION SERVICE: PERSONAL SOCIAL SERVICES STATISTICS ACTUALS.** **Main/Corp** Chartered Institute of Public Finance and Accountancy. **Added/Corp** Society of County Treasurers. (19??)-. Statistical Publication. English. an. £63.00. Chartered Institute of Public Finance and Accountancy, 2 3 Robert Street, London WC2N 6BH England. **Tel** 011 44 1 895 8823. **LC** HV249.E86; C45a. **DD** 362.6/2/0942.

US/0090-6565
**STATISTICAL REPORT - CITY OF LOS ANGELES. SOCIAL SERVICE DEPARTMENT.** (STATISTICAL REPORT.). [Stat. rep. - City Los Angel., Soc. Serv. Dept.]. **Main/Corp** Los Angeles (Calif). Dept. of Social Service. (19??)-. Statistical Publication. English. Los Angeles Department of Social Service, 313 North Figueroa Street, Los Angeles CA 90012. **LC** HV87.L7; A23. **DD** 360/.9794/93.

US/0163-6898
**STATISTICAL REPORT - SOUTH CAROLINA DEPARTMENT OF SOCIAL SERVICES.** **Added/Corp** South Carolina. Dept. of Social Services. **VFOAT** Statistics - South Carolina Department of Social Service. Vol. 35, No. 11 (May 1972)-. Statistical Publication. English. mo. Free on request. Department of Social Services / South Carolina, Columbia SC 29201. **Tel** (803)758-5749. **LC** HV98.S6; S6. **NLM** W2 AS6 S72P. ***Continues*** *Public Welfare Statistics - South Carolina Department of Public Welfare.*

US
**STATISTICAL REPORT (VIRGINIA. DEPT. OF SOCIAL SERVICES. BUREAU OF RESEARCH AND REPORTING).** (STATISTICAL REPORT - VIRGINIA. DEPT. OF SOCIAL SERVICES. BUREAU OF RESEARCH AND REPORTING.). **VFOAT** Public Welfare Statistics. Vol. 44, No. 1 (Sept. 1982)-. Statistical Publication. English. qt. Department of Social Services / Virginia, Blair Building, 8007 Discovery Drive, Richmond VA 23288. **LC** HV86; .V82. **DD** 362/.9755/021. ***Continues*** *Statistical Report (Virginia. Dept. of Welfare. Bureau of Research and Reporting).*

IT
**STATISTICHE DELLA PREVIDENZA, DELLA SANITA E DELL'ASSISTENZA SOCIALE.** **Added/Corp** Istituto Centrale di Statistica (Italy). Vol. 25 (1987)-. Italian. an. L18000. Istituto Nazionale Statistica, GBP SEZ4 Via Cesare Balbo 16, 00184 Rome Italy. **Tel** 011 39 6 46735118. **LC** HD7182; .A9. ***Continues*** *Annuario Statistico della Previdenza, della Sanita e dell'Assistenza Sociale.*

US/0362-0360
**STATISTICS : CALENDAR YEAR REVIEW.** **Main/Corp** North Dakota. Social Service Board. (19??)-. English. an. Social Service Board of North Dakota, c/o Bureau of Governmental Affairs, Box 7176, Grand Forks ND 58201. **LC** HV86; .N9384. **DD** 362/.9784. ***Continues*** *North Dakota Welfare Statistics, Calendar Year Review, 0549-8449.*

US/0163-1403
**STATISTICS ON SOCIAL WORK EDUCATION IN THE UNITED STATES.** **Added/Corp** Council on Social Work Education. (1974)-. English. an. $135.00 Comes with Council on Social Work Education membership Plan A. Council on Social Work Education, 1600 Duke Street, Alexandria VA 22314. **Tel** (703)683-8080. **LC** HV11; .S74. **DD** 361/.007/1173. ***Continues*** *Statistics on Graduate Social Work Education in the United States, 0091-7192.*

US/0361-896X
**STATISTICS - STATE OF TENNESSEE, DEPARTMENT OF HUMAN SERVICES.** (STATISTICS - DEPARTMENT OF HUMAN SERVICES.). **Main/Corp** Tennessee. Dept. of Human Services. April 1975-. English. mo. State Office Building, Hartford CT 06115. **LC** HV86; .T24. **DD** 362/.0768. ***Continues*** *Tennessee. Dept. of Public Welfare. Statistics.*

FI/0780-7554
**STATISTIK OVER PENSIONSTAGARNA I FINLAND.** **VFOAT** Statistical Yearbook of Pensioners in Finland. Swedish (summaries and/or abstracts in English). an. Elaketurvakeskus Tilasto Osasto, PO Box 11, 00521 Helsinki Finland. **Tel** 90-1511, FAX 1481172, telex 1481172. **(Subscription address:** Kansanelakelaitos, PO Box 450, 00101 Helsinki Finland**) ED** Heidi Saila. **LC** HD7197.3; .A46. **Circ:** 3,100 (ctrl).
**Desc:** Statistical yearbook based on Pension Registers of the National and Employment Pensions Schemes.

FI
**SUOMEN VIRALLINEN TILASTO. XXI B, SOSIAALIHUOLTO.** **VFOAT** Sosiaalihuolto; Socialvard; Social Welfare; Finlands Officiella Statistik. XXI B, Socialvard; Official Statistics of Finland. XXI B, Social Welfare. Began with: 14 (1970). English (Finnish and Swedish). **NLM** W2 GF5 S86s. ***Continues*** *Suomen Virallinen Tilasto. XXI B, Sosiaalihuoltotilaston Vuosikirja.*

US/0193-4252
**UTAH REPORT OF MEDICAID STATISTICS.** V. 1- 1977/78-. English. an. Department of Social Services / Utah, Division of Family Services, 333 South 2nd East, Salt Lake City UT 84111. **LC** HD7102.U5; U88. **DD** 362.1/04252/09792.

●US/1077-2197
**VIOLENCE AND ABUSE ABSTRACTS.** No. 1 (Jan. 1995)-. Abstracting/Indexing Service. English. qt (Jan., Apr., July, Oct.). $196.00. SAGE Periodical Press, 2455 Teller Road, Thousand Oaks CA 91320. **Tel** (805)499-0721, FAX (805)499-0871, telex 100799.
**Desc:** Covers current literature on interpersonal violence including, hate crimes against ethnic minorities and homosexuals, physical and sexual abuse against women and children, gang violence, etc.

US/0000-1325
**VOLUNTEERISM (NEW YORK, N.Y.).** (VOLUNTEERISM : DIRECTORY OF ORGANIZATIONS, TRAINING, PROGRAMS AND PUBLICATIONS.). [Volunteerism]. 3rd Ed. (1991)-. Directory. English. ir. $119.00. R R Bowker, A Reed Reference Publishing Company, Part of Reed International PLC, PO Box 31, 121 Chanlon Drive, New Providence NJ 07974. **Tel** (908)464-6800, (800)521-8110, FAX (908)665-6688, telex 138-755. **ED** Harriet Clyde Kipps. **LC** HN90.V64; C65. **DD** 361.8/025/73. ***Continues*** *Community Resources Directory (Detroit, Mich.), 1042-2315.*
**Desc:** Unique directory of more than 5,300 of America's volunteer organizations that will guide you through the full range of national and local volunteer resources, programs and training events.

SZ
**WORLD STATISTICAL DIRECTORY OF VOLUNTEER AND DEVELOPMENT SERVICE ORGANISATIONS.** **VFOAT** Repertoire Statistique Mondial des Organisations de Volontaires et de Service pour le Developpement; Repertorio Estadistico Mundial de las Organizaciones de Voluntarios y de Servicio para el Desarrollo. Statistical Publication. Multiple languages (English, French and Spanish). **LC** HV7; .W67. **DD** 361/.0025.

## MANNERS AND CUSTOMS

CM/0001-3102
**ABBIA.** ***Ceased.*** [Abbia]. **Added/Corp** Cameroon. Ministry of Information and Culture. Cameroun. Ministry of Education, Culture and Vocational Training. University of Yaounde. Universite Federale du Cameroun. (Feb. 1963)-(19??). Periodical. French (English). ir. African

Sociology —Manners and Customs

Imprint Library Service, 410 W Falmouth Highway, Box 350, West Falmouth MA 02574. **Tel** (617)540-5378. **Ind/Abst** MLA Int. Bibl. Books Artic. Mod. Lang. Lit.

US/0002-3949
**AKWESASNE NOTES.** ***Suspended.*** [Akwesasne notes]. Began in 1969-?. Periodical. English. bm. $15.00 US; $18.00 Canada; $30.00 other. Mohawk Nation, PO Box 196, Rooseveltown NY 13683. **Tel** (518)358-9531, (518)358-9535. **ED** Douglas George. **LC** E75; .A39. **Bk Rev.** **Ad Acc.** **Circ:** 15,000. available on microfilm and microfiche from University Microfilms International (UMI). ***Absorbed** Akwesasne News; Longhouse News.*
**Desc:** Native American journal for natives and natural people, self-sufficiency, native philosophy, issues as natives view them, etc. Includes North, South and Central American poetry, art and book reviews.
**Ind/Abst** Altern. Press Index; Anthropol. Index; Hum. Rights Intern. Rep.

US/1055-9191
**AMERICAN HOLIDAY & LIFE.** [Am. holiday life]. **VFOAT** American Holiday and Life. Vol. 1, No. 1 (1991)-. Periodical. English. Six times a year. $11.95. American Holiday & Life, Montessano 800 2nd Avenue, 9th Floor, New York NY 10017. **Tel** (212)983-6100. **LC** E169.04; .A528. **DD** 917.30492/05. Index available.

US/0193-6859
**AMERICAN POPULAR CULTURE.** (1980)-. Monographic series. English. ir. Price varies per volume. Greenwood Press Inc., PO Box 5007, Westport CT 06881-5007. **Tel** (203)226-3571, FAX (203)222-1502.

BE/0772-2125
**BINDTEKEN.** [Bindteken]. (1984)-. Periodical. Dutch. qt. 300.00F. Vrijzinnige Koepel Vzw, Inquisitiestraat 20, 1040 Brussel Belgium. **Tel** 02 735 011 72, FAX 02 735 04 06. **ED** Mareel Bulckaert. Index available. cum. index. **Bk Rev.** **Ad Acc.** **Circ:** 1,000.

PO/0870-0761
**BOLETIM CULTURAL - ASSEMBLEIA DISTRITAL DE LISBOA.** (1977)-. Bulletin. Portuguese. an. **UDC** 946.9.
**Ind/Abst** BHA : Biblio. Hist. Art.

PO/0870-0478
**BOLETIM CULTURAL / CAMARA MUNICIPAL DO PORTO.** **Added/Corp** Porto (Portugal). Camara Municipal. Vol. 1, (Mar. 1938)-. Bulletin. Portuguese. an.
**Ind/Abst** BHA : Biblio. Hist. Art.

CN/0840-464X
**BRITISH COLUMBIA'S WEDDING BELLS.** **See** Family and Marriage.

US/0271-9096
**CALENDAR OF FESTIVALS.** [Cal. festiv.]. Began in 1977. English. $3.25 single issue. National Council for the Traditional Arts, 1346 Connecticut Avenue North 1118, Washington DC 20036. **LC** GT4802; .C34. **DD** 394.2/6973. ***Continues** Calendar of Folk Festivals & Related Events, 0360-3334.*

JA
**CHANOYU QUARTERLY (KYOTO, JAPAN : 1976).** (CHANOYU QUARTERLY.). **Added/Corp** Urasenke Foundation of Kyoto. Urasenke Foundation of Hawaii. **VFOAT** Chanoyu. No. 13 (1976)-. Periodical. English. qt (Feb., May, Aug., Nov.). $25.00. Urasenke Chanoyu Center, 153 East 69th Street, New York NY 10021. **Tel** (212)988-6161, FAX (212)517-7594. **ED** Gretchen Mittwer. **LC** GT2910; .C56. **DD** 394.1/5. **Bk Rev.** **Circ:** 2,000. available on microfilm and microfiche from University Microfilms International (UMI). ***Continues** Chanoyu.*
**Desc:** Articles and original translations on Japanese aesthetics, fine and applied arts, history, literature, philosophy and religion in relation to Chanoyu, the "Tea Ceremony."
**Ind/Abst** ARTbibliogr. Mod. (1980-).

US/0740-5286
**CHASE'S ANNUAL EVENTS.** [Chase's Annu. events]. **VFOAT** Annual Events. (1984)-. English. an. $49.70. Contemporary Books, Two Prudential Plaza, Suite 1200, Chicago IL 60601. **Tel** (312)540-4565. **ED** William D. and Helen M. Chase. **LC** GT4803; .C48. **DD** 394.2/6/05. ***Continues** Chases' Calendar of Annual Events.*
**Desc:** List of 9,000 holidays, holy days, ethnic and national days, seasons, fairs, festivals, and other special events from around the world; lists at least seven facts or events for each day of the year.

US
**CHRISTMAS : AN AMERICAN ANNUAL OF CHRISTMAS LITERATURE AND ART.** Vol. 1, (1931)-. English. an. $16.99. Augsburg Fortress Publishers, 426 South Fifth Street, Box 1209, Minneapolis MN 55440. **Tel** (800)328-4648, (612)330-3300. **ED** R. E. Haugan.

FR/0069-4290
**CIVILISATIONS ET SOCIETES.** **Added/Corp** Paris. Ecole Pratique des Hautes Etudes. Section des Sciences Economiques et Sociales. 1 (1965)-. Monographic series. French. ir. Price varies per volume. Walter de Gruyter Inc. / Hawthorne, 200 Saw Mill River Road, Hawthorne NY 10532. **Tel** (914)747-0110, GERMANY: 011/49/30/260050, FAX (914)747-1326, telex 646677. **DD** 300.

IT/0069-4371
**CIVILTA VENEZIANA. SAGGI.** 11- 1962-. Periodical. Italian. ir. Casa Editrice Leo S. Olschki, Viuzzo del Pozzetto, Casella Postale 66, 50126 Florence Italy. **Tel** 011 39 55 6530684, FAX 011 39 55 6530214. ***Continues** Saggi Historici, Saggi Storici.*

US/0892-1598
**COMMUNITY STORYTELLERS QUARTERLY NEWSLETTER, THE.** ***Ceased.*** **VFOAT** Community Storytellers. Vol. 1, No. 1 (1983)-?. Newsletter. English. qt. Community Storytellers, 4780-D LaVilla Marina, Marina Del Rey CA 90292.

US/0892-340X
**CULT OBSERVER, THE.** [Cult obs.]. Vol. 1, No. 1 (June 1984)-. Periodical. English. Ten times a year. $30.00 US; $35.00 Canada; $42.00 other. American Family Foundation, PO Box 2265, Bonita Springs FL 33959. **Tel** (813)495-3136. **DD** 291. **Circ:** 2,500. available on microfilm. ***Continues** Advisor (Weston, Mass.), 0740-1167.*
**Desc:** Reviews media investigations and reports on cultic groups and psychological manipulation.

AA/0257-6074
**CULTURE POPULAIRE ALBANAISE.** (CULTURE POPULAIRE ALBANAISE / ACADEMIE DES SCIENCES DE LA RPS D'ALBANIE, INSTITUT DE CULTURE POPULAIRE.). [Cult. pop. alb.]. **Added/Corp** Instituti i Kultures Popullore (Akademia e Shkencave e RPS te Shqiperise). (1981)-. French (English).
**Ind/Abst** MLA Int. Bibl. Books Artic. Mod. Lang. Lit.

US/1043-9722
**DIRECTORY OF SEASONAL/HOLIDAY CRAFT BOUTIQUES.** [Dir. seas./holiday craft boutiques]. **VFOAT** Directory of Seasonal Holiday Craft Boutiques. (1990)-. Directory. English. an. $6.95 (single issue). Front Room Publishers, PO Box 1541, Clifton NJ 07015-1541. **DD** 338.

US/0098-2601
**EIGHTEENTH-CENTURY LIFE.** [Eighteenth-century life]. **Added/Corp** University of Pittsburgh. University Center for International Studies. College of William and Mary. Vol. 1 (Sept. 1974)-. Periodical. English. Three times a year (February, May, November). $39.00 US; $43.50 Canada and Mexico; $45.00 other. Johns Hopkins University Press, 2715 North Charles Street, Baltimore MD 21218-4319. **Tel** (410)516-6987, FAX (410)516-6968. **ED** Robert P. Maccubbin. **LC** HN1; .E42. **DD** 309.1/03. **[CCC].** available on microfilm and microfiche from University Microfilms International (UMI). Documents available from The Genuine Article.
**Desc:** Interdisciplinary publication on eighteenth century studies. Features book-length collections on special themes.
**Ind/Abst** Abstr. Engl. Stud.; Am. Hist. Life (1974-); Annu. Bibliogr. Engl. Lang. Lit.; Arts Humanit. Citation Index [Full Cov.]; BHA : Biblio. Hist. Art; Br. Humanit. Index; Child. Lit. Abstr. (19??-); Curr. Contents Arts Humanit.; Index Book Rev. Relig.; Lit. Crit. Regist.; MLA Int. Bibl. Books Artic. Mod. Lang. Lit.; Relig. Index One Period.; Res. Alert [Full Cov.]; Romant. Move.

US/0276-2072
**FAT TUESDAY.** [Fat Tuesday]. V. 1, No. 1-. Periodical. English. sa. $5.00. Fat Tuesday Publications, 7215 Hillside #6, Los Angeles CA 90046.

XR/0015-1068
**FILM A DOBA.** (FILM A DOBA; MESICNIK PRO FILMOVOU KULTURU.). [Film doba]. 19 -. Periodical. Czech. mo. $66.30. **(Subscription address:** Artia Pegas Press Ltd., Palac Metro Narodni Trida 25, 11210 Prague 1 Czech Republic.)
**Ind/Abst** Film Lit. Index.

US
**FOLKLORE OF AMERICAN HOLIDAYS, THE.** **See** Folklore.

US
**FOOT WORSHIP NEWS.** English. ir (once every four weeks). $15.00 US; $35.00 other. B & D Company, Box 7109, Van Nuys CA 91409. **Tel** (818)503-0289. **Bk Rev.** **Ad Acc.** **Circ:** 12,000.
**Desc:** Special publication for those interested in foot worship.

●UK/0966-369X
**GENDER, PLACE AND CULTURE: A JOURNAL OF FEMINIST GEOGRAPHY.** Vol. 1 (1994)-. English. sa (January and June). £68.00. Carfax Publishing Company, PO Box 25 Abingdon, Oxfordshire OX14 3UE England. **Tel** 011 44 235 555335, FAX (0279)31067, telex 817484. **(Subscription address:** US and Canada/ PO Box 2025, Dunnellon, FL 34430-2025; telephone:(904)489-6996) **ED** Liz Bondi & Mona Domosh. Index available. available on microfiche.
**Desc:** Covers geographical variations in gender divisions and structures of patriarchy.

US/0886-0793
**GOURMET FOOD & WINE FESTIVALS OF NORTH AMERICA.** [Gourmet food wine festiv. North Am.]. **VFOAT** Gourmet Food and Wine Festivals of North America. 1st Ed.; Jan. 1986-. English. be. Printwheel Press, 2674 East Main Street / Suite C-124, Ventura CA 93003. **Tel** (805)643-0965. **LC** TX633; .G695. **DD** 394.1/097.

US/8755-6855
**GRASS ROOTS INTERNATIONAL FOLK RESOURCE DIRECTORY.** [Grass roots int. folk resour. dir.]. **VFOAT** Grass Roots Intl Folk Resource Directory. (1985)-. Directory. English. an. $12.95. Grass Roots Productions, 4444 West 54th Street, New York NY 10019. **Tel** (212)957-8386. **ED** Leslie Berman and Heather Wood. **LC** ML12; .G72. **DD** 781.7/025. **Circ:** 2,000.
**Desc:** Over 5,000 listings covering the field of folk music worldwide, plus articles on the business of folk music. Contact information for festivals, societies, publications, etc.

SP/0017-4181
**GRIAL.** **See** The Arts.

JA
**GYOJI SAMBYAKU-ROKUJUGONICHI.** (1972)-. Japanese. ¥1300. Mainichi Shimbun Sha, (Mainichi Newspapers), 1-1-1 Hitotsubashi Chiyoda-ku, Tokyo 100-51 Japan. **Tel** 03 3212 0321, FAX 03 3216 2574. **LC** GT4884.A2; D35. ***Continues** Gyoji Saijiki.*

US/0888-6938
**HAIR (NEW YORK, N.Y.).** ***Ceased.*** (HAIR.). [Hair]. Vol. 1, No. 1 (Jan. 1987)-(1990). Periodical. English. qt. Go Stylish, 475 Park Avenue South, New York NY 10016. **DD** 391.

SZ
**HEIMATLEBEN. COSTUMES ET COUTUMES.** **Added/Corp** Schweizerische Trachtenvereinigung. **VFOAT** Costumes et Coutumes. (March 1976)-. Periodical. French (German). Three times a year. 21.00F. Schweizerische Trachtenvereinigung, Postfach Muehlegasse 15, CH 3400 Burgdorf, Switzerland. **Tel** 034 22239, FAX 034 22239. **LC** GT1240; .H46. **DD** 391/.009494. **Circ:** 23,000. ***Formed by the union of** Heimatleben **and** Costumes et Coutumes.*

JA/0385-6046
**HOPPO BUNKA KENKYU.** **See** The Arts.

●US/1062-7006
**HORIZONS OF VIETNAMESE THOUGHT AND EXPERIENCE.** [Horiz. Vietnam. thought exp.]. **VFOAT** Horizons. (1992)-. Periodical. English. qt. $12.00. Horizons Publications, 45 South Park, Victoria, Suite 350, Milpitas CA 95035. **LC** F869.M63; H67. **DD** 305.

AT
**ICPS NEWLETTER / INSTITUTE FOR CULTURAL POLICY STUDIES.** (19??)-. English. sa. 350.00Aus$ (corporations), 120.00Aus$ (institutions), 30.00Aus$ (individuals). Institute of Cultural Policy Studies, Division of Humanities, Griffith University, Nathan Queensland 4111 Australia. **Tel** 011 61 7 2757111, FAX 07 875 7730. **ED** Jennifer Craik. **Ad Acc**, **Adv Mgr:** Sharon Clifford.

●US/1065-643X
**INTERNATIONAL TATTO ART.** (1992)-. Periodical. English. qt. $14.95. Butterfly Publications, 462 Broadway, New York NY 10013.

JA/0910-4607
**INTERSECT.** **See** Philosophy.

FR
**INTRODUCTION TO AFRICAN CULTURE.** **VFOAT** Introduction a la Culture Africaine. 1-. Monographic series. English (French). Price varies per volume. UNESCO / United Nations Educational Scientific and Cultural Organization, 7 Place de Fontenoy, 75700 Paris France. **Tel** 011 33 1 456610000.

US/0883-6620
**IPADE ALAGBARA.** Periodical. English (English). mo (ten no. a year). $10.50. IPADE Alagbara, Kameleon Publications, PO Box 1534 Los Angeles CA 90028. **Tel** (310)468-9165. **ED** Taivina Songobunmi. **DD** 306. **Bk Rev.** **Ad Acc.** **Circ:** 3,000 (ctrl).
**Desc:** An international journal of African traditional arts and lifestyles of Africans in the new world. Features healing, herbology, divination, astrology, dance, music, rituals. Total traditional arts.

# Sociology—Social Services and Welfare

JA
**KOBE ZEIKAN. / KOBE CUSTOMS.**
**Main/Corp** Japan. Zeikan, Kobe. **VFOAT** Kobe Customs. (19??)-. Periodical. Japanese (English). Kobe Zeikan, Kanocho 6-chome Ikuta-ku (650), Kobe Japan. **LC** HJ7276.Z7; K66a.

US/0736-4903
**LC FOLK ARCHIVE FINDING AID.** (LC FOLK ARCHIVE FINDING AID : LCFAFA.). [LC Folk Arch. find. aid]. **Main/Corp** Archive of Folk Culture (U.S.). **VFOAT** LCFAFA; Finding Aids. **VAT** Library of Congress Folk Archive Finding Aid. No. 1-. English. ir. Free. Archive of Folk Culture, Library of Congress, Washington DC 20540. **Tel** (202)707-5510. **ED** Joseph C Hickerson. **LC** ML156.4.F5; A7. **DD** 016.78162/0026/6. **Circ**: 2,000 (ctrl).
**Desc**: Periodic publication of discographies and related lists covering recorded and other materials contained in the collections of the Archive of Folk Culture.

US/0023-9836
**LEAVES OF TWIN OAKS, THE. Ceased.**
Vol.1 (1967)-Ceased ?. Periodical. English. qt. Harvest Forum, 22400 Skyline Box 7, LaHonda CA 94020. **Tel** (703)894-2126. **Circ**: 700.
**Desc**: A newsletter describing events, ideas, issues and attitudes of the Twin Oaks community.

FR
**MONDE ALPIN ET RHODANIEN, LE.**
**Added/Corp** Centre Alpin et Rhodanien d'Ethnologie (France). No. 1 (1973)-. Periodical. French (summaries and/or abstracts in English, German and Italian). Four times a year. 200.00F. Centre Alpin et Rhodanien Ethnologie Musee Dauphinois, 30 rue Maurice Gignoux, Grenoble Cedex France. **Tel** 011 33 76 876677. **LC** GN585.F8; M66. **Bk Rev. ctrl circ.**
**Ind/Abst** BHA : Biblio. Hist. Art.

US/8756-9965
**MOTC'S NOTEBOOK.** See Family and Marriage.

CN/0703-9069
**NEWSLETTER - MEMORIAL SOCIETY OF EDMONTON AND DISTRICT. Main/Corp** Memorial Society of Edmonton and District. (Oct 1975)-. Newsletter. English. an. Single copies free upon request. Memorial Society of Edmonton and District, 3516 13th Avenue, Edmonton Alberta T6L 3B3 Canada. **Tel** (403)461-7456. **ED** Mae Cox. **DD** 393/.06/271233. **Ad Acc. Circ**: 5,000. **Supersedes** Memorial Society of Edmonton. Newsletter, 0703-9050.
**Desc**: Current information on funeral practices, consumer concerns of special interest to memorial society members.

SP/0213-3105
**NOSA TERRA, A. Added/Corp** Promocions Culturais Galegas. (1984)-. Periodical. Gallegan. wk. 7500ptas (Spain); 8500ptas (Europe); 10900ptas (other). Promocions Culturais Gallegas, Provendre 4 5, 36201 Vigo Spain. **Tel** 34 86 222405, FAX 011 34 86 223101. **LC** DP302.G157; A2. **Ad Acc**, **Adv Mgr**: Cesar Pazos, **Tel** 43-86-433830. **Circ**: 10,500.

US/0030-1892
**OKLAHOMA TODAY.** See History(General)-History of North, South, and Central America.

US
**OSCAR ISRAELOWITZ'S GUIDE TO JEWISH NEW YORK CITY. Ceased.**
(1987)-(19??). English. Israelowitz Publishing, Box 228, Brooklyn NY 11229. **Tel** (718)951-7072, FAX (718)951-7072. Index available. **Bk Rev. Ad Acc. Circ**: 2,000 (ctrl).

US/1047-1499
**OUTLAW BIKER TATTOO REVUE.** English. $21.95 US; $31.95 other. Outlaw Biker Enterprises, 450 7th AveSte 2305, New York NY 10001. **Tel** (212)564-0112, FAX (212)465-8350. **Separated from** Outlaw Biker, 0885-2030.

US/1056-8131
**OUTLAW BIKER TATTOO REVUE SPECIALS.** [Outlaw biker tattoo rev. spec.]. Vol. 1, No.1 (1991)-. Periodical. English. qt. $15.00. Outlaw Biker Enterprises, 450 7th AveSte 2305, New York NY 10001. **Tel** (212)564-0112, FAX (212)465-8350. **DD** 391.

FR
**PAYS DE DINAN, LE.** See The Arts.

UK/0048-3672
**PHAROS. Main/Corp** Cremation Society of Great Britain and the International Cremation Federation. English. qt. Cremation Society of Great Britain, 16/16A Albion Place, Brecon House, Maidstone Kent ME14 5DZ England.

US
**PUBLIC HOLIDAYS IN 154 INDEPENDENT COUNTRIES.** (PUBLIC HOLIDAYS ... IN 154 INDEPENDENT COUNTRIES OF EUROPE, AFRICA & THE NEAR EAST, NORTH & SOUTH AMERICA, ASIA & THE PACIFIC AREA.).
Periodical. English. an. $6.00 public libraries, $10.00 other. Executive Handbooks, 98 Riverside Drive, New York NY 10024. **ED** Richard E Forrest. Index available.
**Desc**: Lists by country public holidays of the world.

CN/0821-1299
**RESEARCH PAPER - RESEARCH GROUP ON LEISURE AND CULTURAL DEVELOPMENT, UNIVERSITY OF WATERLOO.** (RESEARCH PAPER.). [Res. Pap. - Res. Group Leis. Cult. Dev. Univ. Waterloo]. **VFOAT** Research Papers on Leisure and Cultural Development. No. 1-. Monographic series. English. Price varies per volume. Research Group on Leisure and Cultural Development, Department of Recreation, University of Waterloo, Waterloo Ontario N2L 3G1 Canada. **DD** 306.

UK/0267-6834
**REVIEW OF SCOTTISH CULTURE.** See History(General)-History of Europe.

CN/0822-8701
**REVUE DE PRESSE DU ... FESTIVAL D'ETE DE QUEBEC, LA.** [Rev. presse - Festiv. ete Que.]. **Main/Corp** Festival d'Ete de Quebec. 16th (July 1/17, 1983)-. French. an. Festival d'Ete de Quebec, C P 24 Station B, Quebec Quebec G1K 7A1 Canada. **DD** 394.2/5/09714471. **Continues** Festival d'Ete de Quebec. Revue de Presse, 0822-8701.

JA
**RONSHU. Main/Corp** Tokyo Gaikokugo Daigaku. **VFOAT** Area and Culture Studies. (1951)-. Multiple languages.
**Ind/Abst** MLA Int. Bibl. Books Artic. Mod. Lang. Lit.

FR
**SAISON EN EUROPE ET DANS LE MONDE FESTIVALS.** French. an. 18.00F France; 26.50 US and Canada; 27.00F other. ANDC, 5 rue Bellart, 75015 Paris France. **Tel** 011 33 1 47833358.

SZ/0080-732X
**SCHRIFTEN DER SCHWEIZERISCHEN GESELLSCHAFT FUER VOLKSKUNDE.** See Folklore.

SZ/0048-9522
**SCHWEIZER VOLKSKUNDE.** See Folklore.

US/0899-594X
**SOUTHERN FOLKLORE.** See Folklore.

US
**SPIRIT OF CHRISTMAS. VFOAT** Spirit of Christmas Newsletter. Periodical. English. ir. Spirit of Christmas, PO Box 1255, Santa Ana CA 92701.

US/0896-8063
**TATTOO ADVOCATE.** Vol. 1, Issue No. 1; Spring 1988-. Periodical. English. sa. $20.00 US; $23.50 Canada. Tattoo Advocate, PO Box 8390, Haledon NJ 07538-0390. **Tel** (201)790-0429. **ED** Shotsei Gorman. **LC** FT2345; .T37. **DD** 391/.65/05. **Ad Acc.**
**Desc**: Presents historical, medical, ethnographic, psychological and social elements associated with the art, as well as its pop culture aspect.

CN/0831-2184
**TORONTO'S WEDDING BELLS.** See Family and Marriage.

US
**TRIQUARTERLY SERIES ON CRITICISM AND CULTURE.** No. 1 (1985)-. Monographic series. English.
**Ind/Abst** Annu. Bibliogr. Engl. Lang. Lit.

GW/0566-2753
**UNTERSUCHUNGEN UBER GRUPPEN UND VERBANDE.** (1964)-. Monographic series. German. ir. Price varies per volume. Duncker und Humblot Verlag, Postfach 410329, D-12113 Berlin Germany. **Tel** 011 49 30 79000012, 011 49 30 79000613. **DD** 301.4.

US/0890-832X
**VITAL CONNECTIONS.** (VITAL CONNECTIONS : THE NEWSLETTER OF THE FOUNDATION FOR GRANDPARENTING.). [Vital connect.]. **Added/Corp** Foundation for Grandparenting (Jay, N.Y.). (198?)-. Newsletter. English. qt. comes with membership. Foundation for Grandparenting, PO Box 97, Jay NY 12941. **Tel** (518)946-2177. **DD** 392.

CC/0511-4772
**WEN WU. VFOAT** Cultural Relics. (1950)-. Periodical. Chinese. Twelve times a year. $129.24. **(Subscription address:** China International Book Trading Corporation, PO Box 399, Library Service Department, Beijing 100044 People's Republic of China.) available on microfilm from University Microfilms International (UMI).
**Ind/Abst** Am. Hist. Life; Numis. Lit.

US/1045-0564
**WORLD CULTURES.** (WORLD CULTURES [COMPUTER FILE]). [World cult.]. **VFOAT** World Cultures Electronic Journal. Vol. 1, No. 1 (Mar. 1985)-. Periodical. English. qt. $60.00 (regular), $40.00 (student rate). World Cultures, PO Box 12524, La Jolla CA 92037-0650. **DD** 306.

JA
**YASURAGI.** Vol. 1 (1975)-. Periodical. Japanese. mo. ¥400. Geijutsu Bunkasha, c/o Daini Tanko Building, Horikawadori Kuramaguchi Noboru, Kita-ku 603 Kyoto Japan. **LC** GT2910; .Y35.

US/1056-3806
**YOUR PRESENCE.** (YOUR PRESENCE : A GUIDE FOR THE DISCERNING GIFT GIVER / THE REGISTRY GROUP.). [Your presence]. **Added/Corp** Registry Group. (Spring/Summer 1991)-. Periodical. English. qt. Free. The Registry Group, Inc., 85 Old Long Ridge Road, Stamford CT 06903. **DD** 394.

## SOCIAL SERVICES AND WELFARE

CN
**65 A L'HEURE.** V. 1- Oct. 1972-. Periodical. French. mo. 3.00Can$. Ministere des Affaires, Edifice Parlementaire, 1005 Chemin Ste Foy, Quebec Quebec G1A 1C3 Canada. **LC** HV109.Q44; S64. **DD** 362/.9714.

●US/1061-3056
**1992 DIRECTORY OF AGING RESOURCES.** [Dir. aging resour.]. **Added/Corp** Business Publishers. (1992)-. Directory. English. ir. $97.00. Business Publishers Inc., 951 Pershing Drive, Silver Spring MD 20910-4464. **Tel** (301)587-6300, (800)274-0122, FAX (301)585-9075. **ED** Nancy Aldrich. **LC** HV1457; .D53. **DD** 362.6/3/02573. **NLM** WT 22; AA1 D59.
**Desc**: Seven sections bring you detailed information on federal government agencies and programs, US Congress committees and subcommittees, national organizations, associations, and foundations, as well as advocacy and public interest groups, universities and colleges conducting gerontology or geriatrics research, major corporations and businesses that sponsor eldercare initiatives and more.

US
**A.I.M.** See Senior Citizens.

AU/0001-2947
**A.W.R. BULLETIN. Main/Corp** Association for the Study of the World Refugee Problem. **Added/Corp** Fuerst Franz Josef von Liechtenstein Stiftung. **VFOAT** AWR Bulletin. Vol. 1 (1963)-. Periodical. English (French, German and Italian). qt. S450.00 Austria; S495.00 others. Wilhelm Braumueller, Servitengasse 5, A 1092 Vienna, Austria. **Tel** 011 43 1 3191482, 3191159. **ED** Wilhelm Braumuller. **LC** HV640; .A25. **Bk Rev. Ad Acc. Circ**: 1,000 (ctrl). **Continues** Integration (Augsburg, Germany).
**Desc**: Publication on refugee problems.
**Ind/Abst** Hum. Rights Intern. Rep.

US/0887-896X
**ABA JUVENILE & CHILD WELFARE LAW REPORTER.** See Law-Family Law.

CN/0832-7890
**ABILITY AND ENTERPRISE.** See Physically Impaired.

PE/0258-2678
**ACCION CRITICA. Added/Corp** Centro Latinoamericano de Trabajo Social. ALAESS (Association). Vol. 1 (Dec. 1976)-. Periodical. Spanish. Twice a year. $13.00 Latin America; $18.00 other. Centro Latinoamericano de Trabajo Social, Apartado 1262, Lima 18 Peru. **Tel** 011 51 14 403092, 402186. **LC** HV110.5; .A45.

FR
**ACTION SOCIALE DES CAISSES D'ALLOCATIONS FAMILIALES, L'.**
**Main/Corp** Caisse Nationale des Allocations Familiales. **VFOAT** Statistiques Concernant l'Action Sociale des Caisses d'Allocations Familiales. 1971-. French. **LC** HD4925.5.F8; C33A. **DD** 362.5. **Continues** Statistiques Concernant l'Activite des Caisses et Services Particuliers d'Allocations Familiales.

FR/1145-8690
**ACTUALITES SOCIALES HEBDOMADAIRES.** (1955)-. Periodical. French. Forty-seven times a year. 333.01F France; 520.00F other. Actualites Sociales, 14 Boulevard Montmartre, 75311 Paris Cedex 09 France. **Tel** 011 33 1 47708459. **UDC** 362 (44).

US
**ACTUARIAL STUDY (UNITED STATES. SOCIAL SECURITY ADMINISTRATION. OFFICE OF THE ACTUARY).** (ACTUARIAL STUDY.). No. 1-. Monographic series. English. Price varies per volume. Social Security Administration, 6401

Security Boulevard, Baltimore MD 21235. **Tel** (410)965-8822, FAX (410)966-1463. **LC** HD7106.U5; A36. **DD** 368.4/3/00973.

US
**ADAMIS ANNUAL REPORT.** Fiscal Year 1983-. English. an. Missouri Department of Mental Health, 2002 Missouri Boulevard, Jefferson City MO 65101. **LC** HV5297.M8; A36. **DD** 362.2/928/09778.

US/0894-587X
**ADMINISTRATION AND POLICY IN MENTAL HEALTH.** [Adm. policy ment. health]. **Added/Corp** Human Sciences Press. Vol. 16, No. 1 (Fall 1988)-. Periodical. English. bm. £45.00 (individual), £210.00 (institution) UK & Europe; $265.00 US; $310.00 other. Human Sciences Press, PO Box 735, 233 Spring Street, New York NY 10013. **Tel** (212)620-8000, FAX (212)807-1047, telex 23421139. **(Subscription address:** Eurospan Ltd., Journals and Serials Division, 3 Henrietta Street, Covent Garden, London WC2E 8LU England.**) ED** Saul Feldman. **LC** RA790.A1; A43. **DD** 362.2/05. **NLM** W1; AD328. **CODEN** APMHEM. **[CCC].** available on microfilm and microfiche from University Microfilms International (UMI). Documents available from The Genuine Article. ***Continues*** *Administration in Mental Health, 0090-1180.*
**Desc:** The aim of this journal is to improve the effectiveness of all mental health and related human service programs, making administration more viable as a professional career and a field of knowledge. Examines such topics as demands for accountability, shifts in funding, legal challenges, compliance with new government policies, and related fields of interest.
**Ind/Abst** Curr. Contents Soc. Behav. Sci.; EMBASE; Linguist. Lang. Behav. Abstr.; Psychol. Abstr. (1973-); PsycINFO (1990-); Res. Alert [Full Cov.]; Soc. Plann. Policy Dev. Abstr.; Soc. Sci. Cit. Index [Full Cov.]; Soc. Work Abstr. [Select. Cov.]; Sociol. Abstr.

US/0364-3107
**ADMINISTRATION IN SOCIAL WORK.** [Adm. soc. work]. Vol. 1 (Spring 1977)-. Periodical. English. qt. $210.00 US; $294.00 other. The Haworth Press Inc, 10 Alice Street, Binghamton NY 13904-1580. **Tel** (607)722-5857, (800)3-HAWORTH, FAX (607)722-1424. **ED** Simon Slavin (editor's address: Hunter College School of Social Work, City University of New York, 129 East 79th Street, New York, NY 10021). **LC** HV1; .A27. **DD** 658/.91/361005. **NLM** W1 AD339S. **CODEN** ASWODB. **Bk Rev. Ad Acc. Pr Rev. Acid Free. Circ:** 1,065. available on microfilm and microfiche from University Microfilms International (UMI). Documents available from The Genuine Article, UMI Article Clearinghouse, Haworth Document Delivery Service.
**Desc:** The source for authoritative and pertinent material of vital interest to administrators, supervisors, managers and sub-executives in social work and related human services fields.
**Ind/Abst** ABI/INFORM Glob. Ed.; ABI Inform Ondisc (Spring 1985-); Appl. Soc. Sci. Index Abstr.; Curr. Contents Soc. Behav. Sci.; Gen. BusinessFile (1992-); Health Plan. Adminis.; Hospit. Health Admin. Index; Hum. Resour. Abstr.; Index Period. Artic. Relat. Law; Linguist. Lang. Behav. Abstr.; Middle East Abstr. Index; Psychol. Abstr.; PsycINFO (Fall,Winter 198?-); PsycLit; Ref. Z.; Res. Alert [Full Cov.]; Sage Fam. Stud. Abstr. (?-?); Soc. Plann. Policy Dev. Abstr.; Soc. Sci. Cit. Index [Full Cov.]; Soc. Work Abstr. [Full Cov.]; Sociol. Abstr.

US
**ADMINISTRATIVE DIRECTIVE - DEPARTMENT OF SOCIAL SERVICES.** **Main/Corp** New York (State). Dept. of Social Services. (1977)-. Periodical. English. Department of Social Services / New York, 135 Western Avenue, Albany NY 12222. **Tel** (518)442-5731. ***Continues*** *Administrative Letter - Department of Social Services.*

US
**ADOLESCENT PREGNANCY PREVENTION AND SERVICES PROGRAM, ANNUAL REPORT / PREPARED BY THE NEW YORK STATE DEPARTMENT OF SOCIAL SERVICES.** **Added/Corp** New York (State). Dept. of Social Services. (1991)-. English. Department of Social Services / New York, 135 Western Avenue, Albany NY 12222. **Tel** (518)442-5731.

US/0899-5591
**ADOLESCENT PREGNANCY PREVENTION CLEARINGHOUSE.** ***Title Change.*** [Publ. adolesc. pregnancy prev. clgh.]. **VFOAT** Adolescent Pregnancy Prevention Clearinghouse. (1985)-?. Monographic series. English. bm. Children's Defense Fund, 122 C Street NW, Washington DC 20001. **Tel** (202)628-8787. **ED** Ray Perez. **DD** 362. ***Continued by*** *CDF's Child, Youth, Family Futures Clearinghouse, 1055-9221.*
**Desc:** Examines a specific aspect of America's teen pregnancy crisis and strategies for prevention.
**Ind/Abst** Curr. Lit. Fam. Plan. (19??-199?).

UK/0308-5759
**ADOPTION & FOSTERING.** [Adopt. foster.]. **Added/Corp** Association of British Adoption and Fostering Agencies. **VAT** Adoption and Fostering. (1976)-. Periodical. English. Four times a year (Apr., July, Sept., Dec.). £20.00 UK; £25.00 other. British Agencies for Adoption & Fostering, 11 Southwark Street, London SE1 1RQ England. **Tel** 011 41 71 407 8800. **ED** Barbara Fletcher. **LC** HV875; .C445. **DD** 362.7/33/0941. Index available. cum. index. **Bk Rev. Ad Acc. Circ:** 5,000. ***Continues*** *Child Adoption.*
**Desc:** Social work, legal and medical issues concerning children and families. Articles, news items, research, statistics, reports of legal cases and book reviews included.
**Ind/Abst** Appl. Soc. Sci. Index Abstr.; Int. Bibliogr. Sociol.; Psychol. Abstr. (1980-); PsycINFO; PsycLit; Soc. Work Abstr. (Summer 1987-) [Select. Cov.].

CN/1181-845X
**ADOPTION HELPER.** [Adopt. help.]. No. 1 (Sept. 1990)-. Periodical. English. Four times a year (Mar., June, Sept., Dec.). 28.00Can$ (one year); 56.00Can$ (two years). Adoption Helper, 189 Springdale Boulevard, Toronto Ontario M4C 1Z6 Canada. **Tel** (416)463-9412, FAX (416)463-9412. **ED** Katherine Jones. **DD** 362.7/34/097105. Index available (Dec.). cum. index. **Bk Rev**, (Qty: 4). **Circ:** 700. available on an online database from Internet.
**Desc:** Coverage of international adoption. Contains in-depth reports, adoption studies and research, and post-adoption issues.

US/1055-6109
**ADOPTION THERAPIST.** (ADOPTION THERAPIST : A PUBLICATION OF HOPE COTTAGE ADOPTION CENTER.). [Adopt. ther.]. **Added/Corp** Hope Cottage Adoption Center. Vol. 1, No. 1 (May 1990)-. Periodical. English. sa. $20.00. Hope Cottage Adoption Center, 4209 McKinney Avenue, Suite 200, Dallas TX 75205. **DD** 362.

US
**ADOPTIONS IN CALIFORNIA, AGENCY, INDEPENDENT, INTERCOUNTRY. ANNUAL STATISTICAL REPORT.** **Added/Corp** California. Dept. of Social Services. **VFOAT** Annual Statistical Report; Adoptions in California. (June 1991)-. Statistical Publication. English. California Health and Welfare Agency Department of Social Services, 744 P Street, Sacramento CA 95814. **LC** HV875.65.C2; A367. ***Continues*** *Adoptions in California, Relinquishment, Independent, Iintercountry. Annual Statistical Report.*

US
**ADOPTIONS - STATE OF VERMONT, DEPARTMENT OF SOCIAL AND REHABILITATION SERVICES.** **Main/Corp** Vermont. Dept. of Social and Rehabilitation Services. English. Vermont Department of Social and Rehabilitation Services, State Office Building, 109 State Street, Montpelier VT 05602. **LC** HV883.V5; A3. **DD** 362.7/34/09743. ***Continues*** *Vermont Adoptions.*

●US/1076-1020
**ADOPTIVE FAMILIES.** **Added/Corp** Adoptive Families of America, Inc. (1994)-. English. Six times a year (Jan., Mar., May, July, Sept., Nov.). $24.00 US; $34.00 Canada; $42.00 others. Adoptive Families of America Inc., 3333 Highway 100 North, Minneapolis MN 55422. **Tel** (612)353-4829, (800)372-3300, FAX (612)535-7808. **ED** Jolene Roehlkepartain. Index available. cum. index. **Bk Rev**, (Qty: 18-24). **Ad Acc, Adv Mgr:** Sue Slominski, **Tel** (612)535-4829. **Pr Rev. Circ:** 25,000. ***Continues*** *Ours (Minneapolis, Minn.), 0899-9333.*
**Desc:** Publishes in-depth articles on parenting adopted children at various development ages. Provides problem solving assistance and information about the challenges of adoption to adoptive and prospective families.

US/0885-4572
**ADULT DAY CARE LETTER.** [Adult day care lett.]. **Added/Corp** Health Resources Publishing. Vol. 1, No. (July 1985)-. Periodical. English. Twelve times a year. $147.00 (one year), $264.00 (two years), $375.00 (three years); $97.00 (introductory subscription). Health Resources Publishing, 3100 Highway 138, Wall Township NJ 07719-1442. **Tel** (908)681-1133, FAX (908)681-0490. **DD** 362. **[CCC].**
**Desc:** Monthly newsletter containing critical management information, reports on trends and new developments, and above all, a linkage with other adult day care programs across the country.

US/1053-0606
**ADVANCES IN LONG-TERM CARE.** [Adv. long term care]. **VFOAT** Advances in Long Term Care. Vol. 1 (1991)-. English. ir. $44.95 (per copy). Springer Publishing Company, 536 Broadway, New York NY 10012-3955. **Tel** (212)431-4370, FAX (212)941-7842. **LC** RA644.5; .A38. **DD** 362.1/6/05. **NLM** W1; AD658.

CN/0847-2890
**ADVOCATE (EDMONTON).** (THE ADVOCATE : NEWSPAPER OF THE ALBERTA ASSOCIATION OF SOCIAL WORKERS.). [Advocate]. **Added/Corp** Alberta Association of Social Workers. Vol. 1, No. 1 (Spring 1976)-. Periodical. English. Four times a year (Mar., June, Sept., Dec.). 20.00Can$. Alberta Association of Social Workers, 52 9912 106 Street, Edmonton Alta T5K 1C5 Canada. **Tel** (403)421-1167, FAX (403)421-1167. **ED** Lyle Weiss (phone: (403)436-8092). **DD** 361.3/097123. **Ad Acc, Adv Mgr:** Gladys, **Tel** (403)421-1167. **Circ:** 1,500 (ctrl).

US/0893-6587
**AEROMED WEEK.** ***Ceased.*** [Aeromed week]. **VFOAT** Aeromedweek. Vol. 1, No. 1 (April 17, 1987)-Ceased (Dec. 1989). Periodical. English. wk. Aeromed Week, 53 West 1800 South, Orem UT 84058. **DD** 362.

US/0886-1099
**AFFILIA.** [Affilia]. **VFOAT** Affilia Journal of Women and Social Work. Vol. 1, No. 1 (Spring 1986)-. Periodical. English. qt (Feb., May, Aug., Nov.). $128.00. SAGE Periodical Press, 2455 Teller Road, Thousand Oaks CA 91320. **Tel** (805)499-0721, FAX (805)499-0871, telex 100799. **ED** Carol H. Meyer, Columbia University. **LC** HV1442; .A33. **DD** 361.3/2/082. Index available. **Ad Acc. Acid Free. Circ:** 307. available on microfilm and microfiche from University Microfilms International (UMI). Documents available from UMI Article Clearinghouse.
**Desc:** A publication for and about women social workers and their clients. Its intent is to bring insight and knowledge to the field of social work from a feminist perspective and to provide the research and tools necessary to make significant changes and improvements in the delivery of social services.
**Ind/Abst** Educ. Adm. Abstr. (?-?); Expand. Acad. Index (1992-); Hum. Resour. Abstr.; Linguist. Lang. Behav. Abstr.; Newsp. Period. Abstr. (1992-); Sage Fam. Stud. Abstr.; Soc. Plann. Policy Dev. Abstr.; Soc. Work Abstr. (Spring 1987-) [Full Cov.]; Sociol. Abstr.; Stud. Women Abstr.; Women Stud. Abstr. (1991-).

TG/0379-7074
**AFRICAN NEWS SHEET / INTERNATIONAL SOCIAL SECURITY ASSOCIATION.** **Added/Corp** International Social Security Association. African Regional Office. Vol. 1, No. 1 (Jan. 1981)-. Periodical. English (French). Twice a year. Free. International Social Security Association, Case Postale 1, CH-1211 Geneva 22 Switzerland. **Tel** 011 41 22 7996617, FAX 011 41 22 7986385. **LC** HD7237; .A14. **DD** 368.4/0096.

SZ
**AFRICAN SOCIAL SECURITY DOCUMENTATION.** ***Title Change.*** **Main/Corp** International Social Security Association. General Secretariat. (1977)-?. English. ir. International Social Security Association, Case Postale 1, CH-1211 Geneva 22 Switzerland. **Tel** 011 41 22 7996617, FAX 011 41 22 7986385. **LC** HD7237; .A28A. **DD** 368.4/0096. **Circ:** 500. ***Continued by*** *Social Security Documentation: African Series.*
**Desc:** Studies of various aspects or problems of social protection in African countries.
**Ind/Abst** Int. Labour Doc.; LABORDOC.

US/8756-3010
**AFTERWORDS.** (19??)-. Periodical. English. Four times a year. $15.00 US; $20.00 Canada; $25.00 other. Afterwords, 5124 Grove Street, Minneapolis MN 55436. **Tel** (612)929-6448. **ED** Adina Wrobleski. **DD** 361. **Circ:** 2,000.

US/0161-1151
**AGED CARE & SERVICES REVIEW.** ***Title Change.*** [Aged care serv. rev.]. **VAT** Aged Care and Services Review. Vol. 1 (Jan./Feb. 1978)-(19??). Periodical. English. qt (4 issues). The Haworth Press Inc, 10 Alice Street, Binghamton NY 13904-1580. **Tel** (607)722-5857, (800)3-HAWORTH, FAX (607)722-1424. **NLM** ZWT 100.3 A26. **CODEN** ACSRDO. **Acid Free.** available on microfiche. Documents available from Haworth Document Delivery Service. ***Absorbed by*** *Clinical Gerontologist, 0731-7115.*
**Ind/Abst** Health Plan. Adminis.; Psychol. Abstr. (1978-); Soc. Plann. Policy Dev. Abstr.; Sociol. Abstr. (?-?).

US/0163-5158
**AGEING INTERNATIONAL.** **Added/Corp** International Federation on Ageing. Vol. 1, Winter (1973/74)-. Periodical. English (Spanish). qt. $20.00 (individual), $40.00 (institution) North America; $25.00 (individual), $45.00 (institution) other. International Federation on Ageing, 601 E Street Northwest, Washington DC 20049. **Tel** (202)434-2430, FAX (202)434-6458. **ED** Charlotte Nusberg. **NLM** W1 AG326I. Index available. cum. index. **Bk Rev. Circ:** 2,000 (ctrl).
**Desc:** Provides practitioners in the field of ageing with crosscultural information on program innovation and new ideas in service delivery, research results in social gerontology, developments in ageing within international organizations, action by elderly in their own behalf, and activities of voluntary agencies engaged in service delivery or advocacy functions.
**Ind/Abst** Abstr. Soc. Gerontol.; Curr. Index J. Educ. (March 1990); Index Period. Lit. Aging.

US/0147-4383
**AGENCY DIRECTORY - AMERICAN HUMANE.** **Main/Corp** American Humane Association. **Added/Corp** American Humane Association. American Humane Agency Directory. **VFOAT** American Humane Agency Directory. (19??)-. Directory. English. American Humane, 5351 South Roslyn Street, Englewood CO 80110. **LC** HV4763; .A443. **DD** 179/.3/02573.

US/1045-4969
**AGENDA NEW YORK.** [Agenda N. Y.]. (June/July 1989)-. Periodical. English. Four times a year. $39.95. Agenda New York, 155 East 55th Street, Suite E, New York NY 10022. **Tel** (212)759-8010. **ED** Michael Schau. **DD** 361. **Ad Acc. Circ:** 6,000.
**Desc:** Covers how to run events more creatively and professionally.

US/1050-3188
**AGING ACTION ALERT.** ***Title Change.*** [Aging action alert]. (1985)-No. 92/6 (June 16, 1992). Periodical. English. mo. CD Publications, 8204 Fenton Street, Silver Spring MD 20910. **Tel** (800)666-6380, (301)588-6380, FAX (301)588-6385. **DD** 362. ***Continues*** *Aging Alert (Silver Springs, Md.).* ***Continued by*** *Aging News Alert.*

JA
**AICHI-KEN CHIIKI BOSAI KEIKAKU. FUZOKU SHIRYO.** **Added/Corp** Aichi Bosai Kaigi. (1963)-. Japanese. Aichi Bosai Kaigi, 1-ban 2-go Sannomaru, 3-chome Naku-ku, Nagoya Japan. **LC** HV555.J3; A537.

US
**AID TO FAMILIES WITH DEPENDENT CHILDREN.** **Added/Corp** Minnesota. Dept. of Public Welfare. Research and Statistics Division. Minnesota. Dept. of Public Welfare. (19??)-. English. be. Department of Public Welfare / Minnesota, Centennial Office Building, St Paul MN 55155. **LC** HV699; .M53. **DD** 326.8/2/09776. ***Continues*** *Minnesota Aid to Families with Dependent Children for Fiscal Year ... .*

US/1059-8847
**AIDSMONTHLY (BUSINESS AND FINANCE ED.).** ***Title Change.*** (AIDSMONTHLY.). [AIDSmonthly]. **VFOAT** AIDS Monthly. **VAT** Acquired Immune Deficiency Syndrome Monthly. Business and Finance Edition. (Jan. 1992)-(19??). Periodical. English. mo. CW Henderson, PO Box 5528, Atlanta GA 30307-0528. **Tel** (404)377-8895, FAX (404)378-5411. **DD** 362. ***Merged into*** *AIDS Weekly, 1069-1456.*

CN/0824-4715
**AISPICH CHAKWAN.** (AISPICH CHAKWAN : THE INFORMATION BULLETIN OF THE CONSEIL CRI DE LA SANTE ET DES SERVICES SOCIAUX DE LA BAIE JAMES : THE INFORMATION BULLETIN OF THE CREE BOARD OF HEALTH AND SOCIAL SERVICES OF JAMES BAY.). [Aispich chakwan]. **Added/Corp** Cree Board of Health and Social Services of James Bay. **VFOAT** Information Bulletin of the Conseil Cri de la Sante et des Services Sociaux de la Baie James; The Information Bulletin of the Cree Board of Health and Social Services of James Bay. Vol. 1, No. 1 (May 1983)-. Periodical. English. Four times a year. Free. Cree Board of Health and Social Services of James Bay, PO Box 420, Chisasibi James Bay, Chisasibi Quebec J0M 1E0 Canada. **Tel** (819)855-2844, FAX (819)855-2098. **ED** Helen Bobbish Atkinson. **DD** 361/.97141. **Circ:** 2,000 (ctrl).
**Desc:** Issues which are of interest to the native population, special programmes of activities performed by the Cree Board of Health and Social Services of James Bay for the population.

US/0279-6929
**AJL NEWSLINE.** (AJL NEWSLINE : NEWS ABOUT VOLUNTEERING, VOLUNTEERS, & THE ASSOCIATION OF JUNIOR LEAGUES.). **VAT** Association of Junior Leagues Newsletter. Vol. 1, No. 1 (Feb. 1981)-. Periodical. English. bm. Association of Junior Leagues Inc, 660 First Avenue, New York NY 10016. **Tel** (212)683-1515, FAX (212)481-7196.

CN/0848-399X
**ALBERTA HEALTH AND SOCIAL SERVICE EDUCATION PROGRAMS INVENTORY.** [Alta. health soc. serv. educ. programs inventory]. Program Coordination Branch, Alberta Advanced Education, 7th Floor/Devonian Building, 11160 Jasper Avenue, Edmonton Alberta T5K 0L1 Canada.

CN/0713-8067
**ALBERTA PERSPECTIVE.** ***Suspended.*** [Alta. perspect.]. **Added/Corp** Alberta Association for the Mentally Retarded. Alberta Association of Mentally Handicapped. Alberta Association for Community Living. Vol. 1, No. 1 (Fall 1981)-(19??). Periodical. English. qt. $5.00 members, $8.00 nonmembers. Alberta Association of the Mentally Handicapped, 11728 Kingsway Avenue, Edmonton Alberta TSG 0X5 Canada. **Tel** (403)451-3055. **ED** Carol M Peters. **DD** 362.3/097123. **Bk Rev. Ad Acc. Circ:** 1,200 (ctrl). ***Continues*** *New Horizon, 0028-5366.*
**Desc:** Articles of interest to the mentally handicapped, their families and support people. Current and upcoming events.

UK/0002-5623
**ALL THE WORLD. [A QUARTERLY REVIEW OF THE WORLD-WIDE WORK OF THE SALVATION ARMY].** **Added/Corp** Salvation Army. Vol.1 (Jan./Mar. 1938)-. Periodical. English. qt. £4.75. Salvationist Publishing and Supplies, 117-121 Judd St Kings Cross, London WC1H 9NN England. **Tel** 11 44 71 3871656, FAX 11 44 71 3873768. **ED** Barbara Bolton. **LC** BX9701; .A4. **DD** 267.1505. **Circ:** 20,000.
**Desc:** Articles describing remedical work undertaken in all classes of homes, institutions, and hospitals by the Salvation Army world-wide.

US
**ALTERNATIVE CHILD CARE PROGRAMS.** **Main/Corp** California. State Dept. of Education. Office of Child Development. English. an. California State Department of Education, PO Box 944272, 721 Capitol Mall, Sacramento CA 94244. **Tel** (916)657-2451, (916)445-7608, FAX (916)657-3000. **LC** HV857.C2; C35B. **DD** 362.7/1.

●US/1070-5112
**ALZHEIMER'S CARE GUIDE.** [Alzheimer's care guide]. (1993)-. Periodical. English. Twelve times a year. $24.00. Publication Services, Inc., 940 Matley Lane #8 / Box 11885, Reno NV 89510. **Tel** (702)333-6651, (800)354-3371, FAX (702)323-2770. **ED** Maureen Eng. **DD** 362. **Circ:** 2,000.

US/0893-5394
**AMERICAN INDIAN AND ALASKA NATIVE MENTAL HEALTH RESEARCH.** (AMERICAN INDIAN AND ALASKA NATIVE MENTAL HEALTH RESEARCH : JOURNAL OF THE NATIONAL CENTER.). [Am. Indian Alsk. native ment. health res.]. **Added/Corp** National Center for American Indian and Alaska Native Mental Health Research (U.S.). Vol. 1, No. 1 (June 1987)-. Periodical. English. Three times a year. $35.00. University Press of Colorado, PO Box 849, Niwot CO 80544. **Tel** (303)530-5337, FAX (303)530-5306. **ED** Spero M. Manson. **LC** RC451.5.I5; W47. **DD** 362.1/9/08997. **NLM** W1; AM4355. **Ad Acc. Pr Rev. Circ:** 300. Documents available from The Genuine Article. ***Continues*** *White Cloud Journal of American Indian Mental Health, 0886-5027.*
**Desc:** A professionally refereed scientific journal containing articles in the field of the behavioral, social and health sciences relating to the mental health of American Indians and Alaska Natives.
**Ind/Abst** Curr. Contents Soc. Behav. Sci.; Curr. Index J. Educ. (March 1990-); Health Plan. Adminis.; Linguist. Lang. Behav. Abstr.; Psychol. Abstr. (1987-); PsycINFO (1990-); Res. Alert [Full Cov.]; Soc. Plann. Policy Dev. Abstr.; Sociol. Abstr.

●US/1065-3457
**AMERICAN JOURNAL OF ADOPTION REFORM.** [Am. j. adopt. reform]. Vol. 1, No. 1 (Aug. 24, 1992)-. Periodical. English. bw. $40.00. American Journal of Adoption Reform, 1139 Bal Harbor Boulevard, Suite 184, Punta Gorda FL 33950. **DD** 362.

US/1049-9091
**AMERICAN JOURNAL OF HOSPICE AND PALLIATIVE CARE, THE.** [Am. j. hospice palliat. care]. **VFOAT** American Journal of Hospice & Palliative Care. Vol. 7, No. 2 (March/April 1990)-. Periodical. English. bm. $66.00 (individual), $86.00 (institution) US; $76.00 (individual), $96.00 (institution) Canada; $86.00 (individual), $106.00 (institution) other. Prime National Publishing Corporation, 470 Boston Post Road, Weston MA 02193. **Tel** (617)899-2702. **ED** Randy Gates. **LC** R726.8; .A47. **DD** 362.1/75. **NLM** W1; AM454KG. **Bk Rev**, (Qty: 12/yr). **Ad Acc. Pr Rev. Circ:** 2200. ***Continues*** *American Journal of Hospice Care, 0749-1565.*
**Desc:** Professional journal for hospice and palliative care.
**Ind/Abst** Health Plan. Adminis.; Int. Nurs. Index (1990-).

US/0362-4048
**AMERICAN REHABILITATION.** (AMERICAN REHABILITATION : AR.). [Am. rehabil.]. **Added/Corp** United States. Rehabilitation Services Administration. Vol. 1, No. 1 (Sept./Oct. 1975)-. Government Publication. English. qt. $9.00 US; $11.25 other. Superintendent of Documents, US Government Printing Office, Washington DC 20402. **Tel** (202)275-3328, FAX (202)786-2377. **LC** HD7255.A2; A19. **DD** 362.8/5. **NLM** W1 AM7435. available on microfilm and microfiche from University Microfilms International (UMI); available on an online database (file 149/Full-Text) from DIALOG.
**Desc:** The official publication of the Rehabilitation Services Administration, comments on all aspects of life affecting handicapped people and brings program, treatment, news, and legislative and technical matters of interest to a wide range of professional and consumer groups.
**Ind/Abst** Acad. Abstr. Full Text Elite (Jan. 1992-) [Full Txt.]; Acad. Abstr. (Jan. 1992-); Acad. Search (Jan. 1992-); Except. Child Educ. Resour.; Health Index (1989-); Health Period. Database [Full Txt.]; Health Ref. Cent. (Jan. 1989-) [Full Txt.] [Full Cov.]; Health Source (Jan. 1992-) [Full Txt.]; INFO-SOUTH Abstr.; Mag. Artic. Summar. Elite (Jan. 1992-) [Full Txt.]; Mag. Artic. Summar. Select (Jan. 1992-); Mag. Artic. Summar. CD-ROM (Jan. 1992-); Mag. Search; Vocat. Search (Jan. 1992-) [Full Txt.].

US/1048-4965
**AMERICA'S NEW FOUNDATIONS.** [Am. new found.]. **Added/Corp** Taft Group (Rockville, Md.). 4th Ed. (1990)-. English. an (published in Dec. of the prior year). $170.00. Taft Group, 835 Penobscott Building, Customer Service, Detroit MI 48226. **Tel** (800)877-8238, FAX (313)961-6083. **(Subscription address:** Taft Group, PO Box 71701, Chicago, IL 60694; telephone: (800)877-8238 ext. 1716) **LC** HV87; .A6. **DD** 361. ***Continues*** *America's Newest Foundations.*
**Desc:** Uncovers hard-to-find facts on recently created philanthropies, enabling fund raisers to be among the first to request grants.

CN/0844-5761
**AMETHYST MATTERS : NEWSLETTER OF AMETHYST WOMEN'S ADDICTION CENTRE.** [Amethyst matters]. No. 4 (1987)-. Newsletter. English. qt. 488 Wilbrod Street, Ottawa Ontario K1N 5M6 Canada. **DD** 362.2/9/06071384. ***Continues*** *Amethyst News & Views, 0834-1257.*

PR
**ANALISIS (SAN JUAN, P.R.).** (ANALISIS.). Vol. 1, No. 1 (Jan./June 1982)-. Periodical. English (Spanish). sa. Analisis, Revista de Planificacion, Apartado 8085, Santurce, Puerto Rico 00910. **LC** H97; .A52. **DD** 361.6/1/097295.

CN/0228-6610
**ANALYSE DE LA CAMPAGNE / CENTRAIDE CANADA.** **Main/Corp** United Way of Canada. **VFOAT** Campaign Analysis. 1978-. English (French). an. Free. United Way of Canada, 150 Kent Street/Suite 600, Ottawa Ontario K1P 5P4 Canada. **DD** 361.7/0971. ***Continues in part*** *United Way of Canada. Information and Statistics, 0383-9826.*

GR
**ANAPERIKON VEMA.** Periodical. Greek, Modern. qt. Pankyprios Organoses Ap Anaperon, Penetlis 50 Strovolos/Nicosia, Leukosia Greece. **LC** HV1551; .A52.

GW
**ANGESTELLTEN-VERSICHERUNG, DIE.** Vol. 1 (May 1954)-. German. mo. BFA Dezernat Presse, Oeffentlichkeitsarbeit PF, W 1000 Berlin 88 F R Germany. **Tel** 011 49 30 86524536. **LC** HD7116.M42; G42.

IT/0392-5870
**ANIMAZIONE SOCIALE.** [Animaz. soc.]. (1971)-. Periodical. Italian. Ten times a year. L80000 (institutions), L65000 (individuals) Italy; L105000.00 other. Associazione Gruppo Abele, Via Giolitti 21, 10123 Turin Italy. **Tel** 011 39 11 8142745, FAX 011 39 8395577. **UDC** 304. **Ad Acc, Adv Mgr:** Lulena Ortauda, **Tel** 011 814 2748.

CN/0823-0188
**ANNUAIRE DES FEMMES DE MONTREAL, L'.** [Annu. femmes Montr.]. **Added/Corp** Centre d'Information & de Reference pour Femmes. **VFOAT** Montreal Women's Directory. (1982)-. French (English). an. 14.95Can$ (add 1.00Can$ for postage). Les Editions Communiquelles, 3585 rue St-Urbain Street, Montreal Quebec H2Z 2N6 Canada. **Tel** (514)844-1761. **ED** Jacquie Manthorne. **DD** 362.8/3/02571427. **Ad Acc. Circ:** 5,000. ***Continues*** *Pages Jaunes des Femmes de Montreal, 0706-828X;* ***Absorbed*** *Montreal Women's Directory.*

CN/0835-3360
**ANNUAIRE DES RESSOURCES COMMUNAUTAIRES DE LILE DE MONTREAL.** ***Title Change.*** [Annu. ressour. communaut. Ile Montr.]. No. 1 (1987)-(1992). French. Annuaire des Ressources Communautaires du Montreal Metropolitain, a/s Info-Pop, 524 rue de Castelneau, Montreal Quebec H2R 1R5 Canada. **Tel** (514)270-9489. **DD** 361/.0025/71427. ***Continues*** *Annuaire des Ressources Communautaires du Montreal Metropolitain., 0822-6318.* ***Absorbed by*** *Blanchard, Andre, 1947-Annuaire des Ressources Communautaires du Quebec, 1183-0913.*

BE
**ANNUAIRE STATISTIQUE DE LA SECURITE SOCIALE (BRUSSELS, BELGIUM : 1981).** (STATISTISCH JAARBOEK VAN DE SOCIALE ZEKERHEID.). Dutch. an. Ministerie Van Sociale Voorzorg, Zwarte Lievevrouwstraat 3C, B-1000 Brussels Belgium. **LC** HD7186; .A74. ***Continues in part*** *Annuaire Statistique de la Securite Sociale.*

# Sociology —Social Services and Welfare

CN/0713-8555
**ANNUAL BRIEF SUBMITTED BY THE QUEBEC ASSOCIATION FOR THE MENTALLY RETARDED TO THE GOVERNMENT OF QUEBEC. Main/Corp** Quebec Association for the Mentally Retarded. Nov. 1976-. English. an. $1.25 per vol. Quebec Association for the Mentally Retarded, Suite 407/5890 Monkland Avenue, Montreal Quebec H4A 1G2 Canada. **DD** 362.3/09714.

US/0091-0724
**ANNUAL CAUSES & CONDITIONS OF POVERTY IN SOUTH DAKOTA. Main/Corp** South Dakota. State Economic Opportunity Office. English. an. State Economic Opportunity Office / South Dakota, State Capital Building, 500 East Capitol, Pierre SD 57501. **LC** HC107.S83; P62A. **DD** 301.44/1.

US
**ANNUAL REPORT. Main/Corp** Kentucky. Dept. of Child Welfare. (19??)-. English. an. Kentucky Department of Child Welfare, Frankfort KY 40601. **LC** HV742.K4; A32. **DD** 362.7/09769.

II
**ANNUAL REPORT. Main/Corp** India. Ministry of Health and Family Welfare. (19??)-. English. an. Ministry of Health and Family Welfare / India, Government of India, New Delhi. **LC** RA311; .B16. **DD** 354.540084/1/06. **Continues** India. Ministry of Health and Family Welfare. Report.

US
**ANNUAL REPORT / ALABAMA DEPARTMENT OF MENTAL HEALTH AND MENTAL RETARDATION. Main/Corp** Alabama. Department of Mental Health and Mental Retardation. Alabama Department of Mental Health, Department of Mental Health, 135 South Union Street, Montgomery AL 36130.

AT
**ANNUAL REPORT / AUSTRALIAN COUNCIL OF SOCIAL SERVICE. Main/Corp** Australian Council of Social Service. (19??)-. English. an. Australian Council of Social Service, 8-24 Kippax Street, Surry Hills 2010, New South Wales Australia. **Tel** 011 61 2 2123277. **LC** WMLC L 83/6978.

US
**ANNUAL REPORT / CALIFORNIA OFFICE OF EMERGENCY SERVICES. Main/Corp** California. Office of Emergency Services. English. an. California Office of Emergency Services, 2800 Meadowview Road, Sacramento CA 95832. **Tel** (916)427-4990. **LC** HV555.U62; C35A. **DD** 353.97940075/4/06.

CN/1185-9660
**ANNUAL REPORT - CANADIAN COUNCIL OF MINISTERS OF THE ENVIRONMENT.** (RAPPORT ANNUEL.). [Annu. rep. - Can. Counc. Minist. Environ.]. **Main/Corp** Conseil Canadien des Ministres de l'Environnement. **VFOAT** Annual Report; Programme National d'Assainissement des Lieux Contaminés. **VAT** Rapport Annuel - Conseil Canadien des Ministres de l'Environnement. (1991)-. French (English). Le Conseil Canadien des Ministres l'Environnement, Winnipeg Canada. **DD** 363.7/0971.

US/0412-1058
**ANNUAL REPORT - CHILD WELFARE LEAGUE OF AMERICA, INC. Main/Corp** Child Welfare League of America. (19??)-. English. an. Free on request. Child Welfare League of America, 440 1st Street Northwest, Suite 310, Washington DC 20001. **Tel** (202)638-2952, FAX (202)638-4004. **LC** HV741; .C5345b. **DD** 362.7/06/073. **Circ:** 2,500.
**Desc:** Annual report.

AT
**ANNUAL REPORT / DEPARTMENT OF COMMUNITY SERVICES. Main/Corp** Queensland. Dept. of Community Services. (19??)-. English. an. Queensland Department of Community Services, Brisbane Australia. **LC** GN667.Q4; Q43a. **DD** 305.8/9915/05.

US
**ANNUAL REPORT - DEPARTMENT OF HEALTH & WELFARE. Title Change. Main/Corp** Idaho. Dept. of Health and Welfare. (19??)-(19??). English. an. **LC** HV86; .I217. **DD** 353.9/796/008405. **Continued by** Idaho. Dept. of Health and Welfare. Annual Report and Guide to Programs.

US
**ANNUAL REPORT - DEPARTMENT OF SOCIAL SERVICES, DIVISION OF DATA PROCESSING (MISSOURI). Main/Corp** Missouri. Dept. of Social Services. Division of Data Processing. 1977-. English. an. Department of Social Services / Missouri, Broadway State Office Building, Jefferson City MO 65102. **LC** HV98.M8; M46A. **DD** 353.97780084/028/54.

CN/0383-4808
**ANNUAL REPORT - DEPARTMENT OF SOCIAL SERVICES (HALIFAX).** (ANNUAL REPORT - DEPARTMENT OF SOCIAL SERVICES.). **Main/Corp** Nova Scotia. Dept. of Social Services. (1974)-. English. an. Department of Social Sciences, PO Box 696, Johnston Building, Prince Street, Halifax Nova Scotia B3J 2T7 Canada. **LC** HV109.N9; A43. **DD** 354/.716/008405. **Supersedes** Nova Scotia. Dept. of Public Welfare. Annual Report, 0550-1776.

US
**ANNUAL REPORT - DEPARTMENT ON AGING (CONNECTICUT). Main/Corp** Connecticut. Dept. on Aging. English. an. Connecticut Department on Aging, 175 Main Street, Hartford CT 06106-1818. **LC** HV1468.C8; A34. **DD** 353.97460084/6/06. **Continues** Report to the Governor and General Assembly - Department on Aging, 0090-6077.

●NZ
**ANNUAL REPORT / DEPT. OF SOCIAL WELFARE, NEW ZEALAND. Main/Corp** New Zealand. Dept. of Social Welfare. (1992)-. Government Publication. English. an. 4.40NZ$. Government Printing Office / New Zealand, 10 Mulgrave Street, Wellington New Zealand. **Tel** 011 64 4 4737211, FAX 011 64 4 734943, telex GOVPRINT NZ 31320. **LC** HV515.5; .A4a. **DD** 354/.931/0084. **Continues** New Zealand. Dept. of Social Welfare. Report of the Department of Social Welfare for the Year Ended ... .

US/0149-1539
**ANNUAL REPORT - DIVISION OF LONG-TERM CARE.** [Annu. rep. - Div. Long-Term Care]. **Main/Corp** United States. Health Resources Administration. Division of Long-Term Care. (1975-76)-. English. an. US Department of Health and Human Services, 200 Independence Avenue Southwest, Washington DC 20201. **LC** RA644.6; .U56a. **DD** 353.008/41/6.

US
**ANNUAL REPORT FOR THE YEAR ENDED AUGUST 31 ... / CENTRAL OFFICE. Main/Corp** Texas. Dept. of Mental Health and Mental Retardation. Central Office. English. an. **LC** RA790.65.T4; T48D. **DD** 353.97640084/2.

US
**ANNUAL REPORT / FOSTER CARE REVIEW BOARD. Main/Corp** Maryland. Foster Care Review Board. (19??)-. English. an. Maryland Citizen Board for Review of Foster Care of Children, 101 West Read Street/Suite 621, Baltimore MD 21201. **LC** HV883.M3; M37a. **DD** 362.7/33/09752.

SZ
**ANNUAL REPORT - INTERNATIONAL COMMITTEE OF THE RED CROSS. Main/Corp** International Committee of the Red Cross. (19??)-. English. an. Kr12.00. International Committee of the Red Cross, 19 Ave de la Paix, Geneva Switzerland. **Tel** 011 41 22 734 6001. **LC** HV560; .R376a. **DD** 361.7/7. **NLM** W1 RE156TR.

US
**ANNUAL REPORT - LOS ANGELES COUNTY AREA AGENCY ON AGING, ADVISORY COUNCIL. Main/Corp** Los Angeles County Area Agency on Aging. Advisory Council. (1979)-. English. an. **LC** HV1471.L72; L674a. **DD** 352.94/46/0979493.

US
**ANNUAL REPORT / MASSACHUSETTS DEPARTMENT OF SOCIAL SERVICES. Main/Corp** Massachusetts. Dept. of Social Services. 1983-. English. an. Department of Social Services / Massachusetts, 150 Causeway Street, Boston MA 02114. **LC** HV98.M39; M39A.

CN/1183-997X
**ANNUAL REPORT / MENTAL HEALTH COMMISSION OF NEW BRUNSWICK. See** Public Health and Safety.

US
**ANNUAL REPORT ... / MINNESOTA PROGRAM FOR VICTIMS OF SEXUAL ASSAULT, MINNESOTA DEPARTMENT OF CORRECTIONS. Main/Corp** Minnesota Program for Victims of Sexual Assault. English. an. Minnesota Department of Correction, 450 North Syndicate Street, Bigelow Building, Suite 300, St Paul MN 55104. **Tel** (612)642-0282, FAX (612)642-0223. **LC** HV6250.3.U5; M55A. **DD** 362.8/8.

US/0732-9148
**ANNUAL REPORT ... - MONTANA. FIRE MARSHAL BUREAU.** (ANNUAL REPORT / FIRE MARSHAL BUREAU.). **Main/Corp** Montana. Fire Marshal Bureau. English. an. Fire Marshal Bureau / Helena, 1409 Helena Avenue, Helena MT 59601. **LC** HV8079.A7; M64A. **DD** 353.97860078/2/06. **Circ:** 700.
**Desc:** Contains reports on the years activities of the Montana Fire Marshall Bureau and selected statistics from the Montana Fire Information Reporting System.

US
**ANNUAL REPORT - NEW JERSEY. STATE AGENCY FOR SOCIAL SECURITY. Main/Corp** New Jersey. State Agency for Social Security. English. an. State Agency for Social Security, 20 West Front Street, Trenton NJ 08625. **LC** HD7126.N37; N46A. **DD** 368.4/009749. **Continues** Annual Report - New Jersey State Agency for Old Age and Survivors' Insurance Service.

US
**ANNUAL REPORT / NEW MEXICO, GOVERNOR'S COMMITTEE ON CONCERNS OF THE HANDICAPPED. Main/Corp** New Mexico. Governor's Committee on Concerns of the Handicapped. (1982). English. an. New Mexico Governor's Committee on Concerns of the Handicapped, Bataan Memorial Building/Room 309, Santa Fe NM 87503. **LC** HV1555.N6; N48a. **DD** 353.97890084/4/06.

US/0091-0996
**ANNUAL REPORT OF THE DEPARTMENT OF SOCIAL AND REHABILITATION SERVICES TO THE GOVERNOR OF MONTANA.** (ANNUAL REPORT.). **Main/Corp** Montana. Dept. of Social and Rehabilitation Services. 1971/72-. English. an. Department of Social and Rehabilitation Service, State Capitol, Helena MT 59601. **LC** HV86; .M92. **DD** 353.9/786/0084. **Continues** Montana. State Dept. of Public Welfare. Report.

KE
**ANNUAL REPORT OF THE DIRECTOR OF SOCIAL SERVICES & HOUSING FOR THE YEAR - MOMBASA KENYA. Main/Corp** Mombasa (Kenya). Social Services and Housing Dept. 1976-. English. an. Social Services and Housing Department / Kenya, Mombasa 904410 Kenya. **LC** HV449.K44; M655. **DD** 352.84/09676/23. **Continues** Annual Report - Social Services and Housing Department.

US/0090-3051
**ANNUAL REPORT OF THE DIVISION OF SOCIAL SERVICES OF THE DEPARTMENT OF HEALTH AND SOCIAL SERVICES.** (ANNUAL REPORT.). **Main/Corp** Delaware. Division of Social Services. 1970-. English. an. Delaware Division of Social Services, PO Box 309, Wilmington DE 19899. **LC** HV86; .D28. **DD** 353.9/751/008405.

US/0882-5203
**ANNUAL REPORT OF THE U.S. DEPARTMENT OF HEALTH AND HUMAN SERVICES TO THE CONGRESS OF THE UNITED STATES ON SERVICES PROVIDED TO HANDICAPPED CHILDREN IN PROJECT HEAD START. VFOAT** Status of Handicapped Children in Head Start Programs. 8th-. English. an. Administration for Children & Families, 370 L'Enfant Promenade SW, 6th Floor, Washington DC 20447. **Tel** (202)401-9200, FAX (202)252-4683. **LC** LC4031. **DD** 371.9/0973. **NLM** W2; A A13a. **Continues** Annual Report of the U.S. Department of Health, Education, and Welfare to the Congress of the United States on Services Provided to Handicapped Children in Project Head Start, 0093-3430.

AT
**ANNUAL REPORT OF THE UNDER SECRETARY, DEPARTMENT OF COMMUNITY SERVICES. Main/Corp** Queensland. Dept. of Community Services. (19??)-. Government Publication. English. an. Department of Community Services, Brisbane Queensland Australia. **LC** HV474.Q4; Q43a. **DD** 354.9430084/06.

US/0277-8289
**ANNUAL REPORT - OKLAHOMA. DEPT. OF HUMAN SERVICES.** (ANNUAL REPORT.). **Main/Corp** Oklahoma. Dept. of Human Services. (1980). English. an. Free on request. Oklahoma Department of Human Services, PO Box 25352, Oklahoma City OK 73125. **LC** HV86; .O516a. **DD** 353.97660084/06. **NLM** W2; AO5 D5a. **Continues** Oklahoma. Dept. of Institutions, Social and Rehabilitative Services. Annual Report, 0270-6008.
**Ind/Abst** Stat. Ref. Index.

SZ
**ANNUAL REPORT ON CHILD WELFARE, FOR THE ... SESSION OF THE ADVISORY COMMITTEE ON SOCIAL QUESTIONS. Main/Corp** League of Nations. Child Welfare Information Centre. 3rd Session

# Sociology —Social Services and Welfare

(June 19, 1939)-. English. an. *Continues* Summary of Annual Reports Received from Governments Between ..., and the ... Session of the Advisory Committee on Social Questions.

US/0363-9673
**ANNUAL REPORT ON THE PROVISION OF CHILD WELFARE SERVICES IN NEW YORK STATE.** **Main/Corp** New York (State). Dept. of Social Services. (1975)-. English. an. Department of Social Services / New York, 135 Western Avenue, Albany NY 12222. **Tel** (518)442-5731. **LC** HV86; .N7643 subser; HV742.N7. **DD** 361/.9747 S; 362.7/09747.

US/0749-9337
**ANNUAL REPORT ON THE STATUS OF POVERTY IN CALIFORNIA, AN.** *Title Change.* (AN ANNUAL REPORT ON THE STATUS OF POVERTY IN CALIFORNIA / STATE OF CALIFORNIA, OFFICE OF ECONOMIC OPPORTUNITY.). [Annu. rep. status pover. Calif.]. **Added/Corp** California. Office of Economic Opportunity. **VFOAT** California's Poor. (19??)-?. English. an. Office of Economic Opportunity, Sacramento CA 95814. **Tel** (916)322-2940. **DD** 362. **Circ:** 1,500. *Continued by* Status of Poverty in California ... a Report.
**Desc:** Identifies the extent and distribution of California's poor by examining data on the types of individuals and groups who are at risk from social and economic deprivation.

CN/0833-7659
**ANNUAL REPORT - PUBLIC SAFETY SERVICES (ALBERTA).** **See** Public Health and Safety.

US
**ANNUAL REPORT / RS, REHABILITATION SERVICES, WEST VIRGINIA STATE BOARD OF REHABILITATION.** **Main/Corp** West Virginia. Rehabilitation Services. (1987)-. English. West Virginia Division of Vocational Rehabilitation, State Capitol Building, Charleston WV 25305. **LC** HD7256.U6; W473a. **DD** 353.97540083/4. *Continues* Annual Report of the West Virginia Division of Vocational Rehabilitation for the period ... .

US/0581-4766
**ANNUAL REPORT - SAMUEL H. KRESS FOUNDATION.** (ANNUAL REPORT.). **Main/Corp** Samuel H. Kress Foundation. (19??)-. English. **LC** HV97.S25; S25. **DD** 361.7/6.

US/0362-4218
**ANNUAL REPORT - STATE OF NEW JERSEY, DEPARTMENT OF INSTITUTIONS AND AGENCIES, DIVISION OF MEDICAL ASSISTANCE AND HEALTH SERVICES-MEDICAID.** **See** Insurance.

US
**ANNUAL REPORT, STATISTICAL SUPPLEMENT / NEW YORK STATE DEPARTMENT OF SOCIAL SERVICES.** *Title Change.* **Main/Corp** New York (State). Dept.of Social Services. (1983)-(1984). Statistical Publication. English. an. **LC** HV98.N7; N53e. **DD** 353.97470084/06. *Continues* Statistical Supplement to Annual Report, 0364-4715. *Continued by* Statistical Supplement to the ... Annual Report of the New York State Department of Social Services.

US
**ANNUAL REPORT TO THE CONGRESS FOR FISCAL YEAR ... / SOCIAL SECURITY.** **Main/Corp** United States. Social Security Administration. **VFOAT** Annual Report to the Congress. 1979/80-. English. an. Social Security Administration, 6401 Security Boulevard, Baltimore MD 21235. **Tel** (410)965-8822, FAX (410)966-1463. **LC** HD7123; .S53A. **DD** 353.0082/56. available on microfiche (Vols. for (1985-) distributed to depository libraries). *Continues* Annual Report of the Social Security Administration, 0098-6380.

US
**ANNUAL REPORT TO THE GOVERNOR / TEXAS PLANNING COUNCIL FOR DEVELOPMENTAL DISABILITIES.** **Main/Corp** Texas Planning Council for Developmental Disabilities. English. an. **LC** HV1555.T4; T5A. **DD** 362.1/968. *Continues* Biennial Report to the Governor / Texas Planning Council for Developmental Disabilities.

US
**ANNUAL REPORT / UIA, UNITED ISRAEL APPEAL, INC.** **Main/Corp** United Israel Appeal. (1978)-. English. an. United Israel Appeal, 515 Park Avenue, New York NY 10022. **LC** HV3191; .U53a. **DD** 361.7/63. *Continues* United Israel Appeal. Report to the Annual Meeting of the Board of Trustees ..., 1041-374X.

US
**ANNUAL REPORT / VIRGINIA ASSOCIATION OF COMMUNITY SERVICES BOARDS, INC.** **Main/Corp** Virginia Association of Community Services Boards. English. an. Virginia Association of Community Services Boards Inc, 7641 Hull Street Road/Suite 205, Richmond VA 23235-6401. **LC** RA790.65.V54; V58A. **DD** 353.97550084/2.

US
**ANNUAL REPORT - VIRGINIA STATE OFFICE ON VOLUNTEERISM.** *Title Change.* **Main/Corp** Virginia. State Office on Volunteerism. (1976/77)-?. English. an. Virginia State Office on Volunteerism, Fourth Street Office Building, 205 North 4th Street, Richmond VA 23219. **LC** HV86; .V857. **DD** 353.97550084. *Continued by* Annual Report.

US/0093-7665
**ANNUAL REPORT - WAYNE COUNTY DEPARTMENT OF SOCIAL SERVICES.** (ANNUAL REPORT.). **Main/Corp** Wayne Co., Mich. Dept. of Social Services. (19??)-. English. an. Wayne County Department of Social Services, 640 Temple, Detroit MI 48201. **LC** HV86.M58; W33. **DD** 362/.9774/73.

US/0160-7200
**ANNUAL REPORT - WILLIAM T. GRANT FOUNDATION.** **Main/Corp** William T. Grant Foundation. 1975/76-. English. an. William T Grant Foundation, 130 East 59th Street, New York NY 10022. **LC** HV97; .G7. **DD** 362.7/0973. **NLM** W1 WI549J. *Continues* Annual Report - Grant Foundation, 0147-4138.

UK
**ANNUAL REVIEW / BRITISH AGENCIES FOR ADOPTION AND FOSTERING.** **Main/Corp** British Agencies For Adoption and Fostering. 1980-81-. English. an. British Agencies for Adoption & Fostering, 11 Southwark Street, London SE1 1RQ England. **Tel** 011 41 71 407 8800. **ED** Prue Chennells. **LC** HV875; .B73A. **DD** 362.7/33/06041. **Circ:** 5,000.
**Desc:** Presentation of educational, research, consultancy and publishing activities to promote high standards of practice in adoption, fostering and child care.

UK
**ANNUAL REVIEW - NATIONAL CHILDREN'S BUREAU.** **Main/Corp** National Children's Bureau. English. an. National Childrens Bureau Information Services, 8 Wakley Street, Islington, London EC1V 7QE England. **Tel** 011 44 71 2789441. **LC** HV751.A255; A25. **DD** 362.7/0942. *Continues* National Children's Bureau. Annual Report.

US
**ANNUAL SERVICES PLAN - DEPARTMENT OF SOCIAL SERVICES.** **Main/Corp** South Dakota. Dept. of Social Services. English. an. Department of Social Services / South Dakota, State Office Building, 700 Governors Drive, Pierre SD 57501. **Tel** (605)773-4855. **LC** HV98.S8; S67A. **DD** 361.6/2/09783.

US/0093-6715
**ANNUAL STATISTICAL REPORT - DIVISION OF FAMILY SERVICES.** **See** Sociology-Abstracting, Bibliographies and Statistics.

US/0146-2148
**ANNUAL STATISTICAL REPORT. MENTAL HEALTH SERVICES. MENTAL RETARDATION SERVICES. VETERANS' HOMES SERVICE (NEBRASKA).** **See** Sociology-Abstracting, Bibliographies and Statistics.

US/0147-6467
**ANNUAL STATISTICAL REPORT - SOUTH DAKOTA DEPARTMENT OF SOCIAL SERVICES.** **See** Sociology-Abstracting, Bibliographies and Statistics.

●US
**ANNUAL STATISTICAL SUPPLEMENT, ... TO THE SOCIAL SECURITY BULLETIN.** **Added/Corp** United States. Social Security Administration. **VFOAT** Annual Statistical Supplement; Social Security Bulletin, Annual Statistical Supplement. (1992)-. Statistical Publication. English. an. $33.00. Superintendent of Documents, US Government Printing Office, Washington DC 20402. **Tel** (202)275-3328, FAX (202)786-2377. **(Subscription address:** US Government Bookstore / O'Neil Building, 2023 3rd Avenue North, Birmingham AL 35203.**)** *Continues* Social Security Bulletin. Annual Statistical Supplement, 0098-6259.
**Desc:** Reports current data on the operations of the Social Security Administration and the results of research and analysis pertinent to the social security program.
**Ind/Abst** Acad. Search; Bus. Source; Index Med.; INFO-SOUTH Abstr.; Mag. Search.

CR
**ANUARIO ESTADISTICO - DEPTO ACTUARIAL Y ESTADISTICO.** *Ceased.* **Main/Corp** Caja Costarricense de Seguro Social. (19??)-?. Spanish. an. Caja Costarricense de Seguro Social, Apartado 10105, San Jose Costa Rica. **Tel** 011 506 234033. **LC** HD7134; .C37b. **DD** 368.4/0097286.

BL
**ANUARIO ESTATISTICO.** **See** Sociology-Abstracting, Bibliographies and Statistics.

BL
**ANUARIO ESTATISTICO - SERVICO SOCIAL DO COMERCIO, ADMINISTRACAO REGIONAL EM MINAS GERAIS.** **See** Sociology-Abstracting, Bibliographies and Statistics.

II
**ANUDANOM KIMANGEM, SAMAJA KAJANA MANTRALAYA.** **Main/Corp** India. Ministry of Social Welfare. **VFOAT** Demands for Grants of Ministry of Social Welfare. (1980-81)-. Periodical. English (Hindi). Government of India Press / General Manager, Minto Road, New Delhi India. *Continues in part* Anudanom Ki Mangem.

CN/1185-1996
**APERCU, L'.** [Apercu]. **Added/Corp** Centre Hospitalier Regional de Lanaudiere. Service de Readaptation et d'Integration Communautaire. Vol. 1, No 1 (Mar 1991)-. Periodical. French. qt. Limited free distribution. Service de Readaptation et D'Integration Communautaire, Centre Hospitalier Regional de Lanaudiere, 3E Etage, 432 Rue Notre Dame, Joliette Quebec J6E 3H4 Canada. **DD** 362.2.

UK/0141-2205
**APEX (KIDDERMINSTER).** (APEX.). [Apex]. Periodical. English. qt. **NLM** W1 AP115B.
**Ind/Abst** Appl. Soc. Sci. Index Abstr.

US/1043-2809
**APPALACHIAN READER, THE.** [Appalach. read.]. **Added/Corp** Appalachian Community Resource Service. Vol. 1, No. 1 (Mar. 1988)-. Periodical. English. Four times a year (Mar., July, Sept., Dec.). $10.00. Appalachian Reader, PO Box 697, Salyersville KY 41465. **Tel** (606)349-2593. **ED** Liz McGeachy, (editor's address: PO Box 533, Whitesburg, KY 41858, phone: (606)633-3968). **DD** 363. **Bk Rev**, (Qty: 4). **Circ:** 500 (ctrl).

GW/0341-7840
**ARBEITS- UND SOZIALSTATISTIK. HAUPTERGEBNISSE / DER BUNDESMINISTER FUR ARBEIT UND SOZIALORDNUNG.** **See** Economics-Labor.

NE
**ARBO KNIPSELKRANT.** Ned Inst Arbeidsomstandigheden, Postbus 75665, 1070 AR Amsterdam Netherlands. **Tel** 011 31 20 5498611.

●US
**ARC TODAY, THE.** **Added/Corp** Arc (U.S.). Vol. 41, No. 1 (Jan./Feb. 1992)-. Periodical. English. Six times a year. Free to (members); $15.00 (non-members). The Arc - National Headquarters, 500 East Border Street, Suite 300, PO Box 1047, Arlington TX 76004. **Tel** (817)261-6003, FAX (817)277-3491. **ED** Jim Humphrey. **LC** HV891; .M4475. **Ad Acc.** ctrl circ. *Continues* Arc, 0199-9435.
**Desc:** Devoted to news of the association and the field of mental retardation.

FR/0003-9691
**ARCHIVES DES MALADIES PROFESSIONNELLES DE MEDECINE DU TRAVAIL ET SECURITE SOCIALE.** **See** Medical Science and Technology.

US/0885-9787
**ARETE.** (ARETE / GRADUATE SCHOOL OF SOCIAL WORK, UNIVERSITY OF SOUTH CAROLINA.). [Arete]. **Added/Corp** University of South Carolina. Graduate School of Social Work. University of South Carolina. College of Social Work. Vol. 1, No. 1 (Spring 1970)-. Periodical. English. Twice a year (June, Dec.). $15.00. University of South Carolina College of Social Work, Columbus SC 29208. **Tel** (803)777-5291. **ED** Miriam Freeman. **LC** HV1; .A74. **DD** 361. **Pr Rev. Circ:** 1,000 (ctrl).
**Desc:** A professional journal concerned with problems, new developments, and issues in social work practice, social work education and social welfare.
**Ind/Abst** Linguist. Lang. Behav. Abstr.; Soc. Plann. Policy Dev. Abstr.; Soc. Work Abstr. [Full Cov.]; Sociol. Abstr.

US/0363-2903
**ARETE (SAN FRANCISCO).** (ARETE.). (19??)-. Periodical. English. qt. $5.50. C F Debor, 830 Hyder Street/No 6, San Francisco CA 94109. **LC** PN6099.6; .A73. **DD** 811/.5/405.

US/0092-0215
**ARKANSAS SOCIAL SERVICES ANNUAL REPORT.** (ANNUAL REPORT.). **Main/Corp** Arkansas. Social Services. Research and Statistics. (1972)-. English. an. Welfare Employment Security Building, State Capitol Mall, Little Rock AR 72203. **LC** HV86.A88. **DD** 362/.9767. **NLM** W2; AA8 S6ac. ***Continues*** *Arkansas. State Dept. of Public Welfare. Arkansas Department of Public Welfare Annual Report.*

US
**ARNOVA NEWS.** **Main/Corp** Association for Research on Nonprofit Organizations and Voluntary Action. Vol. 18, No. 3/4 (1990)-. English. Four times a year. $110.00 Comes with Association for Research on Nonprofit Organizations and Voluntary Action membership. Arnova, Route 2 Box 696, Pullman WA 99163. **Tel** (509)332-3417, FAX (509)332-3417, (509)335-2863. **ED** Carl Milofsky. **Circ:** 500. ***Continues*** *Association of Voluntary Action Scholars. AVAS Newsletter.*

NE/0168-2857
**AS. MAANDBLAD AKTIVITEITENSEKTOR.** (AS.). [AS, Maandbl. akt.sekt.]. **VFOAT** Maandblad Aktiviteitensektor. (1980)-. Periodical. Dutch. mo (11 issues). Fl93.87. Infolio BV, Postbus 16500, 2500 BM Den Haag Netherlands. **Tel** 011 31 70 3819900, FAX 011 31 70 3632338. **UDC** 615.85. ***Absorbed*** *Ligament, 0024-3264.*

II/0518-8881
**ASIAN NEWS SHEET.** [Asian news sheet]. **Added/Corp** International Social Security Association. Regional Office for Asia and Oceania. (1975)-. English. Four times a year (Jan., Apr., July, Oct.). Free. International Social Security Association, Case Postale 1, CH-1211 Geneva 22 Switzerland. **Tel** 011 41 22 7996617, FAX 011 41 22 7986385. **LC** HD7090; .A8. **DD** 368.4/0095. ***Continues*** *Asian News Sheet (New Delhi, India : 1959).*
**Desc:** Describes trends and developments in social security programs in the region.
**Ind/Abst** Int. Labour Doc.; LABORDOC.

US
**ASSISTANCE PAYMENTS STATISTICS.**
**See** Sociology-Abstracting, Bibliographies and Statistics.

IT/0392-1026
**ASSISTENZA SOCIALE, L'.** [Assist. soc.]. **Added/Corp** Patronato Nazionale per l'Assistenza Sociale. INCA (Organization) Confederazione Generale Italiana del Lavoro. Vol. 1 (Jan. 1947)-. Periodical. Italian. bm. L40000 Italy; L80000 other. Ediesse / Rome, Via Dei Frentani 4A, 00185 Rome Italy. **Tel** 011 39 6 44870286, 44870288, FAX 011 39 6 4481260. **LC** HV4; .A83. **DD** 360.5.
**Ind/Abst** Saf. Health Work.

CN/0316-9332
**ASSOCIATION FOR RETARDED CHILDREN OF BRITISH COLUMBIA. ANNUAL CONFERENCE (MINUTES).** ***Title Change.*** (ANNUAL CONFERENCE.). **Main/Corp** Association for Retarded Children of British Columbia. Conference. Began publication with 1958 issue. Periodical. English. an. British Columbis Association for the Mentally Retarded, 221-119 West Pender Street, Vancouver BC V6B 1S5. **DD** 362.3/06/2711. ***Continued by*** *British Columbia Association for the Mentally Retarded. Conference. Annual Conference.*

ET
**ASWEA: JOURNAL FOR SOCIAL WORK EDUCATION IN AFRICA.** **Main/Corp** Association for Social Work Education in Africa. **VFOAT** Journal for Social Work Education in Africa. V. 1- June 1974-. English. an. PO Box 1176, Addis Ababa Ethiopia. **Tel** 126827 ADDIS ABALA. **LC** HV11; .A752A. **DD** 361/.007/116. **Circ:** 200 (ctrl). ***Supersedes*** *Association for Social Work Education in Africa. Newsletter. Bulletin.*

FR/0985-0120
**ATHAREP.** (BULLETIN DE L'ATHAREP.). **VFOAT** Association pour le Travail des Handicapes dans la Recherche Publique. (1986)-. Bulletin. French. sa. 140.00F. Atharep, 3 rue Michel Ange, 75794 Paris Cedex 16 France. **Tel** 011 33 1 44275970. **UDC** 362.4. **Circ:** 150 (ctrl).
**Desc:** Association activities, news, and studies on special subjects dealing with employment of handicapped persons.

US
**AUDIT GUIDE AND STANDARDS FOR COMMUNITY DEVELOPMENT BLOCK GRANT RECIPIENTS.** Government Publication. English. ir. US Department of Housing and Urban Development, 451 Seventh Street SW, Washington DC 20401. **Tel** (202)708-0980, FAX (202)708-0299.

AT/0725-3109
**AUSTRALIAN BUSINESS INDEX.** [Aust. bus. index]. (1981)-. Periodical. English. mo. 880.00Aus$. Australian Business Index, PO Locked Bag 2100, South Yarra, Victoria 3141 Australia. **Tel** 011 61 3 8827344, FAX 011 61 3 8826837, telex 70508. **DD** 016.338005. Index available (free). **Circ:** 350. available on microfiche. ***Absorbed*** *Austalasian Industry Reporter.*
**Desc:** Reference guide featuring news on all aspects of Australian industries.
**Ind/Abst** APAIS, Aust. Public Aff. Inf. Ser. (1977-19??).

AT/0312-8970
**AUSTRALIAN CHILD AND FAMILY WELFARE.** ***Title Change.*** [Aust. child fam. welf.]. (1???)-(19??). Periodical. English. qt. The Children's Bureau Australia, PO Box 686, Mulgrave NO VIC 3170 Australia. **Tel** 61 3 5589100. **DD** 362.70994. ***Continued by*** *Children Australia, 1035-0772.*
**Ind/Abst** APAIS, Aust. Public Aff. Inf. Ser. (1977-19??).

AT/0157-6321
**AUSTRALIAN JOURNAL OF SOCIAL ISSUES, THE.** [Aust. j. soc. issues]. **Added/Corp** Committee for Post-Graduate Study in Social Work. Australian Council of Social Service. Vol. 1 (Spring 1961)-. Periodical. English. qt. 75.00Aus$ Australia; 95.00Aus$ other (institutions); 45.00Aus$ Australia; $65.00Aus$ other (individuals). Australian Council of Social Service, 8-24 Kippax Street, Surry Hills 2010, New South Wales Australia. **Tel** 011 61 2 2123277. **ED** Sheila Shaver. **LC** HN841; .A88. Index available. cum. index. **Bk Rev. Ad Acc. Pr Rev. Circ:** 1,000 (ctrl). available on microfilm and microfiche from University Microfilms International (UMI). Documents available from The Genuine Article.
**Desc:** A forum for discussion to stimulate debate and action on significant and controversial social issues currently of public concern.
**Ind/Abst** APAIS, Aust. Public Aff. Inf. Ser. (1963-); Appl. Soc. Sci. Index Abstr.; Aust. Educ. Index; Aust. Leg. Mon. Dig.; Crim. Justice Abstr.; Curr. Contents Soc. Behav. Sci.; Geogr. Abstr. Human Geogr. (?-?); Int. Labour Doc.; Linguist. Lang. Behav. Abstr.; Res. Alert [Full Cov.]; Soc. Plann. Policy Dev. Abstr.; Soc. Sci. Cit. Index [Full Cov.]; Soc. Work Abstr. (Summer 1987-) [Select. Cov.]; Sociol. Abstr.

AT/0312-407X
**AUSTRALIAN SOCIAL WORK.** [Aust. soc. work]. **Added/Corp** Australian Association of Social Workers. Vol. 24, No. 3/4 (Sept./Dec. 1971)-. Periodical. English. qt. 80.00Aus$. Australian Association of Social Workers, PO Box 84, Hawker Australian Capital Territory 2614 Australia. **Tel** 011 61 6 2551626. **ED** Elizabeth Rabbitts. Index available. cum. index. **Bk Rev. Ad Acc. Pr Rev. Circ:** 3,500. ***Continues*** *Australian Journal of Social Work, ISSN 0004-9565.*
**Desc:** The theory and practice of social work.
**Ind/Abst** APAIS, Aust. Public Aff. Inf. Ser. (1971-); Appl. Soc. Sci. Index Abstr.; Multicult. Educ. Abstr.; Soc. Work Abstr. [Full Cov.]; Spec. Educ. Needs Abstr.

CN/0824-5193
**BAN THONG TIN (NANAIMO REFUGEE CO-ORDINATION SOCIETY).** (BAN THONG TIN / HOI GIUPNGI TY NAN NANAIMO.). (1981)-. Periodical. Vietnamese. bm. $0.50 per no. Nanaimo Refugee Co-Ordination Society, Suite 225/228 Community Services Facility, 285 Prideaux Street, Nanaimo British Columbia V9R 2N2 Canada. **DD** 362.8/7/0971. ***Continues*** *Ban Thong Tin Cua Hoi Gip Ngi Ty Nan Tai Nanaimo, 0824-5215.*

US/8750-2151
**BAPTIST HOSPITAL FUND BULLETIN.** [Baptist Hosp. Fund bull.]. V. 7, No. 4 (Sept./Oct. 1963)-. Bulletin. English. bm. Baptist Hospital Fund Inc, 1700 University Avenue, St Paul MN 55104. **DD** 362. ***Continues*** *Baptist Hospital Bulletin.*

SW
**BARNOMSORGEN I SIFFROR.** **Added/Corp** Sweden. Socialstyrelsen. (1981)-. Swedish. an. **LC** HV790; .A134.

BE/0775-0234
**BELGISCH TIJDSCHRIFT VOOR SOCIALE ZEKERHEID.** (19??)-. Periodical. Dutch. qt. 900F. Ministerie Van Sociale Voorzor, Zwarte Lievevrouwstraat 3C, 1000 Brussels Belguim. **Tel** 011 32 2 512 7860. Index available. **Bk Rev. Circ:** 2,000.
**Desc:** Upper level scientific journal concentrating on problems relevant to Belgian social security.

CN/1183-1553
**BENEVOLONS! (ST-TITE).** (BENEVOLONS!.). [Benevolons!]. **Added/Corp** Centre d'Action Benevole Normandie. Vol. 1, No 1 (April/May/June 1990)-. Periodical. French. qt. Limited free distribution. Centre d'Action Benevole Normandie, CP 341, St-Tite, Quebec G0X 3H0 Canada. **DD** 361.7.

UK
**BEREAVEMENT.** (19??)-. Monographic series. English. ir. $35.00. International Universities Press Inc., 59 Boston Post Road, PO Box 1524, Madison CT 06443-1524. **Tel** (203)245-4000, FAX (203)245-0775, telex 282986 IUP BK.

US/1071-7366
**BEREAVEMENT & LOSS RESOURCES.**
**See** Psychology.

UK/0268-2621
**BEREAVEMENT CARE.** [Bereave. care]. (1982)-. Periodical. English. Three times a year (Mar., July, Aug.). £11.00 (individuals), £20.00 (institutions) UK; £13.00 (individuals), £23.00 (institutions) Europe; £20.00 (individuals), £30.00 (institutions) other. Cruse-Bereavement Care, 126 Sheen Road, Richmond Surrey TW9 1UR, England. **Tel** 081 940 4818. **ED** Dr. Colin Murray Parkes and Dr. Dora Black. **DD** 362.8. Index available (Dec. iss.). cum. index. **Bk Rev**, (Qty: 16). **Ad Acc, Adv Mgr:** P. Scowen. **Pr Rev. Circ:** 2,000.
**Desc:** Information on helping increase understanding of bereavement.

DK
**BERETNING - SOCIAL- OG SUNDHEDSFORVALTNINGEN I KBENHAVN.** **Main/Corp** Copenhagen. Social- Og Sundhedsforvaltningen. 1976-. Danish. Planlaegningsafdelingen, Svendborggade 5, 2100 Kobenhavn Denmark. **LC** HV325.C6; C67A.

AU/0587-2200
**BERICHT UBER DIE SOZIALE LAGE. SOZIALBERICHT, TATIGKEITSBERICHT DES BUNDESMINISTERIUMS FUER SOZIALE VERWALTUNG.** **Main/Corp** Austria. Bundesministerium fur Soziale Verwaltung. (19??)-. German. an. Free on request. Bundesministerium fuer Soziale Verwaltung, Stubenring 1, A-1010 Vienna Austria. **Tel** 011 43 1 75006232. **LC** WMLC L 83/2070.

BL
**BIBLIOGRAFIA ANALITICA EM BEM-ESTAR SOCIAL.** 1- 1974-. Portuguese. Secretaria de Benn-Estar Social, rua Pedro de Toledo 1529, 04039 Sao Paulo Brazil. **LC** Z7164.C4; B47; HV40.

SZ/0006-1476
**BIBLIOGRAPHIE UNIVERSELLE DE SECURITE SOCIALE.** [Bibliogr. univers. secur. soc.]. **VFOAT** World Bibliography of Social Security; Bibliografia Mundial de Seguridad Social; Weltbibliographie der Sozialen Sicherheit. Vol. 1 (1963)-. Multiple languages (French, English, German and Spanish). sa. 50.00F Switzerland; $24.74 US. Association Internationale de Securite Sociale, Case Postale 1, CH-1211 Geneva 22 Switzerland. **LC** Z7164.L1; B52; HD7091. **DD** 016.3684. ***Continues in part*** *Bulletin of the International Social Security Review.*

US/0147-3492
**BIENNIAL BUDGET REQUEST - WISCONSIN DEPARTMENT OF HEALTH AND SOCIAL SERVICES.** **Main/Corp** Wisconsin. Dept. of Health and Social Services. English. be. Department of Health & Social Services / Wisconsin, 1 West Wilson Street, PO Box 309, Madison WI 53701. **LC** HV86; .W622. **DD** 353.9/775/0084.

US/0146-2423
**BIENNIAL REPORT - GOVERNOR'S ADVOCACY COMMITTEE FOR CHILDREN AND YOUTH.** **Main/Corp** Wisconsin. Governor's Advocacy Committee for Children and Youth. English. be. Governor's Advocacy Committee for Children and Youth, 106 East Doty Street, Suite 208, Madison WI. **LC** HV742.W5; W56A. **DD** 362.7/09775.

SZ/0253-0406
**BIENNIAL REPORT - LEAGUE OF RED CROSS SOCIETIES.** [Bienn. rep. - Leag. Red Cross Soc.]. **Main/Corp** League of Red Cross Societies. 1977/78-. English. be. League of Red Cross Societies, Case Postale 276, 1211 Geneva 19 Switzerland. **LC** HV560; .L4. **DD** 361.7/7. **NLM** W1 LE264C. ***Continues*** *Annual Report - League of Red Cross Societies.*

US/0093-3988
**BIENNIAL REPORT - NORTH CAROLINA. STATE DEPARTMENT OF SOCIAL SERVICES OF THE DEPARTMENT OF HUMAN RESOURCES.** (BIENNIAL REPORT.). **Main/Corp** North Carolina. Dept. of Social Services. English. be. Department of Social Services / North Carolina, 325 North Salisbury Street, Raleigh NC 27611. **LC** HV86; .N8482. **DD** 353.9/756/0084.

US
**BIENNIAL REPORT / NORTH DAKOTA, DEPT. OF HUMAN SERVICES.** **Main/Corp** North Dakota. Dept. of Human Services. **VFOAT** North Dakota Human Services. (1987)-. English. be. North Dakota Department of Human Services, State Capitol, 600 East Boulevard, Bismarck ND 58505. **Tel** (701)224-2310, FAX (701)224-2359. **LC** HV98.N9; N68A. **DD** 353.97840084/06. **Circ:** 600 (ctrl). ***Continues*** *Human Services in North Dakota, 8755-1659.*

**Desc:** Report describes function, evaluation, program inventory and cost analysis summary of the Department of Human Services.

CN/1186-818X
**BILAN SOCIO-ECONOMIQUE, REGION DE LA GASPESIE--ILES-DE-LA-MADELEINE.** [Bilan socio-econ. reg. Gaspesie-Iles-de-la-Madeleine]. **Added/Corp** Office de Planification et de Developpement du Quebec. (1991)-. French. ir. **DD** 361.6.

CN/0700-8198
**BJULETEN SUSPILNOJI SLUZLY KANADY.** (BIULETEN SUSPILNOI SLUZHBY UKRAINTSIV KANADY. BULLETIN, UKRAINIAN CANADIAN SOCIAL SERVICES.). **Added/Corp** Suspilna Sluzhba Urkaintsiv Kanady. **VFOAT** Bulletin, Ukrainian Canadian Social Services. (197?)-. Bulletin. Ukrainian (summaries and/or abstracts in English). sa. Ukrainian Canadian Social Services, 2445 Bloor Street West, Toronto Ontario M6S 1P7 Canada. **DD** 361.7/06/271. ***Supersedes*** *Biuleten Ukrainskoi Kanadskoi Suspilnoi Sluzhby, 0700-818X.*

US/0732-7269
**BLACK CAUCUS.** ***Suspended.*** (BLACK CAUCUS : THE JOURNAL OF THE NATIONAL ASSOCIATION OF BLACK SOCIAL WORKERS.). Vol. 13, No. 1 (Spring 1982)-Suspended. Periodical. English. sa. National Association of Black Social Workers, 642 Beckwith Ct SW, Atlanta GA 30314. ***Continues*** *Black Caucus Journal.*

US
**BLACK CHILD ADVOCATE.** **Added/Corp** National Black Child Development Institute. Black Child Development Institute. Vol. 1 (1972)-. Periodical. English. qt. $12.50. National Black Children's Development Institution Inc, 1023 15th Street NW, Suite 600, Washington DC 20005. **Tel** (202)387-1281. **ED** Merlene Alicia Vassall. **Circ:** 1,500.
**Desc:** Issues affecting black children and families in education, child care, child welfare, health, and public policy.

CN/1180-4912
**BLOOD DONOR DIGEST.** (BLOOD DONOR DIGEST : A PUBLICATION OF THE TORONTO CENTRE OF THE CANADIAN RED CROSS.). [Blood donor dig.]. **Added/Corp** Canadian Red Cross Society. Toronto Centre. Vol. 1, No. 1 (Summer 1990)-. Periodical. English. qt. Limited free distribution. Canadian Red Cross Society, Blood Programme, 95 Wellesley Street East, Toronto Ont. M4Y 1H6. **DD** 362.1/784/0971354105.

US/1049-7986
**BNA'S MEDICARE REPORT.** [BNA's medicare rep.]. **Added/Corp** Bureau of National Affairs (Washington, D.C.). **VFOAT** Medicare Report. Vol. 1, No. 1 (May 18, 1990)-. Periodical. English. bw. $662.00. Bureau of National Affairs Inc., 9435 Key West Avenue, Rockville MD 20850. **Tel** (800)372-1033, (301)258-1033, FAX (301)948-5823. **DD** 368. **[CCC].**

SP/0212-7180
**BOLETIN DE ESTADISTICAS LABORALES.** **See** Economics-Labor.

UY
**BOLETIN ESTADISTICO - ASIGNACIONES FAMILIARES.** **Main/Corp** Asignaciones Familiares (Uruguay). No. 1- July 1976-. Spanish. Asignaciones Familiares Oficina Central, San Jose 1132, Montevideo Uruguay. **LC** HV700.U7; A83A. **DD** 362.8/282/09895.

MX
**BOLETIN INFORMATIVO (INTER-AMERICANA CONFERENCE ON SOCIAL SECURITY).** (BOLETIN INFORMATIVO / CONFERENCIA INTERAMERICANA DE SEGURIDAD SOCIAL.). **Added/Corp** Inter-Americana Conference on Social Security. (19??)-. Periodical. Spanish. bm. Secretaria General del Comite Permanente, Interamericano de Seguridad Social Unidad Independencia, San Jeronimo Lidice, Apartado Postal 20532 Mexico 20 DF. **LC** HD7090; .B64. **DD** 368.4/0097.

IT
**BOLLETTINO STATISTICO QUADRIMESTRALE (ISTITUTO NAZIONALE DELLA PREVIDENZA SOCIALE (ITALY)).** (BOLLETTINO STATISTICO QUADRIMESTRALE / ISTITUTO NAZIONALE DELLA PREVIDENZA SOCIALE.). Italian. Three times a year. **LC** HD7184; .I84A. **DD** 368.4/00945. ***Continues*** *Bollettino Statistico Quadrimestrale (Istituto Nazionale della Previdenza Sociale (Italy). Servizio Statistico Attuariale).*

UK/0965-450X
**BOOTH'S NIC BRIEF.** **See** Insurance.

JA
**BOSAI ROPPO.** **Main/Corp** Japan. **Added/Corp** Japan. Shobocho. Bosai Kyukyuka. Japan. Shobocho. Bosaika. (19??)-. Periodical. Japanese. ¥2500. Zenkoku Kajo Horei Shuppan Company Ltd., Dai 1 Zenkoku Biru 18 Saneicho, Shinjukuku Tokyoto 160 Japan. **LC** LAW.

US
**BREAD AND JUSTICE.** **Added/Corp** Interfaith Hunger Coalition of Southern California. Vol. 1, Issue 1 (March 1989)-. Periodical. English. bm (Jan., Mar., May, July, Sept., Nov.). $15.00 (one year), $25.00 (two year). Bread & Justice, 1010 South Flower Street/500, Los Angeles CA 90015. **Tel** (213)746-7500. ***Continues*** *Bread & Justice, 0890-8613.*

US/1045-1005
**BREAD FOR THE WORLD NEWSLETTER.** [Bread World newsl.]. **Added/Corp** Bread for the World (Organization). Vol. 1, No. 1 (July/Aug. 1989)-. Periodical. English. Eight times a year. $25.00. Bread for the World, 1100 Wayne Avenue, Suite 1000, Silver Springs MO 20910. **Tel** (301)608-2400, FAX (301)608-2401. **ED** Carole Zimmerman. **DD** 363. **Circ:** 41,000. ***Formed by the union of*** *Bread* ***and*** *Action Alert.*
**Desc:** News of the hunger movement. Progress of hunger legislation and background articles on issues relevant to workship, hunger and proverty.

CN/0713-4266
**BREAKING THE SILENCE (OTTAWA, ONT.).** ***Ceased.*** **See** Women's Interests.

CN/0384-9058
**BRISE DE L'EST, LA.** First issue in Sept. 1971. Periodical. French. ir. $2.00. Les Retraites a l'Action, c/o M Gertrude Genest, 337 rue Moreault, Rimouski Quebec G5L 1P4 Canada. **DD** 362.6/3/0971477.

CN/0849-9888
**BRITISH COLUMBIA ASSOCIATION FOR COMMUNITY LIVING NEWS.** **See** Medical Science and Technology-Psychiatry.

UK/0045-3102
**BRITISH JOURNAL OF SOCIAL WORK, THE.** [Br. j. soc. work]. **Added/Corp** British Association of Social Workers. Vol. 1, No. 1 (Apr. 1971)-. Periodical. English. bm. £88.00 UK and Europe; $165.00 other. Oxford University Press, Walton Street, Oxford OX2 6DP England. **Tel** 011 44 865 56767, FAX 011 44 865 267773, telex 837330 OXPRES G. **(Subscription address:** Oxford University Press / USA, Journals Marketing Department, Oxford University Press, 2001 Evans Road, Cary NC 27513.**) ED** Barbara L. Hudson. **LC** HV1; .B67. **DD** 361/.005. **NLM** W1 BR636. **CODEN** BJSWAS. **[CCC].** Index available. **Bk Rev. Ad Acc. Pr Rev.** available on microfilm and microfiche from University Microfilms International (UMI). Documents available from The Genuine Article. ***Formed by the union of*** *British Journal of Psychiatric Social Work* ***and*** *Social Work.*
**Desc:** Covers every aspect of social work, with papers reporting research, discussing practice and examining principles and theories. An essential reading for social workers, social services administrators and social work educators who wish to keep abreast of theoretical and empirical developments in the field. Includes abstracts from law, psychology and psychiatry, sociology, etc.
**Ind/Abst** Appl. Soc. Sci. Index Abstr.; Cumul. Index Nurs. Allied Health Lit.; Curr. Contents Soc. Behav. Sci.; Hum. Resour. Abstr.; Int. Bibliogr. Sociol.; Linguist. Lang. Behav. Abstr.; Middle East Abstr. Index; Psychol. Abstr. (1971-); PsycINFO; PsycLit; Res. Alert [Full Cov.]; Sage Fam. Stud. Abstr.; Sage Race Relat. Abstr.; Soc. Plann. Policy Dev. Abstr.; Soc. Sci. Cit. Index [Full Cov.]; Soc. Work Abstr. (Spring, Summer 1987-) [Full Cov.]; Sociol. Abstr.; Sociol. Educ. Abstr.; Stud. Women Abstr.

IS/0334-4525
**BRYNWT WSTYH HBRTYT.** [brynwt wstyh hbrtyt]. **VFOAT** Crime and Social Deviance. (1972)-. Periodical. Hebrew. qt. $14.00. Bar-Ilan University Press, Department of Criminology, Ramat-Gan 52900 Israel. **Tel** 011 972 3 5318355, FAX 011 972 3 3476 01. **ED** Israel Nachshon. **UDC** 343.9. Index available. **Bk Rev. Ad Acc. Circ:** 500.
**Ind/Abst** Crim. Justice Abstr.; Sociol. Abstr.

US
**BUDGET RECOMMENDATIONS. EXECUTIVE SUMMARY / MASSACHUSETTS EXECUTIVE OFFICE OF HUMAN SERVICES.** **Main/Corp** Massachusetts. Executive Office of Human Services. **VFOAT** Executive Summary. (19??)-. English. **LC** HV86; .M4643a. **DD** 353.97440072/22.

CN/1183-269X
**BULLETIN DBSF.** [Bull. DBSF]. **Added/Corp** Groupe DBSF. Vol. 1, No 1 (1991)-. Bulletin. French. Limited free distribution. Groupe DBSF, 3573 Est Rue Ontario, Montreal Quebec H1W 1R8 Canada. **DD** 362.6.

CN/1187-5038
**BULLETIN DE L'AMIE.** ***Title Change.*** (BULLETIN DE L'AMIE / AIDE MEDICALE INTERNATIONALE A L'ENFANCE.). [Bull. AMIE]. **Added/Corp** Aide Medicale Internationale a l'Enfance. **VAT** Bulletin de l'Aide Medicale Internationale a l'Enfance. Vol. 1, No 1 (Oct. 1991)-Vol. 1 (1992). Bulletin. French. ir. Aide Medicale Internationale a l'Enfance, CP 282, La Pocatiere, Quebec G0R 1Z0 Canada. **DD** 362.7/08/609172405. ***Continues*** *Amie (La Pocatiere, Quebec)., 1184-0846.* ***Continued by*** *Revue de l'AMIE, 1192-3636.*

CN/0226-9880
**BULLETIN DE L'AQDR, LE.** [Bull. AQDR]. Bulletin. French. bm. Free. Association Quebecoise pour la Defense des Retraites et Pre-Retraites, 1850 rue Bercy Bureau/Suite 113A, Montreal Quebec H2K 2V2 Canada. **DD** 362.6/06/0714.

CN/1189-3524
**BULLETIN DE LIAISON ACCESSSIBLE.** [Bull. liaison access.]. **Added/Corp** Alliance des Communautes Culturelles Pour l'Egalite Dans l Sante et les Services Sociaux. **VFOAT** Accesssible; Accessible. Vol. 1, No 1 (Mar 1991)-. Bulletin. French (summaries and/or abstracts in English). qt. Limited free distribution. Alliance des Communautes Culturelles pour L'Egalite dans la Sante et les Services Sociaux, Bureau 331, 3680 Jeanne-Mance, Montreal Quebec H2X 2K5 Canada. **DD** 362.

CN/0316-4454
**BULLETIN DE L'INSTITUT DE READAPTATION DE MONTREAL, LE.** [Bull. Inst. readapt. Montr.]. V. 27, No. 1, (Aug. 1983)-. Bulletin. French (English). qt. Free. Rehabilitation Institute of Montreal, 6300 Darlington Avenue, Montreal Quebec H3S 2J4 Canada. **ED** Claude Tessier. **DD** 362.4/06/0714. **Ad Acc. Circ:** 8,500 (ctrl). ***Continues*** *Rehabilitation Institute of Montreal. Bulletin.*
**Desc:** Information on IRM operations, services and research.

CN/1186-8759
**BULLETIN DE L'IRDAP : UN SERVICE D'INFORMATION DE L'INSTITUT DE RECHERCHES EN DONS ET EN AFFAIRES PUBLIQUES.** [Bull. IRDAP]. **Added/Corp** Institut de Recherches en Dons et en Affaires Publiques. **VAT** Bulletin de l'Institut de Recherches en Dons et en Affaires Publiques. Vol. 1, No 1 (Spring 1991)-. Bulletin. French. Three times a year. Free for Members. L'Institut de Recherches en dons et en Affaires Publiques, 255 Chemin Smyth, Ottawa Ontario K1H 8M7 Canada. **DD** 361.7.

CN/0713-4290
**BULLETIN DE NOUVELLES - CORPORATION PROFESSIONNELLE DES TRAVAILLEURS SOCIAUX DU QUEBEC.** (BULLETIN DE NOUVELLES.). [Bull. nouv. - Corp. prof. trav. soc. Que.]. **Added/Corp** Corporation Professionnelle des Travailleurs Sociaux du Quebec. No. 1, (April 1982)-. Bulletin. French (English; summaries and/or abstracts in English). Five times a year. Bulletin de Nouvelles, c/o Corporation Professionnelle des Travailleurs Sociaux du Quebec, 5757 Avenue Descelles, Montreal Quebec H3S 2C3 Canada. **Tel** (514)731-3925. **ED** Germaine Dionne. **DD** 361.006/0714. **Ad Acc. Circ:** 2,500 (ctrl). ***Continues*** *Corporation Professionnelle des Travailleurs Sociaux du Quebec. Bulletin, 0318-9627.*

FR
**BULLETIN DU SERVICE SOCIAL DES CAISSES D'ASSURANCE MALADIE.** **See** Insurance.

SZ
**BULLETIN / INTERNATIONAL COMMITTEE OF THE RED CROSS.** **Added/Corp** International Committee of the Red Cross. **VFOAT** ICRC Bulletin. (19??)-. Bulletin. English. mo.
**Ind/Abst** Hum. Rights Intern. Rep.

CN/0822-9309
**BULLETIN NATIONAL DU CCA.** [Bull. natl. CCA]. **VFOAT** Bulletin National CCA; Bulletin National. **VAT** Bulletin National du Conseil Canadien des Aveugles; Bulletin National - Conseil Canadien des Aveugles. Bulletin. French. Conseil Canadien des Aveugles, Bureau 610/220 rue Dundas, London Ontario N6A 1H3 Canada. **DD** 362.4/1/06071. ***Continues*** *Bulletin de Nouvelles National du CCA, Communis., 0826-2551.*

CN/0317-8021
**BULLETIN OF CANADIAN WELFARE LAW.** Vol. 1; Feb. 1972-. Bulletin. English. ir. Free. National Council of Welfare, Brooke Claxton Building, Ottawa Ontario K1A 0K9 Canada.

CN/1187-4996
**BULLETIN - ONTARIO. SOCIAL ASSISTANCE REVIEW BOARD.** (BULLETIN / COMMISSION DE REVISION DE L'AIDE SOCIALE.). [Bull. - Ont., Soc. Assist. Rev. Board]. **Main/Corp** Ontario. Commission de revision de l'Aide Sociale. **VFOAT** Bulletin. **VAT** Bulletin - Ontario. Commission de Revision de l'Aide Sociale. Vol. 1, No 1 (Oct. 1991)-. Bulletin. French (English). sa. **DD** 354.7130084.

CN/0822-5699
**BULLETIN SSQ RESPECTING SOCIAL LAWS.** See Law.

CN/0713-8431
**BULLETIN SSQ SUR LES LOIS SOCIALES. FRANCAIS.** (BULLETIN SSQ SUR LES LOIS SOCIALES.). [Bull. SSQ lois soc.]. **VAT** Bulletin Services de Sante du Quebec sur les Lois Sociales. Vol. 9, No. 1 (Jan. 1980)-. Bulletin. French (English). an. Free. Mutuelle d'Assurance Groupe, 2525 Boulevard Laurier, CP 10500, Sainte-Foy Quebec G1V 4H6 Canada. **Tel** (418)651-7000, FAX (418)657-8426. **ED** Gerard A Boudreau. **DD** 344.714/02. **Circ:** 85,000 French, 5,000 English (ctrl). ***Continues*** *Bulletin SSQ, 0713-0120.*
**Desc:** Provides information (up-to-date on January 1st. of each year) on Canadian and Quebec social laws.

US
**BULLETIN / STATE COMMUNITIES AID ASSOCIATION.** **Added/Corp** State Communities Aid Association. **VFOAT** SCAA Bulletin. Vol. 1, No. 1 (Jan. 1986)-. Bulletin. English. Twelve times a year. $40.00 US; $75.00 others. State Communities Aid Association, 1 Columbia Place, Albany NY 12207. **Tel** (518)463-1896. ***Formed by the union of*** *Albany Bulletin on Health and Welfare Legislation of the State Communities Aid Association. Bulletin* ***and*** *SCAA Activity Update.*

IO
**BULLETIN STATISTIK DEPARTEMEN SOSIAL (INDONESIA).** **Main/Corp** Indonesia. Departemen Sosial. Bulletin. Indonesian. D/A Biro Perencanaan & Evaluasi, Jl Ir H Juanda No 36, Jakarta Indonesia. **LC** HV401; .D45C.

●CN/1195-9231
**C-JEUNES.** (C-JEUNES : BULLETIN D'INFORMATION DES CENTRES JEUNESSE DE MONTREAL.). [C-jeunes]. **Added/Corp** Centres Jeunesse de Montreal. **VFOAT** Cjeunes; Ces Jeunes. (1993)-. Periodical. French. ir. Free. CSSMM / Centre de Services Sociaux du Montreal Metropolitain, 1001 Est de Maison Neuve, Montreal Quebec H2L 4R5 Canada. **Tel** (514)527-2761. **DD** 362.7. ***Continues*** *Info 9., 0228-2453.*

US/0192-0618
**C/O : JOURNAL OF ALTERNATIVE HUMAN SERVICES.** **VFOAT** Journal of Alternative Human Services. V. 1- Aug. 1973-. Periodical. English. qt. $12.00. Community Congress of San Diego, 1172 Morena Blvd., San Diego CA 92110. **LC** HV89; .C2. **DD** 361/.005.

US/1052-3103
**CACD JOURNAL.** [CACD j.]. **VFOAT** C.A.C.D. Journal. **VAT** California Association for Counseling and Development Journal. Vol. 5 (1983/84)-. Periodical. English. an. $8.00. California Association for Counseling and Development, 654 East Commonwealth Avenue, Fullerton CA 92631. **Tel** (714)871-6460. **ED** Dr Patricia Wickwire. **DD** 361. **Bk Rev. Ad Acc. Circ:** 3,000 (ctrl). ***Continues*** *News Journal (California Association for Counseling and Development).*

FR/1148-4683
**CAHIERS DE L'EUROPE PARIS.** (CAHIERS DE L'EUROPE ET DE LA FRANCOPHONIE.). **Main/Corp** Union Nationale des Associations de Parents d'enfants Inadaptes. (1990)-. Periodical. French. Five times a year. 200.00F France; 260.00F other. UNAPEI, 15 rue Coysevox, 75876 Paris Cedex 18 France. **Tel** 011 33 1 42638433. **UDC** 364.26.
**Desc:** Legislation for mentally disabled persons in Europe and French speaking countries. International events and demonstrations about mentally disabled persons.

CN/1188-4045
**CAHIERS PROFESSIONNELS, LES.** [Cah. prof.]. **Added/Corp** Centre des Services Sociaux Richelieu. Vol. 1, No 1 (May 1991)-. Periodical. French. Limited Free Distribution. Centre des Services Sociaux Richelieu, 25 Boulevard Lafayette, Longueuil Quebec J4K 5C8 Canada. **DD** 362.7.

CN/0824-5444
**CALGARY COMMUNITY SERVICES DIRECTORY.** [Calg. community serv. dir.]. **Added/Corp** Calgary (Alta.). AID Centre. (1978)-. Directory. English. an. 25.00Can$. City of Calgary Public Information Department, P.O Box 2100, 8113 Station M, Calgary Alberta T2P 2M5 Canada. **Tel** (403)268-4656, telex 4220031. **DD** 361/.0025/71233. Index available. cum. index. **Circ:** 1,500.
**Desc:** Directory of more than 340 non-profit agencies located in Calgary which provide social or related services; includes alphabetical and subject indexes.

US/0190-1591
**CALIFORNIA CRIPPLED CHILDREN SERVICES STATISTICAL REPORT.** See Sociology-Abstracting, Bibliographies and Statistics.

US
**CALIFORNIA STATE PLAN FOR REHABILITATION FACILITIES.** **Main/Corp** California. Dept. of Rehabilitation. Community Resources Development Section. English. an. California Department of Rehabilitation, 1500 Fifth Street, Sacramento CA 95814. **LC** HD7256.U6; C27D. **DD** 362/.0425.

US
**CALIFORNIA UPDATE : LEGISLATION, REGULATIONS AND NEWS AFFECTING INDIVIDUALS WITH SPECIAL NEEDS / EDITED BY DOUGLAS BRITTON.** (19??)-. Periodical. English. Ten times a year (Except Jan. & Aug.). $104.00 (regular); $154.00 combination of Human Service Moneysource & California Update. California Update, 4019 Glenolive Court, Sacramento CA 95821. **Tel** (916)483-6397.

SP
**CAMPANA CONTRA EL HAMBRE EN EL MUNDO.** Spanish. qt. 350.00ptas Europe; 400.00ptas other. Comite Catolico, Alfonso XI 4 2, Madrid 14 Spain.

CN/0842-3202
**CANADA HEALTH ACT ANNUAL REPORT.** [Can. Health Act, annu. rep.]. **Main/Corp** Canada. Health and Welfare Canada. **VFOAT** Loi Canadienne sur la Sante, Rapport Annuel. (1984/1985)-. English (French). an. Free. Health and Welfare of Canada Information Directorate, Ottawa Ontario K1A 0K9 Canada. **Tel** (613)954-8576. **LC** HD7102.C2; C265. **DD** 362.1/0971. **NLM** W2; DC2 H34ce. **Circ:** 1,200 (ctrl). ***Formed by the union of*** *Hospital Insurance and Diagnostic Services, Annual Report, 0713-0430* ***and*** *Medical Care, Annual Report, 0710-8613.*
**Desc:** Annual report on the operation of provincial/territorial health care insurance plans.

CN/0226-0409
**CANADIAN BOOK OF CHARITIES.** (THE CANADIAN BOOK OF CHARITIES. LE VOLUME CANADIEN DES OEUVRES DE CHARITE.). [Can. book charities]. **VFOAT** Le Volume Canadien des Oeuvres de Charite. (1979)-. English (French). an. 14.95Can$. Mavora Publications, Canadian Book of Charities, 51 Bucks Place, Woodbridge Ontario L4L 3P9 Canada. **Tel** (905)851-0555. **(Subscription address:** Interantional Press Publishers, 90 Nolan Court #23, Markham, Ontario L3R 4L9 Canada.**)** **DD** 361/.0025/71. **Circ:** 13,000 (ctrl).

CN/0847-947X
**CANADIAN EMERGENCY NEWS.** See Public Health and Safety.

CN/0713-3936
**CANADIAN JOURNAL OF COMMUNITY MENTAL HEALTH.** [Can. j. community ment. health]. **VFOAT** Revue Canadienne de Sante Mentale Communautaire. Vol. 1, No. 1 (March 1982)-. Periodical. English (French; summaries and/or abstracts in French). sa. 40.00Can$ Canada; $36.00 US; $40.00 other. Wilfrid Laurier University Press, 75 University Avenue West, Waterloo Ontario N2L 3C5 Canada. **Tel** (519)884-1970, FAX (519)725-1399. **ED** Edward M. Bennett, Maurice Payette and Barry Trute. **DD** 362.2/0971. **Bk Rev. Ad Acc. Circ:** 500.
**Desc:** An interdisciplinary journal with interest in the promotion of positive mental health and the prevention of mental health problems in the community setting.
**Ind/Abst** Child Dev. Abstr. Bibliogr.; EMBASE; Hum. Resour. Abstr. (?-?); PAIS Int. Print (1991); Psychol. Abstr. (1983-); PsycINFO; PsycLit; Soc. Work Abstr. [Select. Cov.].

CN/0836-303X
**CANADIAN REVIEW OF SOCIAL POLICY (1987).** (CANADIAN REVIEW OF SOCIAL POLICY: JOURNAL OF THE SOCIAL POLICY AND ADMINISTRATION NETWORK.). [Can. rev. soc. policy]. **Added/Corp** Social Policy and Administration Network. University of Regina. Social Administration Research Unit. **VFOAT** Revue Canadienne de Politique Sociale. No. 16/17 (Oct. 1986/Jan. 1987)-. Periodical. English (French). Twice a year (May, Oct.). $20.00 (individuals); $30.00 (institutions). Carleton University / School of Social Work, Ottawa Ontario K1S 5B6 Canada. **Tel** (613)786-7511, FAX (613)788-7496. **ED** Gillian Walker (phone: (613)788-5601). **DD** 361.6/1/0971. **Bk Rev. Ad Acc, Adv Mgr:** Gerald de Montigny, **Tel** (613)788-2600 Ext. 5601. **Pr Rev. Circ:** 500 (ctrl). ***Continues*** *SPAN (Social Policy and Administration Network), 0836-3080.*
**Desc:** Assesses and reports on current issues, developments and debates in Canadian social policy and administration. Includes updates on research and publications.

CN/0820-909X
**CANADIAN SOCIAL WORK REVIEW.** [Can. soc. work. rev.]. **Added/Corp** Canadian Association of Schools of Social Work. **VFOAT** Revue Canadienne de Service Social. (1983)-. Periodical. English (French). sa. 36.00Can$ Canada; $41.00 other. Wilfrid Laurier University Press, 75 University Avenue West, Waterloo Ontario N2L 3C5 Canada. **Tel** (519)884-1970, FAX (519)725-1399. **ED** Shan Kar Yelaia and Robert Mayer. **LC** HV105; .C275. **DD** 361/.00971. **CODEN** CSWRE9. **Bk Rev. Ad Acc. Circ:** 350. ***Continues*** *Canadian Journal of Social Work Education, 0316-8565.*
**Desc:** Provides knowledge regarding issues, trends and inquiries relevant to Canadian social work theory, practice, policy, administration and education.
**Ind/Abst** Linguist. Lang. Behav. Abstr.; Soc. Plann. Policy Dev. Abstr.; Soc. Work Abstr. [Select. Cov.]; Sociol. Abstr.

CN
**CANADIAN SUICIDE RATIOS BY LOCAL AREAS AND BY URBAN CENTRES.** **Main/Corp** Canada. Statistics Canada. Vital Statistics Section. **VFOAT** Taux de Suicide du Canada, par Localite et par Centre Urbain. 1970/72-. English (French). ir. $0.70. Information Canada, 171 Slater Street, Ottawa Ontario K1A 0S9 Canada. **Tel** (819)997-1095. **LC** HV6548.C3; C35A. **DD** 312/.276.

US/1042-2285
**CAPITAL CONSORTIUM'S NORTH CAROLINIA GIVING.** [Cap. Consort. N.C. giv.]. **VFOAT** North Carolinia Giving. Vol. 1, No. 1 (Spring 1989)-. Periodical. English. qt. $58.00. Capital Consortium Inc, PO Box 2918, Raleigh NC 27602. **ED** Anita Gunn. **DD** 361. **Circ:** 500.

UK
**CARE IN PLACE: THE INTERNATIONAL JOURNAL OF NETWORKS AND COMMUNITY.** (19??)-. English. Three times a year. $90.00 (US & Canada); £60.00 (UK); £65.00 (other). Routledge, 11 New Fetter Lane, London EC4P 4EE England. **Tel** 071 583 9855, FAX 071 842 2298. **(Subscription address:** Kinokuniya Company Ltd., 38-1 Sakuragaoka 5, chome Setagaya-ku, Tokyo 156 Japan.**)**

GW/0008-6622
**CARITAS-KORRESPONDENZ.** [Caritas-Korresp.]. (1950)-. Periodical. German. mo. DM60.00. Lambertus-Verlag GmbH, Postfach 1026, 79010 Freiburg, Germany. **Tel** 011 49 761 3 68 25 0, FAX 011 49 761 3 70 64. **UDC** 266.3.

CN/0821-0128
**CARP NEWS.** (CARP NEWS / CANADIAN ASSOCIATION OF REHABILITATION PERSONNEL.). [CARP news]. **VAT** Canadian Association of Rehabilitation Personnel News. Periodical. English (French). qt. Canadian Association of Rehabilitation Personnel, Suite 305, 160 Eglinton Avenue East, Toronto Ontario M4P 1G3 Canada. **DD** 362.4/06/071.

UK/0955-7989
**CASE STUDIES FOR PRACTICE.** (1988)-. Monographic series. English. ir. Price varies per volume. Jessica Kingsley Publishers, 118 Pentonville Road, London N1 9JN England. **Tel** 011 44 71 833 2307, FAX 011 44 71 837 2917. **ED** Philip Seed. **NLM** W1; CA901J.
**Desc:** This series draws together case material based on social network analysis to illuminate and explore issues in social work policy and practice.

US/0566-0009
**CASELOAD STATISTICS : STATE VOCATIONAL REHABILITATION AGENCIES.** See Sociology-Abstracting, Bibliographies and Statistics.

US/0731-7433
**CAUSE & FUNCTION.** **VFOAT** Cause and Function. Vol. 1, No. 1 (Fall 1980)-. Periodical. English. sa. 525 West Redwood Street, Box 598, Baltimore MD 21201. **LC** HV1; .C36. **DD** 361/.005.

US/0276-6531
**CDF REPORTS.** [CDF rep.]. **Added/Corp** Children's Defense Fund (U.S.). **VAT** Children's Defense Fund Reports. (19??)-. Periodical. English. mo. $29.95. Children's Defense Fund, 122 C Street NW, Washington DC 20001. **Tel** (202)628-8787. **ED** Virginia Witt. **Circ:** 4,000.
**Desc:** Comprehensive news on education, child care, child health and mental health, foster care and adoption, child abuse and neglect, child nutrition, and child poverty.
**Ind/Abst** Curr. Lit. Fam. Plan.

US/1055-9221
**CDF'S CHILD, YOUTH, AND FAMILY FUTURES CLEARINGHOUSE.** ***Ceased.*** [CDF's child youth fam. futur. clgh.]. **Added/Corp** Children's Defense Fund (U.S.). **VFOAT** Child, Youth, and Family Futures Clearinghouse. **VAT** Children's Defense Fund's Child, Youth, and Family Futures Clearinghouse. (Jan. 1991)-(19??). Monographic series. English. bm. Children's Defense Fund, 122 C Street NW, Washington DC 20001. **Tel** (202)628-8787. **DD** 362. ***Continues*** *Publication of the Adolescent Pregnancy Prevention Clearinghouse, 0899-5591.*

US/0362-0778
**CENSUS OF REQUESTS FOR CHILD WELFARE SERVICES.** ***Ceased.*** **Main/Corp** Child Welfare League of America. Research Center. (19??)-(19??). English. Child Welfare League of America, 440 1st Street Northwest, Suite 310, Washington DC 20001. **Tel** (202)638-2952, FAX (202)638-4004. **LC** HV741; .C5352a. **DD** 362.7/0973.

CN/0381-8152
**CENTRE (CHICOUTIMI).** ***Title Change.*** (LE CENTRE.). [Centre]. **Main/Corp** Conseil de la Sante et des Services Sociaux, Region Saguenay-Lac-St-Jean (Quebec). Vol. 1 (Aug./Sept. 1974)-(1992). Periodical. French. bm. Conseil de la Sante et des Services Sociaux, Region Saguenay-Lac-St-Jean, 930 Est rue J-Cartier, Chicoutimi Quebec G7H 2B1 Canada. **DD** 362/.9714/16. ***Continued by*** *Epicentre, 1192-5019.*

KO
**CHAEHWAL YONGU.** **See** Physically Impaired.

US/0528-7928
**CHALLENGE (HARRISBURG), THE.** (THE CHALLENGE.). V. 1- May 1957-. Periodical. English. bm. **LC** HV98.P4; C5. **NLM** W2 AP4 D7C.
**Desc:** Helps meet the challenge of helping gifted children.
**Ind/Abst** Peace Res. Abstr. J. (1965-1967).

●US/0892-1504
**CHANGES (DEERFIELD BEACH, FLA.).** (CHANGES. THE MAGAZINE FOR PERSONAL GROWTH.). [Changes]. **VFOAT** Changes Magazine. Vol. 1, No. 1 (Feb. 1992)-. English. Six times a year (Jan., Mar., May, July, Sept., Nov.). $18.00. Changes, 3201 Southwest 15th Street, Deerfield Beach FL 33442-9879. **Tel** (305)360-0909. ***Continues*** *Changes (Pompano Beach, Fla.), 0892-1504.*

CN/1184-9339
**CHANTIERS JEUNESSE.** (CHANTIERS JEUNESSE : [BULLETIN].). [Chantiers jeun.]. **Added/Corp** Chantiers Jeunesse. Vol. 5, No 1 (Spring 1991)-. Periodical. French. qt. Limited free distribution. Chantiers Jeunesse, 4545 Avenue Pierre-De-Coubertin, CP 1000, Succursale M, Montreal Quebec H1V 3R2 Canada. **DD** 361.8/06/0714. ***Continues*** *Chantiers en Mouvement, 0849-0015.*

US/0149-1792
**CHARACTERISTICS OF STATE PLANS FOR AID TO FAMILIES WITH DEPENDENT CHILDREN UNDER THE SOCIAL SECURITY ACT, TITLE IV-A, AND FOR GUAM, PUERTO RICO, & VIRGIN ISLANDS.** **Added/Corp** United States. Social Security Administration. Assistance Payments Administration. United States. Office of Family Assistance. State Data and Program Characteristics Branch. **VFOAT** Aid to Families with Dependent Children; Characteristics of State Plans for AFDC. **VAT** Characteristics of State Plans for Aid to Families with Dependent Children Under the Social Security Act, Title Four-A. (197?)-. English. an. Social Security Administration / Washington DC, 4301 Connecticut Avenue NW, Washington DC 20008. **Tel** (202)282-7206, FAX (202)282-7219. **LC** HV95; .N34b. **DD** 362.7/1. ***Continues*** *Aid to Families with Dependent Children, 0363-5686.*

UK/0590-9783
**CHARITIES DIGEST.** [Charities dig.]. **Added/Corp** Family Welfare Association. (19??)-. Periodical. English. an. £15.95. Family Welfare Association, 501 505 Kingsland Road, Dalston London E8 4AU England. **Tel** 011 44 71 2546251. **DD** 361. **NLM** HV 245.A2 A615. ***Continues*** *Annual Charities Digest.*

US/0364-0760
**CHARITIES USA.** [Charities USA]. **Added/Corp** National Conference of Catholic Charities (U.S.). **VAT** Charities United States of America. Vol. 1 (Sept./Oct. 1974)-. Periodical. English. qt. $25.00. Catholic Charities USA, 1731 King Street, Alexandria VA 22314. **Tel** (703)549-1390, FAX (703)549-1656. **ED** Alexandra Peeler. **LC** HV530; .C46. **DD** 360.6. **Bk Rev. Ad Acc, Adv Mgr:** C. Anderson, **Tel** (703)549-1390. **Circ:** 3,500. ***Supersedes*** *Aging News Notes; Catholic Charities Newsletter.*
**Desc:** For professionals in Catholic social services, parishes and outreach ministries in United States and Canada.

US/0009-1723
**CHARITY AND CHILDREN.** Periodical. English. sm. $2.00. Baptist Childrens Home of North Carolina, 515 Watson Avenue, Box 338, Thomasville NC 27360. **Tel** (919)476-6183. **ED** Marianna Boucher. **Circ:** 58,000.
**Desc:** Focuses on family issues and information about Baptist children's homes of NC. Includes editorials, and opinion poll, alumni news and a children's page.

UK
**CHARITY TRENDS.** **Added/Corp** Charities Aid Foundation. (1986/87)-. English. an. £20.00. Charities Aid Foundation, 48 Penbury Road, Tonbridge Kent TN9 2JD England. **Tel** 011 44 732 771333, FAX 011 44 732 350570. **LC** HV245; .C587. **DD** 361.8/0941/021. ***Continues*** *Charity Statistics.*

US/0197-0429
**CHARTBOOK OF FEDERAL PROGRAMS IN AGING.** (CHARTBOOK OF FEDERAL PROGRAMS IN AGING / IRMA SCHECHTER.). **VFOAT** Chartbook on Aging. **VAT** Chart Book of Federal Programs in Aging. (1980)-. English. Twice a year. $29.00. Business Publishers Inc., 951 Pershing Drive, Silver Spring MD 20910-4464. **Tel** (301)587-6300, (800)274-0122, FAX (301)585-9075. **ED** Irma Schechter. **LC** HV1457; .S33. **DD** 362.6.
**Desc:** An authoritative and practical compilation of federal aging programs and contacts. Provides services for our aging population.

US
**CHECKPOINTS FOR CHILDREN / REGIONAL INSTITUTE OF SOCIAL WELFARE RESEARCH.** Vol. 1, No. 1 (Spring 1976)-. Periodical. English. bm. $20.00. Regional Institute of Social Welfare Research, Box 152, Athens GA 30603. **Tel** (404)542-7614.

US/0145-2134
**CHILD ABUSE & NEGLECT.** [Child abuse neglect]. **Added/Corp** International Society for the Prevention of Child Abuse and Neglect. **VFOAT** Child Abuse and Neglect. Vol. 1 No. 1 (1977)-. Periodical. English (French). Twelve times a year. $619.00 The Americas; £415.00 other. Pergamon Press, An Imprint of Elsevier Science Ltd., The Boulevard, Langford Lane, Kidlington, Oxford OX5 1GB United Kingdom. **Tel** 011 44 865 843000, 011 44 865 843699, FAX 011 44 865 843010. **(Subscription address:** Elsevier Science Ltd. Oxford Fulfillment Centre, PO Box 800, Kidlington, Oxford OX5 1DX United Kingdom.**) ED** Richard D. Krugman. **LC** HV713; .C3815. **DD** 362.7/1. **NLM** W1 CH642N. **CODEN** CABND3. **[CCC]. Pr Rev.** available on microfilm and microfiche from University Microfilms International (UMI). Documents available from The Genuine Article, BIOSIS Document Express, UMI Article Clearinghouse.
**Desc:** Provides a multidisciplinary forum on all aspects of child abuse and neglect including sexual abuse, with special emphasis on prevention and treatment.
**Ind/Abst** Abstr. Res. Pastor. Care Couns. (19??-); AGRICOLA ( -1987); Appl. Soc. Sci. Index Abstr.; Biol. Abstr. (1991-); Br. Educ. Index; Crim. Justice Abstr.; Crim. Penol. Police Sci. Abstr.; Curr. Contents Soc. Behav. Sci.; Curr. Index J. Educ.; Dev. Med. Child Neurol.; Educ. Index (1992-); EMBASE; Except. Child. Educ. Abstr.; Except. Child Educ. Resour.; Expand. Acad. Index (1992-); Health Plan. Adminis.; Index Med. (1982-); Index Period. Artic. Relat. Law; Int. Nurs. Index; Linguist. Lang. Behav. Abstr.; Middle East Abstr. Index; Newsp. Period. Abstr. (1992-); Physic. Medline Plus; Psychol. Abstr. (1980-); PsycINFO; PsycLit; Res. Alert [Full Cov.]; Soc. Plann. Policy Dev. Abstr.; Soc. Sci. Cit. Index [Full Cov.]; Soc. Work Abstr. [Select. Cov.]; Sociol. Abstr.

US/0195-8836
**CHILD ABUSE AND NEGLECT GRANTS PROGRAM.** **Main/Corp** United States. Administration for Children, Youth, and Families. (19??)-. English. an. Administration for Children & Families, 370 L'Enfant Promenade SW, 6th Floor, Washington DC 20447. **Tel** (202)401-9200, FAX (202)252-4683. **LC** HV741; .U5b. **DD** 362.7/1.

US/0146-9665
**CHILD ABUSE AND NEGLECT PROGRAMS.** **Added/Corp** United States. Dept. of Health, Education, and Welfare. (June 1976)-. Periodical. English. sa. $11.00. National Technical Information Service - NTIS, Room 2027S, 5285 Port Royal Road, Springfield VA 22161. **Tel** (703)487-4630, (703)487-4660, (703)487-4650, FAX (703)321-8547, telex 89-9405. **LC** HV741; .C455. **DD** 362.7/3. **NLM** WA 22 AA1 C4.

US/0145-3025
**CHILD ABUSE AND NEGLECT RESEARCH.** (CHILD ABUSE AND NEGLECT RESEARCH: PROJECTS AND PUBLICATIONS.). **Added/Corp** United States. Dept. of Health, Education, and Welfare. (May 1976)-. English. sa. $25.00. National Technical Information Service - NTIS, Room 2027S, 5285 Port Royal Road, Springfield VA 22161. **Tel** (703)487-4630, (703)487-4660, (703)487-4650, FAX (703)321-8547, telex 89-9405. **LC** HV741; .C456. **DD** 362.7/1/0973. **NLM** ZWA 320 C536.
**Desc:** An extensive collection of information on child abuse and neglect research includes informative abstracts of about 1,100 published documents and descriptions of about 110 on-going researchs.

US
**CHILD ABUSE AND NEGLECT STATISTICS.** **See** Sociology-Abstracting, Bibliographies and Statistics.

US/0145-2134
**CHILD ABUSE & NEGLECT [MICROFORM].** **Added/Corp** International Congress on Child Abuse & Neglect. **VAT** Child Abuse and Neglect. Vol. 1, No. 1 (1977)-. Academic Scholarly Publication. English. bm. Elsevier Science Publishers Ltd, Crown House, Linton Road, Barking Essex IG11 8JU England. **Tel** 011 44 81 5947272, FAX 081-594-5942, telex 896950. **[CCC].**

US/0148-5601
**CHILD ABUSE REPORT (HARRISBURG, PA.).** (CHILD ABUSE REPORT.). **Added/Corp** Pennsylvania. Bureau of Child Welfare. Pennsylvania. Office of Children and Youth. Pennsylvania. Dept. of Public Welfare. Pennsylvania. Bureau of Public Education. Pennsylvania. Dept. of Public Welfare. Office of Systems Development. (1976)-. Periodical. English. an. Department of Public Welfare / Pennsylvania, Harrisburg PA 17120. **LC** HV742.P4; P42a. **DD** 362.7/1.

UK/0952-9136
**CHILD ABUSE REVIEW.** ***Title Change.*** (CHILD ABUSE REVIEW : JOURNAL OF THE BRITISH ASSOCIATION FOR THE STUDY AND PREVENTION OF CHILD ABUSE AND NEGLECT.). [Child abuse rev.]. **Added/Corp** British Association for the Study and Prevention of Child Abuse and Neglect. (1985)-(?). Periodical. English. tq. John Wiley & Sons Ltd., Baffins Lane, Chichester West Sussex PO19 1UD England. **Tel** 0243 779777, FAX 0243 776128 BTG:JWP001, telex 86290 WIBOOKG. **(Subscription address:** North, South and Central America/ John Wiley & Sons, Inc., PO Box 7247-8491, Philadelphia, PA 19170-8491**) ED** Dr. Kevin Browne and Dr. Margaret Lynch. **CODEN** CABEEB. **[CCC].** ***Continued by*** *Child Abuse Review (Chichester, England : 1992).*
**Desc:** Builds on the success of the BASPCAN Newsletter to reflect current child welfare issues and concerns. It will make topical research and new intervention strategies available and accessible to the practitioner through reviews, action research and practice, key articles and abstracts from a range of journals, news and events.

●UK
**CHILD ABUSE REVIEW : JOURNAL OF THE BRITISH ASSOCIATION FOR THE STUDY AND PREVENTION OF CHILD ABUSE AND NEGLECT.** **Added/Corp** British Association for the Study and Prevention of Child Abuse and Neglect. Vol. 1, No. 1 (Apr. 1992)-. Periodical. English. Five times a year. $105.00. John Wiley & Sons Ltd., Baffins Lane, Chichester West Sussex PO19 1UD England. **Tel** 0243 779777, FAX 0243 776128 BTG:JWP001, telex 86290 WIBOOKG. **(Subscription address:** John Wiley / Philadelphia, PO Box 7247, Philadelphia PA 19170.**) ED** Dr. Kevin Browne and Dr. Margaret A. Lynch. **LC** HV6626.5; .C496. **DD** 362.7/6/094105. **NLM** W1; CH642RL. ***Continues*** *Child Abuse Review, 0952-9136.*
**Desc:** Builds on the success of the BASPCAN Newsletter to reflect current child welfare issues and concerns. Key articles and abstracts from a range of journals, news and events.

US
**CHILD ANALYSIS.** **See** Psychology.

US/0738-0151
**CHILD & ADOLESCENT SOCIAL WORK JOURNAL.** (CHILD & ADOLESCENT SOCIAL WORK JOURNAL : C & A.). [Child adolesc. soc. work j.]. **VFOAT** C & A; C and A; Child and Adolescent Social Work. Vol. 1, No. 1 (Spring 1984)-. Periodical. English. Six times a year. £42.00 (individuals); £199.00 (institutions) UK & Europe; $255.00 US; $300.00 other. Human Sciences Press, PO Box 735, 233 Spring Street, New York NY 10013. **Tel** (212)620-8000, FAX (212)807-1047, telex 23421139. **(Subscription address:** Eurospan Ltd., Journals and Serials Division, 3 Henrietta Street, Covent Garden, London WC2E 8LU England.**) ED** Florence Lieberman. **LC** HV701; .C45. **DD** 362.7/05. **NLM** W1; CH642T. **CODEN** CASWDD. **[CCC].** available on microfilm and microfiche from University Microfilms International (UMI). Documents available.
**Desc:** An informative new journal which features original articles focusing on clinical social work practice with children, adolescents, and their families.
**Ind/Abst** Abstr. Res. Pastor. Care Couns. (19??-); Appl. Soc. Sci. Index Abstr.; Linguist. Lang. Behav. Abstr.; Psychol. Abstr. (1984-); PsycINFO; PsycLit; Soc. Plann. Policy Dev. Abstr.; Soc. Work Abstr. [Full Cov.]; Sociol. Abstr.

US/0741-2312
**CHILD AND FAMILY POLICY.** [Child fam. policy]. Vol. 2 (1983)-. Monographic series. English. ir. Price varies per volume. Ablex Publishing Corporation, 355 Chestnut Street, Norwood NJ 07648. **Tel** (201)767-8450, (201)767-8455 (Customer Service), FAX (201)767-6717. **ED** Ron Haskins and James Gallagher. **NLM** W1 CH643DC. ***Continues*** *Advances in Child and Family Policy.*
**Desc:** Six book series on various aspects of social policy as it affects children.

US/0899-093X
**CHILD AND YOUTH CARE ADMINISTRATOR / NOVA UNIVERSITY, THE.** [Child youth care adm.]. **Added/Corp** Nova University. Master's Program for Child and Youth Care Administrators. Vol. 1 (Spring 1988)-. Periodical. English. sa. $25.00. Child and Youth Care Administrator, Nova University, 3301 College Avenue, Fort Lauderdale FL 33314. **Tel** (305)475-7080. **DD** 362. **CODEN** CYCAE2.

US/1053-1890
**CHILD AND YOUTH CARE FORUM.** [Child youth care forum]. **Added/Corp** Human Sciences Press. **VFOAT** Child and Youth Care Forum. Vol. 20, No. 1 (Feb. 1991)-. Periodical. English. bm. £42.00 (individuals), £199.00 (institutions) UK & Europe; $255.00 US; $300.00 other. Human Sciences Press, PO Box 735, 233 Spring Street, New York NY 10013. **Tel** (212)620-8000, FAX (212)807-1047, telex 23421139. **(Subscription address:** Eurospan Ltd., Journals and Serials Division, 3 Henrietta Street, Covent Garden, London WC2E 8LU England.**) ED** Jerome Beker. **LC** HV701; .C513. **DD** 362.7/1/0973. **NLM** W1; CH643DCF. **CODEN** CYCFEH. **[CCC].** available on microfilm and microfiche from University Microfilms International (UMI). Documents available from The Genuine Article. ***Continues*** *Child & Youth Care Quarterly, 0893-0848.*
**Desc:** An independent, professional publication, is committed to the advancement of this field and the improvement of child care practice in a variety of day and residential settings. Child care workers, their supervisors, instructors and students, and other personnel in child care settings will benefit from this interactive medium of communication and debate on practice, selection and training theory and research, and professional issues.
**Ind/Abst** AGRICOLA [Select. Cov.]; Educ. Index; Except. Child Educ. Resour.; Psychol. Abstr. (1965-); PsycINFO; PsycScan: Develop. Psych.; Res. Alert [Full Cov.]; Sage Fam. Stud. Abstr.; Soc. Sci. Cit. Index [Full Cov.]; Spec. Educ. Needs Abstr.

US/0145-935X
**CHILD & YOUTH SERVICES.** [Child youth serv.]. **VFOAT** Child and Youth Services. Vol. 1 (1977)-. Periodical. English. Twice a year. $200.00 US; $280.00 other. The Haworth Press Inc, 10 Alice Street, Binghamton NY 13904-1580. **Tel** (607)722-5857, (800)3-HAWORTH, FAX (607)722-1424. **ED** Jerome Beker (editor's address: Center for Youth Development and Research, 386 McNeal Hall, University of Minnesota, 1985 Buford Avenue, St Paul MN 55108). **LC** HV701; .C47. **DD** 362.7/05. **NLM** W1 CH644. **CODEN** CYSEDP. Index available (bound in last issue). **Bk Rev. Ad Acc. Pr Rev. Acid Free. Circ:** 199. available on microfilm and microfiche from University Microfilms International (UMI). Documents available from Haworth Document Delivery Service.
**Desc:** Provides in-depth coverage of one particular topic regarding the conditions of young people in our society. The journal provides all professionals with a working knowledge of the developments in the child and youth services field.
**Ind/Abst** Abstr. Res. Pastor. Care Couns. (19??-); Child Dev. Abstr. Bibliogr.; Crim. Justice Abstr.; Crim. Justice Period. Index; Crim. Penol. Police Sci. Abstr.; Curr. Index J. Educ.; Except. Child Educ. Resour.; Linguist. Lang. Behav. Abstr.; Multicult. Educ. Abstr.; Psychol. Abstr. (1977-); PsycINFO; PsycLit; Ref. Z.; Sage Fam. Stud. Abstr. (?-?); Soc. Plann. Policy Dev. Abstr.; Soc. Work Abstr. [Select. Cov.]; Sociol. Abstr.; Sociol. Educ. Abstr.; Spec. Educ. Needs Abstr.; Stud. Women Abstr.

US/0889-4558
**CHILD CARE CENTER.** ***Ceased.*** [Child care cent.]. Vol. 1, No. 1 (Sept. 1986)-?. Periodical. English. bm. Scholastic Inc, 730 Broadway, New York NY 10003. **Tel** (416)883-5300, FAX (212)505-3653. **DD** 362.

US/0164-8527
**CHILD CARE INFORMATION EXCHANGE.** [Child care inf. exch.]. **VFOAT** Exchange. (1978)-. Periodical. English. bm (Jan., Mar., May, July, Sept., Nov.). $37.87 Washington residents; $35.00 other. Exchange Press Inc, PO Box 2890, Redmond WA 98073. **Tel** (206)883-9394, FAX (206)883-9683. **LC** HV854; .C46. **DD** 362.7/12/068. Index available (Free). **Bk Rev**, (Qty: varies). **Ad Acc. Circ:** 20,000. available on microfilm and microfiche from University Microfilms International (UMI).
**Desc:** Management magazine providing directors of child care centers, ideas on managing staff, money, marketing, and evaluation.
**Ind/Abst** Curr. Index J. Educ.; Educ. Index.

UK
**CHILD CARE LAW FOR PRACTITIONERS IN SOCIAL WORK, HEALTH & EDUCATION.** (1994)-. Periodical. English. sa. £52.00 Europe; £55.00 Other (Institutions). Longman Group Ltd., Fourth Avenue, Longman House, Harlow Essex CM19 5SR England. **Tel** 011 44 279 429655, FAX 011 44 279 431059, telex 81259.

US
**CHILD CARE REVIEW.** Vol. 2, No. 5 (April 1987)-. English. bm. $20.00. Child Care Review, PO Box 578, Metairie LA 70004. **Tel** (504)831-9662. ***Continues*** *Kiddie Kare Magazine.*
**Desc:** News magazine for directors and administrators. Offers statistical analysis, in-depth research and practical advice on the operation and management of child care centers.

US/0741-2398
**CHILD CARE WORK.** (CHILD CARE WORK : A QUARTERLY PUBLICATION OF THE NATIONAL ORGANIZATION OF CHILD CARE WORKER ASSOCIATIONS, INC.). [Child care work]. **Added/Corp** National Organization of Child Care Worker Associations (U.S.). (1983)-. Periodical. English. Four times a year (Mar., June, Sept., Dec.). $10.00. National Organization of Child Care Workers Association, 601 Pennsylvania Avenue Northwest, 9th Floor, Washington DC 20041. **Tel** (202)232-4171.

US/0093-8009
**CHILD DEVELOPMENT STATE PLAN (PENNSYLVANIA). Main/Corp** Pennsylvania. Commonwealth Child Development Committee. English. Commonwealth Child Development Committee, 512 Finance Building, Harrisburg PA 17120. **LC** HV742.P4; P43A. **DD** 362.7/09748.

US
**CHILD HEALTH PLUS, HEALTH PLAN FOR KIDS : ANNUAL REPORT TO THE GOVERNOR & LEGISLATURE, CHILD HEALTH INSURANCE PLAN.** **See** Insurance.

US/0251-5547
**CHILD REFERENCE BULLETIN.** (CHILD REFERENCE BULLETIN : A UNITED NATIONS CHILDREN'S FUND PUBLICATION ON ACTION FOR CHILDREN.). [Child ref. bull.]. No. 1 (May 1981)-. Bulletin. English. qt. Child Reference Bulletin, UNICEF United Nations, New York NY 10017.

US/0009-4021
**CHILD WELFARE.** [Child welf.]. **Added/Corp** Child Welfare League of America. Vol. 27, No. 7 (July 1948)-. Periodical. English. Six times a year. $55.00 (individuals), $70.00 (institutions). Transaction Publishers / Rutgers State University, New Brunswick NJ 08903. **Tel** (908)932-2280 Ext. 105, FAX (908)932-3138. **ED** Carl Schoenberg. **DD** 362. **NLM** W1 CH692. **CODEN** CHWFA. **[CCC].** Index available. cum. index. **Bk Rev. Ad Acc. Pr Rev. Circ:** 12,000 (ctrl). available on labels; available on microfilm and microfiche from University Microfilms International (UMI). Documents available from The Genuine Article, UMI Article Clearinghouse. ***Continues*** *Child Welfare League of America. Bulletin.*
**Desc:** A journal of policy, practice and program devoted essentially to the needs and goals of personnel associated with the field of child welfare. It covers all phases of child welfare that affect the health, education and psychological needs of children, offering theoretical concepts as well as practical ideas and strategies.
**Ind/Abst** Abstr. Res. Pastor. Care Couns. (19??-); Acad. Abstr. Full Text Elite (July 1990-); Acad. Abstr. (July 1990-); Acad. Ind. [Computer File] (1987-); Acad. Search (July 1990-); AGRICOLA [Select. Cov.]; Appl. Soc. Sci. Index Abstr.; Chicano Index; Child Dev. Abstr. Bibliogr.; Crim. Justice Abstr.; Crim. Penol. Police Sci. Abstr.; Cumul. Index Nurs. Allied Health Lit.; Curr. Contents Soc. Behav. Sci.; Curr. Index J. Educ.; Curr. Lit. Fam. Plan.; Educ. Index; Except. Child Educ. Resour.; Expand. Acad. Index (1987-); Health Plan. Adminis.; Index Med.; Index Period. Artic. Relat. Law; INFO-SOUTH Abstr.; Linguist. Lang. Behav. Abstr.; Mag. Search; Newsp. Period. Abstr. (1986-); PAIS Int. Print (1991-); Psychol. Abstr. (1973-); PsycINFO; PsycLit; Res. Alert [Full Cov.]; Soc. Plann. Policy Dev. Abstr.; Soc. Sci. Source (Jul. 1990-); Soc. Sci. Cit. Index [Full Cov.]; Soc. Sci. Index; Soc. Sci. Index Fulltext (Nov. 1988-) [Full Txt.]; Soc. Work Abstr. [Full Cov.]; Sociol. Abstr.; Spec. Educ. Needs Abstr.; Women Stud. Abstr.

US
**CHILDCARE NEWS.** English. Four times a year (Jan., Apr., July, Oct.). $20.00. Alliance of Business Childcare Development, 600 Wilshire Boulevard, Suite 440, Los Angeles CA 90017. **Tel** (213)624-7018, FAX (213)345-8321.
**Desc:** News and information on childcare.

US/0882-942X
**CHILDREN & TEENS TODAY.** ***Ceased.*** [Child. teens today]. **VFOAT** Children and Teens Today. Vol. 5, No. 9 (May 1985)-(October 1991). Periodical. English. mo. Manisses Communications Group Inc., PO Box 3357, Providence RI 02906-0757. **Tel** (401)831-6020, (800)333-7771, FAX (401)861-6370. **ED** Suzanne Prescod. **DD** 305. **Bk Rev. Ad Acc. Circ:** 2,500 (ctrl). ***Continues*** *Children & Teens in Crisis, 0732-7420.*
**Desc:** A newsletter for professionals in the fields of child welfare and child advocacy.

US
**CHILDREN AND THE LAW COMMITTEE NEWSLETTER.** (19??)-. English. tq (3 issues). $8.00. American Bar Association, 750 North Lake Shore Drive, Chicago IL 60611. **Tel** (312)988-5522, (312)988-5241, FAX (312)988-5528, telex 270593. ***Continues*** *Legal Response : Child Advocacy and Protection.*

●US/1063-892X
**CHILDREN & YOUTH FUNDING REPORT.** [Child. youth funding rep.]. **VFOAT** Children and Youth Funding Report. (1992)-. Periodical. English. sm. $249.00. CD Publications, 8204 Fenton Street, Silver Spring MD 20910. **Tel** (800)666-6380, (301)588-6380, FAX (301)588-6385. **DD** 361. ***Absorbed*** *Public Assistance Funding Report, 1069-1340.*

US/0190-7409
**CHILDREN AND YOUTH SERVICES REVIEW.** [Child. youth serv. rev.]. Vol. 1 (Spring 1979)-. Academic Scholarly Publication. English. bm. $328.00 The Americas; £220.00 other. Pergamon Press, An Imprint of Elsevier Science Ltd., The Boulevard, Langford Lane, Kidlington, Oxford OX5 1GB United Kingdom. **Tel** 011 44 865 843000, 011 44 865 843699, FAX 011 44 865 843010. **(Subscription address:** Elsevier Science Ltd. Oxford Fulfillment Centre, PO Box 800, Kidlington, Oxford OX5 1DX United Kingdom.**) ED** Duncan Lindsey. **LC** HV701; .C575. **DD** 362.7/05. **NLM** W1 CH694Q. **[CCC]. Pr Rev.** available on microfilm and microfiche from University Microfilms International (UMI). Documents available from The Genuine Article.
**Ind/Abst** Appl. Soc. Sci. Index Abstr.; Chicano Index; Crim. Justice Abstr.; Curr. Contents Arts Humanit.; Curr. Contents Soc. Behav. Sci.; EMBASE; Except. Child Educ. Resour.; Index Period. Artic. Relat. Law (19??-19??); Linguist. Lang. Behav. Abstr.; Psychol. Abstr. (1979-); PsycINFO; PsycLit; Res. Alert [Full Cov.]; Sage Fam. Stud. Abstr.; Soc. Plann. Policy Dev. Abstr.; Soc. Sci. Cit. Index [Full Cov.]; Sociol. Abstr.; Spec. Educ. Needs Abstr.

AT/1035-0772
**CHILDREN AUSTRALIA.** (19??)-. English. qt. 45.00Aus$ (Australia); 60.00Aus$ (other). The Children's Bureau Australia, PO Box 686, Mulgrave NO VIC 3170 Australia. **Tel** 61 3 5589100. ***Continues*** *Australian Child & Family Welfare, 0312-8970.*
**Ind/Abst** APAIS, Aust. Public Aff. Inf. Ser. (19??-).

UK/0260-5473
**CHILDREN IN CARE OR UNDER SUPERVISION, SCOTLAND.** [Child. care superv. Scotl.]. (1979)-. Bulletin. English. an. £2.00. Social Work Services Group, Statistics Branch, 43 Jeffrey Street / Room 422, Edinburgh EH1 1DG Scotland. **Tel** 031 244 5431, FAX 031 244 5387. ***Continues in part*** *Scottish Social Work Statistics, 0307-9597.*

●UK/0968-4050
**CHILDREN LOOKED AFTER BY LOCAL AUTHORITIES IN WALES / WELSH OFFICE / PLANT Y GOFELIR AM DANYNT GAN AWDURDODAU LLEOL CYMRU / Y SWYDDFA GYMREIG.** **Added/Corp** Great Britain. Welsh Office. **VFOAT** Plant Y Gofelir am Danynt gan Awdurdodau Lleol Cymru. (1992)-. Government Publication. English. an. £4.00. Statistical Directorate Publication Unit, Welsh Office, New Crown Building, Cathays Park, Cardiff CF1 3NQ Wales England. **Tel** (0222)825087. **ED** E. Swires-Hennessy. **LC** HV1149.W34; G74a. **DD** 362.7/32/09429. **Ad Acc. Circ:** 450 (ctrl). ***Continues*** *Children in Care or Under Supervision Orders in Wales, 0263-2667.*

US/0361-4336
**CHILDREN TODAY.** [Child. today]. **Added/Corp** United States. Children's Bureau. United States. Office of Human Development Services. Vol. 1, No. 1 (Jan./Feb. 1972)-. Government Publication. English. bm. $8.00 domestic; $10.00 other. Superintendent of Documents, US Government Printing Office, Washington DC 20402. **Tel** (202)275-3328, FAX (202)786-2377. **LC** HV741; .C5362. **DD** 362.7/05. **NLM** W1 CH694V. **CODEN** CHTDA. available on microfilm and microfiche from University Microfilms International (UMI); available on an online database (file 647/Full-Text) from DIALOG. Documents available from UMI Article Clearinghouse. ***Formed by the union of*** *Children (Washington, D.C.).*
**Desc:** Reports on federal, state, and local services for children, child development, health and welfare laws, and other news pertinent to child welfare in the United States.
**Ind/Abst** Acad. Abstr. Full Text Elite (Jan. 1984-) [Full Txt.]; Acad. Abstr. (Jan. 1984-); Acad. Ind. [Computer File] (1984-); Acad. Search (Jan. 1984-); AGRICOLA [Select. Cov.]; Appl. Soc. Sci. Index Abstr.; Book Rev. Index; Consum. Index Prod. Eval. Inf. Source; Cumul. Index Nurs. Allied Health Lit.; Curr. Index J. Educ.; Curr. Lit. Fam. Plan.; Educ. Index; Except. Child Educ. Resour. (19??-19??); Expand. Acad. Index (1984-); Gen. Period. Index (1985-); Guide Soc. Sci. Relig. (1977-); Health Ref. Cent. (1987-) [Full Txt.] [Select. Cov.]; Hospit. Health Admin. Index; Index Med.; INFO-SOUTH Abstr.; Mag. Artic. Summar. Elite (Jan. 1984-) [Full Txt.]; Mag. Artic. Summar. Select (Jan. 1984-) [Full Txt.]; Mag. Artic. Summar. CD-ROM (Jan. 1984-); Mag. ASAP Plus [Full Txt.]; Mag. ASAP Sel. [Full Txt.]; Mag. Express (1988-) [Full Txt.]; Mag. Index Plus (1989-); Mag. Index. Sel. (1986-); Mag. Search; Middle East Abstr. Index; Mid. Search (Jan. 1984-) [Full Txt.]; Newsp. Period. Abstr. (1988-); Prim. Search (Jan. 1984-); Read. Guide Abstr. Select Ed.; Read. Guide Period. Lit.; Resource/One Ondisc; Sage Fam. Stud. Abstr. (?-?); Soc. Sci. Source

(Jan. 1984-) [Full Txt.]; Soc. Work Abstr. (Spring, Summer 1987-) [Select. Cov.]; Mag. Index (1978-); Women Stud. Abstr.

US/0739-425X
**CHILDREN'S ADVOCATE, THE.** [Child. advocate]. **Added/Corp** Berkeley Children's Services (Calif.). (197?)-. Periodical. English. Six times a year (Jan., Mar., May, July, Sept., Nov.). $12.00 (one year); $34.00 (two years). Action Alliance for Children, The Hunt House, 1201 Martin Luther King Jr. Way, Oakland CA 94612. **Tel** (510)444-7136, FAX (510)444-7138. **ED** Anglea Gennino. Index available. cum. index. **Bk Rev**, (Qty: 6). **Ad Acc, Adv Mgr:** A. Gennino. **Circ:** 10,000.
**Desc:** Provides comprehensive coverage and expert analysis of trends and public policy issues affecting children and their families.

US
**CHILDREN'S MONITOR.** (19??)-. Periodical. English. qt. Free on request. Child Welfare League of America, 440 1st Street Northwest, Suite 310, Washington DC 20001. **Tel** (202)638-2952, FAX (202)638-4004.

US
**CHILDREN'S TRUST FUND OF PENNSYLVANIA ANNUAL REPORT, THE.** **Main/Corp** Pennsylvania. Children's Trust Fund. **VFOAT** Pennsylvania Annual Report. (1990)-. Periodical. English. **LC** WMLC 91/4302.

US
**CHILDREN'S VOICE.** [Children's voice]. **Added/Corp** Child Welfare League of America. Vol. 1, No. 1 (Fall 1991)-. Periodical. English. qt (4 issues). $50.00 (institution), $35.00 (individual). Child Welfare League of America, 440 1st Street Northwest, Suite 310, Washington DC 20001. **Tel** (202)638-2952, FAX (202)638-4004. **LC** HV741; .C5378. **DD** 362. **NLM** W1; CH699TR. ***Continues** Children's Voice, 1057-736X.*
**Desc:** Offers child welfare practitioners a focus on a range of child welfare news, policy, and practice issues.

AT
**CHILDREN'S WELFARE ASSOCIATION OF VICTORIA NEWSLETTER.** Newsletter. English. qt (Mar., June, Sept., Dec.). 30.00Aus$. Children's Welfare Association of Victoria, 35 Victoria Parade, Collingwood Victoria 3066 Australia. **Tel** 011 61 3 4190588, FAX 011 61 3 4161375. **ED** Margaret Roberts. **Ad Acc. Circ:** 300 (ctrl).
**Desc:** Mainly reports from projects officers and Executive Director.

●CN/1188-8172
**CHOICES (LONDON, ONT.).** (CHOICES / HEART AND STROKE FOUNDATION OF ONTARIO.). [Choices]. **Added/Corp** Heart and Stroke Foundation of Ontario. Vol. 1, No. 1 (Mar. 1992)-. Periodical. English. qt. Limited free distribution. Heart and Stroke Foundation of Ontario / London, c/o Colleen Bradley, 245 Pall Mall Street, London Ontario N6A 1P4 Canada. **DD** 361.7.

●CN/1191-3339
**CHRYSALIS CONNECTION.** [Chrysalis connect.]. **Added/Corp** Western Industrial Research and Training Centres. (Spring 1992)-. Periodical. English. Three times a year. Limited free distribution. Chrysalis, Alberta Society for Citizens with Disabilities, 13325 St. Albert Trail, Edmonton Alberta T5L 4R3 Canada. **DD** 362.4/0484. ***Continues** Western Industrial Connection., 0849-6900.*

CN/0823-616X
**CITEPHILE.** (CITEPHILE : JOURNAL DES ADEPTES DE LA CITE DE LA SANTE DE LAVAL.). [Citephile]. V. 1, No. 1, (Aug. 1981)-. Periodical. French. ir. Cite de la Sante de Laval, 1755 Boulevard, Rene-Laennec Laval, Quebec H7M 3L9 Canada. **DD** 362.1/1/09714271.

US/1071-2321
**CITIZEN ADVOCACY FORUM.** [Citiz. advocacy forum]. (1991)-. Periodical. English. Four times a year (Feb., May, Aug., Nov.). $20.00 (individuals); $25.00 (institutions). Citizen Advocacy Forum, PO Box 86, Beaver PA 15009. **ED** Adam J. Hildebeard (phone: (412)775-4121). **DD** 362. **Bk Rev**, (Qty: 1-2). **Circ:** 300.
**Desc:** The purpose is aim at citizen advocacy offices, those who run them, and citizen advocacy leaders, including board members, coordinators, funders, and others who have or will have leadership roles in making Citizen Advocacy a reality in local communities.

US/0360-5698
**CITIZEN PARTICIPATION AND VOLUNTARY ACTION ABSTRACTS.** **Added/Corp** Association of Voluntary Action Scholars (U.S.). **VFOAT** Voluntary Action Abstracts. No. 1 (1974)-. English. ir. $110.00 Comes with Association for Research on Nonprofit Organizations and Voluntary Action membership. Arnova, Route 2 Box 696, Pullman WA 99163. **Tel** (509)332-3417, FAX (509)332-3417, (509)335-2863. **ED** Carl Milofsky. **Circ:** 500.

US/0199-0330
**CITY LIMITS.** **See** Housing and Urban Development.

CN/0229-706X
**CIVIC (OTTAWA).** (THE CIVIC.). **VFOAT** Civique. **VAT** Civique (Ottawa). Fall 1979-. Periodical. English (French). qt. Ottawa Civic Hospital, 1053 Carling Avenue, Ottawa Ontario K1Y 4E9 Canada. **DD** 362.1/1/0971384.

CN/0821-2252
**CLIN D'OEIL - CENTRE HOSPITALIER DES BOIS-FRANCS.** (CLIN D'OEIL / CHBF.). [Clin oeil - Cent. hosp. Bois-Francs]. **Added/Corp** Centre hospitalier des Bois-Francs. (1979)-. Periodical. French. qt. Limited free distribution. Centre Hospitalier des Bois-Francs, 61 Avenue de L-Ermitage, Victoriaville Quebec G6P 6X4 Canada. **DD** 362.1/6. ***Continues** Etincelle (Victoriaville, Quebec).*
**Ind/Abst** Point Repere (19??-19??).

US/0501-798X
**CLINICAL PROGRAMS FOR MENTALLY RETARDED CHILDREN.** **See** Medical Science and Technology-Pediatrics.

US/0091-1674
**CLINICAL SOCIAL WORK JOURNAL.** [Clin. soc. work j.]. **Added/Corp** National Federation of Societies for Clinical Social Work. Vol. 1 (Spring 1973)-. Periodical. English. qt. £37.00 (individuals), £180.00 (institutions) UK & Europe; $225.00 US; $265.00 other. Human Sciences Press, PO Box 735, 233 Spring Street, New York NY 10013. **Tel** (212)620-8000, FAX (212)807-1047, telex 23421139. **(Subscription address:** Eurospan Ltd., Journals and Serials Division, 3 Henrietta Street, Covent Garden, London WC2E 8LU England.**)** **ED** Jean Sanville. **LC** HV1; .C63. **DD** 361.3/05. **NLM** W1 CL784K. **CODEN** CSWJBG. **[CCC]. Pr Rev.** available on microfilm and microfiche from University Microfilms International (UMI). Documents available from The Genuine Article, UMI Article Clearinghouse.
**Desc:** Devoted exclusively to clinical social work theory an and practice, the journal is interdisciplinary in authorship, scope and content.
**Ind/Abst** Acad. Abstr. Full Text Elite (Jan. 1992-); Acad. Abstr. (Jan. 1992-); Acad. Search (Jan. 1992-); Appl. Soc. Sci. Index Abstr.; Curr. Contents Soc. Behav. Sci.; Expand. Acad. Index (1989-); INFO-SOUTH Abstr.; Linguist. Lang. Behav. Abstr.; Mag. Search; Middle East Abstr. Index; Newsp. Period. Abstr. (1991-); Psychol. Abstr. (1973-); PsycINFO; PsycLit; Res. Alert [Full Cov.]; Sage Fam. Stud. Abstr.; Soc. Plann. Policy Dev. Abstr.; Soc. Sci. Source (Jan. 1992-); Soc. Sci. Cit. Index [Full Cov.]; Soc. Sci. Index; Soc. Sci. Index Fulltext (Fall 1988-) [Full Txt.]; Soc. Work Abstr. (1977-) [Full Cov.]; Sociol. Abstr.; Spec. Educ. Needs Abstr.

CN/1182-6665
**CLIPPING SERVICE.** [Clipp. serv.]. **Added/Corp** Suicide Information and Education Centre. **VFOAT** Newspaper Clipping Service. (Aug. 1990)-. Periodical. English. bm (6 issues). 30.00Can$. Suicide Information & Education Center, #201-1615 10th Avenue Southwest, Calgary Alberta T3C 0J7 Canada. **Tel** (403)283-3900. **DD** 362.2/8/05. **Ad Acc. Circ:** 200. ***Continues** Newspaper Clipping Service., 0823-8359.*
**Desc:** Compilation of current newspaper/newsletter clippings on suicide.

CN/0838-4347
**CLSC EXPRESS.** [CLSC express]. **Added/Corp** Federation des Centres Locaux de Services Communautaires du Quebec. **VAT** Centres Locaux de Services Communautaires du Quebec Express. Vol. 1, No. 3 (April/May 1988)-. Periodical. French. bm (6 issues). 27.00Can$. Federation des CLSC du Quebec, 550 West Sherbrooke Street 2060, Montreal Quebec H3A 1B9 Canada. **Tel** (514)842-5141. **DD** 362/.9714. ***Continues** Fede Express, 0225-1124.*

CN/0715-5654
**CMHA FOCUS.** [CMHA focus]. **VAT** Canadian Mental Health Association Focus; Focus - Canadian Mental Health Association. Vol. 1, No. 1 (April 1982)-. Periodical. English. $10.00. Canata Mental Health Association, Central Alberta REgion, 207-4921 49th Street, Red Deer Alta. T4N 1V2 Canada. **DD** 362.2/097123/3.

FR
**CODES DE LA SANTE PUBLIQUE DE LA FAMILLE ET DE L'AIDE SOCIALE.** **Main/Corp** France. (1975)-. French. be. Dalloz, 35 rue Tournefort, 75240 Paris Cedex 05 France. **Tel** 011 33 1 40515434 or 40515454, FAX 45 87 37 48, telex 206 446 F. **LC** KJV5302.A22; F7. ***Continues in part** France. Code de la Securite Sociale .; **Continues** Codes de la Securite Sociale, de la Sante Publique et de l'Aide Sociale.*

FR
**CODES DE LA SECURITE SOCIALE ET DE LA MUTUALITE, MUTUALITE SOCIALE AGRICOLE.** **Main/Corp** France. **VFOAT** Mutualite Sociale Agricole; Code de la Securite Sociale, Code de la Mutualite, Mutualite Sociale Agricole. (1976)-. French. an. 215.48F. Dalloz, 35 rue Tournefort, 75240 Paris Cedex 05 France. **Tel** 011 33 1 40515434 or 40515454, FAX 45 87 37 48, telex 206 446 F. **LC** KJV3512.2; .F73. **DD** 344.44/02; 344.4042. ***Continues in part** France. Code de la Securite Sociale. **and** Codes de la Securite Sociale, de la Sante Publique et de l'Aide Sociale.*

CN/0834-2121
**COFAQ'TUALITE : BULLETIN DE LIAISON DE LA CONFEDERATION DES ORGANISMES FAMILIAUX DU QUEBEC.** [COFAQ'tualite]. **VAT** Confederation des Organismes Familiaux du Quebec Actualite. (April 1984)-. Bulletin. French. qt. Free. Confederation des Organismes Familiaux du Quebec, Bureau 310, 2335 Quest rue Sherbrooke, Montreal Quebec H3H 1G6 Canada. **DD** 362.8/2/060714. ***Continues** Ofaqtualitie, 0318-5524.*

FR/0010-0811
**COLLECTIVITES EXPRESS.** ***Title Change.*** [Collect. express]. (1954)-(1992). Periodical. French. wk. Editions Max Brezol Sarl, 9 rue Labie, 75838 Paris Cedex 17 France. **Tel** 011 33 1 45742162. **UDC** 33. ***Absorbed** Vie Collective, 0042-5370. **Continued by** Collectivites Hotellerie et Restauration, 1242-2126.*

FR/1242-2126
**COLLECTIVITES HOTELLERIE ET RESTAURATION PARIS.** (COLLECTIVITES HOTELLERIE ET RESTAURATION.). (1992)-. Periodical. French. Nine times a year. 333.00F France; 510.00F other. Editions Max Brezol Sarl, 9 rue Labie, 75838 Paris Cedex 17 France. **Tel** 011 33 1 45742162. **UDC** 64.022(44). ***Continues** Collectivites Express, 0010-0811.*

BE/0773-0357
**COMM - EUROPEAN REGIONAL CLEARING HOUSE FOR COMMUNITY WORK.** ***Suspended.*** [Comm - Eur. Reg. Clg. H. Community Work]. **VFOAT** Community Work and Communication - European Regional Clearing House for Community Work. (1979)-(1990). Periodical. Multiple languages (English and French). Three times a year. 1200.00F Belgium; 1450.00F Europe; 1830.00F other. Inst Europeen Interuniv Action Soc, 179 rue du Debarcadere, B-6001 Marcinelle Belgium. **Tel** 011 32 71 366273. ***Continues** Community Work Abstracts, 0773-0365.*

CN/0319-7468
**COMMUNIQUE - CHILDREN'S AID SOCIETY OF OTTAWA.** (COMMUNIQUE - SOCIETE DE L'AIDE A L'ENFANCE D'OTTAWA.). **Main/Corp** Societe de l'Aide a l'Enfance d'Ottawa. March 1974-. Periodical. Multiple languages (English and French). qt. Free. 1370 rue Bank, Ottawa Ontario K1H 7Y3 Canada. **ED** Valerie Bruneau. **Bk Rev**. ctrl circ. ***Supersedes** The CAS Record, 0045-6675.*
**Desc:** Communication of this organization's role, mandate goals. Sharing of new developments (activities, policies, programs) expression of needs.

US/0736-2099
**COMMUNITY (ALEXANDRIA, VA. : 1982).** ***Ceased.*** (COMMUNITY.). [Community]. (19??)-(19??). Periodical. English. bm. United Way of America, 701 North Fairfax Street, Alexandria VA 22314. **Tel** (703)836-7100. **ED** Roberta A Lindsay and Patricia Ward. **LC** HV88; .U662. **DD** 361/.973. Index available. cum. index. **Circ:** 6,400 (ctrl). ***Continues** Community Focus.*
**Desc:** Ideas in the area of health and human services, voluntarism and the nonprofit sector.

US/1052-7656
**COMMUNITY ALTERNATIVES.** [Community altern.]. Vol. 1, No. 1 (Spring 1989)-. Periodical. English. sa (Apr. and Oct.). $30.00 (1 year), $54.00 (2 year), $72.00 (3 year). Human Service Associates, 336 North Robert, Suite 1520, St Paul MN 55101. **Tel** (612)224-8967, FAX (612)224-6057. **ED** Curt Anderson. **LC** HV697; .C66. **DD** 360. **CODEN** CALTE4. **Bk Rev. Ad Acc. Pr Rev.** ctrl circ.
**Desc:** Forum for persons engaged in research or practice in specialist foster family care. Includes articles, interviews, brief notes on policies and programs, and book reviews.
**Ind/Abst** Linguist. Lang. Behav. Abstr.; Psychol. Abstr. (1989-); PsycINFO; PsycLit; Soc. Plann. Policy Dev. Abstr.; Soc. Work Abstr. [Select. Cov.]; Sociol. Abstr.

US
**COMMUNITY CARE.** **Main/Corp** Illinois. Dept. on Aging. Sept. 1982-. English. an. Illinois Department of Aging, 421 East Capitol Avenue, Springfield IL 62706. **LC** HV1468.I3; I443C. **DD** 362.6/042. ***Continues** Illinois. Dept. on Aging. Community Care for the Elderly.*
**Ind/Abst** Appl. Soc. Sci. Index Abstr.; Sage Race Relat. Abstr.

UK/0307-5508
**COMMUNITY CARE.** (19??)-. Periodical. English. wk. $132.00. Reed Business Publishing / West Sussex, England, Perrymount Road, Haywards Heath, West Sussex RH16 3DH England. **Tel** 011 44 81 6523500. **LC** HV241; .C66. **DD** 361.942/05. **NLM** W1; CO428EC. available on microfilm and microfiche from University Microfilms International (UMI). ***Absorbed** Social Work Today, 0037-8070.*

●UK
**COMMUNITY CARE BULLETIN.** (1990)-. Bulletin. English. an. £2.00. Social Work Services Group, Statistics Branch, 43 Jeffrey Street / Room 422, Edinburgh EH1 1DG Scotland. **Tel** 031 244 5431, FAX 031 244 5387.

US/1052-6552
**COMMUNITY HEALTH FUNDING REPORT.** [Community health funding rep.]. (19??)-. Periodical. English. Twenty-four times a year. $249.00. CD Publications, 8204 Fenton Street, Silver Spring MD 20910. **Tel** (800)666-6380, (301)588-6380, FAX (301)588-6385. **ED** Mary Hensel Lehman. **DD** 362. Index available. cum. index. **Bk Rev.**
**Desc:** Reviews of public and private health grant opportunities including elegibility requirements, funding levels, deadlines and more.

UK/0951-9815
**COMMUNITY LIVING.** [Community living]. (1987)-. Periodical. English. Four times a year. £19.50 (individuals), £18.00 (health authorities) UK; £27.00 Europe & Eire; £36.00 other. Hexagon Publishing, 5 Dickerage Lane, New Malden, Surrey KT3 3RZ England. **Tel** 011 44 81 336-0220, FAX 011 44 81 336-0235.

NZ/0112-3599
**COMMUNITY MENTAL HEALTH IN NEW ZEALAND.** [Community ment. health N. Z.]. **Added/Corp** Mental Health Foundation of New Zealand. Vol. 1, No. 1 (July 1984)-. Periodical. English. sa (June and Dec.). 40.00NZ$ (institutions), 25.00NZ$ (individuals) New Zealand; 45.00NZ$ other. Mental Health Foundation of New Zealand, PO Box 37-438, Parnell Auckland 1 New Zealand. **Tel** (011-64-9)303-1517. **ED** Max Abbott and Barbara Risley. **NLM** W1; CO429M. cum. index. **Circ:** 500.
**Desc:** The journal's aim is to stimulate research and discussion on community health issues, especially in the areas of prevention, mental health promotion and education, community services, political and legal issues relating to mental health, the epidemiology of mental health, issues surrounding deinstitutionalization and multicultural issues in mental health.
**Ind/Abst** Psychol. Abstr. (1984-); PsycINFO; PsycLit.

US/0010-3853
**COMMUNITY MENTAL HEALTH JOURNAL.** [Commmunity ment. health j.]. **Added/Corp** National Council of Community Mental Health Centers (U.S.). Vol. 1 (Spring 1965)-. Academic Scholarly Publication. English. Six times a year. $255.00 US; $300.00 other. Human Sciences Press, PO Box 735, 233 Spring Street, New York NY 10013. **Tel** (212)620-8000, FAX (212)807-1047, telex 23421139. **(Subscription address:** Eurospan Ltd., Journals and Serials Division, 3 Henrietta Street, Covent Garden, London WC2E 8LU England.**) ED** David Cutler. **LC** RA790.A1; C53. **DD** 614.58/05. **NLM** W1 CO429N. **CODEN** CMHJAY. **[CCC]. Pr Rev.** available on microfilm and microfiche from University Microfilms International (UMI). Documents available from The Genuine Article, UMI Article Clearinghouse.
**Desc:** Internationally recognized for its pioneering efforts to coordinate emergent approaches to mental health and social well-being.
**Ind/Abst** Acad. Ind. [Computer File] (1992-); Acad. Search (July 1993-); Appl. Soc. Sci. Index Abstr.; Chicano Index; Crim. Justice Abstr.; Cumul. Index Nurs. Allied Health Lit.; Curr. Contents Soc. Behav. Sci.; EMBASE; Expand. Acad. Index (1989-); Health Plan. Adminis.; Health Source (Jul. 1993-); Hospit. Health Admin. Index; Hum. Resour. Abstr.; Index Med.; INFO-SOUTH Abstr.; J. Plan. Lit.; Linguist. Lang. Behav. Abstr.; Mag. Search; Med. Rev. Dig.; Middle East Abstr. Index; Multicult. Educ. Abstr.; Newsp. Period. Abstr. (1991-); Life Sci. Collect.; Pollut. Abstr. Indexes; Psychol. Abstr. (1973-); PsycINFO; PsycLit; Res. Alert [Full Cov.]; Sage Fam. Stud. Abstr. (?-?); Soc. Plann. Policy Dev. Abstr.; Soc. Sci. Source (Jul. 1993-); Soc. Sci. Cit. Index [Full Cov.]; Soc. Sci. Index; Soc. Sci. Index Fulltext (Winter 1988-) [Full Txt.]; Soc. Work Abstr. [Select. Cov.]; Sociol. Abstr.; Spec. Educ. Needs Abstr.

CN/1185-5347
**COMMUNITY SCENE.** [Community scene]. **Main/Corp** Saskatchewan. Saskatchewan Community Services. (Feb. 1991)-. Periodical. English. **DD** 363/.097124/05.

UK
**COMMUNITY SERVICE.** (19??)-. Bulletin. English. an. £2.00. Social Work Services Group, Statistics Branch, 43 Jeffrey Street / Room 422, Edinburgh EH1 1DG Scotland. **Tel** 031 244 5431, FAX 031 244 5387.

US
**COMMUNITY SOCIAL SERVICES ACT ... EFFECTIVENESS REPORT.** 1980-. English. an. Minnesota Department of Public Welfare, Centennial Office Building, St Paul MN 55155. **LC** HV98.M65; C65. **DD** 353.97760084.

UK/0307-6067
**COMMUNITY WORK.** ***Ceased.*** [Community work]. Vol. 1 (1974)-(19??). English. ir. Routledge, 11 New Fetter Lane, London EC4P 4EE England. **Tel** 071 583 9855, FAX 071 842 2298. **(Subscription address:** Kinokuniya Company Ltd., 38-1 Sakuragaoka 5, chome Setagaya-ku, Tokyo 156 Japan.**) LC** HN400.C6; C65. **DD** 309.2/6/0941.

US/0895-7118
**COMPACT (CHICAGO, ILL.).** ***Ceased.*** (COMPACT.). [Compact]. Vol. 1, No. 1 (1987)-?. Periodical. English. mo. S-N Publications, 103 N Second Street/Suite 200, West Dundee IL 60118. **DD** 362.
**Ind/Abst** Am. Hist. Life (1972-1976).

BE
**COMPENDIUM OF COMMUNITY PROVISIONS ON SOCIAL SECURITY / COMMISSION OF THE EUROPEAN COMMUNITIES.** **Added/Corp** Commission of the European Communities. 1st Ed. (1980)-. English. an. £16.60 UK; 18.00p Ireland. Office for Official Publications of the European Communities, 2 Rue Mercier, 2985 Luxembourg Luxembourg. **Tel** 011 352 499281, FAX 011 352 488573. **LC** KJE3281.A72; C66. **DD** 344.4/02/05; 344.04205.
**Desc:** Compiles the official texts and all information relating to social security for migrant workers.

US/0738-1034
**COMPENSATION & BENEFITS REPORT.** **See** Economics-Labor.

US
**COMPREHENSIVE ANNUAL SERVICES PROGRAM PLAN - (ARKANSAS).** **Main/Corp** Arkansas. Office of Title XX Service. 1978/79-. English. an. Arkansas Department of Human Services, Financial Support Systems/Slot 3350, PO Box 1437, Little Rock AR 72203. **LC** HV86; .A876. **DD** 361.6/2/09767. ***Continues*** *Arkansas. Social Services. Comprehensive Annual Services Program Plan.*

US
**COMPREHENSIVE ANNUAL SERVICES PROGRAM PLAN - (NEVADA).** **Main/Corp** Nevada. Dept. of Human Resources. Welfare Division. English. an. Nevada Department of Human Resources, 308 North Curry Street, Carson City NV 89701. **LC** HV86; .N353. **DD** 361.6/09793.

US
**COMPREHENSIVE SERVICES PROGRAM PLAN.** Program year July 1, 1981-June 30, 1983-. English. be. Nevada Department of Human Resources, 308 North Curry Street, Carson City NV 89701. **LC** HV86; .N353. **DD** 361.6/09793. ***Continues*** *Comprehensive Annual Services Program Plan.*

US/0889-6194
**COMPUTER USE IN SOCIAL SERVICES NETWORK : NEWSLETTER.** ***Title Change.*** **See** Computers.

US/0740-445X
**COMPUTERS IN HUMAN SERVICES.** **See** Computers.

CN/0319-4523
**COMSERVANT, THE.** Issue 1- Sept. 1973-. Periodical. English. qt. Saskatchewan Association for the Mentally Retarded, 3031 Louise Street, Saskatoon Sask. S7J 3LI Canada. **Tel** (306)955-3344. **DD** 362.1/097124.

CN/0226-5729
**CONCERTACTION.** [Concertaction]. **Added/Corp** Conseil Regional de la Sante et des Services Sociaux, Region sud de Montreal (6c) (Quebec). **VFOAT** Concert Action. Vol. 1, (March 1979)-. Periodical. French. Conseil Regional de la Sante et des Services Sociaux de la Region Sud de Montreal, Concertaction Secretariat, General/Communications, CRSS 6-C 125 Boulevard Sainte-Foy, Longueuil Quebec J4J 1W7 Canada. **DD** 361/.97143. ctrl circ.

BL
**CONJUNTURA SOCIAL.** Periodical. Portuguese. MPAS, rua Pedro Lessa 36 12 Andar, Rio de Janeiro Brazil. **LC** HV193; .C65. **DD** 361.6/0981.

US
**CONNECTICUT TITLE XX COMPREHENSIVE ANNUAL SERVICES PROGRAM PLAN.** **Main/Corp** Connecticut. Dept. of Human Resources. **VFOAT** Connecticut Human Resource Department Annual Services Plan. 1980/81-. English. an. Connecticut Department of Human Resources, PO Box 786, 1179 Main Street, Hartford CT 06101. **LC** HV86; .C865A. **DD** 353.97460084/05. ***Continues*** *Connecticut Comprehensive Title XX Social Services Program Plan.*

US
**CONNECTIONS.** **Added/Corp** Washington (State). Dept. of Social and Health Services. Vol. 1, No. 1 (Spring 1987)-. Periodical. English. qt. Office of Public Affairs / Olympia, Department of Social & Health Services, OB-44Q, Olympia WA 98504. **Tel** (206)753-2745. ***Continues*** *Overview.*

US
**CONSOLIDATED FEDERAL FUNDS REPORT. VOLUME I, COUNTY AREAS.** **Added/Corp** United States. Bureau of the Census. United States. Office of Management and Budget. **VFOAT** County Areas. (1983)-. English. an. $15.50. Superintendent of Documents, US Government Printing Office, Washington DC 20402. **Tel** (202)275-3328, FAX (202)786-2377. **(Subscription address:** US Government Bookstore / O'Neil Building, 2023 3rd Avenue North, Birmingham AL 35203.**) LC** HJ9; .C66. **DD** 336.1/85.

US/8750-9652
**CONTEMPORARY LONGTERM CARE.** **VFOAT** Contemporary Longtermcare; Contemporary Long-Term Care; Contemporary LTC. Vol. 8, No. 1 (Jan. 1985). Periodical. English. mo. $60.00. Bill Communications Inc., 355 Park Avenue South, New York NY 10010-1789. **Tel** (800)821-6897, (212)592-6262, FAX (212)592-6209. **ED** John Mitchell. **DD** 362. **NLM** W1; CO769MTD. **[CCC]. Ad Acc. Circ:** 33,000 (ctrl). available on microfilm and microfiche from University Microfilms International (UMI). ***Continues*** *Contemporary Administrator for Long-Term Care, 0745-2837.*
**Ind/Abst** Health Plan. Adminis.; Hospit. Health Admin. Index (1985-); Int. Pharm. Abstr.

US/0147-1082
**CONTEMPORARY PROBLEMS OF CHILDHOOD.** **See** Psychology.

AT/0313-6124
**CONTEMPORARY SOCIAL WORK EDUCATION.** [Contemp. soc. work educ.]. Vol. 1 (1977)-. Periodical. English. Australia International Press and Publications, 397 Little Collins Street, Melbourne VIC 3000 Australia.
**Ind/Abst** APAIS, Aust. Public Aff. Inf. Ser. (1978-); Soc. Work Abstr. (?-?).

US/1057-428X
**CONTINUING CARE.** [Contin. care]. Vol. 5, No. 10 (Nov. 1986)-. Periodical. English. Ten times a year. $58.50 US; $77.50 Canada; $71.50 Mexico; $88.50 other. Stevens Publishing Corporation, 225 North New Road, Waco TX 76702-2604. **Tel** (800)727-7573, (817)776-9000. **(Subscription address:** Stevens Publishing Corp., PO Box 2573, Waco TX 76702.**) DD** 363. **NLM** W1; CO775D. **[CCC]. *Continues*** *Continuing Care Coordinator.*
**Ind/Abst** Int. Pharm. Abstr.

●US
**CONTINUING CARE CONNECTION : LINKING LONG-TERM, HOME AND COMMUNITY CARE SYSTEMS.** **Added/Corp** Healthcare Association of New York. **VFOAT** Connection. Vol. 1, No. 1 (Jan 14, 1994)-. Periodical. English. Twenty-six times a year. $100.00 nonmembers; $40.00 members. Hospital Association of New York State, 74 North Pearl Street, Albany NY 12207. **Tel** (518)431-7600, FAX (518)431-7915. ***Formed by the union of*** *Home Care Update* ***and*** *Long-Term Care News.*

US/1070-9444
**CONTRIBUTIONS (NEWTON CENTER, NEWTON, MASS.).** (CONTRIBUTIONS / CAMBRIDGE FUND RAISING ASSOCIATES.). [Contributions]. **Added/Corp** Cambridge Fund Raising Associates. Vol. 1, No. 1 (Jan. 1987)-. Periodical. English. bm. $24.00 (one year), $36.00 (two year). Contributions, 634 Commonwealth Avenue, Suite 201, Newton Center MA 02159. **Tel** (617)964-2688. **ED** Jerry Cianciolo. **DD** 658. **Bk Rev**, (Qty: 20-30). **Ad Acc, Adv Mgr:** Kathleen Brennan. **Circ:** 16,500.
**Desc:** Focuses on fund raising, nonprofit management, and marketing. Includes columns on direct mail, planned giving, major gifts, legal matters, board development, and prospect research.

UK
**CORACLE (GLASGOW, STRATHCLYDE).** (THE CORACLE.). **Added/Corp** Iona Community. No. 1 (Summer 1980)-. Periodical. English. bm (6 issues). £10.00. Candlemakers Hall Pearce Institute, Iona Community Comm House Govan, Glasgow G51 1AT Scotland. **Tel** 041 427 6731. ***Continues*** *Coracle (Edinburgh, Lothian).*

CN/0225-7033
**CORD (HAMILTON).** (THE CORD.). [Cord]. **Added/Corp** Regional Association of Coordinators of Volunteers. Vol. 1 (Nov. 1977)-. Periodical. English. Three times a year. Regional Association of Co-Ordinators of Volunteers, Publicity Director, 1051 Upper James Street, Hamilton Ontario L9C 3A6 Canada. **DD** 361.3/7/06071352. ctrl circ.

●US/1061-1274
**CORPORATE AND FOUNDATION GRANTS.** **See** Business.

US/0747-8003
**CORPORATE GIVING WATCH.** [Corp. giv. watch]. **Added/Corp** Taft Corporation. Vol. 1, Issue 1 (April 1981)-. English. mo. $149.00 (includes Corporate

Giving Profiles). Taft Group, 835 Penobscott Building, Customer Service, Detroit MI 48226. **Tel** (800)877-8238, FAX (313)961-6083. **(Subscription address:** Taft Group, PO Box 71701, Chicago, IL 60694; telephone: (800)877-8238 ext. 1716) **ED** David W. Grant. **LC** HV97.A3; C645. **DD** 361.7/65/0973. **Bk Rev. Ad Acc. Circ:** 3,200.
**Desc:** News and ideas for nonprofit organizations seeking corporate funds.
**Ind/Abst** Curr. Lit. Fam. Plan. (19??-199?).

●US/1058-689X
**CORPORATE GIVING YELLOW PAGES (1992).** (CORPORATE GIVING YELLOW PAGES.). [Corp. giv. yellow pages]. **Added/Corp** Taft Group (Rockville, Md.). (1992)-. English. an (published in Oct. of prior year). $88.00. Taft Group, 835 Penobscott Building, Customer Service, Detroit MI 48226. **Tel** (800)877-8238, FAX (313)961-6083. **(Subscription address:** Taft Group, PO Box 71701, Chicago, IL 60694; telephone: (800)877-8238 ext. 1716) **DD** 361. ***Continues*** *Taft Guide to Corporate Giving Contacts, 1048-0374.*

US/0738-8144
**CORRECTIONS COMPENDIUM.** [Correct. compend.]. **Added/Corp** Contact, Inc. (197?)-. Periodical. English. mo. $48.00 US; $60.00 Canada & Mexico; $64.00 other. Contact Publications Inc., PO Box 81826, Lincoln NE 68501. **Tel** (402)464-0602, FAX (402)404-5931. **ED** Su Perk Davis. **DD** 365. Index available. **Circ:** 1,250.
**Desc:** For corrections professionals. Features in-depth articles, legal issue case reports, news updates and monthly surveys unique in this field.
**Ind/Abst** Crim. Justice Abstr.

SZ/0538-8295
**COST OF SOCIAL SECURITY. LE COUT DE LA SECURITE SOCIALE. EL COSTO DE LA SEGURIDAD SOCIAL, THE.** **Main/Corp** International Labour Office. **Added/Corp** International Social Security Association. International Labour Office Cout de la Securite Sociale. International Labour Office Costo de la Seguridad Social. **VFOAT** Cout de la Securite Sociale; Le Cout de la Securite Sociale; El Costo de la Seguridad Social. (1951)-. English (French and Spanish). ir (every four years). Price varies. International Labour Office - ILO, Publications Sales Service, CH-1211 Geneva 22 Switzerland. **Tel** 011 41 22 7996111. **(Subscription address:** International Labor Office / Albany, NY, 49 Sheridan Avenue, Albany NY 12210.) **LC** HD7091; .I57. **DD** 368.4.
**Desc:** A world-wide comparison of social security expenditures.

US/0193-7375
**COUNSELING AND HUMAN DEVELOPMENT.** Vol. 10, No. 1 (Sept. 1977)-. Periodical. English. mo (except June-Aug.). $40.00 (institutions), $30.00 (individuals). Love Publishing Company, 1777 South Bellaire Street, Denver CO 80222. **Tel** (303)757-2579. **ED** Stanley F. Love. **Bk Rev. Ad Acc. Circ:** 2,000. available on microfilm and microfiche from University Microfilms International (UMI). ***Continues*** *Focus on Guidance.*
**Desc:** For counselors and those engaged in human services.

UK
**COUNSELLING : THE JOURNAL OF THE BRITISH ASSOCIATION FOR COUNSELLING.** English. qt. £33.00 Europe; £30.00 other. British Association for Counselling, 1 Regent Place, Rugby CV21 2PJ England. **Tel** 011 44 788 578328, FAX 011 44 788 562189.
**Ind/Abst** Appl. Soc. Sci. Index Abstr.

US/1047-7314
**COUNSELOR (ARLINGTON, VA.), THE.** **See** Drug Abuse and Alcoholism.

US/1052-2573
**CREATIVE FORECASTING.** (CREATIVE FORECASTING : A MONTHLY PUBLICATION FOR ACTIVITY PROFESSIONALS.). [Creat. forecast.]. (19??)-. Periodical. English. mo. $30.00 US; $35.00 other. Creative Forecasting Inc., 2607 Farragut Circle, Colorado Springs CO 80907. **Tel** (719)633-3174. **ED** Mary Anne Clagett & Regi Schlis. **DD** 649. **Ad Acc. Circ:** 5,000 (ctrl).
**Desc:** This publication is for activity professionals who work in nursing homes, adult day care centers, retirement facilities, and hospitals.

●US/1064-5136
**CRISIS INTERVENTION AND TIME-LIMITED TREATMENT.** (1994)-. Periodical. English. Three times a year. Harwood Academic Publishers / New York, PO Box 786, Cooper Station, New York NY 10276. **Tel** (212)206-8900, (201)643-7500. **CODEN** CITTEW.
**Desc:** Focusing on the latest clinical innovations and research of those working in crisis intervention.

BL
**CRITICA SOCIAL.** No. 1- Dec. 1974-. Portuguese. Escola de Servicio Social, Universidade Catolica de Minas Gerais, Av Dom Jose Gaspar 500, Belo Horizonte 30.000 Brazil. **LC** HV4; .C74.

US
**CROSSLINK, THE.** V. 13, No. 3- ; Nov. 1978-. Periodical. English. Greater Buffalo Chapter, American Red Cross, 786 Delaware Avenue, Buffalo NY 14209. **Tel** (716)886-7500. **ED** Deborah Williams, Peggy J Klimek. **Circ:** 14,500. ***Continues*** *ARC/Rays.*
**Desc:** Newsletter focusing on news of Red Cross Chapter and blood region.

US/1044-5544
**CROSSROADS (SPRINGDALE, ARK.).** (CROSSROADS.). **Added/Corp** Orphan Train Heritage Society of America. (198?)-. Periodical. English. qt. $20.00. Orphan Train Heritage Society of America, 4912 Trout Farm Road, Springdale AR 72764. **Tel** (501)756-2780. **ED** Mary Ellen Johnson. **LC** HV986; .C76. **DD** 362.7/34/097305. cum. index. **Bk Rev. Ad Acc.**
**Desc:** True experiences told by living orphan train riders plus research information on the era.

CN/0701-8967
**CRSSS 09.** (CRSSS 09 : BULLETIN D'INFORMATION.). [CRSSS 09]. **VAT** Bulletin d'Information - CRSSS 09; Conseil Regional de la Sante et des Services Sociaux 09. Vol. 1, No. 1 (31 Jan. 1978)-. Bulletin. French. Free. Direction Des Communications, Conseil Regional De La Sante Et Des Services, 09 896, Rue De Puyjalon, Hauterive Quebec G5C 1N1. **DD** 361/.971417. ctrl circ.

MX/0186-5617
**CUESTION SOCIAL (MEXICO CITY , MEXICO : 1985).** (CUESTION SOCIAL.). No. 1 (Summer/Autumn 1985)-. Periodical. Spanish. qt. IMSS, Avenida San Jeronimo Esquina con san Ramon, Sin Numero, San Jeronimo Lidice, CP 10100 Mexico DF Mexico. **LC** HD7131. **NLM** W1; CU294. ***Continues*** *Cuestion Social.*

AT/0314-7320
**CURRENCY.** ***Ceased.*** [Currency]. (1977)-(Dec. 1992). Periodical. English. Twenty-five times a year. Alcohol & Drug Foundation, PO Box 269, Woden ACT 2606 Australia. **Tel** 61 062 82 1002. **DD** 378.9452.
**Ind/Abst** Aust. Educ. Index.

US/0162-5780
**CURRENT INTERESTS OF THE FORD FOUNDATION.** **Main/Corp** Ford Foundation. (1974/1975)-. English. be. Free. Office of Communications, 320 East 43rd Street, New York NY 10017. **ED** William Rust. **LC** HV97.F62; F67a. **DD** 361.7/6/0973. **Circ:** 10,000.
**Desc:** A report in the Foundation's plans and programs, including information in grant applications.

SZ/0379-0290
**CURRENT RESEARCH IN SOCIAL SECURITY.** **Added/Corp** International Social Security Association. **VFOAT** Recherches en Securite Sociale; Forschungen in der Sozialen Sicherheit; Investigaciones en la Seguridad Social. (1978)-. Periodical. English (French, German and Spanish). sa. Free upon request. International Social Security Association, Case Postale 1, CH-1211 Geneva 22 Switzerland. **Tel** 011 41 22 7996617, FAX 011 41 22 7986385. **LC** HD7088; .C87. **DD** 368.4/005. ***Continues*** *International Social Security Association. Lists of Research Reports.*
**Ind/Abst** Hum. Rights Intern. Rep.; Trop. Dis. Bull.

US/0146-874X
**CURRENTS (PHILADELPHIA).** (CURRENTS.). Periodical. English. qt. Horizon House Publications, 1019 Stafford House, 5555 Wissahicken Avenue, Philadelphia PA 19144. **LC** RA790.6; .C88. **DD** 362.2/0973. **NLM** W1 CU826B.

GW
**DATEN ZUR SOZIALSTRUKTUR: DIE MATERIELLE LEBENSSICHERUNG.** **See** Economics.

US/0885-6400
**DAV MAGAZINE (1985).** (DAV MAGAZINE : THE OFFICIAL VOICE OF THE DISABLED AMERICAN VETERANS AND DAV AUXILIARY.). **Added/Corp** Disabled American Veterans. DAV Auxiliary. **VFOAT** DAV. **VAT** Disabled American Veterans (1985). Vol. 27, Issue 6 (June 1985)-. Periodical. English. mo. $4.00. Disabled American Veterans, 3725 Alexandria Pike, Cold Springs KY 41076. **Tel** (606)441-7300. **ED** Frank Norberg. **Circ:** 1,100,000. available on audiocassette. ***Continues*** *DAV (Cold Spring, KY.), 0276-7465.*
**Desc:** News and information of interest to combat disabled veterans and their families. It focuses on legislative initiatives for veterans, programs and services provided by the Veterans Administration and DAV service programs.

CN/0711-7930
**DAY CARE CENTRES AND NURSERY SCHOOLS HAMILTON-WENTWORTH.** [Day care cent. nurs. sch., Hamilt.-Wentworth]. 1981-. Periodical. English. Free. Day Care Centres and Nursery Schools Hamilton-Wentworth, Community Information Service, Hamilton-Wentworth/6th Floor, 155 James Street South, Hamilton Ontario L8P 3A4 Canada. **DD** 362.7/12/02571352. ***Continues*** *Day Care Directory, 0382-0645.*

CN/0821-4360
**DAY CARE FOR CHILDREN (KITCHENER).** (DAY CARE FOR CHILDREN.). [Day care child.]. 1982/83-. English. an. $0.50 Per No. Community Information Centre, Waterloo Region, 10 Water Street North, Kitchener Ontario N2H 5A5. **DD** 362.7/12/02571344.

US
**DAY CARE INFORMATION SERVICE.** Vol. 11, No. 3 (Feb. 15, 1982). English. bw. $184.00 US; $209.00 other. United Communications Group, 11300 Rockville Pike, Suite 1100, Rockville MD 20852. **Tel** (301)816-8950 ext. 223, FAX (301)816-8945. ***Continues*** *Day Care & Child Development Reports, 0191-6726.*

US/0732-7889
**DAY CARE JOURNAL.** ***Ceased.*** (DAY CARE JOURNAL : VOICE OF THE DAY CARE COUNCIL OF AMERICA.). [Day care j.]. **Added/Corp** Day Care Council of America. Vol. 1, No. 1 (Summer 1982)-?. Periodical. English. bm. Day Care Council of America, 1602 17th Street NW, Washington DC 20009. **Tel** (202)638-2316. **LC** HV854; .D384. **DD** 362.7/12/0973.

CN/0384-1537
**DAY CARE (TORONTO).** (DAY CARE.). **Added/Corp** Ontario Welfare Council. Action Committee on Day Care. No. 1 (Jan. 1970)-. Periodical. English. Ontario Welfare Council, Suite 404, 1240 Bay Street, Toronto Ontario M5R 2A7. **DD** 362.7/1.

US
**DELPHI, THE.** Vol. 1, No. 1 (Jan. 1980)-. Periodical. English. qt. $8.00 (individuals), $15.00 (institutions). Southern California Rape Prevention Center, 2113 West Loma Vista Place, Los Angeles CA 90039.
**Desc:** Provides a link between research and service related to sexual violence issues: legal, medical, psychological, sociocultural and political.

US
**DEPARTMENT OF HEALTH AND SOCIAL SERVICES QUARTERLY MAGAZINE.** **Main/Corp** Alaska. Dept. of Health and Social Services. **VFOAT** Alaska Health and Social Services Quarterly. (19??)-. Periodical. English. qt. Pouch H-81, Juneau AK 99811. **LC** HV86; .A412. **DD** 361/.9798. ***Continues*** *Alaska. Dept. of Health and Social Services. HSS Quarterly.*

US
**DEPENDENCY.** **Added/Corp** New York (N.Y.). Human Resources Administration. Office of Policy and Economic Research. No. 1 (Apr. 1985)-. Periodical. English. sa. Human Resources Administration Economic Research, 71 Worth Street/4th Floor, New York NY 10013. **Tel** (212)334-7847. **LC** HC108.N7; D47. **DD** 361.9747/1021. ***Formed by the union of*** *New York City Social Report; Quarterly Public Assistance Report for ...; Medicaid Data Report; Quarterly Rent Report* ***and*** *Small Area Demographic Report.*

CL/0716-7865
**DERECHO A LA INFANCIA.** **Added/Corp** Fundacion Para la Proteccion de la Infancia Danada por los Estados de Emergencia. (19??)-. Periodical. Spanish. bm (6 issues). $18.00. Fundacion Pidee, Holanda 3607 Nunoa, Santiago Chile. **Tel** 011 56 2 2258752. **LC** HV747.L3; D47. **DD** 362.7/098/05.

CN/1186-8953
**DESTINATION INTEGRATION.** [Destin. integr.]. **Added/Corp** National Access Awareness Week Committee (Canada). **VFOAT** Destination Integration. (1991)-. Periodical. English (French). qt. Free. National Access Awareness Week Committee (Canada), Room 13-A5, Jules Leger Building, 25 Eddy Street, Hull Quebec K1A 0M5 Canada. **DD** 362.4/048/097105.

CN/1186-8953
**DESTINATION INTEGRATION.** [Destin. integr.]. **Added/Corp** Comite de la Semaine Nationale pour l'Integration des Personnes Handicapees (Canada). **VFOAT** Destination Integration. (1991)-. Periodical. French (English). qt. Free. Comite de la Semaine Nationale pour L'Integration des Personnes Handicapees, Salle 13-A5, Edifice Jules Leger, 25 Rue Eddy, Hull Quebec K1A 0M5 Canada. **DD** 362.4/048/097105.

DK
**DET CENTRALE HANDICAPRADS VIRKSOMHED I ... .** **Main/Corp** Centrale Handicaprad (Denmark). **VFOAT** Arsberetning. 1980-. Danish. an. Socialstyrelsen, Kristineberg 6 Postboks 2555, 2100 Kobenhavn Denmark. **LC** HV1559.D4; C44A.

# Sociology —Social Services and Welfare

II/0376-8279
**DETAILED DEMAND FOR GRANTS OF LABOUR AND SOCIAL WELFARE DEPARTMENT.** *Title Change.* **See** Economics-Labor.

GW/0012-0332
**DEUTSCHE JUGEND.** (Apr. 1953)-. Academic Scholarly Publication. German. mo. DM74.00. Juventa Verlag GmbH, Ehretstrasse 3, D 69469 Weinheim Germany. **Tel** 011 49 6201 61035, FAX 011 49 6201 13135. **ED** Gerd Brenner. **DD** 301. Index available. **Bk Rev. Ad Acc.** Full Page (B&W) DM1200.00. Half Page (B&W) DM600.00. **Circ:** 4,000.
 **Desc:** Covers youth, social work, problems of adolescence, sociology and psychology of adolescence, and politics concerning adolescents. A practical guide to social work.

SZ
**DEUTSCHES ROTES KREUZ DER DEUTSCHEN DEMOKRATISCHEN REPUBLIK. Main/Corp** Red Cross. Germany (Democratic Republic) Deutsches Rotes Kreuz. Periodical. German. mo. Deutscher Judo Verband, Redaktion Ippon Segewaldweg 40, D 12557 Berlin Germany. **Tel** 011 49 711 210770, telex 051 678. **LC** HV580.G3; R42B. **DD** 361.7/7/0943.

US
**DEVELOPMENTAL DISABILITIES STATE PLAN. Main/Corp** Minnesota State Planning Agency. Developmental Disabilities Planning Office. English. Governor's Planning Council on Developmental Disabilities, 300 Centennial Office Building, St. Paul MN 55155. **LC** HV3006.M58; M48A. **DD** 362.3/09776.

US/0092-5470
**DEVELOPMENTS IN HUMAN SERVICES.** *Ceased.* [Dev. hum. serv.] Vol. 1 (1973)-(19??). English. ir. Human Sciences Press, PO Box 735, 233 Spring Street, New York NY 10013. **Tel** (212)620-8000, FAX (212)807-1047, telex 23421139. **LC** HV13; .D47. **DD** 361/.005. **NLM** W1 DE997W.

CN/0822-7128
**DEVELOPPEMENT SOCIAL EN PERSPECTIVES.** (DEVELOPPEMENT SOCIAL EN PERSPECTIVES / CONSEIL CANADIEN DE DEVELOPPEMENT SOCIAL.). [Dev. soc. perspect.]. **VFOAT** Perspectives. **VAT** Perspectives - Conseil Canadien de Developpement Social. Vol. 1, No. 1-. Periodical. French. Four times a year. Free to members only. Conseil Canadien de Developpement Social, 55 Av Parkdale, Ottawa Ontario K1Y 4G1 Canada. **Tel** (613)728-1865, FAX (613)728-9387. **ED** Carolyn Brown. **DD** 361/.971. **Circ:** 3,000 (ctrl). **Continues in part** Social Development, 0316-313X.
 **Desc:** Provides a review of social issues, trends and programs in Canada; keeps you up to date on CCSD activities and projects.

US/8755-8858
**DIABETIC DIARY.** *Suspended.* [Diabt. diary]. Vol. 1, Issue 1 (Nov./Dec. 1984)-?. Periodical. bm (every two months: Nov., Jan., March, May, July, and Sept.). $15.00. Diabetic Diary, PO Box 836, Enfield CT 06012. **DD** 616.

CN/0383-8528
**DIALECT. Added/Corp** Saskatchewan Association for the Mentally Retarded. Saskatchewan Association for Community Living. Vol. 1 (Feb. 1, 1976)-. Periodical. English. Six times a year. Free. Saskatchewan Association for the Mentally Retarded, 3031 Louise Street, Saskatoon Sask. S7J 3LI Canada. **Tel** (306)955-3344. **DD** 362.3/06/27124.

AT/0725-2455
**DIARY OF SOCIAL LEGISLATION AND POLICY. Added/Corp** University of Melbourne. Institute of Applied Economic and Social Research. Institute of Family Studies (Australia) University of New South Wales. Social Welfare Research Centre. (1980)-. Periodical. English. an. 10.00Aus$. Australian Institute of Family Studies, 300 Queen Street, Melbourne Victoria 3000 Australia. **Tel** 61 3 6086888, FAX 61 3 6000886. **LC** LAW. **DD** 344.94; 349.404.
 **Desc:** Summarizes the year's legislative and administrative changes made by the Australian Federal government, and to a lesser extent by the State State governments, in the social policy field.

US/0146-9088
**DIGEST OF SELECTED REPORTS - UNITED WAY OF AMERICA.** *Ceased.* (DIGEST OF SELECTED REPORTS.). **Main/Corp** United Way of America. Information Center. Vol. 2, No. 2 (Oct. 1973)-No. 1 (1992). English. sa. United Way of America, 701 North Fairfax Street, Alexandria VA 22314. **Tel** (703)836-7100. **LC** HV91; .U6a. **DD** 361/.973. **Circ:** 2,000 (ctrl). **Continues** Digest of Current Reports & Publications Catalog.
 **Desc:** Abstracts local United Way Organization reports in planning, allocations, research and social welfare.

US
**DIRECT LOAN PROGRAM FOR THE ELDERLY OR HANDICAPPED.** Government Publication. English. ir. US Department of Housing and Urban Development, 451 Seventh Street SW, Washington DC 20401. **Tel** (202)708-0980, FAX (202)708-0299.

US
**DIRECTIONS; HUMAN RESOURCES DIRECTORY OF SAN DIEGO-IMPERIAL COUNTIES & TIJUANA. Added/Corp** United Way of San Diego County. Community Contact Services. **VFOAT** Human Resources Directory of San Diego-Imperial Counties & Tijuana. Vol. 1 (Spring 1974)-. Periodical. English. be. $39.00. United Way of San Diego County, PO Box 23543, San Diego CA 92193-0543. **Tel** (619)531-4799. Index available (free). **Supersedes** Directory of Organizations Meeting Human Needs in San Diego County.

US/0091-1003
**DIRECTORY : DIOCESAN AGENCIES OF CATHOLIC CHARITIES, UNITED STATES, PUERTO RICO, AND CANADA.** Directory. English. an. $2.00. National Conference of Catholic Charities, 1346 Connecticut Avenue NW, Washington DC 20036. **LC** HV89; .N25. **DD** 361.7/5. **Continues** Directory of Diocesan Agencies of Catholic Charities in the United States and Canada.

US/0195-9859
**DIRECTORY OF ADULT DAY CARE CENTERS.** 1977-. Directory. English. Health Care Financing Administration, 6325 Security Boulevard, Room 700, Baltimore MD 21207. **Tel** (410)966-3000, FAX (410)966-5267. **NLM** WT 22 AA1 D4.

US
**DIRECTORY OF AGENCIES : U.S. VOLUNTARY, INTERNATIONAL VOLUNTARY, INTERGOVERNMENTAL.** *Ceased.* **Added/Corp** National Association of Social Workers. (19??)-(19??). Directory. English. ir. National Association of Social Workers, 750 First Street Northeast, Suite 700, Washington DC 20002-4241. **Tel** (800)638-8799, (202)408-8600, FAX (301)587-1321.

US
**DIRECTORY OF APPROVED PROVIDERS OF TRAINING IN THE IDENTIFICATION AND REPORTING OF CHILD ABUSE AND INFORMATION PERTAINING TO EXEMPTIONS. Added/Corp** University of the State of New York. Division of Professional Education. **VFOAT** Approved Providers of Training in Child Abuse Recognition and Reporting. (1991)-. Directory. English. New York Education Department, Publication Distribution Unit, Albany NY 12234.

US/0163-6065
**DIRECTORY OF BLOOD ESTABLISHMENTS REGISTERED UNDER SECTION 510 OF THE FOOD, DRUG, AND COSMETIC ACT.** 1976-. Directory. English. an. US Food and Drug Administration / FDA, 5600 Fishers Lane, Room 14-71, Rockville MD 20857. **Tel** (301)443-2410, FAX (301)443-0755. **LC** RM172; .D54. **DD** 362.1. **NLM** WH 22 AA1 D4.

US/0147-4405
**DIRECTORY OF CHILD CARE CENTERS.** Directory. English. Department of Social Services / Michigan, 300 South Capitol Avenue, Lansing MI 48026. **LC** HV857.M5; D57. **DD** 362.7/1.

US/0096-3054
**DIRECTORY OF COMMUNITY-BASED MENTAL RETARDATION SERVICES.** Directory. English. be. free. Office of Mental Retardation, State House Station Box 94728. **LC** HV3006.N2; D57. **DD** 362.3/025/782. **Circ:** 1,000.
 **Desc:** Directory of community based mental retardation services in Nebraska.

US/0361-6282
**DIRECTORY OF COMMUNITY CARE FACILITIES.** March 1975-. Directory. English. Sacramento Department of Health Facilities Licensing Section, 744 P Street/Room 440, Sacramento CA 95814. **LC** HV742.C2; D57. **DD** 362/.025/794. **NLM** WA 22 AC2 D4D.

CN/0316-1099
**DIRECTORY OF COMMUNITY (HAMILTON).** *Title Change.* (DIRECTORY OF COMMUNITY SERVICES.). 1966/67-. Directory. English. Social Planning and Research Council of Hamilton and District, 153 1/2 King Street East, Hamilton Ontario L8N 1B1 Canada. **Tel** (416)522-1148. **DD** 361/.0025/71352. **Continues** Directory of Community Services of Hamilton and District, 0316-1102. **Continued by** Directory of Community Services for Hamilton and District, 0702-0171.

CN/0826-7391
**DIRECTORY OF COMMUNITY SERVICES FOR HAMILTON-WENTWORTH.** [Dir. community serv. Hamilt-Wentworth]. **Added/Corp** Community Information Service Hamilton Wentworth. 8th Edition (1983)-. Directory. English. an. $40.00. Community Information Service Hamilton-Wentworth, Public Library, 55 York Boulevard, Hamilton Ontario L8N 4E4 Canada. **Tel** (416)528-0104. **DD** 361/.0025/71352. **Continues** Directory of Community Services, 0702-018X.
 **Desc:** Information on public welfare, charities and social aid.

CN/0713-4681
**DIRECTORY OF COMMUNITY SERVICES FOR WATERLOO REGION.** [Dir. community serv. Waterloo reg.]. Directory. English. an. 25.00Can$. Directory of Community Services, c/o Community Information Centre, 10 Water Street North, Kitchener Ontario N2H 5A5 Canada. **Tel** (519)579-3800. **DD** 361/.0025/71344. Index available. **Circ:** 1,000.
 **Desc:** A comprehensive guide to community services in Waterloo region, including details about hundreds of nonprofit and government organizations.

US/0070-5306
**DIRECTORY OF COMMUNITY SERVICES IN MARYLAND.** [Dir. community serv. Md.]. Directory. English. be. Community Services in Maryland, 200 East Lexington Street, Baltimore MD 21202. **LC** HV98.M3; D57. **DD** 361/.0025/752.

CN/0315-0631
**DIRECTORY OF COMMUNITY SERVICES IN METROPOLITAN TORONTO.** [Dir. community serv. Metrop. Tor.]. **Added/Corp** Community Information Centre of Metropolitan Toronto. **VFOAT** Community Services in Metropolitan Toronto. (1979)-. Directory. English. an. 50.00Can$. Community Information Center of Metropolitan Toronto, 590 Jarvis Street 5th Floor, Toronto Ontario M4Y 2J4 Canada. **Tel** (416)392-4575. **ED** Beth White. **DD** 361/.0025/713541. **Ad Acc. Circ:** 5,000. available on an online database. **Continues** Community Services in Metropolitan Toronto (1974)., 0315-0631.
 **Desc:** Directory of social service organizations in metropolitan Toronto with program details.

CN/0823-6046
**DIRECTORY OF COMMUNITY SERVICES IN REGIONAL NIAGARA.** [Dir. community serv. reg. Niagara]. **Added/Corp** Information Niagara. **VFOAT** Regional Niagara Directory of Services. (19??)-. English. an (Jan.). 28.00Can$. Information Niagara, 125 Welland Avenue, St. Catharine L2R 2N5 Ontario Canada. **Tel** (905)682-6611. **DD** 361/.0025/71338. **Circ:** 1,000.
 **Desc:** A directory of human service agencies in the Niagara region in Ontario Canada. Special sections on mental health, addiction treatment service, long-term care services and services for children with special needs.

CN/0381-629X
**DIRECTORY OF COMMUNITY SERVICES (NEW WESTMINSTER).** (DIRECTORY OF COMMUNITY SERVICES.). Began with 1973 issue?. Directory. English. an. United Good Neighbour Fund, 105, 26 Lorne Street, New Westminister BC V3M 3L7 Canada. **DD** 361/.0025/71133. **Supersedes** Introduction to Agency Services.

US
**DIRECTORY OF COMMUNITY SERVICES (NEW YORK PUBLIC LIBRARY).** (DIRECTORY OF COMMUNITY SERVICES.). **Added/Corp** New York Public Library. **VFOAT** Directorio de Servicios Para la Comunidad. (1980)-. Directory. English. an. $40.00. New York Public Library, Office of Branch Libraries, 455 Fifth Avenue, New York NY 10016. **Tel** (212)340-0909. **ED** Beth Wladis. **LC** F128.18; .D57. **DD** 917.47/0025. **Continues in part** New York Public Library Directory of Community Services, 0191-6629. **Absorbed in part by** Directory of Community Services (New York Public Library). Spanish. Directorio de Servicios para la Comunidad, 1981.
 **Desc:** Covers of over 2,500 community organizations and their services.

CN/0705-7075
**DIRECTORY OF COMMUNITY SERVICES, OTTAWA-CARLETON.** **VFOAT** Ottawa-Carleton, Repertoire des Services Communautaires. 1976/77-. Directory. French (English). an. Centre d'Information Communautaire, 377 rue Rideau, Ottawa Ontario K1N 5Y6 Canada. **DD** 361/.0025/71384. **Continues** Directory of Social Services, Ottawa-Carleton, 0318-9686.

## Sociology —Social Services and Welfare

CN/0709-0749
### DIRECTORY OF COMMUNITY SERVICES (SUDBURY). Title Change.
(DIRECTORY OF COMMUNITY SERVICES.). [Dir. community serv.]. **Main/Corp** Sudbury Public Library. **VFOAT** Repertoire des Services Communautaires. (1975)-. Directory. English. an. Information and Reference Department, Sudbury Public Library, Civic Square West Tower, 200 Brady Street, Sudbury Ontario P3E 5K3 Canada. **Tel** (705)675-1155. **ED** Michaele Mueller. **DD** 361/.0025/713133. **Circ**: 500. *Continued by* Repertoire des Services Communautaires, 0823-891X.
**Desc**: A list of social service agencies. Covers health, housing, counselling, legal employment, and vocational services, in the regional municipality of Sudbury.

US/8755-7118
### DIRECTORY OF COOPERATING AGENCIES.
(DIRECTORY OF COOPERATING AGENCIES / UNITED STATES DEPARTMENT OF AGRICULTURE, FOOD AND NUTRITION SERVICE.). [Dir. coop. agencies]. Directory. English. ir. United States Department of Agriculture Food & Nutrition Service, 3101 Park Center Drive, Room 803, Alexandria VA 22302. **Tel** (703)305-2062, FAX (703)305-2908. **LC** HV696.F6; D57. **DD** 363.8/83/02573.

●US
### DIRECTORY OF CORPORATE AND FOUNDATION GIVERS, THE. Added/Corp
Taft Group (Rockville, Md.). **VFOAT** Corporate and Foundation Givers. (1992)-. Directory. English. an (published in Nov. of prior year). $225.00. Taft Group, 835 Penobscott Building, Customer Service, Detroit MI 48226. **Tel** (800)877-8238, FAX (313)961-6083. **(Subscription address:** Taft Group, PO Box 71701, Chicago, IL 60694; telephone: (800)877-8238 ext. 1716) **LC** HG4028.C6; D567. **DD** 361.7/65/02573.

US/0277-0873
### DIRECTORY OF EVALUATION TRAINING.
(DIRECTORY OF EVALUATION TRAINING / EVALUATION RESEARCH SOCIETY.). [Dir. eval. train.]. Directory. English. Pintail Press, 4122 Edmunds Street NW, Washington DC 20007. **LC** H62.5.U5; D567. **DD** 361.6/1/071073.

US/8755-593X
### DIRECTORY OF FACILITIES OBLIGATED TO PROVIDE UNCOMPENSATED SERVICES BY STATE AND CITY. See Medical Science and
Technology-Hospital Administration and Medical Centers.

US/0148-5091
### DIRECTORY OF FEDERAL DROUGHT ASSISTANCE. Directory. English. Institute For
Policy Research, Western Governors, 2480 West 26th Avenue, Denver CO 80211. **LC** HD1759; .D57. **DD** 362.5.

US
### DIRECTORY OF GOVERNORS AND STATE OFFICIALS RESPONSIBLE FOR DISASTER OPERATIONS. Government
Publication. English. an. US Department of Housing and Urban Development, 451 Seventh Street SW, Washington DC 20401. **Tel** (202)708-0980, FAX (202)708-0299. **LC** HV555.U6; D55. **DD** 361.5/025/73. available on microfiche (Vols. for (1979) distributed to depository libraries).

US
### DIRECTORY OF GRANTS FOR ORGANIZATIONS SERVING PEOPLE WITH DISABILITIES. See Physically Impaired.

US/0149-0788
### DIRECTORY OF HALFWAY HOUSES AND GROUP HOMES FOR TROUBLED CHILDREN. Directory. English. $1.00. Journal of
Drug Issues, PO Box 4021, Tallahassee FL 32315. **Tel** (904)386-6551. **LC** HV9091; .D56. **DD** 362.7/4.

US
### DIRECTORY OF HEALTH, WELFARE AND RECREATION SERVICES FOR GREATER DALLAS. 1969-. Directory. English.
Community Cnl Greater Dallas, 2121 Main Street/Suite 500, Dallas TX 75201. **Tel** (214)741-5851. *Continues* Directory of Health, Welfare, and Recreation Services for Dallas County, Texas.

US/0364-4766
### DIRECTORY OF HUMAN SERVICE ORGANIZATIONS. Directory. English. Legislative
Council - Alaska, State Capitol, Juneau AK 99811. **Tel** (406)444-3064. **LC** HV98.A4; D57. **DD** 361/.0025/798.

US
### DIRECTORY OF HUMAN SERVICES IN THE KALAMAZOO AREA. Directory. English.
an. $6.75. Library Office of Publications, Desk Kalamazoo Public Library, 315 South Rose Street, Kalamazoo MI 49007. **Tel** (616)342-9837. **ED** Margean Gladysz. **LC** HV99.K27; D57. **DD** 362/.025/77417. Each issue contains an index to its own contents (no volume index)--loose.
**Circ**: 1,000 (ctrl).
**Desc**: Contains area providers of non-profit human services; that is health and medical care plus financial and other aid sources.

US/0749-050X
### DIRECTORY OF INFORMATION AND REFERRAL SERVICES IN THE UNITED STATES AND CANADA. [Dir. inf. ref. serv. U.S.
Can.]. (1975). Directory. English. ir. $33.00 non member; $25.00 members. Alliance of Information and Referral Services, 1100 West 42nd Street, Suite 310, Indianapolis IN 46208. **LC** HV89; .D48. **DD** 361/.025/73.

US/0741-8140
### DIRECTORY OF INTERPRETERS FOR THE DEAF IN TEXAS. Added/Corp Texas
Commission for the Deaf. (1983)-. Directory. English. an. Texas Commission for the Deaf, PO Box 12904 Capitol Station, Austin TX 78711. **LC** HV2402; .T48a. **DD** 362.4/283. *Continues* Texas Commission for the Deaf. Directory of Commission-Qualified Interpreters for the Deaf.

US/0271-0277
### DIRECTORY OF JEWISH FAMILY & CHILDREN'S AGENCIES. VFOAT AJFCA
Directory of Jewish Family & Children's Agencies. **VAT** Directory of Jewish Family and Children's Agencies. Directory. English. $3.50. Association of Jewish Family and Children's Agencies, 200 Park Avenue South/6th Floor, New York NY 10003. **LC** HV3191; .D568. **DD** 362.8/49240273.

US/1042-9042
### DIRECTORY OF MEMBER AGENCIES - CHILD WELFARE LEAGUE OF AMERICA (1986). (DIRECTORY OF MEMBER
AGENCIES / CHILD WELFARE LEAGUE OF AMERICA.). [Dir. memb. agencies - Child Welf. Leag. Am.]. **Main/Corp** Child Welfare League of America. (1987)-. Directory. English. be. $14.00. Child Welfare League of America, 440 1st Street Northwest, Suite 310, Washington DC 20001. **Tel** (202)638-2952, FAX (202)638-4004. **LC** HV741; .C5345c. **DD** 362. **NLM** WA 22; AA1 C5. *Continues* Child Welfare League of America. CWLA Directory of Member and Associate Agencies, 0737-786X.
**Desc**: Lists affiliated agencies and includes the program of activities, membership requirements, definitions of child welfare services, and its regional training conference schedule.

US/1045-1684
### DIRECTORY OF MEMBER AGENCIES IN THE UNITED STATES AND CANADA. [Dir.
memb. agencies U. S. Can.]. **Main/Corp** Family Service America. **VFOAT** Directory of Member Agencies. (1987)-. Directory. English. an. $35.00. Family Service America, PO Box 6649, Syracuse NY 13217. **Tel** (414)359-1040, FAX (414)359-1074. **ED** Mary L. Cronce. **DD** 362. **Bk Rev. Ad Acc**. ctrl circ. *Continues* Directory of Member Agencies / Family Service America.
**Desc**: Lists the nearly 300 member agencies of Family Service America in the US and Canada. Also includes addresses, telephone numbers, and geographic areas served. Appendix lists which agencies offer service in each of 15 common service areas.

US
### DIRECTORY OF MEMBERS / AMERICAN ASSOCIATION OF HOMES FOR THE AGING. Main/Corp American Association of Homes
for the Aging. **VFOAT** AAHA Directory of Members. (1984)-. English. an (Mar.). $10.00 (AAHA members), $40.00 (non-profit organizations government agencies & libraries), $200.00 (business firms) Comes with American Association of Homes for the Aging membership. American Association of Homes for the Aging, 901 E Street Northwest, Suite 500, Washington DC 20004. **Tel** (202)783-2242, FAX (202)783-2255. **ED** Miriam B. Washington. **Ad Acc. Circ**: 6,000 (ctrl). *Continues* American Association of Homes for the Aging. Membership Directory, 0160-2055.
**Desc**: This directory is offering you a instant access to a nationwide network of some 5,000 not-for-profit nursing homes, retirement communities and senior housing facilities.

US/0892-9262
### DIRECTORY OF MICROCOMPUTER SOFTWARE IN THE HUMAN SERVICES, A. See Computers-Software.

US/0090-5658
### DIRECTORY OF PROGRAMS AND SERVICES FOR OLDER ADULTS : STATE OF OREGON BY COUNTIES.
Directory. English. Portland State University, PO Box 751, Portland OR 97207. **LC** HV1468.O7; D56. **DD** 362.6/09795.

ET
### DIRECTORY OF REGIONAL SOCIAL WELFARE ACTIVITIES. Main/Corp United
Nations. Economic Commission for Africa. Social Development Section. 1964-. Directory. English. United Nations Economic Commission for Africa, PO Box 3001, Addis Ababa Ethiopia. **Tel** (212)754-8302, telex 21029 VNECA ET. **LC** JX1977; .A2. **DD** 361.06.

US/0362-9562
### DIRECTORY OF RESOURCE ORGANIZATIONS AND MEDIA SERVING MINORITY COMMUNITIES IN CONNECTICUT. See Economics-Labor.

US/0094-1441
### DIRECTORY OF RESOURCES FOR OLDER PEOPLE IN NEW HAMPSHIRE.
**Added/Corp** New Hampshire State Council on Aging. 1st Ed., (1972)-. Directory. English. New Hampshire State Council on Aging, 71 South Main Street, PO Box 786, Concord NH 03301. **LC** HV1468.N4; D57. **DD** 362.6/025/742.

CN/0824-5398
### DIRECTORY OF RESOURCES FOR SENIOR CITIZENS OF OTTAWA-CARLETON. [Dir. resour. sr. citiz.
Ottawa-Carleton]. **VFOAT** Repertoire des Services pour Personnes Agees d'Ottawa-Carleton. Directory. English (French). be. Ottawa Senior Citizens Council, Room 508, 294 Albert Street, Ottawa Ontario K1P 6E6 Canada. **Tel** (613)234-8044. **DD** 362.6/025/71383.

US
### DIRECTORY OF SERVICES. Added/Corp
United States. Office of Elementary and Secondary Education. Office of Migrant Education. (Mar. 1991)-. Government Publication. English. US Department of Education, 400 Maryland Avenue SW, Room 4181, Washington DC 20202. **Tel** (202)401-1576, FAX (202)272-5447.

CN/1184-1753
### DIRECTORY OF SERVICES. [Dir. serv. - Inf.
Serv. Vanc. Vanc. B.C.]. **Added/Corp** Information Services Vancouver (Vancouver, B.C.). **VFOAT** Red Book. (1987)-. Directory. English. an. 57.50Can$. Information Services Vancouver, 3102 Main Street, Suite 202, Vancouver British Columbia V5T 3G7 Canada. **Tel** (604)875-6431. **DD** 361/.0025/71133. *Continues* Directory of Services for Greater Vancouver., 0319-0242.

US/0362-7179
### DIRECTORY OF SERVICES FOR MIGRANT FAMILIES. VFOAT Directorio de
Servicios Para Familias Migrantes. 1975-. Directory. Multiple languages (English and Spanish). Illinois Office of Education, 100 East Edwards Street, Springfield IL 62704. **LC** HV98.I15; D57. **DD** 362.8/5.

US/0164-0550
### DIRECTORY OF SERVICES - TEXAS DEPARTMENT OF MENTAL HEALTH AND MENTAL RETARDATION. Directory.
English. Texas Department of Mental Health, PO Box 12668 Capitol Station, Austin TX 78711. **NLM** WM 22 AT4 D5. *Continues* Directory of Mental Health and Mental Retardation Services for Texas.

CN/0226-0905
### DIRECTORY OF SOCIAL SERVICE ADMINISTRATORS OF LOCAL MUNICIPALITIES. [Dir. soc. serv. adm. local
munic.]. **VAT** Directory of Social Service Administrators of Local Municipalities in Ontario. Began publication in 1976?. Directory. English. an. Ontario Ministry of Community & Social Services, 12th Floor/700 Bay Street, Toronto Ontario M7A 1E9 Canada. **DD** 352.94/4/025713.

CN/0318-9686
### DIRECTORY OF SOCIAL SERVICES. OTTAWA-CARLETON. (DIRECTORY OF
SOCIAL SERVICES, OTTAWA-CARLETON. REPERTOIRE DES OEUVRES, OTTAWA-CARLETON.). **Added/Corp** Centre d'Information Communautaire (Ottawa-Carleton, Ont.). Conseil de Planification Sociale d'Ottawa et de la Region. Service d'Information Communautaire. **VFOAT** Repertoire des Oeuvres, Ottawa-Carleton. (1971)-. Periodical. French (English). an. Centre d'Information Communautaire, 377 rue Rideau, Ottawa Ontario K1N 5Y6 Canada. **DD** 361/.0025/71383. *Continues* Directory of Social Services.

ET
### DIRECTORY OF SOCIAL WELFARE ACTIVITIES IN AFRICA. Added/Corp
Association for Social Work Education in Africa. (19??)-. English. Association for Social Work Education in Africa, c/o College of Social Sciences, Addis Ababa University, PO Box 1176, Addis Ababa Ethiopia. **LC** HV438.A2; D57. **DD** 362/.025/6.

## Sociology —Social Services and Welfare

US/0093-9501
**DIRECTORY OF SPECIAL PROGRAMS FOR MINORITY GROUP MEMBERS; CAREER INFORMATION SERVICES, EMPLOYMENT SKILLS BANKS, FINANCIAL AID.** (1974)-. Directory. English. te (every three years). $30.00. Garrett Park Press, PO Box 190 F, Garrett Park MD 20896. **Tel** (301)946-2553. **LC** HD5724; .D56. **DD** 331.7/02/02573.

●CN/1188-4886
**DIRECTORY OF SUBSTANCE ABUSE ORGANIZATIONS IN CANADA.** See Drug Abuse and Alcoholism.

US/0743-9725
**DIRECTORY OF VOLUNTARY AGENCIES.** [Dir. volunt. agencies]. 1984 Y-. Directory. English. be. Immigration and Naturalization Service, INS Outreach Program, 425 I Street NW, Washington DC 20536. **LC** HV89; .D53. **DD** 362.8.

CN
**DIRECTORY, SERVICES FOR VICTIMS OF CRIME.** See Law-Law Enforcement and Criminology.

US/0731-9509
**DIRECTORY, UNITED WAY AFFILIATED INFORMATION AND REFERRAL SERVICES.** **VFOAT** United Way Affiliated Information and Referral Services; Directory of United Way Affiliated Information and Referral Services; United Way Affiliated Directory Information and Referral Services. Directory. English. ir. $2.50. United Way of America, 701 North Fairfax Street, Alexandria VA 22314. **Tel** (703)836-7100. **LC** HV97.U553; D57. **DD** 361.8/025/73. **Circ:** 2,000.
**Desc:** Name, address and phone number of United Way Affiliated Information and Referral Services; also notes whether an in house I&R program or a separate agency of United Way.

CN/1183-9678
**DISABILITY DIGEST.** *Suspended.* [Disabl. dig.]. **Added/Corp** Disability Network (Canada). Vol. 1, No. 1 (Mar./Apr. 1991)-(19??). Periodical. English. mo. Centre for Independent Living in Toronto, PO Box 500, Station A, Ontario M5W 1E6 Canada. **Tel** (416)975-2366. **DD** 362.4/0971/05.

●US/1069-1359
**DISABILITY FUNDING NEWS.** [Disabil. funding news]. (1993)-. Periodical. English. sm. $249.00. CD Publications, 8204 Fenton Street, Silver Spring MD 20910. **Tel** (800)666-6380, (301)588-6380, FAX (301)588-6385. **DD** 362.

UK/0267-4645
**DISABILITY, HANDICAP & SOCIETY.** *Title Change.* **VFOAT** Disability, Handicap and Society. Vol. 1, No. 1 (1986)-(199?). Periodical. English. qt. Carfax Publishing Company, PO Box 25 Abingdon, Oxfordshire OX14 3UE England. **Tel** 011 44 235 555335, FAX (0279)31067, telex 817484. **(Subscription address:** US and Canada/ PO Box 2025, Dunnellon, FL 34430-2025; telephone:(904)489-6996**)** **LC** HV1551; .D57. **DD** 362.4/05. **NLM** W1; DI726. **CODEN** DHSOEG. **[CCC].** available on microfiche. *Continued by* Disability & Society.
**Ind/Abst** Appl. Soc. Sci. Index Abstr.; Except. Child Educ. Resour.; Linguist. Lang. Behav. Abstr.; Psychol. Abstr. (1986-?); PsycINFO (1990-?); PsycLit; Soc. Plann. Policy Dev. Abstr.; Sociol. Abstr.; Spec. Educ. Needs Abstr.

US
**DISASTER RECOVERY JOURNAL.** Vol. 1, No. 1 (1987)-. Periodical. English. Four times a year (Jan., Apr., July, Oct.). Free to qualified subscribers in the U.S. and Canada; $10.00 US; $24.00 Canada; $47.00 other (non-qualified subscribers). Systems Support Inc., PO Box 510110, St. Louis MO 63151. **Tel** (314)894-0276, FAX (314)894-7474. **ED** Michael Beckerle. **LC** WMLC 93/1407. **CODEN** DREJEZ. **Ad Acc, Adv Mgr:** Patti Fitzgerald, **Tel** same as publisher. **Circ:** 35,000.

UK/0361-3666
**DISASTERS.** [Disasters]. **Added/Corp** London Technical Group. Relief and Development Institute (London, England). Vol. 1 (1977)-. Academic Scholarly Publication. English. Four times a year (Mar., June, Sept., Dec.). $151.00 North America; £97.50 others. Basil Blackwell Publishers Ltd, 108 Cowley Road, Oxford OX4 1JF England. **Tel** 011 44 865 791100, FAX 011 44 865 791347, telex 837022 OXBOOK G. **(Subscription address:** Blackwell Publishers / UK, Marston Book Services, PO Box 87, Oxford OX2 0DT England.**) ED** Charles Melville. **LC** HV553; .D57. **DD** 361.5/05. **NLM** W1 DI742T. **[CCC].** Index available. **Bk Rev. Ad Acc. Pr Rev. Circ:** 700. available on microfilm and microfiche from University Microfilms International (UMI). Documents available from The Genuine Article.
**Desc:** Multi-disciplinary journal covering all aspects of disasters, including sudden onset disasters, food emergencies, refugees, disasters and developments.

**Ind/Abst** Abstr. J. Earthq. Eng.; Archit. Period. Index; Commun. Abstr.; Curr. Contents Soc. Behav. Sci.; EMBASE; Geogr. Abstr. Human Geogr.; Geol. Abstr.; GeoRef; Health Saf. Sci. Abstr.; Int. Bibliogr. Sociol.; Int. Civil Eng. Abstr.; Int. Dev. Abstr.; J. Plan. Lit.; Leis. Recreat. Tour. Abstr.; Linguist. Lang. Behav. Abstr.; Nutr. Abstr. Rev., Ser. B, Live Feeds and Feed.; Nutr. Abstr. Rev., Ser. A, Hum. Exp.; PAIS Int. Print (1991-); Pollut. Abstr. Indexes; Res. Alert [Full Cov.]; Rice Abstr.; Risk Abstr. (19??-19??); Rural Dev. Abstr.; Soc. Plann. Policy Dev. Abstr.; Soc. Sci. Cit. Index [Full Cov.]; Sociol. Abstr.; Trop. Dis. Bull.; World Agric. Econ.

US/0886-9359
**DONOR BRIEFING.** *Ceased.* [Donor brief.]. (1986)-Vol. 9, No. 2 (19??). Periodical. English. bw. Capitol Publications, 1101 King Street, Suite 444, Alexandria VA 22314. **Tel** (703)683-4100, (800)655-5597. **DD** 361. *Absorbed Nonprofit Marketing Insider.*
**Desc:** Concise news briefs on major awards, plus lists of grants from numerous philanthropic foundations. Each issue contains detailed, how-to articles on fundraising, non-profit management, and philanthropic giving.
**Ind/Abst** Curr. Lit. Fam. Plan. (19??-199?).

US
**DORS OPENERS.** See Physically Impaired.

US/0360-4357
**DPI YELLOW PAGES.** **Main/Corp** Nebraska. Dept. of Public Institutions. **VAT** Department of Public Institutions Yellow Pages. English. an. Department of Public Institutions, State of Nebraska, Lincoln NE 68509. **LC** HV86; .N2668. **DD** 362/.025/782.

US/1058-8396
**EARLY INTERVENTION.** [Early interv.]. **Added/Corp** Illinois Public Health Association. Illinois Early Childhood Intervention Clearinghouse. Vol. 1, No. 1 (Nov. 1986)-. Periodical. English. qt (Jan., Apr., July, Oct.). Free. Early Childhood Intervention Clearinghouse, 830 South Spring Street, Springfield IL 62704. **Tel** (217)785-1364. **ED** Chet Brandt. **DD** 362. **Bk Rev**, (Qty: 12). **Circ:** 4,000 (ctrl).
**Desc:** Devoted to the issues related to early childhood intervention. Emphasis on disability and family support. Features articles are news items, book and audiovisual reviews and a conference calendar.

US/1059-2253
**EARTHLETTER.** [Earthletter]. Vol. 1, No. 1 (Mar. 1991)-. Periodical. English. qt. $20.00. Lita Lee, 2061 Hampton Avenue, Redwood City CA 94601. **DD** 363.

CN/0844-5559
**EASTER SEALER.** [Easter seal.]. Vol. 1, No. 1 (Aug. 1988)-. Periodical. English. qt. Free. Easter Sealer, 200-250 Ferrand Drive, Don Mills Ontario M3C 3P2 Canada. **Tel** (416)421-8377. **DD** 362.4/383/088054. **Circ:** 12,500 (ctrl). *Continues Horizons, 0380-4046.*

CN/0382-7194
**ECHO (OTTAWA).** (ECHO.). Nov. 1972-. Periodical. English (French). Hopital pour Enfants de l'Est de l'Ontario, 401 Chemin Smyth Canada. **DD** 362.7/8/110971384.

US/0013-0206
**ECONOMIC OPPORTUNITY REPORT.** Vol. 1 (1966)-. Periodical. English. Fifty times a year. $365.00. Business Publishers Inc., 951 Pershing Drive, Silver Spring MD 20910-4464. **Tel** (301)587-6300, (800)274-0122, FAX (301)585-9075. **ED** Anne Pavuk. **[CCC].**
**Desc:** Congressional and agency actions affecting federal antipoverty programs and community action agencies. Low-income energy aid, weatherization, food stamps, child nutrition, JTPA, Head Start, and more.

●CN/1188-6145
**EDITIONS AVIS DE RECHERCHE, LES.** [Ed. avis rech.]. Vol. 1, No 1 (May 1992)-. Periodical. French. bm. 3.95Can$ per number. Les Editions Avisde Recherche, 10 Rue Suzie, Victoriaville Quebec G6P 7S3 Canada. **DD** 362.82/98/0971405.

US/1040-0729
**EDUCATING AT-RISK YOUTH.** [Educ. at-risk youth]. **Added/Corp** National Professional Resources, Inc. **VFOAT** Educating at Risk Youth. Vol. 1, No. 1 (Fall 1988)-. Periodical. English. mo (except July and Aug.). $68.00 (one year), $99.00 (two year) US; $72.00 (one year), $107.00 (two year) Canada; $76.00 (one year), $115.00 (two year) other. National Professional Resources, PO Box 1479, 25 South Regent Street, Port Chester NY 10573. **Tel** (914)937-8879, FAX (914)937-9327. **ED** Janet Simon. **DD** 362. **Bk Rev**. ctrl circ.

NE
**EISS YEARBOOK / ANNUAIRE EISS.** **Added/Corp** European Institute for Social Security. **VFOAT** Annuaire Eiss. (19??)-. Periodical. English (French). an. Kluwer Law and Taxation Publishers, Staverenstraat 32015, PO Box 23, 7400 GA Deventer Netherlands. **Tel** 011 31 5700 47261. **(Subscription address:** Kluwer Law & Taxation, 675 Massachusetts Avenue, Cambridge MA 02139.**) LC** HD7164; .A25. **DD** 368.4/0094.
**Ind/Abst** LABORDOC.

FI
**ELATUSTUKI.** **Main/Corp** Finland. Sosiaalihallitus. Suunnittelu- Ja Tilastotoimisto. **VFOAT** Underhallsstod. Finnish (Swedish). Tilastokeskus, PL 504, Annankatu 44, 00101 Helsinki Finland. **Tel** 358-0-17341, FAX 358-0-17342474, telex 1002111 TILASTO SF. **LC** HV700.F5; F56A.

US/0891-9275
**ELDERLY HEALTH SERVICES LETTER.** [Elder. health serv. lett.]. Vol. 1, No. 1 (Oct. 1986)-. Periodical. English. Twelve times a year. $147.00 (one year), $264.00 (two years), $375.00 (three years); $127.00 (introductory subscription). Health Resources Publishing, 3100 Highway 138, Wall Township NJ 07719-1442. **Tel** (908)681-1133, FAX (908)681-0490. **DD** 362. **[CCC].**
**Desc:** Newsletter on trends and projections for health services with will be provided the elderly: Inpatient care, long term care, outpatient, home care, primary care, ambulatory care, day care, health promotion, disease prevention, support groups, health education, even residential care.

CN/0825-7531
**EMPATHIC PARENTING.** (EMPATHIC PARENTING : JOURNAL OF THE CANADIAN SOCIETY FOR THE PREVENTION OF CRUELTY TO CHILDREN.). [Empath. parent.]. **Added/Corp** Canadian Society for the Prevention of Cruelty to Children. Vol. 7, Issue 3 (Summer 1984)-. Periodical. English. Four times a year. 10.00Can$ (one year), 25.00Can$ (three years) Comes with Canadian Society for the Prevention of Cruelty to Children membership. Canadian Society for the Prevention of Cruelty to Children, Box 700, Midland Ontario L4R 4P4 Canada. **Tel** (705)526-5647, FAX (705)526-0214. **DD** 362.7/1/05. *Continues Canadian Society for the Prevention of Cruelty to Children. Journal of the CSPCC, 0705-6591.*
**Ind/Abst** Can. Index; Can. Period. Index (19??-).

US/0071-0237
**ENCYCLOPEDIA OF SOCIAL WORK.** **Added/Corp** National Association of Social Workers. (1965)-. English. ir (every 10 years). $90.00. National Association of Social Workers, 750 First Street Northeast, Suite 700, Washington DC 20002-4241. **Tel** (800)638-8799, (202)408-8600, FAX (301)587-1321. **(Subscription address:** NASW Press / National Association of Social Workers, PO Box 431, Annapolis JCT MD 20701.**) LC** HV35; .S6. **DD** 361/.003. **NLM** HV 35 E56. *Continues Social Work Year Book.*

US
**ENERGY CREDIT PROGRAM / OHIO DEPARTMENT OF TAXATION.** 1980-81 Heating Season-. English. an. Department of Taxation / Ohio, Research and Statistics Section, PO Box 530, Columbus OH 43216. **LC** HV1468.O3; E53. **DD** 363.5/8. *Continues Residential Heating Bill Discount and Cash Payment Program.*

US
**ENROLLMENTS IN EDUCATIONAL PROGRAMS OPERATED BY THE DEPARTMENT OF HEALTH AND SOCIAL SERVICES, THE DEPARTMENT OF CORRECTION, AND THE DEPARTMENT OF SERVICES FOR CHILDREN, YOUTH, AND THEIR FAMILIES.** See Education-Special Education and Rehabilitation.

CN/0829-8815
**ENTOURAGE (DOWNSVIEW, ONT.).** (ENTOURAGE.). [Entourage]. **Added/Corp** National Institute on Mental Retardation. Canadian Association for Community Living. Institut quebecois de la deficience mentale. Vol. 1, No. 1 (Winter 1986)-. Periodical. English (French). qt. 18.00Can$ (one year), 32.00Can$ (two year), 48.00Can$ (three year) Canada; 20.00Can$ (one year), 36.00Can$ (two year), 52.00Can$ (three year) other. G Allan Roeher Institute, York U, 4700 Keele Street, Kinsmen Building North York Ontario M3J 1P3, Canada. **Tel** (416)661-9611, FAX (416)661-5701. **ED** Laura Code. **DD** 362.3/0971. **Bk Rev**, (Qty: 5). **Ad Acc**. *Formed by the union of Revue Canadienne de la Deficience Mentale, 0826-4090 and Canadian Journal on Mental Retardation, 0826-4082.*
**Desc:** Promoting community living for persons with a mental handicap and disabilities.
**Ind/Abst** Can. Period. Index (19??-); Except. Child Educ. Resour.; Spec. Educ. Needs Abstr.

PO
**ESTATISTICAS DA ORGANIZACAO CORPORATIVA E PREVIDENCIA : CONTINENTE E ILHAS ADJACENTES.** **VFOAT** Statistiques de l'Organisation Corporative et Continent et Iles Adjacentes Prevoyance: Continent et Iles Adjacentes. Began with 1966 Vol. Multiple languages (French and Portuguese). ir. Instituto Nacional de Estatistica, Servicos Centrais, Avenida Antonio Jose de

Almeida 1, 1078 Lisbon Portugal. **Tel** 80 20 80, FAX 8489480, telex 63738 PCDINE. **LC** HV346; .A33. ***Continues*** *Estatistica da Organizacao Corporativa E Previdencia Social.*

CN
**ESTIMATES. PART III, HEALTH AND WELFARE CANADA, HEALTH AND SOCIAL SERVICES PROGRAM, INCOME SECURITY PROGRAM, FITNESS AND AMATEUR SPORT PROGRAM.** **Main/Corp** Canada. **VFOAT** Budget des Depenses. Partie III, Sante et Bien-etre Social Canada, Programme des Services Sanitaires et Sociaux, Programme de la Securite du Revenue, Programme de Condition Physique et Sport Amateur. (19??)-. English (French). $12.00 Canada; $14.40 other. Canada Communication Group Publishers, Order Processing, Ottawa Ontario K1A 0S9 Canada. **Tel** (819)956-4800, (819)956-4802. **LC** HD7102.C2; C25a. **DD** 354.710084/1.

CN/0226-9783
**ETINCELLE (LAVAL).** (L'ETINCELLE.). [Etincelle]. Vol. 1, No. 1 Mar. 1981-. Periodical. French. ir. $7.00. l'Etincelle, 3165 Circle de Paris, Laval Quebec H7E 3E7 Canada. **DD** 362.8/286.

SZ
**ETUDES ET RECHERCHES.** English (French, German and Spanish). ir (one or two volumes a year). 25.00F. International Social Security Association, Case Postale 1, CH-1211 Geneva 22 Switzerland. **Tel** 011 41 22 7996617, FAX 011 41 22 7986385.
**Desc:** Reports of specialized conferences and meetings as well as studies related to ISSA social security research programs.

AU
**EUROSOCIAL NEWSLETTER.** ir. Free. European Center for Social Welfare Train & Research, Berggasse 17, 1090 Vienna Austria. **Tel** 222 316505.

US/0149-7189
**EVALUATION AND PROGRAM PLANNING.** [Eval. program plann.]. **VFOAT** Journal of Evaluation and Program Planning. Vol. 1 (Jan. 1978)-. Academic Scholarly Publication. English. qt. $321.00 The Americas; £215.00 other. Pergamon Press, An Imprint of Elsevier Science Ltd., The Boulevard, Langford Lane, Kidlington, Oxford OX5 1GB United Kingdom. **Tel** 011 44 865 843000, 011 44 865 843699, FAX 011 44 865 843010. **(Subscription address:** Elsevier Science Ltd. Oxford Fulfillment Centre, PO Box 800, Kidlington, Oxford OX5 1DX United Kingdom.**) ED** Jonathan A. Morrell. **LC** H62.A1; E93. **DD** 300./7/2. **NLM** W1 EV13G. **[CCC]. Pr Rev.** available on microfilm and microfiche from University Microfilms International (UMI); Microfilms International Marketing Corp.; and Pergamon Press. Documents available from The Genuine Article.
**Ind/Abst** Commun. Abstr.; Contents Pages Educ.; Crim. Justice Abstr.; Cumul. Index Nurs. Allied Health Lit.; Curr. Contents Soc. Behav. Sci.; Curr. Index J. Educ.; Educ. Adm. Abstr. (?-?); EMBASE; High. Educ. Abstr. (1986-); Hospit. Health Admin. Index (1978-1989); Hum. Resour. Abstr. (?-?); PAIS Int. Print (1991-); Psychol. Abstr. (1978-); PsycINFO; PsycLit; Res. Alert [Full Cov.]; Sage Public Adm. Abstr. (?-?); Soc. Plann. Policy Dev. Abstr.; Soc. Sci. Cit. Index [Full Cov.]; Sociol. Abstr.; Soc. Res. Methodol. Abstr. (1980-).

US/0095-6813
**EXPENDITURES FOR STAFF DEVELOPMENT AND TRAINING ACTIVITIES.** **Main/Corp** National Center for Social Statistics. English. National Center for Social Statistics, Washington DC 20201. **LC** HV91; .N25l. **DD** 353.008/4.

CN/0822-8213
**EXPRESSION (OTTAWA).** (EXPRESSION : NEWSLETTER OF THE NATIONAL ADVISORY COUNCIL ON AGING.). [Expression]. **Main/Corp** Canada. National Advisory Council on Aging. **VFOAT** Expression. Vol. 1, No. 1 (winter 1984)-. Newsletter. English (French). Four times a year. Free on request. National Advisory Council on Aging, 473 Albert Street, Trebla Building #355, Ottawa Ontario K1A 0K9 Canada. **Tel** (613)957-1968. **ED** Louise Plouffe. **DD** 362.6/0971. **Circ:** 6,000.
**Desc:** Covers various aspects of the life of aging Canadians.

CN/0821-3356
**EXTRA TO THE ONTARIO WELFARE REPORTER.** (EXTRA TO THE ONTARIO WELFARE REPORTER : A NEWS BULLETIN TO UPDATE AND PREVIEW THE BI-MONTHLY ISSUES.). [Extra Ont. welf. report.]. **Added/Corp** Ontario Welfare Council. (1979)-. Periodical. English. Ontario Welfare Council, Suite 404, 1240 Bay Street, Toronto Ontario M5R 2A7. **DD** 361.6/09713.

US/0098-7964
**FACT SHEET BOOKLET.** (STATE VOCATIONAL REHABILITATION AGENCY : FACT SHEET BOOKLET.). **Main/Corp** United States. Rehabilitation Services Administration. English. an. Rehabilitation Services Administration, 330 Independence Avenue SW, Washington DC 20201. **LC** HD7256.U5; U58C. **DD** 362.8/5. **NLM** W2 A R3S.

PK
**FAIZULISLAM.** **VFOAT** Faiz-Ul-Islam. Periodical. Urdu. mo. Rs30.00 Pakistan; $12.00 US, Australia, Canada and other European countries; £5.00 Saudi Arabia, UAR countries, India, Sri Lanka, All Middle East countries. Monthly Faizul Islam, B-210 Iqbal Road, Rawalpindi City Pakistan. **Tel** 72909. **ED** Abdul Hamid Qamar Rueni. **LC** BP1; .F3. **Bk Rev. Ad Acc. Circ:** 3,000 (ctrl).
**Desc:** Short articles and literature on Islam biographical subjects, Anjuman Faizul Islam's activities and monthly accounts of donations received for Anjumanis Orphanage.

●US/1075-3184
**FAMILIES IN CRISIS FUNDING REPORT.** [Fam. crisis funding rep.]. No. 94-04 (Feb. 1994)-. Periodical. English. sm. $249.00. CD Publications, 8204 Fenton Street, Silver Spring MD 20910. **Tel** (800)666-6380, (301)588-6380, FAX (301)588-6385. **DD** 362.

US/1044-3894
**FAMILIES IN SOCIETY.** (FAMILIES IN SOCIETY : THE JOURNAL OF CONTEMPORARY HUMAN SERVICES.). [Fam. soc.]. **Added/Corp** Family Service America. **VFOAT** Journal of Contemporary Human Services. Vol. 71, No. 1 (Jan. 1990)-. Periodical. English. Ten times a year. $79.00 US; $84.00 Canada; $99.00 other. Family Service America, PO Box 6649, Syracuse NY 13217. **Tel** (414)359-1040, FAX (414)359-1074. **ED** Ralph J. Burant. **LC** HV1; .J56. **DD** 362.82/0973/05. **NLM** W1; FA426. **CODEN** FASOEN. **[CCC].** Index available. cum. index. **Bk Rev. Ad Acc. Pr Rev. Circ:** 7,000. available on microfilm and microfiche from University Microfilms International (UMI). Documents available from The Genuine Article, UMI Article Clearinghouse. ***Continues*** *Social Casework, 0037-7678.*
**Desc:** A practice and issues-related journal directed to human service professionals.
**Ind/Abst** Abstr. Soc. Gerontol.; Acad. Abstr. Full Text Elite (Jan. 1992-); Acad. Abstr. (Jan. 1992-); Acad. Ind. [Computer File] (1990-); Acad. Search (Jan. 1992-); Book Rev. Index; Curr. Contents Soc. Behav. Sci.; Expand. Acad. Index (1990-); INFO-SOUTH Abstr.; Int. Bibliogr. Sociol.; Mag. Search; Newsp. Period. Abstr. (1990-); Psychol. Abstr. (1946-); PsycINFO (1990-); PsycLit; Res. Alert [Full Cov.]; Sage Fam. Stud. Abstr.; Soc. Plann. Policy Dev. Abstr.; Soc. Sci. Source (Jan. 1992-); Soc. Sci. Cit. Index [Full Cov.]; Soc. Sci. Index; Soc. Sci. Index Fulltext (Jan. 1990-) [Full Txt.]; Soc. Work Abstr. [Full Cov.]; Spec. Educ. Needs Abstr.

US/1054-8726
**FAMILY DYNAMICS OF ADDICTION QUARTERLY.** ***Ceased.*** **See** Drug Abuse and Alcoholism.

●US/1060-9172
**FAMILY PLANNING MANAGER, THE.** [Fam. plan. manag.]. **Added/Corp** United States. Agency for International Development. Family Planning Management Development (Firm). Vol. 1, No. 1 (Mar./Apr. 1992)-. Periodical. English. bm. Free. Family Planning Management Development, 400 Centre Street, Newton Corner MA 02158. **DD** 362. **NLM** W1; FA453CP.

US/0361-4158
**FAMILY SERVICES IN UTAH.** (FAMILY SERVICES IN UTAH : ANNUAL REPORT.). [Fam. serv. Utah]. **Main/Corp** Utah. Dept. of Social Services. Division of Family Services. English. an. Department of Social Services / Utah, Division of Family Services, 333 South 2nd East, Salt Lake City UT 84111. **LC** HV86; .U79. **DD** 362.8/2/09792.

CN/1184-6801
**FAMILY TIMES (TORONTO).** (FAMILY TIMES.). [Fam. times]. **Added/Corp** Ontario Association of Family Service Agencies. Aug. (1990)-. Periodical. English. bm. Rhode Island Department of Health, Room 408 William Waters, Providence RI 02908. **Tel** (401)277-2901. **DD** 362.82/09713. ***Continues*** *News letter (Ontario Association of Family Service Agencies)., 0227-6771.*

US/1067-7283
**FAMILY VIOLENCE & SEXUAL ASSAULT BULLETIN.** [Fam. violence sex. assault bull.]. **Added/Corp** Family Violence & Sexual Assault Institute. **VFOAT** Family Violence and Sexual Assault Bulletin; FVSAB. Vol. 7, No. 4 (Winter 1991)-. Bulletin. English. qt. $40.00 (institutions), $25.00 (individuals). Family Violence and Sexual Assault Institute, 1310 Clinic Drive, Tyler TX 75701. **Tel** (903)595-6600. **LC** HV6626.2; .F36. **DD** 362.82/92/05. **NLM** W1; FA454NG. **CODEN** FVSBET. ***Continues*** *Family Violence Bulletin, 1055-7938.*
**Ind/Abst** Soc. Plann. Policy Dev. Abstr.

US/0273-3366
**FANON CENTER JOURNAL.** ***Ceased.*** [Fanon Cent. j.]. **Main/Corp** Fanon Research and Development Center. V. 1- May 1980-Ceased. Periodical. English. sa. Fanon Research and Development Center, 12714 S Avalon Boulevard/Suite 303, Los Angeles CA 90061. **Tel** (310)603-3121. **LC** RC451.5.N4; F36A. **DD** 362.2/08996073.

US
**FINAL COMPREHENSIVE ANNUAL SERVICES PROGRAM PLAN FOR TITLE XX - SOCIAL SECURITY ACT.** **Main/Corp** Florida. Dept. of Health and Rehabilitative Services. Office of the Assistant Secretary for Program Planning and Development. **VFOAT** State of Florida Final Comprehensive Annual Services Program Plan for Social Security Act Title XX. English. an. Florida Department of Health and Rehabilitative Services, 1323 Winewood Boulevard, Building 1, Room 115, Tallahassee FL 32399. **Tel** (904)488-7721, FAX (904)488-2112. **LC** HV86; .F64214. **DD** 361.6/09759.

US
**FINAL COMPREHENSIVE ANNUAL SOCIAL SERVICE PROGRAM PLAN.** **Main/Corp** Missouri. Division of Family Services. 1975/76-. English. an. Missouri Division of Family Service, Broadway State Office Building, Jefferson City MO 65101. **LC** HV86; .M797. **DD** 361/.9778.

US
**FINAL NEBRASKA COMPREHENSIVE ANNUAL SERVICES PLAN.** **Main/Corp** Nebraska. Dept. of Public Welfare. **VFOAT** Title XX Nebraska Comprehensive Social Services Plan. English. Department of Public Welfare / Nebraska, PO Box 95026, Lincoln NE 68509. **LC** HV86; .N2669. **DD** 362/.9782. ***Continues*** *Title XX Comprehensive Annual Services Program Plan, 0362-7616.*

US
**FINAL TITLE XX COMPREHENSIVE ANNUAL SERVICES PLAN FOR NORTH CAROLINA.** **Main/Corp** North Carolina. Dept. of Human Resources. Title XX Branch. **VFOAT** Final Title 20 Comprehensive Annual Services Plan for North Carolina; Final Title Twenty Comprehensive Annual Services Plan for North Carolina. English. an. State Department of Human Resources / North Carolina, 701 Barbour Street, Raleigh NC 27603. **Tel** (919)733-4283. **LC** HV86; .N84832A. **DD** 361.6/09756. ***Continues*** *Final Comprehensive Annual Services Plan for North Carolina Pursuant to Title XX of the Federal Social Security Act.*

US/0896-7792
**FINANCIAL AID FOR VETERANS, MILITARY PERSONNEL, AND THEIR DEPENDENTS.** [Financ. aid veterans mil. pers. their depend.]. **Added/Corp** Reference Service Press (San Carlos, Calif.). (1988/89)-. English. be. $41.50. Reference Service Press, 1100 Industrial Road/Suite 9, San Carlos CA 94070. **Tel** (415)594-0743, FAX (415)594-0411. **ED** Gail A Schlachter and R David Weber. **LC** UB403; .F47. **DD** 362.8.
**Desc:** Identifies the hundreds of scholarships, fellowships, loans, grants-in-aid, awards, and internships designed exclusively for military related personnel.

US/0147-8508
**FINANCIAL REPORT ON REGISTERED CHARITABLE ORGANIZATIONS.** **Main/Corp** Wisconsin. Dept. of Regulation and Licensing. (19??)-. Periodical. English. sa. Department of Regulation and Licensing / Wisconsin, 1400 East Washington Avenue, Madison WI 53702. **LC** HV86; .W6254. **DD** 338.4/3.

US/0090-7081
**FISH DIRECTORY.** 1973-. Directory. English. Jarrow Press Inc, 552 de Haro Street, San Francisco CA 94107. **LC** HV7; .F57. **DD** 361.8.

US/0887-3038
**FLORIDA FUNDING.** **See** Business-General Management.

CN/1183-6326
**FNV : LE MAGAZINE DE LA FONDATION NOR-VAL.** [FNV, Fond. Nor-Val]. **Added/Corp** Fondation Nor-Val. **VAT** Fondation Nor-Val. Vol. 1, No 1 (May 1991)-. French. 10.00Can$. Fondation Nor-Val, 26 Rue St-Jean-Baptiste, Victoriaville Quebec G6P 4C7 Canada. **DD** 362.3.

US/0195-5705
**FOCUS (MADISON).** **See** Economics.

UK
**FOOD AID CONVENTION.** (REPORT ON SHIPMENTS BY MEMBERS OF THE CONVENTION IN ...). March 1988-. English. an. £15.00 UK; $30.00 US. International Wheat Council, One Canada Square, Canary Wharf, London E14 5AE England. **Tel** 011 44 71 513 1122, FAX 011 44 71 712 0071, telex 8813241.
**Desc:** Detailed statistical information on shipments of food aid by members of the Food Aid Convention.

US/0895-3090
**FOOD FIRST DEVELOPMENT REPORT.** [Food first dev. rep.]. No. 1 (Sept. 1987)-. Monographic series. English. ir. Price varies per volume. Food First

Books, 145 Ninth Street, San Francisco CA 94103. **Tel** (415)864-8555. **LC** HV696.F6; F64. **DD** 363.8/83/05. **Ad Acc.**

●BG
**FOOD SITUATION REPORT FOR THE MONTH OF ... [MICROFORM]. Added/Corp** Bangladesh. Food Planning and Monitoring Unit. (1992)-. Periodical. English. mo. **LC** Microfiche (o) 92/62005.

US/0276-0320
**FOOD STAMP PROGRAM : STATISTICAL SUMMARY OF OPERATIONS. See** Sociology-Abstracting, Bibliographies and Statistics.

US/0736-0010
**FOODLINES.** (FOODLINES: NEWS ON FEDERAL FOOD PROGRAMS AND BUDGET ISSUES FROM THE FOOD RESEARCH & ACTION CENTER (FRAC).). [Foodlines]. **Added/Corp** Food Research and Action Center. **VFOAT** Food Lines. Vol. 1, No. 1 (Jan. 1983)-. Periodical. English. Six times a year. $25.00. Food Research & Action Center / Washington, DC, 1875 Connecticut Avenue NW, Suite 540, Washington DC 20009. **Tel** (202)986-2200, FAX (202)986-2525. **ED** Christin Driscoll. **Ad Acc. Circ:** 2,000 (ctrl).
**Ind/Abst** AGRICOLA.

CN/0046-4767
**FOSTER PARENT.** ***Title Change.*** **See** Family and Marriage.

US/0145-6067
**FOUNDATION 500. Added/Corp** Douglas M. Lawson Associates. **VAT** Foundation Five Hundred. (19??)-. Periodical. English. ir (every 3 to 10 years). Douglas M Lawson Associates, 545 Madison Avenue, New York NY 10022. **Tel** (212)759-5660, (800)238-0004, FAX (212)759-1893. **ED** David M. Lawson. **LC** HV97.F66; F68. **DD** 361.7/025/73.

US/1055-4998
**FOUNDATION REPORTER (1990).** (FOUNDATION REPORTER.). [Found. rep.]. **Added/Corp** Taft Group (Rockville, Md.). **VFOAT** Taft Foundation Reporter. 22nd Ed. (1991)-. English. an (published in Sept. of prior year). $365.00. Taft Group, 835 Penobscott Building, Customer Service, Detroit MI 48226. **Tel** (800)877-8238, FAX (313)961-6083. **(Subscription address:** Taft Group, PO Box 71701, Chicago, IL 60694; telephone: (800)877-8238 ext. 1716**) LC** HV97.A3; T323. **DD** 361.7/632/02573. **NLM** HV 97.A3; T124. Index available (free). ***Continues*** *Taft Foundation Reporter, 0730-6237.*

CN/0821-638X
**FRIENDS (HALIFAX).** (FRIENDS : THE VOICE OF RED CROSS IN NOVA SCOTIA.). [Friends]. Vol. 1, No. 1 (Sept. 1981)-. Periodical. English. qt. Free. Nova Scotia Red Cross, PO Box 366, Halifax Nova Scotia B3J 2P8 Canada. **Tel** (902)423-9181, FAX (902)422-6247. **ED** Kathleen Stirling. **DD** 361.7/634/09716. **Circ:** 4,100 (ctrl). ***Absorbed*** *A.I.D. News; Canadian Red Cross Society. Nova Scotia Division. Blood Donor Service. Blood Programme, 0712-6484; Link Up (Halifax, N.S.), 0229-9763; Red Cross Goes to School, 0229-9828; Sand and Surf, 0315-677X.*
**Desc:** An informative newsletter used to keep Red Cross members and the general public informed on activities of Red Cross.

CN/0709-6259
**FRIENDSHIP FORUM.** Began with July 1978 issue?. Periodical. English. ir. Free. Big Sister Association of Guelph, Suite 2, 107 Quebec Street, Guelph Ontario N1H 2T5 Canada. **DD** 362.7. ctrl circ. ***Continues*** *Big Sister Association of Guelph. Newsletter, 0709-6267.*

US/0734-1601
**FROM THE STATE CAPITALS. PUBLIC ASSISTANCE & WELFARE TRENDS (NEW HAVEN, CONN.).** (FROM THE STATE CAPITALS. PUBLIC ASSISTANCE & WELFARE TRENDS.). [From state cap., Public assist. welf. trends]. **VFOAT** Public Assistance & Welfare Trends; Public Assistance and Welfare Trends. (1982)-. Periodical. English. wk. $211.50 (one year), $235.00 (two year) public and institutional libraries; $378.00 (one year), $420.00 (two year) other. Wakeman Walworth Inc., 300 North Washington Street #204, Alexandria VA 22314. **Tel** (703)549-8606. **DD** 351. **[CCC]. *Continues*** *From the State Capitals. Public Assistance, 1062-6689.*
**Desc:** Reviews the administration and financing of public aid programs in states across the country. Includes welfare, aid to families with dependent children and services for the elderly and disabled.

US/0748-8157
**FRONTIERS OF HEALTH SERVICES MANAGEMENT. Added/Corp** W.K. Kellogg Foundation. Vol. 1, No. 1 (Sept. 1984)-. Periodical. English. Four times a year (Feb., June, Aug., Nov.). $65.00. American College of Healthcare Executives, 840 North Lake Shore Drive, c/o J. Flory, Chicago IL 60611. **Tel** (312)943-0544 ext. 3000, FAX (312)943-3791. **(Subscription address:** FDN American College of Healthcare Executives, Order Processing Center, 1951 Cornell Avenue, Melrose Park IL 60160.**) ED** Douglas A. Conrad. **LC** RA971; .F77. **DD** 362.1/1/068. **NLM** W1; FR946EF. **[CCC]. Circ:** 2,500. available on microfilm and microfiche from University Microfilms International (UMI). Documents available from UMI Article Clearinghouse.
**Desc:** Each issue focuses on a single topic of immediate interest to forward-looking health services executives.
**Ind/Abst** ABI/INFORM Glob. Ed.; ABI Inform Ondisc (Winter 1987-); Health Plan. Adminis.; Hospit. Health Admin. Index (Vol. 1, No. 1, 1984-); Hospit. Manage. Rev.; Hum. Resour. Abstr. (?-?); UMI ABI/Inform--Bus. Period. Ondisc (Winter 1987-) [Full Txt.].

CN/0228-3891
**FUND RAISING EVENT REPORT.** [Fund rais. event rep.]. Vol. 1, No. 1 (Sept. 1980)-. Periodical. English. mo. $75.00. Fundraising Event Report, 287 Macpherson Avenue, Toronto Ontario M4V 1A4. **DD** 361.7.

●US/1058-1235
**FUNDING DECISION MAKERS.** (FUNDING DECISION MAKERS: A GUIDE TO PHILANTHROPIC CONNECTIONS.). [Funding decis. mak.]. **Added/Corp** Taft Group (Rockville, Md.). **VFOAT** Decision Makers. 1st ed. (1992)-. English. $165.00. Taft Group, 835 Penobscott Building, Customer Service, Detroit MI 48226. **Tel** (800)877-8238, FAX (313)961-6083. **LC** HV27; .F87. **DD** 361.7/092/273.

US/1047-191X
**FUTURE CHOICES.** ***Ceased.*** (FUTURE CHOICES : TOWARD A NATIONAL YOUTH POLICY.). [Future choices]. **Added/Corp** Youth Policy Institute (Washington, D.C.). Premier Edition (Spring 1989)-Vol. 4, No. 1 (Fall 1992). Periodical. English. Three times a year. Youth Policy Institute, 1221 Massachusetts Avenue Northwest, Suite B, Washington DC 20005. **Tel** (202)638-2144. **DD** 362.
**Desc:** A collection of essays that discuss crucial issues affecting the nation's children, youth and families.
**Ind/Abst** AGRICOLA [Select. Cov.]; PAIS Int. Print (1991-).

US/1054-8289
**FUTURE OF CHILDREN / CENTER FOR THE FUTURE OF CHILDREN, THE DAVID AND LUCILE PACKARD FOUNDATION, THE.** [Future child.]. **Added/Corp** Center for the Future of Children. Vol. 1, No. 1 (Spring 1991)-. Periodical. English. qt. Free. Center for the Future of Children, 300 Second Street, Suite 102, Las Altos CA 94022. **DD** 362. **NLM** W1; FU616.
**Ind/Abst** Curr. Index J. Educ.

CN/0842-1986
**GARDAVUE (LONGUEUIL).** (GARDAVUE.). [Gardavue]. **Added/Corp** Association des Services de Garde en Milieu Scolaire du Quebec. (1988)-. Periodical. French. Four times a year. Free (members); 15.00F other. Association des Services de Garde en milieu scolaire du Quebec inc., 13, rue St-Laurent Est, Longueuil, Quebec J4H 4B7. **Tel** (514)646-2753, FAX (514)646-1807. **DD** 362.7/12/09714. ***Continues*** *Bulletin la Ribambelle., 0838-715X.*

CN/0711-3528
**GAZETTE DE LA BUTTE, LA.** [Gaz. Butte]. V. 1, No. 1, (Dec. 23, 1968)-. Periodical. French. ir. Hotel-Dieu d'Alma, 300 Boulevard Champlain, Alma Quebec G8B 5W3 Canada. **DD** 362.1/1/06071414.

UK
**GEORGETOWN JOURNAL ON FIGHTING POVERTY.** (19??)-. English. Twice a year (Fall, Summer). $25.00 US; $30.00 Other. Georgetown University Law Center, 600 New Jersey Avenue NW, Washington DC 20009. **Tel** (202)662-9468, FAX (202)662-9444.

GW
**GESETZLICHE RENTENVERSICHERUNG, DIE.** German. 33.00. Leitfadenverlag Dieter Sunholt, Germany. **LC** KK3387.A24; G47. **DD** 344.43/02; 344.3042.

BE/0378-4657
**GIDS OP MAATSCHAPPELIJK GEBIED.** [Gids Maatsch. Geb.]. (1902)-. Academic Scholarly Publication. Dutch. Ten times a year. 1,300F Belgium; 1,400F other. De Gids Op Maatschappelijk, Wetstraat 121, 1040 Brussels Belgium. **Tel** 02 237 31 11, FAX 02 237 37 00. **ED** Algemeen Christelyk Werknemersverbond. Index available. cum. index. **Bk Rev**, (Qty: 80). **Circ:** 2,000.
**Desc:** Articles about social, cultural and trade union problem.

US/0146-8340
**GLAD DIRECTORY OF RESOURCES AVAILABLE TO DEAF & HARD-OF-HEARING PERSONS IN THE SOUTHERN CALIFORNIA AREA. Main/Corp** Greater Los Angeles Council on Deafness. **VFOAT** Directory of Resources Available to Deaf & Hard-of-Hearing Persons in the Southern California Area. **VAT** Greater Los Angeles Council on Deafness Directory of Resources Available to Deaf and Hard-of-Hearing Persons in the Southern California Area. Directory. English. qt. $10.00 North America; $15.00 other. Greater Los Angeles Council on Deafness, 2222 Laverna Avenue, Los Angeles CA 90041. **Tel** (213)478-8000, FAX (213)383-3803. **ED** Marge Klugman. **LC** HV2561.C2; G74A. **DD** 362.4/2/0257949. available in braille.

CN/0820-7518
**GOELAND (MONTREAL).** (LE GOELAND.). [Goeland]. (Fall 1982)-. Periodical. French. Four times a year. 27.00Can$ (one year), 50.00Can$ (two year) institutions; 13.50Can$ (one year), 25.00Can$ (two year) individuals. Le Goeland, 3761A Rue Normandin, Chomdy Laval Quebec H7T2N1 Canada. **Tel** (514)686-8178. **ED** Jules Danseneau. **DD** 362.4/09714.

CN/0709-9142
**GOVERNMENT REPORT FOR NONPROFITS. ONTARIO.** (GOVERNMENT REPORT FOR NONPROFITS.). [Gov. rep. nonprofits, Ont.]. V. 1- Sept. 1979-. Periodical. English. sm. $37.50 individuals and non-profit organizations, $75.00 corporations. Government Report for Nonprofits, 287 Macpherson Avenue, Toronto Ontario M4V 1A4. **DD** 361.7/63/09713.

US
**GOVERNOR'S YOUTH CONFERENCE. Added/Corp** Nevada Advisory Council on Children and Youth. (19??)-. English. an. **LC** HQ796; .G698. **DD** 362.7/042/09793.

●US
**GRANT$ FOR HEALTH PROGRAMS FOR CHILDREN AND YOUTH. Added/Corp** Foundation Center. **VFOAT** Grants for Health Programs for Children and Youth; Health Programs for Children and Youth. (1992)-. English. ***Continues*** *Children & Youth, Health Programs.*

●US
**GRANT$ FOR MENTAL HEALTH, ADDICTIONS & CRISIS SERVICES. See** Philanthropy.

●US
**GRANT$ FOR SOCIAL SERVICES. See** Philanthropy.

US
**GRANT$ FOR THE AGED / THE FOUNDATION CENTER. See** Philanthropy.

●US
**GRANT$ FOR THE HOMELESS. See** Philanthropy.

US/0094-1387
**GRANTS - U.S. DEPARTMENT OF HEALTH, EDUCATION, AND WELFARE. OFFICE OF HUMAN DEVELOPMENT. OFFICE OF YOUTH DEVELOPMENT.** (GRANTS.). **Main/Corp** United States. Office of Youth Development. English. Office of Youth Development, Washington DC 20201. **LC** HV9103; .O34A. **DD** 364.36/0973.

US/0739-2001
**GRAY PANTHER NETWORK.** (GRAY PANTHER NETWORK; AGE AND YOUTH IN ACTION.). [Gray Panther netw.]. **Added/Corp** Gray Panthers. Gray Panther Project Fund. **VFOAT** Gray Panther network; Network. (1977)-. Periodical. English. ir (new frequency not yet determined). $35.00 (institutions), $20.00 (individuals). Gray Panthers, 2025 Pennsylvania Avenue Nortwest, #821, Washington DC 20036. **Tel** (202)466-3132, FAX (202)466-3133. **LC** WMLC 93/355. **Ad Acc.** ctrl circ. ***Continues*** *Network (Gray Panthers).*
**Ind/Abst** Altern. Press Index (199?-).

US/0196-9870
**GREEN PAGES REHAB SOURCEBOOK, THE. VFOAT** Green Pages. **VAT** Green Pages Rehab Source Book. Began in 1976. English. an. $20.00. Sourcebook Publications, Box 1586, Winter Park FL 32790. **LC** RD755; .G74. **DD** 362.4/048/02573.

US/0883-6876
**GRIT (CAYUGA, IND.).** (GRIT : THE OFFICIAL PUBLICATION OF DELTA THETA TAU SORORITY, INC.). [Grit]. Periodical. English. qt. Delta Theta Tau Sorority, Inc., 201 Third Street, Cayuga IN 47928. **DD** 361.

UK/0951-824X
**GROUPWORK LONDON.** (GROUPWORK). [GroupworkLond.]. (1987)-. Periodical. English. tq. $80.00. Whiting and Birch, 90 Dartmouth Road Forest Hill, London SE23 3HZ England. **Tel** 011 44 81 244-2421. **DD** 361.4. **[CCC].**
**Ind/Abst** Int. Bibliogr. Sociol.; Soc. Plann. Policy Dev. Abstr.; Soc. Work Abstr. [Select. Cov.].

US
**GROWING TOGETHER.** English. mo. $30.00. Dunn & Hargitt Inc, 22 North 2nd Street, PO Box 1100,

Lafayette IN 47901. **Tel** (317)423-2624. **ED** Nancy Kleckner.
**Desc:** A monthly newsletter of reliable information and practical advice for young parents.

CN/0383-2457
**GUIDE TO ACCREDITATION OF CANADIAN MENTAL HEALTH SERVICES.** (1975)-. Periodical. English. Canadian Council on Hospital Accreditation, 1815 Alta Vista Drive, Ottawa Ontario K1G 3Y6 Canada. **DD** 362.2/0971. ***Supersedes*** *Standards for Accreditation of Canadian Mental Hospitals, 0383-2465.*

US/0163-4623
**GUIDE TO CALIFORNIA FOUNDATIONS. Added/Corp** San Francisco Study Center. Northern California Grantmakers. Northern California Foundations Group. (1976)-. English. be. $53.75. Northern California Grantmakers, 116 New Montgomery Street/Suite 742, San Francisco CA 94105. **Tel** (415)777-5761. **LC** HV98.C3; G84. **DD** 361.7/6/025794.

UK
**GUIDE TO YOUTH HOSTELS AROUND THE WORLD, A. Added/Corp** International Youth Hostel Federation. **VFOAT** Guide des Auberges de Jeunesse du Monde Entier. (19??)-. English. an. $10.95. American Youth Hostels, 733 15th Street Northwest, Suite 840, Washington DC 20005. **Tel** (202)783-6161, FAX (202)783-6171.

CN/0714-7066
**HACTION.** [Haction]. Vol. 2, No. 6 (June 1982)-. Periodical. English. bm. $10.00. Handicapped Action Committee, 835 Humboldt, Victoria British Columbia V8V 2Z6 Canada. **Tel** (604)383-4105. **DD** 362.4/09711/34. **Bk Rev. Ad Acc. Circ:** 5,000. ***Continues*** *H.A.C.-ing Away, 0715-3163.*
**Desc:** The newspaper of the Handicapped Action Committee serving the disabled community.

AU
**HANDBUCH DER OSTERREICHISCHEN SOZIALVERSICHERUNG FUER DAS JAHR. Added/Corp** Hauptverband der Osterreichischen Sozialversicherungstrager. (1977)-. Periodical. German. ir. S110.00 (Volume 1), S140.00 (Volume 2) Austria; S130.00 (Volume 1), S165.00 (Volume 2) other. Hauptverband der Oesterreichischen Sozialversi, Kundmanngasse 21 Cherungstraeg, A 1030 Vienna Austria. **LC** HD7169; .S8. **DD** 368.4/009436. ***Continues*** *Statistisches Handbuch der Osterreichischen Sozialversicherung.* ***Continued in part by*** *Statistisches Handbuch der Osterreichischen Sozialversicherung (1992).*

IO
**HASIL PENENELITIAN I.E. PENELITIAN KESEJAHTERAAN SOSIAL ANAK / KANTOR STATISTIK PROPINSI DKI JAKARTA. VFOAT** Hasil Penelitian Kesejahteraan Social Anak. Indonesian. Biro Pusat Statistik, JLN Dr Sutomo 8 Kotak, Pos 1003, Jakarta 10710 Indonesia. **Tel** 3728007, 374908. **LC** HV800.I56; J343.

US/1062-8096
**HAZARDOUS EMERGENCY RESPONSE.** ***Title Change.*** [Hazard. emerg. response]. Vol. 1, No. 1 (Feb. 1992)-(19??). Periodical. English. mo. Stevens Publishing Corporation, 225 North New Road, Waco TX 76702-2604. **Tel** (800)727-7573, (817)776-9000. **DD** 363. ***Merged into*** *HAZMAT News.*
**Ind/Abst** Foods Adlibra (1992-).

US/0017-8721
**HEAD START NEWSLETTER. Main/Corp** Project Head Start (U.S.). Newsletter. English. Project Head Start, Office of Economic Opportunity, Washington DC 20506.

●US/1065-8289
**HEALING WOMAN, THE.** [Heal. woman]. (1992)-. Periodical. English. mo. $25.00. The Healing Woman, PO Box 3038, Moss Beach CA 94038. **DD** 362.
**Desc:** A newsletter providing solid information, self-help and support for women survivors of childhood sexual abuse.

UK/0307-0824
**HEALTH AND PERSONAL SOCIAL SERVICES STATISTICS FOR ENGLAND WITH SUMMARY TABLES FOR GREAT BRITAIN. See** Sociology-Abstracting, Bibliographies and Statistics.

UK/0307-0840
**HEALTH AND PERSONAL SOCIAL SERVICES STATISTICS FOR WALES. See** Sociology-Abstracting, Bibliographies and Statistics.

●UK/0966-0410
**HEALTH & SOCIAL CARE IN THE COMMUNITY. VFOAT** Health and Social Care in the Community. Vol. 1, No. 1 (Jan. 1993)-. Academic Scholarly Publication. English. bm (6 issues). $151.00 (institutions), $57.00 (individuals) US & Canada; £88.50 (institutions), £33.00 (individuals) Europe; £97.50 (institutions), £36.50 (individuals) other. Blackwell Scientific Publications Ltd, Marston Book Services, PO Box 87, Oxford OX2 ODT UK. **Tel** 011 44 865 791155, FAX 011 44 865 791927, telex 837 515 MARDIS G. **NLM** W1; HE265D. **[CCC].**

US/0360-7283
**HEALTH & SOCIAL WORK.** [Health soc. work]. **Added/Corp** National Association of Social Workers. **VFOAT** Health and Social Work. Vol. 1 (Feb. 1976)-. Periodical. English. qt. $40.00 NASW members; $76.00 (institutions), $60.00 (individuals). National Association of Social Workers, 750 First Street Northeast, Suite 700, Washington DC 20002-4241. **Tel** (800)638-8799, (202)408-8600, FAX (301)587-1321. **(Subscription address:** NASW Press / National Association of Social Workers, PO Box 431, Annapolis JCT MD 20701.**) ED** Thomas Owen Carlton. **LC** HV687.5.U5; H4. **DD** 362.1/04/25. **NLM** W1 HE266S. **CODEN** HSWODK. **[CCC].** Index available. **Bk Rev. Ad Acc. Circ:** 5,000. available on microfilm and microfiche from University Microfilms International (UMI). Documents available from UMI Article Clearinghouse.
**Ind/Abst** Acad. Abstr. Full Text Elite (Jan. 1992-); Acad. Abstr. (Jan. 1992-); Acad. Ind. [Computer File] (1992-); Acad. Search (Jan. 1992-); AGRICOLA; Annals Behav. Med.; Appl. Soc. Sci. Index Abstr.; Crim. Penol. Police Sci. Abstr.; Cumul. Index Nurs. Allied Health Lit.; Expand. Acad. Index (1989-); Health Plan. Adminis.; Health Source (Jan. 1992-); Index Med.; INFO-SOUTH Abstr.; Mag. Search; Multicult. Educ. Abstr.; Newsp. Period. Abstr. (1991-); Psychol. Abstr. (1976-); PsycINFO; PsycLit; Soc. Plann. Policy Dev. Abstr.; Soc. Sci. Source (Jan. 1992-); Soc. Sci. Index; Soc. Sci. Index Fulltext (Summer 1988-) [Full Txt.]; Soc. Work Abstr. (Spring, Summer 1987-) [Full Cov.]; Spec. Educ. Needs Abstr.

SZ/0254-9263
**HEALTH FOR ALL SERIES.** [Health for all ser.]. **Added/Corp** World Health Organization. No. 1 (1978)-. Monographic series. English. ir. Price varies per volume. World Health Organization, Distribution and Sales, 20 Avenue Appia, CH-1211 Geneva 27 Switzerland. **Tel** 011 41 22 7912111, FAX 011 41 22 7880401. **LC** UNC. **DD** 362.1. **NLM** W1 HE3365M.

CN/1180-3045
**HEALTH REPORTS. SUPPLEMENT. LIST OF RESIDENTIAL CARE FACILITIES IN CANADA.** ***Title Change.*** (HEALTH REPORTS. NO. 7, SUPPLEMENT. LIST OF RESIDENTIAL CARE FACILITIES IN CANADA / STATISTICS CANADA, CANADIAN CENTRE FOR HEALTH INFORMATION.). [Health rep., Suppl., List resid. care facil. Can.]. **Added/Corp** Canadian Centre for Health Information. **VFOAT** List of Residential Care Facilities in Canada; Liste des Etablissements de Soins Pour Beneficiaires Internes au Canada; Rapports sur la Sante. No 7, Liste des Etablissements de Soins Pour Beneficiaires Internes au Canada. (1989)-(19??). English (French). an. Statistics Canada, Publications Sales & Services, Main Building Room 1710, Ottawa Ontario K1A 0T6 Canada. **Tel** (613)951-5078, (800)267-6677, FAX (613)951-1584, telex 053-3585. **LC** RA998.C3; H38. **DD** 362.1/6/02571. ***Continues*** *List of Residential Care Facilities in Canada, 0831-7321.* ***Continued by*** *List of Residential Care Facilities, 1180-3045.*

CN/1181-8832
**HEALTH REPORTS. SUPPLEMENT. RESIDENTIAL CARE FACILITIES.** ***Title Change.*** (HEALTH REPORTS. SUPPLEMENT. RESIDENTIAL CARE FACILITIES, MENTAL DISORDERS / STATISTICS CANADA, CANADIAN CENTRE FOR HEALTH INFORMATION.). [Health rep., Suppl., Resid. care facil.]. **Added/Corp** Canadian Centre for Health Information. **VFOAT** Residential Care Facilities, Mental Disorders; Etablissements de Soins Speciaux Pour Beneficiaires Internes, Troubles Mentaux; Rapports sur la Sante. Etablissements de Soins Speciaux Pour Beneficiaires Internes, Troubles Mentaux. (1987/1988)-(19??). English (French). an. Statistics Canada, Publications Sales & Services, Main Building Room 1710, Ottawa Ontario K1A 0T6 Canada. **Tel** (613)951-5078, (800)267-6677, FAX (613)951-1584, telex 053-3585. **LC** RA790.7.C2; H44. **DD** 362.2/3/0971021. ***Continues in part*** *Health Reports. Supplement. Residential Care Facilities, 1180-2375.* ***Continued by*** *Residential Care Facilities, Mental, 1195-4175.*
**Desc:** Focuses only on facilities for mental disorders which includes facilities for the psychiatrically disabled, mentally retarded, emotionally disturbed children and centres for those with drug/alcohol problems.

US/0731-6607
**HEALTH SERVICES DIRECTORY. See** Medical Science and Technology-Hospital Administration and Medical Centers.

US/0161-2417
**HEARINGS IN PUBLIC ASSISTANCE. Main/Corp** National Center for Social Statistics. Jan./June 1976-. Periodical. English. sa. US Department of Health and Human Services, 200 Independence Avenue Southwest, Washington DC 20201. **LC** HV91.N25B. **DD** 361.6/2/0973. ***Continues*** *Fair Hearings in Public Assistance, 0145-9422.*

US
**HELPER (AMERICAN SOCIAL HEALTH ASSOCIATION). See** Public Health and Safety.

US/0073-1706
**HELPING PERSON IN THE GROUP.** Vol. 1 (1966)-. English. Syracuse University / Social Work, School of Social Work, Syracuse NY 13244. **ED** M Casper.

US/1064-2080
**HERE'S HELP (RENO, NEV.).** (HERE'S HELP : FOR PEOPLE WHO WORK WITH THE AGING.). [Here's help]. (19??)-. Periodical. English. mo. $49.00. Eymann Publications, PO Box 3577, Reno NV 89505. **Tel** (702)333-6651. **DD** 618. ***Continues*** *Health Care Articles, 1041-2174.*

IS
**HEVRAH U-REVAHAH. VFOAT** Society and Welfare. V. 1- March 1978-. Periodical. Hebrew (summaries and/or abstracts in English). qt. IL30.00 Israel; $18.00 US. Misrad Ha-Avodah, Veha-Revahah Jerusalem Israel. **Tel** 02 708174. **ED** Shimou E Spiro, Geula Altman. **LC** HV378.5; .H48. **DD** 361/.95694/05. Index available. cum. index. **Bk Rev. Circ:** 2,000 (ctrl). ***Supersedes*** *Israel. Misrad Ha-Saad. Saad.*
**Desc:** A social work journal publishing papers based on research, innovations in practice and theoretical work.

US
**HHS FELLOWS PROGRAM, THE. Main/Corp** United States. Dept. of Health and Human Services. **VAT** Health and Human Services Fellows Program. 1981-82-. English. an. HHS Fellows Program, 330 Independence Avenue SW, Washington DC 20201. ***Continues*** *HEW Fellows Program.*

JA
**HIBAKUSHA.** No. 1 ('82-12)-. Periodical. Japanese. ¥500 single issue. Genbaku Higaisha Sodanin No Kai, 11 Hatchobori, 7 Naku-ku, Hiroshima-shi 730 Japan. **LC** HV639; .H5.

US
**HIGHWAY PATROLMEN'S FUND, STATEMENT TO EMPLOYEES. Main/Corp** Minnesota State Retirement System. Began in 1973. English. an. Minnesota State Retirement System, 529 Jackson at 10th Street, St Paul MN 55101. **LC** HV8145.M6; M58A. **DD** 353.97760074.

●US/1063-1704
**HMO PERFORMANCE DIGEST.** [HMO perform. dig.]. **Added/Corp** Health Care Investment Analysts, Inc. KPMG Peat Marwick. (1992)-. English. $199.00. HCIC, 300 East Lombard Street, Baltimore MD 21202. **DD** 362.

US/0891-6624
**HMO PRACTICE.** [HMO pract.]. **Added/Corp** HMO Group (U.S.). **VAT** Health Maintenance Organization Practice. Vol. 1, No. 1 (1987)-. Periodical. English. Four times a year. $150.00. Daniel Wolfson, HMO Group, 100 Albany Street, Suite 130, New Brunswick NJ 08901. **Tel** (908)220-1388, FAX (908)220-0298. **(Subscription address:** HMO Practice, PO Box 133, Circulation Department, West Seneca, NY 14224**) ED** L. Katz M.D. & S. Yox Ed.D (editor's address: HMO Practice, 900 Guaranty Building, Buffalo, NY 14202). **DD** 362. **NLM** W1; HM676T. Index Available published separately, bound from publisher, free-automatically sent. **Bk Rev,** (Qty: 12). **Ad Acc, Adv Mgr:** Hank Townsend, PMI, **Tel** (212)685-5010. **Circ:** 15,000. available on microfilm and microfiche from University Microfilms International (UMI).
**Ind/Abst** Health Plan. Adminis.; Hospit. Health Admin. Index (1989-).

JA
**HOIKU HAKUSHO. Added/Corp** Zenkoku Hoiku Dantai Godo Kenkyu Shukai. (1976)-. Periodical. Japanese. ¥900. Sodo Bunka, 10-6 Gobancho Chiyoda-ku 102, Tokyo Japan. **LC** HV861.J3; H6.

US/0891-9364
**HOME CARE ECONOMICS.** ***Ceased.*** [Home care econ.]. **Added/Corp** American Health Consultants. Vol. 1, No. 1 (Winter 1987)-(19??). Periodical. English. qt. American Health Consultants, 3525 Piedmont Road, Suite 400, Atlanta GA 30305. **Tel** (800)688-2421, (404)262-7436. **LC** WMLC 93/1380. **DD** 362. **NLM** W1; HO502H.
**Ind/Abst** Health Plan. Adminis. (?-?); Hospit. Health Admin. Index (1987-1988).

●US/1058-7934
**HOME CARE SALARY & BENEFITS REPORT.** [Home care salary benefits rep.]. **Added/Corp** Hospital Compensation Service. **VFOAT** Home Care Salary and Benefits Report. (1992)-. English. an (Published in October). $250.00. Hospital & Healthcare Compensation Service, PO Box 376, 69 Minnehaha Blvd., Oakland NJ 07436. **Tel** (201)405-0075, FAX (201)405-1258. **LC** RA645.35; .H654. **DD**

331.2/8136214/0973021.
**Desc:** Covers Salary and bonus data on sixty-three management, nursing, therapy, and clerical jobs according to auspice, state, geographical region, and principal city.

CN/0847-2378
**HOME CARE TODAY.** ***Ceased.*** [Home care today]. **VFOAT** Homecare Today. Vol. 1, No. 1 (Oct. 1989)-(19??). Periodical. English (French). Twice a year (Apr. and Dec.). G. C. I. Communications, Place DU Canada Bureau 1850, Montreal Que H3B 2N2 Canada. **Tel** (514)861-1621, FAX (514)861-1473. **DD** 362.1/4/097105. **Bk Rev.**
**Desc:** About the home care services and nursing.

●US/1061-0227
**HOME CARING.** (HOME CARING: THE NEWSLETTER FOR THE HOME DAY CARE PROFESSIONAL.). [Home caring]. Vol. 1, No. 1 (Spring 1992)-. Newsletter. English. qt. $15.00. Welch Group Publications, PO Box 8241, Bossier City LA 71113-8241. **DD** 362.

US/0162-1424
**HOME HEALTH CARE SERVICES QUARTERLY.** [Home health care serv. q.]. Vol. 1 (Spring 1979)-. Periodical. English. qt. $265.00 US; $371.00 other. The Haworth Press Inc, 10 Alice Street, Binghamton NY 13904-1580. **Tel** (607)722-5857, (800)3-HAWORTH, FAX (607)722-1424. **ED** Brahna Trager (editor's address: PO Box 96, San Geronimo, CA 94963). **LC** RA645.3; .H65. **DD** 362.1/4/05. **NLM** W1 HO502R. **Bk Rev. Ad Acc. Pr Rev. Acid Free. Circ:** 435. available on microfilm and microfiche from University Microfilms International (UMI). Documents available from Haworth Document Delivery Service.
**Desc:** Covering all major areas of concern to policy makers, planners, and providers of home health care and related services. This journal focuses on research policy issues, topics related to the training of professionals and paraprofessionals and innovative approaches to services provision and delivery systems.
**Ind/Abst** Abstr. Soc. Gerontol.; AGRICOLA [Select. Cov.]; Cumul. Index Nurs. Allied Health Lit.; Health Plan. Adminis.; Hospit. Health Admin. Index; Index Period. Lit. Aging; Int. Pharm. Abstr.; Psychol. Abstr. (1988-); PsycINFO (1990-); PsycLit; Soc. Plann. Policy Dev. Abstr.; Soc. Work Abstr. [Select. Cov.]; Sociol. Abstr.

CN/0822-9406
**HOME SUPPORT SERVICES IN METROPOLITAN TORONTO.** [Home support serv. Metrop. Tor.]. 1983-. English. be. Community Information Centre of Metropolitan Toronto, 590 Jarvis Street, Toronto Ontario M4Y 2J4 Canada. **Tel** (416)392-4575, FAX (416)392-4404. **DD** 362.4/0483. ***Continues*** *Home Services and Transportation, 0711-4192.*

US/0882-2700
**HOMECARE (LOS ANGELES, CALIF.).** (HOMECARE.). [Homecare]. **VFOAT** Home Care. (198?)-. Periodical. English. mo. Free, qualified professionals; $48.00 (one year), $84.00 (two year) other. Miramar Publishing Company, 6133 Bristol Parkway, PO Box 3640, Culver City CA 90231. **Tel** (800)543-4116, (310)337-9717. **ED** Andria Segedy. **DD** 362. **Bk Rev. Ad Acc. Circ:** 15,000 (ctrl). ***Continues*** *Homecare Rental/Sales, 0192-1673.*
**Desc:** A business news magazine for firms involved in the rental and sale of home health care products.

US/0896-355X
**HOMEWORDS (WASHINGTON, D.C.).** ***Ceased.*** (HOMEWORDS : A QUARTERLY OF THE HOMELESSNESS INFORMATION EXCHANGE.). [Homewords]. **Added/Corp** Homelessness Information Exchange. **VFOAT** Home Words. Vol. 1, No. 1 (Jan. 1988)-Vol. 4, No. 3. Periodical. English. qt. Homelessness Information Exchange, 1830 Conn Avenue NW/4th Floor, Washington DC 20009. **Tel** (202)462-7551. **ED** Sean Burns. **DD** 363. **Circ:** 3,000.

CN/0701-1490
**HORIZON D'OR.** **Added/Corp** Conseil de l'Age d'or Region Sud-ouest du Quebec. (Jan. 1972)-. Periodical. French. ir. 0.25Can$ per no. Conseil De L'age D'or Region Sud-Ouest Du Quebec, 50 Avenue Grand-Ile, Salaberry De Valleyfield, Quebec J6S 3L8 Canada. **DD** 362.6/3.

US/0891-3781
**HOSPICE FORUM.** [Hosp. forum]. **Added/Corp** Hospice Association of America. (19??)-. Periodical. English. sm. $105.00 US; $120.00 other. Hospice Association of America, 519 C Street Northeast, Washington DC 20002. **Tel** (202)546-4759. **DD** 362.
**Desc:** Keeps hospice professionals up-to-date with issues affecting the industry. Contains legislative and regulatory updates, research news, marketing strategies and general information on the hospice world.

US/0742-969X
**HOSPICE JOURNAL, THE.** [Hosp. j.]. **Added/Corp** National Hospice Organization (U.S.). Vol. 1, No. 1 (Spring 1985)-. Periodical. English. qt. $150.00 US; $210.00 other. The Haworth Press Inc, 10 Alice Street, Binghamton NY 13904-1580. **Tel** (607)722-5857, (800)3-HAWORTH, FAX (607)722-1424. **ED** Madalon O'Rawe (editor's address: 5512 Northumberland Street, Pittsburgh, PA 15217). **LC** R726.8; .H6716. **DD** 362.1/75. **NLM** W1; HO69H. **Bk Rev. Ad Acc. Pr Rev. Acid Free. Circ:** 2,906. available on microfilm and microfiche from University Microfilms International (UMI). Documents available from Haworth Document Delivery Service.
**Desc:** Focusing on terminal and palliative care, this is the first comprehensive, refereed, multidisciplinary forum for clinical and research articles from all aspects of care for the dying.
**Ind/Abst** Abstr. Res. Pastor. Care Couns. (19??-); Cumul. Index Nurs. Allied Health Lit.; Health Saf. Sci. Abstr.; Health Plan. Adminis.; Hospit. Health Admin. Index (1985-); Int. Nurs. Index; Int. Pharm. Abstr.; Nurs. Abstr.; Psychol. Abstr. (1985-); PsycINFO (1990-); PsycLit; Sage Fam. Stud. Abstr.; Soc. Plann. Policy Dev. Abstr.; Soc. Work Abstr. [Select. Cov.].

US/0895-3171
**HOTLINE - CHILDREN'S RIGHTS OF NEW YORK (ORGANIZATION).** (HOTLINE.). [Hotline - Child. Rights N. Y. (Organ.)]. **VFOAT** Hot Line. Periodical. English. qt. Children's Rights of New York Inc, 19 Maple Avenue, Stony Brook NY 11790. **DD** 362.

US/0273-5946
**HOTLINE (SPRINGFIELD, ILL.).** (HOTLINE / ILLINOIS DEPARTMENT OF CHILDREN AND FAMILY SERVICES.). [Hotline]. **Added/Corp** Illinois. Dept. of Children and Family Services. Vol. 1, No. 1 (Spring 1981)-. Periodical. English. Four times a year. Free on request. Illinois Department of Children and Family Services, 1 North Old State Capital Place, Springfield IL 62706. **Tel** (217)785-2670. ***Continues*** *Together, 0199-1841.*

US/1050-3234
**HOUSING THE ELDERLY REPORT.** **See** Senior Citizens.

US/0091-4584
**HOW FEDERAL AGENCIES HAVE SERVED THE HANDICAPPED.** **See** Physically Impaired.

●US/1063-9071
**HOW TO ADOPT YOUR BABY PRIVATELY.** [How adopt your baby priv.]. (1993)-. English. $11.95. Adoption Advocates Press, 1921 Ohio Street NE, Palm Bay FL 32907. **DD** 362.

US/8755-1241
**HSA/NENY NEWS.** (HSA/NENY NEWS / HEALTH SYSTEMS AGENCY OF NORTHEASTERN NEW YORK.). [HSA/NENY news]. **Main/Corp** Health Systems Agency of Northeastern New York. **VFOAT** H.S.A./N.E.N.Y. **VAT** Health Systems Agency of Northeastern New York News. Periodical. English. Health Systems Agency of Northeastern New York, Washington Avenue Ext Pine West Pl 2, Albany NY 12205. **DD** 362.

US
**HUERFANO.** V. 1- 1973-. Periodical. English. sa.

US/0099-2453
**HUMAN RESOURCES ABSTRACTS.** **See** Economics-Abstracting, Bibliographies and Statistics.

US
**HUMAN RESOURCES AND SERVICES, DIRECTORY.** **Added/Corp** Nebraska. State Office of Planning and Programming. (19??)-. English. Office of Planning and Programming, PO Box 94601, Lincoln NE 68509. **LC** HV98.N2; H85. **DD** 362/.025/782.

US
**HUMAN SERVICE MONEY SOURCE.** (19??)-. English. Twelve times a year. $70.00 (regular); $154.00 combination of Human Service Moneysource & California Update. California Update, 4019 Glenolive Court, Sacramento CA 95821. **Tel** (916)483-6397. ***Continues*** *Human Service Business Journal.*

US/1051-5844
**HUMAN SERVICE YELLOW PAGES OF MASSACHUSETTS.** ***Title Change.*** [Hum. serv. yellow pages Mass.]. **Added/Corp** Human Service Yellow Pages (Firm). (1989)-(1992). Periodical. English. be. George D. Hall Company, 50 Congress Street, Boston MA 02109. **Tel** (800)446-1215, (617)523-3745. **DD** 361. ***Continues*** *Human Service Yellow Pages of Greater Boston, 0898-6347.* ***Merged with*** *Human Service Yellow Pages of Rhode Island, 1061-0944* ***to form*** *Human Service Yellow Pages of Massachusetts & Rhode Island.*

●US
**HUMAN SERVICE YELLOW PAGES OF MASSACHUSETTS & RHODE ISLAND.** **VFOAT** Human Service Yellow Pages of Massachusetts and Rhode Island. (1993)-. Directory. English. ir (every 1-2 years). $24.90. George D. Hall Company, 50 Congress Street, Boston MA 02109. **Tel** (800)446-1215, (617)523-3745. **LC** HV98.M4; H86. ***Formed by the union of*** *Human Service Yellow Pages of Massachusetts, 1051-5844* ***and*** *Human Service Yellow Pages of Rhode Island, 1061-0944.*

CN/0823-8480
**HUMAN SERVICES DIRECTORY (SAINT JOHN).** (HUMAN SERVICES DIRECTORY / SAINT JOHN HUMAN DEVELOPMENT COUNCIL.). [Hum. serv. dir.]. **Added/Corp** Saint John Human Development Council. No. 1 (1983)-. Directory. English. be. $17.00 (add $3.00 shipping). Saint John Human Development Council, PO Box 6125 Station A John, New Brunswick E2L 4R6, Canada. **Tel** (506)634-1673. **DD** 361/.0025/71532. Index available. ***Continues*** *Directory of Community Services, 0318-6474.*
**Desc:** Descriptions of human services in greater Saint John area.

US/0193-9009
**HUMAN SERVICES IN THE RURAL ENVIRONMENT.** [Human serv. rural environ.]. **Added/Corp** University of Tennessee, Knoxville. School of Social Work. Inland Empire School of Social Work and Human Services. University of Wisconsin--Extension. Center for Social Service. (1976)-. Periodical. English. qt. $35.00 (institutions), $25.00 (individuals). Human Services in the Rural Environment, Mail Stop 19, Eastern Washington University, Cheney WA 99004. **Tel** (509)359-6474. **ED** Lynne C. Morris. **LC** HV85; .H85. **DD** 361/.973. **Bk Rev. Ad Acc. Circ:** 1,000. available on microfilm and microfiche from University Microfilms International (UMI).
**Desc:** A professional journal dedicated to the concerns of people living in rural areas. Its purpose is to serve as an information exchange and communication forum among those interested in rural service settings by focusing on policy and legislative developments programs, models research and evaluation projects, and innovative efforts to document aspects of rural life.
**Ind/Abst** AGRICOLA [Select. Cov.]; Curr. Index J. Educ.; Soc. Work Abstr. (Spring 1987-) [Select. Cov.].

US
**HUMAN SERVICES MONOGRAPH SERIES (PROJECT SHARE).** (HUMAN SERVICES MONOGRAPH SERIES.). **Added/Corp** Project Share. United States. Dept. of Health, Education, and Welfare. United States. Dept. of Health and Human Services. No. 1 (1976)-. Monographic series. English. ir (3 issues). $20.00. Project Share, PO Box 2309, Rockville MD 20852. **Tel** (301)984-9400. **NLM** W1 HU465.

US
**HUMAN SERVICES NEWS.** Periodical. English. bm. Lincoln Action Program Public Affairs Office, 2202 South 11th Street, Lincoln NE 68502.

US/0745-2616
**HUMAN SERVICES (WOODHAVEN, N.Y.).** (HUMAN SERVICES.). [Hum. serv.]. Periodical. English. bw. $15.00. Human Services, 80-34 Jamaica Avenue, Woodhaven NY 11421. **Tel** (212)296-2860.

FR
**HUMANISME.** **Added/Corp** Freemasons. Grand Orient de France. Centre de Documentation du Grand Orient de France. No. 54 (Nov./Dec. 1965)-. Periodical. French. bm. 930.46F France; 1000.00F other. AAELP, 77 rue de Villiers, 92523 Nuelly Cedex France. **Tel** 011 33 1 46437611. **LC** HS355; .F84a. **DD** 366/.1/05. ***Continues*** *Centre de Documentation du Grand Orient de France. Bulletin.*

CN/0712-2780
**HUMANITE (MONTREAL).** (HUMANITE : ORGANE OFFICIEL DE L'ASSOCIATION NATIONALE D'AIDE AUX HANDICAPES.). [Humanite]. Vol. 1, No. 1-. Periodical. French. Humanite, Bureau 404/140 Ouest Place Cremazie, Montreal Quebec H2P 1C3 Canada. **DD** 362.4/06/0714.

US
**HUNGER NOTES.** **Added/Corp** World Hunger Education Service. (June 1975)-. Periodical. English. qt. $45.00 (institutions), $18.00 (individuals) US; $51.00 (institutions), $24.00 (individuals) other. World Hunger Education Services, PO Box 29056, Washington DC 20017. **Tel** (202)269-1075. **ED** Patricia L. Kutzner Ph.D. **Bk Rev**, (Qty: 3-4). **Circ:** 1,000.

US/0743-6416
**HUNGER PROJECT PAPERS, THE.** [Hunger Proj. pap.]. **Added/Corp** Hunger Project. No. 1 (May 1984)-. Monographic series. English (French). Twice a year. Price varies per volume. Hunger Project, 1388 Sutter Street, San Francisco CA 94103. **Tel** (415)928-8700. **ED** Beverly Tangri. **DD** 363. **Circ:** 25,000 (ctrl).
**Desc:** Occasional papers that present technical/professional analyses of subjects related to ending hunger.

FI/0355-4759
**HUOLTOAPU.** **Main/Corp** Finland. Sosiaalihallitus. Suunnittelu- Ja Tilastotoimisto. **VFOAT** Socialhjalp; Social Assistance. Began with Vol. for 1969. Finnish (Swedish; summaries and/or abstracts in English). Valtion Painatuskeskus, PO Box 516, SF 00101 Helsinki Finland. **Tel** 011 358 0 5660266. **LC** HA1448; HV315.5. **NLM** W2 GF5 S86H. ***Continues** Huoltotilasto.*

CN/1192-7755
**I.D.E.E (BRIGHAM).** (L'I.D.E.E : BULLETIN DE LIAISON DE L'INSTITUT DES ERABLES, CENTRE DE RECHERCHES ET DE FORMATION EN DEFICIENCE INTELLECTUELLE.). [I.D.E.E]. **Added/Corp** Institut des Erables. **VFOAT** Idee. **VAT** Institut des Erables (Brigham). Vol. 1, No 1 (Autumn 1990)-. Bulletin. French. Four times a year (During seasons). 25.00Can$. Institute des Erables, 278 Avenue des Erables, CP 40, Brigham Quebec J0E 1J0 Canada. **Tel** (514)263-3545, FAX (514)263-1148. **ED** Henri-Marvin Laval. **DD** 362.3. **Bk Rev**, (Qty: 12). **Pr Rev. Circ:** 750 (ctrl).

US
**IARCA JOURNAL.** **Added/Corp** IARCA. **VFOAT** Journal. **VAT** International Association of Residential and Community Alternatives Journal. Vol. 2, No. 4 (Dec. 1989)-. Periodical. English. qt. Free to members. International Association of Residential and Community Alternatives, PO Box 1987, La Crosse WI 54602. **Tel** (608)785-0200. ***Continues** IHHA News.*

US/0098-8278
**IASSW DIRECTORY.** (IASSW DIRECTORY; MEMBER SCHOOLS AND ASSOCIATIONS.). **Main/Corp** International Association of Schools of Social Work. **VAT** International Association of Schools of Social Work Directory. Multiple languages. International Association of Schools of Social Work, 345 East 46th Street, New York NY 10017. **LC** HV6; .I42. **DD** 361/.007/1. ***Continues** Directory of Members and Constitution.*

US/0889-4000
**IBFAN NEWS.** (IBFAN NEWS / INTERNATIONAL BABY FOOD ACTION NETWORK.). [IBFAN news]. **Added/Corp** International Baby Food Action Network. **VAT** International Baby Food Action Network News. (19??)-. Periodical. English. Ten times a year. $15.00 (individuals); $16.00 (non-profit making groups); $50.00 (profit making groups). IBFAN News / Action Corporate Accountability, 3255 Hennepin Avenue South, Suite 255, Minneapolis MN 55408. **Tel** (617)823-1571. **DD** 360. **Bk Rev. Circ:** 2,000.
**Desc:** Reports on developments in the international campaign to improve infant health through the promotion and protection of breast feeding and appropriate young child weaning.
**Ind/Abst** Trop. Dis. Bull.

CN/1198-3795
**ICIDH AND ENVIRONMENTAL FACTORS INTERNATIONAL NETWORK.** (19??)-. English (French). Three times a year (Mar., July and Dec.). 45.00Can$. Societe Canadienne de la CIDIH, CP 225, St. Charles Quebec G0A 2H0 Canada. **Tel** (418)529-9141 ext.6202, FAX (418)529-7318. **Ad Acc**, **Adv Mgr Tel** (418)529-9141 ext. 6274. **Circ:** 500. ***Continues** ICIDH International Network, 1182-5049.*
**Desc:** For persons and organizations interested by the International Classification of Impairments, Disabilities and Handicaps and by the propositions of our organization.

CN/1182-5049
**ICIDH INTERNATIONAL NETWORK.** ***Title Change.*** [ICIDH int. netw.]. **Added/Corp** I.C.I.D.H. International Network. Canadian Society for the ICIDH. I.C.I.D.H. International Network. Quebec Committee on the ICIDH. **VFOAT** I.C.I.D.H. International Network; QCICIDH Bulletin. **VAT** International Classification of Impairments, Disabilities and Handicaps International Network. (1988)-(199?). Periodical. English (summaries and/or abstracts in French). Three times a year. Societe Canadienne de la CIDIH, CP 225, St. Charles Quebec G0A 2H0 Canada. **Tel** (418)529-9141 ext.6202, FAX (418)529-7318. **DD** 362.4/06/01. **Ad Acc. Circ:** 500-1000. ***Continues** Reseau International CIDIH.* ***Continued by** ICIDH and Environmental Factors International Network, 1198-3795.*
**Desc:** Information on research and clinical or institutional applications or development of disablement terminology or classification.

US/1058-0514
**IDAHI VELFAIYAR JARNAL.** [Idahi velfaiyar jarnal]. **Added/Corp** Idahi Intarnaishnal Faundeshan. **VFOAT** EDHI Welfare Journal; Welfare Journal. (1991)-. Periodical. Urdu (English). mo. Edhi Welfare Journal, 42-07 National Street, Corona NY 11368. **DD** 305.

CN/0826-8142
**IDENTIFICATION CANADA.** [Identif. Can.]. **Added/Corp** Canadian Identification Society. Vol. 8, No. 1 (Jan. 1985)-. Periodical. English (summaries and/or abstracts in French). qt (Jan., Apr., July, Oct.). 40.00Can$. Canadian Identification Society, 12 Ross Wood Crescent, Scarborough Ontario M1P 3N2 Canada. **Tel** (416)757-8322, FAX (416)757-0104. **DD** 363.2/58/0971. ***Continues** Identification Newsletter., 0829-4577.*

US
**IFAD STUDIES IN RURAL POVERTY.** **Added/Corp** International Fund for Agricultural Development. **VAT** International Fund for Agricultural Development Studies in Rural Poverty. No. 1 (1991)-. Monographic series. English. ir. Price varies per volume. International Fund for Agricultural Development / IFAD, Via del Serafico 107, 00142 Rome Italy. **Tel** 011 39 396 54591, FAX 011 39 396 5043463, telex 620330.

UY
**IINFANCIA : BOLETIN DEL INSTITUTO INTERAMERICANO DEL NINO-OEA.** **Added/Corp** Interamerican Children's Institute. **VFOAT** Boletin del Instituto Interamericano del Nino; Infancia. T. 63, No. 230 (Jul. 1990)-. Periodical. Spanish. **LC** HV703; .A552. **DD** 382.7/098/05. ***Continues** Boletin del Instituto Interamericano del Nino, 0020-4056.*
**Desc:** Information on children and child welfare.

US
**ILLINOIS HOME ENERGY ASSISTANCE PROGRAM FY ... ANNUAL REPORT.** **Added/Corp** Illinois. Dept. of Commerce and Community Affairs. (1982)-. English. an. Illinois Department of Commerce & Community Affairs, 620 East Adams Street, Springfield IL 62701. **Tel** (217)782-7500, FAX (217)785-6454. **LC** HC107.I33; P632. **DD** 362.5/82.

US/0275-4096
**ILLINOIS INSIGHTS.** Vol. 1, 1976-. Periodical. English. Governor's Information Center for Asian Assistance, 100 West Randolph Street 16-600, Chicago IL 60601-3218.

US
**IMPACT (SAVE THE CHILDREN (U.S.)).** (IMPACT.). Vol. 1, No. 1 (Spring 1988)-. English. qt. Save the Children Federation, 54 Wilton Road, Westport CT 06880. **Tel** (203)226-7271, FAX (203)222-1067. **ED** Lee Mullane. **Circ:** 150,000 (ctrl). ***Continues** Lifeline.*

IT
**IN-FORMAZIONE.** (19??)-. Italian. bm (6 issues). L30000.00. Labos, Viale Liegi 14, 00198 Rome Italy. **Tel** 011 39 68543568.

US/0092-0169
**INCIDENTS OF SUSPECTED CHILD ABUSE IN MARYLAND.** [Incid. suspected child abuse Md.]. **Main/Corp** Maryland. Social Services Administration. English. Maryland Social Services Administration, 1315 St.Paul Street, Baltimore MD 21202. **LC** HV742.M3; M34A. **DD** 362.7/1/09752.

US
**INCOME ASSISTANCE, SOCIAL SERVICES, AND MEDICAL ASSISTANCE / WASHINGTON STATE, DEPARTMENT OF SOCIAL & HEALTH SERVICES.** **Added/Corp** Washington (State). Dept. of Social and Health Services. Vol. 35, No. 9 (Mar. 1990)-. Periodical. English. mo. **LC** HV86; .W359. **DD** 361.6/09797. ***Continues** Income Assistance, Community Social Services, and Medical Assistance.*

US
**INCOME MAINTENANCE BULLETIN / COMMONWEALTH OF PENNSYLVANIA, DEPARTMENT OF PUBLIC WELFARE.** **Main/Corp** Pennsylvania. Dept. of Public Welfare. (19??)-. English. ir. Free on request. Legislative Reference Bureau - Pennsylvania, Main Capitol Building, Room 641, Harrisburg PA 17120.

CN/0707-3283
**INCOME SECURITY PROGRAMS.** **VFOAT** Income Security. English. $6.00. Government Services, Publications and Statutes, 11510 Kingsway Avenue, Edmonton Alberta T5G 2Y5 Canada. **LC** HV109.A5; S6. **DD** 361.6/097123. ***Continues** Social Services, Income Security Programs.*

US
**INDIAN ECONOMIC EMPLOYMENT ASSISTANCE PROGRAM, PROGRESS REPORT.** **Main/Corp** Washington (State). Indian Assistance Division. English. be. Indian Assistance Division, 1677 2nd Avenue, Tumwater WA 98504. **LC** E78.W3; W28B. **DD** 362.5.

II/0302-1610
**INDIAN JOURNAL OF PSYCHIATRIC SOCIAL WORK.** [Indian j. psychiatr. soc. work]. **Added/Corp** Indian Society of Psychiatric Social Workers. Vol. 1 (July 1972)-. Academic Scholarly Publication. English. an. $3.00. Hospital for Mental Diseases, Kanke, Ranchi 6 India. **ED** R.K. Upadhyay. **LC** HV689; .I45. **DD** 362.2/0954. **Bk Rev. Ad Acc. Circ:** 1,000.

II/0019-5634
**INDIAN JOURNAL OF SOCIAL WORK, THE.** [Indian j. soc. work]. **Added/Corp** Tata Institute of Social Sciences. Vol. 1 (June 1940)-. Periodical. English. qt. $35.00. Tata Institute of Social Sciences, Sion Trombay Road Deonar, Bombay 400 088 India. **Tel** 551-0400. **(Subscription address:** Prints India, 11 Darya Ganj, New Delhi, 110002 India, (Phone: 011 91 11 3268645)) **ED** Armaity Desai. **LC** HV1; .I5. **DD** 360.5. **NLM** W1 IN234S. **CODEN** IJSWA3. Index available. cum. index. **Bk Rev. Ad Acc. Circ:** 900. available on microfilm and microfiche from University Microfilms International (UMI). Documents available from The Genuine Article.
**Desc:** Articles are based on social work, welfare development, personnel management, industrial relations, organizational behavior, social legislation and audio-visual reviews.
**Ind/Abst** Appl. Soc. Sci. Index Abstr.; Curr. Contents Soc. Behav. Sci.; Int. Bibliogr. Sociol.; Leis. Recreat. Tour. Abstr.; Multicult. Educ. Abstr.; Psychol. Abstr. (1941-); Res. Alert [Full Cov.]; Rural Dev. Abstr.; Soc. Plann. Policy Dev. Abstr.; Soc. Sci. Cit. Index [Full Cov.]; Soc. Work Abstr. (Summer 1987-) [Select. Cov.]; Sociol. Abstr. (?-?); Sociol. Educ. Abstr.; Stat. Theory Method Abstr. (1959-1963); Stud. Women Abstr.; Women Stud. Abstr.; World Agric. Econ.

IO
**INDIKATOR KESEJAHTERAAN RAKYAT / WELFARE INDICATORS.** **Added/Corp** Indonesia. Biro Pusat Statistik. **VFOAT** Welfare Indicators. (1979)-. English (Indonesian). an. Rp7,000 Indonesia; $5.00 US. Central Bureau of Statistics / Indonesia, c/o Dr. Sutomo, 8 Jalan, PO Box 3, Jakarta Indonesia. **Tel** 372808 374908 Ext.342. **LC** HN704; .I54a. **DD** 305/.09598. **Bk Rev. Ad Acc.** ctrl circ. ***Continues** Indonesia. Biro Pusat Statistik. Indikator Sosial.*

SP
**INFANCIA Y SOCIEDAD.** **See** Public Health and Safety.

CN/0228-2453
**INFO 9.** ***Title Change.*** [Info 9]. **Added/Corp** Centre de Services Sociaux du Montreal Metropolitain. **VFOAT** Info Neuf. (1977)-(1993). Periodical. French. ir (21/year). CSSMM / Centre de Services Sociaux du Montreal Metropolitain, 1001 Est de Maison Neuve, Montreal Quebec H2L 4R5 Canada. **Tel** (514)527-2761. **DD** 361/.9714281. ***Continues** Information 9.* ***Continued by** C-Jeunes, 1195-9231.*

CN/1188-1356
**INFO-FAC.** [Info-fac]. **Added/Corp** Centre de Services Sociaux du Montreal Metropolitain. Direction des Bureaux de Services Sociaux. No 1 (Oct. 21, 1991)-. Periodical. French. qt. Limited free distribution. Centre de Services Sociaux du Montreal Metropolitain, 1001 East Boulevard de Maisonneuve, Montreal Quebec H2L 4R5 Canada. **DD** 362.7/33/0971428/05.

CN/0820-7429
**INFO-R.A.A.Q.** (INFO-R.A.A.Q. / REGROUPEMENT DES AVEUGLES ET AMBLYOPES DU QUEBEC.). [Info-R.A.A.Q.]. **VAT** Info-Regroupement des Aveugles et Amblyopes du Quebec. Vol. 1, No. 1 (Mar. 1980). Periodical. French. mo. Free. Info R A A Q, 2ME Etage 3740 rue Berri, Montreal Quebec H2L 4G9 Canada. **DD** 362.4/1/09714.

US
**INFOLINE (BETHESDA, MD.).** (INFOLINE.). **VFOAT** NBREP Infoline. Periodical. English. Three times a year. 4733 Bethesda Avenue, Suite 530, Bethesda MD 20814.

CN/0229-4338
**INFORMACCUEIL, L'.** [InFormAccueil]. V. 1, No. 2 (May 1978)-. Periodical. French. Free. Federation Des Familles D'Accueil Du Quebec, Edifice Blouin Ville-Vanier, Quebec G1M 1E3 Canada. **DD** 362.7/33/09714. ctrl circ. ***Continues** Federation des Familles d'Accueil du Quebec : Journal, 0229-432X.*

CU/0864-0122
**INFORMACION LABORAL (HAVANA, CUBA).** **See** Economics-Labor.

US/0278-2383
**INFORMATION AND REFERRAL.** (INFORMATION AND REFERRAL : THE JOURNAL OF THE ALLIANCE OF INFORMATION AND REFERRAL SYSTEMS.). [Inf. ref.]. **Added/Corp** Alliance of Information and Referral Systems (U.S.). Vol. 1, No. 1 (Spring 1979)-. Periodical. English. an. $30.00 institutions non members; $25.00 individuals non members. The Alliance of Information and Referral Systems, PO Box 3546, Joliet IL 60434-3546. **Tel** (815)744-6922. **ED** Dick Manikowski. **LC** HV85; .I54. **DD** 361/.973/07. **CODEN** IREFD9. **Bk Rev. Ad Acc. Pr Rev. Circ:** 500. Documents available from Ask*IEEE.
**Desc:** Concerned with practical and theoretical issues related to the impact of information and referral systems on the design and delivery of human services.
**Ind/Abst** Inf. Sci. Abstr.; INSPEC (Winter 1981-); Libr. Inf. Sci. Abstr.; PAIS Int. Print (1991-?); Soc. Plann. Policy Dev. Abstr.; Sociol. Abstr.

CN/0315-3150
**INFORMATION - CANADIAN ASSOCIATION OF SOCIAL WORKERS.** **Main/Corp** Canadian Association of Social Workers. V. 1- Mar. 1971-. Periodical. English (French). 23.00Can$ Canada; 27.50Can$ other. Myropen Publishers Ltd., 383 Parkdale Avenue, Suite 402, Ottawa Ontario K1Y 4R4 Canada. **Tel** (613)729-6668, FAX (613)729-9608. **ED** Sherri Resin Torjman. **Bk Rev**. **Ad Acc**. **Circ:** 10,000 (ctrl).
**Desc:** Contains articles of interest to professional social workers and information on conferences and developments in the social welfare field.

CN/0705-8101
**INFORMATION - FEDERATION DES C. L. S. C. DU QUEBEC. SUPPLEMENT, L'.** **Main/Corp** Federation des Centres Locaux de Services Communautaires du Quebec. **VAT** Information - Federation des Centres Locaux de Services Communautaires du Quebec. Supplement. No. 1- Sept. 1977-. Periodical. French. Federation Des C.L.S.C. Du Quebec, Bureau 410, 7333, Anjou Quebec H1M 2X6 Canada. **DD** 362/.9714.

CN/0228-3123
**INFORMATION FOR SENIORS.** [Inf. sr.]. Began publication in 1973?. English. be. Free. Community Information Centre of Metropolitan Toronto, 590 Jarvis Street, Toronto Ontario M4Y 2J4 Canada. **Tel** (416)392-4575, FAX (416)392-4404. **DD** 362.6/09713/541.

US/0092-9476
**INFORMATION PAMPHLET - DEPARTMENT OF EMPLOYMENT AND SOCIAL SERVICES (BALTIMORE).** (INFORMATION PAMPHLET.). **Main/Corp** Maryland. Dept. of Employment and Social Services. English. Department of Employment and Social Services / Maryland, 1315 Saint Paul Street, Baltimore MD 21202. **LC** KFM1549.A73; E4. **DD** 344/.752/03.

US
**INFORMATION SHARING INDEX.** Began with: Jan. 17, 1979. English. an. Office of Child Support Enforcement, 370 L'Enfant Promenade SW, Mail Stop OCSE-RC, Washington DC 20447. **LC** HV741; .I54. **DD** 362.7/95/0973. **NLM** ZWA 320; I43.

US
**INFORMATIONAL LETTER - NEW YORK (STATE). DEPT. OF SOCIAL SERVICES.** **Main/Corp** New York (State). Dept. of Social Services. Periodical. English. Department of Social Services / New York, 135 Western Avenue, Albany NY 12222. **Tel** (518)442-5731.
**Desc:** An informational letter informs local districts of potential developments in the Social Sciences field, or of actual or potential developments in collateral fields of interest.

IT
**INFORMAZIONI SOCIALI.** (19??)-. Periodical. Italian. Twelve times a year. L35000.00 Italy; L50000.00 other. Informazioni Sociali SRL, V Gattamelata 130, 35128 Padua Italy. **Tel** 011 39 49 8074811.

CN/0827-4789
**INITIATIVE.** ***Suspended.*** (INITIATIVE : THE SELF-HELP NEWSLETTER.). [Initiative]. **Added/Corp** Canadian Council on Social Development. **VFOAT** Self-Help Newsletter. **VAT** Bulletin d'entraide. Vol. 1, No. 2 (Dec. 1984)-(19??). English (French). qt. Free. Canadian Council of Social Development, 55 Avenue Parkdale, Box 3505 Station C, Ottawa Ontario K1Y 4G1 Canada. **DD** 361.7. ***Continues*** *Self-Help (Ottawa, Ont.)., 0827-4797.*

US/0095-4519
**INNOVATIONS (PALO ALTO).** (INNOVATIONS.). [Innovations]. **Added/Corp** American Institutes for Research National Institute of Mental Health. Mental Health Services Development Branch. Vol. 1 (Fall 1973)-. Periodical. English. **NLM** W1 IN455B.
**Ind/Abst** Health Plan. Adminis.; Hospit. Health Admin. Index (Fall 1977-Fall 1980).

CN/1183-4749
**INSERVICE QUARTERLY.** [Inserv. q.]. Vol. 1, No. 1 (Winter [1991])-. Periodical. English. qt. $21.00 per year. Health Horizons, PO Box 784, Owen Sound Ontario N4K 5W9 Canada. **DD** 362.6/1/05.

US/1058-8671
**INSIDE JAPANESE SUPPORT.** ***Ceased.*** (INSIDE JAPANESE SUPPORT : DESCRIPTIVE PROFILES AND OTHER INFORMATION ON JAPANESE CORPORATE GIVING AND FOUNDATION GIVING PROGRAMS.). [Inside Jpn. support]. **VFOAT** IJS. (1992)-(1994 edition). English. an (published in Oct. of prior year). Taft Group, 835 Penobscott Building, Customer Service, Detroit MI 48226. **Tel** (800)877-8238, FAX (313)961-6083. **(Subscription address:** Taft Group, PO Box 71701, Chicago, IL 60694; telephone: (800)877-8238**)** **LC** HG4028.C6; I57. **DD** 361.7/65/095205.

BL
**INTER-LEX.** Periodical. Portuguese. Retra Publicacoes E Repr Ltda, rua Voluntarios Da Patria 57 30 Andar, Porto Alegre Brazil. **LC** HD7154; .I585.

CN/0835-5819
**INTERACTION - CANADIAN CHILD DAY CARE FEDERATION.** (INTERACTION.). [Interact. - Can. Child Day Care Fed.]. **Added/Corp** Canadian Child Day Care Federation. **VFOAT** Interaction. Vol. 1, No. 1 (Autumn 1987)-. Periodical. English (French). Four times a year (Jan., Apr., July, Oct.). 25.00Can$ students; 30.00Can$ individuals; 45.00Can$ programs; 85.00Can$ organizations; $40.00 (non-members only). Canadian Child Care Federation, 120 Holland Avenue #401-306, Ottawa ONT K1Y 0X6 Canada. **Tel** (613)729-5289, FAX (613)729-3159. **ED** Susan Vaughn. **DD** 362.7/12/06071. **Bk Rev**, (Qty: 16). **Ad Acc**, **Adv Mgr:** T. Wittur. **Pr Rev. Circ:** 2,000 (ctrl).
**Desc:** Provide up-to-date information on a wide variety of child care concerns. These are the professionals who sent in information that are well researched , high quality, in-depth articles in the child care field.

●US/1065-6669
**INTERCHANGE (CARRBORO, N.C.).** (INTERCHANGE / IPAS.). [Interchange]. **Added/Corp** IPAS. Program Management Division. (May 1992)-. Periodical. English. qt. Free. Interchange / North Carolina, PO Box 100, Carrboro NC 27510. **DD** 362.

CN/0835-5681
**INTERCHANGE - CITIZENSHIP DEVELOPMENT BRANCH (TORONTO).** (INTERCHANGE.). [Interchange - Citizsh. Dev. Branch]. **Added/Corp** Ontario. Citizenship Development Branch. Issue No. 26 (Winter 1987)-. Periodical. English. tq. **DD** 362.84. ***Continues*** *Interchange (Ontario. Newcomer Services Branch)., 0712-5267.*

US/0730-5354
**INTERNATIONAL DIRECTORY (ALEXANDRIA, VA.).** (INTERNATIONAL DIRECTORY - UNITED WAY OF AMERICA.). [Int. dir.]. **Main/Corp** United Way of America. **VFOAT** Directory. Began with 1974-75 issue. Directory. English. an. United Way of America, 701 North Fairfax Street, Alexandria VA 22314. **Tel** (703)836-7100. **LC** HV97.U553; U54B. **DD** 361.8/025.

CN/1183-1359
**INTERNATIONAL FORUM : BULLETIN OF THE JEANNE SAUVE YOUTH FOUNDATION.** [Forum int.]. **Added/Corp** Jeanne Sauve Youth Foundation. **VFOAT** Forum International. **VAT** International Forum (Montreal. 1991). No. 1 (Oct. 1991)-. Bulletin. English (French). sa. Limited free distribution. Jeanne Suave Youth Foundation, Suite 330, 680 West Sherbrooke Street, Montreal Quebec H3A 2S6 Canada. **DD** 327.1/7/05.

UK/0267-3843
**INTERNATIONAL JOURNAL OF ADOLESCENCE AND YOUTH.** **See** Family and Marriage.

US/0161-2522
**INTERNATIONAL MEALS ON WHEELS DIRECTORY.** 1978-. Directory. English. an. Capitol Hill United Methodist Church, 421 Seward Square SE, Washington DC 20003. **LC** HV696.F6; I57. **DD** 362.6/3.

SZ/0020-8604
**INTERNATIONAL REVIEW OF THE RED CROSS.** **Added/Corp** International Committee of the Red Cross. No. 1 (April 1961)-. Periodical. English (Spanish, Arabic and German). bm. 30.00F English, Spanish and Arabic editions; 10.00F German edition. International Committee of Red Cross, 19 Avenue de la Paix, CH 1202 Geneva Switzerland. **Tel** 011 41 22 734 6001, FAX 011 41 22 733 2057, telex 22269. **ED** Jacques Meurant. Index available. **Bk Rev**, (Qty: 15). **Circ:** 2,800 (ctrl). ***Supersedes*** *Revue Internationale de la Croix-Rouge. English Supplement.*
**Desc:** Articles on international humanitarian law and other humanitarian subjects; summary of Red Cross activities and happenings in the Red Cross world.
**Ind/Abst** Hum. Rights Intern. Rep.

●US/1065-2302
**INTERNATIONAL SEARCH AND RESCUE TRADE ASSOCIATION (INSARTA).** (INTERNATIONAL SEARCH AND RESCUE TRADE ASSOCIATION (INSARTA) : [NEWSLETTER].). [Int. Search Rescue Trade Assoc. (INSARTA)]. **Added/Corp** International Search and Rescue Trade Association. Emergency Response Institute (Tacoma, Wash.). **VFOAT** International Search and Rescue Trade Association (INSARTA) Newsletter; INSARTA Newsletter. Vol. 1, No. 1 (Spring 1992)-. Periodical. English. qt. $50.00 (agencies). INSARTA, 4537 Foxhall Drive NE, Olympia WA 98506. **DD** 363.

SZ/0020-871X
**INTERNATIONAL SOCIAL SECURITY REVIEW (ENGLISH EDITION).** (INTERNATIONAL SOCIAL SECURITY REVIEW.). [Int. soc. secur. rev.]. **Added/Corp** International Social Security Association. Vol. 20, No. 1 (1967)-. Academic Scholarly Publication. English (French and German). qt. 50.00F. International Social Security Association, Case Postale 1, CH-1211 Geneva 22 Switzerland. **Tel** 011 41 22 7996617, FAX 011 41 22 7986385. **LC** HD7090; .I662. **NLM** W1 IN841W. Index available. **Bk Rev**. **Circ:** 1,600. available on microfilm and microfiche from University Microfilms International (UMI). ***Continues*** *Bulletin of the International Social Security Association, 1013-7858.*
**Desc:** Contains articles and studies by leading social security experts, descriptive studies of social security schemes in various countries, analysis of technical and administrative aspects of social insurance, and summaries and comments on new social security legislation; reports on international activities in the field of social security and presents a complete record of the work of international social security.
**Ind/Abst** Appl. Soc. Sci. Index Abstr.; CIS Abstr.; EMBASE; Hum. Resour. Abstr.; Index Period. Lit. Aging; Int. Labour Doc.; LABORDOC; Middle East Abstr. Index; PAIS Int. Print (1991-); Public Aff. Inf. Serv. Bull.; Saf. Health Work; Soc. Work Abstr. [Select. Cov.]; Stud. Women Abstr.

UK/0020-8728
**INTERNATIONAL SOCIAL WORK.** [Int. soc. work]. **Added/Corp** International Council on Social Welfare. International Association of Schools of Social Work. International Conference of Social Work (Society) International Federation of Social Workers. Vol. 1 (Jan. 1958)-. Periodical. English (French). qt. £99.00. Sage Publications Ltd., 6 Bonhill Street, London EC2A 4PU, UK. **Tel** 071 374 0645, FAX 071 374 8741, telex 296207 SAGE G. **ED** Francis Turner. **LC** HV1; .I63. Index available. cum. index. **Bk Rev**. **Ad Acc**. **Acid Free.** available on microfilm and microfiche from University Microfilms International (UMI). ***Continues*** *Social Welfare in South-East Asia.*
**Desc:** Designed to extend knowledge and promote communication in the fields of social development, social welfare and human services.
**Ind/Abst** Appl. Soc. Sci. Index Abstr.; Geogr. Abstr. Human Geogr. (?-?); Int. Dev. Abstr. (?-?); Middle East Abstr. Index; PsycINFO; PsycLit; Soc. Plann. Policy Dev. Abstr.; Soc. Work Abstr. (Spring 1987-) [Full Cov.].

US/0896-565X
**INTERNATIONAL WORKCAMP DIRECTORY / VOLUNTEERS FOR PEACE.** 1985-. Directory. English. an. $10.00. VFP Inc, 43 Tiffany Road, Belmont VT 05730. **Tel** (802)259-2759, FAX (802)259-2922, telex 361011. **ED** Peter Coldwell. **DD** 361. **Circ:** 4000. ***Continues*** *International Workcamp Listing.*
**Desc:** Contains listings of international workcamps in 36 countries.

CN/0047-1321
**INTERVENTION.** [Intervention]. **Added/Corp** Corporation des Travailleurs Sociaux Professionnels de la Province de Quebec. Corporation Professionnelle des Travailleurs Sociaux du Quebec. (19??)-. Periodical. French (English). Three times a year. 40.00Can$ (institution); 30.00Can$ (individual) Canada; 45.00Can$ (institution); 35.00Can$ (individual) other. Professional Corporation of Social Workers of Quebec, 5757 Decelles Avenue/Suite 335, Montreal Quebec H3S 2C3 Canada. **Tel** (514)731-3925, FAX (514)731-6785. **ED** Josie Louise Jette. **Bk Rev**. ctrl circ.
**Desc:** Articles of interest to social workers and psychologists that are in the fields of health and social services.

US/0148-6802
**INVEST YOURSELF.** **Added/Corp** Commission on Voluntary Service and Action. (19??)-. English. an. $9.50. Commission on Voluntary Service and Action, PO Box 117, New York NY 10009. **Tel** (212)974-2405. **ED** Susan Angus. **LC** HV89; .I58. **DD** 361.7/0973. **Ad Acc**. **Circ:** 10,000.
**Desc:** Definitive reference book to full-time non-government voluntary service opportunities in North America and throughout the world. Provides descriptive listings of agencies and opportunities.

UK
**IPPF OPEN FILE.** **See** Birth Control.

US/0894-928X
**ISIE.** (ISIE : NEWSLETTER / INCEST SURVIVOR INFORMATION EXCHANGE.). [ISIE]. **Added/Corp** Incest Survivor Information Exchange (U.S.). **VFOAT** I.S.I.E. **VAT** Incest Survivor Information Exchange. (198?)-. Newsletter. English. Four times a year (Mar., June, Sept., Dec.). $12.00 (individuals); $15.00 (institutions) & professionals. Incest Survivor Information Exchange, PO Box 3399, New Haven CT 06515. **Tel** (203)389-5166. **ED** Angela L. Swanger. **DD** 158. **Bk Rev**, (Qty: 4). **Circ:** 500 (ctrl).
**Desc:** About incest survivors.

US
**ISSUE BRIEF : A MONTHLY PUBLICATION FROM THE PUBLIC POLICY INSTITUTE OF AARP.** **Added/Corp** Public Policy Institute (American Association of Retired Persons). No. 1 (Jan. 1991)-. Periodical. English. mo. AARP, 1909 K Street NW, Washington DC 20049. **LC** HQ1064.U5; I85. **DD** 362.6/0973/05.

US/1043-8823
**ISSUES IN CHILD ABUSE ACCUSATIONS.** [Issues child abuse accusations]. **Added/Corp** Institute for Psychological Therapies (Minneapolis, Minn.). Vol. 1, No. 1 (Winter 1989)-. Periodical. English. Four times a year. $50.00 US; $70.00 other. Institute for Psychological Therapies, 13200 Cannon City Boulevard, Northfield MN 55057. **Tel** (507)645-8881, FAX (507)645-8883. **ED** Hollida Wakefield. **LC** HV8079.C48; I87. **DD** 363.2/595554/097305. **CODEN** ICCAEG. **Bk Rev**, (Qty: 75). **Pr Rev. Circ:** 350.
**Desc:** Provides a multi-disciplinary forum on all aspects of child abuse, with special emphasis on research and commentary that question the methods and conventional wisdoms of the child abuse establishment.
**Ind/Abst** Sociol. Abstr.

UK/0261-4154
**ISSUES IN SOCIAL WORK EDUCATION.** **Added/Corp** Association of Teachers in Social Work Education (London, England). Vol. 1, No. 1 (Summer 1981)-. Academic Scholarly Publication. English. Twice a year (July, Dec.). £20.00 UK; £33.00 other. Association Teachers in Social Work Education, University of Sheffield, Department of Social Studies, Sheffield S10 2TN England. **Tel** 44 742 768555 Ext. 332. **ED** Steven Sharolow. Index available. **Bk Rev. Ad Acc. Pr Rev. Circ:** 400 (ctrl).
**Desc:** Scholarly contributions toward theory, research practice and policy in the area of social work education.
**Ind/Abst** Appl. Soc. Sci. Index Abstr.

NE
**JAARVERSLAG - HARMONISATIERAAD WELZIJNSBELEID.** **Main/Corp** Harmonisatieraad Welzijnsbeleid (Netherlands). Dutch. Harmonisatieraad Welzijnsbeleid, Lange Voorhout 19, 2514 Gravenhage Netherlands. **LC** HV306; .H37A.

NE
**JAARVERSLAG - SOCIALE VERZEKERINGSRAAAD.** **Main/Corp** Netherlands (Kingdom, 1815- ). Sociale Verzekeringsraad. (19??)-. Dutch. **LC** HD7190; .S66a. ***Continues*** *Verslag Van de Werkzaamheden Van de Sociale Verzekeringsraad.*

GW
**JAHRBUCH - DEUTSCHES ROTES KREUZ.** **Main/Corp** Red Cross. Germany (Federal Republic). Deutsches Rotes Kreuz. (19??)-. German. an. Prasidium des Deutschen Roten Kreuzes, Friedrich-Ebert-Allee 7, 5380 Bonn Germany. **Tel** 0228/5411, FAX 0228/541290, telex 886619. **ED** Parl-Walfes Baner. **LC** HV580.G3; R42a. **Circ:** 6,500 (ctrl).

SZ
**JAHRESBERICHT / SCHWEIZERISCHES ROTES KREUZ.** **Main/Corp** Schweizerisches Rotes Kreuz. German. an. Schweizerisches Rotes Kreuz, Rainmattstrasse 10, Bern Switzerland. **LC** HV580.S9; S38A.

US/0021-6712
**JEWISH SOCIAL WORK FORUM, THE.** [Jew. soc. work forum.]. **Added/Corp** Wurzweiler School of Social Work. Alumni Association. Vol. 1, (Fall 1963)-. English. an (May). $9.00. Jewish Social Work Forum, Yeshiva University, 2495 Amsterdam Avenue, New York NY 10033. **Tel** (212)960-0841. **ED** Norman Linzer. **LC** HV3190; .J39. **DD** 362.8/4924. **Bk Rev. Ad Acc. Circ:** 800 (ctrl).
**Desc:** The focus is on issues pertaining to social work, social welfare and social work education, and the organized Jewish community and Jewish communal service.
**Ind/Abst** Middle East Abstr. Index; PAIS Int. Print; Soc. Plann. Policy Dev. Abstr.; Soc. Work Abstr. [Full Cov.]; Sociol. Abstr.

JA
**JIDO FUKUSHI ROPPO.** **Main/Corp** Japan. **Added/Corp** Japan. Koseisho. Jido Kateikyoku. (19??)-. Periodical. Japanese. ¥2800. Law and Statutes, 27-4 Yoyogi 2, Shibayu-ku, Tokyo 151 Japan. **LC** LAW.

CN/0715-8602
**JOURNAL - CANADIAN RED CROSS SOCIETY. BLOOD PROGRAMME.** (JOURNAL : NEWS OF THE BLOOD PROGRAMME IN CANADA.). [J. - Can. Red Cross Soc, Blood Programme]. Feb. 1983-. Periodical. English (French). qt. Free. Canadian Red Cross Society, Blood Programme, 95 Wellesley Street East, Toronto Ont. M4Y 1H6. **DD** 362.1/784. ctrl circ.

CN/0228-3425
**JOURNAL - CONSEIL REGIONAL DE LA SANTE ET DES SERVICES SOCIAUX, REGION 01.** [J. - Cons. reg. sante serv. soc., reg. 01]. **Main/Corp** Centre Regional de la Sante et des Services Sociaux. Region 01. No. 10- Jan./Feb. 1980-. Periodical. French. bm. Free. Conseil Regional de la Sante et des Services Sociaux, 274 rue Potvin, Rimouski Quebec G5L 7P5 Canada. **DD** 361/.971477. ctrl circ.

CN/0704-7029
**JOURNAL DE L'AGE D'OR, LE.** V. 1, No. 1- Dec. 1974-. Periodical. French. qt. $5.00. R D Publication Ltee, CP 327 Succursale K, Montreal Quebec H1N 3L3 Canada. **DD** 362.6/09714.

US/8750-3328
**JOURNAL FOR THE OFFICE OF MENTAL RETARDATION & DEVELOPMENTAL DISABILITIES, THE.** [J. Off. Ment. Retard. Dev. Disabil.]. **VFOAT** Journal. Vol. 1, No. 1 (July/Aug. 1984)-. Periodical. English. bm. Office of Mental Retardation and Developmental Disabilities, 12229. **DD** 362. **NLM** W1; JO355. ***Continues*** *Giant Steps, 0199-1868.*

US/1055-324X
**JOURNAL OF AMERICAN HEALTH POLICY, THE.** ***Title Change.*** [J. Am. health policy]. **Added/Corp** Faulkner & Gray, Inc. Vol. 1. No. 1 (July/Aug. 1991)-(19??). Periodical. English. bm. Faulkner & Gray Inc., 11 Penn Plaza, 17th Floor, New York NY 10001. **Tel** (212)967-7000, (800)535-8403. **LC** RA395.A3; J67. **DD** 362.1/0973/05. **NLM** W1; JO535I. ***Continued by*** *The Journal of the American Health Care, 1078-6856.*
**Ind/Abst** Health Plan. Adminis. (?-?); Hospit. Health Admin. Index (1991-); Hospit. Manage. Rev. (199?-); Soc. Sci. Cit. Index (?-?) [Full Cov.].

●US/1052-9950
**JOURNAL OF ANALYTIC SOCIAL WORK.** [J. anal. soc. work]. Vol. 1, No. 1 (1993)-. Periodical. English. qt. $60.00 US; $84.00 other. The Haworth Press Inc, 10 Alice Street, Binghamton NY 13904-1580. **Tel** (607)722-5857, (800)3-HAWORTH, FAX (607)722-1424. **ED** Jerrolo R. Brandell. **LC** HV40; .J687. **DD** 362. **CODEN** JASWEN. **Acid Free.** Documents available from Haworth Document Delivery Service. ***Continues*** *Journal of Independent Social Work, 0883-7562.*
**Desc:** Provides social work clinicians and clinical educators with highly informative and stimulating articles relevant to the practice of psychoanalytic social work with the individual client.
**Ind/Abst** Soc. Work Abstr. [Select. Cov.].

US/0146-4310
**JOURNAL OF APPLIED SOCIAL SCIENCES, THE.** [J. appl. soc. sci.]. **Added/Corp** Case Western Reserve University. School of Applied Social Sciences. (19??)-. Periodical. English. sa (July & Dec.). $35.00 (institutions), $20.00 (individuals) US; $70.00 (institutions), $60.00 (individuals) other. Mandel School of Applied Social Science Case, Case Western University, 10900 Euclid Avenue, Cleveland OH 44106-7164. **Tel** (216)368-8672, FAX (216)368-8670. **ED** Patricia Choby Bornstein. **LC** HV1; .J54. **DD** 361/.005. Index available. cum. index. **Bk Rev**, (Qty: 7). **Ad Acc. Pr Rev. Circ:** 300.
**Ind/Abst** Appl. Soc. Sci. Index Abstr.; J. Plan. Lit.; Middle East Abstr. Index; Psychol. Abstr. (1978-); PsycINFO (1978-); PsycLit; Soc. Plann. Policy Dev. Abstr.; Soc. Work Abstr. [Select. Cov.].

CN/0840-982X
**JOURNAL OF CHILD AND YOUTH CARE.** [J. child youth care]. Vol. 4, No. 1 (1989)-. Periodical. English. qt. $71.50 (institutions), $49.50 (individuals), $38.50 (Child Care Association member). University of Calgary Press, 2500 University Drive Northwest, Calgary Alberta T2N 1N4 Canada. **Tel** (403)220-7578. **ED** Gerry Fewster and Chris Bagley. **DD** 362.7/0971. **Bk Rev. Ad Acc.** ***Continues*** *Journal of Child Care, 0715-5883.*
**Desc:** A publication for child care practitioners. This journal is primarily intended for the child worker. It is recognized, however, that the issues of child care are universal and the journal is committed to the dessemination of information and knowledge for the benefit of all who assume the responsibility for the well being of children.
**Ind/Abst** Psychol. Abstr. (1982-); PsycINFO; PsycLit.

US/0741-9481
**JOURNAL OF CHILD AND YOUTH CARE WORK.** [J. child youth care work]. **Added/Corp** National Organization of Child Care Worker Associations (U.S.). Vol. 1, No. 1 (March 1984)-. Periodical. English. an. $10.00. National Organization of Child Care Workers Association, 601 Pennsylvania Avenue Northwest, 9th Floor, Washington DC 20041. **Tel** (202)232-4171. **(Subscription address:** Child and Youth Care Learning Center, PO Box 413, Milwaukee WI 53201.**)** **DD** 362.

US/1066-1468
**JOURNAL OF CHILD-CARE ADMINISTRATION.** [J. child-care adm.]. **VFOAT** Journal of Child Care Administration. (1990)-. Periodical. English. Six times a year. $55.00 US; $65.00 others. Kalbaugh Communications, 202 Cirrus Road, Holbrook NY 11741. **Tel** (516)472-9033, FAX (516)472-5908. **ED** Christine Kalbaugh. **DD** 362. ***Continues*** *Journal of Day Care Administration.*
**Desc:** Covering all aspects of operating a child-care center. Covers every aspect of the operation, with emphasis on business and practical matters. Interviews with the leading authors, educators, child-care professionals, business executives and other experts; reference source for students interested in the child-care field.

●US/1053-8712
**JOURNAL OF CHILD SEXUAL ABUSE.** [J. child sex. abuse]. Vol. 1, No. 1 (1992)-. Periodical. English. qt. $60.00 US; $84.00 other. The Haworth Press Inc, 10 Alice Street, Binghamton NY 13904-1580. **Tel** (607)722-5857, (800)3-HAWORTH, FAX (607)722-1424. **ED** Robert Geffner (editor's address: 801 Top Hill Drive, Tyler, TX 75703). **LC** HV6570; .J68. **DD** 364.1/536. **NLM** W1; JO584P. **CODEN** JCABEK. **Bk Rev. Ad Acc. Pr Rev. Acid Free.** available on microfiche. Documents available from Haworth Document Delivery Service.
**Desc:** Interdisciplinary in nature and will interface among researchers, academicians, clinicians, and practitioners. Divided into sections to provide the clearest information possible. Covers research issues, clinical issues, case studies, and brief reports. Focuses on three subject groups - child and adolescent victims of sexual abuse or incest, adult survivors of childhood sexual abuse or incest, and sexual abuse or incest offenders.
**Ind/Abst** Abstr. Anthropol. (19??-); Annals Behav. Med.; Except. Child Educ. Resour.; Soc. Work Abstr. [Select. Cov.]; Stud. Women Abstr.

US/0276-0878
**JOURNAL OF CONTINUING SOCIAL WORK EDUCATION.** **See** Education.

US
**JOURNAL OF DAY CARE ADMINISTRATION.** ***Title Change.*** (19??)-(19??). English. bm. Kalbaugh Communications, 202 Cirrus Road, Holbrook NY 11741. **Tel** (516)472-9033, FAX (516)472-5908. ***Continued by*** *Journal of Child-Care Administration, 1066-1468.*
**Desc:** Keeps directors at the forefront of child care. It features interviews with leading authors, child care professionals, business executives and experts from many other fields. The emphasis is on business management.

US/0894-6566
**JOURNAL OF ELDER ABUSE & NEGLECT.** [J. elder abuse negl.]. **Added/Corp** National Committee for the Prevention of Elder Abuse. **VFOAT** Journal of Elder Abuse and Neglect; Elder Abuse & Neglect; Elder Abuse and Neglect. Vol. 1, No. 1 (1989)-. Periodical. English. qt. $140.00 US; $196.00 other. The Haworth Press Inc, 10 Alice Street, Binghamton NY 13904-1580. **Tel** (607)722-5857, (800)3-HAWORTH, FAX (607)722-1424. **ED** Rosalie S. Wolf (editor's address: Institute on Aging, 119 Belmont Street, Worchester, MA 01605); Suzan McMurray-Anderson (editor's address: 12 Hadwen Road, Worchester, MA 01602). **LC** HV6626.3; .J68. **DD** 362.6. **NLM** W1; JO634. **CODEN** JEANE2. **Bk Rev. Ad Acc. Pr Rev. Acid Free. Circ:** 637. available on microfilm and microfiche from University Microfilms International (UMI). Documents available from Haworth Document Delivery Service.
**Desc:** Devoted to the study of the causes, treatment, effects, and prevention of the mistreatment of older people. As a forum for the discussion of scientific investigation, program developments, policy initiatives, and personal commentary about elder abuse and neglect, the journal plays a significant role in the education of professionals and the public concerning this serious social problem.
**Ind/Abst** Abstr. Soc. Gerontol.; Crim. Justice Abstr.; Index Period. Lit. Aging (19??-19??); Sage Fam. Stud. Abstr.; Soc. Plann. Policy Dev. Abstr.; Soc. Work Abstr. [Select. Cov.].

●US/1052-2158
**JOURNAL OF FAMILY SOCIAL WORK.** (1992)-. Periodical. English. qt. $48.00 US; $67.20 other. The Haworth Press Inc, 10 Alice Street, Binghamton NY 13904-1580. **Tel** (607)722-5857, (800)3-HAWORTH, FAX (607)722-1424. **ED** Thomas Edward Smith. **CODEN** JFSWEO. **Pr Rev. Acid Free.** Documents available from Haworth Document Delivery Service.
**Desc:** Social work journal devoted to ecosystemic theory, research, and practice with couples and families.
**Ind/Abst** Abstr. Anthropol.; Abstr. Soc. Gerontol.; Abstr. Res. Pastor. Care Couns.; Appl. Soc. Sci. Index Abstr.; Child Dev. Abstr. Bibliogr.; Crim. Justice Abstr.; Crim. Penol. Police Sci. Abstr.; Educ. Adm. Abstr.; Hum.

Resour. Abstr.; Index Period. Artic. Relat. Law; Linguist. Lang. Behav. Abstr.; Psychol. Abstr.; Sage Fam. Stud. Abstr.; Soc. Plann. Policy Dev. Abstr.; Soc. Work Abstr. [Select. Cov.]; Sociol. Abstr.; Stud. Women Abstr.

US/0885-7482
**JOURNAL OF FAMILY VIOLENCE. See** Family and Marriage.

US/1050-5350
**JOURNAL OF GAMBLING STUDIES.** (JOURNAL OF GAMBLING STUDIES / CO-SPONSORED BY THE NATIONAL COUNCIL ON PROBLEM GAMBLING AND INSTITUTE FOR THE STUDY OF GAMBLING AND COMMERCIAL GAMING.). [J. gambl. stud.]. **Added/Corp** National Council on Problem Gambling (U.S.) University of Nevada, Reno. Institute for the Study of Gambling and Commercial Gaming. Vol. 6, No. 1 (Spring 1990)-. Periodical. English. qt. $215.00 US; $250.00 other. Human Sciences Press, PO Box 735, 233 Spring Street, New York NY 10013. **Tel** (212)620-8000, FAX (212)807-1047, telex 23421139. **(Subscription address:** Eurospan Ltd., Journals and Serials Division, 3 Henrietta Street, Covent Garden, London WC2E 8LU England.**) ED** Henry Lesieur. **LC** RC569.5.G35; J68. **DD** 306. **CODEN** JGSTEM. **[CCC].** available on microfilm and microfiche from University Microfilms International (UMI). ***Continues*** *Journal of Gambling Behavior, 0742-0714.*
**Desc:** Interdisciplinary forum for the dissemination of information on the many aspects of gambling behavior, both controlled and pathological , as well as a variety of problems attendant to or resultant from gambling behavior, including alcoholism, suicide, crime, and a number of other mental health problems. Articles published in the journal are representative of a cross-section of disciplines including psychiatry, psychology, sociology, political science, criminology, and social work, and are of interest to the professional and layperson alike.
**Ind/Abst** Psychol. Abstr. (1985-); PsycINFO; PsycLit; Soc. Plann. Policy Dev. Abstr.; Soc. Work Abstr. [Select. Cov.].

●US/1053-8720
**JOURNAL OF GAY & LESBIAN SOCIAL SERVICES. See** Homosexuality.

US/0163-4372
**JOURNAL OF GERONTOLOGICAL SOCIAL WORK.** [J. gerontol. soc. work]. Vol. 1 (Fall 1978)-. Academic Scholarly Publication. English. qt (Published during the academic year). $225.00 US; $315.00 other. The Haworth Press Inc, 10 Alice Street, Binghamton NY 13904-1580. **Tel** (607)722-5857, (800)3-HAWORTH, FAX (607)722-1424. **ED** Rose Dobrof (editor's address: School of Social Work, Brookdale Center on Aging, Hunter College, 440 East 26th Street, New York, NY 10010). **LC** HV1451; .J68. **DD** 362.6/0973. **NLM** W1 JO669NS. **Bk Rev. Ad Acc. Pr Rev. Acid Free. Circ:** 748. available on microfilm and microfiche from University Microfilms International (UMI). Documents available from The Genuine Article, UMI Article Clearinghouse, Haworth Document Delivery Service.
**Desc:** Devoted exclusively to social work practice, theory, administration and consultation in the field of aging. Oriented towards the practice need of social work administrators, practitioners and consultants in a wide variety of settings.
**Ind/Abst** Abstr. Soc. Gerontol.; Abstr. Res. Pastor. Care Couns.; Acad. Search (July 1993-); Annals Behav. Med.; Appl. Soc. Sci. Index Abstr.; Cumul. Index Nurs. Allied Health Lit.; Curr. Contents Soc. Behav. Sci.; EMBASE; Expand. Acad. Index (1989-); Index Period. Lit. Aging; INFO-SOUTH Abstr.; Mag. Search; Newsp. Period. Abstr. (1991-); Psychol. Abstr. (1978-); PsycINFO; PsycLit; Res. Alert [Full Cov.]; Soc. Plann. Policy Dev. Abstr.; Soc. Sci. Source (Jul. 1993-); Soc. Sci. Cit. Index [Full Cov.]; Soc. Sci. Index; Soc. Sci. Index Fulltext (1987-) [Full Txt.]; Soc. Work Abstr. [Full Cov.]; Sociol. Abstr.

US/0160-4198
**JOURNAL OF HEALTH AND HUMAN RESOURCES ADMINISTRATION.** [J. health human resour. adm.]. **Added/Corp** Southern Public Administration Education Foundation (U.S.). Vol. 1 (Aug. 1978)-. Periodical. English. Four times a year. $50.00 (institutions), $31.00 (individuals). Southern Public Administration Education Foundation, PO Box 632, Randallstown MD 21133. **Tel** (410)665-2137. **LC** RA1; .J68. **DD** 362.1/05. **NLM** W1 JO6694H. **Bk Rev. Circ:** 800 (ctrl).
**Desc:** Focuses on administrative and policy issues faced by health and human service professionals and academics.
**Ind/Abst** Cumul. Index Nurs. Allied Health Lit.; EMBASE; Hospit. Health Admin. Index; Hospit. Manage. Rev. (19??-19??); Hum. Resour. Abstr. (1978-); PAIS Int. Print; Sage Fam. Stud. Abstr.; Soc. Work Abstr. [Select. Cov.].

US/0897-7186
**JOURNAL OF HEALTH & SOCIAL POLICY. See** Public Health and Safety.

US/0897-8018
**JOURNAL OF HOME HEALTH CARE PRACTICE.** [J. home health care pract.]. **VFOAT** JHHCP. Vol. 1, No. 1 (Nov. 1988)-. Periodical. English. qt. $68.00 US. Aspen Publishers Inc., 7201 McKinney Circle, Frederick MD 21701. **Tel** (800)234-1660, (301)698-7100, FAX (301)251-5784, telex 5106014543. **(Subscription address:** Aspen Publishers Inc., PO Box 990, Frederick MD 21701.**) LC** RA645.3; .J67. **DD** 649. **NLM** W1; JO671L. **[CCC].** available on microfilm and microfiche from University Microfilms International (UMI).
**Desc:** A multidisciplinary journal that provides home health care professionals with information to foster expert clinical practice in home health care and to increase their ability to meet the physiological, psychological and social needs of patients in the home setting.

US/0898-5847
**JOURNAL OF INTERNATIONAL AND COMPARATIVE SOCIAL WELFARE.** [J int. comp. soc. welf.]. **Added/Corp** Louisiana State University (Baton Rouge, La.). School of Social Work. International Fellowship for Social and Economic Development. Vol. 1, No. 1 (Fall 1984)-. Periodical. English. sa. $45.00. Dialogues, PO Box 19955, Baton Rouge LA 70893. **Tel** (504)388-1345. **ED** Brij Mohan. **LC** HV1; .J38. **DD** 361/.005. **Bk Rev. Ad Acc. Pr Rev. Circ:** 200.
**Ind/Abst** Soc. Plann. Policy Dev. Abstr.; Soc. Work Abstr. (?-?).

US/0886-2605
**JOURNAL OF INTERPERSONAL VIOLENCE.** [J. interpers. violence]. Vol. 1, No. 1 (March 1986)-. Periodical. English. bm. $170.00. SAGE Periodical Press, 2455 Teller Road, Thousand Oaks CA 91320. **Tel** (805)499-0721, FAX (805)499-0871, telex 100799. **ED** Jon R. Conte (University of Washington). **DD** 303. **NLM** W1; JO719C. **[CCC].** Index available. cum. index. **Ad Acc. Acid Free. Circ:** 1,565. available on microfilm and microfiche from University Microfilms International (UMI). Documents available from The Genuine Article, UMI Article Clearinghouse.
**Desc:** Provides a forum for discussion of the concerns and activities of professionals and researchers working in domestic violence, child sexual assault, physical child abuse, and violent crime.
**Ind/Abst** Crim. Justice Abstr.; Curr. Contents Soc. Behav. Sci.; Newsp. Period. Abstr. (1992-); Psychol. Abstr. (1986-); PsycINFO (1990-); PsycLit; Res. Alert [Full Cov.]; Sage Fam. Stud. Abstr.; Soc. Plann. Policy Dev. Abstr.; Soc. Sci. Cit. Index [Full Cov.]; Soc. Work Abstr. (Summer 1987-) [Select. Cov.]; Spec. Educ. Needs Abstr.; Stud. Women Abstr.

US/0882-7893
**JOURNAL OF INTERPRETATION (SILVER SPRING, MD.).** ***Ceased.*** (JOURNAL OF INTERPRETATION.). [J. interpret.]. **Added/Corp** Registry of Interpreters for the Deaf, Inc. Vol. 2 (June 1985)-(1994). Periodical. English. an. Registry Interpreters for the Deaf, 8719 Colesville Road, Suite 310, Rockville MD 20910. **Tel** (301)608-0050. **LC** HV2402; .J68. **DD** 362.4/283. **CODEN** JOINEA. ***Continues*** *Professional Interpreting Journal of Registry of Interpreters for the Deaf, Inc., 0277-6480.*

●UK
**JOURNAL OF INTERPROFESSIONAL CARE. See** Medical Science and Technology-Homeopathy.

US/0092-8623
**JOURNAL OF MENTAL HEALTH ADMINISTRATION.** [J. mental health adm.]. **Added/Corp** Association of Mental Health Administrators. Vol. 1 (Spring 1972)-. Academic Scholarly Publication. English. qt (Feb., May, Aug., Nov.). $119.00. SAGE Periodical Press, 2455 Teller Road, Thousand Oaks CA 91320. **Tel** (805)499-0721, FAX (805)499-0871, telex 100799. **ED** Bruce L. Levin. **DD** 362. **NLM** W1 JO76KE. Index available. **Bk Rev. Ad Acc. Pr Rev. Acid Free. Circ:** 3,000. available on microfilm and microfiche from University Microfilms International (UMI).
**Desc:** A multidisciplinary journal that publishes articles on the organization, financing and delivery of behavioral health services. The journal also publishes articles on mental health planning, policy analysis, service delivery systems, marketing, law, financing, organizational structure, information systems and evaluation of mental health services.
**Ind/Abst** EMBASE; Health Plan. Adminis.; Hospit. Health Admin. Index; PAIS Int. Print; Psychol. Abstr. (1986-); PsycINFO; PsycLit; Soc. Sci. Cit. Index [Full Cov.]; Soc. Work Abstr. [Select. Cov.].

US/1040-2861
**JOURNAL OF MENTAL HEALTH COUNSELING.** [J. ment. health couns.]. **Added/Corp** American Mental Health Counselors Association. Vol. 9, No. 3 (July 1987)-. Periodical. English. qt (4 issues). $119.00 (institution), $61.00 (individual) US. American Counseling Association, 5999 Stevenson Avenue, Alexandria VA 22304. **Tel** (703)823-9800, (800)347-6647, FAX (703)823-0252. **(Subscription address:** American Counseling Association, Subscription Office, PO Box 2513, Birmingham AL 35201-2513.**) ED** Lawrence Gerstein. **LC** BF637.C6; A42a. **DD** 362.2/04256/05. **NLM** W1; JO76LD. **Ad Acc. Circ:** 423. available on microfilm. ***Continues*** *AMHCA Journal, 0193-1830.*
**Desc:** Devoted to traditional data-based research, this journal is read by mental health counselors in private practice, community agencies, business and industry, and rehabilitation who deal with a wide range of issues such as family counseling, employee assistance, and substance abuse.
**Ind/Abst** Abstr. Soc. Gerontol.; Curr. Index J. Educ.; Hum. Resour. Abstr.; Psychol. Abstr. (1983-); PsycINFO (1990-); PsycLit; Sage Fam. Stud. Abstr.; Soc. Work Abstr. [Select. Cov.].

US/1042-8224
**JOURNAL OF MULTICULTURAL SOCIAL WORK.** [J. multicult. soc. work]. Vol. 1 (Spring 1991)-. Periodical. English. qt. $75.00 US; $105.00 other. The Haworth Press Inc, 10 Alice Street, Binghamton NY 13904-1580. **Tel** (607)722-5857, (800)3-HAWORTH, FAX (607)722-1424. **ED** Paul Keys. **LC** HV3176; .J68. **DD** 362.84/00973/05. **CODEN** JMSWE5. **Bk Rev. Ad Acc. Acid Free. Circ:** 158. available on microfilm and microfiche from University Microfilms International (UMI). Documents available from Haworth Document Delivery Service.
**Desc:** Dedicated to the examination of multicultural social issues as they relate to social work policy, research, theory and practice from an international perspective. The goal of this journal is to develop knowledge and promote understanding of the impact of culture, ethnicity, race, and class on the individual, group, organization, and community on the delivery of human services.
**Ind/Abst** Hum. Resour. Abstr.; Sage Fam. Stud. Abstr.; Soc. Plann. Policy Dev. Abstr.; Soc. Work Abstr. [Full Cov.].

US/1050-9674
**JOURNAL OF OFFENDER REHABILITATION. See** Law-Law Enforcement and Criminology.

CN/0825-8597
**JOURNAL OF PALLIATIVE CARE.** [J. palliat. care]. **Added/Corp** Palliative Care Foundation. Vol. 1 (1985)-. Periodical. English. qt. $70.00 (individuals), $110.00 (institutions) Canada; 80.00Can$ (individuals), 120.00Can$ (institutions) other. Clinical Research Institute, 110 Pine Avenue West, Montreal Quebec H2W 1R7 Canada. **Tel** (514)987-5617, (514)987-5615, FAX (514)987-5695. **ED** David J. Roy. **DD** 362.1/75/05. **[CCC]. Bk Rev,** (Qty: 10-15). **Pr Rev. Circ:** 1,000 (ctrl). available on microfilm from University Microfilms International (UMI).
**Desc:** Scientific research in the field of palliative / hospice care, combining scientific validation with humanistic concerns.
**Ind/Abst** Can. Index; Can. Period. Index (19??-); Cumul. Index Nurs. Allied Health Lit.; Index Med. (Vol. 1, 1985-); Psychol. Abstr. (1985-); PsycINFO (1990-); PsycLit; Trop. Dis. Bull.

US/1042-8232
**JOURNAL OF PROGRESSIVE HUMAN SERVICES.** [J. progress. hum. serv.]. Vol. 1, No. 1 (1990)-. Periodical. English. sa. $48.00 US; $67.20 other. The Haworth Press Inc, 10 Alice Street, Binghamton NY 13904-1580. **Tel** (607)722-5857, (800)3-HAWORTH, FAX (607)722-1424. **ED** Mimi Abramovitz (editor's address: School of Social Work, Hunter College, 113 W 60th Street, New York, NY 10021). **LC** HV85; .J68. **DD** 362/.05. **CODEN** JPHSER. **Bk Rev. Ad Acc. Pr Rev. Acid Free. Circ:** 1,033. available on microfilm and microfiche from University Microfilms International (UMI). Documents available from Haworth Document Delivery Service. ***Continues*** *Catalyst (New York, N.Y. : 1978), 0191-040X.*
**Desc:** Deals with social problems and human services from the progressive perspective. Aims to stimulate debate about major social issues and contribute to the development of the analytic tools needed for building a society based on equality and justice for all. Contributors examine oppressed and vulnerable groups, struggles by workers and clients on the job and in the community, dilemmas of practice in a conservative period and strategies for ending racism, sexism, agism, heterosexism and discrimination against the disabled and the psychologically distressed. They also share critiques of leading social issues, fresh insights about direct practice and reports on innovative human services in different societies.
**Ind/Abst** Left Index (199?-); PAIS Int. Print (1991-?); Soc. Plann. Policy Dev. Abstr.; Soc. Work Abstr. [Select. Cov.].

US/0022-4154
**JOURNAL OF REHABILITATION.** [J. rehabil.]. **Added/Corp** National Rehabilitation Association. Vol. 11, (1945)-. Periodical. English. qt. $40.00 US; $50.00 Canada; $60.00 other. National Rehabilitation Association, 633 South Washington Street, Alexandria VA 22314. **Tel** (703)836-0850, , FAX (703)836-0850. **ED** Dick Dietl. **DD** 362. **NLM** W1 JO866R. **Bk Rev. Ad Acc. Pr Rev. Circ:** 15,000 (ctrl). available in braille; available on microfilm and microfiche from University Microfilms International (UMI). Documents available from The Genuine Article, UMI Article Clearinghouse. ***Continues*** *National Rehabilitation*

*News, 0093-1756.*
**Desc:** Contains articles of interest to both professionals and consumers in the field of rehabilitation.
**Ind/Abst** Acad. Abstr. Full Text Elite (Jan. 1992-); Acad. Abstr. (Jan. 1992-); Acad. Ind. [Computer File] (1992-); Acad. Search (Jan. 1992-); Appl. Soc. Sci. Index Abstr.; Cumul. Index Nurs. Allied Health Lit.; Curr. Index J. Educ.; Energy Res. Abstr. (1982-); Except. Child Educ. Resour.; Expand. Acad. Index (1988-); Health Period. Database [Full Txt.]; Health Source (Jan. 1992-); INFO-SOUTH Abstr.; Mag. Search; Newsp. Period. Abstr. (1991-); Res. Alert [Full Cov.]; Saf. Health Work; Soc. Sci. Source (Jan. 1992-); Soc. Sci. Cit. Index [Full Cov.]; Soc. Sci. Index; Soc. Sci. Index Fulltext (Oct. 1988-) [Full Txt.]; SportSearch; Work Relat. Abstr.

●US/1053-0789
**JOURNAL OF SOCIAL DISTRESS AND THE HOMELESS.** [J. soc. distress homeless]. **VFOAT** Social Distress and the Homeless. Vol. 1, No. 1 (Jan. 1992)-. Periodical. English. qt. $115.00 US; $135.00 other. Human Sciences Press, PO Box 735, 233 Spring Street, New York NY 10013. **Tel** (212)620-8000, FAX (212)807-1047, telex 23421139. **(Subscription address:** Eurospan Ltd., Journals and Serials Division, 3 Henrietta Street, Covent Garden, London WC2E 8LU England.**)** **ED** R. W. Rieber. **LC** HN1; .J58. **DD** 361. **CODEN** JSDHET. **[CCC].**
**Desc:** An interdisciplinary forum for the publication of research reports, case studies, theoretical papers, and historical reviews on psychosocial distress and its related problems. Offers a unique approach to understanding social distress by exploring its links to specific issues such as homelessness, violence, and racial tension, among others, and its institutionalization in modern society.
**Ind/Abst** Soc. Work Abstr. [Select. Cov.].

UK/0047-2794
**JOURNAL OF SOCIAL POLICY.** [J. soc. policy]. **Added/Corp** Social Administration Association (Great Britain). Vol. 1, Pt. 1 (Jan. 1972)-. Academic Scholarly Publication. English. qt (4 issues). $146.00 US, Canada and Mexico; £79.00 other. Cambridge University Press, The Edinburgh Building, Shaftesbury Road, Cambridge CB2 2RU United Kingdom. **Tel** 011 44 223 312393, FAX 011 44 223 325959. **(Subscription address:** Cambridge University Press / North America, 110 Midland Avenue, Port Chester NY 10573.**)** **ED** Gilbert Smith. **LC** HV1; .J57. **DD** 361.2/5/05. **NLM** W1 JO888M. **[CCC]. Bk Rev. Ad Acc. Pr Rev. Circ:** 2,000. available on microfilm and microfiche from University Microfilms International (UMI). Documents available from The Genuine Article, UMI Article Clearinghouse.
**Desc:** The journal of the Social Policy Association. Publishes review articles on all aspects of social policy and administration, both in the United Kingdom and in other countries. Particular emphasis is placed on articles which seek to contribute to the debate on the future direction of social policy, to advance theory or conceptual rigor, or to identify and analyze issues in the implementation of social policies. "Social Digest" is a feature of the journal that appears in each issue and provides commentary on changes in social welfare legislation in the United Kingdom, and a review of the major reports and surveys published by government departments, local authorities and voluntary bodies.
**Ind/Abst** ABC POL SCI; Acad. Abstr. Full Text Elite (Jan. 1992-); Acad. Abstr. (Jan. 1992-); Acad. Search (Jan. 1992-); Appl. Soc. Sci. Index Abstr.; Curr. Contents Soc. Behav. Sci.; Expand. Acad. Index (1989-); Geogr. Abstr. Human Geogr.; Hospit. Health Admin. Index; INFO-SOUTH Abstr.; Int. Bibliogr. Sociol.; Int. Labour Doc.; Int. Polit. Sci. Abstr.; J. Plan. Lit.; LABORDOC; Mag. Search; Middle East Abstr. Index; Newsp. Period. Abstr. (1991-); PAIS Int. Print (1991-); Res. Alert [Full Cov.]; Soc. Plann. Policy Dev. Abstr.; Soc. Sci. Source (Jan. 1992-); Soc. Sci. Cit. Index [Full Cov.]; Soc. Sci. Index; Soc. Sci. Index Fulltext (July 1988-) [Full Txt.]; Sociol. Abstr.; Sociol. Educ. Abstr.; Stud. Women Abstr.; Trop. Dis. Bull.

US/0148-8376
**JOURNAL OF SOCIAL SERVICE RESEARCH.** [J. soc. serv. res.]. **Added/Corp** George Warren Brown School of Social Work. Vol. 1 (Fall 1977)-. Periodical. English. qt. $200.00 US; $280.00 other. The Haworth Press Inc, 10 Alice Street, Binghamton NY 13904-1580. **Tel** (607)722-5857, (800)3-HAWORTH, FAX (607)722-1424. **ED** Shanti K. Khinduka (editor's address: George Warren Brown School of Social Work, Washington University, PO Box 1196, St Louis, MO 63130). **LC** HV1; .J58. **DD** 361/.005. **NLM** W1 JO888U. **CODEN** JSSRDV. **Bk Rev. Ad Acc. Pr Rev. Acid Free. Circ:** 441. available on microfilm and microfiche from University Microfilms International (UMI). Documents available from Haworth Document Delivery Service.
**Desc:** Devoted exclusively to empirical research and its application to the design, delivery, and management of the social services. The journal is invaluable not only to researchers but to administrators and planners whose responsibilities include the effective delivery of social services.
**Ind/Abst** Abstr. Res. Pastor. Care Couns. (19??-); Appl. Soc. Sci. Index Abstr.; Crim. Justice Abstr.; Crim. Justice Period. Index; Crim. Penol. Police Sci. Abstr.; Hum. Resour. Abstr.; J. Plan. Lit.; Psychol. Abstr. (1977-); PsycINFO; PsycLit; Sage Fam. Stud. Abstr.; Sage Public Adm. Abstr. (?-?); Soc. Plann. Policy Dev. Abstr.; Soc. Work Abstr. [Full Cov.]; Sociol. Abstr.

UK/0141-8033
**JOURNAL OF SOCIAL WELFARE & FAMILY LAW. See** Law-Family Law.

US/0276-3850
**JOURNAL OF SOCIAL WORK & HUMAN SEXUALITY.** ***Title Change.*** [J. soc. work hum. sex.]. **VFOAT** Journal of Social Work and Human Sexuality. Vol. 1 No. 1 (Fall/Winter 1982)-Vol. 8, No. 2 (19??). Periodical. English. sa. The Haworth Press Inc, 10 Alice Street, Binghamton NY 13904-1580. **Tel** (607)722-5857, (800)3-HAWORTH, FAX (607)722-1424. **ED** David Shore (editor's address: 2807 Alyssa Court, Naperville, IL 60565). **LC** HV1; .J595. **DD** 361.3. **NLM** W1 JO889D. **CODEN** JSWSDK. **Bk Rev. Ad Acc. Pr Rev. Circ:** 58. available on microfilm and microfiche from University Microfilms International (UMI). Documents available from BIOSIS Document Express, Haworth Document Delivery Service. ***Continued by*** *Journal of Family Social Work.*
**Desc:** The landmark journal devoted exclusively to social work practice, research theory, and education as they relate to issues in human sexuality.
**Ind/Abst** Abstr. Res. Pastor. Care Couns. (19??-); Biol. Abstr.; Crim. Justice Abstr. (-1989); Crim. Penol. Police Sci. Abstr.; Psychol. Abstr. (1982-); PsycINFO; PsycLit; Soc. Plann. Policy Dev. Abstr.; Soc. Work Abstr. [Full Cov.]; Stud. Women Abstr.

IS/0334-9977
**JOURNAL OF SOCIAL WORK AND POLICY IN ISRAEL. VFOAT** Avodah Sotsyalit U-Mediniyut Hevratit Be-Yisrael. Vol. 1 (1987)-. Periodical. English (summaries and/or abstracts in Hebrew; table of contents in Hebrew). Each issue is sold individually. Current issue $17.00. Bar-Ilan University Press, Ramat-Gan 52900 Israel. **Tel** 011 972 3 5318355, FAX 011 972 3 3476 01. **LC** HV378.5; .A17. **DD** 361/.95694.
**Ind/Abst** Index Jew. Period. (199?-); Soc. Work Abstr. [Select. Cov.].

US/1043-7797
**JOURNAL OF SOCIAL WORK EDUCATION.** [J. soc. work educ.]. **Added/Corp** Council on Social Work Education. Vol. 21, No. 1 (Winter 1985)-. Academic Scholarly Publication. English. Three times a year. $180.00 (Plan A); $100.00 (Plan B) Comes with Council on Social Work Education Library Plan A & B membership. Council on Social Work Education, 1600 Duke Street, Alexandria VA 22314. **Tel** (703)683-8080. **ED** Anne E. Fortune, Ivon Katz and Carlton Munson. **LC** HV11; .J66. **DD** 361/.0071. Index available. cum. index. **Bk Rev. Ad Acc. Circ:** 3,000 (ctrl). available on microfilm and microfiche from University Microfilms International (UMI). Documents available from The Genuine Article. ***Continues*** *Journal of Education for Social Work, 0022-0612.*
**Desc:** A scholarly devoted to research and theory of social work education and administration.
**Ind/Abst** Acad. Search (July 1993-); Appl. Soc. Sci. Index Abstr.; Chicano Index; Contents Pages Educ.; Curr. Contents Soc. Behav. Sci.; Curr. Index J. Educ.; Educ. Index; INFO-SOUTH Abstr.; Mag. Search; Middle East Abstr. Index; Res. Alert [Full Cov.]; Res. High. Educ. Abstr.; Soc. Plann. Policy Dev. Abstr.; Soc. Sci. Cit. Index [Full Cov.]; Soc. Sci. Index; Soc. Work Abstr. (Spring 1987-) [Full Cov.]; Sociol. Abstr.; Spec. Educ. Needs Abstr.; Stud. Women Abstr.

UK/0265-0533
**JOURNAL OF SOCIAL WORK PRACTICE. Added/Corp** Group for the Advancement of Psychodynamics and Psychotherapy in Social Work. **VFOAT** J. Social Work Practice. Vol. 1, No. 1 (Nov. 1983)-. Periodical. English. sa (May and November). £78.00. Carfax Publishing Company, PO Box 25 Abingdon, Oxfordshire OX14 3UE England. **Tel** 011 44 235 555335, FAX (0279)31067, telex 817484. **(Subscription address:** US and Canada/ PO Box 2025, Dunnellon, FL 34430-2025; telephone:(904)489-6996**)** **NLM** W1; JO887R. **CODEN** JSWPEC. **[CCC].** Index available. **Bk Rev. Ad Acc. Circ:** 500-600. available on microfiche.
**Desc:** Provides a unique forum for the application of current understanding of unconscious processes to social work practice with individuals, couples, families and other caretakers. Publishes articles where these ideas are related to institutional life and the contradictions of social policy. Seeks to link the psychodynamic tradition with other theoretical orientations. Fosters inter-cultural dialogue.
**Ind/Abst** Appl. Soc. Sci. Index Abstr.; Soc. Plann. Policy Dev. Abstr.; Soc. Work Abstr. [Select. Cov.].

US/0191-5096
**JOURNAL OF SOCIOLOGY AND SOCIAL WELFARE.** [J. sociol. soc. welf.]. (Fall 1973)-. Periodical. English. qt (Feb., May, Aug., Oct.). $28.00 (individuals), $59.00 (institutions) US; $34.00 (individuals), $67.00 (institutions) other. Journal of Sociology & Social Work, West Michigan University, School of Social Work, Kalamazoo MI 49008-5034. **Tel** (616)387-3185, Gary Matthews, FAX (616)387-0958. **ED** Stanley Robin-editors telephone (616) 387-3607. **LC** HN1; .J63. **DD** 301/.05. **[CCC]. Bk Rev. Ad Acc, Adv Mgr:** Barbara Dennison, **Tel** (717) 867-6336. **Pr Rev. Circ:** 600. available on microfilm and microfiche from University Microfilms International (UMI).
**Desc:** Sociological approach to social welfare issues and policies, special thematic issues.
**Ind/Abst** Appl. Soc. Sci. Index Abstr.; Middle East Abstr. Index; Psychol. Abstr. (1974-); PsycINFO; PsycLit; Soc. Plann. Policy Dev. Abstr.; Soc. Work Abstr. [Full Cov.]; Sociol. Abstr.

US/0884-1233
**JOURNAL OF TEACHING IN SOCIAL WORK.** [J. teach. soc. work]. Vol. 1, No. 1 (Spring/Summer 1987)-. Periodical. English. sa. $90.00 US; $126.00 other. The Haworth Press Inc, 10 Alice Street, Binghamton NY 13904-1580. **Tel** (607)722-5857, (800)3-HAWORTH, FAX (607)722-1424. **ED** Florence Vigilante and Harold Lewis (editor's address: Hunter College/Employee Assistance Program, 129 East 79th Street, New York, NY 10021). **LC** HV11; .J68. **DD** 361.3/2/071073. **Bk Rev. Ad Acc. Pr Rev. Acid Free. Circ:** 279. available on microfilm and microfiche from University Microfilms International (UMI). Documents available from Haworth Document Delivery Service.
**Desc:** Qualitative as well as quantitative studies, philosophical and historical insights are among the few topics addressed in this journal. Focuses on the educational process in social work, recognizing that all social workers employ the skills of a teacher in their profession. Aims to be a forum for lively discussion on those skills and their most effective use in practice.
**Ind/Abst** Appl. Soc. Sci. Index Abstr.; Contents Pages Educ.; Soc. Plann. Policy Dev. Abstr.; Soc. Work Abstr. [Full Cov.]; Sociol. Educ. Abstr.; Spec. Educ. Needs Abstr.; Stud. Women Abstr.

●US/1078-6856
**JOURNAL OF THE AMERICAN HEALTH CARE, THE.** (1994)-. Periodical. English. bm. $129.95 US, Canada & Mexico; $155.00 other. Faulkner & Gray Inc., 11 Penn Plaza, 17th Floor, New York NY 10001. **Tel** (212)967-7000, (800)535-8403. ***Continues*** *Journal of American Health Policy, 1055-324X.*

US/0733-6535
**JOURNAL OF VOLUNTEER ADMINISTRATION, THE.** [J. volunt. adm.]. **Added/Corp** Association for Volunteer Administration (U.S.). Vol. 1, No. 1 (Fall 1982)-. Periodical. English. Four times a year (Jan., Apr., July, Oct.). $29.00 US; $32.00 Canada & Mexico; $40.00 others. Association of Volunteer Administration, PO Box 4584, Boulder CO 80306. **Tel** (303)541-0238, FAX (303)541-0277. **ED** Connie Baird. **LC** HV91; .J68. **DD** 361.3/7/0973. cum. index. **Bk Rev. Ad Acc, Adv Mgr:** M. Martin. **Circ:** 2,300. ***Continues*** *Volunteer Administration, 0362-773X.*
**Desc:** Features articles on practical concerns, philosophical issues, and significant research to help you do your job. There are special features to save you time and broaden your knowledge, such as abstracts of related articles and adaptable training designs.
**Ind/Abst** Abstr. Soc. Gerontol. (?-?); AGRICOLA [Select. Cov.]; Health Plan. Adminis.; Hospit. Health Admin. Index; Hum. Resour. Abstr.; Soc. Work Abstr. (Summer 1987-) [Select. Cov.]; Work Relat. Abstr.

US/0895-2841
**JOURNAL OF WOMEN & AGING. See** Women's Interests.

CN/0030-283X
**JOURNAL - ONTARIO ASSOCIATION OF CHILDREN'S AID SOCIETIES. Main/Corp** Ontario Association of Children's Aid Societies. **VFOAT** Journal of the Ontario Association of Children's Aid Societies. Vol. 9, No. 7 (Sept. 1966)-. Periodical. English. qt. 26.50Can$. Ontario Children's Aid Society, 75 Front Street East Suite 203, Suite 203 Toronto, Ontario M5E 1V9 Canada. **Tel** (416)366-8115, FAX (416)366-8317. **ED** Diane Cresswell. **DD** 362.7/09713. **NLM** W1; JO944B. **Bk Rev. Ad Acc, Adv Mgr:** S. Devine. **Circ:** 7,000. ***Continues*** *Journal of the Ontario Children's Aid Societies, 0381-985X.*
**Desc:** A compilation of articles dealing with the care and protection of children.

US/0883-8100
**JOURNAL / WORLD RESOURCES INSTITUTE.** ***Ceased.*** [J. - World Resour. Inst.]. **Added/Corp** World Resources Institute. (1984)-(19??). English. an. WRI Publications, PO Box 4852, Baltimore MD 21211. **Tel** (800)822-0504. **DD** 363.

GW
**JUGENDHILFE.** Periodical. German. mo. Deutscher Judo Verband, Redaktion Ippon Segewaldweg 40, D 12557 Berlin Germany. **Tel** 011 49 711 210770, telex 051 678. **LC** HV763; .A15.

GW
**JUGENDHILFE IN NORDRHEIN WESTFALEN, DIE.** German. an. DM11.00. Landesamt fuer Datenverarbeitung und Statistik Nordrhein-Westfalen, Postfach 101105, 40002

## Sociology — Social Services and Welfare

Duesseldorf Germany. **Tel** (0211)944901, FAX (0211)442006, telex 8586654 LDST D. **LC** HV771.N67; J84.

JA/0911-484X
**KAIGAI SHAKAI HOSHO JOHO.**
**Added/Corp** Shakai Hosho Kenkyujo. **VFOAT** Overseas Social Security News. (19??)-. Periodical. Japanese. Four times a year. $95.00. PCO MA, Forest Research Institute Malaysia, PO Box 201 Kepong, 52109 Kuala Lumpur Malaysia. **Tel** 011 60 3 6342633. **(Subscription address:** Maurzen Co. Ltd. PO Box 5050, Tokyo, 100 31 Japan (phone: 011 81 3 32789224) **LC** HD7088; .K34.

FI/0355-483X
**KANSANELAKELAITOKSEN JULKAISUJA. ML.** See Education-Special Education and Rehabilitation.

US
**KANSAS FINAL COMPREHENSIVE SOCIAL SERVICE PLAN, TITLE XX SOCIAL SECURITY ACT. Main/Corp** Kansas. Dept. of Social and Rehabilitation Services. **VFOAT** Final Comprehensive Social Services Plan, Title XX Social Security Act. Periodical. English. an. Kansas Department of Social and Rehabilitation Service, Topeka KS 66612. **LC** HV86; .K23. **DD** 361.6/09781.

FI
**KASVATUSNEUVOLATOIMINTA. VERKSAMHETEN VID RADGIVNINGSBYRAER FOR UPPFOSTRINGSFRAGOR. Main/Corp** Finland. Sosiaalihallitus. Sunnnittelu- Ja Tilastotoimisto. **VFOAT** Verksamheten Vid Radgivningsbyraer for Uppfostringsfragor. Finnish (Swedish). Sosiaalihallitus, Suunnittelu Ja Tilastotoimisto, Valtion Painatuskeskus, Pl 516, 00101 Helsinki 10 Finland. **LC** HV799.F5; F57B.

FI
**KEHITYSVAMMAISTEN ERITYISHUOLTO. Added/Corp** Finland. Sosiaalihallitus. Suunnitteluosasto. **VFOAT** Specialomsorger om Utvecklingsstorda. (1984)-. Finnish (Swedish). an. **LC** HV3008.F5; F55b. **Continues** Finland. Sosiaalihallitus. Suunnittelu- Ja Tilastotoimisto. Kehitysvammahuolto.

JA
**KENKYU HOKOKU SHU - TOKYO-TO SHINSHIN SHOGAISHA FUKUSHI SENTA. Main/Corp** Tokyo-To Shinshin Shogaisha Fukushi Senta. (19??)-. Periodical. Japanese. Tokyo-to Shinshin Shogaisha Fukushi Senta, 43 Toyamamachi, Shinjuku-ku Tokyo Japan. **LC** HV3024.J3; T64a.

US/0894-8720
**KID CARE MAGAZINE.** [Kid care mag.]. **VFOAT** Kid Care. Vol. 1, No. 1 (Fall 1987)-. Periodical. English. qt. Verdego Media Inc, PO Box 1058, Clackamas OR 97015. **DD** 362.

UK
**KIDS.** (1972)-. Periodical. English. £2.00. Children's Rights Publications, Stewarts Grove SW3, PO Box 70, London England. **LC** HV751; .A12. **DD** 362.7/0942. **Continues** Children's Rights.

US/1057-2996
**KIDS (STORRS, CONN.).** (KIDS / COOPERATIVE EXTENSION SYSTEM, UNIVERSITY OF CONNECTICUT, COLLEGE OF AGRICULTURE AND NATURAL RESOURCES IN COORDINATION WITH THE CONNECTICUT DEPARTMENT OF HUMAN RESOURCES.). [Kids]. **Added/Corp** Connecticut. Dept. of Human Resources. University of Connecticut. Cooperative Extension System. **VFOAT** Kids Newsletter. (19??)-. Periodical. English. **DD** 649.
**Ind/Abst** AGRICOLA [Full Cov.].

JA/0387-3064
**KIKAN SHAKAI HOSHO KENKYU.**
**Added/Corp** Shakai Hosho Kenkyujo. **VFOAT** Quarterly of Social Security Research; Shakai Hosho Kenkyu. (19??)-. Japanese (summaries and/or abstracts in English). qt. $97.00. Shakai Hosho Kenkyujo, 3-4 Kasumigaseki, 1-chome Chiyoda-ku, Tokyo Japan. **(Subscription address:** Maruzen Company Ltd., PO Box 5050, Import & Export Department, Tokyo 100 31 Japan.) **LC** HD7227; .A52.

NE
**KINDERCENTRA / CENTRAAL BUREAU VOOR DE STATISTIEK. Main/Corp** Netherlands. Centraal Bureau Voor de Statistiek. **VFOAT** Public Nurseries. 1977-. Periodical. Dutch. Fl10.25. Centraal Bureau voor de Statistiek, AFD ALG Zaken, Postbus 959, 2270 AZ Voorburg Netherlands. **Tel** 011 31 70 3373800, FAX 011 31 038 7429, telex 32692 CBS NL. **LC** HV861.N4; K56.

US/0023-1703
**KINSHIP.** Periodical. English. qt. $5.00. Kinship of Ohio, Morning Star, PO Box 39188, Cincinnati OH 45239. **Tel** (513)741-8866. **ED** Sister Christine Beckett. **Circ:** 12,000.

FI
**KODINHOITOAPU. Main/Corp** Finland. Sosiaalihallitus Sunnnittelu- Ja Tilastotoimisto. **VFOAT** Hemvardshjalp; Home Help. Began with Vol. for 1971. Finnish (Swedish; summaries and/or abstracts in Finnish, Swedish and English). Valtion Painatuskeskus, PO Box 516, SF 00101 Helsinki Finland. **Tel** 011 358 0 5660266. **LC** HA1448; .F4 subser; HV315.5.

GR
**KOINONIKOS PROYPOLOGISMOS ETOUS ... / HYPOURGEIO HYGEIAS, PRONOIAS, KAI KOINONIKON ASPHALISEON, GENIKE GRAMMATEIA KOINONIKON ASPHALISEON, D/NSE EPITHEORESES. Main/Corp** Greece. Genike Grammateia Koinonikon Asphaliseon. D/NSE Epitheoreses. Greek, Modern. an. **LC** HD7211.83; .A26A.

YU
**KORISNICI I OBLICI SOCIJALNE ZASTITE . USERS AND FORMS OF SOCIAL WELFARE / SOCIJALISTICKA FEDERATIVNA REPUBLIKA JUGOSLAVIJA, SAVEZNI ZAVOD ZA STATISTIKU. Added/Corp** Savezni Zavod za Statistiku (Yugoslavia). **VFOAT** Users and Forms of Social Welfare. Serbo-Croatian (Roman). **LC** HA1631; .A33 subser.; HD7211.6.

JA
**KYUKYU SHOROPPO / SHOBOCHO YOBO KYUKYUKA HEN. Main/Corp** Japan. Japanese. ¥2300. Zenkoku Kajo Horei Shuppan Company Ltd., Dai 1 Zenkoku Biru 18 Saneicho, Shinjukuku Tokyoto 160 Japan. **LC** LAW.

US
**LABORERS' BENEFITS REVIEW. VFOAT** Benefits Review. Vol. 1, No. 1 (June 1988)-. Periodical. English. Laborers International Union of North America, 905 16th Street NW, Washington DC 20006. **Tel** (202)737-8320.
**Ind/Abst** Work Relat. Abstr. (-19??).

SW
**LAGEN OM ALLMAN FORSAKRING OCH ANDRA FORFATTNINGAR OM SOCIALFORSAKRING M.M. Main/Corp** Sweden. Swedish. Riksforsakringsverket Forsakringskasseforbundet, Box 1751, 111 87 Stockholm Sweden. **LC** LAW.

CN/0715-4739
**LANARK, LEEDS AND GRENVILLE COMMUNITY INFORMATION DIRECTORY.** [Lanark, Leeds Grenville community inf. dir.]. 1st Ed. (Jan. 1982)-. Directory. English. te. $10.70 per vol. Lanark, Leeds and Grenville Information BAnk, Box 172, Smiths Falls Ontario K7A 4T1. **DD** 361/.0025/71373.

GW
**LANDESJUGENDPLAN : DURCHFUHRUNGSPLAN. Main/Corp** Rhineland-Palatinate. (Germany). Ministerium fur Soziales, Gesundheit und Sport. German. an. Ministerium fur Soziales Gesundheit und Sport, Bauhofstrasse 4 65, Mainz Germany. **LC** HV771.R47; R47A.

SW
**LANDSTINGENS PLANER. Main/Corp** Svenska Landstingsforbundet. 1914. Swedish. sm. $16.17. Landstingsforbundet, PO Box 6606, 11384 Stockholm Sweden. **Tel** 08 2365 60. **ED** Ake Ingelmo. **LC** HV338; .S86A. **DD** 361.6/09485. **Bk Rev**. **Ad Acc**.
**Desc:** Concerns the county councils and their functions (health and medical care, dental service, culture, finances, administration, public transportation etc.)

IO
**LAPORAN KEGIATAN KANTOR WILAYAH DEP. SOSIAL & DINAS SOSIAL PROPINSI DAERAH TINGKAT I LAMPUNG. Main/Corp** Indonesia. Departemen Sosial. Kantor Wilayah Propinsi Lampung. **Added/Corp** Lampung, Indonesia. Dinas Sosial. **VAT** Laporan Kegiatan Kantor Wilayah Departemen Sosial Dan Dinas Sosial Propinsi Daerah Tingkat Satu Lampung. (19??)-. Indonesian. Jln Golak Galik, Teluketung Indonesia. **LC** HV404.L35; I5a.

IO
**LAPORAN KERJA - PERWAKILAN DEPARTEMEN SOSIAL DAERAH TINGKAT I SUMATERA SELATAN.**
**Main/Corp** Indonesia. Departemen Sosial. Perwakilan Daerah Tingkat I Sumatera Selatan. **VFOAT** Laporan Kerja - Perwakilan Departemen Sosial Daerah Tingkat Satu Sumatera Selatan. Indonesian. Perwakilan Daerah Tingkat I Sumatera Selatan, Jalan Kapien Anwar Sastro, Palembang Indonesia. **LC** HV404.S96; I54A.
**Desc:** Vols. for 1974-75 include the work program for the following year.

IO
**LAPORAN PELAKSANAAN TUGAS-TUGAS & I.E. DAN PEDOMAN PELAKSANAAN TUGAS-TUGAS.**
**Main/Corp** Indonesia. Direktorat Jenderal Bantuan Sosial. 1976/77-. Indonesian. **LC** HV401; .D518A.
**Continues** Evaluasi Pelaksanaan Tugas Direktorat Jenderal Bantuan Sosial.
**Desc:** Vols. for 1976/77-(1977/78) include projections for the following year.

IO
**LAPORAN TAHUNAN / DINAS SOSIAL DAERAH TINGKAT I SUMATERA UTARA. Main/Corp** Sumatera Utara (Indonesia). Dinas Sosial. (197?)-. Indonesian. Jalan Jenderal A Yani VII/29, Medan Indonesia. **LC** HV405.S85; S85a.
**Continues** Progress Report Dinas Sosial Propinsi Sumatera Utara.

FI
**LAPSILISA. VFOAT** Barnbidrag. 1979-. Finnish (Swedish). an. Sosiaalihallitus, Suunnittelu Ja Tilastotoimisto, Valtion Painatuskeskus, Pl 516, 00101 Helsinki 10 Finland. **LC** HV799.F5; F57A. **Continues** Lapsilisatilasto. Statistik over Barnbidrag.

US/0892-6921
**LATER YEARS (LAFAYETTE, IND.), THE. Suspended.** (THE LATER YEARS.). [Later years]. **Added/Corp** Dunn & Hargitt, Inc. (April 1987)-Suspended. Periodical. English. mo. $120.00. Dunn & Hargitt Inc, 22 North 2nd Street, PO Box 1100, Lafayette IN 47901. **Tel** (317)423-2624. **DD** 362.

IT
**LAVORO E SICUREZZA SOCIALE.**
**Added/Corp** Confederazione Italiana dei Dirigenti di Azienda. (May 1959)-. Italian. Four times a year (Jan., Apr., July, Oct.). L110000 Italy; L150000 other. Franco Angeli Riviste SRL, Viale Monza 106, 20127 Milan Italy. **Tel** 011 39 2 2827651, 011 39 2 289562.
**Ind/Abst** PAIS Int. Print.

US/0148-4494
**LAWS RELATED TO THE DEPARTMENT OF SOCIAL SERVICES, PASSED DURING THE LEGISLATIVE SESSION.** See Law.

US/1060-6653
**LEAD ABATEMENT NEWS. Ceased.** (LEAD ABATEMENT NEWS : GOVERNMENT, BUSINESS, TECHNOLOGY.). [Lead abat. news]. (1991)-(Jan. 1992). Periodical. English. mo. Business Publishers Inc., 951 Pershing Drive, Silver Spring MD 20910-4464. **Tel** (301)587-6300, (800)274-0122, FAX (301)585-9075. **DD** 362.

●US
**LEADERSHIP. Added/Corp** Points of Light Foundation. (Jan./Mar. 1993)-. Periodical. English. Four times a year (Jan., Apr., July, Oct.). $20.00 (one year), $38.00 (two year), $56.00 (three year). Points of Light Foundation, 1737 H Street NW, Washington DC 20006. **Tel** (202)223-9186, FAX (202)223-9256. **Continues** Voluntary Action Leadership, 0149-6492.

US/1055-9108
**LEADERSHIP (FORT WORTH, TEX.).**
(LEADERSHIP / HARRIS METHODIST FORT WORTH.). [Leadersh.]. **Added/Corp** Harris Methodist Fort Worth. Vol. 1 No. 1 Winter (1991)-. Periodical. English. Three times a year. Free. Leadership, Harris Methodist Fort Worth, 1301 Pa. Avenue, Fort Worth TX 76104. **DD** 362.

US/0732-6394
**LEGISLATIVE HISTORY OF TITLES I-XX OF THE SOCIAL SECURITY ACT.** See Law.

CN/1186-0367
**LEXIQUE - ONTARIO. MINISTERE DES SERVICES SOCIAUX ET COMMUNAUTAIRES.** (LEXIQUE). [Lex. - Ont., Minist. servic. soc. communaut.]. **Added/Corp** Ontario. Ministere des Services Sociaux et Communautaires. **VFOAT** Lexicon. **VAT** Lexicon - Ontario. Ministry of Community and Social Services. (1991)-. Periodical. English (French). Ontario Ministry of Community & Social Services, 12th Floor/700 Bay Street, Toronto Ontario M7A 1E9 Canada. **DD** 361.6/09713.

CN/1186-0367
**LEXIQUE - ONTARIO. MINISTERE DES SERVICES SOCIAUX ET COMMUNAUTAIRES.** (LEXIQUE). [Lex. - Ont., Minist. servic. soc. communaut.]. **Added/Corp** Ontario. Ministry of Community and Social Services. **VFOAT** Lexicon. (1991). Periodical. French (English). Ontario Ministry of Community & Social Services, 12th Floor/700 Bay Street, Toronto Ontario M7A 1E9 Canada. **DD** 361.6/09713.

IT
**LIBERETA.** (19??)-. Italian. mo. L20000.00 Italy; L40000.00 other. Edispi Srl, Via Dei Frentani 4A, 00185 Rome Italy. **Tel** 011 39 6 444811. ***Continues*** *Pensionato d'Italia.*

CN/0712-9599
**LIBEREZ LES VACANCES.** (LIBEREZ LES VACANCES : PUBLICATION DU MOUVEMENT QUEBECOIS DES CAMPS FAMILIAUX.). No. 1-. Periodical. French. Three times a year. Free. Mouvement Quebecois Des Campus, Familiaux, 49 Est, Rue Ste-Catherine, Montreal Quebec H2X 1K7 Canada. **DD** 362.5/8/09714. ctrl circ.

US
**LIBRARY BULLETIN - CENTER ON SOCIAL WELFARE POLICY AND LAW.** **Main/Corp** Center on Social Welfare Policy and Law. (19??)-. English. Twenty-six times a year. Free. Center on Social Welfare Policy & Law, 95 Madison Avenue, New York NY 10016. **Tel** (212)679-3709.

US
**LIBRARY NOTES / SOCIAL SECURITY ADMINISTRATION.** **Main/Corp** United States. Social Security Administration. Periodical. English. mo. Social Security Administration, 6401 Security Boulevard, Baltimore MD 21235. **Tel** (410)965-8822, FAX (410)966-1463.

US
**LIGHT.** Began publication with V. 3 (Nov. 1931). Periodical. English. qt. **LC** HV1571; .L5.
**Ind/Abst** Work Relat. Abstr.

US/1040-3469
**LINK (ASHLAND, MASS.).** (THE LINK.). **Added/Corp** International Society of Fire Service Instructors. Vol. 9, Issue 30 (Aug. 5, 1988)-. Periodical. English. wk. $45.00 members; $90.00 nonmembers. International Society of Fire Service Instructors, 20 Main Street, Ashland MA 01721. **Tel** (508)881-5800, FAX (508)881-6829. **DD** 363. ***Continues*** *Communications Link, 0739-4535.*

●US/1065-5832
**LINK (DURHAM, N.C.), THE.** (THE LINK : A QUARTERLY BY AND FOR PEOPLE WITH CHRONIC FATIGUE SYNDROME.). (1992)-. Periodical. English. qt. $15.00. The Link, PO Box 51952, Durham NC 27717-1952.

CN/1183-6091
**LINK'AGE (TORONTO).** (LINK*AGE / CARNET, THE CANADIAN AGING RESEARCH NETWORK). [Link'age]. **Added/Corp** CARNET-the Canadian Aging Research Network. **VFOAT** Linkage. Vol. 1, No. 1 (Spring 1991)-. Periodical. English. Three times a year. $13.00 per year. CARNET, The Canadian Aging Research Network, Centre for Studies of Aging, University of Toronto, Suite 305, 455 Spadina Avenue, Toronto Ontario M5S 2G8 Canada. **DD** 362.6/072071.

US/0163-2205
**LINKS (SACRAMENTO).** (LINKS.). **Added/Corp** National Association of Private Residential Facilities for the Mentally Retarded. (197?)-. Periodical. English. mo. $45.00. Links-NAPRR, PO Box 163270, Sacramento CA 95816. **Tel** (916)455-0723. **ED** Charles W Skoien Jr. **Ad Acc. Circ:** 10,000 (ctrl).
**Desc:** National and state educational information that pertains to services for the mentally disabled.
**Ind/Abst** Br. Educ. Index.

CN/1180-3045
**LIST OF RESIDENTIAL CARE FACILITIES / STATISTICS CANADA, CANADIAN CENTRE FOR HEALTH INFORMATION.** **Added/Corp** Canadian Centre for Health Information. **VFOAT** Liste des Etablissements de Soins pour Beneficiaires Internes au Canada. (19??)-. English (French). 31.00Can$ Canada; $32.00 other. Statistics Canada, Publications Sales & Services, Main Building Room 1710, Ottawa Ontario K1A 0T6 Canada. **Tel** (613)951-5078, (800)267-6677, FAX (613)951-1584, telex 053-3585. **LC** RA998.C3; H38. **DD** 362.1/6/02571. ***Continues*** *Health Reports. Supplement. No. 7, List of Residential Care Facilities in Canada, 1180-3045.*

●UK
**LOCAL AUTHORITY SOCIAL WORK EXPENDITURE.** (1992)-. Bulletin. English. an. £2.00. Social Work Services Group, Statistics Branch, 43 Jeffrey Street / Room 422, Edinburgh EH1 1DG Scotland. **Tel** 031 244 5431, FAX 031 244 5387.

II
**LOKAYAN BULLETIN.** **Added/Corp** Lokayan (Delhi, India). (198?)-. Bulletin. English. bm. $45.00. Lokayan Bulletin, 13 Alipur Road, Delhi 110 054 India. **Tel** 011 91 11 2523930. **(Subscription address:** Prints India, 11 Darya Ganj, New Delhi 110002 India.) **LC** JQ201; .L66. **DD** 361.6/1/095456.
**Ind/Abst** Hum. Rights Intern. Rep.

US
**LONG-TERM CARE NEWS / HOSPITAL ASSOCIATION OF NEW YORK STATE.** ***Title Change.*** **Added/Corp** Hospital Association of New York State. **VFOAT** Long Term Care News. (19??)-(1993). Periodical. English. bw. Hospital Association of New York State, 74 North Pearl Street, Albany NY 12207. **Tel** (518)431-7600, FAX (518)431-7915. ***Merged with*** *Home Care Update* ***to form*** *Continuing Care Connection.*

US/0024-6425
**LOOKOUT (NEW YORK), THE.** (THE LOOKOUT.). **Added/Corp** Seamen's Church Institute of New York and New Jersey. Seaman's Church Institute of New York. (19??)-. Periodical. English. Four times a year. $5.00. Seamans Church Institute of New York & New Jersey, 241 Water Street, New York NY 10038. **Tel** (212)349-9090, FAX (212)349-8342. **ED** Andrea Laine. **Bk Rev**, (Qty: 1-2). **Circ:** 9,000 (ctrl).

II
**LUCKNOW UNIVERSITY JOURNAL OF SOCIAL WORK.** **Added/Corp** Lucknow University. Social Work Alumni Association. Lucknow University. Dept. of Social Work. **VFOAT** Journal of Social Work. (19??)-. English. an. $50.00. Lucknow University / Social Work Alumni Association, Lucknow 226 016 India. **(Subscription address:** Prints India, 11 Darya Ganj, New Delhi 110002 India.) **LC** HV1; .L82.

NE
**LVNW NIEUWS.** Dutch. qt. Fl35.00 Netherlands; $30.00 US. Netherlands Association of Social Workers, Leidseweg 80, 3531 BE Utrecht Netherlands. **Tel** 30 948603. **ED** P E Roosenstein. **Bk Rev. Ad Acc. Circ:** 2,000.

AG
**MADRES DE PLAZA DE MAYO : [BOLETIN].** **Added/Corp** Madres de Plaza de Mayo (Association). **VFOAT** Madres. (Sept. 1980)-. Periodical. Spanish. mo. Casa De Las Madres, Hipolito Yrigoyen 1442, 1089 Buenos Aires Argentina. **LC** HV6433.A7; M33. **DD** 323.4/9/0982. ***Continues*** *Madres de Plaza de Mayo de la Plata.*
**Ind/Abst** Hum. Rights Intern. Rep.

CN/0383-7297
**MAILLON, LE.** June 1975-. Periodical. French. mo. Conseil de l'Age d'Or Region de Laval, 765 Roland Forget Duvernay, Laval Quebec H7E 4C1 Canada. **DD** 362.6/3.

US
**MAIN STREET MEMORANDUM, THE.** English. qt. $25.00. Rockford Institute, 934 North Main Street, Rockford IL 61103. **Tel** (815)964-5053, FAX (815)965-1826.

US/0147-2585
**MAINE MENTAL HEALTH PLAN.** **See** Public Health and Safety.

US/0161-3979
**MAINE'S STATE PLAN ON DEVELOPMENTAL DISABILITIES.** **Main/Corp** Maine. Council on Developmental Disabilities. **VFOAT** State Plan of the Developmental Disabilities Planning Council. English. an. 411 State Office Building, Augusta ME 04333. **LC** HV3006.M2; M32A. **DD** 362.3/09741.

US/1061-6764
**MAJOR CHANGES IN STATE MEDICAID PROGRAMS.** [Major chang. state Medicaid programs]. **Added/Corp** George Washington University. Intergovernmental Health Policy Project. (1990)-. English. an. $25.00. Intergovernmental Health Policy Project, 2021 K Street NW, Suite 800, Washington DC 20006. **Tel** (202)872-1445, FAX (202)785-0114. **LC** HD7102.U4; R38. **DD** 362.1/04252/097305. ***Continues*** *Major Canges in Sate Medicaid and Idigent Care Programs.*

●US/1064-5454
**MANAGED CARE QUALITY.** **See** Economics-Industry and Production.

●US/1063-035X
**MANAGING SENIORCARE.** [Manag. sr.care]. **VFOAT** Managing Senior Care. Vol. 1, No. 1 (June 1992)-. Periodical. English. mo. $210.00. Business Publishers Inc., 951 Pershing Drive, Silver Spring MD 20910-4464. **Tel** (301)587-6300, (800)274-0122, FAX (301)585-9075. **DD** 362. **NLM** W1; MA581D.

CN/0715-3481
**MANITOBA SOCIAL WORKER.** [Manit. soc. work.]. **Added/Corp** Manitoba Association of Social Workers. (1971)-. Periodical. English. Eight times a year. 20.00Can$. Manitoba Association of Social Workers, 2015 Portage Avenue, Suite 103, Winnipeg Manitoba R3J OK3 Canada. **Tel** (204)888-9477. **DD** 361/.97127.

CN/0318-5427
**MANUAL OF SOCIAL SERVICES IN MANITOBA.** Began with 1972/73 issue. English. Social Planning Council of Winnipeg, 501-177 Lombard Avenue, Winnipeg Manitoba R3B 0W5. **LC** HV109.M4. **DD** 361/.0025/7127.

CN/0836-0081
**MATURITE.** (MATURITE : BULLETIN DE L'ASSOCIATION INTERNATIONALE FRANCOPHONE DES AINES.). [Maturite]. Vol. 1, No. 1 (Dec. 1987)-. Bulletin. French. qt. Free. Association Internationale Francophone des Aines / Quebec, 129 Cote de la Montagne, Quebec G1k 4E6 Canada. **DD** 362.6/06/01.

CN/1183-8329
**MCDONALD QUARTERLY.** [McDonald q.]. **Added/Corp** Cross Cultural Communications International, Inc. (Sept. 1990)-. Periodical. English. Four times a year (Mar., June, Sept., Dec.). 40.00Can$ non-profit organizations; 80.00Can$ others. Cross Cultural Comm. Intl. Inc., 114-131 Provenncher Boulevard, Winnipeg MANI R2H OG2 Canada. **Tel** (204)233-6239, FAX (204)233-5632. **ED** (phone: (204)949-1144). **DD** 362. **Bk Rev. Circ:** 700.
**Desc:** A topical report on diversity issues.

US/1048-3314
**MCKNIGHT'S LONG-TERM CARE NEWS.** [McKnight's long-term care news]. **VFOAT** McKnight's Long Term Care News; Long-Term Care News; Long Term Care News. (198?)-. Periodical. English. mo. $44.95 (one year), $69.95 (two year). McKnight Medical Communications Inc, 1419 Lake Cook Road, Suite 110, Deerfield IL 60015. **Tel** (708)647-0259, (800)451-7838. **(Subscription address:** Hallmark Data Systems, PO Box 1165, Skokie IL 60076.) **ED** Sue Powills. **DD** 363. **NLM** W1; MC999. **Ad Acc. Circ:** 34,000 (ctrl). ***Continues*** *Today's Nursing Home & Retirement Housing Today Quarterly, 1041-3189.*
**Desc:** News publication for administrators, directors of nursing, retirement housing directors and consultant pharmacists.

US/0193-9483
**MEDICAL ASSISTANCE, MEDICAID (LANSING).** (MEDICAL ASSISTANCE (MEDICAID).). English. an. Department of Social Services / Michigan, 300 South Capitol Avenue, Lansing MI 48026. **LC** HV86; .M536 subser; HD7102.U5. **DD** 361/.9774 S 362.1/04/25.

US
**MEDICAL ASSISTANCE PROGRAM.** **Main/Corp** Illinois. Dept. of Public Aid. (1982-84)-. English. Illinois Department of Public Aid, 316 South Second Street, Springfield IL 62762. **LC** HD7102.U5; I285a. **DD** 368.4/2/00977305. ***Continues*** *Medical Assistance Program Annual Report.*

US/0897-9634
**MEDICARE ADVISOR.** [Medicare advis.]. (Oct. 1987)-. Periodical. English. mo. $105.00. Medicare Advisor, 9441 LBJ Fwy, #510 Box 2, Dallas TX 75243. **Tel** (214)644-0159, FAX (214)644-1538. **ED** Ellen Bradley. **LC** KF3826.N8; A136. **DD** 344.73/0226; 347.304226. ctrl circ.
**Desc:** Covers crucial shifts in policies, trends, and changes in regulations directed to nursing and long-term care facilities.

US/0743-5959
**MEDICARE AND MEDICAID DATA BOOK, THE.** **Added/Corp** United States. Health Care Financing Administration. Office of Research and Demonstrations. (1981)-. English. an. $15.00 US; $18.75 other. ORD Publications, Room 1A9/Oak Meadows Building, 6325 Security Boulevard, Baltimore MD 21207. **Tel** (410)966-6573. **ED** Alice Young. **LC** HD7102.U4; D27. **DD** 362.1/04252/0973. **NLM** W2; A l4d. **Circ:** 3,000 (ctrl). ***Continues*** *Data on the Medicaid Program.*
**Desc:** Provides statistics on medicare and medicaid programs including eligibility, benefits, service coverage and limitations, utilization, expenditures, financing and administration.

●US/1068-1019
**MEDICARE AND MEDICAID LAW BULLETIN.** **See** Insurance.

US/1060-5355
**MEDICARE AND MEDICAID LAW REPORTER.** ***Ceased.*** **See** Law.

US
**MEDICARE COVERAGE ISSUES MANUAL.** **Added/Corp** United States. Health Care Financing Administration. **VFOAT** Coverage Issues Manual. (1985)-. Government Publication. English. ir. $68.00 US; $85.00 other. Superintendent of Documents, US Government Printing Office, Washington DC 20402. **Tel** (202)275-3328, FAX (202)786-2377.

US/0733-4672
**MEDICARE EXPLAINED.** **See** Insurance.

US/0730-143X
**MEDICARE, HEALTH INSURANCE FOR THE AGED AND DISABLED. SUMMARY-UTILIZATION AND REIMBURSEMENT BY PERSON.** ***Title Change.*** **Added/Corp** United States. Health Care Financing Administration. Office of Research, Demonstrations, and Statistics. **VFOAT** Summary-Utilization and Reimbursement by Person. (1975)-(19??). English. Health Care Financing

## Sociology —Social Services and Welfare

Administration, 6325 Security Boulevard, Room 700, Baltimore MD 21207. **Tel** (410)966-3000, FAX (410)966-5267. **NLM** W2 A S63ME. *Continues Medicare, Health Insurance for the Aged and Disabled. Section 1.2, Summary Utilization-and Reimbursement by Person. Continued by Annual Medicare Program Statistics, 0741-0190.*

US
**MEDICARE HOME HEALTH AGENCY MANUAL. Added/Corp** United States. Health Care Financing Administration. **VFOAT** Home Health Agency Manual. (19??)-. Government Publication. English. ir. $135.00 US; $168.75 other. Superintendent of Documents, US Government Printing Office, Washington DC 20402. **Tel** (202)275-3328, FAX (202)786-2377.

US/0896-4815
**MEDICARE-MEMORANDUM (OUTPATIENT CLINIC ED.).** (MEDICARE-MEMORANDUM.). [Medicare-memo.]. **VFOAT** Medicare Memorandum. (1987)-. Periodical. English. mo. $109.00. Medicare-Memorandum, PO Box 181524, Dallas TX 75218. **Tel** (214)226-5501. **DD** 362. **Ad Acc.** ctrl circ.
*Desc:* Medicare information updates.

US
**MEDICARE PART A INTERMEDIARY MANUAL. PART 3, CLAIMS PROCESS, HCFA PUBLICATION, 13 3.** Government Publication. English. ir. $616.00 US; $770.00 other. Superintendent of Documents, US Government Printing Office, Washington DC 20402. **Tel** (202)275-3328, FAX (202)786-2377.

US
**MEDICARE PROGRAM STATISTICS. SELECTED STATE DATA / HEALTH CARE FINANCING ADMINISTRATION.** See Sociology-Abstracting, Bibliographies and Statistics.

US
**MEDICARE PROVIDER REIMBURSEMENT MANUAL. Added/Corp** United States. Health Care Financing Administration. **VFOAT** Provider Reimbursement Manual. (19??)-. Government Publication. English. ir. $113.00 US; $141.25 other. Superintendent of Documents, US Government Printing Office, Washington DC 20402. **Tel** (202)275-3328, FAX (202)786-2377.

US
**MEDICARE SKILLED NURSING FACILITY MANUAL. Added/Corp** United States. Health Care Financing Administration. **VFOAT** Skilled Nursing Facility Manual. (19??)-. Government Publication. English. ir. $227.00 US; $283.75 other. Superintendent of Documents, US Government Printing Office, Washington DC 20402. **Tel** (202)275-3328, FAX (202)786-2377.

US/0538-2793
**MEETING - INTER-AFRICAN CONFERENCE ON RURAL WELFARE. Main/Conf** Inter-African Conference on Rural Welfare. First conference held in 1953. English. **LC** HN772.A1; I5. **DD** 301.35.

US
**MEMBERSHIP DIRECTORY / INTERNATIONAL ASSOCIATION OF RESIDENTIAL AND COMMUNITY ALTERNATIVES. Main/Corp** IARCA. Directory. English. an. IARCA, PO Box 1987, La Crosse WI 54602.

PN
**MEMORIA QUE PRESENTA EL DIRECTOR GENERAL ... A LA HONORABLE ASAMBLEA DE REPRESENTANTES DE CORREGIMIENTOS. Main/Corp** Caja de Seguro Social (Panama). Spanish. **LC** HD7138; .A15A. **DD** 354.72870082/56.

UK/0261-9997
**MENTAL HANDICAP : JOURNAL OF THE BRITISH INSTITUTE OF MENTAL HANDICAP.** Vol. 10, No. 1 (March 1982)-. Periodical. English. qt. £23.00 UK; $50.00 other. BIMH Publications, Foley Industrial Park, Stourport Road, Kidderminster Worcs DY11 7QG England. **Tel** (0562)824933. **ED** S J Newbould. **NLM** W1 ME9229P. cum. index (annual). **Bk Rev. Ad Acc. Circ:** 3,750. *Continues Apex (Kidderminster, Hereford and Worcester).*
*Desc:* Presents original articles on mental and multiple handicaps. Of practical application to professionals and families providing services to people with mental handicaps. Includes book reviews and letters.
**Ind/Abst** Br. Educ. Index; Spec. Educ. Needs Abstr.

●US/1070-7298
**MENTAL HEALTH AND SOCIAL WORK CAREER DIRECTORY. See** Medical Science and Technology-Physicians and Medical Personnel.

US/1062-7235
**MENTAL HEALTH FUNDING NEWS.** *Title Change.* [Ment. health funding news]. (19??)-(1994). Periodical. English. sm. CD Publications, 8204 Fenton Street, Silver Spring MD 20910. **Tel** (800)666-6380, (301)588-6380, FAX (301)588-6385. **DD** 362. *Continued by Mental Health News Alert.*

●US
**MENTAL HEALTH NEWS ALERT.** (1994)-. English. sm (24 issues). $249.00. CD Publications, 8204 Fenton Street, Silver Spring MD 20910. **Tel** (800)666-6380, (301)588-6380, FAX (301)588-6385. *Continues Mental Health Funding News, 1062-7235.*

●US/1065-7525
**MENTAL HEALTH RAP.** (MENTAL HEALTH RAP : RECIPIENTS AND PROVIDERS.). [Ment. health RAP]. **Added/Corp** Mental Health Association of Albany County. Transitional Employment Program. **VFOAT** Mental Health RAP, The Vocational Lifeline. (1992)-. Periodical. English. qt. Transitional Employment Program, Mental Health Association, 95 Central Avenue, Albany NY 12206. **DD** 363.

US/0146-7905
**MENTAL HEALTH STATE PLAN. Main/Corp** South Dakota. Dept. of Social Services. English. Department of Social Services / South Dakota, State Office Building, 700 Governors Drive, Pierre SD 57501. **Tel** (605)773-4855. **LC** RA790.65.S8; S68A. **DD** 362.2/09783.

CN/0821-3305
**MENTAL HEALTH (TORONTO. 1979).** (MENTAL HEALTH : NATIONAL NEWSLETTER OF THE CANADIAN MENTAL HEALTH ASSOCIATION.). [Ment. health]. **VFOAT** Sante Mentale. **VAT** Sante Mentale (Toronto). Vol. 3, No. 1 (Sept. 1979)-. Newsletter. English (French). qt. **DD** 362.2/06/071. *Continues Mental Health News (Toronto, Ont. : 1977), 0705-811X.*

US
**MINNESOTA AID TO FAMILIES WITH DEPENDENT CHILDREN FOR FISCAL YEAR ... .** English. an. **LC** HV699; .M53. **DD** 362.7/13/09776. *Continues Aid to Families with Dependent Children.*

US
**MINNESOTA CHILDREN UNDER STATE GUARDIANSHIP AS DEPENDENT/NEGLECTED, YEAR ENDING JUNE 30 ... ANNUAL REPORT.** 1980-. English. an. **LC** HV990.M6; M55A. **DD** 362.7/3/09776. *Continues Minnesota Children Under State Guardianship as Dependent and/or Neglected, 0148-2262.*

US
**MINNESOTA GENERAL ASSISTANCE AND WORK READINESS ANNUAL REPORT, FISCAL YEAR ... . Added/Corp** Minnesota. Dept. of Human Services. Assistance Payments Division. Report and Statistics. English. Minnesota Department of Human Services, Chemical Dependency Program Division, Human Services Building, 444 Lafayette Road, St Paul MN 55155-3823. **Tel** (612)296-3991. **LC** HV98.M65; M49a. **DD** 361.6/09776. *Continues Minnesota General Assistance Annual Report.*

US/0085-347X
**MINNESOTA MEDICAL ASSISTANCE BIENNIAL REPORT DATA. Main/Corp** Minnesota. Dept. of Public Welfare. Research and Statistics Division. Income Maintenance Section. Periodical. English. be. Department of Public Welfare / Minnesota, Centennial Office Building, St Paul MN 55155. **LC** HD7102.U5; M56. **DD** 362.1/04252/09776.

US
**MINNESOTA MEDICAL ASSISTANCE (TITLE XIX) FOR FISCAL YEAR ... . Main/Corp** Minnesota. Dept. of Public Welfare. Operations Review Division. Reports and Statistics. (1980/1981)-. English. an. Department of Public Welfare / Minnesota, Centennial Office Building, St Paul MN 55155. **LC** HD7102.U5; M57a. **DD** 362.1/04252/09776. *Continues Minnesota. Dept. of Public Welfare. Operations Review Division. Reports and Statistics. Minnesota Medical Assistance (Title XIX) Biennium Report for Fiscal Years ... .*

US/0198-9898
**MINNESOTA WOMAN'S YEARBOOK.** 1978/79-. English. an. $6.70. Sprague Publications, 430 Oak Grove Street, Suite B-10, Minneapolis MN 55403. **LC** HV1446.M6; M56. **DD** 362.8/38/025776.

US/1047-3300
**MINORITY FUNDING REPORT.** [Minor. funding rep.]. **Added/Corp** Government Information Services. Vol. 1, No. 1 (Apr. 1989)-. Periodical. English. mo. $128.00. Government Information Services / Virginia, 4301 North Fairfax Drive, Suite 875, Arlington VA 22203. **Tel** (703)528-1820, FAX (703)528-6060, telex RCA 263591 GIS UR. **ED** Donald Hoffman. **DD** 361. **[CCC]**.
*Desc:* Reports on federal and private financial aid opportunities for programs for minority and disadvantaged groups.

JA
**MINSEI IIN JIDO IIN NO TEBIKI. Main/Corp** Tokyo. Minseikyoku. (19??)-. Periodical. Japanese. Tokyo-to Minseikyoku, 8-1 Marunouchi-3 Chome, Chiyoda-ku, Tokyo Japan. **LC** HV415.T6; T55b.

CN/0822-9619
**MISSION IMPOSSIBLE.** (MISSION IMPOSSIBLE : JOURNAL INTERNE DU CENTRE DE SERVICES SOCIAUX DU CENTRE DU QUEBEC.). **Main/Corp** Centre de Services Sociaux du Centre du Quebec. Vol. 1, No 1 (Oct. 1983)-. Periodical. French. ir. Free. CSSCQ, CP 1330, Trois-Rivieres, Quebec G9A 5L2 Canada. **DD** 361/.971445.

US
**MISSOURI TITLE XX PROPOSED COMPREHENSIVE SERVICE PLAN. Main/Corp** Missouri. Dept. of Social Services. **VFOAT** Title 20 Proposed Comprehensive Service Plan; Title Twenty Proposed Comprehensive Service Plan. (1982)-. English. an. Department of Social Services / Missouri, Broadway State Office Building, Jefferson City MO 65102. **LC** HV98.M8; M46b. **DD** 353.97780084/06. *Continues Missouri. Dept. of Social Services. Proposed Comprehensive Annual Social Services Program Plan.*

US/0277-8637
**MIT PRESS SERIES IN HEALTH AND PUBLIC POLICY.** [MIT Press ser. health public policy]. **VFOAT** M.I.T. Press Series in Health and Public Policy; Health and Public Policy. **VAT** Massachusetts Institute of Technology Press Series in Health and Public Policy. (1981)-. Monographic series. English. ir. Price varies per volume. Massachusetts Institute of Technology (MIT) Press, 55 Hayward Street, Cambridge MA 02142-1399. **Tel** (617)253-2889, (617)625-8481, FAX (617)258-6779. **ED** Jeffrey Harris. **DD** 362.1. **NLM** W1 MI938.

US/0748-8556
**MITCHELL GUIDE. NEW YORK CITY, THE. VFOAT** Mitchell New York City. English. be. $145.00. Mitchell Guide, 195 Nassau Street, PO Box 413, Princeton NJ 08540. **LC** HV99.N59; M57. **DD** 361.7/632/0257471.

GW
**MITTEILUNGEN - ARBEITSGEMEINSCHAFT FUER JUGENDHILFE. Main/Corp** Arbeitsgemeinschaft fur Jugendhilfe. Periodical. German. Haager Weg 44, 5300 Bonn 1 Germany. **LC** HV763; .A13.

US/1043-8157
**MONDAY DEVELOPMENTS.** (MONDAY DEVELOPMENTS : A BIWEEKLY PUBLICATION OF INTERACTION.). [Monday dev.]. **Added/Corp** InterAction (Organization : U.S.). (Feb 1983)-. Periodical. English. bw. $275.00 (institutions), $65.00 (individuals). Interaction, 1717 Massachusetts Ave Nothwest, 8th Floor, Washington DC 20036. **Tel** (202)667-8227, FAX (202)667-8236. **ED** Tracy Geoghegan. **DD** 361. **Bk Rev,** (Qty: 50). **Ad Acc. Circ:** 2,500.
*Desc:* Provides news and commentary on changing global events affecting the work of PVOs, included are policy updates,coming events, reports on meetings and conferences, newly available resources and employment opportunities.

US/0891-8651
**MONDAY MORNING REPORT.** [Monday morning rep.]. **Added/Corp** Alcohol Research Information Service (Lansing, Mich.). (1977)-. Periodical. English. Twenty-four times a year. $30.00. Alcohol Research Information Service, 1106 East Oakland Avenue, Box 10212, Lansing MI 48906. **Tel** (517)485-9900. **DD** 362.
*Desc:* A newsletter covering significant issues, events and opinions in the alcohol problems field.

US/0883-7643
**MONOGRAPH - UNIVERSITY OF WASHINGTON. CENTER FOR SOCIAL WORK RESEARCH.** (MONOGRAPH / CENTER FOR SOCIAL WELFARE RESEARCH, SCHOOL OF SOCIAL WORK, UNIVERSITY OF WASHINGTON.). [Monogr. - Univ. Wash., Cent. Soc. Welf. Res.]. No. 1-. Monographic series. English. Price varies per volume. Center for Social Welfare Research, University of Washington, School of Social Work JH-30, Seattle WA 98195. **DD** 361.

US/0270-3823
**MONTANA AGING SERVICES PROGRAM BOOK.** **Main/Corp** Montana. Aging Services Bureau. **VFOAT** Aging Services Bureau Resource Book. English. an. Aging Services Bureau, PO Box 4210, 111 Sanders, Helena MT 59601. **LC** HV1468.M9; M66A. **DD** 362.6/025/786. ***Continues*** *Montana State Aging Services Bureau Resource Book, 0097-7551.*

US/0160-595X
**MONTANA HUMAN SERVICES DIRECTORY.** Directory. English. Montana State University / Montana Human Service Directory, Bozeman MT 59717. **LC** HV98.M85; M65. **DD** 361/.0025/786. ***Continues*** *Montana Social Service, Health and Recreational Directory, 0096-3151.*

CN/1182-1574
**MONTFORT A LA UNE.** [Montfort une]. **Added/Corp** Montfort Hospital (Ottawa, Ont.). Vol. 1, No. 1 (Feb. 1990)-. Periodical. English (French). tq. Pulsation, Hopital Monrfort, Ottawa Ontario K1K 0T2 Canada. **DD** 362.1/1/0971384. ***Continues*** *Pulsation (Ottawa, Ont.), 0712-6131.*
**Ind/Abst** Am. Hist. Life (1964-1988).

US
**MONTHLY STATISTICAL REPORT - NEW YORK (CITY). HUMAN RESOURCES ADMINISTRATION.** **See** Sociology-Abstracting, Bibliographies and Statistics.

FR
**MUTUALITE SOCIALE AGRICOLE, STATISTIQUES, LA.** **Main/Corp** Union des Caisses Centrales de la Mutualite Agricole. (19??)-. French. 8-10 rue d'Astorg, Paris 8 Eme France. **LC** HD7116.A3; F87. **DD** 368.4.

GW/0012-1185
**NACHRICHTENDIENST.** **Main/Corp** Deutscher Verein fuer Offentliche and Private Fursorge. (1920)-. Periodical. German. Twelve times a year. DM40.00. Deutscher Verein fuer Oeffentliche und Private Fuersorge, Am Stockborn 1-3, 60439 Frankfurt Main Germany. **Tel** 011 49 69 95807-211, FAX 011 49 69 95807-381. **ED** Dr. Manfred Wienand and Ralt Mulot. **LC** HV24; .D44. Index available. cum. index. **Bk Rev**, (Qty: 20). **Ad Acc**, **Adv Mgr:** Ralt Mulot. **Pr Rev. Acid Free. Circ:** 7,800 (ctrl).
**Desc:** Information of the German association public private welfare since 1920, comprises the whole field of social welfare including social work education and further education.

CN/0820-7364
**NAPO NEWS.** [NAPO news]. **Added/Corp** National Anti-Poverty Organization. **VFOAT** Echo de l'ONAP. **VAT** National Anti-Poverty Organization News; Echo de l'Organisation Nationale Anti-Pauvrete. No. 1 (Winter 1983)-. Periodical. English (French). qt. Free to members, 10.00Can$ others. National Anti-Poverty Organization, 316 256 King Edward Avenue, Ottawa Ontario K1N 7M1 Canada. **Tel** (613)789-0096. **ED** Havi Echenberg. **DD** 362.5/0971. **Circ:** 1,500 (ctrl). ***Continues*** *NAPO Info News, 0225-7130.*
**Desc:** Newsletter concerning issues of relevance to low income Canadians; includes national news and regional reports.

US/0027-6022
**NASW NEWS.** [NASW news]. **Main/Corp** National Association of Social Workers. **Added/Corp** National Association of Social Workers. News. **VAT** National Association of Social Workers News. (1955)-. Periodical. English. Ten times a year. $25.00. National Association of Social Workers, 750 First Street Northeast, Suite 700, Washington DC 20002-4241. **Tel** (800)638-8799, (202)408-8600, FAX (301)587-1321. **(Subscription address:** NASW Press / National Association of Social Workers, PO Box 431, Annapolis JCT MD 20701.**) ED** Lucy Norman de Sanchez, M Scott Moss, Jon Hiratsuka, and Lyn Fredrickson Carter. **LC** HV1; .N2. **DD** 361. **Ad Acc. Circ:** 100,000 (ctrl). available on microfilm and microfiche from University Microfilms International (UMI). ***Absorbed*** *Personnel Information.*
**Desc:** The News is the primary means of communicating with the membership about association activities and developments in professional practice and social policy.

US/0277-0695
**NASW REGISTER OF CLINICAL SOCIAL WORKERS.** **Main/Corp** National Association of Social Workers. **Added/Corp** National Association of Social Workers. Register of Clinical Social Workers. **VAT** National Association of Social Workers Register of Clinical Social Workers. 1st Ed. (1976)-. English. be. $60.00. National Association of Social Workers, 750 First Street Northeast, Suite 700, Washington DC 20002-4241. **Tel** (800)638-8799, (202)408-8600, FAX (301)587-1321. **(Subscription address:** NASW Press / National Association of Social Workers, PO Box 431, Annapolis JCT MD 20701.**) LC** HV89; .N223a. **DD** 361/.0025/73. **NLM** HV 89 N1112.

UK
**NATIONAL CHILDREN'S BUREAU /ALL EXCEPT UK AND WALES /REGUALR DELIVERY.** English. ir. £22.00 Individual Members; £31.00 Other Europe; £30.00 Other. National Childrens Bureau Information Service, 8 Wakley Street Islington, London EC1V 7QE. **Tel** 011 44 71 2789441, FAX 011 44 71 2789512.
**Desc:** Promotes the interests of all children and young people and to improve their status in a diverse society. Collects and disseminates information about children and promotes good practice in children's services.

US/0738-9159
**NATIONAL COUNCIL NEWS (ROCKVILLE, MD.).** (NATIONAL COUNCIL NEWS / NATIONAL COUNCIL OF COMMUNITY MENTAL HEALTH CENTERS.). [Natl. Counc. news]. **Added/Corp** National Council of Community Mental Health Centers (U.S.). (197?)-. Periodical. English. Eleven times a year. $21.00. National Council of Community Mental Health Centers, 12300 Twinbrook Parkway, Suite 320, Rockville MD 20852. **Tel** (301)984-6200.
**Desc:** The only tabloid that covers news from a community mental health perspective.

US/0097-479X
**NATIONAL DIRECTORY OF CHILD ABUSE SERVICES AND INFORMATION.** 1st Ed.; 1974-. Directory. English. $4.00. National Committee For Prevention Of Child Abuse, Room 510, 111 East Wacker Drive, Chicago IL 60601. **LC** HV741; .N3155A. **DD** 362.7.

●US/1072-902X
**NATIONAL DIRECTORY OF CHILDREN, YOUTH & FAMILIES SERVICES.** [Natl. dir. child. youth fam. serv.]. **VFOAT** National Directory of Children, Youth and Families Services. (1992)-. Directory. English. an. $78.00. National Directory of Children and Youth Services, PO Box 1837, Longmont CO 80502. **Tel** (303)776-7539. **LC** HV741; .N3157. **DD** 362.7/025/73. **NLM** WA 22; AA1 N22. ***Continues*** *National Directory of Children & Youth Services, 0190-7476.*

US/0147-3476
**NATIONAL DIRECTORY OF MEDICARE HOME HEALTH AGENCIES.** **See** Insurance.

US
**NATIONAL DIRECTORY OF PRIVATE SOCIAL AGENCIES.** (1964)-. Directory. English. mo (10 issues). $79.90. Croner Publications Inc., 34 Jericho Turnpike, Jericho NY 11753. **Tel** (516)333-9085. **ED** Helga B. Croner. Index available. **Circ:** 500.
**Desc:** Listing of private social agencies throughout the country.

CN/0709-8677
**NATIONAL LIFELINER, THE.** V. 12, No. 2-July 1979-. Periodical. English. qt. Royal Life Saving Society Canada / National Office, National Office, 550 Church Street, Toronto Ontario M4Y 2E1 Canada. **DD** 363.1/0971.

CN/0713-0511
**NATIONAL NEWS LETTER - FEDERATION OF MILITARY AND UNITED SERVICES INSTITUTES OF CANADA.** **See** Military and Defense.

CN/0824-5045
**NATIONAL NEWSLETTER - CANADIAN ASSOCIATION OF SEXUAL ASSAULT CENTRES.** (THE NATIONAL NEWSLETTER.). **VFOAT** Les Nouvelles Nationales; Nouvelles Nationales. Newsletter. English. bm. Canadian Association of Sexual Assault Centres, 4-45 Kingsway, Vancouver BC V5T 3H7 Canada. **DD** 362.8/83/0971.

US
**NATIONAL REGISTRY OF COMMUNITY MENTAL HEALTH SERVICES.** **Added/Corp** National Council of Community Mental Health Centers (U.S.). (1985)-. English. be. $25.00. National Council of Community Mental Health Centers, 12300 Twinbrook Parkway, Suite 320, Rockville MD 20852. **Tel** (301)984-6200. **ED** Thomas R. Willis. **Circ:** 1,500.
**Desc:** Directory of Mental Health Centers, listing area served, services provided, satellite locations and key individuals.

US/0896-3002
**NATIONAL REPORT ON WORK & FAMILY.** [Natl. rep. work fam.]. **VFOAT** National Report on Work and Family. Vol. 1, No. 1 (Dec. 15, 1987)-. Periodical. English. bw. $528.00. Business Publishers Inc., 951 Pershing Drive, Silver Spring MD 20910-4464. **Tel** (301)587-6300, (800)274-0122, FAX (301)585-9075. **ED** Richard Hagan. **LC** HD4904.25; .N38. **DD** 306.3/6/05. **[CCC].**
**Desc:** Covers work and family issues, such as parental leave, elder care, care for sick children, flexible work time etc.

US/1059-4922
**NATIONAL SERVICE NEWSLETTER.** [Natl. serv. newsl.]. **Added/Corp** National Service Secretariat (U.S.). No. 1, Aug. (1966)-. Newsletter. English. sa. $10.00. 5140 Sherier Place NW, Washington DC 20016. **Tel** (202)244-5828. **ED** Donald J Eberly. **DD** 343. **Bk Rev. Circ:** 1,300 (ctrl).
**Desc:** Describes latest developments in youth services and conservation corps.

US/1045-0394
**NAVSO NEWS.** [NASVO news]. (1989)-. Periodical. English. mo. $20.00. NAVSO, PO Box 40460, St Petersburg FL 33743. **DD** 362.

US
**NBA FAMILY TALK.** (19??)-. English. sa. Free on request. National Benevolent Association, 11780 Borman Drive, Suite 200, St. Louis MO 63146. **Tel** (314)993-9000, FAX (314)993-9018. **ED** Arthur Buell. ctrl circ.
**Desc:** Prints stories about NBA care facilities and residents.

AT/0313-4133
**NCOSS NEWS.** **Main/Corp** Council of Social Service of New South Wales. English. Council of Social Services of New South Wales, 66 Albion Street, Surrey Hills, New South Wales, 2010 Australia. **Tel** 011 61 2 211 2599.

CN/0824-4820
**NCSA NEWSLETTER.** ***Ceased.*** [NCSA newsl.]. (April 18, 1984). Newsletter. English. bm. Native Counselling Services of Alberta, 9912-106 Street, Edmonton Alberta T5K 1C5 Canada. **Tel** (403)423-2141. **ED** Francis A Campbell. **DD** 362.5/8. Index available. **Bk Rev. Circ:** 350 (ctrl). ***Continues*** *Native Counselling Services of Alberta News, 0824-4820.*
**Desc:** An agency information tool designed to share information ideas regarding programs, people and community events with HCSA Staff and other interested individuals and agencies.

UK/0955-2170
**NCVO NEWS.** [NCVO news]. **VFOAT** National Council for Voluntary Organisations News. (1989)-. English. Ten times a year (except Jan. and Aug.). £25.00 volunteers and individuals; £50.00 statutory institutions; £15.00 local development agencies. National Council Voluntary Organisation, Regents Wharf 8 All Saints Street, London N1 9RL England. **Tel** 011 44 71 7136161, FAX 011 44 71 7136300, telex 817484. **ED** Anne Davies. **DD** 361.70941. **Bk Rev**, (Qty: 200-300). **Ad Acc, Adv Mgr:** Anne Hodgson. **Circ:** 2,700.
**Desc:** Reports on NCVO's work and on other issues affecting the voluntary sector.

US/1070-8316
**NEBRASKA JUVENILE COURT REPORT.** (NEBRASKA JUVENILE COURT REPORT / NEBRASKA CRIME COMMISSION.). [Neb. juv. court rep.]. **Added/Corp** Nebraska Commission on Law Enforcement and Criminal Justice. Statistical Analysis Center. **VFOAT** Juvenile Court Report. (198?)-. English. **DD** 364. ***Continues*** *Nebraska Commission on Law Enforcement and Criminal Justice. Juvenile Court Report, 0362-918X.*

NE/0166-4751
**NEDERLANDS TIJDSCHRIFT VOOR ERGOTHERAPIE.** [Ned. tijdschr. ergother.]. (1973)-. Periodical. Dutch. bm. Fl61.32 Netherlands; Fl73.11 other. Nve Pa Adm Centrum Netherlands, PO Box 500, 2600 AM Delft The Netherlands. **Tel** 011 015 123941. **UDC** 615.851.3. ***Continues*** *Nederlands Tijdschrift Voor Arbeids-Ergotherapie.*

JA
**NENKIN FUKUSHI JIGYODAN NEMPO.** **Main/Corp** Nenkin Fukushi Jigyodan. (1982)-. Japanese. Nenkin Fukushi Jigyodan, 4-1 Kasumigaseki 1-chome, Chiyoda-ku 100 Tokyo Japan. **LC** HD7227; .A525A. ***Formed by the union of*** *Gyomu Tokei* ***and*** *Gyomu Nempo.*

JA
**NENKIN KENKYU NENPO.** Vol. 1 published in 1979. Japanese. Nenkin Seido Kenkyu Kaihatsu Kikin, c/o Nenkin Kikin Sentra Shinjuku-ku, Tokyo-to 160 Japan. **LC** HD7227; .A23.

US/0897-9847
**NETWORK (CHARLOTTE, N.C.), THE.** (THE NETWORK : THE NEWSLETTER OF THE NORTH CAROLINA COALITION ON ADOLESCENT PREGNANCY.). [Network]. **Added/Corp** North Carolina Coalition on Adolescent Pregnancy. (198?)-. Periodical. English. qt. $15.00. North Carolina Coalition on Adolescent Pregnancy, 429B East Boulevard, Charlotte NC 28203. **Tel** (704)335-1313. **DD** 362.
**Ind/Abst** Law Office Inf. Serv.

US/1061-9615
**NETWORK CONNECTION.** **See** Religion and Theology.

CN/0844-2959
**NETWORK NEWS / NATIONAL DAY CARE RESEARCH NETWORK.** [Netw. news - Natl. Day Care Res. Netw.]. (Nov. 1984)-. Periodical. English. ir. Free. National Day Care Research Network, School of Child Care, University of Victoria, PO Box 1700, Victoria British Columbia V8W 2Y2 Canada. **DD** 362.7/12/0971. ***Continues*** *Network News and Information (National Day Care Research Network), 0844-2940.*

CN/0827-2417
**NETWORK (NIAGARA FALLS).** (NETWORK : NIAGARA'S HUMAN SERVICES NEWSLETTER.). [Network]. **VFOAT** Niagara's Human Services Newsletter. Vol. 1, No. 1 (Summer 1984)-. Newsletter. English. qt. Free. Information Niagara, 125 Welland Avenue, St. Catharine L2R 2N5 Ontario Canada. **Tel** (905)682-6611. **ED** Jean Chagnon, Steve Elson, Bev Goodman, and Ellen Gregory. **DD** 362/.9713/38. **Circ:** 2,000.
**Desc:** Niagara region Human services newsletter.

GW/0342-9857
**NEUE PRAXIS.** [Neue Prax.]. (1971)-. Academic Scholarly Publication. German. bm. DM120.00. Hermann Luchterhand Verlag, Postfach 2352, D 56513 Neuwied Germany. **Tel** 011 49 2631 8010. **LC** HV275; .N46. **[CCC].**
**Ind/Abst** Crim. Penol. Police Sci. Abstr.; EMBASE.

●US/1061-2157
**NEW CHOICES FOR RETIREMENT LIVING.** [New choices retire. living]. **VFOAT** Choices; New Choices. Vol. 32, No. 1 (Feb. 1992)-. Periodical. English. Ten times a year. $18.97. R D Publications, 28 West 23rd Street, New York NY 10010. **Tel** (800)365-5005, (212)366-8630. **(Subscription address:** CDS / SIFD Agency Control, 1901 Bell Avenue, Des Moines IA 50315.) **LC** HQ1060; .H36. **DD** 305. **CODEN** NCRLE9. available on microfilm and microfiche from University Microfilms International (UMI). Documents available from UMI Article Clearinghouse. ***Continues*** *New Choices for the Best Years, 1041-6277.*
**Desc:** An informative, up-to-date publication serving the active lifestyle of our growing population of mature adults. Lively articles on travel, medical news, fashion and finances. Plus leisure-time pursuits, entertaining and health recipes to try.
**Ind/Abst** Abr. Read. Guide Period. Lit. (Feb. 1992-); Acad. Abstr. Full Text Elite (Jan. 1989-); Acad. Abstr. (Jan. 1989-); Acad. Search (Jan. 1989-); AGRICOLA; Foods Adlibra (1992-); Gen. Period. Index (1992-); Mag. Artic. Summar. Elite (Jan. 1989-); Mag. Artic. Summar. Select (Jan. 1989-); Mag. Artic. Summar. CD-ROM (Jan. 1989-); Mag. Index Plus (1992-); Mag. Index. Sel. (1992-); Newsp. Period. Abstr. (1988-); Read. Guide Period. Lit.; Resource/One Ondisc (1992-); Mag. Index (?-?); Vocat. Search (Jan. 1989-).

US/0193-9416
**NEW DIRECTIONS FOR MENTAL HEALTH SERVICES.** [New dir. ment. health serv.]. (1979)-. Periodical. English. qt. $78.00 institutions; $56.00 individuals. Jossey Bass Inc., 350 Sansome Street, San Francisco CA 94104. **Tel** (415)433-1767, FAX (415)433-0499. **ED** H. Richard Lamb. **LC** RA790.A1; N43. **DD** 616.89/005. **NLM** W1 NE374E. **CODEN** NMHSEG. **Circ:** 500 (ctrl). available on microfilm and microfiche from University Microfilms International (UMI).
**Desc:** Describes new mental health treatment techniques and approaches. Offers guidance on providing effective services in light of recent social and legal developments.
**Ind/Abst** Abstr. Res. Pastor. Care Couns. (19??-); Index Med.; Psychol. Abstr. (1980-); PsycINFO; PsycLit.

●US/1072-172X
**NEW DIRECTIONS FOR PHILANTHROPIC FUNDRAISING.** (NEW DIRECTIONS FOR PHILANTHROPIC FUNDRAISING / SPONSORED BY THE FUND RAISING SCHOOL, INDIANA UNIVERSITY, CENTER ON PHILANTHROPY.). [New dir. philanthr. fundrais.]. **Added/Corp** Indiana University. Fund Raising School. No. 1 (Fall 1993)-. Periodical. English. qt. $79.00 institutions; $59.00 individuals. Jossey Bass Inc., 350 Sansome Street, San Francisco CA 94104. **Tel** (415)433-1767, FAX (415)433-0499. **DD** 361.

US/0164-7989
**NEW DIRECTIONS FOR PROGRAM EVALUATION.** [New dir. program eval.]. No. 1 (Spring 1978)-. Periodical. English. qt. $78.00 institutions; $56.00 individuals. Jossey Bass Inc., 350 Sansome Street, San Francisco CA 94104. **Tel** (415)433-1767, FAX (415)433-0499. **ED** William Shadish. **LC** H62.A1; N4. **DD** 361.6/1/072073. **NLM** W1 NE374ET. **Circ:** 600 (ctrl). available on microfilm and microfiche from University Microfilms International (UMI).
**Desc:** Outlines techniques and procedures for conducting useful evaluation studies of all types of programs, from educational curricular to welfare projects.
**Ind/Abst** Acad. Search (July 1993-); Contents Pages Educ.; Curr. Index J. Educ.; Curr. Lit. Fam. Plan. (19??-199?); Educ. Index (-1992); INFO-SOUTH Abstr.; Mag. Search; Soc. Plann. Policy Dev. Abstr.

CN/0712-2101
**NEW DIRECTIONS (WINNIPEG).** (NEW DIRECTIONS.). [New dir.]. Vol. 1, No. 1 (Oct. 1980)-. Periodical. English. bm. Free with membership. New Directions CAMR, 46-825 Sherbrooke Street, Winnipeg Manitoba R3A 1M5 Canada. **DD** 362.3/097127/4.

US/0277-996X
**NEW ENGLAND JOURNAL OF HUMAN SERVICES.** [New Engl. j. human serv.]. **VFOAT** Human Services. Vol. 1, Issue 1 (Winter 1981)-. Periodical. English. Four times a year (Seasonally). $24.00 (individuals); $44.00 (institutions). New England Journal of Human Services, PO Box 529, Canton MA 02021. **ED** W. Robert Curtis and Mark R. Yessian. **LC** HV1; .N45. **DD** 362/.974. **NLM** W1 NE387T. Index available. cum. index. **Bk Rev. Ad Acc. Circ:** 2,000. available on microfilm and microfiche from University Microfilms International (UMI).
**Desc:** Addresses human services policy and management issues from a broad perspective, taking into account social, political, and economic developments.
**Ind/Abst** Crim. Justice Abstr.; Hospit. Health Admin. Index; J. Plan. Lit.; PAIS Int. Print (1991-); Soc. Plann. Policy Dev. Abstr.; Soc. Work Abstr. (Spring, Summer 1987-) [Select. Cov.]; Sociol. Abstr.; Urban Aff. Abstr.

US/0896-6478
**NEW MEXICO PROGRESS, THE.** [N. M. prog.]. **Added/Corp** New Mexico School for the Deaf. New Mexico Asylum for the Deaf and Dumb. Vol. 1 (Mar. 1909)-. Periodical. English. Five times a year (during school year). Free. New Mexico School for the Deaf, 1060 Cerrillos Road, Sante Fe NM 87503. **Tel** (505)827-6747, (505)982-9756. **ED** Lester Graham. **LC** HV2561; .N63. **DD** 371. **Circ:** 900.
**Desc:** A newsletter intended to inform parents of the hearing impaired and others interested in the field, of news of the school and developments in the education of the hearing impaired.

US/0190-1168
**NEW SPIRIT.** Feb. 1979-. Periodical. English. mo. $10.00. National Center for Community Action, 1328 New York Avenue NW, Washington DC 20005. **LC** HV95; .N337A. **DD** 361.6/0973.
**Desc:** Vols. for Feb. 1979 include section: The National Center Reporter.

US/0191-6629
**NEW YORK PUBLIC LIBRARY DIRECTORY OF COMMUNITY SERVICES, THE.** ***Title Change.*** **Added/Corp** New York Public Library. **VFOAT** Directorio de Servicios para la Comunidad; Directory of Community Services. (1978)-?. Directory. English (Spanish). Community Information Project, Office of Adult Services, 8 East 40th Street, New York NY 10016. **LC** F128.18; .N37a. **DD** 917.47/0025. ***Split into*** *Directory of the Community Services (New York Public Library)* ***and*** *Directory of the Community Services (New York Public Library. Spanish. Directorio de Servicios para la Comunidad.*

●US
**NEW YORK STATE PLAN FOR COORDINATION OF TRAINING, EMPLOYMENT AND RELATED PROGRAMS.** **Added/Corp** New York State Job Training Partnership Council. (1992)-. English. be. ***Continues*** *Governor's Coordinaton and Special Services Plan for JTPA and Related Programs in New York State.... .*

US/1064-6493
**NEWS AND ISSUES (NEW YORK, N.Y.).** (NEWS AND ISSUES / NATIONAL CENTER FOR CHILDREN IN POVERTY, COLUMBIA UNIVERSITY SCHOOL OF PUBLIC HEALTH.). [News issues]. **Added/Corp** Columbia University. National Center for Children in Poverty. (Spring 1991)-. Periodical. English. Three times a year (Spring, Fall & Winter). Free. National Center for Children in Poverty, 154 Haven Avenue, New York NY 10032. **Tel** (212)927-8792, FAX (212)927-9162. **DD** 362.

US
**NEWS AND ROUND TABLE.** V. 1- 19 -. Periodical. English. bm. $25.00. United Neighborhood Ctrs Amer, 1319 F Street NW/Suite 603, Washington DC 20004. **Tel** (212)677-9600. **ED** Walter L Smart. **Bk Rev. Circ:** 1,200 (ctrl).
**Desc:** Articles related to the national organization and its local affiliates and other social welfare news.

US/1042-5160
**NEWS & VIEWS (PITTSBURGH, PA.).** **See** Environmental Issues-Pollution and Waste Management.

US/0736-1459
**NEWS - ASSISTANCE LEAGUE OF SOUTHERN CALIFORNIA.** (NEWS / ASSISTANCE LEAGUE OF SOUTHERN CALIFORNIA.). **Main/Corp** Assistance League of Southern California. Vol. 1, No. 1 (Mar. 1982)-. Periodical. English. qt. Assistance League of Southern California, 1370 North Street, Andrews Place, Los Angeles CA 90028. ***Continues*** *Assistance League News.*

CN/0225-0446
**NEWS FROM THE CENTRE - INSTITUTE FOR NONPROFIT ORGANIZATIONS.** [News centre - Inst. Nonprofit Organ.]. **Main/Corp** Institute for Nonprofit Organizations. Began publication in 1979 (V. 1, No. 4). Periodical. English. ir. Free to members. Institute for Nonprofit Organizations, 3rd Floor, 287 Macpherson Avenue, Toronto Ontario M4V 1A4. **DD** 361.7/63/0971. ***Continues*** *Management and Fund Raising Centre. News from the Centre, 0225-0470.*

II
**NEWS LETTER - INDIA (REPUBLIC). DEPT. OF SOCIAL WELFARE, THE.** **Main/Corp** India. Dept. of Social Welfare. (19??)-. Periodical. English. Room No 633/A Wing, Shastri Bhavan 110001 India. **LC** HV391; .D46a. **DD** 362/.954.

US/0028-9299
**NEWS OF THE WORLD'S CHILDREN (UNITED STATES COMMITTEE FOR UNICEF).** (NEWS OF THE WORLD'S CHILDREN.). Periodical. English. qt. US Committee for UNICEF, 331 East 38th Street, New York NY 10016. **Tel** (212)686-5522.

CN/1183-644X
**NEWS - ONTARIO. MINISTRY OF COMMUNITY AND SOCIAL SERVICES.** (NEWS.). [News - Ont., Minist. Community Soc. Serv.]. **Main/Corp** Ontario. Ministry of Community and Social Services. Vol. 1, No. 1 (April 1991)-. Periodical. English. mo. **DD** 361.6.

US
**NEWS / OXFAM AMERICA.** **Added/Corp** Oxfam America. (19??)-. Periodical. English. qt. Oxfam America, 115 Broadway, Boston MA 02116.
**Ind/Abst** Hum. Rights Intern. Rep.

AT/030-794X
**NEWSBEAT.** English. qt. Free. Sydney City Mission, 28 Regent Street, Chippendale 2008 Australia. **Tel** (02)212-6277, FAX 281-3854. **ED** Kenneth Harrison. **Circ:** 20,000 (ctrl).
**Desc:** Issues related magazine covering the social services and welfare of the Sydney City Mission and Mission Australia. Dealing with social issues and some case histories distributed among donors and those interested in the work of the organization for awareness.

CN/1184-1478
**NEWSLETTER / B.C. ALLIANCE CONCERNED WITH EARLY PREGNANCY AND PARENTHOOD.** [Newsl. - B.C. Alliance Concern. Early Pregnancy Parent.]. **Added/Corp** B.C. Alliance Concerned with Early Pregnancy and Parenthood. Vancouver YWCA. **VAT** Newsletter - British Columbia Alliance Concerned with Early Pregnancy and Parenthood. (Spring 1990)-. Newsletter. English. Three times a year. comes with membership. Vancouver YWCA, 580 Burrard Street, Vancouver British Columbia V6C 2K9 Canada. **Tel** (604)683-2531. **DD** 362.83/92/08352. ***Continues*** *Newsletter (B.C. Task Force on Teenage Pregnancy and Parenthood)., 0820-4713.*

CN/0712-2950
**NEWSLETTER (HUMANE SOCIETY OF OTTAWA-CARLETON).** (NEWSLETTER / THE HUMANE SOCIETY OF OTTAWA-CARLETON.). Newsletter. English. Three times a year. Free to Members. Humane Society of Ottawa-Carleton, 101 Champagne Avenue South, Ottawa Ontario K1S 4P3 Canada. **DD** 179/.3/06071383.

CN/1194-6180
**NEWSLETTER - INFANT FEEDING ACTION COALITION.** (NEWSLETTER / INFACT CANADA.). [Newsl. - Infant Feed. Action Coalit.]. **Added/Corp** Infant Feeding Action Coalition. **VFOAT** INFACT Canada Newsletter. (1981)-. Periodical. English. qt. $30.00. INFACT Canada, 10 Trinity Square, Toronto Ontario M5G 1B1 Canada. **Tel** (416)595-9819, FAX (416)598-0292. **ED** Elisabeth Sterken. **DD** 649/.3. **Circ:** 5,000.

CN/0229-8759
**NEWSLETTER - MONTREAL JOINT HOSPITAL INSTITUTE.** (NEWSLETTER.). [Newsl. - Montr. Jt. Hosp. Inst.]. **Main/Corp** Montreal Joint Hospital Institute. Vol. 1 No. 1 (May 1977)-. Newsletter. English. mo. Free. Montreal Joint Hospital Institute, 1110 Pine Street West, Montreal Quebec H3A 1A3. **DD** 362.1/1/09714281.

CN/0821-6509
**NEWSLETTER - NATIONAL ASSOCIATION OF FRIENDSHIP CENTRES.** (NAFC NEWSLETTER.). [Newsl. - Natl. Assoc. Friendsh. Cent.]. **Main/Corp** National Association of Friendship Centres. **VAT** National Association of Friendship Centres Newsletter. Newsletter. English. mo. National Association of Friendship Centres, Suite 3, 200 Cooper Street, Ottawa Ontario K2P 0G1 Canada. **DD**

362.8/497071/06071.
**Desc:** Information update/news of interest monthly to membership.

US/0745-3531
**NEWSLETTER - NATIONAL ASSOCIATION OF SOCIAL WORKERS. WASHINGTON STATE CHAPTER.** (NEWSLETTER / NASW, WASHINGTON STATE CHAPTER). **Main/Corp** National Association of Social Workers. Washington State Chapter. **VFOAT** NASW Newsletter, Washington State Chapter; NASW Newsletter. (19??)-. Newsletter. English. qt. $15.00. **ED** Lucy Norman de Sanchez. **Ad Acc. Circ:** 100,000.
**Desc:** The official newspaper of NASW, is a compendium of current events in social work and related fields.

CN/0229-2742
**NEWSLETTER / NIAGARA CHILDREN'S SERVICES COMMITTEE.** [Newsl. - Niagara Child. Serv. Comm.]. **Main/Corp** Niagara Children's Services Committee. Vol. 1, 1 (Oct. 1979)-. Newsletter. English. qt. Free. Niagara Children's Services Committee, 205 King Street, St. Catharines Ontario L2R 3J5. **DD** 362.7/06/071338.

CN/0712-3132
**NEWSLETTER (OPEN DOOR SOCIETY OF OTTAWA).** (NEWSLETTER / THE OPEN DOOR SOCIETY OF OTTAWA, INC.). [Newsl. - Open Door Soc. Ottawa]. Newsletter. English. Open Door Society, Ottawa Branch, 1370 Bank Street, Ottawa Ontario K1H 7Y3 Canada. **DD** 362.7/34.

CN/0823-7999
**NEWSLETTER (S.U.C.C.E.S.S.).** (NEWSLETTER / S.U.C.C.E.S.S. : UNITED CHINESE COMMUNITY ENRICHMENT SERVICES SOCIETY.). [Newsl. - S.U.C.C.E.S.S.]. **VFOAT** S.U.C.C.E.S.S. Newsletter. No. 1-. Newsletter. English (Chinese). qt. Free. S U C C E S S, 449 East Hastings Street, Vancouver British Columbia V6A 1P5 Canada. **DD** 362.8/49510711/006071133.

US/0560-3870
**NEWSLETTER-SOCIAL WELFARE HISTORY GROUP.** **Main/Corp** Social Welfare History Group. No. 1 (1956)-. Periodical. English. Three times a year (Apr., Aug., Dec.). $10.00. East Carolina University / Social Work, Ragsdale 134, Greenville NC 27858. **Tel** (919)757-4208, FAX (919)962-0890. **ED** Gary R. Lowe. **Bk Rev**, (Qty: 1-2). **Circ:** 280.

US
**NEWSLETTER - TEXAS UNITED COMMUNITY SERVICES.** **Main/Corp** Texas United Community Services, Inc. Newsletter. English. Texas United Community Services, PO Box 15164, Austin TX 78761.

CN/0708-3599
**NEWSLETTER / U.N.B. TEMPERANCE UNION.** **Main/Corp** U.N.B. Temperance Union. **VAT** U.N.B. Temperance Union Newsletter; University of New Brunswick Temperance Union Newsletter; Newsletter - University of New Brunswick Temperance Union. Newsletter. English. ir. $1.00 to members. UNB Temperance Union, c/o Department of History, University of New Brunswick, Fredericton New Brunswick Canada. **DD** 362.2/92/0671551.

AU
**NIEDEROSTERREICHISCHE SOZIALHILFE UND JUGENDWOHLFAHRTSPFLEGE.** **Main/Corp** Lower Austria (Austria). (1974)-. German. an. Amt der Niederosterreichischen, Landesregierung Pressedienst Statistik, Herrengasse 11-13, 1014 Vienna Austria. **Tel** 02236/84986. **(Subscription address:** Amt der no Landesregierung, AB R/2 Sachgehiet Statistik, A-2344 Enzersdorf Sudstadtzentrum, 4/4 Austria.**)** **LC** HV259.A9; A13. **Ad Acc. Circ:** 200. ***Continues*** *Niederosterreichische Fursorgestatistik.*

US/8756-601X
**NIH ALMANAC.** **See** Public Health and Safety.

JA
**NIHON FUKUSHI NENKAN.** (1977)-. Periodical. Japanese. ¥5500. Rippu Shobo, 9-5 Kudan Kita 1 chome, Chiyodaku Tokyoto 102 Japan. **LC** HV413.A2; N54.

DK
**NOGET OM SOCIALE FORHOLD, ADMINISTRATION OG POLITISKE INSTITUTIONER.** Danish. an. Aalborg Universitetsforlag, Postbox 159, 9100 Aalborg Denmark. **LC** HN547; .N64.

US/1066-1018
**NON-PROFIT LEGAL & TAX LETTER.** **See** Public Administration-Public Finance and Taxation.

US/0550-8401
**NON-PROFIT ORGANIZATION TAX LETTER.** ***Title Change.*** [Non-profit organ. tax lett.]. **Added/Corp** Organization Management, Inc. (19??)-(199?). Periodical. English. ir (18 per year). Organization Management Inc., 13231 Pleasantview Lane, Fairfax VA 22033. **Tel** (703)968-7039, FAX (703)818-0259. **(Subscription address:** PO Box 944, 7600 Carter Court, Bethesda MD 20817**)** **ED** George D Webster, Hugh Webster, and John W Hazard Jr. **LC** KF6449.A73; N6. **DD** 343.73052. ***Continues*** *Non-Profit Tax Letter.* ***Continued by*** *Non-Profit Legal & Tax Letter, 1066-1018.*
**Desc:** Complete reporting of non-profit development. Written for non-profit organizations, their management and professional advisors.

●US/1060-7889
**NONPROFIT ALMANAC.** [Nonprofit alm.]. **Added/Corp** Independent Sector (Firm). (1992-1993)-. Periodical. English. ir. $49.95 (paper copy). Jossey Bass Inc., 350 Sansome Street, San Francisco CA 94104. **Tel** (415)433-1767, FAX (415)433-0499. **LC** HD2769.2.U6; D55. **DD** 361.7/0973/021. ***Continues*** *Dimensions of the Independent Sector, 0887-9893.*
**Desc:** Includes state-by-state data on nonprofits, as well as financial profiles of nonprofit organizations classified into areas.

US/0899-7640
**NONPROFIT AND VOLUNTARY SECTOR QUARTERLY.** [Nonprofit volunt. sect. q.]. **Added/Corp** Association of Voluntary Action Scholars (U.S.). Vol. 18, No. 1 (Spring 1989)-. Periodical. English. Four times a year (Apr., July, Oct., Dec.). $88.00 institutions; $58.00 individuals. Jossey Bass Inc., 350 Sansome Street, San Francisco CA 94104. **Tel** (415)433-1767, FAX (415)433-0499. **LC** HV1; .J63. **DD** 361.7/05. **CODEN** NVSQEQ. available on microfilm and microfiche from University Microfilms International (UMI). ***Continues*** *Journal of Voluntary Action Research, 0094-0607.*
**Ind/Abst** AGRICOLA [Select. Cov.]; Int. Bibliogr. Sociol.; J. Plan. Lit.; Soc. Plann. Policy Dev. Abstr.

US/1051-9602
**NONPROFIT MANAGEMENT STRATEGIES.** [Nonprofit managem. strateg.]. **Added/Corp** Taft Group (Rockville, Md.). (19??)-. Periodical. English. mo. $150.00. Taft Group, 835 Penobscott Building, Customer Service, Detroit MI 48226. **Tel** (800)877-8238, FAX (313)961-6083. **(Subscription address:** Taft Group, PO Box 71701, Chicago, IL 60694; telephone: (800)877-8238 ext. 1716**)** **DD** 658. ***Continues*** *Taft Nonprofit Executive, 0882-5521.*
**Desc:** An extensive review/summary of over 75 key resources for non-profit executives and volunteers.

US
**NONPROFIT WORLD.** **Added/Corp** Society for Nonprofit Organizations (U.S.). Vol. 4, No. 1 (Jan./Feb. 1986)-. Periodical. English. Six times a year (Jan., Mar., May, July, Sept., Nov.). $79.00 US; $99.00 Canada, Western Hemisphere and Europe; $104.00 other. Society for Nonprofit Organization, 6314 Odana Road/Suite 1, c/o K. Burnham, Madison WI 53719. **Tel** (608)274-9777, (800)424-7367, FAX (608)274-9978. **ED** Jill Muehrcke. **LC** HD62.6; .N69. **DD** 361.7/63/05. Index available. cum. index. **Bk Rev**, (Qty: 6). **Ad Acc**, **Adv Mgr:** Dave Hilsenhoff, **Tel** (608)274-9777. **Pr Rev. Circ:** 15,000. available on microfilm and microfiche from University Microfilms International (UMI); available on an online database (file 15/Full-Text) from DIALOG. Documents available from UMI Article Clearinghouse. ***Continues*** *Nonprofit World Report, 8755-7614.*
**Desc:** Contains original articles and regular columns on all aspects of running an effective nonprofit organization; focuses on leadership and management issues, including fund raising, income generation, legal advice and legal updates, to provide a forum for exchange of information on strengthening and increasing productivity in nonprofit organizations.
**Ind/Abst** ABI/INFORM Glob. Ed.; ABI Inform Ondisc (Jan. 1986-); UMI ABI/Inform--Bus. Period. Ondisc (Nov. 1987-) [Full Txt.].

NO/0333-1342
**NORDISK SOSIALT ARBEID.** **Added/Corp** Nordiske Sosionomforbunds Samarbeidskomite. Vol. 1 (1981)-. Periodical. Multiple languages (Norwegian, Danish and Swedish; summaries and/or abstracts in English and Finnish). qt. Kr450.00, $76.00. Scandinavian University Press, PO Box 2959 Toeyen, N 0608 Oslo 6 Norway. **Tel** 011 47 2 2575400, FAX 011 47 2 2575353, telex 71896 UROR N. **(Subscription address:** Scandinavian University Press, 200 Meacham Ave., Elmont NY 11003.**)** **ED** Gret Stang, Sven Hessle, Gitte Vesterlund, Synnoeve Karvinen, Elisabet Bjarnadottir. **LC** HV333; .N73. **Circ:** 2,000.
**Desc:** Professional journal for social workers in all the Scandinavian countries.

US/0091-1070
**NORTH DAKOTA STATE PLAN FOR DEVELOPMENTAL DISABILITIES SERVICES AND FACILITIES CONSTRUCTION.** **Main/Corp** North Dakota. State Dept. of Health. English. North Dakota State Department of Health & Consolidated Laboratories, 600 East Boulevard Avenue, Bismarck ND 58505. **Tel** (701)224-2372, FAX (701)224-3000. **LC** HV3006.N9; N6A. **DD** 362.3/09784.

CN/0316-6953
**NORTH WIND (VANCOUVER).** (THE NORTH WIND.). V. 1- Jan. 1975-. English. The North Wind, PO Box 65583, Vancouver British Columbia V5N 5K5 Canada. **DD** 367/.9711/33.

IT
**NOTIZIE STATISTICHE / ISTITUTO NAZIONALE DELLA PREVIDENZA SOCIALE.** **Added/Corp** Istituto Nazionale della Previdenza Sociale (Italy) Istituto Nazionale della Previdenza Sociale (Italy). Servizio Statistico Attuariale. (19??)-. Periodical. Italian. ir. Free on request. Istituto Nazionale della Previdenza Sociale, Via Ciro il Grande 21, CP 10024, 00144 Rome Italy. **Tel** 011 39 6 59054090. **LC** HD7182; .N67. **DD** 368.4/00945/021.

CN/0821-0381
**NOUS TOUTES.** (NOUS TOUTES : BULLETIN DE L'ASSOCIATION DE GARDIENNAGE DE MONTREAL-NORD.). [Nous toutes]. Bulletin. French. bm. Free. L'Association De Gardiennage De Montreal-Nord, 6338 Rue Fiset, Montreal-Nord, Quebec H1G 2B2 Canada. **DD** 362.7/12/06071428.

BE/0378-2735
**NOUVELLES - CICIAMS.** **See** Religion and Theology-Catholicism.

CN/0382-7992
**NOUVELLES DES PETITS FRERES.** First issue in 1972. Periodical. French (English). sa. Les Petits Freres des Pauvres, 4624 rue Garnier, Montreal Quebec H2J 3S7 Canada. **DD** 362.6/3/09714281.

CN/1183-6458
**NOUVELLES - ONTARIO. MINISTERE DES SERVICES SOCIAUX ET COMMUNAUTAIRES.** (NOUVELLES.). [Nouv. - Ont., Minist. serv. soc. communaut.]. **Main/Corp** Ontario. Ministere des Services Sociaux et Communautaires. Vol. 1, No 1 (Apr 1991)-. Periodical. French. ir. free. Commission des Doits Personne, 360 rue St. Jaques, Montreal, Quebec H2Y 1P5, Canada. **Tel** (514)873-5146. **DD** 361.6.

CN/0843-4468
**NOUVELLES PRATIQUES SOCIALES.** [Nouv. prat. soc.]. Vol. 1, No 1 (1988)-. Periodical. French. Twice a year. 25.23Can$ (institutions), 17.76Can$ (individuals) Canada 33.00Can$ other. Les Presses de L'Universite de Quebec, 2875 Boulevard Laurier, St. Foy Quebec G1V 2M3 Canada. **Tel** (418)657-4390 Ext. 2860. **DD** 361/.9714.
**Ind/Abst** Point Repere (1991-).

●US
**NRCCSA NEWS / NATIONAL RESOURCE CENTER ON CHILD SEXUAL ABUSE OF THE NATIONAL CENTER ON CHILD ABUSE AND NEGLECT.** **Added/Corp** National Resource Center on Child Sexual Abuse (U.S.). **VAT** National Resource Center on Child Sexual Abuse News. Vol. 1, No. 1 (May/June 1992)-. Periodical. English. bm. Free. National Resource Center on Child Sexual Abuse (NRCCSA), 107 Lincoln Street, Huntsville AL 35801.

US/0196-3295
**NSFRE JOURNAL.** ***Title Change.*** [Natl. Soc. Fund Rais. Exec. j.]. **Main/Corp** National Society of Fund Raising Executives. **VAT** National Society of Fund Raising Executives Journal. Periodical. English. National Society of Fund Raising, 1101 King Street/Suite 3000, Alexandria VA 22314. **Tel** (703)684-0410, FAX (703)684-0540. **LC** HG177; .N37B. **DD** 658.1/5224. ***Continued by*** *Journal (National Society of Fund Raising Executives), 1056-2443.*

US
**NURSING HOME PRACTITIONER.** (19??)-. English. bm. $50.00 (one year), $75.00 (two year) US; $55.00 (one year), $85.00 (two year) Canada and Mexico; $60.00 (one year), $95.00 (two year) other. Medquest Communications Inc., 629 Euclid Avenue, Suite 500, Cleveland OH 44114. **Tel** (216)522-9700. **ED** Richard Peck.
**Desc:** Focusing on the needs and interests of long-term care medical staff, especially physicians and pharmacists. Also covers reimbursement, medicolegal exposure, residents' quality of life, and other topics.

CN/0846-0701
**NWT HELP DIRECTORY.** (THE NWT HELP DIRECTORY / PRODUCED BY THE CANADIAN MENTAL HEALTH ASSOCIATION, NWT DIVISION IN CO-OPERATION WITH ALCOHOL, DRUGS AND COMMUNITY MENTAL HEALTH, DEPARTMENT OF SOCIAL SERVICES, GOVERNMENT OF THE NORTHWEST TERRITORIES.). [NWT help dir.]. **Added/Corp** Northwest Territories. Alcohol, Drugs and Community Mental Health. Canadian Mental Health

Association. NWT Division. **VFOAT** Help, Northwest Territories Directory. **VAT** Northwest Territories Help Directory. (1991)-. Directory. English. **DD** 362.2/025/7192.

CN
**OBJECTIFS DANS LE DOMAINE DES AFFAIRES SOCIALES ET DE LA FAMILLE, LES.** **Main/Corp** Family and Social Affairs Council. 1973/74-. French. Family and Social Affairs Council, 2700 Boul Laurier, Sainte-Foy Quebec Canada. **LC** HV700.C3; F36A. **DD** 362/.971.

US/0894-2811
**OCCUPATIONAL AND ENVIRONMENTAL MEDICINE REPORT, THE.** (THE OCCUPATIONAL AND ENVIRONMENTAL MEDICINE REPORT : THE OEM REPORT.). [Occup. environ. med. rep.]. **VFOAT** OEM Report. Vol. 1, No. 1 (Apr. 1987)-. Periodical. English. Twelve times a year. $149.00 one year; $265.00 two years. OEM Information Inc., 181 Elliott Street, Suite 814, Beverly MA 01915-3080. **Tel** (800)533-8046 (508)921-7300, FAX (508)921-0304. **ED** Robert J. McCunney M.D., M.P.H. **DD** 362. Index available (Bound in 1st issue, in Dec.). cum. index. **Bk Rev**, (Qty: 10). **Circ:** 1,000.
**Desc:** This covers articles in occupational and environmental medicine.

CN/0229-8023
**ODYSSEE (MONTREAL).** (L'ODYSSEE : JOURNAL DES USAGERS DE LA MAISON ST-JACQUES.). [Odyssee]. Periodical. French. Free. Usagers de la Maison, St-Jacques 1629 rue St-Hubert, Montreal Quebec H2L 3Z1 Canada. **DD** 362.2/0425/09714281.

CN/0702-8024
**OEIL DE FEU.** **Added/Corp** Comite Provincial des Malades. Vol. 1, (Jan. 1976)-. Periodical. French. Five times a year. $8.00. Comite Provincial des Malades, CP 458 Complexe Desjardins, Montreal Quebec H5B 1B5 Canada. **Tel** (514)842-3991. **DD** 362.1/1/062714.

CN/0821-7033
**OEIL OUVERT.** (L'OEIL OUVERT / ASSOCIATION D'ENTRAIDE POUR LE BIEN-ETRE EMOTIONNEL.). [Oeil ouvert]. Periodical. French. mo. Free. Association d'Entraide pour le Bien-Etre Emotionnel du Quebec, Montreal Quebec H4J 2M8 Canada. **DD** 362.2/06/0714. ctrl circ.

FR
**OFFICIEL DES COMITES D'ENTERPRISE ET SERVICES SOCIAUX, L'.** (19??)-. Periodical. French. Eleven times a year. 450.00F France; 550.00F other. Editions Garon, 60 Rue du Landy, 93210 Plaine Saint Denis, France. **Tel** 011 33 1 48299959.

US
**OHA LAW JOURNAL.** **Added/Corp** United States. Social Security Administration. Office of Hearings and Appeals. **VAT** Office of Hearings and Appeals Law Journal. Vol. 1, No. 1 (Nov. 1990)-. Government Publication. English. qt. $16.00 US; $20.00 other. Superintendent of Documents, US Government Printing Office, Washington DC 20402. **Tel** (202)275-3328, FAX (202)786-2377. **LC** K15; .H48. **DD** 344.73/02; 347.3042. ***Continues*** *OHA Law Reporter, 0898-7637.*
**Ind/Abst** Index Leg. Period. (1992-).

●US/1064-1793
**O'KEEFE'S GUIDE. MID-ATLANTIC REGIONAL DIRECTORY.** [O'Keefe's guide. Mid-Atl. reg. dir.]. **VFOAT** Mid-Atlantic Regional Directory. (1992)-. Directory. English. Philip O'Keefe Co., Inc., 2200 Sansom Street, Philadelphia PA 19108. **DD** 363.

RU/0131-2618
**OKHRANA TRUDA I SOTSIALNOE STRAKHOVANIE.** **See** Industrial Health and Safety.

CN/0712-3388
**OLD AGE SECURITY, GUARANTEED INCOME SUPPLEMENT, SPOUSE'S ALLOWANCE.** **See** Insurance.

CN/0821-7882
**ON RECORD (TORONTO).** (ON RECORD.). [On rec.]. **Added/Corp** Family Service Association of Metropolitan Toronto. (196?)-. Periodical. English. Three times a year. Free. Family Service Association of Metropolitan Toronto, 22 Wellesley Street East, Toronto Ontario M4Y 1G3 Canada. **Tel** (416)922-3126. **ED** Maria J Muszynska and Margery Griffiths. **DD** 362.8/2/09713541. **Circ:** 2,500 (ctrl). ***Continues*** *Neighbourhood Workers Association. N W A on Record.*
**Desc:** Focuses on current affairs in the social service sector, ie. housing, hunger, poverty, income, daycare, etc., as they affect our clients.

●US/1061-9291
**ON TAP (MORGANTOWN, W.VA.).** (ON TAP: DRINKING WATER NEWS FOR AMERICA'S SMALL COMMUNITES: A PUBLICATION OF THE NATIONAL DRINKING WATER CLEARINGHOUSE, SPONSORED BY FARMERS HOME ADMINISTRATION.). [On tap]. **Added/Corp** United States. Farmers Home Administration. National Drinking Water Clearinghouse (U.S.). Vol. 1, Issue 1 (Mar. 1992)-. Periodical. English. qt. Free. West Virginia University Water Research Institute, Morgantown WV 26506. **DD** 363.

CN/0827-8717
**ON YOUR OWN, A DIRECTORY FOR WOMEN.** [On your own dir. women]. Sept. 1982-. Directory. English. an. $0.50 each volume. Young Women's Christian Association of Metropolitan Toronto, 80 Woodlawn Avenue East, Toronto Ontario M4T 1C1 Canada. **Tel** (416)961-8100. **DD** 362.7/93/025713541.

CN/0827-8725
**ON YOUR OWN, A DIRECTORY FOR YOUNG MEN.** [On your own dir. young men]. Sept. 1983-. Directory. English. an. $0.50 each volume. Young Women's Christian Association of Metropolitan Toronto, 80 Woodlawn Avenue East, Toronto Ontario M4T 1C1 Canada. **Tel** (416)961-8100. **ED** Rochelle Rabinowicz. **DD** 362.7/92/025713541.
**Desc:** Directory of services for young men on their own in Toronto.

CN/1187-0389
**ONTARIO SOCIAL ACTION NEWSLETTER, THE.** [Ont. soc. action newsl.]. **Added/Corp** Multiple Sclerosis Society of Canada. Ontario Division. Vol. 1 No. 2 (Jan. 1991)-. Newsletter. English. Multiple Sclerosis Society of Canada, Ontario Division, 250 Bloor Street East Suite 1000, Toronto Ontario M4W 3P9 Canada. **Tel** (416)922-6065, FAX (416)922-7538. **DD** 362.1. ***Continues*** *MS Ontario Social Ation Newsletter., 1187-0370.*

CN/0381-1522
**ORGANISATION POPULAIRE.** V. 1- Feb. 1975-. Periodical. French. mo. Association Quebecoise pour la Defense des Retraites et Pre-Retraites, 1850 rue Bercy Bureau/Suite 113A, Montreal Quebec H2K 2V2 Canada. **DD** 362.5/09714/281. ***Supersedes*** *Droit Populaire.*

US
**ORS NOTE.** **Added/Corp** United States. Social Security Administration. Office of Research and Statistics. (1987)-. Periodical. English. ***Continues*** *ORSIP Note.*

PL/0209-2182
**ORZECZNICTWO SADU NAJWYZSZEGO. IZBA CYWILNA I ADMINISTRACYJNA ORAZ IZBA PRACY I UBEZPIECZEN SPOECZNYCH.** **Main/Corp** Poland. Sad Najwyzszy. **Added/Corp** Poland. Sad Najwyzszy. Izba Cywilna i Administracyjna. Poland. Sad Najwyzszy. Izba Pracy i Ubezpieczen Spoecznych. **VFOAT** Izba Cywilna i Administracyjna oraz Izba Pracy i Ubezpieczen Spoecznych. (19??)-. Polish. mo. $78.00. **(Subscription address:** ARS Polona, PO Box 1001, 00068 Warsaw Poland.**)** **LC** KKP496.3 Db .O79.

US/0888-5508
**OSERS NEWS IN PRINT.** (OSERS NEWS IN PRINT / OFFICE OF SPECIAL EDUCATION AND REHABILITATIVE SERVICES, U.S. DEPARTMENT OF EDUCATION.). [OSERS news print]. **Added/Corp** United States. Office of Special Education and Rehabilitative Services. **VFOAT** O!. **VAT** Office of Special Education and Rehabilitative Services News in Print. Vol. 1, No. 1 (Autumn 1985)-. Periodical. English. Four times a year. Free. OSERS, 330 C Street, SWOFC of Special Education, Washington DC 20202. **Tel** (202)205-8723. **DD** 362. **Bk Rev**. ***Continues*** *Programs for the Handicapped, 0565-2804.*
**Desc:** Contains information on federal and state initiatives in disability field.

AU
**OSTERREICHISCHE SOZIALVERSICHERUNG, DIE.** 1971-. German. Hauptverband der Osterreichischen Sozialversicherungstrager, Kundmanngasse 21, 1030 Vienna Austria. **LC** HD7169; .O35. **DD** 368.4/009436. ***Supersedes in part*** *Jahrbuch der Osterreichischen Sozialversicherung.*

CN/0700-995X
**OTTAWA NEWSLETTER.** **Main/Corp** Canadian Loyalists' Association. No. 1- 197--. Newsletter. English. C L A Newsletter, PO Box 3084 Station C, Ottawa Ontario K1Y 3B5 Canada. **DD** 369/.2/71.

US/0899-9333
**OURS (MINNEAPOLIS, MINN.).** ***Title Change.*** (OURS.). [Ours]. (1969)-(19??). Periodical. English. Six times a year (Jan., Mar., May, July, Sept., Nov.). Adoptive Families of America Inc., 3333 Highway 100 North, Minneapolis MN 55422. **Tel** (612)353-4829, (800)372-3300, FAX (612)535-7808. **ED** Jolene L. Roehlkepartain. **DD** 362. Index available (bound in issue). **Bk Rev**, (Qty: 6). **Ad Acc**, **Adv Mgr:** Sue Slominski. **Circ:** 15,000. ***Continues*** *News of Ours.* ***Continued by*** *Adoptive Families, 1076-1020.*
**Desc:** A practical adoption magazine that provides problem solving assistance and information about the challenges of adoption to members of adoptive and prospective adoptive families.

US/0737-5131
**PAEDOVITA.** [Paedovita]. **Added/Corp** Eterna International (Organization). Vol. 1, No. 1 (Jan. 1984)-. Periodical. English. Four times a year. Price varies. Eterna Press, PO Box 157941, Chicago IL 60615. **Tel** (312)969-0318. **ED** Stephen B. Parrish. **DD** 362. **NLM** W1; PA267.
**Ind/Abst** Int. Nurs. Index (Vol. 1, No. 1, 1984-); PsycINFO.

US/0031-0336
**PALESTINE REFUGEES TODAY.** **Added/Corp** United Nations Relief and Works Agency for Palestine Refugees in the Near East. (19??)-. English (Arabic, French, German and Spanish). sa. Free. United Nations Relief and Works Agency, Vienna International Centre, PO Box 700, A-1400 Vienna Austria. **Tel** FAX 43-1-237283, telex 135310 UNRA A. **ED** Lynn Failing. **LC** HV640.5.A6; P36. **Bk Rev. Circ:** 12,500.
**Desc:** Describes living conditions of Palestine refugees in Jordan, Lebanon, Syria, West Bank and Gaza; covers the work of UNRWA in providing health, education and welfare services to refugees in these areas.

US/0092-8720
**PAMPHLET - DEPARTMENT OF EMPLOYMENT AND SOCIAL SERVICES (BALTIMORE).** (PAMPHLET.). **Main/Corp** Maryland. Dept. of Employment and Social Services. English. Department of Employment and Social Services / Maryland, 1315 Saint Paul Street, Baltimore MD 21202. **LC** KFM1549.A73; E43. **DD** 344/.752/03.

CN/0824-1341
**PAPER - PACIFIC GROUP FOR POLICY ALTERNATIVES.** (PAPER.). [Pap. - Pac. Group Policy Altern.]. No. P-84-1-. Monographic series. English. Price varies per volume. Pacific Group for Policy Alternatives, 22 East 8th Avenue, Vancouver British Columbia V5T 1R4 Canada. **DD** 361.6/1/09711.

US/0890-3859
**PARENTING FOR PEACE AND JUSTICE NETWORK : [NEWSLETTER].** [Parent. Peace Justice Netw.]. **Added/Corp** Parenting for Peace and Justice Network. Institute for Peace and Justice (U.S.). **VFOAT** Parenting for Peace and Justice Network Newsletter; Parenting for Peace and Justice; Parenting for Peace & Justice Network Newsletter; PPJN Newsletter. (19??)-. Periodical. English. Six times a year. $25.00. Institute for Peace and Justice, 4144 Lindell Boulevard, Suite 221, St Louis MO 63108. **Tel** (314)533-4445. **DD** 361.

CN/1191-1727
**PARENTS DE COEUR.** [Parents coeur]. **Added/Corp** Hopital General de Montreal. Departement de Sante Communautaire. Centre de Services Sociaux Ville Marie. **VFOAT** Parents at Heart. Vol. 1, No 1 (Winter 1991)-. Periodical. French (English). qt. Free. Hopital General de Montreal, Depratement de Sante Communautaire, Bureau 300-A, 980 Rue Guy, Montreal Quebec H3H 2K3 Canada. **DD** 362.7/33/05.

US/1041-3243
**PBI EXCHANGE.** ***Title Change.*** [PBI exch.]. **Added/Corp** American Bar Association. Consortium on Legal Services and the Public. Private Bar Involvement Project (American Bar Association). **VFOAT** Exchange. **VAT** Private Bar Involvement Exchange. Vol. 6, No. 1 (Spring 1988)-Vol. 11, No. 1 (1993). Periodical. English. qt. American Bar Association, 750 North Lake Shore Drive, Chicago IL 60611. **Tel** (312)988-5522, (312)988-5241, FAX (312)988-5528, telex 270593. **LC** KF336.A3; P33. **DD** 347.73/017/05; 347.3071705. ***Continues*** *PBI Activation Exchange, 0737-7614.* ***Merged with*** *PBI Bulletin Board, 1055-0585* ***to form*** *ABA Center for Pro Bono Exchange, 1041-3243.*

US/0195-5926
**PEDIATRIC SOCIAL WORK.** **See** Medical Science and Technology-Pediatrics.

IO/0126-3692
**PELITA BPKS.** **Main/Corp** Balai Penelitian Kesejahteraan Sosial. **VAT** Pelita Balai Penelitian Kesejahteraan Sosial. Periodical. Indonesian (English). bm. free. Balai Penelitian Kesejahteraan Sosial, Tromolpos 65, Yogyakarta Indonesia. **Tel** 3265. **ED** Y B Suparlan. **LC** HV11; .B28A. **Bk Rev. Circ:** 300 (ctrl).
**Desc:** Social science, social work, family, marriage, women, children and youth, humanities, etc.

IO
**PENELITIAN MASALAH KESEJAHTERAAN SOSIAL ANAK PROPINSI JAWA BARAT.** **Added/Corp** Indonesia. Kantor Statistik Propinsi Jawa Barat. (1982)-. Indonesian. **LC** HV800.I56; J386.

# Sociology —Social Services and Welfare

MY
**PENITENTES, LOS.** Periodical. Spanish. Editores Mexicanos Asociados, Lago Chalco No 156, Mexico 17 D F Mexico. **ED** Francisco Ochoa Gonzalez.

IO
**PENYULUH SOSIAL. Added/Corp** Indonesia. Direktorat Penyuluhan dan Bimbingan Sosial. Direktorat Bimbingan dan Penyuluhan Sosial. **VFOAT** Majalah Penyuluh Sosial. (Oct./Nov. 1972)-. Indonesian. ir. Direktorat Jenderal Bira Sosial, Jl Ir H Juanda 36, Jakarta Indonesia. **LC** HV403; .P44. **Continues** Penjuluh Sosial.

US/0145-2932
**PEOPLE (RALEIGH).** (PEOPLE.). Periodical. English. qt. 325 North Salisbury Street, Raleigh NC 27611. **LC** HV86. **DD** 362/.9756.

US/1047-6598
**PEOPLE SEARCHING NEWS.** (PEOPLE SEARCHING NEWS : A REFERENCE MAGAZINE FOR ADOPTION, GENEALOGICAL & MISSING PERSON SEARCHES.). [People search. news]. **VFOAT** PSN. Vol. 1, No. 1 (Oct. 1986)-. Periodical. English. qt (Jan., Apr., July, Oct.). $20.00 US; $29.50 Canada; $39.00 other. JE Carlson & Associates, PO Box 22611, Fort Lauderdale FL 33335. **Tel** (305)370-7100. **DD** 362.

US/0094-8462
**PEOPLE (ST. PAUL).** (PEOPLE.). V. 25, No. 3/4- Winter 1973/74-. Periodical. English. qt. Centennial Office Building, St Paul MN 55155. **LC** HV86; .M67487. **DD** 361.6/2/09776. **Formed by the union of** Minnesota Mental Health Mental Retardation Newsletter, 0092-2730; **Rap and** Minnesota Welfare, 0026-5705.
**Desc:** Vol for 197 includes Biennial report to the Governor.

US/0097-255X
**PEOPLE'S YELLOW PAGES OF AMERICA.** Began publication with 1974 issue. English. $5.00. Heller, 90 Daisy Farms Drive, New Rochelle NY 10804. **LC** HV89; .P45. **DD** 362/.025/73.

CN/0704-5263
**PERCEPTION (OTTAWA).** (PERCEPTION.). [Perception]. **Added/Corp** Canadian Council on Social Development. Vol. 1 (Sept./Oct. 1977)-. Periodical. English (French). qt (4 issues). 20.00Can$ Canada; 23.00Can$ US; 25.00Can$ other; also comes with Canadian Council on Social Development membership. Canadian Council on Social Development, 55 Parkdale Avenue, Ottawa Ontario K1Y 4G1 Canada. **Tel** (613)728-1865, FAX (613)728-9387. **ED** Carolyn Brown. **LC** HV1; .P37. **DD** 361/.005; 309.1/71/064. **Bk Rev Ad Acc. Pr Rev. Circ:** 3,500 (ctrl). available on microfilm and microfiche from University Microfilms International (UMI). **Formed by the union of** C W, Canadian Welfare, 0008-5332 **and** Digeste Social, 0382-6287.
**Desc:** Canadian magazine of social comment. Published by the Canadian Council on Social Development to provide information on the social policy field. Deals in areas of interest to social, health and education professionals as well as the voluntary sector.
**Ind/Abst** Can. Period. Index; Multicult. Educ. Abstr.; PAIS Int. Print (1991-); Sage Race Relat. Abstr.; Spec. Educ. Needs Abstr.

II
**PERFORMANCE BUDGET - DEPARTMENT OF WOMAN AND CHILD WELFARE. Main/Corp** Andhra Pradesh (India). Dept. of Woman and Child Welfare. (19??)-. English. an. **LC** HJ65.A65; D46a. **DD** 354.54/8400722253.

US
**PERMANENCY REPORT / CWL/PERMANENT FAMILIES FOR CHILDREN. Ceased.** Vol. 1, No. 1 (Summer 1983)-(Jan. 1987). Periodical. English. qt. Permanent Families for Children, 67 Irving Place, New York NY 10003. **Continues** Adoption Report.

UK
**PERSONAL SOCIAL SERVICES STATISTICS, ESTIMATES. See** Sociology-Abstracting, Bibliographies and Statistics.

CN/0712-8223
**PERSPECTIVES STATISTIQUES (QUEBEC).** (PERSPECTIVES STATISTIQUES : REVUE STATISTIQUE ANNUELLE DE LA REGIE DES RENTES DU QUEBEC.). [Perspect. stat.]. **Added/Corp** Regie des Rentes du Quebec. Direction de la Recherche et de la Statistique. Vol. 1, (1981)-. French. an. Regie des Rentes du Quebec, Case Postale 5200, Quebec Quebec G1K 7S9 Canada. **Tel** (418)643-8309. **LC** HD7130.Q4; P47. **DD** 368.4/009714. **Continues** Bulletin Statistique (Regie des Rentes du Quebec).

CN/0712-8576
**PETIT A PETIT.** (PETIT A PETIT : PUBLICATION DE L'OFFICE DES SERVICES DE GARDE A L'ENFANCE.). [Petit petit]. **Added/Corp** Quebec (Province). Office des Services de Garde -a l'Enfance. Vol. 1, No. 1 (May 1982)-. Periodical. French. bm (Jan., Mar., May, July, Sept., Nov.). free. L'Office Services de Garde a l'Enfance, 100 Sherbrooke Est, Montreal Quebec H2X 1C3 Canada. **Tel** (514)873-2323. **DD** 362.7/12/09714.

CN/1181-6910
**PHONE LINK : THE OFFICIAL NEWSLETTER OF KIDS HELP PHONE.** [Phone link]. **Added/Corp** Kids Help Phone (Organization). Vol. 1, No. 1 (Jan. 1991)-. Newsletter. English. Three times a year. Free. Kids Help Phone, PO Box 513, Suite 100, 2 Bloor Street West, Toronto Ontario M4W 3E2 Canada. **DD** 362.2/04256/083.

US/0748-8211
**PHYSICIANS DRG NEWSLETTER. Ceased.** [Phys., DRG newsl.]. **VFOAT** Physicians D.R.G. Newsletter. Vol. 1, No. 1 (April 1984)-?. Newsletter. English. mo. Current Health Concepts, 2049 Century Park East/Suite 5117, Los Angeles CA 90067. **DD** 362.

US/0032-0412
**PLAIN RAPPER, THE. Ceased.** (PLAIN RAPPER / PROJECT EDEN, INC.). **Added/Corp** Project Eden (Hayward, Calif.). (1970)-(19??). Periodical. English. qt. Project Eden, 680 West Tennyson Road, Hayward CA 94544. **Tel** (510)887-0566. **ED** Linda Cherry. **Bk Rev. Ad Acc. Circ:** 2,400 (ctrl).
**Desc:** Newsletter of substance abuse, education, prevention, and counseling program for youth and families in Hayward, Castro Valley, and San Lorenzo (Alameda County), California.

CN/0700-9011
**PLAN CANADA NEWS. Added/Corp** Foster Parents Plan of Canada. (Spring 1974)-. Periodical. English. sa. Limited free distribution. Foster Parents Plan of Canada, 153 St Clair Avenue West, Toronto Ontario M4V 1P8 Canada. **DD** 362.7/1/06271.

US
**PLANNING FOR THE DEVELOPMENTALLY DISABLED. Main/Corp** West Virginia. State Commission on Mental Retardation. (19??)-. English. Charleston Commission on Mental Retardation, State Capitol, Charleston WV 25305. **LC** HV3006.W4; W47a. **DD** 362.3/09754.

KO
**POGON SAHOE NONJIP. See** Population Studies.

KO
**POGON YONGAM. See** Public Health and Safety.

IT
**POLITICHE SOCIALI E SERVIZI / CENTRO DI DOCUMENTAZIONE SUI SERVIZI SOCIALI GIOVANNI MARIA CORNAGGIA MEDICI.** Periodical. Italian. Vita e Pensiero, Pubblic University, Largo Gemelli 1, 20123 Milan Italy. **Tel** 011 39 2 72342310, 011 39 2 72342370. **LC** HV286; .P65.

CN/0225-3593
**PORTE-VOIX, LE.** [Porte-voix]. **VFOAT** Journal Communautaire Joli-Mont. V. 1, No. 6- Dec. 1979-. Periodical. French. bm. Free. Comite Promoteur du Journal Communautaire Joli-Mont, CP 270, Saint-Theodore de Chertsey Quebec J0K 3K0 Canada. **DD** 361/.97141. ctrl circ. **Continues** CLSC Joli-Mont, 0708-3122.

UK/0032-5856
**POVERTY.** [Poverty]. **Added/Corp** Child Poverty Action Group. No. 1 (Winter 1966)-. Periodical. English. Three times a year (Apr., Aug., Dec.). £14.00 UK; $16.00 other. Child Poverty Action Group, 1 Bath Street, London EC1V 9P4 England. **Tel** 011 44 71 253 3406. **ED** Fran Bennett and Julia Lewis. **LC** HC260.P63; P6. **DD** 330.942. **Bk Rev. Ad Acc. Circ:** 6,250.
**Desc:** Features articles on citizens rights, poverty, diary facts and figures, reviews and publications digest.
**Ind/Abst** Appl. Soc. Sci. Index Abstr.

●US/1014-9783
**POVERTY AND SOCIAL POLICY PAPER. Added/Corp** International Bank for Reconstruction and Development. **VFOAT** Poverty and Social Policy Paper Series. (1992)-. Monographic series. English. Price varies per volume. World Bank Publications, 1818 H Street Northwest, Washington DC 20433. **Tel** (202)473-1155, (202)473-1155, FAX (202)522-3224, telex WUI 64145 WORLDBANK.

US/0278-9108
**PPG INDUSTRIES FOUNDATION : REPORT. Main/Corp** PPG Industries Foundation. **VFOAT** P.P.G. Industries Foundation. **VAT** Pittsburgh Plate Glass Industries Foundation. English. PPG Industries Inc, 440 College Park Drive, Monroeville PA 15146. **LC** HV97.P67; P676A. **DD** 361.7/65/0973.

US/1068-8897
**PPT EXPRESS.** (PPT EXPRESS : A NEWSLETTER FOR TEACHERS AND OTHERS WORKING WITH PREGNANT AND PARENTING TEENS.). [PPT expr.]. **VAT** Pregnant and Parenting Teens Express. Vol. 1, No. 1 (Feb. 1991)-. Newsletter. English. qt (Feb., May, Aug., Nov.). $15.00. Morning Glory Express Inc., 6595 San Harold Way, Buena Park CA 90620. **Tel** (714)828-1998, FAX (714)828-2049. **ED** Jeanne Lindsay. **DD** 362. **Bk Rev.** (Qty: varies). **Circ:** 10,000.
**Desc:** Investigates teenage parenting.

UK/0950-3153
**PRACTICE BIRMINGHAM.** (PRACTICE.). [Practice Birm.]. (1987)-. Periodical. English. qt. $80.00 (one year), $144.00 (two year), $204.00 (three year). British Association of Social Workers, 16 Kent Street, Birmingham B5 6RD England. **Tel** 011 44 1699 0914. **DD** 361.30941. [CCC].
**Ind/Abst** Soc. Plann. Policy Dev. Abstr.; Soc. Work Abstr.

YU
**PRAVNE SVESKE. See** Insurance.

US/1049-023X
**PREHOSPITAL AND DISASTER MEDICINE. See** Medical Science and Technology.

US/0886-6694
**PREVENTING SEXUAL ABUSE. Ceased.** (PREVENTING SEXUAL ABUSE : A NEWSLETTER OF THE NATIONAL FAMILY LIFE EDUCATION NETWORK.). [Prev. sex. abuse]. Vol. 1, No. 1 (Spring 1986)-Vol. 2, No. 3 (19??). Newsletter. English. qt. SAFE Institute, 1225 Northwest Murray Road/Suite 213, Portland OR 97229. **DD** 362.
**Desc:** A multi-disciplinary journal addressing the medical, psychological, legal, educational and cultural issues of concern to professionals dealing with child sexual abuse.

US/0882-5513
**PREVENTION UPDATE NEWSLETTER.** [Prev. update newsl.]. **VFOAT** Prevention Update. Vol. 1, No. 1-. Newsletter. English. bm. $25.00. Health Promotion Publications, 2952 Mesquite Drive, Riverside CA 92503. **DD** 362.

BL
**PREVIDENCIA SOCIAL, URBANA E RURAL.** Periodical. Portuguese. Caixa Postal 326, Cep 13 100 Campinas Brazil.

●US/1071-2496
**PRIMARY CARE NEWSLETTER.** [Prim. care newsl.]. (1992)-. Newsletter. English. Nine times a year. $103.00 (individuals), $157.00 (institutions) US; $115.00 (individuals), $169.00 (institutions) other. Williams & Wilkins Company, 428 East Preston Street, Baltimore MD 21202-3993. **Tel** (410)528-4000, (800)638-6423, FAX (410)528-8596, telex 87669. **(Subscription address:** Williams & Wilkins, PO Box 64380, Baltimore MD 21264.) **ED** Dr. Michael K. Rees. **DD** 362. **Ad Acc.** Documents available from Quick Copies.
**Desc:** Emphasizes the "nuts and bolts" of adult ambulatory care. Excludes tertiary acute care topics. Assures you of an excellent review of what is basic and what is new in office/ambulatory primary care medicine. Current standard of care is emphasized.

US
**PRIMETIME / PARENTAL RESOURCES FOR INVOLVEMENT IN MIGRANT EDUCATION PROJECT. See** Education.

CN/0317-2341
**PRISM (OTTAWA).** (PRISM.). **Added/Corp** Carleton University. School of Social Work. Vol. 1 (Mar. 1975)-. Periodical. English. ir. Carleton University School of Social Work, Ottawa Ontario K1S 5B6 Canada. **Tel** (613)788-7511. **DD** 361/.007/1171384.

US/1059-0048
**PRO-FUND NOTES.** [PRO-fund notes]. **VFOAT** PRO Fund Notes. Vol. 1, No. 1 (Sept. 1991)-. Periodical. English. bm. $120.00. Profund, PO Box 130, Wellsburg WV 26070-0130. **DD** 361.

UK
**PROBATION JOURNAL. See** Law-Law Enforcement and Criminology.

US
**PROCEEDINGS OF THE ANNUAL MEETING - FLORIDA GROUP CHILD CARE ASSOCIATION. Main/Corp** Florida Group Child Care Association. **Added/Corp** Florida. State Dept. of Public Welfare. Proceedings. English. Florida Department of Health and Rehabilitative Services, 1323 Winewood Boulevard, Building 1, Room 115, Tallahassee FL 32399. **Tel** (904)488-7721, FAX (904)488-2112. **LC** HV741; .A243. **DD** 362.7062759.

US
**PROCEEDINGS OF THE ... INTERNATIONAL CONFERENCE ON SOCIAL WELFARE. Main/Conf** International Conference on Social Welfare. Began publication with 14th in 1968?. Proceedings. English (French).

5301

# Sociology — Social Services and Welfare

International Conference on Social Welfare, Koestlergasse 1129, A-1060 Vienna Austria. **Tel** 0222/587 81 64. **Continues** *Proceedings of the ... Assembly of the International Conference of Social Work.*

FR
**PROCES-VERBAL DE LA REUNION DU ... / MINISTERE DE LA SANTE ET DE LA SECURITE SOCIALE, COMMISSION DES COMPTES DE LA SECURITE SOCIALE.** **Main/Corp** France. Commission des Comptes de la Securite Sociale. English. **LC** HD7173; .F68C. **DD** 354.440072.

US/0887-3798
**PRODUCTIVE AGING NEWS.** [Prod. aging news]. No. 1 (Mar. 1986)-. Periodical. English. Ten times a year. $97.00 (non-profit organizations and individuals); $147.00 (other). Mount Sinai Journal of Medicine, Box 1094 50 East 98th Street, New York NY 10029. **Tel** (212)241-6108, . **ED** Mal Schechter, Box 1070, Mount Sinai, New York, New York 10029 (212)241-4653. **DD** 362. **Bk Rev. Circ:** 500.
**Desc:** Focusing on issues of longevity or population aging in the US and abroad including health trends, geriatrics, economics, and labor force trends, and social and housing services.

US/0884-9110
**PROFILES OF REGULATORY COMPLIANCE.** [Profiles regul. compliance]. Vol. 1, No. 1 (1985)-. Periodical. English. Twenty-four times a year. $225.00 US & Canada & Mexico; $300.00 Corporate Rate, (10 copies each issue); $377.00 other. International Profiles Inc., PO Box 1457, Largo FL 34640. **Tel** (813)399-1168, FAX (813)397-9919. **ED** R. Shannon. **DD** 362. **Continues** *483 Validation Monitor.*
**Desc:** Contains FDA regulatory compliance case histories and medical device firms.

US/0194-3871
**PROGRAM ADMINISTRATION REVIEW OF THE SOCIAL SECURITY DISABILITY INSURANCE AND THE SUPPLEMENTAL SECURITY INCOME VOCATIONAL REHABILITATION PROGRAMS.** **See** Economics-Labor.

US/0091-0511
**PROGRAM INFORMATION SERIES REPORT.** English. Department of Social Welfare, Management Information Service P Street, Sacramento CA 95814. **LC** HV98.C3; A334. **DD** 361./4/09794.

US/0093-7835
**PROGRAM STATISTICS - MICHIGAN DEPARTMENT OF SOCIAL SERVICES.** **See** Sociology-Abstracting, Bibliographies and Statistics.

US/0363-0625
**PROGRAMS AND PROGRESS.** **Main/Corp** New York (State). Office for the Aging. English. an. Office for the Aging, Agency Building 2 Empire Plaza, Albany NY 12223. **LC** HV1468.N7; N5A. **DD** 362.6/09747.

US/0272-4448
**PROGRAMS PROVIDING SERVICES TO BATTERED WOMEN.** (PROGRAMS PROVIDING SERVICES TO BATTERED WOMEN / COMPILED BY CENTER FOR WOMEN POLICY STUDIES, RESOURCE CENTER ON FAMILY VIOLENCE.). English. National Clearinghouse on Domestic Violence, PO Box 2309, Rockville MD 20852. **LC** HV699; .P76. **DD** 362.8/3. **NLM** HV 6626 P964.

US/0091-2883
**PROGRESS REPORT - MICHIGAN DEPARTMENT OF SOCIAL SERVICES. OFFICE OF YOUTH SERVICES.** (PROGRESS REPORT.). **Main/Corp** Michigan. Office of Youth Services. 1971/72-. English. an. Department of Social Services / Michigan, 300 South Capitol Avenue, Lansing MI 48026. **LC** HV86; .M536 subser; HV1435.M5. **DD** 362.7/09774.

IO
**PROGRESS REPORT PELITA P.K3A.** **Main/Corp** Jakarta Raya (Indonesia). Dinas Sosial. **VAT** Progres Report Pembangunan Lima Tahun Pembinaan Kegiatan Kesejahteraan Keluarga dan Anak. Indonesian (Indonesian). Dinas Sosial, J1 Gunung Sahari II/6, Jakarta Indonesia. **LC** HV800.I56; J344.

CN/0708-5710
**PROJECT INFORMATION EXCHANGE (SELECTED DOCUMENTS).** (PROJECT INFORMATION EXCHANGE.). **VFOAT** Project Information Echange-Renseignements; Canadian Social Action Documents. 1976-. Periodical. English (French). Micromedia Limited, 20 Victoria Street, Toronto Ontario M5C 2N8 Canada. **Tel** (416)362-5211, (800)387-2689, FAX (416)362-6161, telex 06524668. **DD** 360.

IO
**PROJECT STATEMENT DAN PEDOMAN PELAKSANAAN D.I.K. & D.I.P.** **Main/Corp** Indonesia. Direktorat Jenderal Bina Karya. **VAT** Project Statement dan Pedoman Pelaksanaan Daftar Isian Kegiatan dan Daftar Isian Proyek. (19??)-. Indonesian. Direktorat Jenderal Bira, Karya Indonesia. **LC** HV401; .D52b.

FR/0033-0884
**PROJET.** **See** Economics-International Economics.

US/0148-317X
**PROPOSED COMPREHENSIVE ANNUAL SERVICE PROGRAM PLAN FOR THE STATE OF HAWAII.** [Propos. compr. annu. serv. program plan State Hawaii]. **Main/Corp** Hawaii. Dept. of Social Services and Housing. English. an. Services Program Development Administrator, 1390 Miller Street, Honolulu HI 96813. **LC** HV86; .H336. **DD** 353.9/969/0084.

US/0147-6157
**PROPOSED COMPREHENSIVE ANNUAL SERVICES PLAN (INDIANAPOLIS).** (PROPOSED COMPREHENSIVE ANNUAL SERVICES PLAN / PREPARED BY THE INDIANA OFFICE OF SOCIAL SERVICES.). **Main/Corp** Indiana Office of Social Services. **VFOAT** State of Indiana Proposed Comprehensive Annual Services Plan. Began with vol. for 1979/80. English. an. Indiana Office of Social Services, 964 North Pennsylvania, Indianapolis IN 46204. **LC** HV86; .I75A. **DD** 353.97720084. **Continues** *Indiana. State Dept. of Public Welfare. Proposed Comprehensive Annual Services Plan, 0147-6157.*

US
**PROPOSED COMPREHENSIVE ANNUAL SERVICES PROGRAM PLAN.** **Main/Corp** Louisiana. Dept. of Health and Human Resources. **Added/Corp** Louisiana. Dept. of Health and Human Resources. Proposed Title XX Comprehensive Annual Services Program Plan for the State of Louisiana. **VFOAT** Proposed Title XX Comprehensive Annual Services Program Plan for the State of Louisiana. (19??)-. English. an. Louisiana Department of Health and Human Resources, 755 Riverdale North, PO Box 3776, Baton Rouge LA 70821. **Tel** (504)342-2297. **LC** HV86; .L823a. **DD** 353.97630084.

US
**PROPOSED COMPREHENSIVE ANNUAL SERVICES PROGRAM PLAN.** **Main/Corp** Minnesota. Dept. of Public Welfare. (1979)-. English. an. Gary Haselhuhn, Division of Social Services, Department of Public Welfare, Centennial Office Building, St Paul MN 55155. **LC** HV86; .M674878. **DD** 353.97760084/05. **Continues** *Comprehensive Annual Services Program Plan. Proposed Plan, Title XX.*

US
**PROPOSED COMPREHENSIVE ANNUAL SERVICES PROGRAM PLAN.** **Main/Corp** Arkansas. Office of Title XX Services. **Added/Corp** Arkansas. Office of Title XX Services. Title XX Proposed Comprehensive Annual Services Program Plan. **VFOAT** Title XX Proposed Comprehensive Annual Services Program Plan. (1979)-. English. an. Office of Title XX Services, Department of Human Resources, PO Box 1427, Little Rock AR 72203. **LC** HV98.A65; A46a. **DD** 361.6/09767. **Continues** *Proposed Comprehensive Annual Services Program Plan.*

US
**PROPOSED COMPREHENSIVE ANNUAL SOCIAL SERVICES PLAN.** **Main/Corp** Alaska. Dept. of Health and Social Services. (19??)-. English. an. Department of Health and Social Services / Office of Alcoholism and Drug Abuse, Pouch H-05F, Juneau AK 99811. **LC** HV86; .A413. **DD** 361.6/2/09798.

US
**PROPOSED COMPREHENSIVE ANNUAL SOCIAL SERVICES PROGRAM PLAN FOR THE STATE OF WASHINGTON.** **Main/Corp** Washington (State). Dept. of Social and Health Services. (19??)-. English. an. David J Holloman, Department of Social and Health Services, Administration and Management, Mail Stop OB-41K, Olympia WA 98504. **LC** HV86; .W3593. **DD** 361.6/09797.

US/0160-2101
**PROPOSED CONNECTICUT STATE PLAN ON AGING.** **Main/Corp** Connecticut. Dept. of Aging. English. Department of Aging, 90 Washington Street, Hartford CT 06115. **LC** HV1468.C8; C63B. **DD** 362.6/09746.

US/0362-7446
**PROPOSED MICHIGAN ANNUAL SOCIAL SERVICES PLAN.** **Main/Corp** Michigan. Dept. of Social Services. (1975/76)-. English. an. Department of Social Services / Michigan, 300 South Capitol Avenue, Lansing MI 48026. **LC** HV86; .M5367. **DD** 362/.9774.

US
**PROPOSED MICHIGAN ANNUAL TITLE XX SERVICES PLAN.** **Main/Corp** Michigan. Dept. of Social Services. Title XX Administration Division. 1980/81-. English. an. Title XX Administration, Office of Planning Budget and Evaluation, Michigan Department of Social Services, 300 South Capitol Avenue, PO Box 30037, Lansing MI 48909. **LC** HV86; .M53727A. **DD** 361.6/09774. **Continues** *Proposed Michigan Annual Title XX Services Plan.*

US/0149-5097
**PROPOSED, STATE OF CALIFORNIA, ANNUAL STATEWIDE SOCIAL SERVICES PLAN.** **Title Change.** **Main/Corp** California. Dept. of Health. Social Services Division. English. an. Sacramento Social Services Division, Department of Health and Welfare, 744 P Street/Room 576, Sacramento CA 95814. **LC** HV86; .C5118. **DD** 361.6/2/09794. **Continues** *Proposed, State of California, Comprehensive Annual Services Program Plan.* **Continued by** *Proposed Comprehensive Annual Services Program Plan for the State of California.*

US
**PROPOSED TITLE XX COMPREHENSIVE SERVICES PROGRAM PLAN.** **Main/Corp** Arkansas. Office of Title XX Services. (19??)-. English. Office of Title XX Services, Department of Human Resources, PO Box 1427, Little Rock AR 72203. **LC** HV98.A65; A46a. **DD** 361.6/09767. **Continues** *Proposed Comprehensive Annual Services Program Plan.*

US
**PROPOSED TITLE XX SOCIAL SERVICES: COMPREHENSIVE ANNUAL SERVICES PROGRAM PLAN FOR THE STATE OF TEXAS.** **Added/Corp** Texas. State Dept. of Public Welfare. Texas. Dept. of Human Resources. (1977)-. English. an. Texas Department of Human Resources, PO Box 2960, Austin TX 78769. **LC** HV98.T5; P76. **Continues** *Proposed Title XX Comprehensive Annual Services Program Plan for Texas.*

IT
**PROSPETTIVE ASSISTENZIALI.** (19??)-. Italian. Four times a year. L40000 Italy; L60000 other. Coop Promozione Sociale, Via Artisti 36, 10124 Turin Italy. **Tel** 011 39 11 8122327, 011 39 11 8124469.

US/0893-4231
**PROTECTING CHILDREN.** [Prot. child.]. **Added/Corp** American Humane Association. Children's Division. Vol. 1, No. 1 (Winter 1984)-. Periodical. English. qt (4 issues). $35.00. American Humane Association / Children's Division, 63 Inverness Drive East, Englewood CO 80112. **Tel** (303)792-9900. **DD** 179. Index available (bound in first issue).

US/0888-0352
**PROVIDER (WASHINGTON, D.C.).** (PROVIDER.). [Provider]. **Added/Corp** American Health Care Association. Vol. 12, No. 3 (Mar. 1986)-. Periodical. English. mo. $48.00 US; $61.00 Canada and Mexico; $85.00 other. American Health Care Association, PO Box 96906, Washington DC 20090. **Tel** (202)842-4444. **ED** Sheran Hartwell and Deborah Dasch. **LC** RA973.5; .A37a. **DD** 362.1/6/05. **NLM** W1; PR838D. Index available. **Bk Rev. Ad Acc. Circ:** 22,000 (ctrl). available on microfilm and microfiche from University Microfilms International (UMI). **Continues** *Journal - American Health Care Association, 0360-4969.*
**Desc:** Covers the progress of long term health care, who is involved and how and where it is happening.
**Ind/Abst** Abstr. Soc. Gerontol.; Cumul. Index Nurs. Allied Health Lit. (March 1986-); Health Plan. Adminis.; Hospit. Health Admin. Index (1986-).

CN/0824-9946
**PROVINCIAL NEWSJOURNAL - INFANT DEVELOPMENT PROGRAMMES OF B.C.** (PROVINCIAL NEWSJOURNAL / INFANT DEVELOPMENT PROGRAMME OF B.C.). [Prov. newsj. - Infant Dev. Programmes B.C.]. **VAT** Newsjournal; Infant Development Programme of B.C. Newsjournal. Vol. 2, No. 1 (May 1983)-. Periodical. English. sa. 10.00Can$. Provincial Advisor Infant Development Programme Berwick UBC, 2765 Osoyoos Crescent, Vancouver British Columbia V6T 1X7 Canada. **Tel** 228-4014. **ED** Dana L Brynelsen. **DD** 362.4/088054. **Bk Rev. Circ:** 2,000 (ctrl). **Continues** *Newsletter (Infant Development Programme of B.C.), 0823-9924.*
**Desc:** Provides parents and professionals with up to date information on development in infancy, handicapping conditions, and resources. Parental and professional perspectives are shared.

UK/0144-4212
**PSLG. PUBLIC SERVICE & LOCAL GOVERNMENT.** **See** Public Administration.

CN/0823-6135
**P'TIT ROBERT, LE.** [P'tit Robert]. No. 1-. Periodical. French. bw. Centre Hospitalier Robert-Giffard Service d'Audio-Visuel, 2601 de la Canardiere, Beauport Quebec G1J 2G3 Canada. **DD** 362.2/0971447. ***Absorbed** Reseau (Beauport, Quebec), 0712-2144.*

US/0090-7138
**PUBLIC ASSISTANCE FOR MINNESOTA INDIANS. See** Ethnic Interests.

US/1069-1340
**PUBLIC ASSISTANCE FUNDING REPORT.** ***Title Change.*** (PUBLIC ASSISTANCE FUNDING REPORT : THE INDEPENDENT NEWSLETTER FOR SOCIAL WELFARE AND HOMELESS SERVICE PROFESSIONALS.). [Public assist. funding rep.]. No. 93-3 (Feb. 2, 1993)-(1993). Newsletter. English. sm. CD Publications, 8204 Fenton Street, Silver Spring MD 20910. **Tel** (800)666-6380, (301)588-6380, FAX (301)588-6385. **DD** 361. ***Continues** Public Assistance Report (Silver Spring, Md.), 1056-7100. **Merged into** Children and Youth Funding Report, 1069-892X.*

US
**PUBLIC ASSISTANCE RECIPIENT AND EXPENDITURE STUDY. Main/Corp** Alaska. Dept. of Health and Social Services. Office of Information Systems. English. sa. Office of Information Systems, Pouch H81, Juneau AK 99811. **LC** HV86; .A414. **DD** 353.97980072/31.

US/1056-7100
**PUBLIC ASSISTANCE REPORT (SILVER SPRING, MD.).** ***Title Change.*** (PUBLIC ASSISTANCE REPORT.). [Public assist. rep.]. (1991)-(199?). Periodical. English. sm. CD Publications, 8204 Fenton Street, Silver Spring MD 20910. **Tel** (800)666-6380, (301)588-6380, FAX (301)588-6385. **DD** 361. ***Continues** Public Assistance Success, 1050-3447. **Continued by** Public Assistance Funding Report, 1069-1340.*

CN/0381-4327
**PUBLIC CONTRIBUTIONS ACT ... ANNUAL REPORT ..., THE. Main/Corp** Alberta. Alberta Consumer and Corporate Affairs. English. an. Alberta Consumer and Corporate Affairs, Office of the Minister, 104 Legislative Building, Edmonton Alberta T5K 2B6 Canada. **Tel** (403)427-6941. **LC** HV109.A5; D56B. **DD** 354.71230084; 361. 7/63/097123. ***Continues** Alberta. Alberta Social Services and Community Health. Public Contributions Act Annual Report, 0381-4327.*

US/0360-6600
**PUBLIC WELFARE ACTIVITIES IN ARIZONA. Main/Corp** Arizona. State Dept. of Public Welfare. English. mo. Department of Public Welfare / Arizona, State Office Building, Phoenix AZ 85009. ***Continues** Public Welfare Statistics.*

US/0163-8297
**PUBLIC WELFARE DIRECTORY, THE.** 1940-. Directory. English. an. $65.00 (members), $70.00 (nonmembers). American Public Welfare Association, 810 First Street Northeast, Suite 500, Washington DC 20002. **Tel** (202)682-0100, FAX (202)289-6555. **ED** Amy Weinstein. **LC** HV89; .A55. **DD** 360.58. **NLM** HV 89 P976. **Circ:** 7,000.
**Desc:** Information on federal, state, territorial, and local public welfare and related agencies in the U.S. and Canada lists agencies, key staff, addresses, telephone and fax numbers. Describes the structure and functions of agencies and reciprocal agreements between agencies. Gives correspondence procedures with Canada. Appendixes include additional information on programs and interstate compacts.

US/0033-3816
**PUBLIC WELFARE (WASHINGTON).** (PUBLIC WELFARE.). [Public welf.]. **Added/Corp** American Public Welfare Association. Vol. 1 (Jan. 1943)-. Periodical. English. qt. $30.00 US and Canada; $40.00 other. American Public Welfare Association, 810 First Street Northeast, Suite 500, Washington DC 20002. **Tel** (202)682-0100, FAX (202)289-6555. **ED** Bill Detweiler. **LC** HV1; .P75. **DD** 360.5. **NLM** W1 PU64. **[CCC]. Bk Rev. Ad Acc. Pr Rev. Circ:** 8,600 (ctrl). available on microfilm and microfiche from University Microfilms International (UMI). Documents available from The Genuine Article, UMI Article Clearinghouse. ***Supersedes** Public Welfare News.*
**Desc:** Articles range from commentary by national leaders to practical features by human service administrators. Research reports and opinion columns.
**Ind/Abst** Acad. Abstr. Full Text Elite (Jan. 1991-); Acad. Abstr. (Jan. 1991-); Acad. Search (Jan. 1991-); Am. Hist. Life (1969-1978); Curr. Contents Soc. Behav. Sci.; Curr. Lit. Fam. Plan.; Expand. Acad. Index (1989-); Hospit. Health Admin. Index; INFO-SOUTH Abstr.; J. Plan. Lit.; Mag. Search; Newsp. Period. Abstr. (1988-); Res. Alert [Full Cov.]; Soc. Plann. Policy Dev. Abstr.; Soc. Sci. Source (Jul. 1990-); Soc. Sci. Cit. Index [Full Cov.]; Soc. Sci. Index; Soc. Sci. Index Fulltext (Fall 1988-) [Full Txt.]; Soc. Work Abstr. (Spring 1987-) [Full Cov.]; Urban Aff. Abstr.; Women Stud. Abstr.

US/0278-0143
**PUBLICATION CATALOG OF THE U.S. DEPARTMENT OF HEALTH AND HUMAN SERVICES.** [Publ. cat. U.S. Dep. Health Hum. Serv.]. **Main/Corp** United States. Dept. of Health and Human Services. **VFOAT** Publications Catalog. **VAT** Publication Catalog of the United States Department of Health and Human Services. Jan. 1979-Dec. 1979-. Catalog. English. an. US Department of Health and Human Services, 200 Independence Avenue Southwest, Washington DC 20201. **LC** Z7164.C4; U48A; HV97.U5. **DD** 016.361. **NLM** ZWA 100 U525c. ***Continues** Publication Catalog of the U.S. Department of Health, Education, and Welfare, 0275-8210.*

CN/0710-0329
**PUBLICATION SERIES. MONOGRAPH SERIES (UNIVERSITY OF TORONTO. FACULTY OF SOCIAL WORK).** (PUBLICATION SERIES. MONOGRAPH SERIES / FACULTY OF SOCIAL WORK, UNIVERSITY OF TORONTO.). [Publ. ser., Monogr. ser. - Fac. Soc. Work, Univ. Tor.]. **VAT** Monograph Series - Faculty of Social Work. University of Toronto. 1-. Monographic series. English. Price varies per volume. Faculty of Social Work, University of Toronto, 246 Bloor Street West, Toronto Ontario M5S 1A1 Canada. **Tel** (416)978-6314. **DD** 361/.005. ***Continues in part** Occasional Papers in Social Work, 0317-8382.*

CN/0710-0299
**PUBLICATION SERIES. WORKING PAPERS ON SOCIAL WELFARE IN CANADA.** (PUBLICATION SERIES. WORKING PAPERS ON SOCIAL WELFARE IN CANADA / FACULTY OF SOCIAL WORK, UNIVERSITY OF TORONTO.). [Publ. ser., Work. pap. soc. welf. Can.]. **VFOAT** Working Papers on Social Welfare in Canada. **VAT** Publication Series. Working Papers on Social Work in Canada. 1-. Monographic series. English. Price varies per volume. Faculty of Social Work, University of Toronto, 246 Bloor Street West, Toronto Ontario M5S 1A1 Canada. **Tel** (416)978-6314. **DD** 361/.971. ***Continues in part** Occasional Papers in Social Work, 0317-8382.*

UK/0269-297X
**QUALITY ASSURANCE ABSTRACTS.** ***Ceased.*** [Qual. assur. abstr.]. (1986)-Vol. 6 (1992). Periodical. English. Twelve times a year. Department of Health and Social Security Library, PO Box 21, Stanmore, Middlesex HA7 1AY England. **Tel** 011 44 71 9722000, 9728161, FAX 011 44 71 972 3765. **DD** 016.36210685.

US/0892-6174
**QUALITY CARE ADVOCATE.** [Qual. care advocate]. **Added/Corp** National Coalition for Nursing Home Reform. Vol. 1, No. 1 (Jan./Feb. 1986)-. Periodical. English. bm. $45.00. National Citizens Coalition for Nursing Home Reform, 1224 M Street Northwest, Number 301, Washington DC 20005. **Tel** (202)797-0657. **ED** Janet C Wells. **DD** 362. **Bk Rev.** ctrl circ.

US/0361-2643
**QUALITY CONTROL : STATES' CORRECTIVE ACTION ACTIVITIES. Main/Corp** United States. Social and Rehabilitation Service. Office of Management. English. Social Rehabilitation Service, Washington DC 20202. **LC** HV85; .S58D. **DD** 362/.973.

US
**QUARTERLY REPORT / NEBRASKA DEPARTMENT OF SOCIAL SERVICES. Added/Corp** Nebraska. Dept. of Social Services. Vol. 46, No. 1 (July/Sept. 1983)-. English. qt. Department of Public Welfare / Nebraska, PO Box 95026, Lincoln NE 68509. **LC** HV86; .N368. **DD** 361.6/09782. ***Continues** Quarterly Report - Nebraska Department of Public Welfare.*

US
**QUARTERLY SUMMARY OF TITLE XX SERVICES AND EXPENDITURES IN NORTH CAROLINA / DEPARTMENT OF HUMAN RESOURCES, DIVISION OF PLANS AND OPERATIONS.** Vols. 1, No. 1 (Oct./Dec. 1977)-. Periodical. English. qt. State Department of Human Resources / North Carolina, 701 Barbour Street, Raleigh NC 27603. **Tel** (919)733-4283. **LC** HV98.N8; Q37. **DD** 361.6/09756.

CN/0228-6238
**QUOI DE 9.** (QUOI DE 9 / CENTRE HOSPITALIER SACRE-COEUR.). **VAT** Quoi de Neuf. Periodical. French. mo. Productions Claude Savoie, 327 Boul St-Joseph, Hull Quebec J8Y 3Z1 Canada. **Tel** (819)776-6533. **DD** 362.1/1/09714221.

CN/1187-5658
**QUOI DE NEUF? / OMPAC, ORGANISATION MONTREALAISE DES PERSONNES ATTEINTES DE CANCER.** [Quoi neuf? - Organ. montr. pers. atteintes cancer]. **Added/Corp** Organisation Montrealaise des Personnes Atteintes de Cancer. Vol. 1, No 1 (1991)-. Periodical. French. qt. Organisation Montrealaise des Personnes Atteintes de Cancer, 6653 Rue St-Denis, Montreal Quebec H2S 2S1 Canada. **DD** 362.1.

CN/0822-9279
**R.A.P.H.A.T. REGROUPEMENT DES ASSOCIATIONS DE PERSONNES HANDICAPEES DE L'ABITIBI-TEMISCAMINGUE.** (R.A.P.H.A.T. : BULLETIN D'INFORMATION DU REGROUPEMENT DES ASSOCIATIONS DE PERSONNES HANDICAPEES DE L'ABITIBI-TEMISCAMINGUE.). [R.A.P.H.A.T. Regroup. assoc. pers. handicap. Abiti-Temiscamingue]. **VAT** Regroupement des Associations de Personnes Handicapees de l'Abitibi-Temiscamingue. Vol. 1, No. 1-. Bulletin. French. qt. Free. RAPHAT, 330 Est rue Perrault, Rouyn Quebec J9X 3J7 Canada. **DD** 362.4/09714/13.

AT/0300-3515
**RALLY (MELBOURNE).** ***Ceased.*** (RALLY.). (1969)-(19??). Periodical. English. mo. Salvation Army Auxiliary Company Australia, 69 Bourke Street, Melbourne Victoria Australia.

FR
**RAPATRIES : BILAN ANNUEL DU SECRETARIAT D'ETAT AUPRES DU PREMIER MINISTRE CHARGE DES RAPATRIES.** French. an. 14 Bd de la Madeleine, 75008 Paris France. **LC** HV640.4.F7; R36. **DD** 362.8/7/0944.

CN/0228-8435
**RAPPORT ANNUEL - COMMISSION QUEBECOISE DES LIBERATIONS CONDITIONNELLES. Main/Corp** Quebec (Province). Commission Quebecoise des Liberations Conditionnelles. 1978/79-. French. an. Editeur Officiel du Quebec, 1283 Boul Charest Ouest, Quebec Quebec G1N 2C9 Canada. **LC** HV9278; .Q43A. **DD** 354.7140084/93.

CN/0710-2305
**RAPPORT ANNUEL - CONSEIL REGIONAL DE LA SANTE ET DES SERVICES SOCIAUX DE QUEBEC.** [Rapp. annu. - Cons. reg sante serv. soc. Que.]. **Main/Corp** CRSS de Quebec (Quebec). **VAT** Rapport Annuel - CRSS de Quebec; Rapport Annuel - Region 03. Conseil de la Sante et des Services Sociaux de la Region de Quebec; Rapport Annuel - Conseil de la Sante et des Services Sociaux. Region 03. 1972-. French. an. Conseil Regional de la Sante et des Services Sociaux, 274 rue Potvin, Rimouski Quebec G5L 7P5 Canada. **LC** HV110.Q4; C66A. **DD** 354.7140084.

CN/0715-7770
**RAPPORT ANNUEL / OFFICE DE LA SECURITE DU REVENU DES CHASSEURS ET PIEGEURS CRIS.** [Rapp. annu. - Off. secur. revenu chasseurs piegeurs cris]. **Main/Corp** Office de la Securite du Revenu des Chasseurs et Piegeurs Cris (Quebec). **VFOAT** Annual Report. 1978-79-. French (English). an. Editeur Officiel du Quebec, 1283 Boul Charest Ouest, Quebec Quebec G1N 2C9 Canada. **LC** HD7116.F642; C226A. **DD** 354.7140084/84.

BE
**RAPPORT ANNUEL - ONSS. Main/Corp** Belgium. Office National de Securite Sociale. 1st (1944/1945)-. French (Dutch). an. 613.21F. Office National de Securite Social, Boulevard de Waterloo 76, 1000 Brussels Belgium. **Tel** 011 32 2 5093111. **LC** HD7186; .A37. **DD** 354.4930082/56. **Bk Rev.**
**Desc:** Financial report, social laws, and statistics of employment.

CN/0380-4585
**RAPPORT ANNUEL - REGIE DES RENTES DU QUEBEC. See** Insurance.

CN/0380-5387
**RAPPORT ANNUEL, REGIME DES ALLOCATIONS FAMILIALES DU QUEBEC. Main/Corp** Regie des Rentes du Quebec. 1976/77-. French. an. Regie des Rentes du Quebec, Case Postale 5200, Quebec Quebec G1K 7S9 Canada. **Tel** (418)643-8309. **LC** HV700.C3; Q46A. **DD** 354.7140084/82.

SZ
**RAPPORT ANNUEL SUR L'ASSURANCE-VIEILLESSE, SURVIVANTS ET INVALIDITE FEDERALE ET SUR LE REGIME DES ALLOCATIONS EN FAVEUR DES MILITAIRES ET DES PERSONNES ASTREINTES A SERVIR DANS L'ORGANISATION DE LA PROTECTION CIVILE. Main/Corp** Switzerland. Bundesamt fur Sozialversicherung. French. 7.00. Office Federal des Assurances Sociales, 3000 Berne Switzerland. **LC** HD7210; .A36A.

# Sociology — Social Services and Welfare

CN/1180-503X
**RAPPORT / CITIZEN ADVOCACY, OTTAWA-CARLETON.** [Rapp. - Citiz. Advocacy Ott.-Carlet.]. **Added/Corp** Citizen Advocacy (Ottawa-Carleton). No. 1 (1990)-. Periodical. English. qt. Limited free distribution. Citizen Advocacy (Ottawa-Carleton), 202-119 Ross Avenue, Ottawa, Ontario K1Y 0N6 Canada. **DD** 362.1.

BE
**RAPPORT GENERAL SUR LA SECURITE SOCIALE. Main/Corp** Belgium. Ministere de la Prevoyance Sociale. (1966)-. French. an. 437.50F. Ministere de la Prevoyance Sociale, rue de la Vierge Niore 3C, 1000 Brussels Belgium. **LC** HD7186; .B44a. **DD** 368.3/009493.

CN/1180-0178
**RAPPORT SUR LES PROJETS / LA SOCIETE CANADIENNE DE LA CROIX-ROUGE.** [Rapp. proj. - Soc. can. Croix-Rouge]. **Main/Corp** Societe Canadienne de la Croix-Rouge. **VFOAT** Mise a Jour des Projets de Developpement International. (1991)-. French. Free. Societe Canadienne de la Croix-Rouge, 1800 Promenade Alta Vista, Ottawa Ontario K1G 4J5 Canada. **DD** 361.7/7/097105.

IT/1120-2831
**RASSEGNA DI PENSIONISTICA.** [Rass. pension.]. (1969)-. Periodical. Italian. bm (6 issues). L32000 Italy; L60000 other. Rassegna Pensionistica, Via Segesta 31, 00179 Rome Italy. **Tel** 011 39 6 7820029. **UDC** 331.25.

IT/0033-9601
**RASSEGNA DI SERVIZIO SOCIALE.** [Rass. serv. soc.]. (1962)-. Periodical. Italian. qt. L45000.00 Italy; L50000.00 other. EISS Ente Italiano Servizio Sociale, Sociale Ferdinando Baldelli 41, 00146 Rome Italy. **Tel** 011 39 6 5410603, 011 39 6 5402762, FAX 011 39 2 5402762. **UDC** 36.

IT
**RASSEGNA STAMPA HANDICAP.** L60.000 Italy; L75.000 other. AIAS Assoc Ital Assis Spastici, Via Degli Orti 60, 40139 Bologna Italy. **Tel** 011 39 51 6234945.

GW
**RAUMORDNUNGSBERICHT ... DER BUNDESREGIERUNG. Added/Corp** Germany. Bundesministerium fur Raumordnung, Bauwesen und Stadtebau. (1991)-. German. **LC** HT395.G4; G3725a. **DD** 361.6/0943. **Continues** Raumordnungsbericht (Bonn, Germany : 1986).

FR/1156-833X
**RECHERCHES, HANDICAPS ET VIE CHRETIENNE.** (1990)-. Periodical. French. Four times a year. 150.00F France; 180.00F other. Recherches, 7 Place Saint-Irenee, F 69005 Lyon France. **Tel** 011 33 78 363203, FAX 011 33 72 570469. **ED** Jean Mesny. **UDC** 364.26. **Circ**: 500. available via Internet. **Continues** Recherches, Conscience Chretienne et Handicap, 0337-9019.
**Desc:** Aimed at those who meet or work with people in difficult or handicapped situations - employs a biblical or theological Christian approach to questions about daily life.

US/0360-4608
**RECORD - TENNESSEE DEPARTMENT OF HUMAN SERVICES, THE.** [Rec. - Tenn. Dep. Human Serv.]. **Main/Corp** Tennessee. Dept. of Human Services. (19??)-. Periodical. English. Six times a year. Free. Tennessee Department of Human Services, 111 Seventh Avenue North, Nashville TN 37203. **LC** HV86; .T23. **DD** 361/.09768. **Continues** Tennessee. Dept. of Public Welfare. Tennessee Public Welfare Record.
**Ind/Abst** Am. Hist. Life.

US/1061-7191
**RECOVERY TODAY.** (RECOVERY TODAY : THE NEWSMAGAZINE FOR TODAY'S RECOVERING COMMUNITY.). [Recovery today]. (1991)-. Periodical. English. mo. $24.00 US; $30.00 Canada; $41.00 other. Recovery Today, 1313 South Military Trail, #314, Deerfield Beach FL 33442. **Tel** (305)428-757, FAX (305)428-7797. **DD** 362.

SZ
**RED CROSS, RED CRESCENT : THE INTERNATIONAL MAGAZINE OF THE LEAGUE OF RED CROSS AND RED CRESCENT SOCIETIES. Added/Corp** League of Red Cross and Red Crescent Societies. (Jan. 1987)-. Periodical. English (French and Spanish). Three times a year. Free on request to libraries; $15.00 other. League of Red Cross and Red Crescent Societies, Box 372, 1211 Geneva 19 Switzerland. **Tel** 011 41 56 345580. **LC** HV560; .R427. **DD** 361.7/634/05. **Continues** League (Geneva, Switzerland).

CN/0711-4044
**RED CROSS TODAY / BRITISH COLUMBIA-YUKON DIVISION.** [Red Cross today]. Nov. 1980-. Periodical. English. qt. British Columbia-Yukon Division, Canadian Red Cross Society, 4750 Oak Street, Vancouver British Columbia V6H 2N9 Canada. **DD** 361.7/63. **Continues** Across (Vancouver, B.C.), 0711-4036.

AT
**RED TAPE.** (19??)-. Newsletter. English. bm (6 issues). Free to individuals; 25.00Aus$ institutions. Welfare Rights Unit, 193 Smith Street, 1st Floor, Fitzroy VIC 3065 Australia. **Tel** 011 61 03 4163552, FAX 011 61 03 4193552. **ED** Dale Nelson.
**Desc:** Newsletter of the Welfare Rights Unit. Acts as a resource base for the community sector by providing information regarding changes to social security legislation, policy & practice.

UK
**REFERRALS OF CHILDREN TO REPORTERS AND CHILDREN'S HEARINGS.** (1976)-. Bulletin. English. an. £2.00. Social Work Services Group, Statistics Branch, 43 Jeffrey Street / Room 422, Edinburgh EH1 1DG Scotland. **Tel** 031 244 5431, FAX 031 244 5387.

CN/0229-5113
**REFUGE (TORONTO. ENGLISH EDITION).** (REFUGE : CANADA'S NATIONAL NEWSLETTER ON REFUGEES.). [Refuge]. No. 1 (May 1981)-. Newsletter. English. ir (ten times a year). Operation Lifeline, 2nd Floor, 8 York Street, Toronto Ontario M5J 1R2 Canada. **DD** 362.8/7/0971.
**Ind/Abst** Hum. Rights Intern. Rep.; PAIS Int. Print.

US/0735-8334
**REFUGEE RESETTLEMENT PROGRAM. Main/Corp** United States. Office of Refugee Resettlement. (19??)-. English. an. Social Security Administration / Washington DC, 4301 Connecticut Avenue NW, Washington DC 20008. **Tel** (202)282-7206, FAX (202)282-7219. **LC** HV640.4.U54; U57a. **DD** 362.8/7/0973. available on microfiche (Vols. for fiscal years 1980 and 1982 distributed to depository libraries).

CN/0317-5782
**REGINA FRIENDSHIP CENTRE NEWSLETTER. Main/Corp** Regina Friendship Centre. 1- May 6, 1974-. Newsletter. English. mo. Regina Friendship Centre, 1689 Toronto Street, Regina Sask, S4P 1M3. **DD** 362.8/4.

US/0886-277X
**REGISTER OF NATIONAL CERTIFIED COUNSELORS. Title Change.** [Regist. natl. certif. couns.]. **Added/Corp** National Board for Certified Counselors (U.S.). (Jan. 1983 / March 1985)-(19??). English. be. NBCC / National Board for Certified Counselors, 3-D Terrace Way, Greensboro NC 27403. **Tel** (910)547-0607. **LC** BF637.C6; R44. **DD** 361.3/23/02573. **Continued by** National Directory of Certified Counselors.

US
**REGISTRY OF CHARITABLE ORGANIZATIONS.** 1977-. English. an. Department of Licensing, PO Box 9649, Olympia WA 98504. **LC** HV98.W3; R43. **DD** 361.7/63/025797.

US
**REHABILITATION & HEALTHCARE MARKETING. See** Business-Marketing.

BL
**RELATORIO ANNUAL - SERVICO SOCIAL DO COMERCIO, ADMINISTRACAO REGIONAL NO ESTADO DO PARA. Main/Corp** Servico Social do Comercio. Administracao Regional no Estado do Para. Portuguese. an. Servico Social do Comercio Administracao Regional No Estado do Para, Rua Senador Mandel Barata 1873, Balem Brazil. **LC** HV194.P33; S47A.

BL
**RELATORIO ANUAL. Main/Corp** Servico Social do Comercio. Administracao Regional no Estado de Sao Paulo. (1946)-. Government Publication. Portuguese. an. Free on request. Servico Social do Comercio, Administracao Regional no Estado de Sao Paulo, Av. Paulista 119, Caixa Postal 6643, CEP 01311-903 Sao Paulo, Brazil. **Tel** (011)284-2111, FAX (011)288-6206, telex (011)23423. **ED** Danilo Santos de Miranda. **LC** HV194.S34; S45a.

BL
**RELATORIO ANUAL DE ATIVIDADES. Main/Corp** Servico Social da Industria. Departamento Regional do Rio Grande do Norte. (19??)-. Portuguese. an. Av Rio Branco, 571 Edif. Barao do rio branco, 7O. Andar, Natal Brazil. **LC** HD6957.B82; R627a. **DD** 354.81/32008485/06. **Continues** Servico Social da Industria.; Relatorio Anual de Atividades Referente ao Exercicio de ... .

BL
**RELATORIO ANUAL / SERVICO SOCIAL DO COMERCIO, ADMINISTRACAO NACIONAL. Main/Corp** Servico Social do Comercio. Administracao Nacional. (19??)-. Portuguese. an. Servico Social do Comercio / Rio de Janeiro, Av General Justo 307, Rio de Janeiro Brazil. **LC** HV193; .S46a. **DD** 354.810084/06.

BL
**RELATORIO DE ATIVIDADES - FUNDACAO PARA O LIVRO DO CEGO NO BRASIL. Main/Corp** Fundacao Para o Livro do Cego no Brasil. (19??)-. Portuguese. an. Fundacao Para O Livro do Cego No Brasil, rua Dr Diogo de Faria 558, 04037 Sao Paulo Brazil. **Tel** 571-3825. **LC** HV1892; .F817. **DD** 362.4/183. Index available. **Ad Acc**. **Circ**: 500 (ctrl). **Continues** Relatorio - Fundacao Para o Livro do Cego no Brasil.
**Desc:** Annual activities of the services of the foundation.

BL
**RELATORIO DE ATIVIDADES - SERVICO SOCIAL DO COMERCIO, ADMINISTRACAO REGIONAL NO ESTADO DE GOIAS. Main/Corp** Servico Social do Comercio. Administracao Regional no Estado de Goias. (19??)-. Portuguese. Servico Social do Comercio Administracao Regional No Estado de Goias, Av Universitaria 1749 Cx Postal, Goiania 309 Brazil. **LC** HV194.G6; S47b.

BL
**RELATORIO SETORIAL, GOVERNO DO ESTADO DE SAO PAULO. Main/Corp** Sao Paulo (Brazil : State). Secretaria da Promocao Social. Social. Portuguese. Secretaria da Promocao Social, Avenida Casper Libero 464, Sao Paulo Brazil. **LC** HV194.S3; S45A. **DD** 354.81/610084/06.

FR/0992-9215
**RENCONTRE - MOUVEMENT CHRETIEN DE PROFESSIONS SOCIALES.** (RENCONTRE.). (1972)-. Periodical. French. Four times a year. 112.63F France; 135.00F other. MCPS / Mouvement Chretien de Professions Sociales, 16 rue de Tiphaine, 75015 Paris France. **Tel** 011 33 1 45753470. **UDC** 368. **Continues in part** UCSS Pages Documentaires, 0500-8786.

FR
**REPERTOIRE ANALYTIQUE DU BULLETIN JURIDIQUE / UCANSS, UNION DES CAISSES NATIONALES DE SECURITE SOCIALE. Added/Corp** Union des Caisses Nationales de Securite Sociale (France). (19??)-. French. an. 320.00F France; 450.00F other. Tour Maine-Montparnasse, 33 Avenue du Maine Boites 45 et 46, 75755 Paris Cedex 15 France. **Tel** 45.38.81.44, telex 203604F. **LC** LAW. **DD** 344.44/02/02648; 344.404202648. Index available. cum. index. **Bk Rev**.

CN/0226-0492
**REPERTOIRE DES CENTRES RESIDENTIELS COMMUNAUTAIRES AU CANADA.** 1975-. French. be. Ministere du Solliciteur General du Canada, Ottawa Ontario K1A 0T6 Canada. **DD** 362.8/025/71.

CN/1184-020X
**REPERTOIRE DES RESSOURCES EN SEXUALITE, LE. See** Sexual Life.

CN/0315-8357
**REPERTOIRE DES SERVICES COMMUNAUTAIRES DE GRANBY ET DES ENVIRONS.** First issue in 1971?. Periodical. French. Centre De Reference Et D'Information De Granby, C.P. 332, Granby Quebec. **DD** 361/.0025/71463.

CN/0712-1237
**REPERTOIRE DES SERVICES COMMUNAUTAIRES DE LA REGION ST-HYACINTHE-BELOEIL-MONT ST-HILAIRE.** [Repert. serv. communaut. reg. St-Hyacinthe-Beloeil-Mont St-Hilaire]. **Added/Corp** Centre de Reference et d'Information Familiale (Saint-Hyacinthe, Quebec). (1981)-. French. an. $7.00. Centre de Reference et d'Information Familiale, CP 190, 1900 Ouest rue Girouard, St-Hyacinthe Quebec J2S 7B4 Canada. **DD** 361/.0025/714523. **Continues** Repertoire des Services Communautaires de la Region St-Hyacinthe-Beloeil, 0712-1229.

CN/0319-258X
**REPERTOIRE DES SERVICES COMMUNAUTAIRES DU GRAND MONTREAL. BIEN-ETRE. SANTE. LOISIRS.** (DIRECTORY OF COMMUNITY SERVICES OF GREATER MONTREAL.). **VFOAT**

# Sociology —Social Services and Welfare

Repertoire des Services Communautaires du Grand Montreal. Directory. English (French). be. Fondation du Centre de Refer, 1800 Dorchester Boulevard, West Canada, Montreal Quebec H2L 1Y8 Canada. **Tel** (514)527-1375. LC HV110.M6; D57. **DD** 362/.025/714281; 361/. 0025/714281.

CN/0823-891X
### REPERTOIRE DES SERVICES COMMUNAUTAIRES (SUDBURY).
(REPERTOIRE DES SERVICES COMMUNAUTAIRES.). [Repert. serv. commun.]. 1983/84-. English (French). an. $10.00. Information and Reference Department, Sudbury Public Library, Civic Square West Tower, 200 Brady Street, Sudbury Ontario P3E 5K3 Canada. **Tel** (705)675-1155. **DD** 361/.0025/713133. Index available. *Separated from Directory of Community Services, 0709-0749.*

UK
### REPORT & ACCOUNTS / BRITISH AGENCIES FOR ADOPTION AND FOSTERING.
**Main/Corp** British Agencies for Adoption and Fostering. **VFOAT** Report of the Management Committee and Accounts. 1980/81-. English. an. British Agencies for Adoption & Fostering, 11 Southwark Street, London SE1 1RQ England. **Tel** 011 41 71 407 8800. **ED** Prue Chennells. LC HV887.G7; B74A. **DD** 354.410072/3/05. **Circ:** 5,000.
**Desc:** Reports and accounts for the year ending on the thirty-first of March.

●CN/1188-2034
### REPORT - CANADIAN RED CROSS SOCIETY. NEW BRUNSWICK DIVISION.
(REPORT.). [Rep. - Can. Red Cross Soc., N.B. Div.]. **Main/Corp** Canadian Red Cross Society. New Brunswick Division. (1992)-. English. Limited free distribution. Canadian Red Cross Society / New Brunswick, New Brunswick Division, PO Box 39, Saint John, New Brunswick E2L 3Y3 Canada. **DD** 361.7.

II
### REPORT - KARNATAKA LEGISLATURE, COMMITTEE ON THE WELFARE OF SCHEDULED CASTES & SCHEDULED TRIBES.
**Main/Corp** Karnataka, India. Legislature. Committee on the Welfare of Scheduled Castes and Scheduled Tribes. English. a. Karnataka Legislative Secretariat, Vidhana Soudha, Bangalore 560001 India. LC HN690.M9; M95A. **DD** 362.8. *Continues Report - Committee on the Welfare of Scheduled Castes and Scheduled Tribes.*

US
### REPORT - KENTUCKY. DEPT. OF ECONOMIC SECURITY.
**Main/Corp** Kentucky. Dept. of Economic Security. 1948/49-. English. an. Kentucky Department of Economic Security, Frankfort KY 40601. LC HV86; .K463. **DD** 360.61769.

MY
### REPORT - MALAYA (FEDERATION) DEPT. OF SOCIAL WELFARE. *Title Change.*
**Main/Corp** Malaya (Federation). Dept. of Social Welfare. English. LC HV394.M3. **DD** 360.61595. *Superseded by Annual Report of the Ministry of Labour and Social Welfare.*

II
### REPORT - MEGHALAYA LEGISLATIVE ASSEMBLY, COMMITTEE ON PETITIONS.
**Main/Corp** Meghalaya, India. Legislative Assembly. Committee on Petitions. 1st- 1973-. English. Meghalaya Legislative Assembly Secretariat, Legislative Assembly, Meghalaya Shillong India. LC HV395.M4; M43A. **DD** 362/.954/16.

US/0090-2233
### REPORT OF ACHIEVEMENTS OF PROGRAMS FOR THE AGING.
**Main/Corp** Hawaii. Commission on Aging. 1970/71-. English. an. Hawaii Commission on Aging, 250 South King Street, Honolulu HI 96813. LC HV1468.H3; A25. **DD** 362.6/09969/3.

AT
### REPORT OF THE DEPARTMENT OF COMMUNITY SERVICES FOR THE YEAR ENDED 30 JUNE.
**Main/Corp** Victoria. Dept. of Community Services. **VFOAT** Annual Report. 1985-. English. an. Department of Community Welfare Services, 55 Swanston Street, Melbourne 3000 Australia. LC HV474.V5; V52A. **DD** 354.9450084/06. *Continues Report of the Department of Community Welfare Services for the Year Ended 30 June ... .*

AT/0728-0645
### REPORT OF THE DIRECTOR - DEPARTMENT OF CHILDREN'S SERVICES.
**Main/Corp** Queensland. Dept. of Children's Services. **VFOAT** Annual Report - Department of Children's Services. 1967-. English. a. LC HV802.Q4; A24. **DD** 362.7/09943. **NLM** W2; KA8.1 Q3D3r.

*Continues Queensland. State Children Dept. Annual Report of the Director, State Children Department for the Year ... .*

UY
### REPORT OF THE GENERAL DIRECTOR - INTERAMERICAN CHILDREN'S INSTITUTE.
**Main/Corp** Interamerican Children's Institute. English. an. Interamerican Children's Institute, Avda 8 de Octubre 2904, Montevideo 2904 Uruguay. LC HV703; .I553. **DD** 362.7/098.

US/0098-2717
### REPORT OF THE GOVERNOR'S EARTHQUAKE COUNCIL.
[Rep. Gov. Earthq. Counc.]. **Main/Corp** California. Governor's Earthquake Council. English. Governor's Earthquake Council, Resources Building/Room 1115, 1416 9th Street, Sacramento CA 98517. LC TA654.6; .C3A. **DD** 363.3/4. **Ind/Abst** GeoRef.

US/0362-8248
### REPORT ON DEPARTMENT OF HEALTH, OFFICE OF MENTAL RETARDATION, NORTH CENTRAL REGIONAL CENTER.
**Main/Corp** Connecticut. Auditors PF Public Accounts. (19??)-. English. be. Auditors of Public Accounts, State Capitol, Hartford CT 06106. LC HV3006.C72; B63a. **DD** 353.9/746/00843.

US
### REPORT ON DEPARTMENT OF SOCIAL SERVICES.
**Main/Corp** Connecticut. Auditors of Public Accounts. **Added/Corp** Connecticut. Dept. of Social Services. (1977)-. Periodical. English. an. Connecticut Auditors of Public Accounts, State Capitol, Hartford CT 06106. LC HV86; .C8635a. **DD** 353.97460084. *Supersedes Connecticut. Auditors of Public Accounts. Report on State Welfare Department.*

●US/1063-1968
### REPORT ON HUMAN RESOURCES COMPENSATION.
(REPORT ON HUMAN RESOURCES COMPENSATION / WYATT DATA SERVICES, ECS.). [Rep. human resour. compens.]. **Added/Corp** Executive Compensation Service (U.S.). **VFOAT** Human Resources Compensation. (1992)-. English. an. $190.00. ECS, Executive Compensation Service, Wyatt Data Services, 218 Route 17 North, Roselle Park NJ 07662-9832. **Tel** (201)843-1177, FAX (201)843-0101. LC HF5549.2.U5; R46. **DD** 331.2/816583/00973021.

US
### REPORT ON LEGISLATIVE ACTIVITIES OF THE COMMITTEE ON LABOR AND HUMAN RESOURCES, UNITED STATES SENATE DURING THE ... CONGRESS ... : PURSUANT TO SECTION 136 OF THE LEGISLATIVE REORGANIZATION ACT OF 1946, AS AMENDED BY THE LEGISLATIVE REORGANIZATION ACT OF 1970. *See Public Health and Safety.*

US/1046-6150
### REPORT ON LITERACY PROGRAMS.
[Rep. lit. programs]. (1989)-. Periodical. bw (26 issues). $260.00. Business Publishers Inc., 951 Pershing Drive, Silver Spring MD 20910-4464. **Tel** (301)587-6300, (800)274-0122, FAX (301)585-9075. **DD** 362. **[CCC]**.
**Desc:** Every issue follows the legislation, funding, agencies and resources involved in adult literacy. It covers the Department of Education and Labor (especially amendments to the Job Training Partnership Act), and reports on funding for literacy-related projects. In addition, the journal reports on efforts to teach basic skills to children before they enter the workforce, innovative strategies to keep "at-risk" youth in school, programs within correctional institutions, and bilingual education and migrant education programs.

CN/1191-3398
### REPORT ON THE BUDGET FOR THE DEVELOPMENT USES OF UNEMPLOYMENT INSURANCE. *Title Change.*
[Rep. budg. dev. uses unempl. insur.]. **Main/Corp** Canadian Labour Force Development Board. **VFOAT** Rapport Sur le Budget de Pour les Utilisations a des Fins Productives de L'Assurance-Chomage. (1992-(19??). English (French). Canada Labour Force Development Board, 23-66 Slater Street, Ottawa, Ontario K1P 5H1 Canada. **DD** 331.13/77/0971. *Continued by Canadian Labour Force Development Board. Report of the Canadian Labour Force Development Board on the Unemployment Insurance (UI) Developmental Uses Plan for ..., 1189-9441.*

US/0277-660X
### REPORT TO COUNCIL ON AGING.
(REPORT TO COUNCIL ON PROGRAM / NATIONAL INSTITUTE ON AGING.). **Main/Corp** National Institute on Aging. English. an. National Institute on Aging, National Institutes of Health, Room B4NB08 Building 31, Bethesda MD 20205. **Tel** (301)496-1789. LC HQ1060. **DD** 362.6/07/1173. **NLM** W2; A N2226r.

AT
### REPORT UPON THE OPERATIONS OF THE SUB-DEPARTMENTS OF NATIVE AFFAIRS, EVENTIDE (SANDGATE), EVENTIDE (CHARTERS TOWERS), EVENTIDE (ROCKHAMPTON), INSTITUTION FOR INEBRIATES (MARBURG), AND QUEENSLAND INDUSTRIAL INSTITUTION FOR THE BLIND (SOUTH BRISBANE).
**Added/Corp** Queensland. Dept. of Health and Home Affairs. **VFOAT** Reports Upon the Operations of Certain Sub-Departments of the Department of Health and Home Affairs. (19??)-. English. an. Government Printer / Queensland, Box 680 GPO, 102 George Street, Brisbane Queensland 4001 Australia. LC WMLC L 83/6953.

US/0091-8482
### REPORT - WORKSHOP FOR CHILD CARE STAFF OF FLORIDA'S CHILD CARING FACILITIES.
(REPORT.). **Main/Conf** Workshop for Child Care Staff of Florida's Child Caring Facilities. English. an. $1.00 per copy. Stetson University, 1401 61st Street South, Gulf Port FL 33707. LC HV742.F6; W65A. **DD** 362.7/32/09759.

UK
### REPORTED DECISIONS OF THE SOCIAL SECURITY COMMISSIONER. SOCIAL SECURITY, CHILD BENEFIT, FAMILY INCOME SUPPLEMENTS, AND SUPPLEMENTARY BENEFIT ACTS / DEPARTMENT OF HEALTH AND SOCIAL SECURITY.
**Main/Corp** Great Britain. Dept. of Health and Social Security. **VFOAT** Social Security and Child Benefit Acts, Commissioner's Decisions. Vol. 9 (1980 to 1982)-. English. LC KD3196.A2; H4. **DD** 344.41/02/02646; 344.104202646. *Continues Great Britain. Dept. of Health and Social Security. Reported Decisions of the Commissioner Under the Social Security and Child Benefit Acts.*

US/0271-2784
### RESEARCH AND DEVELOPMENT PROJECTS IN AGING.
[Res. dev. proj. aging]. **Main/Corp** United States. Administration on Aging. **VAT** Research & Development Projects in Aging. English. Administration on Aging, 330 Independence Avenue SW, Washington DC 20201. LC HV1457; .U5A. **DD** 362.6/072073. **NLM** WT 22 AA1 R4.

US/0362-8221
### RESEARCH, DEMONSTRATION AND EVALUATION STUDIES ON CHILD ABUSE AND NEGLECT.
**Main/Corp** United States. Dept. of Health, Education, and Welfare. Intradepartmental Committee on Child Abuse and Neglect. (1974)-. Government Publication. English. an. $0.80. Superintendent of Documents, US Government Printing Office, Washington DC 20402. **Tel** (202)275-3328, FAX (202)786-2377. LC HV741; .U524a. **DD** 362.7/8/1971.

US
### RESEARCH GRANTS / [PREPARED BY NATIONAL INSTITUTES OF HEALTH, DIVISION OF RESEARCH GRANTS, STATISTICS AND ANALYSIS BRANCH].
*See Medical Science and Technology.*

●US
### RESEARCH IN PROGRESS.
**Added/Corp** Indiana University. Center on Philanthropy. (1989/1992)-. English. Indiana University Center on Philanthropy, Journals Division, Indiana University Press, 601 North Morton Street, Bloomington IN 47404. *Continues in part Research-In-Progress (Washington, D.C. : 1983), 0882-6692.*

US/1049-7315
### RESEARCH ON SOCIAL WORK PRACTICE.
[Res. soc. work pract.]. (1991)-. Periodical. English. qt (Jan., Apr., July, Oct.). $127.00. SAGE Periodical Press, 2455 Teller Road, Thousand Oaks CA 91320. **Tel** (805)499-0721, FAX (805)499-0871, telex 100799. **ED** Bruce A. Thyer (University of Georgia). LC HV1; .R47. **DD** 361.3/2/05. **CODEN** RSWPEW. Acid Free. Documents available from The Genuine Article.
**Desc:** Devoted to the publication of empirical research concerning methods and outcomes of social work practice. Social work practice is broadly interpreted to refer to the application of intentionally designed social work intervention programs to problems of societal and/or interpersonal importance.
**Ind/Abst** Curr. Contents Soc. Behav. Sci.; Hum. Resour. Abstr.; Psychoanal. Abstr.; Psychol. Abstr. (1991-); PsycScan: Appl. Exp. Eng. Psych.; PsycScan: LD/MR;

PsycScan: Neuropsych.; Res. Alert [Full Cov.]; Sage Fam. Stud. Abstr.; Soc. Plann. Policy Dev. Abstr.; Soc. Sci. Cit. Index [Full Cov.]; Soc. Work Abstr. [Full Cov.].

US/0091-5823
**RESEARCH REPORT AFDC.** [Res. rep. A.F.D.C.]. **Main/Corp** Colorado. Dept. of Social Services. Research and Statistics Section. English. Department of Social Services / Colorado, Research and Statistics, Denver CO. **LC** HV742.C6; C57A.

CN/1195-4175
**RESIDENTIAL CARE FACILITIES, MENTAL / STATISTICS CANADA, CANADIAN CENTRE FOR HEALTH INFORMATION.** **Added/Corp** Canadian Centre for Health Information. **VFOAT** Etablissements de Soins Speciaux pour Beneficiaires Internes, Troubles Mentaux. (19??)-. English (French). 15.00Can$ Canada; $18.00 US; $21.00 other. Statistics Canada, Publications Sales & Services, Main Building Room 1710, Ottawa Ontario K1A 0T6 Canada. **Tel** (613)951-5078, (800)267-6677, FAX (613)951-1584, telex 053-3585. **LC** RA790.7.C2; H44. **DD** 362.2/3/0971021. ***Continues*** *Health Reports. Supplements. Residential Care Facilities.*

US/0886-571X
**RESIDENTIAL TREATMENT FOR CHILDREN & YOUTH.** [Resid. treat. child. youth]. **VFOAT** Residential Treatment for Children and Youth. Vol. 4, No. 1 (Fall 1986)-. Academic Scholarly Publication. English. qt. $160.00 US; $224.00 other. The Haworth Press Inc, 10 Alice Street, Binghamton NY 13904-1580. **Tel** (607)722-5857, (800)3-HAWORTH, FAX (607)722-1424. **ED** Gordon Northrup (editor's address: R R 1, Box 561, Lee, MA 01238-9602). **LC** HV59; .R48. **DD** 362.7/32/05. **NLM** W1; RE245V. **CODEN** RTCYEY. **Bk Rev. Ad Acc. Pr Rev. Acid Free. Circ:** 399. available on microfilm and microfiche from University Microfilms International (UMI). Documents available from BIOSIS Document Express, Haworth Document Delivery Service. ***Continues*** *Residential Group Care & Treatment, 0731-7123.*
**Desc:** Serves as an active and contemporary forum for those engaged in the interdisciplinary task of the residential group care of children and youth. Provides a national exchange of scientific views, innovative practices and perspectives on current issues and developments in the field.
**Ind/Abst** Abstr. Res. Pastor. Care Couns. (19??-); Biol. Abstr.; Child Dev. Abstr. Bibliogr.; Crim. Justice Abstr. (Fall 1986-); Crim. Penol. Police Sci. Abstr.; EMBASE (Fall 1986-); Except. Child Educ. Resour.; Hum. Resour. Abstr. (?-?); Pollut. Abstr. Indexes (Fall 1986-); Psychol. Abstr. (Fall 1986-); PsycINFO (1990-); PsycLit; Sage Fam. Stud. Abstr.; Soc. Plann. Policy Dev. Abstr.; Soc. Work Abstr. [Select. Cov.]; Sociol. Abstr. (Fall 1986-); Sociol. Educ. Abstr.; Spec. Educ. Needs Abstr.

CN/0225-5804
**RESILOG.** [Resilog]. **Added/Corp** Canada. Environmental Impact Control Directorate. Waste Management Branch. **VFOAT** Resilog. No. 1 (Dec. 1978)-. Periodical. English (French). Four times a year. Environment Canada / Emergencies Science Division, Ottawa Ontario K1A 0H3 Canada. **Tel** (819)998-9622. **DD** 363.7/28/0971. ***Supersedes*** *Collator.*

US/0892-0818
**RESOURCES IN AGING.** [Resour. aging]. **Added/Corp** American Association of Adult and Continuing Education. Education and Aging Unit. Institute of Lifetime Learning (American Association of Retired Persons) Boca Institute on Aging (Florida). (1???)-. Periodical. English. bm. $25.00. Demko Publishing, 21946 Pine Trace, Boca Raton FL 33428. **Tel** (407)482-6271. **ED** David Demko. **DD** 362. Index available. cum. index. **Bk Rev. Ad Acc. Pr Rev. Circ:** 3,200 (ctrl).
**Desc:** New developments in aging. Learning resources (print, film, video) program innovations, research reports, periodicals, resource directories, forthcoming seminars/conference and funding sources.

US/0894-7597
**RESPONSE TO THE VICTIMIZATION OF WOMEN AND CHILDREN.** ***Title Change.*** (RESPONSE TO THE VICTIMIZATION OF WOMEN AND CHILDREN : JOURNAL OF THE CENTER FOR WOMEN POLICY STUDIES.). [Response victim. women child.]. **Added/Corp** Center for Women Policy Studies. **VFOAT** Response. Vol. 7, No. 4 (Fall 1984)-(199?). Periodical. English. qt. Response Inc., 4136 Leland Street, Chevy Chase MD 20815. **Tel** (301)951-0039. **ED** Jane Roberts Chapman. **DD** 362. **CODEN** RVWCEE. available on microfilm and microfiche from University Microfilms International (UMI). ***Continues*** *Response to Violence in the Family & Sexual Assault, 0737-8300.* ***Merged into*** *Violence Update, 1052-2689.*
**Desc:** Presents the state of the art of intervention, prevention, and assessment as well as the social, political, and legislative trends that profoundly affect the victims of interpersonal violence.
**Ind/Abst** Crim. Justice Abstr. (199?-); Int. Bibliogr. Sociol.; Psychol. Abstr. (1985-); PsycINFO (1990-); PsycLit; Soc. Plann. Policy Dev. Abstr.

UK
**REVIEW OF ... / BRITISH RED CROSS.** **Main/Corp** British Red Cross Society. English. British Red Cross Society, 9 Grosvenor Crescent, London SW1X 7EJ England. **Tel** (01)235-5454, FAX (01)245-6315, telex 918657. **LC** HV580.G6; B75a. **DD** 361.7/634/0941. ***Continues*** *Annual Review of the British Red Cross Society.*

●US/1063-1356
**REVIEW - PATIENT FOCUSED CARE ASSOCIATION.** (REVIEW/ PATIENT FOCUSED CARE ASSOCIATION.). [Rev. - Patient Focus. Care Assoc.]. **Added/Corp** Patient Focused Care Association. **VFOAT** PFCA Review. (1992)-. Periodical. English. qt. $300.00. Patient Focused Care Association, 4239 Farnam, Suite 28, Omaha NE 68131. **DD** 362.

BL
**REVISTA DE PREVIDENCIA SOCIAL.** Portuguese. bm. 2350. Editora Previdenciarai Ltda, Caixa Postal 9117, CEP 01047 Sao Paulo SP Brazil. **LC** HV193; .R48. **DD** 361/.981.

SP
**REVISTA DE SEGURIDAD SOCIAL.** Began with Jan./Mar. 1979 issue. Periodical. Spanish. $30.00. Ministerio de Sanidad y Consumo, Paseo del Prado 18 20, 28071 Madrid Spain. **Tel** 011 34 1 420-2227, 420-2051. **LC** HD7088; .R48.
**Ind/Abst** LABORDOC.

BL
**REVISTA - INSTITUTO NACIONAL DE PREVIDENCIA SOCIAL. PROCURADORIA-GERAL.** **Main/Corp** Instituto Nacional de Previdencia Social. Procuradoria-Gera. V. 1- Jan./Feb. 1970-. Portuguese. bm. Rua Sao Jose 90, 14O. Andar Sala 1.411-E, Guanabara Brazil.

BL
**REVISTA PROMOCAO SOCIAL SAO PAULO.** **Added/Corp** Sao Paulo (Brazil : State). Secretaria da Promocao Social. No. 1, (May 1975)-. Portuguese. **LC** HV194.S3; S44.

BE/0771-1530
**REVUE BELGE DE SECURITE SOCIALE.** [Rev. belge secur. soc.]. **Added/Corp** Belgium. Ministere de la Prevoyance Sociale. Vol. 1 (Jan./Feb. 1954)-. Periodical. French. Four times a year. 900F. Ministerie Van Sociale Voorzor, Zwarte Lievevrouwstraat 3C, 1000 Brussels Belguim. **Tel** 011 32 2 512 7860. **LC** HD7186; .A36. **DD** 368.4/009493. Index available. **Bk Rev. Circ:** 1,000. ***Supersedes in part*** *Revue Belge de Securite Sociale;* ***Continues*** *Belgium. Office National de Coordination des Allocations Familiales. Revue des Allocations Familiales.*
**Desc:** Upper level scientific journal concentrating on problems which are relevant to Belgian social security.
**Ind/Abst** Foreign Lang. Index; Int. Labour Doc.; LABORDOC.

BE
**REVUE D'ACTION SOCIALE : AS.** **VFOAT** AS. Periodical. French. bm. 1000F Belgium; 1600F other. rue des Augustins 30, 4000 Liege Belgium. **Tel** 041/23 3804. **LC** HV303; .R48. **DD** 362/.9493. **Circ:** 6,000.

●CN/1192-3636
**REVUE DE L'AMIE.** (LA REVUE DE L'AMIE / AIDE MEDICALE INTERNATIONALE A L'ENFANCE.). [Rev. AMIE]. **Added/Corp** Aide Medicale Internationale a l'Enfance. **VFOAT** Revue de l'Aide Medicale Internationale a l'Enfance. Vol. 1, (1992)-. Periodical. French. ir. Aide Medicale Internationale a l'Enfance, CP 282, La Pocatiere, Quebec G0R 1Z0 Canada. **DD** 362.7/08/6. ***Continues*** *Bulletin de l'AMIE (La Pocatiere, Quebec)., 1187-5038.*

FR
**REVUE FRANCAISE DE SERVICE SOCIAL, LA.** **Added/Corp** Association Nationale des Assistantes Sociales et des Assistants Sociaux. Association Nationale des Asistants de Service Social. No. 1 (19??)-. Periodical. French. Four times a year (Mar., June, Sept., Dec.). 250.00F France; 290.00F others. Association Nationale des Assistants de Service Social, 15 rue de Bruxelles, 75009 Paris France. **Tel** 011 33 1 45263379. **Ad Acc. Circ:** 4,000 (ctrl).
**Desc:** Journal of studies concerning thought and communication on French social service.

SZ/0379-0312
**REVUE INTERNATIONALE DE SECURITE SOCIALE.** [Rev. int. secur. soc.]. (1967)-. Periodical. French (English, German and Spanish). qt. 50.00F. International Social Security Association, Case Postale 1, CH-1211 Geneva 22 Switzerland. **Tel** 011 41 22 7996617, FAX 011 41 22 7986385.
**Desc:** Reports on international activities in the field of social security. Presents a complete record of the work of the ISSA.
**Ind/Abst** LABORDOC.

IT/0035-6522
**RIVISTA DI SERVIZIO SOCIALE, LA.** [Riv. serv. soc.]. (1961)-. Periodical. Italian. qt. L60000.00 Italy; L75000.00 Europe; L88000.00 other. Rivista di Servizio Sociale, Vle di Villa Pamphili 84, 00152 Rome Italy. **Tel** 011 39 6 5897179. **UDC** 36.

JA
**ROKYOIKU KAGAKU.** **VFOAT** Soundless World. Japanese. qt. ¥600 individual membership. Ro-Kyoiku Kagaku-kai, c/o Kyoto Daigaku Bungakubu Sonohara Kenkyushitsu, Yoshida Sakyo-ku Kyoto Japan. **LC** HV2350; .R63.

PL
**ROLNIK SPOLDZIELCA.** Periodical. Polish. wk. $65.00. **(Subscription address:** ARS Polona, PO Box 1001, 00068 Warsaw Poland.)

US
**RULINGS. CUMULATIVE EDITION : SOCIAL SECURITY RULINGS ON FEDERAL OLD-AGE, SURVIVORS, DISABILITY, SUPPLEMENTAL SECURITY INCOME, AND BLACK LUNG BENEFITS.** **Main/Corp** United States. Social Security Administration. **VFOAT** Social Security Rulings; SSR. 1980-. English. an. US Department of Health and Human Services, 200 Independence Avenue Southwest, Washington DC 20201. **LC** KF3646.A2; S6. **DD** 344.73/023. ***Continues*** *Social Security Rulings on Federal Old-Age, Survivors, Disability, Supplemental Security Income, and Black Lung Benefits. Cumulative Edition.*

●US/1062-2640
**S.H.A.R.E. (TUKWILA, WASHINGTON).** (S.H.A.R.E.: SUPPORT HELP AND RESOURCES EXCHANGE.). [S.H.A.R.E.]. **VFOAT** Support Help and Resources Exchange; SHARE. (1992)-. Periodical. English. bm. $30.00. S.H.A.R.E., PO Box 88722, Tukwila WA 98138-2722. **DD** 362.

US/0891-866X
**S.O.S.** [S.O.S.]. **VFOAT** SOS. **VAT** Survivors of Suicide. Periodical. English. qt. $8.00. American Association of Suicidology, 2459 South Ash, Denver CO 80222. **Tel** 303 692-0985, FAX 303 756-3299. **DD** 362.

IS
**SAAD.** English. Ministry of Social Welfare, Jerusalem Israel. **LC** HV4; .S22. **DD** 361/.0095694.

US
**SAGE HUMAN SERVICES GUIDES.** Vol. 1 (1977)-. Monographic series. English. ir. Price varies per volume. SAGE Periodical Press, 2455 Teller Road, Thousand Oaks CA 91320. **Tel** (805)499-0721, FAX (805)499-0871, telex 100799. **Acid Free.**

KO
**SAHOE POKCHI.** **VFOAT** Social Welfare. Periodical. Korean (Korean). qt. Hanguk Sahoe Pokchi Hyobuihoe, 427-5 Kongduk-dong Mapo-ku, Seoul Korea. **LC** HV415.5.A44.

US
**SALARY STUDY.** **Added/Corp** Child Welfare League of America. (1991)-. Periodical. English. an. $34.95. Child Welfare League of America, 440 1st Street Northwest, Suite 310, Washington DC 20001. **Tel** (202)638-2952, FAX (202)638-4004. **LC** HV741; .A17. **DD** 331.2/8136132/0973021. **NLM** W1; SA31M. ***Continues*** *CWLA Salary Study.*
**Desc:** Covers social and child welfare workers.

US/0744-5083
**SALVATION ARMY YOUTH.** (SALVATION ARMY YOUTH : SAY.). **VFOAT** SAY; S.A.Y.; SAY Magazine. Periodical. English. mo. $3.00. Salvation Army / Headquarters, National Headquarters, 799 Bloomfield Avenue, Verona NJ 07044.

CN/1184-0188
**SANG-LIENS.** (SANG-LIENS / MOUVEMENT RETROUVAILLES, ADOPTE(E)S, NON-ADOPTE(E)S, PARENTS.). [Sang-liens]. **Added/Corp** Mouvement Retrouvailles. **VFOAT** Sans Liens. No. 1 (1990)-. Periodical. French. Three times a year. Free. Mouvement Retrouvailles, CP211, Limoilou, Quebec G1L 4V1 Canada. **DD** 362.82/98/0971405.

CN/0832-8048
**SANTE SOCIETE.** ***Ceased.*** [Sante soc.]. **Added/Corp** Quebec (Province). Ministere de la Sante et des Services Sociaux. Vol. 7, No. 4 (Autumn 1985)- Vol. 14, No. 4 (Dec. 1992). Periodical. French. qt. Ministere de la Sante Services Sociaux, 25 Boulevard Taschereau, Bureau 201, Greenfield PK QC J4V2G8 Canada. **Tel** (418)643-9395, (418)643-7167. **DD** 361/.9714/05. ***Continues*** *Carrefour des Affaires Sociales., 0226-6849.*

CN
**SASKATCHEWAN ASSOCIATION OF SOCIAL WORKERS NEWSLETTER.** (19??)-. Newsletter. English. Four times a year. 20.00$Can. Saskatchewan Association of Social

Workers, 2341 McIntyre Street, Regina, Saskatchewan, S4P 2S3 Canada. **Tel** (306)545-1922, FAX (306)545-1895. **ED** Morgan Williams. **Bk Rev**, (Qty: 6). **Ad Acc**, **Adv Mgr:** M. Hicks, **Tel** same as publisher. **Pr Rev. Circ:** 750 (ctrl).

US/8756-1476
**SATERN.** (SATERN : SATELLITE ASSISTED EMERGENCY RESCUE NEWS.). [SATERN]. **VFOAT** Satellite-Assisted Emergency Assisted Emergency Rescue News. No. 1 (Summer 1984)-. Periodical. English. qt. $20.00. Satern, 427 Haverhill Road, Joppa MD 21085. **DD** 363.

●US/1063-9004
**SATISFACTION (EVANS, GA.). See** Medical Science and Technology-Hospital Administration and Medical Centers.

FR/0036-5041
**SAUVEGARDE DE L'ENFANCE.** **Added/Corp** Union Nationale des Associations Regionales pour la Sauvegarde de l'Enfance et de l'Adolescence. Association Francaise pour la Sauvegarde de l'Enfance et de l'Adolescence. (May 1946)-. Periodical. French. ir (5 issues per year). 390.00F France; 460.00F other. Expansion Scientifique Francaise, 31 Boulevard de la Tour-Maubourg, 75007 Paris France. **Tel** 011 33 1 40 62 64 00, 011 33 1 40626439. **LC** HV761; .A16. **DD** 362.7/0944. **NLM** W1 SA979. **Bk Rev**.
**Desc:** Includes normal and pathological psychology, sociology, education and assistance of the maladjusted child.

●DK/0907-2055
**SCANDINAVIAN JOURNAL OF SOCIAL WELFARE.** (1992)-. English. qt. kr760.00 (institution), kr485.00 (individual) US, Canada and Japan; kr710.00 (institution), kr435.00 (individual) other. Munksgaard International Publishers Ltd, PO Box 2148, DK-1016 Copenhagen K Denmark. **Tel** 011 45 33 12 70 30, FAX 011 45 33 12 93 87, telex 19431 MUNKS DK. **ED** Sven Hessle. **[CCC]**. **Bk Rev**. **Ad Acc**. **Pr Rev**.
**Desc:** Publishes original articles in English on social work and welfare. Focuses on research in Scandinavia but welcomes contributions from elsewhere, especially comparative articles.

SZ/0255-9072
**SCHWEIZERISCHE ZEITSCHRIFT FUER SOZIALVERSICHERUNG UND BERUFLICHE VORSORGE. See** Insurance.

US
**SEA-TOWN CRIER. VFOAT** Sea Town Crier; Crier. Vol. 1, No. 1 (Apr. 1, 1991)-. Periodical. English (Spanish). mo. **LC** HV4506.S6; S415.

UK/0958-3467
**SEARCH YORK.** (1989)-. English. qt. Joseph Rowntree Foundation, The Homestead, 40 Water End, York Y03 6LP England. **Tel** 0904 629241, FAX 0904 620072. **ED** Roland Hurst. **Bk Rev**. **Pr Rev. Circ:** 7,000 (ctrl).
**Desc:** Articles and information highlighting recent work from JRF's research and development project.

US/0092-7740
**SECURITY REGISTER.** ***Suspended.*** (Nov. 1973)-?. Periodical. English. bm. $12.00. Nickerson & Collins, 850 Busse Highway, Park Ridge IL 60068-2382. **Tel** (312)298-6210. **LC** HV8290; .S38. **DD** 658.4/7/05.

US/0194-4495
**SEEDS (DECATUR, GA.). See** International Assistance and Development.

US
**SELECTED CHARACTERISTICS OF PUBLIC ASSISTANCE RECIPIENTS IN NEW YORK CITY BY COMMUNITY DISTRICT.** **Main/Corp** New York (N.Y.). Human Resources Administration. Division of Policy and Economic Research. (19??)-. English. **LC** HV87.N5; H84b. **DD** 362.5/2/097471.

US/0740-7548
**SELF-HELP GROUP DIRECTORY.** (THE SELF-HELP GROUP DIRECTORY.). [Self-help group dir.]. **VFOAT** Self Help Group Directory. 1984-85-. Directory. English. an. $15.00. New Jersey Self-Help Clearinghouse, Saint Clares Riverside Medical Center, Denville NJ 07834. **Tel** (201)625-7101. **ED** A Meese. **LC** HV547; .S43. **DD** 361.7/025/73. **Circ:** 2,000.
**Desc:** Comprehensive guide to self-help groups in New Jersey and national organizations.

IT
**SEMPRE.** (19??)-. Italian. mo. L25000.00 Italy; L35000.00 other. Assn Papa Giovanni XXIII, Via Tiberio 6, 47037 Rimini Italy. **Tel** 011 39 541 55025.

CN/0824-135X
**SERIES - PACIFIC GROUP FOR POLICY ALTERNATIVES.** (SERIES.). [Ser. - Pac. Group Policy Altern.]. Vol. 1 (Feb. 1984)-. Monographic series. English. Price varies per volume. Pacific Group for Policy Alternatives, 22 East 8th Avenue, Vancouver British Columbia V5T 1R4 Canada. **DD** 361.6/1/09711.

US/0744-2807
**SERTOMAN.** **Added/Corp** Sertoma International. (19??)-. Periodical. English. bm. $1.50. Sertoma International, 1912 East Meyer Boulevard, Kansas City MO 64132. **Tel** (816)333-8300. **ED** Arthur F. Bisson. **Bk Rev. Circ:** 30,000 (ctrl).

CN/0712-7642
**SERVICE CLUBS IN HAMILTON-WENTWORTH.** [Serv. clubs Hamilt.-Wentworth]. Oct. 1979-. English. an. $2.00 per vol. Community Information Service Hamilton-Wentworth, Public Library, 55 York Boulevard, Hamilton Ontario L8N 4E4 Canada. **Tel** (416)528-0104. **DD** 361/.0025/71352. ***Continues*** *Service Club Directory of Hamilton and District, 0384-1529.*

BE/0037-2641
**SERVICE SOCIAL DANS LE MONDE.** [Serv. soc. monde]. (1942)-. Periodical. French (English, Spanish, German and Portuguese; summaries and/or abstracts in French, Spanish, German and English). Four times a year. 800F Belgium; 950F other. Service Sociale dans le Monde, rue du Gouvernement 50, 7000 Mons Belgium. **Tel** 011 32 2 3569318, 5120511. **UDC** 335.6. ***Continues*** *Bulletin d'Information.*

CN/0037-2633
**SERVICE SOCIALE (QUEBEC).** (SERVICE SOCIAL.). [Serv. soc.]. **Added/Corp** Universite Laval. Ecole de Service Social. (April 1951)-. Periodical. French. Three times a year. 40.00Can$ (institutions), 28.00Can$ (individuals) Canada; 37.00Can$ (institutions), 27.00Can$ (individuals) US; 39.00Can$ (institutions), 31.00Can$ (individuals) other. Universite Laval / Departement de Sociologie, Faculte de Sciences Sociales, Pavillon Charles de Koninck, Quebec QUE G1K 7P4 Canada. **Tel** (418)656-2131 ext. 4452, FAX (418)656-3266. **LC** HV2; .S4. ctrl circ. available on microfilm from University Microfilms International (UMI).
**Desc:** Deals with social science, social problems with housing, and deviations and delinquency in Canada.
**Ind/Abst** PAIS Int. Print; Point Repere (1983-).

CN/0227-034X
**SERVICE (TORONTO).** (SERVICE.). [Service]. **Added/Corp** Canadian Red Cross Society. Vol. 38, No. 3 (1977)-. English (French). Four times a year. Free on request. Ontario Division - Canadian Red Cross, 5700 Canross Court, Mississauga Ontario L5R 3E9 Canada. **Tel** (905)890-1000. **DD** 361.7/7. ***Formed by the union of*** *Service (Toronto, Ont.). English, 0227-034X* ***and*** *Service (Toronto, Ont.). French, 0227-0358.*

UK
**SERVICES FOR CHILDREN.** (1990)-. Bulletin. English. £2.00. Social Work Services Group, Statistics Branch, 43 Jeffrey Street / Room 422, Edinburgh EH1 1DG Scotland. **Tel** 031 244 5431, FAX 031 244 5387.

CN/0820-8530
**SERVICES FOR SENIORS.** [Serv. sr.]. **Added/Corp** Community Information Centre, Waterloo Region. (1983)-. English. an. $1.00. Community Information Centre, Waterloo Region, 10 Water Street North, Kitchener Ontario N2H 5A5. **DD** 362.6/09713/44.
**Desc:** Comprehensive guide to services for seniors available in Waterloo region.

US
**SERVICES FOR TEXAS CHILDREN / TEXAS DEPARTMENT OF COMMUNITY AFFAIRS, CHILDREN AND YOUTH SERVICES DIVISION.** **Added/Corp** Texas. Dept. of Community Affairs. Children and Youth Services Division. Texas. Dept. of Community Affairs. Children and Youth Services Division. Annual Report. (19??)-. English. TDCA, Children and Youth Services Division, Box 13166, Capitol Station, Austin TX 78711. **LC** HV742.T4; S46. **DD** 362.7/95/025764.
**Desc:** Includes the Annual report of the Division.

SP
**SERVICIOS SOCIALES Y POLITICA SOCIAL.** Spanish. Three times a year. 1375.00ptas Spain; 1500.00ptas other. Revista de Servicios Sociales y Politica Social, Dr Cortezo 11-2, 18012 Madrid Spain.

BL/0101-6628
**SERVICO SOCIAL E SOCIEDADE.** [Serv. soc. soc.]. Vol. 1, No. 1, (Sept. 1979)-. Periodical. Portuguese. Three times a year. $45.00. Cortez e Editora, 387 rue Bartira 05009, Sao Paulo SP Brazil. **ED** Antonio de Paulo Silva. **LC** HV193; .S47. **DD** 361/.981. **Circ:** 5,000.
**Desc:** For the social services professionals. Aims to provoke the developments of critical thought and ideas.

JA
**SHAKAI FUKUSHI NO DOKO.** **Main/Corp** Zenkoku Shakai Fukushi Kyogikai. **Added/Corp** Japan. Koseisho. Shakaikyoku. (19??)-. Japanese. ¥320. Zenkoku Shakai Fukushi Kyogikai, 3-3-4 Kasumigaseki Chiyoda-ku, Tokyo Japan. **LC** HV413.A2; Z43a.

JA
**SHAKAI FUKUSHI ROPPO / KOSEISHO SHAKAIKYOKU JIDO KATEIKYOKU ENGOKYOKU KANSHU.** **Main/Corp** Japan. Japanese. ¥3400. Shin Nihon Hoki Shuppan Kabuskiki Kaisha, 6 Ichigaya Sadohara-cho 2-chome, Shinjuku-ku 162, Tokyo-to Japan. **LC** LAW.

JA
**SHAKAI FUKUSHI SHISETSU CHOSA KOKOKU.** **Main/Corp** Tokyo. Minseikyoku. Somubu. Kikakuka. Japanese. Minseikyoku, Somubu Kikakuka, Tokyo-to 81 Marunouchi, Chiyoda-ku 100, Tokyo Japan. **LC** HV413; .T63A.

JA
**SHAKAI HOKEN ROMU HANDOBUKKU.** Japanese. Chuo Keizaisha, 31-2 Kanda Jinbocho 1, Chiyoda-ku 101, Tokyo Japan.

JA
**SHAKAI MONDAI KENKYU.** **VFOAT** Journal of Social Problems. Began with July 1951 issue. Periodical. Japanese (Japanese). Osaka Shakai Jigyo Tanki Daigaku, Yuhigoaka Tennoji-ku 543, Osaka Japan. **LC** HV4; .S45.

CH
**SHE HUI FU LI CHIH PIAO. SOCIAL WELFARE INDICATORS REPUBLIC OF CHINA.** **Added/Corp** China (Republic of China). Ching Chi She Chi Wei Yuan Hui. Tsung ho Chi Hua Chu. **VFOAT** Social Welfare Indicators, Republic of China. (19??)-. Multiple languages (Chinese and English). **LC** HV426; .C46a.

CH
**SHE HUI PAO HSIEN NIEN KAN.** **Main/Corp** Chung-Kuo She Hui Pao Hsien Hsueh Hui. **VFOAT** Annual Report of Social Insurance. First published in- ; 1976-. Chinese (English). Chung-Kuo She Kui Pao Hsien Hsueh Hui, Labor Insurance Building/Room 605, 42 Chi Nana Road Section 2, Taipei Taiwan. **LC** HD7090; .C37A.

US/0734-3078
**SHELTER SENSE.** **Added/Corp** Humane Society of the United States. National Humane Education Center. (April 1978)-. Periodical. English. Ten times a year. $8.00 one year; $12.00 two years. Humane Society of the United States, 2100 L Street NW, Washington DC 20037. **Tel** (202)452-1100. **ED** Susan Bury Stauffer. **Bk Rev. Circ:** 3,000.
**Desc:** A newsletter for humane and animal control workers that helps them increase their professionalism, reduce animal suffering, and solve community animal problems.
**Ind/Abst** Urban Aff. Abstr.

JA
**SHUKAN SHAKAI HOSHO.** **VFOAT** Shakai Hosho. Began with: Vol. 17, No. 196 (April 1, 1963). Japanese. ¥20000. Shakai Hoken Hoki Kenkyukai, 10-1 Ginza 1-chome Chuo-ku, Tokyo-to 104 Japan. **LC** HD7227; .A545. **NLM** W1; SH644R. ***Formed by the union of*** *Gekkan Shakai Hosho* ***and*** *Shakai Hosho Shuho.*

GW/0170-8694
**SIFKU-INFORMATIONEN.** Periodical. English (German). qt. 7.00 each issue. Verein Fur Sozialwissenschaftliche Katastrophen-Und Unfallforschung, 2300 Kiel 1, Holtenauer Str 82, Kiel Germany. **LC** HV553; .S49. **DD** 363.3/4/05.

AT
**SITREP.** English. qt. New South Wales St Emergency, Box 42, Queen Victoria Building, Sydney New South Wales 2000 Australia. **LC** HV555.A8; S57. **DD** 361.5/09944. ***Formed by the union of*** *New South Wales. State Emergency Services. Bulletin* ***and*** *New South Wales. Bush Fire Council. Bulletin.*

US
**SKILLED WORKER EMERITUS PROGRAM / NEW YORK STATE JOB TRAINING PARTNERSHIP COUNCIL.** **Added/Corp** New York State Job Training Partnership Council. **VFOAT** New York State Skilled Worker Emeritus Program. (1990/1991)-. English.

US/0037-7317
**SMITH COLLEGE STUDIES IN SOCIAL WORK.** [Smith Coll. stud. soc. work]. **Main/Corp** Smith College. School for Social Work. **Added/Corp** Smith College. School for Social Work. Studies in Social Work. Vol. 1 (Sept. 1930)-. Periodical. English. Three times a year (Mar., Jun., Nov.). $16.00. Smith College School for Social Work, Lilly Hall, Northampton MA 01063. **Tel** (413)585-7950, (413)585-7974. **ED** John Laird. **LC** HV1; .S55. **DD** 360.5. **NLM** W1 SM401. **CODEN** SMSWAW. Index available (June issue). **Bk Rev. Pr Rev. Circ:** 1,350 (ctrl). Documents available from The Genuine Article.
**Desc:** Psychoanalytic, psychological scholarship and research in mental health and clinical social work issues.
**Ind/Abst** Am. Hist. Life (1969-1976); Appl. Soc. Sci.

Index Abstr.; Arts Humanit. Citation Index [Select. Cov.]; Curr. Contents Soc. Behav. Sci.; Hum. Resour. Abstr.; Middle East Abstr. Index; Psychol. Abstr. (1930-); PsycINFO; PsycLit; Res. Alert [Full Cov.]; Sage Fam. Stud. Abstr. (?-?); Soc. Plann. Policy Dev. Abstr.; Soc. Sci. Cit. Index [Full Cov.]; Soc. Work Abstr. (Summer 1987-) [Full Cov.]; Sociol. Abstr.; Women Stud. Abstr.

NE/0920-2870
**SOCIAAL RECHT.** (NEDERLANDS TIJDSCHRIFT VOOR SOCIAAL RECHT.). [Soc. recht]. (1986)-. Periodical. Dutch. Twelve times a year. Fl198.50. Kluwer BV, Postbus 23, 7400 GA Deventer Netherlands. **Tel** 011 31 5700 33155, 011 31 5700 48999, FAX 011 31 5700 11504, telex 42829. **UDC** 349.3.

US/0092-5128
**SOCIAL AND REHABILITATIVE SERVICES (CRANSTON).** (SOCIAL AND REHABILITATIVE SERVICES.). **Main/Corp** Rhode Island. Dept. of Social and Rehabilitative Services. 1970/71-. English. an. Aime, J Forand Building, 600 New London Avenue, Cranston RI 02920. **LC** HV86; .R4223. **DD** 362/.9745.

II/0049-0857
**SOCIAL CHANGE.** [Soc. change]. **Added/Corp** Council for Social Development (India). Vol. 1 (Apr. 1971)-. Periodical. English. Four times a year. $24.00. Council of Social Development, New Delhi, India. **(Subscription address:** Prints India, 11 Darya Ganj, New Delhi 110002 India.**)** **LC** HN681; .S588.

GW/0176-1714
**SOCIAL CHOICE AND WELFARE.** [Soc. choice welfare]. Vol. 1, No. 1 (May 1984)-. Periodical. English. Four times a year. DM360.00. Springer-Verlag GmbH & Company KG, Heidelberger Platz 3, D 14197 Berlin Germany. **Tel** 011 49 30 8207223, FAX 011 49 30 8214091, telex 183 319 SPBLN D. **(Subscription address:** Springer Verlag New York Inc. / for North America, 44 Hartz Way, Secaucus NJ 07096.**)** **ED** W Gaertner, J S Kelly, P K Pattanaik, and M Salles. **[CCC]. Bk Rev. Ad Acc. Pr Rev. Circ:** 161. available on microfilm and microfiche from University Microfilms International (UMI). Documents available from The Genuine Article.
**Desc:** Publishes original research, survey papers and book reviews on the ethical and positive aspects of welfare economics and collective choice theory.
**Ind/Abst** Curr. Contents Soc. Behav. Sci.; Econ. Lit. Index; Int. Bibliogr. Sociol.; J. Econ. Lit. (1984-); Math. Rev. (1985-); Res. Alert [Full Cov.]; Soc. Plann. Policy Dev. Abstr.; Soc. Sci. Cit. Index [Full Cov.]; Zentralbl. Math. Ihre Grenzgeb.

US/0147-1473
**SOCIAL DEVELOPMENT ISSUES.** [Soc. dev. issues]. **Added/Corp** University of Iowa. School of Social Work. Vol. 1 (Spring 1977)-. Periodical. English. Three times a year (3 issues per volume). $45.00 (institution), $30.00 (individual). University of Iowa / Publications Order Department, Oakdale Hall, Iowa City IA 52242. **Tel** (319)335-4645, FAX (319)335-4039. **ED** Martin B. Tracy and Wayne D. Johnson. **LC** HV1; .S564. **DD** 361/.005. **Bk Rev. Ad Acc. Circ:** 400 (ctrl).
***Supersedes*** *Iowa Journal of Social Work.*
**Desc:** Promotes issues that impact social justice and the development and well-being of individuals and their communities.
**Ind/Abst** Acad. Search (July 1993-); Geogr. Abstr. Human Geogr.; INFO-SOUTH Abstr.; Int. Dev. Abstr.; LABORDOC; Mag. Search; Soc. Plann. Policy Dev. Abstr.; Soc. Work Abstr. (Spring 1987-) [Select. Cov.]; Sociol. Abstr.

TH
**SOCIAL DEVELOPMENT NEWSLETTER (BANGKOK (THAILAND)).** (SOCIAL DEVELOPMENT NEWSLETTER / ECONOMIC AND SOCIAL COMMISSION FOR ASIA AND THE PACIFIC.). **Added/Corp** United Nations. Economic and Social Commission for Asia and the Pacific. No. 1 (Sept. 1980)-. Periodical. English. ir. Free on request. Economic and Social Commission for Asia and the Pacific, United Nations Building, Rajdamnern Avenue, Bangkok 2 Thailand. **Tel** 011 66 2 2829161. **LC** HN651; .S65. **DD** 354.50081/8. ***Continues*** *Social Work Education and Development Newsletter.*

CN/0822-711X
**SOCIAL DEVELOPMENT OVERVIEW.** (SOCIAL DEVELOPMENT OVERVIEW / CANADIAN COUNCIL ON SOCIAL DEVELOPMENT.). **Added/Corp** Canadian Council on Social Development. **VFOAT** Overview. **VAT** Overview - Canadian Council on Social Development. (1983)-. Periodical. English. ir. 50.00Can$ membership. Canadian Council on Social Development, 55 Parkdale Avenue, Ottawa Ontario K1Y 4G1 Canada. **Tel** (613)728-1865, FAX (613)728-9387. **DD** 361/.971. ***Continues in part*** *Social Development, 0316-313X.*
**Ind/Abst** Can. Index (?-?).

UK
**SOCIAL HOUSING.** English. mo. £120.00 UK; £135.00 Europe & North America; £145.00 Australia. Financial Information Centre Ltd, 40 Bowling Green Lane, London EC1R 0NE England. **Tel** 011 44 71 278-0333, FAX 011 44 71 833-5660. **ED** Tim Roberts. **Ad Acc. Circ:** 1,000.
**Desc:** Analysis of finance for low cost housing.

AT
**SOCIAL INDICATORS.** **Main/Corp** Australian Bureau of Statistics. No. 1 (1976)-. English. ir. 55.00Aus$. Australian Bureau of Statistics, PO Box 10, Belconnen Australian Capital Territory, 2616 Australia. **Tel** 011 61 6 2527911, FAX 011 61 6 2516009. **LC** HN844; .A95a. **DD** 309.1/94. **Circ:** 4,000.
**Desc:** A selection of social indicators and other statistics providing a broad background to social issues in Australia. Presents information on population, families, health, education, working life, crime and justice, housing and welfare.

US/0740-3127
**SOCIAL ISSUES RESOURCES SERIES.** [Soc. issues resour. ser.]. **VFOAT** SIRS. 1977-. Monographic series. English. an. Price varies per volume. Social Issues Resources Series Inc, PO Box 2348, Boca Raton FL 33427. **Tel** (800)327-0513, (407)994-0079. **ED** Eleanor Goldstein. Index available. cum. index. **Pr Rev. Circ:** 11,000. available on microfiche; available on CD-ROM.
**Desc:** Contains article reprints on government documents and journals, popular and professional journals and newspapers.

US/1042-8380
**SOCIAL PLANNING, POLICY & DEVELOPMENT ABSTRACTS.** **See** Sociology-Abstracting, Bibliographies and Statistics.

UK/0144-5596
**SOCIAL POLICY & ADMINISTRATION.** **See** Public Administration.

UK
**SOCIAL POLICY REVIEW.** (1988/89)-. English. an. Longman Group Ltd., Fourth Avenue, Longman House, Harlow Essex CM19 5SR England. **Tel** 011 44 279 429655, FAX 011 44 279 431059, telex 81259. **(Subscription address:** Fourth Avenue, Harlow Essex CM19 5AA England**)** ***Continues*** *Year Book of Social Policy.*
**Ind/Abst** LABORDOC.

CN/0835-9296
**SOCIAL RESOURCES INVENTORY. CALGARY REGION.** [Soc. resour. inventory South Calg. reg.]. **Added/Corp** Alberta Social Resources Inventory. 3rd. Ed. (1987)-. Periodical. English. Alberta Social Resources Inventory, #3 12227-107 Avenue, Edmonton Alberta T5M 1Y9 Canada. **DD** 361/.0025/71233. ***Formed by the union of*** *Social Resources Inventory. Calgary Region., 0228-1279* ***and*** *Social Resources Inventory. South Region., 0715-9625.*

CN/0228-1333
**SOCIAL RESOURCES INVENTORY. EDMONTON REGION.** [Soc. resour. inventory, Edmont. reg.]. 1983-. English. an. 9.50Can$ Canada; $22.50 US. Alberta Social Resources Inventory, #3 12227-107 Avenue, Edmonton Alberta T5M 1Y9 Canada. **LC** HV109.A5; S65. **DD** 361.8/025/7123.

CN/0228-1325
**SOCIAL RESOURCES INVENTORY. NORTHEASTERN REGION.** [Soc. resour. inventory Northeast. reg.]. **VFOAT** Northeastern Region. 1st Ed. (Nov. 1982)-. English. be. 9.50Can$. Alberta Social Resources Inventory / Planning Secretariat, 10030-107 Street, Edmonton Alta T5J 3E4. **ED** Belle Pannul. **LC** HV109.A5; S63. **DD** 361/.0025/71232. Index available. **Circ:** 1,200 (ctrl).
**Desc:** Covers social resource information for Alberta. Cross-referenced and indexed.

US/0037-7910
**SOCIAL SECURITY BULLETIN (WASHINGTON, D.C. : 1938).** (SOCIAL SECURITY BULLETIN.). [Social secur. bull.]. **Added/Corp** United States. Social Security Board. United States. Social Security Administration. Vol. 1, No. 1-3 (March 1938)-. Government Publication. English. mo (annual statistical supplement). $24.00. Superintendent of Documents, US Government Printing Office, Washington DC 20402. **Tel** (202)275-3328, FAX (202)786-2377. **LC** HD7123; .S56. **DD** 368.4/00973. **NLM** W2 A S6S. **CODEN** SSYBA. **Pr Rev.** available on microfilm and microfiche from University Microfilms International (UMI); available on an online database (file 648/Full-Text) from DIALOG. Documents available from The Genuine Article, UMI Article Clearinghouse, Documents on Demand. ***Continues*** *Social Security Bulletin (Washington, D.C. : 1937), 0037-7910;* ***Absorbed*** *Monthly Benefit Statistics (Washington, D.C.), 0364-040X.*
**Desc:** Analytical articles and current statistics on old-age, survivors and disability insurance, supplemental security income, and aid to families with dependent children programs. Reports current data on the operations of the Social Security Administration and the results of research and analysis pertinent to the social security program.
**Ind/Abst** ABI/INFORM Glob. Ed.; ABI Inform Ondisc (Jan. 1984-); Abstr. Soc. Gerontol.; Am. Stat. Index; Bus. ASAP (1990-) [Full Txt.]; Bus. Index (1985-); Bus. Period. Index; Curr. Contents Soc. Behav. Sci.; Curr. Law Index (1980-); Econ. Lit. Index; Expand. Acad. Index (1992-); Gen. BusinessFile (1985-); Gen. Period. Index (1985-); Index Med.; Index Period. Artic. Relat. Law (19??-19??); Index Period. Lit. Aging; J. Econ. Lit.; Leg. Resour. Index (1980-); LegalTrac (1980-); Newsp. Period. Abstr. (1992-); PAIS Int. Print; Res. Alert [Full Cov.]; Soc. Sci. Source (Jul. 1993-) [Full Txt.]; Soc. Sci. Cit. Index [Full Cov.]; Soc. Work Abstr. [Select. Cov.]; UMI ABI/Inform--Bus. Period. Ondisc (Oct. 1987-) [Full Txt.]; Wilson Bus. Abstr.; Work Relat. Abstr.

SZ/0379-704X
**SOCIAL SECURITY DOCUMENTATION. AFRICAN SERIES.** (SOCIAL SECURITY DOCUMENTATION : AFRICAN SERIES / GENERAL SECRETARIAT OF THE INTERNATIONAL SOCIAL SECURITY ASSOCIATION.). [Soc. secur. doc., Afr. ser.]. **Added/Corp** International Social Security Association. General Secretariat. No. 3 (1980)-. Monographic series. English. ir. Price varies per volume. International Social Security Association, Case Postale 1, CH-1211 Geneva 22 Switzerland. **Tel** 011 41 22 7996617, FAX 011 41 22 7986385. ***Continues*** *African Social Security Documentation.*
**Ind/Abst** Int. Labour Doc.

II
**SOCIAL SECURITY DOCUMENTATION : ASIAN SERIES.** English. Regional Office for Asia and the Pacific, International Social Security Association, B-66 Defence Colony, New Delhi 110024 India. **Tel** 62-5001. cum. index.
**Desc:** Reports and summaries of discussions of ISSA meetings on social security issues of special relevance to schemes in the region.

US/0277-0539
**SOCIAL SECURITY EXPLAINED.** [Soc. secur. explain.]. **Added/Corp** Commerce Clearing House. (19??)-. English. ir. Commerce Clearing House Inc., 4025 West Peterson Avenue, Chicago IL 60646-6085. **Tel** (312)583-8500, FAX (708)940-4600. **ED** A.E. Schechter. **LC** KF3649; .C66. **DD** 344.73/023; 347.30423. **NLM** W 32.5; AA1 S59. ***Continues in part*** *Social Security and Medicare Explained, 0162-6361.*

US/0735-3812
**SOCIAL SECURITY FORUM.** (SOCIAL SECURITY FORUM / NATIONAL ORGANIZATION OF SOCIAL SECURITY CLAIMANTS' REPRESENTATIVES.). [Soc. secur. forum]. **Added/Corp** National Organization of Social Security Claimants' Representatives (U.S.). **VFOAT** N.O.S.S.C.R. Forum; NOSSCR Social Security Forum; NOSSC Forum; N.O.S.S.C.R. Social Security Forum. Vol. 1, No. 1 (July 1979)-. Periodical. English. mo. $100.00. National Organization of Social Security Claimants' Representatives, 6 Prospect Street, Midland Park NJ 07432. **Tel** (800)431-2804, (201)444-1415. **ED** Nancy Garvin Shor. **LC** KF3642; .S63. **DD** 344.73/023; 347.30423.

AT/0726-1195
**SOCIAL SECURITY JOURNAL.** [Soc. secur. j.]. **Added/Corp** Australia. Dept. of Social Security. (1981)-. Government Publication. English. Four times a year. 40.00Aus$. Australian Government Publishing Service, GPO Box 84, Canberra ACT 2601 Australia. **Tel** 011 61 6 2954411, FAX 011 61 6 2954455. **LC** HD7250; .A45. **DD** 368.4/00994. ***Continues*** *Social Security, 0159-6349.*
**Ind/Abst** APAIS, Aust. Public Aff. Inf. Ser. (1973-); Aust. Educ. Index (1976-); Int. Bibliogr. Sociol.

US/0148-1967
**SOCIAL SECURITY MANUAL.** **Main/Corp** National Underwriter Company. (19??)-. English. an. $14.95. National Underwriter Company, 505 Gest Street, Cincinnati OH 45203-0874. **Tel** (513)721-2140, (800)543-0874. **LC** KF3650; .N32. **DD** 344/.73/02.
**Desc:** Guide to Social Security rights and rules projecting Social Security benefits and eligibility. For individuals and professionals.

AT
**SOCIAL SECURITY REPORTER.** No. 1 (June 1981)-. English. bm. 35.00Aus$ Australia, 47.00Aus$ other. Legal Service Bulletin Co-Operative Ltd, Faculty of Law, Monash University, Clayton Victoria 3168 Australia. **Tel** 011 61 3 5440974, FAX (03)563-7820.

UK/0950-7515
**SOCIAL SECURITY STATISTICS.** **See** Sociology-Abstracting, Bibliographies and Statistics.

US
**SOCIAL SERVICE JOBS.** (19??)-. Periodical. English. Twenty-four times a year. $127.00. ELSS - Employment Listing Social Services, 10 Angelica Drive, Framingham MA 01701. **Tel** (508)626-9389, FAX (508)626-8389. **Ad Acc.** ctrl circ.
**Desc:** National listing of current human service job openings for social workers, psychologists, counselors, and administrators.

●US
**SOCIAL SERVICE RESOURCE DIRECTORY FOR LOS ANGELES COUNTY.** **VFOAT** Resource Directory for Los Angeles County; Los Angeles County, Social Service Resource Directory. (1992)-. Directory. English. $49.95. Resource Directory, 1038 North Tustin, Suite 241, Orange CA 92667. ***Continues*** *Riddick-Norton, Glenda. Glenda Riddick Presents The Resource Directory for Los Angeles County.*

US/0037-7961
**SOCIAL SERVICE REVIEW (CHICAGO), THE.** (THE SOCIAL SERVICE REVIEW.). [Soc. serv. rev.]. **Added/Corp** University of Chicago. Graduate School of Social Service Administration. Vol. 1 (Mar. 1927)-. Academic Scholarly Publication. English. qt (4 issues). $64.00 institution, $33.00 individual, $23.00 UC SSA alumni and students. University of Chicago Press / Journals Division, PO Box 37005, 5720 South Woodlawn, Chicago IL 60637. **Tel** (312)753-3347, FAX (312)753-0811. **(Subscription telephone:** (312)753-8083**) ED** John R. Schuerman. **LC** HV1; .S6. **DD** 361/.005. **NLM** W1 SO133. **CODEN** SSRVA. **[CCC].** cum. index. **Pr Rev. Acid Free.** available on microfilm and microfiche from University Microfilms International (UMI). Documents available from The Genuine Article, UMI Article Clearinghouse.
**Desc:** Committed to an examination of social welfare practice and to an evaluation of its effects. Publishes articles poverty, ethnicity, income distribution, family conflict, social welfare policy, mental health services, community development and deviancy.
**Ind/Abst** Acad. Abstr. Full Text Elite (Jan. 1992-); Acad. Abstr. (Jan. 1992-); Acad. Search (Jan. 1992-); Am. Hist. Life (1963-); Appl. Soc. Sci. Index Abstr.; Book Rev. Index; Crim. Justice Abstr.; Crim. Penol. Police Sci. Abstr.; Curr. Contents Soc. Behav. Sci.; EMBASE; Expand. Acad. Index (1989-); Hospit. Health Admin. Index; Index Period. Artic. Relat. Law (19??-19??); Int. Bibliogr. Sociol.; Mag. Search; Middle East Abstr. Index; Newsp. Period. Abstr. (1991-); PAIS Int. Print; Res. Alert [Full Cov.]; Sage Fam. Stud. Abstr.; Soc. Plann. Policy Dev. Abstr.; Soc. Sci. Source (Jan. 1992-); Soc. Sci. Cit. Index [Full Cov.]; Soc. Sci. Index; Soc. Sci. Index Fulltext (Sept. 1988-) [Full Txt.]; Soc. Work Abstr. (Spring, Summer 1987-) [Full Cov.]; Sociol. Abstr.; Spec. Educ. Needs Abstr.; Urban Aff. Abstr.; Vocat. Search (Jan. 1992-); Women Stud. Abstr.

US
**SOCIAL SERVICES BLOCK GRANT APPLICATION, WASHINGTON STATE.** English. an. Washington State Department of Social and Health Services, Olympia WA 98504. **LC** HV98.W3; S65. **DD** 353.97970084.

US/1054-3384
**SOCIAL SERVICES EMPLOYMENT BULLETIN.** [Soc. serv. employ. bull.]. Vol. 1, No. 1 (Jan. 11, 1991)-. Periodical. English. sm (24 issues). $42.00 (school); $56.00 other. Social Services Employment Bulletin, PO Box 50303, Provo UT 84605. **Tel** (801)423-2546, FAX (801)226-5550. **ED** Dennis Corbett. **DD** 331. **Ad Acc. Circ:** 900.
**Desc:** National job bulletin for the social services.

US/0099-2070
**SOCIAL SERVICES PERSONNEL IN NORTH CAROLINA COUNTIES. Main/Corp** North Carolina. Division of Social Services. 1972/73-. English. an. State Department of Human Resources / North Carolina, 701 Barbour Street, Raleigh NC 27603. **Tel** (919)733-4283. **LC** HV86; .N848. **DD** 331.7/61/3629756. ***Continues*** *Social Services Personnel in North Carolina, 0092-3613.*

UK/0265-6957
**SOCIAL SERVICES RESEARCH JOURNAL.** (1972)-. Periodical. English. qt. £49.00 UK; £55.00 other. University of Birmingham / England, Edgbaston, Center for Byzantine Ottoman, Greek Street, Birmingham B15 2TT England. **Tel** 011 44 21 414 5733, FAX 011 44 21 414 5726. **ED** Nicholas Deakin & Martin Willis. Index available. cum. index. **Bk Rev. Ad Acc, Adv Mgr:** Helen Harris. **Circ:** 230 (ctrl). Documents available from BLDSC.

●US
**SOCIAL THOUGHT: JOURNAL OF RELIGION IN THE SOCIAL SERVICES.** **See** Religion and Theology.

II/0037-8038
**SOCIAL WELFARE. Added/Corp** India (Republic) Central Social Welfare Board. (1954)-. Periodical. English (Hindi). mo. $20.00. Central Social Welfare Board, Jeevan Deep Building, Parliament Street, New Delhi 1 India. **Tel** 312637. **(Subscription address:** Prints India, 11 Darya Ganj, New Delhi 110002 India.**) ED** G Ravindran Nair. **LC** HV1; .S642. **Bk Rev. Ad Acc. Circ:** 4,000.
**Desc:** Concerned with welfare activities in the field of social welfare. Published to create awareness among the public of the need for monitoring the evil effects of of alcoholism, drugs, etc. Covers all social subjects, such as welfare of the handicapped, etc.
**Ind/Abst** Int. Labour Doc.

SI
**SOCIAL WORK.** V. 1- 1971-. English. Department of Social Work & Social Administration, University of Singapore, Bukit Timah Road, Singapore 10 Singapore. **LC** HV1; .S645. **DD** 361/.9595/2.
**Ind/Abst** Curr. Index J. Educ.

●US/1070-5317
**SOCIAL WORK ABSTRACTS. See** Sociology-Abstracting, Bibliographies and Statistics.

US/0737-5778
**SOCIAL WORK AND CHRISTIANITY.** **Added/Corp** National Association of Christians in Social Work (U.S.). **VFOAT** SWC,. Vol. 6, No. 1 (Spring 1979)-. Periodical. English. sa. $10.00. North American Association of Christians in Social Work, Box S-90, St Davids PA 19087. **Tel** (215)687-5777. **ED** David Sherwood. **LC** HV530; .S58. **DD** 361.7/5/05. Index available. cum. index. **Bk Rev. Ad Acc. Circ:** 1,100 (ctrl). ***Continues*** *Paraclete.*
**Desc:** Integration of Christian faith and social work practice.
**Ind/Abst** Christ. Period. Index; Guide Soc. Sci. Relig.; Soc. Work Abstr. [Select. Cov.].

UK/0953-5225
**SOCIAL WORK AND SOCIAL SCIENCES REVIEW.** **VFOAT** Social Work and Social Sciences Review. (1989/90)-. Periodical. English. Three times a year. $95.00. Whiting and Birch Ltd., 90 Dartmouth Road Forest Hill, London SE23 3HL England. **Tel** 011 44 81 2442421. **CODEN** SWSREN. **[CCC].**
**Ind/Abst** Int. Bibliogr. Sociol.; Psychoanal. Abstr.; Psychol. Abstr. (1989-); PsycINFO; PsycScan: Appl. Exp. Eng. Psych.; PsycScan: LD/MR; PsycScan: Neuropsych.; Soc. Plann. Policy Dev. Abstr.; Soc. Work Abstr. [Select. Cov.].

UK/0261-5479
**SOCIAL WORK EDUCATION.** [Soc. work educ.]. **Main/Corp** Royal Institute of Public Administration. Social Work Education Committee. Vol. 1, No. 1 (Autumn 1981)-. Periodical. English. Three times a year. $80.00. Whiting and Birch, 90 Dartmouth Road Forest Hill, London SE23 3HZ England. **Tel** 011 44 81 244-2421. **DD** 007.1141. **[CCC].**
**Ind/Abst** Br. Educ. Index; Int. Bibliogr. Sociol.; Soc. Plann. Policy Dev. Abstr.; Soc. Work Abstr. [Select. Cov.].

US
**SOCIAL WORK EDUCATION REPORTER.** **Added/Corp** Council on Social Work Education. Vol. 13 Mar. (1965)-. Periodical. English. Three times a year. $75.00. Council on Social Work Education, 1600 Duke Street, Alexandria VA 22314. **Tel** (703)683-8080. **ED** Ivon Katz. **Ad Acc. Circ:** 3,000 (ctrl). available on microfiche. ***Continues*** *Social Work Education.*
**Desc:** Newsletter of the council on social work education. Serves to inform membership of CSWE activities and news affecting social work education.

US/0162-7961
**SOCIAL WORK IN EDUCATION.** [Soc. work educ.]. **Added/Corp** National Association of Social Workers. Vol. 1 (Oct. 1978)-. Periodical. English. qt. $34.00 NASW members; $74.00 (institutions), $53.00 (individuals). National Association of Social Workers, 750 First Street Northeast, Suite 700, Washington DC 20002-4241. **Tel** (800)638-8799, (202)408-8600, FAX (301)587-1321. **(Subscription address:** NASW Press / National Association of Social Workers, PO Box 431, Annapolis JCT MD 20701.**) ED** Paula Allen-Meares. **LC** LB3013.4; .S62. **DD** 371.2/02. **CODEN** SOWEEG. **[CCC].** Index available. **Bk Rev. Ad Acc. Circ:** 2,000. available on microfilm and microfiche from University Microfilms International (UMI).
**Desc:** A journal that focuses on social work services in schools and social work in education.
**Ind/Abst** Appl. Soc. Sci. Index Abstr.; Br. Educ. Index; Contents Pages Educ.; Educ. Index (1992-); Multicult. Educ. Abstr.; Psychol. Abstr. (1982-); School Organ. Manage. Abstr.; Soc. Plann. Policy Dev. Abstr.; Soc. Work Abstr. (Spring, Summer 1987-) [Full Cov.]; Sociol. Educ. Abstr.; Spec. Educ. Needs Abstr.; Stud. Women Abstr.

US/0098-1389
**SOCIAL WORK IN HEALTH CARE.** [Soc. work health care]. Vol. 1 (Fall 1975)-. Academic Scholarly Publication. English. qt. $160.00 US; $224.00 other. The Haworth Press Inc, 10 Alice Street, Binghamton NY 13904-1580. **Tel** (607)722-5857, (800)3-HAWORTH, FAX (607)722-1424. **ED** Sylvia Clarke (editor's address: Department of Social Work, The Mount Sinai Hospital, 1 Gustave L, Levy Place, New York, NY 10029). **LC** HV687.A2; S6. **DD** 362.1/05. **NLM** W1 SO135P. **CODEN** SWHCDO. **Bk Rev. Ad Acc. Pr Rev. Acid Free. Circ:** 1,567. available on microfilm and microfiche from University Microfilms International (UMI). Documents available from The Genuine Article, BIOSIS Document Express, Haworth Document Delivery Service.
**Desc:** Devoted to social work theory, practice, and administration in a wide variety of health care settings.
**Ind/Abst** Abstr. Soc. Gerontol.; Annals Behav. Med.; Appl. Soc. Sci. Index Abstr.; Biol. Abstr.; Cumul. Index Nurs. Allied Health Lit.; Curr. Contents Soc. Behav. Sci.; EMBASE; Energy Res. Abstr. (1982-); Hum. Resour. Abstr.; Index Med.; Psychol. Abstr. (1975-); PsycINFO; PsycLit; Res. Alert [Full Cov.]; Soc. Plann. Policy Dev. Abstr.; Soc. Sci. Cit. Index [Full Cov.]; Soc. Work Abstr. (Summer 1987-) [Full Cov.]; Sociol. Abstr.; Spec. Educ. Needs Abstr.

UK/0144-0969
**SOCIAL WORK INFORMATION BULLETIN.** ***Ceased.*** [Soc. work inf. bull]. (1976)-(Mar. 1992). English. bw. Libraries & Information Service, Information Centre, Bishop Street, Leicester LE1 6AA England. **Tel** 011 44 553 556699. **DD** 016.361.

PH/0583-7057
**SOCIAL WORK (MANILA).** ***Suspended.*** (SOCIAL WORK.). (1956)-Suspended Vol. 31. Periodical. English. qt. PSSC Central Subscription Service, PO Box 205 UP Diliman, Quezon City 1101 Philippines. **Tel** 011 63 2 9229621. **ED** Thelma Lee Mendoza. **LC** HV1; .S6453. **DD** 361.3/05. **NLM** W1 SO135M. **Bk Rev. Ad Acc. Circ:** 1,000.
**Desc:** Prints articles and papers on social development and welfare.
**Ind/Abst** Soc. Sci. Cit. Index [Full Cov.].

US/0037-8046
**SOCIAL WORK (NEW YORK).** (SOCIAL WORK.). [Soc. work]. **Added/Corp** National Association of Social Workers. Vol. 1 (Jan. 1956)-. Periodical. English. bm. $85.00 (institutions), $61.00 (individuals). National Association of Social Workers, 750 First Street Northeast, Suite 700, Washington DC 20002-4241. **Tel** (800)638-8799, (202)408-8600, FAX (301)587-1321. **(Subscription address:** NASW Press / National Association of Social Workers, PO Box 431, Annapolis JCT MD 20701.**) ED** Ann Hartman. **LC** HV1; .S644. **DD** 361.3/05. **NLM** W1 SO135. **CODEN** SOWOA. **[CCC].** Index available. **Bk Rev. Ad Acc. Pr Rev. Circ:** 110,000. available on microfilm and microfiche from University Microfilms International (UMI). Documents available from The Genuine Article, UMI Article Clearinghouse. ***Supersedes*** *Social Work Journal.*
**Desc:** Covers social issues, new techniques, research, and education for social work.
**Ind/Abst** Abstr. Soc. Gerontol. (Vol. 35 No. 1, 1990-); Acad. Abstr. Full Text Elite (July 1990-); Acad. Abstr. (July 1990-); Acad. Ind. [Computer File] (1987-); Acad. Search (July 1990-); Am. Hist. Life (1969-1972); Book Rev. Index; Cumul. Index Nurs. Allied Health Lit.; Curr. Contents Soc. Behav. Sci.; Curr. Index J. Educ.; Except. Child Educ. Resour.; Expand. Acad. Index (1987-); Health Plan. Adminis.; Hospit. Health Admin. Index (v23n2, 1978-); Index Med. (v35n1, 1990-); Index Philip. Period. (-199?); INFO-SOUTH Abstr.; Int. Nurs. Index; Mag. Artic. Summar. Elite (July 1990-); Mag. Artic. Summar. Select (July 1990-); Mag. Artic. Summar. CD-ROM (July 1990-); Mag. Search; Multicult. Educ. Abstr.; Newsp. Period. Abstr. (1989-); PAIS Int. Print; Psychol. Abstr. (1956-); PsycINFO; PsycLit; Res. Alert [Full Cov.]; Sage Race Relat. Abstr.; Soc. Plann. Policy Dev. Abstr.; Soc. Sci. Source (Jul. 1990-); Soc. Sci. Index; Soc. Sci. Index Fulltext (Nov. 1988-) [Full Txt.]; Soc. Work Abstr. [Full Cov.]; Sociol. Abstr.; Spec. Educ. Needs Abstr.; Stud. Women Abstr.; Vocat. Search (July 1990-).

US/0272-9016
**SOCIAL WORK PAPERS OF THE SCHOOL OF SOCIAL WORK, UNIVERSITY OF SOUTHERN CALIFORNIA.** ***Ceased.*** [Soc. work pap. School Soc. Work, Univ. South. Calif.]. **Main/Corp** Los Angeles. University of Southern California. School of Social Work. Vol. 12 (1974)-(19??). Monographic series. English. an. University of Southern California School of Social Work, University Park, Los Angeles CA 90089. **Tel** (213)743-8312. **ED** Elizabeth McBroom. **LC** HV13; .L6. ***Continues*** *Social Work Papers of the Faculty, Alumni and Students.*
**Desc:** Each issue covers a special topic of current social work interest. Recent issues have covered industrial social work topics.
**Ind/Abst** Soc. Work Abstr. [Select. Cov.].

●US/1070-5309
**SOCIAL WORK RESEARCH.** [Soc. work res.]. **Added/Corp** National Association of Social Workers. Vol. 18, No. 1 (Mar. 1994)-. Abstracting/Indexing Service. English. qt. $38.00 (NASW members), $84.00 (institutions), $60.00 (individuals). National Association of Social Workers, 750 First Street Northeast, Suite 700, Washington DC 20002-4241. **Tel** (800)638-8799, (202)408-8600, FAX (301)587-1321. **(Subscription address:** NASW Press / National Association of Social

Workers, PO Box 431, Annapolis JCT MD 20701.) **DD** 361. **NLM** W1; SO137KM. ***Continues in part*** *Social Work Research and Abstracts, 0148-0847.*

US/0148-0847
**SOCIAL WORK RESEARCH & ABSTRACTS.** ***Title Change.*** **See** Sociology-Abstracting, Bibliographies and Statistics.

NZ/0111-7351
**SOCIAL WORK REVIEW (NEWTON, AUCKLAND, N.Z.).** (SOCIAL WORK REVIEW : MAGAZINE OF THE NEW ZEALAND ASSOCIATION OF SOCIAL WORKERS.). **Added/Corp** NZASW, Inc. **VFOAT** NZSW Review. Vol. 1, No. 1 (July 1988)-. Periodical. English. qt (Mar., June, Sept., Dec.). 80.00NZ$ New Zealand; 90.00NZ$ (surface), 100.00NZ$ (air) other. NZASW Publications, PO Box 41-083 St. Lukes, Auckland New Zealand. **Tel** 011 64 9 309530. **ED** Mary Nash. **LC** HV515.5; .A47. **DD** 361.3/09931/05. **[CCC]**. **Bk Rev**, (Qty: 15). **Ad Acc. Circ:** 1,000. ***Formed by the union of*** *New Zealand Social Work Journal* ***and*** *News and Views in Social Work.*

SA/0037-8054
**SOCIAL WORK STELLENBOSCH.** [Social Work Stellenbosch]. **VFOAT** Maatskaplike Werk. (1965)-. Periodical. Multiple languages. Four times a year (Mar., June, Sept., Dec.). R50.00 (individuals), R100.00 (institutions). Social Work / Maatskaplike Werk, Box 223, Stellenrosch South Africa. **Tel** 011 27 2231 772070, 011 27 2231 772489. **ED** Professor J. I. Cronje. **DD** _a360. **Bk Rev**. **Ad Acc**. **Pr Rev. Circ:** 2,000.

UK/0037-8070
**SOCIAL WORK TODAY.** ***Title Change.*** (SOCIAL WORK TODAY : JOURNAL OF THE BRITISH ASSOCIATION OF SOCIAL WORKERS.). [Soc. work today]. **Added/Corp** British Association of Social Workers. **VFOAT** SWT; S.W.T. Vol. 1, No. 1 [(Apr. 1970)]-Vol. 25, No. 5 (4 Feb. 1993). Periodical. English. wk. Macmillan Magazines Ltd., Houndmills, Basingstoke, Hampshire RG21 2XS England. **Tel** 011 44 256 29242, FAX 011 44 256 812358, telex 858493. **(Subscription address:** PO Box 500, Leicester LE99 0AA England; telephone: 0858-410510**)** **ED** David Hagland. **LC** HV1; .S648. **DD** 361.3/05. **NLM** W1 SO137M. **Bk Rev**. **Ad Acc. Circ:** 27,000 (ctrl). available on microfilm and microfiche from University Microfilms International (UMI). ***Continues*** *Case Conference; Medical Social Work (London, England); Mental Welfare; Association of Moral Welfare Workers. Bulletin of the Association of Moral Welfare Workers; ASW News.* ***Absorbed by*** *Community Care, 0307-5508.*
**Desc:** Produced for professional social workers involved in all fields of social services activity and related areas.
**Ind/Abst** Appl. Soc. Sci. Index Abstr.; Sage Race Relat. Abstr.

US/0160-9513
**SOCIAL WORK WITH GROUPS (NEW YORK. 1978).** (SOCIAL WORK WITH GROUPS.). [Soc. work groups]. Vol. 1, No. 1 (Spring 1978)-. Periodical. English. qt. $200.00 US; $280.00 other. The Haworth Press Inc, 10 Alice Street, Binghamton NY 13904-1580. **Tel** (607)722-5857, (800)3-HAWORTH, FAX (607)722-1424. **ED** Roselle Kurland (editor's address: School of Social Work, Hunter College, 129 E 79th Street, New York, NY 10021). **LC** HV45; .S63. **DD** 361.4/05. **NLM** W1 SO137MB. **CODEN** SWGRDU. **Bk Rev**. **Ad Acc**. **Pr Rev**. **Acid Free. Circ:** 837. available on microfilm and microfiche from University Microfilms International (UMI). Documents available from The Genuine Article, Haworth Document Delivery Service.
**Desc:** Covers the areas of group work in psychiatric, rehabilitative and multipurpose social work, with articles on social service agencies, crisis theory and groupwork.
**Ind/Abst** Appl. Soc. Sci. Index Abstr.; Arts Humanit. Citation Index [Select. Cov.]; Curr. Contents Soc. Behav. Sci.; Hum. Resour. Abstr.; Psychol. Abstr. (1979-); PsycINFO; PsycLit; Res. Alert [Full Cov.]; Soc. Plann. Policy Dev. Abstr.; Soc. Sci. Cit. Index [Full Cov.]; Soc. Work Abstr. (Spring 1987-) [Full Cov.]; Sociol. Abstr.; Spec. Educ. Needs Abstr.

CN/0037-8089
**SOCIAL WORKER. TRAVAILLEUR SOCIAL. Added/Corp** Canadian Association of Social Workers. **VFOAT** Travailleur Social. Vol. 1 (1932)-. Periodical. English (French). qt (4 issues). 37.00Can$; 40.00Can$ US. Myropen Publishers Ltd., 383 Parkdale Avenue, Suite 402, Ottawa Ontario K1Y 4R4 Canada. **Tel** (613)729-6668, FAX (613)729-9608. **ED** Penny Sipkes (managing editor). Index available (index). **Bk Rev**, (Qty: 9). **Ad Acc**, **Adv Mgr:** same as editor. **Circ:** 13,500. available on microfilm and microfiche from University Microfilms International (UMI).
**Desc:** Contains information on: the sharing of social work information, knowledge, skills and research with social workers and with the general public; the examination of social issues; the discussion of regional, national, and international issues in social work and social welfare.
**Ind/Abst** Abstr. Res. Pastor. Care Couns.; Can. Index; Middle East Abstr. Index; Soc. Plann. Policy Dev. Abstr.; Soc. Work Abstr. (Spring, Summer 1987-) [Full Cov.].

NE
**SOCIALE VERSEKERING, PENSIOENVERSEKERING, LEVENSVERZEKERING / CENTRAAL BUREAU VOOR DE STATISTIEK. VFOAT** Social Security, Pension Funds, and Life Insurance. 1955-1964-. Dutch (summaries and/or abstracts in English). an. Fl20.25. W Haan, Staatsuitgeverij, S-Gravenhage Netherlands. **LC** HD7190; .S58.

SW
**SOCIALFORSAKRING / RIKSFORSAKRINGSVERKET. Added/Corp** Sweden. Riksforsakringsverket. **VFOAT** National Insurance. (1990)-. Swedish (summaries and/or abstracts in English). be. **LC** HA1521; .F6582. **DD** 368.4/009485. ***Continues*** *Allman Forsakring MM.*

BE
**SOCIALISTISCHE WELZIJNSWERK.** (19??)-. qt. 600.00F. VSW, Brogniezstr 46, 1070 Brussels Belgium.

SW/0283-1929
**SOCIONOMEN 1987.** (SOCIONOMEN.). (1987)-. Periodical. Swedish. Seven times a year. Kr245.00 (individuals), Kr565.00 (institutions). Socionomen, Mariedalsvagen 4, S-122 51 Stockholm Sweden. **Tel** 011 46 8 6174441. **UDC** 331.105.44. Index available. **Bk Rev**. **Pr Rev. Circ:** 6,200 (ctrl). available on audiocassette.
**Desc:** Analyzing articles, reports, reviews and research on social work and welfare.

CN/0229-3889
**SOLEIL DE TRIEST.** (SOLEIL DE TRIEST / CENTRE D'ACCUEIL PIERRE-JOSEPH TRIEST.). [Soleil Triest]. Periodical. French. Free. Centre d'Accueil Pierre-Joseph Triest, 4900 Boulevard LaPointe, Montreal H1K 4W9 Quebec Canada. **Tel** (514)353-1220. **DD** 362.6/09714/281.

FR/0755-7000
**SOMMAIRES DE SECURITE SOCIALE.** [Somm. secur. soc.]. (1968)-. Periodical. French. mo (except Aug. & Sept.). 651.32F. Editions de l'Avenir, 18 Ave de la Marne, 92600 Asnieres France. **Tel** 011 33 1 47930588. **UDC** 368.4.

FI
**SOSIAALIMENOT VUONNA ... . VFOAT** Socialutgifterna Ar ...; Social Security Expenditure in ... . English (Finnish and Swedish). an. Valtion Painatuskeskus, PO Box 516, SF 00101 Helsinki Finland. **Tel** 011 358 0 5660266. **LC** HD7197.3; .A45. **DD** 362.94897/021/05. ***Continues*** *Sosiaalimenot Vuonna ... Seka Ennakkotiedot Vuodelle ... .*

NO
**SOSIAL TRYGD. Added/Corp** Norges Trygdekasselag. (19??)-. Periodical. Norwegian. mo. Kr315.00, $64.00. Scandinavian University Press, PO Box 2959 Toeyen, N 0608 Oslo 6 Norway. **Tel** 011 47 2 2575400, FAX 011 47 2 2575353, telex 71896 UROR N. **(Subscription address:** Scandinavian University Press, 200 Meacham Ave., Elmont NY 11003.**)** **LC** HD7200; .S65.

US/0740-4549
**SOURCE BOOK (NEW YORK, N.Y. 1983), THE.** (THE SOURCE BOOK.). [Source book]. **VFOAT** Sourcebook. (1984/85)-. English. ir. $52.50 North America; $63.00 other. Oryx Press, 4041 North Central Avenue, #700, Phoenix AZ 85012-3397. **Tel** (800)279-ORYX, (602)265-2651, FAX (602)265-6250, (800)279-4663, (800)279-6799. **ED** Nancy Leeyn-Kirby. **LC** HV99.N59; S56. **DD** 361/.0025/7471.
**Desc:** Contains information on 1,721 agencies operating 11,861 service programs at 4,472 locations. Includes emergency telephone numbers and agency profiles.

●CN/1188-4428
**SOURCE (MONTREAL. 1992).** (LA SOURCE.). [Source]. **Added/Corp** Association des Centres Hospitaliers et des Centres d'Accueil Prives du Quebec. (Febr. 1992)-. Periodical. French. qt. Limited free distribution. Association des Centres Hospitaliers et des Centres d'Acceuil Prives du Quebec, Bureau 1021, CP1083, Succursale Place du Parc, Montreal Quebec H2W 2P4 Canada. **DD** 362.1/6/0971405.

US
**SOURCES OF VOLUNTARY AGENCY INCOME / SUSAN HADDOW, MARY ANN JONES.** ***Ceased.*** **Added/Corp** Child Welfare League of America. Research Center. (19??)-(19??). Periodical. English. Child Welfare League of America, 440 1st Street Northwest, Suite 310, Washington DC 20001. **Tel** (202)638-2952, FAX (202)638-4004. **LC** HV741; .S694. **DD** 362.7/95.

CN/0384-8779
**SOURD QUEBECOIS, LE.** V. 5, No. 2- Oct. 1975-. Periodical. French. ir. 50.00Can$ per no. Centre Des Loisirs Des Sourds De Montreal, CP 328, Succursale R, Montreal Quebec H2S 3K9. **DD** 362.4/2/097114. ***Continues*** *Penseur du Sourd, 0384-8760.*

US/0360-9022
**SOUTH DAKOTA COUNTY POOR RELIEF. Main/Corp** South Dakota. Dept. of Social Services. English. an. Free. Department of Social Services / South Dakota, State Office Building, 700 Governors Drive, Pierre SD 57501. **Tel** (605)773-4855. **LC** HV86; .S786. **DD** 362.5/09783. **Circ:** 225 (ctrl).

US/0094-372X
**SOUTH DAKOTA INDIAN RECIPIENTS OF SOCIAL WELFARE. Main/Corp** South Dakota. Dept. of Social Services. (19??)-. English. an. Free. Department of Social Services / South Dakota, State Office Building, 700 Governors Drive, Pierre SD 57501. **Tel** (605)773-4855. **LC** E78.S63; S585a. **DD** 362.8/4. **Circ:** 65 (ctrl).

US/1044-6168
**SOUTHERN CALIFORNIA TDD COMMUNITY DIRECTORY.** [South. Calif. TDD community dir.]. **VAT** Southern California Telephone Device for the Deaf Community Directory. (1988/89)-. Directory. English. an. $5.00. Eye Festival Communications Inc, 4717 Laurel Canyon Boulevard, #210, North Hollywood CA 91607-3944. **Tel** 800 735-2922 ask for (818)760-3292, FAX (818)760-3391. **DD** 362.

GW/0490-1606
**SOZIALE ARBEIT.** [Soz. Arb.]. **Added/Corp** Arbeitsgemeinschaft fuer Oeffentliche und Freie Wohlfahrtspflege. Berlin (West Berlin) Der Senator fuer Sozialwesen. Vol. 1 (Oct. 1951)-. Periodical. German. Eleven times a year. DM82.00. Deutsches Zentralinst Soziale Fragen, Bernadottestrasse 94, D 141951 Berlin Germany. **Tel** 011 49 30 8324041. **LC** HV3; .S6.
**Ind/Abst** EMBASE.

GW/0490-1630
**SOZIALE SICHERHEIT (KOLN).** (SOZIALE SICHERHEIT.). [Soz. Sicherh.]. **Added/Corp** Deutscher Gewerkschaftsbund. (Jan. 1952)-. Academic Scholarly Publication. German. qt. DM98.00 Germany; DM112.00 other. Bund Verlag GmbH, Postfach 900840, D 51118 Cologne Germany. **Tel** 011 49 2203 934758. **LC** HD7177.A1; D43. **DD** 368.4/00943. **[CCC]**.
**Ind/Abst** EMBASE.

AU/0038-6065
**SOZIALE SICHERHEIT (WIEN).** (SOZIALE SICHERHEIT.). [Soz. Sicherh.]. 1.- Yearly volume; June 1948-. Periodical. German. mo. S170.00 Austria; S259.50 other. Soziale Sicherheit, Kundmanngasse 21, 1030 Vienna Austria. **Tel** 0222/71 132-1120, FAX 0222-71132-3777, telex 136682 HVSVT A. **ED** Ralph Mace. **LC** HD7090; .S68. **DD** 368.4/009436. cum. index. **Bk Rev**. **Ad Acc. Circ:** 7,500.
**Desc:** Social life and social security in Austria.
**Ind/Abst** Saf. Health Work.

GW/0173-394X
**SOZIALLEISTUNGEN. REIHE 1: VERSICHERTE IN DER KRANKEN- UND RENTENVERSICHERUNG. Main/Corp** Germany (West). Statistisches Bundesamt. **Added/Corp** Germany (West). Statistisches Bundesamt. Versicherte in der Kranken- und Rentenversicherung. **VFOAT** Fachserie 13. (1976)-. German. an. DM6.90. **LC** HD7177; .S57b. **NLM** W2 GG4 S9S. ***Continues*** *Bevolkerung und Kultur. Reihe 6, Erwerbstatigkeit. 2: Versicherte in der Gesetzlichen Kranken- und Rentenversicherung, 0340-7543.*

GW/0936-9198
**SOZIALVERSICHERUNGS-BERATER.** [Soz.versicher.-Berat.]. (1989)-. German. bm. DM220.00. Verlag Rentrop, Theodor-Heuss- Str 4, W-5300 Bonn 2 Germany. **Tel** 0228 18205 0, FAX 0228 1 364411, telex 17228309 TTXD. **ED** Norman Rentrop. **UDC** 368.4. **Bk Rev**.
**Desc:** Advisory on social security for entrepreneurs.

US/0749-9442
**SPECIAL PUBLICATION - UNIVERSITY OF COLORADO, BOULDER. NATURAL HAZARDS RESEARCH AND APPLICATIONS INFORMATION CENTER.** (SPECIAL PUBLICATION / NATURAL HAZARDS RESEARCH AND APPLICATIONS INFORMATION CENTER.). [Spec. publ. - Univ. Colo. Boulder, Nat. Hazards Res. Appl. Inf. Cent.]. (1981)-. Monographic series. English. ir. Price varies per volume. University of Colorado / Campus Box 482, Campus Box 482, Boulder CO 80309. **Tel** (303)492-6818, FAX (303)492-2151. **DD** 363.
**Ind/Abst** GeoRef.

## Sociology —Social Services and Welfare

US
**SPECIAL REVIEW OF THE DEPARTMENT OF HEALTH AND SOCIAL SERVICES, DIVISION OF PUBLIC ASSISTANCE, MEDICAL ASSISTANCE PAYMENTS FOR ABORTIONS, A.** English. G L Wilkerson CPA Legislative Auditor, Division of Legislative Audit Pouch W, Juneau AK 99811. **LC** HD7102.U5; A47. **DD** 353.97980082/56.

CN/0226-9228
**SPECTRUM (TORONTO. 1981).** (SPECTRUM.). [Spectrum]. Vol. 1, No. 1 (June/July 1981)-. Periodical. English. bm. $10.00 for 6 issues. Spectrum / Canada, c/o Pedowie Publishers, 632 Queen Street West, Toronto Ontario M6J 1E Canada. **DD** 362.4/0971.

US/0891-9720
**SPRINGER SERIES ON SOCIAL WORK.** [Springer ser. soc. work]. Vol. 1-. Monographic series. English. Price varies per volume. Springer-Verlag New York Inc., 175 5th Avenue, New York NY 10010. **Tel** (212)460-1500, telex 232 235 SPB UR. **(Subscription address:** Springer Verlag New York Inc. / for North America, 44 Hartz Way, Secaucus NJ 07096.) **ED** Albert R Roberts. **DD** 361. **NLM** W1; SP685SFB.

US
**SSI RECIPIENTS BY STATE AND COUNTY. Added/Corp** United States. Social Security Administration. Office of Research and Statistics. **VFOAT** Supplemental Security Income Recipients by State and County. (19??)-. English. **Continues** Supplemental Security Income, State and County Data, 0736-8216.
**Desc:** Information on the supplemental security income program, public assistance, and social security.

CN/0380-8181
**ST. JOHN NEWS. VFOAT** Journal St-Jean. **VAT** Journal St-Jean. Began with April 1952 issue. Periodical. English (French). qt. Free. St John Ambulance, PO Box 388 Station A, Ottawa Ontario K1N 8V4 Canada. **Tel** (613)236-7461. **ED** Rosemary Walsh. **DD** 362.1'8. **Circ:** 6,000.
**Desc:** Purpose is to applaud the achievements of St. John Ambulance people in Canada and to inform readers about the nation-wide activities of our organization. St. John Ambulance is a national, non-profit organization which provides first aid and health care courses and volunteer services.

CN/0848-7340
**STAFF DEVELOPMENT CALENDAR - ALBERTA. ALBERTA FAMILY AND SOCIAL SERVICES. STAFF DEVELOPMENT.** (STAFF DEVELOPMENT CALENDAR.). [Staff dev. cal. - Alta., Alta. Fam. Soc. Serv., Staff Dev.]. **Main/Corp** Alberta. Alberta Family and Social Services. Staff Development. (Sept. 1990/June 1991)-. English. **DD** 354.7110084/071. **Continues** Alberta. Alberta Social Services. Staff Development. Staff Development Calendar., 0837-4996.

UK/0144-5081
**STAFF OF SCOTTISH SOCIAL WORK DEPARTMENTS. Added/Corp** Great Britain. Scottish Education Dept. Social Work Services Group. (1976)-. English. an. £2.00. Social Work Services Group, Statistics Branch, 43 Jeffrey Street / Room 422, Edinburgh EH1 1DG Scotland. **Tel** 031 244 5431, FAX 031 244 5387. **LC** HV249.S5; S73. **DD** 331.12/513616/09411.

UK
**STAFF OF SOCIAL SERVICES DEPARTMENTS ... / WELSH OFFICE.**
**Main/Corp** Great Britain. Welsh Office. (19??)-. Statistical Publication. English. an. Welsh Office Publications Unit, Crown Building, Cathay's Park, Cardiff CF1 3NQ Wales. **Tel** 011 44 222 825111. **LC** HV250.W34; G73a. **DD** 354.4290084.
**Desc:** Information about staff of local authority social services departments in Wales.

US/0095-3660
**STATE AND REGIONAL DATA, FEDERALLY FUNDED COMMUNITY MENTAL HEALTH CENTERS. Main/Corp** United States. National Institute of Mental Health. Division of Biometry. Survey and Reports Branch. (19??)-. English. National Institute of Mental Health / Survey and Reports Branch, Survey and Reports Branch, Division of Biometry, 5600 Fishers Lane, Rockville MD 20852. **LC** RH790.6; U56b. **DD** 362.2/2/0973.

US
**STATE CHILD WELFARE SERVICES PLAN, STATE OF TENNESSEE.** Tennessee Department of Human Services, 111 Seventh Avenue North, Nashville TN 37203.

US/0092-5543
**STATE FACILITIES PLAN (OLYMPIA).** (STATE FACILITIES PLAN.). **Main/Corp** Washington (State). Vocational Rehabilitation Services Division. English. Vocational Rehabilitation Services Division, PO Box 1788, Olympia WA 98504. **LC** HD7256.U6; W285A. **DD** 362.8/5.

US/1070-7719
**STATE HOUSE WATCH. See** Public Administration.

US/0743-7676
**STATE MENTAL RETARDATION FACILITY DATA.** (STATE MENTAL RETARDATION FACILITY DATA FOR THE FISCAL YEAR ...). [State ment. retard. facil. data]. English. an. MIS and Data Services Division, Department of Mental Health and Mental Retardation, PO Box 1797, Richmond VA 23214.

US/1055-9213
**STATE OF AMERICA'S CHILDREN. Title Change.** [State Am. child.]. **Added/Corp** Children's Defense Fund (U.S.). (1991)-(1992). English. Children's Defense Fund, 122 C Street NW, Washington DC 20001. **Tel** (202)628-8787. **LC** HV741; .C5375. **DD** 362.7/95/0973; 362. **NLM** W1; ST314WG. **Continues** Children's Defense Budget, 0736-6701. **Continued by** State of America's Children Yearbook.

●US
**STATE OF AMERICA'S CHILDREN YEARBOOK, THE. Added/Corp** Children's Defense Fund (U.S.). **VFOAT** State of America's Children. (1994)-. English. $12.95. Children's Defense Fund, 122 C Street NW, Washington DC 20001. **Tel** (202)628-8787. **LC** HV741; .C5375. **Continues** State of America's Children, 1055-9213.

US
**STATE OF FLORIDA PROPROSED COMPREHENSIVE ANNUAL SERVICES PROGRAM PLAN FOR SOCIAL SECURITY ACT TITLE XX. Main/Corp** Florida. Dept. of Health and Rehabilitative Services. **VFOAT** Proposed Comprehensive Annual Services Program Plan for Title XX--Social Security Act. English. $5.65. Florida Department of Health and Rehabilitative Services, 1323 Winewood Boulevard, Building 1, Room 115, Tallahassee FL 32399. **Tel** (904)488-7721, FAX (904)488-2112. **LC** HV86; .F642. **DD** 361.6/2/09759.

US
**STATE OF INDIANA FINAL COMPREHENSIVE ANNUAL SERVICES PLAN. Main/Corp** Indiana. Office of Social Services. 1978/79-. English. an. Indiana Office of Social Services, 964 North Pennsylvania, Indianapolis IN 46204. **LC** HV86; .I685A. **DD** 361.6/09772. **Continues** State of Indiana Final Comprehensive Annual Services Plan.

US/0265-718X
**STATE OF THE WORLD'S CHILDREN (OXFORD).** (THE STATE OF THE WORLD'S CHILDREN.). [State world's child.]. **Added/Corp** UNICEF. (1980)-. Periodical. English. an. $8.00 (latest edition). **(Subscription address:** Oxford University Press / USA, Journals Marketing Department, Oxford University Press, 2001 Evans Road, Cary NC 27513.) **Tel** (919)677-0977. **LC** HQ792.2; .S73. **DD** 362.7/1/091724. **NLM** W1; ST315CH.

US
**STATE PLAN ANNUAL REVISION, DEVELOPMENTAL DISABILITIES SERVICES AND FACILITIES CONSTRUCTION ACT OF 1970. Main/Corp** California. Developmental Disabilities Planning and Advisory Council. English. an. State Planning and Advisory Council for Developmental Disabilities, 926 J Street/Room 522, Sacramento CA 95814. **LC** HV3006.C2; C32B. **DD** 362.3/09794.

US/0146-5740
**STATE PLAN FOR CHILD WELFARE SERVICES. Main/Corp** South Dakota. Dept. of Social Services. (19??)-. English. an. Department of Social Services / South Dakota, State Office Building, 700 Governors Drive, Pierre SD 57501. **Tel** (605)773-4855. **LC** HV742.S8; S68a. **DD** 362.7/09783.

US/0148-9240
**STATE PLAN FOR PROGRAMS ON AGING UNDER TITLE III AND TITLE VII OF THE OLDER AMERICANS ACT OF 1965 AS AMENDED FOR THE STATE OF NEW HAMPSHIRE. Main/Corp** New Hampshire State Council on Aging. **VAT** State Plan for Programs on Aging Under Title Three and Title Seven on the Older Americans Act of Nineteen Hundred and Sixty-Five as Amended for the State of New Hampshire. English. an. Administration on Aging, 330 Independence Avenue SW, Washington DC 20201. **LC** HV1468.N4; N49A. **DD** 353.9/742/00846.

US
**STATE PLAN ON AGING FOR THE STATE OF NEBRASKA. Main/Corp** Nebraska. Commission on Aging. English. ir (every five years). Nebraska Department on Aging, 301 Centennial Mall South, Lincoln NE 68509. **Tel** (402)471-2306. **LC** HV1468.N6; N23A. **DD** 362.6/3/09782. **Circ:** 1,000 (ctrl).
**Desc:** A plan for aging services in the state of Nebraska.

US
**STATE PLAN ON AGING UNDER TITLE III OF THE OLDER AMERICANS ACT FOR SOUTH CAROLINA.** Fiscal Years 1981-83-. English. an. South Carolina Commission on Aging, 400 Arbor Lake Drive/#B-500, Columbia SC 29223-4535. **LC** HV1468.S6; S75. **DD** 362.6/09757. **Continues** State Plan on Aging for the State of South Carolina for Fiscal Year ... .

US
**STATE PLAN ON AGING UNDER TITLE III OF THE OLDER AMERICANS ACT FOR STATE OF SOUTH DAKOTA / DEPARTMENT OF SOCIAL SERVICES, OFFICE OF ADULT SERVICES & AGING. Main/Corp** South Dakota. Office of Adult Services and Aging. English. ir (every four years). Free. Department of Social Services / South Dakota, State Office Building, 700 Governors Drive, Pierre SD 57501. **Tel** (605)773-4855. **LC** HV1468.S8; S68A. **DD** 362.6/09783. **Circ:** 50 (ctrl). **Continues** South Dakota. Office of Adult Services and Aging. State Plan on Aging.

US/0147-0914
**STATE VOCATIONAL REHABILITATION AGENCY PROGRAM DATA. Main/Corp** United States. Rehabilitation Services Administration. Periodical. English. an. Rehabilitation Services Administration, 330 Independence Avenue SW, Washington DC 20201. **LC** HD7256.U5; U58F. **DD** 362.8/5. **NLM** W2 A R3SE.
**Desc:** Publication provides (1) public accountability for funds appropriated for fiscal year and (2) basic data for evaluating program performance and goal attainment.

UK
**STATISTICAL INFORMATION SERVICE: PERSONAL SOCIAL SERVICES STATISTICS ACTUALS. See** Sociology-Abstracting, Bibliographies and Statistics.

US/0090-6565
**STATISTICAL REPORT - CITY OF LOS ANGELES. SOCIAL SERVICE DEPARTMENT. See** Sociology-Abstracting, Bibliographies and Statistics.

US/0163-6898
**STATISTICAL REPORT - SOUTH CAROLINA DEPARTMENT OF SOCIAL SERVICES. See** Sociology-Abstracting, Bibliographies and Statistics.

US
**STATISTICAL REPORT (VIRGINIA. DEPT. OF SOCIAL SERVICES. BUREAU OF RESEARCH AND REPORTING). See** Sociology-Abstracting, Bibliographies and Statistics.

IT
**STATISTICHE DELLA PREVIDENZA, DELLA SANITA E DELL'ASSISTENZA SOCIALE. See** Sociology-Abstracting, Bibliographies and Statistics.

US/0362-0360
**STATISTICS : CALENDAR YEAR REVIEW. See** Sociology-Abstracting, Bibliographies and Statistics.

US/0163-1403
**STATISTICS ON SOCIAL WORK EDUCATION IN THE UNITED STATES. See** Sociology-Abstracting, Bibliographies and Statistics.

US/0361-896X
**STATISTICS - STATE OF TENNESSEE, DEPARTMENT OF HUMAN SERVICES. See** Sociology-Abstracting, Bibliographies and Statistics.

GW
**STATISTIK IN DER RENTENVERSICHERUNG.** Seminar 1-. Periodical. German. an. Verband Deutscher Rentenversicherungstrager, Eysseneckstr 55, Frankfurt Am Main Germany. **Tel** 069/1522-0, telex 412-536 VDR. **LC** HD7177; .S56. **DD** 368.4/00943. Index available. cum. index. **Bk Rev**. **Ad Acc**. ctrl circ.

# Sociology — Social Services and Welfare

IO
**STATISTIK KRIMINALITAS DKI JAKARTA.** **VFOAT** Statistik Kriminalitas D.K.I. Jakarta. Indonesian. Kantor Sensus dan Statistik Dki Jakarta, Jl Medan Merdeka Selatan 8-9, Lantai XX, Jakarta Indonesia. **LC** HV7104.J34; S7.

FI/0780-7554
**STATISTIK OVER PENSIONSTAGARNA I FINLAND.** See Sociology-Abstracting, Bibliographies and Statistics.

US/1069-5478
**STREET BEAT (PITTSBURGH, PA.).** See Literature.

US/1047-014X
**STROKE CONNECTION.** (STROKE CONNECTION : A COURAGE CENTER STROKE PUBLICATION.). [Stroke connect.]. **Added/Corp** Courage Stroke Center (Golden Valley, Minn.) Courage Stroke Network. (1980)-. Periodical. English. bm. $8.00. American Heart Association, 7272 Greenville Avenue, Dallas TX 75231-4596. **Tel** (214)706-1310, (214)373-6300, FAX (214)691-6342. **(Subscription address:** AHA Stroke Connection, 7272 Greenville Avenue, Dallas TX 75231.) **ED** Pat Kasell. **DD** 362. **Bk Rev**, (Qty: 6). **Ad Acc. Circ:** 5,000. **Desc:** The purpose of the Stroke Connection is to link stroke survivors, their family members, and the professionals who serve them by providing a forum for sharing knowledge and experiences related to living with stroke.

US/0891-849X
**STUDIES IN HEALTH AND HUMAN SERVICES.** See Public Health and Safety.

UK
**STUDIES IN SOCIAL POLICY AND WELFARE.** Began in 1976. Monographic series. English. Price varies per volume. Heinemann Educational Books Ltd, 22 Bedford Square, London WC1B 3HH England.

US/8755-5360
**STUDIES IN SOCIAL WELFARE POLICIES AND PROGRAMS.** [Stud. soc. welf. policies programs]. No. 1 (1985)-. Monographic series. English. ir. Price varies per volume. Greenwood Press Inc., PO Box 5007, Westport CT 06881-5007. **Tel** (203)226-3571, FAX (203)222-1502. **DD** 360.

US/0149-2586
**STUDIES IN WELFARE POLICY.** No. 1-. Monographic series. English. Price varies per volume. Department of Social Services / Michigan, 300 South Capitol Avenue, Lansing MI 48026. **NLM** W2 AM5 D6S.

US
**SUBJECTS FROM DECISIONS OF DEPARTMENTAL APPEALS BOARD / U.S. DEPARTMENT OF HEALTH AND HUMAN SERVICES.** Ceased. **Added/Corp** United States. Dept. of Health and Human Services. Departmental Appeals Board. **VFOAT** DAB Decisions; DAB Subject Index. (198?)-(Aug. 1993). Periodical. English. an. Index Publications Inc, PO Box 1729, Olympia WA 98507. **Tel** (206)754-8063. **LC** KF3720.5.A58; S83. **DD** 344.73/0316; 347.304316.

CN/1185-877X
**SUMMARIES OF DECISIONS / SOCIAL ASSISTANCE REVIEW BOARD.** [Summ. decis. - Soc. Assist. Rev. Board]. **Main/Corp** Ontario. Social Assistance Review Board. Vol. 1, No. 1 (Oct. 1991)-. Periodical. English. qt. **DD** 344.713.

US/0145-7314
**SUMMARY INFORMATION ON MASTER OF SOCIAL WORK PROGRAMS.** **Main/Corp** Council on Social Work Education. English. an. Council on Social Work Education, 1600 Duke Street, Alexandria VA 22314. **Tel** (703)683-8080. **LC** HV11; .C772A. **DD** 361/.007/1173.

UK
**SUMMARY OF HEALTH AND PERSONAL SOCIAL SERVICES ACCOUNTS.** See Public Health and Safety.

FI
**SUOMEN VIRALLINEN TILASTO. XXI B, SOSIAALIHUOLTO.** See Sociology-Abstracting, Bibliographies and Statistics.

CN/0820-6643
**SURETE.** (SURETE : LE MAGAZINE DE LA SURETE DU QUEBEC.). [Surete]. V. 12, No. 4 (April 1982)-. Periodical. French. mo. Surete du Quebec, Service des Communications, 1701 rue Parthenais/Bureau 730, Montreal Quebec H2L 4K7 Canada. **DD** 363.2/09714. Continues *La Revue de la Surete du Quebec, 0381-2758*.
**Ind/Abst** Point Repere (1983-).

US
**T.E.A.M.** **VFOAT** Turtle and Tortoise Education and Adoption Media, T.E.A.M. Periodical. English. mo. $10.00 US; $12.00 other. 3245 Military Avenue, Los Angeles CA 90034. **ED** Ray Lewis and Felice Rood. ctrl circ.

US/1048-0374
**TAFT GUIDE TO CORPORATE GIVING CONTACTS.** *Title Change.* [Taft guide corp. giv. contacts]. **Added/Corp** Taft Corporate Information Service. **VFOAT** Corporate Giving Yellow Pages. 6th Ed. (1989)-(19??). English. Taft Group, 835 Penobscott Building, Customer Service, Detroit MI 48226. **Tel** (800)877-8238, FAX (313)961-6083. **LC** HV89; .C683. **DD** 361.7//632/097471. Continues *Corporate Giving Yellow Pages, 0894-6310*. Continued by *Corporate Giving Yellow Pages (Rockville, Md. : 1992), 1058-689X*.

JA
**TAISHOKUKIN TEINENSEI OYOBI NENKIN JIJO CHOSA.** **Main/Corp** Japan. Chuo Rodo Iinkai. (19??)-. Japanese. 5-32 Shiba Koen 1, Minato-ku 105, Tokyo Japan. **LC** HD7106.J3; J33a.

●US
**TCA JOURNAL.** **Added/Corp** Texas Counseling Association. Vol. 20, No. 2 (Fall 1992)-. Periodical. English. sa. **LC** BF637.C6; T46a. **DD** 158/.3/05. Continues *TACD Journal, 1046-171X*.

US/0735-7966
**TECHNICAL NOTES - UNITED STATES. DEPT. OF HEALTH AND HUMAN SERVICES. DIVISION OF CHILDREN, YOUTH, AND FAMILY POLICY.** (TECHNICAL NOTES.). [Tech. notes - U. S., Dep. Health Hum. Serv., Div. Child., Youth, Fam. Policy]. Fiscal Year 1980-. English. an. Division of Children Youth and Family Policy, Office of Social Services, Policy Office of the Assistant Secretary for Planning and Evaluation, US Department of Health and Human Services, Room 416E/Hubert Humphrey Building, 200 Independence Avenue SW, Washington DC 20201. **LC** HV85; .T43. **DD** 361.6/0973. **NLM** W2 A D3816T. Continues *Technical Notes (United States. Dept of Health, Education, and Welfare. Office of the Assistant Secretary for Planning and Evaluation)*.

US/0896-8586
**TECHNOLOGY UPDATE (PALO ALTO, CALIF.).** See Physically Impaired.

US
**TELEPHONE DIRECTORY.** **Main/Corp** United States. Dept. of Health and Human Services. **VFOAT** Directory. (Spring 1980)-. Directory. English. an. $29.00 US; $36.25 other. US Department of Health and Human Services, 200 Independence Avenue Southwest, Washington DC 20201. Continues *Telephone Directory (United States. Dept. of Health, Education, and Welfare), 0276-1238*.

CU/0256-2863
**TEMAS DE TRABAJO SOCIAL.** (TEMAS DE TRABAJO SOCIAL / HOSPITAL PSIQUIATRICO DE LA HABANA.). [Temas trab. soc.]. **Added/Corp** Hospital Psiquiatrico de la Habana. (1979)-. Periodical. Spanish. Twice a year (Jan., July). Hspt Psiquiatrico de la Habana, Ministerio de Salud Publica, Habana Cuba. **Tel** 45-16-88. **ED** Dr. Edward Bernabe Ordazy and Manuel Toymil. **NLM** W1; TE305PH. Index available. **Bk Rev Circ:** 2,000.

SP
**TEORIA Y PRACTICA.** Periodical. Spanish. 1,500. Santa Teresa 6, Madrid Spain. **LC** HN1; .T46.

US
**TEXAS FRONT IN THE NATION'S STRUGGLE AGAINST POVERTY : ANNUAL REPORT OF THE TEXAS DEPARTMENT OF COMMUNITY AFFAIRS' ECONOMIC OPPORTUNITY DIVISION, THE.** **Main/Corp** Texas. Economic Opportunity Division. English. an. Texas Department of Community Affairs, PO Box 13166 Capitol Station, Austin TX 78711. **LC** HV86; .T38. **DD** 361.6/2/09764. Continues *Texas Front in the Nation's Struggle Against Poverty: Annual Report of Texas Department of Community Affairs' Texas Office of Economic Opportunity*.

TH
**THAI DEVELOPMENT NEWSLETTER.** **Added/Corp** Khanakammakan Phiphr l Songsm Nganphattmana. Thai Development Information Service (London, England). (Dec. 1982)-. Newsletter. English. Three times a year. $12.00. Thai Development Support Committee, 530 Soi St Louis 3 S Sathorn, Yannawa Bangkok 10120 Thailand. **Tel** 011 66 2 2110906, 2120542, FAX 011 66 2 217584. **ED** Suntaree Kiatiprajuk. **LC** HN700.55.Z9; C68. **Circ:** 800.
**Desc:** Covers an overview of social problems, development work and alternative development activities carried out by non-governmental organizations in Thailand.
**Ind/Abst** Hum. Rights Intern. Rep.

US/0741-8213
**THREE-YEAR REPORT / FUND FOR THE CITY OF NEW YORK.** **Main/Corp** Fund for the City of New York. (19??)-. English. te. **LC** HV99.N6; F953a. **DD** 361.7//632/097471.

BE
**TIJDSCHRIFT VOOR WELZIJNSWERK.** (19??)-. Bulletin. Dutch. Ten times a year. 1000F. Verbond van Instellingen voor Welzijnswerk, Marnixlaan 19, Bus 6B, B-1050 Brussels Belgium. **Tel** 02 513 2803, FAX 02 511 7979. **Bk Rev**, (Qty: 20). **Ad Acc.** Full Page (B&W) 10000F. Half Page (B&W) 5000F. **Circ:** 1,200 (ctrl). Continues *Welzijnswerk Kroniek*.

●CN/1187-967X
**TIRE TALK.** [Tire talk]. **Main/Corp** British Columbia. FIRST Program. (Mar. 1992)-. Periodical. English. qt. **DD** 363.72/88.

US
**TITLE XX COMPREHENSIVE ANNUAL SERVICES PROGRAM PLAN.** **Main/Corp** California. Health and Welfare Agency. **VFOAT** Title 20 Comprehensive Annual Services Program Plan; Title Twenty Comprehensive Annual Services Program Plan; Comprehensive Annual Services Program Plan. Began in 1976. English. an. California Health and Welfare Agency Department of Social Services, 744 P Street, Sacramento CA 95814. **LC** HV86; .C58185. Continues *California. Dept. of Social Services. Adult and Family Division. Comprehensive Annual Services Program Plan*.

US
**TITLE XX FINAL COMPREHENSIVE I.E. COMPREHENSIVE ANNUAL SERVICES PLAN.** **Main/Corp** South Dakota. Dept. of Social Services. English. an. Department of Social Services / South Dakota, State Office Building, 700 Governors Drive, Pierre SD 57501. **Tel** (605)773-4855. **LC** HV86; .S788A. **DD** 361.6/09783.

US
**TITLE XX NEEDS ASSESSMENT, FISCAL YEAR ... - BUREAU OF PLANNING ANALYSIS, DIVISION OF PLANNING SERVICES, IOWA DEPARTMENT OF SOCIAL SERVICES.** 1st (1978/79)-. English. an. Free. Department of Social Services / Iowa, Hoover State Office Building, Des Moines IA 50319. **LC** HV98.I8; T57. **DD** 362/.9777.
**Desc:** Summary: Information about Title XX services and clients. Title XX provides federal funding for social services delivered at the local level ... .

US
**TITLE XX, SOCIAL SERVICES.** **Main/Corp** Texas. Dept. of Human Resources. English. an. Texas Department of Human Resources, PO Box 2960, Austin TX 78769. **LC** HV86.T55; .T57.

US
**TITLE XX SOCIAL SERVICES BLOCK GRANT REPORT.** **VFOAT** Title 20 Social Services Block Grant Report; Title Twenty Social Services Block Grant Report. English. Department of Social Services / Missouri, Broadway State Office Building, Jefferson City MO 65102. **LC** HV98.M8; T58. **DD** 353.97780084/05.

CN/0824-5177
**TOWARZYSTWO D/S UCHOCZCOW W NANAIMO.** (TOWARZYSTWO D/S UCHODZCOW W NANAIMO : [NEWSLETTER].). **VAT** Wiadomosci Towarzystwa D/S Uchodzchow W Nanaimo. Vol. 8, No. 4 (Listop./Grudz. 1982)-. Periodical. English (summaries and/or abstracts in Polish). bm. Nanaimo Refugee Co-Ordination Society, Suite 225/228 Community Services Facility, 285 Prideaux Street, Nanaimo British Columbia V9R 2N2 Canada. **DD** 362.8/7/0971.

SP/1130-2976
**TRABAJO SOCIAL Y SALUD.** [Trab. soc. salud]. **Added/Corp** Ociacion Espanola de Trabajo Social y Salud. **VFOAT** Revista de Trabajo Social y Salud. (1987)-. Periodical. Spanish. tq (Jan., July, Dec.). 5150ptas. Hospital Clinico Universitario, Madre Vedruna 18 30 IZQ, 50008 Zaragoza Spain. **Tel** 011 34 976 356400. **(Subscription address:** Fundacion El Ciervo, Calle Madre Vedruna 18 Pal Izq., 50008 Zaragoza Spain.) **UDC** 364. **Circ:** 1,000 (ctrl).

US/0161-8288
**TRAINING AND MANPOWER DEVELOPMENT ACTIVITIES.** (TRAINING AND MANPOWER DEVELOPMENT ACTIVITIES SUPPORTED BY THE ADMINISTRATION ON AGING UNDER TITLE IV-A OF THE OLDER AMERICANS ACT OF 1965, AS AMENDED). **Main/Corp** United States. Administration on Aging. Division of Manpower Resources. English. US Department of Health and

Human Services, 200 Independence Avenue Southwest, Washington DC 20201. **LC** HQ1060; .U545A. **DD** 362.6/07/1173.

US
### TRAINING FOR SOCIAL WELFARE.
**Main/Corp** United Nations. Dept. of Economic and Social Affairs. 5th (1971)-. Government Publication. English. ir. United Nations Publications, 2 United Nations Plaza, Room DC2 0853, Department 007C, New York NY 10017. **Tel** (212)963-8303, (800)253-9646. ***Continues*** *United Nations. Dept. of Economic and Social Affairs. Training for Social Work.*

FR/0767-1822
### TRAITE DE LA SECURITE SOCIALE.
(1953)-. French. qt. UCANSS, 33 Avenue du Maine, BP 45 & 46, 75755 Paris Cedex 15 France. **Tel** 011 33 1 45388149, 011 33 1 45388148. **UDC** 368.4 : 34.

SZ/0255-9641
### TRAVAIL SOCIAL 1981.
[Trav. soc. 1981]. (1981)-. Periodical. French. mo. 100.00F Switzerland; 110.00F other. Zentralsekretariat SBS, Postfach, CH 3000 Bern 27 Switzerland. **Tel** 011 41 31 3822822, FAX 011 41 31 3821125. **ED** Hans Ellenberger. **UDC** 361.

FR/0753-9711
### TRAVAIL SOCIAL ACTUALITES PARIS.
[Trav. soc. actual.Paris]. **VFOAT** T.S.A. Travail Social Actualites (Paris). (1983)-. Periodical. French. Forty-seven times a year (weekly except Aug.). 530.00F (one year), 970.00F (two years) France; 650.00F Dom-Tom; 961.00F other. Travail Social Actualites, 67 Rue De L'Aqueduc, 75010 Paris France. **Tel** 33 1 40359540, FAX 33 1 40351711. **ED** M Bance. **UDC** 331. **Bk Rev. Ad Acc, Adv Mgr:** M Villeneuve. ctrl circ.

US/1052-3995
### TREATING ABUSE TODAY.
(TREATING ABUSE TODAY : THE INTERNATIONAL NEWSJOURNAL OF ABUSE, SURVIVORSHIP, AND THERAPY.). [Treat. abuse today]. Vol. 1, No. 1 (Mar./Apr. 1991)-. Periodical. English. Six times a year (Jan., Mar., May, July, Sept., Nov.). $55.00 (institutions), $36.00 (individuals) US; add $10.00 postage Canada; add $20.00 postage other. Clinical Training Publications, Inc., 2722 Eastlake Avenue East, Suite 300, Seattle WA 98102. **Tel** (206)329-9101, FAX (206)329-8462. **ED** David L. Calof. **LC** RC569.5.C55; T737. **DD** 616.85/822. **NLM** W1; TR316. Index available. cum. index. **Bk Rev. Ad Acc, Adv Mgr:** Anna Machan, **Tel** (206)466-5654. **Circ:** 8,000 (ctrl).
**Desc:** An international newsjournal presenting recent developments and practical applications about abuse survivorship, therapy and related subjects.

US/1050-8031
### TRILOGY (LEXINGTON, KY.). *Suspended.*
(TRILOGY : THE MAGAZINE OF OUTDOOR COMMITMENT.). [Trilogy]. (1989)-(19??). Periodical. English. sa. $10.00. Trilogy, PO Box 11546, 805 D Newtown Circle, Lexington KY 40511. **Tel** (606)231-8522. **LC** GV191.2; .T75. **DD** 790/.05.

IT/0393-7798
### TUTELA.
[Tutela]. (1985)-. Periodical. Italian. Four times a year. L30000 Italy; L60000 other. Edizioni Inas Servizi Tutela, Viale Regina Margherita 83D, 00198 Rome Italy. **Tel** 011 39 6 84438325. **UDC** 33. Index available. **Pr Rev. Circ:** 2,000 (ctrl).
**Desc:** Produced for social study (old age, pensions, immigration, social security).

US/0749-5005
### U.S. REGULATORY REPORTER.
[U.S. regul. rep.]. **Added/Corp** Parexel International Corporation. **VFOAT** United States Regulatory Reporter. (198?)-. Periodical. English. Twelve times a year. $395.00 North America; $425.00 Europe; $455.00 other. Parexel International Corporation, 195 West Street, c/o Victoria Wong, Waltham MA 02154. **Tel** (617)487-9900. **ED** Mark Mathieu. **DD** 363. **NLM** W1; U8305. **Circ:** 1,000 (ctrl).
**Desc:** Regulatory information for the pharmaceutical, chemical, medical device, food, and allied industries. Focuses on regulation and regulatory processes of the FDA and EPA.

SZ
### UNICEF HISTORY SERIES.
**Added/Corp** UNICEF. **VFOAT** UNICEF History Series Monograph. Monograph 1, (1986)-. Monographic series. English. ir. Price varies per volume. US Committee of UNICEF, 331 East 38th Street, New York NY 10016. **Tel** (212)686-5522.

MX
### UNIDAD DE PROMOCION VOLUNTARIA DEL IMSS : REVISTA.
**VFOAT** Volunteer Advancement Unit of the Mexican Institute of Social Security; The Voluntary Promotion Unit of the Mexican Institute of Social Security: Review. Yearly V. 1, No. 4, (May/June/July 1979)-. Periodical. English (Spanish). qt. Reforma No 476 8O Piso, Mexico 6 DF Mexico. **LC** HD7131; .A24. **DD** 368.4/00972. ***Continues*** *Grupo de Promotoras Sociales Voluntarias del IMSS.*

BL
### UNIDADES OPERACIONAIS: ENDERECOS.
**Main/Corp** Servico Social do Comercio. (19??)-. Portuguese. Servico Social do Comercio / Rio de Janeiro, Av General Justo 307, Rio de Janeiro Brazil. **LC** HV193.A2; S45a.

US/0890-8648
### UNITED STATES OF ACORN.
(UNITED STATES OF ACORN : USA / ACORN.). [U. S. ACORN]. **Added/Corp** ACORN (Organization). **VFOAT** USA. **VAT** United States of Association of Community Organizations for Reform Now. (19??)-. Periodical. English. Four times a year. ACORN, 401 Howard Avenue, New Orleans LA 70130. **DD** 361.

US
### UNITED STATES. REHABILITATION SERVICES ADMINISTRATION. ANNUAL REPORT TO THE PRESIDENT AND CONGRESS, FISCAL YEAR.
(19??)-. Periodical. English. an. US Department of Education Rehabilitation Services Administration, Office of Special Education & Rehabilitative Services, Washington DC 20202. ***Continues*** *Annual Report of the Rehabilitation Services Administration to the President and the Congress on Federal Activities Related to the Administration of the Rehabilitation Act of 1973, as Amended., 0272-8753.*

CN/0843-3704
### UNITED WAY RESEARCH SERVICES BULLETIN.
[United Way res. serv. bull.]. Bulletin. United Way Social Planning and Research, 1625 West 8th Avenue V6J 1T9 Canada.

AU
### UNRWA : RESUME DU RAPPORT.
**Main/Corp** United Nations Relief and Works Agency for Palestine Refugees in the Near East. (19??)-. French (French). an. Free. United Nations Relief and Works Agency, Vienna International Centre, PO Box 700, A-1400 Vienna Austria. **Tel** FAX 43-1-237283, telex 135310 UNRA A. **LC** HV640.5.A6; U474a. **DD** 362.8/7. **Circ:** 5,000 (ctrl).
**Desc:** Illustrated summary of commissioner - general's report to U.N. general assembly.

CN/0315-2944
### UP TO THE NECK. *Title Change.*
Periodical. English. mo. Up to the Neck, 3553 St. Urbain Street, Montreal Quebec H2X 2N6 Canada. **DD** 362.5/09714/281. ***Continued by*** *Up To The Neck, Action, 0315-8624.*

CN/0315-8624
### UP TO THE NECK, ACTION.
**VFOAT** Action. V. 1 (May 1974)-. Periodical. English. mo. 0.25Can$ each number. Up to the Neck/Action, 3553 Street Urbain Street, Montreal Quebec H2X 2N6 Canada. **DD** 362.5/09714/281. ***Supersedes*** *Up to the Neck, 0315-2944.*
**Desc:** An English-language monthly which will report the activities of movements for progressive social change in Montreal.

●US/1065-822X
### URBAN ISSUES IN SOCIAL WORK.
[Urban issues soc. work]. Vol. 1, Issue 1 (Oct. 1992)-. Periodical. English. mo. $39.00. Wilbon Associates, 1000 Connecticut Avenue NW, Suite 9, Washington DC 20036. **DD** 361.

US
### UTAH DEVELOPMENTAL DISABILITIES STATE PLAN.
**Main/Corp** Utah Council for Handicapped and Developmentally Disabled Persons. English. $3.00. Utah Council for Handicapped and Developmentally Disabled Persons, PO Box 1958, Salt Lake City UT 84110-1958. **Tel** (801)533-6770. **LC** HV3006.U8; U84A. **DD** 362.3/09792.

US/0193-4252
### UTAH REPORT OF MEDICAID STATISTICS.
**See** Sociology-Abstracting, Bibliographies and Statistics.

AT/1031-4997
### V.C.O.S.S. NOTICEBOARD.
[V.C.O.S.S. noticeboard]. **VFOAT** Victorian Council of Social Service Noticeboard. (1988)-. Periodical. English. mo (except Jan. and Dec.). 60.00Aus$. Victorian Council of Social Service, 290-292 Wellington Street, Collingwood VIC 3066 Australia. **Tel** 011 61 3 677 7096. **DD** 361.9945.

SW
### VAL & VE : SOCIALSTYRELSENS TIDNING.
**Added/Corp** Sweden. Socialstyrelsen. **VFOAT** Val Och Ve. No. 1 (Sept 1990)-. Periodical. Swedish. sm. **LC** HN571; .V34. ***Formed by the union of*** *Socialnytt **and** Vigor (Stockholm, Sweden).*

SW/0280-1418
### VALFARDS BULLETINEN / SCB.
**Added/Corp** Sweden. Statistiska Centralbyran. **VFOAT** Valfardsbulletinen. (19??)-. Periodical. Swedish. qt. Kr85.00. Valfardsbulletinen, Statistics Sweden Utredningsinstitut, 115 81 Stockholm Sweden. **Tel** 019-176000. **ED** Lars G. Anderson. **LC** HV338; .V34. **Bk Rev. Ad Acc. Circ:** 1,300 (ctrl).
**Desc:** Analysis of welfare in Sweden based on facts from statistics about individuals collected mainly by Statistics Sweden.

SW
### VAR TRYGGHET.
Swedish. an. Kr35.00. Folksam Forlagsservice, 10660 Stockholm Sweden. **Tel** (08)7726000. **LC** HD7203; .V3. Index available. cum. index. **Bk Rev. Circ:** 80,000.
**Desc:** Handbook on the social rights in Sweden.

CN/0712-6824
### VEILLEUR, LE.
[Veilleur]. V. 1, No 2 (Feb. 1982)-. Periodical. French. ir. Free to members, $7.00 others. Veilleur, 930 rue St Jacques, Longueuil Quebec J4H 3E2 Canada. **DD** 362.6/09714/37. ***Continues*** *Journal des Retraites de Longueuil, 0712-6816.*

CN
### VICTIMS OF VIOLENCE REPORT.
Victims of Violence Society, 151 Slater Street, Suite B150, Ottawa Ontario K1P 5H3 Canada.

US/0890-2658
### VIEWPOINT / ASSOCIATION OF REHABILITATION PROGRAMS IN DATA PROCESSING.
[Viewpoint]. **Added/Corp** Association for Rehabilitation Programs in Data Processing. **VFOAT** ARPDP Viewpoint. (19??)-. Periodical. English. Four times a year. Centre for Information Resources, 4025 Chestnut Street, 3rd Floor, Philadelphia PA 19104. **Tel** (215)898-8108. **DD** 362.

●US/1077-2197
### VIOLENCE AND ABUSE ABSTRACTS.
**See** Sociology-Abstracting, Bibliographies and Statistics.

VI
### VIRGIN ISLANDS DIRECTORY OF SERVICES FOR THE AGING.
**VFOAT** Directory of Services for the Elderly. Directory. English. PO Box 5138, St Thomas US Virgin Islands 00801. **LC** HV1478.V5; V57. **DD** 362.6/042.

US/1055-9213
### VISION FOR AMERICA'S FUTURE: AN AGENDA FOR THE 1990S, A.
English. an. $12.95. Children's Defense Fund, 122 C Street NW, Washington DC 20001. **Tel** (202)628-8787. Index available. **Bk Rev. Circ:** 27,000.
**Desc:** A comprehensive analysis of the status of American children, youth, and families. Chapters include family income, health, childcare and development, education, teen pregnancy, homelessness, and vulnerable children and their families.

CN/1185-5940
### VISIONS / CANADIAN MENTAL HEALTH ASOCIATION, B.C. DIVISION.
**See** Public Health and Safety.

US/1055-9159
### VISTAS (LUBBOCK, TEX.).
(VISTAS : TEXAS TECH RESEARCH.). [Vistas]. **Added/Corp** Texas Tech University. Office of News and Publications. Vol. 1, No. 1 (Spring 1991)-. Periodical. English. Three times a year. $2.00. Texas Tech University / News & Publications, Office of News and Publications, 212 Administration Building, Lubbock TX 79409-2022. **DD** 362.

US/0096-1426
### VOCATIONAL REHABILITATION INDEX.
English. Rehabilitation Research Institute, Box 208, J Hills Miller Health Center, University of Florida, Gainesville FL 32610. **LC** Z7164.V6; V63; HD7256.U5. **DD** 016.3628/5.

US/0149-6492
### VOLUNTARY ACTION LEADERSHIP. *Title Change.*
[Volunt. action leadersh.]. **Added/Corp** National Center for Voluntary Action. Volunteer: The National Center for Citizen Involvement. Volunteer-The National Center. National Volunteer Center. Points of Light Foundation. (19??)-(Fall 1992). Periodical. English. qt. Volunteer The National Center, 1111 N 19th Street/Suite 500, Arlington VA 22209. **Tel** (703)276-0542. **LC** HV91; .V63. **DD** 361.7. ***Absorbed*** *Voluntary Action News, 0300-6638.* ***Continued by*** *Leadership (Washington, D.C. : 1993).*
**Ind/Abst** AGRICOLA [Select. Cov.]; Hospit. Health Admin. Index (winter 1978-fall 1990).

CN/0828-6566
### VOLUNTEER OPPORTUNITIES.
1982-. English. be. Community Information Centre, 18 Queen Street North, Kitchener Ontario N2H 2G8 Canada. **DD** 361.3/7/02571344.

US/0275-3030
### VOLUNTEERING.
**Added/Corp** Volunteer: The National Center for Citizen Involvement. (1980)-. English. an. $3.00 single issue. Volunteer: The National Center for Citizen Involvement, 1111 North 19th Street/Suite 500, Arlington VA 22209. **LC** HV1; .V64. **DD** 361.3/7/0973.

CN/0824-1848
**VOLUNTEERS IN ACTION.** (VOLUNTEERS IN ACTION / THE CANADIAN RED CROSS SOCIETY, PRINCE EDWARD ISLAND DIVISION.). Vol. 1, No. 1 (Jan. 1983)-. Periodical. English. ir. Free. Canadian Red Cross Society / Prince Edward Island, Prince Edward Island Division, 62 Prince Street, Charlottetown Prince Edward Island C1A 4R2 Canada. **Tel** (902)894-8551. **ED** Hartwell Daley. **DD** 361.7/634/09717. **Circ:** 5,000 (ctrl).
**Desc:** Short history of the people and events of the P.E.D. Division of the Canadian Red Cross Society.

US/0090-4465
**VRA BULLETIN BOARD.** **See** Public Administration.

US/0163-8300
**W-MEMO.** **See** Public Administration.

JA
**WAKARIYASUI KOSEI NENKIN HOKEN HO : KAISETSU TO SODAN.** **VFOAT** Kosei Nenkin Hoken Ho. Japanese. ¥1100. Chuo Keizaisha, 31-2 Kanda Jinbocho 1, Chiyoda-ku 101, Tokyo Japan. **LC** LAW.

US/8756-0399
**WANTED MISSING PERSONS.** **VFOAT** Missing Persons Magazine. Sept. 1984-. Periodical. English. mo. $2.50 each issue. Missing Person Publishing Company, PO Box 1006, Port Jervis NY 12771. **DD** 363.

US/0043-0234
**WAR CRY (NEW YORK, N.Y.), THE.** (THE WAR CRY.). [War cry]. **Added/Corp** Salvation Army. **VFOAT** War Cry of the Salvation Army. (1880)-. Periodical. English. Twenty-six times a year. $7.50 (one year), $14.00 (two years), $20.00 (three years). Salvation Army, 10 W Algonquin Road, Des Plaines IL 60016. **Tel** (708)294-2000. **ED** Henry Gariepy. **LC** BX9701; .W7. **Bk Rev. Circ:** 400,000 (ctrl).
**Desc:** Inspiration evangelism and information on the Salvation Army.

US/0043-0722
**WASHINGTON REPORT.** **Main/Corp** American Foundation for the Blind. Jan./Feb. 1968-). Periodical. English. bm. American Foundation for the Blind, 15 West 16th Street, New York NY 10011. **Tel** (212)620-2000, (800)829-0500.

US
**WASHINGTON REPORT - AMERICAN ASSOCIATION OF HOMES FOR THE AGING.** **Added/Corp** American Association of Homes for the Aging. **VFOAT** AAHA Washington Report. (19??)-. Periodical. English. bw. American Association of Homes for the Aging, 901 E Street Northwest, Suite 500, Washington DC 20004. **Tel** (202)783-2242, FAX (202)783-2255.

US
**WASHINGTON (STATE) DIVISION OF VOCATIONAL REHABILITATION STATE FACILITIES PLAN.** Department of Social and Health Services / Washington, Mail Stop OB-41K, Olympia WA 98504.

AT/0310-4869
**WELFARE IN AUSTRALIA.** [Welf. Aust.]. (1971)-. Periodical. English. an. 15.00Aus$. Australia Institute of Welfare Workers, PO Box 2557, Canberra City 2601 Australia. **Tel** 61 6 2991111. **DD** _a361.994. Index available. **Bk Rev**, (Qty: 1). **Ad Acc. Circ:** 1,500 (ctrl).

UK/0269-879X
**WELFARE MANCHESTER.** [Welfare Manch.]. (1985)-. Periodical. English. Three times a year. £15.00. The Institute of Welfare Officers, 254 The Corn Exchange, Hanging Ditch, Manchester M4 3ES England. **Tel** 011 44 061 8321374, FAX 011 44 061 8332969. **ED** Marian Maclean-Ives. **DD** 361.94105. **Bk Rev. Ad Acc. Circ:** 2,000 (ctrl). ***Continues*** *Welfare & Social Services Journal, 0261-4049.*

UK/0263-2098
**WELFARE RIGHTS BULLETIN.** (19??)-. English. bm (6 issues). £10.00 UK; £12.00 other. Child Poverty Action Group, 1 Bath Street, London EC1V 9P4 England. **Tel** 011 44 71 253 3406. **Bk Rev. Circ:** 6,250.
**Desc:** Features articles on welfare rights, and benefits.

●US/1060-5622
**WELFARE TO WORK.** (1992)-. Periodical. English. Twenty-four times a year. $252.00. MII Subscriptions Center, 1211 Connecticut Avenue Northwest, Suite 402, Washington DC 20036. **Tel** (800)524-8960 or (202)293-1740, FAX (202)293-0377. **ED** Mildred Charley Green. **Bk Rev**, (Qty: 20). **Ad Acc.**

NE/0169-0639
**WELZYNSWEEKBLAD 1981.** [Welzynsweekblad 1981]. (1981)-. Periodical. Dutch. wk. Fl193.40 Netherlands; $124.91 other. Stichting TMW, Postbus 6307, 2001 HH Haarlem Netherlands. **Tel** 011 31 23 275354, FAX (023)254394. **ED** J. J. Lagendijk. **UDC** 364.442. Index available. **Bk Rev. Ad Acc.** available on audiocassette. ***Continues*** *TMW Welzijnsweekblad, 0165-117X.*
**Desc:** Topics on social welfare.

US/8755-4534
**WESTCHESTER HUMAN SERVICES DIRECTORY.** Directory. English. Westchester Community Services Council, 175 Clearbrook Road, Elmsford NY 10523. **LC** HV98.N7; W46. **DD** 361/.9747277.

US
**WESTERN WIRE.** **Main/Corp** Western Rural Development Center. No. 1 (Sept. 1975)-. Periodical. English. qt.
**Ind/Abst** Irr. Drain. Abstr.; Soils Fert.; World Agric. Econ.

US
**WHEN YOU GET SOCIAL SECURITY DISABILITY BENEFITS : WHAT YOU NEED TO KNOW.** **Added/Corp** United States. Social Security Administration. (Mar. 1991)-. English. Social Security Administration, 6401 Security Boulevard, Baltimore MD 21235. **Tel** (410)965-8822, FAX (410)966-1463. ***Continues*** *Your Social Security Rights and Responsibilities. Disability Benefits.*

US
**WHEN YOU GET SSI : WHAT YOU NEED TO KNOW.** **Added/Corp** United States. Social Security Administration. **VFOAT** When You Get Supplemental Security Income. (Mar. 1991)-. English. Social Security Administration, 6401 Security Boulevard, Baltimore MD 21235. **Tel** (410)965-8822, FAX (410)966-1463.

CN/1185-6238
**WHITBY COMMUNITY SERVICES DIRECTORY.** [Whitby community serv. dir.]. **Added/Corp** Information Whitby. (1991)-. Directory. English. $15.00 per volume. Information Whitby, 405 Dundas Street West, Whitby Ontario L1N 6A1 Canada. **DD** 361. ***Continues*** *Directory of Ccommunity Services for Whitby., 1185-622X.*

US/1056-7402
**WIDE SMILES.** [Wide smiles]. Vol. 1, Issue 1 (Summer 1991)-. Periodical. English. qt. $18.00 (1 year), $34.00 (2 year) US; $22.00 (1 year), $40.00 (2 year) other. Wide Smiles, PO Box 5153, Joanne Green, Stockton CA 95205. **ED** Joanne Green. **DD** 362. Index available. cum. index. **Bk Rev**, (Qty: 4-8). **Ad Acc. Circ:** 1,000.
**Desc:** For families with children born with a craniofacial disorder. Provides education, inspiration, and support.

US/0738-8012
**WORD FROM WASHINGTON.** **Added/Corp** United Cerebral Palsy Associations. (19??)-. Periodical. English. Twelve times a year. $55.00. UCPA Governmental Act Office, 1522 K Street Northwest, Suite 1112, Washington DC 20005. **Tel** (800)872-5827, (202)842-1266.

US
**WORKERS' COMPENSATION DESK BOOK.** **See** Insurance.

US/1064-8585
**WORKING TOGETHER (SEATTLE, WASH.).** (WORKING TOGETHER : TO PREVENT SEXUAL AND DOMESTIC VIOLENCE.). [Work. together]. **Added/Corp** Center for the Prevention of Sexual and Domestic Violence (Seattle, Wash.). (19??)-. Periodical. English. Four times a year. $20.00. Center for the Prevention of Sexual & Domestic Violence, 1914 North 34th Street, Suite 105, Seattle WA 98103. **Tel** (206)634-1903, FAX (206)634-0115. **ED** Thelma Burgonid-Watson. **DD** 362. **Bk Rev**, (Qty: 5). **Ad Acc. Circ:** 30,000.
**Desc:** A newsjournal for the prevention of sexual and domestic violence. Articles on justice for the crime, the church legal liabilities, and consultation and other reviews.

SZ
**WORLD STATISTICAL DIRECTORY OF VOLUNTEER AND DEVELOPMENT SERVICE ORGANISATIONS.** **See** Sociology-Abstracting, Bibliographies and Statistics.

NE
**WVC DOCUMENTATIE / MINISTERIE VAN WELZIJN, VOLKSGEZONDHEID EN CULTUUR.** **Added/Corp** Netherlands. Ministerie van Welzijn, Volksgezondheid en Cultuur. **VFOAT** Documentatie. Vol. 19, No. 1, (Jan. 1983)-. Periodical. Dutch. Twenty-four times a year. Fl81.01. SDU Uitgeverij, Postbus 20014, Christoffel Plan, 2500 EA Den Haag Netherlands. **Tel** 011 31 70 3789911. **LC** Z936.A12; R55a; HN511. ***Continues*** *Netherlands. Ministerie van Cultuur, Recreatie en Maatschappelijk Werk. CRM Documentatie.*

US/0148-8570
**YEAR OF ACHIEVEMENT.** **Main/Corp** United States. Office of Human Development. English. an. Administration for Children & Families, 370 L'Enfant Promenade SW, 6th Floor, Washington DC 20447. **Tel** (202)401-9200, FAX (202)252-4683. **LC** HV85; .O35A. **DD** 353.008/4.

UK
**YHA ACCOMODATION GUIDE. ENGLAND & WALES / YHA.** **Added/Corp** Youth Hostels Association (England and Wales). **VFOAT** YHA Accomodation Guide. England and Wales; England & Wales. (1989)-. Directory. English. an. £5.99. Youth Hostels Association, Trevelyan House, 8 St Stephens Hill, St Albans Herts AL1 2DY England. **Tel** 0727 855215, FAX 0727 844126, telex 265258 YHAEWG. **ED** Suby Dubowski, Hellen Barnes and Anneliese Kraemer. **LC** TX907.5.G7; Y47. **DD** 647.944207. **Ad Acc, Adv Mgr:** Vicki King. **Circ:** 300,000 (ctrl). ***Continues*** *YHA ... Guide.*
**Desc:** A guide book to youth hostels in England and Wales.

US
**YMCA DIRECTORY.** (19??)-. English. an. $50.00. YMCA of the USA, 101 North Wacker Drive, Chicago IL 60606. **Tel** (312)269-0505, FAX (312)977-9063. ***Continues*** *YMCA Year Book and Official Rosters.*

UK
**YOUNG PEOPLE NOW.** English. mo. £22.80. National Youth Agency, 17-23 Albion Street, Leicester LE1 6GD England. **Tel** 011 44 533 471200, FAX 011 44 533 471043. **ED** Jackie Scott. **Bk Rev. Ad Acc. Circ:** 15,000.
**Desc:** Magazine for everyone concerned with young people, social and political education and youth affairs.
**Ind/Abst** Appl. Soc. Sci. Index Abstr.

CN/0317-3429
**YOUR QUEBEC PENSION PLAN.** 1965-. Periodical. English. an. 8.00. CCH Canadian Ltd., 6 Garamond Court, Don Mills Ontario M3C 1Z5 Canada. **Tel** (416)441-2992, FAX (416)441-3418. **DD** 368.4/3/009714.
**Desc:** Pocket-size booklet explaining Quebec Pension Plan, revisions to Old Age Security Pension, Guaranteed Income Supplement, Spouse's Allowance.

UK/0307-1790
**YOUTH IN SOCIETY.** ***Ceased.*** (Sept./Oct. 1973)-(Dec. 1988). Periodical. English. mo. National Youth Agency, 17-23 Albion Street, Leicester LE1 6GD England. **Tel** 011 44 533 471200, FAX 011 44 533 471043. **ED** Jackie Scott. **LC** HV1441.G7; Y58. **DD** 362.7/0941. **Bk Rev. Ad Acc. Circ:** 3,500.
**Desc:** Interprofessional journal for everyone concerned with young people, social and political education and youth affairs.
**Ind/Abst** Appl. Soc. Sci. Index Abstr.; Br. Educ. Index; Sage Race Relat. Abstr.; School Organ. Manage. Abstr.; Sociol. Educ. Abstr.; Tech. Educ. Train. Abstr.

US
**YOUTH POLICY.** [Youth policy]. (19??)-. English. Thirty-six times a year. $127.00 US, Canada & Mexico; $237.00 others. Youth Policy Institute, 1221 Massachusetts Avenue Northwest, Suite B, Washington DC 20005. **Tel** (202)638-2144. **ED** David Fleming. **Bk Rev. Ad Acc. Circ:** 500 (ctrl). ***Continues*** *The America Family, 0161-1178.*
**Desc:** Monitors federal policy affecting youth. Includes legislation people and organizations, book reviews, bibliography, and meetings. The publication is non-partisan.
**Ind/Abst** AGRICOLA [Select. Cov.]; PAIS Int. Print; Urban Aff. Abstr.

US
**YOUTH PROGRAMS (WALTHAM, MASS.).** (YOUTH PROGRAMS : A PUBLICATION OF THE CENTER FOR EMPLOYMENT AND INCOME STUDIES, BRANDEIS UNIVERSITY.). **Added/Corp** Florence Heller Graduate School for Advanced Studies in Social Welfare. Center for Employment and Income Studies. (19??)-. Periodical. English. Four times a year. $25.00 (individuals), $50.00 (institutions). Brandeis University / Center of Human Resources, 60 Turner Street, PO Box 9110, Waltham MA 02254-9110. **Tel** (617)736-3770, (800)343-4705. **ED** Alan Melchir. **Circ:** 10,000 (ctrl).
**Desc:** Information on policies and "best practices" for youth employment and education practitioners.

US/0196-9668
**YOUTH-SERVING ORGANIZATIONS DIRECTORY.** [Youth-serv. organ. dir.]. **VAT** Youth Serving Organizations Directory. 1st- Ed. Directory. English. ir. $72.00. Gale Research Inc., 835 Penobscot Building, Detroit MI 48226. **Tel** (800)877-GALE, (313)961-2242, FAX (313)961-6083, telex TWX 810-221-7086. **ED** A Brewer. **LC** HS17.
**Desc:** In a single alphabetic sequence, detailed entries, describe relevant special libraries and information centers, research centers, and national associations in the United States.

CN/0830-9221
**YOUTH UPDATE (REXDALE, ONT.).** See Law-Law Enforcement and Criminology.

GW/0044-4278
**ZENTRALBLATT FUER SOZIALVERSICHERUNG, SOZIALHILFE UND VERSORGUNG.** [Zentralbl. sozialversicher., sozialhilfe versorg.]. **VFOAT** Zentralblatt fur Sozialversicherung und Versorgung. Periodical. German. mo. Asgard Verlag, Einsteinstrasse 10 Postfach 3080, 5205 Saint Augustin Germany. **NLM** W1 ZE794.
**Ind/Abst** Saf. Health Work.

## SOUND RECORDINGS AND SYSTEMS

US/8756-7717
**1/1 (SAN FRANCISCO, CALIF.).** See Music.

US/0097-1138
**ABSOLUTE SOUND, THE.** (1973)-. Periodical. English. Eight times a year. $46.00 (one year), $96.00 (two year), $135.00 (three year) US; $55.00 (one year), $126.00 (two year), $180.00 (three year) Canada; $70.00 (one year), $156.00 (two year), $225.00 (three year) other. Pearson Publishing Empire, PO Box 357, Sea Cliff NY 11579. **Tel** (800)222-3201, (516)676-2830. **(Subscription address:** 202 Twin Oaks Drive, Syracuse, NY 13206) **ED** Harry Pearson. **LC** TK7881.4; .A22. **DD** 621.389/3/05. Index available. cum. index. **Ad Acc. Circ:** 10,000.
**Desc:** The high end journal for the discriminating viewer. Reviews state of the art video components and accessories.
**Ind/Abst** Music Artic. Guide.

US/0148-8856
**ACE INTERNATIONAL. ENGLISH EDITION.** (ACE INTERNATIONAL.). **VAT** Audio/Consumer Electronics International. English Edition. V. 1- June 1977-. Periodical. English. bm. $35.00. ACE Publishing Ltd, 20 Atwood Street, Newburyport MA 01950. **Tel** (617)46500206. **LC** HD9696.A92; A14. **DD** 380.1/45/62138933094. available on an online database.

US
**AES : JOURNAL OF THE AUDIO ENGINEERING SOCIETY, AUDIO/ACOUSTICS/APPLICATIONS.** **Added/Corp** Audio Engineering Society. **VFOAT** Journal of the Audio Engineering Society, Audio/Acoustics/Applications. Vol. 34, No. 1/2 (Jan./Feb. 1986)-. Periodical. English. Ten times a year (Jan./Feb & July/Aug. issues combined). $125.00 (surface mail); $170.00 (airmail); $125.00 Comes with Audio Engineering Society Membership;. Audio Engineering Society Inc, 60 East 42nd Street, Room 2520, New York NY 10165. **Tel** (212)661-8528, (800)541-7299, FAX (212)682-0477. ***Continues*** *Audio Engineering Society. Journal of the Audio Engineering Society.*
**Desc:** Devoted exclusively to audio technology.
**Ind/Abst** Curr. Biotechnol.

BE/0777-6268
**AGENDA DES FESTIVALS AUDIOVISUELS EN EUROPE, L'.** [Agenda festiv. audiov. Eur.]. **VFOAT** Agenda of Audio-Visual Festivals in Europe. (1990)-. Periodical. French. an. Edimedia ASBL, rue de la Constitution 22, 1030 Brussels Belgium. **Tel** 011 32 2 2180031. **UDC** 654.02. **Ad Acc.** ***Continues in part*** *Videodoc (Bruxelles), 0775-3179.*

SP/1130-4855
**ALTA FIDELIDAD EN AUDIO Y EN VIDEO.** See Communication-Broadcasting.

US/0162-0312
**AMERICAN PHONOGRAPH JOURNAL.** V. 1- Mar. 1978-. Periodical. English. qt. $7.00. Tim Christen, PO Box 265, Belmont CA 94002. **LC** TS2301.P3. **DD** 621.389/33.

US/0003-0716
**AMERICAN RECORD GUIDE.** [Am. rec. guide]. **VFOAT** ARG. Vol. 11, No. 2 (Oct. 1944)-. Periodical. English. Six times a year. $36.00 institutions; $29.00 individuals. American Record Guide, 4412 Braddock Street, Cincinnati OH 45204. **Tel** (513)941-1116. **ED** G. Wolf. **LC** ML1; .A725. **DD** 780.5. Index available (bound in Nov. issue). **Bk Rev. Ad Acc. Circ:** 5,000. available on microfilm and microfiche from University Microfilms International (UMI). Documents available from UMI Article Clearinghouse. ***Continues*** *Listener's Record Guide;* ***Absorbed*** *Musical America.*
**Desc:** Covers classical recordings with detailed, informed and forthright reviews; also makes comparisons with other recordings to help in making competent buying decisions.
**Ind/Abst** Bibliogr. Mission. (1959-); Gen. Period. Index (1985-); Mag. Index Plus (1989-); Mag. Search; Music Artic. Guide; Music Index; Newsp. Period. Abstr. (1988-); Pop. Period. Index; Read. Guide Period. Lit.; Mag. Index (1977-).

UK
**ANTIQUE RECORDS.** Nov. 1972-. Periodical. English. J Hall, KT7 OLH Ditton England. **LC** ML5; .A5965. **DD** 789.9/12/075.

CN/1187-2705
**ARIA NEWS.** (ARIA NEWS : THE OFFICIAL PUBLICATION OF THE ALBERTA RECORDING INDUSTRY ASSOCIATION.). [ARIA news]. **Added/Corp** Alberta Recording Industry Association. **VFOAT** ARIA Newsletter. **VAT** Alberta Recording Industry Association News. Vol. 5, No. 4 (Apr. 1991) or Vol. 5, No. 5 (May 1991)-. Periodical. English. mo. Alberta Recording Industry Association, #102, 10550-102 Street, Edmonton Alberta T5H 2T3 Canada. **DD** 338.4/778149/0607123. ***Continues*** *ARIA Newsletter., 0843-3747.*

US
**ARSC JOURNAL.** **Added/Corp** Association for Recorded Sound Collections. Vol. 17, No. 1/3 (1985)-. Periodical. English. Twice a year (Sring and Fall). $30.00 Comes with Association for Recorded Sound Collections membership. Association for Recorded Sound Collections, PO Box 543, Annapolis MD 21401. **Tel** (401)757-0488. **ED** Barry Ashpole, (editor's address: 377 Soudan Avenue, Toronto, Ontario, Canada, phone: (416)362-4804). **LC** ML1; .A84. **Bk Rev**, (Qty: 18). **Ad Acc, Adv Mgr:** Gary Thalheimer. **Pr Rev. Circ:** 1,000. ***Continues*** *Association for Recorded Sound Collections. Journal - Association for Recorded Sound Collections, 0004-5438;* ***Absorbed*** *Association for Recorded Sound Collections. Bulletin.*
**Desc:** Results of major research, technical developments, discographies, record and book reviews, and a current bibliography of related articles in other publications.
**Ind/Abst** MLA Int. Bibl. Books Artic. Mod. Lang. Lit.; Music Index (?-19??); RILM Abstr.

US/0004-7546
**AUDIO AMATEUR.** Vol. 1, (Winter 1970)-. Periodical. English. Four times a year. $20.00 (individuals), $25.00 (institutions) US & Canada; $35.00 (individuals), $40.00 (institutions) others. Audio Amateur Publications, PO Box 576, Peterborough NH 03458. **Tel** (603)924-9464, FAX (603)924-9467. **ED** Edward T. Dell Jr. **LC** TK7881.7; .A9. **DD** 621.389/3/05. **Bk Rev. Circ:** 5,500. available on microfilm and microfiche from University Microfilms International (UMI).
**Desc:** Design, construction and modification of sound reproduction equipment.
**Ind/Abst** Index Inf. (1990-).

US/0164-8985
**AUDIO & ELECTRONICS DIGEST.** **VAT** Audio and Electronics Digest. Periodical. English. mo. $20.00 US; $30.00 other. International Audio Club, PO Box 660, Beverly Hills CA 90213.

UK
**AUDIO ARTS MAGAZINE SOUND RECORDING.** (Oct. 1973)-. Periodical. English (German). Four times a year. £30.00 UK; £35.00 Europe; £40.00 US & Canada; £43.00 other. Audio Arts, 6 Briarwood Road, London SW4 9PX England. **Tel** 011 44 71 720 9129. available on audiocassette.
**Desc:** Provides a medium for the articulation and dissemination of debate, theory and practice in relation to contemporary art. Includes collaborations with leading international artists, interviews, discussions, art works, documentation, reportage and archive recordings.

US/0146-4701
**AUDIO CRITIC, THE.** [Audio crit.]. Vol. 1, (Jan./Feb. 1977)-. Periodical. English. Four times a year (Feb., May, Aug., Nov.). $24.00. The Audio Critic, PO Box 978, Quakertown PA 18951. **Tel** (215)538-9555. **ED** Peter Aczel (phone: (215)536-8884). **LC** TK7881.4; .A9. **DD** 621. cum. index. **Ad Acc. Circ:** 10,000.

US/0883-8437
**AUDIO (DURANGO, COLO.).** (AUDIO.). [Audio]. **Added/Corp** Orion Research Corporation. **VFOAT** Audio Blue Book; Orion Audio Blue Book. (1984)-. English. an (Dec.). $164.00. Orion Research Corporation, 14555 North Scottsdale Road, Suite 330, Scottsdale AZ 85260. **Tel** (800)844-0759, (602)951-1114, FAX (602)951-1117. **ED** Roger Rohrs. **LC** TK7881.4; .A93. **DD** 621.389/3/029473. **Bk Rev. Ad Acc.** ***Continues*** *Audio Reference Guide, 0277-3562.*
**Desc:** Hardbound, 700-page book lists more than 41,000 products, including receivers, amps, speakers, cassettes, tuners, equalizers and digital and digital equipment.

US/0004-752X
**AUDIO (PHILADELPHIA, PA.).** (AUDIO.). [Audio]. Vol. 38, No. 3 (March 1954)-. Periodical. English. mo. $24.00. Hachette Magazines Inc., 1633 Broadway, New York NY 10019. **Tel** (212)767-6000. **(Subscription address:** Neodata / Colorado, PO Box 2606, Boulder Boulder CO 80322.) **ED** Eugene Pitts III. **LC** TK6540; .R17. **DD** 621. available on microfilm and microfiche from University Microfilms International (UMI). Documents available from UMI Article Clearinghouse, Magazine Collection. ***Continues*** *Audio Engineering, 0275-3804.*
**Desc:** Magazine for high fidelity enthusiasts. Gives highly specialized information and guidance for the true audiophile. Includes comprehensive reviews on equipment, records and compact discs. Features by columnists include car stereo, digital technology, new products and exclusive interviews.
**Ind/Abst** Acad. Ind. [Computer File] (1984-1988); Appl. Sci. Technol. Index; Consum. Index Prod. Eval. Inf. Source; Expand. Acad. Index (1984-1988); Gen. Period. Index (1985-); Mag. Index Plus (1989-); Mag. Index. Sel. (1986-); Mag. Search; Music Index; Newsp. Period. Abstr. (1988-); Mag. Index (1977-).

SW/0282-6364
**AUDIO VIDEO.** ***Ceased.*** (19??)-(19??). Periodical. Swedish. Affarsforlaget, PO Box 3188, S-103-63 Stockholm Sweden. **Tel** +4687365650, FAX +468319038. **LC** TK7881.4; .A95.

US/1041-5378
**AUDIO/VIDEO INTERIORS.** [Audio/video inter.]. **VFOAT** Audio Video Interiors. **VAT** Audio video interiors. (1989)-. Periodical. English. mo. $23.95 (one year), $47.90 (two year), $71.85 (three year). AVCOM, 21700 Oxnard Street, Suite 1600, Woodland Hill CA 91367. **Tel** (818)593-3900. **ED** Chris Esse. **LC** TK7881.8; .A93. **DD** 747/.9. **Circ:** 130,000.
**Desc:** A guide for consumers who want to know what audio or video products fit their budget and home lifestyle.

NE/0922-2367
**AUDIO VIDEO TOTAAL.** See Consumer Interests.

UK
**AUDIO VISUAL DIRECTORY.** (19??)-. Directory. English. mo. £33.00 UK; £65.00 Europe; £75.00 other. EMAP Readerlink, Audit House, 260 Field End Road, Ruislip Middlesex HA4 9LT England. **Tel** 011 44 081 868 4499, FAX 011 44 081 429 3117. **ED** Peter Lloyd. **LC** HD9697.A843; G72 SUPPL. **DD** 338.7/62138/04402541. **Ad Acc.**
**Desc:** Directory of UK audio-visual businesses broken down by product sector.

CN/0821-5529
**AUDIO-VISUAL PRESENTATIONS / CANADIAN JEWISH CONGRESS, AUDIO-VISUAL DEPARTMENT.** [Audio-v. present. - Can. Jew. Congr., Audio-v. Dep.]. **Main/Corp** Canadian Jewish Congress. Audio-Visual Dept. **VFOAT** Presentations Audio-Visuelles. English (Yiddish and French). an. Free. Audio-Visual Department, Canadian Jewish Congress, 1590 Dr Penfield Avenue, Montreal Quebec H3G 1C5 Canada. **DD** 016.909/04924. ctrl circ.

US/1044-7601
**AUDIO WEEK.** [Audio week]. Vol. 1, No. 1 (June 19, 1989)-. Periodical. English. wk. $590.12 Washington DC; $554.00 other US, Canada, and Mexico; $596.00 other. Warren Publishing, Inc., 2115 Ward Court NW, Washington DC 20037. **Tel** (202)872-9200, FAX (202)293-3435. **DD** 338. available on an online database (files 16,636/Full-Text) from DIALOG.
**Ind/Abst** PROMT [Full Txt.]; PTS Newsl. Database [Full Txt.].

US/1055-9566
**AUDIO'S GUIDE TO SURROUND SOUND.** **VFOAT** Guide to Surround Sound; Audio/Surround Sound. **VAT** Audio Surround Sound. (1990)-. Periodical. English. Audio, PO Box 52548, Boulder CO 80321-2548. **LC** IN PROCESS. **DD** 621.

AT/0816-9330
**AUDIOVISION AND PROSOUND.** [Audiov. prosound]. (1984)-. Periodical. English. bm. Horwitz Grahame Pty Ltd, 506 Miller Street, Cammeray New South Wales, 2062 Australia. **Tel** 011 61 2 9296144, FAX 011 61 2 9571814. **DD** 338.47621380440994. ***Continues*** *Audio Vision (Sydney), 0727-4165.*

IT/0303-7622
**AUDIOVISIONE (ROMA).** (AUDIOVISIONE.). (Feb. 1973)-. Periodical. Italian. mo. L4000. Viale Degli Ammiragli 71, Rome 00136 Italy. **LC** TK7881.7; .A94.

US/0362-1162
**AUDIVIDEO INTERNATIONAL.** (19??)-. Periodical. English. Twelve times a year. Free to trade, $30.00 non-trade (surface mail); $40.00 Canada & Mexico, $65.00 others (airmail). Dempa Publications Inc., 1 11 15 Higashi Gotanda, Shinagawa Ku Tokyo 141 Japan. **Tel** 011 81 3 34456111. **(Subscription address:** Dempa Publications, 275 Madison Avenue, New York NY 10016.) **ED** Steve T. Mason. **LC** TK7800; .A83. **DD** 621.38/05. **Ad Acc. Circ:** 42,000 (ctrl). ***Continues*** *Audiovideo.*
**Desc:** Serves retailers, distributors and manufacturers of consumer electronics products.

US/0194-8679
**AUTOSOUND & COMMUNICATIONS.** ***Ceased.*** **VAT** Autosound and Communications. Vol. 1 (June 1979)-(March 1990). Periodical. English. ir. CES Publishing Company, 345 Park Avenue South, Bernard Rock, New York NY 10010. **Tel** (212)686-7744. ***Supersedes*** *Communications Retailing.*

# Sound Recordings and Systems

**NE/0923-7054**
**AVPROF AMSTERDAM.** (AVPROF).
[AVprofAmst.]. **VFOAT** AudioVideoprof (Amsterdam). (1987)-. Periodical. Dutch. mo (11 issues per year). Fl180.20. Wegener Tijl Tijdschriften Group, Postbus 9943, 1006 AP Amsterdam Netherlands. **Tel** 011 31 20 5182828. **UDC** 621.39.

**US/0195-0908**
**B.A.S. SPEAKER, THE. Main/Corp** Boston Audio Society. **VAT** Boston Audio Society Speaker. (19??)-. Periodical. English. bm (6 issues). $35.00. Boston Audio Society, PO Box 211, Boston MA 02126. **Tel** (617)232-9654. **ED** Mark P. Fishman. **Circ:** 500.
**Desc:** Reports on meetings and activities of the Boston Audio Society and promotes highest quality music reproduction in the home and high standards of recording and transmission.

**NE**
**BEELD EN GELUID.** Dutch. mo. TWF Publicity, PO Box 71933, 1008 EC Amsterdam Netherlands. **Tel** 011 31 20 6461727.

**NE**
**BEELD EN GELUID OPINIE.** Dutch. mo (11 issues). F59.50. TWF Publicity, PO Box 71933, 1008 EC Amsterdam Netherlands. **Tel** 011 31 20 6461727.
**Continues** Beeld en Geluid.

**GW**
**BIELEFELDER KATALOG SCHALLPLATTEN, COMPACT DISCS, MUSICASSETTEN KLASSIK. VFOAT**
Bielefelder Katalog Schallplatten, Compact Discs. Klassik; Bielefelder Katalog (K); Bielefelder Katalog. Klassik. (1985)-. English (German). sa. Vereinigte Motor Verlag GmbH, Motor Presse, POB 106036, D 70049 Stuttgart Germany. **Tel** 011 49 711 1821506, 011 49 711 1821545. **Continues** Bielefelder Katalog Schallplatten, Compact Discs. Klassik.

**FR/0338-9405**
**BULLETIN D'AUDIOPHONOLOGIE BESANCON.** [Bull. audiophonol. Besancon]. (1971)-. Periodical. French. Six times a year. 390.00F France; 430.00F other. Assn Franc Comtoise, Audiophonologie 4 PI St Jacque, 25030 Besancon Cedex France. **Tel** 011 33 81 811145 ext. 692. **UDC** 534.75 : 534.78. **Continues** Annales Scientifiques de l'Universite de Franche-Comte-Besancon. Medecine, Pharmacie, 0224-5264.

**UK**
**BULLETIN OF THE NFGS. VFOAT** Bulletin of the National Federation of Gramophone Societies; Bulletin. Began in 1947. Bulletin. English. sa.

**US/0090-9033**
**BUYER'S GUIDE TO THE WORLD OF TAPE. VFOAT** World of Tape. (19??)-. English. $1.50 single issue. Billboard Publications Inc., 1515 Broadway Billboard, New York NY 10036. **Tel** (212)764-7300, FAX (305)755-7048, telex WU TWX 710-581-6279. **LC** TK7881.6; .B88. **DD** 621.389/32.

**US/0272-2291**
**BUYING GUIDE TO CAR STEREO SYSTEMS.** Consumer Publication. English. $2.95. ABC Leisure Magazine Inc, 825 7th Avenue, New York NY 10019. **Tel** (212)265-8360. **LC** TK7881.85; .B88. **DD** 629.2/77.

**CN/0381-9507**
**CANADIAN L P & TAPE CATALOGUE, THE. VAT** The Canadian Long Play and Tape Catalogue. V. 1- Summer 1975-. English. M J MacArthur Wrightman, 33 Seguin Street, Ottawa Ontario K1J 6P2 Canada. **LC** ML156.2; .C25. **DD** 016.7899/12.

**US/0898-3720**
**CAR AUDIO AND ELECTRONICS.** [Car audio electron.]. **VFOAT** Car Audio. Vol. 1, No. 1 (July 1988)-. Periodical. English. mo. $21.95. AVCOM, 21700 Oxnard Street, Suite 1600, Woodland Hill CA 91367. **Tel** (818)593-3900. **(Subscription address:** Neodata / Colorado, PO Box 2606, Boulder Boulder CO 80322.) **ED** William Burton. **LC** WMLC 93/1278. **DD** 621.
**Desc:** Geared toward teenagers and young urban professionals and advises readers how to buy and enjoy electronics for their cars. Editorial covers audio equipment, radar detectors, security systems and car telephones and includes product test reports.

**US/0894-3443**
**CAR STEREO REVIEW (LOS ANGELES, CALIF.).** (CAR STEREO REVIEW.). [Car stereo rev.]. Vol. 1, No. 1 (Fall 1987)-. Periodical. English. bm (6 issues). $18.00. Hachette Magazines Inc., 1633 Broadway, New York NY 10019. **Tel** (212)767-6000. **(Subscription address:** Neodata / Colorado, PO Box 2606, Boulder Boulder CO 80322.) **DD** 621.

**US/0008-7289**
**CASH BOX, THE.** [Cash box]. (19??)-. Periodical. English. wk. $180.00 North America; $225.00 other. Cash Box Publishing Company Inc., 6464 Sunset Boulevard, Hollywood CA 90028. **Tel** (213)464-8241. **ED** Mark Albert. **LC** ML1; .C325. **DD** 789.9/1/05. **Ad Acc. Circ:** 18,000.
**Desc:** An international trade publication concerned with news coverage information and reviews and various national charts regarding today's music, video and home entertainment industries.
**Ind/Abst** Music Index.

**US/0193-5801**
**CATALOG OF TELEVISION AND AUDIOVISUAL MATERIALS. See** Communication-Broadcasting.

**FR**
**CATALOGUE DISQUES. See** Music.

**US**
**CD PUBLISHER NEWS.** (19??)-. English. Meridian Data, 5615 Scotts Valley Drive, Scotts Valley CA 95066. **Tel** (408)138-3100.

**IT**
**CHI E - DOV' E; ANNUARIO DELL'INDUSTRIA FONOGRAFICA E DELL'EDITORIA MUSICALE IN ITALIA.**
**VFOAT** Chi & Dove; Chi E Dove. (19??)-. Italian. L600. Musica e Dischi / M. De Luigi, Via de Amicis 47, 20123 Milan Italy. **Tel** 011 39 2 89402837, FAX 011 39 2 8323843. **LC** ML21; .C52. **DD** 380.1/45/7802545.

**US/0149-5860**
**CHICOREL INDEX TO VIDEO TAPES AND CASSETTES.** English. an. $125.00. American Library Publishing Corporation, PO Box 2014, Sedona AZ 86336. **Tel** (602)284-1162. **ED** Marietta S Chicorel. **LC** LB1044.7.Z9; C47. **DD** 011.
**Desc:** Over 4,000 tapes listed by title. Gives specs and descriptive summary of each program.

**UK/0961-5237**
**CLASSICAL CATALOGUE. Title Change.**
38th Yr., No. 150 (Dec. 1990)-(1993). English. Twice a year (June., Dec.). General Gramophone Publishers Ltd., 177-179 Kenton Road, Harrow Middlesex HA3 0HA England. **Tel** 011 44 81 907 4476, FAX 011 44 81 907 0073, telex 265871 MONREF G MUS027. **LC** ML156.2; .G675. **Formed by the union of** Gramophone Compact Disc Digital Audio Guide and Catalogue, 0267-2162 **and** Gramophone Classical Catalogue, 0309-4367. **Continued by** Gramophone Classical Catalogue (Harrow, London, England : 1993).

**US/0888-7381**
**CMRR REPORT.** [CMRR rep.]. **Added/Corp** University of California, San Diego. Center for Magnetic Recording Research. **VFOAT** C.M.R.R. Report. **VAT** Center for Magnetic Recording Research Report. (1984)-. Periodical. English. ir. Free on request. University of California Magnetic Recording Research, Research 0401, 9500 Gilman Drive, La Jolla CA 92093. **Tel** (619)534-6199. **DD** 621.

**US**
**COMPACT DISC BUYERS' GUIDE. VFOAT** Stereo Review's Compact Disc Buyers' Guide; CD Buyers' Guide; Stereo Review Presents Compact Disc Buyers' Guide. (198?)-. Consumer Publication. English. an. Hachette Magazines Inc., 1633 Broadway, New York NY 10019. **Tel** (212)767-6000. **LC** TK7881.75; .C65. **DD** 621.389/3.

**US/0270-627X**
**COMPLETE BUYER'S GUIDE TO STEREO/HI-FI EQUIPMENT, THE. VFOAT** Speakers. **VAT** Complete Buyer's Guide to Stereo HiFi Equipment. Periodical. English. bm (seven no. a year). $2.50. Service Communications, 50 Rockefeller Plaza, New York NY 10020. **LC** TK7881.8; .C6. **DD** 621.389/334.

**CN/0709-7166**
**COUNTERPOINT CLASSICAL RECORD REVIEW. See** Music.

**CN/0709-7158**
**COUNTERPOINT'S BASIC CLASSICAL RECORD LIBRARY GUIDE. See** Music.

**CN/0229-1533**
**CUE TRACK. See** Music.

**FR**
**DIAPASON. See** Music.

**FR/0765-5983**
**DIAPASON HARMONIE. Title Change. See** Music.

**BE**
**DIFFUSION DES PROGRAMMES AUDIOVISUELS, LA. See** Photography and Video.

**US/8755-738X**
**DIGITAL & AUDIO/VIDEO DISCONTINUED DEVICES. Ceased.** [Dig. audio/video discont. devices]. **VFOAT** Digital and Audio/Video Discontinued Devices; Digital & Audio Video Discontinued Devices; Digital & Audio/Video I.C.'s Discontinued Devices. Ceased with 5th Ed. English. an. DATA Business Publishing, PO Box 6510, 15 Inverness Way East, Englewood CO 80155. **Tel** (800)447-4666, (303)799-0381, FAX (303)799-4082. **ED** Steven D Adolf. **LC** TK7874.5; .D53. **DD** 621.381/73/0216.
**Desc:** Contains specifications on 21,100 devices no longer in production from 143 manufacturers.

**UK**
**DIRECTORY OF MEMBER ARCHIVES.**
Directory. English. Kr60.00 (members), Kr90.00 (non-members). International Association of Sound Archives, c/o Marit Grimstad, Programarkivet NRK, N-0340 Olso, Norway. **ED** Grace Koch. **LC** CD941; .D57. **DD** 027.5/025.

**US**
**DIRECTORY OF SPOKEN-VOICE AUDIO-CASSETTES. See** Music.

**UK**
**DISCO 45. See** Music.

**CN/0706-7763**
**DISCO FEVER. See** Music.

**IT**
**DISCOTECA ALTA FEDELTA.** Began with No. 12, 1971. Periodical. Italian. $11.00. Casa Editrice l'Esperto, Via Martignoni 1, Milan 20124 Italy. **LC** ML5; .D63. **DD** 384. **Continues** Discoteca.
**Ind/Abst** RILM Abstr.

**IT**
**DISCOTECA HI-FI. Suspended.** Periodical. Italian. mo. $14.85. Ed Portoria Spa, Corso Venezia 8, 20121 Milan Italy. **LC** ML5; .D63. **DD** 789.9/12/05. **Continues** Discoteca Alto Fedelata.

**US/0197-2626**
**DON CLEARY'S RECORD COLLECTORS DIRECTORY.** (19??)-. Directory. English. Don Cleary's Record Collectors Directory, PO Box 16265, Ft Lauderdale FL 33318. **LC** ML12; .C6. **DD** 789.9/12/075.

**FR**
**EDITION PHONOGRAPHIQUE EN FRANCE D'APRES LE DEPOT LEGAL / BIBLIOTHEQUE NATIONALE, DEPARTMENT DE LA PHONOTHEQUE NATIONALE ET DE L'AUDIOVISUEL, L'.**
French. an. Bibliotheque Nationale, 58 rue de Richelieu, 75084 Paris Cedex 02 France. **Tel** 011 33 1 47038385. **LC** ML111.5; .P25. **DD** 338.4/7780266/0944. **Continues** Edition Phonographique d'Apres le Depot Legal.

**US/0091-7591**
**FIND CATALOG. See** Music.

**NE**
**FONOWEEK 40.** Periodical. Dutch. 94.85. Koning Wilhelminalaan 12, Amersfoort Netherlands. **LC** TK7881.7; .F67.

**CN/0702-8393**
**FUGUE. See** Music.

**NE/0925-9406**
**GELUID ALPHEN AAN DEN RIJN.** (GELUID). [Geluid Alphen Rijn]. (1991)-. Periodical. Dutch. qt (4 issues). Fl79.72. Samson Bedrijfsinformatie, Postbus 4, 2400 MA Alphen Rij Netherlands. **Tel** 011 31 1 72066633. **(Subscription address:** Intermedia BV, Postbus 4, 2400 MA Alphen Rijn Netherlands; telephone: 011 31 1720 66481) **UDC** 534. **Continues** Geluid en Omgeving, 0165-2982.

●**UK**
**GRAMOPHONE CLASSICAL CATALOGUE, THE. VFOAT** Classical Catalogue. (Dec. 1993)-. English. sa. £55.00. General Gramophone Publishers Ltd., 177-179 Kenton Road, Harrow Middlesex HA3 0HA England. **Tel** 011 44 81 907 4476, FAX 011 44 81 907 0073, telex 265871 MONREF G MUS027. **LC** ML156.2; .G675. **Continues** Classical Catalogue, 0961-5237.

**UK/0017-310X**
**GRAMOPHONE INCLUDING COMPACT DISC NEWS AND REVIEWS. Title Change.**
Periodical. English. mo. General Gramophone Publications Ltd, 177-179 Kenton Road, Harrow Middlesex HA3 0HA England. **Tel** 01-907 4476, FAX +44 1 907 0073, telex 265871 MONREF G MUS027. **ED** Christopher Pollard. **LC** ML5; .G65. **DD** 789.9/13/05. Index available. **Bk Rev. Ad Acc. Circ:** 69,248. **Continues** Gramophone, 0017-310X. **Continued by** Gramophone.

# Sound Recordings and Systems

**Desc:** News and detailed reviews of new classical recordings, new release listings and hi-fi equipment reports.

US/0147-8494
**GRAMOPHONE NEWS, THE.** (19??)-. Periodical. English. The Gramophone News, 1163 Cherry Avenue, San Jose CA 95125. **LC** ML1; .G924. **DD** 621.389/33/05.

UK
**GRAMOPHONE. SPOKEN WORD AND MISCELLANEOUS CATALOGUE.** **Suspended.** (1969)-?. English. an. £4.45 UK; $5.31 North America; £4.70 other. General Gramophone Publications Ltd, 177-179 Kenton Road, Harrow Middlesex HA3 0HA England. **Tel** 01-907 4476, **FAX** +44 1 907 0073, telex 265871 MONREF G MUS027. **Ad Acc**. **Circ:** 9,000.
**Desc:** Detailed listing of recorded works on records and cassettes which fall outside musical categories.

UK
**GRAMOPHONE, WIRELESS & TALKING MACHINE NEWS.** **Added/Corp** League of British Artists. **VAT** Gramophone, Wireless and Talking Machine News. Vol. 15, No. 389B (Mar. 1923)-. Periodical. English. mo. **LC** ML156.9; .T25. **DD** 789.9/1/05. **Continues** Talking Machine News & Journal of Amusements.

BE
**GUIDE DU PRODUCTEUR DE DISQUES, LE.** (19??)-. French. 1200F Belgium & Luxembourg; 320F France; 2200F other. Edimedia ASBL, rue de la Constitution 121, 1030 Brussels Belgium. **Tel** 011 32 2 2180031. **Bk Rev**. **Ad Acc**.

FR
**HI-FI.** French (French). 10.00. Societe des Editions Radio, 17 rue Bucci, Paris 75006 France. **LC** TK7881.7; .H285. **DD** 621.389/33/05. **Continues** Haute-Fidelite.

UK
**HI-FI ANSWERS.** **Title Change.** Periodical. English. mo. Haymarket Publishing Ltd., 12 14 Ansdell Street, London W8 5TR England. **Tel** 011 44 483 733800, **FAX** 011 44 483 776573. **LC** TK7881.7; .H47. **DD** 621.389/33. **Continued by** Audiofile.

UK/0142-6230
**HI-FI NEWS & RECORD REVIEW.** [Hi-fi news rec. rev.]. **VFOAT** Hi-fi News and Record Review. **VAT** High Fidelity News and Record Review. Vol. 16, No. 1 (1971)-. Periodical. English. Twelve times a year. £30.00 UK; £42.50 Europe; £40.00 other. **(Subscription address:** United Magazine Subscriptions, 1st Floor, Stephenson House, Brunel C, Milton Keynes, MK2 2EW England; telephone: 11 44 908 371981) **ED** Steve Harris. Index available (bound in issue). **Continues** Hi-Fi News Incorporating Record Review.
**Desc:** Internationally respected high quality magazine for hi-fi enthusiasts.

NE
**HI FI VIDEO TEST.** (19??)-. Dutch. mo (11 issues). Fl79.50. Hi Fi Video, POB 6130, 7401 JC Deventer Netherlands. **Tel** 011 31 5700 14014.

FR/0337-1891
**HIFI STEREO, VIDEO.** See Music.

UK
**HIGH FIDELITY.** **Title Change.** (19??)-(19??)-. English. mo. Haymarket Publishing Ltd., 12 14 Ansdell Street, London W8 5TR England. **Tel** 011 44 483 733800, **FAX** 011 44 483 776573. **Absorbed** New HI-FI Sound. **Absorbed by** What HI-FI?.

US/0198-7224
**HIGH FIDELITY'S BUYING GUIDE TO STEREO COMPONENTS.** **VFOAT** Buying Guide to Stereo Components. Consumer Publication. English. an. ABC Leisure Magazine Inc, 825 7th Avenue, New York NY 10019. **Tel** (212)265-8360. **LC** TK7881.8; .H53. **DD** 621.389/334/029473.

US/0161-4371
**HIGH FIDELITY'S BUYING GUIDE TO TAPE SYSTEMS.** **VFOAT** Buying Guide to Tape Systems. Consumer Publication. English. $1.95 single copy. ABC Leisure Magazine Inc, 825 7th Avenue, New York NY 10019. **Tel** (212)265-8360. **LC** TK7881.6; .H53. **DD** 621.389/32.

US/0277-1357
**HIGH PERFORMANCE REVIEW.** Vol. 1, No. 1 (Spring 1981)-. Periodical. English. qt. $29.97 (one year), $54.97 (two years), $79.97 (three years) US; $38.97 (one year), $72.97 (two years), $106.97 (three years) other. High Performance Review, PO Box 346, 76 Quassuk Road, Woodbury CT 06798. **Tel** (203)266-0084. **ED** David H Tarumoto. **LC** TK7881.7; .H55. **DD** 621.389/332/05. **[CCC]**. Index available. **Bk Rev**. **Ad Acc**. **Circ:** 18,000.
**Desc:** Definitive magazine for audiophiles and music lovers. Reviews of stereo components and recordings. Contains 100-plus CD, LP and cassette reviews in each issue.

US/0896-7172
**HOME & STUDIO RECORDING.** **Title Change.** [Home stud. rec.]. **VFOAT** Home and Studio Recording; H&SR. (1987)-Vol. 7, No. 9 (June 1994). Periodical. English. mo. Music Maker Publications Inc, 7318 Topanga Canyon Boulevard, Suite 200, Canoga CA 91303. **Tel** (818)346-0744, **FAX** (818)346-0882. **(Subscription address:** Kable Publishers Aide, 308 East Hitt Street, Subscription Department, Mt. Morris IL 61054-1473.) **LC** TK7881.4; .H65. **DD** 621.389/3. **Absorbed** Music Technology, 0896-2480. **Continued by** Recording.

US/0273-9518
**IAR HOTLINE.** **VFOAT** I.A.R. Hotline. **VAT** International Audio Review Hotline. No. 1/2 (Oct. 1980)-. Periodical. English. Twelve times a year. $38.00. Institute for Research / California, PO Box 4271, International Audio Review, Berkeley CA 94704. **Tel** (510)547-2284. **LC** TK7881.7; .I27. **DD** 621.389/332/05.

●HU/1021-562X
**IASA JOURNAL / INTERNATIONAL ASSOCIATION OF SOUND ARCHIVES.** **Added/Corp** International Association of Sound Archives. No. 1 (May 1993)-. Periodical. English (German). an (May). $40.00. International Association Sound Archives, PO Box 27890, ALB Anna M. Foyer, S 115 93 Stockholm Sweden. **LC** ML5; .P363. **Continues** Phonographic Bulletin.

●US/1063-6676
**IEEE TRANSACTIONS ON SPEECH AND AUDIO PROCESSING.** (IEEE TRANSACTIONS ON SPEECH AND AUDIO PROCESSING : A PUBLICATION OF THE IEEE SIGNAL PROCESSING SOCIETY.). [IEEE trans. speech audio process.]. **Added/Corp** IEEE Signal Processing Society. **VFOAT** Transactions on Speech and Audio Processing; Speech and Audio Processing. **VAT** Institute of Electrical and Electronics Engineers Transactions on Speech and Audio Processing. Vol. 1, No. 1 (Jan. 1993)-. Periodical. English. Six times a year. $180.00. IEEE, Institution of Electrical and Electronics Engineers, Inc., 345 East 47th Street, New York NY 10017-2394. **Tel** (908)981-1393, **FAX** (908)981-9667. **(Subscription address:** IEEE / Institute of Electrical and Electronics Engineers, 445 Hoes Lane, PO Box 1331, Piscataway NJ 08855-1331.) **LC** TK7882.S65; I38. **DD** 621.382. **NLM** W1; IE447. **CODEN** IESPEJ.
**Desc:** Major forum for research in speech and audio processing. Topics include transmission and storage, enhancement and noise reduction, speech recognition, analysis and synthesis, speaker recognition, system evaluation, language modeling, active sound control and acoustic noise reduction, psychoacoustics and perception, and hardware for speech and audio processing.

US/0277-8424
**INDEX TO AUDIO EQUIPMENT REVIEWS.** **Ceased.** (INDEX TO AUDIO EQUIPMENT REVIEWS / BY ARNE JON ARNESON AND STUART MILLIGAN.). [Index audio equip. rev.]. **Added/Corp** Music Library Association. (19??)-(19??)-. English. an. Music Library Association, PO Box 487, Canton MA 02021. **Tel** (617)828-8450, **FAX** (617)828-8915. **LC** Z5838.H5; I5; TK7881.7. **DD** 016.621389/33.

US
**INTERNATIONAL BUYER'S GUIDE.** See Music.

US/0889-4922
**INTERNATIONAL RECORDING EQUIPMENT & STUDIO DIRECTORY.** [Int. rec. equip. stud. dir.]. **VFOAT** International Recording Equipment and Studio Directory; Recording Equipment and Studio Directory; International Billboard Recording Equipment & Studio Directory; Billboard ... International Recording Equipment and Studio Directory. (1984/85)-. Directory. English. $53.00 US; $58.00 other. Billboard Publications Inc., 1515 Broadway Billboard, New York NY 10036. **Tel** (212)764-7300, **FAX** (305)755-7048, telex WU TWX 710-581-6279. **(Subscription address:** Billboard Publications, 1695 Oak Street, Lakewood, NJ 08701) **LC** TK7881.4; .I57. **DD** 338.7/6621389/3025. **Continues** International Billboard Recording Studio & Equipment Directory, 0889-4914.
**Desc:** Provides information on professional recording equipment, recording studios and recording studio equipment.

US/0270-4048
**JAZZ RAG.** See Music.

●US/1063-1887
**JOURNAL WATCH (SOUND RECORDING).** (JOURNAL WATCH [SOUND RECORDING] : THE AUDIO CASSETTE SERVICE.). (1992)-. Periodical. English. sm. $195.00. Audio-Digest Foundation, 1577 Chevy Chase Drive, Glendale CA 91206. **Tel** (213)245-8505, (800)423-2308, **FAX** (818)240-7379.

US/0749-5250
**LASER DISC NEWSLETTER, THE.** [Laser disc newsl.]. (1984)-. Newsletter. English. mo. $35.00. Laser Disc Newsletter, PO Box 420, East Rockaway NY 11518. **Tel** (516)594-9304, **FAX** (516)594-9307. **ED** Douglas Pratt. **DD** 004. **Circ:** 2,000.

US/0148-3544
**LISTENING POST (CITY OF INDUSTRY).** See Music.

BE
**MARCHE MONDIAL DE L'AUDIOVISUEL, LE.** See Photography and Video.

CN/0714-7422
**MARKETNEWS.** [Marketnews]. Vol. 8, Issue 4 (Apr. 1982)-. Periodical. English. mo. Hunter-Nichols Publishing, 2282 Queen Street East, Toronto Ontario M4E 1G6. **DD** 338.4/76213893/05. **Continues** Audio Marketnews, 0382-6120.

NE
**MB PRODUCTIETECHNIEK.** See Computers.

US/0195-6191
**MEAN MOUNTAIN MUSIC.** See Music.

SP
**MEDIOS AUDIO-VISUALES.** See Motion Picture.

US/0164-9957
**MIX (BERKELEY, CALIF.), THE.** (THE MIX.). [Mix]. (197?)-. Periodical. English (summaries and/or abstracts in Spanish). Twelve times a year. $49.80 New York residents; $46.00 other US; $66.00 Canada; $86.00 other. Cardinal Business Media, Inc., 6400 Hollis Street, Suite 12, Emeryville CA 94608. **Tel** (510)653-3307, **FAX** (510)653-5142. **ED** George Pearson. **LC** HD9697.P563; U55. **DD** 338.4/76213893/0973. **Ad Acc**, **Adv Mgr:** Robin Boyce. **Circ:** 42,721 (ctrl).
**Desc:** The magazine for recording music and audio production. Provides information on latest equipment, choosing quality gear, behind the scenes look at artists in the studio, profiles of studios around the world, developments in digital audio and new audio formats.
**Ind/Abst** Music Artic. Guide (?-?).

US/0277-2533
**MODERN HI-FI AND MUSIC.** (19??)-. Periodical. English. mo. Maco Publishing Company, 699 Madison Avenue, New York NY 10021. **Tel** (212)490-0172. **LC** ML1; .M1775. **DD** 780. **Continues** Modern Hi-Fi & Stereo Guide (Quarterly).

US/0273-8511
**MODERN RECORDING & MUSIC.** **Suspended.** [Mod. rec. music]. **VFOAT** Modern Recording and Music. **VAT** Modern Recording and Music. Vol. 5, No. 10 (July 1980)-Suspended. Periodical. English. mo. $18.00. Modern Recording & Music, 1120 Old Country Road, Plainview NY 11803. **Tel** (516)883-6200. **ED** Larry Zide and Jeff Tamarkin. **LC** ML1; .M1795. **DD** 621.389/3. **Ad Acc**. **Circ:** 25,000 (ctrl). **Continues** Modern Recording, 0361-0004.
**Desc:** Published for the small recording studio operator and musician. Features focus on audio equipment and its usage. Artist producer profiles; test reports; new product listings.

US/0276-9239
**MODERN RECORDING & MUSIC'S BUYER'S GUIDE.** (MODERN RECORDING & MUSIC'S ... BUYER'S GUIDE.). [Mod. rec. music's buy. guide]. **VAT** Modern Recording and Music's Buyer's Guide. (1981)-. English. an. $2.95. Modern Recording & Music, 1120 Old Country Road, Plainview NY 11803. **Tel** (516)883-6200. **LC** TK7881.4; .M62. **DD** 381/.456213893/0973. **Continues** Modern Recording's Buyer's Guide, 0161-1496.

CN/0823-0498
**MONDE DU ROCK.** See Music.

US
**MUSIC AND RECORDINGS.** See Music.

US/0894-1238
**MUSIC & SOUND RETAILER, THE.** See Music.

US/1055-5536
**MUSIC CATALOG (WASHINGTON, D.C.), THE.** See Music.

US/1048-2741
**MUSIC LIBRARY. MUSICAL SOUND RECORDINGS.** (MUSIC LIBRARY. MUSICAL SOUND RECORDINGS [COMPUTER FILE].). [Music libr., Music. sound rec.]. **Added/Corp** OCLC. **VFOAT** Musical Sound Recordings. (1990)-. English. an. $350.00; $300.00 (OCLC members). OCLC Asia Pacific Services, 6565 Frantz Road, Dublin OH 43017. **Tel** (800)848-5878, (614)764-6394 or 6000, **FAX** (614)764-6096. **DD** 780.
**Desc:** System requirements: OCLC workstation or IBM

# Sound Recordings and Systems

PC XT, AT, PS/2 or compatible, 640K RAM, hard disk drive, CD-ROM drive, MS-DOS 2.0 or higher, OCLC Search CD software.

UK
**MUSIC MASTER.** (19??)-. English. an. John Humphries Publishing Ltd., 1 De Cham Avenue, Hastings E. Sussex TN37 6HE, England. **Tel** 011 44 424 715181. **LC** ML156.9; .M85. **DD** 016.7899/12/0941.

UK/0265-1548
**MUSIC WEEK (1983). See** Music.

CN/0709-7174
**MUSICAL NEWS (TORONTO). See** Music.

GW
**MUSIK REPORT; DAS KRITISCHE HANDBUCH DER KLASSISCHEN MUSIKSCHALLPLATTE. See** Music.

US/1051-5097
**NARAS JOURNAL.** [NARAS j.]. **Added/Corp** National Academy of Recording Arts and Sciences (U.S.). National Education Dept. NARAS Foundation. Vol. 1, No. 1 (1990)-. Periodical. English. sa (Apr., and Oct.). NARAS Foundation, 303 North Glenoaks Boulevard, Suite 140, Burbank CA 91502. **Tel** (818)843-8233, FAX (213)849-2529. **LC** ML1055; .N37. **DD** 384.
**Ind/Abst** Music Index.

US/0028-4181
**NEW AMBEROLA GRAPHIC, THE. Added/Corp** New Amberola Phonograph Company. (19??)-. Periodical. English. Four times a year (Jan., Apr., July, oct.). $8.00 (two years). The New Amberola Phonograph Company, 37 Caledonia Street, Saint Johnsbury VT 05819. **Tel** (802)748-9264. **ED** Martin F. Bryan. **LC** ML156.9; .N4. **DD** 789.9/12/05. **Bk Rev**, (Qty: 8-10). **Ad Acc. Circ:** 1,050.
**Desc:** Publication devoted to the history of sound recordings covering the four decades between 1895 and 1935. Articles, discographies, biographies, book reviews, advertisements, etc.

UK
**NEW HI-FI SOUND. Title Change. VFOAT** HI-FI Sound. Periodical. English. m. Haymarket Publishing Ltd., 12 14 Ansdell Street, London W8 5TR England. **Tel** 011 44 483 733800, FAX 011 44 483 776573. **ED** Nevillie Farmer. **LC** TK7881.7; .N47. **DD** 621.389/3/05. **Ad Acc. Circ:** 28,556. **Continues** Popular HI-FI (Teddington, Middlesex). **Continued by** High Fidelity.

US/0733-6586
**NEWS TALK. See** Encyclopedias and General Reference Books.

US
**NEWSLETTER : CONCERT RECORDINGS. See** Music.

DK/0108-2914
**NORDIC SOUNDS.** [Nord. sounds]. (1982)-. Periodical. English. Four times a year. Free. MIC Dansk Musik Information Center, Vimmelskaftet 48 DK 1161, Copenhagen K Denmark. **Tel** 01 11 47 11. **ED** Anders Beyer. **DD** 780.948. **Bk Rev. Circ:** 5,000. **Continues** Nomus Nytt, 0345-8504.
**Desc:** Classical and comtemporary nordic music. Articles on portraits and reviews.

FR
**NOUVELLE REVUE DU SON, DES IDEES, DES NOUVEAUTES, TOUS LES PRIX, LA.** Periodical. French. mo. 180.00F France; 260.00F (add 80.00F for postage) other. Editions Frequences, 1 Boulevard Ney, 75018 Paris France. **Tel** 011 33 1 40360197, FAX 011 33 1 40361196. **LC** TK7888.4; .N68. **DD** 621/389/3/05.

US
**NTIS ALERT. PHOTOGRAPHY & RECORDING DEVICES. See** Photography and Video.

US
**NUMERICAL LISTING OF SUPRAPHON LP RECORDS / SUPRAPHON. See** Music.

US/0890-782X
**OFFICIAL VIDEO DIRECTORY & BUYER'S GUIDE, THE.** [Off. video dir. buy. guide]. **VFOAT** Official Video Directory and Buyer's Guide. 1987-. Directory. English. an. $53.00 US and Canada. Palm Springs Media Inc, PO Box 2740, Palm Springs CA 92262. **Tel** (619)322-3050. **LC** HD9696.V533; U546. **DD** 338.7/621388332/02573.

SW/0030-5642
**ORKESTER JOURNALEN. See** Music.

US/0360-2109
**PAUL'S RECORD MAGAZINE. See** Music.

US/0743-8621
**PERCUSSIONER INTERNATIONAL AUDIO MAGAZINE.** [Percuss. int. audio mag.]. **VFOAT** Percussioner International. Vol. 1, No. 1 (June 1984)-. Periodical. English. bm. $50.00. Sal Sofia Industries Inc, 6 Avenue J, Brooklyn NY 11230. **Tel** (718)258-0066. **ED** Sal Sofia, Angela Sofia. **DD** 789. Index available. cum. index. **Bk Rev. Ad Acc. Circ:** 85,000.
**Desc:** Informative interviews with artists that discuss their views on music, the industry and lifestyles. Plus, artists write an educational column which is also played on an accompanying cassette by the artist themselves.

US/0895-4143
**PERFECT VISION, THE. See** Communication-Broadcasting.

BL
**PESQUISA BRASILEIRA DO DISCO.** (19??)-. Periodical. Portuguese. mo. $50.00. Editora Pesquisa Brasileira do Disco, rua Timbiras 502 30 Conj 307, Sao Paulo Brazil. **LC** ML5; .P25. **DD** 789.9/12/05.

BL
**PESQUISA NACIONAL DO SUCESSO. See** Music.

●US/1073-4724
**PETERSEN'S AUTOTRONICS.** (PETERSEN'S AUTOTRONICS : THE COMPLETE GUIDE TO AUTOSOUND AND ACCESSORIES.). **VFOAT** Autotronics. (1994)-. Periodical. English. mo. $19.94 US; $30.97 Canada; $29.94 other. Petersen Publishing Company, 6420 Wilshire Boulevard, Los Angeles CA 90048. **Tel** (213)782-2485.

AU
**PHONO.** Vol. 1 (Fall 1954)-. Periodical. German. bm. **LC** ML5; .P35.
**Desc:** Phonographic journal published out of Vienna, Austria.

GW
**PHONO PRESS. Added/Corp** Bundesverband der Phonographischen Wirtschaft. (19??)-. German. ir (two or four issues per year). Free to the press and interested institutions. Bundesverband der Phonographischen Wirschaft, Grelckstr 36, W-2000 Hamburg 54 Germany. **Tel** 040-3675 13, FAX 582842. **ED** Norbert Thurozo and Peter Zombik. **LC** ML5; .P355. **DD** 789.9/12. **Circ:** 1,600.
**Desc:** Press information bulletin of Bundesverband Phono (German Federation of Phonographic Industry).

UK/0253-004X
**PHONOGRAPHIC BULLETIN. Title Change.** [Phonogr. bull.]. **Added/Corp** International Association of Sound Archives. No. 1-61 (Summer 1971)-(Nov. 1992). Periodical. English (French and German). Three times a year. International Association Sound Archives, PO Box 27890, ALB Anna M. Foyer, S 115 93 Stockholm Sweden. **LC** ML5; .P36. **DD** 789.9/12. **Continued by** IASA Journal.
**Ind/Abst** Libr. Inf. Sci. Abstr.

US
**PREPRINTS OF PAPERS PRESENTED AT THE AES CONVENTIONS. Main/Corp** Audio Engineering Society. (19??)-. English. Ten times a year. Audio Engineering Society Inc, 60 East 42nd Street, Room 2520, New York NY 10165. **Tel** (212)661-8528, (800)541-7299, FAX (212)682-0477. **ED** Jesse Klapholz. **CODEN** AESPDW. Index available. cum. index. **Bk Rev. Ad Acc. Circ:** 12,000. (ctrl). available on microfilm.
**Desc:** Documents scientific knowledge in the audio and engineering field and its allied arts, includes theoretical and practical applications.
**Ind/Abst** Bioeng. Abstr.

UK/0269-4735
**PRO SOUND NEWS (EUROPEAN ED.).** (PRO SOUND NEWS.). [Pro sound news]. Vol. 1, No. 1 (June 23, 1986)-. Periodical. English. mo. $50.00. Pro Sound News Publications, Link House Dingwall Avenue, Croydon CR9 2TA England.
**Ind/Abst** Trade Ind. Index.

US/0164-6338
**PRO SOUND NEWS (INTERNATIONAL ED.).** (PRO SOUND NEWS.). (19??)-. English. mo. $30.00 (one year), $50.00 (two year), $70.00 (three year) US and Canada; $60.00 (one year), $110.00 (two year), $160.00 (three year) other. PSN Publications, 2 Park Avenue, Suite 1820, New York NY 10016. **Tel** (212)213-3444, FAX (212)213-3484. **LC** WMLC L 83/9175. **Continues** Pro Sound News. US Ed., 0164-6338.

US/0164-6338
**PRO SOUND NEWS (U.S. ED.). Title Change.** (PRO SOUND NEWS.). [Pro sound news]. No. 1 (Nov. 1978)-(19??). Periodical. English. mo. 220 Westbury Avenue, Carle Place, New York NY 11514. **Tel** (516)324-7880. **ED** Randy Savicky. **DD** 338. **Ad Acc. Circ:** 15,000 (ctrl). **Continued by** Pro Sound News (International Ed.), 0164-6338.
**Desc:** Trade newsmagazine for the professional sound production industry.

US/0747-752X
**PROFESSIONAL AUDIO BUYERS REFERENCE GUIDE.** Consumer Publication. English. an. $14.95. SIE Publishing, 976 Fernhill Avenue, Newbury Park CA 91320.

US/1058-9678
**R.E.P. (OVERLAND PARK, KAN.). Ceased.** (R.E.P.). [R. E. P.]. **VFOAT** REP; Recording, Engineering, Production. Vol. 21, No. 6 (June 1990)-(1992). Periodical. English. mo. Intertec Publishing Corporation, 9800 Metcalf, Overland Park KS 66212. **Tel** (913)341-1300. **LC** TK7881.6; .R4. **DD** 621.389/3. **Continues** Recording Engineer/Producer, 0034-1673.

US/0099-0817
**RECORD COLLECTORS JOURNAL, THE.** V. 1- July 1975-. Periodical. English. mo. $10.00. Markell Publishing Company, PO Box 1200, Covina CA 91722. **LC** ML1; .R284. **DD** 789.9/12/05.

US/1071-4170
**RECORD ROUNDUP (NORTH CAMBRIDGE, MASS.). See** Music.

US/0034-1622
**RECORD WORLD.** (19??)-. Periodical. English. wk. Record World, 1697 Broadway, New York NY 10019.

US/0361-5855
**RECORDER REVIEW.** English. Nitka, 2343 East 28th Street, Brooklyn NY 11229. **LC** ML1; .R465. **DD** 788/.53/05.

US/0276-6078
**RECORDING INDUSTRY INDEX.** (RECORDING INDUSTRY INDEX / NARM.). Jan. 1977-Dec. 1977-. English. an. $20.00. National Association of Recording Merchandisers, 1060 Kings Highway North, Cherry Hill NJ 08034. **LC** Z7164.S76; R42; HD9697.P56. **DD** 016.3384/778991/0973.

●US
**RECORDING : THE MAGAZINE FOR THE RECORDING MUSICIAN. VFOAT** Recording Magazine. Vol. 7, No. 10 (July 1994)-. Periodical. English. mo. $20.00. Music Maker Publications Inc, 7318 Topanga Canyon Boulevard, Suite 200, Canoga CA 91303. **Tel** (818)346-0744, FAX (818)346-0882. **(Subscription address:** Publishers Creative Systems, PO Box 460996, Escondido CA 92046.) **LC** TK7881.4; .H65. **DD** 621.389/3. **Continues** Home and Studio Recording, 0896-7172.

SP
**REVISTA DE ACUSTICA.** Yearly V. 1- July/Sept. 1970-. Periodical. English (summaries and/or abstracts in Spanish). ir. $10.00. Revista de Acustica, Serrano 144, Madrid 6 Spain. **Tel** 261 88 06.

US/0162-2447
**SAMS TAPE RECORDER SERVICE DATA. Main/Corp** Howard W. Sams & Co. English. Howard Sams & Company, Inc., 2647 Waterfront Parkway E Drive, Indianapolis IN 46214. **Tel** (800)428-7267, (317)298-5400. **LC** TK7881.6; .S24. **DD** 621.389/32. **Continues** Sams Photofact Tape Recorder Series.

US
**SAMS VIDEOCASSETTE RECORDER SERVICE DATA. VFOAT** Sams V.C.R. Service Data; Sams Videocassette Recorder Photofact Service Data; Sams VCR Service Data. VCR45 (Apr. 1981)-. English. H W Sams & Company, 4300 West 62nd Street, PO Box 7092, Indianapolis IN 46268. **LC** TK6655.V5; V15. **DD** 621.388/332/0288. **Continues** Videocassette Recorder Service Data.

PL/1230-395X
**SAT AUDIO VIDEO.** [Sat Audio Video]. (1991)-. Periodical. Polish. Eleven times a year. Price on Request. **(Subscription address:** ARS Polona, PO Box 1001, 00068 Warsaw Poland.) **UDC** 681.84. **Continues** Audio Video Hi Fi, 0239-8435.

●US/1066-2138
**SCHWANN OPUS.** [Schwann opus]. Vol. 4, No. 1 (1993)-. Periodical. English. qt. $29.95. Schwann Publications, PO Box 5529, Santa Fe NM 87502. **Tel** (800)446-3563, (505)982-2366, FAX (818)718-8482. **(Subscription address:** Johnson Press, 49 Sheridan Avenue, Albany NY 12210.) **LC** ML156.2; .068. **DD** 016. **Continues** Opus (Chatsworth, Calif.), 1047-2355.

●US/1065-9161
**SCHWANN SPECTRUM.** [Schwann spectr.]. Vol. 4, No. 1 (Winter 1992/93)-. Periodical. English. qt. $24.95. Schwann Publications, PO Box 5529, Santa Fe NM 87502. **Tel** (800)446-3563, (505)982-2366, FAX (818)718-8482. **(Subscription address:** Johnson Press, 49 Sheridan Avenue, Albany NY 12210.) **LC** ML156.2; .S69. **DD** 016.78026/605. **Continues** Spectrum (Chatsworth, Calif.), 1047-2371.

US/0199-4654
**SENSIBLE SOUND, THE.** (1977)-. Periodical. English. qt (4 issues). $20.00 US, Canada and Mexico; $30.00 other. Sensible Sound, 403 Darwin Drive, Snyder NY 14226. **Tel** (716)681-3513, FAX (716)681-3518. **ED** Karl Nehring (editor's telephone: (716)839-2199). Index available. **Bk Rev. Ad Acc. Circ:** 10,900.
**Desc:** A candid audio equipment review journal. Evaluations equate sonic purity with economic reality.

CN/0831-0785
**SON HI-FI VIDEO.** Vol. 6, No. 33 (1984)-. Periodical. French. Six times a year. 18.00Can$ Canada; 28.00Can$ other. Publications Transcontinental Inc, 1100 Rene-Levesque, 24Fl Boulevard West, Montreal Quebec H3B 4X9 Canada. **Tel** (514)392-9000, FAX (514)392-4724. **ED** Francine Tremblay, Claude Gervais, and Dominique Lamarche. **DD** 621.389/332/05. ***Continues*** *Son Hi-Fi Magazine, 0708-1588.*
**Desc:** Aimed at stereo buffs. Includes an annual buying guide. Articles focus on new products and new stereo and video techniques.
**Ind/Abst** Point Repere.

FR/1148-4322
**SON, MUSIQUE, VIDEO MAG.** **See** Photography and Video.

FR/0765-3530
**SON, VIDEO MAGAZINE.** ***Title Change.*** (19??)-(19??). Periodical. French. mo. Editions Frequences, 1 Boulevard Ney, 75018 Paris France. **Tel** 011 33 1 40360197, FAX 011 33 1 40361196. **LC** PAR. **Bk Rev. Ad Acc. Circ:** 30,000. ***Continues*** *Son Magazine.* ***Continued by*** *Son, Musique, Video Mag, 1148-4322.*
**Desc:** Sound (general), video, music, (jazz, rock, classic), audio and video synthesizers, laboratory tests on sound (hi-fi) and video (VTR-camcorders).

US/0741-1715
**SOUND & VIDEO CONTRACTOR.** (SOUND & VIDEO CONTRACTOR : S&VC.). [Sound video contract.]. **VFOAT** Sound and Video Contractor; S&VC; S. & V. C. Vol. 1, No. 1 (Sept. 1983)-. Periodical. English. mo. $27.06 US; $50.59 other. Intertec Publishing Corporation, 9800 Metcalf, Overland Park KS 66212. **Tel** (913)341-1300. **(Subscription address:** Intertec Publishing Corporation, PO Box 2901, Overland Park KS 66282.**) ED** Fred Ampel and Darryll Fortune. **DD** 729. **[CCC]. Ad Acc. Circ:** 20,000 (ctrl).
**Desc:** Features technical and management information, covering topics as sound and video technology, business tips and information news.

FR
**SOUND CREATIVE. CD ROM.** English (French). $266.00. CDR Informatique, BP 32, 91470 Limours France. **Tel** 011 33 1 64912676.
**Desc:** Presents all kinds of applications such as sound research or the building of a sound bank.

UK/0144-6037
**SOUND INTERNATIONAL.** **VFOAT** Sound International Incorporating Beat Instrumental. 1978-. Periodical. English. mo. Link House Magazines Ltd., Link House, Dingwall Avenue, Croydon Surrey CR9 2TA England. **Tel** 011 44 81 686 2599, FAX 011 44 81 760 5154, telex 947709. ***Absorbed*** *Beat Instrumental, Songwriting & Recording.*

CN/0847-1223
**SOUND RECORDING.** (SOUND RECORDING / STATISTICS CANADA, EDUCATION, CULTURE AND TOURISM DIVISION.). [Sound rec.]. **Added/Corp** Statistics Canada. Education, Culture and Tourism Division. **VFOAT** Enregistrement Sonore. (1987/1988)-. English (French). an. 24.00Can$ Canada; $39.00 US; $44.00 other. Statistics Canada, Publications Sales & Services, Main Building Room 1710, Ottawa Ontario K1A 0T6 Canada. **Tel** (613)951-5078, (800)267-6677, FAX (613)951-1584, telex 053-3585. **LC** ML3790; .C84. **DD** 338.4/780266/0971021. ***Continues*** *Culture Statistics, Sound Recording Preliminary Statistics.*
**Desc:** Provides details on all aspects of the Sound Recording Survey including highlights and methodology.

US/1059-0897
**SOUND TIMES.** (SOUND TIMES [SOUND RECORDING].). [Sound times]. Began in Aug. 1991-. Periodical. English. wk. $131.88. Sound Marketing Inc., Chatsworth CA. **DD** 051.

US/0163-4607
**SOUND TRAX.** **See** Music.

BE/0771-6303
**SOUNDTRACK.** [Soundtrack !]. (1982)-. Periodical. English. qt. 600F. Luc Van de Ven, Astridlaan 171, 2800 Mechelen Belgium. **Tel** 011 32 15414107, FAX 011 32 15414107. **ED** Luc Van de Ven. **UDC** 78. **Bk Rev. Ad Acc.**

US/1042-0649
**SOUNDTRACK (RINGWOOD, N.J.).** (SOUNDTRACK : THE JOURNAL OF THE INDEPENDENT MUSIC ASSOCIATION.). [Soundtrack]. (19??)-. Periodical. English. Six times a year. $75.00 US; $80.00 Canada & Mexico; $85.00 others. Soundtrack Publishing, 317 Skyline Lake Drive, Box 609, Ringwood NJ 07456. **Tel** (201)831-1317. **ED** Don Kulak. **DD** 780. Index available. cum. index. **Bk Rev. Ad Acc. Circ:** 10,000. available on diskette.
**Desc:** Business information on marketing and distributing and independent release, running a small record label and recording technology.

US/0199-7920
**SPEAKER BUILDER.** [Speak. build.]. (Feb. 1980)-. Periodical. English. Six times a year. $25.00 (individuals), $30.00 (institutions) US & Canada; $40.00 (individuals), $45.00 (institutions) others. Audio Amateur Publications, PO Box 576, Peterborough NH 03458. **Tel** (603)924-9464, FAX (603)924-9467. **ED** Edward T. Dell Jr. **LC** TK5983; .S64. **DD** 621.389/332. **Bk Rev. Ad Acc. Circ:** 6,000. available on microfilm.
**Desc:** To help build audio speakers.
**Ind/Abst** Index Inf.

US/0278-1387
**SPEAKERS.** [Speakers]. English. an. $1.95. ABC Leisure Magazine Inc, 825 7th Avenue, New York NY 10019. **Tel** (212)265-8360. **LC** TK5983; .H53. **DD** 621.38/0282. ***Continues*** *High Fidelity's Buying Guide to Speaker Systems, 0147-7676.*

CN/0712-5151
**SPECIALISTE (GATINEAU, QUEBEC).** (LE SPECIALISTE.). [Specialiste]. Vol. 1, No 1 (Summer 1982)-. Periodical. French. qt. Free. Specialiste, a/s Camera RL, 368 rue Main, Gatineau Quebec J8P 5K7 Canada. **DD** 770/.6/0714221.

GW/0340-0778
**STEREO.** (1973)-. Periodical. German. Twelve times a year. DM81.60 Germany; DM108.00 other. SZV Spezialzeitschriftenverlag, Postfach 401629, D 80716 Munich Germany. **Tel** 011 49 89 237260. **(Subscription address:** Presse Marketing Services, Postfach 290180, D 47261 Duisburg Germany.**) LC** ML5; .S77. **DD** 780/.5. ***Absorbed*** *Hifi Exklusiv, 0172-3235.* ***Continued in part by*** *Hifi Exklusiv (1986), 0935-4174.*

US
**STEREO.** (19??)-. English. an. High Fidelity, Publishing House, Great Barrington MA 02130. **LC** TK7882.S7; S75.
**Ind/Abst** Music Artic. Guide (?-?).

US/0090-6786
**STEREO DIRECTORY & BUYING GUIDE.** **VAT** Stereo Directory and Buying Guide. (19??)-. Directory. English. bm. $7.50. Hachette Magazines Inc., 1633 Broadway, New York NY 10019. **Tel** (212)767-6000. **LC** TK7881.8; .S73. **DD** 338.4/7/621393302573. ***Continues*** *Stereo/Hi-Fi Directory.*

US/0039-1220
**STEREO REVIEW.** [Stereo rev.]. Vol. 21, No. 5] (Nov. 1968)-. Periodical. English. mo. $18.00. Hachette Magazines Inc., 1633 Broadway, New York NY 10019. **Tel** (212)767-6000. **(Subscription address:** Neodata / Colorado, PO Box 2606, Boulder Boulder CO 80322.**) LC** ML1; .H43. **DD** 780/.5. available on microfilm and microfiche from University Microfilms International (UMI); available on an online database (files 647,648/Full-Text) from DIALOG. Documents available from UMI Article Clearinghouse. ***Continues*** *HiFi/Stereo Review, 1045-3474;* ***Absorbed*** *High Fidelity (Great Barrington, Mass. : 1959), 0018-1455.*
**Desc:** Designed and edited for those people who have a serious interest in a broadrange range and reproduction equipment. Features reviews of classical, popular, jazz, folk and rock music, records and tapes, plus extensive coverage and tests of equipment including turntables, amps, receivers, speakers, tape decks and more.
**Ind/Abst** Abr. Read. Guide Period. Lit.; Acad. Abstr. Full Text Elite (Feb. 1984-) [Full Txt.]; Acad. Abstr. (Feb. 1984-); Acad. Ind. [Computer File] (1984-); Acad. Search (Feb. 1984-); Book Rev. Index; Consum. Index Prod. Eval. Inf. Source; Expand. Acad. Index (1984-); Gen. Period. Index (1985-); INFO-SOUTH Abstr.; Mag. Artic. Summar. Elite (Feb. 1984-) [Full Txt.]; Mag. Artic. Summar. Select (Feb. 1984-) [Full Txt.]; Mag. Artic. Summar. CD-ROM (Feb. 1984-); Mag. ASAP Plus [Full Txt.]; Mag. ASAP Sel. [Full Txt.]; Mag. Index Plus (1989-); Mag. Index. Sel. (1986-); Mag. Search; Music Artic. Guide; Music Index; Newsp. Period. Abstr. (1988-); Read. Guide Abstr. Select Ed.; Read. Guide Period. Lit.; Resource/One Ondisc (1988-); RILM Abstr.; Mag. Index (1977-); TOM Gen. Index (1985-) [Full Txt.]; Vocat. Search (Feb. 1984-) [Full Txt.].

US/0736-6515
**STEREO REVIEW'S STEREO ... BUYERS GUIDE.** ***Title Change.*** [Stereo rev. Stereo buy. guide]. **VFOAT** Stereo Buyer's Guide. (19??)-(19??). English. an. Diamandis Communications Inc, 1499 Monrovia Avenue, New Port Beach CA 92663. **Tel** (714)720-5300. **ED** William Burton. **LC** TK7881.8; .S737. **DD** 621.389/334/029473. **Ad Acc.** ***Continued by*** *Stero Buyers' Guide, 1060-8133.*
**Desc:** Descriptions, features, specifications, and prices on stereo receivers, amplifiers, tuners, turntables, cartridge, tonearms, cassette decks, open-reel decks, blank tape, accessories, speakers, headphones, pocket stereo, signal processors, and compact disc players.

US
**STEREO REVIEWS TAPE RECORDING BUYERS' GUIDE.** **VFOAT** Tape Recording Buyers Guide. Consumer Publication. English. an. $3.95. CBS Publications, 1515 Broadway, New York NY 10036. **Tel** (212)503-5064. **LC** TK7881.6; .S73. **Ad Acc.**
**Desc:** Product listings of tape-recording equipment, articles on buying and using audio and video gear, test reports on tape decks and VCR's plus glossary and directory of manufacturers.

US/0194-1844
**STEREO TEST REPORTS.** 1979-. Periodical. English. $2.95 each. 1330 Avenue of the Americas, New York NY 10019. **LC** TK7881.8; .S738. **DD** 621.389/3/05.

SP/0211-7045
**STEREOFONIA.** [Stereofonia]. (1981)-. Periodical. Spanish. Eleven times a year. 3600ptas Spain; 4590ptas other. Stereofonia SA, C Card H Oria 171, Ciud Period, 28034 Madrid, Spain. **Tel** 011 34 1 7307177. **UDC** 681.8.

US/0585-2544
**STEREOPHILE.** [Stereophile]. **VFOAT** Stereophile Magazine. (1962)-. Periodical. English. mo. $35.00 (1 year), $60.00 (2 year), $75.00 (3 year) US and Canada; $75.00 (1 year), $150.00 (2 year), $225.00 (3 year) other. Stereophile, PO Box 5529, Santa Fe NM 87502. **Tel** (505)982-2366, (800)334-8152, (619)745-2809, FAX (505)989-8791. **ED** Gordon Holt. **LC** TK7881.8; .S739. **DD** 621.389/334. **Ad Acc. Circ:** 20,000.
**Desc:** Reviews high-end audio, stereo equipment.

GW
**STEREOPLAY.** No. 1 (Jan. 1984)-. Periodical. German. mo. DM84.00. Vereinigte Motor Verlag GmbH, Motor Presse, POB 106036, D 70049 Stuttgart Germany. **Tel** 011 49 711 1821506, 011 49 711 1821545. available on microfilm from University Microfilms International (UMI). ***Continues*** *Hifi Stereophonie, 0018-1382.*
**Ind/Abst** Music Index.

UK/0144-5944
**STUDIO SOUND AND BROADCAST ENGINEERING.** [Stud. sound boradcast eng.]. **VFOAT** Studio Sound. (1973)-. Periodical. English. mo. £24.00 UK; £30.50 other. Link House Magazines Ltd., Link House, Dingwall Avenue, Croydon Surrey CR9 2TA England. **Tel** 011 44 81 686 2599, FAX 011 44 81 760 5154, telex 947709. **(Subscription address:** Link House Magazines Ltd., 120 126 Lavendar Avenue, Mitcham Surrey CR4 3HP England.**) ED** Keith Spencer-Allen. **LC** TK7881.4; .S78. **DD** 621.389/32. Index available. **Bk Rev. Ad Acc. Circ:** 22,000 (ctrl). ***Continues*** *Studio Sound;* ***Absorbed*** *Broadcast Systems International.*
**Desc:** A technical journal for those professionally involved in sound recording industry and related areas.

US/1041-7699
**STUDIO SOUND (SHAWNEE MISSION, KAN.).** (STUDIO SOUND.). **Added/Corp** Bill Daniels Co. (1991)-. Periodical. English. an. Bill Daniels' Illustrated Trade References, 9101 Bond, Shawnee Mission KS 66214.

UK
**TAPE.** (19??)-. Periodical. English. mo. Seymour Press Ltd, 6 Woodland Rise, London N10 3UH United Kingdom. **LC** TK7881.6; .T29. **DD** 621.389/32/05. ***Supersedes*** *Sound & Picture Tape Recording Magazine.*

US/0164-4602
**TAPE DECK.** V. 1- Jan./Feb. 1979-. Periodical. English. an. $4.95. Hampton International Comm Inc, 60 East 42nd Street/Suite 3415, New York NY 10017. **Tel** (212)682-7320.

US
**TAPE/DISC DIRECTORY / BILLBOARD.** **VFOAT** Tape Disc Directory; Billboard's Tape Disc Directory; Billboard's Tape/Disc Directory. (1991)-. Directory. English. an. $43.00. Billboard Publications Inc., 1515 Broadway Billboard, New York NY 10036. **Tel** (212)764-7300, FAX (305)755-7048, telex WU TWX 710-581-6279. **LC** TK7881.6; .B53; TK7881.6; .B532. **DD** 621.389/32/0294. ***Continues*** *Billboard's International Manufacturing & Packaging Directory for the Record, CD, and Audio/Video Tape Industries, 1045-1641.*
**Desc:** Product and service listings for the tape/disc industry. Covers everything from jewel boxes to shrinkwrap.

US/0093-996X
**TAPE RECORDING & BUYING GUIDE.** ***Suspended.*** (STEREO REVIEW'S TAPE RECORDING & BUYING GUIDE.). **VFOAT** Tape Recording & Buying Guide. (1973)-Suspended (19??). Consumer Publication. English. an. $1.50. Stereo Review Tape and Record Buying Guide, PO Box 603, Holmes PA 19043. **Tel** (212)719-6187. **LC** TK7881.6; .T33. **DD** 621.389/32. ***Continues*** *Stereo Review's Tape Recorder Guide, 0737-2361.*

GW
**TON REPORT.** Periodical. German (German). Ring der Tonbandfreunde, Postfach 22 34, W-2970 Emden 1 Germany. **Tel** 0208-42 64 44. **ED** Lutz Koester. **LC** TK7881.6; .T65. **Bk Rev.** ctrl circ.

# Sound Recordings and Systems

CN/0847-1851
**UHF. ULTRA HIGH FIDELITY.** (ULTRA HIGH FIDELITY MAGAZINE : UHF.). [UHF, Ultra high fidel.]. **VFOAT** UHF. No. 19 (Feb. 1989)-. Periodical. English. Six times a year (Mar., May, July, Sept., Oct., Dec.). 21.50Can$ Canada; 30.00Can$ others. Broadcast Canada, Box 65085 Place Longueuil, Longueuil Quebec J4K 5J4 Canada. **Tel** (514)651-5720, FAX (514)651-5720. **ED** Gerard Rejskind. **DD** 621.389/3/05. **Bk Rev**, (Qty: 3). **Ad Acc**, **Adv Mgr:** R. Lessard, **Tel** (514)651-5720. **Circ:** 11,000. **Continues** Hi-Fi Sound Magazine, 0821-4875.
 **Desc:** Reviews, advice, opinions, and records reviews are the many topics for this magazine.

US/0193-9602
**VIDEOLOG : PROGRAMS FOR GENERAL INTEREST AND ENTERTAINMENT, THE.** See Communication-Broadcasting.

US/0090-3922
**VIDEOPLAYER.** Periodical. English. bm. $10.00. Videoplayer, 13272 Ventura Blvd., Suite 213, Studio City CA 91604. **LC** TK6655.V5; V56. **DD** 778.59.

UK/0042-6369
**VINTAGE JAZZ MART.** See Music.

US/0278-5455
**VINYL EDITION, THE.** See Music.

AU
**VOX (VIENNA, AUSTRIA).** See Music.

UK
**WHAT HI-FI?.** (19??)-. English. Thirteen times a year. £29.00 UK; £59.00 Eire & Europe; £77.00 America, Middle East, Africa & India; £84.00 Australia, New Zealand & Japan; £49.00 other. Haymarket Publishing Ltd., 12 14 Ansdell Street, London W8 5TR England. **Tel** 011 44 483 733800, FAX 011 44 483 776573. **Absorbed** High Fidelity and New Hi Fi Sound.

CH
**YIN HSIANG CHIH NAN.** **VFOAT** Audio Guide Book. Chinese (Chinese). an. $15.00. Tai-Pei Shih Tien Chi Shang Yeh Tung Yeh Kung Hui, 131 Sung-Chiang Road, Taipei Taiwan. **LC** TK7881.8; .Y56.

CH
**YIN YUEH YU YIN HSIANG.** **VFOAT** Music & Audiophile. (1973)-. Chinese (Chinese). Twelve times a year. $80.00. Music and Audiophile, 6F1 271 Sec 2 Chin I Rd, Taipei Taiwan. **Tel** 011 886 2 393 7201. **LC** ML5; .Y549.

---

## ABSTRACTING, BIBLIOGRAPHIES AND STATISTICS

GW/0721-7153
**BIELEFELDER KATALOG KLASSIK.** [Bielef. Kat., Klass.]. **VFOAT** Bielefelder Katalog (K). 1979-. German. sa. G Braun Verlag, Postfach 1709, D 76006 Karlsruhe Germany. **Tel** 011 49 721 165392. **LC** ML156.2; .B52. **DD** 016.7899/12/05. **Continues** Bielefelder Katalog.

---

## STATISTICS

US/0094-7970
**AAP-AUPS UNIVERSITY PRESS STATISTICS.** **VFOAT** University Press Statistics. English. Dessauer, Inc., 1 Park Avenue, New York NY 10016. **LC** Z231.5.U6; A15. **DD** 338.4/7/0705730973.

CN/0709-9541
**ABS NEWSTATS.** [ABS newstats]. **Main/Corp** Alberta. Bureau of Statistics. **VAT** Alberta Bureau of Statistics Newstats. Vol. 1 (Jan. 6, 1978)-. Periodical. English. ir. Free. Alberta Bureau of Statistics / Canada, Alberta Treasury, 7th Floor/9811-109 Street, Edmonton Alberta T5K OC8 Canada. **Tel** (403)427-3058, FAX (403)427-0409. **DD** 310/.5.

BB/0522-3725
**ABSTRACT OF STATISTICS - BARBADOS. STATISTICAL SERVICE.** (ABSTRACT OF STATISTICS.). **Main/Corp** Barbados. Statistical Service. **VFOAT** Abstract of the Statistics of Barbados. No. 1- 1956-. English. Bridgetown Statistical Service, Barbados West Indies. **LC** HA865.

PP
**ABSTRACT OF STATISTICS (PAPUA NEW GUINEA NATIONAL STATISTICAL OFFICE).** (ABSTRACT OF STATISTICS / PAPUA NEW GUINEA NATIONAL STATISTICAL OFFICE.). Dec. Quarter 1980-. Statistical Publication. English. qt. k.6.00 Papua New Guinea; k7.00 (surface mail); k.12.00 (airmail) other. National Statistical Office, PO Wards Strip NCO, Papua New Guinea. **Tel** 011 675 27182 271172, FAX 011 657 255057, telex FINANCE NE 22312. **LC** HA4007.P3; A25A. **DD** 319.5/3. **Continues** Abstract of Statistics - Bureau of Statistics, Papua New Guinea, 0303-934X.

CN/0848-659X
**ABSTRACTS - ALBERTA. BUREAU OF STATISTICS.** (ABSTRACTS : THE ALBERTA BUREAU OF STATISTICS NEWSLETTER.). [Abstr. - Alta., Bur. Stat.]. **Main/Corp** Alberta. Bureau of Statistics. Vol. 1, No. 1 (Mar. 1990)-. Newsletter. English. Three times a year. **DD** 354.71230081/9.

US/0744-1010
**ADDRESS LIST / NATIONAL CLEARINGHOUSE FOR CENSUS DATA SERVICES.** Jan. 1981-. Government Publication. English. US Department of Commerce / Bureau of the Census, Data User Services Division, Customer Services, Washington DC 20233-0800. **Tel** (301)763-4100. (**Subscription address:** Superintendent of Documents, US Government Printing Office, Washington DC 20402.) **LC** HA37; .U112. **DD** 310/.6/073. **Continues** Summary Tape Processing Centers and State Data Centers.
 **Desc:** Lists, by state, all registrants in the National Clearinghouse for Census Data Services including name, address, and telephone number.

NE
**ADVANCED STUDIES IN THEORETICAL AND APPLIED ECONOMETRICS.** Vol. 1 (1982)-. Monographic series. English. ir. Price varies per volume. Kluwer Academic Publishers, Postbus 322, 3300 AH Dordrecht, The Netherlands. **Tel** 011 (31) 78 524400, FAX 011 31 78 183273, telex 20083.
 **Ind/Abst** Math. Rev. (1988-); Zentralbl. Math. Ihre Grenzgeb.

US/1045-6821
**ADVANCES IN STATISTICAL ANALYSIS AND STATISTICAL COMPUTING.** [Adv. stat. anal. stat. comput.]. Vol. 1 (1986)-. Statistical Publication. English. an. $73.25. JAI Press Inc., 55 Old Post Road, Suite 2, PO Box 1678, Greenwich CT 06836-1678. **Tel** (203)661-7602, FAX (203)661-0792. **ED** Roberto S. Mariano. **LC** QA276.A1; A38. **DD** 519.5/05.

ET
**AFRICAN STATISTICAL YEARBOOK. ANNUAIRE STATISTIQUE POUR L'AFRIQUE.** **Added/Corp** United Nations. Economic Commission for Africa. **VFOAT** Annuaire Statistique pour l'Afrique. (1974)-. Statistical Publication. English (French). ir. $50.00. United Nations Publications, 2 United Nations Plaza, Room DC2 0853, Department 007C, New York NY 10017. **Tel** (212)963-8303, (800)253-9646. **LC** HA1955; .U5. **DD** 330.96/00212. **Bk Rev**. **Ad Acc**. **Circ:** 1,500 (ctrl). **Continues** United Nations. Economic Commission for Africa. Statistical Yearbook; Annuaire Statistique / Commission Economique pour l'Afrique.
 **Desc:** Contains data with a maximum of 48 ten-year time series tables under nine socio-economic chapters for each African country.

JA
**AJIA SHOKOKU YORAN.** **Added/Corp** Japan. Gaimusho. Ajiakyoku. (19??)-. Statistical Publication. Japanese. Gaimusho / Ajiakyoku, 2-1 Kasumigaseki 2-chome, Chiyoda-ku 100 Tokyo Japan. **LC** HA1665; .A35.

SU
**AL-ARD AL-IQTISADI WA-AL-MALI.** **Main/Corp** Bank Al-Sudan. Maslahat Al-Ihsa. Arabic. qt. Bank Al-Sudan, Maslahat Al-Ihsa, PO Box 313, Al-Khartum Sudan. **LC** HA2275.S8; B35A.

MU
**AL-NASHRAH AL-SHAHRIYAH LIL-IHSA - IDARAT AL-IHSAAT WA-AL-DIRASAT AL-IQTISADIYAH.** **Main/Corp** Mauritania. Direction de la Statistique et des Etudes Economiques. **VFOAT** Bulletin Mensuel Statistique- Direction de la Statistique et des Etudes Economiques. French (French). 20.00. B P 240, Nouakchott Mauritania. **LC** HA2096.5; .A2B. **DD** 316.6/1.

US/1065-5301
**ALABAMA IN PERSPECTIVE.** (ALABAMA IN PERSPECTIVE : A STATISTICAL VIEW OF THE "HEART OF DIXIE STATE".). [Ala. perspect.]. **Added/Corp** Morgan Quinto Corporation. (1990)-. Statistical Publication. English. $18.00. Morgan Quinto Corporation, PO Box 1656, 512 East 9th Street, Lawrence KS 66044. **Tel** (800)457-0742, (913)841-3534, FAX (913)841-3534. **DD** 317.
 **Desc:** Reports on the state's data and rank for each of the categories featured in State Rankings.

US/0095-3431
**ALABAMA'S VITAL EVENTS.** **Added/Corp** Alabama. Division of Vital Statistics. (1972)-. English. an. $10.00. Special Services Administration, 434 Monroe Street, Montgomery AL 36130. **Tel** (205)242-5095. **LC** HA221; .A37. **DD** 312/.09761. **NLM** W2 AA4 D6A. available on microfiche. **Absorbed** Look at Infant Deaths from Linked Records, Alabama.
 **Ind/Abst** Stat. Ref. Index.

US/1065-531X
**ALASKA IN PERSPECTIVE (LAWRENCE, KAN.).** (ALASKA IN PERSPECTIVE : A STATISTICAL VIEW OF "THE LAST FRONTIER STATE".). [Alsk. perspect.]. **Added/Corp** Morgan Quinto Corporation. (1990)-. Statistical Publication. English. $18.00. Morgan Quinto Corporation, PO Box 1656, 512 East 9th Street, Lawrence KS 66044. **Tel** (800)457-0742, (913)841-3534, FAX (913)841-3534. **DD** 317. **Continues** Alaska in Perspective (Elmwood, Neb.), 1065-531X.
 **Desc:** Reports on the state's data and rank for each of the categories featured in State Rankings.

CN/0317-3917
**ALBERTA STATISTICAL REVIEW (ANNUAL ED.).** (ALBERTA STATISTICAL REVIEW.). **Added/Corp** Alberta. Treasury Dept. Alberta. Bureau of Statistics. (Apr. 1973)-. Statistical Publication. English. Four times a year. Free. Alberta Bureau of Statistics / Canada, Alberta Treasury, 7th Floor/9811-109 Street, Edmonton Alberta T5K OC8 Canada. **Tel** (403)427-3058, FAX (403)427-0409. **LC** HA747.A79; A4. **DD** 317.123.

GW/0002-6018
**ALLGEMEINES STATISTISCHES ARCHIV.** [Allg. stat. arch.]. **Added/Corp** Arbeitsgemeinschaft fuer Gemeindliche Statistik. Deutsche Statistische Gesellschaft. Vol. 1 (1890)-. Periodical. German. Four times a year. DM140.00. Vandenhoeck & Ruprecht, Robert Bosch Breite 6, D-37079 Goettingen Germany. **Tel** 011 49 551 695911, FAX 011 49 551 695917, telex 965226 VAN d. **LC** HA1; .A4. **NLM** W1 AL824C. **CODEN** ALSAAX. [CCC]. cum. index.
 **Ind/Abst** Coal Abstr.; Int. Bibliogr. Sociol.; Math. Rev.; Stat. Theory Method Abstr. (1959-1967).

SW/0039-7253
**ALLMAN MANADSSTATISTIK.** **Main/Corp** Sweden. Statistiska Centralbyran. **Added/Corp** Sweden. Statistiskal Centralbyran. Monthly Digest of Swedish Statistics. **VFOAT** Monthly Digest of Swedish Statistics. Vol. 1 (1963)-. Periodical. Swedish (English and Swedish). Twelve times a year. Kr760.00. Statistics Sweden Publishing Service, S-70189 Orebro Sweden. **Tel** 011 46 19176800, telex 15261 SWESTATS. **ED** Agneta Sverkel-Osterberg. **LC** HA1523; .A38. Index available. **Circ:** 3,000 (ctrl). **Supersedes in part** Kommersiella Meddelanden.
 **Desc:** Statistical data and index series for the last two years and annual data for the last five years.
 **Ind/Abst** Chicano Index.

US/0003-1305
**AMERICAN STATISTICIAN, THE.** [Am. stat.]. **Added/Corp** American Statistical Association. Vol. 1 (Aug. 1947)-. Periodical. English. qt. $60.00. American Statistical Association, 1429 Duke Street, Alexandria VA 22314. **Tel** (703)684-1221, (202)393-3253, FAX (703)684-2037 (orders). **LC** .A614. **DD** 310.6273. **NLM** HA 1 A517. **CODEN** ASTAAJ. [CCC]. cum. index. **Ad Acc**. **Pr Rev. Circ:** 16,000. available on microfilm and microfiche from University Microfilms International (UMI). Documents available from The Genuine Article, Ask*IEEE, UMI Article Clearinghouse. **Continues** Bulletin of the American Statistical Association.
 **Desc:** Brief papers of immediate interest, teachers' aids, and statistical computing.
 **Ind/Abst** ABI/INFORM Glob. Ed.; ABI Inform Ondisc (Oct. 1971-Oct. 1972); Acad. Search (July 1993-); Biostatistica; Bus. Source (Jul. 1993-); Compumath Citation Index [Full Cov.]; Curr. Contents Phys. Chem. Earth Sci.; Curr. Index Stat.; Expand. Acad. Index (1989-); GeoRef; INSPEC (Feb. 1982-Feb. 1983); Int. Aerosp. Abstr.; J. Plan. Lit.; Mag. Search; Math. Rev.; Newsp. Period. Abstr. (1991-); Pollut. Abstr. Access.; Qual. Control Appl. Stat.; Res. Alert [Full Cov.]; Sci. Cit. Index; SCISEARCH; Soc. Sci. Cit. Index [Select. Cov.]; Soc. Sci. Index; Soc. Sci. Index Fulltext (Nov. 1988-) [Full Txt.]; Soc. Res. Methodol. Abstr. (1982-); Stat. Theory Method Abstr. (1959-1963, 1969, 1986); Zentralbl. Math. Ihre Grenzgeb.

US/0163-9617
**AMSTAT NEWS.** [AMSTAT news]. **Main/Corp** American Statistical Association. **VAT** American Statistical Association News. No. 1 (Jan. 1974)-. Periodical. English. Eleven times a year. $40.00. American Statistical Association, 1429 Duke Street, Alexandria VA 22314. **Tel** (703)684-1221, (202)393-3253, FAX (703)684-2037 (orders). **DD** 519. **Ad Acc**. **Circ:** 15,500.
 **Desc:** Membership magazine of the ASA.
 **Ind/Abst** Abstr. Bull. Inst. Pap. Sci. Tech.

GW/0170-2696
**AMTLICHE NACHRICHTEN DER BUNDESANSTALT FUER ARBEIT. ARBEITSSTATISTIK ... JAHRESZAHLEN.** **VFOAT** Arbeitsstatistik ... Jahreszahlen. German. DM100.00. Bundesanstalt fuer Arbeit, Regensburger Strasse 104, 8500 Nuernberg Germany. **LC** HD5777; .A67. **DD** 331.1/0943/021. ***Continues*** *Bundesanstalt fur Arbeit (Germany). Jahreszahlen, Arbeitsstatistik.*

YU/0300-2543
**ANKETA O PORODICNIM BUDZETIMA RADNICKIH DOMACINSTAVA.** **Main/Corp** Savezni Zavod za Statistiku (Yugoslavia). Serbo-Croatian (Roman). 4.00 Din per issue. Savezni Zavod za Statistiku, Kneza Milosa 20, Belgrad Yugoslavia. **LC** HA1631; .A33 subser; HD7045.5.

YU
**ANKETA O SEOSKIM DOMACINSTVIMA.** **Main/Corp** Savezni Zavod za Statistiku (Yugoslavia). Serbo-Croatian (Roman). 5.00 Din. Savezni Zavod za Statistiku, Kneza Milosa 20, Belgrad Yugoslavia. **LC** HA1631; .A33 subser; HN631.

US/0090-5364
**ANNALS OF STATISTICS, THE.** [Ann. stat.]. **Added/Corp** Institute of Mathematical Statistics. Vol. 1 (Jan. 1973)-. Periodical. English. Six times a year. $150.00. Institute of Mathematical Statistics, 3401 Investment Boulevard, Suite 7, Hayward CA 94545-3819. **Tel** (510)783-8141, FAX (510)783-4131. **ED** Arthur Cohen. **LC** HA1; .A83. **DD** 519.5/05. **CODEN** ASTSC7. **[CCC].** Index available. **Bk Rev. Ad Acc. Pr Rev. Circ:** 4,800. available on microfilm and microfiche from University Microfilms International (UMI). Documents available from The Genuine Article. ***Supersedes in part*** *Annals of Mathematical Statistics, 0003-4851.*
**Desc:** Presents contributions to the theory of statistics and its applications.
**Ind/Abst** Biostatistica; Compumath Citation Index [Full Cov.]; Curr. Contents Phys. Chem. Earth Sci.; Curr. Index Stat.; Math. Rev.; Qual. Control Appl. Stat.; Res. Alert [Full Cov.]; Risk Abstr. (19??-19??); Sci. Cit. Index; SCISEARCH; Soc. Sci. Cit. Index [Select. Cov.]; Stat. Theory Method Abstr. (1973-1984, 1986-1987); Zentralbl. Math. Ihre Grenzgeb.

US/0278-9221
**ANNOTATED BIBLIOGRAPHY OF STATISTICAL METHODOLOGY.** [Annot. bibliogr. stat. methodol.]. **Added/Corp** National Center for Health Statistics (U.S.). (19??)-. Statistical Publication. English. an. US Department of Health and Human Services, 200 Independence Avenue Southwest, Washington DC 20201. **LC** Z7553.M43; A55; RA409. **DD** 362.1/0723. **NLM** ZWA 950 A615.

FR
**ANNUAIRE ABREGE DE STATISTIQUES AGRICOLES, REGION RHONE-ALPES.** **See** Agriculture-Abstracting, Bibliographies and Statistics.

BE/0770-0369
**ANNUAIRE DE STATISTIQUES REGIONALES.** (1976)-. French. 360F Belgium; 480F other. Institut National de Statistique / Belgium, rue de Louvain, 44, Centre Albert, 8e Etage, 1000 Brussels Belgium. **Tel** 011 32 2 5486211. **LC** HA1393; .A7. **DD** 314.93. **Bk Rev. Ad Acc. Circ:** 900 (ctrl).
**Desc:** General statistics about the regions, provinces and arrondissements in Belgium.

CG/0304-5692
**ANNUAIRE DES STATISTIQUES DU COMMERCE EXTERIEUR (KINSHASA).** (ANNUAIRE DES STATISTIQUES DU COMMERCE EXTERIEUR.). [Annu. stat. commer. exter.]. French. mo. Free. Institut National de la Statistique / Zaire, Kinshasa Zaire. **Tel** 33313-33313. **(Subscription address:** Institut National de la Statistique, BP 20, Kinshasa Gombe) **LC** HF270.5; .A5. **DD** 382/.09675/1. **Bk Rev. Ad Acc.**

FR
**ANNUAIRE REGIONAL - SERVICE CENTRAL DES ENQUETES ET ETUDES STATISTIQUES, REGION DE PROGRAMME BOURGOGNE.** **See** Agriculture-Abstracting, Bibliographies and Statistics.

FR
**ANNUAIRE RHONE-ALPES.** French. an. 12.00F. CNGP INSEE - Institut National de la Statistique et des Estudes Economiques, BP 2718, 1 rue V Auriol, F 80027 Amiens Cedex 1 France. **Tel** 011 33 22 927322. **LC** HA1228.R55; A55. **DD** 314.4/582.

FT
**ANNUAIRE STATISTIQUE DE DJIBOUTI / REPUBLIQUE DE DJIBOUTI, MINISTERE DU COMMERCE, DES TRANSPORTS ET DU TOURISME, DIRECTION NATIONALE DE LA STATISTIQUE.** **VFOAT** Annuaire de Statistique. 1981-. French. an. Ministere du Commerce, des Transports et du Tourisme, Direction Nationale de la Statistique, BP 1846 Republic of Djibouti. **LC** HA4691; .A13. **DD** 316.7/71. ***Continues*** *Annuaire Statistique (Djibouti, Djibouti).*

BE/0066-3646
**ANNUAIRE STATISTIQUE DE LA BELGIQUE.** **Added/Corp** Institut National de Statistique (Belgium). Vol. 81 (1960)-. French (Dutch). an. 1250F Belgium; 1560F other. Institut National de Statistique / Belgium, rue de Louvain, 44, Centre Albert, 8e Etage, 1000 Brussels Belgium. **Tel** 011 32 2 5486211. **LC** HA1393; .A34. **DD** 314.93. **NLM** W2 GB4 I5AB. **Bk Rev. Ad Acc. Circ:** 1,350 (ctrl). ***Continues*** *Annuaire Statistique de la Belgique et du Congo Belge.*
**Desc:** General statistics about Belgium.

AE
**ANNUAIRE STATISTIQUE DE L'ALGERIE.** **Added/Corp** Algeria. Wizarat al-Takhtit wa-al-Tahyiah al-Umraniyah. Algeria. Niyabat Mudiriyat al-Ihsaat. Algeria. Mudiriyat al-Ihsaat. Algeria. Mudiriyat al-Ihsaat wa-al-Muhasabah al-Wataniyah. (19??)-. French (Arabic and English). an. 1,000AD. Office of National Statistiques, 8 10 rue des Movsebilines, Algiers Algeria. **Tel** 64-77-90, telex 67-190. **LC** HA2071; .A32. **DD** 316.5. Index available. cum. index. **Bk Rev. Ad Acc. Circ:** 10,000. available on microfiche.

BE/0067-5431
**ANNUAIRE STATISTIQUE DE POCHE - INSTITUT NATIONAL DE STATISTIQUE.** (ANNUAIRE STATISTIQUE DE POCHE.). **Main/Corp** Institut National de Statistique (Belgium). 1965-. French. an. 125F Belgium; 160F other. Institut National de Statistique / Belgium, rue de Louvain, 44, Centre Albert, 8e Etage, 1000 Brussels Belgium. **Tel** 011 32 2 5486211. **LC** WMLC L 83/658. **Bk Rev. Ad Acc. Circ:** 1,200 (ctrl).
**Desc:** General statistics about Belgium.

MR
**ANNUAIRE STATISTIQUE DU MAROC (RABAT, MOROCCO : 1982).** (ANNUAIRE STATISTIQUE DU MAROC / ROYAUME DU MAROC, MINISTERE DU PLAN, DE LA FORMATION DES CADRES ET DE LA FORMATION PROFESSIONELLE.). **Added/Corp** Morocco. Wizarat al-Takhtit wa-al-Takwin al-Utur wa-al-Takwin al-Mihni. Mudiriyat al-Ihsa. Morocco. Wizarat al-Takhtit. Mudiriyat al-Ihsa. Morocco. Wazir al-Awwal. (19??)-. French. an. 165.00MD Morocco; 174.50MD other. Direction de la Statistique, Boite Postale 178, Rabat Morocco. **Tel** 011 212 77 73606, FAX 011 212 77 73217, telex 32774. **LC** HA4682; .A13. **Ad Acc.** ctrl circ. ***Continues*** *Nashriyah Al-Ihsaiyah Al-Sanawiyah Lil-Maghrib.*

TG
**ANNUAIRE STATISTIQUE DU TOGO.** French. an. Secretariat la Presidence Charge du Commerce de Industrie et du Plan, Direction de la Statistique, BP 118, Lome Togo. **LC** HA2126; .A24. **DD** 316.6/81.

DM
**ANNUAIRE STATISTIQUE (INSTITUT NATIONAL DE LA STATISTIQUE ET DE L'ANALYSE ECONOMIQUE).** (ANNUAIRE STATISTIQUE.). No. 6 (1980)-. French. an. Direction Generale de l'INSAE, BP 323, Cotonou Dahomey. **LC** HA2111.D34; A54. **DD** 316.6/83. ***Continues*** *Annuaire Statistique de la Republique Populaire du Benin.*

UK/0533-2117
**ANNUAL ABSTRACT OF GREATER LONDON STATISTICS.** Vol. 1 (1966)-. English. an. £20.00. Greater London Council, The County Hall, London SE1 7PB England. **Tel** (01)633-7139. **ED** M Minors. **LC** HA1139; .L696. **DD** 314.21. **Circ:** 1,400.
**Desc:** Collection of statistics relating to administration and infrastructure of greater London.

UK/0072-5730
**ANNUAL ABSTRACT OF STATISTICS.** **Main/Corp** Great Britain. Central Statistical Office. **Added/Corp** Gt. Brit. Board of Trade. Great Britain. Board of Trade. Statistical Abstract for the United Kingdom. Great Britain. Board of Trade. Statistical Department. (1840)-. Statistical Publication. English. an. £19.95. Her Majesty's Stationery Office, 51 Nine Elms Lane, London SW8 5DR England. **Tel** 011 44 71 873 8459, 011 44 71 873 8499, FAX 011 44 71 873 8499, 011 44 71 873 8456, telex 297138. **(Subscription address:** Her Majesty's Stationery Office, PO Box 276, Publications Centre, London SW8 5DT England.) **[CCC].**

NR/0078-0626
**ANNUAL ABSTRACT OF STATISTICS - NIGERIA. FEDERAL OFFICE OF STATISTICS.** (ANNUAL ABSTRACT OF STATISTICS - FEDERATION OF NIGERIA, FEDERAL OFFICE OF STATISTICS.). **Main/Corp** Nigeria. Federal Office of Statistics. V. 1- 1960-. English. an. N25.00 Nigeria; $25.00 (add $5.00 postage) other. Federal Office of Statistics / Nigeria, Director PMB 12528, Lagos Nigeria. **Tel** 011 234 1 601710. **LC** HA1977.N5; A22. **Ad Acc. Circ:** 10,000. ***Supersedes in part*** *Nigeria. Federal Office of Statistics. Digest of Statistics.*

MM/0256-8047
**ANNUAL ABSTRACTS OF STATISTICS - CENTRAL OFFICE OF STATISTICS (VALLETTA).** (ANNUAL ABSTRACT OF STATISTICS / CENTRAL OFFICE OF STATISTICS, MALTA.). [Annu. abst. stat. - Cent. Off. Stat.]. **Main/Corp** Malta. Office of Statistics. **Added/Corp** Malta. Central Office of Statistics. **VFOAT** Abstract; Abstract, an Annual Statistical Review. (19??)-. English. an. Department of Information / Malta, Publications Section, Valletta Malta. **LC** HA1117.M3; A3. **DD** 314.58/5. **NLM** W2 GM3 C3S. **Bk Rev.** ***Continues*** *Malta. Office of Statistics. Statistical Abstract of the Maltese Islands.*

FR
**ANNUAL AND QUARTERLY ENERGY PRICE AND TAX STATISTICS.** English (French). Four times a year. $1,745.00 (magnetic tape). OECD Publications and Information Center, 2 rue Andre-Pascal, 75775 Paris Cedex 16 France. **Tel** 011 33 1 45248167, US:(202)785-6323, FAX 011 33 1 45248500 OR 45248176, telex 620 160 OCDE. **(Subscription address:** OECD Publications Center, 2001 L Street, Suite 700, Washington DC 20036.)

US
**ANNUAL PLANNING INFORMATION. CHARLESTON, WEST VIRGINIA STANDARD METROPOLITAN STATISTICAL AREA.** **VFOAT** Charleston, West Virginia Standard Metropolitan Statistical Area; Charleston Standard Metropolitan Statistical Area for ...; Charleston Metropolitan Statistical Area and Kanawha County; Vice Delivery Area for ... . Fiscal Year 1983-. Statistical Publication. English. an. Free. West Virginia Employment Programs Bureau, 112 California Avenue, Charleston WV 25305. **Tel** (304)558-2630, FAX (304)348-0301. **LC** HD5726.C37; W48A. **DD** 331.12/09754/38. **Circ:** 250 (ctrl). ***Continues*** *Charleston, West Virginia Standard Metropolitan Statistical Area, Annual Planning Information.*
**Desc:** Provides comprehensive information relating to projected estimates of manpower statistics based upon previous labor market conditions and current indicators. Updated data provided.

CN/0703-2633
**ANNUAL REPORT - STATISTICS CANADA.** ***Ceased.*** (THE ... ANNUAL REPORT OF STATISTICS CANADA / PREPARED BY COMMUNICATIONS DIVISION.). [Annu. rep. - Stat. Can.]. **Main/Corp** Statistics Canada. Communications Division. **VFOAT** Annual Report; Rapport Annuel de Statistique Canada. (1986/87)-(March 1993). English (French). an. Statistics Canada, Publications Sales & Services, Main Building Room 1710, Ottawa Ontario K1A 0T6 Canada. **Tel** (613)951-5078, (800)267-6677, FAX (613)951-1584, telex 053-3585. **LC** HA742; .A35. **DD** 354.710081/9. ***Continues*** *Annual Report of Statistics Canada., 0703-2633.*
**Desc:** The annual report reviews the accomplishments of the Agency in the fiscal year under review. Featuring an overview and introduction to Statistics Canada, it profiles activities in social and economic statistics, presents new developments in methodology and highlights key products and services.

US/0733-0979
**ANNUAL STATISTICAL BULLETIN. PUBLIC UNIVERSITY LIBRARY STATISTICS.** **VFOAT** Public University Library Statistics. Statistical Publication. English. an. Washington State University / Library, Washington Library Network AJ-11W, Olympia WA 98504. ***Continues in part*** *Annual Statistical Bulletin - Washington State Library.*

SQ/0300-2098
**ANNUAL STATISTICAL BULLETIN - SWAZILAND. CENTRAL STATISTICAL OFFICE.** (ANNUAL STATISTICAL BULLETIN.). **Main/Corp** Swaziland. Central Statistical Office. (19??)-. Statistical Publication. English. an. $2.00. Economics Statistics Library, PO Box 456, Mbabane Swaziland. **Tel** 011 43765. **LC** HA1977.S9; A24. **DD** 316.8/3. Index available. **Ad Acc. Circ:** 1,000. ***Continues*** *Swaziland. Dept. of Statistics. Annual Statistical Bulletin - Swaziland.*

TR/0564-2604
**ANNUAL STATISTICAL DIGEST - CENTRAL STATISTICAL OFFICE (PORT-OF-SPAIN).** (ANNUAL STATISTICAL DIGEST / ISSUED BY THE CENTRAL STATISTICAL OFFICE.). **Added/Corp** Trinidad and Tobago. Central Statistical Office. No. 1 (1951)-. Statistical Publication. English. an. Price varies. Government Printery / Trinidad, 110 Henry Street, Port of Spain Trinidad. **LC** HA867; .A35. **DD** 317.298/3. **NLM** W2 DT7 C3A. **Circ:** 1,000.
**Desc:** Contains data on labour and employment, justice and crime, social conditions, transport and communication, industrial production, agriculture, mining and refining, national income and expenditure, overseas trade, prices and banking.

US/0364-2372
**ANNUAL SUMMARY OF VITAL STATISTICS, KANSAS (1969).** (ANNUAL SUMMARY OF VITAL STATISTICS, KANSAS.). **Added/Corp** Kansas. Division of Registration and Health Statistics Services. Kansas. Division of Registration and Health Statistics. Kansas. Bureau of Registration and Health Statistics. Kansas. Dept. of Health and Environment. (1969)-. English. an. Free. Kansas Department of Health and Environment, Office of Research and Analysis, 109 Southwest 9th Street, Suite 400A, Topeka KS 66612-2219. **Tel** (913)296-0632. **ED** Janet Marquis. **LC** HA381; .K36. **DD** 304.6/09781/021. **NLM** W2 AK3 D85AC. **Circ:** 750 (ctrl). ***Continues*** *Annual Summary of Vital Statistics, State of Kansas.*
**Desc:** Compilation of data collected on births, deaths, marriages, divorces, abortions and stillbirths reported through the vital statistics registration system of Kansas.

MX
**ANNUARIO DE ESTADISTICAS ESTATALES.** (1984)-. Statistical Publication. Spanish. an. Inst Nacional Estadistica Geog, Advd Insur Sur #795-PH Col Nap, 03810 Mexico DF Mexico. **LC** HA762; .A3. **DD** 317.2.

IT/0066-4545
**ANNUARIO STATISTICO ITALIANO.** **Added/Corp** Italy. Direzione Generale di Statistica. Italy. Direzione della Statistica Generale. Italy. Direzione Generale della Statistica. Italy. Direzione Generale della Statistica e del Lavoro. Italy. Ufficio Centrale di Statistica. Istituto Centrale di Statistica del Regno d'Italia. Istituto Centrale di Statistica (Italy). (1878)-. Italian. an. L55000. Istituto Nazionale Statistica, GBP SEZ4 Via Cesare Balbo 16, 00184 Rome Italy. **Tel** 011 39 6 46735118. **LC** HA1367; .A3. **NLM** W2; GI8 I5AU.

SP
**ANUARI ESTADISTIC DE LA CIUTAT DE BARCELONA.** (1987)-. Catalan. an. **LC** HA1559.B3; A58. **DD** 314.6/72/05.

EC
**ANUARIO DE ESTADISTICA.** **Main/Corp** Instituto Nacional de Estadistica (Ecuador). Statistical Publication. Spanish. ir. Instituto Nacional de Estadistica y Censos, Avda 10 de Agosto 229, Quito Ecuador. **Tel** 51.95.97/51.93.20, telex 21421 INFEC ED. **Circ:** 1,500.
**Desc:** Summary of major statistics of The National Institute of Statistics and Census of Ecuador, especially important statistics on hospitals, industry, transport, internal commerce and services, price indexes and more.

SP
**ANUARIO DE ESTADISTICA AGRARIA.** **See** Agriculture-Abstracting, Bibliographies and Statistics.

CL
**ANUARIO ESTADISTICO DE AMERICA LATINA Y EL CARIBE.** **Added/Corp** United Nations. Economic Commission for Latin America and the Caribbean. **VFOAT** Statistical Yearbook for Latin America and the Caribbean. (1985)-. Government Publication. Spanish (English). an. F535.00. United Nations Publications, 2 United Nations Plaza, Room DC2 0853, Department 007C, New York NY 10017. **Tel** (212)963-8303, (800)253-9646. **LC** HA751; .A58; HA751; .U52. **DD** 318/.05. ***Continues*** *Anuario Estadistico de America Latina.*

CK/0120-3495
**ANUARIO ESTADISTICO DE ANTIOQUIA.** Spanish. an. Free (institutions). Planeacion Departamental, CAD Jose Maria Cordova, La Alpujarra piso 11, Medellin Antioquia Colombia. **LC** HA1017.A6; A42. **DD** 318.61/2. Index available. **Circ:** 1,500 (ctrl). ***Continues*** *Anuario Estadistico de Antioquia.*

SP
**ANUARIO ESTADISTICO DE ESPANA.** **Added/Corp** Instituto Nacional de Estadistica (Spain) Instituto Geografico y Estadistico (Spain) Spain. Servicio General de Estadistica. Instituto Geografico, Catastral y de Estadistica (Spain) Spain. Direccion General de Estadistica. (1912)-. Spanish. an. Instituto Nacional Estadistico Spain, Paseo de la Castellana 183, 28046 Madrid Spain. **Tel** 011 34 1 583 9100. **LC** HA1543; .A5.

AG
**ANUARIO ESTADISTICO (INSTITUTO NACIONAL DE ESTADISTICA Y CENSOS (ARGENTINA)).** (ANUARIO ESTADISTICO.). **Added/Corp** Instituto Nacional de Estadistica y Censos (Argentina). **VFOAT** Anuario Estadistico de la Republica Argentina. (1980)-. Spanish. ir. $50.00 (latest edition). Instituto Nacional de Estadistica y Censos Argentina 12 OF 1209, AV Pte Julio A Roco 609 Piso 9, 1067 Buenos Aires Argentina. **Tel** 011 54 1 9529860 2403 4050. **(Subscription address:** SEC Programa Economica INDEC, AV Pte Julio A Roco 609 Piso 9, 1067 Buenos Aires Argentina, telephone: 011 54 1 9529860**)** **LC** HA954; .A57. **DD** 318.2. Index available. ctrl circ. ***Continues*** *Anuario Estadistico de la Republica Argentina.*
**Desc:** Includes geographical, climatological, seismological and geomagnetical data and general information on the country, such as population, employment and unemployment, community organizations and social and economic sectors. Includes statistical information and census returns.

BL
**ANUARIO ESTATISTICO - COMISSAO DE FINANCIAMENTO DA PRODUCAO, DEPARTAMENTO DE PESQUISAS ECONOMICAS.** **See** Agriculture-Abstracting, Bibliographies and Statistics.

BL
**ANUARIO ESTATISTICO DO AMAPA.** Portuguese. Divisao de Geografia E Estatistica, Av Fab 1316, Mecape Brazil. **LC** HA988.A45; A3. **DD** 318.1/1. ***Continues*** *Anuario Estatistico do Amapa.*

BL/0100-1299
**ANUARIO ESTATISTICO DO BRASIL / MINISTERIO DA AGRICULTURA, INDUSTRIA E COMMERCIO, DIRECTORIA GERAL DE ESTATISTICA.** **Added/Corp** Brazil. Directoria Geral de Estatistica. Instituto Nacional de Estatistica (Brazil) Instituto Brasileiro de Geografia e Estatistica. Instituto Brasileiro de Estatistica. Fundacao Instituto Brasileiro de Geografia e Estatistica. **VFOAT** Annuaire Statistique du Bresil; Anuario Estatistico do Brasil. No. 1, (1912)-. Portuguese (French). an. $100.00. Instituto Brasileiro de Geografia e Estatistica, Rua General Canabarro 666 AN2, 20271 Rio de Janeiro RJ Brazil. **Tel** 011 55 21 2847690, 011 55 21 2342043. **LC** HA971; .A32. **NLM** W2 DB8 D5A. Index available. **Circ:** 7,000 (ctrl). available in microform.
**Desc:** Presents information and data on social, cultural, economic, physical, demographic, administrative and political aspects of the country.

BL/0100-8730
**ANUARIO ESTATISTICO DO ESTADO DE SAO PAULO.** [Anu. estat. Estado Sao Paulo]. Vol. 56 (1979)-. Portuguese. an. $18.00 (seamail), $32.00 (airmail). Fundacao Sistema Estadual de Analise de Dados, Caixa Postal 8223, 01033 Sao Paulo Brazil. **Tel** (011)229-2433, telex (011)31390 SEAD BR. **LC** HA988.S2; A76. **DD** 318.1/61. **Bk Rev. Circ:** 1,200. ***Continues*** *Anuario Estatistico (Sao Paulo (Brazil : State). Departamento de Estatistica).*
**Desc:** Gathers tables and charts which characterize the state of Sao Paulo in its social, demographic and physical aspects.

BL
**ANUARIO ESTATISTICO DO ESTADO DO RIO DE JANEIRO.** 1978-. Portuguese. Secplan, Fiderj - Palacio Guanabara, Edificio Anexo 20. Andar, Rio de Janeiro Brazil. **LC** HA988.R6; A75.

RM
**ANUARUL STATISTIC AL ROMANIEI.** **Added/Corp** Romania. Comisia Nationala Pentru Statistica. **VFOAT** Anuarul Statistic. (1990)-. Romanian. an. $70.00. **(Subscription address:** Orion Press SRL, SPL Independentei 202-A, Bucharest 6 Romania.**)** **LC** HA1641; .A58. ***Continues*** *Anuarul Statistic al Republicii Socialiste Romania.*

UK/0035-9254
**APPLIED STATISTICS.** [Appl. stat.]. **Added/Corp** Royal Statistical Society (Great Britain). Royal Statistical Society (Great Britain). Journal of the Royal Statistical Society. Series C (Applied Statistics). **VFOAT** Journal of the Royal Statistical Society. Series C; Journal of the Royal Statistical Society. Vol. 1 (March 1952)-. Academic Scholarly Publication. English. Four times a year. £49.00 UK and Europe; $87.50 North America; £56.00 other. Basil Blackwell Publishers Ltd, 108 Cowley Road, Oxford 0X4 1JF England. **Tel** 011 44 865 791100, FAX 011 44 865 791347, telex 837022 OXBOOK G. **(Subscription address:** Blackwell Publishers / UK, Marston Book Services, PO Box 87, Oxford OX2 0DT England.**)** **ED** I R Dunsmore and D J Hand. **NLM** W1 AP53. **CODEN** APSTAG. **[CCC].** Index available. **Bk Rev. Ad Acc. Pr Rev. Circ:** 5,500 (ctrl). available on microfilm and microfiche from University Microfilms International (UMI). Documents available from The Genuine Article, Ask*IEEE.
**Desc:** Papers are motivated by practical problems, concerned with applications of statistical methods and relevant algorithms.
**Ind/Abst** Agric. Eng. Abstr.; Biostatistica; Compumath Citation Index [Full Cov.]; Contents Pages Manage. (1968-); Curr. Contents Phys. Chem. Earth Sci.; Curr. Index Stat.; Curr. Technol. Index (1968-); GeoRef; INSPEC (1968-); Math. Rev.; Life Sci. Collect.; Qual. Control Appl. Stat.; Res. Alert [Full Cov.]; Sci. Cit. Index; Selec. Coop. Index Manage. Period; SCISEARCH; Soc. Sci. Cit. Index [Select. Cov.]; Soils Fert.; Soc. Res. Methodol. Abstr. (1975-); Stat. Theory Method Abstr. (1959-1963, 1966-1977, 1980-1984, 1986-1987); Trop. Dis. Bull.; World Agric. Econ.

GW
**ARBEITSSTATTEN DES GROSSHANDELS UND DER HANDELSVERMITTLUNG IN RHEINLAND-PFALZ, DIE.** German. DM9.20. Statistisches Landesamt Rheinland-Pfalz, Postfach Mainzer Strasse 15/16, 5427 Bad Ems Germany. **LC** HA1320; .R453 subser; HF3569.R55. **DD** 314.3/43.

DK/0901-4527
**ARBEJDSDIREKTORATETS OG ARBEJDSFORMIDLINGENS ARSSTATISTIK FOR ... .** 1984-. Danish. an. Arbejdsdirektoratet, Adelgade 13, 1304 Kbenhavn K Denmark. ***Continues in part*** *Arbejdsdirektoratets Beretning om Arbejdsformidlingen Og Arbejdslshedsforsikringen M. V. for Regnskabsaret ... .*

SW/0348-6729
**ARETS TRYCK.** **Main/Corp** Sweden. Statistiska Centralbyran. **VFOAT** Publications of the Year. Swedish (English and Swedish). SCB Statistiska Centralbyran, 11581 Stockholm Sweden. **LC** Z7165.S8; S94A; HA1523.
**Desc:** The publication is listing all publications produced by Statistics Sweden during that particular year.

US/1065-5328
**ARIZONA IN PERSPECTIVE.** (ARIZONA IN PERSPECTIVE : A STATISTICAL VIEW OF THE "GRAND CANYON STATE".). [Ariz. perspect.]. **Added/Corp** Morgan Quitno Corporation. (1990)-. Statistical Publication. English. $18.00. Morgan Quitno Corporation, PO Box 1656, 512 East 9th Street, Lawrence KS 66044. **Tel** (800)457-0742, (913)841-3534, FAX (913)841-3534. **DD** 317. ***Continues*** *Arizona in Perspective, 1065-5328.*
**Desc:** Reports on the state's data and rank for each of the categories featured in State Rankings.

US/1045-4195
**ARIZONA STATISTICAL ABSTRACT : A ... DATA HANDBOOK.** [Ariz stat. abstr.]. **Added/Corp** University of Arizona. Division of Economic and Business Research. (1979)-. Statistical Publication. English. ir. University of Arizona / Business, College of Business and Public Administration, Tucson AZ 85721. **Tel** (602)621-2155. **LC** HA241; .S85. **DD** 317.91/05. ***Continues*** *Statistical Abstract of Arizona.*
**Desc:** Reference source for statistics pertaining to Arizona and its political subdivisions.

US/1065-5336
**ARKANSAS IN PERSPECTIVE.** (ARKANSAS IN PERSPECTIVE : A STATISTICAL VIEW OF THE "LAND OF OPPORTUNITY STATE".). [Ark. perspect.]. **Added/Corp** Morgan Quitno Corporation. (1990)-. Statistical Publication. English. $18.00. Morgan Quitno Corporation, PO Box 1656, 512 East 9th Street, Lawrence KS 66044. **Tel** (800)457-0742, (913)841-3534, FAX (913)841-3534. **DD** 317. ***Continues*** *Arkansas in Perspective, 1065-5336.*
**Desc:** Reports on the state's data and rank for each of the categories featured in State Rankings.

GW
**AUSLANDER.** **Main/Corp** Niedersachsisches Landesverwaltungsamt. German. an. DM3.60. Niedersachsisches Landesverwaltungsamt, Postfach 107, 3000 Hannover Germany. **Tel** (0511)108-9466. **LC** HA1248.S28; S284A.

GW
**AUSSENHANDEL. REIHE S. 6, SYSTEMATIKEN IN DER AUSSENHANDELSSTATISTIK / STATISTISCHES BUNDESAMT.** **Added/Corp** Germany (West). Statistisches Bundesamt. **VFOAT** Systematiken in der Aussenhandelsstatistik; Fachserie 7. (1990)-. German. Hermann Leins GmbH & Co., Verlags-KG, Holzwiesenstr 2, 7408 Kusterdingen.

AT/0067-1754
**AUSTRALIAN CAPITAL TERRITORY STATISTICAL SUMMARY.** ***Title Change.*** **Added/Corp** Australian Bureau of Statistics. (19??)-(199?). Statistical Publication. English. an. Australian Bureau of Statistics, PO Box 10, Belconnen Australian Capital Territory, 2616 Australia. **Tel** 011 61 6 2527911, FAX 011 61 6 2516009. **LC** HA3008.A9; A25. **DD** 319.4/7. ***Continues*** *Australian Capital Territory Statistical Summary, 0067-1754.* ***Continued by*** *Australian Capital Territory in Focus, 1039-6594.*
**Desc:** Information on the population and its characteristics; social statistics and demography, primary production, labor, wages and prices, retail trade, building and transport.

AT/0004-9581
**AUSTRALIAN JOURNAL OF STATISTICS.** [Aust. j. stat.]. **Added/Corp** Statistical Society of New South Wales. Statistical Society of Australia. Vol. 1 (April 1959)-. English. Three times a year (Apr., Aug., Dec.). 75.00Aus$ (surface mail); 105.00Aus$ (airmail). Australian Statistical Publishing Association Inc,

GPO Box 573, Canberra ACT 2601 Australia. **Tel** 011 61 6249889, FAX 011 61 6 2498266, telex 62337. **ED** C. A. McGilchrist. **LC** HA1; .A87. **DD** 310/.994. **NLM** HA 1 A938. **CODEN** AUJSA3. Index available. cum. index. **Bk Rev. Circ:** 1,600 (ctrl). ***Supersedes*** *Statistical Society of New South Wales. Bulletin.*
**Desc:** Papers on statistics.
**Ind/Abst** Biostatistica; Curr. Index Stat.; Int. Bibliogr. Sociol.; Math. Rev.; Qual. Control Appl. Stat.; Stat. Theory Method Abstr. (1959-1963, 1966-1979, 1983-1984, 1986-1987); Zentralbl. Math. Ihre Grenzgeb.

TU
**AYLK ISTATISTIK BULTENI. VFOAT** Monthly Statistical Bulletin. (Jan./Feb. 1990)-. Periodical. English (Turkish). bm. Central Bank / Turkey, Republic of Turkey, Ankara Turkey. **LC** HG187.T9; I78. ***Continues*** *Istatistik ve Degerlendirme Bulteni.*

NO/0333-1504
**BANK- OG KREDITTSTATISTIKK: AKTUELLE TALL. Added/Corp** Norway. Statstisk Sentralbyra. No. 1 (March 30, 1981)-. Periodical. Norwegian. ir. Kr440.00. Central Bureau of Statistics / Norway, PO Box 8131 DEP, N-0033 Oslo 1 Norway. **Tel** 011 47 2 2864964, FAX 011 47 2 864973. ***Continues in part*** *Kvartalshefte for Private OG Offentlige Banker.*

BE/0081-4873
**BASIC STATISTICS OF THE COMMUNITY.** (BASIC STATISTICS OF THE COMMUNITY / STATISTICAL OFFICE OF THE EUROPEAN COMMUNITIES.). **Added/Corp** Statistical Office of the European Communities. (196?)-. Statistical Publication. English (French, Italian, Dutch and German). an. £7.10 UK; 7.70p Ireland. Office for Official Publications of the European Communities, 2 Rue Mercier, 2985 Luxembourg Luxembourg. **Tel** 011 352 499281, FAX 011 352 488573. **(Subscription address:** US: UNIPUB, 4611 F Assembly Drive, Lanham, MD 20706) **LC** HA1107.5; .A12. **DD** 314. ***Continues*** *Basic Statistics for Fifteen European Countries.*
**Desc:** Key statistics for the Community Member States plus comparisons with those of other European states, Canada, US, Japan, etc.

GW
**BAUWIRTSCHAFT UND BAUTATIGKEIT IN NORDRHEIN-WESTFALEN. Main/Corp** North Rhine-Westphalia (Germany). Landesamt fur Datenverarbeitung und Statistik. 1973-. German. an. DM12.00. Landesamt fuer Datenverarbeitung und Statistik Nordrhein-Westfalen, Postfach 101105, 40002 Duesseldorf Germany. **Tel** (0211)944901, FAX (0211)442006, telex 8586654 LDST D. **LC** HA1320.N6; A32 subser; HD9715.G3 G33. **DD** 314.3/55 S; 338.4/7/690094355. **Circ:** 250. ***Continues*** *Bauwirtschaft und Bautatigkeit in Nordrhein-Westfalen.*
**Desc:** Statistical returns on the building boom, building measures, planning and building permission and house building.

DK/0070-3478
**BEFOLKNINGENS BEVGELSER. VFOAT** Vital Statistics. Danish. an. kr60.66 (plus kr35.00 postage). Danmarks Statistik, Sejrgade 11, DK-2100 Copenhagen Denmark. **Tel** 011 45 3 9173917, FAX 011 45 31 18 48 01, telex 1 62 36. **LC** HA1473; .B43.

●UK/1350-7265
**BERNOULLI.** (1994)-. English. qt. $170.00 US and Canada; £100.00 Europe; £115.00 Other. Chapman & Hall, 2-6 Boundary Row, London SE1 8HN England. **Tel** 011 44 71 865 0066, FAX 011 44 71 522 9623, telex 290164 Chapmag. **(Subscription address:** Chapman & Hall, Cheriton House, North Way, Andover, Hampshire, SP10 5BE England.)

GW
**BESCHAFTIGTENENTWICKLUNG IN NORDRHEIN-WESTFALEN. ERGEBNISSE EINER REGIONAL DISAGGREGIERTEN ANALYSE, DIE. VFOAT** Ergebnisse Einer Regional Disaggregierten Analyse. (1983)-. German. Landesamt fuer Datenverarbeitung und Statistik Nordrhein-Westfalen, Postfach 101105, 40002 Duesseldorf Germany. **Tel** (0211)944901, FAX (0211)442006, telex 8586654 LDST D. **LC** HA1320.N6; A32 subser; HD5780.N.

FR
**BILAN ANNUEL BRETAGNE.** French. an. 36 Place du Colombier, Rennes France. **LC** HA1228.B7; O27 SUPPL. **DD** 314.4/1.

US/0006-341X
**BIOMETRICS.** [Biometrics]. **Added/Corp** Biometric Society. American Statistical Association. Biometrics Section. Vol. 3 (March 1947)-. Periodical. English (French and German). Four times a year. $90.00. Biometric Society, 1429 Duke Street/Suite 401, Alexandria VA 22314-3402. **Tel** (703)836-8311. **ED** K Hinkelmann. **NLM** W1 BI859. **CODEN** BIOMB6. **[CCC].** Index available. cum. index. **Bk Rev. Ad Acc. Pr Rev. Circ:** 7,500 (ctrl). available on microfilm and microfiche from University Microfilms International (UMI). Documents available from The Genuine Article, Ask*IEEE. ***Continues*** *Biometrics Bulletin, 0099-4987.*
**Desc:** A scientific journal which emphasizes the role of mathematics in use of mathematical and statistical methods in pure and applied biological sciences by describing developments in these methods and their applications in a form readily assimilable by experimental scientists.
**Ind/Abst** Anim. Breed. Abstr.; Biol. Agric. Index; Biostatistica; Compumath Citation Index [Full Cov.]; Comput. Rev.; Curr. Aware. Biol. Sci., CABS; Curr. Contents, Agric. Biol. Environ. Sci.; Curr. Contents Life Sci.; Curr. Index Stat.; Dairy Sci. Abstr.; Ecol. Abstr.; EMBASE; Energy Res. Abstr.; Fish Rev.; Food Sci. Technol. Abstr.; For. Prod. Abstr.; For. Abstr.; Geogr. Abstr. Phys. Geogr.; Health Plan. Adminis.; Hortic. Abstr.; Index Med.; Index Vet.; INIS Atomindex [Micro.]; INSPEC (June 1982-1985); Int. Aerosp. Abstr.; Int. Dev. Abstr. (?-?); Key Word Index Wildl. Res.; Math. Rev.; Life Sci. Collect.; Pig News Inf.; Plant Breed. Abstr.; Popul. Index (?-?); Poult. Abstr.; Protozoolog. Abstr.; Qual. Control Appl. Stat.; Ref. Upd. Deluxe Ed.; Res. Alert [Full Cov.]; Rev. Med. Vet. Entomol.; Rev. Plant Pathol.; Risk Abstr. (19??-19??); Sci. Cit. Index; SCISEARCH; Soc. Sci. Cit. Index [Select. Cov.]; Soils Fert.; Stat. Theory Method Abstr. (1959-1963, 1966-1984, 1986-1987); Vet. Bull.; Wheat Barley Trit. Abstr.; Wildl. Rev.; Zentralbl. Math. Ihre Grenzgeb.

US/0363-1281
**BIRTHS AND DEATHS BY JURISDICTION OF RESIDENCE. MARRIAGES AND DIVORCES BY COUNTY. Main/Corp** Ohio. Division of Vital Statistics. English. an. Ohio Department of Health, 246 North High Street, Columbus OH 43266. **Tel** (614)466-2253, FAX (614)644-8526. **LC** HA571; .D58A. **DD** 312/.09771.

PL/0006-4025
**BIULETYN STATYSTYCZNY. Main/Corp** Poland. Glowny Urzad Statystyczny. (Jan 1957)-. Polish (Russian; table of contents in English and Russian). mo. Price on Request. Zaklad Wydawnictw Statystycznych, Al Niepodleglosci 208, 00-925 Warszawa Poland. **Tel** 253241, telex 814581A GUS. **LC** HA1451; .A16. **DD** 314.38. **Ad Acc. Circ:** 2,250 (ctrl).
**Desc:** Statistical data bulletin of Poland.

AO/1010-4151
**BOLETIM MENSAL DE ESTATISTICA.** [Bol. mens. estad. - Inst. nac. estad.]. **Main/Corp** Angola. Direcao Provincial dos Servicos de Estatistica. Vol. 25-1969-. Bulletin. Portuguese. mo. 13500$00 Portugal; 20000$00 other. Caixa Postal 1215, Luanda Angola. **LC** HA2211; .A37. ***Continues*** *Boletim Mensal de Estatistica.*

MH
**BOLETIM MENSUAL DE ESTATISTICA. Main/Corp** Macao. Reparticao dos Servicos de Estatistica. **VFOAT** Monthly Bulletin of Statistics. Jan. 1976-. Bulletin. Portuguese (Chinese). mo. Free. Direccao de Servicos de Estatistica e Censos, PO Box 3022, Macao. **Tel** 550935. **LC** HA1950.M3; A27A. **DD** 315.1/26. Index available. **Circ:** 400 (ctrl).

PO/0303-1705
**BOLETIM TRIMESTRAL DE ESTATISTICA (FUNCHAL).** (BOLETIM TRIMESTRAL DE ESTATISTICA.). [Bol. trimest. estat.]. Vol. 1- 1st Quarter 1972-. Bulletin. Portuguese. qt. 900$00. Edificio da Junta-Geral, Av Arriaga, Funchal Portugal. **Tel** 27454. **LC** HA1577.M3; P65A. **DD** 314.69/8. **Ad Acc. Circ:** 500 (ctrl).
**Desc:** Autonomous region of Madeira.

SF/0303-1675
**BOLETIM TRIMESTRAL DE ESTATISTICA - INSTITUTO NACIONAL DE ESTATISTICA. DELEGACAO SE S. TOME E PRINCIPE.** (BOLETIM TRIMESTRAL DE ESTATISTICA.). **Main/Corp** Sao Tome e Principe. Reparticao Provincial dos Servicos de Estatistica. Yearly V. 1- 1st Quarter 1971-. Bulletin. Portuguese. qt. 120.00. Reparticao Provincial dos Servicos de Estatistica, Caixa Postal No 256, Sao Tome E Principe. **LC** HA2204.S27; S27A.

EC
**BOLETIN ANUARIO - BANCO CENTRAL DEL ECUADOR. Main/Corp** Banco Central del Ecuador. No. 1- 1978-. Spanish. an. Museo Antropologico, Banco Central de Ecuador, Secretaria General, PO Box 1331, Guayaquil Ecuador. **Tel** 011 593 4 517717, telex 043257 BCOCNG ED MUSEO. **LC** HA1025; .B36A. Index available. **Bk Rev. Ad Acc.** ctrl circ.

CK/0120-6281
**BOLETIN DE ESTADISTICA (BOGOTA, COLOMBIA).** (BOLETIN DE ESTADISTICA.). No. 1 (Jan./March 1985)-. Statistical Publication. Spanish. qt. 4000Col$. Departamento Administrativo Nacional de Estadistica, Apartado Aereo 80043, Bogota Colombia. **Tel** 011 57 1 2223273, 011 57 1 2224318. **LC** HA1011; .B64. **DD** 318.61. ***Continues*** *Boletin Mensual de Estadistica.*
**Ind/Abst** PAIS Int. Print (1991-?).

PN
**BOLETIN DE ESTADISTICA (UNIVERSIDAD DE PANAMA. DEPARTAMENTO DE ESTADISTICA).** (BOLETIN DE ESTADISTICA / UNIVERSIDAD DE PANAMA, DIRECCION DE PLANIFICACION UNIVERSITARIA, DEPARTAMENTO DE ESTADISTICA.). No. 26 (Dec. 1985)-. Statistical Publication. Spanish. Ciudad Universitaria / Panama, Panama. **Tel** 64-1572. ***Continues*** *Boletin - Universidad de Panama, Direccion de Planificacion Universitaria.*

MX
**BOLETIN DE INFORMACION ESTADISTICA / SISTEMA ESTATAL DE INFORMACION, COPLADE-CHIHUAHUA. Added/Corp** Chihuahua (Mexico : State). Sistema Estatal de Informacion. No. 1 (Jan. 1990)-. Statistical Publication. Spanish. bm. **LC** HA767.C5; B65. **DD** 317.2/16/05.

ES
**BOLETIN ESTADISTICO - DIRECCION GENERAL DE ESTADISTICA Y CENSOS. Main/Corp** El Salvador. Direccion General de Estadistica Y Censos. (19??)-. Statistical Publication. Spanish. qt. Direccion General de Estadistica y Censos / El Salvador, Rasale Contreras 145, San Salvador El Salvador. **LC** HA841; .A34. **DD** 317.284. ***Continues*** *Salvador. Direccion General de Estadistica. Boletin Estadistico.*

AG/0325-1969
**BOLETIN ESTADISTICO TRIMESTRAL - INSTITUTO NACIONAL DE ESTADISTICA Y CENSOS. *Suspended.*** (BOLETIN ESTADISTICO TRIMESTRAL.). [Bol. estad. trimest. - Inst. nac. estad. censos]. **Main/Corp** Instituto Nacional de Estadistica y Censos (Argentina). Jan./March 1973-Suspended Jan 1991. Periodical. Spanish. qt. Inst Nacional Estadist Censos Arg, Av Pte Julio a Roca 609 Piso 9, 1067 Buenos Aires Argentina. **Tel** 011 54 1 9529860. **LC** HA943; .A73A.

SP
**BOLETIN MENSUAL DE ESTADISTICA. Main/Corp** Instituto Nacional de Estadistica (Spain). Vol. 1, No. 1 (Feb. March 1939)-. Statistical Publication. Spanish. mo. Secretaria General Tecnica, Centro de Publicaciones, Gran Via, 76, Planta 8, 28013 Madrid, Spain. **Tel** 5479833, 5475422.

●SP
**BOLETIN MENSUAL DE ESTADISTICA/ INSTITUTO NACIONAL DE ESTADISTICA. Added/Corp** Instituto Nacional de Estadistica (Spain). No. 1 (Enero 1992)-. Statistical Publication. Spanish. mo. ***Continues*** *Boletin de Estadistica (Madrid, Spain: 1980), 0212-6664.*

IT/0021-3136
**BOLLETTINO MENSILE DI STATISTICA - ISTITUTO CENTRALE DI STATISTICA.** (BOLLETTINO MENSILE DI STATISTICA.). [Boll. mens. stat. - Ist. cent. stat.]. **Added/Corp** Istituto Centrale di Statistica (Italy) Istituto Nazionale di Statistica (Italy) Italy. Gazzetta Ufficiale del Regno d'Italia. Italy. Gazzetta Ufficiale della Repubblica Italiana. Year 1 (Nov. 1926)-. Italian. mo. L138000 Italy; L170000 other. Istituto Nazionale Statistica, GBP SEZ4 Via Cesare Balbo 16, 00184 Rome Italy. **Tel** 011 39 6 46735118. **LC** HA1360; .A23.

UK/0068-1210
**BRITISH AID STATISTICS. Main/Corp** Great Britain. Ministry of Overseas Development. **Added/Corp** Great Britain. Ministry of Overseas Development. Great Britain. Overseas Development Administration. (1966)-. English. an. £8.00. Overseas Development Administration / Glasgow, Abercombie House, Eaglesham Road, Glasgow G75 8EA Scotland. **Tel** 011 31 355 843599. **LC** HC60; .G693. **DD** 338.91/172/4041. **[CCC]. *Continues*** *British Aid Statistics, 0068-1210.*
**Desc:** Annual publication showing flows of UK overseas aid for economic and social development. Gives information for year in question (usually 2 years pre pub date) and previous years for comparison.

HU/0438-2242
**BUDAPEST STATISZTIKAI ZSEBKONYVE.** 1956-. Hungarian. an. 45.00ft. Statisztikai Kiado Vallalat, PO Box 99, H-1033 Budapest 3 Hungary. **Tel** 803-311, telex 22-6699-SKV-H. **LC** HA1208; .B938. **DD** 314.39. **NLM** W2 GH8 K7b. **Circ:** 1,500.
**Desc:** A statistical pocket-book of Budapest; reviews yearly the development of economic and social life of the Hungarian capital.

HU
**BUDAPESTI STATISZTIKAI TAJEKOZTATO.** Hungarian. qt. 200.00ft. Statisztikai Kiado Vallalat, PO Box 99, H-1033 Budapest 3 Hungary. **Tel** 803-311, telex 22-6699-SKV-H. **LC**

HA1208.B8; B83. **Circ:** 800.
**Desc:** Statistical bulletin of Budapest population, social and economic data.

IO
**BUKU SAKU STATISTIK INDONESIA.**
**VFOAT** Statistical Pocketbook of Indonesia. English (Indonesian). an. Rp6500 Indonesia; $4.50 US. Central Bureau of Statistics / Indonesia, c/o Dr. Sutomo, 8 Jalan, PO Box 3, Jakarta Indonesia. **Tel** 372808 374908 Ext.342. **LC** HA1811; .A34. **DD** 315.98. **Bk Rev.** ctrl circ. ***Continues*** *Statistik Indonesia.*
**Desc:** Statistics on population, transportation and financing.

II/0008-0683
**BULLETIN - CALCUTTA STATISTICAL ASSOCIATION.** (CALCUTTA STATISTICAL ASSOCIATION BULLETIN.). [Bull. - Calcutta Stat. Assoc.]. **Main/Corp** Calcutta Statistical Association. Vol. 1, No. 1 (Aug. 1947)-. Statistical Publication. English. qt. $35.00. Calcutta Statistical Association, 35 Ballygunge Circle Road, New Science Building/5th Floor, Calcutta 700019 India. **(Subscription address:** Prints India, 11 Darya Ganj, New Delhi, 110002 India, (Phone: 011 91 11 3268645)) **ED** S K Chatterjee. **LC** HA1; .C35. **NLM** HA 1 C144. **CODEN** CSTBAA. **Bk Rev. Circ:** 355 (ctrl).
**Desc:** Publishes articles dealing with advances and critical appraisals relating to various branches of theoretical and applied statistics and allied fields.
**Ind/Abst** Curr. Index Stat.; Math. Rev.; Stat. Theory Method Abstr. (1968-1975, 1977, 1979, 1982-1984, 1986-1987); Zentralbl. Math. Ihre Grenzgeb.

CD
**BULLETIN DE STATISTIQUE (CHAD).**
***Title Change.*** **Main/Corp** Chad. Sous-Direction de la Statistique. Bulletin. French. qt. Bulletin de Statistique, BP 453, Ndjamena Chad. **LC** HA2086; .A26. **DD** 330.9/67/4304. ***Continues*** *Bulletin de Statistique / CHAD. Direction de la Statistique et des Etudes Economiques.* ***Continued by*** *Bulletin de Statistique (Chad. Direction de la Statistique, des Etudes Economiques et Demographiques).*

RW/0304-9426
**BULLETIN DE STATISTIQUE - DIRECTION DE LA STATISTIQUE ET DE LA DOCUMENTATION (RWANDA).** ***Title Change.*** **Main/Corp** Rwanda. Direction de la Statistique et de la Documentation. (19??)-(19??). Bulletin. French. BP 46, Kigala Rwanda. **LC** HA4695; A25a. **DD** 316.7/571. ***Continues*** *Bulletin des Statistique - Direction de l'Office General des Statistiques. Rwanda, 0557-5583.* ***Continued by*** *Bulletin de Statistique - Direction Generale de la Documentation et de la Statistique Generale, 0304-9426.*

RW
**BULLETIN DE STATISTIQUE - DIRECTION DE LA STATISTIQUE ET DE LA DOCUMENTATION. SUPPLEMENT ANNUEL (RWANDA).** **Main/Corp** Rwanda. Direction de la Statistique et de la Documentation. No. 1-1974-. Bulletin. French. an. $7.00. Direction de la Statistique et de la Documentation, BP 46, Kigali Rwanda. **LC** HA2124.R8; A15A. **DD** 316.7/571.

BE/0045-1703
**BULLETIN DE STATISTIQUE - INSTITUT NATIONAL DE STATISTIQUE.** (BULLETIN DE STATISTIQUE.). [Bull. stat. - Inst. natl. stat.]. **Added/Corp** Institut National de Statistique (Belgium). (1940)-. Periodical. French (Dutch). mo. 1,410.00F Belgium; 1,760.00F other. Institut National de Statistique / Belgium, rue de Louvain, 44, Centre Albert, 8e Etage, 1000 Brussels Belgium. **Tel** 011 32 2 5486211. ***Continues*** *Bulletin de Statistique / Belgium. Office Central de Statistique.* ***Continued in part by*** *Statistiques Sociales (Brussels, Belgium), 0067-5563.*
**Ind/Abst** Foreign Lang. Index.

NG
**BULLETIN DE STATISTIQUE - REPUBLIQUE DU NIGER, MINISTERE DU DEVELOPPEMENT ET DE LA COOPERATION, DIRECTION DE LA STATISTIQUE.** ***Title Change.*** **Main/Corp** Niger. Ministere du Developpement et de la Cooperation. Direction de la Statistique. **VFOAT** Bulletin Trimestriel de Statistique - Republique du Niger, Ministere du Developpement et de la Cooperation, Direction de la Statistique. Bulletin. French. qt. Compte Bceao No 1-16-13, Monsieur le Tresorier General de la Republique du Niger, Niamey Nigeria. **LC** HA2097; .A3. **DD** 316.6/26. ***Continues*** *Niger. Service de la Statistique. Bulletin Trimestriel de Statistique.* ***Continued by*** *Bulletin de Statistique (Niger. Direction de la Statistique et des Comptes Nationaux).*

US/0146-3942
**BULLETIN - INSTITUTE OF MATHEMATICAL STATISTICS.** [Bull. - Inst. Math. Stat.]. **Main/Corp** Institute of Mathematical Statistics. **VFOAT** Institute of Mathematical Statistics Bulletin; IMS Bulletin. Vol. 1 (Jan. 1972)-. Periodical. English. bm. $50.00. Institute of Mathematical Statistics, 3401 Investment Boulevard, Suite 7, Hayward CA 94545-3819. **Tel** (510)783-8141, FAX (510)783-4131. **ED** George P.H. Styan. **LC** QA276.A1; I5. **DD** 519.5/05. **CODEN** ISMBCV. Index available. **Bk Rev. Ad Acc. Circ:** 4,300. available on microfilm and microfiche from University Microfilms International (UMI).
**Desc:** Carries the abstracts of all contributed papers presented at the meetings of the Institute and publishes news items of interest to mathematical statisticians and probabilists.
**Ind/Abst** Biostatistica (19??-); Math. Rev.; Stat. Theory Method Abstr. (1967-).

FR/0007-4713
**BULLETIN MENSUEL DE STATISTIQUE.** [Bull. mens. stat.]. **Main/Corp** Institut National de la Statistique et des Etudes Economiques (France). **Added/Corp** Institut National de la Statistique et de Etudes Economiques (France) Etudes Statistique. (Jan. 1950)-. Periodical. French. Twelve times a year. 433.00F. CNGP INSEE - Institut National de la Statistique et des Estudes Economiques, BP 2718, 1 rue V Auriol, F 80027 Amiens Cedex 1 France. **Tel** 011 33 22 927322. ***Continues*** *Institut National de la Statistique et de ,etudes Economiques (France) Bulletin de la Statistique Generale de la France.*
**Ind/Abst** Foreign Lang. Index; Predicasts.

TI
**BULLETIN MENSUEL DE STATISTIQUE - INSTITUT NATIONAL DE LA STATISTIQUE (AL-MAHAD).** **Main/Corp** Al-Mahad Al Qqwmi Lil-Ihsa. Bulletin. French. mo. 0.2TD. Institut National de la Statistique / Tunisia, 70 rue Eccham, 1002 Tunis Belvedere Tunisia. **Tel** 011 216 1 282500, 285339. **LC** HA2076; .S48A. **DD** 316.1/1. ***Continues*** *Tunisia. Service des Statistiques. Bulletin Mensuel de Statistique.*

TG
**BULLETIN MENSUEL DE STATISTIQUE (LOME, TOGO).** (BULLETIN MENSUEL DE STATISTIQUE / REPUBLIQUE TOGOLAISE, MINISTERE DU COMMERCE, DE L'INDUSTRIE, DU TOURISME ET DU PLAN, DIRECTION DE LA STATISTIQUE.). Bulletin. French. mo. 2,000CFAF. Ministere du Plan, BP 118, Lome Togo. **LC** HA2126; .M55A.

ML
**BULLETIN MENSUEL DE STATISTIQUE / REPUBLIQUE DU MALI, MINISTERE D'ETAT CHARGE DU PLAN ET DE LA COORDINATION DES AFFAIRES ECONOMIQUES ET FINANCIERES, SERVICE DE LA STATISTIQUE GENERALE ET DE LA COMPTABILITE ECONOMIQUE NATIONALE.** **Main/Corp** Mali (Republic). Service de la Statistique Generale et de la Comptabilite Economique Nationale. **Added/Corp** Mali. Service de la Statistique Generale, de la Comptabilite Nationale et de la Mecanographie. Mali. Direction Nationale de la Statistique et de l'Informatique. (Jan. 1964)-. Bulletin. French. mo. 400.00F. Service de la Statistique / Mali, General et de la Comptabilite Economique National, BP 12, Bamako Republic of Mali. **Tel** 22 24 55. **LC** HA2096; .A32a. **DD** 316.6/23. ***Continues*** *Mali (Republic). Service Statistique. Bulletin Statistique Mensuel.*

GO
**BULLETIN MENSUEL DE STATISTIQUES (GABON. DIRECTION COMMERCIALE ET DE L'EXPLOITATION).** (BULLETIN MENSUEL DE STATISTIQUES / DIRECTION COMMERCIALE ET DE L'EXPLOITATION.). **Added/Corp** Gabon. Direction Commerciale et de l'Exploitation. **VFOAT** Bulletin Statistique. (19??)-. Bulletin. French. mo.

CG
**BULLETIN MENSUEL DES STATISTIQUES - DIRECTION DE LA STATISTIQUE ET DE LA COMPTABILITE ECONOMIQUE (CONGO (BRAZZAVILLE)).** **Main/Corp** Congo (Brazzaville). Direction de la Statistique et de la Comptabilite Economique. Bulletin. French. qt. $18.10 US. Brazzaville Republique Populaire du Congo, Vice-Presidente du Conseil d'Etat, Commissariat General au Plan, Direction de la Statistique et de la Compatabilite Economique, Boite Postal 2031, Braze Congo. **Tel** 81-43-24. **LC** HA2088; .A2. **DD** 316.7/24. **Circ:** 300. ***Continues*** *Congo (Brazzaville). Service de la Statistique. Bulletin Mensuel de Statistique.*

GW/0074-8609
**BULLETIN OF THE INTERNATIONAL STATISTICAL INSTITUTE.** (BULLETIN DE L'INSTITUT INTERNATIONAL DE STATISTIQUE.). [Bull. Internat. Statist. Inst.]. **Added/Corp** International Statistical Institute. International Statistical Institute. Comptes Rendu de la ... Session de l'Institut International de Statistique. International Statistical Institute. Actes de la ... Session de l'Institut International de Statistique. International Statistical Institute. Proceedings of the ... Session. **VFOAT** Bulletin of the International Statistical Institute. Vol. 1, No. 1, 2nd Ed. (1886)-. English (French, German and Italian). be. Fl175.00. International Statistical Institute, 428 Prinses Beatrixlaan, 2270 AZ Voorburg Netherlands. **Tel** 011 31 70 3375737, FAX 011 31 70 3860025, telex 32260 ISI NL. **LC** HA11; .I5. **DD** 310.621. **NLM** W1 BU539T. **CODEN** BIISAR. **Circ:** 2,500 (ctrl).
**Desc:** Proceedings of the biennial session, all papers presented.
**Ind/Abst** Math. Rev.; Stat. Theory Method Abstr. (1966); Zentralbl. Math. Ihre Grenzgeb.

BD
**BULLETIN STATISTIQUE.** **Added/Corp** Institut National de Statistiques et des Etudes Economiques (Burundi). No. 106 (1989)-. Bulletin. French. qt. Republique du Burundi, Ministere du Plan, Service National des Etudes et Statistiques, B P 1 156, Bujumbura Burundi. **LC** HC557.B8; A15a. ***Continues*** *Bulletin Statistique (Burundi. Service National des Etudes Etstatistiques), 1016-2402.*

CX
**BULLETIN TRIMESTRIEL DE STATISTIQUE (BANGUI, CENTRAL AFRICAN REPUBLIC).** (BULLETIN TRIMESTRIEL DE STATISTIQUE.). Bulletin. French. Ministere de l'Economie et des Finances, Secretariat General, Direction of la Statistique Generale et des Etudes Economiques, BP 954, Bangui Central African Republic. **LC** HA2084; .A14a. ***Continues*** *Bulletin Mensuel de Statistique.*

AE
**BULLETIN TRIMESTRIEL DE STATISTIQUES - DIRECTION DES STATISTIQUES ET DE LA COMPTABILITE NATIONALE.** **Main/Corp** Algeria. Mudiriyat Al-Ihsaat Wa-Al-Muhasabah Al-Wataniya. **Added/Corp** Algeria. Mudiriyat al-Ihsaat wa-al-Muhasabah al-Wataniyah. Nashrah al-Fasliyah lil-Ihsaat. **VFOAT** Nashrah Al-Fasliyah Lil-Ihsaat. (Jan./March 1975)-. Periodical. French. qt. 60.00AD. Ministry Plan Amen Territ, BP 478 IBN Badis al-Mouiz, El Biar Algeria. **LC** HA2071; .M83a. **DD** 316.5. ***Continues*** *Bulletin Trimestriel de Statistiques - Direction des Statistiques.*

TR
**BULLETIN (TRINIDAD AND TOBAGO. CENTRAL STATISTICAL OFFICE).** (BULLETIN / CENTRAL STATISTICAL OFFICE.). **Added/Corp** Trinidad and Tobago. Central Statistical Office. Vol. 12, No. 8 (Jan. 1983)-. Statistical Publication. English. Central Statistical Office / Trinidad and Tobago, PO Box 98, 23 Park Street, Port of Spain Trinidad. **Tel** 62-54970, FAX 62-53802. **LC** HA867; .A35A. **DD** 317.298/3. ***Continues*** *Statistical Bulletin / Trinidad and Tobago. Central Statistical Office.*

UK/0967-6392
**BUSINESS STATISTICS LONDON.** [Bus. stat.Lond.]. (1990)-. English. ir (every 2 years). £89.00 UK; $179.00 other. Headland Business Information, 1 Henry Smiths Terrace, Headland Cleveland, TS24 0PD England. **Tel** 011 44 429 231902, FAX 011 44 429 861403.

US/0895-5913
**CA SELECTS: FOOD & FEED ANALYSIS.** **See** Chemistry-Abstracting, Bibliographies and Statistics.

FR/0339-3097
**CAHIERS DE L'ANALYSE DES DONNEES, LES.** [Cah. anal. donnees]. **VFOAT** Analyse des Donnees. Vol. 1 (1976)-. Periodical. French (summaries and/or abstracts in English). Four times a year. 520.00F France; 730.00F other. Dunod Gauthier Villars, 15 rue Gossin, 92543 Montrouge cedex France. **Tel** 011 33 1 46 56 52 66, FAX 011 33 1 46 57 40 69. **(Subscription address:** Centrale des Revues, 11 rue Gossin, 92543 Montrouge Cedex France.) **ED** J. Benzecri. **CODEN** CADODG. **[CCC].** Index available. **Bk Rev. Ad Acc. Circ:** 900.
**Desc:** Publishes results of specific studies, statistics and programs designed for data analysis.
**Ind/Abst** Br. Archaeol. Bibliogr. (?-?); Energy Res. Abstr. (April 1982-); GeoRef; Stat. Theory Method Abstr. (1978-1983, 1986-1987); Zentralbl. Math. Ihre Grenzgeb.

US/0748-4402
**CALIFORNIA ALMANAC.** **Added/Corp** Pacific Data Resources, Inc. (1985)-. English. be. $17.95. ABC Clio Press, PO Box 1911, 130 Cremona, Santa Barbara CA 93117. **Tel** (805)968-1911, (800)422-2546, FAX (805)685-9685. **LC** HA261; .C29. **DD** 317.94.

US/1065-5344
**CALIFORNIA IN PERSPECTIVE.** (CALIFORNIA IN PERSPECTIVE : A STATISTICAL VIEW OF THE "GOLDEN STATE" / KATHLEEN O'LEARY MORGAN, SCOTT MORGAN AND NEAL QUITNO, EDITORS.). [Calif. perspect.]. **Added/Corp**

Morgan Quitno Corporation. (1990)-. Statistical Publication. English. $18.00. Morgan Quitno Corporation, PO Box 1656, 512 East 9th Street, Lawrence KS 66044. **Tel** (800)457-0742, (913)841-3534, FAX (913)841-3534. **DD** 317. ***Continues*** *California in Perspective, 1065-5344.*
**Desc:** Reports on the state's data and rank for each of the categories featured in State Rankings.

US/0575-6200
**CALIFORNIA STATISTICAL ABSTRACT.** **Added/Corp** California. Legislature. Senate. Economic Development Agency of the State of California. California. Dept. of Finance. California. Legislature. Senate. Fact-Finding Committee on Commerce and Economic Development. Report. (1958)-. Statistical Publication. English. an (Oct.). Free on request. California Department of Finance, 915 L Street, 8th Floor, Finance-Economic Research, Sacramento CA 95814. **Tel** (916)322-2263. **ED** Cecily Palada (editor's telephone: (916)322-2263 ext. 29). **LC** HA261; .C3. **DD** 317.94. **Circ:** 2000.
**Desc:** A compilation of data on social, economic and physical aspects of the state of California.

CN/0319-5724
**CANADIAN JOURNAL OF STATISTICS, THE.** [Can. j. stat.]. **VFOAT** Revue Canadienne de Statistique. Vol. 1 (Dec. 1973)-. Periodical. English (French). Four times a year (Mar., June, Sept., Dec.). 99.00Can$. Canadian Journal of Statistics, 26 Stapleton Crescent D Krewski, Nepean Ontario K2H 9L3 Canada. **Tel** (613)545-9275. **ED** David Bray. **Ad Acc. Pr Rev. Circ:** 1,300. Documents available from The Genuine Article.
**Desc:** Publishes original work in the theory and application of statistics in the social physical, biological and engineering sciences.
**Ind/Abst** Biostatistica; Compumath Citation Index [Full Cov.]; Curr. Index Stat.; Math. Rev.; Oper. Res./Manag. Sci.; Qual. Control Appl. Stat.; Res. Alert [Full Cov.]; SCISEARCH; Stat. Theory Method Abstr. (1976-1977, 1979, 1983-1984, 1986-1987); Zentralbl. Math. Ihre Grenzgeb.

FR/0762-2929
**CARNETS STATISTIQUES - CAISSE NATIONALE DE L'ASSURANCE MALADIE DES TRAVAILLEURS SALARIES.** (CARNETS STATISTIQUES.). (1983)-. Monographic series. French. qt. 390.00F. Caisse Nationale Assurance Maladie Travailleurs Salaries, 75694 Paris Cedex 14 France. **UDC** 31. ***Formed by the union of*** *Statistiques - Caisse Nationale de l'Assurance Maladie des Travailleurs Salaries, 0767-4406; Le Secteur Liberal des Professions de Sante, 0767-4392; Statistiques des Regimes d'Assurance Maladie, 0761-3261* ***and*** *Demographie des Professions de Sante, 0756-7561.*

AT/1032-805X
**CATALOGUE OF PUBLICATIONS.** **Main/Corp** Australian Bureau of Statistics. (198?)-. English. an. 4.00Aus$. Australian Bureau of Statistics, PO Box 10, Belconnen Australian Capital Territory, 2616 Australia. **Tel** 011 61 6 2527911, FAX 011 61 6 2516009. **LC** Z7554.A77; A93a; HA3001. **DD** 016.3194. Index available. **Circ:** 6,000. ***Continues*** *Catalogue of Publications - Australian Bureau of Statistics.*
**Desc:** Lists publications and other standard products and services available from the Bureau.

PP
**CATALOGUE OF STATISTICAL INFORMATION ON PAPUA NEW GUINEA.** **Main/Corp** Papua New Guinea. Bureau of Statistics. Statistical Publication. English. Bureau of Statistics / Papua New Guinea, PO Box 2032, Konedobu Papua New Guinea. **LC** HA37; .P413A. **DD** 016.3195.

US
**CATFISH PROCESSING / NATIONAL AGRICULTURAL STATISTICS SERVICE, UNITED STATES DEPT. OF AGRICULTURE.** **See** Fish and Fisheries.

IT/1121-0958
**CAUSE DI MORTE (1989).** (CAUSE DI MORTE.). [Cause morte]. **Added/Corp** Istituto Centrale di Statistica (Italy) Istituto Nazionale di Statistica (Italy). (1985)-. Monographic series. Italian. ir. L3500000. Istituto Nazionale Statistica, GBP SEZ4 Via Cesare Balbo 16, 00184 Rome Italy. **Tel** 011 39 6 46735118. **LC** RA407.5.I8; C38. **DD** 614.4/245/021. ***Continues in part*** *Statistiche Sanitarie, 1121-1008.*

US
**CENSUS HIGHLIGHTS.** ***Ceased.*** **Added/Corp** University of Virginia. Center for Public Service. University of Virginia. Center for Public Service. Demographics Research Section. No. 1 (July 1991)-(1992). Periodical. English. mo. Center for Public Service, 2015 Ivy Road, Fourth Floor, University of Virginia, Charlottesville VA 22903-1795. **Tel** (804)924-0944. **LC** HA681; .C46. **DD** 304.6/09755/05.

●US/1060-1465
**CHARTS, GRAPHS & STATS INDEX.** [Charts, graphs stats index]. **VFOAT** Charts, Graphs and Stats; Charts, Graphs and Stats Index. (1992). English. an. $42.00. Highsmith Press, W 5527 Highway 106, Ft. Akinson WI 53538. **Tel** (800)558-2110, FAX (414)563-7395. **LC** AI3; .C43. **DD** 310. Index available.
**Desc:** Access to graphics and statistics in "Newsweek", "Time", "US News and World Report", "Black Enterprise", "Bulletin of Atomic Scientists", "Business Week", "FDA Consumer", "Ms" and "Scholastic Update".

JA
**CHIIKI TOKEI TEIYO.** **Added/Corp** Kokuritsu Kokkai Toshokan (Japan). Chosa Rippo Kosakyoku. (1975)-. Statistical Publication. Japanese. Kokuritsu Kokkai Toshokan, (National Diet Library), 1-10-1 Nagatacho Chiyoda-ku, Tokyo 100 Japan. **Tel** 03 3581-2331, FAX 03 3597-9104. **LC** HA1844; .C53.

●CC
**CHINA MONTHLY STATISTICS / CHINA STATISTICAL INFORMATION AND CONSULTANCY SERVICE CENTRE.** **Added/Corp** China Statistical Information & Consultancy Service Centre. International Centre for the Advancement of Science & Technology. (1992)-. Statistical Publication. English. mo. $300.00 university libraries, $353.00 other, US; $335.00 university libraries, $388.00 other, Europe; $350.00 university libraries, $403.00 other, Australia and Asia. China Statistical Information & Consultancy, 38 Yeutan Nanjie Sanlihe, Beijing 100826, People's Republic of China. **Tel** 011 86 1 8515074, FAX 011 86 1 8515078. **LC** HA4631; .C49. ***Continues*** *Chung-kuo Tung Chi Yueh Pao. English. China statistics monthly, 0897-7224.*

HK/1052-9225
**CHINA STATISTICAL YEARBOOK.** [China stat. yearb.]. **Added/Corp** China. Kuo chia tung chi chu. China Statistical Information & Consultancy Service Centre. International Centre for the Advancement of Science & Technology. University of Illinois at Chicago. China Statistics Archives. (1988)-. Statistical Publication. English. an. $130.00 (1 year), $234.00 (2 year) US; $165.00 (1 year), $269.00 (2 year) Europe; $180.00 (1 year), $284.00 (2 year) Australia and Asia. China Statistical Information & Consultancy, 38 Yeutan Nanjie Sanlihe, Beijing 100826, People's Republic of China. **Tel** 011 86 1 8515074, FAX 011 86 1 8515078. **LC** HA4631; .S83. **DD** 315.1/05. ***Continues*** *Statistical Yearbook of China, 0255-6766.*

US/0897-7224
**CHINA STATISTICS MONTHLY.** ***Ceased.*** [China stat. mon.]. **VFOAT** Chun-Kuo Tung Chi. (1988)-(1992). Periodical. English. mo. China Statistics Archives, 1033 West Van Buren Street, Chicago IL 60607. **Tel** (312)413-0007. **LC** HA4631; .C49.
**Desc:** The most comprehensive and current source in English for official statistical information on China.

CC
**CHUNG-KUO CHENG SHIH TUNG CHI NIEN CHIEN.** **Added/Corp** China. Kuo Chia Tung Chi Chu. Tsung Ho Ssu. Chung-kuo Tung Chi Hsin Hsi Tzu Hsun Fu Wu Chung Hsin. (1985)-. Chinese. an. $29.00. China Statistical Information & Consultancy, 38 Yeutan Nanjie Sanlihe, Beijing 100826, People's Republic of China. **Tel** 011 86 1 8515074, FAX 011 86 1 8515078. **LC** HA4631; .C455. **DD** 315.1/05.

XR/0578-3208
**CISLA PRO KAZDEHO.** Periodical. Czech. an. SNTL - Nakladatelstvi Technicke Literatury, Technical Literature, Spalena 51, 113 02 Prague 1 Czech Republic. **Tel** (2)297670. **LC** HA1191.

IT
**COLLANA DOCUMENTAZIONE STATISTICA E NOTIZIARIO STATISTICO REGIONALE.** (19??)-. Italian. mo. L150000.00. Tesoreria Regione Lombardia Rimb Spese Documenti, V Pirelli 12, 20124 Milan Italy. **Tel** 011 39 2 67654305.

US/1065-5352
**COLORADO IN PERSPECTIVE.** (COLORADO IN PERSPECTIVE : A STATISTICAL VIEW OF THE "CENTENNIAL STATE".). [Colo. perspect.]. **Added/Corp** Morgan Quitno Corporation. (1990)-. Statistical Publication. English. $18.00. Morgan Quitno Corporation, PO Box 1656, 512 East 9th Street, Lawrence KS 66044. **Tel** (800)457-0742, (913)841-3534, FAX (913)841-3534. **DD** 317. ***Continues*** *Colorado in Perspective, 1065-5352.*
**Desc:** Reports on the state's data and rank for each of the categories featured in State Rankings.

UK/0262-5334
**COMMERCIAL AND INDUSTRIAL FLOORSPACE STATISTICS, WALES.** ***Ceased.*** **Added/Corp** Great Britain. Welsh Office. (19??)-(19??). English. an. Economic and Statistical Services, CP2 Welsh Office, New Crown Building, Cathays Park, Cardiff CF1 3NQ Wales England. **Tel** (0222)825087. **ED** E Swires-Hennessy. **LC** HD1393.5; .C65. **DD** 333.3/8. **Bk Rev. Ad Acc. Circ:** 300.
**Desc:** Contains detailed information, including gross and percentage changes for the latest year and since 1974, presented by counties, statistical sub-divisions and districts for seven non-domestic, use classes.

TU
**COMMUNICATIONS DE LA FACULTE DES SCIENCES DE L'UNIVERSITE D'ANKARA. SERIES AB1S, MATHEMATICS AND STATISTICS.** **See** Mathematics.

US/0361-0918
**COMMUNICATIONS IN STATISTICS : SIMULATION AND COMPUTATION.** **See** Computers-Simulation.

US/0882-0287
**COMMUNICATIONS IN STATISTICS : STOCHASTIC MODELS.** [Commun. stat., stoch. models]. **Added/Corp** Operations Research Society of America. **VFOAT** Stochastic Models. Vol. 1, No. 1 (1985)-. Periodical. English. Four times a year. $385.00 US; $399.00 other; $2,195.00 US, $2,265.00 other (combination of Theory and Methods, Simulation and Computation, and Stochastic Models). Marcel Dekker Inc., 270 Madison Avenue, New York NY 10016. **Tel** (212)696-9000, (800)228-1160, FAX (212)685-4540, telex 421419. **(Subscription address:** Marcel Dekker Inc, PO Box 5017, Monticello NY 12701.**) ED** Marcel F. Neuts. **LC** QA274.A1; C65. **DD** 519.2. **[CCC]. Bk Rev. Ad Acc.** available on microfiche.
**Desc:** This journal presents contributions on mathematical methodology ranging from structural, analytic, and algorithmic to experimental approaches. Offering an interdisciplinary presentation on the uses of probability theory, this journal discusses the practical applications of stochastic models to diverse areas such as biology, computer science/telecommunications modeling, inventories and dams, reliability, storage, queueing theory, and operations research.
**Ind/Abst** Biostatistica (19??-); Curr. Index Stat.; Int. Abstr. Oper. Res. [Select. Cov.]; Math. Rev.; Stat. Theory Method Abstr. (1986-1987); Zentralbl. Math. Ihre Grenzgeb.

BE/0771-0364
**COMMUNIQUE HEBDOMADAIRE (INSTITUT NATIONAL DE STATISTIQUE (BELGIUM) : 1982).** (COMMUNIQUE HEBDOMADAIRE / INSTITUT NATIONAL DE STATISTIQUE.). **Added/Corp** Institut National de Statistique (Belgium). No. 1922 (1982)-. Periodical. French. wk (51 issues). 1400F Belgium; 1750F other. Institut National de Statistique / Belgium, rue de Louvain, 44, Centre Albert, 8e Etage, 1000 Brussels Belgium. **Tel** 011 32 2 5486211. **LC** HA1391; .C65. **DD** 314.93. ***Continues in part*** *Communique Hebdomadaire (Institut National de Statistique (Belgium) : 1963).*

BE/0771-0410
**COMMUNIQUE HEBROMADAIRE (INSTITUT NATIONAL DE STATISTIQUE (BELGIUM) : 1982).** (WEEKBERICHT / NATIONAL INSTITUUT VOOR DE STATISTIEK.). Periodical. Dutch (French). wk. 650F Belgium; 870F other. Institut National de Statistique / Belgium, rue de Louvain, 44, Centre Albert, 8e Etage, 1000 Brussels Belgium. **Tel** 011 32 2 5486211. **LC** HA1393; .C65. **Bk Rev. Ad Acc. Circ:** 500 (ctrl). ***Continues in part*** *Communique Hebdomadaire (Institut National de Statistique (Belgium) : 1963).*
**Desc:** General statistics about Belgium.

PR
**COMPENDIO DE ESTADISTICAS SOCIALES / ESTADO LIBRE ASOCIADO DE PUERTO RICO, OFICINA DEL GOBERNADOR, JUNTA DE PLANIFICACION.** 1979-. Statistical Publication. Spanish. an. Junta de Planificacion, PO Box 41119, San Juan Puerto Rico 000940. **Tel** (809)742-2840. **LC** HA901; .C65. **DD** 317.295. ctrl circ. ***Continues*** *Compendio Estadisticas Sociales.*

IT/0301-8628
**COMPENDIO STATISTICO ITALIANO.** **Added/Corp** Istituto Centrale di Statistica (Italy). (1927)-. Italian. an. L25000. Istituto Nazionale Statistica, GBP SEZ4 Via Cesare Balbo 16, 00184 Rome Italy. **Tel** 011 39 6 46735118. **LC** HA1362; .A32. **NLM** W2 GI8 I5c.

●GW
**COMPUTATIONAL STATISTICS.** **See** Mathematics.

PL
**CONCISE STATISTICAL YEARBOOK OF POLAND.** **Added/Corp** Poland. Gowny Urzad Statystyczny. (19??)-. Statistical Publication. English. **(Subscription address:** ARS Polona, PO Box 1001, 00068 Warsaw Poland.**) LC** HA1451; .C66. **DD** 314.38.

US/1065-5360
**CONNECTICUT IN PERSPECTIVE.** (CONNECTICUT IN PERSPECTIVE : A STATISTICAL

VIEW OF THE "CONSTITUTION STATE".). [Conn. perspect.]. **Added/Corp** Morgan Quitno Corporation. (1990)-. Statistical Publication. English. $18.00. Morgan Quitno Corporation, PO Box 1656, 512 East 9th Street, Lawrence KS 66044. **Tel** (800)457-0742, (913)841-3534, FAX (913)841-3534. **DD** 317. ***Continues*** *Connecticut in Perspective, 1065-5360.*
**Desc:** Reports on the state's data and rank for each of the categories featured in State Rankings.

IV
**COTE D'IVOIRE EN CHIFFRES, LA.**
**VFOAT** Annuaire Statistique de la Cote d'Ivoire. (1975)-. French. Societe Africaine d'Edition, BP 1877 20 rue Mohamed V, Dakar Senegal. **Tel** 32216. **LC** HC547.I8; C63. **DD** 316.66/8.

US/1057-8781
**COUNTY & CITY DATA BOOK (CD-ROM ED.).** (COUNTY & CITY DATA BOOK [COMPUTER FILE].). [Cty. city data book]. **Added/Corp** United States. Bureau of the Census. Data User Services Division. **VFOAT** County and City Data Book. (1988)-. Government Publication. English. $125.00 US; $156.25 other. US Department of Commerce, 14th Street & Constitution Avenue NW, Washington DC 20230. **Tel** (202)482-2000, FAX (202)482-3772. **LC** HA202; .A36c. **DD** 317. available in print (As: County & City Data Book); available on microfiche.
**Desc:** Contains demographic, economic, and governmental data from both the federal government and private agencies, presented for the purpose of multi-area comparisons or single area profiles. Current estimates and benchmark census results are included. System requirements: CD-ROM reader; CD-ROM software such as Microsoft CD-ROM extensions 2.0 or higher; IBM PC, XT, AT or compatible microcomputer or the IBM PS/2 family system; DOS 3.1 or higher; 640K RAM. (ISO 9660 format.)

●US/1059-9096
**COUNTY AND CITY EXTRA.** (COUNTY AND CITY EXTRA : ANNUAL METRO, CITY AND COUNTY DATA BOOK.). **VFOAT** Annual Metro, City, and County Data Book. (1992)-. English. an. $89.95. Bernan Associates, 4611-F Assembly Drive, Lanham MD 20706-4391. **Tel** (301)459-7666, (800)274-4447 US, (800)233-0504 CANADA, FAX (301)459-0056, telex 7108260418. **ED** Courtenay M. Slater & George E. Hall. **LC** HA203; .C68. **DD** 917.3/05. available on CD-ROM.
**Desc:** Includes data from the Census Bureau, FBI, Bureau of Economic Analysis, and National Weather Service to provide a variety of information on the states, counties, cities and metropolitan areas of the US.

US
**COUNTY AND CITY STATISTICS ANNUAL CD-ROM.** English. an. $745.00. Slater Hall Information Products, 1301 Pennsylvania Avenue Northwest, Washington DC 20004. **Tel** (202)393-2666.

US/0362-4269
**CURRENT TREND REVIEW.** English. Florida Ocean Sciences Institute, 1500 SE 3rd Court, Suite 101, Deerfield Beach FL 23441. **LC** HA214; .C86. **DD** 309.1/73/092.

SP
**DADES BALEARS / CONSELL GENERAL INTERINSULAR, CONSELLERIA D'ECONOMIA I HISENDA.** 1980-. Spanish (Spanish). an. Conselleria d'Economia I Hisenda, Institut Balear d'Economia, Apartado Postal 1.438, 07071 Palma de Mallorca Spain. **LC** HA1558.B3; D33. **DD** 314.6/75.

IO
**DAFTAR PENERBITAN PENERBITAN BIRO PUSAT STATISTIK.** **Main/Corp** Indonesia. Biro Pusat Statistik. **VFOAT** List of Publications Issued by CBS. English (Indonesian). Biro Pusat Statistik, JLN Dr Sutomo 8 Kotak, Pos 1003, Jakarta 10710 Indonesia. **Tel** 3728007, 374908. **LC** Z7165.I65; I53A; HA1811. **Bk Rev.**

DK/0107-7139
**DANMARK I TAL.** Danish. an. Danmarks Statistik, Sejrgade 11, DK-2100 Copenhagen Denmark. **Tel** 011 45 3 9173917, FAX 011 45 31 18 48 01, telex 1 62 36. **LC** HA1473; .D36.

US
**DATA BOOK.** **Added/Corp** Washington (State). Office of Financial Management. **VFOAT** Washington State ... Data Book. (1991)-. English. be. Office of Financial Management, Insurance Building AQ-44, Olympia WA 98504. **Tel** (206)456-4775. **LC** HA693; .A26. ***Continues*** *State of Washington Data Book.*

US/0147-7064
**DATA USER EDUCATION & TRAINING ACTIVITIES.** ***Title Change.*** **Main/Corp** United States. Bureau of the Census. Data User Services Division. **VAT** Data User Education and Training Activities. Government Publication. English. US Department of Commerce / Bureau of the Census, Data User Services Division, Customer Services, Washington DC 20233-0800. **Tel** (301)763-4100. **LC** HA35; .U53A. **DD** 001.4/33. ***Continued by*** *Catalog of Training Activities.*

XV
**DELAVCI V ZDRUZENEM DELU / ZAVOD SR SLOVENIJE ZA STATISTIKO.** Slovenian. Zavod Sr Slovenije za Statistiko, Vozarski Pot 12, Ljubljana Slovenia. **LC** HD5811.6.S58; D45.

US/1065-5379
**DELAWARE IN PERSPECTIVE.** (DELAWARE IN PERSPECTIVE : A STATISTICAL VIEW OF THE "FIRST STATE".). [Del. perspect.]. **Added/Corp** Morgan Quitno Corporation. (1990)-. Statistical Publication. English. $18.00. Morgan Quitno Corporation, PO Box 1656, 512 East 9th Street, Lawrence KS 66044. **Tel** (800)457-0742, (913)841-3534, FAX (913)841-3534. **DD** 317. ***Continues*** *Delaware in Perspective, 1065-5379.*
**Desc:** Reports on the state's data and rank for each of the categories featured in State Rankings.

NE
**DEMOGRAFISCHE GEGEVENS.**
**Main/Corp** Rotterdam. Gemeentelijk Bureau voor Onderzoek en Statistiek. Dutch. an. Gemeentelijk bur voor Onder Zoek en Stat, Postbus 70018, 3000 KX Rotterdam Netherlands. **LC** HA1388.R6; R65A.

CN/0840-8491
**DEMOGRAPHIC AND INCOME STATISTICS FOR POSTAL AREAS, CANADA.** ***Ceased.*** (DEMOGRAPHIC AND INCOME STATISTICS FOR POSTAL AREAS, CANADA / STATISTICS CANADA, SMALL AREA AND ADMINISTRATIVE DATA DIVISION). [Demogr. income stat. post. areas Can.]. **Added/Corp** Statistics Canada. Small Area and Administrative Data Division. **VFOAT** Statistiques Demographiques et Sur le Revenu par Regions Postales, Canada. (1987)-(19??). English (French). an. Statistics Canada, Publications Sales & Services, Main Building Room 1710, Ottawa Ontario K1A 0T6 Canada. **Tel** (613)951-5078, (800)267-6677, FAX (613)951-1584, telex 053-3585. **DD** 339.2/2/0971021. ***Continues*** *Urban FSA and Rural Postal Code Summary Data, Canada., 0833-529X.*
**Desc:** This publication brings together various demographic and socio-economic characteristics of tax filers for more than 7000 postal areas across Canada.

US/8755-2744
**DETAILED MORTALITY STATISTICS, SOUTH CAROLINA.** [Detail. mortal. stat., S.C.]. **VFOAT** Detailed Mortality Statistics, S.C. 1979-. English. an. Office of Vital Records and Public Health Statistics, South Carolina Department of Health and Environmental Control, 2600 Bull Street, Columbia SC 29201. **Tel** (803)734-4860. **LC** RA407.4.S57. **DD** 614.4/2757/021. **NLM** W2; AS6 D35d. **Circ:** 200 (ctrl).
**Desc:** Vital statistics for S.C. (mortality data).

DK/0417-0164
**DETAILPRISER.** **Main/Corp** Denmark. Danmarks Statistik. Periodical. Dutch. qt. kr48.36, (add kr35.00 for postage); kr14.75 (per copy). Danmarks Statistik, Sejrgade 11, DK-2100 Copenhagen Denmark. **Tel** 011 45 3 9173917, FAX 011 45 31 18 48 01, telex 1 62 36. **Circ:** 775. ***Continues*** *Detailpriser.*
**Desc:** Average prices for 41 local municipalities collected for 81 items of the Danish consumer price indices.

US/1066-9477
**DEVELOPMENTAL POLICY STUDIES.** ***Ceased.*** (DEVELOPMENTAL POLICY STUDIES : THE NEWSLETTER-JOURNAL OF THE REGIONAL PSO'S.). [Dev. policy stud.]. **Added/Corp** Policy Studies Organization. Vol. 1, Issue 1 (Sept. 1991)-(1992). Newsletter. English. qt. Policy Studies Organization, 361 Lincoln Hall, University of Illinois, Urbana IL 61801. **Tel** (217)359-8541. **DD** 338.

ET
**DIRECTORY OF AFRICAN STATISTICIANS / ECONOMIC COMMISSION FOR AFRICA.** **Added/Corp** United Nations. Economic Commission for Africa. **VFOAT** Repertoire des Statisticiens Africains. (19??)-. Directory. English (French). be. Free. United Nations Economic Commission for Africa, PO Box 3001, Addis Ababa Ethiopia. **Tel** (212)754-8302, telex 21029 VNECA ET. **LC** HA37; .A318. **DD** 310/.25/6. **Circ:** 1,800. ***Continues*** *African Directory of Statisticians.*
**Desc:** Directory of african statisticians.

US/0740-7181
**DIRECTORY OF MEMBERS - AMERICAN STATISTICAL ASSOCIATION; BIOMETRIC SOCIETY. EASTERN NORTH AMERICAN REGION. BIOMETRIC SOCIETY. WESTERN NORTH AMERICAN REGION.** (DIRECTORY OF MEMBERS.). [Dir. memb. - Am. Stat. Assoc., Biom. Soc., East North Am. Reg., Biom. Soc., West. North Am. Reg.]. **Main/Corp** American Statistical Association. **Added/Corp** Biometric Society. Eastern North American Region. Biometric Society. Western North American Region. Statistical Society of Canada. Institute of Mathematical Statistics. **VFOAT** Directory of Statisticians. (1981)-. Directory. English. ir (every three years). $125.00. American Statistical Association, 1429 Duke Street, Alexandria VA 22314. **Tel** (703)684-1221, (202)393-3253, FAX (703)684-2037 (orders). **LC** HA1; .D52. **DD** 310/.25/73. ***Continues*** *Directory of Statisticians, 0278-405X.*
**Desc:** Combined listing of the 23,000 members of the ASA, the Institute of Mathematical Statistics, the Eastern and Western North American Regions of the Biometric Society, the Statistical Society of Canada and the Bernoulli Society.

FR
**DIRECTORY OF MEMBERS - INTERNATIONAL ASSOCIATION OF SURVEY STATISTICIANS.** ***Title Change.*** **Main/Corp** International Association of Survey Statisticians. **Added/Corp** International Association of Survey Statisticians. Liste des Membres - Association Internationale des Statisticiens d'Enquetes. **VFOAT** Liste des Membres - Association Internationale des Statisticiens d'Enquetes. (19??)-(199?). Directory. Multiple languages (English and French). International Association of Survey Statisticians, 18 Boulevard A Pinard, Paris 75675 France. **LC** HA1; .I544. **DD** 310/.6/21. ***Continued by*** *International Association of Survey Statisticians. Membership Directory.*

●CN/1193-7580
**DIRECTORY OF STATISTICS IN CANADA.** (DIRECTORY OF STATISTICS IN CANADA / REPERTOIRE DES STATISTIQUES DU CANADA.). [Dir. stat. Can.]. **VFOAT** Repertoire des Statistiques du Canada; DSC; RSC. (1992)-. Directory. English (summaries and/or abstracts in French). an. Micromedia Limited, 20 Victoria Street, Toronto Ontario M5C 2N8 Canada. **Tel** (416)362-5211, (800)387-2689, FAX (416)362-6161, telex 06524668. **DD** 016.3171. ***Continues*** *Canadian Statistics Index, 0832-655X.*

II/0523-3456
**DISTRICT STATISTICAL HANDBOOK - (INDIA).** **Main/Corp** Bihar, India (State). District Statistical Office, Monghyr. Statistical Publication. English. District Statistical Office, Patna India.

VE/0577-2567
**DOCUMENTOS - CENTRO DE INFORMACION Y DOCUMENTACION PARA AMERICA LATINA.** **Main/Corp** Centro de Informacion y Documentacion Para America Latina. 1-1967-). Periodical. Spanish. Quinta Campoamor, Dir de Biblio Infor Docu y Pub, Caracas Venezuela.

FR/0395-8280
**DONNEES STATISTIQUES DU LIMOUSIN.** [Donnees stat. Limousin]. **Added/Corp** Institut National de la Statistique et des Etudes Economiques (France). (July 1971)-. Periodical. French. Four times a year. Price varies. CNGP INSEE - Institut National de la Statistique et des Estudes Economiques, BP 2718, 1 rue V Auriol, F 80027 Amiens Cedex 1 France. **Tel** 011 33 22 927322. **LC** HA1228.L5; A32. **Bk Rev.** ***Supersedes*** *Bulletin de Statistique: Limousin (Correze, Creuse, Haute-Vienne), 0150-8342.*
**Desc:** Analyses of subjects of an economic and social nature based on the review of a great number of writings.

CN/0715-1055
**DONNEES SUR LA POPULATION ACTIVE : QUEBEC, ONTARIO ET CANADA.** [Donnees popul. act.: Que. Ont. Can.]. Periodical. French. mo (also quarterly). 99.46Can$ (monthly), 43.82Can$ (quarterly). Bureau of Statistics / Quebec, Publications, 117 rue Saint Andre, Quebec Quebec G1K 3Y3 Canada. **Tel** (418)691-2401, (800)463-4090. **DD** 331.11/0971. **Circ:** 125 (ctrl).
**Desc:** Statistics on manpower.

UK
**ECONOMIST BOOK OF VITAL WORLD STATISTICS, THE.** English. £20.99 UK; £23.50 other. Economist, Diary Department, 25 St James Street, London SW1A 1HG England. **Tel** (44)4023 81555, FAX (44)4023 81211, telex 927809. ***Continues*** *World in Figures.*
**Desc:** A unique source of facts about the modern world: essential reading for decision-makers; fascinating and illuminating browsing for everyone; a companion volume to The Economist Atlas.

FI/0785-4218
**ENNAKKOTIETOJA TEOLLISUUDESTA / TILASTOKESKUS.** **Added/Corp** Finland. Tilastokeskus. **VFOAT** Forhandsuppgifter Over Industrin. (1988)-. Finnish (Swedish; summaries and/or abstracts in English). an. Fmk169.00. Tilastokeskus, PL 504, Annankatu 44, 00101 Helsinki Finland. **Tel** 358-0-17341, FAX 358-0-17342474, telex 1002111 TILASTO SF. **ED** Mr. Heikki Pihlaja. **LC** HC337.F5; F4245a. ***Continues*** *Finland. Tilastokeskus. Ennakkotietoja Suomen Teollisuudesta.*

●UK/1352-8505
**ENVIRONMENTAL AND ECOLOGICAL STATISTICS.** See Environmental Issues-Ecology.

FI/0357-6825
**ESPOON KAUPUNGIN TILASTOLLINEN VUOSIKIRJA.** **VFOAT** Statistisk Arsbok for Esbo Stad; Espoo/Esbo Tilastollinen Vuosikirja. Began with Vol. for 1970. Finnish (Swedish). an. Fmk55.00 Finland. Espoo City Statistical Bureau, Espoonkatu 3, SF-02770 Espoo Finland. **LC** HA1450.5.Z9; E865. **Circ:** 600.

US/0014-1135
**ESTADISTICA.** [Estadic.]. **Added/Corp** Inter American Statistical Institute. Vol. 1 (March 1943)-. Statistical Publication. Multiple languages (English and Spanish). sa. $50.00 (institutions), $30.00 (individuals). Inter-American Statistical Institute, Apartado Postal 5139, Panama 5 Panama. **Tel** 011 507 641349, 011 507 6413367, FAX 011 507 644601. **ED** Federico O'Reilly. **LC** HA1; .E8. **DD** 310.627. **NLM** HA 1 E79. **CODEN** ESTDA4. cum. index. **Ad Acc. Circ:** 1,500. available on microfilm and microfiche from University Microfilms International (UMI).
**Ind/Abst** Math. Rev.; Popul. Index (?-?).

SP
**ESTADISTICA DEL SUICIDIO EN ESPANA.** **Main/Corp** Spain. Instituto Nacional de Estadistica. (19??)-. Statistical Publication. Spanish. ir. **LC** HB1323.S8; S5. ***Continues*** *Estadistica del Suicidio en Espana.*

SP/0014-1151
**ESTADISTICA ESPANOLA.** [Estad. esp.]. **Added/Corp** Instituto Nacional de Estadistica (Spain). No. 1 (Oct./Dec. 1958)-. Statistical Publication. Spanish. Three times a year. 1400ptas Spain; $25.00 US. Instituto Nacional Estadistico Spain, Paseo de la Castellana 183, 28046 Madrid Spain. **Tel** 011 34 1 583 9100. **ED** Daniel Pena. **LC** HA1; .E82. **NLM** W2 GS6 I46EA. **CODEN** ESTEA7. Index available. cum. index. **Bk Rev. Pr Rev. Circ:** 1,000 (ctrl).
**Desc:** Publishes research articles in areas of methodological and applied statistics.
**Ind/Abst** Curr. Index Stat.; Math. Rev.; Stat. Theory Method Abstr. (1966-1969, 1974-1976, 1979-1984, 1986-1987).

PN
**ESTADISTICA PANAMENA; BOLETIN SEMANAL.** **Main/Corp** Panama. Direccion de Estadistica y Censo. (1???)-. Statistical Publication. Spanish. ir. Free. Direccion de Estadistica y Censo, Contraloria General, Apartado 5213, Panama 5 Panama. **Tel** 011 507 640777 Ext. 269 or 203, . **ED** Amilcar Villarreal L. **Circ:** 850 (ctrl).
**Desc:** Provides the diffusion of the activities related with the services producing statistics. Publishes specific themes and analytic studies.

UY
**ESTADISTICAS AGROPECUARIAS.** Statistical Publication. Spanish. Comcorde Secretaria Tecnica, Avda Rondeau 1908, Montevideo Uruguay.

SP/0214-3240
**ESTADISTICO DE ENCUESTAS.** [Estad. encuestas]. **Added/Corp** Ociacion Internacional de Estadisticos de Encuestas. **VFOAT** Statisticien d'Enquetes; Survey Statistician. (1982)-. Periodical. Spanish. sa. 700ptas Spain; 3462ptas other. Inst Natl Estadistica Dep Publ, Paseo Castellano 183, Madrid 28046 Spain. **Tel** 011 34 1 58395080, FAX 011 34 1 2792713, telex 43247 ESTD E. **UDC** 31. Index available. **Circ:** 650.
**Desc:** The Spanish version of statistics survey.

BL
**ESTADO DA PARAIBA, ANUARIO ESTATISTICO.** **Added/Corp** Fundacao Instituto de Planejamento da Paraiba. **VFOAT** Anuario Estatistico P.B.; Anuario Estatistico PB. (19??)-. Portuguese. an. Fundacao Instituto de Planejamento da Paraiba, rua 1O de Maio 417, Joao Pressoa PB Brazil. **Tel** (083)221-4430. **LC** HA988.P33; E78. **DD** 318.1/33. **Bk Rev. Ad Acc. Circ:** 500.
**Desc:** Statistical yearbook of the state of Paraiba, cost of living index, social indicators of Paraiba and others.

SP
**ESTUDIOS FRANCISCANOS.** (19??)-. Periodical. Spanish. Three times a year. 3000ptas Spain and Portugal; 3500ptas other. Convento de Capuchinos Admin, Diagonal 450, 08006 Barcelona 6 Spain. **Tel** 011 34 3 2175812. **Bk Rev.** ***Continues*** *Revista de Estudios Franciscanos.*
**Desc:** Studies on the Church and the Franciscan Order with the Iberian peninsula viewed as their sphere of influence.
**Ind/Abst** Am. Hist. Life (1955-1968); Bibliogr. Mission.; Indice Hist. Esp. (1955-1968); New Testam. Abstr.

BE/0522-7585
**ETUDES STATISTIQUES (BRUSSELS, BELGIUM).** (ETUDES STATISTIQUES.). **Added/Corp** Institut National de Statistique (Belgium). No. 15 (19??)-. Periodical. French. ir. 240F Belgium; 300F other. Institut National de Statistique / Belgium, rue de Louvain, 44, Centre Albert, 8e Etage, 1000 Brussels Belgium. **Tel** 011 32 2 5486211. **Bk Rev. Ad Acc. Circ:** 1,000 (ctrl). ***Continues*** *Etudes Statistiques et Econometriques.*
**Desc:** General statistical studies.

UK
**EUROPEAN COMMUNITY : FACTS AND FIGURES, THE.** English. **LC** HA1107.5; .A14. **DD** 309.1/4/055.

UK/0953-0258
**EUROPEAN DIRECTORY OF NON-OFFICIAL STATISTICAL SOURCES.** **Added/Corp** Euromonitor Publications Limited. **VFOAT** Directory of Non-Official Statistical Sources. 1st Ed. (1988)-. Statistical Publication. English. an. $335.00. Euromonitor Publications Ltd., 87-88 Turnmill Street, London EC1M 5QU England. **Tel** 011 44 71 2518024, FAX 011 44 71 6083149, telex 21120. **(Subscription address:** US: Gale Research Co., 835 Penobscot Building, Detroit, MI 48226**) ED** David Mort. **LC** HA37; .E914. **DD** 310/.6/04.
**Desc:** Details on the key non-official statistical sources in Western Europe. Provides over 2,000 published reports from a variety of sources including trade associations, banks, professional bodies, market researchers, consultants, stockbrokers, academic institutions and private companies.

LU
**EUROSTAT CATALOGUE : PUBLICATIONS AND ELECTRONIC SERVICES.** **Main/Corp** Statistical Office of the European Communities. **Added/Corp** Office for Official Publications of the European Communities. (198?)-. Catalog. English (French and German). an. Eurostat Information Office, L-2920 Luxembourg. **Tel** (352)43013-45 67, FAX (352)43 64 04. ***Continues*** *Statistical Office of the European Communities. Catalogue of Eurostat Publications.*
**Desc:** Comprises monographs, collections, CD-ROMs and computer output products.

US
**FACT BOOK : TABLES AND CHARTS ON THE NEW YORK METROPOLITAN REGION.** **Main/Corp** New York City Council on Economic Education. 1970-. English. be. $19.95. New York City Council on Economic Education, 17 Lexington Avenue, Box 405 Baruch College, New York NY 10010. **Tel** (212)725-4431. **ED** Albert Alexander. **Bk Rev. Circ:** 1,000 (ctrl).
**Desc:** A concise one-volume unique collection of selected economic and related statistics about New York City and the surrounding region.

●NZ
**FACTS NEW ZEALAND.** **Added/Corp** New Zealand. Dept. of Statistics. (1992)-. English. ***Continues*** *New Zealand Pocket Digest of Statistics.*

RE
**FAITS ET CHIFFRES REUNIONNAIS.** French. 25.00F. Institut de Developpement Regional, 18 rue Milius, 97400 St-Denis Reunion. **LC** HA2307; .A17.

SW
**FARSKA FAKTA OCH SORTERADE SIFFRUR.** **Main/Corp** Sweden. Statistiska Centralbyran. **VFOAT** Publikationer Fran Statistiska Centralbyran. (19??)-. Swedish. an. SCB Statistiska Centralbyran, 11581 Stockholm Sweden. **LC** Z7554.S8; S93a; HA1523. **DD** 016.31485.
**Desc:** General catalog of publications and databases available each year from the Swedish Central Statistics Office.

US
**FCCAA STATISTICAL REPORTING SERVICE / MEN'S BASEBALL.** See Recreation, Leisure-Sports.

US
**FLORIDA ACCIDENTAL DEATH STATISTICS.** **Main/Corp** Florida. Dept. of Health and Rehabilitative Services. English. $2.64. Florida Department of Health and Rehabilitation Services, 1317 Winewood Boulevard, Tallahassee FL 32399. **Tel** (904)359-6960. **LC** HB1355.F6; F55A. **DD** 312/.27/09759.

US/1065-5387
**FLORIDA IN PERSPECTIVE.** (FLORIDA IN PERSPECTIVE : A STATISTICAL VIEW OF THE "SUNSHINE STATE".). [Fla. perspect.]. **Added/Corp** Morgan Quitno Corporation. (1990)-. Statistical Publication. English. $18.00. Morgan Quitno Corporation, PO Box 1656, 512 East 9th Street, Lawrence KS 66044. **Tel** (800)457-0742, (913)841-3534, FAX (913)841-3534. **DD** 317. ***Continues*** *Florida in Perspective, 1065-5387.*
**Desc:** Reports on the state's data and rank for each of the categories featured in State Rankings.

US/0071-6022
**FLORIDA STATISTICAL ABSTRACT.** **Added/Corp** University of Florida. Bureau of Economic and Business Research. 1st Ed. (1967)-. Statistical Publication. English. an (Dec.). University of Florida Press, 15 Northwest 15th Street, Gainesville FL 32611. **Tel** (904)392-5717, (800)226-3822. **ED** Anne Shoemyen. **LC** HA311; .F55. **DD** 317.59. **Circ:** 3,000.
**Desc:** A 700 page compilation of the latest data available from many sources about Florida, its counties and metropolitan areas in twenty-five subject categories.
**Ind/Abst** Stat. Ref. Index.

SZ
**FORUM STATISTICUM / VERBAND SCHWEIZERISCHER STATISTISCHER AMTER.** Periodical. French (German and Italian). Eidgenossisches Statistisches Amt, Hallwylstrasse 15, CH-3003 Bern Switzerland. **LC** HA37; .S914. **DD** 314.94.

FR
**FRANCHE-COMTE EN QUELQUES CHIFFRES, LA.** French. an. CNGP INSEE - Institut National de la Statistique et des Estudes Economiques, BP 2718, 1 rue V Auriol, F 80027 Amiens Cedex 1 France. **Tel** 011 33 22 927322. **LC** HA1228.F7; F73. **DD** 314.4/45.

GW
**GABUN : WIRTSCHAFTLICHE ENTWICKLUNG.** **Main/Corp** Bundesstelle fur Aussenhandelsinformation (Germany). 1968/73-. German. Bundesstelle fuer Aussenhandelsinformation, Agrippastr 87 93, D 50676 Cologne Germany. **Tel** 011 49 221 2057316, FAX 011 49 221 2057212. **LC** HA2090.

US/1051-2616
**GALLUP POLL MONTHLY, THE.** (GALLUP POLL MONTHLY.). [Gallup poll mon.]. No. 291 (Dec. 1989)-. Periodical. English. mo (12 issues). $65.00 US $95.00 ohter (institutions); $110.00 other. Gallup Poll, PO Box 628, Princeton NJ 08542. **Tel** (609)924-9600. **LC** HM261.A1; G34. **DD** 303. Documents available from UMI Article Clearinghouse. ***Continues*** *Gallup Report (Princeton, N.J. : 1981), 0731-6143.*
**Ind/Abst** Acad. Ind. [Computer File] (1992-); Expand. Acad. Index (1992-); Newsp. Period. Abstr. (1989-); PAIS Int. Print; Stat. Ref. Index.

US/0736-9514
**GALLUP REPORT INTERNATIONAL.** [Gallup rep. int.]. **Added/Corp** Gallup Organization. (1982)-. Periodical. English. bm. $95.00. Gallup Poll, PO Box 628, Princeton NJ 08542. **Tel** (609)924-9600.

GW
**GEMEINDEDATEN.** **Main/Corp** Bayerisches Statistisches Landesamt. German. sa. DM22.00. Bayerisches Statistisches, Neuhauserstr 511, W-8000 Munchen 2 Germany. **Tel** 089/2119-205. **LC** HA1261; .S7A. **DD** 314.3/3. Index available. ctrl circ.

GW
**GEMEINDEN NORDRHEIN-WESTFALEN, DIE.** **Main/Corp** Landesamt fur Datenverarbeitung und Statistik Nordrhein-Westfalen. (19??)-. German. an. DM13.00. Landesamt fuer Datenverarbeitung und Statistik Nordrhein-Westfalen, Postfach 101105, 40002 Duesseldorf Germany. **Tel** (0211)944901, FAX (0211)442006, telex 8586654 LDST D. **LC** HA1320.N6; N67a. **Circ:** 1,200.
**Desc:** Selected statistical returns on the 396 communities of Nordrhein-Westfalen.

US/1044-0976
**GEORGIA COUNTY GUIDE, THE.** [Ga. cty. guide]. **Added/Corp** University of Georgia. Rural Development Center. University of Georgia. Cooperative Extension Service. (1981)-. English. an (June). $15.00. Georgia County Guide, D Bachtel, 325 Hoke Smith Annex, University of Georgia, Athens GA 30602. **Tel** (404)542-8938, FAX (404)542-8845. **(Subscription address:** Georgia Country Guide, 203 Conner Hall AG, Business University of Georgia, Athens GA 30602.**) ED** Doug Bachtel and Sue Boatright. **LC** HA321; .G416. **DD** 917.58/05.
**Desc:** Contains data tables and maps covering a wide range of topics for all 159 of Georgia's counties.

US/1065-5395
**GEORGIA IN PERSPECTIVE.** (GEORGIA IN PERSPECTIVE : A STATISTICAL VIEW OF THE "PEACH STATE".). [Ga. perspect.]. **Added/Corp** Morgan Quitno Corporation. (1990)-. Statistical Publication. English. $18.00. Morgan Quitno Corporation, PO Box 1656, 512 East 9th Street, Lawrence KS 66044. **Tel** (800)457-0742, (913)841-3534, FAX (913)841-3534. **LC** HA321; .G47. **DD** 317. ***Continues*** *Georgia in Perspective, 1065-5395.*
**Desc:** Reports on the state's data and rank for each of the categories featured in State Rankings.

US
**GEORGIA MORTALITY VITAL STATISTICS REPORT.** **Added/Corp** Georgia. Vital Records and Health Statistics Unit. Georgia Center for Health Statistics. **VFOAT** Vital Statistics Data of the

State of Georgia; Mortality. (1988)-. English. ir. $18.05 (per copy). Vital Records & Health Statistics, 878 Peachtree Street Northeast, Suite 200, Atlanta GA 30309. **NLM** W2; AG4 V8g. ***Separated from*** *Georgia Vital Statistics Report.*

US/0085-1043
**GEORGIA STATISTICAL ABSTRACT.** **Added/Corp** University of Georgia. Bureau of Business and Economic Research. University of Georgia. Graduate School of Business Administration. Division of Research. University of Georgia. College of Business Administration. Division of Research. (1970)-. Statistical Publication. English. be. $25.00. University of Georgia Economic Growth Center, Terry College of Business, Athens GA 30602. **Tel** (706)542-4085, FAX (706)542-3835. **ED** Lorena M. Akioka, (706)542-3856. **LC** HA321; .G4. **DD** 317.58. Index available. **Circ:** 800 (ctrl). ***Continues*** *Georgia Statistical Abstract.*
**Desc:** State statistics pertaining to population, income, wealth, production, manufacturing, agriculture, health, education, etc. Comparisons by county and with other southeastern states and US.

US
**GEORGIA VITAL AND MORBIDITY STATISTICS.** **Main/Corp** Georgia. Dept. of Human Resources. English. an. 47 Trinity Avenue SW, Atlanta GA 30334. **LC** HA321; .A3. **DD** 312/.0975. ***Continues*** *Georgia Vital and Morbidity Statistics.*

UK
**GLIM NEWSLETTER, THE.** **Added/Corp** Royal Statistical Society (Great Britain). Working Party on Statistical Computing. Numerical Algorithms Group Limited. (19??)-. Newsletter. English. Twice a year. £16.00. Numerical Algorithms Group Ltd., Wilkinson House Jordan Hill Road, Oxford 0X2 8DR England. **Tel** 011 44 865 511245, FAX 011 44 865 310139, telex 83354 NAGUKG. **ED** B. Francis and A.J. Stalenski. **Bk Rev. Ad Acc. Circ:** 400 (ctrl).
**Desc:** Newsletter for users of Generalised Linear Interactive Modelling (GLIM).

PP
**GROSS DOMESTIC PRODUCT AND EXPENDITURE.** English. an. k200 New Guinea; k3.00 other. National Statistical Office, PO Wards Strip NCO, Papua New Guinea. **Tel** 011 675 27182 271172, FAX 011 657 255057, telex FINANCE NE 22312. **(Subscription address:** Publication Officer, National Statistical Office, P.O. Wards Strip, N.C.B. Papua New Guinea**) ED** Nick Suvulo. **Ad Acc. Circ:** 150.
**Desc:** Provides an analysis of all economic activity in New Guinea. Includes tables, a six year time series of expenditure on cost structure, etc.

FR/0762-0-95
**GUIDE DES RATIOS DES REGIONS / MINISTERE DE L'INTERIEUR, LE SECRETAIRE D'ETAT AUPRES DU MINISTRE DE L'INTERIEUR CHARGE DES COLLECTIVITES TERRITORIALES, DIRECTION GENERALE DES COLLECTIVITES LOCALES, MISSION D'ETUDES ET DE STATISTIQUES.** **Added/Corp** France. Direction Generale des Collectivites Locales. Mission d'Etudes et de Statistiques. (1986)-. French. Documentation Francaise, 29 Quai Voltaire, 75344 Paris Cedex 7 France. **Tel** 011 33 1 40157000, FAX 011 33 1 40157230, telex 204 826 DOCFRAN.

UK
**GUIDE TO OFFICIAL STATISTICS.** **Main/Corp** Great Britain. Central Statistical Office. (1976)-. English. ir. Her Majesty's Stationery Office, 51 Nine Elms Lane, London SW8 5DR England. **Tel** 011 44 71 873 8459, 011 44 71 873 8499, FAX 011 44 71 873 8499, 011 44 71 873 8456, telex 297138. **(Subscription address:** UNIPUB, 4611 F Assembly Drive, Lanham MD 20706.**) LC** HA37; .G5816. **DD** 016.3141.

II
**HANDBOOK OF BASIC STATISTICS OF MAHARASHTRA STATE.** **Main/Corp** Maharashtra, India (State). Directorate of Economics and Statistics. (1974)-. English. an. Rs3.90. Directory of Economics and Statistics / Bombay India, DD Building, Old Custom House, Bombay 400023 India. **ED** S.M. Vidwans. **LC** HA1728.M3; A3. **DD** 315.4/792. ***Continues*** *Maharashtra, India (State). Bureau of Economics and Statistics. Handbook of Basic Statistics.*

NE/0169-7161
**HANDBOOK OF STATISTICS.** [Handb. stat.]. Vol. 1-. Monographic series. English. Price varies per volume. Elsevier Science Publishers BV, PO Box 211, 1000 AE Amsterdam Netherlands. **Tel** 011 31 20 5803642, FAX 011 31 20 5862696, telex 15682. Documents available from Ask*IEEE.
**Ind/Abst** INSPEC; Math. Rev.; Zentralbl. Math. Ihre Grenzgeb.

US
**HAWAII FACTS AND FIGURES.** ***Ceased.*** (1946/47)-Ceased ?. English. an. Chamber of Commerce of Hawaii, 735 Bishop Street, Suite 220, Honolulu HI 96813. **Tel** (808)522-8813. **ED** C L Hodge. ***Continues*** *General Information about Honolulu, Hawaii, U.S.A. and the Territory, Combined with Business Statistics.*

US/1065-5409
**HAWAII IN PERSPECTIVE.** (HAWAII IN PERSPECTIVE : A STATISTICAL VIEW OF THE "ALOHA STATE".). [Hawaii perspect.]. **Added/Corp** Morgan Quitno Corporation. (1990)-. Statistical Publication. English. $18.00. Morgan Quitno Corporation, PO Box 1656, 512 East 9th Street, Lawrence KS 66044. **Tel** (800)457-0742, (913)841-3534, FAX (913)841-3534. **DD** 317. ***Continues*** *Hawaii in Perspective, 1065-5409.*
**Desc:** Reports on the state's data and rank for each of the categories featured in State Rankings.

FI/0357-3370
**HELSINGIN VAESTO.** **VFOAT** Helsingfors Befolkning. Finnish. an. Toolontorinkatu 2 B, 00260 Helsinki 26 Finland. **Tel** FAX 358 0 4029454. **LC** HA1450.5.Z9; H443.

GR
**HENA.** **VFOAT** Ena. (1983)-. Periodical. Greek, Modern (Greek, Modern). wk. Grammi SA, 15 Voukourestiou St, 106 71 Athens Greece. **LC** AP85; .H37.

CN/0712-5828
**HIGHLIGHTS (LONDON, ONT.).** (HIGHLIGHTS / POPULATION STUDIES CENTRE, DEPARTMENT OF SOCIOLOGY ; CENTRE FOR CANADIAN POPULATION STUDIES.). [Highlights]. **Added/Corp** Centre for Canadian Population Studies. University of Western Ontario. Population Studies Centre. **VFOAT** PSC-CCPS Newsletter; PSC-CCPS Highlights. **VAT** Population Studies Centre - Centre for Canadian Population Studies Highlights. Vol. 1, No. 1 (Sept. 1982)-. Periodical. English. Twice a year (Apr. & Sept.). Free. Population Studies Centre, University of Western Ontario, Social Science Building, London ONT N6A 5C2 Canada. **Tel** (519)661-3819, FAX (519)661-3200. **ED** Suzanne Shiel. **DD** 304.6/07/1171326. **Circ:** 200.
**Desc:** Announcements of activities of the centre and its researchers and students. Also includes a list of recent publications.

US
**HISPANIC POPULATION IN THE UNITED STATES. ADVANCE REPORT, THE.** Government Publication. English. an. US Department of Commerce, 14th Street & Constitution Avenue NW, Washington DC 20230. **Tel** (202)482-2000, FAX (202)482-3772. ***Continues*** *Persons of Spanish Origin in the United States ... Advance Report.*

HU
**HUNGARIAN STATISTICAL YEARBOOK / HUNGARIAN CENTRAL STATISTICAL OFFICE.** **Added/Corp** Hungary. Koezponti Statisztikai Hivatal. (1990)-. Statistical Publication. English. Four times a year. $29.00. Hungarian Central Statistical Office, Keleti Karoly Utca, PO Box 51, H-1525 Budapest Hungary. **Tel** 011 36 1 2024011. **(Subscription address:** Kultura, PO Box 149, H 1389 Budapest 62 Hungary.**) LC** HA1201; .S83. **DD** 314.39/05. ***Continues*** *Statisztikai Evkoenyv. English & Russian. Statistical Yearbook, 0237-1901.*

HU/0230-5755
**HUNGARY, STATISTICAL DATA / CENTRAL STATISTICAL OFFICE OF HUNGARY.** Statistical Publication. English (Hungarian, German and Russian). an. 42.00ft. Statistical Publishing House, PO Box 99, H-1300 Budapest Hungary. **Tel** 803-311, telex 22-6699-SKU-H. **(Subscription address:** KULTURA, PO Box 149, H-1389 Budapest Hungary**) LC** HA1201; .H86. **DD** 314.39. **Circ:** 15,000.
**Desc:** This popular small-format book gives a comprehensive picture on Hungary's economic and social development by way of thousands of statistical data; in Hungarian, English, German and Russian.

II/0970-0102
**IAPQR TRANSACTIONS.** (IAPQR TRANSACTIONS : JOURNAL OF THE INDIAN ASSOCIATION FOR PRODUCTIVITY, QUALITY & RELIABILITY.). [IAPQR trans.]. **Added/Corp** Indian Association for Productivity, Quality & Reliability. (1976)-. Periodical. English. sa. $15.00. Indian Association for Productivity, Quality, and Reliability, Calcutta, India. **(Subscription address:** Prints India, 11 Darya Ganj, New Delhi, 110002 India, (Phone: 011 91 11 3268645)**) UDC** 658.5.
**Ind/Abst** Math. Rev.; Zentralbl. Math. Ihre Grenzgeb.

US/1065-5417
**IDAHO IN PERSPECTIVE.** (IDAHO IN PERSPECTIVE : A STATISTICAL VIEW OF THE "GEM STATE".). [Ida. perspect.]. **Added/Corp** Morgan Quitno Corporation. (1990)-. Statistical Publication. English. $18.00. Morgan Quitno Corporation, PO Box 1656, 512 East 9th Street, Lawrence KS 66044. **Tel** (800)457-0742, (913)841-3534, FAX (913)841-3534. **DD** 317. ***Continues*** *Idaho in Perspective, 1065-5417.*
**Desc:** Reports on the state's data and rank for each of the categories featured in State Rankings.

US/1065-5425
**ILLINOIS IN PERSPECTIVE.** (ILLINOIS IN PERSPECTIVE : A STATISTICAL VIEW OF THE "LAND OF LINCOLN STATE".). [Ill. perspect.]. **Added/Corp** Morgan Quitno Corporation. (1990)-. Statistical Publication. English. $18.00. Morgan Quitno Corporation, PO Box 1656, 512 East 9th Street, Lawrence KS 66044. **Tel** (800)457-0742, (913)841-3534, FAX (913)841-3534. **DD** 317. ***Continues*** *Illinois in Perspective, 1065-5425.*
**Desc:** Reports on the state's data and rank for each of the categories featured in State Rankings.

CY/0253-858X
**IMPORTS AND EXPORTS STATISTICS.** **Added/Corp** Cyprus. Tmema Statistikes kai Ereunon. **VFOAT** Imports & Exports Statistics. (19??)-. English. an. Department of Statistics and Research / Cyprus, 13 Lord Byron Avenue, Nicosia 162 Cyprus. **Tel** 011 357 2 303286. **LC** HF259.C9; A3. **DD** 382/.095645/0021. **Circ:** 550. ***Continues*** *Statistics of Imports and Exports, 0253-858X.*

YU/0513-0689
**INDEKS; MESECNI PREGLED PRIVREDNE STATISTIKE FNRJ.** **Added/Corp** Savezni Zavod za Statistiku (Yugoslavia) Savezni Zavod za Statistiku (Yugoslavia). **VFOAT** Index; Monthly Review of Yugoslav Economic Statistics. Vol. 1 (April 1952)-. Serbo-Croatian (Roman). Twelve times a year. $30.00. Federal Institute for Statistics, Kneza Milosa 20, 11000 Belgrad Republic of Yugoslavia. **LC** HA1631; .I55.

US/0737-4461
**INDEX TO INTERNATIONAL STATISTICS.** (INDEX TO INTERNATIONAL STATISTICS : IIS.). [Index int. stat.]. **Added/Corp** Congressional Information Service. **VFOAT** IIS; I.I.S. Index to International Statistics; IIS Index to International Statistics. Vol. 1, No. 1 (Jan. 1983)-. Periodical. English. mo. Congressional Information Service Inc, 4520 East-West Highway, Suite 800, Bethesda MD 20814-3389. **Tel** (800)638-8380, (301)654-1550, FAX (301)654-4033, telex 292386 CIS UR. **LC** Z7552; .I53; HA155. **DD** 310/.16. available on CD-ROM.

US/0886-330X
**INDIANA FACTBOOK (BLOOMINGTON, IND.).** **See** General Interest-General Interest-North America.

US/1065-5433
**INDIANA IN PERSPECTIVE.** (INDIANA IN PERSPECTIVE : A STATISTICAL VIEW OF THE "HOOSIER STATE."). [Indiana perspect.]. **Added/Corp** Morgan Quitno Corporation. 1st Ed. (1990)-. Statistical Publication. English. $18.00. Morgan Quitno Corporation, PO Box 1656, 512 East 9th Street, Lawrence KS 66044. **Tel** (800)457-0742, (913)841-3534, FAX (913)841-3534. **DD** 317. ***Continues*** *Indiana in Perspective, 1065-5433.*
**Desc:** Reports on the state's data and rank for each of the categories featured in State Rankings.

IT/0390-6620
**INDICATORI MENSILI / ISTAT, ISTITUTO CENTRALE DI STATISTICA.** **Main/Corp** Istituto Centrale di Statistica (Italy). **Added/Corp** Istituto Centrale di Statistica (Italy) Istituto Nazionale di Statistica (Italy). (1971). Italian. mo. 3500000L Italy; 4500000L other. Istituto Nazionale Statistica, GBP SEZ4 Via Cesare Balbo 16, 00184 Rome Italy. **Tel** 011 39 6 46735118. **LC** HA1363; .A242. ***Continues*** *Sintesi Grafica della Vita Economica Italiana, 0393-5396.*

FI
**INDUSTRIAL STATISTICS.** English, Swedish and Finnish. ir. Academic Bookstore Akateeminen, Postilokero 23, FIN-00371 Helsinki Finland. **Tel** 011 358 0 12141.

GW
**INDUSTRIE IN NORDRHEIN-WESTFALEN, DIE.** **Main/Corp** North Rhine-Westphalia (Germany). Landesamt fur Datenverarbeitung und Statistik. German. 9.50. Landesamt fuer Datenverarbeitung und Statistik Nordrhein-Westfalen, Postfach 101105, 40002 Duesseldorf Germany. **Tel** (0211)944901, FAX (0211)442006, telex 8586654 LDST D. **LC** HA1320.N6; A32 subser; HC287.N6 N6.

YU
**INDUSTRIJSKA PREDUZECA.** **Main/Corp** Savezni Zavod za Statistiku (Yugoslavia). Serbo-Croatian (Roman). 5.00. Savezni Zavod za Statistiku, Kneza Milosa 20, Belgrad Yugoslavia. **LC** HA1631; .A33 subser; HC407.Y6.

NO/0078-1886
**INDUSTRISTATISTIKK. HEFTE 1, NRINGSTALL.** **VFOAT** Industrial Figures; Manufacturing Statistics. Volume 1, Industrial Figures. (1982)-. Norwegian (English). an. Kr24.00. Central Bureau of Statistics / Norway, PO Box 8131 DEP, N-0033

Oslo 1 Norway. **Tel** 011 47 2 2864964, FAX 011 47 2 864973. **LC** HA1501 subser; HC361. **DD** 314.81 S; 338.4/767/09481021. ***Continues in part*** *Industristatistikk.*

MX
**INFORMACIONES ESTADISTICAS DOMINICANAS.** **Main/Corp** Dominican Republic. Direccion General de Estadistica y Censos. Statistical Publication. Spanish. ir. Iztapalapa Av Michoacan Puris, 09340 Mexico DF Mexico. ***Continues*** *Dominican Republic. Direccion General de Estadistica. Informaciones Estadisticas Dominicanas.*

RE/0336-3791
**INFORMATIONS STATISTIQUES RAPIDES (INSTITUT NATIONAL DE LA STATISTIQUE ET DES ETUDES ECONOMIQUES (FRANCE)).** (INFORMATIONS STATISTIQUES RAPIDES.). French. mo. 2F single issue. I.N.S.E.E., BP 2718, 80027 Amens Cedex France. **LC** HA2307; .A2. **DD** 316.9/81.

CL/0577-8514
**INFORMATIVO ESTADISTICO.** **Main/Corp** Chile. Universidad, Santiago. Instituto de Investigaciones Estadisticas. No. 1- 19 -. Periodical. Spanish. Santiago Univ de Chile, Casilla 10220, Santiago Chile.

CK
**INFORME SOBRE CHILE.** Spanish. an. 17,400Chil$ Chile. Editorial Gestion, Avda Los Leones 2279, Santiago Chile. **Tel** 251 31 72, FAX 274 54 94, telex 34036 PB VTRCK. **LC** HA993; .I53. **DD** 318.3. **Ad Acc.** ctrl circ.

FR/0998-4844
**INSEE. CADRAGE ET INSEE RESULTATS EMPLOIS REVENUS.** French. Institut National de la Statistique et des Etudes Economiques, 18 Bd Adolphe Pinard, 75675 Paris 14 France.

FR/0998-4836
**INSEE. CADRAGE ET INSEE RESULTATS SYSTEME PRODUCTIF.** French. Institut National de la Statistique et des Etudes Economiques, 18 Bd Adolphe Pinard, 75675 Paris 14 France.

US/1059-3810
**INTERNATIONAL REFERENCE.** [Int. ref.]. **Added/Corp** BTA Economic Research Institute. (1991)-. English. Economic Research Institute, 16770 Northeast 79th Street, Suite 104, Redmond WA 98052. **Tel** (800)627-3697, (206)627-3697, FAX (206)885-5091. **LC** HA154; .I58. **DD** 310/.5.

US/0098-5643
**INTERNATIONAL RESEARCH DOCUMENT.** [Int. res. doc.]. No. 1- 1975-. Government Publication. English. US Department of Commerce / Bureau of the Census, Data User Services Division, Customer Services, Washington DC 20233-0800. **Tel** (301)763-4100. **(Subscription address:** Superintendent of Documents, US Government Printing Office, Washington DC 20402.**)** **LC** HA42; .I57A. **DD** 310/.8.
**Ind/Abst** Popul. Index (?-?).

NE/0306-7734
**INTERNATIONAL STATISTICAL REVIEW.** (INTERNATIONAL STATISTICAL REVIEW / REVUE IINTERNATIONALE DE STATISTIQUE.). [Int. stat. rev.]. **Added/Corp** International Statistical Institute. **VFOAT** Revue Internationale de Statistique. Vol. 40, No. 1 (Apr. 1972)-. Statistical Publication. English (French). Three times a year (Apr., Aug. & Dec.). $78.13. International Statistical Institute, 428 Prinses Beatrixlaan, 2270 AZ Voorburg Netherlands. **Tel** 011 31 70 3375737, FAX 011 31 70 3860025, telex 32260 ISI NL. **ED** D. J. Trewin (Australia) and B. W. Silverman (UK). **DD** 519.5/05. **NLM** HA 1 I61R. **CODEN** ISTRDP. Index available. **Ad Acc. Circ:** 3,000 (ctrl). Documents available from The Genuine Article, Ask*IEEE. ***Continues*** *Revue de l'Institut Internationale de Statistique.* ***Continued in part by*** *Short Book Reviews.*
**Desc:** Provides a comprehensive view of work in statistics, over the whole spectrum of the statistical profession and including the most relevant aspects of probability. Publishes original research papers of wide interest, integrated critical surveys of particular fields of statistics or probability, history of statistics and probability and reports on recent developments in statistics, computer facilities, survey programs and teaching methods and experience.
**Ind/Abst** Biostatistica; Compumath Citation Index [Full Cov.]; Contents Pages Manage.; Curr. Contents Phys. Chem. Earth Sci.; Curr. Index Stat.; GeoRef; INSPEC (April 1982-); Math. Rev.; Qual. Control Appl. Stat.; Res. Alert [Full Cov.]; Sci. Cit. Index; SCISEARCH; Soc. Sci. Cit. Index [Select. Cov.]; Stat. Theory Method Abstr. (1978-1984); Zentralbl. Math. Ihre Grenzgeb.

US/1065-5441
**IOWA IN PERSPECTIVE.** (IOWA IN PERSPECTIVE : A STATISTICAL VIEW OF THE "HAWKEYE STATE" / KATHLEEN O'LEARY MORGAN, SCOTT MORGAN AND NEAL QUITNO, EDITORS.). [Iowa perspect.]. **Added/Corp** Morgan Quitno Corporation. (1990)-. Statistical Publication. English. $18.00. Morgan Quitno Corporation, PO Box 1656, 512 East 9th Street, Lawrence KS 66044. **Tel** (800)457-0742, (913)841-3534, FAX (913)841-3534. **DD** 317. ***Continues*** *Iowa in Perspective, 1065-5441.*
**Desc:** Reports on the state's data and rank for each of the categories featured in State Rankings.

II/0258-1736
**ISI LECTURE NOTES.** [ISI lect. notes]. **Added/Corp** Indian Statistical Institute. No. 1 (1978)-. Monographic series. English. **LC** UNC.
**Ind/Abst** Math. Rev.; Zentralbl. Math. Ihre Grenzgeb.

IT/0021-2849
**ITALIA SCACCHISTICA, L'.** **Added/Corp** Federazione Scacchistica Italiana. Vol. 1 No. 1 (1911)-. Periodical. Italian. Eleven times a year. L70000 Italy; L100000 others. Italia Scacchistica, via Lamarmora 40, 20122 Milan Italy. **Tel** 011 39 2 55019079.

RU/0202-7488
**ITOGI NAUKI I TEHNIKI - VSESOJUZNYI INSTITUT NAUCNOJ I TEHNICESKOJ INFORMACII. SERIJA TEORIJA VEROJATNOSTEJI, MATEMATICESKAJA STATISTIKA, TEORETICESKAJA KIBERNETIKA.** **See** Mathematics.

NE
**JAARBOEK (AMSTERDAM (NETHERLANDS). BESTUURSINFORMATIE. AFDELING STATISTIEK).** (JAARBOEK : UITGAVE VAN BESTUURSINFORMATIE, AFDELING STATISTIEK.). 11. (1980)-. Dutch. an. Bestuursinformatie, Afdeling Onderzoek en Statistiek, PO Box 202, 1000 AE Amsterdam Netherlands. **LC** HA1388.A5; A72A. ***Continues*** *Jaarboek (Amsterdam (Netherlands). Bureau van Statistiek).*

GW/0408-1706
**JAHRBUCHER FUR STATISTIK UND LANDESKUNDE VON BADEN-WURTTEMBERG.** **Main/Corp** Statistisches Landesamt Baden-Wurttemberg. V. 1- ; 1954/55-. German. ir. St Landesamt Baden, Wurttemberg Germany. **Tel** 0711/64 65 463, telex 7 22 815 STALA D. **Circ:** 500.

IO
**JAKARTA PUSAT DALAM ANGKA STATISTIK.** **Main/Corp** Jakarta Pusat, Indonesia. Walikota. Indonesian. Walikota Jakarta Pusat, Jl Pegangsaan Barat, Jakarta Indonesia. **LC** HA1818.J34; J32A.

JA
**JAPAN (JAPAN. SORIFU. TOKEIKYOKU).** (JAPAN.). 1979-. English. Statistics Bureau / Management and Coordination Agency, 19-1 Wakamatsu-cho, Shinjuku-ku, 162 Tokyo Japan. **LC** HA4621; .J36. **DD** 952/.005.

IO
**JAWA BARAT DALAM ANGKA.** (1983)-. Indonesian. an. Biro Pusat Statistik, JLN Dr Sutomo 8 Kotak, Pos 1003, Jakarta 10710 Indonesia. **Tel** 3728007, 374908. **LC** HA1817.J35; J35A. ***Continues*** *Statistik Jawa Barat.*

IO
**JAWA TENGAH DALAM ANGKA.** Began with 1971 Vol. English (Indonesian). an. Kantor Statistik Propinsi Jateng, UL Pahlawan No 6, Semarang Indonesia. **LC** HA4607.J385; J38. ***Continues*** *Djawa Tengah Dalam Angka.*

FR/0037-914X
**JOURNAL DE LA SOCIETE DE STATISTIQUE DE PARIS.** **Main/Corp** Societe de Statistique de Paris. **Added/Corp** Centre National de la Recherche Scientifique (France). Vol. 1 (1860)-. Periodical. French. qt (4 issues). 380.00F France; 420.00F other. Societe de Statistique de Paris, 18 Boulevard Pinard, 75675 Paris Cedex 14 France. **LC** HA1; .S6. **NLM** W1 JQ317Q. (free). cum. index.
**Ind/Abst** Int. Bibliogr. Sociol.; Popul. Index; Stat. Theory Method Abstr. (1967, 1976-1983, 1986).

●US/1067-5817
**JOURNAL OF APPLIED STATISTICAL SCIENCE.** [J. appl. statist. sc.]. (1993)-. Statistical Publication. English. Four times a year. $115.00. Nova Science Publishers Inc., 6080 Jericho Turnpike, Suite 207, Commack NY 11725-2808. **Tel** (516)499-3103, (516)499-3106, FAX (516)499-3146. **LC** QA276.A1; J56. **DD** 519.5/05.

UK/0266-4763
**JOURNAL OF APPLIED STATISTICS.** **VFOAT** Applied Statistics. Vol. 11, No. 1 (Jan. 1984)-. Periodical. English. Six times a year (Plus special double issue). £208.00. Carfax Publishing Company, PO Box 25 Abingdon, Oxfordshire OX14 3UE England. **Tel** 011 44 235 555335, FAX (0279)31067, telex 817484. **(Subscription address:** US and Canada/ PO Box 2025, Dunnellon, FL 34430-2025; telephone:(904)489-6996**)** **ED** Gopal K. Kanji. **LC** QA276.A1; J57. **DD** 519.5/05. **[CCC].** Index available. available on microfiche. ***Continues*** *Bulletin in Applied Statistics.*
**Ind/Abst** Biostatistica (19??-); Curr. Index Stat.

●US/1063-8539
**JOURNAL OF COMBINATORIAL DESIGNS.** **See** Mathematics.

●US/1061-8600
**JOURNAL OF COMPUTATIONAL AND GRAPHICAL STATISTICS.** (JOURNAL OF COMPUTATIONAL AND GRAPHICAL STATISTICS: A JOINT PUBLICATION OF AMERICAN STATISTICAL ASSOCIATION, INSTITUTE OF MATHEMATICAL STATISTICS, INTERFACE FOUNDATION OF NORTH AMERICA.). [J. comput. graph. stat.]. **Added/Corp** American Statistical Association. Institute of Mathematical Statistics. Interface Foundation of North America. (1992)-. Statistical Publication. English. qt. $95.00 (library). American Statistical Association, 1429 Duke Street, Alexandria VA 22314. **Tel** (703)684-1221, (202)393-3253, FAX (703)684-2037 (orders). **LC** QA276.4; .J68. **DD** 519.5/0285.
**Desc:** Designed to improve and extend the use of computational and graphical methods in statistics and data analysis.
**Ind/Abst** Curr. Index Stat. (199?-).

US/1048-5252
**JOURNAL OF NONPARAMETRIC STATISTICS.** [J. nonparametr. stat.]. Vol. 1, No. 1/2 (1991)-. Periodical. English. qt. $302.00 (academic institutions), $472.00 (corporate institutions). Gordon & Breach Science Publishers, Inc., PO Box 786, Cooper Station, New York NY 10276. **Tel** (212)206-8900, FAX (212)645-2459. **(Subscription address:** International Publishers Distributor at one of the following addresses: 820 Town Center Drive, Langhorne, PA 19047; or PO Box 90, Reading Berkshire RG1 8JL UK; or Kent Ridge PO Box 1180, Singapore 9111, Republic of Singapore**)** **LC** QA278.8; .J68. **DD** 519.5. **CODEN** NOSTEK. **[CCC].**
**Ind/Abst** Curr. Index Stat.

SW/0282-423X
**JOURNAL OF OFFICIAL STATISTICS.** [J. off. stat.]. **Added/Corp** Sweden. Statistiska Centralbyran. **VFOAT** JOS. Vol. 1 (1985)-. Periodical. English. Four times a year. Kr400.00. Statistics Sweden Publishing Service, S-70189 Orebro Sweden. **Tel** 011 46 19176800, telex 15261 SWESTATS. **(Subscription address:** Akademika AS, PO Box 84, Blindern OSLA 0314 Norway.**)** **ED** Lars Lyberg. **LC** HA1523; .A4. **DD** 314.85. **CODEN** JOFSEA. Index available. **Bk Rev. Circ:** 1,200 (ctrl). ***Continues*** *Sweden. Statistiska Centralbyran. Statistisk Tidskrift.*
**Desc:** Articles on methodology and policy related to statistics produced by national offices and other statistical organizations.
**Ind/Abst** Biostatistica; Curr. Index Stat.; Qual. Control Appl. Stat.; Selec. Coop. Index Manage. Period; Stat. Theory Method Abstr. (1986-1987).

PH/0022-3603
**JOURNAL OF PHILIPPINE STATISTICS.** [J. Philipp. stat.]. **Added/Corp** Philippines. Bureau of the Census and Statistics. Philippines. National Census and Statistics Office. Vol. 1 (July 1941)-. Periodical. English. qt. $60.00 Philippines; $81.00 other. National Statistics Office of Manila, PO Box 779, Manila Philippines. **Tel** 011 63 613645. **LC** HA1821; .J68. **DD** 319.14. **Circ:** 250 per quarter.
**Ind/Abst** Index Philip. Period. (-199?); PAIS Int. Print (1991-).

US/0094-9655
**JOURNAL OF STATISTICAL COMPUTATION AND SIMULATION.** **See** Computers-Simulation.

BG/0256-422X
**JOURNAL OF STATISTICAL RESEARCH - UNIVERSITY OF DACCA. INSTITUTE OF STATISTICAL RESEARCH AND TRAINING.** (JOURNAL OF STATISTICAL RESEARCH.). [J. stat. res. - Univ. Dacca, Inst. Stat. Res. Train.]. **Added/Corp** University of Dacca. Institute of Statistical Research and Training. Vol. 4, No. 1 (Jan. 1970)-. Statistical Publication. English. Twice a year. $6.00. University of Dhaka, Institute of Statistical Research and Training, Dhaka 1000 Bangladesh. **Tel** 011 880 501298, 503811. **ED** M. Ali, Ehsanes Saleh, M. Masoom Ali, G. Rabbani and M.H. Kabir. **Bk Rev. Circ:** 200 (ctrl). ***Continues*** *Bulletin of the Institute of Statistical Research and Training.*
**Desc:** This is a core journal on statistical theory and methods.
**Ind/Abst** Math. Rev.; Stat. Theory Method Abstr. (1971-1973, 1977-1979, 1983, 1986-1987).

US/0162-1459
**JOURNAL OF THE AMERICAN STATISTICAL ASSOCIATION.** [J. Am. Stat. Assoc.]. **Added/Corp** American Statistical Association. **VFOAT** J.A.S.A.; JASA. Vol. 18 (Mar. 1922), New Series No. 137-. Statistical Publication. English. qt (Mar., June, Sept., Dec.). $230.00. American Statistical Association, 1429 Duke Street, Alexandria VA 22314. **Tel** (703)684-1221, (202)393-3253, FAX (703)684-2037 (orders). **LC** HA1; .A6. **NLM** HA 1 A512. **CODEN** JSTNAL. **[CCC]**. Index available (bound in Dec. issue). cum. index. **Bk Rev. Ad Acc. Pr Rev. Circ:** 17,000. available on microfilm and microfiche from University Microfilms International (UMI). Documents available from The Genuine Article, Ask*IEEE, UMI Article Clearinghouse. ***Continues*** *Quarterly Publication of the American Statistical Association.*
**Desc:** Articles on theoretical and applied aspects of statistics.
**Ind/Abst** Acad. Search (July 1993-); Biostatistica (Sept. 1971-Sept. 1972); Bus. Index (1985-); Compumath Citation Index [Full Cov.]; Comput. Rev. (1981-); Contents Pages Manage.; Curr. Contents Phys. Chem. Earth Sci.; Curr. Index Stat.; Econ. Lit. Index (19??-); EMBASE; Expand. Acad. Index (1992-); Gen. BusinessFile (1985-); Gen. Period. Index (1985-); Hortic. Abstr.; INSPEC (March 1982-); Int. Aerosp. Abstr.; Int. Bibliogr. Sociol.; Int. Polit. Sci. Abstr.; J. Econ. Lit.; Mag. Search; Math. Rev.; Newsp. Period. Abstr. (1992-); Pollut. Abstr. Indexes; Popul. Index; Qual. Control Appl. Stat. (March 1982-); Res. Alert [Full Cov.]; Sci. Cit. Index; Selec. Coop. Index Manage. Period; SCISEARCH; Soc. Sci. Cit. Index [Select. Cov.]; Soc. Res. Methodol. Abstr. (1975-); Stat. Theory Method Abstr. (1959-1963, 1966-1984, 1986-1987); Trade Ind. Index (1981-?); Trop. Dis. Bull.; Zentralbl. Math. Ihre Grenzgeb.

II/0537-2585
**JOURNAL OF THE INDIAN STATISTICAL ASSOCIATION.** [J. Indian Stat. Assoc.]. **Main/Corp** Indian Statistical Association. (1963)-. Statistical Publication. English. an. $30.00. Indian Statistical Association, University of Poona, c/o Department of Statistics, Poona 411007 India. **(Subscription address:** Prints India, 11 Darya Ganj, New Delhi, 110002 India, (Phone: 011 91 11 3268645)**)** **ED** S R Adke. **LC** HA1; .I5. **CODEN** ISAJB6. Index available. **Bk Rev. Ad Acc.**
**Desc:** Research papers in statistics.
**Ind/Abst** Math. Rev.; Stat. Theory Method Abstr. (1963, 1966-1970, 1972, 1977-1978, 1982-1984, 1986-1987).

JA/0915-2350
**JOURNAL OF THE JAPANESE SOCIETY OF COMPUTATIONAL STATISTICS. See** Mathematics.

UK/0035-9238
**JOURNAL OF THE ROYAL STATISTICAL SOCIETY. SERIES A (GENERAL).** **Main/Corp** Royal Statistical Society (Great Britain). **Added/Corp** Statistical Society of London. Vol. 1 (1839)-. Statistical Publication. English. Three times a year. £49.00 UK and Europe; $87.00 North America; £56.00 other. Basil Blackwell Publishers Ltd, 108 Cowley Road, Oxford 0X4 1JF England. **Tel** 011 44 865 791100, FAX 011 44 865 791347, telex 837022 OXBOOK G. **(Subscription address:** Blackwell Publishers / UK, Marston Book Services, PO Box 87, Oxford OX2 0DT England.**)** **ED** C Chilvers and H Goldstein. **[CCC]**. Index available. cum. index. **Bk Rev. Ad Acc. Pr Rev. Circ:** 5,350. Documents available from The Genuine Article.
**Ind/Abst** Biostatistica (19??-); Contents Pages Manage.; Curr. Index Stat.; Econ. Lit. Index (19??-); Index Med.; Int. Bibliogr. Sociol.; Int. Pharm. Abstr.; J. Econ. Lit.; Math. Rev.; PAIS Int. Print; Popul. Index; Res. Alert [Full Cov.]; SCISEARCH; Soc. Res. Methodol. Abstr. (1975-); Stat. Theory Method Abstr. (1959-1966), (1977-1981); Trop. Dis. Bull.; Zentralbl. Math. Ihre Grenzgeb.

UK
**JOURNAL OF THE ROYAL STATISTICAL SOCIETY. SERIES A: (STATISTICS IN SOCIETY).** **Added/Corp** Royal Statistical Society (Great Britain). **VFOAT** Statistics in Society. Vol. 151, Pt. 1 (1988)-. Statistical Publication. English. Three times a year. $87.00 North America. Basil Blackwell Publishers Ltd, 108 Cowley Road, Oxford 0X4 1JF England. **Tel** 011 44 865 791100, FAX 011 44 865 791347, telex 837022 OXBOOK G. **(Subscription address:** Blackwell Publishers / UK, Marston Book Services, PO Box 87, Oxford OX2 0DT England.**)** **LC** HA1; .R8. **NLM** W1; JO951M. **CODEN** JSSAEF. Index available (bound in last issue). **Bk Rev. Ad Acc. Pr Rev. Circ:** 5,800 (ctrl). available on microfilm from University Microfilms International (UMI). ***Continues*** *Royal Statistical Society (Great Britain). Journal of the Royal Statistical Society. Series A, (General), 0035-9238.*
**Desc:** Publishes original papers on statistical topics of general interest, reviews and papers presented for discussion by the society.
**Ind/Abst** Compumath Citation Index [Full Cov.]; Curr. Contents Phys. Chem. Earth Sci.; J. Econ. Lit.; Math. Rev.; Plant Breed. Abstr.; Sci. Cit. Index; Soc. Sci. Cit. Index [Select. Cov.].

UK/0035-9246
**JOURNAL OF THE ROYAL STATISTICAL SOCIETY. SERIES B (METHODOLOGICAL).** [J. R. Stat. Soc. Ser. B. Methodol.]. **Main/Corp** Royal Statistical Society (Great Britain). Vol. 10 (1948)-. Statistical Publication. English. Four times a year. £49.00 UK and Europe; $87.00 North America; £56.00 other. Basil Blackwell Publishers Ltd, 108 Cowley Road, Oxford 0X4 1JF England. **Tel** 011 44 865 791100, FAX 011 44 865 791347, telex 837022 OXBOOK G. **(Subscription address:** Blackwell Publishers / UK, Marston Book Services, PO Box 87, Oxford OX2 0DT England.**)** **ED** R L Smith and J T Kent. **LC** HA1; .R803. **DD** 310/.5. **NLM** W1 JO951JA. **CODEN** JSTBAJ. **[CCC]**. Index available. **Ad Acc. Pr Rev. Circ:** 4,600 (ctrl). available on microfilm and microfiche from University Microfilms International (UMI). Documents available from The Genuine Article. ***Continues*** *Supplement to the Journal of the Royal Statistical Society.*
**Desc:** Covers theory and methodology of statistics.
**Ind/Abst** Compumath Citation Index [Full Cov.]; Curr. Contents Phys. Chem. Earth Sci.; Curr. Index Stat.; Math. Rev.; Res. Alert [Full Cov.]; Sci. Cit. Index; SCISEARCH; Soc. Sci. Cit. Index [Select. Cov.]; Stat. Theory Method Abstr. (1959-1966, 1977-1981); Trop. Dis. Bull.; Zentralbl. Math. Ihre Grenzgeb.

IE/0081-4776
**JOURNAL OF THE STATISTICAL AND SOCIAL INQUIRY SOCIETY OF IRELAND.** [J. stat. soc. inq. soc. Irel.]. **Added/Corp** Statistical and Social Inquiry Society of Ireland. Vol. 3, Pt. 18/25 (Jan. 1861/Dec. 1863)-. Statistical Publication. English. an. $10.00. Statistical and Social Inquiry Society, Central Statistics Office, Ardee Road, Rathmines Dublin 6 Ireland. **Tel** 011 353 1 767531. ***Continues*** *Journal of the Dublin Statistical Society.*
**Ind/Abst** Stat. Theory Method Abstr. (1959-1963, 1969).

JM
**JOURNAL OF THE STATISTICAL INSTITUTE OF JAMAICA.** **Added/Corp** Statistical Institute of Jamaica. Vol. 1 (1988)-. Statistical Publication. English. sa. Statistical Institute of Jamaica, 9 Swallowfield Road, PO Box 643, Kingston 5 Jamaica. **Tel** (809)92-62175-6, FAX (809)92-64859. **LC** HA35.3.J35; J68. **DD** 317.292/05.
**Desc:** Deals with issues relating to the interpretation of statistics and their application to theory and policy.

IS
**JUDEA, SAMARIA, AND GAZA AREA STATISTICS QUARTERLY.** **VFOAT** Judaea, Samaria, and Gaza Area Statistics; Rivon Statisti Li-Yehudah, Shomron, Ve-Hevelazah; Statistikah Shel Yehudah, Shomron, Ve-Hevelazah; Statistics of Judaea, Samaria, and the Gaza Area. Periodical. English (Hebrew). Central Bureau of Statistics / Israel, PO Box 13015, 91 130 Hakirya Jerusalem Israel. **Tel** 011-972-2-553553. **LC** DS127.6.O3; A23. **DD** 956/.046. ***Continues*** *Rivon Statisti La-Shetahim Ha-Muhzakim.*

IO
**KABUPATEN GRESIK DALAM ANGKA.** **Added/Corp** Indonesia. Kantor Statistik Kabupaten Gresik. Bappeda Kabupaten Daerah Tk. II Gresik. **VFOAT** Kabupaten Gresik Dalam Tahun ... . (1981)-. Indonesian. an. Kantor Statistik Kabupaten Gresik, JL Kyai Haji Wakhid Hasyim No 9A, Gresik Indonesia. **LC** HA4607.S87; S75. ***Continues*** *Statistik Kabupaten Daerah Tingkat II Gresik.*

IO
**KABUPATEN KENDAL DALAM ANGKA.** **Added/Corp** Indonesia. Kantor Statistik Kabupaten Kendal. (19??)-. Indonesian. an. Biro Pusat Statistik, JLN Dr Sutomo 8 Kotak, Pos 1003, Jakarta 10710 Indonesia. **Tel** 3728007, 374908. **(Subscription address:** Kantor Statistik Kabupaten Kendal Jl, Raya Barat No 42 A, Kendal 51314 Indonesia**)** **LC** HA1817.K46; K46a. ***Continues*** *Kabupaten Daerah Tingkat II Kendal Dalam Angka.*
**Desc:** Regional statistical data and tables.

US/1065-545X
**KANSAS IN PERSPECTIVE.** (KANSAS IN PERSPECTIVE : A STATISTICAL VIEW OF THE "SUNFLOWER STATE."). [Kans. perspect.]. **Added/Corp** Morgan Quitno Corporation. (1990)-. Statistical Publication. English. $18.00. Morgan Quitno Corporation, PO Box 1656, 512 East 9th Street, Lawrence KS 66044. **Tel** (800)457-0742, (913)841-3534, FAX (913)841-3534. **DD** 317. ***Continues*** *Kansas in Perspective, 1065-545X.*
**Desc:** Reports on the state's data and rank for each of the categories featured in State Rankings.

US/0453-2600
**KANSAS STATISTICAL ABSTRACT.** (19??)-. Statistical Publication. English. an. $27.00. University of Kansas Institute for Public Policy and Business, 1 Jayhawk Boulevard, 607 Blake Hall, Lawrence KS 66044. **Tel** (913)864-3701, FAX (913)864-3683. **ED** Thelma Helyar. **LC** HA385; .K36. **DD** 317.81. **Circ:** 750.
**Desc:** Summary data on Kansas covering seventeen areas, including population, vital statistics, employment, income, education, elections, government finances, crime, agriculture, business and industry.

●GW/0943-8769
**KAPITALMARKTSTATISTIK / DEUTSCHE BUNDESBANK. See** Business-Abstracting, Bibliographies and Statistics.

MY
**KATALOG.** **Main/Corp** Malaysia. Jabatan Perangkaan. English (Malay). Kentua Perangkawan, Jabatan Perangkaan, Jl Cenderasari Kuala Lumpur Malaysia. **Tel** 2922133. **LC** Z7554.M24; M34A; HA4600.6. **DD** 016.31595. **Circ:** 500. ***Continues*** *Malaysia. Jabatan Perangkaan. Katalok.*

US/1065-5468
**KENTUCKY IN PERSPECTIVE.** (KENTUCKY IN PERSPECTIVE : A STATISTICAL VIEW OF THE BLUE-GRASS STATE.). [Ky. perspect.]. **Added/Corp** Morgan Quitno Corporation. (1990)-. Statistical Publication. English. $18.00. Morgan Quitno Corporation, PO Box 1656, 512 East 9th Street, Lawrence KS 66044. **Tel** (800)457-0742, (913)841-3534, FAX (913)841-3534. **DD** 317. ***Continues*** *Kentucky in Perspective, 1065-5468.*
**Desc:** Reports on the state's data and rank for each of the categories featured in State Rankings.

KE
**KENYA STATISTICAL DIGEST.** Vol. 1, No. 1 (Sept. 1963)-. Statistical Publication. English. qt. $4.06. Government Printer of Kenya, Box 30128, Nairobi Kenya. **Tel** 334075. **LC** HA1977.K4; A25. **DD** 316.76/2. ***Continues*** *Kenya Trade and Supplies Bulletin.*

NZ/0114-2119
**KEY STATISTICS / DEPARTMENT OF STATISTICS, NEW ZEALAND.** **Added/Corp** New Zealand. Dept. of Statistics. (Feb. 1989)-. English. Eleven times a year. 355.00Aus$ Australia & South Pacific; 455.00Aus$ others. Department of Statistics / New Zealand, PO Box 2922, Wellington New Zealand. **Tel** 011 64 4 4954600. **(Subscription address:** GP Legislation Services, PO Box 12 418, Wellington New Zealand.**)** **LC** HA3032; .A3. **DD** 319.31. ***Continues*** *Monthly Abstract of Statistics (Wellington, N.Z.), 0027-0180.*

IO
**KLATEN DALAM ANGKA.** **Added/Corp** Indonesia. Kantor Statistik Kabupaten Klaten. (19??)-. Indonesian. an. Biro Pusat Statistik, JLN Dr Sutomo 8 Kotak, Pos 1003, Jakarta 10710 Indonesia. **Tel** 3728007, 374908. **LC** HA1817.K57; S8. ***Continues*** *Kabupaten Klaten Dalam Angka.*

KO
**KOREA STATISTICAL HANDBOOK.** **Added/Corp** Korea (South). Kyongje Kihoegwon. Chosa Tonggyeguk. (1977)-. Statistical Publication. English. an. National Bureau of Statistics, Economic Planning Board, 90 Gyeongwun-dong Jongro-gu, Seoul South Korea. **LC** HA4630.5; .A18. **DD** 315.19/5. ***Continues*** *Statistical Handbook of Korea.*

GW
**KREISFREIE STADTE UND LANDKREISE IN ZAHLEN.** (1981)-. German. an. DM7.50. Niedersachsisches Landesverwaltungsamt, Postfach 107, 3000 Hannover Germany. **Tel** (0511)108-9466. **LC** HA1248.L69; S73 subser. **DD** 314.3/59. **Bk Rev. Circ:** 400.
**Desc:** Important statistical results of the regions and important towns in Niedersaechsen (Lower-Saxony).

GW
**KREISSTANDARDZAHLEN.** **Main/Corp** North Rhine-Westphalia. Landesamt fur Datenverarbeitung und Statistik. **Added/Corp** North Rhine-Westphalia. Landesamt fur Datenverarbeitung und Statistik. Statistisches Angaben fur Kreisfreie Stadte und Kreise des Landes Nordrhein-Westfalen. **VFOAT** Statistisches Angaben fur Kreisfreie Stadte und Kreise des Landes Nordrhein-Westfalen. (19??)-. Statistical Publication. German. an. DM10.00. Landesamt fuer Datenverarbeitung und Statistik Nordrhein-Westfalen, Postfach 101105, 40002 Duesseldorf Germany. **Tel** (0211)944901, FAX (0211)442006, telex 8586654 LDST D. **LC** HA1320.N6; A5213. **Circ:** 1,200. ***Continues*** *Statistisches Landesamt Nordrhein-Westfalen. Kreisstandardzahlen des Landes Nordrhein-Westfalen.*
**Desc:** Statistical returns on areas subdivided into the 54 districts of Nordrhein-Westfalen.

XV
**KULTURNO-UMETNISKA IN PROSVETNA DEJAVNOST.** **Main/Corp** Zavod Sr Slovenije za Statistiko. (19??)-. Slovenian. an. Zavod Sr Slovenije za Statistiko, Vozarski Pot 12, Ljubljana Slovenia. **LC** HA1634.S58; S57f.

AT
**LABOUR FORCE. See** Economics-Labor.

## Statistics

GW/0939-690X
**LAENDERBERICHT. TSCHAD / STATISTISCHES BUNDESAMT.**
**Added/Corp** Germany. Statistisches Bundesamt. (1990)-. Statistical Publication. German (table of contents in French). W Kohlhammer Verlag GmbH, Postfach 800430, D 70549 Stuttgart Germany. **Tel** 011 49 711 78631, FAX 011 49 711 7863263, telex 7-255820. **LC** HA4718; .A26. *Continues Statistik des Auslandes. Laenderbericht. Tschad, 0177-3690.*

GW/0938-5398
**LANDERBERICHT. AFGHANISTAN / [STATISTISCHES BUNDESAMT].**
**Added/Corp** Germany (West). Statistisches Bundesamt. (1989)-. German (table of contents in English). Hermann Leins GmbH & Co., Verlags-KG, Holzwiesenstr 2, 7408 Kusterdingen. **LC** HA1675; .G44. **DD** 315.81/05. *Continues Allgemeine Statistik des Auslandes. Landerberichte. Afghanistan, 0072-2138.*

GW
**LANDERBERICHT. ANGOLA / STATISTISCHES BUNDESAMT.**
**Added/Corp** Germany. Statistisches Bundesamt. (1991)-. German (table of contents in English). Hermann Leins GmbH & Co., Verlags-KG, Holzwiesenstr 2, 7408 Kusterdingen. **LC** HA4710; .A25. **DD** 316.7/3. *Continues Statistik des Auslandes. Landerbericht. Angola, 0179-3292.*

GW
**LANDERBERICHT. BOLIVIEN / STATISTISCHES BUNDESAMT.**
**Added/Corp** Germany. Statistisches Bundesamt. (1991)-. German (table of contents in English). Hermann Leins GmbH & Co., Verlags-KG, Holzwiesenstr 2, 7408 Kusterdingen. **LC** HA961; .S7. **DD** 318.4. *Continues Statistik des Auslandes. Landerbericht. Bolivien, 0179-7786.*

GW/0940-0907
**LANDERBERICHT. BRASILIEN / STATISTISCHES BUNDESAMT.**
**Added/Corp** Germany. Statistisches Bundesamt. (1991)-. German (table of contents in English). Hermann Leins GmbH & Co., Verlags-KG, Holzwiesenstr 2, 7408 Kusterdingen. **LC** HA984; .S73. **DD** 318.1/05. *Continues Statistik des Auslandes. Landerbericht. Brasilien, 0179-7549.*

GW
**LANDERBERICHT. BULGARIEN / STATISTISCHES BUNDESAMT.**
**Added/Corp** Germany. Statistisches Bundesamt. (1991)-. German (table of contents in English). Hermann Leins GmbH & Co., Verlags-KG, Holzwiesenstr 2, 7408 Kusterdingen. **LC** HA1625; .S72. **DD** 314.977/05. *Continues Statistik des Auslandes. Landerbericht. Bulgarien, 0173-3060.*

GW
**LANDERBERICHT. COTE D'IVOIRE / STATISTISCHES BUNDESAMT.**
**Added/Corp** Germany. Statistisches Bundesamt. (1991)-. German (table of contents in French). Hermann Leins GmbH & Co., Verlags-KG, Holzwiesenstr 2, 7408 Kusterdingen. **LC** HA2096; .G43. **DD** 316.668/05. *Continues Statistik des Auslandes. Landerbericht. Cote d'Ivoire.*

GW
**LANDERBERICHT : GABUN.** *Title Change.*
**Main/Corp** Germany (Federal Republic, 1949- ). Statistisches Bundesamt. German. W Kohlhammer Verlag GMBH, Postfach 800430, D70549 Stuttgart Germany. **Tel** 011 49 711 78631. **LC** HA2090; .G45B. *Continued by Statistik des Auslandes. Landerbericht. Gabun.*

GW
**LANDERBERICHT. GOLFSTAATEN / STATISTISCHES BUNDESAMT.**
**Added/Corp** Germany. Statistisches Bundesamt. (1991)-. German (table of contents in English). Hermann Leins GmbH & Co., Verlags-KG, Holzwiesenstr 2, 7408 Kusterdingen. **LC** HA4562; .A27.

GW
**LANDERBERICHT. GRIECHENLAND / STATISTISCHES BUNDESAMT.**
**Added/Corp** Germany (West). Statistisches Bundesamt. (1990)-. German (table of contents in English). Hermann Leins GmbH & Co., Verlags-KG, Holzwiesenstr 2, 7408 Kusterdingen. **LC** HA1351; .S73. **DD** 314.95. *Continues Statistik des Auslandes. Landerbericht. Griechenland, 0179-1362.*

GW
**LANDERBERICHT. INDIEN / STATISTISCHES BUNDESAMT.**
**Added/Corp** Germany. Statistisches Bundesamt. (1991)-. German (table of contents in English). Hermann Leins GmbH & Co., Verlags-KG, Holzwiesenstr 2, 7408 Kusterdingen. **LC** HA4581; .S7. **DD** 315.4. *Continues Statistik des Auslandes. Landerbericht. Indien, 0175-9132.*

GW/0938-4472
**LANDERBERICHT. INDONESIEN.**
**Added/Corp** Germany (West). Statistisches Bundesamt. VFOAT Indonesien. 1990-. German (table of contents in English). W Kohlhammer Verlag GmbH, Postfach 800430, D 70549 Stuttgart Germany. **Tel** 011 49 711 78631, FAX 011 49 711 7863263, telex 7-255820. **LC** HA4601; .S72. *Continues Statistik des Auslandes. Landerbericht. Indonesien, 0178-8469.*

GW
**LANDERBERICHT. IRAN / STATISTISCHES BUNDESAMT.**
**Added/Corp** Germany. Statistisches Bundesamt. (19??)-. German (table of contents in English). Hermann Leins GmbH & Co., Verlags-KG, Holzwiesenstr 2, 7408 Kusterdingen. **LC** HA1864; .G4. **DD** 315.5. *Continues Statistik des Auslandes. Landerbericht. Iran, 0178-8477.*

GW
**LANDERBERICHT. KAMBODSCHA / STATISTISCHES BUNDESAMT.**
**Added/Corp** Germany. Statistisches Bundesamt. (1991)-. German (table of contents in French). Hermann Leins GmbH & Co., Verlags-KG, Holzwiesenstr 2, 7408 Kusterdingen. **LC** HA4600.3; .A35. *Continues Statistik des Auslandes. Landerbericht. Kamputschea, 0931-1246.*

GW
**LANDERBERICHT. KAP VERDE / STATISTISCHES BUNDESAMT.**
**Added/Corp** Germany (West). Statistisches Bundesamt. (1990)-. German (table of contents in English). Hermann Leins GmbH & Co., Verlags-KG, Holzwiesenstr 2, 7408 Kusterdingen. **LC** HA4738.9; .A24.

GW/0937-9975
**LANDERBERICHT. KOREA, DEMOKRATISCHE VOLKSREPUBLIK.**
**Added/Corp** Germany (West). Statistisches Bundesamt. VFOAT Korea, Demokratische Volksrepublik. (1989)-. German (table of contents in English). DM8.60. W Kohlhammer Verlag GmbH, Postfach 800430, D 70549 Stuttgart Germany. **Tel** 011 49 711 78631, FAX 011 49 711 7863263, telex 7-255820. **LC** HA4630.6; .A34. *Continues Statistik des Auslandes. Landerbericht. Demokratische Volksrepublik Korea, 0931-3389.*

GW
**LANDERBERICHT. LESOTHO / STATISTISCHES BUNDESAMT.**
**Added/Corp** Germany. Statistisches Bundesamt. (1991)-. German (table of contents in English). Hermann Leins GmbH & Co., Verlags-KG, Holzwiesenstr 2, 7408 Kusterdingen. **LC** HA4704; .A23. **DD** 316.81/6. *Continues Statistik des Auslandes. Landerbericht. Lesotho, 0931-3443.*

GW
**LANDERBERICHT. MADAGASKAR / STATISTISCHES BUNDESAMT.**
**Added/Corp** Germany. Statistisches Bundesamt. (1991)-. German (table of contents in French). Hermann Leins GmbH & Co., Verlags-KG, Holzwiesenstr 2, 7408 Kusterdingen. **LC** HA4699; .A36. *Continues Statistik des Auslandes. Landerbericht. Madagaskar.*

GW/0937-7972
**LANDERBERICHT. MALAYSIA / STATISTISCHES BUNDESAMT.**
**Added/Corp** Germany. Statistisches Bundesamt. (1989)-. German (table of contents in English). Hermann Leins GmbH & Co., Verlags-KG, Holzwiesenstr 2, 7408 Kusterdingen. **LC** HA4600.6; .A3. **DD** 315.95/021. *Continues Statistik des Auslandes. Landerbericht. Malaysia, 0179-7972.*

GW
**LANDERBERICHT. MALI / STATISTISCHES BUNDESAMT.**
**Added/Corp** Germany. Statistisches Bundesamt. (1990)-. German (table of contents in French). Hermann Leins GmbH & Co., Verlags-KG, Holzwiesenstr 2, 7408 Kusterdingen. **LC** HA4727; .A3. **DD** 316.6/23. *Continues Statistik des Auslandes. Landerbericht. Mali, 0179-8405.*

GW
**LANDERBERICHT. NICARAGUA / STATISTISCHES BUNDESAMT.**
**Added/Corp** Germany. Statistisches Bundesamt. (1991)-. German (table of contents in English). Hermann Leins GmbH & Co., Verlags-KG, Holzwiesenstr 2, 7408 Kusterdingen. **LC** HA835; .G45a. *Continues Statistik des Auslandes. Landerbericht. Nicaragua, 0178-5990.*

GW/0938-474X
**LANDERBERICHT. NIEDERLANDE / STATISTISCHES BUNDESAMT.**
**Added/Corp** Germany (West). Statistisches Bundesamt. (1990)-. German (table of contents in English). Hermann Leins GmbH & Co., Verlags-KG, Holzwiesenstr 2, 7408 Kusterdingen. **LC** HA1381; .S77. **DD** 314.92/05. *Continues Statistik des Auslandes. Landerbericht. Niederlande, 0934-7844.*

GW
**LANDERBERICHT. NORWEGEN / STATISTISCHES BUNDESAMT.**
**Added/Corp** Germany. Statistisches Bundesamt. (1991)-. German (table of contents in English). Hermann Leins GmbH & Co., Verlags-KG, Holzwiesenstr 2, 7408 Kusterdingen. **LC** HA1501; .S73. **DD** 314.81/05. *Continues Statistik des Auslandes. Landerbericht. Norwegen, 0932-092X.*

GW
**LANDERBERICHT. OSTASIATISCHE STAATEN / STATISTISCHES BUNDESAMT.** **Added/Corp** Germany (West). Statistisches Bundesamt. VFOAT Ostasiatische Staaten. (1991)-. German (table of contents in English). Hermann Leins GmbH & Co., Verlags-KG, Holzwiesenstr 2, 7408 Kusterdingen.

GW
**LANDERBERICHT. SOMALIA / STATISTISCHES BUNDESAMT.**
**Added/Corp** Germany. Statistisches Bundesamt. (1991)-. German (table of contents in English). Hermann Leins GmbH & Co., Verlags-KG, Holzwiesenstr 2, 7408 Kusterdingen. **LC** HA4690; .A3. **DD** 316.7/73. *Continues Statistik des Auslandes. Landerbericht. Somalia, 0179-8413.*

GW
**LANDERBERICHT. STAATEN MITTEL- UND OSTEUROPAS / EUROSTAT [UND] STATISTISCHES BUNDESAMT.**
**Added/Corp** Statistical Office of the European Communities. Germany. Statistisches Bundesamt. Overseas Development Institute (London, England). (1991)-. German (table of contents in English). Hermann Leins GmbH & Co., Verlags-KG, Holzwiesenstr 2, 7408 Kusterdingen.

●GW
**LANDERBERICHT. SUDAMERIKANISCHE STAATEN / STATISTISCHES BUNDESAMT.**
**Added/Corp** Germany. Statistisches Bundesamt. VFOAT Sudamerikanische Staaten. (1992)-. German (table of contents in English). Hermann Leins GmbH & Co., Verlags-KG, Holzwiesenstr 2, 7408 Kusterdingen.

GW
**LANDERBERICHT. TOGO / EUROSTAT [UND] STATISTISCHES BUNDESAMT.**
**Added/Corp** Statistical Office of the European Communities. Germany. Statistisches Bundesamt. Deutsches Institut Fur Entwicklungspolitik. (1991)-. German. Hermann Leins GmbH & Co., Verlags-KG, Holzwiesenstr 2, 7408 Kusterdingen. **LC** HA2128; .S72. **DD** 316.681/05. *Continues Statistik des Auslandes. Landerbericht. Togo, 0173-3052.*

GW
**LANDERBERICHT : UNGARN.** *Title Change.*
**Main/Corp** Germany (West). Statistisches Bundesamt. VFOAT Ungarn. German. W Kohlhammer Verlag GMBH, Postfach 800430, D70549 Stuttgart Germany. **Tel** 011 49 711 78631. **LC** HA1205; .G46A. *Merged with Statistik Des Auslandes. Landerkurzbericht. Ungarn to form Statistik des Auslandes. Landerbericht. Ungarn.*

GW
**LANDERKURZBERICHT : NAMIBIA (SUDWESTAFRIKA).** **Main/Corp** Germany (West). Statistisches Bundesamt. VFOAT Namibia (Sudwestafrika). German. W Kohlhammer Verlag GMBH, Postfach 800430, D70549 Stuttgart Germany. **Tel** 011 49 711 78631. **LC** HA1977.N3; .G47A.

GW
**LANDERKURZBERICHTE : BAHAMAS.**
**Main/Corp** Germany (West). Statistisches Bundesamt. German. W Kohlhammer Verlag GMBH, Postfach 800430, D70549 Stuttgart Germany. **Tel** 011 49 711 78631. **LC** HA861; .G47A. **DD** 317.29/6.

GW
**LANDERKURZBERICHTE : BAHRAIN, KATAR.** **Main/Corp** Germany (West). Statistisches Bundesamt. German. DM2.00 single issue. W Kohlhammer Verlag GMBH, Postfach 800430, D70549 Stuttgart Germany. **Tel** 011 49 711 78631. **LC** HA1950.B3; G47A. **DD** 315.3/65.

GW
**LANDERKURZBERICHTE : BOLIVIEN.**
**Main/Corp** Germany (West). Statistisches Bundesamt. German. W Kohlhammer Verlag GmbH, Postfach 800430, D 70549 Stuttgart Germany. **Tel** 011 49 711 78631, FAX 011 49 711 7863263, telex 7-255820. **LC** HA965; .G45. **DD** 318.4.

GW
**LANDERKURZBERICHTE : FRANZ. -GUAYANA.** **Main/Corp** Germany (West). Statistisches Bundesamt. German. DM3.40. W Kohlhammer Verlag GMBH, Postfach 800430, D70549 Stuttgart Germany. **Tel** 011 49 711 78631. **LC** HA1037.F7; G47A. **DD** 318.8/2.

GW
**LANDERKURZBERICHTE : HONG KONG.** **Main/Corp** Germany (Federal Republic, 1949). Statistisches Bundesamt. German. an. DM3.00. W Kohlhammer Verlag GmbH, Postfach 800430, D 70549 Stuttgart Germany. **Tel** 011 49 711 78631, FAX 011 49 711 7863263, telex 7-255820. **LC** HA1950.H6; G47A. **DD** 315.1/25.

GW
**LANDERKURZBERICHTE : JORDANIEN.** **Main/Corp** Germany (West). Statistisches Bundesamt. German. W Kohlhammer Verlag GMBH, Postfach 800430, D70549 Stuttgart Germany. **Tel** 011 49 711 78631. **LC** HA1950.J6; G45A. **DD** 315.695.

GW
**LANDERKURZBERICHTE : KONGO.** **Main/Corp** Germany (West). Statistisches Bundesamt. German. W Kohlhammer Verlag GMBH, Postfach 800430, D70549 Stuttgart Germany. **Tel** 011 49 711 78631. **LC** HA2088; .G45. ***Continues*** *Landerkurzberichte: Kongo (Brazzaville).*

GW/0072-2871
**LANDERKURZBERICHTE: KUBA.** **Main/Corp** Germany (West). Statistisches Bundesamt. **VFOAT** Kuba. (19??)-. German. W Kohlhammer Verlag GmbH, Postfach 800430, D 70549 Stuttgart Germany. **Tel** 011 49 711 78631, FAX 011 49 711 7863263, telex 7-255820. **LC** HA875; .G45. **DD** 317.291.

GW
**LANDERKURZBERICHTE : NEPAL.** **Main/Corp** Germany (West). Statistisches Bundesamt. **VFOAT** Nepal. German. W Kohlhammer Verlag GMBH, Postfach 800430, D70549 Stuttgart Germany. **Tel** 011 49 711 78631. **LC** HA1950 .N5; G45A. **DD** 315.49/6.

GW
**LANDERKURZBERICHTE : PANAMA.** **Main/Corp** Germany (West). Statistisches Bundesamt. **VFOAT** Panama. German. W Kohlhammer Verlag GmbH, Postfach 800430, D 70549 Stuttgart Germany. **Tel** 011 49 711 78631, FAX 011 49 711 7863263, telex 7-255820. **LC** HA853; .G45A. **DD** 317.287.

GW/0072-3274
**LANDERKURZBERICHTE : PERU.** **Main/Corp** Germany (West). Statistisches Bundesamt. **VFOAT** Peru. German. an. W Kohlhammer Verlag GmbH, Postfach 800430, D 70549 Stuttgart Germany. **Tel** 011 49 711 78631, FAX 011 49 711 7863263, telex 7-255820. **LC** HA1064; .G45A. **DD** 318.5.

GW
**LANDERKURZBERICHTE : REPUBLIK KOREA.** **Main/Corp** Germany (West). Statistisches Bundesamt. **VFOAT** Republik Korea. German. DM3.40. W Kohlhammer Verlag GMBH, Postfach 800430, D70549 Stuttgart Germany. **Tel** 011 49 711 78631. **LC** HA1855; .G46B. **DD** 315.19.

GW/0072-369X
**LANDERKURZBERICHTE : VENEZUELA.** **Main/Corp** Germany (West). Statistisches Bundesamt. German. be. W Kohlhammer Verlag GmbH, Postfach 800430, D 70549 Stuttgart Germany. **Tel** 011 49 711 78631, FAX 011 49 711 7863263, telex 7-255820. **LC** HA1095; .G45A. **DD** 318.7.

GW
**LANDERKURZBERICHTE : ZYPERN.** **Main/Corp** Germany (West). Statistisches Bundesamt. **VFOAT** Zypern. German. W Kohlhammer Verlag GMBH, Postfach 800430, D70549 Stuttgart Germany. **Tel** 011 49 711 78631. **LC** HA1950.C9; G45. **DD** 315.64/5.

IO
**LAPORAN KEPALA KANTOR SENSUS DAN STATISTIK DKI JAKARTA.** **Main/Corp** Jakarta Raya (Indonesia). Kantor Sensus dan Statistik. 1977/78-. Indonesian. an. Kantor Sensus dan Statistik Dki Jakarta, Jl Medan Merdeka Selatan 8-9, Lantai XX, Jakarta Indonesia. **LC** HA1818.J34; J34A. ***Continues*** *Laporan Kantor Sensus & I.E. dan Statistik D.K.I. Jakarta.*

GW/0930-0325
**LECTURE NOTES IN STATISTICS (BERLIN, WEST).** (LECTURE NOTES IN STATISTICS.). [Lect. notes stat.]. (1980)-. Monographic series. English. ir. Price varies per volume. Springer-Verlag GmbH & Company KG, Heidelberger Platz 3, D 14197 Berlin Germany. **Tel** 011 49 30 8207223, FAX 011 49 30 8214091, telex 183 319 SPBLN D. **(Subscription address:** Springer Verlag New York Inc. / for North America, 44 Hartz Way, Secaucus NJ 07096.**)** Documents available from Ask*IEEE.
**Desc:** Contains notes on statistics.
**Ind/Abst** For. Abstr.; INSPEC; Math. Rev.; Zentralbl. Math. Ihre Grenzgeb.

US/0749-2170
**LECTURE NOTES-MONOGRAPH SERIES.** (LECTURE NOTES-MONOGRAPH SERIES / INSTITUTE OF MATHEMATICAL STATISTICS.). [Lect. notes-monogr. ser.]. **Added/Corp** Institute of Mathematical Statistics. Vol. 2 (1982)-. Monographic series. English. ir. Price varies per volume. Institute of Mathematical Statistics, 3401 Investment Boulevard, Suite 7, Hayward CA 94545-3819. **Tel** (510)783-8141, FAX (510)783-4131. **DD** 519. ***Continues*** *Lecture Notes Series (Institute of Mathematical Statistics), 0749-2189.*

LO
**LESOTHO STATISTICAL YEARBOOK / COMPILED AND ISSUED BY BUREAU OF STATISTICS.** **Added/Corp** Lesotho. Bureau of Statistics. **VFOAT** Statistical Yearbook; Statistical Yearbook of the Kingdom of Lesotho. (1987)-. Statistical Publication. English. an. R20.00 Lesotho; R48.00 others in Africa; R58.00 others. Bureau of Statistics / Lesotho, PO Box 455, Maseru 100 Lesotho. **LC** HA1977.B35; A27. **DD** 316.885. **Ad Acc.** ***Continues*** *Annual Statistical Bulletin (Lesotho. Bureau of Statistics).*

HU
**LETMINIMUM / KOZPONTI STATISZTIKAI HIVATAL.** **Added/Corp** Hungary. Kozponti Statisztikai Hivatal. Eletszinvonal es Emberi Eroforras Statisztikai Foosztaly. (1991)-. Hungarian.

NE
**LIST OF MEMBERS OF THE INTERNATIONAL STATISTICAL INSTITUTE.** **Main/Corp** International Statistical Institute. **VFOAT** Liste des Membres de l'Institut International de Statistique. Statistical Publication. English (French). Institut International de Statistique, 428 Prinses Beatrixlaan, Voorburg Netherlands. **LC** HA11; .I624. **DD** 310/.6/21. **Circ:** 1,500 (ctrl).

US/1065-5476
**LOUISIANA IN PERSPECTIVE.** (LOUISIANA IN PERSPECTIVE : A STATISTICAL VIEW OF THE "PELICAN STATE".). [La. perspect.]. **Added/Corp** Morgan Quitno Corporation. (1990)-. Statistical Publication. English. $18.00. Morgan Quitno Corporation, PO Box 1656, 512 East 9th Street, Lawrence KS 66044. **Tel** (800)457-0742, (913)841-3534, FAX (913)841-3534. **DD** 317. ***Continues*** *Louisiana in Perspective, 1065-5476.*
**Desc:** Reports on the state's data and rank for each of the categories featured in State Rankings.

NE
**MAANDBULLETIN BUITENLANDSE HANDEL EEG.** SDU Uitgeverij, Postbus 20014, Christoffel Plan, 2500 EA Den Haag Netherlands. **Tel** 011 31 70 3789911.

NE
**MAANDSCHRIFT CBS.** (19??)-. Periodical. Dutch. Twelve times a year. Fl174.50. SDU Uitgeverij, Postbus 20014, Christoffel Plan, 2500 EA Den Haag Netherlands. **Tel** 011 31 70 3789911.

US/1065-5484
**MAINE IN PERSPECTIVE.** (MAINE IN PERSPECTIVE : A STATISTICAL VIEW OF THE "PINE TREE STATE".). [Maine perspect.]. **Added/Corp** Morgan Quitno Corporation. (1990)-. Statistical Publication. English. $18.00. Morgan Quitno Corporation, PO Box 1656, 512 East 9th Street, Lawrence KS 66044. **Tel** (800)457-0742, (913)841-3534, FAX (913)841-3534. **DD** 317. ***Continues*** *Maine in Perspective, 1065-5484.*
**Desc:** Reports on the state's data and rank for each of the categories featured in State Rankings.

MW
**MALAWI MONTHLY STATISTICAL BULLETIN.** ***Title Change.*** Statistical Publication. English. mo. National Statistical Office, PO Wards Strip NCO, Papua New Guinea. **Tel** 011 675 27182 271172, FAX 011 657 255057, telex FINANCE NE 22312. **LC** HA1977.M3; A3. **DD** 316.897. ***Continued by*** *Monthly Statistical Bulletin (Zomba, Mayawi).*

MW
**MALAWI STATISTICAL YEARBOOK.** **Added/Corp** Malawi. National Statistical Office. (1972)-. Statistical Publication. English. an. $12.00 Malawi; $17.00 others. Malawi National Statistical Office, PO Box 333, Zomba Malawi. **Tel** 011 265 522377, FAX 011 265 523130. **LC** HA1977.M3; M33. **DD** 316.89/7. ***Continues*** *Compendium of Statistics for Malawi.*

PL/0079-2608
**MALY ROCZNIK STATYSTYCZNY.** No. 1 (1958)-. Polish. an. Z11.00 Poland; Z17.00 North America; Z16.00 other. Zaklad Wydawnictw Statystyczych, AL Niepodleglosci 208, 00-925 Warszawa Poland. **Tel** 253241, telex 814581A GUS. **LC** HA1451; .A19. **Circ:** 50,000 (ctrl).

US/1065-5492
**MARYLAND IN PERSPECTIVE.** (MARYLAND IN PERSPECTIVE : A STATISTICAL VIEW OF THE "FREE STATE".). [Md. perspect.]. **Added/Corp** Morgan Quitno Corporation. (1990)-. Statistical Publication. English. $18.00. Morgan Quitno Corporation, PO Box 1656, 512 East 9th Street, Lawrence KS 66044. **Tel** (800)457-0742, (913)841-3534, FAX (913)841-3534. **DD** 317. ***Continues*** *Maryland in Perspective, 1065-5492.*
**Desc:** Reports on the state's data and rank for each of the categories featured in State Rankings.

US/0580-9029
**MARYLAND STATISTICAL ABSTRACT.** ***Title Change.*** **Main/Corp** Maryland. Dept. of Economic and Community Development. (1973)-(19??). Statistical Publication. English. be. Maryland Statistical Abstract, Division of Public Affairs, 45 Calvert Street, Annapolis MD 21401. **Tel** (301)333-6600. **ED** Irene Tashlick. **LC** HA421; .D46a. **DD** 317.52. **Circ:** 700. ***Continues*** *Maryland Statistical Abstract, 0580-9029.* ***Continued by*** *Maryland. Dept. of Economic and Employment Development. Maryland Statistical Abstract.*
**Desc:** The 1988-89 Maryland statistical abstract is a comprehensive presentation of numerous economic/demographic characteristics for Maryland and its subdivisions.

II
**MASIKA ANKARA SARA. MONTHLY ABSTRACT OF STATISTICS.** **Main/Corp** India. Central Statistical Organisation. **VFOAT** Monthly Abstract of Statistics. Vol. 30, No. 1/2 (Jan./Feb. 1977)-. Periodical. English (Hindi). mo. Rs720.00 India; $259.20 US. Deputy Director, Government of India, Ministry of Planning, Department of Statistics, Central Statistical Organisation, Industrial Statistics Wing 1, Council House Street, Calcutta-700001 India. **Tel** 23-6534. Index available. **Circ:** 700 (ctrl). ***Continues*** *India. Central Statistical Organisation. Monthly Abstract of Statistics.*
**Desc:** Presents key statistical data pertaining to various facets of the Indian economy. Subject coverage is periodically reviewed and attempts made to improve it, keeping in view comparability and continuity. The journal has a standing of more than 35 years.

US/1065-5506
**MASSACHUSETTS IN PERSPECTIVE.** (MASSACHUSETTS IN PERSPECTIVE : A STATISTICAL VIEW OF THE "BAY STATE".). [Mass. perspect.]. **Added/Corp** Morgan Quitno Corporation. (1990)-. Statistical Publication. English. $18.00. Morgan Quitno Corporation, PO Box 1656, 512 East 9th Street, Lawrence KS 66044. **Tel** (800)457-0742, (913)841-3534, FAX (913)841-3534. **DD** 317. ***Continues*** *Massachusetts in Perspective, 1065-5506.*
**Desc:** Reports on the state's data and rank for each of the categories featured in State Rankings.

US/0888-6083
**MASSACHUSETTS MUNICIPAL PROFILES.** (1987)-. Periodical. English. an. $75.00. Information Publications, 3790 El Camino Real/Suite 162, Palo Alto CA 94306. **Tel** (415)965-4449. **ED** Alfred N. Garwood. **LC** HA431; .M37. **DD** 317.44.
**Desc:** Collection of one page data profiles for every city and town in Massachusetts, alphabetically arranged, town by town, displays over 100 items on population, housing, government, finances, taxes and schools.

PL/0867-0846
**MATERIALY I OPRACOWANIA STATYSTYCZNE.** Polish. an. $8.00 US; $7.00 other. Zaklad Wydawnictw Statystycznych, Al Niepodleglosci 208, 00-925 Warszawa Poland. **Tel** 253241, telex 814581A GUS. ctrl circ.

PL
**MAY ROCZNIK STATYSTYKI MIEDZYNARODOWEJ.** 1972-. Polish. an. Z13.00 Poland; Z16.00 North America; Z15.00 other. Zaklad Wydawnictw Statystycznych, Al Niepodleglosci 208, 00-925 Warszawa Poland. **Tel** 253241, telex 814581A GUS. **(Subscription address:** CHZ Ars-Polona, Ul Krakowskie Przedmiescie 7, 00-068 Warszawa Poland**)** **LC** HA173.P6; A24 subser. **Circ:** 1,600.
**Desc:** Principal data on socio-development of major countries as well as a comparison with Poland.

FR
**MEMENTO DE STATISTIQUE AGRICOLE : DORDOGNE.** **See** Agriculture-Abstracting, Bibliographies and Statistics.

IT/0026-1424
**METRON.** Vol. 1 (July 1920)-. Periodical. English (Italian, French and German). Twice a year. L185000 Italy; $190.00 others. ESIA Books and Journals, Via Palestro 30, 00185 Rome Italy. **Tel** 011 39 6 4441220, 011 39 6 4441221, FAX 011 39 6 4747743. **ED** Carlo Benedetti. **LC** HA1; .M4. **DD** 310/.5. **CODEN** MRONAM. **Bk Rev. Circ:** 1,000. Documents available from BIOSIS Document Express.
**Desc:** Presents contributions of most significant mathematicians, statisticians and economists. Topics in statistics applied to demography, physics, biology and medicine.

**Ind/Abst** Biol. Abstr.; Math. Rev.; Stat. Theory Method Abstr. (1959-1963, 1966-1973, 1979, 1982-1984, 1986-1987); World Ceram. Abstr.; Zentralbl. Math. Ihre Grenzgeb.

FI/0784-929X
**METSATYONTEKIJOIDEN VUOSIANSIOT / TILASTOKESKUS.** **Added/Corp** Finland. Tilastokeskus. (19??)-. Finnish. an. Fmk55.00. Tilastokeskus, PL 504, Annankatu 44, 00101 Helsinki Finland. **Tel** 358-0-17341, FAX 358-0-17342474, telex 1002111 TILASTO SF. **ED** Mr. Jarmo Hyrkko. **LC** PAR.

HU/0238-7891
**MEZOGAZDASAGI ELELMISZERIPARI STATISZTIKAI ZSEBKONYU / LOZPONTI STATISZTIKAI HIVATAL.** **VFOAT** Mezogazdasagi Zsebkonyv. Hungarian. an. 71.00ft. Statisztikai Kiado Vallalat, PO Box 99, H-1033 Budapest 3 Hungary. **Tel** 803-311, telex 22-6699-SKV-H. **LC** HD1940.5; .A28. **Ad Acc. Circ:** 3,500.
**Desc:** Statistical data on farming results such as the value, sale and price of agricultural products. It also includes information on the cultivation of plants, livestock farming, forestry, food industry and weather conditions.

US/1065-5514
**MICHIGAN IN PERSPECTIVE.** (MICHIGAN IN PERSPECTIVE : A STATISTICAL VIEW OF THE "GREAT LAKE STATE" / KATHLEEN O'LEARY MORGAN, SCOTT MORGAN AND NEAL QUITNO, EDITORS.). [Mich. perspect.]. **Added/Corp** Morgan Quitno Corporation. (1990)-. Statistical Publication. English. $18.00. Morgan Quitno Corporation, PO Box 1656, 512 East 9th Street, Lawrence KS 66044. **Tel** (800)457-0742, (913)841-3534, FAX (913)841-3534. **DD** 317. ***Continues*** *Michigan in Perspective, 1065-5514.*
**Desc:** Reports on the state's data and rank for each of the categories featured in State Rankings.

JA
**MINI TOKEI HANDO BUKKU.** **Added/Corp** Japan. Sorifu. Tokeikyoku. (19??)-. Japanese. Sorifu Tokeikyoku, 95 Wakamatsu-cho Shinjuku-ku, Tokyo-to 162 Japan. **LC** HA4621; .M55.

US/1065-5522
**MINNESOTA IN PERSPECTIVE.** (MINNESOTA IN PERSPECTIVE : A STATISTICAL VIEW OF THE "NORTH STAR STATE".). [Minn. perspect.]. **Added/Corp** Morgan Quitno Corporation. (1990)-. Statistical Publication. English. $18.00. Morgan Quitno Corporation, PO Box 1656, 512 East 9th Street, Lawrence KS 66044. **Tel** (800)457-0742, (913)841-3534, FAX (913)841-3534. **DD** 317. ***Continues*** *Minnesota in Perspective, 1065-5522.*
**Desc:** Reports on the state's data and rank for each of the categories featured in State Rankings.

US/0093-9668
**MINNESOTA STATISTICAL ABSTRACT.** **Main/Corp** Minnesota State Planning Agency. Office of Local and Urban Affairs. 1973-. Statistical Publication. English. Minnesota State Planning Agency, 300 Centennial Office Building, St Paul MN 55155-1600. **LC** HA451; .S73A. **DD** 317.76.

US
**MINNESOTA STATISTICAL PROFILE.** **Main/Corp** Minnesota. Dept. of Economic Development. Research Division. 1976-. Statistical Publication. English. 480 Cedar Street, St Paul MN 55101. **LC** HA451; .D46A. **DD** 317.76. ***Continues*** *Minnesota Profile.*

US/1065-5530
**MISSISSIPPI IN PERSPECTIVE.** (MISSISSIPPI IN PERSPECTIVE : A STATISTICAL VIEW OF THE "MAGNOLIA STATE".). [Miss. perspect.]. **Added/Corp** Morgan Quitno Corporation. (1990)-. Statistical Publication. English. $18.00. Morgan Quitno Corporation, PO Box 1656, 512 East 9th Street, Lawrence KS 66044. **Tel** (800)457-0742, (913)841-3534, FAX (913)841-3534. **DD** 317. ***Continues*** *Mississippi in Perspective, 1065-5336.*
**Desc:** Reports on the state's data and rank for each of the categories featured in State Rankings.

US/0745-2535
**MISSISSIPPI MORBIDITY REPORT.** (MISSISSIPPI MORBIDITY REPORT / MISSISSIPPI STATE DEPARTMENT OF HEALTH.). [Miss. morb. rep.]. Periodical. English. mo. Mississippi Department of Health, PO Box 1700, Jackson MS 39215. **Tel** (601)960-7634, FAX (601)960-7948. **LC** RA407.4.M7; M57.

US
**MISSISSIPPI STATISTICAL ABSTRACT.** **Added/Corp** Mississippi State University. College of Business and Industry. Division of Research. Mississippi Research and Development Center. (1969)-. Statistical Publication. English. an. $35.00. Mississippi State University / Mississippi Statistical Abstract, PO Drawer 5288, Mississippi State MS 39762. **Tel** (601)325-3817. **ED** Janis Bryant. **LC** HA465; .A25. **DD** 317.62. **Circ:** 600. ***Continues*** *Statistical Abstract of Mississippi.*
**Desc:** Compilation of statistical data on the state of Mississippi.

US/1065-5549
**MISSOURI IN PERSPECTIVE (LAWRENCE, KAN.).** (MISSOURI IN PERSPECTIVE : A STATISTICAL VIEW OF THE "SHOW ME STATE".). [Mo. perspect.]. **Added/Corp** Morgan Quitno Corporation. (1990)-. Statistical Publication. English. $18.00. Morgan Quitno Corporation, PO Box 1656, 512 East 9th Street, Lawrence KS 66044. **Tel** (800)457-0742, (913)841-3534, FAX (913)841-3534. **DD** 317. ***Continues*** *Missouri in Perspective (Elmwood, Neb.), 1065-5549.*
**Desc:** Reports on the state's data and rank for each of the categories featured in State Rankings.

US/0098-1974
**MISSOURI VITAL STATISTICS.** **Main/Corp** Missouri Center for Health Statistics. 1973-. English. an. Missouri Vital Statistics, Box 570, Jefferson City MO 65102-0570. **Tel** (314)751-8074. **ED** Wayne Schramm. **LC** HA471; .C45A. **DD** 312/.09778. **NLM** W2 AM8 B9V. **Circ:** 700 (ctrl). ***Continues*** *Missouri Vital Statistics.*
**Desc:** Missouri vital statistic data in the state containing a short two or three page analytical article relating to public health data of interest.

SZ
**MONATSBLATTER.** **Added/Corp** Statistisches Amt der Stadt Zurich. (1991)-. German. mo. Statistisches Amt der Stadt Zurich, Napfgasse 6, 8001 Zurich Switzerland. **LC** HA1609.Z87; M66. **DD** 314.94/57/021. ***Continues*** *Monatsheft (Statistisches Amt der Stadt Zurich).*

UK/0960-6696
**MONOGRAPHS ON STATISTICS AND APPLIED PROBABILITY.** [Monogr. stat. appl. probab.]. (1975)-. Monographic series. English.
**Ind/Abst** Zentralbl. Math. Ihre Grenzgeb.

US/1065-5557
**MONTANA IN PERSPECTIVE.** (MONTANA IN PERSPECTIVE : A STATISTICAL VIEW OF THE "TREASURE STATE".). [Mont. perspect.]. **Added/Corp** Morgan Quitno Corporation. (1990)-. Statistical Publication. English. $18.00. Morgan Quitno Corporation, PO Box 1656, 512 East 9th Street, Lawrence KS 66044. **Tel** (800)457-0742, (913)841-3534, FAX (913)841-3534. **DD** 317. ***Continues*** *Montana in Perspective, 1065-5557.*
**Desc:** Reports on the state's data and rank for each of the categories featured in State Rankings.

CH/0256-2324
**MONTHLY BULLETIN OF STATISTICS, THE REPUBLIC OF CHINA.** [Mon. bull. stat. - Repub. China]. **Main/Corp** China (Republic : 1949-). Hsing Cheng Yuan. Vol. 1 (July 1975)-. English. Twelve times a year. $35.00. Cheng Chung Shu Chu, 20 Heng Yang Road, Taipei Taiwan. **Tel** 011 886 2 3813825. **LC** HA1710.5; .A183b. **DD** 315.1/249.

US/0041-7432
**MONTHLY BULLETIN OF STATISTICS - UNITED NATIONS.** (MONTHLY BULLETIN OF STATISTICS / STATISTICAL OFFICE OF THE UNITED NATIONS.). [Mon. bull. stat. - U. N.]. **Added/Corp** United Nations. Statistical Office. **VFOAT** Bulletin Mensuel de Statistique. Vol. 1, No. 1 (Jan. 1947)-. Statistical Publication. English (French). mo. $225.00; $450.00 (commercial). United Nations Publications, 2 United Nations Plaza, Room DC2 0853, Department 007C, New York NY 10017. **Tel** (212)963-8303, (800)253-9646. **(Subscription address:** United Nations Publications, Subscription Office, PO Box 361, Birmingham AL 35201-0361.**)** **LC** HC57; .U66. **DD** 330.9/0021. available on microfilm and microfiche from University Microfilms International (UMI). ***Continues*** *Monthly Bulletin of Statistics (United Nations. Statistical Office : 1946).*
**Desc:** Provides statistics from over 200 countries and territories on more than 70 subjects such as population, food, trade, production, finance and national income.

SI
**MONTHLY DIGEST OF STATISTICS.** **Main/Corp** Singapore. Dept. of Statistics. Vol. 1 (Jan. 1962)-. English. Twelve times a year. 111.60Sing$ (surface mail); 132.00Sing$ Taiwan, Korea, and Hong Kong, 152.40Sing$ US, (airmail). Chief Statistician Singapore, 8 Shenton Way 10 01 Treasury B, Singapore 0106 Singapore. **Tel** 011 65 3239686, telex 20826 STATS RS. **LC** HA1797.S5; A34. **DD** 315.95/7. **Circ:** 900. ***Supersedes*** *Malayan Statistics; Digest of Economic and Social Statistics.*
**Desc:** It gives the latest available data on the demographic and economic characteristics of Singapore.

ZA/0027-0377
**MONTHLY DIGEST OF STATISTICS.** **Main/Corp** Zambia. Central Statistical Office. Vol. 1 (Apr. 19640-. English. mo. Central Statistical Office / Zambia, PO Box 1908, Lusaka Zambia. **Tel** 211231. **DD** 316. **Circ:** 1,000 (ctrl). ***Supersedes*** *Northern Rhodesia. Central Statistical Office. Monthly Digest of Statistics.*
**Desc:** Time series of data on population and migration, agriculture, employment, production, external trade transport, government accounts, money and banking, prices, national accounts education, and health.

UK/0017-3622
**MONTHLY DIGEST OF STATISTICS.** **Main/Corp** Great Britain. Central Statistical Office. No. 1 (Jan. 1946)-. Periodical. English. mo. £85.00. Her Majesty's Stationery Office, 51 Nine Elms Lane, London SW8 5DR England. **Tel** 011 44 71 873 8459, 011 44 71 873 8499, FAX 011 44 71 873 8499, 011 44 71 873 8456, telex 297138. **(Subscription address:** Her Majestys Stationery Offic, PO Box 276 Public Centre, London SW8 5DT England**)** **LC** HC251; .A32. **DD** 330.942.

HK
**MONTHLY MARKET STATISTICS.** Chinese. mo. HK$120.00 Hong Kong; HK$204.00 Asia; HK$216.00 other. Stock Exchange Hong Kong Ltd., Exchange Square, Box 8888, Hong Kong, Hong Kong. **Tel** 011 852 5221122.

MW
**MONTHLY STATISTICAL BULLETIN.** **Added/Corp** Malawi. National Statistical Office. (19??)-. Statistical Publication. English. mo. $15.00 Malawi; $21.00 other. Malawi National Statistical Office, PO Box 333, Zomba Malawi. **Tel** 011 265 522377, FAX 011 265 523130. **Bk Rev.** ctrl circ. ***Continues*** *Malawi Monthly Statistical Bulletin.*

BG/0377-1555
**MONTHLY STATISTICAL BULLETIN OF BANGLADESH.** **Main/Corp** Bangladesh. Bureau of Statistics. Vol. 1 (March 1972)-. Statistical Publication. English. Twelve times a year. $120.00. Bangladesh Bureau of Statistics, Ministry of Planningstats Division, Dacca 1000 Bangladesh. **Tel** 011 880 23000 29312081. **LC** HA1730.8; .A23. **DD** 315.49/2. **Circ:** 300. ***Continues*** *Monthly Bulletin of Statistics / East Pakistan. Bureau of Statistics.*

CN/0837-8649
**MONTHLY STATISTICAL REVIEW - SASKATCHEWAN. BUREAU OF STATISTICS (1978).** (MONTHLY STATISTICAL REVIEW / GOVERNMENT OF SASKATCHEWAN, BUREAU OF STATISTICS.). [Mon. stat. rev. - Sask., Bur. Stat.]. **Main/Corp** Saskatchewan. Bureau of Statistics. **Added/Corp** Saskatchewan. Bureau of Statistics. Vol. 4 (Jan. 1978)-. Statistical Publication. English. Twelve times a year. Free on request. Bureau of Statistics / Saskatchewan, 3475 Albert Street, TC Douglas Building, Regina Sask S4S 6X6 Canada. **Tel** (306)565-6333. **LC** HA747.S3; S25a. **DD** 317.124. **Circ:** 600. ***Continues*** *Saskatchewan Monthly Statistical Review, 0837-8630.*
**Desc:** Economic and social statistics for the province of Saskatchewan.

BG
**MONTHLY SUMMARY OF JUTE GOODS STATISTICS.** **Main/Corp** Bangladesh Jute Mills Association. English. 6.00. Bangladesh Jute Mills Association, 62/63 Motijheel, Dacca Bangladesh. **LC** HD9156.J8; P45. **DD** 338.4/7/67713095492. ***Continues*** *Monthly Summary of Jute Goods Statistics.*

AT
**MONTHLY SUMMARY OF STATISTICS, AUSTRALIA.** **Main/Corp** Australian Bureau of Statistics. (July 1979)-. English. Twelve times a year. 244.80Aus$. Australian Bureau of Statistics, PO Box 10, Belconnen Australian Capital Territory, 2616 Australia. **Tel** 011 61 6 2527911, FAX 011 61 6 2516009. **LC** HC601; .A32. **DD** 330.994/005. ***Continues*** *Monthly Review of Business Statistics, 0311-9025.*
**Desc:** Data on a wide range of items classified in varying degree of details for population and vital statistics, employment and unemployment, internal and overseas trade, etc.

AT/0314-2094
**MONTHLY SUMMARY OF STATISTICS, TASMANIA / AUSTRALIAN BUREAU OF STATISTICS.** **Added/Corp** Australian Bureau of Statistics. Tasmanian Office. No. 396 (June 1978)-. English. mo. 22.30Aus$. Australian Bureau Statistics / Tasmanian Office, Commonwealth Government Centre, 188 Collins Street, Hobart GPO Box 66A, Hobart Tasmania 7001 Australia. **Tel** (002)205889. **LC** HA3007.T37; M66. **DD** 319.46. ***Continues*** *Monthly Summary of Statistics (Australian Bureau of Statistics. Tasmania Office).*
**Desc:** Contains tables dealing with: population and vital statistics, employment and unemployment, wages and prices, production statistics, building, finance and trade.

RU/0259-5133
**MOSKVA V CIFRAH.** (MOSKVA V TSIFRAKH.). [Mosk. cifrah]. **Main/Corp** Statisticheskoe Upravlenie Goroda Moskvy. (19??)-. Russian. an. 0.65rub. Izdatelstvo Finansy I Statistika, Ulitsa Chernyshvskogo 7, K-142, 101000 Moscow Russia. **LC** HA1449.M8; M58a. **CODEN** MTSFE2.

FI/0357-6507
**MUISTIO (FINLAND. TILASTOKESKUS).** (MUISTIO.). Monographic series. Finnish. Price varies per volume. **LC** HA37; .F516.

II
**MUNICIPAL YEAR BOOK, KERALA.**
English. Government of Kerala / Bureau of Economics and Statistics, Trivandrum India. **LC** HA4587.K47; M86. **DD** 315.4/83.

UN/0258-0780
**NARODNOE HOZAJSTVO UKRAINSKOJ SSR. STATISTICESKIJ EZEGODNIK.** (NARODNOE KHOZIAISTVO UKRAINSKOI SSR.). [Nar. hoz Ukr. SSR. Stat. ezegod.]. **Added/Corp** Ukraine. TSentralne Statystychne Upravlinnia. (19??)-. Russian. Tekhnika, Pushkinskaia 28, Kiev Ukraine. **Tel** 282243. **LC** HA1448.U6; N33.

RU
**NARODNOE KHOZIAISTVO LENINGRADA I LENINGRADSKOI OBLASTI. Main/Corp** Leningrad, Russian S. F. S. R. Statisticheskoe Upravlenie. (19??)-. Russian. 1.05rub. Fontanka 59, St. Petersburg Russia. **LC** HA1448.L4; L38a.

RU
**NARODNOE KHOZIAISTVO SOTSIALISTICHESKIKH STRAN V ... GODU : SOOBSHCHENIIA TSSU / INSTITUT EKONOMIKI MIROVOI SOTSIALISTICHESKOI SISTEMY AN SSSR, SEKTOR STATISTIKI. Added/Corp** Institut Ekonomiki Mirovoi Sotsialisticheskoi Sistemy (Akademiia Nauk SSSR). Sektor Statistiki. Institut Ekonomiki Mirovoi Sotsialisticheskoi Sistemy (Akademiia Nauk SSSR). (1961)-. Russian. an. Izdatelstvo Ekonomika, Berezhkovskaia Nab., 6, 121864 Moscow Russia. **LC** PAR.

US/1065-5565
**NEBRASKA IN PERSPECTIVE.** (NEBRASKA IN PERSPECTIVE : A STATISTICAL VIEW OF THE "CORNHUSKER STATE".). [Neb. perspect.]. **Added/Corp** Morgan Quitno Corporation. (1990)-. Statistical Publication. English. $18.00. Morgan Quitno Corporation, PO Box 1656, 512 East 9th Street, Lawrence KS 66044. **Tel** (800)457-0742, (913)841-3534, FAX (913)841-3534. **DD** 317. ***Continues** Nebraska in Perspective, 1065-5565.*
**Desc:** Reports on the state's data and rank for each of the categories featured in State Rankings.

US/1065-559X
**NEVADA IN PERSPECTIVE.** (NEVADA IN PERSPECTIVE : A STATISTICAL VIEW OF THE "SAGEBRUSH STATE".). [Nev. perspect.]. **Added/Corp** Morgan Quitno Corporation. (1990)-. Statistical Publication. English. $18.00. Morgan Quitno Corporation, PO Box 1656, 512 East 9th Street, Lawrence KS 66044. **Tel** (800)457-0742, (913)841-3534, FAX (913)841-3534. **DD** 317. ***Continues** Nevada in Perspective, 1065-559X.*
**Desc:** Reports on the state's data and rank for each of the categories featured in State Rankings.

US
**NEVADA STATISTICAL ABSTRACT. Added/Corp** Nevada. Governor's Office of Planning Coordination. Nevada. Dept. of Administration. (1977)-. Statistical Publication. English. be. $20.00. Nevada State Offices, Office of Community Services, Capitol Complex, Carson City NV 89710. **Tel** (702)687-4065. **(Subscription address:** State of Nevada Department of Administration, Planning Division, Capitol Complex, Carson City NV 89710.**) ED** Peter D. Christiansen and John B. Walker. **LC** HA501; .N48. **DD** 317.93. **Bk Rev. Ad Acc. Circ:** 1,000 (ctrl).
**Desc:** Statistical and demographic data on Nevada. Topics include: population, housing employment and earnings, energy, government and taxes, education, etc. Data available to county level.

US/1065-5581
**NEW HAMPSHIRE IN PERSPECTIVE.** (NEW HAMPSHIRE IN PERSPECTIVE : A STATISTICAL VIEW OF THE "GRANITE STATE".). [N.H. perspect.]. **Added/Corp** Morgan Quitno Corporation. (1990)-. Statistical Publication. English. $18.00. Morgan Quitno Corporation, PO Box 1656, 512 East 9th Street, Lawrence KS 66044. **Tel** (800)457-0742, (913)841-3534, FAX (913)841-3534. **DD** 317. ***Continues** New Hampshire in Perspective, 1065-5581.*
**Desc:** Reports on the state's data and rank for each of the categories featured in State Rankings.

US/1065-5573
**NEW JERSEY IN PERSPECTIVE.** (NEW JERSEY IN PERSPECTIVE : A STATISTICAL VIEW OF THE "GARDEN STATE".). [N.J. perspect.]. **Added/Corp** Morgan Quitno Corporation. (1990)-. Statistical Publication. English. $18.00. Morgan Quitno Corporation, PO Box 1656, 512 East 9th Street, Lawrence KS 66044. **Tel** (800)457-0742, (913)841-3534, FAX (913)841-3534. **DD** 317. ***Continues** New Jersey in Perspective, 1065-5573.*
**Desc:** Reports on the state's data and rank for each of the categories featured in State Rankings.

US/1065-5794
**NEW MEXICO IN PERSPECTIVE.** (NEW MEXICO IN PERSPECTIVE : A STATISTICAL VIEW OF THE "LAND OF ENCHANTMENT STATE".). [N.M. perspect.]. **Added/Corp** Morgan Quitno Corporation. (1990)-. Statistical Publication. English. $18.00. Morgan Quitno Corporation, PO Box 1656, 512 East 9th Street, Lawrence KS 66044. **Tel** (800)457-0742, (913)841-3534, FAX (913)841-3534. **DD** 317. ***Continues** New Mexico in Perspective, 1065-5794.*
**Desc:** Reports on the state's data and rank for each of the categories featured in State Rankings.

US/1065-5603
**NEW YORK IN PERSPECTIVE.** (NEW YORK IN PERSPECTIVE : A STATISTICAL VIEW OF THE "EMPIRE STATE".). [N.Y. perspect.]. **Added/Corp** Morgan Quitno Corporation. (1990)-. Statistical Publication. English. $18.00. Morgan Quitno Corporation, PO Box 1656, 512 East 9th Street, Lawrence KS 66044. **Tel** (800)457-0742, (913)841-3534, FAX (913)841-3534. **DD** 317. ***Continues** New York in Perspective, 1065-5603.*
**Desc:** Reports on the state's data and rank for each of the categories featured in State Rankings.

US
**NEW YORK STATE BUSINESS STATISTICS. QUARTERLY SUMMARY. Added/Corp** New York (State). Bureau of Business Research. (Jan.-Mar. 1989)-. Periodical. English. qt. New York Department of Commerce, 99 Washington Avenue, Albany NY 12245. **Tel** (518)474-6950, (518)474-5027. ***Continues** Business Statistics, New York State. Quarterly Summary.*

US/0077-9334
**NEW YORK STATE STATISTICAL YEARBOOK.** [N. Y. State stat. yearb.]. **Added/Corp** New York (State). Division of the Budget. Office of Statistical Coordination. New York (State). Division of the Budget. Technical Services Unit. New York (State). Division of the Budget. Budget Services Unit. Nelson A. Rockefeller Institute of Government. 1st Ed. (1967)-. Statistical Publication. English. an (July). $54.00. Rockefeller Institute, 411 State Street, Albany NY 12203. **Tel** (518)443-5522, FAX (518)443-5788. **ED** Michael Cooper (editor's telephone: (518)443-5258). **LC** HA541; .N48. **DD** 317.47. Index available. **Circ:** 3,000. available on microfiche from Congressional Information Service.
**Desc:** Over 450 pages of statistical tables prepared with cooperation of 70 state agencies. Also contains a complete description of every state agency, as well as names and phone numbers of agency contacts.

NZ/0111-9176
**NEW ZEALAND STATISTICIAN, THE. Added/Corp** New Zealand Statistical Association. (1966)-. Periodical. English. sa. 30.00NZ$. New Zealand Statistical Association, PO Box 1731, Wellington New Zealand. **Tel** 011 64 4 190448. **[CCC].**
**Ind/Abst** Curr. Index Stat.

NZ
**NEW ZEALAND VISITOR STATISTICS.** (NEW ZEALAND VISITOR STATISTICS. THE AMERICAS.). 1987/88-. English. an. $50.00. New Zealand Tourist and Publicity Department, Head Office 256 Lambton Quay, PO Box 95, Wellington New Zealand. **Tel** 728 860, FAX 781 736, telex NZ 3491. **LC** G155.N5; N47. **DD** 338.4/791930437021. ***Continues in part** New Zealand Visitor Statistics.*

NZ
**NEW ZEALAND VISITOR STATISTICS. ASIA.** 1987/88-. English. an. Free. New Zealand Tourist and Publicity Department, Head Office 256 Lambton Quay, PO Box 95, Wellington New Zealand. **Tel** 728 860, FAX 781 736, telex NZ 3491. **LC** G155.N5; N474. **DD** 338.4/791930437/021. Index available. **Ad Acc. Circ:** 100 (ctrl). ***Continues in part** New Zealand Visitor Statistics.*
**Desc:** Annual visitor arrival statistics.

NZ
**NEW ZEALAND VISITOR STATISTICS. AUSTRALIA AND PACIFIC.** 1987/88-. English. an. Free. New Zealand Tourist and Publicity Department, Head Office 256 Lambton Quay, PO Box 95, Wellington New Zealand. **Tel** 728 860, FAX 781 736, telex NZ 3491. **LC** G155.N5; N475. **DD** 338.4/791930437/021. Index available. **Ad Acc. Circ:** 100 (ctrl). ***Continues in part** New Zealand Visitor Statistics.*
**Desc:** Annual visitor arrival statistics.

NZ
**NEW ZEALAND VISITOR STATISTICS. EUROPE.** 1987/88-. English. an. Free. New Zealand Tourist and Publicity Department, Head Office 256 Lambton Quay, PO Box 95, Wellington New Zealand. **Tel** 728 860, FAX 781 736, telex NZ 3491. **LC** G155.N5; N48. **DD** 338.4/791930437/021. Index available. **Ad Acc. Circ:** 100 (ctrl). ***Continues in part** New Zealand Visitor Statistics.*
**Desc:** Annual visitor arrival statistics.

NZ
**NEW ZEALAND VISITOR STATISTICS. TOTAL VISITORS.** 1987/88-. English. an. Free. New Zealand Tourist and Publicity Department, Head Office 256 Lambton Quay, PO Box 95, Wellington New Zealand. **Tel** 728 860, FAX 781 736, telex NZ 3491. **LC** G155.N5; N485. **DD** 338.4/791930437/021. Index available. **Ad Acc. Circ:** 100 (ctrl). ***Continues in part** New Zealand Visitor Statistics.*
**Desc:** Annual visitor arrival statistics.

US/0014-9225
**NEWSLETTER - FEDERAL STATISTICS USERS' CONFERENCE.** [Newsl. - Fed. Stat. Users' Conf.]. **Main/Corp** Federal Statistics Users' Conference. Newsletter. English. mo. $30.00. Federal Statistics Users' Conference, 1030 Fifteenth Street NW, Washington DC 20005.

AT/0314-6820
**NEWSLETTER - STATISTICAL SOCIETY OF AUSTRALIA.** [Newsl. - Stat. Soc. Aust.]. (1977)-. Newsletter. English. qt. 8.00Aus$. Australian Statistical Publishing Association Inc, GPO Box 573, Canberra ACT 2601 Australia. **Tel** 011 61 6249889, FAX 011 61 6 2498266, telex 62337. **DD** 001.42206294.
**Ind/Abst** AESIS Q.

JA
**NEYAGAWA-SHI TOKEISHO. Main/Corp** Neyagawa-Shi (Japan). (19??)-. Statistical Publication. Japanese. an. Neyagawa Shiyakusho, 1-1 Honmachi, Neyagawa 582 Japan. **LC** HA1849.N47; N47a.

GW
**NIEDERSACHSEN IN ZAHLEN.** German. an. DM2.00. Niedersachsisches Landesverwaltungsamt, Postfach 107, 3000 Hannover Germany. **Tel** (0511)108-9466. **LC** HA1301; .N53. **Circ:** 17,000.
**Desc:** Statistical dates about population, economy and the country of lower saxony.

JA/0303-6065
**NIHON HYOJUN SANGYO BUNRUI; GOJUON SAKUIN HYO.** [Nihon hyojun sangyo bunrui. Gojuon sakuin hyo]. Began in 1949. Japanese. ir. ¥1600. Zenkoku Tokei Kyokai Rengokai, 3-1-1 Kasumigaseki Chiyoda-ku, Tokyo Japan. **LC** HA40.I6; N483.

JA/0389-5602
**NIHON TOKEI GAKKAISHI (TOKYO. 1970).** (NIHON TOKEI GAKKAI SHI.). [Nihon Tokei Gakkaishi]. **Added/Corp** Nihon Tokei Gakkai. **VFOAT** Journal of the Japan Statistical Society. Vol. 1, No. 1 (1970)-. English (Japanese). sa. $114.00. Nihon Tokei Gakkai, c/o Tokei Suri Kenkyujo, 4-6-7 Minami Azabu, Minato-ku, Tokyo Japan 106. **Tel** 03-442-5801. **(Subscription address:** Kyowa Book Company Inc., 1-38 Kanda Jinbo-Cho, Chiyoda-Ku Tokyo 101, Japan**) ED** Naoto Kunitomo. **LC** HA1; .N5. **Bk Rev. Circ:** 1,350.
**Ind/Abst** Curr. Index Stat.; Math. Rev.

JA
**NIHON TOKEI GEPPO. Added/Corp** Japan. Sorifu. Tokeikyoku. Monthly Statistics of Japan. Nihon Tokei Kyokai. **VFOAT** Monthly Statistics of Japan. (July 1961)-. Periodical. Japanese (table of contents in English). mo. $230.00. Somucho Tokeikyoku, (Statistics Bureau, Management & Coordination Agency), 19-1, Wakamatsucho, Shinjukuku, Tokyoto 162 Japan. **(Subscription address:** Kyowa Book Company Inc., 1 38 Kanda Jinbocho Chiyoda-ku, Tokyo 101 Japan.**)** ***Supersedes** Japan. Sorifu. Tokeikyoku. Tokei Geppo.*

JA/0389-9004
**NIHON TOKEI NENKAN.** [Nihon tokei nenkan]. **Added/Corp** Japan. Sorifu. Tokeikyoku. **VFOAT** Japan Statistical Yearbook. (1949)-. Statistical Publication. English (Japanese). an. Price varies per volume. Japan Statistical Association, 19 1 Wakamatuchu, Shinjuku, Tokyo Japan. **(Subscription address:** Taylor & Francis Inc., 1900 Frost Road, Suite 101, Bristol PA 19007-1598.**) DD** 315.2. ***Continues** Dai Nihon Teikou Tokei Nenkan.*

BL
**NORDESTE EM NUMEROS. Main/Corp** Brazil. Superintendencia do Desenvolvimento do Nordeste. Divisao de Comercio. Portuguese. Av Prof Moraes Rego, S/N Cidade Universitaria, Recife Brazil. **LC** HA973; .B72A.

US/1065-5611
**NORTH CAROLINA IN PERSPECTIVE.** (NORTH CAROLINA IN PERSPECTIVE : A STATISTICAL VIEW OF THE "TARHEEL STATE."). [N.C. perspect.]. **Added/Corp** Morgan Quitno Corporation. (1990)-. Statistical Publication. English. $18.00. Morgan Quitno Corporation, PO Box 1656, 512 East 9th Street, Lawrence KS 66044. **Tel** (800)457-0742, (913)841-3534, FAX (913)841-3534. **DD** 317. ***Continues** North Carolina in Perspective, 1065-5611.*
**Desc:** Reports on the state's data and rank for each of the categories featured in State Rankings.

# Statistics

US/1065-562X
**NORTH DAKOTA IN PERSPECTIVE (LAWRENCE, KAN.).** (NORTH DAKOTA IN PERSPECTIVE : A STATISTICAL VIEW OF THE "PEACE GARDEN STATE".). [N.D. perspect]. **Added/Corp** Morgan Quitno Corporation. (1990)-. Statistical Publication. English. $18.00. Morgan Quitno Corporation, PO Box 1656, 512 East 9th Street, Lawrence KS 66044. **Tel** (800)457-0742, (913)841-3534, FAX (913)841-3534. **DD** 317. **Continues** North Dakota in Perspective, 1065-562X.
**Desc:** Reports on the state's data and rank for each of the categories featured in State Rankings.

IE/0267-6044
**NORTHERN IRELAND ANNUAL ABSTRACT OF STATISTICS.** [North. Irel. annu. abstr. stat.]. **Added/Corp** Northern Ireland. Dept. of Finance and Personnel. Policy Planning and Research Unit. (1982)-. English. an. £16.50. Statistics and Social Division / Policy Planning and Research Unit, Department of Finance & Personnel, Room 250, Parliament Buildings, Stormont, Belfast BT4 3SW Northern Ireland. **Tel** 0232 521538, FAX 0232 521660. **CODEN** NIRSE4. **Circ:** 500.

CM
**NOTE ANNUELLE DE STATISTIQUE - DIRECTION DE LA STATISTIQUE ET DE LA COMPTABILITE NATIONALE.** **Main/Corp** Cameroon. Dept. of Statistics and National Accounts. Yearly V. 1973/74–. French. 7500CFAF. Department of Statistics and National Accounts / Cameroon, Boite Postale No 660, Yaounde Cameroon. **Tel** 22-04-45. **LC** HA2141; .D46A. **DD** 316.7/11.

FR/0005-559X
**NOTES D'INFORMATION ET STATISTIQUES.** [Notes inf. stat.]. **Main/Corp** Banque Centrale des Etats de l'Afrique de l'Ouest. **Added/Corp** Institut d'Emission de l'Afrique Occidentale Francaise et du Togo. (1956)-. Periodical. French. Eleven times a year. $40.00. Banque Centrale des Etats de l'Afrique de l'Ouest, Siega Avenue du Barachois Boite, Postale 3108, Dakar Senegal.

IT
**NOTIZIARIO ISTAT. SERIE 1 : ATTIVITA PRODUTTIVA. FOGLLIO 14 : STATISTICA DEL COMMERCIO CON L'ESTERO.** **Ceased.** **Main/Corp** Istituto Centrale di Statistica (Italy). (19??)-(Dec. 1993). Italian. mo. Istituto Nazionale Statistica, GBP SEZ4 Via Cesare Balbo 16, 00184 Rome Italy. **Tel** 011 39 6 46735118.

IT
**NOTIZIARIO ISTAT. SERIE 2: STATISTICHE DELL ATTIVITA PRODUTTIVA.** **Ceased.** (19??)-(Dec. 1993). Italian. Istituto Nazionale Statistica, GBP SEZ4 Via Cesare Balbo 16, 00184 Rome Italy. **Tel** 011 39 6 46735118.

IT
**NOTIZIARIO ISTAT. SERIE 3 : POPOLAZIONE. FOGLIO 31 : ANDAMENTO DEMOGRAFICO.** **Ceased.** **Main/Corp** Istituto Centrale di Statistica (Italy). (19??)-(Dec. 1993). Periodical. Italian. mo. Istituto Central Statistica, GPB Sez4, Via Cesare Balbo 16, 00184 Rome Italy.

IT
**NOTIZIARIO ISTAT. SERIE 4: ARGOMENTI VARI.** **Ceased.** (19??)-(Dec. 1993). Italian. ir. Istituto Nazionale Statistica, GBP SEZ4 Via Cesare Balbo 16, 00184 Rome Italy. **Tel** 011 39 6 46735118.

IT
**NOTIZIARIO STATISTICO INAIL.** (19??)-. Italian. Three times a year. L16400. Inail Direz Generale, Serv Rel Int Est, Via IV Noviembre 144, 00187 Rome Italy. **Tel** 011 39 6 672041.

US
**NUNG KUNG SHANG PU TUNG CHI PIAO.** **Main/Corp** China. Nung Kung Shang Pu. Chinese. Center for Chinese Research Materials / Washington DC, Association of Research Libraries, 1527 New Hampshire Avenue, Washington DC 20036. **LC** HA1701; .N86A. **DD** 315.1.

II/0258-0853
**NYADARSA PAMJIKARANA BULETINA.** (SAMPLE REGISTRATION BULLETIN.). [Nyadarsa pamjikarana buletina]. **Added/Corp** India. Vital Statistics Division. **VFOAT** Saimpala Rajistrikarana Buletina; SRS Bulletin. (19??)-. Bulletin. English (Hindi). qt. Office of the Registrar General, Vital Statistics Division, West Block No. 1, R. K. Puram, New Delhi 110 066 India. **LC** HA1721; .A35. **DD** 312/.0954.
**Ind/Abst** Popul. Index.

●US
**OCCUPATIONAL COMPENSATION SURVEY--PAY AND BENEFITS. ST. LOUIS, MISSOURI-ILLINOIS, METROPOLITAN AREA / U.S. DEPARTMENT OF LABOR, BUREAU OF LABOR STATISTICS.** **See** Economics-Labor.

PL
**OCHRONA SRODOWISKA; PROGNOZOWANIE I PLANOWANIE ROZWOJU NAUKI I TECHNIKI. KONFERENCJA NAUKOWA, WROCLAW, 4-6 II 1971.** Polish. Zaklad Wydawnictw Statystycznych, Al Niepodleglosci 208, 00-925 Warszawa Poland. **Tel** 253241, telex 814581A GUS.

PL
**OCHRONA SRODOWISKA - RACHUNEK STRAT I KORZYSCI SPOLECZNYCH.** Polish. Zaklad Wydawnictw Statystycznych, Al Niepodleglosci 208, 00-925 Warszawa Poland. **Tel** 253241, telex 814581A GUS.

PL
**OCHRONA SRODOWISKA : REFLEKSJE PRAWNE, EKONOMICZNE I SOCIOLOGICZNE.** Polish. Zaklad Wydawnictw Statystycznych, Al Niepodleglosci 208, 00-925 Warszawa Poland. **Tel** 253241, telex 814581A GUS.

US/1065-5638
**OHIO IN PERSPECTIVE.** (OHIO IN PERSPECTIVE : A STATISTICAL VIEW OF THE "BUCKEYE STATE."). [Ohio perspect.]. **Added/Corp** Morgan Quitno Corporation. (1990)-. Statistical Publication. English. $18.00. Morgan Quitno Corporation, PO Box 1656, 512 East 9th Street, Lawrence KS 66044. **Tel** (800)457-0742, (913)841-3534, FAX (913)841-3534. **DD** 317.71/05. **Continues** Ohio in Perspective, 1065-5638.
**Desc:** Reports on the state's data and rank for each of the categories featured in State Rankings.

JA
**OKINAWA-KEN TOKEI NENKAN.** **Added/Corp** Okinawa (Prefecture). Tokeika. Vol. 46, No. 16 (1971)-. Periodical. Japanese. Okinawa-ken, 2-32 1-chome Izumizaki, Naha-shi 900 Japan. **LC** HA1848.R9; A34. **Continues** Ryukyu Tokei Nenkan.

US/1065-5646
**OKLAHOMA IN PERSPECTIVE.** (OKLAHOMA IN PERSPECTIVE : A STATISTICAL VIEW OF THE "SOONER STATE".). [Okla. perspect.]. **Added/Corp** Morgan Quitno Corporation. (1990)-. Statistical Publication. English. $18.00. Morgan Quitno Corporation, PO Box 1656, 512 East 9th Street, Lawrence KS 66044. **Tel** (800)457-0742, (913)841-3534, FAX (913)841-3534. **DD** 317. **Continues** Oklahoma in Perspective, 1065-5646.
**Desc:** Reports on the state's data and rank for each of the categories featured in State Rankings.

NE/0168-454X
**ONDERZOEK HUISHOUDENS MET EENMALIGE UITKERING / CENTRAAL BUREAU VOOR DE STATISTIEK, HOOFDAFDELING STATISTIEKEN VAN INKOMEN EN CONSUMPTIE.** **VFOAT** Survey of Households Receiving Non-Recurrent Benefit. Periodical. Dutch. an. Fl8.40. Centraal Bureau voor de Statistiek, AFD ALG Zaken, Postbus 959, 2270 AZ Voorburg Netherlands. **Tel** 011 31 70 3373800, FAX 011 31 038 7429, telex 32692 CBS NL. **LC** HC329.5.I5; O53.

CI
**OPSTINE U SR SRBIJI.** **Main/Corp** Republicki Zavod za Statistiku SR Srbije. (19??)-. Serbo-Croatian (Cyrillic). 400.00 Din. Republicki Zavod za Statistiku, Central Bureau of Statistics of the Republic of Croatia, Ilica 3, Zagreb Croatia. **Tel** 011 385 41 45 44 22, FAX 011 385 41 42 94 13, 011 385 41 42 37 11, telex 21130 DZSTAT RH. **LC** HA1651; .A36. **Continues** Republicki Zavod za Statistiku SR Srbije. Statisticki Pokazatelji o Opstinama.

US/1065-5654
**OREGON IN PERSPECTIVE.** (OREGON IN PERSPECTIVE : A STATISTICAL VIEW OF THE "BEAVER STATE".). [Or. perspect.]. **Added/Corp** Morgan Quitno Corporation. (1990)-. Statistical Publication. English. $18.00. Morgan Quitno Corporation, PO Box 1656, 512 East 9th Street, Lawrence KS 66044. **Tel** (800)457-0742, (913)841-3534, FAX (913)841-3534. **DD** 317. **Continues** Oregon in Perspective, 1065-5654.
**Desc:** Reports on the state's data and rank for each of the categories featured in State Rankings.

CN
**OVERVIEW.** **Added/Corp** Statistics Canada. Communications Division. **VFOAT** Vue d'Ensemble. Vol. 1, No. 1 (Spring 1989)-. English (French). qt. Free on request. Statistics Canada, Publications Sales & Services, Main Building Room 1710, Ottawa Ontario K1A 0T6 Canada. **Tel** (613)951-5078, (800)267-6677, FAX (613)951-1584, telex 053-3585.
**Desc:** This newsletter provides data users with in-depth information on statistics on canadian products and services and on changes in departmental programs and policies.

NR
**OYO STATE OF NIGERIA STATISTICAL HANDBOOK.** **VFOAT** Statistical Handbook. Statistical Publication. English. Ministry of Finance & Economic Development, Statistics Division, Abeokuta Nigeria.

PK
**PAKISTAN JOURNAL OF STATISTICS.** Vol. 1, No. 1 & 2 (July 1985)-. Periodical. English. $5.00 (students), $10.00 (teachers), $40.00 (institutions). University of Punjab Social Sciences Research Centre, New Campus, Lahore 20 Pakistan. **LC** QA276.A1; P35. **DD** 519.5/05.
**Ind/Abst** Curr. Index Stat.; Math. Rev. (1987-); Zentralbl. Math. Ihre Grenzgeb.

PK/0078-8023
**PAKISTAN STATISTICAL YEARBOOK.** (1952)-. Statistical Publication. English. an (Aug.). Price varies. NGM Communication, PO Box 2627, Karachi 75900 Pakistan. **Tel** 011 92 21 428625. **LC** HA1730.5.

SY
**PALESTINIAN STATISTICAL ABSTRACT / PALESTINE LIBERATION ORGANIZATION, PALESTINE NATIONAL FUND, CENTRAL BUREAU OF STATISTICS.** **VFOAT** Majmuah Alihsaiyah Al-Filastiniyah. No. 1 (1979)-. Statistical Publication. Arabic (English). an. £Syr500.00 Syria; $50.00 US; $40.00 other. PO Box 7309, Damascus Syria. **Tel** 448288, 443505, telex 411943 SUNDUK. **LC** HA4560; .A28. **DD** 315.695/1. Index available. **Circ:** 1,000.
**Desc:** Presents statistical data and indicators reflecting demographic and socio-economic characteristics related to the Palestinian Arab people in occupied Palestine Arab countries and other parts of the world.

PN
**PANAMA EN CIFRAS / DIRECCION DE ESTADISTICA Y CENSO.** **Added/Corp** Panama. Direccion de Estadistica y Censo. (1960)-. Statistical Publication. Spanish. an. available on exchange basis only. Direccion de Estadistica y Censo, Contraloria General, Apartado 5213, Panama 5 Panama. **Tel** 011 507 640777 Ext. 269 or 203, . **ED** Amilcar Villarreal L. **LC** HA851; .N83. **DD** 317.287. **NLM** W2 DP2 D5P. Index available. **Circ:** 5,000. available on microfiche. **Continues** Nuestro Progreso en Cifras.
**Desc:** Statistical compendium containing important information about the basic statistics produced by the different services in the Republic of Panama.

IO
**PENDUDUK JAWA-BARAT, HASIL REGISTRASI PENDUDUK.** **Main/Corp** Jawa Barat, Indonesia. Kantor Sensus dan Statistik. 1972-. Indonesian. Kantor Sensus & Statistik Java-Barat, Jalan Jendral Gatotsubroto 77, Bandung Indonesia. **LC** HA1817.J35; J35B.

IO
**PENDUDUK JAWA TENGAH, HASIL REGISTRASI PENDUDUK.** **VFOAT** Penduduk Jawa Tengah. Indonesian. (024)311195. Biro Pusat Statistik, JLN Dr Sutomo 8 Kotak, Pos 1003, Jakarta 10710 Indonesia. **Tel** 3728007, 374908. **LC** HA1817.J38; J38A . ctrl circ. **Continues** Penduduk Jawa Tengah, Hasil Registrasi.

IO
**PENDUDUK SUMATERA UTARA.** **Main/Corp** Indonesia. Kantor Sensus Dan Statistik Propinsi Sumatera Utara. 1973-. Indonesian. Kantor Sensus dan Statistik, Jln Sukamulia 13 Atas, Medan Indonesia. **LC** HA1817.S9; S85B.

●US
**PENNSYLVANIA ABSTRACT / PREPARED BY THE PENNSYLVANIA STATE DATA CENTER.** **Added/Corp** Pennsylvania State Data Center. (1992)-. English. an. $400.00. Pennsylvania State Data Center, 777 West Harrisburg Pike, Middletown PA 17057-4898. **Tel** (717)948-6336. **LC** HA607; .P4. **DD** 317.48. **Continues** Pennsylvania Statistical Abstract, 0476-1103.
**Desc:** A publication of facts which provide information to the business community and other individuals seeking to learn more about Pennsylvania.

US
**PENNSYLVANIA COUNTY DATA BOOK.** 1979-. English. an. **Circ:** 600. **Continues** Pennsylvania County Industry Report.

# Statistics

**Desc:** Overall statistical view of Pennsylvania counties. Individual report published for each of Pennsylvania's 67 counties.

US/1065-5662
**PENNSYLVANIA IN PERSPECTIVE.** (PENNSYLVANIA IN PERSPECTIVE : A STATISTICAL VIEW OF THE "KEYSTONE STATE".). [Pa. perspect.]. **Added/Corp** Morgan Quinto Corporation. (1990)-. Statistical Publication. English. $18.00. Morgan Quitno Corporation, PO Box 1656, 512 East 9th Street, Lawrence KS 66044. **Tel** (800)457-0742, (913)841-3534, FAX (913)841-3534. **DD** 317. **Continues** Pennsylvania in Perspective, 1065-5662.
**Desc:** Reports on the state's data and rank for each of the categories featured in State Rankings.

BL
**PERFIL MUNICIPAL.** **Main/Corp** Sao Paulo (Brazil : State). Fundacao Sistema Estadual de Analise de Dados. V. 1- 1979-. Portuguese. an. $300. Fundacao Sistema Estadual de Analise de Dados, Caixa Postal 8223, 01033 Sao Paulo Brazil. **Tel** (011)229-2433, telex (011)31390 SEAD BR. **LC** HA988.S2; S28A.
**Desc:** Socio-economic data regarding the 572 cities of the state of Sao Paulo.

US
**PERSPECTIVES '93.** English. an. $25.00 member, $40.00 non-member US; $35.00 member; $50.00 non-member other. American Productivity & Quality Center, 123 North Post Oak Lane, Houston TX 77024. **ED** Steve Scheffler. **Acid Free. Circ:** 3,200 (ctrl).
**Desc:** Statistical abstract of U.S. competitiveness on quality and production.

FR
**PETIT GUIDE STATISTIQUE DE LA LORRAINE.** **Main/Corp** Institut National de la Statistique et des Etudes Economiques. Observatoire Economique de l'Est. French. 34 Quai Claude Lorrain, Nanncy France. **LC** HA1228.L65; F7A.

IO
**PETUNJUK KELURAHAN WILAYAH JAKARTA BARAT.** **Main/Corp** Jakarta Raya, Indonesia. Kantor Sensus dan Statistik. 1977-. Indonesian. Kantor Sensus dan Statistik Dki Jakarta, Jl Medan Merdeka Selatan 8-9, Lantai XX, Jakarta Indonesia. **LC** HA1818.J34; J34F. **Continues** Buku Petunjuk Kelurahan Wilayah Jakarta Barat.

IO
**PETUNJUK KELURAHAN WILAYAH JAKARTA PUSAT.** **Main/Corp** Jakarta Raya, Indonesia. Kantor Sensus dan Statistik. (1977)-. Indonesian. an. Kantor Sensus dan Statistik Dki Jakarta, Jl Medan Merdeka Selatan 8-9, Lantai XX, Jakarta Indonesia. **LC** HA1818.J34; J34d. **Continues** Buku Petunjuk Kelurahan Wilayah Jakarta Pusat.

IO
**PETUNJUK KELURAHAN WILAYAH JAKARTA SELATAN.** **Main/Corp** Jakarta Raya, Indonesia. Kantor Sensus dan Statistik. 1977-. Periodical. Indonesian. Kantor Sensus dan Statistik Dki Jakarta, Jl Medan Merdeka Selatan 8-9, Lantai XX, Jakarta Indonesia. **LC** HA1818.J34; J34E. **Continues** Buku Petunjuk Kelurahan Wilayah Jakarta Selatan.

IO
**PETUNJUK KELURAHAN WILAYAH JAKARTA TIMUR.** **Main/Corp** Jakarta Raya, Indonesia. Kantor Sensus dan Statistik. 1977-. Indonesian. Kantor Sensus dan Statistik Dki Jakarta, Jl Medan Merdeka Selatan 8-9, Lantai XX, Jakarta Indonesia. **LC** HA1818.J34; J34C. **Continues** Buku Petunjuk Kelurahan Wilayah Jakarta Timur.

IO
**PETUNJUK KELURAHAN WILAYAH JAKARTA UTARA.** **Main/Corp** Jakarta Raya, Indonesia. Kantor Sensus dan Statistik. 1977-. Indonesian. Kantor Sensus dan Statistik Dki Jakarta, Jl Medan Merdeka Selatan 8-9, Lantai XX, Jakarta Indonesia. **LC** HA1818.D5; A25. **Continues** Buku Petunjuk Kelurahan Wilayah Jakarta Utara.

IS
**PEULOT U-FIRSUMIM STATISTIYIM HADASHIM BE-YISRAEL.** **VFOAT** New Statistical Projects and Publications in Israel. Periodical. Multiple languages (English and Hebrew). qt. IL20.00. Government Publishing House, Street B/No 29 Hakirya, Tel-Aviv Israel. **Tel** (00-972)2-211400. **LC** HA37; .I714A. **Continues** Peulot Statistiyot Hadashot.

PH/0031-7829
**PHILIPPINE STATISTICIAN, THE.** **Added/Corp** Philippine Statistical Association. Vol. 1 (June 1952)-. Periodical. English. Twice a year. $30.00. PSSC Central Subscription Service, PO Box 205 UP Diliman, Quezon City 1101 Philippines. **Tel** 011 63 2 9229621. **ED** Burton T Onate. **Bk Rev. Ad Acc. Circ:** 1,000.
**Desc:** Presents papers and articles on theoretical and applied statistics.
**Ind/Abst** Index Philip. Period.; Philip. Sci. Technol. Abstr.; Stat. Theory Method Abstr. (1968, 1984).

PH
**PHILIPPINE YEARBOOK.** **Added/Corp** Philippines. National Census and Statistics Office. (1971)-. English. be. $90.00. National Statistics Office of Manila, PO Box 779, Manila Philippines. **Tel** 011 63 613645. **Continues** Philippine Statistics Yearbook.

PH
**POCKETBOOK OF PHILIPPINE STATISTICS.** **Added/Corp** Philippines. National Economic and Development Authority. (19??)-. English. ir. National Economic and Development Authority, PO Box 419, Greenhills Metro Manila Philippines. **Tel** 011 63 2 6313281. **LC** HA4611; .P63. **DD** 315.99.

FR
**POINT ECONOMIQUE DE L'AUVERGNE, LE. See** Sociology.

PL/0860-6811
**POLSKA, DANE STATYSTYCZNE.** Polish (English). an. Z2.00 Poland; Z3.00 North America; Z2.50 other. Zaklad Wydawnictw Statystycznych, Al Niepodleglosci 208, 00-925 Warszawa Poland. **Tel** 253241, telex 814581A GUS. **LC** HA1451; .P66. **Circ:** 4,500 (ctrl).
**Desc:** Data of Poland.

GW/0178-8051
**PROBABILITY THEORY AND RELATED FIELDS. See** Mathematics.

UK
**PROCEEDINGS OF THE ANNUAL CONFERENCE : ESOMAR.** **Main/Corp** Esomar. Proceedings. English. an. ESOMAR Central Secretariat, J J Viottastraat 29, 1071 JP Amsterdam Netherlands. **Tel** 011 31 20 6642141. **LC** HM261.A1; E822.

US
**PROCEEDINGS OF THE SECTION ON QUALITY AND PRODUCTIVITY.** (19??)-. Proceedings. English. ir. $30.00. American Statistical Association, 1429 Duke Street, Alexandria VA 22314. **Tel** (703)684-1221, (202)393-3253, FAX (703)684-2037 (orders).
**Ind/Abst** Curr. Index Stat. (199?-).

US/0733-1282
**PROCEEDINGS OF THE SECTION ON STATISTICAL EDUCATION - AMERICAN STATISTICAL ASSOCIATION. SECTION ON STATISTICAL EDUCATION.** (PROCEEDINGS OF THE SECTION ON STATISTICAL EDUCATION / AMERICAN STATISTICAL ASSOCIATION.). [Proc. Sect. Stat. Educ. - Am. Stat. Assoc., Sect. Stat. Educ.]. **Main/Corp** American Statistical Association. Section on Statistical Education. (19??)-. Statistical Publication. English. an. $48.50. American Statistical Association, 1429 Duke Street, Alexandria VA 22314. **Tel** (703)684-1221, (202)393-3253, FAX (703)684-2037 (orders).
**Ind/Abst** Curr. Index Stat.

US/1048-5635
**PROCEEDINGS OF THE SECTION ON STATISTICAL GRAPHICS.** [Proc. Sect. Stat. Graph.]. **Main/Corp** American Statistical Association. Section on Statistical Graphics. (19??)-. Statistical Publication. English. an. $33.50. American Statistical Association, 1429 Duke Street, Alexandria VA 22314. **Tel** (703)684-1221, (202)393-3253, FAX (703)684-2037 (orders). **DD** 001.
**Ind/Abst** Curr. Index Stat.

US/0066-0752
**PROCEEDINGS OF THE SOCIAL STATISTICS SECTION (WASHINGTON).** (PROCEEDINGS OF THE SOCIAL STATISTICS SECTION.). [Proc. Soc. Stat. Sect.]. **Main/Corp** American Statistical Association. Social Statistics Section. 1st (1958)-. Proceedings. English. an (Summer). $71.50. American Statistical Association, 1429 Duke Street, Alexandria VA 22314. **Tel** (703)684-1221, (202)393-3253, FAX (703)684-2037 (orders). **LC** HA1; .A669. **DD** 310/.6/073. **NLM** W1 PR5863. available on microfilm and microfiche from University Microfilms International (UMI).
**Ind/Abst** Curr. Index Stat.

US/1059-7328
**PROCEEDINGS - UNITED STATES. BUREAU OF THE CENSUS.** (PROCEEDINGS : ... ANNUAL RESEARCH CONFERENCE / BUREAU OF THE CENSUS.). [Proc. - U. S., Bur. Census]. **Added/Corp** United States. Bureau of the Census. **VFOAT** Annual Research Conference; Research Conference. March 20-23, (1985)-. Government Publication. English. an. Free. US Department of Commerce / Bureau of the Census, Data User Services Division, Customer Services, Washington DC 20233-0800. **Tel** (301)763-4100. **(Subscription address:** Superintendent of Documents, US Government Printing Office, Washington DC 20402.**) LC** HA37; .U124. **DD** 351.
**Ind/Abst** Curr. Index Stat.

FR
**PROFILS.** (19??)-. French. Five times a year. 420.00F (1-5 subjects). CTBA, 10 Avenue de Sainte Mande, F-75012 Paris, France. **Tel** 011 33 1 40194905. **Continues** Revue Documentaire, 0295-5717.

XV
**PRVI STATISTICNI PODATKI ZA LETO ... (Z OCENO) IN SPREMLJANJE RESOLUCIJE O POLITIKI IZVAJANJA DRUZBENEGA PLANA SR SLOVENIJE V LETU ... / ZAVOD SR SLOVENIJE ZA STATISTIKO.** Slovenian. an. Zavod Sr Slovenije za Statistiko, Vozarski Pot 12, Ljubljana Slovenia. **LC** HA1634.S58; P778.

PL/0033-2372
**PRZEGLAD STATYSTYCZNY.** [Prz. stat.]. **Added/Corp** Polskie Towarzystwo Ekonomiczne. Sekcja Statystyki. Polska Akademia Nauk. Komitet Statystyki i Ekonometrii. Vol. 1 (1954)-. Periodical. Polish (summaries and/or abstracts in English and Russian; table of contents in Russian and English). qt. $54.00. **(Subscription address:** ARS Polona, PO Box 1001, 00068 Warsaw Poland.**) LC** HA1; .P73. **DD** 310/.5. **CODEN** PZSTAD. Documents available from Ask*IEEE.
**Ind/Abst** INSPEC (1985-); Int. Abstr. Oper. Res. [Select. Cov.]; Int. Bibliogr. Sociol.; Math. Rev.; Stat. Theory Method Abstr. (1959-1963); Zentralbl. Math. Ihre Grenzgeb.

IT
**PUBBLICAZIONI DEL CENTRO STATISTICA AZIENDALE.** Italian. ir. L300000.00. Centro Statistica Aziendale, Via Baldesi 18, 50131 Florence Italy. **Tel** 011 39 55 576041, FAX 011 39 55 576265.

US/1050-5067
**PUBLIC PERSPECTIVE, THE.** (THE PUBLIC PERSPECTIVE : A ROPER CENTER REVIEW OF PUBLIC OPINION AND POLLING.). [Public perspect.]. **Added/Corp** Roper Public Opinion Research Center. Vol. 1, No. 1 (Nov./Dec. 1989)-. Periodical. English. bm. $105.00 (US), $135.00 (other) institutions & libraries; $55.00 (US), $85.00 (other). University of Connecticut Roper Center, PO Box 440, Storrs CT 06268. **Tel** (203)486-4440, FAX (203)486-6308. **ED** Everett Ladd. **LC** HM261; .P84. **DD** 303.3/8/05. Index available. cum. index. **Bk Rev** (Qty: up to 6 per year). **Circ:** 2,300.
**Desc:** Devoted to public opinion and polling. Articles in the journal are authored by a distinguished roster of business, media and academic leaders interested in the application of polling to public policy issues.
**Ind/Abst** PAIS Int. Print.

UK/0549-0782
**PUBLICATIONS. See** Library and Information Sciences.

FR/0553-2930
**PUBLICATIONS DE L'INSTITUT DE STATISTIQUE DE L'UNIVERSITE DE PARIS.** [Publ. Inst. stat. Univ. Paris]. **Main/Corp** Institut de Statistique des Universites de Paris. **Added/Corp** Institut Henri Poincare. (1952)-. Periodical. French. Twice a year. 300.00F France; 350.00F other. Lab Statistique Theorique Appl, Tour 45 55 E3, 4 Place Jussieu, 75252 Paris Cedex 05 France. **Tel** 011 33 1 44273302. **LC** HA1; .P332. **CODEN** PBSPA3.
**Ind/Abst** Math. Rev.; Stat. Theory Method Abstr. (1959-1963, 1967-1971, 1973, 1977, 1979-1983, 1986-1987); Zentralbl. Math. Ihre Grenzgeb.

AT/0312-4819
**PUBLICATIONS OF THE AUSTRALIAN BUREAU OF STATISTICS.** **Main/Corp** Australian Bureau of Statistics. English. an. The Commonwealth Statistician, Cameron Offices, PO Box 10, Belconnen Australian Capital Territory 2616 Australia. **LC** Z7554.A77; A93A; HA37.A8. **DD** 016.3194. **Continues** Publications of the Commonwealth Bureau of Census and Statistics.

FR
**PUBLICATIONS STATISTIQUES DES ADMINISTRATIONS.** **Main/Corp** Institut National de la Statistique et des Etudes Economiques (France). French. 8.00F. CNGP INSEE - Institut National de la Statistique et des Etudes Economiques, BP 2718, 1 rue V Auriol, F 80027 Amiens Cedex 1 France. **Tel** 011 33 22 927322. **LC** Z7554.F7; F73A; HA1213. **DD** 016.3144.

ZA
**QUARTERLY AGRICULTURAL STATISTICAL BULLETIN. See** Agriculture-Abstracting, Bibliographies and Statistics.

# Statistics

US
**QUARTERLY AIRCRAFT OPERATING COSTS AND STATISTICS.** See Aeronautics, Astronautics.

MM
**QUARTERLY DIGEST OF STATISTICS.** **Main/Corp** Malta. Office of Statistics. No. 1 (Mar. 1960)-. English. Four times a year. £M80.0. Central Office of Statistics / Malta, Auberge de Castille, Merchants Street, Valletta Malta. **LC** HA1117.M3; A28. **DD** 314.58/5.
**Desc:** Records changes in the main sector of the economy. Statistical information in respect of previous periods for analysis and comparative purposes.

RH
**QUARTERLY DIGEST OF STATISTICS (ZIMBABWE. CENTRAL STATISTICAL OFFICE).** (QUARTERLY DIGEST OF STATISTICS.). **Added/Corp** Zimbabwe. Central Statistical Office. (Sept. 1983)-. Periodical. English. qt. 40.00Zin$ Zimbabwe; 42.93Zin$ Africa; 51.10Zin$ Europe; 43.06Zin$ Americas and Asia. Central Statistical Office / Zimbabwe, PO Box 8063, Causeway Salisbury Harare, Zimbabwe. **Tel** 011 263 0 706681. **LC** HA4702; .A25. **DD** 316.891.
**Continues in part** Monthly Digest of Statistics (Zimbabwe. Central Statistical Office).

US/0093-3481
**R & S REPORT (HONOLULU).** (R & S REPORT.). No. 1- Jan. 1973-. English. Research and Statistics Office, PO Box 3378, Honolulu HI 96801. **LC** HB3525.H3; H33A. **DD** 312/.09969. **NLM** W2 AH3 D45R.

YU
**RADNE ORGANIZACIJE VANPRIVREDNIH DELATNOSTI.** **Main/Corp** Savezni Zavod za Statistiku (Yugoslavia). Serbo-Croatian (Roman). 4.00. Savezni Zavod za Statistiku, Kneza Milosa 20, Belgrad Yugoslavia. **LC** HA1631; .A33 subser; HA1632.

CM
**RAPPORT D'ACTIVITE - SERVICE PROVINCIAL DE STATISTIQUE DU CENTRE-SUD.** **Main/Corp** Cameroon. Service Provincial de Statistique du Centre-Sud. French. Service Provincial de Statistique du Centre-Sud, BP 1501, Yaounde Cameroon. **LC** HA2141; .S468A. **DD** 316.67/11/05.

CN/1185-5460
**RAPPORT D'ACTIVITES / LE BUREAU DE LA STATISTIQUE DU QUEBEC.** [Rapp. act. - Bur. stat. Que.]. **Main/Corp** Bureau de la Statistique du Quebec. (1991)-. French. Statistique Quebec, 117 rue Saint Andre, Quebec Quebec G1K 3Y3 Canada. **Tel** (514)283-2642. **DD** 354.7140081/9.

CX
**RAPPORT D'ACTIVITES - REPUBLIQUE UNIE DU CAMEROUN, SERVICE PROVINCIAL STATISTIQUE DU NORD CAMEROUN.** **Main/Corp** Cameroon. Service Provincial Statistique du Nord Cameroun. French. Service Provincial Statistique du Nord Cameroun, BP 251, Garoua, Cameroun Africa. **LC** HA2141; .S47A. **DD** 316.7/112.

FR
**RECUEIL STATISTIQUE DU POITOU-CHARENTES.** French. an. Direction Regionale de l'INSEE, 5 rue Sainte-Catherine, 86021 Poitiers France. **LC** HA1228.P6; R4. **DD** 944/.65.

FR
**RECUEIL STATISTIQUES.** Monographic series. French. ir. Price varies per volume. SESSI Ministere de l'Industrie, 85 Boulevard du Montparnasse, 75270 Paris Cedex 06 France. **Tel** 011 33 1 43194118.

UK
**REGIONAL TRENDS / CENTRAL STATISTICAL OFFICE.** **Added/Corp** Great Britain. Central Statistical Office. 16 (1981 Ed.)-. Statistical Publication. English. an. £26.00. Her Majesty's Stationery Office, 51 Nine Elms Lane, London SW8 5DR England. **Tel** 011 44 71 873 8459, 011 44 71 873 8499, FAX 011 44 71 873 8499, 011 44 71 873 8456, telex 297138. **(Subscription address:** Her Majesty's Stationery Office, PO Box 276, Publications Centre, London SW8 5DT England.) **LC** HA1123; .C44a. **DD** 314.1. **Continues** Regional Statistics (Great Britain. Central Statistical Office).

GW
**REGIONALSTRUKTUR BADEN-WURTTEMBERG: GEMEINDEN.** **Main/Corp** Statistisches Landesamt Baden-Wurttemberg. (19??)-. German. ir. Statistisches Landesamt Baden-Wuerttemberg, Postfach 10 60 33, 70049 Stuttgart Germany. **Tel** 011 49 771 6410, FAX 011 49 711 6412440. **LC** HA1320.B2; A32 subser; HA1248.B32. **Circ:** 900.

**Desc:** Covers statistical subjects: population, education, employment, agriculture, industries, communal finances. Presented in tabular form and graphically.

IT
**REGIONI IN CIFRE, LE.** **Main/Corp** Italy. Istituto Centrale di Statistica. **Added/Corp** Istituto Centrale di Statistica (Italy) Istituto Nazionale Di Statistica (Italy). (19??)-. Italian. an. Free. Istituto Nazionale Statistica, GBP SEZ4 Via Cesare Balbo 16, 00184 Rome Italy. **Tel** 011 39 6 46735118. **LC** HA1362; .I87a.

CE/0254-0924
**REPORT OF THE REGISTRAR-GENERAL OF CEYLON ON VITAL STATISTICS FOR ... .** [Rep. Regist.-Gen. Ceylon vital stat.]. 1950-. English. an. **NLM** W2 JC4 R3V. **Continues** Report on Vital Statistics for the Year, 0254-0916.

BB
**REPORT ON VITAL STATISTICS & REGISTRATIONS.** **Main/Corp** Barbados. Registration Office. (19??)-. English. Barbados Government Printing Office, Bridgetown Barbados West Indies. **LC** HA865; .A28. **DD** 312/.09729/81.

UK/0414-0532
**REPORTS : ST.** **Main/Conf** Inter-African Conference on Statistics. **Added/Corp** Commission for Technical Co-operation in Africa South of the Sahara. Scientific Council for Africa South of the Sahara. **VFOAT** Reports: Statistics. 1 (1955)-. Periodical. English. Europa Publications Ltd, 18 Bedford Square, London WC1B 3JN England. **Tel** 011 44 71 5808236, telex 21540 EUROPA G. **DD** 316.

US
**RESIDENT & RECORDED LIVE BIRTHS, INFANT DEATHS, AND DEATHS FOR ILLINOIS LARGER CITIES / ILLINOIS DEPARTMENT OF PUBLIC HEALTH.** **VFOAT** Resident and Recorded Live Births, Infant Deaths, and Deaths for Illinois Larger Cities. 1979-. English. an. Illinois Department of Public Health, 535 West Jefferson Street, 5th Floor, Springfield IL 62761. **Tel** (217)785-8830. **LC** HA341; .R47. **DD** 312/.09773. **Continues** Resident and Recorded Live Births, Infant Deaths, and Deaths for the Larger Cities in Illinois.

US/0091-3758
**RESOURCE-DATA BOOK.** English. an. Capital Area Planning Council, 2520 Interstate Highway, 35 South/Suite 100, Austin TX 78704. **LC** HA651; .R48. **DD** 317.64.

BL/0034-7175
**REVISTA BRASILEIRA DE ESTATISTICA.** [Rev. bras. estat.]. **Added/Corp** Fundacao Instituto Brasileiro de Geografia e Estatistica. Departamento de Divulgacao Estatistica. Conselho Nacional de Estatistica (Brazil) Sociedade Brasileira de Estatistica. No. 1 (Jan./Mar. 1940)-. Periodical. Portuguese. qt. $60.00. Instituto Brasileiro de Geografia e Estatistica, Rua General Canabarro 666 AN2, 20271 Rio de Janeiro RJ Brazil. **Tel** 011 55 21 2847690, 011 55 21 2342043. **LC** HA984; .R4. **DD** 330.981. **NLM** W1 RE317. **Supersedes** Revista de Economia e Estatistica.
**Ind/Abst** Popul. Index.

CK/0120-1751
**REVISTA COLOMBIANA DE ESTADISTICA.** [Rev. Colomb. Estad.]. (1968)-. Periodical. Spanish. ir. **DD** 310.
**Ind/Abst** Zentralbl. Math. Ihre Grenzgeb.

RM
**REVISTA ROMANA DE STATISTICA : ORGAN AL COMISIEI NATIONALE PENTRU STATISTICA.** **Added/Corp** Romania. Comisia Nationala Pentru Statistica. No. 1 (1990)-. Periodical. Romanian. mo. DM210.00. **(Subscription address:** Kubon & Sagner, ABT Zeitschriftenimport, D 80328 Munich Germany.) **LC** HA1; .R38. **Continues** Revista de Statistica, 0556-6398.

FR/0035-175X
**REVUE DE STATISTIQUE APPLIQUEE.** [Rev. stat. appl.]. **Added/Corp** Universite de Paris. Institut de Statistique. Universite de Paris. Centre de Formation aux Applications Industrielles de la Statistique. (1953)-. Periodical. French. qt (Jan., Mar., Sept., Nov.). 490.00F France; 550.00F other. Revue de Statistique Appliquee, 11 rue Pierre et Marie Curie, 75231 Paris Cedex 05 France. **Tel** 011 33 1 44276660. **ED** Pierre Cazes. **NLM** W1 RE805G. **CODEN** RVSTA7. Index available. cum. index. **Bk Rev. Circ:** 800.
**Desc:** Publishes papers on applied statistics.
**Ind/Abst** Energy Res. Abstr.; Math. Rev.; Stat. Theory Method Abstr. (1959-1963, 1966-1972, 1977-1982, 1984, 1986-1997); Zentralbl. Math. Ihre Grenzgeb.

FR/0295-5717
**REVUE DOCUMENTAIRE - CENTRE TECHNIQUE DU BOIS ET DE L'AMEUBLEMENT.** **Title Change.** [Revue doc.- Centre tech. bois ameubl.]. (1985)-(1992). Periodical.

French. bm. CTBA, 10 Avenue de Sainte Mande, F-75012 Paris, France. **Tel** 011 33 1 40194905. **UDC** 674(051). **Continues** Bulletin Bibliographique - Centre Technique du Bois et de l'Ameublement, 0755-2696. **Continued by** Les Profils.

CN/0823-311X
**REVUE STATISTIQUE DU CANADA. SUPPLEMENT.** **Added/Corp** Canada. Dominion Bureau of Statistics. Busines Statistics Section. No. 1 (1953)-. Periodical. French. be. Canadian Bureau of Statistics, Publications Distribution, Ottawa Ontario K1A 0T6 Canada. **Tel** (613)951-7276, (808)267-6677, telex 053-3585. **LC** HA745; .R48 Suppl. **DD** 317.1.

US/1065-5670
**RHODE ISLAND IN PERSPECTIVE.** (RHODE ISLAND IN PERSPECTIVE : A STATISTICAL VIEW OF THE "OCEAN STATE".). [R.I. perspect.]. **Added/Corp** Morgan Quitno Corporation. (1990)-. Statistical Publication. English. $18.00. Morgan Quitno Corporation, PO Box 1656, 512 East 9th Street, Lawrence KS 66044. **Tel** (800)457-0742, (913)841-3534, FAX (913)841-3534. **DD** 317. **Continues** Rhode Island in Perspective, 1065-5670.
**Desc:** Reports on the state's data and rank for each of the categories featured in State Rankings.

IT/0035-6549
**RIVISTA DI STATISTICA APPLICATA.** [Riv. stat. appl.]. (1967)-. Periodical. Italian. qt. L90000.00. Rocco Curto Editore, Vico Sant Aniello Caponapoli 6, 80138 Naples Italy. **Tel** 011 39 81 449636. **UDC** 31.

PL
**ROCZNIK STATYSTYCZNY.** **Main/Corp** Poland. Gowny Urzad Statystyczny. (1930)-. Polish. an. Zaklad Wydawnictw Statystycznych, Al Niepodleglosci 208, 00-925 Warszawa Poland. **Tel** 253241, telex 814581A GUS. **Circ:** 28,000 (ctrl).

PL
**ROCZNIK STATYSTYCZNY / GOWNY URZAD STATYSTYCZNY.** Polish. an. **(Subscription address:** ARS Polona, PO Box 1001, 00068 Warsaw Poland.) **NLM** W2 GP6 G5RC. **Continues** Maly Rocznik Statystyczny.

PL
**ROCZNIK STATYSTYCZNY KULTURY.** $10.00 Poland; $12.00 US; $11.00 other. Zaklad Wadawnictw Statystycznych, Al Niepodleglosci 208, 00-925 Warszawa Poland. **Tel** 253241 ext. 210, telex 814581A GUS PL. **Circ:** 1,500 (ctrl).
**Desc:** Yearbook on Polish culture.

PL/0208-838X
**ROCZNIK STATYSTYCZNY MIAST / GOWNY URZAD STATYSTYCZNY.** [Rocz. Stat. Miast]. 1980-. Polish. an. Z90.00. 00-068 Warszawa, Ksiegarnia Naukowa Im Bolesawa Prusa, Ul Krakowskie Przedmiescie 7, Warszawa Poland. **LC** HA1451; .R63.

PL
**ROCZNIK STATYSTYCZNY MIASTA NYSY.** V. 1 (1971)-. Polish. Z20.00 single issue. Gowna Ksiegarnia Naukowa Im B Prusa, Ul Krakowskie Przedmiescie 7, Warszawa Poland. **LC** HA1458.N9; R6.

PL
**ROCZNIK STATYSTYCZNY MIASTA PIOTRKOWA TRYBUNALSKIEGO.** V. 1 (1971)-. Polish. Z20. Gowna Ksiegarnia Naukowa Im B Prusa, Ul Krakowskie Przedmiescie 7, Warszawa Poland. **LC** HA1458.P5; R6.

PL
**ROCZNIK STATYSTYCZNY POWIATU KROSNO.** V. 1- 1971-. Polish. 20.00. Powiatowy Inspektorat Statystyczwy, Warszawa Cowna Ksiegarnia Naukowa Im B Prusa, UL Krakowskie Przedmiescie 7, Krosno Poland. **LC** HA1457.K75; R6.

PL
**ROCZNIK STATYSTYCZNY PRACY.** Title Change. **Added/Corp** Poland Gowny Urzad Statystyczny. (19??)-(19??). Polish (table of contents in English and Russian). Zaklad Wydawnictw Statystycznych, Al Niepodleglosci 208, 00-928 Warszawa Poland. **Tel** 253241 ext. 210, telex 814581A GUS PL. **LC** HD5797.7.A6; R6. **Circ:** 1,200 (ctrl). **Continued by** Roczniki Statystyczne. Praca.
**Desc:** Labor yearbook for Poland.

PL/0208-9300
**ROCZNIK STATYSTYCZNY WOJEWODZTW.** [Rocz. Stat. Woj.]. 1976-. Polish. be. Z21.00 Poland; Z25.50 North America; Z24.00 other. Zaklad Wydawnictw Statystycznych, Al Niepodleglosci 208, 00-925 Warszawa Poland. **Tel** 253241, telex 814581A GUS. **LC** HA1451; .G58A. **Circ:** 1,300 (ctrl). **Continues** Statystyka Wojewodztw.

PL
**ROCZNIK STATYSTYCZNY WOJEWODZTWA WROCAWSKIEGO I MIASTA WROCAWIA / WOJEWODZKI URZAD STATYSTYCZNY WE WROCAWIU.** Began with vol. for 1976. Polish. an. 40.00. Ksiegarnia Im Marchlewskiego, Rynek 60, 50-116 Wroclaw Poland. **LC** HA1457.W76; R62. ***Formed by the union of*** *Rocznik Statystyczny Wojewodztwa Wrocawskiego* ***and*** *Rocznik Statystyczny Miasta Wrocawia.*

PL
**ROCZNIK STATYSTYKI MIEDZYNARODOWEJ.** **Main/Corp** Poland. Gowny Urzad Statystyczny. (1965)-. Polish. te. $17.00 Poland; $20.00 North America; $19.00 other. Zaklad Wydawnictw Statystycznych, Al Niepodleglosci 208, 00-925 Warszawa Poland. **Tel** 253241, telex 814581A GUS. **LC** HA173.P6; P64A. **DD** 310/.5. **Circ:** 1,800 (ctrl).

PL/0867-082X
**ROCZNIKI STATYSTYCZNE.** Polish. an. $17.00 US; $16.00 other. Zaklad Wydawnictw Statystyczych, AL Niepodleglosci 208, 00-925 Warszawa Poland. **Tel** 253241, telex 814581A GUS. **Circ:** 50,000 (ctrl).

CI
**ROENI U SR SRBIJI / SOCIJALISTICKA REPUBLIKA SRBIJA, REPUBLICKI ZAVOD ZA STATISTIKU.** Began with vol. for 1970-1976. Serbo-Croatian (Roman). 80.00 Din. Republicki Zavod za Statistiku, Central Bureau of Statistics of the Republic of Croatia, Ilica 3, Zagreb Croatia. **Tel** 011 385 41 45 44 22, FAX 011 385 41 42 94 13, 011 385 41 42 37 11, telex 21130 DZSTAT RH. **LC** HA1651; .A334 subser; HA1634.S4 S47.

US/1057-2570
**ROOTS & BRANCHES.** [Roots branches]. **Added/Corp** Garfield County Genealogists. **VFOAT** Roots and Branches. Vol. 14, No. 1 (Spring 1991)-. Periodical. English. qt. Garfield County Genealogists Inc, PO Box 427, Enid OK 73701. **LC** F702.G25; G28. **DD** 929. ***Continues*** *Garfield County Roots & Branches, 0737-9242.*

GW
**SAARLAND HEUTE.** **Added/Corp** Saarland (Germany) Statistiches Amt. (19??)-. German. an. Statistisches Amt des Saarlandes, Postfach 409 Hardenbergstr 3, W-6600 Saarbrucken Germany. **LC** HA1320.S24; S22. **DD** 314.3/42.

GW/0486-7890
**SAARLANDISCHE KREISZAHLEN.** **Added/Corp** Saarland (Germany). Statistisches Amt. (August 1981)-. German. Statistisches Amt des Saarlandes, Postfach 409 Hardenbergstr 3, W-6600 Saarbrucken Germany. **LC** HA1248.S23; S22. **DD** 314.3/42.

YU
**SAMOUPRAVLJANJE U USTANOVAMA DRUSTVENIH SLUZBI.** **Main/Corp** Savezni Zavod Za Statistiku (Yugoslavia). Serbo-Croatian (Roman). 10.00. Savezni Zavod za Statistiku, Kneza Milosa 20, Belgrad Yugoslavia. **LC** HA1631; .A33 subser; HD5660.Y8.

US
**SAMPLE SURVEYS OF CURRENT INTEREST.** **Added/Corp** United Nations. Statistical Office. (Feb. 28, 1949)-. Government Publication. English. ir. United Nations Publications, 2 United Nations Plaza, Room DC2 0853, Department 007C, New York NY 10017. **Tel** (212)963-8303, (800)253-9646. **LC** HA13; .U5; JX1977; .A2. **DD** 311.22. cum. index.

II/0581-572X
**SANKHYA. SERIES A.** (SANKHYA. SERIEA A. METHODS AND TECHNIQUES.). [Sankhya, Ser. A]. **Added/Corp** Indian Statistical Institute. **VFOAT** Sankhya A. Vol. 23 (Feb. 1961)-. Periodical. English. Three times a year. $75.00. Statistical Publishing Society Road, Calcutta 700 035 India. **(Subscription address:** Prints India, 11 Darya Ganj, New Delhi, 110002 India, (Phone: 011 91 11 3268645)) **CODEN** SANABS. **Pr Rev.** Documents available from The Genuine Article. ***Supersedes in part*** *Sankhya.*
**Ind/Abst** Compumath Citation Index [Full Cov.]; Curr. Index Stat.; Math. Rev.; Res. Alert [Full Cov.]; Zentralbl. Math. Ihre Grenzgeb.

II/0581-5738
**SANKHYA. SERIES B.** (SANKHYA. SERIES B. METHODOLOGICAL.). [Sankhya. Ser. B]. **Added/Corp** Indian Statistical Institute. **VFOAT** Sankhya B. Vol. 23 (Dec. 1960)-. Periodical. English. Three times a year. $75.00. Statistical Publishing Society Road, Calcutta 700 035 India. **(Subscription address:** Prints India, 11 Darya Ganj, New Delhi, 110002 India, (Phone: 011 91 11 3268645)) **CODEN** SANBBV. **Pr Rev.** Documents available from The Genuine Article. ***Supersedes in part*** *Sankhya.*
**Ind/Abst** Compumath Citation Index [Full Cov.]; Curr. Index Stat.; Math. Rev.; Res. Alert [Full Cov.]; Soc. Sci. Cit. Index [Select. Cov.]; Zentralbl. Math. Ihre Grenzgeb.

YU
**SAOBRACAJ I VEZE.** **Main/Corp** Savezni Zavod za Statistiku (Yugoslavia). Serbo-Croatian (Roman). 30.-. Kneza Milosa 20, Belgrad Yugoslavia. **LC** HA1631; .A33 subser.

II
**SARVEKSHANA.** **Added/Corp** National Sample Survey Organisation. Vol. 1 (July 1977)-. Periodical. English (summaries and/or abstracts in Hindi). qt. $10.00. Chief Executive Officer, National Sample Survey Organisation, Sardar Patel Bhavan Parliament Street, New Delhi 110001 India. **LC** HA1724; .S27. **DD** 315.4. Index available in last issue of volume--attached.

SW/0303-6898
**SCANDINAVIAN JOURNAL OF STATISTICS.** (SCANDINAVIAN JOURNAL OF STATISTICS, THEORY AND APPLICATIONS.). [Scand. j. stat.]. **Added/Corp** Dansk Selskab for Teoretisk Statistik. Vol. 1 (1974)-. Academic Scholarly Publication. English. Four times a year. £80.00 UK and Europe; $132.00 North America; £85.00 other. Basil Blackwell Publishers Ltd, 108 Cowley Road, Oxford 0X4 1JF England. **Tel** 011 44 865 791100, FAX 011 44 865 791347, telex 837022 OXBOOK G. **(Subscription address:** Blackwell Publishers / UK, Marston Book Services, PO Box 87, Oxford OX2 0DT England.**)** **ED** Benat Rosen. **LC** QA276.A1; S28. **DD** 519.5/05. **NLM** W1 SC154BN. **CODEN** SJSADG. **[CCC]. Ad Acc. Pr Rev. Circ:** 1,000. Documents available from The Genuine Article, Ask*IEEE.
**Desc:** Publishes research papers on statistical theory and its applications including relevant aspects of probability.
**Ind/Abst** Biostatistica; Compumath Citation Index [Full Cov.]; Curr. Index Stat.; INSPEC (1975-); Math. Rev.; Qual. Control Appl. Stat.; Res. Alert [Full Cov.]; Sci. Cit. Index; Selec. Coop. Index Manage. Period; SCISEARCH; Zentralbl. Math. Ihre Grenzgeb.

SZ
**SCHWEIZ IN KURVEN, DIE.** **VFOAT** La Suisse en Diagrammes. Periodical. French (German). 85.00F. Economica Verlag AG, Dorneckstr 105, 4143 Dornach Switzerland. **LC** HA1604; .S28. **DD** 314.94.

UK
**SCOTTISH ABSTRACT OF STATISTICS.** **Added/Corp** Great Britain. Scottish Office. No. 1 (1971)-. English. an. £22.00. Scottish Office Library, Room 1-44 New St. Andrews House, Edinburgh EH1 3TG Scotland. **Tel** 011 44 31 2444771, FAX 011 44 31 2444785. **LC** HA1151; .A32. **DD** 314.1. ***Continues in part*** *Digest of Scottish Statistics.*

US
**SELECTED PERINATAL STATISTICS.** English. an. $5.00. Center for Health Statistics, State Office Building, 434 Monroe Street, Montgomery AL 36130. **Tel** (205)242-5253. **ED** Dale E Quinney. **Circ:** 300 (ctrl).

XV
**SEZNAM PREJETIH STATISTICNIH PUBLIKACIJ, KNJIG IN REVIJ V ... / ZAVOD SR SLOVENIJE ZA STATISTIKO.** Periodical. Slovenian. mo. **LC** Z7555; .S49; HA154. ***Continues*** *Seznam Prejetih Knjig, Revij in Statisticnih Pulikacij V ... .*

JA
**SHUTOKEN TOKEI YORAN.** **Added/Corp** Japan. Kokudocho. Daitoshiken Seibikyoku. (1974)-. Statistical Publication. Japanese. Kokudocho Daitoshiken Seibikyoku, 6-19 Azabudai 1-chome Minato-ku, Tokyo Japan. **LC** HA1849.T6; S57.

MY
**SIARAN PERANGKAAN TAHUNAN, SABAH. ANNUAL BULLETIN OF STATISTICS, SABAH.** **Main/Corp** Malaysia. Jabatan Perangkaan. **VFOAT** Annual Bulletin of Statistics, Sabah. Bulletin. Malay (English). Department of Statistics / Malaysia, Jalan Cenderasari, 50514 Kuala Lumpur Malaysia. **Tel** 011 60 3 2922133. ***Continues*** *Annual Bulletin of Statistics, Sabah.*

LU/1018-5739
**SIGMA : THE BULLETIN OF EUROPEAN STATISTICS.** **Added/Corp** Statistical Office of the European Communities. No. 1 (Sept./Oct. 1991)-. Bulletin. English. qt. Free on request. Office for Official Publications of the European Communities, 2 Rue Mercier, 2985 Luxembourg Luxembourg. **Tel** 011 352 499281, FAX 011 352 488573. **LC** HA1107.5; .A26c. **DD** 314. ***Continues*** *Statistical Office of the European Communities. Eurostat News, 0378-4207.*

SI/0217-4316
**SINGAPORE STATISTICAL NEWS : SSN.** Vol. 6, No. 1-. Statistical Publication. English. qt. Free. Singapore Statistical News, Robinson Road, PO Box 3010, Singapore 9050 Singapore. **Tel** 3209689, telex RS20826 STATS RS. **ED** Khoo Chian Kim, Leow Bee Geok, Robert Hia. **LC** HA4600.67; .A23A. **Bk Rev. Circ:** 2,150 (ctrl). ***Continues*** *NSC Statistical News.*
**Desc:** Contains a feature article, summary results of surveys, notes on statistical publications, overseas seminar/courses attended and key statistical personnel in the public sector.
**Ind/Abst** PAIS Int. Print (?-?).

BL
**SINOPSE ESTATISTICA DA REGIAO NORTE / SECRETARIA DE PLANEJAMENTO DA PRESIDENCIA DA REPUBLICA, FUNDACAO INSTITUTO BRASILEIRO DE GEOGRAFIA E ESTATISTICA, IBGE.** **Added/Corp** Fundacao Instituto Brasileiro de Geografia e Estatistica. (1981)-. Portuguese. $25.00 US (back issues). Instituto Brasileiro de Geografia e Estatistica, Rua General Canabarro 666 AN2, 20271 Rio de Janeiro RJ Brazil. **Tel** 011 55 21 2847690, 011 55 21 2342043. **LC** HA973; .S56. **DD** 318.1. Index available. **Ad Acc.** ctrl circ.
**Desc:** Focuses on geophysical, demographic, social, cultural, economic and political/administrative aspects that are fundamental and particular to each region.

BL
**SINOPSE ESTATISTICA DA REGIAO SUL / SECRETARIA DE PLANEJAMENTO DA PRESIDENCIA DA REPUBLICA, FUNDACAO INSTITUTO BRASILEIRO DE GEOGRAFIA E ESTATISTICA, IBGE.** 1982-. Portuguese. an. Instituto Brasileiro de Geografia e Estatistica, Rua General Canabarro 666 AN2, 20271 Rio de Janeiro RJ Brazil. **Tel** 011 55 21 2847690, 011 55 21 2342043. **LC** HA988.S68; S57. **DD** 318.1/6.
**Desc:** Focuses on geophysical, demographic, social, cultural, economic and political/administrative aspects that are fundamental and particular to each region.

GW
**SONDERHEFTE ZUM ALLGEMEINEN STATISTISCHEN ARCHIV.** **Added/Corp** Deutsche Statistische Gesellschaft. **VFOAT** Allgemeines Statistisches Archiv. Sonderhefte zum Allgemeinen Statistischen Archiv. (1970)-. Monographic series. German. cum. index.
**Ind/Abst** Zentralbl. Math. Ihre Grenzgeb.

US/1065-5689
**SOUTH CAROLINA IN PERSPECTIVE.** (SOUTH CAROLINA IN PERSPECTIVE : A STATISTICAL VIEW OF THE "PALMETTO STATE".). [S.C. perspect.]. **Added/Corp** Morgan Quitno Corporation. (1990)-. Statistical Publication. English. $18.00. Morgan Quitno Corporation, PO Box 1656, 512 East 9th Street, Lawrence KS 66044. **Tel** (800)457-0742, (913)841-3534, FAX (913)841-3534. **DD** 317. ***Continues*** *South Carolina in Perspective, 1065-5689.*
**Desc:** Reports on the state's data and rank for each of the categories featured in State Rankings.

US/0739-9308
**SOUTH CAROLINA STATISTICAL ABSTRACT.** 1972-. Statistical Publication. English. an. $17.00. South Carolina Budget and Control Board, Division of Research & Statistical Services, 1000 Assembly Street/Room 425, Columbia SC 29201. **Tel** (803)734-3788. **ED** Joyce A Hallenbeck. **LC** HA621; .S68. **DD** 317.57. **Circ:** 850. ***Supersedes in part*** *Economic Report, the State of South Carolina, 0145-3637.*
**Desc:** Single-source reference for demographic and economic data on South Carolina. Statistics from federal, state, local and private sources on agriculture, banking and finance, business and industry, climate, education, employment, energy, government, health, housing, income, law enforcement, recreation and tourism, transportation, and vital statistics. Includes S.C. rankings among all states.

US/0094-6338
**SOUTH CAROLINA VITAL AND MORBIDITY STATISTICS.** [S.C. vital morb. stat.]. **Main/Corp** South Carolina. Division of Biostatistics. (1974)-. English. 2600 Bull Street, Columbia SC 29201. **Tel** (803)734-4860, FAX (803)754-5554. **LC** HA621; .O34a. **DD** 312/.09757. **NLM** W2 AS6 D65S. **Circ:** 500. ***Continues*** *South Carolina Vital and Morbidity Statistics, 0094-6338.*
**Desc:** Vital statistics for South Carolina.
**Ind/Abst** Stat. Ref. Index.

US/1065-5697
**SOUTH DAKOTA IN PERSPECTIVE.** (SOUTH DAKOTA IN PERSPECTIVE : A STATISTICAL VIEW OF THE "COYOTE STATE".). [S.D. perspect.]. **Added/Corp** Morgan Quitno Corporation. (1990)-. Statistical Publication. English. $18.00. Morgan Quitno Corporation, PO Box 1656, 512 East 9th Street, Lawrence KS 66044. **Tel** (800)457-0742, (913)841-3534, FAX (913)841-3534. **DD** 317. ***Continues*** *South Dakota in Perspective, 1065-5697.*
**Desc:** Reports on the state's data and rank for each of the categories featured in State Rankings.

CI
**SREDNJE USMERENO OBRAZOVANJE (PO REGIONIMA I OPSTINAMA) / SOCIJALISTICKA REPUBLIKA SRBIJA, REPUBLICKI ZAVOD ZA STATISTIKU.** **Added/Corp** Republicki Zavod za Statistiku SR Srbije. (1981)-. Serbo-Croatian (Roman). 80.00. Republicki Zavod za Statistiku, Central Bureau of Statistics of the Republic of Croatia, Ilica 3, Zagreb Croatia. **Tel** 011 385 41 45 44 22, FAX 011 385 41 42 94 13, 011 385 41 42 37 11, telex 21130 DZSTAT RH. **LC** HA1651; .A334 subser.; LA1009.S47.

US/0362-5397
**STANDARD METROPOLITAN STATISTICAL AREAS.** **Main/Corp** United States. Office of Management and Budget. Statistical Policy Division. Statistical Publication. English. Office of Management and Budget, Executive Office Building, Washington DC 20503. **Tel** (202)395-3080. **LC** HT334.U5; U53A. **DD** 317.3.

US
**STAT BANK COMPUTER FILE.** **Added/Corp** NewsBank, Inc. Issue 9 (1991)-. Periodical. English. Four times a year. $1,195.00. Newsbank Inc, 58 Pine Street, New Canaan CT 06840. **Tel** (800)243-7694, (800)762-8182, FAX (203)966-6254. ***Continues*** *Stat Fact.*
**Desc:** Contains over one-half million statistics and facts on all 50 states and the District of Columbia in one easy-to-search database. System requirements: IBM PC or compatible, 256K, CD-ROM drive. Accompanied by access and retrieval software.

US/0276-6566
**STATE AND METROPOLITAN AREA DATA BOOK.** **Added/Corp** United States. Bureau of the Census. (1979)-. English. ir. $27.30 US; $32.50 other. CW Associates, PO Box 34099, Bethesda MD 20827. **Tel** (301)340-9399. **LC** HA202; .S84. **DD** 317.3. **NLM** W2 A B9S.

US
**STATE DATA CENTER DATA DEVELOPMENTS BULLETIN / STATE OF NEW YORK, DEPARTMENT OF COMMERCE.** No. 1 (Jan. 1983)-. Bulletin. English. mo. Free. New York Department of Commerce, 99 Washington Avenue, Albany NY 12245. **Tel** (518)474-6950, (518)474-5027. **ED** Leonard M Gaines. **LC** HA37.U7; N717. **DD** 310/.6/0747. **Circ:** 1,200.
**Desc:** Newsletter containing news about the release of data and reports from the US Census Bureau or other sources regarding New York state.

US/0073-1080
**STATE OF HAWAII DATA BOOK.** (THE STATE OF HAWAII DATA BOOK : A STATISTICAL ABSTRACT PUBLISHED BY THE OFFICE OF INFORMATION, DEPARTMENT OF PLANNING AND ECONOMIC DEVELOPMENT, STATE OF HAWAII.). **Main/Corp** Hawaii. Dept. of Planning And Economic Development. **Added/Corp** Hawaii. Dept. of Planning and Economic Development. Office of Information. Hawaii. Dept. of Planning and Economic Development. Office of Information and Public Services. Hawaii. Dept. of Planning and Economic Development. Hawaii. Dept. of Business and Economic Development. (1967)-. Statistical Publication. English. an. $8.00 Hawaii; $12.00 others. Hawaii Department of Business and Economic Development, PO Box 2359, Honolulu HI 96804. **Tel** (808)586-2423. **(Subscription address:** Dbedt Information, Attention: Data Book Request, PO Box 2359, Honolulu HI 96804.) **ED** Robert C. Schmitt. **LC** HA329.1; .H35a. **DD** 319.69. **Bk Rev. Ad Acc. Circ:** 3,000 (ctrl). ***Continues*** *Hawaii. Dept. of Planning and Research. Statistical Abstract of Hawaii.*
**Desc:** Serves as the statistical abstract and guide to sources of Hawaii statistics.
**Ind/Abst** Stat. Ref. Index.

US/0090-3787
**STATE OF ILLINOIS STATISTICAL REPORT.** **Main/Corp** Illinois. Office of Planning and Analysis. 1972-. Statistical Publication. English. Illinois Office of Planning & Analysis, Springfield IL 62706. **LC** HA341; .A38. **DD** 317.73.

US/1057-3623
**STATE RANKINGS (LAWRENCE, KAN.).** (STATE RANKINGS : A STATISTICAL VIEW OF THE 50 UNITED STATES.). [State rank.]. **Added/Corp** Morgan Quitno Corporation. (1990)-. Statistical Publication. English. an (Apr.). $43.95. Morgan Quitno Corporation, PO Box 1656, 512 East 9th Street, Lawrence KS 66044. **Tel** (800)457-0742, (913)841-3534, FAX (913)841-3534. **LC** HA203; .U17. **DD** 317.3. ***Continues*** *U.S. Statistical Rankings, 0743-0833.*
**Desc:** Contains a variety of tables that compare the 50 United States in 527 categories.

US/1053-7740
**STATES IN PROFILE.** (STATES IN PROFILE : THE STATE POLICY REFERENCE BOOK.). [States profile]. **Added/Corp** Brizius & Foster. State Policy Research, Inc. (1990)-. English. be (June and Dec.). $99.95 (one edition), $129.95 (both editions). Brizius & Foster, RD 1 Box 445D, McConnellsburg PA 17233. **Tel** (717)485-5348. **(Subscription address:** US Data on Demand Inc., RD 1, Box 445-D, McConnellsburg PA 17233.) **LC** HA203; .S74. **DD** 317.3/05. ***Continues*** *State Policy Data Book.*

IT/0390-590X
**STATISTICA.** [Statistica]. Year 1, No. 1 (Jan./March 1941)-. Periodical. Italian. qt. L47000 Italy; L62000 other. Clueb Coop Libraria Univ Edi, Bologna Via Marsala 24, 40126 Bologna Italy. **Tel** 011 39 51 220736, 224780, FAX 011 39 51 237758. **NLM** HA 1 S797. **CODEN** STATDJ. cum. index. ***Supersedes*** *Nuovi Problemi di Politica, Storia ed Economia. Supplemento Statistico.*
**Ind/Abst** Int. Bibliogr. Sociol.; J. Econ. Lit.; Math. Rev.; Popul. Index; Stat. Theory Method Abstr. (1959-1963, 1966, 1972, 1979, 1982-1984, 1986-1987); Zentralbl. Math. Ihre Grenzgeb.

IT/0390-6566
**STATISTICA ANNUALE DEL COMMERCIO CON L'ESTERO. TOMO 2. MERCI PER PAESI.** [Stat. annu. commer. estero Tomo 2]. (1964)-. Periodical. Italian. an. L124000.00. Istituto Nazionale Statistica, GBP SEZ4 Via Cesare Balbo 16, 00184 Rome Italy. **Tel** 011 39 6 46735118. **UDC** 382. ***Continues*** *Statistica Annuale del Commercio con l'Estero, 0075-1871.*

IT/0075-188X
**STATISTICA DEGLI INCIDENTI STRADALI.** [Stat. incid. str.]. (1953)-. Periodical. Italian. an. L23000.00. Istituto Nazionale Statistica, GBP SEZ4 Via Cesare Balbo 16, 00184 Rome Italy. **Tel** 011 39 6 46735118. **UDC** 31 : 614.84.

NE/0039-0402
**STATISTICA NEERLANDICA.** [Stat. neerl.]. Year 9, No. 1/2-. Academic Scholarly Publication. Dutch (English). Three times a year. $126.00 North America; £81.00 other. Basil Blackwell Publishers Ltd, 108 Cowley Road, Oxford 0X4 1JF England. **Tel** 011 44 865 791100, FAX 011 44 865 791347, telex 837022 OXBOOK G. **(Subscription address:** Blackwell Publishers / UK, Marston Book Services, PO Box 87, Oxford OX2 0DT England.) **LC** HA1; .V433. **[CCC]. Bk Rev.** ***Continues*** *Statistics (Vereniging voor Statistiek).*
**Desc:** Scientific statistical research journal including review papers on subfields of probability and statistics.
**Ind/Abst** Biostatistica; Curr. Index Stat.; Int. Abstr. Oper. Res. [Select. Cov.]; Math. Rev.; Qual. Control Appl. Stat.; Stat. Theory Method Abstr. (1966-1975, 1977-1981, 1983-1984, 1986-1987); Zentralbl. Math. Ihre Grenzgeb.

KU
**STATISTICAL ABSTRACT - CENTRAL STATISTICAL OFFICE.** **Main/Corp** Kuwait (State). Al-idarah Al-Markaziyah Lil-ihsa. **Added/Corp** Kuwait (State). Majlis al-Takhtit. Kuwait (State). Idarat al-Ihsa al-Markaziyah. (1964)-. Statistical Publication. English. an. $8.00. Central Statistical Office / Kuwait, Box 26188, Kuwait 13122 Kuwait. **Tel** 011 965 5628231, 011 965 2428200. **LC** HA1950.K8; A3.

TZ
**STATISTICAL ABSTRACT (DAR ES SALAAM, TANZANIA).** (STATISTICAL ABSTRACT.). **Added/Corp** East Africa High Commission. East African Statistical Dept. Tanganyika Office. East Africa High Commission. East African Statistical Dept. Tanganyika Unit. Tanganyika. Economics and Statistics Division. Tanzania. Maktaba ya Takwimu. Directorate of Development and Planning. (1938/1951)-. Statistical Publication. English. an. Government Printer / Tanzania, PO Box 2483, Dar es Salaam Tanzania. **LC** HA2131; .A3. **DD** 316.78. available on microfiche.

IE/0790-8970
**STATISTICAL ABSTRACT DUBLIN. 1986.** [Stat. abstr. Dublin, 1986]. **VFOAT** Ireland Statistical Abstract. (1986)-. Abstracting/Indexing Service. English. an. Government Publications, 4 5 Harcourt Road, Dublin 2 Ireland. **Tel** 011 353 1 6613111 Ext.4005. **DD** 314.7. **Circ:** 2,000. ***Continues*** *Statistical Abstract of Ireland, 0081-4660.*

ET
**STATISTICAL ABSTRACT - ETHIOPIA. CENTRAL STATISTICAL OFFICE.** ***Title Change.*** **Main/Corp** Ethiopia. Central Statistical Office. **Added/Corp** Ethiopia. YaStatistiks Taqlay Sehfat Bet. **VFOAT** Ethiopia Statistical Abstract; Statistical Abstract of Ethiopia. (1963)-(1964). Statistical Publication. English. **LC** HA1961; .A3. ***Continued by*** *Ityopya, Amatawi Yastatistiks Mashet.*

II
**STATISTICAL ABSTRACT, INDIA.** **Main/Corp** India (Republic). Central Statistical Organisation. **VFOAT** Statistical Abstract. New Ser., V. 1-1949-. Statistical Publication. English. $90.00. Controller of Publications / Civil Lines, Government of India, Civil Lines, New Delhi 110054 India. **Tel** 3015984, telex 3166415. **LC** HA1713. **DD** 315.4. ***Supersedes*** *India. Dept. of Commercial Intelligence and Statistics. Statistical Abstract for British India, with Statistics, when Available, Relating to Certain Indian States.*

US/0364-9202
**STATISTICAL ABSTRACT OF COLORADO.** **Added/Corp** University of Colorado, Boulder. Business Research Division. (1976/77)-. Statistical Publication. English. be. $45.00. University of Colorado, Business Research Division, Campus Box 420, Boulder CO 80309. **Tel** (303)492-8227. **LC** HA275; .S73. **DD** 317.88.

IS/0081-4679
**STATISTICAL ABSTRACT OF ISRAEL.** [Snaton statisti le-Yiserael]. **Added/Corp** Israel. Lishkah ha-Merkazit Li-Statistikah. Israel. Lishkah ha-Merkazit Li-Statistikah Ule-Mehkar Kalkali. **VFOAT** Shenaton Statisti Le-Yisrael. No. 1, (1950)-. Statistical Publication. Multiple languages (English and Hebrew). an. $69.00. Central Bureau of Statistics / Israel, PO Box 13015, 91 130 Hakirya Jerusalem Israel. **Tel** 011-972-2-553553. **LC** HA1931; .A35. **DD** 315.694. **NLM** W2 JI9 C399S. Index available.
**Desc:** Presents data on population, economics and society in Israel, all in one volume. Covers demography, vital statistics, climate, finance, manpower, prices, agriculture, construction, commerce, transport, education, welfare, health, industry, society and macroeconomics.

US/0081-4687
**STATISTICAL ABSTRACT OF LATIN AMERICA.** [Stat. abstr. Lat. Am.]. **Added/Corp** University of California, Los Angeles. Committee on Latin American Studies. University of California, Los Angeles. Center of Latin American Studies. University of California, Los Angeles. Latin American Center. UCLA Latin American Center. 1st Ed. (1955)-. Statistical Publication. English. an. $250.00. Regents of the University of California at Los Angeles, 405 Hilgard Avenue, Los Angeles CA 90024-1447. **Tel** (310)825-6634. **ED** James W. Wilkie and Enrique Ochoa. **LC** HA935; .S8. Index available. **Circ:** 600.
**Desc:** A basic statistical reference on Latin America for more than twenty years. It is a standard source of information for scholars, researchers, businesses and governments.
**Ind/Abst** Stat. Ref. Index.

US/0081-4695
**STATISTICAL ABSTRACT OF LOUISIANA / COMPILED UNDER THE DIRECTION OF JAMES R. BOBO.** **Added/Corp** Louisiana State University in New Orleans. Division of Business and Economic Research. University of New Orleans. Division of Business and Economic Research. Louisiana. State Planning Office. First Ed. (1965)-. Statistical Publication. English. ir (every 3 years). $22.00. University of New Orleans Division of Business and Economic Research, New Orleans LA 70148. **Tel** (504)286-6248. **ED** Vincent Maruggi. **LC** HA401; .S74. **DD** 317.63. **Circ:** 1,000.

II
**STATISTICAL ABSTRACT OF MAHARASHTRA STATE.** 1960/61-. Statistical Publication. English. an. Government of Maharashtra / Economics and Statistics, Directorate of Economics and Statistics, Bombay 34WB India. **LC** HA1728.M3; S74. **DD** 315.4/79. ***Supersedes*** *Statistical Abstract of Bombay State.*

US
**STATISTICAL ABSTRACT OF OHIO.** **Main/Corp** Ohio. Dept. of Industrial and Economic Development. 1st- Ed.; 1960-. Statistical Publication. English. an. 65 South Front Street, Columbus OH 43215. **LC** HA571; .A523. **DD** 317.71.

US/0191-0310
**STATISTICAL ABSTRACT OF OKLAHOMA (1972).** (STATISTICAL ABSTRACT OF OKLAHOMA.). **Added/Corp** University of Oklahoma. Center for Economic and Management Research. University of Oklahoma. Bureau for Business and Economic Research. (1972)-. Statistical Publication. English. an (Sept.). $22.00. University of Oklahoma CEMR, 307 West Brooks / Room 4, College of Business Administration, Norman OK 73019. **Tel** (405)325-2931. **ED** Neil Dikeman. **LC** HA581; .U54a. **DD** 317.66. Index available. **Circ:** 350 (ctrl). ***Continues*** *Oklahoma Data Book, 0078-4354.*
**Desc:** Reference for economic and demographic statistical data pertaining to Oklahoma.

US/0081-4741
**STATISTICAL ABSTRACT OF THE UNITED STATES.** (STATISTICAL ABSTRACT OF THE UNITED STATES / PREPARED BY THE CHIEF OF THE BUREAU OF STATISTICS, TREASURY DEPARTMENT.). [Stat. abstr. U. S.]. **Added/Corp** United States. Dept. of the Treasury. Bureau of Statistics. United States. Dept. of Commerce and Labor. Bureau of Statistics. United States. Bureau of Foreign and Domestic Commerce. United States. Bureau of the Census. 1st No. (1878)-. Statistical Publication. English. an. $37.85. Claitors Law Books, 3165 South Acadian, Baton Rouge

LA 70808. **Tel** (504)344-0476, (800)274-1403. **(Subscription address:** Claitors Law Books, PO Box 3333, Baton Rouge, LA 70821**) LC** HA202. **DD** 317.3. **NLM** HA 202 A1. available on microfilm and microfiche from University Microfilms International (UMI).

●US/1063-1690
**STATISTICAL ABSTRACT OF THE UNITED STATES (ENLARGED PRINT ED.).** (STATISTICAL ABSTRACT OF THE UNITED STATES / U.S. DEPT. OF COMMERCE, ECONOMICS AND STATISTICS ADMINISTRATION, BUREAU OF THE CENSUS.). [Stat. abstr. U.S.]. **Added/Corp** United States. Economics and Statistics Administration. United States. Bureau of the Census. **VFOAT** National Data Book. 112th Ed. (1992)-. Statistical Publication. English. an. $38.00 (cloth), $32.00 (paper). Bernan Associates, 4611-F Assembly Drive, Lanham MD 20706-4391. **Tel** (301)459-7666, (800)274-4447 US, (800)233-0504 CANADA, FAX (301)459-0056, telex 7108260418. **DD** 317.
**Ind/Abst** Predicasts Forecasts.

CY/0590-4862
**STATISTICAL ABSTRACT - STATISTICS AND RESEARCH DEPARTMENT (NICOSIA).** (STATISTICAL ABSTRACT - REPUBLIC OF CYPRUS, STATISTICS AND RESEARCH DEPARTMENT.). **Main/Corp** Cyprus. Statistics and Research Dept. **VFOAT** Statistical Abstract - Republic of Cyprus, Statistics and Research Department, Ministry of Finance. No. 5 (1959)-. Statistical Publication. English. an. $10.00. Department of Statistics and Research / Cyprus, 13 Lord Byron Avenue, Nicosia 162 Cyprus. **Tel** 011 357 2 303286. **DD** 314. **Circ:** 420. ***Continues*** *Cyprus. Statistical Service. Statistical Abstract - Cyprus Statistical Service.*
**Desc:** Summarized analysis providing statistical data on economic and social conditions in Cyprus. Includes comparative international statistics.

IE/0790-8334
**STATISTICAL BULLETIN. Added/Corp** Ireland. Central Statistics Office. **VFOAT** Feasachan Staidrimh. Vol. 62, No. 1 (Mar. 1987)-. Statistical Publication. English. Four times a year. 27p. Central Statistical Office, Sun Alliance House, Molesworth Street, Dublin 2 Ireland. **Tel** 011 353 1767531. **LC** HF189; .A52. **DD** 314.17. ***Continues*** *Irish Statistical Bulletin, 0021-1370.*

BS
**STATISTICAL BULLETIN / REPUBLIC OF BOTSWANA.** Vol. 1, No. 1 (June 1976)-. Statistical Publication. English. qt. P8.00 Botswana; P2.00 US. Government Printer / Botswana Government, Private Bag 0081, Gaberone Republic of Botswana. **Tel** 09267-315551. **LC** HA4706; .A26. **DD** 316.81/1. **Circ:** 600 (ctrl).
**Desc:** Update of the most recent demographic, social and economic statistics for Botswana.

UK
**STATISTICAL CHANGES IN 1992 / CENTRAL STATISTICAL OFFICE.**
**Added/Corp** Great Britain. Central Statistical Office. Great Britain. Government Statistical Service. Statistical Publication. English. sa. Central Statistical Office Library, Govn Building, Cardiff Road, Newport, Newport Gwent NP9 1XG England.

II
**STATISTICAL HANDBOOK - WEST BENGAL. BUREAU OF APPLIED ECONOMICS AND STATISTICS. Main/Corp** West Bengal. Bureau of Applied Economics and Statistics. Statistical Publication. English. an. Rs5.88. Government of West Bengal / Economics & Statistics, Bureau of Applied Economics & Statistics, Calcutta West Bengal India. **LC** HA1728.B42; A36. **DD** 315.4/14. ***Continues West Bengal.*** *State Statistical Bureau. Statistical Hand Book.*

NE/0167-8000
**STATISTICAL JOURNAL OF THE UNITED NATIONS ECONOMIC COMMISSION FOR EUROPE.** [Stat. j. U.N. Econ. Comm. Eur.]. **Added/Corp** United Nations. Economic Commission for Europe. Vol. 1 No. 1 (June 1982)-. Statistical Publication. English. qt. Fl449.00. United Nations Publishers Geneva, Palais des Nations, C115 Services Ventes, CH-1211 Geneva 10 Switzerland. **Tel** 011 41 227988400, 7985850. **(Subscription address:** IOS International Organisations SVC BV, Van Diemenstraat 94, 1013 CN Amsterdam Netherlands**) LC** HA1; .S67. **DD** 310/.6/01. **CODEN** SJUED4. Documents available from Ask*IEEE.
**Desc:** Informs the professional world of statisticians, whether involved with theoretical or practical problems, of the work of the Conference of European Statisticians. Established a forum for critical discussion of the entire range of problems organizational, methodological, analytical or conceptual facing statistical services.
**Ind/Abst** Curr. Index Stat. (1989-); Econ. Lit. Index (199?-); INSPEC (1989-); J. Econ. Lit.; Stat. Theory Method Abstr. (1986-1987).

US
**STATISTICAL MASTERFILE [COMPUTER FILE]. Added/Corp** Congressional Information Service. **VFOAT** CIS Statistical Masterfile. Statistical Publication. English. qt. Congressional Information Service Inc, 4520 East-West Highway, Suite 800, Bethesda MD 20814-3389. **Tel** (800)638-8380, (301)654-1550, FAX (301)654-4033, telex 292386 CIS UR. **LC** Z7552. **DD** 310. Index available. cum. index. **Bk Rev**. ctrl circ. available on microfiche.
**Desc:** Covers statistical publications issued by federal and state government agencies, international organizations, and the private sector. System requirements: IBM PC, AT, or PS/2; book free memory and hard disk; DOS 3.1 or higher; CD-ROM drive with Microsoft extensions.

UK/0017-3630
**STATISTICAL NEWS (GREAT BRITAIN. CENTRAL STATISTICAL OFFICE).** (STATISTICAL NEWS.). **Added/Corp** Great Britain. Central Statistical Office. No. 1 (May 1968)-. Statistical Publication. English. qt. £30.00. Her Majesty's Stationery Office, 51 Nine Elms Lane, London SW8 5DR England. **Tel** 011 44 71 873 8459, 011 44 71 873 8499, FAX 011 44 71 873 8499, 011 44 71 873 8456, telex 297138. **(Subscription address:** Her Majestys Stationery Offic, PO Box 276 Public Centre, London SW8 5DT England**) CODEN** STANE2. **[CCC].** available on microfilm and microfiche from University Microfilms International (UMI).
**Desc:** Provides a comprehensive account of current developments in British official statistics to help all who use or would like to use official statistics.
**Ind/Abst** Geogr. Abstr. Human Geogr. (?-?); Manage. Market. Abstr.

GW/0932-5026
**STATISTICAL PAPERS (BERLIN, GERMANY).** (STATISTICAL PAPERS.). **VFOAT** Statistische Hefte. Vol. 29, No. 1 (1988)-. Statistical Publication. German. Four times a year. DM288.00. Springer-Verlag GmbH & Company KG, Heidelberger Platz 3, D 14197 Berlin Germany. **Tel** 011 49 30 8207223, FAX 011 49 30 8214091, telex 183 319 SPBLN D. **(Subscription address:** Springer Verlag New York Inc. / for North America, 44 Hartz Way, Secaucus NJ 07096.**) CODEN** STPAE4. **[CCC].** available on microfilm and microfiche from University Microfilms International (UMI). ***Continues*** *Statistische Hefte, 0039-0631.*
**Desc:** Addresses itself to all persons and organizations that have to deal with statistical methods in their own field of work. Attempts to provide a forum for the presentation and critical assessment of statistical methods, in particular for the discussion of their methodological foundations as well as their potential applications.
**Ind/Abst** Compumath Citation Index [Full Cov.]; Soc. Sci. Cit. Index [Select. Cov.].

NP
**STATISTICAL POCKET BOOK, NEPAL.**
**Main/Corp** Nepal. Central Bureau of Statistics. (1974)-. Statistical Publication. English. be. $10.31, $0.61 per issue (add $2.00 for postage). Central Bureau of Statistics / Nepal, Kathmandu Nepal. **Tel** 2-12606. **LC** HA1950.N5; A14a. **DD** 315.49/6. **Circ:** 5,000 (ctrl).
**Desc:** Covers area and population, forest, mineral production, water, power and irrigation, education, health, tourism, transport and communication, climate, food and agriculture, industry, government, finance, and prices.

AF
**STATISTICAL POCKET-BOOK OF AFGHANISTAN. Added/Corp** Afghanistan. Dept. of Statistics. (1972)-. Statistical Publication. English. Department of Statistics, Kabul Afghanistan. **LC** HA1675; .S7. **DD** 315.8/1.

BG
**STATISTICAL POCKET BOOK OF BANGLADESH. Added/Corp** Bangladesh. Parisamkhyana Byuro. **VFOAT** Bamladesa Parisamkhyana Paketa Bai. (1978)-. Statistical Publication. Bengali (English). an. $12.00. Bangladesh Bureau of Statistics, Ministry of Planningstats Division, Dacca 1000 Bangladesh. **Tel** 011 880 23000 29312081. **LC** HA4590.6; .A25. **DD** 315.49/2. **Circ:** 1,730.

CE/0585-1777
**STATISTICAL POCKET BOOK OF THE DEMOCRATIC SOCIALIST REPUBLIC OF SRI LANKA.** [Stat. pocket book Democr. Social. Repub. Sri Lanka]. **Added/Corp** Sri Lanka. Janalekhana ha Sankhyalekhana Departamentuva. 11th, (1978)-. Statistical Publication. English. an. Rs20.00 Sri Lanka; $5.45 US. PO Box 563, Colombo 7 Sri Lanka Ceylon. **Tel** 595291. **LC** HA1697; .A23. **DD** 315.49/3. **Circ:** 3,932. ***Continues*** *Statistical Pocket Book of the Republic of Sri Lanka (Ceylon).*
**Desc:** Contains statistical data on population and vital statistics on agriculture, social conditions, education, health, national accounts, public finance, geography, etc.

YU/0585-1815
**STATISTICAL POCKET-BOOK OF YUGOSLAVIA. VFOAT** Statistical Pocket Book of Yugoslavia. 1955-. Statistical Publication. English. an. Federal Institute for Statistics, Kneza Milosa 20, 11000 Belgrad Republic of Yugoslavia. **LC** HA1631. **DD** 314.

US/0885-6834
**STATISTICAL REFERENCE INDEX.** [Stat. ref. index]. **Added/Corp** Congressional Information Service. **VFOAT** S.R.I.; SRI. Vol. 1 (Jan. 1980)-. Abstracting/Indexing Service. English. ir. Congressional Information Service Inc, 4520 East-West Highway, Suite 800, Bethesda MD 20814-3389. **Tel** (800)638-8380, (301)654-1550, FAX (301)654-4033, telex 292386 CIS UR. **ED** Lynne Marble. **DD** 016.

US/0278-694X
**STATISTICAL REFERENCE INDEX ... ANNUAL.** [Stat. ref. index annu.]. **VFOAT** SRI ... Annual Index. 1980-. Statistical Publication. English. an. Congressional Information Service Inc, 4520 East-West Highway, Suite 800, Bethesda MD 20814-3389. **Tel** (800)638-8380, (301)654-1550, FAX (301)654-4033, telex 292386 CIS UR. **LC** Z7554.U5; S73; HA203. **DD** 016.3173.
**Ind/Abst** Stat. Ref. Index.

YU
**STATISTICAL REPORT. See** Business-Abstracting, Bibliographies and Statistics.

US/0081-5020
**STATISTICAL RESEARCH MONOGRAPHS.** Vol. 1-. Statistical Publication. English. ir. Price varies per volume. University of Chicago Press / Book Department, 11030 South Langley Avenue, Chicago IL 60628. **Tel** (800)621-2736, (312)568-1550, FAX (312)753-0811, telex 23933.

JM
**STATISTICAL REVIEW (JAMAICA. DEPT. OF STATISTICS).** (STATISTICAL REVIEW.). **Added/Corp** Jamaica. Dept. of Statistics. (Aug. 1981)-. Statistical Publication. English. qt. $15.00. Statistical Institute of Jamaica, 9 Swallowfield Road, PO Box 643, Kingston 5 Jamaica. **Tel** (809)92-62175-6, FAX (809)92-64859. **LC** HA891; .S7. **DD** 317.292.

US/0883-4237
**STATISTICAL SCIENCE.** (STATISTICAL SCIENCE : A REVIEW OF JOURNAL OF THE INSTITUTE OF MATHEMATICAL SCIENCES.). [Stat. sci.]. **Added/Corp** Institute of Mathematical Statistics. Vol. 1, No. 1 (Feb. 1986)-. Statistical Publication. English. qt. $75.00. Institute of Mathematical Statistics, 3401 Investment Boulevard, Suite 7, Hayward CA 94545-3819. **Tel** (510)783-8141, FAX (510)783-4131. **ED** Carl N. Morris. **LC** QA276.A1; S73. **DD** 519.5/05. **CODEN** STSCEP. **[CCC].** Index available. **Bk Rev. Ad Acc. Pr Rev. Circ:** 5,800. available on microfilm and microfiche from University Microfilms International (UMI).
**Desc:** Presents contemporary statistical thought at a technical level accessible to the community of practitioners, teachers, researchers, and students in statistics, probability, and related fields.
**Ind/Abst** Biostatistica; Curr. Index Stat.; Math. Rev. (1986-); Qual. Control Appl. Stat.; Soc. Sci. Cit. Index [Select. Cov.]; Soc. Res. Methodol. Abstr. (1986-); Stat. Theory Method Abstr. (1987); Zentralbl. Math. Ihre Grenzgeb.

US/0732-6971
**STATISTICAL SERVICES DIRECTORY.** ***Ceased.*** [Stat. serv. dir.]. **VFOAT** Directory to Statistical Services. First Ed., Issue No. 1 (June 1982)-Ceased with 3rd Ed. Statistical Publication. English. ir. Gale Research Inc., 835 Penobscot Building, Detroit MI 48226. **Tel** (800)877-GALE, (313)961-2242, FAX (313)961-6083, telex TWX 810-221-7086. **LC** HA37; .U137. **DD** 310/.25/73.
**Desc:** The new edition of this directory provides over 2,000 detailed entries leading researchers to the primary gatherers and disseminators of statistics in numerous industries and areas of interest.

GW/0173-5896
**STATISTICAL SOFTWARE NEWSLETTER. See** Mathematics.

US/0147-5525
**STATISTICAL SOURCE DIRECTORY FOR NEW JERSEY STATE GOVERNMENT.** [Stat. source dir. N. J. State gov.]. 1977-. Statistical Publication. English. be. Division of Labor Market and Demographic Research, New Jersey Department of Labor, CN 388, Trenton NJ 08625-0388. **Tel** (609)292-0076, FAX (609)984-6833. **LC** HA37.U7; N47. **DD** 310/.6/1749.

XR
**STATISTICAL SURVEY OF CZECHOSLOVAKIA.** (1973)-. Statistical Publication. English. Orbis Publishing House, Prague Czech Republic. **LC** HA1195; .S78. **DD** 314.37. ***Continues*** *Czechoslovakia Statistical Abstract, 0591-0587.*

UK/0039-0518
**STATISTICAL THEORY AND METHOD ABSTRACTS.** [Stat. theory method abstr.]. **Added/Corp** International Statistical Institute. Vol. 5 (1964)-. Abstracting/Indexing Service. English. qt. $183.00. International Statistical Institute, 428 Prinses

Beatrixlaan, 2270 AZ Voorburg Netherlands. **Tel** 011 31 70 3375737, FAX 011 31 70 3860025, telex 32260 ISI NL. **ED** C. van Eeden, J. Mijnheer. **LC** HA1; .S764. **DD** 001.4/22/05. **NLM** Z 7551 S797. Index Available, published separately, free-automatically sent. **Ad Acc. Circ:** 1,200. ***Continues*** *International Journal of Abstracts: Statistical Theory and Method.*
**Desc:** Provides world-wide coverage of published articles on mathematical statistics and probability. Gives valuable information on new developments in all fields of probability theory, estimation, linear models, stochastic processes, operations research, testing of hypothesis, experimental design and time series analysis. About 4,000 abstracts are published each year, classified into 16 main sections and subdivided into 300 subsections.
**Ind/Abst** Math. Rev.

CN/1189-038X
**STATISTICAL UPDATE.** [Stat. update]. **Added/Corp** Ontario. Addiction Research Foundation. Statistical Information Service. Vol. 1, No. 1 (1991)-. Statistical Publication. English. **DD** 362.29/09713/05.

TH
**STATISTICAL YEAR BOOK, THAILAND.** **Main/Corp** Thailand. National Statistical Office. **Added/Corp** Thailand. Ministry of Commerce (1916?-1926). Statistical Year Book of the Kingdom of Siam. Thailand. Dept. of General Statistics. Statistical Year Book of the Kingdom of Siam. Thailand. Bureau of General Statistics. Statistical Year Book of the Kingdom of Siam. Thailand. Central Service of Statistics. Statistical Year Book of the Kingdom of Siam. Thailand. Central Statistical Office. (1916)-. Statistical Publication. Multiple languages (English and Thai). ir. National Statistical Office, PO Wards Strip NCO, Papua New Guinea. **Tel** 011 675 27182 271172, FAX 011 657 255057, telex FINANCE NE 22312. **Circ:** 1,000 (ctrl).
**Desc:** Area population, public health, and vital statistics on immigration, education, public justice, agriculture, fisheries, forestry, mining industry, business enterprises, transport and communication.

UK
**STATISTICAL YEARBOOK.** **Main/Corp** Central Electricity Generating Board. **VFOAT** CEGB Statistical Yearbook for the Year Ended 31 March ... . (1988/89)-. Statistical Publication. English. Central Electricity Generating Board, Courtney House 18 Warwick Lane, London EC4P England. **LC** WMLC L 83/441. ***Continues*** *CEGB Statistical Yearbook, 0577-0777.*

US/0082-8459
**STATISTICAL YEARBOOK / ANNUAIRE STATISTIQUE / DEPARTMENT OF ECONOMIC AND SOCIAL INFORMATION AND POLICY ANALYSIS, STATISTICAL DIVISION.** **Main/Corp** United Nations. Statistical Office. **Added/Corp** United Nations. Statistical Division. **VFOAT** Annuaire Statistique. 38th issue (1990/91)-. Statistical Publication. English (French). an. Price varies per volume. United Nations Publications, 2 United Nations Plaza, Room DC2 0853, Department 007C, New York NY 10017. **Tel** (212)963-8303, (800)253-9646. **LC** HA12.5; .U63. ***Continues*** *United Nations. Statistical Office. Statistical Yearbook, 0082-8459.*
**Desc:** Provides statistical data for more than 270 countries and territories on economic and social subjects.

TH
**STATISTICAL YEARBOOK FOR ASIA AND THE PACIFIC.** **Added/Corp** United Nations. Economic and Social Commission for Asia and the Pacific. **VFOAT** Annuaire Statistique pour l'Asie et le Pacifique. (1973)-. Statistical Publication. English (French). an. $70.00. United Nations Publications, 2 United Nations Plaza, Room DC2 0853, Department 007C, New York NY 10017. **Tel** (212)963-8303, (800)253-9646. **LC** HA1665; .S73. **DD** 315. ***Continues*** *Statistical Yearbook for Asia and the Far East.*
**Desc:** Contains a wealth of statistics covering population, manpower, national accounts, agriculture, forestry and fishing, industry, energy supplies, consumption, transport and communication, internal and external trade, wages and banking.

BG
**STATISTICAL YEARBOOK OF BANGLADESH.** **Added/Corp** Bangladesh. Parisamkhyana Byuro. **VFOAT** Bamladesa Parisamkhyana Barshagrantha. (1975)-. Statistical Publication. English. an. $40.00. Bangladesh Bureau of Statistics, Ministry of Planningstats Division, Dacca 1000 Bangladesh. **Tel** 011 880 23000 29312081. **LC** HA4590.6; .A26. **DD** 315.49/2. ***Continues*** *Statistical Digest of Bangladesh.*

JM
**STATISTICAL YEARBOOK OF JAMAICA.** **Added/Corp** Jamaica. Central Planning and Development Division. Information Section. (1973)-. Statistical Publication. English. an. $60.00. Statistical Institute of Jamaica, 9 Swallowfield Road, PO Box 643, Kingston 5 Jamaica. **Tel** (809)92-62175-6, FAX (809)92-64859. **LC** HA891; .C45a. **DD** 317.292.

UK
**STATISTICAL YEARBOOK OF MEMBER STATES OF THE COUNCIL FOR MUTUAL ECONOMIC ASSISTANCE.** **Main/Corp** Sovet Ekonomicheskoi Vzaimopomoshchi. **Added/Corp** Council for Mutual Economic Assistance. Secretariat. (19??)-. Statistical Publication. English (Russian). an. $38.31. Reed Business Publishing / West Sussex, England, Perrymount Road, Haywards Heath, West Sussex RH16 3DH England. **Tel** 011 44 81 6523500. **LC** HA1107; .S65a. **DD** 314.7.

NE/0303-6448
**STATISTICAL YEARBOOK OF THE NETHERLANDS.** **Added/Corp** Netherlands. Centraal Bureau voor de Statistiek. (1969/70)-. Statistical Publication. English. an. Fl33.96. SDU Uitgeverij, Postbus 20014, Christoffel Plan, 2500 EA Den Haag Netherlands. **Tel** 011 31 70 3789911. **LC** HA1381; .S75. **DD** 314.92. **NLM** W2 GN4 C3J. ***Continues*** *Jaarcijfers voor Nederlanden.*

CH
**STATISTICAL YEARBOOK OF THE REPUBLIC OF CHINA.** Statistical Publication. English. an. $56.00. Cheng Chung Shu Chu, 20 Heng Yang Road, Taipei Taiwan. **Tel** 011 886 2 3813825.

YU/0585-1858
**STATISTICAL YEARBOOK OF THE SOCIALIST FEDERAL REPUBLIC OF YUGOSLAVIA / SOCIALIST FEDERAL REPUBLIC OF YUGOSLAVIA, FEDERAL STATISTICAL OFFICE.** [Stat. yearb. Social. Fed. Repub. Yugosl.]. **VFOAT** Statistical Yearbook of the SFRY. 1963-. Statistical Publication. English (Serbo-Croatian (Roman)). an. $40.00. PO Box 650279, Vero Beach FL 33965. **Tel** (407)562-9186. **ED** Allan Benz. ***Continues*** *Statistical Yearbook of the Federal People's Republic of Yugoslavia.*

RM/0377-5739
**STATISTICAL YEARBOOK OF THE SOCIALIST REPUBLIC OF ROMANIA.** (STATISTICAL YEARBOOK OF THE SOCIALIST REPUBLIC OF ROMANIA; TRANSLATION OF TEXTS.). **Added/Corp** Romania. Directia Centrala de Statistica. (1966)-. Statistical Publication. English (Romanian). an. lei500 Romania; $70.00 North America; $60.00 other. Statistical Yearbook of Romania, Central Statistical Board, Bucharest Romania. **Tel** 158200, FAX 145560, telex 11153, 11430. **DD** 314. **NLM** W2 GR8 D5AA. **Bk Rev. Ad Acc.** ***Continues*** *Statistical Yearbook of the R.P.R., 0485-6147.*
**Desc:** Statistical yearbook of Romania.

RH
**STATISTICAL YEARBOOK OF ZIMBABWE.** **Added/Corp** Zimbabwe. Central Statistical Office. **VFOAT** Statistical Year Book of Zimbabwe; Statistical Year Book; Statistical Yearbook. (1985)-. Statistical Publication. English. Central Statistical Office / Zimbabwe, PO Box 8063, Causeway Salisbury Harare, Zimbabwe. **Tel** 011 263 0 706681. **LC** HA4702; .A26. **DD** 316.891.

FR/0082-7541
**STATISTICAL YEARBOOK (UNESCO).** (STATISTICAL YEARBOOK.). **Added/Corp** Unesco. **VFOAT** Annuaire Statistique; Anuario Estadistico; Unesco Statistical Yearbook. (1963)-. Statistical Publication. English (French). an. $80.00. UNESCO / France, 31 rue Francois Bonvin, 75732 Paris Cedex 15 France. **Tel** 011 33 1 45684564, 011 33 1 45684565, FAX 011 33 1 42733007, telex 204461 Paris. **(Subscription address:** UNIPUB, 4611 F Assembly Drive, Lanham MD 20706.**)** **NLM** W2 MU7 S7. **CODEN** SYUNDY. ***Continues*** *Basic Facts and Figures (Unesco).*
**Desc:** Reference tables, education, science and technology, and culture and communication, including linguistics.
**Ind/Abst** F&S Index Plus Text, Int. [Select. Cov.]; Predicasts Forecasts.

IT
**STATISTICHE CULTURALI.** **Added/Corp** Istituto Centrale di Statistica (Italy). Vol. 26 (1986)-. Italian. an. L18000. Istituto Nazionale Statistica, GBP SEZ4 Via Cesare Balbo 16, 00184 Rome Italy. **Tel** 011 39 6 46735118. **LC** HA40.C8; I8. ***Continues*** *Istituto Centrale di Statistica (Italy). Annuario Delle Statistiche Culturali, 0075-1677.*

IT
**STATISTICHE GIUDIZIARIE.** Italian. an. L33,500. Istituto Nazionale Statistica, GBP SEZ4 Via Cesare Balbo 16, 00184 Rome Italy. **Tel** 011 39 6 46735118. **LC** KKH30; .S73. ***Continues*** *Annuario di Statistiche Giudiziarie.*

BU
**STATISTICHESKI GODISHNIK NA REPUBLIKA BULGARIIA / TSENTRALNO STATISTICHESKO UPRAVLENIE.** **Added/Corp** Bulgaria. TSentralno Statistichesko Upravlenie. (1990)-. Statistical Publication. Bulgarian. an. 7.28lv. **(Subscription address:** Hemus Foreign Trade Organization, 6 Tzar Osvobodite l Boulevard, 1000 Sofia Bulgaria.**)** **LC** HA1621; .S8. **CODEN** SGRBES. **Circ:** 2,000. ***Continues*** *Statisticheski Godishnik na Narodna Republika Bulgariia, 0204-4838.*

BU
**STATISTICHESKI IZVESTIIA.** **Added/Corp** Bulgaria. Durzhavno Upravlenie za Informatsiia. Bulgaria. Tsentralno Statistichesko Upravlenie. (1970)-. Periodical. Bulgarian. Four times a year. DM166.00. **(Subscription address:** Kubon & Sagner, ABT Zeitschriftenimport, D 80328 Munich Germany.**)**

UN
**STATISTICHESKII BIULLETEN / VSEUKRAINSKII SOVET PROFESSIONALNHYKH SOIUZOV, NARODNYI KOMISSARIAT TRUDA UKRAINY.** **Added/Corp** Vseukrainskii Sovet Professionalnhykh Soiuzov. Periodical. Russian. mo. **LC** WMLC 91/5.

RU
**STATISTICHESKII EZHEGODNIK.** **Added/Corp** Soviet Union. Tsentralnoe Statisticheskoe Upravlenie. **VFOAT** Annuaire Statistique. Vol. 1 (1918/1920)-. Russian (French). an. **LC** HA1431; .A37 subser.

UK/0039-0526
**STATISTICIAN, THE.** [Statistician]. Vol. 12 (1962)-. Academic Scholarly Publication. English. qt. £125.00 UK & Europe; $225.00 North America; £145.00 other. Basil Blackwell Publishers Ltd, 108 Cowley Road, Oxford 0X4 1JF England. **Tel** 011 44 865 791100, FAX 011 44 865 791347, telex 837022 OXBOOK G. **(Subscription address:** Blackwell Publishers / UK, Marston Book Services, PO Box 87, Oxford OX2 0DT England.**)** **ED** R R Harris. **LC** HA1; .A853. **CODEN** STTNAP. **[CCC]. Bk Rev. Ad Acc. Pr Rev.** Documents available from The Genuine Article, Ask*IEEE. ***Continues*** *Incorporated Statistician.*
**Desc:** Publishes articles encouraging the application of statistical principles to administrative and research problems.
**Ind/Abst** Biostatistica; Compumath Citation Index [Full Cov.]; Contents Pages Manage.; Curr. Index Stat.; EMBASE; Geogr. Abstr. Phys. Geogr.; Geogr. Abstr. Human Geogr.; GeoRef; INSPEC (March 1973-); Int. Bibliogr. Sociol.; Int. Dev. Abstr.; Oper. Res./Manag. Sci.; Qual. Control Appl. Stat.; Res. Alert [Full Cov.]; Soc. Sci. Cit. Index [Select. Cov.]; SportSearch; Stat. Theory Method Abstr. (1967, 1969-1978, 1980-1984, 1986-1987).

YU/0039-0534
**STATISTICKA REVIJA.** V. 1- March 1951-. Periodical. Slovak (summaries and/or abstracts in French and English). qt. **(Subscription address:** Jugoslovenska Knjiga, PO Box 36, YU 11001 Belgrade Yugoslovia.**)** **LC** HA37.Y83.
**Ind/Abst** MLA Int. Bibl. Books Artic. Mod. Lang. Lit.; Soc. Plann. Policy Dev. Abstr.; Sociol. Abstr. (?-?); Stat. Theory Method Abstr. (1959-1963, 1970-1972, 1974-1975, 1983).

YU
**STATISTICKI GODISNJAK.** ***Title Change.*** **Main/Corp** Stara Pazova, Serbia (District). Narodni Odbor. (1952)-(19??). Serbo-Croatian (Roman) (English). an. **(Subscription address:** Jugoslovenska Knjiga, PO Box 36, YU 11001 Belgrade Yugoslovia.**)** **LC** HA1657.S7; S7a. ***Merged with*** *Statistical Yearbook of the Socialist Federal Republic of Yugoslavia* ***to form*** *Statisticki Godisnjak Jugoslavije. Statistical Yearbook of Yugoslavia.*
**Desc:** Giving data on social and economic course; social structure, social products, national income, consumption (general, collective investment), prices, etc. Illustrated with charts and interesting for persons work in field of analysis and plan.

CI/0585-1920
**STATISTICKI GODISNJAK JUGOSLAVIJE.** (STATISTICKI GODISNJAK JUGOSLAVIJE / SOCIJALISTICKA FEDERATIVNA REPUBLIKA JUGOSLAVIJA, SAVEZNI ZAVOD ZA STATISTIKU.). [Stat. god. Jugosl.]. **Added/Corp** Savezni Zavod za Statistiku (Yugoslavia). **VFOAT** Statisticki Godisnjak SFRJ. (1968)-. Serbo-Croatian (Roman). ir. **(Subscription address:** Jugoslovenska Knjiga, PO Box 36, YU 11001 Belgrade Yugoslovia.**)** **LC** HA1631; .A34. **CODEN** SGJUEB. ***Continues*** *Statisticki Godisnjak SFRJ.*

CI
**STATISTICKI GODISNJAK SRBIJE.** **Added/Corp** Republicki Zavod za Statistiku (Serbia). (1991)-. Serbo-Croatian (Cyrillic). Republicki Zavod za Statistiku, Central Bureau of Statistics of the Republic of Croatia, Ilica 3, Zagreb Croatia. **Tel** 011 385 41 45 44 22, FAX 011 385 41 42 94 13, 011 385 41 42 37 11, telex 21130 DZSTAT RH. **LC** HA1634.S67; S73. ***Continues*** *Statisticki Godisnjak SR Srbije.*

# Statistics

**XV**
**STATISTICNI LETOPIS REPUBLIKE SLOVENIJE / REPUBLIKA SLOVENIJA, ZAVOD REPUBLIKE SLOVENIJE ZA STATISTIKO.** **Added/Corp** Zavod SR Slovenije za Statistiko. (1990)-. Slovenian. **LC** HA1634.S6; S73. *Continues StatistiEcni Letopis SR Slovenije.*

**GW**/0721-2631
**STATISTICS & DECISIONS.** [Stat. decis.]. **VFOAT** Statistics and Decisions. Vol. 1, No. 1 (1982)-. Periodical. English. qt. DM296.00. R Oldenbourg Verlag, Postfach 801360, D 81613 Munich Germany. **Tel** 011 49 89 450190, FAX 011 49 89 45019305. **ED** E.J. Dudewicz, D. Plachky and P.K. Sen. [**CCC**] **Bk Rev**. **Ad Acc**. **Circ:** 250.
**Desc:** Theoretical and applied aspects of decision theoretically oriented mathematical statistics. Topics covered include classical and multiple statistical decision procedures and asymptotic and nonparametric statistical procedures.
**Ind/Abst** Curr. Index Stat.; Math. Rev.; Stat. Theory Method Abstr. (1983-1984, 1986-1987); Zentralbl. Math. Ihre Grenzgeb.

**GW**
**STATISTICS & DECISIONS. SUPPLEMENT ISSUE.** **VFOAT** Supplement Issues of Statistics & Decisions; Statistics and Decisions. Supplement Issue. (1984)-. English. Four times a year. DM298.80 Germany; DM303.80 other. R Oldenbourg Verlag, Postfach 801360, D 81613 Munich Germany. **Tel** 011 49 89 450190, FAX 011 49 89 45019305.

**TR**
**STATISTICS AT A GLANCE / REPUBLIC OF TRINIDAD AND TOBAGO, CENTRAL STATISTICAL OFFICE.** (1986)-. Statistical Publication. English. Central Statistical Office / Trinidad and Tobago, PO Box 98, 23 Park Street, Port of Spain Trinidad. **Tel** 62-54970, FAX 62-53802. **LC** HA867; .A388A. **DD** 317.298/3. *Continues Statistical Pocket Digest - Trinidad and Tobago, Central Statistical Office.*

**NZ**/0113-1133
**STATISTICS PUBLICATIONS CATALOGUE.** *Title Change.* [Stat. publ. cat.]. **Main/Corp** New Zealand. Dept. of Statistics. **VFOAT** Publications Catalogue. Oct. (1986)-(19??). English. an. Enquiries Section, Information Services Division, Department of Statistics, Wellington New Zealand. **Tel** 729-119. **LC** Z7554.N5; N48a; HA3173. **DD** 016.31931. *Continues Descriptive List of Publications as at 30 September ... / Department of Statistics, 0111-5855. Continued by New Zealand. Dept. of Statistics. Catalogue.*
**Desc:** A list of official publications that are issued by the Department of Statistics.

**CN**/0225-9907
**STATISTICS QUARTERLY - BUREAU OF STATISTICS (YELLOWKNIFE).** (STATISTICS QUARTERLY.). [Stat. q. - Bur. Stat.]. **Added/Corp** Northwest Territories. Bureau of Statistics. **VAT** Statistics Quarterly - Northwest Territories. (Dec. 1979)-. Periodical. English. Four times a year (Mar., June, Sept., Dec.). 40.00Can$. Bureau of Statistics / Yellow Knife, Government of Northwest Territories, Yellow Knife Northwest Territories, X1A 2L9 Canada. **Tel** (403)873-7653. **LC** HA747.N6; S82. **DD** 317.19/2/05. **Circ:** 900.
**Desc:** Provides statistical data on the Northwest Territories.

**US**/0585-198X
**STATISTICS SOURCES.** 1st Ed. (1962)-. English. ir. $360.00. Gale Research Inc., 835 Penobscot Building, Detroit MI 48226. **Tel** (800)877-GALE, (313)961-2242, FAX (313)961-6083, telex TWX 810-221-7086. **ED** Jacqueline Wasserman O'Brien and Steven R. Wasserman. **LC** Z7551; .S83; HA1. **DD** 016.31. **NLM** Z 7551; S798.
**Desc:** More than 20,000 highly specific topics with more than 95,000 citations and over 2,000 statistic sources, including national and international, print and non-print, published and non-published sources.

**US**/1040-0672
**STATISTICS, TEXTBOOKS AND MONOGRAPHS.** [Stat. textb. monogr.]. Vol. 1 (1972)-. Monographic series. English. Price varies per volume. Marcel Dekker Inc., 270 Madison Avenue, New York NY 10016. **Tel** (212)696-9000, (800)228-1160, FAX (212)685-4540, telex 421419. **(Subscription address:** Marcel Dekker Inc, PO Box 5017, Monticello NY 12701.**) DD** 519. **CODEN** STMOEV. Documents available from BIOSIS Document Express.
**Desc:** Each volume presents information of value to those involved with statistics. Topics include probability and econometrics, and more.
**Ind/Abst** Biol. Abstr. (1988-); Zentralbl. Math. Ihre Grenzgeb.

●**US**/1062-3507
**STATISTICS USERS NETWORK.** [Stat. users netw.]. **Added/Corp** New Vistas Information Services. Vol. 1, No. 1 (Feb. 1992)-. Periodical. English. Twelve times a year. $45.00. New Vistas Information Services, PO Box 6483, Bloomington IN 47407. **Tel** (812)331-0148. **DD** 310.

**AT**/1033-8640
**STATISTICS WEEKLY.** [Stat. w.]. **Added/Corp** Australian Bureau of Statistics. (1989)-. Periodical. English. wk. 4.20Aus$. Australian Bureau of Statistics, PO Box 10, Belconnen Australian Capital Territory, 2616 Australia. **Tel** 011 61 6 2527911, FAX 011 61 6 2516009. **DD** 319.94.
**Desc:** Presents statistical feature articles for each of the week's major releases, together with up-to-date reference tables containing figures for major national and State economic indicators.

**NE**/0921-0083
**STATISTIEK VAN HET BEROEPSONDERWIJS. BEROEPSBEGELEIDEND ONDERWIJS EN VORMINGSEREK, CURSORISCH ONDERNEMERSONDERWIJS / CBS, CENTRAAL BUREAU VOOR DE STATISTIEK, HOOFDAFDELING STATISTIEKEN VAN ONDERWIJS EN WETENSCHAPPEN.** **VFOAT** Beroepsbegeleidend Onderwijs en Vormingswerk, Cursorisch Ondernemersonderwijs. 1985/'86-. Dutch. an. Staatsuitgeverij, Christoffel Plantijnstraat 1, 2515 TZ'S Gravenhage Netherlands. **Tel** 070/78-95-70. *Formed by the union of Statistiek van het Beroepsonderwijs. Beroepsbegeleidend Onderwijs, Leerlingwezen and Statistiek van het Vormingswerk voor Jongeren Statistiek van het Participatieonderwijs.*

**SA**
**STATISTIEKE VAN PLAASLIKE OWERHEDE, ORANJE-VRYSTAAT, TRANSVAAL.** **Main/Corp** South Africa. Dept. of Statistics. **VFOAT** Local Government Statistics, Orange Free State, Transvaal. Multiple languages. 3.75. Department of Statistics / South Africa, The Government Printer, Bosman Street, Private Bag X85, Pretoria South Africa. **LC** HA2221; .D46A.

**IO**
**STATISTIK BIOSKOP & REKREASI.** **VFOAT** Statistik Bioskop dan Rekreasi. 1981-. Indonesian. an. Kantor Sensus dan Statistik Dki Jakarta, Jl Medan Merdeka Selatan 8-9, Lantai XX, Jakarta Indonesia. **LC** PN1993.5.I84; S73.

**GW**
**STATISTIK DES AUSLANDES. LANDERBERICHT. EG-STAATEN / HERAUSGEBER STATISTICHES BUNDESAMT.** **VFOAT** Landerbericht. Eg-Staaten; Landerbericht. Eg Staaten. German. DM7.70. W Kohlhammer Verlag, Postfach 800430, D 70549 Stuttgart Germany. **Tel** 011 49 711 78631, FAX 011 49 711 7863263, telex 7-255820. **LC** HA1107.5; .A27. **DD** 314.

**GW**
**STATISTIK DES AUSLANDES. LANDERBERICHT. KOLOMBIEN / HERAUSGEBER STATISTISCHES BUNDESAMT.** **VFOAT** Landerbericht. Kolumbien. German. DM7.70. W Kohlhammer Verlag GmbH, Postfach 800430, D 70549 Stuttgart Germany. **Tel** 011 49 711 78631, FAX 011 49 711 7863263, telex 7-255820. **LC** HA1015; .G45A. **DD** 318.61. *Continues Germany (West). Statistisches Bundesamt. Landerberichte: Kolumbien.*

**GW**
**STATISTIK DES AUSLANDES. LANDERBERICHT. OMAN / HERAUSGEBER STATISTISCHES BUNDESAMT.** **VFOAT** Landerbericht. Oman; Oman. German. DM7.70. W Kohlhammer Verlag GmbH, Postfach 800430, D 70549 Stuttgart Germany. **Tel** 011 49 711 78631, FAX 011 49 711 7863263, telex 7-255820. **LC** HA4565; .A27.

**GW**
**STATISTIK DES AUSLANDES. LANDERBERICHT. SAMBIA / HERAUSGEBER STATISTISCHES BUNDESAMT.** **VFOAT** Landerbericht. Sambia. German. DM9.70. W Kohlhammer Verlag GmbH, Postfach 800430, D 70549 Stuttgart Germany. **Tel** 011 49 711 78631, FAX 011 49 711 7863263, telex 7-255820.

**GW**
**STATISTIK DES AUSLANDES. LANDERBERICHT. ZYPERN / HERAUSGEBER STATISTISCHES BUNDESAMT.** **VFOAT** Landerbericht. Zypern; Zypern. German. DM7.70. W Kohlhammer Verlag GmbH, Postfach 800430, D 70549 Stuttgart Germany. **Tel** 011 49 711 78631, FAX 011 49 711 7863263, telex 7-255820. **LC** HA4557; .A27. **DD** 315.645.

**GW**
**STATISTIK DES AUSLANDES. LANDERKURZBERICHT. KARIBISCHE STAATEN / HERAUSGEBER STATISTISCHES BUNDESAMT.** **VFOAT** Landerkurzbericht. Karibische Staaten. German. DM5.10. W Kohlhammer Verlag GmbH, Postfach 800430, D 70549 Stuttgart Germany. **Tel** 011 49 711 78631, FAX 011 49 711 7863263, telex 7-255820. **LC** HA855.5; A27. **DD** 317.29.

**GW**
**STATISTIK DES AUSLANDES. LANDERKURZBERICHT. PAZIFISCHE STAATEN / HERAUSGEBER STATISTISCHES BUNDESAMT.** **Added/Corp** Germany (West). Statistisches Bundesamt. **VFOAT** Landerkurzbericht. Pazifische Staaten. (19??)-. German. DM5.40. W Kohlhammer Verlag GMBH, Postfach 800430, D70549 Stuttgart Germany. **Tel** 011 49 711 78631. **LC** HA4001; .S74. **DD** 319.

**IO**/0126-2912
**STATISTIK INDONESIA. STATISTICAL YEARBOOK OF INDONESIA.** **Added/Corp** Indonesia. Biro Pusat Statistik. **VFOAT** Statistical Yearbook of Indonesia. (1975)-. Statistical Publication. Multiple languages (English and Indonesian). an. $55.50. Central Bureau of Statistics / Indonesia, c/o Dr. Sutomo, 8 Jalan, PO Box 3, Jakarta Indonesia. **Tel** 372808 374908 Ext.342. **(Subscription address:** Yasmin, PO Box 510, KBY, Jakarta Selatan Indonesia.**) LC** HA1811; .B57c. **Ad Acc**. ctrl circ.

**AU**
**STATISTIK - KAMMER DE GEWERBLICHEN WIRTSCHAFT FUR WIEN.** *Title Change.* **Main/Corp** Kammer der Gewerblichen Wirtschaft fur Wien (Austria) Wien. (19??)-(19??). German. an. Stubenring 8-10, Vienna I Austria. **LC** HA1189.V6; V56A. *Continued by Statistik--Wirtschaftskammer Wien.*

**IO**
**STATISTIK KOTAMADYA PASURUAN.** 1980-. Indonesian. an. Kantor Statistik Kotamadya Pasuruan, Jl Panglima Sudirman No 84, Pasuruan Indonesia. **LC** HA4608.P37; P37A. *Continues Statistik Kotamadya Daerah Tingkat II Pasuruan.*

**DK**
**STATISTIK OVER LUFTFARTSAKTIVITETER / LUFTFARTSDIREKTORATET.** Danish. qt. Statens Luftfartsvsen Luftfartsdirektoratet, Gammel Kongevej 60, 1850 Kbenhavn V Denmark.

**SW**
**STATISTIK (SWEDEN. STATISTISKA CENTRALBYRAN).** (STATISTIK.). **VFOAT** Statistics ..., A Plan for the Publication of the Official Statistics of Sweden. 1981-. Swedish. an. SCB Statistiska Centralbyran, 11581 Stockholm Sweden.

**IO**
**STATISTIK WILAYAH DKI JAKARTA.** (1972)-. Indonesian. an. Biro Pusat Statistik, JLN Dr Sutomo 8 Kotak, Pos 1003, Jakarta 10710 Indonesia. **Tel** 3728007, 374908. **LC** HA1818.J34; J34B. **Circ:** 100. *Continues DCI Djakarta, Statistik Wilajah.*

**AU**
**STATISTIK--WIRTSCHAFTSKAMMER WIEN.** (19??)-. German. an. Stubenring 8-10, Vienna I Austria. *Continues Statistik--Kammer de Gewerblichen Wirtschaf fur Wien.*

**BU**
**STATISTIKA.** **Main/Corp** Bulgaria. Glavna Direktsiia Na Statistikata. (1???)-. Periodical. Bulgarian. bm. **(Subscription address:** Hemus Foreign Trade Organization, 6 Tzar Osvoboditel Boulevard, 1000 Sofia Bulgaria.**) LC** HA1621; .A42.
**Ind/Abst** Stat. Theory Method Abstr. (1983).

**XR**/0585-2013
**STATISTIKA.** **Added/Corp** Dansk Arbejdsgiverforening. (1964)-. Periodical. Czech (summaries and/or abstracts in English and Russian). mo. **(Subscription address:** Artia Pegas Press Ltd., Palac Metro Narodni Trida 25, 11210 Prague 1 Czech Republic.**) LC** HA1; .S77. *Continues in part Statistika a Kontrola, 0011-619X.*

**GR**/0072-7431
**STATISTIKE EPETERIS TES HELLADOS.** (STATISTIKE EEPETERIS TES HELLADOS / GENIKE STATISTIKE HYPERESIA TES HELLADOS). **Added/Corp** Ethnike Statistike Hyperesia tes Hellados. Genike Statistike Hyperesia (Greece). **VFOAT** Annuaire Statistique de la Greece; Statistical

Yearbook of Greece; Synoptike Statistike Epeteris Tes Hellados. (1930)-. English (French and Greek, Modern). an. Dr1,000 Greece; $20.00 US. National Statistical Service of Greece, 14 Lycourgou Street, GR 10166 Athens Greece. **Tel** 3244-746, telex 216-734 ESYE GR. **LC** HA1351; .S75. **DD** 314.95. **NLM** W2 GG6 G8S. **Circ:** 3,500.
**Desc:** Presents concise statistical data on population, employment, education, agriculture, industry, external trade, public finance, etc.

DK/0107-0851
**STATISTIKKEN. ARBEJDERLN.** **VFOAT** Arbejderln; Dansk Arbejdsgiverforenings Statistik. 1978-. Danish. qt. **LC** HD5049; .A53. ***Continues in part*** *Statistikken, 0011-619X.*

FR
**STATISTIQUE AGRICOLE : REGION PARISIENNE.** **See** Agriculture-Abstracting, Bibliographies and Statistics.

CN/0227-0668
**STATISTIQUE - BUREAU DE LA STATISTIQUE DU QUEBEC (1981).** (STATISTIQUES.). [Stat. - Bur. Stat. Que.]. **Added/Corp** Bureau de la Statistique du Quebec. Vol. 1, No. 1 (Mar. 1981)-. French. qt. 85.00Can$. Les Publications du Quebec, CP 1190, Outremont Quebec H2V 4S7 Canada. **Tel** (514)948-1222, (800)463-2100, FAX (514)278-3030. **LC** HA747; .Q33. **DD** 317.14. ***Continues*** *Revue Statistique du Quebec.*
**Ind/Abst** Foreign Lang. Index; Point Repere.

FR/0750-7364
**STATISTIQUE ET ANALYSE DES DONNEES.** [Stat. anal. donnees]. (1976)-. Periodical. French. Association des Statisticiens Universitaires, Grenoble France. **UDC** 31.
**Ind/Abst** Zentralbl. Math. Ihre Grenzgeb.

FR/0396-0099
**STATISTIQUES & ETUDES : MIDI-PYRENEES.** [Stat. etud. Midi-Pyren.]. June 1971-. Periodical. French. qt. 80.00F France. CNGP INSEE - Institut National de la Statistique et des Estudes Economiques, BP 2718, 1 rue V Auriol, F 80027 Amiens Cedex 1 France. **Tel** 011 33 22 927322. **LC** HA1228.A78. **Bk Rev. Circ:** 900. ***Supersedes*** *Bulletin de Statistique: Midi-Pyrenees (Ariege, Aveyron, Haute-Garonne, Gers, Lot, Hautes-Pyrenees, Tarn, Tarn-et-Garonne).*
**Desc:** Fundamental articles on economic and social life of the mid-Pyrenees region. Short articles on various current topics. A selection of information and documentary references.

PO
**STATISTIQUES DES SOCIETES.** **See** Business.

PO/0870-3205
**STATISTIQUES DES SOCIETES. ESTATISTICAS DAS SOCIEDADES.** ***Title Change.*** **Main/Corp** Instituto Nacional de Estatistica (Portugal). Servicos Centrais. **Added/Corp** Instituto Nacional de Estatistica (Portugal) Instituto Nacional de Estatistica (Portugal). Servicos Centrais. Estatisticas das Sociedades. **VFOAT** Estatisticas das Sociedades. (1970)-(19??). French (Portuguese). ir. Imprensa Nacional, Av Antonie Jose de al Eida, 1078 Lisbon Codex Portugal. **LC** HD2889; .A152a. **DD** 338.7/09469/01. ***Continues*** *Instituto Nacional de Estatistica (Portugal). Servicos Centrais. Estatisticas das Sociedades.* ***Continued by*** *Statistiques des Societes (Instituto Nacional de Estatistica (Portugal).*

NE
**STATISTISCH BULLETIN - CENTRAAL BUREAU VOOR DE STATISTIEK.** **Main/Corp** Netherlands. Centraal Bureau voor de Statistiek. (19??)-. Bulletin. Dutch. wk (51 issues per year). Fl115.00. Centraal Bureau voor de Statistiek, AFD ALG Zaken, Postbus 959, 2270 AZ Voorburg Netherlands. **Tel** 011 31 70 3373800, FAX 011 31 038 7429, telex 32692 CBS NL. **(Subscription address:** Central Bureau Statistiek, Postbus 4481, Kloosterweg 1, 6401 CZ Heerlen Netherlands.) **LC** HA1381; .A26.

BE
**STATISTISCH TYDSCHRIFT.** Multiple languages (French and Dutch). mo. 1695F. National Instituut voor Statistiek, Leuvenseweg 44, 1000 Brussels Belgium. **Tel** 02 513 46 50, FAX 01 5139510. available on diskette.

GW/0418-8322
**STATISTISCHE BEIHEFTE ZU DEN MONATSBERICHTEN DER DEUTSCHEN BUNDESBANK. REIHE 3 : ZAHLUNGSBILANZSTATISTIK.** ***Title Change.*** **Main/Corp** Deutsche Bundesbank. **Added/Corp** Deutsche Bundesbank. **VFOAT** Zahlungsbilanzstatistik. (1968)-(1992). Periodical. German (English; summaries and/or abstracts in English). mo. Deutsche Bundesbank Presse, Information Wilh Epsteinstrasse 14, D 60431 Frankfurt Germany. **Tel** 011 49 69 1583509 or 1583455, telex 41 227 OR 414 431. **LC** HG3883.G3; .D4. **DD** 382. ***Continued by*** *Zahlungsbilanzstatistik, 0943-8777.*

GW
**STATISTISCHE BERICHTE DES STATISTISCHEN AMTES DES SAARLANDES.** ***Title Change.*** **Main/Corp** Saarland (Germany). Statistisches Amt. (19??)-(19??). Monographic series. German. Hardenbergstrasse 3, Saarbrucken Germany. **LC** HA1320.S24; A25a. **Circ:** 400-500. ***Continued by*** *Statistische Berichte (Saarland (Germany). Statistisches Landesamt).*

GW/0175-7350
**STATISTISCHE MITTEILUNGEN.** German. Statistisches Landesamt Bremen 14/16, W-2800 Bremen 1 Germany. **LC** HA1271; .A326. ***Continues*** *Statistische Mitteilungen Freier Hansestadt Bremen.*

AU/0029-9960
**STATISTISCHE NACHRICHTEN - OSTERREICHISCHES STATISTISCHES ZENTRALAMT.** (STATISTISCHE NACHRICHTEN.). [Stat. Nachr. - Osterr. Stat. Zent.amt]. **Main/Corp** Osterreichisches Statistisches Zentralamt. **Added/Corp** Austria. Bundesamt Fur Statistik. (Apr. 1923)-. Periodical. German. Twelve times a year. $131.12. Verlag der Oesterreichischen, Staatsdruckerei Rennweg 12A, A-1037 Vienna Austria. **Tel** 011 43 1 797893766. **LC** HA1173; .A24. **Circ:** 2,000. ***Supersedes*** *Austria. Bundesamt Fur Statistik. Mitteilungen des Bundesamtes Fur Statistik.*
**Desc:** Most recent data including frequent commentaries on national accounts, currency, financing, banking, prices, wages, agriculture, industrial production, energy, construction, foreign and internal trade, transport, tourism and population.

GW
**STATISTISCHE NACHRICHTEN (SAARLAND, GERMANY).** (STATISTISCHE NACHRICHTEN.). **Added/Corp** Saarland (Germany). Statistisches Amt. (1981)-. German. qt. 10.00. Statistisches Amt des Saarlandes, Postfach 409 Hardenbergstr 3, W-6600 Saarbrucken Germany. **LC** HA1248.S23; S72. **DD** 314.3/42. **Circ:** 500.

GW/0431-6983
**STATISTISCHER WOCHENDIENST.** **Main/Corp** Germany (West). Statistisches Bundesamt. (Oct. 1950)-. German. Fifty-two times a year. DM135.00. Metzler Poeschel Verlag Veroeffen, Statist Bundesamt Kernerstr 43, D 70182 Stuttgart Germany. **Tel** 011 49 7071 935350. **(Subscription address:** Metzler Poeschel H Leins GmbH, Postfach 1152, D 72125 Kusterdingen Germany.) **LC** HA1231; .A36. **[CCC].**

AU
**STATISTISCHES HANDBUCH FUER DIE REPUBLIK OESTERREICH.** ***Title Change.*** **Main/Corp** Osterreichisches Statistisches Zentralamt. **Added/Corp** Austria. Bundesamt fuer Statistik. Austria. Statistische Zentralkommission. Vol. 1-17, (1920)-(1937);Vol. 1 (1950)-(19??). German. ir. Verlag der Osterreichischen, Staatsdruckerei Rennweg 12A, A 1037 Vienna Austria. **Tel** 011 43 1 797893766. **LC** HA1171; .C3. ***Continued by*** *Statistisches Jahrbuch fuer die Republik Oesterreich.*
**Desc:** This handbook documents the most current statistics available on an annual basis covering culture, economy and voting results. Also covered are vacation travel by the Austrian population, labor statistics, exports, tourism, etc.

GW
**STATISTISCHES JAHRBUCH BERLIN.** German. an. DM55.00 Germany; $32.00 US. Kulturbuch-Verlag, Passauer Strasse 4, W-1000 Berlin 30 Germany. **Tel** (030)2136071. **LC** HA1330; .B52. Index available. cum. index. **Bk Rev. Ad Acc. Circ:** 1,500 (ctrl). ***Continues*** *Statistisches Jahrbuch der Stadt Berlin.*
**Desc:** Statistical numbers of the growth in Berlin: economy, peoples, culture, law and security, etc.

SZ/0081-5330
**STATISTISCHES JAHRBUCH DER SCHWEIZ.** (STATISTISCHES JAHRBUCH DER SCHWEIZ / HERAUSGEGEBEN VOM STATISTISCHEN BUREAU DES EIDG. DEPARTEMENTS DES INNERN.). [Stat. Jahrb. Schweiz]. **Added/Corp** Switzerland. Eidgenossisches Statistisches Amt. Switzerland. Eidgenossisches Statistisches Bureau. Switzerland. Eidgenossisches Statistisches Amt. Switzerland. Bundesamt fuer Statistik. **VFOAT** Annuaire Statistique de la Suisse. Vol. 1 (1891)-. German (French). an (Dec.). 95.00F Switzerland; 106.80F Europe; 115.00F other. Buchverlag Neue Zuercher, Zeitung Postfach, CH 8021 Zurich Switzerland. **Tel** 011 41 1 2581505, FAX 011 41 1 2581399. **NLM** W2; GS9 S7S. cum. index.

GW/0081-5349
**STATISTISCHES JAHRBUCH DEUTSCHER GEMEINDEN.** Vol. 1 (1890)-. German. an. DM105.00. JP Bachem Verlag GmbH, Ursulaplatz 1, Bachemhaus, W5000 Cologne 1 Germany. **Tel** 011 49 221 1619122, FAX (0221)3771-128. **Circ:** 2,200.
**Desc:** Statistics of towns and cities.

●AU
**STATISTISCHES JAHRBUCH FUER DIE REPUBLIK OESTERREICH / HERAUS-GEGELEN VON OESTERREICHISCHEN STATISTISCHEN ZENTRALANT.** **Added/Corp** Oesterreichisches Statistisches Zentralamt. **VFOAT** Statisches Jahrbuch. Vol. 43 (1992)-. Statistical Publication. German (English). an. S785.00. Verlag der Osterreichischen, Staatsdruckerei Rennweg 12A, A 1037 Vienna Austria. **Tel** 011 43 1 797893766. **LC** HA1171; .C3. ***Continues*** *Statistisches Handbuch fuer die Republik Oesterreich (1950).*

GW/0468-656X
**STATISTISCHES JAHRBUCH NORDRHEIN-WESTFALEN.** Vol. 16- 1974-. German. an. DM39.00. Landesamt fuer Datenverarbeitung und Statistik Nordrhein-Westfalen, Postfach 101105, 40002 Duesseldorf Germany. **Tel** (0211)944901, FAX (0211)442006, telex 8586654 LDST D. **Circ:** 2,000. ***Continues*** *Statistisches Jahrbuch Nordrhein-Westfalen.*
**Desc:** Statistical returns.

AU
**STATISTISCHES MONATSHEFT / OESTERREICHISCHE NATIONALBANK.** **Added/Corp** Oesterreichische Nationalbank. (1990)-. German. mo. S1000.00. Oesterreichische Nationalbank, Otto Wagner Platz 3, A 1090 Vienna 9 Austria. **Tel** 011 43 4117209. **LC** HG3014; .A34. **Circ:** 2,650. ***Continues*** *Oesterreichische Nationalbank. Mitteilungen des Direktoriums der Oesterreichischen Nationalbank, 0029-9332.*

GW
**STATISTISCHES TASCHENBUCH.** **Main/Corp** Hamburg. Statistisches Landesamt. (1967)-. Periodical. German. an. DM12.00 (latest edition). Statistisches Landesamt Hamburg, Steckelhoern 12, D-20457 Hamburg Germany. **Tel** 011 49 40 36811721. ctrl circ.
**Desc:** Most important results from all areas of official statistics concerning population, education, culture, public health, commerce, harbor traffic and the finances of the city of Hamburg.

DK
**STATISTISK ARBOG.** **Main/Corp** Denmark. Danmarks Statistik. (1896)-. Danish (Danish and English). an. kr103.28. Danmarks Statistik, Sejrgade 11, DK-2100 Copenhagen Denmark. **Tel** 011 45 3 9173917, FAX 011 45 31 18 48 01, telex 1 62 36. **Bk Rev. Ad Acc. Circ:** 15,000 (ctrl).
**Desc:** Covers population, housing, agriculture, manufacturing, external trade, social security, elections, public finance and national accounts in Denmark, the Faeroe Islands and Greenland.

NO
**STATISTISK ARBOG FOR NORGE (MICROFICHE).** (STATISTICK ARBOK FOR NORGE.). **Main/Corp** Norway. Statistisk Sentralbyra. **VFOAT** Annuaire Statistique de la Norvege; Statistical Yearbook of Norway. (1879)-. Norwegian (French and English). an. Kr95.00. Central Bureau of Statistics / Norway, PO Box 8131 DEP, N-0033 Oslo 1 Norway. **Tel** 011 47 2 2864964, FAX 011 47 2 864973. cum. index. **Bk Rev. Circ:** 45,000.
**Desc:** Main statistical data on population, socioeconomic topics, labour, mining and manufacturing, trade, transport and communication, national accounts, finance, education, agriculture.

NO/0078-1932
**STATISTISK ARBOK.** (STATISTISK ARBOK / STATISTICAL YEARBOOK OF NORWAY.). **Main/Corp** Norway. Statistisk Sentralbyra. **Added/Corp** Norway. Statistisk Sentralbyra. **VFOAT** Statistical Yearbook of Norway; Statistical Yearbook. (1964)-. Statistical Publication. English (Norwegian). an (Fall). KR70.00 (latest edition). Scandinavian University Press, PO Box 2959 Toeyen, N 0608 Oslo 6 Norway. **Tel** 011 47 2 2575400, FAX 011 47 2 2575353, telex 71896 UROR N. **(Subscription address:** Scandinavian University Press, 200 Meacham Ave., Elmont NY 11003.) **NLM** W2 GN6 S6SA. **[CCC]. Circ:** 45,000. ***Continues*** *Statistisk Arbok for Norge.*
**Desc:** Contains main statistical data on environment, population, social economic topics, trade, production, transport and communication, national accounts, finance, education, agriculture and international table.

SW/0081-5381
**STATISTISK ARSBOK FOER SVERIGE.** **Added/Corp** Sweden. Statistiska Centralbyran. **VFOAT** Annuaire Statistique de la Suede; Statistical Abstract of Sweden. Vol. 1 (1914)-. Swedish (French and English). an. Fritzes Information Center, Regeringsgatan 12, S 106 47 Stockholm Sweden. **Tel** 011 46 8 6909090. **LC**

HA1523; .A46. **NLM** W2 GS8 S7SC. ***Supersedes*** *Sweden. Statistiska Centralbyran. Sveriges Officiella Statistik i Sammandrag.*

NO/0029-3636
**STATISTISK MANEDSHEFTE. Main/Corp** Norway. Statistisk Sentralbyra. **Added/Corp** Norway. Statistisk Sentralbyra. Meddelelser. Norway. Statistisk Sentralbyra. Statistiske Meddelelser. Norway. Statistisk Sentralbyra. Statistiske Meldinger. Vol. 1 (1882/83)-. Norwegian (English). mo. Kr415.00. Central Bureau of Statistics / Norway, PO Box 8131 DEP, N-0033 Oslo 1 Norway. **Tel** 011 47 2 2864964, FAX 011 47 2 864973. **LC** HA1503; .A5. cum. index. **Bk Rev. Circ:** 4,400. available on diskette.
**Desc:** Economic statistics (indexes finance trade).
**Ind/Abst** Predicasts F&S Index, U. S. Annu. Ed.

SW/0039-7261
**STATISTISK TIDSKRIFT. Main/Corp** Sweden. Statistiska Centralbyrían. **VFOAT** Statistical Review. (1860)-. Swedish (summaries and/or abstracts in English). ir. cum. index.
**Ind/Abst** Selec. Coop. Index Manage. Period.

SW
**STATISTISKA MEDDELANDEN. Main/Corp** Gothenburg, Sweden. Stadskontoret. **VFOAT** Statistical Review. Swedish. Fredsgatan 1, Fack 1510, 401 10 1 Goteborg Sweden. **LC** HA1539.G6; G67A. ***Continues*** *Meddelanden.*

DK/0108-5530
**STATISTISKE EFTERRETNINGER. BEFOLKNING OG VALG. VFOAT** Befolkning og Valg. Vol. 1 (1983)-. Monographic series. Danish. Price varies per volume. Danmarks Statistik, Sejrgade 11, DK-2100 Copenhagen Denmark. **Tel** 011 45 3 9173917, FAX 011 45 31 18 48 01, telex 1 62 36. **LC** HB3611; .S72. ***Continues in part*** *Danmarks Statistik. Statistiske Efterretninger.*
**Desc:** Statistics on population size, foreign nationals, births and deaths, internal and external migration, marriages and divorces, families, households, adoptions, legal abortions, population forecasts, housing conditions, national elections and local government elections.

DK/0108-5549
**STATISTISKE EFTERRETNINGER. BYGGE- OG ANLGSVIRKSOMHED. VFOAT** Bygee- og Anlgsvirksomhed. Vol. 1 (1983)-. Monographic series. Danish. Price varies per volume. Danmarks Statistik, Sejrgade 11, DK-2100 Copenhagen Denmark. **Tel** 011 45 3 9173917, FAX 011 45 31 18 48 01, telex 1 62 36. **LC** HD9715.D4; S72. ***Continues in part*** *Danmarks Statistik. Statistiske Efterretninger.*
**Desc:** Statistics on employment and labor costs, with building cost indexes, construction cost indexes for civil engineering projects, tendency surveys, accounts statistics and sales and assessments of real property.

DK/0108-5557
**STATISTISKE EFTERRETNINGER. FRERNE OG GRNLAND. VFOAT** Frerne og Grnland. Vol. 1 (1983)-. Monographic series. Danish. Price varies per volume. Danmarks Statistik, Sejrgade 11, DK-2100 Copenhagen Denmark. **Tel** 011 45 3 9173917, FAX 011 45 31 18 48 01, telex 1 62 36. **LC** HF3649.F3; S72. ***Continues in part*** *Danmarks Statistik. Statistiske Efterretninger.*
**Desc:** Statistics on population size and changes, external trade, prices and incomes for the Faroe Islands and Greenland.

DK/0108-5573
**STATISTISKE EFTERRETNINGER. GENEREL ERHVERVSSTATISTIK OG HANDEL. VFOAT** Generel Erhvervsstatistik og Handel. Vol. 1 (1983)-. Monographic series. Danish. Price varies per volume. Danmarks Statistik, Sejrgade 11, DK-2100 Copenhagen Denmark. **Tel** 011 45 3 9173917, FAX 011 45 31 18 48 01, telex 1 62 36. **LC** HF3641; .S72. ***Continues in part*** *Danmarks Statistik. Statistiske Efterretninger.*
**Desc:** Statistics on accounts, joint-stock companies and business units registered by VAT settlement, with register-based workplace statistics, sales by non-agricultural industries and an index of retail sales.

DK/0108-5506
**STATISTISKE EFTERRETNINGER. UDENRIGSHANDEL / DANMARKS STATISTIK. Added/Corp** Danmarks Statistik. **VFOAT** Udenrigshandel. Vol. 1 (1983)-. Monographic series. Danish. ir. Price varies per volume. Danmarks Statistik, Sejrgade 11, DK-2100 Copenhagen Denmark. **Tel** 011 45 3 9173917, FAX 011 45 31 18 48 01, telex 1 62 36. **LC** HF3641; .S73. ***Continues in part*** *Danmarks Statistik. Statistiske Efterretninger;* ***Formed by the union of*** *Danmarks Statistik. Manedsstatistik Over Udenrigshandelen.*
**Desc:** Statistics on imports and exports, with quantity indexes; the terms of trade; distributions by countries, commodity groups and modes of transport; and EAGGF subsidies.

HU/0018-781X
**STATISZTIKAI HAVI KOZLEMENYEK. Main/Corp** Hungary. Kozponti Statisztikai Hivatal. (19??)-. Periodical. Hungarian. Twelve times a year. $74.00. Statistical Publishing House, PO Box 99, H-1300 Budapest Hungary. **Tel** 803-311, telex 22-6699-SKU-H. **(Subscription address:** Kultura, PO Box 149, H-1389 Budapest 62 Hungary, phone: 011 36 1 359370**) ED** Gy Holka. **LC** HA1201; .A524. **DD** 314. **Ad Acc. Circ:** 1,800 (ctrl).
**Desc:** Reports the results of the monthly and quarterly data-collections. Gives information on Hungarian demographical population changes, employment, national economy, branches of money, social and cultural situation.

SA
**STATS.** (May 30, 1964)-. English. Twelve times a year. R182.40 South Africa; R180.00 APU countries; R200.00 other. George Warman Publications Pty, PO Box 704, Cape Town 8000 South Africa. **Tel** 011 27 21 245320, FAX 011 27 21 261332, telex 5-21849. **ED** R.E. Pretorius. cum. index.
**Desc:** Supplies updated economic trend indicators; also statistics from a wide range of sources on a variety of subjects.

US/1053-8607
**STATS (ALEXANDRIA, VA.).** (STATS.). [Stats]. **Added/Corp** American Statistical Association. No. 1 (Spring 1989)-. Periodical. English. sa (Apr. and Oct.). $20.00. American Statistical Association, 1429 Duke Street, Alexandria VA 22314. **Tel** (703)684-1221, (202)393-3253, FAX (703)684-2037 (orders). **LC** QA276.A1; S747. **DD** 519.5.
**Desc:** Contains feature stories, career information, student experiences and humor.

AU/0039-1093
**STEIRISCHE STATISTIKEN / AMT DER STEIERMAERKISCHEN LANDESREGIERUNG, PRAESIDIALABTEILUNG, REFERAT STATISTIK. Added/Corp** Styria (Austria). Abteilung fuer Wirtschaft und Statistik. Styria (Austria). Referat Statistik. (19??)-. Bulletin. German. qt. S120.00. Amt der Steiermarkischen Landesregierung, Praesidialabteilung, Referat Statistik, Burgring 4, A-8010 Graz, Austria. **ED** Ernst Burger. **LC** HA1188.S8; A27. **DD** 314.36/5. Index available. **Circ:** 500. available with charts.

PP/0377-5844
**SUMMARY OF STATISTICS. BUREAU OF STATISTICS, KONEDOBU.** (SUMMARY OF STATISTICS.). English. an. The Statistician, National Statistical Office, PO Wards Strip/Waigani, Port Moresby City, Papua New Guinea. **LC** HA4007.P3; A3. **DD** 319.5/3.

FI
**SUOMEN TILASTOLLINEN VUOSIKIRJA. VFOAT** Statistisk Arsbok for Finland; Statistical Yearbook for Finland. New Series, 49- (1953)-. English (Finnish and French). an. Fmk240.00 Europe; Fmk245.00 other. Central Statistical Office, PO Box 504, SF-00101 Helsinki Finland. **Tel** 358-0-17347, 1002111 TILASTO SF, FAX 358-0-17342279. **ED** Eila Laakso. **LC** HA1448; .F537C. **DD** 314.71. **NLM** W2 GF5 T5SA. **Circ:** 4,000. available in microform (by CIS). ***Continues*** *Suomen Tilastollinen Vuosikirja;* ***Absorbed*** *Statistisk Arsbok for Finland.*
**Desc:** Covers Finnish demography, agriculture, forestry, industry, construction, trade, banking, transport, communications, national accounts, prices, labor, education, social affairs and elections.

US/0503-4019
**SUPPLEMENT TO THE STATISTICAL YEARBOOK AND THE MONTHLY BULLETIN OF STATISTICS. *Ceased.*** **Main/Corp** United Nations. Statistical Office. 1967-?. Statistical Publication. English. ir. United Nations Publications, 2 United Nations Plaza, Room DC2 0853, Department 007C, New York NY 10017. **Tel** (212)963-8303, (800)253-9646. **LC** HA36; .U415. **DD** 310/.5. ***Supersedes*** *Monthly Bulletin of Statistics; Supplement, Definitions and Explanatory Notes / United Nations Statistical Office.*
**Desc:** Possibly the most complete statistical reference book in existence, it provides a wealth of statistical data for more than 270 countries and territories on economic and social subjects.

FR
**SURVEY STATISTICIAN. Added/Corp** International Association of Survey Statisticians. No. 1 (Feb. 1979)-. Periodical. English. ir. 130.00F Comes with International Association of Survey Statisticians Membership. Insee Aise, C/O Mrs. Ancelmi, 18 BLD Adolphie Pinard BUR 919, 75014 Paris France. **Tel** 011 33 1 41175300. **LC** HA1; .S93. **DD** 310/.6. ***Supersedes*** *Newsletter - International Association of Survey Statisticians.*

US/0737-545X
**SURVEYS, POLLS, CENSUSES, AND FORECASTS DIRECTORY. *Ceased.*** [Surv. polls censuses forecasts dir.]. **VFOAT** Surveys, Polls, Censuses & Forecasts Directory. Issue No. 1, Oct. (1983)-Ceased 1st Ed. (1983). Directory. English. Three times a year. Gale Research Inc., 835 Penobscot Building, Detroit MI 48226. **Tel** (800)877-GALE, (313)961-2242, FAX (313)961-6083, telex TWX 810-221-7086. **LC** Z7554.U5; S95; HA203. **DD** 016.0014/33/0973.
**Desc:** Provides access to a wide range of surveys, polls censuses, and forecasts that are available through public and private organizations.

FI/0784-8323
**SVT. JULKINEN TALOUS. VFOAT** Julkinen Talous; Offentlig Ekonomi; Public Economy; SVT. Vol. 1 (1988)-. Monographic series. Finnish (Swedish). ir. Price varies per volume. Central Statistical Office, PO Box 504, SF-00101 Helsinki Finland. **Tel** 358-0-17347, 1002111 TILASTO SF, FAX 358-0-17342279.

TZ
**TAARIFA YA TAKWIMU ROBO MWAKA. VFOAT** Quarterly Statistical Bulletin. English (Swahili). qt. **LC** HA2131; .B87A. ***Continues*** *Taarifa ya Tarakimu.*

TZ
**TAARIFA YA TARAKIMU. *Title Change.*** **Main/Corp** Tanzania. Bureau of Statistics. **VFOAT** Quarterly Statistical Bulletin. Multiple languages (Swahili and English). qt. Bureau of Statistics / Tanzania, PO Box 796, Dar es Salaam Tanzania. **LC** HA2131; .B87A. ***Continues*** *Monthly Statistical Bulletin.* ***Continued by*** *Taarifa ya Takwimu Robo Mwaka.*

NL
**TABLEAUX DE L'ECONOMIE CALEDONIENNE.** French. Three times a year. 1800CFPF Caledonia; 2500CFPF other. Institut Territorial de la Statistique et des Etudes Economiques, BP 823, Noumea Nouvelle-Caledonie. **Tel** (27 54 81. **LC** HA4015; .A35. cum. index. **Bk Rev. Circ:** 2,000.
**Desc:** The principal reference work of the ITSEE, with condensed information about government, demography, health, building, education, employment, agriculture, mining, overseas transactions, tourism, etc.

FR
**TABLEAUX DE L'ECONOMIE CHAMPENOISE / INSEE, OBSERVATOIRE ECONOMIQUE DE CHAMPAGNE-ARDENNE. VFOAT** T.E.C.; TEC. French. 32. Direction Regionale de Reims, 1 rue de l'Arbalete, 51079 Reims Ce France. **Tel** 26882412. **LC** HA1228.C5; T32. **DD** 314.4/3. **Circ:** 1,000.
**Desc:** Our main subjects are local studies about population, industry, education, housing and urban development in Champagne Ardenne.

CH
**TAIWAN STATISTICAL DATA BOOK. Added/Corp** China. Hsing Cheng Yuan. Mei Yuan Yun Yung Wei Yuan Hui. Economic Research Center. China. Kuo Chi Ching Chi Ho Tso Fa Chan Wei Yuan Hui. Hsing Cheng Yuan Ching Chi Chien She Wei Yuan Hui (China). (19??)-. Statistical Publication. English (Chinese). an. $11.00 Taiwan; $14.90 other. Council for Economic Planning and Development, Nanjing E Road Sec 2 9th Floor 87, Taipei 10408 Taiwan. **Tel** 02 522 5403. **LC** HA1710.5; .T35. **DD** 315.1/249. **Ad Acc. Circ:** 1,000 (ctrl).
**Desc:** Statistics for area; population, national income, agriculture, industry, transportation, communication, banking, prices, external trade, etc.

US/0082-9544
**TECHNICAL PAPER - U.S. DEPARTMENT OF COMMERCE, SOCIAL AND ECONOMICS STATISTICS ADMINISTRATION, BUREAU OF THE CENSUS.** (TECHNICAL PAPER (UNITED STATES. BUREAU OF THE CENSUS).). **Added/Corp** United States. Bureau of the Census. **VAT** Technical Paper - United States Department of Commerce, Social and Economics Statistics Administration, Bureau of the Census. No. 1 (1953)-. Government Publication. English. Price varies per volume. US Department of Commerce, 14th Street & Constitution Avenue NW, Washington DC 20230. **Tel** (202)482-2000, FAX (202)482-3772.

CN/0823-1664
**TECHNICAL REPORT SERIES OF THE LABORATORY FOR RESEARCH IN STATISTICS AND PROBABILITY.** **See** Mathematics.

FR/0754-1627
**TENDANCES DE LA CONJONCTURE. CAHIER 1, GRAPHIQUES SUR 10 ANS.** [Tendances de la conjonct., Cah. 1, Graph. 10 ans]. **VFOAT** Graphiques sur 10 Ans; Graphiques sur Dix Ans. No. 1 (June 1981)-. Periodical. French. qt. PGM, 5 rue

des Morillons, 75015 Paris France. **Tel** 011 33 1 45300319. **LC** HC271; .T46. ***Continues in part*** *Tendances de la Conjoncture, 0497-2007.*

FR/0754-1619
**TENDANCES DE LA CONJONCTURE. CAHIER 2, GRAPHIQUES SUR 20 ANS.** [Tendances conjonct., Cah. 2, Graph. 20 ans]. **Added/Corp** Institut National de la Statistique et des Etudes Economiques (France). **VFOAT** Graphiques sur 20 Ans; Graphiques sur Vingt Ans. No. 1 (Jan. 8, 1982)-. Periodical. French. Twelve times a year. 146.91F France; 260.00F others. Excelsior Publications, 1 rue du Colonel Pierre Avia, 75503 Paris Cedex 15 France. **Tel** 011 33 1 46484848, FAX 011 33 1 46484793. **LC** HC271; .T47. ***Continues in part*** *Tendances de la Conjoncture, 0497-2007.*

US/1065-5700
**TENNESSEE IN PERSPECTIVE.** (TENNESSEE IN PERSPECTIVE : A STATISTICAL VIEW OF THE "VOLUNTEER STATE".). [Tenn. perspect.]. **Added/Corp** Morgan Quitno Corporation. (1990)-. Statistical Publication. English. $18.00. Morgan Quitno Corporation, PO Box 1656, 512 East 9th Street, Lawrence KS 66044. **Tel** (800)457-0742, (913)841-3534, FAX (913)841-3534. **DD** 317. ***Continues*** *Tennessee in Perspective.*
**Desc:** Reports on the state's data and rank for each of the categories featured in State Rankings.

US/0082-2760
**TENNESSEE STATISTICAL ABSTRACT.** **Added/Corp** University of Tennessee, Knoxville. Center for Business and Economic Research. (1969)-. Statistical Publication. English. an. $36.00. University of Tennessee Center for Business and Economic Research, Suite 100 Glocker Building, Knoxville TN 37996. **Tel** (615)974-5441. **ED** Betty B. Vickers. **LC** HA641; .T43. **DD** 317.68. Index available. **Circ:** 1,200 (ctrl).
**Desc:** A compendium of economic and demographic data on Tennessee, its six metropolitan statistical areas, counties, and cities.
**Ind/Abst** Stat. Ref. Index.

●SP/1133-0686
**TEST (MADRID).** (1992)-. Spanish. ir (2-3 issues). 8200ptas Latin America; 13000ptas other. Sociedad de Estadistica e Investigacion Operativa, Hortaleza 104-2 IZDA, 28004 Madrid Spain. **Tel** 011 34 1 3082474. ***Continues in part*** *Trabajos de Estadistica (Madrid. 1986), 0213-8190.*

US/1065-5719
**TEXAS IN PERSPECTIVE.** (TEXAS IN PERSPECTIVE : A STATISTICAL VIEW OF THE "LONE STAR STATE" / KATHLEEN O'LEARY MORGAN, SCOTT MORGAN AND NEAL QUITNO, EDITORS.). [Tex. perspect.]. **Added/Corp** Morgan Quitno Corporation. (1990)-. Statistical Publication. English. $18.00. Morgan Quitno Corporation, PO Box 1656, 512 East 9th Street, Lawrence KS 66044. **Tel** (800)457-0742, (913)841-3534, FAX (913)841-3534. **DD** 317. ***Continues*** *Texas in Perspective, 1065-5719.*
**Desc:** Reports on the state's data and rank for each of the categories featured in State Rankings.

FI/0015-2390
**TILASTOKATSAUKSIA.** **Main/Corp** Finland. Tilastokeskus. **VFOAT** Statistiska Oversikter; Bulletin of Statistics. 46, No. 3-. English (Finnish, Swedish and English). qt. Fmk192.00 Europe; Fmk200.00 other. Statistikcentralen, PB 504, SF-00101 Helsinki 10 Finland. **Tel** 358017341. **LC** HA1450.5; .A34A. **DD** 314.897. **Circ:** 2,000. ***Continues*** *Tilastokatsauksia.*
**Desc:** Statistical data in population, production, commerce, banking, transport, communication, national accounts, prices, wages, labour, state finances, etc., seasonally adjusted series included.

FI/0358-6243
**TILASTOTIEDOTUS. VL.** **VFOAT** VL; Statistisk Rapport. VL. **VAT** Tilastotiedotus. Vaesto- Ja Asuntolaskenta. Monographic series. Finnish (Swedish). ir. Price varies per volume. Central Statistical Office, PO Box 504, SF-00101 Helsinki Finland. **Tel** 358-0-17347, 1002111 TILASTO SF, FAX 358-0-17342279. **LC** HB3608.3.A3; T56.

FI
**TILK : NELJANNESVUOSIKATSAUS.** **Main/Corp** Helsinki (Finland). Telastokeskus. **VFOAT** Tilk: Kvartalsoversikt; Tilk: Quarterly Review. 1979-. Finnish (Swedish; summaries and/or abstracts in English). qt. Fmk90.00 Finland. Helsingin Kaupunki, Tilstokeskus, Toolontorinkatu 2 B, 00260 Helsinki 26 Finland. **ED** Iero Holstila. **LC** HA1450.5.Z9; H444A. **Circ:** 900. ***Continues*** *Tilastollisia Kuukausitietoja Helsingista.*

JA
**TOKEI CHOSA SORAN.** Japanese. an. ¥5300. Statistical Standards Department, Statistics Bureau, Management and Coordination Agency, 19-1 Wakamatsu-cho Shinjuku-ku, Tokyo 162 Japan. **LC** Z7554.J3; T63; HA1844. Index available. **Circ:** 2,500 (ctrl).

JA
**TOKYO-TO TOKEI CHOSA ICHIRAN.** **Main/Corp** Tokyo. Somukyoku. Tokeibu. Japanese. Tokyo-To Somukyoku, 5-1 Marunouchi 3, Chiyoda-ku, Tokyo Japan. **LC** Z7554.J3; T67A; HA1849.T6.

YU
**TROMESECNI PREGLED MEUNARODNE STATISTIKE.** **Main/Corp** Savezni Zavod za Statistiku (Yugoslavia). Vol. 6-Jan./March 1973-. Serbo-Croatian (Roman). 120.00 Din. Savezni Zavod za Statistiku, Kneza Milosa 20, Belgrad Yugoslavia. **LC** HA173.Y8; A26. ***Continues*** *Mesecni Pregled Meunarodne Statistike.*

TU
**TURKIYE ISTATISTIK YLL. STATISTICAL YEARBOOK OF TURKEY.** **Added/Corp** Devlet Istatistik Enstitusu (Turkey). **VFOAT** Statistical Yearbook of Turkey; Annuaire Statistique de la Turquie. (19??)-. Statistical Publication. Multiple languages (English and Turkish). an. Free on request. Turkish State Institute of Statistics, Necatibey Cadessi 114, Ankara 016100 Turkey. **Tel** 1188719, FAX 125 33 87, telex 46347 DIETR. **LC** HA1911; .A3 subser. **NLM** W2 GT8 I8T. **Bk Rev. Circ:** 7,500. ***Continues*** *Devlet Istatistik Enstitusu (Turkey). Annuaire Statistique.*

FI
**TYOMARKKINATIETOJA.** **Added/Corp** Finland. Ammatinvalinnanohjaustoimisto. (19??)-. Finnish. Central Statistical Office, PO Box 504, SF-00101 Helsinki Finland. **Tel** 358-0-17347, 1002111 TILASTO SF, FAX 358-0-17342279. **LC** L456; .A25 subser; HF5382.5.F5.

US
**U.S. EXPORT AND IMPORT PRICE INDEXES.** **Main/Corp** United States. Bureau of Labor Statistics. **VAT** United States Export and Import Price Indexes. (19??)-. Government Publication. English. Four times a year. Free. US Department of Labor / Bureau of Labor Statistics, 441 G Street NW, Washington DC 20212. **Tel** (202)606-7800, FAX (202)606-7797. **(Subscription address:** Superintendent of Documents, US Government Printing Office, Washington DC 20402.**)**

US/8755-7398
**U.S. REGIONAL.** [U. S. Reg.]. **VFOAT** US Regional. **VAT** United States Regional. English. DRI McGraw Hill, 24 Hartwell Avenue, Lexington MA 02173. **Tel** (617)863-5100. **LC** HA37; .U184. **DD** 016.3173.

US/0888-7926
**U.S. STATISTICS.** [U.S. stat.]. **Added/Corp** Federal Statistics Users Group (U.S.). **VAT** United States Statistics. (1985)-. Statistical Publication. English. mo. $95.00 US; $110.00 Canada. US Statistics Inc, PO Box 816, Alexandria VA 22313. **Tel** (703)979-9699, FAX (703)548-4585. **ED** Cynthia L. Rosacker. **DD** 317. **Circ:** 1,000.
**Desc:** Purpose is to help organizations with access to and use of Federal and related statistics.

RU/0503-0021
**UCHENYE ZAPISKI PO STATISTIKE.** [Uc. zap. stat.]. **Added/Corp** Tsentralnyi Ekonomiko-Matematicheskii Institut (Akademiia Nauk SSSR). Akademiia Nauk SSSR. Otdelenie Ekonomicheskikh, Filosofskikh i Pravovykh Nauk. Vol. 1 (1955)-. Academic Scholarly Publication. Russian. Izdatelstvo Nauka / Akademiia Nauk, Publishing House of the Russian Academy of Sciences, Leninskii Porspekt 14, 117901 Moscow Russia. **Tel** 011 95 954-21-53, FAX 011 95 938-21-44, telex 411964. **LC** HA1.A38; A15.
**Ind/Abst** Math. Rev.

FI
**ULKOMAISET TILASTOKAUSIJULKAISUT.** **Main/Corp** Tilastokirjasto (Finland). **VFOAT** Utlandska Statistiska Periodica. Finnish (Swedish). Tilastokeskus, PL 504, Annankatu 44, 00101 Helsinki Finland. **Tel** 358-0-17341, FAX 358-0-17342474, telex 1002111 TILASTO SF. **LC** Z7552; .T55A; HA154.

UK
**UNITED KINGDOM BALANCE OF PAYMENTS.** **Main/Corp** Great Britain. Central Statistical Office. **Added/Corp** Great Britain. Treasury. Great Britain. Central Statistical Office. (1947)-. English. an (Aug.). £13.25. Her Majesty's Stationery Office, 51 Nine Elms Lane, London SW8 5DR England. **Tel** 011 44 71 873 8459, 011 44 71 873 8499, FAX 011 44 71 873 8499, 011 44 71 873 8456, telex 297138. **(Subscription address:** Her Majesty's Stationery Office, PO Box 276, Publications Centre, London SW8 5DT England.**)** **LC** HF3501; .A235. **DD** 382/.17/094105. ***Continues*** *United Kingdom Balance of Payments.*

IE
**UNIVERSITY STATISTICS (DUBLIN, IRELAND).** (UNIVERSITY STATISTICS.). English. Government Publications, 4 5 Harcourt Road, Dublin 2 Ireland. **Tel** 011 353 1 6613111 Ext.4005. **LC** WMLC L 83/6639.

US/1185-2488
**USA FACTS.** [USA facts]. **VFOAT** United States of America Facts. (1991)-. English. $9.95 per volume. **LC** HA203; .U82. **DD** 330.973/0927.

US
**USA STATE FACTBOOK. CD-ROM.** English. an. $54.95. Quanta Press, Inc., 1313 Fifth Street Southeast, Suite 208C, Minneapolis MN 55414. **Tel** (612)379-3956, FAX (612)623-4570.
**Desc:** Guide to the U.S. states, territories, and protectorates. Major areas include geography, vital statistics, state governments, economics, communications, and other state specific information. Available in DOS and MAC formats.

US/0148-7760
**USSR FACTS & FIGURES ANNUAL.** **VFOAT** U.S.S.R. Facts and Figures Annual. **VAT** Union of Soviet Socialist Republics Facts and Figures Annual. Vol. 1 (1977)-. English. an. $71.00 (standing orders), $91.50 (separate volumes). Academic International Press, Box 1111, Gulf Breeze FL 32561. **ED** Alan P. Pollard. **LC** HA1446; .U17. **DD** 314.7. **NLM** DK 1 U11. **Bk Rev.** ctrl circ.
**Desc:** Based on a vast array of official, private and international sources, and on specialist literature in many fields. Organized into 29 main categories: government, republics, demography, agriculture, foreign trade, energy, etc.

US/1065-5727
**UTAH IN PERSPECTIVE.** (UTAH IN PERSPECTIVE : A STATISTICAL VIEW OF THE "BEEHIVE STATE".). [Utah perspect.]. **Added/Corp** Morgan Quitno Corporation. (1990)-. Statistical Publication. English. $18.00. Morgan Quitno Corporation, PO Box 1656, 512 East 9th Street, Lawrence KS 66044. **Tel** (800)457-0742, (913)841-3534, FAX (913)841-3534. **DD** 317. ***Continues*** *Utah in Perspective, 1065-5727.*
**Desc:** Reports on the state's data and rank for each of the categories featured in State Rankings.

US
**UTAH'S VITAL STATISTICS, BIRTHS ... .** **Added/Corp** Utah. Center for Health Information. (1986)-. English. an. Utah Department of Health, Center for Health Information, PO Box 16700, Salt Lake City UT 84116-0700. ***Continues in part*** *Utah Vital Statistics, Annual Report (Salt Lake City, Utah : 1977), 0736-4601.*

DK/0109-8314
**VEJVISER I STATISTIKKEN.** Danish. kr53.28. Danmarks Statistik, Sejrgade 11, DK-2100 Copenhagen Denmark. **Tel** 011 45 3 9173917, FAX 011 45 31 18 48 01, telex 1 62 36. **LC** Z7554.D3; V43; HA1471. **Bk Rev. Ad Acc. Circ:** 3,500 (ctrl). ***Continues*** *Vejviser I Danmarks Statistiske Publikationer, 0107-1009.*
**Desc:** Description of contents and collection methods in the various fields of statistics such as surveys, censuses, analyses, compilations, etc.

GW
**VERARBEOTEMDES GEWERBE.** **Added/Corp** Statistisches Landesamt Baden-Wurttemberg. (19??)-. German. Statistisches Landesamt Baden-Wuerttemberg, Postfach 10 60 33, 70049 Stuttgart Germany. **Tel** 011 49 771 6410, FAX 011 49 711 6412440. **LC** HA1320.B2; A32 subser.; HC287.B23. **DD** 314.3/46; 338.0943/46.

US/0092-5144
**VERMONT FACTS AND FIGURES.** **Main/Corp** Vermont. Office of Statistical Coordination. 1st ed. (1972)-. English. **LC** HA671; .O33a. **DD** 317.43.

US/1065-5735
**VERMONT IN PERSPECTIVE.** (VERMONT IN PERSPECTIVE : A STATISTICAL VIEW OF THE "GREEN MOUNTAIN STATE".). [Vt. perspect.]. **Added/Corp** Morgan Quitno Corporation. (1990)-. Statistical Publication. English. $18.00. Morgan Quitno Corporation, PO Box 1656, 512 East 9th Street, Lawrence KS 66044. **Tel** (800)457-0742, (913)841-3534, FAX (913)841-3534. **DD** 317. ***Continues*** *Vermont in Perspective, 1065-5735.*
**Desc:** Reports on the state's data and rank for each of the categories featured in State Rankings.

GW
**VEROEFFENTLICHUNGEN DES STATISTISCHEN LANDESAMTES BADEN-WUERTTEMBERG.** **Main/Corp** Statistisches Landesamt Baden-Wuerttemberg. (19??)-. Statistical Publication. German. Statistisches Landesamt Baden-Wuerttemberg, Postfach 10 60 33, 70049 Stuttgart Germany. **Tel** 011 49 771 6410, FAX 011 49 711 6412440. **LC** Z7554.G3; B2a; HA1320.B2. **DD** 016.3143/46/021. ***Continues*** *Statistisches Landesamt Baden-Wuerttemberg. Veroeffentlichungsverzeichnis.*

GW
**VEROFFENTLICHUNGEN DES HESSISCHEN STATISTISCHEN LANDESAMTES.** **Main/Corp** Hesse. Statistisches Landesamt. (19??)-. Catalog. German. be. Free. Hessisches Statistisches Landesamt, Rheinstrasse 35/37, D 65175 Wiesbaden Germany. **Tel** 0644 3802 0,

FAX 0644 3802 990. **LC** HA1320.H6; A25b. **DD** 314.3/41.
**Desc:** List of publications of the Hesse Statistical Department.

GW
**VEROFFENTLICHUNGEN DES LANDESAMTES FUER DATENVERARBEITUNG UND STATISTIK NORDRHEIN-WESTFALEN.** **Main/Corp** Landesamt fEur Datenverarbeitung und Statistik Nordrhein-Westfalen. (19??)-. German. be. Free. Landesamt fuer Datenverarbeitung und Statistik Nordrhein-Westfalen, Postfach 101105, 40002 Duesseldorf Germany. **Tel** (0211)944901, FAX (0211)442006, telex 8586654 LDST D. **LC** Z7165.G3; N67a; HA1320.N6. **DD** 016.3143/55. **Circ:** 2,000.

RU/0042-4692
**VESTNIK STATISTIKI.** **Added/Corp** Russia (1917- R.S.F.S.R.) T Sentralnoe Statisticheskoe Upravlenie. Russia (1923- U.S.S.R.) T Sentralnoe Statisticheskoe Upravlenie. (1919)-. Periodical. Russian. mo. $139.95. **(Subscription address:** East View Publications Inc., 3020 Harbor Lane North, Suite 110, Minneapolis MN 55447.**)** **LC** HA1431; .V4. cum. index. available on microfilm from University Microfilms International (UMI).
**Ind/Abst** Popul. Index (?-?); Curr. Dig. Post Sov. Press.

RU/0320-8168
**VESTNIK STATISTIKI : ORGAN TSSU SSSR.** [Vestn. statistiki]. **Added/Corp** Soviet Union. Sentralnoe Statisticheskoe Upravlenie. (Jan./Feb. 1949)-. Periodical. Russian. mo. $139.95 (No America); $149.95 (So America & Europe); $159.95 (other). **(Subscription address:** Victor Kamkin, 4956 Boiling Brook Parkway, Rockville MD 20852.**)** **LC** HA1431. cum. index. ***Continues in part*** *Planovoe Khoziaistvo, 0370-0356.*
**Ind/Abst** Popul. Index.

US/0360-3830
**VIRGINIA AGRICULTURAL STATISTICS.** **See** Agriculture-Abstracting, Bibliographies and Statistics.

US/1065-5743
**VIRGINIA IN PERSPECTIVE.** (VIRGINIA IN PERSPECTIVE : A STATISTICAL VIEW OF THE "OLD DOMINION STATE".). [Va. perspect.]. **Added/Corp** Morgan Quitno Corporation. Williams' Market Analysis. (19??)-. Statistical Publication. English. $18.00. Morgan Quitno Corporation, PO Box 1656, 512 East 9th Street, Lawrence KS 66044. **Tel** (800)457-0742, (913)841-3534, FAX (913)841-3534. **LC** HA681; .V55. **DD** 317.
**Desc:** Reports on the state's data and rank for each of the categories featured in State Rankings.

US/0083-2073
**VITAL AND HEALTH STATISTICS. SERIES 4, DOCUMENTS AND COMMITTEE REPORTS.** [Vital health stat., Ser. 4, Doc. comm. rep.]. **Added/Corp** National Center for Health Statistics (U.S.). **VFOAT** Vital & Health Statistics. Series 4, Documents and Committee Reports; Documents and Committee Reports. No. 1 (1965)-. English. ir. Free on request for libraries. US Department of Health and Human Services, 200 Independence Avenue Southwest, Washington DC 20201. **LC** HA37; .U1693. **DD** 312/.0973. **NLM** W2 A N148VD.
**Ind/Abst** Energy Res. Abstr. (Aug. 1982-); Index Med. (19??-).

US/0737-1896
**VITAL STATISTICS (CONCORD, N.H.).** (VITAL STATISTICS / NEW HAMPSHIRE.). 1980-. English. an. Bureau of Vital Resources and Health Statistics, Division of Public Health Services, Health and Welfare Building, Haxen Drive, Concord NH 03301. **LC** HA5111; .N48. **DD** 312/.09742. **NLM** W2 AN3 S4P. ***Continues*** *Vital Statistics Report for the State of New Hampshire, 0270-3378.*

US/0164-0151
**VITAL STATISTICS (EUGENE).** (VITAL STATISTICS.). (1978)-. Periodical. English. qt. $12.00. Wolf Run Books, PO Box 10671, Eugene OR 97440. **Tel** (503)343-9391.

US/0097-9449
**VITAL STATISTICS OF NEW YORK STATE.** [Vital stat. N.Y. State]. **Added/Corp** New York (State). Dept. of Health. New York (State). Bureau of Health Statistics. **VFOAT** Vital statistics for New York State. (1970)-. English. an. Free on request. New York Vital Statistics Review, New York State Department of Health, Empire State Plaza, Albany NY 12237. **LC** HA541; .V57a. **DD** 304.6/09747/021. **NLM** W2 AN6 D3S. ***Continues*** *Vital Statistics for New York State, 0098-0374.*
**Desc:** Publishes information concerning births, deaths, fetal deaths, marriages and dissolutions of marriages in the state of New York.

US/0083-6710
**VITAL STATISTICS OF THE UNITED STATES.** [Vital stat. U.S.]. **Added/Corp** National Center for Health Statistics (U.S.). Division of Vital Statistics. United States. National Vital Statistics Division. United States. National Office of Vital Statistics. United States. Bureau of the Census. Vital Statistics Division. (1937)-. English. ir. Superintendent of Documents, US Government Printing Office, Washington DC 20402. **Tel** (202)275-3328, FAX (202)786-2377. **LC** HA203; .A22. **DD** 312/.0973. **NLM** W2; A N25VI. ***Continues in part*** *Birth, Stillbirth, and Infant Mortality Statistics for the Continental United States, the Territory of Hawaii, the Virgin Islands; United States. Bureau of the Census. Mortality Statistics ... Annual Report, 1057-4328.*

PH/0116-2675
**VITAL STATISTICS REPORT.** **Main/Corp** Philippines. National Statistics Office. (1984)-. English. an. $30.00 Phillipines; $40.50 US. National Statistics Office of Manila, PO Box 779, Manila Philippines. **Tel** 011 63 613645. **Circ:** 200 (ctrl). ***Continues*** *Vital Statistics Report.*
**Desc:** Publication presents vital data related to births, death's, and marriages that occurred and were registered in the Philippines during the reference year.

FR/0395-9473
**VUES SUR L'ECONOMIE D'AQUITAINE.** [Vues econ. Aquitaine]. **Added/Corp** Institut National de la Statistique et des Etudes Economiques (France). (May 1971)-. Periodical. French. bm. 70.00F. CNGP INSEE - Institut National de la Statistique et des Etudes Economiques, BP 2718, 1 rue V Auriol, F 80027 Amiens Cedex 1 France. **Tel** 011 33 22 927322. **LC** HA1228.A75; A332. ***Supersedes*** *Bulletin de Statistique: Aquitaine (Dordogne, Gironde, Landes, Lot-et-Garonne, Pyrnees-Atlantiques), 0150-8369.*
**Desc:** Publishes socio-economic information on the Bordeaux region of France in an accessible format with concise analysis of statistics.

NE
**VVS BULLETIN.** Bulletin. Dutch (English). Ten times a year. Fl114.00. Verenging Voor Statistiek en Operations Research, Postbus 282, 1850 AG Heiloo Netherlands. **Tel** 3115 781635. **ED** S de Lange and B C van Zomeren (editor's address: FWI, Mekelweg 4, 2628 CD Delft Netherlands). **Bk Rev**. **Ad Acc**. **Circ:** 1,500 (ctrl).
**Desc:** Informal newsletter of the society.

US/0095-4330
**WASHINGTON AGRICULTURAL STATISTICS.** **See** Agriculture-Abstracting, Bibliographies and Statistics.

US/1065-5751
**WASHINGTON IN PERSPECTIVE.** (WASHINGTON IN PERSPECTIVE : A STATISTICAL VIEW OF THE "EVERGREEN STATE".). [Wash. perspect.]. **Added/Corp** Morgan Quitno Corporation. (1990)-. Statistical Publication. English. $18.00. Morgan Quitno Corporation, PO Box 1656, 512 East 9th Street, Lawrence KS 66044. **Tel** (800)457-0742, (913)841-3534, FAX (913)841-3534. **DD** 317. ***Continues*** *Washington in Perspective, 1065-5751.*
**Desc:** Reports on the state's data and rank for each of the categories featured in State Rankings.

US/1065-576X
**WEST VIRGINIA IN PERSPECTIVE.** (WEST VIRGINIA IN PERSPECTIVE : A STATISTICAL VIEW OF THE "MOUNTAIN STATE".). [W.Va. perspect.]. **Added/Corp** Morgan Quitno Corporation. (1990)-. Statistical Publication. English. $18.00. Morgan Quitno Corporation, PO Box 1656, 512 East 9th Street, Lawrence KS 66044. **Tel** (800)457-0742, (913)841-3534, FAX (913)841-3534. **DD** 317. ***Continues*** *West Virginia in Perspective, 1065-576X.*
**Desc:** Reports on the state's data and rank for each of the categories featured in State Rankings.

PL
**WIADOMOSCI STATYSTYCZNE (WARSAW, POLAND : 1956).** (WIADOMOSCI STATYSTYCZNE.). Vol. 1, No. 1, (July/Aug. 1956)-. Periodical. Polish. mo. $51.00. Zaklad Wydawnictw Statystycznych, Al Niepodleglosci 208, 00-925 Warszawa Poland. **Tel** 253241, telex 814581A GUS. **Ad Acc**. **Circ:** 1,700 (ctrl). ***Continues*** *Wiadomosci Statystyczne (Warsaw, Poland : 1923).*
**Desc:** Covers statistical novelties and theoretical problems.
**Ind/Abst** Popul. Index.

GW/0043-6143
**WIRTSCHAFT UND STATISTIK.** [Wirtsch. stat.]. **Added/Corp** Germany. Statistisches Reichsamt. Germany (West). Statistisches Bundesamt. Germany (Territory Under Allied Occupation, 1945-1955. Vereinigtes Wirtschaftsgebiet). Statistisches Amt. Vol. 1-27, 1921-1944 (April 1949)-. Periodical. German. mo. DM189.00. Metzler Poeschel Verlag Veroeffen, Statist Bundesamt Kernerstr 43, D 70182 Stuttgart Germany. **Tel** 011 49 7071 935350. **(Subscription address:** Metzler Poeschel H Leins GmbH, Postfach 1152, D 72125 Kusterdingen Germany.**)** **LC** HC281; .A24. **[CCC]**. cum. index.
**Desc:** Furnishes, by means of texts, figures and charts, the latest information of official statistics on economic and social life in West Germany. Statistical figures inform at a glance about major benchmark data and their changes over time. Selected tables present results from statistics which became available in the reference month, and may also provide additional information for the articles.
**Ind/Abst** Energy Res. Abstr. (March 1982-); Popul. Index; Stat. Theory Method Abstr. (1959-1963).

US/1065-5778
**WISCONSIN IN PERSPECTIVE.** (WISCONSIN IN PERSPECTIVE : A STATISTICAL VIEW OF THE "BADGER STATE".). [Wis. perspect.]. **Added/Corp** Morgan Quitno Corporation. (1990)-. Statistical Publication. English. $18.00. Morgan Quitno Corporation, PO Box 1656, 512 East 9th Street, Lawrence KS 66044. **Tel** (800)457-0742, (913)841-3534, FAX (913)841-3534. **DD** 317. ***Continues*** *Wisconsin in Perspective, 1065-5778.*
**Desc:** Reports on the state's data and rank for each of the categories featured in State Rankings.

US
**WORLD STATISTICS IN BRIEF.** **Added/Corp** United Nations. Statistical Office. **VFOAT** United Nations Statistical Pocketbook. 1st Ed. (1976)-. Government Publication. English. an. $7.50. United Nations Publications, 2 United Nations Plaza, Room DC2 0853, Department 007C, New York NY 10017. **Tel** (212)963-8303, (800)253-9646. **LC** JX1977; .A2 subser. **DD** 310/.5 S; 310/.5.
**Desc:** Pocketsize reference book giving statistical data from 156 countries on demography, labor force, national accounts, agriculture, industry, trade, finance, tourism, transport, communication, education, health and nutrition.

US
**WYOMING DATA HANDBOOK.** **Main/Corp** Wyoming. Dept. of Administration and Fiscal Control. English. Wyoming Research DAFC, 302 Emerson Building, Cheyenne WY 82002. **Tel** (307)777-7201. **LC** HA721; .D46A. **DD** 317.87.
**Ind/Abst** Stat. Ref. Index.

US/1065-5786
**WYOMING IN PERSPECTIVE.** (WYOMING IN PERSPECTIVE : A STATISTICAL VIEW OF THE "EQUALITY STATE".). [Wyo. perspect.]. **Added/Corp** Morgan Quitno Corporation. (1990)-. Statistical Publication. English. $18.00. Morgan Quitno Corporation, PO Box 1656, 512 East 9th Street, Lawrence KS 66044. **Tel** (800)457-0742, (913)841-3534, FAX (913)841-3534. **DD** 317. ***Continues*** *Wyoming in Pperspective, 1065-5786.*
**Desc:** Reports on the state's data and rank for each of the categories featured in State Rankings.

US
**WYOMING STATISTICAL REVIEW.** **VFOAT** Employment Security Statistical Review, Wyoming. Statistical Publication. English. an. Free. Wyoming Statistical Review, PO Box 2760, Casper WY 82602. **Tel** (307)235-3296. **ED** Deana Hauf. **LC** HD7096.U6; W868. **DD** 368.4/4/009787. Index available. **Circ:** 75. available on diskette.
**Desc:** Contains historical data for Wyoming concerning job openings, work applications, job placements, claims for unemployment insurance benefits, and payments of unemployment insurance benefits act.

IS/0021-1982
**YARHON HA-STATISTI LE-YISRAEL, HA-.** **Main/Corp** Israel. Lishkah Ha-Merkazit Li-Statistitkah. **Added/Corp** Israel. Lishkah ha-Merkazit li-Statistikah. Statistical Bulletin of Israel. Israel. Lishkah ha-Merkazit li-Statistikah. Monthly Bulletin of Statistics. **VFOAT** Statistical Bulletin of Israel; Monthly Bulletin of Statistics. Vol. 18, (Jan. 1967)-. Multiple languages (English and Hebrew). Twelve times a year. $95.00. Central Bureau of Statistics / Israel, PO Box 13015, 91 130 Hakirya Jerusalem Israel. **Tel** 011-972-2-553553. **LC** HA1931; .L58b. ***Formed by the union of*** *Israel. Lishkah ha-Merkazit li-Statistikah. Yarhon ha-Statisti le-Yisrael, Helek A: Hevrah* ***and*** *Israel. Lishkah ha-Merkazit li-Statistikah. Yarhon ha-Statisti le-Yisrael, Helek B: Kalkalah.*
**Desc:** Periodic official statistics on various branches of Israel's society, demography and economy.

IS
**YARHON HA-STATISTI LE-YISRAEL. MUSAF, HA-.** **Main/Corp** Israel. Lishkah Ha-Merkazit Li-Statistikah. **VFOAT** Statistical Bulletin of Israel Supplements; Monthly Bulletin of Statistics Supplement. Vol. 18 (Jan. 1967)-. Multiple languages (English and Hebrew). Government Printing House, Street B No 29 Hakirya, Yerushalayim Israel. **LC** HA1931; .L58C.

AT/0810-8633
**YEAR BOOK, AUSTRALIA.** [Yearb. Aust.]. **Added/Corp** Australian Bureau of Statistics. **VFOAT** Yearbook Australia. No. 62 (1977 and 1978)-. English. an (July). 70.00Aus$. Australian Bureau of Statistics, PO Box 10, Belconnen Australian Capital Territory, 2616 Australia. **Tel** 011 61 6 2527911, FAX 011 61 6 2516009. **LC** HA3001; .B5. **DD** 319.4. **NLM** W2 KA8 B9O. Index available. **Bk Rev**. **Ad Acc**. **Circ:** 7,000. available on microfiche. ***Continues*** *Official Year Book of Australia, 0312-4746.*
**Desc:** Includes statistical material illustrated by maps, pictures and graphs.
**Ind/Abst** Energy Res. Abstr. (Sept. 1982-).

SW/0078-1088
**YEARBOOK OF NORDIC STATISTICS.** (YEARBOOK OF NORDIC STATISTICS. NORDISK STATISTISK AARSBOK.). **Added/Corp** Nordic Council. Nordic Council of Ministers. Nordic Statistical Secretariat. **VFOAT** Nordisk Statistisk Arsbok. (1962)-. English (Swedish). an. Kr472.00. Almqvist & Wiksell International, PO Box 4627, S-11691 Stockholm Sweden. **Tel** 011-46-8-6408800. **LC** DL1; .N63; HA1465. **DD** 314.8. **NLM** W1 YE278.

SI/0583-3655
**YEARBOOK OF STATISTICS: SINGAPORE.** **Added/Corp** Singapore. Dept. of Statistics. (1967)-. English. an. $12.40. Singapore National Printers, 303 Upper Serangoon Road, Singapore 1334 Singapore. **Tel** 011 65 2820611. **LC** HA1797.S5; A35. **DD** 315.95/7. **NLM** W2 JS6 D4Y.

GW
**ZAHLENSPIEGEL.** **Main/Corp** Germany (Federal Republic, 1949- ). Bundesministerium fur Innerdeutsche Beziehungen. German (English and French). ir (every four to five years). Free. Bundesministerium fur Innerdeutsche Beziehungen, Postfach 16 40, 5300 Bonn 1 Germany. **Tel** 0228/207-235, telex 886 776 BGAD. **LC** HA1233; .B87A. **Circ:** 235,000.
**Desc:** Intended for teaching in schools and for instruction of youth and adults; of interest to educators concerned with the German Democratic Republic and the divided Germany.

ZA
**ZAMBIA IN FIGURES.** **Main/Corp** Zambia. Central Statistical Office. English. Central Statistical Office / Zambia, PO Box 1908, Lusaka Zambia. **Tel** 211231. **LC** HA4703; .A16A. **DD** 316.894.

GW
**ZEITSCHRIFT DES BAVERISCHEN STATISTISCHEN LANDESAMTS.** **Main/Corp** Bayerisches Statistisches Landesamt. German. mo. DM12.00 Germany. Bayerisches Statistisches, Neuhauserstr 511, W-8000 Munchen 2 Germany. **Tel** 089/2119-205. **LC** HA1261; .B. **NLM** W2 GG4.1 B3S7Z. Index available. ctrl circ. ***Continues*** *Zeitschrift des Koniglich Bayerischen Statistischen Bureau.*
**Desc:** Statistical office.

PL
**ZMIANY CEN W GOSPODARCE NARODOWEJ ... .** **Added/Corp** Poland. Gowny Urzad Statystyczny. Departament Cen. (1989)-. Polish. an. $8.00 US; $7.00 other. Zaklad Wydawnictw Statystycznych, Al Niepodleglosci 208, 00-925 Warszawa Poland. **Tel** 253241, telex 814581A GUS. ctrl circ.

JA
**ZUSETSU EPOKA TOKEI SHIRYO.** **VFOAT** Epoka Tokei Shiryo. (19??)-. Statistical Publication. Japanese. Obunsha Publishing Company Ltd., 55 Yokoderacho Shinjukuku 162, Tokyo Japan. **Tel** 03 2666101, FAX 03 2666175. **LC** HA1844; .Z87.

# TEXTILES

HK/1015-8138
**A.T.A. JOURNAL.** [A.T.A. j.]. **VFOAT** Asia on Textile & Apparel Journal. (1990)-. Periodical. English (Chinese). bm. $48.00 Asia; $54.00 other. Adsale Publishing Company, 14/F Devon House Taikoo Place, 979 King's Road, Quarry Bay, Hong Kong. **Tel** 011 852 811 8897, FAX 011 852 516 5119. **ED** Benjamin Heung and Lisa Li. **UDC** 677. **Photos**. **Ad Acc**, **Adv Mgr:** Erica Cheng, Esther Chan and Janette Li. **Pr Rev. Circ:** 12,300 (ctrl).
**Desc:** Aims at channeling information to Asia from countries around the world, especially Europe, the US and Japan, which possess advanced technology and at the same time are the most important textile markets for Asian exporters.

US/0734-8894
**AATCC TECHNICAL MANUAL.** [AATCC tech. man.]. **Added/Corp** American Association of Textile Chemists and Colorists. **VFOAT** Technical Manual of the American Association of Textile Chemists and Colorists; Technical Manual. **VAT** American Association of Textile Chemists and Colorists Technical Manual. Vol. 39 (Sept. 1963)-. English. an. $82.00. American Association of Textile Chemists and Colorists, PO Box 12215, Research Triangle Park NC 27709. **Tel** (919)549-8141, FAX (919)549-8933. **LC** TP890; .A5. **DD** 667/.3/05. **[CCC].** Index available (Free). available in microform (from Information Handling Services). ***Continues*** *Technical Manual of the American Association of Textile Chemists and Colorists, 0883-4539.*
**Desc:** Contains all AATCC test methods plus AATCC research and administrative committee rosters and reports.
**Ind/Abst** Art Archaeol. Tech. Abstr.

UK
**ACCOUNTS.** **Main/Corp** Textile Institute (Manchester, England). English. Textile Institute International Headquarters, 10 Black Friars Street, Manchester M35 DR United Kingdom. **Tel** 061 834 8457, FAX 061 835 3087, telex 668297 TEXINS. **LC** TS1300; .T216b. **DD** 677/.006041. ***Continues in part*** *Annual Report and Accounts for ... .*

GW/0323-7648
**ACTA POLYMERICA.** [Acta polym.]. Vol. 30 (Jan. 1979)-. Academic Scholarly Publication. German (English, German and Russian). bm. $425.00. VCH Gesellschaft GmbH, Postfach 101161, D 69451 Weinheim Germany. **Tel** 011 49 6201 606459, FAX 011 49 6201 606184. **(Subscription address:** VCH Publishers Inc., 303 Northwest 12th Avenue, Journals Department, Deerfield FL 33442.) **LC** TS1300; .F34. **DD** 668.9/05. **CODEN** ACPODY. **[CCC]. Pr Rev.** Documents available from The Genuine Article, CASDDS. ***Continues*** *Faserforschung und Textiltechnik.*
**Ind/Abst** Abstr. Bull. Inst. Pap. Sci. Tech.; Art Archaeol. Tech. Abstr.; Chem. Abstr.; Chem. Titles; Curr. Biotechnol.; Curr. Contents Phys. Chem. Earth Sci.; Energy Res. Abstr. (Jan. 1981-); Eng. Mater. Abstr.; Leadscan; Polymer Contents; Res. Alert [Full Cov.]; Sci. Cit. Index; SCISEARCH; Sug. Indus. Abstr.; Text. Technol. Dig.; World Text. Abstr.

UK/0144-7521
**AFRICAN TEXTILES.** [Afr. text.]. **VFOAT** Directory ... African Buyer's Guide to Textile Machinery; Annuaire de. (June 1980)-. Periodical. English (table of contents in French). Six times a year. $75.00. Alain Charles Publishing Ltd., 27 Wilfred Street, London SW1E 6PR England. **Tel** 011 44 71 834 7676, FAX 011 44 71 973 0076, telex 297166/7.
**Ind/Abst** Anim. Breed. Abstr.; Cot. Trop. Fibr. Abstr. Bibliogr.; Text. Technol. Dig.; World Text. Abstr.

US
**AGENT, THE.** (19??)-. Periodical. English. sa. Halper Publishing, 600 Central Avenue, Suite 200, Highland Park IL 60035. **Tel** (708)831-6678. **LC** TS1312; .A35. **DD** 677.058.

US/0092-2811
**AMERICAN COIN-OP.** [Am. coin-op]. Vol. 14, No. 2 (Feb. 1973)-. Periodical. English. Twelve times a year. $33.00. Crain Associates Enterprises Inc, 500 North Dearborn Street, Chicago IL 60610. **Tel** (312)337-7700. **LC** HD9999.L38; C6. **DD** 338.4/7/66713. available on microfilm from University Microfilms International (UMI). ***Continues*** *Coin-Op.*

US/0002-8258
**AMERICAN DRYCLEANER.** [Am. dryclean.]. **VFOAT** American Dry Cleaner. Began with April 1934 issue. Periodical. English. mo. $20.00. Crain Associates Enterprises Inc, 500 North Dearborn Street, Chicago IL 60610. **Tel** (312)337-7700. **LC** HD9999.C48. **DD** 338.4/7/667120973. **[CCC].** available on microfilm from University Microfilms International (UMI). ***Continues*** *Cleaners and Dyers Advertiser.*
**Ind/Abst** Art Archaeol. Tech. Abstr.; Text. Technol. Dig.

US/0002-8266
**AMERICAN DYESTUFF REPORTER.** [Am. dyest. report.]. **Added/Corp** American Association of Textile Chemists and Colorists. Proceedings. Vol. 1 (Oct. 8, 1917)-. Periodical. English. Twelve times a year. $33.00 US; $35.00 Canada; $55.00 others. SAF International Publishing Inc., Promenade A Suite 2, Harmon Cove Towers, Secaucus NJ 07094. **Tel** (201)867-9230, FAX (201)867-0545, telex 955-329. **ED** Edward Fox. **LC** TP890; .A6. **DD** 667/.2/05. **CODEN** ADREAI. Index available. cum. index. **Bk Rev**. **Ad Acc**. **Circ:** 11,500 (ctrl). available on microfilm and microfiche from University Microfilms International (UMI). Documents available from Article Express International, CASDDS. ***Absorbed*** *Textile Colorist and Converter, 0096-591X.*
**Desc:** Edited for management in dyehouses, finishing facilities and textile mills. Feature articles cover the range of technical and non-technical chemical, dyeing and equipment applications relating to these plants.
**Ind/Abst** Abstr. Bull. Inst. Pap. Sci. Tech.; Appl. Sci. Technol. Index; Bioeng. Abstr.; Biogr. Index; Chem. Abstr.; Ei Page One; EMBASE; Eng. Index Annu.; F&S Index Plus Text, Int. [Select. Cov.]; PROMT; Text. Technol. Dig.; World Text. Abstr.

US
**AMERICAN FABRICS AND FASHIONS (1984).** ***Ceased.*** (AMERICAN FABRICS AND FASHIONS.). **VFOAT** American Fabrics and Fashions Magazine. No. 130 (1984)-(Sept./Oct. 1986). Periodical. English. bm. American Fabrics, 343 Lexington Avenue, New York NY 10016. ***Continues*** *AFF.*
**Ind/Abst** Art Index.

US/0002-9718
**AMERICAN LAUNDRY DIGEST.** [Am. laund. dig.]. (19??)-. Periodical. English. Twelve times a year. $33.00. Crain Associates Enterprises Inc, 500 North Dearborn Street, Chicago IL 60610. **Tel** (312)337-7700. **DD** 338. **[CCC].** available on microfilm and microfiche from University Microfilms International (UMI).
**Ind/Abst** Health Plan. Adminis.; Hospit. Health Admin. Index; Text. Technol. Dig.

US/0890-9970
**AMERICA'S TEXTILES INTERNATIONAL.** [Am. text. int.]. **Added/Corp** Textile Quality Control Association (U.S.). **VFOAT** America's Textiles. Vol. 15, No. 4 (April 1986)-. Academic Scholarly Publication. English. mo. $43.00 US; $53.00 (surface mail), $115.00 (airmail) other. Billian Publishing Inc., 2100 Powers Ferry Road, Atlanta GA 30339. **Tel** (404)955-5656, FAX (404)952-0669. **LC** TS1300; .A36. **DD** 677/.00973. **CODEN** ATINEE. **Bk Rev**. **Ad Acc**. **Circ:** 35,250 (ctrl). available on microfilm from University Microfilms International (UMI). Documents available from CASDDS. ***Continues*** *America's Textiles (Greenville, S.C. : 1983), 0737-0040.*
**Desc:** Edited for the spinning and weaving industries, including man-made fiber producers, texturizers, tufted, nonwovens, knitting, industrial fabrics, carpet mills, dyeing and finishing plants and other operations allied to the field. All aspects of textile manufacturing are covered. Also covers international developments that affect textiles in North America: finance, technology, etc.
**Ind/Abst** Chem. Abstr. (1986-); Chem. Ind. Notes (1986-); Nonwovens Abstr.; Text. Technol. Dig.; Trade Ind. Index.

PO
**ANITAF DIRECTORY.** **Main/Corp** ANITAF (Organization). **VFOAT** A.N.I.T.A.F. Directory. Directory. English (French, German and Portuguese). Associacao Nacional das Industrias Texteis, Algodoeiras E Fibras, rue de Goncalo Cristovao, 96-1O E 2O, Porto Portugal. **LC** HD9865.P66; A54A. **DD** 677/.0029/4469.

US/1051-3337
**ANNIE'S QUICK & EASY PATTERN CLUB.** [Annie's quick easy pattern club]. **VFOAT** Pattern Club. Periodical. English. bm. $14.95. Annie's Attic, Dept CA01, Route 2, Box 212B, Big Sandy TX 75755. **Tel** (903)636-4303. **DD** 746. ***Continues*** *Annie's Pattern Club Newsletter, 0199-7106.*

US/0162-7651
**ANNOTATED DIRECTORY OF SELF-PUBLISHED TEXTILE BOOKS.** 1977-. Directory. English. Sommer, PO Box 1133, Forest Hills NY 11375. **LC** Z6153.T4; A55; TT699. **DD** 016.746.

II
**ANNUAL REPORT - AHMEDABAD TEXTILE MILL'S ASSOCIATION.** **Main/Corp** Ahmedabad Textile Mills' Association. (19??)-. English. Ahmedabad Textile Mills' Association Ranchhodlal, Marg Ashram Road, Ahmedabad 380009 India. **LC** HD9866.I64; A43a. **DD** 338.4/7677/00605475.

UK
**ANNUAL REPORT / THE TEXTILE INDUSTRY.** **Main/Corp** Textile Institute (Manchester, England). **VFOAT** Textile Institute Annual Report. English. Textile Institute International Headquarters, 10 Black Friars Street, Manchester M35 DR United Kingdom. **Tel** 061 834 8457, FAX 061 835 3087, telex 668297 TEXINS. **LC** TS1300; .T216c. **DD** 677/.006041. ***Continues in part*** *Annual Report and Accounts for ... / Textile Institute (Manchester England).*

IT
**ANNUARIO ... DELL'INDUSTRIA ITALIANA DELLA MAGLIERIA E DELLA CALZETTERIA / MAGLIECALZE.** **Added/Corp** Magliecalze (Association). **VFOAT** Annuaire de la Bonneterie Italienne; Yearbook of the Italian Knitting Industry. (19??)-. English (French, German, English and Spanish). an. L90.000. Gesto S R L, Via Cesare Battisti 21, 20122 Milan Italy. **Tel** (02)798155, FAX 39-2-5465310. **LC** HD9969.K7; I83. **DD** 338.4/7677/002545. Index available. **Ad Acc. Circ:** 15,000. available on diskette.
**Desc:** Yearbook is the official directory of Italian producers of hosiery and knitwear, and their suppliers of yarns, machinery and services.

US
**APPAREL DIGEST.** **Added/Corp** Institute of Textile Technology (Charlottesville, Va.). (1984)-. Periodical. English. mo. $75.00. Institute of Textile Technology, 2551 Ivy Road, Charlottesville VA 22903-4641. **Tel** (804)296-5511, FAX (804)977-5400.

PK
**APTMA DIRECTORY OF MEMBERS - ALL PAKISTAN TEXTILE MILLS ASSOCIATION.** **Main/Corp** All Pakistan Textile Mills Association. **VAT** All Pakistan Textile Mills Association Directory of Members. Directory. English. Rs0.05. All Pakistan Textile Mills Association, Mohammedi House/3rd Floor, I I Chundrigar Road, Karachi Pakistan. **LC** HD9886.P14; A43A. **DD** 338.4/7/677210255491.

IO/0518-4010
**ARENA TEKSTIL.** [Arena tekstil]. V. 1 (1969)-. Academic Scholarly Publication. Multiple languages (English and Indonesian). Institut Teknologi Tekstil, Jl Jenderal A Yani 318, Bandung Indonesia. **LC** TS1300;

.A74. **CODEN** ARTKDB. Documents available from CASDDS.
**Ind/Abst** Chem. Abstr. (1969-1981).

IT/0393-4462
**ARREDO. TESSILI-COMPLEMENTI.** [Arredo, Tess. - complementi]. (1982)-. Periodical. Multiple languages. mo (10 issues per year). $100.00. Nuove Tecniche Editoriali Srl, Via San Siro 27, 20149 Milan Italy. **Tel** 011 39 2 481-2213, 498-0532. **UDC** 677.07. ***Absorbed*** *Arredo Biancheria Casa.*

CN/0824-9091
**ARS TEXTRINA. Added/Corp** Charles Babbage Research Centre. **VFOAT** Art of Weaving. Vol. 1 (Dec. 1983)-. Periodical. English. sa. $80.00. Charles Babbage Research Centre, PO Box 272 St Norbert Postal Station, Winnipeg Manitoba R3V 1L6 Canada. **Tel** (204)474-8313, (204)772-2612. **ED** R. G. Stanton and J. A. Hoskins. **DD** 677/.028242/05. Index available. **Circ:** 250.
**Desc:** Investigation of mathematical patterns associated with weaving, interest in the history, theory, practice, and development of textile knowledge in general.
**Ind/Abst** Am. Hist. Life (1985-).

IT
**ARTE TESSILE : RIVISTA-ANNUARIO DEL CENTRO ITALIANO PER LO STUDIO DELLA STORIA DEL TESSUTO.** **Added/Corp** Centro Italiano per lo Studio della Storia del Tessuto (Milan, Italy). No. 1 (Feb 1990)-. Italian (summaries and/or abstracts in English). an. **LC** NK8800; .A68. **DD** 746/.05.
**Ind/Abst** BHA : Biblio. Hist. Art.

BE/0776-3670
**ARTES TEXTILES. Added/Corp** Vereniging voor de Geschiedinis van de Textiele Kunsten. Rijksuniversiteit te Gent. Centrum voor de Geschiedenis van de Tapijtkunst. Rijksuniversiteit te Gent. Centrum voor de Geschiedenis van de Textiele Kunsten. Centrum voor de Geschiedenis van de Tapijtkunst. (1953)-. Periodical. Dutch.
**Ind/Abst** BHA : Biblio. Hist. Art.

II/0971-3425
**ASIAN TEXTILE JOURNAL.** (1992)-. English. mo. $120.00. **(Subscription address:** Prints India, 11 Darya Ganj, New Delhi 110002 India.**)**

US/1047-692X
**ATI DIRECTORY.** (ATI DIRECTORY : THE TEXTILE RED BOOK.). [ATI dir.]. **VFOAT** Textile Red Book. **VAT** America's Textile International Directory. (1988)-. Directory. English. an. $91.50 US; $95.00 Canada; $109.00 Europe and South America; $114.00 The Orient and India. Billian Publishing Inc., 2100 Powers Ferry Road, Atlanta GA 30339. **Tel** (404)955-5656, FAX (404)952-0669. **LC** TS1312; .A86. **DD** 677/.002573.

II/0378-8148
**ATIRA TECHNICAL DIGEST.** [ATIRA tech. dig.]. **Added/Corp** Ahmedabad Textile Industry's Research Association. **VFOAT** A.T.I.R.A. Technical Digest. **VAT** Ahmedabad Textile Industry's Research Association Technical Digest. (19??)-. Academic Scholarly Publication. English. ir. $5.00 (latest issue). Indian Books and Periodicals, 2429 Tilak Street, Pahar Ganj, New Delhi 110005 India. **CODEN** ATTDD4. **Bk Rev.** Documents available from CASDDS.
**Ind/Abst** Chem. Abstr. (1966-1982); World Text. Abstr.

AT/0725-086X
**AUSTRALASIAN TEXTILES.** [Australas. text.]. **Added/Corp** Society of Dyers and Colourists of Australia and New Zealand. Textile Society of Australia. (1981)-. Periodical. English. bm. 47.00Aus$ Australia; 57.00Aus$ New Zealand; 105.00Aus$ other. Australasian Textiles Publishers, 11 Woodlands Drive, Ocean Grove Victoria 3226 Australia. **Tel** 011 61 52 552699, FAX 011 61 52 561668. **(Subscription address:** Australasian Textiles Publishers, PO Box 286, Belmont Victoria 3216 Australia**)** **ED** Stan Boston. Index available. cum. index. **Bk Rev. Ad Acc. Circ:** 2,350 (ctrl).
**Ind/Abst** AGRICOLA [Select. Cov.]; Art Archaeol. Tech. Abstr.; Text. Technol. Dig.; World Text. Abstr.

AT
**AUSTRALIAN APPAREL MANUFACTURER.** ***Title Change.*** **VFOAT** AAM; A.A.M. Vol. 59, No. 4 (June/July 1985)-(19??). Periodical. English. bm. National Library of Australia, Parkes Place, Canberra ACT, 2600 Australia. **Tel** 011 61 6 2621374, FAX 011 61 6 2731084. **ED** Glenn Thiele. **Circ:** 3,679. ***Continues*** *Textile & Apparel Manufacturer.* ***Continued by*** *Apparel Industry.*
**Desc:** Covers the latest technological and production techniques, market and fashion trends, new fabrics and equipment, plus government and labor matters.
**Ind/Abst** Text. Technol. Dig.

NE/0168-4914
**BANDINDUSTRIE EN OVERIGE TEXTIELINDUSTRIE / CENTRAAL BUREAU VOOR DE STATISTIEK, HOOFDAFDELING STATISTIEKEN VAN INDUSTRIE EN BOUWNIJVERHEID.** **Added/Corp** Netherlands. Centraal Bureau voor de Statistiek. Hoofdafdeling Statistieken van Industrie en Bouwnijverheid. **VFOAT** Manufacture of Narrow Fabrics and of Other Textiles. (19??)-. Dutch (summaries and/or abstracts in English). FI10.15. Centraal Bureau voor de Statistiek, AFD ALG Zaken, Postbus 959, 2270 AZ Voorburg Netherlands. **Tel** 011 31 70 3373800, FAX 011 31 038 7429, telex 32692 CBS NL. **LC** HD9865; .N64; B36.

BG/0253-5424
**BANGLADESH JOURNAL OF JUTE & FIBRE RESEARCH.** [Bangladesh j. jute fibre res.]. **Added/Corp** Bangladesh Jute Research Institute. **VAT** Bangladesh Journal of Jute and Fibre Research. July (1976)-. Academic Scholarly Publication. English. sa. TK250.00 Bangladesh; $8.50 US. Bangladesh Jute Research Institute, Sher-e-Banlanagar, Dhaka 15 Bangladesh. **CODEN** BJJRD5. Documents available from CASDDS.
**Ind/Abst** Chem. Abstr.

SP
**BOLETIN INTEXTAR DEL INSTITUTO DE INVESTIGACION TEXTIL Y DE COOPERACION INDUSTRIAL. Added/Corp** Universidad Politecnica de Catalunya. Instituto de Investigacion Textil y de Cooperacion Industrial. **VFOAT** Intextar; Boletin Intextar. (198?)-. Periodical. Spanish. sa. **LC** TS1300; .I66a. Documents available from CASDDS. ***Continues*** *Universidad Politecnica de Catalunya. Instituto de Investigacion Textil y de Cooperacion Industrial. Boletin del Instituto de Investigacion Textil y de Cooperacion Industrial.*
**Ind/Abst** Chem. Abstr.

US/0892-2713
**BOOK OF PAPERS - AMERICAN ASSOCIATION OF TEXTILE CHEMISTS AND COLORISTS. INTERNATIONAL CONFERENCE & EXHIBITION.** (BOOK OF PAPERS / INTERNATIONAL CONFERENCE & EXHIBITION, AATCC.). [Book pap. - Am. Assoc. Text. Chem. Color., Int. Conf. Exhib.]. **Main/Corp** American Association of Textile Chemists and Colorists. (1984)-. Academic Scholarly Publication. English. an (October). $61.00. American Association of Textile Chemists and Colorists, PO Box 12215, Research Triangle Park NC 27709. **Tel** (919)549-8141, FAX (919)549-8933. **LC** TP890.5; .N37a. **DD** 667/.3. **CODEN** BPIAEQ. **[CCC].** Documents available from Article Express International, CASDDS. ***Continues*** *Book of Papers / National Technical Conference, AATCC, 0192-4699.*
**Ind/Abst** AGRICOLA [Select. Cov.]; Bioeng. Abstr.; Chem. Abstr. (1985-); Ei Page One; Eng. Index Annu.

CN/0228-8710
**BREF (ASSOCIATION DES TISSERANDS D'ICI), EN.** (EN BREF : JOURNAL DE L'ASSOCIATION DES TISSERANDS D'ICI.). **Added/Corp** Association des Tisserands d'ICI. V. 1, No. 1 (Winter 1979/80)-. Periodical. French. ir. $2.00 per number. Association des Tisserands d'Ici, 402 Est rue St-Paul, Montreal Quebec H2Y 1H4 Canada. **DD** 746.1/4/09714.

US/0730-0905
**BROADWOVEN GRAY FABRIC PRODUCTION. SEASONAL ADJUSTMENT SUPPLEMENT.** (CURRENT INDUSTRIAL REPORTS. MQ-22T, BROADWOVEN GRAY FABRIC PRODUCTION, SEASONAL ADJUSTMENT SUPPLEMENT / U.S. DEPARTMENT OF COMMERCE, BUREAU OF THE CENSUS.). **VFOAT** Broadwoven Gray Fabric Production, Seasonal Adjustment Supplement. Government Publication. English. US Department of Commerce / Bureau of the Census, Data User Services Division, Customer Services, Washington DC 20233-0800. **Tel** (301)763-4100. **(Subscription address:** Superintendent of Documents, US Government Printing Office, Washington DC 20402.**)** **LC** HD9851; .C87. **DD** 338.4/7677/00973021.

FR
**BULLETIN DU CIETA. Added/Corp** Centre International d'Etude des Textiles Anciens. **VFOAT** Bulletin de Liaison; Bulletin. **VAT** Bulletin du Centre International d'Etude des Textiles Anciens. No. 67 (1989)-. Bulletin. English (French). $100.00 (museums/institutions), $50.00 (libraries), $45.00 (individuals). Bulletin de Liaison Centre, 34 rue de la Charite, 69002 Lyon France. ***Continues*** *Textiles Anciens.*
**Desc:** Information on textile fabrics.

US
**BULLETIN / INTERNATIONAL OLD LACERS.** ***Title Change.*** **Main/Corp** International Old Lacers. **VFOAT** Bi-Monthly Bulletin for Members. 1952. Bulletin. English. qt. International Old Lacers Inc, 2409 South 9th, Carolyn Regnier, Lafayette IN 47905. **Tel** (317)474-1176. **ED** Robert C Ridell. **Bk Rev. Ad Acc. Circ:** 2,100 (ctrl). ***Continues*** *International Old Lacers Inc. Bulletin, 0740-6746.* ***Continued by*** *International Old Lacers Inc., Bulletin, 0740-6746.*
**Desc:** Lace articles, patterns, pictures of lace exhibits, club activities, advertising of lace related materials, and information on the yearly convention.

US/0065-7352
**BUYER'S GUIDE - AMERICAN ASSOCIATION OF TEXTILE CHEMISTS AND COLORISTS. Main/Corp** American Association of Textile Chemists and Colorists. **VFOAT** AATCC Buyer's Guide. (1978)-. English. an. $33.00 (members). American Association of Textile Chemists and Colorists, PO Box 12215, Research Triangle Park NC 27709. **Tel** (919)549-8141, FAX (919)549-8933. ***Continues*** *Products.*
**Desc:** Lists sources for dyes, pigments, chemical specialties, machinery and equipment.

US/1049-1376
**C2C ABSTRACTS JAPAN. TEXTILES.** **See** Textiles-Abstracting, Bibliographies and Statistics.

CN/0008-5170
**CANADIAN TEXTILE JOURNAL.** [Can. text. j.]. **VFOAT** Revue du Textile Canadien. Vol. 25 (1908)-. Periodical. English (French; summaries and/or abstracts in French). mo. CTJ Inc., 1 rue Pacifique, Sainte-Anne-de-Bellevue, Quebec H9X 1C5 Canada. **Tel** (514)457-2347, FAX (514)457-2147. **CODEN** CTJOA6. Documents available from CASDDS. ***Continues*** *Canadian Journal of Fabrics.*
**Ind/Abst** AGRICOLA [Select. Cov.]; Art Archaeol. Tech. Abstr.; Chem. Abstr.; Chem. Ind. Notes; World Text. Abstr.

UK/0263-4236
**CARPET & FLOORCOVERINGS REVIEW.** [Carpet floorcoverings rev.]. **VFOAT** Carpet and Floorcoverings Review. Vol. 1, No. 1 (Sept. 9, 1982)-. Periodical. English. sm (23 issues). £59.00 UK; £79.00 other. Benn Publications Ltd., Sovereign Way, Tonbridge TNQ 1RW England. **Tel** 011 44 732 364422, FAX 011 44 732 361534, telex 0732 95132 BENTON G. available on an online database (file 16/Full-Text) from DIALOG. ***Continues*** *Carpet Review Weekly, 0308-4507.*
**Ind/Abst** PROMT [Full Txt.]; World Text. Abstr.

UK/0069-0767
**CARPET ANNUAL. See** Economics-Industry and Production.

US
**CARPET MANAGEMENT : A QUARTERLY REVIEW OF THE INTERNATIONAL CARPET AND RUG INDUSTRY.** (19??)-. Newsletter. English. Four times a year. $200.00. Carpet Management, 3707 Bonita Court, Johns Island SC 29455. **Tel** (803)768-3632, FAX (803)768-3632. **ED** Robert J. Saunders. **UDC** 68. **Circ:** 1,000 (ctrl).
**Desc:** For carpet industry executives.

US/0095-6457
**CARPET SPECIFIER'S HANDBOOK, THE. Main/Corp** Carpet and Rug Institute. (1974)-. English. an. $10.00. Carpet and Rug Institute, Box 2048, Dalton GA 30720. **Tel** (404)278-3176, FAX (404)278-8835. **LC** TS1772; .C29a. **DD** 677/.643/05. cum. index. **Ad Acc.**
**Desc:** Guide to assist in writing a set of specifications, and understanding the basic factors affecting a carpet selection. Discusses carpet composition, manufacturing techniques, comparison with floor coverings, and maintenance.

CN/0831-2907
**CARRIAGE TRADE (SARNIA, ONT.).** (THE CARRIAGE TRADE.). [Carriage trade]. Vol. 1 (1981)-. Periodical. English. qt. $15.95 US; $15.95 other. The Carriage Trade, 20 Dalrymple RR #2, Box 18, Camlachie Ontario N0N 1E0 Canada. **Tel** (519)869-4079, FAX (519)542-4854. **ED** Ruth Johnson. **DD** 746.43/2. Index available. cum. index. **Bk Rev. Ad Acc. Circ:** 3,000 (ctrl).
**Desc:** Contains machine knitting patterns, questions and answers and Cook's Corner. Machine knitting techniques, profiles, letters to the editor.

IT/0394-882X
**CASA TESSIL REPORTER.** (CASA TESSILREPORTER.). **VFOAT** Casa Tessil Reporter. (1987)-. Periodical. Italian. Eleven times a year (July/Aug. issues combined). L90000.00 Italy; L170000.00 other. EDI Team SNC, Via Montecassino, 20021 Baranzate Bollate Italy. **Tel** 011 39 2 38200080, FAX 011 39 2 38200082. **UDC** 645.48. **Bk Rev. Ad Acc, Adv Mgr:** Za AL Tessile, **Tel** 02 38200080 1. **Circ:** 25,000.
**Desc:** This magazine carries current news and information about the textiles industries. Articles are included such as, housewares, designs and fashions, and the retail industry.

XO/0528-9432
**CHEMICHE VLAKNA.** [Chem. vlakna]. (1951)-. Academic Scholarly Publication. Czech (Czech). qt. Dm104.00. **(Subscription address:** Slovart GTG Ltd., Krupinska 4, 852 99 Bratislava Slovakia.**)** **CODEN** CMVLA8. Documents available from CASDDS.
**Ind/Abst** Abstr. Bull. Inst. Pap. Sci. Tech.; Chem. Abstr.; World Text. Abstr.

GW/0340-3343
**CHEMIEFASERN, TEXTILINDUSTRIE.** **VFOAT** Chemiefasern/Textilindustrie; Chemiefasern, Textilindustrie. Vol. 29, No. 1 (Jan. 1979)-. Academic Scholarly Publication. German (English; translations available in English). Twelve times a year. DM213.94 Germany; DM240.10 other. Deutscher Fachverlag GmbH, Verlagsgruppe, D 60264 Frankfurt Germany. **Tel** 011 49 69 75951001, telex 411 862. **CODEN** CFTXAJ. Documents available from CASDDS. ***Continues*** *Chemiefasern, Textil-Industrie.*
**Ind/Abst** Chem. Abstr.; F&S Index Plus Text, Int. [Select. Cov.]; Infomat Int. Bus.; World Text. Abstr.

KO
**CHESA TONGGYE YONBO.** **VFOAT** Year Book of Raw Silk Statistics. English (Korean). mo. Hanguk Saengsa Suchul Chohap, 1-426 Youido-dong, Yongdungpo-ku, Seoul South Korea. **LC** HD9926.K6; C47. **DD** 338.4/7677391/095195.

HK
**CHINA TEXTILE.** Chinese. Seven times a year. HK$273.00 Hong Kong; $77.00 other. Adsale Publishing Company, 14/F Devon House Taikoo Place, 979 King's Road, Quarry Bay, Hong Kong. **Tel** 011 852 811 8897, FAX 011 852 516 5119. **ED** Linus Wu. **Ad Acc. Circ:** 35,000 (ctrl).
**Desc:** A specialized industrial magazine designed to introduce to China advanced foreign technology, machinery and processing materials in the textile and apparel mart.

US/1042-6442
**CLEANFAX (COLUMBUS, OHIO).** (CLEANFAX : THE OFFICIAL PUBLICATION OF THE UNITED CARPET CLEANERS INSTITUTE, INC.). [Cleanfax]. **Added/Corp** United Carpet Cleaners Institute. (1986)-. Trade Publication. English. Six times a year (Jan., Mar., May, July, Sept., Nov.). $19.00 (one year), $29.00 (two year). Cleanfax Publications Inc, PO Box 565, Granville OH 43023. **Tel** (614)366-0750. **ED** John Downey (phone: (614)587-1393). **DD** 667. **Ad Acc, Adv Mgr:** Bill Yeadon, **Tel** (800)669-0803. **Circ:** 30,000.
**Desc:** A trade magazine for professional carpet cleaning industry.

UK
**CLEANING & MAINTENANCE.** English. £44.00 UK; £57.00 other. Turret Group, 177 Hagden Lane, Watford Herts WD1 8LN United Kingdom. **Tel** 011 44 923 228577, FAX 011 44 923 221346.

US/0886-9901
**CLEANING AND RESTORATION.** (CLEANING AND RESTORATION : THE OFFICIAL PUBLICATION OF ASCR INTERNATIONAL.). **Added/Corp** Association of Specialists in Cleaning and Restoration. (Jan. 1986)-. Periodical. English. mo (12 issues). $27.00. Association of Specialists in Cleaning and Restoration, 10830 Annapolis Junction Road, Suite 312, Annapolis MD 00701-1111. **Tel** (301)604-4411. **ED** Kimberly Howard. **Bk Rev. Ad Acc, Adv Mgr:** Collen Carpenter, **Tel** (410)235-6500. **Circ:** 2,500. ***Continues*** *Voice (Falls Church, VA.), 0747-0533.*
**Desc:** Education-oriented toward cleaning and restoration of rugs, carpet, upholstery, draperies; restoration after fire, smoke, water, vandalism problems. Technical articles also cover these areas.

UK/0961-4729
**CLEANING INDUSTRY YEARBOOK.** [Clean. ind. yearb.]. (1990)-. Directory. English. an. £33.00 UK; £35.00 Europe; £37.00. Turret Group, 177 Hagden Lane, Watford Herts WD1 8LN United Kingdom. **Tel** 011 44 923 228577, FAX 011 44 923 221346. **DD** 648.5.

UK
**CLOTH DIRECTORY.** **See** Clothing Industry and Fashion.

US/0887-2937
**CLOTHING AND TEXTILE ARTS INDEX, THE.** **See** Clothing Industry and Fashion.

US/0887-302X
**CLOTHING AND TEXTILES RESEARCH JOURNAL.** [Cloth. text. res. j.]. **Added/Corp** Association of College Professors of Textiles and Clothing. Vol. 1 (1982)-. Academic Scholarly Publication. English. Four times a year. $45.00 (institutions) US; $52.00 (institutions) Canada and Mexico; $55.00 (institutions) others; $75.00 (individuals). International Textile and Apparel Association, PO Box 1360, Monument CO 80132. **Tel** (719)488-3716. **ED** Joan Laughlin, (editor's address: UNL College of Home Economics, Lincoln, NE 68583-0800, (phone: (402)472-2913). **DD** 646. **CODEN** CTRJEZ. Index available. **Pr Rev. Circ:** 1,300 (ctrl).
**Desc:** Scholarly articles, both research and theoretical, on textiles and clothing subject matter.
**Ind/Abst** AGRICOLA [Select. Cov.]; Am. Hist. Life (1989-); Linguist. Lang. Behav. Abstr.; Psychol. Abstr. (1987-); PsycINFO (1990-); PsycLit; Soc. Plann. Policy Dev. Abstr.; Sociol. Abstr.; Text. Technol. Dig.

II/0530-0495
**COIR.** ***Ceased.*** **Added/Corp** India (Republic). Coir Board. Vol. 1 (Aug. 1956)-(1993). Periodical. English. qt. Coir Board, PO Box 1752, Ernakulam South Cochen 16 India. **(Subscription address:** Prints India, 11 Darya Ganj, New Delhi 110002 India.**)** **LC** TS1544.C6; C6. **DD** 338.1; 634.

II/0010-1826
**COLOURAGE.** [Colourage]. (1954)-. English. mo. $60.00. Colour Publications Private, 126A Dhuruwadi Off, c/o Dr. Nariman, Bombay 400025 India. **Tel** 011 91 22 4309318 6319, telex 71242 CEPE. **(Subscription address:** Prints India, 11 Darya Ganj, New Delhi 110002 India.**)** **ED** R V Raghavan. **LC** TP890; .C62. **DD** 667/.3/05. **CODEN** COLOBG. **Bk Rev. Ad Acc. Circ:** 6,400. available on microfilm and microfiche from University Microfilms International (UMI). Documents available from The Genuine Article, CASDDS.
**Desc:** Technical articles, special columns and news reports pertaining to the textile wet processing and dyestuffs industries.
**Ind/Abst** Art Archaeol. Tech. Abstr.; Chem. Abstr.; Res. Alert [Select. Cov.]; SCISEARCH; Text. Technol. Dig.; World Text. Abstr.

II/0588-5108
**COLOURAGE ANNUAL.** [Colour. annu.]. (1967)-. English. an. Colour Publications Private, 126A Dhuruwadi Off, c/o Dr. Nariman, Bombay 400025 India. **Tel** 011 91 22 4309318 6319, telex 71242 CEPE. **LC** TP890; .C63. **DD** 667/.2/05. **CODEN** COLAB8. Documents available from CASDDS.
**Ind/Abst** Chem. Abstr.

BE
**COMITEXTIL. BULLETIN.** **Added/Corp** Comite de Coordination des Industries Textiles de la Communaute Economique Europeenne. **VFOAT** COMITEXTIL. (1975)-. Bulletin. English (French). Six times a year. 3750F (textile firms); 4250F (other). Comitextil, 24 rue Montoyer, 1040 Bruxelles Belgium. **Tel** 011 32 2 2309580, FAX 011 32 2 2306054, telex 0222380. Index available. **Circ:** 400 (ctrl). ***Supersedes*** *Comitextil. Documents; Comitextil. Information* ***and*** *Comitextil. Presse.*
**Desc:** Bulletin on the European textile industry, giving information on economics, politics, external trade and monographies on textile and clothing at international levels.
**Ind/Abst** Text. Technol. Dig.; World Text. Abstr.

US/0890-0027
**COMMERCIAL CARPET DIGEST.** [Commer. carpet dig.]. (Dec. 1980)-. Periodical. English. Ten times a year. $49.00 US & Canada; $69.00 other. Infosource, Division of RBI International, PO Box 1607, Dalton GA 30722. **Tel** (404)623-5183, (404)278-1375, FAX (404)278-3536, telex 543-420. **ED** Anthony King. **DD** 338. ctrl circ.

BE
**CON TEXT MAGAZINE.** **See** Clothing Industry and Fashion.

NE/0010-5449
**CONFECTIE.** **See** Economics-Industry and Production.

US/1063-746X
**CORDAGE NEWS.** [Cord. News]. **Added/Corp** Cordage Institute (U.S.). (Jan./Feb. 1988)-. Periodical. English. bm. $50.00 US, Canada, and Mexico; $100.00 others. Cordage Institute, 350 Lincoln Street, Hingham MA 02043. **Tel** (617)749-1016, FAX (617)749-9783. **ED** G.P. Foster. **DD** 338. **Bk Rev. Ad Acc. Circ:** 1,000 (ctrl).

US
**CORRELATION, TEXTILE, AND APPAREL CATEGORIES WITH TARIFF SCHEDULES OF THE UNITED STATES ANNOTATED / PREPARED BY INTERNATIONAL AGREEMENTS AND MONITORING DIVISION.** **Added/Corp** United States. International Trade Administration. Office of Textiles and Apparel. International Agreements and Monitoring Division. United States. Domestic and International Business Administration. Office of Textiles. United States. Industry and Trade Administration. Office of Textiles. United States. International Trade Administration. Office of Textiles and Apparel. Trade and Data Division. **VFOAT** Textile and Apparel Categories with Staff Schedules of the United States Annotated; Textile and Apparel Categories by Tariff Schedules of the United States Annotated; Textile and Apparel Categories with Tariff Schedules of the United States Annotated, Cotton, Wool, Manmade Fibers. (19??)-. English. an. $30.00. US Department of Commerce / International Trade Administration, 14th Street & Constitution Avenue NW, Hoover Building, Room 3850, Washington DC 20230. **Tel** (202)482-2867, FAX (202)482-5933. **LC** HF2651.T42; U53. **DD** 382/.45677/00973021.

UK
**COTLOOK DAILY.** (19??)-. English. ir (720 per year). $2625.00. Cotlook Ltd. / Outlook House, 458 New Chester Road, Rock Ferry, Bir Merseyside L42 2AE England. **Tel** 011 44 51 644 6400.
**Desc:** Telex service for the cotton industry.

UK
**COTLOOK PRISCOPE.** (19??)-. Trade Publication. English. ir (360 per year). $1229.00. Cotlook Ltd. / Outlook House, 458 New Chester Road, Rock Ferry, Bir Merseyside L42 2AE England. **Tel** 011 44 51 644 6400.
**Desc:** Telex service for the cotton industry.

US
**COTTON COUNTS ITS CUSTOMERS.** **Main/Corp** National Cotton Council of America. Utilization Research Division. Market Research Section. Periodical. English. National Cotton Council, PO Box 12285, Memphis TN 38112. **Tel** (901)274-9030.
**Ind/Abst** Predicasts Forecasts.

US/0090-2462
**COTTON DIGEST INTERNATIONAL, THE.** [Cotton dig. int.]. **VFOAT** Cotton Digest. (19??)-. Periodical. English. Twelve times a year. $40.00 one year; $60.00 two years. Cotton Digest International, PO Box 820768, Houston TX 77282. **Tel** (713)977-1644, FAX (713)467-6935. **(Subscription address:** P.O. Box 820768, Houston, TX 77282-0768**)** **ED** Elizabeth E. Abbey. **CODEN** CTDGAK. **Ad Acc, Adv Mgr:** Anderson. **Circ:** 5,500.
**Desc:** Represented merchants, ginners, transportation banks, commodity brokers, ports, wholesale and compress that deal with cotton in the US and around the world.
**Ind/Abst** Text. Technol. Dig.

US/0566-5469
**COTTON FIBER AND PROCESSING TEST RESULTS.** English. ir. $11.00. Agricultural Marketing Service Test Cotton Division, PO Box 67, Clemson SC 29631. **LC** TS1542; .U35. **DD** 677/.21/305. Documents available from Documents on Demand. ***Continues*** *United States. Consumer and Marketing Service. Cotton Division. Cotton Fiber and Processing Results.*
**Ind/Abst** Am. Stat. Index; Text. Technol. Dig.

US/0010-9800
**COTTON GIN AND OIL MILL PRESS, THE.** [Cotton gin oil mill press]. **Added/Corp** National Cottonseed Products Association. Vol. 48, No. 10 (May 17, 1947)-. Periodical. English. bw. $7.50 (one year), $10.00 (two year), $15.00 (three year) US; $25.00 (one year), $30.00 (two year), $35.00 (three year) other. Cotton Gin & Oil Mill Press, 3638 Executive Boulevard, Mesquite TX 75149. **Tel** (214)288-7511, FAX (214)285-4881. **ED** Don Swanson. **Ad Acc. Circ:** 1,800 (ctrl). available on microfilm and microfiche from University Microfilms International (UMI). ***Continues*** *Cotton and Cotton Oil Press.*
**Desc:** This is primarily a publication pertaining to the cotton and oilseed industry.
**Ind/Abst** AGRICOLA; Text. Technol. Dig.

US/0070-0673
**COTTON INTERNATIONAL.** [Cotton int.]. (1970)-. Periodical. English. an. $21.00 US; $22.50 other. Meister Publishing Company, 37733 Euclid Avenue, Willoughby OH 44094-5992. **Tel** (216)942-2000, (800)572-7740, FAX (216)942-0662. **LC** TS1550; .C825. **DD** 677/2/05. **[CCC].** ***Continues*** *Cotton (International Ed.), 1059-1850.*
**Desc:** Focused on the international market for cotton. Covers a variety of information on growing, harvesting, production technology, and market trends for the worldwide cotton industry.
**Ind/Abst** AGRICOLA [Full Cov.]; Text. Technol. Dig.

US
**COTTON: MONTHLY REVIEW OF THE WORLD SITUATION.** **Main/Corp** International Cotton Advisory Committee. (Aug. 1949)-. Periodical. English. mo. $50.00 US; $70.00 Argentina, Australia, Belgium, Brazil, Cameroon, Chad, China, Taiwan, Colombia, Cote D'Ivoire, Denmark, Finland, Egypt, France, Germany, Greece, Guatemala, India, Iran, Israel, Italy, Japan, Republic of Korea, Mexico, Netherlands, Nicaragua, Norway, Pakistan, Paraguay, Peru, Philippines, Poland, Russia, Senegal, South Africa, Spain, Sudan, Sweden, Switzerland, Syria, Tanzania, Turkey, Uganda, UK, Uzbekistan, and Zimbabwe; $135.00 other. International Cotton Advisory Committee, 1629 K Street NW, Suite 702, Washington DC 20006. **Tel** (202)463-6660, FAX 463-6950.
**Ind/Abst** Predicasts Forecasts.

UK
**COTTON OUTLOOK.** Periodical. English. wk. $715.82 North America; $1063.67, £509.00 Europe and USSR; $973.31, £465.76 Middle East; $1002.06, £479.52 Far East and Southeast Asia; $919.48, £440.00 UK; $980.91, £469.40 other. Outlook Ltd, Outlook House, 458 New Chester Road Rockferry 2AE England. **Tel** (011 44) 51 644-6400. ***Continues*** *Cotton and General Economic Review.*
**Desc:** Review of events in cotton around the world.

Includes production, consumption, trading and cotton price information from the world's foremost private source.

US/0098-7026
**COTTON QUALITY CROP.** (COTTON QUALITY CROP OF ...). **Added/Corp** United States. Agricultural Marketing Service. Cotton Division. United States. Consumer and Marketing Service. Cotton Division. (1960)-. English. an. $11.00 US; $12.00 Canada; $13.00 other. US Department of Agriculture / Tennessee, Agricultural Marketing Service, 4841 Summer Avenue, Memphis TN 38122. **Tel** (901)766-2934. **LC** TS1565.U6; C65. **DD** 677/.21/30973.

US
**COTTON QUALITY. SUPPLY, DISAPPEARANCE, CARRY-OVER. See** Agriculture-Crop Production and Soil.

AT/0312-5211
**CSIRO TEXTILE NEWS.** [CSIRO text. news]. **Main/Corp** Commonwealth Scientific and Industrial Research Organization. Wool Research Laboratories. No. 1 (Nov. 1975)-. Periodical. English. ir. Free on request. CSIRO Publications, PO Box 89, 314 Albert Street, East Melborne Victoria 3002 Australia. **Tel** 011 61 3 4187333, 4187217, FAX 011 61 3 4190459, telex AA 30236. ***Supersedes*** *C.S.I.R.O. Wool Textile News.*
**Ind/Abst** Art Archaeol. Tech. Abstr.; Text. Technol. Dig.; World Text. Abstr.

AT
**CSIRO TEXTILE PHYSICS. Added/Corp** Commonwealth Scientific and Industrial Research Organization (Australia). Division of Textile Physics. **VFOAT** Textile Physics. (19??)-. Periodical. English. an. CSIRO Publications, PO Box 89, 314 Albert Street, East Melborne Victoria 3002 Australia. **Tel** 011 61 3 4187333, 4187217, FAX 011 61 3 4190459, telex AA 30236. **LC** TS1547; .C78. **DD** 677/.317.

US
**CURRENT INDUSTRIAL REPORTS. M22P, CONSUMPTION ON THE COTTON SYSTEM AND STOCKS / U.S. DEPARTMENT OF COMMERCE, ECONOMICS AND STATISTICS ADMINISTRATION, BUREAU OF THE CENSUS.** ***Title Change.*** **See** Agriculture-Crop Production and Soil.

US
**CURRENT INDUSTRIAL REPORTS. MQ22P, CONSUMPTION ON THE COTTON SYSTEM AND STOCKS.** ***Title Change.*** **Added/Corp** United States. Bureau of the Census. **VFOAT** Consumption on the Cotton System and Stocks. 1st quarter (1991)-(1991). Government Publication. English. mo (summary issue). US Department of Commerce / Bureau of the Census, Data User Services Division, Customer Services, Washington DC 20233-0800. **Tel** (301)763-4100. Documents available from Documents on Demand. ***Continues*** *Current Industrial Reports. M22P, Consumption on the Cotton System and Stocks, 0731-020x.* ***Continued by*** *Current Industrial Reports. M22P, Consumption on the Cotton System and Stocks (Washington, D.C.).*
**Ind/Abst** Am. Stat. Index.

US
**DAILY SPOT COTTON QUOTATIONS / UNITED STATES DEPARTMENT OF AGRICULTURE, AGRICULTURAL MARKETING SERVICE, COTTON DIVISION. See** Agriculture-Crop Production and Soil.

AT
**DALGETY FARMERS' ANNUAL WOOL DIGEST. See** Textiles-Abstracting, Bibliographies and Statistics.

US/0363-5252
**DAVISON'S "SALESMAN'S BOOK.".** 63rd Ed. (1974)-. English. an. $60.00. Davison Publishing Company, PO Box 477, Ridgewood NJ 07451. **Tel** (201)445-3135, FAX (201)445-4397. **ED** Bruce W. Nealy. **LC** TS1312; .D3. **DD** 338.4/7/677002573. **Ad Acc.** ctrl circ. ***Continues*** *Davison's Textile Directory for Executives and Salesmen.*
**Desc:** Reference for anyone selling, servicing or supplying the textile industry.

US/0070-2951
**DAVISON'S TEXTILE "BLUE BOOK".** (1888)-. English. an. $124.95 (east of Mississippi River), $129.00 (west of Mississippi) US; $130.00 Canada; $138.00 Europe; $140.00 Asia, Australia, and South Africa. Davison Publishing Company, PO Box 477, Ridgewood NJ 07451. **Tel** (201)445-3135, FAX (201)445-4397. **ED** Bruce W. Nealy. **LC** TS1312; .B6. **DD** 677. Index available. **Ad Acc, Adv Mgr:** Carol Nealy. available on CD-ROM.
**Desc:** Published for those interested in the textile industry in the United States, Canada and Mexico. Textile mills, dyers, finishers and bleachers are arranged alphabetically by city and state, with names of personnel, machinery, types of goods manufactured or processed, number of employees, branches and sales outlets. Mills are classified by product.

US
**DAVISON'S TEXTILE BLUE BOOK. EUROPE. VFOAT** Textile Blue Book. Europe; Europe. 1st Ed. (1991)-. English. an. $125.00. Davison Publishing Company, PO Box 477, Ridgewood NJ 07451. **Tel** (201)445-3135, FAX (201)445-4397. **LC** HD9865.A1; D38. **DD** 338.7/677/002944.
**Desc:** Comprehensive directory of European textile companies listing weavers, knitters, spinners, non-woven mills, dyers and finishers. Hoisery and carpet mills are also included.

US
**DAVISON'S TEXTILE BLUE BOOK : UNITED STATES AND CANADA. VFOAT** Textile Blue Book. 26th Annual Edition (1913-1914)-. English. an. $90.00. PO Box 477, Ridgewood NJ 07451. **Tel** (201)445-3135, FAX (201)445-4397. **LC** TS1312; .B6. Index available. **Ad Acc. Circ:** 5,000. available on diskette; available on labels. ***Continues*** *Blue Book Textile Directory of the United States and Canada;* ***Absorbed*** *Dockham's American Report and Directory of the Textile Manufacturer and Dry Goods Trade.*
**Ind/Abst** Text. Technol. Dig.

US/0734-4708
**DAVISON'S TEXTILE BUYERS GUIDE (1980).** (DAVISON'S TEXTILE BUYERS GUIDE.). [Davison's text. buyers guide]. **VFOAT** Davison Textile Buyers Guide. (1980)-. Consumer Publication. English. an. $54.25 (east of Mississippi), $59.00 (west of Mississippi) US. Davison Publishing Company, PO Box 477, Ridgewood NJ 07451. **Tel** (201)445-3135, FAX (201)445-4397. **LC** HD9850.3; .D39. **DD** 681/.7677/029473. ***Continues*** *Davison's Textile Buyers Guide and Buyer's Guide, 0730-5990.*
**Desc:** Lists companies that supply new and used equipment, or that repair, rebuild or purchase used equipment.

US/0069-0740
**DIRECTORY AND REPORT / CARPET AND RUG INSTITUTE. Main/Corp** Carpet and Rug Institute. 1969/70-. Directory. English. an. $10.00. Carpet and Rug Institute, Box 2048, Dalton GA 30720. **Tel** (404)278-3176, FAX (404)278-8835. **LC** HD9937.U5; C35A. **DD** 338.4/7/67764302573.

SZ
**DIRECTORY - INTERNATIONAL TEXTILE MANUFACTURERS FEDERATION. Main/Corp** International Textile Manufacturers Federation. 9th Ed. (1979)-. Directory. English. be. International Textile Manufacturers Federation, Postfach 289, CH-8039 Zurich Switzerland. **Tel** 011 41 1 2017080, 011 41 1 2017747, telex 56798 ITMF CH. **LC** HD9870.3; .I14. **DD** 338.7/677/0025. ***Continues*** *Directory / International Federation of Cotton and Allied Textile Industries.*

II
**DIRECTORY OF WOOL, HOSIERY & FABRICS. VAT** Directory of Wool, Hosiery and Fabrics. 1972-. Directory. English. $3.00. Manek Mahal, 6th Floor/90 Veer Nariman Road, Churchgate Bombay-20 India. **LC** HD9906.I4; I5. **DD** 380.1/45/6773102554. ***Continues*** *India & Pakistan Wool, Hosiery & Fabrics.*

UK/0012-3811
**DISPOSABLES AND NONWOVENS.** [Dispos. nonwovens]. **VFOAT** Disposables & Nonwovens. Vol. 1-5, (July 1970)-. Periodical. English. Six times a year. £25.00 UK; £35.00 other; $70.00 US. Chandler Publications Ltd, 10 South Street, Totnes Devon TQ9 5DZ England. **Tel** 0803 864668, FAX 0803 805049, telex 42928. **ED** J. R. D. Heming. **LC** TS1828; .D53. **Bk Rev. Ad Acc. Circ:** 2,000.
**Desc:** A news sheet for the disposable markets covering manufacture, formulation, conversion and industrial news.
**Ind/Abst** Nonwovens Abstr.; Text. Technol. Dig.; World Text. Abstr.

GW/0011-507X
**DNZ INTERNATIONAL.** (DNZ INTERNATIONAL; DIE NAHMASCHINEN-ZEITUNG.). [DNZ int.]. **Added/Corp** Internationale Vereinigung des Nahmaschinenhandels und-Handwerks. **VFOAT** Nahmaschinen-Zeitung; Sewing Maching Review; Revue de la Machine a Coudre. (1966)-. Periodical. German (summaries and/or abstracts in English and French). mo. DM140.00. Bielefelder Verlagsanstalt KG, Niederwall 53, D 33602 Bielefeld Germany. **Tel** 011 49 521 595520. ctrl circ.
**Ind/Abst** World Text. Abstr.

US/0012-6802
**DRYCLEANER NEWS.** [Dryclean. news]. (19??)-. Periodical. English. mo (12 issues). Free to trade organizations; $36.00 other. Zackin Publications Inc, PO Box 2180, Waterbury CT 06722. **Tel** (203)755-0158. **ED** Jack Goldberg. **DD** 338. **Bk Rev. Ad Acc. Circ:** 9,000 (ctrl).
**Desc:** Business, industry and technical advice for drycleaners in the Northeast.

CN
**ESTIMATED POUNDAGE EQUIVALENTS. Main/Corp** Canadian Textiles Institute. **VFOAT** Study of Canadian Imports of Manufactured Textiles. 1975/76-. English. an. Canadian Textiles Institute, 1002 Commerce House, 1808 Beaver Hall Hill, Montreal Quebec H2Z 1T6 Canada. ***Continues in part*** *Canadian Textiles Institute. Pounds and Square Yards Study, 0318-3408.*

UK
**FABRIC INTELLIGENCE : THE INTERNATIONAL FABRIC DIRECTORY.** Directory. English. an. £75.00. Sterling Publications Ltd., PO Box 799, Brunel House, London W2 1XR England. **Tel** 011 44 71 2580066, FAX 011 44 71 4026441, telex 295819 ESPEEL G. **ED** Sue Peverill.

US/0733-1843
**FABRICNEWS.** [Fabricnews]. **Added/Corp** Arthur J. Imparato Associates. **VAT** Fabric News. Vol. 1, No. 9 (June/July 1980)-. Periodical. English. Twice a year. FabricNews, 80 Park Avenue, Suite 6K, New York NY 10016. **Tel** (212)697-5780. ***Continues*** *Fabricnews to the Trade, 0199-493X.*

US/1045-0483
**FABRICS & ARCHITECTURE. See** Architecture.

US/0097-2495
**FABRICS-FASHIONS. Main/Corp** IFI Research Center. No. FF-219- 1973-. English. bm. Available to members only. International Fabricare Institute, 12251 Tech Road, Silver Spring MD 20904. **Tel** (301)622-1900. **ED** Lynn Schweizer. **LC** TP932.3; .I56C. **DD** 667/.12/05. **Pr Rev. Circ:** 10,000 (ctrl). ***Continues*** *Fabrics-Fashions.*
**Desc:** Textile bulletin of identification , uses and proper handling and cleaning. Also includes problems and spotting procedure.

US/1067-7062
**FAIRCHILD'S TEXTILE & APPAREL FINANCIAL DIRECTORY.** [Fairchild's text. appar. financ. dir.]. **VFOAT** Fairchild's Textile and Apparel Financial Directory; Textile & Apparel Financial Directory; Textile and Apparel Financial Directory. (1974)-. English. an (published in October). $102.90 Alaska, Hawaii & Puerto Rico; $93.95 other US; $111.85 other. Fairchild Publications Inc, 7 West 34th Street, 4th Floor, New York NY 10001. **Tel** (212)630-4230. **ED** Robert Benjamin. **DD** 338. **Circ:** 1,000 (ctrl). ***Continues*** *Fairchild's Textile & Apparel Financial Fact Book & Directory.*
**Desc:** Presents financial profiles of more than 200 publicly-owned textile and apparel manufacturers.
**Ind/Abst** Text. Technol. Dig.

CC/0254-6469
**FANGZHI GONGCHENG XUEKAN.** (FANG CHIH KUNG CHENG HSUEH KAN.). [Fangzhi gongcheng xuekan]. **Added/Corp** Feng-Chia Kung Shang Hsueh Yuan. Fang Chih Kung Cheng Yen Chiu So. **VFOAT** Journal of Textile Engineering. (1973)-. Periodical. Chinese. an. **LC** TS1300; .F328. **DD** 677/.005. **CODEN** FCKKDI. Documents available from CASDDS.
**Ind/Abst** Chem. Abstr.

CC/0251-0804
**FANGZHI KEXUE.** (FANG CHIH KO HSUEH. TEXTILE SCIENCE.). [Fangzhi kexue]. **Added/Corp** Feng-Chia Kung Shang Hsueh Yuan Fang Chih Cheng Yen Chiu Hsueh Hui. **VFOAT** Textile Science. (May 1965)-. Chinese. **LC** TS1300; .F327. **CODEN** FCKHD9. Documents available from CASDDS.
**Ind/Abst** Chem. Abstr.

CH/0253-9721
**FANGZHI XUEBAO.** (FANG CHIH HSUEH PAO.). [Fangzhi xuebao]. **VFOAT** Journal of China Textile Engineering Association; Journal of Textile Research. Began in 1980. Academic Scholarly Publication. Chinese (Chinese). mo. NT$0.40. Science Press, 16 Donghuangchenggen North Street, Beijing 100707, People's Republic of China. **Tel** 011 86 1 4019821, 011 86 1 4010642, FAX 011 86 1 4012180, 011 86 1 4019810, telex 210147. **LC** TS1300; .F3245 . **DD** 677/.005. **CODEN** FCHPDI. available on microfilm from University Microfilms International (UMI). Documents available from CASDDS.
**Ind/Abst** Chem. Abstr.; World Text. Abstr.

US
**FASHION INTERNATIONAL. See** Clothing Industry and Fashion.

CN/0318-8701
**FASHION TEXTILES MODE.** ***Title Change.*** **VFOAT** Textiles Mode. Vol. 1 (Summer 1973)-?. Periodical. Multiple languages (English and French). qt. Fashion Textiles Mode, 3445 de Gaspe/Suite 101, Montreal Quebec H2T 3B2 Canada. **DD** 677/.0286/0971. ***Continued by*** *Fem Ego, 0318-871X.*

US
**FIBER ORGANON.** **Added/Corp** Fiber Economics Bureau. Vol. 60, No. 4 (Apr. 1989)-. Periodical. English. mo. $175.00, $75.00 (schools & non-profit). Fiber Economics Bureau, Inc., 101 Eisenhower Parkway, Roseland NJ 07068. **LC** HD9929.5.U6; T4. **DD** 338.4/76774/021. **CODEN** FIOREY. ***Continues** Textile Organon (1952), 0040-5132.*
**Ind/Abst** F&S Index Plus Text, Int. [Select. Cov.].

US/0748-0733
**FIBER WORLD.** [Fiber world]. Began with Issue for Jan. (1984)-. Periodical. English. qt. (only available as an insert in Americas Textiles International). Billian Publishing Inc., 2100 Powers Ferry Road, Atlanta GA 30339. **Tel** (404)955-5656, FAX (404)952-0669. **DD** 338. ***Continues** Fiber Producer, 0361-4921.*

US/0164-324X
**FIBERARTS. See** Sewing and Needlework.

US/0198-8387
**FIBERSCOPE.** [Fiberscope]. Vol. 1 (1979)-. Periodical. English. an. $18.00. Interweave Press, 201 East 4th Street, Loveland CO 80537. **Tel** (303)669-7672. **ED** L. Jane Patrick. **LC** N6494.F47; F53. **DD** 746/.09/04. **Bk Rev**. **Ad Acc. Circ:** 35,000.
**Desc:** Handwoven designs, full color photography, complete project instructions to encourage the beginner and challenge the experienced weaver. In-depth features, outstanding craftsmen.

US/8756-7121
**FIBERWORKS QUARTERLY.** ***Ceased.*** Vol. 1, No. 1 (1985)-(1993). Periodical. English. Four times a year (Jan., Apr., July, Oct.). Fiberworks Quarterly, PO Box 49770, Austin TX 78765. **Tel** (512)343-6112. **DD** 746. **Bk Rev**, (Qty: 25). **Ad Acc**.

US/0015-0541
**FIBRE CHEMISTRY.** [Fibre chem.]. **Added/Corp** Consultants Bureau. Vol. 1 (Jan./Feb. 1969)-. Trade Publication. English (Russian). bm. $1035.00 US; $1210.00 other. Consultants Bureau, A Division of Plenum Publishing Corporation, 233 Spring Street, New York NY 10013. **Tel** (212)620-8000, (212)620-8466, FAX (212)463-0742, telex 23/421139. **ED** G. I. Kudryavtsev. **LC** TS1548.5; .F514. **CODEN** FICYAP. **[CCC]**. Index available. available on microfilm and microfiche from University Microfilms International (UMI). Documents available from Article Express International.
**Desc:** Presents important and accurate appraisal of recent developments in theoretical and practical aspects of the basic science, engineering and textile technology of the synthetic fibre industry.
**Ind/Abst** AGRICOLA [Full Cov.]; Bioeng. Abstr.; Ei Page One; EMBASE; Eng. Index Annu.; Text. Technol. Dig.

US/0046-3728
**FIBRE MARKET NEWS.** [Fibre mark. news]. (19??)-. Periodical. English. wk (published every Fri.). $115.00 US; $145.00 Canada; $170.00 other; $297.00 airmail. GIE Publishing Company, 4012 Bridge Avenue, Cleveland OH 44113. **Tel** (216)961-4130, (800)456-0707, FAX (216)961-0364. **ED** Daniel Sandowal. **Ad Acc, Adv Mgr:** M Gladstone. **Circ:** 1,500.
**Desc:** Covers all aspects of recycling secondary fibres. Offers market reviews and prices.

UK
**FIBRE REPORT.** **Added/Corp** Wigglesworth & Co. Limited. (19??)-. Periodical. English. Six times a year (Jan., Mar., May, July, Sept., Nov.). £25.00. Wigglesworth and Company Ltd, 69 Southwark Bridge Road, London SE1 0NG England. **Tel** (011 71 4031919, telex 8952396. **ED** V. J. Landon. ctrl circ.

US/0276-3389
**FINISHED BROADWOVEN FABRIC PRODUCTION. See** Manufacturing.

US/0272-5509
**FINISHED FABRICS. PRODUCTION, INVENTORIES, AND UNFILLED ORDERS. See** Manufacturing.

US/0361-6320
**FLAME RETARDANCY OF POLYMERIC MATERIALS.** [Flame retardancy polym. mater.]. Vol. 1 (1973)-. English. an. $275.00. Business Communications Inc., 25 Van Zant Street, Suite 13, Norwalk CT 06855. **Tel** (203)853-4266. **ED** W. C. Kuryla. **CODEN** FRPMBG. Documents available from CASDDS.
**Ind/Abst** Chem. Abstr. (1973-1979).

US/0882-4983
**GEOTECHNICAL FABRICS REPORT.** [Geotech. fabr. rep.]. **Added/Corp** Industrial Fabrics Association International. Vol. 1, No. 1 (Summer 1983)-. Periodical. English. ir (9 times per year). $30.00 US; $35.00 Canada and Mexico; $42.00 other. Industrial Fabrics Association International, 345 Cedar Street, Suite 800, St Paul MN 55101. **Tel** (612)222-2508, (800)225-4324, FAX (612)222-8215, telex TWX (612)222-7862. **ED** Peter Ausenhus. **DD** 677. cum. index. **Bk Rev**. **Ad Acc. Circ:** 12,000 (ctrl). Documents available from Article Express International.
**Desc:** Gives detailed reports and case histories on latest geosynthetic product developments, techniques and applications. Written for the civil engineer, installer, designer and specifier.
**Ind/Abst** AGRICOLA; Ei Page One; Eng. Index Annu.; Fluid Abstr., Civil Eng.; Fluid Abstr. Proc. Eng.; FLUIDEX; Geotech. Abstr.; Nonwovens Abstr.; Text. Technol. Dig.; World Text. Abstr.

UK/0142-0798
**HALI.** (HALI; THE INTERNATIONAL JOURNAL OF ORIENTAL CARPETS AND TEXTILES.). [Hali]. **VFOAT** Hali. Vol. 1 (Spring 1978)-. Periodical. English (German). Six times a year. £56.00 UK; DM178.00 Germany; £60.00 Europe; $104.00 US; $140.00 or £75.00 other. HALI, Kingsgate House, Kingsgate Place, London NW6 4TA England. **Tel** 011 44 71 3289341, FAX 011 44 71 3725924. **ED** Alan Marcuson. **LC** NK2808; .H17. **DD** 746.7/5/05. **Bk Rev**. **Ad Acc. Circ:** 15,000.
**Desc:** Devoted to the history and market for antique oriental rugs and textiles.
**Ind/Abst** AGRICOLA; Art Archaeol. Tech. Abstr.; ARTbibliogr. Mod. (1984-); Ethnoarts Index; Index Islam. Lit.

US/0198-8212
**HANDWOVEN.** [Handwoven]. (1979)-. Periodical. English. ir (5 issues). $21.00. Interweave Press, 201 East 4th Street, Loveland CO 80537. **Tel** (303)669-7672. **ED** Linda C. Ligon. **LC** TT848; .H356. **DD** 746.1/4/05. **Bk Rev**. **Ad Acc. Circ:** 32,000. ***Absorbed** Interweave, 0198-8220.*
**Desc:** Presents handwoven designs to encourage the beginner and challenge the experienced weaver. Includes full-color photography, complete instructions, yarn recommendations, history and more.
**Ind/Abst** Index Inf. (1980-).

KO/0253-6420
**HANGUG SEMNYU GONHAGHOIJI.** (HAN'GUK SOMYU KONGHAKHOE CHI.). [Hangug semnyu gonhaghoiji]. **Main/Corp** Han'guk Somyu Konghakhoe. **VFOAT** Journal of the Korean Society of Textile Engineers and Chemists. Academic Scholarly Publication. Korean (summaries and/or abstracts in English). **LC** TS1300; .H36A. **CODEN** HSKCDQ. Documents available from CASDDS. ***Continues** Somyu Konghakhoe Chi.*
**Ind/Abst** Chem. Abstr.

KO
**HAN'GUK UIRYU HAKHOE CHI. See** Clothing Industry and Fashion.

GW/0343-6853
**HAUSTEX.** (19??)-. German. Twelve times a year. DM108.00 Europe; DM168.00 other. Westdeutsche Verlagsanstalt GmbH, Ahmser Strasse 190, 32052 Herford Germany. **Tel** 011 49 05221 7750, FAX 011 49 05221 775 215. **(Subscription address:** Westdeutsche Verlagsanstalt GmbH, Postfach 3054, D 32046 Herford Germany.**)** ***Continues in part** Heimtex Aktuell, Haustex, 0172-2409; **Continues** Aussteuer, Bett & Couch, 0004-8259; **Absorbed** Das Betten-Magazin, 0005-9285.*

FR/0989-4985
**HEBDO-TEX, L'.** (1988)-. Periodical. French. Eleven times a year. 411.36F France; 450.00F other. Editions Belouze, BP 5/68 rue des Tricots, 92144 Clamart Cedex France. **Tel** 011 33 1 46382000, FAX 011 33 1 46388774. **UDC** 677 : 331.

UK/0144-5871
**HIGH PERFORMANCE TEXTILES.** [High perform. text.]. **Added/Corp** Shirley Institute. Vol. 1, No. 1 (July 1980)-. Periodical. English. Twelve times a year. $404.00 The Americas; £271.00 other. Elsevier Advanced Technology, An Imprint of Elsevier Science Ltd., The Boulevard, Langford Lane, Kidlington, Oxford OX5 1GB United Kingdom. **Tel** 011 44 865 843000, 011 44 865 843699, FAX 011 44 865 843010. **(Subscription address:** Elsevier Science Ltd. Oxford Fulfillment Centre, PO Box 800, Kidlington, Oxford OX5 1DX United Kingdom.**)** **ED** Peter Lennox-Kerr. **[CCC]**. available on microfilm from University Microfilms International (UMI); available on an online database (file 636/Full-Text) from DIALOG.
**Desc:** Provides the essential link between textile user and manufacturer, allowing each to gauge the needs and capabilities of the other and to keep up with the latest research across the field.
**Ind/Abst** AGRICOLA; Art Archaeol. Tech. Abstr.; F&S Index Plus Text, Int. [Select. Cov.]; Nonwovens Abstr.; PTS Newsl. Database [Full Txt.]; Text. Technol. Dig.; World Text. Abstr.

IT
**HOME.** Italian (English). mo (10 issues). L70000.00 Italy; L95000.00 other. Editoriale Galfa, Viale Monza 57, 20125 Milan Italy. **Tel** 011 39 2 2891452, FAX 011 39 2 2840574, telex 315614. **ED** Carla M. Braccini. **Ad Acc, Adv Mgr:** Ernesto Cipriani. **Circ:** 8,000 (ctrl).

US/0195-3184
**HOME TEXTILES TODAY.** [Home text. today]. Vol. 1 (Sept. 1979)-. Periodical. English. wk (50 issues). $89.97 US, Canada & Mexico; $250.00 (surface mail), $495.00 (airmail) other. Cahners Publishing Company, 249 West 17th Street, New York NY 10011. **Tel** (212)645-0067, FAX (212)242-6987. **(Subscription address:** Cahners Publishing Company / North Carolina, Circulation Department, PO Box 2754, High Point NC 27261-2754.**)** **ED** Marge Axelrod. **DD** 338. **Ad Acc. Circ:** 11,000. available on microfilm from University Microfilms International (UMI).
**Desc:** Edited for senior management in all retail channels of home textile distribution. The focus is on the business and fashion news that home textile industry leaders need in order to make timely and accurate decisions regarding their merchandising and marketing objectives.

US/0742-8065
**HOSIERY NEWS / NATIONAL ASSOCIATION OF HOSIERY MANUFACTURERS.** [Hosiery news]. Vol. 61, No. 6 (Apr. 1982)-. Periodical. English. mo. National Association of Manufacturer, 447 S Sharon Amity Road, Charlotte NC 28211. **LC** HD9969.H6; H6. **DD** 338.4/76873/0973. ***Continues** Hosiery Newsletter, 0018-540X.*
**Ind/Abst** Text. Technol. Dig.; World Text. Abstr.

US
**HOSIERY STATISTICS / NAHM.** **Added/Corp** National Association of Hosiery Manufacturers (U.S.). (19??)-. English. $40.00. National Association of Hosiery Manufacturers, 447 South Sharon Amity Road, Charlotte NC 28211. **LC** HD9969.H8; U55. ***Continues** Quarterly Statistical Bulletin of the Hosiery Industry.*
**Ind/Abst** Predicasts Forecasts.

UK/0952-0708
**ICA. INTERNATIONAL COLOUR AUTHORITY.** [ICA, Int. colour auth.]. **VFOAT** International Colour Authority. (1968)-. Multiple languages. sa. $920.00 US; £440.00 Europe; £460.00 other. International Textile Benjamin Dent Ltd, 23 Bloomsbury Square, London WC1A 2P England. **Tel** 011 44 71 637 2211, FAX 011 44 71 637 2248, telex 8954884.
**Desc:** Color prediction service published 24 months ahead of the season.

UK/0269-1450
**ICB CARPET DIRECTORY.** 4th Ed. (1986)-. Directory. English. £61.05 UK; £66.31 Irish Republic; £74.74 Europe; £84.21 (surface mail), £106.31 (airmail) US. World Textile Publications Ltd, Caidan House, Canal Road, Altrincham Cheshire WA14 1TD England. **Tel** 011 44 061 9763636. ***Continues** ICB Directory.*

UK/0268-2966
**ICB. INTERNATIONAL CARPET BULLETIN.** [ICB, Int. carpet bull.]. **VFOAT** International Carpet Bulletin. (1970)-. Newsletter. English. ir. £88.89 UK; £105.56 Europe; £144.45 other. World Textile Publications Ltd., 76 Kirkgate, Bradford West Yorkshire, BD1 1TB England. **Tel** 011 44 274 726357, 011 44 274 731907, FAX 011 44 274 735045, telex 517617 WOOLMN G. **(Subscription address:** W R Publications Ltd., Caidan House, Canal Road, Altrincham, Chesire WA14 1TD UK**)** **Ad Acc, Adv Mgr:** Julie Smith, **Tel** same as publisher.

US
**INDA JOURNAL OF NONWOVENS RESEARCH.** English. qt. $48.00 (Inda members), $60.00 (nonmembers) US; $96.00 (other). Rodman Publishing Corp, 17 S Franklin Turnpike, Ramsey NJ 07446. **Tel** (201)825-2552.
**Ind/Abst** Abstr. Bull. Inst. Pap. Sci. Tech.

II/0971-0426
**INDIAN JOURNAL OF FIBRE & TEXTILE RESEARCH.** [Indian j. fibre text. res.]. **Added/Corp** Council of Scientific & Industrial Research (India). Publications & Information Directorate. **VFOAT** Indian Journal of Fibre and Textile Research. Vol. 15, No. 1 (March 1990)-. Academic Scholarly Publication. English. qt. $80.00. Council of Scientific & Industrial Research, Publications & Information Director, Hillside Road, New Delhi 110012 India. **Tel** FAX 011 91 11 5731353. **(Subscription address:** Prints India, 11 Darya Ganj, New Delhi, 110002 India, (Phone: 011 91 11 3268645)**)** **LC** TS1540; .I52. **CODEN** IJFRET. Documents available from The Genuine Article, CASDDS. ***Continues** Indian Journal of Textile Research, 0377-8436.*
**Ind/Abst** Abstr. Bull. Inst. Pap. Sci. Tech.; Chem. Abstr.; Res. Alert [Full Cov.].

II/0019-6355
**INDIAN SILK.** **Added/Corp** India (Republic). Central Silk Board. Vol. 1 (May 1962)-. Periodical. English. mo. $40.00. Central Sericulture Research & Training Institute, Central Silk Board, Manandavadi Road, Mysore 570 008 India. **Tel** 0821 21406 24408. **(Subscription address:** Prints India, 11 Darya Ganj, New Delhi, 110002 India, (Phone: 011 91 11 3268645)**)** **LC** HD9910.1; .I45.

II/0537-0078
**INDIAN TEXTILE BULLETIN.** **Added/Corp** India (Republic) Office of the Textile Commissioner. (1955)-. Bulletin. English. qt. Price varies. Government of India / Ministry of Urban Development, Department of Publication, Civil Lines, Delhi 110054 India. **(Subscription address:** Prints India, 11 Darya Ganj, New Delhi, 110002 India, (Phone: 011 91 11 3268645)**)** **LC** HD9850.1; .I54.

II/0019-6436
**INDIAN TEXTILE JOURNAL, THE.** [Indian text. j.]. (1890)-. Periodical. English. mo. $55.00. Indian Textile Journal Pvt Ltd Fort, Bombay 400 023 India. **(Subscription address:** Prints India, 11 Darya Ganj, New Delhi, 110002 India, (Phone: 011 91 11 3268645)) **ED** S Laxminazain. **LC** TS1300; .I55. **CODEN** INTJAV. Index available. **Ad Acc.** Documents available from CASDDS. ***Absorbed*** *Indian Import and Export Trades Journal; Indian Industries & Power.*
**Ind/Abst** Art Archaeol. Tech. Abstr.; Chem. Abstr. (1890-1977); Cot. Trop. Fibr. Abstr. Bibliogr.; World Text. Abstr.

IT/0019-7491
**INDUSTRIA COTONIERA.** [Ind. coton.]. **Added/Corp** Associazione Cotoniera Italiana. Vol. 1 (1966)-. Periodical. Italian. ir (8 issues per year). L88000. IASAT, Viale Sarca 223, 20126 Milan, Italy. **Tel** 011 39 2 66103838. **ED** Roberto Diegi. cum. index. **Ad Acc. Circ:** 2,000. ***Supersedes*** *Rivista Dell'Industria Cotoniera Italiana.*
**Desc:** Publishes technical, economic, and trade union information. Also includes other matters of interest concerning the cotton industry.
**Ind/Abst** World Text. Abstr.

IT
**INDUSTRIA TESSILE.** (19??)-. Italian. mo. Free on request. Ediba, Via Ponte Rotto, 21056 Induno Olona, Va Italy. **Tel** 0332 201101.

RM
**INDUSTRIA USOARA.** (INDUSTRIA USOARA. TEXTILE, TRICOTAJE, CONFECTII TEXTILE.). [Ind. usoara]. **Added/Corp** Institutul de Cercetari Textile (Romania) Romania. Ministerul Industriei Usoare. **VFOAT** Textile, Tricotaje, Confectii Textile; Industria Usoara - Textile; Revista Industria Usoara. Textile, Tricotaje, Confectii Textle. Vol. 25, No. 7 (July 1974)-. Academic Scholarly Publication. Romanian (summaries and/or abstracts in English, French, German and Russian). bm (6 issues). DM172.00. **(Subscription address:** Kubon & Sagner, ABT Zeitschriftenimport, D 80328 Munich Germany.) **LC** TS1300; .I58. **CODEN** IUSAAE. Documents available from CASDDS. ***Continues*** *Industria Usoara. Seria A. Textila.*
**Desc:** Studies and articles in the field of the light industry.
**Ind/Abst** Art Archaeol. Tech. Abstr.; Ceram. Abstr.; Chem. Abstr.; Saf. Health Work; World Text. Abstr.

US/0019-8307
**INDUSTRIAL FABRIC PRODUCTS REVIEW.** [Ind. fabr. prod. rev.]. **Added/Corp** Industrial Fabrics Association International. Canvas Products Association International. V. 42, No. 10 (Feb. 1966)-. Trade Publication. English. mo (except 2 issues in April). $34.00 US; $39.00 Canada and Mexico; $90.00 other. Industrial Fabrics Association International, 345 Cedar Street, Suite 800, St Paul MN 55101. **Tel** (612)222-2508, (800)225-4324, FAX (612)222-8215, telex TWX (612)222-7862. **ED** Sue Hagen. **LC** HD9938; .U5C3. **DD** 677. Index available. **Bk Rev. Ad Acc. Circ:** 6,000 (ctrl). ***Continues*** *Canvas Products Review.*
**Desc:** Trade magazine for end product manufacturers and suppliers in industrial fabrics industry.
**Ind/Abst** Text. Technol. Dig.; World Text. Abstr.

US
**INDUSTRIAL FABRIC PRODUCTS REVIEW BUYERS GUIDE.** Consumer Publication. English. an. $25.00. Industrial Fabrics Association International, 345 Cedar Street, Suite 800, St Paul MN 55101. **Tel** (612)222-2508, (800)225-4324, FAX (612)222-8215, telex TWX (612)222-7862.

US/0046-9211
**INDUSTRIAL LAUNDERER.** [Ind. laund.]. **Added/Corp** Institute of Industrial Launderers. (19??)-. Periodical. English. mo. $50.00 (non-members), $30.00 (members). Institute Industrial Launderer, 1730 M Street NW, Washington DC 20036. **Tel** (202)296-6744, FAX (202)296-2309. **ED** Kenneth Koepper. **Ad Acc, Adv Mgr:** Mittie Spruill. **Circ:** 2,700 (ctrl).
**Desc:** Wide range of general management and specific how-to articles tailored to the industrial laundry industry.
**Ind/Abst** Text. Technol. Dig.

FR/0019-9176
**INDUSTRIE TEXTILE (PARIS).** (L'INDUSTRIE TEXTILE.). [Ind. text.]. (19??)-. Academic Scholarly Publication. French. mo. 690.00F France and Monaco; 950.00F other. L'Industrie Textile, 16 rue Ballu, Hall Calais, 75009 Paris France. **Tel** 011 33 1 48741596, telex 641438 EDITEXT. **ED** P S Robin. **CODEN** INTPAF. Index available. **Bk Rev. Ad Acc. Circ:** 6,000. Documents available from CASDDS.
**Ind/Abst** AGRICOLA; Art Archaeol. Tech. Abstr.; Chem. Abstr. (1885-1983); EMBASE; F&S Index Plus Text, Int. [Select. Cov.]; Nonwovens Abstr.; PROMT; Saf. Health Work; Text. Technol. Dig.; World Text. Abstr.

US
**INDUSTRY REVIEW.** **See** Textiles-Abstracting, Bibliographies and Statistics.

FR
**INFORMATION SUR LES TEXTILES SYNTHETIQUES ET CELLULOSIQUES.** **Added/Corp** International Rayon and Synthetic Fibres Committee. **VFOAT** Information on Man-Made Fibres. (1972)-. English (French and German). an. 29 rue de Courcelles, 75008 Paris France. **LC** HD9929.2.A1; I53. **DD** 338.4/76774/021. ***Continues*** *Information sur les Textiles Cellulosiques et Synthetiques.*
**Ind/Abst** Predicasts Forecasts.

US/0733-8244
**INSIDE TEXTILES.** (198?)-. Periodical. English. Twenty-four times a year. $167.00 North America; $197.00 other. Point Publishing, PO Box 1309, Point Pleasant NJ 08742. **Tel** (201)295-8258. **ED** Noreen Heimbold. **[CCC].**
**Desc:** Covers manufacturing and marketing of textiles and apparel.
**Ind/Abst** Text. Technol. Dig.

UK/0954-1438
**INTERIOR LONDON.** (INTERIOR). [InteriorLond.]. (1988)-. Periodical. English. tq (April, Aug., Dec.). $170.00. International Textile Benjamin Dent Ltd, 23 Bloomsbury Square, London WC1A 2P England. **Tel** 011 44 71 637 2211, FAX 011 44 71 637 2248, telex 8954884. **DD** 747. ***Continues*** *International Textiles Interior, 0020-8922.*

SZ/0538-6829
**INTERNATIONAL COTTON INDUSTRY STATISTICS.** **See** Textiles-Abstracting, Bibliographies and Statistics.

UK
**INTERNATIONAL DYER.** **Added/Corp** Society of Dyers and Colourists. **VFOAT** International Dyer with SDC News. Vol. 176, No. 8 (Aug. 1991)-. Periodical. English. Twelve times a year. £53.34 UK; £59.43 Europe; £56.01 (surface mail), £67.43 (airmail) other. World Textile Publications Ltd., 76 Kirkgate, Bradford West Yorkshire, BD1 1TB England. **Tel** 011 44 274 726357, 011 44 274 731907, FAX 011 44 274 735045, telex 517617 WOOLMN G. ***Continues*** *International Dyer, Textile Printer, Bleacher and Finisher, 0020-658X.*
**Desc:** Specialized coverage of the dyeing, printing and finishing industry.

US/1049-801X
**INTERNATIONAL FIBER JOURNAL.** [Int. fiber j.]. **VFOAT** IFJ. (198?)-. Periodical. English. bm (6 issues). $25.00. International Fiber Journal, 2919 Spalding Drive, Atlanta GA 30350. **Tel** (404)394-6098, FAX (404)393-0161. **ED** Ann Snider. **DD** 677. **Bk Rev. Ad Acc. Circ:** 9,000 (ctrl).
**Desc:** News, technical data, marketing information and anything to assist international man-made fiber producers.

US
**INTERNATIONAL FIBER SCIENCE AND TECHNOLOGY SERIES.** (1983)-. Monographic series. English. Price varies per volume. Marcel Dekker Inc., 270 Madison Avenue, New York NY 10016. **Tel** (212)696-9000, (800)228-1160, FAX (212)685-4540, telex 421419. **(Subscription address:** Marcel Dekker Inc, PO Box 5017, Monticello NY 12701.)
**Desc:** Covers topics in fiber science such as carbon fibers and the chemical processing of fibers and fabrics.

UK/0955-6222
**INTERNATIONAL JOURNAL OF CLOTHING SCIENCE AND TECHNOLOGY.** **See** Clothing Industry and Fashion.

US
**INTERNATIONAL NONWOVENS DIRECTORY.** **Added/Corp** Association of the Nonwoven Fabrics Industry. European Disposables & Nonwovens Association. (1988/89)-. Directory. English. Association of the Nonwoven Fabrics Industry, 1001 Winstead Drive/Suite 460, Cary NC 27513. **Tel** (919)467-4632, FAX (919)481-0942. ***Continues*** *International Directory of the Nonwoven Fabrics Industry, 0095-683X.*

US/0740-6746
**INTERNATIONAL OLD LACERS INC., BULLETIN.** [Int. Old Lacers Inc. bull.]. **Added/Corp** International Old Lacers. (198?)-. Bulletin. English. qt. $15.00 US; $22.00 other. International Old Lacers Inc, 2409 South 9th, Carolyn Regnier, Lafayette IN 47905. **Tel** (317)474-1176. **ED** Susan Penner. **Bk Rev**, (Qty: 20). **Ad Acc. Circ:** 1,500. ***Continues*** *International Old Lacers. Bulletin.*
**Desc:** Provides handmade lace makers with information on lace, classes, other members, lace books, and etc.

SZ/1012-8417
**INTERNATIONAL TEXTILE BULLETIN. DYEING/PRINTING/FINISHING.** [Int. text. bull., Dye. print. finish.]. **Added/Corp** International Textile Club. International Textile Institute of Technology and Management. International Textile Service. **VFOAT** Dyeing/Printing/Finishing; I.T.S. Bulletin. Dyeing/Printing/Finishing; I.T.B. Dyeing/Printing/Finishing; ITS Bulletin. Dyeing/Printing/Finishing; ITB. Dyeing/Printing/Finishing. **VAT** International Textile Service Bulletin. Dyeing/Printing/Finishing. (19??)-. Bulletin. German (English, French, Italian, Spanish and Chinese). qt. 65.00F (1 year), 120.00F (2 year) Europe; $55.00 (1 year), $100.00 (2 year) surface mail; $85.00 (1 year), $160.00 (2 year) airmail. International Textile Service Ltd, Kesslerstrasse 9/PO Box 8952, Schlieren Switzerland. **Tel** 011 41 1 7305856, FAX 011 41 1 7308183, telex 827758. **CODEN** ITBFD8. **Ad Acc. Circ:** 26,500 (ctrl). Documents available from Article Express International. ***Continues*** *International Textile Bulletin. Dying/Finishing.*
**Desc:** Deals with machines, accessories and technology of the following fields: preparation, dyeing, printing, finishing, dyestuffs, auxiliary products.
**Ind/Abst** Bioeng. Abstr.; Ei Page One; Eng. Index Annu.; Nonwovens Abstr.; Print. Abstr.; World Text. Abstr.

SZ/1012-8425
**INTERNATIONAL TEXTILE BULLETIN. FABRIC FORMING.** ***Title Change.*** [Int. text. bull., Fabr. form.]. **Added/Corp** International Textile Service. International Textile Institute of Technology and Management. International Textile Club. **VFOAT** Fabric Forming; I.T.S. Bulletin. Fabric Forming; ITS Bulletin. Fabric Forming. **VAT** International Textile Service Bulletin. Fabric Forming. 1st Quarter (1983)-(19??). Periodical. German (English, French, Italian, Spanish and Chinese). qt. International Textile Service Ltd, Kesslerstrasse 9/PO Box 8952, Schlieren Switzerland. **Tel** 011 41 1 7305856, FAX 011 41 1 7308183, telex 827758. **Ad Acc. Circ:** 45,700 (ctrl). ***Formed by the union of*** *International Textile Bulletin. Weaving* ***and*** *International Textile Bulletin. Knitting/Hosiery/Embroidery/Making-Up.* ***Merged into*** *International Textile Bulletin Yarn and Fabric Forming.*
**Desc:** Deals with machines, accessories and technology of the following fields: weaving, knitting, hosiery, embroidery, including preparation and yarn processing.
**Ind/Abst** Bioeng. Abstr.; Nonwovens Abstr.; Print. Abstr.; Text. Technol. Dig.; World Text. Abstr.

SZ
**INTERNATIONAL TEXTILE BULLETIN. YARN AND FABRIC FORMING.** (19??)-. Bulletin. German (English, French, Italian, Spanish and Chinese). qt. $70.00. International Textile Service Ltd, Kesslerstrasse 9/PO Box 8952, Schlieren Switzerland. **Tel** 011 41 1 7305856, FAX 011 41 1 7308183, telex 827758. ***Absorbed*** *International Textile Bulletin Fabric Forming and Yarn Forming.*

SZ
**INTERNATIONAL TEXTILE BULLETIN. YARN FORMING/NONWOVEN.** (198?)-. Bulletin. English (German, French, Spanish, Italian and Chinese). qt (Feb., May, Aug., Nov.). 65.00F (1 year), 120.00F (2 year) Switzerland; $55.00 (1 year), $100.00 (2 year) surface mail; $85.00 (1 year), $160.00 (2 year) airmail. International Textile Service Ltd, Kesslerstrasse 9/PO Box 8952, Schlieren Switzerland. **Tel** 011 41 1 7305856, FAX 011 41 1 7308183, telex 827758. ***Continues*** *International Textile Bulletin.*

SZ
**INTERNATIONAL TEXTILE BULLETIN. YARN FORMING/NONWOVENS.** **VFOAT** Yarn Forming/Nonwovens; Yarn Forming, Nonwovens; Yarn Forming; ITB. Yarn Forming. Bulletin. English. qt. ***Continues*** *International Textile Bulletin. Yarn Forming, 1012-9596.*
**Ind/Abst** Print. Abstr.

UK/0263-5879
**INTERNATIONAL TEXTILE CALENDAR / TEXTILE INSTITUTE.** **Added/Corp** Textile Institute (Manchester, England). (19??)-. Periodical. English. bm. £75.00 UK; £130.00 US and Canada. Textile Institute, 10 Blackfriars Street, Manchester M3 5DR England. **Tel** 11 44 61 834 8457, FAX 11 44 61 835 3087, telex 668297 G.

SZ/1012-9545
**INTERNATIONAL TEXTILE MANUFACTURING.** [Int. text. manuf.]. V. 1-1978-. English. an. 50.00F Switzerland; $40.00 US. International Textile Manufacturers Federation, Postfach 289, CH-8039 Zurich Switzerland. **Tel** 011 41 1 2017080, 011 41 1 2017747, telex 56798 ITMF CH. **ED** Herwig Strolz. **LC** HD9850.1; .I62. **DD** 338.4/7677/005. **CODEN** ITXMAY. **Circ:** 800. Documents available from Article Express International. ***Supersedes*** *Cotton and Allied Textile Industries.*
**Desc:** Matters related to the International Textile Industry.
**Ind/Abst** Bioeng. Abstr.; Ei Page One; Eng. Index Annu.; World Text. Abstr.

NE/0020-8914
**INTERNATIONAL TEXTILES.** Vol. 1 (1933)-. Periodical. English (Dutch, English, French, German and Spanish). mo (10 issues). $445.00 US; £150.00 Europe; £230.00 other. International Textile Benjamin Dent Ltd, 23 Bloomsbury Square, London WC1A 2P England. **Tel** 011 44 71 637 2211, FAX 011 44 71 637 2248, telex 8954884. **ED** Stephen Higginson. **LC** TS1300; .I63. Index

available. **Bk Rev.** **Ad Acc.** **Circ:** 10,000 (ctrl). available on microfilm and microfiche from University Microfilms International (UMI). ***Absorbed*** *Textile Forecast.*
**Desc:** Promotes women's and men's yarns, fabrics and fibres for the fashion and textile industries.
**Ind/Abst** AGRICOLA.

NE/0020-8922
**INTERNATIONAL TEXTILES INTERIOR.** **Added/Corp** International Textiles. **VFOAT** Interior. (1960)-. Periodical. English (French and German). Three times a year. Fl170.00. International Textile Benjamin Dent Ltd, 23 Bloomsbury Square, London WC1A 2P England. **Tel** 011 44 71 637 2211, FAX 011 44 71 637 2248, telex 8954884. available on microfilm from University Microfilms International (UMI).

SP/0302-5268
**INVESTIGACION E INFORMACION TEXTIL Y DE TENSIOACTIVOS.** ***Ceased.*** [Invest. inf. textil tensioact.]. **Added/Corp** Instituto de Tecnologia Quimica y Textil (Spain). (1972)-(19??). Academic Scholarly Publication. Spanish (summaries and/or abstracts in English, French and German). qt. Investigacion e Informacion, Jorge Girona Salgado S/N, Barcelona 34 Spain. **LC** TS1300; .I696. **CODEN** IITTCS. **[CCC].** Documents available from CASDDS. ***Continues*** *Investigacion e Informacion Textil.*
**Ind/Abst** AGRICOLA; Art Archaeol. Tech. Abstr.; Chem. Abstr.; World Text. Abstr.

JA/0285-869X
**ISHIKAWA-KEN KOGYO SHIKENJO SHIKENJO HOKOKU.** (SHIKENJO HOKOKU.). [Ishikawa-ken Kogyo Shikenjo shikenjo hokoku]. **Main/Corp** Ishikawa-ken Kogyo Shikenjo. **VAT** Shikenjo Hokoku - Ishikawa-Ken Kogyo Shikenjo. Academic Scholarly Publication. Japanese. **(Subscription address:** Japan Publications Trading Company, Ltd., PO Box 5030, Tokyo International, Tokyo 100-31 Japan.**)** **LC** TS1300; .I77A. **CODEN** IKSHD2. Documents available from CASDDS.
**Ind/Abst** Chem. Abstr.

US/1067-2850
**ITAA PROCEEDINGS. NATIONAL MEETING.** [ITAA proc., Natl. meet.]. **Main/Corp** International Textile and Apparel Association. **VFOAT** National Meeting; International Textile and Apparel Association Proceedings; Proceedings. 48th Year (1991)-. Proceedings. English. $22.00 US; $25.00 other. International Textile and Apparel Association, PO Box 1360, Monument CO 80132. **Tel** (719)488-3716. **LC** TS1300; .A85b. **DD** 677/.005. **Pr Rev. Circ:** 1,100. ***Continues*** *Association of College Professors of Textiles and Clothing. ACPTC Proceedings. National Meeting, 1051-1466.*

RU/0021-3497
**IZVESTIJA VYSSIH UCEBNYH ZAVEDENIJ. TEHNOLOGIJA TEKSTILNOJ PROMYSLENNOSTI.** ***Ceased.*** (IZVESTIIA VYSSHIKH UCHEBNYKH ZAVEDENII. TEKHNOLOGIIA TEKSTILNOI PROMYSHLENNOSTI.). [Izv. vyss. ucebn. zaved. Tehnol. tekst. prom-sti]. **Added/Corp** Soviet Union. Ministerstvo Vysshego Obrazovaniia. Soviet Union. Ministerstvo Vysshego i Srednego Spetsialnogo Obrazovaniia. Soviet Union. Gosudarstvennyi Komitet po Narodnomu Obrazovaniiu. Russia (Federation). Ministerstva Nauki, Vysshei Shkoly i Tekhnicheskoi Politiki. Komitet po Vysshei Shkole Ivanovskii Tekstilnyi Institut Imeni M.V. Frunze. **VFOAT** Tekhnologiia Tekstilnoi Promyshlennosti. (Nov. 1957)-(1992). Academic Scholarly Publication. Russian (table of contents in English and German). bm. **(Subscription address:** Victor Kamkin, 4956 Boiling Brook Parkway, Rockville MD 20852.**)** **LC** TS1300; .R8. **CODEN** IVTTAF. Documents available from CASDDS.
**Ind/Abst** Abstr. Bull. Inst. Paper Chem.; Abstr. Bull. Inst. Pap. Sci. Tech.; AGRICOLA; Art Archaeol. Tech. Abstr.; Chem. Abstr.

FR/0021-8197
**JOURNAL DU TEXTILE 1964.** [J. text. 1964]. (1964)-. Periodical. French. Forty-three times a year. 925.56F France; 1235.00F other. Hennessen, 61 rue de Malte, 75541 Paris Cedex 11 France. **Tel** 011 33 1 43572189. **UDC** 677.

UK
**JOURNAL FOR WEAVERS, SPINNERS & DYERS, THE.** **Added/Corp** Association of the Guilds of Weavers, Spinners, and Dyers (Great Britain). **VFOAT** Journal of Weavers, Spinners and Dyers. No. 131 (1984)-. Periodical. English. qt. £11.80 UK; £14.25 other. Journal for Weavers and Spinners, 39 Sandown Drive, Hereford HR4 9LU England. **Tel** 011 44 432 359066. ***Continues*** *Weavers Journal.*
**Ind/Abst** AGRICOLA [Select. Cov.].

II
**JOURNAL - INDIAN COTTON MILLS' FEDERATION.** **Main/Corp** Indian Cotton Mills' Federation. Began with May 1964 issue. Periodical. English. mo. Rs100.00. Indian Cotton Mills' Federation, Textile Center, P D Mello Road, Bombay 400 009 India. **Tel** 86 20 43, telex 75426. **ED** C V Radhakrishnan. **LC** HD9086.I4. **DD** 338.4/7/677210954. Index available. cum. index. **Circ:** 2,000.
**Desc:** Deals with matters of textiles. Contains special articles, reports and statistical tables connected with textiles, etc.

US/0093-4658
**JOURNAL OF COATED FABRICS.** [J. coated fabrics]. Vol. 3 (July 1973)-. Academic Scholarly Publication. English. qt. $220.00 (one year), $430.00 (two year), $640.00 (three year). Technomic Publishing Company, Inc., 851 New Holland Avenue, Box 3535, Lancaster PA 17604. **Tel** (717)291-5609, (800)233-9936, FAX (717)295-4538. **ED** Peter Larcombe. **LC** TS1512; .J65. **DD** 677/.02864. **CODEN** JCTFAL. **[CCC].** cum. index. **Circ:** 350. available on microfilm and microfiche from University Microfilms International (UMI). Documents available from Article Express International, CASDDS. ***Continues*** *Journal of Coated Fibrous Materials.*
**Desc:** Reports exclusively on new developments in the international coating and laminating industry. Presents research papers on materials, techniques and markets. Provides a forum for discussion among researchers, production personnel, marketers, and consultants. An international patents digest provides summaries of relevant patents from major countries. Also covers industry news, standards, regulatory aspects, safety, and environmental concerns.
**Ind/Abst** Abstr. Bull. Inst. Pap. Sci. Tech.; AGRICOLA [Select. Cov.]; Bioeng. Abstr.; Chem. Abstr.; Ei Page One; EMBASE; Eng. Index Annu.; Nonwovens Abstr.; Text. Technol. Dig.; World Text. Abstr.

PK
**JOURNAL OF TEXTILE INDUSTRY.** (1967)-. Periodical. English. qt. $4.00 Pakistan; $8.00 other. Journal of Textile Industry, V E 1516 Nazimabad, Karachi Pakistan. **LC** HD9866.P3; J68. **DD** 338.4/7/677095491.

II/0368-4636
**JOURNAL OF THE TEXTILE ASSOCIATION.** (JOURNAL.). [J. Text. Assoc.]. **Main/Corp** Textile Association (India). Vol. 33 (March 1972)-. Periodical. English. bm. $60.00. Textile Association India, 72 A Santosh, Dadar Bombay 400 028 India. **Tel** 011 91 22 461145. **(Subscription address:** Prints India, 11 Darya Ganj, New Delhi, 110002 India, (Phone: 011 91 11 3268645)**)** **LC** TS1300; .T213. **DD** 677/.005. **CODEN** JTXAA9. Documents available from CASDDS. ***Continues*** *Textile Digest.*
**Ind/Abst** Chem. Abstr.; Cot. Trop. Fibr. Abstr. Bibliogr.; Text. Technol. Dig.; World Text. Abstr.

UK/0040-5000
**JOURNAL OF THE TEXTILE INSTITUTE.** [J. text. inst.]. **Main/Corp** Textile Institute (Manchester, Greater Manchester). **Added/Corp** Textile Institute (Manchester, England). **VFOAT** Textile Bibliography. Vol. 1 (1910)-. Academic Scholarly Publication. English. Four times a year. £105.00 UK; $180.00 US and Canada. Textile Institute, 10 Blackfriars Street, Manchester M3 5DR England. **Tel** 11 44 61 834 8457, FAX 11 44 61 835 3087, telex 668297 G. **LC** TS1300; .T215. **CODEN** JTINA7. cum. index. Documents available from Article Express International, The Genuine Article, CASDDS. ***Superseded in part by*** *Textile Institute and Industry* ***and*** *Textile Abstracts.*
**Ind/Abst** Abstr. Bull. Inst. Pap. Sci. Tech.; AGRICOLA [Select. Cov.]; Art Archaeol. Tech. Abstr.; Bioeng. Abstr.; Chem. Abstr.; Curr. Contents Eng. Tech. Appl. Sci.; Ei Page One; EMBASE; Eng. Index Annu.; Nonwovens Abstr.; Res. Alert [Full Cov.]; Sci. Cit. Index; SCISEARCH; Soc. Sci. Cit. Index [Select. Cov.]; Text. Technol. Dig.; World Text. Abstr.

JA/0040-5043
**JOURNAL OF THE TEXTILE MACHINERY SOCIETY OF JAPAN.** (JOURNAL.). [J. Text. Mach. Soc. Jpn.]. **Main/Corp** Nihon Seni Kikai Gakkai. **VFOAT** Journal of the Textile Machinery Society of Japan. Vol. 1 (March 1955)-. Academic Scholarly Publication. English. Four times a year. $77.00. Nihon Seni Kikai Gakkai, (Textile Machinery Soc. of Japan), Osaka Kagaku Gijutsu Senta Biru, 8-4, Utsubo Honmachi 1 Chome, Nishiku, Osakashi, Osakafu 550 Japan. **(Subscription address:** Japan Publications Trading Company, Ltd., PO Box 5030, Tokyo International, Tokyo 100-31 Japan.**)** **LC** TS1300; .N5. **CODEN** JTMJAF. Documents available from Article Express International, CASDDS.
**Ind/Abst** Art Archaeol. Tech. Abstr.; Bioeng. Abstr.; Chem. Abstr.; Ei Page One; Eng. Index Annu.; World Text. Abstr.

JA
**JSN INTERNATIONAL.** (19??)-. Periodical. English. mo. $60.00 (one year), $120.00 (three year). JSN International Inc., Dia Plc 501 4 9 Lidabashi 4 CH, Chiyoda Ku Tokyo 102 Japan. **Tel** 011 81 3 32656488, FAX 011 81 3 32639078. **Ad Acc. Circ:** 8,000-10,000 (ctrl).
**Ind/Abst** Text. Technol. Dig.; World Text. Abstr.

JA
**JTN.** [JTN]. **Added/Corp** Osaka Seni Kenkyusha. Gaikokubu. No. 276 (Nov. 1977)-. Academic Scholarly Publication. English. mo. $130.00 Hong Kong; $170.00 other. Osaka Senken Ltd., 4 9 Bingomachi, 3-chome Chuo-ku, Osaka 541 Japan. **Tel** 011 81 6 2027891. **LC** HD9866.J3; J35. **DD** 338.4/7/67700952. **CODEN** JTNNDZ. Documents available from CASDDS. ***Continues*** *Japan Textile News, 0021-4752.*
**Ind/Abst** Chem. Abstr. (1977-1985); Nonwovens Abstr.; Text. Technol. Dig.; World Text. Abstr.

BG/1010-3791
**JUTE AND JUTE FABRICS, BANGLADESH.** [Jute jute fabr.--Bangladesh]. **Added/Corp** Bangladesh Jute Research Institute. Newsletter 1 (Jan. 1975)-. Periodical. English. mo. £12.00. Bangladesh Jute Research Institute, Sher-e-Banlanagar, Dhaka 15 Bangladesh. **LC** HD9156.J8; B2544. **DD** 338.1/7354/095492. ***Continues*** *Jute and Jute Fabrics Pakistan.*
**Ind/Abst** AGRICOLA; Art Archaeol. Tech. Abstr.; Text. Technol. Dig.

JA/0368-475X
**KASEN GEPPO.** [Kasen geppo]. **Added/Corp** Nippon Kagaku Seni Kyokai. **VFOAT** Japan Synthetic Textile Monthly; Japan Chemical Fibres Monthly. Vol. 1 (Nov. 1948)-. Academic Scholarly Publication. Japanese. mo. $192.00. Seni Sogo Kenkyujo, (Fiber & Textile Research Inst.), 1-20, Nihonbashi Muromachi, 3 Chome, Chuoku, Tokyoto 103, Japan. **(Subscription address:** Kyowa Book Company Inc., 1 38 Kanda Jinbocho Chiyoda-ku, Tokyo 101 Japan.**)** **CODEN** KAGEAI. Documents available from CASDDS.
**Ind/Abst** Chem. Abstr.

GW/0047-3405
**KETTENWIRK-PRAXIS.** [Kettenwirk-Prax.]. (1967)-. Periodical. German (translations available in English). qt. DM57.50 (German issue), DM92.00 (with English translation) Germany; DM63.00 (German issue), DM96.50 (with English translation) other. Verlag Karl Mayer Gmbh, POB 1120, 63166 Obertshausen Germany. **Tel** 011 49 6104 402042, FAX 011 49 6104 43574. **ED** Rolf Hufschlager.

JA/0285-0567
**KIITO KENSA KENKYU HOKOKU.** (KIITO KENSA KENKYU HOKOKU / NORIN SUISANSHO, YOKOHAMA NORIN KIKAKU KENSASHO ; KOBE NORIN KIKAKU KENSASHO.). [Kiito kensa kenkyu hokoku]. **Added/Corp** Yokohama Norin Kikaku Kensasho. Kobe Norin Kikaku Kensasho. **VFOAT** Research Reports of the Raw Silk Testing. (1981)-. Japanese. an. **CODEN** KKHUD8. Documents available from CASDDS. ***Continues*** *Kiito Kensajo Kenkyu Hokoku.*
**Ind/Abst** Chem. Abstr.

US/0145-4900
**KNIT FABRIC PRODUCTION.** (CURRENT INDUSTRIAL REPORTS. MA-22K, KNIT FABRIC PRODUCTION.). [Knit fabr. prod.]. **Added/Corp** United States. Bureau of the Census. **VFOAT** Knit Fabric Production. (19??)-. Government Publication. English. an. $1.00. US Department of Commerce / Bureau of the Census, Data User Services Division, Customer Services, Washington DC 20233-0800. **Tel** (301)763-4100. **(Subscription address:** Superintendent of Documents, US Government Printing Office, Washington DC 20402.**)** **LC** HD9969.K7; U58. **DD** 338.4/7677661/0973021.
**Desc:** Presents timely data on the production, inventories, and orders of approximately 5,000 products, which represents 40 percent of all US manufacturing.
**Ind/Abst** Text. Technol. Dig. (19??-199?).

US/0160-6336
**KNITOVATIONS.** Periodical. English. Woolknit Associates Ins., 501 Madison Avenue, New York NY 10022. **LC** TT679; .K63. **DD** 338.4/7/687.

UK/0266-8394
**KNITTING INTERNATIONAL.** [Knitting int.]. Vol. 81, No. 961 (1974)-. Periodical. English. mo. $200.00 US; £75.00 Europe; £110.00 other. International Textile Benjamin Dent Ltd, 23 Bloomsbury Square, London WC1A 2P England. **Tel** 011 44 71 637 2211, FAX 011 44 71 637 2248, telex 8954884. **ED** John T. Millington. Index available. cum. index. **Bk Rev.** **Ad Acc.** **Circ:** 5,000 (ctrl). ***Continues*** *Hosiery Trade Journal, 0018-5434.*
**Desc:** Provides news on the latest developments in technology, production, marketing, yarns, fabrics, fashions, people and companies.
**Ind/Abst** Curr. Technol. Index; World Text. Abstr.

HU
**KOTOIPARI SZEMLE.** **See** Clothing Industry and Fashion.

JA/0368-6280
**KYOTO DAIGAKU NIHON KAGAKU SENI KENKYUJO KOENSHU.** [Kyoto Daigaku Nippon Kagakusen'i Kenkyusho koenshu]. **VFOAT** Annual Report of the Research Institute for Chemical Fibers, Japan; Nippon Kagakusen-I Kenkyusho Koen Shu. Academic Scholarly Publication. Japanese (Japanese). ir. Nippon Kagaku Seni Kenkyujo, (Research Inst. for Chemical Fibers, Japan), Kyoto Daigaku, Yoshida Honcho, Sakyoku, Kyotoshi, Kyotofu 606, Japan. **(Subscription address:** Japan Publications Trading Company, Ltd., PO Box 5030, Tokyo International, Tokyo

100-31 Japan.) **LC** TS1548.5; .K96. **CODEN** KNKKAB. Documents available from CASDDS.
**Ind/Abst** Chem. Abstr.

IT
**LANIERA.** Giuseppe Mendella Publ Edizioni, Via Stradivari 10, 20131 Milan Italy.

US/0164-5765
**LAUNDRY NEWS.** [Laund. news]. (19??)-. Periodical. English. mo. Free to US qualified buyers of institutional laundry products; $24.00 US nonqualified buyers; $36.00 other. Mill Hollow Corporation, 19 West 21st Street, New York NY 10010. **Tel** (212)741-2095, FAX (212)633-9367.
**Ind/Abst** Hospit. Health Admin. Index (1977-1987-).

US/0892-743X
**LDB INTERIOR TEXTILES.** [LDB inter. text.]. **VFOAT** Linens, Domestics & Bath Products/Interior Textiles; Linens, Domestics and Bath Products/Interior Textiles; LDB/Interior Textiles. Vol. 84, No. 1 (Jan. 1987)-. Periodical. English. mo. $40.00 (1 year), $55.00 (2 year) US; $75.00 other. Columbia Communications Inc., 370 Lexington Avenue, New York NY 10017. **Tel** (212)532-9290. **LC** HD9850.1; .L32. **DD** 338.4/76843/0973. ***Formed by the union of*** *Linens, Domestics & Bath Products, 0024-3833* ***and*** *Interior Textiles, 0740-6703.*
**Ind/Abst** Trade Ind. Index.

IT
**LETTERA QUOTIDIANA : SETTORE TESSILE I+C.** Agenzia Lettera Quotidiana, Via San Lucio 32, 00165 Rome Italy.

CN/0068-9858
**LLOYD'S CANADIAN TEXTILE DIRECTORY.** **Added/Corp** Lloyd Publications of Canada. 41st Ed. (1964)-. Directory. English. an. 30.00Can$ Canada; 50.00Can$ US; 60.00Can$ other. Sentinel Business Publications, 7575 Trans Canada Highway, Suite 500, St. Laurent Quebec H4T 1V6 Canada. **Tel** (514)333-1116, FAX (514)631-8858. **ED** Carol Clifford. **LC** WMLC L 83/4358. **DD** 338.4/7/677. **Ad Acc. Circ:** 4,500 (ctrl). ***Continues*** *Wilson's Canadian Textile Directory.*
**Desc:** Directory of product listings and suppliers to Canada's textile industry.

US/0565-2022
**LONG STAPLE COTTON REVIEW. See** Agriculture-Crop Production and Soil.

UK/0266-8505
**MACHINE KNITTING NEWS.** [Mach. knitting news]. **VFOAT** Litharne's Machine Knitting News. (1984)-. Periodical. English. mo. £20.40 UK; £27.00 other. Litharne Ltd, PO Box 9, Stratford-upon-Avon, Warwickshire CV37 8RS England. **Tel** 011 44 789 7206040, FAX 011 44 789 720888. **DD** 746.432.

HU/0025-0309
**MAGYAR TEXTILTECHNIKA.** [Magy. textiltech.]. **Added/Corp** Textilipari Muszaki es Tudomanyos Egyesulet. (1947)-. Academic Scholarly Publication. Hungarian (summaries and/or abstracts in German, English and Russian). Twelve times a year. $114.00. Textilipari Muszaki es Tudomanyos Egyesulet, Lapkiado Vallalat, Lenin korut 9-11, 1073 Budapest 7 Hungary. **Tel** 222-408, FAX 361-561215, telex 22-4343. **(Subscription address:** Kultura, PO Box 149, H 1389 Budapest 62 Hungary; telephone: 011 36 1 359370**) LC** TS1300; .T68. **Ad Acc.** Documents available from CASDDS.
**Ind/Abst** Abstr. Bull. Inst. Pap. Sci. Tech.; AGRICOLA; Art Archaeol. Tech. Abstr.; Chem. Abstr.; Text. Technol. Dig.; World Text. Abstr.

JA/0303-7215
**MAN-MADE FIBERS OF JAPAN.** **Added/Corp** Nihon Kinu Kasen Yushutsu Kumiai. Nippon Kagaku Seni Kyokai. (19??)-. Periodical. English. ir. Free on request. Japan Chemical Fibers Association, 1 11 Nihonbashi Honcho 3-chome, Chuoku Tokyo 103 Japan. **Tel** 011 81 3 32412311. **LC** HD9866.J3; M35. **DD** 338.4/7/67740952.

II/0377-7537
**MAN-MADE TEXTILES IN INDIA.** [Man-made text. India]. **Added/Corp** Silk and Art Silk Mills' Research Association. Vol. 16, No. 8 (Aug. 1973)-. Periodical. English. mo. $50.00. Silk & Art Silk Mills Research Association, Dr. Annie Beasant Road, Worli Bombay 400 025 India. **Tel** 011 91 22 4935351, FAX 011 91 22 4930225. **ED** Prof. D. B. Ajgaonkar. **LC** TS1640; .S55. **DD** 677/.4/0954. **CODEN** MMTIBW. (published in Dec. issue). **Bk Rev**, (Qty: 12). **Ad Acc. Circ:** 1,500 (ctrl). Documents available from CASDDS. ***Continues*** *Silk and Rayon Industries of India, (OCoLC)1765558.*
**Desc:** Deals with all aspects of the man-made fibre and textile industry. It also deals with the latest machinery developments in the industry and new technology.
**Ind/Abst** Chem. Abstr.; Curr. Lit. Sci. Sci.; Nonwovens Abstr.; World Text. Abstr.

US/0885-9949
**MARINE TEXTILES.** [Mar. text.]. **Added/Corp** Industrial Fabrics Association International. (Jan/Feb. 1986)-. Periodical. English. Nine times a year. $28.00 US & Canada; $85.00 others. RCM Enterprises, 173 South Lakeview Lane, PO Box 720, Wayzata MN 55391. **Tel** (612)473-5088, FAX (612)475-1602. **ED** Susan Klemond. **DD** 677. Index available. **Ad Acc, Adv Mgr:** Jim Penningroth, **Tel** (612)473-5088. **Circ:** 5,500 (ctrl).
**Desc:** Focuses on textiles, products and furnishings used in boats, pleasure boats, commerical boats, passenger ships and military vessels.

US/1057-0160
**MATERIAL INFORMATION.** (MATERIAL INFORMATION / BY MARCI COHEN.). [Mater. inf.]. (1990)-. Periodical. English. mo. Material Information, 928 Broadway, New York NY 10010. **DD** 677.

NE/0266-2078
**MEDICAL TEXTILES. See** Medical Science and Technology.

GW/0341-0781
**MELLIAND-TEXTILBERICHTE (1976).** (MELLIAND TEXTILBERICHTE.). [Melliand-Textilberichte]. **Added/Corp** Verein der Textilchemiker und Coloristen (Germany). **VFOAT** Textiltechnik, Textilmaschinen, Textilveredlung, Textilchemie, Textilindustrie; International Textile Reports. No. 57, Issue 1 (Jan. 1976)-. Academic Scholarly Publication. German (summaries and/or abstracts in English). mo. DM480.00 English Edition; DM240.00 German Edition; DM328.00 (US, Canada, Central America, Africa, Near and Middle East, India, Bangladesh and Thailand), DM355.00 (South America and Far East), DM381.00 (Australia and New Zealand) airmail. Melliand Textilberichte GmbH, Rohrbacherstrasse 76, D-69115 Heidelberg, 1 Germany. **Tel** 011 49 6221 21865, FAX 011 49 6221 166763, telex 461876. **LC** TS1300; .M38. **DD** 677/.005. **CODEN** MTIRDL. **[CCC]**. Documents available from CASDDS. ***Continues*** *Melliand Textilberichte International (Heidelberg, Germany), 0375-9350;* ***Absorbed*** *Melliand Textilberichte (Heidelberg, Germany : 1976). English; Textiltechnik, 0323-3804.*
**Ind/Abst** Abstr. Bull. Inst. Pap. Sci. Tech.; Art Archaeol. Tech. Abstr.; Chem. Abstr.; Cot. Trop. Fibr. Abstr. Bibliogr.; Curr. Biotechnol.; EMBASE; Energy Res. Abstr. (Jan. 1976-); PROMT; Text. Technol. Dig.; World Text. Abstr.

KO
**MERIYASU KONGOP YONBO. VFOAT** Annual on Korean Knitting Industry. Korean (Korean). **LC** HD9969.K7; K795.

II/0377-1490
**MODERN FIBRES.** **Added/Corp** Association of Man-Made Fibre Industry. (19??)-. English. ir. Association of Synthetic Fibre Industry, Raj Mahal 1st/84 Veer Nariman, Bombay 400 020 India. **Tel** 011 91 22 2048075, telex 4323. **LC** HD9929.2.I5; M6. **DD** 338.4/7/67740954.

AT
**MOHAIR AUSTRALIA.** **Added/Corp** Angora Mohair Association of Australia. Vol. 7, No. 3 (Sept. 1977)-. Periodical. English. Six times a year (Five times a year plus 1 annual published in May). 25.00Aus$ Australia; 37.00Aus$ New Zealand & Asia; 40.60Aus$ others. Angora Mohair Breeder Australian Ltd, PO Box 14426 MCMC, Melbourne VIC 3000 Australia. **Tel** 011 61 6 391244. **ED** T.S. Manifold. **Ad Acc. Circ:** 1,000 (ctrl).

US/0027-0318
**MONTHLY COTTON LINTERS REVIEW. See** Agriculture-Crop Production and Soil.

●US
**MUNDO TEXTIL.** (1994)-. Periodical. English. qt. $35.00. MacLean Hunter Publishing Corporation / Chicago, IL, 29 North Wacker Drive, Chicago IL 60606-3298. **Tel** (312)726-2802, FAX (312)726-3091.

CN/0705-3681
**NAN'S KNIT-KNACKS. VFOAT** Knit-Knacks. **VAT** Knit-Knacks (Montebello). V. 1- Apr. 1977-. Periodical. English (French). qt. The Knitting Loft, 7 Henri Bourassa, Monbebello Quebec J0V 1L0 Canada. **Tel** (416)487-5914. **DD** 746.4/32.

US/0149-032X
**NARROW FABRICS. See** Manufacturing.

US/0744-6306
**NATIONAL CLOTHESLINE (MIDWEST ED.), THE.** (THE NATIONAL CLOTHESLINE.). Periodical. English. mo. $15.00. The National Clothesline, 717 E Chelten Avenue, Philadelphia PA 19144. **Tel** (215)843-9795. **ED** Hal Horning. **Ad Acc. Circ:** 41,500 (ctrl).
**Desc:** For drycleaners, launderers, management and personnel.

●US/1062-0648
**NATURAL FIBERS FACT BOOK.** (1992)-. English. $15.00. Bureau of Business Research / Texas, University of Texas at Austin, Box 7459, Austin TX 78713. **Tel** (512)471-1616, FAX (512)471-1063.

●US/1065-5247
**NEW NONWOVENS WORLD, THE.** [New nonwovens world]. Vol. 1, No. 1 (Summer 1992)-. Periodical. English. qt. $45.00. M/TS Publications, 4100 South 7th Street, Kalamazoo MI 49009. **Tel** (616)375-1236, FAX (616)375-6710. **ED** James P. Hanson. **LC** WMLC 93/1949. **DD** 677. ***Continues*** *Nonwovens World, 0888-1979.*

NZ/0113-2792
**NEW ZEALAND WOOL MARKET REVIEW.** ***Title Change.*** (WOOL MARKET REVIEW.). [N.Z. wool mark. rev.]. **VFOAT** Wool Market Review. (1987)-(1992). Periodical. English. Twenty-five times a year. Wools of New Zealand, PO Box 3225, Wellington New Zealand. **Tel** 011 64 4 4726888. **ED** Economic Section, New Zealand Wool Board, Box 3225, Wellington, New Zealand. **DD** 338.176363145099305. cum. index. **Bk Rev. Ad Acc.** ctrl circ. ***Continued by*** *Wool Market Review, 1171-9672.*

US
**NEWSLETTER OF THE TEXTILE MUSEUM ASSOCIATION OF SOUTHERN CALIFORNIA.** Newsletter. English. ir. $25.00 libraries and individual, $100.00 other. Textile Museum Association of California, PO Box 3893 / David Goldberg, Manhattan Beach CA 90266. **Tel** (714)883-6161 Clara Gresham. **Bk Rev**, (Qty: 4). ctrl circ.

UK/9036-1234
**NONWOVENS ABSTRACTS. See** Textiles-Abstracting, Bibliographies and Statistics.

US/0163-4429
**NONWOVENS INDUSTRY. See** Economics-Industry and Production.

US
**NONWOVENS INDUSTRY EXECUTIVE REPORT.** (19??)-. Trade Publication. English. Twenty-four times a year. $325.00 US; $360.00 other. Rodman Publications Corporation, 17 S Franklin Turnpike, PO Box 555, Ramsey NJ 07446. **Tel** (201)825-2552, FAX (201)825-0553. **(Subscription address:** Rodman Publishing Corporation, PO Box 555, Ramsey NJ 07446.) ***Continues*** *Executive Summary.*

US
**NONWOVENS MARKETS.** (19??)-. English. Twenty-five times a year. $489.00. Miller Freeman Inc., 600 Harrison Street, San Francisco CA 94107. **Tel** (415)905-2337, FAX (415)905-2240, telex 278273. ***Continues*** *Nonwovens Markets and Fiber Structures Report, 1053-9832.*

US/1053-9832
**NONWOVENS MARKETS AND FIBER STRUCTURES REPORT.** ***Title Change.*** [Nonwovens mark. fiber struct. rep.]. **VFOAT** Nonwovens Markets. (19??)-(19??). English. Twenty-five times a year. Miller Freeman Inc., 600 Harrison Street, San Francisco CA 94107. **Tel** (415)905-2337, FAX (415)905-2240, telex 278273. **DD** 338. **CODEN** NMFRE3. ***Continued by*** *Nonwovens Markets.*
**Ind/Abst** Infomat Int. Bus. (?-?); Nonwovens Abstr. (?-?).

UK/0953-1092
**NONWOVENS REPORT INTERNATIONAL.** [Nonwovens rep. int.]. No. 85 (May 1978)-. Periodical. English. mo. £78.00 UK and Ireland; $165.00 North and Latin America; £85.00 other. Texpress, Merridale House, Mauldeth Road, Stockport SK4 3NT England. **Tel** 44 61 4321005, FAX 44 61 4431421. **ED** Derek T Ward. ***Continues*** *Nonwovens Report.*
**Desc:** Commercial, product, technical developments in world nonwovens industries.
**Ind/Abst** Abstr. Bull. Inst. Pap. Sci. Tech.; Nonwovens Abstr.; Pap. Board Abstr.; Text. Technol. Dig.; World Text. Abstr.

NO/0029-2168
**NORSK TEKSTILTIDENDE.** [Nor. tekstiltid.]. (1920)-. Periodical. Norwegian. mo. **LC** TS1300; .N67.
**Ind/Abst** Int. Packag. Abstr.; World Text. Abstr.

IT
**NOTIZIARIO TESSILE ABBIGLIAMENTO.** Italian (English). qt. L16.00 Italy; L32.00 other. Bisiachi Irene, Via Filippo Turati 28, 20121 Milan Italy. **Tel** 02 627825, FAX 02 6272999, telex 331871 PEDUS MI. **(Subscription address:** Notizario Tessile Abbigliamento ĺCorso Rosmini 78/A, 38068 Rovereto TN Italy) **ED** Irene Bisiachi. **Bk Rev. Ad Acc. Circ:** 6,000.
**Desc:** Contains brief news flashes and press releases from the fashion, textiles, clothing and accessories field as well as informative editorials and commentary from Italy and abroad.

UK/0309-2097
**OE REPORT.** [OE rep.]. (1976)-. Periodical. English. bm. £50.00 Europe; £55.00 other. OE Report, 1 London Place New Mills, Stockport SK12 4ER England. **Tel** 011 44 663 742005, FAX 011 44 663 747657, telex 668520.

FR
**OFFICIEL DES TEXTILES.** French. 450.00F France; 540.00F other. Publications Mandel, 43 BD Vauban, 78182 St. Quen Yvl Cedex France. **Tel** 011 33 1 34834230.

AU
**OSTERREICHISCHE TEXTILE-ZEITUNG.** (19??)-. Periodical. German. wk. Osterreichische Textil Zeitung, Perchtoldsdorf Austria. **Tel** 86-49-21.

UK
**PAPERS OF THE ... ANNUAL CONFERENCE OF THE TEXTILE INSTITUTE.** **Main/Corp** Textile Institute (Manchester, England). Conference. (19??)-. Academic Scholarly Publication. English. an (published in October). £50.00. Textile Institute, 10 Blackfriars Street, Manchester M3 5DR England. **Tel** 11 44 61 834 8457, FAX 11 44 61 835 3087, telex 668297 G. **CODEN** ACTIAX. Documents available from CASDDS.
**Ind/Abst** Chem. Abstr.

US/0886-4268
**PRECIOUS FIBERS.** ***Ceased.*** (1985)-?. Periodical. English. mo. Graphicom Inc, PO Box 8246, Madeira Beach FL 33738. **Tel** (606)986-1495. **ED** Lea Schultz. **DD** 677. **Bk Rev. Ad Acc. Circ:** 2,000 (ctrl).
**Desc:** For those who rear fiber producing animals and process the fleece into yarns. Wool, mohair, angora, llama, alpach, silk, and flax are our targets.

US
**PREDI-BRIEFS : TEXTILES & FIBERS.** ***Ceased.*** **Added/Corp** Predicasts, Inc. **VFOAT** Textiles and Fibers. (March 1977)-(Dec. 1992). Periodical. English. mo. Predicasts Inc., A Ziff Communications Company, 11001 Cedar Avenue, Cleveland OH 44106. **Tel** (800)321-6388, (216)795-3000, FAX (216)229-9944, telex 985 604. **(Subscription address:** Information Access Company, PO Box 61000, Department 1851, San Francisco, CA 94161; Phone: (800)321-6388**)** Index available. cum. index.

CN/0835-0043
**PRIMARY TEXTILE INDUSTRIES.** (PRIMARY TEXTILE INDUSTRIES / STATISTICS CANADA, INDUSTRY DIVISION, CENSUS OF MANUFACTURES SECTION.). [Prim. text. ind.]. **Added/Corp** Statistics Canada. Census of Manufactures Section. Statistics Canada. Industry Division. Statistics Canada. Annual Survey of Manufactures Section. **VFOAT** Industries Textiles de Premiere Transformation. (1985)-. English (French). an. 38.00Can$ Canada; $46.00 US; $54.00 other. Statistics Canada, Publications Sales & Services, Main Building Room 1710, Ottawa Ontario K1A 0T6 Canada. **Tel** (613)951-5078, (800)267-6677, FAX (613)951-1584, telex 053-3585. **LC** HD9864.C2; F53. **DD** 338.4/7677/00971021. ***Continues*** *Fibre, Yarn and Cloth Mills, 0319-8901.*
**Desc:** Annual census of manufacturers.

US/0898-3313
**PRINTWEAR MAGAZINE.** [Printwear mag.]. **VFOAT** Print Wear Magazine.; Printwear. (19??)-. Periodical. English. mo. $26.00 US; $45.00 Canada & Mexico; $70.00 other. National Business Media Inc, PO Box 1416, Broomfield CO 80020. **Tel** (303)469-0424, FAX (303)469-5730. **ED** Mark Buchanan. **DD** 746. **Ad Acc. Circ:** 22,000.
**Ind/Abst** Abstr. Bull. Inst. Pap. Sci. Tech.

PL/0860-7427
**PROBLEMS IN TEXTILE GEOGRAPHY / INTERNATIONAL STANDING WORKING GROUP ON TEXTILE GEOGRAPHY.** **VFOAT** Problemes de Geographie des Textiles. Periodical. English (French; summaries and/or abstracts in Polish; table of contents in Polish). an. **LC** HD9850.1; .P76. **DD** 338.4/7677/005.

II
**PROCEEDINGS OF THE TECHNOLOGICAL CONFERENCE.** **Main/Corp** Ahmedabad Textile Industry's Research Association. **Added/Corp** South India Textile Research Association. Bombay Textile Research Association. 1st (1959)-. Proceedings. English. an. $9.00 (surface mail); $13.00 (airmail). Ahmedabad Textile Indian Research Association, PO Polytechnic, Ahmedabad 380 015 India. **Tel** 442671. **Bk Rev. Circ:** 2,000.
**Desc:** Papers in the field of textiles and allied subjects.
**Ind/Abst** Text. Technol. Dig.; World Text. Abstr.

CN/0825-8031
**PROTEXTILE.** (PROTEXTILE : LE CENTRE QUEBECOIS DE PRODUCTIVITE DU TEXTILE.). [Protextile]. **Added/Corp** Protextile (Firm). (June/July 1984)-. Periodical. English. bm. Free. Textile Technology Centre, 3000 Boulle Street, Saint Hyacinthe Quebec J2S 1H9 Canada. **Tel** (514)778-1870, FAX (514)773-9971. **DD** 338.4/7677/009714.

PL/0033-2410
**PRZEGLAD WOKIENNICZY; MIESIECZNIK NAUKOWO-TECHNICZNY.** (1958)-. Academic Scholarly Publication. Polish. mo. $168.00. **(Subscription address:** ARS Polona, PO Box 1001, 00068 Warsaw Poland.**)** **CODEN** PRZWAZ. Documents available from CASDDS. ***Continues*** *Prezemys Wokienniczy.*
**Ind/Abst** Abstr. Bull. Inst. Pap. Sci. Tech.; Ceram. Abstr. (19??-); Chem. Abstr.; Cot. Trop. Fibr. Abstr. Bibliogr.; World Text. Abstr.

IT
**RAPPORTO SULLA INDUSTRIA COTONIERA LINIERA / ASSOCIAZIONE COTONIERA LINIERA E DELLE FIBRE AFFINI.** **Added/Corp** Associazione Cotoniera Liniera e delle Fibre Affini (Italy). (1991)-. Italian. **LC** HD9885.I8; A832a. **DD** 338.1/7351/0945. ***Continues*** *Associazione Cotoniera Italiana. Rapporto sulla Industria Cotoniera Italiana.*
**Desc:** Concerned with the cotton trade and linen industry.

GW
**READYWEAR. INTERNATIONAL TRADE INFORMATION SERVICE FOR CLOTHING MANUFACTURERS.** (19??)-. Periodical. English. Twice a year. DM75.00 Germany; DM80.50 other. SN Verlag Michael Steinert, An der Alster 21, W 2000 Hamburg 1 F R Germany. **Tel** 011 49 40 240852, FAX 011 49 40 2803788.

GW/0034-3625
**REINIGER + WASCHER.** (REINIGER + I.E. UND WASCHER.). [Reinig. + Wasch.]. **Added/Corp** Deutscher Wascherei-Verband. Bundesfachverband Chemischreinigung-Farberei. **VAT** Reiniger und Wascher. Vol. 23, No. 4, (April 1970)-. Academic Scholarly Publication. German. mo. DM102.00 Germany; DM120.00 other. Verlag Neuer Merkur GmbH, Postfach 460805, D 80916 Munich Germany. **Tel** 011 49 89 3189050. **ED** Jorg Lingenberg, Kurt W. Bruninghais and Peter Focht. **LC** TP932; .W33. Index available. **Bk Rev. Ad Acc. Circ:** 6,000 (ctrl). ***Continues*** *Wascher + I.E. und Reiniger.* ***Absorbed in part by*** *Chemischreiniger, Wascher, Farber Zeitung,, 0009-3009.*
**Desc:** A German trade journal for dry cleaning, laundry, linen supply, textile rental, leather and carpet cleaning.
**Ind/Abst** EMBASE; Saf. Health Work; Text. Technol. Dig.

HK
**REPORT ON TEXTILE PRODUCTION STATISTICS.** (19??)-. English. qt. HK$10.00 Hong Kong; HK$24.00 other. Hong Kong Government Information Service, Beaconsfield House, 4 Queens Road, Hong Kong Hong Kong. **Tel** 011 852 8428801 4, telex 61190 HKGIS. **(Subscription address:** Government Information Service, Publications Office, 1 Battery Path, Hong Kong Hong Kong.**)**

SP/0300-3418
**REVISTA DE QUIMICA TEXTIL.** [Rev. quim. text.]. **Added/Corp** Asociacion Espanola de Quimicos y Coloristas Textiles. (1966)-. Periodical. Spanish. ir. 6800ptas Spain; 16000ptas other. Revista de Quimica Textil, Gran Via 670 6A, 08010 Barcelona Spain. **CODEN** RQTED3. **[CCC].** Documents available from CASDDS.
**Ind/Abst** Chem. Abstr.; Nonwovens Abstr.; World Text. Abstr.

IT/0394-5413
**RIVISTA DELLE TECNOLOGIE TESSILI.** [Riv. tecnol. tess.]. (1987)-. Periodical. Italian. Eleven times a year. L85000.00 Italy; L140000.00 other. Stammer Spa, Via della Liberazione 1, 20068 Peschiera Borromeo, Italy. **Tel** 011 39 2 55302606, FAX 011 39 2 55302700, telex 321083. **ED** Girolamo Bellina. **UDC** 677. **Bk Rev. Ad Acc. Pr Rev. Circ:** 14,700 (ctrl).
**Desc:** Textiles, machinery, commerce , marketing and general management.

US
**RN & WPL ENCYCLOPEDIA / THE SALESMAN'S GUIDE, INC.** **Added/Corp** Salesman's Guide, Inc. **VFOAT** RN and WPL Encyclopedia. (1984)-. English. an. $191.50. PS Press, 620 Herndon Pkwy, Suite20, Herndon VA 22070. **Tel** (703)481-9810. **ED** Patricia Swygert. **LC** HD9940.U3; R5. **DD** 338.7/687/02573. Index available. cum. index. available on diskette; available on audiocassette. ***Continues*** *RN & WPL Directory.*
**Desc:** This directory is a comprehensive reference book that can be used to locate suppliers and sources, follow competition, and find news of the latest trends.

US/0278-9795
**RUG NEWS.** (19??)-. Periodical. English. mo (July/Aug. issue is combined). $44.00 US; $57.00 Canada; $96.00 other. Museum Books Inc, 34 West 37th Street, New York NY 10018. **Tel** (212)563-2770, FAX (212)563-2798. **ED** Suzanne Cummings. **Ad Acc.**

SA/0258-4565
**SAWTRI SPECIAL PUBLICATION.** ***Title Change.*** [SAWTRI spec. publ.]. **VFOAT** S.A.W.T.R.I. Special Publication. **VAT** South African Wool and Textile Research Institute Special Publication. Academic Scholarly Publication. English. ir. South African Wool Textile Research Institute, Box 1124, Port Elizabeth 6000 South Africa. **Tel** (041)53-2131, telex 24 5183. **ED** P Horn. **CODEN** SASPDW. **Circ:** 230 (ctrl). Documents available from CASDDS. ***Continued by*** *TexReport.*
**Desc:** Textile related topics such as the physical and chemical properties of natural fibers or blends of wool, cotton and mohair with synthetics of one another.
**Ind/Abst** Chem. Abstr. (1982); Text. Technol. Dig.; World Text. Abstr.

JA/0037-9875
**SENI GAKKAI SHI.** [Seni Gakkaishi]. **Added/Corp** Seni Gakkai (Japan). **VFOAT** Seni Gakkaishi; Journal of the Society of Fiber and Technology, Japan. (1944)-. Academic Scholarly Publication. Japanese. mo. $288.00. Sen'i Gakkai, (Soc. of Fiber Science & Technology, Japan), 3-9-208, kamiosaki 3 Chome, Shinagawaku, Tokyoto 141, Japan. **(Subscription address:** Kyowa Book Company Inc., 1 38 Kanda Jinbocho Chiyoda-ku, Tokyo 101 Japan.**)** **CODEN** SENGA5. Documents available from CASDDS. ***Supersedes*** *Seni Kogyo Gakkai Shi;* ***Absorbed*** *Seni to Kogyo.*
**Ind/Abst** Abstr. Bull. Inst. Pap. Sci. Tech.; Chem. Abstr.; Curr. Biotechnol.; Polymer Contents; Text. Technol. Dig.

JA/0286-987X
**SENI KAGAKU.** [Seni Kagaku]. **Added/Corp** Nihon Seni Senta. (1960)-. Periodical. Japanese. mo. $236.00. **(Subscription address:** Japan Publications Trading Company, Ltd., PO Box 5030, Tokyo International, Tokyo 100-31 Japan.**)** **CODEN** SEKAB7.

JA/0371-0580
**SENI KIKAI GAKKAI SHI.** [Seni Kikai Gakkaishi]. **Main/Corp** Nihon Seni Kikai Gakkai. **Added/Corp** Nihon Seni Kikai Gakkai. Journal. **VFOAT** Journal of the Textile Machinery Society of Japan. (1972)-. Periodical. Japanese (summaries and/or abstracts in English). mo. $288.00. **(Subscription address:** Japan Publications Trading Company, Ltd., PO Box 5030, Tokyo International, Tokyo 100-31 Japan.**)** **LC** TS1300; .S4. ***Continues*** *Nihon Seni Kikai Gakkai. Seni Kogaku.* ***and*** *Nihon Seni Kikai Gakkai. Seni Kikai Gakkai Rombun Shu.*
**Ind/Abst** World Text. Abstr.

JA/0371-0807
**SENI KOBUNSHI ZAIRYO KENKYUSHO KENKYU HOKOKU.** ***Title Change.*** (KENKYU HOKOKU / BULLETIN OF RESEARCH INSTITUTE FOR POLYMERS AND TEXTILES.). [Seni Kobunshi Zairyo Kenkyusho kenkyu hokoku]. **Added/Corp** Seni Kobunshi Zairyo Kenkyu Jo (Japan). **VFOAT** Bulletin of Research Institute for Polymers and Textiles. No. 88 (1969)-No. 175 (1992). Academic Scholarly Publication. Japanese (summaries and/or abstracts in English; table of contents in English). qt. Research Institute of Polymers & Textiles, 1 1 4 Yatabe Higashi, Tsukuba Ibaraki 305 Japan. **Tel** 0298 54 6229. **CODEN** SKZHA8. Documents available from CASDDS. ***Continues*** *Kenkyu Hokoku (Sen'i Kogyo Shikenjo).* ***Merged with*** *Kagaku Gijutsu Kenkyujo Hokoku, 0388-3213; Seihin Kagaku Kenkyujo (Japan). Seihin Kagaku Kenkyujo Kenkyu Hokoku; Busshitsu Kogaku Kogyo Gijutsu Kenkyujo Hokoku, 0919-7087.*
**Ind/Abst** Abstr. Bull. Inst. Pap. Sci. Tech.; Chem. Abstr.; Text. Technol. Dig.; World Text. Abstr.

JA/0037-2072
**SENI SEIHIN SHOHI KAGAKU.** (SENI SEIHI SHOHI KAGAKU.). [Seni seihin shohi kagaku]. **Added/Corp** Nihon Seni Seihin Shohi Kagakkai. **VFOAT** Shohi Kagaku; Journal of the Japan Research Association for Textile End-Uses; Senshoshi. (1960)-. Academic Scholarly Publication. Japanese (summaries and/or abstracts in English). Twelve times a year. $220.00. Nihon Sen'i Seihin Shohi Kagakkai, (Japan Research Assoc. for Textile End-Uses), 11-5-201, Doshin 2 Chome, Kitaku, Osakashi, Osakafu 530, Japan. **(Subscription address:** Kyowa Book Company Inc., 1 38 Kanda Jinbocho Chiyoda-ku, Tokyo 101 Japan.**)** **LC** TS1300; .S418. **CODEN** SESKB9. **[CCC].** Documents available from CASDDS.
**Ind/Abst** Art Archaeol. Tech. Abstr.; Chem. Abstr.; Text. Technol. Dig.; World Text. Abstr.

SP
**SERIE DE INGENIERIA DE LA CALIDAD.** Spanish. Asociacion de Investigacion Textil Algodonera, Avda Jose Antonio 670, Barcelona Spain. **LC** HD9885.S69; A84 subser.

US/0145-496X
**SHEETS, PILLOWCASES, AND TOWELS.** ***Ceased.*** (CURRENT INDUSTRIAL REPORTS. MQ-23X, SHEETS, PILLOWCASES, AND TOWELS.). [Sheets pillowc. towels]. (19??)-(199?). Government Publication. English. qt (Summary Issue). Superintendent of Documents, US Government Printing Office, Washington DC 20402. **Tel** (202)275-3328, FAX (202)786-2377. **LC** HD9969.H833; U543. **DD** 338.4/768. Documents available from Documents on Demand.

**Desc:** Detailed statistics on textiles, apparel, and footwear.
**Ind/Abst** Am. Stat. Index.

II
**SILK EXPORT BULLETIN.** See Business-Commerce.

US/1051-7928
**SITUATION AND OUTLOOK REPORT. COTTON AND WOOL.** (SITUATION AND OUTLOOK REPORT. COTTON AND WOOL / UNITED STATES DEPARTMENT OF AGRICULTURE, ECONOMIC RESEARCH SERVICE.). [Situat. outlook rep., Cotton wool]. **Added/Corp** United States. Dept. of Agriculture. Economic Research Service. United States. World Agricultural Outlook Board. **VFOAT** Cotton and Wool; Cotton and Wool Situation and Outlook; Cotton and Wool Situation and Outlook Report. (May 1986)-. Periodical. English. mo. $31.00. Economic Research Service USDA, 341 Victory Drive, Herndon VA 22070. **Tel** (800) 999-6779. **LC** HD9074.; U47a. **DD** 338.1/7351/0973021. ***Continues*** *Outlook and Situation Report. Cotton and Wool, 1051-8894.*
**Ind/Abst** F&S Index Plus Text, Int. [Select. Cov.]; World Agric. Econ.

UK
**SKINNER'S BRITISH TEXTILE REGISTER.** **VFOAT** British Textile Register. 1st- Ed.; 1973-. Multiple languages (English, French, German and Spanish). £10.50. RAC House, Lansdowne Road, Croydon CR9 2HH England. **LC** TS1312; .S55. **DD** 338.4/7/677002542. ***Formed by the union of*** *British Textile Industry; Lancashire Textile Industry; Skinner's Cotton and Man-Made Fibres Directory of the World; Skinner's Hosiery and Knit Goods Directory; Skinner's Wool Trade Directory of the World* ***and*** *Yorkshire Textile Industry.*

KO
**SOMYU YONGAM.** **Added/Corp** Hanguk Somyu Sanop Yonhaphoe. **VFOAT** Textile Year Book. (1980)-. Korean. an. Hanguk Somyu Snaop, Yonhaphoe 10-1, 2 Ka Hoehyon-dong, Chung-ku, Seoul Korea. **LC** HD9866.K65; S66.

SA
**SOUTHERN AFRICA TEXTILES.** ***Title Change.*** **VFOAT** SA Textiles. Aug. 1952-. Academic Scholarly Publication. English. mo. The Phoenix Group, PO Box 69264, Bryanston 2021 Republic South Africa. **LC** TS1300; .S627. **CODEN** TISADK. Documents available from CASDDS. ***Merged with*** *Dyers Digest* ***and*** *Textile Industries Southern Africa* ***to form*** *Textile Industries Dyegest Southern Africa, 0254-0533.*
**Ind/Abst** Chem. Abstr.

US/0038-4607
**SOUTHERN TEXTILE NEWS.** [South. text. news]. (1945)-. Newspaper. English. Fifty times a year (Mon.). $25.00 US; $35.00 Canada & Mexico; $50.00 others. Southern Textile News, PO Box 241028, Charlotte NC 28224. **Tel** (704)527-5111, (800)738-5111, FAX (704)527-5114. **ED** Marjorie T. Richardson. **DD** 382. **Ad Acc, Adv Mgr:** David O'Neal. **Circ:** 6,500. available on microfilm.
**Desc:** Dedicated to management level personnel of the textile manufacturing and allied industries. Covers major industry events, technological changes, market news, legislation, business conditions, mergers, acquisitions, personnel, and trends.
**Ind/Abst** Text. Technol. Dig.

US/0198-8239
**SPIN-OFF (LOVELAND, COLO.).** (SPIN OFF.). Vol. 1 (1977)-. English. qt. $18.00. Interweave Press, 201 East 4th Street, Loveland CO 80537. **Tel** (303)669-7672. **ED** Lee Raven. **LC** TT847; .S677. **DD** 746.1/2/05. **Bk Rev. Ad Acc. Circ:** 13,500 (ctrl).
**Desc:** How-to's, history, fiber use and properties, news and technical information on handspun designs, plus articles and photography.

US/0277-0733
**SPUN YARN PRODUCTION.** See Manufacturing.

US/1046-820X
**STATISTICAL YEARBOOK / CHICAGO MERCANTILE EXCHANGE.** [Stat. yearb. - Chic. Merc. Exch.]. **Added/Corp** Chicago Mercantile Exchange. Chicago Mercantile Exchange. International Monetary Market Division. **VFOAT** Yearbook; Chicago Mercantile Exchange Yearbook. (1984)-. Statistical Publication. English. an. Chicago Mercantile Exchange, 30 South Wacker Drive, Chicago IL 60606. **Tel** (312)930-8210. **DD** 332. ***Formed by the union of*** *Year Book - Chicago Mercantile Exchange, 0577-7259; International Monetary Market Year Book, 0195-9980* ***and*** *Yearbook (Chicago Mercantile Exchange. Index and Option Market), 0884-3686.*

US/0899-5893
**STITCHES MAGAZINE.** [Stitches mag.]. **VFOAT** Stitches. (19??)-. Periodical. English. mo. $54.12 US; $64.71 Canada & Mexico; $74.12 other. Intertec Publishing Corporation, 9800 Metcalf, Overland Park KS 66212. **Tel** (913)341-1300. **(Subscription address:** Intertec Publishing Corporation, PO Box 2901, Overland Park KS 66282.**)** **LC** TS1783; .S75. **DD** 677/.77/05. **[CCC].**

CN/1180-3908
**STOCKLISTS AND NEWS SERVICE FOR CARPET AND FLOORCOVERING BUYERS, THE.** [Stockl. news serv. carpet floorcover. buy.]. **VFOAT** Stocklists. No. 1 (Apr. 1990)-. Periodical. English. bm. $20.00. Mayville Publishing (Canada) Ltd., PO Box 113, 10 Mill Street, Bloomfield, Ontario K0K 1G0 Canada. **DD** 380.1/45677643/097105.

US/0149-0583
**STOCKS OF WOOL AND RELATED FIBERS.** (CURRENT INDUSTRIAL REPORTS. MA-22M, STOCKS OF WOOL AND RELATED FIBERS / U.S. DEPARTMENT OF COMMERCE, BUREAU OF THE CENSUS.). Government Publication. English. be. $1.00. US Department of Commerce / Bureau of the Census, Data User Services Division, Customer Services, Washington DC 20233-0800. **Tel** (301)763-4100. **(Subscription address:** Superintendent of Documents, US Government Printing Office, Washington DC 20402.**)** **LC** HD9891; .S84. ***Continues*** *Current Industrial Reports. M22M, Stocks of Wool and Related Fibers.*
**Desc:** Information on raw wool, tops, noils, and related fibers, including synthetic staple, owned or held on consignment for growers or US agents of foreign exporters.

XR
**STROJIMPORT.** **Added/Corp** Strojimport Foreign Trade Corp. Vol. 1, No. 1 (March 1984)-. Periodical. English (French, Spanish, German and Spanish). Four times a year. $17.30. **(Subscription address:** Artia Pegas Press Ltd., Palac Metro Narodni Trida 25, 11210 Prague 1 Czech Republic.**)** ***Continues in part*** *Strojimport, Investa.*
**Desc:** Information on the textile machinery industry, leather industry and trade, and the sewing-machine industry.
**Ind/Abst** Text. Technol. Dig.

●NE/0924-7696
**STUDIES IN TEXTILE AND COSTUME HISTORY.** [Stud. text. costume hist.]. (1992)-. Monographic series. English. ir. Price varies per volume. E. J. Brill, Postbus 9000, 2300 PA Leiden Netherlands. **Tel** 011 31 71 312624, FAX 011 31 71 317532, telex 39296 BRILL NL. **UDC** 677 + 646.43 :94/99.

US/0565-2030
**SUMMARY OF COTTON FIBER AND PROCESSING TEST RESULTS.** **Added/Corp** United States. Agricultural Marketing Service. Cotton Division. United States. Consumer and Marketing Service. Cotton Division. (19??)-. English. Standards Section, Cotton Division AMS, USDA, 4841 Summer Avenue, Memphis TN 38122. **LC** TS1542; .S9. **DD** 677/.21/30973.

US/0197-4483
**SURFACE DESIGN JOURNAL.** [Surf. des. j.]. **Added/Corp** Surface Design Association (U.S.). **VFOAT** SDJ. Vol. 2, No. 3 (Summer 1978)-. Periodical. English. Four times a year (Mar., June Sept., Dec.). $45.00 (one year); $85.00 (two years); $125.00 (three years) Comes with Surface Design Association membership. Surface Design Association, PO Box 20799, Oakland CA 94620. **Tel** FAX (707)829-3285. **ED** Patricia Malarcher (editor's address: 93 Ivy Lane, Englewood, NJ 07631, phone: (201)568-1084). **Bk Rev**, (Qty: 4). **Ad Acc, Adv Mgr:** Joy Stocksdale, **Tel** (510)841-2008. **Circ:** 3,000 (ctrl). ***Continues*** *Surface Design.*
**Desc:** For those interested in the coloring and patterning of fabric and fiber with dyes, pigments, or manipulation.
**Ind/Abst** Index Inf.

CN/0847-0553
**SURFACING (TORONTO).** (SURFACING.). [Surfacing]. **Added/Corp** Textile Dyers and Printers Association. (1979)-. Periodical. English. qt. Free to members (membership $20.00 per year). Surfacing Textile Dyers Printers Association, PO Box 6828 Station A, Toronto ONT M5W 1X6 Canada. **DD** 746.6/06/0713.

II
**SYNTHETIC FIBRES / ASSOCIATION OF SYNTHETIC FIBRE INDUSTRY.** (June 1972)-. Periodical. English. Four times a year (Feb., May, Aug., Nov.). $48.00. Association of Synthetic Fibre Industry, Raj Mahal 1st/84 Veer Nariman, Bombay 400 020 India. **Tel** 011 91 22 2048075, telex 4323. **(Subscription address:** Prints India, 11 Darya Ganj, New Delhi 110002 India.**)** cum. index. **Ad Acc. Circ:** 1,000 (ctrl).
**Ind/Abst** World Text. Abstr.

HU
**SZOVETKEZETI IPAR.** **Added/Corp** Kisipari Szovetkezetek Orszagos Szovetsege. (19??)-. Periodical. Hungarian. bm. Ikisz, Budapest V Pesti Barnabas UTCA 6, Budapest Hungary. **LC** HD9865.H9; S98.

US/0095-666X
**TECHNICAL BULLETIN - IFI RESEARCH CENTER.** **Main/Corp** IFI Research Center. No. T-486 (March 1973)-. Bulletin. English. IFI Research Center, 12251 Tech Road, Silver Spring MD 20904. **LC** TP932; .N33. **DD** 667/.12/05. ***Continues*** *Technical Bulletin - International Fabricare Institute, Drycleaning Division.*
**Ind/Abst** Art Archaeol. Tech. Abstr.

US/0065-7069
**TECHNICAL REVIEW & REGISTER.** **Main/Corp** American Association for Textile Technology. **VFOAT** AATT Technical Review and Register. 1968-. English. an. Rayon Publishing Company, 303 5th Avenue, New York NY 10016. **LC** TS1300.A16. **DD** 677/.005. ***Continues*** *American Association for Textile Technology. Annual Conference.*

UK
**TECHNICAL TEXTILES.** **Added/Corp** Textile Institute (Manchester, England). No. 1 (Nov. 1989)-. Academic Scholarly Publication. English. Elsevier Science Publishers BV, PO Box 211, 1000 AE Amsterdam Netherlands. **Tel** 011 31 20 5803642, FAX 011 31 20 5862696, telex 15682.
**Ind/Abst** Abstr. Bull. Inst. Pap. Sci. Tech.

●UK/0964-5993
**TECHNICAL TEXTILES INTERNATIONAL.** [Tech. text. int.]. (1992)-. Periodical. English. Ten times a year. $164.00 The Americas; £110.00 other. Elsevier Advanced Technology, An Imprint of Elsevier Science Ltd., The Boulevard, Langford Lane, Kidlington, Oxford OX5 1GB United Kingdom. **Tel** 011 44 865 843000, 011 44 865 843699, FAX 011 44 865 843010. **(Subscription address:** Elsevier Science Ltd. Oxford Fulfillment Centre, PO Box 800, Kidlington, Oxford OX5 1DX United Kingdom.**)** **ED** Nick Butler. **DD** 338.4767705. **[CCC]. Ad Acc.**
**Desc:** Reports on commercial and technological aspects from all sectors of the technical textiles industry, and features focusing on critical and topical subjects. Fibres, fabrics, machinery, finishing processes, and applications are included.

IT/0392-8136
**TECNICA DELLA CONFEZIONE E DELLA MAGLIERIA.** (1975)-. Periodical. Italian. bm (6 issues). L55000 Italy; L100000 other. Tecnica della Confezione Srl, Via Fabio Filzi 27, 20124 Milan Italy. **Tel** 011 39 2 6690677. **UDC** 677.

SP/0040-1900
**TECNICA TEXTIL INTERNACIONAL.** [Tec. text. int.]. (1972)-. Periodical. Spanish. bm. $90.00 Europe; $110.00 other. Etecnes, Travesera de Gracia 15, Barcelona 08021 Spain. **Tel** FAX 011 34 3 2096918. **UDC** 677. **Bk Rev. Ad Acc. Pr Rev. Circ:** 7,500 (ctrl). ***Continues*** *Tecnica Textil, 0210-1599.*
**Desc:** Contains articles on different aspects of the textile industry.

FR/0040-2206
**TEINTURE ET APPRETS.** [Teint. apprets.]. Began in 1948. Academic Scholarly Publication. French. bm. Siege Social et Bureaux, 97 rue du Bas-Saut, 60230 Chambly France. **CODEN** TNAPA7. Documents available from CASDDS.
**Ind/Abst** Chem. Abstr. (1948-1977).

FI/0785-0549
**TEKSTIILI- JA VAATETUSTEOLLISUUS.** **VFOAT** Textil- Och Bekladnadsindustri. Finnish (Swedish). an. Tilastokeskus, PL 504, Annankatu 44, 00101 Helsinki Finland. **Tel** 358-0-17341, FAX 358-0-17342474, telex 1002111 TILASTO SF. **LC** HD9865.F5; T45.

FI
**TEKSTIILILEHTI.** **Added/Corp** Suomen Tekstiilimiesten Liitto. (1937)-. Periodical. Finnish. Six times a year. $64.86. Textile-Technical Association Finland, Suvantokatu 1A, SF 33100 Tampere Finland. **Tel** 011 358 31 12835. **LC** TS1300; .T1216.

FI
**TEKSTIILITEOLLISUUDEN KONEKANTA. TEXTILINDUSTRINS MASKINER.** **Main/Corp** Finland. Tilastokeskus. (1969)-. Multiple languages (Finnish and Swedish). Tilastokeskus, PL 504, Annankatu 44, 00101 Helsinki Finland. **Tel** 358-0-17341, FAX 358-0-17342474, telex 1002111 TILASTO SF. **LC** HD9865.F5; F55A.

FI
**TEKSTIILITEOLLISUUDEN VUOSIKIRJA. TEXTILINDUSTRINS ARSBOK. THE TEXTILE INDUSTRY YEARBOOK.** **Added/Corp** Tekstiiliteollisuuden Tyonantajaliitto. Tekstiiliteollisuusyhdistys Tekstiilivaltuuskunta. **VFOAT** Textilindustrins Arsbok; The Textile Industry Yearbook. (19??)-. Finnish (Swedish; summaries and/or abstracts in English). Tekstiiliteollisuuden Tyonantajaliitto, Aleksis Kivenkatu 10 33210, Tampere 21 Finland. **LC** TS1395.F5; T44.

CI/0492-5882
**TEKSTIL.** (1952)-. Periodical. Multiple languages. mo. Savez Inzenjera i Tehnicara Tekstilaca Hrvatske, Novakova 8-11, PP 829, Zagreb Croatia. **UDC** 677. **Ind/Abst** Soc. Sci. Cit. Index [Select. Cov.].

RU/0040-2397
**TEKSTILNAJA PROMYSLENNOST.** (TEKSTILNAIA PROMYSHLENNOST.). [Tekst. prom.]. **Added/Corp** Soviet Union. Narodnyi Komissariat Tekstilnoi Promyshlennosti. Soviet Union. Ministerstvo Tekstilnoi Promyshlennosti. Soviet Union. Ministerstvo Legkoi Promyshlennosti. Soviet Union. Ministerstvo Promyshlennykh Tovarov Shirokogo Potrebleniia. Soviet Union. Gosudarstvennyi Nauchno-Tekhnicheskii Komitet. Profsoiuz Rabochikh Tekstilnoi i Legkoi Promyshlennosti (Soviet Union). TSK. Nauchno-Tekhnicheskoe Obshchestvo Legkoi Promyshlennosti (Soviet Union). TSentralnoe Pravlenie. Soviet Union. Gosudarstvennyi Komitet po Koordinatsii Nauchno-Issledovatelskikh Rabot. Soviet Union. Gosudarstvennyi Komitet po Legkoi Promyshlennosti. (1941)-. Academic Scholarly Publication. Russian (table of contents in English, French and German). mo. $99.95. **(Subscription address:** East View Publications Inc., 3020 Harbor Lane North, Suite 110, Minneapolis MN 55447.**)** **LC** TS1300; .T122. **CODEN** TTLPA2. Documents available from CASDDS. ***Formed by the union of*** *Promyshlennost Lubianykh Volokon; Khlopchatobumazhnaia Promyshlennost; Shelk* ***and*** *Sherstianoe Delo.*
**Ind/Abst** Abstr. Bull. Inst. Pap. Sci. Tech.; Art Archaeol. Tech. Abstr.; Chem. Abstr.; World Text. Abstr.

SP
**TET : THE EAST TRADE. See** Interior Design.

IT
**TEX HOME.** Italian (English). mo (10 issues). L70000.00 Italy; L95000.00 other. Editoriale Galfa, Viale Monza 57, 20125 Milan Italy. **Tel** 011 39 2 2891452, FAX 011 39 2 2840574, telex 315614. **ED** Sergio Coccia. **Ad Acc**, **Adv Mgr:** Aldo Gerbert. **Circ:** 8,000 (ctrl).

BE
**TEX - TEXTILIS, DE. Added/Corp** Nationale Groepering van Textielingenieurs en Textielbedrijfsleiders. Association des Ingenieurs Sortis de l'ecole Superieure des Textiles de Verviers. Nederlands Textielinstituut. No. 6 (June 1973)-. Periodical. Multiple languages (Dutch and French). bm. $14.83. De Tex Textiles, 92 Savaanstraat, Ghent Belgium. ***Continues*** *De Tex Textilis.*
**Ind/Abst** Art Archaeol. Tech. Abstr.; Nonwovens Abstr.

II
**TEXINCON. Added/Corp** National Information Centre for Textile and Allied Subjects (India). **VFOAT** Textile Information Condensed. Vol. 1, No. 1 (Jan. 1989)-. Periodical. English. qt. $40.00. National Information Centre for Textile and Allied Subjects (NICTAS), Third Floor, At Atira, Ahmedabad 380 015 India. **Tel** 442671, telex 121-6571. **(Subscription address:** Prints India, 11 Darya Ganj, New Delhi, 110002 India, (Phone: 011 91 11 3268645)**)**

II/0970-5686
**TEXINCON AHMEDABAD.** (TEXINCON - TEXTILE INFORMATION CONDENSED.). [Texincon Ahmedabad]. **VFOAT** Textile Information Condensed. (1989)-. Periodical. English. qt. Rs300.00 India; $50.00 other. National Information Centre for Textile and Allied Subjects (NICTAS), Third Floor, At Atira, Ahmedabad 380 015 India. **Tel** 442671, telex 121-6571. **(Subscription address:** Prints India, 11 Darya Ganj, New Delhi 110002 India.**)** **ED** P. C. Shah. **UDC** 677. Index available. cum. index. **Bk Rev**. **Ad Acc**. **Pr Rev. Circ:** 1,000. available on diskette.
**Desc:** Summaries of textile related articles, books, etc.

NE
**TEXPRESS.** VNU Business Publications BV, Postbus 9479, 1006 AC Amsterdam Netherlands. **Tel** 011 31 20 5102911, 011 31 20 5102879, FAX 011 31 20 6170291.

SA
**TEXREPORT.** (19??)-. English. ir. R20.00 South Africa; R24.00 other (per report). Division of Textile Technology, Port Elizabeth 6000 South Africa. **Tel** 27 41 532131, FAX 27 41 532325, telex 24 5183. **ED** P. Horn. **Circ:** 230 (ctrl). ***Continues*** *SAWTRI Special Publication, 0258-4565.*
**Desc:** Textile related topics such as the physical and chemical properties of natural fibers or blends of wool, cotton and mohair with synthetics of one another.

NE
**TEXTIEL BEHEER.** (1990)-. Periodical. Dutch. bm. Stichting Vakblad Textielreiniging, Rembrandtlaan 67, 3723 BH Bilthoven Netherlands. **Tel** 011 31 30 456338. ***Absorbed*** *Textielverzorging, 0169-5584.*

XR/0040-4829
**TEXTIL.** [Textil]. (1946)-. Periodical. Czech. mo. $58.60. **(Subscription address:** Artia Pegas Press Ltd., Palac Metro Narodni Trida 25, 11210 Prague 1 Czech Republic.**)**
**Ind/Abst** Abstr. Bull. Inst. Pap. Sci. Tech.; Saf. Health Work; World Text. Abstr.

HU/0209-9578
**TEXTIL- ES TEXTILRUHAZATI IPARI SZAKIRODALMI TAJEKOZTATO.** (1981)-. Periodical. Hungarian. mo. 6.200ft. Orszagos Muszaki Informacios Kozpont es Konyvtar (O.M.I.K.K.), National Technical Information Centre and Library Museum, u 17, PO Box 12, 1428 Budapest, Hungary. **Tel** (361)118-1994, FAX (361)138-2414, telex 22-4944 OMIKK H. **ED** Gatai Gyorgyne. **UDC** 016. Index available. cum. index. **Bk Rev**. **Ad Acc**. **Circ:** 115 (ctrl).
**Desc:** Information on the textile industry.

GW
**TEXTIL MITTEILUNGEN : TM.** (19??)-. German. wk. DM235.00 Germany; DM320.00 other. Branche & Business Fachverlag, Postfach 101701, D 40008 Duesseldorf Germany. **Tel** 011 49 211 132375.

GW/0040-4853
**TEXTIL PRAXIS INTERNATIONAL.** ***Ceased.*** [Text.-Prax. int.]. (1971)-(Oct. 1994). Academic Scholarly Publication. German (English). mo. Konradin Verlagsgruppe, Postfach 100252, Ernst Mey Str 8, W-7022 Leinfelden Echterdingen 1 Germany. **Tel** (0711)75940, telex 7 255 421. **ED** Horst Meyrahn. **LC** TS1300; .T126. **DD** 677/.005. **CODEN** TXPIAT. **[CCC]**. **Bk Rev**. **Ad Acc**. **Circ:** 7,088. Documents available from CASDDS. ***Continues*** *Textil-Praxis.*
**Desc:** Magazine for practice and research in spinning, twisting, weaving, non-wovens, fabric manufacturing, dyeing, and finishing industries.
**Ind/Abst** Art Archaeol. Tech. Abstr.; Chem. Abstr.; EMBASE; F&S Index Plus Text, Int. [Select. Cov.]; Nonwovens Abstr.; PROMT; Saf. Health Work; Text. Technol. Dig.

GW/0040-487X
**TEXTIL-WIRTSCHAFT (FRANKFURT).** (TEXTIL-WIRTSCHAFT.). [Text.-Wirtsch.]. **Added/Corp** Bundesverband des Deutschen Textileinzelhandels. European Association of National Textile Retailers' Organizations. (1946)-. Periodical. German. wk. DM360.89 Germany; DM386.55 Austria; DM527.85 other. Deutscher Fachverlag GmbH, Verlagsgruppe, D 60264 Frankfurt Germany. **Tel** 011 49 69 75951001, telex 411 862.
**Ind/Abst** F&S Index Plus Text, Int. [Select. Cov.]; PROMT.

US/0894-8267
**TEXTILE ANALYSIS BULLETIN SERVICE.** (TEXTILE ANALYSIS BULLETIN SERVICE : TABS / INTERNATIONAL FABRICARE INSTITUTE.). [Text. anal. bull. serv.]. **Added/Corp** International Fabricare Institute. **VFOAT** TABS; T.A.B.S. (19??)-. Bulletin. English. ir. 15.00Can$. Textile Analysis Service, 315 B Printing Service Building, Edmonton Alberta 26G 2N1 Canada. **Tel** (403)432-3832. **DD** 667.
**Ind/Abst** AGRICOLA [Select. Cov.].

US/1051-4090
**TEXTILE & TEXT.** ***Ceased.*** [Text. text]. **Added/Corp** Fashion Institute of Technology (New York, N.Y.). **VFOAT** Textile and Text. Vol. 12, No. 1 & 2 (1989)-Vol. 15, No. 2. Periodical. English. qt. Fashion Institute of Technology, 7th Avenue 27th Street, New York NY 10001. **Tel** (212)760-7970. **DD** 746. **Circ:** 500. ***Continues*** *Textile Booklist, 0149-5682.*
**Ind/Abst** BHA : Biblio. Hist. Art.

HK/0049-3554
**TEXTILE ASIA.** [Text. Asia]. **VFOAT** Ya-Chou Fang Chih Yueh Kan. Vol. 1 (Oct. 1970)-. Academic Scholarly Publication. English. mo. 398.00HK$ Hong Kong; 475.00HK$ Macau & China; $95.00 other. Business Press Ltd, California Tower/11th Floor, 30-32 D'Aguilar Street, GPO Box 185, Hong Kong. **Tel** 011 852 5 5-233744, 5-247467, 5-247523, 5-247441, FAX 011 825 8106966, telex 60275 TEXIA HX. **ED** Kayser Sung. **LC** TS1399; .T44. **DD** 338.4/7/677095. **CODEN** TASIDM. Index available (Published separately). **Bk Rev**. **Ad Acc**. **Pr Rev. Circ:** 17,000. Documents available from CASDDS.
**Desc:** Includes textile and clothing technology, reports on and analyses of international textile trade, management features, new equipment reports, fashion trends, news about textile companies and people.
**Ind/Abst** Chem. Abstr. (1970-1983); Cot. Trop. Fibr. Abstr. Bibliogr.; Nonwovens Abstr.; Text. Technol. Dig.; World Text. Abstr.

HK
**TEXTILE ASIA INDEX.** English. an (Edition year published March of following year). 120.00HK$ Hong Kong & Macau; $19.00 other. Business Press Ltd, California Tower/11th Floor, 30-32 D'Aguilar Street, GPO Box 185, Hong Kong. **Tel** 011 852 5 5-233744, 5-247467, 5-247523, 5-247441, FAX 011 825 8106966, telex 60275 TEXIA HX. **ED** Kayser Sung. **Ad Acc**. **Pr Rev. Circ:** 15,500.
**Desc:** Covers policies, economics, interviews, technology, trade, markets, exhibitions, fashion trends, management features and development of new machinery, plant equipment and processes for the textile industry.

US/0739-0491
**TEXTILE BUSINESS OUTLOOK.** [Text. bus. outlook]. **Added/Corp** Statistikon Corp. (19??)-. English. sa. $985.00. Statistikon Corporation, PO Box 246, East Norwich NY 11732. **Tel** (516)922-0882, FAX (516)624-3145. **ED** Jordan P Yale.
**Desc:** Short (monthly) and intermediate (2 years) term computer forecasts of textile-time series for the U.S.A., and around the world (by select country and geographic area). Textile consumer marketing trends, analysis of textile financial trends, other color graphics.

US/0270-0786
**TEXTILE CHALLENGER. See** Economics-Labor.

US/0040-490X
**TEXTILE CHEMIST AND COLORIST.** [Text. chem. color.]. **Added/Corp** American Association of Textile Chemists and Colorists. Vol. 1 (Jan. 1969)-. Academic Scholarly Publication. English. Twelve times a year (July issues is published as buyer's guide). $30.00 US & Canada; $40.00 other; $50.00 (senior), $61.00 (associate) Comes with American Assoication of Textile Chemists & Colorist membership. American Association of Textile Chemists and Colorists, PO Box 12215, Research Triangle Park NC 27709. **Tel** (919)549-8141, FAX (919)549-8933. **ED** Jack Kissiah. **LC** TP890; .T28. **DD** 677/.02825/05. **CODEN** TCCOB6. **[CCC].** cum. index. **Bk Rev**. **Ad Acc**. **Pr Rev. Circ:** 10,200 (ctrl). available on microfilm and microfiche from University Microfilms International (UMI). Documents available from Article Express International, The Genuine Article, CASDDS.
**Desc:** Contains current news and features on all phases of textile wet processing, plus in-depth reports on AATCC activities.
**Ind/Abst** Abstr. Bull. Inst. Pap. Sci. Tech.; AGRICOLA [Select. Cov.]; Art Archaeol. Tech. Abstr.; Bioeng. Abstr.; Chem. Abstr.; Curr. Contents Eng. Tech. Appl. Sci.; Ei Page One; EMBASE; Eng. Index Annu. [Select. Cov.]; Res. Alert [Full Cov.]; Soc. Sci. Cit. Index [Select. Cov.]; Text. Technol. Dig.; World Text. Abstr.

US/0094-5781
**TEXTILE CLEANING TECHNOLOGY.** **Main/Corp** International Fabricare Institute. (19??)-. Periodical. English. mo. $40.00. International Fabricare Institute, 12251 Tech Road, Silver Spring MD 20904. **Tel** (301)622-1900. **LC** TP932.3; .I56a. **DD** 667/.12/05.

II/0040-4926
**TEXTILE DYER & PRINTER.** [Text. dyer print.]. Vol.1 (1967)-. Academic Scholarly Publication. English. Twenty-six times a year. $36.00 (surface mail); $75.00 (airmail). Sevak Publications, 306 Shri Hanuman Ind, Est Gd Ambekar Road, Wadala 400 031, Bombay India. **Tel** 91 22 4120743, 91 22 4131198, telex 1176053 CWLY IN. **(Subscription address:** Prints India, 11 Darya Ganj, New Delhi, 110002 India, (Phone: 011 91 11 3268645)**)** **ED** R Raghavan. **LC** TP890; .T34. **CODEN** TDYPAN. **Bk Rev**, (Qty: 26). **Ad Acc**. **Circ:** 10,000 (ctrl). Documents available from CASDDS.
**Desc:** Devoted to textile wet processing industry.
**Ind/Abst** Art Archaeol. Tech. Abstr.; Chem. Abstr.; Text. Technol. Dig.; World Text. Abstr.

II
**TEXTILE DYER & PRINTER : ANNUAL NUMBER.** English. Sevak Publications, 306 Shri Hanuman Ind, Est Gd Ambekar Road, Wadala 400 031, Bombay India. **Tel** 91 22 4120743, 91 22 4131198, telex 1176053 CWLY IN. **LC** TP890; .T35. **DD** 667/.3/05.

JA
**TEXTILE EXPORTS OF JAPAN : COUNTRY BY COMMODITY. Main/Corp** Yushutsu Seni Tokei Kyokai (Japan). **VFOAT** Seni Yushutsu Tokei Geppyo: Kunibetsu Shohinbetsu. Multiple languages (English and Japanese). Yushutsu Seni Tokei Kyokai, c/o Textile Exporters' House 4 Higashi-ku, Osaka 540 Japan. **LC** HD9866.J3; Y87A. **DD** 382/.45677/00952.

AT/0818-6308
**TEXTILE FIBRE FORUM. Added/Corp** Australian Forum for Textile Arts. **VFOAT** Fibre Forum. Vol. 6, Issue 1 (1987)-. Periodical. English. Three times a year (Mar., July, Nov.). 18.00Aus$ one year; 35.00Aus$ two years. Australian Forum Textile Arts, PO Box 38, The Gap Queensland 4061 Australia. **Tel** 011 61 7 3006491. **ED** Janet de Boer. cum. index. **Bk Rev**, (Qty: 30). **Ad Acc**. **Pr Rev. Circ:** 8,000 (ctrl). ***Continues*** *Fibre Forum, 0725-9565.*

US/1054-982X
**TEXTILE FINANCIAL OUTLOOK. ENGINEERING.** [Text. financ. outlook]. **VFOAT** TFO. (1991)-. English. an. $3,985.00. Statistikon Corporation, PO Box 246, East Norwich NY 11732. **Tel** (516)922-0882, FAX (516)624-3145. **LC** IN PROCESS. **DD** 338.
**Desc:** Evaluation and analysis of the textile industry's quarterly balance sheet income statement. Trend evaluations of aggregate costs - raw materials, energy, labor, and investments.Also trend evaluations of aggregate fabrication prices - fibers, yarns, fabrics and end uses.

US/0738-9620
**TEXTILE FLAMMABILITY DIGEST.** ***Ceased.*** [Text. flammabl. dig.]. Vol.1, (1973)-Ceased with Vol. 15, Dec. (1987). Periodical. English. mo. LeBlanc Research Corporation, PO Box 391, Tallulah LA

71284-0391. **Tel** (318)574-4343. **ED** R Bruce LeBlanc. **Bk Rev. Ad Acc. Circ:** 200 (ctrl).
**Desc:** Abstracts of all literature, patents, meetings, and other information on textile flammability and flame resistance.

UK/0040-4969
**TEXTILE HISTORY.** [Text. hist.]. **Added/Corp** Pasold Research Fund Ltd. Vol. 1, No. 1 (Dec. 1968)-. Periodical. English. Twice a year (July, & Dec.). £48.00 (institutions), £24.00 (individuals). W. S. Maney and Son Ltd., Hudson Road, Leeds LS9 7DL England. **Tel** 011 44 532 497481, FAX 011 44 532 486983. **LC** HD9850.1; .T52. **DD** 338.4/7677/005. **[CCC].**
**Desc:** Textile history.
**Ind/Abst** Am. Hist. Life (1989-); Anim. Breed. Abstr.; Art Archaeol. Tech. Abstr.; Art Index; ARTbibliogr. Mod.; BHA : Biblio. Hist. Art; Br. Archaeol. Bibliogr.; Br. Humanit. Index; Text. Technol. Dig.; World Text. Abstr.

●UK/1351-0266
**TEXTILE HORIZONS. VFOAT** TH. (1994)-. English. Six times a year. $180.00 US; £65.00 Europe; £95.00 other. International Textile Benjamin Dent Ltd, 23 Bloomsbury Square, London WC1A 2P England. **Tel** 011 44 71 637 2211, FAX 011 44 71 637 2248, telex 8954884. ***Continues*** *Textile Horizons International.*
**Desc:** Specialist textiles and management journal distributed to all members of the Textile Institute and others involved in the textile industry all over the world.

UK/1351-0266
**TEXTILE HORIZONS INTERNATIONAL.** ***Title Change.*** **Added/Corp** Textile Institute (Manchester, England). **VFOAT** Textile Horizons; TH. Vol. 12, No. 1 (Jan. 1992)-Vol. 13, No. 6 (Dec. 1993). Academic Scholarly Publication. English. mo. International Textile Benjamin Dent Ltd, 23 Bloomsbury Square, London WC1A 2P England. **Tel** 011 44 71 637 2211, FAX 011 44 71 637 2248, telex 8954884. **LC** HD9850.1; .T527. Documents available from Article Express International. ***Continues*** *Textile Horizons, 0260-6518.* ***Continued by*** *Textile Horizons (London, England).*
**Ind/Abst** Abstr. Bull. Inst. Paper Chem.; Abstr. Bull. Inst. Pap. Sci. Tech.; Bioeng. Abstr.; Ei Page One; EMBASE; Eng. Index Annu.; Predicasts; World Text. Abstr.

SA/0254-0533
**TEXTILE INDUSTRIES DYEGEST OF SOUTHERN AFRICA.** [Text. ind. dyegest, South. Afr.]. **Added/Corp** Dyers and Finishers Association (South Africa) Textile Institute (Manchester, England). East London. Textile Institute (Manchester, England). Eastern. Textile Institute (Manchester, England). Natal. Textile Institute (Manchester, England). Transvaal. Textile Institute (Manchester, England). Western. **VFOAT** Textile Industries Dyegest S.A.; Textiles Industries Dyegest. Vol. 1, No. 1 (June 1982)-. Academic Scholarly Publication. English. Twelve times a year. R75.24 South Africa; R80.00 APU countries; R96.00 other. George Warman Publications Pty, PO Box 704, Cape Town 8000 South Africa. **Tel** 011 27 21 245320, FAX 011 27 21 261332, telex 5-21849. **ED** Tony Walker. **CODEN** TIDADD. **Ad Acc. Circ:** 1,750 (ctrl). Documents available from CASDDS. ***Formed by the union of*** *Textile Industries Southern Africa; Dyers Dyegest* ***and*** *Southern Africa Textiles.*
**Ind/Abst** Art Archaeol. Tech. Abstr.; Chem. Abstr. (1982-1983); Nonwovens Abstr.; Text. Technol. Dig.; World Text. Abstr.

II/0040-4993
**TEXTILE INDUSTRY & TRADE JOURNAL.** [Text. ind. trade j.]. (Jan. 1963)-. Periodical. English. mo. $25.00. Indian Export Trade Journal, Savajuganj, Baroda 5 India. **Tel** 329158. **(Subscription address:** Prints India, 11 Darya Ganj, New Delhi, 110002 India, (Phone: 011 91 11 3268645)) **ED** C M Pandit and B V Pandit. **LC** TS1300; .T21394. **DD** 677/.005. **Bk Rev. Ad Acc. Circ:** 4,500.
**Desc:** Includes information on textile technology, weaving, spinning, processing, fabrics, garments, silk, wool, rayon, and man-made fabrics.
**Ind/Abst** Art Archaeol. Tech. Abstr.; Text. Technol. Dig.

SZ
**TEXTILE LEADER. Added/Corp** International Textile Service. **VFOAT** ITS Textile Leader. **VAT** International Textile Service Textile Leader. (1989?)-. Periodical. English (German, Chinese and Spanish). sa. $55.00 (1 year), $100.00 (2 year). International Textile Service Ltd, Kesslerstrasse 9/PO Box 8952, Schlieren Switzerland. **Tel** 011 41 1 7305856, FAX 011 41 1 7308183, telex 827758. ***Continues*** *ITS Textile Leader.*

II/0040-5078
**TEXTILE MAGAZINE, THE.** Vol. 1 (1959)-. Periodical. English. Twelve times a year. Rs1800. Textile Magazine, Gr Complex 407, 408 Mount Road, Madras 600035 India. **Tel** 11 91 44 452892, FAX 011 91 044 457579. **(Subscription address:** Prints India, 11 Darya Ganj, New Delhi 110002 India.) **ED** R. Kalidusan. **LC** TS1300; .T498. **Bk Rev**, (Qty: 12). **Ad Acc. Circ:** 20,000 (ctrl).

CN/0381-551X
**TEXTILE MANUAL.** (TEXTILE MANUAL. MANUEL DU TEXTILE.). **VFOAT** Manuel du Textile; Manual of the Textile Industry of Canada. (1969)-. English (French). an. $7.50. Canadian Textile Journal, 1 Pacifique Ste. Anne De Bellevue, Quebec H9X 1C5. **LC** TS1326; .M3. **DD** 338.4/7/67700971. **CODEN** TXMNBU. ***Continues*** *Manual of the Textile Industry of Canada, 0076-4183.*

UK
**TEXTILE MANUFACTURER & KNITTING WORLD. VFOAT** Knitting World & Textile Manufacturer. V. 102, No. 1202- May 1975-. Periodical. English. mo. £10.00. 33 King Street, London M2 6AA England. **LC** TS1300; .T226. **DD** 338.4/7/67700941. available on microfilm and microfiche from University Microfilms International (UMI). ***Supersedes in part*** *Textile Manufacturer; British Knitting Industry.*

US/1065-1713
**TEXTILE MANUFATURING.** [Textile manuf.]. (Jan. 1988)-. Periodical. English. bm (6 issues). $30.00 US; $36.00 Canada & Mexico; $42.00 other. Merit Publications Inc, 12 Perimeter Park Drive, Suite 102, Atlanta GA 30341. **Tel** (404)451-4990, FAX (404)451-4880. **ED** Steve Barnes. **DD** 338. **Bk Rev. Ad Acc. Circ:** 16,500 (ctrl).

UK/0040-5116
**TEXTILE MONTH.** [Text. mon.]. (Jan. 1968)-. Periodical. English. Twelve times a year. £65.56 UK; £72.00 Ireland; £84.58 Europe; £82.29 (surface mail), £106.29 (airmail) other. World Textile Publications Ltd., 76 Kirkgate, Bradford West Yorkshire, BD1 1TB England. **Tel** 011 44 274 726357, 011 44 274 731907, FAX 011 44 274 735045, telex 517617 WOOLMN G. **LC** TS1300; .T312. **DD** 677/.005. **CODEN** TXMOAW. available on microfilm and microfiche from University Microfilms International (UMI). Documents available from Article Express International. ***Formed by the union of*** *Man-Made Textiles, 0369-0989* ***and*** *Textile Recorder, 0372-1094.*
**Desc:** Comprehensive coverage of the latest world textile news and major machinery and processing developments.
**Ind/Abst** Bioeng. Abstr.; Curr. Technol. Index; Ei Page One; EMBASE; Eng. Index Annu.; F&S Index Plus Text, Int. [Select. Cov.]; Nonwovens Abstr.; Predicasts; PROMT; Text. Technol. Dig.; World Text. Abstr.

US/0083-7407
**TEXTILE MUSEUM JOURNAL. See** Museums and Galleries.

UK/0268-4764
**TEXTILE OUTLOOK INTERNATIONAL.** (TEXTILE OUTLOOK INTERNATIONAL / THE ECONOMIST PUBLICATIONS.). [Text. outlook int.]. **Added/Corp** Economist Publications (Firm) Economist Intelligence Unit (Great Britain). (1985)-. Periodical. English. bm. $562.50 (schools and educational libraries), $750.00 (other)*North America. The Economist Intelligence Unit, 40 Duke Street, London W1A 1DW England. **Tel** 011 44 71 8301000. **(Subscription address:** Economist Intelligence Unit / North America Subscriptions, 111 West 57th Street, New York NY 10019.) **LC** HD9850.1; .T45. **DD** 338.4/7677/005. **CODEN** TOINEI.
**Ind/Abst** Text. Technol. Dig.

US/0739-4144
**TEXTILE PRICING OUTLOOK. Added/Corp** Statistikon Corp. (19??)-. Periodical. English. Twice a year. $985.00. Statistikon Corporation, PO Box 246, East Norwich NY 11732. **Tel** (516)922-0882, FAX (516)624-3145. **ED** Jordan P. Yale.
**Desc:** Evaluation and prediction of short term price trends for fiber raw materials, textiles (yarns, fibers, fabrics), apparel.

CN/0319-891X
**TEXTILE PRODUCTS INDUSTRIES.** (TEXTILE PRODUCTS INDUSTRIES / STATISTICS CANADA, MANUFACTURING AND PRIMARY INDUSTRIES DIVISION, FOODS, BEVERAGES, TEXTILES AND MISCELLANEOUS INDUSTRIES SECTION.). [Text. prod. ind.]. **Added/Corp** Statistics Canada. Foods, Beverages, Textiles and Miscellaneous Industries Section. Statistics Canada. Census of Manufactures Section. Statistics Canada. Industry Division. Statistics Canada. Annual Survey of Manufactures Section. **VFOAT** Industrie de Produits Textiles; Industries des Produits Textiles. (1981)-. English (French). an. 38.00Can$ Canada; $46.00 US; $54.00 other. Statistics Canada, Publications Sales & Services, Main Building Room 1710, Ottawa Ontario K1A 0T6 Canada. **Tel** (613)951-5078, (800)267-6677, FAX (613)951-1584, telex 053-3585. **LC** HD9864.C2; T49. **DD** 338.4/7677/00971021. ***Formed by the union of*** *Canvas Products and Cotton and Jute Bags Industries, 0700-0278; Cordage and Twine Industry (Statistics Canada : Final), 0527-4990; Miscellaneous Textile Industries (Final), 0300-0257* ***and*** *Felt and Fibre Processing Mills, 0700-0731;* ***Absorbed*** *Carpet, Mat and Rug Industry (Final), 0527-4893.*
**Desc:** Annual census of manufacturers.

UK/0040-5167
**TEXTILE PROGRESS.** (TEXTILE PROGRESS / THE TEXTILE INSTITUTE.). [Text. prog.]. **Added/Corp** Textile Institute (Manchester, England). Vol. 1, No. 1 (March 1969)-. Periodical. English. qt. £60.00 UK; $120.00 US and Canada. Textile Institute, 10 Blackfriars Street, Manchester M3 5DR England. **Tel** 11 44 61 834 8457, FAX 11 44 61 835 3087, telex 668297 G. **(Subscription address:** Textile Progress / North America Subscriptions, PO Box 1897, Lawrence KS 66044-8897.) **LC** TS1300; .T316. **DD** 677/.005. **CODEN** TXPRAM. Index available in last issue of volume--attached. available on microfilm and microfiche from University Microfilms International (UMI). Documents available from Article Express International.
**Ind/Abst** Abstr. Bull. Inst. Pap. Sci. Tech.; Bioeng. Abstr.; Ei Page One; Eng. Index Annu.; Text. Technol. Dig.; World Text. Abstr.

UK
**TEXTILE RECORDER BOOK OF THE YEAR, THE.** 1947/48-. English. an. **LC** TS1301; .T45. **DD** 677.05. ***Continues*** *Textile Recorder Year Book.*

US/0195-0118
**TEXTILE RENTAL.** [Text. rent.]. **Added/Corp** Textile Rental Services Association of America. (197?)-. Periodical. English. mo. $90.00 (one year). Textile Rental Services Association of American, 1130 East Beach Boulevard/Suite B, Hallandale FL 33008. **Tel** (305)457-7555, FAX (305)457-3890. ***Continues*** *Linen Supply News, 0024-3825.*
**Ind/Abst** Health Plan. Adminis.; Hospit. Health Admin. Index; Predicasts.

US/0040-5175
**TEXTILE RESEARCH JOURNAL.** [Tex. res. j.]. Vol. 15, No. 2; Feb. 1945-. Academic Scholarly Publication. English. mo. $130.00. Textile Research Institute, PO Box 625, Princeton NJ 08540. **Tel** (609)924-3150. **ED** Ludwig Rebenfeld. **LC** TS1300; .T43. **DD** 677. **CODEN** TRJOA9. **[CCC].** Index available. **Bk Rev. Pr Rev. Circ:** 2,000. available on microfilm and microfiche from University Microfilms International (UMI). Documents available from Article Express International, The Genuine Article, CASDDS. ***Continues*** *Textile Research, 0096-5928.*
**Desc:** Contains fundamental and applied scientific information in the physical, chemical, and engineering sciences related to the textile and allied industries.
**Ind/Abst** Abstr. Bull. Inst. Pap. Sci. Tech.; AGRICOLA [Select. Cov.]; Appl. Sci. Technol. Index; Art Archaeol. Tech. Abstr.; Bioeng. Abstr.; Chem. Abstr.; Cot. Trop. Fibr. Abstr. Bibliogr.; Curr. Contents Eng. Tech. Appl. Sci.; Ei Page One; EMBASE; Eng. Index Annu.; F&S Index Plus Text, Int. [Select. Cov.]; Int. Aerosp. Abstr.; Nonwovens Abstr.; Life Sci. Collect.; Polymer Contents; PROMT; Res. Alert [Full Cov.]; Sci. Cit. Index; SCISEARCH; Text. Technol. Dig.; World Text. Abstr.

US/0040-5191
**TEXTILE TECHNOLOGY DIGEST. See** Textiles-Abstracting, Bibliographies and Statistics.

UK/0953-2404
**TEXTILE TECHNOLOGY INTERNATIONAL.** [Text. technol. int.]. (1988)-. English. an. £55.00. Sterling Publications Ltd., PO Box 799, Brunel House, London W2 1XR England. **Tel** 011 44 71 2580066, FAX 011 44 71 4026441, telex 295819 ESPEEL G.

II/0040-5205
**TEXTILE TRENDS.** (1???)-. Periodical. English. mo. $13.92 India; $100.00 other. Eastland Publications Pr Ltd, 44 Chittaranjan Avenue, Calcutta 700 012 India. **Tel** 11 91 33 273096. **(Subscription address:** Prints India, 11 Darya Ganj, New Delhi, 110002 India, (Phone: 011 91 11 3268645)) **ED** Malay Chakrabarti. **LC** TS1300; .T46. **Bk Rev. Ad Acc. Circ:** 4,000.
**Desc:** Various articles, news, write-ups on textile and allied industries for the textile and allied industries exclusively served by us.
**Ind/Abst** Art Archaeol. Tech. Abstr.; Nonwovens Abstr.; Text. Technol. Dig.

NE
**TEXTILE VIEW MAGAZINE. See** Clothing Industry and Fashion.

US/0161-9713
**TEXTILE WEEK.** V. 1- May 22, 1978-. Periodical. English. wk. $156.00. McGraw Hill Publishing Company, Inc., 1221 Avenue of the Americas, New York NY 10020. **Tel** (212)512-6410, (800)525-5003, FAX (212)512-6111. **LC** HD9851; .T46. **DD** 338.4/7/67700973.

US/0040-5213
**TEXTILE WORLD.** [Text. world]. Vol. 59, No. 6 (Feb. 5, 1921)-. Periodical. English. mo. $45.00 (one year), $75.00 (two year), $105.00 (three year) US & Canada; $80.00 (one year), $135.00 (two year), $190.00 (three year) other. MacLean Hunter Publishing Corporation / Chicago, IL, 29 North Wacker Drive, Chicago IL 60606-3298. **Tel** (312)726-2802, FAX (312)726-3091. **CODEN** TEWOAH. **[CCC]. Ad Acc.** ctrl circ. available on microfilm and microfiche from University Microfilms International (UMI); available on an online database (file 648/Full-Text) from DIALOG. Documents available from Article Express International, UMI Article Clearinghouse, CASDDS. ***Continues*** *Textile World Journal, 0096-5936;* ***Absorbed*** *Posselt's Textile Journal, 0096-8358; Textiles; Textile Advance News.*
**Ind/Abst** ABI/INFORM Glob. Ed.; ABI Inform Ondisc

(June 1988-); Acad. Search (July 1993-); Appl. Sci. Technol. Index; Art Archaeol. Tech. Abstr.; Bioeng. Abstr.; Bus. ASAP (1990-) [Full Txt.]; Bus. Index (1985-); Bus. Period. Index; Bus. Source (Jul. 1993-); Chem. Abstr.; Chem. Ind. Notes; Ei Page One; EMBASE; Eng. Index Annu.; F&S Index Plus Text, Int. [Select. Cov.]; Gen. BusinessFile (1985-); Gen. Period. Index (1985-); INFO-SOUTH Abstr.; Mag. Search; Nonwovens Abstr.; Plant Breed. Abstr.; PROMT; Saf. Health Work; Stat. Ref. Index; Text. Technol. Dig.; Trade Ind. ASAP [Full Txt.]; Trade Ind. Index [Full Txt.]; Wilson Bus. Abstr.; World Text. Abstr.

UK/0306-0748
**TEXTILES.** [Textiles]. **Added/Corp** Shirley Institute. British Textile Technology Group. Vol. 1 (Feb. 1972)-. Periodical. English. Four times a year. £25.00 UK; $36.00 US and Canada. Textile Institute, 10 Blackfriars Street, Manchester M3 5DR England. **Tel** 11 44 61 834 8457, FAX 11 44 61 835 3087, telex 668297 G. **(Subscription address:** Textiles / North America Subscriptions, PO Box 1897, Lawrence KS 66044-8897.**)** **ED** Maureen Sawbridge. **LC** TS1300; .T4. cum. index. **Bk Rev. Ad Acc. Circ:** 5500 (ctrl). ***Continues** Shirley Link.*
**Desc:** Descriptions in non-technical language of science and technology of fibres, textile materials, clothing, industrial and other fibre-containing products.
**Ind/Abst** Abstr. Bull. Inst. Pap. Sci. Tech.; AGRICOLA [Select. Cov.]; Art Archaeol. Tech. Abstr.; Ei Page One; Text. Technol. Dig.; World Text. Abstr.

US
**TEXTILES AND APPAREL. APPAREL.** English. wk. $20.0. Wall Street Transcript, 100 Wall Street, New York NY 10005. **Tel** (212)747-9500.

US
**TEXTILES AND APPAREL. TEXTILES.** English. wk. $20.00. Wall Street Transcript, 100 Wall Street, New York NY 10005. **Tel** (212)747-9500.

II/0047-1119
**TEXTILES NEWS / INTERNATIONAL PRESS CUTTING SERVICE.** **Added/Corp** International Press Cutting Service. **VFOAT** Textile News. No. 1 (1986)-. English. mo. $56.00. International Press Cutting, PO Box 121, Allahabad 211001 India. **(Subscription address:** Prints India, 11 Darya Ganj, New Delhi 110002 India.**)**

US/0049-3570
**TEXTILES PANAMERICANOS.** [Text. panam.]. Vol. 1 (May 1941)-. Periodical. Spanish. bm (6 issues). $40.00 US; $48.00 (surface mail), $70.00 (airmail) other. Billian Publishing Inc., 2100 Powers Ferry Road, Atlanta GA 30339. **Tel** (404)955-5656, FAX (404)952-0669. **ED** Jim Woodroffe. **LC** TS1300; .T5. **DD** 677. **Ad Acc. Circ:** 11,511 (ctrl).
**Desc:** Covers all facets of the textile/apparel industry throughout Latin America with extensive circulation in all 19 countries. New technology, manufacturing processes, new products and modern management methods discussed in each issue.
**Ind/Abst** Text. Technol. Dig.

SP
**TEXTILES PARA EL HOGAR.** (19??)-. Spanish. bm. $91.00. Publica SA, Ecuador 75 Entresuelo, 08029 Barcelona Spain. **Tel** 011 34 3 3215046, 4391027.

SZ/0040-5248
**TEXTILES SUISSES.** **VFOAT** Swiss Textiles. (19??)-. Multiple languages (French, English and German). Four times a year (Mar., June, Sept., Dec.). 84.00F, 74.00F (libraries, schools, advertisers) Switzerland; 91.00F, 101.00F (libraries, schools, advertisers) other. Office Suisse d'Expansion Commericale, Avenue de l Avant Poste 4, CP 1128, CH-1001 Lausanne Switzerland. **Tel** 011 41 21 3203231, FAX 011 41 21 207337, telex 455 425 OSEC CH. **ED** Peter Pfister. **Ad Acc. Circ:** 13,000 (ctrl).
**Desc:** Devoted to Swiss clothing fabrics and their use. Covers accessories and company profiles.

GW
**TEXTILFORUM.** **VFOAT** Deutsches Textilforum. (March, 1990)-. German (English). Four times a year (Mar., June, Sept., Dec.). DM70.00 Germany; DM80.00 other. Textilforum, Postfach 5944, D-30059 Hannover Germany. **Tel** 011 49 511 815120, FAX 011 49 511 813108. **ED** Beatrijs Sterk and Dietmar Laue. **Ad Acc. Circ:** 5500. ***Continues** Deutsches Textilforum.*

HU/0133-2082
**TEXTILIPARI KUTATO INTEZET KOZLEMENYEI.** [Textilip. kut. Intez. kozl.]. Began in 1976. Academic Scholarly Publication. Hungarian (Hungarian). bm. Price varies per volume. **CODEN** TKIKDE. Documents available from CASDDS.
**Ind/Abst** Chem. Abstr.; World Text. Abstr.

HU
**TEXTILIPARI TERVGAZDAG.** (19??)-. English. bm (6 issues). $23.00. **(Subscription address:** Kultura, PO Box 149, H 1389 Budapest 62 Hungary**)**

SZ/0040-5310
**TEXTILVEREDLUNG.** [Textilveredlung]. Yearly Vol. 1 Jan. 1966-. Academic Scholarly Publication. German (summaries and/or abstracts in English). mo. 87.00F Switzerland; 104.00F other. Geschaftsstelle Basel, Postfach 146, CH-4013 Basel Switzerland. **Tel** (061)243265. **ED** A Barthold. **LC** TS1510; .T46. **DD** 677/.005. **CODEN** TXLVAE. Index available. **Bk Rev. Ad Acc. Circ:** 3,000 (ctrl). Documents available from CASDDS.
**Desc:** Magazine for people working in the textile industry, the chemical industry (dyestuffs, finishes) and the machine industry (machines for the texture finishing industry). Also for schools of textile engineering and universities (chemistry of dyestuffs).
**Ind/Abst** Abstr. Bull. Inst. Pap. Sci. Tech.; Art Archaeol. Tech. Abstr.; Chem. Abstr.; EMBASE; Saf. Health Work; Text. Technol. Dig.; World Text. Abstr.

US/0495-3789
**TEXTRACTS.** ***Ceased.*** No. 1, July (1953)-Ceased with Dec. (1988). Periodical. English. mo. Varley Textile Associates, 32 West 40th Street, New York NY 10018. **Tel** (212)840-7022. **ED** Gerald M Varley. **Bk Rev.**
**Desc:** A summary of domestic and international textile, apparel, industrial news, and technology.

US/0272-7439
**TEXTURED YARN PRODUCTION.** ***Ceased.*** **See** Manufacturing.

US/0882-7370
**THREADS MAGAZINE.** [Threads mag.]. **VFOAT** Threads. (Oct./Nov. 1985)-. Periodical. English. bm (Feb., Apr, June, Aug., Oct., Dec.). $28.00 (one year), $48.00 (two year), $64.00 (three year). Taunton Press, 63 South Main Street, PO Box 5506, Newtown CT 06470-5506. **Tel** (203)426-8171, (800)283-7252, FAX (203)426-3434, telex 5106004860. **ED** Betsy Levine, Amy Yanagi, Alice Kovach and David Page. **LC** TT697; .T48. **DD** 746/.05. Index available. **Bk Rev. Ad Acc. Circ:** 125,000.
**Desc:** The only magazine devoted to making beautiful things of fiber and fabric.
**Ind/Abst** AGRICOLA [Select. Cov.]; Art Archaeol. Tech. Abstr.; Index Inf.

UK
**TI NEWS / THE TEXTILE INSTITUTE.** **Added/Corp** Textile Institute (Manchester, England). **VAT** Textile Institute News. (19??)-. Periodical. English. mo. Textile Institute, 10 Blackfriars Street, Manchester M3 5DR England. **Tel** 11 44 61 834 8457, FAX 11 44 61 835 3087, telex 668297 G. **ED** Roger T. Bogg. **Circ:** 9,000 (ctrl).

IT/0040-7984
**TINCTORIA.** [Tinctoria]. **Added/Corp** Associazione Nazionale Industriali Tintori, Stampatori e Finitori. (1900)-. Academic Scholarly Publication. Italian. Twelve times a year. L100000 Italy, L125000 others (surface mail); L247678.02 US & Africa & Asia, L185758.51 Europe & Mediterranean, L286377.71 others (airmail). Edizione Ariminum, Via Negroli 51, 20133 Milan Italy. **Tel** 011 39 2 70102026, FAX 011 39 2 717346. **CODEN** TINCAW. Index available. cum. index. **Bk Rev. Ad Acc. Circ:** 3,000. Documents available from CASDDS.
**Desc:** Technical magazine on ennoblement of textiles dyeing and finishing.
**Ind/Abst** Abstr. Bull. Inst. Pap. Sci. Tech.; Art Archaeol. Tech. Abstr.; Chem. Abstr.; Text. Technol. Dig.; World Text. Abstr.

US
**TRI NEWS AND RESEARCH BRIEFS.** **VAT** Textile Research Institute News and Research Briefs. Periodical. English. ir. Textile Research Institute, PO Box 625, Princeton NJ 08540. **Tel** (609)924-3150. ctrl circ.
**Ind/Abst** World Text. Abstr.

US/0748-7142
**TRSA ORGANIZATION.** (TRSA ORGANIZATION / LEADERSHIP/STAFF SERVICES, TEXTILE RENTAL SERVICES ASSOCIATION OF AMERICA.). [TRSA org.]. **Main/Corp** Textile Rental Services Association of America. **VAT** Textile Rental Services Association of America Organization. English. Textile Rental Association, 1130 E Hallandale Beach Boulevard/Suite C, Hallandale FL 33009.

FR/1161-9317
**TUT. TEXTILES A USAGES TECHNIQUES.** (TUT.). **VFOAT** Textiles a Usages Techniques (Paris). (1991)-. Periodical. French (English). Four times a year. 100.00F (single issue). Industrie Textile, 16 Rue Balle Hall Calais, 75009 Paris France. **Tel** 011 33 1 48741596. **UDC** 677.
**Desc:** This magazine is about the technical textile end-users.

US/0093-4429
**UNITED STATES COTTON QUALITY REPORT FOR GINNINGS.** **See** Agriculture-Crop Production and Soil.

GW/0935-6347
**VLIESSTOFF NONWOVEN INTERNATIONAL.** [Vliesst. Nonwoven int.]. **VFOAT** VNI. Vliesstoff, Nonwoven International. (1986)-. Periodical. English. mo. DM133.00 Germany; DM160.00 other. VNI USA Verlag GmbH, Usinger STR 115, D 61239 Ober Moerlen Germany. **Tel** 011 49 6002 7823. **UDC** 677-486.6.

JA
**WAGA KUNI NO KOKOGYO : SENI KOGYO HEN; SENI RYUTSU HEN.** **Main/Corp** Japan. Tsusho Sangyosho. Daijin Kambo. Chosa Tokeibu. (19??)-. Periodical. Japanese. Daijin Kanbo, 8-9, Ginza 2-chome, Chuo-ku Tokyo 104 Japan. **LC** HD9866.J3; J28a.

US/0732-6890
**WARP AND WEFT (MCMINNVILLE, OR.).** (WARP AND WEFT.). [Warp weft]. (Nov. 1947)-. Periodical. English. mo (except July and August). $12.00. Warp & Weft, 533 North Adams Street, McMinnville OR 97128. **Tel** (503)472-5760. **ED** Russell E. Groff. **Bk Rev. Ad Acc. Circ:** 500 (ctrl).
**Desc:** For handweavers with 4-harness looms. A sample with directions on how-to-weave each month, and other articles concerning handweaving.

US/1042-7643
**WEAVER'S (SIOUX FALLS, S.D.).** (WEAVER'S.). [Weaver's]. (Spring 1988)-. Periodical. English. qt (Mar., June, Sept., Dec.). $18.00 (one year), $34.00 (two years). Golden Fleece Publications, PO Box 1525, Sioux Falls SD 57101. **Tel** (605)338-2450, FAX (605)338-2994. **LC** TT848; .P69. **DD** 746.1/4/05. **Ad Acc, Adv Mgr:** Karen Bright. ***Continues** Prairie Wool Companion, 0743-8907.*

US/0145-0360
**WEEKLY COTTON MARKET REVIEW.** **See** Agriculture-Crop Production and Soil.

UK
**WEEKLY MARKET REPORT - ENGLAND.** (19??)-. Newsletter. English. wk (Thursday). £116.67 UK; £135.56 other. World Textile Publications Ltd., 76 Kirkgate, Bradford West Yorkshire, BD1 1TB England. **Tel** 011 44 274 726357, 011 44 274 731907, FAX 011 44 274 735045, telex 517617 WOOLMN G. **(Subscription address:** Wool Record Ltd., Caidan House, Canal Road, Altrincham, Chesire WA14 1TD UK) available via fax.

AT/1320-4122
**WEEKLY WOOL INTERNATIONAL.** (19??)-. Newsletter. English. wk (Forty-four issues per year). Wool International, Wool House / 369 Royal Pde, Parkville Victoria 3052 Australia. **Tel** 011 61 3 3419408, FAX 011 61 3 3419409, telex AA30548HWOOL. **ED** W.R. Watkins. **Circ:** 1,000. ***Continues** Wool Market News. Weekly Market Summary.*
**Desc:** Summary of wool sold at auction around Australia during a specific week. Includes comment on the major price movements, description of wool sold in Australia, New Zealand and South Africa. Detail of Wool International sales, Australian market indicators, and summary quotes.

KO
**WOLGAN SOMYU.** **VFOAT** Somyu; The Monthly Textile; Monthly Textile. Periodical. Korean (Korean). mo. W2,000. **LC** HD9866.K6; W65.

PK
**WOOL & CARPET REVIEW.** **VFOAT** Wool and Carpet Review. Vol. 1, No. 1 (1981)-. Periodical. English. qt. Rs280.00. Naeem Tahir, 23 Carvan Building Link McLeod Road, PO Box 1834, Lahore Pakistan. **LC** HD9937.P18; W66. **DD** 338.4/7677643/095491.

US
**WOOL AND MOHAIR / CROP REPORTING BOARD, ECONOMICS AND STATISTICS SERVICE, U.S. DEPARTMENT OF AGRICULTURE.** **Added/Corp** United States. Crop Reporting Board. (1964)-. Government Publication. English. an. $5.00 (one year), $9.00 (two year), $13.00 (three year). US Department of Agriculture / National Agricultural Statistics Service (NASS), Room 5829 South Building, Washington DC 20250. **Tel** (202)720-4020, FAX (314)875-5231. **(Subscription address:** ERS NASS, 341 Victory Drive, Herndon VA 22070.**)** ***Continues** Wool Production and Value.*

II/0043-7808
**WOOL & WOOLLENS OF INDIA.** [Wool woolens India]. **Added/Corp** Indian Woolen Mills' Federation. **VFOAT** Wool and Woollens of India. (1964)-. Academic Scholarly Publication. English. qt. $25.00. Indian Woollen Mills Federation, Churchgate Chambers, 7th Floor, 5 New Marine Lines, Bombay 400020 India. **Tel** 91 22 2624372, FAX 91 22 2624675, telex 011-83067. **(Subscription address:** Prints India, 11 Darya Ganj, New Delhi 110002 India.**)** **ED** K V A Warrier. **CODEN** WWIDA5. **Ad Acc, Adv Mgr:** same as editor. **Circ:** 450. Documents available from CASDDS.
**Ind/Abst** Anim. Breed. Abstr.; Art Archaeol. Tech. Abstr.; Chem. Abstr.; Text. Technol. Dig.; World Agric. Econ.; World Text. Abstr.

AT/1322-3992
**WOOL INTERNATIONAL INSIGHT.** (19??)-. Newsletter. English. mo (Eleven issues per year). Wool International, Wool House / 369 Royal Pde, Parkville Victoria 3052 Australia. **Tel** 011 61 3 3419408, FAX 011 61 3 3419409, telex AA30548HWOOL. **ED** Chris

Cunningham. ***Continues*** *Wool Market News Monthly Perspective.*
**Desc:** Market intelligence of the wool industry specifically identifying Australian production, demand factors and the futures market.

AT
**WOOL MARKET NEWS MONTHLY PERSPECTIVE.** ***Title Change.*** **VFOAT** Monthly Perspective. (198?)-(1994). Periodical. English. mo. Australian Wool Corporation, Wool House/369 Royal Pde, Parkville Victoria 3052 Australia. ***Continued by*** *Wool International Insight, 1322-3992.*

AT
**WOOL MARKET NEWS. WEEKLY MARKET SUMMARY.** ***Title Change.*** **VFOAT** Weekly Market Summary. (1???)-(1994). Periodical. English. wk. Australian Wool Corporation, Wool House/369 Royal Pde, Parkville Victoria 3052 Australia. ***Continued by*** *Weekly Wool International, 1320-4122.*

NZ/1171-9672
**WOOL MARKET REVIEW.** [Wool mark. rev.]. (1992)-. Periodical. English. Twenty-five times a year. 50.00NZ$ New Zealand; 75.00NZ$ other. Wools of New Zealand, PO Box 3225, Wellington New Zealand. **Tel** 011 64 4 4726888. **DD** 338.1763145099305. ***Continues*** *New Zealand Wool Market Review, 0113-2792.*

NZ/0110-6015
**WOOL (PALMERSTON NORTH).** (WOOL.). [Wool]. **Added/Corp** Massey Wool Association. Massey College Wool Association. Massey Wool Association of New Zealand. (1948)-. English. an. 10.00NZ$. Massey Wool Association Inc, PO Box 421, Palmerston North New Zealand. **Tel** 011 64 63 69099, FAX 011 64 63 505622. Index available. cum. index. **Bk Rev. Ad Acc. Circ:** 1,200 (ctrl).
**Desc:** Publication sent to members covering papers presented at the annual conferences.
**Ind/Abst** AGRICOLA; Text. Technol. Dig.; World Agric. Econ.

UK/0142-1921
**WOOL QUARTERLY. See** Textiles-Abstracting, Bibliographies and Statistics.

UK/0263-6131
**WOOL RECORD (BRADFORD, WEST YORKSHIRE : 1982).** (WOOL RECORD.). [Wool rec.]. **VFOAT** Wool Record and Textile World. Vol. 141, No. 3447 (Jan. 1982)-. Periodical. English. Twelve times a year. £65.56 UK; £73.15 Ireland; £97.15 Europe; £90.29 (surface mail), £116.58 (airmail) other. World Textile Publications Ltd., 76 Kirkgate, Bradford West Yorkshire, BD1 1TB England. **Tel** 011 44 274 726357, 011 44 274 731907, FAX 011 44 274 735045, telex 517617 WOOLMN G. ***Continues*** *Wool Record & Textile World, 0043-7832.*
**Desc:** Reports on the world's wool industry including market notes and trade updates.
**Ind/Abst** Art Archaeol. Tech. Abstr.; F&S Index Plus Text, Int. [Select. Cov.]; Infomat Int. Bus.; Predicasts; PROMT; Text. Technol. Dig.; World Text. Abstr.

UK
**WOOL RECORD WEEKLY MARKET REPORT.** (197?)-. Trade Publication. English. wk. World Textile Publications Ltd., 76 Kirkgate, Bradford West Yorkshire, BD1 1TB England. **Tel** 011 44 274 726357, 011 44 274 731907, FAX 011 44 274 735045, telex 517617 WOOLMN G. **ED** Michael Mallett. **Ad Acc, Adv Mgr:** Wynn Home, **Tel** 0274 726357. available via fax from World Textile Publications Ltd. ***Continues*** *Weekly Wool Chart and Private Business Report (45.8 W855).*
**Desc:** Commentary of wool and yarn prices and wool futures markets around the world.
**Ind/Abst** World Text. Abstr.

NZ/0112-6059
**WOOL REPORT NEW ZEALAND.** [Wool rep. N.Z.]. **Added/Corp** New Zealand Wool Board. **VFOAT** Wool Report; New Zealand Wool Report. (1985)-. Periodical. English. Four times a year (Mar., June, Sept., Dec.). 22.00NZ$ New Zealand; 30.00NZ$ other. Wools of New Zealand, PO Box 3225, Wellington New Zealand. **Tel** 011 64 4 4726888. **ED** Justine Riegen. **Bk Rev. Ad Acc.** ctrl circ. ***Continues*** *Wool World, 0110-0823.*

UK/0043-7859
**WOOL SCIENCE REVIEW.** [Wool sci. rev.]. **Added/Corp** International Wool Secretariat. Technical Center. (Aug. 1948)-. Academic Scholarly Publication. English. an. Free. Wool Bureau Inc., 225 Crossways Park Dr, Woodbury NY 11797. **Tel** (516)364-0890. **CODEN** WOSRA7. Documents available from CASDDS.
**Ind/Abst** Chem. Abstr.; World Text. Abstr.

UK
**WORLD FIBRE NEWS.** Periodical. English. wk. $18.00. Hughes Sanders & Howard Ltd., 25 Camp Road, Farnborough CU12 C England. **LC** HD9850.1; .W67. **DD** 338.4/7/677. ***Absorbed*** *Jute Markets & Prices; Textile Production.*

UK/0043-9118
**WORLD TEXTILE ABSTRACTS. See** Textiles-Abstracting, Bibliographies and Statistics.

UK
**WORLD TEXTILES.** (19??)-. Abstracting/Indexing Service. English. Available through DIALOG - usage charges vary. Elsevier Geo Abstracts, An Imprint of Elsevier Science Ltd., The Boulevard, Langford Lane, Kidlington, Oxford OX5 1GB United Kingdom. **Tel** 011 44 865 843000, 011 44 865 843699, FAX 011 44 865 843010. available in print.
**Desc:** Features a truly international overview of publications, specialist coverage of textile related patents and the use of specialist staff in the selection and preparation of material.

US/0043-9827
**WYOMING WOOL GROWER. See** Agriculture-Livestock and Poultry.

IS/0372-7777
**YALKUT LE-SIVIM, TEKHNOLOGYAH U-MINHAL SHEL TEKSTIL.** [Yalkut Le-sivim, Tekhnol. U-minhal Shel Tekst.]. **VFOAT** Yalkut for Fibres and Textile Technology. (19??)-. Hebrew. ir. **CODEN** YLTUAM. Documents available from CASDDS.
**Ind/Abst** Chem. Abstr.

US/0882-7982
**YARN MARKET NEWS.** ***Ceased.*** [Yarn mark. news]. Periodical. English. bm. Butterick Company Inc., 2900 Beale Avenue, Altoona PA 16603. **Tel** (814)943-5281, (800)766-3619. **DD** 338.
**Ind/Abst** AGRICOLA [Select. Cov.].

CC/1000-1476
**ZHONGGUO FANGZHI DAXUE XUEBAO.** (CHUNG-KUO FANG CHIH TA HSUEH HSUEH PAO.). [Zhongguo fangzhi daxue xuebao]. **Added/Corp** Chung-kuo Fang Chih Ta Hsueh. **VFOAT** Zhongguo Fangzhi Daxue Xuebao; Journal of China Textile University. (1986)-. Academic Scholarly Publication. Chinese (summaries and/or abstracts in English). qt. $20.00. Zhongguo Fangzhi Daxue / China Textile University, 1882 Yan'an Xilu, Shanghai 200051 People's Republic of China. **Tel** 2199898. **LC** TS1300; .C55. **DD** 677/.02864/05. **CODEN** ZFDXEQ. Documents available from Article Express International, CASDDS, BLDSC, CASDDS. ***Continues*** *Hua Tung Fang Chih Kung Hsueh Yuan Hsueh Pao, 0253-2433.*
**Ind/Abst** Chem. Abstr. (1986-); Ei Page One; Eng. Index Annu.

CC/1000-632X
**ZHONGGUO MIANHUA. VFOAT** China Cottons. (1958)-. Periodical. Chinese. bm. **DD** 633.51.
**Ind/Abst** Plant Breed. Abstr.; Rev. Plant Pathol.

## ABSTRACTING, BIBLIOGRAPHIES AND STATISTICS

AT/0311-9882
**AUSTRALIAN WOOL SALE STATISTICS; STATISTICAL ANALYSIS. Added/Corp** Australian Wool Corporation. Vol. 1 (1971)-. Statistical Publication. English. an. 85.00Aus$ Australia; 105.00Aus$ other. Wool International, Wool House / 369 Royal Pde, Parkville Victoria 3052 Australia. **Tel** 011 61 3 3419408, FAX 011 61 3 3419409, telex AA30548HWOOL. **ED** Mark Gabrys.
**Desc:** Statistical summary on wool offered at auction.
**Ind/Abst** Text. Technol. Dig.

US/1049-1376
**C2C ABSTRACTS JAPAN. TEXTILES.** [C2C abstr. Jap., Text.]. **VFOAT** Textiles. Vol. 1, No. 1 (Feb. 1990)-. English. mo. $200.00. SCAN C2C Inc, Attn Carol G Heffernan Marketing Director, 500 E Street Southwest, Suite 800, 8th Floor, Washington DC 20024. **Tel** (202)863-3850, (800)525-3865, FAX (202)863-3855. **DD** 620. Index available. cum. index. available on CD-ROM from DIALOG; available on an online database from ORBIT; DATA-STAR; and DIALOG.
**Desc:** English abstracts of over 500 Japanese science, technical and business journals in the field of textiles.

US
**COTTON : WORLD STATISTICS. VFOAT** Coton : Statistiques Mondiales; Algodon : Estadisticas Mundiales. Periodical. English (Spanish and French). qt. $40.00. International Cotton Advisory Committee, 1629 K Street NW, Suite 702, Washington DC 20006. **Tel** (202)463-6660, FAX 463-6950. ctrl circ. ***Continues*** *Cotton : Quarterly Statistical Bulletin.*
**Ind/Abst** F&S Index Plus Text, Int. [Select. Cov.]; Predicasts Forecasts; Text. Technol. Dig.; World Text. Abstr.

AT
**DALGETY FARMERS' ANNUAL WOOL DIGEST. Added/Corp** Dalgety Farmers (Firm). **VFOAT** Annual Wool Digest. (1984)-. English. an. Free. Public Relations Department of Dalgety Farmers Ltd, GPO Box 261, Sydney New South Wales 2001 Australia. **Tel** (02)238-2000, FAX (02)238 2850, telex 126663. **ED** Terence C. Anderson. **Circ:** 15,000 (ctrl). ***Continues*** *Dalgety-N.Z.L. Annual Wool Digest.*
**Desc:** A digest of the Australian wool market statistics and information and summary of New Zealand and South African wool markets.

II
**HANDBOOK OF STATISTICS ON COTTON TEXTILE INDUSTRY.** II. English. an. Textile Center, P d'Mello Road, Bombay 400009 India. **Tel** 86 20 43. **LC** HD9886.I4; H36. **DD** 338.4/767721/0954. Index available. **Circ:** 2,500 (ctrl).

US
**INDUSTRY REVIEW. Added/Corp** Carpet and Rug Institute. (19??)-. English. an. $15.00. Carpet and Rug Institute, Box 2048, Dalton GA 30720. **Tel** (404)278-3176, FAX (404)278-8835. **ED** Betty Hickman. **LC** HD9937.U5; C37. **DD** 338.4/7/7367973. **Bk Rev. Circ:** 600. ***Continues*** *Review: State of the Industry, 0092-0495.*
**Desc:** Statistical report presenting seven year summary of carpet industry shipments in square yards and dollars; import, export data; and information on fiber consumption, backing, and artificial turf.

SZ/0538-6829
**INTERNATIONAL COTTON INDUSTRY STATISTICS. Added/Corp** International Federation of Cotton and Allied Textile Industries. International Textile Manufacturers Federation. Vol. 1 (1958)-. English. an. 70.00F Switzerland; $50.00 US. International Textile Manufacturers Federation, Postfach 289, CH-8039 Zurich Switzerland. **Tel** 011 41 1 2017080, 011 41 1 2017747, telex 56798 ITMF CH. **ED** Herwig Strolz. **LC** HD9870.4; .I55. **Circ:** 500. ***Continues*** *International Cotton Loom Statistics.*
**Desc:** Detailed information on installed capacities, capacity utilization and raw materials consumption in the world's cotton system spinning and weaving industries.
**Ind/Abst** Text. Technol. Dig.

SZ
**INTERNATIONAL TEXTILE MACHINERY SHIPMENT STATISTICS. Added/Corp** International Textile Manufacturers Federation. (1978)-. English. an. 150.00F. International Textile Manufacturers Federation, Postfach 289, CH-8039 Zurich Switzerland. **Tel** 011 41 1 2017080, 011 41 1 2017747, telex 56798 ITMF CH. **LC** HD9850.1; .I56. **DD** 382/.456817677/0212. ***Continues*** *International Cotton Industry Statistics Supplement.*

UK/9036-1234
**NONWOVENS ABSTRACTS. Added/Corp** Pira (Association). Vol. 1, No. 1 (Jan. 1989)-. Abstracting/Indexing Service. English. mo. $504.00 (one year), $957.60 (two year) The Americas; £305.00 (one year), £579.00 (two year) other. Pira International, Randalls Road, Leatherhead, Surrey KT22 7RU England. **Tel** 011 44 372 376161, FAX 011 44 372 377526. **ED** Diana Deavin. **Bk Rev. Pr Rev. Circ:** 300. available on CD-ROM; available on an online database. Documents available.
**Desc:** Covers all aspects of nonwovens business, technology and end-uses. Sections include: nonwovens industry in general; market and company information; new materials (synthetic fibres, inorganic fibres, etc.); process technologies; composites; products and end-uses (healthcare, clothing, etc.); and environment.

NZ/0110-1242
**STATISTICAL HANDBOOK / NEW ZEALAND WOOD BOARD.** 1977/78 Season-. Statistical Publication. English. an. 20.00NZ$ New Zealand. Wools of New Zealand, PO Box 3225, Wellington New Zealand. **Tel** 011 64 4 4726888. **LC** HD9908.N45; N48A. **DD** 338.1/763145. **Circ:** 2,000. ***Continues*** *Statistical Handbook (New Zealand Wool Marketing Corporation).*
**Desc:** Statistics and economic commentary on New Zealand wool production, exports, sales and other aspects of wool industry.

US/0040-5191
**TEXTILE TECHNOLOGY DIGEST.** [Text. technol. dig.]. **Added/Corp** Institute of Textile Technology (Charlottesville, Va.). Vol. 1, No. 1 (June 1944)-. Abstracting/Indexing Service. English. mo. $475.00. Institute of Textile Technology, 2551 Ivy Road, Charlottesville VA 22903-4641. **Tel** (804)296-5511, FAX (804)977-5400. **ED** Dennis C. Loy, Del Kolberg Jr, Marc J. Vassallo, Meredith Bennett, Doug Lane. **LC** TS1300; .T35. **DD** 016.677. **[CCC].** Index available. cum. index. **Bk Rev. Ad Acc.** available on microfilm and microfiche from University Microfilms International (UMI); available on an online database from DIALOG; available on CD-ROM from the publisher.
**Desc:** Provides abstracts of published literature focusing on fiber, yarn and fabric production, dyeing, finishing, testing and control, apparel production, home furnishings, geotextiles, pollution, environment, health and safety, textile mill management, and general textile information about research, education, and the industry.
**Ind/Abst** Abstr. Bull. Inst. Pap. Sci. Tech.; World Text. Abstr.

NO
**TJENESTEYTING, FORRETNINGSMESSIG TJENESTEYTING, UTLEIE AV MASKINER OG UTSTYR, RENOVASJON OG REINGJRING, VASKERI- OG RENSERIVIRKSOMHET.**
**VFOAT** Services, Business Services, Machinery and Equipment Rental and Leasing, Sanitary and Similar Services, Laundries, Laundry Services and Cleaning and Dyeing Plants. English (Norwegian). an. 18.00. **LC** HA1501; subser: HD9986.N8. **DD** 314.81; 338.4/7/0009481.

UK/0142-1921
**WOOL QUARTERLY.** [Wool q.]. **Added/Corp** Commonwealth Secretariat. International Wool Study Group. International Wool Textile Organisation. Vol. 1 (Jan. 1979)-. Periodical. English. Four times a year. £100.00. Commonwealth Secretariat / London, Marlborough House, Pall Mall, London SW1Y 5HX England. **Tel** 44 71 8393411, telex 27678. **ED** M. Godfrey.
**Desc:** Deals with world wool, wool textile situation outlook and summary developments affecting wool supplies and markets. Also comprises detailed analytical statistical tables on all countries with an interest in sector.
**Ind/Abst** World Text. Abstr.

UK
**WOOL STATISTICS.** 1948-. English. an. $18.38. Commonwealth Secretariat / London, Marlborough House, Pall Mall, London SW1Y 5HX England. **Tel** 44 71 8393411, telex 27678. **ED** M J Godfrey.
**Desc:** Reviews world wool and wool textile situations and outlook. Contains comprehensive up-to-date statistics on sheep numbers, raw wool production, consumption, trade and prices.

UK/0043-9118
**WORLD TEXTILE ABSTRACTS.** [World text. abstr.]. **Added/Corp** Shirley Institute. Vol. 1 (Jan. 15, 1969)-. Abstracting/Indexing Service. English. mo. $686.00 The Americas; £460.00 other. Elsevier Geo Abstracts, An Imprint of Elsevier Science Ltd., The Boulevard, Langford Lane, Kidlington, Oxford OX5 1GB United Kingdom. **Tel** 011 44 865 843000, 011 44 865 843699, **FAX** 011 44 865 843010. **(Subscription address:** Elsevier Science Ltd. Oxford Fulfillment Centre, PO Box 800, Kidlington, Oxford OX5 1DX United Kingdom.) **ED** M.J. Oakes. **LC** TS1300; W94. **DD** 677/.005. **CODEN** WTXAA. **[CCC].** Index available. **Bk Rev. Ad Acc.** available on microfilm from University Microfilms International (UMI); available on an online database (as World Textiles) from DIALOG. **Supersedes** *Textile Abstracts*.
**Desc:** Summary of world literature relevant to science, technology and technical economics of textile and related industries. Includes British, European and US patent literature.
**Ind/Abst** Abstr. Bull. Inst. Pap. Sci. Tech.; Anal. Abstr.; Nonwovens Abstr.; Pap. Board Abstr.; Print. Abstr.

# THEATER

CN/1188-2506
**2 MONDES.** (LES 2 MONDES : BULLETIN D'INFORMATION DE THEATRE DE LA MARMAILLE.). [2 mondes]. **Added/Corp** Theatre de la Marmaille. **VFOAT** Deux Mondes. Vol. 1, No 1 (Nov. 1991)-. Bulletin. French. Free for members. Theatre de Marmaille, Bureau 2, 1895 Rue Everett, Montreal Quebec H2E 1P1 Canada. **DD** 792/.0971428/05.

II
**ABHINAYA.** See Literature.

FR
**ACTEURS/AUTEURS.** Ceased. **VFOAT** Revue du Theatre; Acteurs Auteurs. (March 1988)-(1992). Periodical. French. qt. **Continues** *Nouvel Acteurs Theatre*.

GW
**ACTIEN BOERSE.** (19??)-. German. wk. DM540.00. Bernecker & Cie, Koenigsallee 50, D 40212 Duesseldorf Germany. **Tel** 011 49 211 320426.

US/1070-9274
**ACTS FACTS.** See Industrial Health and Safety.

UA
**AL-SINIMA WA-AL-MASRAH.** See Motion Picture.

UK
**AMATEUR STAGE.** English. mo. £16.50 (one year), £32.00 (two years) UK; £26.00 (one year), £50.00 (two years) Europe; £35.00 (one year), £65.00 (two years) other. Platform Publications, PO Box 83, George Street, London W1H 5PL England. **Tel** 44 71 4861732, **FAX** 44 71 2242215, telex 918647.

US/1061-0057
**AMERICAN DRAMA.** [Am. drama]. **Added/Corp** American Drama Institute. **VFOAT** AD. Vol. 1, No. 1 (Fall 1991)-. Periodical. English. Twice a year (May & Nov.). $25.00 (institutions), $15.00 (individuals). American Drama Institute, University of Cincinnati, Department of English, ML 69, Cincinnati OH 45221. **Tel** (513)556-3914. **LC** PS350; .A53. **DD** 812.009/05.

US/8750-3255
**AMERICAN THEATRE.** [Am. theatr.]. **Added/Corp** Theatre Communications Group. Vol. 1, No. 1 (April 1984)-. Periodical. English. Ten times a year (May/June and July/Aug issues combined). $35.00 (one year), $70.00 (two year) US; $50.00 (one year) $85.00 (two year) other. Theatre Communications Group, 355 Lexington Avenue, New York NY 10017. **Tel** (212)697-5230, **FAX** (212)983-4847. **ED** Jim O'Quinn. **LC** PN2000; .A52. **DD** 792/.0973. **Bk Rev. Ad Acc. Circ:** 16,500. Documents available from UMI Article Clearinghouse. **Continues** *Theatre Communications, 0275-5971*.
**Desc:** Serves as a forum for the professional theatre. Regular columns include: production schedules, plays and playwrights, government, funding in print, management, stages, and people. Features articles by leading theatre critics, artists and professionals.
**Ind/Abst** Acad. Ind. [Computer File] (1992-); Access (1984-); Book Rev. Index; Expand. Acad. Index (1992-); Newsp. Period. Abstr. (1989-).

UK/0140-7740
**ANIMATIONS.** [Animations]. **Main/Corp** Puppet Centre Trust. (1977)-. English. Six times a year. £25.00 (institutions), £15.00 (individuals) UK; £25.00 other. Puppet Centre Trust, Battersea Arts Center, Lavender Hill, London SW11 5TN England. **Tel** 011 44 71 2285335. **Continues** *Bulletin - Puppet Centre Trust*.

CN/0827-0198
**ANNUAIRE THEATRAL, L'.** [Annu. theatr.]. (1985)-. French. sa. 23.33Can$ (one year), 41.67Can$ (two year). Societe Histoire Theatre du Quebec, PO Box 4691, Outremont d'Leblanc, Montreal Quebec, H2V 4N3 Canada. **Tel** (514)343-6111. **DD** C842/.0099714.

US/0885-3940
**ANNUAL - THEATRE HISTORICAL SOCIETY (U.S.).** (ANNUAL FOR ... / THEATRE HISTORICAL SOCIETY.). [Annu. - Theatre Hist. Soc. (U. S.)]. **Added/Corp** Theatre Historical Society (U.S.). **VFOAT** Publication. (1973)-. English. **LC** NA6821; .T44. **DD** 725. cum. index.
**Ind/Abst** Avery Index Archit. Period. Suppl. Colum. Univ. (1990-).

US/1063-620X
**APPLAUSE/BEST PLAYS THEATER YEARBOOK, THE.** *Title Change.* (THE APPLAUSE/BEST PLAYS THEATER YEARBOOK OF ... : FEATURING THE TEN BEST PLAYS OF THE SEASON.). [Applause/best plays theater yearb.]. **VFOAT** Applause Best Plays Theater Yearbook of ...; Theater Yearbook of ...; Theater Yearbook ... (1991)-(1992). English. an. Limelight Editions, 118 East 30th Street, New York NY 10016. **Tel** (212)532-5525. **LC** PN6112; .B45. **DD** 792. **Continues** *Burns Mantle Theater Yearbook of ... Featuring the Ten Best Plays of the Season*. **Continued by** *Best Plays of ..., 1071-6971*.

US
**APPLAUSE THEATRE BOOK REVIEW & CATALOG, THE.** See The Arts-Performing Arts.

CL
**APUNTES.** See Literature.

GW
**ARCHIV FUER URHEBER-, FILM-, FUNK- UND THEATERRECHT.** **VFOAT** UFITA. (1928)-. Periodical. German. ir. Staempfli & Cie SA, Postfach 8326, CH-3001 Bern Switzerland. **Tel** 011 41 31 3006666, telex 031 911 515 EDMZ CH.
**Ind/Abst** Index Foreign Leg. Per.

IT
**ARCHIVIO DEL TEATRO ITALIANO.** No. 1 (1968)-. Periodical. Italian. ir. Edizioni Polifilo, Via Borgonuovo 21, 20121 Milan Italy. **Tel** 011 39 2 6551549.

IT
**ARIEL : QUADRIMESTRALE DI DRAMMATURGIA DELL'ISTITUTO DI STUDI PIRANDELLIANI E SUL TEATRO ITALIANO CONTEMPORANEO.** **Added/Corp** Istituto di Studi Pirandelliani. Vol. 1, No. 1 (Apr. 1986)-. Periodical. Italian. Three times a year. L80000.00 Italy; L90000.00 other. Bulzoni Editore Srl, Via dei Liburni 14, 00185 Rome Italy. **Tel** 011 39 6 445-5207, **FAX** 011 39 6 445-0355. **LC** PN2005; .A74. **DD** 792/.0945/05.

FR/0297-2557
**ART DU THEATRE (PARIS, FRANCE : 1985).** Ceased. (L'ART DU THEATRE.). No. 1 (Spring 1985)-?. Periodical. French. Three times a year. Chaillot, Le Theatre National, 1 Place de Trocadero, 75116 Paris France.

US/0742-5457
**ASIAN THEATRE JOURNAL.** See The Arts-Performing Arts.

IS/0334-5963
**ASSAPH. SECTION C. STUDIES IN THE THEATRE.** [Assaph, Sect. C, Stud. theatre]. **Added/Corp** Universitat Tel-Aviv. Fakultah le-Omanuyot. **VFOAT** Studies in the Theatre; ASSAPH. Studies in the Arts. No. 1 (1984)-. Periodical. English. an. $14.50 (institutions); $9.50 (individuals). Tel Aviv University / Visual & Performing Arts, Faculty of Visual & Performing Arts, Ramat Aviv, 69978 Tel Aviv Israel. **Tel** 011 972 3 420612. **LC** PN2001; .A87. **DD** 792/.05.
**Ind/Abst** MLA Int. Bibl. Books Artic. Mod. Lang. Lit.

US/0044-7927
**ASTR, AMERICAN SOCIETY FOR THEATRE RESEARCH NEWSLETTER.** [ASTR]. **Main/Corp** American Society for Theatre Research. **VFOAT** ASTR Newsletter. **VAT** American Society for Theatre Research Newsletter. No. 1-, 1957-71; New Ser., V. 1- 1972-. Newsletter. English. sa. $30.00. P T Dircks, C W Post Center Greenvale, Long Island NY 11548. **Tel FAX** (516)299-2391. **ED** Phyllis Dircks. **LC** PN2000; .A64. **DD** 792. **Circ:** 700 (ctrl).
**Desc:** Matters of professional interest to members of ASTR.

US/1074-0740
**AUSTIN CHRONICLE, THE.** See General Interest-General Interest-North America.

AT/0810-4123
**AUSTRALASIAN DRAMA STUDIES.** Vol. 1, No. 1 (Oct. 1982)-. Periodical. English. Twice a year (Apr., Oct.). 30.00Aus$ Australia; 40.00Aus$ other. University of Queensland / Department of English, St. Lucia QLD 4067 Australia. **Tel** 011 61 7 3772147, **FAX** 3719578. **ED** Veronica Kelly and Richard Fotheringham. **LC** PN3010; .A9. **DD** 790.2/0994. **Bk Rev. Ad Acc. Pr Rev. Circ:** 500.
**Desc:** Theatre documentation and criticism with an emphasis on Australian and New Zealand drama.
**Ind/Abst** Annu. Bibliogr. Engl. Lang. Lit.; APAIS, Aust. Public Aff. Inf. Ser.; Aust. Educ. Index (1982-); MLA Int. Bibl. Books Artic. Mod. Lang. Lit.

AT
**AUSTRALIAN & NEW ZEALAND THEATRE RECORD : ANZTR.** **Added/Corp** University of New South Wales. Australian Theatre Studies Centre. International Theatre Institute. Australian Centre. **VFOAT** ANZTR; Australian and New Zealand Theatre Record. (April 1988)-. Periodical. English. mo. 80.00Aus$ Australia; 95.00Aus$ (seamail), 110.00Aus$ (airmail) New Zealand; 110.00Aus$ (seamail), 140.00Aus$ (airmail) North America. University of New South Wales, PO Box 1, Kensington New South Wales, 2033 Australia. **Tel** 011 61 2 697-3362, **FAX** 011 61 2 662-6616. **ED** Jeremy Eccles. **LC** PN3014; .A78. **DD** 792.9/5/099405. Index available. cum. index. **Bk Rev. Ad Acc. Circ:** 275 (ctrl). **Continues** *Australian Theatre Record, 0819-1182*.
**Desc:** Details, reviews and photos of professional theater productions presented in Australia and New Zealand.

NE/0921-2531
**AUSTRALIAN PLAYWRIGHTS.** No. 1 (1987)-. Monographic series. English. Price varies per volume. Editions Rodopi BV, Keizersgracht 302-304, 1016 Ex Amsterdam Netherlands. **Tel** 011 31 20 6227507, **FAX** 011 31 20 380948. **ED** Ortrun Zuber-Skerritt.
**Desc:** Series contributes to the promotion, analysis and better understanding of Australian drama both in Australia and overseas. Gives an overview of a particular playwright's life and work and a critical analysis of his/her plays. Each contains a transcript of associated video program.
**Ind/Abst** MLA Int. Bibl. Books Artic. Mod. Lang. Lit.

IT
**AUTOBUS.** See Literature.

FR/0045-1169
**AVANT-SCENE, THEATRE, L'.** **VFOAT** Theatre, l'Avant-Scene. No. 238 (March 1, 1961)-. Periodical. French. Twenty times a year. 705.19F France; 906.00F other; 1098.92F France, 1485.00F other Comes with Avant Scene Cinema. L'Avant Scene, 6 rue Git le Couer, 75006 Paris France. **Tel** 011 33 1 46342820, **FAX** 011 33 1 43545014. **LC** PN6113; .A9. **DD** 808.82/005. **Continues** *Avant-Scene, Femina-Theatre*.

IS/0045-138X
**BAMAH (JERUSALEM, ISRAEL).** (BAMAH.). (June 1959)-. Periodical. Hebrew (summaries and/or abstracts in English). Four times a year. $35.00. Bamah

Theatrical Review, POB 24290, Jerusalem 91240 Israel. **Tel** (02)883989, FAX (02)883989. **ED** Professor D. Gilula. **DD** 792. **Circ:** 1,500. ***Continues*** *Bamah.*

US/0067-6225
**BEST AMERICAN PLAYS.** Ser.1 (1930/39); Ser.2 (1939/46); Ser.3 (1945/51); Ser.4 (1951/57); Ser.5 (1957/63); Ser.6 (1963/67); Ser. 7 (1967/73)-. English. ir. $37.50. Random House Inc., 400 Hahn Road, Westminster MD 21157. **Tel** (800)726-0600, (800)733-3000, FAX (800)659-2436.

US/1062-7561
**BEST AMERICAN SHORT PLAYS, THE.** [Best Am. short plays]. (1990)-. Periodical. English. an. $29.95 cloth; $14.95 paper. Applause Theater & Book Publs, 212 West 71st Street, New York NY 10023. **Tel** (212)595-4735, FAX (212)721-2856. **LC** PN6111; .B47. **DD** 812. ***Continues*** *Best Short Plays (Dodd, Mead & Company), 0067-6284.*

US
**BEST MEN'S STAGE MONOLOGUES, THE.** **VFOAT** Men's Stage Monologues. (1990)-. English. $6.95. Smith and Kraus, Inc, Main Street, PO Box 10, Newbury VT 05051. **LC** PN4305.M6; B47.

US/1071-6971
**BEST PLAYS OF ..., THE.** [Best plays]. **VFOAT** Otis Guernsey Burns Mantle Theater Yearbook; Theater Yearbook. (1992-1993)-. Periodical. English. an. $45.00. Limelight Editions, 118 East 30th Street, New York NY 10016. **Tel** (212)532-5525. **LC** PN6112; .B45. **DD** 792. ***Continues*** *Applause/Best Plays Theater Yearbook of ..., 1063-620X.*

SP
**BIBLIOTECA ANTONIO MACHADO DE TEATRO.** Vol. 1 (1986)-. Monographic series. Spanish. Price varies per volume.

IT
**BIBLIOTECA TEATRALE (BULZONI EDITORE).** (BIBLIOTECA TEATRALE.). Monographic series. Italian. ir. Price varies per volume. Casa di Goldoni, S Toma 2794, 30125 Venice Italy. **Desc:** Publication for study and research of theatrical performance.

US/0360-2516
**BILLBOARD INDEX.** (19??)-. English. wk. University Microfilms International, 300 North Zeeb Road, Ann Arbor MI 48106-1346. **Tel** (313)761-4700, (800)521-0600 Exts. 2490, 2491, FAX (313)973-1540. **LC** PN2000; .B517. **DD** 338.4/7/789912.

US/0006-2510
**BILLBOARD [MICROFORM].** Vol. 75, No. 1 (Jan. 5, 1963)-. Periodical. English. $50.00 per reel. Kraus International Publishing, Route 100, Millwood NY 10546. **Tel** (914)761-9600, telex 6711564. **[CCC].** ***Continues*** *Billboard Music Week.*

US/0887-7580
**BLACK MASKS.** [Black masks]. Vol. 1, No. 1 (Sept. 1984)-. Periodical. English. Six times a year (Jan., Mar., May, July, Sept., Nov.). $17.00 (one year); $47.00 (three years). Black Masks, PO Box 2, Riverdale Station, Bronx NY 10471. **Tel** (212)304-8900, FAX (212)304-8900. **ED** Beth Turner. **DD** 792. Index available. cum. index. **Bk Rev**, (Qty: 1-2). **Ad Acc, Adv Mgr:** B. Turner. **Circ:** 1,000. **Desc:** Black performing and visual arts across the United States. It features profiles of Black artists, Black arts groups and important Black arts issues.

BL
**BOLETIM INFORMATIVO DO INSTITUTO NACIONAL DE ARTES CENICAS / INACEN, MINISTERIO DA EDUCACAO E CULTURA, SECRETARIA DA CULTURA.** **Added/Corp** Instituto Nacional de Artes Cenicas (Brazil). **VFOAT** INACEN; Boletim Informativo. (198?)-. Bulletin. Portuguese. **LC** PN2470; .B65. **DD** 790.2/0981.

UK/0142-5218
**BRITISH ALTERNATIVE THEATRE DIRECTORY.** [Br. altern. theatre dir.]. Began in 1979-?. Directory. English. an. $12.18. John Offord Publications, 12 The Avenue, Eastbourne East Sussex BN21 3YA England. **Tel** 0323 645871. **ED** Cathy Itzin. **LC** PN2595; .B73. **DD** 792./02/9541. **Ad Acc. Circ:** 2,000. ***Continued in part by*** *Directory of Playwrights, Directors, Designers.* **Desc:** Comprehensive guide to UK fringe and alternative theatre.

UK
**BRITISH THEATRE REVIEW.** 1974-. English. an. John Offord Publications, 12 The Avenue, Eastbourne East Sussex BN21 3YA England. **Tel** 0323 645871. **LC** PN2580; .B74. **DD** 792/.0941.

US/0068-2748
**BROADSIDE (NEW YORK, N.Y. : 1940).** (BROADSIDE : NEWSLETTER OF THE THEATRE LIBRARY ASSOCIATION.). Vol. 1, No. 1 (1940); New Ser. Vol. 1, No. 1 (Summer 1973)-. Newsletter. English. qt. Free to members, $20.00 personal, $25.00 institutions. Theatre Library Association, 111 Amsterdam Avenue, New York NY 10023. **Tel** (212)870-1670. **ED** Alan J Pally. **DD** 026.792. Index available. **Bk Rev. Circ:** 500 (ctrl). **Desc:** Includes information about Theatre Library Association sponsored events, book reviews, articles about exhibitions and collections related to the performing arts, and other items of interest in the fields of theatre, film and dance worldwide.

GW/0007-3091
**BUEHNENTECHNISCHE RUNDSCHAU.** [Buehnentech. Rundsch.]. Vol. 1, No. 1 (1907)-. Periodical. German. Six times a year. DM75.00 (latest editon). Erhard Friedrich Verlag, Postfach 100150, D 30917 Seelze Germany. **Tel** 011 49 511 4000452. **ED** W. Unruh. **LC** WMLC L 83/1180. available on microfilm. **Ind/Abst** Archit. Period. Index (1961-).

AU/0007-3075
**BUHNE (VIENNA, AUSTRIA : 1958).** (DIE BUHNE.). **Added/Corp** Wiener Buhnenverein. Vol. 1 (Oct. 1958)-. Periodical. German. mo. S620.00 (Austria); S745.45 (other). Orac Verlag, Schoenbrunner Str 58-61, 1050 Vienna Austria. **Circ:** 132,500.

CN/0228-8079
**BULLETIN PROVINCIAL (CANADIAN CHILD AND YOUTH DRAMA ASSOCIATION. NEW BRUNSWICK).** (BULLETIN PROVINCIAL / L'ASSOCIATION CANADIENNE DU THEATRE POUR LE JEUNESSE DU NOUVEAU-BRUNSWICK.). [Bull. prov. - Assoc. can. theatre jeun. N.-B.]. **VFOAT** Provincial Newsletter / New Brunswick Canadian Child and Youth Drama Association. Fall 1979-. Bulletin. English. qt. Free. New Brunswick Canadian Child and Youth Drama Association Newsletter, c/o R Hallum, 248 Wellington Street, Fredericton New Brunswick E3B 3A5 Canada. **DD** 792/.0226/09715. ctrl circ.

●US/1064-475X
**BUSINESS THEATER.** (1993)-. Periodical. English. qt. $110.00 (includes monthly bulletins). Second Chance Communications, PO Box 538, Antioch TN 37011.

FR/0759-125X
**CAHIERS / COMEDIE-FRANCAISE, LES.** **Added/Corp** Comedie-Francaise. **VFOAT** Cahiers de la Comedie-Francaise. No 1 (Automne 1991)-. Periodical. French. qt. POL, 8 Villa d'Alesia, 75014 Paris France. **Tel** 011 33 1 45627721.

●CN/1188-1461
**CAHIERS DE LA NCT.** [Cah. NCT]. **Added/Corp** Nouvelle Compagnie Theatrale. **VFOAT** Cahiers de la Nouvelle Compagnie Theatrale. New series No. 1 (Jan. 1992)-. Periodical. French. Free for members. Nouvelle Compagnie Theatrale, 4353 Est rue Ste-Catherine, Montreal Quebec H1V 1Y2 Canada. **DD** 792/.09714/2805. ***Continues*** *Le Magazine NCT., 1181-7550.*

BE/0771-4653
**CAHIERS THEATRE LOUVAIN.** ***Ceased.*** (1986)-(1993). French. Four times a year. Cahiers Theatre Louvain, Ferme de Blocry, 1348 Louvain la Neuve Belgium. **Tel** 011 32 10 400500. **LC** Z2174.D7; B5; PN1563; .B52.

GW
**CALDERONIANA.** **Added/Corp** Hamburg. Universitat. Romanisches Seminar. Vol. 1 (1968)-. Monographic series. German. ir. Price varies per volume. Walter de Gruyter Inc., PO Box 303421, D 10728 Berlin Germany. **Tel** 011 49 30 260050, FAX 011 49 30 26005251. **(Subscription address:** Walter de Gruyter Inc., 200 Saw Mill River Road, Hawthorne NY 10532.**)**

US/0733-5806
**CALIFORNIA THEATRE ANNUAL.** (1980/81)-. Periodical. English. an. $35.00. Performing Arts Network Mag, 3539 Motor Ave, Los Angeles CA 90034-4800. **Tel** (310)273-8161. **LC** PN2275.C3; C34. **DD** 792/.09794.

US/1064-0703
**CALL BOARD (SAN FRANCISCO, CALIF.).** (CALL BOARD.). [Call board]. **Added/Corp** Theatre Bay Area, Inc. **VFOAT** Callboard. (19??)-. Periodical. English. mo. $35.00 (institution); $32.00 (individual). Theatre Bay Area, 657 Mission Street, Suite 402, San Francisco CA 94105. **Tel** (415)957-1557, FAX (415)957-1556. **ED** Belinda Taylor. **DD** 792. **Bk Rev**, (Qty: 10-15 / year). **Ad Acc.** ctrl circ.

CN
**CALLBOARD.** **VAT** Call Board. Periodical. English. qt. 15.00Can$ Canada; $11.61 US; 20.00Can$ other. Nova Scotia Drama League, 5516 Spring Garden Road/Suite 305, Halifax Nova Scotia B3J 1G6 Canada. **Tel** (902)425-3876, FAX (902)425-5606. **ED** Eva Moore. **Bk Rev. Ad Acc. Circ:** 1,200 (ctrl). **Desc:** A publication of news and reviews of theatre activity, local and national.

CN/0380-9455
**CANADA ON STAGE.** [Can. stage]. **Added/Corp** York University (Toronto, Ont.). Faculty of Fine Arts. Professional Association of Canadian Theatres. Communications Centre. **VFOAT** Canadian Theatre Review Yearbook. (1975)-. English. ir. $40.00. PACT Communications Centre, 64 Charles Street East, Toronto Ontario M4Y 1T1 Canada. **Tel** (416)968-3033, FAX (416)968-3035. **ED** Beverly A.B. Sweeting. **DD** 792/.0971. ***Supersedes*** *Canadian Theatre Review Yearbook, 0316-1323.* **Desc:** The only published record of professional theatre production in Canada.

CN/1183-1243
**CANADIAN JOURNAL OF DRAMA AND THEATRE, THE.** ***Ceased.*** [Can. j. drama theatre]. Vol. 1, Issue 1 (1991)-(Jan. 1993). Periodical. English. sa. University of Calgary Press, 2500 University Drive Northwest, Calgary Alberta T2N 1N4 Canada. **Tel** (403)220-7578. **DD** 792/.0971. **[CCC].**

CN/1184-2695
**CANADIAN STAGE PRESS.** ***Ceased.*** [Can. stage press]. **Added/Corp** Canadian Stage Company. **VFOAT** Stage Press. (1990)-(199?). Periodical. English. Canadian Stage Company, 26 Berkeley Street, Toronto, Ontario M5A 2Z5 Canada. **DD** 792/.09713/54105. ***Continues*** *Stage Free Press., 0847-1665.*

CN/0315-0836
**CANADIAN THEATRE REVIEW.** [Can. theatre rev.]. **Added/Corp** York University (Toronto, Ont.). Faculty of Fine Arts. CTR 1 (Winter 1974)-. Academic Scholarly Publication. English (French). qt (Mar., June, Sep., Dec.). $50.00. University of Toronto Press, 5201 Dufferin Street, Downsview Ontario M3H 5T8 Canada. **Tel** (416)667-7781, (416)667-7782, FAX (416)667-7803. **ED** A. Filewood and N. Rewa. **LC** PN2009; .C35. **DD** 792/.05. **[CCC]. Bk Rev. Ad Acc. Circ:** 1,500 (ctrl). available on microfiche from University Microfilms International (UMI); and Micromedia Limited. Documents available from The Genuine Article. **Desc:** Committed to serving both the practicing and the scholarly theatre communities of the country. Publishes playscripts as well as essays on issues of concern to Canadian theatre professionals; analyzes trends and developments in both Canadian and international theatre; features interviews with playwrights, directors, actors and designers; documents workshops, conferences, productions and festivals; and more. **Ind/Abst** Annu. Bibliogr. Engl. Lang. Lit.; Arts Humanit. Citation Index (19??-19??) [Full Cov.]; Can. Index; Can. Period. Index; Curr. Contents Arts Humanit.; Middle East Abstr. Index; MLA Int. Bibl. Books Artic. Mod. Lang. Lit.; Res. Alert [Full Cov.].

CN/0829-3627
**CANPLAY.** **Added/Corp** Playwrights Union of Canada. Vol. 1, No. 2 (Dec. 1984)-. Newsletter. English. Six times a year. 24.20Can$ (one year), 42.10Can$ (two year). Playwrights Union of Canada, 54 Wolseley Street, 2nd Floor, Toronto, Ontario M5T 1A5 Canada. **Tel** (416)947-0201. **ED** Jodi Armstrong. **DD** C812/.54/06071. **Ad Acc. Circ:** 700. ***Continues*** *Newsletter (Playwrights Union of Canada), 0827-3073.* **Desc:** Newsletter focusing on the playwrights' role in Canadian theatre.

IT
**CASTELLO DI ELSINORE, IL.** (1988)-. Periodical. Italian. Three times a year. 6200000L Italy; 9000000L other Europe; 10500000L other. Rosenberg & Sellier, Via Andrea Doria 14, 10123 Turin Italy. **Tel** 011 39 11 8127808, telex 224202 ROSSELI.

US
**CATALOG OF THE THEATRE AND DRAMA COLLECTIONS.** **Main/Corp** New York Public Library. Research Libraries. **Added/Corp** New York Public Library. Research Libraries. Dictionary Catalog of the Theatre and Drama Collections. (1967)-. Catalog. English. ir. GK Hall & Co, 100 Front Street, Riverside NJ 08075. **Tel** (800)257-5755 ext. 2223.

US
**CENTER STAGE (NEW YORK).** (CENTER STAGE.). English. mo. $25.00. Lesbian & Gay Community Services Center Inc, 208 West 13th Street, New York NY 10011. **Tel** (212)620-7310. **Bk Rev. Ad Acc. Circ:** 25,000 (ctrl). **Desc:** Theatre news and features in New York.

CN/0380-4720
**CENTRE STAGE MAGAZINE.** V. 1- Sept. 1975-. Periodical. English. Royal Alexandra Theatre, 260 King Street West, Toronto Ontario M5V 1H9 Canada. **DD** 792/.0299.

XR
**CESKE DIVADLO.** **Added/Corp** Divadelni Ustav (Prague, Czechoslovakia). (1979)-. Periodical. Czech. ir. kcs25.00-kcs30.00. Divadelni Ustav, Celetna 17, Prague 1 Czech Republic. **Tel** 232 88 24, 232 88 11. **LC** PN2859.C9; C433. **Circ:** 1,500-2,000.

CH
**CHU TAN.** **VFOAT** Jutan. First published in 1982. Periodical. Chinese. bm. NT$0.35. Post Office Tien-Chin, Tien-Chin, People's Republic of China. **LC** PN2870; .C47. **DD** 792/.0951.

CN/0317-364X
**CITADEL SCENE, THE.** **Main/Corp** Citadel Theatre. V. 1- Jan./Feb. 1975-. English. Citadel Theatre, 10018-102 Street, Edmonton Alta T5J 0V7 Canada. **DD** 792/.097123/3.

CN/1185-1627
**CITT NEWSLETTER.** [CITT newsl.]. **Added/Corp** Canadian Institute for Theatre Technology. **VAT** Canadian Institute for Theatre Technology Newsletter. Vol. 1, No. 1 (Nov. 1990)-. Newsletter. English. qt. Free to members. Canadian Institute for Theatre Technology, 2500 University Drive, Calgary, Alberta T2N 1N4 Canada. **DD** 792.

US/0748-237X
**CLIPPER STUDIES IN THE AMERICAN THEATER.** [Clipp. stud. Am. theater]. No. 1 (1987)-. Monographic series. English. ir. Price varies per volume. Borgo Press, PO Box 2845, San Bernardino CA 92406. **Tel** (714)884-5813, (714)885-1161. **DD** 792.
**Desc:** Monographs and anthologies on American and European theatre, from its beginnings to modern times.

SP/0587-9957
**COLECCION TEATRO.** No. 1- 1951-. Periodical. Spanish. Ediciones Alfil, Comandante Azcarraga, Madrid 16 Spain.

FR
**COMEDIE FRANCAISE.** (19??)-. French. mo. 300.00F France; 350.00F other. Comedie Francaise, Place Colette, F 75001 Paris France. **Tel** 011 33 1 42961024. **ED** Jean-Loup Riviere. Index available. cum. index. **Circ:** 3,000 (ctrl).
**Desc:** Presents studies in new French comedy, events in French & foreign theater, research on theatrical comedy and the history of French comedy.

US/0740-8943
**COMMUNICATIONS FROM THE INTERNATIONAL BRECHT SOCIETY.** **See** Literature.

US/0010-4078
**COMPARATIVE DRAMA.** [Comp. drama]. Vol. 1 (Spring 1967)-. Periodical. English. qt. $30.00 US; $32.50 other. Comparative Drama, Medieval Institute Publications, Western Michigan University, Kalamazoo MI 49008-3851. **Tel** (616)387-2572, FAX (616)387-3999. **ED** Clifford Davidson and John H. Stroupe. **LC** PN1601; .C66. **DD** 809.2. Index available. **Bk Rev**. **Circ:** 1,000 (ctrl). available on microfilm and microfiche from University Microfilms International (UMI). Documents available from The Genuine Article, UMI Article Clearinghouse.
**Ind/Abst** Abstr. Engl. Stud.; Acad. Search (July 1993-); Am. Bibliogr. Slavic East Europ. Stud.; Annu. Bibliogr. Engl. Lang. Lit.; Arts Humanit. Citation Index [Full Cov.]; Book Rev. Index; Curr. Contents Arts Humanit.; Expand. Acad. Index (1989-); Humanit. Index; Humanit. Source (Jul. 1993-); INFO-SOUTH Abstr.; Lit. Crit. Regist.; Mag. Search; Middle East Abstr. Index; MLA Int. Bibl. Books Artic. Mod. Lang. Lit.; Newsp. Period. Abstr. (1990-); Res. Alert [Full Cov.]; Romant. Move.

UK/1050-3919
**CONTEMPORARY DRAMATISTS.** **See** Biographies.

SZ/1049-6513
**CONTEMPORARY THEATER STUDIES.** (1991)-. Monographic series. English. Price varies per volume. Harwood Academic Publishers, PO Box 90, Reading RG1 8JL England. **Tel** 011 44 734 560080. **(Subscription address:** International Publishers Distributor at one of the following addresses: 820 Town Center Drive, Langhorne, PA 19047; or PO Box 90, Reading Berkshire RG1 8JL UK; or Kent Ridge PO Box 1180, Singapore 9111, Republic of Singapore**)** **ED** Franc Chamberlain.
**Desc:** Forum for the more interesting developments in theatre arts research. Keeps a finger on the pulse of current trends on the international theatre scene.

●SZ/1048-6801
**CONTEMPORARY THEATRE REVIEW.** [Contemp. theatre rev.]. Vol. 1, Pt. 1 (1992)-. Periodical. English. £53.00. Harwood Academic Publishers, PO Box 90, Reading RG1 8JL England. **Tel** 011 44 734 560080. **(Subscription address:** International Publishers Distributor at one of the following addresses: 820 Town Center Drive, Langhorne, PA 19047; or PO Box 90, Reading Berkshire RG1 8JL UK; or Kent Ridge PO Box 1180, Singapore 9111, Republic of Singapore**)** **ED** Franc Chamberlain. **LC** PN2000.A1; C66. **DD** 791. **CODEN** CTHRE9. **[CCC]**.
**Desc:** Journal for research in the field of performance. It is concerned with all aspects of the theatre event.

US/0163-3821
**CONTRIBUTIONS IN DRAMA AND THEATRE STUDIES.** No. 1 (1979)-. Monographic series. English. ir. Price varies per volume. Greenwood Press Inc., PO Box 5007, Westport CT 06881-5007. **Tel** (203)226-3571, FAX (203)222-1502. **ED** Joseph Donohue. **LC** UNC.

US/0045-9070
**CRITICAL DIGEST.** V. 1- Sept. 7, 1947-. Periodical. English. sm. $95.00. Critical Digest, 225 West 34th Street/Room 918, New York NY 10001. **Tel** (212)361-4400. **ED** Ted M Kraus. **Bk Rev**. available on microfilm from Xerox; available on microfilm and microfiche from University Microfilms International (UMI).
**Desc:** Digest of news, reviews, comments on NYC and London theatre.

DR
**CUADERNOS DE POSTGRADO : PUBLICACIONES DE LA UNIVERSIDAD AUTONOMA DE SANTO DOMINGO.** No. 1-. Periodical. Spanish. Editora de la UASD, Apartado Postal No 1355, Santo Domingo Republica Dominicana. **LC** PAR.

SP/0214-1388
**CUADERNOS DE TEATRO CLASICO.** **Added/Corp** Compania Nacional de Teatro Clasico (Spain). No. 1 (1988)-. Monographic series. Spanish. sa. Price varies per volume. Compania Nacional de Teatro Clasico, Principe, 14 3 Izda, 28012 Madrid Spain. **LC** PQ6098.7; .C8.
**Ind/Abst** MLA Int. Bibl. Books Artic. Mod. Lang. Lit.

US/0197-7962
**CUE (HOLLAND PATENT), THE.** (THE CUE.). Periodical. English. $2.50. Steffen Publishing, Holland Patent NY 13354. ***Continues** Cue of Theta Alpha Phi.*

US/0011-5509
**DAILY VARIETY.** **See** Motion Picture.

GW
**DEUTSCHE BUHNE, DIE.** **Added/Corp** Deutscher Buhnenverein. (1929)-. Periodical. German. mo. DM105.40. Erhard Friedrich Verlag, Postfach 100150, D 30917 Seelze Germany. **Tel** 011 49 511 4000452. **ED** Wolfgang Ruf. **LC** PN2004; .D28. **DD** 792/.0943. Index available. cum. index. **Bk Rev**. **Ad Acc**. **Circ:** 3,000.
**Desc:** Informs and discusses on all aspects of German (and international) theater including opera, dance and general questions of management and culture politics.

BE
**DIDASCALIES : CAHIERS OCCASIONNELS DE L'ENSEMBLE THEATRAL MOBILE.** **VFOAT** Textes pour Didascalies. Periodical. French. 400F. Ensemble Theatral Mobile, 88 rue de la Caserne, 1000 Bruxelles Belgium. **Tel** 32.2.513.73.00. **ED** Marc Liebens. **LC** PQ1223; .D53.
**Desc:** All subjects in connection with theater: contemporary, theater's texts, analysis, critique, photography, etc.

AG
**DIOGENES : ANUARIO CRITICO DEL TEATRO LATINOAMERICANO.** **Added/Corp** Asociacion de Trabajadores e Investigadores del Nuevo Teatro (New York, N.Y.) Instituto de Cooperacion Iberoamericana (Madrid, Spain) Comision Nacional del Quinto Centenario del Descubrimiento de America (Spain) Grupo Editor Latinoamericano (Buenos Aires, Argentina). Vol. 1 (1985)-. Spanish (English). an (Published in June of following year). $12.50 individuals; $22.50 institutions. Grupo Editor Latinoamericano SRL, Laprida 1183, Buenos Aires Argentina. **Tel** 011 54 1 9627172. **(Subscription address:** Latin American Studies, University of California, 4128 Sproul Hall, Riverside CA 92521.**)** **LC** PN2309; .D56. **DD** 792/.098/05.
**Desc:** Information on Latin American drama and theater.

IT
**DIONISO.** V. 3, No. 1, 1931-. Periodical. Italian (English, French, German and Spanish). sa. L80000. Instituto Nazionale Drama Antico, Siracusa Italy. **Tel** 0331/67415. Index available. cum. index. **Bk Rev**. **Ad Acc**. ctrl circ. ***Continues** Istituto Nazionale del Dramma Antico. Bollettino.*

CN/0709-8421
**DIRECTORY OF CANADIAN THEATRE SCHOOLS, A.** 1979-. Directory. English. be. $2.50 per vol. Canadian Theatre Review Publications, 4700 Keele Street, Downsview Ontario M3J 1P3 Canada. **DD** 792/.07/1071.

●US
**DIRECTORY OF DOCTORAL PROGRAMS IN THEATRE STUDIES IN THE U.S.A. AND CANADA.** **Added/Corp** American Society for Theatre Research. (1992)-. Directory. English. be. $8.95 (U.S.), $9.95 (Canada). Simon Williams, Department of Dramatic Art, University of California, Santa Barbara CA 93106. **LC** PN2078.U6; D571.

US/0194-178X
**DIRECTORY OF NIGHTCLUBS, HOTELS, THEATRES, LOUNGES & DISCOTHEQUES.** **VFOAT** Talent & Booking's Nightclub Directory. **VAT** Directory of Nightclubs, Hotels, Theatres, Lounges and Discotheques. (1980)-. Directory. English. an. $25.00. Talent & Booking Publishing Company, PO Box 2772, Palm Springs CA 92263. **LC** PN1968.U5; D55. **DD** 792.7/02/9573.

US/1041-7273
**DIRECTORY OF THEATRE FACULTIES IN COLLEGES AND UNIVERSITIES, U.S. AND CANADA.** [Dir. theatre fac. coll. univ. U. S. Can.]. **VFOAT** Directory of Theatre Faculties. 1st. Edition (1986/1988)-. English. an. $55.00 (two years). College Music Society / CMS Publications, 202 West Spruce Street, Missoula MT 59802. **Tel** (406)728-2002, (800)729-0235. **ED** Robby D. Gunstream. **LC** PN2078.U6; D53. **DD** 792.071/173. Index available. **Circ:** 500.
**Desc:** A listing of institutions in alphabetical order within each state or province. Lists by teaching specializations. Contains an international alphabetical listing, an index to graduate degrees in theatre, and an alphabetical listing of institutions.

US/1041-5211
**DIRECTORY OF THEATRE TRAINING PROGRAMS.** (DIRECTORY OF THEATRE TRAINING PROGRAMS : PROFILES OF COLLEGE AND CONSERVATORY PROGRAMS THROUGHOUT THE UNITED STATES.). [Dir. theatre train. programs]. **Added/Corp** Dorset Theatre Festival & Colony House. 1st (1987)-. English. $17.50. Director of Theatre Training Programs, PO Box 519, Friday Harbor WA 98250. **Tel** (206)378-4191. **ED** J. Charles. **LC** PN2078.U6; D56. **DD** 792/.07/1173. Each issue contains an index to its own contents (no volume index)--loose.
**Desc:** Specialized career directory that follow the usual pattern of college guides, arranging schools of institutes first by state, then alphabetically by name.

●XR
**DIVADELNI NOVINY.** **Added/Corp** Divadelni Ustav (Prague, Czechoslovakia). Vol. 1 (1992)-. Periodical. Czech. bw. Divadelni Ustav, Celetna 17, Prague 1 Czech Republic. **Tel** 232 88 24, 232 88 11.

XR
**DIVADLO.** **Added/Corp** Czechoslovak Republic. Ministerstvo Skolstvi a Kultury. Svaz Ceskoslovenskych Spisovatelu. (1???)-. Periodical. Czech. ir. **(Subscription address:** Artia Pegas Press Ltd., Palac Metro Narodni Trida 25, 11210 Prague 1 Czech Republic.**)** **LC** PN2859.C9; D6.

AT/0727-971X
**DO IT.** **See** History(General).

UK/0012-5946
**DRAMA.** ***Ceased.*** (DRAMA, THE QUARTERLY THEATRE REVIEW.). [Drama]. **Added/Corp** British Theatre Association. British Drama League. No. 1 (Summer 1946)-?. Periodical. English. qt. British Theatre Association, Regents College, Inner Circle, Regents Park, London NW1 4NW England. **Tel** 01935 2571. **ED** Christopher Edwards. **LC** PN2001; .D64. **DD** 792.0941. Index available. cum. index. **Bk Rev**. **Ad Acc**. **Circ:** 7,000. available on microfilm and microfiche from University Microfilms International (UMI). Documents available from UMI Article Clearinghouse. ***Supersedes** Interim Drama.*
**Desc:** Includes reviews, articles and features on subsidized, commercial, experimental, fringe and young people's theatre and theatre personalities in the UK and abroad.
**Ind/Abst** Abstr. Engl. Stud.; Book Rev. Index; Expand. Acad. Index (1989-); Humanit. Index; Newsp. Period. Abstr. (1989-1989); Mag. Index (?-?).

UK/0261-1651
**DRAMA BROADSHEET.** [Drama broadsh.]. (1979)-. Periodical. English. Three times a year (Apr., Aug., Dec.). £15.00 UK & Europe; £20.00 surface mail, £25.00 airmail, other. Drama Broadsheet, 8 Boningale Close Stirchley, Telford Shrop TF3 1RA England. **Tel** 011 44 952 595188. **Bk Rev**, (Qty: 6). **Ad Acc**.
**Desc:** This contains articles on drama in education and theatre in education.

US/1056-4349
**DRAMA CRITICISM (DETROIT, MICH. : 1991).** (DRAMA CRITICISM.). [Drama crit.]. Vol. 1 (1991)-. English. an. $75.00. Gale Research Inc., 835 Penobscot Building, Detroit MI 48226. **Tel** (800)877-GALE, (313)961-2242, FAX (313)961-6083, telex TWX 810-221-7086. **ED** Lawrence J. Trudeau. **LC** PN1601; .D59. **DD** 809.2/005. Index available. cum. index.
**Desc:** Provides excerpts from significant commentary on the most widely studied dramatists from antiquity to contemporary times.

YU/0353-0701
**DRAMA INFORMER, THE.** **VFOAT** YU Drama Informer. **VAT** Yugoslav Drama Informer. Vol. 1 (1987)-. Periodical. English. sa. Sterijino Pozorje, 21000 Novi Sad, Zmaj Jovina 22/1, Yugoslavia. **LC** PG571; .D73. **DD** 891.8/1.

US/0272-2720
**DRAMA-LOGUE.** **VFOAT** Hollywood Drama-Logue. Periodical. English. wk (except last week in Dec.). $55.00. Drama Logue Inc, PO Box 38771, Hollywood CA 90038. **Tel** (310)464-5079. **ED** Lee Melville. **Bk Rev**. **Ad Acc**. **Circ:** 19,000.
**Desc:** Theatrical newspapers specializing in casting information for actors and entertainers.

US/1046-5022
**DRAMA/THEATRE TEACHER, THE.** [Drama theatre teach.]. **Added/Corp** American Alliance for Theatre and Education. **VFOAT** Drama Theatre Teacher. Vol. 1, No. 1 (Fall 1988)-. Periodical. English. Three times a year. $25.00. American Alliance for Theatre Education, Department of Theatre, Arizona State University, Tempe AZ 85287. **Tel** (602)965-6064. **ED** Judith Rethwisch. **DD** 792. **Bk Rev**. **Ad Acc**. **Circ:** 1,100 (ctrl).
**Desc:** Articles of interest to drama/theatre teachers K-12.
**Ind/Abst** Curr. Index J. Educ.; Educ. Index (1992-).

UK
**DRAMATHERAPY (NEWSLETTER).** (DRAMATHERAPY : THE NEWSLETTER OF THE BRITISH ASSOCIATION FOR DRAMATHERAPY.). **Added/Corp** British Association of Dramatherapy. (19??)-. Newsletter. English. Four times a year (Jan., May, July, Nov.). £32.00 Comes with British Association of Dramatherapists membership. British Association of Dramatheraphists, 2 Sunnyvale Village Durlston Swana, Dorset BH19 2HY Scotland. **ED** David Powley. Index available. cum. index. **Bk Rev**. **Ad Acc**. **Circ:** 300.
**Desc:** A newsletter containing dramatherapy news, book reviews and advertising forthcoming events, short courses and employment vacancies in dramatherapy.

UK
**DRAMATHERAPY : THE JOURNAL OF THE BRITISH ASSOCIATION OF DRAMATHERAPY.** **Added/Corp** British Association of Dramatherapy. Vol. 1, No. 1 (Summer 1977)-. Periodical. English. Three times a year. £32.00 Comes with British Association of Dramatherapists membership. British Association of Dramatheraphists, 2 Sunnyvale Village Durlston Swana, Dorset BH19 2HY Scotland. **Bk Rev**, (Qty: 2 or 3). **Ad Acc**. **Circ:** 400 (ctrl).

US/0012-5989
**DRAMATICS.** **Added/Corp** National Thespian Society (U.S.). Vol. 1 (Jan. 1929)-. English. Nine times a year. $18.00 (one year), $32.00 (two year), $45.00 (three year). Educational Theatre Association, 3368 Central Parkway, Cincinnati OH 45225. **Tel** (513)559-1996. **ED** Don Corathers. **LC** PN3175.A1; H5. **DD** 371.89505. Index available. **Bk Rev**. **Ad Acc**. **Circ:** 35,000. available on microfilm and microfiche from University Microfilms International (UMI).
**Desc:** Offers new plays, how-to articles on everything from auditioning and acting technique to building a set on a budget. Feature articles that offer insight into all aspects of the performing arts, and interviews with people ranging from struggling unknowns to theater legends.

US/0012-6004
**DRAMATISTS GUILD QUARTERLY, THE.** **Added/Corp** Author's League of America. Dramatists' Guild. Vol. 1 (Spring 1964)-. Periodical. English. Four times a year (Feb., May, Aug., Nov.). $65.00. Dramatists Guild Inc., 234 West 44th Street, New York NY 10036. **Tel** (212)398-9366, FAX (212)944-0420. **LC** PN2000; .D84. **DD** 792/.0973. **Bk Rev**. **Circ:** 7,000 (ctrl). ***Supersedes** Dramatists Bulletin.*

US/0733-1606
**DRAMATISTS SOURCEBOOK.** **Added/Corp** Theatre Communications Group. **VFOAT** T.C.G.'s Dramatists Sourcebook; TCG's Dramatists Sourcebook. (1982)-. English. an (Aug.). $17.45. Consortium Sales & Book Dist., 1045 Westgate Drive, St. Paul MN 55114. **Tel** (800)283-3572. **ED** M. Elizabeth Osborn. **LC** PN2289; .D73. **DD** 792/.025/73. ***Continues** Information for Playwrights.*
**Desc:** Comprehensive annual guide to professional opportunities. Current information on script submissions, contests, publishing outlets, workshops, conferences and service organizations.

US/0013-1997
**EDUCATIONAL THEATRE NEWS.** ***Ceased.*** **Added/Corp** American Educational Theatre Association. Southern California District. Vol. 1 (Feb. 1954)-Vol. 40, No. 6 (June 1993). Periodical. English. bm. George Gunkle Theatre Department, Cal State University at Northridge, Northridge CA 91330.

CN/0317-4964
**ELIZABETHAN THEATRE, THE.** [Elizab. theatre]. **Main/Conf** International Conference on Elizabethan Theatre. **Added/Corp** University of Waterloo. (1969)-. English. ir. Price varies per volume. PD Meany Company Limited, PO Box 118, Streetsville ONT L5M2B7 Canada. **Tel** (613)547-2619. **LC** PN2589; .I49a. **DD** 792/.0942.
**Ind/Abst** MLA Int. Bibl. Books Artic. Mod. Lang. Lit.

II/0013-6980
**ENACT.** **VFOAT** Enactment. No. 1 (Jan. 1967)-. Periodical. English (translations available in Multiple languages). Ten times a year. $15.00. Enact, c/o Pauls Peers, E44-11 Okhla Industrial Area, New Delhi 110020 India. **LC** PN2001; .E5.

US/0071-0164
**ENCORE.** **Added/Corp** National Association of Dramatics and Speech Arts. (1???)-. Periodical. English. an (Apr.). $15.00 (regular), $25.00 (sustaining), $45.00 (organizational) Comes with National Association of Dramatics and Speech Arts membership. National Association of Dramatic Speech Arts, 208 Cherokee Drive, Blacksburg VA 24060. **Tel** (703)231-5805. **ED** Dr. H. D. Flowers, II. Index available. cum. index. **Bk Rev**. **Ad Acc**. **Circ:** 2,000. available on microfilm and microfiche from University Microfilms International (UMI).
**Desc:** A magazine designed by theatricians in historically black institutions on the history and innovation in ethnic theatre. New plays, research and innovative theatre projects featured.

JA
**ENGEKIGAKU / HENSHU WASEDA DAIGKU ENGEKI GAKKAI.** **VFOAT** Studies on Theatre Arts. Japanese. an. ¥1000 Japan. Waseda Daigaku Engeki Gakkai, Waseda University, Faculty of Literature, Division of Theatre, 1-24-1 Toyama, Shinjuku-ku Tokyo 162 Japan. **Tel** (03)203-4141 (ext. 72-2465). **LC** PN2009; .E52. **Bk Rev**. **Circ:** 1,400 (ctrl).
**Desc:** Organ of the Waseda Daigaku Engeki Gakkai; deals mainly with the Japanese traditional theaters (Kabuki, Bunraku, folkloric performing arts), but also theaters in general, movies and television.

US/1054-4690
**ENSEMBLE (SANTA ANA, CALIF.).** (ENSEMBLE : EASTERN BOYS PRODUCTIONS THEATRICAL NEWSLETTER.). **Added/Corp** Eastern Boys Productions. Vol. 1, No. 1 (Mar. 15, 1991)-. Newsletter. English. mo. Free. Eastern Boys Productions, PO Box 12567, Santa Ana CA 92712.

UK/0143-8980
**ENTERTAINMENT & ARTS MANAGEMENT.** **VFOAT** Entertainment and Arts Management. 1982-. Periodical. English. mo. John Offord Publications, 12 The Avenue, Eastbourne East Sussex BN21 3YA England. **Tel** 0323 645871.

NQ
**ESCENA.** Vol. 1, No. 0 (Feb. 1990)-. Periodical. Spanish. **LC** JL1616; .E8.

AG/0840-5891
**ESCENA LATINOAMERICANA, LA.** ***Suspended.*** [Escen, latinoam.]. **Added/Corp** Instituto Internacional de Teoria y Critica de Teatro Latinoamericano. **VFOAT** EL. No. 1 (April 1989)-(19??). Periodical. Spanish. sa. $28.00 US per year. IITCTL, Charcas 3741, 1425 Buenos Aires Argentina. **Tel** 011 54 1 711739. **LC** PN2309; .E8. **DD** 792/.09805.

CN/0821-4425
**ESSAYS IN THEATRE.** [Essays theatre]. **Added/Corp** University of Guelph. Dept. of Drama. **VFOAT** Etudes Theatrales. Vol. 1, No. 1 (Nov. 1982)-. Periodical. English. Twice a year. 20.00Can$ institutions, 15.00Can$ individuals Canada; $20.00 institutions, $15.00 individuals other. University of Guelph / Department of Drama, Guelph Ontario N1G 2W1 Canada. **Tel** (519)824-4120 Ext. 3147, FAX (519)824-0560. **ED** Prof. A. Wilson and Prof. H. Lane. **DD** 792/.05. **Bk Rev**, (Qty: approx. 12/year). **Ad Acc**. **Pr Rev**. **Circ:** 375. Documents available from The Genuine Article. ***Absorbed** Canadian Drama, 0317-9044.*
**Desc:** A journal of theatre and drama; dramatic theory, literature, aesthetics, history and practice.
**Ind/Abst** Arts Humanit. Citation Index [Full Cov.]; Curr. Contents Arts Humanit.; MLA Int. Bibl. Books Artic. Mod. Lang. Lit.; Res. Alert [Full Cov.].

US/0097-8663
**ESTRENO.** (ESTRENO CUADERNOS DEL TEATRO ESPANOL CONTEMPORANEO INCLUDES FREE INDEX). [Estreno]. **Added/Corp** McMicken College of Arts and Sciences. Dept. of Romance Languages and Literatures. Vol. 1 (Winter 1975)-. Periodical. Spanish (English). sa (March and October). $26.00. Estreno, 350 North Burrowes Building, University Park PA 16802. **Tel** (814)238-0270, (814)865-4252, FAX (814)863-7944. **ED** Professor Martha Halsey, (phone: (814)865-1122. **DD** 862. **Bk Rev**, (Qty: 30). **Ad Acc**. **Pr Rev**. **Circ:** 550.
**Desc:** Unpublished Spanish plays, research articles, reviews of plays and books and material of interest to scholars or professionals of 20th Century Spanish theater.
**Ind/Abst** Arts Humanit. Citation Index [Full Cov.]; Curr. Contents Arts Humanit.; MLA Int. Bibl. Books Artic. Mod. Lang. Lit.; Res. Alert [Full Cov.].

SP/0212-3819
**ESTUDIS ESCENICS.** (ESTUDIS ESCENICS : QUADERNS DE L'INSTITUT DEL TEATRE DE LA DIPUTACIO DE BARCELONA.). [Estud. escen.]. 22 (March 1983)-. Periodical. Catalan (summaries and/or abstracts in English, French and Spanish). Edicions Proa, Tuset 3, Barcelona Spain. **LC** PQ6098.7; .E83. **DD** 792/.05. ***Continues** Estudios Escenicos.*
**Ind/Abst** MLA Int. Bibl. Books Artic. Mod. Lang. Lit.

XV/0353-7161
**EUROMASKE: THE EUROPEAN THEATRE QUARTERLY.** (EUROMASKE.). **VFOAT** Euro Maske. No. 1 (Fall 1990)-. Periodical. English. Four times a year. $9.75. **(Subscription address:** Euromaske Inc., LBS Bank of New York, 101 East 52nd Street, New York NY 10022.**)** **ED** Dusan Jovanovic and Dragan Klaic.

CN/0315-4165
**EXIL (TROIS- RIVIERES).** ***Title Change.*** (EXIL.). V. 1-2. Periodical. French. mo. Groupe De Planifications Des Derives Urbaines, C.P 1443, Succursale B, Hull Quebec J8X 3Y3. **DD** 792'.05. ***Continued by** Derive Urbaine, 0702-8830.*

UK
**FIGHT DIRECTOR, THE.** Periodical. English. Three times a year. £5.00 (membership). The Society of British Fight Directors, 111 Queens Crescent, London NW5 England. **Tel** 01 82-1030. **Bk Rev**. **Ad Acc**. **Circ:** 150.
**Desc:** Professional journal for directors of fights on stage and screen. Contains news of fights and fight direction, with technical articles on various styles of fighting.

GW/0930-5874
**FORUM MODERNES THEATER.** (1986)-. Periodical. German (English and French). sa. DM48.00. Gunter Narr Verlag, Dishingerweg 5, D 72070 Tuebingen Germany. **Tel** 011 49 7071 78091, FAX (07071)75288. Documents available from The Genuine Article.
**Ind/Abst** Arts Humanit. Citation Index [Full Cov.]; Curr. Contents Arts Humanit.; Res. Alert [Full Cov.]; Soc. Sci. Cit. Index [Select. Cov.].

GW
**FRIELING THEATER-JAHRBUCH.** (1991)-. German.

US/1040-483X
**GESTOS (IRVINE, CALIF.).** (GESTOS.). [Gestos]. **Added/Corp** University of California, Irvine. Dept. of Spanish and Portuguese. (April 1986)-. Periodical. Spanish (English). sa. $35.00 (insitutions), $20.00 (individuals). University of California - Irvine, Gestos / Revista de Teoria y, Department of Spanish and Portuguese, Irvine CA 92717. **Tel** (714)856-7171, FAX (714)725-2803. **ED** Juan Villegas. **LC** PQ6098.7; .G47. **DD** 862.009/05. Index available. cum. index. **Bk Rev**. **Ad Acc**.
**Ind/Abst** MLA Int. Bibl. Books Artic. Mod. Lang. Lit.

YU/0351-9120
**GODISNJAK JUGOSLOVENSKIH POZORISTA.** [God. jugosl. pozor.]. **VFOAT** Godisnjak Jugoslovenskih Kazalista. Began with issue for 1978/79. Serbo-Croatian (Roman). an. $5.00 Yugoslavia; $15.00 North America; $10.00 other. Sterijno Pozorje, Zmaj-Jovina 22/l, 2100 Novi Sad Yugoslavia. **Tel** 021/23 161. **LC** PN2850; .G63. Index available. cum. index.

GW
**GRIMM & GRIPS.** **Added/Corp** International Association of Theatre for Children and Young People. Sektion Bundesrepublik Deutschland. **VFOAT** Grimm und Grips. Vol. 1 (1987/88)-. German. an.

UK
**GUIDE TO SELECTING PLAYS, THE.** **See** Literature.

US/0145-3750
**GUTHRIE NEW THEATER.** V. 1- 1976-. English. an. $4.95 single issue. Grove Press Inc, 841 Broadway/4th Floor, New York NY 10003. **Tel** (212)529-3600, telex 6720753. **LC** PS634; .G86. **DD** 812/.5/408.

GW
**HAMBURGER JAHRBUCH FUER THEATER UND MUSIK.** (194?)-. German. an. **ED** P.T. Hoffmann.

II/0256-2480
**HAMLET STUDIES.** **See** Literature.

US/0739-9839
**HANDBOOK - NATIONAL ASSOCIATION OF SCHOOLS OF THEATRE (U.S.).** (HANDBOOK / NAST.). [Handb. - Natl. Assoc. Sch. Theatre (U.S.)]. **Main/Corp** National Association of Schools of Theatre (U.S.). 1984-1985-. English. be. $7.00. National Association of Schools of Theatre, 11250 Roger Bacon Drive/Suite 21, Reston VA 22090. **Tel** (703)437-0700. **ED** David Bading. **LC**

PN2078.U6; N37A. **DD** 792/.07/073. **Circ:** 500.
**Desc:** Standards for accreditation for educational programs in theatre.

CC
**HSI CHU : CHUNG YANG HSI CHU HSUEH YUAN HSUEH PAO.** **Added/Corp** Chung Yang Hsi Chu Hsueh Yuan (China). **VFOAT** Drama. (19??)-. Periodical. Chinese. qt. RMBY1.00. Science Press, 16 Donghuangchenggen North Street, Beijing 100707, People's Republic of China. **Tel** 011 86 1 4019821, 011 86 1 4010642, FAX 011 86 1 4012180, 011 86 1 4019810, telex 210147. **LC** PN2009; .H73. **DD** 792/.05.

CH
**HSI CHU HSUEH HSI / CHUNG YANG HSI CHU HSUEH YUAN PIEN.** **See** Literature.

CC
**HSI CHU I SHU.** **Added/Corp** Shang-Hai Hsi Chu Hsueh Yuan. **VFOAT** Theatre Arts; Xi Ju Yi Shu. (Mar. 1978)-. Periodical. Chinese. Four times a year. $18.22. Science Press, 16 Donghuangchenggen North Street, Beijing 100707, People's Republic of China. **Tel** 011 86 1 4019821, 011 86 1 4010642, FAX 011 86 1 4012180, 011 86 1 4019810, telex 210147. **(Subscription address:** China International Book Trading Corporation, PO Box 399, Library Service Department, Beijing 100044 People's Republic of China.**)** **LC** PN2009; .H74. **DD** 792/.05.

CC
**HSI CHU LUN TSUNG.** **VFOAT** Xijuluncong; Selected Essays of Theatre. 1957-. Periodical. Chinese. qt. RMBY0.65. Hsin Hua Shu Tien, Beijing, People's Republic of China. **Tel** 551253. **LC** PN2870; .H79. **DD** 792/.0951.

CH/0258-3283
**HUAXUE SHIJI.** (HUA HSUEH SHIH CHI.). [Huaxue shiji]. **VFOAT** Chemical Reagents. Began in 1979. Academic Scholarly Publication. Chinese (Chinese). bm. $4.73. Science Press, 16 Donghuangchenggen North Street, Beijing 100707, People's Republic of China. **Tel** 011 86 1 4019821, 011 86 1 4010642, FAX 011 86 1 4012180, 011 86 1 4019810, telex 210147. **ED** Zhang Tai. **LC** QD77; .H78. **CODEN** HUSHDR. **Bk Rev.** **Ad Acc.** **Circ:** 20,000. Documents available from CASDDS.
**Desc:** Preparations, syntheses, applications of chemical reagents and fine chemicals.
**Ind/Abst** Anal. Abstr.; Chem. Abstr.; Chem. Titles.

CN/0848-1482
**IMPACT - PROFESSIONAL ASSOCIATION OF CANADIAN THEATRES.** (IMPACT.). [Impact - Prof. Assoc. Can. Theatres]. **Added/Corp** Professional Association of Canadian Theatres. Vol. 1, No. 1 (Summer 1989)-. Periodical. English. qt. 25.00Can$. PACT Communications Centre, 64 Charles Street East, Toronto Ontario M4Y 1T1 Canada. **Tel** (416)968-3033, FAX (416)968-3035. **ED** Beverly A.B. Sweeting. **DD** 792/.0971. ***Continues*** *PACT News (Toronto, Ont.), 0820-5051.*
**Desc:** News from professional theatres across Canada.

GW
**IN KULTUR : DAS MAGAZIN DER HAMBURGER VOLKSBUHNE.** **Added/Corp** Hamburger Volksbuhne. (1991)-. Periodical. German. mo. **LC** PN2656.H17; V8. ***Continues*** *Buhne (Hamburg, Germany).*

US/0019-3763
**INDEPENDENT SHAVIAN, THE.** **See** Literature.

●US
**INDUSTRY RESOURCES / THEATER CRAFTS.** (1992)-. Periodical. English. **LC** PN2289; .T53. ***Continues*** *Theatre Crafts Directory.*

US/0882-9446
**INTERNATIONAL BIBLIOGRAPHY OF THEATRE.** **See** Theater-Abstracting, Bibliographies and Statistics.

IE/0791-105X
**IRISH STAGE & SCREEN.** [Ir. stage screen]. **VFOAT** Irish Stage and Screen. (1988)-. Periodical. English. Irish Stage and Screen, 9-11 St Andrews Lane, Exchequer Street, Dublin 2 Ireland.

AT
**ITI INTERNATIONAL NEWS ROUND UP.** **See** The Arts-Performing Arts.

AU
**JACOBEAN DRAMA STUDIES.** **Added/Corp** Salzburg. Universitat. Institut fur Englische Sprache und Literatur. (1972)-. Monographic series. English.
**Ind/Abst** MLA Int. Bibl. Books Artic. Mod. Lang. Lit.

AU/0377-0354
**JAHRBUCH DER WIENER GESELLSCHAFT FUER THEATERFORSCHUNG.** **Added/Corp** Wiener Gesellschaft fuer Theaterforschung. (1974)-. German. be. Verband der Wissenschaftlichen Gesellschaften Osterreichs, Lindengasse 37, A-1070 Vienna Austria. **Tel** 011 43 1 932166, 011 43 1 934756, telex 847/134981. **ED** Otto Schindler. **LC** PN2616.V5; V54. **DD** 792/.09436/13. **Circ:** 500. ***Continues*** *Jahrbuch der Gesellschaft fuer Wiener Theaterforschung.*
**Desc:** Articles about different details of the history of theatre, about playwriters or actors; listings of performances in Austria.

SP
**JANUS.** English (Spanish). qt. Free. Inst Nac Seguridad Higiene Trabajo, Calle Dulcet 2 10, 08034 Barcelona Spain. **Tel** 011 34 3 2800102.
**Ind/Abst** HILITES.

XO
**JAVISKO.** Periodical. Slovak. ir. 30.00. PNS - Ustredna Expedicia Tlace V Bratislave Czechoslovakia. **LC** PN2859.C93; S54.

CN/0382-0335
**JEU.** **VFOAT** Cahiers de Theatre Jeu. (Winter 1976)-. Periodical. French. qt. 48.00Can$ (institutions), 38.00Can$ (individuals) Canada; 58.00Can$ (institutions), 47.00Can$ (individuals) other. Cahiers de Theatre Jeu Inc, 426 rue Sherbrooke Est, Bur 102, Montreal Quebec H2L 1J6 Canada. **Tel** (514)288-2808. **(Subscription address:** Periodica Inc., PO Box 444, 1155 Ducharme, Outrement Quebec H2V 4R6 Canada.**)** **ED** Lorraine Camerlain. **LC** PN2305.Q4; J48. **DD** 792/.09714. **Bk Rev.** **Ad Acc.** **Circ:** 1,500.
**Desc:** Informs about various tendencies of contemporary theatre in Quebec and other countries. Editorial promotes circulation of theatrical testimonies by practitioners and, through socio-political questioning, the historicization of the theatrical practice.
**Ind/Abst** Point Repere (19??-).

●CN/1189-5071
**JOURNAL DU VILLAGE D'EMILIE, LE.** [J. Village Emilie]. **Added/Corp** Corporation du Centre de la Culture de Grand'Mere. No 1 (1992)-. French. 1.25Can$. Corporation du Centre de la Culture de Grand'Mere, 15 6E Avenue, Grand'Mere Quebec G9T 2G1 Canada. **DD** 792.45/7.

US/1044-937X
**JOURNAL OF AMERICAN DRAMA AND THEATRE, THE.** [J. Am. drama theatre]. **Added/Corp** Center for Advanced Study in Theatre Arts. Vol. 1, No. 1 (Spring 1989)-. Periodical. English. Three times a year. $12.00. Center for Advanced Theatre Arts, 33 West 42nd Street, CUNY Graduate Center, New York NY 10036. **Tel** (212)642-2225, FAX (212)642-2642. **LC** PS332; .J66. **DD** 792.

US/0888-3203
**JOURNAL OF DRAMATIC THEORY AND CRITICISM.** [J. dram. theory crit.]. **Added/Corp** University of Kansas. Division of Communication and Theatre. Joyce and Elizabeth Hall Center for the Humanities. Vol. 1, No. 1 (Fall 1986)-. Periodical. English. sa (May and December). $25.00 (institution) US and Canada; $30.00 (institution) other. Journal of Dramatic Theory & Criticism, University of Kansas, 211 Watkins Home, Lawrence KS 66044. **Tel** (913)864-4798. **LC** PN1601; .J68. **DD** 809.2/005.

US/0145-5516
**JOURNAL OF THE ILLINOIS SPEECH & THEATRE ASSOCIATION.** **Main/Corp** Illinois Speech & Theatre Association. **VAT** Journal of the Illinois Speech and Theatre Association. (19??)-. English. an. $25.00. Illinois Speech and Theatre Association, Bradley University, Central Office, Peoria IL 61625. **Tel** (309)677-2364, FAX (309)677-2330. **ED** Dr. Mary Pelias. **LC** PN4073; .I5813. **DD** 808.5/08. **Pr Rev.** **Circ:** 400 (ctrl).

US/0892-4899
**KENTUCKY MARQUEE.** (Sept. 1986)-. Periodical. English. ir. Kentucky Marquee, 118 Bauer Avenue, Louisville KY 40207. **Tel** (502)896-9797. **ED** Leigh Anne Howard. **DD** 792. **Ad Acc.** **Circ:** 60,000 (ctrl).

AT
**KINO / JOURNAL OF THE AUSTRALIAN THEATRE HISTORICAL SOCIETY.** English. Four times a year. 40.00Aus$. Australian Theatre Historical Society, PO Box 447, Campbelltown NSW 2560 Australia. **Tel** 011 61 02 6311867. **ED** Les Tod. Index available (published separately). **Circ:** 250.

GW/0176-8905
**KLEINE SCHRIFTEN DER GESELLSCHAFT FUER THEATERGESCHICHTE.** [Kleine Schr. Ges. Theatergesch.]. **Added/Corp** Gesellschaft fur Theatergeschichte (Berlin, Germany). (1906)-. Monographic series. German. **LC** PN2640; .G3. cum. index. ***Continues in part*** *Archiv fur Theatergeschichte.*

JA
**KOKURITSU GEKIJO ENGEIJO.** Began with No. 1 (March/April 1979). Periodical. Japanese. ir. Kokuritsu Gekijo 4-ban, 1-go Hayabusa-cho Chiyoda-ku, Tokyo-to 102 Japan. **LC** PN2920; .K63.

US/0023-8813
**LATIN AMERICAN THEATRE REVIEW.** [Lat. Am. theatre rev.]. **Added/Corp** University of Kansas. Center of Latin American Studies. Vol. 1 (Fall 1967)-. Periodical. English (Spanish and Portuguese). Twice a year (June and December). $15.00 individuals, $30.00 institutions, $5.00 Latin America. Center of Latin American Studies, The University of Kansas, Lawrence KS 66045. **Tel** (913)864-4213, FAX (913)864-4555. **ED** George Woodyard, (editor's address: International Studies, University of Kansas, 108 Lippincott Hall, Lawrence, KS 66045 phone: (913)864-4141). **LC** PN2309; .L37; F1401; .K3 subser. Index available (Every 5 years). cum. index. **Bk Rev.** **Circ:** 1,200. Documents available from The Genuine Article.
**Desc:** Studies of Latin American theatre.
**Ind/Abst** Arts Humanit. Citation Index [Full Cov.]; Curr. Contents Arts Humanit.; HAPI Hisp. Am. Period. Index; MLA Int. Bibl. Books Artic. Mod. Lang. Lit.; Res. Alert [Full Cov.].

IT/0024-144X
**LETTURE.** [Letture]. (1946)-. Periodical. Italian. Ten times a year (monthly with June/July & Aug./Sep. issues combined). L45000 Italy; $70.00 other. Letture, Piazza San Fedele 4, 20121 Milan Italy. **Tel** 011 39 2 722711, FAX 011 39 2 72023481. **ED** Gesuiti di San Fedele. **LC** AS221; .L47. Index available. cum. index. **Bk Rev**, (Qty: 350). **Ad Acc.** **Circ:** 5,000 (ctrl).
**Desc:** A presentation about a writer, director or producer and up dates on literary works, theater, experimental films and religion.
**Ind/Abst** MLA Int. Bibl. Books Artic. Mod. Lang. Lit.; Romant. Move.

US
**LHAT BULLETIN.** **See** Architecture.

CN/0227-227X
**LIAISON (THEATRE-ACTION).** (LIAISON.). [Liaison]. **Added/Corp** Theatre-Action. No. 1 (Summer 1978)-. Periodical. French. Five times a year. 20.56Can$ (1 year), 37.38Can$ (2 year) institutions; 16.82Can$ (1 year), 29.91Can$ (2 year) individuals. Editions L'Interligne, 28 Rue Dupuis Suite 202, Vanier Ontario K1L 7H9 Canada. **Tel** (613)748-0850, FAX (613)748-0852. **ED** Paul-Francois Sylvestre. **DD** 792/.09713. Index available. cum. index. **Bk Rev**, (Qty: 25-30). **Ad Acc.** **Circ:** 1,300.
**Desc:** Informative and critical look at all forms of creativity by French-Canadians outside Quebec, especially those of Ontario; interviews with artists, feature articles on current issues concerning Franco-Ontarians, in-depth analysis of dossiers four times a year, and a creative writing issue once a year.

IT
**LINEA TEATRALE.** No. 1 (1985)-. Periodical. Italian. Three times a year. L18000. Stilema, Corso Brescia 4 Bis 2, 10152 Turin Italy. **Tel** 011 39 11 859398.

UK
**LONDON THEATRE GUIDE.** (1925)-. English. bw. £10.00 UK; £22.00 North America; £14.00 Europe. Society of London Theatre, Bedford Chambers, The Piazza, Covent Garden, London WC2E 8HQ England. **Tel** 011 44 71 836 0971, FAX 011 44 71 497 2543. **ED** Howard Watson. **Ad Acc, Adv Mgr:** David Burns. **Circ:** 169,000 (ctrl).
**Desc:** Comprehensive listing of all London's west end theatres, including performance times, prices, theatreland map, how to book and general information for theatre goers.

US/1064-0312
**LONDON THEATRE NEWS.** (LONDON THEATRE NEWS : WITH NOTES FROM NEW YORK.). [Lond. theatre news]. **VFOAT** LTN. (198?)-. Periodical. English. Ten times a year. $60.00 (one year), $95.00 (two year). London Theatre News Limited, 12 East 86th Street, Suite 620, New York NY 10028. **Tel** (212)517-8608, FAX (212)249-9371. **ED** Roger Harris. **DD** 792. Index available. cum. index. **Bk Rev**, (Qty: 4). **Ad Acc, Adv Mgr:** Ellen Wilk-Harris.
**Desc:** Comprehensive guide to London theatre. Provides exclusive opening night reviews, recommendations, interviews, restaurant reviews, and more.

US/1040-2292
**LOS ANGELES THEATRE & ENTERTAINMENT REVIEW.** [Los Angel. theatre entertain. rev.]. **VFOAT** L.A. Review; Theatre and Entertainment Review; Los Angeles Theatre and Entertainment Review. Vol. 1, No. 1 (July 13-26, 1988)-. Periodical. English. bw. $45.00. R&R Communications, PO Box 2085, Hollywood CA 90028. **DD** 791.

US
**MARQUEE (WASHINGTON, D.C.).** (MARQUEE : THE JOURNAL OF THE THEATRE HISTORICAL SOCIETY.). [Marquee]. **Added/Corp** Theatre Historical Society (U.S.). Vol. 1 (Feb. 1969)-. Periodical. English. Five times a year. $40.00 US,

Canada, & Mexico; $50.00 other. Theatre Historical Society of America, 152 North York Road, Suite 200, Elmhurst IL 60126. **Tel** (708)782-1800. **ED** John Fischer (editor's address: 3128 Walton Boulevard, Suite 136, Rochester Hills, MI 48309, (313)651-4563). **Bk Rev. Ad Acc. Circ:** 1,000 (ctrl). available on microfilm and microfiche from University Microfilms International (UMI).
**Desc:** Records the history of the world of theater through the design and function of its architectural heritage.
**Ind/Abst** Avery Index Archit. Period. Suppl. Colum. Univ. (1989-).

US/0731-3403
**MEDIEVAL & RENAISSANCE DRAMA IN ENGLAND. VFOAT** Medieval and Renaissance Drama in England. (1984)-. English. an. $57.50. AMS Press Inc., 56 East 13th Street, New York NY 10003. **Tel** (212)777-4700, FAX (212)995-5413, telex 710 581 2302. **ED** J Leeds Barroll and Paul Werstine. **LC** PR621; .M65. **DD** 822/.009.
**Desc:** Historical investigations and critical studies in English drama from the beginnings to 1642.
**Ind/Abst** MLA Int. Bibl. Books Artic. Mod. Lang. Lit.

UK/0143-3784
**MEDIEVAL ENGLISH THEATRE. Added/Corp** University of Lancaster. Vol. 1 (Oct. 1979)-. Periodical. English. sa. £7.00 UK; £10.00 other. University of Lancaster Department of English, Lancaster LA1 4TY England. **ED** Meg Twycross, Peter Meredith, and Sarah Carpenter. **LC** PN2587; .M43. **DD** 792/.0942/0902. Index available. **Circ:** 400 (ctrl).
**Desc:** Practices of theatre in England in Middle Ages; Anglo-Saxon period to late sixteenth-century; mysteries, moralities, mummings, interludes, etc.
**Ind/Abst** Annu. Bibliogr. Engl. Lang. Lit.; MLA Int. Bibl. Books Artic. Mod. Lang. Lit.

US/0145-787X
**MIME JOURNAL. Added/Corp** Pomona College (Claremont, Calif.). Theater Dept. Mime School (Fayetteville, Ark.) University of Arkansas, Fayetteville. Dept. of Speech and Dramatic Art. Valley Studio (Spring Green, Wis.) Grand Valley State Colleges. Performing Arts Center. No. 1 (1974)-. Periodical. English. an. $12.00 (individual); $25.00 (institutions). Pomona Claremont Colleges, Theatre Department, 333 North College Way, Claremont CA 91711. **Tel** (909)621-8186, FAX (909)621-8403. **ED** Thomas Leabhart. **LC** PN1985; .M555. **DD** 792.3/05. **Circ:** 500.
**Desc:** A illustrated monograph published on mime and movement theater. Recent topics include Decroux, Copeau, Noh masks and essays on modern and post-modern mime.

SZ
**MIMOS : MITTEILUNGEN DER SCHWEIZERISCHEN GESELLSCHAFT FUER THEATERKULTUR. Added/Corp** Schweizerische Gesellschaft fuer Theaterkultur. **VFOAT** Mitteilungen der Schweizerischen Gesellschaft fuer Theaterkultur; Communications de la Societe Suisse du Theatre; MIMOS : Communications de la Societe Suisse du Theatre. (19??)-. Periodical. French (German). Dr. L. Benz-Burger, Geschaftsstelle SGTK, Herenholzweg 33, CH-8906 Bonstetten Switzerland. **LC** PN2800; .M56. **DD** 792/.09494/05.

US/0076-9142
**MINNESOTA DRAMA EDITIONS. *Ceased.*** (19??)-Completed Series Vol. 9 (19??). Monographic series. English. ir. University of Minnesota Press, 2037 University Avenue Southeast, Minneapolis MN 55414. **Tel** (612)642-2516, (612)624-0005. **ED** Michael Langham. **[CCC].**

CN/0026-7694
**MODERN DRAMA.** [Mod. drama]. **Added/Corp** University of Toronto. Graduate Centre for Study of Drama. Vol. 1 (May 1958)-. Periodical. English. qt (Mar., June, Sep., Dec.). $40.00. University of Toronto Press, 5201 Dufferin Street, Downsview Ontario M3H 5T8 Canada. **Tel** (416)667-7781, (416)667-7782, FAX (416)667-7803. **ED** Dorthy Parker. **DD** 809.2/005. **[CCC].** cum. index. **Bk Rev. Ad Acc. Pr Rev. Circ:** 2,100 (ctrl). available on microfilm and microfiche from University Microfilms International (UMI). Documents available from The Genuine Article, UMI Article Clearinghouse.
**Desc:** Focuses exclusively on world drama since 1850. Students of drama find essays which analyze texts and contexts, along with interviews with famous theatrical creators. Publishes articles by international critics and scholars.
**Ind/Abst** Abstr. Engl. Stud. (1982-); Acad. Abstr. Full Text Elite (Dec. 1990-); Acad. Abstr. (Dec. 1990-); Acad. Ind. [Computer File] (1987-); Acad. Search (Dec. 1990-); Am. Bibliogr. Slavic East Europ. Stud.; Annu. Bibliogr. Engl. Lang. Lit.; Arts Humanit. Citation Index [Full Cov.]; Can. Index; Can. Period. Index (19??-); Curr. Contents Arts Humanit.; Expand. Acad. Index (1987-); Film Lit. Index; Humanit. Index; INFO-SOUTH Abstr.; Lit. Crit. Regist. (1982-); Mag. Search; Middle East Abstr. Index; MLA Int. Bibl. Books Artic. Mod. Lang. Lit.; Newsp. Period. Abstr. (1990-); Res. Alert [Full Cov.]; Romant. Move.

US/0026-7856
**MODERN INTERNATIONAL DRAMA. See** Literature.

IE
**MODERN IRISH PLAYS.** (1982)-. Monographic series. English. ir. Price varies per volume. **LC** UNC.

AT/0157-471X
**MONASH NINETEENTH-CENTURY DRAMA SERIES.** [Monash ninet.-century drama ser.]. (1977)-. Monographic series. English. ir. 3.00Aus$. Monash University, Centre for Southeast Asian Studies, Clayton Victoria 3168 Australia. **Tel** 011 61 3 541 2135. **DD** _a808.82034.

US/1065-1519
**MOVEMENT THEATRE QUARTERLY.** (MOVEMENT THEATRE QUARTERLY : MTQ.). [Mov. theatre q.]. **Added/Corp** National Movement Theatre Association (U.S.). **VFOAT** MTQ. (19??)-. Periodical. English. Four times a year. $20.00. National Movement Theatre Association, PO Box 1437, Portsmouth NH 03802-1437. **Tel** (603)436-6660. **ED** Marguerite Mathews. **DD** 792. **Bk Rev**, (Qty: 4-5). **Ad Acc. Circ:** 400. ***Continues*** *Mime News (Claremont, Calif.), 0892-4910.*
**Desc:** A journal devoted to informing its membership, providing insight into the artistic work of movement theatre artists, and promoting the field to the general public. This journal acts as a forum for movement theatre artists and a tool for creating visibility in the outside world. News of festivals, interviews, articles, and reviews appear regularly.

SZ
**MUSIK & THEATER (SAINT GALL, SWITZERLAND). See** Music.

RU
**NASHI DEBIUTANTY.** (19??)-. Periodical. Russian. 0.20rub. Izdatelstvo Iskusstvo, Vorotnikovskii Pereulok 11, 103009 Moscow Russia. **LC** PG3240.5; .N34.

CN/0383-1256
**NATIONAL THEATRE SCHOOL OF CANADA. Main/Corp** National Theatre School of Canada. **VFOAT** Ecole National de Theatre du Canada. (1961)-. English (French). an. Free. National Theatre School of Canada, 5030 St Denis Street, Montreal Quebec H2J 2L8 Canada. **DD** 792/.07/10714281. ctrl circ.

US/0279-120X
**NATO NEWS AND VIEWS.** [NATO news views]. **Added/Corp** National Association of Theatre Owners. **VFOAT** NATO News and Views. **VAT** National Association of Theatre Owners News and Views. (19??)-. Periodical. English. mo. $50.00 US; $65.00 other. National Association of Theatre Owners, 4605 Lankershim Blvd, Suite 340, North Hollywood CA 91602. **Tel** (818)506-1778, FAX (818)506-0269. **ED** Jim Kozak. **DD** 369. **Circ:** 2,400 (ctrl). ***Continues*** *NATO Flash Bulletin.*
**Desc:** News and information of interest to motion picture theatre owners and executives.

US
**NEW AMERICAN PLAYS. See** Literature.

US/0896-1506
**NEW ENGLAND ENTERTAINMENT DIGEST. VFOAT** NEED. Vol. 1, No. 1 (Aug. 6, 1979)-. Periodical. English. mo. $15.00 (1 year), $28.00 (2 year). Taylor Publishing / Portland, PO Box 313, Portland CT 06480. **Tel** (203)342-4730, FAX (203)342-1977. **ED** Bob Taylor. **LC** PN2001; .N45. **Bk Rev**, (Qty: 6). **Ad Acc. Circ:** 3,500.
**Desc:** Covers performing arts throughout New England.

US
**NEW ENGLAND ENTERTAINMENT DIGEST [MICROFORM]. VFOAT** NEED. Vol. 1, No. 1 (Aug. 6, 1979)-. Periodical. English. mo. $15.00 (one year); $28.00 (two year). Taylor Publishing / Portland, PO Box 313, Portland CT 06480. **Tel** (203)342-4730, FAX (203)342-1977. **ED** Paul J. Reale. **Bk Rev. Ad Acc. Circ:** 10,000 (ctrl).
**Desc:** Promotes theater, music, dance, and film video.

US/1050-9720
**NEW ENGLAND THEATRE JOURNAL.** [N. Engl. theater j.]. **Added/Corp** New England Theatre Conference. **VFOAT** New England Theater Journal; Theatre Journal; Theater Journal; NETJ. Vol. 1, No. 1 (1990)-. Periodical. English. an (June). $10.00. New England Theatre Conference, Dep Theatre, 360 Huntington Avenue, Waltham MA 02115. **Tel** (617)424-9275. **ED** Jeffrey Martin (address: 78 Bristol Ferry Road, Portsmouth, RI, 02871) (phone: (401)683-0367). **LC** PN2000; .N443. **DD** 792/.05. **Bk Rev**, (Qty: 10). **Ad Acc, Adv Mgr:** Corey. **Circ:** 1,000.
**Desc:** Scholarly journal of theatre history, pedagogy, and performance practice.
**Ind/Abst** MLA Int. Bibl. Books Artic. Mod. Lang. Lit.

US/8755-0598
**NEW FREEDOM QUARTERLY.** Periodical. English. qt. $15.00. New Freedom Theater Inc, 1346 N Broad Street, Philadelphia PA 19121.

UK/0266-464X
**NEW THEATRE QUARTERLY : NTQ.** [NTQ, New theatre q.]. **VFOAT** NTQ. Vol. 1, No. 1 (Feb. 1985)-. Academic Scholarly Publication. English. qt. $76.00 US, Canada and Mexico; £43.00 other. Cambridge University Press, The Edinburgh Building, Shaftesbury Road, Cambridge CB2 2RU United Kingdom. **Tel** 011 44 223 312393, FAX 011 44 223 325959. **(Subscription address:** Cambridge University Press / North America, 110 Midland Avenue, Port Chester NY 10573.**) ED** Clive Barker and Simon Trussler. **LC** PN2001; .T435. **DD** 792/.05. **[CCC].** available on microfilm and microfiche from University Microfilms International (UMI). Documents available from The Genuine Article, UMI Article Clearinghouse. ***Continues*** *Theatre Quarterly, 0049-3600.*
**Desc:** Provides a vital international literary forum where theatrical scholarship and practice can meet, and where prevailing dramatic assumptions can be subjected to vigorous critical questioning. Shows that theatre history is intrinsic to theatre studies, that theatre needs a philosophy, theatre studies need a methodology and criticism needs a language. The journal publishes news, analysis and debate within the field of theatre studies.
**Ind/Abst** Acad. Search (Jan. 1994-); Am. Hist. Life (1991-); Arts Humanit. Citation Index [Full Cov.]; Br. Humanit. Index; Curr. Contents Arts Humanit.; Expand. Acad. Index (1989-); Humanit. Index; Humanit. Source (Jul. 1993-); INFO-SOUTH Abstr.; Mag. Search; MLA Int. Bibl. Books Artic. Mod. Lang. Lit.; Newsp. Period. Abstr. (1991-); Res. Alert [Full Cov.].

US/0028-7784
**NEW YORK THEATRE CRITICS' REVIEWS.** [N. Y. theatre crit. rev.]. **VFOAT** Theatre Critics' Reviews. (1943)-. Periodical. English. Twenty-two times a year. $122.00 ; $137.50 (bound volumes). New York Theatre Critics Reviews, 37-15 61st Street, Woodside NY 11377. **Tel** (718)492-6674, FAX (718)492-6672. **ED** Joan Marlowe and Betty Blake. **LC** PN2000; .N76. Index available. cum. index. ***Continues*** *Critics' Theatre Reviews.*
**Desc:** Brings the complete reviews from these New York publications and stations when covered: New York Daily News, Wall Street Journal, Time, etc.

US/0160-0583
**NEW YORK TIMES THEATER REVIEWS, THE.** (1885)-. English. an. $165.00. Garland Publishing, 1000A Sherman Avenue, Hamden CT 06514. **Tel** (800)627-6273, (203)281-4487, FAX (203)230-1186. **LC** PN2266; .N48. **DD** 792/.0973.

CN/0821-4476
**NEWS / THEATRE ONTARIO.** [News - Theatre Ont.]. **Added/Corp** Theatre Ontario. **VFOAT** Theatre Ontario News. No. 1 (1981)-. Periodical. English. ir (5 issues). Comes with Theatre Ontario membership. Theatre Ontario, 344 Bloor Street West, 6th Floor, Toronto Ontario M5S 3A7 Canada. **Tel** (416)964-6771. **ED** Angie Bahr Fostaty. **DD** 792/.09713. **Bk Rev. Circ:** 2,500 (ctrl).
**Desc:** Features profiles, articles, and on stage listings on professional, community and educational theatre in Ontario.

CN/1193-7564
**NEWSLETTER / ASSOCIATION FOR CANADIAN THEATRE RESEARCH.** [Newsl. - Assoc. Can. Theatre Res.]. **Main/Corp** Association for Canadian Theatre Research. **Added/Corp** Association for Canadian Theatre Research. Vol. 15, No. 2 (Fall 1991)-. Periodical. English (French; summaries and/or abstracts in French). Twice a year. 50.00Can$ Comes with Association for Canadian Theatre Research membership. Association for Canadian Theatre Research, University of Lethbridge, Department of Drama Arts, Lethbridge Alt T1K 3M4 Canada. **Tel** (403)329-2671, FAX (403)382-7127. **ED** Doug McCallum and Andre Loiselle, (editor's address: Department of Theatre, University of British Columbia, Vancouver, British Columbia, V67 1Z2 Canada, phone: (604)822-5985 Fax). **LC** PN2009; .A78. **DD** 792/.0971. **Bk Rev**, (Qty: 10). **Pr Rev. Circ:** 250-300. ***Continues*** *Newsletter (Association for Canadian Theatre History), 0705-7989.*

CN/0708-9597
**NEWSLETTER - ASSOCIATION OF BRITISH COLUMBIA DRAMA EDUCATORS. *Title Change.*** [Newsl. - Assoc. B.C. Drama Educ.]. Sept./Oct. 1978-. Newsletter. English. Association of British Columbia Drama Educators, c/o British Columbia Teachers Federation, 2235 Burrard Street, Vancouver British Columbia V6J 3H9 Canada. **DD** 792/.07/0711. ***Continues*** *W A D E, 0708-9589.* ***Continued by*** *ABCDE Newsletter, 0829-3775.*

UK
**NEWSLETTER / THE COSTUME SOCIETY. Added/Corp** Costume Society. (19??)-. Newsletter. English. Free to members of the Costume Society. Costume Society, 21 Oak Road, Woolston SO19 9BQ United Kingdom. **Tel** 011 44 703 442011. **LC** GT730; .N48.

NR/1115-201X
**NIGERIAN STAGE, THE.** **Added/Corp** Innovation Theatre (Ilorin, Nigeria) University of Ilorin. Theatre Study Group. Vol. 1, No. 1 (Mar. 1990)-. Periodical. English. sa. Nigerian Stage, Department of Performing Arts, University of Ilorin, Ilorin Nigeria. **LC** IN PROCESS; PN2993; .N54.

JA
**NIHON NO JIDO ENGEKI.** **VFOAT** Children's Theatre in Japan. 1982-. Japanese (Japanese). an. Nihon Jido Engeki Kyokai, 19-3 Jingumae 6 Shibuya-ku, Tokyo-to 150 Japan. **LC** PN3159.J3; N52.

US/0893-3766
**NINETEENTH CENTURY THEATRE.** [Ninet. century theatre]. **VFOAT** 19th Century Theatre. Vol. 15, No. 1 (Summer 1987)-. Periodical. English. sa. $12.00 (individuals), $20.00 (institutions). Nineteenth Century Theatre, Department of English, University of Massachusetts, Amherst MA 01003. **Tel** (413)545-0498. **ED** Joseph Donohue. **LC** PN1851; .N55. **DD** 809.2/034. Index available. cum. index. **Bk Rev. Ad Acc. Circ:** 500 (ctrl). available on microfilm from University Microfilms International (UMI). ***Continues** Nineteenth Century Theatre Research, 0316-5329.*
**Desc:** A journal of theater studies concentrating on Western theater in the period 1789-1914.
**Ind/Abst** Abstr. Engl. Stud. (1987-); Am. Hist. Life (1986-); Am. Humanit. Index; Lit. Crit. Regist.; MLA Int. Bibl. Books Artic. Mod. Lang. Lit.

DK/0904-6380
**NORDIC THEATRE STUDIES.** (1988)-. English. ir. kr187.30. Munksgaard International Publishers Ltd, PO Box 2148, DK-1016 Copenhagen K Denmark. **Tel** 011 45 33 12 70 30, FAX 011 45 33 12 93 87, telex 19431 MUNKS DK. **(Subscription address:** DBK Bogdistribution, Siljangade 2 8 , DK 2300 Cophenhagen S Denmark) **LC** PN2730; .N66.

GW
**OFFENE TOR, DAS.** **See** Music.

US/0020-5885
**OFFICIAL BULLETIN OF THE THEATRICAL STAGE EMPLOYEES AND MOVING PICTURE MACHINE OPERATORS OF THE UNITED STATES AND CANADA.** **Main/Corp** International Alliance of Theatrical Stage Employees and Moving Picture Machine Operators of the United States and Canada. Bulletin. English. qt. International Alliance of Theatrical Stage Employees and Moving Picture Machine Operators of the United States and Canada, 1515 Broadway/Suite 601, New York NY 10036. **LC** WMLC L 82/230.
**Ind/Abst** Work Relat. Abstr. (-19??).

●US/1065-805X
**OLLANTAY THEATER MAGAZINE.** **Added/Corp** Ollantay Center for the Arts. (1993)-. Periodical. English. sa. $25.00 (institutions). Ollantay Theater Magazine, PO Box 556, Jackson Heights NY 11372.

US/0749-1549
**ON-STAGE STUDIES.** (ON-STAGE STUDIES / COLORADO SHAKESPEARE FESTIVAL.). [On-stage stud.]. **Added/Corp** Colorado Shakespeare Festival. **VFOAT** On Stage Studies. No. 3 (1979)-. English. an. $16.00 (institutions), $11.00 (individuals). University of Colorado / Campus Box 261, Campus Box 261, Boulder CO 80309. **Tel** (303)492-7355, FAX (303)492-5105. **ED** Judith Bock (editor's phone: (303)444-3520). **LC** PR2885; .O5. **DD** 822.3/3. **Ad Acc, Adv Mgr:** same as editor. **Circ:** 200. ***Continues** Colorado Shakespeare Festival Annual, 0198-831X.*
**Desc:** Insights into Shakespeare texts and production methods by those engaged in the production of Shakespeare's plays.
**Ind/Abst** Annu. Bibliogr. Engl. Lang. Lit.

CN/0030-3062
**OPAL, THE.** ***Ceased.*** **Added/Corp** Ontario Puppetry Association. (1???)-(1???). Periodical. English. bm. Ontario Pupperty Association, 171 Avondale, Willowdale Ontario M2N 2V4 Canada.

US
**OPENING NIGHT ON BROADWAY.** (19??)-. Periodical. English. $65.00. New York Theatre Critics Reviews, 37-15 61st Street, Woodside NY 11377. **Tel** (718)492-6674, FAX (718)492-6672.

UK
**ORIGINAL BRITISH THEATRE DIRECTORY, THE.** **VFOAT** British Theatre Directory. 16th Ed. (1987/88)-. English. an. £20.95. Richmond House Publishing Company, 9-11 Richmond Buildings, London W1Y 5AF England. **Tel** 011 44 71 437 9556. ***Continues** British Theatre Directory, 0306-4107.*

CN/1180-5137
**P.O.V. : A NEWSLETTER FOR MANITOBA ACTORS.** [P.O.V., newsl. Manit. actors]. **Added/Corp** Alliance of Canadian Cinema, Television and Radio Artists. Manitoba Performers' Branch. **VFOAT** Newsletter for Manitoba Actors. **VAT** Point of View, a Newsletter for Manitoba's Actors. Vol. 1, No. 1 (May 1990)-. Newsletter. English. mo. Free to members. Manitoba Performers' Branch, Alliance of Canadian Cinema, Television and Radio Artists, Suite 110, 388 Donald Street, Winnipeg, Manitoba R3B 2J4 Canada. **DD** 791.4/097127.

US/1061-8112
**PASSING SHOW (NEW YORK, N.Y.).** (THE PASSING SHOW : NEWSLETTER OF THE SHUBERT ARCHIVE.). Vol. 1, No. 1 (Winter 1977)-. Newsletter. English. sa. Lyceum Theatre, 149 West 45th Street, New York NY 10036. **Tel** (212)944-3895. **LC** WMLC L 83/506. cum. index. **Bk Rev. Circ:** 1,200 (ctrl).
**Desc:** Descriptive essays on holdings, project reports, music, scripts, ephemera of Shubert broadway productions, correspondence, business records, costume and set designs, architectural plans.

US/0554-3037
**PLAY INDEX.** (1949/1952)-. Monographic series. English. ir. Price varies per volume. H W Wilson Company, 950 University Avenue, Bronx NY 10452. **Tel** (800)367-6770, (718)588-8400, FAX (718)590-1617, telex 4990003 HWILSON. **LC** Z5781; .P53.
**Desc:** Comprehensive record of the plays published during the time period covered. Author, title, subject, and dramatic style entries for each play are offered.

US
**PLAY SOURCE.** English. qt. $20.00 US and Canada; $35.00 other. Theatre Communications Group, 355 Lexington Avenue, New York NY 10017. **Tel** (212)697-5230, FAX (212)983-4847.

US/0551-0678
**PLAYBILL.** Vol. 1, No. 1 (Sept. 30, 1957)-. Periodical. English. ir. $150.00 US; $200.00 other. Playbill Inc., 52 Vanderbuilt Avenue, 11th Floor, New York NY 10017. **Tel** (212)557-5757, FAX (323)682-2932. **ED** Joan Alleman. **Ad Acc, Adv Mgr:** B Charles. **Circ:** 13,000 (ctrl).
**Desc:** Theatre magazine for general public includes articles on dance, actors, and etc; the actual program distributed in the theatre on opening night.

UK/0032-1559
**PLAYS AND PLAYERS.** [Plays & play]. **VFOAT** Plays & Players. Began with V. 1, 1953. Periodical. English. mo. £26.00 UK; £33.00 (surface mail), £39.00 (airmail) other. Plusloop Ltd, Magnum Dist Ltd, Cloister Ct, 22 26 Farringdon, London EC1R 6HU England. **Tel** 011 44 1 253 3456, 081 953 5433. **(Subscription address:** Unit 4, Durham Road, Borehamwood, Herts WD6 1LW England) **LC** PN2001; .P57. **DD** 792/.0941. available on microfilm and microfiche from University Microfilms International (UMI). ***Absorbed** Plays (London, England); Theatre World; Encore (London, England).*
**Ind/Abst** Humanit. Index.

US
**PLAYS & PLAYWRIGHTS.** **See** Literature.

US/0032-1540
**PLAYS (BOSTON).** (PLAYS.). Vol. 1 (Sept. 1941)-. English. Seven times a year (Oct.-May). $28.00 (one year), $52.00 (two year), $75.00 (three year). Plays Inc., 120 Boylston Street, Boston MA 02116. **Tel** (617)423-3157. **ED** Sylvia K. Burack. **LC** PN1601; .P6. **DD** 371.8952. Index available in last issue of volume--attached. **Bk Rev. Ad Acc. Circ:** 20,300. available on microfilm and microfiche from University Microfilms International (UMI). ***Absorbed** One Act Play Magazine and Radio-Drama Review.*
**Desc:** Presents one-act plays and programs for young people in lower grades through high school, to perform in schools, drama groups, libraries and clubs. Plays includes comedies, holiday plays, dramatized classics, special occasion plays, skits, creative drama, puppet plays, etc.
**Ind/Abst** Child. Mag. Guide (1981-); Gen. Period. Index (Jan. 1985-Dec. 1985); Mid. Search (Jan. 1994-); Read. Guide Period. Lit.; Mag. Index (1977-Dec. 1985).

UK
**PLAYS BY WOMEN.** English. ir. Reed Book Service, Northampton Road, Rushden Nhts NN10 9PU England. **Tel** 011 44 71 933-5821.

US/0736-0711
**PLAYS IN PROCESS.** ***Ceased.*** **Added/Corp** Theatre Communications Group. (19??)-Vol. 13, No. 12 (1993). Monographic series. English. mo. Theatre Communications Group, 355 Lexington Avenue, New York NY 10017. **Tel** (212)697-5230, FAX (212)983-4847. **ED** James Leverett. **LC** PS634; .P6144. **DD** 812.008/005. **Circ:** 370.
**Desc:** A national script circulation service that offers a first-hand look at some of America's most important new dramatic writing.

UK/0268-2028
**PLAYS INTERNATIONAL.** [Plays int.]. Vol. 1, No. 1 (Aug. 1985)-. Periodical. English. mo. $55.00. Plays International Limited, F6 Greenwood Court Harlescott, Shrewsbury SY1 3TB England. **Tel** 011 44 743 351278.

US/0887-1507
**PLAYWRIGHT'S COMPANION, THE.** (198?)-. English. an. $18.95, $16.95 (libraries). Feedback Theatre, 305 Madison Avenue, Suite 1146, New York NY 10165. **Tel** (212)687-4185 or, (207)359-2781. **ED** Mollie Ann Meserve. **LC** PN2289; .P57. **DD** 792/.02573. Index available. **Ad Acc. Circ:** 8,000.
**Desc:** A submission guide to theatres, contests, play publishers and special programs for playwrights; introduction gives tips on marketing, script format, scenarios, synopses, query/cover letters, and resumes.

SP/0032-8367
**PRIMER ACTO.** No. 1 (Abr. 1957)-. Periodical. Spanish. Five times a year. 3375.00ptas Spain; 4000.00ptas Latin America; 4575.00ptas rest of Europe; 4650.00ptas other. Primer Acto, C Cervantes 21 1 of 3, 28014 Madrid Spain. **Tel** 011 34 1 4203050, 011 34 1 3555867.
**Desc:** Covers the theater and Spanish drama.

PO
**PROGRAMA.** No. 1- July 1978-. Portuguese (Portuguese). 50.00 each issue. Teatro do Grupo de Campolide, Av D Carlos I N 61-1, Lisbon Portugal. **LC** PN2796.L52; G786.

IT
**PROSCENIO.** (1984)-. Monographic series. Italian. Price varies per volume. Societa Editrice il Mulino, Strada Maggiore 37, 40125 Bologna Italy. **Tel** 011 39 51 256011, FAX 011 39 51 256034.

US/0033-443X
**PUPPETRY JOURNAL, THE.** **See** The Arts-Performing Arts.

AU/0259-0786
**QUELLEN ZUR THEATERGESCHICHTE.** Vol. 1-. German. ir. Verband der Wissenschaftlichen Gesellschaften Osterreichs, Lindengasse 37, A-1070 Vienna Austria. **Tel** 011 43 1 932166, 011 43 1 934756, telex 847/134981. **ED** Otto Schindler. **LC** PN2616.V5; V54 subser. **Circ:** 400.
**Desc:** Monographs of edited sources and documents concerning different periods in the history of the theatre.

CN/0825-7507
**REACH TH' PEOPLE.** [Reach people]. **Added/Corp** Black Theatre Canada. Vol. 1 No. 1 (Apr 1984)-. Periodical. English. Free to members. Black Theatre Canada, 109 Vaughan Road, Toronto Ontario M6C 2L9. **DD** 792/.08996.

CN/0700-9283
**RECORDS OF EARLY ENGLISH DRAMA.** (RECORDS OF EARLY ENGLISH DRAMA : NEWSLETTER.). [Rec. early Engl. drama]. **Added/Corp** Records of Early English Drama (Firm). **VFOAT** REED Newsletter. (June 1976)-. Newsletter. English. Twice a year (Aug. & Dec.). $10.00. Records of Early English Drama Newsletter, University of Ontario, c/o S. Levitt, 150 Charles Street West, Toronto Ontario M5S 1K9 Canada. **Tel** (416)585-4504, FAX (416)585-4594. **ED** Prof. Helen Ostovich (editor's telephone: (905)525-9140). **LC** PR641; .R43. **DD** 822/.009. Index available. cum. index. **Bk Rev**, (Qty: 450). **Ad Acc. Pr Rev. Circ:** 450 (ctrl).
**Desc:** Documents dealing with Medieval and Renaissance English drama.
**Ind/Abst** Am. Hist. Life (1988-); Annu. Bibliogr. Engl. Lang. Lit.; MLA Int. Bibl. Books Artic. Mod. Lang. Lit.

US/1041-9411
**REGIONAL THEATRE DIRECTORY.** [Reg. theatre dir.]. **Added/Corp** Dorset Theatre Festival & Colony House. (1985/1986)-. Directory. English. an. $17.70. Theatre Directories, PO Box 519, Dorset VT 05251. **Tel** (802)867-2223, FAX (802)867-0144. **ED** Jill Charles. **LC** PN2289; .R44. **DD** 792/.025/73. **Ad Acc. Circ:** 15,000.
**Desc:** Profiles about 400 professional theatre companies which run Fall/Winter/Spring seasons. Employment guide for theatre professionals, internship opportunities for students.

US/0486-3739
**RENAISSANCE DRAMA.** [Renaiss. drama]. (1964)-. English. an. $45.95. Northwestern University Press, PO Box 1093, Evanston IL 60201. **Tel** (708)491-5313, FAX (708)491-8150. **ED** Mary Beth Rose. **LC** PN1785; .R4. **DD** 809.2/09/02. ***Continues** Renaissance Drama: A Report on Research Opportunities. **Continued in part by** Research Opportunities in Renaissance Drama, 0098-647X.*
**Desc:** Drama of all nations in the 15th, 16th, and 17th Century.
**Ind/Abst** Abstr. Engl. Stud.; Annu. Bibliogr. Engl. Lang. Lit. (19??-19??); MLA Int. Bibl. Books Artic. Mod. Lang. Lit.

MX
**REPORTE TEATRAL / COORDINACION GENERAL DE EXTENSION UNIVERSITARIA Y DIFUSION CULTURAL, EL.** **Added/Corp** Universidad Autonoma de Coahuila. Coordinacion General de Extension Universitaria y Difusion Cultural. Vol. 1 No. 1 (Sept. 15 1991)-. Periodical. Spanish. sm.

US/0098-647X
**RESEARCH OPPORTUNITIES IN RENAISSANCE DRAMA.** See Literature.

US/0034-5822
**RESTORATION AND 18TH CENTURY THEATRE RESEARCH.** [Restor. 18th century theatre res.]. **Added/Corp** Loyola University of Chicago. **VFOAT** Restoration and Eighteenth Century Theatre Research. **VAT** Restoration and Eighteenth Century Theatre Research. Vol. 2 (May 1963);New Series Vol. 1 (July 1986)-. Periodical. English. sa (June & Dec.). $8.00. Loyola University of Chicago, 6525 North Sheridan Road, Department of English, Chicago IL 60820. **Tel** (312)915-6718. **DD** 822. ***Continues*** *17th and 18th Century Theatre Research.*
**Ind/Abst** Am. Hist. Life (1973-1977,1986-); Annu. Bibliogr. Engl. Lang. Lit.; MLA Int. Bibl. Books Artic. Mod. Lang. Lit.

BL/0034-8953
**REVISTA DE TEATRO.** **Added/Corp** Sociedade Brasileira de Autores Teatrais. No. 285 (1955)-. Periodical. Portuguese. qt. $40.00. Sociedade Brasileira de Autores Teatrais, Rua da Quitanda 194, Salas 1008, 20091 Rio de Janeiro Brazil. **Tel** 011 55 21 2637856. **LC** WMLC L 83/47; PN2008; .S3. ***Continues*** *SBAT Boletim.*
**Ind/Abst** HAPI Hisp. Am. Period. Index (19??-); MLA Int. Bibl. Books Artic. Mod. Lang. Lit.

FR/0035-2373
**REVUE D'HISTOIRE DU THEATRE.** [Rev. hist. theatre]. **Added/Corp** Societe d'Histoire du Theatre (Paris, France). **VFOAT** Revue de la Societe d'Histoire du Theatre. Vol. 1, (1948/49)-. Periodical. French. Four times a year (Mar., June, Sept., Dec.). 340.00F France, 360.00F EEC Countries, 380.00F others (surface mail); 420.00F (airmail). Societe D Histoire du Theatre, 98 Boulevard Kellermann, 75013 Paris France. **Tel** 011 33 1 45884655. **LC** PN2003; .R38. **DD** 792. Index available (bound in issue). **Bk Rev**. **Ad Acc**. Documents available from The Genuine Article. ***Supersedes*** *Societe d'Histoire du Theatre. Bulletin.*
**Desc:** Each issue contains unpublished studies and documents about theater in France and abroad. Also, international bibliography of performance arts, summaries of books and exhibitions.
**Ind/Abst** Am. Hist. Life (1975-); Annu. Bibliogr. Engl. Lang. Lit.; Arts Humanit. Citation Index [Full Cov.]; BHA : Biblio. Hist. Art; Curr. Contents Arts Humanit.; MLA Int. Bibl. Books Artic. Mod. Lang. Lit.; Res. Alert [Full Cov.]; Romant. Move.; Soc. Sci. Cit. Index [Select. Cov.].

IT
**RIDOTTO.** **Added/Corp** Societa Italiana Autori Drammatici. (1951)-. Periodical. Italian. ir (10 issues). L40000 Italy; L50000 other. SIAD, Via Po 10, 00198 Rome Italy. **Tel** 011 39 6 8416970, FAX 011 39 6 8558860. **Bk Rev**.
**Desc:** Distribution of theatrical texts.
**Ind/Abst** MLA Int. Bibl. Books Artic. Mod. Lang. Lit.

IT
**RIVISTA ILLUSTRATA DEL MUSEO TEATRALE ALLA SCALA, LA.** **Added/Corp** Museo Teatrale Alla Scala. Vol. 1, No.1 (1988/89)-. Periodical. Italian. qt. L50000 Italy; L65000 other Europe; L85000 other. Nuova Diffusione Lombarda SAS di Pieraldo Campagnoni & C, Via Numa Pompilio 12, 20123 Milan Italy. **Tel** 011 39 2 48195522. **LC** ML1733.8.M5; R58. **DD** 792.5/0945/2105.

UK/0142-9434
**ROYAL SHAKESPEARE COMPANY; A COMPLETE RECORD OF THE YEAR'S WORK.** **Main/Corp** Royal Shakespeare Company. Periodical. English. an. $5.75. Royal Shakespeare Company BKSP, England. **LC** PN2596.S82; R687. **DD** 792/.0941.05.

●US/1068-8161
**RUSSIAN THEATRE ARCHIVE.** (1993)-. Monographic series. English. Price varies per volume. Harwood Academic Publishers / New York, PO Box 786, Cooper Station, New York NY 10276. **Tel** (212)206-8900, (201)643-7500. **(Subscription address:** International Publishers Distributor at one of the following addresses: 820 Town Center Drive, Langhorne, PA 19047; or PO Box 90, Reading Berkshire RG1 8JL UK; or Kent Ridge PO Box 1180, Singapore 9111, Republic of Singapore**)** **ED** Anatoly Smeliansky, John Freedman, Leon Gitelman.
**Desc:** Aims to make available avantgarde plays, from the pre-Revolutionary period to the present day.

RU
**RUSSKII VODEVIL.** (1967)-. Periodical. Russian. 0.22rub. Izdatelstvo Iskusstvo, Vorotnikovskii Pereulok 11, 103009 Moscow Russia. **LC** PG3253; .R88.

US/0146-9576
**SAN FRANCISCO THEATRE.** Periodical. English. qt. $8.00. San Francisco Theatre Magazine, 408 Columbus Avenue, San Francisco CA 94133.

PL
**SCENA.** **Added/Corp** Towarzystwo Kultury Teatralnej. (19??)-. Periodical. Polish. bm. Price on Request. **(Subscription address:** ARS Polona, PO Box 1001, 00068 Warsaw Poland.**)** **LC** PN2859.P6; S28. ***Continues*** *Teatr Ludowy.*

CN/0381-8098
**SCENE CHANGES.** V. 1- Feb. 1973-. Periodical. English. mo. Theatre Ontario, 344 Bloor Street West, 6th Floor, Toronto Ontario M5S 3A7 Canada. **Tel** (416)964-6771. **DD** 792/.09713. ***Continues*** *Dialog (Theatre Ontario), 0708-7667.*

US/0748-2558
**SHAKESPEARE BULLETIN.** [Shakespeare bull.]. **Added/Corp** New York Shakespeare Society (1982- ) Lafayette College (Easton, Pa.). Vol. 2, Nos. 5, 6 (Nov./Dec. 1983)-. Periodical. English. qt. $15.00. Lafayette College, English Department, Easton PA 18042. **Tel** (610)250-5245, (215)250-5245, FAX (215)250-9850. **ED** James P. Lusardi and June Schlueter. **LC** PR3091; .B77. **DD** 792.9/5/05. Index available. **Bk Rev**, (Qty: 25-30). **Ad Acc. Pr Rev. Circ:** 1,000. ***Continues*** *Bulletin of the New York Shakespear Society, 1075-1661;* ***Absorbed*** *Shakespeare on Film Newsletter, 0739-6570.*
**Desc:** A journal of performance criticism and scholarship. Provides commentary on Shakespeare and Renaissance drama through feature articles and through theatre and book reviews.
**Ind/Abst** Abstr. Engl. Stud.; Lit. Crit. Regist.; MLA Int. Bibl. Books Artic. Mod. Lang. Lit.

SA/1011-582X
**SHAKESPEARE IN SOUTHERN AFRICA : JOURNAL OF THE SHAKESPEARE SOCIETY OF SOUTHERN AFRICA.** **Added/Corp** Shakespeare Society of Southern Africa. Vol. 1 (1987)-. English. an. R30.00. Shakespeare Society of Southern Africa, PO Box 94 ISEA, Rhodes University, Grahamstown 6140 South Africa. **Tel** 011 27 461 22023, FAX 011 27 461 25642. **ED** Lawrence Wright. **Bk Rev. Ad Acc. Pr Rev. Circ:** 400.
**Desc:** Publishes articles, commentary and reviews on all aspects of Shakespearean studies and performance, with a particular emphasis on the response to Shakespeare in Southern Africa. Scholarly notes of a factual nature are also welcome.
**Ind/Abst** MLA Int. Bibl. Books Artic. Mod. Lang. Lit.

UK
**SHAKESPEARE QUARTO FACSIMILES.** **Main/Corp** Shakespeare Association (Great Britain). **VFOAT** Shakespeare Quartos in Collotype Facsimile. (1939)-. Monographic series. English. ir. Price varies per volume. Oxford University Press, Walton Street, Oxford OX2 6DP England. **Tel** 011 44 865 56767, FAX 011 44 865 267773, telex 837330 OXPRES G.

CC
**SHAN-HSI HSI CHU.** **VFOAT** Shanxixiju. (19??)-. Periodical. Chinese. mo. Post Office / China, People's Republic of China. **LC** PN2875.S54; S53. **DD** 792/.0951/43.

CC
**SHANG-HAI HSI CHU.** **VFOAT** Shanghai Xiju. (1959)-. Periodical. Chinese. bm. $13.68. Science Press, 16 Donghuangchenggen North Street, Beijing 100707, People's Republic of China. **Tel** 011 86 1 4019821, 011 86 1 4010642, FAX 011 86 1 4012180, 011 86 1 4019810, telex 210147. **LC** PN2009; .S5. **DD** 792/.0951.

US/0083-9403
**"SHORT PLAY" SERIES, THE.** No. 1 (1966)-. Monographic series. English. ir. Price varies per volume. Proscenium Press, PO Box 361, Newark DE 19711. **Tel** (302)764-8477.

FR/0151-979X
**SHOW MAGAZINE.** French. sm (except Aug.). 680.00F France; 1100.00F other. Show Magazine, 41-43 rue Paul Bert, 92100 Boulogne Billanct France. **Tel** 011 33 1 48255222.

US/8755-9560
**SHOW MUSIC.** See Music.

AT
**SHOWCAST.** See The Arts-Performing Arts.

IT
**SIPARIO.** Vol. 1, No. 1 (1946). Periodical. Italian. ir (9 issues). L70000 Italy; L135000 Europe; L170000 others. CAMA, Via San Marco 34, 20121 Milan Italy. **Tel** 011 39 2 6572654, 011 39 2 6559915.
**Desc:** Theater and motion pictures.
**Ind/Abst** MLA Int. Bibl. Books Artic. Mod. Lang. Lit.

●US/1069-2800
**SLAVIC AND EAST EUROPEAN PERFORMANCE.** (SLAVIC AND EAST EUROPEAN PERFORMANCE : DRAMA, THEATRE, FILM.). [Slav. East Eur. perform.]. **Added/Corp** Center for Advanced Study in Theatre Arts. Institute for Contemporary East European Drama and Theatre. **VFOAT** SEEP. Vol. 12, No. 1 (Spring 1992)-. Periodical. English. Three times a year. $10.00. CASTA / Center for Advanced Study in Theatre Arts, CUNY Graduate Center, 33 West 42nd Street, New York NY 10036. **Tel** (212)642-2225. **LC** PN2720; .S65. **DD** 792/.0947/05. ***Continues*** *Soviet and East European Performance, 1047-0018.*
**Ind/Abst** Am. Bibliogr. Slavic East Europ. Stud.

XO/0037-699X
**SLOVENSKE DIVADLO.** [Slov. divad.]. **Added/Corp** Slovenska Akademia Vied. Vol. 2 (1954)-. Periodical. Slovak. qt. Veda, Publishing House of the Slovak Academy of Sciences, Klemensova 19, 814 30 Bratislava Slovakia. **Tel** (7)583-15. **(Subscription address:** Kubon & Sagner, ABT Zeitschriftenimport, D 80328 Munich Germany.**)** **ED** Milos Mistrik. **LC** PN2859.C93; S5. **Bk Rev. Ad Acc. Circ:** 750 (ctrl). ***Continues*** *Divadelnovedny Sbornik Slovenskej Akademie Vied.*
**Desc:** Focuses on all questions of the Slovak theatre. Carries articles dealing with aesthetical and theoretical subjects as well as problems of contemporary stage art in drama, opera, operetta and ballet.
**Ind/Abst** MLA Int. Bibl. Books Artic. Mod. Lang. Lit.

US/0272-6459
**SO & SO.** See Literature-Poetry.

SA
**SOUTH AFRICAN THEATRE JOURNAL : SATJ.** **Added/Corp** University of the Witwatersrand. School of Dramatic Art. **VFOAT** SATJ. Vol. 1, No. 1 (May 1987)-. Periodical. English (Afrikaans). sa (May & Sept.). R38.50. SATJ / South African Theatre Journal, PO Box 6054, 7612 Uniedal South Africa. **Tel** 011 27 2231 773216, FAX 011 27 21 808 4336. **ED** Temple Hauptfleisch and Ian Steadman. **LC** PN2001; .S68. Index available. cum. index. **Bk Rev**, (Qty: 8-10). **Ad Acc, Adv Mgr Tel** 021 808 3216. **Circ:** 250.
**Desc:** Journal of theatre and performance studies, with emphasis on history, theory, and practice of performance and the performing arts in Southern Africa.
**Ind/Abst** MLA Int. Bibl. Books Artic. Mod. Lang. Lit.

US/0584-4738
**SOUTHERN THEATRE.** **Added/Corp** Southeastern Theatre Conference (U.S.). Vol. 7, (Fall 1963)-. Periodical. English. qt. $10.00. Southeastern Theatre Conference, PO Box 9868G Street, Greensboro NC 27429-0868. **Tel** (919) 272-3645, FAX (919) 272-8810. **ED** Darwin Honeycutt. **Bk Rev. Ad Acc. Circ:** 3,400 (ctrl). ***Continues*** *Southern Theatre News.*
**Desc:** Popular Magazine of timely articles for theatre people in the southeastern region of the country.

RU
**SOVETSKIE KHUDOZHNIKI TEATRA I KINO.** (19??)-. Periodical. Russian. 2.37rub. Izdatelstvo Sovetskii Khudozhnik, Ulitsa Cherniakhovskogo 4a, 12319 Moscow Russia. **LC** PN2091.S8; S664.

RU
**SOVETSKII TEATR.** ***Ceased.*** **Added/Corp** Vsesoiuznoe Agentstvo po Avtorskim Pravam. (1983)-Ceased with Dec. (1991). Periodical. Russian. qt. VAAP-Inform, B Bronnaia 6A, 103104 Moscow Russia. **LC** PN2724; .V2. ***Continues*** *V Sovetskom Teatre.*

CN/0703-5640
**SPECIAL BULLETIN - THEATRE CANADA.** **Main/Corp** Theatre Canada. **VFOAT** Bulletin Special - Theatre Canada. Began publication in 1973?. Bulletin. English (French). Theatre Canada, 45 Rideau Street, Ottawa Ontario K1N 5W8 Canada. **DD** 792/.0971.

UK/0038-7142
**SPEECH AND DRAMA.** **Added/Corp** Society of Teachers of Speech and Drama. (1951)-. English. Twice a year. £6.00. Society of Teachers of Speech and Drama, 23 High Ash Avenue, c/o Linda Gregory, Leeds West York LS17 8RS England. **Tel** 11 44 91 0532-684519. **ED** Dr. Paul Ranger, 43 Fane Road, Oxford OX3 OSA England, Telephone:11 44 91 0865-728304. **LC** PN4071; .S73. **DD** 001.54. Each issue contains an index to its own contents (no volume index)--loose. **Bk Rev. Ad Acc. Circ:** 1,500 (ctrl).
**Desc:** Teaching and performing of speech, educational drama, theatre arts, poetry, prose, articles, book reviews, advertisements, forthcoming events.
**Ind/Abst** Br. Educ. Index.

CN/1189-3397
**SPOTLIGHTING PLAYS ON ALCOHOL AND OTHER DRUGS.** [Spotlight. plays alcohol other drugs]. **Added/Corp** Saskatchewan Alcohol and Drug Abuse Commission. Spring (1991)-. English. **DD** 016.812/54.

UK/0038-9099
**STAGE AND TELEVISION TODAY, THE.** (Feb. 19, 1959)-. Periodical. English. wk. £44.20 UK; £58.20 other. Carson & Comerford Ltd, Stage House, 47 Bermondsey Street, London Bridge London SE1 3XT England. **Tel** 01-403 1818, FAX 011 44 71 378 0480. **ED** Jeremy Jehu. **Bk Rev. Ad Acc, Adv Mgr:** C. Finnlpy, **Tel** 071-11031818. **Circ:** 39,341 (ctrl). ***Continues*** *Stage.*
**Desc:** All matters relating to the interest of theatre and television, for all of the professionals and serious students.

US/1047-1901
**STAGE DIRECTIONS (WEST SACRAMENTO, CALIF.).** (STAGE DIRECTIONS.). [Stage dir.]. (1988)-. Periodical. English. Ten times a year (Except July & Dec.). $26.00 US; $33.00 Canada & Mexico; $42.00 others. SMW Communications / Stage Directions, 3101 Poplarwood Court, Suite 310, Raleigh NC 27604. **Tel** (919)872-7888, FAX (919)872-6888. **ED** Stephen Peithman and Neil Offen. **LC** PN2267; .S72. **DD** 792/.0973/05. **Ad Acc**, **Adv Mgr:** Lori Viffa.
**Desc:** A newsletter for people involved in community, academic and semi-professional/regional theater; provides practical ideas on directing, acting, audience development, fund raising, sets, costuming, lighting...sound, useful information on artistic techniques and management topics for theater.

US/1041-6048
**STAGES (NORWOOD, N.J.).** (STAGES.). [Stages]. Vol. 1, No. 1 (Mar. 1984)-. Periodical. English. Six times a year. $15.00. Stages, 301 West 45th Street, Suite 5A, New York NY 10036. **Tel** (212)245-9186. **ED** Frank Scheck. **DD** 792. **Bk Rev**.

CN/1183-966X
**STEPTEXT (TORONTO).** (STEPTEXT.). [Steptext]. **VFOAT** Step Text. Vol. 1, Issue 1 (1991)-. Periodical. English. qt. Steptext, 846 College Street, Toronto Ontario M6H 1A2 Canada. **DD** 792.8.

CN/0085-6789
**STRATFORD FESTIVAL STORY, THE.** **Main/Corp** Stratford Festival (Ont.). Began in 1953/61. Periodical. English. an. Stratford Festival, PO Box 520, Stratford Ontario N5A 6V2 Canada. **Tel** (519)271-4040. **LC** PN2306.S77; S767A. **DD** 792/.09713/23. ***Continues*** *Story of the Stratford Festival, Canada, 0318-2975.*

CN/0822-9066
**STRATFORD FOR STUDENTS.** [Stratf. stud.]. **Added/Corp** Stratford Festival (Ont.). (1978)-. Periodical. English. sa. Free. Stratford Festival, PO Box 520, Stratford Ontario N5A 6V2 Canada. **Tel** (519)271-4040. **ED** Pat Quigley. **DD** 822.3/3. **Circ:** 7,000 (ctrl). ***Continues*** *Stratford School Newsletter, 0317-2082.*

US/0081-6051
**STUBS.** Began publication in 1942. English. Meyer Schattner, 246 West 44th Street, New York NY 10036. **LC** PN2277.N5; S8. **DD** 792/.0295/7472.

US/0886-7097
**STUDIES IN AMERICAN DRAMA, 1945-PRESENT.** ***Suspended.*** [Stud. Am. drama 1945-present]. Vol. 1 (1986)-(19??). Academic Scholarly Publication. English. sa. $32.00 (library/institution), $16.00 (individual) $10.50 (student), US; $35.00 (library/instituition), $19.00 (individual) $13.50 (student) other. Ohio State University Press, 1070 Carmack Road, 180 Pressey Hall, Columbus OH 43210. **Tel** (614)292-6930, (614)292-1407, FAX (614)292-2065. **ED** Philip C. Kolin. **LC** PS352; .S78. **DD** 812/.54/09. **[CCC]. Ad Acc. Pr Rev. Circ:** 500. available on microfilm and microfiche from University Microfilms International (UMI).
**Desc:** Scholarly articles and resource materials on contemporary American drama.
**Ind/Abst** Am. Humanit. Index; Lit. Crit. Regist.; MLA Int. Bibl. Books Artic. Mod. Lang. Lit.

●US/1062-0591
**STUDIES IN FRENCH THEATRE.** (1992)-. Monographic series. English. Price varies per volume. Peter Lang Publishing, 62 West 45th Street, 4th Floor, New York NY 10036. **Tel** (212)764-1471, (800)770-5264, telex 6973364 PLNY.

US/0884-5840
**SUMMER THEATRE DIRECTORY (DORSET, VT.).** (SUMMER THEATRE DIRECTORY.). [Summer theatre dir.]. **Added/Corp** Dorset Theatre Festival & Colony House. (1984)-. Directory. English. an (Published in Dec.). $17.70. Theatre Directories, PO Box 519, Dorset VT 05251. **Tel** (802)867-2223, FAX (802)867-0144. **ED** Jill Charles. **LC** PN2289; .S8. **DD** 792/.025/73. **Ad Acc**, **Adv Mgr:** Gene Siratof. **Pr Rev. Circ:** 15,000. Documents available.
**Desc:** An employment guide for professionals seeking work in summer and regional theatre.

US
**SUMMER THEATRES.** **VFOAT** Leo Shull's Summer Theatres. English. an. Leo Shull Publications, 1501 Broadway/29th Floor, New York NY 10036. **Tel** (212)354-7600. **LC** PN2269. **DD** 792.

US/0887-3119
**SUNCOAST THEATRE GRAPEVINE, THE.** (19??)-. Periodical. English. Twelve times a year. $20.00. The Suncoast Theatre, PO Box 1002, Palm Harbor FL 34682. **Tel** (813)942-6015. ***Continues*** *Lary Crews Theatre Grapevine.*

HU/0039-8136
**SZINHAZ.** [Szinhaz]. Vol. 1 (1968)-. Periodical. Hungarian. mo. $32.00. Lapkiado Vallalat, Lenin Korut 9-11, 1073 Budapest 7, Hungary. **Tel** 222-408. **(Subscription address:** Kultura, PO Box 149, H 1389 Budapest 62 Hungary.) **ED** I. Boldizsar. Index available. cum. index. **Bk Rev. Circ:** 2,500 (ctrl).
**Desc:** Covers important trends in theatrical art in Hungary and abroad. Includes theater critique, interviews on theater, theatrical book reviews and debates on the theater.
**Ind/Abst** MLA Int. Bibl. Books Artic. Mod. Lang. Lit.

CU
**TABLAS.** **Added/Corp** Centro de Investigacion y Desarrollo de las Artes Escenicas (Cuba). **VFOAT** Revista Tablas. (1982)-. Periodical. Spanish. qt. Ediciones Cubanas, Obispo 527, Altos ESQ Bernaza, CP 10100 Havana Cuba. **Tel** 011 632980, 631942, FAX 011 631011, telex 512337, 6540. **Circ:** 10,000 (ctrl).
**Desc:** Spreads the image of current Cuban theater and serves as a vehicle of orientation and criticism. Permanent sections of general interest in the theatrical arts.

●US/1062-5453
**TAFT AND UNIVERSITY OF CINCINNATI SERIES IN LATIN AMERICAN AND HISPANIC AMERICAN THEATRE.** **Added/Corp** University of Cincinnati. Charles Phelps Taft Memorial Fund. Charles Phelps Taft Memorial Fund. (1993)-. Monographic series. English. Price varies per volume. Peter Lang Publishing, 62 West 45th Street, 4th Floor, New York NY 10036. **Tel** (212)764-1471, (800)770-5264, telex 6973364 PLNY.

US
**TCG THEATRE DIRECTORY.** **Added/Corp** Theatre Communications Group. **VFOAT** T.C.G. Directory. Vol. 8 (1980/1981)-. Directory. English. an. $7.95. Theatre Communications Group, 355 Lexington Avenue, New York NY 10017. **Tel** (212)697-5230, FAX (212)983-4847. **(Subscription address:** Consortium Book Sales and Distribution, 1045 Westgate Drive, St. Paul MN 55114.) **Circ:** 4,000. ***Continues*** *Theatre Directory.*
**Desc:** Contact information for nonprofit professional theatres and related art organizations in the US.

●US/1063-9497
**TCI (NEW YORK, N.Y.).** (TCI : THE BUSINESS OF ENTERTAINMENT TECHNOLOGY & DESIGN.). [TCI]. **VFOAT** Theatre Crafts International. Vol. 26, No. 7 (Aug./Sept. 1992)-. Periodical. English. Ten times a year (published monthly with Jun./Jul. and Aug./Sept. issues combined). $40.00 (one year), $72.00 (two year), $96.00 (three year). Theatre Crafts Association, 32 West 18th Street, New York NY 10011-4612. **Tel** (212)229-2965, FAX (212)229-2084. **(Subscription address:** TCI, PO Box 470, Mt. Morris IL 61054.) **LC** PN2000; .T48. **DD** 792. Documents available from The Genuine Article, UMI Article Clearinghouse. ***Formed by the union of*** *Theatre Crafts, 0040-5469* ***and*** *Theatre Crafts International, 1060-3042.*
**Ind/Abst** Acad. Abstr. (Aug. 1992-); Acad. Search (Aug. 1992-); Arts Humanit. Citation Index [Full Cov.]; Book Rev. Index; Curr. Contents Arts Humanit.; Mag. Artic. Summar. Elite (Aug. 1992-); Mag. Artic. Summar. CD-ROM (Aug. 1992-); Mag. Search; Newsp. Period. Abstr. (1988-); Read. Guide Period. Lit.; Res. Alert [Full Cov.]; Resource/One Ondisc (1992-); Mag. Index; TOM Gen. Index (1992-) [Full Txt.].

US/1052-6765
**TD&T (NEW YORK, N.Y.).** (TD&T.). [TD&T]. **Added/Corp** United States Institute for Theatre Technology. **VFOAT** TD and T; Theatre Design and Ttechnology; Theatre Design & Technology. Vol. 26, No. 1 (Spring 1990)-. Periodical. English. Five times a year. $40.00 (institutions); comes with membership (individuals). US Institute for Theatre Technology, 10 West 19th Street, Suite 5A, New York NY 10011. **Tel** (212)924-9088. **LC** NA1; .T45. **DD** 725/.822/05. cum. index. available on microfilm and microfiche from University Microfilms International (UMI). ***Continues*** *Theatre Design & Technology, 0040-5477.*

US/1054-2043
**TDR (1988).** (TDR.). [TDR]. **Added/Corp** Tisch School of the Arts. **VFOAT** Drama Review. Vol. 32, No. 1 (Spring 1988)-. Periodical. English. qt. $32.00 (individuals), $90.00 (institutions). Massachusetts Institute of Technology (MIT) Press, 55 Hayward Street, Cambridge MA 02142-1399. **Tel** (617)253-2889, (617)625-8481, FAX (617)258-6779. **ED** Richard Schechner. **DD** 792. Documents available from The Genuine Article. ***Continues*** *Drama Review, 0012-5962.*
**Desc:** Examining and debating the range of performance: theatre, dance, rituals, politics, performance art, sports, performance in everyday life. Contents include articles, interviews, plays, manifestos, reports, and historical documents.
**Ind/Abst** Abstr. Engl. Stud.; Acad. Abstr. Full Text Elite (Dec. 1990-); Acad. Abstr. (Dec. 1990-); Acad. Ind. [Computer File] (1984-); Acad. Search (Dec. 1990-); Am. Bibliogr. Slavic East Europ. Stud.; Annu. Bibliogr. Engl. Lang. Lit.; Arts Humanit. Citation Index [Full Cov.]; Book Rev. Index; Expand. Acad. Index (1984-); Gen. Period. Index (1985-); Humanit. Index; Humanit. Source (Jul. 1990-); Mag. Index Plus (1989-); Mag. Index. Sel. (1986-); Mag. Search; MLA Int. Bibl. Books Artic. Mod. Lang. Lit.; Res. Alert [Full Cov.]; Mag. Index (1988-).

YU
**TEATAR.** (19??)-. Serbo-Croatian (Roman). **LC** WMLC L 83/5476.
**Ind/Abst** Annu. Bibliogr. Engl. Lang. Lit.

DK/0902-8234
**TEATERRAADETS INDSTILLINGER, FORSLAG OG KONKLUSIONER.** **Main/Corp** Denmark. Teaterrĺadet. (1986/87)-. Danish. an. Free on request. Danish Theater Council / Ministry of Culture, Vesterbrogade 24, 4th, Copenhagen V 1620 Denmark. **Tel** 011 45 33 247304. **LC** IN PROCESS. ***Continues*** *Teaterraadets Indstilling, 0107-248X.*

SW
**TEATERTIDNINGEN.** No. 49 (1990)-. Periodical. Swedish. qt. ***Continues*** *Nya Teatertidningen, 0348-0119.*

PL
**TEATR.** Vol. 13, No. 9 (May 1958)-. Periodical. Polish. mo. $27.00. **(Subscription address:** ARS Polona, PO Box 1001, 00068 Warsaw Poland.) ***Continues*** *Teatr i Film.*

RU
**TEATR.** **Added/Corp** Informtsentr po Problemam Kultury i Iskusstva (Soviet Union). (19??)-. Russian (Multiple languages). mo. $169.95. **(Subscription address:** East View Publications Inc., 3020 Harbor Lane North, Suite 110, Minneapolis MN 55447.) **LC** Z2504.D7; N68; PN2724. ***Continues*** *Novosti Nauchnoi Literatury: Teatr.*

RU
**TEATRALNYI LENINGRAD (LENINGRAD, R.S.F.S.R. : 1956).** (TEATRALNYI LENINGRAD.). **Added/Corp** Leningradskii Gorodskoi Sovet Deputatov Trudiashchikhsia. Direktsiia Teatralnykh Kass. (1956)-. Periodical. Russian. wk. ***Continues*** *Leningradskie Teatry.*

GW
**TEATRO DEL SIGLO DE ORO.** **VFOAT** Bibliografias y Catalogos. 1983-. Monographic series. Spanish. Price varies per volume.

IT
**TEATRO E STORIA.** Vol. 1, No. 1 (Oct. 1986)-. Periodical. Italian (summaries and/or abstracts in English). sa. L54000 Italy; L90000 (surface mail), L120000 (airmail) other. Societa Editrice il Mulino, Strada Maggiore 37, 40125 Bologna Italy. **Tel** 011 39 51 256011, FAX 011 39 51 256034.

IT
**TEATRO IN EUROPA : TE.** ***Suspended.*** **VFOAT** TE; Theatre en Europe. (1987)-Suspended with Vol. 8, No. 9 (1990). Periodical. Italian. qt. Elemond Arte SRL, Via Trentacoste 7, 20134 Milan Italy. **Tel** 011 39 2 215631.

IT
**TEATRO IN ITALIA.** **Added/Corp** Societa Italiana Degli Autori ed Editori. (1987)-. Italian. an. L25000. Societa Italiana Degli Autori, Viale della Letteratura 30, 00144 Rome Italy. **Tel** 011 39 6 5990630. **LC** PN2684; .T37. ***Continues*** *Teatro Italiano.*

IT
**TEATRO, STUDI E TESTI.** Monographic series. Italian. Price varies per volume. Casa Editrice Leo S. Olschki, Viuzzo del Pozzetto, Casella Postale 66, 50126 Florence Italy. **Tel** 011 39 55 6530684, FAX 011 39 55 6530214.

RM
**TEATRUL AZI.** **Added/Corp** Romania. Ministerul Culturii. No. 1 (1990)-. Periodical. Romanian (summaries and/or abstracts in English, French and Italian). Twelve times a year. DM162.00. **(Subscription address:** Kubon & Sagner, ABT Zeitschriftenimport, D 80328 Munich Germany.) **LC** PN2844; .T43. ***Continues*** *Teatrul, 0040-0815.*

US/1053-8860
**TECHNICAL BRIEF (YALE SCHOOL OF DRAMA. DEPT. OF TECHNICAL DESIGN AND PRODUCTION).** **See** The Arts-Performing Arts.

CN/0317-5243
**TEL QUE NOUS LE PENSONS ET AVONS ENVIE DE LE DIRE.** V. 1-. French. Edition Jeunesse Quebec, 801, 12E Rue, Quebec, Quebec G1J 2N1.

US/1054-724X
**TEXT AND PRESENTATION.** [Text present.]. (1980)- Vol. 14 (1993)-. Periodical. English. an (March). $20.00. Maupin House Publishing, PO Box 90148, Gainesville FL 32607. **Tel** (904)336-9290. **ED** Karelisa Hartigan, Ph.D (904)377-2178. **DD** 808. **Ad Acc**, **Adv Mgr:** J. Grady, **Tel** (800)524-0634. **Circ:** 1000.
**Desc:** Referred papers of the conference (international drama) text and presentation featuring worldwide theatre and drama.

GW
**THEATER.** (19??)-. Academic Scholarly Publication. German. Twelve times a year. DM19.20. Erhard Friedrich Verlag, Redaktion Theater heute, Lutzowplatz 7, D-10785 Berlin Germany. **Tel** 030 261 70 03. **LC** PN2004; .T46. Index available. **Bk Rev**. **Ad Acc**, **Adv Mgr:** Marion Schaduthe. Full Page (B&W) DM4000.00. Half Page (B&W) DM2000.00. **Circ:** 15,000.

GW/0040-5418
**THEATER DER ZEIT.** [Theater Zeit]. **Added/Corp** Verband der Theaterschaffenden der DDR. Vol. 1 (July 1946)-. Periodical. German. bm. DM68.00 Germany; DM83.00 other. Theater der Zeit, Puschkinallee 5, D-12435 Berlin Germany. **LC** PN2004; .T53. **DD** 792/.05. Index available (yearly). Documents available from The Genuine Article.
**Ind/Abst** Arts Humanit. Citation Index (19??-19??) [Full Cov.]; Res. Alert [Full Cov.]; RILM Abstr.

GW/0040-5507
**THEATER HEUTE.** Vol. 1- Sept. 1960-. Periodical. German. mo. 195.00F. Bouvier GMBH & Company KG ABT Verlag, Am HOF 28, D53113 Bonn Germany. **Tel** 011 49 228 7290141. **LC** PN2004; .T54. **DD** 792/.05. **[CCC]**. Documents available from The Genuine Article.
**Ind/Abst** Arts Humanit. Citation Index [Full Cov.]; Curr. Contents Arts Humanit.; Res. Alert [Full Cov.]; Romant. Move.

AU
**THEATER IN OSTERREICH / WIENER GESELLSCHAFT FUER THEATERFORSCHUNG, INSTITUT FUER THEATERWISSENSCHAFT AN DER UNIVERSITAT WIEN.** **Added/Corp** Wiener Gesellschaft fuer Theaterforschung. Universitat Wien. Institut fuer Theaterwissenschaft. Verband der Wissenschaftlichen Gesellschaften Osterreichs. (1980/81)-. German. Verband der Wissenschaftlichen Gesellschaften Osterreichs, Lindengasse 37, A-1070 Vienna Austria. **Tel** 011 43 1 932166, 011 43 1 934756, telex 847/134981. **ED** Oto G. Schindler. **LC** PN2616.V5; V54 subser; PN2614. **DD** 792/.9436 S; 792/.02/95436. **Bk Rev**. **Ad Acc**. **Circ:** 400 (ctrl).
**Desc:** Lists performances on Austrian stages for the season.

US/0161-0775
**THEATER (NEW HAVEN, CONN.).** (THEATER.). [Theater]. **Added/Corp** Yale School of Drama. Yale Repertory Theatre. Vol. 9 (Fall 1977)-. Periodical. English. Three times a year (Mar., July, Nov.). $22.00 (individuals), $35.00 (institutions). Yale University School of Drama, Yale Repertory Theatre, 222 York Street, New Haven CT 06520. **Tel** (203)432-1568, FAX (203)432-1550. **ED** Erika Munk. **LC** PN2000; .Y34. **DD** 792/.05. Index available. **Bk Rev**. **Ad Acc**, **Adv Mgr Tel** (203)432-9664. **Circ:** 2,500. available on microfilm and microfiche from University Microfilms International (UMI). Documents available from The Genuine Article, UMI Article Clearinghouse. ***Continues** Yale/Theatre, 0044-0167.*
**Desc:** Publishes the most noted American and international critics, playwrights, and scholars. Each issue contains a group of essays, a major new playscript, reports from abroad, interviews with renowned theater professionals, fine performance photographs, and theatre and reviews.
**Ind/Abst** Arts Humanit. Citation Index [Full Cov.]; Curr. Contents Arts Humanit.; Expand. Acad. Index (1992-); Film Lit. Index; MLA Int. Bibl. Books Artic. Mod. Lang. Lit.; Newsp. Period. Abstr. (1992-); Res. Alert [Full Cov.].

GW
**THEATER RUNDSCHAU.** German. Twelve times a year. DM44.00 Germany; DM51.00 other. Theater Rundschau Verlagsges, MBH / Bonner Talweg 10, D-53113 Bonn Germany. **Tel** 011 49 228 915031, FAX 011 49 2289150350. **Bk Rev**, (Qty: 30/year). **Ad Acc**. **Circ:** 58,000.
**Desc:** Information on the theatre in Germany, Switzerland and Austria.

US/1052-0511
**THEATER THREE.** ***Ceased.*** [Theater three]. **VFOAT** Theater 3. No. 1, Fall (1986)-Ceased with Iss. 10. Periodical. English. sa. Carnegie Melon U, Drama Department, Pittsburgh PA 15213. **LC** PN2000; .T315. **DD** 792/.05.
**Ind/Abst** Lit. Crit. Regist.

US/0896-1956
**THEATER WEEK.** [Theater week]. **VFOAT** Theaterweek. (198?)-. Periodical. English. wk. $59.00 US; $84.00 other. That New Magazine Inc., 28 West 25th Street, 4th Floor, New York NY 10159. **Tel** (212)627-2120, FAX (212)727-9321. **ED** Charles L. Ortleb. **DD** 792. cum. index. **Bk Rev**. **Ad Acc**, **Adv Mgr:** Wendy Daigneault. **Circ:** 12,000.
**Desc:** Guide to American and British theater for theater insiders, professionals and fans. Each issue includes features, news, interviews, profiles, gossip, and book and record reviews.

US/0735-1895
**THEATERWORK MAGAZINE.** **VFOAT** Theater Work Magazine. Vol. 2, No. 5 (July/Aug. 1982)-. Periodical. English. bm. $9.00 US; $15.00 other. 120 South Broad Street, Mankato MN 56001. **LC** PN2000; .T32. **DD** 792/.05. ***Continues** Theaterwork, 0736-1130.*

GW/0723-1172
**THEATERZEITSCHRIFT.** **See** The Arts-Performing Arts.

UK
**THEATRE.** 1954/55-. English. an. **ED** I Brown. **LC** PN2580. **DD** 792.0942. Each issue contains an index to its own contents (no volume index)--loose.

FR/0563-3966
**THEATRE, LE.** 1- 1968-. Periodical. French. Christian Bourgeois, 8 rue Garanciere, Paris 6EME France. **ED** Fernando Arrabal.

UK
**THEATRE & THERAPY.** ***Ceased.*** (19??)-(19??). English. sa. Dramatherapy Consultants, PO Box 32, Stratford Upon Avon CV37 6GU England. **Tel** 011 44 789 68558. **ED** Sue Jennings. **Bk Rev**. **Ad Acc**. **Pr Rev**. ctrl circ.
**Desc:** Articles, research, reviews and interviews on clinical practice and theatre development of drama and therapy.

US/0082-3821
**THEATRE ANNUAL, THE.** [Theatr. annu.]. **Added/Corp** Theatre Library Association. (1942)-. English. an (Fall). $10.00. Theatre Annual, College of William and Mary, Williamsburg VA 23187. **Tel** (804)221-2668, FAX (804)221-1287. **ED** John V. Falconieri. **LC** PN2012; .T5. **DD** 792.058. Index available (every ten years). **Pr Rev**. **Circ:** 250 (ctrl).
**Desc:** A traditional focus on the theatre to include all performances for a public audience. Articles from scholars in music, popular culture, anthropology, dance, philosophy, history, folklore, and theatre, and especially from researchers who cross these and other disciplinary lines.
**Ind/Abst** Abstr. Engl. Stud.; MLA Int. Bibl. Books Artic. Mod. Lang. Lit.

US
**THEATRE CLASSICS : THE LEAGUE OF HISTORIC AMERICAN THEATRES ANNUAL PUBLICATION.** **Added/Corp** League of Historic American Theatres. (19??)-. English. an. $7.00. League of Historic American Theatres, 1511 K Street Northwest, Suite 923, Washington DC 20005. **Tel** (202)783-6966, FAX (202)393-2141. **ED** Tara Schroeder. **LC** PN2221; .T48. **DD** 792/.0973/05. ctrl circ.
**Desc:** A journal of case studies of various historic theatre restoration projects.

US/0040-5469
**THEATRE CRAFTS.** ***Title Change.*** [Theatre crafts]. **VFOAT** TC. Vol. 1 (Mar. 1967)-Vol. 26 No. 6 (July 1992). Periodical. English. mo (ten issues per year). Theatre Crafts Associates, 135 Fifth Avenue, New York NY 10010-7193. **Tel** (212)677-5997, FAX (212)677-3857. **(Subscription address:** PO Box 470, Mt Morris, IL 61054**) ED** Patricia Mackay and David Barbour. **LC** PN2000; .T48. **DD** 792/.05. **Bk Rev**. **Ad Acc**. **Circ:** 27,500. available on microfilm and microfiche from University Microfilms International (UMI). Documents available from UMI Article Clearinghouse, Magazine Collection. ***Merged with** Theatre Crafts International, 1060-3042 **to form** TCI, 1063-9497.*
**Desc:** Covers the people and products that make the performing arts work. Lighting and sound, set and costume design, and more.
**Ind/Abst** Acad. Abstr. Full Text Elite (Jan. 1989-June 1992); Acad. Abstr. (Jan. 1989-June 1992); Acad. Search (Jan. 1989-June 1992); Arts Humanit. Citation Index (19??-19??) [Full Cov.]; Book Rev. Index; Film Lit. Index (19??-); Gen. Period. Index (1985-); Humanit. Source (Jan. 1989-Aug. 1992); INFO-SOUTH Abstr.; Mag. Artic. Summar. Elite (Jan. 1989-June 1992); Mag. Artic. Summar. Select (Jan. 1989-); Mag. Artic. Summar. CD-ROM (Jan. 1989-June 1992); Mag. Index Plus (1989-); Mag. Index Sel. Microfiche (1986-) [Full Txt.]; Mag. Index. Sel. (1986-); Mag. Search; Read. Guide Abstr. Select Ed.; Read. Guide Period. Lit.; Resource/One Ondisc (1988-1992); Mag. Index (1977-); TOM Gen. Index (1985-?) [Full Txt.].

US
**THEATRE CRAFTS DIRECTORY.** ***Title Change.*** (1980-1992). Directory. English. an. Theatre Crafts Associates, 135 Fifth Avenue, New York NY 10010-7193. **Tel** (212)677-5997, FAX (212)677-3857. **(Subscription address:** PO Box 639, Holmes, PA 19043**) LC** PN2289; .T53. **Bk Rev**. **Ad Acc**. **Circ:** 27,500. ***Continues** Theatre Crafts. **Continued by** Industry Resources.*
**Desc:** Covers theatre, film and video for the professional with the emphasis on how things get done: lighting, sound, costume design, make-up, construction, etc.

US/1060-3042
**THEATRE CRAFTS INTERNATIONAL.** ***Title Change.*** [Theatre crafts int.]. **VFOAT** Theatre Crafts. (May 1990)-(199?). Periodical. English. Ten times a year. Theatre Crafts Association, 32 West 18th Street, New York NY 10011-4612. **Tel** (212)229-2965, FAX (212)229-2084. **LC** PN2000; .T484. **DD** 792/.05. **Bk Rev**. **Ad Acc**. **Circ:** 27,000. available on microfiche; available in microform. ***Merged with** Theatre Crafts, 0040-5469 **to form** TCI, 1063-9497.*

XR
**THEATRE, CZECH & SLOVAK.** **Added/Corp** Divadelni Ustav (Prague, Czechoslovakia). **VFOAT** Theatre, Czech and Slovak; Theatre; Theatre, Tcheque & Slovaque; Theatre, Tcheque et Slovaque. (1991)-. Periodical. English (French). sa.

US/0737-0172
**THEATRE DIRECTORY OF THE SAN FRANCISCO BAY AREA.** [Theatre dir. San Franc. Bay Area]. (1984)-. Directory. English. be. $14.50. Theatre Bay Area, 657 Mission Street, Suite 402, San Francisco CA 94105. **Tel** (415)957-1557, FAX (415)957-1556. **ED** Jean Schiffman. **LC** PN2275.C3; T47. **DD** 790.2/09794/6. **Bk Rev**. **Ad Acc**. ctrl circ. ***Continues** Theatre Directory of the Bay Area, 0730-9260.*
**Desc:** Resource guide to the San Francisco Bay area theatre scene, including complete descriptions of over 100 resident theatre companies.

US
**THEATRE/DRAMA ABSTRACTS.** Vol. 2 (April 1975)-. Periodical. English. Three times a year. Theatre/Drama Speech Information Center, 1 Erin Court, Pleasant Hill CA 94523. ***Supersedes in part** Theatre/Drama & Speech Index.*

PL/0040-5493
**THEATRE EN POLOGNE, LE.** [Theatre Pol.]. **Added/Corp** International Theatre Institute. Polish Centre. Authors Agency. **VFOAT** Theatre in Poland. Yearly Vol. 1, No. 1/2, (Sept./Oct. 1958)-. Periodical. French (English and French). qt. Price on Request. **(Subscription address:** ARS Polona, PO Box 1001, 00068 Warsaw Poland.**) LC** PN2859.P6; T5. cum. index.

CN/0226-5761
**THEATRE HISTORY IN CANADA.** ***Title Change.*** [Theatre hist. Can.]. **Added/Corp** University of Toronto. Graduate Centre for Study of Drama. Queen's University (Kingston, Ont.). Dept. of Drama. Association for Canadian Theatre History. **VFOAT** Histoire du Theatre au Canada. Vol. 1, No. 1 (Spring 1980)-Volume 13 (1992). Periodical. English (French). sa. University of Toronto, Graduate Centre for the Study of Drama, 214 College Street, Toronto Ontario M5T 2Z9 Canada. **Tel** (416)971-1378. **LC** PN2009; .T473. **DD** 792/.0971. Index available. cum. index. **Bk Rev**. **Pr Rev**. ctrl circ. Documents available from The Genuine Article. ***Continued by** Theatre Research in Canada.*
**Desc:** Lively, illustrated journal; focuses on all aspects of the history of theatre in Canada from its earliest years. Publishes articles on a broad range of topics, including resident and touring companies, individuals who have contributed to the theatre, its craft and criticism, analyses plays and performance records, as well as newly uncovered scripts and historical documents.
**Ind/Abst** Arts Humanit. Citation Index (19??-19??) [Full Cov.]; Can. Index (1985-1986); Can. Period. Index (19??-); Curr. Contents Arts Humanit.; MLA Int. Bibl. Books Artic. Mod. Lang. Lit.; Res. Alert [Full Cov.].

US/0733-2033
**THEATRE HISTORY STUDIES.** [Theatre hist. stud.]. Vol. 1 (1981)-. Periodical. English. an. $8.00 (one year), $15.00 (two year). University of North Dakota, Grand Forks ND 58202. **Tel** (701)777-2941. **ED** Ron Engle. **LC** PN2000; .T49. **DD** 792/.09. **Bk Rev**. **Ad Acc**. **Circ:** 600. Documents available from The Genuine Article.
**Desc:** Illustrated theatre history journal devoted to research in all areas and fields of interest in national and international theatre history.
**Ind/Abst** Am. Hist. Life (1990-); Am. Bibliogr. Slavic East Europ. Stud. (19??-19??); Arts Humanit. Citation Index (19??-19??) [Full Cov.]; Curr. Contents Arts Humanit.; MLA Int. Bibl. Books Artic. Mod. Lang. Lit.; Res. Alert [Full Cov.].

US/0040-5515
**THEATRE INFORMATION BULLETIN.** 1944-. Bulletin. English. wk. $225.00 (one year), $375.00 (two year), $475.00 (three year) US; $245.00 (one year), $415.00 (two year), $535.00 (three year) Canada; $275.00 (one year), $475.00 (two year), $625.00 (three year) other. Corporate Information Services, PO Box 1041, Darien CT 06820. **Tel** (203)656-3300, FAX (203)656-3382. **ED** Joan Marlowe and Betty Blake.
**Desc:** Desk guide to current and advance theatrical activity. Broadway, on and off broadway, regional theatre, cross country, and summer theatre--the answers at a glance.

US
**THEATRE INSIGHT.** Vol. 1, No. 1 (Autumn 1988)-. Periodical. English. Twice a yearTri-quarterly. $20.00 (institutions), $10.00 (individuals). Theatre Insight Association, Windship Building, University of Texas - Austin, Austin TX 78712. **Tel** (512)471-5793. **ED** Michael Barnes. **LC** PN2000; .T5. **Bk Rev**. **Ad Acc**. **Circ:** 150.
**Desc:** Written and edited by graduate students and junior faculty on the subjects of performance, theater and drama.

IE/0263-6344
**THEATRE IRELAND.** ***Ceased.*** (1982)-(1993). Periodical. English. qt. Theatre Ireland, 29 Main Street Castlerock, Co Derry BT51 4RA, Northern Ireland. **Tel** 353-265-848130, FAX 353-0265-40903. **ED** Lynda Henderson. **LC** PN2601; .T53. **Bk Rev. Ad Acc. Circ:** 7,000.
**Desc:** The definitive magazine for contemporary theatre in Ireland. Its function is to serve the debating ground between the academic and the practical, to encourage new innovative theatre throughout the island and to reflect on the international status of irish theatre.

US/0192-2882
**THEATRE JOURNAL (WASHINGTON, D.C.).** (THEATRE JOURNAL.). [Theatre j.]. **Added/Corp** University and College Theatre Association (U.S.) American Theatre Association. **VFOAT** TJ. Vol. 31 (March 1979)-. Periodical. English. Four times a year (March, May, October, December). $55.00 US; $59.00 Canada & Mexico; $65.30 other. Johns Hopkins University Press, 2715 North Charles Street, Baltimore MD 21218-4319. **Tel** (410)516-6987, FAX (410)516-6968. **(Subscription address:** John Hopkins University Press, Journals Publishing Division, PO Box 19966, Baltimore MD 21211.**)** **ED** Enoch Brater and Janelle Reineit. **LC** PN3171; .E38. **DD** 792/.05. **[CCC]. Bk Rev. Ad Acc. Circ:** 2,150. available on microfilm and microfiche from University Microfilms International (UMI). Documents available from The Genuine Article, UMI Article Clearinghouse. ***Continues*** *Educational Theatre Journal, 0013-1989.*
**Desc:** Publishes articles on a range of topics, from social and historical studies, to production reviews, to theoretical inquiries that illuminate dramatic text and production.
**Ind/Abst** Abstr. Engl. Stud.; Acad. Search (Jan. 1994-); Am. Bibliogr. Slavic East Europ. Stud.; Arts Humanit. Citation Index [Full Cov.]; Book Rev. Index; Curr. Contents Arts Humanit.; Curr. Contents Soc. Behav. Sci.; Curr. Index J. Educ.; Educ. Index; Expand. Acad. Index (1989-); Humanit. Index; Humanit. Source (Jul. 1993-); INFO-SOUTH Abstr.; Lit. Crit. Regist.; Mag. Search; Middle East Abstr. Index; MLA Int. Bibl. Books Artic. Mod. Lang. Lit.; Newsp. Period. Abstr. (1991-); Res. Alert [Full Cov.].

UK/0040-5523
**THEATRE NOTEBOOK.** [Theatre noteb.]. **Added/Corp** Society for Theatre Research. Vol. 1 (Oct. 1945)-. Periodical. English. Three times a year (Jan., May, Sept.). £12.00 UK; £13.00 other. The Society for Theater Research, Theatre Museum, 1E Tavistock Street, London WC2E 7PA England. **ED** Russell Jackson, Michael Booth, & Katherine Worth. Index available (Published separately). cum. index. **Bk Rev. Ad Acc. Circ:** 1,450 (ctrl). Documents available from The Genuine Article.
**Desc:** History and technique of British theatre.
**Ind/Abst** Abstr. Engl. Stud. (1980-); Annu. Bibliogr. Engl. Lang. Lit.; Archit. Period. Index (1945-); Arts Humanit. Citation Index [Full Cov.]; Br. Humanit. Index; Curr. Contents Arts Humanit.; Humanit. Index; Index Book Rev. Humanit.; MLA Int. Bibl. Books Artic. Mod. Lang. Lit.; Res. Alert [Full Cov.]; Romant. Move.

US/0040-5531
**THEATRE ORGAN (1970). See** Music.

US/0361-7947
**THEATRE PROFILES. Added/Corp** Theatre Communications Group. Vol. 1 (1973)-. English. ir. price varies per volume. Theatre Communications Group, 355 Lexington Avenue, New York NY 10017. **Tel** (212)697-5230, FAX (212)983-4847. **(Subscription address:** Consortium Book Sales and Distribution, 1045 Westgate Drive, St. Paul MN 55114.**)** **ED** Laura Ross. **LC** PN2266; .T48. **DD** 792/.0973. **Circ:** 4,000.
**Desc:** Illustrated; artistic profiles plus financial and production information on over 175 theatres across the US.

FR/0335-2927
**THEATRE/PUBLIC. Added/Corp** Ensemble Theatral de Gennevilliers. Theatre de Gennevilliers. **VFOAT** Theatre, Public. **VAT** Theatre, Public. (Sept./Oct. 1974)-. Periodical. French. Four times a year (Jan., Apr., May, July, Nov.). 325.00F France; 355.00F other (postage included). Theatre Public, 41 Avenue des Gresillons, 92230 Gennevilliers France. **Tel** 011 33 1 47 932630, FAX 011 33 1 40 861744. **ED** A. Girault. cum. index. **Ad Acc, Adv Mgr:** A. Girault. **Pr Rev. Circ:** 2,000.

CN/0825-4494
**THEATRE QUEBEC.** [Theatre Que.]. **Added/Corp** Centre d'Essai des Auteurs Dramatiques (Montreal, Quebec). Vol. 1, No. 1 (1984)-. Periodical. English. ir. Limited free distribution. Centre d'Essai des Auteurs Dramatiques, Bureau 300/426 Est rue Sherbrooke, Montreal Quebec H2L 1J6 Canada. **DD** 792/.09714/281. ctrl circ.

CN/0705-0453
**THEATRE (QUEBEC).** (THEATRE.). **VFOAT** Trident. V. 1, No 2- Oct./Nov. 1976-. Periodical. French. bm. Free. Theatre du Trident, Edifice Palais Montcalm, 975 Place d'Youville, Quebec Quebec G1R 3P1 Canada. **DD** 792/.09714/471. ***Continues*** *Theatru du Trident, 0705-0445.*

UK/0962-1792
**THEATRE RECORD.** Vol. 11, Issue 1 (Jan. 1-14, 1991)-. Periodical. English. Twenty-six times a year. £130.00 UK; £160.00 others. London Theatre Record, 4 Cross Deep Gardens Twickenham, Middlesex TW1 4QU England. **Tel** 011 44 81 8926087. **ED** Iam Jerbert. **LC** PN2596.L6; L66. Index available. **Bk Rev. Ad Acc.** ***Continues*** *London Theatre Record, 0261-5282.*

●CN/1196-1198
**THEATRE RESEARCH IN CANADA.** [Theatre res. Can.]. **Added/Corp** University of Toronto. Graduate Centre for Study of Drama. Queen's University (Kingston, Ont.). Dept. of Drama. **VFOAT** Recherches Theatrales au Canada. Vol. 13, No. 1/2 (Spring/Fall 1992)-. Periodical. English (French). Twice a year (June, & Dec.). 22.00Can$ (institutions), 15.00Can$ (individuals) Canada; 24.50Can$ (institutions), 17.50Can$ (individuals) other; 50.00Can$ Comes with Association for Canadian Theatre Research membership. University of Toronto, Graduate Centre for the Study of Drama, 214 College Street, Toronto Ontario M5T 2Z9 Canada. **Tel** (416)971-1378. **ED** Helene Beauchamp, Stephen Johnson, and Robert Nunn. **LC** PN2009; .T473. **DD** 792/.0971. Index available (Free on request). **Bk Rev**, (Qty: 10). **Pr Rev. Circ:** 300-350. available on microfilm and microfiche from Micromedia Limited. ***Continues*** *Theatre History in Canada, 0226-5761.*
**Desc:** A full range of critical approaches applied to the study of theatre as a multidisciplinary art, in the context of the cultures of Canada and Quebec.
**Ind/Abst** Arts Humanit. Citation Index [Full Cov.]; Can. Index.

UK/0307-8833
**THEATRE RESEARCH INTERNATIONAL.** [Theatre res. int.]. **Added/Corp** Oxford University Press. International Federation for Theatre Research. Vol. 1 (Oct. 1975)-. Periodical. Multiple languages (English; summaries and/or abstracts in French). tq. £56.00 UK and Europe; $107.00 other. Oxford University Press, Walton Street, Oxford OX2 6DP England. **Tel** 011 44 865 56767, FAX 011 44 865 267773, telex 837330 OXPRES G. **(Subscription address:** Oxford University Press / USA, Journals Marketing Department, Oxford University Press, 2001 Evans Road, Cary NC 27513.**)** **ED** Claude Schumacher. **LC** PN2001; .T436. **DD** 790.2/05. **[CCC].** Index available. cum. index. **Bk Rev. Ad Acc. Circ:** 1,000. available on microfilm and microfiche from University Microfilms International (UMI). Documents available from The Genuine Article, UMI Article Clearinghouse. ***Formed by the union of*** *Theatre Research, 0040-5566* ***and*** *New Theatre Magazine, 0028-6893.*
**Desc:** Covers the history of criticism of drama conceived as the art of the theatre, providing both a medium of communication for scholars and a service to students of art, architecture, design, music and dramatic literature.
**Ind/Abst** Acad. Search (July 1993-); Am. Hist. Life (1977-); Annu. Bibliogr. Engl. Lang. Lit.; Arts Humanit. Citation Index [Full Cov.]; Br. Humanit. Index; Curr. Contents Arts Humanit.; Expand. Acad. Index (1989-); Humanit. Index; Humanit. Source (Jul. 1993-); INFO-SOUTH Abstr.; Mag. Search; Middle East Abstr. Index; MLA Int. Bibl. Books Artic. Mod. Lang. Lit.; Newsp. Period. Abstr. (1991-); Res. Alert [Full Cov.]; Romant. Move.

UK
**THEATRE REVIEW.** (1973)-. Periodical. English. an. £4.00. W.H. Allen Company, 44 Hill Street, WIX 8LB London England. **LC** PN2580; .T38. **DD** 792.9.

US/0743-5452
**THEATRE SOUTHWEST.** V. 1- Feb. 1975-. Periodical. English. Three times a year. $8.00. Theatre Southwest, 102 Seretean OSU, Stillwater OK 74078. **Tel** (405)624-6094. **ED** Kenneth D Cox. **LC** PN2000; .T714. **DD** 792/.05. **Bk Rev. Ad Acc. Circ:** 1,200 (ctrl).
**Desc:** Scholarship and features of southwestern American and world theatre. Approximately 40-8 1/2 x 11 pages.

US/0362-0964
**THEATRE STUDIES.** [Theatre stud.]. **Added/Corp** Ohio State University. Theatre Research Institute. No. 18 (1971/1972)-. English. an (June). $10.00 (institutions), $8.00 (individuals). Theatre Studies, 1430 Lincoln Tower, 1800 Cannon, Columbus OH 43210. **Tel** (614)292-6614. **ED** Beth A. Kattelman. **LC** PN1620.O45; A3. **DD** 792/.05. **Bk Rev**, (Qty: 25). **Pr Rev. Circ:** 400. available on microfilm. Documents available from The Genuine Article. ***Continues*** *Ohio State University Theatre Collection Bulletin, 0030-1175.*
**Desc:** A journal which publishes new research in the area of theatre history, literature, criticism, and theory by graduate scholars in the field.
**Ind/Abst** Abstr. Engl. Stud.; Am. Humanit. Index; Annu. Bibliogr. Engl. Lang. Lit.; Arts Humanit. Citation Index [Full Cov.]; Curr. Contents Arts Humanit.; Lit. Crit. Regist. (1972-); MLA Int. Bibl. Books Artic. Mod. Lang. Lit.; Res. Alert [Full Cov.].

US/0040-5574
**THEATRE SURVEY.** [Theatre surv.]. **Added/Corp** American Society for Theatre Research. (1960)-. Periodical. English. Twice a year (May and Nov.). $40.00 membership; $20.00 students. Gordon S. Armstrong, University of Rhode Island, Department of Theatre, F.A.C., Kingston RI 02881-0824. **ED** Michael L. Quinn. **LC** PN2000; .T716. **DD** 792/.05. cum. index. **Bk Rev. Ad Acc. Circ:** 1,200 (ctrl). available on microfilm and microfiche from University Microfilms International (UMI). Documents available from The Genuine Article, UMI Article Clearinghouse.
**Desc:** A theatre history journal with a broadly-conceived historical orientation, including most performance-centered studies, regardless of culture or critical methodology, as well as historiographic studies.
**Ind/Abst** Abstr. Engl. Stud.; Acad. Search (July 1993-); Am. Hist. Life (1978-); Annu. Bibliogr. Engl. Lang. Lit.; Arts Humanit. Citation Index [Full Cov.]; Curr. Contents Arts Humanit.; Expand. Acad. Index (1989-); Humanit. Index; Humanit. Source (Jul. 1993-); INFO-SOUTH Abstr.; Lit. Crit. Regist.; Mag. Search; MLA Int. Bibl. Books Artic. Mod. Lang. Lit.; Newsp. Period. Abstr. (1990-); Res. Alert [Full Cov.]; Romant. Move.; Soc. Sci. Cit. Index [Select. Cov.].

●US/1065-4917
**THEATRE SYMPOSIUM.** (THEATRE SYMPOSIUM : A JOURNAL OF THE SOUTHEASTERN THEATRE CONFERENCE.). **Added/Corp** Southeastern Theatre Conference. (1993)-. Periodical. English. $40.00. Southeastern Theatre Conference, PO Box 9868G Street, Greensboro NC 27429-0868. **Tel** (919) 272-3645, FAX (919) 272-8810.

US/0732-300X
**THEATRE TIMES.** ***Suspended.*** (THEATRE TIMES : A PUBLICATION OF THE ALLIANCE OF RESIDENT THEATRES/NEW YORK.). Vol. 1, No. 1-?. Periodical. English. bm. $15.00. Alliance of Resident Theatres, 131 Varicle Street/Room 904, New York NY 10013. **Tel** (212)989-5257, FAX (212)989-4880. **ED** Mindy N Levine. **Bk Rev. Ad Acc. Circ:** 3,000 (ctrl).
**Desc:** The trade newspaper of New York City's nonprofit theatre. Reports on artistic and management issues important to off and on-broadway theatre.

US/1054-8378
**THEATRE TOPICS.** [Theatre top.]. **Added/Corp** Association for Theatre in Higher Education (U.S.). (1991)-. Periodical. English. Twice a year. $27.00 US; $30.00 Canada & Mexico; $31.00 other. Johns Hopkins University Press, 2715 North Charles Street, Baltimore MD 21218-4319. **Tel** (410)516-6987, FAX (410)516-6968. **ED** Beverly Byers-Pevitts. **LC** PN2000; .T52. **DD** 792/.05. **[CCC]. Ad Acc. Pr Rev.**
**Desc:** Addresses the concerns of scholars and artists in the areas of performance studies and drama.

US/8756-4335
**THEATRE (WASHINGTON, D.C.).** (THEATER / NATIONAL ENDOWMENT FOR THE ARTS.). Fiscal Year 1980-. English. an. National Endowment for the Arts, 1100 Pennsylvania Avenue Northwest, Washington DC 20506. **Tel** (202)682-5400, (202)682-5435. **LC** PN2044.U6; N36A. **DD** 792/.079. ***Continues*** *Theatre (Washington, D.C.), 8756-4335.*

US
**THEATRE WORLD (NEW YORK, N.Y. : 1981).** ***Ceased.*** (THEATRE WORLD.). **VFOAT** John Willis Theatre World. Vol. 37 (1981)-(19??). English. an. Crown Publishers Inc, 34 Engelhard Avenue, Avenel NJ 07001. **Tel** (201)382-7600. **ED** J Willis. available on microfilm from University Microfilms International (UMI). ***Continues*** *John Willis' Theatre World.*

●US/1060-5320
**THEATREFORUM (LA JOLLA, CALIF.).** (THEATREFORUM.). **Added/Corp** University of California, San Diego. Theatre Dept. **VFOAT** Theatre Forum. (1992)-. Periodical. English. sa. $25.00 (institutions). University of California, San Diego, Theatre Department 0344, 9500 Gilman Drive, La Jolla CA 92093-0344.

UK/0265-2609
**THEATREPHILE.** Vol. 1, No. 1 (Dec. 1983)-. Periodical. English. Four times a year. Theatrephile, 2 Goodwins Court, London WC2N 4LL England. **ED** D. F. Chesmire and Sean McCarthy. **LC** PN2001; .T445. **DD** 792/.09. **Ad Acc. Circ:** 1,000.
**Desc:** History of theatre, popular theatre and leisure entertainments of all periods to present day.
**Ind/Abst** Archit. Period. Index.

US/1046-9869
**THEATRICAL INDEX.** [Theatr. index]. (1964)-. Periodical. English. wk. $295.00. Price Berkley, 888 8th Avenue, New York NY 10019. **Tel** (212)586-6343. **LC** PN2277.N5; T48. **DD** 792/.09747/1/05.

GR
**THEATRIKA.** Periodical. Greek, Modern. mo. Ekdoseis Choros, Aiginitou 9, Athens Greece. **LC** PN2009; .T475.

CN/0838-5696
**THEATRUM (TORONTO).** (THEATRUM: A THEATRE JOURNAL.). [Theatrum]. Issue #1 (Apr. 1985)-. Periodical. English. mo. 20.00Can$ (1 year), 38.00Can$ (2 year) institutions, Canada; 20.00Can$ (1 year), 30.00Can$ (2 year) individual, Canada; 25.00Can$ (1 year), 43.00Can$ (2 year) institutions, other; 23.00Can$ (1 year), 35.00Can$ (2 year) individual, other

## Theater

(All US and foreign subscribers must pay in US funds.). Theatrum, PO Box 688 Station C, Toronto Ont M6J 3S1 Canada. **Tel** (416)297-9292. **DD** 792/.05.
**Ind/Abst** Can. Index; Can. Period. Index (1990-).

GR
**TO TETARTO.** Vol. 1 (May 1985)-. Periodical. Greek, Modern. mo. Voukourestiou 15, Athens 106 71 Greece.

CN/0225-638X
**TORONTO THEATRE REVIEW.** Vol. 1 (Feb. 1977)-. Periodical. English. $6.00 Canada and US, $10.00 other. Toronto Theatre Review, Box 41, Station P, Toronto Ont. M5S 2S6. **DD** 792/.09713/541.

MX
**TRAMOYA. Added/Corp** Universidad Veracruzana. Rutgers University--Camden. (Oct./Dec. 1975)-. Periodical. Spanish. Four times a year. $20.00. Dr. E. Cortes, Rutgers University, Camden NJ 08102. **Tel** (609)757-6114, (609)757-6136. **LC** WMLC L 83/1027; PQ7183; .T73.

US/0738-4009
**UBU REPERTORY THEATER PUBLICATIONS. VFOAT** UBU. Vol. 1-. Monographic series. English (translations available in French). qt. Price varies per volume. UBU Repertory Theater, 15 W 28 Street, New York NY 10001. **Tel** (212)925-0999. **ED** Catherine Temerson.
**Desc:** Contemporary French-language plays in English translation.

UN
**UKRAINSKYI TEATR. Added/Corp** Ukraine. Ministerstvo Kultury. Ukrainske Teatralne Tovarystvo. (1936)-. Periodical. Ukrainian. bm. **LC** PN2725.U4; U4.

US/0042-2738
**VARIETY. See** Motion Picture.

US
**VARIETY.** Vol. 1 (Dec. 16, 1905)-. Periodical. English. $50.00 per reel. Kraus Reprint and Periodicals, 358 Saw Mill River Road, Millwood NY 10546. **Tel** (914)762-2200, (800)223-8323, FAX (914)762-1195, telex 6818112. **LC** Microfilm 03722 PN; PN2000. available in print.

●US/1064-1300
**WANT'S THEATRE DIRECTORY. VFOAT** Theatre Directory. (1993)-. Directory. English. $25.50. Want Publishing Company, 1511 K Street Northwest, Suite 635, Washington DC 20005. **Tel** (202)783-1887, FAX (202)393-5106.

GW
**WER SPIELTE WAS?. Added/Corp** Germany (East). Direktion feur das Buhnenrepertoire. (1977)-. German. an. Direktion fur das Buhnenrepertoire, Griechische Allee, Berlin Germany. **LC** PN2640; .D7. **DD** 792/.0943. **Continues** Dramatiker und Komponisten auf den Buhnen der Deutschen Demokratischen Republik.

US/0740-770X
**WOMEN & PERFORMANCE.** [Women perform.]. **Added/Corp** Tisch School of the Arts. Women & Performance Project. **VFOAT** Women and Performance. Vol. 1 No. 1 (Spring/Summer 1983)-. Periodical. English. sa. $25.00 US; $28.00 Canada; $31.00 other (institutions); $14.00 US; $17.00 Canada; $20.00 other (individual). Department of Performance Studies, 721 Broadway, 6th Floor, New York NY 10003. **ED** J. Burns, J. Rosenthal. **Bk Rev**, (Qty: 2-6/yr). **Ad Acc. Pr Rev. Circ:** 1000.
**Ind/Abst** Altern. Press Index (197?-); Left Index; MLA Int. Bibl. Books Artic. Mod. Lang. Lit.

US/0749-7768
**WORD PLAYS. Ceased.** (WORD PLAYS : AN ANTHOLOGY OF NEW AMERICAN DRAMA.). [Word plays]. **VFOAT** Wordplays. 1st Ed- (1980)-?. English. ir. Performing Arts Journal Publications, 131 Varick Street, Suite 902, New York NY 10013. **Tel** (212)243-3974. **DD** 812.

UK
**YEARBOOK OF THE SOCIETY FOR PIRANDELLO STUDIES, THE. Added/Corp** Society for Pirandello Studies. **VFOAT** Pirandello Yearbook. No. 11 (1991)-. Periodical. English (Italian). an. **LC** PQ4835.I7; Z96. **DD** 852/.912. **Continues** Yearbook of the British Pirandello Society, 0260-9215.

US/0892-9092
**YOUTH THEATRE JOURNAL.** [Youth theatre j.]. **Added/Corp** American Association of Theatre for Youth. Vol. 1 No. 1 (Summer 1986)-. Periodical. English. Four times a year (Mar., June, Sept., Dec.). $25.00 Comes with American Alliance Theatre & Education membership. American Alliance for Theatre and Education, Department of Theatre, Arizona State University, Tempe AZ 85287. **Tel** (602)965-6064. **ED** Susan Pearson Davis. **LC** PN3157; .Y68. **DD** 792/.0226/05. **Bk Rev. Ad Acc. Pr Rev. Circ:** 1,000. **Continues** Children's Theatre Review, 0009-4196.
**Desc:** Includes research, educational theory and methods, history, special populations, K-12 curriculum, film and television for young people and professional children's theatre.
**Ind/Abst** Curr. Index J. Educ. (March 1990).

RU
**ZHENSHCHINAKH, O.** (1970)-. Periodical. Russian. an. 0.35rub. Izdatelstvo Iskusstvo, Vorotnikovskii Pereulok 11, 103009 Moscow Russia. **LC** PG3255.A42; O23.

## ABSTRACTING, BIBLIOGRAPHIES AND STATISTICS

US/0360-2788
**BIBLIOGRAPHIC GUIDE TO THEATRE ARTS. Main/Corp** New York Public Library. Research Libraries. **Added/Corp** New York Public Library. Research Libraries. Catalog of the Theatre and Drama Collections. (1975)-. English. an. $195.00. GK Hall & Co, 100 Front Street, Riverside NJ 08075. **Tel** (800)257-5755 ext. 2223. **LC** Z6935; .N46a; PN1584. **DD** 016.792.

US/0882-9446
**INTERNATIONAL BIBLIOGRAPHY OF THEATRE.** (INTERNATIONAL BIBLIOGRAPHY OF THEATRE / SPONSORED BY THE AMERICAN SOCIETY FOR THEATRE RESEARCH, AND THE INTERNATIONAL ASSOCIATION OF LIBRARIES AND MUSEUMS OF THE PERFORMING ARTS IN COOPERATION WITH THE INTERNATIONAL FEDERATION FOR THEATRE RESEARCH.). [Int. bibliogr. theatr.]. **Added/Corp** Brooklyn College. Theatre Research Data Center. American Society for Theatre Research. International Association of Libraries and Museums of the Performing Arts. International Federation for Theatre Research. **VFOAT** IBT. (1987)-. Bibliography. English. ir. Price varies per volume. Theatre Research Data Center, Brooklyn College, Brooklyn NY 11210. **Tel** (718)951-5999. **LC** Z6935; .I53; PN1561. **DD** 016.79/02.

US/0023-8813
**LATIN AMERICAN THEATRE REVIEW. See** Theater.

GW
**SCHAUSPIELFUHRER, DER.** (1953)-. German. Anton Hiersemann Verlag, Rosenbergstrasse 113, D 70193 Stuttgart Germany. **Tel** 011 49 711 638264 5. **Ad Acc. Circ:** 3,000.
**Desc:** To date, description of 2,300 theatre plays of all languages (countries).

## TOBACCO

FR/0399-0206
**ANNALES DU TABAC. SECTION 1, RECHERCHE ET DEVELOPPEMENT.** Periodical. French (summaries and/or abstracts in English and German). 53 Quai d'Orsay, 75340 Paris Cedex 07 France. **Tel** (1)45 55 91 50. **ED** C Joigny. **LC** TS2220; .A56. **DD** 679/.7/05. **Circ:** 1,000. **Continues** Annales du Tabac. Section 1, Recherche et Ingegnierie.
**Desc:** Technology of tobacco manufacturing and analytical chemistry applied to tobacco, tobacco products or tobacco smoke.

FR/0399-0354
**ANNALES DU TABAC. SECTION 2. Added/Corp** France. Service d'Exploitation Industrielle des Tabacs et Allumettes. Institut Experimental du Tabac (Bergerac, France) Societe Nationale d'Exploitation Industrielle des Tabacs et Allumettes (France). (1976)-. Periodical. French (summaries and/or abstracts in English, German and Russian). **LC** SB273; .A55. **DD** 633.7/1/05. **CODEN** ATSED2. Documents available from CASDDS. **Continues in part** Tabac.
**Ind/Abst** Chem. Abstr.

IT/0391-4836
**ANNALI DELL'ISTITUTO SPERIMENTALE PER IL TABACCO.** [Ann. Ist. Sper. Tab.]. **Main/Corp** Istituto Sperimentale per il Tabacco. Vol. 1 (1973/74)-. Academic Scholarly Publication. Italian. an. **CODEN** AISTD4. Documents available from CASDDS.
**Ind/Abst** Chem. Abstr.; Nematol. Abstr.; Plant Grow. Reg. Abstr.

US
**ANNUAL REPORT - TOBACCO WORKING GROUP, NATIONAL INSTITUTES OF HEALTH. Main/Corp** National Cancer Institute. Tobacco Working Group. (19??)-. Periodical. English. an. National Cancer Institute, NCI Building Room, 10A 18, Bethesda MD 20892. **Tel** (800)422-6237, (301)496-8774.

AT/0567-1159
**AUSTRALIAN TOBACCO GROWERS' BULLETIN. Added/Corp** Australia. Dept. of Primary Industry Tobacco Secretariat. (1961)-. Periodical. English. Tobacco Secretariat / Division of Agricultural Production, Department of Primary Industry, Canberra ACT Australia.
**Ind/Abst** Field Crop Abstr.; Grasslands For. Abstr.; Soils Fert.

GW/0173-783X
**BEITRAEGE ZUR TABAKFORSCHUNG INTERNATIONAL.** [Beitr. tab.forsch. int.]. V. 9, No. 4 (July 1978)-. Academic Scholarly Publication. German (summaries and/or abstracts in English, French and German). sa. free. Verband der Cigarettenindustrie, Harvestehuder Weg 88, Konigswinterer Strabe 550, D-5300 Bonn 3. **Tel** (0228)44 90 60, FAX (0228)44 25 82.
**(Subscription address:** F Adlkofer, H Emlenhorst, W Fink, C R Green, L O Hjern, H Kaneko, E Kausch, H Klus, T S Osdene, W Rhan, O Stuhl, R E Thornton. T C Tso and K Wegman) **LC** TS2220; .B45. **DD** 679/.7/05. **NLM** W1; BE461J. **CODEN** BTAID3. Index available. cum. index. **Pr Rev. Circ:** 1,100 (ctrl). available on microfilm; available on microfiche. Documents available from The Genuine Article, BIOSIS Document Express, CASDDS. **Continues** Beitrage zur Tabakforschung.
**Ind/Abst** AGRICOLA [Select. Cov.]; Anal. Abstr.; BioBusiness; Biol. Abstr.; Chem. Abstr.; Curr. Contents, Agric. Biol. Environ. Sci.; EMBASE; Field Crop Abstr.; Grasslands For. Abstr.; Life Sci. Collect.; Plant Breed. Abstr.; Postharvest News Inf.; Protozoolog. Abstr.; Res. Alert [Full Cov.]; Rev. Agric. Entomol.; Sci. Cit. Index; SCISEARCH.

CN/0835-0019
**BEVERAGE AND TOBACCO PRODUCTS INDUSTRIES. See** Food and Food Industry-Beverage Industry.

II
**BHARATIYA TAMBAKU. Ceased. Added/Corp** India (Republic). Directorate of Tobacco Development. V. 1- April/June 1971-. Hindi (Hindi). qt. Tambaku Vikasa Nidesalaya, 3-A Eldams Road, Teynampet Madrasa 600018 India. **LC** SB278.I58; B45.

BL
**BOLETIM INFORMATIVO : COMERCIO EXTERIOR - EXPORTACAO DE FUMO EM FOLHAS. Main/Corp** Instituto Bahiano do Fumo. Bulletin. Portuguese. Rua de Belgica, 2-Ed Roosevelt Lo Andar, Salvador Brazil. **LC** HD9144.B73; B353A.

●US/1065-710X
**BREATHE! (LA QUINTA, CALIF.). See** Public Health and Safety.

FR/0525-6240
**BULLETIN D'INFORMATION. INFORMATION BULLETIN. Main/Corp** Cooperation Centre for Scientific Research Relative to Tobacco. **VFOAT** Information Bulletin. (1957)-. Bulletin. French (English). qt. Coresta, 53 Quai D'Orsay, 75007 Paris France. **Tel** 33 1 45566019.
**Ind/Abst** Rev. Plant Pathol.

CN/0008-5189
**CANADIAN TOBACCO GROWER, THE.** (1953)-. Periodical. English. qt (Feb., Apr., July, Oct.). 8.00Can$ Canada; 38.00Can$ other. NCC Publishing, 222 Argyle Avenue, Delhi Ontario N4B 2Y2 Canada. **Tel** (519)582-2513, FAX (519)582-4040. **ED** David MacLaren. **Ad Acc, Adv Mgr:** Bill Arts. **Circ:** 3,500 (ctrl).
**Desc:** Serving growers of flue-cured tobacco in Canada.

CU/1013-9869
**CIENCIA Y TECNICA EN LA AGRICULTURA. TABACO.** [Cienc. t,ec. agric., Tabaco]. **Added/Corp** Centro de Informacion y Documentacion Agropecuario (Cuba) Centro de Informacion y Divulgacion Agropecuario (Cuba) Estacion Central de Tabaco (Cuba). **VFOAT** Tabaco. (197?)-. Spanish (summaries and/or abstracts in English; table of contents in English). Ediciones Cubanas, Obispo 527, Altos ESQ Bernaza, CP 10100 Havana Cuba. **Tel** 011 632980, 631942, FAX 011 631011, telex 512337, 6540. **CODEN** CATBEO. Documents available from BIOSIS Document Express.
**Ind/Abst** Biol. Abstr. (1986-); Field Crop Abstr.; Plant Breed. Abstr.; Plant Grow. Reg. Abstr.; Rev. Plant Pathol.; Soils Fert.

●US/1063-7885
**CIGAR AFICIONADO.** [Cigar afic.]. Vol. 1, No. 1 (Autumn 1992)-. Periodical. English. qt. $12.95 (one year), $22.95 (two year), $32.95 (three year) US; $16.94 Canada; £12.00 UK; $22.95 other. M. Shanken Communications, Inc., 387 Park Avenue South, New York NY 10016. **Tel** (212)684-4224, FAX (212)684-5424, telex 422687 MSHANK UI. **(Subscription address:** Neodata / Colorado, PO Box 2606, Boulder Boulder CO 80322.) **LC** TS2260; .C52. **DD** 394.1/4. **Ad Acc, Adv Mgr:** James Archambault, **Tel** (212)684-4224.
**Desc:** Knowledge and appreciation of cigars. Covers dining and entertaining, world travel, and the arts.

# Tobacco

**CU**
**CUBA TABACO.** Periodical. Spanish. Amargura No. 103, Esq A San Ignacio, Zona 1 Ciudad Habana Cuba. **LC** HD9144.C9; C82.

US/0015-4512
**FLUE CURED TOBACCO FARMER, THE.** [Flue cured tob. farmer]. (1964)-. Periodical. English. ir (November-June). $10.00 US; $36.00 other. Specialized Agriculture Publications, 3000 Highwoods Boulevard/Suite 300, Raleigh NC 27625. **Tel** (919)872-5040. **ED** Dayton Matlick. **Ad Acc. Circ:** 25,000 (ctrl).
**Desc:** Serves commercial tobacco producers.
**Ind/Abst** AGRICOLA.

US/0965-2051
**FOREST.** (1981)-. English. bm. FOREST, 2 Grosvenor Gardens, SW1W 0DH London England. **Tel** 71 823 6550, **FAX** 71 823 4534.
**Desc:** The goal of the magazine is not to promote smoking but to defend adult freedom of choice against prohibitionists, social authoritarians and medical paternalists. It is not the role of the state to restrict the non-violent lifestyles of the individual, even if they involve a degree of risk.

**FR**
**FRANCE TABAC. Added/Corp** Societe de Presse et d'Edition Tabacole. No. 1 (Jan. 1985)-. Periodical. French. Eleven times a year. 102.84F. Societe Presse Edit Tabacole, 19 rue Ballu, 75009 Paris France. **Tel** 011 33 1 44534800. **Continues** Voix des Cultures.
**Ind/Abst** Agric. Eng. Abstr.; Field Crop Abstr.; Seed Abstr.

**JA**
**GYOTEI HOKOKU - NIHON SEMBAI KOSHA UTSUNOMIYA TABAKO SHIKENJO. Main/Corp** Utsunomiya Tabako Shikenjo. **Added/Corp** Utsunomiya Tabako Shikenjo. Tabako Shikenjo Gyotei Hokoku. **VFOAT** Tabako Shikenjo Gyotei Hokoku. (19??)-. Periodical. Japanese. Utsunomiya Tabako Shikenjo, 1900 Oaza Izui, Koyama 323 Japan. **LC** SB278.J3; U86a.

**KO**
**HANGUK YONCHO HAKHOE CHI. Added/Corp** Hanguk Yoncho Hakhoe. **VFOAT** Journal of the Korean Society of Tobacco Science. (19??)-. Periodical. Korean (summaries and/or abstracts in English). Tong Hakhoe, 112 Inui-dong, Chongno-ku, Seoul South Korea. **LC** TS2249; .H29.
**Ind/Abst** Rev. Plant Pathol.

**JA**
**HATABAKO KENKYU.** Japanese. Tabako Sangyo Kosaikai Bunka Jigyobu, (Japan Tabacco Foundation), 3-13, Toranomon 2 Chome, Minatoku, Tokyoto 105 Japan. **LC** SB278.J3; H35A.

II/0445-7951
**INDIAN TOBACCO.** [Indian tob.]. English. World Trade Centre, 123-C Mount Road, 600006 Madras India. **LC** HD9146.I4; I69. **DD** 338.1/7/3710954.

**II**
**INDIAN TOBACCO (GUNTUR, INDIA).** (INDIAN TOBACCO.). 1981-. English. Post Bag No 451, Lakshmipuram, Guntur 522007 India. **LC** HD9146.I4; I7. **DD** 633.7/1/029454.

UK/0959-2431
**JOURNAL OF SMOKING-RELATED DISORDERS, THE.** See Medical Science and Technology-Toxicology.

JA/0369-4372
**KENKYU HOKOKU.--NIHON SEMBAI KOSHA CHUO KENKYUJO. Main/Corp** Nihon Sembai Kosha. **Added/Corp** Nihon Sembai Kosha. Chuo Kenkyujo. Scientific Papers of the Central Research Institute, Japan Tobacco & Salt Public Corporation. **VFOAT** Scientific Papers of the Central Research Institute, Japan Tobacco & Salt Public Corporation. (19??)-. Academic Scholarly Publication. Multiple languages (Japanese and English). Nihon Sembai Kosha / Yokohama, Umegaoka Midori-Ku, Yokohama Japan. **LC** TS2220; .N55a. **CODEN** NISHA6. Documents available from CASDDS.
**Ind/Abst** AGRICOLA; Chem. Abstr. (1925-1984).

**JA**
**KOKUNAISAN HATABAKO KAISETSUSHO. Main/Corp** Nihon Semabi Kosha. Genryo Hombu. (1975)-. Periodical. Japanese. Nihon Sembai Kosha / Yokohama, Umegaoka Midori-Ku, Yokohama Japan. **LC** SB278.J3; N54. **Continues** Kokunaisan Hatabako Kaisetsusho.

US/0886-0122
**MEALEY'S LITIGATION REPORT. TOBACCO.** Title Change. See Law.

**US**
**NEWS LETTER / FLUE-CURED TOBACCO COOPERATIVE STABILIZATION CORPORATION. Added/Corp** Flue-Cured Tobacco Cooperative Stabilization Corporation. **VFOAT** Newsletter. (Jan. 4, 1954)-. Periodical. English. mo.

**US**
**NORTH CAROLINA INTEGRATED TOBACCO PEST MANAGEMENT ... ANNUAL REPORT.** 1974-. English. an. **Continues** North Carolina Tobacco Pest Management Annual Report.

**IT**
**NOTIZIARIO TECNICO TESSILE.** (19??)-. Italian. Four times a year. L20000 Italy; L40000 other. Assn Ex-Allievi Ist Nazionale Setificio, Via Castelnuovo 1, 22100 Como Italy. **Tel** 011 39 31 276175.

CN/0708-336X
**PRODUCTION AND DISPOSITION OF TOBACCO PRODUCTS.** [Prod. dispos. tob. prod.]. **Added/Corp** Statistics Canada. Manufacturing and Primary Industries Division. Statistics Canada. Industry Division. **VFOAT** Production et Disposition des Produits du Tabac. Vol. 7, No. 1 (Jan. 1978)-. Periodical. English (French). mo. 60.00Can$ Canada; $72.00 US; $84.00 other. Statistics Canada, Publications Sales & Services, Main Building Room 1710, Ottawa Ontario K1A 0T6 Canada. **Tel** (613)951-5078, (800)267-6677, **FAX** (613)951-1584, telex 053-3585. **DD** 338.4/76797/0971.
**Continues** Tobacco and Tobacco Products., 0705-4270.
**Desc:** Provides monthly and cumulative production, sales and inventory of cigarettes, cigars and cut tobacco.

US/0361-1612
**REPORT OF THE COUNCIL FOR TOBACCO RESEARCH--U.S.A., INC. Main/Corp** Council for Tobacco Research--U.S.A. English. an. Council for Tobacco Research USA, 900 3rd Avenue, New York NY 10022. **Tel** (212)421-8885. **LC** R850.A1; C68A. **DD** 615.9/52/379. **NLM** W1 CO955B.

**JA**
**SHISHA CHIHOKYOKU TABAKO KOSAKU SHIKEH SEISEKI. Main/Corp** Nihon Sembai Kosha. Seisan Hombu. (19??)-. Japanese. Nihon Sembai Kosha Seisan Hombu, 2 Akasaka Aoicho, Minato-ku, Tokyo 107 Japan. **LC** SB278.J3; N53a. **Continues** Nihon Sembai Kosha. Seisan Hombu. Chihokyoku Tabako Kosaku Shiken Seiseki.

US/0893-8946
**SITUATION AND OUTLOOK REPORT. TOBACCO.** [Situat. outlook rep., Tob.]. **Added/Corp** United States. Dept. of Agriculture. Economic Research Service. United States. World Agricultural Outlook Board. **VFOAT** Situation and Outlook Yearbook. Tobacco; Tobacco Situation and Outlook Report. TS-195 (June 1986)-. Government Publication. English. qt. $11.00 US; $13.75 other. Superintendent of Documents, US Government Printing Office, Washington DC 20402. **Tel** (202)275-3328, **FAX** (202)786-2377. **LC** HD9131; .T63. **DD** 338.1/7371/0973. Documents available from Documents on Demand. **Continues** Outlook and Situation Report. Tobacco, 0889-7948.
**Ind/Abst** Am. Stat. Index; F&S Index Plus Text, Int. [Select. Cov.]; Predicasts Forecasts; Trade Ind. ASAP [Full Txt.]; Trade Ind. Index [Full Txt.]; World Agric. Econ.

US/0146-9266
**SMOKESHOP.** See Business.

US/0081-0363
**SMOKING AND HEALTH BULLETIN.** See Public Health and Safety.

US/0300-6239
**SOUTHERN TOBACCO JOURNAL.** [South. tob. j.]. Periodical. English. mo. Southern Trade Publications Company, PO Box 18343, Greensboro NC 27419. **Tel** (919)854-3033.

US/1064-0851
**STAT NEWS.** (STAT NEWS : A NEWSLETTER FOR THE MEMBERS OF STAT.). [STAT news]. **Added/Corp** STAT (Organization). **VAT** Stop Teenage Addiction to Tobacco News. (19??)-. Periodical. English. Twice a year. $25.00 Comes with Stop Teenage Addiction to Tobacco / STAT, 511 East Columbus Avenue, Springfield MA 01105. **Tel** (413)732-7828, **FAX** (413)734-4219. **ED** Caudette Carveth. **DD** 362.

CN/0713-5467
**TABAC AU CANADA.** (LE TABAC AU CANADA ... : UN RAPPORT.). [Tab. Can.]. 1981-. French (English). an. Free. Conseil Canadien des Fabricants des Produits du Tabac, Canadian Tobacco Manufacturers Council, 701-99 Bank Street, Ottawa Ontario K1P 6B9 Canada. **Tel** (514)937-7428, **FAX** (514)937-6380. **DD** 338.4/76797/0971. **Circ:** 100 (ctrl)
**Desc:** Articles on tobacco in Canada.

CH/0379-4199
**TAIWAN SHENGYANJIU GONGMAIJU YONGYE SHIYAN-SUO YANJIU HUIBAO.** (TAI-WAN SHENG YEN CHIU KUNG MAI CHU YEN YEH SHIH YEN SO YEN CHIU HUI PAO.). [Taiwan shengyanjiu gongmaiju yongye shiyan-suo yanjiu huibao]. **Main/Corp** Tai-Wan Sheng Yen Chiu Kung Mai Chu. Yen Yeh Shih Yen So. **VFOAT** Bulletin of the Tobacco Research Institute, Taiwan Tobacco & Wine Monopoly Bureau; Report of Tobacco Research Institute, Taiwan Tobacco & Wine Monopoly Bureau. No. 3- Aug. 1974-. Academic Scholarly Publication. Chinese (summaries and/or abstracts in English). sa. Tobacco Research Institute, Taiwan Tobacco & Wine Monopoly Bureau, Taichung, Taiwan. **CODEN** BTRBDX. Documents available from BIOSIS Document Express, CASDDS.
**Ind/Abst** AGRICOLA; Biodeter. Abstr.; Biol. Abstr.; Chem. Abstr.; Crop Physiol. Abstr.; EMBASE; Field Crop Abstr.; Postharvest News Inf.; Rev. Agric. Entomol.; Rev. Plant Pathol.

**KO**
**TAMBAE (HANGUK YONCHO HAKHOE).** (TAMBAE.). **VFOAT** Tobacco Korea. Periodical. Korean (Korean). Tong Hakhoe, 112 Inui-dong, Chongno-ku, Seoul South Korea. **LC** SB273; .T19.

**KO**
**TAMBAE YONGU NONMUNJIP. VFOAT** Research Papers of Tobacco. Periodical. English (Korean). Hanguk Insam Yoncho Yonguso, 112 Inui-dong, Chongno-ku, Seoul South Korea. **LC** SB278.K6; T35.

US/0563-6191
**TAX BURDEN ON TOBACCO, THE.** V. 1- 1966-. English. an. **LC** HD9130.1; .T62A. **DD** 336.2/78/67970973.
**Ind/Abst** Stat. Ref. Index.

GW/0721-5185
**TJI : TOBACCO JOURNAL INTERNATIONAL.** [TJI. Tob. Tab. Tab. Tab. Tab.-J. int.]. **VFOAT** Tobacco Journal International; T.J.I. (19??)-. Periodical. English (Dutch, French, German, Italian and Spanish). Six times a year (Feb., Apr., June, Aug., Oct., Dec.). DM150.00 Germany; $97.00 US. Rhein Main Zeitschriften, Rheinallee 3 a, 55116 Mainz, Postfach 3120, 55021 Mainz. **Tel** (0 61 31)144-282, **FAX** (0 61 31)23 44 72. **ED** Hans-Gerd Koenen, Hans Georg Poehl and Barbara Horne. **LC** HD9130.1; .T53. **DD** 338.1/7371/05. **CODEN** TJOIAS. **Bk Rev. Ad Acc. Circ:** 4,200. **Continues** Tabak-Journal International, 0039-0748.
**Desc:** This publication is about tobacco trade and industry.
**Ind/Abst** BioBusiness; Int. Packag. Abstr.

UK/0040-8271
**TOBACCO.** (1881)-. Periodical. English. bm. £47.00 UK; £55.00, $98.00 other. Argus Press Group, Queensway House, 2 Queensway Redhill, Surrey RH1 1QS England. **Tel** 011 44 737 768611, 011 44 737 761685, **FAX** 011 44 737 760510, telex 948669 TOPJNL G. **LC** HD9130.1; .T595. **DD** 338.476791371.
**Desc:** Covers the UK tobacco market.

US/0040-8298
**TOBACCO ABSTRACTS.** Vol. 1 (1957)-. Periodical. English. ir. $39.50. Tobacco Literature Service, Box 8009, 2314 D H Hill Library, North Carolina State University, Raleigh NC 27695-7111. **Tel** (919)515-2836. **ED** Pamela E. Puryear. Index available. **Circ:** 700 (ctrl).
**Desc:** Tobacco culture, chemistry, genetics, production, product manufacture, economics, properties; molecular biology and biotechnology relative to tobacco.

**US**
**TOBACCO ALLOTTED, BY COUNTIES AND KINDS.** Government Publication. English. an. Department of Agriculture / Washington, 14th Street and Independence Avenue SW, Washington DC 20250. **Tel** (202)720-2791.

●US/1064-8577
**TOBACCO & HEALTH.** [Tob. health]. **VFOAT** Tobacco and Health. (1992)-. Periodical. English. mo. $170.00 US; $190.00 other. James Publications, PO Box 5, Media PA 19063. **Tel** (215)328-5623, **FAX** (215)328-9073. **ED** Patricia Peters. **DD** 616.
**Desc:** This publication contains articles dealing with the medical and psychological effects of tobacco products and smoking.

**US**
**TOBACCO FARMER / GEORGIA AGRICULTURAL COMMODITY COMMISSION FOR TOBACCO. --, THE. Added/Corp** Georgia Agricultural Commodity Commission for Tobacco. (19??)-. Periodical. English. Four times a year. Georgia Agricultural Commodity Commission, PO Box 396, Lifton GA 31794.

●US/1064-2072
**TOBACCO-FREE YOUTHREPORTER.** (TOBACCO-FREE YOUTHREPORTER : A QUARTERLY PUBLICATION OF STAT--STOP TEENAGE ADDICTION TO TOBACCO.). [Tob.-free youthreport.]. **Added/Corp** STAT (Organization). **VFOAT** Tobacco Free Youth Reporter. (1992)-. Periodical. English. Four times a year. $25.00 Comes with Stop Teenage Addiction to Tobacco membership. Stop Teenage Addiction of Tobacco / STAT, 511 East Columbus Avenue, Springfield MA 01105. **Tel** (413)732-7828, FAX (413)732-4219. **ED** Caudette Carveth. **DD** 362. **Circ:** 65,000 (ctrl). ***Continues*** *Tobacco and Youth Reporter, 1064-086X.*

US/8756-4750
**TOBACCO GROWER, THE.** (THE TOBACCO GROWER : THE OFFICIAL PUBLICATION OF THE TOBACCO GROWERS ASSOCIATION OF NORTH CAROLINA, INC.). [Tob. grow.]. **Added/Corp** Tobacco Growers Association of North Carolina. Vol. 1, No. 1 (July 1984)-. Periodical. English. Nine times a year. $15.00. TGANC, 3700 National Drive/Suite 212, Raleigh NC 27612. **Tel** (919)781-2307. **ED** Chris Bickers. **DD** 633. **Circ:** 3,000.
**Desc:** Latest information on political developments, especially Washington, management practices, agronomy and economics affecting tobacco growers.

CN/0713-5459
**TOBACCO IN CANADA.** (TOBACCO IN CANADA ... : A REPORT.). [Tob. Can.]. 1981-. English (French). an. Free. Canadian Tobacco Manufacturers Council, Robert F Clarke, 1808 Sherbrooke Street West, Montreal Quebec H3H 1E5 Canada. **Tel** (514)937-7428, FAX (514)937-6380. **DD** 338.4/76797/0971. **Circ:** 100 (ctrl).
**Desc:** Summary of the tobacco industry in Canada. Reports on growing, production, and taxation.

US/0887-7831
**TOBACCO INDUSTRY LITIGATION REPORTER.** **See** Law.

US/0049-3945
**TOBACCO INTERNATIONAL.** [Tob. int.]. Vol. 172 (Jan. 8, 1971)-. Periodical. English. bw. $34.00 (1 year), $47.00 (2 year), $60.00 (3 year) US; $55.00 (1 year), $77.00 (2 year), $99.00 (3 year) other. Lockwood Trade Journal Co Inc, 130 West 42nd Street 22nd Floor, New York NY 10036. **Tel** (212)391-2060. **LC** HD9130.1; .T594. **DD** 338.4/76797/05. **CODEN** TBCIAETBCIA. available on microfilm and microfiche from University Microfilms International (UMI); available on an online database (file 648/Full-Text) from DIALOG. Documents available from CASDDS. ***Continues*** *Tobacco, 0040-828X.*
**Ind/Abst** AgBiotech News Inf.; AGRICOLA; Bibliogr. Mission.; BioBusiness; Chem. Abstr. (-1987); Crop Physiol. Abstr.; EMBASE; F&S Index Plus Text, Int. [Select. Cov.]; Field Crop Abstr.; Int. Aerosp. Abstr.; Int. Packag. Abstr.; Nematol. Abstr.; Plant Breed. Abstr.; Plant Grow. Reg. Abstr.; Postharvest News Inf.; Potato Abstr.; Predicasts Forecasts; Rev. Agric. Entomol.; Rev. Plant Pathol.; Weed Abstr.; Wheat Barley Trit. Abstr.

US/0742-1869
**TOBACCO MARKET REVIEW. BURLEY.** (TOBACCO MARKET REVIEW. BURLEY / UNITED STATES DEPARTMENT OF AGRICULTURE, AGRICULTURAL MARKETING SERVICE.). **Added/Corp** United States. Agricultural Marketing Service. **VFOAT** Burley. TOB-LA-26 (1981 Crop)-. Government Publication. English. an. $3.00 North America; $6.00 other. US Department of Agriculture / Tobacco Market, PO Box 44085, Enfant Plaza Station, Washington DC 20026. **LC** HD9134; .A3825. **DD** 381/.413717. available on microfiche (Vols. for 1982- distributed to depository libraries). ***Continues*** *Tobacco Market Review. Light Air-Cured. Burley, Type 31, 0196-8688.*

US/0272-2771
**TOBACCO MARKET REVIEW. FIRE-CURED AND DARK AIR-CURED.** (TOBACCO MARKET REVIEW. FIRE-CURED AND DARK AIR-CURED / UNITED STATES DEPARTMENT OF AGRICULTURE, AGRICULTURAL MARKETING SERVICE.). [Tob. mark. rev., Fire-cured dark air-cured]. **Added/Corp** United States. Agricultural Marketing Service. **VFOAT** Fire-Cured and Dark Air-Cured; Fire Cured and Dark Air Cured. TOB-FDA-19, 1975 Crop, season of (1976-76)-. Government Publication. English. an. $3.00 North America; $6.00 other. US Department of Agriculture / Tobacco Market, PO Box 44085, Enfant Plaza Station, Washington DC 20026. **LC** HD9134; .A38182. **DD** 338.1/7371. available on microfiche (Vols. for (1981-) distributed to depository libraries). ***Continues*** *Fire-Cured and Dark Air-Cured Tobacco Market Review, 0498-2150.*

US/0193-6514
**TOBACCO MARKET REVIEW. FLUE-CURED.** (TOBACCO MARKET REVIEW. FLUE-CURED / UNITED STATES DEPARTMENT OF AGRICULTURE, AGRICULTURAL MARKETING SERVICE.). [Tob. mark. rev., Flue-cured]. **VFOAT** Flue-Cured; Flue Cured. Began with: TOB-FL-19 (1975 Crop). Government Publication. English. an. $2.00. US Department of Agriculture / Tobacco Market, PO Box 44085, Enfant Plaza Station, Washington DC 20026. **LC** HD9134; .A3822. **DD** 338.1/7/371. ***Continues*** *Flue-Cured Tobacco Market Review, 0498-1782.*

US/0364-7420
**TOBACCO MARKET REVIEW. SOUTHERN MARYLAND.** (TOBACCO MARKET REVIEW. SOUTHERN MARYLAND / UNITED STATES DEPARTMENT OF AGRICULTURE, AGRICULTURAL MARKETING SERVICE.). [Tob. mark. rev., South. Md.]. **VFOAT** Southern Maryland. Began with: Tob-La (1974 Crop). Government Publication. English. an. US Department of Agriculture / Agricultural Marketing Service / Washington, DC, Market News Branch, Fruit and Vegetable Division, Washington DC 20250. **Tel** (202)720-2745, (202)720-3343, FAX (202)720-7502. **LC** HD9137.M3; U53A. **DD** 381/.41/371097524. ***Continues in part*** *Light Air-Cured Tobacco Market Review, 0094-4572.*

●RH
**TOBACCO NEWS.** Vol. 1, No. 1 (Jan. 1992)-. Periodical. English. Twelve times a year. R94.95 South Africa; R99.85 others. Thomson Publications Zimbabwe PVT Ltd., Box 1683, Harare Zimbabwe. **Tel** 011 263 4 736835, FAX 011 263 4 706055. ***Continues in part*** *Zimbabwe Tobacco Today.*

II
**TOBACCO NEWS / TOBACCO BOARD INDIA.** (1977)-. English. bm. $12.00. Tobacco Board, PO Box 451, Guntur 522007 India. **Tel** 32434, telex 0471-264. **Ad Acc.** ***Continues*** *Indian Tobacco.*
**Ind/Abst** Field Crop Abstr.

UK/0142-1913
**TOBACCO QUARTERLY.** ***Ceased.*** Vol. 1, No. 1, Jan. (1979)-Ceased with Nov. (1990). Periodical. English. qt. Commonwealth Secretariat / London, Marlborough House, Pall Mall, London SW1Y 5HX England. **Tel** 44 71 8393411, telex 27678. **ED** K. D. Sharma. **Circ:** 500 (ctrl).
**Desc:** Providing detailed information on tobacco leaf production, exports, imports, stocks, prices and consumption. Also gives data on production, consumption, exports and imports of cigarettes, cigars/cigarillos, and other tobacco manufacturers' products.

US/0040-8328
**TOBACCO REPORTER.** **VFOAT** TR. Vol. 93, No. 6 (June 1966)-. Periodical. English. mo. Edgell Communications, Two Illinois Center, 24th Floor, 233 North Michigan Avenue, Chicago IL 60601. **Tel** (312)938-2381, FAX (312)938-4854. **LC** HD9130.1; .W5. **DD** 338.1/7/37105. ***Continues*** *Western Tobacco Journal.*
**Ind/Abst** Trade Ind. Index.

US/0743-4707
**TOBACCO REPRINT SERIES.** ***Ceased.*** [Tob. repr. ser.]. **Added/Corp** North Carolina Agricultural Research Service. North Carolina Agricultural Experiment Station. North Carolina State University. (1954)-(19??). Periodical. English. ir. Tobacco Literature Service, Box 8009, 2314 D H Hill Library, North Carolina State University, Raleigh NC 27695-7111. **Tel** (919)515-2836. **LC** SB273; .T65. **DD** 633. **Circ:** 400 (ctrl).
**Desc:** Reprints of published NCSU tobacco related research.

II/0379-055X
**TOBACCO RESEARCH.** [Tob. res.]. **Added/Corp** Tobacco Research Workers' Association of India. Vol. 1 (June 1975)-. Academic Scholarly Publication. English. sa. $25.00. Indian Society Tobacco Science Institute, Rajahmundry 533104 India. **(Subscription address:** Prints India, 11 Darya Ganj, New Delhi, 110002 India, (Phone: 011 91 11 3268645)) **CODEN** TRESDX. Documents available from CASDDS.
**Ind/Abst** Agrofor. Abstr. (1991-); Chem. Abstr.; Crop Physiol. Abstr.; Field Crop Abstr.; Irr. Drain. Abstr.; Nematol. Abstr.; Plant Breed. Abstr.; Rev. Agric. Entomol.; Rev. Plant Pathol.; Soils Fert.

US
**TOBACCO STOCKS.** **See** Business-Investments.

US
**TOBACCO TAX GUIDE.** **Main/Corp** United States. Internal Revenue Service. **VFOAT** Tobacco Tax Guide. Transmittal. Periodical. English. Internal Revenue Service, 1111 Constitution Avenue NW, Washington DC 20224.

UK/0954-9773
**TOBACCO TRADE MARKETING DIRECTORY.** Directory. English. an. £38.00 UK; £48.00, $81.00 other. Argus Press Group, Queensway House, 2 Queensway Redhill, Surrey RH1 1QS England. **Tel** 011 44 737 768611, 011 44 737 761685, FAX 011 44 737 760510, telex 948669 TOPJNL G. ***Continues*** *Tobacco Trade Directory and Diary.*

●US
**TOBACCO, WORLD MARKETS & TRADE / UNITED STATES DEPARTMENT OF AGRICULTURE, FOREIGN AGRICULTURAL SERVICE.** **Added/Corp** United States. Foreign Agricultural Service. United States. World Agricultural Outlook Board. **VFOAT** Tobacco, World Markets and Trade. FT-94-1 (Jan. 1994)-. Government Publication. English. mo. $66.00. US Department of Agriculture / Foreign Agricultural Service, 14th Street & Independence Avenue Southwest, Washington DC 20250. **Tel** (202)720-9445, FAX (202)720-7729. **(Subscription address:** NTIS, 5285 Port Royal Road, Springfield VA 22161.) **LC** HD9130.1; .F67. **DD** 382/.41371/0973021. **Bk Rev.** **Ad Acc.** **Circ:** 724. ***Continues*** *World Tobacco Situation.*
**Desc:** Report highlights latest information on imports and exports of tobacco, world prices, world developments affecting tobacco demand and supply, and US tobacco industry and trade developments.
**Ind/Abst** F&S Index Plus Text, Int. [Select. Cov.]; Predicasts Forecasts.

FI/0784-8412
**TUPAKKATILASTO.** **VFOAT** Tobacco Statistics. Finnish (Finnish). an. Tilastokeskus, PL 504, Annankatu 44, 00101 Helsinki Finland. **Tel** 358-0-17341, FAX 358-0-17342474, telex 1002111 TILASTO SF. **LC** HD9145.F5; T86.

FI
**TUPAKKATUOTTEIDEN KULUTUS.** **VFOAT** Tobakskonsumtion; Tobakskonsumtionen; Consumption of Tobacco Products. 1960-1978-. English (Finnish and Swedish). an. Government Printing Centre, PO Box 516, SF-00101 Helsinki 10 Finland. **LC** HB3608.3.A3; T55 subser.

PL
**WIADOMOSCI TYTONIOWE.** Periodical. Polish. mo. $54.00. **(Subscription address:** ARS Polona, PO Box 1001, 00068 Warsaw Poland.**)**

US/0161-7672
**WORLD SMOKING & HEALTH.** (WORLD SMOKING & HEALTH : AN AMERICAN CANCER SOCIETY JOURNAL.). **Added/Corp** American Cancer Society. **VFOAT** World Smoking and Health. **VAT** World Smoking and Health. (Fall/Winter 1976)-. Periodical. English. Three times a year (Mar., July, Nov.). Free. American Cancer Society Institute Activities, 1599 Clifton Road Northeast, Atlanta GA 30329. **ED** Adele Paroni. **LC** RA1242.T6; W68. **DD** 613.8/5/05. **NLM** W1 WO899. **Circ:** 10,000 (ctrl).
**Desc:** Presents articles discussing the world smoking epidemic and the harmful effects of smoking. Includes epidemiologic studies and cessation suggestions.

UK/0043-9126
**WORLD TOBACCO.** [World tob.]. No. 1 (June 1963)-. Periodical. English (summaries and/or abstracts in French, German and Spanish). bm. £89.00 UK; £98.00, $178.00 other. Argus Press Group, Queensway House, 2 Queensway Redhill, Surrey RH1 1QS England. **Tel** 011 44 737 768611, 011 44 737 761685, FAX 011 44 737 760510, telex 948669 TOPJNL G. **ED** George Gaye. **LC** SB273; .W64. **Bk Rev.** **Ad Acc.** **Circ:** 4,389. available on microfilm and microfiche from University Microfilms International (UMI); available on an online database (file 648/Full-Text) from DIALOG.
**Desc:** A journal for managers and key decision makers involved in the international tobacco and allied industries.
**Ind/Abst** F&S Index Plus Text, Int. [Select. Cov.]; Infomat Int. Bus.; Int. Packag. Abstr.; PROMT.

UK/0084-2273
**WORLD TOBACCO DIRECTORY.** [World tob. dir.]. (1972/73)-. Directory. English. an. £90.00 UK; £100.00, $184.00 other. Argus Press Group, Queensway House, 2 Queensway Redhill, Surrey RH1 1QS England. **Tel** 011 44 737 768611, 011 44 737 761685, FAX 011 44 737 760510, telex 948669 TOPJNL G. ***Continues*** *Costa's World Tobacco Directory.*

US
**WORLD TOBACCO SITUATION / UNITED STATES DEPARTMENT OF AGRICULTURE, FOREIGN AGRICULTURAL SERVICE.** ***Title Change.*** **Added/Corp** United States. Foreign Agricultural Service. United States. World Agricultural Outlook Board. **VFOAT** Foreign Agriculture Circular. World Tobacco Situation. (Jan. 1987)-(Dec. 1993). Government Publication. English. mo. Department of Agriculture / Foreign Agricultural Service, 14th Street and Independence Avenue SW, Washington DC 20250-1000. **Tel** (202)720-3935, FAX (202)720-7729. **LC** HD9130.1; .F67. **DD** 382/.41371/0973021. **Bk Rev.** **Ad Acc.** **Circ:** 724 (ctrl). available on microfiche (Vols. for 1987- distributed to depository libraries). ***Continues*** *Foreign Agriculture Circular. Tobacco. World Tobacco Situation.* ***Continued by*** *Tobacco, World Markets & Trade.*
**Desc:** Report highlights latest information on imports and exports of tobacco, world prices, world developments affecting tobacco demand and supply, and US tobacco industry and trade developments.
**Ind/Abst** F&S Index Plus Text, Int. [Select. Cov.]; Predicasts Forecasts.

KO
**YON YONCHO.** **Added/Corp** Yop Yoncho Saengsan Chohap Yonhaphoe (Korea). (19??)-. Periodical. Korean. ir. Yop Yoncho Saengsan Chohap Yonhaphee, 86 Chunghak-dong Chongno-ku, Seoul South Korea. **LC** SB278.K6; Y65.

RH
**ZIMBABWE TOBACCO NEWS.** English. mo. Thomson Publications Zimbabwe PVT Ltd., Box 1683, Harare Zimbabwe. **Tel** 011 263 4 736835, **FAX** 011 263 4 706055. *Continues Zimbabwe Tobacco Today.*

## ABSTRACTING, BIBLIOGRAPHIES AND STATISTICS

US/0747-5314
**ANNUAL REPORT ON TOBACCO STATISTICS (1980).** (ANNUAL REPORT ON TOBACCO STATISTICS / UNITED STATES DEPARTMENT OF AGRICULTURE, AGRICULTURAL MARKETING SERVICE.). [Annu. rep. tob. stat.]. **Added/Corp** United States. Agricultural Marketing Service. (1980)-. Government Publication. English. an. $3.00 North America; $6.00 other. US Department of Agriculture / Tobacco Market, PO Box 44085, Enfant Plaza Station, Washington DC 20026. **LC** HD9134; .A38. **DD** 338.1/7371/0973. *Continues Annual Report on Tobacco Statistics, 0747-5314.*

## TRANSPORTATION

●US/1055-6311
**1:87 SCALE.** [1:87 scale]. **VFOAT** 1 to 87 Scale; One to Eighty-Seven Scale. No. 1 (Jan./Feb. 1992)-. Periodical. English. bm. $5.00. RPM Publishing, PO Box 7916, La Verne CA 91750. **DD** 625.

US/0001-0154
**AAMVA BULLETIN / AMERICAN ASSOCIATION OF MOTOR VEHICLE ADMINISTRATORS.** **Added/Corp** American Association of Motor Vehicle Administrators. **VAT** American Association of Motor Vehicle Administrators Bulletin. Vol. 31, No. 1 (Jan. 1966)-. Periodical. English. Six times a year. $25.00. American Association of Motor Vehicle Administration, 4200 Wilson Boulevard, Suite 1100, Arlington VA 22203. **Tel** (703)522-4200, FAX (703)522-1553. **ED** Jamie P. Lacey. **LC** HE5623.A1; A55. **Circ:** 1,500 (ctrl). *Continues American Association of Motor Vehicle Administrators. Bulletin.*
**Desc:** An association of state and provincial officials responsible for the administration and enforcement of motor vehicle and traffic laws in the United States and Canada.

US
**AASHTO JOURNAL.** English. $150.00 US; $175.00 other. American Association St. Hwy. Tran. Official, 444 North Capitol Street, Suite 225, Washington DC 20001. **Tel** (202)624-5800, FAX (202)624-5806, telex 4900009580. *Continues Transportation Journal.*

US/0147-4847
**AASHTO QUARTERLY.** **Main/Corp** American Association of State Highway and Transportation Officials. **Added/Corp** American Association of State Highway and Transportation Officials. Quarterly. **VAT** American Association of State Highway and Transportation Officials Quarterly. Vol. 55, No. 2 (Apr. 1976)-. Periodical. English. Four times a year. $10.00. AASHTO / American Association State Highways Transportation Official, 444 North Capitol Street Northwest, Suite 249, Washington DC 20001. **Tel** (202)624-5800, FAX (202)624-5806. **ED** Mariann Humphreys. **LC** TE1; .A67. **DD** 388/.0973. **Circ:** 6,200. *Continues American Highway & Transportation Magazine, 0147-4820.*
**Desc:** Articles cover topics of wide variety relating to planning, building and maintaining the nation's transportation systems.
**Ind/Abst** Urban Aff. Abstr.

US/0360-6090
**ACCELERATION AND PASSING ABILITY.** **Main/Corp** United States. National Highway Traffic Safety Administration. English. US Department of Transportation / National Highway Traffic Safety Administration, 400 7th Street SW, Washington DC 20590. **LC** TL1; .C66 subser; TL154. **DD** 629.28/3/2.

FR
**ACTIVITES DE L'INSTITUT DE RECHERCHE DES TRANSPORTS.** **Main/Corp** Institut de Recherche des Transports (France). (19??)-. French. Four times a year. 391.77F France; 500.00F others. Institut National de Recherche sur les Transports et Leur Securite, 2 Avenue du General Malleret-Joinville, F - 94114 Arcueil Cedex France. **Tel** 011 33 1 47 40 70 00, FAX 011 33 1 45 47 56 06. **LC** TA1071; .I58a.

II
**ADMINISTRATION REPORT - KARNATAKA STATE ROAD TRANSPORT CORPORATION.** **Main/Corp** Karnataka State Road Transport Corporation. 12th-1972/73-. English. Transport House, Shanthinagar 27, Bangalore India. **LC** HE5691.M9; A32. **DD** 388.1./1. *Continues Mysore State Road Transport Corporation. Administration Report.*

US
**ADVISORY BULLETIN - OFFICE OF PIPELINE SAFETY OPERATIONS.** **Main/Corp** United States. Office of Pipeline Safety Operations. Bulletin. English. mo. US Department of Transportation / Materials Transportation Bureau, Office of Pipeline Safety Operations, 400 7th Street SW, Washington DC 20590.

US/0745-5100
**AIR CARGO WORLD.** (AIR CARGO WORLD : A PUBLICATION OF COMMUNICATION CHANNELS, INC.). [Air cargo world]. Vol. 73, No. 1 (Jan. 1983)-. Periodical. English. Twelve times a year. $48.00 surface mail; $108.00 airmail. Argus Business, 6151 Powers Ferry Road, Atlanta GA 30339. **Tel** (404)995-2500, (800)233-3359. **ED** Linda Parham. **LC** HE9788; .C37. **DD** 387.7/44/05. **[CCC].** Bk Rev. Ad Acc. **Circ:** 22,000 (ctrl). available on microfilm and microfiche from University Microfilms International (UMI); available on an online database (file 648/Full-Text) from DIALOG. *Continues Air Cargo Magazine, 0148-7469.*
**Desc:** Edited for shippers and form orders who frequently use air transportation. Coverage is also given to air cargo carriers and airports.
**Ind/Abst** Aviat. Tradescan [Full Cov.]; Trade Ind. ASAP [Full Txt.]; Trade Ind. Index [Full Txt.].

US/0890-2925
**AIR CHARTER GUIDE, THE.** [Air chart. guide]. (Fall/Winter 1986/87)-. Periodical. English. sa (Jan., July). $185.00 US; $205.00 other. The Air Charter Guide, PO Box 2387, Cambridge MA 02238. **Tel** (617)547-5811, FAX (617)868-5335. **DD** 387. Ad Acc, Adv Mgr: Meara McLaughlin. **Circ:** 7,000.
**Desc:** This publication is a buyer's guide of all air charter operators and their aircraft. It provides the information necessary to research and contract a charter flight.

US/0092-2870
**AIR FREIGHT DIRECTORY.** **Added/Corp** Air Cargo, inc. (19??)-. Directory. English. bm. $79.50 US; $102.00 other. Air Cargo Incorporated, 1819 Bay Ridge Avenue, Annapolis MD 21403. **Tel** (410)280-5576, FAX (410)280-5588. **ED** Stephanie Wilkins. **LC** HE9788.5.U5; A6. **DD** 387.7/44/0973. **Circ:** 5,000. *Continues Air Freight Directory of Points in the United States Served Directly by Air and by Pick-Up and Delivery Service and by Connecting Motor Carriers.*

US/0190-552X
**AIR TRANSPORT (WASHINGTON).** See Aeronautics, Astronautics.

UK/0951-7782
**AIRCARGO NEWS INTERNATIONAL.** [Aircargo news int.]. **VFOAT** Air Cargo News International. (1983)-. Periodical. English. Twenty-five times a year. £40.00 UK; £57.00 Europe; £68.00 other. Tabmag Publishing Ltd, Grove House, 31 37 Church Road, Asford Middlesex TW15 2UE England. **Tel** 011 44 784 255000.
**Ind/Abst** Fluid Abstr., Civil Eng.; Fluid Abstr. Proc. Eng.; FLUIDEX (19??-).

US/1057-5537
**AIRPORT OPERATIONS.** See Aeronautics, Astronautics.

US/0002-4384
**ALABAMA TRUCKER.** Ceased. [Ala. truck.]. **Added/Corp** Alabama Trucking Association. Motor Vehicle Association of Alabama. Vol. 1, No. 1 (March 1952)-Ceased (Sept./Oct. 1988). Periodical. English. bm. Alabama Trucker, 660 Adams Avenue/Suite 247, Montgomery AL 36104. **Tel** (205)834-3983. **ED** James I Ritchie.

CN/1186-7558
**ALASKA TRANSPORTER : THE OFFICIAL PUBLICATION OF THE ALASKA TRUCKING ASSOCIATION, INC.** [Alsk. transp.]. **Added/Corp** Alaska Trucking Association. (1991)-. English. bm. Naylor Communications Ltd, 100 Sutherland Avenue, Winnipeg Manitoba R2W 3C7 Canada. **Tel** (204)947-0222, FAX (604)985-7399. **DD** 388.3/24/09798.

CN/0821-7718
**ALBERTA TRANSPORTATION (CALGARY).** (ALBERTA TRANSPORTATION.) [Alta. transp.]. **VFOAT** Western Canada Oil & Gas Directory. **VAT** Western Canada Oil & Gas Directory. Alberta Transportation. No. 1 (1983)-. English. Five times a year. Free. Alberta Transportation, Twin Atria Building, 4999-98 Avenue, Edmonton Alberta T6B 2X3 Canada. **DD** 380.5/24/0257123.

SW/0280-7645
**ALCOHOL, DRUGS, AND TRAFFIC SAFETY : CURRENT RESEARCH LITERATURE.** See Drug Abuse and Alcoholism.

CN/0834-0102
**ALL POINTS BULLETIN.** [All points bull.]. Vol. 1, No. 2 (March 1986)-. Periodical. English. Six times a year. Wadham Publications, Division of Southam Communications Ltd, 1450 Don Mills Road, Don Mills Ontario M3B 2X7 Canada. **Tel** (416)445-6641, (416)442-2213. **DD** 388.3/24/0971. *Separated from Driver/Owner, 0829-0512.*

US/1043-5824
**ALLSTATE MOTOR CLUB RV SALES, RENTAL & SERVICE DIRECTORY.** **VFOAT** Allstate Motor Club RV Sales, Rental, and Service Directory. **VAT** Allstate Motor Club Recreational Vehicle Sales, Rental, and Service Directory; Recreational Vehicle Sales, Rental, and Service Directory. (1990)-. Directory. English. an. $10.95. Macmillan Publishing Co. / Indiana, 201 West 103rd Street, Indianapolis IN 46290. **Tel** (800)428-5331, (800)858-7674.

IO
**ALMANAK PERHUBUNGAN DAN PARIWISATA INDONESIA.** 1982-. Indonesian. an. Cv Sandaan, JL Cipinang Sodong Raya, No 27, Jakarta-Timur Indonesia. **LC** HE275; .A713.

US
**AMERICAN ASSOCIATION OF STATE HIGHWAY OFFICIALS PROCEEDINGS.** Proceedings. English. American Association St. Hwy. Tran. Official, 444 North Capitol Street, Suite 225, Washington DC 20001. **Tel** (202)624-5800, FAX (202)624-5806, telex 4900009580.

US/0146-0811
**AMERICAN MCD. NEW ENGLAND EDITION.** Title Change. (AMERICAN MCD : AMERICAN MOTOR CARRIER DIRECTORY.). **Added/Corp** American Trucking Associations. American Trucking Associations. ATA American Motor Carrier Directory. **VFOAT** American Motor Carrier Directory; ATA American Motor Carrier Directory. **VAT** American Motor Carrier Directory. New England Edition; American Trucking Associations American Motor Carrier Directory. (19??)-(19??). English. an. K III Press Inc., 424 West 33rd Street, New York NY 10001. **Tel** (212)714-3100, (800)221-5488. *Merged into American Motor Carrier Directory.*

US/0146-082X
**AMERICAN MCD. PACIFIC STATES EDITION.** Title Change. (AMERICAN MCD : AMERICAN MOTOR CARRIER DIRECTORY.). **Added/Corp** American Trucking Associations. American Trucking Associations. ATA American Motor Carrier Directory. **VFOAT** American Motor Carrier Directory; ATA American Motor Carrier Directory. **VAT** American Motor Carrier Directory. Pacific States Edition; American Trucking Associations American Motor Carrier Directory. (19??)-(19??). Directory. English. an. K III Press Inc., 424 West 33rd Street, New York NY 10001. **Tel** (212)714-3100, (800)221-5488. *Absorbed by American Motor Carrier Directory.*

US/0003-0066
**AMERICAN MOTOR CARRIER.** (19??)-. Periodical. English. bm. American Motor Carrier, 473 Hemlock Drive, Marietta GA 30064. **Tel** (404)427-6362. **ED** W.H. Hooker. Ad Acc. **Circ:** 28,000 (ctrl).
**Desc:** Activities of trucking companies and individual truckers and official information from state public service commissions and from the Interstate Commerce Commission.

US/0897-0807
**AMERICAN MOTOR CARRIER DIRECTORY (NORTH AMERICAN EDITION).** (AMERICAN MOTOR CARRIER DIRECTORY : MCD.). [Am. motor carr. dir.]. **VFOAT** MCD. (19??)-. Periodical. English. sa. $315.00 US & Mexico; $413.00 other. K III Press Inc., 424 West 33rd Street, New York NY 10001. **Tel** (212)714-3100, (800)221-5488. **DD** 338. *Continues American MCD, 0569-6356.*

●US/1072-4893
**AMERICAN RIDER.** (1993)-. English. qt. $9.98. TL Enterprises, 29901 Agoura Road, Agoura CA 91301. **Tel** (800)234-3450, (805)389-0300. **ED** Buzz Buzzelli.
**Desc:** Focuses on Harley-Davidson motorcycles and includes articles, road-test results, and interviews.

BE
**ANALYSIS AND FORECASTS.** **VFOAT** Europa Transport. Observation of Transport Markets. 1st-. English. an. Directorate-General for Transport,

●US/1072-

Transportation

# Transportation

Commission of the European Communities, 200 rue de la Loi, 1049 Brussels Belgium. **LC** HE199.E87; A52. **DD** 380.5/24/094.

CN/0711-9453
**ANALYSIS OF BICYCLE/MOTOR VEHICLE COLLISIONS REPORTED IN MANITOBA, JANUARY 1,-DECEMBER 31 ..., AN.** [Anal. bicycle/mot. veh. collis. rep. Manit.]. English. Free. Manitoba Department of Highways and Transportation, Motor Vehicle Branch, 1075 Portage Avenue, Winnipeg Manitoba R3G 0S1 Canada. **LC** HE5614.5.C2; M35A. **DD** 388.3/14. **Circ:** 300.
**Desc:** Statistical breakdown of reported accidents in Manitoba involving collisions between bicycles and motor vehicles.

US
**ANALYSIS OF MOTOR CARRIER ACCIDENTS INVOLVING VEHICLE DEFECTS OR MECHANICAL FAILURE.** English. an. US Department of Transportation - Federal Highway Administration, 400 Seventh Street Southwest, Washington DC 20590. **Tel** (202)366-0660. **LC** WMLC L 83/7074. **Continues** Analysis of Motor Carrier Accidents Involving Mechanical Defects.

FR
**ANNALES STATISTIQUES DE TRANSPORT / CONFERENCE EUROPEENNE DES MINISTRES DES TRANSPORTS. Added/Corp** European Conference of Ministers of Transports. **VFOAT** Statistical Trends in Transport. (1983)-. English (French). an. $38.00. OECD Publications and Information Center, 2 rue Andre-Pascal, 75775 Paris Cedex 16 France. **Tel** 011 33 1 45248167, US:(202)785-6323, FAX 011 33 1 45248500 OR 45248176, telex 620 160 OCDE. **(Subscription address:** OECD Publications Center, 2001 L Street, Suite 700, Washington DC 20036.**) LC** HE242.A15; A56. **DD** 380.5/094. **Continues in part** Annales Statistiques de Transport. Evolution des Investissements, des Infrastructures, des Materiels, et des Trafics.

CN/0701-1636
**ANNUAIRE - ASSOCIATION DES ROUTES ET TRANSPORTS DU CANADA. Title Change.** (ANNUAIRE - ASSOCIATION DES ROUTES ET TRANSPORTS DU CANADA. DIRECTORY - ROADS AND TRANSPORTATION ASSOCIATION OF CANADA.). [Annu. - Assoc. routes transp. Can.]. **Main/Corp** Roads and Transportation Association of Canada. **VFOAT** Directory - Roads and Transportation Association of Canada. (1976)-(19??). Directory. English (French). an. Roads & Transportation Association of Canada, 1765 St Laurent Boulevard, Ottawa Ontario K1G 3V4 Canada. **Tel** (613)521-4052. **ED** Gilbert C Morier. **DD** 388.1/06/271. **Circ:** 550 (ctrl). **Continues** Roads and Transportation Association of Canada. Membership Directory, 0382-4381. **Continued by** Directory, 0828-2021.
**Desc:** Directory of RTAC members; also contains general information on the Association.

US/0066-3859
**ANNUAL BULLETIN OF TRANSPORT STATISTICS FOR EUROPE. BULLETIN ANNUEL DE STATISTIQUES DE TRANSPORTS POUR L'EUROPE. EZHEGODNYI BIULLETEN' EVROPEISKOI STATISTIKI TRANSPORTA. Main/Corp** United Nations. Economic Commission for Europe. **Added/Corp** United Nations. Economic Commission for Europe. Bulletin Annuel de Statistiques de Transports pour l'Europe. United Nations. Economic Commission for Europe. Ezhegodnyi Biulleten' Evropeiskoi Statistiki Transporta. United Nations. Economic Commission for Europe. Bulletin annuel de Statistiques de Transports Europeens. **VFOAT** Bulletin Annuel de Statistiques de Transports pour l'Europe; Ezhegodnyi Biulleten' Evropeiskoi Statistiki Transporta; Bulletin Annuel de Statistiques de Transports Europeens. (1954)-. Government Publication. English. an. $60.00. United Nations Publications, 2 United Nations Plaza, Room DC 2 0853, Department 007C, New York NY 10017. **Tel** (212)963-8303, (800)253-9646. **CODEN** ABTSEQ. **Continues** Annual bulletin of Transport Statistics for Europe. Bulletin de Statistiques de Transports Europeens.
**Desc:** Statistics and brief studies on transport plus tables on energy consumption for transport are included.

CN/0705-677X
**ANNUAL CONFERENCE PROCEEDINGS - INSTITUTE OF TRANSPORTATION ENGINEERS, CANADA. Main/Corp** Institute of Transportation Engineers. District 7, Canada. 1976-. Proceedings. English. an. Institute of Transportation Engineers District 7 Canada, PO Box 96 Station K, Toronto Ontario M4P 2G1 Canada. **DD** 388.3/1.

US
**ANNUAL FINANCIAL REPORT FOR THE FISCAL YEAR ENDING AUGUST 31 ... - TEXAS. STATE DEPT. OF HIGHWAYS AND PUBLIC TRANSPORTATION. Main/Corp** Texas. State Dept. of Highways and Public Transportation. English. an. State Department of Highways and Public Transportation / Texas, Austin TX 78701. **Tel** (512)483-3689. **LC** HE28.T4; S7A. **DD** 353.97640072/32.

US
**ANNUAL FINANCIAL REPORT, STATE OWNED TOLL BRIDGES. Main/Corp** California. Dept. of Transportation. (19??)-. English. an. California Transportation Commission, 1120 North Street, PO Box 1139, Sacramento CA 95805. **Tel** (916)445-1690. **LC** HE376.A2; C33a. **DD** 388.1/14.

CN/0316-7933
**ANNUAL MEETING. PROCEEDINGS. CANADIAN URBAN TRANSIT ASSOCIATION.** (PROCEEDINGS - CANADIAN URBAN TRANSIT ASSOCIATION, MEETING.). **Main/Corp** Canadian Urban Transit Association. Meeting. 68th (1972/1973)-. Proceedings. English. an. 20.00Can$ (latest edition). Canadian Urban Transit Association, 55 York Street, Suite 901, Toronto Ontario M5J 1R7 Canada. **Tel** (416)365-9800, FAX (416)365-1295. **LC** HE4501; .C36a. **DD** 388.4/06/271. **Continues in part** Canadian Transit Association. Meeting. Proceedings, 0316-7941.

US
**ANNUAL PROGRESS REPORT - MICHIGAN DEPARTMENT OF TRANSPORTATION. Main/Corp** Michigan. Dept. of Transportation. 27th- 1977-. English. an. Department of Transportation / Michigan, Transportation Building, 425 West Ottawa, Box 30050, Lansing MI 48909. **LC** HE356.M5; M45A. **DD** 388.1/09774. **Continues** Annual Progress Report - Michigan Department of State Highways and Transportation.

CN/0836-1509
**ANNUAL REPORT - ALBERTA TRANSPORTATION AND UTILITIES.** (ANNUAL REPORT.). [Annu. rep. - Alta. Transp. Util.]. **Main/Corp** Alberta. Alberta Transportation and Utilities. (1986/87)-. English. Alberta Transportation, Twin Atria Building, 4999-98 Avenue, Edmonton Alberta T6B 2X3 Canada. **DD** 354.71230087. **Formed by the union of** Annual Report / Alberta. Alberta Transportation, 0702-7702 **and** Annual Report / Alberta Utilities, 0839-573X.

AT/0313-6833
**ANNUAL REPORT - AUSTRALIAN ROAD RESEARCH BOARD.** [Annu. rep. - Aust. Road Res. Board]. (1976)-. Periodical. English. an. Price varies. Australian Road Research Board, PO Box 156, Nunawading VIC 3131 Australia. **Tel** 011 61 3 8811555, FAX 011 61 3 8878104, telex AA 33113. **DD** 625.707294.
**Ind/Abst** AESIS Q.

CN/0824-8265
**ANNUAL REPORT / CANADIAN NATIONAL.** [Annu. rep. - Can. Natl.]. **Main/Corp** Canadian National. 1979-. English. an. Free. Corporate Communications Canadian National, PO Box 8100, Montreal Quebec H3C 3N4 Canada. **Tel** (514)877-4758. **LC** HE2801; .C34A. **DD** 385/.065/71. **Circ:** 40,000 (ctrl). **Continues** Canadian National Railways. Annual Report, 0225-1868.
**Desc:** Covers financial reviews and outlook for this integrated transport and communications company, operating throughout Canada and with international links.

AT/1032-1896
**ANNUAL REPORT / DEPARTMENT OF TRANSPORT AND COMMUNICATIONS. Main/Corp** Australia. Dept. of Transport and Communications. **Added/Corp** Australian Government Publishing Service. (1987/1988)-. Corporate Report. English. an. Department of Transport and Communications, GPO Box 594, Canberra Australian Capital Territory 2601 Australia. **Tel** (062)687111, FAX (062)572505, telex 62018. **LC** HE289.A15; A95a. **DD** 354.940087/5/006. Index available. **Circ:** 1,500 (ctrl). **Formed by the union of** Annual Report / Australia. Dept. of Aviation, 0729-7424 **and** Annual Report / Australia. Dept. of Transport, 0812-5384.

US
**ANNUAL REPORT - DEPT. OF TRANSPORTATION AND PUBLIC FACILITIES. Main/Corp** Alaska. Dept. of Transportation and Public Facilities. 1977-. English. an. **LC** HE28.A4; D46A. **DD** 353.9/798/087505. **Formed by the union of** Alaska. Dept. of Highways. Annual Report **and** Alaska. Dept. of Public Works. Annual Report.

US
**ANNUAL REPORT / GEORGIA DEPARTMENT OF TRANSPORTATION. Main/Corp** Georgia. Dept. of Transportation. Fiscal Year (1983)-. English. an. Free. Georgia Dept of Transportation, 2 Capitol Square, Public Affairs Office 114, Atlanta GA 30334. **LC** HE213.G4; G42a. **DD** 353.97580087/5/006. **Continues** Georgia. Dept. of Transportation. Georgia Department of Transportation Annual Report, FY ... .

US/0082-710X
**ANNUAL REPORT - METROPOLITAN TRANSIT COMMISSION. Main/Corp** Metropolitan Transit Commission. (1975)-. English. an. Metropolitan Transit Commission, 330 Metro Square, St Paul MN 55101. **LC** HE310.T85; T85a. **DD** 352/.91/8409776579. **Continues** Metropolitan Transit Commission. Annual Report (1973).

US
**ANNUAL REPORT, MICHIGAN TRANSPORTATION FUND. Main/Corp** Michigan. State Transportation Commission. Fiscal year ending Sept. 30, 1979-. English. an. Michigan Department of Transportation, Transportation Commission, Transportation Building, 425 West Ottawa, PO Box 30050, Lansing MI 48909. **LC** HE356.M5; A35. **DD** 353.97740086/42/06. **Continues** Michigan. State Transportation Commission. Annual Report, Motor Vehicle Highway Fund.

US
**ANNUAL REPORT - MILWAUKEE COUNTY TRANSIT BOARD. Main/Corp** Milwaukee County Transit Board. No. 1, (1975)-. Periodical. English. Milwaukee County Transit Board, Milwaukee WI 53233.

US/0363-3330
**ANNUAL REPORT OF THE COMMISSIONER OF TRANSPORTATION TO THE GOVERNOR.** (ANNUAL REPORT OF THE COMMISSIONER OF TRANSPORTATION TO THE GOVERNOR - TENNESSEE.). **Main/Corp** Tennessee. Dept. of Transportation. **VFOAT** Annual Report to the Governor by the Commissioner. English. an. Department of Transportation / Tennessee, Andrew Jackson State Office Building, Nashville TN 37219. **LC** HE28.T2; D46A. **DD** 353.9/768/0087505. **Absorbed** Tennessee. Bureau of Mass Transit. Annual Report of the Bureau of Area Mass Transit of the Tennessee Department of Transportation.

AT
**ANNUAL REPORT OF THE DEPARTMENT OF TRANSPORT FOR THE YEAR ENDED JUNE 30 ... . Main/Corp** Western Australia. Dept. of Transport. 1st (1986)-. English. an. Department of Transport / Western Australia, 136-138 Stirling Highway, Nedlands WA 6009 Australia. **Tel** FAX 011 61 3 3865119. **LC** HE289.Z7; W485a. **DD** 354.9410087/5/006.

CN/0701-9971
**ANNUAL REPORT OF THE ONTARIO HIGHWAY TRANSPORT BOARD.** [Annu. rep. Ont. Hwy. Transp. Board]. **Main/Corp** Ontario. Highway Transport Board. 1971-. English. an. **LC** HE5635.O5; A3. **DD** 354/.713/00878305. **Continues in part** Ontario. Dept. of Transport. Annual Report.

US/0090-6247
**ANNUAL REPORT - OFFICE OF DIRECTOR. OREGON DEPARTMENT OF TRANSPORTATION.** (ANNUAL REPORT.). **Main/Corp** Oregon. Dept. of Transportation. Office of Director. English. an. Oregon Department of Transportation, Office of Director, State Highway Building, Salem OR 97310. **LC** HE28.O7; A32. **DD** 353.9/795/0087.

US
**ANNUAL REPORT ON HAZARDOUS MATERIALS TRANSPORTATION : HAZARDOUS MATERIALS TRANSPORTATION ACT (TITLE I, PUBLIC LAW 93-633). See** Law.

CN/0843-4042
**ANNUAL REPORT / ONTARIO, MINISTRY OF TRANSPORTATION.** [Annu. rep. - Ont., Minist. Transp.]. **Main/Corp** Ontario. Ministry of Transportation. **VFOAT** Rapport Annuel. **VAT** Rapport Annuel - Ontario. Ministere des Transports. (1988)-. English (French). an. M T O Publications, 880 Bay Street, Toronto, Ontario. M7A 1N8 Canada. **LC** HE215.Z7; O56a. **DD** 354.7130087/5/006. **Continued in part by** Ontario. Ministry of Transportation Annual Report, 0843-4042.

## Transportation

SA
**ANNUAL REPORT / THE SOUTH AFRICAN TRANSPORT SERVICES.** **Main/Corp** South African Transport Services. (1980/81)-. English (Afrikaans). an. Office of the General Manager, South African Transport Services, Johannesburg South Africa. **Tel** 773 5549. **(Subscription address:** The Manager, Public Relations Transnet, PO Box 72501, Parkview 2122 South Africa) **ED** Mrs. Alrika Hefers. **LC** HE3459.S7; S6. **DD** 354.680087/5/006. Index available. ctrl circ. **Continues** South African Railways and Harbours. Annual Report.
 **Desc:** Business operations of Transnet LTD (formerly SATs) and financial statements/reports.

US
**ANNUAL REPORT TO CALIFORNIA LEGISLATURE / CALIFORNIA TRANSPORTATION COMMISSION.** **Main/Corp** California Transportation Commission. 1st (1984)-. English. an. California Transportation Commission, 1120 North Street, PO Box 1139, Sacramento CA 95805. **Tel** (916)445-1690. **ED** Robert Remen. **Circ:** 900.
 **Desc:** Summary of policies of California transportation commission, major upcoming issues for consideration by California legislature, and monitoring of highway program's implementation.

US/0161-0759
**ANNUAL REPORT TO CONGRESS ON THE IMPLEMENTATION OF PUBLIC LAW 94-413, THE ELECTRIC & HYBRID VEHICLE RESEARCH, DEVELOPMENT & DEMONSTRATION ACT OF 1976.** **Main/Corp** United States. Office of Electric and Hybrid Vehicle Systems. 1st- 1977-. English. an. Iowa Department of Corrections, 523 East 12th Street, Capitol Annex, Des Moines IA 50319. **Tel** (515)281-4811, FAX (515)281-7345. **LC** TL220; .U55A. **DD** 629.22/93/05.

US
**ANNUAL REPORT TO DIRECTOR ... / RESEARCH SECTION, DIVISION OF PLANNING AND PROGRAMMING, DEPT. OF TRANSPORTATION (ALASKA).** **Main/Corp** Alaska. Dept. of Transportation and Public Facilities. Research Section. English. an. **LC** TA1024.A4; A44A. **DD** 629.04/0720798.

US
**ANNUAL REPORT / U.S. DEPARTMENT OF TRANSPORTATION.** **Main/Corp** United States. Dept. of Transportation. **VFOAT** U.S. Department of Transportation Annual Report. (1967)-. Government Publication. English. an. Free. Superintendent of Documents, US Government Printing Office, Washington DC 20402. **Tel** (202)275-3328, FAX (202)786-2377. **LC** HE206.3; .A3. **DD** 353.008/75. **Absorbed** United States. Federal Aviation Agency. Annual Report to the President and the Congress.

US/0360-0246
**ANNUAL REPORT - WEST VIRGINIA GOVERNOR'S HIGHWAY SAFETY ADMINISTRATION.** See Public Administration.

CN/0845-1109
**... ANNUAL REVIEW OF THE NATIONAL TRANSPORTATION AGENCY OF CANADA, THE.** [Annu. rev. Natl. Transp. Agency Can.]. **VFOAT** Annual Review; Examen Annuel de l'Office National des Transports du Canada; NTA Annual Review. **VAT** Annual Review - National Transportation Agency of Canada Examen Annuel - Office National des Transports du Canada. 1st (1988)-. English (French). an. **LC** HE215.A15; A56. **DD** 354.710087/5/005.

US
**ANNUAL SUMMARY OF SPEED LIMIT 55 MONITORING PROGRAM / MINNESOTA, DEPARTMENT OF TRANSPORTATION.** **Main/Corp** Minnesota. Dept. of Transportation. English. an. Minnesota Department of Transportation, John Ireland Boulevard/Room 810, St Paul MN 55155. **LC** HE5620.S6; M56A. **DD** 388.3/144/09766.

SP
**ANO DEL TRANSPORTE, EL.** No. 1- 1975/76-. Spanish. 1000. Edisport S L, Isaac Peral 12, Madrid 15 Spain. **LC** HE8; .A49.

FR/0395-8582
**ANTENNE MARSEILLE, L'.** (1947)-. Periodical. French. da. 1956.00F France; 2530.77 other. Antenne, 17 rue Venture, PO Box 1811, 13221 Marseille Cedex 1, France. **Tel** (33)91 33 25 81, FAX (33)91 55 58 97, telex 400865F. **UDC** 330. **Ad Acc. Circ:** 10,000. **Continues** L'Antenne de Marseille, 1153-8473.

CL
**ANUARIO ESTADISTICO DE TRANSPORTE TERRESTRE.** **Added/Corp** Chile. Ministerio de Transportes y Telecomunicaciones. Spanish. **LC** HE234.A15; A58. **Continues** Anuario Estadistico de Transporte.

US
**APPLICATION AND INSTRUCTIONS FOR VEHICLE PRORATION.** **Main/Corp** Illinois. Office of Secretary of State. Commercial and Farm Truck Division. (19??)-. English. an. free. Office of the Secretary of State, Commercial and Farm Truck Division, Centennial Building/Room 300, Springfield IL 62756. **Tel** (217)782-4815, (217)782-4816. **Circ:** 13,000.
 **Desc:** Describes how to participate in the International Registration plan in the state of Illinois. Basically a reference manual for prorate applications.

UK
**ARABIAN TRANSPORT.** **Title Change.** English. an. Beacon Publishing, Weston Favell, Northampton NN3 4NW England. **LC** HE268.6.A15; A73. **DD** 380.5/025/53. **Continues** Arabian Transport Directory. **Continued by** Arabian Transport Guide.

US/0195-5632
**ARMY MOTORS.** See Military and Defense.

AT/0158-071X
**ARRB RESEARCH REPORT ARR.** **Title Change.** [ARRB res. rep. ARR]. **Main/Corp** Australian Road Research Board. **VAT** Australian Road Research Board Research Report ARR. Academic Scholarly Publication. English. ir. Australian Road Research Board, PO Box 156, Nunawading VIC 3131 Australia. **Tel** 011 61 3 8811555, FAX 011 61 3 8878104, telex AA 33113. **CODEN** ARBODZ. **Circ:** 500. available on microfiche. Documents available from CASDDS. **Continues** ARR Report. **Continued by** Research Report ARR.
 **Desc:** Covers technical reports describing research performed at the Australian Road Research Board.
 **Ind/Abst** Chem. Abstr.

DK
**ARSBERETNING.** **Main/Corp** Hovedstadsomradets Trafikselskab (Hovedstadsradet). Danish (summaries and/or abstracts in English). an. **LC** HE4859.C6; H68. **Continues in part** Beretning og Regnskab Hovedstadsomradets Trafikselskab.

CH/1021-3740
**ASIAN AIR TRANSPORT.** [Asian air transp.]. (1992)-. Periodical. English. mo (12 issues). $65.00. Tseng Brothers Information Group, 4F 5 551 Kuang Fu S Road, Taipei, Taiwan. **Tel** 011 886 2 7251904. **UDC** 388.9.

CN/0842-9596
**ATLANTIC TRANSPORTATION JOURNAL.** [Atl. transp. j.]. Vol. 1, No. 1 (Sept. 1988)-. Periodical. English. Four times a year. 18.00Can$ Canada; 24.00Can$ others. Bilby Holdings Ltd., 6029 Cunard Street, Halifax Nova Scotia B3K 1E5 Canada. **Tel** (920)420-0437, FAX (920)423-8212. **DD** 380.5/09715.

CN/0830-1808
**ATLANTIC TRUCKING.** [Atl. truck.]. **Added/Corp** Atlantic Provinces Trucking Association. Vol. 1, No. 1 (Spring 1986)-. Periodical. English. Four times a year (Mar., June, Sept., Dec.). 18.00Can$. Atlantic Provinces Trucking Association, 1 Trites Rd, Exec 1 Building Suite 14, Riverview NB E1B 2V5 Canada. **Tel** (506)387-4413, FAX (506)387-7424. **ED** Gregory Kero. **DD** 388.3/24/09715. **Ad Acc. Circ:** 1,200.
 **Desc:** News and information of Canada's views of the transportation industry.

AT
**ATN: AUSTRALIAN TRANSPORT NEWS.** See Business-Commerce.

CN/0829-6154
**ATV CANADA.** See Engineering.

AT
**AUSTRALASIAN BUS AND COACH.** English. mo (except January). 35.00Aus$ Australia; 65.00Aus$ other. Publishing Services Pty Ltd, 21 Baxter Street, Fortitude Valley, Brisbane Queensland 4006 Australia. **Tel** (617)854-1286, FAX (617)252-4579. **ED** Andrew Stewart. **Bk Rev**. **Ad Acc**. **Pr Rev. Circ:** 3,500 (ctrl).
 **Desc:** A business/management publication for the owners of bus and coach operations and vehicle equipment manufacturers.

AT/0005-0385
**AUSTRALIAN TRANSPORT.** **Added/Corp** Institute of Transport. Institute of Transport. Australian Journal. (1975)-. Periodical. English. Eleven times a year (monthly Feb. through Dec.). 80.00Aus$ Australia; Box Q398, Queen Victoria Boulevard, Sydney New South Wales, 2000 Australia. **Tel** 011 61 2 2615451, telex 170857. **ED** A Dallow (editor's address: PO Box 20, Chelsea Victoria 3196 Australia; editor's phone: 61 3 5870888). **Ad Acc, Adv Mgr:** J Balodis, **Tel** 61 3 5870888. **Circ:** 3,000.

**Desc:** Circulated to senior executives in the Australian transport industry and covers all information on shipping, airlines and highway transportation.
 **Ind/Abst** APAIS, Aust. Public Aff. Inf. Ser. (1963-).

US/1042-7414
**AUTO SERVICE TODAY.** **Title Change.** [Auto serv. today]. (Dec. 1988)-?. Periodical. English. bw. ATCOM Inc., 2315 Broadway, New York NY 10024-4397. **Tel** (800)521-7004, (212)873-5900, FAX (212)799-1728. **DD** 629. **Continued by** Auto Service Insider, 1053-4318.
 **Desc:** Newsletter for professionals involved in all aspects of car and truck service, repair and reconditioning.

IT/1120-4133
**AUTOTRASPORTO DI MERCI, L'.** [Autotrasp. merci]. (1978)-. Periodical. Italian. sm (24 issues per year). L312000. Egaf Edizioni SAS, Via F Guarini 2, 47100 Forli Italy. **Tel** 011 39 543 782278, FAX 011 39 543 782255. **UDC** 656.13. Index available. cum. index. **Circ:** 2,000. available on diskette.
 **Desc:** Contains information on freight transportation by road.

FR
**AUXILIAIRES DES TRANSPORTS TERRESTRES.** **Title Change. Main/Corp** France. Departement des Statistiques des Transports. French. an. Department des Statistiques des Transport, 21 rue Mathurin Regnier, 75732 Paris Cedex 15 France. **LC** HE199.F8; F72B. **DD** 380.5/24/0944. **Continued by** Auxiliaires des Transports Terrestres et Fluviaux.

US/1048-9819
**BADGER TRUCKER.** [Badger truck.]. (1980)-. Periodical. English. mo. Allied Publication Inc, 7355 North Woodland Drive, PO Box 603, Indianapolis IN 46206. **DD** 388. **Continues** Badger Truck Exchange.

US/0195-9727
**BAGNALL'S VPO INDUSTRY NEWS.** **VFOAT** VPO Industry News; VPO; Van Pickup & Off-Road Industry News. **VAT** Van Pickup and Off Road Industry News. Periodical. English. mo. $10.00 US; $15.00 other. Bagnall Brothers Publishing Company, 4262 Campus Drive, Suite A, Newport Beach CA 92660.

SP/0304-8993
**BALANCE PREVENTIVO - SOCIEDAD PRIVADA MUNICIPAL TRANSPORTES DE BARCELONA.** **Main/Corp** Sociedad Privada Municipal Transportes de Barcelona. Spanish. Sociedad Privada Municipal Transportes de Barcelona, Luchana 99, Barcelona 5 Spain. **LC** HE4899.B4; S642.

US/0883-1777
**BARRETT TRANSPORTATION NEWSLETTER.** [Barrett transp. newsl.]. (19??)-. Periodical. English. mo. $175.00. Barrett Transportation Consultants, 12166 Holly Knoll Circle, Great Falls VA 22066. **Tel** (703)444-4611. **ED** Colin Bonett. **DD** 380.

DK
**BERETNING OG REGNSKAB - KBENHAVNS SPORVEJE.** **Main/Corp** Kbenhavns Sporveje. Danish (summaries and/or abstracts in English). **LC** HE4859.C7; K6324A. **Continues** Arsberetning / Kbenhavns Sporve.

BE
**BIBLIO EXPRESS.** (19??)-. French (English and German). Twelve times a year. Free to UITP members; 3000F Europe, 3200F others (non-members). International Union of Public Transport, Avenue de l'Uruguay 19, B 1050 Brussels Belgium. **Tel** 011 32 2 6733325, FAX 011 32 2 6607072, telex (046)63916 UITP B. **Continues** Biblio Index UITP, 0041-5146.

US
**BIENNIAL REPORT / LEGISLATIVE ADVISORY COMMITTEE TO THE REGIONAL TRANSPORTATION AUTHORITY.** **Main/Corp** Illinois. General Assembly. Legislative Advisory Committee to the Regional Transportation Authority. June 1984-. English. be. Illinois Legislative Advisory Committee to the Regional Transportation Authority, 2049 Stratton Building, Springfield IL 62706. **LC** HE4487.I4; I43A. **DD** 388.4/09773.

US
**BIENNIAL REPORT - NORTH CAROLINA DEPARTMENT OF TRANSPORTATION.** **Main/Corp** North Carolina. Dept. of Transportation. English. be. North Carolina Department of Transportation, PO Box 25201, Raleigh NC 27611. **LC** HE213.N8; N67A. **DD** 353.97560087/5/005.

US/0147-8362
**BIENNIAL REPORT - STATE DEPARTMENT OF HIGHWAYS AND PUBLIC TRANSPORTATION.** (BIENNIAL REPORT - STATE DEPARTMENT OF HIGHWAYS AND PUBLIC TRANSPORTATION, FINANCE DIVISION.). **Main/Corp** Texas. State Dept. of Highways and Public

# Transportation

Transportation. Finance Division. 30th- 1974/76-. Periodical. English. be. Texas State Department of Highway/Public Transportation, Austin TX 78701. **LC** HE356.T4; T33A. **DD** 353.9/764/008781. *Continues Biennial Report - State Highway Department of Texas, 0147-8370.*

US
**BIENNIAL REPORT - STATE OF MINNESOTA DEPARTMENT OF PUBLIC SERVICE.** See Public Administration.

US
**BIENNIAL STATEWIDE TRANSPORTATION NEEDS REPORT TO THE ARIZONA LEGISLATURE. Main/Corp** Arizona. Dept. of Transportation. 1st- 1976-. English. be. Arizona Department of Transportation, 205 South 17th Avenue, 614 East, Phoenix AZ 85007. **Tel** (602)255-7724. **LC** HE356.A7; A7A. **DD** 388.1/09791. *Supersedes* Arizona. Highway Dept. Planning Survey Division. Inventory of Highway Needs (Excluding Interstate System); Arizona. Dept. of Transportation. Status of Road Systems Mileages.

CN/1180-1204
**BILAN SAINT-LAURENT.** [Bilan Saint-Laurent]. **Added/Corp** Centre Saint-Laurent. (May 1990)-. Periodical. French. **DD** 386/.5/0971405.

GW
**BINNENSCHIFFAHRT UND BUNDESWASSERSTRASSEN JAHRESBERICHT.** (1988)-. German. an. Bundesminister fur Verkehr, Abteilung Binnenschiffahrt und Wasserstrassen, Postfach 20 01 00, Robert-Schuman-Platz 1, W-5300 Bonn 2 Germany. **LC** HE669; .A2826. *Continues Bundeswasserstrassen und Schiffahrt, 0172-8377.*

GW/0939-1916
**BINNENSCHIFFAHRT : ZEITSCHRIFT FEUR BINNENSCHIFFAHRT UND WASSERSTRASSEN. Added/Corp** Bundesverband der Deutschen Binnenschiffahrt. Verein feur Binnenschiffahrt und Wasserstrassen. **VFOAT** Binnen Schiffahrt; Binnenschiffahrt-ZfB. No. 1/2 (Jan. 18, 1991)-. Periodical. German. sm. **LC** HE669; .A128. *Formed by the union of BW and Binnenschiffahrts-Nachrichten.*

BL
**BOLETIM DA PROCURADORIA GERAL.** See Law.

FR
**BOTTIN DU TRANSPORT.** 1975-. French. Societe Didot-Bottin, 28 rue du Docteur-Finlay, 75738 Cedex 15 Paris France. **LC** HE199.F8; B68.

US
**BRIDGE AND FERRY DIRECTORY : INCLUDING TOLL BRIDGES, FERRIES, DOMESTIC STEAMSHIP LINES AND AUTO/PASSENGER LAND CARRIERS. Added/Corp** American Automobile Association. Highway Information Services. (1986)-. English. an. $12.50. American Automobile Association, 1000 AAA Drive, Heathrow FL 32746. **Tel** (407)444-7000. **LC** IN PROCESS. *Continues Directory of Toll Bridges, Ferries, Domestic Steamship Lines and Auto/Passenger Land Carriers, 0149-757X.*

●CN/1189-4717
**BRITISH COLUMBIA SCHOOL BUS.** [B.C. sch. bus.]. **Added/Corp** Association of School Transportation Supervisors of B.C. (1992)-. English. Free to members. Naylor Communications Ltd, 100 Sutherland Avenue, Winnipeg Manitoba R2W 3C7 Canada. **Tel** (204)947-0222, FAX (604)985-7399. **DD** 371.8.

US/0147-7382
**BUDGET - NATIONAL TRANSPORTATION SAFETY BOARD. Main/Corp** United States. National Transportation Safety Board. English. an. US National Transportation Safety Board, 800 Independence Avenue SW, Washington DC 29594. **LC** HE17; .N37A. **DD** 353.0087/5/00289. *Continues United States. National Transportation Safety Board. Budget Estimates.*

US
**BULLETIN : A VDOT MONTHLY NEWSPAPER. Main/Corp** Virginia. Dept. of Transportation. Vol. 53, No. 13 (Feb. 1987)-. Bulletin. English. mo. Virginia Department of Transportation, 1401 East Broad Street, Richmond VA 23219. **Tel** (804)786-4243, FAX (804)786-6250. **ED** Roxanne S Llewellyn. **LC** TE24.V8; V5. **DD** 353.97550086/4. **Circ:** 17,000 (ctrl). *Continues Bulletin - Virginia Department of Highways and Transportation, 0360-9413.*

FR/1157-1055
**BULLETIN DES TRANSPORTS ET DE LA LOGISTIQUE PARIS.** (BULLETIN DES TRANSPORTS ET DE LA LOGISTIQUE.). (1991)-. Bulletin. French. Forty-seven times a year. 898.23F France; 1010.00F others. Editions Lamy SA, 187-189 Quai de Valmy, 75490 Paris Cedex 10 France. **Tel** 011 33 1 44721200, 011 33 1 44721212, FAX 011 33 1 44721395. **UDC** 656(44). *Continues Bulletin des Transports, 0007-4519.*

CN/1181-7941
**BULLETIN D'INFORMATION DE L'APCRIQ. Title Change.** (BULLETIN D'INFORMATION DE L'APCRIQ : L'ORGANE OFFICIEL DE L'ASSOCIATION DES PROPRIETAIRES DE CAMIONS REMORQUES INDEPENDANTS DU QUEBEC.). [Bull. inf. APCRIQ]. **Added/Corp** Association des Proprietaires de Camions Remorques Independants du Quebec. **VFOAT** Bulletin d'Information de l'Association des Proprietaires de Camions Remorques Independants du Quebec. Vol. 1, No 1 (Nov./Dec. 1990)-Vol. 2, No 3 (July./Aug. 1992). Bulletin. French. bm. Association des Proprietaires de Camions Remorques Independants du Quebec, Bureau 104, 2700 Thimens, St-Laurent, Quebec H4R 1T4 Canada. **DD** 388.3. *Continued by Camionneurs/Truckers Magazine, 1192-3857.*

US/0028-5838
**BULLETIN - NEW JERSEY MOTOR TRUCK ASSOCIATION. Main/Corp** New Jersey Motor Truck Association. **VFOAT** NJMTA Bulletin. (1914)-. Bulletin. English. mo. $25.00. New Jersey Motor Truck Association, c/o Joyce Clark, 160 Tices Lane, East Brunswick NJ 08816. **Tel** (201)254-5000. **ED** Robert J. Behre. **Ad Acc. Circ:** 2,800 (ctrl).
**Desc:** Publishes news and feature stories that relate to the trucking industry, particularly in New Jersey.

FR/0427-2129
**BULLETIN OFFICIEL DES DOUANES.** [Bull. off. douanes]. (1954)-. Periodical. French. da (312 issues). 1072.48F France; 1645.00F other. Imprimerie Nationale / France, BP 514, 59505 Douai Cedex France. **Tel** 011 33 27 937090. **UDC** 336.41.

UK
**BUS AND COACH STATISTICS, GREAT BRITAIN.** English. Department of Transport / England, 2 Marsham Street, London SW1P 3EB England. **Tel** 011 44 71 2765082. **LC** HE5663; .A13. **DD** 388.3/22/0941021.

FR/0399-2535
**BUS ET CAR.** (1976)-. Periodical. French. Forty-Five times a year. 666.01F France; 780.00F other. Compagnie Gen Developpement, 11 rue Godefroy Cavaignac, 75541 Paris Cedex 11 France. **Tel** 011 33 1 43790630, FAX 011 33 1 43791775, telex 211351. **UDC** 65.

US/0192-8902
**BUS RIDE.** (19??)-. Trade Publication. English. bm (eight no. a year). $20.00. Friendship Publications Inc, PO Box 1472, Spokane WA 99210. **Tel** (509)328-9181, (800)332-2670, FAX (509)325-5396, telex 910250 7640. **ED** William A Luke. **DD** 051. **Bk Rev. Ad Acc. Circ:** 12,700 (ctrl).
**Desc:** Trade journal for the bus industry.
**Ind/Abst** Highw. Res. Abstr.

US/0363-3764
**BUS RIDE: BUS INDUSTRY DIRECTORY. VFOAT** Bus Industry Directory. (1965)-. Directory. English. Nine times a year. $35.00 (surface), $55.00 (air mail) US and Mexico; $40.00 (surface), $62.00 (air mail) Canada; $45.00 (surface), $75.00 (air mail) other. Friendship Publications Inc, PO Box 1472, Spokane WA 99210. **Tel** (509)328-9181, (800)332-2670, FAX (509)325-5396, telex 910250 7640. **ED** William A Luke. **LC** HE5623.A45; B86. **DD** 388.3/22/02573. **Bk Rev. Ad Acc. Circ:** 2,000 (ctrl).
**Desc:** Bus industry directory.

GW
**BUS VERKEHR. VFOAT** Busverkehr. Periodical. German. mo. DM4,780 Germany; $36.00 US. Kirschbaum Verlag, Siegfriedstr 28, Postfach 210209, D 53157 Bonn Germany. **LC** HE5669.A6; B86. **DD** 388.3/22/0943. Index available. **Bk Rev. Ad Acc. Circ:** 7,000 (ctrl).

US/0162-9689
**BUS WORLD.** Vol. 1, No. 1 (1978)-. Periodical. English. Four times a year. $14.00 (one year); $26.00 (two years). Stauss Publications, PO Box 39, Woodland Hills CA 91365. **Tel** (818)710-0208. **ED** Ed Stauss. **LC** TL232; .B853. **DD** 388.34/233/05. **Bk Rev**, (Qty: varies). **Ad Acc. Circ:** 5,500 (ctrl).
**Desc:** Enthusiast journal of buses and bus systems. Reports on new and old buses; intercity, transit and school buses.

UK/0007-6392
**BUSES SHEPPERTON.** [BusesShepperton]. (1968)-. Periodical. English. mo. £17.40 UK; £24.00 other. Ian Allan Ltd, Coombelands Lane, Addlestone Weybridge, KT15 1HY England. **Tel** 011 44 932 858511, 855909, FAX 011 44 932 232366, 854750. **ED** Stephen Morris. [CCC]. **Bk Rev. Ad Acc. Continues** Buses Illustrated *and* Passenger Transport Journal.

**Desc:** News and features about the road passenger transport industry in Britain.
**Ind/Abst** Highw. Res. Abstr.

UK
**BUSES YEARBOOK. VFOAT** Buses Year Book. (1989)-. Consumer Publication. English. an. £10.99. Ian Allan Ltd, Coombelands Lane, Addlestone Weybridge, KT15 1HY England. **Tel** 011 44 932 858511, 855909, FAX 011 44 932 232366, 854750. **ED** S. J. Brown. **Ad Acc. Continues** Buses Annual.
**Desc:** Features articles on local passenger transport.

US
**BUYER'S GUIDE REPORTS. TRUCK & VAN PRICES. Title Change. VFOAT** Truck & Van Prices; Truck and Van Prices; New and Used Truck and Van Prices; New Truck & Van Prices; Buyer's Guide Reports. New and Used Truck and Van Prices; Buyer's Guide Reports. Truck and Van Prices; Buyer's Guide Reports. New Truck & Van Prices. Periodical. English. bm. Pace Publications Inc., 1020 North Broadway, Suite 111, Milwaukee WI 53202. **Tel** (414)272-9977, FAX (414)297-9973. **LC** TL230.A1; B89. **DD** 629.223/029673. *Continues Buyer's Guide Reports/Carfacts. New and Used Truck and Van Prices, 0740-1310. Continued by Pace Buyer's Guides. Domestic & Foreign Truck & Van Prices New & Used, 1050-7272.*

US/0732-1236
**CAB FARE.** Vol. 1 (1991)-. Periodical. English. bm. Heanue System, 115 Broad Street, Boston MA 02110.

FR/1150-8809
**CAHIERS SCIENTIFIQUES DU TRANSPORT CAEN, LES.** See Economics.

●CN/1183-7853
**CALGARY & AREA AVIATION BUSINESS DIRECTORY.** [Calg. area aviat. bus. dir.]. **VFOAT** Calgary and Area Aviation Business Directory. (1991/92)-. Directory. English. $7.50 per volume. Business Directories International #107, 5621-11 St. Northeast, Calgary Alta. T2E 6Z7 Canada. **DD** 387.7. *Continues Calgary & Area Airport Business Directory., 0823-8219.*

US/1049-1023
**CALIFORNIA TRUCKER.** (CALIFORNIA TRUCKER : SERVING ARIZONA, CALIFORNIA, NEVADA, AND HAWAII.). [Calif. truck.]. (1979)-. Periodical. English. Twelve times a year. $12.00. Construction Digest Incorporated, PO Box 603, 7355 North Woodland Drive, Indianapolis IN 46206. **Tel** (317)297-5500. **DD** 629. **Ad Acc.**

US/0736-1939
**CAMPING TRAILER & TRAVEL TRAILER TRADE-IN-GUIDE. Title Change.** [Camping trailer travel trailer trade-in-guide]. **Added/Corp** Intertec Publishing Corporation. Technical Publications Division. **VFOAT** Camping Trailer and Travel Trailer Trade-In Guide; Camping and Travel Trailer Trade-In Guide; Camping & Travel Trailer Trade-In Guide. (19??)-(199?). English. an. Intertec Publishing Corporation, 9800 Metcalf, Overland Park KS 66212. **Tel** (913)341-1300. **ED** Tom Fournier. **LC** HD9710.38.A2; C35. **DD** 629.2/26/029473. **Bk Rev. ctrl circ. Merged with** Motor Home & Truck Camper Trade-In Guide **to form** Intertec Recreational Vehicle Trade-In Guide, 1064-3079.
**Desc:** Valuation guide for fold-down camping trailers and travel trailers; includes specifications, prices and trade-in values.

CN/1191-0577
**CANADA IN TRANSIT.** [Can. transit]. (1991)-. English. Free to members. **DD** 388.

CN/0828-2161
**CANADIAN AUTOMOTIVE FLEET.** [Can. automot. fleet.]. Vol. 1, No. 1 (Oct./Nov. 1984)-. Periodical. English. Seven times a year. 30.00Can$ (one year), 35.00Can$ (two years). Bobit Publishing, 2512 Artesia Boulevard, Redondo Beach CA 90278. **Tel** (310)376-8788, (800)334-8152, FAX (213)376-9043. **DD** 388.3/2/068.

US/1187-5356
**CANADIAN AUTOMOTIVE FLEET. FACT BOOK.** (FACT BOOK / AUTOMOTIVE FLEET.). [Can. automot. fleet, Fact book]. Began with 1985 issue, (1985)-. English. $35.00. Bobit Publishing, 2512 Artesia Boulevard, Redondo Beach CA 90278. **Tel** (310)376-8788, (800)334-8152, FAX (213)376-9043. **DD** 388.3/2/068.

CN/0702-8733
**CANADIAN HIGHWAY CARRIERS GUIDE. Ceased. VFOAT** Le Guide des Transporteurs Routiers Canadiens. (1976)-Ceased ?. English (French). an. Southam Information and Technology Group Inc., 1450 Don Mills Road, Don Mills Ontario M3B 2X7 Canada. **Tel** (416)445-6641, (800)668-2374, FAX (416)442-2261. **ED** Rob Robertson. **DD** 388.3/24/02571. **Bk Rev. Ad Acc. Circ:** 3,000. **Supersedes** Highway

*Carriers Guide, 0315-7520.*
**Desc:** A listing of all cities, towns, and villages in Canada with the names of highway carriers serving each.

CN/0710-4405
**CANADIAN RECREATIONAL VEHICLE GUIDE.** (CANADIAN RECREATIONAL VEHICLE GUIDE / GUIDE CANADIEN DU VEHICULE RECREATIF.). [Can. recreat. veh. guide]. **VFOAT** Guide Canadien du Vehicule Recreatif. (1981)-. English (French). ir. $35.00. Canadian Recreational Vehicle Guide, 1208 Beaupre Avenue, Ste Foy Quebec G1W 4C1 Canada. **DD** 381/.45629226/029471.

CN
**CANADIAN TRANSPORTATION LOGISTICS GUIDE.** an. 39.95Can$. Southam Information and Technology Group Inc., 1450 Don Mills Road, Don Mills Ontario M3B 2X7 Canada. **Tel** (416)445-6641, (800)668-2374, FAX (416)442-2261.

CN/0826-1954
**CANALS CANADA.** (CANALS CANADA : NEWSLETTER OF THE CANADIAN CANAL SOCIETY.). [Canals Can.]. **Added/Corp** Canadian Canal Society. Issue No. 1 (Jan. 1983)-. Periodical. English. ir. 10.00Can$. Canadian Canal Society, PO Box 1652, St Catharines Ontario L2R 7K1 Canada. **Tel** (905)682-0253. **DD** 386/.4/06071.

●US
**CAPITAL IMPROVEMENT PROGRAM.** **Main/Corp** Alaska. Dept. of Transportation and Public Facilities. (1987-1993)-. English. Alaska Department of Transportation and Public Facilities, PO Box 7, Juneau AK 99811. **LC** HE213.A4; A56c. **DD** 388/.09798/05. ***Continues*** *Six-Year Capital Improvement Program.*

US/0278-0801
**CARGO FACTS.** (CARGO FACTS. A SERVICE OF AIR CARGO MANAGEMENT GROUP.). **Added/Corp** Air Cargo Management Group (Bellevue, Wash.). (198?)-. Periodical. English. Twelve times a year. $250.00 US & Canada; $270.25 Washington; $295.00 other. Cargo Facts, 1601 Fifth Avenue, Suite 525, Seattle WA 98101. **Tel** (206)587-6537, FAX (206)587-6540. **ED** Steven Swedin. **Ad Acc**, **Adv Mgr:** John Riley, **Tel** (206)587-6538.
**Desc:** Covers development in the air freight and express industry worldwide.

UK/0306-0985
**CARGO SYSTEMS INTERNATIONAL.** [Cargo syst. int.]. **Added/Corp** International Cargo Handling Coordination Association. **VFOAT** Cargo Systems. Vol. 1, (Nov. 1973)-. Periodical. English. Twelve times a year. £220.00 (one year), US & Canada; £65.00 UK, £75.00 Europe, £95.00 others. CS Publications Ltd., Markets Towers 2nd Floor, 1 Nine Elms Lane, London SW8 5NQ England. **Tel** 011 44 71 344 3800. **ED** Clive Woodbridge. **LC** TA1215; .C35. **DD** 380.5/2. **CODEN** CSYIBN. **Bk Rev**. **Ad Acc**. **Circ:** 8,000. Documents available from Article Express International. ***Supersedes*** *ICHCA Monthly Journal.*
**Desc:** Ports and terminal operations, container industry; ships and shipping, intermodalism, and cargo handling.
**Ind/Abst** Bioeng. Abstr.; BMT Abstr.; Coal Abstr.; Ei Page One; EMBASE; Eng. Index Annu.; Fluid Abstr., Civil Eng.; Fluid Abstr. Proc. Eng.; FLUIDEX (1973-).

HK/0252-9610
**CARGONEWS ASIA.** (1977)-. English. bw. 198.90HK$; $25.50 airmail Asia; $59.50 airmail other. Far East Trade Press Ltd, BL C 10 F Seaview E, 2 8 Watson, North Point Hong Kong. **Tel** 011 852 5 5668381. **ED** Martin Savery. **UDC** 38. **[CCC]**. **Ad Acc**, **Adv Mgr:** Chris Michaelides. **Circ:** 13,000 (ctrl).
**Desc:** Asia's first and multimodel freighting magazine.

US/0360-4586
**CARLOAD WAYBILL STATISTICS.** (CARLOAD WAYBILL STATISTICS. STATEMENT TD-1, TERRITORIAL DISTRIBUTION, TRAFFIC, AND REVENUE BY COMMODITY CLASSES.). **Added/Corp** United States. Interstate Commerce Commission. Bureau of Transport Economics and Statistics. United States. Interstate Commerce Commission. Bureau of Economics. United States. Office of Rail Systems Analysis and Program Development. United States. Office of Rail Systems Analysis and Information. United States. Federal Railroad Administration. Office of Information and Statistics Division. United States. Federal Railroad Administration. Office of Policy. **VFOAT** Territorial Distribution, Traffic, and Revenue by Commodity Classes. (1953)-. English. an. Association of American Railroads, 50 F Street Northwest, Room 5401, Washington DC 20001. **Tel** (202)639-2550. **LC** HE2704; .A23. **DD** 385/.24/0973. ***Continues*** *Carload Waybill Statistics. Territorial Distribution, Traffic, and Revenue by Commodity Classes, Terminations in ... .*

US
**CARRIER REPORT.** English. qt. $35.00. Carrier Report, PO Box 39, Lubec ME 04652. **Tel** (207)733-2856. **ED** Richard W. Honer. **Ad Acc.** ctrl circ.
**Desc:** Financial reports of the largest regulated trucking companies operating in the US.

FR/0750-8131
**CARROSSERIE.** [Carrosserie]. (1958)-. Periodical. French. ir. 280.00F France; 320.00F other. Fedn Francaise de Carrosse, 35 rue des Renaudes, 75017 Paris France. **Tel** 011 33 1 47630368. **(Subscription address:** Compagnie Francaise de Presse, 2 Bis rue Mercoeur, 75011 Paris France**)** **UDC** 629.11.011.5.

NE
**CBS WEGVERVOERVERWANTE BEDRIJVEN / CENTRAAL BUREAU VOOR DE STATISTIEK, HOOFDAFDELING STATISTIEKEN VAN VERKEER EN VERVOER.** **VFOAT** C.B.S. Wegvervoerverwante Bedrijven; Supporting Services to Road Transport. Dutch (summaries and/or abstracts in English). an. Fl7.50. Centraal Bureau voor de Statistiek, AFD ALG Zaken, Postbus 959, 2270 AZ Voorburg Netherlands. **Tel** 011 31 70 3373800, FAX 011 31 038 7429, telex 32692 CBS NL. **LC** HE5674; .A14.

US/0162-8275
**CDE STOCK OWNERSHIP DIRECTORY: TRANSPORTATION INDUSTRY.** **Main/Corp** Corporate Data Exchange, Inc. **VFOAT** Stock Ownership Directory: Transportation Industry. **VAT** Corporate Data Exchange Stock Ownership Directory: Transportation Directory. (1976)-. English. Corporate Data Exchange Inc., 198 Broadway, Room 707, New York NY 10038. **LC** HE196.5; .C67a. **DD** 338.7/61/38050973.

US
**CENSUS OF TRANSPORTATION.** **Main/Corp** United States. Bureau of the Census. **VFOAT** Commodity Transportation Survey. 1963-. Government Publication. English. ir. US Department of Commerce / Bureau of the Census, Data User Services Division, Customer Services, Washington DC 20233-0800. **Tel** (301)763-4100. **(Subscription address:** Superintendent of Documents, US Government Printing Office, Washington DC 20402.**)**

CN/1183-7098
**CHARLTON STANDARD CATALOGUE OF CANADIAN TIRE CASH BONUS COUPONS, THE.** [Charlton stand. cat. Can. Tire cash bonus coupons]. **Added/Corp** Canadian Tire Corporation. **VFOAT** Canadian Tire Cash Bonus Coupons. 1st Ed. (1991)-. English. be. 9.95Can$ per volume. Charlton Press, 2010 Yonge Street, Toronto Ontario M4S 1Z9. **Tel** (416)488-4653. **DD** 769.5/5.

CH
**CHIAO TUNG CHIEN SHE.** Periodical. Chinese. mo. $30.00. Chung Kuo Chiao Tung Chien She Hsueh Hui, 4 Lane 77 Chin Shan St, Taipei Taiwan. **LC** HE7; .C458. **DD** 380.5/05.

US/1062-0060
**CHILTON'S COMMERCIAL CARRIER JOURNAL FOR PROFESSIONAL FLEET MANAGERS.** (CHILTON'S COMMERCIAL CARRIER JOURNAL FOR PROFESSIONAL FLEET MANAGERS : CCJ.). [Chilton's commer. carr. j. prof. fleet manag.]. **Added/Corp** Chilton Company. **VFOAT** CCJ; Commercial Carrier Journal for Professional Fleet Managers; Chilton's Commercial Carrier Journal; Commercial Carrier Journal. Vol. 147, No. 9 (Sept. 1990)-. Periodical. English. mo. $45.00 US; $75.00 other. Chilton Company, 201 King of Prussia Road, Radnor PA 19089. **Tel** (610)964-4122, (800)695-1214, FAX (610)964-4978, telex 6851035 CHILTON UW. **LC** TL1; .C57. **DD** 388.3/24/0973. ***Continues*** *Commercial Carrier Journal for Professional Fleet Managers, 1062-0052.*
**Ind/Abst** F&S Index Plus Text, Int. [Select. Cov.].

US/1057-9710
**CHILTON'S DISTRIBUTION (1986).** ***Title Change.*** (CHILTON'S DISTRIBUTION.). [Chilton's distrib.]. **Added/Corp** Chilton Company. **VFOAT** Distribution. Vol. 85 No. 1 (Jan. 1986)-Vol. 91 No. 8 (Aug. 1992). Periodical. English. mo. Chilton Company, 201 King of Prussia Road, Radnor PA 19089. **Tel** (610)964-4122, (800)695-1214, FAX (610)964-4978, telex 6851035 CHILTON UW. **LC** HF5487; .A26. **DD** 388. available on microfilm and microfiche from University Microfilms International (UMI). ***Continues*** *Chilton's Distribution for Traffic & Transportation Decision Makers, 0273-6721.* ***Continued by*** *Distribution (Radnor, Pa. : 1992), 1066-8489.*
**Ind/Abst** Bus. ASAP (1990-) [Full Txt.]; Bus. Index (1985-); Bus. Period. Index; Gen. BusinessFile (1985-); Gen. Period. Index (1985-); Stat. Ref. Index; Trade Ind. ASAP [Full Txt.]; Trade Ind. Index [Full Txt.]; Vocat. Search (July 1993-); Wilson Bus. Abstr.

US
**CHILTON'S OWNER OPERATOR.** [Owner oper.]. **VFOAT** Chilton's Owner Operator. Vol. 20, No. 8 (Oct. 1990)-. Periodical. English. bm. $30.00 US; $50.00 other. Chilton Company, 201 King of Prussia Road, Radnor PA 19089. **Tel** (610)964-4122, (800)695-1214, FAX (610)964-4978, telex 6851035 CHILTON UW. **ED** Leon Witconis. **LC** HE5601; .O85. **DD** 388. **Ad Acc. Circ:** 90,515 (ctrl). available on microfilm and microfiche from University Microfilms International (UMI). ***Continues*** *Owner Operator.*
**Desc:** Publication for owners and operators of one-to-ten heavy duty, over-the-road trucks. Contents: new products, business management, taxes, how-to-do-it, technical, legislation and news.

US/0194-1410
**CHILTON'S TRUCK & OFF-HIGHWAY INDUSTRIES.** [Chilton's truck off-highw. ind.]. **VFOAT** Chilton's Truck and Off-Highway Industries. Vol. 1, No. 4 (July/Aug. 1979)-. Periodical. English. bm. $75.00. Chilton Company, 201 King of Prussia Road, Radnor PA 19089. **Tel** (610)964-4122, (800)695-1214, FAX (610)964-4978, telex 6851035 CHILTON UW. **ED** John McElroy. **LC** TL230.A1. **DD** 338.4/76292/240973. **CODEN** TOINDH. **Ad Acc. Circ:** 33,000 (ctrl). available on microfilm and microfiche from University Microfilms International (UMI). Documents available from Article Express International. ***Continues*** *Truck & Off-Highway Industries, 0164-3436.*
**Desc:** Covers the heavy-duty truck and off-highway equipment industry.
**Ind/Abst** Bioeng. Abstr.; Ei Page One; Eng. Index Annu.

IT/1120-4141
**CIRCOLAZIONE STRADALE.** ***Title Change.*** [Circ. str.]. (1987)-(19??). Periodical. Italian. bw. Egaf Edizioni SAS, Via F Guarini 2, 47100 Forli Italy. **Tel** 011 39 543 782278, FAX 011 39 543 782255. **UDC** 656.1. Index available. cum. index. **Circ:** 2,000. available on an online database. ***Continued by*** *Codice Della Strada, 1121-6840.*
**Desc:** Contains highway codes, street laws and some circulars from the ministry.

CN/1184-7840
**CITL MEMBERSHIP DIRECTORY.** [CITL membsh. dir.]. **Main/Corp** Canadian Industrial Transportation League. **VFOAT** Canadian Shipper/CITL Directory. **VAT** Canadian Industrial Transportation League Membership Directory. (1990)-. Directory. English. Canadian Industrial Transportation League, 706-480 University Avenue, Toronto, Ontario M5G 1V2 Canada. **DD** 388. ***Continues*** *Canadian Industrial Transportation League. Membership Directory and Information Guide., 0836-5334.*

CN/0227-5708
**CITT NEWS.** [CITT news]. **VAT** Canadian Institute of Traffic and Transportation News. Periodical. English. mo. Canadian Institute of Traffic and Transportation, Suite 515, 44 Victoria Street, Toronto Ontario M5C 1Y2 Canada. **DD** 380.5/06/071.

UK/0263-0850
**CLASSIC MOTOR CYCLE, THE.** [Class. mot. cycle]. **VFOAT** Classic Motorcycle. (June/July 1981)-. Periodical. English. Twelve times a year. £20.50 UK & Eire; £22.50 others. EMAP National Publications Ltd, Farndon Road, Market Harborough, Leicestershire, LE16 9NR England. **Tel** 011 44 733 555161. **LC** WMLC L 83/8915.

UK
**COACH AND BUS OPERATIONS.** (19??)-. Periodical. English. bm. £138.70. Croner Publ Ltd, Croner House, London Road, Kingston upon Thames, Surrey KT2 6SR England. **Tel** 011 44 81 5473333, FAX 081 547-2637.

US/0732-8397
**COAL TRANSPORTATION REPORT.** [Coal transp. rep.]. **Added/Corp** Energy Bureau Inc. (1982)-. Periodical. English. bw. $595.00 US & Canada; $660.00 other. Fieldston Publications, 1920 North Street Northwest, Suite 210, Washington DC 20036. **Tel** (202)775-0240, FAX (202)872-8045. **ED** James N Heller. **Bk Rev**.
**Desc:** Only newsletter in US on coal transportation. Covers technical, legislative, regulatory, legal, and marketing aspects of coal transport by rail, barge, truck, and slurry.

US
**COAST MARINE & TRANSPORTATION DIRECTORY.** (19??)-. Directory. English. an. $95.00 US, Canada & Mexico; $110.00 other. K III Press Inc., 424 West 33rd Street, New York NY 10001. **Tel** (212)714-3100, (800)221-5488. **ED** Barbera Krueger. **Ad Acc. Circ:** 2,500. ***Absorbed*** *Pacific Coast Directory of Transportation.*
**Desc:** Regional transportation markets on the West Coast including British Columbia, Hawaii and Alaska.

US
**CODE OF FEDERAL REGULATIONS. 49, TRANSPORTATION.** **See** Law.

●IT/1121-6840
**CODICE DELLA STRADA.** [Codice str.]. (1992)-. Periodical. Italian. sm (24 issues per year). L390000. Egaf Edizioni SAS, Via F Guarini 2, 47100 Forli Italy. **Tel** 011 39 543 782278, FAX 011 39 543 782255. **UDC** 342.9. ***Continues*** *Circolazione Stradale, 1120-4141.*

# Transportation

**CK**
**CODIFICACION DE NORMAS DE TRANSITO Y TRANSPORTES - (COLOMBIA).** Spanish. $60.00. Apartado Aereo 9188, Bogota Colombia.

CN/1185-9326
**COMCAR REVIEW.** [Comcar rev.]. **Added/Corp** Com Car Owner Operators' Association. **VFOAT** Com Car Review; Common Carrier Review. Vol. 1, No. 1 (1991)-. English. Naylor Communications Ltd, 100 Sutherland Avenue, Winnipeg Manitoba R2W 3C7 Canada. **Tel** (204)947-0222, FAX (604)985-7399. **DD** 388.3.

**US**
**COME BACK SAFELY.** English. mo. $7.68. Bureau of Business Practice, 24 Rope Ferry Road, Waterford CT 06386. **Tel** (800)243-0876, (203)442-4365, (800)876-9105, FAX (203)443-1123. **ED** Linda Mileski. **Circ**: 14,000 (ctrl).
**Desc**: Cartoon-illustrated safety publication for truck drivers with safety and health tips in an informal, friendly format. Provides truck drivers with an ongoing motivational message to make road safety a priority.

**II**
**COMMERCE YEARBOOK OF ROAD TRANSPORT.** English. an. Rs50.00. Commerce Publications Ltd, NKM International House, 178 Backbay Reclamation, Bombay 400 020 India. **LC** HE5691.A45; C65. **DD** 338.3/0954.

**SA**
**COMMERCIAL TRANSPORT.** **Added/Corp** Motor Transport Owners' Association of South Africa. (19??)-. Periodical. English. mo. R78.00 South Africa; R118.00 other. Thomson Publications Pty, PO Box 56182, Pinegowrie 2123 South Africa. **Tel** 011 27 11 7892144. **LC** HE5601; .C64. **DD** 388.3/24/05. *Continues Commercial Transport and Freight, 0376-5849.*

US/0895-4437
**COMMUNITY TRANSPORTATION REPORTER : CTR.** (COMMUNITY TRANSPORTATION REPORTER.). [Community transp. report.]. **Added/Corp** Rural America, Inc. Center for Community Transportation. Community Transportation Association of America. **VFOAT** Community Transportation; CTR. Vol. 5, No. 2 (Feb. 1987)-. Periodical. English. Ten times a year. $35.00. Community Transport Association, 1440 New York Avenue Northwest 440, Washington DC 20005. **Tel** (202)628-1480. **ED** Scott Bogren. **DD** 388. **Ad Acc**, **Adv Mgr**: Bill Shoemaker, **Tel** (302)436-4375. **Circ**: 10000. *Continues Rural Transportation Reporter.*

**US**
**COMMUTED RATE SCHEDULE.** **Added/Corp** United States. General Services Administration. (198?)-. English. General Services Administration, General Services Building, Eighteenth and F Streets NW, Washington DC 20405. **Tel** (202)655-4000. *Continues Commuted Rate Schedule for Transportation of Household Goods.*

**US**
**COMMUTED RATE SCHEDULE FOR TRANSPORTATION OF HOUSEHOLD GOODS.** **Title Change**. **Added/Corp** United States. General Services Administration. (19??)-(198?). English. General Services Administration, General Services Building, Eighteenth and F Streets NW, Washington DC 20405. **Tel** (202)655-4000. *Continued by Commuted Rate Schedule.*

US/1054-7436
**COMMUTER AIR INTERNATIONAL.** **Title Change**. [Commut. air int.]. **Added/Corp** Communication Channels, Inc. **VFOAT** International Commuter Air; Commuter Air. (March 1990)-(1993). Periodical. English. mo. Argus Business, 6151 Powers Ferry Road, Atlanta GA 30339. **Tel** (404)995-2500, (800)233-3359. **LC** TL726; .C64. **DD** 387.7/42. available on microfilm and microfiche from University Microfilms International (UMI); available on an online database (file 648/Full-Text) from DIALOG. *Continues Commuter Air, 0199-2686. Continued by Regional Air International, 1070-065X.*
**Ind/Abst** Aviat. Tradescan [Full Cov.].

US/0734-3817
**COMMUTER (COLLEGE PARK, MD.), THE.** (THE COMMUTER : A PUBLICATION OF THE NATIONAL CLEARINGHOUSE FOR COMMUTER PROGRAMS.). **Added/Corp** National Clearinghouse for Commuter Programs (U.S.). (19??)-. Periodical. English. qt (Mar., June, Sept., Dec.). comes with National Clearinghouse Commuter Program Membership. National Clearinghouse for Commuter Programs, University of Maryland, 1195 Student Union, College Park MD 20742. **Tel** (301)454-5274. **ED** Barbara Jacoby. Index available. cum. index. **Bk Rev**. **Ad Acc**. **Circ**: 500 (ctrl).
**Desc**: Provides information concerning services, programs, advocacy, and research for commuter students in higher education.

US/1040-5402
**COMMUTER / REGIONAL AIRLINE NEWS.** [Commut./reg. airl. news]. **VFOAT** Commuter Regional Airline News; C/R News. (1982)-. Periodical. English. wk (50 issues). $595.00. Phillips Business Information, Inc., 1201 Seven Locks Road, Potomac MD 20854. **Tel** (301)424-3338, (800)777-5006, FAX (301)309-3847. **ED** Kelly Murphy. **DD** 387. **[CCC]**. Index available. **Ad Acc**. **Circ**: 300.
**Ind/Abst** PROMT [Full Txt.]; PTS Newsl. Database [Full Txt.]; Trade Ind. ASAP [Full Txt.]; Trade Ind. Index [Full Txt.].

US/1056-0254
**COMMUTER / REGIONAL AIRLINE NEWS INTERNATIONAL.** See Aeronautics, Astronautics.

UK/0267-8519
**COMPANY CAR.** (19??)-. English. mo. £72.00 UK; $83.00, $151.00 other. Argus Press Group, Queensway House, 2 Queensway Redhill, Surrey RH1 1QS England. **Tel** 011 44 737 768611, 011 44 737 761685, FAX 011 44 737 760510, telex 948669 TOPJNL G.
**Desc**: Journal for fleet-car operators.

**US**
**COMPLIANCE STRATEGIES REVIEW.** (19??)-. English. sm (24 issues). $675.00 US & Canada; $740.00 other. Fieldstone Publications, 1920 North Street Northwest, Suite 210, Washington DC 20036. **Tel** (202)775-0240, FAX (202)872-8045.

US/0090-8460
**CONNECTICUT MASTER TRANSPORTATION PLAN.** **Main/Corp** Connecticut. Dept. of Transportation. **Added/Corp** Charles A. Maguire and Associates. (1971)-. English. an. Connecticut Department of Transportation, Wethersfield CT 06109. **LC** HE28.C8; C63a. **DD** 380.5/09746.

**AG**
**CONSULTOR.** Periodical. Spanish. $50.00. Republica Argentina Centro de Informaciones del Transporte Internacional, Cerrito 40 - 1 B, Buenos Aires Argentina. **LC** HE7; .C66. **DD** 380.5/05. cum. index.

US/0010-7360
**CONTAINER NEWS.** [Contain. news]. Vol. 1 (1966)-. Periodical. English. Twelve times a year. $39.00. Argus Business, 6151 Powers Ferry Road, Atlanta GA 30339. **Tel** (404)995-2500, (800)233-3359. (Subscription address: Hallmark Data Systems, PO Box 1147, Skokie, IL 60076) **ED** James Elphick. **LC** TA1215; .C5934. **DD** 380.5/2. **[CCC]**. **Circ**: 30,000. available on microfilm and microfiche from University Microfilms International (UMI); available on an online database (file 648/Full-Text) from DIALOG. Documents available from UMI Article Clearinghouse.
**Ind/Abst** ABI/INFORM Glob. Ed.; ABI Inform Ondisc (Sept. 1973-Oct. 1973); Int. Packag. Abstr.

**FR**
**CONTAINERS.** See Packaging.

**IT**
**CORRIERE DEI TRASPORTI.** Italian. Fifty-two times a year (Mon.). L6000 Italy; L120000 others. Corriere Dei Trasporti, Salita Viale 1 Int 21, 16128 Genoa Italy. **Tel** 011 39 10 565946, FAX 011 39 10 564962.

**US**
**COST OF TRANSPORTING FREIGHT BY CLASS I AND CLASS II MOTOR COMMON CARRIERS OF GENERAL COMMODITIES, BY REGIONS OR TERRITORIES.** **Title Change**. **Main/Corp** United States. Interstate Commerce Commission. Bureau of Accounts. English. Interstate Commerce Commission / Bureau of Accountants, Room 3349 ICC Building, Washington DC 20423. **Tel** (202)275-7351. *Continued by Cost of Transporting Freight by Class I and Class II Motor Common Carriers of General Commodities.*

**US**
**COST OF TRANSPORTING FREIGHT BY CLASS I AND CLASS II MOTOR COMMON CARRIERS OF GENERAL COMMODITIES. CENTRAL REGION.** See Business-Commerce.

US/0499-6909
**COST OF TRANSPORTING FREIGHT BY CLASS I AND CLASS II MOTOR COMMON CARRIERS OF GENERAL COMMODITIES. EASTERN-CENTRAL TERRITORY.** See Business-Commerce.

**US**
**COST OF TRANSPORTING FREIGHT BY CLASS I AND CLASS II MOTOR COMMON CARRIERS OF GENERAL COMMODITIES : MIDDLE ATLANTIC REGION, SOUTHERN (INTRA) REGION, EAST-SOUTH TERRITORY, SOUTH-CENTRAL TERRITORY.** See Business-Commerce.

**US**
**COST OF TRANSPORTING FREIGHT BY CLASS I AND CLASS II MOTOR COMMON CARRIERS OF GENERAL COMMODITIES. TRANSCONTINENTAL TERRITORY, ROCKY MOUNTAIN REGION, MIDDLEWEST REGION, SOUTHWEST REGION, PACIFIC REGION.** See Business-Commerce.

**US**
**COST OF TRANSPORTING FREIGHT; CLASS I AND CLASS II MOTOR COMMON CARRIERS OF GENERAL COMMODITIES. NEW ENGLAND REGION - GROUP I, NEW ENGLAND REGION- GROUP II, CENTRAL REGION, EASTERN CENTRAL TERRITORY.** See Business-Commerce.

UK/0070-1610
**CRONER'S ROAD TRANSPORT OPERATION (OF GOODS VEHICLES IN THE UNITED KINGDOM AND ON THE CONTINENT OF EUROPE).** (1967)-. Periodical. English. mo. £181.55. Croner Publ Ltd, Croner House, London Road, Kingston upon Thames, Surrey KT2 6SR England. **Tel** 011 44 81 5473333, FAX 081 547-2637.

●**US**
**CSAH APPORTIONMENT DATA.** (1993)-. Periodical. English. an. Minnesota Department of Transportation, John Ireland Boulevard/Room 810, St Paul MN 55155. *Continues County State Aid Highway Apportionment Data.*

US/0361-2791
**CTA QUARTERLY.** **Main/Corp** Chicago Transit Authority. **VAT** Chicago Transit Authority Quarterly. V. 1- Autumn 1974-. Periodical. English. qt. Public Affairs Department, Chicago Transit Authority, Merchandise Mart Plaza, PO Box 3555, Chicago IL 60654. **LC** HE310.C45; C59A. **DD** 388.4/09773/11. *Continues in part Chicago Transit Authority. Annual Report (1972), 0733-5083.*

US/0011-3654
**CURRENT LITERATURE IN TRAFFIC AND TRANSPORTATION.** [Curr. lit. traffic transp.]. **Added/Corp** Northwestern University (Evanston, Ill.). Transportation Center. Library. Vol.1 (Jan./Feb. 1960)-. Periodical. English. qt. $18.00 US; $21.00 other. Transportation Library, Northwestern University, Library, Evanston IL 60208-2300. **Tel** (708) 491-5275. **ED** Mary McCreudie. **LC** Z7164.T8; C8; HE151. **DD** 016.3805. **Circ**: 550. available on microfilm and microfiche from University Microfilms International (UMI). *Supersedes Current Literature in Transportation.*
**Desc**: Periodical of publications dealing in traffic and transportation.

XR/0011-4650
**CZECHOSLOVAK MOTOR REVIEW.** (1955)-. Periodical. Multiple languages (English, French, German, Russian and Serbo-Croatian (Roman)). mo. $22.50. Rapid / Czech Republic, 28 Rijna 13, 112 79 Prague 1 Czech Republic. **Tel** (2)2319111, FAX (2)2327520. (Subscription address: Artia Pegas Press Ltd., Palac Metro Narodni Trida 25, 11210 Prague 1 Czech Republic.) **UDC** 629.113. **CODEN** 796.7.

CN/0710-0914
**DANGEROUS GOODS : NEWSLETTER.** [Danger. goods: newsl.]. **Added/Corp** Canada. Transport of Dangerous Goods Branch. (1980)-. Newsletter. English (French). qt (4 issues). Free on request. Transport Dangerous Goods Dir, 344 Slater Street, 14th Floor, Canada Building, Ottawa Ontario K1A 0N5 Canada. **Tel** (613)990-1151, FAX (613)952-1338. **ED** Helene Beaulieu (telephone: (613)990-1157). **DD** 363.1/756/0971. **Bk Rev**, (Qty: occasionally). **Ad Acc**. **Circ**: 18,000 (English), 5,500 (French) (ctrl).

CN/0256-3223
**DANGEROUS GOODS REGULATIONS.** See Public Health and Safety.

SP/0376-8112
**DATOS - SOCIEDAD PRIVADA MUNICIPAL TRANSPORTES DE BARCELONA.** **Main/Corp** Sociedad Privada Municipal Transportes de Barcelona. Spanish. Sociedad Privada Municipal Transportes de Barcelona, Luchana 99, Barcelona 5 Spain. **LC** HE4899.B4; S643.

# Transportation

SZ/0011-4820
**DDR VERKEHR.** Began publication with 1, Jan. 1968. Periodical. German (table of contents in Russian, English and French). mo. Deutscher Judo Verband, Redaktion Ippon Segewaldweg 40, D 12557 Berlin Germany. **Tel** 011 49 711 210770, telex 051 678. **LC** HE5. **DD** 380.5/0943/1.
**Ind/Abst** Coal Abstr.

BE
**DE LLOYD / LE LLOYD.** (19??)-. Newspaper. Multiple languages (French and Dutch). ir. 7750.00F Belgium; 11500.00F other. Editions Lloyd Anversois, Uleminckstraat 18, B-2000 Antwerpen Belgium. **Tel** 03 234 05 50, FAX 03 234 2593, telex 31446. **Ad Acc, Adv Mgr:** Koen Heinen. Full Page (B&W) 6335F. Half Page (B&W) 3000F. **Circ:** 10,600.
**Desc:** Daily newspaper for transport economics.

US/0011-7625
**DEFENSE TRANSPORTATION JOURNAL.** See Military and Defense.

US/0277-1136
**DELAWARE VALLEY GUIDE TO TRANSPORTATION.** English. $2.00 members of the Chamber of Commerce, $5.00 for nonmembers. Penjerdel Corporation, 1528 Walnut Street, Philadelphia PA 19102. **Continues** Delaware Valley Transportation Facts & Facilities.

US/0148-298X
**DEPARTMENT OF TRANSPORTATION, STATE OF RHODE ISLAND. Main/Corp** Rhode Island. Dept. of Transportation. 1974/75-. English. Room 210, State Office Building. **Tel** (401)277-2481. **LC** HE28.R4; A3. **DD** 353.9/745/0087505. **Continues** Transportation.

US/0279-8468
**DESTINATIONS.** Periodical. English. mo. American Bus Association, 1025 Connecticut Avenue NW, Washington DC 20036.

US/0093-4062
**DIGEST OF MOTOR LAWS.** See Law.

US/0092-7449
**DIRECTION.** Vol. 55, No. 3 (March 1973)-. English. mo. $30.00 (members), $42.00 (non-members) US; $36.00 (members), $48.00 (non-members). National Moving & Storage Association, 124 South Royal Street, Alexandria VA 22314. **Tel** (703)549-9263, FAX (703)548-5082, telex 901803 NMSA WASH. **ED** Joyce McDowell. **LC** HF5487; .A25. **DD** 658.7/85. **Bk Rev. Ad Acc. Circ:** 2,200. **Continues** Directions.
**Desc:** Informative articles slanted toward the moving and storage industry, as well as regular columns on sales and management.

CN/0714-8658
**DIRECTORY - BRITISH COLUMBIA MOTOR TRANSPORT ASSOCIATION.** (DIRECTORY.). [Dir. - B.C. Mot. Transp. Assoc.]. **Main/Corp** British Columbia Motor Transport Association. **VFOAT** British Columbia Motor Transport Directory; B.C. Motor Transport Directory. **VAT** British Columbia Motor Transport Directory (1981). (1981)-. Directory. English. an. 29.95Can$ (members); 39.95Can$ (non-members). Naylor Communications Ltd, 100 Sutherland Avenue, Winnipeg Manitoba R2W 3C7 Canada. **Tel** (204)947-0222, FAX (604)985-7399. **(Subscription address:** Naylor Communications Ltd., 124 West 8th Street, North Vancouver British Columbia, V7M 3H2 Canada.) **DD** 388.3/24/025711. **Bk Rev. Ad Acc. Circ:** 1,700. **Continues** British Columbia Motor Transport Association. B.C. Motor Transport Directory., 0714-8666.
**Desc:** Shippers guide to truck transportation services available in British Columbia.

US
**DIRECTORY OF COMPUTER SOFTWARE APPLICATIONS. TRANSPORTATION, A.** See Computers-Software.

US
**DIRECTORY OF METROPOLITAN PLANNING ORGANIZATIONS AND STATE TRANSPORTATION AGENCIES.** **VFOAT** Metropolitan Planning Organizations & State Transportation Agencies, Directory. 1980-. Directory. English. an. US Department of Transportation / Technology Sharing Program, DRT-1, Washington DC 20590. **Circ:** 1,500.

US
**DIRECTORY OF NATIONAL DEFENSE EXECUTIVE RESERVISTS ON ASSIGNMENT TO OFFICE OF SECRETARY OF TRANSPORTATION, U.S. DEPARTMENT OF TRANSPORTATION. Main/Corp** United States. Dept. of Transportation. Office of the Secretary. **VFOAT** Directory, National Defense Executive Reserve, Office of Secretary of Transportation. Directory. English. US Department of Transportation / Office of the Secretary, 400-7th Street SW, Washington DC 20590.

US
**DIRECTORY OF STANDARD MULTI-MODAL CARRIER AND TARIFF AGENT'S CODES. SCAC AND STAC.** English. qt (Mar., June, Sept., Dec.). $110.00. National Motor Freight Traffic Association Inc., 2200 Mill Road, Alexandria VA 22314. **Tel** (703)838-1822, FAX (703)683-1094. **Continues** Standard Carrier Alpha Code SCAS.

US/0360-5078
**DIRECTORY OF THE TRANSPORTATION RESEARCH BOARD. Main/Corp** National Research Council (U.S.). Transportation Research Board. (1974)-. English. an. $35.00 North America, $40.00 other. Transportation Research Board, Box 289, Washington DC 20055. **Tel** (202)334-3218, FAX (202)334-2519. **LC** TE12; .N2513. **DD** 380.5/025/73. **Continues** Directory of the Highway Research Board.

IO/0126-4613
**DIRECTORY PERUSAHAAN BIS (ANTAR PROPINSI).** Directory. Indonesian. an. Rp3,000 Indonesia; $3.20 US. Central Bureau of Statistics / Indonesia, c/o Dr. Sutomo, 8 Jalan, PO Box 3, Jakarta Indonesia. **Tel** 372808 374908 Ext.342. **LC** HE5695.A45; D57. ctrl circ.

IO/0216-700X
**DIREKTORI PERUSAHAAN TRUK (ANTAR PROPINSI) DI JAWA.** 1981-. Indonesian. an. Biro Pusat Statistik, JLN Dr Sutomo 8 Kotak, Pos 1003, Jakarta 10710 Indonesia. **Tel** 3728007, 374908. **LC** HE5695.A1; D57. **Continues** Directory Perusahaan Truck (Antar Propinsi) di Jawa.

US/0743-7269
**DISPATCH (ROCKVILLE, MD.).** (DISPATCH / INTERNATIONAL TAXICAB ASSOCIATION.). [Dispatch]. Periodical. English. mo. International Taxicab Association, 3849 Farragut Avenue, Kensington MD 20895. **Tel** (301)946-5700. **ED** Joan P Rood. **Ad Acc. Circ:** 600 (ctrl).
**Desc:** A business newsletter, circulated to members only, to keep them up-to-date on current and critical issues that affect the industry.

●US/1066-8489
**DISTRIBUTION (RADNOR, PA. 1992).** (DISTRIBUTION.). [Distribution]. Vol. 91, No. 9 (Sept. 1992)-. Periodical. English. Thirteen times a year. $65.00. Chilton Company, 201 King of Prussia Road, Radnor PA 19089. **Tel** (610)964-4122, (800)695-1214, FAX (610)964-4978, telex 6851035 CHILTON UW. **LC** HF5487; .A26. **DD** 388. **Continues** Chilton's Distribution (Radnor, Pa. : 1986), 1057-9710.

BE
**DRIVE.** (19??)-. French. qt (4 issues). 330.00F Netherlands; 350.00F Belgium. Uitgeverij Pelckmans NV, Kapelsestraat 222, C 2950 Kapellen Belgium. **Tel** 011 32 3 6645320, FAX 011 32 3 6650263.

US/0097-8655
**DRIVERS LICENSES. Main/Corp** United States. Federal Highway Administration. English. US Department of Transportation - Federal Highway Administration, 400 Seventh Street Southwest, Washington DC 20590. **Tel** (202)366-0660. **LC** HE5623; .A24A. **DD** 388.3.

US/0093-9528
**DUN & BRADSTREET REFERENCE BOOK OF TRANSPORTATION. VFOAT** Reference Book of Transportation. English. Trinc Transportation Consultants, Suite 4200, 485 L'Enfant Plaza SW, Washington DC 20024. **LC** HE5623.A45; D82. **DD** 380.5/2/02573. **Supersedes** Dun's Reference Book of Transportation.

GW/0342-166X
**DVZ DEUTSCHE VERKEHRS-ZEITUNG.** (DEUTSCHE VERKEHRS-ZEITUNG : DVZ.). [DVZ Dtsch. Verkehrs-Ztg.]. **VFOAT** DVZ; D.V.Z. (19??)-. German. ir. DM384.00 Germany; DM593.60 other. Deutscher Verkehrs Verlag GmbH, Nordkanalstr 36 PF 101609, D 20097 Hamburg Germany. **Tel** 011 49 40 2371401. **ED** Wolfhart Schlichting and Herbert Zernikow. **LC** Discard. **Bk Rev. Ad Acc. Circ:** 13,000 (ctrl).
**Desc:** Forwarding, warehousing, transhipment, traffic by surface, air or sea, inland navigation, container and trailer exchange, foreign country sections, and register of forwarding agents.
**Ind/Abst** Energy Res. Abstr. (May 1979-).

CN/0705-7040
**ECHO DU TRANSPORT, L'.** Vol. 1 (May 1977)-. Periodical. French. Ten times a year. 52.95Can$ US; 42.80Can$ Canada. Editions Bomart LTEE, 7493 RTE Transcanadienne 103, Montreal Quebec H4T 1T3 Canada. **Tel** (514)337-9043. **DD** 388.3/24/09714.

●CN/1183-7861
**EDMONTON & AREA AVIATION BUSINESS DIRECTORY.** [Edmont. area aviat. bus. dir.]. **VFOAT** Edmonton and Area Aviation Business Directory. 1991/92-. Directory. English. $7.50 per v. Consolidated Communications, 807 Manning Road Northeast, Suite 200, Calgary Alberta T2E 7M8 Canada. **Tel** (403)569-9520, FAX (403)569-9590. **DD** 387.7. **Continues** Edmonton & Area Airport Business Directory., 0823-8200.

US
**ELECTRIC AND HYBRID VEHICLES PROGRAM.** English. an. National Technical Information Service - NTIS, Room 2027S, 5285 Port Royal Road, Springfield VA 22161. **Tel** (703)487-4630, (703)487-4660, (703)487-4650, FAX (703)321-8547, telex 89-9405. **LC** TL220; .U47A. **DD** 629.2/293/05. **Continues** Annual Report to Congress for FY ... Electric and Hybrid Vehicle Program.

UK/0141-9811
**ELECTRIC VEHICLE DEVELOPMENTS.** **Suspended.** (ELECTRIC VEHICLE DEVELOPMENTS : EVD.). [Electr. veh. dev.]. **VFOAT** EVD; E.V.D. (March 1979)-(19??). Periodical. English. qt (January, April, July and October). £67.00. Research Applications Limited, Rosedale House, Rosedale Road, Richmond Surrey TW9 2SZ United Kingdom. **Tel** 011 44 359 70744. **CODEN** EVDEDJ. **[CCC].** Index available. **Bk Rev. Ad Acc.** Documents available from Ask*IEEE.
**Desc:** Reports on technical advances in electric road transport made by researchers, manufactures and operators of all electric vehicles. This includes battery powered, hybrid, dual mode and tracked systems vehicles.
**Ind/Abst** Coal Abstr.; Curr. Titles Electrochem.; Energy Res. Abstr. (Oct. 1979-); INSPEC (March 1979-); Leadscan.

IT/1121-7995
**ELEVATORI MODERNI : SOLLEVAMENTO E TRASPORTO A FUNE.** (1992)-. Periodical. Italian. Six times a year. L35000.00 Italy; L73000.00 (airmail) Europe; L53000.00 other. Volpe Editore, Via Pacinotti 4, 20090 Segrate Milan Italy. **Tel** 11 39 2 26922454, FAX 11 39 2 26922511, telex 313661. Index available in last issue of volume--attached. **Bk Rev.** (Qty: 10). **Ad Acc. Adv Mgr:** Arch. Colonna, **Tel** 11 39 2 27203245. **Circ:** 2,500 (ctrl). **Continues** Elevatori Moderni, 1120-1289.
**Desc:** Contains articles of interest in the field of international transport, i.e., elevators, rides, escalators.

NE
**ELSEVIER.** (1987)-. Periodical. Dutch. wk. BV Uitgeversmaatschappij Bonaventura, PO Box 2158, 1000 CD Amsterdam Netherlands. **Tel** 011 31 20 6914111, 011 31 20 5674911. **Continues** Elseviers Magazine.

FR
**ENQUETE ANNUELLE D'ENTREPRISES.** (ENQUETE ANNUELLE D'ENTREPRISES. LES ENTREPRISES DE TRANSPORT EN ...). **VFOAT** Entreprises de Transport en .... French. an. Ministere de l'Equipement, 21 rue Mathuring-Regnier, 75732 Paris Cedex 15 France. **LC** HE248.A15; E57.

FR
**ENQUETE PERMANENTE SUR L'UTILISATION DES VEHICULES DE TRANSPORT EN COMMUN DE PERSONNES EN ... / DEPARTEMENT DES STATISTIQUES DES TRANSPORTS.** French. an. Ministere des Transports, Departement des Statistiques des Transports, 55 rue Brillat-Savarin, 75658 Paris Cedex 13 France. **LC** HE5668; .A23. **DD** 388.3/22/0944.

US/1072-2416
**ENVIROLINE (FINDLAY, OHIO).** See Environmental Issues.

CN
**ESTIMATES. PART III, NATIONAL TRANSPORTATION AGENCY OF CANADA. Main/Corp** Canada. **VFOAT** Estimates. Part 3, National Transportation Agency of Canada; Budget des Depenses. Partie III, Office National des Transports du Canada. (19??)-. English (French). an. Canada Communication Group Publishers, Order Processing, Ottawa Ontario K1A 0S9 Canada. **Tel** (819)956-4800, (819)956-4802. **LC** HE215.A15; C35b. **DD** 354.710087/5/05. **Continues** Canada. Estimates. Part III, Canadian Transport Commission.

CN
**ESTIMATES. PART III, TRANSPORT CANADA. Main/Corp** Canada. **VFOAT** Budget des Depenses, Partie III, Transports Canada. (19??)-. English (French). $12.00 Canada; $14.40 other. Canada Communication Group Publishers, Order Processing, Ottawa Ontario K1A 0S9 Canada. **Tel** (819)956-4800, (819)956-4802. **LC** HE215.A15; C35c. **DD** 354.710087/5.

# Transportation

**CN**
**ESTIMATES. PART III, TRANSPORT CANADA, DEPARTMENTAL ADMINISTRATIVE PROGRAM, MARINE TRANSPORTATION PROGRAM, SURFACE TRANSPORTATION PROGRAM.** **Main/Corp** Canada. **VFOAT** Budget des Depenses. Partie III, Transports Canada, Programme de l'Administration Centrale, Programme des Transports par Eau, Programme des Transports de Surface. (19??)-. English (French). $12.00 Canada; $14.40 other. Canada Communication Group Publishers, Order Processing, Ottawa Ontario K1A 0S9 Canada. **Tel** (819)956-4800, (819)956-4802. **LC** HE215.A15; C35a. **DD** 354.710087/5.

●**SP**
**ESTUDIOS DE TRANSPORTES.**
**Added/Corp** Spain. Ministerio de Obras Publicas y Transportes. No. 57 (Jul. a Dic. 1992)-. Periodical. Spanish. sa. Centro Publicaciones del MTTC, Almagro 36 3, 28010 Madrid Spain. **LC** HE261.A15; B64. **DD** 380.5/068. **Continues** TTC.

**FR**
**ETUDES DE TRANSPORT EN ..., LES.**
French. 244 Boulevard Saint-Germain VIIE, 75775 Paris Cedex 16 France. **LC** HE192.55.F8; E87. **DD** 380.5/072044.

**BE/0252-239X**
**EUROPA TRANSPORT. KONJUNKTURERHEBUNG. Ceased.** [Eur. transp., Konjunkturerheb.]. **VFOAT** Konjunkturerhebung; Transport Survey; Europa Transport; Observation of the Transport Markets. (1981)-(1992). Periodical. German (English and French). qt. Office for Official Publications of the European Communities, 2 Rue Mercier, 2985 Luxemburg Luxembourg. **Tel** 011 352 499281, **FAX** 011 352 488573.

**UK**
**EUROPEAN AGREEMENT CONCERNING THE INTERNATIONAL CARRIAGE OF DANGEROUS GOODS BY ROAD.** **See** Environmental Issues-Pollution and Waste Management.

**UK**
**EUROPEAN FREIGHT MANAGEMENT.**
English. sm. £365.00 UK; £385.00 other. Financial Times Business Information Ltd., Tower House, Southampton Street, London WC2E 7HA England. **Tel** 011 44 71 353 1040.

**BE/0014-3154**
**EUROPEAN TRANSPORT LAW. See** Law.

**CN/1183-6423**
**EXPERIENCE TRILLIUM : THE OFFICIAL PUBLICATION OF TRILLIUM TERMINAL 3 - TORONTO, CANADA.** [Exp. Trillium]. **VFOAT** Trillium. No. 1 (1991)-. Periodical. English. Three times a year. Free. ADC Studios, 340 College Street, Suite 405, Toronto Ontario M5T 3A9 Canada. **DD** 387.7/36/0971354105.

**AU**
**FAHRPLANE.** **Main/Corp** Austria. Generaldirektion der Osterreichischen Bundesbahnen. (19??)-. Periodical. German. sa. S40.00. Generaldirektion der Osterreichischen Bundesbahnen, Offentlichkeitsarbeit, Werbung und Design, A-1010 Wien, Elisabethstrasse 9, Vienna 1010 Austria. **Tel** 011 43 0222 5800. **LC** HE9.A8; A3. **Continues** Amtliches Osterreichisches Kursbuch.

**US/0360-3024**
**FAMILY MOTOR COACHING. Added/Corp** Family Motor Coach Association. (19??)-. Periodical. English. Twelve times a year. $24.00 one year; $44.00 two years; $60.00 three years. Family Motor Coaching Association, PO Box 44144, 8291 Clough Pike, Cincinnati OH 45244. **Tel** (513)474-3622 (800)543-3622. **ED** Pamela Kay. **LC** TL298; .F25. **DD** 796.7. Index available. **Ad Acc. Circ:** 80,000 (ctrl).

**IT**
**FATTURATO, PRODOTTO LORDO, INVESTIMENTI DELLE IMPRESE INDUSTRIALI, DEL COMMERCIO, DEI TRASPORTI E COMUNICAZIONI E DI ALTRI TIPI DI SERVIZI. Added/Corp** Istituto Centrale di Statistica (Italy). (19??)-. Italian. an. **LC** HC301; .F33. **DD** 314.5/05.

**US/0093-0180**
**FEDERAL MOTOR VEHICLE FLEET REPORT FOR THE FISCAL YEAR ENDING ... .** (1972)-. English. an. Free. Fleet Management Service, Crystal Mall 4 Room 105, Arlington VA 22202. **Tel** (703)557-1273. **LC** JK1677.M7; A66. **DD** 353.0071/34. **Circ:** 2,800. **Continues** Annual Motor Vehicle Report.
**Desc:** The report contains inventory, cost, and operational information on commercial design motor vehicles operated by the Federal Government.
**Ind/Abst** F&S Index Plus Text, Int. [Select. Cov.].

**US/0364-6858**
**FEDERAL MOTOR VEHICLE SAFETY STANDARDS AND REGULATIONS.**
(FEDERAL MOTOR VEHICLE SAFETY STANDARDS AND REGULATIONS, WITH AMENDMENTS AND INTERPRETATIONS.). **Main/Corp** United States. National Highway Traffic Safety Administration. (19??)-. Periodical. English. an (supplements). $149.00 US; $186.25 other. Department of Transportation, 400 Seventh Street SW, Washington DC 20590. **Tel** (202)426-4000. **(Subscription address:** Superintendent of Documents, US Government Printing Office, Washington DC 20402.)
**Desc:** Contains three sections: procedural rules and regulations; standards; and rulings and additional regulations.

**CN/0708-3300**
**FERRIES, BRIDGES, CRUISES.** [Ferries, bridges, cruises]. **Added/Corp** Canadian Government Travel Bureau. Canadian Government Office of Tourism. **VAT** Ferries, Bridges & Cruises; Ferries, Bridges and Cruises. (19??)-. Periodical. an. Canadian Government Travel Bureau, 235 Queen Street/4th Floor East, Ottawa Ontario K1A 0H6 Canada. **DD** 386/.242/02571. **Continues** Ferries, Bridges, Boat Tours, 0711-0332.

**US**
**FIELD & STREAM GUIDE TO CAMPING ON WHEELS.** **See** Recreation, Leisure-Outdoor Life.

**US/0099-2445**
**FINANCIAL ANALYSIS OF THE MOTOR CARRIER INDUSTRY.** **Ceased. Added/Corp** American Trucking Associations. ( )-(1987). English. American Trucking Association, 2200 Mill Road, Alexandria VA 22314. **Tel** (703)838-1772. **LC** HE5623; .F55. **DD** 388.3/24.
**Ind/Abst** Stat. Ref. Index.

**US/0145-2924**
**FINANCIAL STATEMENT AFTER ALLOCATION.** (FINANCIAL STATEMENT AFTER ALLOCATION - FLORIDA. DEPT. OF TRANSPORTATION.). **Main/Corp** Florida. Dept. of Transportation. English. an. Florida Department of Transportation, The Capitol, Tallahassee FL 32304. **LC** HE28.F6; D46A. **DD** 353.9/759/0087.

**US/0885-8837**
**FIRE APPARATUS JOURNAL. See** Fire Prevention.

**CN/0820-8859**
**FIRST CHOICE CANADA.** [First choice Can.]. Vol. 1, No. 1 (Nov. 1981)-. Periodical. English (French; summaries and/or abstracts in Arabic, Chinese and Spanish). bm. 75.00Can$. FCM Communications Inc., 3662 Adam Street, Montreal Quebec H1W 1Z2 Canada. **Tel** (514)522-6146. **ED** James Parry. **LC** HD9709.C2; F57. **DD** 338.4/7629046/0971. Index available. cum. index. **Bk Rev**, (Qty: 6). **Ad Acc. Circ:** 23,500.

**US/0278-2987**
**FISCAL YEAR BUDGET ESTIMATES - DEPT. OF TRANSPORTATION, OFFICE OF THE SECRETARY.** **Main/Corp** United States. Dept. of Transportation. Office of the Secretary. English. an. Department of Transportation Office of the Secretary, 400 Seventh Street SW, Washington DC 20590.

**US/0747-2544**
**FLEET EQUIPMENT.** [Fleet equip.]. Vol. 10, No. 4 (April 1984)-. Periodical. English. mo (12 issues). $82.00 US and Possessions; $100.00 other. Maple Publishing, 134 West Slade, Palatine IL 60067. **Tel** (708)359-6100, **FAX** (708)359-6420. **(Subscription address:** 6201 West Howard Street, Room 207, Niles, IL 60648) **ED** Tom Gelinas. **LC** TL230.2; .F53. **DD** 629.28/74/05. **[CCC]. Ad Acc, Adv Mgr:** Bill White. **Circ:** 62,000 (ctrl). available on microfilm and microfiche from University Microfilms International (UMI); available on an online database (file 15/Full-Text) from DIALOG. Documents available from UMI Article Clearinghouse. **Continues** Fleet Maintenance and Specifying, 0095-3245.
**Desc:** Written for professional truck fleet equipment managers. Subject areas covered are equipment technology, equipment management techniques, feature articles on top fleets, new products and technology. Primary focus is on reducing equipment operating costs.
**Ind/Abst** ABI/INFORM Glob. Ed.; ABI Inform Ondisc (April 1988-); UMI ABI/Inform-Bus. Period. Ondisc (Apr. 1988-) [Full Txt.].

**US**
**FLEET MANAGEMENT.** English. Twelve times a year. $247.00. Skyline Publishing Co., 3239 Madison Avenue, Brookfield IL 60513. **Tel** (708)485-6015, **FAX** (708)485-4237.

**US/1042-1769**
**FLEET MANAGEMENT NEWS (PORT READING, N.J.).** (FLEET MANAGEMENT NEWS.). [Fleet manag. news]. (19??)-. Periodical. English. mo. $39.00. Fleet Management News, 48 Marion Street, Port Reading NJ 07064. **Tel** (908)937-0058. **ED** Donna Simeone. **DD** 388. **Ad Acc, Adv Mgr:** J. Dickenson. **Circ:** 1,000.
**Desc:** Facts and information pertaining to auto/fleet management.

**UK**
**FLEET NEWS.** (19??)-. English. wk. Free to those who qualify, £60.00 UK; £110.00 other. EMAP Response Publishing, Wentworth House, Wentworth Street, Peterborough PE1 IDS England. **Tel** 011 44 733 63100, **FAX** 011 44 733 66437. **ED** Mike Gunnell. **Bk Rev. Ad Acc. Circ:** 26,600 (ctrl).
**Ind/Abst** Infomat Int. Bus.

**US**
**FLEET OWNER.** (1989)-. Periodical. English. mo. $40.00 US; $49.41 Canada; $69.41 other. Intertec Publishing Corporation, 9800 Metcalf, Overland Park KS 66212. **Tel** (913)341-1300. **(Subscription address:** Intertec Publishing Corporation, PO Box 2901, Overland Park KS 66282.) **Formed by the union of** Fleet Owner (Big Fleet Ed.), 0731-9622 **and** Fleet Owner (Small Fleet Ed.), 0162-1025.

**US**
**FLEET RENTING AND LEASING.** (1993)-. Directory. English. Twice a year. $95.00. Transportation Technical Services, 225 West 34th Street, New York NY 10122. **Tel** (800)666-4887, **FAX** (703)899-1948. available on magnetic tape; available on diskette.

**AT/0312-4681**
**FLEETLINE.** [Fleetline]. (1975)-. Periodical. English. Twelve times a year. 49.00Aus$. Historic Commerical Vehicle Association, PO Box 1010, Sydney NSW 2001 Australia. **Tel** 011 61 2 5856368, **FAX** 011 61 2 8581137. **ED** Les Pascoe. **DD** 388.342330994. Index available (Bound in Dec. iss.). **Bk Rev**, (Qty: 6). **Continues** H.C.V.A. Newsheet.
**Desc:** Current news concerning buses in Australia.

**US**
**FLIGHT GUIDE : EASTERN MANUAL.**
English. $16.50. Air Guide Publications, PO Box 1288, Long Beach CA 90713. **Tel** (213)437-3210.

**US**
**FLIGHT GUIDE : WESTERN MANUAL.**
(19??)-. English. $15.50. Air Guide Publications, PO Box 1288, Long Beach CA 90713. **Tel** (213)437-3210.

**US/0015-4334**
**FLORIDA TRUCK NEWS. Added/Corp** Florida Trucking Association, Inc. Vol. 1 (Sept. 1947)-. Periodical. English. Twelve times a year. $14.00. Florida Trucking Association Inc, 350 East College Avenue, Tallahassee FL 32301. **Tel** (904)222-9900, **FAX** (904)222-9363. **ED** Tom Webb Jr. **Bk Rev**, (Qty: 2). **Ad Acc. Circ:** 2,300 (ctrl).

**US/0015-4849**
**FLYING MODELS. See** Hobbies.

**AT/1037-9088**
**FOREIGN TRADE AUSTRALIA, INTERNATIONAL CARGO. See** Transportation-Abstracting, Bibliographies and Statistics.

**CN/1183-2282**
**FORUM - CANADIAN URBAN TRANSIT ASSOCIATION.** (FORUM.). [Forum - Can. Urban Transit Assoc.]. **Added/Corp** Association Canadienne du Transport Urbain. Vol. 1, No. 1 (Jan. 1991)-. Periodical. French (English). mo. Limited free distribution. Association Canadienne du Transport Urbain, Bureau 901, 55 Rue York, Toronto Ontario M5J 1R7 Canada. **DD** 388.4. **Continues** Transit Topics., 1185-2208.

**CN/1183-2282**
**FORUM - CANADIAN URBAN TRANSIT ASSOCIATION.** (FORUM.). [Forum - Can. Urban Transit Assoc.]. **Added/Corp** Canadian Urban Transit Association. **VAT** Forum - Association Canadienne du Transport Urbain. Vol. 1, No. 1 (Jan. 1991)-. Periodical. English (French). mo. Limited free distribution. Canadian Urban Transit Association, 55 York Street, Suite 901, Toronto Ontario M5J 1R7 Canada. **Tel** (416)365-9800, **FAX** (416)365-1295. **DD** 388.4. **Continues** Transit Topics., 1185-2208.

**US/0015-9123**
**FOUR WHEELER.** [Four wheel.]. (19??)-. Periodical. English. mo. $17.87. General Media Publishing Company, 1965 Broadway, New York NY 10023. **Tel** (212)496-6100. **(Subscription address:** CDS

# Transportation

Agency Hard Copy, PO Box 4966, Des Moines IA 50340.) **ED** Rich Johnson. **DD** 629. **Ad Acc. Circ:** 213,310.
**Desc:** Includes late breaking news in the world of hard driving 4WD vehicles. Includes current trends, valuable maintenance tips, advice, outstanding photography, unusual rigs, and hot new models from here and abroad.

AT
**FOUR WHEELER.** (19??)-. Periodical. English. qt. 22.00Aus$ Australia; 26.40Aus$ New Zealand; 37.80Aus$ other. Australian Consolidated Press Ltd, GPO Box 5252, Sydney New South Wales 2001 Australia. **Tel** 011 61 2 2600000.

UK/0016-0873
**FREIGHT MANAGEMENT.** [Freight manag.]. **VFOAT** Freight Management and Distribution Today. (1966)-. Periodical. English. mo. £25.00 UK; £30.00 Europe; £40.00 US. Ravenshead Pr Ltd, Concept House, 1-3 Oakridge Road, Downham Bromely, Kent BR1 5QW England. **Tel** 011 44 81 650-5051, **FAX** 011 44 81 695-5423. **DD** 380.5. **Bk Rev. Ad Acc. Circ:** 9,842 (ctrl). available on microfilm and microfiche from University Microfilms International (UMI).
**Desc:** Contains articles on the freight and distribution industry.

UK/0965-4704
**FREIGHT MANAGEMENT INTERNATIONAL.** [Freight manag. Int.]. (1991)-. Periodical. English. Ten times a year (Jan./Feb. & Nov./Dec. issues combined). £32.50 UK; £39.00 others. Aldwych Publishing, A. Clark, 230-234 Long Lane, London SE1 4QE England. **Tel** 11 44 71 4034353, 011 44 71 4077541, **FAX** 11 44 71 4030233. **ED** Stephen Taylor. **DD** 388.044. **Ad Acc.**

UK
**FREIGHT NEWS (1983).** (FREIGHT NEWS.). Periodical. English. $26.05. Link House Magazines Ltd., Link House, Dingwall Avenue, Croydon Surrey CR9 2TA England. **Tel** 011 44 81 686 2599, **FAX** 011 44 81 760 5154, telex 947709. **Continues** Freight News International Weekly.

UK
**FREIGHT NEWS EXPRESS. Ceased.** (19??)-(Dec. 1992). Periodical. English. bw. Triangle Communications Ltd, 35-39 Castle Street, High Wycombe HP13 6RN England. **Tel** 011 44 1 494464448, telex 296032. **ED** Roger Tilleray. **Bk Rev. Ad Acc. Circ:** 14,800 (ctrl). **Continues** Freight News (1983).
**Desc:** Journal for shippers, forwarders and operators, with special sections on imports, express, shipping and airfreight.

US/0278-5404
**FREIGHT SERVICE DIRECTORY. CHICAGO EDITION.** (FREIGHT SERVICE DIRECTORY.). **Added/Corp** Equipment Interchange Association (U.S.) Illinois Trucking Associations. Vol. No. 1 (Aug. 1981)-. Directory. English. sa. $26.00. Equipment Interchange Association, 1616 P Street NW, Washington DC 20036. **LC** HE5623; .A17. **DD** 388.3/24/02573.

US/0749-2774
**FROM THE STATE CAPITALS. TRANSPORTATION POLICIES.** [From state cap., Transp. policies]. **VFOAT** Transportation Policies. (198?)-(19??). Periodical. English. mo. $125.00, $75.00 (libraries). Wakeman Walworth Inc., 300 North Washington Street #204, Alexandria VA 22314. **Tel** (703)549-8606. **ED** Emily Novick. **DD** 351. *Formed by the union of From the State Capitals. Parking Regulations,* 0741-3513 *and From the State Capitals. Urban Transit,* 0741-3564. **Merged into** *From the State Capitals. Economic Development.*
**Desc:** Mass transit funding, traffic and parking regulations, roadway financing, urban transit fare structures, commuter lines, financing and grants for roadway and terminal construction, equipment purchase and rehabilitation, efficiency measures and expanded services.

CN/0225-9214
**FUEL CONSUMPTION GUIDE.** See Transportation-Automobiles.

CN/0822-2142
**FUELSAVER.** [Fuelsaver]. **Added/Corp** Ontario. Transportation Technology and Energy Branch. Vol. 8, Issue 2 (Spring 1991)-. Periodical. English. qt. **DD** 388.4. **Continues** Fuelsaver for Fleet Managers and Driving Instructors., 0822-2142.

●US/1065-8661
**GAS TRANSPORTATION REPORT.** See Petroleum and Natural Gas.

GW/0016-5808
**GEFAEHRLICHE LADUNG.** (GEFAEHRLICHE LADUNG, DANGEROUS CARGO.). [Gefaehrl. lad.]. **VFOAT** Dangerous Cargo. (1971)-. Multiple languages (English and German). Twelve times a year. DM177.57 Germany; DM219.57 other. KO Storck & Co Verlag & Druck, Stahltwiete 7, D 22761 Hamburg Germany. **Tel** 011 49 40 8500071. **ED** H. Meder and U. Heins. **LC** T55.3.H3; G43. **Bk Rev. Ad Acc. Circ:** 4,000.

**Desc:** Covers transport, storage and handling of hazardous cargos by all modes. Includes coverage of fire and disaster prevention and oil spill prevention.
**Ind/Abst** Energy Res. Abstr. (March 1982-).

US/0731-5473
**GETTING THERE BY TRAIN, TRANSIT, BOAT & BUS.** **VFOAT** Getting There. Vol. 1, No. 1 (Summer 1981)-. Periodical. English. qt. $7.00 US; $8.00 other. Transport Research and Communications, PO Box 3175, Saxonville Station MA 01701. **LC** WMLC L 83/616.

NE
**GEVAARLIJKE STOFFEN.** Dutch. ir. Set-Point, Mgr Nolensplein 14, 4812 JC Breda Netherlands. **Tel** 011 31 76 224000.

CN/0225-9842
**GO SYSTEM TIMETABLE.** [GO syst. timetable]. Periodical. English. Toronto Area Transit Operating Authority, Toronto Ontario Canada. **DD** 380.5/22/09713541.

US/0090-6492
**GRANT AWARDS - U.S. DEPARTMENT OF TRANSPORTATION.** (GRANT AWARDS / U.S. DEPARTMENT OF TRANSPORTATION, OFFICE OF THE SECRETARY OF TRANSPORTATION.). **Added/Corp** United States. Dept. of Transportation. Office of the Secretary. (19??)-. Periodical. en. US Department of Transportation / Assistant Secretary for Administration, Office of Installations and Logistics, Washington DC 20590. **LC** HE17; .A28. **DD** 380.5.

US/0731-9819
**GREEN GUIDE FOR ELECTRIC LIFT TRUCKS.** [Green guide electr. lift trucks]. (19??)-. English. an. $417.00. K III Press Inc., 424 West 33rd Street, New York NY 10001. **Tel** (212)714-3100, (800)221-5488.

US/0731-9827
**GREEN GUIDE FOR LIFT TRUCKS.** [Green guide lift trucks]. (19??)-. English. an. $417.00. K III Press Inc., 424 West 33rd Street, New York NY 10001. **Tel** (212)714-3100, (800)221-5488.

US/0731-9835
**GREEN GUIDE FOR OFF-HIGHWAY TRUCKS & TRAILERS.** [Green guide off-highw. trucks trailers]. **VAT** Green Guide for Off Highway Trucks and Trailers. (19??)-. Periodical. English. ir. $329.00. K III Press Inc., 424 West 33rd Street, New York NY 10001. **Tel** (212)714-3100, (800)221-5488.

GW/0017-5137
**GUETERVERKEHR, DER.** **VFOAT** Der Gueterverkehr (Bonn). (1952)-. Periodical. German. mo. DM42.00. Kirschbaum Verlag, Siegfriedstr 28, Postfach 210209, D 53157 Bonn Germany. **Tel** 011 49 228 954530. **UDC** 656.025.4. **CODEN** 658.788.5. **[CCC]**.

CK
**GUIA COLOMBIANA DEL TRANSPORTE.** 1977-. Spanish. Apartado Aereo 8010, Bogota Colombia. **LC** HE235; .G84.

BL
**GUIA NACIONAL DO TRANSPORTE RODOVIARIO DE CARGA.** Portuguese. Associacao Nacional das Empresas de Transportes, rua Araujo 216 - 10 Andar, Sao Paulo Brazil. **LC** HE5653.A1; G84.

CN/0844-1871
**GUIDE DU PORT DE MONTREAL & REPERTOIRE DU TRANSPORT.** [Guide port Montr. repert. transp.]. **Added/Corp** Montreal Board of Trade. **VFOAT** Montreal Port Guide & Transportation Register. (1987)-. French (English and French). **DD** 387.1/025/714281. **Continues** Transport Montreal., 0229-2408.

CN/0706-9995
**GUIDE DU TRANSPORT PAR CAMION INC.** (GUIDE DU TRANSPORT PAR CAMION INC. TRUCK TRANSPORT GUIDE INC.). **VFOAT** Truck Transport Guide Inc. (1???)-. English (French). an (November). 85.00Can$. Guide du Transport par Camion, 7493 Transcanadienne Suite 103, Saint-Laurent Quebec H4T 9Z9 Canada. **Tel** (514)337-9043, **FAX** (514)337-1862. **DD** 388.3/24/02571. **Ad Acc, Adv Mgr:** Raymond Patry. **Circ:** 5,500.
**Desc:** Publicity on transportation means for Canada and USA, transportation guide.

US/1062-6026
**HAZMAT TRANSPORTATION MANAGEMENT. Title Change.** [Hazmat transp. manag.]. **VFOAT** Hazardous Transportation Management. Vol. 1, No. 1 (Feb. 21, 1992)-(1993). Periodical. English. mo. Stevens Publishing Corporation, 225 North New Road, Waco TX 76702-2604. **Tel** (800)727-7573, (817)776-9000. **(Subscription address:** PO Box 253, Waco TX 76702)**. DD** 363. **Merged into** Hazmat News.

US/0017-9434
**HEAVY DUTY TRUCKING.** [Heavy duty truck.]. **VFOAT** HDT. (Jan. 1968)-. Periodical. English. mo. free to qualified owners, $45.00 other. Newport Publications, PO Box 1058, Newport Beach CA 92658. **Tel** (714)261-1636 or, (714)261-2580. **ED** Doug Condra. **LC** HE5601; .M65. **DD** 388.3/24/05. **Circ:** 97,054. **Continues** Western Trucking and Motor Transportation.
**Desc:** Written for heavy truck fleets operating tractor-trailer combinations and straight trucks of Class 7 and 8 weight size. Recipients are corporate officers, owners, managers and maintenance executives.

US/0272-8591
**HEAVY TRUCK COLLISION ESTIMATING GUIDE: CHEVROLET, DIAMOND REO, DODGE, FORD, FREIGHTLINER, GMC, INTERNATIONAL, KENWORTH, MACK, PETERBILT, WHITE.** **Main/Corp** Mitchell Manuals, Inc. (19??)-. English. an. $124.00. Mitchell International Inc, PO Box 26260, San Diego CA 92126-0260. **Tel** (619)578-6550, (800)648-8010, **FAX** (619)578-4752. **(Subscription address:** Mitchell International Inc., PO Box 71654, Chicago IL 60694.) **LC** TL230.2; .M58b. **DD** 629.28/74.

US/0364-3468
**HIGHWAY & URBAN MASS TRANSPORTATION.** [Highw. urban mass transp.]. **VAT** Highway and Urban Mass Transportation. Periodical. English. Department of Transportation, 400 Seventh Street SW, Washington DC 20590. **Tel** (202)426-4000. **LC** HE308; .A3. **DD** 388.4/0973. **Continues** Highway Transportation.

CN/0701-8568
**HIGHWAY TRANSPORT BOARD BULLETIN.** (HIGHWAY TRANSPORT BOARD BULLETIN / THE AUTOMOTIVE TRANSPORT ASSOCIATION OF ONTARIO.). **VFOAT** Highw. Transp. Board bull.]. No. 57/26 (July 2, 1957)-. Bulletin. English. wk. Free. Ontario Trucking Association, 555 Dixon Road, Rexdale Ontario M9W 1H8 Canada. **Tel** (416)249-7401, **FAX** (416)245-6152. **DD** 388.3/24/09713. ctrl circ. **Continues** Members' Bulletin (Automotive Transport Association of Ontario), 0229-9755.

UK
**HIGHWAYS EXPENDITURE / SOCIETY OF COUNTY TREASURERS AND COUNTY SURVEYORS' SOCIETY.** English. an. Society of County Treasurers, County Hall, Truro TR1 3BD England. **LC** WMLC L 83/1323.

HK
**HONG KONG DEPARTMENTAL REPORT BY THE COMMISSIONER FOR TRANSPORT.** **Main/Corp** Hong Kong. Transport Dept. English. $8.00. J R Lee, Government Printer, Java Road, Hong Kong Hong Kong. **LC** HE96.H6; T7A. **DD** 354/.51/250087.

US
**HOW TO RECOVER FOR LOSS OR DAMAGE TO GOODS IN TRANSIT.** 1976-. English. ir. Matthew Bender & Company Inc., 1275 Broadway, Albany NY 12204. **Tel** (800)833-9844, (518)487-3000. Index Available Published separately--free--upon request.

IT/0391-2019
**HP ENERGIA TRASPORTI.** [HP Energ. trasp.]. (1974)-. Periodical. Italian. Eleven times a year. L25000 Italy; L50000 other. Editrice del Automobile, V le Regina Margherita 290, 00198 Rome Italy. **Tel** 011 39 6 440-2061. **UDC** 388. **Continues** Segnalazioni Stradali, 0037-0959.

US/0898-6894
**HPV NEWS (INDIANAPOLIS, IND.).** See Engineering.

IT
**I F TRASPORTI E COMUNICAZIONE.** (19??)-. Italian. mo. L150000. Editoria e Informatica, Pza Villa Fiorelli 1 15, 00182 Rome Italy. **Tel** 011 39 6 7014703.

UK/0032-5007
**IFW. INTERNATIONAL FREIGHTING WEEKLY.** (INTERNATIONAL FREIGHTING WEEKLY : IFW.). [IFW, Int. freight. wkly.]. **VFOAT** IFW; I.F.W. Began publication in 1962. Periodical. English. wk. $68.96. Maclean Hunter Canada / Montreal, 1001 bvd. de Maisonneuve W., Montreal, Quebec H3A 3E1 Canada. **Tel** 514-845-5141, **FAX** 514-845-4302, telex 055-60604. **ED** Derek North. **Ad Acc. Circ:** 20,679 (ctrl). available on an online database (file 648/Full-Text) from DIALOG. Documents available from UMI Article Clearinghouse. **Absorbed** Ports and Terminals/International Freighting.
**Desc:** Read by personnel responsible for the movement and handling of international cargo. The UK's only weekly

freight newspaper.
**Ind/Abst** ABI/INFORM Glob. Ed.; F&S Index Plus Text, Int. [Select. Cov.]; Infomat Int. Bus.; PROMT.

US
**ILLINOIS APPLICATIONS, INSTRUCTIONS, AND FEES, INTERNATIONAL REGISTRATION PLAN.** **Added/Corp** Illinois. Commercial & Farm Truck Division. English. Secretary of State / Illinois Commercial & Farm Truck Division, Springfield IL 62756. **Tel** (217)782-4815. **LC** HE5633.I3; A66. **DD** 353.97730087/834. ***Continues*** *Applications and Instructions for the International Registration Plan.*

US/0019-2309
**ILLINOIS TRUCK NEWS.** **Added/Corp** Illinois Trucking Associations. (19??)-. Periodical. English. mo. Illinois Trucking Associations, Western Spring IL 60558-1501.

US
**IMPLEMENTATION DIVISION ACTIVITIES REPORT / FEDERAL HIGHWAY ADMINISTRATION, OFFICES OF RESEARCH AND DEVELOPMENT.** English. an. US Department of Transportation - Federal Highway Administration, 400 Seventh Street Southwest, Washington DC 20590. **Tel** (202)366-0660. ***Continues*** *Implementation Division Activities, 0161-2239.*

US/0019-3291
**IN TRANSIT (WASHINGTON).** (IN TRANSIT.). **Added/Corp** Amalgamated Association of Street, Electrical Railway and Motor Coach Employees of America. Amalgamated Transit Union. Vol. 65, No. 2 (Feb. 1957)-. Periodical. English. mo. $5.00 (surface mail). Amalgamated Transit Union, 5025 Wisconsin Avenue, Washington DC 20016. **Tel** (202)537-1645. **ED** Shawn T. Perry. **Bk Rev. Ad Acc. Circ:** 165,000 (ctrl).
**Ind/Abst** Work Relat. Abstr.

CN/0840-3945
**INDEPENDENT TRUCKER.** ***Ceased.*** [Indep. truck.]. Vol. 8, No. 7 (Sept. 1988)-Ceased (Dec. 1991). Periodical. English. ir. Southam Business Communications Inc, 1450 Don Mills Road, Don Mills Ontario M3B 2X7 Canada. **Tel** (416)445-6641. **DD** 388.3/24/0971. ***Continues*** *Trucking Canada (Don Mills, Ont.), 0832-9087;* ***Absorbed*** *Driver/Owner, 0829-0512.*

CN/0822-6776
**INFO PREVENTION.** [Info prev.]. Vol. 1, No. 1 (Nov./Dec. 1983)-. Periodical. French. bw. Free. Travail Du Secteru Transport Et Entreposage, 1550 Est, Boul, St. Joseph, Montreal, Quebec H2J 1M7. **DD** 363.1/193805/09714. ctrl circ.

FR/0397-6440
**INFORMATION DU VEHICULE, L'.** [Inf. veh.]. (1970)-. Periodical. French. Twenty-seven times a year. Free, auto manufacturers; 1650.00F France; 1880.00F other. Interpress, 64 rue des Mathurins, 75008 Paris France. **Tel** 011 31 1 42681824, FAX 011 33 1 47428628, telex 215668. **UDC** 629.

CN/0319-1818
**INFORMATION - L'ASSOCIATION QUEBECOISE DU TRANSPORT ET DES ROUTES.** **Main/Corp** Association Quebecoise du Transport et des Routes. V. 1- May 1975-. Periodical. French. Four times a year. 50.00Can$ Canada; $60.00 other. L'Association Quebecoise du Transport et des Routes Inc, c/o Ecole Polytechnique, CP 6079 Succursale A, Montreal Quebec H3C 3A7 Canada. **Tel** (514)274-3573, FAX (514)274-9608. **DD** 380.5/06/2714. Index available. cum. index. **Ad Acc. Circ:** 1,500.
**Desc:** Aims to be the link between industry and all those who are interested in all aspects of transport.

US/0148-8473
**INFORMATION SERIES. GROUP 2: DESIGN AND CONSTRUCTION OF TRANSPORTATION FACILITIES.** **Added/Corp** National Research Council (U.S.). Transportation Research Board. **VAT** Information Series. Group Two. Design and Construction of Transportation Facilities. (19??)-. Periodical. English. Transportation Research Board, Box 289, Washington DC 20055. **Tel** (202)334-3218, FAX (202)334-2519.

PO
**INQUERITO AO TRANSPORTE RODOVIARIO DE MERCADORIAS. FOLHA SINTESE.** Portuguese. Instituto Nacional de Estatistica, Servicos Centrais, Avenida Antonio Jose de Almeida 1, 1078 Lisbon Portugal. **Tel** 80 20 80, FAX 8489480, telex 63738 PCDINE. **LC** HE5681; .A25. **DD** 388.3/24/0946905.

US/1050-818X
**INSIDE DOT & TRANSPORTATION WEEK.** [Indside DOT transp. week]. **VFOAT** Inside DOT and Transportation Week. **VAT** Inside Department of Transportation and Transportation Week. Vol. 1, No. 1 (May 17, 1990)-. Periodical. English. wk (50 issues). $697.00. King Publishing Group, 627 National Press Building, Washington DC 20045. **Tel** (202)638-4260, FAX (202)662-9744. **ED** Rupert Welch. **DD** 384. **[CCC]. Circ:** 500. available on an online database (file 636/Full-Text) from DIALOG. ***Absorbed*** *ATC Week.*
**Desc:** For current developments shaping the transportation industry. Monitors the Department of Transportation, its disbursement of funds, and its regulatory policy.
**Ind/Abst** PTS Newsl. Database [Full Txt.].

●US/1061-4494
**INSIDE FLYER.** [Inside fly.]. Vol. 1, Issue 1 (Jan. 1992)-. Periodical. English. mo. Flightplan, 4715-C Town Center Drive, Colorado Springs CO 80916. **DD** 387. ***Continues*** *Frequent Update, 1048-5759.*

US/1054-2647
**INSIDE IVHS.** (INSIDE IVHS : INTELLIGENT VEHICLE / HIGHWAY SYSTEMS UPDATE.). [Inside IVHS]. **VFOAT** Inside Intelligent Vehicle Highway Systems Update. **VAT** Inside Intelligent Vehicle/Highway Systems Update. Vol. 1, No. 1 (Jan. 7, 1991)-. Periodical. English. Twenty-four times a year. $495.00. Waters Information Services, PO Box 2248, Binghamton NY 13902-2248. **Tel** (607)770-8535, FAX (607)798-1692. **ED** Philip Alling. **DD** 388. available on an online database (files 16,636/Full-Text) from DIALOG.
**Desc:** Business aspects of smart car and smart highway prototypes and projects.
**Ind/Abst** PROMT [Full Txt.]; PTS Newsl. Database [Full Txt.].

CN/1180-4602
**INSIDE ROUTES.** [Inside routes]. **Main/Corp** Ontario. Ministry of Transportation. Vol. 1, No. 1 (Sept. 1990)-. Periodical. English. MTO Communications Services Branch, 1201 Wilson Avenue, Downsview Ontario M3M 1J8 Canada. **DD** 354.7130687/5/05. ***Continues*** *Routes, 0847-1894.*

US/1061-4311
**INTELLIMOTION (RICHMOND, CALIF.).** (INTELLIMOTION : KEEPING UP WITH PATH RESEARCH IN INTELLIGENT TRANSPORTATION SYSTEMS.). [Intellimotion]. **Added/Corp** Partners for Advanced Transit and Highways (Calif.). Vol. 1, No. 1 (Fall 1991)-. Periodical. English. qt. Free. Path Publications, Univeristy of California, Berkeley, Institute of Transportation Studies - Path Building, 452 Richmond Field Station, 1301 South 46th Street, Richmond CA 94804. **DD** 388. ***Continues*** *PATH Progress.*

US/0882-8059
**INTERMODAL REPORTER.** **Added/Corp** Traffic Service Corporation. (1985)-. Periodical. English. sm. $297.00 US & Mexico; $335.00 other. K III Press Inc., 424 West 33rd Street, New York NY 10001. **Tel** (212)714-3100, (800)221-5488. **ED** Kurt Hoffman. **DD** 380. **Ad Acc.**

UK/0260-1087
**INTERNATIONAL BULK JOURNAL : IBJ.** [Int. bulk j.]. **VFOAT** IBJ; I.B.J. (1981)-. Periodical. English. mo. $310.00 (1 year), $580.00 (2 year), $840.00 (3 year). IBJ Associates, Ranmore House/ 19 Ranmore Road, Darking Surrey RH4 1HE England. **Tel** 011 44 306 740447, FAX (0306)883650, telex 859597. **ED** Richard G Peckham. **Bk Rev. Ad Acc. Circ:** 7,500 (ctrl).
**Desc:** All aspects of seaborne dry bulk trade, transport and handling.
**Ind/Abst** Coal Abstr.; Fluid Abstr., Civil Eng.; Fluid Abstr. Proc. Eng.; FLUIDEX (1981-).

BE
**INTERNATIONAL CONGRESS PROCEEDINGS.** **Main/Corp** International Union of Public Transport. (19??)-. English (French and German). be. International Union of Public Transport, Avenue de l'Uruguay 19, B 1050 Brussels Belgium. **Tel** 011 32 2 6733325, FAX 011 32 2 6607072, telex (046)63916 UITP B. **LC** TF701; .I5. **DD** 388/.042/05. ***Continues*** *International Congress of Public Transport. Proceedings.*
**Desc:** Proceedings of the international congresses held by the UITP dealing with urban and regional public transport.

UK
**INTERNATIONAL FREE TRADE ZONE.** ***Title Change.*** **VFOAT** Lloyd's International Free Trade Zones. 1st Ed. (1989)-. English. an (November). Lloyd's of London Press Ltd, Sheepen Place, Colchester, Essex, CO3 3LP England. **Tel** 011 44 206 772113, US: (212)529-9500, US: (800)955-6937, FAX 011 44 206 772880, US: (212)529-9826, telex 987321 LLOYDS G. **ED** P Baxter. **Ad Acc. Circ:** 4,500 (ctrl). ***Absorbed by*** *Absorbed into Lloyd's Ports of the World.*
**Desc:** Provides essential details of each operational zone, monitors their most recent developments, planned and actual, providing an independent, unbiased assessment to aid decision making about international trade activity

●US/1065-5174
**INTERNATIONAL JOURNAL OF TRANSPORTATION POLICY.** (1993)-. English. Gordon & Breach Science Publishers, Inc., PO Box 786, Cooper Station, New York NY 10276. **Tel** (212)206-8900, FAX (212)645-2459. **(Subscription address:** International Publishers Distributor at one of the following addresses: 820 Town Center Drive, Langhorne, PA 19047; or PO Box 90, Reading Berkshire RG1 8JL UK; or Kent Ridge PO Box 1180, Singapore 9111, Republic of Singapore**)**
**Desc:** Focuses on transportation policy issues and approaches, seeks to be a leading source of ideas in the world on major transportation issues.

SZ
**INTERNATIONAL TRANSPORT JOURNAL OVERSEAS DIGEST.** English. wk. 170.00F. Rittman Ltd, Spalentorweg 9, 4003 Basel Switzerland. **Tel** 011 41 61 258830.

US
**INTERNATIONAL TRANSPORT POLICY / UNITED STATES COUNCIL OF THE INTERNATIONAL CHAMBER OF COMMERCE INC.** Periodical. English. ir. 1212 Avenue of the Americas, New York NY 10036. **Tel** (212)354-4480.
**Desc:** Reports on international air and sea transport policy developments in intergovernmental organizations, in labor, business, and trade groups, and in the US government.

SZ/0020-9341
**INTERNATIONALE TRANSPORT ZEITSCHRIFT.** **VFOAT** Journal Pour le Transport Internationale. French and German. wk. 200.00F Switzerland; 256.00F Europe; 270.00F other. Rittman Ltd, Spalentorweg 9, 4003 Basel Switzerland. **Tel** 011 41 61 258830.

GW/0020-9511
**INTERNATIONALES VERKEHRSWESEN.** [Int. Verkehrswes.]. **Added/Corp** Deutsche Verkehrswissenschaftliche Gesellschaft. (19??)-. Academic Scholarly Publication. German (summaries and/or abstracts in English and French). Twelve times a year. DM135.00. Tetzlaff Verlag GmbH, Postfach 101609, D-20010 Hamburg Germany. **Tel** 011 49 40 2371401, telex 419258. **LC** HE5; .I53. **DD** 380.5/05. **[CCC].** Index available. **Bk Rev. Ad Acc. Circ:** 4,100 (ctrl). ***Continues*** *IV.*
**Desc:** Technical, economic, legal, and political aspects of international transportation.
**Ind/Abst** EMBASE; Highw. Res. Abstr.; Int. Civil Eng. Abstr.; Soft. Abstr. Eng.

US/0884-8394
**INTERSTATE INFORMATION REPORT.** **See** Law.

US/0094-2707
**IRT DIGEST.** **Main/Corp** Institute for Rapid Transit (U.S.). English. IRT Digest, 1612 K Street NW, Wasington DC 20006. **LC** HE4201; .I45A. **DD** 388.4/0973.

AU
**ISR, INTERNATIONLE BERG- UND SEILBAHNRUNDSCHAU. INTERNATIONAL AERIAL TRAMWAY REVIEW.** **See** Engineering-Mechanical Engineering and Machinery.

US/0162-8178
**ITE JOURNAL.** [ITE j.]. **Main/Corp** Institute of Transportation Engineers. **Added/Corp** Institute of Transportation Engineers. Journal. **VFOAT** Journal. **VAT** Institute of Transportation Engineers Journal. Vol. 48, No. 6 (June 1978)-. Academic Scholarly Publication. English. mo. $50.00 (1 year), $120.00 (3 year) US, Canada, and Mexico; $70.00 (1 year), $160.00 (3 year) other. Institute of Transportation Engineers, 525 School Street SW/Suite 410, Washington DC 20024. **Tel** (202)554-8050, FAX (202)863-5486, telex 467943. **ED** Kathryn Harrington-Hughes. **LC** HE331; .T7. **DD** 380.5/05. **CODEN** ITEJDZ. Index available. cum. index. **Bk Rev. Ad Acc. Pr Rev. Circ:** 10,400. available on microfilm and microfiche from University Microfilms International (UMI). Documents available from Article Express International, The Genuine Article, Documents on Demand. ***Continues*** *Transportation Engineering, 0148-0170.*
**Ind/Abst** Appl. Sci. Technol. Index; Bioeng. Abstr.; Curr. Contents Eng. Tech. Appl. Sci.; Ei Page One; EMBASE; Energy Inf. Abstr.; Energy Res. Abstr. (March 1979-); Eng. Index Annu. [Select. Cov.]; Environ. Abstr.; Geogr. Abstr. Phys. Geogr.; Geogr. Abstr. Human Geogr.; Highw. Res. Abstr.; INIS Atomindex [Micro.]; Int. Dev. Abstr.; J. Plan. Lit.; Leadscan; Res. Alert [Select. Cov.]; Sage Urban Stud. Abstr; SCISEARCH; Soc. Sci. Cit. Index [Select. Cov.]; Urban Aff. Abstr.

RU/0134-7799
**ITOGI NAUKI I TEKHNIKI. SERIIA ORGANIZATSIIA UPRAVLENIIA TRANSPORTOM.** **Added/Corp** Vsesoiuznyi Institut Nauchnoi i Tekhnicheskoi Informatsii (Soviet Union). **VFOAT** Seriia Organizatsiia Upravleniia Transportom; Itogi Nauki I Tekhniki: Organizatsiia Upravleniia Transportom. (1978)-. Monographic series. Russian. Price varies per volume. VINITI - Vsesoyuznyi Institut Nauchno-Tekhnicheskoi Informatsii, All-Union

Scientific and Technical Information Institute, Baltiiskaia Ulitsa 14, 125219 Moscow Russia. **Tel** 238-46-00, FAX 9430060, telex 411160. **LC** HE255; .I85. **CODEN** INOTE6.

FR/0754-4618
**J.T.R. INFORMATIONS. VFOAT** J.T.R. Info; Journees des Transporteurs Routiers Informations. (1982)-. Periodical. French. ir. 837.41F France; 965.00F others. Compagnie Gen Developpement, 11 rue Godefroy Cavaignac, 75541 Paris Cedex 11 France. **Tel** 011 33 1 43790630, FAX 011 33 1 43791775, telex 211351. **UDC** 656.1.

NE
**JAARVERSLAG - NEDERLANDSCHE SCHEEPVAART UNIE. Main/Corp** Nederlandsche Scheepvaart Unie. Dutch. Dr H Colinjnlaan, 204 Rijsuijk Netherlands. **LC** HE945.N63; N4A.

UK
**JANE'S CONTAINERISATION DIRECTORY. Added/Corp** Jane's Information Group. Jane's Transport Data. **VFOAT** Containerisation Directory. (1988/89)-. Directory. English. an. $285.00 US and Mexico; $349.00 Central and South America. Jane's Information Group, Sentinel House, 163 Brighton Road, Coulsdon Surrey CR3 2NX England. **Tel** 011 44 81 763 1030, FAX 011 44 81 763 1006. **ED** Patrick Hicks. **LC** TA1215; .J34. **DD** 388/.044. ***Continues*** *Jane's Freight Containers, 0075-3033.*

●UK
**JANE'S MILITARY VEHICLES AND LOGISTICS. See** Military and Defense.

UK
**JANE'S URBAN TRANSPORT SYSTEMS. VFOAT** Urban Transport Systems. 1st Ed. (1982)-. English. an. $285.00 US & Mexico; $349.13 Central & South America. Jane's Information Group, Sentinel House, 163 Brighton Road, Coulsdon Surrey CR3 2NX England. **Tel** 011 44 81 763 1030, FAX 011 44 81 763 1006. **ED** Chris Bushell and Peter Stonham. **LC** HE4201; .J36. **DD** 388.4. **Ad Acc.**
**Desc:** Reference book covering world's major urban transport systems, including metro, light rail, tram, bus and trolleybus. Also lists manufacturers, products, consultants and their projects.

US/0021-6003
**JET CARGO NEWS.** (19??)-. Periodical. English. mo. $30.00 US; $45.00 other. Hagall Publishing Co., PO Box 920952 #398, Houston TX 77292. **Tel** (713)681-4760, FAX (713)682-3871. **(Subscription address:** Jet Cargo News, Subscription Service Center, PO Box 3304, Southeastern, PA 19398**) ED** Patricia M. Chandler. **DD** 387.7/44/05. **Ad Acc. Circ:** 22,300 (ctrl). available on an online database (file 16/Full-Text) from DIALOG.
**Desc:** Covers development of air cargo-related technologies, containerization, regulation, and documentation, market opportunities, routing, rates, trends, and interviews with industry executives worldwide.
**Ind/Abst** F&S Index Plus Text, Int. [Full Txt.] [Select. Cov.]; PROMT [Full Txt.].

JA
**JIDOSHA CHOSA NENPO. Added/Corp** Japan. Unyusho. Daijin Kanbo. Tokei Chosabu. Japan. Unyusho. Joho Kanribu. Nihon Jidosha Kaigisho. (19??)-. Periodical. Japanese. Nihon Jidosha Kaigisho, (Japan Automobile Chamber of Commerce and Industries), 8-3 Marunouchi 1 chome Chiyodaku, Tokyoto 100 Japan. **LC** HE5697.A1; J5.

US/0197-6729
**JOURNAL OF ADVANCED TRANSPORTATION.** [J. adv. transp.]. **Added/Corp** Institute for Transportation (Durham, N.C.) Advanced Transit Association (Washington, D.C.). Vol. 13, (Spring 1979)-. Periodical. English. Three times a year. $80.00 US & Canada; $90.00 others. Institute for Transportation, PO Box 90304, Duke University, Durham NC 27708. **Tel** (919)660-5312, FAX (919)660-8963. **ED** C. M. Harman. **LC** TF1300; .H53. **DD** 388/.05. **CODEN** JATRDC. **Pr Rev. Circ:** 450. available on microfilm and microfiche from University Microfilms International (UMI). Documents available from Article Express International. ***Continues*** *High Speed Ground Transportation Journal, 0018-1501.*
**Desc:** Urban mass transportation is emphasized. Engineering aspects include structures, vehicles and control. Economics, planning and socio-political aspects of transportation included. A journal for professionals and scholars concerned with urban mass transportation and advanced transportation.
**Ind/Abst** Bioeng. Abstr.; Ei Page One; Energy Res. Abstr. (Jan. 1980-); Eng. Index Annu. [Select. Cov.]; Fluid Abstr., Civil Eng.; Fluid Abstr. Proc. Eng.; FLUIDEX (1979-); Highw. Res. Abstr.; Int. Abstr. Oper. Res. [Select. Cov.]; Int. Aerosp. Abstr.; J. Plan. Lit.; Pollut. Abstr. Indexes.

US/0735-3766
**JOURNAL OF BUSINESS LOGISTICS.** [J. bus. logist.]. **Added/Corp** Council of Logistics Management (U.S.) Ohio State University. College of Administrative Science. National Council of Physical Distribution Management. **VFOAT** Business Logistics. Vol. 1 (Spring 1978)-. Periodical. English. sa. $25.00 US; $30.00 Canada and Mexico; $40.00 other. Council of Logistics Management, 2803 Butterfield Road, Suite 380, Oak Brook IL 60521. **Tel** (708)574-0985, FAX (708)574-0989. **ED** Bernard J. La Londe. **LC** HD38.5; .J68. **DD** 658.5/005. **Pr Rev. Circ:** 5,000. available on microfilm and microfiche from University Microfilms International (UMI). Documents available from UMI Article Clearinghouse.
**Desc:** Provides information, new theory or techniques, and researched generalizations about thought and practice in transportation and distribution. Presents views and syntheses which impact the future.
**Ind/Abst** ABI/INFORM Glob. Ed.; ABI Inform Ondisc (1987-); UMI ABI/Inform--Bus. Period. Ondisc (1987-) [Full Txt.].

US/1046-1469
**JOURNAL OF THE TRANSPORTATION RESEARCH FORUM.** [J. Transp. Res. Forum]. **Added/Corp** Transportation Research Forum. Canadian Transportation Research Forum. Vol. 28, No. 1 (1987)-. English. sa. $50.00; $60.00 (membership). Transportation Research Forum, 1730 North Lynn St. #502, Arlington VA 22209. **Tel** (703)525-1191, FAX (703)276-8196. **LC** HE11; .T75a; HE1; .T7762. **DD** 388/.05. ***Continues*** *Proceedings / Transportation Research Forum, 0091-2468.*
**Ind/Abst** J. Plan. Lit.; Maize Abstr.; PAIS Int. Print.

UK/0022-5258
**JOURNAL OF TRANSPORT ECONOMICS AND POLICY.** [J. transp. econ. policy]. **Added/Corp** London School of Economics and Political Science. University of Bath. Vol. 1 (Jan 1967)-. Periodical. English. Three times a year (Jan., May, and Sept.). £48.00 UK; $94.00 US. Journal of Transport Economics & Policy, Claverton Down, Bath BA2 7AY England. **Tel** 011 44 225 826302, FAX 011 44 225 826767, telex 449097. **ED** S. Glaister, C. Nash. **LC** HE1; .J597. **CODEN** JTEPEV. **Bk Rev. Ad Acc. Pr Rev. Circ:** 1,350. Documents available from The Genuine Article, UMI Article Clearinghouse.
**Desc:** Articles range from fundamental studies making original contributions to analysis to those exploring innovations in policy. Topics have included liner freight rates, air navigation, Urban traffic, vehicle ownership and operating costs, shipping and port costs, deregulation and infrastructure finance, contributors include economists, practising consultants operational research analysts, and administrators.
**Ind/Abst** ABI/INFORM Glob. Ed.; ABI Inform Ondisc (Jan. 1981-); Appl. Soc. Sci. Index Abstr.; Aviat. Tradescan [Select. Cov.]; Br. Humanit. Index; Contents Recent Econ. J.; Curr. Contents Soc. Behav. Sci.; Econ. Lit. Index; Gen. BusinessFile (1992-); Geogr. Abstr. Human Geogr.; Highw. Res. Abstr.; Int. Abstr. Oper. Res. [Select. Cov.]; J. Econ. Lit.; Leis. Recreat. Tour. Abstr.; PAIS Int. Print (1991-); Res. Alert [Full Cov.]; Risk Abstr.; Soc. Sci. Cit. Index [Full Cov.].

UK/0022-5266
**JOURNAL OF TRANSPORT HISTORY, THE.** [J. transp. hist.]. Vol. 1, No. 1 (May 1953)-. Periodical. English. sa. £60.00 (institution), £27.50 (individual) UK; $120.00 (institution), $55.00 (individual) other. Manchester University Press, Journals Dept, Oxford Road, Manchester M13 9PL England. **Tel** 011 44 061 2735539, FAX 011 44 061 2743346, telex 668932. **ED** John Armstrong. **LC** HE1; .J6. **DD** 380.5/09. **[CCC]. Bk Rev. Ad Acc. Circ:** 472. available on microfilm from University Microfilms International (UMI).
**Desc:** Covers all aspects of the social and economic history of transportation.
**Ind/Abst** Am. Hist. Life (1955-); Br. Humanit. Index; Geogr. Abstr. Human Geogr.; Int. Dev. Abstr.; J. Plan. Lit.; Middle East Abstr. Index.

US/0733-947X
**JOURNAL OF TRANSPORTATION ENGINEERING. See** Engineering-Civil Engineering.

US
**KARPOWER COMPUTERIZED USED CAR GUIDE.** English. bm. $299.00. Kelley Blue Book, PO Box 19691, Irvine CA 92713. **Tel** (714)770-7704.

US
**KELLEY BLUE BOOK EARLY MODEL CAR GUIDE.** English. sa. $49.00. Kelley Blue Book, PO Box 19691, Irvine CA 92713. **Tel** (714)770-7704.

US
**KELLEY BLUE BOOK MOTORCYCLE GUIDE.** English. Three times a year. $45.00 continental US; $49.00 other US; $55.00 other. Kelley Blue Book, PO Box 19691, Irvine CA 92713. **Tel** (714)770-7704.

HU/0023-4362
**KOEZLEKEDESTUDOMANYI SZEMLE.** [Koezlekedestud. szle.]. **Added/Corp** Koezlekedestudomanyi Egyesuelet. **VFOAT** Scientific Review of Communication. Vol. 1 (Jan. 1951)-. Periodical. Multiple languages (English, French, German and Russian). mo. $38.00. Lapkiado Vallalat, Lenin Korut 9-11, 1073 Budapest 7, Hungary. **Tel** 222-408. **(Subscription address:** Kultura, PO Box 149, H 1389 Budapest 62 Hungary.**) LC** TA1001; .K6. **CODEN** KOSZAZ. Documents available from Ask*IEEE. ***Supersedes*** *Magyar Koezlekedes, Mely- es Vizepites.*
**Ind/Abst** INSPEC (July 1973-).

FI/0782-5315
**KOTIMAAN VESILIIKENNE.** Finnish. an. **LC** HE675.3; .A23.

JA
**KOTSU ANZEN KOGAI KENKYUJO NEMPO. Main/Corp** Kotsu Anzen Kogai Kenkyujo. 1970/71-. Japanese. an. ¥200. 38-1 Shinkawa 6-chome, Tokyo Japan. **Tel** 011-81-422-48-3866. **LC** HE5614.5.J3; K665A. **Circ:** 1,000.

JA
**KOTSU SHOROPPO. Main/Corp** Japan. **Added/Corp** Japan. Keisatsucho. Kotsu Kikakuka. Japan. Keisatsucho. Kotsukyoku. (1961)-. Periodical. Japanese. ¥950. Taisei Shuppansha, 1-7-11 Hanegi 1, Setagaya-ku, Tokyo-to Japan.

JA
**KOTSUGAKU KENKYU: KENKYU NEMPO. Added/Corp** Nihon Kotsu Gakkai. (1957)-. Japanese. Nikon Kotsu Kuokai, 5-6 Izumicho 2 Kokubunji (185), Kokubunji Japan. **LC** HE7; .K67.

JA
**KYUSHU UNYU YORAN. RIKUUN HEN. Added/Corp** Japan. Kyushu Unyukyoku. **VFOAT** Rikuun Hen. (1986)-. Japanese. **LC** HE5697.K93; J35a. ***Continues*** *Rikuun yoran.*

FR
**LAMY TRANSPORT (SOCIETE LAMY). See** Law.

US
**LARGE CLASS I HOUSEHOLD GOODS CARRIERS SELECTED EARNINGS DATA. Main/Corp** United States. Interstate Commerce Commission. Bureau of Accounts. Periodical. English. qt. Free. Interstate Commerce Commission / Bureau of Accountants, Room 3349 ICC Building, Washington DC 20423. **Tel** (202)275-7351. **Circ:** 550.
**Desc:** Report showing latest earnings and traffic volume data of certain large class I household goods carriers.

US
**LARGE CLASS I MOTOR CARRIERS OF PROPERTY SELECTED EARNINGS DATA. Main/Corp** United States. Interstate Commerce Commission. Bureau of Accounts. English. Interstate Commerce Commission / Bureau of Accountants, Room 3349 ICC Building, Washington DC 20423. **Tel** (202)275-7351.

CN/0709-7093
**LEISURE WHEELS.** [Leis. wheels]. V. 10 - May 1979-. Periodical. English. bm. $10.00. Murray Publications Ltd, PO Box 7302 Station E, Calgary Alberta T3C 3M2 Canada. **Tel** (403)263-2707. **ED** M Gimbel. **DD** 796.7/9/05. **Bk Rev. Ad Acc. Circ:** 25,000 (ctrl). ***Continues*** *Taylor's Leisure Wheels, 0318-3467.*

XV
**LETNI PREGLED PROMETA IN ZVEZ. Main/Corp** Zavod Sr Slovenije Za Statistiko. 1978-. Slovenian. an. Zavod Sr Slovenije za Statistiko, Vozarski Pot 12, Ljubljana Slovenia. **LC** HE80.5; .S5. ***Continues*** *Letni Pregled Prometa.*

US/1056-893X
**LGB TELEGRAM.** [LGB telegr.]. **VAT** Lehmann Gross Bahn Telegram. (July 1991)-. Periodical. English. qt. $18.00. Buffington Associates, Inc., 4171 King George Drive, Suite E, Harrisburgh PA 17109. **DD** 625.

US
**LIGHT, MEDIUM, HEAVY TRUCK SHOP MANUAL.** English. Ford Parts & Service Division, 20000 Rotunda Drive, Dearborn MI 48121. **LC** TL230.5.F57; L53. **DD** 629.28/74/05.

FI/0784-8463
**LIIKENTEEN TILINPAATOSTILASTO. Added/Corp** Finland. Tilastokeskus. **VFOAT** Bokslutsstatistik Over Samfardsel Financial; Statements Statistics of; Transport Communication. (19??)-?. Finnish (Swedish; summaries and/or abstracts in English). an. Tilastokeskus, PL 504, Annankatu 44, 00101 Helsinki Finland. **Tel** 358-0-17341, FAX 358-0-17342474, telex 1002111 TILASTO SF. **LC** HE255.3.A15; L55. ***Continued in part by*** *Puhelinyritysten Tilinpaatostilasto, 0788-3080.*

US/8750-7374
**LIMOUSINE & CHAUFFEUR.** **VFOAT** Limousine and Chauffeur. (1983)-. Periodical. English. Seven times a year. $28.00 (one year), $38.00 (two years), $51.00 (three years) US; $38.00 (one year), $51.00 (two years), $69.00 (three years) Canada; $50.00 (one year), $67.00 (two years), $90.00 (three years) other. Bobit Publishing, 2512 Artesia Boulevard, Redondo Beach CA 90278. **Tel** (310)376-8788, (800)334-8152, FAX (213)376-9043. **ED** Scott Fletcher. **LC** TL232.7; .L56. **DD** 388.4/1321/05. **Circ:** 8,170.

US
**LINEUP.** English. qt. $12.00. Motorcar Operators West, 8672 Fairmont Way, Fair Oaks CA 95628. **ED** Michael J Raposa (Editor's Address: PO Box 51002, Palo Alto, CA 94303-0679; Editor's Phone: (415)496-7315).
**Desc:** Aimed towards those that have an interest in railroad motorcar restoration and operation, primarily for recreational railroad transportation and enthusiast/hobby use.

CN/0256-4742
**LIVE ANIMALS REGULATIONS / IATA.** [Live anim. regul.]. **Main/Corp** International Air Transport Association. **VFOAT** IATA Live Animals Regulations. **VAT** International Air Transport Association Live Animals Regulations. English. an. $46.00. International Air Transport Association / Montreal, 2000 Peel Street, Room 3050, Montreal Quebec H3A 2R4 Canada. **Tel** (514)844-6311 ext. 232, FAX (514)844-5286, telex 05-267627. **DD** 387.7/44.
**Desc:** Contains detailed provisions for preparation of live animals prior to dispatch, container specifications, handling and storage, standards of handling, including information on health and hygiene.

NE
**LLOYD, DE.** LLoyd, L Heyman, Postbus 161, 3190 AD Hoogvliet Netherlands.

UK
**LLOYD'S LOADING LIST.** (1853)-. English. wk (52 issues). £98.00. Lloyd's of London Press Ltd, Sheepen Place, Colchester, Essex, CO3 3LP England. **Tel** 011 44 206 772113, US: (212)529-9500, US: (800)955-6937, FAX 011 44 206 772880, US: (212)529-9826, telex 987321 LLOYDS G. **(Subscription address:** Lloyd's of London Press Inc. / North America, 611 Broadway, Suite 308, New York NY 10012.**) ED** Keith Wright. **LC** HE568; .L6. **DD** 387.51/656. **Bk Rev. Ad Acc. Circ:** 5,000. ***Continues*** *General Weekly Shipping List.*
**Desc:** A weekly directory of export services available from the United Kingdom by road, sea and air to over 1,200 destinations overseas. Plus weekly transportation news, special features, etc. Supplements on related subjects are distributed free of charge to subscribers.

UK/0962-6220
**LOCAL TRANSPORT TODAY.** (?989)-. English. sm. £56.00 UK; £72.00 other. Landor Holdings Ltd, Quadrant House, 250 Kennington Lane, London SE11 5RD England. **Tel** 011 44 71 735 5058, FAX 011 44 71 587 0497. **Bk Rev. Ad Acc.** ctrl circ.
**Desc:** Provides coverage of the total urban and regional UK transport scene from the viewpoint of planners, policy makers, traffic engineers, and economic and environmental analysts with particular reference to those in local government, public authorities, consultancies and research institutions.

CN/0047-4991
**LOGISTICS AND TRANSPORTATION REVIEW, THE.** [Logist. transp. rev.]. **Added/Corp** University of British Columbia. Faculty of Commerce and Business Administration. (1972)-. Periodical. English. qt. 45.00Can$ Canada; $45.00 US; $49.00 (surface mail), $69.00 (air mail) other. University of British Columbia Faculty Commerce Business Administration, 1924 West Mall, Room 100, Vancouver British Columbia V6T 1Z2 Canada. **Tel** (604)822-4977, FAX (604)822-8521. **ED** W G Waters II. **LC** U168; .L6. **DD** 355.4/11/05. **CODEN** LGTRA5. **[CCC].** Index available. **Bk Rev. Pr Rev. Circ:** 1,000 (ctrl). available on microfilm and microfiche from University Microfilms International (UMI); available on an online database (file 648/Full-Text) from DIALOG. Documents available from The Genuine Article, UMI Article Clearinghouse, Ask*IEEE, Documents on Demand. ***Continues*** *Logistics Review, 0024-5844.*
**Desc:** University-based journal dealing specifically with important issues in transport topics, new approaches to logistics problems, managerial problems and government's role in transportation.
**Ind/Abst** ABI/INFORM Glob. Ed.; ABI Inform Ondisc (March 1979-); Acad. Search (Jan. 1993-); Bus. ASAP (1990-) [Full Txt.]; Bus. Index (1985-); Contents Pages Manage.; Curr. Contents Eng. Tech. Appl. Sci.; Econ. Lit. Index; Environ. Abstr.; Gen. BusinessFile (1985-); Gen. Period. Index (1985-); Geogr. Abstr. Human Geogr.; Highw. Res. Abstr.; INFO-SOUTH Abstr.; INSPEC (1972-);; Int. Abstr. Oper. Res. [Select. Cov.]; Int. Aerosp. Abstr.; J. Econ. Lit. (1983); J. Plan. Lit.; Mag. Search; Manage. Contents (1974-); Manage. Contents; Postharvest News Inf.; Res. Alert [Select. Cov.]; SCISEARCH; Soc. Sci. Cit. Index [Select. Cov.]; UMI ABI/Inform--Bus. Period. Ondisc (Dec. 1987-) [Full Txt.]; Vocat. Search (Jan. 1993-); World Agric. Econ.

GW/0173-6213
**LOGISTIK HEUTE.** [Logist. heute]. (19??)-. Periodical. German. ir. DM60.00 Germany; DM70.00 other. Huss Verlag GmbH, Postfach 460480, W 8000 Munich 46 Germany. **Tel** 011 49 89 32391315. **UDC** 658.78.

US/0894-7473
**M & S TIMES.** [M&S times]. **VFOAT** M and S Times. **VAT** Moving and Storage Times. Periodical. English. wk. National Moving and Storage Association, 1500 North Beauregard Street, Alexandria VA 22311-1715. **Tel** (703)941-1770. **DD** 338. ***Continues*** *National Moving & Storage Times, 0747-3877.*

NE
**MAANDSTATISTIEK INTERNATIONAL WEGVERVOER.** **Added/Corp** Netherlands. Centraal Bureau voor de Statistiek. **VFOAT** Monthly Statistical Bulletin of International Transport by Road. No. 1 (Jan. 1966)-. Dutch. mo. **LC** HE5674; .A236. ***Continues*** *Maandstatistiek ven het Grensoverschrijdend Goederenvervoer Over de weg.*

CN/1186-7639
**MAGAZINE DES VEHICULES UTILITAIRES ANCIENS, LE.** [Mag. veh. util. anc.]. **VFOAT** Vehicules Utilitaires Anciens. Vol. 1, No. 1 (Mar/Apr. 1991)-. Periodical. French. bm. 4.50Can$ per issue. Magazine des Vehicules Utilitaires Anciens, 8180 de la Croix, Montreal Quebec H1P 2V2 Canada. **DD** 629.22.

US/0047-5548
**MAINE TRAIL, THE.** **Added/Corp** Maine Good Roads Association. (19??)-. Periodical. English. bm. $20.00. Maine Better Transportation Association, 146 State Street, Augusta ME 04330. **Tel** (207)622-0526.

US/0890-1791
**MAINTENANCE (NEWSLETTER FOR PROFESSIONAL TRUCK DRIVER/OWNERS).** (MAINTENANCE : THE NEWSLETTER FOR PROFESSIONAL TRUCK DRIVERS/OWNERS.). [Maintenance]. **Added/Corp** American Trucking Associations. Maintenance Council. Vol. 1, No. 1 (Oct. 1986)-. Newsletter. English. mo. $58.00 (members), $85.00 (non-members). American Trucking Association, 2200 Mill Road, Alexandria VA 22314. **Tel** (703)838-1772. **DD** 629.
**Desc:** Specializes in trucking management and equipment issues, focusing heavily on government, legislative and regulatory issues, cost control, shop productivity, and future technological possibilities.

US/0890-1775
**MAINTENANCE (NEWSLETTER FOR PROFESSIONAL TRUCK EQUIPMENT MANAGERS).** (MAINTENANCE : THE NEWSLETTER FOR PROFESSIONAL TRUCK EQUIPMENT MANAGERS / THE MAINTENANCE COUNCIL.). [Maintenance]. **Added/Corp** American Trucking Associations. Maintenance Council. Vol. 1, No. 1 (Oct. 1986)-. Periodical. English. mo. $75.00 (nonmember); $48.00 (members). American Trucking Association, 2200 Mill Road, Alexandria VA 22314. **Tel** (703)838-1772. **DD** 629.
**Desc:** Specializes in trucking management and equipment issues, focusing heavily on government, legislative and regulatory issues, cost control, shop productivity, and future technology possibilities.

US/0890-1783
**MAINTENANCE (NEWSLETTER FOR PROFESSIONAL TRUCK EQUIPMENT SUPERVISORS).** (MAINTENANCE : THE NEWSLETTER FOR PROFESSIONAL TRUCK EQUIPMENT SUPERVISORS / THE MAINTENANCE COUNCIL.). [Maintenance]. **Added/Corp** American Trucking Associations. Maintenance Council. Vol. 1, No. 1 (Oct. 1986)-. Periodical. English. mo. $75.00, $48.00 (members). American Trucking Association, 2200 Mill Road, Alexandria VA 22314. **Tel** (703)838-1772. **DD** 629.
**Desc:** Specializes in trucking management and equipment issues, focusing heavily on government, legislative and regulatory issues, cost control, shop productivity, and future technological possibilities.

US/0890-1767
**MAINTENANCE : THE NEWSLETTER FOR PROFESSIONAL TRUCK EQUIPMENT EXECUTIVES.** [Maintenance]. Vol. 1, No. 1 (Sept. 1986)-. Newsletter. English. mo. $75.00, $48.00 (members). Maintenance Council ATA, 2200 Mill Road, Alexandria VA 22314. **DD** 629.
**Desc:** Specializes in trucking management and equipment issues, focusing heavily on government, legislative and regulatory issues, cost control, shop productivity, and future technological possibilities.

US/0025-312X
**M&R. MARINE AND RECREATION NEWS.** ***Ceased.*** **See** Boats and Boating.

UK/0264-2697
**MARICHEM.** (MARICHEM / CONFERENCE ON THE MARINE TRANSPORTATION, HANDLING AND STORAGE OF BULK CHEMICALS.). [MariChem]. **VFOAT** Proceedings. (1977)-. Academic Scholarly Publication. English. be. London RAI, Glen House, 200/208 Tottenham Court Road, London W1P 9LA England. **Tel** 44 0 71 436 9774, FAX 44 0 71 436 5694. **CODEN** MARID8. Index available. **Bk Rev. Circ:** 1,000 (ctrl). Documents available from CASDDS.
**Desc:** Covering all modes of transportation including road, river, rail, and sea as related to storage, commerce, training, safety, distribution, policy, technical innovation, and regulatory isues.
**Ind/Abst** Chem. Abstr.

US/0364-3484
**MASS TRANSIT (WASHINGTON, D.C.).** (MASS TRANSIT.). [Mass transit]. **VFOAT** MT. Vol. 1 (June 1974)-. Periodical. English. Six times a year. $40.00 US & Canada; $65.00 other. PTN Publishing Company, 445 Broad Hollow Road, Melville NY 11747. **Tel** (516)845-2700, FAX (516)845-7109. **ED** Patricia S. Brucato, Thomas S. Kapinos. **LC** HE4201; .M35. **DD** 388.4/05. **Ad Acc.** available on microfilm and microfiche from University Microfilms International (UMI); available on an online database (file 648/Full-Text) from DIALOG.
**Desc:** International publication dealing with issues, products, systems and legislation concerning the mass transit.
**Ind/Abst** Acad. Search (July 1993-); Appl. Sci. Technol. Index; Avery Index Archit. Period. Suppl. Colum. Univ. (1990-); Bus. ASAP (1990-) [Full Txt.]; Bus. Index (1985-); Bus. Period. Index; Bus. Source (Jul. 1993-); Gen. BusinessFile (1985-); Gen. Period. Index (1985-); Highw. Res. Abstr.; Mag. Search; Trade Ind. ASAP [Full Txt.]; Trade Ind. Index (1981-) [Full Txt.]; Urban Aff. Abstr.; Vocat. Search (July 1993-); Wilson Bus. Abstr.

US/0092-1254
**MASTER PLAN FOR TRANSPORTATION (TRENTON).** (A MASTER PLAN FOR TRANSPORTATION.). **Main/Corp** New Jersey. Dept. of Transportation. 1968-. English. Department of Transportation / Trenton, 1035 Parkway Avenue, Trenton NJ 08625. **LC** HE28.N5; D46A. **DD** 711/.73/09749.

US
**MBTA BUDGET, REPORT OF ADVISORY BOARD BUDGET COMMITTEE.** **Main/Corp** Massachusetts Bay Transportation Authority. Budget Committee. 1978-. English. Massachusetts Bay Transportation Authority, 50 High Street, Boston MA 02110. **LC** HE310 .B6; M36A. **DD** 352.1/252. ***Continues*** *MBTA Itemized Budget and Report of Advisory Budget Committee, 0363-1346.*

US/0733-6012
**MCD. MIDDLE ATLANTIC EDITION.** (MCD.). **VFOAT** M.C.D.; American Motor Carrier Directory. **VAT** Motor Carrier Directory. Middle Atlantic Edition. English. an. $40.00 single issue. American Motor Carrier, 473 Hemlock Drive, Marietta GA 30064. **Tel** (404)427-6362.

UK
**MET, MIDDLE EAST TRANSPORTATION.** **VFOAT** Middle East Transportation. Periodical. English. mo. Free to qualified, $62.00 other. **LC** HE268.2.A1; M17. **DD** 380.5/0956.

CN/0714-4776
**METRO GUIDE (MONTREAL, QUEBEC).** (METRO GUIDE.). [Metro guide]. 1981/82-. French. an. Free. Publications Metro Guide, Bureau 1405/3637 East Boulevard Cremazie, Montreal Quebec H1Z 2J9 Canada. **DD** 388.4/28/09714281.

US/1057-8196
**METRO MAGAZINE.** **VFOAT** Metropolitan. Vol. 81, No. 3 (May/June 1985)-. Periodical. English. Seven times a year. $25.00 (one year), $34.00 (two years), $46.00 (three years) US; $30.00 (one year), $41.00 (two years), $55.00 (three years) Canada; $38.00 (one year), $51.00 (two years), $69.00 (three years) other. Bobit Publishing, 2512 Artesia Boulevard, Redondo Beach CA 90278. **Tel** (310)376-8788, (800)334-8152, FAX (213)376-9043. available on microfilm and microfiche from University Microfilms International (UMI). ***Continues*** *Metro (Redondo Beach, Calif.), 0162-6221; Metropolitan Public Transportation Administration and Planning.*
**Ind/Abst** Highw. Res. Abstr.

RU
**METROSTROI.** **Added/Corp** Metrostroi, Moscow. (19??)-. Periodical. Russian. mo. $16.00. **(Subscription address:** Victor Kamkin, 4956 Boiling Brook Parkway, Rockville MD 20852.**) LC** TF845; .M47.

US/0097-8744
**MICHIGAN SCHOOL BUS ACCIDENTS.** **Main/Corp** Michigan. Dept. of State Police. English. an. Michigan Department of State Police, 714 South Harrison Road, East Lansing MI 48823. **LC** HE5614.3.M4; M49A. **DD** 388.3/14.

US/0746-2298
**MICHIGAN SNOWMOBILER.** (19??)-. Periodical. English. Six times a year. $6.00 (1 year), $8.00 (2 year), $10.00 (3 year) US; $11.00 (1 year), $18.00 (2 year), $25.00 (3 year) Canada; $9.00 (1 year), $12.50 (2 year), $16.00 (3 year) other. Michigan Snowmobiler, PO Box 417, Jordan MI 49727. **Tel** (616)536-2371. **ED** Lyle K Shipe. **Ad Acc. Circ:** 29,300 (ctrl).
**Desc:** Covers snowmobiling related subjects.

US/0741-5451
**MICROCOMPUTERS IN TRANSPORTATION. SOFTWARE AND SOURCE BOOK.** (MICROCOMPUTERS IN TRANSPORTATION. SOFTWARE AND SOURCE BOOK / U.S. DEPARTMENT OF TRANSPORTATION.). [Microcomput. transp., Softw. source book]. **VFOAT** Software and Source Book; MTPS; M.T.P.S. Jan. 1983-. Periodical. English. US Department of Transportation / Urban Mass Transportation Administration, Methods Division, National Technical Information Service, 5285 Port Royal Road, Springfield VA 22161. **Tel** (800)553-6847, (703)487-4812. **LC** HE147.6; .M53. **DD** 388.4/028/5425. ***Continues** Microcomputers in Transportation. Information Source Book.*

UK/0261-1473
**MIDDLE EAST INDUSTRY & TRANSPORT.** ***Ceased.*** [Middle East ind. transp.]. **VFOAT** Middle East Industry and Transport. Issue No. 34 (Jan./Feb. 1981)-?. Periodical. English. bm. IC Publications Ltd., 7 Coldbath Square, London EC1R 4LQ England. **Tel** 011 44 71 713-7711, FAX 011 44 71 713-7898, telex 8811757. **ED** Norma Di Marco. **LC** HE268.2 .A15; M43. **DD** 380.5/0956. **Bk Rev. Ad Acc. Circ:** 6,500 (ctrl). ***Continues** Middle East Transport.*

US/0199-2317
**MILK AND LIQUID FOOD TRANSPORTER.** Vol. 18, No. 5 (April 1978)-. Periodical. English. mo. Milk & Liquid Food Transporter Avenue, PO Box 878, Menomonee Falls WI 53051. **Tel** (414)255-0108. **ED** Linda Mittag. **Ad Acc. Circ:** 6,000 (ctrl). ***Continues** Milk Hauler and Liquid Food Transporter.*
**Desc:** Articles of interest to those involved in the transportation and processing of bulk milk and liquid foods.

US/0094-7466
**MINERALS TRANSPORTATION. See** Earth Sciences-Mineralogy.

US
**MINNESOTA MOTOR VEHICLE LAW. See** Law.

●CN/1193-2651
**MINUTES OF PROCEEDINGS AND EVIDENCE OF THE SUB-COMMITTEE ON THE ST. LAWRENCE SEAWAY OF THE STANDING COMMITTEE ON TRANSPORT.** [Minutes proc. evid. Sub-Comm. St. Lawrence Seaw. Standing Comm. Transp.]. **Main/Corp** Canada. Parliament. House of Commons. Sub-Committee on the St. Lawrence Seaway. **VFOAT** St. Lawrence Seaway; Proces-Verbaux et Temoignages du Sous-Comite sur lla Voie Maritime du Saint-Laurent du Comite Permanent des Transports. (1992)-. Proceedings. English (French). **DD** 386/.5/09714.

●CN/1193-2651
**MINUTES OF PROCEEDINGS AND EVIDENCE OF THE SUB-COMMITTEE ON THE ST. LAWRENCE SEAWAY OF THE STANDING COMMITTEE ON TRANSPORT (FRENCH EDITON).** [Minutes proc. evid. Sub-Comm. St. Lawrence Seaw. Standing Comm. Transp.]. **Main/Corp** Canada. Parlement. Chambre des Communes. Sous-Comite sur la Voie Maritime du Saint-Laurent. **VFOAT** La Voie Maritime du Saint-Laurent; Proces-Verbaux et Temoignages du Sous-Comite sur la Voie Maritime du Saint-Laurent du Comite Permanent des Transports. (1992)-. Proceedings. French (English). **DD** 386/.5/09714.

US
**MITCHELL DOMESTIC LIGHT TRUCKS AND VANS SERVICE AND REPAIR.** (1990)-. Periodical. English. an. Mitchell International Inc, PO Box 26260, San Diego CA 92126-0260. **Tel** (619)578-6550, (800)648-8010, FAX (619)578-4752. ***Continues** Domestic Light Trucks and Vans Service and Repair.*

US/1054-8076
**MOBILE HOME & RV TRAILER GUIDE, NEW & USED VALUES. Main/Corp** Kelley Blue Book Co. **VFOAT** Mobile Home and RV Trailer Guide, New and Used Values. **VAT** Mobile Home and Recreational Vehicle Trailer Guide, New & Used Value. (19??)-. English. $20.00. Kelley Blue Book, PO Box 19691, Irvine CA 92713. **Tel** (714)770-7704. **LC** HD9710.A1; K44a. **DD** 381/.45/6292260973.

US
**MOBILITY TRENDS.** (1980)-. Periodical. English. qt. Allied Van Lines Inc, PO Box 4403, Chicago IL 60680.

US/0891-6187
**MODEL T TIMES.** [Model T times]. Periodical. English. bm. $16.00 (membership) US; $19.00 (membership) other. Model T Ford Club International, PO Box 438315, Chicago IL 60643-8315. **DD** 388.

SA
**MOMENTUM (JOHANNESBURG, SOUTH AFRICA).** ***Ceased.*** (MOMENTUM.). **Added/Corp** South African Transport Services. (Summer 1984)-(19??). Periodical. Afrikaans (English). qt. PTP Publishing Services, PO Box 31753, Braamfontein 2017 South Africa. **LC** HE284.3.A15; M66.

US/0545-025X
**MOODY'S TRANSPORTATION MANUAL. VFOAT** Transportation Manual. (1954)-. Periodical. English. an. $1625.00. Moody's Investors Service, 99 Church Street, New York NY 10007. **Tel** (212)553-0547, (212)553-0435, FAX (212)553-4700. **LC** HG4971; .M74. **DD** 380.5/0973. ***Continues in part** Moody's Manual of Investments, American and Foreign. Transportation.*

AT
**MOTOR.** (19??)-. Periodical. English. mo. 67.20Aus$ Australia; 80.30Aus$ New Zealand; 121.20Aus$ other. Australian Consolidated Press Ltd, GPO Box 5252, Sydney New South Wales 2001 Australia. **Tel** 011 61 2 2600000. ***Continues** Modern Motor.*

NZ/0550-5089
**MOTOR ACCIDENTS IN NEW ZEALAND.** Periodical. English. an. 12.50NZ$ New Zealand; 10.00NZ$ other. Land Transport Division, Ministry of Transport, PO Box 27-459, Wellington New Zealand. **Tel** 828 300, FAX 855699. **LC** HE5614.5.N45; M65. **DD** 388.3/14. **Circ:** 500.
**Desc:** Tables of road accident data for a given calender year.

US/0160-4570
**MOTOR CARRIER ANNUAL REPORTS.** (MOTOR CARRIER ANNUAL REPORT / FINANCIAL & OPERATING STATISTICS.). **Main/Corp** American Trucking Associations. **Added/Corp** American Trucking Associations. American Trucking Associations. Financial & Operating Statistics. **VFOAT** Motor Carrier Annual Reports. (19??)-. English. an. American Trucking Association, 2200 Mill Road, Alexandria VA 22314. **Tel** (703)838-1772. **LC** HE5623.A1; A652a. **DD** 388.3/24/0973.

US
**MOTOR CARRIER FREIGHT FORWARDER DIGEST SERVICE. INCLUDES SUPPLEMENTS.** (1937)-. English. Twelve times a year. $330.00. Hawkins Publishing Company, PO Box 480, Mayo MD 21106. **Tel** (410)798-1677. available in Loose-leaf.
**Desc:** Analysis of reports of the Interstate Commerce Commission.

US/0739-117X
**MOTOR COACH AGE.** [Mot. coach age]. **Added/Corp** Motor Bus Society. (19??)-. Periodical. English. mo (12 issues). $25.00 (comes with membership to Motor Bus Society). Motor Bus Society Inc, PO Box 10503, New Brunswick NJ 08906. **LC** HE5601; .M5515. Index available. cum. index. **Bk Rev.**
**Desc:** Information on bus lines.

UK/0027-1853
**MOTOR CYCLE NEWS PETERBOROUGH.** [Mot. cycle news Peterb.]. **VFOAT** Motorcycle News. (1955)-. Periodical. English. Fifty-two times a year. £45.50 UK, £55.50 others (surface mail); £58.00 Europe, £69.00 Middle East & North Africa; £81.00 others, £93.00 Pacific Island, Australasia & Far East (airmail). EMAP National Publications Ltd, Farndon Road, Market Harborough, Leicestershire, LE16 9NR England. **Tel** 011 44 733 555161. **DD** 796.7. **[CCC].**

US/0886-8778
**MOTOR FREIGHT CONTROLLER.** [Motor freight control.]. **VFOAT** Controller. Periodical. English. mo. National Accounting & Finance Council, 2200 Mill Road, Alexandria VA 22314. **DD** 388.

US
**MOTOR HOMES, CAMPERS, VAN CONVERSIONS, SURFER VANS. VFOAT** Kelley Blue Book RV Guide. (19??)-. English. ir. $33.00. Kelley Blue Book, PO Box 19691, Irvine CA 92713. **Tel** (714)770-7704. **LC** HD9710.U5; K44a. **DD** 380.1/45690879/0973.

UK
**MOTOR INDUSTRY OF GREAT BRITAIN, THE.** ***Title Change.*** 1930-?. English. an. Society of Motor Manufacturers & Traders, Forbes House, Halkin Street, London SW1X 7DS England. **Tel** 01-550-3231. **ED** M Murphy. **Circ:** 900. ***Continued by** Motor Industry of Great Britain ..., World Automotive Statistics.*
**Desc:** Covers vehicles in use, vehicles in production, new registrations, United Kingdom production by model and UK exports by manufacturer, plus miscellaneous information related to the motor industry.

US
**MOTOR LIGHT TRUCK TUNE UP & REPAIR MANUAL.** ***Title Change.*** **VFOAT** Motor Light Truck Tune Up and Repair Manual; Light Truck Tune Up & Repair Manual; Light Truck Tune Up and Repair Manual. (1986)-(19??). English. an. Hearst Corporation, c/o Ronald Powell, 817 Round Hill Road, Pelham AL 35124. **Tel** (205)663-0353, (800)288-6828. **LC** TL230.2; .M69. **DD** 629.28/73. ***Continues** Motor Light Truck & Van Repair Manual.* ***Continued by** Motor Truck Engine Tune-Up & Electronic Manual.*

UK
**MOTOR SPECIFICATIONS AND PRICES. VFOAT** Stone & Cox Motor Specifications & Prices. Began in 1922. Periodical. English. an. £10.00 UK; $15.00 US. Stone & Cox Ltd Publishers, 111 Peter Street, Suite 202, Toronto Ontario M5V 2H1 Canada. **Tel** (416)599-0772. **ED** Ernest Holland. **LC** HD9710.G7; .M57. **Ad Acc. Circ:** 1,000.
**Desc:** Specifications, prices and recommended insurance group ratings for all models of UK manufactured and non-UK private cars and motorcycles for the past four years.

US/0027-206X
**MOTOR TRANSPORT [MICROFORM].** (1905)-. English. wk. $119.00 US and Canada. Reed Business Publishing / West Sussex, England, Perrymount Road, Haywards Heath, West Sussex RH16 3DH England. **Tel** 011 44 81 6523500. **(Subscription address:** Computer Action Ltd., Central House, 27 Park Street, Croyden Surrey CR0 1YD England**) LC** Microfilm 02080. ***Continues** Bus & Coach.*
**Ind/Abst** Fluid Abstr., Civil Eng.; Fluid Abstr. Proc. Eng.; FLUIDEX (19??-); Infomat Int. Bus.; PROMT.

CN/0027-2108
**MOTOR TRUCK.** [Mot. truck]. Vol. 33, No. 6 (June 1964)-. Periodical. English. mo. 30.00Can$ (one year), 49.00Can$ (two year) Canada; 47.00Can$ (one year), 75.00Can$ (two year) other. Southam Information and Technology Group Inc., 1450 Don Mills Road, Don Mills Ontario M3B 2X7 Canada. **Tel** (416)445-6641, (800)668-2374, FAX (416)442-2261. **DD** 388.3/24/0971. available on microfilm and microfiche from University Microfilms International (UMI). ***Continues** Motor Truck & Coach, 0380-0849.*

US
**MOTORCYCLE AND ATV MARKET REVIEW.** English. Motorcycle Industry Council Inc, 2 Jenner Street/Suite 150, Irvine CA 92718. **Tel** (714)727-4211. **LC** HD9710.5.U5; M67. **DD** 381/.456292275/0973.

US/0164-9256
**MOTORCYCLIST'S POST, THE.** 1967. Periodical. English. mo. $10.00 US; $16.00 other. Motorcyclist Post, PO Box 154, Rochdale MA 01542. **Tel** (617)885-5221. **ED** Stephen D Henry and Robert F Frink. **Bk Rev. Ad Acc. Circ:** 10,060. available on CD-ROM; available on an online database.
**Desc:** Motorcycle activity and sport riding in New England area.

US/0744-074X
**MOTORHOME.** [MotorHome]. **VFOAT** Motor Home. Vol. 19, No. 1 (Jan. 1982)-. Periodical. English. mo. $26.00. TL Enterprises, 29901 Agoura Road, Agoura CA 91301. **Tel** (800)234-3450, (805)389-0300. **(Subscription address:** Neodata / Colorado, PO Box 2606, Boulder Boulder CO 80322.**) ED** Bob Livingston. **LC** TX1100; .M67. **DD** 643/.2. **Circ:** 119,546. ***Continues** Motorhome Life (Agoura, Calif.), 0164-503X.*
**Ind/Abst** Consum. Index Prod. Eval. Inf. Source.

IT/1120-415X
**MOTORIZZAZIONE, LA.** [Motorizzazione]. (1981)-. Periodical. Italian. sm. L129000.00. Egaf Edizioni SAS, Via F Guarini 2, 47100 Forli Italy. **Tel** 011 39 543 782278, FAX 011 39 543 782255. **UDC** 656.1. Index available. cum. index. **Circ:** 4,000. available on diskette.
**Desc:** Contains updates of national transport and all newly issued laws.

US/0279-0971
**MOVING HOUSE AND HOME (NEW YORK, N.Y.).** (MOVING HOUSE AND HOME.). (198?)-. Periodical. English. qt. Moving Market Inc., 420 Lexington Avenue / Suite 2616, New York NY 10170.

US
**N.A.D.A. MOTORCYCLE, SNOWMOBILE, ATV, AND PERSONAL WATERCRAFT APPRAISAL GUIDE. Added/Corp** National Automobile Dealers Association. **VFOAT** NADA Motorcycle Snowmobile ATV Personal Watercraft; Motorcycle, Snowmobile, ATV, Personal Watercraft Appraisal Guide; N.A.D.A. Appraisal Guide; N.A.D.A. Motorcycle Appraisal Guide. **VAT** National Automobile Dealers Association Motorcycle, Snowmobile,

ATV, Personal Watercraft Appraisal Guide. (Jan./April 1988)-. English. Three times a year. $45.00. NADA Appraisal Guides, PO Box 7800, Costa Mesa CA 92628. **Tel** (714)556-8511, (800)966-6232, FAX (714)556-8715. **ED** Lenny Sims and Bob Marsh. **LC** HD9710.5.A1; N16. **DD** 629.22/042. ***Continues*** *N.A.D.A. Motorcycle-Moped-ATV-Personal Watercraft Appraisal Guide.*
**Desc:** Lists used wholesale and used retail values for all motorcycles, ATV's, personal watercraft and snowmobiles.

US
**N.A.D.A. OFFICIAL OLDER USED CAR GUIDE : AN OFFICIAL N.A.D.A. VALUE GUIDE.** **Added/Corp** National Automobile Dealers Association. **VFOAT** NADA Official Older Used Car Guide; Official Older Used Car Guide; Older Used Car Guide. (198?)-. English. Three times a year. $50.00. NADA Appraisal Guides, PO Box 7800, Costa Mesa CA 92628. **Tel** (714)556-8511, (800)966-6232, FAX (714)556-8715. **ED** Lynn Weaver. ***Continues in part*** *N.A.D.A. Older Car, RV, Motorcycle.*
**Desc:** Lists used trade-in, average loan, and used retail values for domestic and imported cars. Also includes light duty trucks.

US/0092-4601
**N.A.D.A. RECREATION VEHICLE APPRAISAL GUIDE.** **Main/Corp** National Automobile Dealers Association. **Added/Corp** Recreational Vehicle Dealers of America. National Automobile Dealers Association. Recreation Vehicle Appraisal Guide. (19??)-. English. Three times a year. $95.00. NADA Appraisal Guides, PO Box 7800, Costa Mesa CA 92628. **Tel** (714)556-8511, (800)966-6232, FAX (714)556-8715. **ED** Lenny Sims. **LC** HD9715.7.U6; N39a. **DD** 381/.45/6292260973.
**Desc:** Lists used wholesale and used retail values for all types of RV's. Also shows suggested list prices.

US/0194-939X
**NATIONAL BUS TRADER.** (Dec. 1977)-. Periodical. English. mo (12 issues). $20.00 US; $25.00 other. National Bus Trader Inc, 9698 West Judson Road, Polo IL 61064. **Tel** (815)946-2341, FAX (815)946-2347. **ED** Larry Plachno. **LC** TL232; .N275. **DD** 629.2/2233/0973. Index available. **Bk Rev**, (Qty: 1-2). **Ad Acc, Adv Mgr:** J. Plachno. **Circ:** 6,000.

US
**NATIONAL MOTOR FREIGHT CLASSIFICATION.** (1952)-. English. ir. $49.55 per copy. American Trucking Association, 2200 Mill Road, Alexandria VA 22314. **Tel** (703)838-1772.

US/0889-0749
**NATIONAL SCHOOL BUS REPORT.** ***Title Change.*** [Natl. sch. bus rep.]. **Added/Corp** National Association of School Bus Contract Operators. National School Transportation Association. Vol. 1 (June/July 1971)-(Dec. 1991). Periodical. English. qt. National School Transportation Association, PO Box 2639, Springfield VA 22152. **Tel** (703)644-0700. **LC** LB2864; .N338. **DD** 371.8/7/0973. ***Continued by*** *NSTA Bi-Weekly Newsletter.*

US/0077-586X
**NATIONAL TANK TRUCK CARRIER DIRECTORY.** **Added/Corp** National Tank Truck Carriers, inc. (1955)-. Directory. English. an (January). $42.00 members; $62.00 nonmembers. National Truck Carriers Inc, 2200 Mill Road, Alexandria VA 22314. **Tel** (703)838-1960. **LC** HE5623.A45; N33. **DD** 388. **Ad Acc. Circ:** 3,000.
**Desc:** Listing of for hire Bulk Carriers (tank truck carriers) in the US, Canada, and several other nations.

US/0094-761X
**NATIONAL TRANSPORTATION SAFETY BOARD DECISIONS.** **Main/Corp** United States. National Transportation Safety Board. Vol. 1 (Apr. 1, 1967-Dec. 31, 1972)-. English. Department of Transportation, 400 Seventh Street SW, Washington DC 20590. **Tel** (202)426-4000. **LC** KF2172.A2; T7. **DD** 344/.73/047.

US/0148-222X
**NATIONAL TRUCK CHARACTERISTIC REPORT.** **Main/Corp** United States. Office of Highway Planning. Planning Services Branch. English. an. US Department of Transportation - Federal Highway Administration, 400 Seventh Street Southwest, Washington DC 20590. **Tel** (202)366-0660. **LC** TL230.A1; U56A. **DD** 629.22/4.

US/1040-2284
**NATSO TRUCKERS NEWS.** [NATSO truck. news]. **Added/Corp** National Association of Truck Stop Operators (U.S.). **VFOAT** Truckers News. **VAT** National Association of Truck Stop Operators Truckers News. (198?)-. Periodical. English. mo. $13.00. National Association of Truck Stop Operators (NATSO), 1199 North Fairfax Street, Suite 101, Alexandria VA 22313. **Tel** (703)549-2100. **DD** 388. Index available. **Ad Acc. Circ:** 210,000 (ctrl).

US/0148-8457
**NEW CONCEPTS IN URBAN TRANSPORTATION.** ***Ceased.*** Vol. 2 (July 15, 1972)-?. Periodical. English. ir. Transportation Research Board, Box 289, Washington DC 20055. **Tel** (202)334-3218, FAX (202)334-2519. ***Continues*** *Personal Rapid Transit.*

US
**NEW HAMPSHIRE SELECTED MOTOR VEHICLE AND BOATING LAWS.** **See** Law.

US/0148-8511
**NEWSLINE (WASHINGTON).** (NEWSLINE.). **Added/Corp** National Research Council (U.S.). Transportation Research Board. (19??)-. Periodical. English. Three times a year. Free on request. Transportation Research Board, Box 289, Washington DC 20055. **Tel** (202)334-3218, FAX (202)334-2519. **Ind/Abst** Print. Abstr.

NE
**NIEUWSBLAD TRANSPORT.** Nieusblad Transport, Postbus 30180, 3001 DD Rotterdam Netherlands.

●US/1061-8090
**NORTHEAST JOURNAL OF TRANSPORTATION, THE.** **VFOAT** N.E. Journal of Transportation. (1992)-. Newspaper. English. wk. $82.00 US; $102.00 Canada. Northeast Journal of Transportation, PO Box 404, 31 Fargo Street, Boston MA 02127. **Tel** (617)695-1660, FAX (617)695-1665. ***Continues*** *New England Journal of Transportation, 1062-4309.*
**Desc:** Weekly newspaper serving the shipping, trucking, air freight, and railroad industries in the Northeast.

US/0550-0974
**NOTES FROM UNDERGROUND.** ***Suspended.*** No. 1 (1964)-Vol. 18 (1988). English. mo. $20.00. Committee Better Transit Inc, PO Box 3106, Long Island City NY 11103. **Tel** (718)728-0091. **ED** Stephen B. Dobro. **LC** AP2; .N887. **Bk Rev. Ad Acc. Circ:** 2,400. available in microform. ***Continues*** *Renaissance.*
**Desc:** News and views on urban transportation, with special emphasis on the New York-New Jersey metropolitan area.

US
**NSTA BI-WEEKLY NEWSLETTER.** (1992)-. Newsletter. English. Twenty-six times a year. $2000.00 (manufacturer membership), $1200.00 (suppler & public affiliate membership), $500.00 (single state supplier), $125.00 (individual public membership). National School Transportation Association, PO Box 2639, Springfield VA 22152. **Tel** (703)644-0700. ***Continues*** *National School Bus Report., 0880-0749.*

US
**NTIS ALERT. TRANSPORTATION.** (19??)-. Periodical. English. Twenty-four times a year. $145.00 US; $210.00 other. National Technical Information Service - NTIS, Room 2027S, 5285 Port Royal Road, Springfield VA 22161. **Tel** (703)487-4630, (703)487-4660, (703)487-4650, FAX (703)321-8547, telex 89-9405. Index available. ***Continues*** *Transportation / NTIS, 0163-1527.*
**Desc:** Provides information on metropolitan rail transportation, global navigation systems, safety, etc.

US/0745-9874
**NTSB REPORTER.** [NTSB report.]. **VFOAT** N.T.S.B. Reporter. **VAT** National Transportation Safety Board Reporter. Vol. 1, No. 1 (1983)-. Periodical. English. mo. $36.00. Peter Katz Productions Inc, PO Box 831, White Plains NY 10602. **Tel** (914)949-7443.

GW
**NUTZFAHRZEUG, DAS.** (Jan. 1949)-. Periodical. German. mo. DM102.80 Germany; DM114.20 other. Vogel Fachzeitschriften GmbH, Neumarkter Str 18, D 81664 Munich Germany. **Tel** 011 49 89 431800. **ED** Theo Delfried Dolmina. **LC** TL3; .N8. Index available. cum. index. **Bk Rev. Ad Acc. Circ:** 5,000 (ctrl).
**Desc:** Covers fleet operating, vehicle specifications, test reports on trucks and trailers and transport business information.

US/0191-152X
**OAG AIR CARGO GUIDE.** **VFOAT** Air Cargo Guide. (19??)-. English. Twelve times a year. $117.00. Official Airline Guides, 2000 Clearwater Drive, Oak Brook IL 60521. **Tel** (800)323-3537. **(Subscription address:** Neodata / Colorado, PO Box 2606, Boulder Boulder CO 80322.) **ED** Alex Igyarto. **Ad Acc. Circ:** 9,000. available on microfilm and microfiche from University Microfilms International (UMI).
**Desc:** Reference publication for worldwide commercial airfreight schedules and related information.

CN/0712-1067
**OCCASIONAL PAPER (UNIVERSITY OF BRITISH COLUMBIA. CENTRE FOR TRANSPORTATION STUDIES).** (AN OCCASIONAL PAPER / THE CENTRE FOR TRANSPORTATION STUDIES, UNIVERSITY OF BRITISH COLUMBIA.). Monographic series. English. Price varies per volume. Centre for Transportation Studies, University of British Columbia, Vancouver British Columbia B6T 1W5 Canada. **DD** 380.5/07/2.

CN/0229-9704
**OCCASIONAL STUDENT PAPER (UNIVERSITY OF BRITISH COLUMBIA. CENTRE FOR TRANSPORTATION STUDIES).** (AN OCCASIONAL STUDENT PAPER / THE CENTRE FOR TRANSPORTATION STUDIES, UNIVERSITY OF BRITISH COLUMBIA.). [Occas. stud. pap. - Cent. Transp. Stud., Univ. B.C.]. **VFOAT** Student Paper. **VAT** Student Paper - Centre for Transportation Studies. University of British Columbia. English. qt. Centre for Transportation Studies, University of British Columbia, Vancouver British Columbia B6T 1W5 Canada. **DD** 380.5/0971.

GW/0172-4185
**OFF ROAD MUNCHEN.** (1978)-. Periodical. German. Twelve times a year. DM81.60. DSB Abonnements Verwaltung GMB, Kochendorfer STR 40, PF 1163 W 7107, Neckarsulum, Germany. **Tel** 011 49 7132 385238, FAX 011 49 7132 385243. **ED** Alfons Gerny & Berhard Weinbacher. **UDC** 621.11:379.8. **Ad Acc, Adv Mgr:** R. Muhlberger. **Circ:** 183,800 (ctrl).

US
**OFFICAL INTERMODAL GUIDE : DIRECTORY OF INTERMODAL SERVICES, FACILITIES AND PERSONNEL, THE.** Vol. 1, No. 1 (Spring/Summer 1983)-. Directory. English. sa. $220.00 US & Mexico; $226.00 other. K III Press Inc., 424 West 33rd Street, New York NY 10001. **Tel** (212)714-3100, (800)221-5488. **LC** HE9.U5; O43. **DD** 380.5/24/02573.

US/0192-2629
**OFFICIAL DIRECTORY OF INDUSTRIAL AND COMMERCIAL TRAFFIC EXECUTIVES, THE.** **VFOAT** Directory of Industrial and Commercial Traffic Executives; Industrial and Commercial Traffic Executives. (19??)-. Directory. English. an. $157.00 US & Mexico; $195.00 other. K III Press Inc., 424 West 33rd Street, New York NY 10001. **Tel** (212)714-3100, (800)221-5488. **ED** Crista Byrne. **Ad Acc. Circ:** 4,000. ***Continues*** *Official Directory of Commercial Traffic Executives, with an Appendix of Transportation Commissions and Organizations.*
**Desc:** A directory of executives in the traffic and transportation distribution profession in the U.S. and Canada. Also lists consultants, government agencies, and associations involved in the profession.

US
**OFFICIAL FINANCIAL STATEMENT.** **Main/Corp** Florida. Dept. of Transportation. June 1980-. English. an. Florida Department of Transportation, Fiscal Mail Station 42, Tallahassee FL 32301. **LC** HE28.F6; D46B. **DD** 353.97590072/31. ***Continues*** *Florida. Dept. of Transportation. Official Financial Statements.*

US/0190-6690
**OFFICIAL INTERMODAL EQUIPMENT REGISTER, THE.** (1969)-. Periodical. English. qt. $106.00 US & Mexico; $187.00 other. K III Press Inc., 424 West 33rd Street, New York NY 10001. **Tel** (212)714-3100, (800)221-5488. **Ad Acc.**
**Desc:** Dimensions and capacities tariff for containers, trailers and chassis in intermodal use by listed companies. Covers reporting marks, and type codes series.

CN/0713-8776
**OFFICIAL MANITOBA SHIP-BY-TRUCK DIRECTORY (1983).** (THE OFFICIAL MANITOBA SHIP-BY-TRUCK DIRECTORY.). [Off. Manit. ship-by-truck dir.]. **Added/Corp** Manitoba Trucking Association. **VFOAT** Manitoba Ship-by-Truck Directory; M.T.A Ship-by-Truck Directory. (1983)-. Directory. English. an. 27.00Can$. Manitoba Trucking Association, 25 Bunting Street, Winnipeg R2X 2P5 Man Canada. **Tel** (204)632-6600, FAX (204)694-7134. **ED** Bob Wilks. **DD** 388.3/24/0257127. **Ad Acc. Circ:** 1,600. ***Continues*** *SBTD : Manitoba Ship-by-Truck Directory, 0228-7315.*
**Desc:** Contains complete information on shipping and truck services in Manitoba for carriers, shippers, receivers and traffic managers.

US/0472-6243
**OFFICIAL MOTOR CARRIER DIRECTORY.** Began in Autumn 1958. Directory. English. sa. $31.50. Official Motor Carrier Directory Inc, 1130 South Canal Street, Chicago IL 60607. **Tel** (312)939-1434 OR (800)621-4650. **ED** Laura M Stukus. **LC** HE5623.A45; O4. **DD** 388.3/24/02573. **Bk Rev. Ad Acc. Circ:** 5,000.
**Desc:** Alphabetical listing of motor and air carriers. Provides general office information, terminals etc. Also lists organizations related to transportation.

FR/1156-3133
**OFFICIEL DES TRANSPORTS PARIS, L'.** (L'OFFICIEL DES TRANSPORTEURS.). (1991)-. Periodical. French. Forty-six times a year. 680.00F France; 795.00F other. Compagnie Gen Developpement,

11 rue Godefroy Cavaignac, 75541 Paris Cedex 11 France. **Tel** 011 33 1 43790630, FAX 011 33 1 43791775, telex 211351. **UDC** 656. ***Continues*** *Officiel des Transporteurs et Garagistes., 1163-0736.*

US
**OHIO MOTOR VEHICLE LAWS.** **See** Law.

US
**OHIO MOTORISTS ASSOCIATION.** English. $39.00 (individual), $17.00 (associate). Ohio Motorists Association, PO Box 6150, Cleveland OH 44101. **Tel** (216)361-6000.

US
**ON THE MOVE (BUFFALO, N.Y.).** (ON THE MOVE / NIAGARA FRONTIER TRANSPORTATION AUTHORITY.). Vol. 1, No. 1 (Jan. 1981)-. Periodical. English. qt. Free. Niagara Frontier Transportation Authority, 181 Ellicott Street, Buffalo NY 14205. **Tel** (716)855-7657, telex ESL 6290-6025. **ED** Larry Schieber. **Circ:** 7,500 (ctrl).
**Desc:** Reports on progress and activities on Niagara Frontier Transportation Authority.

NE/0030-3461
**OPENBAAR VERVOER.** [Openbaar vervoer]. (19??)-. Academic Scholarly Publication. Dutch. mo (10 issues). Fl30.00 (institutions); Fl40.00 other. Albracht, Postbus 50, 3417 ZH Montfoort Netherlands. **Tel** 011 03484-2544. **LC** HE7; .O64.
**Ind/Abst** EMBASE.

CN/0831-8212
**OPERATING COSTS OF TRUCKS IN CANADA.** (OPERATING COSTS OF TRUCKS IN CANADA / TRIMAC CONSULTING SERVICES LTD. [FOR] MINISTRY OF TRANSPORT.). [Oper. costs trucks Can.]. **Added/Corp** Canada. Transport Canada. Surface. Trimac Consulting Services. Canada. Motor Carrier Branch. (1972)-. Monographic series. English. ir. Price varies per volume. Receiver General for Canada / Ottawa, Canada Comm Group Publishing, Ottawa Ontario K1A 0S9 Canada. **Tel** (819)956-4802, (800)661-2868. **LC** HE5635; .A43. **DD** 388.3/24.

UK
**OPERATIONAL COSTINGS FOR TRANSPORT MANAGEMENT.** (19??)-. Periodical. English. £114.50. Croner Publ Ltd, Croner House, London Road, Kingston upon Thames, Surrey KT2 6SR England. **Tel** 011 44 81 5473333, FAX 081 547-2637.

PO
**ORCAMENTO DA DESPESA PARA ... 1, CLASSIFICACAO ORGANICA, FUNCIONAL E ECONOMICA / REPUBLICA PORTUGUESA, MINISTERIO DA HABITACAO, OBRAS PUBLICAS E TRANSPORTES, DEPARTAMENTO DOS TRANSPORTES.** **Main/Corp** Portugal. Departamento dos Transportes. **VFOAT** Orcamento da Despesa para ... Um, Classificacao Organica, Funcional e Economica; Classificacao Organica, Funcional e Economica. Portuguese. **LC** HE262.A15; P67A. **DD** 354.4690087/5.

US/0148-9704
**OREGON TRANSPORTATION COMMISSION POLICIES.** **Main/Corp** Oregon Transportation Commission. English. an. Department of Transportation / Oregon, State Highway Building, Salem OR 97310. **LC** HE28.O7; T73A.

CN/0824-2224
**OTA VIEWPOINT.** [OTA viewp.]. **VAT** Ontario Trucking Association Viewpoint. Periodical. English. Free to members. Ontario Trucking Association, 555 Dixon Road, Rexdale Ontario M9W 1H8 Canada. **Tel** (416)249-7401, FAX (416)245-6152. **DD** 388.3/24/09713.

US/0030-7394
**OVERDRIVE.** (1961)-. Periodical. English. mo. $29.00. Randall Publishing, 3200 Rice Mine Road, Tuscaloosa AL 35403. **Tel** (800)777-3748, (205)349-2990. **Circ:** 58,289.
**Ind/Abst** Acad. Search (July 1993-); Bus. Index (Jan. 1985-Dec. 1985); Gen. BusinessFile (Jan. 1985-Dec. 1985); Gen. Period. Index (Jan. 1985-Dec. 1985); Mag. Search.

AT
**OVERSEAS ARRIVALS AND DEPARTURES, AUSTRALIA.** **See** Transportation-Abstracting, Bibliographies and Statistics.

US
**OVERWEIGHT VEHICLES- PENALTIES & PERMITS : REPORT TO CONGRESS FROM THE SECRETARY OF TRANSPORTATION.** **VAT** Overweight Vehicles-Penalties and Permits. Nov. 1981-. Government Publication. English. an. US Department of Agriculture, 14th Street and Independence Avenue SW, Washington DC 20250. **Tel** (202)720-5457. available on microfiche (Vols. for 1981- distributed to depository libraries). ***Continues*** *Overweight Vehicle Penalties and Permits.*

US/1050-7272
**PACE BUYER'S GUIDES. DOMESTIC & FOREIGN TRUCK & VAN PRICES NEW & USED.** ***Title Change.*** [Pace buy. guides, Domest. foreign truck van prices new used]. **VFOAT** Domestic & Foreign Truck & Van Prices New & Used; Domestic and Foreign Truck and Van Prices New and Used; Truck & Van Prices; Truck and Van Prices; Pace Buyer's Guides. New and Used Truck and Van Prices; Buyer's Guide Reports. Truck & Van Prices. (19??)-(199?). English. bm. Pace Publications Inc., 1020 North Broadway, Suite 111, Milwaukee WI 53202. **Tel** (414)272-9977, FAX (414)297-9973. **LC** TL230.A1; B89. **DD** 629.223/029/673. ***Continues*** *Buyer's Guide Reports. Truck & Van Prices.* ***Continued by*** *Pace Buyer's Guide. Domestic & Foreign Truck, Van, 4x4 Prices, New and Used, 1064-4628.*

GW/0724-8490
**PACKUNG & TRANSPORT.** [Pack. Transp.]. **VFOAT** Packung und Transport. Vol. 5 (1983)-. Periodical. German. mo. DM72.00. Handelsblatt GmbH, Postfach 102716, D-40018 Duesseldorf Germany. **Tel** 011 49 211 8871730. **LC** TS195.A1; P3. ***Continues*** *Packung & Transport in Chemie, Kosmetik, Pharmazie.*
**Ind/Abst** Chem. Bus. Bull.; Chem. Bus. NewsBase (1989-); Chem. Bus. Update; F&S Index Plus Text, Int. [Select. Cov.]; Infomat Int. Bus.; Int. Packag. Abstr.; PROMT.

AT
**PAPERS OF THE AUSTRALASIAN TRANSPORT RESEARCH FORUM.** **Main/Conf** Australasian Transport Research Forum. Vol. 15 (1990)-. English. ***Continues*** *Australasian Transport Research Forum. Forum Papers.*

US/1055-890X
**PARKING TECHNOLOGY.** [Park. technol.]. Vol. 1, No. 1 (July, 1991)-. Periodical. English. Ten times a year. Free (qualified subscribers), $33.00 others. Witter Publishing Company Inc., 84 Park Avenue, Flemington NJ 08822. **Tel** (908)788-0343. **LC** WMLC 91/2245. **DD** 388.

FR/1146-5166
**PASCAL. F 25, TRANSPORTS TERRESTRES ET MARITIMES.** ***Ceased.*** **VFOAT** PASCAL. F 25, Ground and Sea Transportations; PASCAL. F Vingt-Cinq, Transports Terrestres et Maritimes. (1990)-(199?). Periodical. Multiple languages. mo. Institut de l'Information Scientique et Technique (INIST), 2 Allee du Parc de Brabois, 54514 Vandoeuvre Nancy Cedex France. **Tel** 011 33 83 504600, FAX 011 33 83 504650. **UDC** 011. ***Continues*** *Pascal Folio. F25: Transports Terrestres et Maritimes.*

CN/0383-5766
**PASSENGER BUS AND URBAN TRANSIT STATISTICS.** (PASSENGER BUS AND URBAN TRANSIT STATISTICS / STATISTICS CANADA, TRANSPORTATION AND PUBLIC UTILITIES DIVISION, TRANSPORTATION SECTION.). [Passeng. bus urban transit stat.]. **Added/Corp** Statistics Canada. Transportation Section. Statistics Canada. Surface Transport Section. Statistics Canada. Surface and Marine Transport Section. Statistics Canada. Transportation Section. Statistiques du Transport des Voyageurs par Autobus et du Transport Urbain. **VFOAT** Statistique du Transport des Voyageurs par Autobus et du Transport Urbain. (1974)-. English (French). an. 36.00Can$ Canada; $44.00 US; $51.00 other. Statistics Canada, Publications Sales & Services, Main Building Room 1710, Ottawa Ontario K1A 0T6 Canada. **Tel** (613)951-5078, (800)267-6677, FAX (613)951-1584, telex 053-3585. **ED** Dan Calof (editor's phone number: (613)951-2519, FAX: (613)951-0579). **LC** HE5635; .A37. **DD** 388.3/22/0971. Index available. **Circ:** 460. ***Formed by the union of*** *Urban Transit (Annual), 0576-0046* ***and*** *Passenger Bus Statistics, 0527-6012.*
**Desc:** Data on investment, operating revenues, expenses and other data on inter-city and rural bus companies and urban transit systems.

CN/0829-1756
**PASSENGER BUS AND URBAN TRANSIT STATISTICS (MONTHLY ED.).** (PASSENGER BUS AND URBAN TRANSIT STATISTICS.). [Passeng. bus urban transit stat.]. **Added/Corp** Statistics Canada. **VFOAT** Statistique du Transport des Voyageurs par Autobus et du Trasport Urbain. Vol. 37, No. 3 (March 1985)-. Periodical. English (French). mo. 80.00Can$ Canada; $96.00 US; $112.00 other. Statistics Canada, Publications Sales & Services, Main Building Room 1710, Ottawa Ontario K1A 0T6 Canada. **Tel** (613)951-5078, (800)267-6677, FAX (613)951-1584, telex 053-3585. **ED** Yasmin Sheikh (editor's telephone number: (613)951-2518, FAX: (613)951-0579. **DD** 338.4/0971. **Circ:** 320. ***Continues*** *Urban Transit (Monthly), 0380-5948.*
**Desc:** Data on urban transit and inter-city bus companies with gross annual operating revenues from urban transit operations exceeding $500,000.00. Includes data on number of passengers carried and distance travelled.

US/0364-345X
**PASSENGER TRANSPORT.** Vol. 1, (Apr. 30 1943)-. Periodical. English. Fifty times a year. $77.00 North America; $113.75 other, Surface mail; $137.00 airmail. American Public Transit Association, 1201 New York Avenue Northwest, Suite 400, Washington DC 20005. **Tel** (202)898-41194128, FAX 9202)898-4095. **ED** Dennis M. Kouba. **LC** HE4441; .P32. **DD** 388.305. Index available. **Ad Acc, Adv Mgr:** Cecilia Barber, **Tel** (202)898-4122. **Circ:** 5,000.
**Desc:** Newspaper of transit industry, keeps you in touch with capitol hill actions, ridership increases, people in the industry, UMTA grants, and updates on individual systems.
**Ind/Abst** Highw. Res. Abstr.; Urban Aff. Abstr.

IT/1120-4176
**PATENTE DI GUIDA, LA.** [Pat. guida]. (1990)-. Periodical. Italian. Twenty-four times a year. L248.000. Egaf Edizioni SAS, Via F Guarini 2, 47100 Forli Italy. **Tel** 011 39 543 782278, FAX 011 39 543 782255. **UDC** 656.09.

UK/0268-4942
**PERFORMANCE BIKES.** [Perform. bikes]. **VFOAT** Performance Bikes & Mechanics. (1985)-. Periodical. English. Twelve times a year. £19.20 UK, £29.50 others (surface mail); £26.00 Europe, £29.50 Middle East & North Africa; £37.00 Pacific Island, Australasia & Far East £34.50 others, (airmail). EMAP National Publications Ltd, Farndon Road, Market Harborough, Leicestershire, LE16 9NR England. **Tel** 011 44 733 555161. **DD** 629.227505. ***Continues*** *Mechanics (Peterborough), 0263-8274.*

HU/0303-7800
**PERIODICA POLYTECHNICA : TRANSPORTATION ENGINEERING. TRANSPORT.** [Period. polytech., Transp. eng., Transp.]. **Added/Corp** Budapesti Muszaki Egyetem. **VFOAT** Transportation Engineering; Transport. Vol. 1 (1973)-. Periodical. Multiple languages. ir (2 issues). $11.00. **(Subscription address:** Kultura, PO Box 149, H 1389 Budapest 62 Hungary.**)** **LC** TA1001; .P47.
**Ind/Abst** Ei Page One; Fluid Abstr., Civil Eng.; Fluid Abstr. Proc. Eng.; FLUIDEX (1973-); Int. Aerosp. Abstr.

US/0898-6371
**PFEIFFER'S OFFICIAL FREQUENT FLYER GUIDE.** **VFOAT** Official Frequent Flyer Guide. 1989-. Periodical. English. bm. Pegasus Press, 8535 Production Avenue, San Diego CA 92121.

US/0090-2896
**PHYSICAL CONDITION REPORT OF COMMERCIAL DRIVERS INVOLVED IN ACCIDENTS.** **Main/Corp** United States. Bureau of Motor Carrier Safety. English. an. Free single copy. US Department of Transportation - Federal Highway Administration, 400 Seventh Street Southwest, Washington DC 20590. **Tel** (202)366-0660. **LC** HE5614.2; .U55A. **DD** 614.8/62. **NLM** W2 A U8702P.

US/0747-1041
**PICKUPS 'N PANELS IN PRINT.** **VFOAT** Pickups and Panels in Print. Periodical. English. mo. Pickups N Panels in Print, PO Box 607458, Orlando FL 32860.

FR
**PILOTE.** ***Ceased.*** ( )-(Nov. 1989). Periodical. French. mo. Dargaud Editeur, 12 rue Blaise Pascal, 92200 Neuilly/Seine France.

SP
**PLAN DE EMPRESA.** ***Ceased.*** **Main/Corp** TMB (Agency : Barcelona, Spain). (198?)-(1992). Periodical. Spanish. an.

US
**PLANNING AND RESEARCH PROGRAM.** **Main/Corp** Iowa. Dept. of Transportation. (197?)-. English. Department of Transportation / Iowa, 800 Lincoln Way, Ames IA 50010. **LC** HE213.I8; I64a. **DD** 353.97770087/5/006.

CN/0701-1725
**PLEINS FEUX SUR LE TAXI.** First issue in 1973?. Periodical. French (English). 0.25Can$ per number. Pleins Feux sur le Taxi, 5310 Boulevard Couture, Montreal Quebec H1R 1CM Canada. **DD** 388.4/1321.

US/1064-7686
**PORT OF HOUSTON.** (PORT OF HOUSTON / PORT OF HOUSTON AUTHORITY.). [Port Houst.]. **Added/Corp** Port of Houston Authority. **VFOAT** Port of Houston Magazine. Vol. 31, No. 1 (Jan. 1987)-. Periodical. English. Twelve times a year. Free. Port of Houston Authority, PO Box 2562, Houston TX 77252. **LC** HE554.H65; P65. **DD** 387. ***Continues*** *Port of Houston Magazine, 0032-4825.*
**Ind/Abst** Fluid Abstr., Civil Eng.; Fluid Abstr. Proc. Eng.; FLUIDEX (19??-).

US/0032-8871
**PRIVATE CARRIER.** (THE PRIVATE CARRIER.). **Added/Corp** Private Carrier Conference. National Private

# Transportation

Truck Council. **VFOAT** TPC. Vol. 1 (Jan. 1964)-. Periodical. English. mo. free on request. National Private Truck Council, 66 Canal Ceter Plaza, Suite 600, Alexandria VA 22314. **Tel** (703)683-1300. **ED** Donald E. Tepper. **LC** HE5623.A1; P75. **DD** 388.3/243. **Bk Rev**. **Ad Acc. Circ:** 35,000 (ctrl).
**Desc:** Information regarding legal, legislative, regulatory, technical, safety and operational developments in the field of private carriage.

●US/1061-4761
**PRIVATE FLEET DIRECTORY, THE.** (THE PRIVATE FLEET DIRECTORY: A TRANSPORTATION TECHNICAL SERVICES PUBLICATION, IN COOPERATION WITH FLEET OWNER MAGAZINE AND THE NATIONAL PRIVATE TRUCK COUNCIL.). [Priv. fleet dir.]. **Added/Corp** Transportation Technical Services, Inc. National Private Truck Council. (1992)-. Directory. English. an (May). $395.00. Transportation Technical Services, 225 West 34th Street, New York NY 10122. **Tel** (800)666-4887, FAX (703)899-1948. **DD** 388. **Acid Free.** available on magnetic tape; available on diskette.
**Desc:** Provides key information on 19,000 of the nation's top private fleets.

PL
**PROBLEMY PRAWA PRZEWOZOWEGO / WNIWERSYTET SLASKI. See** Law.

CN/1183-2770
**PROCEEDINGS ... ANNUAL MEETING OF THE CANADIAN TRANSPORTATION RESEARCH FORUM.** [Proc. annu. meet. Can. Transp. Res. Forum]. **Main/Corp** Canadian Transportation Research Forum. Meeting. **Added/Corp** Canadian Transportation Research Forum. **VFOAT** Proceedings of the ... Annual Meeting of the Canadian Transportation Research Forum; C.T.R.F. Proceedings. (196?)-. Proceedings. English (summaries and/or abstracts in French). an. 50.00Can$ Comes with Canadian Transportation Research Forum Membership. Canadian Transportation Research Forum, 209-15 Innovation Boulevard, Saskatoon SK S7N 2X8 Canada. **Tel** (306)668-2828, FAX (306)668-7603. **DD** 388/.0971/05. **Circ:** 400 (ctrl). **Continues** Canadian Transportation Research Forum. Meeting. Papers Presented to the Annual Meeting.

●UK/0965-092X
**PROCEEDINGS OF THE INSTITUTION OF CIVIL ENGINEERS, TRANSPORT. See** Engineering-Civil Engineering.

UK/0954-4097
**PROCEEDINGS OF THE INSTITUTION OF MECHANICAL ENGINEERS. PART F, JOURNAL OF RAIL AND RAPID TRANSIT. See** Engineering-Mechanical Engineering and Machinery.

US/1043-4712
**PROCEEDINGS OF THE INTERNATIONAL AIR CARGO FORUM.** [Proc. Int. Air Cargo Forum]. **Added/Corp** Society of Automotive Engineers. American Institute of Aeronautics and Astronautics. American Society of Mechanical Engineers. (1986)-. Proceedings. English. be. Society of Automotive Engineers, 400 Commonwealth Drive, Warrendale PA 15096. **Tel** (412)776-4841, (412)772-7106, FAX (412)776-5760. **LC** HE9788; .I5. **DD** 387.7/44/05. **Continues** International Forum for Air Cargo. Conference Proceedings of the ... International Forum for Air Cargo, 0737-8424.
**Desc:** Information on commercial aeronautics.

CN/1189-2005
**PROCEEDINGS OF THE STANDING SENATE COMMITTEE ON TRANSPORT AND COMMUNICATIONS. See** Communication.

US/0735-0805
**PROCEEDINGS - SOUTHEASTERN ASSOCIATION OF STATE HIGHWAY AND TRANSPORTATION OFFICIALS (U.S.). MEETING.** (PROCEEDINGS.). **Main/Corp** Southeastern Association of State Highway and Transportation Officials (U.S.). Meeting. Proceedings. English. an. Virginia Department of Highways and Transportation, 1221 East Broad Street, Richmond VA 23219. **LC** HE208; .S68A. **DD** 380.5/0975.

US/0272-1767
**PRODUCTS LIABILITY AND TRANSPORTATION LEGAL DIRECTORY. See** Law.

GW
**PROGNOSEBERICHT ZUR VERKEHRSENTWICKLUNG.** German. Pressestelle des Bundesministers fur Verkehr, Kennedyallee 72, W-5300 Bonn 2 Germany. **LC** HE249.A15; P76. **DD** 388/.0943/01.

IV
**PROGRAMME DE RECHERCHE - INSTITUT DE RECHERCHE DES TRANSPORTS. Main/Corp** Institut de Recherche des Transports. French. 2 Avenue du General Malleret-Joinville, B P 28, Arcrieil 94114 France. **LC** HE192.5; .I58A. **DD** 380.5/07/2044.

US/0092-6159
**PROGRESS REPORT ON TRIP ENDS GENERATION RESEARCH COUNTS (SAN FRANCISCO).** (PROGRESS REPORT ON TRIP ENDS GENERATION RESEARCH COUNTS.). **Main/Corp** California. Dept. of Transportation. English. California Department of Transportation, PO Box 3366, Rincon Annex, San Francisco CA 94119. **LC** HE373.U53; S23A. **DD** 388.3/14/09794.

US/0149-6328
**PROGRESS REPORT TO THE GOVERNOR'S HIGHWAY SAFETY OFFICE. Main/Corp** University of North Carolina (System) Highway Safety Research Center. **Added/Corp** North Carolina. Governor's Highway Safety Program. (19??)-. Periodical. English. qt. University of North Carolina Press, 116 South Boundary Street, PO Box 2288, Chapel Hill NC 27515-2288. **Tel** (919)966-3561, FAX (919)966-3829. **LC** HE5614.3.N6; U54a. **DD** 614.8/62/09756.

CI
**PROMET I VEZE / SOCIJALISTICKA REPUBLIKA HRVATSKA, REPUBLICKI ZAVOD ZA STATISTIKU.** Serbo-Croatian (Roman). an. 130.00. Republicki Zavod za Statistiku, Central Bureau of Statistics of the Republic of Croatia, Ilica 3, Zagreb Croatia. **Tel** 011 385 41 45 44 22, FAX 011 385 41 42 94 13, 011 385 41 42 37 11, telex 21130 DZSTAT RH. **LC** HE265.5.Z7; C77.

PL
**PRZEGLAD KOMUNIKACYJNY.** Vol. 1 (1962)-. Periodical. Polish (table of contents in Russian, English and French). mo. Price on Request. (**Subscription address:** ARS Polona, PO Box 1001, 00068 Warsaw Poland.) **LC** HE7; .P718.

US
**PTI JOURNAL.** English. bm. $28.00 (one year), $38.00 (two year). SR Consultants, 1666 Newport Boulevard #141, Costa Mesa CA 92627. **Tel** (714)752-1292. **ED** Steven B. Rooney. **Ad Acc.** ctrl circ.
**Desc:** A journal of innovations in the area of public transportation.

UK
**PTRC PROCEEDINGS.** (19??)-. Proceedings. English. an. Planning Transport Research and Computation, Glenthorne House, Hammersmith Road, London W6 0LG England. **Tel** 011 44 081 1516.

US/0148-4087
**PUBLIC TRANSIT REPORT.** *Title Change.* (1973)-(199?). Periodical. English. bw. Business Publishers Inc., 951 Pershing Drive, Silver Spring MD 20910-4464. **Tel** (301)587-6300, (800)274-0122, FAX (301)585-9075. **ED** Dede Ryan. *Continued by* Urban Transport News, 0195-4695.
**Desc:** A report on public transit systems throughout the US, with information from Washington (Capital Hill and the Department of Transportation) as well as local transit companies.

BE/1016-796X
**PUBLIC TRANSPORT INTERNATIONAL. VFOAT** Offentliche Nahverkehr in der Welt; Transport Public International. Vol. 1 (Feb./May 1990)-. Periodical. English (French and German). Six times a year. 2000F. International Union of Public Transport, Avenue de l'Uruguay 19, B 1050 Brussels Belgium. **Tel** 011 32 2 6733325, FAX 011 32 2 6607072, telex (046)63916 UITP B. **LC** HE4201; .I5. **DD** 388.4/05. Index available. **Ad Acc. Circ:** 10,000.
**Desc:** Aimed at all those who are interested in public transport. The articles are specially written for this publication and deal with technical, organizational and commercial aspects of public transport.
**Ind/Abst** Ei Page One; Highw. Res. Abstr.

US/0147-359X
**PUBLIC UTILITIES AND TRANSPORTATION NEWSLETTER. See** Public Administration.

CN/0709-9851
**PUBLICATION / UNIVERSITE DE MONTREAL, CENTRE DE RECHERCHE SUR LES TRANSPORTS.** [Publ. - Cent rech transp., Univ. Montr.]. **Added/Corp** Universite de Montreal. Centre de Recherche sur les Transports. (197?)-. Monographic series. English (French). ir. Price varies per volume. Universite de Montreal Centre de Recherche sur les Transport, Montreal Quebec H3C 3J7 Canada. **DD** 380.5/07/24.

US
**PUBLICATIONS CATALOG. Main/Corp** National Research Council (U.S.). Transportation Research Board. **VFOAT** Transportation Research Board Publications Catalog. (198?)-. Catalog. English. ir. $1,275.00 North America; $1,400.00 others. Transportation Research Board, Box 289, Washington DC 20055. **Tel** (202)334-3218, FAX (202)334-2519. **LC** WMLC L 83/3393. **Continues** National Research Council (U.S.) Transportation Research Board. Catalog of Publications.

US/0730-5443
**PUPIL TRANSPORTATION NEWS.** (198?)-. Periodical. English. mo. $72.00 US; $74.40 other. Pupil Transportation News, PO Box 191, Fords NJ 08863. **Tel** (908)541-9302. **ED** Donna Simeone (editor's phone: (908)937-0058). **Ad Acc. Pr Rev. Circ:** 825.
**Desc:** Provides facts and information regarding the pupil transportation industry.

US/0092-4644
**PUPIL TRANSPORTATION STATISTICS, ILLINOIS PUBLIC SCHOOLS. See** Education-Abstracting, Bibliographies and Statistics.

US/1058-1251
**PURCHASING PERFORMANCE BENCHMARKS FOR THE U.S. TRANSPORTATION INDUSTRY / CAPS, CENTER FOR ADVANCED PURCHASING STUDIES.** [Purch. perform. benchmarks U.S. transp. ind.]. **Added/Corp** Center for Advanced Purchasing Studies (Tempe, Ariz.). **VFOAT** Purchasing Performance Benchmarks. (1991)-. English. Free. National Association of Purchasing Management, 2055 East Centennial Circle, PO Box 22160, Tempe AZ 85285-2160. **DD** 658.

CN/0317-6347
**PURCHASING PREFERENCE SURVEY : TRAFFIC/TRANSPORTATION. See** Business-Purchasing.

AT
**QUARTERLY BULLETIN. Main/Corp** Co-ord. Transport Industries Research Council of Australia. (19??)-. Periodical. English. qt. $0.80. Transport Industries Research Council of Australia, 14 Kennington Road, Camp Hill Australia. **LC** HE192.5; .C65a. **DD** 380.5/072.

US
**RAIL CARRIER SERVICE. INCLUDES SUPPLEMENTS.** (1927)-. English. Twelve times a year. $330.00. Hawkins Publishing Company, PO Box 480, Mayo MD 21106. **Tel** (410)798-1677. available in Loose-leaf.
**Desc:** Analysis of reports of the Interstate Commerce Commission, relating to rail, rail-water, express, pipeline carrier and water carrier.

CN
**RAPPORT ANNUEL / CANADIAN NATIONAL. Main/Corp** Canadian National. French. an. Free. Corporate Communications Canadian National, PO Box 8100, Montreal Quebec H3C 3N4 Canada. **Tel** (514)877-4758. **LC** HE2801; .C34B. **DD** 385/.065/71. **Circ:** 10,000 (ctrl). *Continues in part* Canadian National Railways; **Continues** Annual Report / Canadian National Railways.
**Desc:** Covers financial review and outlook for this integrated transport and communications company, operating throughout Canada and with international links.

CN/0702-0996
**RAPPORT ANNUEL - COMMISSION DES TRANSPORTS DU QUEBEC. Main/Corp** Quebec (Province). Commission des Transports. 1977/78-. French. an. Editeur Officiel du Quebec, 1283 Boul Charest Ouest, Quebec Quebec G1N 2C9 Canada. **LC** HE30.Q4; T7A. **DD** 354.7140087/5/006. *Continues* Rapports des Activites de la Commission des Transports du Quebec, 0318-5303.

RU
**RASPISANIE DVIZHENIIA RECHNYKH PASSAZHIRSKIKH SUDOV OSNOVNYKH TRANSPORTNYKH LINII NA NAVIGATSIIU. Added/Corp** Russian S.F.S.R. Ministerstvo Rechnogo Flota. (19??)-. Russian. Transport / Moscow, Basmannyi Tup 6A, Moscow Russia. **LC** HE675; .A23a.

FR/1168-3392
**RATP SAVOIR FAIRE PARIS.** (RATP SAVOIR FAIRE.). (1992)-. Periodical. French. qt (4 issues). 200.00F. Regie Auto Transport Parisien, 53Ter Quai d'Grands Augustins, 75271 Paris Cedex 06 France. **Tel** 346 33 33, telex 200000. (**Subscription address:** RATP, Miriam Pinsard, 8 Avenue des Minimes, 94300 Vincennes France) **ED** J. Aubrun. **UDC** 087.7. **CODEN** 656.34(443.611). ctrl circ.

# Transportation

FR/0304-3320
**RECHERCHE EN MATIERE D'ECONOMIE DES TRANSPORTS.** See Economics.

FR/0761-8980
**RECHERCHE, TRANSPORTS, SECURITE.** [Rech. transp. secur]. **VFOAT** RTS. Recherche, Transports, Securite. (1984)-. Periodical. French. qt. 360.00F France; 460.00F other. Inst Recherche des Transports, BP 34, 94114 Arceuil Cedex France. **Tel** 011 33 1 47407000. **UDC** 629.11. **Continues** Recherche Transports, 0291-8439.

US/0733-4745
**RECREATIONAL VEHICLE BLUE BOOK.** [Recreat. veh. blue book]. (19??)-. Periodical. English. Three times a year. $110.00. MacLean Hunter Publishing Corporation / Chicago, IL, 29 North Wacker Drive, Chicago IL 60606-3298. **Tel** (312)726-2802, **FAX** (312)726-3091. **(Subscription address:** Maclean Hunter Market Reports, 29 North Wacker Drive, Chicago IL 60606.) **LC** TL298; .R4. **DD** 629.2/26/029473.

RU
**REFERATIVNYI ZHURNAL: PROMYSHLENNYI TRANSPORT.** **Added/Corp** Akademiia Nauk SSSR. Institut Nauchnoi Informatsii. **VFOAT** Promyshlennyi Transport. (Jan. 1962)-. Periodical. Russian (summaries and/or abstracts in English; table of contents in English). mo. $159.95. VINITI - Vsesoyuznyi Institut Nauchno-Tekhnicheskoi Informatsii, All-Union Scientific and Technical Information Institute, Baltiiskaia Ulitsa 14, 125219 Moscow Russia. **Tel** 238-46-00, **FAX** 9430060, telex 411160. **(Subscription address:** East View Publications Inc., 3020 Harbor Lane North, Suite 110, Minneapolis MN 55447.) **Supersedes in part** Referativnyi Zhurnal: Transport.

CN/0227-4558
**REFLET.** (REFLET : BULLETIN DE LA COMMISSION DE TRANSPORT DE LA RIVE SUD DE MONTREAL.). [Reflet]. **Main/Corp** Commission de Transport de la Rive sud de Montreal. V. 1, No. 1 (June 1978)-. Bulletin. French. bm. Free to employees. Reflet CTRSM, Bureau 100 1000 rue de Serigny, Longueuil Quebec J4K 5B1 Canada. **DD** 388.4/065/71437.

US/0034-3129
**REFRIGERATED TRANSPORTER.** [Refrig. transp.]. (19??)-. Periodical. English. mo (12 issues). $25.00 US; $40.00 other. Tunnell Publications, PO Box 66010, Houston TX 77266. **Tel** (713)523-8124, **FAX** (713)523-8384. **ED** Gary Macklin. **Bk Rev. Ad Acc. Circ:** 15,000 (ctrl). **Desc:** Equipment specifications, maintenance of equipment, operating refrigerated truck fleets. **Ind/Abst** Bus. Index (1981-?).

CN/0849-2921
**REGULATION UPDATE & OPERATING AUTHORITY BULLETIN. Ceased.** [Regul. update oper. auth. bull.]. **Added/Corp** Alberta Trucking Association. **VFOAT** Trux Law. **VAT** Regulation Update and Operating Authority Bulletin. No. 8 (Feb. 27, 1990)-(199?). Bulletin. English. wk. Alberta Trucking Association, PO Box 5520 Station A, Calgary Alberta T2H 1X9 Canada. **Tel** (403)253-8401. **DD** 343.712309/483. **Continues** Operating Authority Bulletin, 0383-8994.

BL
**RELATORIO DAS ATIVIDADES - EMPRESA BRASILEIRA DE PLANEJAMENTO DE TRANSPORTES.** **Main/Corp** Empresa Brasileira de Planejamento de Transportes. Portuguese. Setor de Autarquias Sul Quadra, Brazil. **LC** HE233; .E45A. **DD** 354/.81/00875.

BL
**RELATORIO DE ATIVIDADES / GOVERNO DO ESTADO DA PARAIBA, SECRETARIA DOS TRANSPORTES E OBRAS.** **Main/Corp** Paraiba (Brazil : State). Secretaria dos Transportes e Obras. (19??)-. Portuguese. **LC** HE233.Z7; P366a. **DD** 354.81/330875/06.

AT
**REPORT AND STATEMENT OF ACCOUNTS FOR THE YEAR ENDED 30TH JUNE, ... / METROPOLITAN (PERTH) PASSENGER TRANSPORT TRUST.** **Main/Corp** Metropolitan (Perty) Passenger Transport Trust. **VFOAT** Annual Report. English. an. Perth Metropolitan Passenger Transport Trust, 10 Adelaide Terrace, Perth Western Australia. **LC** HE311.A852; P475A. **DD** 352.91/84/099411.

US/0093-8947
**REPORT NO. TES.** See Environmental Issues-Pollution and Waste Management.

US
**REPORT OF OPERATIONS : HIGHWAYS, BUSES, AERONAUTICS, RAILROADS.** **Main/Corp** New Jersey. Dept. of Transportation. English. Department of Transportation / Trenton, 1035 Parkway Avenue, Trenton NJ 08625. **LC** HE28.N5; A285. **DD** 380.5/09749.

US/0731-6194
**REPORT OF THE JOINT LEGISLATIVE COMMITTEE ON MOTOR VEHICLES, HIGHWAY AND TRAFFIC SAFETY TO THE LEGISLATURE OF THE STATE OF NEW YORK. Title Change. Main/Corp** New York (State). Legislature. Joint Legislative Committee on Motor Vehicles, Traffic, and Highway Safety. **VFOAT** Report of the Joint Legislative Committee on Motor Vehicles, Traffic and Highway Safety; Report of the New York State Joint Legislative Committee on Motor Vehicles, Traffic and Highway Safety. 1965-1968. English. New York Legislature, State Legislative Office Building, Albany NY 12224. **Continues** Report of the Joint Legislative Committee on Motor Vehicles and Traffic Safety. **Continued by** Annual Report of the Joint Legislative Committee on Mass Transportation to the Legislature of the State of New York, 0548-8141.

NZ
**REPORT OF THE MINISTRY OF TRANSPORT.** **Main/Corp** New Zealand. Ministry of Transport. **VFOAT** Report of the Ministry of Transport ... for the year ended ... . (19??)-. English. **LC** HE297.5.A1; N44a. **DD** 354/.931/0087.

SL
**REPORT OF THE ROAD TRANSPORT DEPARTMENT - SIERRA LEONE.** **Main/Corp** Sierra Leone. Road Transport Dept. 1947-. English. Government Printing Department / Sierra Leone, Freetown Sierra Leone. **LC** HE5704.S5; A3. **DD** 388.3.

US/0360-750X
**REPORT TO CONGRESS CONCERNING THE DEMONSTRATION OF FARE-FREE MASS TRANSPORTATION.** **Main/Corp** United States. Urban Mass Transportation Administration. 1975-. English. an. US Department of Transportation - Federal Highway Administration, 400 Seventh Street Southwest, Washington DC 20590. **Tel** (202)366-0660. **LC** HE17; .U7A. **DD** 388.4.

US/0098-0617
**REPORT TO THE CONGRESS OF THE UNITED STATES ON URBAN TRANSPORTATION POLICIES & ACTIVITIES.** [Rep. Congr. U. S. urban transp. policies act.]. **Main/Corp** United States. Dept. of Transportation. **VFOAT** Urban Transportation Policies & Activities. English. US Department of Transportation - Federal Highway Administration, 400 Seventh Street Southwest, Washington DC 20590. **Tel** (202)366-0660. **LC** HE308; .U55A. **DD** 388.4/0973.

●US
**REPORT, WASHINGTON STATE TRANSPORTATION PLAN UPDATE.** **Added/Corp** Washington (State). Dept. of Transportation. **VFOAT** Washington State Transportation Plan Update. (1995)-. English. be. Washington State Department of Transportation, Transportation Building, Olympia WA 98504. **Tel** (206)753-6028. **LC** HE213.W2; R46. **DD** 380.5/068.

US
**RESEARCH & TECHNOLOGY TRANSPORTER / U.S. DEPARTMENT OF TRANSPORTATION, FEDERAL HIGHWAY ADMINISTRATION. Added/Corp** United States. Federal Highway Administration. Turner-Fairbank Highway Research Center. **VFOAT** Research and Technology Transporter; Transporter. (April 1991)-. Periodical. English. qt. Department of Transportation, 400 Seventh Street SW, Washington DC 20590. **Tel** (202)426-4000. **Continues** TFHRC Update.

UK/0266-5247
**RESEARCH REPORT - TRANSPORT AND ROAD RESEARCH LABORATORY.** [Res. rep. - Transp. Road Res. Lab.]. **VFOAT** TRRL Research Report. (1984)-. Monographic series. English. ir. Price varies per volume. **Ind/Abst** Geogr. Abstr. Human Geogr.; Int. Dev. Abstr.

CN/0316-7984
**RESEARCH REPORT - UNIVERSITY OF MANITOBA, CENTRE FOR TRANSPORTATION STUDIES. Main/Corp** University of Manitoba. Centre for Transportation Studies. (1969)-. Monographic series. English. ir. Price varies per volume. University of Manitoba Center for Transportation Studies, Winnipeg Manitoba R3T 2N2 Canada. **DD** 380.5. **Continues** University of Manitoba. Centre for Transportation Studies. Research Progress Report, 0316-7976.

US/1048-1311
**RESULTS ... ANNUAL SURVEY OF CORPORATE RELOCATION POLICIES.** See Business.

SP/0378-3294
**REVISTA A.I.T.** [Rev. A.I.T.]. **VFOAT** Revista Asociacion de Investigacion del Transporte. (1976)-. Periodical. Spanish. bm. $33.00 US, Pan America, Canada, and Europe; $22.35 other. Asociacion Investigacion del Transporte, Alberto Alcocer 38, Madrid 16 Spain. **UDC** 629.

BL
**REVISTA BRASILEIRA DE TRANSPORTES. Added/Corp** Brazil. Grupo Executivo de Integracao da Politica de Transportes. No. 1 (July/Sept. 1966)-. Periodical. Portuguese. qt. Grupo Executivo de Integracao da Politica de Transportes, R Alcindo Guanabara, 24 S/814 GB ZC-06, Rio de Janeiro Brazil. **LC** HE7; .B717. **DD** 380.5/0981.

RM/0379-2390
**REVISTA TRANSPORTURILOR SI TELECOMUNICATIILOR.** [Rev. transp. telecomun.]. **Added/Corp** Romania. Ministerul Transporturilor si Telecomunicatiilor. Consiliul National al Inginerilor si Tehnicienilor din Republica Socialista Romania. **VFOAT** RTTc. (1974)-. Periodical. Romanian (summaries and/or abstracts in English, French, German and Russian). mo. $87.00. Ministerul Transporturilor si Telecomunicatiilor, Calea Grivitei 193B, 78141 Bucharest Romania. **(Subscription address:** Rompresfilatelia, PO Box 12 201, Bucharest Romania.) **LC** TA1001; .R42. **Desc:** Publishes studies from the transport and telecommunication field. **Ind/Abst** Coal Abstr.; Int. Aerosp. Abstr.

IT/0303-5247
**RIVISTA INTERNAZIONALE DI ECONOMIA DEI TRASPORTI.** See Economics.

IT
**RIVISTA TRASPORTI.** Rivista Trasporti, Viale Miramare 309, 34122 Trieste Italy.

US/1055-7725
**ROAD & REC.** [Road rec]. **Added/Corp** Air Force Inspection and Safety Center (U.S.). **VFOAT** Road and Rec; Road & Recreation. Vol. 1, No. 1 (Dec. 1988)-. Periodical. English. qt. Road & Rec, HQ AFISC/SEPP, Norton Air Force Base CA 92409-7001. **DD** 629. **Continues in part** Driver, 0002-2373.

CN/0703-654X
**ROAD MOTOR VEHICLES. FUEL SALES.** (ROAD MOTOR VEHICLES--FUEL SALES / STATISTICS CANADA, TRANSPORTATION AND COMMUNICATIONS DIVISION, SURFACE TRANSPORT SECTION.). [Road mot. veh., Fuel sales]. **Added/Corp** Statistics Canada. Surface Transport Section. **VFOAT** Vehicules Automobiles-Ventes de Carburants. (1975)-. English (French). an. 25.00Can$; $30.00 US; $35.00 other. Statistics Canada, Publications Sales & Services, Main Building Room 1710, Ottawa Ontario K1A 0T6 Canada. **Tel** (613)951-5078, (800)267-6677, **FAX** (613)951-1584, telex 053-3585. **ED** Yasmin Sheikh. **LC** HD9574.C2; R6. **DD** 381/.4566553827/0971021. Index available. **Circ:** 435. **Continues** Statistics Canada. Surface Transport Section. Motor Vehicle, 0527-5830. **Desc:** Data presented on sales of gasoline, diesel oil and liquified petroleum gas used for automotive purposes. Breakdowns provided by year and month, province and territory.

US/1067-8697
**ROAD RIDER'S MOTORCYCLE CONSUMER NEWS. Title Change.** [Road rider's motorcycle consum. news]. **VFOAT** Motorcycle Consumer News; Road Rider/Motorcycle Consumer News; RR/MCN; RR/MCNews. Vol. 24, No. 1 (Jan. 1993)-Vol. 24, No. 10 (Oct. 1993). Periodical. English. mo. RR/MCNews, Subscription Department, PO Box 488, Mt Morris IL 61054-0488. **LC** TL440.5; .R6. **DD** 796.7. **Continues** Road Rider, 0035-7243. **Continued by** Motorcycle Consumer News, 1073-9408.

UK
**ROAD TRANSPORT OPERATION; EMPLOYMENT LAW.** (19??)-. English. £100.30. Croner Publ Ltd, Croner House, London Road, Kingston upon Thames, Surrey KT2 6SR England. **Tel** 011 44 81 5473333, **FAX** 081 547-2637.

UK
**ROAD WAY, THE.** Began in 1935. Periodical. English. mo. £18.00 UK; £28.00 other. Road Haulage

Association, Roadway House, 35 Monument Hill, Weybridge Surrey KT13 8RN England. **Tel** 0932 841515. **LC** HE5601; .R6. **DD** 388.3. **Ad Acc. Circ:** 14,000 (ctrl).

PL
## ROCZNIK STATYSTYCZNY TRANSPORTU.
1945/66-. Polish. Z17.00 Poland; Z20.00 North America; Z19.00 other. Zaklad Wydawnictw Statystycznych, Al Niepodleglosci 208, 00-925 Warszawa Poland. **Tel** 253241, telex 814581A GUS. **LC** HE255.7; .R63. **DD** 380.5/09438. Index available. **Circ:** 1,000 (ctrl).
**Desc:** Yearbook of the polish transport.

CN/0319-3780
## ROUTES ET TRANSPORTS.
[Routes transp.]. **Added/Corp** Association quebecoise du transport et des routes. No. 14 (May 1975)-. French. Four times a year. 50.00Can$ Canada; 60.00Can$ other. Association Quebecoise du Tran Routes, 6455 Avenue Christophe Colomb #300, Montreal Quebec H4K 1K5 Canada. **Tel** (514)274-3573, FAX 9514)274-9608. **ED** Catherine Hirou. **DD** 625.7/09714. **Ad Acc. Circ:** 1,400. ***Continues*** *Routes du Quebec, 0318-6245.*
**Desc:** Publishes articles in research, development and technology transfer in the field of all modes of transportation. Addresses engineers and specialized technicians.
**Ind/Abst** Point Repere (1983-).

US/1060-5932
## ROVER REGISTER, THE.
(THE ROVER REGISTER : OFFICIAL PUBLICATION OF THE ROVER OWNERS CLUB OF NORTH AMERICA.). [Rover regist.]. **Added/Corp** Rover Owners Club of North America. Vol. 1, No. 1 (Oct. 1991)-. English. bm. $28.00. Rover Owners Club of North America, PO Box 43005, Tuscon AZ 85719. **DD** 629.

US
## RUNZHEIMER GUIDE TO FLEET MANAGEMENT.
English. be. $195.00. Runzheimer International / Wisconsin, Runzheimer Park, Rochester WI 53167. **Tel** (414)767-2200, FAX (414)767-2254, (800)558-1702.

US/0730-8655
## RUNZHEIMER REPORTS ON TRANSPORTATION.
***Title Change.*** [Runzheimer rep. transp.]. (198?)-(19??). Periodical. English. mo. Runzheimer International / Wisconsin, Runzheimer Park, Rochester WI 53167. **Tel** (414)767-2200, FAX (414)767-2254, (800)558-1702. **ED** Adlore Chaudier. **[CCC]. Bk Rev. Ad Acc.** ctrl circ. ***Absorbed*** *Runzheimer Reports on Automotive Alternatives.* ***Continued by*** *Runzheimer Reports on Fleet Management.*
**Desc:** Covers all aspects of corporate fleet management.

US/0036-0171
## RUSSELL'S OFFICIAL NATIONAL MOTOR COACH GUIDE.
***Title Change.*** (RUSSELL'S OFFICIAL NATIONAL MOTOR COACH GUIDE FOR UNITED STATES, CANADA, MEXICO, CENTRAL AMERICA.). Vol. 9 (Oct. 1936)-(198?). Periodical. English. mo. Russells Guides Inc, 834 Third Avenue Southeast, PO Box 278, Cedar Rapids IA 52406. **Tel** (319)364-6138, FAX (319)364-4853. **ED** Tom Whitters. **LC** HE5623.A1; R8. **DD** 388.3/221/097. **Bk Rev. Ad Acc. Circ:** 9,000 (ctrl). ***Continues*** *Russell's National Motor Coach Guide.* ***Continued by*** *Russell's Official National Motor Coach Guide.*
**Desc:** Bus schedules throughout the US and Canada.

US/0036-0171
## RUSSELL'S OFFICIAL NATIONAL MOTOR COACH GUIDE.
**VFOAT** Official Bus Guide. (198?)-. Periodical. English. mo. ***Continues*** *Russell's Official National Motor Coach Guide for United States, Canada, Mexico, Central America.*
**Desc:** This publication provides a guide to bus lines.

US/0742-6208
## RV BUYERS GUIDE.
**VFOAT** R.V. Buyers Guide. (19??)-. Consumer Publication. English. an. $5.95. TL Enterprises, 29901 Agoura Road, Agoura CA 91301. **Tel** (800)234-3450, (805)389-0300. **LC** TL298; .R8. **DD** 629.2/26/029.
**Desc:** Information on recreational vehicles.

US/0745-0389
## RV TRADE DIGEST (CHICAGO, ILL. 1981).
(RV TRADE DIGEST.). [RV trade dig.]. **VAT** Recreational Vehicle Trade Digest. (1981)-. Periodical. English. mo. $36.00 US; $72.00 other. Continental Publishing Company, PO Box 1805, Elkhart IN 46515. **Tel** (219)295-1962, FAX (219)295-7574. **ED** Tom Russell and Chuck Stolberg. **DD** 338. **Ad Acc. Circ:** 14,000 (ctrl).
**Desc:** Edited to reach the entire audience of trade professionals which include the nation's recreational vehicle dealerships, manufacturers, and industry suppliers. Editorial is an upbeat approach of positive articles aimed to aid in the marketing sales of RV's.

US
## RV WORLD.
**See** Recreation, Leisure.

US/0744-9569
## RVBUSINESS / FROM THE EDITORS OF TL ENTERPRISES.
[RVBusiness]. **VFOAT** RV Business. **VAT** Recreational Vehicle Business. Vol. 33, No. 5 (Aug. 1982)-. Periodical. English. Thirteen times a year. $24.00 US; $48.00 Canada; $96.00 other. TL Enterprises, 29901 Agoura Road, Agoura CA 91301. **Tel** (800)234-3450, (805)389-0300. **LC** TL298; .R17. **DD** 338.4/7629226. ***Continues*** *Recreational Vehicle Dealer, 0886-0041.*
**Ind/Abst** Bus. Index (1985-); Gen. BusinessFile (1985-); Gen. Period. Index (1985-); Mag. Search; Trade Ind. Index (1982-); Vocat. Search (Jan. 1993-).

FR
## S.I.T.R.A.M. RESULTATS GENERAUX, TRAFIC INTERIEUR ET INTERNATIONAL / MINISTERE DES TRANSPORTS, DEPARTEMENT DES STATISTIQUES DES TRANSPORTS.
**Added/Corp** France. Departement des Statistiques des Transports. **VFOAT** SITRAM. Resultats Generaux, Trafic Interieur et International; Resultats Generaux, Trafic Interieur et International; Systeme d'Information sur les Transports Marchandises. Resultats Generaux, Trafic Interieur et International. (19??)-. French. Ministere des Transports, Departement des Statistiques des Transports, 55 rue Brillat-Savarin, 75658 Paris Cedex 13 France. **LC** HE199.F8; S18. **DD** 380.5/24/0944.

FR/0762-0616
## S.I.T.R.A.M., TRAFIC INTERNATIONAL / MINISTERE DE L'EQUIPEMENT, DU LOGEMENT, DE L'AMENAGEMENT DU TERRITOIRE ET DES TRANSPORTS, DEPARTEMENT DES SYNTHESES STATISTIQUES ET ECONOMIQUES.
**VFOAT** SITRAM, Trafic International; Trafic International. **VAT** Systeme d'Information sur les Transports de Marchandises, Trafic International. Vol. 1 1987-. French. qt. Ministere des Transports, Departement des Statistiques des Transports, 55 rue Brillat-Savarin, 75658 Paris Cedex 13 France. **LC** HE597.F8; S57. ***Continues*** *S.I.T.R.A.M., Trafic International. Resultats Trimestriels.*

US
## SAILING DIRECTIONS (ENROUTE) FOR NOVA SCOTIA, AND THE ST. LAWRENCE.
**Main/Corp** Defense Mapping Agency. Hydrographic Center. (1976)-. English. ir. US Department of Defense Defense Mapping Agency, 8613 Lee Highway, Fairfax VA 22031. **Tel** (703)285-9290, FAX (703)285-9374.

NO/0332-8988
## SAMFERDSEL (1979).
(SAMFERDSEL.). [Samferdsel]. **Added/Corp** Transportkonomisk Institutt. No. 1 (Febr. 1979)-. Periodical. Norwegian. mo (10 issues). Kr400.00 Norway; Kr425.00 Nordic countries; Kr450.00 other. Institute of Transport Economics, PO Box 6110 Etterstad, N 0602 Oslo Norway. **Ad Acc. Circ:** 2,800 (ctrl). ***Continues*** *Samferdsel Transport.*

NO/0036-3774
## SAMFERDSEL TRANSPORT.
V. 1- ; Jan. 1969-. Periodical. Norwegian. ir. **LC** HE363.N6; S25. ***Absorbed*** *Samferdsel; Norsk Vegtidsskrift.*

●CN/1187-4562
## SANFORD EVANS GOLD BOOK, OFFICIAL SNOWMOBILE DATA AND USED PRICES.
[Sanford Evans gold book off. snowmob. data used prices]. **Added/Corp** Sanford Evans Communications Ltd. **VFOAT** Official Snowmobile Data and Used Prices; Gold Book Official Snowmobile Guide. (1992)-. English. Sanford Evans Communications Ltd., Box 6900, 1700 Church Avenue, Winnipeg Manitoba R3C 3B1 Canada. **Tel** (204)632-2768, FAX (204)694-2347. **DD** 629.2. ***Continues*** *Sanford Evans Gold Book of Snowmobile Data and Used Prices., 0318-9422.*

JA
## SANGYO SHARYO.
***Ceased.*** **Added/Corp** Nihon Sangyo Sharyo Kyokai. (19??)-?. Japanese. mo. Nihon Sangyo Sharyo Kyokai, (Japan Industrial Vehicles Assoc.), 5-26, Motoakasaka 1 Chome, Minatoku, Tokyoto 107, Japan. **(Subscription address:** Maruzen Company Ltd., PO Box 5050, Import & Export Department, Tokyo 100 31 Japan.) **ED** Terada. **LC** TJ1350.A1; S25. **Ad Acc. Circ:** 1,000 (ctrl).
**Desc:** Publishes research data concerned with rationalization of transportation. Introduces new products of industrial vehicles and statistics.

US/0163-2833
## SAR STATISTICS.
**See** Transportation-Abstracting, Bibliographies and Statistics.

US/0036-6501
## SCHOOL BUS FLEET.
(19??)-. Periodical. English. Seven times a year. $25.00 US; $30.00 Canada; $38.00 other. Bobit Publishing, 2512 Artesia Boulevard, Redondo Beach CA 90278. **Tel** (310)376-8788, (800)334-8152, FAX (213)376-9043. **ED** Bill Paul. **Circ:** 17,500 (ctrl). ***Continues*** *School Bus Transportation.*
**Ind/Abst** Highw. Res. Abstr.; Stat. Ref. Index.

US
## SCHOOL BUS FLEET FACT BOOK.
English. $25.00. Bobit Publishing, 2512 Artesia Boulevard, Redondo Beach CA 90278. **Tel** (310)376-8788, (800)334-8152, FAX (213)376-9043.

US
## SCHOOL BUS PURCHASES.
**See** Education-School Organization and Administration.

US/0273-0936
## SCHOOL TRANSPORTATION.
Vol. 1, No. 1 (Dec. 11, 1980)-. Periodical. English. Twenty-two times a year (published twice monthly except Aug and Dec). $107.00. Federal News Services Inc., PO Box 13460, Silver Spring MD 20911. **Tel** (301)608-9322, FAX (301)608-9057. **[CCC].**
**Desc:** News of federal, state and local developments which can affect local school transportation safety, funding, or management practices.

US/1070-3586
## SCHOOL TRANSPORTATION NEWS.
(SCHOOL TRANSPORTATION NEWS : STN.). [Sch. transp. news]. **VFOAT** STN. (19??)-. Periodical. English. mo. $24.00. BP Communications, PO Box 930, Redondo Beach CA 90277. **Tel** (310)792-2226, FAX (310)792-2231. **ED** William Paul (editor's address: 1926 South Pacific Coast Highway, #103, Redondo Beach, CA 90277. **DD** 371. **Ad Acc. Circ:** 15,500.
**Desc:** Written for readers professionally involved in school transportation. Provides coverage of the latest news affecting the industry.

US
## SCTA HI LIGHTS.
English. Twelve times a year. $5.00. South Carolina Trucking, 2425 Devine Street, Columbia SC 29208. **Tel** (803)799-4306.

US
## SECRETARY'S SEMIANNUAL REPORT TO THE CONGRESS, THE.
**Main/Corp** United States. Dept. of Transportation. Office of the Secretary. **Added/Corp** United States. Dept. of Transportation. Office of Management Planning. Vol. 1, No. 1 (Oct. 1, 1989-Mar. 30, 1990)-. English. sa. US Department of Transportation - Federal Highway Administration, 400 Seventh Street Southwest, Washington DC 20590. **Tel** (202)366-0660.

US/0145-9309
## SELECTED LIBRARY ACQUISITIONS.
**See** Library and Information Sciences.

CN/0229-8627
## SELECTED PAPERS FROM THE TRANSPORTATION SEMINAR SERIES.
[Sel. pap. transp. semin. ser.]. **VFOAT** Transportation Seminar Series. Periodical. English. Free. University of New Brunswick Department of Civil Engineering, Fredericton New Brunswick E3B 5A3 Canada. **DD** 380.5/0971. ctrl circ.

US/8755-4836
## SEMIANNUAL REPORT TO THE CONGRESS - UNITED STATES. DEPT. OF TRANSPORTATION. OFFICE OF INSPECTOR GENERAL (1981).
(SEMIANNUAL REPORT TO THE CONGRESS / INSPECTOR GENERAL.). **Main/Corp** United States. Dept. of Transportation. Office of Inspector General. **VFOAT** Semi-Annual Report to the Congress. April 1, 1981-Sept. 30, 1981-. English. sa. US Department of Transportation / Office of Inspector General, Washington DC 20590. **LC** HE206.3; .U53D. **DD** 353.86/06. available on microfiche (Vols. for (1981-) distributed to depository libraries). ***Continues*** *United States. Dept. of Transportation. Office of Inspector General. Semiannual Report, 8755-4488.*

US/0196-6405
## SERVICE AND METHODS DEMONSTRATION PROGRAM ANNUAL REPORT. EXECUTIVE SUMMARY.
**Added/Corp** United States. Office of Transportation Management and Demonstrations. United States. Urban Mass Transportation Administration. Office of Service and Methods Demonstrations. (19??)-. English. an. National Technical Information Service - NTIS, Room 2027S, 5285 Port Royal Road, Springfield VA 22161. **Tel** (703)487-4630, (703)487-4660, (703)487-4650, FAX (703)321-8547, telex 89-9405. **LC** HE308; .U565a. **DD** 388.4/0973.

AT
## SERVICE STATION.
English. mo (Dec./Jan. issue combined). 49.00Aus$ Australia; 110.00Aus$ other. Berg Bennett & Assiociates Party Ltd, 73 Mullens Street, Balmain 2041 Australia. **Tel** 011 61 2 5551355, FAX 011 61 2 5551434. **ED** Phil Grose. **Ad Acc, Adv Mgr:** M. Malone. **Circ:** 11,000.

CN/0711-303X
**SHIP-BY-TRUCK OFFICIAL ONTARIO DIRECTORY AND BUYER'S GUIDE.** [Off. Ont. dir. buy. guide]. **VFOAT** Official Ontario Directory and Buyer's Guide; Ship-By-Truck; Official Ontario "Ship-By-Truck" Directory. **VAT** Official Ontario Ship-By-Truck- Directory and Buyers' Guide. Vol. 38 (1981)-. Directory. English. an. $44.95 (OTA members), $74.95 (non-members). Ontario Trucking Association, 555 Dixon Road, Rexdale Ontario M9W 1H8 Canada. **Tel** (416)249-7401, FAX (416)245-6152. **DD** 388.3/24/025713. **Ad Acc.** ***Continues*** *O T A Official Ontario Ship-by-Truck Directory, 0226-5680.*
**Desc:** A concise listing of all for-hire carriers operating in Ontario, including detailed descriptions of their operating licenses.

CN/0228-3824
**SIGNAL (WINNIPEG).** (THE SIGNAL.). [Signal]. **Added/Corp** Manitoba. Dept. of Education. Transportation Branch. Manitoba. Manitoba Education. Transportation Branch. Manitoba. Manitoba Education. Transportation Section. Manitoba. Manitoba Education and Training. Pupil Transportation Section. Signal No. 1 (Feb. 1977)-. Periodical. English. Manitoba Department of Education, Legislative Building, Winnipeg Manitoba R3C 0V8 Canada. **DD** 371.8/72/097127. ***Continues*** *Transportation Bulletin (Manitoba. Dept. of Education).*

SI
**SINGAPORE SHIPPING & AIR TRANSPORTATION INDUSTRIES DIRECTORY.** (1975)-. Directory. English. bm. $46.00. **(Subscription address:** Victor Kamkin, 4956 Boiling Brook Parkway, Rockville MD 20852.**) LC** HE884.6.S52; S5. **DD** 387.5/44/0255952.
**Ind/Abst** Appl. Mech. Rev.; Int. Aerosp. Abstr.; Math. Rev.

US
**SIX-YEAR CAPITAL IMPROVEMENT PROGRAM, THE.** ***Title Change.*** **Main/Corp** Alaska. Dept. of Transportation and Public Facilities. **VFOAT** Six Year Capital Improvement Program. (1987-1992). English. ***Continued by*** *Capital Improvement Program.*

US
**SOUTHWEST HARBOR NEWS.** **Added/Corp** Port of Seattle. 1st Ed. (Fall 1991)-. Periodical. English. qt. **LC** HE554.S5; S68.

US/0360-859X
**SPECIAL REPORT - TRANSPORTATION RESEARCH BOARD, NATIONAL RESEARCH COUNCIL.** [Spec. rep. - Transp. Res. Board, Natl. Res. Counc.]. **Main/Corp** National Research Council (U.S.). Transportation Research Board. (1974)-. Monographic series. English. ir. $67.00 US & Canada; $ 77.00 other. Transportation Research Board, Box 289, Washington DC 20055. **Tel** (202)334-3218, FAX (202)334-2519. **CODEN** SRTBDC. Documents available from Article Express International, CASDDS. ***Continues*** *National Research Council (U.S.). Highway Research Board. Special Report.*
**Ind/Abst** Bioeng. Abstr.; Chem. Abstr.; Ei Page One; Eng. Index Annu.; GeoRef; Highw. Res. Abstr.

CN/1180-1220
**ST. LAWRENCE UPDATE.** [St. Lawrence update]. **Added/Corp** St. Lawrence Centre. (May 1990)-. Periodical. English. **DD** 386/.5/0971405.

GW
**STADTVERKEHR, DER.** (Mar. 1956)-. Periodical. German. Ten times a year (Except July and November). DM80.00. Eisenbahn Kurier, Mercystrasse 15, D-79100 Freiburg, Breis Germany. **Tel** 011 49 761 703100, FAX 011 49 761 7031050. **LC** TA1001; .S75.
**Desc:** Public transportation in the city.

US
**STANDARD TRANSPORTATION COMMODITY CODE. HAZARDOUS MATERIALS OR SUBSTANCES OR HAZARDOUS WASTES.** **See** Environmental Issues-Pollution and Waste Management.

US
**STARKS OFF HIGHWAY LEDGER.** (19??)-. Periodical. English. bw. $695.00. JC Communications Co Inc, 176 West Adams Street, Chicago IL 60603. **Tel** (312)236-5122, FAX (312)236-3297. **ED** John A. Stark.
**Desc:** Covers the production, sales, and inventories of trucks, farm & construction machinery.

US
**STATE GUIDE FOR RV MANUFACTURERS.** **See** Manufacturing.

DK/0108-5484
**STATISTISKE EFTERRETNINGER. SAMFRDSEL OG TURISME.** **VFOAT** Samfrdsel Og Turisme. Monographic series. Danish. Price varies per volume. Danmarks Statistik, Sejrgade 11, DK-2100 Copenhagen Denmark. **Tel** 011 45 3 9173917, FAX 011 45 31 18 48 01, telex 1 62 36. **LC** HE257; .A15. ***Continues in part*** *Statistiske Efterretninger.*
**Desc:** Statistics on motor vehicle stock and regulations, goods transport by road, vehicle inspections, road traffic accidents; ships, sea transport, shipping; holidays and travel, nights spent in hotels and travelers' currency.

US
**STATUS OF OHIO'S CAPITAL AND OPERATING NEEDS FOR PUBLIC TRANSPORTATION, THE.** **Main/Corp** Ohio. Dept. of Transportation. English. an. Ohio Department of Transportation, 25 South Front Street, PO Box 899, Columbus OH 43216. **LC** HE309.O36; O42A. **DD** 388.4/042.

US/0039-0844
**STEAMBOAT BILL (1958).** **See** History(General)-History of North, South, and Central America.

US/0039-1298
**STEERING WHEEL (AUSTIN).** ***Ceased.*** (STEERING WHEEL.). [Steer. wheel]. **Added/Corp** Texas Motor Transportation Association. (1936)-(1992). Periodical. English. sw. Texas Motor Transportation Association, PO Box 1669, Austin TX 78767. **Tel** (512)478-2541. **ED** Cathy Brandervie. **DD** 338. **Bk Rev. Ad Acc. Circ:** 3,500 (ctrl).
**Desc:** News on truck and bus equipment, safety, public relations, related economic and government issues, personnel management and news about association activities.

AT/0810-0187
**STREET MACHINE SYDNEY.** [Street mach. Syd.]. (1982)-. Periodical. English. Eight times a year. 42.00Aus$ Australia; 45.40Aus$ New Zealand; 82.00Aus$ other. Australian Consolidated Press Ltd, GPO Box 5252, Sydney New South Wales 2001 Australia. **Tel** 011 61 2 2600000. **DD** 629.22220994. ***Continues*** *Street Machine & Van Wheels, 0810-0195.*

SZ/0039-2510
**STROM + SEE.** German. Seven times a year. 55.00F. Verlag Schiffart and Weltverkehr, Suedquaistrasse 14, 4019 Basel Switzerland. **Tel** 0041 61 65 27 27, FAX 0041 61 651483. **Bk Rev. Ad Acc. Circ:** 3,000.
**Desc:** All problems of international transportation.

SZ/1016-8664
**STRUCTURAL ENGINEERING INTERNATIONAL : JOURNAL OF THE INTERNATIONAL ASSOCIATION FOR BRIDGE AND STRUCTURAL ENGINEERING (IABSE).** **Added/Corp** International Association for Bridge and Structural Engineering. **VFOAT** SEI; S. E. I. Vol. 1, No. 1 (Feb. 1991)-. Periodical. English (French and German). Four times a year (Feb., May., Aug., Nov.). 120.00F. International Association for Bridge and Structural Engineering, Eth-Honggerberg, CH 8093 Zurich Switzerland. **Tel** 011 41 1 3772647, FAX 011 41 1 371213, telex 822186. **ED** Roy Greenspan. **LC** TA630; .S826. **DD** 624.1/05. Index available. **Bk Rev. Ad Acc. Circ:** 4,000 (ctrl). ***Continues*** *International Association for Bridge and Structural Engineering. IABSE Periodica.*
**Ind/Abst** J. Ferrocement.

US/0161-6080
**SUCCESSFUL DEALER, THE.** Vol. 1 (Nov. 1978)-. Periodical. English. Six times a year. $50.00. Kona Communications, 707 Lake Cook Road, Suite 300, Deerfield IL 60015. **Tel** (312)498-3180.

US
**SUMMARY OF ACTIVITIES, OFFICE OF RESEARCH.** **Main/Corp** Connecticut. Dept. of Transportation. Office of Research. **VFOAT** Summary of Activities. Began with 1976/77 issue. English. an. Connecticut Department of Transportation, Wolcott Hill Road, PO Drawer A, Wethersfield CT 06109. **LC** HE213.C6; C65B. **DD** 380.5/0720746.

US
**SUMMARY OF AWARDS, ... PROGRAM OF UNIVERSITY RESEARCH.** **VFOAT** University Research Summary of Awards. Began with 1976/77. English. an. US Department of Transportation / Research and Special Programs Administration / Transportation Programs Bureau, Office of University Research, Washington DC 20590. **LC** HE192.5; .U49B. **DD** 380.5/07/2073. ***Continues*** *Summary of Awards & Published Reports, 0147-4340.*

CN
**SUMMARY OF CANADIAN TRANSIT STATISTICS.** (19??)-. Periodical. English. an. 30.00Can$. Canadian Urban Transit Association, 55 York Street, Suite 901, Toronto Ontario M5J 1R7 Canada. **Tel** (416)365-9800, FAX (416)365-1295. ***Continues*** *Urban Transit Facts in Canada, 0821-2996.*

US/0740-9427
**SUMMARY OF LEGISLATIVE ACTIVITIES - UNITED STATES. CONGRESS. HOUSE. COMMITTEE ON PUBLIC WORKS AND TRANSPORTATION.** **See** Law.

US/0277-5859
**SUMMARY OF UMTA'S TRANSIT ASSISTANCE PROGRAM.** **Main/Corp** United States. Urban Mass Transportation Administration. Office of Transit Assistance. **VFOAT** Summary of U.M.T.A.'s Transit Assistance Program. **VAT** Summary of Urban Mass Transportation Administration's Transit Assistance Program. English. US Department of Transportation / Urban Mass Transportation, Administration Office of Tranist Assistance, Washington DC 20590. **LC** HE308; .U565B. **DD** 338.4/042.

US/8750-0124
**SUPPLY LINE.** **See** Military and Defense.

CN/0828-2897
**SURFACE AND MARINE TRANSPORT.** (SURFACE AND MARINE TRANSPORT / TRANSPORTATION DIVISION.). [Surf. mar. transp.]. **Added/Corp** Statistics Canada. Transportation Division. **VFOAT** Transports Terrestre et Maritime. Vol. 1, No. 1 (1985)-. Periodical. English (French). Eight times a year. 80.00Can$ Canada; $96.00 US; $112.00 other. Statistics Canada, Publications Sales & Services, Main Building Room 1710, Ottawa Ontario K1A 0T6 Canada. **Tel** (613)951-5078, (800)267-6677, FAX (613)951-1584, telex 053-3585. **ED** Jim Cain (editor's telephone number: (613)951-0581, FAX: (613)951-0579). **LC** HE215.A15; S84. **DD** 380.5/0971/021. Index available. **Circ:** 325. ***Formed by the union of*** *Railway Transport (Service Bulletin), 0700-2211; Road Transport (Statistics Canada), 0702-8121* ***and*** *Water Transport, 0380-0350.*
**Desc:** Presents timely analytical data, time series analysis, and special tabulations covering trucking, rail, bus, urban transit, marine transportation and highway infrastructure.

US/0743-4499
**SURVEY OF STATE INVOLVEMENT IN PUBLIC TRANSPORTATION.** (SURVEY OF STATE INVOLVEMENT IN PUBLIC TRANSPORTATION : A REPORT OF THE STANDING COMMITTEE ON PUBLIC TRANSPORTATION.). **Added/Corp** American Association of State Highway and Transportation Officials. Standing Committee on Public Transportation. (1980)-. English. an. $11.00. American Association of State Highway and Transportation Officials, 444 North Capital Street, Suite 249, Washington DC 20001. **Tel** (202)624-5800. **LC** HE4401; .S9. **DD** 388.4/042.

HK
**SURVEY OF TRANSPORT & RELATED SERVICES / TRANSPORT AND SERVICES STATISTICS SECTION, CENSUS AND STATISTICS DEPARTMENT, HONG KONG.** **Added/Corp** Hong Kong. Census and Statistics Dept. Transport and Services Statistics Section. **VFOAT** Survey of Transport and Related Services. (19??)-. Government Publication. English. an. $21.00. Hong Kong Government Information Service, Beaconsfield House, 4 Queens Road, Hong Kong Hong Kong. **Tel** 011 852 8428801 4, telex 61190 HKGIS. **LC** HE281.A15; S866. **DD** 380.5/0951/25021.

US/0547-5570
**SYNTHESIS OF HIGHWAY PRACTICE.** (SYNTHESIS OF HIGHWAY PRACTICE / NATIONAL COOPERATIVE HIGHWAY RESEARCH PROGRAM.). [Synth. highw. pract.]. **Main/Corp** National Cooperative Highway Research Program. **Added/Corp** National Cooperative Highway Research Program. National Research Council (U.S.). Highway Research Board. National Research Council (U.S.). Transportation Research Board. American Association of State Highway Officials. United States. Bureau of Public Roads. American Association of State Highway and Transportation Officials. United States. Federal Highway Administration. (1969)-. Monographic series. English. ir. Price varies. Transportation Research Board, Box 289, Washington DC 20055. **Tel** (202)334-3218, FAX (202)334-2519. **CODEN** NCHSBB. Documents available from Article Express International.
**Ind/Abst** Bioeng. Abstr.; Ei Page One; Eng. Index Annu.; GeoRef.

CN/1183-5532
**T.A.C. NEWS.** [T.A.C. news]. **Added/Corp** Transportation Association of Canada. **VAT** Transportation Association of Canada News. Vol. 16, No. 5 (Sept./Oct. 1990)-. Periodical. English. bm. Free to members. Roads & Transportation Association of Canada, 1765 St Laurent Boulevard, Ottawa Ontario K1G 3V4 Canada. **Tel** (613)521-4052. **DD** 388/.06/071. ***Continues*** *RTAC News, 0317-1280.*

IT/1120-8732
**T & T. TRASPORTI E TRAZIONE.** [T T, Trasp. trazione]. **VFOAT** T e T. Trasporti e Trazione; Trasporti e Trazione. (1988)-. Periodical. Italian. bm.

L72500 Italy. Masson S.P.A, Via Statuto 2/4, 20121 Milan Italy. **Tel** 011 39 2 63671, FAX 011 39 2 6367211. **ED** Ernesto Stagni. **UDC** 656. **Circ:** 2,000.
**Desc:** Technical-scientific articles that deal with public transportation, rolling stock and traction equipment, town-planning, and waterways.

CN/0703-6906
**T 'N T, TRUCK 'N TRAILER.** **VFOAT** Truck 'n Trailer; Truck and Trailer. No. 6 (May 10, 1976)-. Periodical. English. ir. $5.50. Pace Publishing Ltd, 150 Lakeshore Road West, Suite 36 Mississauga, Ontario L5H 3R2 Canada. **Tel** (905)274-4883, FAX (905)274-8686. **DD** 388.3/24/0971. ***Continues*** *Truck & Trailer, 0319-7492.*

●CN/1188-8709
**TAC TECHNICAL BULLETIN.** [TAC tech. bull.]. **Added/Corp** Transportation Association of Canada. Transportation Association of Canada. Technical Information Service. **VFOAT** Transportation Association of Canada Technical Bulletin. No. 1 (June 1992)-. Periodical. English. qt. Free to members. Transportation Association of Canada, 2323 St. Laurent Boulevard, Ottawa Ontario K1G 4K6 Canada. **Tel** (613)736-1350, FAX (613)736-1395. **DD** 625.7/05.

NE
**TACT : THE AIR CARGO TARIFF.** English (Spanish, Italian and French). Six times a year. Fl450.00. Tact The Air Cargo Tariff, PO Box 903, 2130 EA Hoofddorp Netherlands. **Tel** (0)2503-73520, FAX (0)2503-73515. Index available. **Bk Rev**. **Ad Acc**. **Pr Rev.** ctrl circ. available on diskette; available on magnetic tape.
**Desc:** Provides information on the subject of air cargo rates and the rules to apply these rates. The rates published are either IATA rates or carriers own rates. Domestic and international are published.

US/0039-968X
**TARHEEL WHEELS.** Periodical. English. qt. $3.14. Tarheel Wheels, PO Box 2977, Raleigh NC 27602. **Circ:** 3,000.
**Desc:** TARHEEL WHEELS deals with the trucking industry and its news, mainly in North Carolina. It list North Carolina safety award winners, conferences, meetings and trucking industry leaders.

US/1064-4199
**TARIFF NEWS.** [Tariff news]. **Added/Corp** Eastern States Traffic Service. Vol. 1, No. 1 (1989)-. Periodical. English. ir (at least once a month). $375.00. Eastern States Traffic Service, PO Box 330, Rockport MA 01966. **Tel** (508)546-6081. **DD** 388.

JO
**TARIQ AL-SALAMAH / AL-JAMIYAH AL-URDUNIYAH LIL-WIQAYAH MIN HAWADITH AL-TURUQ.** Periodical. Arabic. qt. 0.250JD Jordan; $10.00 US. Al-Jamiyah Al-Urduniyah Lil-Wiqayah Min Hawadith Al-Turuq Shari Al-Kulliyah Al-Arabiyah, Hayy Al-Madinah Al-Riyadiyah SB 9480, Amman Jordan. **Tel** 666412, telex 23888 DAROTL JO. **ED** Nizar Aabidi, Fauzeddin el Bassoumy, Ahmad Shaker. **LC** HE5614.5.J6; T37. **Bk Rev**. **Ad Acc**. **Circ:** 5,000.
**Desc:** Covers road traffic safety.

CN/0700-3099
**TAYLOR'S INDUSTRY DIGEST.** **See** Economics-Industry and Production.

SW/1100-4231
**TEKNIK I TRANSPORT.** (1989)-. Periodical. Swedish. ir. Indufa AB, Box 601, S 25106, Helsingborg, Sweden. **Tel** 011 46 42 173500, FAX 011 46 42 173600. **UDC** 621.8. ***Continues*** *Skandinavisk Transportteknik, 0284-074X.*

US/0887-3526
**TENNESSEE TRUCKER, THE.** (19??)-. Periodical. English. mo. $12.00. Tennessee Trucker Inc, PO Box 248, Buckner KY 40010. **Tel** (502)222-0146, (800)626-6409. **Ad Acc**. **Circ:** 16,000 (ctrl).

CN/0229-0065
**THIS BUSINESS OF TRUCKING.** Periodical. English. bm. Free. Saskatchewan Trucking Association, 1335 Wallace Street, Regina Saskatchewan S4N 3Z5 Canada. **DD** 388.3/24/097124. ctrl circ.

SA
**THIS IS SAR & H : ROAD TRANSPORT HANDBOOK.** **Main/Corp** South African Railways and Harbours. English. ir. Thomson Publications Pty, PO Box 56182, Pinegowrie 2123 South Africa. **Tel** 011 27 11 7892144. **LC** HE5704.4; .A29A. **DD** 388.3/2/0968.

NE/0040-7623
**TIJDSCHRIFT VOOR VERVOERSWETENSCHAP.** [Tijdschr. vervoerswet.]. **Added/Corp** Nederlands Vervoerswetenschappelijk Instituut. (1965)-. Academic Scholarly Publication. Dutch (English). Four times a year. Fl121.80. Nieuwsblad Transport, Postbus 30180, 3001 DD Rotterdam Netherlands. **Tel** 011 31 10 4053130. **ED** C.M.L. van der Velde. **LC** HE7; .T48. **Bk Rev**. **Ad Acc**. **Circ:** 500.
**Desc:** A multidisciplinary and multi-model journal covering all facets of transport. Provides a forum for the practising researcher and the decision maker at political and business levels.
**Ind/Abst** EMBASE; Highw. Res. Abstr.

US/0731-0722
**TIME-SENSITIVE DELIVERY GUIDE.** ***Ceased.*** **VFOAT** TSDG. Issue No. 1 (Fall 1981)-Ceased Dec. 1991. English. ir. Pitney Bowes Smart Mail, 1 Parrott Drive, Shelton CT 06484. **Tel** (203)925-5255. **LC** HE5895; .T54. **DD** 380.5/2.

CN/0381-9345
**TIPS & TOPICS.** **Added/Corp** Atlantic Provinces Transportation Commission. Maritimes Transportation Commission. Vol. 1 (June 1961)-. Periodical. English. Twelve times a year. Free. Atlantic Provinces Transportation Commission, 1133 St. George Boulevard, Suite 330, Moncton New Brunswick, E1E 4E1 Canada. **Tel** (506)857-2820, FAX (506)857-2835. **ED** Jack MacQuerrie. **Circ:** 2,500.
**Desc:** News and information of the transportation commission.

CN/0837-1512
**TODAY'S TRUCKING.** [Today's truck.]. Vol. 1, No. 1 (July/Aug. 1987)-. Periodical. English. mo (10 issues). 28.00Can$ Canada; 81.00Can$ Europe; 36.00Can$ other. New Communications Group Inc, 452 Attwell Suite 100, Etobicoke Ontario M9W 5C3 Canada. **Tel** (416)798-2977. **ED** Rolf Lockwood. **DD** 388.3/24/0971. **[CCC]**. **Bk Rev**. **Ad Acc**. **Circ:** 30,000 (ctrl).
**Desc:** Business magazine for trucking fleets.

US/0890-7129
**TOWPATHS.** [Towpaths]. **Added/Corp** Canal Society of Ohio. (196?)-. Periodical. English. qt. $20.00 non-profit corporations and families; $30.00 profit corporations and contributing members; $20.00 sustaining members; $50.00 patrons; $18.00 individuals; $10.00 students. Canal Society of Ohio, 550 Copley Road, c/o Corresponding Secretary, Akron OH 44320. **ED** Edith McNally (Editor's Address: 1382 Elbur Avenue #21, Cleveland, OH 44107-2746). **DD** 386. **Circ:** 400 (ctrl).

US/0275-3766
**TOXIC MATERIALS TRANSPORT.** ***Title Change.*** [Toxic mater. transp.]. (1980)-(1986). Periodical. English. bw. Business Publishers Inc., 951 Pershing Drive, Silver Spring MD 20910-4464. **Tel** (301)587-6300, (800)274-0122, FAX (301)585-9075. **ED** Andrew Stephens. **[CCC]**. Index available. **Bk Rev**. available on an online database (file 636/Full-Text) from DIALOG. ***Continued by*** *Hazmat Transport News.*
**Desc:** Coverage of both federal and local issues and legislation regulation of carriers. Focus also on accident response, routing, requirements technological developments, compliance efforts and costs.

US/0738-6826
**TR NEWS.** [TR news]. **Added/Corp** National Research Council (U.S.) Transportation Research Board. **VFOAT** T.R. News. No. 104 (Jan.-Feb. 1983)-. Periodical. English. Six times a year. $45.00 North America; $55.00 other. Transportation Research Board, Box 289, Washington DC 20055. **Tel** (202)334-3218, FAX (202)334-2519. **(Subscription address:** Transportation Research Board, Box 289, Washington DC 20055.**)** **LC** TE1; .H57. **DD** 380.5/072073. **Bk Rev**. **Ad Acc**. **Circ:** 8,000 (ctrl). ***Continues*** *Transportation Research News, 0095-2656.*
**Desc:** Discussions of the activities and programs of the Board, government, and industry. Features articles on timely subjects, abstracts of current transportation literature, and announcements of TRB publications and meetings.
**Ind/Abst** Ei Page One; J. Plan. Lit.

US/0730-5400
**TRACTION YEARBOOK.** [Tract. yearb.]. 1981-. English. an. $38.00 US; $39.00 other. Traction Slides International, Box 123, Bank Plaza Station, Merrick NY 11566. **Tel** (516)379-9797. **ED** Joseph P Saitta. **LC** TF701; .T68. **DD** 388.4/2/05. **Bk Rev**. **Circ:** 3,000. ***Continues*** *Traction Fan's Directory, 0496-0076.*
**Desc:** Comprehensive news and photo information concerning latest developments in street railways, subways and trolleybuses, worldwide.

UK/0041-0683
**TRAFFIC ENGINEERING & CONTROL.** [Traffic eng. control]. **Added/Corp** World Touring and Automobile Organisation. **VFOAT** Traffic Engineering + Control; Traffic Engineering and Control; Traffic Engineering Plus Control. Vol. 2, No. 1 (May 1960)-. Academic Scholarly Publication. English. Eleven times a year (Summer issue combined). £50.00 UK; £58.00 others; $110.00 (surface mail), $120.00 (airmail) US & Canada. Traffic Engineering Control Subs Bureau, Queen Street / March, Cambridgeshire PE15 8SN England. **Tel** 011 44 354 58080, FAX 011 44 354 53965. **ED** Keith Lumley. **LC** HE331; .T72. **DD** 388.3/1/05. **CODEN** TENCA4. **Bk Rev**. **Ad Acc**. **Circ:** 2,500 (ctrl). available in microform from University Microfilms International (UMI). Documents available from Article Express International, Ask*IEEE. ***Absorbed*** *International Road Safety; Traffic Review.*
**Desc:** Road testing and safety information.
**Ind/Abst** Bioeng. Abstr.; Curr. Technol. Index; Ei Page One; EMBASE; Eng. Index Annu.; Ergon. Abstr.; Geogr. Abstr. Human Geogr.; Highw. Res. Abstr.; INSPEC (March 1970-); Int. Abstr. Oper. Res. [Select. Cov.]; Int. Civil Eng. Abstr.; Int. Dev. Abstr. (?-?); J. Plan. Lit.; Middle East Abstr. Index; Soft. Abstr. Eng.

US/0041-0691
**TRAFFIC MANAGEMENT.** [Traffic manage.]. Vol. 1 (Jan. 1962)-. Periodical. English. mo. $75.00 US; $112.00 Canada; $105.00 Mexico; $135.00 (surface mail) other. Cahners Publishing Company, 249 West 17th Street, New York NY 10011. **Tel** (212)645-0067, FAX (212)242-6987. **(Subscription address:** Cahners Publishing Company / Colorado, Paid Subscription Service Center, PO Box 7610, Highlands Ranch CO 80126-7610.**)** **ED** Francis J. Quinn. **LC** HE1; .T62. **CODEN** TRMADJ. **[CCC]**. **Ad Acc**. **Circ:** 70,000 (ctrl). available on microfilm and microfiche from University Microfilms International (UMI); available on an online database (file 648/Full-Text) from DIALOG. Documents available from UMI Article Clearinghouse, Ask*IEEE.
**Desc:** Concentrates on operations management and corporate management in addition to its largest reader group of traffic managers. Editorial is designed to help readers cope with issues of deregulation, computerization and new customer service pressures.
**Ind/Abst** ABI/INFORM Glob. Ed.; ABI Inform Ondisc (Oct. 1972-); ABI/INFORM Ondisc: Expr. Ed.; Acad. Search (July 1993-); Aviat. Tradescan [Select. Cov.]; Bus. Index (1985-); Bus. Period. Index; Bus. Source (Jul. 1993-); Gen. BusinessFile (1985-); Gen. Period. Index (1985-); INFO-SOUTH Abstr.; INSPEC (Sept. 1980-); Mag. Search; Stat. Ref. Index; Trade Ind. ASAP [Full Txt.]; Trade Ind. Index [Full Txt.]; Wilson Bus. Abstr.

US/0735-7613
**TRAFFIC TOPICS.** ***Ceased.*** (TRAFFIC TOPICS : CURRENT NEWS ON TRANSPORTATION / NRMA.). [Traffic top.]. **Added/Corp** National Retail Association. **VFOAT** Current News on Transportation. (1975)-(19??). Periodical. English. qt. National Retail Federation, 325 7th Street NW Suite 1000, Washington DC 20004. **Tel** (202)626-8146. **ED** Beatrice Cohen. **DD** 380. **Bk Rev**. ctrl circ.
**Desc:** Covers regulatory matters pertaining to transportation and responsibilities of traffic managers such as transportation, cost routing, modes of transportation, loss and damage claims.

US/0041-073X
**TRAFFIC WORLD, THE.** **Added/Corp** Traffic Service Corporation. Traffic Service Bureau. Vol. 11, No. 1 (Jan. 4, 1913)-. Periodical. English. wk. $159.00 US, Canada & Mexico; $224.00 other. Journal of Commerce Inc, 445 Marshall Street, Phillipsburg NJ 08865. **Tel** (800)222-0356, (908)859-1300. **(Subscription address:** Traffic World, Box 5570 GPO, New York NY 10087.**)** **ED** Ruput Welch. **[CCC]**. Index available. cum. index. **Bk Rev**. **Ad Acc**. **Circ:** 11,000. available on microfilm and microfiche from University Microfilms International (UMI); available on an online database (files 16,637/Full-Text) from DIALOG. ***Continues*** *Traffic World and Traffic Bulletin;* ***Absorbed*** *Federal Trade Reporter.*
**Desc:** News magazine of transportation and distribution management.
**Ind/Abst** Acad. Search (July 1993-); Aviat. Tradescan [Select. Cov.]; Bus. Period. Index; Bus. Source (Jul. 1993-); Highw. Res. Abstr.; INFO-SOUTH Abstr.; J. Plan. Lit.; Mag. Search; PROMT [Full Txt.]; Wilson Bus. Abstr.

CN/0229-6497
**TRAFIC ROUTIER (MONTREAL. 1981).** (TRAFIC ROUTIER.). [Trafic rout.]. V. 1, No. 1, (April 1981)-. Periodical. French. ir. $2.50 each number. Publications Amylitho Inc, 4270 rue Papineau, Montreal Quebec H2H 1S9 Canada. **DD** 388.3/24/09714.

US/0041-0772
**TRAILER/BODY BUILD.** (TRAILER/BODY BUILDERS.). [Trailer/body build.]. **VFOAT** Trailer Body Builders. 1953. Periodical. English. mo. Trailer Body Builders, 1602 Harold Street, Houston TX 77006. **Tel** (713)523-8124, FAX (713)523-8384. **ED** Paul Shenck. Index available. **Bk Rev**. **Ad Acc**. **Circ:** 12,000 (ctrl).
**Desc:** For manufacturers and distributors of truck trailers, truck bodies and related equipment and components.

NE/0168-5775
**TRAM- EN AUTOBUSBEDRIJVEN / CENTRAAL BUREAU VOOR DE STATISTIEK, HOOFDAFDELING STATISTIEKEN VAN VERKEER EN VERVOER.** **VFOAT** Tram- and Buscompanies. Dutch (summaries and/or abstracts in English). an. Fl7.50. Centraal Bureau voor de Statistiek, AFD ALG Zaken, Postbus 959, 2270 AZ Voorburg Netherlands. **Tel** 011 31 70 3373800, FAX 011 31 038 7429, telex 32692 CBS NL. **LC** HE4821; .C46A.

US
**TRANS ACTION / CALIFORNIA DEPARTMENT OF TRANSPORTATION, DISTRICT 7.** **Added/Corp** California. Dept. of Transportation. District 7. **VFOAT** Transaction. (19??)-.

English.
**Ind/Abst** Calif. Period. Index (19??-); Calif. Period. Microfi. (19??-).

FR/0766-8007
**TRANS RURAL EXPRESS.** (1984)-. Periodical. French. bw. 220.00F (individuals), 330.00F (schools & universities), 440.00F other. AFIP Editions Diffusion, 2 rue Paul Escudier, 75009 Paris France. **Tel** 14 874 5288. **UDC** 63 : 070.431.

CN/0714-8100
**TRANSACTION. See** Religion and Theology-Protestantism.

AT/0818-5204
**TRANSIT AUSTRALIA.** [Transit Aust.]. (1987)-. Periodical. English. Twelve times a year. 51.00Aus$ Australia; 63.00Aus$ Asia/Oceania; 65.00Aus$ other. Transit Australia Publishing, GPO Box 1017, Sydney NSW 2001 Australia. **Tel** 011 61 2 9494424. **DD** 388.40994. Index available in last issue of volume--attached. ***Continues** ET (Sydney), 0013-4163.*

US/0149-3132
**TRANSIT FACT BOOK (WASHINGTON, D.C.).** (TRANSIT FACT BOOK.). [Transit fact book]. **Added/Corp** American Public Transit Association. American Transit Association. (19??)-. English. an. $5.00. American Public Transit Association, 1201 New York Avenue Northwest, Suite 400, Washington DC 20005. **Tel** (202)898-41194128, FAX 9202)898-4095. **ED** Long H. Pham. **LC** HE4441; .A55. **DD** 388.4/0973. **Circ:** 10,000.
**Desc:** Contains statistical reference of trends in transit finance and operation in North America.
**Ind/Abst** Predicasts Forecasts.

US/0149-0656
**TRANSIT LAW REVIEW. Added/Corp** American Public Transit Association. Vol. 1 (Spring/Summer 1977)-. Periodical. English. American Public Transit Association, 1201 New York Avenue Northwest, Suite 400, Washington DC 20005. **Tel** (202)898-41194128, FAX 9202)898-4095. **LC** K24; .R28. **DD** 343/.73/09805.
**Ind/Abst** LegalTrac (1980-1981).

CN/0712-8355
**TRANSIT NEWS CANADA. *Ceased.*** [Transit news Can.]. No. 1 (Jan. 1982)-(199?). Periodical. English (French). bm. Transit News Canada, TNC Publishers, 651 Wavell Avenue, Ottawa Ontario K1A 3A9 Canada. **DD** 388.4/0971.

US/0361-6371
**TRANSIT OPERATING REPORT. Main/Corp** American Public Transit Association. Statistical Dept. English. an. American Public Transit Association, 1201 New York Avenue Northwest, Suite 400, Washington DC 20005. **Tel** (202)898-41194128, FAX 9202)898-4095. **LC** HE308; .A65A. **DD** 388.4/0973.

US/0748-7347
**TRANSIT PULSE. Added/Corp** Trans21(Firm). **VFOAT** Transitpulse. (1983)-. Periodical. English. bm (Jan., Mar., May, July, Sept., and Nov.). $75.00 (one year) $135.00 (two year); $90.00 (one year) $160.00 (two year) other. Trans 21, PO Box 249, Fields Corner Station, Boston MA 02122. **Tel** (617)825-2318.

●US/1062-9483
**TRANSIT RESEARCH ABSTRACTS (1992).** (TRANSIT RESEARCH ABSTRACTS.). [Transit res. abstr.]. **Added/Corp** National Research Council (U.S.). Transportation Research Board. (1992)-. English. an. $82.00 North America; $89.00 other. Transportation Research Board, Box 289, Washington DC 20055. **Tel** (202)334-3218, FAX (202)334-2519. **LC** HE305; .U696. **DD** 388.4/05. ***Continues** Urban Transportation Abstracts, 0734-0648.*

US/0278-2804
**TRANSITIONS (CINCINNATI, OHIO).** (TRANSITIONS.). **Added/Corp** ATE Management and Service Company. (Spring 1980)-. Periodical. English. Three times a year. $18.00. ATE Management and Service Company, 617 Vine Street/Suite 800, Cincinnati OH 45202. **Tel** (513)381-7424. **ED** Donna Kathman. **Bk Rev. Circ:** 1,500 (ctrl).
**Desc:** Articles in journal format on topics of interest to public transit professionals. Such topics include operations, funding, marketing, labor relations, insurance, maintenance, and service alternatives.
**Ind/Abst** Curr. Lit. Fam. Plan. (19??-199?).

FR/0764-809X
**TRANSPAC ACTUALITES.** (1983)-. Periodical. French. Four times a year. Free. Transpac, 87 rue du Gouverneur Eboue, 92441 Issy l'Moulineaux France. **Tel** 011 33 1 46481515. **UDC** 654:681.3.

CN/0706-3954
**TRANSPO. *Suspended.*** (TRANSPO / TRANSPORT CANADA.). Vol. 1, No. 1 (Summer 1978)-?. Periodical. English (French). Three times a year. Free. Transport Canada / Public Affairs Branch, Ottawa Ontario K1A 0N5 Canada. **Tel** (613)991-2309. **ED** Peter Twidale. **LC** HE215; .T7. **DD** 380.5/0971. **Circ:** 6,000 (ctrl). ***Continues** Transport Canada.*
**Desc:** Canadian transportation, mainly involving Transport Canada, the Federal Government Department.

CN/0227-3020
**TRANSPORT-ACTION.** [Transp.-action]. **Added/Corp** Transport 2000 Canada. No. 5 (Summer 1980)-. Newsletter. English (French). bm. 22.00Can$ Canada; 25.00Can$ US; 27.00Can$ other. Transport Action, Box CP 858 Station B, Ottawa Ontario K1P 5P9 Canada. **Tel** (613)594-3290. **ED** Roy Jamieson. **DD** 380.5/0971. **Bk Rev. Circ:** 2,500. ***Continues** Trans-Action, 0226-5966.*
**Desc:** Covers public transportation policy, technology and operation with an emphasis on consumer advocacy.

AT/1033-9752
**TRANSPORT AND COMMUNICATIONS INDICATORS.** (1988)-. Government Publication. English. qt. 17.00Aus$. Australian Government Publishing Service, GPO Box 84, Canberra ACT 2601 Australia. **Tel** 011 61 6 2954411, FAX 011 61 6 2954455.

II
**TRANSPORT & TOURISM JOURNAL.** Periodical. English. Rs8.00. 1969 Ganj Mir Khan Daryaganj, New Delhi-6 India. **LC** HE7; .T66. **DD** 338.4/7/915404505.

US/0733-0197
**TRANSPORT (DE)REGULATION REPORT. VFOAT** Transport Deregulation Report. (19??)-. Periodical. English. mo. $167.00 US; $181.00 other. Transportation Services, 960 Broadway, Hicksville NY 11801. **Tel** (516)822-1183, FAX (516)822-1126. **ED** Anthony N. Nuzio.
**Desc:** Monthly source of news analysis and forecasts on all matters effecting freight transportation throughout the US and the world.

GW
**TRANSPORT-DIENST + WIRTSCHAFTS-CORRESPONDENT.** ***Ceased.*** **VFOAT** Transport-Dienst und Wirtschafts-Correspondent; Transport Dienst + Wirtschafts Correspondent; Transport Dienst und Wirtschafts Correspondent. (19??)-(Dec. 1992). Periodical. German. mo. Schiffahrts-Verlag, PO Box 11 03 29, Stubbenhuk 10, W-2000 Hamburg 11 Germany. **Tel** (040)373964, FAX 040 36 49 85, telex 040 36 49 812 13 075 HANSA D. **LC** HE5; .T66. **DD** 380.5/24/05. Index available. **Bk Rev. Ad Acc. Circ:** 12,500 (ctrl). ***Continues** Transport-Dienst.*
**Desc:** Reports and informs on shipping, ports, air transport, rail and road transport, forwarding, international transport and transport engineering.

BE/0009-6083
**TRANSPORT ECHO ED. BILINGUE.** (1970)-. Periodical. Dutch (French). mo. 7300.00F. Transmedia PVBA, Cuylitsstraat 39, B-2018 Antwerpen Belgium. **Tel** 011 32 3 2385836, FAX 03 216 4488, telex 71726. **ED** Nicole Martinet, Dominique L'Hoost, Jef Van de Keybus, Marc Van de Perre, Jan Proot, and Annemie Morbee. Index available. **Bk Rev. Ad Acc. Circ:** 22,500.
**Desc:** Magazine and weekly newsletter for shippers, freight forwarders and transport companies.

US/0041-1434
**TRANSPORT ECONOMICS.** Aug. 1941-. Periodical. English. mo. Interstate Commerce Commission / Bureau of Economics, 1112 ICC Building, Washington DC 20423. **LC** HE17; .A37. **DD** 385. cum. index. available on microfilm and microfiche from University Microfilms International (UMI).

NE
**TRANSPORT EN OPSLAG. See** Business.

UK/0020-3122
**TRANSPORT ENGINEER, THE. See** Engineering.

UK/0041-1469
**TRANSPORT HISTORY.** [Trans. hist.]. (Mar. 1968)-. Periodical. English. Three times a year. Graphmitre Ltd, 1 West Street, Tavistock Devon PL19 8DS England. **Tel** 0822-612785, FAX 0822-612078. Index available. **Bk Rev. Ad Acc. Circ:** 2,000 (ctrl).
**Desc:** History of all forms of communication worldwide.
**Ind/Abst** Am. Hist. Life (1972-).

NE/0929-9645
**TRANSPORT LOGISTICS.** (19??)-. English. qt. DM250.00. VSP International Science Publishers, Godfried van Seystlaan 47, 3703 BR Zeist Netherlands. **Tel** 011 31 3404 25790, FAX 011 31 3404 32081, telex 40217 USP NL. **(Subscription address:** VSP International Science Publishers, PO Box 346, 3700 AH Zeist Netherlands.**)**

UK/0144-3453
**TRANSPORT (LONDON. 1980).** (TRANSPORT.). [Transport]. Vol. 1, No. 1 (Mar./Apr. 1980)-. Periodical. English. mo (ten issues per year; bi-monthly Jan./Feb. and July/August). £75.00. Fitzalan Publications Ltd, 100 Great Portland Street, London W1N 5PD United Kingdom. **Tel** (1)0480-861266, FAX (1)0480-861212. **(Subscription address:** The Chairman's Office, Tilbrook Hall, Tilbrook, Huntingdon, Cambridgeshire PE18 0JS England**) ED** David Robinson. **LC** HE1; .T775. **DD** 380.5/05. Index available. **Bk Rev. Ad Acc. Circ:** 20,000. ***Continues** Chartered Institute of Transport. Journal, 0020-3181.*
**Desc:** Content includes features, book reviews, letters, case studies, technology, personal profiles, news digest and special reports.
**Ind/Abst** Curr. Technol. Index; Energy Res. Abstr. (Dec. 1980-); Geogr. Abstr. Human Geogr.; Highw. Res. Abstr.; Int. Civil Eng. Abstr.; PAIS Int. Print.

FR/1162-387X
**TRANSPORT MAGAZINE PARIS.** (TRANSPORT MAGAZINE.). (1991)-. Periodical. French. mo (11 issues). 309.00F France; 425.00F other. Editions du Monde, 2 Bis rue Mercoeur, 75011 Paris, France. **Tel** 011 33 1 43676424. **UDC** 656(44). ***Continues** Camions Magazine, 0756-4643.*

UK/0041-1515
**TRANSPORT MANAGEMENT; THE BRITISH JOURNAL OF TRADE AND TRANSPORT.** (1945)-. Periodical. English. Six times a year (Feb., April, June, Aug., Oct., Dec.). £18.00. Institute Transport Administration, 32 Palmerston Road, Southampton SO1 41LL England. **Tel** 0703 631380, FAX 0703 634165. **ED** N. H. Tilsley. **Bk Rev**, (Qty: 6). **Ad Acc, Adv Mgr:** MMA Associates, **Tel** 0580 753221. **Pr Rev. Acid Free. Circ:** 4,500 (ctrl). available in print.

UK
**TRANSPORT MANAGER'S HANDBOOK, THE.** English. an. $16.95. Kogan Page Ltd., 120 Pentonville Road, London N1 9BR England. **Tel** 011 44 71 2780433, FAX 011 44 71 8376348, telex 263088 KOGAN G. **ED** David Lowe. **LC** KD2579.A1; T7. **DD** 343/.42/0948.
**Desc:** Includes new material on changes to the EEC driving hours law, and regulations concerning the fitting of anti-spray equipment and the classification, packaging and labeling of dangerous substances.

PL/0209-0333
**TRANSPORT MIEJSKI.** (198?)-. Periodical. Polish. mo. Price on Request. **(Subscription address:** ARS Polona, PO Box 1001, 00068 Warsaw Poland.**) LC** HE311.P7; T7.

US
**TRANSPORT OF DANGEROUS GOODS. Main/Corp** United Nations. Committee of Experts on the Transport of Dangerous Goods. (1953-1956). **Added/Corp** United Nations. Committee of Experts on the Transport of Dangerous Goods (1957- ). (1964)-. Government Publication. English. ir. $80.00. United Nations Publications, 2 United Nations Plaza, Room DC2 0853, Department 007C, New York NY 10017. **Tel** (212)963-8303, (800)253-9646. **LC** JX1977; .A2; HE595.D3; U5.
**Desc:** Contains significant recommendation on transporting dangerous goods, definitions, instructions and technical information of relevance to international shippers and inspection authorities.

CN/0822-580X
**TRANSPORT OF THUNDER BAY.** [TransP. Thunder Bay]. **Added/Corp** Lakehead Harbour Commission (Canada). Thunder Bay Harbour Commissioin (Canada). **VFOAT** Port of Thunder Bay. Vol. 1, No. 1 (Spring 1983)-. Periodical. English. Three times a year (Feb., June, Oct.). Free. Thunder Bay Harbour Commission, PO Box 2266, Thunder Bay Ontario P78 5E8 Canada. **Tel** (807)345-6400. **ED** Nora Logan. **DD** 387.1/09713/12. Index available. cum. index. **Circ:** 3,000 (ctrl).

●UK/0967-070X
**TRANSPORT POLICY.** Vol. 1, No. 1 (Oct. 1993)-. Periodical. English. Four times a year. $194.00 The Americas; £130.00 other. Butterworth Heinemann Publishers, Linacre House, Jordan Hill, Oxford OX2 8DP England. **Tel** 011 44 865 310366. **(Subscription address:** Elsevier Science Ltd. Oxford Fulfillment Centre, PO Box 800, Kidlington, Oxford OX5 1DX United Kingdom.**) LC** HE193; .T648. **CODEN** TRPOE9.
**Desc:** It reflects the concerns of policy makers in government, industry and voluntary organisations providing independent, original and rigorous analysis in order to understand all aspects of transport policy decision making.

NE/0166-1957
**TRANSPORT POLICY AND DECISION MAKING.** [Transp. policy decis. mak.]. V. 1-. Academic Scholarly Publication. English. qt. Martinus Nijhoff Publishers, Subsidiary of Kluwer Academic Publishers, Koraalrood 50, 2718 SC Zoetermeer Netherlands. **Tel** 011 31 79 684400.
**Ind/Abst** EMBASE; Int. Dev. Abstr. (?-?).

FR/0249-5643
**TRANSPORT PUBLIC.** [Transp. public]. (1981)-. Periodical. French. mo. 411.36F France; 490.00F other. Union des Transports Publics, 5 7 rue d Aumale, 75009 Paris France. **Tel** 011 33 1 48746351. **UDC** 629.1-45.

*Continues Revue des Transports Publics Urbains et Regionaux, 0397-474X.*
**Ind/Abst** Highw. Res. Abstr.

UK/0265-9301
**TRANSPORT RESEARCH & CONSULTANCY BRIEFING.** [Transp. res. consult. brief.]. **VFOAT** Transport Research and Consultancy Briefing. (1983)-. Periodical. English. mo. £52.00 UK; £68.00 others. Landor Holdings Ltd, Quadrant House, 250 Kennington Lane, London SE11 5RD England. **Tel** 011 44 71 735 5058, FAX 011 44 71 587 0497. **DD** 380.505.

UK
**TRANSPORT REVIEW.** No. 5084- Mar. 12, 1976-. Periodical. English. sm. £10.00 UK; £16.00 other. 205 Euston Road, London NW1 England. **Tel** (01)387-4771. **ED** J Finney. **LC** HD6668.R3; R3. **DD** 380.5/0941. **Bk Rev. Ad Acc.** ctrl circ. ***Continues*** *Railway Review.*

UK/0144-1647
**TRANSPORT REVIEWS.** [Transp. rev.]. Vol. 1, No. 1 (Jan./March 1981)-. Periodical. English (summaries and/or abstracts in French, German and Spanish). qt. £124.00 UK; $205.00 other. Taylor & Francis Ltd., Rankine Road, Basingstoke Hampshire, RG24 8PR United Kingdom. **Tel** 011 44 256 840366, FAX 011 44 256 479438, telex 858540. **(Subscription address:** Taylor & Francis Inc., 1900 Frost Road, Suite 101, Bristol PA 19007-1598.**) ED** S. M. A. Banister. **LC** WMLC 93/517. **[CCC]. Pr Rev.** available on microfilm from University Microfilms International (UMI). Documents available from The Genuine Article.
**Desc:** Covers all modes of transport. Each paper is of interest and relevance to people concerned with transport in many nations and written for readers not expert in the author's discipline. The journal has built a series of papers on the following topics: transport organization and policies in countries, national policies toward cars, transport in major cities and computers in transport.
**Ind/Abst** Curr. Contents Soc. Behav. Sci.; Ergon. Abstr.; Geogr. Abstr. Human Geogr.; Highw. Res. Abstr.; Int. Abstr. Oper. Res. [Select. Cov.]; Int. Dev. Abstr.; Res. Alert [Full Cov.]; Soc. Sci. Cit. Index [Full Cov.].

CN/0049-447X
**TRANSPORT ROUTIER DU QUEBEC.** ***Ceased.*** **VFOAT** Quebec Road Transport. (1942)-(May 1992). Periodical. French (English). mo. Transport Routier du Quebec, 4837 rue Boyer Bureau 100, Montreal Quebec H2J 3E6 Canada. **Tel** (514)527-1359. **ED** M Jacques Alary. **Ad Acc. Circ:** 10,000 (ctrl).
**Desc:** New rules in transportation, new products available for trucks and cars.

US/0041-1558
**TRANSPORT TOPICS.** [Transp. top.]. **Added/Corp** American Trucking Associations. (1935)-. Periodical. English. Fifty-two times a year. $69.00 US; $79.00 others. American Trucking Association, 2200 Mill Road, Alexandria VA 22314. **Tel** (703)838-1772. **ED** Oliver Patton. **LC** HE5601; .T6. **DD** 388.3. **[CCC]. Bk Rev. Ad Acc. Circ:** 32,000. available on microfilm and microfiche from University Microfilms International (UMI). ***Continues*** *A.T.A. News Bulletin.*
**Desc:** National business newspaper of the trucking industry-- national, state and local news concerning management of operations and maintenance of for-hire and private truck fleets.

US/0197-3320
**TRANSPORTATION AND TRAVEL : OFFICIAL TABLE OF DISTANCES, FOREIGN TRAVEL. See** Travel and Tourism.

US/0273-2602
**TRANSPORTATION (BOCA RATON).** (TRANSPORTATION.). [Transportation]. V. 1, Article 1-. English. an. Social Issues Resources Series Inc, PO Box 2348, Boca Raton FL 33427. **Tel** (800)327-0513, (407)994-0079. **ED** Eleanor C Goldstein. **LC** HE202.5; .T7. **DD** 380.5/0973.
**Desc:** Interdisciplinary resource material consisting of reprinted articles from popular and professional journals, newspapers, magazines and government documents.

US/1043-4054
**TRANSPORTATION BUILDER.** [Transp. build.]. **Added/Corp** American Road & Transportation Builders Association. Vol. 1, No. 1 (First Quarter 1989)-. Periodical. English. Twelve times a year. $30.00 (members), $50.00 (non-members) Comes with American Road & Transportation Builder Association membership. American Road & Transportation Builders Association / ARTBA, 1010 Massachusetts Avenue, Washington DC 20001. **Tel** (202)289-4434. **ED** Angelin M. Donohue. **LC** TE1; .T64. **DD** 625.7/0973. **Ad Acc. Circ:** 10,000. ***Continues*** *American Transportation Builder, 0149-4511.*
**Ind/Abst** Highw. Res. Abstr.; Trade Ind. Index.

US/1041-9136
**TRANSPORTATION (CLEVELAND, OHIO).** (TRANSPORTATION.). [Transportation]. **Added/Corp** Predicasts, Inc. (19??)-. Periodical. English. mo. $225.00. Predicasts Inc., A Ziff Communications Company, 11001 Cedar Avenue, Cleveland OH 44106. **Tel** (800)321-6388, (216)795-3000, FAX (216)229-9944, telex 985 604. **(Subscription address:** Information Access Company, PO Box 61000, Department 1851, San Francisco, CA 94161; Phone: (800)321-6388**) DD** 380.

US
**TRANSPORTATION COMMISSION UPDATE.** English. Six times a year. Free on request. Mississippi Department of Transportation, PO Box 1850, Jackson MS 39215-1850. **Tel** (601)359-1217. **ED** Donna M. Lum.
**Desc:** A bi-monthly report from the Mississippi Department of Transportation.

US/0091-1410
**TRANSPORTATION; CURRENT LITERATURE. Added/Corp** United States. Dept. of Transportation. Library Services Division. Vol. 51, No. 1 (Jan. 5, 1972)-. English. wk. US Department of Transportation / Library Services Division, 400 Sixth Street, Washington DC 20590. **LC** Z7295; .H55. **DD** 016.38/05. ***Continues*** *Highways. Current Literature.*

NE/0049-4488
**TRANSPORTATION (DORDRECHT).** (TRANSPORTATION.). [Transportation]. Vol. 1 (May 1972)-. Periodical. English. qt. $389.00. Kluwer Academic Publishers, Postbus 322, 3300 AH Dordrecht, The Netherlands. **Tel** 011 (31) 78 524400, FAX 011 31 78 183273, telex 20083. **ED** Martin G Richards, David Hartgen, Ryuichi Kitamura, James Scott, and William Young. **LC** HE7; .T685. **DD** 380.5/05. **CODEN** TRPOB6. **[CCC]. Bk Rev. Ad Acc. Pr Rev. Acid Free. Circ:** 750 (ctrl). available on microfilm and microfiche from University Microfilms International (UMI). Documents available from Article Express International, The Genuine Article, Documents on Demand.
**Desc:** Focuses on issues of direct relevance to those concerned with policy formulation, preparation and evaluation of plan, and day-to-day operational management of transport systems. It concerns itself with the policies and systems themselves, as well as with their impacts on and relationship with other aspects of the social, economic and physical environment.
**Ind/Abst** Appl. Sci. Technol. Index; Avery Index Archit. Period. Suppl. Colum. Univ. (1989-); Bioeng. Abstr.; Curr. Contents Eng. Tech. Appl. Sci.; Curr. Contents Soc. Behav. Sci.; Ei Page One; Energy Res. Abstr. (June 1977-); Eng. Index Annu.; Environ. Abstr.; Highw. Res. Abstr.; Int. Abstr. Oper. Res. [Select. Cov.]; Int. Aerosp. Abstr.; Int. Civil Eng. Abstr.; J. Plan. Lit.; Res. Alert [Full Cov.]; Soc. Sci. Cit. Index [Full Cov.]; Soft. Abstr. Eng.; Transp. Res. Abstr.

US/0885-8330
**TRANSPORTATION ENERGY RESEARCH.** [Transp. energy res.]. **Added/Corp** United States. Dept. of Energy Office of Scientific and Technical Information. United States. Dept. of Energy. Office of Conservation and Renewable Energy. United States. Dept. of Energy. Office of Transportation Systems. **VFOAT** TER. Doe/Ter-86/1 (Jan. 15, 1986)-. Government Publication. English. mo. $165.00 North America; $330.00 other. US Department of Energy, 1000 Independence Avenue SW, Washington DC 20585. **Tel** (202)586-5000, FAX (202)586-4073. **(Subscription address:** National Technical Information Service, 5285 Port Royal Road, Springfield, VA 22161**) ED** Lila Smith and Barry Steele. **DD** 629.

CN/0835-0140
**TRANSPORTATION EQUIPMENT INDUSTRIES (1986).** (TRANSPORTATION EQUIPMENT INDUSTRIES / STATISTICS CANADA, INDUSTRY DIVISION, CENSUS OF MANUFACTURES SECTION.). [Transp. equip. ind.]. **Added/Corp** Statistics Canada. Census of Manufactures Section. Statistics Canada. Industry Division. **VFOAT** Industries du Materiel de Transport. (1985)-. English (French). an. 38.00Can$ Canada; $46.00 US; $54.00 other. Statistics Canada, Publications Sales & Services, Main Building Room 1710, Ottawa Ontario K1A 0T6 Canada. **Tel** (613)951-5078, (800)267-6677, FAX (613)951-1584, telex 053-3585. **LC** HD9709.C2; T72. **DD** 338.4/7629046/097105. ***Formed by the union of*** *Aircraft and Aircraft Parts Manufacturers (Final), 0384-2711; Motor Vehicle Parts and Accessories Manufacturers (Final), 0527-5857; Railroad Rolling Stock Industry (Final), 0575-9579; Truck Body and Trailer Manufacturers, 0527-6365; Shipbuilding and Boatbuilding, 0319-8987* ***and*** *Motor Vehicle Industries, 0319-9088.*

US/0098-0129
**TRANSPORTATION FOCUS.** English. Department of Transportation / Sacramento, Room 4113/1120 N Street, Sacramento CA 95814. **LC** HE1; .T857. **DD** 380.5/05.

US/0889-0889
**TRANSPORTATION IN AMERICA. See** Transportation-Abstracting, Bibliographies and Statistics.

US/0041-1612
**TRANSPORTATION JOURNAL.** [Transp. j.]. **Added/Corp** American Society of Traffic and Transportation. Vol. 1 (Fall 1961)-. Periodical. English. Four times a year (Apr., July, Oct., Dec.). $50.00 US, Canada and Mexico; $55.00 other. American Society of Transportation and Logistics, 216 East Church Street, Lock Haven PA 17745. **Tel** (717)748-8515, FAX (717)748-9118. **ED** John C. Spychalski. **LC** HE1; .T826. **DD** 380.5/05. **CODEN** TRNJA. Index available. **Bk Rev. Pr Rev. Circ:** 3,000 (ctrl). available on microfilm and microfiche from University Microfilms International (UMI); available in reprints. Documents available from The Genuine Article, UMI Article Clearinghouse, Documents on Demand.
**Desc:** Publication of articles designed to advance the traffic, transportation and physical distribution management profession.
**Ind/Abst** ABI/INFORM Glob. Ed.; ABI Inform Ondisc (Fall 1987-); Acad. Search (Jan. 1993-); Aviat. Tradescan [Select. Cov.]; Bus. ASAP (1992-) [Full Txt.]; Bus. Index (1985-); Bus. Period. Index; Bus. Source (Jan. 1993-); Coal Abstr.; Curr. Contents Soc. Behav. Sci.; Energy Res. Abstr. (Aug. 1975-); Environ. Abstr.; Environ. Period. Bibliogr.; Expand. Acad. Index (1992-); Gen. BusinessFile (1985-); Gen. Period. Index (1985-); Highw. Res. Abstr.; INFO-SOUTH Abstr.; J. Plan. Lit.; Mag. Search; Middle East Abstr. Index; Newsp. Period. Abstr. (1992-); PAIS Int. Print; Res. Alert [Full Cov.]; Soc. Sci. Cit. Index [Full Cov.]; Trade Ind. ASAP [Full Txt.]; Trade Ind. Index [Full Txt.]; Vocat. Search (Jan. 1993-); Wilson Bus. Abstr.

US/0049-450X
**TRANSPORTATION LAW JOURNAL, THE. See** Law.

US
**TRANSPORTATION LINES OF THE UNITED STATES.** 1983/84-. English. an. District Engineer, US Army Engineer District New Orleans, New Orleans LA 70160. ***Formed by the union of*** *Transportation Lines On the Great Lakes System, 0361-8978* ***and*** *Transportation Lines On the Atlantic, Gulf, and Pacific Coasts, 0361-9125 Transportation Lines On the Mississippi River System and the Gulf Intracoastal Waterway, 0361-8986.*

US/0162-699X
**TRANSPORTATION MONITORING REPORT. Main/Corp** Data Resources, Inc. Transportation Service. V. 1- May 1978-. English. mo. DRI McGraw Hill, 24 Hartwell Avenue, Lexington MA 02173. **Tel** (617)863-5100. **LC** HE203; .D37A. **DD** 380.5/2.

US/1047-062X
**TRANSPORTATION NEWS DIGEST, THE.** [Transp. news dig.]. (1986)-. Periodical. English. Twelve times a year. $45.00 one year; $80.00 two year. Transportation News Digest, PO Box 10751, White Bear Lake MN 55110. **Tel** (612)426-9530, FAX (612)426-9530. **ED** M. J. Anuta. **DD** 380. **Pr Rev. Circ:** 1,000 (ctrl).
**Desc:** Industrial truck, rail, air, and water transportation current news and anaylsis.

US/0308-1060
**TRANSPORTATION PLANNING AND TECHNOLOGY.** [Transp. plann. technol.]. Vol. 1, No. 1 (April 1972)-. Academic Scholarly Publication. English. qt. £183.00. Gordon & Breach Science Publishers, Inc., PO Box 786, Cooper Station, New York NY 10276. **Tel** (212)206-8900, FAX (212)645-2459. **(Subscription address:** International Publishers Distributor at one of the following addresses: 820 Town Center Drive, Langhorne, PA 19047; or PO Box 90, Reading Berkshire RG1 8JL UK; or Kent Ridge PO Box 1180, Singapore 9111, Republic of Singapore**) ED** N J Ashford. **CODEN** TPLTAK. **[CCC]. Bk Rev. Ad Acc.** Documents available from Article Express International, Ask*IEEE.
**Ind/Abst** Bioeng. Abstr.; Ei Page One; EMBASE; Eng. Index Annu.; Highw. Res. Abstr.; INSPEC (April 1972-); Int. Abstr. Oper. Res. (1987-1989) [Select. Cov.]; Int. Dev. Abstr. (1987-1989); J. Plan. Lit.; Math. Rev.

UK/0966-7146
**TRANSPORTATION PLANNING SYSTEMS.** (19??)-. English. Four times a year. £60.00. Landor Holdings Ltd, Quadrant House, 250 Kennington Lane, London SE11 5RD England. **Tel** 011 44 71 735 5058, FAX 011 44 71 587 0497.
**Desc:** Provides a forum for the in-depth discussion of important issues facing those in public authorities, consultancies, and academic research institutions as they address urban, regional and national transportation planning questions, and gives an opportunity for the pooling of information which will enhance professional understanding and expertise.

US/8756-9302
**TRANSPORTATION PRACTITIONERS JOURNAL.** [Transp. pract. j.]. Vol. 52, No. 1 (Fall 1984)-. Periodical. English. qt. $55.00 US; $60.00 Canada; $65.00 other. Association of Transportation Practitioners, 19564 Club House Road, Gaithersburg MD

20879-3002. **Tel** (301)670-6733, FAX (301)670-6735. **LC** K24; .R295. **Ad Acc. Continues** *ICC Practitioners' Journal, 0018-8859.*
**Desc:** Covers all modes of transportation, including labor, antitrust, safety, and environmental issues. Reports on recent developments at state and federal regulatory agencies and the courts.
**Ind/Abst** Account. Art.; Curr. Law Index (1980-); Fed. Tax Artic.; Index Leg. Period.; J. Plan. Lit.; Leg. Resour. Index (1980-); LegalTrac (1984-).

US/0278-9434
**TRANSPORTATION QUARTERLY.** [Transp. q.]. **Added/Corp** Eno Foundation for Transportation. Vol. 36, No. 1 (Jan. 1982)-. Periodical. English. qt (Jan., Apr., July, Oct.). $40.00 (one year), $60.00 (two year) US; $50.00 (one year), $80.00 (two year) other. ENO Transportation Foundation, 44211 Slatestone Court, Lansdowne VA 22075. **Tel** (703)729-7200, FAX (703)729-7219. **ED** Charles Snyder. **LC** HE331; .T74. **DD** 380.5/05. **CODEN** TRQUDV. **Ad Acc. Pr Rev. Circ:** 2,000. available on microfilm and microfiche from University Microfilms International (UMI). Documents available from Article Express International, The Genuine Article, UMI Article Clearinghouse, Documents on Demand. **Continues** *Traffic Quarterly, 0041-0713.*
**Desc:** Broad range of transportation topics from authors in academic, government and industrial fields.
**Ind/Abst** Acad. Abstr. Full Text Elite (July 1990); Acad. Abstr. (July 1990-); Acad. Search (July 1990-); Appl. Sci. Technol. Index; Avery Index Archit. Period. Suppl. Colum. Univ. (1989-); Aviat. Tradescan [Select. Cov.]; Bioeng. Abstr.; Bus. Source (Jul. 1990-); Curr. Contents Soc. Behav. Sci.; Ei Page One; Energy Res. Abstr. (Feb. 1982-); Eng. Index Annu. [Select. Cov.]; Environ. Abstr.; Expand. Acad. Index (1992-); Geogr. Abstr. Human Geogr.; Highw. Res. Abstr.; INFO-SOUTH Abstr.; Int. Abstr. Oper. Res. [Select. Cov.]; Int. Dev. Abstr.; J. Plan. Lit.; Mag. Search; Middle East Abstr. Index; Newsp. Period. Abstr. (1990-); PAIS Int. Print; Pollut. Abstr. Indexes; Res. Alert [Full Cov.]; Sage Urban Stud. Abstr; Soc. Sci. Cit. Index [Full Cov.]; Urban Aff. Abstr.; Vocat. Search (July 1990-).

●US/0965-8564
**TRANSPORTATION RESEARCH. PART A, POLICY AND PRACTICE. VFOAT** Policy and Practice; Transportation Research-A. Vol. 26A, No. 1 (Jan. 1992)-. Periodical. English. bm. $425.00 (regular subscription), $787.00 (combination subscription with Part B), $1058.00 (combination subscription with Parts B & C) The Americas; £285.00 (regular subscription), £528.00 (combination subscription with Part B), £710.00 (combination subscription with Parts B & C) other. Pergamon Press, An Imprint of Elsevier Science Ltd., The Boulevard, Langford Lane, Kidlington, Oxford OX5 1GB United Kingdom. **Tel** 011 44 865 843000, 011 44 865 843699, FAX 011 44 865 843010. **(Subscription address:** Elsevier Science Ltd. Oxford Fulfillment Centre, PO Box 800, Kidlington, Oxford OX5 1DX United Kingdom.**) LC** HE192.5; .T682. **DD** 380.5/05. **CODEN** TRPPEC. **Continues** *Transportation Research. Part A: General, 0191-2607.*
**Ind/Abst** Bus. Source (Jan. 1993-); Mag. Search; Sage Urban Stud. Abstr; SCISEARCH; Soc. Sci. Cit. Index [Full Cov.].

UK/0191-2615
**TRANSPORTATION RESEARCH. PART B, METHODOLOGICAL.** [Transp. res., Part B: methodol.]. **VFOAT** Transportation Research-B. Vol. 13B (Mar. 1979)-. Academic Scholarly Publication. English. bm. $425.00 (regular subscription), $787.00 (combination subscription with Part A), $1058.00 (combination subscription with Parts A & C) The Americas; £285.00 (regular subscription), £528.00 (combination subscription with Part A), £710.00 (combination subscription with Parts A & C) other. Pergamon Press, An Imprint of Elsevier Science Ltd., The Boulevard, Langford Lane, Kidlington, Oxford OX5 1GB United Kingdom. **Tel** 011 44 865 843000, 011 44 865 843699, FAX 011 44 865 843010. **(Subscription address:** Elsevier Science Ltd. Oxford Fulfillment Centre, PO Box 800, Kidlington, Oxford OX5 1DX United Kingdom.**) ED** Frank Haight. **LC** HE192.5; .T68. **DD** 380.5/07/2. **CODEN** TRBMDY. **[CCC]. Pr Rev.** available on microfilm and microfiche from University Microfilms International (UMI). Documents available from Article Express International, The Genuine Article, Ask*IEEE. **Continues in part** *Transportation Research, 0041-1647.*
**Ind/Abst** Appl. Sci. Technol. Index; Bioeng. Abstr.; Coal Abstr.; Curr. Contents Eng. Tech. Appl. Sci.; Curr. Contents Soc. Behav. Sci.; Ei Page One; EMBASE; Energy Res. Abstr. (July 1979-); Eng. Index Annu.; Environ. Period. Bibliogr.; Geogr. Abstr. Human Geogr.; Highw. Res. Abstr.; INSPEC (Sept. 1979-); Int. Abstr. Oper. Res. [Full Cov.]; Int. Aerosp. Abstr.; Int. Dev. Abstr.; J. Plan. Lit.; Math. Rev.; Res. Alert [Full Cov.]; Sage Urban Stud. Abstr; Sci. Cit. Index; SCISEARCH; Soc. Sci. Cit. Index [Full Cov.].

●US/0968-090X
**TRANSPORTATION RESEARCH. PART C, EMERGING TECHNOLOGIES. VFOAT** Emerging Technologies. Vol. 1C, No. 1 (Mar. 1993)-. Periodical. English. Six times a year. $425.00 (regular subscription), $1058.00 (combination subscription with Parts A & B) The Americas; £285.00 (regular subscription), £710.00 (combination subscription with Parts A & B) other. Pergamon Press, An Imprint of Elsevier Science Ltd., The Boulevard, Langford Lane, Kidlington, Oxford OX5 1GB United Kingdom. **Tel** 011 44 865 843000, 011 44 865 843699, FAX 011 44 865 843010. **(Subscription address:** Elsevier Science Ltd. Oxford Fulfillment Centre, PO Box 800, Kidlington, Oxford OX5 1DX United Kingdom.**) LC** HE1; .T867. **DD** 388/.05. **[CCC].**

US/0361-1981
**TRANSPORTATION RESEARCH RECORD.** [Transp. res. rec.]. **Added/Corp** National Research Council (U.S.). Transportation Research Board. No. 480 (1974)-. Monographic series. English. ir. $1,172.00 North America; $1,240.00 other. Transportation Research Board, Box 289, Washington DC 20055. **Tel** (202)334-3218, FAX (202)334-2519. **LC** TE7; .H5. **DD** 380.5/08. **CODEN** TRREDM. **Circ:** 3,000. Documents available from Article Express International, CASDDS. **Continues** *Highway Research Record, 0073-2206.*
**Desc:** Contains several technical papers on a given subject. The papers are usually prepared for an annual meeting and accepted for publication through a technical review process.
**Ind/Abst** Bioeng. Abstr.; Chem. Abstr.; Coal Abstr.; Ei Page One; Eng. Index Annu. [Select. Cov.]; Fish Rev. (Jan. 1989-July 1992); GeoRef; Geotech. Abstr.; Int. Civil Eng. Abstr.; Soft. Abstr. Eng.; Wildl. Rev. (Jan. 1989-July 1992).

US/0197-419X
**TRANSPORTATION REVIEW.** [Transp. rev.]. **VFOAT** Data Resources Transportation Review. Periodical. English. DRI McGraw Hill, 24 Hartwell Avenue, Lexington MA 02173. **Tel** (617)863-5100. **LC** HE1; .T87. **DD** 380.5/05.

US/0041-1655
**TRANSPORTATION SCIENCE.** [Transp. sci.]. **Added/Corp** Operations Research Society of America. Transportation Science Section. Vol. 1 (Feb. 1967)-. Periodical. English. qt. $93.00 (institutions), $37.00 (individuals). Operations Research Society of America, 1314 Guilford Avenue, Baltimore MD 21202. **Tel** (410)850-0300, (800)850-0300. **ED** Mark S. Daskin. **LC** TA1001; .T73. **DD** 380.5/05. **CODEN** TRSCBJ. **[CCC].** Index available. **Bk Rev. Ad Acc. Pr Rev. Circ:** 1,500. available on microfilm and microfiche from University Microfilms International (UMI). Documents available from Article Express International, The Genuine Article, Ask*IEEE.
**Desc:** Covers methodology and practice, and occasional research papers. Contains research on all modes of transportation, and includes a bibliographical section.
**Ind/Abst** Appl. Sci. Technol. Index; Bioeng. Abstr.; Curr. Contents Soc. Behav. Sci.; Ei Page One; Eng. Index Annu.; Highw. Res. Abstr.; INSPEC (Nov. 1971-); Int. Abstr. Oper. Res. [Full Cov.]; Int. Aerosp. Abstr.; Int. Civil Eng. Abstr.; J. Plan. Lit.; Math. Rev.; Oper. Res./Manag. Sci.; Pollut. Abstr. Indexes; Res. Alert [Full Cov.]; Soc. Sci. Cit. Index [Full Cov.]; Soft. Abstr. Eng.; Zentralbl. Math. Ihre Grenzgeb.

US/0741-2266
**TRANSPORTATION SYSTEM MANAGEMENT REPORT FOR NORTHEASTERN ILLINOIS, THE.** **Main/Corp** Chicago Area Transportation Study. (1982)-. English. an. Chicago Area Transportation Study, 300 West Adams Street, Chicago IL 60606. **LC** HE310.C45; C57c. **DD** 388/.068. **Continues** *Chicago Area Transportation Study. Transportation System Management Plan for Northeastern Illinois, 0743-6092.*

US
**TRANSPORTATION TELEPHONE TICKLER. Added/Corp** Journal of Commerce. (19??)-. English. an. $79.95. Journal of Commerce Inc, 445 Marshall Street, Phillipsburg NJ 08865. **Tel** (800)222-0356, (908)859-1300. **(Subscription address:** Journal of Commerce, PO Box 5570, New York NY 10087.**) LC** HE9.U5; N7. **DD** 385.1. **Ad Acc.** ctrl circ. **Continues** *The Journal of Commerce Transportation Telephone Tickler, 0447-9181.*
**Desc:** A 4-volume set of over 25,000 North American suppliers of 130 different freight services. Includes name, address, telephone, fax, line-of-business and contact names.

CU
**TRANSPORTE Y VIAS DE COMUNICACION. Added/Corp** Instituto Superior Politecnico "Jose Antonio Echeverria". (19??)-. Periodical. Spanish (summaries and/or abstracts in English). Ediciones Cubanas, Obispo 527, Altos ESQ Bernaza, CP 10100 Havana Cuba. **Tel** 011 632980, 631942, FAX 011 631011, telex 512337, 6540. **Continues** *Ciencias Tecnicas. Transporte y Vias de Comunicacion, 0254-8526.*

SP
**TRANSPORTES, EL TURISMO Y LAS COMUNICACIONES EN ... Y PRIMER SEMESTRE DE, LOS. VFOAT** Transportes, el Turismo y las Comunicaciones en ... y Avance de ... . 1981 ... 1982-. Spanish. an. Ministerio de Sanidad y Consumo, Paseo del Prado 18 20, 28071 Madrid Spain. **Tel** 011 34 1 420-2227, 420-2051. **LC** HE261.A15; T73.

US/0883-0932
**TRANSPORTING PERSONAL FIREARMS.** [Transp. pers. firearms]. English. Sparrow Publishing House, PO Box 121, Boulder City NV 89005. **LC** KF3941.Z95; T7. **DD** 344.73/0533.

GW/0174-559X
**TRANSPORTRECHT. See** Law.

FR/0564-1373
**TRANSPORTS.** Vol. 1 (Jan. 1956)-. Periodical. French. Six times a year. 752.00F France; 861.00F others. Les Editions Techniques et Economiques, 3 rue Soufflot, 75005 Paris France. **Tel** 33 1 46341030, FAX 33 1 46345583, telex 260 717 F. **ED** E Epstein. **LC** HE3; .T73. **[CCC].** cum. index. **Bk Rev**, (Qty: 6). **Ad Acc, Adv Mgr:** Epstein.
**Ind/Abst** Highw. Res. Abstr.

FR
**TRANSPORTS ACTUALITES.** French. ir. 330.00F France; 457.00F other. CEP Information Professions, 1 Cite Bergere, 75311 Paris Cedex 09 France. **Tel** 011 33 1 44695550.

FR
**TRANSPORTS ROUTIERS DE MARCHANDISES. Main/Corp** France. Departement des Statistiques des Transports. **VFOAT** Enquete Annuelle d'Entreprise. (19??)-. French. Ministere de l'Equipement, 21 rue Mathuring-Regnier, 75732 Paris Cedex 15 France. **LC** HE5668; .A27a. **DD** 388.3/24/0944.

FR/0397-6521
**TRANSPORTS URBAINS.** (1974)-. Periodical. French. Four times a year. 280.00F France; 300.00F other. Groupement l'Etudes Transports, 173 Rue Armand Silvestre, F 92400 Courbevoie France. **ED** Mr. Alain Sutter. **UDC** 656. cum. index. **Bk Rev**, (Qty: 4). **Ad Acc. Pr Rev. Circ:** 2,000 (ctrl).

IT/0041-1809
**TRASPORTI INDUSTRIALI.** [Trasp. ind.]. (1967)-. Periodical. Italian. mo. L100000.00 Italy; L155000.00 other. Etas SRL, Via Mecenate 89, 20138 Milan Italy. **Tel** 011 39 2 580841. **UDC** 380. **CODEN** TRIND4. **Continues** *Trasporti Industriali Nella Tecnica Della Produzione, 0496-1196.*

IT
**TRASPORTI NEWS.** Ediz Trasporti Internazionali, Piazza Duca d'Aosta 6, 20124 Milan Italy.

US/0145-3785
**TRAVEL TRAILERS, 5TH WHEEL TRAILERS, CAMPING TRAILERS RV GUIDE, NEW & USED VALUES. Main/Corp** Kelley Blue Book Co. **VAT** Travel Trailers, Fifth Wheel Trailers, Camping Trailers Recreational Vehicle Guide, New and Used Values. (19??)-. English. $20.00. Kelley Blue Book, PO Box 19691, Irvine CA 92713. **Tel** (714)770-7704. **LC** TL297; .K43a. **DD** 629.2/26/029473.

US/0890-5029
**TROLLEY COACH NEWS.** Began Jan. 1969. Periodical. English. ir (at least four issues a year). $12.00 US; $15.00 Canada. Trolley Coach News, 1042 Bardstown Road, Louisville KY 40204-1318. **LC** TL232; .T72. **DD** 388.4/13223/05.

US/8756-5129
**TRUCK & TRAILER BUYER'S GUIDE.** ***Suspended.*** [Truck trailer buy. guide]. **VFOAT** Truck and Trailer Buyer's Guide. Suspended (May, 1990). Periodical. English. mo. $15.00. PO Box 153873, Irving TX 75015. **LC** TL230.A1; T6885. **DD** 629.2/24/029473.

NE
**TRUCK & TRANSPORT.** ***Title Change.*** (19??)-(199?). Misset Uitgeverij BV, Postbus 9000, 6800 DA Arnhem Netherlands. **Tel** 011 31 85 209911. ***Continued by*** *Truck & Transport Management.*

AT
**TRUCK AUSTRALIA.** (19??)-. English. Eleven times a year. 56.00Aus$ Australia; 77.00Aus$ New Zealand, Papua New Guinea; 81.00Aus$ Malaysia, Indonesia, Fiji; 82.00Aus$ Japan, India, Hong Kong; 91.00Aus$ US, Canada, Lebanon; 100.00Aus$ Europe, Africa, former USSR. Thomson Publications / Australia, 47 Chippen Street, Chippendale New South Wales, 2008 Australia. **Tel** 011 61 2 6992411, FAX 011 61 2 698 3920, telex 122226. **(Subscription address:** Thomson Publications Australia, PO Box 815, Strawberry Hills, New South Wales, 2012 Australia.**)**

US/8756-4041
**TRUCK BLUE BOOK LEASE GUIDE, RESIDUAL PROJECTIONS, THE. Added/Corp** National Market Reports, Inc. **VFOAT** Truck Blue Book Lease Guide. Vol. 1, No. 1 (Jan. 1-Mar. 31, 1985)-. Periodical. English. qt. $65.00. MacLean Hunter Publishing Corporation / Chicago, IL, 29 North Wacker Drive, Chicago IL 60606-3298. **Tel** (312)726-2802, FAX

(312)726-3091. **(Subscription address:** Maclean Hunter Market Reports, 29 North Wacker Drive, Chicago IL 60606.**)** **DD** 629.

US/0362-5737
**TRUCK BROKER DIRECTORY.** Directory. English. ir. J. J. Keller & Associates, PO Box 548, Neenah WI 54957-0368. **Tel** (800)558-5011, (414)722-2848. **LC** HE5623.A1; T75. **DD** 388.3/24/02573.

US/0749-4548
**TRUCK CAMPER TRADE-IN GUIDE.** ***Ceased.*** (19??)-(19??). English. an. Intertec Publishing Corporation, 9800 Metcalf, Overland Park KS 66212. **Tel** (913)341-1300. **LC** HD9710.U52; O35. **DD** 629.2/26. ***Continues*** *Official Truck Camper Trade-in Guide, 0094-1131.*

CN/0315-5501
**TRUCK CANADA.** V. 21, No. 5- May 1973-. Periodical. English. mo. $27.09. Sentinel Business Publications, 7575 Trans Canada Highway, Suite 500, St. Laurent Quebec H4T 1V6 Canada. **Tel** (514)333-1116, FAX (514)631-8858. **ED** Carole Clifford. **Bk Rev. Ad Acc. Circ:** 21,500 (ctrl). ***Continues*** *Truck Transportation Canada, 0315-551X.*
**Desc:** Technical data maintenance, fleet operations, and product information on heavy-duty trucks.

NE
**TRUCK EN TRANSPORT MANAGEMENT.** (19??)-. Dutch. ir. Fl143.20 (latest issue). Misset Uitgeverij BV, Postbus 9000, 6800 DA Arnhem Netherlands. **Tel** 011 31 85 209911.

US/0162-3435
**TRUCK LUBRICATION GUIDE.** (19??)-. English. an. $35.80. H.M Gousha & Company, PO Box 49006, 2001 The Alameda, San Jose CA 95161. **Tel** (800)662-6277. **Circ:** 2,600.
**Desc:** Covers periodic maintenance and lubrication of all sizes of on-highway trucks, in tabular data form.

CN/0712-2683
**TRUCK NEWS (TORONTO).** (TRUCK NEWS.). [Truck news]. Vol. 1, Issue 1 (May 1981)-. Periodical. English. Twelve times a year. 24.00Can$ (one year), 36.00Can$ (two year) Canada; 48.00Can$ other. Southam Information and Technology Group Inc., 1450 Don Mills Road, Don Mills Ontario M3B 2X7 Canada. **Tel** (416)445-6641, (800)668-2374, FAX (416)442-2261. **DD** 388.3/24/0971.

NZ
**TRUCK OPERATING COSTS. Main/Corp** New Zealand. Ministry of Transport. Economics Division. 1975-. English. an. 5.00NZ$. Ministry of Transport / New Zealand, Private Bag, Wellington 1 New Zealand. **Tel** 721-253 Ext. 747. **LC** HE5717.5; .A23A. **DD** 388.3/24. **Circ:** 1,000. ***Supersedes*** *Car and Truck Operating Costs.*
**Desc:** A breakdown of the private economic costs of operating different sized trucks in New Zealand. Two broad components: running and standing costs.

US/1047-7535
**TRUCK SAFETY NEWS.** [Truck saf. news]. (1986)-. Periodical. English. Twelve times a year. $150.00. Truck Safety News, PO Box 65081, Washington DC 20035. **Tel** (301)229-3267. **ED** B. C. Walton. **DD** 363.
**Desc:** Government responses of truck safety standards and agreements among the international countries that comes in the US for the highway and truck safety.

US/1053-5942
**TRUCK SALES & LEASING.** [Truck sales leas.]. **VFOAT** Truck Sales and Leasing. Vol. 8, No. 5 (Sept./Oct. 1990)-. Periodical. English. bm. $30.00. Heavy Truck Salesman, 1800 East Deere Avenue, Santa Ana CA 92705. **Tel** (714)261-1636, FAX (714)261-2904. **LC** HD9710.35.U6; H4. **DD** 629.224/068/8. ***Continues*** *Heavy Truck Salesman, 0740-3941.*

US/0517-5666
**TRUCK TAXES BY STATES.** English. an. American Trucking Association, 2200 Mill Road, Alexandria VA 22314. **Tel** (703)838-1772. **LC** HE5623; .A22. **DD** 336.2/78388324/0973.

US/0145-5001
**TRUCK TRAILERS.** ***Title Change.* See** Manufacturing.

US/0364-703X
**TRUCK WEIGHT STUDY (JACKSON).** (TRUCK WEIGHT STUDY.). **Main/Corp** Mississippi. Transportation Planning Division. English. an. Mississippi State Highway Department, PO Box 1850, Jackson MS 39215-1850. **LC** TL230.A1; M58A. **DD** 629.22/4.

US/0360-7399
**TRUCK WEIGHT SURVEY. Main/Corp** Tennessee. Dept. of Transportation. Bureau of Planning and Programming. English. an. Bureau of Planning, Department of Transportation, Nashville TN. **LC** TL230.A1; T44A. **DD** 388.3/24.

US/0743-5525
**TRUCKER'S ALMANAC.** 1984-. English. an. $7.95. J. J. Keller & Associates, PO Box 548, Neenah WI 54957-0368. **Tel** (800)558-5011, (414)722-2848. **LC** HE5623; .A225. **DD** 388.3/24/0973.

US/0897-9219
**TRUCKERS/USA (TUSCALOOSA, ALA.).** (TRUCKERS/USA.). **VFOAT** Truckers USA. (198?)-. Periodical. English. Twelve times a year (Tues.). $19.95. Truckers USA, PO Box 3168, Tuscaloosa AL 35403. **Tel** (205)394-2993, FAX (205)758-2236. **ED** Bobby Scale. **Ad Acc.**

US/0277-5743
**TRUCKIN.** (19??)-. Periodical. English. Twelve times a year. $23.95 (one year), $37.95 (two years). McMullen Publishing Inc, 2145 West La Palma Avenue, PO Box 70015, Anaheim CA 92801-1785. **Tel** (714)572-2255, FAX (714)572-1864. **ED** Steve Stillwell.

AT/0155-9648
**TRUCKIN' LIFE.** (1976)-. Periodical. English. mo. 53.00Aus$ Australia; 88.00Aus$ New Zealand & Papua New Guinea; 112.00Aus$ US & Canada; 119.00Aus$ Europe & Africa; 94.00Aus$ Singapore, Malaysia, Indonesia; 103.00Aus$ other. Federal Publishing Co Pty Ltd, PO Box 199, 180 Bourke Road, Alexandria New South Wales, 2015 Australia. **Tel** 011 61 2 693 6666, FAX 011 61 2 693 9935. **(Subscription address:** Federal Publishing Co. Pty Ltd., PO Box 199, Alexandria NSW 2015 Australia.**)**

CN/0829-8947
**TRUCKING IN CANADA.** (TRUCKING IN CANADA / STATISTICS CANADA, TRANSPORTATION DIVISION, SURFACE AND MARINE TRANSPORT SECTION.). [Truck. can.]. **Added/Corp** Statistics Canada. Surface and Marine Transport Section. **VFOAT** Camionnage au Canada. (1984)-. English (French). an. 50.00Can$ Canada; $60.00 US; $70.00 other. Statistics Canada, Publications Sales & Services, Main Building Room 1710, Ottawa Ontario K1A 0T6 Canada. **Tel** (613)951-5078, (800)267-6677, FAX (613)951-1584, telex 053-3585. **ED** Kathryn Davidson (editor's telephone number: (613)951-8779, FAX: (613)951-0579). **LC** HE5635; .A44. **DD** 388.3/24/0971. Index available. **Circ:** 900. ***Continues*** *Motor Carriers, Freight and Household Goods Movers, 0705-5978.*
**Desc:** Comprehensive overview of the Canadian trucking industry, both for hire and private or on account. Data includes revenues and expenses, equipment operated, investment, employment, and commodities transported from point of origin to point of destination.

US/0884-8947
**TRUCKS. *Ceased.* VFOAT** Trucks Magazine. Vol. 1, No. 1 (Jan. 1986)-(19??). Periodical. English. bm. Trucks Magazine Inc, 20 Waterside Plaza, New York NY 10010. **Tel** (212)532-1392. **ED** John Stevens, Chris Krieg.

US/0146-9622
**TRUCKS 26,000 PLUS. VAT** Trucks Twenty-Six Thousand Plus. V. 5- Feb. 1977-. Periodical. English. bm. $15.00. McGraw Hill Publishing Company, Inc., 1221 Avenue of the Americas, New York NY 10020. **Tel** (212)512-6410, (800)525-5003, FAX (212)512-6111. **LC** HE5623.A1; T85. **DD** 388.3/24/0973. available on microfilm from University Microfilms International (UMI). ***Continues*** *26 Plus, 0091-410X.*

US/0894-962X
**TRUCKSTOP WORLD.** (TRUCKSTOP WORLD : TW.). [Truck. world]. **VFOAT** TW; Truck Stop World. Issue 1 (Sept. 1987)-. Periodical. English. Six times a year. $18.00. Newport Publications, PO Box 1058, Newport Beach CA 92658. **Tel** (714)261-1636 or, (714)261-2580. **ED** Jack Thiessen. **DD** 338. **Ad Acc. Circ:** 18,000 (ctrl).
**Desc:** Addresses the concerns of owners, general managers and department managers of truckstop areas.

US/0888-2266
**TRUSST TIMES. Added/Corp** Trucking Support Services Team (San Mateo, Calif.). **VAT** Trucking Support Services Team Times. (19??)-. Periodical. English. bw. $86.00. Trusst Times, PO Box 1608, Placerville CA 95667. **Tel** (916)644-5485.

CN/0820-5655
**TRUXBOOK. See** Business-Commerce.

SZ
**TT REVUE / HERAUSGEBER, VERBAND OFFENTLICHER VERKEHR VOV ... ET AL. Added/Corp** Verband Offentlicher Verkehr (Switzerland). **VAT** Transport Tourismus Revue. (19??)-. Periodical. French (German). mo. 55.00F. Buechler Grafino Ltd, Seftigenstrasse 310, CH 3084 Wabern Switzerland. **Tel** 011 41 31 9608111, FAX 011 41 31 962282. **LC** HE5; .O33. ***Continues*** *VST Revue.*

US/1056-0440
**TTS BLUE BOOK OF TRUCKING COMPANIES.** [TTS blue book truck. co.]. **Added/Corp** Transportation Technical Services, Inc. **VFOAT** Blue Book of Trucking Companies. **VAT** Transportation Technical Services Blue Book of Trucking Companies. (1990/1991)-. Directory. English. $195.00. Transportation Technical Services, 225 West 34th Street, New York NY 10122. **Tel** (800)666-4887, FAX (703)899-1948. **LC** HE5623; .A227. **DD** 388.3/24/0973021. **Ad Acc, Adv Mgr:** Thomas R. Fugee. **Acid Free.** available on magnetic tape; available on diskette.
**Desc:** Balance sheets, income statements, operating expenses and key ratios of the top 2,000 for-hire motor carriers.

US/1061-477X
**TTS NATIONAL MOTOR CARRIER DIRECTORY.** [TTS natl. mot. carr. dir.]. **Added/Corp** Transportation Technical Services, Inc. **VFOAT** National Motor Carrier Directory. **VAT** Transportation Technical Services National Motor Carrier Directory. (1991)-. Directory. English. an. $395.00. Transportation Technical Services, 225 West 34th Street, New York NY 10122. **Tel** (800)666-4887, FAX (703)899-1948. **LC** HE5623.A45; T78. **DD** 388.3/24/02573. **Ad Acc, Adv Mgr:** Thomas R. Fugee. **Acid Free.** available on magnetic tape; available on diskette. ***Continues*** *National Motor Carrier Directory.*
**Desc:** Key information on 28,000 US and Canadian for-hire motor carriers.

IT/1121-5593
**TUTTO TRASPORTI PASSEGGERI.** [Tutto trasp. passegg.]. (1991)-. Periodical. Italian. Six times a year. L25000.00 Italy; L56000.00 other. Editoriale Domus, Via Achille Grandi 5-7, 20089 Rozzano Milan Italy. **Tel** 011 39 2 82472276, FAX 011 39 2 8255033. **UDC** 629.1-46.

US/0145-1308
**U.S. GREAT LAKES PORTS.** [U. S. Great Lakes ports]. **VAT** United States Great Lakes Ports. Periodical. English. qt. US Department of Transportation / St. Lawrence Seaway Development Corporation, Washington DC 20591.

BE/0041-5146
**UITP BIBLIO-INDEX. TRANSPORT-VERKEHR. *Title Change.*** **Added/Corp** Union Internationale des Transports Publics. **VFOAT** Transport-Verkehr. **VAT** Union Internationale des Transports Publics Biblio-Index. (1963)-(19??). Periodical. French (English and German). qt. International Union of Public Transport, Avenue de l'Uruguay 19, B 1050 Brussels Belgium. **Tel** 011 32 2 6733325, FAX 011 32 2 6607072, telex (046)63916 UITP B. **Bk Rev. Circ:** 2,700. ***Continued by*** *Biblio Express.*
**Desc:** Bibliographical journal dealing with all urban and regional public transport problems.

UN
**UKRAINSKA RSR. VFOAT** Ukrainskaia SSR; Ukrainian SSR. English (Russian and Ukrainian). Tekhnika, Pushkinskaia 28, Kiev Ukraine. **Tel** 282243. **ED** Mariya Georgievna Pisarenko. **LC** HA1448.U6; A36. **DD** 314.7/71. **Ad Acc. Circ:** 3,000,000.
**Desc:** Literature for workers in industry, transportation and service (reference books, textbooks, and applied monographs).

US/0739-7100
**UMTRI RESEARCH REVIEW, THE.** [UMTRI res. rev.]. **Added/Corp** University of Michigan. Transportation Research Institute. **VFOAT** U.M.T.R.I. Research Review. **VAT** University of Michigan Transportation Research Institute Research Review. Vol. 13, No. 1 & 2 (July-Aug./Sept.-Oct. 1982)-. Periodical. English. bm. $35.00. Transportation Research Institute, The University of Michigan, 2901 Baxter Road, Ann Arbor MI 48109. **Tel** (313)936-1073, FAX (313)936-1081. **ED** Robert Sweet. **NLM** W1; UM159H. **Circ:** 1400 (ctrl). available on microfilm from University Microfilms International (UMI). ***Continues*** *University of Michigan. Highway Safety Research Institute. HSRI Research Review, 0146-8545.*
**Desc:** Articles on research findings in automotive safety-data analyses, restraint systems, vehicle dynamics, biomechanics, human factors, and public policy studies.
**Ind/Abst** Energy Res. Abstr. (July 1982-); PAIS Int. Print; Psychol. Abstr. (1982-); PsycINFO; PsycLit; PsycScan: Appl. Psych.; Public Aff. Inf. Serv. Bull.

GW/0722-8333
**UNFALLVERHUTUNGSBERICHT STRASSENVERKEHR : BERICHT DES BUNDESMINISTERS FUER VERKEHR UBER MASSNAHMEN AUF DEM GEBIET DER UNFALLVERHUTUNG IM STRASSENVERKEHR. VFOAT** Bericht des Bundesministers fuer Verkehr Uber Massnahmen auf dem Gebiet der Unfallverhutung im Strassenverkehr. German. Bundesminister fuer Verkehr, Abteilung Binnenschiffahrt und Wasserstrassen, Postfach 20 01 00, Robert-Schuman-Platz 1, W-5300 Bonn 2 Germany. **LC** HE5614.5.G3; U53.

US/0361-9079
**UNIFIED WORK PROGRAM. Main/Corp** Illinois. Dept. of Transportation. Office of Planning, Programming, and Environmental Science. (19??)-.

English. an. Illinois Department of Transportation, Auditorium, 2300 South Dirksen Parkway, Springfield IL 62764. **LC** HE28.I3; D46a. **DD** 309.2/5/09773.

CN/0841-2472
**UPDATE - ONTARIO TRUCKING ASSOCIATION.** (UPDATE.). [Update - Ont. Truck. Assoc.]. Vol. 7, No. 7-9 (Feb. 11/March 3, 1989)-. Periodical. English. wk. Free. Ontario Trucking Association, 555 Dixon Road, Rexdale Ontario M9W 1H8 Canada. **Tel** (416)249-7401, FAX (416)245-6152. **ED** Terri Albrecht. **DD** 388.3/24/09713. **Ad Acc. Circ:** 1,500 (ctrl). ***Continues*** *Ontario Trucking Update, 0713-8482.*
**Desc:** Industry newsletter.

CN/0821-2996
**URBAN TRANSIT FACTS IN CANADA.** ***Title Change.*** [Urban transit facts Can.]. **Added/Corp** Canadian Urban Transit Association. (1983)-(19??). Periodical. English. an. Canadian Urban Transit Association, 55 York Street, Suite 901, Toronto Ontario M5J 1R7 Canada. **Tel** (416)365-9800, FAX (416)365-1295. **LC** HE4501; .U73. **DD** 388.4/0971. ***Continues in part*** *Transit Fact Book and Membership Directory, 0706-7658.* ***Continued by*** *Summary of Canadian Transit Statistics, 1199-1755.*

UK/0953-7139
**URBAN TRANSPORT INTERNATIONAL.** [Urban transp. int.]. (1988)-. Periodical. English. Six times a year. £24.00 UK; £32.00 Europe; £42.00 others. Landor Holdings Ltd, Quadrant House, 250 Kennington Lane, London SE11 5RD England. **Tel** 011 44 71 735 5058, FAX 011 44 71 587 0497. **DD** 388.4.

US/0195-4695
**URBAN TRANSPORT NEWS.** (19??)-. Periodical. English. bw. $338.00. Business Publishers Inc., 951 Pershing Drive, Silver Spring MD 20910-4464. **Tel** (301)587-6300, (800)274-0122, FAX (301)585-9075. **ED** Robert M. Loebelson. **[CCC].** available on an online database (file 636/Full-Text) from DIALOG. ***Continues*** *Public Transit Report, 0148-4087.*
**Desc:** Coverage of developments in public transportation. This includes buses, subways, light rail, commuter rail and the manufacturers and the operators of mass transit equipment.
**Ind/Abst** PTS Newsl. Database [Full Txt.].

US/1040-4880
**URBAN TRANSPORTATION MONITOR, THE.** [Urban transp. monit.]. (198u)-. Periodical. English. bw. $195.00. Lawley Publications, PO Box 12300, Burke VA 22009. **Tel** (703)764-0512, FAX (703)764-0516. **ED** Daniel B. Rathbone. **DD** 388. **Bk Rev. Ad Acc, Adv Mgr:** C. Reeves. ctrl circ.
**Desc:** Publishes current news and information on all modes and aspects related to urban transportation. Includes analysis and insight into the latest trends and developments in transportation planning, traffic engineering and transit.

US/0278-7253
**URBAN TRANSPORTATION OFFICIALS.** Mar. 1981 -. English. an. Free to members. US Conference of Mayors, 1620 Eye Street NW, Washington DC 20006. **Tel** (202)293-7330, FAX (202)293-2352. **LC** HE308; .U697. **DD** 352.91/84/02573.

US/0742-4523
**U.S. MOPED, 3 & 4 WHEELER, MOTOR SCOOTERS, ETC. IMPORTS. VFOAT** US Moped, Three and Four Wheeler, Motor Scooters, etc., Imports. (19??)-. English. mo. price varies per volume. W. C. Single, 6040 Boulevard East, 18D, West New York NY 07093. **Tel** (201)868-2446.

FR
**UTILISATION DES VEHICULES DE TRANSPORT ROUTIER DE MARCHANDISES EN, L'. Added/Corp** Observatoire Economique et Statistique des Transports (France). (19??)-. French. 100F. Observatoire Economique et Statistique des Transports, 55 rue Brillat Savarin, 75013 Paris France. **LC** HE5668; .A298.

US/0747-5063
**VACUUM CIRCUITS.** (VACUUM CIRCUITS : DOMESTIC CARS, LIGHT TRUCKS & VANS, IMPORTED CARS & TRUCKS.). **Added/Corp** Mitchell Manuals, Inc. **VFOAT** Mitchell Vacuum Circuits. (1978)-. English. ir. $159.00. Mitchell International Inc, PO Box 26260, San Diego CA 92126-0260. **Tel** (619)578-6550, (800)648-8010, FAX (619)578-4752. **(Subscription address:** Mitchell International Inc., PO Box 71654, Chicago IL 60694.**) ED** Dan Kelley. **LC** TL275; .V27. **DD** 629.2/528. **Ad Acc.** ctrl circ.
**Desc:** Contains vacuum circuit diagrams; information on tune-ups, emission and air conditioning servicing easier. Covers domestic and imported cars and light trucks.

IT/0042-2096
**VADO E TORNO.** [Vado torno]. (1962)-. Periodical. Italian. mo (except Feb. and Aug.). L42000.00 (1 year), L82000.00 (2 year) Italy; L75000.00 other. Vado e Torno Edizioni SRL, V Lattanzio 77, 20137 Milan Italy. **Tel** 011 39 2 55193629, FAX 011 39 2 55193660. **UDC** 388. Index available. **Ad Acc. Circ:** 50,000.

HU/0133-0314
**VAROSI KOZLEKEDES.** [Var. kozlek.]. **Main/Corp** Budapesti Kozlekedesi Vallalat. **VFOAT** VK. Varosi Kozlekedes. (1968)-. Bulletin. Hungarian. Two issues per month. Kozlekedesi Vallalat, Postafiok 11, Budapest VII Akacfa u. 15, Levelcim, Budapest 8 Hungary. **Tel** 011 36 1 422-130/1932, telex 226325. **ED** Dr. Rudolf Nagy. **LC** HE311.H82; B82a. **UDC** 656 (1-22). Index available. **Bk Rev,** (Qty: approx. 10). **Pr Rev. Circ:** 1,200 (ctrl). ***Continues*** *Fovarosi Villamosvasut Muszaki Szemle, 0324-458X.*
**Desc:** Introduces the science of city transport, and the results and problems of engineering, construction and operation. Also profiles of the pedestrian and public transport and individual motor car traffic as well as other problems related to transportation.

II
**VARSHIKA KARYA-VIVARANA / UTTARA PRADESA RAJYA SARAKA PARIVAHANA NIGAMA. Main/Corp** Uttara Pradesa Rajya Saraka Parivahana Nigama. Hindi (Hindi). an. Free. **LC** HE365.I44; U888A.

US
**VEHICLE AND TRAFFIC LAW. See** Law.

US
**VEHICLE LEASING TODAY.** English. bm. $29.00. National Vehicle Leasing Association, 3710 South Robertson Boulevard, Suite 220, Culver City CA 90232. **Tel** (310)838-3170, FAX (310)838-3160. **ED** Rodney J. Couts. Index available. **Ad Acc, Adv Mgr:** Deborah Dember. **Circ:** 4,500 (ctrl).
**Desc:** Focuses on the latest trends in leasing, highlights upcoming events and activities, legal issues affecting vehicle lessors, etc.

US
**VEHICLE WEIGHT AND USE DATA COLLECTED ON MINNESOTA ROADS. Main/Corp** Minnesota. Dept. of Transportation. English. be. Minnesota Department of Transportation, John Ireland Boulevard/Room 810, St Paul MN 55155. **LC** TL230.A1; M54A. **DD** 388.34/4/09776.

GW
**VERKEHRSWIRTSCHAFT, DIE. See** Transportation-Abstracting, Bibliographies and Statistics.

GW
**VERKEHRSWIRTSCHAFTLICHE ZAHLEN.** German. an. Free. Breitenbachstr 1, 6 Frankfurt Main 93 Germany. **Tel** 069 7919 365, FAX 069 7919265, telex 04 11627. **ED** Georg Dierschke. **LC** HE249; .V394A. **Circ:** 4,500 (ctrl).
**Desc:** Statistics of goods transport in, from, and to West Germany.

SA
**VERSLAG VAN DIE RAAD VAN SUID-AFRIKAANSE VERVOERDIENSTE VIR DIE JAAR GEEINDIG ... . Main/Corp** South African Transport Services Board. **VFOAT** Report of the South African Transport Services Board for the Year Ended ... . 1981-. Afrikaans (English). an. **LC** HE284.4.A15; S68a. **DD** 354.680087/.5/006.

XR
**VESTNIK DOPRAVY. Main/Corp** Czechoslovakia. Federalni Ministerstvo Dopravy. Czech. Nakladatelstvi Dopravy a Spoju, Transport and Communications, Hybernska 5, 11578 Prague 1 Czech Republic. **Tel** (2) 2365774, FAX (2) 2356772. **LC** HE7; .C94A.

RU/0042-4749
**VESTNIK VSESOJUZNOGO NAUCNO-ISSLEDOVATELSKOGO INSTITUTA ZELEZNODOROZNOGO TRANSPORTA.** (VESTNIK VSESOIUZNOGO NAUCHNO-ISSLEDOVATELSKOGO INSTITUTA ZHELEZNODOROZHNOGO TRANSPORTA.). [Vestn. Vses. naucno-issled. inst. zeleznodorozn. transp.]. **Added/Corp** Vsesoiuznyi Nauchno-Issledovatelskii Institut Zheleznodorozhnogo Transporta (Soviet Union). **VFOAT** Vestnik Vniizht. (Aug. 1956)-. Academic Scholarly Publication. Russian. Eight times a year. $89.95. **(Subscription address:** East View Publications Inc., 3020 Harbor Lane North, Suite 110, Minneapolis MN 55447.**) CODEN** VVNZAA. Documents available from CASDDS. ***Continues*** *Tekhnika Zheleznykh Dorog.*
**Ind/Abst** Chem. Abstr. (1956-1983).

●US
**VIA INTERNATIONAL PORT OF NEW YORK-NEW JERSEY. Added/Corp** Port Authority of New York and New Jersey. Vol. 44, No. 3 (Mar. 1992)-. Periodical. English. mo. The Port Authority of New York and New Jersey, One World Trade Center, New York NY 10048. ***Continues*** *Via Port of New York-New Jersey.*
**Ind/Abst** PAIS Int. Print.

IT
**VIE E TRASPORTI.** (19??)-. Periodical. Italian. bm. L60000 Italy; L90000 other. Casa Editrice la Fiaccola, Via C Ravizza 62, 20149 Milan Italy. **Tel** 011 39 2 481-4355, 481-4939, FAX 011 39 2 481-4834, telex 335512 COSTRU I. **ED** Sig. Giuseppe Saronni. **LC** TE4; .A68. Index available. cum. index. **Ad Acc. Circ:** 7,500 (ctrl). ***Continues*** *Rivista Della Strada.*
**Desc:** Technical magazine on transport problems (road, rail, air, sea and waterway), construction and use of equipment and organization of transport systems of people and goods.

NE
**VOICE OF THE PEDESTRIAN, THE.** ***Suspended.*** **See** Housing and Urban Development.

GW/0340-4536
**V+T. VERKEHR UND TECHNIK.** (VERKEHR UND TECHNIK.). [V+T, Verk. Tech.]. **Added/Corp** Verband Offentlicher Verkehrsbetriebe. (1966)-. Academic Scholarly Publication. German. Twelve times a year. DM184.00. Erich Schmidt Verlag GmbH, Postfach 304240, D 10724 Berlin Germany. **Tel** 011 49 30 25008525. **LC** TF3; .V45. **Bk Rev. Ad Acc. Circ:** 3,236 (ctrl).
**Desc:** Traffic and technical science magazine.
**Ind/Abst** EMBASE.

US
**WASHINGTON LETTER ON TRANSPORTATION.** (19??)-. Newsletter. English. Fifty-one times per year. $295.00. Washington Letter, 1225 I Street Northwest, Suite 300, Washington DC 20005. **Tel** (202)682-3901, FAX (202)842-0621. **ED** James Young.
**Desc:** A weekly newsletter on federal transportation programs, legislation and regulations, including related clean air, budget, and court actions.

US/0091-5734
**WASHINGTON TRANSPORTATION NEWSLETTER. Added/Corp** Washington Transportation Associates. (19??)-. Newsletter. English. wk. Washington Letter, 1225 I Street Northwest, Suite 300, Washington DC 20005. **Tel** (202)682-3901, FAX (202)842-0621. **LC** HE1; .W35.

US/0043-1524
**WATERWAYS JOURNAL, THE.** (Apr. 1887)-. Periodical. English. wk (Publish on Monday). $28.00 one year; $52.00 two year; $76.00 three year. Waterways Journal, 319 North 4th Street, Suite 650, St Louis MO 63102. **Tel** (314)241-7354, FAX (314)241-4207. **ED** Jack Simpson. **LC** HE623; .W3. **DD** 386.20973. **Ad Acc. Circ:** 5,500.
**Desc:** Weekly marine newspaper relating to the inland waterways of the U.S.

UK/0267-8160
**WELSH TRANSPORT STATISTICS / YSTADEGAU TRAFNIDIAETH CYMRU. Added/Corp** Great Britain. Welsh Office. Economic & Statistical Services. **VFOAT** Ystadegau Trafnidiaeth Cymru. No. 1 (1985)-. Statistical Publication. English (Welsh). Welsh Office Publications Unit, Crown Building, Cathay's Park, Cardiff CF1 3NQ Wales. **Tel** 011 44 222 825111. **LC** HE244.A15; W44. **DD** 380.5/09429/021. available with charts.

CN/0229-6268
**WESTERN TRUCK NEWS.** [West. truck news]. Vol. 1, No. 5 (June 1980)-. Periodical. English. mo. $6.00. Western Truck News, PO Box 4653, Edmonton Alberta T6E 5G5 Canada. **DD** 388.3/24/097123. ***Continues*** *Western Truck, 0229-625X.*

JA
**WHEEL EXTENDED, THE. Added/Corp** Toyota Jidosha Hanbai Kabushiki Kaisha. Vol. 1 (Spring 1971)-. Periodical. English. qt. Free on request. Toyota Motor Corporation, 1 Toyota Cho, Toyota Shi Aichi Japan. **Tel** 03 3817 9933, FAX 03 3817 9017. **ED** S. Imamura. **LC** HE277.A1; W48. **DD** 380.5/0952. Index available. cum. index. **Circ:** 12,000.
**Desc:** Focusing on the issues relating to urban transportation.
**Ind/Abst** Avery Index Archit. Period. Suppl. Colum. Univ. (1990-).

AT/0043-4779
**WHEELS (AUSTRALIA).** (WHEELS.). (19??)-. Periodical. English. mo. 67.20Aus$ Australia; 80.30Aus$ New Zealand; 121.20Aus$ other. Australian Consolidated Press Ltd, GPO Box 5252, Sydney New South Wales 2001 Australia. **Tel** 011 61 2 2600000.

US
**WHEELS ETC.** Periodical. English (Spanish). wk. $125.00. WANT AD Publications, Inc., 740 Boston Post Road, Sudbury MA 01776-3397. **Tel** (508)443-4778, FAX (508)443-5293.
**Desc:** Information on bikes, boats, cars, planes, RVs, trailers, trucks, vans, etc.

US/0738-565X
**WHEELS OF TIME.** (WHEELS OF TIME / AMERICAN TRUCK HISTORICAL SOCIETY.). [Wheels time]. **Added/Corp** American Truck Historical Society. Vol. 1, No. 1 (Oct. 1980)-. Periodical. English. Six times a year (Jan., Mar., May, July, Sept., Nov.). $30.00 Comes with American Truck Historical Society membership.

# Transportation

American Truck Historical Society, 300 Office Park Drive, PO Box 531168, Birmingham AL 35223. **Tel** (205)870-0566, FAX (205)870-3069. **ED** E. E. Addor. **LC** TL230.A1; W45. **DD** 629.2/24/0973. Index available. cum. index. **Bk Rev. Ad Acc. Circ:** 14,500 (ctrl).
 **Desc:** Dedicated to the collection and preservation of the dynamic history of trucks, the trucking industry and its pioneers.

JA
**WHITE PAPER ON TRANSPORTATION SAFETY IN JAPAN / TRAFFIC SAFETY POLICY OFFICE, PRIME MINISTER'S OFFICE.** 1983-. English. an. IATSS 6-20, 2-chome Yaesu, Chuo-ku Tokyo 104 Japan. **LC** HE5614.5.J3; J36B. **DD** 363.1/2/0952. *Continues* Japan. Sorifu. Japanese Government White Paper on Transportation Safety.

US/0162-7015
**WOODALL'S RV BUYER'S CATALOG.**
 **Main/Corp** Woodall Publishing Company. **VFOAT** RV Buyer's Catalog. Catalog. English. $5.95. Woodall Publishing Company, 28167 North Keith Drive, Lake Forest IL 60015. **Tel** (708)362-6700. **LC** TL298; .W66A.

US/0162-7368
**WOODALL'S RV BUYER'S GUIDE.**
 **Main/Corp** Woodall Publishing Company. **Added/Corp** Woodall Publishing Company. RV Buyer's Guide. **VAT** Woodall's Recreational Vehicle Buyer's Guide. (19??)-. English. an. Woodall Publishing Company, 28167 North Keith Drive, Lake Forest IL 60015. **Tel** (708)362-6700. **LC** TL298; .W66b. **DD** 629.22/6.

US/0192-4532
**WOODALL'S RV OWNER'S HANDBOOK.** **VFOAT** RV Owner's Handbook. **VAT** Woodall's Recreational Vehicle Owner's Handbook. V. 1-. English. an. Woodall Publishing Company, 28167 North Keith Drive, Lake Forest IL 60015. **Tel** (708)362-6700.

UK/0951-8673
**WORLD AIRLINE FLEETS NEWS.**
 **Added/Corp** Aviation Data Centre. No. 1 (1 July 1987)-. Periodical. English. mo. £30.00 UK; £34.00 Europe; £36.00 other. Aviation Data Centre, PO Box 92, Feltham Middlesex TW13 4SA England. **Tel** 011 44 81 7513317. *Continues* Airline Data News.

●US
**WORLD IVHS MARKET.** (1994)-. English. Four times a year. $1025.00. Forecast International / DMS Inc., 22 Commerce Road, Newtown CT 06470. **Tel** (203)426-0800, FAX (203)426-1964, telex 467615.

●UK/1355-2554
**WORLD TRANSPORT POLICY & PRACTICE.** (1995)-. Periodical. English. Four times a year. £99.00. MCB University Press, 60 62 Toller Lane, Bradford West Yorkshire BD8 9BX England. **Tel** 011 44 274 499821, FAX 011 44 274 547143, telex 51317 MCBUNI G. **ED** Dr. John Whitelegg.
 **Desc:** Information on transport policy including passenger transport, global and local issues, car-free cities, high-speed rail networks, regional airports, land use planning issues, the design of cities and rural areas, international links, the economy and environment.

US
**WYOMING URBAN AREAS ... ANNUAL REPORT.** 1982-. English. Urban Transportation Planning Unit Wyoming Highway Department, PO Box 1708, Cheyenne WY 82002-9019. **LC** HE309.W8; W9. **DD** 338.4/09787.

US/0362-6725
**YEARBOOK / TIRE AND RIM ASSOCIATION, INC.** [Year b. - Tire Rim Assoc.]. **Added/Corp** Tire and Rim Association. (19??)-. English. an (Feb.). $32.00 US; $33.00 others. Tire and Rim Association, 175 Montrose Avenue West, Suite 150, Copley OH 44321. **Tel** (216)666-8121. **LC** TL270; .A23. **DD** 678. *Continues* Yearbook (Tire and Rim Association of America).
 **Desc:** Includes standards on tires, rims, and valves for interchangeability.

PL
**ZAGADNIENIA TRANSPORTU.** Polish (summaries and/or abstracts in English). 42.00 each issue. Panstwowe Wydawn Naukowe, Miodowa 10, PO Box 391, 00251 Warsaw Poland. **LC** HE7; .Z3.

AU
**ZEITSCHRIFT FUER VERKEHRSRECHT.** Vol. 1, (Jan. 1956)-. Periodical. German. Twelve times a year. S1,040.00. Manzsche Verlagsbuchhandlung, Kohlmarkt 16 Postfach 163, A 1014 Vienna Austria. **Tel** 011 43 222 5316171. **LC** LAW. **Ad Acc.**

GW/0044-3670
**ZEITSCHRIFT FUER VERKEHRSWISSENSCHAFT.** [Z. Verkehrswiss.]. 1. Volume, No. 1. Academic Scholarly Publication. German. bm. DM58.00. Verkehrs Verlag J Fischer, Postfach 140265, D 40072 Dusseldorf Germany. **Tel** 011 49 211 991930. **LC** HE5; .Z4. **DD** 380.5/05. **Bk Rev. ctrl circ.**
 **Ind/Abst** EMBASE; Ergon. Abstr. (?-?); Int. Bibliogr. Sociol.; PAIS Int. Print.

## ABSTRACTING, BIBLIOGRAPHIES AND STATISTICS

US/0740-8676
**AFTERMARKET STATISTICAL YEARBOOK.** (AFTERMARKET STATISTICAL YEARBOOK / NATIONAL AFTERMARKET AUDIT CO.). **VFOAT** Aftermarket Yearbook. 1st Ed. (1984)-. Statistical Publication. English. an. $225.00. National Aftermarket Audit Company, PO Box 1509, Duxbury MA 02331. **Tel** (617)934-6577. **ED** A C McKendry. **LC** HE5623; .A119. **DD** 388.3/422/0973021; 629. Index available.
 **Desc:** Car and truck registration statistics by make and year at state level.

US
**ANALYSIS OF CLASS 1 RAILROADS.** **Added/Corp** Association of American Railroads. Economics and Finance Dept. **VFOAT** Analysis of Class I Railroads; Analysis of Class One Railroads. (19??)-. English. an (Sept.). $200.00 (nonmembers), $100.00 (members). Association of American Railroads, 50 F Street Northwest, Room 5401, Washington DC 20001. **Tel** (202)639-2550. **Bk Rev. Ad Acc.** available on magnetic tape. *Absorbed* Operating & Traffic Statistics, 0738-0003.
 **Desc:** Financial and operating statistics for Class 1 Railroads within the following categories: fuel consumption, net worth, investment base, revenue expenses, income and employment.

MX
**ANUARIO ESTADISTICO DEL COMERCIO EXTERIOR DE LOS ESTADOS UNIDOS MEXICANOS.** **Main/Corp** Mexico. Direccion General de Estadistica. 1920/22-. Spanish. Sec Indust y Comer Div de Adm, Direccion General de Estadistica, Avenida Cuauhtemoc 80, Mexico 7DT Mexico. **LC** HF131. **DD** 382.0972.

BL
**ANUARIO ESTATISTICO DAS FERROVIAS DO BRASIL.** V. 1- 1977-. Portuguese. Ministerio dos Transportes, Rede Ferroviaria Federal, Praca Procopio Ferreira/B6, 20-021 Rio de Janeiro RJ Brazil. **Tel** 533 3094, telex (021)30939. **LC** HE2921; .A85. **DD** 385/.0981. **Circ:** 1,200 (ctrl). *Supersedes* Estatistica das Estradas de Ferro do Brasil.
 **Desc:** Covers railroads, transportation, traffic accidents, revenues and expenses, statistics, etc.

BL
**ANUARIO ESTATISTICO DOS TRANSPORTES.** Portuguese. an. Pra Ca Duque de Caxias 86-9, Andar ZC-14, 20.224 Rio de Janeiro Brazil. **LC** HE48; .A36. **DD** 380.5/0981. *Continues* Brazil. Servico de Estatistica dos Transportes. Anuario Estatistico dos Transports.

UK
**BASIC ROAD STATISTICS.** **Added/Corp** British Road Federation. (19??)-. English. an. **LC** HE363.G7; B3. **DD** 388.1/0941.

FR
**BIBLIOGRAPHIE D'ECONOMIE DES TRANSPORTS.** Began in 1971. French. Institut de L'Information Scientifique et Technique, 54 Boulevard Raspail, PB 140, 75260 Paris Cedex 06 France. **Tel** 45 44 38 49 F. **LC** Z7164.T8; B5; HE 3.

US/0148-849X
**BIBLIOGRAPHY (NATIONAL RESEARCH COUNCIL (U.S.) TRANSPORTATION RESEARCH BOARD).** (BIBLIOGRAPHY - TRANSPORTATION RESEARCH BOARD.). (1974)-. English. ir. $10.00. Transportation Research Board, Box 289, Washington DC 20055. **Tel** (202)334-3218, FAX (202)334-2519. **LC** UNC. **Circ:** 3,000. *Continues* National Research Council. Highway Research Board. Bibliography.
 **Desc:** Generally developed by TRB Library or by committees of the Board.

BL
**BOLETIM ESTATISTICO - ADMINISTRACAO DO PORTO DO RECIFE.** **Main/Corp** Administracao do Porto do Recife. Bulletin. Portuguese. mo. Administracao do Porto do Recife, Setor Comercial, Sub-Setor de Controle e Estatistica, Praca Artur Oscar S/No, Recife PE Brazil. **LC** HE556.R4; A3A. **DD** 387.1/0981/3.

BL
**BOLETIM ESTATISTICO / ESTADO DE SANTA CATARINA, SECRETARIA DOS TRANSPORTES E OBRAS, ADMINISTRACAO DO PORTO DE SAO FRANCISCO DO SUL.** **Main/Corp** Administracao do Porto de Sao Francisco do Sul. **VFOAT** Estatistica. Bulletin. Portuguese. mo. Administracao do Porto de Sao Francisco do Sul Assessoria de Planejamento Servico de Estatistica, Rua Babitonga 99 CP 7, Sao Francisco do Sul Santa Catarina. **LC** HE563.B8; A344A. **DD** 387.1/0981/64.

CE
**BULLETIN ON MOTOR VEHICLE STATISTICS.** 1978-. Bulletin. English. ir. Rs30.00. Department of Census and Statistics / Sri Lanka, PO Box 563, Colombo 7 Sri Lanka. **Tel** 595291. **LC** HE5689.8; .A13. **DD** 354.549/30087834. **Circ:** 468.
 **Desc:** Contains statistical data pertaining to the present motor vehicle population of the Island classified by districts and by type, fare, payload and other important variables.

UK/0141-0687
**CARGO HANDLING ABSTRACTS / INTERNATIONAL CARGO HANDLING CO-ORDINATION ASSOCIATION.** **Added/Corp** International Cargo Handling Coordination Association. (1978)-. Periodical. English. qt. £25.00 (surface mail); £21.00 (air mail) members; £30.00 (surface mail); £40.00 (air mail) other. International Cargo Holding Coordination Association, 71 Bondway, London SW8 1SH England. **Tel** 011 44 71 7931022, FAX 011 44 71 8201703, telex 261106.

US
**COMPARATIVE MOTOR VEHICLE TRAFFIC ACCIDENT STATISTICS IN CITIES OF 5,000 POPULATION AND OVER / STATE OF ILLINOIS, DEPARTMENT OF PUBLIC WORKS AND BUILDINGS, DIVISION OF HIGHWAYS, BUREAU OF TRAFFIC.** Periodical. English. sa. Department of Public Works & Buildings, Bureau of Traffic, Springfield IL 62706. **LC** HE5614.3.I4; C65. **DD** 312/.44/09773.
 **Desc:** First issue of each year compares first half of current year with first half of previous year; second issue each year compares entire current year with entire previous year.

US/0363-9983
**CONTINENTAL DIRECTORY NMF. STANDARD POINT LOCATION CODES SPLC.** (CONTINENTAL DIRECTORY OF STANDARD POINT LOCATION CODES (SPLC) / NATIONAL MOTOR FREIGHT TRAFFIC ASSOCIATION, INC.). **Added/Corp** National Motor Freight Traffic Association. **VFOAT** Continental Directory, Standard Point Location Codes, SPLC; Standard Point Location Codes, SPLC; Continental Directory of SPLC. **VAT** Continental Directory National Motor Freight. Standard Point Location. (1975)-. Directory. English. Four times a year. $115.00. National Motor Freight Traffic Association Inc., 2200 Mill Road, Alexandria VA 22314. **Tel** (703)838-1822, FAX (703)683-1094. **ED** Paul G. Levine. **LC** HE202; .C66. **DD** 388.3/24/02573. **Circ:** 1,300.
 **Desc:** A compilation of numeric place identification codes. Also available on 9-track tape.

BL
**DADOS ESTATISTICOS DA MOVIMENTACAO DE CARGA E PASSAGEIROS.** **Added/Corp** Empresa de Navegacao da Amazonia. Setor de Processamento de Dados Estatisticos. **VFOAT** Dados Estatisticos da Navegacao. (19??)-. Portuguese. Av P Vargas 41, Caixa Postal 1068, Belem Brazil. **LC** HE563.B8; D3.

BL
**ESTATISTICA / EMPRESA DE PORTOS DO BRASIL S/A, PORTOBRAS, ADMINISTRACAO DO PORTO DO RECIFE, SETOR COMERCIAL, SUB-SETOR DE CONTROLE E ESTATISTICA.** **Main/Corp** Administracao do Porto do Recife. Sub-Setor de Controle e Estatistica. Portuguese. Administracao do Porto do Recife, Setor Comercial, Sub-Setor de Controle e Estatistica, Praca Artur Oscar S/No, Recife PE Brazil. **LC** HE563.B8; A36A. **DD** 387.1/0981/34.

KE
**ESTIMATES OF REVENUE AND EXPEDITURE - EAST AFRICAN RAILWAYS CORPORATION.** **Main/Corp** East African Railways Corporation. (19??)-. English. **LC** HE3419.E3; E382b. **DD** 385/.1.

PK
**EXPLANATORY MEMORANDUM AND STATISTICAL SUPPLEMENT, PAKISTAN RAILWAY BUDGET.** **Main/Corp** Pakistan. Railway Board. **VFOAT** Railway Budget: Explanatory Memorandum and Statistical Supplement. Statistical Publication. English. Government of Pakistan / Ministry of Railways, Railway Board, Karachi 15 3 Pakistan. **LC** HE3300.5; .A363A. **DD** 353.9/549/100875.

CN
**FACTS AND FIGURES OF THE AUTOMOBILE INDUSTRY. Added/Corp** Canadian Automobile Chamber of Commerce. English. Canadian Automobile Chamber of Commerce, 2 Carlton Street, Toronto Ontario Canada. **LC** HD9710.C2; F2. **DD** 338.476292.

CN/0316-3504
**FACTS AND FIGURES OF THE AUTOMOTIVE INDUSTRY (ANNUAL EDITION).** (FACTS AND FIGURES OF THE AUTOMOTIVE INDUSTRY.). 1958-. Periodical. English. an. American Automobile Manufacturers Association, PO Box 11170, Detroit MI 48211. **Tel** (313)872-4311. **DD** 338.4/7/6292. ***Continues*** *Facts and Figures of the Automobile Industry, 0316-3555.*

US/0362-9317
**FINANCIAL AND OPERATING STATISTICS CLASS I MOTOR CARRIERS OF PASSENGERS. Main/Corp** United States. Interstate Commerce Commission. Bureau of Accounts. **VAT** Financial and Operating Statistics Class One Motor Carriers of Passengers. Jan./June 1975-. English. sa. Interstate Commerce Commission / Bureau of Accountants, Room 3349 ICC Building, Washington DC 20423. **Tel** (202)275-7351. **LC** HE5623; .A267. **DD** 388.3/22. ***Continues*** *Revenues, Expenses, other Income, and Statistics of Class I Motor Carriers of Passengers.*

AT/1037-9088
**FOREIGN TRADE AUSTRALIA, INTERNATIONAL CARGO.** (1991)-. English. qt. 9.70Aus$. Australian Bureau of Statistics, PO Box 10, Belconnen Australian Capital Territory, 2616 Australia. **Tel** 011 61 6 2527911, FAX 011 61 6 2516009. ***Continues*** *Shipping and Air Cargo Commodity Statistics, Australia, 0814-138X.*
**Desc:** Information on gross weight and value of inward and outward cargo classified by commodity, mode of transport and place of loading and discharge.

US/0194-0562
**FREIGHT COMMODITY STATISTICS. MOTOR CARRIERS OF PROPERTY. VFOAT** Freight Commodity Statistics of Class 1 Motor Carriers of Property Operating in Intercity Service--Common and Contract, in the United States; Motor Carriers of Property. 1968-. Periodical. English. an. Interstate Commerce Commission / Bureau of Accountants, Room 3349 ICC Building, Washington DC 20423. **Tel** (202)275-7351. **LC** HE5623; .A273C. **DD** 388.3/24/0973. ***Continues*** *Freight Commodity Statistics.*

US/0364-0825
**HIGHWAY TRAFFIC STATISTICS. Main/Corp** North Carolina. Division of Highways. Planning and Research Branch. English. North Carolina Department of Transportation and Highway Safety, PO Box 25201, Raleigh NC 27611. **LC** HE371.N75; N67A. **DD** 388.3/14/09756.

UK/0260-9894
**HIGHWAYS AND TRANSPORTATION STATISTICS ... ESTIMATES.** 1981-82-. English. an. £9.00. Chartered Institute of Public Finance and Accountancy, 2 3 Robert Street, London WC2N 6BH England. **Tel** 011 44 1 895 8823. **LC** HE243.A15; H53. **DD** 388/.049.

BE
**JAARSTATISTIEK OVER DE INTERNATIONALE TRAFIEK DER HAVENS. Main/Corp** Institut National de Statistique (Belgium). Dutch. an. 690F Belgium; 1490F other. Koninkrijk Belgie, Ministerie van Economische Zaken, Nationaal Instituut voor de Statistiek, Leuvenseweg 44, 1000 Brussel Belgium. **Tel** 02/513 96 50. **LC** HE563.B3; B44A. **Circ:** 400 (ctrl). ***Supersedes in part*** *Institut National de Statistique (Belgium). Statistique Annuelle de Trafic International des Ports; Chiffres Definitifs.*

US
**KANSAS HIGHWAY & TRAFFIC STATISTICS / GOVERNOR'S COMMITTEE ON CRIMINAL ADMINISTRATION, STATISTICAL ANALYSIS CENTER. VFOAT** Kansas Highway and Traffic Statistics; Highway and Traffic Statistics. 1978-. Statistical Publication. English. an. Kansas Bureau of Investigation, Statistical Analysis Center, 3420 Van Buren, Topeka KS 66611. **LC** HE5614.3.K3; K34. **DD** 363.1/252/09781021.

NE
**MAANDSTATISTIEK VAN VERKEER EN VERVOER / CENTRAAL BUREAU VOOR DE STATISTIEK. DE. Added/Corp** Netherlands. Centraal Bureau voor de Statistiek. **VFOAT** Monthly Bulletin of Transport Statistics. Vol. 47 No. 8 (Aug. 1984)-. Periodical. Dutch. mo. Fl100.00. Centraal Bureau voor de Statistiek, AFD ALG Zaken, Postbus 959, 2270 AZ Voorburg Netherlands. **Tel** 011 31 70 3373800, FAX 011 31 038 7429, telex 32692 CBS NL. **LC** HE69; .A3. ***Continues*** *CBS Maandstatistiek Van Verkeer en Vervoer.*

US/0096-333X
**MISSISSIPPI FINANCIAL STATISTICS FOR HIGHWAY PLANNING ON STATE HIGHWAYS COUNTY ROADS CITY STREETS.** English. an. Mississippi State Highway Department, PO Box 1850, Jackson MS 39215-1850. **LC** HE356.M7; M5. **DD** 388.1/1/09762.

US/0196-5352
**MOTOR CARRIER STATISTICAL SUMMARY. Main/Corp** American Trucking Associations. Division of Research and Economics. 1977-. Statistical Publication. English. qt. American Trucking Association, 2200 Mill Road, Alexandria VA 22314. **Tel** (703)838-1772. ***Continues*** *Truck Beat; Intercity Truck Tonnage, 0569-8839.*

US/0741-1723
**NATIONAL ACCIDENT SAMPLING SYSTEM.** (NATIONAL ACCIDENT SAMPLING SYSTEM / U.S. DEPARTMENT OF TRANSPORTATION, NATIONAL HIGHWAY SAFETY ADMINISTRATION.). [Natl. accid. sampl. syst.]. English. an. Department of Transportation, 400 Seventh Street SW, Washington DC 20590. **Tel** (202)426-4000. **LC** HE5614.2; .N25. **DD** 312/.445/0973.

US/0275-3286
**NATIONAL HIGHWAY AND AIRWAY CARRIERS AND ROUTES.** (19??)-. English. Twice a year. $181.90 Illinois; $170.00 other. National Highways Carriers Directory, PO Box 6099, Buffalo Grove IL 60089. **Tel** (312)541-6565. **Ad Acc. Circ:** 10,500. ***Continues*** *National Highway Carriers Directory and Routes, Including Air Cargo Transports.*
**Desc:** Guide for routing freight between all points in U.S. and Canada; includes terminal locations and phone numbers, company officials, type of service and states served.

US/0161-8628
**NATIONAL TRANSPORTATION STATISTICS. Added/Corp** Transportation Systems Center. Statistical Information Reporting Branch. Transportation Systems Center. Information Management Branch. Center for Transportation Information (U.S.) United States. Dept. of Transportation. Research and Special Programs Administration. Transportation Systems Center. (1977)-. Government Publication. English. an. $23.00. Superintendent of Documents, US Government Printing Office, Washington DC 20402. **Tel** (202)275-3328, FAX (202)786-2377. **LC** HE203; .T76a. **DD** 380.5/0973. available on microfiche (Vols. for (1981-) distributed to depository libraries). ***Formed by the union of*** *Summary of National Transportation Statistics, 0145-2541* ***and*** *Energy Statistics, 0360-8980.*
**Ind/Abst** Predicasts Forecasts.

US/0737-2981
**NATIONAL URBAN MASS TRANSPORTATION STATISTICS.** (NATIONAL URBAN MASS TRANSPORTATION STATISTICS : ANNUAL REPORT, SECTION 15 REPORTING SYSTEM.). [Natl. urban mass transp. stat.]. **VFOAT** Section 15 Reporting System; Section 15 Annual Report. 1st (fiscal years ending between July 1, 1978 and June 30, 1979)-. English. an. National Technical Information Service - NTIS, Room 2027S, 5285 Port Royal Road, Springfield VA 22161. **Tel** (703)487-4630, (703)487-4660, (703)487-4650, FAX (703)321-8547, telex 89-9405. **LC** HE4401; .N37. **DD** 338.4/0973. available on microfiche (Vols. for (1978/79) distributed to depository libraries).

US/0731-017X
**NEW MEXICO ... HIGHWAY STATISTICS AND RELATED INFORMATION. VFOAT** Highway Statistics. English. an. New Mexico State Highway Department, Planning Research Section, PO Box 1149, Santa Fe NM 87503. **LC** HE356.N6; N47C. ***Continues*** *Highway Statistics and Related Information, 0363-3993.*

CN/0705-5595
**NEW MOTOR VEHICLE SALES (MONTHLY ED.).** (NEW MOTOR VEHICLE SALES / PREPARED IN THE INDUSTRY AND MERCHANDISING DIVISION.). [New mot. veh. sales]. **Added/Corp** Canada. Dominion Bureau of Statistics. Industry and Merchandising Division. Canada. Dominion Bureau of Statistics. Merchandising and Services Division. Statistics Canada. Merchandising and Services Division. Statistics Canada. Retail Trade Section. **VFOAT** Ventes de Vehicules Automobiles Neufs. Vol. 33, No. 1 (Jan. 1961)-. Periodical. English (French). mo. 160.00Can$ Canada; $192.00 US; $224.00 other. Statistics Canada, Publications Sales & Services, Main Building Room 1710, Ottawa Ontario K1A 0T6 Canada. **Tel** (613)951-5078, (800)267-6677, FAX (613)951-1584, telex 053-3585. **DD** 381/.456292/0971. ***Continues*** *New Motor Vehicle Sales and Motor Vehicle Financing, 0705-5609;* ***Absorbed*** *New Motor Vehicle Sales (Annual), 0575-920X.*

IT
**NOTIZIARIO STATISTICO - ANFIA. Main/Corp** Associazione Nazionale Fre Industrie Automobilistiche. **VAT** Notiziario Statistico - Associazione Nazionale Fre Industrie Automobilistiche. Vol. 19 (Jan. 1977)-. Periodical. Italian. Eleven times a year. L430000. ANFIA, Corso Galileo Ferraris 61, 10128 Turin Italy. **Tel** 011 39 11 5613901, telex 221334 ANFIA. **LC** HD9710.I8; A8. Index available. **Circ:** 290 (ctrl). ***Continues*** *Associazione Nazionale fra Industrie Automobilistiche. Bollettino Statistico.*
**Desc:** Bulletin of the motor industry; presents detailed statistics on Italian production, market and foreign trade, with statistics for the main foreign countries.

AT
**OVERSEAS ARRIVALS AND DEPARTURES, AUSTRALIA. Main/Corp** Australian Bureau of Statistics. (19??)-. English. qt. 14.30Aus$. Australian Bureau of Statistics, PO Box 10, Belconnen Australian Capital Territory, 2616 Australia. **Tel** 011 61 6 2527911, FAX 011 61 6 2516009.
**Desc:** Travellers classified according to category (settlers, Australian residents, visitors), type of movement, country or Australian State of last or intended residence, country of birth, citizenship, State of clearance, purpose of journey, intended or actual length of stay, mode of transport, age and sex.

US
**PENNSYLVANIA MASS TRANSIT STATISTICAL REPORT. VFOAT** Mass Transit Statistical Report. Statistical Publication. English. an. Pennsylvania Department of Transportation, Room 1215 Transportation & Safety Building, Harrisburg PA 17120. **LC** HE4487.P4; P45. **DD** 338.4/09748.

UK/0263-9149
**PORT STATISTICS. *Ceased.* Added/Corp** British Ports Association. Great Britain. Dept. of Transport. British Ports Federation. (1980)-(1992). English. an. British Ports Federation, Victoria House, Vernon Place, London WC1B 4LL England. **LC** HE557.G7; P62. **DD** 387.1/0941/021. ***Continues*** *Annual Digest of Port Statistics.*
**Desc:** Contains detailed comments on the 120 pages of tables and 10 pages of charts and graphs which cover the main features and activities of British Ports.

US/0093-2140
**RAILROAD ACCIDENTS IN OREGON.** (RAILROAD ACCIDENTS IN OREGON, STATISTICS SUMMARY AND ANALYSIS.). **Main/Corp** Oregon. Public Utility Commissioner. English. an. Public Utility Commissioner, Labor and Industries Building, Salem OR 97310. **Tel** (503)378-6351. **ED** David J Astle. **LC** HE1780.5.O7; A3. **DD** 312/.4/4. **Circ:** 600 (ctrl). ***Continues*** *Statistical Report, Railroad Accidents.*
**Desc:** Statistics and analysis of accidents at rail crossings in Oregon. Also includes section on railroad employee accidents.

FR
**RAPPORT STATISTIQUE SUR LES ACCIDENTS DE LA ROUTE EN ... / CONFERENCE EUROPEENNE DES MINISTRES DES TRANSPORTS. Added/Corp** European Conference of Ministers of Transport. **VFOAT** Statistical Report on Road Accidents in ... . (1983)-. English (French). an. OECD Publications and Information Center, 2 rue Andre-Pascal, 75775 Paris Cedex 16 France. **Tel** 011 33 1 45248167, US:(202)785-6323, FAX 011 33 1 45248500 OR 45248176, telex 620 160 OCDE. **(Subscription address:** US/OECD Publications Center, 2001 L Street Northwest, Suite 700, Washington, DC 20036; telephone: (202)785-6323) **LC** HE5614.5.E8; R36. **DD** 363.12/52/094021. **NLM** W2; GA1 E8r. ***Continues in part*** *Annales Statistiques de Transport. Evolution des Investissements, des Infrastructures, des Materiels, et des Trafics.*
**Desc:** Contains statistics on road accidents in OECP member countries.

RU
**REFERATIVNYI ZHURNAL: ORGANIZATSIIA I BEZOPASNOST DOROZHNOGO DVIZHENIIA. Added/Corp** Vsesoiuznyi Institut Nauchnoi i Tekhnicheskoi Informatsii (Soviet Union). **VFOAT** Organizatsiia I Bezopasnost Dorozhnogo Divzheniia. (1974)-. Abstracting/Indexing Service. Russian. mo. $66.00. VINITI - Vsesoyuznyi Institut Nauchno-Tekhnicheskoi Informatsii, All-Union Scientific and Technical Information Institute, Baltiiskaia Ulitsa 14, 125219 Moscow Russia. **Tel** 238-46-00, FAX 9430060, telex 411160. **(Subscription address:** Victor Kamkin, 4956 Boiling Brook Parkway, Rockville MD 20852.) **LC** HE5601; .R43.
**Ind/Abst** Abstr. Bull. Inst. Pap. Sci. Tech.

IS
**RIVON LI-STATISTIKAH SHEL TAHBURAH.** **Main/Corp** Israel. Lishkah Ha-Merkazit Li-Statistikah. **VFOAT** Quarterly Transport Statistics. Vol. 1- 1974-. Multiple languages (English and Hebrew). $13.75. Ha-Lishkah Ha-Merkazit Li-Statistikah, PO Box 13015, Jerusalem 91130 Israel. **Tel** (00-972)2-211400. **LC** HE96.I8; L58A.
**Desc:** Periodic official statistics on all divisions of Israel's land, air and sea transportation and various special surveys.

II
**ROAD STATISTICS IN KARNATAKA STATE.** **Main/Corp** Karnataka (India). Public Works Dept. Statistical Unit. (19??)-. English. Public Works Department / Bangalore, Statistical Unit, Communications and Buildings Central Office 1, Bangalore India. **LC** HE365.I44; M97. **DD** 388.1/0954/87. ***Continues*** *Mysore. Public Works Dept. (Communications and Buildings). Road Statistics in Mysore State.*

YU
**SAOBRACAJNE NEZGODE NA PUTEVIMA.** **Main/Corp** Yugoslavia. Savezni Zavod za Statistiku. **VFOAT** Transport Accidents on Roads. Serbo-Croatian (Roman). 15.00 Din. Savezni Zavod za Statistiku, Kneza Milosa 20, Belgrad Yugoslavia. **LC** HA1631; .A3 subser; HE5614.5.Y8 Y8.

US/0163-2833
**SAR STATISTICS.** (SAR STATISTICS / DEPARTMENT OF TRANSPORTATION, COAST GUARD.). **VFOAT** S.A.R. Statistics. **VAT** Search and Rescue Statistics. English. an. Commandant (G-OSR-3), US Coast Guard, Washington DC 20593. **LC** TL553.8; .U482A. **DD** 361.5/8.

CN/0318-2819
**SASKATCHEWAN PROVINCIAL HIGHWAYS ACCIDENT STATISTICS.** **VFOAT** Accident Statistics. **VAT** Accidents Statistics (Regina.). Began publication 1973?. English. an. Free. Saskatchewan Highways & Transportation, 9th Floor, 1855 Victoria Avenue, Regina Saskatchewan S4P 3V5 Canada. **Tel** (306)787-4756, FAX (306)787-1007. **DD** 388.3/14. **Circ:** 4,000 (ctrl).
**Desc:** A summary of all the motor vehicle traffic accidents occurring within the province of Saskatchewan.

SW
**SCBS BILKALENDER.** **VFOAT** S.C.B.S Bilkalender. V. 1 (1983)-. Swedish. an. SCB Statistiska Centralbyran, 11581 Stockholm Sweden. **LC** HD9710.S8; S33.

IO/0445-9474
**SERI STATISTIK PENGANGKUTAN KERETA API. RAILWAYS STATISTICS.** **VFOAT** Statistik Pengangkutan Kereta Api; Railway Statistics. Indonesian (English). an. Rp1500 Indonesia; $1.00 US. Central Bureau of Statistics / Indonesia, c/o Dr. Sutomo, 8 Jalan, PO Box 3, Jakarta Indonesia. **Tel** 372808 374908 Ext.342. **LC** HE3331; .A63A. ctrl circ.
**Desc:** Railway statistics.

GW
**SHIPPING STATISTICS.** **Main/Corp** Institut fur Serverkehrswirtschaft Bermen. **Added/Corp** Institut fur Seeverkehrswirtschaft Bremen. Statistik der Schiffahrt. **VFOAT** Statistik der Schiffahrt. (19??)-. English (German). mo. DM265.00. Institute of Shipping Economics and Statistics, Universitatsallee GW1 Blockade, D 28359 Bremen Germany. **Tel** 011 49 421 2209611, FAX 011 49 421 2209655, telex 244840. **ED** Christel Heideloff and Manfred Zachcial. **LC** HE561; .I52a. **DD** 387.5/021/2. Index available. **Bk Rev. Circ:** 600.
**Desc:** Presentation of supply and demand indicators for the shipping industry, continuous acquisition of freight rate indices, statistical analysis of the shipbuilding markets, processing and sorting of port statistics worldwide.

UK/0306-1817
**SHIPPING STATISTICS AND ECONOMICS.** [Shipp. stat. econ.]. **Added/Corp** H.P. Drewry (Shipping Consultants) Limited. **VFOAT** SSE. Shipping Statistics and Economics. No. 1 (Nov. 1970)-. Periodical. English. mo. £510 Europe; £550.00 other. Drewry Shipping Consultants Ltd, 11 Heron Quay, London E14 4JF England. **Tel** 011 44 71 5380191, FAX 01-987-9396, telex 21167 HPDLDG. **ED** A B Carpenter.
**Desc:** Monthly updated record of the whole tanker and dry cargo charter markets, extensive data on shipping demand, fleet developments, freight rates with tables/charts.

FJ
**SHIPPING STATISTICS OF FIJI.** English. 1.00Fij$. Government of Fiji / Bureau of Statistics, Box 2221, Suva Fiji Islands. **Tel** 011 679 315144. **LC** HE933.5; .S5. **DD** 387.5/0996/11021. **Circ:** 96. ***Continues*** *Shipping Statistics (Suva, Fiji).*
**Desc:** International shipping, type of vessels, exports and imports, origin and destination of cargo, domestic shipping, recording of shipping data on a port by port basis for both overseas and domestic shipping.

US/0160-1970
**STATISTICAL PROFILE - IOWA DEPARTMENT OF TRANSPORTATION.** ***Title Change.*** (STATISTICAL PROFILE - DEPARTMENT OF TRANSPORTATION.). **Main/Corp** Iowa. Dept. of Transportation. Statistical Publication. English. an. Iowa Department of Transportation, 800 Lincoln Way, Ames IA 50010. **Tel** (515)239-1528. **LC** HE28.I8; D46B. **DD** 380.5/09777. ***Continued by*** *Iowa Transportation System Facts.*

US/0093-2418
**STATISTICAL REPORT OF ACCIDENTS (CHARLESTON).** (STATISTICAL REPORT OF ACCIDENTS.). **Main/Corp** West Virginia. Safety Responsibility Division. Statistical Publication. English. 1800 Washington Street East, Charleston WV 25305. **LC** HE5614.3.W4; W45A. **DD** 312.4/4.

NE
**STATISTIEK VAN DE SCHEEPVAARTBEWEGING / CENTRAAL BUREAU VOOR DE STATISTIEK, HOOFDAFDELING STATISTIEKEN VAN VERKEER EN VERVOER.** **Added/Corp** Netherlands. Centraal Bureau voor de Statistiek. Hoofdafdeling Statistieken van Verkeer en Vervoer. **VFOAT** Census of Inland Shipping at Docks and Bridges. (19??)-. Dutch. an. Staatsuitgeverij, Christoffel Plantijnstraat 1, 2515 TZ'S Gravenhage Netherlands. **Tel** 070/78-95-70. **LC** HE674; .A233. ***Continues*** *Statistiek van de Scheepvaartbeweging in Nederland.*

NE
**STATISTIEK VAN HET AUTOPARK.** **Main/Corp** Netherlands (Kingdom, 1815- ). Centraal Bureau voor de Statistiek. Dutch. Centraal Bureau voor de Statistiek, AFD ALG Zaken, Postbus 959, 2270 AZ Voorburg Netherlands. **Tel** 011 31 70 3373800, FAX 011 31 038 7429, telex 32692 CBS NL. **LC** HE5674; .A242B.

SA
**STATISTIEKE VAN MOTOR- EN ANDER VOERTUIE SOOS OP ... / REPUBLIEK VAN SUID-AFRIKA, SENTRALE STATISTIEKDIENS.** **VFOAT** Statistics of Motor and Other Vehicles as at ... . June 30, 1981-. Afrikaans (English). an. R2.50. Government Printer / South Africa, Bosman Street, Private Bag X85, Pretoria 0001 South Africa. **Tel** 011 27 12 3239731 Ext. 262. **LC** HE5704.4; .A28B. ***Continues*** *Statistieke van Motor- en Ander Voertuie, Alle Voertuie.*

SA
**STATISTIEKE VAN NUWE VOERTUIE GELISENSIEER.** **Main/Corp** South Africa. Dept. of Statistics. **VFOAT** Statistics of New Vehicles Licensed. Multiple languages (Afrikaans and English). The Government Printer, Bosman Street, Private Bag X85, Pretoria 0001 South Africa. **Tel** 012-323-9731, FAX 012-323-0009. **LC** HE5704.4; .A28A.

IO
**STATISTIK KENDARAAN BERMOTOR DAN PANJANG JALAN.** **Main/Corp** Indonesia. Biro Pusat Statistik. Indonesian. Biro Pusat Statistik, JLN Dr Sutomo 8 Kotak, Pos 1003, Jakarta 10710 Indonesia. **Tel** 3728007, 374908. **LC** HE5695; .A23.

BE
**STATISTIQUE ANNUELLE DES VEHICULES NEUFS IMMATRICULES EN BELGIQUE. JAARLIJKSE STATISTIEK DER NIEUWE VOERTUIGEN IN BELGIE INGESCHREVEN.** **VFOAT** Jaarlijkse Statistiek der Nieuwe Voertuigen in Belgie Ingeschreven. Dutch (French). Febiac, Boulevard de la Woluwe 46 Bie 6, B-1200 Bruxelles Belgium. **LC** HE5673.A45; S75.

BE
**STATISTIQUE DU TRAFIC INTERNATIONAL DES PORTS, U.E.B.L. / ROYAUME DE BELGIQUE, MINISTERE DES AFFAIRES ECONOMIQUES, INSTITUT NATIONAL DE BELGIQUE.** **Added/Corp** Institut National de Statistique (Belgium). (1981)-. French. qt. 600F Belgium; 800F other. Institut National de Statistique / Belgium, rue de Louvain, 44, Centre Albert, 8e Etage, 1000 Brussels Belgium. **Tel** 011 32 2 5486211. **LC** HF3601.5; .S82. **DD** 380.1/09493. **Bk Rev. Ad Acc. Circ:** 295 (ctrl). ***Continues*** *Statistique du Trafic International (U.E.B.L.) des Ports.*
**Desc:** Statistics about the international traffic in the Belgian seaports.

PO/0377-2292
**STATISTIQUES DES TRANSPORTS ET COMMUNICATIONS : CONTINENT, AZORES ET MADERE.** **Main/Corp** Instituto Nacional de Estatistica (Portugal). Servicos Centrais. **VFOAT** Estatisticas dos Transportes e Comunicacoes : Continente, Acores e Madeira. 1976-. French (Portuguese). an. Instituto Nacional de Estatistica, Servicos Centrais, Avenida Antonio Jose de Almeida 1, 1078 Lisbon Portugal. **Tel** 80 20 80, FAX 8489480, telex 63738 PCDINE. **LC** HE77; .I57A. **DD** 380.3/05. ***Continues*** *Statistiques des Transports: Continente et Iles Adjacentes.*

SW/0082-0334
**STATISTISKA MEDDELANDEN. T.** **VFOAT** Statistiska Meddelanden. Serie T. Monographic series. Swedish. Price varies per volume. SCB Statistiska Centralbyran, 11581 Stockholm Sweden. **LC** HE260.A15; S7.

AT
**SURVEY OF MOTOR VEHICLE USE.** **Added/Corp** Australian Bureau of Statistics. (1985)-. English. Three times a year. 19.00Aus$. Australian Bureau of Statistics, PO Box 10, Belconnen Australian Capital Territory, 2616 Australia. **Tel** 011 61 6 2527911, FAX 011 61 6 2516009. ***Continues*** *Australian Bureau of Statistics. Survey of Motor Vehicle Usage.*
**Desc:** Comprises final statistics, by State or Territory of registration or area of operation, for private and commerical vehicles.

IE
**TRADE AND SHIPPING STATISTICS.** **Added/Corp** Irish Free State. Department of Industry and Commerce. Ireland (Eire). Department of Industry and Commerce. Ireland. Central Statistics Office. (1930)-. Periodical. English. Government Publications, 4 5 Harcourt Road, Dublin 2 Ireland. **Tel** 011 353 1 6613111 Ext.4005. **LC** HF189; .A54. **DD** 382.09415.

BS
**TRANSPORT STATISTICS.** **Main/Corp** Botswana. Ministry of Works and Communications. Statistics Unit. Began 1976/78. English. Botswana Government, PO Box 51, Information Service, Gaborone Botswana Africa. **LC** HE99.9.A3; B68A. **DD** 380.5/09681/1021.

US
**TRANSPORT STATISTICS IN THE UNITED STATES.** 68th (1954)-. English. an. Government Printing Office / Washington, Washington DC 20402. **Tel** (202)783-3238. **LC** HE2708. **DD** 380.5/0973. ***Continues*** *Annual Report on the Statistics of Railways in the United States.*

US/0889-0889
**TRANSPORTATION IN AMERICA.** [Transp. Am.]. **Added/Corp** Transportation Policy Associates. 1st Ed. (March 1983)-. English. an (Mar., includes supplements published in Aug. & Dec.). $55.00. End Transportation Foundation, 44211 Slatestone Court, Landsdowne VA 22075. **Tel** (703)729-7200, FAX (703)729-7219. **ED** Rosalyn Wilson. **LC** HE203; .T73. **DD** 380.5/0973. Index available. **Circ:** 1500. ***Continues*** *Transportation Facts & Trends, 0564-1292.*
**Desc:** Statistical analysis of freight and passenger transport by modes and including current and historical data. Other articles includes outlays, traffic distribution, employment and wage fringe levels and capital outlays number of units.
**Ind/Abst** Stat. Ref. Index.

FR/0525-9363
**TRANSPORTS EN EUROPE; BIBLIOGRAPHIE, LES.** **VFOAT** Transport in Europe; Bibliography. Vol. 1 (March 1954)-. French (English). Europe Information Service, rue de Geneve 6, 1140 Brussels Belgium. **Tel** 011 32 2 242 6020, FAX 011 32 2 242 9549. **LC** Z7164.T8.

GW
**VERKEHRSWIRTSCHAFT, DIE.** **Main/Corp** Statistisches Landesamt Baden-Wurttemberg. (19??)-. German. Statistisches Landesamt Baden-Wuerttemberg, Postfach 10 60 33, 70049 Stuttgart Germany. **Tel** 011 49 771 6410, FAX 011 49 711 6412440. **LC** HA1320.B2; A32 subser; HE249.Z7B25. **Circ:** 400.

US/0886-5175
**WARD'S AUTOMOTIVE REPORTS.** [Ward's automot. rep.]. **VFOAT** Automotive Reports. (19??)-. Periodical. English. wk. $1,045.00. Ward's Communications Inc., 3000 Town Center, Suite 2750, Southfield MI 48075. **Tel** (810)357-0800. **LC** HD9710.U5; W28. **DD** 338. Index available.
**Desc:** Industry's leading statistical newsletter, provides weekly industry production updates, sales and inventory statistics, and late-breaking news.
**Ind/Abst** F&S Index Plus Text, Int. [Select. Cov.]; PROMT; Trade Ind. Index.

UK
**WORLD SHIPPING STATISTICS.** **Added/Corp** H.P. Drewry (Shipping Consultants) Limited. Research Division. (1975)-. Statistical Publication. English. an. $220.00. Fairway Publications Ltd., 20 Ullswater Crescent, Ullswater Business Park, Coulsdon Surrey CR5 2HR England. **LC** HE563.A3; W67. **DD** 387.5/44/0212.

## AUTOMOBILES

●US/1073-4740
**5.0 MUSTANG.** **VFOAT** Five Point Zero Mustang. (1994)-. Periodical. English. bm (6 issues). $13.95 US; $24.56 Canada; $23.95 other. Petersen Publishing Company, 6420 Wilshire Boulevard, Los Angeles CA 90048. **Tel** (213)782-2485. **(Subscription address:** Neodata / Colorado, PO Box 2606, Boulder Boulder CO 80322.**)**

●US/1068-1256
**1949-50-51 FORD/MERCURY OWNERS MAGAZINE.** [1949-50-51 Ford/Mercury own. mag.]. **VFOAT** 1949, 50, 51 Ford Mercury Owners Magazine; Nineteen Forty-Nine, Fifty, Fifty-One Ford/Mercury Owners Magazine; 49-50-51 Ford/Mercury Owners Magazine; Ford/Mercury Owners Magazine. No. 97 (Jan. 1993)-. Periodical. English. mo. Shoebox Ford Enterprises, PO Box 30647, Midwest City OK 73140-3647. **DD** 629. **Continues** 49-50-51 Ford Owners Newsletter, 0890-4146.

UK
**AA CAMPING AND CARAVANNING IN BRITAIN.** See Recreation, Leisure-Outdoor Life.

ZA
**AA HANDBOOK.** **Main/Corp** Automobile Association of Zambia. (19??)-. English. Associated Reviews Ltd, Lufunsa Avenue, Box 717, Ndola Zambia. **LC** TL119.Z34; A85a. **DD** 916.89/4/044.

US/0744-6535
**AAA TRAVELER. MUSKINGUM AAA EDITION, THE.** (THE AAA TRAVELER.). **VFOAT** A.A.A. Traveler. **VAT** American Automobile Association Traveler. Muskingum AAA Edition. Periodical. English. bm. $1.00. Ohio Automobile Club, 1120 Maple Avenue, Zanesville OH 43701. **Continues** Motor Travel, 0279-5779.

US/1063-3863
**AAA WORLD (ALASKA, HAWAII ED.).** See Travel and Tourism.

US/0731-8723
**AAA WORLD. HAWAII.** Title Change. See Travel and Tourism.

US/0743-0736
**AAA WORLD (LOUISIANA ED.).** Title Change. See Travel and Tourism.

US/1063-3871
**AAA WORLD (LOUISIANA, MISSISSIPPI ED.).** See Travel and Tourism.

US/0277-1039
**AAA WORLD. MASSACHUSETTS.** Title Change. See Travel and Tourism.

US/1063-388X
**AAA WORLD (MASSACHUSETTS, NEW HAMPSHIRE ED.).** See Travel and Tourism.

US/0743-0663
**AAA WORLD (MISSISSIPPI EDITION).** Title Change. See Travel and Tourism.

US/0277-1012
**AAA WORLD. NEW HAMPSHIRE.** Title Change. See Travel and Tourism.

US/0279-0270
**AAA WORLD. POTOMAC.** See Travel and Tourism.

US/1063-3898
**AAA WORLD (TEXAS, NEW MEXICO, OKLAHOMA ED.).** See Travel and Tourism.

US/1058-5052
**AAA WORLD (VIRGINIA ED.).** See Travel and Tourism.

US/0277-1411
**AAA WORLD. WISCONSIN.** See Travel and Tourism.

US/0001-0154
**AAMVA BULLETIN / AMERICAN ASSOCIATION OF MOTOR VEHICLE ADMINISTRATORS.** See Transportation.

SZ/0272-5088
**ACCELERATORS AND STORAGE RINGS.** [Accel. storage rings]. Vol. 1 (1978)-. Academic Scholarly Publication. English. ir. Price varies per volume. Harwood Academic Publishers, PO Box 90, Reading RG1 8JL England. **Tel** 011 44 734 560080. **ED** J. P. Blewett and F. T. Cole. **DD** 539. **CODEN** ASRGDU. Documents available from CASDDS. **Ind/Abst** Chem. Abstr.

US/1057-8153
**ACCIDENT RECONSTRUCTION JOURNAL.** [Accid. reconstr. j.]. **Added/Corp** National Association of Professional Accident Reconstruction Specialists. (Jan./Feb. 1989)-. Periodical. English. bm. $39.00 (1 year) $66.00 (2 year), $89.00 (3 year) US; $43.00 (1 year), $72.00 (2 year), $101.00 (3 year) other. Accident Reconstruction Journal, P.O.Box 234, Waldorf MD 20604. **Tel** (301)843-1371, **FAX** (301)884-5066. **DD** 363.

FR/0001-7418
**ACTION AUTOMOBILE ET TOURISTIQUE, L'.** [Action automob. tour.]. (1945)-. Periodical. French. Eleven times a year. 203.72F France; 268.00F other. Excelsior Publications, 1 rue du Colonel Pierre Avia, 75503 Paris Cedex 15 France. **Tel** 011 33 1 46484848, **FAX** 011 33 1 46484793. **UDC** 796.7. **Continues** L'Action Automobile, 0758-3168.

US/0044-6092
**ACTION ERA VEHICLE, THE.** [Action era veh.]. **VFOAT** AEV. Periodical. English. bm. Contemporary Historical Vehicle Association, PO Box 4416, Redding CA 96099. **DD** 629.

US/0898-2538
**ACTIONLINE (SOUTHFIELD, MICH.).** (ACTIONLINE.). [Actionline]. **Added/Corp** Automotive Industry Action Group. **VFOAT** Action Line. (1988)-. Periodical. English. Twelve times a year. Free to (members); $80.00 (non-members). Automotive Industry Action Group, 26200 Lahser Road, Suite 200, Southfield MI 48034. **Tel** (313)358-3570. **DD** 629.

US/0899-9171
**AFAS QUARTERLY OF THE AUTOMOTIVE FINE ARTS SOCIETY.** [AFAS q. Automot. Fine Arts Soc.]. **Added/Corp** Automotive Fine Arts Society. **VFOAT** AFAS Quarterly. **VAT** Automotive Fine Arts Society Quarterly. Vol. 1, No. 1 (Winter 1988)-. Periodical. English. Four times a year (Jan., Apr., July, Oct.). $16.00. GP Publishing, 4140 South Lapeer Road, Orion MI 48359. **Tel** (313)373-2500, **FAX** (313)373-0565. **ED** Michael Sheridan. **LC** WMLC 93/357. **DD** 629. **Bk Rev**. **Ad Acc**. **Pr Rev**. **Circ:** 5,000. **Desc:** Devoted to automotive fine art and automotive art collecting. Includes coverage of events, auctions, collectors and artists.

US/0162-6604
**AFTERMARKET EXECUTIVE.** V. 1- Oct. 1978-. Periodical. English. bm. $25.00. Automotive Parts and Accessories Association, 1025 Connecticut Avenue NW, Washington DC 20036. **LC** HD9710.3.A1; A34. **DD** 658.89/6292/0973.

AT/0044-5681
**AIM. AUTOMOTIVE INDUSTRY MATTERS.** [AIM, Automot. ind. matters]. **VFOAT** Automotive Industry Matters. (1967)-. Periodical. English. Twenty-three times a year. 343.00Aus$ Australia; 493.00Aus$ others. Automotive Industry Matters Ltd., PO Box 184, Albert Park 3206 Australia. **Tel** 011 61 59 898440, **FAX** 011 61 59 898686. **ED** Trevor Dawson-Grove. **DD** 338.476292. **Ad Acc**.

US
**AIR COOLED NEWS.** **Added/Corp** H. H. Franklin Club. (1953)-. Periodical. English. Three times a year. H H Franklin Club, PO Box 535, Cumberland MD 21502. **LC** TL215.F85; A7.

US/0160-3019
**AIRSTREAM SERVICE MANUAL.** **Main/Corp** Airstream, Inc. English. Airstream Inc, Jackson Center OH 45334. **LC** TL297; .A37A. **DD** 629.28/7/6.

US/0090-8614
**ALA SIGHTS TO SEE BOOK.** **Main/Corp** Automobile Legal Association. 1973-. English. an. ALA Auto and Travel Club, National Headquarters, 888 Worcester Street, Wellesley MA 02181. **Tel** (617)237-5200. **LC** E158; .A9A. **DD** 917.3/04/9205. **Continues** A.L.A. Green Book.

●US/1061-8295
**ALABAMA AUTOMOTIVE REPORT.** (1992)-. Periodical. English. mo. Free (qualified subscribers). Autographic Publishing Company, 5751 Old Hickory Blvd., #205, Hermitage TN 37076-2929.

US/0364-930X
**ALFA OWNER.** [Alfa own.]. Periodical. English. mo. Alfa Romeo Owners, 2468 Gumtree Lane, Fallbrook CA 92028-2530. **Tel** (714)259-8240. **ED** Julie Nichols. **LC** TL215.A35; A42. **DD** 629.22/22. **Bk Rev**. **Ad Acc**. **Circ:** 5,800.

US/1058-9082
**ALIGNMENT TECH/TALK.** **VFOAT** Alignment Tech Talk. (1990)-. Periodical. English. Twelve times a year. $69.00 US; $80.00 other. M D Publications Inc, PO Box 2210, Springfield MO 65801. **Tel** (800)274-7890, (417)866-3917, **FAX** (417)866-2781. **ED** Ron Henningsen. **DD** 629. **Circ:** 1,000. **Desc:** Technical newsletter detailing repair procedures of auto steering components and alignment techniques.

US/0898-8986
**ALL CHEVY.** **VFOAT** All Chevrolet. (1987)-. Periodical. English. Twelve times a year. $15.98 (one year), $29.98 (two years). McMullen Publishing Inc, 2145 West La Palma Avenue, PO Box 70015, Anaheim CA 92801-1785. **Tel** (714)572-2255, **FAX** (714)572-1864. **DD** 629. **Continues** Popular Cars; Super Street Machines.

CN/0821-7505
**ALMANACH DE L'AUTO (MONTREAL).** (ALMANACH DE L'AUTO.). [Alm. Auto]. (1982)-. French. an. 11.95Can$. Quebecor Inc, 7 Bates Rd. Outremont, PQ H2V 1A6 Canada. **Tel** (514)270-1100, **FAX** (514)276-5120. **DD** 629.2/222/05.

US/0095-1811
**AMERICAN CLEAN CAR.** See Business.

US/1055-9833
**AMERICAN DREAM CARS, 1946-1972.** Ceased. [Am. dream cars, 1946-1972]. **Added/Corp** Edmund Publications Corporation. (1991)-(19??). English. Edmund Publications Corporation / Massachusetts, 1740 Massachusetts Avenue, Boxborough MA 01719. **LC** TL162; .A46. **DD** 629.222/075.

US/1041-3138
**AMERICAN RODDER.** [Am. rodder]. **VFOAT** American Rodder Magazine. (1987)-. Periodical. English. mo. $30.00. Paisano Publications, 28210 Dorothy Drive, Agoura Hills CA 91301-2693. **Tel** (818)889-8740, **FAX** (818)889-4726. **DD** 796. **Desc:** Geared to hot rod and custom-car enthusiasts. Written for the person highly involved in the hobby of modifying classic cars.

US/0274-8215
**AMERICAN TOWMAN, THE.** Periodical. English. Eleven times a year (11 issues). $40.00 (one year); $75.00 (two year). American Towman Publishing Company, 629 Amboy Avenue, 3rd Floor, Edison NJ 08837. **Tel** (908)738-5900.

US
**AMERICAN TRUCKING TRENDS.** **Added/Corp** American Trucking Associations. Dept. of Research and Transport Economics. American Trucking Associations. Public Relations Dept. (1957)-. English. an. $20.00. American Trucking Associations, 2200 Mill Road, Alexandria VA 22314. **Tel** (703)838-1772. **Continues** Trends Showing the Year-To-Year Changes in the Pattern of Many Phases of Motor Truck Operation. **Ind/Abst** Predicasts Forecasts.

AT/1032-6499
**AMERICAR AUSTRALIA.** [Americar Aust.]. (1989)-. Periodical. English. qt. 21.00Aus$ Australia; 30.00Aus$ New Zealand; 33.00Aus$ other. Eddie Ford Publications, Private Bag, Newstead Victoria 3462 Australia. **Tel** (054)762212, **FAX** (054)762592. **ED** Eddie Ford. **DD** 629.222205. **Ad Acc**. **Desc:** Caters for the American car enthusiast in Australia and includes technical articles on converting American cars to RHD, importing cars to Australia and full color features.

US/0148-6861
**ANNUAL NATIONAL VEHICLE POPULATION PROFILE : IMPORT CARS.** [Annu. natl. veh. popul. profile import cars]. **Main/Corp** R.L. Polk & Co. English. an. R. L. Polk & Company, 1155 Brewery Park Boulevard, Detroit MI 48207. **Tel** (313)393-0880. **LC** HE5623.A1; P64A. **DD** 388.34/0973.

US/0148-6276
**ANNUAL NATIONAL VEHICLE POPULATION PROFILE : LIGHT TRUCKS.** **Main/Corp** R.L. Polk & Co. English. an. R. L. Polk & Company, 1155 Brewery Park Boulevard, Detroit MI 48207. **Tel** (313)393-0880. **LC** HE5623.A1; P64B. **DD** 629.22.

US/0196-6723
**ANNUAL REPORT - STATE OF NEW YORK, DEPARTMENT OF MOTOR VEHICLES.** **Main/Corp** New York (State). Dept. of Motor Vehicles. 1st- 1961-. English. an. New York State Department of Motor Vehicles, Albany NY 12228. **Tel** (518)473-8603. **LC** HE5633.N7; A255. **DD** 388.3/09747. **Continues** New York (State). Bureau of Motor Vehicles. Annual Report.

US
**ANNUAL REPORT / STATE OF OHIO, STATE PARKING COMMISSION.** **Main/Corp** Ohio. State Parking Commission. (1988)-. English. 60 East State Street, Columbus OH 43215. **LC** HE5633.O3; A24. **DD** 353.97710087/8474/06. **Continues** Annual Report -State of Ohio, the State Underground Parking Commission, 0145-7764.

SW
**ANNUAL REPORT - VOLVO. Main/Corp** Volvo, Aktiebolaget. English. AB Volvo, S-405 08 Gotenburg Sweden. **LC** HD9710.S84; V643A. **DD** 338.7/62/9209485. ***Continues*** *Annual Report for ... / Volvo Aktiebolaget.*

US/0747-9786
**ANTIQUE & CLASSIC CARS, TRUCKS, MOTORCYCLES. VFOAT** Antique and Classic Cars, Trucks, Motorcycles; Cars, Trucks and Motorcycles; Cars, Trucks & Motorcycles. 1st Ed.-. English. an. $3.50. Random House Inc., 400 Hahn Road, Westminster MD 21157. **Tel** (800)726-0600, (800)733-3000, FAX (800)659-2436. **LC** TL7.A1; A57. **DD** 629.2/2/075.

US/0003-5831
**ANTIQUE AUTOMOBILE, THE.** 1937. Periodical. English. bm. Comes with membership. Antique Auto Club of America, PO Box 417, 501 West Governor Road, Hershey PA 17033. **Tel** (717)534-1910. **ED** William H. Smith. **LC** TL1; .A472. **DD** 629.2/222/075. Index available. **Bk Rev. Ad Acc. Circ:** 40,000 (ctrl). available on microfilm and microfiche from University Microfilms International (UMI). ***Continues*** *Bulletin of the Antique Automobile Club of America.*
**Desc:** Contains historical articles, tour accounts, technical and restoration articles, and advertisements of cars, parts and literature for sale or wanted.

US/0164-7237
**ANTIQUE CAR TIMES. See** Antiques.

BL
**ANUARIO DA INDUSTRIA BRASILEIRA DE AUTOPECAS. VFOAT** Yearbook of the Brazilian Industry of Automotive Parts. 1976/77-. Portuguese (English). G & C Gomes, Av Paulista 807 9 Andar Conj 911, 01311 Sao Paulo Brazil. **LC** HD9710.3.B7; A58. **DD** 338.4/7/62920981.

FR
**ARGUS DE L'AUTOMOBILE & DES LOCOMOTIONS, L'.** French. Argus de l Automobile, 1 Place Boieldieu, 75002 Paris France.

●US
**ASIA/PACIFIC AUTOMOTIVE BULLETIN.** (1994)-. Bulletin. English. Twelve times a year. $645.00. Forecast International / DMS Inc., 22 Commerce Road, Newtown CT 06470. **Tel** (203)426-0800, FAX (203)426-1964, telex 467615.

JA
**ASIAN AUTOTECH REPORT.** (19??)-. English. sm. $978.00 US and Europe. AI Publishing Co. Ltd., 3-4-2-202 Akatsutsumi, Setagayaku Tokyo 156 Japan. **Tel** 011 81 3 3325 4660. ***Continues*** *Japan Autotech Report.*

US
**ASIAN COLLISION ESTIMATING GUIDE.** (19??)-. Periodical. English. bm. $132.00. Mitchell International Inc, PO Box 26260, San Diego CA 92126-0260. **Tel** (619)578-6550, (800)648-8010, FAX (619)578-4752. **(Subscription address:** Mitchell International Inc., PO Box 71654, Chicago IL 60694.**)**

IT
**ATA INGEGNERIA AUTOMOTORISTICA. Added/Corp** Associazione Tecnica dell'Automobile. **VFOAT** ATA; Ingegneria Automotoristica. (19??)-. Periodical. Italian. Eight times a year. $82.00. Associazione Technica Automob, Strada Torino 32, 10043 Orbassano to Italy. **Tel** 011 39 11 9032364. **LC** TL4; .A116. **DD** 629.2/05. ***Continues*** *ATA.*
**Ind/Abst** Fluid Abstr., Civil Eng.; Fluid Abstr. Proc. Eng.; FLUIDEX (19??-).

●US/1066-6494
**ATD, N.A.D.A. OFFICIAL HEAVY DUTY TRUCK GUIDE.** [ATD N.A.D.A. offic. heavy duty truck guide]. **Added/Corp** American Truck Dealers (Association) National Automobile Dealers Association. **VFOAT** N.A.D.A. Official Heavy Duty Truck Guide; Official Heavy Duty Truck Guide; N.A.D.A. Heavy Duty Truck Guide; ATD/N.A.D.A. Official Heavy Duty Truck Guide. (1993)-. Periodical. English. bm (6 issues). $90.00. National Automobile Dealers Association, 8400 West Park Drive, McLean VA 22102. **Tel** (703)749-4700, (800)544-6232, FAX (703)821-7269. **DD** 629.

GW/0001-2785
**ATZ. AUTOMOBILTECHNISCHE ZEITSCHRIFT.** (AUTOMOBILTECHNISCHE ZEITSCHRIFT.). [ATZ, Automobiltech. Z.]. **Added/Corp** Automobil- und Flugtechnische Gesellschaft. **VFOAT** ATZ. (1929)-. German. mo. DM289.45 Germany; DM296.95 other. Franckhsche Verlagshandlung Kosmos Verlag, Postfach 106011, D-70049 Stuttgart Germany. **Tel** 011 49 711 2191332. **ED** Karl-Ernst Hailer. **CODEN** AUTZA6. **[CCC].** Index available. **Bk Rev. Ad Acc. Circ:** 3,900 (ctrl). ***Formed by the union of*** *Motorwagen, 0369-1330* ***and*** *Auto-Technik, 0365-8090.*
**Desc:** A technical journal for engineers, constructors and the management of the automobile industry.
**Ind/Abst** Bioeng. Abstr.; Ei Page One; EMBASE; Energy Res. Abstr. (March 1976-); Fluid Abstr., Civil Eng.; Fluid Abstr. Proc. Eng.; FLUIDEX (1973-); Saf. Health Work; Shock Vibr. Dig.; Stat. Theory Method Abstr. (1972).

AT
**AUSTRALASIAN BUS AND COACH. See** Transportation.

AT
**AUSTRALIAN DESIGN RULES.** English. ir. 95.00Aus$ (new), 35.00Aus$ (renewal). Department of Transport and Communications, GPO Box 594, Canberra Australian Capital Territory 2601 Australia. **Tel** (062)687111, FAX (062)572505, telex 62018.

AT/1036-3254
**AUSTRALIAN ROAD AND TRACK.** (1990)-. Periodical. English. Twelve times a year. 70.00Aus$ Australia; 130.00Aus$ Asia and Oceania; 190.00Aus$ other. Stop Press Publishing Pty Ltd, PO Box 666, Balgowlah New South Wales, 2093 Australia. **Tel** 011 61 2 9070133, FAX 011 61 2 9070195. **ED** Robin William Luck (editor's address: 51 Jackson Street, Balgowlah NSW 2093 Australia). **Bk Rev**, (Qty: varies). **Ad Acc, Adv Mgr:** D. McLeod, **Tel** same as publisher. **Circ:** 20,000 (ctrl). ***Continues*** *Chequered Flag.*

IT
**AUTO.** (19??)-. Italian. mo. L68000 Italy; L120000 other. Conti Editore, Via del Lavoro 7, 40068 S Lazzaro Savena Italy. **Tel** 011 39 51 6227111, FAX 011 39 51 6258112, telex 510283.

US/0885-8292
**AUTO ADVERTISING REPORT. See** Business-Advertising and Public Relations.

●US/1070-8294
**AUTO AGE DEALER BUSINESS.** [Auto age deal. bus.]. **VFOAT** Dealer Business. Vol. 27, No. 1 (Sept. 1992)-. Periodical. English. mo. $36.00 (one year), $65.00 (two year) US; $55.00 (one year), $95.00 (two year) Canada; $80.00 (one year), $145.00 (two year) other. MacLean Hunter Publishing Corporation / Chicago, IL, 29 North Wacker Drive, Chicago IL 60606-3298. **Tel** (312)726-2802, FAX (312)726-3091. **DD** 381. ***Continues*** *Auto Age (Van Nuys, Calif.), 0894-1270.*

US/0894-1270
**AUTO AGE (VAN NUYS, CALIF.).** ***Title Change.*** (AUTO AGE.). [Auto age]. Vol. 20 No. 12 (July 1986)-Vol. 26 No. 12 (Aug. 1992). Periodical. English. mo. MacLean Hunter Publishing Corporation / Chicago, IL, 29 North Wacker Drive, Chicago IL 60606-3298. **Tel** (312)726-2802, FAX (312)726-3091. **DD** 381. available on microfilm and microfiche from University Microfilms International (UMI); available on an online database (file 648/Full-Text) from DIALOG. ***Continues*** *Automotive Age, 0005-1470.* ***Continued by*** *Auto Age Dealer Business, 1070-8294.*
**Ind/Abst** Trade Ind. ASAP [Full Txt.]; Trade Ind. Index [Full Txt.].

IT/0393-8387
**AUTO AND DESIGN.** (1979)-. Periodical. English (Italian). bm. $127.00. Auto & Design Srl, Corso Francia 161, 10139 Turin Italy. **Tel** 011 39 11 758810.

IT
**AUTO & SPORT.** (19??)-. Italian. mo. L80000 Italy; L130000 other. Cazzola Alfredo Editore, Via C Colombo 21, 40131 Bologna Italy. **Tel** 011 39 51 325991. ***Continues*** *Rombo.*

US/1065-6685
**AUTO & TRUCK INTERNATIONAL.** [Auto truck int.]. **VFOAT** Auto and Truck International. (19??)-. Periodical. English. Six times a year. $50.00. Hunter Publishing Company Inc., 25 Northwest Point Boulevard, Suite 800, Elk Grove Village IL 60007-1036. **Tel** (708)427-9512, FAX (708)427-2097. **DD** 629. ***Continues*** *Automobile International, 0099-2615.*

US/1065-6693
**AUTO & TRUCK INTERNATIONAL EN ESPANOL.** [Auto truck int. esp.]. **VFOAT** Auto and Truck International en Espanol. (19??)-. Periodical. Spanish. Six times a year. $50.00. Hunter Publishing Company Inc., 25 Northwest Point Boulevard, Suite 800, Elk Grove Village IL 60007-1036. **Tel** (708)427-9512, FAX (708)427-2097. **DD** 629. ***Continues*** *Automovil Internacional, 0193-0907.*

GW
**AUTO BILD.** (19??)-. German. wk (52 issues). DM120.00 (latest issue). Axel Springer Verlag Ag, Brieffach 2460, D 20350 Hamburg Germany. **Tel** 011 49 40 34724503. **(Subscription address:** DBS ABO Betreuung GmbH, D 74168 Neckarsulm Germany; telephone: 011 49 7132 9590**)**

US/0746-8504
**AUTO CLUB NEWS (LOS, ANGELES CALIF.).** (AUTO CLUB NEWS.). **Added/Corp** Automobile Club of Southern California. (19??)-. Periodical. English. Six times a year. $1.00. Automobile Club of Southern California, 2601 South Figueroa Street, Los Angeles CA 90007. **Tel** (310)741-4410. ***Continues*** *Auto Club News Pictorial, 0005-0725.*

NE
**AUTO EN MOTORTECHNIEK.** Misset Uitgeverij BV, Postbus 9000, 6800 DA Arnhem Netherlands. **Tel** 011 31 85 209911.

SZ
**AUTO EXKLUSIV.** Periodical. German. mo. 68.00. Tobinium-Verlag, Henzmannstr 27, 4800 Zofingen Switzerland. **LC** TL3; .A734. **DD** 629.222/05.

FR/0150-7230
**AUTO EXPERTISE.** [Auto expert.]. (1973)-. Periodical. French. bm. 744.37F France; 875.00F other. Editions Techniques pour l'Automobile et l'Industrie (ETAI), 94 96 rue de Paris, 92100 Boulogne Billancourt France. **Tel** 011 33 1 46992424. **UDC** 629.113 : 368.21. ***Continues*** *Assurances & Techniques de l'Expertise Automobile, 0150-7370.*

SP
**AUTO HEBDO SPORT.** Spanish. wk. 9800ptas. Auto Hebdo Sport, Calle Alcala 248, 28027 Madrid Spain. **Tel** 011 34 1 4052314.

SZ
**AUTO INDEX.** French and German. mo. 261.00F. Hallwag AG, Nordring 4, CH-3001 Bern Switzerland. **Tel** 011 41 31 3323131, FAX 031/414133, telex 912661 HAWA CH.

US/0145-6776
**AUTO INDEX, THE.** (1974)-. English. Six times a year. $6.00. The Auto Index, 7 Clinton Place, Suffern NY 10901. **Tel** (914)357-3695. **ED** David F. Plump. ctrl circ.
**Desc:** Specialized index of automotive periodicals for consumers, do-it-yourselfers, and writers/researchers. 14 periodicals (Road and Track, Car and Driver, Hot Rod, Popular Mechanics, etc.) are covered.

NE
**AUTO-INDUSTRIE EN ASSEMBLAGEBEDRIJVEN, AUTO-ONDERDELENINDUSTRIE, VLIEGTUIGBOUW- EN VLIEGTUIGREPARATIEBEDRIJVEN / CENTRAAL BUREAU VOOR DE STATISTIEK, HOOFDAFDELING STATISTIEKEN VAN INDUSTRIE EN BOUWNIJVERHEID. VFOAT** Manufacture and Assembly of Motor Vehicles, Manufacture of Parts and Accessories for Motor Vehicles, Manufacture and Repair or Aircraft. 1981-. Dutch (summaries and/or abstracts in English). an. 10.55. Centraal Bureau voor de Statistiek, AFD ALG Zaken, Postbus 959, 2270 AZ Voorburg Netherlands. **Tel** 011 31 70 3373800, FAX 011 31 038 7429, telex 32692 CBS NL. **LC** HD9710.N4; N47B. ***Continues*** *Netherlands. Centraal Bureau voor de Statistiek. Auto-Industrie en Assemblagebedrijven, Auto-Onderdelenindustrie, Vliegtuigreparatiebedrijven Produktiestatistieken.*

AT
**AUTO INDUSTRY AUSTRALIA.** (199?)-. Periodical. English. Eleven times a year. 55.00Aus$ individuals; Free to Australia institutions, schools and colleges. Victoria Auto Chamber of Commerce, 464 St. Kilda Road / 7th Floor, Melbourne VIC 3004 Australia. **Tel** 11 61 3 8291111, FAX 11 61 3 8203401. **ED** Brian Adams (editor's phone: 011 61 3 8291159). **Bk Rev**, (Qty: 15-20 per year). **Ad Acc, Adv Mgr:** Bette Billett, **Tel** 011 61 3 8291156. **Circ:** 5,500. ***Continues*** *Motor Industry Journal, 0729-0799.*

US/0746-3774
**AUTO INDUSTRY MAGAZINE.** Vol. 1, No. 1 (July 1983)-. Periodical. English. mo. $12.00. Target Publishing Inc / New Jersey, Rd 1 Box 470, Newton NJ 07860.

FR/0005-0768
**AUTO-JOURNAL (PARIS), L'.** (L'AUTO-JOURNAL.). [Auto-j. (Paris)]. (Jan. 15, 1950)-. French. Twenty-three times a year. 341.82F France; 480.00F other. Soc Presse Auto Journal, 8 10 rue Pierre Brossolette, 92300 Lavallois Perret France. **Tel** 011 33 1 40874181. **LC** TL2; .A79. **DD** 629.22/22/05. **Ad Acc.** ctrl circ.

GW
**AUTO KATALOG.** (19??)-. German. an (1 issue). Vereinigte Motor Verlag GmbH, Motor Presse, POB 106036, D 70049 Stuttgart Germany. **Tel** 011 49 711 1821506, 011 49 711 1821545. **(Subscription address:** Deutscher Pressevertrieb Buch., POB 101602, Hansa GmbH D-20010 Hamburg Germany; telephone: 011 49 40 237110**)**

US/0005-0776
**AUTO LAUNDRY NEWS.** [Auto laund. news]. (19??)-. Periodical. English. Twelve times a year. $25.00 US; $60.00 other. Columbia Communications Inc., 370 Lexington Avenue, New York NY 10017. **Tel** (212)532-9290. **ED** Ralph Monti. **LC** HD9999.C27; A98. **DD** 338. **Bk Rev. Ad Acc. Circ:** 15,000 (ctrl). ***Continues*** *ALN; Auto Laundry News.*
**Desc:** Contains articles on developments and improvements in carwash operations, equipment and

# Transportation —Automobiles

supplies; solutions to operating problems; case history reports on successful carwash facilities; trends in costs, energy requirements, water treatment and reclamation; technical articles; progress reports on the industry; new products and literature; editorial and general news.

HK
**AUTO MAGAZINE.** Chinese. mo. $42.00. Sisters Press Ltd, Room 903 8 9F, Kodak House II, 321 Java Road, North Point Hong Kong. **Tel** 011 852 5908738.

AT/1035-1051
**AUTO MARKET REPORT.** (1990)-. Periodical. English. Twelve times a year. 254.00Aus$. Autospec Pty. Ltd., PO Box 143, Caulfield East Victoria 3145 Australia. **Tel** 011 61 3 5721858, FAX 011 61 3 5717427. **ED** Richard Reid. Index available. cum. index. ctrl circ. available on an online database from the publisher. Documents available from the publisher.

US/0192-186X
**AUTO MERCHANDISING NEWS.** See Business.

CN/0822-1006
**AUTO MODIFIEE, L'.** See Recreation, Leisure-Sports.

GW/0005-0806
**AUTO, MOTOR UND SPORT.** **VFOAT** Auto + Motor und Sport; Auto und Motor und Sport; Auto + Motor und Sport. (Stuttgarter Ausg.). (1951)-. Periodical. German. bw. $140.00. Vereinigte Motor Verlag GmbH, Motor Presse, POB 106036, D 70049 Stuttgart Germany. **Tel** 011 49 711 1821506, 011 49 711 1821545. **UDC** 629.113. **CODEN** 796.7.

FR/0992-8154
**AUTO PLUS PARIS.** (AUTO PLUS). (1988)-. Periodical. French. wk (Published every Tuesday). 317.34F France; 540.00F other. Editions Mondiales, 9 11 13 Rue du Col Pierre Avia, 75754 Paris Cedex 15 France. **Tel** 011 33 1 46622162. **(Subscription address:** Auto Plus, BP 52 F-77932 Perthes France (telephone 011 33 64 380103)**)** UDC 629.11.

CN/0825-4990
**AUTO PREVENTION.** (AUTO PREVENTION : BULLETIN D'INFORMATION DE L'ASSOCIATION SECTORIELLE, SERVICES AUTOMOBILES.). [Auto prev.]. **VFOAT** Bulletin d'Information de l'Association Sectorielle, Services Automobiles. V. 1, No. 1 (Mar./Apr. 1984)-. Bulletin. English. bm. Free. Association Sectorielle, Services Automobiles, Bureau 340, 1425, Rue De La Montagne, Montreal Quebec H3G 1Z3. **DD** 363.1/19338476292222/09714.

US/1042-6205
**AUTO PRICES ALMANAC.** [Auto prices alm.]. **VFOAT** Auto Price Almanac; Autoprice Almanac. (1987)-. English. Seven times a year. $26.95 US; $44.95 Canada & Mexico; $56.95 Europe & Western Hemisphere; $66.95 Africa & Asia & Pacific Rim. Pace Publications Inc., 1020 North Broadway, Suite 111, Milwaukee WI 53202. **Tel** (414)272-9977, FAX (414)297-9973. **LC** HD9710.U5; A77. **DD** 629.222/129/473.

CN/0821-7343
**AUTO-QUEBEC.** (AUTO-QUEBEC : REVUE OFFICIELLE DE LA FEDERATION AUTO-QUEBEC.). [Auto-Que.]. Periodical. French. bm. Federation Auto-Quebec, 1415 Est rue Jarry, Montreal Quebec H2E 2Z7 Canada. **DD** 796.7/2/09714.

US/0090-8029
**AUTO RACING DIGEST.** See Recreation, Leisure-Sports.

US/0743-7129
**AUTO RACING MEMORIES & MEMORABILIA.** See Recreation, Leisure-Sports.

US/8756-9353
**AUTO RACING/USA (DALLAS, TEX.).** See Recreation, Leisure-Sports.

US/0164-369X
**AUTO RACING USA (FRANKLIN LAKES, N.J.).** See Recreation, Leisure-Sports.

LU
**AUTO REVUE LUXEMBOURG.** German. mo. 985.00F. Auto Revue Merfra, 78 Grand rue, Luxembourg L-1660 Luxembourg.

US/1053-4318
**AUTO SERVICE INSIDER.** [Auto serv. insid.]. Periodical. English. bw. $195.00. ATCOM Inc., 2315 Broadway, New York NY 10024-4397. **Tel** (800)521-7004, (212)873-5900, FAX (212)799-1728. **DD** 629. **Continues** Auto Service Today, 1042-7414.

US/1065-0792
**AUTO SOUND & SECURITY.** [Auto sound secur.]. **VFOAT** Auto Sound and Security. Vol. 1, No. 1 (Nov. 1990)-. Periodical. English. Twelve times a year. $19.95 (one year), $29.95 (two years). McMullen

Publishing Inc, 2145 West La Palma Avenue, PO Box 70015, Anaheim CA 92801-1785. **Tel** (714)572-2255, FAX (714)572-1864. **LC** WMLC 91/6429. **DD** 629.

JA
**AUTO SPORT.** Japanese. sm (24 issues). ¥44460.00. Nippon IPS Co. Ltd., 11 6 3 Chome Iidabashi, Chiyodaku Tokyo 102 Japan. **Tel** 011 81 3 3238 0700.

CN/0714-7104
**AUTO SPORT.** See Recreation, Leisure-Sports.

FR/0245-4548
**AUTO STEREO PARIS.** (1980)-. Periodical. French. Eleven times a year. 265.00F. Neomedia, 5 7 rue de l'Amiral Courbet, 94160 Saint Mande France. **Tel** 011 33 1 43982222. **UDC** 681.

US/1049-9601
**AUTO TRIM & RESTYLING NEWS.** [Auto trim restyling news]. **Added/Corp** National Association of Auto Trim Shops (U.S.). **VFOAT** Auto Trim and Restyling News; Auto Trim news. Vol. 38, Issue 1 (Jan. 1990)-. Periodical. English. mo. $30.00 US, $51.00 Canada and Mexico, $82.00 other. Shore Communications Inc., 6255 Barfield Road, Suite 200, Atlanta GA 30328. **Tel** (404)252-8831, ((800)241-9034, FAX (404)252-4436. **DD** 629. **Continues** Auto Trim News, 0005-0865.

FR/0222-3996
**AUTO VERTE PARIS. 1979.** (1979)-. Periodical. French. mo. 274.24F France; 330.00F other. Editions Lariviere Naryse Menn, 15 17 Quai de l Oise Sec. Abonn., 75166 Paris Cedex 19 France. **Tel** 011 33 1 40342207, FAX 33 1 40358441, telex 211678. **UDC** 796.71.

UK/0955-5889
**AUTOCAR & MOTOR.** **VFOAT** Autocar and Motor. Vol. 177, No. 10 (Sept. 7, 1988)-. Periodical. English. wk. £70.00 UK; £90.00 Europe and Ireland; £130.00 America, Africa, and India; £180.00 Australia, New Zealand, and Japan; £90.00 other. Haymarket Publishing Ltd, 12 14 Ansdell Street, London W8 5TR England. **Tel** 011 44 483 733800, FAX 011 44 483 776573. **(Subscription address:** Haymarket Publishing Ltd, PO Box 219, Subscriptions Department, Woking Surrey GU21 1ZW, United Kingdom.**)** LC TL1; .A52. **DD** 629.222. **Formed by the union of** Motor (Sutton, Surrey), 0143-6945 **and** Autocar, 0005-092X. **Ind/Abst** Curr. Technol. Index.

AG
**AUTOCLUB.** **VFOAT** Auto Club. No. 1- ; Oct. 1961- . Periodical. Spanish. bm. Auto Club, Avda Del Libertado 1850, Buenos Aires Argentina.

US/1047-2061
**AUTOGLASS (MCLEAN, VA.).** See Glass and Ceramics.

US/1047-5559
**AUTOINC.** [AutoInc.]. **Added/Corp** Automotive Service Association. **VFOAT** Auto Inc. Vol. 37, No. 10, Oct. (1989)-. Periodical. English. mo. $20.00 US; $45.00 Canada; $90.00 other (one year); $35.00 US; $75.00 Canada; $160.00 other. Independent Automotive Service Association, PO Box 929, Bedford TX 76021. **Tel** (817)283-6205. **DD** 629. **Continues** Automotive Independent, 0199-6908.

●US/1065-9137
**AUTOINTELLIGENCE. VOL. 1, SMALL CARS, SPORTY CARS, MID-SIZE SEDANS.** **VFOAT** Auto Intelligence; Small Cars, Sporty Cars, Mid-Size Sedans. (1993)-. English. $12.00. Random House Inc., 400 Hahn Road, Westminster MD 21157. **Tel** (800)726-0600, (800)733-3000, FAX (800)659-2436.

●US/1065-9145
**AUTOINTELLIGENCE. VOL. 2, LARGE, LUXURY & HIGH PERFORMANCE CARS, SPORT UTILITY VEHICLES, STATION WAGONS & COMPACT VANS.** **VFOAT** Auto Intelligence; Large, Luxury & High Performance Cars, Sport Utility Vehicles, Station Wagons & Compact Vans; Large, Luxury and High Performance Cars, Sport Utility Vehicles, Station Wagons & Compact Vans. (1993)-. English. $12.00. Random House Inc., 400 Hahn Road, Westminster MD 21157. **Tel** (800)726-0600, (800)733-3000, FAX (800)659-2436.

HU/0587-2243
**AUTOKOZLEKEDES (BUDAPEST. 1964).** (AUTOKOZLEKEDES.). (1964)-. Periodical. Hungarian. mo. 60.00. Lapkiado Vallalat, Lenin Korut 9-11, 1073 Budapest 7, Hungary. **Tel** 222-408. **LC** HE5601; .A86.

GW/0005-1306
**AUTOMOBIL-INDUSTRIE.** Vol. 1 (1956)-. Periodical. English. bm. DM165.00 Germany; DM175.00 other. Vogel Verlag, Postfach 6740, D-97064 Wuerzburg Germany. **Tel** 011 49 931 4182145, 011 49 931 4182483, FAX 011 49 931 4182670, telex 641 680131. **ED** Ing Rolf Gnadler. **[CCC]**. Index available. **Bk Rev**. **Ad Acc**. **Circ**: 4,000 (ctrl). **Desc**: Articles of high technical standard focus on

fundamental problems in research and development, design and production, as they arise in the production of motor vehicles.

SA/0304-8721
**AUTOMOBIL (JOHANNESBURG).** (AUTOMOBIL). V. 55, No. 4- Apr. 1975-. Periodical. Afrikaans (English). Mead and McGrouther, PO Box 741, Johannesburg South Africa. **LC** HD9710.S7; S682. **DD** 338.4/7/6292220968. **Continues** Automobile in Southern Africa.

GW/0934-0394
**AUTOMOBIL-PRODUKTION.** [Automob.-Prod.]. (1986)-. Periodical. German. bm. DM168.00 Germany; DM171.00 other. Verlag Moderne Industrie, Justus von Liebigstrasse 1, D 86899 Landsberg Lech Germany. **Tel** 011 49 8191 125453. **UDC** 629.

FR
**AUTOMOBILE, L'.** No. 1 (Sept. 1946)-. Periodical. French. Fifteen times a year. 352.60F France; 511.00F other. Soc Edns Tech & Tour de France, 60 62 rue Danjou, 92100 Boulogne, Cedex France. **Tel** 011 33 1 46099596. **(Subscription address:** Automobile Magazine Service, Abonnements B 340, 60732 St. Genevieve Cedex France; Phone: 011 33 44 034499)**)** LC TL2; .A814. **Bk Rev**

UK/0309-0817
**AUTOMOBILE ABSTRACTS (NUNEATON. 1975).** (MIRA AUTOMOBILE ABSTRACTS.). [Automob. abstr.]. **Added/Corp** Motor Industry Research Association. **VFOAT** M.I.R.A. Automobile Abstracts; Automobile Abstracts. (1975)-. Periodical. English. mo. £225.00 (air mail), £220.00 (surface mail). Motor Industry Research Association, Watling Street, Nuneaton Warwickshire CV10 0TU England. **Tel** 011 44 203 348541, FAX 011 44 203 343772, telex 311277. **LC** TL1; .M92452. **DD** 629.2/05. Index available. **Bk Rev**. **Ad Acc**. **Circ**: 600. **Continues** MIRA Abstracts.
**Desc**: References to world literature on automotive research.
**Ind/Abst** BMT Abstr. (1973-); Fluid Abstr., Civil Eng.; Fluid Abstr. Proc. Eng.; FLUIDEX (1973-1990)(1973-).

US/0067-2513
**AUTOMOBILE ALMANAC.** (1967)-. English. an. $6.95. Automobile Almanac, Box 160, Orangeburg NY 10962. **Tel** (914)353-1500. **ED** Ray Fluddy. Index available. cum. index. **Bk Rev**. **Ad Acc**. **Circ**: 200,000.
**Desc**: A comprehensive automotive reference. Over 300 fact filled pages covering all officially sanctioned motorsport competition past and present plus major new car reviews and extensive significant historical data. Complete with illustrative photographs and diagrams.

II
**AUTOMOBILE BUYERS' GUIDE.** 1968-. Consumer Publication. English. Mel Martin Enterprises, PO Box 22505, Houston TX 77027. **LC** TL12. **DD** 338.4/7/629202554.

UK/0955-1328
**AUTOMOBILE (COBHAM).** (THE AUTOMOBILE.). [Automob.]. (198?)-. Periodical. English. mo. £28.00 England; £45.00 other Europe; £56.00 other. Enthusiast Publishing Ltd, Holmerise Seven Hills Road, Cobham Surrey KT11 1ES England. **Tel** 011 44 932 864212, FAX 0932 862340.
**Desc**: Devoted exclusively to cars manufactured before 1950 and commercial vehicles; includes a classified section of pre-1950 cars for sale.

CN/0005-1330
**AUTOMOBILE (DON MILLS).** (L'AUTOMOBILE.). [Automobile]. Periodical. French. bm (6 issues). 13.00Can$ (one year), 21.00Can$ (two year), 35.00Can$ (three year) Canada; 21.00Can$ (one year), 27.50Can$ (two year), 35.00Can$ (three year) other. Southam Information and Technology Group Inc., 1450 Don Mills Road, Don Mills Ontario M3B 2X7 Canada. **Tel** (416)445-6641, (800)668-2374, FAX (416)442-2261. **ED** Jean-Marie Germain. **Circ**: 12,000 (ctrl).
**Desc**: Editorial surrounding news as it pertains to the automotive aftermarket.
**Ind/Abst** Point Repere (1983-).

US/0198-781X
**AUTOMOBILE INDUSTRY TRENDS.** Periodical. English. qt. Sanford C Bernstein & Company, 22nd Floor/767 Fifth Avenue, New York NY 10153.

US/0093-0466
**AUTOMOBILE INSURANCE LOSSES COLLISION COVERAGES VARIATIONS BY MAKE AND SERIES.** See Insurance.

US/0099-2615
**AUTOMOBILE INTERNATIONAL.** *Title Change*. (19??-19??). Periodical. English. ir. Johnston International Publishing, Vine House Fairgreen, Reach, Cambridge CB50JD England. **Tel** (011)638-743688. **ED** Bernard Zinober. **Ad Acc**. **Circ**: 28,046 (ctrl).
**Absorbed** Fleet International; Automobile World.
**Continued by** Auto & Truck International, 1065-6685.

**Desc:** Serves the vehicle aftermarket outside of North America with service-oriented articles addressed to repair shops, vehicle distributors, fleets and parts dealers.

FR/0982-9156
**AUTOMOBILE MAGAZINE, L'.** (1981)-. Periodical. French. mo (Plus 3 special issues). 352.60F France; 511.00F other. Soc Edns Tech & Tour de France, 60 62 rue Danjou, 92100 Boulogne, Cedex France. **Tel** 011 33 1 46099596. **UDC** 796.7. ***Continues*** *L'Automobile., 0758-6957.*

US/0897-8360
**AUTOMOBILE (NEW YORK, N.Y. : 1988).** (AUTOMOBILE.). [Automobile]. **VFOAT** Automobile Magazine. Vol. 2, No. 11 (Feb. 1988)-. Periodical. English. mo. $20.00. K 3 Magazine Corporation, 200 Madison Avenue 8th Floor, New York NY 10016. **Tel** (212)447-4700, (212)447-4732. **(Subscription address:** Neodata / Colorado, PO Box 2606, Boulder Boulder CO 80322.**)** **DD** 629. ***Continues*** *Automobile Magazine (New York, N.Y. : 1986), 0894-3583.*

US/0005-1438
**AUTOMOBILE QUARTERLY.** [Automob. q.]. **Added/Corp** Princeton Institute for Historic Research. Vol. 1 (Spring 1962)-. Periodical. English. Four times a year. Price varies. Automobile Quarterly, PO Box 348, Kutztown PA 19530-0348. **Tel** (215)683-7341, FAX (215)683-5616. **ED** Jonathan Stein, Julie Fenster and John Heilg. **LC** TL1; .A588. **DD** 629.205. Index available. cum. index. **Circ:** 19,500. available on microfilm and microfiche from University Microfilms International (UMI).
**Desc:** Contains articles on contemporary, modern, classic, collectible, historic, special interest, sports, racing, postwar and pre-war cars. Offers its readers the full, complete coverage of the wonderful world of the automobile that no other magazine can match.
**Ind/Abst** Appl. Sci. Technol. Index.

US/0736-7953
**AUTOMOBILE RED BOOK.** (AUTOMOBILE RED BOOK / NATIONAL MARKET REPORTS, INC.). [Automob. red book]. **Added/Corp** National Market Reports, Inc. **VFOAT** Red Book. (198?)-. Periodical. English. Eight times a year. $49.50. MacLean Hunter Publishing Corporation / Chicago, IL, 29 North Wacker Drive, Chicago IL 60606-3298. **Tel** (312)726-2802, FAX (312)726-3091. **(Subscription address:** Maclean Hunter Market Reports, 29 North Wacker Drive, Chicago IL 60606.**)** **LC** HD9710.U5; N37. **DD** 629.2/222/029473. ***Continues*** *Red Book (Chicago, Ill. : 1979), 0484-1697.*

SZ
**AUTOMOBILE REVUE.** **VFOAT** Revue Automobile. German. Fifty-two times a year. 93.00F Switzerland; 148.80F other. Hallwag AG, Nordring 4, CH-3001 Bern Switzerland. **Tel** 011 41 31 3323131, FAX 031/414133, telex 912661 HAWA CH.

SZ
**AUTOMOBILE YEAR.** English (French and German). an. 79.00F. Editions Jr, c/o J R Piccard, Boulevard de Grancy 12, CH-1006 Lausanne Switzerland. **Tel** 41 21 27 88 00, FAX 41 21 27 88 54. **(Subscription address:** l'Annee Automobile, Case Postale 81, CH-1001 Lausanne Switzerland**)** **ED** David Hodges. **Ad Acc. Circ:** 23,000. ***Continues*** *Annual Automobile Review.*
**Desc:** International annual on production cars, automobile industry and car racing.

FR
**AUTOMOBILES CITROEN. RAPPORT.** **Main/Corp** Automobiles Citroen (Firm). French. Mundoprint-France, 75 Avenue de la Grande Armee, Paris 16E France. **LC** HD9710.F74; A872. **DD** 338.7/62/920944.

FR/0759-6065
**AUTOMOBILES CLASSIQUES.** [Automob. class.]. (1983)-. Periodical. French. bm. $65.00. Les Editions Conde Nast, Service Abonnements B620, 60732 S Genevieve Cedex 9 France. **Tel** 011 33 45 673505, 44 034400. **UDC** 796.71.

US/0742-7417
**AUTOMOBILES CLASSIQUES (ENGLISH EDITION).** (AUTOMOBILES CLASSIQUES.). [Automob. class.]. No. 1 (Spring/Summer 1984)-. Periodical. English. qt. Automobiles Classiques, 500 Fifth Avenue, Suite 1423, New York NY 10110.

US/0194-0023
**AUTOMOTIVE AIR CONDITIONING AND HEATING SERVICE MANUAL : BOOK SUPPLEMENT.** **Main/Corp** Mitchell Manuals, Inc. **VFOAT** Automotive Air Conditioning and Heating Service Manual: Supplement; Air Conditioning and Heating Service Manual. Trade Publication. English. an. Mitchell International Inc, PO Box 26260, San Diego CA 92126-0260. **Tel** (619)578-6550, (800)648-8010, FAX (619)578-4752. **(Subscription address:** 9889 Willow Creek Road, San Diego CA 92131**)** **ED** Larry Laumann. **LC** TL271; .M57A. **DD** 629.2/77. **Circ:** 10,000.
**Desc:** Repairing air conditioning and heating in automobiles.

●US/1071-1430
**AUTOMOTIVE & TRANSPORTATION INTERIORS.** [Automot. transp. inter.]. **VFOAT** Automotive and Transportation Interiors. (1994)-. Periodical. English. mo. $30.00 US; $51.00 Canada and Mexico; $82.00 other. Shore Communications Inc., 6255 Barfield Road, Suite 200, Atlanta GA 30328. **Tel** (404)252-8831, ((800)241-9034, FAX (404)252-4436. **DD** 388.

US/0192-0995
**AUTOMOTIVE BODY REPAIR NEWS.** [Autom. body repair news]. (19??)-. Periodical. English. mo. $52.00. Chilton Company, 201 King of Prussia Road, Radnor PA 19089. **Tel** (610)964-4122, (800)695-1214, FAX (610)964-4978, telex 6851035 CHILTON UW. **LC** TL255; .A95. **DD** 629.2/6/0288. ***Continues*** *Automotive Service and Body News.*
**Desc:** Targets the body shop market. This publication reaches more than 62,000 independent and franchised business establishments involved in body repair, refinishing and restoration, providing, for many, the only regularly used source of product information and general industry news.

US/0191-6459
**AUTOMOTIVE BOOSTER OF CALIFORNIA, THE.** Periodical. English. mo. McAnally & Associates Inc, PO Box 765, Lacanada CA 91011. **Tel** (818)790-6554. **ED** Don McAnally. **Circ:** 3,700.

US
**AUTOMOTIVE, BURGLARY PROTECTION, MECHANICAL EQUIPMENT DIRECTORY.** **Added/Corp** Underwriters' Laboratories. (1978)-. Directory. English. an (Oct.). $9.00. Underwriters Laboratories Inc., 333 Pfingsten Road, Northbrook IL 60062. **Tel** (708)272-8800 Ext.3542, FAX (708)272-8129, telex 6502543343. ***Continues*** *Underwriters' Laboratories. Accident, Automotive, Burglary Protection Equipment Directory.*

UK
**AUTOMOTIVE BUSINESS NEWS.** **See** Business.

US/0746-2077
**AUTOMOTIVE CHAIN STORE (NEW YORK, N.Y.).** (AUTOMOTIVE CHAIN STORE.). Began in 1983. Periodical. English. mo. $25.00. Automotive Chain Store, 77 North Miller Road, Akron OH 44313. **LC** HD9710.A1; A78. **DD** 381/.456292/068. available on microfilm from University Microfilms International (UMI). ***Continues*** *ACS Magazine, 0738-663X.*

US/0005-1497
**AUTOMOTIVE COOLING JOURNAL : ACJ.** [Automot. cool. j.]. **Added/Corp** National Automotive Radiator Service Association. Mobile Air Conditioning Society (Harleysville, Pa.). **VFOAT** ACJ. (1958)-. Trade Publication. English. Twelve times a year. $30.00 US; $48.50 Canada; $75.00 other. National Automotive Radiator Service Association, PO Box 97, East Greenville PA 18041. **Tel** (215)541-4500, FAX (215)679-4977. **ED** Richard Krisher & Wayne Juchno. **DD** 629. Index Bound in First Issue. **Ad Acc. Circ:** 10,000.
**Desc:** Information on the specialized fields of automotive and commercial heat exchange and cooling.

US/1054-4828
**AUTOMOTIVE ELECTRONICS JOURNAL.** ***Ceased.*** [Automot. electron. j.]. (Oct. 9 1989)-(Sept. 1990). Periodical. English. bw. Automotive Electronic News, 7 East 12th Street, New York NY 10003. **Tel** (212)741-4184. **LC** TL272.5; .A983. **DD** 629.25/49. ***Continues*** *Automotive Electronic News, 1041-9934.*

UK/0307-6490
**AUTOMOTIVE ENGINEER.** [Automot. eng.]. Vol. 1 (Oct. 1975)-. Periodical. English. bm (6 issues). $139.00 Western Hemisphere. Mechanical Engineering Publications, PO Box 24, Northgate Avenue, Bury St. Edmunds, Suffolk IP32 6BW England. **Tel** 011 44 284 763277, telex 817376. **(Subscription address:** Mechanical Engineering Publications / Western Hemisphere Subscriptions, Subscription Office, PO Box 361, Birmingham AL 35201-0361.**)** **ED** Ralph Goss. **LC** TL1; .A596. **DD** 629.2/05. **[CCC]. Bk Rev. Ad Acc.** available on microfilm and microfiche from University Microfilms International (UMI). Documents available from Article Express International. ***Formed by the union of*** *JAE, Journal of Automotive Engineering, 0307-1820* ***and*** *Automotive Design Engineering.*
**Desc:** Coverage includes research design, development and production in the automotive industry. Topics encompass the manufacture of various vehicles based on automotive engineering principles and technology.
**Ind/Abst** Acoust. Abstr.; Agric. Eng. Abstr.; Alum. Ind. Abstr.; Bioeng. Abstr.; Coal Abstr.; Curr. Technol. Index; Ei Page One; EMBASE; Energy Res. Abstr. (Oct. 1976-); Eng. Mater. Abstr.; Eng. Index Annu. [Select. Cov.]; Fluid Abstr., Civil Eng.; Fluid Abstr. Proc. Eng.; FLUIDEX (1975-); Highw. Res. Abstr.; Lit. Pat. Abstr., Oilfield Chem. (1972-1989); Lit. Abstr., Catal. Catal.; Lit. Abstr., Health Environ.; Lit. Abstr., Pet. Refin. Petrochem.; Lit. Abstr., Pet. Substit.; Lit. Abstr., Transp. Storage; Met. Abstr.; Pollut. Abstr. Indexes.

US/0195-1564
**AUTOMOTIVE EXECUTIVE (1979).** (AUTOMOTIVE EXECUTIVE : AE.). **Added/Corp** National Automobile Dealers Services Corp. National Automobile Dealers Association. **VFOAT** AE; A.E. Vol. 1, No. 1 (Sept. 1979)-. Periodical. English. mo. $24.00. National Automobile Dealers Association, 8400 West Park Drive, McLean VA 22102. **Tel** (703)749-4700, (800)544-6232, FAX (703)821-7269. **ED** Joe Phillips, Joan Mooney, and Roberta Maynard. **LC** HD9710.U5; A836. **DD** 629.2/068. **Ad Acc. Circ:** 22,500. available on microfilm from University Microfilms International (UMI). ***Continues*** *Cars & Trucks, 0027-5778.*
**Desc:** Serves the retail auto and truck market. 95 percent of circulation includes franchised new car and truck dealers. Content is business management information for dealerships.

US/0005-1519
**AUTOMOTIVE FLEET.** (1961)-. Periodical. English. Six times a year. $35.00 US; $42.00 Canada; $53.00 others. Bobit Publishing, 2512 Artesia Boulevard, Redondo Beach CA 90278. **Tel** (310)376-8788, (800)334-8152, FAX (213)376-9043. **ED** Edward Bobit and Tom Bezzi. **Circ:** 19,967.
**Ind/Abst** Stat. Ref. Index.

UK/0951-158X
**AUTOMOTIVE INDUSTRY DATA LTD.** [Automot. Ind. Data Ltd.]. (1983)-. Periodical. English. sm (24 issues per year). £340.00 Europe; £370.00 other. Automotive Industry Data Ltd, City House 2-4 Dam St, Lichfield Staffs WS13 6AA England. **Tel** 011 44 5432 57295, FAX (0)543-256884. Index available (Free index).
**Desc:** In-depth industry and critical market reporting on the automobile industry in the main world automotive regions, with a key emphasis on Western Europe.

UK
**AUTOMOTIVE INDUSTRY DATA YEARBOOK.** (1984)-. English. an. £130.00. Automotive Industry Data Ltd, City House 2-4 Dam St, Lichfield Staffs WS13 6AA England. **Tel** 011 44 5432 57295, FAX (0)543-256884. available on diskette.

UK/0967-0386
**AUTOMOTIVE INTERIORS INTERNATIONAL.** [Automot. inter. int.]. (1991)-. Periodical. English. qt. £55.00 UK; £60.00 (surface), £65.00 (air mail) other. Turret Group, 177 Hagden Lane, Watford Herts WD1 8LN United Kingdom. **Tel** 011 44 923 228577, FAX 011 44 923 221346.

US/0898-2155
**AUTOMOTIVE INVESTOR.** [Automot. invest.]. Vol. 1, No. 1 (Aug. 1988)-. Newsletter. English. mo. $108.00. Mary Ann Liebert Inc., 1651 Third Avenue, New York NY 10128. **Tel** (212)289-2300, (800)M-LIEBERT, FAX (212)289-4697. **DD** 629.
**Desc:** For buyers, sellers and collectors of vintage, classic and special-interest cars from 1925 to 1975. Reports current market activities and trends and analyzes future investment opportunities by make. Covers cars to buy, sell, and hold. Ten-year price projections with rates of return are listed. Also provides contacts for technical information on all makes featured.

US
**AUTOMOTIVE LEASE GUIDE.** English. bm. $42.00. First National Lease Systems / Automotive Lease Guide, 1328 de la Vina Street, Santa Barbara CA 93101. **Tel** (805)965-1403. **UDC** 68.
**Desc:** Convenient method of determining residual value of vehicles at the end of lease term.

US/0732-9350
**AUTOMOTIVE LITERATURE INDEX.** (AUTOMOTIVE LITERATURE INDEX / A. WALLACE, COMPILER.). [Automot. lit. index]. (1947/1976)-. English. ir (issued every five years). Automotive Literature Index, 2307 Shoreland, Toledo OH 43611. **Tel** (419)729-9065. **ED** A. Wallace. **LC** Z5170; .A84; TL145. **DD** 016.6292/05. Index available. cum. index. **Circ:** 5,000.
**Desc:** Index to American automotive journals (historical).

US/0733-2084
**AUTOMOTIVE MARKET REPORT.** **See** Business-Marketing.

CN/0702-8318
**AUTOMOTIVE MARKETER.** ***Ceased.*** [Automot. mark.]. Issue No. 18 (Fall 1976)-(1991). Periodical. English. an. Wadham Publications, Division of Southam Communications Ltd, 1450 Don Mills Road, Don Mills Ontario M3B 2X7 Canada. **Tel** (416)445-6641, (416)442-2213. **DD** 338.4/7/62920971. ***Continues*** *Automotive Mass Marketer, 0067-2572.*

US/0005-1551
**AUTOMOTIVE NEWS.** [Automot. news]. (19??)-. Periodical. English. Fifty-two times a year. $80.00 US; $125.00 Canada. Crain Communications Inc., 1400 Woodbridge, Detroit MI 48207. **Tel** (313)446-6000, (800)992-9970. **ED** Andrew McGill. **LC** TL1; .A865. **DD** 338.4/7/62922205. **[CCC]. Ad Acc. Circ:** 65,000.

available on an online database (thru NEXIS - file AIR); available on microfilm and microfiche from University Microfilms International (UMI). Documents available from UMI Article Clearinghouse. ***Absorbed*** *Automotive Service;* ***Continues*** *Automotive Daily News.*
**Ind/Abst** Acad. Ind. [Computer File] (1984-); Bus. Index (1985-); Bus. Period. Index; Bus. Source (Jan. 1993-); Expand. Acad. Index (1984-); F&S Index Plus Text, Int. [Full Txt.] [Select. Cov.]; Gen. BusinessFile (1985-); Gen. Period. Index (1985-); Infobank (Jan. 1969-); Mag. Search; Mark. Advert. Ref. Serv. [Full Txt.]; Newsp. Period. Abstr. (1990-); PROMT [Full Txt.]; Stat. Ref. Index; Trade Ind. Index (1981-); Vocat. Search (Jan. 1993-); Wilson Bus. Abstr.

US
**AUTOMOTIVE NEWS. MARKET DATA BOOK.** **VFOAT** Automotive News. Market Data Book Issue; Market Data Book; Market Data Book Issue. (1976)-. English. an. $19.95. Crain Communications Inc., 1400 Woodbridge, Detroit MI 48207. **Tel** (313)446-6000, (800)992-9970. **ED** Andrew R McGill. **Ad Acc. Circ:** 64,000. available on an online database (file 16/Full-Text) from DIALOG. ***Continues*** *Automotive News. Almanac Issue.*
**Desc:** Comprehensive data on 1985 automotive calendar year and 1986 model cars and trucks. Includes statistics and analysis of motor vehicle production, sales and registrations, products and specs, prices, options, equipment and much more.

US/0896-3614
**AUTOMOTIVE PARTS INTERNATIONAL.** ***Title Change.*** [Automot. parts int.]. (198?)-(199?). Periodical. English. bw. International Trade Services, PO Box 50120, Washington DC 20004. **Tel** (202)857-8454. **DD** 338. available on an online database (file 636/Full-Text) from DIALOG. ***Absorbed by*** *Autoparts Report, 1045-1978.*
**Desc:** Reports on international trade and investment trends in automotive parts industry worldwide.

US/8750-4103
**AUTOMOTIVE PRODUCTS REPORT.** ***Ceased.*** [Automot. prod. rep.]. Vol. 1, No. 1 (Oct. 1984)-?. Periodical. English. bm. Irving-Cloud Publishing Company, 417 North Hough Street, Barrington IL 60010. **Tel** (708)382-3405, FAX (708)674-7015. **(Subscription address:** 6201 W Howard Street, Room 207, Niles, IL 60648**) ED** Nancy Austin. **DD** 629. **Ad Acc. Circ:** 35,000 (ctrl). ***Continues*** *Automotive Volume Distribution, 0745-3043.*
**Desc:** Product information for buyers of retail automotive products.

US/0196-0156
**AUTOMOTIVE Q & A.** **Main/Corp** Williams, Doug. **VFOAT** Q & A. **VAT** Automotive Questions and Answers; Automotive Q&A. Periodical. English. sm. Automotive Q & A, 20420 Briarcliff, Detroit MI 48221. **Tel** (313)341-0654.

US/0567-2317
**AUTOMOTIVE REBUILDER.** Vol. 1 (Oct. 1964)-. Periodical. English. mo. $45.00 US, Canada, and Mexico; $91.00 other. Babcox Publications Inc., 11 South Ford Street, Akron OH 44304. **Tel** (216)535-7011. **ED** Becky Babcox. **LC** TL1; .A885. **DD** 658/.92/9287. **Ad Acc. Circ:** 24,000 (ctrl).
**Desc:** To aid readers in the profitable operation of their volume rebuilding business.

US/1058-9376
**AUTOMOTIVE RECYCLING.** (AUTOMOTIVE RECYCLING : THE OFFICIAL MAGAZINE OF THE AUTOMOTIVE DISMANTLERS & RECYCLERS ASSOCIATION.). [Automot. recycl.]. **Added/Corp** Automotive Dismantlers and Recyclers Association. (Jan./Feb. 1991)-. Periodical. English. Six times a year. $30.00. Automobiles Dismantlers & Recycling Association, 3975 Fairbridge Drive, Suite 20, Fairfax VA 22033. **Tel** (703)385-1001. **LC** TL154; .D53. **DD** 629.28/7. ***Continues*** *Dismantlers Digest, 0192-0316.*

US
**AUTOMOTIVE RESEARCH. LONG-TERM FORECAST REPORT.** **Added/Corp** WEFA Group. Automotive Service. (Summer/Fall 1990)-. English. sa. WEFA Group, 401 City Avenue, Suite 300, Bala Cynwyd PA 19004. **LC** HD9710.U5; W44. **DD** 338.4/76292/0973. ***Continues*** *WEFA Group/Ward's Research Automotive Long-Term Review.*

CN/0005-1578
**AUTOMOTIVE RETAILER (VANCOUVER).** (AUTOMOTIVE RETAILER.). [Automot. retail.]. **Added/Corp** Automotive Retailers' Association. (1???)-. Periodical. English. Twelve times a year. 24.00Can$ (one year), 46.00Can$ (two year), 66.00 (three year). Automotive Retailer Publishing, 120 4281 Canada Way, Burnaby British Columbia V5G 4P1 Canada. **Tel** (604)432-7987, FAX (604)432-1756. **ED** R. Romero. **Ad Acc, Adv Mgr:** Lea Allen. **Circ:** 5,000.

CN/0705-6281
**AUTOMOTIVE SERVICE DATA BOOK.** [Automot. serv. data book]. **VAT** Data Book (Toronto). (1978)-. English. an. 28.00Can$. Southam Information and Technology Group Inc., 1450 Don Mills Road, Don Mills Ontario M3B 2X7 Canada. **Tel** (416)445-6641, (800)668-2374, FAX (416)442-2261. **DD** 629.28/7/2. ***Continues*** *Canadian Service Data Book, 0068-9629.*
**Desc:** Contains specifications for domestic and imported automobiles for the current and preceding five years.

US/0273-7477
**AUTOMOTIVE SERVICE REPORTS.** Periodical. English. mo. Automotive Service Councils, 188 Industrial Drive/Suite 112, Elmhurst IL 60126.

UK/0957-2481
**AUTOMOTIVE SPECIAL REPORT.** [Automot. spec. rep.]. (1984)-. Monographic series. English. ir. Price varies per volume. Economist Intelligence Unit / Essex, PO Box 14 Harold Hill, Romford RM3 8EQ, Essex England. **Tel** 011 44 322 289194. **(Subscription address:** Business International Ltd., PO Box 154, Unit 151, Dartford Kent DA1 1QB England.**)**

US/0889-3918
**AUTOMOTIVE WEEK.** [Automot. week]. (19??)-. Periodical. English. Forty-eight times a year. $125.00 US, Canada & Mexico; $200.00 others. Automotive Week Publishing Company, PO Box 3495, Wayne NJ 07470-3495. **Tel** (201)694-7792, FAX (201)694-2817. **ED** Chuck Laverty. **DD** 338. Index available (semi-annually). **Ad Acc.** ***Continues*** *Automotive Buyer.*
**Desc:** Retailing of automotive accessories, parts and service. Covers trends, acquisitions, new market entries, bankruptcies and litigation.

US/0163-6448
**AUTOMOTIVE WHOLESALING : FINANCIAL OPERATION AND PERFORMANCE ANALYSIS.** **See** Economics-Industry and Production.

UK
**AUTONEWS.** ***Ceased.*** (19??)-(Dec. 1993). English. sa. Institution of Mechanical Engineers, Auto Division, 1 Birdcage Walk, London SW1H 9JJ England. **Tel** 011 44 71 222 7899, FAX 011 44 71 222 4557, telex 917944. **ED** Gordon Shearer and Maria Taylor. **Circ:** 15,000 (ctrl).

US/1045-1978
**AUTOPARTS REPORT, THE.** [Autoparts rep.]. **VFOAT** Auto Parts Report. (1987)-. Periodical. English. sm. $297.00 North America; $357.00 other. Automotive Parts International, PO Box 5950, Bethesda MD 20824. **Tel** (202)857-8454. **ED** Kate Victory. **DD** 338. available on an online database (files 16,636/Full-Text) from DIALOG. ***Absorbed*** *Automotive Parts International, 0896-3614.*
**Desc:** Auto parts, manufacturing, distribution, and retail.
**Ind/Abst** PTS Newsl. Database [Full Txt.].

CN/0836-1630
**AUTOPINION (OTTAWA).** (AUTOPINION.). [Autopinon]. **Added/Corp** Canadian Automobile Association. (1988)-. English. an. $6.95 Canada; $8.95 US; $14.95 other. Canadian Automobile Association, 1775 Courtwood Crescent, Ottawa Ontario K2C 3J2 Canada. **Tel** (613)226-7631, FAX (613)225-7383, telex 053-4440. **DD** 629.2/222/029471. ***Continues*** *Canadian Motorist Car Facts, 0834-0846.*

SP/0567-2392
**AUTOPISTA.** [Autopista]. (1961)-. Periodical. Spanish. wk. 17300ptas Spain; 31800ptas Europe; 40300ptas other. Luike Motorpress, Calle Ancora 40, 28045 Madrid Spain. **Tel** 011 34 1 3470157. **(Subscription address:** G & J Subscripciones, Marques de Villamagna 4, 28001 Madrid Spain.**) UDC** 629.113.

SP/0005-1961
**AUTOREVISTA.** Spanish. wk. 17300ptas Spain; 23800ptas other. Tecnipublicaciones SA, C Fernando VI No 27, 28004 Madrid Spain. **Tel** 011 34 1 3197889, FAX 341 4101069, telex 43905 YEBE E. **ED** Julian Guerrero. **Bk Rev. Ad Acc. Circ:** 39,000.
**Desc:** Full coverage of auto industry developments.

UK/0269-946X
**AUTOSPORT (TEDDINGTON).** (AUTOSPORT.). [Autosport]. **VFOAT** Auto Sport. (19??)-. Periodical. English. wk (52 issues). £90.00 UK; £97.00 Europe and Ireland; £131.00 America, Africa, Middle East and India; £169.00 Australia, New Zealand, and Japan. Haymarket Publishing Ltd., 12 14 Ansdell Street, London W8 5TR England. **Tel** 011 44 483 733800, FAX 011 44 483 776573. **(Subscription address:** Haymarket Publishing Ltd, PO Box 219, Subscriptions Department, Woking Surrey GU21 1ZW, United Kingdom.**) ED** Andy Hallbery. **Bk Rev**, (Qty: 52). **Ad Acc, Adv Mgr:** Matthew Newell, **Tel** (908)665-7811.

IT/0005-1748
**AUTOSPRINT.** Italian. wk (52 issues). L140000.00 Italy; L200000.00 other. Conti Editore, Via del Lavoro 7, 40068 S Lazzaro Savena Italy. **Tel** 011 39 51 6227111, FAX 011 39 51 6258112, telex 510283.

UK/0308-7476
**AUTOTRADE.** [Autotrade]. (1973)-. Periodical. English. mo. £75.00 UK and Northern Ireland; $185.00 other. Morgan Grampian, 40 Beresford Street Woolwich, London SE18 6BQ England. **Tel** 011 44 81 855 7777, FAX 011 44 81 855 5548, telex 896238. available in microform.

US/0192-9674
**AUTOWEEK.** [AutoWeek]. **VFOAT** Auto Week. (19??)-. Periodical. English. Fifty-two times a year. $28.00 US and possessions; $60.00 other. Crain Communications Inc., 1400 Woodbridge, Detroit MI 48207. **Tel** (313)446-6000, (800)992-9970. **(Subscription address:** Crain Communications, 965 East Jefferson Avenue, Detroit, MI 48207, telephone: (800)678-9595 or (313)446-1616**) ED** Leon Mandell. **DD** 338. **[CCC]. Ad Acc. Circ:** 160,000. available on microfilm and microfiche from University Microfilms International (UMI); available on an online database from NEXIS; and (file 16/Full-Text) DIALOG. ***Continues*** *Autoweek and Competition Press.*
**Desc:** Written and edited for the enthusiast looking for state-of-the-art information on new cars, prototypes, classic cars, and racing cars. Includes technical updates, mechanical advice, travel planners and information on wheels, tires, accessories, car care, electronics and sound systems.
**Ind/Abst** F&S Index Plus Text, Int. [Full Txt.] [Select. Cov.]; Mag. Search; PROMT [Full Txt.]; Vocat. Search (July 1993-).

NE
**AUTOWEEK.** English. wk (52 issues). Fl111.80. Medianet BV, Postbus 6298, 2001 LN Haarlem Netherlands. **Tel** 011 31 23 173311.

GW
**AUTOZEITUNG.** (19??)-. German. bw (26 issues). $100.00 US. Heinrich Bauer Verlag, Burchardstr 11, D-20095 Hamburg Germany. **Tel** 011 49 40 30190. **(Subscription address:** US/ German Language Publ. Inc., 153 South Deanstreet, Englewood, NJ 07631; telephone: (201)871-1010**)**

US
**AVION OWNER'S MANUAL.** **Main/Corp** Avion Coach Corporation. English. PO Box 7300, Riverside CA 92516. **LC** TL297; .A95A. **DD** 643.

RU
**AVTOEXPORT ROUND-UP.** (19??)-. Periodical. English. qt. V/O Avtoexport, 14 Ui Volkhonda, 119902 Moscow Russia. **LC** HD9710.R9; A87. **DD** 338.4/76292/0947.

RU/0005-2337
**AVTOMOBILNAJA PROMYSLENNOST.** (AVTOMOBILNAIA PROMYSHELNNOST.). [Avtomob. prom.]. **Added/Corp** Soviet Union. Ministerstvo Avtomobilnoi Promyshlennosti, Traktornogo i Selskokhoziaistvennogo Mashinostroeniia. (1958)-. Periodical. Russian. mo. $89.95. **(Subscription address:** East View Publications Inc., 3020 Harbor Lane North, Suite 110, Minneapolis MN 55447.**)** Documents available from CASDDS. ***Continues*** *Avtomobilnaja i Traktornaia Promyshlennost.*
**Ind/Abst** Alum. Ind. Abstr.; Chem. Abstr.; Eng. Mater. Abstr.; Met. Abstr.; Surf. Treat. Technol. Abstr.

KZ
**AVTOMOBILNYI TRANSPORT KAZAKHSTANA.** **Added/Corp** Kazakh S.S.R. Ministerstvo Avtomobilnogo Transporta. Profsoiuz Rabochikh Avtomobilnogo Transporta i Shosseinykh Dorog. Kazakhskii Respublikanskii Komitet. (19??)-. Periodical. Russian. mo. $18.00. 83 GSP-1 Pr Seifullina 460, Alma-Ata Kazakhstan. **LC** HE5699.K3; A9.

US
**BIENNIAL REPORT - VIRGINIA DIVISION OF MOTOR VEHICLES.** **Main/Corp** Virginia. Division of Motor Vehicles. English. be. Virginia Division of Motor Vehicles, 2220 West Broad Street, Richmond VA 23220. **LC** HE5633.V8; V57A. **DD** 353.9/755/008783.

DK
**BILEN, MOTOR OG SPORT.** Periodical. Danish. mo. Palle Fogtdal, Nrre Farimagsgade 49, 1364 Kbenhavn Denmark. **LC** TL4; .B52. ***Continues*** *Bilen Og Baden.*

US/0747-4393
**BLACK BOOK. OLD CAR ... MARKET GUIDE.** [Black book, Old car mark. guide]. **VFOAT** Old Car ... Market Guide; Black Book. Periodical. English. mo. $36.00. Black Book, PO Box 758, Gainesville GA 30503. **DD** 629.

CN/0318-9368
**BLACK BOOK USED SPECIALTY VEHICLE AND TRUCK GUIDE.** Jan./Feb. 1975-. English (French). bm. $30.00. National Auto Research Canada, 67 Ellesmere Road, Scarborough Ontario M1R 4B8 Canada. **DD** 338.4/3/6292230971. ***Supersedes*** *Black Book Used Truck Guide, 0318-935X.*

UK/0006-5501
**BODY LEEDS.** (BODY.). [Body Leeds]. (1966)-. Periodical. English. Ten times a year. £30.00 UK; £46.00 Europe; £60.00 US, Australia and Pacific rim; £55.00 other. VBRA, Belmont House, Gildersome, Leeds LS27 7TW England. **Tel** 11 44 532 538333, FAX 11 44 532

380496. **ED** Nicola Keane (editor's address: 28 Finkle Lane, Gildersome Leeds LS27 7TW England). Each issue contains an index to its own contents (no volume index)--loose. **Ad Acc, Adv Mgr:** Sally Barlow. **Pr Rev. Circ:** 5,000. ***Continues*** *VBRA Journal.*
**Desc:** Managerial information for the vehicle body repair and commercial vehicle bodybuilding industries.

CN/0045-2319
**BODYSHOP.** Vol. 1 (Jan./Feb. 1970)-. Periodical. English. bm (6 issues). 13.00Can$ (one year), 21.00Can$ (two year), 27.50Can$ (three year) Canada; 21.00Can$ (one year), 27.50Can$ (two year), 35.00Can$ (three year) other. Southam Information and Technology Group Inc., 1450 Don Mills Road, Don Mills Ontario M3B 2X7 Canada. **Tel** (416)445-6641, (800)668-2374, FAX (416)442-2261.

US/0730-7241
**BODYSHOP BUSINESS. VFOAT** Body Shop Business. Vol. 1, No. 1 (Mar. 1982)-. Periodical. English. ir (13 issues). $45.00 US, Canada and Mexico; $91.00 other (includes Lift Guide and Annual Industry Profile). Babcox Publications Inc., 11 South Ford Street, Akron OH 44304. **Tel** (216)535-7011. **ED** Denise Lloyd. **Circ:** 44,300.
**Desc:** Bodyshop business delivers management and technical information that can be directly applied in running a more efficient and profitable collision repair shop.
**Ind/Abst** Mag. Search; Vocat. Search (Jan. 1993-).

US/0193-726X
**BRAKE & FRONT END. VFOAT** Brake and Front End. (19??)-. Periodical. English. mo. $45.00 US, Canada & Mexico; $91.00 other. Babcox Publications Inc., 11 South Ford Street, Akron OH 44304. **Tel** (216)535-7011. **ED** Jeffrey S. Davis. **LC** TL275.A1; B75. **DD** 629.2/46/0288. **Bk Rev. Ad Acc. Circ:** 29,000 (ctrl). ***Continues*** *Brake and Front End Service.*
**Desc:** For auto repair shops engaged in brake, steering and suspension service. Semi-technical descriptions of mechanical systems and repair techniques, plus management articles, product reviews and industry news.

US/1058-3610
**BRAKE TECH/TALK.** [Brake tech/talk]. **VFOAT** Brake Tech Talk; Brake Tech Talk Newsletter; Brake Tech/Talk Newsletter. (1990)-. Periodical. English. Twelve times a year. $69.00 US; $80.00 other. M D Publications Inc., PO Box 2210, Springfield MO 65801. **Tel** (800)274-7890, (417)866-3917, FAX (417)866-2781. **ED** Ron Henningsen. **DD** 629. **Circ:** 1,000.
**Desc:** Technical newsletter detailing repair/replacement procedures of auto brake systems.

US/0095-1854
**BRAKES.** **See** Public Health and Safety.

US
**BRANHAM AUTOMOBILE REFERENCE BOOK, SHOWING IN ILLUSTRATED FORM THE LOCATION OF MOTOR AND SERIAL NUMBERS ON ALL PASSENGER CARS AND TRUCKS.** (192?)-. English. an. $41.70. Branham Publishing Company, PO Box 1948, Santa Monica CA 90406. **Tel** (310)394-8585, (310)394-8956. **LC** TL151; .B75. **DD** 629.2085.

US/1052-0929
**BRITISH CAR.** [Br. car]. (198?)-. Periodical. English. Six times a year. $22.95 US; $26.00 Canada & Mexico; $35.00 others. British Car, 22026 Gault Street, Canoga Park CA 91303. **Tel** (818)710-1234, FAX (818)710-1877. **(Subscription address:** PO Box 9099, Canoga Park, CA 91309**)** **DD** 388.

US/1056-8468
**BRITISH MARQUE CAR CLUB NEWS.** [Br. marque car club news]. **VFOAT** British Marque; British Marque Club News. (1990)-. Periodical. English. mo. $10.00 US; $15.00 Canada. Hull Associates, 633 East Washington Street, North Attleboro MA 02760. **DD** 796.

CN/0045-3226
**BROKEN SPOKE, THE. Added/Corp** Calgary Sports Car Club. **VFOAT** Rayon Casse; Gebrochene Speiche; Raggi Della Ruota Sono Rotti; Brocken Egern. (Jan. 1959)-. Newsletter. English. bm (6 issues). 10.00Can$. Calgary Sports Car Club, PO Box 61143, Kensington Postal Station, Calgary Alberta T2P 4S6 Canada. **Tel** (403)285-1177, FAX (403)289-7256. **ED** Akio Nagatomi, Steve Barry. **DD** 796.7/7/05. **Ad Acc. Circ:** 200 (ctrl).
**Desc:** Covers both club and motorsport news. Also provides information on coming events.

US
**BUICK ... ELECTRICAL SYSTEMS MANUAL. PARK AVENUE, PARK AVENUE ULTRA.** ***Title Change.*** **Added/Corp** General Motors Corporation. Buick Motor Division. **VFOAT** Electrical Systems Manual. Park Avenue, Park Avenue Ultra; Park Avenue, Park Avenue Ultra; Park Avenue/Park Avenue Ultra. (1991)-(199?). English. **LC** TL215.B84; B854. **DD** 629.25/4. ***Continues*** *Buick ... Electrical SyMtems manual. LeSabre, Electra/Park Avenue.* ***Continued by*** *Electrical Systems Manual. Park Avenue, LeSabre.*

AT/0155-0535
**BUSHDRIVER.** (BUSHDRIVER.). [Bushdriver]. (1977)-. Periodical. English. bm. 26.00Aus$ (Australia); 30.00Aus$ (New Zealand, New Guinea, & Papua); 35.00Aus$ (other). Richard Williams & Associates, 25 Valley Park Crescent, Turramurra New South Wales, 2074 Australia. **Tel** 02 488-9900. **ED** Ric Williams. **DD** 629.220994. **Ad Acc. Circ:** 22,000.
**Desc:** Information for four-wheel drivers including road tests, outback and international travel.

CN/0381-9906
**C. A. S. C. RACE REGULATIONS.** **See** Recreation, Leisure-Sports.

US/1042-9603
**CALIFORNIA REPORT ON AUTOMOTIVE MARKETING, THE.** (THE CALIFORNIA REPORT ON AUTOMOTIVE MARKETING / J.D. POWER ASSOCIATES.). [Calif. rep. automot. market.]. **Added/Corp** J.D. Power and Associates. **VFOAT** California Report. (198?)-. Periodical. English. mo. $202.80 (1 year), $364.00 (2 year), $483.60 (3 year) Michigan; $195.00 (1 year), $350.00 (2 year), $465.00 (3 year) other. J D Powers & Associates Publishing, 30401 Agoura Road, Agoura Hills CA 91301. **Tel** (818)889-6330, FAX (818)889-3719. **ED** John Rettie. **DD** 629. **Circ:** 1,400. ***Continues*** *Power California Market Report.*

US/0747-0223
**CALIFORNIA SPORTSCAR CLUB NEWS. VFOAT** California Sports Car Club News; California Sports Car. Vol. 5, No. 1 (Jan. 1984)-. Periodical. English. mo. $15.00. California Sports Car Club of American Inc, 12444 Victory Boulevard/#405A, Victory Square, North Hollywood CA 91606. ***Continues*** *Finish Line, 0199-5936.*

●US/1059-5740
**CAMAROS (LOS ANGELES, CALIF.).** (CAMAROS.). (1992)-. Periodical. English. $3.95. Petersen Publishing Company, 6420 Wilshire Bouldevard, Los Angeles CA 90048. **Tel** (213)782-2485.

●CN/1192-3857
**CAMIONNEURS/TRUCKERS MAGAZINE.** [Camion./truck. mag.]. **Added/Corp** Association des Proprietaires de Camions Remorques Independants du Quebec. **VFOAT** Truckers Magazine. Vol. 1, No 1 (Sept./Oct. 1992)-. Periodical. French (summaries and/or abstracts in English). bm. 18.00Can$. Communications JSSR, 4274 Est Boulevard Henri-Bourassa, Montreal-Nord, Quebec H1H 1L6 Canada. **DD** 388.3. ***Continues*** *Bulletin d'Information de l'APCRIQ., 1181-7941.*

CN/0821-2651
**CANADIAN AFTERMARKET, THE.** V. 1, No. 1 (April/May 1982)-. Periodical. English. bm. $10.00. Wheelspin News, 3045 Universe Drive, Mississauga Ontario L4X 2E2. **DD** 338.4/76292/0971.

CN/1180-2065
**CANADIAN AUTOMOTIVE TECHNICIAN.** ***Title Change.*** (CANADIAN AUTOMOTIVE TECHNICIAN : C A T.). [Can. automot. tech.]. **VFOAT** CAT. (April 1990)-(1992). Periodical. English. qt. Southam Information and Technology Group Inc., 1450 Don Mills Road, Don Mills Ontario M3B 2X7 Canada. **Tel** (416)445-6641, (800)668-2374, FAX (416)442-2261. **DD** 629.222. ***Continues*** *Canadian Automotive Training, 1180-1093.* ***Merged into*** *Service Station & Garage Management, 0381-548X.*

●CN/1192-2745
**CANADIAN AUTOWORLD.** [Can. autoworld]. **VAT** Canadian Auto World. Vol. 1, No. 1 (Oct. 1992)-. Periodical. English. Twelve times a year. 18.00Can$. World of Wheels Publishing, Inc., 1200 Markham Road 220, Scarborough Ontario M1H 3C3 Canada. **Tel** (416)438-7777, FAX (416)438-5333. **DD** 338.4. **Ad Acc.**

CN/0705-6966
**CANADIAN BLACK BOOK.** 1978/1971-. English. ir. William Ward Publications Ltd, 85 Ellesmere Road/Suite 201, Scarborough Ontario M1R 4B8 Canada. **Tel** (416)447-8545. **DD** 629.22/2/0212. ***Continues*** *Black Book Vehicle Identification Guide, 0316-4896.*

CN/0384-8434
**CANADIAN BLACK BOOK. ONTARIO.** (CANADIAN BLACK BOOK; OFFICIAL USED CAR MARKET GUIDE.). Sept. 20, 1976-. Periodical. English (French). bm. National Auto Research Canada, 67 Ellesmere Road, Scarborough Ontario M1R 4B8 Canada. **DD** 338.4/7/62920971. ***Supersedes*** *Black Book; Official Used Car Market Guide, 0047-875X.*
**Desc:** Confidential information for dealers, banks, finance companies and insurance adjusters on the cash value of used cars.

CN/1187-4376
**CANADIAN BLACK BOOK, USED TRUCK AND VAN GUIDE.** [Can. black book used truck van guide]. (Sept 1991)-. Periodical. English. mo. $48.15 per year, Canada. William Ward Publications Ltd, 85 Ellesmere Road/Suite 201, Scarborough Ontario M1R 4B8 Canada. **Tel** (416)447-8545. **DD** 338.4/3629223/029471. ***Continues*** *Canadian Black Book Used Specialty Vehicle and Truck Valuations., 0822-5176.*

CN/0711-3064
**CANADIAN MOTORSPORT ANNUAL ..., THE.** [Can. motorsport annu.]. 1980/81-. English. an. $3.00. Wheelspin News, 3045 Universe Drive, Mississauga Ontario L4X 2E2. **DD** 796.7/05.

CN/0843-2392
**CANADIAN PLASTICS AUTOMOTIVE DIRECTORY.** [Can. plast. automot. dir.]. **Added/Corp** Society of the Plastics Industry of Canada. **VFOAT** Automotive Directory. (1986)-. English. an. Society of the Plastics Industry of Canada, 1262 Don Mills Road, Suite 104, Don Mills Ontario, M3B 2W7 Canada. **Tel** (416)449-3444, FAX (416)449-5685, telex 06-966739. **DD** 338.4/76292.

CN/0045-527X
**CANADIAN RED BOOK. Added/Corp** Federation of Automobile Dealer Associations of Canada. Vol. 1, (June/Aug. 1958)-. Periodical. English (French). Twelve times a year. 80.00Can$ Canada; 97.00Can$ others. MacLean Hunter Publ. Limited / Toronto, 777 Bay Street, 8th Floor Agency Control, Toronto Ontario M5W 1A7 Canada. **Tel** (416)596-5000, (800)268-6811, FAX (416)596-5526.

UK
**CAP BLACK BOOK. VFOAT** Cap Black Book/ Cars Trade and Retail Values. Consumer Publication. English (French). mo. £120.00. Cap Nationwide Motor Research, Cap House, Carlton Road, Skipton North BD23 2BE England. **Tel** 011 44 756 700666.

UK
**CAP BLACK BOOK. CARS, TRADE & RETAIL VALUES.** English. mo. £130.00. Cap Nationwide Motor Research, Cap House, Carlton Road, Skipton North BD23 2BE England. **Tel** 011 44 756 700666.

UK/0008-5987
**CAR.** English. mo. $72.00. F F Publishing Ltd, PO Box 2 DISS, Norfolk IP22 3AP England.

UK
**CAR AND ACCESSORY TRADER.** (19??)-. English. mo (12 issues). £27.00 UK; £35.00 Eire & Europe; £63.00 America, Middle East, Africa & India; £74.00 Australia, New Zealand & Japan; £35.00 other. Haymarket Publishing Ltd., 12 14 Ansdell Street, London W8 5TR England. **Tel** 011 44 483 733800, FAX 011 44 483 776573. **(Subscription address:** Haymarket Publishing Ltd, PO Box 219, Subscriptions Department, Woking Surrey GU21 1ZW, United Kingdom.**)**

US/0008-6002
**CAR AND DRIVER.** [Car driv.]. Vol. 6, No. 10 (Apr. 1961)-. Periodical. English. mo. $20.00. Hachette Magazines Inc., 1633 Broadway, New York NY 10019. **Tel** (212)767-6000. **(Subscription address:** Neodata / Colorado, PO Box 2606, Boulder Boulder CO 80322.**)** **LC** TL236; .S664. **DD** 629. **Ad Acc.** available on microfilm and microfiche from University Microfilms International (UMI); available on an online database (file 647/Full-Text) from DIALOG; and NEXIS. Documents available from UMI Article Clearinghouse, Magazine Collection. ***Continues*** *Sports Cars Illustrated.*
**Desc:** Examines automobiles and automotive topics, and covers both domestic and imported products. The magazine gives some attention to motor sports and personalities, but 80 percent of its coverage is pure car, including road tests.
**Ind/Abst** Acad. Abstr. Full Text Elite (Jan. 1984-) [Full Txt.]; Acad. Abstr. (Jan. 1984-); Acad. Ind. [Computer File] (1984-1988); Acad. Search (Jan. 1984-); Consum. Index Prod. Eval. Inf. Source; Expand. Acad. Index (1984-1988); Gen. Period. Index (1985-); Highw. Res. Abstr.; Mag. Artic. Summar. Elite (Jan. 1984-) [Full Txt.]; Mag. Artic. Summar. Select (Jan. 1984-) [Full Txt.]; Mag. Artic. Summar. CD-ROM (Jan. 1984-); Mag. ASAP Plus [Full Txt.]; Mag. ASAP Sel. [Full Txt.]; Mag. Index Plus (1989-); Mag. Index Sel. Microfiche (1990-) [Full Txt.]; Mag. Index. Sel. (1986-); Mag. Search; Mid. Search (Jan. 1988-) [Full Txt.]; Newsp. Period. Abstr. (1986-); Read. Guide Abstr. Select Ed.; Read. Guide Period. Lit.; Mag. Index (1981-); TOM Gen. Index (1985-) [Full Txt.]; Vocat. Search (Jan. 1984-) [Full Txt.].

US
**CAR AND DRIVER BUYERS GUIDE TO ... NEW CARS. VFOAT** Car and Driver Buyers Guide to New Cars.; Buyers Guide to New Cars. (19??)-. English. an. $7.50. Hachette Magazines Inc., 1633 Broadway, New York NY 10019. **Tel** (212)767-6000. **(Subscription address:** STB, PO Box 7085, Brick NJ 08723.**)**

JA
**CAR AND DRIVER JAPAN.** (19??)-. Periodical. Japanese. sm. $156.00. **(Subscription address:** Maruzen Company Ltd., PO Box 5050, Import & Export Department, Tokyo 100 31 Japan.**)**

US/8755-626X
**CAR AND DRIVER ROAD TEST ANNUAL.** [Car driv. road test annu.]. **VFOAT** Road Test Annual. (198?)-. English. an. $4.95. Hachette Magazines Inc., 1633 Broadway, New York NY 10019. **Tel** (212)767-6000. **ED** William Jeanes. **LC** TL1; .C27. **DD** 629.28/24/05. **Bk Rev. Ad Acc. Circ:** 250,000.

US/1050-9682
**CAR AND DRIVER YEARBOOK (DANBURY, CONN.).** (CAR AND DRIVER YEARBOOK.). (1991)-. English. $15.00. Grolier Enterprises, Sherman Turnpike, Danbury CT 06816. **DD** 629.

US/0893-1208
**CAR BOOK, THE.** (THE CAR BOOK / BY JACK GILLIS.). [Car book]. (1982)-. English. $9.95. Harper Collins Publishers, Keystone Industrial Park, Scranton PA 18512. **Tel** (800)242-7737, (800)233-4727, FAX (800)822-4090. **LC** TL162; .G55. **DD** 629.2/222.

US/0275-391X
**CAR CARE.** [Car care]. **VFOAT** Money Saving Car Care. Periodical. English. an. $2.25. Performance Publications Inc, PO Box 99, Amawalk NY 10501. **LC** TL152; .C356. **DD** 629.28/722/05.

US/0162-3443
**CAR CARE GUIDE. Added/Corp** H.M. Gousha (Firm). (1973)-. English. an. $55.95. H.M Gousha & Company, PO Box 49006, 2001 The Alameda, San Jose CA 95161. **Tel** (800)662-6277. **ED** Robert Colver. **LC** TL152; .C3575. **DD** 629.28/722. **Circ:** 30,000.
**Desc:** Ten years of automotive maintenance services, comprehensive lubrication recommendations and popular automotive systems specifications including a service bulletin highlighting current technology, service, manufacturers updates.

US
**CAR CARE MALL NEWS.** English. mo. Automotive Week Publishing Company, PO Box 3495, Wayne NJ 07470-3495. **Tel** (201)694-7792, FAX (201)694-2817. **ED** Chuck Laverty. **Ad Acc. Circ:** 6,000 (ctrl).
**Desc:** Development and marketing of automotive service malls.

US/1042-7406
**CAR COLLECTING & INVESTING. *Ceased.*** [Car collect. invest.]. **VFOAT** Car Collecting and Investing. (1988)-(Dec. 1993). Periodical. English. bw. Mary Ann Liebert Inc., 1651 Third Avenue, New York NY 10128. **Tel** (212)289-2300, (800)M-LIEBERT, FAX (212)289-4697. **DD** 629.
**Desc:** Newsletter for individuals interested in collecting, restoring and selling collectible and investment-grade vehicles.

●US
**CAR COLLECTOR & CAR CLASSICS.** **VFOAT** Car Collector and Car Classics; Car Collector. Vol. 16, No. 1 (Jan. 1993)-. Periodical. English. mo. $32.00. Car Collector, 8601 Dunwoody Place/Suite 144, Atlanta GA 30338. **Tel** (404)442-1952. **LC** TL1; .C3116. ***Continues*** *Car Collector & Car Classics Magazine, 1057-4441.*
**Desc:** Covers the antique, classic, special interest and sports car fields. Generous use of color. Includes classifieds.

US/1057-4441
**CAR COLLECTOR & CAR CLASSICS MAGAZINE. *Title Change.* VFOAT** Car Collector and Car Classics Magazine; Car Collector. (1991)-(1992). Periodical. English. mo. Car Collector, 8601 Dunwoody Place/Suite 144, Atlanta GA 30338. **Tel** (404)442-1952. **ED** Don Peterson. **LC** TL1; .C3116. **DD** 629. **Bk Rev. Ad Acc. Circ:** 43,087 (ctrl). ***Continues*** *Car Collector and Car Classics, 0164-5552.* ***Continued by*** *Car Collector & Car Classics (Roswell, Ga. : 1993).*
**Desc:** Covers the antique, classic, special interest and sports car fields. Generous use of color. Includes classifieds.

US/1045-7216
**CAR CORRAL. *Title Change.*** [Car corral]. (1989)-(1992). Periodical. English. mo. Krause Publications, 700 East State Street, Iola WI 54990-0001. **Tel** (715)445-2214, FAX (715)445-4087, telex 55 6461. **ED** John Gunnell. **DD** 338. **Ad Acc. Circ:** 41,000. ***Absorbed by*** *Old Cars, 0048-1637.*
**Desc:** A marketplace for buyers and sellers of both collectors and late model cars. Unique listings of classified ads are arranged alphabetically by type of make and model and then listed by model year. Buyers can pinpoint the location of the vehicles they want to buy quickly and easily.

US/0008-6010
**CAR CRAFT.** [Car craft]. (1953)-. Periodical. English. mo. $19.94 US; $28.83 Canada; $27.94 other. Petersen Publishing Company, 6420 Wilshire Bouldevard, Los Angeles CA 90048. **Tel** (213)782-2485. **(Subscription address:** Neodata / Colorado, PO Box 2606, Boulder Boulder CO 80322.**) ED** Jeff Smith. **Circ:** 407,741. available on microfilm and microfiche from University Microfilms International (UMI). ***Continues*** *Honk.*
**Desc:** Read by auto enthusiasts interested in modifying, restoring and improving the performance of their musclecars and street machines. Each issue contains car features, new-car tests and practical how-to articles on all aspects of performance modifications...from bolt-ons to complete engine rebuilding, and more.

US/0743-3182
**CAR CRAFT ANNUAL.** [Car craft annu.]. Periodical. English. an. $4.95 US; $5.95 Canada. Petersen Publishing Company, 6420 Wilshire Bouldevard, Los Angeles CA 90048. **Tel** (213)782-2485. **LC** TL210; .C32. **DD** 629.2/28/05.

US/1052-407X
**CAR DEALER INSIDER (1990).** (CAR DEALER INSIDER.). [Car deal. insid.]. (1990)-. Periodical. English. Fifty times a year. $285.00 (one year), $560.00 (two year). United Communications Group, 11300 Rockville Pike, Suite 1100, Rockville MD 20852. **Tel** (301)816-8950 ext. 223, FAX (301)816-8945. **DD** 338. ***Continues*** *Car & Truck Dealer Insider Newsletter, 1043-6456.*

UK/0008-6037
**CAR MECHANICS.** (1958)-. Periodical. English. mo. £23.50 UK and Eire; £25.00 Europe; £31.00 other. Kelsey Publishing Limited, Kelsey House, 77 High Street, Beckenham Kent BR3 1AN, England. **Tel** 44 81 6583531, FAX 44 81 6508035. **[CCC].**

CN/0712-8614
**CAR (MONTREAL, QUEBEC).** (CAR : CLUB AUTOMOBILE ROUTIER.). [Car, Club automob. rout.]. **Added/Corp** CAR (Organisation). **VFOAT** Club Automobile Routier. (Autumn 1981)-. Periodical. French. ir. Free to members. Des Routiers Du Quebec, Bureau 208, 3019 Est, Sherbrooke, Montreal Quebec H1W 1B3. **DD** 629.2/222/060714.

US/0739-1722
**CAR PRICES. *Ceased.*** [Car prices]. **VFOAT** Car Prices Magazine. (1966)-(1992). Periodical. English. an. Peoples Publishing Company, 5440 Ericson Way, PO Box 1095, Arcata CA 95521. **Tel** (707)822-8442, FAX (707)822-0973. **ED** Rosemary Anderson. **DD** 629. **Ad Acc. Circ:** 100,000.
**Desc:** Car price catalogue.

US/1052-4118
**CAR RENTAL & LEASING INSIDER.** [Car rent. leas. insid.]. **VFOAT** Car Rental and Leasing Insider. (1990)-. Periodical. English. Twelve times a year. $245.00. United Communications Group, 11300 Rockville Pike, Suite 1100, Rockville MD 20852. **Tel** (301)816-8950 ext. 223, FAX (301)816-8945. **DD** 388. ***Continues*** *Car & Truck Rental/Leasing Insider Newsletter, 1043-6561.*

US/0743-6084
**CAR SERVICE MANUAL.** (CAR SERVICE MANUAL / MOBIL.). [Car serv. man.]. **Added/Corp** Mobil Oil Corporation. Products Dept. Mobil Oil Corporation. Technical Publications. **VFOAT** Mobil Car Service Manual. (19??)-. English. an. Mobil Oil Corporation / Technical Publications, Technical Publications, 3225 Gallows Road, Fairfax VA 22037. **LC** TL152; .C366. **DD** 629.28/722.

US/1046-3852
**CAR STEREO (DURANGO, COLO.).** (CAR STEREO.). English. an. $99.00. Orion Research Corporation, 14555 North Scottsdale Road, Suite 330, Scottsdale AZ 85260. **Tel** (800)844-0759, (602)951-1114, FAX (602)951-1117. **LC** TK7881.85; .C38. **DD** 629.2/77.

US/0272-7943
**CAR STEREO (NEW YORK). See** Engineering-Electricity, Electrical Engineering, Electronics.

JA
**CAR STYLING.** (Sept. 1987)-. Periodical. English (Japanese). bm. $129.75 US; $141.75 other. Kaneko Enterprises Inc, 16421 D Gothard Street, Huntington Beach CA 92647-3616. **Tel** (714)842-4332, FAX (714)848-7693. Index available. ***Continues*** *Car Styling Quarterly.*

CN/0384-9309
**CARGUIDE.** [Carguide]. **VFOAT** Carguide Preview. (197?)-. English (French). Six times a year (Jan., Mar., May, July, Sept., Nov.). 12.99Can$ (one year), 21.99Can$ (two year) Canada; 20.99Can$ (one year), 37.99Can$ (two year) other. Formula Publications Ltd, 447 Speers Road, Suite 4, Oakville ONT L6K 3S7 Canada. **Tel** (905)842-6591, FAX (905)842-6843. **ED** Alan McPhee and Tim Lindsay. **DD** 629.22/22/05. **Ad Acc, Adv Mgr:** Grant Wells or Al Henderson. **Circ:** January-English 229,500; others, 80,000, January-French 97,800; others, 40,000.
**Desc:** All of these issues contains articles on road testing, touring articles, new and exciting reviews, technical information, automotive history, automotive trivia, and more to keep you informed on what's happening in the automotive industry.

FR/0750-8131
**CARROSSERIE. See** Transportation.

US
**CARS.** Periodical. English. $10.00. Popular Publications / New York, 420 Lexington Avenue, New York NY 11017. **LC** TL236; .H425. **DD** 629.22/8. ***Continues*** *Hi-Performance Cars.*

US
**CARS.** (1985)-. Periodical. English. an. $3.95. Kiplinger Washington Editors, 1729 H Street Northwest, Washington DC 20006. **Tel** (202)887-6400, (800)544-0155, FAX (202)331-1206. **LC** TL162; .C397. **DD** 629.2/222.

US/0008-6975
**CARS & PARTS. VFOAT** Cars and Parts. **VAT** Cars and parts. (19??)-. Periodical. English. mo. $22.00 (one year), $38.00 (two years) US; $27.00 (one year), $48.00 (two years) other. Amos Press, PO Box 29, Sidney OH 45365. **Tel** (513)498-0802, (800)448-7293, FAX (513)498-0812. **ED** Robert J Stevens. **LC** TL7.A1; C39. **DD** 629.2/222/075. Index available. **Bk Rev. Ad Acc. Circ:** 120,000.
**Desc:** Readers collect cars from all eras. Editorial focus is on authenticity, restoration, history. How-to's, swap meets, questions answered, classified marketplace for cars, parts, accessories and services.

US
**CARS & PARTS ANNUAL. VFOAT** Cars and Parts Annual. (19??)-. Periodical. English. an (Sept.). $4.95. Amos Press, PO Box 29, Sidney OH 45365. **Tel** (513)498-0802, (800)448-7293, FAX (513)498-0812. **LC** TL7; .C28. **DD** 629.2/222/075.

UK
**CARS IN PROFILE.** Collection 1- 1973-. English. £4.00. **LC** TL236; .C344. **DD** 629.22/22/0904.

NE
**CBS CARROSSERIE-, AANHANGWAGEN- EN OPLEGGERINDUSTRIE / CENTRAAL BUREAU VOOR DE STATISTIEK, HOOFDAFDELING STATISTIEKEN VAN INDUSTRIE EN BOUWNIJVERHEID.** **VFOAT** C.B.S. Carrosserie, Aanhangwagen- en Opleggerindustrie; Manufacture of Bodies for Motor Vehicles, of Trailers and Semitrailers. 1980-. Dutch (summaries and/or abstracts in English). an. Fl10.55. Staatsuitgeverij, Christoffel Plantijnstraat 1, 2515 TZ'S Gravenhage Netherlands. **Tel** 070/78-95-70. **LC** HD9710.3.N4; N47. ***Continues*** *Carrosserie-, Aanhangwagen- en Opleggerindustrie Produktiestatistieken.*

●US/1066-4734
**CC PERFORMANCE CAR. VFOAT** C C Performance Car. **VAT** Car Craft Performance Car. (1993)-. Periodical. English. $3.95. Peterson Publishing Company, 6725 Sunset Boulevard, Los Angeles CA 90028.

CN/0702-8369
**CENTRE LINE (TORONTO).** (CENTRE LINE.). Began publication in 1969?. Periodical. English. Ontario Motor League, 2 Carlton Street, Toronto Ontario M5B 1K4 Canada. **DD** 388.3/09713.

JA/0915-1702
**CG. CAR GRAPHIC.** (CAR GRAPHIC.). [CG. Car graph.]. **VFOAT** Car Graphic; Car Guraffiku. (1962)-. Periodical. Japanese. mo. $222.00. Nigensha, (Nigensha Publishing Co., Ltd.), 4-6, Misakicho 2 Chome, Chiyodaku, Tokyoto 101 Japan. **(Subscription address:** Maruzen Company Ltd., PO Box 5050, Import & Export Department, Tokyo 100 31 Japan.**) DD** 629.22.

KO
**CHABOTAP. See** Insurance.

KO
**CHADONGCHA CHONOL. Added/Corp** Kyotong Sinmunsa. **VFOAT** Monthly Car Journal. Vol. 23 No. 6 (1991)-. Periodical. Korean. mo. Kyotong Sinmunsa, 81-2 2-Ka Hangangno, Yongsan-Ku, Seoul 140-012 Korea. **LC** HE277.5.A15; W64. ***Continues*** *Wolgan Kyotong.*

KO
**CHADONGCHA SAENGHWAL. VFOAT** Car Life. V. 1- (1984, 9)-. Periodical. Korean (Korean). mo. W30,800. **LC** TL4; .C4.

US
**CHASSIS SERVICE & REPAIR. DOMESTIC CARS. Added/Corp** Mitchell Manuals, inc. **VFOAT** Domestic Cars; Mitchell Chassis Service & Repair, Domestic Cars. **VAT** Chassis Service

Transportation —Automobiles

and Repair, Domestic Cars. (1976)-. English. ir. $159.00. Mitchell International Inc, PO Box 26260, San Diego CA 92126-0260. **Tel** (619)578-6550, (800)648-8010, FAX (619)578-4752. **(Subscription address:** Mitchell International Inc., PO Box 71654, Chicago IL 60694.**)**

US/0747-2080
**CHECKPOINT (IRVING, TEX.).** (CHECKPOINT : THE OFFICIAL PUBLICATION OF THE UNITED STATES AUTO CLUB, MOTORING DIVISION, INC. / UNITED STATES AUTO CLUB MOTORING DIVISION.). **VFOAT** Check Point. Periodical. English. qt. United States Auto Club, Motoring Division, 250 East Carpenter Freeway, Irving TX 75062.

US/1056-2974
**CHEVY ACTION.** [Chevy action]. **VFOAT** Muscle Review Presents Chevy Action. Vol. 1, No. 1 (Spring 1991)-. Periodical. English. bm. $4.95 (single issue). Dobbs Publications, PO Box 455, Lakeland FL 33807. **Tel** (813)646-5744. **LC** WMLC 91/1764. **DD** 796.

US/1062-192X
**CHEVY HIGH PERFORMANCE.** [Chevy high perform.]. (199?)-. Periodical. English. mo. $19.94 US; $30.97 Canada; $29.94 other. Petersen Publishing Company, 6420 Wilshire Bouldevard, Los Angeles CA 90048. **Tel** (213)782-2485. **(Subscription address:** Neodata / Colorado, PO Box 2606, Boulder Boulder CO 80322.**)** **DD** 629. ***Continues*** *Chevrolet High Performance, 1052-5491.*

CC
**CHI CHE KUNG CHENG. QICHE GONGCHENG.** **Added/Corp** Chung-kuo Chi Hsieh Kung Cheng Hsueh Hui (Peking, China). Chi Che Hsueh Hui. **VFOAT** Qiche Gongcheng. (19??)-. Trade Publication. Chinese (summaries and/or abstracts in English). qt. ¥21. Zhongguo Qiche Gongcheng Xuehui, (Society of Automotive Engineers), 16 Fuxingmenwai Street, Beijing 100860, People's Republic of China. **Tel** 86-1-860262, FAX 86-1-3263605. **(Subscription address:** China International Book Trading Corporation, PO Box 399, Library Service Department, Beijing 100044 People's Republic of China.**)** **ED** Wu Huile. **LC** TL4; .C45. **DD** 629.2/05. **Circ:** 4,000.

US/1046-6142
**CHICAGO USED CAR SELLER'S GUIDE, THE.** **VFOAT** Used Car Seller's Guide. (1991)-. Periodical. English. $6.95. Green Light Press, 545 West Golf Road, Arlington Heights IL 60005.

US/1055-5560
**CHILTON'S AIR CONDITIONING AND HEATING LABOR GUIDE.** [Chilton's air cond. heat. labor guide]. **Added/Corp** Chilton Book Company. **VFOAT** Air Conditioning and Heating Labor Guide; Chilton Motor/Age ... Air Conditioning and Heating Labor Guide. (1991)-. English. be. $15.00. Chilton Book Company, 1 Chilton Way, Radnor PA 19089. **Tel** (215)964-4000, (800)695-1214, FAX (215)964-4273, telex 6851035 CHILTON UW. **DD** 629.

US/1053-1114
**CHILTON'S AIR CONDITIONING AND HEATING MANUAL.** [Chilton's air cond. heat. manual]. **VFOAT** Air Conditioning and Heating Manual. (1991)-. English. be. $59.00. Chilton Book Company, 1 Chilton Way, Radnor PA 19089. **Tel** (215)964-4000, (800)695-1214, FAX (215)964-4273, telex 6851035 CHILTON UW. **DD** 629. ***Continues*** *Chilton's Auto Heating, Air Conditioning Manual, 1042-4911.*

US/0069-3634
**CHILTON'S AUTO REPAIR MANUAL.** [Chilton's auto repair man.]. **VFOAT** Auto Repair Manual. (1968)-. Periodical. English. an. $26.95. Chilton Company, 201 King of Prussia Road, Radnor PA 19089. **Tel** (610)964-4122, (800)695-1214, FAX (610)964-4978, telex 6851035 CHILTON UW. **LC** TL152. **[CCC].** Each issue contains an index to its own contents (no volume index)--loose. ***Continues*** *Glenn's Auto Repair Manual.*

US/0273-656X
**CHILTON'S AUTOMOTIVE INDUSTRIES (1976).** (CHILTON'S AUTOMOTIVE INDUSTRIES.). [Chilton's automot. ind.]. **VFOAT** Automotive Industries; Chilton's International Automotive Industries. Vol. 154 (Jan. 1, 1976)-. Periodical. English. mo. $70.00. Chilton Company, 201 King of Prussia Road, Radnor PA 19089. **Tel** (610)964-4122, (800)695-1214, FAX (610)964-4978, telex 6851035 CHILTON UW. **ED** John McElroy and Lindsay Brooke. **LC** TL1; .A6. **DD** 629.2/05. **CODEN** CAUIEG. **[CCC].** Index available. **Ad Acc. Circ:** 89,000 (ctrl). available on microfilm and microfiche from University Microfilms International (UMI). Documents available from Documents on Demand. ***Continues*** *Automotive Industries, 0886-4675.*
**Desc:** Circulation of more than 81,500 reaches the decision makers within the worldwide vehicle producing industries; topics include news, management, marketing, engineering, design, manufacturing, hi-tech, off-highway, materials and new products.
**Ind/Abst** Appl. Sci. Technol. Index; Bus. ASAP (1990-) [Full Txt.]; Bus. Index (1985-); Bus. Period. Index; Ei Page One; EMBASE; Energy Inf. Abstr.; Energy Res. Abstr. (March 1976-); Environ. Abstr.; F&S Index Plus Text, Int. [Select. Cov.]; Gen. BusinessFile (1985-); Gen. Period. Index (1985-); Infomat Int. Bus.; Mag. Search; PROMT; Trade Ind. ASAP [Full Txt.]; Trade Ind. Index (1981-) [Full Txt.]; Vocat. Search (July 1993-); Wilson Bus. Abstr.

US/0193-3264
**CHILTON'S AUTOMOTIVE MARKETING.** [Chilton's automot. mark.]. **VFOAT** Automotive Marketing. Vol. 7 (Jan. 1978)-. Periodical. English. mo. $50.00. Chilton Company, 201 King of Prussia Road, Radnor PA 19089. **Tel** (610)964-4122, (800)695-1214, FAX (610)964-4978, telex 6851035 CHILTON UW. **ED** Charles Haberstroh. **DD** 381. **[CCC].** **Ad Acc. Circ:** 26,621 (ctrl). available on microfilm and microfiche from University Microfilms International (UMI). ***Continues*** *Chilton's AM: Automotive Marketing, 0045-107X.*
**Desc:** Serves the automotive retail aftermarket; reaches decision-making buyers of parts, accessories, chemicals, oil and equipment. Editorial direction is business marketing, merchandising and news. Winner of four Neal Awards in the last five years.
**Ind/Abst** Bus. ASAP (1990-) [Full Txt.]; Bus. Index (1985-); Gen. BusinessFile (1985-); Gen. Period. Index (1985-); Mag. Search; Trade Ind. ASAP [Full Txt.]; Trade Ind. Index (1981-) [Full Txt.]; Vocat. Search (Jan. 1993-).

●US/1072-7507
**CHILTON'S CASCADE EMISSION CONTROL APPLICATION GUIDE.** (1994)-. English. be. Chilton Company, 201 King of Prussia Road, Radnor PA 19089. **Tel** (610)964-4122, (800)695-1214, FAX (610)964-4978, telex 6851035 CHILTON UW.

US/1056-1285
**CHILTON'S CHASIS ELECTRONICS SERVICE MANUAL. ASIAN CARS AND TRUCKS.** **VFOAT** Asian Cars and Trucks. (1991)-. English. be. $72.00. Chilton Book Company, 1 Chilton Way, Radnor PA 19089. **Tel** (215)964-4000, (800)695-1214, FAX (215)964-4273, telex 6851035 CHILTON UW. ***Continues in part*** *Chilton's Chassis Electronics Service Manual.*

●US/1065-660X
**CHILTON'S CHASSIS ELECTRONIC SERVICE MANUAL. CHRYSLER.** **VFOAT** Chassis Electronic Service Manual. Chrysler; Chrysler. (1993)-. English. be. $95.00. Chilton Book Company, 1 Chilton Way, Radnor PA 19089. **Tel** (215)964-4000, (800)695-1214, FAX (215)964-4273, telex 6851035 CHILTON UW. ***Continues*** *Chilton's Chasis Electronics Service Manual. Ford/Chrysler/Jeep-Eagle Cars and Light Trucks.*

●US/1065-6618
**CHILTON'S CHASSIS ELECTRONIC SERVICE MANUAL. FORD.** **VFOAT** Chassis Electronic Service Manual. Ford; Ford. (1993)-. English. be. $95.00. Chilton Book Company, 1 Chilton Way, Radnor PA 19089. **Tel** (215)964-4000, (800)695-1214, FAX (215)964-4273, telex 6851035 CHILTON UW. ***Continues*** *Chilton's Chasis Electronics Service Manual. Ford/Chrysler/Jeep-Eagle Cars and Light Trucks.*

●US/1072-7469
**CHILTON'S DRIVEABILITY MANUAL. ASIAN.** **VFOAT** Driveability Manual. Asian. (1994)-. English. be. Chilton Company, 201 King of Prussia Road, Radnor PA 19089. **Tel** (610)964-4122, (800)695-1214, FAX (610)964-4978, telex 6851035 CHILTON UW. ***Continues*** *Chilton ... Motor/Age Professional Electronic Engine Controls Manual. Asian, 1050-1207.*

●US/1072-7477
**CHILTON'S DRIVEABILITY MANUAL. CHRYSLER.** **VFOAT** Driveability Manual. Chrysler; Chrysler. (1994)-. English. be. Chilton Company, 201 King of Prussia Road, Radnor PA 19089. **Tel** (610)964-4122, (800)695-1214, FAX (610)964-4978, telex 6851035 CHILTON UW. ***Continues in part*** *Chilton's Electronic Engine Controls Manual. Ford, Chrysler, Jeep-Eagle Cars and Light Trucks.*

●US/1072-7485
**CHILTON'S DRIVEABILITY MANUAL. EUROPEAN.** **VFOAT** Driveability Manual. European. (1994)-. English. be. Chilton Company, 201 King of Prussia Road, Radnor PA 19089. **Tel** (610)964-4122, (800)695-1214, FAX (610)964-4978, telex 6851035 CHILTON UW. ***Continues*** *Chilton's Electronic Engine Controls Manual. Audi, BMW, Jaguar, Mercedes-Benz, Merkur, Peugeot, Porsche, Saab, Sterling, Volkswagen, Volvo, Yugo, 1050-1134.*

●US/1072-7493
**CHILTON'S DRIVEABILITY MANUAL. FORD.** **VFOAT** Driveability Manual. Ford; Ford. (1994)-. English. be. Chilton Company, 201 King of Prussia Road, Radnor PA 19089. **Tel** (610)964-4122, (800)695-1214, FAX (610)964-4978, telex 6851035 CHILTON UW. ***Continues in part*** *Chilton's Electronic Engine Controls Manual. Ford, Chrysler, Jeep-Eagle Cars and Light Trucks.*

US/1050-1134
**CHILTON'S ELECTRONIC ENGINE CONTROLS MANUAL. EUROPEAN CARS AND LIGHT TRUCKS.** [Chilton's electron. engine controls man., Audi BMW Jaguar Mercedes-Benz Merkur Peugeot Porsche Saab Sterling Volkswagen Volvo Yugo]. **VFOAT** Electronic Engine Controls Manual European Cars and Light Trucks. (1990)-. English. be. $72.00 (single issue). Chilton Book Company, 1 Chilton Way, Radnor PA 19089. **Tel** (215)964-4000, (800)695-1214, FAX (215)964-4273, telex 6851035 CHILTON UW. **DD** 629. ***Continues in part*** *Chilton's Electronic Engine Controls Manual. Import Cars and Trucks, 1042-4903.*

US/1053-2196
**CHILTON'S EMISSION CONTROL MANUAL.** **VFOAT** Emission Control Manual. (1991)-. English. be. $80.00. Chilton Book Company, 1 Chilton Way, Radnor PA 19089. **Tel** (215)964-4000, (800)695-1214, FAX (215)964-4273, telex 6851035 CHILTON UW.

US/1053-2188
**CHILTON'S EMISSION CONTROLS APPLICATION GUIDE.** **VFOAT** Emission Controls Application Guide. (1991)-. English. be. $19.00. Chilton Book Company, 1 Chilton Way, Radnor PA 19089. **Tel** (215)964-4000, (800)695-1214, FAX (215)964-4273, telex 6851035 CHILTON UW.

US/1050-1169
**CHILTON'S EMISSION, DIAGNOSIS, TUNE-UP AND SERVICE MANUAL. DOMESTIC CARS AND LIGHT TRUCKS.** **VFOAT** Emission, Diagnosis, Tune-Up and Service Manual. Domestic Cars and Light Trucks. (1990)-. English. be. $40.00 (single issue). Chilton Book Company, 1 Chilton Way, Radnor PA 19089. **Tel** (215)964-4000, (800)695-1214, FAX (215)964-4273, telex 6851035 CHILTON UW.

US/1055-6834
**CHILTON'S GEARBOX FLUID SERVICE LOCATOR.** **VFOAT** Gearbox Fluid SeLvice locator. (1991)-. English. be. $45.00. Chilton Book Company, 1 Chilton Way, Radnor PA 19089. **Tel** (215)964-4000, (800)695-1214, FAX (215)964-4273, telex 6851035 CHILTON UW. **DD** 629.

US/1053-1823
**CHILTON'S GUIDE TO CHASSIS ELECTRONIC CONTROLS AND POWER ACCESSORIES. IMPORT CARS AND TRUCKS.** **VFOAT** Import Cars and Trucks. (1991)-. English. be. $19.95. Chilton Book Company, 1 Chilton Way, Radnor PA 19089. **Tel** (215)964-4000, (800)695-1214, FAX (215)964-4273, telex 6851035 CHILTON UW. ***Continues in part*** *Chilton's Guide to Chassis Electronics and Power Accessories, 1049-8478.*

US/1053-1130
**CHILTON'S GUIDE TO CHASSIS ELECTRONICS & POWER ACCESSORIES. FORD/CHRYSLER/JEEP/EAGLE.** [Chilton's guide chass. electron. power accessories, Ford/Chrysler/Jeep/Eagle]. **VFOAT** Chassis Electronics & Power Accessories. Ford/Chrysler/Jeep/Eagle; Chassis Electronics and Power Accessories. Ford/Chrysler/Jeep/Eagle; Ford/Chrysler/Jeep/Eagle; Ford, Chrysler, Jeep, Eagle. (1991)-. English. be. $19.95. Chilton Book Company, 1 Chilton Way, Radnor PA 19089. **Tel** (215)964-4000, (800)695-1214, FAX (215)964-4273, telex 6851035 CHILTON UW. **DD** 629. ***Continues in part*** *Chilton's Guide to Chassis Electronics and Power Accessories, 1049-8478.*

US/1053-6302
**CHILTON'S GUIDE TO CHASSIS ELECTRONICS AND POWER ACCESSORIES. GENERAL MOTORS.** [Chilton's guide chass electron. power accessories, Gen. Mot.]. **VFOAT** Guide to Chassis Electronics and Power Accessories. General Motors; General Motors. (1989/91)-. English. be. $19.95. Chilton Book Company, 1 Chilton Way, Radnor PA 19089. **Tel** (215)964-4000, (800)695-1214, FAX (215)964-4273, telex 6851035 CHILTON UW. **DD** 629. ***Continues in part*** *Chilton's Guide to Chassis Electronics and Power Accessories, 1049-8478.*

●US/1061-740X
**CHILTON'S GUIDE TO FUEL INJECTION AND ELECTRONIC ENGINE CONTROLS. BUICK, OLDS, PONTIAC CARS AND TRUCKS.** [Chilton's guide fuel inject. electron. engine controls, Buick, Olds, Pontiac cars trucks]. **Added/Corp** Chilton Book Company. **VFOAT** Chilton's Guide to Fuel Injection & Electronic Engine Controls. Buick, Olds, Pontiac Cars and trucks; Guide to Fuel Injection and Electronic Engine Controls. Buick, Olds, Pontiac Cars and trucks; Guide to Fuel Injection & Electronic Engine Controls. Buick, Olds, Pontiac Cars and

trucks; Fuel Injection & Electronic Engine Controls. Buick, Olds, Pontiac Cars and Trucks; Fuel Injection and Electronic Engine Controls. Buick, Olds, Pontiac Cars and Trucks; Chilton Fuel Injection & Electronic Engine Controls. Buick, Olds, Pontiac Cars and Trucks. (1993)-. English. be. Chilton Book Company, 1 Chilton Way, Radnor PA 19089. **Tel** (215)964-4000, (800)695-1214, FAX (215)964-4273, telex 6851035 CHILTON UW. ***Separated from*** *Chilton's Guide to Fuel Injection and Electronic Engine Controls. General Motors, 1052-9144.*

●US/1061-7418
**CHILTON'S GUIDE TO FUEL INJECTION AND ELECTRONIC ENGINE CONTROLS. CHEVROLET CARS AND TRUCKS.** [Chilton's guide fuel inject. electron. engine controls, Chevrolet cars trucks]. **Added/Corp** Chilton Book Company. **VFOAT** Chilton's Guide to Fuel Injection & Electronic Engine Controls. Chevrolet Cars and trucks; Guide to Fuel Injection and Electronic Engine Controls. Chevrolet Cars and Trucks; Guide to Fuel Injection & Electronic Engine Controls. Chevrolet Cars and Trucks; Fuel Injection & Electronic Engine Controls. Chevrolet Cars and Trucks; Fuel Injection and Electronic Engine Controls. Chevrolet Cars and Trucks; Chilton Fuel Injection & Electronic Engine Controls. Chevrolet Cars and Trucks. (1992)-. English. be. Chilton Book Company, 1 Chilton Way, Radnor PA 19089. **Tel** (215)964-4000, (800)695-1214, FAX (215)964-4273, telex 6851035 CHILTON UW. ***Separated from*** *Chilton's Guide to Fuel Injection and Electronic Engine Controls. General Motors, 1052-9144.*

●US/1061-7388
**CHILTON'S GUIDE TO FUEL INJECTION AND ELECTRONIC ENGINE CONTROLS. CHRYSLER CARS AND TRUCKS.** [Chilton's guide fuel inject. electron. engine controls, Chrysler cars trucks]. **Added/Corp** Chilton Book Company. **VFOAT** Chilton's Guide to Fuel Injection & Electronic Engine Controls. Chrysler Cars and trucks; Guide to Fuel Injection and Electronic Engine Controls. Chrysler Cars and trucks; Guide to Fuel Injection & Electronic Engine Controls. Chrysler Cars and trucks; Fuel Injection & Electronic Engine Controls. Chrysler Cars and trucks; Fuel Injection and Electronic Engine Controls. Chrysler Cars and trucks; Chilton Fuel Injection & Electronic Engine Controls. Chrysler Cars and Trucks. (1992)-. English. be. Chilton Book Company, 1 Chilton Way, Radnor PA 19089. **Tel** (215)964-4000, (800)695-1214, FAX (215)964-4273, telex 6851035 CHILTON UW. ***Separated from*** *Chilton's Guide to Fuel Injection and Electronic Engine Controls. Ford/Chrysler, 1053-7635.*

●US/1061-7396
**CHILTON'S GUIDE TO FUEL INJECTION AND ELECTRONIC ENGINE CONTROLS. FORD CARS AND TRUCKS.** [Chilton's guide fuel inject. electron. engine controls, Ford cars trucks]. **Added/Corp** Chilton Book Company. **VFOAT** Chilton's Guide to Fuel Injection & Electronic Engine Controls. Ford Cars and trucks; Guide to Fuel Injection and Electronic Engine Controls. Ford Cars and Trucks; Guide to Fuel Injection & Electronic Engine Controls. Ford Cars and Trucks; Fuel Injection & Electronic Engine Controls. Ford Cars and Trucks; Fuel Injection and Electronic Engine Controls. Ford Cars and Trucks; Chilton Fuel Injection & Electronic Engine Controls. Ford Cars and Trucks. (1992)-. English. be. Chilton Book Company, 1 Chilton Way, Radnor PA 19089. **Tel** (215)964-4000, (800)695-1214, FAX (215)964-4273, telex 6851035 CHILTON UW. ***Separated from*** *Chilton's Guide to Fuel Injection and Electronic Engine Controls. Ford/Chrysler, 1053-7635.*

●US/1065-6626
**CHILTON'S HEAVY DUTY TRUCK SERVICE MANUAL.** **VFOAT** Heavy Duty Truck Service Manual. (1992)-. English. be. $95.00. Chilton Book Company, 1 Chilton Way, Radnor PA 19089. **Tel** (215)964-4000, (800)695-1214, FAX (215)964-4273, telex 6851035 CHILTON UW.

US/0742-0323
**CHILTON'S IMPORT LABOR GUIDE AND PARTS MANUAL.** **Added/Corp** Chilton Book Company. **VFOAT** Import Labor Guide and Parts Manual; Chilton Motor/Age Professional Import Labor Guide and Parts Manual. (1981)-. English. ir. $95.00 (latest edition). Chilton Company, 201 King of Prussia Road, Radnor PA 19089. **Tel** (610)964-4122, (800)695-1214, FAX (610)964-4978, telex 6851035 CHILTON UW. **LC** TL152; .C5293. **DD** 338.4/3629/28722.

US/0749-5579
**CHILTON'S LABOR GUIDE AND PARTS MANUAL (1980).** ***Ceased.*** (CHILTON'S ... LABOR GUIDE AND PARTS MANUAL.). [Chilton's labor guide parts man.]. **Added/Corp** Chilton Book Company. **VFOAT** Chilton ... Motor/Age Professional Labor Guide and Parts Manual. (1980)-(19??). English. an. Chilton Company, 201 King of Prussia Road, Radnor PA 19089. **Tel** (610)964-4122, (800)695-1214, FAX (610)964-4978, telex 6851035 CHILTON UW. **LC** TL152; .C5517. **DD** 338.4/3629/28722. ***Continues*** *Chilton's Motor/Age Professional Labor Guide and Parts Manual, 0361-9397.*

●US/1060-4405
**CHILTON'S MEDIUM/HEAVY DUTY TRUCK SERVICE MANUAL.** **VFOAT** Chilton's Medium Heavy Duty Truck Service Manual. (1992)-. Periodical. English. be. $75.00 (single issue). Chilton Book Company, 1 Chilton Way, Radnor PA 19089. **Tel** (215)964-4000, (800)695-1214, FAX (215)964-4273, telex 6851035 CHILTON UW.

US/0193-7022
**CHILTON'S MOTOR/AGE (1970).** (CHILTON'S MOTOR/AGE.). [Chilton's motor/age]. **VFOAT** Chilton's Motor Age; Motor/Age; Motor Age. Vol. 89 (Jan. 1970)-. Periodical. English. mo. $44.00. Chilton Company, 201 King of Prussia Road, Radnor PA 19089. **Tel** (610)964-4122, (800)695-1214, FAX (610)964-4978, telex 6851035 CHILTON UW. **ED** Stanley Stephenson. **DD** 388. **[CCC]. Ad Acc. Circ:** 136,000 (ctrl). available on microfilm and microfiche from University Microfilms International (UMI). ***Continues*** *Motor Age.*
**Desc:** Serves the automotive aftermarket, general and specialty repair shops, service stations, car dealerships, collusion repair facilities plus their wholesale suppliers. Editorial focuses on mechanical, management and merchandising themes helping shop owners repair the nation's automobiles and maintain business profitability.
**Ind/Abst** Bus. ASAP (1990-) [Full Txt.]; Mag. Search; Trade Ind. ASAP [Full Txt.]; Trade Ind. Index (1981-) [Full Txt.]; Vocat. Search (July 1993-).

US/0737-2663
**CHILTON'S MOTOR/AGE ... PROFESSIONAL MECHANIC'S REFERENCE GUIDE.** [Chilton's motor/age prof. mech. ref. guide]. **VFOAT** Professional Mechanic's Reference Guide. **VAT** Chilton's Motor Age Professional Mechanic's Reference Guide. English. Chilton Book Company, 1 Chilton Way, Radnor PA 19089. **Tel** (215)964-4000, (800)695-1214, FAX (215)964-4273, telex 6851035 CHILTON UW. **LC** TL152; .C5518. **DD** 629.28/722/0212.

●US/1060-4413
**CHILTON'S NISSAN REPAIR MANUAL.** (1992)-. Periodical. English. be. $24.95 (single issue). CEM Chilton's Control Equipment Master, Chilton Company, Chilton Way, Radnor PA 19089. **Tel** (215)964-4000, (800)695-1214, FAX (215)964-4273, telex 6851035 CHILTON UW.

US/1055-6842
**CHILTON'S QUICK LUBRICATION GUIDE.** [Chilton's quick lubr. guide]. **VFOAT** Quick Lubrication Guide. (1991)-. Periodical. English. be. $45.00 (single issue). H.M. Gousha Company, PO Box 49006, 2001 The Alameda, San Jose CA 95161. **Tel** (800)662-6277. **DD** 629.

●US/1065-6634
**CHILTON'S TRANSMISSION DIAGNOSTIC MANUAL.** **VFOAT** Transmission Diagnostic Manual. (1993)-. English. be. $95.00. Chilton Book Company, 1 Chilton Way, Radnor PA 19089. **Tel** (215)964-4000, (800)695-1214, FAX (215)964-4273, telex 6851035 CHILTON UW.

GW/0412-3417
**CHRISTOPHORUS STUTTGART.** (1952)-. Periodical. German. bm. $27.00. Dr Ing HCF Porsche AG, Postfach 400640, W-7000 Stuttgart Germany. **Tel** 011 49 7141 398314. **(Subscription address:** Porsche Cars North America Inc., 200 South Virginia Street, Reno NV 89501.) **ED** Jurgen Pippig. **UDC** 629.113. **Ad Acc.**
**Desc:** Magazine for clients and friends of Porsche, car tests, reports on new technical developments, and actual information.

US
**CHRYSLER / AMC COLLISION ESTIMATING GUIDE.** (19??)-. Periodical. English. qt. $104.00. Mitchell International Inc, PO Box 26260, San Diego CA 92126-0260. **Tel** (619)578-6550, (800)648-8010, FAX (619)578-4752. **(Subscription address:** Mitchell International Inc., PO Box 71654, Chicago IL 60694.)

UK
**CLASSIC AND SPORTSCAR.** English. mo (12 issues). £25.00 UK; £39.00 Eire & Europe; £67.00 America, Middle East, Africa & India; £82.00 Australia, New Zealand & Japan; £39.00 other. Haymarket Publishing Ltd., 12 14 Ansdell Street, London W8 5TR England. **Tel** 011 44 483 733800, FAX 011 44 483 776573. **(Subscription address:** Eric Waiter Associates, PO Box 188, Berkely Heights, NJ 07922; Telephone: (800)272-2670 or (908)665-7811) **ED** Ian Bond. Index available. cum. index. **Bk Rev**, (Qty: 24). **Ad Acc, Adv Mgr:** Matthew Newell, **Tel** (908)665-7811. **Circ:** 100,000.
**Desc:** Every issue has over 200 pages of interviews, club and auction news, classic/antique, club valuation and reviews of past/present sportscars.

US/1042-5683
**CLASSIC AUTO RESTORER.** [Class. auto restor.]. (June 1989)-. Periodical. English. mo. $25.97. Fancy Publications, PO Box 6050, Mission Viejo CA 92690. **Tel** (714)855-8822, (800)426-2516, FAX (714)855-3045. **(Subscription address:** Palm Coast Data, PO Box 420235, Agency Department, Palm Coast FL 32142.) **LC** WMLC L 83/6669. **DD** 629.

US/0009-8310
**CLASSIC CAR.** **Added/Corp** Classic Car Club of America. Vol. 1 (Jan. 1953)-. Periodical. English. qt. $28.00 US; $34.00 Canada; $33.10 Mexico; $35.20 other. Classic Car Club, 2300 East Devon Avenue, Suite 126, Des Plaines IL 60018. **Tel** (708)390-0443. **LC** TL7; .C5. **Circ:** 5,000 (ctrl).
**Desc:** Hobby magazine for classic car collectors.

US/0740-4794
**CLASSIC CAR BIMONTHLY.** [Class. car bimon.]. **VFOAT** Classic Car Series. (19??)-. Periodical. English. bm. $3.50 single issue. Consumer Guide, 3841 West Oakton Street, Skokie IL 60076. **Tel** (312)676-3470, telex 280084. **LC** TL1; .C56. **DD** 629.222.

US
**CLASSIC CAR DIGEST.** (199?)-. English. qt. $24.00. BEMIS Communication Group Inc., 118 Pleasant Street, Marblehead MA 01945. **Tel** (617)639-3000. ***Continues*** *Carrozzeria, 0896-3061.*

US/0098-2741
**CLASSIC MG YEARBOOK, THE.** Began with Vol. for 1973. English. an. $13.95. R L Knudson, 21 Franklin Street, Oneonta NY 13820. **LC** TL215.M2; C55. **DD** 629.22/22.

UK/0953-8240
**COACH AND BUS WEEK.** (19??)-. Periodical. English. wk. £49.00 UK; £92.00 Europe; £124.00 other. EMAP Response Publishing, Wentworth House, Wentworth Street, Peterborough PE1 IDS England. **Tel** 011 44 733 63100, FAX 011 44 733 66437.

US/0742-812X
**COLLECTIBLE AUTOMOBILE.** [Collect. automob.]. Vol. 1, No. 1 (May 1984)-. Periodical. English. bm. $28.50 (1 year), $57.00 (2 year), $85.50 (3 year). Publications International Ltd., 7373 North Cicero Avenue, Lincolnwood IL 60646. **Tel** (708)676-3470. **ED** Duane Mackie and Chris Poole. **Bk Rev. Ad Acc. Circ:** 90,000.
**Desc:** Points out pros and cons and assesses the collectibility of cars. Color photos throughout.

US
**COLLECTIBLE TRUCKS.** **VFOAT** Cars & Parts Collectible Trucks. Vol. 1, No. 1 (1991)-. Periodical. English. **LC** WMLC 91/4455.

US/0888-1944
**COLLECTOR CAR NEWS.** **See** Hobbies.

UK
**COLLECTOR'S CAR.** **See** Hobbies.

US/0739-7437
**COLLISION.** (197?)-. Periodical. English. Ten times a year (every six weeks). $28.00 (one year), $58.00 (three year). Collision Magazine, PO Box M, Franklin MA 02038. **Tel** (508)528-6211. **ED** J.A. Kruza. **Bk Rev**, (Qty: 20 or more per year). **Ad Acc. Circ:** 24,000.
**Desc:** Written for the auto body manager and repairman, covering news, technical, and legislative matters as well as insurance policies towards claims.

US
**COLLISION ESTIMATING GUIDE DOMESTIC.** **Added/Corp** Mitchell International. **VFOAT** Chrysler Motors, Jeep-Eagle Collision Estimating Guide Domestic; Mitchell Collision Estimating Guide Domestic. Vol. 30/13 (Oct. 1988)-. Periodical. English. Sixteen times a year. $244.00. Mitchell International Inc, PO Box 26260, San Diego CA 92126-0260. **Tel** (619)578-6550, (800)648-8010, FAX (619)578-4752. **(Subscription address:** Mitchell International Inc., PO Box 71654, Chicago IL 60694.) **LC** TL152; .M5a. **DD** 629.28/722/029473. ***Continues*** *Mitchell Collision Estimating Guide Domestic, 0735-9039.*

US/0883-3117
**COLLISION ESTIMATING GUIDE, DOMESTIC OLDER MODELS.** **Added/Corp** Mitchell Manuals, Inc. **VFOAT** Mitchell Collision Estimating Guide, Domestic Older Models; Older Domestic Collision Estimating Guide. Vol. 23, No. 4 (Oct. 1981)-. Periodical. English. qt. $99.00. Mitchell International Inc, PO Box 26260, San Diego CA 92126-0260. **Tel** (619)578-6550, (800)648-8010, FAX (619)578-4752. **(Subscription address:** Mitchell

International Inc., PO Box 71654, Chicago IL 60694.) **LC** TL255; .C642. **DD** 629.28/722/029473. ***Continues*** *Collision Estimating Guide. Older Models. Domestic Edition, 0735-1224.*

US
**COLLISION ESTIMATING GUIDE. EARLY MODELS.** **Added/Corp** Mitchell Information Services. **VFOAT** Mitchell Collision Estimating Guide. (19??)-. English. ir. Mitchell International, PO Box 26260, San Diego CA 92126. **Tel** 800 648-8010, 800 854-7030. **LC** TL152; .C5695.

US
**COLLISION ESTIMATING GUIDE. FORD MOTOR CO.** (19??)-. Periodical. English. bm. $104.00. Mitchell International Inc, PO Box 26260, San Diego CA 92126-0260. **Tel** (619)578-6550, (800)648-8010, FAX (619)578-4752. **(Subscription address:** Mitchell International Inc., PO Box 71654, Chicago IL 60694.)

US/0735-858X
**COLLISION ESTIMATING GUIDE IMPORTED.** (MITCHELL COLLISION ESTIMATING GUIDE IMPORTED.). Vol. 22, No. 10 (Oct. 1981)-. English. mo. $90.00. Mitchell International Inc, PO Box 26260, San Diego CA 92126-0260. **Tel** (619)578-6550, (800)648-8010, FAX (619)578-4752. **LC** TL152; .I48. **DD** 629.28/722. ***Continues*** *Imported Collision Estimating Guide, 0730-2398.*

US/0735-7826
**COLLISION ESTIMATING GUIDE, IMPORTED OLDER MODELS.** (MITCHELL COLLISION ESTIMATING GUIDE, IMPORTED OLDER MODELS.). **Added/Corp** Mitchell Manuals, inc. **VFOAT** Collision Estimating Guide, Imported Older Models. Vol. 2, No. 4 (Oct. 1981)-. English. qt. $99.00. Mitchell International Inc, PO Box 26260, San Diego CA 92126-0260. **Tel** (619)578-6550, (800)648-8010, FAX (619)578-4752. **(Subscription address:** Mitchell International Inc., PO Box 71654, Chicago IL 60694.) **LC** TL152; .M49. **DD** 629.28/722. ***Continues*** *Mitchell Collision Estimating Guide. Older Models. Imported Edition, 0277-3147.*

UK/0010-3063
**COMMERCIAL MOTOR, THE.** [Commer. mot.]. **VFOAT** CM. Vol. 1, No. 1 (Mar. 16, 1905)-. Periodical. English. Fifty-one times per year. £122.45. Reed Business Publishing / West Sussex, England, Perrymount Road, Haywards Heath, West Sussex RH16 3DH England. **Tel** 011 44 81 6523500. **[CCC].** available on microfilm and microfiche from University Microfilms International (UMI). ***Absorbed*** *Commercial Vehicles.* **Ind/Abst** Curr. Technol. Index; Highw. Res. Abstr.; Infomat Int. Bus.; Saf. Health Work.

CN/0380-6987
**COMMUNIQUE - CANADIAN AUTOMOBILE ASSOCIATION.** **Main/Corp** Canadian Automobile Association. V. 1- Nov. 1970-. Periodical. English. ir. Canadian Automobile Association, 1775 Courtwood Crescent, Ottawa Ontario K2C 3J2 Canada. **Tel** (613)226-7631, FAX (613)225-7383, telex 053-4440. **DD** 388.3/0971.

UK/0267-8519
**COMPANY CAR.** [Co. car. Redhill]. (1984)-. Periodical. English. mo. £72.00 UK; £83.00, $151.00 other. Argus Press Group, Queensway House, 2 Queensway Redhill, Surrey RH1 1QS England. **Tel** 011 44 737 768611, 011 44 737 761685, FAX 011 44 737 760510, telex 948669 TOPJNL G. ***Continues*** *Car Fleet Management, 0263-6077.*

US/1054-9056
**COMPASS (SYRACUSE, N.Y.).** (COMPASS : PUBLICATION OF THE AUTOMOBILE CLUB OF SYRACUSE.). **Added/Corp** Automobile Club of Syracuse. Vol. 1, No. 1 (Jan./Feb. 1991)-. Periodical. English. bm. $1.00 (single issue). Compass / Syracuse, 514 West Onondaga Street, Syracuse NY 13204-3299. ***Continues*** *AAA Today (Syracuse, N.Y.), 0890-801X.*

US/1064-055X
**COMPETITION PLUS.** (COMPETITION PLUS : THE R/C CAR MAGAZINE.). [Compet. plus]. Vol. 1, No. 1 (Sept. 1982)-. Periodical. English. mo. $26.00 (one year), $48.00 (two years), $66.00 (three years) US; $39.00 Canada; $68.00 other. Competition Plus, 23182 Alcalde, Suite K, Laguna Hills CA 92653. **Tel** (714)830-2290. **ED** Peter Barana. **LC** WMLC 91/5899. **DD** 793.

UK
**COMPLETE CAR.** (19??)-. Periodical. English. mo. $119.11. Perry Motorpress ltd, 22 Redan Place, Compass House, London W2 4SZ, England. **Tel** 011 44 71 2297799.

US/1060-8400
**COMPLETE CAR BUYER'S GUIDE, THE.** [Complete car buy. guide]. **VFOAT** Road & Track ... Complete Car Buyer's Guide; Car Buyer's Guide. (1991)-. English. an. $6.70. Hachette Magazines Inc., 1633 Broadway, New York NY 10019. **Tel** (212)767-6000. **(Subscription address:** Neodata / Colorado, PO Box 2606, Boulder Boulder CO 80322.) **DD** 629. ***Continues*** *Road & Track Car Buyer's Guide, 1058-5125.*

US/1045-2206
**COMPLETE CAR COST GUIDE, THE.** [Complete car cost guide]. **Added/Corp** Intelligent Choice Information Company. IntelliChoice, Inc. **VFOAT** Car Cost Guide. (1987 Ed.)-. English. $30.00. IntelliChoice Inc., 1135 South Saratoga Sunnyvale Road, San Jose CA 95129. **Tel** (408)554-8711, (800)227-2665, FAX (408)253-4822. **LC** TL151.5; .C66. **DD** 629.

US
**COMPUTERIZED ENGINE CONTROLS. IMPORTED CARS & TRUCKS.** **Added/Corp** Mitchell International. (1986)-. English. Mitchell International Inc, PO Box 26260, San Diego CA 92126-0260. **Tel** (619)578-6550, (800)648-8010, FAX (619)578-4752. **LC** TL214.C64; C64. **DD** 629.2/58. ***Continues in part*** *Computerized Engine Controls. Domestic Cars, Light Trucks & Vans; Imported Cars & Trucks, 0884-0415.*

US
**CONCERNING CARS.** English. Six times a year. $20.00. Concerning Cars, PO Box 450, Pound Ridge NY 10576. **Tel** (914)764-8260.

CN/0228-9083
**CONDUCTEUR AVERTI.** Vol. 1, No. 1-. Periodical. French. mo. Ligue de Securite du Quebec, 6785 Ouest rue St-Jacques, Montreal Quebec H4B 1V3 Canada. **DD** 629.28/3/05.

US/1045-8956
**CONSUMER ADVANTAGE INSIDERS VEHICLE MARKET DIGEST.** (1991)-. Periodical. English. mo. $69.95. Consumer Advantage Reference Services, Inc., 40074 Eagle Drive, Sterling Heights MI 48310.

US/0097-8337
**CONSUMER GUIDE : AUTO.** (19??)-. English. an. $125.00 (Consumer Guide subscription package). Publications International Ltd., 7373 North Cicero Avenue, Lincolnwood IL 60646. **Tel** (708)676-3470. **ED** Rick Popely. **LC** TL5; .C65. **DD** 629.22/22/05. **Circ:** 200,000. Documents available from UMI Article Clearinghouse.
**Ind/Abst** Acad. Search (Jan. 1992-); Mag. Search; Newsp. Period. Abstr. (1992-).

US/0364-0809
**CONSUMER GUIDE : CARS.** **See** Consumer Interests.

US/0573-8164
**CONTINENTAL COMMENTS.** Periodical. English. qt. $25.00 US; $35.00 other. Lincoln Continental Owners Club Inc, PO Box 549, Nogales AZ 85628. Index available. **Bk Rev. Circ:** 4,000 (ctrl).

UK/0589-5413
**CONTINENTAL HANDBOOK & GUIDE TO WESTERN EUROPE.** **Added/Corp** Royal Automobile Club (Great Britain). **VFOAT** Continental Handbook and Guide to Western Europe. (1932)-. English. an. RAC Motoring Services Ltd, RAC House, PO Box 100, South Croydon Surrey CR2 6XW England. **LC** GV1025.A2; C23. **DD** 914/.04/55.

US/0895-1047
**CONVENIENT AUTOMOTIVE SERVICES RETAILER.** [Conv. automot. serv. retail.]. **VFOAT** CAS Retailer. (1987)-. Periodical. English. mo. $37.00 US & Canada; $90.00 other. GCI Publishing, 1801 Rockville Pike, Suite 330, Rockville MD 20852. **Tel** (301)984-7333. **Ad Acc. Circ:** 5,500 (ctrl).

US/0045-8554
**CORMORANT NEWS BULLETIN, THE.** [Cormorant news bull.]. **VFOAT** Cormorant News-Bulletin. Bulletin. English. mo. $25.00 US; $35.00 other. The Packard Club, Box 2808, Oakland CA 94618. **ED** Alan Adams. **DD** 629. **Bk Rev. Ad Acc. Circ:** 3,100 (ctrl).
**Desc:** Ads and contents aimed toward preservation of the Packard automobile 1899-1958.

US/0195-1661
**CORVETTE FEVER MAGAZINE.** [Corvette fever mag.]. **VFOAT** Corvette Fever. Vol. 1 (Oct. 1978)-. Periodical. English. mo. $19.97 US; $29.97 other. Dobbs Publishing Group, 3816 Industry Boulevard, Lakeland FL 33811. **Tel** (813)646-5743, FAX (813)648-1187. **ED** Paul Zazarine. **LC** WMLC L 83/1800. **Ad Acc, Adv Mgr:** Curt Patterson. **Circ:** 100,000.
**Desc:** Primary emphasis is on third- and fourth-generation Corvettes. For anyone who owns, drives, maintains, or simply enjoys the Corvette. Spans all eras of Corvette production.

US/0897-4179
**CORVETTE QUARTERLY.** [Corvette q.]. **VFOAT** Corvette. Vol. 1, No. 1 (Spring 1988)-. Periodical. English. Four times a year (Seasonally). Free to Chevrolet Employees; $8.00 others. The Aegis Group, 30400 Van Dyke Avenue, Warren MI 48093-2316. **Tel** (313)575-9100. **DD** 629. ***Continues*** *Corvette News.*

US
**CORVETTE SERVICE MANUAL.** **Added/Corp** General Motors Corporation. Chevrolet Motor Division. English. Chevrolet Motor Division, General Motors Corporation, Detroit MI 48203. **LC** TL215.C6; S47. **DD** 629.28/722. ***Continues*** *Corvette Shop Manual.*

US/0739-3695
**COUNTERMAN.** (1983)-. Periodical. English. mo. $25.00. Babcox Publications Inc., 11 South Ford Street, Akron OH 44304. **Tel** (216)535-7011.

CN/0702-0376
**COURRIER DES FAMILLES, LE.** V. 1- Fall 1978-. Periodical. French. qt. $1.00 per no. Le Courrier des Familles, C P 3 Succursale F, Montreal Quebec H3J 2K8 Canada. **DD** 338.4/7/9171404.

US/0897-8751
**CPI (BALTIMORE, MD.).** (CPI : CARS OF PARTICULAR INTEREST.). **VAT** Cars of Particular Interest. (19??)-. Periodical. English. qt (Jan., Apr., July, Oct.). $20.00 US; $23.00 Canada; $30.00 Other. CPI, PO Box 3190, Laurel MD 20709. **Tel** (301)317-4228. **DD** 629. **Ad Acc.**
**Desc:** Value guide to cars of particular interest.

US/0742-2350
**CUMULATIVE INDEX OF SAE TECHNICAL PAPERS.** [Cumul. index SAE tech. pap.]. **Added/Corp** Society of Automotive Engineers. **VFOAT** Cumulative Index of S.A.E. Technical Papers. **VAT** Cumulative Index of Society of Automotive Engineers Technical Papers. 5th Ed. (1965-1978)-. English. ir. $195.00. Society of Automotive Engineers, 400 Commonwealth Drive, Warrendale PA 15096. **Tel** (412)776-4841, (412)772-7106, FAX (412)776-5760. **(Subscription address:** SAE / Society of Automotive Engineers, Department L1094P, Pittsburgh PA 15264.) **LC** TL1; .C83. **DD** 016.6292. **[CCC].** Index available. cum. index. ***Continues*** *Cumulative Index ... SAE Technical Papers, 0742-2350.*
**Desc:** Lists by subject, author, and chronologically, all SAE technical papers published from 1965-1985.

●US/1073-4732
**CUSTOM & CLASSIC TRUCKS.** [Cust. class. trucks]. **Added/Corp** Petersen Publishing Company. **VFOAT** Custom and Classic Trucks. Vol. 1, No. 1 (Apr. 1994)-. Periodical. English. bm (6 issues). $13.95 US; $24.56 Canada; $23.95 other. Petersen Publishing Company, 6420 Wilshire Bouldevard, Los Angeles CA 90048. **Tel** (213)782-2485. **(Subscription address:** Neodata / Colorado, PO Box 2606, Boulder Boulder CO 80322.) **LC** WMLC 93/4904. **DD** 629.

UK/0591-2334
**CUSTOM CAR.** [Custom car]. (1970)-. Periodical. English. Twelve times a year. £24.00 UK, £33.50 Europe, £32.00 others (regular delivery); £42.20 (airmail). United Magazine Subscriptions, 1st Floor Stephenson House, Brunel C, Milton Keynes MK2 2EW England. **Tel** 011 44 908 747008.

●US/1059-5732
**CUSTOM PAINT & BODY.** **VFOAT** Custom Paint and Body. (1992)-. Periodical. English. $3.95. Petersen Publishing Company, 6420 Wilshire Bouldevard, Los Angeles CA 90048. **Tel** (213)782-2485.

US/1076-3678
**CUSTOM RODDER.** [Custom rodder]. **VFOAT** Custom Rodder Magazine. (1990)-. Periodical. English. Six times a year. $16.50 (one year), $33.00 (two years). McMullen Publishing Inc, 2145 West La Palma Avenue, PO Box 70015, Anaheim CA 92801-1785. **Tel** (714)572-2255, FAX (714)572-1864. **DD** 629.

US/8755-6936
**DETROIT AUTOMOTIVE SERVICES. NEW CAR INVOICE GUIDE.** **VFOAT** New Car Invoice Guide. English. National Auto Research, PO Box 758, Gainesville GA 30503. **LC** HD9710.U5; D47. **DD** 629.2/22/029473.

US/8755-0881
**DIEMEX-WHARTON. PROYECTO AUTOMOTRIZ. PROYECCIONES PREVIAS A LA JUNTA.** **VFOAT** Proyecto Automotriz. Proyecciones Previas a la Junta; Proyecciones Previas a la Junta. English. WEFA / Philadelphia, PO Box 8500, Suite 1995, Philadelphia PA 19178. **Tel** (215)667-6000, telex 710 6700575. **LC** HD9710.M4; D53. **DD** 338.4/76292/0972.

UK/0956-3806
**DIESEL CAR.** [Diesel car]. (1988)-. Periodical. English. Twelve times a year. £26.40 UK; £37.00 Europe; £59.00 other. Merricks Publishing Ltd, 4 Wessex Building, Somerton, Somerset TA11 6SB England. **Tel** 011 44 45 874447, FAX 011 44 45 874059. **ED** John Kerswill. **DD** 629.2222. Index available. **Ad Acc, Adv Mgr:** Helen

# Transportation — Automobiles

Kirkhope.
**Desc:** News on diesel car models and maintenance information for diesel car owners.

US/0160-7065
**DIESEL CAR DIGEST. Ceased.** Periodical. English. qt. Diesel Car Digest, PO Box 160253, Sacramento CA 95816. LC TL229.D5; D54. DD 629.22.

US/0272-3611
**DIESEL FUEL DIRECTORY.** Directory. English. an. H.M. Gousha Company, PO Box 49006, 2001 The Alameda, San Jose CA 95161. **Tel** (800)662-6277. LC TL153; .D49. DD 629.28/6/029473. **Supersedes** Edna Connelly's Diesel Fuel and Truck Stop Guide, 0098-2172.

US/0485-3695
**DIRECTORY AND REGISTER / ROLLS-ROYCE OWNERS' CLUB.**
**Main/Corp** Rolls-Royce Owners' Club. Directory. English. sa. Rolls-Royce Owners Club Inc, 191 Hempt Road, Mechanicsburg PA 17055. **Tel** (717)697-4671. **ED** John E N Blair. LC TL215.R6; F54 SUPPL. DD 629.2/222. **Ad Acc. Circ:** 6,500 (ctrl).

US
**DIRECTORY. AUTOMOBILE DEALERS, NEW. Added/Corp** American Business Directories, Inc. **VFOAT** Automobile Dealers, New; Directory of Automobile Dealers, New. (198?)-. Trade Publication. English. an. $420.00. American Business Directory, 5711 South 86th Circle, Omaha NE 68127. **Tel** (402)593-4600, FAX (402)331-5481. LC HD9710.U5; D55. DD 381/.4562929/02573. **Continues** New Car Dealers Directory.

US/0736-0452
**DIRECTORY OF AUTO AFTERMARKET SUPPLIERS.** [Dir. auto aftermark. suppliers]. **VFOAT** Directory of Automotive Aftermarket Suppliers; Auto Aftermarket Suppliers; Chain Store Guide; Auto Aftermarket Suppliers. (1984)-. Periodical. English. be (Sept.). $230.00 continental US; $240.00 other US; $255.00 other. Lebhar Friedman Inc., 3922 Coconut Palm Drive, Tampa FL 33619. **Tel** (800)927-9292, (813)664-6707. **ED** Paul Smith. LC HD9710.3.U5; D57. DD 629.2/029/473. **Continues** Directory of Auto Supply Chains, 0730-2533.
**Desc:** Complete company profiles on 1,900 jobber/retailers operating 17,500 stores, 900 warehouse distributors and their branch offices, and 20 distribution groups serving 45,000 stores.

UK
**DIRECTORY OF MEMBERS - VEHICLE BUILDERS & REPAIRERS ASSOCIATION. Main/Corp** Vehicle Builders & Repairers Association. **VFOAT** V.B.R.A. Directory of Members; VBRA Directory of Members. Directory. English. Vehicle Builders and Repairers Association, Belmont House, 102 Finkle Lane, Gildersome Leed LS27 7TW England. LC TL12; .V5. DD 629.2/06/041. **Continues** Vehicle Builders & Repairers Association. Directory.

US/1059-0072
**DIRECTORY OF NATURAL GAS VEHICLE REFUELING STATIONS, PRODUCTS, AND SERVICES.** (DIRECTORY OF NATURAL GAS VEHICLE REFUELING STATIONS, PRODUCTS, AND SERVICES / PREPARED BY THE PLANNING & ANALYSIS GROUP, AMERICAN GAS ASSOCIATION.). **Added/Corp** American Gas Association. Planning and Analysis Group. (Feb. 1991)-. Directory. English. American Gas Association / Virginia, 1515 Wilson Boulevard, Arlington VA 22209. **Tel** (703)841-8400, (703)841-8559, FAX (703)841-8697. DD 629.

US/0145-1782
**DISTRIBUTION OF MOTOR VEHICLE REGISTRATION FEES AND FUEL TAXES TO OHIO CITIES. Main/Corp** Ohio. Dept. of Taxation. English. Research and Statistics Section, PO Box 530, Columbus OH 43216. LC HJ5359; .O36A. DD 336.1/85.

US
**DOMESTIC AND IMPORTED EARLY MODEL ESTIMATING GUIDE.** (19??)-. Periodical. English. $64.00. Mitchell International Inc, PO Box 26260, San Diego CA 92126-0260. **Tel** (619)578-6550, (800)648-8010, FAX (619)578-4752. **(Subscription address:** Mitchell International Inc., PO Box 71654, Chicago IL 60694.)

US/0735-0333
**DOMESTIC AND IMPORTED VEHICLES TOWING MANUAL.** (DOMESTIC AND IMPORTED VEHICLES TOWING MANUAL / AAA.). English. an. $8.95. American Automobile Association, 1000 AAA Drive, Heathrow FL 32746. **Tel** (407)444-7000. LC TL154; .A582A. DD 629.28/6. **Continues** Domestic Vehicles Towing Manual, 0272-8125.

US
**DOMESTIC CAR AND LIGHT TRUCK TRANSMISSION MANUAL.** English. ir (annual or biennial). $124.00. Mitchell International Inc, PO Box 26260, San Diego CA 92126-0260. **Tel** (619)578-6550, (800)648-8010, FAX (619)578-4752. **(Subscription address:** Mitchell International Inc., PO Box 71654, Chicago IL 60694.)

US
**DOMESTIC CARS REPAIR MANUAL MECHANICAL PARTS AND LABOR ESTIMATING MANUAL.** (19??)-. Periodical. English. an. $89.00. Mitchell International Inc, PO Box 26260, San Diego CA 92126-0260. **Tel** (800)648-8010, FAX (619)578-4752. **(Subscription address:** Mitchell International Inc., PO Box 71654, Chicago IL 60694.)

US/1041-4290
**DOMESTIC CARS SERVICE & REPAIR.** [Domest. cars serv. repair]. **Added/Corp** Mitchell International. **VFOAT** Domestic Cars Service and Repair. (1987)-. English. ir. Mitchell International Inc, PO Box 26260, San Diego CA 92126-0260. **Tel** (619)578-6550, (800)648-8010, FAX (619)578-4752. LC TL152; .D553. DD 629.28/722. available on CD-ROM. **Continues** Domestic Cars Tune-up Mechanical Service & Repair.

US
**DOMESTIC CARS SERVICE AND REPAIR MANUAL. ELECTRICAL.** (19??)-. Periodical. English. ir. $245.00. Mitchell International Inc, PO Box 26260, San Diego CA 92126-0260. **Tel** (619)578-6550, (800)648-8010, FAX (619)578-4752. **(Subscription address:** Mitchell International Inc., PO Box 71654, Chicago IL 60694.)

US
**DOMESTIC CARS SERVICE AND REPAIR MANUAL. ELECTRICAL COMPONENT LOCATOR.** (19??)-. Periodical. English. an. $159.00. Mitchell International Inc, PO Box 26260, San Diego CA 92126-0260. **Tel** (619)578-6550, (800)648-8010, FAX (619)578-4752. **(Subscription address:** Mitchell International Inc., PO Box 71654, Chicago IL 60694.)

US
**DOMESTIC CARS SERVICE AND REPAIR MANUAL. ENGINE PERFORMANCE.** (19??)-. Periodical. English. an. $245.00. Mitchell International Inc, PO Box 26260, San Diego CA 92126-0260. **Tel** (619)578-6550, (800)648-8010, FAX (619)578-4752. **(Subscription address:** Mitchell International Inc., PO Box 71654, Chicago IL 60694.)

US
**DOMESTIC CARS SERVICE AND REPAIR MANUAL. HEATING AND AIR CONDITIONING.** (19??)-. Periodical. English. ir. $169.00. Mitchell International Inc, PO Box 26260, San Diego CA 92126-0260. **Tel** (619)578-6550, (800)648-8010, FAX (619)578-4752. **(Subscription address:** Mitchell International Inc., PO Box 71654, Chicago IL 60694.)

US
**DOMESTIC LIGHT TRUCKS AND VANS SERVICE AND REPAIR MANUAL. ANNUAL DATA ENGINE PERFORMANCE / ELECTRICAL / MECHANICAL.** (19??)-. Periodical. English. an. $140.00. Mitchell International Inc, PO Box 26260, San Diego CA 92126-0260. **Tel** (619)578-6550, (800)648-8010, FAX (619)578-4752. **(Subscription address:** Mitchell International Inc., PO Box 71654, Chicago IL 60694.)

US
**DOMESTIC LIGHT TRUCKS AND VANS SERVICE AND REPAIR MANUAL ELECTRICAL.** (19??)-. Periodical. English. an. $199.00. Mitchell International Inc, PO Box 26260, San Diego CA 92126-0260. **Tel** (619)578-6550, (800)648-8010, FAX (619)578-4752. **(Subscription address:** Mitchell International Inc., PO Box 71654, Chicago IL 60694.)

US
**DOMESTIC LIGHT TRUCKS AND VANS SERVICE AND REPAIR MANUAL ENGINE PERFORMANCE.** (19??)-. Periodical. English. an. $199.00. Mitchell International Inc, PO Box 26260, San Diego CA 92126-0260. **Tel** (619)578-6550, (800)648-8010, FAX (619)578-4752. **(Subscription address:** Mitchell International Inc., PO Box 71654, Chicago IL 60694.)

US
**DOMESTIC TRANSMISSIONS, SERVICE & REPAIR. VFOAT** Transmission Service & Repair, Domestic Cars. 1972-. English. an. Mitchell International Inc, PO Box 26260, San Diego CA 92126-0260. **Tel** (619)578-6550, (800)648-8010, FAX (619)578-4752.

CN/1183-7314
**DRIVER/EDUCATION (TORONTO).** (DRIVER/EDUCATION.). [Driv./educ.$b]. Vol. 1, Issue No. 1 (June 1991)-. Periodical. English. Four times a year. $35.00 (institutions), $25.00 (individuals). PDE Publications, 310-5334 Yonge Street, Toronto Ontario M2N 6M2 Canada. **Tel** (416)767-4885, FAX (416)767-7425. **ED** Dan Keegan. DD 629.28/3/07071. **Bk Rev**, (Qty: 5-10). **Ad Acc. Circ:** 700-1,000 (ctrl).
**Desc:** Target readership is innovators, decision makers, and policy makers in field of driver improvement, traffic safety, driver training/education. Content is issue-oriented with researched articles.

PP
**DRIVERS AND RIDERS LICENCES / BUREAU OF STATISTICS.** English. National Statistical Office, PO Wards Strip NCO, Papua New Guinea. **Tel** 011 675 27182 271172, FAX 011 657 255057, telex FINANCE NE 22312. LC HE5717.8; .A23A. DD 354.95/300878321. **Continues** Drivers and Riders Licenses Issued.

US/0012-7132
**DUNE BUGGIES AND HOT VWS.** [Dune bug. hot VWs]. **VFOAT** Hot VWs. **VAT** Dune Buggies and Hot Volkswagens. (1970)-. Periodical. English. mo. $19.97 (one year), $36.97 (two year). Wright Publishing Company Inc, Box 2260, Costa Mesa CA 92628. **Tel** (714)533-4083. **ED** Lane Evans. LC TL236.7; .D8. DD 629.22/22. **Bk Rev. Ad Acc. Circ:** 113,430. **Continues** Dune Buggies.
**Desc:** Edited for Volkswagen owners, off-road enthusiasts, racers and general automotive enthusiasts. Includes technical articles, how-to-do-it's and competition coverage.

US/0748-3341
**DUQUETTE'S SHOW CAR QUARTERLY. VFOAT** Show Car Quarterly. No. 1 (July 1984)-. Periodical. English. qt. $12.00. Jim and Brenda Duquette, 7901 Northeast 10th, Suite 204, Midwest City OK 73110. DD 629.

RU/0320-1074
**DVIGATELI VNUTRENNOGO SGORANIJA (OMSK).** (DVIGATELI VNUTRENNOGO SGORANIIA.). [Dvigateli vnutr. sgoranija]. **Added/Corp** Sibirskii Avtomobilno-Dorozhnyi Instut. (1969)-. Academic Scholarly Publication. Russian. **CODEN** DVSGDL. Documents available from CASDDS.
**Ind/Abst** Chem. Abstr. (?-1974).

US/1047-076X
**EDMUND'S CAR SAVVY.** [Edmund's car savvy]. **VFOAT** Car Savvy. (1986)-. English. an. $3.50. Edmund's Publications Corporation / California, 300 North Sepulveda Boulevard, Suite 2050, El Segundo CA 90245. **Tel** (310)640-7840, (914)962-6297. LC TL151; .E34A. DD 629.2/222. **Continues** Edmund's Auto-Pedia, 0270-5354.

US/0732-5835
**EDMUND'S ECONOMY CAR BUYING GUIDE.** (EDMUND'S ... ECONOMY CAR BUYING GUIDE.). [Edmund's. econ. car buy. guide]. **VFOAT** Economy Car Buying Guide. (Summer 1982)-. Consumer Publication. English. Edmund's Publications Corporation / California, 300 North Sepulveda Boulevard, Suite 2050, El Segundo CA 90245. **Tel** (310)640-7840, (914)962-6297. LC TL162; .E338. DD 629.2/222/029473.

US/1048-9738
**EDMUND'S ... IMPORT CAR PRICES. Title Change.** [Edmund's import car prices]. **Added/Corp** Edmund Publications Corporation. **VFOAT** Import Car Prices. Vol. 24, No. 3 (July 1990)-(19??)-. English. Three times a year. Edmund's Publications Corporation / California, 300 North Sepulveda Boulevard, Suite 2050, El Segundo CA 90245. **Tel** (310)640-7840, (914)962-6297. **(Subscription address:** Edmund Publications, PO Box 338, Shrub Oak, NY 10588) LC IN PROCESS. DD 338. **Continues** Edmund's Foreign Car Prices, 0531-7886. **Merged with** Edmund's New Car Prices **to form** Edmund's New Cars American and Imports.

US/1047-0751
**EDMUND'S NEW CAR PRICES. Title Change.** [Edmund's new car prices]. **VFOAT** New Car Prices. (1968)-(19??). Periodical. English. Six times a year. Edmund's Publications Corporation / California, 300 North Sepulveda Boulevard, Suite 2050, El Segundo CA 90245. **Tel** (310)640-7840, (914)962-6297. DD 338. **Merged with** Edmund's Import Car Prices **to form** Edmund's New Cars American and Imports.

## Transportation — Automobiles

**UK**
**EDMUND'S NEW CARS AMERICAN AND IMPORTS.** (19??)-. English. $12.00. Edmund's Publications Corporation / California, 300 North Sepulveda Boulevard, Suite 2050, El Segundo CA 90245. **Tel** (310)640-7840, (914)962-6297. *Formed by the union of Edmund's New Car Prices, 1047-0751 and Edmund's Import Car Prices, 1048-9738.*

US/1055-2200
**EDMUND'S PRESENTS ... CAR SAVVY.** **VFOAT** Car Savvy. (1991)-. English. $4.95. Edmund Publications Corp, 200 Baker Avenue, Concord MA 01742.

US/1055-2197
**EDMUND'S PRESENTS ... CAR, VAN & TRUCK PREVIEW.** **VFOAT** Car, Van and Truck Preview; Car, Van & Truck Preview; Edmund's Presents Car, Van, and Truck Preview. (1991)-. English. $4.95. Edmund Publications Corp, 200 Baker Avenue, Concord MA 01742.

US/1055-2170
**EDMUND'S PRESENTS ... ECONOMY CAR BUYING GUIDE.** [Edmund's presents econ. car buy. guide]. **VFOAT** Economy Car Buying Guide. (1991)-. English. $4.95. Edmund Publications Corp, 200 Baker Avenue, Concord MA 01742. **DD** 629.

US/1055-2219
**EDMUND'S PRESENTS ... MUSCLE CAR BUYER'S GUIDE.** [Edmund's presents muscle car buy. guide]. **VFOAT** Muscle Car Buyer's Guide. (Sept. 1991)-. English. $4.95. Edmund Publications Corp, 200 Baker Avenue, Concord MA 01742. **LC** WMLC 91/4938. **DD** 629.

US/1055-2189
**EDMUND'S PRESENTS ... NEW CAR PRICE ANNUAL.** **VFOAT** New Car Price Annual. (1991)-. English. $4.95. Edmund Publications Corp, 200 Baker Avenue, Concord MA 01742.

US/0424-5059
**EDMUND'S USED CAR PRICES.** [Edmund's used car prices]. **VFOAT** Used Car Prices. (1967)-. Periodical. English. Six times a year. $16.00. Edmund's Publications Corporation / California, 300 North Sepulveda Boulevard, Suite 2050, El Segundo CA 90245. **Tel** (310)640-7840, (914)962-6297. **(Subscription address:** Edmund Publications, PO Box 338, Shrub Oak, NY 10588**) DD** 338.

●US/1077-2111
**EDMUND'S VAN, PICKUP, SPORT UTILITY.** **Added/Corp** Edmund Publications Corporation. **VFOAT** Van, Pickup, Sport Utility; Edmund's Van, Pickup, Sport Utility Buyer's Guide. (Feb. 1994)-. English. tq. $12.00. Edmund's Publications Corporation / California, 300 North Sepulveda Boulevard, Suite 2050, El Segundo CA 90245. **Tel** (310)640-7840, (914)962-6297. **LC** TL162; .V36. **DD** 629.223. *Continues Van, Pickup, Sport Utility Buyer's Guide, 1043-8270.*

**SZ**
**EINGEFUHRTE MOTORFAHRZEUGE.** **Main/Corp** Switzerland. Eidgenossisches Statistisches AMT. **VFOAT** Vehicules a Moteur Importes. Multiple languages (French and German). Publikationsdienst, Hallurylstrasse 11, CH-3003 Bern Switzerland. **LC** HD9710.S9; S9A. **DD** 314.94 S; 382/.45/629209494. *Continues in part Eingefuhrte Motorfahrzeuge.*

US/0199-5804
**EJAG NEWS MAGAZINE, THE.** [EJAG news mag.]. (19??)-. Periodical. English. mo. EJAG Publications, Box J, Carlisle MA 01741.

●US/1064-1254
**ELECTRIC VEHICLE DIGEST.** (1992)-. Periodical. English. mo. $175.00. Electric Vehicle Digest, 301 Scola Road, Brookhaven PA 19015.

AT/0818-8491
**ELECTRIC VEHICLE NEWS MELBOURNE.** [Electr. veh. news Melb.]. **Added/Corp** Australian Electric Vehicle Association. **VFOAT** EV News. (1974)-. Periodical. English. mo. 40.00Aus$ Australia, 60.00Aus$ others (ordinary); 120.00Aus$ Australia, 300.00Aus$ others (corporate). Australian Electric Vehicle Association, PO Box 4622SS, Melbourne 3001, Australia. **Tel** 11 61 3 6914094. **DD** 629.22930994. *Absorbed Melbourne Branch Newsletter, 0817-9166.*

US/0743-6076
**ELECTRICAL COMPONENT LOCATOR. DOMESTIC CARS, LIGHT TRUCKS & VANS, IMPORTED CARS & TRUCKS.** **Added/Corp** Mitchell Manuals, inc. Mitchell International Inc, PO Box 26260, San Diego CA 92126-0260. **Tel** (619)578-6550, (800)648-8010, FAX (619)578-4752. **ED** Dan Kelley. **LC** TL272; .E38. **DD** 629.2/54/05. **Ad Acc.** ctrl circ. available on CD-ROM.

**Desc:** Locator charts and illustrations guide you to electrical components on 1978-85 domestic cars and light trucks, or 1977-84 imported cars and light trucks.

**US**
**ELECTRICAL COMPONENT LOCATOR. IMPORTED CARS & TRUCKS / MITCHELL.** **Added/Corp** Mitchell Manuals, inc. Mitchell Information Services. Mitchell International. **VFOAT** Imported Cars & Trucks; Imported Cars and Trucks; Electrical Component Locator. Imported Cars, Light Trucks & Vans; Imported Cars, Light Trucks & Vans; Imported Cars, Light Trucks, and Vans. (19??)-. English. ir. $159.00. Mitchell International Inc, PO Box 26260, San Diego CA 92126-0260. **Tel** (619)578-6550, (800)648-8010, FAX (619)578-4752. **(Subscription address:** Mitchell International Inc., PO Box 71654, Chicago IL 60694.**) LC** TL272; .E384. **DD** 629.2/548.

US/0741-6334
**ELECTRONIC FUEL INJECTION, DIAGNOSIS & TESTING.** [Electron. fuel inj., diagn. test.]. **Added/Corp** Mitchell Manuals, inc. **VFOAT** Electronic Fuel Injection. (19??)-. English. an. $45.00. Mitchell International Inc, PO Box 26260, San Diego CA 92126-0260. **Tel** (619)578-6550, (800)648-8010, FAX (619)578-4752. **(Subscription address:** Mitchell International Inc., PO Box 71654, Chicago IL 60694.**) ED** Dan Kelley. **LC** TL214.F78; E4. **DD** 629.2/53. **Ad Acc.** ctrl circ.

**Desc:** Diagnose, test, adjust and repair 1975-86 domestic and 1968-85 imported car and light truck electronic fuel injection systems with this guide.

**US**
**EMISSION CONTROL APPLICATIONS GUIDE.** **Added/Corp** Mitchell International. (19??)-. English. an. $59.00. Mitchell International Inc, PO Box 26260, San Diego CA 92126-0260. **Tel** (619)578-6550, (800)648-8010, FAX (619)578-4752. **(Subscription address:** Mitchell International Inc., PO Box 71654, Chicago IL 60694.**) LC** TL214.P6; E535. **DD** 629.25/28.

US/0489-5606
**ENGINEERING KNOW-HOW IN ENGINE DESIGN.** See Engineering-Mechanical Engineering and Machinery.

CN/0225-9222
**ENONCES DE PRINCIPE - ASSOCIATION CANADIENNE DES AUTOMOBILISTES.** [Enonces princ. - Assoc. can. automob.]. **Main/Corp** Association Canadienne des Automobilistes. Publication began with 1974/75?. French (English). an. Association Canadienne des Automobilistes / Ottawa, 1775 Courtwood Crescent, Ottawa Ontario K2C 3J2 Canada. **Tel** (613)226-7631, FAX (613)225-7383, telex 053-4440. **ED** Michael S McNeil. **DD** 388/.0971. **Circ:** 3,000.

**US**
**EUROPEAN AUTOMOTIVE BULLETIN.** (19??)-. Bulletin. English. Twelve times a year. $645.00. Forecast International / DMS Inc., 22 Commerce Road, Newtown CT 06470. **Tel** (203)426-0800, FAX (203)426-1964, telex 467615.

US/1056-8476
**EUROPEAN CAR.** [Eur. car]. Vol. 22, No. 8 (Aug. 1991)-. Periodical. English. mo. $18.80. Argus Publishers Corporation, 12100 Wilshire Boulevard, Suite 250, Los Angeles CA 90025. **Tel** (310)820-3601, FAX (310)207-9388. **(Subscription address:** Kable Publishers Aide, 308 East Hitt Street, Subscription Department, Mt. Morris IL 61054-1473.**) LC** TL55; .V93. **DD** 629.222/094. *Continues VW & Porsche, 0273-6748.*

**US**
**EUROPEAN COLLISION ESTIMATING GUIDE.** (19??)-. Periodical. English. bm. $132.00. Mitchell International Inc, PO Box 26260, San Diego CA 92126-0260. **Tel** (619)578-6550, (800)648-8010, FAX (619)578-4752. **(Subscription address:** Mitchell International Inc., PO Box 71654, Chicago IL 60694.**)**

UK/0267-8233
**EUROPEAN MOTOR BUSINESS.** [Eur. motor bus.]. **VFOAT** EIU European Motor Business. No. 1 (May 1985)-. Periodical. English. qt. $641.25 (schools and educational libraries), $885.00 (other)"North America. The Economist Intelligence Unit, 40 Duke Street, London W1A 1DW England. **Tel** 011 44 71 8301000. **(Subscription address:** Economist Intelligence Unit / North America Subscriptions, 111 West 57th Street, New York NY 10019.**) ED** Arthur Way. **LC** HD9710.E8; E9. **DD** 338.4/76292/094. available on microfilm from World Microfilm Publications Ltd. *Continues in part Motor Business, 0027-1802.*

**Desc:** A research publication analysing the activity of the automotive industries of Western Europe and their national and international markets.

**Ind/Abst** Contents Pages Manage.

**IT**
**EUROTAX DUE RUOTE.** (19??)-. Periodical. Italian. Twice a year. L56.000. Sanguinetti Editore, Via Hoepli 7, 20121 Milan Italy. **Tel** 011 39 2 86462726.

US/0896-0798
**EXCELLENCE (ROSS, CALIF.).** (EXCELLENCE.). [Excellence]. **VFOAT** Excellence Magazine. Vol. 1, No. 6 (Nov/Dec. 1987)-. Periodical. English. bm. $20.00 (one year), $35.00 (two year), $49.00 (three year). Excellence Magazine, PO Box 1529, Ross CA 94957. **Tel** (415)382-0580, FAX (415)382-0587. **ED** Tom Toldrian (editor's address: 42 Digital Drive, #5, Novato, CA 94949. **LC** WMLC L 83/4377. **DD** 629. **Ad Acc. Circ:** 40,000. *Continues Porsche Magazine, 0894-2587.*

**Desc:** Magazine about Porsche cars.

**BE**
**EXERCICE - CHAMBRE SYNDICALE DES CONSTRUCTEURS D'AUTOMOBILES ET DE MOTOCYCLES DE BELGIQUE ET FEDERATION BELGE DES INDUSTRIES DE L'AUTOMOBILE ET DU CYCLE REUNIES.** See Economics-Industry and Production.

AT/1030-2077
**EXHAUST AND UNDERCAR.** (1987)-. Periodical. English. Six times a year. 30.00Aus$ Australia; 60.00Aus$ New Zealand; 80.00Aus$ other. Exhaust Publications, PO Box 303, Fairy Meadows NSW 2519 Australia. **Tel** 61 42 832500, FAX 61 42 832737. **DD** 621.4370288. *Continues Exhaust (Fairy Meadow), 1030-2069.*

US/1054-8084
**EXOTIC CARS QUARTERLY.** [Exot. cars q.]. **VFOAT** Road & Track's Exotic Cars Quarterly. Vol. 2, No. 1 (Spring 1991)-. Periodical. English. qt. $14.95 (US), $19.95 (Canada). Diamandis Communications Inc, 1499 Monrovia Avenue, New Port Beach CA 92663. **Tel** (714)720-5300. **LC** TL236; .R562. **DD** 629.222. *Continues Road & Track's Exotic Cars Quarterly, 1047-4501.*

US/0885-4750
**FABULOUS MUSTANGS & EXOTIC FORDS.** *Ceased.* **VFOAT** Fabulous Mustangs and Exotic Fords. (19??)-(Dec. 1993). English. bm. Argus Publishers Corporation, 12100 Wilshire Boulevard, Suite 250, Los Angeles CA 90025. **Tel** (310)820-3601, FAX (310)207-9388. **LC** TL215.M8; F3. **DD** 629.2/222.

AT/1033-7369
**FAST FOURS & ROTARIES.** [Fast fours rotaries]. (1988)-. Periodical. English. Twelve times a year. 53.00Aus$ Australia; 88.00Aus$ New Zealand & Papua New Guinea; 112.00Aus$ US & Canada; 119.00Aus$ Europe & Africa; 94.00Aus$ Singapore, Malaysia & Indonesia; 103.00Aus$ other. Federal Publishing Co Pty Ltd, PO Box 199, 180 Bourke Road, Alexandria New South Wales, 2015 Australia. **Tel** 011 61 2 693 6666, FAX 011 61 2 693 9935. **(Subscription address:** Federal Publishing Co. Pty Ltd., PO Box 199, Alexandria NSW 2015 Australia.**) DD** 629.22805.

●US/1072-8422
**FASTEST STREET CARS IN AMERICA.** **Added/Corp** Petersen Publishing Company. (1994)-. English. $3.95. Petersen Publishing Company, 6420 Wilshire Boulevard, Los Angeles CA 90048. **Tel** (213)782-2485.

US/1057-0330
**FAT FENDERED STREET RODS.** *Ceased.* **VFOAT** Fendered Street Rods. (1991)-(199?). Periodical. English. qt. Challenge Publications Inc., 7950 Deering Avenue, Canoga Park CA 91304. **Tel** (818)887-0550. **DD** 629.

GW/0933-050X
**FAT-SCHRIFTENREIHE.** (FAT SCHRIFTENREIHE / FORSCHUNGSVEREINIGUNG AUTOMOBILTECHNIK E.V.). [FAT-Schr.reihe]. **Added/Corp** Forschungsvereinigung Automobiltechnik (Germany). **VAT** Forschungsvereinigung Automobiltechnik e.V. Schriftenreihe. (1974)-. Academic Scholarly Publication. German. ir (occasionally 2-3 per year). DM25.00. Forschungsvereinigung Automobiltechnik E V, Postfach 170563, 60079 Frankfurt/M 17 Germany. **Tel** 069 7570 (0) 247, 069 7570 0 248, FAX 069 7570-209. **CODEN** FASCEL. **Pr Rev. Circ:** 500. Documents available from CASDDS.

**Ind/Abst** Chem. Abstr.

US/0364-6858
**FEDERAL MOTOR VEHICLE SAFETY STANDARDS AND REGULATIONS.** See Public Administration.

Transportation —Automobiles

GW
**FERNVERKEHR DEUTSCHER LASTKRAFTFAHRZEUGE ... IN SEINER BEWEGUNG NACH VERKEHRSGEBIETEN, GUTERHAUPTGRUPPEN UND WICHTIGEREN GUTERGRUPPEN : GEMEINSAMER BERICHT DER BUNDESANSTALT FUR DEN GUTERFERNVERKEHR UND DES KRAFTFAHRT-BUNDESAMTES.** **VFOAT** BAG/KBA Fermverlejr Deutscher Lastkraftfahrzeuge-Guterbewegung. German. an. **LC** HE5669; .A24. **DD** 388.3/24/0943.

UK/0958-7462
**FERRARI WORLD.** [Ferrari world]. (1989)-. Periodical. English. bm. £21.00 UK; $45.00 North America; £32.00 other. Hyde Park Publications Ltd., Stephenson House, First Floor, Bletchley Milton Keynes, MK2 2EW England. **Tel** 011 44 908 371981, FAX 011 44 81-874-2150. **(Subscription address:** Accolade Subscription Department, 2001 West Main Street, Plaza W-140, Stanford CT 06902.) **ED** Alessandro Giudice. **Bk Rev. Ad Acc. Circ:** 50,000.
**Desc:** Devoted exclusively to Ferrari, the man, the machine, and the history. Exclusive photography, authoritative articles from sources close to and within Maparello. Topics from design to technology, from classic to the latest models.

FR
**FICHIER CENTRAL DES AUTOMOBILES, PARC ET IMMATRICULATIONS / MINISTERE DES TRANSPORTS, DIRECTION DES AFFAIRES ECONOMIQUES, FINANCIERES ET ADMINISTRATIVES, DEPARTEMENT DES STATISTIQUES DES TRANSPORTS.** French. an. Ministere des Transports, Departement des Statistiques des Transports, 55 rue Brillat-Savarin, 75658 Paris Cedex 13 France. **LC** HE5668; .A25. **DD** 388.3/4/0944021. *Formed by the union of* Parc des Vehicules Utilitaires Immatricules *and* Immatriculations des Vehicules Utilitaires.

US
**FINANCIAL STATEMENTS AND SUPPLEMENTAL SCHEDULES FOR THE YEARS ENDED SEPTEMBER 30 ... AND INDEPENDENT AUDITOR'S REPORT.** **Main/Corp** Public Parking Authority of Pittsburgh (Pa.). (1989/1990)-. English. *Continues* Public Parking Authority of Pittsburgh (Pa.). Financial Statements and Schedules, Years Ended September 30, ... With Independent Auditor's Report Thereon.

US
**FISCAL YEAR ... ALABAMA TRANSIT DATA REPORT / MASS TRANSPORTATION DIVISION, BUREAU OF URBAN PLANNING, ALABAMA HIGHWAY DEPARTMENT.** English. an. **LC** HE5633.A2; F57. **DD** 388.3/22/09761.

US/0071-5697
**FIX YOUR VOLKSWAGEN.** English. an. Goodheart-Willcox Company Inc., 123 West Taft Drive, South Holland IL 60473. **Tel** (800)323-0440, (708)333-7200. **ED** Larry Johnson.

CN/0710-0663
**FORESIGHT (TORONTO).** See Public Health and Safety.

UK
**FRENCH RIVIERA. COTE D'AZUR.** 1st- Ed.; 1957-. English. **LC** GV1025.F7; F73.

US/0884-9889
**FRIENDS (WARREN, MICH.).** Ceased. (FRIENDS.). [Friends]. (May 1939)-(19??). Periodical. English. ir. The Aegis Group, 30400 Van Dyke Avenue, Warren MI 48093-2316. **Tel** (313)575-9100. **DD** 051. **Ind/Abst** Index Free Period.

US/0016-1810
**FROM THE STATE CAPITALS. MOTOR VEHICLE REGULATION.** [From state cap., Motor veh. regul.]. **VFOAT** Motor Vehicle Regulation. (19??)-. Periodical. English. wk. $211.50 (one year), $235.00 (two year) public and institutional libraries; $378.00 (one year) $420.00 (two year) other. Wakeman Walworth Inc., 300 North Washington Street #204, Alexandria VA 22314. **Tel** (703)549-8606. **ED** Emily Novick. **DD** 351. **[CCC]**.
**Desc:** Examines state motor vehicle safety regulations, inspections, emission standards, drunken driving laws, motorist licensing, insurance and education.

CN/0225-9214
**FUEL CONSUMPTION GUIDE.** [Fuel consum. guide]. **VFOAT** Guide de Consommation de Carburant; Guide sur la Consommation de Carburant. 1st Ed. (1980)-. English (French). an. Free. Transport Canada / Road Safety, Ottawa Ontario K1A 0N5 Canada. **DD** 629.2/53. **Ad Acc. Circ:** 600,000 (ctrl). available on diskette.

US/1056-4330
**GALE'S AUTO SOURCEBOOK.** Ceased. [Gale's auto sourceb.]. **VFOAT** Gale's Auto. 1st Ed. (1991)-(1992). English. Gale Research Inc., 835 Penobscot Building, Detroit MI 48226. **Tel** (800)877-GALE, (313)961-2242, FAX (313)961-6083, telex TWX 810-221-7086. **LC** TL162; .G35. **DD** 629.222.
**Desc:** Guide to information on cars and light trucks.

US/0890-149X
**GALVES AUTO PRICE LIST (AMERICAN USED CARS ED.).** (GALVES AUTO PRICE LIST.). [Galves auto price list]. (1957)-. Periodical. English. wk. $92.22 New Jersey; $87.00 other. Galves Auto Price List Incorporated, 430 Industrial Avenue, Teterboro NJ 07608. **Tel** (201)393-0051, FAX (201)393-0508. **DD** 388.

UK
**GARAGE NEWS.** English. mo (12 issues). £27.00 UK; £35.00 Eire & Europe; £63.00 America, Middle East, India & Africa; £74.00 Australia, New Zealand & Japan; £35.00 other. Haymarket Publishing Ltd., 12 14 Ansdell Street, London W8 5TR England. **Tel** 011 44 483 733800, FAX 011 44 483 776573. **(Subscription address:** Haymarket Publishing Ltd, PO Box 219, Subscriptions Department, Woking Surrey GU21 1ZW, United Kingdom.) **ED** D. Jenkinson.

US/0196-7630
**GENERAL COMPETITION RULES (DENVER).** (GENERAL COMPETITION RULES.). [Gen. compet. rules]. **Main/Corp** Sports Car Club of America. (19??)-. English. Free to members; $55.00 membership. Sports Car Club of America, PO Box 3278, Englewood CO 80155. **LC** GV1030; .S66a. **DD** 796.7/20973.

US
**GENERAL MOTORS COLLISION ESTIMATING GUIDE.** (19??)-. Periodical. English. bm. $104.00. Mitchell International Inc, PO Box 26260, San Diego CA 92126-0260. **Tel** (619)578-6550, (800)648-8010, FAX (619)578-4752. **(Subscription address:** Mitchell International Inc, PO Box 71654, Chicago IL 60694.)

US
**GENUINE CORVETTE BLACK BOOK, THE.** (19??)-. Periodical. English. $9.95. Michael Bruce Associates Inc, PO Box 396, Powell OH 43065. **ED** M.B. Antonick. **Bk Rev.**
**Desc:** Contains details for all Corvette models.

US
**GEO STORM SERVICE MANUAL.** **Added/Corp** General Motors Corporation. Chevrolet-Pontiac-Canada Group. **VFOAT** Storm Service Manual; Geo Service Manual. Storm. English. Chevrolet Motor Division, General Motors Corporation, Detroit MI 48203. **LC** TL215.G4534; G46. **DD** 629.28/722.

UK
**GLASS CAR GUIDE.** English. mo. £110.00. Glass's Guide Service Ltd., Elgin House St. George Avenue, Weybridge Sur K13 0BX England. **Tel** 011 44 932 853211.

US/1070-9975
**GLOBAL AUTOMOTIVE REVIEW AND OUTLOOK.** [Global automot. rev. outl.]. **Added/Corp** Global Automotive Information Services (Bloomfield, Mich.). (19??)-. Periodical. English. mo. $295.00 US; $310.00 Canada and Mexico; $325.00 other. Global Automotive Information Service, 4813 Pelican Way, West Bloomfield MI 48323. **Tel** (313)683-2686. **ED** R. L. Fornshell. **DD** 338. ctrl circ.

US/1057-0535
**GOLD BOOK. CONTEMPORARY VEHICLES, THE.** [Gold book, Contemp. veh.]. **VFOAT** Contemporary Vehicles. Vol. 12, No. 1 (Jan./Feb. 1991)-. Periodical. English. Six times a year. $66.00. Gold Book Inc, 1400 Hearn Drive, 2nd Floor E, Atlanta GA 30319. **Tel** (404)847-6503, (800)842-6848. **(Subscription address:** The Gold Book Inc., PO Box 105068, Atlanta GA 30348.) **DD** 629. *Continues in part* Gold Book (El Paso, Tex.).

US
**GOLD BOOK (EL PASO, TEX.), THE.** Title Change. (THE GOLD BOOK.). (19??)-(19??). Periodical. English. qt. Quentin Craft, 6242 Vanderbilt Drive, El Paso TX 79935. **Tel** (915)592-5713. **ED** Q Craft. *Split into* Gold Book. Older Vehilces, 1057-0136; Gold Book. Classics & Antiques; Gold Book. Contemporary Vehicles, 1057-0535 *and* Gold Book. Special Interest, Imports & Domestics, 1062-0974.

US/1057-0136
**GOLD BOOK. OLDER VEHICLES, THE.** [Gold book, Older veh.]. **VFOAT** Older Vehicles. Vol. 12, No. 1 (Jan./Feb./Mar. 1991)-. English. Four times a year. $51.00. Gold Book Inc, 1400 Lake Hearn Drive, 2nd Floor E, Atlanta GA 30319. **Tel** (404)847-6503, (800)842-6848. **DD** 629. *Continues in part* Gold Book (El Paso, Tex.).

CN/0822-5222
**GRAND PRIX LABATT DU CANADA. REGLEMENTS.** (REGLEMENTS.). [Grand Prix Labatt Can., Reglem.]. **Main/Corp** Grand Prix du Canada. **VFOAT** Regulations. **VAT** Grand Prix Labatt du Canada. Regulations. English (French). an. Grand Prix du Canada, Bassin Olympiquell Ile Notre-Dame, Montreal Quebec H3C 1A0 Canada. **DD** 796.7/2/09714.

●US/1064-2404
**GRAY'S SPECIALTY CAR VALUE GUIDE.** **VFOAT** Specialty Car Value Guide. (1992)-. English. qt $24.95. Gray's Specialty Publishing, PO Box 4115, Deerfield Beach FL 33364.

●US/1059-6143
**GREEN CAR JOURNAL.** [Green car j.]. Vol. 1, No. 1 (Jan. 1992)-. Periodical. English. mo. $320.00 North America; $360.00 other. Green Car Media, 1334-D North Benson Avenue, Upland CA 81786. **Tel** (909)985-9700, FAX (909)946-0664. **ED** Ron Cogan. **DD** 629. **CODEN** GCJOE3. Index available (published separately). cum. index. **Bk Rev.**
**Desc:** Contains information on the electric and alternative fuel vehicle industries.

CN/0820-8964
**GUIDE D'ACHAT DE LA VOITURE USAGEE.** [Guide achat voiture usager]. French (English). an. 3.95Can$ Canada; $3.00 US. Association Canadienne des Automobilistes / Quebec, c/o CAA Quebec, 2600 Laurier Boulevard, Ste Foy Quebec G1V 2L1 Canada. **Tel** (418)653-2600. **DD** 629.2/222. **Ad Acc. Circ:** 75,450.

CN/0315-9205
**GUIDE DE L' AUTO (MONTREAL).** (LE GUIDES DE L'AUTO.). 1967-. Periodical. French. an. $3.00. Editions La Presse, 4550 Rue Hockelaga, Montreal H1V 1C6. **LC** TL2; .D88.

CN/0228-9776
**GUIDE DE L' AUTOMOBILE AMERICAINE, LE.** 1981-. French. an. $2.95 per no. Editions & Publications Heraud, Bureau 11/1459 Belanger, Montreal Quebec H2G 1A5 Canada. **ED** Daniel Heraud. **DD** 629.2/22/05. *Continues* Guide de l'Automobile Nord-Americaine, 0226-1960.

FR
**GUIDE DE L'EQUIPEMENT ET DE L'OUTILLAG.** French. 350.00F France. F Editions Techniques pour l'Automobile et l'Industrie, 20-22 rue de la Saussiere, 92100 Boulogne-Billancourt France. **Tel** 33 1 4604 8113, FAX 33 1 4825 5042, telex 204850 F. **ED** Jean Graudens. **Ad Acc. Circ:** 55,000.
**Desc:** Supplies jobber store owner/manager with names of products and locations of suppliers of all equipment related to cars, vans and trucks.

CN/1186-9321
**GUIDE DES AUTOS USAGEES, LE.** [Guide autos usagees]. **VFOAT** Carnet de Route; Livre Jaune. (1991)-. French. 9.95Can$ Canada. Guide des Autos Usagees, BP 597, Saint-Lambert Quebec J4P 3RS Canada. **DD** 629.222/2.

CN/0706-9995
**GUIDE DU TRANSPORT PAR CAMION INC.** See Transportation.

US/0160-1318
**GUIDE MOTOR CLUB'S ANNUAL EMERGENCY ROAD SERVICE GUIDE.** **Main/Corp** Guide Motor Club. **VFOAT** Emergency Road Service Guide. No. 1- 1977-. English. an. Hagstrom Company, 450 West 33rd Street, New York NY 10001. **LC** TL153; .G85A. **DD** 629.28/6/025747.1

JA
**GUIDE TO JAPAN'S AUTO INDUSTRY, FACTS & INFO.** **Added/Corp** Automotive Herald Co. (19??)-. Periodical. English. an. Y10460 North & Central America & West Indies; Y7500 Japan; Y10240 Asia & Oceania; Y10680 other. Jan Corporation, 2 17 Hamanatsu Cho 1 Chome, Minato Ky Tokyo 105 Japan. **Tel** 011 81 3 34380361.

US/0895-6782
**GUIDE TO MUSCLE CARS.** Ceased. [Guide muscle cars]. (19??)-(June 1992). Periodical. English. qt. Argus Publishers Corporation, 12100 Wilshire Boulevard, Suite 250, Los Angeles CA 90025. **Tel** (310)820-3601, FAX (310)207-9388. **LC** TL1; .G83. **DD** 629.2/5.

JA
**GUIDE TO THE MOTOR INDUSTRY OF JAPAN.** **Added/Corp** Jidosha Kogyo Shinkokai. **VFOAT** Motor Industry of Japan. (1960)-. Periodical. English. an. ¥6620.00 Japan; ¥6500.00 other. Japan

Motor Industrial Federation Inc., Otemachi Building 6 1 1 Chome, Chiyoda ku Tokyo 100 Japan. **Tel** 011 81 3 32118731. **ED** Toshiro Kikuchi. **LC** TL5; .G85. **Bk Rev. Ad Acc. Circ:** 20,000.
**Desc:** Covers the Tokyo Motor Show, automobile manufacturers, general catalogues, specifications, motor vehicle statistics with a directory of organizations and manufacturers.

US/1064-4822
**HAMMER & DOLLY.** [Hammer dolly]. **Added/Corp** Washington Metropolitan Auto Body Association. (19??)-. Trade Publication. English. Twelve times a year. $18.00 (one year), $30.00 (two years) US; $30.00 (one year), $50.00 (two years) other. Hammer & Dolly, 5303 Connecticut Avenue NW, Washington DC 20015. **Tel** (202)363-1858, FAX (202)244-0178. **ED** Sheila Loftus. **DD** 629. **Bk Rev. Ad Acc, Adv Mgr:** Scott DeSimone. **Circ:** 5,000.
**Desc:** Trade magazine for auto collision repair industry.

US/0163-1055
**HANDBOOK AND DIRECTORY - CLASSIC CAR CLUB OF AMERICA. Main/Corp** Classic Car Club of America. Directory. English. qt. Classic Car Club, 2300 East Devon Avenue, Suite 126, Des Plaines IL 60018. **Tel** (708)390-0443. **Circ:** 5,000 (ctrl).
**Desc:** Hobby magazine for classic car collectors.

CN/0229-6667
**HEADLAMP (ARMDALE).** (HEADLAMP / DETA.). [Headlamp]. Vol. 1, No. 1 (Feb. '79)-. Periodical. English. qt. Free to members. Headlamp, c/o Deta Nova Scotia Teachers' Union, PO Box 1060, Armdale Nova Scotia B3L 4L7 Canada. **DD** 629.28/32/07.

US
**HEMMINGS MOTOR NEWS.** (19??)-. Periodical. English. mo. $65.00 US; $82.24 Canada; $88.00 Mexico. Hemmings Motor News, Box 100, Bennington VT 05201. **Tel** (802)442-3101, FAX (802)447-1561. **Ad Acc.**
**Desc:** Advertisements for antique auto flea markets, car shows, etc.

US/0745-5941
**HIGH-PERFORMANCE PONTIAC. VFOAT** High Performance Pontiac. Periodical. English. bm (Feb., Apr., Jun., Aug., Oct., Dec.). $16.00. CSK Publishing Company, 299 Market Street, Saddle Brook NJ 07662. **Tel** (201)712-9300, FAX (201)712-9899. **ED** Cliff Gromer and Jim Koscs. **Ad Acc. Circ:** 38,000. ***Continues*** *Thunder AM Magazine, 0199-1957.*
**Desc:** Magazine is edited for the Pontiac enthusiast and covers collecting, restoring, performance modifications and customizing. Pontiac features them all, from 1950's fuelies to 1987 high techers.

US/1041-5416
**HIGH SPEED DIESELS & DRIVES.** [High speed diesels drives]. **VFOAT** High Speed Diesels and Drives. Vol. 8, No. 1 (Jan./Feb. 1989)-. Periodical. English. bm. $30.00. Diesel & Gas Turbine Publishers, 13555 Bishops Court, Brookfield WI 53005. **Tel** (414)784-9177, (800)558-4322, FAX (414)784-8133, telex 275398 DIESL UR. **LC** TJ795.A1; H53. **DD** 621.43/6/05. ***Continues*** *High Speed Diesel Report, 0730-5303.*

US
**HIGHWAY USER REVENUES AND DISTRIBUTION FOR THE CALENDAR YEAR ENDING ... / ARKANSAS STATE HIGHWAY AND TRANSPORTATION DEPARTMENT, PLANNING DIVISION.** English. **LC** HE5633.A8; H53. **DD** 388.1/14.

UK
**HISTORICAL SERIES / ROLLS-ROYCE HERITAGE TRUST. See** History(General).

US/0018-5213
**HORSELESS CARRIAGE GAZETTE.** V. 17, No. 4-. Periodical. English. bm. $20.00 (one year), $60.00 (three year). Horseless Carriage Club, 128 S Cypress Street, Orange CA 92666. **Tel** (818)704-4253. **ED** Brad Haugaard. **LC** TL1; .H83. **DD** 388.3/21/09. **Circ:** 5,500. available on microfilm from University Microfilms International (UMI). ***Continues*** *Horseless Carriage Club Gazette.*

US/0018-6031
**HOT ROD.** [Hot rod]. Vol. 6, No. 5 (May 1953)-. Periodical. English. mo. $19.94 US; $28.83 Canada; $28.94 other. Petersen Publishing Company, 6420 Wilshire Bouldevard, Los Angeles CA 90048. **Tel** (213)782-2485. **(Subscription address:** Neodata / Colorado, PO Box 2606, Boulder Boulder CO 80322.**) ED** Leonard Emanuelson. **LC** TL236; .H55. **Ad Acc. Circ:** 509,000. available on microfilm and microfiche from University Microfilms International (UMI); available on an online database (file 647/Full-Text) from DIALOG. Documents available from UMI Article Clearinghouse, Magazine Collection. ***Continues*** *Hot Rod Magazine.* ***Absorbed in part by*** *Rod & Custom, 0161-150X.*
**Desc:** Covers the world of performance automobiles--including colorful features on street rods, musclecars and modern performance machines. Every issue contains money-saving how-to tips on maintenance, restoration, rebuilding, paint and graphics, bolt-on parts, improving performance, etc.
**Ind/Abst** Abr. Read. Guide Period. Lit.; Access (1980-1987); Gen. Period. Index (1985-); Mag. Artic. Summar. Elite (Feb. 1984-); Mag. Artic. Summar. Select (Jan. 1987-); Mag. Artic. Summar. CD-ROM (Feb. 1984-); Mag. Index Plus (1989-); Mag. Index Sel. Microfiche (1990-) [Full Txt.]; Mag. Index. Sel. (1986-); Mag. Search; Mid. Search (Jan. 1987-); Newsp. Period. Abstr. (1988-); Prim. Search (Jan. 1987-); Read. Guide Period. Lit.; Mag. Index (1977-); TOM Gen. Index (1985-) [Full Txt.].

US/0735-083X
**HOT ROD ... ANNUAL.** [Hot rod annu.]. **VFOAT** Petersen's Hot Rod Annual. 1982-. English. an. $6.95 US, $8.50 Canada. Petersen Publishing Company, 6420 Wilshire Bouldevard, Los Angeles CA 90048. **Tel** (213)782-2485. **LC** TL236; .H573. **DD** 629.2/28. **Ad Acc. Circ:** 200,000. available on microfilm and microfiche from University Microfilms International (UMI).

US/0271-0919
**HOT ROD MAGAZINE CHEVROLET.** [Hot rod mag. Chevrolet]. **VFOAT** Hot Rod Chevrolet. (19??)-. Periodical. English. $2.50 US; $3.25 Canada. Petersen Publishing Company, 6420 Wilshire Bouldevard, Los Angeles CA 90048. **Tel** (213)782-2485. **LC** TL215.C5; H67. **DD** 629.2/222. **Ad Acc. Circ:** 200,000.

US/0273-0383
**HOT ROD MAGAZINE CORVETTE. VFOAT** Corvette. Periodical. English. $2.50 US; $3.50 Canada. Petersen Publishing Company, 6420 Wilshire Bouldevard, Los Angeles CA 90048. **Tel** (213)782-2485. **LC** TL215.C6; H66. **DD** 629.2/222.

US/0730-4811
**HOT ROD MAGAZINE ENGINES.** ***Title Change.*** [Hot rod mag. engines]. **VFOAT** Engines; HR Engines. (19??)-(19??). English. Petersen Publishing Company, 6420 Wilshire Bouldevard, Los Angeles CA 90048. **Tel** (213)782-2485. **LC** TL210; .H683. **DD** 629.2/5. **Ad Acc. Circ:** 200,000. ***Continued by*** *Engines (Los Angeles, Calif.), 1059-258X.*

US/0731-3314
**HOT ROD MAGAZINE KIT CAR. VFOAT** H.R. Kit Car Annual; HR Kit Car Annual. Periodical. English. an. Petersen Publishing Company, 6420 Wilshire Bouldevard, Los Angeles CA 90048. **Tel** (213)782-2485. **ED** Dave Fults. **LC** TL240; .H66. **DD** 629.222. **Ad Acc. Circ:** 150,000. ***Continues*** *Hot Rod Magazine Kit Car Annual.*

US/0730-5044
**HOT ROD MAGAZINE PICKUPS & MINI-TRUCKS.** (HOT ROD MAGAZINE PICKUPS & MINI-TRUCKS / BY THE EDITORS OF HOT ROD MAGAZINE.). **VFOAT** Pickups & Mini-Trucks; HR Pickups & Mini-Trucks. **VAT** Hot Rod Magazine Pickups and Mini-Trucks. (19??)-. English. $2.50 US; $3.25 Canada. Petersen Publishing Company, 6420 Wilshire Bouldevard, Los Angeles CA 90048. **Tel** (213)782-2485. **LC** TL230; .H68. **DD** 629.82/73.

US/0196-7010
**HOT ROD PERFORMANCE AND CUSTOM DIRECTORY. VFOAT** Hot Rod Directory. Directory. English. an. $4.95 single copy. Petersen Publishing Company, 6420 Wilshire Bouldevard, Los Angeles CA 90048. **Tel** (213)782-2485. **LC** TL12; .H67. **DD** 338.4/76292/02573.

US/1057-5006
**HOUSEHOLD VEHICLES ENERGY CONSUMPTION. See** Energy.

US/1042-6434
**HOW TO AVOID RIPPING YOUR HAIR OUT WHEN PURCHASING NEW OR USED FOREIGN OR DOMESTIC TAX FREE CARS DIRECT STATESIDE, OVERSEAS OR CANADA. VFOAT** Tax Free Cars Direct. (1990)-. Periodical. English. an. $24.95. Bos Corp, Three 1st National Plaza/Suite 1960, Chicago IL 60602.

UK/0306-2910
**IBCAM.** [I.B.C.A.M.]. **Main/Corp** Institute of British Carriage and Automobile Manufacturers. **Added/Corp** Institute of British Carriage and Automobile Manufacturers. Institute Journal. **VFOAT** Institute Journal. Vol. 1 (Jan. 1974)-. Periodical. English. mo. Institute of British Carriage and Automobile Manufacturing, Thames Meadow, 59 Henley Road, Shillingford OX9 8EZ England. **LC** TL1; .I563a. ***Continues*** *Institute of British Carriage and Automobile Manufacturers. Institute Bulletin.*

US/0162-4989
**IMPACT (WASHINGTON). See** Law.

US/0199-4468
**IMPORT AUTOMOTIVE PARTS & ACCESSORIES. VFOAT** IAPA. **VAT** Import Automotive Parts and Accessories. Vol.1 (Jan. 1980)-. Periodical. English. mo. $34.00 US; $50.00 Canada and Mexico; $85.00 other. Meyers Publishing Corporation, 6211 Van Nuys Blvd, Suite 200, Van Nuys CA 91401. **Tel** (818)785-3900, FAX (818)785-4397, telex 650-292300 MCI. **ED** Steve Relyea. **Ad Acc, Adv Mgr:** Lana Meyers, **Tel** (818)761-4272. **Circ:** 32,000 (ctrl).
**Desc:** Designed as a forum for the parts and accessories market. Content focuses on recent automotive technological developments, new product listings, international trade update automotive association news and general industry happenings.

US
**IMPORT CAR AND TRUCK TRANSMISSION MANUAL.** (19??)-. Periodical. English. an. $119.00. Mitchell International Inc, PO Box 26260, San Diego CA 92126-0260. **Tel** (619)578-6550, (800)648-8010, FAX (619)578-4752. **(Subscription address:** Mitchell International Inc., PO Box 71654, Chicago IL 60694.**)**

US
**IMPORT COLLISION ESTIMATING GUIDE.** (19??)-. Periodical. English. mo. $244.00. Mitchell International Inc, PO Box 26260, San Diego CA 92126-0260. **Tel** (619)578-6550, (800)648-8010, FAX (619)578-4752. **(Subscription address:** Mitchell International Inc., PO Box 71654, Chicago IL 60694.**)**

US/0896-5722
**IMPORT SERVICE.** [Import serv.]. Vol. 1, No. 1 (Nov./Dec. 1987)-. Periodical. English. mo. $48.00. Import Service Magazine, 306 North Cleveland-Massillon Road, Akron OH 44333. **Tel** (216)666-9553, FAX (216)666-8912. **DD** 382. ctrl circ.
**Desc:** Repair information for technicians who repair import vehicles.

●US/1069-4714
**IMPORTCAR (1993).** (IMPORTCAR : SERVICE AND PARTS FOR IMPORT VEHICLES.). [ImportCar]. **VFOAT** Import Car. Vol. 15, No. 4 (Apr. 1993)-. Periodical. English. mo. $45.00 US, Canada & Mexico; $91.00 other. Babcox Publications Inc., 11 South Ford Street, Akron OH 44304. **Tel** (216)535-7011. **LC** TL159; .B3. **DD** 629.222. ***Continues*** *ImportCar & Truck, 1040-5267.*

US/1040-5267
**IMPORTCAR & TRUCK.** ***Title Change.*** **VFOAT** Import Car & Truck; ImportCar and Truck; Import Car and Truck. Vol. 10, No. 7 (July 1988)-(19??). Periodical. English. mo. Babcox Publications Inc, 11 South Forge Street, Akron OH 44304. **Tel** (216)535-6117. **LC** TL159; .B3. **DD** 629.222. ***Continues*** *ImportCar (Akron, Ohio : 1982), 0735-7877.* ***Continued by*** *ImportCar (Akron, Ohio : 1993), 1069-4714.*

US
**IMPORTED CAR REPAIR MANUAL PARTS / LABOR ESTIMATING MANUAL.** (19??)-. Periodical. English. an. $89.00. Mitchell International Inc, PO Box 26260, San Diego CA 92126-0260. **Tel** (619)578-6550, (800)648-8010, FAX (619)578-4752. **(Subscription address:** Mitchell International Inc., PO Box 71654, Chicago IL 60694.**)**

US
**IMPORTED CARS & TRUCKS, ELECTRICAL SERVICE & REPAIR. VFOAT** Mitchell Manuals for Automotive Professionals. Electrical Service & Repair, Imported Cars & Trucks; Electrical Service & Repair, Imported Cars & Trucks. **VAT** Imported Cars and Trucks, Electrical Service and Repair. English. an. Mitchell International Inc, PO Box 26260, San Diego CA 92126-0260. **Tel** (619)578-6550, (800)648-8010, FAX (619)578-4752. **ED** Dan Kelley. **Ad Acc.** ctrl circ.
**Desc:** Testing, servicing, and repair of alternators, starters, regulators, ignition systems and others electrical components on 1975-84 imported cars and light trucks. Wiring diagrams included.

US/0741-0158
**IMPORTED CARS & TRUCKS, TRANSMISSION SERVICE & REPAIR. VFOAT** Imported Cars and Trucks, Transmission Service & Repair. English. an. Mitchell International Inc, PO Box 26260, San Diego CA 92126-0260. **Tel** (619)578-6550, (800)648-8010, FAX (619)578-4752. **ED** Dan Kelley. **LC** TL262; .M57A. **DD** 629.2/44/05. **Ad Acc.** ctrl circ. ***Continues*** *Transmission Service & Repair, Imported Cars & Trucks.*
**Desc:** This manual explains servicing, trouble shooting and overhaul of manual and automatic transaxles and transmissions for 1975-84 imported cars and light trucks.

US
**IMPORTED CARS, LIGHT TRUCKS, AND VANS SERVICE AND REPAIR MANUAL. ANNUAL DATA ENGINE PERFORMANCE / ELECTRICAL / MECHANICAL.** (19??)-. Periodical. English. an. $236.00. Mitchell International Inc, PO Box 26260, San Diego CA 92126-0260. **Tel** (619)578-6550, (800)648-8010, FAX (619)578-4752. **(Subscription address:** Mitchell International Inc., PO Box 71654, Chicago IL 60694.**)**

US
**IMPORTED CARS, LIGHT TRUCKS, AND VANS SERVICE AND REPAIR MANUAL. ELECTRICAL.** (19??)-. Periodical. English. an. $269.00. Mitchell International Inc, PO Box 26260, San Diego CA 92126-0260. **Tel** (619)578-6550, (800)648-8010, FAX (619)578-4752. **(Subscription address:** Mitchell International Inc., PO Box 71654, Chicago IL 60694.**)**

US
**IMPORTED CARS, LIGHT TRUCKS, AND VANS SERVICE AND REPAIR MANUAL ENGINE PERFORMANCE.** (19??)-. Periodical. English. an. $269.00. Mitchell International Inc, PO Box 26260, San Diego CA 92126-0260. **Tel** (619)578-6550, (800)648-8010, FAX (619)578-4752. **(Subscription address:** Mitchell International Inc., PO Box 71654, Chicago IL 60694.**)**

US
**IMPORTED CARS, LIGHT TRUCKS, AND VANS SERVICE AND REPAIR MANUAL. HEATING AND AIR CONDITIONING.** (19??)-. Periodical. English. an. $169.00. Mitchell International Inc, PO Box 26260, San Diego CA 92126-0260. **Tel** (619)578-6550, (800)648-8010, FAX (619)578-4752. **(Subscription address:** Mitchell International Inc., PO Box 71654, Chicago IL 60694.**)**

CN/0702-5785
**IN THE DRIVER'S SEAT. Added/Corp** Ontario Safety League. (19??)-. Periodical. English. mo. Ontario Safety League, 21 Four Seasons Place, Suite 100, Etobiocoke Ontario M9B 6J8 Canada. **DD** 629.2/04/205. ctrl circ.

LH
**IN VERKEHR GESETZTE NEUE MOTORFAHRZEUGE. Main/Corp** Liechtenstein. Amt fur Volkswirtschaft. German. Free. Amt fur Volkswirtshaft des Furstentums Liechtenstein, Fl 9490 Liechtenstein, Vaduz Liechtenstein. **Tel** 075/66 111, telex REPI FL 88 92 90. **LC** HE5667.9; .A19A. **DD** 388.3/2/0943648. **Circ:** 300 (ctrl).
**Desc:** Motor vehicles newly registered and rolling stock of motor vehicles.

US/1055-3355
**INDIANAPOLIS 500 YEARBOOK, THE.** [Indianap. 500 yearb.]. **VFOAT** Carl Hungness Presents the Indianapolis 500 Yearbook. (1973)-. English. an (Sept.). $23.95. Carl Hungness Publications, PO Box 24308, Speedway IN 46224. **Tel** (317)244-4792. **ED** Carl Hungness. **DD** 796. Index available. **Ad Acc.**

FR/0020-1200
**INGENIEURS DE L'AUTOMOBILE (PARIS).** (INGENIEURS DE L'AUTOMOBILE.). [Ing. automob.]. **Added/Corp** Societe des Ingenieurs de l'Automobile (France). Vol. 32, No. 1 (Jan. 1959)-. Academic Scholarly Publication. French. Eight times a year. 670.00F France; 760.00F other. V B Promotion, 15 Rue Du 19 Janvier, 92380 Garches France. **Tel** 011 33 1 47014474, FAX 011 33 1 47014825. ***Continues** Societe des Ingenieurs de l'Automobile (France). Journal.*
**Ind/Abst** Alum. Ind. Abstr.; EMBASE; Infomat Int. Bus.; Met. Abstr.; Saf. Health Work.

US/0276-6280
**INSURANCE THEFT LOSSES. VANS, PICKUPS AND UTILITY VEHICLES, ... MODELS. See** Insurance.

US/0959-6631
**INTELLIGENT HIGHWAY, THE. See** Transportation-Roads and Traffic.

US
**INTERCHANGE, IMPORTED CARS & TRUCKS.** English. Mitchell International Inc, PO Box 26260, San Diego CA 92126-0260. **Tel** (619)578-6550, (800)648-8010, FAX (619)578-4752.

UK/0262-317X
**INTERNATIONAL AUTO INDUSTRY NEWSLETTER.** [Int. auto ind. newsl.]. (1981)-. Periodical. English. mo. $395.00. Industrial Newsletters, 42 Market Square, Toddington, Dunstable Beds, LU5 6BS United Kingdom. **Tel** 011 44 525 872060, FAX 011 44 525 874759. **DD** 338.47629205. ***Continues** Auto Industry Newsletter.*

UK/0261-2267
**INTERNATIONAL AUTOMOTIVE REVIEW. *Ceased.*** [Int. automat. rev.]. **Added/Corp** Automotive Research & Management Consultants Ltd. (1981)-(19??). Periodical. English. qt. MCB University Press, 60 62 Toller Lane, Bradford West Yorkshire BD8 9BX England. **Tel** 011 44 274 499821, FAX 011 44 274 547143, telex 51317 MCBUNI G. **ED** Peter Cooke, Paul Sleigh, and Mike Woodmansey. **LC** HD9710..A1; I55. **DD** 338.4/76292/05.
**Desc:** Aims to provide international, in-depth coverage of topics of current and coming strategic interest to the automotive industry. Presents a balanced and informed view for management and for those who need to know.

SZ/0143-3369
**INTERNATIONAL JOURNAL OF VEHICLE DESIGN.** (INTERNATIONAL JOURNAL OF VEHICLE DESIGN : THE JOURNAL OF THE INTERNATIONAL ASSOCIATION FOR VEHICLE DESIGN.). [Int. j. veh. des.]. **Added/Corp** Unesco. Vol. 1, No. 1 (Oct. 1979)-. Academic Scholarly Publication. English. bm (6 issues). £170.00 UK; $250.00 North America; DM420.00 other. Inderscience Enterprises Ltd, World Trade Center Building, 110 Avenue Louis Casai, Case Postale 306, CH-1215 Geneva-Aeroport Switzerland. **Tel** 011 41 22 7383437, FAX 011 41 22 7910885, telex 28 99 50. **ED** M. A. Dorgham. **LC** TL1; .I69. **DD** 629.2/31/05. **CODEN** IJVDDW. **[CCC].** Index available. cum. index. **Bk Rev. Ad Acc. Pr Rev. Circ:** 75,000. Documents available from Article Express International, The Genuine Article, Ask*IEEE, Documents on Demand.
**Desc:** Topics include vehicle engineering and components, transport, design, energy, materials, electronics, manufacturing, product planning, aerodynamics, environment, safety, thermo, fluid mechanics, and vibration.
**Ind/Abst** Acoust. Abstr.; Alum. Ind. Abstr.; Bioeng. Abstr.; Curr. Contents Eng. Tech. Appl. Sci.; Curr. Technol. Index; Ei Page One; EMBASE; Energy Inf. Abstr.; Eng. Mater. Abstr.; Eng. Index Annu.; Environ. Abstr.; Ergon. Abstr.; Highw. Res. Abstr.; INSPEC (Feb. 1981-); Int. Aerosp. Abstr.; Leadscan; Met. Abstr.; Pollut. Abstr. Indexes; Res. Alert [Select. Cov.]; SCISEARCH; Shock Vibr. Dig.

SZ/1351-7848
**INTERNATIONAL JOURNAL OF VEHICLE DESIGN SERIES B : HEAVY VEHICLE SYSTEMS.** English. Four times a year. £135.00 UK; $185.00 North America; DM340.00 other. Inderscience Enterprises Ltd, World Trade Center Building, 110 Avenue Louis Casai, Case Postale 306, CH-1215 Geneva-Aeroport Switzerland. **Tel** 011 41 22 7383437, FAX 011 41 22 7910885, telex 28 99 50.
**Desc:** Covers highway transportation technology and heavy vehicle engineering and safety. Coverage includes heavy road, off-road vehicles and buses.

UK/0267-8225
**INTERNATIONAL MOTOR BUSINESS. Added/Corp** Economist Intelligence Unit (Great Britain). No. 122 (Apr. 1985)-. Periodical. English. qt. $577.50 (schools and educational libraries), $770.00 (other)*North America. The Economist Intelligence Unit, 40 Duke Street, London W1A 1DW England. **Tel** 011 44 71 8301000. **(Subscription address:** Economist Intelligence Unit / North America Subscriptions, 111 West 57th Street, New York NY 10019.**) ED** Arthur Way. **LC** HD9710.A1; M65. **DD** 338.4/76292/05. Index available. available on microfilm from World Microfilm Publications Ltd. ***Continues in part** Motor Business, 0027-1802.*
**Desc:** Examines recent developments, current trends and short term prospects for the passenger car and commercial vehicle sectors of the world's principal producing countries.
**Ind/Abst** Contents Pages Manage.

UK/0960-3204
**ITALIAN CARS.** [Ital. cars]. (1990)-. Periodical. English. bm (6 issues). $42.00. **(Subscription address:** US: International Publishers Corporation, 242 West Avenue, Darien, CT 06820**) ED** Phil Ward. **DD** 629.2220945. **Bk Rev. Ad Acc.**
**Desc:** Magazine covering all exotic Italian cars both classic and modern, including motorcycles.

US
**JAGUAR INTERNATIONAL MAGAZINE.** Vol. 3, No. 1 (Oct. 1985)-. Periodical. English. mo. Jaguar International, 1306 South Pope, Benton IL 62812. **LC** WMLC L 83/290. ***Continues** Jags Unlimited Magazine.*

US/0743-3913
**JAGUAR JOURNAL.** [Jaguar j.]. (19??)-. Periodical. English. bm. The Editor Jaguar Journal, 600 Willow Tree Road, Leonia NJ 07605. **ED** John F. Dugdale and Karen Miller. **LC** TL215.J3; J32. **DD** 629.2/222.

JA/0286-5971
**JAMA FORUM, THE. VFOAT** J.A.M.A. Forum. Vol. 1, No. 1 (April 1982)-. Periodical. English (French). qt. Automobiles. Japan Automobile Manufacturers Association Inc, Ohte-Machi Building, 6-1 Ohte-Machi 1-chome Chiyoda-ku, Tokyo 100 Japan. **Tel** 03-216-5777, FAX 03-287-2072, telex 0-222-3410 JAMATK J. **LC** HD9710.J3; J35. **DD** 338.4/76292/0952. **Bk Rev.**
**Ind/Abst** Hum. Resour. Abstr. (?-?).

UK/1355-6118
**JAPAN AUTO DIGEST.** (19??)-. English. mo (12 issues). $595.00 (except Europe). Newspeed, 134 Lots Road, London SW10 0RJ England. **Tel** 011 44 71 3529220, FAX 011 44 71 3529110. **ED** Paul Fisher. Index available (In each issue). **Circ:** 1,000.
**Desc:** Reports on and analyzes the impact of the Asian auto industry worldwide, and covers the activities of western automakers and suppliers in Asia.

JA
**JAPAN AUTOMOBILE LETTER. *Ceased.*** (19??)-(Dec. 1992). English. ir. **(Subscription address:** Maruzen Company Ltd., PO Box 5050, Import & Export Department, Tokyo 100 31 Japan.**)**

JA
**JAPAN AUTOMOTIVE NEWS.** English. mo. $99.00; $34.50 (postage for airmail zone I), $38.50 (postage for airmail zone II). Nikkan Jidosha Shinbunsha, 1-25, Kaigan 2 Chome, Minatoku, Tdokyoto 105 Japan. **(Subscription address:** Maruzen Company Ltd., PO Box 5050, Import & Export Department, Tokyo 100 31 Japan.**)**

JA
**JAPAN AUTOTECH REPORT. *Title Change.*** (19??)-(19??). English. sm. AI Publishing Co. Ltd., 3-4-2-202 Akatsutsumi, Setagayaku Tokyo 156 Japan. **Tel** 011 81 3 3325 4660. ***Continued by** Asian Autotech Report.*

US
**JAPANESE MOTOR BUSINESS / EIU, THE ECONOMIST INTELLIGENCE UNIT. Added/Corp** Economist Intelligence Unit (Great Britain). 1st Issue (Sept. 1984)-. English. qt. $577.50 (schools and educational libraries), $770.00 (other)*North America. The Economist Intelligence Unit, 40 Duke Street, London W1A 1DW England. **Tel** 011 44 71 8301000. **(Subscription address:** Economist Intelligence Unit / North America Subscriptions, 111 West 57th Street, New York NY 10019.**) ED** Arthur Way. **LC** HD9710.J3; J36. **DD** 338.4/76292/0952. available on microfilm from World Microfilm Publications Ltd.
**Desc:** A research bulletin examining the impact of the Japanese on international markets.

JA/0914-5230
**JATI COURIER.** [JATI cour.]. **VFOAT** Japan Automobile Technology Institute Courier. (1982)-. Periodical. English. mo. $192.00. JAT Institute, PO Box 58, Toyonaka-Minami 561 Japan. **ED** S. Fonda. **DD** 629.2.
**Desc:** Reports on new products and technologies. Abstracts from Japanese articles about new products, technologies, materials, trends, etc. in the ever progressing Japanese automotive industry.

JA
**JATMA YEAR BOOK: JAPAN AUTOMOBILE TIRE MANUFACTURERS ASSOCIATION.** Japanese. an. ¥6000.00. Jatma, Executive Managing Direc, No. 1-1-12 Toranomon, Minatoku Tokyo Japan 105. **Tel** 011 81 3 3503 0191.

JA
**JIDOSHA GIJUTSUKAI RONBUNSHU / TRANSACTIONS OF THE SOCIETY OF AUTOMOTIVE ENGINEERS OF JAPAN, INC.** [Jidosha Gijutsukai ronbunshu]. **Added/Corp** Jidosha Gijutsukai. **VFOAT** Transactions of the Society of Automotive Engineers of Japan, Inc. (1970)-. Academic Scholarly Publication. Japanese. qt. $225.00. Jidosha Gijutsukai, (Soc. of Automotive Engineers of Japan), 10-2, Gobancho, Chiyodaku,, Tokyoto 102 Japan. **(Subscription address:** Maruzen Company Ltd., PO Box 5050, Import & Export Department, Tokyo 100 31 Japan.**) CODEN** JGRODZ. Documents available from CASDDS.
**Ind/Abst** Chem. Abstr. (1970-1985).

CN/0021-7050
**JOBBER NEWS (TORONTO).** (JOBBER NEWS.). (1932)-. Periodical. English. mo. 48.00Can$ (one year), 77.00Can$ (two year), 112.00Can$ (three year) Canada; 72.00Can$ (one year), 101.00Can$ (two year), 136.00Can$ (three year) other. Southam Information and Technology Group Inc., 1450 Don Mills Road, Don Mills Ontario M3B 2X7 Canada. **Tel** (416)445-6641, (800)668-2374, FAX (416)442-2261. **ED** Bob Blans. **Ad Acc. Circ:** 11,500 (ctrl).
**Desc:** Canada's leading aftermarket publication serving the key buying and selling personnel of WD's jobbers and new mass merchandisers, hardware chains and national accounts.

US/0148-5792
**JOBBER RETAILER. *Title Change.*** Vol. 1 (Apr. 1977)-(199?). Periodical. English. Thirteen times a year. Bill Communications Inc., 355 Park Avenue South, New York NY 10010-1789. **Tel** (800)821-6897, (212)592-6262, FAX (212)592-6209. **(Subscription address:** Bill Communications, 200 South Route 130, Cinnaminson, NJ 08077**) LC** HD9710.A1; J64. **DD** 338.4/7/629205. available on microfilm from University Microfilms International (UMI). ***Continued by** Parts Business, 1072-5598.*

US/0021-7069
**JOBBER TOPICS.** [Jobber top.]. Began in 1934. Periodical. English. mo. $5.00 (single issue) except July issue $25.00; $50.00 US and Possessions; $60.00 other. Irving-Cloud Publishing Company, 417 North Hough Street, Barrington IL 60010. **Tel** (708)382-3405, FAX (708)674-7015. **(Subscription address:** 6201 W Howard Street, Room 207, Niles, IL 60648**) ED** Bob Weber. **Ad Acc. Circ:** 60,000 (ctrl).
**Desc:** Edited for automotive jobbers, redistributing

jobbers, and automotive warehouse distributors. **Ind/Abst** Bus. Index (Jan. 1985-Dec. 1985); Gen. BusinessFile (Jan. 1985-Dec. 1985); Trade Ind. Index (1981-?).

CN/0840-7754
**JOURNAL OF MOTOR VEHICLE LAW.** **See** Law.

JA/0385-7298
**JOURNAL OF THE SOCIETY OF AUTOMOTIVE ENGINEERS OF JAPAN.** **Added/Corp** Jidosha Gijutsukai. **VFOAT** Jidosha Gijutsu. (19??)-. Academic Scholarly Publication. Japanese. mo. $440.00. Jidosha Gijutsukai, (Soc. of Automotive Engineers of Japan), 10-2, Gobancho, Chiyodaku,, Tokyoto 102 Japan. **(Subscription address:** Kyowa Book Company Inc., 1-38 Kanda Jinbo-Cho, chiyoda-Ku Tokyo 101, Japan**)** **ED** Katsumi Kageyama. **CODEN** JDGJA9. **Circ:** 20,000 (ctrl). Documents available from CASDDS.
**Desc:** Report of technical studies about the car industry. Provides introductions and explanation, announcements of complete cars or excellent parts, and an introduction of documents.
**Ind/Abst** Chem. Abstr.; Coal Abstr.

CN/0702-8555
**JOURNAL PISTES CIRCUITS.** **VFOAT** Pistes et Circuits. (1972)-. Periodical. French (English; summaries and/or abstracts in English). mo. 0.50Can$. Promotions P C, CP 71 Ste-Rose, Laval Quebec H7L 1K8 Canada. **DD** 796.7/2/05.

JA/0389-4304
**JSAE REVIEW.** **Added/Corp** Jidosha Gijutsukai. **VAT** Japanese Society of Automotive Engineers Review. No. 1 (1978)-. Academic Scholarly Publication. English. qt. $168.00. Society of Automotive Engineers, 400 Commonwealth Drive, Warrendale PA 15096. **Tel** (412)776-4841, (412)772-7106, FAX (412)776-5760. **ED** Kiyoshi Fukuchi. **LC** TL240; .J77. **DD** 629.2/0952. **CODEN** JREVDY. **[CCC]**. **Bk Rev**. **Ad Acc**. ctrl circ. Documents available from CASDDS.
**Desc:** Technical magazine that covers the developments in the Japanese automotive industry. Contains abstracts of JSAE papers and reports of the Ministry of Transport.
**Ind/Abst** Acoust. Abstr.; Alum. Ind. Abstr.; Chem. Abstr.; Fluid Abstr., Civil Eng.; Fluid Abstr. Proc. Eng.; FLUIDEX (1978-); Highw. Res. Abstr.; Met. Abstr.

US/0744-5962
**KART SPORT.** [Kart sport]. Vol. 1, No. 1 (May 1982)-. Periodical. English. mo. Kart Sport Inc., 5570 Ashbourne Road, Baltimore MD 21227.

US/0096-3216
**KARTER NEWS.** **See** Recreation, Leisure-Sports.

US/0192-1134
**KARTING DIGEST.** V. 1- Jan. 1975-. Periodical. English. mo. $10.00. K Dee Publishing, PO Box 1659, Opa Locka FL 33055. **LC** GV1029.5; .K326. **DD** 796.7/6/05.

US
**KELLEY BLUE BOOK ADVANCE SHEETS.** English. bm. $20.00. Kelley Blue Book, PO Box 19691, Irvine CA 92713. **Tel** (714)770-7704.

US/0897-6171
**KELLEY BLUE BOOK NEW CAR PRICE MANUAL.** [Kelley blue book new car price man.]. **VFOAT** Blue Book New Car Price Manual; New Car Price Manual; Kelley Blue Book Auto Price Manual; Kelley Blue Book; Blue Book Auto Price Manual. (19??)-. Periodical. English. bm. $96.00 Alaska and Hawaii; $79.00 other US; $139.00 other. Kelley Blue Book, PO Box 19691, Irvine CA 92713. **Tel** (714)770-7704. **DD** 380.

US
**KELLEY BLUE BOOK, OFFICIAL GUIDE FOR OLDER CARS.** **VFOAT** Kelley Blue Book Auto Market Report, Official Guide for Older Cars. (19??)-. Periodical. English. Six times a year. $49.00 US; $65.00 other. Kelley Blue Book, PO Box 19691, Irvine CA 92713. **Tel** (714)770-7704.

US
**KELLEY BLUE BOOK. RESIDUAL VALUE GUIDE.** **Added/Corp** Kelley Blue Book Co. **VFOAT** Kelley Blue Book Residual Value Guide; Residual Value Guide; Kelley Blue Book Auto Residual Guide; Official Residual Value Guide. (198?)-. Periodical. English. bm. $49.00 Continental US; $55.00 Hawaii & Alaska $65.00 other. Kelley Blue Book, PO Box 19691, Irvine CA 92713. **Tel** (714)770-7704. **LC** HD9710.A1; K43. **DD** 629.2/222/0294.
**Desc:** Information on used cars and automobiles.

US
**KELLEY BLUE BOOK. RV MOTOR HOME GUIDE.** **Added/Corp** Kelley Blue Book Co. **VFOAT** RV Motor Home Guide; Official RV Guide; Motor Home & Camper Guide; Kelley Blue Book. Official RV Guide Kelley Blue Book. Motor Home & Camper Guide. (19??)-. Periodical. English. Three times a year. $45.00 US; $55.00 other. Kelley Blue Book, PO Box 19691, Irvine CA 92713. **Tel** (714)770-7704. **LC** TL297; .K42. **DD** 629.2/26/.

US
**KELLEY BLUE BOOK. RV TRAILER GUIDE.** **Added/Corp** Kelley Blue Book Co. Recreation Vehicle Dealers Association of North America. **VFOAT** Kelley Blue Book. Official R.V. Guide; Kelley Blue Book. R.V. Trailer Guide; RV Trailer Guide; R.V. Trailer Guide; Kelley Blue Book Official RV Guide. (19??)-. English. Twice a year. $45.00 US; $55.00 other. Kelley Blue Book, PO Box 19691, Irvine CA 92713. **Tel** (714)770-7704. **LC** TL297; .K43a. **DD** 629.2/26/029473. ***Continues*** *Travel Trailers, 5th Wheel Trailers, Camping Trailers RV Guide, New & Used Values, 0145-3785.*

GW/0047-3049
**KFZ I.E. KRAFTFAHRZEUG-BETRIEB UND AUTOMARKT.** **VFOAT** KFZ-Betrieb und Automarkt. Yearly V. 62- ; 19. Jan. 1972-. Periodical. German. sm. Vogel Verlag, Postfach 6740, D-97064 Wuerzburg Germany. **Tel** 011 49 931 4182145, 011 49 931 4182483, FAX 011 49 931 4182670, telex 841 680131. **LC** TL3; .K683. **DD** 629.22/2/05. ***Formed by the union of*** *KFZ-Betrieb* ***and*** *Automarkt.*

●US/1072-7981
**KIT CAR.** (1993)-. Periodical. English. bm (6 issues). $15.95 US; $22.42 Canada; $20.95 other. Petersen Publishing Company, 6420 Wilshire Bouldevard, Los Angeles CA 90048. **Tel** (213)782-2485. **(Subscription address:** Neodata / Colorado, PO Box 2606, Boulder Boulder CO 80322.**)** ***Continues*** *Specialty Car, 1068-2627.*

US/1062-9610
**KIT CAR ILLUSTRATED.** **See** Hobbies.

JA
**KOTSU ANZEN KOGAI KENKYUJO NEMPO.** **See** Transportation.

GW/0023-4419
**KRAFTFAHRZEUGTECHNIK.** [Kraftfahrzeugtechnik]. **Added/Corp** Kammer der Technik. Kammer der Technik. Fachverband Fahrzeugbau und Verkehr. (Sept. 1950)-. Academic Scholarly Publication. German. Twelve times a year. DM62.40. VPM Verlagsunion Pabel Moewig, Leserservice, D 65175 Wiesbaden Germany. **Tel** 011 49 611 266173. **LC** TL3; .K73.
**Ind/Abst** EMBASE.

US/0192-5458
**KRUSE REPORT.** Periodical. English. qt. $40.00. Kruse International, PO Box 190, Auburn IN 46706. **Tel** (219)925-5600. **ED** Dean V Kruse.
**Desc:** Includes information about Kruse Auctions, interviews with prominent people in the business, and Dean Kruse's personal comments about the car market.

FI
**KUORMA-AUTO LINJALIIKENNE.** **Main/Corp** Finland. Tilastokeskus. **VFOAT** Linjetrafik Med Lastbilar. Multiple languages (Finnish and Swedish). Tilastokeskus, PL 504, Annankatu 44, 00101 Helsinki Finland. **Tel** 358-0-17341, FAX 358-0-17342474, telex 1002111 TILASTO SF. **LC** HE5675.3; .A27B.

NO/0802-7870
**LAST OG BUSS.** [Last buss]. (1969)-. Periodical. Multiple languages. qt. Kr1720.00 Norway; Kr1804.00 Scandinavia; Kr1828.00 Europe. Last og Buss, Postboks 9831 Ila, 0132 Oslo 1 Norway. **DD** 629.22. **Ad Acc**.

●US/1061-4052
**'LECTRIC AUTO NEWS.** **Added/Corp** Technical Education Council. **VFOAT** Electric Auto News. (1992)-. Periodical. English. mo. Technical Education Council, PO Box 739, Havertown PA 19083.

CN/0834-2423
**LEMON-AID (1985).** (LEMON AID MAGAZINE). [Lemon-aid]. **Added/Corp** Automobile Protection Association. Vol. 11 No. 1 (March/May 1985)- Vol. 18 (Mar, 1993)-. Periodical. English (French). Four times a year (Mar., June, Sept., Dec.). 12.00Can$ (one year); 22.00 (two year). Les Publs En Consommation APA, INC 292 BOUL Saint Joseph Quest, Montreal QUE H2V 2N7 Canada. **Tel** (514)273-1662, FAX (514)273-0797. **ED** Antoinette Greco & George Ivy. **DD** 338.4/76292222/05. **Circ:** 30,000. ***Continues*** *Lemon Aid Bulletin, 0827-3456.*
**Desc:** A magazine dedicated to providing up-to-date consumer information regarding the automobile marketplace. Included are ratings of new and used cars, light trucks, and 4x4's.

CN/0714-5861
**LEMON-AID NEW CAR GUIDE.** (LEMON-AID NEW CAR GUIDE ... / C.PHIL EDMONSTON.). **VFOAT** Lemon-Aid New Car Guide. (1982)-. English. an. 15.95Can$. Irwin Publisher, 34 Lesmill Road, Don Mills Ontario M3B 2T6 Canada. **Tel** (416)445-3333. **DD** 629.2/222/05. ***Continues*** *Edmonston, Louis-Philippe, 1944- Lemon-Aid., 0383-7084.*

PP
**LICENCES ISSUED TO DRIVERS AND RIDERS OF MOTOR VEHICLES / BUREAU OF STATISTICS, KONEDOBU, PAPUA.** ***Title Change.*** English. an. **LC** HE5717.8; .A27. **DD** 354.95/30087834. ***Continued by*** *Licences Issued to Drivers of Motor Vehicles and Riders of Motor Cycles.*

US
**LIGHT TRUCK REPAIR MANUAL MECHANICAL PARTS / LABOR ESTIMATING MANUAL.** (19??)-. Periodical. English. an. $59.00. Mitchell International Inc, PO Box 26260, San Diego CA 92126-0260. **Tel** (619)578-6550, (800)648-8010, FAX (619)578-4752. **(Subscription address:** Mitchell International Inc., PO Box 71654, Chicago IL 60694.**)**

US/0199-9362
**LOW RIDER.** **VFOAT** Low Rider Magazine. (19??)-. Periodical. English. mo. $31.00. Low Rider, PO Box 648, Walnut CA 91788. **Tel** (909)598-2300, FAX (909)598-3551. **ED** David Cohen. **Ad Acc. Circ:** 165,000.
**Desc:** Provides readers with information on all aspects of the sport, from vehicle showcases to hands-on technical articles to music and lifestyle features.

●CN/1187-9475
**MAGAZINE CARGUIDE.** (LE MAGAZINE CARGUIDE.). [Mag. carguide]. **VFOAT** Carguide. (Winter 1992)-. French. Six times a year (Jan., Mar., May, July, Sept., Nov.). 12.99 Can$ (one year), 21.99Can$ (two year) Canada; 20.99Can$ (one year); 37.99Can$ (two years) other. Formula Publications Ltd, 447 Speers Road, Suite 4, Oakville ONT L6K 3S7 Canada. **Tel** (905)842-6591, FAX (905)842-6843. **ED** Alan McPhee and Tim Lindsay. **DD** 629.2/222/05. **Ad Acc, Adv Mgr:** Grant Wells or Al Henderson. **Circ:** 300,000 January (English & French), 100,000 Mar., May, July, Sept., Nov. (ctrl). ***Continues*** *L'Annuaire de l'Auto., 0831-2966.*
**Desc:** All of these issues contains articles on road testing, touring articles, new and exciting reviews, technical information, automotive history, automotive trivia, and more to keep you informed on what's happening in the automotive industry.

CN/0821-1329
**MAGAZINE CONTRE-JOUR.** **See** Recreation, Leisure-Sports.

AG
**MANUAL PARA LA REPARACION DE AUTOMOVILES Y CAMIONES, GUIA DEL COMERCIO Y LA INDUSTRIA AUTOMOTOR.** **VFOAT** Guia del Comercio y la Industria Automotor. (19??)-. Spanish. **LC** TL152; .M265. **DD** 338.4/7/629.28702582.

US
**MECHANICAL LABOR ESTIMATING GUIDE.** **Added/Corp** Mitchell International. (1990)-. English. an. $149.00. Mitchell International Inc, PO Box 26260, San Diego CA 92126-0260. **Tel** (619)578-6550, (800)648-8010, FAX (619)578-4752. **(Subscription address:** Mitchell International Inc., PO Box 71654, Chicago IL 60694.**)** **LC** TL152; .M3653. **DD** 629.28/72/0299. ***Continues in part*** *Mechanical Parts/Labor Estimating Guide. Domestic Cars (San Diego, Calif. : 1983); Mechanical Parts/Labor Estimating Guide. Domestic Trucks & Vans (San Diego, Calif. : 1985), 0898-9605; Mechanical Parts/Labor Estimating Guide. Imported Cars & Trucks (1982), 8755-6057.*

US/0884-0156
**MECHANICAL PARTS/LABOR ESTIMATING GUIDE. DOMESTIC GLASS.** [Mech. parts/labor estim. guide, Domest. glass]. **VFOAT** Mitchell Mechanical Parts/Labor Estimating Guide. Domestic Glass; Mechanical Parts Labor Estimating Guide. Domestic Glass; Domestic Glass. English. an. Mitchell International Inc, PO Box 26260, San Diego CA 92126-0260. **Tel** (619)578-6550, (800)648-8010, FAX (619)578-4752. **ED** Bill Jillard. **LC** TL275; .M35. **DD** 629.28/7/029473. **Ad Acc**. ctrl circ.
**Desc:** Mechanical part numbers and prices, estimated labor times for 1974-86 domestic cars. Separate times for combined operations. Skill level codes and model identification illustrations.

CN/0714-8569
**MEMBERS & CARS.** (MEMBERS & CARS / THE ANTIQUE AUTOMOBILE CLUB OF OTTAWA.). [Memb. cars]. **Main/Corp** Antique Automobile Club of Ottawa. 1982-. English. an. Free to members. Antique Automobile Club of Ottawa, PO Box 2525 Station D, Ottawa Ontario K1P 5W6 Canada. **DD** 629.2/222. ***Continues*** *Antique Automobile Club of Ottawa. AACO Membership Roster, 0714-8569.*

## Transportation — Automobiles

**KE**
**MEMBERS' HANDBOOK - AUTOMOBILE ASSOCIATION OF KENYA.** Main/Corp Automobile Association of Kenya. 1979-. English. Free to Members. Media Services, PO Box 50095, Nairobi Kenya. **LC** GV1025.K4; A94A. **DD** 916.76/204/4. Continues AA Guide to Motoring in Kenya.

**CN/1187-3469**
**MEMBERSHIP ROSTER - AUTOMOTIVE RETAILERS ASSOCIATION (WINNIPEG).** (MEMBERSHIP ROSTER / AUTOMOTIVE RETAILERS ASSOCIATION.). [Membsh. roster - Automot. Retail. Assoc.]. Main/Corp Automotive Retailers Association (B.C.). (1991)-. English. Limited free distribution. Automotive Retailers Association, Suite 120, 4281 Canada Way, Burnaby British Columbia V5G 4P1 Canada. **DD** 381/.456292/025711. Continues Membership Roster., 0833-8868.

**US/0735-1798**
**MICHIGAN LIVING.** See Travel and Tourism.

**US/0199-2465**
**MID AMERICAN AUTO RACING NEWS.** See Recreation, Leisure-Sports.

**US/0026-3338**
**MIDWEST AUTOMOTIVE NEWS.** VFOAT Midwest - Pacific Automotive News. Periodical. English. mo. Automotive Publishing, 2900 West Peterson, Chicago IL 60659.

**US/0047-732X**
**MIDWEST RACING NEWS.** See Recreation, Leisure-Sports.

**US**
**MILESTONE CAR, THE.** V. 1- Summer 1972-. Periodical. English. qt. $2.00 each issue. Milestone Car Society, 13150 El Capitan Way, Delhi CA 95315. **LC** TL1; .M54. **DD** 629.22/22/05.

**US/1052-0961**
**MINITRUCKIN' (ANAHEIM, CALIF.).** See Recreation, Leisure-Sports.

**US/1062-2578**
**MINIVAN, PICKUP, AND 4X4 BOOK, THE.** Title Change. (MINIVAN, PICKUP, AND 4X4 BOOK.). VFOAT Minivan, Pickup, and Four by Four Book; Minivan, Pickup, and Four-by-Four Book. (1993)-(1993). English. ir. Harper Collins Publishers, Keystone Industrial Park, Scranton PA 18512. **Tel** (800)242-7737, (800)233-4727, FAX (800)822-4090. **DD** 629. Continues Truck, Van, and 4X4 Book, 1050-9259. Continued by Truck, Van, and 4x4 Book (New York, N.Y. : 1994).

**US**
**MINNESOTA ... MOTOR VEHICLE CRASH FACTS (MINNESOTA. DEPT. OF PUBLIC SAFETY. OFFICE OF TRAFFIC SAFETY : 1982).** (MINNESOTA ... MOTOR VEHICLE CRASH FACTS.). VFOAT Motor Vehicle Crash Facts. 1982-. English. an. Office of Traffic Safety, Department of Public Safety, 207 Transportation Building, St Paul MN 55155. **LC** HE5614.3.M5; .M5A. **DD** 312/.44/09776. Continues Minnesota ... Motor Vehicle Crash Data, 0737-0121.

**US**
**MITCHELL COLLISION ESTIMATING AND REPAIR MANUAL. DOMESTIC VEHICLE DIMENSIONS. VDD.** (19??)-. Periodical. English. ir. $219.00. Mitchell International Inc, PO Box 26260, San Diego CA 92126-0260. **Tel** (619)578-6550, (800)648-8010, FAX (619)578-4752. (Subscription address: Mitchell International Inc., PO Box 71654, Chicago IL 60694.)

**US**
**MITCHELL COLLISION ESTIMATING AND REPAIR MANUAL. IMPORT VEHICLE DIMENSIONS. VDI.** (19??)-. Periodical. English. ir. $219.00. Mitchell International Inc, PO Box 26260, San Diego CA 92126-0260. **Tel** (619)578-6550, (800)648-8010, FAX (619)578-4752. (Subscription address: Mitchell International Inc., PO Box 71654, Chicago IL 60694.)

**US**
**MITCHELL GUIDE TO PROFESSIONAL ESTIMATING.** (19??)-. Periodical. English. an. $19.00. Mitchell International Inc, PO Box 26260, San Diego CA 92126-0260. **Tel** (619)578-6550, (800)648-8010, FAX (619)578-4752. (Subscription address: Mitchell International Inc., PO Box 71654, Chicago IL 60694.)

**US**
**MITCHELL SERVICE AND REPAIR MANUAL. ANNUAL DATA: TUNE-UP / ELECTRICAL / MECHANICAL.** (19??)-. Periodical. English. an. $149.00. Mitchell International Inc, PO Box 26260, San Diego CA 92126-0260. **Tel** (619)578-6550, (800)648-8010, FAX (619)578-4752. (Subscription address: Mitchell International Inc., PO Box 71654, Chicago IL 60694.)

**US/8755-4453**
**MITCHELL TECH SERVICE BULLETIN.** [Mitchell tech serv. bull.]. Added/Corp Mitchell Manuals, Inc. VFOAT Mitchell Tech Service Bulletins. Vol. 1 (1983)-. Bulletin. English. qt. Mitchell International Inc, PO Box 26260, San Diego CA 92126-0260. **Tel** (619)578-6550, (800)648-8010, FAX (619)578-4752. **ED** Dan Kelley. **LC** TL152; .M524. **DD** 629.28/7. Ad Acc. ctrl circ.
Desc: Factory information on fixing computer controlled driveability problems.

**US/0276-2382**
**MITCHELL TECHNICAL SERVICE BULLETIN, COLLISION.** [Mitchell tech. serv. bull., collis.]. Added/Corp Mitchell Manuals, inc. VFOAT Technical Service Bulletin, Collision. Vol. 1, Issue No. 1 (Mar. 1, 1980)-. Periodical. English. Ten times a year. $99.00. Mitchell International Inc, PO Box 26260, San Diego CA 92126-0260. **Tel** (619)578-6550, (800)648-8010, FAX (619)578-4752. (Subscription address: Mitchell International Inc., PO Box 71654, Chicago IL 60694.)

**UK/0267-2715**
**MODEL AUTO REVIEW.** See Hobbies.

**US/0026-8496**
**MODERN TIRE DEALER.** [Mod. tire deal.]. VFOAT MTD. (1919)-. Periodical. English. ir (14 issues). $55.00 US; $90.00 Canada; $80.00 other. Bill Communications Inc., 355 Park Avenue South, New York NY 10010-1789. **Tel** (800)821-6897, (212)592-6262, FAX (212)592-6209. (Subscription address: Bill Communications, 200 South Route 130, Cinnaminson, NJ 08077) available on microfilm and microfiche from University Microfilms International (UMI); available on an online database (file 648/Full-Text) from DIALOG.
Desc: Contains information for executives and tire dealers throughout North America.
Ind/Abst F&S Index Plus Text, Int. [Select. Cov.]; Gen. Period. Index (1985-); Mag. Search; PROMT; Trade Ind. ASAP [Full Txt.]; Trade Ind. Index (1981-) [Full Txt.].

**FR**
**MONDE DE L'AUTOMOBILE.** (19??)-. Periodical. French. Ten times a year. Le Monde de l Automobile, 46 rue de Troyon, 92310 Sevres France. **Tel** 011 33 45 07 02 00. **ED** Esther Slama. Circ: 40,000.

**BE**
**MONITEUR DE L'AUTOMOBILE, LE.** (1979)-. Periodical. French (Dutch). bw (every other Thurs.). 1995F Belgium; 2990F other. Editions Auto Magazine, Chaussee de la Hulpe 181, Bte. 2,, 1170 Brussels, Belgium. **Tel** 011 32 2 660 1920, FAX 011 32 2 643 2200. **ED** Etienne Visart. Circ: 390,000.

**FI**
**MOOTTORIAJONEUVO- JA KUMIKORJAAMOT.** Main/Corp Finland. Tilastokeskus. VFOAT Reparation av Motorfordon, Dack och Slangar. Multiple languages (Finnish and Swedish). Tilastokeskus, PL 504, Annankatu 44, 00101 Helsinki Finland. **Tel** 358-0-17341, FAX 358-0-17342474, telex 1002111 TILASTO SF. **LC** HD9710.F5; F55A.

**GW**
**MOT AUTO-JOURNAL.** (19??)-. Periodical. German. bw. DM166.40. Vereinigte Motor Verlag GmbH, Motor Presse, POB 106036, D 70049 Stuttgart Germany. **Tel** 011 49 711 1821506, 011 49 711 1821545. (Subscription address: Deutscher Pressevertrieb Buch, POB 101602 Hansa GMBH, D 20010 Hamburg Germany.) **LC** TL3; .M58. **DD** 629.2/05. Supersedes MOT; Absorbed Motor Rundschau.

**GW**
**MOT : DIE AUTOZEITSCHRIFT.** Nr. 1 (21 Dez. 1990)-. Periodical. German. bw. DM135.98 Europe. Vereinigte Motor Verlag GmbH, Motor Presse, POB 106036, D 70049 Stuttgart Germany. **Tel** 011 49 711 1821506, 011 49 711 1821545. (Subscription address: Hansa GmbH POB 101602, W 2000 Hamburg 1 F R Germany, Telephone: 011 49 40 237110) **ED** Engelbert Manner and Wolfgang Hecht. Index available. Ad Acc. Circ: 127,175 (ctrl).
Desc: Automotive publication with emphasis on tests, automotive technology and car maintenance.

**SP/0212-9000**
**MOTOR 16.** [Motor 16]. VFOAT Motor Dieciseis. (1983)-. Periodical. Spanish. wk. 15600ptas Spain; 26936ptas Europe; 33176ptas US; 44436ptas other. Motor 16, Hermanos Garcia Noblejas 41, 28037 Madrid, Spain. **Tel** 011 34 1 4072700. **UDC** 629.11. Index available. Ad Acc. Circ: 47,069 (ctrl). available on teletext.
Desc: Road tests, comparisons of similar car models, and sports.

**US/0278-9418**
**MOTOR AGE MECHANICS NEWSLETTER.** VFOAT Mechanics Newsletter; Motor/Age Mechanics Newsletter. (1981)-. Newsletter. English. ir. $30.00. Chilton Company, 201 King of Prussia Road, Radnor PA 19089. **Tel** (610)964-4122, (800)695-1214, FAX (610)964-4978, telex 6851035 CHILTON UW.

**US/0098-1745**
**MOTOR AUTO REPAIR MANUAL.** Added/Corp Motor (New York). (19??)-. English. an. $118.00. The Hearst Corporation, 250 West 55th Street, New York NY 10019. **Tel** (212)649-4014. **LC** TL152; .M815. **DD** 629.28/7/22. Continues Motor's Auto Repair Manual.

**US/0194-9411**
**MOTOR CRASH ESTIMATING GUIDE.** VFOAT Crash Estimating Guide; Motor's Crash Estimating Guide. (19??)-. Periodical. English. Fifteen times a year. $237.00. Hearst Corporation, c/o Ronald Powell, 817 Round Hill Road, Pelham AL 35124. **Tel** (205)663-0353, (800)288-6828. ctrl circ.
Desc: Part numbers, parts prices, and labor news needed to estimate cost of reparing wreck-damaged vehicles.

**US**
**MOTOR DOMESTIC WIRING DIAGRAM & MANUAL.** (19??)-. English. ir. Price varies; $66.00 for the General Motors 1993 volume, $57.00 for the Chrysler 1993 volume. Hearst Corporation, c/o Ronald Powell, 817 Round Hill Road, Pelham AL 35124. **Tel** (205)663-0353, (800)288-6828.

**US/0160-1644**
**MOTOR EARLY MODEL CRASH ESTIMATING GUIDE.** VFOAT Motor's Crash Estimating Guide; Early Model Crash Estimating Guide. (Winter 1977)-. English. Four times a year. $176.00. The Hearst Corporation, 250 West 55th Street, New York NY 10019. **Tel** (212)649-4014. **LC** TL152; .M713. **DD** 338.4/3629/28705.

**US/0743-1031**
**MOTOR EMISSION CONTROL MANUAL.** VFOAT Emission Control Manual. 2 (1975)-. English. an. $61.00. Hearst Corporation, c/o Ronald Powell, 817 Round Hill Road, Pelham AL 35124. **Tel** (205)663-0353, (800)288-6828. **LC** TL214.P6; M666. **DD** 629.2/528/05. Continues Motor's Emission Control Manual, 0743-1031.
Desc: Contains the latest Emission information available for domestic and imported cars.

**AT**
**MOTOR EQUIPMENT NEWS.** (19??)-. English. mo (11 issues). 35.00Aus$. Motor Equipment News, 54 Kellett Street, Kings Cross, PO Box 229, Potts Point NSW 2011 Australia. **Tel** 011 61 2 358 1155, FAX 011 61 2 356 3834.
Desc: Covers all aspects of the automotive service, repair and service station industries.

**US/0094-1514**
**MOTOR HANDBOOK.** Periodical. English. an. Motor Handbook, 250 West 55th Street, New York NY 10019. **LC** TL152; .M73. **DD** 629.28/7/05. Continues Motor's Handbook.

**US/0164-6346**
**MOTOR IMPORTED CAR CRASH ESTIMATING GUIDE.** VFOAT Imported Car Crash Estimating Guide; Motor's Imported Car Crash Estimating Guide. (19??)-. English. Twelve times a year. $255.00 Alabama; $237.00 others. Hearst Corporation, c/o Ronald Powell, 817 Round Hill Road, Pelham AL 35124. **Tel** (205)663-0353, (800)288-6828. **ED** Philip Cunningham. **LC** TL152; .M714. **DD** 338.4/3/629287220973. ctrl circ.
Desc: A complete listing of labor times, part numbers and prices needed to make an accurate repair cost estimate for vehicles damaged in a crash.

**US/0090-1563**
**MOTOR IMPORTED CAR REPAIR MANUAL.** (19??)-. English. an. $136.00. The Hearst Corporation, 250 West 55th Street, New York NY 10019. **Tel** (212)649-4014. **LC** TL152; .M86. **DD** 629.28/722/05. Continues Motor's Imported Car Repair Manual, 0090-1563.

**US/0163-9110**
**MOTOR IMPORTED CAR REPAIR MANUAL. PROFESSIONAL SERVICE TRADE EDITION.** (MOTOR IMPORTED CAR REPAIR MANUAL.). Main/Corp Motor. Added/Corp Motor. Imported Car Repair Manual. (19??)-. English. an. $142.00. Hearst Corporation, c/o Ronald Powell, 817 Round Hill Road, Pelham AL 35124. **Tel** (205)663-0353, (800)288-6828. **LC** TL152; .M7125a. **DD** 629.28/7/2205.

**US**
**MOTOR IMPORTED ENGINE TUNE UP & ELECTRONICS MANUAL.** VFOAT Imported Engine Tune Up & Electronics Manual; Imported Engine Tune Up and Electronics Manual. (1984)-. English. an. Price varies; $61.00 (1991-1994 volume). Hearst

5419

Corporation, c/o Ronald Powell, 817 Round Hill Road, Pelham AL 35124. **Tel** (205)663-0353, (800)288-6828. **LC** TL210; .M648. **DD** 629.2/5/0288.

US
**MOTOR IMPORTED WIRING DIAGRAM & MANUAL.** **VFOAT** Motor Imported Wiring Diagram and Manual; Imported Wiring Diagram Manual; Motor Imported Wiring Diagram Manual. 4th Ed. (1987)-. English. ir. $93.00 for 1993 Volume. Hearst Corporation, c/o Ronald Powell, 817 Round Hill Road, Pelham AL 35124. **Tel** (205)663-0353, (800)288-6828. **LC** TL272; .M722. **DD** 629.2/54. ***Continues*** *Motor Imported Vacuum & Wiring Diagram Manual.*

CN/0027-190X
**MOTOR IN CANADA.** ***Title Change. Suspended.*** [Mot. Can.]. April 1917-?. Periodical. English. mo. Sanford Evans Communications Ltd., Box 6900, 1700 Church Avenue, Winnipeg Manitoba R3C 3B1 Canada. **Tel** (204)632-2768, FAX (204)694-2347. **ED** James Buchok. **Ad Acc. Circ:** 13,500 (ctrl). ***Supersedes*** *Motor and Sport.* ***Continued by*** *Western Autobody, 0842-9855.*
**Desc:** Articles of interest to those involved in the automotive aftermarket mainly in western Canada. Articles include features , service advice, new products and literature.

AT/0729-0799
**MOTOR INDUSTRY JOURNAL.** ***Title Change.*** [Mot. ind. j.]. (1982)-(199?). Periodical. English. Eleven times a year (monthly except Jan.). Victoria Auto Chamber of Commerce, 464 St. Kilda Road / 7th Floor, Melbourne VIC 3004 Australia. **Tel** 11 61 3 8291111, FAX 11 61 3 8203401. **ED** Mitchell Mackey. **DD** 338.4762920994. **Bk Rev. Ad Acc, Adv Mgr:** Betty Billett. **Circ:** 6,000 (ctrl). ***Continues*** *VACC Journal, 0004-8712.* ***Continued by*** *Auto Industry Australia.*

UK
**MOTOR INDUSTRY OF GREAT BRITAIN ..., WORLD AUTOMOTIVE STATISTICS.** **VFOAT** World Automotive Statistics; SMMT Motor Industry of Great Britain, World Automotive Statistics. (1985)-. English. an. £54.00, add £4.00 (surface mail), £14.00 (airmail). Society of Motor Manufacturers & Traders, Forbes House, Halkin Street, London SW1X 7DS England. **Tel** 01-550-3231. **LC** HD9710.G7; S6. **DD** 338.4/76292/0941021. Index available. **Circ:** 1,000. ***Continues*** *Motor Industry of Great Britain.*
**Desc:** Covers vehicles in use, vehicles in production, new registrations, United Kingdom production by model and UK exports by manufacturer, plus miscellaneous information related to the motor industry, overseas registrations, overseas production and vehicles in use.

JA
**MOTOR INDUSTRY OF JAPAN (TOKYO, JAPAN : 1985).** (THE MOTOR INDUSTRY OF JAPAN.). English. an. World Press Inc, 11 11 Shinjuku 1 chome, Shinjuku-ku, Tokyo 160 Japan. **LC** HD9710.J3; M595. **DD** 338.4/76292/095205.

NZ
**MOTOR INDUSTRY YEAR BOOK.** English. an. 40.50NZ$ New Zealand. New Zealand Motor Trade Federation, PO Box 766, Wellington New Zealand. **Tel** (04)856026. **ED** R C Morpeth. **LC** HD9710.N5; N4. **DD** 338.4/7/629209931. Index available. cum. index. **Ad Acc. Circ:** 800. ***Continues*** *New Zealand Motor Trade Year Book.*
**Desc:** Reference book covering statistics related to the motor industry: taxes, sales, licenses, etc.

IT
**MOTOR ITALIA.** (1926)-. Periodical. Italian. qt. $65.00. Stamperia Artistica Nazionale, Corso Siracusa 37, 10136 Turin Italy. **Tel** 011 39 11 3290031. **ED** Gianni Rogliatti. **LC** TL4; .M57. **Bk Rev. Ad Acc. Circ:** 20,000.
**Desc:** Motoring, new car descriptions (both technical and historical). Occasional truck, boat and component descriptions.

JA
**MOTOR MATERIAL : M.M.** **VFOAT** M.M.; MM; M.M. Mota Materiaru; Mota Materiaru. Periodical. Japanese. mo. ¥6500. Mota Materiarusha, (Motor Material Co., Ltd.), 1-64, Kanda Jinbocho, Chiyodaku, Tokyoto 101, Japan. **LC** TL159; .M675.

CN/0229-6128
**MOTOR MINIATURES.** [Mot. miniat.]. Vol. 1, No. 1 (Nov. 1980)-. Periodical. English. qt. $5.95 Canada; $6.95 US. Wheelspin News, 3045 Universe Drive, Mississauga Ontario L4X 2E2. **DD** 629.2/21/05.

SP/0210-5969
**MOTOR MUNDIAL.** [Mot. mund.]. (1944)-. Periodical. Spanish. Eleven times a year. Motor Ediciones SA, Velazquez 121 7 Dcha, 28006 Madrid Spain. **Tel** 011 34 1 5624620, 5624628. **UDC** 629.113.

US/0027-1748
**MOTOR (NEW YORK).** (MOTOR.). [Motor]. Vol. 1, No. 1 (Oct. 1903)-. Periodical. English. mo. $18.00 (one year), $34.00 (two year). Hearst Corporation, c/o Ronald Powell, 817 Round Hill Road, Pelham AL 35124. **Tel** (205)663-0353, (800)288-6828. **LC** TL1; .M85. **DD** 629.2/222/05. available on microfilm and microfiche from University Microfilms International (UMI).

US/0300-6301
**MOTOR NORTH.** Began publication in 1972. Periodical. English. mo. $29.00. R & S, 6420 Zane Avenue North/Suite 201, Minneapolis MN 55429. **Tel** (612)535-8383.

US/0098-1656
**MOTOR PARTS AND TIME GUIDE.** English. mo. The Hearst Corporation, 250 West 55th Street, New York NY 10019. **Tel** (212)649-4014. **LC** TL152; .M82. **DD** 658.8/16. ***Continues*** *Motor's Parts and Time Guide.*

US/0090-2144
**MOTOR RACING YEAR, THE.** **See** Recreation, Leisure-Sports.

GW
**MOTOR REISEN REVUE.** Began with Dec. 1957 issue. Periodical. German. mo. DM15.00. Niederrad Lyoner Strasse 16, Postfach 71 0166, W-6 Frankfurt AM Main Germany. **Tel** 089/2183-8637, telex 523 426 SZD. **LC** TL3; .M615. **Ad Acc. Circ:** 260,000 (ctrl).

UK/0306-6274
**MOTOR REPORT INTERNATIONAL.** ***Ceased.*** [Mot. rep. int.]. (1973)-(Dec. 1993). Periodical. English. Twenty-five times a year. Circlemartin Ltd, PO Box 87, Dorking Surrey, RH4 2YS England. **Tel** 011 44 1 949 3302. available on an online database (file 648/Full-Text) from DIALOG.
**Ind/Abst** F&S Index Plus Text, Int. [Select. Cov.]; PROMT; Trade Ind. ASAP [Full Txt.]; Trade Ind. Index [Full Txt.].

US/0027-1977
**MOTOR SERVICE (CHICAGO, ILL. : 1951).** (MOTOR SERVICE.). [Mot. serv.]. (Sept. 15, 1951)-. Periodical. English. Twelve times a year. $38.00 US; $45.00 Canada & Mexico; $86.00 other. Hunter Publishing Company Inc., 25 Northwest Point Boulevard, Suite 800, Elk Grove Village IL 60007-1036. **Tel** (708)427-9512, FAX (708)427-2097. **ED** Jim Halloran. **LC** TL1; .M938. **DD** 629.28/722/05. **[CCC]. Ad Acc. Circ:** 130,000. ***Continues*** *Motor Service Magazine (Chicago, Ill. : 1950);* ***Absorbed*** *Service Station Management.*
**Desc:** Directed to owners/operators and managers of general and specialty repair shops, new car and truck dealers, fleet-owned repair shops and selected service stations.

US/0091-8822
**MOTOR SPORT YEARBOOK.** **See** Recreation, Leisure-Sports.

UK
**MOTOR SPORTS CAR ROAD TESTS, THE.** **See** Recreation, Leisure-Sports.

AT
**MOTOR TRADE JOURNAL.** English. Eleven times a year (published monthly except Jan.). 48.00Aus$. Motor Trade Association of South Australia Inc, Motor Trade Association of South Australia Inc, Adelaide, South Australia, 5001 Australia. **Tel** 011 08 272 4444, FAX 011 08 373 1724. **Ad Acc.** ctrl circ.

UK/0027-2043
**MOTOR TRADER.** [Mot. trader]. (1905)-. Periodical. English. wk (52 issues). £75.00 UK; £80.00 other. Reed Business Publishing / West Sussex, England, Perrymount Road, Haywards Heath, West Sussex RH16 3DH England. **Tel** 011 44 81 6523500. **DD** 388.3. ***Absorbed*** *Garage, 0016-4526.*
**Ind/Abst** Infomat Int. Bus.

US/0027-2094
**MOTOR TREND.** [Motor trend]. Vol. 1 (Sept. 1949)-. Periodical. English. mo. $19.94 US; $30.97 Canada; $28.94 other. Petersen Publishing Company, 6420 Wilshire Bouldevard, Los Angeles CA 90048. **Tel** (213)782-2485. **(Subscription address:** Neodata / Colorado, PO Box 2606, Boulder Boulder CO 80322.**) ED** Tony Swan. **LC** TL1; .M9447. **DD** 629.205. **Ad Acc. Circ:** 778,000. available on microfilm and microfiche from University Microfilms International (UMI); available on an online database (file 647/Full-Text) from DIALOG. Documents available from UMI Article Clearinghouse, Magazine Collection. ***Absorbed*** *Car Life; Sports Car Graphic; Wheels Afield.*
**Desc:** America's automotive authority filled with road tests, service features, forecasts and racing news.
**Ind/Abst** Abr. Read. Guide Period. Lit.; Acad. Abstr. Full Text Elite (Jan. 1984-); Acad. Abstr. (Jan. 1984-); Acad. Search (Jan. 1984-); Consum. Index Prod. Eval. Inf. Source; Gen. Period. Index (1985-); INFO-SOUTH Abstr.; Mag. Artic. Summar. Elite (Jan. 1984-); Mag. Artic. Summar. Select (Jan. 1984-); Mag. Artic. Summar. CD-ROM (Jan. 1984-); Mag. Express (1986-) [Full Txt.]; Mag. Index Plus (1989-); Mag. Index Sel. Microfiche (1990-) [Full Txt.]; Mag. Index. Sel. (1986-); Mag. Search; Mid. Search (Jan. 1984-); Newsp. Period. Abstr. (1986-); Prim. Search (Jan. 1984-); Read. Guide Abstr. Select Ed.; Read. Guide Period. Lit.; Resource/One Ondisc; Mag. Index (1977-); TOM Gen. Index (1985-) [Full Txt.]; Vocat. Search (Jan. 1984-).

US/0160-8886
**MOTOR TREND NEW CAR BUYER'S GUIDE.** [Motor trend new car buyer's guide]. (19??)-. Periodical. English. an. $5.70. Petersen Publishing Company, 6420 Wilshire Bouldevard, Los Angeles CA 90048. **Tel** (213)782-2485. **LC** TL5; .M7514. **DD** 629.22/2/05.

US/0098-3624
**MOTOR TRUCK REPAIR MANUAL.** ***Title Change.*** Periodical. English. an. Hearst Corporation, c/o Ronald Powell, 817 Round Hill Road, Pelham AL 35124. **Tel** (205)663-0353, (800)288-6828. **LC** TL230.A1; M615. **DD** 629.28/7/405. ***Merged with*** *Motor Truck and Diesel Repair Manual, 0362-6938* ***to form*** *Motor Light Truck & Van Repair Manual.*

US/0273-1029
**MOTOR VACUUM & WIRING DIAGRAM DIAGNOSTIC MANUAL. PROFESSIONAL SERVICE TRADE EDITION.** ***Title Change.*** (MOTOR VACUUM & WIRING DIAGRAM DIAGNOSTIC MANUAL.). [Mot. vac. wiring diagr. diagn. man., Prof. serv. trade ed.]. **Main/Corp** Motor (New York). **VFOAT** Vacuum & Wiring Diagram Diagnostic Manual. **VAT** Motor Vacuum and Wiring Diagram Diagnostic Manual. Professional Service Trade Edition. (19??)-(19??). English. Hearst Corporation, c/o Ronald Powell, 817 Round Hill Road, Pelham AL 35124. **Tel** (205)663-0353, (800)288-6828. **LC** TL272; .M69A. **DD** 629.2/54/0288. ***Continued by*** *Motor Wiring Diagram Manual.*

AT
**MOTOR VEHICLE CENSUS, TASMANIA.** **Main/Corp** Australian Bureau of Statistics. (19??)-. English. ir. Free. Australian Bureau Statistics / Tasmanian Office, Commonwealth Government Centre, 188 Collins Street, Hobart GPO Box 66A, Hobart Tasmania 7001 Australia. **Tel** (002)205889. **LC** HE5709.T37; A93a. **DD** 388.3/4/09946.

CN/0316-6198
**MOTOR VEHICLE DATA BOOK.** [Mot. veh. data book]. **Added/Corp** Sanford Evans Services Ltd. Sanford Evans & Company. (1948)-. Directory. English (French). an. 35.00Can$. Sanford Evans Communications Ltd., Box 6900, 1700 Church Avenue, Winnipeg Manitoba R3C 3B1 Canada. **Tel** (204)632-2768, FAX (204)694-2347. **ED** G.B. Henry. **DD** 629.22/2/0212. ctrl circ.
**Desc:** Contains passenger car statistics for vehicle identification and registration. Includes vehicle weight, wheelbase, serial numbers, engine stats and manufacturers retail prices.

US/0736-8437
**MOTOR VEHICLE IDENTIFICATION.** English. an. American Automobile Manufacturers Association, PO Box 11170, Detroit MI 48211. **Tel** (313)872-4311.

US
**MOTOR VEHICLE STATISTICS. ACCIDENT, LICENSE AND REGISTRATION STATISTICAL DATA.** **See** Transportation-Roads and Traffic.

●US/1055-8233
**MOTOR WORLD (LOS ANGELES, CALIF.).** (MOTOR WORLD.). (1993)-. Periodical. English. qt. $29.99. Publishing & Business Consultants, PO Box 75392, Los Angeles CA 90075. **Tel** (213)732-3477, FAX (213)732-9123. **ED** Andeson Napoleon Atia. **Ad Acc.** Full Page (B&W) $5750.00. Half Page (B&W) $3575.00. Full Page (Color) $8750.00 (2 color). Half Page (Color) $5500.00 (2 color). **Circ:** 170,000 total.
**Desc:** Focused on the active and trendy automotive buyer. Features articles on general trends in the automobile industry, basic maintenance, servicing and repairs.

SZ
**MOTORFAHRZEUGBESTAND IN DER SCHWEIZ NACH KANTONEN UND ORTSCHAFTEN.** **Main/Corp** Switzerland. Statistisches Amt. **VFOAT** Effectif des Vehicules a Moteur en Suisse par Cantons et Localites. Multiple languages (French and German). 24.00. Eidgenossisches Statistisches Amt, Hallwylstrasse 15, CH-3003 Bern Switzerland. **LC** HE5683; .A28.

IT
**MOTORI.** Periodical. Italian. bm. L16000 Italy; L51000 other. Torino Motori, C So Galileo Febraris 155, 10134 Turin Italy. **Tel** 011/318.11.38. **LC** TL4; .T6. **DD** 629.2/222/05. **Ad Acc.** ***Continues*** *Torino Motori.*
**Desc:** Stands as a fair and correct publication on automobiles and transport on wheels.

UK/0027-2264
**MOTORING NEWS LONDON.** **See** Recreation, Leisure-Sports.

US/1056-2532
**MOTORIST (ALLENTOWN, PA.).** (MOTORIST : A PUBLICATION OF LEHIGH VALLEY MOTOR CLUB.). **Added/Corp** Lehigh Valley Motor Club. **VFOAT** AAA motorist. Vol. 67, No. 1 (Jan./Feb. 1991)-. Periodical. English. bm. Lehigh Valley Motor Club, 1020 Hamilton Street, Allentown PA 18101-1085. ***Continues*** *AAA Today (Allentown, Pa.), 0896-4874.*

UK/0027-2302
**MOTORISTS GUIDE TO NEW & USED CAR PRICES.** [Mot. guide new used car prices]. **VFOAT** Motorists Guide to New and Used Car Prices. (1962)-. Periodical. English. Twelve times a year. £23.00 UK; £33.00 Europe; £47.00 other. Foxpride Ltd, 67 Tyrrell Street, Leicester LE3 5SB England. **Tel** 44 533 511393, FAX 44 533 511335. **ED** L J Shoebridge. **DD** 388.3. cum. index. **Ad Acc**, **Adv Mgr:** Adam. **Circ:** 50,000 (ctrl).
**Desc:** New and used car price guide giving values by year, condition and mileage. Useful data is supplied to assist the public in buying and selling a car.

US/0027-2310
**MOTORLAND.** **Added/Corp** California State Automobile Association. Vol. 1 (1921)-. Periodical. English. bm. $3.50. California State Automobile Association, 150 Van Ness Avenue, San Francisco CA 94101. **Tel** (415)565-2451. **ED** John G. Holmgren. **Circ:** 1,650,483.

US/0027-2396
**MOTRIX.** [Motrix]. (19??)-. Periodical. Spanish. Six times a year (Feb., Apr., June, Aug., Oct., Dec.). $30.00. Lineal Publishing Company, 10842 Pine Bark Lane, Boca Raton FL 33428-2852. **Tel** (407)451-9429, FAX (407)776-6649, telex 522-265 LINEAL CO FL. **ED** Jorge Sainz. **Ad Acc. Circ:** 30,000 (ctrl). ***Continues*** *Transporte Moderno, 0041-1698.*
**Desc:** A magazine of self-propelled vehicle service.

US/0891-4796
**MUSCLE CAR REVIEW.** [Muscle car rev.]. **VFOAT** Car Review. (Dec. 1986)-. Periodical. English. mo. $14.97 US; $19.97 other. Dobbs Publishing Group, 3816 Industry Boulevard, Lakeland FL 33811. **Tel** (813)646-5743, FAX (813)648-1187. **DD** 388. ***Continues*** *Popular and Performance Car Review, 0747-1483.*

US/0898-5820
**MUSCLE CARS OF THE ... .** (LEGEND SERIES, MUSCLE CARS OF THE ...). [Muscle cars]. **VFOAT** Muscle Cars of the ... . Vol. 1, No. 1 (1988)-. Periodical. English. Six times a year. $19.95 (one year), $38.90 (two years). Amos Press, PO Box 29, Sidney OH 45365. **Tel** (513)498-0802, (800)448-7293, FAX (513)498-0812. **ED** Robert J Stevens and Kevin C Ross. **LC** TL23; .L374. **DD** 629.222. **Ad Acc. Circ:** 50,000 (ctrl).
**Desc:** For collectors, restorers and admirers of the super cars of yesteryear. Those high performance road warriors that became legends on the roads and dragstrips of America.

US/1054-8912
**MUSCLE MUSTANGS & FAST FORDS.** [Muscle Mustangs fast Fords]. **VFOAT** Muscle Mustangs and Fast Fords; Mustangs & Fast Fords; A.Mustangs and fast Fords. (Fall 1988)-. Periodical. English. Ten times a year. $21.97 US; $30.97 Canada; $32.97 other. CSK Publishing Company, 299 Market Street, Saddle Brook NJ 07662. **Tel** (201)712-9300, FAX (201)712-9899. **DD** 629.

US/0899-1421
**MUSCLECAR CLASSICS.** ***Title Change.*** [Musclecar class.]. **VFOAT** Muscle Car Classics. (1987)-(1992). Periodical. English. bm. Petersen Publishing Company, 6420 Wilshire Bouldevard, Los Angeles CA 90048. **Tel** (213)782-2485. **DD** 796. ***Continued by*** *Petersen's Musclecar Restoration and Performance.*
**Desc:** Written for all automotive enthusiasts interested in the restoration, investment and collectibility of musclecars. Readers get exciting features on the country's hottest musclecars, restoration guides, and hands-on technical advice on aspects of improving musclecars performance, plus much more.

US/0897-0963
**MUSCLECARS (HACKENSACK, N.J.).** (MUSCLECARS.). [Musclecars]. **VFOAT** Muscle Cars. (198?)-. Periodical. English. bm. $16.00. CSK Publishing Company, 299 Market Street, Saddle Brook NJ 07662. **Tel** (201)712-9300, FAX (201)712-9899. **DD** 629.

US/1059-5368
**MUSTANG & FORDS.** **VFOAT** Mustang and Fords. (1991)-. Periodical. English. bm (6 issues). $15.95 US; $22.42 Canada; $20.95 other. Petersen Publishing Company, 6420 Wilshire Bouldevard, Los Angeles CA 90048. **Tel** (213)782-2485. **(Subscription address:** Neodata / Colorado, PO Box 2606, Boulder Boulder CO 80322.) **LC** WMLC 91/2306. **DD** 629. ***Continues*** *Hot Rod's Mustang & Fords, 1057-655X.*

US/0898-8994
**MUSTANG ILLUSTRATED.** [Mustang illus.]. (198?)-. Periodical. English. Six times a year (Feb., Apr., June, Aug., Oct., Dec.). $15.95 (one year), $26.95 (two years). McMullen Publishing Inc, 2145 West La Palma Avenue, PO Box 70015, Anaheim CA 92801-1785. **Tel** (714)572-2255, FAX (714)572-1864. **DD** 629.

US/0894-5179
**MUSTANG (LOS ANGELES, CALIF.).** ***Title Change.*** (MUSTANG.). [Mustang]. **VFOAT** Hot Rod's Mustang. Vol. 1, No. 1 (Spring 1983)-(19??). Periodical. English. bm. Petersen Publishing Company, 6420 Wilshire Bouldevard, Los Angeles CA 90048. **Tel** (213)782-2485. **ED** Lee Kelley. **LC** WMLC 91/2306. **DD** 629. ***Continued by*** *Hot Rod's Mustang & Fords, 1057-655X.*
**Desc:** From the first classic to the '87 convertible, this magazine covers it all - customizing, restorations, technical information, accessories and more.

US/0274-8460
**MUSTANG MONTHLY MAGAZINE.** (MUSTANG MONTHLY.). [Mustang monthly]. **VFOAT** Mustang Monthly Magazine. (19??)-. Periodical. English. mo. $19.97 US; $29.97 other. Dobbs Publishing Group, 3816 Industry Boulevard, Lakeland FL 33811. **Tel** (813)646-5743, FAX (813)648-1187. **ED** Jerry Pitt. **LC** WMLC 93/248. **Ad Acc, Adv Mgr:** Curt Patterson, **Tel** (813)644-7610.

US/0744-2572
**MUSTANG TIMES.** Periodical. English. mo. $25.00 US; $30.00 Canada; $50.00 other. Mustang Club of America Inc, PO Box 447, Lithonia GA 30058-0447. **Tel** (404)482-4822. **ED** Steve McMullan. **Bk Rev. Ad Acc.** ctrl circ.
**Desc:** Restoration and preservation of the Mustang automobile.

US/0272-3395
**MVMA MOTOR VEHICLE FACTS & FIGURES.** [MVMA mot. veh. facts fig.]. **Added/Corp** Motor Vehicle Manufacturers Association of the United States. **VFOAT** MVMA Motor Vehicle Facts and Figures. **VAT** Motor Vehicle Manufacturers Association Motor Vehicle Facts and Figures. (1978)-. English. an (July). $10.00 US, $11.00 Canada & Mexico, $14.00 other, (surface mail); $18.00 Korea, (airmail). Motor Vehicle Manufacturers Association, 7430 Second Avenue, Suite 300, Detroit MI 48202. **Tel** (313)872-4311, FAX (313)872-5400, telex 1009770 AUTOMAKERS DET. **LC** HD9710.U5; M63a. **DD** 338.4/76292/0973021. **Circ:** 30,000. ***Continues*** *Motor Vehicle Facts & Figures, 0146-9932.*
**Ind/Abst** F&S Index Plus Text, Int. [Select. Cov.]; PROMT.

US/0192-7027
**MY LITTLE SALESMAN TRUCK CATALOG.** (197?)-. Catalog. English. mo. $12.00 (US); $42.00 (Canada & Mexico); $90.00 (other). My Little Salesman Inc, PO Box 70208, Eugene OR 97401. **Tel** (503) 342-1201, FAX (503) 342-3307.

US/0027-5794
**N.A.D.A. OFFICIAL USED CAR GUIDE.** **Main/Corp** National Automobile Dealers Association. **VAT** National Automobile Dealers Association Official Used Car Guide. (19??)-. Periodical. English. mo. $47.00. National Automobile Dealers Association, 8400 West Park Drive, McLean VA 22102. **Tel** (703)749-4700, (800)544-6232, FAX (703)821-7269. **ED** Lynn A. Weaver. ctrl circ. ***Continues*** *Blue Book.*
**Desc:** Prices on used cars: domestic, imports and light trucks.

●US/1061-9054
**N.A.D.A. OFFICIAL USED CAR GUIDE (RETAIL CONSUMER ED.).** (N.A.D.A. OFFICIAL USED CAR GUIDE.). **Added/Corp** National Automobile Dealers Association. **VAT** National Automobile Dealers Association Official Used Car Guide. (1992)-. Periodical. English. qt. $9.95 (single issue). Nada Used Car Guide, 8400 Westpark Drive, Mclean VA 22102.

US
**N.A.D.A. TITLE AND REGISTRATION BOOK / THE OFFICIAL TITLE AND REGISTRATION BOOK OF THE NATIONAL AUTOMOBILE DEALERS ASSOCIATION.** **Added/Corp** National Automobile Dealers Association. **VAT** National Automobile Dealers Association Title and Registration Book. (19??)-. English. an. $50.00. NADA Appraisal Guides, PO Box 7800, Costa Mesa CA 92628. **Tel** (714)556-8511, (800)966-6232, FAX (714)556-8715. **ED** Pat Phillips. Index available.
**Desc:** Gives a complete summary of the motor vehicle laws and regulations for all fifty states.

US/0164-3592
**NADA NEWSLETTER.** **Main/Corp** National Automobile Dealers Association. **VAT** National Automobile Dealers Association Newsletter. (19??)-. Periodical. English. mo. $12.00 (members), $50.00 (nonmembers). National Automobile Dealers Association, 8400 West Park Drive, McLean VA 22102. **Tel** (703)749-4700, (800)544-6232, FAX (703)821-7269.

US
**NADA VAN CONVERSION LIMOUSINE APPRAISAL GUIDE.** (19??)-. English. Three times a year. $35.00. NADA Appraisal Guides, PO Box 7800, Costa Mesa CA 92628. **Tel** (714)556-8511, (800)966-6232, FAX (714)556-8715.

US
**NASCAR NEWS.** English. National Association for Stock Car Auto Racing Inc, PO Box K, Daytona Beach FL 32015. **Tel** (904)253-0611.

US
**NATIONAL NEW CAR PRICE GUIDE.** **VFOAT** National Appraisal Guides New Car Price Guide; New Car Price Guide. (19??)-. English. an. National Automobile Dealers Association, 8400 West Park Drive, McLean VA 22102. **Tel** (703)749-4700, (800)544-6232, FAX (703)821-7269.

US/0731-4787
**NEW CAR COST GUIDE.** (NEW CAR COST GUIDE / AIS.). [New car cost guide]. **Added/Corp** Automobile Invoice Service. **VFOAT** AIS New Car Cost Guide; A.I.S. New Car Cost Guide. (1956)-. Periodical. English. Six times a year. $82.00 US; $162.00 other. Automobile Invoice Service, PO Box 49006, San Jose CA 95161. **Tel** (408)296-1060 ext. 210. **ED** Christine Boldt. **Bk Rev. Circ:** 8,000.
**Desc:** Source of information on all domestic and imported cars and light trucks: dealer invoice and manufacturers' suggested retail prices, standard equipment, options and "preferred equipment group" cost, tire styles and prices, destination charges, and more.

US/0279-6384
**NEW DRIVER (HIGHLAND PARK, ILL.).** ***Ceased.*** (NEW DRIVER.). ( )-Vol. 8 (May 1986). Periodical. English. qt. General Learning Corporation, 60 Revere Drive, PO Box 3060, Northbrook IL 60065. **Tel** (800)323-5471, (708)564-4070. **ED** Margaret Mucklo. **Bk Rev. Ad Acc. Circ:** 150,000 (ctrl). ***Continues*** *Scholastic Wheels, 0161-2727.*
**Desc:** A periodical for driver education students stressing behind-the-wheel safety and skill, energy conservation, maintenance, consumer and legal issues. Teacher's guide included with each issue.

US/0745-5860
**NEW KIT CAR MONTHLY, THE.** Periodical. English. mo. Auto Logic Publications Inc, POB 2073, Wilmington DE 19899.

US
**NEW MODEL PRODUCT INFORMATION MANUAL, PONTIAC.** **Main/Corp** General Motors Corporation. Pontiac Motor Division. **VFOAT** Pontiac New Product Information Manual. English. Pontiac Motor Division / Trucks, General Motors Corporation, 660 East South Boulevard, Pontiac MI 48053. **LC** TL215.P68; G45C. **DD** 629.2/222/05.

CN/0705-5595
**NEW MOTOR VEHICLE SALES (MONTHLY ED.).** **See** Transportation-Abstracting, Bibliographies and Statistics.

US/0191-4979
**NEW YORK AUTO REPAIR NEWS.** **VFOAT** Auto Repair News. (19??)-. Periodical. English. mo (12 issues). $3.00. Van Allen Publishing Company, Box 354, Hicksville NY 11502. **Tel** (516)422-5521. **ED** Richard Van Allen. **Bk Rev. Ad Acc. Circ:** 11,300.

US/0028-7385
**NEW YORK MOTORIST.** Periodical. English. mo. $0.50. New York Motorist, 28 East 78th Street, New York NY 10021. **Tel** (212)586-1166. **ED** Sy Oshinsky. **Circ:** 620,000.

US/0149-6301
**NOMAD NEWS.** Periodical. English. mo. $20.00. National Nomad Club, 4691 South Mariposa Drive, Englewood CO 80110. **LC** TL215.N57; N65. **DD** 629.22/22.

FR
**NORMANDIE.** **See** Recreation, Leisure-Sports.

US/0094-078X
**NORTHWESTERN TOUR BOOK.** **See** Travel and Tourism.

SA
**NUWE VOERTUIE GEREGISTREER / REPUBLIEK VAN SUID-AFRIKA, SENTRALE STATISTIEKDIENS.** **VFOAT** New Vehicles Registered. Afrikaans (English). an. R2.50. Government Printer / South Africa, Bosman Street, Private Bag X85, Pretoria 0001 South Africa. **Tel** 011 27 12 3239731 Ext. 262. **LC** HE5704.4; .A23.

US/0192-009X
**O & A MARKETING NEWS.** **VAT** Oil and Automotive Service Marketing News. (19??)-. Periodical. English. Seven times a year. $30.00. Kal Publications, 1037 North Lake Avenue, Pasadena CA 91104. **Tel** (818)398-6848. **Circ:** 9,040.

CN/0383-9028
**O R G A NEWS.** See Petroleum and Natural Gas.

CN/0228-0469
**O R G A NEWSLINE.** [ORGA newsline]. **Main/Corp** Ontario Retail Gasoline and Automotive Service Association. **VAT** Ontario Retail Gasoline and Automotive Service Association Newsline. Vol. 1 (Dec. 1979)-. Periodical. English. Ontario Retail Gasoline and Automotive Service Association West, Suite 102, 101 Queensway West, Mississauga Ontario L5B 2P7 Canada. **DD** 629.28/6/09713. ***Supersedes in part*** *Automotive Review, 0706-506X.*

UK/0953-203X
**OFF ROAD AND 4 WHEEL DRIVE.** [Off road 4 wheel drive]. (1986)-. Periodical. English. mo. £27.60 UK; £37.40 Europe; £35.40 other. Link House Magazines Ltd., Link House, Dingwall Avenue, Croydon, Surrey CR9 2TA England. **Tel** 011 44 81 686 2599, FAX 011 44 81 760 0973, telex 947709. **(Subscription address:** United Magazine Subscriptions, 120-126 Lavender Avenue, Mitcham, Surrey CR4 3HP England.**)** ***Continues*** *Off Road and 4 Wheel Driver, 0268-4586.*

US/0363-1745
**OFF-ROAD (LOS ANGELES).** (OFF-ROAD.). [Off-road]. **VFOAT** Off Road. **VAT** Off Road. (19??)-. Periodical. English. Twelve times a year. $14.98 (one year); $24.96 (two years). Argus Publishers Corporation, 12100 Wilshire Boulevard, Suite 250, Los Angeles CA 90025. **Tel** (310)820-3601, FAX (310)207-9388. **(Subscription address:** Kable Publishers Aide, 308 East Hitt Street, Subscription Department, Mt. Morris IL 61054-1473.**)** **ED** Duane Elliott. **LC** TL235.6; .O334. **DD** 629.22. **Ad Acc. Circ:** 81,413. available on microfilm and microfiche from University Microfilms International (UMI); available on an online database (file 647/Full-Text) from DIALOG. Documents available from UMI Article Clearinghouse, Magazine Collection. ***Continues*** *Off-Road Vehicles and Adventure.*
**Desc:** Serious do it yourself off-road enthusiast newest vehicles and aftermarket products. How-to-articles, off road competition and travel stories.
**Ind/Abst** Consum. Index Prod. Eval. Inf. Source; Mag. Index Plus (1989-); Newsp. Period. Abstr. (1988-); Mag. Index (1977-).

US/8756-1654
**OFFICIAL PRICE GUIDE TO COLLECTOR CARS, THE.** See Hobbies.

US/0736-7988
**OFFICIAL WISCONSIN AUTOMOBILE VALUATION GUIDE.** (OFFICIAL WISCONSIN AUTOMOBILE VALUATION GUIDE : FOR USE IN STATE OF WISCONSIN.). **Main/Corp** Wisconsin Automobile and Truck Dealers Association. **Added/Corp** National Market Reports, Inc. (19??)-. Periodical. English. Eight times a year. $49.50. MacLean Hunter Publishing Corporation / Chicago, IL, 29 North Wacker Drive, Chicago IL 60606-3298. **Tel** (312)726-2802, FAX (312)726-3091. **(Subscription address:** Maclean Hunter Market Reports, 29 North Wacker Drive, Chicago IL 60606.**)**

FR/0030-0454
**OFFICIEL DE L'AUTOMOBILE, L'.** ***Ceased.*** [Off. automob.]. (1970)-(1992). Periodical. French. sm (except Aug.). EDI 7, 6 rue Ancelle, 92525 Neuilly Sur Seine, Cedex France. **Tel** 011 33 1 40886000. **UDC** 629.11.

BL
**OFICINA.** Periodical. Portuguese. 1.00 single issue. Departamento de Circulacao Consultas, Caixa Postal 5095, Sao Paulo Brazil. **LC** TL152; .O27.

US/0030-0985
**OHIO MOTORIST.** **Added/Corp** Ohio Motorists Association. (19??)-. Periodical. English. mo (10 issues). $1.50. Ohio Motorists Association, PO Box 6150, Cleveland OH 44101. **Tel** (216)361-6000. ***Continues*** *Motorist.*

US/0475-1876
**OLD CAR VALUE GUIDE.** ***Ceased.*** English. an. Gold Book Inc, 1400 Lake Hearn Drive, 2nd Floor E, Atlanta GA 30319. **Tel** (404)847-6503, (800)842-6848. **ED** Q Craft. **LC** TL7; .O38. **DD** 629.2/222/075. **Bk Rev. Ad Acc. Circ:** 25,000 (ctrl).
**Desc:** Collector car values, photos, original factory specifications on all cars 1897 to 1980 plus automobile history on 500 makes, classic color section plus over 200 black and white photos.

US/0048-1637
**OLD CARS.** [Old cars]. **VFOAT** Old Cars Weekly. Vol. 1, No. 1 (Oct. 1971)-. Periodical. English. wk. $29.95 US; $38.00 other. Krause Publications, 700 East State Street, Iola WI 54990-0001. **Tel** (715)445-2214, FAX (715)445-4087, telex 55 6461. **ED** Mary Sieber. **DD** 629. **Bk Rev. Ad Acc. Circ:** 77,132. ***Absorbed*** *Car Corral, 1045-7216.*
**Desc:** Contains news and features on collector cars, restoration tips, auction results, car show information. Classified marketplace puts buyers and sellers of collectible automobiles and hard-to-find parts in touch with car enthusiasts.

US/0194-6404
**OLD CARS PRICE GUIDE.** [Old cars price guide]. (1978)-. English. bm. $16.95 US; $23.75 other. Krause Publications, 700 East State Street, Iola WI 54990-0001. **Tel** (715)445-2214, FAX (715)445-4087, telex 55 6461. **ED** Kenneth Buttolph and James Lenzke. **Bk Rev. Ad Acc. Circ:** 106,558.
**Desc:** Lists current values to all American-made automobiles manufactured from 1901-1979 in five grading conditions. Prices established through auction reports and actual collector car sales through advertising in Old Cars Weekly. Special issues focus on nationwide auction results, trucks, foreign makes, and specialty vehicles.

US/1071-5452
**OLDER CAR / TRUCK RED BOOK.** [Older car/truck red book]. **VFOAT** Older Car Truck Red Book; Red Book; Older Car Red Book. (198?)-. Periodical. English. Four times a year. $69.00. MacLean Hunter Publishing Corporation / Chicago, IL, 29 North Wacker Drive, Chicago IL 60606-3298. **Tel** (312)726-2802, FAX (312)726-3091. **(Subscription address:** Maclean Hunter Market Reports, 29 North Wacker Drive, Chicago IL 60606.**)** **DD** 629. ***Continues*** *Older Car Red Book, 0736-6124.*

US/1041-9756
**OLDER TRUCK BLUE BOOK, THE.** [Older truck blue book]. **VFOAT** Blue Book. Vol. 1, No. 1 (Jan. 1/June 30, 1989)-. Periodical. English. Twice a year. $75.00. MacLean Hunter Publishing Corporation / Chicago, IL, 29 North Wacker Drive, Chicago IL 60606-3298. **Tel** (312)726-2802, FAX (312)726-3091. **(Subscription address:** Maclean Hunter Market Reports, 29 North Wacker Drive, Chicago IL 60606.**)** **LC** HD9710.35.U6; O54. **DD** 629.224/029/473.

US/0749-5692
**ON & OFF ROAD MAINTENANCE AND FUEL COST INDEX.** [On off road maint. fuel cost index]. **VFOAT** On-Road and Off-Road Cost Index; On and Off Road Maintenance and Fuel Cost Index; On-Road & Off-Road Cost Index. 1984-. English. an. Cost Research Institute Inc, PO Box 5227, 912 Highland Avenue, Albany GA 31706. **LC** TL151.5; .O5. **DD** 629.28/7042.

US/0279-2737
**ON TRACK (SANTA ANA, CALIF.).** See Recreation, Leisure-Sports.

IT
**OPERATING YEAR ANNUAL REPORT.** **Main/Corp** Fiat (Firm). **VFOAT** Fiat in Pictures; Consolidated Financial Statements of the Fiat Group. English. an. Fiat Corso Marconi 10, Turin Italy. **LC** HD9710.I84; F52. **DD** 338.7/6292/0945. ***Continues*** *Reports of the Board of Directors and Statutory Auditors to Shareholders.*

US
**OREGON TRAFFIC ACCIDENTS ... SUMMARY / OREGON DEPARTMENT PF TRANSPORTATION, MOTOR VEHICLES DIVISION.** **Added/Corp** Oregon. Motor Vehicles Division. **VFOAT** Summary. (1980)-. Periodical. English. Motor Vehicles Division, Department of Transportation, Salem OR 97314. ***Continues*** *Oregon Motor Vehicle Accidents.*

US
**ORGANIZATION CHART MANUAL / STATE OF CALIFORNIA, DEPARTMENT OF MOTOR VEHICLES.** **Main/Corp** California. Dept. of Motor Vehicles. English. an. Department of Motor Vehicles / Staff Services Section: California, Staff Services Section, Division of Administration, PO Box 11828, Sacramento CA 95953. **LC** HE5633.C2; C34B. **DD** 353.97940087/834.

US/1056-1889
**PACE BUYER'S GUIDES. CAR FACTS.** [Pace buy. guides, Car facts]. **VFOAT** Car Facts. (May 1991)-. Periodical. English. bm. $21.95. Pace Publications Inc., 1020 North Broadway, Suite 111, Milwaukee WI 53202. **Tel** (414)272-9977, FAX (414)297-9973. **DD** 629.

US/1064-4628
**PACE BUYER'S GUIDES. DOMESTIC & FOREIGN TRUCK, VAN, 4X4 PRICES, NEW & USED.** ***Title Change.*** (DOMESTIC & FOREIGN TRUCK, VAN, 4X4 PRICES, NEW & USED.). [Pace buyer's guides, Domest. foreign truck van 4x4 prices new used]. **VFOAT** Domestic & Foreign Truck, Van, 4x4 Prices, New & Used; Domestic and Foreign Truck, Van, 4x4 Prices, New and Used; Truck, Van, 4x4 Prices; Truck, Van, Four by Four; Pace Buyer's Guides. Truck, Van, 4x4. (199?)-(199?). English. Seven times a year. Pace Publications Inc., 1020 North Broadway, Suite 111, Milwaukee WI 53202. **Tel** (414)272-9977, FAX (414)297-9973. **DD** 629. ***Continues*** *Domestic & Foreign Truck & Van Prices New and Used, 1050-7272.* ***Continued by*** *New & Used Truck, Van, 4x4 Prices.*

US/1065-6707
**PACE BUYER'S GUIDES. FOREIGN AND JAPANESE CAR PRICES, NEW & USED.** ***Title Change.*** (FOREIGN AND JAPANESE CAR PRICES, NEW & USED.). [Pace buy. guides, Foreign Jpn. car prices new used]. **VFOAT** Foreign and Japanese Car Prices, New and Used; New & Used Foreign and Japanese Car Prices; New and Used Foreign and Japanese Car Prices; Foreign Car Prices; Foreign and Japanese Car Prices. (199?)-(1992). English. bm. Pace Publications Inc., 1020 North Broadway, Suite 111, Milwaukee WI 53202. **Tel** (414)272-9977, FAX (414)297-9973. **LC** HD9710.A1; P32. **DD** 629. ***Continues*** *Foreign Car Prices New & Used, 1050-5423.* ***Continued by*** *New & Used Import Car Prices, 1069-3238.*

US/1050-5423
**PACE BUYER'S GUIDES. FOREIGN CAR PRICES NEW & USED.** ***Title Change.*** [Pace buy. guides, Foreign car prices new used]. **VFOAT** Foreign Car Prices New & Used; Foreign Car Prices New and Used; Buyer's Guide Reports. Foreign Car Prices. (19??)-(199?). English. bm. Pace Publications Inc., 1020 North Broadway, Suite 111, Milwaukee WI 53202. **Tel** (414)272-9977, FAX (414)297-9973. **LC** HD9710.A1; P32. **DD** 629. ***Continued by*** *Pace Buyer's Guides. Foreign and Japanese Car Prices, New & Used, 1065-6707.*

US/1069-3238
**PACE BUYER'S GUIDES. NEW & USED IMPORT CAR PRICES.** ***Ceased.*** **VFOAT** Pace Buyer's Guides. New and Used Import Car Prices; New & Used Import Car Prices; New and Used Import Car Prices; Import Car Prices. (1993)-(199?). English. Seven times a year. Pace Publications Inc., 1020 North Broadway, Suite 111, Milwaukee WI 53202. **Tel** (414)272-9977, FAX (414)297-9973. ***Continues*** *Pace Buyer's Guides. Foreign and Japanese Car Prices, New & Used, 1065-6707.*

US/1049-8583
**PACE BUYER'S GUIDES. NEW CAR PRICES.** [Pace buy. guides, New car prices]. **VFOAT** New Car Prices. (19??)-. English. Seven times a year. $21.95 US, $31.95 Canada & Mexico, $43.95 Europe & Western Hemisphere, $49.95 Africa, Asia, & Pacific Rim (one year); $75.00 US, $115.00 Canada & Mexico, $163.00 Europe & Western Hemisphere, $187.00 Africa, Asia, & Pacific Rim comes with Automotive combination subscription. Pace Publications Inc., 1020 North Broadway, Suite 111, Milwaukee WI 53202. **Tel** (414)272-9977, FAX (414)297-9973. **LC** HD9710.U5; B88. **DD** 629.222/029/473. ***Continues*** *Buyer's Guide Reports. New Car Prices (Milwaukee, Wis. : 1989), 1046-9400.*

US
**PACE BUYER'S GUIDES. TRUCK AND VAN PRICES.** (19??)-. Consumer Publication. English. Seven times a year. $21.95 US, $31.95 Canada & Mexico, $43.95 Europe & Western Hemisphere, $49.95 Africa, Asia, & Pacific Rim (one year); $75.00 US, $115.00 Canada & Mexico, $163.00 Europe & Western Hemisphere, $187.00 Africa, Asia, & Pacific Rim comes with Automotive combination subscription. Pace Publications Inc., 1020 North Broadway, Suite 111, Milwaukee WI 53202. **Tel** (414)272-9977, FAX (414)297-9973.

US/1056-1870
**PACE BUYER'S GUIDES. TRUCK FACTS.** [Pace buy. guides, Truck facts]. **VFOAT** Truck Facts. (Apr. 1991)-. Periodical. English. bm. $21.95. Pace Publications Inc., 1020 North Broadway, Suite 111, Milwaukee WI 53202. **Tel** (414)272-9977, FAX (414)297-9973. **DD** 629.

US/1050-5415
**PACE BUYER'S GUIDES. USED CAR PRICES.** [Pace buy. guides, Used car prices]. **VFOAT** Used Car Prices; Buyer's Guide Reports. Used Car Prices. (19??)-. English. Seven times a year. $21.95 US, $31.95 Canada & Mexico, $43.95 Europe & Western Hemisphere, $49.95 Africa & Asia & Pacific Rim (one year); $75.00 US, $115.00 Canada & Mexico, $163.00 Europe & Western Hemisphere, $187.00 Africa, Asia, & Pacific Rim comes in Automotive combination subscription. Pace Publications Inc., 1020 North Broadway, Suite 111, Milwaukee WI 53202. **Tel** (414)272-9977, FAX (414)297-9973. **LC** HD9710.A1; P33. **DD** 629.222/029/473. ***Continues*** *Buyer's Guide Reports. Used Car Prices (Milwaukee, Wis. : 1988), 1043-9161.*

US/0744-8155
**PACIFIC AUTOMOTIVE NEWS.** **VFOAT** Midwest-Pacific Automotive News. Periodical. English. bm. Automotive Publishing Company, 30312 Grande Vista, Laguna Niguel CA 92677.

US/0362-9368
**PACKARD CORMORANT, THE.** Vol. 22, No. 4, (Winter 1976)-. Periodical. English. qt. The Packard Club, Box 2808, Oakland CA 94618. **ED** Richard Langworth. **LC** TL215.P25; P32. **DD** 629.22/22. Index

# Transportation — Automobiles

available. **Circ:** 3,999 (ctrl). **Continues** Cormorant.
**Desc:** Our publication is dedicated to the information regarding the Packard automobile of 1899-1958.

FR
**PARC ET IMMATRICULATIONS DES VEHICULES UTILITAIRES / MINISTERE DES TRANSPORTS, DEPARTEMENT DES STATISTIQUES DES TRANSPORTS.** French. an. Ministere des Transports, Departement des Statistiques des Transports, 55 rue Brillat-Savarin, 75658 Paris Cedex 13 France. **LC** HE5668; .A28. **DD** 388.3/2/0944.

US/0031-2193
**PARKING (WASHINGTON, D.C.).** (PARKING.). [Parking]. **Added/Corp** National Parking Association. (19??)-. Periodical. English. mo (10 issues - Jan./Feb. and July/Aug. are combined). $95.00. National Parking Association Inc, 1112 16th Street Northwest, Suite 300, Washington DC 20036. **Tel** (202)296-4336, **FAX** (202)331-8523. **ED** Genilee Swope Parente. **LC** HE371.A2; P3. **DD** 388.4/74/0973. **Ad Acc, Adv Mgr:** Dawn Newman. **Circ:** 5,000. **Absorbed** Parking World; Government Affairs Report.
**Desc:** Information on automobile parking and parking garages.
**Ind/Abst** Urban Aff. Abstr.

●US/1072-5598
**PARTS BUSINESS.** [Parts bus.]. **Added/Corp** Bill Communications. Vol. 17, No. 9 (Jan. 1994)-. English. mo. $60.00. Bill Communications Inc, 355 Park Avenue South, New York NY 10010-1789. **Tel** (800)821-6897, (212)592-6262, **FAX** (212)592-6209. **(Subscription address:** Bill Communications, 200 South Route 130, Cinnaminson, NJ 08077) **DD** 338. **Continues** Jobber Retailer, 0148-5792.

●US/1059-2083
**PBC AUTO GUIDE.** **VFOAT** Auto Guide. **VAT** Publishing and Business Consultants Auto Guide. (1992)-. English. $19.95. Publishing & Business Consultants, PO Box 75392, Los Angeles CA 90075. **Tel** (213)732-3477, **FAX** (213)732-9123.

UK/0265-6183
**PERFORMANCE CAR.** [Perform. car]. (1983)-. Periodical. English. mo. Argus Specialist Publications, Queensway House, 2 Queensway Redhill, Surrey RH1 1QS England. **Tel** 0737 768611, **FAX** 0737 773993, telex 948669 TOPJNL G. **[CCC]**. **Continues** Hot Car.

●US
**PERFORMANCE MUSCLECARS.** (May 1994)-. Periodical. English. bm. Petersen Publishing Company, 6420 Wilshire Boulevard, Los Angeles CA 90048. **Tel** (213)782-2485. **LC** WMLC 93/885. **Continues** Petersen's Musclecar Restoration & Performance.

AT
**PERFORMANCE STREET CAR.** (19??)-. Periodical. English. Six times a year. 24.00Aus$ Australia; 44.70Aus$ New Zealand & Papua New Guinea; 57.00Aus$ US & Canada; 60.00Aus$ Europe & Africa; 47.00Aus$ Singapore, Malaysia, Indonesia; 52.00Aus$ Hong Kong, China, Japan, India. Federal Publishing Co Pty Ltd, PO Box 199, 180 Bourke Road, Alexandria New South Wales, 2015 Australia. **Tel** 011 61 2 693 6666, **FAX** 011 61 2 693 9935. **(Subscription address:** Federal Publishing Co. Pty Ltd., PO Box 199, Alexandria NSW 2015 Australia.**)**

US/0730-3580
**PETERSEN'S BIG BOOK OF AUTO REPAIR.** **VFOAT** Big Book of Auto Repair. 1977- Ed. English. an. $14.95 US; $18.50 Canada. Petersen Publishing Company, 6420 Wilshire Boulevard, Los Angeles CA 90048. **Tel** (213)782-2485. **LC** TL152; .P396. **DD** 629.28/722.

US/0092-4512
**PETERSEN'S COMPLETE BOOK OF PLYMOUTH, DODGE, CHRYSLER.** [Petersen's complete book Plymouth Dodge Chrysler]. **VFOAT** Complete Book of Plymouth, Dodge, Chrysler; Plymouth, Dodge, Chrysler Book. 1973-. English. $2.00. Petersen Publishing Company, 6420 Wilshire Boulevard, Los Angeles CA 90048. **Tel** (213)782-2485. **LC** TL215.C55; P47. **DD** 629.22/22.

US/0271-3527
**PETERSEN'S HOW TO TUNE YOUR CAR.** [Petersen's how to tune your car]. 6Th-. Periodical. English. $5.95. Petersen Publishing Company, 6420 Wilshire Boulevard, Los Angeles CA 90048. **Tel** (213)782-2485. **LC** TL210; .H69. **DD** 629.2/504/0288. **Continues** How to Tune Your Car.

US/0883-5705
**PETERSEN'S KIT CAR.** **Title Change.** [Petersen's Kit car]. **VFOAT** Kit Car. (198?)-(199?). Periodical. English. bm. Petersen Publishing Company, 6420 Wilshire Boulevard, Los Angeles CA 90048. **Tel** (213)782-2485. **Continued by** Specialty Car, 1068-2627. **Desc:** Presents kit cars from replicas to rebodies to unusual original designs. Every issue brings to its readers exciting full-color articles featuring the thrill of building and driving specialty cars. Articles include: how-to-assemble tips, buyers' guides, advice on parts, show coverage, and much more.

US/1068-1892
**PETERSEN'S MUSCLECAR RESTORATION & PERFORMANCE.** **Title Change.** [Petersen's musclecar restor. perform.]. **VFOAT** Musclecar Restoration and Performance; Petersen's Musclecar Restoration and Performance; Musclecar Restoration & Performance. (Feb. 1993)-(1993). Periodical. English. bm. Petersen Publishing Company, 6420 Wilshire Boulevard, Los Angeles CA 90048. **Tel** (213)782-2485. **LC** WMLC 93/885. **DD** 629. **Continues** Musclecar Classics, 0899-1421. **Continued by** Performance Musclecars.

US/1045-120X
**PETERSEN'S ROD & CUSTOM.** **Title Change.** [Petersen's rod & cust.]. **VFOAT** Peterson's Rod and Custom; Rod and Custom; Rod & Custom. (Dec. 1988)-?. Periodical. English. bm. Petersen Publishing Company, 6420 Wilshire Boulevard, Los Angeles CA 90048. **Tel** (213)782-2485. **DD** 629. **Continues** Rod & Custom, 0161-150X. **Continued by** Rod & Custom, 1053-2064.

US
**PETERSEN'S WHEELS AFIELD.** **VFOAT** Wheels Afield. V. 1- Feb. 1967-. Periodical. English. mo. Petersen Publishing Company, 6420 Wilshire Boulevard, Los Angeles CA 90048. **Tel** (213)782-2485. **LC** TL298; .P47. **DD** 629.22/6/05.

US
**PICKUP, VAN & 4WD ROAD TEST ANNUAL AND BUYERS' GUIDE.** See Business-Purchasing.

US/0032-1737
**PLYMOUTH BULLETIN.** **Added/Corp** Plymouth 4 & 6 Cylinder Owners Club. (19??)-. Bulletin. English. bm. $18.00. Plymouth Owners Club Incorporated, PO Box 416, Cavalier ND 58220. **Tel** (701)549-3746, **FAX** (204)636-2646. **ED** Lanny Knutson. **Bk Rev. Ad Acc. Circ:** 3,300.
**Desc:** Dedicated to restoration and preservation of Plymouth automobiles, Plymouth trucks and Fargo commercial vehicles. Contains historical retrospectives, data, restoration information, and features of members' vehicles. Includes classified advertising.

FR/0296-9386
**PNEUMATIQUE PARIS, LE.** See Rubber.

US/0149-9637
**PONTIAC; CHASSIS SHOP MANUAL.** **Main/Corp** General Motors Corporation. Pontiac Motor Division. 1960-. English. Pontiac Motor Division, General Motors Corporation, 660 East South Boulevard, Truck Division, Pontiac MI 48053. **LC** TL215.P68; G45B. **DD** 629.2/4/028.

CN/0700-3447
**PONTIAC SHOP MANUAL SUPPLEMENT.** **Main/Corp** General Motors of Canada. **VFOAT** Pontiac Chassis Shop Manual. 1973-. English. an. General Motors of Canada Ltd, 36 Overlea Boulevard, Toronto Ontario M4H 1B7 Canada. **DD** 629.2/87/2. **Supersedes** Pontiac Service Manual, Supplement, 0700-3439.

US/0032-4523
**POPULAR HOT RODDING.** No. 1 (June 1962)-. Periodical. English. Twelve times a year. $16.94 (one year); $29.94 (two years). Argus Publishers Corporation, 12100 Wilshire Boulevard, Suite 250, Los Angeles CA 90025. **Tel** (310)820-3601, **FAX** (310)207-9388. **(Subscription address:** Kable Publishers Aide, 308 East Hitt Street, Subscription Department, Mt. Morris IL 61054-1473.**) ED** Pete Pesterre. **LC** TL236; .P627. **DD** 629.22/8/05. **Ad Acc. Circ:** 238,281.
**Desc:** Covers hot rodding events, races, etc.

US/0360-2273
**POPULAR MECHANICS DO-IT-YOURSELF YEARBOOK.** [Pop. mech. do-it-yours. yearb.]. English. an. The Hearst Corporation, 250 West 55th Street, New York NY 10019. **Tel** (212)649-4014. **LC** TT155; .P79. **DD** 605.

US/0147-3565
**PORSCHE PANORAMA.** Periodical. English. mo. $8.00. Porsche Club of America, 5616 Clermont Drive, Alexandria VA 22310. **LC** TL215.P75; P67. **DD** 629.22/8/05. available on microfilm from University Microfilms International (UMI).

US/1042-9581
**POWER REPORT ON AUTOMOTIVE MARKETING, THE.** [Power rep. automot. mark.]. **Added/Corp** J.D. Power and Associates. **VFOAT** Power Report. (19??)-. Periodical. English. $306.80 (1 year); $520.00 (2 year); $691.60 (3 year) Michigan; $295.00 (1 year); $500.00 (2 year); $665.00 (3 year) other. J D Powers & Associates Publishing, 30401 Agoura Road, Agoura Hills CA 91301. **Tel** (818)889-6330, **FAX** (818)889-3719. **ED** Jack Feuer. **DD** 629. Index available.

US
**POWERSYSTEM.** English. Fourteen times a year. $495.00. Kelley Blue Book, PO Box 19691, Irvine CA 92713. **Tel** (714)770-7704.

CN/0710-0671
**PREVOYANCE.** See Public Health and Safety.

US
**PRIVATE PASSENGER AUTOMOBILE INSURANCE.** See Insurance.

US
**PROCEEDINGS ... OF THE ANNUAL CONVENTION / AUTOMOTIVE ENGINE REBUILDERS ASSOCIATION (U.S.).** **Main/Corp** Automotive Engine Rebuilders Association (U.S.). Proceedings. English. an. **LC** TL1; .A866. **DD** 629.250627.

US
**PROFESSIONAL CARWASHING & DETAILING.** English. mo. $39.00 US; $90.00 other. National Trade Publications, 13 Century Hill Drive, Latham NY 12110. **Tel** (518)783-1281, **FAX** (518)783-1386. **ED** Steve Kane. Index available. **Ad Acc. Circ:** 16,000 (ctrl).
**Desc:** Includes information on professional, commercial car wash operations.

US/0161-7214
**PROFESSIONAL'S TIRE HANDBOOK, THE.** **VFOAT** Modern Tire Dealer's Professional Tire Handbook. English. $4.00 each issue. Hartman Communications, 633 Third Avenue, New York NY 10017. **LC** TL270; .P75. **DD** 629./48.

US
**PROGRESS IN TECHNOLOGY SERIES.** **Added/Corp** Society of Automotive Engineers. (197?)-. Monographic series. English. ir. Price varies per volume. Society of Automotive Engineers, 400 Commonwealth Drive, Warrendale PA 15096. **Tel** (412)776-4841, **FAX** (412)776-5760. **(Subscription address:** SAE / Society of Automotive Engineers, Department L1094P, Pittsburgh PA 15264.**) Continues** Progress in Technology.

GW
**PROMOBIL.** (19??)-. German. mo. DM89.04 Belgium & Netherlands; DM105.00 Denmark; DM85.76 France; DM87.36 Greece & Italy; DM89.88 Ireland & Portugal; DM86.52 Luxembourg & Spain (except Canary Islands); DM84.00 other. Vereinigte Motor Verlag GmbH, Motor Presse, POB 106036, D 70049 Stuttgart Germany. **Tel** 011 49 711 1821506, 011 49 711 1821545. **(Subscription address:** Deutscher Pressevertrieb Buch, POB 101602 Hansa GmbH, D 20010 Hamburg Germany)

IT
**QUATTRORUOTE.** (1956)-. Periodical. Italian. mo. $97.00. Editoriale Domus, Via Achille Grandi 5-7, 20089 Rozzano Milan Italy. **Tel** 011 39 2 82472276, **FAX** 011 39 2 8255033. **ED** Raffaele Mastrostefano. **LC** TL4; .Q38. **Ad Acc. Circ:** 610,000.
**Desc:** World famous motortrade magazine which anticipates Italian and foreign novelties, strict technical tests pointing out merits and faults, up-to-date pricelist for new and second-hand cars.

US/0736-2846
**QUINLAN PRIVATE TRUCK LAW REPORT, THE.** See Law.

UK/0961-1096
**RACECAR ENGINEERING.** (1991)-. Periodical. English. bm. $39.00 (one year), $78.00 (two year), $117.00 (three year) US; $49.00 (one year), $98.00 (two year), $147.00 (three year) Canada and Mexico. Q. Editions Ltd., Banstead Road, Caterham, Surrey CR3 5QG England. **(Subscription address:** Racecar Engineering, 369 Springfield Avenue, Berkeley Heights, NJ 07922) **ED** Quentin Spurring. **Bk Rev**, (Qty: 6). **Ad Acc.**

CN/0713-3928
**RACONTE.** [Raconte]. Vol. 1, No. 8 (Oct./Nov. 1978). Periodical. French. mo. Regie de l'Assurance Auto du Quebec, 1134 Chemin St-Louis, Quebec Quebec G1S 1E5 Canada. **DD** 354.7140087/31. **Continues** Regie de l'Assurance Automobile du Quebec. Raconte R A A Q, 0707-8986.

US/0744-7043
**READING-BERKS AUTO CLUB MAGAZINE.** (READING-BERKS AUTO CLUB MAGAZINE. / AAA.). Periodical. English. bm. Reading-Berks Auto Club, POB 1696, Reading PA 19603. **Tel** (215)374-4531. **ED** Robert R Gerhart. **Circ:** 38,000 (ctrl).

US/0733-530X
**RECREATION VEHICLE FINANCING.** See Public Administration-Public Finance and Taxation.

US
**RECREATION VEHICLE MARKETING REPORT.** English. mo. $175.00. Recreation Vehicle Industry Association, PO Box 2999, 1896 Preston WH Dr., Reston VA 22090-0999. **Tel** (703)620-6003. **Acid Free. Circ:** 1600.
**Desc:** A statistical report produced monthly based on a monthly industry survey of RV production shipments by product type. Compares current month to a year ago. Provides unit size and wholesale price.

US
**REFINISHING MATERIALS GUIDE: DOMESTIC AND IMPORTED.** (19??)-. Periodical. English. $69.00. Mitchell International Inc, PO Box 26260, San Diego CA 92126-0260. **Tel** (619)578-6550, (800)648-8010, FAX (619)578-4752. **(Subscription address:** Mitchell International Inc., PO Box 71654, Chicago IL 60694.**)**

PP
**REGISTERED MOTOR VEHICLES. Main/Corp** Papua New Guinea. Bureau of Statistics. English. Bureau of Statistics / Papua New Guinea, PO Box 2032, Konedobu Papua New Guinea. **LC** HE5718.P3; A23B.

SW
**REGISTRERADE FORDON EFTER FABRIKAT DEN ... . VFOAT** Registered Vehicles by Make on ... . English (Swedish). Liber Distribution, Prenumerationsorder, Forlagsorder 162 89, Stockholm Sweden. **LC** HE260.A15; S7 subser; HE5680.

FI
**REKISTERIIN MERKITYT UUDET MOOTTORIAJONEUVOT. Main/Corp** Finland. Tilastokeskus. **VFOAT** Inregistrerade Nya Motorfordon; Registered New Vehicles; Rekisteriin Merkityt Uudet Ammattimaiset Ajoneuvot. Multiple languages (English, Finnish and Swedish). Tilastokeskus, PL 504, Annankatu 44, 00101 Helsinki Finland. **Tel** 358-0-17341, FAX 358-0-17342474, telex 1002111 TILASTO SF. **LC** HE5675.3; .A27C.

US/0885-1638
**REPAIR CAR/NEW CAR DIRECTORY, THE.** [Repair car/new car dir.]. **VFOAT** Repair Car, New Car Directory. (197?)-. English. an. $30.00. ADCAL Publishing Company, 2206 Fairway Drive, Michigan City IN 46360. **Tel** (219)872-1489. **DD** 625. ***Continues** Repair Car Directory.*

US/1048-1036
**REPLACEMENT ASSEMBLIES ESTIMATING GUIDE.** (REPLACEMENT ASSEMBLIES ESTIMATING GUIDE / MITCHELL.). [Replace. assem. estim. guide]. **Added/Corp** Mitchell International. **VFOAT** Mitchell Replacement Assemblies Estimating Guide. (19??)-. Periodical. English. an. $99.00. Mitchell International Inc, PO Box 26260, San Diego CA 92126-0260. **Tel** (619)578-6550, (800)648-8010, FAX (619)578-4752. **(Subscription address:** Mitchell International Inc., PO Box 71654, Chicago IL 60694.**) LC** TL152; .R444. **DD** 629.28/72.

US/0092-3583
**RESEARCH REPORT - DEPARTMENT OF MOTOR VEHICLES. RESEARCH AND TECHNOLOGY DIVISION (OLYMPIA).** (RESEARCH REPORT.). **Main/Corp** Washington (State). Dept. of Motor Vehicles. Research and Technology. English. Washington State Departmen of Motor Vehicles & Research Technology, Olympia WA 98504. **LC** TL24.W2; W38A. **DD** 629.2/05.

US/0503-5562
**RESEARCH REPORT - U. S. LAND LOCOMOTION RESEARCH LABORATORY, CENTER LINE, MICHIGAN. See** Engineering.

US/0736-5934
**RESTORATION (TUCSON, ARIZ.).** ***Suspended.* See** Antiques.

FR/0150-7214
**REVUE MOTO TECHNIQUE BOULOGNE-SUR-SEINE. See** Economics-Industry and Production.

FR/0017-307X
**REVUE TECHNIQUE AUTOMOBILE.** [Rev. tech. automob.]. (1947)-. Periodical. French. Eleven times a year. 1313.00F. Editions Techniques pour l'Automobile et l'Industrie (ETAI), 94 96 rue de Paris, 92100 Boulogne Billancourt France. **Tel** 011 33 1 46992424. **UDC** 629.11. **[CCC].**

FR/0150-7206
**REVUE TECHNIQUE CARROSSERIE.** [Rev. tech. carross.]. (1968)-. Periodical. French. bm. 685.60F France; 810.00F other. Editions Techniques pour l'Automobile et l'Industrie (ETAI), 94 96 rue de Paris, 92100 Boulogne Billancourt France. **Tel** 011 33 1 46992424. **UDC** 629.113. **[CCC].**

FR/0037-2579
**REVUE TECHNIQUE DIESEL. VFOAT** Service Diesel. (1963)-. Trade Publication. French. bm. 705.00F France; 885.00F other. Editions Techniques pour l'Automobile et l'Industrie (ETAI), 94 96 rue de Paris, 92100 Boulogne Billancourt France. **Tel** 011 33 1 46992424. **ED** Bernard Adam. **LC** TJ795.A1; R48. **DD** 629.2/506/05. **[CCC]. Circ:** 6,600.
**Desc:** How-to information on trucks, public works material and industrial engines.

FR/0223-0135
**REVUE TECHNIQUE MACHINISME AGRICOLE.** (1979)-. Periodical. French. bm. 681.00F France; 760.00F other. Editions Techniques pour l'Automobile et l'Industrie (ETAI), 94 96 rue de Paris, 92100 Boulogne Billancourt France. **Tel** 011 33 1 46992424. **UDC** 631. **[CCC]. Bk Rev. Ad Acc. Circ:** 15,000.
**Ind/Abst** Agric. Eng. Abstr. (1991-).

IT
**RIVISTA GIURIDICA DELLA CIRCOLAZIONE E DEI TRASPORTI : ORGANO DELLA COMMISSIONE GIURIDICA DELL'AUTOMOBILE CLUB D'ITALIA. Added/Corp** Automobile Club d'Italia. Commissione Giuridica. (19??)-. Periodical. Italian. ir (five regular issues plus two notebooks). L80000 Italy; L120000 other. Editrice del Automobile, V le Regina Margherita 290, 00198 Rome Italy. **Tel** 011 39 6 440-2061. **LC** K22; .I796. **DD** 343.45/0944/05; 344.50394405.

US/0035-7189
**ROAD AND TRACK.** [Road track]. **VFOAT** Road & Track; R and T; R & T. Vol. 1, No. 1 (June 1947)-. Periodical. English. mo. $20.00. Hachette Magazines Inc., 1633 Broadway, New York NY 10019. **Tel** (212)767-6000. **(Subscription address:** Neodata / Colorado, PO Box 2606, Boulder Boulder CO 80322.**) LC** TL1; .R56. **DD** 796.7/2/05. **Ad Acc.** available on microfilm and microfiche from University Microfilms International (UMI); available on an online database (file 647/Full-Text) from DIALOG. Documents available from UMI Article Clearinghouse, Magazine Collection.
**Desc:** Contains information about cars and driving blended with wide-ranging feature stories, entertainment and racing coverage. Road tests focus on exciting, well-engineered enthusiast cars. Features on automotive subjects, humor and fiction, industry trends, travel, books and racing events.
**Ind/Abst** Acad. Abstr. Full Text Elite (Jan. 1984) [Full Txt.]; Acad. Abstr. (Jan. 1984-); Acad. Ind. [Computer File] (1984-1988); Acad. Search (Jan. 1984-); Consum. Index Prod. Eval. Inf. Source; Expand. Acad. Index (1984-1988); Gen. Period. Index (1985-); INFO-SOUTH Abstr.; Mag. Artic. Summar. Elite (Jan. 1984-) [Full Txt.]; Mag. Artic. Summar. Select (Jan. 1984-) [Full Txt.]; Mag. Artic. Summar. CD-ROM (Jan. 1984-); Mag. Index Plus (1989-); Mag. Index. Sel. (1986-); Mag. Search; Newsp. Period. Abstr. (1986-); Read. Guide Abstr. Select Ed.; Read. Guide Period. Lit.; Resource/One Ondisc (1986-); Mag. Index (1977-); TOM Gen. Index (1985-) [Full Txt.]; Vocat. Search (Jan. 1984-) [Full Txt.].

US/1053-2064
**ROD & CUSTOM (1990).** (ROD & CUSTOM.). [Rod custom]. **VFOAT** Rod and Custom. (19??)-. Periodical. English. Twelve times a year. $21.94 US; $30.97 Canada; $29.94 other. Petersen Publishing Company, 6420 Wilshire Bouldevard, Los Angeles CA 90048. **Tel** (213)782-2485. **(Subscription address:** Neodata / Colorado, PO Box 2606, Boulder Boulder CO 80322.**) DD** 629. ***Continues** Peterson's Rod & Custom, 1045-120X.*
**Desc:** Showcases the latest street rods, custom cars, '50s classics and vintage racers available in street rodding today. Each issue contains technical how-to advice for maintenance and restoration, as well as extensive buyers' guides, complete coverage of all the latest events, and more.

●US/1060-6831
**ROD & CUSTOM ANNUAL.** [Rod cust. annu.]. **VFOAT** Rod and Custom Annual; Hot Rod Rod & Custom Annual. (1992)-. English. $4.95 (single issue). Petersen Publishing Company, 6420 Wilshire Bouldevard, Los Angeles CA 90048. **Tel** (213)782-2485. **DD** 629.

IT
**ROMBO.** ***Title Change.*** (19??)-(19??). Italian. mo. Edimotor Editor Italiana, Via Milazzo 30, 40121 Bologna Italy. **Tel** 011 39 51 524412. ***Continued by** Auto & Sport.*

US/0194-6439
**ROTARY ROCKET.** Periodical. English. qt. $16.00. RX-7 Club of America Inc, Palos Verdes Drive North/Suite 108, Rolling Hills Estate CA 90274.

CN/0820-0270
**ROULEZ SANS VOUS FAIRE ROULER. GUIDE DES VOITURES D'OCCASION.** (ROULEZ SANS FAIRE ROULER.). [Roulez faire rouler, Guide voitures occas.]. **Added/Corp** Association Pour la Protection des Automobilistes. **VFOAT** Guide des Voitures d'Occasion. 1982-. French. $10,00 le vol. Les Publs en Concummation APA Inc, 292 Boul St Joseph Ouest, Montreal Quebec H2V 2N7 Canada. **DD** 629.2/222/05. ***Continues in part** Roulez Sans Vous Faire Rouler., 0383-7092.*

US/0889-3225
**ROUNDEL.** (ROUNDEL : THE MAGAZINE OF THE BMW CAR CLUB OF AMERICA, INC.). [Roundel]. Periodical. English. mo. $17.50 (membership). BMWCCA Inc, 345 Harvard Street, Cambridge MA 02138. **DD** 796. ***Continues** Blau Mit Weiss Roundel.*

CN/0048-8771
**RUNNING BOARD, THE. Added/Corp** Edmonton Antique Car Club. Vol. 8 (Jan. 1969)-. Periodical. English. mo. 10.00Can$. Edmonton Antique Car Club, Box 102, Edmonton 15 Alberta Canada. ***Continues** Edmonton Antique Car Club Bulletin, 0380-8106.*

US/0730-8647
**RUNZHEIMER ON CARS & LIVING COSTS. See** Consumer Interests.

US
**RVBUSINESS. ANNUAL DIRECTORY AND BUYER'S GUIDE.** Directory. English. an. $9.00. TL Enterprises, 29901 Agoura Road, Agoura CA 91301. **Tel** (800)234-3450, (805)389-0300. **LC** HD9710.37.U6; R85. **DD** 338.4/7629226/02573.

AT/0373-3173
**S.A.E. AUSTRALASIA.** (THE SAE--AUSTRALASIA : JOURNAL OF THE SOCIETY OF AUTOMOTIVE ENGINEERS - AUSTRALASIA.). [SAE Australas.]. **Added/Corp** Society of Automotive Engineers - Australasia. **VFOAT** SAE Australasia; Journal of the Society of Automotive Engineers - Australasia. **VAT** S.A.E. Australasia. (Jan./Feb. 1967)-. Periodical. English. Six times a year. 55.00Aus$ Australia; 80.00Aus$ others. Society of Automotive Engineers, 400 Commonwealth Drive, Warrendale PA 15096. **Tel** (412)776-4841, (412)772-7106, FAX (412)776-5760. **(Subscription address:** Society of Automotive Engineers, 191 Royal Parade, Parkville Victoria 3052 Australia.**) *Continues** Institute of Automotive and Aeronautical Engineers. IAAE Journal.*
**Ind/Abst** Alum. Ind. Abstr.; Fluid Abstr., Civil Eng.; Fluid Abstr. Proc. Eng.; FLUIDEX (199?-); Met. Abstr.

US
**S-R-S; SAFETY RESPONSIBILITY SUSPENSIONS. Main/Corp** Texas. Dept. of Public Safety. **VFOAT** Safety-Responsibility Suspensions. (1???)-. Periodical. English. bm. ***Supersedes** Texas. Dept. of Public Safety. S-R Suspensions by County.*

CN/0381-548X
**S S G M. SERVICE STATION & GARAGE MANAGEMENT.** (S S G M, SERVICE STATION & GARAGE MANAGEMENT.). [S S G M, Serv. stn. garage manage.]. Vol. 5, No. 8 (Aug. 1975)-. Periodical. English. Twelve times a year. 33.00Can$ (one year), 50.00Can$ (two year), 66.00Can$ (three year) Canada; 47.00Can$ other. Southam Information and Technology Group Inc., 1450 Don Mills Road, Don Mills Ontario M3B 2X7 Canada. **Tel** (416)445-6641, (800)668-2374, FAX (416)442-2261. **DD** 658/.91/62928605. ***Continues** Service Station and Garage Management, 0037-2668* ***and** Canadian Automotive Technician, 1180-2065.*

US/0891-995X
**SAE GROUND VEHICLE STANDARDS INDEX.** [SAE ground veh. stand. index]. **Added/Corp** Society of Automotive Engineers. **VFOAT** Ground Vehicle Standards Index. **VAT** Society of Automotive Engineers Ground Vehicle Standards Index. (Feb. 1987)-. Periodical. English. qt. $25.00. Society of Automotive Engineers, 400 Commonwealth Drive, Warrendale PA 15096. **Tel** (412)776-4841, (412)772-7106, FAX (412)776-5760. **DD** 629. **[CCC].**

US/0362-8205
**SAE HANDBOOK.** (S.A.E. HANDBOOK.). **Added/Corp** Society of Automotive Engineers. **VFOAT** SAE Handbook. (192?)-. English. an (February). $350.00. Society of Automotive Engineers, 400 Commonwealth Drive, Warrendale PA 15096. **Tel** (412)776-4841, (412)772-7106, FAX (412)776-5760. **LC** TL151; .S62. **[CCC].**
**Desc:** Contains standards, recommended practices, and information reports for hundreds of interest areas related to vehicle design, manufacture, test, and performance.

US/0741-2029
**SAE TECHNICAL LITERATURE ABSTRACTS.** ***Title Change.* See** Engineering.

US
**SAE TRANSACTIONS. Main/Corp** Society of Automotive Engineers. **VFOAT** SAE Transactions and Literature Developed. **VAT** Society of Automotive Engineers Transactions. English. an. $895.00. Society of Automotive Engineers, 400 Commonwealth Drive, Warrendale PA 15096. **Tel** (412)776-4841, (412)772-7106, FAX (412)776-5760. available on microfiche. Documents available from Article Express International.

**Desc:** Six parts containing over 800 papers judged and selected to have the greatest long term reference value by industry experts. Six special volumes are included in a set or sold separately: volume containing only aerospace papers - volume containing only commercial vehicle related papers - volume containing engines papers - volume containing fuels and lubricants papers - volume containing materials/manufacturing papers - volume containing only passenger car related papers. Also an inclusive plan on microfiche.
**Ind/Abst** Appl. Mech. Rev.; Eng. Index Annu.

US/0096-736X
**SAE TRANSACTIONS.** (S.A.E. TRANSACTIONS.). [SAE transact.]. **Main/Corp** Society of Automotive Engineers. **VFOAT** SAE Transactions. **VAT** Society of Automotive Engineers Transactions. Vol. 22 (1927)-. English. an (published in September). $850.00 (includes annual index of SAE Transactions). Society of Automotive Engineers, 400 Commonwealth Drive, Warrendale PA 15096. **Tel** (412)776-4841, (412)772-7106, FAX (412)776-5760. **LC** TL1; .S6. **DD** 629.106273. **[CCC]. *Continues*** *Society of Automotive Engineers. Transactions of the Society of Automotive Engineers.* ***Continued in part by*** *Annual Index/Abstracts of SAE Technical Papers.*

US
**SAE TRANSACTIONS AND LITERATURE DEVELOPED DURING.** **Added/Corp** Society of Automotive Engineers. **VFOAT** SAE Transactions. **VAT** Society of Automotive Engineers Transactions and Literature. Vol. 74 (1966)-. English. an. $650.00. Society of Automotive Engineers, 400 Commonwealth Drive, Warrendale PA 15096. **Tel** (412)776-4841, (412)772-7106, FAX (412)776-5760. available on microfiche. ***Continues*** *SAE Transactions.*
**Desc:** Contains the outstanding technical papers as judged by special committees comprised of experts in automotive engineering.
**Ind/Abst** Appl. Mech. Rev.

US/0898-8749
**SAFE DRIVER.** (SAFE DRIVER / NATIONAL SAFETY COUNCIL.). [Safe driv.]. **Added/Corp** National Safety Council. (1954)-. English. mo. $19.00. National Safety Council, 1121 Spring Lake Drive, Itasca IL 60143. **Tel** (800)621-7615, (708)775-2294, FAX (708)285-0797. **DD** 629.

US/0146-7026
**SAFETY RELATED RECALL CAMPAIGNS FOR MTOR VEHICLES AND MOTOR VEHICLE EQUIPMENT, INCLUDING TIRES: DETAILED REPORTS.** **Main/Corp** United States. National Highway Traffic Safety Administration. (19??)-. Periodical. English. qt. National Technical Information Service - NTIS, Room 2027S, 5285 Port Royal Road, Springfield VA 22161. **Tel** (703)487-4630, (703)487-4660, (703)487-4650, FAX (703)321-8547, telex 89-9405. **LC** TL242; .U57a. **DD** 629.2/34.

CN/0381-8179
**SANFORD EVANS GOLD BOOK OF USED CAR PRICES.** [Sanford Evans gold book used car prices]. **Added/Corp** Sanford Evans Commmunications Ltd. Sanford Evans Publishing. (July 1969)-. Periodical. English. mo. $72.00. Sanford Evans Communications Ltd., Box 6900, 1700 Church Avenue, Winnipeg Manitoba R3C 3B1 Canada. **Tel** (204)632-2768, FAX (204)694-2347. **ED** G.B. Henry. **Ad Acc.** ctrl circ. ***Continues*** *Sanford Evans Used Car Market Report.*
**Desc:** Reporting service of retail and wholesale prices for used cars and light duty trucks. Nine model years are covered and prices are supplied for three major markets.

US/0147-3506
**SCOUT FOUR WHEEL DRIVE ANNUAL.** (19??)-. English. an. $1.95 single issue. Popular Publications / New York, 420 Lexington Avenue, New York NY 11017. **LC** TL215.S36; S27. **DD** 629.22/22.

US/0731-471X
**SERVICE BULLETIN (SAN JOSE, CALIF.).** (SERVICE BULLETIN / CHEK-CHART.). [Serv. bull.]. **Added/Corp** Chek-Chart Corporation. **VFOAT** Chek-Chart Service Bulletin. Vol. 1 (1929)-. Periodical. English. mo. $15.40. H.M Gousha & Company, PO Box 49006, 2001 The Alameda, San Jose CA 95161. **Tel** (800)662-6277. **ED** Jo Phelps. **Circ:** 20,000 (ctrl).
**Desc:** Automotive repair and maintenance procedures and news. Car manufacturers latest tips and bulletins. Tricks and secrets of the auto repair trade.

US
**SERVICE MANUAL.** **Added/Corp** Saturn Corporation. **VFOAT** Saturn Service Manual. (1991)-. English. **LC** TL215.S27; S47. **DD** 629.28/722.

US/1041-4282
**SERVICE MANUAL. CAMARO.** (CAMARO SERVICE MANUAL.). **Added/Corp** General Motors Corporation. Chevrolet Motor Division. English. Chevrolet Motor Division, General Motors Corporation, Detroit MI 48203. **LC** TL215.C33; S45. **DD** 629.28/722. ***Continues*** *Chevrolet Camaro Shop Manual, 0735-0066.*

AT
**SERVICE STATION.** **See** Transportation.

US/0488-3896
**SERVICE STATION MANAGEMENT.** ***Title Change.*** (SERVICE STATION MANAGEMENT : SSM.). [Serv. stn. manage.]. **VFOAT** SSM. (Mar. 1958)-(May 1993). Periodical. English. bm. Hunter Publishing Company Inc., 25 Northwest Point Boulevard, Suite 800, Elk Grove Village IL 60007-1036. **Tel** (708)427-9512, FAX (708)427-2097. **ED** Jim Halloran. **LC** TL153.A1; S4. **DD** 629. **[CCC]. Bk Rev. Ad Acc. Pr Rev. Circ:** 85,000 (ctrl). ***Absorbed by*** *Motor Service.*
**Desc:** Directed to owners/operators and managers of service stations and truck stops including independently owned, leased or company-owned outlets.

US
**SHOP MANUAL. CAPRICE, MONTE CARLO, EL CAMINO.** **VFOAT** Shop Manual Covering Caprice, Monte Carlo, and El Camino. (1986)-. English. an. Chevrolet Motor Division, General Motors Corporation, Detroit MI 48203. **LC** TL215.I43; I46. **DD** 629.28/722.

US/0164-3509
**SKINNED KNUCKLES.** (19??)-. Periodical. English. Twelve times a year. $16.00 California; $31.00 others. Skinned Knuckles, 175 May Avenue, Monrovia CA 91016. **Tel** (818)358-6255. **ED** Terry Cannon. **Bk Rev. Ad Acc. Circ:** 7,500.
**Desc:** Devoted exclusively to the restoration, operation, and maintenance of all authentic collector vehicles.
**Ind/Abst** Index Inf.

●US/1059-5724
**SMALL BLOCK CHEVY.** (1992)-. Periodical. English. $3.95. Petersen Publishing Company, 6420 Wilshire Bouldevard, Los Angeles CA 90048. **Tel** (213)782-2485.

US/0099-5908
**SOCIETY OF AUTOMOTIVE ENGINEERS.** **See** Engineering.

US
**SOUTH CAROLINA DRIVER'S HANDBOOK.** **Added/Corp** South Carolina. Department of Highways and Public Transportation. **VFOAT** Driver's Handbook. (1977)-. English. ***Continues*** *South Carolina. State Highway Department. South Carolina Driver's Handbook.*

US/0038-4372
**SOUTHERN MOTOR CARGO.** Began in 1945. Periodical. English. mo. $25.00. Southern Motor Cargo Magazine, Box 4169, Memphis TN 38104. **Tel** (901)276-5424. **ED** Tom Stone. **LC** TL230.A1; S6. Index available. **Ad Acc. Circ:** 56,000 (ctrl). available on microfilm from University Microfilms International (UMI).
**Desc:** A tax-paying, independent magazine published for operators of all types of truck fleets located in the South as defined by the Census Bureau, U.S. Department of Commerce.

US/0049-1616
**SOUTHERN MOTORACING.** (19??)-. Periodical. English. bw. $12.50 US; $17.00 Canada. Hank Schoolfield, Box 500, Winston-Salem NC 27102. **Tel** (919)723-5227, FAX (919)722-3757. **ED** Hank Schoolfield. **Ad Acc. Circ:** 18,000 (ctrl).
**Desc:** Aimed primarily at motor racing fans, with coverage emphasis on Southeastern US motor racing.

US/0049-1845
**SPECIAL-INTEREST AUTOS.** (1970)-. Periodical. English. bm. $19.95 (one year), $36.00 (two year). Hemmings Motor News, Box 100, Bennington VT 05201. **Tel** (802)442-3101, FAX (802)447-1561. **ED** David Brownell. **Bk Rev. Ad Acc. Circ:** 38,000 (ctrl).
**Desc:** Covers collectable cars from 1920 to 1970.

US/0193-7278
**SPECIALTY & CUSTOM DEALER.** **VAT** Specialty and Custom Dealer. (19??)-. Periodical. English. mo. $43.00 US, Canada and Mexico; $87.00 other. Babcox Publications Inc., 11 South Ford Street, Akron OH 44304. **Tel** (216)535-7011. **ED** Jim MacQueen. **LC** HD9710.3.U5; S67. **DD** 380.1/456292/05. **Bk Rev. Ad Acc. Circ:** 23,000 (ctrl). ***Continues*** *Speed & Custom Dealer.*
**Desc:** The business management magazine for speed and custom equipment retailers.

●US/1063-0716
**SPECIALTY AUTO MARKETPLACE.** **VFOAT** Specialty Auto Market Place; Specialty Auto. (1992)-. Periodical. English. wk. $1.95 (single issue). Marketplace Publications, Inc., PO box 3049, Danbury CT 06813-3049.

US/0894-7414
**SPECIALTY AUTOMOTIVE PARTS AND ACCESSORIES.** [Spec. automot.]. Periodical. English. qt. Meyers Publishing Corp., 6211 Van Nuys Blvd/Ste 200, Van Nuys CA 91401. **Tel** (818)785-3900. **ED** John Rettie. **Circ:** 25,000.

US/1068-2627
**SPECIALTY CAR.** ***Title Change.*** [Spec. car]. (199?)-(199?). Periodical. English. bm. Petersen Publishing Company, 6420 Wilshire Bouldevard, Los Angeles CA 90048. **Tel** (213)782-2485. **(Subscription address:** Neodata / Colorado, PO Box 2606, Boulder Boulder CO 80322.**) LC** WMLC 93/925. **DD** 629. ***Continues*** *Petersen's Kit Car, 0883-5705.* ***Continued by*** *Kit Car, 1072-7981.*

GW
**SPORT AUTO.** **See** Recreation, Leisure-Sports.

FR/0151-6353
**SPORT AUTO, VIRAGE AUTO, CHAMPION.** **VFOAT** Sport Auto, Virage, Champion; Sport Auto (Paris. 1985); Sport Auto, Champion. (1974)-. Periodical. French. mo. Gerpresse, 8 10 rue Pierre Brossolette, 92300 Levallois Perr France. **Tel** 011 33 1 40874085. **UDC** 790.

US/1062-9629
**SPORT COMPACT CAR.** [Sport compact car]. **VFOAT** Sport Compact Car Magazine. (1989)-. Periodical. English. Six times a year. $16.95 (one year), $30.98 (two years). McMullen Publishing Inc, 2145 West La Palma Avenue, PO Box 70015, Anaheim CA 92801-1785. **Tel** (714)572-2255, FAX (714)572-1864. **DD** 629.

US/1044-7903
**SPORT TRUCK.** [Sport truck]. (198?)-. Periodical. English. mo. $19.94 US; $29.90 Canada; $30.94 other. Petersen Publishing Company, 6420 Wilshire Bouldevard, Los Angeles CA 90048. **Tel** (213)782-2485. **(Subscription address:** Neodata / Colorado, PO Box 2606, Boulder Boulder CO 80322.**) ED** Drew Hardin. **DD** 629. **Ad Acc. Circ:** 200,000.
**Desc:** Covers the entire range of light-duty trucks with an emphasis on performance. Readers get vehicle evaluations and real-world, long-term tests on full-size and mini pick-ups, sport/utilities, vans and specialty vehicles. Offers insights into improving handling, increasing horsepower, and more.

CN/0846-1333
**SPORTING CLASSICS (OTTAWA).** (SPORTING CLASSICS.). [Sport. class.]. Vol. 1, No. I (Jan./Feb. 1991)-. Periodical. English. bm. $19.80 per year. Sporting Classics Magazine, PO Box 160, Manotick Ontario K0A 2N0 Canada. **DD** 629.222.

US/0300-6387
**SPORTS CAR.** [Sports car]. **Added/Corp** Sports Car Club of America. (19??)-. Trade Publication. English. mo. $18.00 (1 year), $30.00 (2 year) US; $28.00 (1 year), $40.00 (2 year) other. Sports Car Club of America, PO Box 3278, Englewood CO 80155.
**Desc:** This publication covers amateur and professional events such as road rallies, autocrosses, and racing. The magazine also includes articles dealing with new products, the car industry, and motorsports news and views.

US/1042-9662
**SPORTS CAR INTERNATIONAL.** [Sports car int.]. (1989)-. Periodical. English. Twelve times a year. $17.95 (one year); $34.00 (two years). Ross Publishing, 42 Digital Drive, Suite 5, Novato CA 94949. **Tel** (415)382-0580. **ED** Jay Lamm. **LC** TL236; .S637. **DD** 629.222. Index available. cum. index. **Ad Acc, Adv Mgr:** Stan. ***Continues*** *Sports Car Illustrated (Atlanta, GA.), 0895-416X.*
**Desc:** The magazine on sports and the performance of cars.

US/0096-3313
**SPORTS CARS IN REVIEW.** English. an. Henry Ford Museum, Dearborn MI 48121. **LC** TL236; .S6683. **DD** 629.22/22.

US
**STAPP CAR CRASH AND FIELD DEMONSTRATION CONFERENCE.** First conference held in 1955. English. ir. **LC** TL6; .S78.

US/0744-155X
**STAR (LAKEWOOD, COLO.), THE.** (THE STAR / MERCEDES-BENZ CLUB OF AMERICA.). [Star]. **Added/Corp** Mercedes-Benz Club of America. **VFOAT** Mercedes-Benz Star. (1956)-. Periodical. English. Six times a year (Jan., Mar., May, July, Sept., Nov.). $35.00 Comes Mercedes Benz Club of America membership. Mercedes-Benz Club of America, 1907 Lelaray Street, Colorado Springs CO 80909. **Tel** (719)633-6427. **DD** 629.

CN/0702-2441
**STATEMENT OF POLICY - CANADIAN AUTOMOBILE ASSOCIATION.** **Main/Corp** Canadian Automobile Association. (1975)-. Periodical. English (French). an. Canadian Automobile Association,

1775 Courtwood Crescent, Ottawa Ontario K2C 3J2 Canada. **Tel** (613)226-7631, FAX (613)225-7383, telex 053-4440. **ED** Michael S. McNeil. **DD** 388/.0971. **Circ:** 3,000. ***Supersedes*** *Canadian Automobile Association. Policies and Resolutions., 0702-2476.*

SA
**STATISTIEKE VAN MOTORVOERTUIE : NUWE VOERTUIE GELISENSIEER.**
**Main/Corp** South Africa. Dept. of Statistics. **VFOAT** Motor Vehicle Statistics: New Vehicles Licensed. Multiple languages (Afrikaans and English). R60. Government Printer / South Africa, Bosman Street, Private Bag X85, Pretoria 0001 South Africa. **Tel** 011 27 12 3239731 Ext. 262. **LC** HE5704.S6; S68A. **DD** 354/.68/0087834.

US/0731-2008
**STOCK CAR CLASSIFICATION GUIDE.**
[Stock car classif. guide]. **Added/Corp** National Hot Rod Association. (19??)-. English. an. $150.00. National Hot Rod Association, 2035 Financial Way, Glendora CA 91740. **Tel** (818)914-4761. **ED** Dave Danish. **LC** TL236; .S754. **DD** 629.2/28/0212. **Circ:** 10,000 (ctrl).
**Desc:** Technical manual of American and international car specifications.

XO/0139-6501
**STOP (BRATISLAVA).** (STOP; AUTO-MOTO REVUE.). (1971)-. Periodical. Slovak. PNS Xustredna Expedicia Tlace, Gottwaldovo Nam 6, 813 81 Bratislava Slovakia. **Tel** 675 71. **ED** Emil Pauliny. **LC** TL4; .S7. **Bk Rev**. **Ad Acc. Circ:** 120,000 (ctrl).

AU
**STRASSENGUTERVERKEHR, DER.**
**Added/Corp** Fachverband des Guterbeforderungsgewerbes. (19??)-. Periodical. German. ir. Osterreichischer Wirtschaftsvg, Nikolsdorfer Gasse 7 11, A 1051 Vienna Austria. **Tel** 011 43 1 555585. **LC** HE5667.A1; S8.

GW/0173-2501
**STRASSENVERKEHRSZAHLUNGEN.**
**Added/Corp** Bundesanstalt fur Strassenwesen (Germany). (1976)-. Monographic series. German. **LC** HE5601; .S89. **DD** 388.3/0943.

UK/0143-5949
**STREET MACHINE (LONDON, ENGLAND).** (STREET MACHINE.). [Str. mach.]. (1979)-. Periodical. English. mo. $48.00 North America; £18.00 other. AGB Business Publs Ltd, Audit House, Field End Road, Ruislip Middlesex HA4 9LT England. **Tel** 011 44 81 868 4499. **(Subscription address:** Expediters of the Printed Word, Dept. St. Machine, PO Box 1305, Long Island City NY 11101.**) ED** Clive Househam. **LC** TL236.3; .S78. **Bk Rev**. **Ad Acc. Circ:** 77,773.

US/0192-1967
**STREET MACHINES & BRACKET RACING.** **VAT** Street Machines and Bracket Racing. Periodical. English. $1.95 each copy. Petersen Publishing Company, 6420 Wilshire Bouldevard, Los Angeles CA 90048. **Tel** (213)782-2485. **LC** TL236; .S783. **DD** 629.22/8.

US/1046-5367
**STREET ROD ACTION.** [Street rod action]. Vol. 18, No. 3 (Mar. 1989)-. Periodical. English. mo. $26.50. Challenge Publications Inc., 7950 Deering Avenue, Canoga Park CA 91304. **Tel** (818)887-0550. **LC** TL236.3; .R63. **DD** 629. ***Continues*** *Rod Action, 0194-7133.*

●US/1067-5256
**STREET ROD PICKUPS.** (1993)-. Periodical. English. Twelve times a year. $21.95. Challenge Publications Inc., 7950 Deering Avenue, Canoga Park CA 91304. **Tel** (818)887-0550.

US/8750-3298
**STREET RODDING ILLUSTRATED.**
***Ceased.*** [Str. rodding illus.]. (198?)-(19??). Periodical. English. bm. McMullen Publishing Inc, 2145 West La Palma Avenue, PO Box 70015, Anaheim CA 92801-1785. **Tel** (714)572-2255, FAX (714)572-1864. **ED** Philippe Danh. **DD** 629. **Ad Acc. Circ:** 80,000.
**Desc:** Covers the building and rebuilding of 1948 and earlier cars using late model engines and suspension. Also covers both outdoor and indoor shows featuring this type of vehicle. Lots of technical information and how-to articles for the home street rod builder.

IO/0126-494X
**STRUKTUR BIAYA BUS DAN TRUK UMUM.** Indonesian. an. Rp1,500 Indonesia; $1.00 US. Central Bureau of Statistics / Indonesia, c/o Dr. Sutomo, 8 Jalan, PO Box 3, Jakarta Indonesia. **Tel** 372808 374908 Ext.342. **LC** HE5695; .A33. ctrl circ.

IT/0039-4254
**STYLE AUTO.** [Style auto]. (1963)-. Periodical. Multiple languages. Four times a year. $14.30 Itlay; $20.00 other. Style Auto Editrice, Corso Adriatico 26, 10129 Turin Italy. **UDC** 388.

US
**SUMMARY OF ... MOTOR VEHICLE LICENSE ISSUE AS COMPARED TO ... / COMMONWEALTH OF VIRGINIA, DIVISION OF MOTOR VEHICLES.** **VFOAT** Summary of Motor Vehicle License and Title Issue. English. an. **LC** HE5633.V8; S96. **DD** 388.3/2/09755021.

PP
**SUMMARY OF NEW MOTOR VEHICLES REGISTERED.** **Main/Corp** Papua New Guinea. Bureau of Statistics. (19??)-. English. Bureau of Statistics / Papua New Guinea, PO Box 2032, Konedobu Papua New Guinea. **LC** HE5718.P3; A23c. **DD** 388.34/0995/3.

US/0896-0437
**SUPER AUTOMOTIVE SERVICE.** ***Ceased.*** [Super automot. serv.]. **VFOAT** Automotive Service. Vol. 116, No. 4 (Oct. 1987)-Ceased Feb .(1991). Periodical. English. mo. Irving-Cloud Publishing Company, 417 North Hough Street, Barrington IL 60010. **Tel** (708)382-3405, FAX (708)674-7015. **(Subscription address:** 6201 W Howard Street, Room 207, Niles, IL 60648**) ED** Bob Weber and Cynthia Savio. **LC** TL153.A1; S8. **DD** 629.28/7/05. Index available. cum. index. **Bk Rev. Ad Acc. Circ:** 114,000 (ctrl). ***Continues*** *Super Service Station, 0039-5676.*
**Desc:** Specifically edited for automotive service technicians with up-to-date information and procedures for servicing and repairing automotive vehicles.
**Ind/Abst** Trade Ind. Index (1987-?).

US/0146-2628
**SUPER CHEVY.** **VFOAT** Super Chevy Magazine. (197?)-. Periodical. English. Twelve times a year. $16.94 (one year); $29.94 (two years). Argus Publishers Corporation, 12100 Wilshire Boulevard, Suite 250, Los Angeles CA 90025. **Tel** (310)820-3601, FAX (310)207-9388. **(Subscription address:** Kable Publishers Aide, 308 East Hitt Street, Subscription Department, Mt. Morris IL 61054-1473.**) ED** Doug Marion. **LC** TL215.C5; S86. **DD** 629.2/222. **Circ:** 137,970.

US/1054-318X
**SUPER FORD.** **VFOAT** Super Ford Magazine. English. mo. $23.97 (one year), $46.00 (two years), $64.00 (three years). Dobbs Publications, PO Box 455, Lakeland FL 33807. **Tel** (813)646-5744. **(Subscription address:** Super Ford Magazine, PO Box 494, Mt Morris, IL 61054**) LC** WMLC L 83/6982. ***Continues*** *Super Ford Magazine, 0279-2184.*

US/0279-2184
**SUPER FORD MAGAZINE.** ***Title Change.*** (19??)-(19??). Periodical. English. mo. Dobbs Publications, PO Box 455, Lakeland FL 33807. **Tel** (813)646-5744. ***Continued by*** *Super Ford, 1054-318X.*

US/0039-5692
**SUPER STOCK & DRAG ILLUSTRATED.** **See** Recreation, Leisure-Sports.

US
**SUPER STREET TRUCK.** ***Ceased.*** **VFOAT** Popular Hot Rodding Magazine's Super Street Truck. Vol. 1, No. 1 (Summer 1990)-(199?). Periodical. English. qt. Argus Publishers Corporation, 12100 Wilshire Boulevard, Suite 250, Los Angeles CA 90025. **Tel** (310)820-3601, FAX (310)207-9388. **LC** WMLC L 90/0007.

US/0278-422X
**SURVEY AND ANALYSIS OF BUSINESS CAR POLICIES & COSTS.** **See** Business.

AT
**SURVEY OF MOTOR VEHICLE USE.** **See** Transportation-Abstracting, Bibliographies and Statistics.

GR
**TAXIDIA STEN EUROPE.** Greek, Modern. 200.00. EKD Hellenews, Platia Karitsy 6, T T 124 Athens Greece. **LC** D923; .T36.

GR
**TAXIDIA STEN HELLADA KAI TEN KYPRO.** Greek, Modern. 60.00. EKD Hellenews, Platia Karitsy 6, T T 124 Athens Greece. **LC** DF727; .T35.

CN/0318-3467
**TAYLOR'S LEISURE WHEELS.** **VFOAT** Leisurewheels. V. 4, No. 6- June 1972-. Periodical. English. mo. Tall-Taylor Publishing, Box 40 Canada. **DD** 796.7/9/05. ***Continues*** *Travel Leisure, 0049-4550.*

US/0092-3680
**TECHNICAL DIGEST - I.E.E.E. VEHICULAR TECHNOLOGY ANNUAL CONFERENCE.** (TECHNICAL DIGEST.). **Main/Conf** IEEE Vehicular Technology Conference. **VAT** Technical Digest - Institute of Electrical and Electronics Engineers Vehicular Technology Annual Conference. (19??)-. English. an. $5.00. Institution of Electrical Engineers / IEE, Michael Faraday House, Six Hills Way, Stevenage Herts SG1 2AY UK. **Tel** 011 44 438 313311, FAX 011 44 438 742840, telex 825578 IEESTV G. **(Subscription address:** IEE / UK, Publications Sales Department, PO Box 96, Stevenage, Herts, SG1 2SD England.**) LC** TL272.5; .I17a. **DD** 388.3/028.

US/0741-2029
**TECHNICAL LITERATURE ABSTRACTS (WARRENDALE, PA. : 1987).** **See** Engineering.

●US/1068-1744
**THIS OLD TRUCK.** (THIS OLD TRUCK : THE OFFICIAL PUBLICATION FOR MEMBERS OF THE LIGHT COMMERCIAL VEHICLE ASSOCIATION.). [This old truck]. **Added/Corp** Light Commercial Vehicle Association. Vol. 1, No. 1 (Feb./Mar. 1993)-. Periodical. English. bm (6 issues). $20.00. Antique Power Inc., PO Box 562, Yellow Springs OH 45387. **Tel** (513)767-1433, (800)767-5828. **LC** WMLC 93/1679. **DD** 629.

UK
**THOROUGHBRED & CLASSIC CARS.**
**VAT** Thoroughbred and Classic Cars. (19??)-. Periodical. English. mo. $60.00. IPC Magazines Ltd., Perrymount Road, Haywards Heath, West Sussex RH16 3DH England. **Tel** 011 44 444 440421. **LC** TL1; .T46. **DD** 629.22/22/09. available on microfilm from University Microfilms International (UMI).

US/0145-4110
**THUNDERBIRD ILLUSTRATED.** V. 1- Fall 1974-. Periodical. English. qt. $15.00. Thunderbird Publications, PO Box 6446, Orange CA 92667. **LC** TL215.T46; T48. **DD** 338.34/2/2.

US/0090-8657
**TIRE SCIENCE & TECHNOLOGY.** [Tire sci. technol.]. **Added/Corp** American Society for Testing and Materials. **VAT** Tire Science and Technology. Vol. 1 (Feb. 1973)-. Periodical. English. qt (4 issues). $100.00 US. Tire Society Inc., PO Box 1502, Akron OH 44309. **Tel** (216)253-8473. **LC** TL270; .T525. **DD** 629.2/48. **CODEN** TSTCAU. Index available (bound in Nov. issue). available on microfilm and microfiche from University Microfilms International (UMI). Documents available from Article Express International.
**Ind/Abst** Bioeng. Abstr.; Ei Page One; Eng. Index Annu.; Fluid Abstr., Civil Eng.; Fluid Abstr. Proc. Eng.; FLUIDEX (19??-); Int. Aerosp. Abstr.

US/0095-2001
**TIRES.** **See** Public Health and Safety.

US/0277-8300
**TRANSMISSION DIGEST.** (TRANSMISSION DIGEST: TD). **VFOAT** TD. Vol. 1, No. 1 (Sept. 1981)-. Periodical. English. Twelve times a year. $34.00 US; $40.00 Canada and Mexico; $82.00 other. M D Publications Inc., PO Box 2210, Springfield MO 65801. **Tel** (800)274-7890, (417)866-3917, FAX (417)866-2781. **ED** Lola Miller. **Ad Acc, Adv Mgr:** Robert Mace. **Circ:** 21,000 (ctrl).
**Desc:** Information for and about the automotive transmission field: manufacturing, distribution, and repair.

US/1058-479X
**TRANSMISSION TECH/TALK.** [Transm. tech talk]. **VFOAT** Transmission Tech Talk. (198?)-. Periodical. English. Twelve times a year. $89.00 US, Canada and Mexico; $100.00 other. M D Publications Inc., PO Box 2210, Springfield MO 65801. **Tel** (800)274-7890, (417)866-3917, FAX (417)866-2781. **ED** Bob Chermay. **DD** 621. **Circ:** 1,000.
**Desc:** Technical newsletter detailing rebuilding techniques for automotive transmissions.

UK
**TRUCK.** (19??)-. Periodical. English. mo. £21.50 UK; £33.00 (air mail) Europe; £26.00 (surface) other. Village Publishing Limited, 24A Mews North/ Paddington, London W2 3BW England. **Tel** 011 44 71 224 9242, FAX 011 44 71 402 3994. **LC** TL230.A1; T687. **DD** 388.3/24/05.

UK/0263-6263
**TRUCK & BUS BUILDER.** **See** Manufacturing.

US/0273-9402
**TRUCK BLUE BOOK.** [Truck blue book]. **Added/Corp** National Market Reports, Inc. **VFOAT** Truck Blue Book and Identification Book. (19??)-. Periodical. English. qt. $120.00. MacLean Hunter Publishing Corporation / Chicago, IL, 29 North Wacker Drive, Chicago IL 60606-3298. **Tel** (312)726-2802, FAX (312)726-3091. **(Subscription address:** Maclean Hunter Market Reports, 29 North Wacker Drive, Chicago IL 60606.**)** ***Continues*** *Blue Book IL.*

CN/0564-3392
**TRUCK DATA BOOK.** [Truck data book]. **Added/Corp** Sanford Evans Services Ltd. Sanford Evans & Company. (1949/50)-. Periodical. English (French). an. 35.00Can$. Sanford Evans Communications Ltd., Box 6900, 1700 Church Avenue, Winnipeg Manitoba R3C 3B1 Canada. **Tel** (204)632-2768, FAX (204)694-2347. **ED** Gary B. Henry. **DD** 629.22/4/0212.
**Desc:** Over 500 pages covering light medium and heavy duty trucks, current model and year and past eight years. Data includes, retail prices, serial numbers, gross and curb weights, wheelbase, number of cylinders, displacement and horsepower.

US/1048-9584
**TRUCK ENGINEERING.** [Truck eng.]. **Added/Corp** Society of Automotive Engineers (U.S.). Vol. 1, No. 1 (Nov. 1989)-. Periodical. English. mo. $20.00. Society of Automotive Engineers, 400 Commonwealth Drive, Warrendale PA 15096. **Tel** (412)776-4841, (412)772-7106, FAX (412)776-5760. **DD** 629. **CODEN** TRENEJ.

US/0889-3888
**TRUCK IDENTIFICATION BOOK.** (TRUCK IDENTIFICATION.). [Truck identif. book]. **Added/Corp** National Market Reports, Inc. (1975)-. Periodical. English. an. $15.00. MacLean Hunter Publishing Corporation / Chicago, IL, 29 North Wacker Drive, Chicago IL 60606-3298. **Tel** (312)726-2802, FAX (312)726-3091. **(Subscription address:** Maclean Hunter Market Reports, 29 North Wacker Drive, Chicago IL 60606.**) LC** TL230.A1; T696. **DD** 629.2/24/027.

US/1050-9259
**TRUCK, VAN, AND 4X4 BOOK, THE.** ***Title Change.*** [Truck van 4X4 book]. **VFOAT** Truck, Van, and Four-by-Four Book. **VAT** Truck, Van, and Four by Four Book. (1991)-(1992). Periodical. English. an. Harper Collins Publishers, Keystone Industrial Park, Scranton PA 18512. **Tel** (800)242-7737, (800)233-4727, FAX (800)822-4090. **LC** TL162; .T78. **DD** 629.223/029/773. ***Continued by*** *Minivan, Pickup, and 4x4 Book, 1062-2578.*

●US/1062-2578
**TRUCK, VAN AND 4X4 BOOK.** (1993). English. ir. Harper Collins Publishers, Keystone Industrial Park, Scranton PA 18512. **Tel** (800)242-7737, (800)233-4727, FAX (800)822-4090. **DD** 629. ***Continues*** *Truck, Van, and 4X4 Book (New York : 1994), 1050-9259.*

CN/1185-3409
**TRUCK WEST (WINNIPEG).** (TRUCK WEST.). [Truck west]. Vol. 1, Issue 1 (Sept. 1990)-. Periodical. English. mo. 24.00Can$ (one year), 36.00Can$ (two year) Canada; 40.00Can$ other. Southam Information and Technology Group Inc., 1450 Don Mills Road, Don Mills Ontario M3B 2X7 Canada. **Tel** (416)445-6641, (800)668-2374, FAX (416)442-2261. **DD** 388.3/24/0971205.

IT/1121-5585
**TUTTOTRASPORTI ROZZANO.** (TUTTOTRASPORTI.). [Tuttotrasporti Rozzano]. (1978)-. Periodical. Italian. Eleven times a year. $90.00. Editoriale Domus, Via Achille Grandi 5-7, 20089 Rozzano Milan Italy. **Tel** 011 39 2 82472276, FAX 011 39 2 8255033. **UDC** 347.763.

GW
**TUV AUTO-REPORT. Main/Corp** Vereinigung der Technischen Uberwachungs-Vereine. **VAT** Technischer Uberwachungs-Vereine Auto-Report. German. Verlag Tuv Rheinlan GmbH, Viktoriastr 26, W-5000 Cologne 90 F R Germany. **Tel** 011 49 2203 170960. **LC** TL3; .V47A.

UK
**TYRES, BATTERIES, AND EXHAUSTS.** English. bm. £25.00 UK and Northern Ireland; $40.00 other. Morgan Grampian, 40 Beresford Street Woolwich, London SE18 6BQ England. **Tel** 011 44 81 855 7777, FAX 011 44 81 855 5548, telex 896238.

US
**U.S. AUTOMOBILE INDUSTRY, THE. Added/Corp** United States International Trade Commission. **VFOAT** US Automobile Industry; U.S. Automotive Industry. **VAT** United States Automobile Industry. (19??)-. Periodical. English. mo. free. United States International Trade Commission, 500 E Street Southwest, Washington DC 20436. **Tel** (202)205-1806. **Circ:** 400.
**Desc:** Contains automobile trade data.

US/0734-6573
**U.S. AUTOMOTIVE SERVICES BULLETIN.** [U. S. automot. serv. bull.]. **VFOAT** US Automotive Services Bulletin. **VAT** United States Automotive Services Bulletin. Bulletin. English. qt. DRI McGraw Hill, 24 Hartwell Avenue, Lexington MA 02173. **Tel** (617)863-5100. **LC** HD9710.U5; U18. **DD** 338.4/76292/0973.

US/0890-040X
**UAW FACTS. See** Economics-Labor.

US/0893-6943
**UNDERCAR DIGEST.** [Undercar dig.]. **VFOAT** New Undercar Digest. Vol. 11, No. 9 (June 1987)-. Periodical. English. Twelve times a year. $34.00 US; $40.00 Canada and Mexico; $82.00 other. M D Publications Inc., PO Box 2210, Springfield MO 65801. **Tel** (800)274-7890, (417)866-3917, FAX (417)866-2781. **ED** Jim Wilder. **DD** 338. **Ad Acc, Adv Mgr:** Larry Dixon. **Circ:** 30,000 (ctrl). ***Continues*** *Muffler Digest, 0164-6044.*
**Desc:** Pertains to repair and replacement of exhaust, brake and chassis parts.

US
**UNIBODY & CHASSIS, DIMENSION & SPECIFICATION CHARTS. DOMESTIC CARS & TRUCKS. Added/Corp** KLM Automotive Publishing Inc. **VFOAT** Unibody and Chassis, Dimension and Specification Charts. Domestic Cars and Trucks; Domestic Cars & Trucks; Domestic Cars and Trucks; KLM Unibody and Chassis, Dimension and Specification Charts; KLM Unibody & Chassis, Dimension & Specification Charts. (19??)-. English. an. $119.00. Mitchell International Inc, PO Box 26260, San Diego CA 92126-0260. **Tel** (619)578-6550, (800)648-8010, FAX (619)578-4752. **(Subscription address:** Mitchell International Inc., PO Box 71654, Chicago IL 60694.**) LC** TL255; .U54. **DD** 629.26.

US
**UNIBODY & CHASSIS, DIMENSION & SPECIFICATION CHARTS. IMPORT CARS & TRUCKS. Added/Corp** KLM Automotive Publishing Inc. **VFOAT** Unibody and Chassis, Dimension and Specification Charts. Import Cars and Trucks; Import Cars & Trucks; Import Cars and Trucks; KLM Unibody and Chassis, Dimension and Specification Charts; KLM Unibody & Chassis, Dimension & Specification Charts. (19??)-. English. an. $119.00. Mitchell International Inc, PO Box 26260, San Diego CA 92126-0260. **Tel** (619)578-6550, (800)648-8010, FAX (619)578-4752. **(Subscription address:** Mitchell International Inc., PO Box 71654, Chicago IL 60694.**) LC** TL255; .U546. **DD** 629.26.

US/0892-4023
**UNMANNED SYSTEMS. See** Engineering-Electricity, Electrical Engineering, Electronics.

●US/1059-5775
**USED 4 X 4 BUYER'S GUIDE. VFOAT** Used Four By Four Buyer's Guide; Used 4x4 Buyer's Guide. (1992)-. English. $3.95. Rev Max A Kapp, Box 1392, Vineyard Haven MA 02568.

US/0895-3899
**USED CAR BOOK (NEW YORK, N.Y.), THE.** (THE USED CAR BOOK.). [Used car book]. (1988)-. Periodical. English. an. $14.35. Harper Collins Publishers, Keystone Industrial Park, Scranton PA 18512. **Tel** (800)242-7737, (800)233-4727, FAX (800)822-4090. **LC** TL162; .U79. **DD** 629.2/222.

US/0279-425X
**USED CAR DEALER, THE.** Periodical. English. mo. National Independent Automobile Dealer Association, c/o Smith & Associates, PO Box 19005, Raleigh NC 27619.

US/1053-2552
**USED CARS INSIDER.** [Used cars insid.]. **VFOAT** Used Cars Insider Newsletter. (19??)-. Periodical. English. Twenty-four times a year. $225.00 (one year), $440.00 (two years) surface mail; $210.00 (one year), $445.00 (two years), $645.00 (three years) airmail. United Communications Group, 11300 Rockville Pike, Suite 1100, Rockville MD 20852. **Tel** (301)816-8950 ext. 223, FAX (301)816-8945. **DD** 388. ***Continues*** *Used Cars Today, 0890-2291.*

US/0890-2291
**USED CARS TODAY.** ***Title Change.*** [Used cars today]. Periodical. English. bw. ATCOM Inc., 2315 Broadway, New York NY 10024-4397. **Tel** (800)521-7004, (212)873-5900, FAX (212)799-1728. **DD** 388. ***Continues*** *Used Cars Today Newsletter, 0740-0055.* ***Continued by*** *Used Cars Insider, 1053-2552.*

US/0745-4562
**UTAH MOTORIST.** (UTAH MOTORIST : OFFICIAL PUBLICATION OF THE AUTOMOBILE CLUB OF UTAH / AAA.). Vol. 1, No. 1 (Winter 1983)-. Periodical. English. bm. $1.00. Automobile Club of Utah, 560 East 5th South, Salt Lake City UT 84404.

US/0274-5003
**V-8 TIMES. VAT** V Eight Times. Periodical. English. bm. Early Ford V8 Club of America, Box 2122, San Leandro CA 94577. **DD** 629.

US/0884-7231
**VAN CONVERSION BLUE BOOK OFFICIAL MARKET REPORT.** [Van convers. blue book off. mark. rep.]. **Added/Corp** National Market Reports, Inc. **VFOAT** Van Conversion Blue Book. (1984)-. Periodical. English. qt. $60.00. MacLean Hunter Publishing Corporation / Chicago, IL, 29 North Wacker Drive, Chicago IL 60606-3298. **Tel** (312)726-2802, FAX (312)726-3091. **(Subscription address:** Maclean Hunter Market Reports, 29 North Wacker Drive, Chicago IL 60606.**) DD** 629.

US/1043-8270
**VAN, PICKUP, SPORT UTILITY BUYER'S GUIDE.** ***Title Change.*** [Van pickup sport util. buy. guide]. **Added/Corp** Edmund Publications Corporation. **VFOAT** Edmund's Van, Pickup, Sport Utility Buyer's Guide. (May 1989)-(1993). English. Six times a year. Edmund's Publications Corporation / California, 300 North Sepulveda Bouldevard, Suite 2050, El Segundo CA 90245. **Tel** (310)640-7840, (914)962-6297. **(Subscription address:** Edmund Publications, PO Box 338, Shrub Oak, NY 10588**) LC** TL162; .V36. **DD** 629.223. ***Continues*** *Edmund's Vans, Pickups, Offroad Buyer's Guide.* ***Continued by*** *Edmund's Van, Pickup, Sport Utility, 1077-2111.*

US
**VEHICLE CODE. Main/Corp** California. **Added/Corp** California. Dept. of Motor Vehicles. **VFOAT** California Vehicle Code. (19??)-. English. an. $3.00. Department of Motor Vehicles / California, Attn S Wiseman, 2415 First Avenue, Sacramento CA 95818. Each issue contains an index to its own contents (no volume index)--loose.

US/8756-940X
**VEHICLE IDENTIFICATION.** [Veh. identif.]. English. be. $42.50. Lee Books, PO Box 906, Novato CA 94948. **Tel** (800)828-3550. **ED** Lee S Cole. **LC** TL154; .V43. **DD** 629.22/22/027. **Bk Rev.** ctrl circ.
**Desc:** Books on vehicle theft, fire fraud and identification procedures and methods.

US
**VEHICLE LEASING TODAY. See** Transportation.

BE
**VEHICULES A MOTEUR NEUFS MIS EN CIRCULATION. Main/Corp** Institut National de Statistique (Belgium). French. 250F Belgium; 300F other. Institut National de Statistique / Belgium, rue de Louvain, 44, Centre Albert, 8e Etage, 1000 Brussels Belgium. **Tel** 011 32 2 5486211. **LC** HE5673; .A26A. **Bk Rev. Ad Acc. Circ:** 165 (ctrl).
**Desc:** Statistics about the new cars in traffic.

US/0199-7890
**VETTE.** [Vette]. (19??)-. Periodical. English. mo. $24.95. CSK Publishing Company, 299 Market Street, Saddle Brook NJ 07662. **Tel** (201)712-9300, FAX (201)712-9899. **ED** D. Randy Riggs. **Ad Acc. Circ:** 50,000.
**Desc:** Covers new technology, restorations, performance modifications, customizing and Corvette shows for Corvette enthusiasts and owners.

US/0279-8476
**VETTE VUES MAGAZINE.** (19??)-. Periodical. English. mo. $20.00. Vette Vues, PO Box 76270, Sandy Springs GA 30328. **Tel** (404)252-2575. **ED** James B. Prather. **Bk Rev. Ad Acc. Circ:** 25,000 (ctrl).
**Desc:** For Chevrolet Corvette owners. Includes cars and parts for sale, articles and events.

US/0194-3294
**VETTE'N USA. VAT** Vette'n United States of America. Periodical. English. mo.

CN/0844-1804
**VIE EN PLEIN AIR.** [Vie plein air]. Vol. 12, No. 1 (Sept./Autumn 1987)-. Periodical. French. ir. 10.00Can$. CRV Publications, 2585 Skymark Ave, Suite 306, Mississauga Ontario L4W 4L5 Canada. **Tel** (416)624-8218, FAX (416)624-6764. **DD** 796.7. ***Continues*** *Magazine Tout Terrain, 0829-4445.*

UK
**VINTAGE CAR ANNUAL.** No. 1- 1979-. English. **LC** TL1; .V56. **DD** 629.2/222/09.

US/0042-6350
**VINTAGE FORD, THE.** V. 1- Mar./Apr. 1966-. Periodical. English. bm. $15.00 US; $20.00 other. Model T Ford Club of America, Box 7400, Burbank CA 91510. **Tel** (818)842-2010. **ED** Bruce W McCalley. **LC** TL215.F7; V53. Index available. cum. index. **Bk Rev. Ad Acc. Circ:** 7,000 (ctrl).
**Desc:** General coverage of the model T Ford, its history and current activities.

UK
**VINTAGE LORRY ANNUAL.** No. 1- 1979-. Periodical. English. an. **LC** TL230.A1; V55. **DD** 629.2/24/0941.

US/0147-9695
**VINTAGE TRIUMPH, THE.** Periodical. English. qt. $20.00. Vintage Triumph Register, Box 36477, Grosse Point MI 48236. **Tel** (203)481-0533. **ED** Steven Rossi. **LC** TL215.T7; V56. **DD** 629.22/22. Index available. **Bk Rev. Circ:** 3,600 (ctrl).
**Desc:** Articles and information to assist and encourage the ownership, operation and enjoyment of Triumph sports cars and motor cars.

US/0049-6723
**VOLKSWAGEN GREATS. VFOAT** VW Greats. Periodical. English. bm. $7.00 US; $9.00 other. Volkswagen Greats, PO Box 49659, Los Angeles CA 90049.

CI
**VOZAC I SAOBRACAJ. Added/Corp** Savez Udruzenja Vozaca I Automehanicara SRH. (19??)-. Periodical. Serbo-Croatian (Roman). mo. Savez

Udrunzenja Vozaca I Automehanicara SRH, Draskoviceva 27/1, Zagreb Croatia. **Tel** (041)417-009. **LC** TL4; .V66. **Ad Acc**. ***Continues*** *Vozac.*

US/8750-3301
**VW TRENDS.** [VW trends]. **VFOAT** VW Trends Magazine. **VAT** Volkswagen Trends. (198?)-. Periodical. English. Twelve times a year. $18.95 (one years), $28.95 (two years). McMullen Publishing Inc, 2145 West La Palma Avenue, PO Box 70015, Anaheim CA 92801-1785. **Tel** (714)572-2255, FAX (714)572-1864. **LC** TL215.V6; V89. **DD** 629.2/222.

US/0043-0315
**WARD'S AUTO WORLD.** [Ward's auto world]. Vol. 5 (Feb. 1969)-. Periodical. English. mo. $48.50. Ward's Communications Inc., 3000 Town Center, Suite 2750, Southfield MI 48075. **Tel** (810)357-0800. **ED** Edward K. Miller. **LC** HD9710.U5; W33. **DD** 338.4/76292220973. **[CCC]**. **Ad Acc**. **Circ:** 86,000 (ctrl). available on microfilm and microfiche from University Microfilms International (UMI); available on an online database from DIALOG; and NEXIS. ***Continues*** *Ward's Quarterly.*
**Desc:** In-depth analysis and reporting on all aspects of the automotive industry, including manufacturing trends; new product technology; materials; advances in electronics, design, and production; interviews with industry leaders; and forecasts of sales and production.
**Ind/Abst** Bus. Index (1985-); Bus. Period. Index; F&S Index Plus Text, Int. [Select. Cov.]; Gen. BusinessFile (1985-); Gen. Period. Index (1985-); Infobank (1979-); Mag. Search; Mark. Advert. Ref. Serv.; PROMT; Trade Ind. ASAP [Full Txt.]; Trade Ind. Index [Full Txt.]; Vocat. Search (Jan. 1993-); Wilson Bus. Abstr.

US/0895-2191
**WARD'S AUTOMOTIVE INTERNATIONAL.** [Ward's automot. int.]. **Added/Corp** Ward's Communications Inc. **VFOAT** Automotive International. (198?)-. Periodical. English. sm. $475.00 US; $505.00 other. Ward's Communications Inc., 3000 Town Center, Suite 2750, Southfield MI 48075. **Tel** (810)357-0800. **LC** HD9710.A1; W37. **DD** 338.4/76292/05.
**Desc:** Features reports on worldwide competition, news, production, technical developments, marketing strategies and governmental policies.
**Ind/Abst** F&S Index Plus Text, Int. (19??-) [Select. Cov.]; PROMT (19??-).

US/0083-7229
**WARD'S AUTOMOTIVE YEARBOOK.** [Ward's automot. yearb.]. **Added/Corp** Ward's Reports, Inc. (1938)-. English. an. $275.00 North America; $305.00 other. Ward's Communications Inc., 3000 Town Center, Suite 2750, Southfield MI 48075. **Tel** (810)357-0800. **LC** HD9710.U5; W3. **DD** 388. **[CCC]**.
**Desc:** The industry's most authoritative source for statistics on domestic and international car and truck production and sales. Details trends in automotive electronics, engines and drivetrains, materials and other related technologies.
**Ind/Abst** F&S Index Plus Text, Int. (19??-) [Select. Cov.]; Predicasts Forecasts (19??-).

US
**WARD'S ENGINE AND VEHICLE TECHNOLOGY UPDATE.** English. Twenty-four times a year. $730.00 US; $755.00 other. Ward's Communications Inc., 3000 Town Center, Suite 2750, Southfield MI 48075. **Tel** (810)357-0800.
**Desc:** Presents coverage of the latest in engine and drivetrain technology including engine design and materials, chassis refinements, electronics and manufacturing techniques. Profiles new and future vehicles.

US
**WARD'S SPECIAL REPORTS.** English. ir. Price varies per title. Ward's Communications Inc., 3000 Town Center, Suite 2750, Southfield MI 48075. **Tel** (810)357-0800.
**Desc:** Offers in-depth single-subject industry reports such as Antilock Braking Systems, Automotive Materials in the 1990s and the US Luxury Vehicle Market in the 1990s.

US/0748-1683
**WAY OF THE ZEPHYR, THE. Added/Corp** Lincoln Zephyr Owner's Club. (19??)-. Periodical. English. bm. $18.00 (membership) U.S., Canada, and Mexico. Lincoln Zephyr Owner's Club, 2107 Steinruck Road, Elizabethtown PA 17022. **LC** TL215.Z46; W39. **DD** 629.2/22.

CN/0842-9855
**WESTERN AUTOBODY.** ***Suspended.*** [West. autobody]. Vol. 4, No. 1 (March 1988)-?. Periodical. English. qt. Free. Western Autobody, POB 6900, Winnipeg Manitoba R3C 3B1 Canada. **DD** 629.2/6/0288. ***Separated from*** *Motor in Canada, 0027-190X.*

US/0510-2626
**WESTERN RACING NEWS.** (19??)-. English. ir (40 issues per year). $35.00 (one year), $50.00 (two year). Pueblo Publishers Inc, 7122 North 59th Avenue, Glendale AZ 85301. **Tel** (602)842-6000. **ED** Ron Rose. **Ad Acc**. **Circ:** 4,000 (ctrl).
**Desc:** Contains auto racing results, news and features.

GW
**WESTEUROPA QUELLEN ZUM KRAFTFAHRZEUGMARKT. Main/Corp** Bundesstelle fur Aussenhandelsinformation (Germany). German. 10.00. Bundesstelle fuer Aussenhandelsinformation, Agrippastr 87 93, D 50676 Cologne Germany. **Tel** 011 49 221 2057316, FAX 011 49 221 2057212. **LC** HD9710.A1; G47A.

US/0043-4434
**WESTWAYS.** [Westways]. **Added/Corp** Automobile Club of Southern California. Vol. 26, No. 1 (Jan. 1934)-. Periodical. English. Twelve times a year. $12.95. Automobile Club of Southern California, 2601 South Figueroa Street, Los Angeles CA 90007. **Tel** (310)741-4410. **ED** Eric Seyfarth. **DD** 917. **Bk Rev**. **Ad Acc, Adv Mgr:** S. Kilets, **Tel** (213)741-4765. **Circ:** 480,000. ***Continues*** *Touring Topics.*
**Ind/Abst** Access (1975-); Am. Hist. Life (1974-1977, 1979-1986); Calif. Period. Index.

UK
**WHAT CAR?.** (19??)-. Periodical. English. mo (13 issues). £28.50 UK; £40.00 Eire & Europe; £80.00 America, Middle East, Africa & India; £90.00 New Zealand, Australia & Japan; £40.00 other. Haymarket Publishing Ltd., 12 14 Ansdell Street, London W8 5TR England. **Tel** 011 44 483 733800, FAX 011 44 483 776573. **(Subscription address:** Haymarket Publishing Ltd, PO Box 219, Subscriptions Department, Woking Surrey GU21 1ZW, United Kingdom.**) LC** TL1; .W45. **DD** 629.22/22/05. Index available. **Bk Rev**. **Ad Acc**. **Circ:** 126,000.
**Desc:** Long-term tests on new cars; informs potential buyers.

US/0882-6676
**WHEEL-O-RAMA.** (WHEEL-O-RAMA : OFFICIAL SHOWTIME MAGAZINE OF THE NCSA.). [Wheel-o-rama]. **VFOAT** NCSA Wheel-O-Rama. Vol. 1, No. 1 (Mar. 1985). Periodical. English. qt. $18.00. National Custom Show Association, 836 South Wayne Avenue, Columbus OH 43204. **Tel** (614)279-2172. **ED** Margaret Frum. **DD** 629. **Ad Acc**. **Circ:** 2,000 (ctrl).
**Desc:** Consists of car pictures and stories about the cars and owners. Also automotive clubs and their members and sponsored events, for sale and wanted car items, and advertisements.

US/0888-1103
**WHEEL (SAN FRANCISCO, CALIF.).** (THE WHEEL.). Periodical. English. mo. $10.00. San Francisco Region of Sports Car Club of America, 3609 Virgin Islands Court, Pleasanton CA 94566.

US/1047-3165
**WHEELS (DETROIT, MICH.).** (WHEELS : JOURNAL OF THE NATIONAL AUTOMOTIVE HISTORY COLLECTION.). [Wheels]. **Added/Corp** National Automotive History Collection (U.S.) Detroit Public Library. Friends. (Mar. 1983)-. Periodical. English. Three times a year. Free. Friends of the Detroit Public Library, 5201 Woodward Avenue, Detroit MI 48202. **LC** TL15; .W45. **DD** 629.222/09.

UK/0267-1816
**WHICH VAN?.** [Which van?]. (1984)-. Periodical. English. bm (6 issues). £15.00 UK; £20.00 Eire & Europe; £28.00 America, Middle East, Africa & India; £32.00 Australia, New Zealand & Japan; £20.00 other. Haymarket Publishing Ltd., 12 14 Ansdell Street, London W8 5TR England. **Tel** 011 44 483 733800, FAX 011 44 483 776573. **(Subscription address:** Haymarket Publishing Ltd, PO Box 219, Subscriptions Department, Woking Surrey GU21 1ZW, United Kingdom.**) DD** 629.2230294.

SA/0257-5426
**WIEL.** [Wiel]. (1978)-. Periodical. Afrikaans. mo. R50.00. Wiel, P.O.Box 1874, Randburg 2125 South Africa. **Tel** 011 27 11 7043046 7, FAX 011 27 11 7043047. **ED** J. Herbst. **UDC** 796.7. **Ad Acc**. **Circ:** 30,000 (ctrl).

US/0149-3175
**WNY MOTORIST.** V. 70, No. 6 (June 1977)-. Periodical. English. mo. Automobile Club of Western New York, 976 Delaware Avenue, Buffalo NY 14240. **LC** TL1; .B8. **DD** 338.3/21/097479. ***Continues*** *Western New York Motorist, 0043-3977.*

KO
**WOLGAN UNJON SEGYE.** ***Title Change.*** **VFOAT** Unjon Segye. 1st Vol. (1984/2)-?. Periodical. Korean. mo. Wolgan Unjon Segye, 48-24 Mia 4-dong Tobong-ku, Seoul Korea. **LC** TL4; .W64. ***Continued by*** *Unjon Segye.*

US/1043-979X
**WOMEN WITH WHEELS.** (WOMEN WITH WHEELS : WWW.). [Women wheels]. **VFOAT** WWW. Vol. 1, No. 1 (Spring 1989)-. Periodical. English. qt (4 issues). $20.00. Women With Wheels, 1718 A Northfield Square, Northfield IL 60093. **Tel** (708)501-3519. **ED** Susan Frissel. **DD** 629. Index available (published in Dec.). **Bk Rev**. **Ad Acc**. **Circ:** 100.
**Desc:** Provides women with information on cars and their maintenance. Features articles on subjects such as anti-lock brakes, women and safety, leasing versus purchasing and dealing with car salesman. Regular columns appear with topics such as interviews, news of research and recalls.

CN/0228-2011
**WORKING PAPER - ROLE OF THE AUTOMOBILE STUDY, TRANSPORT CANADA.** [Work. pap. - Role Automob. Study, Transp. Can.]. **Main/Corp** Canada. Ministry of Transport. Role of the Automobile Study. **VAT** Role of the Automobile Study. Working Paper. No. 1 (1978)-. Monographic series. English (summaries and/or abstracts in French). Price varies per volume. Transport Canada / Strategic Planning Group, Ottawa Ontario K1A 0N5 Canada. **DD** 388.

US
**WORLD AUTOMOTIVE ALTERNATIVE ENERGY & FUELS BULLETIN.** **See** Energy.

US
**WORLD AUTOMOTIVE ENVIRONMENT & SAFETY BULLETIN.** (19??)-. Bulletin. English. Twelve times a year. $525.00. Forecast International / DMS Inc., 22 Commerce Road, Newtown CT 06470. **Tel** (203)426-0800, FAX (203)426-1964, telex 467615.

US
**WORLD AUTOMOTIVE INDUSTRY WEEKLY.** (19??)-. Bulletin. English. Fifty times a year. $1090.00. Forecast International / DMS Inc., 22 Commerce Road, Newtown CT 06470. **Tel** (203)426-0800, FAX (203)426-1964, telex 467615.

US
**WORLD AUTOMOTIVE MARKET, THE.** ***Title Change.*** 39th (1969)-(19??). English. an. Auto International-Johnston International Publishers, 386 Park Avenue South, New York NY 10016. **Tel** (212)689-0120, telex 666811 JONST. **ED** Bernard Zinober. **LC** HD9710.A1; W665. **DD** 380.1/456292/021. **Bk Rev**. **Circ:** 3,000 (ctrl). ***Continues*** *World Automotive Market Survey.* ***Continued by*** *World Automotive Market Report.*
**Desc:** Statistical analysis of worldwide vehicle production, registration, and trade, as well as reports on U.S. exports of automotive products.

US
**WORLD AUTOMOTIVE MARKET REPORT.** (199?)-. English. an. $50.00 US and Canada; $55.00 other. Hunter Publishing Company Inc., 25 Northwest Point Boulevard, Suite 800, Elk Grove Village IL 60007-1036. **Tel** (708)427-9512, FAX (708)427-2097. **LC** HD9710.A1; W665. ***Continues*** *World Automotive Market.*
**Desc:** Information concerning the automobile industry such as trade and supplies.

US
**WORLD AUTOMOTIVE MATERIALS & COMPOSITES BULLETIN.** (19??)-. Bulletin. English. Twelve times a year. $525.00. Forecast International / DMS Inc., 22 Commerce Road, Newtown CT 06470. **Tel** (203)426-0800, FAX (203)426-1964, telex 467615.

US
**WORLD AUTOMOTIVE NEWS SERVICE.** English. wk. £961.55. PRS Consulting Group Inc, 2301 West Big Beaver/Suite 620, Troy MI 48084. **Tel** (313)649-7110.

US
**WORLD AUTOMOTIVE TECHNOLOGY TRACKING.** (19??)-. Bulletin. English. Twelve times a year. $525.00. Forecast International / DMS Inc., 22 Commerce Road, Newtown CT 06470. **Tel** (203)426-0800, FAX (203)426-1964, telex 467615.

US
**WORLD DIESEL & OFF-HIGHWAY NEWS.** (19??)-. Bulletin. English. Twelve times a year. $525.00. Forecast International / DMS Inc., 22 Commerce Road, Newtown CT 06470. **Tel** (203)426-0800, FAX (203)426-1964, telex 467615.

US/0085-8307
**WORLD MOTOR VEHICLE DATA.** [World mot. veh. data]. **Added/Corp** Motor Vehicle Manufacturers Association of the United States. **VFOAT** MVMA. World Motor Vehicle Data, B.. (19??)-. English. an (Aug.). $50.00 US; $60.00 Canada and Mexico; $75.00 other. American Automobile Manufacturers Association, PO Box 11170, Detroit MI 48211. **Tel** (313)872-4311. **LC** HD9710.A1; W67. **DD** 338.4/7/62922.
**Desc:** Contains sections on vehicle production, sales, registration, ownership, usage, and economic and social impact.
**Ind/Abst** Stat. Ref. Index.

CN/0824-5487
**WORLD OF WHEELS.** [World wheels]. Vol. 1, No. 1 (Fall 1983)-. Periodical. English. Six times a year.

## Transportation —Railroads

12.00Can$. World of Wheels Publishing, Inc., 1200 Markham Road 220, Scarborough Ontario M1H 3C3 Canada. **Tel** (416)438-7777, FAX (416)438-5333. **DD** 629.2/222/05.

US/0362-6725
**YEARBOOK / TIRE AND RIM ASSOCIATION, INC. See** Transportation.

UK/0957-6525
**YOUR CLASSIC.** [Your class.]. (1989)-. Periodical. English. mo. £1.70 UK; $4.00 other (per issue). **ED** Ian Bond. **DD** 629.2222. Index available. **Bk Rev. Ad Acc. Pr Rev. Circ:** 70,000. **Continues** Restoring Classic Cars Magazine, 0954-1764.
  **Desc:** Magazine aimed at cheaper classic cars, first-time buyers, enthusiasts, and restorers.

## RAILROADS

US/1046-2147
**3/16 SCALE RAILROADING.** [3/16 "s"cale railr.]. **VFOAT** Three-Sixteenth Scale Railroading; Three-Sixteenth Inch Scale Railroading; S Scale Railroading. Vol. 1, No. 1 (Dec. 1989/Jan. 1990)-. Periodical. English. qt. $27.50 US; $30.00 Canada. Manufacturing Advisors Inc, 1446 Fremont Avenue, Los Altos CA 94024. **LC** WMLC L 83/8476. **DD** 625.

UK
**A.R.P.S. YEAR BOOK & STEAM PRESERVATION GUIDE. Main/Corp** Association of Railway Preservation Societies. **VFOAT** Railway Forum. (19??)-. English. £65.00. 31 Old Croft Road, Walton on the Hill Stafford England. **LC** TF1; .A83. **DD** 625.1/0074/02.

US/0899-2029
**AAR RAILROAD COST INDEXES.** [AAR railr. cost indexes]. **Added/Corp** Association of American Railroads. Economics and Finance Dept. **VAT** Association of American Railroads Railroad Cost Indexes. (Sept. 1986)-. English. qt. $50.00 (nonmembers), $25.00 (members). Association of American Railroads, 50 F Street Northwest, Room 5401, Washington DC 20001. **Tel** (202)639-2550. **DD** 385. **Continues** AAR Railroad Cost Recovery Index, 0734-3620.

US/0163-4674
**ACCIDENT/INCIDENT BULLETIN. See** Public Health and Safety.

US/8750-5762
**AMERICAN RAILS.** [Am. rails]. (1985)-. Periodical. English. Six times a year. $10.00. White Publishing, PO Box 286, Geneseo IL 61254. **Tel** (309)-944-3227. **ED** Frank L. White. **DD** 385. **Ad Acc. Circ:** 400. **Continues** Midwestern Rails, 8750-5819.

US
**AMTRAK MATRIX SYSTEM ANNUAL ORIGIN/DESTINATION PASSENGER COUNT. Main/Corp** United States. Federal Railroad Administration. **Added/Corp** Amtrak. United States. Office of Rail Systems Analysis and Information. (1977)-. English. an. US Department of Transportation / Federal Railroad Administration, 400 Seventh Street SW, Washington DC 20590. **Tel** (202)366-0881, FAX (202)366-7009.

US/0275-9829
**AMTRAK'S INVENTORY AND PROPERTY CONTROLS NEED STRENGTHENING. Main/Corp** United States. General Accounting Office. English. an. US Government Accounting Office, Distribution Section, 441 G Street NW, Washington DC 20548. **LC** HE2791; .A5626A. **DD** 353.0087/5/00687.

PK
**ANNUAL BUDGET STATEMENT OF PAKISTAN RAILWAYS. Main/Corp** Pakistan. Ministry of Railways. English. Government of Pakistan / Ministry of Railways, Railway Board, Karachi 15 3 Pakistan. **LC** HE3300.5; .A334A. **DD** 354.549/10072252.

US/0883-6035
**ANNUAL PROCEEDINGS, PRE-CONVENTION REPORT - LOCOMOTIVE MAINTENANCE OFFICERS ASSOCIATION (U.S.).** (ANNUAL PROCEEDINGS ... PRE-CONVENTION REPORT / LMOA.). [Annu. proc. pre-conv. rep. - Locomot. Maint. Off. Assoc. (U.S.)]. **Main/Corp** Locomotive Maintenance Officers Association (U.S.). **VFOAT** LMOA. Proceedings. English. an. Locomotive Maintenance Officers Association, 1344 Brereton Court, Huntington WV 25705. **LC** TJ675; .L592A. **DD** 625.2/66/05. **Formed by the union of** Locomotive Maintenance Officers Association (U.S.). Pre-Convention Report **and** Locomotive Maintenance Officers Association (U.S.). Annual Proceedings of the Annual Meeting.

JA
**ANNUAL REPORT. Main/Corp** Higashi Nihon Ryokaku Tetsudo Kabushiki Kaisha. (19??)-. English. **(Subscription address:** East Japapn Railway Company, New York Office, 45 Rockefeller Plaza, New York, NY 10111) **Continues in part** Nihon Kokuyu Tetsudo. Facts and Figures.

AT
**ANNUAL REPORT / AUSTRALIAN NATIONAL RAILWAYS COMMISSION. Main/Corp** Australian National Railways Commission. (1975/1976)-. Corporate Report. English. an. Free. Australian National Railways Commission, 1 Richmond Road, Keswick South Australia 5035, Australia. **Tel** 08 217 4775, FAX 08 231 9936. **ED** L. Welsey. **LC** HE3461; .C65a. **DD** 385/.0994. Index available. **Circ:** 3,000 (ctrl). **Continues** Australian National Railways Commission. Report on the Operations of the Commonwealth Railways.
  **Desc:** Contains administrative and statistical reports.

AT
**ANNUAL REPORT FOR YEAR ENDED 30 JUNE ... / QUEENSLAND RAILWAYS.** Title Change. **Main/Corp** Queensland Railways. **VFOAT** Report from the Commissioner for Railways. (19??-19??). English. an. **LC** HE3501; .Q44a. **DD** 385/.065/943. **Continues** Queensland Railways.; Report of the Commissioner for Railways for the Year Ended 30th June ... . **Absorbed by** Queensland. Dept. of Transport.; Annual Report of the Director-General.

KE
**ANNUAL REPORT / KENYA RAILWAYS. See** Public Administration.

US/0748-8750
**ANNUAL REPORT / NORFOLK SOUTHERN. Main/Corp** Norfolk Southern Corporation. 1982-. English. an. Free. Norfolk Southern Corporation, One Commercial Place, Norfolk VA 23510-2191. **Tel** (804)629-2600. **ED** D H Noxon. **LC** HE2791.N816; .A23A. **DD** 385/.065/75. **Circ:** 160,000. **Formed by the union of** Annual Report - Southern Railway Company **and** Norfolk and Western Railroad Company. Annual Report.
  **Desc:** Report to stockholders of Northfolk Southern Corp., a Virginia based holding company (Southern Rwy.; Norfolk and Western Rwy.; North American Van Lines, Inc.).

US
**ANNUAL REPORT OF RAILROAD ACCIDENTS OCCURRING IN CALIFORNIA AND REPORTED UNDER GENERAL ORDER 22-B AND ... / CALIFORNIA PUBLIC UTILITIES COMMISSION, TRANSPORTATION DIVISION, RAILROAD OPERATIONS AND SAFETY BRANCH.** English. an. California Public Utilities Commission, State Building, San Francisco CA 94102. **LC** HE1780.5.C2; A77. **DD** 312/.44/09794. **Continues** Annual Report of Railroad Accidents Reported under General Order No. 22-B for Year ... .

US
**ANNUAL REPORT OF THE NORTH COMMISSION (ALASKA). Main/Corp** Alaska. Northern Operations of Rail Transportation and Highways Commission. (1968)-. Periodical. English. Alaska Northern Operations of Rail Transportation and Highways Commission, Juneau AK 99801. **LC** HE2709; .A34. **DD** 353.9/798/0082.

US/0483-9005
**ANNUAL REPORT - THE RAILWAY & LOCOMOTIVE HISTORICAL SOCIETY, INC. Main/Corp** Railway & Locomotive Historical Society. English. $25.00. Railway and Locomotive Historical Society, 115 I Street B Kleinschmidt, Sacramento CA 95814. **Tel** (916)447-9665, FAX (916)327-5655. cum. index. **Bk Rev**, (Qty: 30). **Ad Acc. Circ:** 3000.
  **Desc:** Leaflets, each containing the early history of a railraod, report of the annual meeting, list of officers, etc.

UK
**ANNUAL REPORT - TRANSPORT USERS CONSULTATIVE COMMITTEE FOR WALES. Main/Corp** Transport Users Consultative Committee for Wales. (1974)-. English. an. **LC** HE59; .A3. **DD** 354.4290087/5/06. **Continues** Transport Users' Consultative Committee for Wales and Monmouthshire. Report.

CN/0706-5698
**ANNUAL REPORT / VIA RAIL CANADA INC. Main/Corp** Via Rail Canada. **VFOAT** Rapport Annuel. **VAT** Rapport Annuel - Via Rail Canada Inc. Began in 1977-. English (French). an. Via Rail Canada Inc, Box 8116, Montreal Quebec H3C 3N3 Canada. **LC** HE2591.C3; V5A. **DD** 385/.22/0971.

JA
**ANNUAL REPORT / WEST JAPAN RAILWAY COMPANY. Main/Corp** West Japan Railway Company. (19??)-. English. **(Subscription address:** West Japan Railway Company, JR Group Overseas Offices, 45 Rockefeller Plaza, New York, NY 10111) **Continues in part** Nihon Kokuyu Tetsudo. Facts and Figures.

US
**ANNUAL TECHNICAL CONFERENCE. Main/Corp** Association of American Railroads. Communication and Signal Division. Technical Conference. **VFOAT** Communication and Signal Division ... Annual Technical Conference; Proceedings ... Annual Technical Conference. English. American Railroads Engineering Association, 50 F Street NW/Suite 7702, Washington DC 20001. **Continues** Annual Meeting / Association of American Railroads. Communication and Signal Division, 0744-2920.

GW/0341-0463
**ARCHIV FUER EISENBAHNTECHNIK; BEIHEFT ZU DER ZEITSCHRIFT EISENBAHN TECHNISCHE RUNDSCHAU. VFOAT** AET. 1952-. Periodical. German. Hestra Verlag Hernincel & Dr Strauss GmbH & Co KG, Postfach 4244, D 64201 Darmstadt Germany. **Tel** 011 49 6151 39070. **CODEN** AEBTAO. **[CCC].** Documents available from Article Express International, Ask*IEEE.
  **Ind/Abst** Bioeng. Abstr.; Ei Page One; Eng. Index Annu.; INSPEC (1968-).

SW
**ARSREDOVISNING / SJ. Main/Corp** Statens Jarnvagar (Sweden). **VFOAT** SJ Arsredovisning. 1980/81-. Swedish. an. SJ Centralforvaltning, 105 50 Stockholm Sweden. **LC** HE3181; .S7A. **Continues** Statens Jarnvagar (Sweden). Verksamhetsberattelse.

US/0092-6515
**AUTO-TRAIN MAGAZINE.** Vol. 1 (Nov. 1973)-. Periodical. English. qt. $3.00. Auto-Train Corporation, 1801 K Street NW, Washington DC 20006. **LC** F206; .A97. **DD** 917.5/04/405.

RU/0005-2329
**AVTOMATIKA, TELEMEHANIKA I SVJAZ.** (AVTOMATIKE, TELEMEKHANIKA I SVIAZ.). [Avtom., telemeh. svjaz]. **Added/Corp** Russia. Ministerstvo Putei Soobshcheniia. Vol. 1 (Jan. 1957)-. Periodical. Russian. mo. $99.95. **(Subscription address:** East View Publications Inc., 3020 Harbor Lane North, Suite 110, Minneapolis MN 55447.) **LC** TF615; .A85. **CODEN** ATSVAG. Documents available from Ask*IEEE.
  **Desc:** Information on railroads, automatic controls, and remote controls.
  **Ind/Abst** INSPEC (1968-); Pollut. Abstr. Indexes.

US
**AWARDS ... FIRST DIVISION, NATIONAL RAILROAD ADJUSTMENT BOARD. Main/Corp** United States. National Railroad Adjustment Board. V. 1- 1936-. Periodical. English. **LC** HD5503; .A3422. **DD** 331.1550973.

US/0362-2711
**B & M BULLETIN. Added/Corp** Boston and Maine Railroad Historical Society. **VAT** Boston and Maine Bulletin. (19??)-. Periodical. English. Four times a year. Boston and Maine Railroad Historical Society, PO Box 223 Harwood Station, Littleton MA 01460. **LC** TF25.B8; B15. **DD** 385/.0974.

US/0146-8707
**BAXTER'S EURAILPASS TRAVEL GUIDE. VFOAT** Eurailpass Travel Guide. 1972/73-. English. an. Rail Europe, PO Box 3255, Alexandria VA 22302. **LC** HE3004; .B284. **DD** 385/.2042/094. **Continues** Eurail, 0146-8723.

SA
**BEGROTING VAN DIE ADDISIONELE BEDRYFSUITGAWE. ESTIMATES OF THE ADDITIONAL WORKING EXPENDITURE. Main/Corp** South African Railways and Harbours. **Added/Corp** South African Railways and Harbours. Estimates of the Additional Working Expenditure. **VFOAT** Estimates of the Additional Working Expenditure. (19??)-. Afrikaans (English). R0.90. **LC** HE3426; .A4a. **DD** 354.680072/2253.

FR
**BILAN / OCTRA, LE. Main/Corp** Octra (Gabon). French. Cabinet Daniel Verpeaux, 35 Quai d'Anjou, 75004 Paris France. **LC** HE3438; .F87 SUPPL. **DD** 354.67/210087/5/06.

IT
**BOLLETTINO COMMERCIALE FF SS.** FF SS, Tesoreria, Cassa Abbon Boll Comm, P ZA Croce Rossa 1, 00161 Rome Italy.

CN/0824-233X
**BRANCHLINE (OTTAWA).** (BRANCHLINE / BYTOWN RAILWAY SOCIETY.). [Branchline]. **Added/Corp** Bytown Railway Society. (1961)-. Periodical. English. mo (except July and Aug. combined). $32.00. Bytown Railway Society, PO Box 141 Station A, Ottawa Ontario K1N 8V1 Canada. **Tel** (613)745-1201. **ED** David Stremes. **DD** 385/.0971. **Circ:** 850.
**Desc:** Contains news, features and numerous photographs of railway activities in Canada, both past and present. Also details changes in the motive power and rolling stock of Canadian railways.

US
**BRITAIN BY BRITRAIL. WRITTEN BY GEORGE WRIGHT FERGUSON. See** Travel and Tourism.

CN/0229-0553
**BRMNA JOURNAL.** (THE BRMNA JOURNAL.). [BRMNA j.]. **Added/Corp** British Railway Modellers of North America. **VAT** British Railway Modellers of North America Journal. (1968)-. Periodical. English. mo. Free. British Railway Modellers of North America, 666 Island Park Drive, Ottawa Ontario K1Y 0B7 Canada. **Tel** (613)728-1491, (613)829-1377. **ED** Graham Parsons. **DD** 625.1/9/05. **Bk Rev. Ad Acc.** ctrl circ. ***Continues*** *British Railway Modellers' Association Journal.*
**Desc:** Publication concerns railway modelling - all scales and aspects.

II/0536-9290
**BUDGET / GOVERNMENT OF INDIA, MINISTRY OF FINANCE. See** Public Administration-Public Finance and Taxation.

US/0003-0694
**BULLETIN - AMERICAN RAILWAY ENGINEERING ASSOCIATION.** [Bull. - Am. Railw. Eng. Assoc.]. **Main/Corp** American Railway Engineering Association. **VFOAT** AREA Bulletin. (1911)-. Bulletin. English. Five times a year (Jan., Mar., May, Oct., Dec.). $79.00 (surface mail); $127.00 (airmail). American Railway Engineering Association, 50 F Street Northwest, Suite 7702, Washington DC 20001. **Tel** (202)639-2190, FAX (202)639-2183. **ED** T. P. Smithberger. **DD** 625. Index available. **Ad Acc. Circ:** 4,200. available on microfilm. ***Continues*** *American Railway Engineering and Maintenance-of-Way Association. Bulletin.*
**Desc:** Contains reports of associations, technical committees, papers on railway engineering, construction, maintenance and research results.
**Ind/Abst** Ei Page One; GeoRef.

FR
**BULLETIN DE DOCUMENTATION ET D'INFORMATION - DIRECTION DES ETUDES GENERALES. Main/Corp** Regie Autonome des Transports Parisiens. Direction des Etudes Generales. **VFOAT** Documentation, Information - RATP. Bulletin. French. qt. Direction des Etudes Generales Augustins, 75271 Paris Cedex 06 France. **LC** HE4769.P33; R42. **DD** 388.4. ***Continues*** *Bulletin d'Information et de Documentation Generale.*

SZ/1011-3797
**BULLETIN DES TRANSPORTS INTERNATIONAUX FERROVIAIRES / ZEITSCHRIFT FUER DEN INTERNATIONALEN EISENBAHNVERKEHR.** [Bull. transp. int. ferrov.]. **Added/Corp** Central Office for International Carriage by Rail. **VFOAT** Zeitschrift fur den Internationalen Eisenbahnverkehr. No. 1/2 (Jan./Feb. 1986)-. Periodical. French (German). bm. Office Central des Transports Internationaux Ferroviaires, Gryphenhubeliweg 30, CH-3006 Berne Switzerland. **Tel** (031)43 17 62, FAX (031)43 11 64, telex 912 063 OCTI CH. ***Continues*** *Bulletin des Transports Internationaux par Chemins de Fer, 1015-2156.*

US/0147-0027
**BULLETIN - RAILROAD STATION HISTORICAL SOCIETY, THE. Main/Corp** Railroad Station Historical Society. (1968)-. Periodical. English. bm. $3.00 US; $5.00 other. J.B. Publishing Company, 430 Ivy Avenue, Crete NE 68333. **Tel** (402)826-3356.

US
**BULLETIN (TOY TRAIN OPERATING SOCIETY : 1973). See** Hobbies.

GW/0007-5876
**BUNDESBAHN, DIE.** ***Title Change.*** [Bundesbahn]. **Added/Corp** Deutsche Bundesbahn. Hauptverwaltung. Deutsche Bundesbahn. Vol. 23 No. 18 (Sept. 1949)-(1992). Academic Scholarly Publication. German. mo. Hestra Verlag Hernincel & Dr Strauss GmbH & Co KG, Postfach 4244, D 64201 Darmstadt Germany. **Tel** 011 49 6151 39070. **ED** Elmar Haas. **LC** HE1001; .R35. **[CCC]. Ad Acc. Circ:** 10,000 (ctrl). ***Continues*** *Reichsbahn.* ***Continued by*** *Deutsche Bahn.*
**Desc:** Official review of the German Federal Railways.
**Ind/Abst** EMBASE; Int. Civil Eng. Abstr.; Soft. Abstr. Eng.

JA
**BUSINESS REPORT. Main/Corp** Japan Freight Railway Company. (19??)-. English. Japan Freight Railway Company, 6-5 Marunouchi 1-Chome, Chiyoda-ku, Tokyo 100 Japan. ***Continues in part*** *Nihon Kokuyu Tetsudo. Facts and Figures.*

CN/0008-4875
**CANADIAN RAIL. Added/Corp** Canadian Railroad Historical Association. No. 135 (July/Aug. 1962)-. Periodical. English (French). bm. 27.00Can$ Canada; $23.00 US. Canadian Railroad Historical Association, 120 rue Staint Pierre, St Constant Quebec, J5A 2G9 Canada. **Tel** (514)484-4815. **ED** Fred Angus. **Bk Rev. Circ:** 1,300. ***Continues*** *Canadian Railroad Historical Association. CRHA News Report.*
**Desc:** Covers the latest in technological developments, historical articles and essays, and photo stories of Canada's railways.

CN/0226-157X
**CANADIAN RAILWAY CLUB NEWS.** [Can. Railw. Club news]. **Main/Corp** Canadian Railway Club. **VFOAT** Nouvelles Club du Rail Canadien. Vol. 1 (Jan. 1979)-. Periodical. English (French). Three times a year (April, August, and December). 15.00Can$. Canadian Railway Club, PO Box 162 Station A, Montreal Quebec H3C 1C5 Canada. **Tel** (514)634-4515. **ED** J. H. Glatzmayer. **DD** 385/.06/071. **Ad Acc. Circ:** 1,600 (ctrl).

CN/0849-2964
**CANADIAN RAILWAY MODELLER.** [Can. railw. model.]. Train 1, Track 1 (May/June 1990)-. Periodical. English. Six times a year (Feb., Apr., June, Aug., Sept., Nov.). 22.00Can$ Canada; 28.00Can$ other. Canadian Railway Modeller, PO Box 28103, 1453 Henderson Way, Winnipeg Manitoba R2G 4E9 Canada. **Tel** (204)668-0168. **ED** Morgan B. Turwey. **DD** 625.1/9/05. Index Available Published separately--free--upon request. cum. index. **Bk Rev. Ad Acc. Pr Rev. Circ:** 4,000.
**Desc:** Model Train Wobby Magazine featuring canadian content with construction with all usual magazine features.

CN/0829-3023
**CANADIAN TRACKSIDE GUIDE.** [Can. trackside guide]. **Added/Corp** Bytown Railway Society. **VFOAT** Trackside Guide. **VAT** Trackside Guide (1985). (1985)-. English. an (March). $15.95. Bytown Railway Society, PO Box 141 Station A, Ottawa Ontario K1N 8V1 Canada. **Tel** (613)745-1201. **ED** David Stremes. **DD** 625.2/0971. ***Continues*** *Trackside Guide., 0825-2408.*
**Desc:** Comprehensive guide to Canadian railways.

CN/0045-5466
**CANADIAN TRANSPORT.** ***Title Change.*** **VFOAT** Transport Canadien. Began publication in 1954. Periodical. English (French). mo. Canadian Brotherhood of Railroad Employees, 2300 Carling Avenue, Ottawa Ontario K2B 2G1 Canada. available on microfilm from University Microfilms International (UMI). ***Continues*** *Canadian Railway Employees' Monthly, 0319-6933.* ***Continued by*** *Transport Canadien.*

US
**CAR AND LOCOMOTIVE CYCLOPEDIA OF AMERICAN PRACTICE. Added/Corp** Association of American Railroads. Mechanical Division. **VFOAT** Car and Locomotive Cyclopedia. (1966)-. English. ir. $69.95. Simmons Boardman Publishing Corporation / Nebraska, 1809 Capitol Avenue, Omaha NE 68102. **Tel** (402)346-4300. **ED** K G Ellsworth. **LC** TF373; .C27. **Ad Acc. Circ:** 5,500. ***Formed by the union of*** *Locomotive Cyclopedia of American Practice* ***and*** *Car Builders' Cyclopedia of American Practice.*
**Desc:** Provides definitions, illustrations and descriptions of railroad cars and locomotives built for domestic and export service and other pertinent data.

US/0008-9532
**CENTRAL RAILWAY CHRONICLE.** Periodical. English. qt. $3.00. Central Railway Club of Buffalo, 39 Paul Place, Buffalo NY 14210. **ED** Clarence M Voll. **Bk Rev. Ad Acc. Circ:** 300 (ctrl).
**Desc:** Reports of meetings, concentrated reports of railroad operation and railroad history.

US
**CHAPTER AND RAIL NEWS AS VIEWED FROM THE OBSERVATION PLATFORM. Main/Corp** Railway and Locomotive Historical Society. Southern California Chapter. (1960)-. Periodical. English. ir (10-12 issues per year). $15.00. Southern California Chapter of RLHS, 6006 Wooster Street, Los Angeles CA 90056. **Tel** (310)670-4235. **ED** Ed Cheetham.

FR/0009-2924
**CHEMINS DE FER : BULLETIN OFFICIEL. Added/Corp** Association Francaise des Amis des Chemins de Fer. (1927)-. Periodical. French. Six times a year. 274.24F France; 320.00F EEC Countries, Austria and Switzerland; 340.00F other. Association Francaise des Amis des Chemins de Fer, Gare de l' Est, Cour Sout Bag 9, 75475 Paris Cedex 10 France. **Tel** 011 33 1 40382092. **Ad Acc. Circ:** 4,000 (ctrl).
**Desc:** Technical and historic studies of France and foreigner railways - national, city lines, and subways.

CC
**CHI CHE TIEN CHUAN TUNG. Added/Corp** Tieh Tao Pu Chu-Chou Tien Li Chi Che Yen Chiu So (China). **VFOAT** Jichedianchuandong; Electric Drive for Locomotive. (19??)-. Periodical. Chinese. Four times a year. $31.20. Guozi Shudian, PO Box 399, Chegongzhuang Xilu 35, Beijing, People's Republic of China. **Tel** 1 8414284, FAX 1 8412023, telex 22496. **(Subscription address:** China International Book Trading Corporation, PO Box 399, Library Service Department, Beijing 100044 People's Republic of China.**)** **ED** Li Guo-Luan, Lou Xiou-Li, Qian Xiou-Hua, Zhang Ji-Gui, Luo Xian-Zhong. **LC** TF975; .C49. **DD** 625.2/63/05. **Circ:** 5,000 (ctrl).
**Desc:** Concerned with the general trend of affairs of railway motive power, scientific and research development in the electrical drive of the electric locomotive unit train and diesel locomotive, as well as their manufacturing, service and maintenance.

KO
**CHOLTO CHARYANG KISUL / ROLLING STOCK ENGINEERING. Added/Corp** Cholto Charyang Kisul Kongsa (Korea). **VFOAT** Rolling Stock Engineering. (19??)-. Periodical. Korean. qt. Not for sale. Cholto Charyang Kisul Kongsa, 17-2 Piltong 2-ka Chung-ku, Seoul Korea. **Tel** (02)275-6591-3. **ED** Kyung Lak Woo. **LC** TF371; .C47. **Circ:** 1,000 (ctrl).

KO
**CHOLTO TONGGYE YONBO.** ***Ceased.*** **Added/Corp** Korea (South). Choltochong. **VFOAT** Statistical Yearbook of Railroad. (19??)-(19??). Korean (English). an. **LC** HE3360.5; .C48. **DD** 385/.09519/5. ***Continues*** *Cholto Yonbo.*

CN/0383-2449
**CIGGT REPORT.** [CIGGT rep.]. **VFOAT** C I G G T Report. **VAT** Canadian Institute of Guided Ground Transport Report. No. 1972-. Monographic series. English. Price varies per volume. Canadian Institute of Guided Ground Transport, Queen's University, Kingston Ontario K7L 3N6 Canada. **DD** 625.1. ***Continues*** *Working Paper Series (Canadian Institute of Guided Ground Transport), 0702-8709.*

US/0148-723X
**CIRCULAR - ASSOCIATION OF AMERICAN RAILROADS, MECHANICAL DIVISION. Main/Corp** Association of American Railroads. Mechanical Division. (19??)-. English. $100.00 (members), $150.00 (nonmembers). Association of American Railroads, 50 F Street Northwest, Room 5401, Washington DC 20001. **Tel** (202)639-2550. **LC** TF340; .A85a.

US
**CLASS I FREIGHT RAILROADS SELECTED EARNINGS DATA / INTERSTATE COMMERCE COMMISSION, BUREAU OF ACCOUNTS. Added/Corp** United States. Interstate Commerce Commission. Bureau of Accounts. **VFOAT** Class 1 Freight Railroads Selected Earnings Data; Class One Freight Railroads Selected Earnings Data. (June 30, 1983)-. Periodical. English. qt. Free on request. Interstate Commerce Commission / Bureau of Accountants, Room 3349 ICC Building, Washington DC 20423. **Tel** (202)275-7351. **LC** HE2355; .C57. **DD** 385/.1. ***Continues*** *Class I Freight Line-Haul Railroads Selected Earnings Data, 0749-548X.*

US/0193-3477
**CLEAR TRACK. Added/Corp** National Railroad Construction and Maintenance Association. (197?)-. Periodical. English. Ten times a year. $20.00 (one year); $36.00 (two years); $54.00 (three years). National Railroad Construction & Maintenance, 9331 Waymond Avenue, Highland IN 46332. **Tel** (219)924-1709.

US/1061-9739
**CN LINES. VFOAT** CN Lines.; Canadian Lines Newsletter. (1991)-. English. qt. $16.00 US; $20.00Can$ Canada; $36.00 (airmail), $24.00 (surface mail) other. CN Lines, 2488 Paige Janette Drive, Harvey LA 70058. **Tel** (504)347-0503. **ED** Mike Christian. **Bk Rev. Circ:** 350 (ctrl).
**Desc:** Publication of the CN Lines Special Interest Group of the National Model Railroad Association. The CN Lines SIG is a non-profit organization founded for the purpose of providing a forum for those sharing a common interest in the Canadian National family of railroads.

US
**COLORADO RAIL ANNUAL.** (19??)-. English. an. $42.95 per copy. Colorado Railroad Museum, PO Box 10, Golden CO 80402. **Tel** (303)279-4591, (800)365-6263, FAX (303)279-4229.

●CN/1189-363X
**CP RAIL SYSTEM NEWS.** [CP Rail Syst. news]. **Added/Corp** CP Rail. **VAT** Canadian Pacific Rail System News. Vol.22, No.1 Feb. (1992)-. Periodical. English. ir (16 issues per year). Limited free distribution. CP Trucks, Public Relations, 2255 Sheppard Ave. E, Suite 335, Willowdale Ontario N2J 4Y1 Canada. **Tel** (514)395-7596. **ED** Tim Humphreys. **DD** 385. **Circ:** 50,000. ***Continues*** *CP Rail News., 0229-8694.*

SZ/0933-7598
**DAMPF & REISE, UBERSEEISCHE BAHNEN.** **VFOAT** Dampf und Reise, Uberseeische Bahnen; Overseas Railways. German. qt. 57.00F. Quellenhof-Verlag, Bahnhofstrasse 47, Postfach 207, CH-9202 Gossau 1 Switzerland. **LC** TF3; .D36. **DD** 385/.05. ***Formed by the union of*** *Dampf & Reise, 0930-6684* ***and*** *Ueberseeische Bahnen, 1010-5093.*

GW
**DB; DEINE BAHN.** **VFOAT** Deine Bahn. Periodical. German. DM45.60 (add DM13.20 for postage). Eisenbahn-Fachverlag GmbH, Postfach 2330, 65 Mainz Germany. **Tel** 06131-222871, FAX 06131-227969. **LC** TF3; .D13. **DD** 625.1/00943. Index available. **Ad Acc.** ctrl circ. ***Formed by the union of*** *Eisenbahnfachmann* ***and*** *Eisenbahner.*

US
**DELAWARE VALLEY RAIL PASSENGER, THE.** (Jan. 1983)-. English. mo. Must order direct from the publisher. Delaware Valley Association of Railroad Passengers, PO Box 7505, Philadelphia PA 19101. **Tel** (215)222-3373. **ED** Matthew Mitchell. Index available (published separately). **Bk Rev**, (Qty: varies). **Ad Acc**, **Adv Mgr:** (same as editor). **Circ:** 1,300. available via electronic mail from Internet.
**Desc:** News and analysis of rail transit commuter rail and other mass transit issues in the greater Philadelphia area.

GW
**DEUTSCHE BAHN, DIE.** ***Ceased.*** **Added/Corp** Deutsche Bundesbahn. Deutsche Reichsbahn (Germany). (May 1992)-(Dec. 1993). German. mo. Hestra Verlag Hernincel & Dr Strauss GmbH & Co KG, Postfach 4244, D 64201 Darmstadt Germany. **Tel** 011 49 6151 39070. **LC** HE1001; .R35. ***Continues*** *Bundesbahn, 0007-5876.*

GW
**DEUTSCHES BUNDESBAHN-ADRESSBUCH. TEIL 2 : GLEISANSCHLUSSBESITZER UND-MITBENUTZER.** **VAT** Deutsches Bundesbahn-Adressbuch. Teil Zwei: Gleisanschlussbesitzer und- Mitbenutzer. German. an. Hestra Verlag Hernincel & Dr Strauss GmbH & Co KG, Postfach 4244, D 64201 Darmstadt Germany. **Tel** 011 49 6151 39070. **LC** TF73; .D44.

UK
**DEVELOPING METROS.** (1985)-. Periodical. English. an. Comes with Subway to Railway Gazette International. Transport Press, Quadrant House, Sutton Surrey SM2 5AS England. **LC** HE4201; .D48. **DD** 308.4/28/05.

US/0732-9873
**DIRECTORY / TOY TRAIN OPERATING SOCIETY.** See Gifts, Toys.

BE
**DOCUMENTATION - SNCB, DIRECTION DU PERSONNEL ET DES SERVICES SOCIAUX.** **Main/Corp** Societe Nationale des Chemins de fer Belges. Direction du Personnel et des Services Sociaux. **VFOAT** Documentatie - NMBS, Directie van het Personnel en de Sociale Diensten; Bulletin Documentation; Documentatiebulletin. Dutch. ir. 750F. Services Generaux, Affaires Generales, Bureau 01 012 Section 80-1, Documentation Bibliotheque, rue de France 85, 1070 Bruxelles Belgium. **Tel** (02)5238080. **LC** Z7231; .S62A. **DD** 016.385/09493. ***Supersedes*** *Bulletin Mensuel de Documentation.*
**Desc:** Railway transportation articles.

US/0883-1831
**DSI-RAIL ROUTING SUPPLEMENT, THE.** [DSI rail routing suppl.]. **VFOAT** DSI Rail Routing Supplement. **VAT** Distribution Sciences Inc. Rail Routing Supplement. English. bm. $15.00. National Railway Publishing Company, 424 West 33rd Street, New York NY 10001. **Tel** (212)714-3100. **LC** HE2353; .D75. **DD** 385/.24/0973.

PL
**DZIENNIK TARYF I ZARZADEN KOLEJOWYCH. WYDAWNICTWO MINISTERSTWA KOMUNIKACJI.** **Main/Corp** Poland. Ministerstwo Komunikacji. Yr. 1- 1. July 1928-. Polish. **LC** HE3139.7; .A285. **DD** 385.09438.

GW/0071-0075
**EISENBAHN INGENIEUR KALENDER.** (1988)-. German. an. DM27.00. Tetzlaff Verlag GmbH, Postfach 101609, D-20010 Hamburg Germany. **Tel** 011 49 40 2371401, telex 419258. **ED** Verband Deutscher. **LC** TP73; .E37. **DD** 625.1/0943. Index available. **Ad Acc.** **Circ:** 9,450. ***Continues*** *Taschenbuch der Eisenbahntechnik.*
**Desc:** Railroad engineering, construction, telecommunication, signaling, machinery and electro-engineering.

GW/0013-2810
**EISENBAHNINGENIEUR, DER.** [Eisenbahningenieur]. Academic Scholarly Publication. German (summaries and/or abstracts in English and French). mo. DM128.40 (subscription); DM12.90 (single copies). Tetzlaff Verlag GmbH, Postfach 101609, D-20010 Hamburg Germany. **Tel** 011 49 40 2371401, telex 419258. **CODEN** ESBGAP. **[CCC]**. Index available. **Bk Rev.** **Ad Acc.** **Circ:** 11,500. Documents available from Ask*IEEE. ***Continues*** *Zeitschrift - Verein Deutscher Eisenbahningenieure;* ***Absorbed*** *Eisenbahnbau; Eisenbahntechnik.*
**Desc:** All questions of engineering in the field of railroad technology are covered.
**Ind/Abst** Ei Page One; EMBASE; Energy Res. Abstr. (Aug. 1972-); INSPEC (April 1981-); Int. Civil Eng. Abstr.

RU/0422-9274
**ELEKTRICESKAJA I TEPLOVOZNAJA TJAGA.** ***Title Change.*** (ELEKTRICHESKAIA I TEPLOVOZNAIA TIAGA.). [Elektr. teplovoz. tjaga]. **Added/Corp** Soviet Union. Ministerstvo Putei Soobshcheniia. **VFOAT** ETT. (1957)-(199?). Periodical. Russian. mo. **(Subscription address:** East View Publications Inc., 3020 Harbor Lane North, Suite 110, Minneapolis MN 55447.**)** **LC** TF4; .E45. **CODEN** ETTYA6. Documents available from Ask*IEEE. ***Continued by*** *Lokomotiv.*
**Ind/Abst** Energy Res. Abstr. (March 1978-); INSPEC (Dec. 1968-1985).

GW/0013-5437
**ELEKTRISCHE BAHNEN.** (ELEKTRISCHE BAHNEN; ZENTRALBLATT FUER ELEKTRISCHEN ZUGBETRIEB UND ALLE ARTEN VON TRIEBFAHRZEUGEN MIT ELEKTRISCHEM ANTRIEB.). [Elektr. Bahnen]. (1925)-. Periodical. English. mo. DM298.00. R Oldenbourg Verlag, Postfach 801360, D 81613 Munich Germany. **Tel** 011 49 89 450190, FAX 011 49 89 45019305. **LC** TF701; .E32. **CODEN** ELBAAQ. **[CCC]**. Index available. **Bk Rev.** **Ad Acc.** **Circ:** 2,000. available on microfilm and microfiche from University Microfilms International (UMI). Documents available from Article Express International, Ask*IEEE. ***Absorbed*** *Zentralblatt fuer den Elektrischen Zugbetrieb.*
**Desc:** Current information on all areas of technology connected with railways, such as machine technology, electrical and information systems and safety.
**Ind/Abst** Bioeng. Abstr.; Coal Abstr.; Ei Page One; Energy Res. Abstr. (Sept. 1976-); Eng. Index Annu.; INSPEC (1968-); Int. Aerosp. Abstr.

GW/0013-2845
**ETR.** (ETR; EISENBAHNTECHNISCHE RUNDSCHAU.). [ETR Eisenbahntech. rundsh.]. **VFOAT** Eisenbahntechnische Rundschau. (1952)-. Academic Scholarly Publication. German (English, French and Spanish). mo (10 issues per year). DM242.40 Germany; DM250.80 other. Hestra Verlag Hernincel & Dr Strauss GmbH & Co KG, Postfach 4244, D 64201 Darmstadt Germany. **Tel** 011 49 6151 39070. **ED** E Schreck, T Hafner. **[CCC]**. **Bk Rev.** **Ad Acc.** **Circ:** 6,050.
**Desc:** German publication for the whole field of railroading.
**Ind/Abst** EMBASE; Energy Res. Abstr. (April 1978-); Highw. Res. Abstr.

US/0085-0330
**EURAIL GUIDE.** (1971)-. English. an (January). $15.84 (public libraries); $16.43 (private libraries). Houghton Mifflin Company, Wayside Road, Burlington MA 01803. **Tel** (800)225-3362, (617)272-1500. **LC** HE3004; .E88. **DD** 914/.0455/05. **Bk Rev.**
**Desc:** Complete information concerning every tourist train ride in the world. Covers 112 countries.

US/0272-7021
**EXAMINATION OF UNITED STATES RAILWAY ASSOCIATION'S FINANCIAL STATEMENTS.** English. US General Accounting Office / District of Columbia, 441 G Street NW, Room 4528, Washington DC 20548. **Tel** (202)275-2812. **LC** HE2714; .U54A. **DD** 353.0087/5/06.

JA
**FACT BOOK.** **Main/Corp** Higashi Nihon Ryokaku Tetsudo Kabushiki Kaisha. **VFOAT** East Japan Railway Company Fact Book. (1990)-. English. East Japan Railway Company, 6-5 Marunouchi 1-Chome, Chiyoda-ku, Tokyo 100 Japan. ***Continues in part*** *Nihon Kokuyu Tetsudo. Facts and Figures.*

US
**FAHRT FREI (MICROFORM).** Began publication in 1949. German. bw. Deutscher Judo Verband, Redaktion Ippon Segewaldweg 40, D 12557 Berlin Germany. **Tel** 011 49 711 210770, telex 051 678. **LC** MICROFILM 05509 HE; HE3080.5. ***Formed by the union of*** *Verkehr: Ausgabe Eisenbahn.*

US
**FEDERAL RAILROAD ADMINISTRATION SPRING PREVIEW.** **Main/Corp** United States. Federal Railroad Administration. English. an. US Department of Transportation / Federal Railroad Administration, 400 Seventh Street SW, Washington DC 20590. **Tel** (202)366-0881, FAX (202)366-7009.

BL
**FERROVIAS DO BRASIL.** 1946-. Portuguese. Ministerio dos Transportes, Rede Ferroviaria Federal, Praca Procopio Ferreira/B6, 20-021 Rio de Janeiro RJ Brazil. **Tel** 533 3094, telex (021)30939. **LC** HE2921; .F4. **DD** 385.

US/0098-3128
**FINANCIAL CONDITION OF PENN CENTRAL TRANSPORTATION COMPANY, THE.** (THE FINANCIAL CONDITION OF PENN CENTRAL TRANSPORTATION COMPANY: ANNUAL REPORT TO THE PRESIDENT AND THE CONGRESS.). **Main/Corp** United States. Dept. of Transportation. (19??)-. English. an. US Department of Transportation - Federal Highway Administration, 400 Seventh Street Southwest, Washington DC 20590. **Tel** (202)366-0660. **LC** HE2791; .P4326. **DD** 385/.1/06574.

US/0271-7638
**FLAGS, DIAMONDS, AND STATUES.** **Added/Corp** Anthracite Railroads Historical Society (U.S.). (19??)-. Periodical. English. qt. $20.00. Anthracite Railroads Historical Society, PO Box 119, Bridgeport PA 19405. **ED** Richard W Jahn. **LC** TF23.1; .F56. **DD** 385/.09748. Index available. **Circ:** 3,000 (ctrl).
**Desc:** Historical articles dealing with the motive power, right-of-way and corporate aspects of the Anthracite railroads of Pennsylvania (LV, RDG, CNJ, DL&W, and LNE).

US/1053-959X
**FLORIDA RAILROAD DIRECTORY.** [Fla. railr. dir.]. (1991)-. Directory. English. $7.95. Forrester Communications, PO Box 421901, Kissimmee FL 34742. **DD** 385.

UK/0264-5769
**FRENCH RAILWAY REVIEW.** [Fr. railw. rev.]. Vol. 1, No. 1 (April 1983)-. Periodical. English (French). bm. $96.00. North Oxford Academic, 242 Banbury Road, Oxford OX2 7DW England. **Tel** 0865 51 1166. **LC** TF1; .R72. **DD** 625.1/005. Documents available from Ask*IEEE.
**Ind/Abst** Ei Page One; INSPEC (April 1983-).

FR
**FUTURAIL : REVUE BIMESTRIELLE DE L'OCTRA - OFFICE DU CHEMIN DE FER TRANSGABONAIS.** Periodical. French. bm. 200F. Cabinet Daniel Verpeaux, 35 Quai d'Anjou, 75004 Paris France. **LC** HE3438; .F87. **DD** 385/.0967/21.

US/0747-0622
**GARDEN RAILWAYS.** [Gard. railw.]. **VFOAT** Garden Railways Magazine. Vol. 1, No. 1 (Jan./Feb. 1984)-. Periodical. English. Six times a year. $21.00 US; $28.00 other. Sidestreet Bannerworks, PO Box 61461, Denver CO 80206. **Tel** (303)733-4779. **ED** Marc Horovitz and Barbara Horovitz. **DD** 625. Index available. **Bk Rev.** **Ad Acc.** **Circ:** 12,000.
**Desc:** For outdoor model railroaders. Features everything of interest to gauge O and gauge I modelers working in the backyard.

AU
**GESCHAFTSBERICHT UND RECHNUNGSABSCHLUSS - STEIERMARKISCHE LANDESBAHNEN.** **Main/Corp** Steiermarkische Landesbahnen. (19??)-. German. Radetzky Strasse 31, A-8010, Graz Austria. **Tel** 011 0043 316 8125 810, FAX 011 0043 316 8125 8125. **LC** HE3060.S74; S74a. available on diskette.

US/1048-8685
**GREAT MODEL RAILROADS.** ***Ceased.*** [Great model railr.]. **VFOAT** Model Railroader Presents Great Model Railroads. (1991)-(19??). Periodical. English. an. Kalmbach Publishing Company, PO Box 1612, Waukesha WI 53187. **Tel** (414)796-8776 ext.411, FAX (414)796-0126. **LC** TF197; .G65. **DD** 625.1/9/05.

●RU
**GUDOK.** (1993)-. Russian. ir. $199.95. **(Subscription address:** East View Publications Inc., 3020 Harbor Lane North, Suite 110, Minneapolis MN 55447.**)**
**Ind/Abst** Curr. Dig. Post Sov. Press.

US/0091-8059
**HEADLIGHTS (NEW YORK).** (HEADLIGHTS.). **Added/Corp** Electric Railroaders' Association. Vol. 23, No. 1 (Jan. 1961)-. Periodical. English. ir. $16.00 US; $19.00 Canada and Mexico; $21.00 other. Electric Railroaders Association, PO Box 3323, New York NY 10163. **Tel** (212)986-4482. **LC** TF701; .E113. **DD** 388.4/2. ***Continues*** *ERA Headlights.*

US
**ILLINOIS RAIL PLAN ... UPDATE.** Began in 1978. English. an. Illinois Department of Transportation, Auditorium, 2300 South Dirksen Parkway, Springfield IL 62764. **LC** HE2709; .I28B. **DD** 385/.068. ***Continues*** *Illinois Rail System Plan, Annual Update.*

II/0019-6266
**INDIAN RAILWAY TECHNICAL BULLETIN.** (1954)-. Periodical. Multiple languages. qt. $20.00. **(Subscription address:** Prints India, 11 Darya Ganj, New Delhi 110002 India.**)** **UDC** 621.1.

II/0019-6274
**INDIAN RAILWAYS. Added/Corp** India (Republic). Railway Board. Vol. 1 (Apr. 1956)-. Periodical. English. mo. $8.50. The Ministry of Railways, Government of India, New Delhi India. **(Subscription address:** Prints India, 11 Darya Ganj, New Delhi 110002 India.**)** **LC** TF4; .I55.

US
**INDIANA RAIL PLAN UPDATE. Added/Corp** Indiana. Division of Railroads. English. Public Service Commission of Indiana, 901 State Office Building, 100 North Senate Avenue, Indianapolis IN 46204. ***Continues*** *Indiana ... State Rail Plan Update.*

IT/0021-3128
**INFORMAZIONI DOC.** [Inf. doc]. (1961)-. Periodical. Multiple languages. bm (6 issues). L60000.00. Ente FS Funz Studi Istit Inter, Bibl Cent P Za Croce Rossa 1, 00161 Rome Italy. **Tel** 011 39 6 8490 2174. **UDC** 625.

UK/0744-5326
**INTERNATIONAL RAILWAY JOURNAL AND RAPID TRANSIT REVIEW.** (INTERNATIONAL RAILWAY JOURNAL AND RAPID TRANSIT REVIEW : IRJ.). [Int. railw. j. rapid transit rev.]. **VFOAT** IRJ; International Railway Journal. Vol. 19, No. 1 (Jan. 1979)-. Academic Scholarly Publication. English (summaries and/or abstracts in French, German and Spanish). mo. $35.00 (one year), $60.00 (two year). Simmons Boardman Publishing Corporation / New York, 345 Hudson Street, New York NY 10014. **Tel** (402)346-4740. **(Subscription address:** Simmons Boardman Publishing Corporation, PO Box 986, Omaha NE 68101.**)** **ED** Mike Knutton. **LC** TF1; .I626. **DD** 385/.05. **[CCC].** Index available (free). **Bk Rev. Ad Acc. Circ:** 9,400 (ctrl). available on microfilm and microfiche from University Microfilms International (UMI). ***Continues*** *International Railway Journal (New York, N.Y.), 0020-8450.*
**Desc:** Worldwide railway developments analysed in business and economic terms for principal officers of railways, and railway equipment manufacturers and suppliers.
**Ind/Abst** EMBASE.

US/0891-7655
**INTERNATIONAL RAILWAY TRAVELER, THE.** (198?)-. Periodical. English. bm. $39.95 US; $41.45 Canada; $45.95 other. International Railway Traveler, 1810 Sils Avenue #306B, Louisville KY 40205. **Tel** (502)454-0277, FAX (502)458-8901. **ED** Gena Holle. **Bk Rev. Ad Acc. Circ:** 3,500.
**Desc:** Covers railways from the traveler's point of view, offering features and hard information on luxury, high-speed, overnight, mountain, Third-World and urban rail journeys worldwide.

US/0147-2178
**INTERSTATE COMMERCE COMMISSION'S REPORT TO THE PRESIDENT AND THE CONGRESS. EFFECTIVENESS OF THE ACT. AMTRAK.** (AMTRAK : EFFECTIVENESS OF THE ACT.). **Main/Corp** United States. Interstate Commerce Commission. **VFOAT** Report on the Effectiveness the Rail Passenger Service Act of 1970 (Public Law 91-518). English. an. $1.50 per issue. Interstate Commerce Commission / Bureau of Accountants, Room 3349 ICC Building, Washington DC 20423. **Tel** (202)275-7351. **LC** HE2708; .I46. **DD** 385/.0973.

US
**IRON HORSE NEWS.** (19??)-. English. bm (6 issues). Free on request. Colorado Railroad Museum, PO Box 10, Golden CO 80402. **Tel** (303)279-4591, (800)365-6263, FAX (303)279-4229.

GW/0075-2479
**JAHRBUCH DES EISENBAHNWESENS.** [Jahrb. Eisenbahnwes.]. (1950)-. German. an. DM39.60. Hestra Verlag Hernincel & Dr Strauss GmbH & Co KG, Postfach 4244, D 64201 Darmstadt Germany. **Tel** 011 49 6151 39070. **LC** HE3071; .A14. **Ad Acc. Circ:** 5,500.
**Desc:** Official yearbook of the German railways.
**Ind/Abst** Energy Res. Abstr. (Dec. 1981-).

UK/0075-3084
**JANE'S WORLD RAILWAYS.** 1st Ed., (1951)-. English. an. $285.00 US & Mexico; $349.13 others. Jane's Information Group, Sentinel House, 163 Brighton Road, Coulsdon Surrey CR3 2NX England. **Tel** 011 44 81 763 1030, FAX 011 44 81 763 1006. **ED** Geoffrey Freeman Allen. **LC** TF1; .J3. **DD** 385.05. **[CCC]. Ad Acc.**
**Desc:** Reference guide to all rail transport. Divided into two main sections- manufacturers and systems. Details cover all types of equipment and rail networks by country.

JA/0448-8938
**JAPANESE RAILWAY ENGINEERING.** [Jpn. railw. eng.]. **Added/Corp** Nihon Tetsudo Gijutsu Kyokai. Vol. 1 (July 1959)-. Periodical. English (summaries and/or abstracts in French and Spanish). sa. $100.00. Japan Railway Engineers Association. **(Subscription address:** Maruzen Company Ltd., PO Box 5050, Import & Export Department, Tokyo 100 31 Japan.**)** **LC** TF4; .J3. **CODEN** JAREBT. ctrl circ. Documents available from Article Express International, Ask*IEEE.
**Desc:** Introduces the techniques of Japanese railways to the world.
**Ind/Abst** Bioeng. Abstr.; Ei Page One; Eng. Index Annu.; INSPEC (1979-).

SW
**JARNVAGSHOBBY.** (1976)-. Periodical. Swedish. Forlag J Jango, Riksradsvagen 78, S-121 60 Johanneshov Sweden. **Tel** 46 8 59 22 77. **ED** Jan Jango. **LC** TF197; .J24. **Circ:** 6,000.
**Desc:** Book series covering all types of railroad hobbies in Sweden; model railroad building, clubs, veteran railroads and private collecting.

UK/0031-5524
**JOURNAL AND REPORT OF PROCEEDINGS - PERMANENT WAY INSTITUTION. See** Engineering-Civil Engineering.

US/1045-067X
**JOURNAL OF RAILWAY TANK CARS.** [J. railw. tank cars]. **Added/Corp** Society of Freight Car Historians. Vol. 1, Pt. 1 (Feb. 1990)-. English. sa. $10.00. Journal of Railway Tank Cars, PO Box 2480, Monrovia CA 91017. **DD** 385.

JA/0447-2322
**JREA.** Periodical. Japanese. mo. ¥450 single issue. Nihon Tetsudo Gijutsu Kyokai Suidobashi Nishiguchi Kaikan Nai, 20-8 Misaki-cho 2-chome Chiyoda-ku, Tokyo-to 101 Japan. **LC** TF4; .J7.

US/0744-4036
**KEYSTONE (PITTSBURGH, PA. 1968), THE.** (THE KEYSTONE : OFFICIAN PUBLICATION OF THE PENNSYLVANIA RAILROAD TECHNICAL ADN HISTORICAL SOCIETY.). [Keystone]. Vol. 1, No. 1 (Apr. 1968)-. Periodical. English. qt. $25.00 US and Canada; $35.00 other. Business Office of Pennsylvania Railroad Technical and Historical Society, PO Box 389, Upper Darby PA 19082. **ED** Charles Blardone, Jr. **Bk Rev. Circ:** 2,700 (ctrl).
**Desc:** Contains articles about locomotives, cars, facilities and operating practices of the Pennsylvania Railroad.

DK
**KREPLAN. Main/Corp** Denmark. Generaldirektratet for Statsbanerne. Danish. 5KR. Generaldirektratet for Statsbanerne, Slvgade 40, 1349 Kbenhavn Denmark. **LC** HE3151; .A53A.

GW
**KURSBUCH - DEUTSCHE BUNDESBAHN. Main/Corp** Deutsche Bundesbahn. (19??)-. German. DM15.00. DBAG, Geschaftsbereich, Fernverkehr, Kaiserstrasse 3, D 55116 Mainz Germany. **Tel** 061 31 15 54 18, FAX 061 31 15 57 65. **LC** HE3074; .A117. available on diskette; available on CD-ROM. ***Continues*** *Amtliches Kursbuch.*

GW
**KURSBUCH: INTERNATIONALER + I.E. UND BINNENVERKEHR. Main/Corp** Deutsche Reichbahn (East Germany). **VFOAT** Kursbuch der Dr Internationaler + I.E. und Binnenverkehr. Multiple languages (English, French, German and Russian). sa. DM3.50 single issue. Wilhelm-Pick-Str 49, 1054 Berlin Germany. **LC** HE3080.5; .A262A. **DD** 385/.2/09431.

US/0364-5177
**LIVE STEAM.** Periodical. English. mo. Live Steam, PO Box 629, Traverse City MI 49684. **Tel** (616)941-7160. **LC** TJ630; .L58. **DD** 621.1/05. available on microfilm and microfiche from University Microfilms International (UMI). ***Continues*** *Live Steam Magazine, 0300-7804.*

US/0891-7647
**LOCOMOTIVE & RAILWAY PRESERVATION.** [Locomot. railw. preserv.]. **VFOAT** Locomotive and Railway Preservation. Vol. 1, No. 1 (Mar. 1986)-. Periodical. English. Six times a year. $21.50. Locomotive & Railway Reserve, PO Box 95, Richmond VT 05477. **Tel** (802)434-2351, FAX (802)343-4803. **(Subscription address:** Pentrex Publishing, PO Box 17095, North Hollywood CA 91615.**)**

US/0898-8625
**LOCOMOTIVE ENGINEER NEWSLETTER, THE.** [Locomot. eng. newsl.]. **VFOAT** Locomotive Engineer. (1987)-. Newsletter. English. mo. Brotherhood of Locomotive Engineers, 1370 Ontario Street, Standard Building MZ, Cleveland OH 44113. **Tel** (216)241-2630. ***Continues in part*** *Locomotive Engineer.*

US/0741-8760
**LOCOMOTIVE (HARTFORD, CONN.), THE.** (THE LOCOMOTIVE.). [Locomotive]. **Added/Corp** Hartford Steam Boiler Inspection and Insurance Company. (1867)-. Periodical. English. Eight times a year. Hartford Company 56, 1 State Street, Hartford CT 06102. **Tel** (203)722-1866. **ED** Nancy E. Bergeron. **LC** TJ1; .L7. **CODEN** LCOVAW. Index available. cum. index. **Circ:** 60,000 (ctrl).
**Desc:** Published for owners and operators of boilers and power equipment; includes new developments and safety procedures.

US/0276-6736
**LOCOMOTIVE QUARTERLY.** [Locom. q.]. (Fall 1976)-. Periodical. English. Four times a year. $40.00. Locomotive Quarterly, PO Box 383, Mount Vernon NY 10552. **LC** TJ605; .L63. **DD** 625.2/6/05.

US/0743-281X
**LOG TRAIN, THE.** (THE LOG TRAIN : JOURNAL OF THE MOUNTAIN STATE RAILROAD & LOGGING HISTORICAL ASSOC.). [Log train]. Vol. 1, No. 1-2 (July/Oct. 1982)-. English. qt. $15.00. PO Box 89, Cass WV 24927. **Tel** (304)456-4362. **ED** Max S Robin. **LC** TF678; .L63. **DD** 385/.54/05. **Bk Rev. Ad Acc. Circ:** 300 (ctrl).
**Desc:** A journal devoted to the history of railroading in West Virginia with emphasis on logging railroads.

GW
**LOK-MAGAZIN.** 1.- 1962. Periodical. German. bm. DM13.50 Germany; DM68.40 US. Franckhsche Verlagshandlung Kosmos Verlag, Postfach 106011, D-70049 Stuttgart Germany. **Tel** 011 49 711 2191332. **ED** Horst J Obermayer. **LC** TJ605; .L664. Index available. **Bk Rev. Ad Acc. Circ:** 9,000.
**Desc:** Technics and history of railroads, especially in Germany and central Europe.

●RU
**LOKOMOTIV. Added/Corp** Russia (Federation). Ministerstvo Putei Soobshcheniia. **VFOAT** ETT; Elektricheskaia i Teplovoznaia Tiaga. (1992)-. Periodical. Russian. mo. $89.95. **(Subscription address:** East View Publications Inc., 3020 Harbor Lane North, Suite 110, Minneapolis MN 55447.**)** **LC** TF4; .E45. ***Continues*** *Elektricheskaia i Teplovoznaia Tiaga.*
**Desc:** Information on electric and diesel railroads.

UK/0309-5428
**LONDON PASSENGER TRANSPORT.** No. 1-. Periodical. English. ir. London Passenger Transport Research Group, 24 Cranbourn Street, London WC2H 7AA England. **LC** HE4719.L82; L64. **DD** 388.4/1/09421.

US/0199-5421
**MAINLINE MODELER.** [Mainline model.]. V. 1, No. 1 (Jan./Feb. 1980)-. English. mo. $36.00 (one year), $72.00 (two year). Hundman Publishing, 5115 Monticello Drive, Edmond WA 98020. **Tel** (206)743-2607. **ED** Jeff Koeller. **LC** TF197; .M218. **DD** 625.1/9/05. **Ad Acc. Circ:** 14,000.
**Desc:** Scale drawings, prototype history. Modeling for the beginner as well as other's, structures, new products, historical society listings, and many other interesting features.

US/0273-0332
**MANAGEMENT COMPENSATION, RAILROADS.** English. an. Charles M Rice, 408 Olive Street, Box 8793 Jefferson Memorial Station, St Louis MO 63102. **LC** HD4965.5.U6; R53. **DD** 331.2/81385. ***Continues*** *Management Compensation in the Railroad Industry, 0160-8657.*

JA
**MANTETSUKAI HO. Main/Corp** Mantetsukai (Japan). Japanese. ir. ¥2000. Mantetsukai, c/o Matsuo Building, 2-4 Ginza 7, Chuo-ku 104 Tokyo Japan. **LC** HE3290.M5; M33A.

US/0065-9940
**MANUAL OF THE AMERICAN RAILWAY ENGINEERING ASSOCIATION. Main/Corp** American Railway Engineering Association. (1???)-. English. ir (2 Vol. sets with binders & supplements). $130.00 US & Canada & Mexico; $222.00 others. American Railway Engineering Association, 50 F Street Northwest, Suite 7702, Washington DC 20001. **Tel** (202)639-2190, FAX (202)639-2183. **ED** Louis T. Cerny. cum. index.
**Desc:** Technical information on various phases of railway engineering, construction and maintenance.

CN/0227-2458
**MILEPOST (WINNIPEG).** (MILEPOST.). [Milepost]. Began publication in Aug. 1975?. Periodical. English. mo. Free to members. Midwestern Rail Association, PO Box 1855, Winnipeg Manitoba R3C 3R1 Canada. **DD** 385/.09712.

JA
**MINTETSU TOKEI NEMPO. Added/Corp** Japan. Unyusho. Tetsudo Kantokukyoku. (1975)-.

Japanese. ¥2500. Seifu Shiryoto Fukyu Chosakai, (Inst. for Dissemination & Research of Government Data), 6-13, Nihonbashi Horidomecho, Chuoku, Tokyoto 103, Japan. **LC** HE3951; .A35. ***Continues** Shitetsu Tokai Nempo.*

US
**MODEL RAILROAD BUYERS GUIDE.** (1976)-. Consumer Publication. English. ir. $6.00. Boynton & Associates, 14101 G. Parke Long Court, Chantilly VA 22021. **Tel** (703)263-0900. **LC** TF197; .M59. **DD** 338.4/7/62519.

GW
**MODELLEISENBAHNER, DER.** (19??)-. Periodical. German. mo. Deutscher Judo Verband, Redaktion Ippon Segewaldweg 40, D 12557 Berlin Germany. **Tel** 011 49 711 210770, telex 051 678. **LC** TF197; .M66.

UK/0026-8356
**MODERN RAILWAYS.** [Mod. railw.]. No. 160 (Jan. 1962)-. Periodical. English. mo. £22.20 UK; £32.00 Europe; £31.20 other. Ian Allan Ltd, Coombelands Lane, Addlestone Weybridge, KT15 1HY England. **Tel** 011 44 932 858511, 855909, FAX 011 44 932 232366, 854750. **(Subscription address:** Ian Allan Ltd., Northbridge Road, Berkhamsted, Herts HP4 1ST United Kingdom.**)** **ED** K. Cordner. **CODEN** MORABC. **[CCC]**. Index available. **Bk Rev. Ad Acc. Circ:** 33,000. available on microfilm and microfiche from University Microfilms International (UMI). Documents available from Ask*IEEE. ***Continues** Trains Illustrated.*
**Desc:** News and feature articles on engineering, economics and operation of British and overseas railroads.
**Ind/Abst** Coal Abstr.; Curr. Technol. Index; Highw. Res. Abstr.; INSPEC (Feb. 1970-Sept. 1981).

CN/0704-1500
**"MOVIN".** **Added/Corp** Canadian National Railways. Freight Sales Dept. Planning and Promotion Section. Vol. 1 (Dec. 1968)-. Periodical. English (French). Six times a year. Free. Movin, PO Box 8100, Montreal Quebec H3C 3N4 Canada. **Tel** (514)399-4240, (514)399-5822.

US/0740-672X
**MUTUAL MAGAZINE (PHILADELPHIA, PA. : 1980), THE.** (THE MUTUAL MAGAZINE.). Began in 1980. Periodical. English. mo. $0.60 members, $1.20 non-members. Mutual Benefit, 1617 JFK Boulevard/Suite 366, Philadelphia PA 19103-1822. **Tel** (215)596-3580. **ED** Stephen M Santarlasci. **LC** HE2791; .P369. **DD** 331.7/61385/0974. **Ad Acc. Circ:** 9,000 (ctrl). ***Continues** Mutual, 0162-2676.*
**Desc:** Fraternal monitor of Railroad Affiliated Insurance Association.

US/1045-5140
**N-SCALE (EDMONDS, WASH.).** (N-SCALE.). **VAT** N scale. Vol. 1, No. 1 (July/Aug. 1989)-. Periodical. English. bm. $24.00$ (one year), $8.00 (two year). Hundman Publishing, 5115 Monticello Drive, Edmond WA 98020. **Tel** (206)743-2607. **ED** Bob Hundman. **LC** TF197; .N22. **DD** 625.1/9/05. **Ad Acc.**

US/0148-2122
**NARROW GAUGE AND SHORT LINE GAZETTE.** (19??)-. Periodical. English. Six times a year. $24.00. Benchmark Publications Ltd, PO Box 26, Los Altos CA 94023. **Tel** (415)941-3823. **ED** Bob Brown. **LC** TF197; .N28. **DD** 625.1/9/05. **Bk Rev**, (Qty: 15). **Ad Acc. Circ:** 16,000.
**Desc:** History and modeling of Narrow Gauge and Short Line Railroads.

US/0885-5099
**NATIONAL RAILWAY BULLETIN.** [Natl. railw. bull.]. Vol. 41 (1976)-. Bulletin. English. ir. $15.00. National Railway Historical Society, PO Box 4059, Oak Park IL 60303. **Tel** (203)623-4280. **LC** HE2715; .N48. **DD** 385/.0973. ***Continues** National Railway Historical Society. Bulletin.*

RH
**NATIONAL RAILWAYS OF ZIMBABWE.** **VFOAT** National Railways of Zimbabwe Magazine. Periodical. English. mo. 3.50. Publicity Office, National Railways of Zimbabwe, Box 596, Bulawayo Zimbabwe Africa. **Tel** (36)3526, FAX 263-9-363502, telex 33173. **ED** J J Mpofu. **LC** HE3419.R4; R39. **DD** 385/.096891. **Bk Rev. Ad Acc. Circ:** 19,500 (ctrl). ***Continues** Rhodesia Railways Magazine.*
**Desc:** House magazine of the National Railways of Zimbabwe.

HU/0300-2330
**NEMZETKOZI VASUTI OESSEZEKOETTETESEK KIVONATOS MENETRENDJE.** **Main/Corp** Hungary. Kozlekedes- es Postaugyi Miniszterium. Vasuti Foosztaly. (19??)-. Hungarian. Vi Nepkoztarsas ag Utja 73-75, Budapest Hungary. **LC** HE3059.5; .A26.

AT/0159-7302
**NETWORK (MELBOURNE (VIC.).** (NETWORK : RAILWAYS OF AUSTRALIA QUARTERLY.). **Added/Corp** Railways of Australia. **VFOAT** Railways of Australia NETWORK; Railways of Australia N.E.T.W.O.R.K. (19??)-. Periodical. English. qt (Jan., Apr., July, Oct.). 20.00Aus$ Australia; 35.00Aus$ other. Star Media Services, GPO Box 2501, Melbourne Victoria 3001 Australia. **Tel** 011 61 3 857-8818, FAX 011 61 3 816-3441. **ED** Maurice Reeves. **LC** TF121; .R336. **DD** 385/.0994. **Bk Rev**, (Qty: 4). **Ad Acc, Adv Mgr:** M. Reeves, **Tel** same as publisher. **Circ:** 10,250 (ctrl). ***Continues** Railways of Australia Network.*
**Desc:** News on matters relating to railways from local and international sources.

US/1048-3845
**NEW ELECTRIC RAILWAY JOURNAL, THE.** [New elec. railw. j.]. **Added/Corp** Free Congress Research and Education Foundation. George Mason University. **VFOAT** Electric Railway Journal. Vol. 1, No. 1 (Autumn 1988)-. Periodical. English. qt. $25.00 (one year), $46.00 (two year). Free Congress Research and Education Foundation, 717 Second Street NE, Washington DC 20002. **Tel** (202)546-3000, (800)525-4992, FAX (202)546-7689. **ED** Richard Kunz. **LC** TF701; .N36. **DD** 388.4/6. **Ad Acc. Circ:** 7,000.
**Desc:** Journal of the electric rail industry.

US/0162-1599
**NEW ENGLAND STATES LIMITED, THE.** Periodical. English. qt. $8.00. PO Box 701, Keene NH 03431. **LC** HE2714; .N48. **DD** 385/.0974.

US
**NEW JERSEY STATE RAIL PLAN. UPDATE.** **Added/Corp** New Jersey. Dept. of Transportation. English. New Jersey Department of Transportation, 1035 Parkway Avenue, Trenton NJ 08625. **Tel** (609)292-1530. ***Continues** Update, New Jersey State Rail Plan.*

NZ/0028-8624
**NEW ZEALAND RAILWAY OBSERVER.** [N.Z. Railw. obs.]. **VFOAT** N.Z. Railway Observer. (1944)-. Periodical. English. qt (Mar., June, Sept., Dec.). 27.00NZ$. New Zealand Railway Locomotive Society Incorporated, 86 Totara Crescent, Lower Hutt New Zealand. **Tel** 011 64 4 5662248, telex NZ3996. **ED** T.A. McGavin. **DD** _a620. **[CCC]**. Index available. **Bk Rev**, (Qty: 12). **Ad Acc. Circ:** 1,300.

CN/0708-028X
**NEWS BULLETIN - SASKATCHEWAN RAIL COMMITTEE.** **Main/Corp** Saskatchewan Rail Committee. 1- Mar. 1977-. Bulletin. English. ir. Free. Saskatchewan Rail Committee, PO Box 3594, Regina Saskatchewan S4P 3L7 Canada. **DD** 385/.06/27124. ctrl circ.

CN/0845-8847
**NEWSLETTER - UPPER CANADA RAILWAY SOCIETY (1980).** ***Title Change.*** (NEWSLETTER / UPPER CANADA RAILWAY SOCIETY.). [Newsl. - Upper Can. Railw. Soc.]. **Added/Corp** Upper Canada Railway Society. Vol. 363 (Jan. 1980)-No. 514 (Aug. 1992). Newsletter. English. mo. Upper Canada Railway Society, PO Box 122 Postal Station A, Toronto Ontario M5W 1A2 Canada. **DD** 385/.0971. ***Continues** Rail and Transit, 0382-9057.* ***Continued by** Rail & Transit (1992), 1193-7971.*

AT/0310-7477
**NEWSRAIL.** **Added/Corp** Australian Railway Historical Society. Victorian Division. (Jan. 1973)-. Newsletter. English. mo. 45.00Aus$. Australian Railway Historical Society, GPO Box 5177AA, Melbourne VIC 3001 Australia. **Tel** 011 61 03 510 6146. **LC** TF122.V5; N48. **DD** 625.1/09945/05. ***Continues** Divisional Diary.*

US/0027-9722
**NMRA BULLETIN.** [NMRA bull.]. **Main/Corp** National Model Railroad Association. **Added/Corp** National Model Railroad Association. Bulletin. **VAT** National Model Railroad Association Bulletin. (1935)-. Bulletin. English. mo. comes with membership. National Model Railroad Association, 4121 Cromwell Road, Chattanooga TN 37421. **Tel** (615)892-2846. available on microfilm from University Microfilms International (UMI).

SW
**NORDENS JARNVAGAR.** Multiple languages (English and Swedish). F Stenvall, Kopenhamnsvagen 47A, S-217 71 Malmo Sweden. **LC** TF88.5; .N67.

SW
**NORDISK JARNBANETIDSKRIFT.** **Added/Corp** Nordiska Jarnvagsmannasallskapet. **VFOAT** Jarnbanetidskrift. (19??)-. Periodical. Swedish. Five times a year. Kr200.00. Nordisk Jarnvagmanasallskapet, SJ Centralforvaltning, S 105 50 Stockholm Sweden. **Tel** 46 87623180, FAX 46 8149431. **ED** Harry Rosengren. **LC** TF4; .N64. **Ad Acc. Circ:** 2,800 (ctrl).
**Desc:** Developments in Scandinavian railroading.

US/0894-0800
**NORTHWESTERNER (LARKSPUR, CALIF.).** (THE NORTHWESTERNER.). [Northwesterner]. **Added/Corp** Northwestern Pacific Railroad Historical Society. Vol. 1, No. 1 (1987)-. Periodical. English. sa (Apr., Oct.). $20.00 US; $25.00 other. Northwestern Pacific Railroad Historical Society, PO Box 667, Santa Rosa CA 95402. **Tel** (707)573-0751. **ED** Dick Murdock. **DD** 385. **Bk Rev. Ad Acc. Circ:** 1,000 (ctrl).
**Desc:** Contains four or five articles, many historic photos and is dedicated to preserving the heritage of Northwestern Pacific Railroad's Redwood Empire Route.

US/0030-0373
**OFFICIAL RAILWAY EQUIPMENT REGISTER, THE.** (19??)-. Periodical. English. qt. $175.00 US & Mexico; $174.77 Canada; $182.00 other. K III Press Inc., 424 West 33rd Street, New York NY 10001. **Tel** (212)714-3100, (800)221-5488.

US/1069-1715
**OFFICIAL RAILWAY GUIDE (FREIGHT SERVICE ED.), THE.** (THE OFFICIAL RAILWAY GUIDE.). [Off. railw. guide]. (19??)-. English. bm. $153.00 US and Mexico; $152.34 Canada; $215.00 other. K III Press Inc., 424 West 33rd Street, New York NY 10001. **Tel** (212)714-3100, (800)221-5488. **DD** 389. ***Continues** Official Railway Guide (North American Freight Service ed.), 0190-6704.*

US/0190-6704
**OFFICIAL RAILWAY GUIDE (NORTH AMERICAN FREIGHT SERVICE EDITION).** ***Title Change.*** (THE OFFICIAL RAILWAY GUIDE.). [Off. railw. guide.]. V. 106, No. 8 (Jan./Feb. 1974)-(19??). Periodical. English. bm. K III Press Inc., 424 West 33rd Street, New York NY 10001. **Tel** (212)714-3100, (800)221-5488. **DD** 389. ***Supersedes in part** Official Guide of the Railways and Steam Navigation Lines of the United States, Puerto Rico, Canada, Mexico and Cuba.* ***Continued by** Official Railway Guide (Freight Service Ed.), 1069-1715.*

US/0273-9658
**OFFICIAL RAILWAY GUIDE. NORTH AMERICAN TRAVEL EDITION. UNITED STATES, CANADA AND MEXICO, THE.** (THE OFFICIAL RAILWAY GUIDE.). [Off. railw. guide, North Am. travel ed.]. (19??)-. Periodical. English. Six times a year. $258.00 US and Mexico; $276.67 Canada; $250.00 other. K III Press Inc., 424 West 33rd Street, New York NY 10001. **Tel** (212)714-3100, (800)221-5488. **LC** HE2727; .O32. **DD** 385/.2042. ***Continues** Official Railway Guide. North American Passenger Travel Edition, 0094-5218.*

US/1057-0268
**OUTDOOR RAILROADER.** [Outdoor railr.]. Vol. 1, No. 1 (Oct./Nov. 1991)-. Periodical. English. bm. $21.00. Westlake Publishing Co., 1574 Kerryglen Street, Westlake Village CA 91361. **DD** 625.

US/8750-8486
**PACIFIC RAIL NEWS.** [Pac. rail news]. **VFOAT** Pacific News; Pacific Railnews. No. 252 (Oct. 1984)-. Periodical. English. Twelve times a year. $30.00. Pentrex, PO Box 94911, Pasadena CA 91109. **Tel** (800)950-9333, (818)793-3400. **ED** James W. Walker Jr. **LC** TF23.6; .P33. **DD** 385/.0978. **Bk Rev. Ad Acc. Circ:** 7,600. ***Continues** Pacific News (Burlingame, Calif.), 0030-879X.*
**Desc:** Covers railways and urban transit west of the Mississippi River with news stories, features and photographs.

RU
**PAROVOZNIK.** No. 1 (Mar. 15, 1936)-. Periodical. Russian. tm (every 10 days). $45.00. **(Subscription address:** Victor Kamkin, 4956 Boiling Brook Parkway, Rockville MD 20852.**)** **LC** WMLC L 83/851.

UK
**PASSENGER TIMETABLE : GREAT BRITAIN INTER-CITY, LOCAL AND SUBURBAN SERVICES, IRISH, CHANNEL ISLAND, COASTAL SERVICES.** **Main/Corp** British Railways Board. English. £1.80. British Railways Board, Euston House, 24 Eversholt Street CP 13, London NW1 1DZ England. **Tel** 011 44 71 9285151. **LC** HE3014; .G74B. **DD** 385/.22/0941.

UK
**PASSENGER TIMETABLE : INTERNATIONAL, INTER-CITY, SEALINK, SEASPEED SERVICES, GREAT BRITAIN-CONTINENT OF EUROPE.** **Main/Corp** British Railways Board. **VFOAT** International, Inter-City, Sealink, Seaspeed Services, Great Britain-Continent of Europe. English. an. £14.00. British Railways Board, Euston House, 24 Eversholt Street CP 13, London NW1 1DZ England. **Tel** 011 44 71 9285151. **LC** HE3014; .G74A. **DD** 385/.22. **Circ:** 180,000.
**Desc:** British rail passenger timetable issued in May and September giving comprehensive details of all train services run in Great Britain.

US/1042-7937
**PASSENGER TRAIN ANNUAL.** [Passeng. train annu.]. (1975)-. English. $17.95. Interurban Press, PO Box 6444, Glendale CA 91225. **Tel** (818)240-9130. **LC** TF570; .P37. **DD** 625.2/0973/05.

US/0160-6913
**PASSENGER TRAIN JOURNAL.** [Passeng. train j.]. (19??)-. Periodical. English. Twelve times a year. $30.00 (one year); $58.00 (two years). Pentrex, PO Box 94911, Pasadena CA 91109. **Tel** (800)950-9333, (818)793-3400. **(Subscription address:** Pentrex Publishing, PO Box 17095, North Hollywood CA 91615.**)** **ED** Mike Schafer. **LC** HE2583; .P37. **DD** 385/.22/0973. **Bk Rev. Ad Acc. Circ:** 18,500. ***Continues*** *PTJ. Passenger Train Journal, 0160-6352.*
**Desc:** News, photos and features on passenger trains, both Amtrak and the nostalgic trains of yesteryear.

US/0743-4448
**PINE TREE FLYER.** (PINE TREE FLYER : PUBLICATION OF THE RAILROAD HISTORICAL SOCIETY OF MAINE.). [Pine tree flyer]. Vol. 1, No. 1 (Fall 1981)-. Periodical. English. qt. Free to members, included in dues. Railroad Historical Society of Maine, Box 8057, Portland ME 04104. **DD** 385.

US/0032-1826
**POCKET LIST OF RAILROAD OFFICIALS, THE.** **VFOAT** Pocket List. Vol. 1 Serial No. 1 (1895)-. English. qt. $110.00 US & Mexico; $109.35 Canada; $154.00 other. K III Press Inc., 424 West 33rd Street, New York NY 10001. **Tel** (212)714-3100, (800)221-5488. **LC** HE2723; .P7.

US/1044-4688
**POCKET LIST OF RAILROAD OFFICIALS (INTERNATIONAL ED.), THE.** (THE POCKET LIST OF RAILROAD OFFICIALS.). [Pocket list railr. off.]. **Added/Corp** International Thomson Transport Press. (1989)-. English. an. $125.00 US and Mexico; $124.30 Canada; $140.00 other. K III Press Inc., 424 West 33rd Street, New York NY 10001. **Tel** (212)714-3100, (800)221-5488. **LC** HE1009; .P63. **DD** 385/.025/73.

US
**PORTFOLIO OF TRACKWORK PLANS.** English. ir. $185.00 US & Canada & Mexico; $305.00 others (A looseleaf book with hardcover binder). American Railway Engineering Association, 50 F Street Northwest, Suite 7702, Washington DC 20001. **Tel** (202)639-2190, FAX (202)639-2183.

US
**PORTFOLIO OF TRACKWORK PLANS. SUPPLEMENT.** English. an (July). $39.00 US & Canada & Mexico; $121.00 others. American Railway Engineering Association, 50 F Street Northwest, Suite 7702, Washington DC 20001. **Tel** (202)639-2190, FAX (202)639-2183.

VE
**PRESUPUESTO PRO PROGRAMA - INSTITUTO AUTONOMO ADMINISTRACION DE FERROCARRILES DEL ESTADO, DIVISION DE PRESUPUESTO.** **Main/Corp** Instituto Autonomo Administracion de Ferrocarriles del Estado (Venezuela). Division de Presupuesto. Spanish. Instituto Autonomo Administracion de Ferrocarriles del Estado, Oficina de Planificacion y Presupuesto, Caracas Venezuela. **LC** HE2991; .I57A. **DD** 354/.87/00875.

US/1047-9473
**PRIVATE VARNISH.** [Priv. varn.]. Periodical. English. bm. $22.00 (one year), $41.00 (two year) US; £3.00 (one year), £6.00 (two year) other. Interurban Publications, PO Box 6128, Glendale CA 91205. **Tel** (818)240-4777, FAX (818)240-5436. **LC** TF455; .P75. **DD** 625.2/3. **Bk Rev. Ad Acc. Circ:** 3,500.
**Desc:** Railroad hobbist magazine covering preservation and movement of privately owned railroad cars.

US
**PROCEEDINGS OF THE AMERICAN RAILWAY ENGINEERING ASSOCIATION.** **Main/Corp** American Railway Engineering Association. Proceedings. English. an. American Railway Engineering Association, 50 F Street Northwest, Suite 7702, Washington DC 20001. **Tel** (202)639-2190, FAX (202)639-2183. ***Continues*** *Proceedings, Technical Conference - American Railway Engineering Association.*

US/0096-0268
**PROCEEDINGS OF THE ANNUAL CONVENTION - AMERICAN RAILWAY ENGINEERING ASSOCIATION.** (PROCEEDINGS OF THE ANNUAL CONVENTION.). **Main/Corp** American Railway Engineering Association. Vol. 1, (1900)-. Proceedings. English. an (Feb. (following yr.)). $47.00 (membership); $78.00 (current volume) Consists of 5 issues of the Bulletin of American Railway Engineering Association bound from the previous year. American Railway Engineering Association, 50 F Street Northwest, Suite 7702, Washington DC 20001. **Tel** (202)639-2190, FAX (202)639-2183. **LC** TF1; .A45 Index. cum. index.

US/0276-7724
**PROCEEDINGS OF THE ANNUAL MEETING AND REGIONAL MEETING - AMERICAN ASSOCIATION OF RAILROAD SUPERINTENDENTS.** (PROCEEDINGS OF THE ANNUAL MEETING AND REGIONAL MEETING.). [Proc. annu. meet. reg. meet. - Am. Assoc. Railr. Supt.]. **Main/Corp** American Association of Railroad Superintendents. Proceedings. English. an. American Association of Railroad Superintendents, 18154 Harwood Avenue, Homewood IL 60430. ***Continues*** *American Association of Railroad Superintendents. Proceedings of the Annual Meeting.*

US
**PROCEEDINGS OF THE ... IEEE/ASME JOINT RAILROAD CONFERENCE.** **Added/Corp** Vehicular Technology Society. American Society of Mechanical Engineers. Rail Transportation Division. (1991)-. Proceedings. English. IEEE Computer Society, 10662 Los Vaqueros Circle, PO Box 3014, Los Alamitos CA 90720-1264. **Tel** (714)821-8380, (800)272-6657, FAX (714)821-4641. **LC** TF858.A2; J66a. ***Continues*** *Technical Papers Presented at the ... IEEE/ASME Joint Railroad Conference, 1054-0253.*

US
**PROCEEDINGS OF THE INTERNATIONAL AND ASSOCIATION RAILWAY OPERATING OFFICERS INC.** Proceedings. English. an. $16.05. International Association Railway Operating Officers, #1 Leo Drive, Bloomington IL 61701.

US
**PROCEEDINGS OF THE NEW ENGLAND RAILROAD CLUB.** **Main/Corp** New England Railroad Club, Boston. Proceedings. English. qt. New England Rail Road Club, Box 445, Pembroke MA 02359. **LC** TF1; .N5.

US
**PROCEEDINGS / SOUTHERN AND SOUTHWESTERN RAILWAY ASSOCIATION.** **Main/Corp** Southern and Southwestern Railway Association. (197?)-. Proceedings. English. qt. $3.00. Southern Southwest Railway Association, Box 1744, Roanoke VA 24008. ***Continues*** *Southern and Southwestern Railway Club. Proceedings.*

US/0033-0817
**PROGRESSIVE RAILROADING.** (PROGRESSIVE RAILROADING : THE EXECUTIVE VIEWPOINT.). Vol. 1 (1958)-. Periodical. English. Twelve times a year. $45.00 US; $50.00 Canada; $75.00 other. Murphy-Richter Publishing Company, 230 West Monroe, Suite 2210, Chicago IL 60606. **Tel** (312)629-1200, FAX (312)629-1304. **ED** Tom Judge. **Ad Acc. Circ:** 19,800 (ctrl).
**Desc:** The railroad technology that is geared to the rail and rail transit officials worldwide.

RU/0131-5560
**PROMYSHLENNYI TRANSPORT.** **See** Manufacturing.

PL
**PRZEGLAD KOLEJOWY ELEKTROTECHNICZNY.** (1953)-. Periodical. Polish. Twelve times a year. **(Subscription address:** ARS Polona, PO Box 1001, 00068 Warsaw Poland.**)** **LC** TF4; .P76. ***Continues in part*** *Przeglad Kolejowy.*

PL/0033-2224
**PRZEGLAD KOLEJOWY MECHANICZNY.** [Prz. kolej. mech.]. Began with Sept. 1953 issue. Periodical. Polish. mo. **(Subscription address:** ARS Polona, PO Box 1001, 00068 Warsaw Poland.**)** **LC** TF340; .P73. ***Continues in part*** *Przeglad Kolejowy.*
**Ind/Abst** Saf. Health Work.

PL
**PRZEGLAD KOLEJOWY PRZEWOZOWY.** Began in 1953. Periodical. Polish. mo. **(Subscription address:** ARS Polona, PO Box 1001, 00068 Warsaw Poland.**)** **LC** TF504; .P75. ***Continues in part*** *Przeglad Kolejowy.*

JA/0033-9008
**QUARTERLY REPORTS - RAILWAY TECHNICAL RESEARCH INSTITUTE.** [Q. rep. Railw. Tech. Res. Inst.]. **Main/Corp** Tetsudo Gijutsu Kenkyujo, Tokyo. **VFOAT** Quarterly Reports of Railway Technical Research Institute; Quarterly Report of RTRI. (Mar. 1960)-. Periodical. English. qt. $214.00. Kenyusha Inc, 1-45-6 Hikaricho Kokubunji-shi, Tokyo Japan. **Tel** 0425 (72) 7157. **(Subscription address:** Maruzen Company Ltd., PO Box 5050, Import & Export Department, Tokyo 100 31 Japan.**)** **LC** TF1; .T48a. **DD** 625.1/005. **CODEN** QRTIA8. cum. index. **Circ:** 550. Documents available from Article Express International, Ask*IEEE.
**Desc:** Covers the activities of the Railway Technical Research Institute, a foundation belonging to the JR Group.
**Ind/Abst** Abstr. J. Earthq. Eng. (?-?); Bioeng. Abstr.; Ei Page One; Eng. Index Annu.; Highw. Res. Abstr.; INSPEC (Dec. 1968-).

US/0743-9075
**RAIL CLASSICS & RAILWAY QUARTERLY.** [Rail class. railw. q.]. **VFOAT** Rail Classics and Railway Quarterly. Vol. 13, No. 3 (May 1984)-. Periodical. English. bm. $17.75. Challenge Publications Inc., 7950 Deering Avenue, Canoga Park CA 91304. **Tel** (818)887-0550. **ED** E. Stauss. **LC** TF1; .R135. **DD** 385/.05. **Bk Rev. Ad Acc.** ctrl circ. ***Formed by the union of*** *Rail Classics, 0194-9187* ***and*** *Railway Quarterly, 0191-1805.*

UK/0141-4615
**RAIL ENGINEERING INTERNATIONAL (1981).** (RAIL ENGINEERING INTERNATIONAL.). [Rail eng. int.]. Vol. 10, No. 4 (Oct./Dec. 1981)-. Academic Scholarly Publication. English. Four times a year. £22.00 (airmail), £18.00 (surface mail). De Rooi Publications, PO Box 543, NL-3900 AM Veenendaal Netherlands. **Tel** 011 31 8385 15012, FAX +31 8385 11243. **ED** W. M. de Rooi. **LC** TF1; .R473. **DD** 625.1/005. **CODEN** REGIAX. **Bk Rev. Ad Acc. Circ:** 3,000. Documents available from Article Express International. ***Continues*** *Railway Engineer International.*
**Desc:** Developments and innovations in railway technology.
**Ind/Abst** Bioeng. Abstr.; Ei Page One; EMBASE (1981-); Eng. Index Annu.; Fluid Abstr., Civil Eng.; Fluid Abstr. Proc. Eng.; FLUIDEX (1981-1990); Pollut. Abstr. Indexes.

US/0197-5315
**RAIL-HIGHWAY CROSSING ACCIDENT/INCIDENT AND INVENTORY BULLETIN.** **VAT** Rail Highway Crossing Accident Incident and Inventory Bulletin. Began with No. 1, 1978. Bulletin. English. an. US Department of Transportation / Federal Railroad Administration, 400 Seventh Street SW, Washington DC 20590. **Tel** (202)366-0881, FAX (202)366-7009. **LC** HE1780; .U53A. **DD** 312/.44/0973. ***Continues*** *Rail-Highway Grade-Crossing Accidents/Incidents Bulletin for the Year Ended December 31, ... .*

US/0738-1778
**RAIL HOBBYIST.** [Rail hobbyist]. September 1984-. Periodical. English. mo. $18.00 US; $26.00 other. Rail Hobbyist, PO Box 789, Hurst TX 76053. **DD** 385.

CN/0843-4530
**RAIL IN CANADA.** (RAIL IN CANADA / STATISTICS CANADA, TRANSPORTATION DIVISION, SURFACE AND MARINE TRANSPORT SECTION.). [Rail Can.]. **Added/Corp** Statistics Canada. Surface and Marine Transport Section. **VFOAT** Transport Ferroviaire au Canada. (1987)-. English (French). an. 45.00Can$ Canada; $54.00 US; $63.00 other. Statistics Canada, Publications Sales & Services, Main Building Room 1710, Ottawa Ontario K1A 0T6 Canada. **Tel** (613)951-5078, (800)267-6677, FAX (613)951-1584, telex 053-3585. **ED** Yasmin Sheikh (editor's phone number: (613)951-2518, FAX: (613)951-0579). **LC** HE2801; .R33. **DD** 385/.0971/05. Index available. **Circ:** 600. ***Formed by the union of*** *Railway Transport in Canada, Commodity Statistics, 0823-3969; Railway Transport, Railway Commodity Origin and Destination Statistics, 0229-883X* ***and*** *Railway Transport in Canada, General Statistics, 0823-3950.*
**Desc:** Data on size and structure of the Canadian rail transport industry; analysis on the economic performance, operating outputs, financial structure and equipment use, provinicial origin and destination.

BE/0020-8442
**RAIL INTERNATIONAL.** [Rail int.]. **Added/Corp** International Railway Congress Association. International Union of Railways. Vol. 1 (1970)-. Periodical. English (French, German and Russian). Eleven times a year. 3200F. International Railway Congress Association, rue de France 85 Sec 10, B 1070 Brussel Belgium. **Tel** 011 32 2 5207831, telex 250 35 RAILCBB. **ED** A. Martems. **LC** TF1; .I623. **DD** 625.1/005. **CODEN** RAIIAF. Index available. **Bk Rev. Ad Acc. Circ:** 12,000 (ctrl). Documents available from Article Express International, Ask*IEEE. ***Supersedes*** *International Railway Congress Association. Monthly Bulletin - International Railway Congress Association; Monthly Bulletin; Cybernetics and Electronics on the Railways; International Union of Railways. Bulletin - International Railway Union; International Union of Railway. Office for Research and Experiments. Bulletin - International Union of Railway, Office for Research and Experiments.*
**Desc:** Publishes articles, original technical papers, dealing with all branches of railway science and management, including economic, financial and social questions.
**Ind/Abst** Bioeng. Abstr.; Ei Page One; Eng. Index Annu.; INSPEC (Jan. 1970-).

US/1070-7751
**RAIL MART, THE.** [Rail mart]. (1986)-. Periodical. English. Twelve times a year. $20.00. Rail Mart, 502 River Bluff Drive, Carpentersville IL 60110. **Tel** (708)428-5899, FAX (708)428-5991. **DD** 381. **Ad Acc.**

Circ: 2,500 (ctrl).
**Desc:** A source for disposition of railcar, parts, motive power available covering North America.

FR/0989-8220
**RAIL PARIS, LE.** (LE RAIL.). Periodical. French (English). Eight times a year. 284.04F France; 290.00F French-speaking Africa; 370.00F other. IA Diffusion, 3 Avenue Hoche, 75008 Paris France. **Tel** 011 33 1 40549893. **ED** Christian Scasso. **UDC** 625.143. **Ad Acc. Pr Rev. Circ:** 17,000.
**Desc:** International railway information.

US/0091-9667
**RAIL PASSENGER STATISTICS IN THE NORTHEAST CORRIDOR. Main/Corp** United States. Federal Railroad Administration. **Added/Corp** United States. Office of High-Speed Ground Transportation. Demonstrations Division. United States. Federal Railroad Administration. (1968)-. English. US Department of Transportation / Federal Railroad Administration, 400 Seventh Street SW, Washington DC 20590. **Tel** (202)366-0881, FAX (202)366-7009. **LC** HE2583; .U55a. **DD** 385/.22/0974.

FR/0150-1313
**RAIL SYNDICALISTE, LE. Added/Corp** Federation Syndicaliste Force Ouvriere des Cheminots. Federation Syndicaliste Force Ouvriere des Travailleurs, Cadres et Techniciens des Chemins de fer de France et de l'Union Francaise. (19??)-. Periodical. French. Ten times a year. Le Rail Syndicaliste, 60 rue Vergniaud, 75640 Paris Cedex 13 France. **LC** HD6681.A1; R3.

US/0360-5272
**RAIL TRANSIT DIRECTORY.** Directory. English. an. Rail Ways of the Americas Inc, Box 1437, Washington DC 20013. **LC** HE1009; .R3. **DD** 385/.0974.

II
**RAIL TRANSPORT. Added/Corp** Institute of Rail Transport (India). **VFOAT** IRT Journal. Vol. 24, No. 2 (Apr./June 1987)-. Periodical. English. qt. $15.00. Institute of Rail Transport, New Delhi, India. **(Subscription address:** Prints India, 11 Darya Ganj, New Delhi 110002 India.) **LC** HE3291; .I57. ***Continues** Journal of the Institute of Rail Transport, 0020-3114.*

US/0163-7266
**RAILFAN & RAILROAD.** [Railfan railr.]. **VAT** Railfan and Railroad. V. 2, No. 10- May 1979-. Periodical. English. mo. $23.00. Carstens Publications Inc, PO Box 700, Newton NJ 07860. **Tel** (201)383-3355, FAX (201)383-4064. **ED** James A Boyd. **LC** TF1; .R145. **DD** 385/.0973. Index available. **Bk Rev. Ad Acc. Circ:** 53,000. ***Formed by the union of** Railroad Magazine, 0033-8761 **and** Railfan (Newton, N.J.), 0098-0714.*
**Desc:** Railroad news magazine of contemporary railroading: rail history, books, video, collecting, traction, narrow gauge, rail museums, posters, movies, fantrips, railroadiana, events.

UK
**RAILNEWS.** (19??)-. Periodical. English. mo. £6.00 UK; £12.00 US and Canada. British Railways Board, Euston House, 24 Eversholt Street CP 13, London NW1 1DZ England. **Tel** 011 44 71 9285151. **(Subscription address:** Checkers, 2 Wood Street, London NW1 1DZ England.)

US/0745-5267
**RAILPACE NEWSMAGAZINE. VFOAT** Railpace Magazine. (198?)-. Periodical. English. mo. $39.00. Railpace Company Inc, PO Box 927, Piscataway NJ 08854. **Tel** (201)463-1091. **ED** Thomas J. Nemeth. **LC** TF1; .R146. **DD** 385/.0973. Index available. **Bk Rev. Ad Acc. Circ:** 7,000.
**Desc:** Contemporary and historical railroad news and feature stories, Northeastern Region of the U.S.

UK/0262-8805
**RAILPOWER.** [Railpower]. (1963)-. Periodical. English. qt. Free on request. Railway Ind. Association / Great Britain, 56 Buckingham Gate, London SW1E 6AW England. **Tel** 011 44 71 8341426. **DD** 385.

US/0160-1261
**RAILROAD ACCIDENT INVESTIGATION REPORTS. Main/Corp** United States. Federal Railroad Administration. Office of Safety. English. US Department of Transportation / Federal Railroad Administration, 400 Seventh Street SW, Washington DC 20590. **Tel** (202)366-0881, FAX (202)366-7009. **LC** HE1780; .U54B. **DD** 614.8/63/0973.

US/0148-0200
**RAILROAD ACCIDENT REPORT. BRIEF FORMAT.** (RAILROAD ACCIDENT REPORTS, BRIEF FORMAT / NATIONAL TRANSPORTATION SAFETY BOARD.). Began with 1976. English. ir. National Technical Information Service - NTIS, Room 2027S, 5285 Port Royal Road, Springfield VA 22161. **Tel** (703)487-4630, (703)487-4660, (703)487-4650, FAX (703)321-8547, telex 89-9405. **LC** HE17; .A47 subser; HE1780. **DD** 629.04/2/08 S 385.

US/0091-5572
**RAILROAD CAR JOURNAL.** No. 1- Aug. 1971-. Periodical. English. $3.50 single issue. Kratville Publications, 516 Farnam Building, Omaha NE 68101. **LC** TF371; .R33. **DD** 625.2/4/05.

US/0742-1850
**RAILROAD FACTS (WASHINGTON, D.C.).** (RAILROAD FACTS.). [Railr. facts]. **Added/Corp** Association of American Railroads. Office of Information and Public Affairs. (1983)-. English. an. Association of American Railroads, 50 F Street Northwest, Room 5401, Washington DC 20001. **Tel** (202)639-2550. **LC** HE2713; .Y4. **DD** 385/.0973. ***Continues** Yearbook of Railroad Facts, 0084-3997.*
**Ind/Abst** Predicasts Forecasts.

US/0090-7847
**RAILROAD HISTORY.** [Railr. hist.]. **Added/Corp** Railway & Locomotive Historical Society. No. 127 (Oct. 1972)-. Periodical. English. Twice a year. $35.00 Comes with Railway & Locomotive Historical Society membership. Railway and Locomotive Historical Society, 115 I Street B Kleinschmidt, Sacramento CA 95814. **Tel** (916)447-9665, FAX (916)327-5655. **LC** TF1; .R22. **DD** 385/.09. available on microfilm and microfiche from University Microfilms International (UMI). ***Continues** Railway and Locomotive Historical Society. Bulletin.*
**Ind/Abst** Am. Hist. Life (1976-).

●US
**RAILROAD RETIREMENT AND UNEMPLOYMENT INSURANCE SYSTEMS HANDBOOK.** **See** Insurance.

US
**RAILROAD REVENUES, EXPENSES, AND INCOME: CLASS I RAILROADS IN THE UNITED STATES. Main/Corp** Association of American Railroads. Economics and Finance Dept. 3rd Qtr. (1967)-. Periodical. English. Four times a year (Feb., May, Aug., Nov.). $25.00 (railroad members), $75.00 (non-railroad members). Association of American Railroads, 50 F Street Northwest, Room 5401, Washington DC 20001. **Tel** (202)639-2550. **Bk Rev. Ad Acc. *Continues** Bureau of Railway Economics, Washington, D.C. Railroad Revenues, Expenses and Income.*
**Desc:** Detailed financial data of most recent quarter and cumulative period of year compared with the same periods of previous year.

US/1041-4746
**RAILROAD TEN-YEAR TRENDS.** [Railr. ten-year trends]. **Added/Corp** Association of American Railroads. Economics and Finance Dept. **VFOAT** Railroad Ten Year Trends. Vol. No. 1 (1984)-. English. an (Sept.). $100.00 (nonmembers), $50.00 (members). Association of American Railroads, 50 F Street Northwest, Room 5401, Washington DC 20001. **Tel** (202)639-2550. **LC** HE2713; .R34. **DD** 385/.0973/021. ***Formed by the union of** Economic ABZ's of the Railroad Industry **and** Association of American Railroads. Economics and Finance Dept. Statistics of Railroads of Class I in the United States, 0091-4894.*
**Desc:** More than 175 tables and graphs describing contemporary railroad economics within the following categories: industry consist; financial statements; financial, traffic, employment and operating statistics; and profiles of railroad-related organizations. The data in each edition represents the ten most recent years' information, when available.

RH
**RAILROADER.** English. mo. 6.00Zin$ Zimbabwe; 9.00Zin$ other. Publicity Office, National Railways of Zimbabwe, Box 596, Bulawayo Zimbabwe Africa. **Tel** (36)3526, FAX 263-9-363502, telex 33173. **(Subscription address:** Public Relations Office, National Railways of Zimbabwe, P.O. Box 596, Bulawayo Aimbabwe Africa) **ED** J J Mpofw and M Gumede. Index available. **Ad Acc. Circ:** 17,800 (ctrl).
**Desc:** Activities of the local railway organization, and its staff. Work of a technical nature carried out and issues of personnel administration.

US/0199-3445
**RAILROADIANA EXPRESS, THE.** **See** Hobbies.

NZ/0110-6155
**RAILS (WELLINGTON).** [Rails Wellington]. (1971)-. Periodical. English. Twelve times a year. 39.60NZ$ New Zealand; 50.00NZ$ other. Southern Press Ltd., R D 1 Porirua, Wellington New Zealand. **Tel** 011 64 4 2399063, FAX 011 64 4 2399063. **ED** R. H. (Bob) Stott. **DD** 385. **[CCC].** Index available (bound in Sept. issue). **Bk Rev,** (Qty: varies). **Ad Acc. Circ:** 4,500.
**Desc:** Commercially oriented, independent rail transport journal.

UK/0267-5943
**RAILWATCH.** [Railwatch]. (1985)-. Periodical. English. Four times a year (Jan., Apr., July, Oct.). £3.30. Railway Development Society, 48 The Park Great Bookham, Surrey KT23 3LS England. **Tel** 011 44 372 452863. **ED** Ray Kins. **Bk Rev,** (Qty: 4). **Ad Acc. Circ:** 4,500. ***Continues** Railway Development News, 0266-724X.*
**Desc:** News and views on railway from the user's point of view.

US/0033-8826
**RAILWAY AGE (BRISTOL).** (RAILWAY AGE.). [Railw. age]. **VFOAT** Railway Age and Railway Review. (1918)-. Periodical. English. mo. $45.00 (one year), $75.00 (two year), $120.00 (three year). Simmons Boardman Publishing Corporation / New York, 345 Hudson Street, New York NY 10014. **Tel** (402)346-4740. **(Subscription address:** Simmons Boardman Publishing Corporation, PO Box 986, Omaha NE 68101.) **LC** TF1; .R2. **DD** 385.05. **CODEN** RAAGA3. **[CCC].** available on microfilm and microfiche from University Microfilms International (UMI); available on an online database (files 15,647,648/Full-Text) from DIALOG. Documents available from Ask*IEEE, UMI Article Clearinghouse, CASDDS, Documents on Demand. ***Continues** Railway Age Gazette, 0096-2317; **Absorbed** Railway Review; Modern Railroads (Cahners Pub. Co. : 1982), 0736-2064.*
**Desc:** Railroadings's magazine of news and interpretation, its editorial content is of special importance to the efficient management and operating of the railroads and rail rapid transit. Its circulation is maintained mainly among executives, managerial and supervisory groups on the railways, but also includes financial groups, shippers, transit groups, and railway equipment supply manufacturers.
**Ind/Abst** ABI Inform Ondisc (Aug. 1991-); Acad. Search (Jan. 1993-); Bus. ASAP (1990-) [Full Txt.]; Bus. Index (1985-); Bus. Period. Index; Chem. Abstr.; Coal Abstr.; Energy Inf. Abstr.; Environ. Abstr.; F&S Index Plus Text, Int. [Select. Cov.]; Fluid Abstr., Civil Eng.; Fluid Abstr. Proc. Eng.; FLUIDEX (1973-1990); Gen. BusinessFile (1985-); Gen. Period. Index (1985-); INFO-SOUTH Abstr.; INSPEC (Nov. 1975-); Mag. ASAP Plus [Full Txt.]; Mag. Index Plus (1989-); Mag. Search; Newsp. Period. Abstr. (1988-); PAIS Int. Print (1973-); PROMT (1977-); Stat. Ref. Index; Mag. Index (1977-); Trade Ind. ASAP [Full Txt.]; Trade Ind. Index [Full Txt.]; Vocat. Search (Jan. 1993-); Wilson Bus. Abstr.

PK
**RAILWAY BUDGET : DEMANDS FOR GRANTS FOR THE PAKISTAN RAILWAYS, THE. Main/Corp** Pakistan. Railway Board. English. Government of Pakistan / Ministry of Railways, Railway Board, Karachi 15 3 Pakistan. **LC** HE3300.5; .A363C. **DD** 353.9/549/100875.

PK
**RAILWAY BUDGET : IMPROVEMENT FUND WORKS PROGRAMME, THE. Main/Corp** Pakistan. Railway Board. English. Government of Pakistan / Ministry of Railways, Railway Board, Karachi 15 3 Pakistan. **LC** HE3300.5; .A363D. **DD** 353.9/5491/00875.

PK
**RAILWAY BUDGET IN BRIEF, THE. Main/Corp** Pakistan. Railway Board. (19??)-. English. Government of Pakistan / Ministry of Railways, Railway Board, Karachi 15 3 Pakistan. **LC** HE3300.5; A363e. **DD** 354/.9549/100875.

CN/0380-6308
**RAILWAY CARLOADINGS (MONTHLY ED.).** (RAILWAY CARLOADINGS.). [Railw. carload.]. **Main/Corp** Canada. Statistique Canada. Section des Transports de Surface. **Added/Corp** Canada. Bureau Federal de la Statistique. Section des Transports. Statistique Canada. Section des Transports. Statistique Canada. Division des Transports et des Communications. Statistique Canada. Section des Transports de Surface. Statistique Canada. Section des Transports de Surface et Maritimes. **VFOAT** Chargements Ferroviaires. Vol. 47, No. 1 (Jan. 1970)-. Periodical. French (English). mo. 100.00Can$ Canada; $120.00 US; $140.00 other. Statistics Canada, Publications Sales & Services, Main Building Room 1710, Ottawa Ontario K1A 0T6 Canada. **Tel** (613)951-5078, (800)267-6677, FAX (613)951-1584, telex 053-3585. **ED** Angus MacLean (editor's phone: (613)951-2484; FAX (613)951-0579. **DD** 385/.24/0971. **Circ:** 285 (ctrl). ***Continues** Carloadings (1948).*
**Desc:** An indicator of current business activity; includes data on cars and tons of revenue freight loaded in Canada, with breakdowns between eastern and western Canada.

US/0033-8850
**RAILWAY CARMEN'S JOURNAL. Added/Corp** Brotherhood Railway Carmen of the United States and Canada. Brotherhood Railway Carmen of America. Vol. 1 (1895)-. Periodical. English. mo. $5.00, nonmembers; Free, members. Brotherhood Railway Carmen of the United States and Canada, 4929 Main Street, Kansas City MO 64112. **LC** HD6350.R25; R5.

CN/0317-3437
**RAILWAY FREIGHT TRAFFIC (OTTAWA. QUARTERLY EDITION).** ***Title Change.*** (RAILWAY FREIGHT TRAFFIC.). [Railw. freight traffic]. **Main/Corp** Statistics Canada. Surface Transport Section. **VFOAT** Trafic Marchandises Ferroviaire. Vol. 52 (1st Quarter 1974)-?. English (French). qt. Statistics Canada, Publications Sales & Services, Main Building Room 1710, Ottawa Ontario K1A 0T6 Canada. **Tel** (613)951-5078,

(800)267-6677, FAX (613)951-1584, telex 053-3585. **LC** HE2801; .A69. **DD** 385/.264/0971. ***Continues*** *Railway Freight Traffic, 0317-3437.* ***Continued by*** *Rail in Canada, 0843-4530.*
**Desc:** Provincial and national data on revenue freight carried by Class I and II railways II Canada.

UK/0373-5346
**RAILWAY GAZETTE INTERNATIONAL.** [Railw. gaz. int.]. Vol. 126, No. 19 (Oct. 1970)-. Periodical. English. Twelve times a year. $73.00 (one year), $124.00 (two years) US & Canada; $42.00 Europe; $68.00 others;. Reed Business Publishing / West Sussex, England, Perrymount Road, Haywards Heath, West Sussex RH16 3DH England. **Tel** 011 44 81 6523500. **LC** TF1; .R5. **DD** 385/.1/05. **CODEN** RWGIAN. **[CCC].** available on microfilm and microfiche from University Microfilms International (UMI). Documents available from Article Express International, Ask*IEEE. ***Continues*** *Railway Gazette, 0033-8907.*
**Ind/Abst** Alum. Ind. Abstr.; Coal Abstr.; Ei Page One; Eng. Mater. Abstr.; Eng. Index Annu.; Highw. Res. Abstr.; INSPEC (Nov. 1970-); Met. Abstr.; Saf. Health Work.

US/0093-8505
**RAILWAY HISTORY MONOGRAPH, THE.** V. 1- Jan. 1972-. Periodical. English. qt. $10.00. J.B. Publishing Company, 430 Ivy Avenue, Crete NE 68333. **Tel** (402)826-3356. **ED** William F Rapp. **LC** TF15; .R34. **DD** 385/.09. **Bk Rev. Circ:** 100.
**Desc:** Presents articles on all phases of railway history.

US/0190-6763
**RAILWAY LINE CLEARANCES.** **Added/Corp** National Railway Publication Company. (19??)-. English. an. $105.00 US & Mexico; $110.00 other. K III Press Inc., 424 West 33rd Street, New York NY 10001. **Tel** (212)714-3100, (800)221-5488. **LC** TF22; .R28. **DD** 385.312/0973.

UK/0033-8923
**RAILWAY MAGAZINE (LONDON).** (THE RAILWAY MAGAZINE.). [Railw. mag.]. (1897)-. Periodical. English. Twelve times a year. £48.00 US & Canada; £20.00 UK, £21.50 others (surface mail); £27.00 Middle East & North Africa, £30.00 Mexico & South America & South Asia, £31.50 Far East Australia & New Zealand & Pacific Ocean Islands, £28.61 Europe & Cyprus (airmail). IPC Magazines Ltd., Perrymount Road, Haywards Heath, West Sussex RH16 3DH England. **Tel** 011 44 444 440421. **LC** TF1; .R57. **[CCC].** available on microfilm from University Microfilms International (UMI).
**Ind/Abst** Br. Humanit. Index; Curr. Technol. Index.

CN/0380-5964
**RAILWAY OPERATING STATISTICS (MONTHLY ED.).** (RAILWAY OPERATING STATISTICS / PREPARED IN THE PUBLIC FINANCE AND TRANSPORTATION DIVISION.). [Railw. oper. stat.]. **Added/Corp** Canada. Dominion Bureau of Statistics. Public Finance and Transportation Section. Canada. Dominion Bureau of Statistics. Transportation and Public Utilities Section. Canada. Dominion Bureau of Statistics. Transportation Section. Statistics Canada. Transportation Section. Statistics Canada. Surface Transport Section. Statistics Canada. Surface and Marine Transport Section. Statistics Canada. **VFOAT** Statistique de l'Exploitation Ferroviaire. Vol. 34, No. 1 (Jan. 1954)-. English (French). mo. 120.00Can$ Canada; $144.00 US; $168.00 other. Statistics Canada, Publications Sales & Services, Main Building Room 1710, Ottawa Ontario K1A 0T6 Canada. **Tel** (613)951-5078, (800)267-6677, FAX (613)951-1584, telex 053-3585. **ED** Angus MacLean (editor's telephone number: (613)951-2484, FAX: (613)951-0579). **LC** HE2801; .R34. **DD** 385/.0971. **Circ:** 325. ***Continues*** *Operating Revenues, Expenses & Statistics, Railways in Canada with Annual Operating Revenues of $500,000 or Over;* ***Absorbed*** *Statistics Canada. Transportation Section. Railway Operating Statistics.*
**Desc:** Data on major railways, including statistics on operating finances and traffic. Data on Canadian National and Canadian Pacific Rail operations are presented separately.

US/0094-2278
**RAILWAY PASSENGER CAR ANNUAL.** V. 1- 1973/74-. English. an. RPC Publication, PO Box 211, Park Forest IL 60466. **LC** TF455; .R3. **DD** 385/.33/0973.

CN
**RAILWAY TRANSPORT.** ***Title Change.*** **Main/Corp** Canada. Statistics Canada. Surface Transport Section. **VFOAT** Transport Ferroviaire. Multiple languages (English and French). an. Statistics Canada, Publications Sales & Services, Main Building Room 1710, Ottawa Ontario K1A 0T6 Canada. **Tel** (613)951-5078, (800)267-6677, FAX (613)951-1584, telex 053-3585. **LC** HE2801; .A3. **DD** 385/.0971. ***Continues*** *Railway Transport.* ***Continued by*** *Rail in Canada, 0843-4530.*

US
**RAILWAY WORLD, THE.** Vol. 1, No. 1 (Jan. 2, 1875)-. Periodical. English. wk. ***Continues*** *United States Railroad and Mining Register.*
**Ind/Abst** Curr. Technol. Index.

UK/0082-5891
**RAILWAY WORLD ANNUAL.** English. an. $8.25. Ian Allan Ltd, Coombelands Lane, Addlestone Weybridge, KT15 1HY England. **Tel** 011 44 932 858511, 855909, FAX 011 44 932 232366, 854750. **ED** Peter Johnson. **Ad Acc. Circ:** 10,000. ***Continues*** *Trains.*
**Desc:** Annual for rail enthusiasts. Varied content, old and new in the style of parent monthly magazine.

SA/0254-2218
**RAILWAYS.** ***Title Change.*** [Railways]. **VFOAT** Railways Southern Africa. (Mar. 1977)-(Feb./Mar. 1992). Periodical. English. bm. Target Communications, PO Box 3445, 2125 Randburg Transvaal, South Africa. **Tel** 011 27 11 886-4583, 886-4584, 886-4585. **ED** R E Bull. **LC** TF1; .R48. **DD** 625.1/005. **Bk Rev. Ad Acc. Circ:** 2,300 (ctrl). Documents available from Ask*IEEE. ***Continues*** *Railway Engineering (Johannesburg), 0033-8885.* ***Continued by*** *Railways Africa.*
**Desc:** Aimed at the decision makers in national railways, mines and industries in Southern Africa. It covers systems, developments, products and people in the railway industry.
**Ind/Abst** INSPEC (1977-).

●SA
**RAILWAYS AFRICA.** **VFOAT** RA. (Apr./May 1992)-. Periodical. English. bm. **LC** TF1; .R48. **DD** 625.1/005. ***Continues*** *Railways, 0254-2218.*

CG
**RAPPORT ANNUEL.** **Main/Corp** Compagnie des Chemins de fer Kinshasa-Dilolo-Lubumbashi. **Added/Corp** Compagnie du Chemin de fer du Bas-Congo au Katanga. (19??)-. French. Compagnie des Chemins de fer Kinshasa-Dilolo-Lubumbashi, Place de la Gare, Lubumbashi Zaire. **LC** HE3460.K5; C65a. **DD** 385/.09675/1.

II
**REPORT OF THE COMPTROLLER AND AUDITOR GENERAL OF INDIA, UNION GOVERNMENT (RAILWAYS).** **Main/Corp** India (Republic). Comptroller and Auditor-General. 1970/71-. English. an. $1.19. Controller of Publications / Civil Lines, Government of India, Civil Lines, New Delhi 110054 India. **Tel** 3015984, telex 3166415. **LC** HE3291; .A37162. **DD** 354/.54/00875. ***Continues*** *Central Government Audit Report, Railways.*

SA
**REPORT OF THE SELECT COMMITTEE ON RAILWAY ACCOUNTS. VERSLAG VAN DIE GEKOSE KOMITEE OOR SPOORWEGREKENINGS.** **Main/Corp** South Africa. Parliament. House of Assembly. Select Committee on Railway Accounts. **Added/Corp** South Africa. Parliament. House of Assembly. Select Committee on Railway Accounts. Verslag van die Gekose Komitee oor Spoorwegrekenings. **VFOAT** Verslag van die Gekose Komitee oor Spoorwegrekenings. (19??)-. Afrikaans (English). an. R8.70. House of Assembly / Select Committee on Railway Acounts, Government Printer, Bosman Street, Private Bag X85, Pretoria 0001 South Africa. **Tel** 012-457531. **(Subscription address:** PO Box 571, 8000 Cape Town Republic of South Africa**)** **LC** HE3419.S8; S665c. **DD** 385/.1. **Circ:** 1,000 (ctrl).

SP
**REVISTA AIT.** **Main/Corp** Asociacion de Investigacion del Transporte (Spain). **VAT** Revista Asociacion de Investigacion del Transporte. Periodical. Spanish (summaries and/or abstracts in English, French and German). Asociacion de Investigacion del Transporte, Alberto Alcocer 38, Madrid-16 Spain. **LC** TF4; .A76A. **DD** 625.1/05.

FR/0760-548X
**REVUE DE L ASSOCIATION FRANCAISE DES AMIS DES CHEMINS DE FER.** **VFOAT** Chemins de Fer(1984). (1979)-. Periodical. French. bm. 290.00F. L'Association Francaise des Amis des Chemins de Fer Gare de l'Est, 75675 Paris Cedex 70 France. **Tel** 011 33 1 42039631 ext AFAC. **UDC** 656.2:367.

FR/0035-3183
**REVUE GENERALE DES CHEMINS DE FER (1924).** (REVUE GENERALE DES CHEMINS DE FER.). [Rev. gen. ch. fer]. (1924)-. Periodical. French. Eleven times a year. 840.00F (institutions), 610.00F (individuals) France; 1050.00F (institutions), 770.00F (individuals) other. Dunod Gauthier Villars, 15 rue Gossin, 92543 Montrouge cedex France. **Tel** 011 33 1 46 56 52 66, FAX 011 33 1 46 57 40 69. **(Subscription address:** Centrale des Revues, 11 rue Gossin, 92543 Montrouge Cedex France.**)** **CODEN** RGCFAI. **[CCC].** Documents available from Article Express International, Ask*IEEE. ***Continues*** *Revue Generale des Chemins de Fer et des Tramways, 0245-9175.*
**Ind/Abst** Bioeng. Abstr.; Ei Page One; EMBASE; Eng. Index Annu.; Highw. Res. Abstr.; INSPEC (1968-).

US
**RT&S, RAILWAY TRACK & STRUCTURES.** **VFOAT** Railway Track & Structures. Vol. 75 (Jan. 1979)-. Periodical. English. mo. $24.00 (non-trade), $12.00 (trade) US, Canada and Mexico; $45.00 other (surface mail). Simmons Boardman Publishing Corporation / New York, 345 Hudson Street, New York NY 10014. **Tel** (402)346-4740. **(Subscription address:** Simmons Boardman Publishing Corporation, PO Box 986, Omaha NE 68101.**)** Index available (free). Documents available from Article Express International. ***Continues*** *Railway Track & Structures.*
**Ind/Abst** Concr. Abstr.; Ei Page One; Eng. Index Annu. [Select. Cov.].

GW/0079-9548
**RTR. RAILWAY TECHNICAL REVIEW.** (19??)-. Periodical. English. an. DM32.00. Hestra Verlag Hernincel & Dr Strauss GmbH & Co KG, Postfach 4244, D 64201 Darmstadt Germany. **Tel** 011 49 6151 39070. **UDC** 629.4. **CODEN** 656.2.

CN/0715-5034
**S & L MUSEUM NEWSLETTER.** **See** Museums and Galleries.

US/0738-9892
**SANTA FE ROUTE, THE.** Vol. 1, No. 1 (Summer 1983)-. Periodical. English. qt. $12.00. Santa Fe Railway, PO Box 92887, Long Beach CA 90809-2887. **Tel** (310)593-2788. **ED** Michael A Martin. **Circ:** 800 (ctrl).
**Desc:** The history of the Santa Fe Railroad and its subsidiaries from its formation to present day operations. Covers all aspects of the Santa Fe Railroad in general.

US/0162-0282
**SHORELINER.** Periodical. English. qt. $8.50. Ronald Hall, 280 North Elm Street, Wallingford CT 06492. **LC** TF25.N726; S46. **DD** 625.1/00974.

US/0162-0746
**SHORELINER SUPPLEMENT.** English. Ronald Hall, 280 North Elm Street, Wallingford CT 06492. **LC** TF25.N726; S46 SUPPL. **DD** 385/.09746.

US/0199-4050
**SHORT LINE, THE.** [Short line]. (19??)-. Periodical. English. Six times a year. $19.00 (US); $20.00 (other). The Short Line, PO Box 607, Pleasant Garden NC 27313. **Tel** (919)674-2168. **ED** Garreth M. McDonald. Index available. cum. index. **Bk Rev**, (Qty: 6). **Pr Rev. Circ:** 1,600.
**Desc:** This emphasis on the news of the shortlines and industries railroads in the North America.

GW/0037-4997
**SIGNAL UND DRAHT.** [Signal + Draht]. **VFOAT** Signal + Draht. (1969)-. Periodical. German (summaries and/or abstracts in English). Twelve times a year. DM178.00. Tetzlaff Verlag GmbH, Postfach 101609, D-20010 Hamburg Germany. **Tel** 011 49 40 2371401, telex 419258. **CODEN** SIGDAN. **[CCC].** Index available. **Bk Rev. Ad Acc. Circ:** 3,000. Documents available from Ask*IEEE.
**Desc:** Signaling, data processing, process control, measuring and regulating, telecommunications, automation and office machines for the railway sector.
**Ind/Abst** Highw. Res. Abstr.; INSPEC (March 1969-).

US/0037-5020
**SIGNALMAN'S JOURNAL, THE.** **Added/Corp** Brotherhood of Railroad Signalmen of America. Vol. 1 (Jan. 1920)-. Periodical. English (French). bm. $10.00. Signalmans Journal, 601 Golf Road, PO Box U, Mt Prospect IL 60056. **Tel** (312)439-3732. **ED** J P Finn. **LC** HD6350.R39; S5. **Ad Acc. Circ:** 15,000 (ctrl).
**Desc:** Edited for the men and women who install, test, inspect and maintain signal equipment and systems on railroads and transit systems.
**Ind/Abst** Work Relat. Abstr.

BL
**SISTEMA FERROVIARIO DO BRASIL / REDE FERROVIARIA FEDERAL, S.A., DIRECTORIA DE PLANEJAMENTO, DEPARTAMENTO GERAL DE ESTATISTICA.** Began with V. for 1964. Portuguese. ir. Free. Rede Ferroviaria Federal SA, Diretoria de Planejamento, Departamento Geral de Estatistica, Centro ZC-14 Caixa Postal 1693, 20.000 Rio de Janeiro Brazil. **Tel** (021)2334541, telex (021.21.372)REFERRO. **LC** HE2921; .S58. **DD** 385/.0981.
**Desc:** Maps of the railroads network of Brazil and the list of the stations.

US/0733-5296
**SOO, THE.** (THE SOO : THE MAGAZINE OF THE SOO LINE HISTORICAL AND TECHNICAL SOCIETY.). **Added/Corp** Soo Line Historical and Technical Society. No. 1 (Sept. 1977)-. Periodical. English. Four times a year (Jan., Apr., July, Oct.). $16.00. Soo Line Historical and Technical Society, 3410 Kasten Court, Middleton WI 53562. **Tel** (414)725-4160. **ED** Larry E. Easton. **LC** TF25.S65; S66. **DD** 385/.0977. Index available. cum. index. **Bk Rev. Ad Acc. Circ:** 1,200 (ctrl).
**Desc:** A publication that deals with the history of the railroad and predecessor lines.

## Transportation —Railroads

US/8756-8853
**SOUTHERN PACIFIC LOCOMOTIVE DIRECTORY.** **VFOAT** Locomotive Directory. 84-. Directory. English. Wordways, PO Box 2592, Menlo Park CA 94026. **LC** TJ603.3.S6; S67. **DD** 625.2/6/0978.

US/0584-4568
**SOUTHERN PACIFIC MOTIVE POWER ANNUAL.** Began with Vol. for 1966-1967. English. ir. Chatham Publishing Company, PO Box 283, Burlingame CA 94010. **LC** TJ603.3.S6; J48. **DD** 625.2/66/0978.

US/0160-6875
**STANDARD TRANSPORTATION COMMODITY CODE.** (STANDARD TRANSPORTATION COMMODITY CODE. ALPHABETICAL-NUMERICAL.). **Main/Corp** Association of American Railroads. **Added/Corp** Association of American Railroads. **VFOAT** STCC Tariff; Tariff STCC; Standard Transportation Commodity Code Tariff. (1963)-. English. Association of American Railroads, 50 F Street Northwest, Room 5401, Washington DC 20001. **Tel** (202)639-2550. **LC** HF1052; .A88a. **DD** 338/.001/2. available on magnetic tape. *Continued in part by* Continued in part by Standard Transportation Commodity Code. Hazardous Materials or Substances or Hazardous Wastes, 1062-2993.

US
**STATE RAIL PLAN, ANNUAL UPDATE.** **Main/Corp** West Virginia Railroad Maintenance Authority. (19??)-. English. an. **LC** TF24.W4; W47a. **DD** 385/.09754.

UK/0958-7373
**STEAM CLASSIC.** [Steam class.]. (1990)-. Periodical. English. Twelve times a year. £21.00 UK; $55.00 other. Argus Specialist Publications, Queensway House, 2 Queensway Redhill, Surrey RH1 1QS England. **Tel** 0737 768611, FAX 0737 773993, telex 948669 TOPJNL G. **DD** 625.2610941.
**Desc:** Covers the history, design, and the past and present performance of locomotives; encompasses the long tradition of the British steam locomotive as well as those types more in active service today.

US/0081-542X
**STEAM PASSENGER SERVICE DIRECTORY.** **Added/Corp** Empire State Railway Museum. **VFOAT** Steam Passenger Directory. (1966)-. Directory. English. an. $10.00. Empire State Railway Museum, PO Box 455, Phoenicia NY 12464. **Tel** (914)688-7501. **ED** Marvin H. Cohen. **LC** TF6.U5; S75. **DD** 385/.22/02573. **Ad Acc**. **Pr Rev. Circ:** 15,000.
**Desc:** Information on tourist type railroads, trolley museums and railway museums in the United States and Canada.

JA
**SUJI DE MIRU MINTETSU.** **Added/Corp** Unyu Keizai Kenkyu Senta. Japan. Unyusho. Tetsudo Kantokukyoku. (19??)-. Periodical. Japanese. ¥200. Unyu Keizai Kenkyu Senta, (Japan Transport Economics Research Center), 6-6 Toranomon 1 chome, Minatoku Tokyoto 105 Japan. **LC** HE3351; S9.

US
**SUMMARY OF ACCIDENTS/INCIDENTS REPORTED BY ALL LINE-HAUL AND SWITCHING AND TERMINAL RAILROAD COMPANIES / DEPARTMENT OF TRANSPORTATION, FEDERAL RAILROAD ADMINISTRATION.**
**Added/Corp** United States. Federal Railroad Administration. (Jan. 1975)-. Periodical. English. mo. US Department of Transportation / Federal Railroad Administration, 400 Seventh Street SW, Washington DC 20590. **Tel** (202)366-0881, FAX (202)366-7009.
*Continues* Summary of Accidents Reported by all Line-Haul Switching and Terminal Railroad Companies for the Month of ..., 0565-5307.

US/0092-2781
**SUMMARY OF ACCIDENTS INVESTIGATED BY THE FEDERAL RAILROAD ADMINISTRATION.** (SUMMARY OF ACCIDENTS INVESTIGATED BY THE FEDERAL RAILROAD ADMINISTRATION IN THE ... / DEPARTMENT OF TRANSPORTATION, FEDERAL RAILROAD ADMINISTRATION, OFFICE OF SAFETY.). English. an. US Department of Transportation / Federal Railroad Administration, 400 Seventh Street SW, Washington DC 20590. **Tel** (202)366-0881, FAX (202)366-7009. available on microfiche (Vols. for calendar year 1983- distributed to depository libraries).

US
**SUMMARY OF O-D TRIPS (ALL TRAINS).** **Main/Corp** Amtrak. **VFOAT** Ranking Summary of O/D Trips. 1977-. English. US Department of Transportation / Federal Railroad Administration, 400 Seventh Street SW, Washington DC 20590. **Tel** (202)366-0881, FAX (202)366-7009.

PK
**SUPPLEMENTARY BUDGET STATEMENT OF PAKISTAN RAILWAYS.** **Main/Corp** Pakistan. Railway Board. English. Government of Pakistan / Ministry of Railways, Railway Board, Karachi 15 3 Pakistan. **LC** HE3300.5; .A363F. **DD** 354/.549/10072254.

US/0730-935X
**TECHNICAL PAPERS PRESENTED AT GENERAL SESSIONS AND COMMITTEE WORKSHOPS. ANNUAL MEETING.** (TECHNICAL PAPERS PRESENTED AT GENERAL SESSIONS AND COMMITTEE WORKSHOPS ... ANNUAL MEETING / COMMUNICATION AND SIGNAL DIVISION, AAR.). **Main/Corp** Association of American Railroads. Communication and Signal Division. Meeting. **VFOAT** Technical Papers and Committee Reports ... Annual Meeting. 19th (1979)-. English. an. American Railroads Engineering Association, 50 F Street NW/Suite 7702, Washington DC 20001. **LC** TF615; .A8A. **DD** 625.1/65/05. *Continues* Association of American Railroads. Communication and Signal Division. Meeting. Technical Papers Presented at General Sessions and Committee Workshops ... Annual Meeting, 0730-935X.

SA
**THIS IS SAR & H : RAILWAYS HANDBOOK.** **Main/Corp** South African Railways and Harbours. **VFOAT** This is South African Railways. English. Thomson Publications Pty, PO Box 56182, Pinegowrie 2123 South Africa. **Tel** 011 27 11 7892144. **LC** HE3419.S8; S68K. **DD** 385/0968.

UK/0952-620X
**THOMAS COOK EUROPEAN TIMETABLE.** **VFOAT** Indicateur Europeen. Jan. 1988-. English (French, German and Spanish). mo. $170.00. Thomas Cook Ltd, PO Box 227, Peterborough PE3 6SB England. **Tel** 011 44 733 268943, FAX 011 44 733 505792, telex 32581. **LC** HE3004; .T48. **DD** 385/.2042/094. Index available. **Ad Acc. Circ:** 16,600. *Continues* Thomas Cook Continental Timetable (Peterborough, Cambridgeshire : 1981), 0144-7467.
**Desc:** Detailed surface transportation schedules for European rail and shipping services.

UK/0144-7475
**THOMAS COOK OVERSEAS TIMETABLE.** See Travel and Tourism.

CC
**TIEH TAO HSUEH PAO.** **Added/Corp** Chung-kuo Tieh Tao Hsueh Hui. **VFOAT** Journal of the China Railway Society. (19??)-. Periodical. Chinese (summaries and/or abstracts in English). qt. China Railway Society, 10 Fuxing Road, PO Box 2499, Beijing, People's Republic of China. **LC** TF4; .T5518. **DD** 625.1/005.
**Ind/Abst** Concr. Abstr.

US/0041-0934
**TRAINS.** Vol. 14, No. 5 (Mar. 1954)-. Periodical. English. mo. $34.95 US; $45.00 other. Kalmbach Publishing Company, PO Box 1612, Waukesha WI 53187. **Tel** (414)796-8776 ext.411, FAX (414)796-0126. **ED** J. David Ingles. **LC** TF1; .T67. **DD** 385/.0973. Index available. **Bk Rev**. **Ad Acc. Circ:** 97,000. available on microfilm from University Microfilms International (UMI). Documents available from UMI Article Clearinghouse. *Continues* Trains & Travel.
**Desc:** News reports on the railroading industry. Features cover operations, locomotive power, rolling stock, and routes.
**Ind/Abst** Gen. Period. Index (1985-); Mag. Index Plus (1989-); Newsp. Period. Abstr. (1988-); Mag. Index (1977-).

PL
**TRAKCJA I WAGONY.** V. 1- Jan. 1978-. Periodical. Polish. Centrala Kolportazu Prasy I Wydawnictw RSW Prasa-Ksiazka-Ruch, Ul Towarowa 28, 00-958 Warszawa Poland. **LC** TF4; .T64.

US
**TRANSIT CONNECTIONS.** English. qt. free to transit professions; $25.00 other. Simmons Boardman Publishing Corporation / New York, 345 Hudson Street, New York NY 10014. **Tel** (402)346-4740. **(Subscription address:** Simmons Boardman Publishing Corporation, PO Box 986, Omaha NE 68101.**)**

CN/0381-5404
**TRANSPORT CANADIEN (1963).** *Ceased*. (TRANSPORT CANADIEN.). **Added/Corp** Fraternite Canadienne des Cheminots, Employes des Transports et Autres Salaries. (1963)-(1??) Periodical. French. Canadian Brotherhood of Railroad Employees, 2300 Carling Avenue, Ottawa Ontario K2B 2G1 Canada. *Separated from* Canadian Transport, 0045-5466.

●US/1049-1422
**TRANSPORT HISTORY MONOGRAPH.**
[Transp. hist. monogr.]. **Added/Corp** Society of Freight Car Historians. (1992)-. Monographic series. English. Price varies per volume. Society Freight Car Historians, PO Box 2480, Monrovia CA 91017. **DD** 385.

IT
**TRENO, IL.** **Main/Corp** Azienda Autonoma Delle Ferrovie Dello Stato (Italy). Italian. L5.000 single issue. Conto Corrente Postale, Intestato A: Banca Nazionale Delle Comunicazione, Ufficio Ragineria Dei Servizi Centrale FS, Rome Italy. **LC** HE3094; .A94A.

US/0148-8406
**TROLLEY TALK.** (Sept. 1954)-. Periodical. English. bm. 59 Euclid Avenue, Cincinnati OH 45215. **LC** TF701; .T76. **DD** 388.4/6/0973.

RU
**TRUDY.** **Main/Corp** Vsesoiuznyi Nauchno-Issledovatelskii Institut Vagonstroeniia. (19??)-. Russian. **LC** TF371; .V8.

RU
**TRUDY INSTITUTOV INZHENEROV ZHELEZNODOROZHNOGO TRANSPORTA.** *Title Change*. **Added/Corp** Moskovskii Institut Inzhenerov Zheleznodorozhnogo Transporta. Academic Scholarly Publication. Russian. **(Subscription address:** Victor Kamkin, 4956 Boiling Brook Parkway, Rockville MD 20852.**)** **LC** TF4; .M57. **CODEN** TIITDR. Documents available from CASDDS. *Continues* Trudy. *Continued by* Mezhvuzovskii Sbornik Nauchnykh Trudov (Moskovskii Institut Inzhenerov Zheleznodorozhnogo Transporta).
**Ind/Abst** Chem. Abstr. (-1982); Math. Rev.

RU/0372-3305
**TRUDY VSESOJUZNOGO NAUCNO-ISSLEDOVATELSKOGO INSTITUTA ZELEZNODOROZNOGO TRANSPORTA.** (TRUDY VSESOIUZNOGO ORDENA TRUDOVOGO KRASNOGO ZNAMENI NAUCHNO-ISSLEDOVATELSKOGO INSTITUTA ZHELEZNODOROZHOGO TRANSPORTA.). [Tr. Vses. naucno-issled. inst. zeleznodorozn. transp.]. **Added/Corp** Vsesoiuznyi Nauchno-Issledovatelskii Institut Zheleznodorozhnogo Transporta (Soviet Union). **VFOAT** Trudy Vsesoiuznogo Ordena Trudovogo Krasnogo Znameni Nauchno-Issledovatelskogo Instituta Zheleznodorozhnogo Transporta. (1946)-. Academic Scholarly Publication. Russian. ir. Price varies per volume. Transport / Moscow, Basmannyi Tup 6A, Moscow Russia. **LC** TF4; .M6. **CODEN** TVZTAU. Documents available from CASDDS.
**Ind/Abst** Chem. Abstr. (1946-1980).

CN/0227-244X
**TURNOUT, THE.** [Turnout]. No. 1 (Sept. 1972)-. Periodical. English. Ten times a year. 14.00Can$. Canadian Railroad Historical Association, 120 rue Staint Pierre, St Constant Quebec, J5A 2G9 Canada. **Tel** (514)484-4815. **ED** Hollie Lowry. **DD** 385/.0971. **Bk Rev**. **Ad Acc. Circ:** 165 (ctrl).
**Desc:** Club newsletter containing regional railroad and historical news and short features. Uses black and white photographs only.

US/0743-7994
**U.S. RAIL NEWS.** *Ceased*. (U.S. RAIL NEWS / UNITED STATES RAIL CORPORATION.). [U.S. rail news]. **VFOAT** United States Rail News. Periodical. English. mo. US Rail News, PO Box 1353, Royal Oak MI 48068. **Bk Rev**. **Ad Acc. Circ:** 1,500 (ctrl).

US/0275-3758
**U.S. RAIL NEWS.** [U.S. rail news]. **VAT** United States Rail News. (1978)-. Periodical. English. bw. $429.00. Business Publishers Inc., 951 Pershing Drive, Silver Spring MD 20910-4464. **Tel** (301)587-6300, (800)274-0122, FAX (301)585-9075. **ED** Andrew Stephens. **LC** Discard. **[CCC]**. available on an online database (file 636/Full-Text) from DIALOG.
**Desc:** Report on all aspects of the US rail industry- legislation, regulation, funding, business news on mergers and acquisitions, labor relations, marketing techniques and successes.
**Ind/Abst** PTS Newsl. Database [Full Txt.].

CN/0383-2015
**UTU NEWS CANADA.** See Economics-Labor.

HU/0231-0767
**VASUTI KOZLEKEDESI SZAKIRODALMI TAJEKOZTATO.** (1983)-. Periodical. Hungarian. mo. 2,200ft. Orszagos Muszaki Informacios Kozpont es Konyvtar (O.M.I.K.K.), National Technical Information Centre and Library Museum, u 17, PO Box 12, 1428 Budapest, Hungary. **Tel** (361)118-1994, FAX (361)138-2414, telex 22-4944 OMIKK H. **(Subscription address:** OMIKK Budapest, POB 12, H-1428 Hungary**)** **ED** Kovacs Agnes Raczne. **UDC** 016. Index available. cum. index. **Bk Rev**. **Ad Acc. Circ:** 360 (ctrl).
**Desc:** Articles on railroad traffic.

FR/0042-5478
**VIE DU RAIL PARIS, LA.** **VFOAT** La Vie du rail, Notre Metier. (1952)-. Periodical. French. wk. La Vie du

## Transportation —Railroads

Rail, 11 rue de Milan, 75440 Paris Cedex 09 France. **Tel** 011 33 1 49701263. **UDC** 656.2. *Continues Notre Metier (Paris), 1149-3763.*

US
**VIRGINIA STATE RAIL PLAN ... UPDATE.** English. an. Rail Transportation Division, Virginia Department of Highways and Transportation, 1401 East Broad Street, Richmond VA 23219. **LC** HE2771.V8; V63. **DD** 385/.068.

CN/0085-8188
**WESTERN CANADIAN STEAM LOCOMOTIVE DIRECTORY.** Began with 1969 issue. Directory. English. be. $1.00 each number. Richard L Coulton, Bentley Alberta T0C 0J0 Canada. **DD** 625.2/61/09712.

US/0149-4996
**WESTERN RAILROADER AND WESTERN RAILFAN.** Periodical. English. mo. $3.00. PO Box 688, San Mateo CA 94401. **LC** TF23.6; .W47. **DD** 385/.0978. available on microfilm and microfiche from University Microfilms International (UMI).

US/0043-4744
**WHEEL CLICKS. Added/Corp** Pacific Railroad Society, Inc. (19??)-. Periodical. English. mo. $20.00. Pacific Railroad Society, PO Box 80726, San Marino CA 91118-8726. **Tel** (310)283-0087, (818)798-5290. **ED** Dick Finley. Index available. **Bk Rev. Circ:** 250.
  **Desc:** Feature articles, news, history, photos, maps of railroads and rail transit systems. Includes facilities, events, passenger services, museums, tourist railways. Occasional book reviews. PRS news.

GW/0373-322X
**ZEITSCHRIFT FUER EISENBAHNWESEN UND VERKEHRSTECHNIK.** (ZEITSCHRIFT FUER EISENBAHNWESEN UND VERKEHRSTECHNIK : ZEV.). [Z. Eisenbahnwes. Verkehrstech.]. **VFOAT** ZEV; Z.E.V.; Z.E.V.-Glas. **Added/Corp** Journal for Railways and Transport; ZEV-Glas. Ann. Vol. 96, Issue 1 (Jan. 1972)-. Academic Scholarly Publication. German (summaries and/or abstracts in English and French). mo. DM238.00. Georg Siemens Verlagsbuchhandlung, Postfach 450169, D-12171 Berlin Germany. **Tel** 011 49 30 7699040, FAX 011 49 30 76990418. **ED** Manfred Benzenberg. **LC** T3; .A6. **CODEN** ZEVGAK. **[CCC].** Index available. cum. index. **Bk Rev. Ad Acc. Circ:** 4,000. Documents available from Article Express International, Ask*IEEE, CASDDS. *Continues Glasers Annalen.*
  **Desc:** The oldest technical scientific journal for railways and transport of Germany.
  **Ind/Abst** Bioeng. Abstr.; Chem. Abstr.; Ei Page One; EMBASE; Energy Res. Abstr. (July 1977-); Eng. Index Annu.; INSPEC (June 1972-); Int. Aerosp. Abstr.

GW/0941-0589
**ZEV, DET, GLASERS ANNALEN, DIE EISENBAHNTECHNIK.** (1990)-. Multiple languages. Twelve times a year. DM234.07 Germany; DM274.00 other. Georg Siemens Verlagsbuchhandlung, Postfach 450169, D-12171 Berlin Germany. **Tel** 011 49 30 7699040, FAX 011 49 30 76990418. **ED** Manfred Benzenberg. Index available. cum. index. **Bk Rev. Ad Acc. Circ:** 4,000.
  **Desc:** Technical scientific journal for railways and transport in Germany.

RU/0044-4448
**ZHELEZNODOROZHNYI TRANSPORT. Added/Corp** Soviet Union. Narodnyi Komissariat Putei Soobshcheniia. Soviet Union. Ministerstvo Putei Soobshcheniia. (1941)-. Periodical. Russian. mo. $89.95. (Subscription address: East View Publications, Inc., 3020 Harbor Lane North, Suite 110, Minneapolis MN 55447.) **LC** HE7; .Z5. *Continues Sotsialisticheskii Transport.*

RU
**ZHELEZNYE DOROGI SSSR. Main/Corp** Soviet Union. Glavnoe Upravlenie Geodezii i Kartografii. (1965)-. Russian. an. Registr SSSR, Glavnoe Upravlenie, Dvortsovaia Naberezhnaia 8, 192041 St. Petersburg Russia.

### ROADS AND TRAFFIC

US
**200TH HIGHEST HOUR TRAFFIC VOLUMES, TENNESSEE / PREPARED BY THE TENNESSEE DEPARTMENT OF TRANSPORTATION, BUREAU OF PLANNING AND DEVELOPMENT, PLANNING DIVISION, MAPPING AND STATISTICS OFFICE, TRAFFIC AND SAFETY PLANNING, IN COOPERATION WITH THE U.S. DEPARTMENT OF TRANSPORTATION, FEDERAL HIGHWAY ADMINISTRATION. Added/Corp** Tennessee. Dept. of Transportation. Traffic and Safety Planning. **VFOAT** Two Hundredth Highest Hour Traffic Volumes, Tennessee; 200 Highest Hour Report. (19??)-. English. Department of Transportation / Tennessee, Andrew Jackson State Office Building, Nashville TN 37219. **LC** HE371.T2; A17. **DD** 388.3/142/09768.

US/1051-4848
**ABERDEEN'S PAVEMENT MAINTENANCE.** [Aberdeen's pavement maint.]. **VFOAT** Pavement Maintenance. Vol. 5, No. 4 (Aug./Sept. 1990)-. Periodical. English. bm. Aberdeen Group, 426 South Westgate, Addison IL 60101. **Tel** (312)543-0870, FAX (708)543-3112. **ED** Allan Heydorn. **DD** 625. *Continues Aberdeen's Pavement Maintenance & Management.*

US/1053-2870
**ABERDEEN'S PAVEMENT MAINTENANCE TRADER.** [Aberdeen's pavement maint. trader]. **Added/Corp** Aberdeen Group. **VFOAT** Pavement Maintenance Trader. Vol. 8, No. 5 (Sept./Oct. 1990)-. Periodical. English. bm. Aberdeen Group, 426 South Westgate, Addison IL 60101. **Tel** (312)543-0870, FAX (708)543-3112. **ED** Allan Heydorn. **DD** 338. **Pr Rev.**

US/0360-9847
**ACCIDENT AND VIOLATION ANALYSIS FOR LICENSED OREGON DRIVERS. Main/Corp** Oregon. Motor Vehicles Division. English. Department of Transportation Motor Vehicle Division, Salem OR 97314. **LC** HE5614.3.O7; O68D. **DD** 363.1/252/09795021.

US/1057-8153
**ACCIDENT RECONSTRUCTION JOURNAL.** See Transportation-Automobiles.

BE/0770-237X
**ACCIDENTS DE LA CIRCULATION SUR LA VOIE PUBLIQUE AVEC TUES OU BLESSES.** [Accid. circ. voie publique tues blesses]. **Added/Corp** Institut Nnational de Statistique (Belgium). (1973)-. French. Institut National de Statistique / Belgium, rue de Louvain, 44, Centre Albert, 8e Etage, 1000 Brussels Belgium. **Tel** 011 32 2 5486211. **LC** HE5614.5.B4; B45a. **NLM** W2 GB4 I5SB. *Continues Accidents de la Circulation sur la Voie Publique.*

CN/0825-5709
**ALBERTA TRAFFIC COLLISION FACTS.** [Alta. traffic collis. facts]. 1982-. English. an. Alberta Transportation, Twin Atria Building, 4999-98 Avenue, Edmonton Alberta T6B 2X3 Canada. **LC** HE5614.5.C2; A44. **DD** 363.1/252/097123. *Continues Alberta Collision Facts, 0825-5695.*

US/0550-7898
**ANNUAL NEVADA STREET AND HIGHWAY CONFERENCE.** (NEVADA STREET AND HIGHWAY CONFERENCE.). **Main/Conf** Nevada Street and Highway Conference. English. an. University of Nevada Civil Engineering Department, Reno NV 89507. **LC** TA1; .E63 subser. **DD** 625.7/09793.

US/1051-0850
**ANNUAL REPORT - COLORADO. DEPT. OF HIGHWAYS.** (ANNUAL REPORT / STATE OF COLORADO, DEPARTMENT OF HIGHWAYS.). [Annu. rep. - Colo., Dep. Highw.]. **Main/Corp** Colorado. Dept. of Highways. (19??)-. English. Colorado Department of Highways, 4201 East Arkansas Avenue, Denver CO 80222. **Tel** (303)757-9011. **DD** 353. *Continues Colorado. Dept. of Highways. Expenditure Report, 0146-7506.*

AT/0155-7084
**ANNUAL REPORT / COMMISSIONER FOR MAIN ROADS. Main/Corp** New South Wales. Dept. of Main Roads. (19??)-. English. an. Roads and Traffic Authority, PO Box K198, Haymarket NSW 2000 Australia. **Tel** 02 218 6888. **LC** TE122.N38; N49a. **DD** 354.9440086/42/06.

US/0095-1994
**ANNUAL REPORT - DEPARTMENT OF SAFETY.** (ANNUAL REPORT - DEPARTMENT OF SAFETY (TENNESSEE). **Main/Corp** Tennessee. Dept. of Safety. English. an. free. Andrew Jackson State Office Building, Nashville TN 37219. **LC** HE5614.3.T2; T45A. **DD** 353.9/768/00783. ctrl circ.
  **Desc:** Activities and accomplishments of the department.

US
**ANNUAL REPORT, HIGHWAY SAFETY IMPROVEMENT PROGRAMS IN VIRGINIA / PREPARED BY THE DIVISION OF TRAFFIC AND SAFETY FOR THE VIRGINIA DEPARTMENT OF HIGHWAYS AND TRANSPORTATION.** See Public Health and Safety.

US
**ANNUAL REPORT / MAINE DEPARTMENT OF TRANSPORTATION, BRIDGE DESIGN SECTION. Main/Corp** Maine. Dept. of Transportation. Bridge Design Section. (1989/1990)-. English. **LC** WMLC 91/2893.

US
**ANNUAL REPORT / MISSOURI HIGHWAY & TRANSPORTATION COMMISSION. Main/Corp** Missouri Highway and Transportation Commission. 1983-. English. an. $1.00. Missouri Highway and Transportation Commission, PO Box 270, Jefferson City MO 65102. **Tel** (314)751-2840. **LC** HE356.M8; M52A. **DD** 353.97780087/5/006. ctrl circ. *Continues Missouri Highway and Transportation Commission. Review.*

US/0098-6364
**ANNUAL REPORT OF THE BOARD OF EXAMINERS FOR COUNTY HIGHWAY AND CITY STREET SUPERINTENDENTS.** (ANNUAL REPORT.). **Main/Corp** Nebraska. Board of Examiners for County Highway and City Street Superintendents. English. an. **LC** HE356.N36; N42A. **DD** 353.9/782/008781.

AT
**ANNUAL REPORT OF THE MOTOR ACCIDENTS BOARD FOR THE YEAR ENDED 30 JUNE ... (VICTORIA). Main/Corp** Victoria. Motor Accidents Board. English. an. **LC** HE5614.5.A8; V4A. **DD** 354.9450087/831.

US
**ANNUAL REPORT OF THE SOUTH CAROLINA DEPARTMENT OF HIGHWAYS AND PUBLIC TRANSPORTATION TO THE GENERAL ASSEMBLY. Main/Corp** South Carolina. Dept. of Highways and Public Transportation. 1976/77-. English. an. 1100 Senate Street, PO Box 191, Columbia SC 29202. **LC** HE356.S5; S64A. **DD** 353.9/757/00878105.

US
**ANNUAL REPORT OF THE TRAFFIC BOARD FOR THE YEAR ENDING JUNE 30 ... (WESTERN AUSTRALIA). Main/Corp** Western Australia. Traffic Board. 1982-. English. an. **LC** HE368.Z6; W47. **DD** 354.9410087/831/06. *Continues Western Australia. Road Report.*

US
**ANNUAL REPORT, SOUTH DAKOTA GOVERNOR'S TRAFFIC SAFETY PROGRAM. Main/Corp** South Dakota. Division of Highway Safety. State & Community Programs. English. an. Department of Public Safety / South Dakota, 118 West Capitol, Pierre SD 57501. **LC** HE5614.3.S8; S68D. **DD** 614.8/62/09783.

US/0748-5077
**ANNUAL REPORT TO THE OKLAHOMA TURNPIKE AUTHORITY.** See Public Administration.

US/0363-9312
**ANNUAL REPORTS - INDIANA STATE HIGHWAY COMMISSION, DIVISION OF ACCOUNTING & CONTROL. Main/Corp** Indiana. State Highway Commission (1961-1981). Division of Accounting and Control. **VAT** Annual Reports - Indiana State Highway Commission, Division of Accounting and Control. English. an. Indiana State Highway Commission, Division of Accounting and Control, Indianapolis IN. **LC** HE356.I6; I5A. **DD** 353.9/772/008781.

US
**ANNUAL SPEED STUDY, WASHINGTON ... AND CERTIFICATION OF 55 MPH ENFORCEMENT / PREPARED BY THE DEPARTMENT OF HIGHWAYS, HIGHWAY PLANNING DIVISION, IN COOPERATION WITH THE U.S. DEPARTMENT OF TRANSPORTATION, FEDERAL HIGHWAY ADMINISTRATION. Added/Corp** Washington (State). Highway Planning Division. Washington (State). Public Transportation and Planning Division. Planning Survey. Washington (State). Public Transportation and Planning Division. Washington (State). Planning, Research, and Public Transportation Division. United States. Federal Highway Administration. (1975)-. English. an. Department of Transportation / Washington State, Highway Administration Building, Olympia WA 98504. **LC** HE371.W2; W35a. **DD** 338.2/144/09797. *Continues Annual Speed Study (Olympia, Wash.).*

## Transportation —Roads and Traffic

US/0095-3385
**ANNUAL WORK PROGRAM - WASHINGTON TRAFFIC SAFETY COMMISSION.** See Public Health and Safety.

AT/1037-051X
**APRG REPORT.** [APRG rep.]. **Added/Corp** Austroads. Australian Pavement Research Group Australian Road Research Board. **VFOAT** Australian Pavement Research Group Report. (1991)-. Monographic series. English. ir. 30.00Aus$. Australian Road Research Board, PO Box 156, Nunawading VIC 3131 Australia. **Tel** 011 61 3 8811555, FAX 011 61 3 8878104, telex AA 33113. **DD** 625.8099405.

US/0360-7720
**ARIZONA TRAFFIC. Main/Corp** Arizona. Dept. of Transportation. Planning Survey Group. English. an. Arizona Department of Transportation, 205 South 17th Avenue, 614 East, Phoenix AZ 85007. **Tel** (602)255-7724. **LC** HE356.A7; A3. **DD** 388.3/14/09791. **Continues** Arizona Traffic.

US/0096-9796
**ARIZONA TRAFFIC ACCIDENT SUMMARY. Main/Corp** Arizona. Office of Highway Safety. (1974)-. English. an. Free. Arizona Department of Transportation, 205 South 17th Avenue, 614 East, Phoenix AZ 85007. **Tel** (602)255-7724. **LC** HE5614.3.A6; A3. **DD** 388.3/14. **Continues** Arizona's Traffic Accident Summary, 0096-9796.

US
**ARKANSAS HIGHWAY COMMISSION ANNUAL REPORT TO THE GOVERNOR OF ARKANSAS.** Title Change. **Main/Corp** Arkansas. State Highway Commission. **Added/Corp** Arkansas. State Highway & Transportation Dept. **VFOAT** Annual Report to the Governor of Arkansas; Annual Report. (19??)-(1984). English. an. State Highway Commission, PO Box 2261, Little Rock AR 72203. **LC** HE28.A8; S69a. **DD** 353.97670086/4/06. **Continued by** Annual Report.

AT/0158-071X
**ARRB RESEARCH REPORT ARR.** Title Change. See Transportation.

BE
**ASPECTS TECHNIQUES DE LA SECURITE ROUTIERE. VFOAT** Technical Aspects of Road Safety. Began with Mar. 1960 Issue. Periodical. French (English, Flemish and German). qt. **LC** HE5601; .A78. **DD** 363.1/25/05. cum. index.

US/1055-9205
**ASPHALT CONTRACTOR, THE.** (THE ASPHALT CONTRACTOR : PAVING AMERICA.). [Asph. contract.]. (19??)-. Periodical. English. Nine times a year. $36.00. Group III Communications, 10229 East Independence Avenue, Independence MO 64053. **Tel** (816)254-8735. **LC** IN PROCESS. **DD** 625.

FR/0395-4366
**AUTO HEBDO PARIS. 1976.** [Auto hebdoParis, 1976]. (1976)-. Periodical. French. wk. 470.13F France; 510.00F other. Soc Francaise d Edition Presse, 48 50 Boulevard Senard, 92210 St Cloud France. **Tel** 011 33 1 47112000. **UDC** 790. **Continues** Scratch, 0395-4358.

FR/0769-8933
**AUTO-MOTO MONTLHERY.** [Auto Moto Montlhery]. (1982)-. Periodical. French. Eleven times a year. 146.91F France; 208.30F other. Circuler Service d'Abonnement, PB 469 08, 75360 Paris Cedex France. **Tel** 011 31 1 69 121852. **UDC** 796.7. **Continues** Prevention Routiere, 0032-8022.

FR
**AUTOHEBDO.** French. Soc Francaise d Edition Presse, 48 50 Boulevard Senard, 92210 St Cloud France. **Tel** 011 33 1 47112000.

IT
**AUTOSTRADE. Added/Corp** Autostrade, Concessioni e Costruzioni Autostrade s.p.a. Vol. 1 (Jan. 1959)-. Periodical. Italian. Four times a year. L60000 Italy; L75000 other. Autostrade Spa, Via Bergamini 50, 00159 Rome Italy. **Tel** 011 39 6 436331, telex 612235. **LC** TE4; .A8. **DD** 338.1/22/05. Index available. cum. index. **Ad Acc. Circ:** 4,500.

US/0094-7415
**AVERAGE DAILY TRAFFIC VOLUMES ON INTERSTATE, ARTERIAL AND PRIMARY ROUTES.** English. an. Division of Traffic and Safety, Richmond VA 23219. **LC** HE371.V8; V45C. **DD** 388.3/14/09755. **Continues** Average Daily Traffic Volumes on Interstate and Primary Routes.

RU/0005-2353
**AVTOMOBILNYE DOROGI.** [Avtomob. dorogi]. **Added/Corp** Soviet Union. Ministerstvo Transportnogo Stroitelstva. (1954)-. Academic Scholarly Publication. Russian. mo. $99.95. **(Subscription address:** East View Publications Inc., 3020 Harbor Lane North, Suite 110, Minneapolis MN 55447.**)** Index available in last issue of volume--attached. Documents available from CASDDS. **Continues** Stroitelstvo Dorog.
**Ind/Abst** Chem. Abstr. (1954-1982); Energy Res. Abstr. (Oct. 1982-).

AU
**BERICHT UBER DIE FORDERUNG VON FORSCHUNGS- UND ENTWICKLUNGSVORHABEN UND UBER DIE ERTEILUNG VON FORSCHUNGS- UND ENTWICKLUNGSAUFTRAGEN. Main/Corp** Austria. Bundesministerium fuer Bauten und Technik. Bundesstrassenverwaltung. **Added/Corp** Austria. Bundesministerium fuer Bauten und Technik. Bundesstrassenverwaltung. Jahresbericht. **VFOAT** Jahresbericht - Bundesministerium fur Bauten und Technik, Bundesstrassenverwaltung. (19??)-. German. ir. Bundesministerium fur Bauten und Technik, Stubenring 1, A-1010 Vienna Austria. **LC** TE192; .A93a.

GW
**BERLIN-VERKEHR, DER. Main/Corp** Berlin (West Berlin). Der Senator fur Verkehr und Betriebe. German. Senator fur Verkear und Betriebe, Nurnberger Strasse 53-55, 1 Berlin 30 Germany. **LC** HE363.G34; B475.

US/0006-0208
**BETTER ROADS.** [Better roads]. **VFOAT** Better Roads Magazine. Vol. 1 (1931)-. Periodical. English. Twelve times a year. $20.00 US, Canada and Mexico; $90.00 other. Better Roads / Department of Circulation, PO Box 558, Park Ridge IL 60068. **Tel** (312)693-7710, FAX (312)696-3445. **ED** William Dannhausen and Ruth W. Stidger. **CODEN** BEROAW. **Ad Acc. Circ:** 40,000 (ctrl). available on microfilm and microfiche from University Microfilms International (UMI). Documents available from Article Express International, Documents on Demand.
**Desc:** Governmental road, street, bridge construction, maintenance, traffic and work zone control safety, funding at federal, state, county, town/township road and city street levels.
**Ind/Abst** Bioeng. Abstr.; Concr. Abstr.; Ei Page One; Eng. Index Annu. [Select. Cov.]; Environ. Abstr.; Highw. Res. Abstr.

US/0146-9037
**BID OPENING REPORT. Main/Corp** United States. Federal Highway Administration. (19??)-. English. US Department of Transportation - Federal Highway Administration, 400 Seventh Street Southwest, Washington DC 20590. **Tel** (202)366-0660. **LC** HE355.A3; A2857b. **DD** 388.1/1.

US
**BIENNIAL REPORT - NORTH DAKOTA STATE HIGHWAY DEPARTMENT. Main/Corp** North Dakota. State Highway Dept. English. be. North Dakota State Highway Department, Capitol Grounds, Bismarck ND 58505. **LC** TE24.N9; A3. **DD** 353.97840086/4/05. **Continues** North Dakota. State Highway Commission. Report.

SP/0210-9085
**BOLETIN DE INFORMACION DEL LABORATORIO DE CARRETERAS Y GEOTECNIA.** [Bol. inf. Lab. Carret. Geotec.]. **Main/Corp** Laboratorio de Carreteras y Geotecnia (Spain). Began with Jan./Feb. 1980 issue. Periodical. Spanish. bm. Laboratorio de Carreteras y Geotecnia Jose Luis Escario, Alfonso XII 3, Madrid-7 Spain. **LC** TE4.M3; A27.
**Ind/Abst** GeoRef.

US/1042-7708
**BULLETIN - ASSOCIATION FOR THE ADVANCEMENT OF AUTOMOTIVE MEDICINE.** (BULLETIN.). [Bull. - Assoc. Adv. Automot. Med.]. **Added/Corp** Association for the Advancement of Automotive Medicine. Vol. 1, No. 1 (Feb. 1988)-. Bulletin. English. bm. $50.00 (U.S./Canada/Mexico). American Association for Automotive Medicine, 2350 East Devon Avenue/Suite 205, Des Plaines IL 60018-4602. **Tel** (312)390-8927. **DD** 616. **NLM** W1; BU478. **Continues** Journal (American Association for Automotive Medicine), 0893-7761.

BE/0777-2572
**BULLETIN CRR.** [Bull. CRR]. **VFOAT** Bulletin Centre de Recherches Routieres. (1988)-. Periodical. French. qt. Centre de Recherches Routieres, Boulevard de la Woluwe 42, 1200 Brussels Belgium. **Tel** 011 32 2 767 5111, FAX 011 32 2 767 1780. **ED** G. Venstermans, B. Guelton, D. Vergaillie. **UDC** 625. **Continues** Technique Routiere, 0040-1277.

FR/0295-608X
**BULLETIN DES AUTOROUTES FRANCAISES.** [Bull. autoroutes fr.]. (1985)-. Periodical. French. Three times a year. Free. Association des Societes Francaises d Autoroutes, 3 rue Edmond Valentin, 75007 Paris France. **Tel** 011 33 1 47533700, FAX 011 33 1 45558488. **UDC** 625.711.3. **Continues** Bulletin des Autoroutes de France, 0761-4772.

UK
**BULLETIN - GREAT BRITAIN DEPARTMENT OF SCIENTIFIC AND INDUSTRIAL RESEARCH. ROAD RESEARCH BOARD. Main/Corp** Great Britain. Dept. of Scientific and Industrial Research. Road Research Board. **Added/Corp** Great Britain. Ministry of Transport. No. 1, (1936)-. Bulletin. English.

UK/0045-5768
**CARE ON THE ROAD BIRMINGHAM.** [Care road Birm.]. (1972)-. Periodical. English. mo. Royal Society for the Prevention of Accidents, Cannon House, Priory Queensway, Birmingham B4 6BS England. **Tel** 011 44 21 200 2461, FAX 021 201 1254. **Continues** Safety News, 0036-2522; Road Accident Statistical Review; Driving Safety Bulletin; Drivers' Digest.
**Ind/Abst** HILITES.

US/0277-6286
**CAUSEWAYS & THEATRE PROJECTS; ANNUAL REPORT. Main/Corp** Jones Beach State Parkway Authority. **VAT** Causeways and Theatre Projects: Annual Report. (19??)-. English. an. Jones Beach State Parkway Authority, Babylon NY 11702.

US
**CENTERLINE. VFOAT** Nebraska Centerline. English. Accident Record Bureau, Lincoln NE 68508. **LC** HE5614.3.N35; C4. **DD** 388.3/14.

CC
**CHUNG-KUO CHIAO TUNG NIEN CHIEN.** (1986)-. Chinese. an. $42.00. China National Publishing Import & Export Corporation, 16 Gongti E Rd., Chaoyang Dist., Beijing 100704, People's Republic of China. **Tel** 011 8601 5630169, 5066688, FAX 011 8601 5063101, 5063010, telex 22313. **LC** HE278.A15; C49. **DD** 380.5/0951.

FR
**CIRCULATION ROUTIERE: FAITS ET CHIFFRES, LA. Main/Corp** Union Routiere de France. (19??)-. French. Union Routiere de France, 54 Avenue Marceau, Paris 75008 France. **LC** HE373.F7; U54a.

US
**CODE OF FEDERAL REGULATIONS. 23, HIGHWAYS.** See Law.

US/0743-1570
**COMPENDIUM OF TECHNICAL PAPERS : INSTITUTE OF TRANSPORTATION ENGINEERS ... ANNUAL MEETING.** [Compend. tech. pap. - Inst. Transp. Eng., Meet.]. **Main/Corp** Institute of Transportation Engineers. Meeting. 46th (1976)-. English (summaries and/or abstracts in Spanish). an. $66.00. Institute of Transportation Engineers, 525 School Street SW/Suite 410, Washington DC 20024. **Tel** (202)554-8050, FAX (202)863-5486, telex 467943. **LC** TA1005; .I52a. **DD** 629.04/05. Documents available from Article Express International. **Continues** Institute of Traffic Engineers. Meeting. Compendium of Technical Papers.
**Ind/Abst** Bioeng. Abstr.; Ei Page One; Eng. Index Annu.

US/0588-9715
**CONCEPTS FOR TRAFFIC SAFETY.** 1- Spring 1968-. Periodical. English. Concepts for Traffic Safety, 151 Farmington Avenue, Hartford CT 06156. **Continues** Drivotrainer Digest.

BL
**CONTAGENS DE TRAFEGO: TEMPORADA DE VERAO. Main/Corp** Rio Grande do Sul, Brazil (State). Departamento Autonomo de Estradas de Rodagem. (1977)-. Portuguese. an. Secretaria dos Transportes, Departamento Autonomo de Estradas de Rodagem, Porto Alegre Brazil. **LC** HE373.B72; R57. **DD** 388.3/14/09816. **Continues** Rio Grande do Sul, Brazil (State). Secretaria dos Transportes. Contagens de Trafego: Temporada de Verao.

US
**CONTINUOUS COUNT TRAFFIC DATA. Main/Corp** Georgia. Dept. of Transportation. (19??)-. Periodical. English. an. **Continues** Georgia. State Highway Data. Continuous Count Traffic Data.

US
**DELAWARE TURNPIKE ANNUAL REPORT. Main/Corp** Delaware Turnpike Administration. **VFOAT** Annual Report. English. an. **LC** HE356.D4; D48A. **DD** 353.97510086/42.

BL
**DER-PE RELATORIO / GOVERNO DO ESTADO DE PERNAMBUCO, SECRETARIA DOS TRANSPORTES, ENERGIA E COMUNICACOES, DEPARTAMENTO DE ESTRADAS DE RODAGEM. Main/Corp** Pernambuco (Brazil). Departamento de Estradas de Rodagem. **VFOAT**

## Transportation —Roads and Traffic

D.E.R.-P.E. Relatorio. 1981-. Portuguese. **LC** HE359.B9; P435A. **DD** 354.81/34008642/06. *Continues Pernambuco (Brazil). Departamento de Estradas de Rodagem. Relatorio Anual.*

II
**DETAILS OF WORKS FOR DEMANDS 39, ROADS AND BRIDGES AND 52, CAPITAL OUTLAY ON ROADS AND BRIDGES FOR THE YEAR ... . Main/Corp** Tamil Nadu (India). **VFOAT** Detailed Roads and Bridges Budget. (1980-81)-. English. an. 4.35. **LC** HE365.I44; T357. **DD** 354.54/8200864. *Continues Tamil Nadu (India). Detailed Roads and Bridges Report.*

UK/0269-8196
**DIGEST OF REPORT - TRANSPORT AND ROAD RESEARCH LABORATORY.** (DIGESTS OF REPORTS.). [Dig. rep. - Transp. Road Res. Lab.]. **Added/Corp** Transport and Road Research Laboratory. **VFOAT** Technical Information and Library Services. (197?)-. Periodical. English. mo. £20.00. Transport and Road Research Lab, Old Wokingham Road, Department of Transportation, Crowthorne BK RG11 6AU England. **Tel** 44 344 773131, FAX 44 344 770356. Index available. cum. index. **Bk Rev. Ad Acc. Circ:** 1,100.
**Desc:** Digest of trial reports.
**Ind/Abst** Fluid Abstr., Civil Eng.; Fluid Abstr. Proc. Eng.; FLUIDEX (1973-1990).

IT
**DIRITTO E TECNICA DELLA CIRCOLAZIONE STRADALE E ASSICURAZIONE OBBLIGATORIA DI RCA.** See Law.

CN/0714-2153
**DISTANCES ROUTIERES.** [Distances rout.]. French. ir. Gouvernement du Quebec, 600 St Amable 4E Etage, Quebec Quebec G1R 4Z1 Canada. **DD** 388.1/2/09714.

US/0899-6717
**DRIVE.** [Drive]. **Added/Corp** South Carolina. Dept. of Highways and Public Transportation. Vol. 1, No. 1 (Fall 1987)-. Periodical. English. qt. Free. Carolina Highways, Box 191, Columbia SC 29202. **LC** HE356.S5; D75. **DD** 388.1/09757. *Continues Carolina Highways, 0008-6789.*

US
**DRIVE SAFELY.** English. mo. Bureau of Business Practice, 24 Rope Ferry Road, Waterford CT 06386. **Tel** (800)243-0876, (203)442-4365, (800)876-9105, FAX (203)443-1123. ctrl circ.
**Desc:** Handy booklet containing articles that go beyond the usual advice to drive defensively.

UK/0142-2952
**ENCYCLOPEDIA OF HIGHWAY LAW AND PRACTICE.** See Law.

GW
**ERFAHRUNGSAUSTAUSCH UBER ERDARBEITEN IM STRASSENBAU.** German. Bundesanstalt fuer Strassenwesen, Bruhler Strasse 324, 5 Koln, Bruler Strasse 1, Radethal Germany. **LC** TE210; .E72.

US/0146-7506
**EXPENDITURE REPORT - STATE OF COLORADO, DEPARTMENT OF HIGHWAYS.** *Title Change.* (EXPENDITURE REPORT - DEPARTMENT OF HIGHWAYS.). [Expend. rep. - State Colo. Dep. Highw.]. **Main/Corp** Colorado. Dept. of Highways. **VFOAT** Annual Report - State of Colorado Department of Highways. English. an. Colorado Department of Highways, 4201 East Arkansas Avenue, Denver CO 80222. **Tel** (303)757-9011. **LC** HE356.C6; C58A. **DD** 353.9/788/008781. *Continued by Annual Report (Colorado Dept. of Highways), 1051-0850.*

US
**FACTS.** **Added/Corp** Insurance Institute for Highway Safety. (1990)-. Periodical. English. Insurance Institute for Highway Safety, 1005 North Glebe Road, Suite 800, Arlington VA 22201. **Tel** (703)247-1500. **LC** HE5614.2; .I33. *Continues IIHS Facts.*

US/0732-9792
**FATAL ACCIDENT REPORTING SYSTEM.** (FATAL ACCIDENT REPORTING SYSTEM / UNITED STATES DEPARTMENT OF TRANSPORTATION, NATIONAL HIGHWAY TRAFFIC SAFETY ADMINISTRATION, NATIONAL CENTER FOR STATISTICS AND ANALYSIS.). [Fatal accid. rep. syst.]. **Added/Corp** National Center for Statistics and Analysis (U.S.) United States. National Highway Traffic Safety Administration. **VFOAT** Decade of Progress; Review of Information on Fatal Traffic Accidents in the U.S. in ... . (1979)-. English. Twice a year. Transportation Research Institute, The University of Michigan, 2901 Baxter Road, Ann Arbor MI 48109. **Tel** (313)936-1073, FAX (313)936-1081. **LC** HE5614.2; .U58b. **DD** 312/.279/0973.

available on microfiche. *Continues National Center for Statistics and Analysis (U.S.). FARS, Fatal Accident Reporting System. Annual Report, 0195-6930.*

US/0737-6332
**FATAL MOTOR VEHICLE ACCIDENT COMPARATIVE DATA REPORT.** [Fatal motor veh. accid. comp. data rep.]. English. an. New Jersey State Police, Fatal Accident Unit, Traffic Bureau, Box 7068, West Trenton NJ 08625. **LC** HE5614.3.N44; N46A. **DD** 312/.44/09749. *Continues New Jersey Fatal Motor Vehicle Accidents and Fatalities Review, Comparative Data Report, 0097-9457.*

US
**FINANCIAL REPORT TO MANAGEMENT. Main/Corp** Kentucky. Bureau of Highways. Division of Accounts. **Added/Corp** Kentucky. Dept. of Transportation. (19??)-. English. sa. Kentucky Department of Transportation, Frankfort KY 40601. **LC** HE28.K4; B87a. **DD** 353.97690072/31.

US/0092-007X
**FLORIDA SUMMARY OF ACCIDENT DATA. Main/Corp** Florida. Dept. of Transportation. Division of Safety. English. Florida Department of Transportation, Division of Safety, Tallahassee FL 32304. **LC** HE5614.3.F6; F57A. **DD** 388.3/14.

GW
**FORSCHUNGSGESELLSCHAFT FUR STRASSEN- UND VERKEHRSWESEN (GERMANY).** (TATIGKEITSBERICHT / FORSCHUNGSGESELLSCHAFT FUER STRASSEN- UND VERKEHRSWESEN.). German. Alfred-Schutte-Allee 10, W-5000 Koln 21 Germany. **LC** TE192; .F67A. **DD** 625.7/05. *Continues Tatigkeitsbericht der Forschungsgesellschaft fur das Strassenwesen.*

GW/0170-5431
**FORSCHUNGSPROGRAMM - BUNDESANSTALT FUR STRASSENWESEN, BEREICH UNFALLFORSCHUNG.** [Forsch.progr. - Bundesanst. Strassenwes., Bereich Unf.forsch.]. **Main/Corp** Bundesanstalt fur Strassenwesen (Germany). Bereich Unfallforschung. German. an. Bundesstelle fuer Aussenhandelsinformation, Agrippastr 87 93, D 50676 Cologne Germany. **Tel** 011 49 221 2057316, FAX 011 49 221 2057212. **LC** HE5614.5.G3; B85. **Circ:** 2,000.
**Desc:** Program of accident research (road safety) of the ministry of transport of the Federal Republic of Germany.

US
**FREEWAY EVOLUTION, THE. Main/Corp** California. Division of Highways. District 7. English. Department of Transportation / Division of Highways, District 7, Los Angeles CA 90053. **LC** HE356.C2; D58A. **DD** 388.1/22/097949.
**Desc:** Consists of the district's annual report.

US/0740-3003
**FREEWAY/L.A.** (FREEWAY/L.A. : NEWSLETTER OF DIGNITY/LOS ANGELES.). **VFOAT** Freeway LA. **VAT** Freeway Los angeles. Newsletter. English. mo. Dignity/LA, PO Box 27516, Los Angeles CA 90026. *Continues Caterpillar.*

US/0016-1705
**FROM THE STATE CAPITALS. HIGHWAY FINANCING AND CONSTRUCTION.** [From state cap., Highw. financ. constr.]. **VFOAT** Highway Financing and Construction. (19??)-. Periodical. English. wk. $292.00 (one year) $325.00 (two year) public and institutional libraries; $526.00 (one year), $585.00 (two year). Wakeman Walworth Inc., 300 North Washington Street #204, Alexandria VA 22314. **Tel** (703)549-8606. **ED** Emily Novick. **DD** 351. [CCC].
**Desc:** Highway financing and construction: furnishes updates on the allocation of funds for highway, street and bridge construction, extension, repair, renovation, replacement, and truck weight limits and fees.

US/1054-4127
**GOUSHA TRUCKER'S ROAD ATLAS.** [Gousha truck. road atlas]. **Added/Corp** H.M. Gousha Company. **VFOAT** Truckers Road Atlas. (1991)-. English. H.M. Gousha Company, PO Box 49006, 2001 The Alameda, San Jose CA 95161. **Tel** (800)662-6277. **DD** 912.

BL
**GUIA DE ENDERECOS DO RIO DE JANEIRO. VFOAT** Enderecos do Rio de Janeiro. No. 1 Ed. (1991)-. Portuguese.

AT
**GUIDE TO STABILISATION IN ROADWORKS / NATIONAL ASSOCIATION OF AUSTRALIAN STATE ROAD AUTHORITIES. Added/Corp** National Association of Australian State Road Authorities. **VFOAT** Guide to Stabilisation in Roadworks. (19??)-. English. National Association of Australian State Road

Authorities, PO Box 489, Milsons Point New South Wales 2061 Australia. **Tel** (02)957-6188, FAX (02)959-4756. **LC** TE210.4; .G85. **DD** 625.7/4.

US
**HAMMOND ROAD ATLAS AMERICA.** See Geography-Cartography.

JA
**HANSHIN KOSOKU DORO KODAN NEMPO. Main/Corp** Hanshin Kosoku Doro Kodan. (1966)-. Periodical. Japanese. an. Hanshin Kosoku Doro Kodan, (Hanshin Expressway Public Corporation), 4-68 Kitakyutarocho, Higashiku Osakashi Osakafu 541 Japan. **LC** HE365.J34; O734.

US/8755-9196
**HIGHWAY ACCIDENT REPORTS. SUMMARY FORMAT.** (HIGHWAY ACCIDENT REPORTS. SUMMARY FORMAT / NATIONAL TRANSPORTATION SAFETY BOARD.). **Added/Corp** United States. National Transportation Safety Board. No. 1 (1980)-. Periodical. English. Three times a year. $150.00. National Technical Information Service - NTIS, Room 2027S, 5285 Port Royal Road, Springfield VA 22161. **Tel** (703)487-4630, (703)487-4660, (703)487-4650, FAX (703)321-8547, telex 89-9405. **LC** HE5614.2; .H525. **DD** 363.

US/1062-5194
**HIGHWAY & HEAVY CONSTRUCTION PRODUCTS.** *Title Change.* [Highw. heavy constr. prod.]. **VFOAT** Highway and Heavy Construction Products. Vol. 135, No. 1 (Feb. 1992)-Vol. 136, no. 1 (Jan. 1993). Periodical. English. bm. Highway & Heavy Construction Products, 44 Cook Street, Denver CO 80206-5800. **LC** TE1; .R7. **DD** 625.7/05. Documents available from Article Express International. *Continues Highway & Heavy Construction, 0362-0506. Continued by Construction Products (Newton, Mass.).*
**Ind/Abst** Appl. Sci. Technol. Index; Bioeng. Abstr.; Bus. Index (1992-); Ei Page One; Eng. Index Annu.; Gen. BusinessFile (1992-); Gen. Period. Index (1992-); Mag. Search; Trade Ind. ASAP [Full Txt.]; Trade Ind. Index [Full Txt.].

US/0161-0325
**HIGHWAY & VEHICLE SAFETY REPORT. VAT** Highway and Vehicle Safety Report. (1974)-. Periodical. English. Twenty-six times a year. $277.00 US & Canada & Mexico; $302.00 other. Highway & Vehicle Safety Report, PO Box 3667, Branford CT 06405. **Tel** (203)488-9808, FAX (203)488-3129. **ED** S. Paul Stamler and Julie Marsh (editor's address: P.O. Box 3367, Branford. CT 06405; phone: (203)488-9808). Index available. **Bk Rev.**
**Desc:** News and analysis of all areas of vehicle and highway safety. Articles are on legislation, regulation, litigation, reports, recalls, defect investigations, and research statistics.

US
**HIGHWAY COMMISSION UPDATE.** English. bm. Mississippi State Highway Department, PO Box 1850, Jackson MS 39215-1850. **ED** Donna M Lunn.

US
**HIGHWAY IMPROVEMENT PROGRAM / INDIANA DEPARTMENT OF TRANSPORTATION. Main/Corp** Indiana. Dept. of Transportation. Division of Program Development. (1990)-. English. an. Indiana Department of Highways, Division of Planning Building, Room 1205/State Office Building, 100 North Senate Avenue, Indianapolis IN 46204. **LC** TE24.I6; I53A. **DD** 388.1/09772/05. *Continues Biennial Highway Improvement Program.*

US/0738-5277
**HIGHWAY SAFETY LITERATURE (1973).** (HIGHWAY SAFETY LITERATURE.). [Highw. saf. lit.]. **Added/Corp** National Research Council (U.S.). Transportation Research Board. National Research Council (U.S.). Highway Research Information Service. (1982-1986); New Series (1993)-. Periodical. English. an. $50.00 North America; $60.00 other. Transportation Research Board, Box 289, Washington DC 20055. **Tel** (202)334-3218, FAX (202)334-2519. **LC** HE5614; .H476. **DD** 363.1/25/05. Documents available from Documents on Demand. *Continues Highway Safety Literature (United States. National Highway Traffic Safety Administration : 1973), 0738-5277.*
**Ind/Abst** Am. Stat. Index.

US/8755-8688
**HIGHWAY SAFETY PERFORMANCE. FATAL AND INJURY ACCIDENT RATES ON PUBLIC ROADS IN THE UNITED STATES.** (HIGHWAY SAFETY PERFORMANCE ... FATAL AND INJURY ACCIDENT RATES ON PUBLIC ROADS IN THE UNITED STATES / PREPARED BY THE OFFICES OF HIGHWAY SAFETY AND HIGHWAY PLANNING.). [Highw. saf. perf., Fatal inj. rates public roads U. S.]. **Added/Corp** United States. Office of Highway Safety. United States. Office of Highway Planning. United States. Federal Highway Administration. Office of Highway Information Management. **VFOAT** Fatal and Injury Accident Rates on Public Roads in the

United States. (1982)-. English. an. Free. US Department of Transportation - Federal Highway Administration, 400 Seventh Street Southwest, Washington DC 20590. **Tel** (202)366-0660. **LC** HE5614.2; .U563a. **DD** 363.1/252/0973021. **NLM** W2; A O225h. available on microfiche (Vols. for (1983-) distributed to depository libraries). ***Continues*** *Fatal and Injury Accident Rates on Federal-Aid and Other Highway Systems, 0565-0437.*

US
**HIGHWAY SAFETY PLAN / OTSC.** **Main/Corp** Oregon Traffic Safety Commission. Began with Vol. for 1978. English. an. Free. Oregon Traffic Safety Commission, 400 State Library Building, Salem OR 97310. **Tel** (503)378-3669, IN OREGON: (800)922-2022. **LC** HE5614.3.O7; O74A. **DD** 363.1/2556/09795. Index available. **Circ:** 100 (ctrl).
**Desc:** Document is Oregon's application for federal '402' traffic safety funds. It summarizes the funded projects and other activities directed towards reducing traffic fatalities and injuries.

US
**HIGHWAY SAFETY PLAN - WASHINGTON (STATE). TRAFFIC SAFETY COMMISSION.** **Main/Corp** Washington (State). Traffic Safety Commission. English. Washington Traffic Safety Commission, PO Box 1399, 1000 South Cherry, Edit Centerline, Olympia WA 98504. **Tel** (206)753-6197. **LC** HE5614.3.W2; W39B. **DD** 363.1/256/09797.

US/0277-2310
**HIGHWAY SAFETY STEWARDSHIP REPORT, THE.** (THE ... HIGHWAY SAFETY STEWARDSHIP REPORT : REPORT OF THE SECRETARY OF TRANSPORTATION TO THE UNITED STATES CONGRESS.). 6th(1980)-. English. an. Office of Highway Safety / Washington DC, Washington DC 20590. **LC** HE5614.2; .H53. **DD** 363.1/256/0973. ***Continues*** *Highway Safety Improvement Programs.*

US/0095-344X
**HIGHWAY STATISTICS.** (HIGHWAY STATISTICS / PUBLIC ROADS ADMINISTRATION, FEDERAL WORKS AGENCY.). **Added/Corp** United States. Public Roads Administration. United States. Bureau of Public Roads. United States. Federal Highway Administration. (1945)-. Statistical Publication. English. ir. Superintendent of Documents, US Government Printing Office, Washington DC 20402. **Tel** (202)275-3328, FAX (202)786-2377. **LC** HE355.A3; A25. **DD** 388.1/0973.
**Ind/Abst** Predicasts Forecasts.

US/0147-9539
**HIGHWAY SUFFICIENCY REPORT.** [Highw. suffic. rep.]. **Main/Corp** Maine. Dept. of Transportation. Bureau of Planning. English. Maine Department of Transportation, Transportation Building, Child Street, Augusta ME 04333. **LC** TE24.M2; M34A. **DD** 388.1/09741.

US/0732-8230
**HIGHWAY TAXES AND FEES.** (HIGHWAY TAXES AND FEES / C.U.S. DEPARTMENT OF TRANSPORTATION, FEDERAL HIGHWAY ADMINISTRATION.). **Added/Corp** United States. Federal Highway Administration. (19??)-. English. US Department of Transportation - Federal Highway Administration, 400 Seventh Street Southwest, Washington DC 20590. **Tel** (202)366-0660. **LC** HE355.A3; A15. **DD** 353.9/372.

US/0092-3389
**HIGHWAY TRANSPORTATION RESEARCH AND DEVELOPMENT STUDIES.** **Main/Corp** United States. Federal Highway Administration. English. $4.20. US Department of Transportation - Federal Highway Administration, 400 Seventh Street Southwest, Washington DC 20590. **Tel** (202)366-0660. **LC** TE1; .U73A. **DD** 625.7/07/2073. ***Continues*** *R & D Highway & Safety Transportation Systems Studies.*

UK/0265-6868
**HIGHWAYS AND TRANSPORTATION.** (HIGHWAYS AND TRANSPORTATION : JOURNAL OF THE INSTITUTION OF HIGHWAYS AND TRANSPORTATION & HTTA.). [Highw. transp.]. Vol. 30, No. 8/9 (Aug./Sept. 1983)-. Academic Scholarly Publication. English. mo (Aug. and Sept. issues combined). £22.00. East Midland Allied Press, 41 Broadway, Peterborough Bretton Court, Bretton PE3 8DZ England. **LC** TE1; .I453. **DD** 625.7/05. **CODEN** HITRED. available on microfilm from University Microfilms International (UMI). Documents available from Article Express International. ***Continues*** *Highway Engineer, 0306-6452.*
**Ind/Abst** Civ. Struct. Eng. Abstr.; Comput. Inf. Syst. Abstr. J. [Full Cov.]; Curr. Technol. Index; Ei Page One; EMBASE; Eng. Index Annu.; Environ. Eng. Abstr.; Ergon. Abstr.; Int. Civil Eng. Abstr.; Mater. Sci. Eng. Abstr.; Mech. Eng. Abstr.

JA/0386-1112
**IATSS RESEARCH.** **Main/Corp** Kokusai Kotsu Anzen Gakkai. Vol. 1 (1977)-. English. Twice a year. $60.00. International Association of Traffic & Safety, 2-6-20 Yaesu Chuo-Ku, Tokyo 104 Japan. **Tel** 011 81 3 3273 7884. **LC** HE5601; .K64a. **DD** 363.1/256/0952.

US
**ILLINOIS TRAFFIC ACCIDENT FACTS AND STATISTICS.** **Added/Corp** Illinois. Dept. of Transportation. (1988)-. English. Illinois Department of Transportation, Auditorium, 2300 South Dirksen Parkway, Springfield IL 62764. ***Formed by the union of*** *Accident Facts. Illinois. Dept. of Transportation* ***and*** *Motorcycle Accident Facts (Springfield, Ill.).*

US/1064-2560
**IMSA JOURNAL.** [IMSA j.]. **Added/Corp** International Municipal Signal Association. Vol. 15, No. 6 (Nov./Dec. 1979)-. Periodical. English. bm (6 issues). $40.00. International Municipal Signal Association, PO Box 539, 1115 North Main Street, Newark NY 14513. **Tel** (315)331-2182, (315)331-2183, FAX (315)331-8205. **ED** Harold Glerum. **DD** 388. **Bk Rev. Ad Acc, Adv Mgr:** Sharon Earl. **Circ:** 5,600 (ctrl). ***Continues*** *Municipal Signals, 1064-4652.*
**Desc:** Articles include information on traffic signals, signs & highway markings, dispatch, work zones, and roadway lighting.

II/0376-7256
**INDIAN HIGHWAYS.** **Added/Corp** Indian Roads Congress. Vol. 1 (July 1973)-. Periodical. English. mo. $20.00. Indian Roads Congress, Jannagar House, Shahjahan Road, New Delhi, India. **Tel** 385395, 381649. **(Subscription address:** Prints India, 11 Darya Ganj, New Delhi 110002 India.**) ED** Shri Ninan Koshi. **LC** TE5; .I44. **DD** 625.7/0954. **Bk Rev. Ad Acc. Pr Rev. Circ:** 6,000 (ctrl). ***Continues*** *Transport-Communications Monthly Review.*
**Desc:** Certain articles on road and road transport including road transport economics, traffic engineering, bridge engineering.
**Ind/Abst** Ei Page One; Highw. Res. Abstr.

US/0959-6631
**INTELLIGENT HIGHWAY, THE.** (THE INTELLIGENT HIGHWAY : RTI/IVHS NEWS.). [Intell. highw.]. **VFOAT** RTI/IVHS News. Issue 1 (April 1990)-. Periodical. English. Twenty-four times a year. $495.00. Waters Information Services, PO Box 2248, Binghamton NY 13902-2248. **Tel** (607)770-8535, FAX (607)798-1692. **DD** 629. Index available (bound in April issue).

UK/0966-4955
**INTERNATIONAL CAR PARK DESIGN & CONSTRUCTION TRENDS.** [Int. car park des. constr. trends]. **VFOAT** International Car Park Design and Construction Trends; Car Park Design & Construction Trends. (198?)-. Periodical. English. sa. £16.00 UK; £24.00 other. Landor Holdings Ltd, Quadrant House, 250 Kennington Lane, London SE11 5RD England. **Tel** 011 44 71 735 5058, FAX 011 44 71 587 0497.
**Desc:** Examines the changing approaches to designing, building, equipping and refurbishing car parks. Designed to provide a review for architects, developers, designers, consultants, planners, engineers and contractors.

US
**IOWA MOTOR VEHICLE TRAFFIC ACCIDENT FACTS.** **Main/Corp** Iowa. Motor Vehicle Division. Research & Statistics Section. English. Research and Statistics Section / Des Moines, Motor Vehicle Division, Iowa Department of Transportation, Grimes State Office Building, Des Moines IA 50319. **LC** HE5614.3.I8; I58A. **DD** 388.3/14.

●SZ/1065-5123
**IVHS JOURNAL.** [IVHS j.]. **Added/Corp** IVHS America. **VAT** Intelligent Vehicle Highway Systems Journal. Vol. 1, No. 1 (Apr. 1993)-. Periodical. English. qt. $216.00 (academic institutions), $336.00 (corporate institutions). Gordon & Breach Science Publishers, Inc., PO Box 786, Cooper Station, New York NY 10276. **Tel** (212)206-8900, FAX (212)645-2459. **(Subscription address:** International Publishers Distributor at one of the following addresses: 820 Town Center Drive, Langhorne, PA 19047; or PO Box 90, Reading Berkshire RG1 8JL UK; or Kent Ridge PO Box 1180, Singapore 9111, Republic of Singapore**) DD** 629. **CODEN** IVJOEM.
**Desc:** Focuses on intelligent vehicle highway systems (IVHS), published in cooperation with IVHS America.

US
**IVHS REVIEW.** English. Four times a year. $19.00 (members); $29.00 (nonmembers) North America; $49.00 (nonmembers) Europe & South America; $59.00 (nonmembers) other. IVHS America, 400 Virginia Avenue SW, Suite 800, Washington DC 20024. **Tel** (202)484-2906.
**Desc:** Contains invited articles that will explore the technical and social implications of IVHS, published in cooperation with IVHS America.

US/0164-1344
**JOURNAL OF TRAFFIC SAFETY EDUCATION.** [J. traffic saf. educ.]. V. 18- Oct. 1970-. Periodical. English. qt. 11.00Can$ Canada; 13.50Can$ to 16.50Can$ depending on area Europe and Asia. c/o Charles Weber, 37639 Robin Lane, Palmdale CA 93550. **Tel** (805)947-9411. **ED** Charles Weber. **LC** HE5614.3.C3; J68. **DD** 614.8/62/07120794. Index available. **Ad Acc. Circ:** 2,500 (ctrl). ***Continues*** *California Journal of Traffic Safety Education.*
**Desc:** Mostly deals with driver and passenger safety, drivers education and training. Also deals with research, engineering and law enforcement.
**Ind/Abst** Educ. Index; Highw. Res. Abstr.

HU/0231-0724
**KOZUTI KOZLEKEDESI SZAKIRODALMI TAJEKOZTATO.** (1983)-. Periodical. Hungarian. mo. 3.800ft. Orszagos Muszaki Informacios Kozpont es Konyvtar (O.M.I.K.K.), National Technical Information Centre and Library Museum, u 17, PO Box 12, 1428 Budapest, Hungary. **Tel** (361)118-1994, FAX (361)138-2414, telex 22-4944 OMIKK H. **ED** Ferenc Sido. **UDC** 016. Index available. cum. index. **Bk Rev. Ad Acc. Circ:** 220 (ctrl).
**Desc:** Information on transportation, automobiles, roads and traffic.

HU/0237-2576
**KOZUTI KOZLEKEDESI SZAKIRODALMI TAJEKOZTATO. UTUGYI SZAKKIADAS.** (1985)-. Periodical. Hungarian. mo. 3.800ft. Orszagos Muszaki Informacios Kozpont es Konyvtar (O.M.I.K.K.), National Technical Information Centre and Library Museum, u 17, PO Box 12, 1428 Budapest, Hungary. **Tel** (361)118-1994, FAX (361)138-2414, telex 22-4944 OMIKK H. **ED** Sido Ferenc. **UDC** 016. **Circ:** 250.
**Desc:** Traffic in general, accidents, roads, building of roads, building materials.

US
**LARGE CLASS I HOUSEHOLD GOODS CARRIERS SELECTED EARNINGS DATA.** **See** Transportation.

US/0075-8159
**LATIN AMERICAN TRAVEL & PAN AMERICAN HIGHWAY GUIDE.** **See** Travel and Tourism.

FR/1164-4079
**MACADAM NICE.** (MACADAM.). (198?)-. Periodical. French. tq. **UDC** 796.073(449.4).
**Ind/Abst** Archit. Period. Index.

US
**MANUAL ON UNIFORM TRAFFIC CONTROL DEVICES FOR STREETS AND HIGHWAYS.** **Main/Corp** United States. National Advisory Committee on Uniform Traffic Control Devices. **Added/Corp** nited States. Federal Highway Adminstration. **VFOAT** Manual on Uniform Traffic Control Devices. (1978)-. Government Publication. English. an. Superintendent of Documents, US Government Printing Office, Washington DC 20402. **Tel** (202)275-3328, FAX (202)786-2377.
**Desc:** Provides detailed uniform standards for all signs, markings and devices placed on, over, or adjacent to a street or highway.

US/0364-2518
**MERGE.** **Main/Corp** Kansas. Highway Safety Coordinating Office. Issue 1- Nov./Dec. 1972-. English. Kansas Highway Safety Coordinating Office, 10th Office Building, Topeka KS 66612. **LC** HE5614.3.K3; K25A. **DD** 388.3/14.

US
**MISSISSIPPI HIGHWAY TRAFFIC REPORT / PREPARED BY THE MISSISSIPPI STATE HIGHWAY DEPARTMENT, TRANSPORTATION PLANNING DIVISION ; IN COOPERATION WITH U.S. DEPARTMENT OF TRANSPORTATION, FEDERAL HIGHWAY ADMINISTRATION.** **Added/Corp** Mississippi. Transportation Planning Division. United States. Federal Highway Administration. Mississippi. Traffic and Planning Division. **VFOAT** Mississippi ... Highway Traffic. (19??)-. English. **LC** HE371.M7; A25. **DD** 388.3/142/09762.

US
**MISSISSIPPI PUBLIC ROAD MILEAGE AS OF DECEMBER 31 / PREPARED BY MISSISSIPPI STATE HIGHWAY DEPARTMENT, TRANSPORTATION PLANNING DIVISION IN COOPERATION WITH U.S. DEPARTMENT OF TRANSPORTATION, FEDERAL HIGHWAY ADMINISTRATION.** **Added/Corp** Mississippi. Transportation Planning Division. United States. Federal Highway Administration. **VFOAT** Mississippi State Highway Department Public Road Mileage as of December 31. (19??)-. English. an. **LC** HE356.M7; M49. **DD** 388.1/09762.

CN/0709-5341
**MOTOR VEHICLE REPORTS.** **See** Law.

# Transportation — Roads and Traffic

US
**MOTOR VEHICLE STATISTICS. ACCIDENT, LICENSE AND REGISTRATION STATISTICAL DATA.** **Added/Corp** New York (State). Dept. of Motor Vehicles. Division of Research and Development. New York (State). Dept. of Motor Vehicles. Division of Research and Evaluation. **VFOAT** Accident, License and Registration Statistical Data. (1984/1983/1982)-. Statistical Publication. English. te. New York State Department of Motor Vehicles, Albany NY 12228. **Tel** (518)473-8603. *Continues* Motor vehicle statistics. Accident and operational statistical data.

CN
**MOTOR VEHICLE TRAFFIC ACCIDENTS.** **Ceased. Main/Corp** Statistics Canada. Transportation Section. **VFOAT** Accidents de la Circulation Routiere. Ceased (1976). Multiple languages (English and French). an. Statistics Canada, Publications Sales & Services, Main Building Room 1710, Ottawa Ontario K1A 0T6 Canada. **Tel** (613)951-5078, (800)267-6677, **FAX** (613)951-1584, telex 053-3585. **LC** HE5614.5.C2; C23A. **DD** 312/.4/4. *Continues* Motor Vehicle Traffic Accidents.

GW/0722-8287
**NAHVERKEHR, DER.** [Nahverkehr]. (1983)-. Periodical. German. Ten times a year. DM180.00 Germany; DM188.40 other Europe; DM217.20 other. Alba Fachverlag GmbH & Co KG, Roemerstrasse 9, D40476 Duesseldorf Germany. **Tel** 011 49 211 469-0161. **UDC** 656.021(1-22). **[CCC].**

US/0077-5614
**NATIONAL COOPERATIVE HIGHWAY RESEARCH PROGRAM REPORT.** (REPORT - NATIONAL COOPERATIVE HIGHWAY RESEARCH PROGRAM.). [Natl. Coop. Highw. Res. Program rep.]. **Added/Corp** National Cooperative Highway Research Program. National Research Council (U.S.). Transportation Research Board National Research Council (U.S.). Highway Research Board. (1964)-. Monographic series. English. ir. Price varies per volume. Transportation Research Board, Box 289, Washington DC 20055. **Tel** (202)334-3218, **FAX** (202)334-2519. **LC** TE7; .N25. **CODEN** NCHRDA. Documents available from Article Express International, CASDDS.
**Ind/Abst** Bioeng. Abstr.; Chem. Abstr.; Ei Page One; Eng. Index Annu.

US
**NEBRASKA SELECTED STATISTICS FOR ...** **VFOAT** Selected Highway Statistics for ... . (1983)-. English. an. Nebraska Department of Roads, Office of Planning Transportation Planning Division, Statistics Unit, Lincoln NE 68509. **LC** HE356.N36; N43B. **DD** 338.1/09782/021. *Continues* Nebraska Highway Statistics: State and Local Road and Street Data.

US/1059-8545
**NEW JERSEY TRAFFIC DIRECTORY (STATEWIDE ED.), THE.** (THE NEW JERSEY TRAFFIC DIRECTORY.). [N.J. traffic dir.]. (1991)-. Directory. English. an (Dec.). $139.00 US. Traffic Directories, Inc., 4 Cornwall Drive, Suite 200, East Brunswick NJ 08816. **Tel** (908)651-1000. **LC** HE371.N5; N48. **DD** 388.3/14/0974905.

US
**NEW YORK STATE'S ... HIGHWAY SUFFICIENCY RATINGS.** **VFOAT** Highway Sufficiency Ratings; New York State's ... Highway Sufficiency Rating. English. New York State Department of Transportation, State Campus Building 4/Room 108, Albany NY 12232. **LC** TE24.N7; N49. **DD** 625.7/09747/021.

SW/1101-5179
**NORDIC ROAD & TRANSPORT RESEARCH.** **VFOAT** Nordic Road and Transport Research. (1989)-. Periodical. English. ir. Free on request. Swedish Road and Transport Institute, S 581 95 Linkoping Sweden. **Tel** 011 46 13 204000. **UDC** 351.81. **Ind/Abst** Geotech. Abstr.

●NO
**NORSK VEG-OG VEGTRAFIKKPLAN.** **Added/Corp** Norway. Vegdirektoratet. Norway. Samferdselsdepartementet. (1990-93)-. Norwegian. **LC** HE363.N6; N67. *Continues* Vegplan.

US/0361-9532
**NORTH CAROLINA MUNICIPAL EXPENDITURES FROM STATE STREET-AID ALLOCATIONS.** **Main/Corp** North Carolina. Division of Highways. Planning and Research Branch. English. an. North Carolina Department of Transportation and Highway Safety, PO Box 25201, Raleigh NC 27611. **LC** HE356.N8; N65B. **DD** 338.4/3.

US/0095-7712
**NORTH DAKOTA ACCIDENT FACTS.** **Main/Corp** North Dakota. Traffic Engineering Division. 1973-. English. North Dakota Highway Safety Improvement Program, Traffic Engineering Division, Bismarck ND. **LC** HE5614.3.N63; N67A. **DD** 388.3/14. *Continues* Traffic Accident Facts and Statistical Report.

US/0361-8099
**NORTH DAKOTA HIGHWAY SAFETY IMPROVEMENT PROGRAM, ANNUAL REPORT.** **Main/Corp** North Dakota. Traffic Engineering Division. English. an. North Dakota Highway Safety Improvement Program, Traffic Engineering Division, Bismarck ND. **LC** HE5614.3.N63; N67B. **DD** 388.3/12.

US
**NORTH DAKOTA HIGHWAY SAFETY PLAN.** **VFOAT** Highway Safety Plan. English. an. North Dakota State Highway Department, Capitol Grounds, Bismarck ND 58505. **LC** HE5614.3.N63; N69. **DD** 363.1/256/09784.

US/0549-852X
**NORTH DAKOTA TRAFFIC REPORT.** **Main/Corp** North Dakota. Transportation Services Division. Began in 1963. English. an. North Dakota State Highway Department, Capitol Grounds, Bismarck ND 58505. **LC** HE371.N8; N65A. **DD** 388.3/14/09784. *Continues* North Dakota Traffic Report.

US
**NORTH DAKOTA VEHICULAR CRASH FACTS.** **Added/Corp** North Dakota. Drivers License and Traffic Safety Division. (1987)-. English. Driver's License & Traffic Safety Division, North Dakota State Highway Department, 600 East Boulevard Avenue, Bismarck ND 59505-0700. **Tel** (701)224-2600. **LC** HE5614.3.N63; N7. **DD** 363.12/52/09784021. *Continues* North Dakota Vehicular Accident Facts, 0362-9171.

US
**OKLAHOMA TRAFFIC ACCIDENT FACTS.** **Main/Corp** Oklahoma. Dept. of Public Safety. Services & Records Division. English. an. Services and Records Division, Department of Public Safety, Box 11415, Oklahoma City OK 73136. **LC** HE5614.3.O5; O38B. **DD** 312/.44/09766.

CN/0702-8040
**ONTARIO TRAFFIC SAFETY. Added/Corp** Ontario. Ministry of Transportation and Communications. Ontario. Dept. of Transportation and Communications. Ontario. Dept. of Transport. Vol. 1 (Apr. 1958)-. English (French). qt (Mar., July, Sept., Dec.). Free upon request. Ministry of Transportation / Canada, 1201 Wilson Avenue, 1st Floor/West Tower, Downsview Ontario M3M 1J8 Canada. **Tel** (905)248-3501. **ED** Terry Dicarlo. **Circ:** 21,000.

US
**OREGON TRAFFIC ACCIDENTS. FOCUS ON MOTORCYCLES. Main/Corp** Oregon. Motor Vehicles Division. 1976-. English. an. Oregon Motor Vehicles Division, 1905 Lana Avenue NE, Salem OR 97314. **LC** HE5614.3.O7; O68B. **DD** 363.1/259. *Continues* Oregon Motorcycle Accidents, 0092-9913.

DK
**OVERSIGT OVER VEJBUDGETTERNE.** Danish. **LC** HE363.D43; E357.

US/0030-8943
**PACIFIC TRAFFIC. Ceased. VFOAT** Pacific Traffic Magazine. (1953)-(July 1988). Periodical. English. mo. Pacific Traffic, 110 West Ocean Boulevard/#323, Long Beach CA 90802-4626. **Tel** (310)822-3132. **ED** Nicole Knowlton. **Ad Acc. Circ:** 13,500 (ctrl).
**Desc:** Serves traffic and distribution managers who ship and/or store goods and merchandise by air, rail, truck or ship throughout the world.

SA
**PADVERKEERBOTSINGS / SENTRALE STATISTIEKDIENS. VFOAT** Road Traffic Collisions. Afrikaans (English). an. R2.50. Staatsdrukker, Bosmanstraat, Privaatsak X85, Pretoria 0001 South Africa. **LC** HE5614.5.S6; S68A. *Continues* Road Traffic Accidents (Pretoria, South Africa).

US/0896-2324
**PARKING PROFESSIONAL, THE.** [Park. prof.]. **Added/Corp** Institutional and Municipal Parking Congress. (198?)-. Periodical. English. mo. $60.00 US, Canada & Mexico; $72.00 other. IMPC, PO Box 7167, Fredericksburg VA 22404. **Tel** (703)371-7535, **FAX** (703)371-8022. **ED** Marie Witmer. **DD** 363. Index available. cum. index. **Ad Acc, Adv Mgr:** Lynne Chiara. **Circ:** 1,800.
**Desc:** Provides news and information on what's in the parking market.

UK/0962-3566
**PARKING REVIEW.** [Parking rev.]. (198?)-. Periodical. English. Ten times a year. £32.00 UK; £42.00 Europe; £52.00 other. Landor Holdings Ltd, Quadrant House, 250 Kennington Lane, London SE11 5RD England. **Tel** 011 44 71 735 5058, **FAX** 011 44 71 587 0497. **DD** 388.474.
**Desc:** Offers news and feature coverage of on and off-street parking policy, car park design and maintenance services, parking meters, pay-and-display machines, tickets, barriers, security systems, advertising facilities, lighting, residents parking management systems, and all other equipment and services used by public and private car park operators.

FR/0986-1793
**PCM LE PONT. VFOAT** Ponts et Chaussees et Mines le Pont. (1987)-. Periodical. French. mo. 440.00F France; 500.00F others. PCM Service Abonnement, 28 rue des Saints Peres, 75007 Paris France. **Tel** 011 33 1 42692533. **UDC** 378 : 62. *Formed by the union of* PCM Ponts et Chaussees et Mines le Pont, 0397-4634 *and* Le Pont (Paris), 0398-0251.

BL
**PLANO RODOVIARIO ESTADUAL. Main/Corp** Maranhao, Brazil (State). Departamento de Estradas de Rodagem. (19??)-. Portuguese. **LC** HE359.B9; M275a. **DD** 388.1/0981/2.

FR
**PREVENTION ROUTIERE INTERNATIONALE : [PUBLICATION TRIMESTRIELLE DE LA PRI], LA. Added/Corp** International Road Safety (Association). **VFOAT** International Road Safety; Internationale Verkehrssicherheit. (197?)-. Periodical. English (German and French). Three times a year. 1400.00F Luxembourg; 1670.00F other. PRI, 75 rue de Mamer BP 40, L-8001 Bertrange Luxembourg. **Tel** 011 352 318341. **LC** HE5614; .P76. **DD** 363.1/25/05.

LU
**PRI REVIEW. INTERNATIONAL ROAD SAFETY.** See Public Health and Safety.

US/0091-5122
**PROCEEDINGS - COMMITTEE ON COMPUTER TECHNOLOGY.** (PROCEEDINGS : NATIONAL CONFERENCE.). [Proc. - Comm. Comput. Technol.]. **Main/Corp** American Association of State Highway Officials Committee on Computer Technology. 1970-. Proceedings. English. an. American Association of State Highway and Transportation Officials, 444 North Capital Street, Suite 249, Washington DC 20001. **Tel** (202)624-5800. **LC** TE5; .A45A. **DD** 625.7/028/54. *Continues* National Conference - A.A.S.H.O Committee on Electronics, 0091-5130.

AT/0572-1431
**PROCEEDINGS [OF THE CONFERENCE]. Main/Corp** Australian Road Research Board. (1962)-. English. be. Price varies per part and set. Australian Road Research Board, PO Box 156, Nunawading VIC 3131 Australia. **Tel** 011 61 3 8811555, **FAX** 011 61 3 8878104, telex AA 33113. **LC** TE121; .A9. **DD** 625. **CODEN** PCABDH. **Circ:** 1,000. available on microfiche. Documents available from Article Express International.
**Desc:** Papers presented at the major conferences held by the Board.
**Ind/Abst** Bioeng. Abstr.; Ei Page One; Eng. Index Annu.; Highw. Res. Abstr.

US/0033-3735
**PUBLIC ROADS.** [Public roads]. **Added/Corp** United States. Federal Highway Administration. United States. Bureau of Public Roads. United States. Federal Highway Administration. Offices of Research, Development, and Technology. United States. Federal Highway Administration. Office of Research and Development (1990)-. (May 1918)-. Government Publication. English. qt. $9.50 US; $11.90 other. Superintendent of Documents, US Government Printing Office, Washington DC 20402. **Tel** (202)275-3328, **FAX** (202)786-2377. **LC** TE23; .P86. **DD** 625. **CODEN** PUROAQ. available on microfiche and hardcopy from University Microfilms International (UMI). Documents available from Article Express International, UMI Article Clearinghouse, CASDDS, Documents on Demand.
**Desc:** Contains articles relating to highway research, engineering, safety on the highways, surfacing, and other subjects in this field.
**Ind/Abst** Am. Stat. Index; Appl. Sci. Technol. Index; Bioeng. Abstr.; Chem. Abstr.; Ei Page One; EMBASE; Eng. Index Annu.; Expand. Acad. Index (1992-); Geogr. Abstr. Human Geogr. (?-); Geol. Abstr.; GeoRef; Highw. Res. Abstr.; Int. Civil Eng. Abstr.; J. Plan. Lit.; Newsp. Period. Abstr. (1989-); Soft. Abstr. Eng.; Trade Ind. ASAP [Full Txt.]; Trade Ind. Index [Full Txt.].

FR
**RAPPORT ANNUEL DE LA CAISSE NATIONALE DES AUTOROUTES. Main/Corp** Caisse Nationale des Autoroutes. French (English). an. Free. Caisse Nationale des Autoroutes, 56

Transportation—Roads and Traffic

rue de Lille, 75007 Paris France. **Tel** 47 53 85 11, FAX 47 53 98 61, telex 200055. **LC** HE363.F7; C33. **DD** 354.440086/42/05. **Circ:** 3,000.
**Desc:** Activity of the CNA Bonds issued during the year.

FR
**RAPPORT ANNUEL DU CONSEIL D'ADMINISTRATION SUR L'ACTIVITE DE LA CAISSE NATIONALE DES AUTOROUTES EN ... . Main/Corp** Caisse Nationale des Autoroutes. Conseil d'Administration. French. an. 56 rue de Lille, 75007 Paris France. **LC** HE363.F7; C33. **DD** 354.44086/42/05. **Continues** Rapport Annuel de la Caisse Nationale des Autoroutes.

RU
**REFERATIVNYI ZHURNAL: ORGANIZATSIIA I BEZOPASNOST DOROZHNOGO DVIZHENIIA. See** Transportation-Abstracting, Bibliographies and Statistics.

US
**REPORT. Main/Corp** Kentucky. Dept. of Highways. (19??)-. English. an. Kentucky Department of Transportation, Frankfort KY 40601. **LC** HE356.K4; A3. **DD** 625.7.

US
**REPORT OF THE MISSISSIPPI RIVER PARKWAY COMMISSION TO THE ... GENERAL ASSEMBLY OF ILLINOIS / MISSISSIPPI RIVER PARKWAY COMMISSION. Main/Corp** Mississippi River Parkway Commission (III.). 1st (1981)-. English. an. Illinois Mississippi River Parkway Commission, Room 121B/Capitol Building, Springfield IL 62706. **LC** HE356.I3; M57A. **DD** 353.97730086/42/06.

CN/0707-1973
**REPORT OF THE SASKATCHEWAN SAFETY COUNCIL PUBLIC OPINION POLL, A. See** Public Health and Safety.

US
**REPORT ON ACTIVITIES UNDER THE HIGHWAY SAFETY ACT OF 1966 AS AMENDED, A. Added/Corp** United States. National Highway Traffic Safety Administration. United States. Federal Highway Administration. **VFOAT** Traffic Safety; Highway Safety. (1974)-. English. an. National Highway Traffic Safety Administration, 400 Seventh Street SW, Washington DC 20590. **LC** HE5614.2; .A332. **DD** 614.8/6. available on microfiche (Vols. for (1983)- distributed to depository libraries). **Continues** Report on Activities of the National Highway Traffic Safety Administration and the Federal Highway Administration Under the Highway Safety Act of 1966.

US/0735-8539
**REPORT ON TRAFFIC ACCIDENTS AND INJURIES.** (REPORT ON TRAFFIC ACCIDENTS AND INJURIES FOR ... / [RESEARCH AND DEVELOPMENT, NATIONAL CENTER FOR STATISTICS AND ANALYSIS].). [Rep. traffic accid. inj.]. **Added/Corp** United States. National Highway Traffic Safety Administration. National Center for Statistics and Analysis. Research and Development. Comsis Corporation. National Accident Sampling System (U.S.). (1979)-. English. an. Department of Transportation, 400 Seventh Street SW, Washington DC 20590. **Tel** (202)426-4000. **LC** HE5614.2; .R46. **DD** 363.1/252/0973. available on microfiche (Vols. for 1979/1980- distributed to depository libraries).

CN/0701-6441
**REPORT ON TRAVEL ON SASKATCHEWAN HIGHWAYS. Added/Corp** Saskatchewan. Traffic Engineering Section. Saskatchewan. Traffic Research Section. Saskatchewan. Traffice Analysis Section. Saskatchewan. Saskatchewan Highways and Transportation. Engineering Support Branch. Saskatchewan. Design and Traffic Safety Branch. Saskatchewan. Traffic Engineering Section. Travel on Saskatchewan Highways. **VFOAT** Travel on Saskatchewan Highways. (1972)-. English. Saskatchewan Highways & Transportation, 9th Floor, 1855 Victoria Avenue, Regina Saskatchewan S4P 3V5 Canada. **Tel** (306)787-4756, FAX (306)787-1007. **LC** HE373.C4; S278a. **DD** 388.3/14/097124. **Continues** Report on ... Travel on Saskatchewan Highways, 0701-6441.

US
**REPORT TO THE PEOPLE. Main/Corp** Oklahoma Highway Safety Office. (19??)-. English. an. Oklahoma Highway Safety Office, G-80 Jim Thorpe Building, Oklahoma City OK 73105. **LC** HE5614.3.O5; O386a. **DD** 614.8/62/09766.

US
**REPRINT. Main/Corp** Virginia Council of Highway Investigation and Research. No. 1 Oct. (1949)-. English.

AT
**RESEARCH REPORT - AUSTRALIAN ROAD RESEARCH BOARD. Main/Corp** Australian Road Research Board. No. 1 (19??)-. English. ir. 30.00Aus$. Australian Road Research Board, PO Box 156, Nunawading VIC 3131 Australia. **Tel** 011 61 3 8811555, FAX 011 61 3 8878104, telex AA 33113. **Circ:** 500. available on microfiche.
**Desc:** Results of research work performed or sponsored by the Australian Road Research Board.

US/0547-5554
**RESEARCH RESULTS DIGEST / NATIONAL COOPERATIVE HIGHWAY RESEARCH PROGRAM. Main/Corp** National Cooperative Highway Research Program. **Added/Corp** National Cooperative Highway Research Program. (Dec. 1968)-. Monographic series. English. ir. Price varies per volume. Transportation Research Board, Box 289, Washington DC 20055. **Tel** (202)334-3218, FAX (202)334-2519. **LC** TE1; .N2516.

DK
**RESULTATER AF MANUELLE TRAFIKTLLINGER I ... I FASTE PUNKTER PA VEJNETTET / VEJDIREKTORATET, ARBEJDSGRUPPEN OM MANUELLE TRAFIKTLLINGER.** 1982-. Danish. an. **LC** HE373.D4; R47.

BL
**REVISTA DO DER PERNAMBUCO. Main/Corp** Pernambuco, Brazil Departamento de Estradas de Rodagem. **VAT** Revista do Departamento de Estradas de Rodagem Pernambuco. Periodical. Portuguese. bm. Caixa Postal 412, Recife Brazil. **LC** HE359.B9; P42. **Continues** Pernambuco, Brazil (State). Departamento de Estradas de Rodagem. Noticias.

BL
**REVISTA RODOVIARIA. Added/Corp** Rio Grande do Sul (Brazil). Departamento Autonomo de Estradas de Rodagem. Vol. 1 (Aug. 1972)-. Periodical. Portuguese. mo. Departamento Autonomo del Estrades Rodagem, Divisiao de Services Especiais, Av. Borges de Medeiras, No. 1555 Porto Alegre Brazil. **LC** TE4; .R495.

UK
**ROAD ACCIDENTS GREAT BRITAIN. Main/Corp** Great Britain. Dept. of Transport. English. £2.25. Directorate of Statistics, STCG3 Division, Department of the Environment, 2 Marsham Street, London SW1P 3EB England. **LC** HE5614.5.G7; G735A. **DD** 388.3/14.

UK/0263-9653
**ROAD ACCIDENTS, WALES. VFOAT** Damweiniau Ffyrdd, Cymru. English (Welsh). an. **LC** HE5614.5; .G7; R73. **DD** 312/.44.

●AT/1037-5783
**ROAD & TRANSPORT RESEARCH : [A JOURNAL OF AUSTRALIAN AND NEW ZEALAND RESEARCH AND PRACTICE]. Added/Corp** Australian Road Research Board. **VFOAT** Road and Transport Research. Vol. 1, No. 1 (Mar. 1992)-. Periodical. English. Four times a year. 95.00Aus$. Australian Road Research Board, PO Box 156, Nunawading VIC 3131 Australia. **Tel** 011 61 3 8811555, FAX 011 61 3 8878104, telex AA 33113. **LC** TE121; .A92. **DD** 625.7/0994. **CODEN** RTRREK. **Continues** Australian Road Research, 0005-0164.
**Ind/Abst** Highw. Res. Abstr.

JA/0917-0863
**ROAD HOME, THE.** [Road home]. (1989)-. Periodical. English. ir (four to six issues per year). International Highway Construction Corporation, 37-13 Udagawa-cho, Shibuya Tokyo 150 Japan. **Tel** (03)3481-5731, FAX (03)3481-5994. **ED** Tateo Yanaoka. **DD** 625.7. **Pr Rev. Circ:** 500.
**Desc:** Aims to promote world peace by proposing to build an international highway that links all nations of the world, including a highway through China and a tunnel connecting Japan and Korea.

UK
**ROAD LAW. Title Change.** Vol. 1, No. 1 (Feb./March 1985)-(19??). Periodical. English. Eight times a year. Barry Rose Law Periodicals Ltd., Little London, Chichester West Sussex PO19 1PG England. **Tel** 011 44 243 787841, 011 44 243 783637, FAX 011 44 243 779174, 011 44 243 779278. **LC** KD2592; .R6. **DD** 343.4109/4/05; 344.1039405. **Continued by** Road Law and Road Law Reports.
**Desc:** Covers all aspects of road law, deregulation, road traffic regulations, competition, tachographs, maintenance, road law reports and aspects of PVC operations.

UK/1352-0717
**ROAD LAW AND ROAD LAW REPORTS.** (19??)-. English. Eight times a year. £50.75 UK; £52.40 other. Barry Rose Law Periodicals Ltd., Little London, Chichester West Sussex PO19 1PG England. **Tel** 011 44 243 787841, 011 44 243 783637, FAX 011 44 243 779174, 011 44 243 779278. **ED** Charles Arnold-Baker. Bk Rev, (Qty: 12). **Ad Acc, Adv Mgr:** Mrs. Curtis. **Continues** Road Law.
**Desc:** Covers all aspects of road law, deregulation, road traffic regulations, competition, tachographs, maintenance, road law reports and aspects of PVC operation. Also covers all relevant and newsworthy road law reports and additional comments, when appropriate.

UK
**ROAD LENGTHS IN GREAT BRITAIN. Added/Corp** Great Britain. Government Statistical Service. Great Britain. Dept. of Transport. (19??)-. English. an. Department of Transport / England, 2 Marsham Street, London SW1P 3EB England. **Tel** 011 44 71 2765082. **LC** PAR.

CN/0706-067X
**ROAD MOTOR VEHICLES. REGISTRATIONS.** (ROAD MOTOR VEHICLES, REGISTRATIONS / STATISTICS CANADA, TRANSPORTATION AND COMMUNICATIONS DIVISION, SURFACE TRANSPORT SECTION.). [Road mot. veh., Regist.]. **Added/Corp** Statistics Canada. Surface Transport Section. Statistics Canada. Surface and Marine Transport Section. **VFOAT** Vehicles Automobiles, Immatriculations. (1975)-. English (French). an. 25.00Can$; $30.00 US; $35.00 other. Statistics Canada, Publications Sales & Services, Main Building Room 1710, Ottawa Ontario K1A 0T6 Canada. **Tel** (613)951-5078, (800)267-6677, FAX (613)951-1584, telex 053-3585. **ED** Yasmin Sheikh (editor's telephone number: (613)951-2518, FAX: (613)951-0579). **LC** HE5635; .A38a. **DD** 354.710087/83. Index available. **Circ:** 540. **Continues** Motor Vehicle. Part III, Registration., 0575-9110.
**Desc:** Data on the registration of motor vehicles, by type. Categories include passenger automobiles, trucks, motorcycles, buses, trailers and others. Also, data on driver's licenses and garage licenses.

AT
**ROAD ROUGHNESS PROFILES. MAIN ROADS / ADVANCE PLANNING SECTION, MAIN ROADS DEPARTMENT, WESTERN AUSTRALIA. Added/Corp** Western Australia. Main Roads Dept. Advance Planning Section. **VFOAT** Main Roads. (19??)-. English. an. **LC** TE153; .R54. **DD** 625.8/028/7.

UK
**ROAD SAFETY AND THE ROAD USER BIENNIAL SYMPOSIUM PROCEEDINGS.** Proceedings. English. University of Salford Department of Civil Engineering, Ms. Charleston, Salford M5 4WT England.

CN/0317-8196
**ROAD SAFETY ANNUAL REPORT. Main/Corp** Canada. Road Safety. **VFOAT** Rapport Annuel, Securite Routiere. (19??)-. English (French). an. Free. Transport Canada / Public Affairs Branch, Ottawa Ontario K1A 0N5 Canada. **Tel** (613)991-2309. **LC** HE5614.5.C2; C27A. **DD** 354.710087/83/0289. **Continues** Traffic Safety Annual Report.

AT
**ROAD TRAFFIC ACCIDENTS INVOLVING CASUALTIES. Title Change. Main/Corp** Australian Bureau of Statistics. Western Australian Office. (19??)-(19??). English. Australian Bureau of Statistics, PO Box 10, Belconnen Australian Capital Territory, 2616 Australia. **Tel** 011 61 6 2527911, FAX 011 61 6 2516009. **LC** HE5614.5.A8; A3. **DD** 312/.274. **Continues** Australia. Commonwealth Bureau of Census and Statistics. Western Australian Office. Western Australia Road Traffic Accidents Involving Casualties. **Continued by** Road Traffic Accidents Involving Casualties Reported to the Police Department, Western Australia, 1032-4577.
**Desc:** Provides detailed national data on road traffic accidents which resulted in deaths or admissions to hospitals.

AT
**ROAD TRAFFIC ACCIDENTS INVOLVING CASUALTIES, TASMANIA. Main/Corp** Australian Bureau of Statistics. Tasmanian Office. (19??)-. English. an. Australian Bureau of Statistics / Tasmanian Office, Commonwealth Government Centre, 188 Collins Street, Hobart GPO Box 66A, Hobart Tasmania 7001 Australia. **Tel** (002)205889. **LC** HE5614.5.A8; A8b. **DD** 312/.44/09946.
**Desc:** Persons killed in road traffic accidents.

SA
**ROAD TRAFFIC ACCIDENTS (PRETORIA, SOUTH AFRICA). Title Change.** (ROAD TRAFFIC ACCIDENTS.). **Main/Corp** South Africa. Dept. of Statistics. **VFOAT** Padverkeerongelukke. Afrikaans (19??)-. English. an. Department of Statistics / South Africa, The Government Printer, Bosman Street, Private Bag X85, Pretoria South Africa. **LC** HE5614.5.S6; S68A. **DD** 312/.4/4. **Continues** Road Traffic Accidents. **Continued by** Road Traffic Collisions.

# Transportation — Roads and Traffic

UK/0265-7937
**ROAD TRAFFIC LAW BULLETIN.** VFOAT
RTLB. Bulletin. English. mo (ten issues per year). £70.00 UK; £129.75 other. Longman Professional, 21-27 Lamb's Conduit Street, London WC1N 3NJ England. **Tel** 01-242-2548. **(Subscription address:** Fourth Avenue, Pinnales, Harlow Essex CM19 5AA England; telephone: 0279-29655) **ED** Susan Marshall and Paul Niekirk. **LC** KD2617.A13; R63. cum. index. **Bk Rev. Ad Acc.** available on microfilm and microfiche from University Microfilms International (UMI).
**Desc:** Provides authoritative analysis of matters currently before the courts and in the news.

UK/0306-5286
**ROAD TRAFFIC REPORTS. Added/Corp**
Great Britain. Courts. (1970)-. English. Ten times a year (Except Aug.& Sept.) £87.50 UK; £91.50 other. Kenneth Mason Publications Ltd, 12A North Street Emsworth, Hampshire P010 7DD England. **Tel** 011 44 243 377977. **ED** L. Norman Williams and Percy Mercalfe. **[CCC].** Index available. cum. index.
**Desc:** Publishes High Court reports.
**Ind/Abst** Aust. Leg. Mon. Dig.

NZ
**ROAD TRAFFIC SAFETY RESEARCH COUNCIL REPORT. Main/Corp** New Zealand. Road Traffic Safety Research Council. English. an. Road Traffic Safety Research Council, PO Box 4140, Wellington New Zealand. **Tel** 04 721-253. **LC** HE5614.5.N45; N48A. **DD** 614.8/62/0720931. **Circ:** 400 (ctrl).
**Desc:** Report on the activities of the Road Traffic Safety Research Council with appendix listing current New Zealand road safety research for the year ending March 31.

US
**ROADS (ALBANY, N.Y. : 1953).** (ROADS / NEW YORK GOOD ROADS ASSOCIATION.). Vol. 3, No. 9 (Sept. 1953)-. Periodical. English. New York Good Roads Association, 116 Washington Avenue, Albany NY 12210. **LC** HE356.N7; R612. **Continues** Roads Bulletin.

SA
**ROBOT. Added/Corp** National Road Safety Council (South Africa). (19??)-. Periodical. Afrikaans (English). Six times a year. Free on request. National Road Safety Council, Private Bag X147, 0001 Pretoria South Africa. **Tel** 011 27 12 285929. **LC** HE5614.5.S6; R6. **DD** 614.8/62/05. Index available. **Ad Acc. Circ:** 20,000 (ctrl).
**Desc:** Journal of South African safety procedures; educational lifestyle for children and adults.

FR/1011-1891
**ROUTES PARIS. 1986. See** Engineering.

CN
**ROUTES QUEBECOISES, LES. Main/Corp**
Quebec (Province). Roads Dept. French. an. Les Routes Quebecoises, 1283 Boul Charest Ouest, Quebec Quebec 61N 2CP Canada. **LC** HE357.Z6; Q47A. **DD** 388.1/.09714.

FR/0243-6795
**ROUTIERS, LES.** [routiers]. (1934)-. Periodical. French. Eleven times a year. 240.00F France; 300.00F other. Les Routiers, 6 rue de l Isly, 75008 Paris France. **UDC** 331.88.

US/1054-5050
**ROY ANDERSON'S ROAD WORK SAFETY REPORT.** [Roy Anderson's road work saf. rep.]. **VFOAT** Road Work Safety Report. Vol. 1, No. 1 (Jan./Feb. 1991)-. Periodical. English. bm. $59.00. TranSafety Inc, PO Box 10735, Burke VA 22009. **Tel** (703)644-0050. **ED** Roy Anderson. **DD** 363. available in Loose-leaf.

US/0147-3743
**SAFETY SADISTICS. Suspended. See** Public Health and Safety.

CN/0711-9178
**SASKATCHEWAN TRAFFIC ACCIDENT FACTS.** [Sask. traffic accid. facts]. 1979-. English. Traffic Safety Engineering Branch, Saskatchewan Highways and Transportation, 1855 Victoria Avenue, Regina Saskatchewan S4P 3V5 Canada. **LC** HE5614.5.C2; S35. **DD** 312/.445/097124. **Continues** Saskatchewan Provincial Highways Accident Statistics, 0318-2819.

US/0737-1969
**SEASONALLY ADJUSTED TRAFFIC AND CAPACITY. MAJORS, SCHEDULED SERVICE, SYSTEM, DOMESTIC AND INTERNATIONAL OPERATIONS.** VFOAT
Majors, Scheduled Service, System, Domestic and International Operations. (Jan. 1981)-. Periodical. English. mo. Civil Aeronautics Board, 1825 Connecticut Avenue NW, Washington DC 20428. **Tel** (202)673-5174. Documents available from Documents on Demand.
**Continues** Seasonally Adjusted Capacity and Traffic. Scheduled Operations, System, Domestic and International Trunks, Plus Local Service Carriers, 0883-3621.
**Ind/Abst** Am. Stat. Index.

US
**SEATTLE TRAFFIC ACCIDENT SUMMARY.** 1980 & 1981-. English. Free. Seattle Engineering Department, 600 Fourth Avenue, Room 910, Seattle WA 98104. **Tel** (206)625-2347. **ED** Elizabeth Whitney. **Circ:** 400 (ctrl). **Continues** Seattle Traffic Collision Summary.
**Desc:** Overview of major vehicle accidents in Seattle; highlighting pedestrian, pedacycle, motorcycle, and DWI accidents.

SZ
**SELECTION OF INTERNATIONAL ROAD TRANSPORT DOCUMENTATION.** (19??)-.
English (French). Twice a year. 50.00F. International Road Transport Union, BP 44, 1211 Geneva 20 Switzerland. **Tel** 011 44 22 341330, telex 27107.
**Desc:** Information on international road transportation.

BL
**SISTEMA RODOVIARIO DO ESTADO DO PARANA / ESTADO DO PARANA, SECRETARIA DE ESTADO DOS TRANSPORTES, DEPARTAMENTO DE ESTRADAS DE RODAGEM. Added/Corp**
Parana (Brazil : State). Departamento de Estradas de Rodagem. (19??)-. Portuguese. an. **LC** HE359.B9; P356. **DD** 388.1/0981/62021.

US
**SOUTH CAROLINA HIGHWAY SAFETY PLAN.** VFOAT Highway Safety Plan. Fiscal Year 1979-. English. an. 1205 Pendleton Street, Columbia SC 29201. **LC** HE5614.3.S6; S57. **DD** 363.1/256/09757.

US
**SOUTH DAKOTA HIGHWAY SAFETY MANAGEMENT SYSTEM PLAN. Main/Corp**
South Dakota. Division of Highway Safety. (19??)-. English. Department of Public Safety / South Dakota, 118 West Capitol, Pierre SD 57501. **LC** HE5614.3.S8; S68b. **DD** 614.8/62/09783.

US/0361-3461
**SOUTH DAKOTA HIGHWAY SAFETY WORK PROGRAM. Main/Corp** South Dakota. Division of Highway Safety. (19??)-. English. Department of Public Safety / South Dakota, 118 West Capitol, Pierre SD 57501. **LC** HE5614.3.S8; S68a. **DD** 614.8/62/0710783. **Continues** South Dakota Highway Safety Work Program, 0361-3461.

US
**SOUTH DAKOTA MOTOR VEHICLE TRAFFIC ACCIDENT SUMMARY.** VFOAT
Motor Vehicle Traffic Accident Summary. English. South Dakota Department of Commerce and Consumer Affairs, State Capitol, 500 East Capitol, Pierre SD 57501. **LC** HE5614.3.S8; S69. **DD** 363.1/252/09783021.

AT/0572-144X
**SPECIAL REPORT - AUSTRALIAN ROAD RESEARCH BOARD.** [Spec. rep. - Aust. Road Res. Board]. (1966)-. Periodical. English. ir. 50.00Aus$. Australian Road Research Board, PO Box 156, Nunawading VIC 3131 Australia. **Tel** 011 61 3 8811555, FAX 011 61 3 8878104, telex AA 33113. **DD** 625.7072.

PR
**SPECIAL REPORT ON PUERTO RICO HIGHWAY AUTHORITY, A. Main/Corp**
Government Development Bank for Puerto Rico. English. Government Development Bank for Puerto Rico, PO Box 42001, San Juan PR 00940. **Tel** (809)722-2525, FAX (809)268-5496. **LC** HE359.P92; G68. **DD** 388.1/097295.

US
**SPEED MONITORING REPORT / PREPARED BY THE DEPARTMENT OF TRANSPORTATION, DIVISION OF DATA BASE GENERATION, BUREAU OF DATA RESOURCES. Added/Corp** New Jersey. Dept. of Transportation. New Jersey. Dept. of Transportation. Bureau of Data Resources. **VFOAT** New Jersey Speed Monitoring Report. 1st Quarter (1976/77)-. Periodical. English. qt. **LC** HE5620.S6; S64. **DD** 388.3/144/09749.

US
**STANDARD HIGHWAY SIGNS / AS SPECIFIED IN THE MANUAL ON UNIFORM TRAFFIC CONTROL DEVICES. Main/Corp** United States. Federal Highway Administration. (19??)-. Government Publication. English. ir. $34.00 US; $42.50 other. Superintendent of Documents, US Government Printing Office, Washington DC 20402. **Tel** (202)275-3328, FAX (202)786-2377.
**Desc:** Shows many typical standard signs approved to use on streets and highways. Also provides detailed information on dimensions and the placement of symbol messages.

US
**STANDARD SPECIFICATIONS FOR HIGHWAY CONSTRUCTION.** English. Chief of Engineering Services, PO Box 1467, Juneau AK 99802.

US/0091-6064
**STATE AID TO MUNICIPALITIES FOR HIGHWAYS AND STREETS (BOSTON).**
(STATE AID TO MUNICIPALITIES FOR HIGHWAYS AND STREETS.). **Main/Corp** Massachusetts. Dept. of Public Works. English. Mr George M Joseph, Principal Federal Aid Engineer, 100 Nashua Street, Boston MA 02114. **LC** HE5633.M4; M35A.

US/0097-000X
**STATE OF COLORADO ANNUAL HIGHWAY SAFETY WORK PROGRAM.**
**Main/Corp** Colorado. Division of Highway Safety. English. an. 4201 East Arkansas Avenue, Denver CO 80222. **LC** HE5614.3.C6; C66A. **DD** 388.3/14.
**Continues** State of Colorado Annual Highway Safety Work Program, 0097-000X.

US/0094-5706
**STATE OF IDAHO ANNUAL WORK PROGRAM. Main/Corp** Idaho. Traffic Safety Commission. English. an. Idaho Traffic Safety Commission, 2419 West State Street, Boise ID 83702. **LC** HE5614.3.I2; I3A. **DD** 614.8/62/09796.

US/0090-1067
**STATE OF WISCONSIN STATE SUMMARY. TYPE AND AMOUNT OF AIDS PAID TO ALL GOVERNMENTAL UNITS AND COUNTIES.** (STATE SUMMARY : TYPE AND AMOUNT OF AIDS PAID TO ALL LOCAL GOVERNMENTAL UNITS AND COUNTIES.). **Main/Corp** Wisconsin. Dept. of Transportation. Division of Planning. English. an. Wisconsin Department of Transportation, PO Box 7916, Design Section Room 651, Madison WI 53707. **Tel** (608)266-1113. **LC** HE356.W5; A25. **DD** 388.1/1.

US/0146-8359
**STATE ROAD ANNUAL REPORT.**
**Main/Corp** Utah. Dept. of Finance. (19??)-. English. an. Utah Finance Division, 2110 State Office Building, Salt Lake City UT 84114. **Tel** (801)538-3082, FAX (801)538-3244. **LC** HE365.U8; U68a. **DD** 388.1/1.

US/0018-988X
**STATUS REPORT - INSURANCE INSTITUTE FOR HIGHWAY SAFETY.**
(STATUS REPORT.). **Main/Corp** Insurance Institute for Highway Safety. Periodical. English. mo. Free. Insurance Institute for Highway Safety, 1005 North Glebe Road, Suite 800, Arlington VA 22201. **Tel** (703)247-1500. **ED** James H Mooney. **LC** HE5614; .I48A. **DD** 614.8/62. Index available. **Bk Rev. Circ:** 14,500 (ctrl). available on microfilm from University Microfilms International (UMI).
**Desc:** A newsletter by the Institute, an independent, nonprofit scientific and educational organization on highway safety.

US/0360-1188
**STATUS REPORT - PENNSYLVANIA TRANSPORTATION INSTITUTE.**
**Main/Corp** Pennsylvania Transportation Institute. (1974)-. English. Pennsylvania Department of Transportation, Room 1215 Transportation & Safety Building, Harrisburg PA 17120. **LC** HE192.5; .P45a. **DD** 380.5/07/20748. **Continues** Pennsylvania Transportation and Traffic Safety Center. Status Report.

SZ
**STRASSE UND VERKEHR. Added/Corp**
Vereinigung Schweizerischer Strassenfachmanner. Schweizerische Vereinigung fur Gesundheitstechnik. **VFOAT** Route et la Circulation Routiere. (19??)-. Periodical. German (French and English). mo. 110.00F Switzerland; 128.00F other Europe; 142.00F other. VSS Verein Schweizerischer Strassenfachleute, Seefeldstrasse 9, CH8008 Zurich Switzerland. **Tel** 011 41 1 2516914, FAX 011 41 1 2523130. **LC** TE3; .S755. Index available. ctrl circ.
**Desc:** Development of road construction and maintenance in Switzerland.

GW/0039-2219
**STRASSEN- VERKEHRSTECHNIK.**
(STRASSENVERKEHRSTECHNIK.). [Str.-verkehrstech.]. **Added/Corp** Forschungsgesellschaft fuer das Strassenwesen (Germany) Bundesvereinigung der Strassenbau- und Verkersingenieure. (1957)-. Academic Scholarly Publication. German. Six times a year. DM81.00. Kirschbaum Verlag, Siegfriedstr 28, Postfach 210209, D 53157 Bonn Germany. **Tel** 011 49 228 954530. **LC** HE363.G29; S87. **CODEN** SVKTAC. **[CCC].** Documents available from Ask*IEEE.
**Ind/Abst** EMBASE; INSPEC (May/June 1974-); Int. Civil Eng. Abstr.

Transportation —Roads and Traffic

AU
**STRASSENVERKEHRSSICHERHEIT IM JAHRE ... / HERAUSGEGEBEN VOM OSTERREICHISCHEN STATISTISCHEN ZENTRALAMT.** **Added/Corp** Osterreichisches Statistisches Zentralamt. (1979)-. Statistical Publication. German. an. S300.00. Kommissionsverlag Osterreichische Staatsdruckerei, Rennweg 12A, 1030 Vienna Austria. **Tel** 0222 787 89 295, FAX 0222 787 89 419. **LC** HA1173; .A27 Subser; HE5614.5.A9. **Pr Rev. Acid Free. Circ:** 300 (ctrl).

GW
**STRASSENVERKEHRSUNFAELLE.** **Main/Corp** Niedersachsisches Landesverwaltungsamt. (19??)-. Periodical. German. an. DM60.00. Niedersachsisches Landesverwaltungsamt, Postfach 107, 3000 Hannover Germany. **Tel** (0511)108-9466. **LC** HE5614.5.G3; S27a. **Bk Rev. Circ:** 250.
**Desc:** Road traffic accidents available for districts in Lower Saxony.

SZ
**STRASSENVERKEHRSUNFALLE IN DER SCHWEIZ.** **VFOAT** Accidents de la Circulation Routiere en Suisse. French (German). an. 26.00F. Bundesamt fuer Statistik, Schwarztorstrasse 96, CH 3003 Bern Switzerland. **Tel** 031 3236011, FAX 031 3236061. **LC** HE5614.5.S9; S65.
**Desc:** Accidents and road traffic in Switzerland.

US
**STREET FINANCE REPORT FOR IOWA CITIES.** **VFOAT** Report of Municipal Street Finance. English. an. Iowa Department of Transportation, 800 Lincoln Way, Ames IA 50010. **Tel** (515)239-1528. **LC** HE356.I8; S77. **DD** 388.4/.042. **Continues** Annual Street Finance Report for the Incorporated Cities and Towns of Iowa.
**Desc:** SUMMARY: Receipts received by cities and towns from the Road Use Tax Fund allocation, and expenditures from the Fund and other state and local revenues.

JA
**SUJI DE MIRU JIDOSHA.** **Added/Corp** Japan. Unyusho. Jidoshakyoku. Nihon Jidosha Kaigisho. (19??)-. Periodical. Japanese. Nihon Jidosha Kaigisho, (Japan Automobile Chamber of Commerce and Industries), 8-3 Marunouchi 1 chome Chiyodaku, Tokyoto 100 Japan. **LC** HE5697.A6; S9.

UK
**SUMMARIES OF LABORATORY NOTES.** **Main/Corp** Road Research Laboratory. Periodical. English.

US/0146-7468
**SUMMARY OF ACCIDENT DATA (RICHMOND). Ceased.** (SUMMARY OF ACCIDENT DATA.). **Main/Corp** Virginia. Division of Traffic & Safety. **Added/Corp** Virginia. Division of Traffic and Planning. Virginia. Dept. of State Police. Virginia. Division of Highway and Traffic Safety. Virginia. Traffic Engineering Division. United States. Federal Highway Administration. **VFOAT** Summary Accident Data. (1961)-(19??). English. an. Virginia Department of Transportation, 1401 East Broad Street, Richmond VA 23219. **Tel** (804)786-4243, FAX (804)786-6250. **LC** HE5614.3.V8; V57a. **DD** 388.3/14. **Continues** Accident Summary of Rural Primary System.

US/0146-1192
**SUMMARY OF ACCIDENTS INVOLVING THE DRINKING DRIVER.** **Main/Corp** Washington State Patrol. English. Washington State Patrol, R & D Section, General Administration Building AX-12, Olympia WA 98504. **Tel** (206)753-4453. **LC** HE5614.3.W2; W38B. **DD** 614.8/62. **Continues** Drinking Driver Accident Summary, 0095-3350.

US
**SUMMARY OF ALL REPORTED MOTOR VEHICLE TRAFFIC ACCIDENTS AND ACTIVITIES OF ALL FIELD PERSONNEL AND DRIVER SERVICES DIVISION IN THE STATE OF MISSISSIPPI.** **Main/Corp** Mississippi. Driver Services Division. Statistical Bureau. **Added/Corp** Mississippi. Driver Services Division. Statistical Bureau. Annual Summary. (19??)-. English. an. Mississippi Highway Safety Patrol, Driver Services Division, PO Box 958, Jackson MS 39205. **Tel** (601)987-1262. **LC** HE5614.3.M55; M57a. **DD** 312/.4/409762.

US
**SUMMARY OF IOWA COUNTY ENGINEERS ANNUAL HIGHWAY REPORTS.** English. an. Free. Iowa Department of Transportation, 800 Lincoln Way, Ames IA 50010. **Tel** (515)239-1528. **LC** HE356.I8; S84. **DD** 388.1/14/09777. ctrl circ.

US/0741-448X
**SUMMARY OF MOTOR VEHICLE TRAFFIC ACCIDENTS. ALEXANDRIA.** (SUMMARY OF MOTOR VEHICLE TRAFFIC ACCIDENTS. ALEXANDRIA / STATE OF LOUISIANA.). Jan.-Dec. 1981-. English. mo. Free. Department of Public Safety / Louisiana, Traffic Records Unit, PO Box 66614, Baton Rouge LA 70896. **LC** HE5614.4.A44; S86. **DD** 312/.44/0976369.

US/0741-4471
**SUMMARY OF MOTOR VEHICLE TRAFFIC ACCIDENTS. BATON ROUGE.** (SUMMARY OF MOTOR VEHICLE TRAFFIC ACCIDENTS. BATON ROUGE / STATE OF LOUISIANA.). Jan.-Dec. 1981-. English. mo. Free. Department of Public Safety / Louisiana, Traffic Records Unit, PO Box 66614, Baton Rouge LA 70896.

US/0741-4455
**SUMMARY OF MOTOR VEHICLE TRAFFIC ACCIDENTS. GRETNA.** (SUMMARY OF MOTOR VEHICLE TRAFFIC ACCIDENTS. GRETNA / STATE OF LOUISIANA.). Jan.-Dec. 1981-. English. mo. Free. Department of Public Safety / Louisiana, Traffic Records Unit, PO Box 66614, Baton Rouge LA 70896. **LC** HE5614.4.G73; S85. **DD** 312/.44/0976338.

US/0741-4366
**SUMMARY OF MOTOR VEHICLE TRAFFIC ACCIDENTS INVESTIGATED / REPORTED BY STATE POLICE.** (SUMMARY OF MOTOR VEHICLE TRAFFIC ACCIDENTS. INVESTIGATED / REPORTED BY STATE POLICE / STATE OF LOUISIANA.). **Added/Corp** Louisiana. Traffic Records Unit. (Jan.-Dec. 1981)-. English. mo. Free. Department of Public Safety / Louisiana, Traffic Records Unit, PO Box 66614, Baton Rouge LA 70896. **LC** HE5614.3.L8; S86. **DD** 312/.44/09763.

US/0741-4439
**SUMMARY OF MOTOR VEHICLE TRAFFIC ACCIDENTS. KENNER.** (SUMMARY OF MOTOR VEHICLE TRAFFIC ACCIDENTS. KENNER / STATE OF LOUISIANA.). Jan.-Dec. 1981-. English. mo. Free. Department of Public Safety / Louisiana, Traffic Records Unit, PO Box 66614, Baton Rouge LA 70896.

US/0741-4404
**SUMMARY OF MOTOR VEHICLE TRAFFIC ACCIDENTS. MONROE.** (SUMMARY OF MOTOR VEHICLE TRAFFIC ACCIDENTS. MONROE / STATE OF LOUISIANA.). Jan./Dec. 1981-. English. mo. Free. Department of Public Safety / Louisiana, Traffic Records Unit, PO Box 66614, Baton Rouge LA 70896. **LC** HE5614.4.M66; S85. **DD** 312/.44/0976387.

US/0741-4390
**SUMMARY OF MOTOR VEHICLE TRAFFIC ACCIDENTS. NEW IBERIA.** (SUMMARY OF MOTOR VEHICLE TRAFFIC ACCIDENTS. NEW IBERIA / STATE OF LOUISIANA.). Jan.-Dec. 1981-. English. mo. Free. Department of Public Safety / Louisiana, Traffic Records Unit, PO Box 66614, Baton Rouge LA 70896. **LC** HE5614.4.N48; S85. **DD** 312/.44/0976349.

US/0741-4374
**SUMMARY OF MOTOR VEHICLE TRAFFIC ACCIDENTS. NEW ORLEANS.** (SUMMARY OF MOTOR VEHICLE TRAFFIC ACCIDENTS. NEW ORLEANS / STATE OF LOUISIANA.). Jan.-Dec. 1981-. English. mo. Free. Department of Public Safety / Louisiana, Traffic Records Unit, PO Box 66614, Baton Rouge LA 70896. **LC** HE5614.4.N49; S86. **DD** 312/.44/0976335.

US/0741-4358
**SUMMARY OF MOTOR VEHICLE TRAFFIC ACCIDENTS. STATEWIDE.** (SUMMARY OF MOTOR VEHICLE TRAFFIC ACCIDENTS. STATEWIDE / STATE OF LOUISIANA.). Jan.-Dec. 1981-. English. mo. Free. Department of Public Safety / Louisiana, Traffic Records Unit, PO Box 66614, Baton Rouge LA 70896.

US/0741-4331
**SUMMARY OF MOTOR VEHICLE TRAFFIC ACCIDENTS. URBAN.** (SUMMARY OF MOTOR VEHICLE TRAFFIC ACCIDENTS. URBAN / STATE OF LOUISIANA.). Jan.-Dec. 1981-. English. mo. Free. Department of Public Safety / Louisiana, Traffic Records Unit, PO Box 66614, Baton Rouge LA 70896. **LC** HE5614.3.L8; S87. **DD** 312/.44/09763.

US/0547-5562
**SUMMARY OF PROGRESS - NATIONAL COOPERATIVE HIGHWAY RESEARCH PROGRAM.** **Main/Corp** National Cooperative Highway Research Program. 1962/66-. English. National Academy of Sciences, 2101 Constitution Avenue NW, Washington DC 20418. **Tel** (202)334-2525, FAX (202)334-2926. **LC** TE153; .N25A. **DD** 388.1/07/2073.

US/0363-4027
**SURVEY OF OUT-OF-STATE PASSENGER CARS AND OUT-OF-STATE CAMPER VEHICLES ON INTERSTATE, ARTERIAL AND PRIMARY HIGHWAYS IN VIRGINIA, A.** **Main/Corp** Virginia. Division of Traffic & Safety. **VFOAT** Virginia Visitor Travel Survey. English. Virginia Department of Transportation, 1401 East Broad Street, Richmond VA 23219. **Tel** (804)786-4243, FAX (804)786-6250. **LC** HE371.V8; V45D. **DD** 388.3/14. ctrl circ.

US
**TABULATION SHOWING ANNUAL AVERAGE DAILY TRAFFIC VOLUME AT RECORDER LOCATIONS AND PERCENT OF CHANGE IN VOLUME OVER PREVIOUS YEARS.** **Main/Corp** Florida. State Road Department. Division of Traffic and Planning. **Added/Corp** United States. Bureau of Public Roads. English. Florida Road Department, Tallahassee FL 32304. **LC** HE371.F6; F58a. **DD** 388.3/14/09759.

AT/0313-895X
**TECHNICAL MANUAL ATM.** [Tech. man. ATM]. (1976)-. Monographic series. English. ir. 30.00Aus$. Australian Road Research Board, PO Box 156, Nunawading VIC 3131 Australia. **Tel** 011 61 3 8811555, FAX 011 61 3 8878104, telex AA 33113. **DD** 6257042.

US
**TECHNICAL REPORTS OF THE NATIONAL HIGHWAY TRAFFIC SAFETY ADMINISTRATION.** **Main/Corp** United States. National Highway Traffic Safety Administration. English. US Department of Transportation / National Highway Traffic Safety Administration, 400 7th Street SW, Washington DC 20590.

US/0093-917X
**TEEN-AGE DRIVERS (OLYMPIA).** (TEEN-AGE DRIVERS.). **Main/Corp** Washington State Patrol. (19??)-. English. Washington State Patrol, R & D Section, General Administration Building AX-12, Olympia WA 98504. **Tel** (206)753-4453. **LC** HE5614.3.W2; W389. **DD** 388.3/14. **Continues** Summary of Traffic Accidents Involving Teen-Age Drivers.

DK/0902-1116
**TEKNISK TRAFIKRAPPORT.** 1985-. Danish. an. **LC** HE373.D4; T45. **Continues** in part Trafikrapport, 0106-7389.

US/0360-5396
**TENNESSEE MOTOR VEHICLE TRAFFIC ACCIDENT FACTS.** **Main/Corp** Tennessee. Dept. of Safety. Planning and Research Section. **VFOAT** Motor Vehicle Traffic Accident Facts. (1974)-. English. an. Free. Department of Safety / Tennessee, Planning & Research Section, 1150 Foster Avenue, Nashville TN 37249. **Tel** (615)251-5229. **LC** HE5614.3.T2; T45b. **DD** 388.3/14. **Circ:** 2,000. **Continues** Fatal Accident Facts, 0363-3373.
**Desc:** Contains data furnished by the Accident Records Section of the Driver Control Division and the Fatal Accident Reporting System (FARS), Unit of the Planning and Research Section of the Tennessee Department of Safety. These are compiled from the Officer's Traffic Accident Report Forms submitted by federal, state county and city law enforcement agencies.

US
**TEXAS TRAFFIC SAFETY REPORT.** **Added/Corp** Texas. Governor's Office of Traffic Safety. (1974)-. English. Ten times a year. Free on request. State Department of Highways and Public Transportation / Texas, Austin TX 78701. **Tel** (512)483-3689.

FI
**TIELIIKENNEONNETTOMUUDET.** **Main/Corp** Finland. Tilastokeskus. **VFOAT** Road Traffic Accidents; Vagtrafikolyckor. 1978-. Finnish (Swedish). Tilastokeskus, PL 504, Annankatu 44, 00101 Helsinki Finland. **Tel** 358-0-17341, FAX 358-0-17342474, telex 1002111 TILASTO SF. **LC** HE5614.5.F5; F55A. **Continues** Tieliikennevahingot.

KO
**TORO KYOTONG.** Periodical. Korean. mo. Toro Kyotong Anjon Hyophoe, 198-16 Kwanhun-dong Chongno-ku, Seoul Korea. **LC** HE5614.K6; T67.

US
**TRAFFIC ACCIDENT FACTS.** **Title Change.** **Added/Corp** Wyoming. Highway Dept. Highway Safety Branch. (19??)-(19??). English. Wyoming Highway Department, Highway Safety Branch, Safety Analysis Section, PO Box 1708, Cheyenne WY 82002-9019. **Merged with** Wyoming. Highway Safety Analysis Section.; Wyoming Truck Accident Facts; Wyoming.

# Transportation —Roads and Traffic

*Highway Safety Analysis Section. and Wyoming's Fatal Accident Facts to form Wyoming's Comprehensive Report on Traffic Accidents, 07747-8771.*

US/0738-3657
### TRAFFIC ACCIDENT FACTS (DOVER, DEL.). (TRAFFIC ACCIDENT FACTS). **Added/Corp** Delaware. Division of State Police. (19??)-. English. an. Department of Public Safety Division of State Police / Delaware, Division of State Police, PO Box 430, Dover DE 19901. **LC** HE5614.3.D3; T7. **DD** 312/.44/09751.

US
### TRAFFIC CRASH DATA / FLORIDA DEPARTMENT OF HIGHWAY SAFETY AND MOTOR VEHICLES. **Title Change.** **Added/Corp** Florida. Dept. of Highway Safety & Motor Vehicles. Office of Management and Planning Services. (1992)-(199?). Government Publication. English. an. Department of Highway Safety & Motor Vehicles, N Kirkman Building A430, Tallahassee FL 32399. **Tel** (904)488-7370. **LC** HE5614.3.F6; A33. **Continues** Florida Traffic Crash Facts. **Continued by** Traffic Crash Facts.

US
### TRAFFIC CRASH FACTS. (199?)-. Government Publication. English. an. Department of Highway Safety & Motor Vehicles, N Kirkman Building A430, Tallahassee FL 32399. **Tel** (904)488-7370.

US
### TRAFFIC DATA FROM AUTOMATIC TRAFFIC RECORDER STATIONS. **Main/Corp** Virginia. Division of Traffic & Safety. **VFOAT** Automatic Traffic Recorder Data. English. an. Virginia Department of Transportation, 1401 East Broad Street, Richmond VA 23219. **Tel** (804)786-4243, FAX (804)786-6250. **LC** HE371.V8; V45A. **DD** 388.3/14/09755. ctrl circ.

US/0893-3030
### TRAFFIC LAW REPORTS. **See** Law.

US/0041-0721
### TRAFFIC SAFETY (CHICAGO, ILL.). (TRAFFIC SAFETY.). [Traffic saf.]. **Added/Corp** National Safety Council. Vol. 50, No. 6 (June 1957)-. Periodical. English. Six times a year. $30.00. National Safety Council, 1121 Spring Lake Drive, Itasca IL 60143. **Tel** (800)621-7615, (708)775-2294, FAX (708)285-0797. (**Subscription address:** National Safety Council, PO Box 429, Itasca IL 60143.) **LC** HV675.A1; P85. available on microfilm and microfiche from University Microfilms International (UMI). **Continues** Public Safety (Chicago, Ill.).
**Ind/Abst** Appl. Sci. Technol. Index; Crim. Justice Period. Index; J. Plan. Lit.; Saf. Health Work.

US
### TRAFFIC SAFETY SERIES. English. ir (two-three editions annually). $19.95 (paper). Transaction Publishers / Rutgers State University, New Brunswick NJ 08903. **Tel** (908)932-2280 Ext. 105, FAX (908)932-3138.
**Desc:** An integrated approach to lowering risks and hazards of automobile, trucking and motorcycle travel. The series deals with issues ranging from drunk driving to seat belt use.

AT
### TRAFFIC VOLUMES AND SUPPLEMENTARY DATA, CENTRAL MOUNTAINS DIVISION AND SHIRE OF HAWKESBURY. **Added/Corp** New South Wales. Dept. of Main Roads. **VFOAT** Central Mountains Division and Shire of Hawkesbury. (19??)-. English. an. Secretary Main Roads Department, GPO Box S 1400, Perth 6001 Western Australia. **LC** HE373.A982; .N47. **DD** 388.3/142/09944.

AT
### TRAFFIC VOLUMES AND SUPPLEMENTARY DATA, CENTRAL MOUNTAINS DIVISION, CITY OF GOSFORD AND SHIRE OF COLO / DMR. **Added/Corp** New South Wales. Dept. of Main Roads. (19??)-. English. an. Roads and Traffic Authority, PO Box K198, Haymarket NSW 2000 Australia. **Tel** 02 218 6888. **LC** HE373.A982; N43c. **DD** 388.3/142/09944. **Continues** Traffic Volumes and Supplementary Data, Central Mountains Division and Colo-Gosford Shires.

US/0145-9813
### TRAFFIC VOLUMES ON THE CALIFORNIA STATE HIGHWAY SYSTEM. (TRAFFIC VOLUMES ON THE CALIFORNIA STATE HIGHWAY SYSTEM / STATE OF CALIFORNIA, BUSINESS AND TRANSPORTATION AGENCY, DEPT. OF PUBLIC WORKS, DIVISION OF HIGHWAYS, PREPARED IN COOPERATION WITH THE DEPT. OF TRANSPORTATION, FEDERAL HIGHWAY ADMINISTRATION, BUREAU OF PUBLIC ROADS.). **Added/Corp** California. Division of Highways. California. Office of Traffic. California. Office of Traffic Engineering. United States. Bureau of Public Roads. California. Division of Traffic Engineering. **VFOAT** Traffic Volumes on California State Highways; Traffic Volumes. (1968)-. Periodical. English. Department of Transportation / California, Division of Operations, Sacramento CA 95802. **Tel** (916)445-5163. **LC** HE371.C2; A312. **DD** 388.3/142/09794. **Continues** Annual Traffic Census.

SW/0347-6359
### TRAFIK-SKADOR. **Added/Corp** Sweden. Statistiska Centralbyran. **VFOAT** Trafik Skador; Trafikskador; Traffic Injuries. (1985)-. Periodical. Swedish (English). an. SCB Statistiska Centralbyran, 11581 Stockholm Sweden. **LC** HE5614.5.S8; S93a. **Ad Acc.** ctrl circ. **Continues** Vagtrafikolyckor Med Personskada.

US/0884-612X
### TRANSAFETY REPORTER. **See** Public Health and Safety.

CN/0381-8284
### TRANSPORTATION RESEARCH IN CANADA. 1973-. English. an. Roads & Transportation Association of Canada, 1765 St Laurent Boulevard, Ottawa Ontario K1G 3V4 Canada. **Tel** (613)521-4052. **DD** 388.1/07/2071. **Supersedes** Road Research in Canada, 0381-8292.

SP
### TRANSPORTES Y LAS COMUNICACIONES / [MOPT, MINISTERIO DE OBRAS PUBLICAS Y TRANSPORTES], LOS. **Added/Corp** Spain. Ministerio de Obras Publicas y Transportes. Instituto de Estudios del Transporte y las Comunicaciones (Spain). (19??)-. Spanish. Four times a year. 3000.00ptas Spain; 4000.00ptas other. MOPT Ministerio de Obras Publicas y Transportes, Paseo de la Castellana 67, 28071 Madrid Spain. **Tel** 011 34 1 5977263. **LC** HE261.A15; T74.
**Desc:** Presents information and studies on communication and traffic.

US
### TRIO. TRAFFIC RULINGS, INTERPRETATIONS, OPINIONS. **Main/Corp** New York (State). Dept. of Motor Vehicles. **VFOAT** Traffic Rulings, Interpretations, Opinions. V. 1- 1961/62-. English. New York Department of Motor Vehicles, Albany NY 12224. **DD** 343.747/0946; 347.4703946.

US/0090-5879
### TWENTY YEAR HIGHWAY NEEDS STUDY. **Main/Corp** Maryland. Dept. of Transportation. English. Maryland Department of Transportation, State Highway Administration, PO Box 717, Baltimore MD 21203. **LC** HE356.M3; A33. **DD** 388.1/09752. **Continues** Twenty Year Highway Needs Study.

UK/0966-1743
### URBAN STREET ENVIRONMENT, THE. [Urban str. environ.]. (1992)-. Periodical. English. bm (6 issues). £24.00 UK; £32.00 Europe; £42.00 other. Landor Holdings Ltd, Quadrant House, 250 Kennington Lane, London SE11 5RD England. **Tel** 011 44 71 735 5058, FAX 011 44 71 587 0497.
**Desc:** Provides a forum for a broad view to be taken of the total design, management and maintenance of roads and pavements, precincts and other public amenity areas.

NE/0377-8495
### VERKEERSKUNDE. [Verkeerskunde]. **Added/Corp** Koninklijke Nederlandse Toeristen Bond ANWB. Vol. 26, No. 6 (June 1975)-. Academic Scholarly Publication. Dutch (summaries and/or abstracts in English). mo. Infolio BV, Postbus 16500, 2500 BM Den Haag Netherlands. **Tel** 011 31 70 3819900, FAX 011 31 70 3632338. **Continues** Verkeers Techniek.
**Ind/Abst** EMBASE.

US
### VOLUME OF TRAFFIC ON THE PRIMARY ROAD SYSTEM OF IOWA. **VFOAT** Volume of Traffic on the Primary Road System. English. be. $12.50. Iowa Department of Transportation, 800 Lincoln Way, Ames IA 50010. **Tel** (515)239-1528. **LC** HE356.I8; V64. **DD** 388.3/142/09777.

UK
### WARTIME ROAD NOTE. **Main/Corp** Road Research Laboratory. English.

US
### WASHINGTON STATE HIGHWAY ACCIDENT REPORT. **Added/Corp** Washington (State). Transportation Data Office. United States. Federal Highway Administration. **VFOAT** Highway Accident Report. (1987)-. English. an. Washington State Department of Transportation, Transportation Building, Olympia WA 98504. **Tel** (206)753-6028. **LC** HE5614.3.W2; A334. **DD** 363.12/52/09797021. **Continues** Highway Traffic Accident Report.

NE
### WEGVERVOER. Dutch. Chrislelijk Vervoers Organisat CVO, Treubstraat 2, 2288 EH Rijswijk Netherlands. **Tel** 011 31 70 3199500.

AT
### WESTERN ROADS : OFFICIAL JOURNAL OF THE MAIN ROADS DEPARTMENT, WESTERN AUSTRALIA. **Added/Corp** Western Australia. Main Roads Dept. Vol. 1, No. 1 (Jan. 1976)-. Periodical. English. qt. Secretary Main Roads Department, GPO Box S 1400, Perth 6001 Western Australia. **LC** TE122.W47; W47. **DD** 388.1/09941.

US/0148-7728
### WISCONSIN ANNUAL HIGHWAY SAFETY WORK PROGRAM. **Main/Corp** Wisconsin. Division of Highway Safety Coordination. English. an. Division of Highway Safety Coordination, James Wilson Plaza, Suite 803, 131 West Wilson Street, Madison WI 53702. **LC** HE5614.3.W5; W57B. **DD** 614.8/62/09775.

US/0043-8529
### WORLD HIGHWAYS. **Added/Corp** International Road Federation. International Road Federation. World Highway Report. (1950)-. Periodical. English. Six times a year. $75.00. International Road Federation / Washington, DC, 525 School Street SW, Suite 302, Washington DC 20024. **Tel** (202)554-2106. (**Subscription address:** Metal Bulletin Inc., 220 Fifth Avenue, 19th Floor, New York NY 10001-7781.) **ED** Hugh M. Gillespie. **Bk Rev. Circ:** 4,800. available on microfilm from University Microfilms International (UMI).
**Desc:** Information on road and transportation projects worldwide; notices of IRF meetings and activities.
**Ind/Abst** Highw. Res. Abstr.

SZ
### WORLD ROAD STATISTICS. **Main/Corp** International Road Federation. **VFOAT** Statistiques Routieres Mondiales; Welt-Strassen-Statistik. English. an. International Road Federation / Geneva, 63 rue de Lausanne, CH-1202 Geneva Switzerland. **Tel** 011 41 22 7317150.

US/0747-8771
### WYOMING'S COMPREHENSIVE REPORT ON TRAFFIC ACCIDENTS. **Title Change.** (WYOMING'S COMPREHENSIVE REPORT ON TRAFFIC ACCIDENTS / WYOMING HIGHWAY DEPARTMENT, HIGHWAY SAFETY BRANCH, SAFETY ANALYSIS SECTION.). **Added/Corp** Wyoming. Highway Safety Analysis Section. **VFOAT** Comprehensive Report on Traffic Accidents. (1982)-(19??). English. an. Wyoming Highway Department, Highway Safety Branch, Safety Analysis Section, PO Box 1708, Cheyenne WY 82002-9019. **LC** HE5614.3.W9; W86. **DD** 312./44/09787. **Formed by the union of** Wyoming. Highway Safety Analysis Section. Wyoming's Fatal Accident Facts **and** Wyoming. Truck Accident Facts Traffic Accident Facts / Wyoming. **Absorbed by** Wyoming. Highway Safety Analysis Section. Wyoming Truck Accident Facts; Traffic Accident Facts.

US/0276-7325
### YEAR'S WORK - INSURANCE INSTITUTE FOR HIGHWAY SAFETY, THE. (THE YEAR'S WORK.). **Main/Corp** Insurance Institute for Highway Safety. 1980-1981-. English. an. Free. Insurance Institute for Highway Safety, 1005 North Glebe Road, Suite 800, Arlington VA 22201. **Tel** (703)247-1500. **ED** Anne Fleming. **LC** HE5614.2; .I54A. **DD** 363.1/25/0973. ctrl circ.

FI
### YHTEENVETO TIELIIKENNEVAHINGOISTA. **VFOAT** Sammandrag AV Vagtrafikolyckorna. Finnish (Swedish). Tilastokeskus, PL 504, Annankatu 44, 00101 Helsinki Finland. **Tel** 358-0-17341, FAX 358-0-17342474, telex 1002111 TILASTO SF. **LC** HE5614.5.F5; Y48.

US/0094-9914
### YOUR HIGHWAY DEPARTMENT, ARKANSAS. (YOUR HIGHWAY DEPARTMENT.). **Main/Corp** Arkansas. State Highway Dept. English. State Highway Department, PO Box 1067, Little Rock AR 72201. **LC** HE356.A8; A74A. **DD** 353.9/767/008781.

GW/0044-3654
### ZEITSCHRIFT FUER VERKEHRSSICHERHET. [Z. Verkehrssicherh.]. **Added/Corp** Deutsche Verkehrswissenschaftliche Gesellschaft. Osterreichische Verkehrswissenschaftliche Gesellschaft. Forschungsgesellschaft fur das Strassenwesen (Germany). Vol. 1, (June/July 1952)-. Periodical. German (English, French and German). Four times a year (Jan., Apr., July, Oct.). DM162.00 Germany; DM172.00 other. Verlag Tuv Rheinlan GmbH, Viktoriastr 26, W-5000 Cologne 90 F R Germany. **Tel** 011 49 2203 170960. **LC** HE331; .Z4.

# Transportation — Ships and Shipping

## SHIPS AND SHIPPING

UK/0266-8971
**100 A1.** [100 A1]. **Added/Corp** Lloyd's Register of Shipping (Firm : 1914-). **VAT** One Hundred A One. No. 1 (June 1958)-. Trade Publication. English. qt. Lloyd's Register of Shipping / New York, 17 Battery Place, New York NY 10004. **Tel** (212)425-8050. **ED** Helen Drummond, Tim Johnston. **LC** VM1; .O63. **Circ:** 30,000 (ctrl).
**Desc:** Industrial/marine trade magazine of Lloyd's Register of Shipping.
**Ind/Abst** Alum. Ind. Abstr.; Fluid Abstr., Civil Eng.; Fluid Abstr. Proc. Eng.; FLUIDEX; Met. Abstr.

UK/0001-0480
**ABC PASSENGER SHIPPING GUIDE.**
*Title Change.* No. 359 (Jan. 1986)-(1993). English. mo. Reed Travel Group / England, World Timetable Center, Church Street, Dunstable, Bedfordshire LU5 4HB England. **Tel** 011 44 582 600111, **FAX** 011 44 582 695348. **LC** HE568; .A23. **DD** 387.5/42/0294. *Continues ABC Shipping Guide. Continued by ABC Cruise and Ferry Guide.*

US
**AISA GUIDE TO SHIPPING COOPERATIVES.** See Economics-Cooperatives.

UA
**AL-NASHRAH AL-SANAWIYAH LIL-MILAHAH WA-AL-NAQL AL-BAHRI / AL-JIHAZ AL-MARKAZI LIL-TABIAH AL-AMMAH WA-AL-IHSA. VFOAT** Annual Bulletin of Sea-Borne Traffic. Began in 1880. Arabic (English). an. Jihaz Al-Markazi Lil-Tabiah Al-Ammah Wa-Al-Ihsa, Tariq Salah Salim Madinatnasr, Al-Qahirah Egypt. **LC** HE702.7; .A2. **DD** 387.5/44/0962.

US/0271-8987
**ALASKA SHIPPERS GUIDE.** [Alsk. shipp. guide]. 1981-. English. an. $19.95. Alaska Northwest Publishing Company, 130 Second Avenue South, Edmonds WA 98020-3588. **Tel** (206)774-4111, (800)533-7381. **LC** HE9.U5; T65. **DD** 380.5/24/025798.

IO
**ALMANAK INSA. Main/Corp** Persatuan Pelayaran Niaga Indonesia. **VFOAT** Almanak I.N.S.A.; Almanak. 1981-. English (Indonesian). Persatuan Pelayaran Niaga Indonesia, Jl Tanah Abang III No 10, Jakarta Pusat Indonesia. **LC** HE887; .P48A.

US/0091-5491
**AMERICAN MARINE REGISTER.** [Am. mar. regist.]. English. ir. $100.00. American Marine Register, PO Box 5468, North Little Rock AR 72119. **LC** HE553; .A62. **DD** 387.1/025/73.

US
**AMERICAN SHIPPER INTERNATIONAL.**
*Title Change.* **VFOAT** American Shipper. Vol. 32, No. 6 (June 1990)-(19??). Periodical. English. mo. Howard Publications Inc., PO Box 4728, Jacksonville FL 32201-4728. **Tel** (904)355-2601, **FAX** (904)791-8836. **LC** HF1; .F55. available on microfilm and microfiche from University Microfilms International (UMI). *Continues American Shipper, 0160-225X. Merged into American Ship Southern Edition, 1074-8350 and American Shipper Northern Edition.*

RM
**ANALELE UNIVERSITATII DIN GALATI. FASCICULA XI.** Bulletin. Romanian (English and French). an. Price varies. Redactia Analelor, 6200 Galati, Str Domneasca Nr. 47 Romania. **Tel** 40 93 413602, **FAX** 40 93 412328.

CM
**ANNUAIRE MARITIME NATIONAL / CONSEIL NATIONAL DES CHARGEURS DU CAMEROUN. Added/Corp** National Shippers Council of Cameroon. (19??)-. French. an. CNCC, BP 1588, Douala Cameroon. **LC** HE905.4; .A44. **DD** 387.5/025/6711.

CN
**ANNUAL CONVENTION OF THE HUDSON BAY ROUTE ASSOCIATION.**
**Main/Corp** Hudson Bay Route Association. (19??)-. English. an. Hudson Bay Route Association, Box 10, Hudson Bay, Saskatchewan Saskatchewan Canada. **LC** HE564.B4; S24a. **DD** 389.5/44/062712.

US/0569-3578
**ANNUAL REPORT / AMERICAN BUREAU OF SHIPPING. Main/Corp** American Bureau of Shipping. (19??)-. English. American Bureau of Shipping, 2 World Trade Center, 106th Floor, New York NY 10048. **Tel** (212)839-5000, **FAX** (201)368-0255, telex RCA 232099. **LC** VK1; .A5213. **DD** 387.5/05.

AT
**ANNUAL REPORT / AUSTRALIAN CHAMBER OF SHIPPING. Main/Corp** Australian Chamber of Shipping. English. an. Free. Australian Chamber of Shipping, 60 Pitt Street, Sydney Australia. **Tel** (02)241-3793, **FAX** (02)231-1719.
(Subscription address: GPO Box 47, Sydney New South Wales 2001 Australia) **LC** HE564.K3; A83A. **DD** 387.5/0994. **Circ:** 1,000.

CY
**ANNUAL REPORT - CYPRUS PORTS AUTHORITY. Main/Corp** Cyprus Ports Authority. (1977)-. Greek, Modern (English). an. Free. Cyprus Ports Authority, 23 Crete Street, PO Box 2007, Nicosia Cyprus. **Tel** 02-450100, **FAX** 02-365420, telex 2833 cypa cy. **LC** HE559.C9; C94a. **DD** 354.56450087/71/05. **Circ:** 1,000 (ctrl).

NO
**ANNUAL REPORT / DET NORSKE VERITAS. Main/Corp** Norske Veritas (Organization). English. an. DNV, PO Box 300, N 1322 Hovik Norway. **Tel** 011 47 67 577250. **ED** R Keith Evans. **LC** HE969.N6; N67A. **Circ:** 20,000 (ctrl).
**Desc:** Contains the board's report, shipping activities, offshore activities, international industry, highlights, and statistics.

AT
**ANNUAL REPORT / MACKAY PORT AUTHORITY. Main/Corp** Mackay Port Authority. English. MacKay Harbour Board, PO Box 96, MacKay Qld 4740 Australia. **Tel** (079)551155, **FAX** (079)552868, telex 46373 MKPORT. **LC** HE560.M24; M23a. **DD** 387.1/09943/6. *Continues Annual Report and Cargo Statistics.*

US/0558-194X
**ANNUAL REPORT / SAINT LAWRENCE SEAWAY DEVELOPMENT CORPORATION. Main/Corp** St. Lawrence Seaway Development Corporation. Began with 1954/55. English. an. Saint Lawrence Seaway Development Corporation, 800 Independence Avenue SW, Washington DC 20591. **LC** HD1694; .A155. **DD** 386/.5/09714. available on microfiche (Vols. for (1978) distributed to depository libraries).

AT
**ANNUAL REPORT - WESTERN AUSTRALIAN COASTAL SHIPPING COMMISSION. Main/Corp** Western Australian Coastal Shipping Commission. (19??)-. Corporate Report. English. Western Australian Coastal Shipping Commission, PO Box 394, Fremantle Western Australia 6160 Australia. **Tel** 011 09 4300200, **FAX** 011 09 4304326, telex AA92054. **LC** HE945.W42; W47a. **DD** 387.5/09941.

BL
**ANUARIO DE PORTOS E NAVIOS.**
Portuguese. an. $3000. Revista Tecnica e Informativa Ltda, CX Postal 2791, Rio de Janeiro Brazil. **LC** HE803; .A66. **DD** 387/.00981.

SP
**ANUARIO DEL PUERTO AUTONOMO DE BARCELONA. Main/Corp** Puerto Autonomo de Barcelona. **VFOAT** Anuario Puerto Barcelona. Spanish. an. Publicaciones El Vigia SA, Plaza Duque de Medinaceli 5, 08002 Barcelona Spain. **LC** HE558.B3; P84A. **DD** 387.1/0946/72.

II
**ANUDANOM KI MANGEM, NAUVAHANA AURA PARIVAHANA MANTRALAYA. Main/Corp** India. Ministry of Shipping and Transport. **VFOAT** Demands for Grants of Ministry of Shipping and Transport; Anudanom ki Mangem; Jahajarani aura Parivahana Mantralaya ki Anudanom ki Mangem. (1977)-. English (Hindi). Government Press / General Manager, Ring Road, Chandigarh India. **LC** HE879; .I5a. *Continues India. Ministry of Shipping and Transport. Nauvahana aura Parivahana Mantralaya ki Anudanom ki Mangem. Continued in part by India. Ministry of Transport. Anudanom ki Mangem, Parivahana Mantralaya.*

UK/0141-4151
**ARAB SHIPPING.** *Title Change.* [Arab shipp.]. **VFOAT** Al-Dalil Al-Bahri Lil-Alam Al-Arabi; Arab Shipping Guide; Seatrade Guide to Arab Shipping. (1978)-?. Arabic (English). an. Seatrade Organisation, 42-48 North Station Road, Colchester CO1 1RJ Essex England. **Tel** 011 44 206 45121, **FAX** 44 206 45190. **LC** PAR. *Continued by Arab Shipping Guide.*

GR
**ARGO.** Periodical. Multiple languages (English and Greek, Modern). $35.00. E Batis, 145 Kountourioutou and King George Strs 7, Peiraieus Greece. **LC** HE561; .A75.

PH
**ASIAN FISHING AND SHIPPING MAGAZINE.** See Fish and Fisheries.

HK
**ASIAN SHIPPING.** No. 1 (Jan. 1978)-. Periodical. English. mo. HK$300.00 (sea mail); HK$460.00 (air mail) US, Europe, Australia, & New Zealand; HK$400.00 (air mail) SE Asia. Asian Shipping, PO Box 20014, Hennessy Road, Hong Kong. **Tel** 5-278532, telex 72727 ASAMM AX. **ED** A G Barnett. **LC** HE873; .A84. **DD** 387.5/095. **Bk Rev. Ad Acc. Circ:** 5,300.
**Desc:** The shipping industry in East and Southeast Asia with associated developments in shipbuilding and marine engineering.
**Ind/Abst** Ocean. Abstr.

AT
**AUSTRALASIAN SHIPPING RECORD.**
**Added/Corp** Australasian Maritime Historical Society. Vol. 1, (19??)-. Periodical. English. Six times a year (Feb., Apr., June, Aug., Oct., Dec.). 17.50Aus$ Australia; 20.00Aus$ other. Australasian Maritime Historical Society, PO Box 89, Lobethal 5241 South Australia. **Tel** 011 61 8 389 4292. **ED** Ronald Parsons. Index available. **Bk Rev**. ctrl circ.
**Desc:** A digest of current happenings in maritime affairs in Australia and New Zealand plus historical material contributed by members.

AT/1032-3449
**AUSTRALASIAN SHIPS & PORTS.**
[Australas. ships ports]. (1989)-. Periodical. English. mo. 70.00Aus$ Australia; 95.00Aus$ other. Baird Publications Pty Ltd, PO Box 460, 573 Chapel Street, South Yarra Victoria, 3141 Australia. **Tel** 11 61 3 826-8741, **FAX** 011 61 3 827-0704, telex AA36720. **ED** Neil Baird. **DD** 387.160994. **Bk Rev**. **Ad Acc**. **Pr Rev**. **Circ:** 4,600 (ctrl).
**Desc:** Newsmagazine of the shipping and port industry in Australia and the Southwest Pacific.

BG
**BANGLADESH SHIPPING DIRECTORY.**
Directory. English. 46.00. Bangladesh Ocean Publications, 1314 A Bangabandhu Road, PO Box 316, Chittagong Bangladesh. **LC** HE880.6; .B35. **DD** 387.5/025/5492.

NR/0189-2029
**BI-LINGUAL MAGAZINE. Main/Corp** Nigerian Ports Authority. Management Services Division. **VFOAT** Revue Bilingue; Nigerian Ports Authority Magazine. 1981-. English (French). an. Management Services Division, Nigerian Ports Authority, 26-28 Marina Lagos Nigeria. **LC** HE559; .N54A. **DD** 354.6690087/71/06.

US/0093-6200
**BIENNIAL REPORT - ARKANSAS WATERWAYS COMMISSION.** (REPORT.).
**Main/Corp** Arkansas. Waterways Commission. English. be. Waterways Commission, 138 National Old Line Building, Little Rock AK 72201. **LC** HE624.A8; A73A. **DD** 353.9/767/00876.

UK
**BIENNIAL REPORT - INTERNATIONAL CARGO HANDLING CO-ORDINATION ASSOCIATION. Main/Corp** International Cargo Handling Co-Ordination Association. English. be. International Cargo Handling Co-ordination Association, 71 Bondway, London SW8 1SH England. **Tel** 011 44 71 7931022. **LC** HE561; .I557A. **DD** 380.5/2.

FR
**BILAN/PERSPECTIVES. Main/Corp** Port Autonome de Paris. **VFOAT** Bilan Perspectives. (19??)-. French. an. Port Autonome de Paris, 2 Quai de Grenelle, Paris Cedex 15 France. **Tel** (1)45.78.61.92, telex 204487. **LC** HE560.P32; P67a.

DK/0901-814X
**BIMCO BULLETIN.** [BIMCO bull.]. **Main/Corp** Baltic and International Maritime Conference. **Added/Corp** Baltic and International Maritime Conference. Baltic and International Maritime Council. **VAT** Baltic and International Maritime Conference Bulletin. (1970)-. Bulletin. English. bm. kr2070.00. Baltic and International Maritime Council (BIMCO), Bagsvaerdvej 161, DK-2880 Bagsvaerdvej Denmark. **Tel** 011 45 44 444500. **ED** Peter Thornton. **LC** HE381.A2; B3. Index available. cum. index. **Bk Rev**. **Ad Acc**. **Circ:** 3,000 (ctrl). *Continues Bulletin (Baltic and International Maritime Conference), 0903-4242.*
**Desc:** Contains articles on the international shipping industry, and developments affecting that industry.

UK/0268-9650
**BMT ABSTRACTS : BRITISH MARITIME TECHNOLOGY ABSTRACTS.** See Naval Science, Navigation-Abstracting, Bibliographies and Statistics.

PL
**BUDOWNICTWO OKRETOWE I GOSPODARKA MORSKA : ORGAN SEKCJI OKRETOWCOW PRZY ZARZADZIE GOWNYM STOWARZYSZENIA INZYNIEROW I TECHNIKOW MECHANIKOW POLSKICH. Added/Corp** Stowarzyszenie Inzynierow i Technikow Mechanikow Polskich. Sekcja

Okretowcow. **VFOAT** Shipbuilding and Maritime Economy; Shipbuilding & Maritime Economy. (1990)-. Periodical. Polish (English). mo. **(Subscription address:** ARS Polona, PO Box 1001, 00068 Warsaw Poland.) ***Formed by the union of*** *Budownictwo Okretowe, 0007-3008* ***and*** *Technika i Gospodarka Morska.*

TI
**BULLETIN ANNUEL DES STATISTIQUES - REPUBLIQUE TUNISIENNE, OFFICE DES PORTS NATIONAUX.** **Main/Corp** Diwan Al-Mawani Al-Qawmiyah. Bulletin. French. CERES - Centre d'Etudes et de Recherches Economiques et Sociales, 23 rue d'Espagne, 1000 Tunis Tunisia. **Tel** 011 216 1 242994, 011 216 1 248053. **LC** HE559.T8; D58B. **DD** 387.1/0961/1.

CM
**CAMEROON INTER-PORTS : ORGANE DE LIAISON ET D'INFORMATION DE L'OFFICE NATIONAL DES PORTS DU CAMEROUN.** Periodical. English (French). ir. Office National des Ports du Cameroun, 5 Boulevard Leclerc, BP 4020, Douala Cameroon Africa. **LC** HE559.C35; C35. **DD** 387.1/0967/113.

CN/0068-9467
**CANADIAN PORTS AND SEAWAY DIRECTORY.** ***Ceased.*** 19th- Ed.; 1963-Ceased ?. Directory. English. an. Southam Information and Technology Group Inc., 1450 Don Mills Road, Don Mills Ontario M3B 2X7 Canada. **Tel** (416)445-6641, (800)668-2374, FAX (416)442-2261. **DD** 387/.0025/71. ***Continues*** *Canadian Ports and Shipping Directory, 0381-8241.*
**Desc:** Including United States ports on the Great Lakes.

CN/0821-5944
**CANADIAN SAILINGS.** [Can. sail.]. (July 5, 1982)-. Periodical. English. wk. 51.93Can$ Canada; 80.00Can$ US; 100.00Can$ other. Canadian Sailings, 4634 St Catherine Street West, Montreal Quebec H3Z 1S3 Canada. **Tel** (514)937-0373, FAX (514)937-4708. **ED** Brian Gallery. **LC** HE561; .C36. **DD** 387.5/44/097105. **Ad Acc. Circ:** 11,000 (ctrl). ***Absorbed*** *Seaports and the Shipping World, 0037-0150.*
**Desc:** Provides a Canadian perspective to international maritime shipping and provide readers with import/export opportunities.

CN/0008-4972
**CANADIAN SAILOR.** **Added/Corp** Seafarers' International Union of Canada. Seafarers' International Union of North America. Canadian District. **VFOAT** Marin Canadien. (1948)-. Periodical. English (French). Six times a year. 12.00Can$. Seafarers International Union of Canada, 1333 St Jacques, Montreal QUE H3C 4K2 Canada. **Tel** (514)931-7859, FAX (514)931-3667, telex 0525473. **ED** Andrew C. Boyle. **Circ:** 1,000 (ctrl).
**Desc:** A review of activities which have occurred in each port and letters to the editor seafarer's training institute graduates.

CN/0836-5164
**CANADIAN SHIPBUILDING, OFFSHORE AND MARINE INDUSTRIES.** [Can. shipbuild. offshore mar. ind.]. **VFOAT** Canadian Shipbuilding and Ship Repairing Association Directory of Services, Products and Facilities; CSSRA Directory of Services, Products and Facilities. 8th Ed. (1987)-. English. an. 7.00Can$ Canada; $10.00 US; 15.00Can$ other. Canadian Maritime Industries Association, 100 Sparks Street/Suite 801, PO Box 1429 Ottawa Ontario K1P 5B7 Canada. **Tel** 232-7127, FAX 232-2490, telex 053-4848. **DD** 338.4/76238/02571. **Circ:** 3,000. ***Continues*** *Canadian Shipbuilding and Allied Industries, 0714-8364.*

CN/1187-4295
**CANADIAN TRANSPORTATION LOGISTICS.** [Can. transp. logist.]. **Added/Corp** Southam Business Publications. Vol. 94, Issue No. 9 (Sept. 1991)-. Periodical. English. mo. 41.95Can$ (one year), 57.95Can$ (two year), 67.95Can$ (three year) Canada; 52.95Can$ (one year), 66.50Can$ (two year) US; 74.00Can$ other. Southam Information and Technology Group Inc., 1450 Don Mills Road, Don Mills Ontario M3B 2X7 Canada. **Tel** (416)445-6641, (800)668-2374, FAX (416)442-2261. **LC** HE1; .C3. **DD** 388/.0971/05. available on microfilm and microfiche from University Microfilms International (UMI). ***Continues*** *Canadian Transportation (Don Mills, Ont. : 1989), 1184-1052.*

US
**CANAL TIMES : NEW YORK STATE CANAL SYSTEM NEWS.** Vol. 1, No. 1 (Spring 1989)-. Periodical. English. qt. Free. Barge Canal Planning and Development Board, 5 Governor Harriman Campus, Albany NY 12232. **Tel** (518)457-6400, FAX (518)457-6506. **ED** Thomas J Ryan. **Ad Acc.**
**Desc:** Promotional and educational publication for New York state waterways.

UK
**CAPITAL FOR SHIPPING / COMPILED BY MARITIME CONSULTANTS LIMITED.** **Added/Corp** Maritime Consultants Limited. (1989)-. English. an (April). Lloyd's of London Press Ltd, Sheepen Place, Colchester, Essex, CO3 3LP England. **Tel** 011 44 206 772113, US: (212)529-9500, US: (800)955-6937, FAX 011 44 206 772880, US: (212)529-9826, telex 987321 LLOYDS G. **(Subscription address:** Lloyd's of London Press Inc. / North America, 611 Broadway, Suite 308, New York NY 10012.)
**Desc:** Provides a comprehensive information package on financial services for shipping. Contents include: arrangers and providers of capital, commercial, merchant and investment banks, specialist ship finance institutions, stockbrokers, government institutions and agencies as well as intermediaries specializing in arranging and sourcing capital. In addition to listing the types of finance they offer, the directory also gives details of the key personnel in these institutions.

UK/0141-0687
**CARGO HANDLING ABSTRACTS / INTERNATIONAL CARGO HANDLING CO-ORDINATION ASSOCIATION.** **See** Transportation-Abstracting, Bibliographies and Statistics.

US
**CARGO / NORTH CAROLINA STATE PORTS AUTHORITY.** **Added/Corp** North Carolina State Ports Authority. Vol. 16, No. 1 1st Quarter (1991)-. Periodical. English. qt. North Carolina State Ports Authority, PO Box 9002, Wilmington NC 28402. **LC** HE554.A3; N65. **DD** 387.1/64/0975605. ***Continues*** *North Carolina Cargo Magazine.*

GW/0172-9314
**CARGOWORLD.** [Cargoworld]. (1980)-. Periodical. English. wk. DM564.00 Europe; DM636.00 other. Deutscher Verkehrs Verlag GmbH, Nordkanalstr 36 PF 101609, D 20097 Hamburg Germany. **Tel** 011 49 40 2371401. **ED** Alison Bailey. **LC** VM1; .N4. **DD** 623.8/24/05. **Bk Rev**, (Qty: 10). **Ad Acc, Adv Mgr:** Peter Waulker, **Tel** 040 23714165. **Circ:** 1,000. ***Continues*** *New Ships.*
**Desc:** Covers all developments and fields of the international transporation industry.

JM
**CARIBBEAN PORTS HANDBOOK.** ***Suspended.*** **Added/Corp** Caribbean Shipping Association. (19??)-(19??). English. be. Creative Communications Inc Ltd, PO Box 105, Kingston 10 Jamaica. **Tel** (809)927-4271, telex 2431 CARISHIP JA. **(Subscription address:** Creative Communications Inc Ltd, 29 Munroe Road, Kingston 6, Jamaica West Indies) **ED** Anthony Gambrill. **LC** HE555.A3; C37. **DD** 387.1/09182/1. **Ad Acc. Pr Rev. Circ:** 1,000.
**Desc:** Designed primarily to provide information for vessel operators/owners, ship charterers, masters and shipping agents. It provides port information on 147 ports in 38 countries in the Caribbean Basin, Gulf of Mexico, and some US ports.

JM
**CARIBBEAN SHIPPING : THE JOURNAL OF THE CARIBBEAN SHIPPING ASSOCIATION.** Periodical. English. qt. $16.00. Creative Communications Inc Ltd, PO Box 105, Kingston 10 Jamaica. **Tel** (809)927-4271, telex 2431 CARISHIP JA. **ED** Anthony Gambrill. **LC** HE785; .C27. **DD** 387.1/64/091821. **Bk Rev. Ad Acc. Circ:** 2,500.
**Desc:** Specifically serves the needs of the shipping and port industries of the Caribbean.

US
**CHADBURN, THE.** **Added/Corp** Great Lakes Historical Society. (Summer 1976)-. Periodical. English. qt. Free to members. Great Lakes Historical Society, 480 Main Street, Vermilion OH 44089. **Tel** (216)967-3467, FAX (216)967-1519. **ED** Rita Howley. **DD** 977/.006/277122. **Circ:** 3,000.
**Desc:** Current events of the Society along with noteworthy news of events along the Great Lakes.

HK
**CHUNG-KUO HAI YUN.** **VFOAT** Maritime China. (1983)-. Periodical. Chinese (English). an. $55.00. Hong Kong Trade Fair Group, 4306 China Resources Building, 26 Harbour Road, Hong Kong. **Tel** 11 852 5 736211, FAX 11 852 8913831, telex 68444. **ED** Terran Wu. **LC** HE894; .C48. **DD** 387.5/0951. **Bk Rev. Ad Acc. Circ:** 6,000 (ctrl).
**Desc:** Keeps China up-to-date with international shipping and informs the rest of the world about the Chinese industry.

II
**COMMERCE YEARBOOK OF PORTS, SHIPPING AND SHIPBUILDING.** (1974)-. English. an. D B Mahatme, 90 Veer Nariman Road, 400 200 Bombay India. **(Subscription address:** Prints India, 11 Darya Ganj, New Delhi 110002 India.) **LC** HE561; .C58. **DD** 387/.0954. ***Continues*** *Commerce Yearbook of Shipping and Shipbuilding.*

US
**COMPARATIVE SUMMARY OF WATER BORNE FOREIGN COMMERCE WITH GRAPHIC CHARTS.** **Added/Corp** United States. Shipping Board. Bureau of Research. United States. Division of Shipping Research. United States. Maritime Commission. Division of Research. English.

UK
**CONFERENCE PROCEEDINGS / INSTITUTE OF MARINE ENGINEERS.** **See** Engineering.

UK/0269-7726
**CONTAINER MANAGEMENT.** [Contain. manage.]. (1984)-. Periodical. English. Eleven times a year. £95.00 (one year), £180.00 (two years) UK; £105.00 (one year), £195.00 (two years) Europe; £120.00 (one year), £220.00 (two years) other. Baltic Publishing Ltd, The Baltic Centre, Great West Road, Brentford Middlesex TW8 9BU England. **Tel** 44 81 8472446, FAX 44 81 569 8688.

IT
**CORRIERE MERCANTILE.** Coop Giornalisti Poligrafici, Via Archimede 169, 16142 Genoa Italy.

US/0893-1240
**CRUISE INDUSTRY NEWS QUARTERLY, THE.** **See** Travel and Tourism.

US/0145-0646
**DAILY DEPOSITORY SHIPPING LIST.** **Added/Corp** United States. Superintendent of Documents. Library Division. United States. Information Dissemination/Superintendent of Documents. Library Division. (1???)-. Government Publication. English. da (except Saturdays, Sundays, and Holidays). $286.00 domestic; $357.50 other. Superintendent of Documents, US Government Printing Office, Washington DC 20402. **Tel** (202)275-3328, FAX (202)786-2377.
**Desc:** List sales and non-sales publications mailed each day from the GPO's Library Programs Service to depository libraries. Over 50,000 titles, representing over 5,000 subject categories, appear on the lists in an average year.

DK
**DANSK ILLUSTRERET SKIBSLISTE.** **Main/Corp** Arhus Havn (Firm). **VFOAT** Danish Illustrated List of Ships. Danish (English). Arhus Havn, Europaplads 2, 8000 Arhus C Denmark. **LC** HE565.D4; A32A.

US
**DETROIT MARINE HISTORIAN.** **Added/Corp** Marine Historical Society of Detroit. Vol. 1, No. 1 (Sept. 1947)-. Periodical. English. Twelve times a year. $20.00. Marine Historical Society of Detroit, 52 Middlebury Court, Dearburn MI 48120. **Tel** (313)441-6805. **ED** Jim Jackson and Mike Nicholls. Index available (In 1994.). **Bk Rev**, (Qty: varies). **Circ:** 1,200 (ctrl).

GW
**DEUTSCHES SCHIFFAHRTSARCHIV.** **Added/Corp** Deutsches Schiffahrtsmuseum Bremerhaven. Vol. 1 (1975)-. Periodical. German. an. Ernst Kabel Verlag, PF 601309, Heubergredder 12/14, D 22297 Hamburg Germany. **Tel** 011 49 40 5112951. Index available.
**Ind/Abst** Art Archaeol. Tech. Abstr.

US/0091-8458
**DIRECTORY : FLORIDA PORTS AND WATERWAYS.** **VFOAT** Florida Ports and Waterways Directory. 1972-. Directory. English. Florida Department of Commerce Development, 107 West Gaines Street, Collins Building, Suite 536, Tallahassee FL 32399. **Tel** (904)488-3104, FAX (904)487-1612. **ED** Wayne Mixson. **LC** HE554.A4; D57. **DD** 387.1/025/759. **Circ:** 10,000 (ctrl).
**Desc:** Florida's major seaports are among the most sophisticated and cost effective in the world. Mode RN ports build for modern shipping needs. The better bottom line.

CN/0845-3039
**DIRECTORY OF OCEAN SHIPPING SERVICES.** [Dir. ocean shipp. serv.]. **VFOAT** Directory of Ocean Shipping Services Between the Ports of Saint John-Halifax and World Ports Including Connecting Services to amd from Newfoundland. 11th Ed. (Nov. 1988)-. Directory. English. be. Atlantic Provinces Transportation Commission, 1133 St. George Boulevard, Suite 330, Moncton New Brunswick, E1E 4E1 Canada. **Tel** (506)857-2820, FAX (506)857-2835. **DD** 387.5/442/025715. ***Continues*** *Directory of Ocean Containership Services Between the Ports of Halifax-Saint John and World Ports, 0319-0137.*

US/0732-5975
**DIRECTORY OF SOUTH CAROLINA PORT SERVICES.** **VFOAT** Directory of Services. Directory. English. South Carolina State Ports Authority, 176 Concord Street, PO Box 817, Charleston SC 29402. **LC** HE553; .D57. **DD** 387.1/6/025757.

NE
**DIRKZWAGER'S GUIDE TO THE NEW WATERWAY, ROTTERDAM, DORDRECHT, EUROPOORT, AND BOTLEK.** (19??)-. English. an. WYT Uitgeefgrouep, Postbus 6438, 3000 AG Rotterdam Netherlands. **Tel** 011 31 10 4762566, 4255944. **LC** HE558.R75; D5. **DD** 387.1/09492. ***Continues*** *Dirkzwager's Guide to the New Waterway, Rotterdam and Dordrecht.*

UK/0012-4419
**DOCK AND HARBOUR AUTHORITY.** (THE DOCK AND HARBOUR AUTHORITY.). [Dock harb. auth.]. Vol. 1 (Nov. 1920)-. Periodical. English. mo. £55.00 UK; £60.00 other. Foxlow Publishing Company, 27 Great James Street, London WC7N 3ES England. **Tel** 011 44 71 4045855, FAX 011 44 71 8311829. **ED** Anthony Burt. **LC** [TC1; .D6]. **CODEN** DHBAAL. **Bk Rev. Ad Acc. Circ:** 2,800. available on microfilm and microfiche from University Microfilms International (UMI). Documents available from Article Express International.
**Desc:** Guide for senior personnel of ports and related industries.
**Ind/Abst** Aquat. Sci. Fish. Abstr. (Computer File); Bioeng. Abstr.; BMT Abstr.; Curr. Technol. Index; Ei Page One; EMBASE; Eng. Index Annu. [Select. Cov.]; Fluid Abstr., Civil Eng.; Fluid Abstr. Proc. Eng.; FLUIDEX (1973-); Geogr. Abstr. Phys. Geogr. (?-?); Geogr. Abstr. Human Geogr. (?-?); Health Saf. Sci. Abstr.; Int. Civil Eng. Abstr.; PAIS Int. Print (1991-); Life Sci. Collect.; Pollut. Abstr. Indexes; Soft. Abstr. Eng.

CN/1185-1783
**DOLPHIN UPDATE.** [Dolphin update]. **Main/Corp** British Columbia Ferry Corporation. **VFOAT** BC Ferries News Update. (Jan. 1991)-. Periodical. English. bm. **DD** 386.

UK/0143-5000
**DRYDOCK.** [Drydock]. Vol. 1, No. 1 (Nov./Dec. 1979)-. Academic Scholarly Publication. English. Four times a year. £15.00 UK; £20.00 other. Marine Publications International Ltd, 4 Hubbard Road, Houndmills, Basingstoke RG21 2UH England. **Tel** 011 44 256 840444.
**Ind/Abst** BMT Abstr.; EMBASE; Ocean. Abstr.; Life Sci. Collect.; Pollut. Abstr. Indexes.

IO
**DUNIA MARITIM.** Indonesian. mo. Rp1100. JL Merdeka Timur 5, Jakarta Indonesia. **LC** HE887; .D85.

IO
**ECONOMIC & SHIPPING REVIEW.** **Added/Corp** Persatuan Pelayaran Niaga Indonesia. Vol. 1 (Jan. 1979)-. Periodical. English. mo. Rp7.500. Insa Jalan Bungar Besar 54, Jakarta Indonesia. **LC** HE561; .E25. **DD** 387.5/09598.

UK
**ECS MARINE FINANCIAL YEAR BOOK.** **VFOAT** Marine Financial Year Book. 1st ed. (1985/86)-. English. an.

UK/0141-4585
**EEC SHIPPING.** **VAT** European Economic Community Shipping. 1978-. English. an. Seatrade Organisation, 42-48 North Station Road, Colchester CO1 1RJ Essex England. **Tel** 011 44 206 45121, FAX 44 206 45190.

NO/0800-1235
**ELSKAPER.** **VFOAT** Yearbook of Scandinavian Shipowners and Ship Managers; Skandinaviske Skipsrederier. 52. Ed. 1987-. English (Norwegian). **LC** HE563.N8; A8. **DD** 387.5/06/048. ***Continues*** *Arbok Over Skandinaviske Skipsrederier.*

FR/0988-2022
**ESPACES ET RESSOURCES MARITIMES.** **VFOAT** Collection Espaces et Ressources Maritimes. (1986)-. Periodical. French. an. 210.00F Europe; 220.00F US & Canada; 236.00F other. Cerdam Editions A. Pedone, 13 rue Sovfflot 13, 75005 Paris France. **Tel** 011 33 93 435-0597, FAX 011 33 93 463-0760. **UDC** 347.79.

US/0743-7404
**EXAMINATION OF THE PANAMA CANAL COMMISSION'S FINANCIAL STATEMENTS.** (EXAMINATION OF THE PANAMA CANAL COMMISSION'S FINANCIAL STATEMENTS FOR THE YEARS ENDED ...). Sept. 30, 1982 and 1981-. English. an. US General Accounting Office / District of Columbia, 441 G Street NW, Room 4528, Washington DC 20548. **Tel** (202)275-2812. **LC** HE538; .A2. **DD** 353.0087/6444. available on microfiche (Vols. for 1982/81- distributed to depository libraries). ***Continues*** *Examination of Financial Statements of the Panama Canal Commission for the Years Ended ... .*

UK
**FAIRPLAY (LONDON, ENGLAND : 1985).** (FAIRPLAY.). **VFOAT** Fairplay International Shipping Weekly. Vol. 292, No. 5289 (Jan. 31, 1985)-. Periodical. English. wk. $265.00 (US & Canada); £145.00 (Europe); £195.00 (other). Fairplay International Publications Ltd, PO Box 96, Coulsdon Surrey CRE 2TE England. **Tel** 011 44 81 6602811, FAX 011 44 81 6602824, telex 884595. ***Continues*** *Fairplay International Shipping Weekly, 0307-0220.*
**Ind/Abst** BMT Abstr. (-199?); Curr. Technol. Index.

UK/0261-2356
**FAIRPLAY WORLD PORTS DIRECTORY.** **VFOAT** World Ports Directory. 39th Ed. (1981/82)-. English. an. $210.00 US; £120.00. Fairplay International Publications Ltd, PO Box 96, Coulsdon Surrey CRE 2TE England. **Tel** 011 44 81 6602811, FAX 011 44 81 6602824, telex 884595. **ED** P Malpas. **LC** HE552; .P58. Index available. **Bk Rev. Ad Acc. Circ:** 3,000. available on diskette. ***Continues*** *Port Dues, Charges, and Accommodation.*
**Desc:** Listing of world's seaports.

UK/0959-3101
**FAIRPLAY WORLD SHIPPING DIRECTORY.** **Added/Corp** Fairplay Information Systems Ltd. **VFOAT** World Shipping Directory. (1990/91)-. English. an. $178.00 US and Canada; £89.00 other. Fairplay International Publications Ltd, PO Box 96, Coulsdon Surrey CRE 2TE England. **Tel** 011 44 81 6602811, FAX 011 44 81 6602824, telex 884595. **LC** HE561; .F56. **DD** 387.5/029/4. ***Continues*** *Fairplay World Shipping Year Book, 0140-5047.*

●US/1065-5069
**FISHING VESSELS OF THE UNITED STATES.** **See** Fish and Fisheries.

US/0884-8548
**FLORIDA SHIPPER, THE.** ***Title Change.*** [Fla. shipp.]. **VFOAT** Florida Shipper Magazine. (19??)-(19??). Trade Publication. English. wk. Florida Shipper Magazine, PO Box 371305, Miami FL 33137. **Tel** (305)567-6766, FAX (305)576-6759. **ED** Alinda Montfort. **DD** 387. **Ad Acc, Adv Mgr:** Brian Neuhart. **Circ:** 2,000. ***Continues*** *South Florida Shipper.* ***Continued by*** *Florida Shipper Magazine, 1067-1455.*
**Desc:** Trade magazine for the transportation industry. Includes listings and schedulings of ships and ports.

US/1067-1455
**FLORIDA SHIPPER MAGAZINE, THE.** [Fla. shipp. mag.]. **VFOAT** Florida Shipper. (19??)-. Periodical. English. wk. Journal of Commerce Inc., Two World Trade Center, New York NY 10048. **DD** 387. ***Continues*** *Florida Shipper Magazine, 0884-8548.*

US/0096-1353
**FORD'S DECK PLAN GUIDE.** **See** Travel and Tourism.

US/0015-7066
**FORD'S INTERNATIONAL CRUISE GUIDE.** [Ford's int. cruise guide]. **VFOAT** International Cruise Guide. 1st- Ed.(Winter 1970/71)-. Periodical. English. qt (Mar., June, Sept., Dec.). $40.00 US; $52.00 other. Fords Travel Guides, 19448 Londelius Street, Northridge CA 91324. **Tel** (818)701-7414, FAX (818)701-7415. **ED** Judith A Howard. **LC** HE568; .F66. **DD** 910./2/02. **Ad Acc. Circ:** 12,000.
**Desc:** The most complete, easy-to-use cruise directory over 200 pages of information includes: pictures and profiles of current sailing ships, plus exclusive "yellow page" section offers quick access to cruises by departure date. White page section is indexed by cruise line, ship, sailing date, point of embarkation, and ports of call.

US/1057-6266
**FROMMER'S COMPREHENSIVE TRAVEL GUIDE. CRUISES.** **See** Travel and Tourism.

KE/0302-8089
**GATEWAYS OF EASTERN AFRICA.** [Gatew. East. Afr.]. **Added/Corp** East African Harbours Corporation. No. 1 (June 1971)-. Periodical. English. bm. East African Harbours Corporation, Omombasa Kenya, PO Box 95009. **LC** HE550; .G37. **DD** 387.1/0967.

US/0016-8149
**GEORGIA ANCHORAGE.** **VFOAT** Anchorage; Georgia Anchor Age. Began Publication with Vol. 1 1960?. Periodical. English. bm. Free. Georgia Ports Authority, PO Box 2406, Savannah GA 31402. **Tel** (912)964-3811, FAX (912)964-3903, telex 804782. **ED** Amy Rhodes. **LC** HE554.A3; G45. **DD** 387.1/09758. **Ad Acc. Circ:** 13,000 (ctrl).
**Desc:** Vessel operations, cargo information, people in the business, noteworthy local events, and transportation industry events and trends.

SZ
**GESCHAFTSBERICHT (SCHWEIZERISCHE REEDEREI UND NEPTUN AG).** **Main/Corp** Schweizerische Reederei und Neptun Ag. 1975-. German. Schweizerische Reederei und Neptun Ag, Wiesandamm 4, Basel 4019 Switzerland. **LC** HE683.Z9; S37. ***Supersedes*** *Schweizerische Reederei A. G., Basel. Geschaftsbericht.*

PL
**GOSPODARKA MORSKA / INSTYTUT MORSKI.** 1982-. Polish. 500.00. Instytut Morski, 80-830 Gdansk, Skrytka Pckzt 82 Poland. **LC** HE848.7; .G65.

●US/1067-4144
**GREAT LAKES LOG.** (1993)-. Periodical. English. bw. $20.00 (one year), $36.00 (two year), $50.00 (three year). Harbor House Publishers, 221 Water Street, Boyne City MI 49712. **Tel** (616)582-2814, FAX (615)582-3392. **ED** David Knight. **Bk Rev. Circ:** 1,300. ***Continues*** *Lake Log Chips, 0270-5680.*
**Desc:** Information on the boats, the cargoes and the people that make up the maritime tradition of the Great Lakes.

CN/0824-8583
**GREAT LAKES NAVIGATION.** [Great Lakes navig.]. (1973)-. English. an (Mar.). 30.00Can$. Canadian Marine Publications, 1434 St. Catherine Street West, Suite 512, Montreal Quebec H3G 1R4 Canada. **Tel** (514)861-6715, FAX (514)861-0966. **ED** Megan Perkins. **LC** HE554.A5; G72. **DD** 386/.5/0977. **Ad Acc. Circ:** 3,228.

GR
**GREEK SHIPPING DIRECTORY.** **VFOAT** Hellenikos Nautikos Hodegos. (1957)-. Directory. English. an. $150.00. Greek Shipping Publications Co, 14 Skouze Street, 185 36 Piraeus Greece. **Tel** 452 1839 59. **LC** HE872.5; .G74. **DD** 387.5/065/495.

US/0072-7490
**GREENWOOD'S GUIDE TO GREAT LAKES SHIPPING.** **VFOAT** Guide to Great Lakes Shipping. 2nd Ed. (1961)-. English. an (April). $66.55 (includes postage). Fresh Water Press Inc., 1701 East 12th Street/Suite 3 K W, Cleveland OH 44114-3201. **Tel** (216)241-0373. **ED** Michael J. Dills. **LC** HE630.G7; G75. **Ad Acc. Circ:** 1,700 (ctrl). ***Continues*** *Guide to Great Lakes Freighters.*
**Desc:** Comprehensive overview of great lakes shipping. Includes all aspects of waterborne commerce.

PO
**GUIA - ADMINISTRACAO-GERAL DO PORTO DE LISBOA.** **Main/Corp** Portugal. Administracao Geral do Porto de Lisboa. 1970-. Portuguese (English). an. Free. Ministerio dos Transportes e Comunicacoes, Cais do Sodre 2, Lisbon Portugal. **Tel** 36 23 21, telex 18 529 P PORLI. **LC** HE558.L45; P67A. **DD** 387.1/09469/42. Index available. **Circ:** 4,000 (ctrl). ***Continues*** *Guia do Porto de Lisboa.*
**Desc:** Collection of general information on the Port of Lisbon, namely physical description of means and equipment and listing of port operators and users as well as technical tables.

UK
**GUIDE TO PORT ENTRY.** (1971)-. English. an (Feb.). £195.00. Shipping Guides Ltd., Shipping Guides House, 75 Bell Street, Reigate Surrey RH2 7AN England. **Tel** 011 44 737-242255, FAX 011 44 737-222449, telex 917070. **ED** Robert Pedlow and Charles Watson. Index available. **Bk Rev. Circ:** 10,000.
**Desc:** Contains over 3,500 pages of comprehensive marine data. Includes late reports and late plans section, many new ports, shipmaster's and reports of conditions experienced.

UK
**GUIDE TO TANKER PORTS.** (19??)-. English. ir. Shipping Guides Services Ltd, 75 Bell Street, Shipping Guides House, Reigate Surrey RH2 7AN England. **Tel** 011 44 737 242255, FAX 0737 222449, telex 917070. **ED** Feargal Hogan. ctrl circ.
**Desc:** Port information and plans.

US
**GUIDE TO THE PORT OF NEW YORK-NEW JERSEY.** ***Title Change.*** **Added/Corp** Port Authority of New York and New Jersey. (1989/1990)-(199?). English. ***Absorbed*** *Scheduled Steamship Services Directory; Port of New York-New Jersey Scheduled Air Cargo Service Directory; Port of New York-New Jersey Container Drayage Service Directory; International Freight Forwarders and Custom House Brokers Directory.* ***Continued by*** *Port of New York & New Jersey Guide.*

UK
**GUIDE TO WORLDWIDE BUNKERING SERVICES.** **VFOAT** Bunkering Guide. (1990)-. English. an. Lloyd's of London Press Ltd, Sheepen Place, Colchester, Essex, CO3 3LP England. **Tel** 011 44 206 772113, US: (212)529-9500, US: (800)955-6937, FAX 011 44 206 772880, US: (212)529-9826, telex 987321 LLOYDS G. **(Subscription address:** Lloyd's of London Press Inc. / North America, 611 Broadway, Suite 308, New York NY 10012.**)** **LC** VK367; .G85. **DD** 623.8/74/025.
**Desc:** Provides a country by country listing of oil companies, bunker suppliers, traders and brokers with contact details, delivery methods and rates.

KO
**HAESA YONGAM.** 1982-. English (Korean). an. 25,000. Koria Swiping Kajetu Sa, 43-1 Tongui-dong, Chongno-ku Seoul Korea. **LC** HE892.5; .H28.

KO
**HAEUN HANGMAN.** Periodical. Korean. Haeun Hangmanchong, 263 Yonji-dong Chongno-ku, Seoul Korea. **LC** HE561; .H25.

KO
**HAEUN YONBO.** Korean. Hanguk Sonju Hyophoe, 95-1 Tangju-dong Chongno-ku, Seoul 110 Korea. **LC** HE892.5; .H345.

CH
**HAI CHIAO SHIH YEN CHIU.** Periodical. Chinese. an. NT$0.50. Fu-Chien Sheng Chuan-Chou, Shih Yu Tien Chu, Fu-Chien, People's Republic of China. **LC** HE894; .H34. **DD** 387.5/0951.

HU/0231-1941
**HAJOZASI SZAKIRODALMI TAJEKOZTATO.** (1983)-. Periodical. Hungarian. bm. 2.700ft. Orszagos Muszaki Informacios Kozpont es Konyvtar (O.M.I.K.K.), National Technical Information Centre and Library Museum, u 17, PO Box 12, 1428 Budapest, Hungary. **Tel** (361)118-1994, FAX (361)138-2414, telex 22-4944 OMIKK H. **(Subscription address:** OMIKK Budapest, POB 12, H-1428 Hungary**)** **ED** Laszlo Fejos. **UDC** 656.6. **Circ:** 49.
**Desc:** Articles on ships and shipping.

US/0744-1061
**HAMPTON ROADS SHIPPING NEWS, THE.** ***Ceased.*** [Hampton Roads shipp. news]. ( )-(1983). Periodical. English. wk. Hampton Roads Shipping News, 740 Duke Street, Duke Grace Building/310, Norfolk VA 23510. **Tel** (804)622-2687. ***Continues*** *Shipping News, 0744-3498.*

CN/0017-7636
**HARBOUR & SHIPPING.** [Harb. & shipp.]. (1918)-. Periodical. English. Twelve times a year. 40.00Can$ Canada; 52.00Can$ US; 68.00Can$ others. Progress Publishing Company Ltd., 1765 Bellevue Avenue, West Vancouver British Columbia, V7V 1A8 Canada. **Tel** (604)922-6717, FAX (604)922-1739. **ED** Liz Bennett. **Bk Rev. Ad Acc. Circ:** 2,000 (ctrl).
**Desc:** A marine journal covering local and worldwide port and shipping news including new construction of ships, marine law and insurance columns, new products and nautical nostalgia.
**Ind/Abst** Fluid Abstr., Civil Eng.; Fluid Abstr. Proc. Eng.; FLUIDEX (1973-).

CN
**HARBOUR & SHIPPING. ANNUAL PORT ISSUE.** (1974)-. English. Progress Publishing Company Ltd., 1765 Bellevue Avenue, West Vancouver British Columbia, V7V 1A8 Canada. **Tel** (604)922-6717, FAX (604)922-1739. **DD** 387.1/09711/33.

CN
**HARBOUR & SHIPPING. ANNUAL SHIPBUILDING EDITION.** **VFOAT** Annual Shipbuilding Edition. 1973-. English. an. Progress Publishing Company Ltd., 1765 Bellevue Avenue, West Vancouver British Columbia, V7V 1A8 Canada. **Tel** (604)922-6717, FAX (604)922-1739. **DD** 338.4/7/62382009711.

CN
**HARBOUR & SHIPPING. ANNUAL SHIPPING DIRECTORY.** **VFOAT** Annual Shipping Directory. 1975-. Directory. English. Progress Publishing Company Ltd., 1765 Bellevue Avenue, West Vancouver British Columbia, V7V 1A8 Canada. **Tel** (604)922-6717, FAX (604)922-1739. **DD** 387.1/025711/33.

UK/0143-6864
**HAZARDOUS CARGO BULLETIN.** [Hazard. cargo bull.]. (Jan. 1980)-. Trade Publication. English. Twelve times a year. £89.00. Intapress Publishing Ltd., 38 Tavistock Street, London WC2E 7PB England. **Tel** 011 44 71 2400837, FAX 011 44 71 8369321, telex 25247. **ED** Michael Corkhill. **LC** WMLC 93/1316. Index available. **Bk Rev. Ad Acc. Circ:** 20,000. Documents available from BLDSC.
**Desc:** News and regulations covering the transport and handling of oils, gases and chemicals.
**Ind/Abst** Coal Abstr.; Energy Res. Abstr. (Jan. 1981-); Fluid Abstr., Civil Eng.; Fluid Abstr. Proc. Eng.; FLUIDEX (1980-); Int. Packag. Abstr.

HK
**HONG KONG SHIPPING STATISTICS.** **Added/Corp** Hong Kong. Shipping Statistics Section. (19??)-. Government Publication. English. qt. HK$44.50. Hong Kong Government Information Service, Beaconsfield House, 4 Queens Road, Hong Kong Hong Kong. **Tel** 011 852 8428801 4, telex 61190 HKGIS. **LC** HE897; .H66. **DD** 387.5/44/095125021.

NE/0923-666X
**HSB INTERNATIONAL.** **VFOAT** Holland Shipbuilding; HSB. Vol. 36, No. 11 (Jan. 1988)-. Periodical. English. Eleven times a year. Fl97.50 Netherlands; Fl150.00 other. Uitgevery Radius C., c/o Radius Publ., PO Box 277, 3300 AG Dordrecht Netherlands. **Tel** 011-31-78-168844, FAX 011-31-78-214975. **ED** Mr. D.A. Vinhoert. **LC** VM77; .H6. **Circ:** 7,300. ***Continues*** *HSB.*
**Ind/Abst** Fluid Abstr., Civil Eng.; Fluid Abstr. Proc. Eng.; FLUIDEX (19??-).

UK
**IMO NEWS.** **Added/Corp** International Maritime Organization. No. 2 (1982)-. Periodical. English. qt. Free. International Maritime Organ, 4 Albert Embankment, London SE1 7SR England. **Tel** 011/44/71/7357611, FAX 011/44/71/5873210. **LC** HE561.5; .I35. **DD** 387.5/05. ***Continues*** *IMCO News.*

US
**INBOUND LOGISTICS.** Vol. 10, No. 4 (Apr. 1990)-. Periodical. English. Twelve times a year. $65.00. Thomas Publishing Company / Food Industry, 5 Penn Plaza, New York NY 10001. **Tel** (212)290-8700. ***Continues*** *Thomas Register's Inbound Logistics, 0888-8493.*

II
**INDIAN MARINE DIRECTORY.** Began with Vol. for 1981. Directory. English. ir. Daily Shipping Times, 5 Gunbow Street, Bombay 400001 India. **ED** Nikhil N Modi. **LC** HE879; .I54. **DD** 387.5/025/54.

II/0970-4299
**INDIAN SHIPPING.** [Indian shipp.]. **Added/Corp** Indian National Steamship Owners' Association. Vol. 1 (1949)-. Periodical. English. mo. $24.00. Indian National Shipowners Association, 22 Maker Tower F Cuffe Parade, Bombay 400005 India. **Tel** (211268)215718. **(Subscription address:** Prints India, 11 Darya Ganj, New Delhi 110002 India.**)** **ED** B V Nilkund. **Bk Rev. Ad Acc. Circ:** 1,000.

IT
**INFORMATORE MARITTIMO.** (19??)-. Italian. mo. L50000 Italy; L70000 other. Informatore Marittimo, Via Campana 198, 80078 Pozzuoli NA Italy. **Tel** 011 39 81 7520711.

ES
**INFORME ESTADISTICO ANUAL. PUERTO DE ACAJUTLA.** **VFOAT** Informe Estadistico del Puerto de Acajulta. Spanish. an. ***Continues in part*** *Estadisticas Portuarias. Puerto de Acajutla.*

US/0198-859X
**INLAND RIVER GUIDE.** (1972)-. English. an. $40.00. Waterways Journal, 319 North 4th Street, Suite 650, St Louis MO 63102. **Tel** (314)241-7354, FAX (314)241-4207. **ED** Dan Owen. **LC** HE627; .I54. **DD** 386/.025/73. **Bk Rev. Ad Acc. Circ:** 3,500 (ctrl).
**Desc:** Quick reference directory covering the inland waterways and Gulf coast; lists barge and towing companies, shipyards, public and private terminals, professional firms, contractors, divers, service firms, etc.

HK
**INTERMODAL ASIA.** (19??)-. English. qt (published as supplement). Included with "Lloyd's List Maritime Asia". Lloyd's of London Press / Far East, 233 Hollywood Road/Room 1101, Hollywood Centre, Hong Kong Hong Kong. **Tel** 011 852 854 3222, FAX 011 852 854 1538, telex 66224 LLPFE HX. **ED** Kevin Chinnery. **Bk Rev. Ad Acc.** ctrl circ.
**Desc:** Reports on trade logistics by land, sea and air from an Asian perspective. Aimed at providers and users of intermodal transport services throughout Asia and amongst Asia's trading partners. It covers topics such as air freight, the freight forwarding, NVOCC and liner industries, JIT inventory control, the economics of intermodalism, EDI, legislation, facilitation and deregulation, the sea-air business - all within the context of Asia's massive trade movement. Supplement to "Lloyd's List Maritime Asia."

UK
**INTERNATIONAL CRUISE AND FERRY REVIEW.** English. Twice a year. £50.00 UK; $110.00 US. Euromoney Publications PLC, Nestor House, Playhouse Yard, London EC4Z 5EX England. **Tel** 011 44 71 779 8888, FAX 011 44 71 779 8617, telex 290700 EUROMON G.
**Desc:** Review of passenger shipping published to provide the industry world-wide with detailed and informative editorial on recent and topical developments in ship services and technology.

CN/0843-8706
**INTERNATIONAL NEWSLETTER OF MARITIME HISTORY.** [Int. newsl. marit. hist.]. **VFOAT** INMH. Vol. 3, No. 1 (March 1989)-. Newsletter. English. sa. Free with subscription of International Journal of Maritime History, $45.00 US. International Journal of Maritime Histroy, Memorial University of Newfoundland, Department of History, St Johns Newfoundland A1C 5S7 Canada. **Tel** (709)737-8424, (709)737-2602, FAX (709)737-4569. **ED** Lewis R Fischer and Helge W Nordvik. **DD** 387.5/05. **Circ:** 500 (ctrl). ***Continues*** *Newsletter of the Maritime Economic History Group, 0835-6955.*

UK/0967-1056
**INTERNATIONAL SHIPPING REVIEW.** [Int. shipp. rev.]. (1992)-. Periodical. English. qt. $110.00. Euromoney Publications PLC, Nestor House, Playhouse Yard, London EC4Z 5EX England. **Tel** 011 44 71 779 8888, FAX 011 44 71 779 8617, telex 290700 EUROMON G. **(Subscription address:** Euromoney Publications Plc, Perrymount Road Haywards Heath, West Sussex RH16 3DH England.**)** **ED** Paul Richardson. **DD** 387.5. ***Continues*** *Scandinavian and European Shipping Review., 0955-4408.*
**Desc:** Comprehensive review of the shipping industry, clearly sectioned into specific topics to address current issues and new developments in ship-building, management, repair.

US/0074-9982
**INTERSTATE PORT HANDBOOK.** **Added/Corp** Chicago Regional Port Commission. **VFOAT** Interstate Port Handbook of Illinois and Indiana. (19??)-(19??). English. $25.00. Vance Publishing Corporation, 400 Knightsbridge Parkway, Lincolnshire IL 60069. **Tel** (800)255-5113, (708)634-2600. **LC** HE554.A5; I5. **DD** 368.2.

US/0097-9341
**INVENTORY OF AMERICAN INTERMODAL EQUIPMENT.** (INVENTORY OF AMERICAN INTERMODAL EQUIPMENT / U.S. DEPARTMENT OF TRANSPORTATION, MARITIME ADMINISTRATION.). [Inventory Am. intermodal equip.]. **Main/Corp** United States. Maritime Administration. English. an. Department of Transportation, 400 Seventh Street SW, Washington DC 20590. **Tel** (202)426-4000. **LC** HE17; .M32A. **DD** 387.5/44. available on microfiche (Vols. for (1984-) distributed to depository libraries).

UK/0260-924X
**IRELAND, PORTS & SHIPPING HANDBOOK.** **VFOAT** Ireland, Ports and Shipping Handbook; Ports & Shipping Handbook; Ports and Shipping Handbook. English. an. £10.00. Charter Publications, 11 London Road, Downham Market, Norfolk PE38 9B England. **Tel** 0366 387344. **ED** J Moriarty. **LC** HE557.I75; I73. **DD** 387.1/09415. **Circ:** 6,000 (ctrl).
**Desc:** Guide to the ports and shipping services of Ireland.

BE
**JAARBOEK VAN DE HAVEN VAN ANTWERPEN. ANNUAIRE DU PORT D'ANVERS. ANTWERP PORT ANNUAL.** **Main/Corp** Port d'Anvers. **Added/Corp** Port d'Anvers. Annuaire du Port d'Anvers. Port d'Anvers. Antwerp Port Annual. **VFOAT** Annuaire du Port d'Anvers; Antwerp Port Annual. (19??)-. Dutch (English, French and German). an. 1850.00F. Antwerpse Lloyd, Vleminckstraat 18, B-2000 Antwerpen Belgium. **Tel** 011 3 234 05 50, FAX 001 3 234 25 93, telex 31446. **LC** HE558.A6; P5632a. **DD** 387.1/09493/2. **Ad Acc, Adv Mgr:** Koen Heinen. **Circ:** 6,000.

FR/0983-0537
**JOURNAL DE LA MARINE MARCHANDE ET DU TRANSPORT MULTIMODAL.** [J. mar. marchande transp. multimodal]. **VFOAT** Journal de la Marine Marchande. Vol. 68E, No. 3463 (Jan./May 1986)-. Academic Scholarly Publication. French. Fifty-two times a year. Price varies. Moreux SA, 190 Boulevard Haussmann, 75008 Paris France. **Tel** 011 33 1 44959992, telex NAVIMAR 290 131 F. **LC** VK2; .J6. **DD** 387.5/0944. ***Continues*** *Journal de la Marine Marchande.*
**Ind/Abst** Coal Abstr. (1986-); EMBASE (1986-); Energy Res. Abstr. (1986-).

TU
**KABOTAJ VE ULUSLARARAS DENIZ TASMAS ISTATISTIKLERI.** **VFOAT** Statistics of Coastwise and International Sea Transportation. (1986)-. English (Turkish). an. **LC** HA1911; .A3 subser; HE563.T8. **DD** 387.5/24/09561021. ***Continues in part*** *Deniz Tastlar, Kabotaj ve Uluslararas Deniz Tasmas Istatistikleri.*

JA
**KAIJO HOAN TOKEI NEMPO.** **Main/Corp** Japan. Kaijo Hoancho. (1950)-. Statistical Publication. Japanese. an. Koaji Hoancho Somubu, (Maritime Safety Agency Administration Dept.), 1-3 Kasumigaseki 2 chome, Chiyodaku Tokyoto 100 Japan. **LC** HE891; .J32a.

JA
**KAINAN SHIMPANCHO SAIKETSU REI SHU.** **Main/Corp** Japan. Koto Kainan Shimpancho. **Added/Corp** Kainan Shinpan Kenkyukai. Kainan Shinpan Kyokai. Vol. 1 (1963)-. Japanese. an. ¥3.600. Kainan Shimpan Kyokai, 1-17-2 Nishi-Shinbashi Minato-ku, Tokyo Japan. **Tel** 03 3502 7278/7279, FAX 03 3506 9559. **LC** LAW. Index available. **Circ:** 600 (ctrl).
**Desc:** Contains information on the international regulations to prevent collision at sea.

JA/0389-9101
**KANSAI ZOSEN KYOKAI SHI / JOURNAL OF THE KANSAI SOCIETY OF NAVAL ARCHITECTS, JAPAN.** **VFOAT** Journal of the Kansai Society of Naval Architects, Japan.

(19??)-. Periodical. Japanese. sa. $180.00. **(Subscription address:** Maruzen Company Ltd., PO Box 5050, Import & Export Department, Tokyo 100 31 Japan.) **Desc:** Covers the shipbuilding industry.

FI
**KAUPPAMERENKULUN SEKA HUOLINTA- JA AHTAUSTOIMINNAN TASETILASTO.** **Main/Corp** Finland. Tilastokeskus. **VFOAT** Balansstatistiken Over Handelssjorarten Samt Speditions- och Stuveriverksamheten; Statistics of Profit and Loss and Balance Sheet Accounts of Sea Transport, Stevedoring and Forwarding. Multiple languages (English, Finnish and Swedish). Tilastokeskus, PL 504, Annankatu 44, 00101 Helsinki Finland. **Tel** 358-0-17341, FAX 358-0-17342474, telex 1002111 TILASTO SF. **LC** HE563.F5; T54A.

GW/0176-473X
**KEHRWIEDER.** Periodical. German. mo. DM20.60, DM2.70 (single issues). Verband Deutscher Reeder, Postfach 33 50 80, W-2 Hamburg 36 Germany. **Tel** 040/4350970, FAX 040/35087211, telex 211407. **(Subscription address:** Schiffahrts Verlag Hansa, C Schroeoterdlo, Stubben Huk 10, 2000 Hamburg 11 West Germany) **ED** Raef Schneider. **LC** HE730; .K44. Index available. **Bk Rev. Ad Acc. Circ:** 9,000. **Desc:** Information for employees of German shipping companies aboard and ashore and the German public, especially opinion leaders on events and problems in the German shipping industry.

UN
**KIBERNETIKA NA MORSKOM TRANSPORTE.** (19??)-. Periodical. Russian. Vyshcha Shkola, Ulitsa Universitetskaia 16, Kharkov Ukraine. **LC** VM480; .K44.

KO
**KOREA SHIPPING GAZETTE.** (19??)-. Periodical. English (Korean). wk. $530.00 North America; $301.00 Far East Asia; $307.00 South Asia; $432.00 other. Korean Shipping Gazette, 43-1 Tongent-dong, Jongro-ku, CPO 3198, Seoul Korea. **Tel** 737-499/23, FAX 737-3771. **LC** HE892.5; .K65.

KO
**KORIA SWIPOJU CHONOL.** **VFOAT** Korea Shippers' Journal. English (Korean). wk. 900 single issue. Koria Swipoju Chonol, 23-1 Cho-dong 1-ka Chung-ku, Seoul Korea. **LC** HE561; .K67.

US/0270-5680
**LAKE LOG CHIPS.** ***Title Change.*** **See** Business-Commerce.

IO
**LALU LINTAS ANGKUTAN ANTAR PULAU MENURUT GOLONGAN BARANG, DAERAH ASAL, DAN TUJUAN.** **VFOAT** Inter Island Cargo Traffic by Commodity Group, Region of Origin, and Region of Destination. English (Indonesian). an. Rp4,500 Indonesia; $3.60 US. Central Bureau of Statistics / Indonesia, c/o Dr. Sutomo, 8 Jalan, PO Box 3, Jakarta Indonesia. **Tel** 372808 374908 Ext.342. **LC** HE887; .L34. ctrl circ.

IO
**LAPORAN PERUSAHAAN - BIRO KLASIFIKASI INDONESIA.** **Main/Corp** Indonesia. Biro Klasifikasi. Indonesian. Jalan Yos Sudarso, No 38-39 Tanjung Priok, Jakarta Indonesia. **LC** HE887; .I45A.

IO
**LAPORAN TAHUNAN - DEPALINDO.** **Main/Corp** Dewan Pemakai Jasa Angkutan Laut Indonesia. 1976-. Multiple languages (English and Indonesian). **LC** HE730; .D48A.

IO
**LAPORAN TAHUNAN DIREKTORAT NAVIGASI.** **Main/Corp** Indonesia. Direktorat Navigasi. (19??)-. Indonesian. Direktorat Nanigasi, JL Merdeka Timur No 5, Jakarta Indonesia. **LC** HE563.I6; I645a.

US/0145-7705
**LIST OF INSPECTED TANK BARGES & TANKSHIPS.** **Main/Corp** United States. Coast Guard. **VAT** List of Inspected Tank Barges and Tankships. English. sa. $9.25. National Technical Information Service - NTIS, Room 2027S, 5285 Port Royal Road, Springfield VA 22161. **Tel** (703)487-4630, (703)487-4660, (703)487-4650, FAX (703)321-8547, telex 89-9405. **LC** HE589.U5; C62A. **DD** 387.2/4/5.

DK
**LIST OF MEMBERS / BALTIC AND INTERNATIONAL MARITIME CONFERENCE.** **Main/Corp** Baltic and International Maritime Conference. (1979)-. English. ir. Bimco, Brasvaerdvej 161, DK 2880 Bagsvaerd Denmark. **Tel** 011 45 44 444500. **LC** HE564.A2; B354. **DD** 387.5/025.

UK
**LIST OF SHIPOWNERS / LLOYD'S REGISTER OF SHIPPING.** [List Shipown.]. **Added/Corp** Lloyd's Register of Shipping (Firm : 1914- ). (1980/81)-. English. an. $245.00. Lloyd's Register of Shipping / London, 71 Senchurch Street, London EC3 M4BS England. **Tel** 011 44 71 7099166. **(Subscription address:** Lloyd's Register of Shipping, 17 Battery Place, New York NY 10004.) ***Continues in part*** *List of Shipowners ... Former Names of Ships, Compound Names of Ships.*

CN/0833-5672
**LIST OF SHIPS.** [List ships]. **Added/Corp** Canada. Transport Canada. **VFOAT** Nomenclature des Navires. (1985)-. Monographic series. English (French). an. Price varies per volume. Canada Communication Group Publishers, Order Processing, Ottawa Ontario K1A 0S9 Canada. **Tel** (819)956-4800, (819)956-4802. **LC** HE565.C2; A2. **DD** 387.2/044/0971. ***Continues*** *List of Shipping, 0701-7588.*

BE
**LISTE OFFICIELLE DES NAVIRES DE MER BELGES ET DE LA FLOTTE DE LA FORCE NAVALE.** **Main/Corp** Belgium. Administration de la Marine et de la Navigation Interieur. French (Dutch). an. 140F. Administration de la Marine et de la Navigation Interieur, rue d'Arlon 104, B-1040 Bruxelles Belgium. **Tel** 02/233 12 11, FAX 02/230 30 02, telex 61 880 VERTRA B. **LC** HE565.B4; B43A. **DD** 387.2/09493. **Bk Rev. Ad Acc. Circ:** 300 French, 450 Dutch.

UK/0966-761X
**LLOYD'S CASUALTY WEEK.** (1992)-. English. wk. £300.00. Lloyd's of London Press Ltd, Sheepen Place, Colchester, Essex, CO3 3LP England. **Tel** 011 44 206 772113, US: (212)529-9500, US: (800)955-6937, FAX 011 44 206 772880, US: (212)529-9826, telex 987321 LLOYDS G. **(Subscription address:** Lloyd's of London Press Inc. / North America, 611 Broadway, Suite 308, New York NY 10012.) ***Continues*** *Lloyd's Weekly Casualty Reports, 0047-4908.*

UK
**LLOYD'S CONFIDENTIAL INDEX OF STEAM AND MOTOR VESSELS.** **VFOAT** Lloyd's Confidential Index; Confidential Index of Steam and Motor Vessels. (19??)-. English. sa. **LC** HE565.A3; L685. **DD** 387.2/4/025. **Desc:** Gives details of ownership management, classification, tonnage, type, flag, year of build and other particulars for 35,000 self-propelled merchant vessels.

UK
**LLOYD'S LIST.** (19??)-. English. da. $545.90 US and Canada; $561.35 other. Lloyd's of London Press Ltd, Sheepen Place, Colchester, Essex, CO3 3LP England. **Tel** 011 44 206 772113, US: (212)529-9500, US: (800)955-6937, FAX 011 44 206 772880, US: (212)529-9826, telex 987321 LLOYDS G. **(Subscription address:** Lloyd's of London Press Inc. / North America, 611 Broadway, Suite 308, New York NY 10012.) **ED** David Gilbertson. Index available. **Bk Rev. Ad Acc. Circ:** 14,800. available on CD-ROM. **Desc:** A daily newspaper for key executives involved in shipping, insurance, energy, trade and finance. **Ind/Abst** Infomat Int. Bus.

●HK/1015-227X
**LLOYD'S LIST MARITIME ASIA.** **Added/Corp** Lloyd's of London Press. **VFOAT** Maritime Asia. (Feb. 1993)-. Trade Publication. English. mo. $12.00. Lloyd's of London Press / Far East, 233 Hollywood Road/Room 1101, Hollywood Centre, Hong Kong Hong Kong. **Tel** 011 852 854 3222, FAX 011 852 854 1538, telex 66224 LLPFE HX. **ED** Kevin Chinnery. **LC** HE873; .L56; HE873; .L566. **Ad Acc, Adv Mgr:** Jonathon Hughes, **Tel** 011 44 71 250 1500. Full Page (B&W) $2263.00. Half Page (B&W) $1250.00. Full Page (Color) $3270.00. Half Page (Color) $2258.00. ***Continues*** *Lloyd's Maritime Asia, 0217-1120.* **Desc:** Reports on and analysis the maritime industry in the Asia-Pacific region. "Intermodal Asia" is published quarterly as a supplement.

HK/0217-1120
**LLOYD'S MARITIME ASIA.** ***Title Change.*** **Added/Corp** Lloyd's of London Press. Vol. 1, No. 1 (Apr. 1985)-(Jan. 1993). Periodical. English. mo. Lloyd's of London Press Inc., 611 Broadway/Suite 308, New York NY 10012. **Tel** (212)529-9500, FAX (212)529-9826, telex 7105812659. **(Subscription address:** UK/ Sheepen Place, Colchester Essex CO3 3LP England, US/ 611 Broadway, Suite 523, New York, NY 10012) **ED** Kevin Chinnery. **LC** HE873; .L56. **Bk Rev. Ad Acc. Circ:** 6,000 (ctrl). ***Continues*** *Maritime Asia.* ***Continued by*** *Lloyd's List Maritime Asia.* **Desc:** The only comprehensive information source on maritime affairs in the Asia-Pacific region. Offers a special insight of regional developments in ship finance, ship operations, ship building and repair, ports, chartering and the liner and bulk trades. **Ind/Abst** Fluid Abstr., Civil Eng.; Fluid Abstr. Proc. Eng.; FLUIDEX.

UK/0076-020X
**LLOYD'S MARITIME ATLAS.** **VFOAT** Maritime Atlas. (1951)-. English. be. $90.00 North America; £40.00 UK; £40.00 other. Lloyd's of London Press Ltd, Sheepen Place, Colchester, Essex, CO3 3LP England. **Tel** 011 44 206 772113, US: (212)529-9500, US: (800)955-6937, FAX 011 44 206 772880, US: (212)529-9826, telex 987321 LLOYDS G. **(Subscription address:** North America/ Lloyds of London Press, Inc., 611 Broadway, Suite 308, New York, NY 10012; telephone: (212)529-9500) **ED** A. K. C. Berisford and H. C. Dobson. **LC** G1060; .L6. Index available. **Circ:** 15,000. **Desc:** Gives reference to over 10,000 ports and shipping places around the world. Contains 64 pages of maps and two indexes of the the world's ports listed alphabetically and geographically. Other useful information covers port facilities, a distance table, weather charts, load line zones and a list of inland container depots.

UK/0268-327X
**LLOYD'S MARITIME DIRECTORY.** [Lloyd's marit. dir.]. **VFOAT** I.S.S.D.; ISSD. (1982)-. English. an (February). $285.00. Lloyd's of London Press Ltd, Sheepen Place, Colchester, Essex, CO3 3LP England. **Tel** 011 44 206 772113, US: (212)529-9500, US: (800)955-6937, FAX 011 44 206 772880, US: (212)529-9826, telex 987321 LLOYDS G. **(Subscription address:** Lloyd's of London Press Inc. / North America, 611 Broadway, Suite 308, New York NY 10012.) **ED** S. Hooke. **LC** HE951; .L56. **DD** 387.2/025. **Ad Acc. Circ:** 3,500. ***Continues in part*** *International Shipping and Shipbuilding Directory.* **Desc:** Reference book on ships, shipbuilders and repairers, and other maritime organizations. Revised each year, it contains over 5,500 shipowners, managers and agents, arranged in alphabetical order under countries, and essential details of the 34,000 vessels under their control. Other sections of the directory provide comprehensive reference lists of Ship Management services.

UK/0266-6189
**LLOYD'S MONTHLY LIST OF LAID UP VESSELS.** [Lloyd's mon. list laid up vessels]. (1975)-. Periodical. English. mo. £300.00. Lloyd's of London Press Ltd, Sheepen Place, Colchester, Essex, CO3 3LP England. **Tel** 011 44 206 772113, US: (212)529-9500, US: (800)955-6937, FAX 011 44 206 772880, US: (212)529-9826, telex 987321 LLOYDS G. **(Subscription address:** Lloyd's of London Press Inc. / North America, 611 Broadway, Suite 308, New York NY 10012.) **ED** C. Fairweather. ***Continues*** *List of Vessels Laid Up at Foreign Ports.* **Desc:** A comprehensive, up-to-date monthly record, compiled from Lloyd's exclusive sources of information, of vessels laid up through lack of employment, with analysis of the listed vessels by type, flag and age. Vessels being used for storage purposes, or detained in port and details of casualties sustained by vessels while laid up are also included.

UK
**LLOYD'S PORTS OF THE WORLD.** **VFOAT** Ports of the World. (1982)-. Directory. English. an. $270.00. Lloyd's of London Press Ltd, Sheepen Place, Colchester, Essex, CO3 3LP England. **Tel** 011 44 206 772113, US: (212)529-9500, US: (800)955-6937, FAX 011 44 206 772880, US: (212)529-9826, telex 987321 LLOYDS G. **(Subscription address:** Lloyd's of London Press Inc. / North America, 611 Broadway, Suite 308, New York NY 10012.) **LC** HE552; .P6. ***Continues*** *Ports of the World (London), 0079-4066.* **Desc:** For those involved in international trade. Ports are listed with information on name and address details of Port authorities and personnel, services available by port, documentation requirements for entry, approach and berthing details, hazards and tides, bunker facilities, storage facilities, level of traffic, wharf capacities and other information.

UK
**LLOYD'S REGISTER ANNUAL REPORT.** **Added/Corp** Lloyd's Register of Shipping. (1985)-. English. an. Lloyd's Register of Shipping / London, 71 Senchurch Street, London EC3 M4BS England. **Tel** 011 44 71 7099166. **(Subscription address:** Lloyd's Register of Shipping, 17 Battery Place, New York NY 10004.) ***Continues*** *Lloyd's Register of Shipping Annual Report.*

UK/0261-2151
**LLOYD'S REGISTER OF SHIPPING.** (CASUALTY RETURN; MERCHANT SHIPS TOTALLY LOST, BROKEN UP, ETC.). [Casualty return. Merch. ships total. lost, broken up, etc]. (19??)-. Periodical. English. an. $110.00. Lloyd's of London Press Ltd, Sheepen Place, Colchester, Essex, CO3 3LP England. **Tel** 011 44 206 772113, US: (212)529-9500, US: (800)955-6937, FAX 011 44 206 772880, US: (212)529-9826, telex 987321 LLOYDS G. **(Subscription address:** North America/ Lloyds of London Press, Inc., 611 Broadway, Suite 308, New York, NY 10012; telephone: (212)529-9500) **Desc:** Summary of all merchant ships totally lost or reported broken up during the year.

UK
**LLOYD'S REGISTER SHIPBUILDING RETURNS : MERCHANT SHIPS OF 100 TONS GROSS AND UPWARDS.** (19??)-. Periodical. English. qt. Free on request. Lloyd's Register of Shipping / New York, 17 Battery Place, New York NY 10004. **Tel** (212)425-8050.
**Ind/Abst** BMT Abstr. (-199?).

UK/0265-2455
**LLOYD'S SHIP MANAGER : LSM. VFOAT** LSM. Vol. 12, No. 2 (May 1990)-. Periodical. English. mo. £86.00. Lloyd's of London Press Ltd, Sheepen Place, Colchester, Essex, CO3 3LP England. **Tel** 011 44 206 772113, US: (212)529-9500, US: (800)955-6937, FAX 011 44 206 772880, US: (212)529-9826, telex 987321 LLOYDS G. **(Subscription address:** Lloyd's of London Press Inc. / North America, 611 Broadway, Suite 308, New York NY 10012.**) LC** HE561; .L73. ***Continues*** *Lloyd's Ship Manager & Shipping News International.*

UK
**LLOYD'S SHIPBUILDING REVIEW.** (19??)-. English. qt. £108.00 UK; $255.00 North America; £116.00 to £125.00 depending on airmail zone. Lloyd's Register of Shipping / New York, 17 Battery Place, New York NY 10004. **Tel** (212)425-8050. **ED** Humphrey Lloyd and David Wrightman. **LC** VM57; .L56. **DD** 623.8/05. Index available. cum. index. **Bk Rev. Circ:** 400.
**Desc:** Meets the requirements of all those involved in the legal and commercial aspects of international construction.

UK/0144-6673
**LLOYD'S SHIPPING ECONOMIST.** [Lloyd's shipp. econ.]. Vol. 1 (Feb. 1979)-. Periodical. English. mo. £480.00 UK; £545.00 Europe. Lloyd's of London Press Ltd, Sheepen Place, Colchester, Essex, CO3 3LP England. **Tel** 011 44 206 772113, US: (212)529-9500, US: (800)955-6937, FAX 011 44 206 772880, US: (212)529-9826, telex 987321 LLOYDS G. **(Subscription address:** Lloyd's of London Press Inc. / North America, 611 Broadway, Suite 308, New York NY 10012.**) ED** Ms. Deborah Seyman. Index available. cum. index. **Ad Acc. Circ:** 1,200.
**Desc:** Provides information and comment upon supply and demand factors in the international shipping markets. Each issue includes an analysis of costs, general cargo carriers and dry bulk carriers, plus commodity data, rates and price information, and financial insight. Regular reports on new buildings, sale and purchase, and government decisions, together with special features on individual countries and companies are also published. An annual directory of financial services for shipping is free to subscribers or may be purchased by non-subscribers. This journal is for shipowners, consultants, bankers and brokers in the shipping industry, shipbuilders, repairers, large public utilities and government bodies.

UK/0144-4549
**LLOYD'S SHIPPING INDEX.** [Lloyd's shipp. index]. **VFOAT** Shipping Index. (1936)-. English. wk (Tues.). £971.00. Lloyd's of London Press Ltd, Sheepen Place, Colchester, Essex, CO3 3LP England. **Tel** 011 44 206 772113, US: (212)529-9500, US: (800)955-6937, FAX 011 44 206 772880, US: (212)529-9826, telex 987321 LLOYDS G. **(Subscription address:** Lloyd's of London Press Inc. / North America, 611 Broadway, Suite 308, New York NY 10012.**) ED** Mr. T.C. Bird. **DD** 387. **Ad Acc. Circ:** 5,000. available on an online database.
**Desc:** Presents the current voyages, latest reported movements and vital particulars of nearly 25,000 merchant ships, together with any casualty or other information reported. Continuous update with thousands of ship movements every day, ensures subscribers have immediate access to the exclusive information from Lloyd's global network of agents, port authorities and maritime exchanges. Also includes changes in vessels' names, particulars and contacts. A market briefing section, published every Monday, highlights the essential changes in the maritime market over the previous week, plus world flag and ship type statistics.
**Ind/Abst** BMT Abstr. (-199?).

UK/0144-4557
**LLOYD'S VOYAGE RECORD.** [Lloyd's voyage rec.]. **Added/Corp** Lloyd's of London Press. **VFOAT** Voyage Record. (19??)-. English. wk (52 issues). £993.00. Lloyd's of London Press Ltd, Sheepen Place, Colchester, Essex, CO3 3LP England. **Tel** 011 44 206 772113, US: (212)529-9500, US: (800)955-6937, FAX 011 44 206 772880, US: (212)529-9826, telex 987321 LLOYDS G. **(Subscription address:** Lloyd's of London Press Inc. / North America, 611 Broadway, Suite 308, New York NY 10012.**) ED** Mr. M.D.S. Rodger. **LC** IN PROCESS. **Ad Acc. Circ:** 800. available on microfiche; available on diskette; available on magnetic tape; available on an online database; available on a computer list.
**Desc:** Provides details of the recent voyage history and ports of call, in chronological order with arrival and departure dates, of nearly 25,000 vessels in commercial service. The last four ports of call are listed for tankers, six for bulk carriers and eight for dry cargo vessels. Other information includes reported casualties, vessels laid up, repairing or converting and vessels renaming or reflagging.

UK
**LLOYD'S WEEKLY CASUALTY REPORTS. *Title Change.*** Vol. 207 (1972)-. English. wk. Lloyd's of London Press Ltd, Sheepen Place, Colchester, Essex, CO3 3LP England. **Tel** 011 44 206 772113, US: (212)529-9500, US: (800)955-6937, FAX 011 44 206 772880, US: (212)529-9826, telex 987321 LLOYDS G. **ED** D Tucker. Index available. cum. index. **Ad Acc. *Continued by*** *Lloyd's Casualty Week, 0047-4908.*
**Desc:** Convenient, easy-to-use weekly journal contains all the vital information on marine, aviation and miscellaneous casualties and incidents. A separate quarterly index aids research and identification.
**Ind/Abst** BMT Abstr. (-199?).

UK
**LLOYD'S WEEKLY LIST OF ALTERATIONS TO THE REGISTER OF SHIPS. Added/Corp** Lloyd's Register of Shipping. (198?)-. Periodical. English. Fifty-two times a year. $365.00. Lloyd's Register of Shipping / London, 71 Senchurch Street, London EC3 M4BS England. **Tel** 011 44 71 7099166. **(Subscription address:** Lloyd's Register of Shipping, 17 Battery Place, New York NY 10004.**)**

GW/0175-7601
**LOGBUCH, DAS. See** Hobbies.

AG
**MARINA MERCANTE IBEROAMERICANA / INSTITUTO DE ESTUDIOS DE LA MARINA MERCANTE, LA. Added/Corp** Instituto de Estudios de la Marina Mercante. Instituto de Estudios de la Marina Mercante Iberoamericana. **VFOAT** Latin American Shipping. (1964)-. Spanish. **LC** HE798; .M32. ***Supersedes*** *Marina Mercante Argentina.*

IT/0025-3103
**MARINA MERCANTILE, LA. *Suspended.*** [Mar. mercant.]. -Suspended with 1990 issue. Periodical. Italian. L50000 Italy; L10000 other. Silvio Basile, Via Lungo Bisagno Istria 34/C, 16141 Genoa Italy. **Tel** 011 39 10 852151. **LC** HE839; .M37.
**Ind/Abst** BMT Abstr.

CN/0318-3017
**MARINE BUYERS' DIRECTORY.** 1974-. Directory. English. Maclean Hunter Canada / Montreal, 1001 bvd. de Maisonneuve W., Montreal, Quebec H3A 3E1 Canada. **Tel** 514-845-5141, FAX 514-845-4302, telex 055-60604. **DD** 338.4/7/6238602571. ***Supersedes*** *Marine Equipment, Buyers' Directory, 0318-3033.*

US
**MARINE DIRECTORY.** Directory. English. an. Marine Engineering, 508 Birch Street, Bristol CT 06010. **LC** HE565.U5. **DD** 338.4/7/6238025. ***Continues*** *Simmons-Boardman Marine Directory.*

US/0897-0491
**MARINE LOG (NEW YORK, N.Y.).** (MARINE LOG.). [Mar. log]. Vol. 92, No. 11 (Nov. 1987)-. Academic Scholarly Publication. English. Eleven times a year. $35.00 (non-trade) US and Canada; $60.00 (non-trade) other. Simmons Boardman Publishing Corporation / New York, 345 Hudson Street, New York NY 10014. **Tel** (402)346-4740. **(Subscription address:** Simmons Boardman Publishing Corporation, PO Box 986, Omaha NE 68101.**) LC** VM1; .M3. **DD** 623.8. Index available (free). available on microfilm and microfiche from University Microfilms International (UMI). Documents available from Documents on Demand. ***Continues*** *Marine Engineering/Log (Bristol, Conn. : 1979), 0732-5460.*
**Ind/Abst** Appl. Sci. Technol. Index (Nov. 1987-1990); Coal Abstr. (Nov. 1987-); EMBASE (Nov. 1987-); Energy Inf. Abstr. (Nov. 1987-); Environ. Abstr. (Nov. 1987-); F&S Index Plus Text, Int. [Select. Cov.]; Life Sci. Collect. (Nov. 1987-); Pollut. Abstr. Indexes (Nov. 1987-); PROMT.

FR/0755-365X
**MARINE MARCHANDE EN ..., LA.** (LA MARINE MARCHANDE.). [Mar. marchande]. **Main/Corp** Comite Central des Armateurs de France, Paris. (19??)-. French. an. Moreux SA, 190 Boulevard Haussmann, 75008 Paris France. **Tel** 011 33 1 44959992, telex NAVIMAR 290 131 F. **LC** HE833; .C66a. **DD** 387.5/0944.
**Ind/Abst** Ship Abstr.

UK
**MARINE NEWS. Added/Corp** World Ship Society. Vol. 1 (1947)-. Periodical. English. mo. £20.00 (membership). World Ship Society, 28 Natland Road, Kendal Cumbria England. **ED** M Crowdy (editor's address: 28 Natland Road, Kendal Cumbria LA9 7LT England). **LC** WMLC L 83/259. Index available. **Bk Rev. Ad Acc.** ctrl circ.
**Ind/Abst** Fluid Abstr., Civil Eng.; Fluid Abstr. Proc. Eng.; FLUIDEX (19??-).

UK/0143-3709
**MARINE PROPULSION INTERNATIONAL.** [Mar. propul. int.]. (1979)-. Periodical. English. bm. £84.00 UK; £95.00, $175.00 other. Argus Press Group, Queensway House, 2 Queensway Redhill, Surrey RH1 1QS England. **Tel** 011 44 737 768611, 011 44 737 761685, FAX 011 44 737 760510, telex 948669 TOPJNL G. **CODEN** MPRIEC.
**Desc:** Provides in-depth coverage of the latest developments in the propulsion of marine craft.
**Ind/Abst** BMT Abstr.; Health Saf. Sci. Abstr.

CN/0829-545X
**MARINER (VANCOUVER, B.C.). *Suspended.*** (THE MARINER.). [Mariner]. Vol. 2, No. 3 (Dec. 1984)-Suspended 1986. Periodical. English. qt. $8.75. KW Publishing Ltd, 1268 West Pender Street, Vancouver British Columbia V6E 2Z8 Canada. **Tel** (604)688-2271, FAX (604)688-2038. **ED** Gilbert Handsbee. **DD** 338.3/72/09711. **Bk Rev. Ad Acc. Circ:** 25,000 (ctrl). ***Continues*** *Pacific Mariner, 0824-6130.*
**Desc:** Canadian commercial marine journal disseminating views of the shipbuilding industry, fishing industries, marine products, technology ports, harbours news and offshore oil and gas.

US/1045-3296
**MARITIME ABSTRACTS.** [Marit. abstr.]. **Added/Corp** National Maritime Research Center. National Maritime Research Center. Maritime Technical Information Facility. **VFOAT** NMRC Abstracts Journal. (June 1986)-. English. mo. $300.00. Maritime Technical Information Facility, Maritime Research Center, Kings Point NY 11024-1699. **DD** 387. Index Available, published separately, free-automatically sent.
**Ind/Abst** BMT Abstr.

UK/0264-6420
**MARITIME GUIDE / LLOYD'S REGISTER OF SHIPPING. Added/Corp** Lloyd's Register of Shipping (Firm : 1914-). (1984)-. English. an. $240.00. Lloyd's Register of Shipping / London, 71 Senchurch Street, London EC3 M4BS England. **Tel** 011 44 71 7099166. **(Subscription address:** Lloyd's Register of Shipping, 17 Battery Place, New York NY 10004.**) LC** HE561; .M327. **DD** 387.5/05. ***Continues*** *Lloyd's Register of Shipping. Appendix.*
**Desc:** Reference work covering worldwide ports facilities (with gazetteer and maps), telegraphic addresses, call sign index, shipbuilders and shipbreakers, UK marine insurance addresses, etc.

US/0161-9373
**MARITIME NEWSLETTER. See** Economics-Labor.

UK/0308-8839
**MARITIME POLICY AND MANAGEMENT.** [Marit. policy manage.]. Vol. 4 (July 1976)-. Periodical. English. qt. £223.00 UK; $368.00 other. Taylor & Francis Ltd., Rankine Road, Basingstoke Hampshire, RG24 8PR United Kingdom. **Tel** 011 44 256 840366, FAX 011 44 256 479438, telex 858540. **(Subscription address:** Taylor & Francis Inc., 1900 Frost Road, Suite 101, Bristol PA 19007-1598.**) ED** Richard Goss and John Evans (editor's address: Department of Maritime Studies, University of Wales College of Cardiff, PO Box 907, Colum Drive, Cardiff CF1 3EU United Kingdom). **LC** HC92; .M37. **DD** 333.9/1/005. **[CCC]. Bk Rev. Circ:** 400. available on microfilm from University Microfilms International (UMI). ***Continues*** *Maritime Studies and Management.*
**Desc:** Multi-disciplinary, international journal brings together papers concerned with many different topics that concern the maritime world, presenting the latest findings and analyses. Emphasis is placed on organizational, economic, sociolegal and management topics at port, community, shipping company and shipboard levels. It also provides notices of conferences, book reviews and short items of interest to research and workers and professionals, ashore and afloat.
**Ind/Abst** Aquat. Sci. Fish. Abstr. (Computer File); BMT Abstr.; CIS Abstr.; Electron. Commun. Abstr. J.; Fluid Abstr., Civil Eng.; Fluid Abstr. Proc. Eng.; FLUIDEX (1976-); Geogr. Abstr. Human Geogr.; ISMEC Bull.; Ocean. Abstr.; Life Sci. Collect.; Pollut. Abstr. Indexes; Risk Abstr.; Saf. Health Work; Saf. Sci. Abstr. J.; Ship Abstr.

UK
**MARITIME STUDIES AND MANAGEMENT.** V. 1- July 1973-. English. an. £8.00. Scientechnica Ltd, 823-825 Bath Road, Bristol BS4 5NU England. **LC** HC92; .M37. **DD** 333.9/1/005. available on microfilm from University Microfilms International (UMI).

FR/0474-5884
**MARITIME TRANSPORT. Added/Corp** Organisation for European Economic Co-Operation. Maritime Transport Committee. Organisation for Economic Co-Operation and Development. Maritime Transport Committee. (Sept. 1954)-. English. ir (1-2 issues per year). $46.00. OECD Publications and Information Center, 2 rue Andre-Pascal, 75775 Paris Cedex 16 France. **Tel** 011 33 1 45248167, US:(202)785-6323, FAX 011 33 1 45248500 OR 45248176, telex 620 160 OCDE. **(Subscription address:** OECD Publications Center, 2001 L Street, Suite 700, Washington DC 20036.**) LC** HE821; .O7.
**Desc:** Information on international shipping developments and detailed data on world seaborne trade, world merchant fleets and the freight market.

US/0025-6129
**MAY DAY PICTORIAL NEWS.** ***Ceased.*** [May day pict. news]. (1961)-?. Periodical. English. mo. May Day Pictorial News, PO Box 23255, Pleasant Hill CA 94523-0255. **Tel** (510)947-2138. **ED** Helen Wion. **DD** 623. **Ad Acc. Circ:** 5,298 (ctrl).
**Desc:** General information on merchant marine ship building, repair ship services and ship supply manufacturers.

US
**MERCHANT FLEETS OF THE WORLD / U.S. DEPARTMENT OF COMMERCE, MARITIME ADMINISTRATION.** **Added/Corp** United States. Maritime Administration. (Dec. 31, 1955)-. English. an. US Department of Transportation / Maritime Administration, 400 7th Street SW, Room 7206, Washington DC 20590. **Tel** (202)366-5812, FAX (202)366-3890. **LC** HE735; .U5. available on microfiche.

FI/0430-5574
**MERENKULKU. KAUPPALAIVASTO.** **VFOAT** Kauppalaivasto; Handelsflottan; Merchant Fleet; Sjofart. Handelsflottan; Navigation. Merchant Fleet. English (Finnish and Swedish). an. Government Printing Centre, PO Box 516, SF-00101 Helsinki 10 Finland. **LC** HA1448; .F4 subser; HE563.F5.

FI/0430-5582
**MERENKULKU. MERILIIKENNE SUOMEN JA ULKOMAIDEN VALILLA.** **VFOAT** Meriliikenne Suomen Ja Ulkomaiden Valilla; Sjofarten Mellan Finland och Utlandet; Shipping Between Finland and Foreign Countries; Sjofart. Sjofarten Mellan Finland och Utlandet; Navigation. Shipping Between Finland and foreign Countries. Finnish (Swedish). an. Government Printing Centre, PO Box 516, SF-00101 Helsinki 10 Finland. **LC** HA1448; .F4 subser; HE563.F5.

BG
**MONTHLY BULLETIN, PORT OF CHITTAGONG.** ***Title Change.*** **Main/Corp** Chittagong Port Authority. **VFOAT** Port of Chittagong Monthly Bulletin. Bulletin. English. mo. Chittagong Port Authority, PO Box 2013, Chittagong Bangladesh. **LC** HE560.C5; C48A. **DD** 387.1/09549/23. ***Continues*** *Monthly Bulletin, Port of Chittagong.* ***Continued by*** *Port Folio, Port of Chittagong.*

UK
**MONTHLY SHIPPING REVIEW : SS&Y RESEARCH SERVICES LTD.** English. SS&Y Research Services Ltd, 28 St Mary Axe, London EC3A 8DR England.

UK/0027-2000
**MOTOR SHIP.** (THE MOTOR SHIP.). [Mot. ship]. No. 449 (Oct. 1957)-. Academic Scholarly Publication. English. mo (12 issues). $127.00. Reed Business Publishing / West Sussex, England, Perrymount Road, Haywards Heath, West Sussex RH16 3DH England. **Tel** 011 44 81 6523500. **LC** VM1; .M57. **DD** 623.8/231. **CODEN** MOSHA3. Index available (free). available on microfilm and microfiche from University Microfilms International (UMI). Documents available from Article Express International, Ask*IEEE. ***Continues*** *British Motor Ship.*
**Ind/Abst** Bioeng. Abstr.; BMT Abstr.; Bus. Index (1985-); Coal Abstr.; Ei Page One; EMBASE; Eng. Index Annu. [Select. Cov.]; Gen. BusinessFile (1985-); Gen. Period. Index (1985-); INSPEC (Feb. 1969-); Ocean. Abstr.; Life Sci. Collect.; Trade Ind. Index (1981-).

UK
**MOTOR SHIP DIRECTORY, THE.** (199?)-. Directory. English. an. $150.00 US and Canada. Reed Business Publishing Group / England, Quadrant House, Quadrant Sutton Surrey, SM2 5AS England. **Tel** 011 44 81 652-3500. **LC** HE565.A3; D5. **DD** 387.5/025. ***Continues*** *Motor Ship Directory of Shipowners & Shipbuilding.*

UK
**MOTOR SHIP DIRECTORY OF SHIPOWNERS & SHIPBUILDING, THE.** ***Title Change.*** **VFOAT** Motor Ship Directory. (1990)-(199?). Directory. English. an. Reed Business Publishing / West Sussex, England, Perrymount Road, Haywards Heath, West Sussex RH16 3DH England. **Tel** 011 44 81 6523500. **LC** HE565.A3; D5. **DD** 387.5/025. **CODEN** MSDSER. ***Continues*** *Directory of Shipowners, Shipbuilders & Marine Engineers.* ***Continued by*** *Motor Ship Directory.*

US/0147-572X
**MRIS ABSTRACTS.** **See** Naval Science, Navigation.

UK
**MULTIHULL INTERNATIONAL.** **See** Engineering.

GR
**NAFTILIAKI.** Year 21, No. 912/3 (July/Aug. 1977)-. Trade Publication. English (Greek, Modern). Three times a year. Dr6000 Greece; $40.00 Europe; $50.00 other. Diorama Publishers Ltd., 4-6 Efplias Street, PO Box 80-162, Piraeus Greece. **Tel** 4282788, FAX 4283193, telex 212310 NAFT GR. **ED** David C. Glass. **LC** HE561; .N38. **DD** 387.5/09495. **Bk Rev. Ad Acc, Adv Mgr:** Natassa Vassilaki. Full Page (Color) $2384.00. Half Page (Color) $1592.00. **Circ:** 3,265. ***Continues*** *Nautiliake, Nautergatike.*
**Desc:** Market information, news and analysis of Greek merchant shipping and shipping-related business.

UK/0305-5701
**NATIONAL PORTS COUNCIL BULLETIN.** ***Ceased.*** [Natl. Ports Counc. bull.]. **VFOAT** Bulletin / National Ports Council. No. 1 (Spring 1972)-(1992). Bulletin. English. British Ports Federation, Victoria House, Vernon Place, London WC1B 4LL England. ***Continues in part*** *Research and Technical Bulletin.*

UK/0306-0209
**NAVAL ARCHITECT.** (THE NAVAL ARCHITECT.). [Nav. archit.]. **Added/Corp** Royal Institution of Naval Architects. (April 1971)-. Periodical. English. Ten times a year. £97.62 UK; £113.89 Europe; £122.02 other. Royal Institution of Naval Architects, 10 Upper Belgrave Street, London SW1X 8BQ England. **Tel** 011 44 71 2354622, FAX 011 44 71 245 6959, telex 265844 SINAI G. **ED** Tim Knaggs. **CODEN** NVARA3. **Ad Acc. Circ:** 6,758. Documents available from Article Express International, The Genuine Article. ***Continues in part*** *Royal Institution of Naval Architects. Transactions, 0035-8967.*
**Desc:** Covers the world of ship design, ship building and marine equipment. High technical content, including six technical papers annually.
**Ind/Abst** Biodeter. Abstr.; Bioeng. Abstr.; BMT Abstr.; Curr. Contents Eng. Tech. Appl. Sci.; Curr. Technol. Index; Ei Page One; Energy Res. Abstr. (Sept. 1976-); Eng. Index Annu.; Fluid Abstr., Civil Eng.; Fluid Abstr. Proc. Eng.; FLUIDEX (19??-); Life Sci. Collect.; Res. Alert [Select. Cov.]; SCISEARCH; SportSearch.

US/0742-2695
**NEW JERSEY AND NEW YORK PORT HANDBOOK.** [N. J. N. Y. port handb.]. **VFOAT** N.J. and N.Y. Port Handbook; NJ and NY Port Handbook. English. $25.00. WWS World Ports, 77 Moehring Drive, Blauvelt NY 10913. **LC** HE767.N5; N48. **DD** 387.1/64/02947471.

NZ/0027-724X
**NEW ZEALAND SHIPPING GAZETTE CHRISTCHURCH.** (NEW ZEALAND SHIPPING GAZETTE.). [N.Z. shipp. gaz. Christch.]. **VFOAT** Shipping Gazette. (1927)-. English. ir (Sat.). 106.95NZ$. Mercantile Gazette of N Z, GPO Box 20-034, Christchurch New Zealand. **Tel** 011 64 006433583 219, FAX 011 64 33584 490. **DD** 387.5. **Ad Acc, Adv Mgr:** H. Driver, **Tel** (09)3094892. ctrl circ.
**Desc:** Information on New Zealand shipping companies, shipping movements around the world, and ships that come to New Zealand.

GR
**NEWSFRONT GREEK SHIPPING INTELLIGENCE.** Diorama Publishers Ltd, 4-6 Efplias Street, POB 80-162, Piraeus Greece.

CN/0820-3911
**NEWSLETTER (MEMORIAL UNIVERSITY OF NEWFOUNDLAND. MARITIME HISTORY GROUP).** (NEWSLETTER / MARITIME HISTORY GROUP.). [Newsl. - Marit. Hist. Group]. Sept. 1, 1982/March 31, 1984-. Newsletter. English. an. Memorial University of Newfoundland / Faculty of Education, Elizabeth Avenue, St John's Newfoundland AIC 5S7, Canada. **Tel** (709)737-8621. **DD** 387.5/09715. ***Continues*** *Atlantic Canada Shipping Project Newsletter, 0710-247X.*

JA/0386-1597
**NIHON ZOSEN GAKKAISHI.** **Added/Corp** Nihon Zosen Gakkai. **VFOAT** Techno Marine; Technomarine; Bulletin of the Society of Naval Architects of Japan. (1915)-. Periodical. Japanese. mo. $185.00. **(Subscription address:** Kyowa Book Company Inc., 1-38 Kanda Jinbo-Cho, Chiyoda-Ku Tokyo 101, Japan**)** **LC** VM4; .N653.

GW
**NORD-OSTSEE-KANAL JAHRESBERICHT.** **Added/Corp** Germany (West). Wasser- und Schiffahrtsdirektion Nord. **VFOAT** Nord Ostsee Kanal Jahresbericht; Nord-Ostsee-Kanal Annual Report. (1980)-. English (German). an. Free. Wasser und Schiffahrtsdirektion Nord, Hindenburgufer 247, 2300 Kiel Germany. **Tel** (0431)385-1, FAX (0431)385-348, telex 1780-WSD N. **LC** HE449.K3; N6. **DD** 386/.47/0943512. **Circ:** 1,000 (ctrl). ***Continues*** *Nord-Ostsee-Kanal.*
**Desc:** Contains statistical information of traffic on the Kiel Canal and traffic regulation.

NE/0168-1753
**NORTH SEA MONITOR.** [North Sea monit.]. Periodical. English. qt. $85.00. John Wiley & Sons Ltd., Baffins Lane, Chichester West Sussex PO19 1UD England. **Tel** 0243 779777, FAX 0243 776128 BTG:JWP001, telex 86290 WIBOOKG. **(Subscription address:** John Wiley / Philadelphia, PO Box 7247, Philadelphia PA 19170.**)** **UDC** 614.7.

US/1061-799X
**OAG CRUISE AND SHIPLINE GUIDE.** [OAG cruise shipline guide]. **Added/Corp** Official Airline Guides, inc. **VFOAT** Cruise and Shipline Guide; OAG Worldwide Cruise and Shipline Guide. **VAT** Official Airline Guides Cruise and Shipline Guide, Worldwide Edition. Vol. 17, No. 3 (May-June 1991)-. English. bm. $97.00. Official Airline Guides / Illinois, 2000 Clearwater Drive, Oak Brook IL 60521. **Tel** (800)323-3537, FAX (312)574-6091, telex 210144 OAGO UR. **LC** HE568; .023. **DD** 387.5/42/025. ***Continues*** *OAG Worldwide Cruise & Shipline Guide, 0097-8779.*

US
**OFFICE EQUIPMENT EXPORTER.** (19??)-. English. an (fall). $10.00 US; $15.00 Canada; $20.00 Mexico; $25.00 other. Penton Publishing, 1100 Superior Avenue, Cleveland OH 44114-2543. **Tel** (216)696-7000, FAX (216)696-0836. **(Subscription address:** Penton Publishing, PO Box 96732, Chicago IL 60693.**)**

US/0094-8454
**OFFICIAL SOUTHERN CALIFORNIA PORTS MARITIME DIRECTORY AND GUIDE.** 1st- Ed.; 1974-. Directory. English. $10.00. 404 South Bixel Street, Los Angeles CA 90051. **LC** HE554.A6; O47. **DD** 387.1/09794.

US/0734-1016
**OFFICIAL STEAMSHIP SERVICE DIRECTORY, THE.** [Off. steamsh. serv. dir.]. June/July/Aug. 1981-. Directory. English. qt. $75.00. Twenty-First Century Publishing Company, PO Box 1148, San Carlos CA 94070. **LC** HE945.A2; O37. **DD** 387.5/025.

DK
**OFFICIEL FORTEGNELSE OVER DANSKE SKIBE MED KENDINGSSIGNALER / UDGIVIT AF HANDELSMINISTERIET.** **VFOAT** Danmarks Skibsliste. Danish. an. Farvandsdirektoratet Nautisk Afdeling, Esplanaden 19, 1263 Copenhagen K Denmark. **LC** HE565.D4; O36.

UK/0309-040X
**OFFSHORE SERVICE VESSEL REGISTER / COMPILED AND PUBLISHED BY H. CLARKSON & COMPANY LIMITED, THE.** **Added/Corp** H. Clarkson & Company. Clarkson Research Studies Limited. (19??)-. English. an. £150.00 Europe; £170.00 others. Clarkson Research Studies Ltd., 12 Camomile Street, London EC3A 7BP England. **Tel** 011 44 71 2838955.

US/0887-6827
**OFFSHORE SERVICE VESSELS. A GUIDE TO THE AMERICAN FLEET.** [Offshore serv. vessels, guide Am. fleet]. **VFOAT** Offshore Service Vessels, American. English. an. Fleet Data Service, PO Box 2576, Nacogdoches TX 75963-2576. **DD** 387. ***Continues*** *Guide to American Offshore Fleets. Offshore Service Vessels, 0197-1131.*

UK
**OLSEN'S FISHERMAN'S NAUTICAL ALMANACK, CONTAINING TIDE TABLES AND DIRECTORY OF BRITISH FISHING VESSELS.** No. 52 (1928)-. English. an. £20.15 UK; £21.65 other. ET Dennis & Sons Ltd, Melrose Street Scarborough, North Yorkshire YO12 7SJ England. **Tel** 011 44 723 500555, FAX 011 44 723 501488. **ED** Captain T. Smith. **Ad Acc, Adv Mgr:** B. Rumford. ctrl circ. ***Continues*** *Fisherman's Nautical Almanack and Tide Tables.*

US/0741-7586
**PACIFIC MARITIME MAGAZINE.** [Pac. marit. mag.]. (1984)-. Periodical. English. mo. $25.00 US (non-trade); $18.00 other. Pacific Maritime Magazine, 1818 Westlake Avenue North, Suite 430, Settle WA 98109. **Tel** (206)284-8285. **ED** Richard H. Philips. **DD** 387. **Bk Rev**, (Qty: 2). **Ad Acc. Circ:** 6,100 (ctrl). ***Continues*** *Port Reporter, 0738-4165.*
**Desc:** Covers marine transportation, construction, and ports on the West Coast of North America. Readership includes operators of tugs, barges, cargo and passenger vessels, dredges, crew and supply boats.

US/0030-8900
**PACIFIC SHIPPER.** [Pac. shipp.]. (19??)-. Periodical. English. wk. $120.00 US & Mexico; $155.00 other. K III Press Inc., 424 West 33rd Street, New York NY 10001. **Tel** (212)714-3100, (800)221-5488. **ED** Robert Bowman. **Ad Acc. Circ:** 7,500.
**Desc:** Contains schedules for worldwide shipping and cargo moving. Editorial ads include maritime, air and intermodal transportation for importers, exporters, traffic managers, FRT forwarder, CHB.

# Transportation — Ships and Shipping

US
**PACIFIC SHIPPER'S TRANSPORTATION SERVICES DIRECTORY : TSD.** **Added/Corp** K-III Information Co. **VFOAT** Transportation Services Directory; TSD; Pacific Shipper's TSD. (1993)-. Directory. English. an. $95.00 US and Mexico; $95.33 Canada; $110.00 other. K III Press Inc., 424 West 33rd Street, New York NY 10001. **Tel** (212)714-3100, (800)221-5488. **LC** HE752.C2; P33. *Continues* Coast Marine & Transportation Directory.

PN/0031-0646
**PANAMA CANAL REVIEW, THE.** V. 1- May 1950-. Periodical. English. ir. $1.50. Panama Canal Review, Box M, Balboa Heights Canal Zone. **LC** HE2830.P2; P3. **DD** 386/.445.

PN/0364-8044
**PANAMA CANAL SPILLWAY, THE.** **VFOAT** Spillway del Canal de Panama. Periodical. English (Spanish). bw. $4.00 (students); $6.00 US; $19.00 (airmail) other. Panama Canal Commission, Public Affairs Office, APO Miami FL 34011-5000. **ED** Jennifer Jones. **LC** HE538; .A37. **DD** 386/.444/05. **Bk Rev. Circ:** 14,450. *Continues* Spillway.
**Desc:** Publication for Panama Canal employees, customers, and other interest groups.

CN
**PAPERS PRESENTED TO THE ... ANNUAL TECHNICAL CONFERENCE / CANADIAN MARITIME INDUSTRIES ASSOCIATION.** [Pap. present. ... annu. tech. conf. - Can. Marit. Ind. Assoc., Tech. Conf.]. **Main/Corp** Canadian Maritime Industries Association. Technical Conference. 40th (February 16, 1988)-. English. $25.00. Conference Papers, c/o Canadian Maritime Industries Association, 100 Sparks/Suite 801, PO Box 1429 Station B, Ottawa Ontario K1P 5B7 Canada. **Tel** (613)232-7127, FAX (613)232-2490, telex 053-4848. *Continues* Papers Presented to the ... Annual Technical Conference, 0820-0556.

FR/0031-3726
**PECHE MARITIME (PARIS, FRANCE).** (LA PECHE MARITIME.). [Peche marit.]. **VFOAT** Peche Maritime, La Peche Fluviale, & La Pisciculture. (1918)-. Periodical. French. Twelve times a year. 568.07F France; 650.00F others. Moreux SA, 190 Boulevard Haussmann, 75008 Paris France. **Tel** 011 33 1 44959992, telex NAVIMAR 290 131 F.
**Ind/Abst** Aquat. Sci. Fish. Abstr. (Computer File); Ocean. Abstr.

FR
**PETIT PERROQUET, LE.** No. 1 (Nov./Dec. 1970)-. Periodical. French. bm. 70.00F. Aux Editions des 4 Seigneurs, 39 rue Marceau, 3800 Grenoble France.

US
**PIKE & FISCHER SHIPPING REGULATION.** (19??)-. English. bw. $2125.00. Pike & Fischer Inc., 4600 East-West Highway, Suite 200, Bethesda MD 20814-1438. **Tel** (301)654-6262, FAX (301)654-6297.

NO
**PLATOU REPORT, THE.** **Main/Corp** Platou (R.S.) A/S. English. PO Box 1357 Vika, 1 Oslo Norway. **LC** HE561; .P56A. **DD** 387.5/44/05.

JM
**PORT BUSTAMANTE ... HANDBOOK.** English. Port Bustamante Handbook, c/o The Shipping Association of Jamaica, 5-7 King Street, Kingston Jamaica West Indies. **LC** HE556.K55; P64. **DD** 387.1/097292.

UK/0267-4823
**PORT DEVELOPMENT INTERNATIONAL.** [Port dev. int.]. **VFOAT** Port Development Int'l. Vol. 1, No. 1 (Feb. 1985)-. Periodical. English. mo. $120.00. Port Development International, 8A West Smithfield, London EC1A 9JR England. **Tel** 011 44 71 236 0246.
**Ind/Abst** Fluid Abstr., Civil Eng.; Fluid Abstr. Proc. Eng.; FLUIDEX (19??-).

BG
**PORT FOLIO, PORT OF CHITTAGONG.** **Main/Corp** Chittagong Port Authority. **Added/Corp** Chittagong Port Authority. Port of Chittagong Monthly Bulletin. **VFOAT** Port of Chittagong Monthly Bulletin July 1978-. (19??)-. Periodical. English. mo. Chittagong Port Authority, PO Box 2013, Chittagong Bangladesh. **LC** HE560.C5; C48a. **DD** 387.1/09549/23. *Continues* Monthly Bulletin, Port of Chittagong.

US/0465-1146
**PORT OF BALTIMORE HANDBOOK.** (HANDBOOK.). [Port Baltimore handb.]. English. be. Maryland Port Administration, Port Promotion Department, The World Trade Center, Baltimore MD 21202. **Tel** (301)333-4550, telex TWX: 710-234-1075. **LC** HE554.B3; H35. **DD** 387.1/09752/6.

US/0149-208X
**PORT OF BOSTON HANDBOOK.** **Main/Corp** Boston Shipping Association. V. 1- 1975/76-. English. $2.50. Port of Boston Handbook, 223 Lewis Wharf, Boston MA 02110. **LC** HE554.B6; B65A. **DD** 387.1/09744/61.

US/0160-5526
**PORT OF DETROIT WORLD HANDBOOK.** English. an. $6.00 (add $2.50 postage). Fourth Seacoast Publishing Company Inc, PO Box 145, St Clair Shores MI 48080. **Tel** (313)779-5570, FAX (313)779-5547. **LC** HE554.D4; P67. **DD** 386/.8/0977434. Index available. **Ad Acc. Pr Rev. Circ:** 6,000 (ctrl).
**Desc:** International reference source on Detroit area firms engaged in all facets of doing domestic and international business such as the container, steamship line and agents, brokers, forwarders, railroads, trucking, ect.

CN/0834-0862
**PORT OF HALIFAX (HALIFAX-DARTMOUTH PORT COMMISSION).** (PORT OF HALIFAX.). [Port Halifax]. **Added/Corp** Halifax-Dartmouth Port Commission. (Feb. 1984)-. Periodical. English. mo. Halifax-Dartmouth Commission, 900 Cogswell Tower, Scotia Square, Halifax Nova Scotia B3J 3K1 Canada. **Tel** (902)429-1400. **DD** 387.1/09716/22. *Continues* Port of Halifax Bulletin, 0380-1497.
**Desc:** Information on ports and harbors.

FI/0359-7431
**PORT OF HELSINKI HANDBOOK.** **Added/Corp** Helsingin Kaupungin Satamalaitos. (19??)-. Trade Publication. English (Swedish). an. Port of Helsinki Authority, Olympiaranta 3, PO Box 193, 00141 Helsinki 14 Finland. **Tel** 358-173-331, FAX 173-33-232, telex 124913 PHAS. **ED** Liisa Melin. **LC** HE558.H45; P67. **DD** 387.1/094897/1. Acid Free. **Circ:** 1,500 (ctrl).
**Desc:** Description of harbour facilities. Detailed information about stevedoring, warehousing, and transportation services in the Port of Helsinki.

JM
**PORT OF KINGSTON HANDBOOK.** English. Shipping Association of Jamaica, PO Box 40, Kingston 15 Jamaica. **LC** HE556.K55; P66. **DD** 387.1/097292.

UK/0030-8064
**PORT OF LONDON.** [Port Lond.]. **Added/Corp** Port of London Authority. Vol. 45, No. 537 (July 1970)-. English. Four times a year. £9.00 UK; £12.00 other. Port of London Authority, Europe House, World Trade Center, London E1 9AA England. **Tel** 011 44 71 4818484. **ED** Roger Mutton. **LC** HE558.L8; P2. **DD** 387.1/09421. Index available. **Bk Rev. Ad Acc. Circ:** 8,000. *Continues* PLA Monthly, 0140-1521.
**Ind/Abst** Fluid Abstr., Civil Eng.; Fluid Abstr. Proc. Eng.; FLUIDEX (1973-).

US/0085-5030
**PORT OF NEW ORLEANS ANNUAL DIRECTORY.** Directory. English. an. Free. Board of Commissioners / Port of New Orleans, PO Box 60046, New Orleans LA 70160. **ED** Paul S McKelvey. **LC** HE554.N4; A28. **DD** 387.1/025/76335. **Ad Acc. Circ:** 20,000 (ctrl).
**Desc:** A description of facilities and operations of the port of New Orleans with a list of more than 1,000 companies and organizations associated with the local maritime community.

JA
**PORT OF TOKYO.** **Added/Corp** Tokyo (Japan). Kowankyoku. (1951)-. Periodical. English. an. Free. Tokyo Metropolitan Government / Port and Harbor Bureau, 8-1 Marunouchi 3-chome, Chiyoda-ku, Tokyo 100-81 Japan. **Tel** 03 3211 7949, telex 33346 PORTOKYO J. **LC** HE560.T6; P67. **DD** 387.1/0952/135. **Circ:** 7,000. available with illustrations.

CN/0477-6410
**PORT OF TORONTO NEWS.** **Added/Corp** Toronto Harbour Commission. Vol. 1 (Summer 1954)-. Periodical. English. ir. Free. Toronto Harbour Commission, 60 Harbour Street, Toronto Ontario M5J 1B7 Canada. **Tel** (416)863-2036, telex 06-219666. **ED** John Jursa and Rosemary Powell. **Bk Rev. Circ:** 7,500.
**Desc:** This publication deals with shipping on the Toronto waterfront, Toronto Island Airport, Port of Toronto and firms that doing business with Toronto Harbour Commission.

CN/0707-2481
**PORTFOLIO (HAMILTON).** (PORTFOLIO.). Spring 1977-. Periodical. English. sa. Free. Hamilton Harbour Commissioners, Hamilton Ontario L8L 1K1 Canada. **Tel** (416)525-4330, telex 061-8638. **ED** Charles A Towsley. *Supersedes* Port of Hamilton Dimension, 0381-0453.
**Desc:** Focuses on shipping, port development and activities in the Port of Hamilton, Ontario, Canada (four color process).

IT
**PORTO DI SAVONA.** **Added/Corp** Ente Portuale Savona-Piemonte. Vol. 1 (Jan. 1956)-. Periodical. Italian. Four times a year. Free on request. Ente Autonomo Porto Savona, Via Gramsci 14, 17100 Savona Italy. **Tel** 011 39 19 85541.

NE/0166-5766
**PORTS AND DREDGING.** **Added/Corp** IHC Holland. (19??)-. Periodical. English. ir. Free. IHC Holland NV, PO Box 204, 3360 AE Sliedrecht Netherlands. **Tel** 011 31 1840 11555. **LC** TC203; .P65. **DD** 627/.2/05. Documents available from Article Express International. *Continues* Ports and Dredging & Oil Report, 0377-2802.
**Ind/Abst** Eng. Index Annu. [Select. Cov.]; Fluid Abstr., Civil Eng.; Fluid Abstr. Proc. Eng.; FLUIDEX (19??-).

JA/0287-7555
**PORTS AND HARBORS.** [Ports harb.]. **Added/Corp** International Association of Ports and Harbors. (1956)-. Periodical. English. mo (10 issues). $138.00. Kokusai Kowan Kyokai, (International Assoc. of Ports & Harbors), 2-8, Toranomon 1 Chome, Minatoku, Tokyo 105, Japan. **(Subscription address:** Maruzen Company Ltd., PO Box 5050, Import & Export Department, Tokyo 100 31 Japan.)
**Ind/Abst** Fluid Abstr., Civil Eng.; Fluid Abstr. Proc. Eng.; FLUIDEX (1973-).

CN/0225-5456
**PORTS ANNUAL. CANADIAN PORTS EDITION.** (PORTS ANNUAL.). [Ports annu., Can. ports ed.]. **VFOAT** Shipping Register. (1978)-. English. an (Aug.). 30.61Can$ Canada; 35.00Can$ others. Canadian Marine Publications, 1434 St. Catherine Street West, Suite 512, Montreal Quebec H3G 1R4 Canada. **Tel** (514)861-6715, FAX (514)861-0966. **DD** 386/.8/0971. *Continues in part* Ports Annual. North American Ports Ed., 0823-5678.

UK/0262-1630
**PORTS / ASSOCIATED BRITISH PORTS.** '83-. English. £5.00. Charter Publications, 11 London Road, Downham Market, Norfolk PE38 9B England. **Tel** 0366 387344. **LC** HE557.G7; P65. **DD** 387.1/0941. *Continues* BTDB Ports.

SZ
**PORTS DESIGNATED IN APPLICATION OF THE INTERNATIONAL HEALTH REGULATIONS.** **Main/Corp** World Health Organization. **Added/Corp** World Health Organization. Ports Notifies en Application du Reglement Sanitaire International. **VFOAT** Ports Notifies en Application du Reglement Sanitaire International. (19??)-. Multiple languages (English, French, Arabic, Chinese, Russian and Spanish). ir. price varies per volume. World Health Organization, Distribution and Sales, 20 Avenue Appia, CH-1211 Geneva 27 Switzerland. **Tel** 011 41 22 7912111, FAX 011 41 22 7880401. **(Subscription address:** World Health Organization, 49 Sheridan Avenue, Albany NY 12210.) **LC** HE951; .W67a. **DD** 387.1. **NLM** W2 MW6 W9PC.

CN/0832-8587
**PORTUS (OTTAWA).** Ceased. (PORTUS.). [Portus]. **Added/Corp** Ports Canada. Vol. 1, No. 1 (Fall 1986)-(19??). Periodical. English (French). qt. **LC** HE550; .P65. **DD** 387.1/0971/05.
**Desc:** Information on harbors.

US/1053-3494
**PROCEEDINGS - AMERICAN MERCHANT MARINE AND MARITIME INDUSTRY CONFERENCE.** (PROCEEDINGS.). [Proc. - Am. Merch. Mar. Marit. Ind. Conf.]. **Main/Conf** American Merchant Marine and Maritime Industry Conference. **Added/Corp** Propeller Club of the United States. Vol. 53 (1987)-. Periodical. English. Propeller Club of the United States, 3927 Old Lee Highway, Highway/#101A, Fairfax VA 22038. **Tel** (201)898-0680. **DD** 387. *Continues* Proceedings - American Merchant Marine Conference, 0364-7374.

FR
**PROGRES REALISE EN SIGNALISATION MARITIME DURANT L'ANNEE ... / ASSOCIATION INTERNATIONALE DE SIGNALISATION MARITIME.** **VFOAT** Development of Aids to Navigation During the Year ... . English (French). an. **LC** VK1000; .P76. **DD** 343.09/66/05.

UK
**PUBLICATIONS OF THE INTERNATIONAL MARITIME ORGANIZATION.** See Naval Science, Navigation.

SP
**PUERTOS ESPANOLES.** Periodical. Spanish. 750ptas. Edificio Astygi, Planta 7A, Madrid Spain. **LC** HE557.S6; P8. **DD** 387.1/0946.

BL
**QUEBRA-MAR.** Periodical. Portuguese. sa. Administracao do Porto do Recife, Setor Comercial,

Sub-Setor de Controle e Estatistica, Praca Artur Oscar S/No, Recife PE Brazil. **LC** HE556.R4; Q4. **DD** 387.1/0981/34.

CM
**RAPPORT ANNUEL - OFFICE NATIONAL DES PORTS DU CAMEROUN.** **Main/Corp** Cameroon National Ports Authority. **VFOAT** Annual Report. English (French). an. National Ports Authority, Bureau de Douala, BP 513, Lome Cameroon. **LC** HE559.C35; N38A. **DD** 387.1/6/096711.

CM
**RAPPORT D'ACTIVITE / NATIONAL SHIPPERS COUNCIL OF CAMEROON.** **Main/Corp** National Shippers Council of Cameroon. French. C N C C, BP 1588, Douala Cameroon. **LC** HE905.4; .N37A. **DD** 387.5/44/096711.

RU
**RECHNOI TRANSPORT.** **Added/Corp** Russia (1923-U.S.S.R.). Narodnyi Komissariat Rechnogo Flota. Russia (1923-U.S.S.R.). Ministerstvo Rechnogo Flota. (1941)-. Periodical. Russian. ir. $229.95. **(Subscription address:** East View Publications Inc., 3020 Harbor Lane North, Suite 110, Minneapolis MN 55447.) **LC** TC601; .R4. ***Supersedes in part*** *Vodnyi Transport;* ***Continues*** *Morksoi Flot.*

US
**RECORD OF THE AMERICAN BUREAU OF SHIPPING.** **Main/Corp** American Bureau of Shipping. (1933)-. English. an. $642.00 New Jersey; $600.00 other. American Bureau of Shipping, 2 World Trade Center, 106th Floor, New York NY 10048. **Tel** (212)839-5000, FAX (201)368-0255, telex RCA 232099. ***Continues*** *Record of American and Foreign Shipping.*
**Desc:** Items include propulsion engine design and number, licensees name, compliance with the Marine Pollution Convention, information on offshore installations classed by ABS.

UK
**REED'S COMMERCIAL SALVAGE PRACTICE.** (1987)-. English. £400.00. Thomas Reed Publications Ltd, 80 Coombe Road, New Malden Surrey KT3 4QS England. **Tel** (081)949 7033, FAX (081)949 0530, telex 883526. **ED** David Hancox. **DD** 627/.703. **Ad Acc. Circ:** 500.
**Desc:** Covers marine salvage practice.

UK
**REGISTER OF OFFSHORE UNITS, SUBMERSIBLES & DIVING SYSTEMS.** **Main/Corp** Lloyd's Register of Shipping. **Added/Corp** Lloyd's Register of Shipping (Firm : 1914- ). **VFOAT** Register of Offshore Units, Submersibles, and Diving Systems; Register of Offshore Units, Submersibles & Underwater Systems; Register of Offshore Units, Submersibles, and Underwater Systems. **VAT** Register of Offshore Units, Submersibles, and Diving Systems. (1977/78)-. English. an. $220.00. Lloyd's Register of Shipping / London, 71 Senchurch Street, London EC3 M4BS England. **Tel** 011 44 71 7099166. **(Subscription address:** Lloyd's Register of Shipping, 17 Battery Place, New York NY 10004.) **LC** VM466.O35; L46a. **DD** 622/.29/028.
**Desc:** Contains sections listing mobile drilling rigs, submersibles, diving systems classed or certified by Lloyd's Register, work units, and owners' addresses.

UK/0141-4909
**REGISTER OF SHIPS (LLOYD'S REGISTER OF SHIPPING).** (REGISTER OF SHIPS.). [Regist. ships]. **Added/Corp** Lloyd's Register of Shipping (Firm : 1914-). (1967)-. English. an. $995.00. Lloyd's Register of Shipping / London, 71 Senchurch Street, London EC3 M4BS England. **Tel** 011 44 71 7099166. **(Subscription address:** Lloyd's Register of Shipping, 17 Battery Place, New York NY 10004.) **LC** HE565.A3; L7. **DD** 623.8/24/05. ***Continues*** *Lloyd's Register of Shipping.*
**Desc:** Three volumes listing comprehensive details of over 76,000 merchant ships in alphabetical order by ship-name.

RU
**REGISTROVAIA KNIGA MORSKIKH SUDOV SSSR / REGISTR SOIUZA SSR / REGISTER BOOK OF SEA-GOING SHIPS OF THE USSR / REGISTER OF SHIPPING OF THE USSR.** **Added/Corp** Registr Soiuza SSR. **VFOAT** Register Book of Sea-Going Ships of the USSR; Registrovaia Kniga Morskikh Sudov Soiuza SSR. (19??)-. English (Russian). Registr SSSR, Glavnoe Upravlenie, Dvortsovaia Naberezhnaia 8, 192041 St. Petersburg Russia. **LC** HE565.S65; R44.

UK
**REPORT AND ACCOUNTS - BRITISH TRANSPORT DOCKS BOARD.** **Main/Corp** British Transport Docks Board. English. an. **LC** HE557.G7.

PK
**REPORT AND ACCOUNTS FOR THE YEAR ENDED 30TH JUNE ... / PAKISTAN NATIONAL SHIPPING CORPORATION.** **Main/Corp** National Shipping Corporation (Pakistan). (19??)-. English. an. PNSC Building, Moulvi Tamizuddin Khan Road, Karachi Pakistan. **LC** HE880.5; .N37a. **DD** 387.5/0655491. ***Continues*** *National Shipping Corporation (Pakistan). _tReport and accounts -National Shipping Corporation.*

SI
**REPORT AND ACCOUNTS / SINGAPORE SHIPPING ASSOCIATION.** **Main/Corp** Singapore Shipping Association. English. Singapore Shipping Association Eng Building, 101 Cecil Street, Singapore Singapore. **LC** HE885; .S56A. **DD** 387.5/06/05957.

FR
**REPORT & ACCOUNTS TO BE SUBMITTED AT THE ANNUAL GENERAL MEETING OF SHAREHOLDERS.** **Main/Corp** Compagnie Financiere de Suez. (1973)-. English. Paris Financiere de Suez, 1 rue d'Astorg, Paris 75008 France. **LC** HE543; .C655d. **DD** 386/.43/065. ***Continues*** *Compagnie Financiere de Suez et de l'Union Parisienne. Report & Accounts to be Submitted at the General Meeting of Shareholders.*

CU/0864-2621
**REVISTA CUBANA DE CONSTRUCCION NAVAL; REVISTA CIENTIFICO TECNICA.** ***Suspended.*** (19??)-(19??). Spanish (summaries and/or abstracts in English). sa. Centro de Proyectos Navales, Calle Oficios No 452, PO Box 116, Habana 1 Cuba. **Tel** 99-02-21. **ED** Norma Cardenas Sarduy. Index available. **Bk Rev. Circ:** 2,000 (ctrl).

FR/0767-094X
**REVUE DE LA NAVIGATION, PORTS & INDUSTRIES.** [Rev. navig. ports ind.]. **VFOAT** Navigation, Ports & Industries; Navigation, Ports et Industries. Vol. 57 No. 5 (March 10, 1985)-. Academic Scholarly Publication. French. Twenty-two times a year. 891.28F France; 1100.00F other. Editions de la Navigation du Rhin, 7 Quai du General Knig, 67085 Strasbourg France. **Tel** 011 33 88 362844. **LC** HE387.R5; N3. Index available. ***Continues*** *Revue de la Navigation Fluviale Europeenne, Ports et Industries, Amenagement du Territoire, 0373-5206.*
**Ind/Abst** EMBASE; Ship Abstr.

SP/0211-2892
**ROTACION.** (1968)-. Spanish. Twelve times a year. $78.43 Spain; $89.64 Europe; $112.05 other. Pedeca, Maria Auxiliadora 5, 28040 Madrid Spain. **Tel** 011 34 1 4508837.

UK
**RULES AND REGULATIONS FOR THE CLASSIFICATION OF SHIPS / LLOYD'S REGISTER OF SHIPPING.** **Added/Corp** Lloyd's Register of Shipping. (1978?)-. English. an. $135.00. Lloyd's Register of Shipping / London, 71 Senchurch Street, London EC3 M4BS England. **Tel** 011 44 71 7099166. **(Subscription address:** Lloyd's Register of Shipping, 17 Battery Place, New York NY 10004.) ***Continues*** *Rules and Regulations for the Construction and Classification of Steel Ships.*

UK
**SAFETY AT SEA INTERNATIONAL.** Issue No. 268 (July 1991)-. Periodical. English. mo. £94.00 UK; £106.00, $195.00 other. Argus Press Group, Queensway House, 2 Queensway Redhill, Surrey RH1 1QS England. **Tel** 011 44 737 768611, 011 44 737 761685, FAX 011 44 737 760510, telex 948669 TOPJNL G. **LC** VK200; .S33. ***Continues*** *Safety at Sea, 0142-0666.*

US
**SAILING DIRECTIONS (ENROUTE) FOR NEWFOUNDLAND, LABRADOR AND HUDSON BAY.** **Main/Corp** Defense Mapping Agency Hydrographic Center. (1976)-. English (French). ir. 17.50Can$ Canada; 21.00Can$ other. Canada Communication Group Publishers, Order Processing, Ottawa Ontario K1A 0S9 Canada. **Tel** (819)956-4800, (819)956-4802.

DK
**SCANDINAVIAN SHIPPING GAZETTE.** Vol. 1 (1916)-. Periodical. English. wk (double issues June-Aug.). Kr600.00 (surface mail); Kr790.00 (airmail) Europe; Kr850.00 (air mail) other. Scandinavian Shipping Gazette, Svensk Sjoefarts Tidning, Box 53090, S-40014 Goetegorg Sweden. **Tel** 011 46 31 178540, FAX 011 46 31 115418. **LC** HE561; .S2.

GW/0938-1643
**SCHIFF & HAFEN/SEEWIRTSCHAFT.** **Added/Corp** Schiffbautechnische Gesellschaft. Germanischer Lloyd. Verband Deutscher Kapitane und Schiffsofiziere. **VFOAT** Schiff und Hafen/Seewirtschaft; Schiff & Hafen, Seewirtschaft; Schiff & Hafen; Seewirtschaft. (1990)-. German (English). Twelve times a year. DM298.00. Seehafen Verlag, Nordkanalstrasse 36, D 20097 Hamburg Germany. **Tel** 011 49 40 2371402. **ED** Hans-Jurgen Witthoft. **LC** VM3; .S22. **DD** 338.4/762382/05. **CODEN** SHASEZ. **Ad Acc, Adv Mgr:** Helmut Moller. **Circ:** 6000 (ctrl). ***Formed by the union of*** *Schiff & Hafen, 0036-603X* ***and*** *Seewirtschaft.*
**Ind/Abst** Fluid Abstr., Civil Eng.; Fluid Abstr. Proc. Eng.; FLUIDEX (19??-).

US
**SEA BREEZE (BOSTON, MASS.).** (THE SEA BREEZE.). 1827. Periodical. English. sa. $1.50. Boston Seamans Friend Society, 45 Church Street, Boston MA 02116. **Tel** (617)426-1665. **Ad Acc. Circ:** 2,600.
**Desc:** Information of activities going on at Seaman's House, programs, meetings, news of various seaman. Also events and happenings on the waterfront.

UK/0036-9977
**SEA BREEZES.** [Sea breezes]. **Added/Corp** Pacific Steam Navigation Company. (1919)-. Periodical. English. Twelve times a year. 53.00Can$ (surface mail), 65.00Can$ (airmail) Canada; 45.00Can$ (surface mail), 60.00Can$ (airmail) US. Jocast Limited, 202 Cotton Exchange, Old Hall Street, Liverpool LE 9LA England. **Tel** 11 44 51 2363935. **ED** H. Milsom. **LC** HE753.P32; S4. Index available. **Bk Rev. Ad Acc, Adv Mgr:** M. Shacklady. **Circ:** 18,000.
**Desc:** Strictly factual yarns of ships and the sea, ship and shipping company histories, personal reminiscences by seamen plus review of current events affecting tugs, sailing ships, coasters and new tonnage. Reader service for answering queries and aiding research.

US/0896-1646
**SEA HISTORY GAZETTE.** [Sea hist. gaz.]. **Added/Corp** National Maritime Historical Society (U.S.). Vol. 1, No. 1 (15 July 1987)-. Periodical. English. mo. $30.00 US; $40.00 other. National Maritime Historical Society, Charles Point Marina, PO Box 68, Peekskill NY 10566. **Tel** (914)737-7878, FAX (914)737-7816. **ED** Kevin Hayden. **DD** 387. **Bk Rev.** ctrl circ.

UK/0037-007X
**SEAFARER (LONDON).** **See** Naval Science, Navigation.

CN/0037-0150
**SEAPORTS AND THE SHIPPING WORLD.** ***Title Change.*** [Seapt. shipp. world]. (Aug. 1968)-(1992). Periodical. English. mo. Gallery Publishers Ltd, 4634 St Catherine Street West, Montreal Quebec H3Z 2W6 Canada. **Tel** (514)934-0373, FAX (514)937-4250. **ED** Brian O'N Gallery. **LC** HE561; .S316. **DD** 387/.05. **Bk Rev. Ad Acc. Circ:** 3,000 (ctrl). ***Supersedes*** *Seaports and the Transport World, 0559-2429.* ***Absorbed by*** *Canadian Sailings, 0821-5944.*
**Desc:** Covers the marine shipping industry in Canada.

CN
**SEAPORTS AND THE SHIPPING WORLD. SPRING ISSUE.** 1969-. English. an. $30.00 (one year), $50.00 (two year), $60.00 (three year) Canada and US; $50.00 (one year) Europe. Gallery Publishers Ltd, 4634 St Catherine Street West, Montreal Quebec H3Z 2W6 Canada. **Tel** (514)934-0373, FAX (514)937-4250. **ED** Brian O Gallery. **DD** 387/.00971. **Ad Acc. Circ:** 3,000 (ctrl). ***Continues*** *Seaports and the Transport World. Spring Issue.*

US/0899-1936
**SEAPORTS OF THE WESTERN HEMISPHERE.** ***Ceased.*** (SEAPORTS OF THE WESTERN HEMISPHERE : AAPA DIRECTORY.). [Seapts. west. hemisph.]. **Added/Corp** American Association of Port Authorities. **VFOAT** AAPA Directory; AAPA Directory, Seaports of the Western Hemisphere. (1986)-(1993). Directory. English. an. K III Press Inc., 424 West 33rd Street, New York NY 10001. **Tel** (212)714-3100, (800)221-5488. **LC** HE553; .S42. **DD** 387.1/025/1812.

●UK/0964-8895
**SEATRADE REVIEW.** **VFOAT** Seatrade. Vol. 21, No. 1 (Jan. 1992)-. Periodical. English. Twelve times a year. $192.00. Seatrade Organisation, 42-48 North Station Road, Colchester CO1 1RJ Essex England. **Tel** 011 44 206 45121, FAX 44 206 45190. **LC** HE561; .S3175. **DD** 387.5/05. ***Continues*** *Seatrade Business Review, 0951-6832;* ***Absorbed*** *Seatrade German Shipping Report.*
**Ind/Abst** PAIS Int. Print.

US/0891-2319
**SEATRADE WEEK.** ***Title Change.*** [Seatrade week]. (198?)-Vol. 12, No. 20 (May 1993). Periodical. English. wk. Seatrade North America Inc, Princeton Forrestal Village, 125 Village Boulevard, Suite 220, Princeton NJ 08540-5703. **Tel** (609)452-9414, FAX (609)452-9374, telex 233629 SEA UR. **LC** HE561; .S32. **DD** 338. ***Absorbed*** *Seatrade, 0037-0428.* ***Continued by*** *Seatrade Week Newsfront.*

●HK
**SEATRADE WEEK NEWSFRONT.** Vol. 12, No. 21 (May 1993)-. Periodical. English. wk (60 issues). $695.00. Seatrade Information Services, 28 Harbour Road, 44th F China Research, Hong Kong Hong Kong. **Tel** 011 852 5 8279128. **(Subscription address:** Seatrade North America Inc., 125 Village Boulevard, Suite 220, Princeton, NJ 08540) **LC** HE561; .S32. ***Continues*** *Seatrade Week, 0891-2319.*

US/0582-3668
**SEAWAY MARITIME DIRECTORY.** [Seaway marit. dir.]. (1960)-. Directory. English. an. $24.30 Michigan; $23.50 other. Fourth Seacoast Publishing Company Inc, PO Box 145, St Clair Shores MI 48080. **Tel** (313)779-5570, FAX (313)779-5547. **ED** Roger J Buysse. **Ad Acc. Circ:** 8,000 (ctrl). ***Continues*** *Official Seaway Maritime Directory.*
**Desc:** General description of entire Great Lakes and St. Lawrence Seaway system. Services and facilities of 35 seaway ports on seaway routes. Description of lock system, and container services at all ports.

US/0037-0487
**SEAWAY REVIEW.** [Seaw. rev.]. Vol. 1 (Spring 1970)-. Periodical. English. qt (March, June, Sept. Dec.). $25.00 (one year), $36.00 (two year), $50.00 (three year). Harbor House Publishers, 221 Water Street, Boyne City MI 49712. **Tel** (616)582-2814, FAX (615)582-3392. **ED** David Knight. **LC** HE381.A2; S4. **DD** 386/.47/09713. **[CCC]. Ad Acc. Circ:** 8,000 (ctrl). available on microfilm, microfiche, and CD-ROM from University Microfilms International (UMI).
**Desc:** For the people who design, build, own, operate and buy for the giant US and Canadian Great Lakes and inland waterways fleets.
**Ind/Abst** Coal Abstr.

JA
**SEMPAKU SETSUBI KANKEI HOREI.** **Added/Corp** Japan. Unyusho. Sempakukyoku. Japan. Norinsho. Japan. Teishinsho. Japan. Unyusho. (1965)-. Japanese. ¥1500. 4-51 Minami Motocho, Shinjuku-ku, Tokyo 160 Japan. **LC** LAW.

JA
**SENKYO KAIUM NEMPO.** **Main/Corp** Nihon Senshu Kyokai. 1956/57-. Japanese. Nihon Senshu Kyokai, (Japanese Ship Owners' Assoc.), Kaiun Biru, 6-4, Hirakawacho 2 Chome, Chiyodaku, Tokyoto 102, Japan. **LC** HE891; .N55A.

JA
**SENPAKU SEIBI KODAN GYOMU YORAN.** **Main/Corp** Senpaku Seibi Kodan (Japan). Japanese. Free. Senpaku Seibi Kodan, 1-1 Uchisaiwai-cho 2, Chiyoda-ku Tokyo-to Japan. **Tel** (03)501-2146. **ED** Jakeshi Mashima. **LC** HE891; .S42A. **Circ:** 200 (ctrl).
**Desc:** Report on history and performance of our corporation.

UK/0037-3834
**SHIP & BOAT INTERNATIONAL.** [Ship boat int.]. **VAT** Ship and Boat International. (1969)-. Academic Scholarly Publication. English. Ten times a year. £50.00 UK; £55.00 Europe; £60.00 other. Royal Institution of Naval Architects, 10 Upper Belgrave Street, London SW1X 8BQ England. **Tel** 011 44 71 2354622, FAX 011 44 71 245 6959, telex 265844 SINAI G. **ED** R.G. White. **LC** VM320; .S45. **DD** 623.8/2/005. **Ad Acc. Circ:** 3,327. ***Continues*** *Ship & Boat Builder International;* ***Absorbed*** *International Tug and Workboat.*
**Desc:** Reports on the commercial small vessel industry.
**Ind/Abst** BMT Abstr.; Curr. Technol. Index; EMBASE; F&S Index Plus Text, Int. [Select. Cov.]; Fluid Abstr., Civil Eng.; Fluid Abstr. Proc. Eng.; FLUIDEX (1973-); Life Sci. Collect.; PROMT.

GW
**SHIP TECHNOLOGY RESEARCH.** **VFOAT** Schiffstechnik. Vol. 36, No. 1 (March 1989)-. Periodical. English. qt. Schiffahrts-Verlag, PO Box 11 03 29, Stubbenhuk 10, W-2000 Hamburg 11 Germany. **Tel** (040)373964, FAX 040 36 49 85, telex 040 36 49 812 13 075 HANSA D. Documents available from Article Express International. ***Continues*** *Schiffstechnik, 0036-6064.*
**Ind/Abst** Ei Page One; Eng. Index Annu.

UK/0142-6680
**SHIPBROKER, THE.** ***Ceased.*** [Shipbroker]. (1931)-(1986). Periodical. English. Ryston Publications, Bank Chambers, Downham Market, Norfolk PE38 9BU England. **Tel** (44)366 387344. **ED** John Ison. **LC** HE610.G7; S5. **Bk Rev. Ad Acc. Circ:** 6,000.
**Desc:** Shippings international business monthly.

UK/0966-8330
**SHIPBUILDING & SHIPREPAIR.** [Shipbuild. shiprep.]. (1991)-. Periodical. English. qt. £65.00. Lloyd's of London Press Ltd, Sheepen Place, Colchester, Essex, CO3 3LP England. **Tel** 011 44 206 772113, US: (212)529-9500, US: (800)955-6937, FAX 011 44 206 772880, US: (212)529-9826, telex 987321 LLOYDS G. **(Subscription address:** Lloyd's of London Press Inc. / North America, 611 Broadway, Suite 308, New York NY 10012.) **DD** 338.476238305.

UK/0263-7944
**SHIPCARE & MARITIME MANAGEMENT.** [Shipcare marit. manage.]. **VFOAT** Ship Care & Maritime Managment; Ship Care and Maritime Management. **VAT** Shipcare and Maritime Management. Vol. 11, No. 9 (Sept. 1979)-. Academic Scholarly Publication. English. bm. £81.00 UK; £84.00, $155.00 other. Argus Press Group, Queensway House, 2 Queensway Redhill, Surrey RH1 1QS England. **Tel** 011 44 737 768611, 011 44 737 761685, FAX 011 44 737 760510, telex 948669 TOPJNL G. **ED** Michael Hood. **Bk Rev. Ad Acc. Circ:** 5,000. ***Formed by the union of*** *Tanker & Bulker Maritime Management* ***and*** *Shipcare International, 0140-8461.*
**Desc:** This journal covers the areas of ship repair, conversions and maintenance, offering shipowners information on the most cost effective way of ship operation.
**Ind/Abst** Aquat. Sci. Fish. Abstr. (Computer File); BMT Abstr.; Curr. Technol. Index; EMBASE; Lit. Pat. Abstr., Oilfield Chem. (1972-); Lit. Abstr., Catal. Catal.; Lit. Abstr., Health Environ.; Lit. Abstr., Pet. Refin. Petrochem.; Lit. Abstr., Pet. Substit.; Lit. Abstr., Transp. Storage; Ocean. Abstr.; Life Sci. Collect.; Pollut. Abstr. Indexes.

SI/0217-1139
**SHIPPERS' TIMES.** Periodical. English (Chinese). bm. Free to all SNSC members. Singapore National Shippers Council, 47 Hill Street, Singapore Chinese Chamber of Commerce & Industry Building, Singapore 0617 Singapore. **Tel** 3372441, telex RS 24473 FRETER. **ED** Goh Ee Beng, Fu Wa Chu, Ong Siong Kai, Kantilal J Shah, Oh Choon Siow. **LC** HE561; .S3415. **DD** 387.5/05. **Ad Acc.** ctrl circ.
**Desc:** Published to educate and to disseminate information and current relevant shipping issues which benefit shippers.

GR
**SHIPPING.** Periodical. English. 89 Kolokotroni Street, Piraeus Greece. **LC** HE561; .S342.
**Ind/Abst** BMT Abstr.

NZ/0110-5698
**SHIPPING AND CARGO MOVEMENTS.** 1980-. English. an. 7.15NZ$. Department of Statistics / New Zealand, PO Box 2922, Wellington New Zealand. **Tel** 011 64 4 4954600. **LC** HE563.N55; S54. **DD** 387.1/09931.
**Desc:** Contains detailed shipping and cargo statistics for the year ended December 1984.

II/0970-0285
**SHIPPING & MARINE INDUSTRIES JOURNAL.** [Shipp. mar. ind. j.]. **VFOAT** Shipping and Marine Industries Journal. Vol. 1 (Oct. 1972)-. Periodical. English. qt. $72.00. Shipping & Marine Inc, 3 Radhe Nivas, 36th Road Bandra, Bombay 400050 India. **Tel** 6427281/273187. **(Subscription address:** Prints India, 11 Darya Ganj, New Delhi, 110002 India, (Phone: 011 91 11 3268645)) **ED** V J Joseph. **LC** HE561; .S3426. **DD** 387.5/05. **Bk Rev. Ad Acc. Circ:** 15,000 (ctrl).
**Desc:** Devoted to shipping and shipbuilding, offshore and underwater activities. A fisheries, ports, oceanography, shipping and marine industries journal.

JA
**SHIPPING & TRADE NEWS.** English. da. $1520.00. **(Subscription address:** Maruzen Company Ltd., PO Box 5050, Import & Export Department, Tokyo 100 31 Japan.)

UK/0958-7683
**SHIPPING BOURNEMOUTH.** (SHIPPING TODAY AND YESTERDAY). [Shipping Bournem.]. (1990)-. Periodical. English. Twelve times a year. £19.20 one year, £36.50 two year, £54.00 three year, UK; £26.00 one year, £48.00 two year, £72.00 three year, Surface Mail; £40.00 airmail. HPC Publishing, Drury Lane Hastings, East Sussex TN34 1XW England. **Tel** 011 44 424 720477, FAX 011 44 424 443693. **DD** 387.5.
**Desc:** This magazine brings news as views on shipping worldwide covering the Merchant and Royal Navies, commerical and passenger industries both past and present.

AT
**SHIPPING, COMMERCE AND INDUSTRY.** **See** Business-Commerce.

US/0037-3893
**SHIPPING DIGEST.** (Mar. 12, 1923)-. Periodical. English. Fifty-two times a year. $46.00 US and Canada; $90.00 other. Geyer-McAllister Publications Inc, 51 Madison Avenue, New York NY 10010. **Tel** (212)689-4411. **LC** HE561; .S4. **DD** 656. **[CCC].**
**Desc:** Complete advance sailing schedules of cargo vessels from U.S. and Canadian ports to world ports, including date of departure, name of vessel, flag, type of vessel, name of company and, for sailings from New York, freight department phone number, pier and pier phone number. Provides current, concise news about foreign trade, ports, intermodal shipping, containerization, tariffs and steamship, railroad and air transportation.

CN/0835-5533
**SHIPPING IN CANADA.** (SHIPPING IN CANADA / STATISTICS CANADA, TRANSPORTATION DIVISION, SURFACE AND MARINE TRANSPORT SECTION.). [Shipp. Can.]. **Added/Corp** Statistics Canada. Surface and Marine Transport Section. **VFOAT** Transport Maritime au Canada. (1986)-. English (French). an. 50.00Can$ Canada; $60.00 US; $70.00 other. Statistics Canada, Publications Sales & Services, Main Building Room 1710, Ottawa Ontario K1A 0T6 Canada. **Tel** (613)951-5078, (800)267-6677, FAX (613)951-1584, telex 053-3585. **ED** Anna MacDonald (editor's telephone number: (613)951-0291, FAX (613)951-0579). **LC** HE563.C2; S55. **DD** 387.5/44/0971021. Index available. **Circ:** 600. ***Formed by the union of*** *International Seaborne Shipping Statistics (Annual), 0828-3230; Coastwise Shipping Statistics (Annual), 0225-1507* ***and*** *Water Transportation (Statistics Canada : Annual), 0380-0342.*
**Desc:** Data on domestic and international shipping at Canadian ports; vessel traffic data and commodity detail by points of loading and unloading and trends in port traffic.

UK/0080-9284
**SHIPPING MARKS ON TIMBER.** [Shipp. marks timber]. (1894)-. English. ir. £35.00. Benn Business Information Service Ltd, Riverbank House, Angel Lane, Tonbridge Kent TN9 1SE England. **Tel** 011 44 732 362666, FAX 011 44 732 770483, telex 95454 BBIS.

●GW
**SHIPPING STATISTICS AND MARKET REVIEW.** **Added/Corp** Institut fuer Seeverkehrswirtschaft und -Logistik (Bremen, Germany). **VFOAT** Monthly Shipping Statistics and Market Review; ISL. Vol. 38, No. 1/2 (Jan./Feb. 1994)-. English. mo. DM390.00. Institute of Shipping Economics and Statistics, Universitatsallee GW1 Blockade, D 28359 Bremen Germany. **Tel** 011 49 421 2209611, FAX 011 49 421 2209655, telex 244840. **LC** HE561; .B73. **DD** 387.5/44/021. ***Continues*** *Shipping Statistics (Bremen, Germany), 0721-3751.*

GW/0721-3220
**SHIPPING STATISTICS YEARBOOK.** **Added/Corp** Institut fuer Seeverkehrswirtschaft und -Logistik (Bremen, Germany). (19??)-. English. an. DM275.00. Institute of Shipping Economics and Statistics, Universitatsallee GW1 Blockade, D 28359 Bremen Germany. **Tel** 011 49 421 2209611, FAX 011 49 421 2209655, telex 244840.
**Desc:** Worldwide information on merchant fleet figures, freight rate indices, statistical information on trading, shipbuilding markets and port traffic development.

GW/0721-3751
**SHIPPING STATISTICS (ZEITSCHRIFT).** ***Title Change.*** (SHIPPING STATISTICS.). [Shipp. stat.]. **Added/Corp** Institut fuer Seeverkehrswirtschaft und -Logistik (Bremen, Germany). (1982)-(19??). English. mo. Institute of Shipping Economics and Statistics, Universitatsallee GW1 Blockade, D 28359 Bremen Germany. **Tel** 011 49 421 2209611, FAX 011 49 421 2209655, telex 244840. **LC** HE561; .B73. **DD** 387.5/44/021. ***Continues*** *Statistik der Schiffahrt, 0520-8939.* ***Continued by*** *Shipping Statistics and Market Review.*

UK/0037-3931
**SHIPPING WORLD & SHIPBUILDER.** [Ship. world shipbuild.]. **VAT** Shipping World and Shipbuilder. (1964)-. Periodical. English. mo. £35.00 UK; £45.00 other (one year), £63.00 UK; £81.00 other (two year). Marine Publications International Ltd, 4 Hubbard Road, Houndmills, Basingstoke RG21 2UH England. **Tel** 011 44 256 840444. **ED** A. Thorpe. **CODEN** SWSBA5. available on microfilm and microfiche from University Microfilms International (UMI). Documents available from Article Express International. ***Absorbed*** *Shipbuilder and Marine Engine Builder;* ***Continues*** *Shipping World and World Shipbuilding.*
**Ind/Abst** Aquat. Sci. Fish. Abstr. (Computer File); Bioeng. Abstr.; BMT Abstr.; Coal Abstr.; Curr. Technol. Index; Ei Page One; Eng. Index Annu.; Ocean. Abstr.; Life Sci. Collect.; Pollut. Abstr. Indexes; Saf. Health Work; World Surf. Coat. Abstr.

UK
**SHIPS ATLAS, THE.** English. be (Nov.). £40.00 UK; £45.00 other. Shipping Guides Ltd., Shipping Guides House, 75 Bell Street, Reigate Surrey RH2 7AN England. **Tel** 011 44 737-242255, FAX 011 44 737-222449, telex 917070. **ED** Robert Pedlow and Feargal Hogan. Index available. **Bk Rev. Ad Acc.** Documents available.

JA
**SHIPS OF THE WORLD: SEKAI NO KANSEN.** Japanese. Fourteen times a year. $246.00. Kaijinsha, (Kaijinsha Co., Ltd.), 9-8, Iidabashi 4 Chome, Chiyodaku, Tokyoto 102, Japan. **(Subscription address:** Kyowa Book Company Inc., 1-38 Kanda Jinbo-Cho, Chiyoda-Ku, Tokyo 101, Japan (Phone: 03-3293-0727))

US/0893-5777
**SHIPWRECKS & TREASURE MAGAZINE.** **Added/Corp** Corporation for Ocean Development (Jersey City, NJ). **VFOAT** Shipwrecks and Treasure Magazine; Shipwrecks and Treasure;

# Transportation —Ships and Shipping

Shipwrecks & Treasure. (1991)-. Periodical. English. qt. Corporation for Ocean Development, 202 Delaware Avenue/1st Floor, Jersey City NJ 07306.

SI
**SINGAPORE SHIPPING 'N' SHIPBUILDER.** Periodical. English. mo. $24.00. Cosmic Media, PO Box 3163, Singapore Singapore. **LC** HE561; .S62. **DD** 387.5/05.

NO/0300-3310
**SKIP.** [Skip]. (1962)-. Periodical. Multiple languages (Danish, Norwegian and Swedish). mo. Kr260.00 Norway; Kr285.00 other. Bjarne H Reenskaug A-S, PO Box 130, 2261 Kirkenaer Norway.

UK/0262-480X
**SMALL SHIPS.** [Small ships]. (19??)-. Periodical. English. bm. £95.00 UK; £104.00, $191.00 other. Argus Press Group, Queensway House, 2 Queensway Redhill, Surrey RH1 1QS England. **Tel** 011 44 737 768611, 011 44 737 761685, FAX 011 44 737 760510, telex 948669 TOPJNL G.
**Desc:** Devoted to the needs of owner/operators of commercial craft not exceeding 100 metres in length.
**Ind/Abst** BMT Abstr.; Fluid Abstr., Civil Eng.; Fluid Abstr. Proc. Eng.; FLUIDEX (-19??).

US/0888-4072
**SOUNDINGS (MILWAUKEE, WIS.).** (SOUNDINGS.). [Soundings]. **Added/Corp** Wisconsin Marine Historical Society. Vol. 1, No. 1 (Oct. 1959)- . Periodical. English. qt. $30.00 (membership, Wisconsin Marine Historical Society). Wisconsin Marine Historical Society, 814 West Wisconsin Avenue, Public Library, Milwaukee WI 53233. **Tel** (414)278-3074. **ED** Gene C. Harrison. **DD** 977. **Bk Rev**. **Circ:** 450 (ctrl).
**Desc:** Relating to the maritime history of the Great Lakes.

SA/0038-2671
**SOUTH AFRICAN SHIPPING NEWS AND FISHING INDUSTRY REVIEW, THE.** [S. Afr. shipp. news fish. ind. rev.]. (Jan. 1946)-. English. Six times a year. R50.16 South Africa; R68.00 APU countries; R80.00 other. George Warman Publications Pty, PO Box 704, Cape Town 8000 South Africa. **Tel** 011 27 21 245320, FAX 011 27 21 261332, telex 5-21849. **ED** Michael Stuttaford. **LC** HE561; .S69. **Bk Rev**. **Ad Acc**. **Circ:** 1,150 (ctrl).
**Desc:** Includes information on industrial shipping, fishing, marine mineral exploitation, and harbours in southern Africa.
**Ind/Abst** Aquat. Sci. Fish. Abstr. (Computer File).

US
**SOUTH CAROLINA STATE PORTS AUTHORITY, CHARLESTON, SOUTH CAROLINA. REPORT OF STATE AUDITOR AND FINANCIAL STATEMENTS.** **Main/Corp** South Carolina. State Auditor. English. South Carolina Office of the State Auditor, PO Box 11333, Columbia SC 29211. **LC** HE554.A3; S58A. **DD** 353.9/757/008771.

US/1054-7150
**SOUTHERN SHIPPER.** *Title Change.* [South. shipp.]. Vol. 40, No. 1 (Jan. 1991)-(19??)-. Periodical. English. mo. Howard Publications Inc., PO Box 4728, Jacksonville FL 32201-4728. **Tel** (904)355-2611 FAX (904)791-8836. **ED** Hayes Howard. **DD** 387. **Ad Acc**, **Adv Mgr:** Bill Barrs, **Tel** (904)355-26013. **Circ:** 7,790 (ctrl). available on microfilm and microfiche from University Microfilms International (UMI). *Continues Seafarer (Jacksonville, Fla.), 0882-7788. Merged into American Shipper Southern Edition, 1074-8350.*

UK/0076-0234
**STATISTICAL TABLES.** **Main/Corp** Lloyd's Register of Shipping (Firm : 1914-). (1954)-. Statistical Publication. English. an. $150.00. Lloyd's Register of Shipping / New York, 17 Battery Place, New York NY 10004. **Tel** (212)425-8050. **LC** HE563.A3; L5.
**Desc:** The world merchant fleet categorised by registration, size, age and ship-type.

IT
**STATISTICHE DEL MOVIMENTO PORTUALE DI LIVORNO.** Italian. an. Camera di Commercio / Modena, Industria Artigianato e Agricoltura, Via Ganaceto 134, 4100 Modena Italy. **LC** HE558.L55; S73.

NE
**STATISTIEK VAN DE BINNENVLOOT.** **Main/Corp** Netherlands. Centraal Bureau voor de Statistiek. Hoofdafdeling Statistieken van Verkeer en Vervoer. **VFOAT** Statistics of the Inland Fleet. 1979-. Dutch. de. Fl10.25. Centraal Bureau voor de Statistiek, AFD ALG Zaken, Postbus 959, 2270 AZ Voorburg Netherlands. **Tel** 011 31 70 3373800, FAX 011 31 038 7429, telex 32692 CBS NL. **LC** HE674; .A256B. *Continues Statistiek van de Binnenvloot.*

NE
**STATISTIEK VAN DE SCHEEPVAARTBEWEGING / CENTRAAL BUREAU VOOR DE STATISTIEK, HOOFDAFDELING STATISTIEKEN VAN VERKEER EN VERVOER.** See Transportation-Abstracting, Bibliographies and Statistics.

IO
**STATISTIK BONGKAR MUAT BARANG DI PELABUHAN INDONESIA.** **Main/Corp** Indonesia. Biro Pusat Statistik. **VFOAT** Cargo Loading and Unloading at Ports in Indonesia. Indonesian (English and Indonesian). an. Rp6000 Indonesia; $4.00 US. Central Bureau of Statistics / Indonesia, c/o Dr. Sutomo, 8 Jalan, PO Box 3, Jakarta Indonesia. **Tel** 372808 374908 Ext.342. **LC** HF247; .I53J. ctrl circ.

IO/0216-6909
**STATISTIK PERHUBUNGAN - BIRO PUSAT STATISTIK (LALU LINTAS ANGKUTAN BARANG ANTAR PULAU MENURUT JENIS PELAYARAN).** (LALU LINTAS ANGKUTAN BARANG ANTAR PULAU MENURUT JENIS PELAYARAN.). [Stat. perhubungan - Biro Pusat Stat. (Lalu Lintas angkutan barang antar p ulau menurut jenis pelayaran)]. **VFOAT** Inter Island Cargo Traffics by Shipping Sector. English (Indonesian). an. Rp2,000 Indonesia; $2.80 US. Central Bureau of Statistics / Indonesia, c/o Dr. Sutomo, 8 Jalan, PO Box 3, Jakarta Indonesia. **Tel** 372808 374908 Ext.342. **LC** HE887; .L35. **Bk Rev**. **Ad Acc**. ctrl circ.

BE
**STATISTIQUE DE LA NAVIGATION MARITIME.** **VFOAT** Statistiek van de Zeevaart. Dutch (French). an. 500F. Secretariat General Benelux, rue de la Regence 39, 1000 Bruxelles Belgium. **Tel** (02)519 38 11, FAX 513 42 06, telex 61540 BENELU B. **ED** P Vandu Meiven. **LC** HE843; .S73. **Circ:** 3,000.
**Desc:** Statistics of maritime transportation originating in or destined to religion and Dutch seaports.

BE
**STATISTIQUE DU TRAFIC INTERNATIONAL DES PORTS.** **Main/Corp** Institut National de Statistique (Belgium). **VFOAT** Statistique du Trafic International (U.E.B.L.) des Ports; Statistique du Trafic International des Ports, U.E.B.L. (19??)-. French. qt. Institut National de Statistique / Belgium, rue de Louvain, 44, Centre Albert, 8e Etage, 1000 Brussels Belgium. **Tel** 011 32 2 5486211. **LC** HE563.A3; I58a. **DD** 387.1/012/2.

UN
**SUDOSTROENIE.** No. 22, (1974)-. Academic Scholarly Publication. Russian. mo. $149.00 domestic airmail; $159.00 international airmail. **(Subscription address:** Victor Kamkin, 4956 Boiling Brook Parkway, Rockville MD 20852.) **LC** VM7; .S9. **CODEN** SUDODQ. Documents available from CASDDS. *Continues Sudostroenie I Morskie Sooruzheniia.*
**Ind/Abst** Chem. Abstr. (1974-1981); Energy Res. Abstr. (Oct. 1982-); Saf. Health Work.

IS
**SUMMARY AND OBJECTIVES.** **Main/Corp** Rashut Ha-Nemalim Be-Yisrael. English. Israel Ports Authority, 74 Petach Tikva Road POB 20, Tel-Aviv 67215 Israel.

FI
**SUOMEN KAUPPALAIVASTO. FINLANDS HANDELSFLOTTA. THE FINNISH MERCHANT MARINE.** **Added/Corp** Finland. Merenkulkuhallitus. Tilasto-ja Rekisteritoimisto. Finland. Merenkulkuhallitus. Tilastokonttori. Finland. Tilasto- ja Alusrekisteritoimisto. **VFOAT** Finlands Handelsflotta; Finland's Mercantile Marine; Finnish Merchant Marine. (1918)-. Finnish (English and Swedish). an. **LC** HE565.F5; S6.

UK/0959-6089
**TANK CONTAINER WORLD.** *Title Change.* Vol. 1, No. 1 (Feb./March 1990)-. Periodical. English. bm. Container Concepts Inc, 7501 Lemont Road/Suite 230, Woodridge IL 60517. *Continued by Tank World.*

UK
**TANK WORLD.** (19??)-. Periodical. English. Eight times a year. £80.00 (one year), £140.00 (two years) UK; £95.00 (one year), £170.00 (two years) Europe; £110.00 (one year), £195.00 (two Years) other. Baltic Publishing Ltd, The Baltic Centre, Great West Road, Brentford Middlesex TW8 9BU England. **Tel** 44 81 8472446, FAX 44 81 569 8688. *Continues Tank Container World, 0959-6089.*

UK/0958-8787
**TANKER CHARTER RECORD.** (1977)-. Academic Scholarly Publication. English. mo. $260.00. Basil Blackwell Publishers Ltd, 108 Cowley Road, Oxford OX4 1JF England. **Tel** 011 44 865 791100, FAX 011 44 865 791347, telex 837022 OXBOOK G. **[CCC]**.

UK
**TANKER MARKET QUARTERLY REPORT.** (1979)-. English. qt. £960.00. Drewry Shipping Consultants Ltd, 11 Heron Quay, London E14 4JF England. **Tel** 011 44 71 5380191, FAX 01-987-9396, telex 21167 HPDLDG.
**Desc:** Comprehensive data and information on the oil and tanker markets, forecasts, data base appendices and the identification of major trends affecting the tanker industry.

UK
**TANKER MARKET REPORT.** English. wk. Free. Galbraiths Limited, Shackelton House, 4 Battle Bridge Lane, London SE1 2HY England. **Tel** 071 378 6363.

UK/0305-179X
**TANKER REGISTER.** **Added/Corp** H. Clarkson & Company. (1960)-. English. an (June). £145.00 Europe; £165.00 other. Clarkson Research Studies Ltd., 12 Camomile Street, London EC3A 7BP England. **Tel** 011 44 71 2838955. **(Subscription address:** Rankine Road, Basingstoke, Hants RG24 0PR United Kingdom) **LC** HE566.T3; R4. **DD** 387.2/45. *Continues Register of Tank Vessels of the World.*

SA
**THIS IS SAR & H : HARBOURS & PIPELINES HANDBOOK.** **Main/Corp** South African Railways and Harbours. **Added/Corp** South African Railways and Harbours. Harbours & Pipelines Handbook. (19??)-. English. Thomson Publications Pty, PO Box 56182, Pinegowrie 2123 South Africa. **Tel** 011 27 11 7892144. **LC** HE559.S6; S67a. **DD** 387.1/0968.

FR
**TRAFIC.** **Main/Corp** Port Autonome de Paris. French. an. Free. Port Autonomi de Paris, 2 Quai de Grenelle, Paris Cedex 15 France. **Tel** (1)45 78 61 92, FAX (1)45 78 08 57, telex 204487. **LC** HE558.P2; P67A. **DD** 387.1/0944/36.

UK
**TRANSACTIONS / INSTITUTE OF MARINE ENGINEERS.** See Engineering.

UK
**TRANSACTIONS / INSTITUTION OF ENGINEERS AND SHIPBUILDERS IN SCOTLAND.** See Engineering.

US/0895-8548
**TRANSPORTATION & DISTRIBUTION.** [Transp. distrib.]. **VFOAT** Transportation and Distribution. Vol. 28, No. 9 (Sept. 1987)-. Periodical. English. Twelve times a year. $45.00 US; $65.00 Canada; $75.00 Mexico; $85.00 other. Penton Publishing, 1100 Superior Avenue, Cleveland OH 44114-2543. **Tel** (216)696-7000, FAX (216)696-0836. **(Subscription address:** Penton Publishing, PO Box 96732, Chicago IL 60693.) **LC** TS149; .H32. **DD** 658. **[CCC]**. available on microfilm and microfiche from University Microfilms International (UMI); available on an online database (files 15,648/Full-Text) from DIALOG. Documents available from UMI Article Clearinghouse. *Continues Handling & Shipping Management, 0194-603X.*
**Ind/Abst** ABI/INFORM Glob. Ed.; ABI Inform Ondisc (Sept. 1983-); Bus. ASAP (1990-) [Full Txt.]; Bus. Index (1987-); Bus. Period. Index; Bus. Source (Jan. 1993-); Gen. BusinessFile (1987-); Gen. Period. Index (1987-); Mag. Search; UMI ABI/Inform--Bus. Period. Ondisc (Sept. 1987-) [Full Txt.]; Vocat. Search (July 1993-); Wilson Bus. Abstr.

US
**TRANSPORTATION LINES OF THE UNITED STATES.** See Transportation.

US/0361-9125
**TRANSPORTATION LINES ON THE ATLANTIC, GULF, AND PACIFIC COASTS.** *Title Change.* **Main/Corp** United States. Army. Corps of Engineers. (19??)-(1992). English. Waterborne Commerce Statistics Center, PO Box 60267, New Orleans LA 70160. **LC** HE565.U68; A3. **DD** 387.5/24/0973. *Continues United States. Board of Engineers for Rivers and Harbors. Transportation Lines on the Atlantic, Gulf, and Pacific Coasts. Merged with Transportation Lines on the Great Lakes System and Transportation Lines on the Mississippi River System and the Gulf Intracoastal Waterway (OCoLC)2441468 to form Transportation Lines of the United States.*

US/0361-8978
**TRANSPORTATION LINES ON THE GREAT LAKES SYSTEM.** *Title Change.* English. an. District Engineer, US Army Engineer District New Orleans, New Orleans LA 70160. **LC** HE565.U71; A3. **DD** 386/.54/0977. *Merged with Transportation Lines on the Mississippi River System and the Gulf Intracoastal Waterway and Transportation Lines on the Atlantic, Gulf, and Pacific Coasts to form Transportation Lines of the United States.*

## Transportation — Ships and Shipping

**US/0361-8986**
**TRANSPORTATION LINES ON THE MISSISSIPPI RIVER SYSTEM AND THE GULF INTRACOASTAL WATERWAY.** **Title Change. Main/Corp** United States. Army. Corps of Engineers. (19??)-(19??). English. Waterborne Commerce Statistics Center, PO Box 60267, New Orleans LA 70160. **LC** HE565.U74; A3. **DD** 386/.35/0977. **Continues** Transportation Lines on the Mississippi River System and the Gulf Intracoastal Waterway. **Merged with** Transportation Lines on the Great Lakes System **and** Transportation Lines on the Atlantic, Gulf, and Pacific Coasts **to form** Transportation Lines of the United States.

**CM**
**TRANSPORTS MARITIMES (NATIONAL SHIPPERS COUNCIL OF CAMEROON).** (TRANSPORTS MARITIMES : REVUE TRIMESTRIELLE PUBLIEE PAR LE CONSEIL NATIONAL DES CHARGEURS DU CAMEROUN.) Dec. 1980-. Periodical. English (French). qt. C N C C, BP 1588, Douala Cameroon. **LC** HE905.4; .T73. **DD** 387.5/44/096711.

**IT**
**TRASPORTI MARE TERRITORIO.** (19??)-. Giuffre Editore SPA, Via Busto Arsizio 40, 20151 Milan Italy. **Tel** 011 398 2 38089200.

**JA**
**TSUKO SEMPAKU JITTAI CHOSA HOKOKUSHO. Main/Corp** Japan. Kaijo Hoancho Keibi Kyunanbu. Koko Anzenka. Kaijo Kostu Kikakushitsu. (19??)-. Periodical. Japanese. Kaijo Hoancho / Keibi Kyunanbu, 1-3 Kasumigaseki 2-chome Chiyoda-ku, Tokyo Japan. **LC** HE497.A1; K34a.

**UK**
**TUG & SALVAGE WORLD.** (19??)-. Periodical. English. Four times a year. £35.00 (one year), £90.00 (three years) Europe; £50.00 (one year), £120.00 (three years) other. TRP Magazines Ltd., Thames Wharf Studios, Rainville Road, London W6 9HA England. **Tel** 44 71 3853344, FAX 44 71 3853183. **ED** David Robinson. **Desc:** To provide subscribers with a much sharper focus on the key issues facing this vital sector of the international maritime industry. To stimulate discussion and debate through a comprehensive supply of news, features and statistical data.

**UK/0266-7193**
**TURKISH SHIPPING.** 1984 -. Periodical. English. Free to seatrade subscribers. Seatrade Organisation, 42-48 North Station Road, Colchester CO1 1RJ Essex England. **Tel** 011 44 206 45121, FAX 44 206 45190. **ED** Mary Bond. **LC** HE873.4; .T57. **DD** 387.5/09561. **Ad Acc. Desc:** Authoritative articles on the Turkish maritime industry; fleet statistics; and listings of Turkish maritime companies and organisations.

**NE**
**UIT EUROPOORTKRINGEN.** (19??)-. mo (12 issues). Fl100.00 (latest issue). Uitgeversmij L A Van Beek BV, Postbus 33050, 3005 EB Rotterdam Netherlands. **Tel** 011 31 10 4613000, 011 31 10 4611416. **Absorbed** Isolatie Energiebesparing.

**US/0161-8830**
**UNITED STATES OCEANBORNE FOREIGN TRADE ROUTES.** Began with 1975/76. Periodical. English. an. Maritime Administration, Washington DC 20590. **LC** HE745; .U48B. **DD** 387.5/1. **Continues** Essential United States Foreign Trade Routes.

**NO**
**VERITAS FORUM: CORPORATE MAGAZINE OF DET NORSKE VERITAS.** No. 1 (March 1987)-. Periodical. English. qt. $2.25 (single issue). DNV, PO Box 300, N 1322 Hovik Norway. **Tel** 011 47 67 577250. **Formed by the union of** Veritas **and** Veritas World. **Ind/Abst** BMT Abstr.

**US/0505-4176**
**VIA PENSACOLA.** Vol. 1 (May 1957)-. Periodical. English. mo. Free on request. Pensacola Port Authority, Pensacola FL 32504. **DD** 387.

**US**
**VIRGINIA MARITIMER. Added/Corp** Virginia Port Authority. Vol. 6, No. 2 & 3 (Dec. 1985/Jan. 1986)-. Periodical. English. mo (ten issues per year). Free. Virginia Maritimer, 600 World Trade Center, Norfolk VA 23510. **Tel** (800)-446-8098, (804)623-8000, FAX 804-623-8500, telex 804-780-881-1231 VA PORT NFK. **ED** Tina Kneisley. **LC** HE752.V8; P67. **DD** 387.1/09755. Index available. **Ad Acc. Circ:** 7,500. **Continues** Ports of Virginia Monthly Log. **Desc:** Publication on Virginia's port interest in international trade and maritime.

**US**
**WASHINGTON LETTER / JOINT MARITIME CONGRESS. Added/Corp** Joint Maritime Congress. **VFOAT** Joint Maritime Congress Washington Letter. Began publication with Vol. 1 in (1979)-. Periodical. English. ir. Free on request. Joint Maritime Congress Washington Letter, 444 North Capitol Street Suite 801, Washington DC 20001. **Tel** (202)638-2405, telex 89479. **ED** William Tuthill. **Circ:** 1,900 (ctrl). **Desc:** Provides a weekly report on events relating to U.S. flag oceanborne transportation with a particular emphasis on Congress and the Administration.

**US/0511-3806**
**WATERWAY GUIDE. SOUTHERN EDITION.** (WATERWAY GUIDE.). [Waterway guide, South. ed.]. (19??)-. English. an. Waterway Guide, 390 5th Avenue, New York NY 10018-8104. **Tel** (212)715-2600. **DD** 797. **Continues** Inland WaterWay Guide. (Southern Edition).

**US/0192-382X**
**WEEKLY BULLETIN. PORT OF NEW ORLEANS. Ceased. Added/Corp** Associated Port Interests of New Orleans. (1??)-(Febr. 1992). Bulletin. English. wk. Kriedt Enterprises LTD, 129 South Cortez Street, New Orleans LA 70119. **Tel** (504)482-3914, FAX (504)482-4205.

**CN/0844-5567**
**WESTCOAST MARINER.** (THE WESTCOAST MARINER.). [Westcoast mar.]. Vol. 1, No. 1 (Mar. 1988)-. Periodical. English. Twelve times a year. 30.00Can$ Canada; 40.00Can$ other. Westcoast Publishing Ltd., 1496 West 72nd Avenue, Vancouver British Columbia V6P 3C8 Canada. **Tel** (800)972-1060, (604)266-7433, FAX (604)263-8620. **ED** Rob Morris (editor's phone: (604)266-8611). **DD** 387/.009711. Index available (bound in Feb. issue).

**UK/1037-3748**
**WORK BOAT WORLD.** See Boats and Boating.

**UK**
**WORLD DIRECTORY OF FREIGHT CONFERENCES.** (19??)-. Directory. English. mo. £144.60. Croner Publ Ltd, Croner House, London Road, Kingston upon Thames, Surrey KT2 6SR England. **Tel** 011 44 81 5473333, FAX 081 547-2637.

**UK**
**WORLD FREIGHT SHIPPER. Ceased.** (19??)-(Mar. 1992). English. mo. Inc Publications, 38 St John Street, London ECIM 4AY England. **Tel** 011 44 71 2518798. **Continues** Freight Forwarding.

●**US**
**WORLD INTERMODAL FREIGHT MARKET.** (1994)-. English. Four times a year. $1025.00. Forecast International / DMS Inc., 22 Commerce Road, Newtown CT 06470. **Tel** (203)426-0800, FAX (203)426-1964, telex 467615.

**US/0502-3343**
**WORLD PORT INDEX.** [World port index]. Began with 1953. English. be. US Department of Defense Defense Mapping Agency, 8613 Lee Highway, Fairfax VA 22031. **Tel** (703)285-9290, FAX (703)285-9374. **LC** HE552; .W67. **DD** 387.1/5/05. available on microfiche (Vols. for (1982)- distributed to depository libraries).

**US/0194-4681**
**WORLD PORTS (1978).** (WORLD PORTS.). V. 1- Sept./Oct. 1978-. Periodical. English. bm. $9.00 US, Canada, Mexico, Central and South America; $20.00 others. World Ports, PO Box 1067 Blair Station, Silver Spring MD 20910. **LC** HE550; .W67. **DD** 387.1/05. **Supersedes in part** World Ports/American Seaport.

**UK**
**WORLD TANKER FLEET REVIEW.** English. sa (Jan., July). 220.00. John I Jacobs PLC, 9 Mandeville Place, London W1M 5LB England. **Tel** 011 44 71 4863000, FAX 44 71 486-2937, telex 851 888081. **Circ:** 600.

●**US/1058-1618**
**WORLD TRADE RESOURCES GUIDE.** See Business-Commerce.

**US/1060-7900**
**WORLD WIDE SHIPPING.** (WORLD WIDE SHIPPING : WWS.). [World wide shipp.]. **Added/Corp** International Cargo Handling Coordination Association. U.S. National Committee. International Cargo Handling Coordination Association. Canadian National Committee. Foreign Commerce Club of New York. **VFOAT** WWS; Worldwide Shipping. Vol. 48, No. 1 (Mar. 1985)-. Periodical. English. Eight times a year. $32.00 US; $47.00 other. World Wide Shipping Guide, 20 South Delaware Drive, Nyack NY 10960. **Tel** (914)358-3813, telex 510-100-4052 WWS. (**Subscription address:** World Wide Shipping, 77 Moehring Drive, Blauvelt NY 10913.) **LC** HE561; .W6. **DD** 387.1/09181/2. **CODEN** WWSHE3. **Continues** WWS/World Ports, 0278-6664. **Ind/Abst** Coal Abstr.; Life Sci. Collect.; Ship Abstr.

**UK**
**WORLDWIDE TANKER NOMINAL FREIGHT SCALE / JOINTLY SPONSORED AND ISSUED BY WORLDSCALE ASSOCIATION (LONDON) LIMITED [AND] WORLDSCALE ASSOCIATION (NYC). Added/Corp** Worldscale Association (London). Worldscale Association (NYC). **VFOAT** Worldscale. (1969)-. English. an (Jan.). $1425.00 US. Worldscale Association, 64 Queens Street, London EC3R 1AD England. **Tel** 011 44 71 248-4747. (**Subscription address:** Worldscale, 17 Battery Place, New York NY 10004.) **LC** HE594; .W67. **DD** 387.5/1. ctrl circ.

**US/0162-0088**
**WWS, WORLD WIDE SHIPPING GUIDE. VFOAT** World Wide Shipping Guide. (19??)-. English. an. $105.00 US; $115.00 other. World Wide Shipping Guide, 20 South Delaware Drive, Nyack NY 10960. **Tel** (914)358-3813, telex 510-100-4052 WWS. **ED** Lee di Paci. **LC** HE561; .W2. **DD** 387.5/44/025. Index available. **Ad Acc. Circ:** 11,500 (ctrl). **Desc:** Directory listing various companies involved in the shipping industry by the city.

**IS**
**YEDION. Main/Corp** Makhon Ha-Yisreeli Le-Heker Ha-Sapanut. **VFOAT** Information Paper. Periodical. Hebrew. mo. IL75.00 Israel; $50.00 other. Wydra Institute of Shipping and Aviation Research, Eshkol Tower, University of Haifa, Haifa 31999 Israel. **Tel** (04)247127, FAX 972-4-342104, telex 46660 UNIHA IL. **ED** Miriam Ofek. **LC** HE730; .M27A. **DD** 387.5/095694. ctrl circ. **Desc:** Summaries of important news and developments worldwide in shipping, aviation, and ports.

**RU/0321-4249**
**ZA RULEM. Added/Corp** DOSAAF SSSR. (Apr. 1928)-. Periodical. Russian. mo. $79.95. (**Subscription address:** East View Publications Inc., 3020 Harbor Lane North, Suite 110, Minneapolis MN 55447.)

**NE/0168-3187**
**ZEEVAARTVERWANTE BEDRIJVEN / CENTRAAL BUREAU VOOR DE STATISTIEK, HOOFDAFDELING STATISTIEKEN VAN VERKEER EN VERVOER. VFOAT** Supporting Services to Maritime Transport. Dutch (summaries and/or abstracts in English). an. Fl7.50. Centraal Bureau voor de Statistiek, AFD ALG Zaken, Postbus 959, 2270 AZ Voorburg Netherlands. **Tel** 011 31 70 3373800, FAX 011 31 038 7429, telex 32692 CBS NL. **LC** HE845; .Z43.

## TRAVEL AND TOURISM

**US/1058-6113**
**2 TO 22 DAYS AROUND THE GREAT LAKES.** [2 22 days Gt. Lakes]. **VFOAT** Two to Twenty-two Days Around the Great Lakes. 1st Ed. (1991)-. English. $9.95. John Muir Publications, PO Box 613, Santa Fe NM 87504. **Tel** (505)982-4078. **ED** Arnold Schuchter. **DD** 917.

●**US/1062-4325**
**2 TO 22 DAYS IN ASIA.** [2 22 days Asia]. **VFOAT** Two to Twenty-Two Days in Asia. (1992)-. English. $9.95. John Muir Publications, PO Box 613, Santa Fe NM 87504. **Tel** (505)982-4078. **DD** 915. **Continues** 22 Days in Asia.

●**US/1062-4333**
**2 TO 22 DAYS IN AUSTRALIA.** [2 22 days Aust.]. **VFOAT** Two to Twenty-Two Days in Australia. (1992)-. English. John Muir Publications, PO Box 613, Santa Fe NM 87504. **Tel** (505)982-4078. **LC** DU95; .A15. **DD** 919. **Continues** 22 Days in Australia.

●**US/1059-2946**
**2 TO 22 DAYS IN EUROPE / RICK STEVES. VFOAT** Two to Twenty-Two Days in Europe. (1992)-. English. $9.95. John Muir Publications, PO Box 613, Santa Fe NM 87504. **Tel** (505)982-4078. **Continues** 22 Days in Europe.

●**US/1062-4341**
**2 TO 22 DAYS IN FLORIDA.** [2 22 days Fla.]. **VFOAT** Two to Twenty-Two Days in Florida. (1992)-. English. $9.95. John Muir Publications, PO Box 613, Santa Fe NM 87504. **Tel** (505)982-4078. **DD** 917. **Continues** 22 Days in Florida.

**US/1059-8278**
**2 TO 22 DAYS IN FRANCE.** [2 22 days Fr.]. **VFOAT** Two to Twenty-two Days in France. (1991)-. English. be. John Muir Publications, PO Box 613, Santa Fe NM 87504. **Tel** (505)982-4078. **DD** 914. **Continues** 22 Days in France.

●**US/1058-6059**
**2 TO 22 DAYS IN GERMANY, AUSTRIA, AND SWITZERLAND. VFOAT** Two to Twenty-Two Days in Germany, Austria, and Switzerland. (1992)-. English. Seatrade Organisation, 42-48 North Station Road, Colchester CO1 1RJ Essex England. **Tel** 011 44 206 45121, FAX 44 206 45190. **Continues** 22 Days in Germany, Austria, and Switzerland, 1058-6016.

frequent travelers who have a special interest in Hawaii and the Pacific. In addition to providing information on destinations, hotels, dining and entertainment. Helps readers understand and appreciate the many cultures and lifestyles of the islands.

SZ
**ALPES, LES.** **VFOAT** Le Alpi; Las Alpas; Die Alpen; Alpi; Alps; Alpen. Jan. 1957-. Periodical. Multiple languages (French, German and Italian). mo. 55.00F. Staempfli & Cie SA, Postfach 8326, CH-3001 Bern Switzerland. **Tel** 011 41 31 3006666, telex 031 911 515 EDMZ CH. **ED** E Gross. **Bk Rev.** **Ad Acc.** **Circ:** 70,000 (ctrl). ***Supersedes in part*** *Alpen. Les Alpes. Le Alpi. Las Alps.*

FR
**AMENAGEMENT DE L'ESPACE ET DU TEMPS ET DEVELOPPEMENT DU TOURISME : ACTES DU CONSEIL SUPERIEUR DU TOURISME.** **VFOAT** Actes du Conseil Superieur du Tourisme. Session 1979-1980-. French. Documentation Francaise, 29 Quai Voltaire, 75344 Paris Cedex 7 France. **Tel** 011 33 1 40157000, FAX 011 33 1 40157230, telex 204 826 DOCFRAN. **LC** G155.F8; A75. **DD** 380.1/45914404838. available in microform.

US/0363-535X
**AMERICAN EXECUTIVE TRAVEL COMPANION.** **Main/Corp** Guides to Multinational Business, Inc. **VFOAT** Guide to Traveling on Business in 50 States. English. an. Guides to Multinational Business, Harvard Square, PO Box 92, Boston MA 02138. **Tel** (617)868-2288. **LC** E158; .G954A. **DD** 917.3/04/92.

US
**AMERICAN EXPRESS ... SURVEY OF BUSINESS TRAVEL, THE.** **Added/Corp** American Express Travel Related Services Co. **VFOAT** Survey of Business Travel. (198?)-. English. be. $190.00. American Express Travel Related Services Company, 200 Vesey Street, 41st Floor, New York NY 10285.
**Desc:** Information on business travel and travel costs.

US/0747-0843
**AMERICAN TRAVELER.** Vol. 7, No. 4 (Spring 1984)-. Periodical. English. qt. Travel Magazine Inc, 28 West 23rd Street/10th Floor, New York NY 10010. **Tel** (212)366-8700. ***Continues*** *September Days, 0746-5009.*

US
**AMERICAN URBAN GUIDENOTES : THE NEWSLETTER OF GUIDEBOOKS.** **VFOAT** Guidenotes : The Newsletter of Guidebooks. Vol. 1, No. 1 (Summer 1979)-. English. Four times a year. American Urban Guides, PO Box 186, 1761 R Street Northwest, Washington DC 20009. **Tel** (202)667-1357. **ED** John Fondersmith. **Bk Rev.** **Circ:** 400.
**Desc:** Deals primarily with current guidebooks, mostly for the United States. Includes some guidebook history.
**Ind/Abst** Avery Index Archit. Period. Suppl. Colum. Univ. (1984-199?).

US/0003-1518
**AMERICAN WAY (DALLAS, TEX.).** **See** Aeronautics, Astronautics.

●US/1070-3365
**AMERICANS TRAVELING ABROAD.** (1994)-. English. te. $39.99. World Travel Institute Press, 8268 Streamwood Drive, PO Box 32674, Baltimore MD 21208. **Tel** (410)922-4903, FAX (410)922-8115. **ED** Gladson J. Nwanna, PhD. Index available (Jan.). **Acid Free.** **Circ:** 20,000.
**Desc:** An encyclopedia of travel resources, information and tips. This book reproduces in one volume, almost all of the available publications of the U.S. Government directed to Americans traveling abroad. Includes tips for travelers to every region of the world. Over 170 countries are profiled.

●US/1063-0007
**AMERICA'S WONDERFUL LITTLE HOTELS & INNS. THE MIDWEST.** **See** Hotels/Motels.

US/0275-5564
**AMOCO TRAVELER.** [Amoco travel.]. V. 1, Issue 1 (Spring 1981)-. Periodical. English. qt. Amoco Traveler, PO Box 9018, Des Moines IA 50306. **DD** 910.

GW/0171-7243
**AMUSEMENT-INDUSTRIE.** **See** Recreation, Leisure.

TU
**ANADOLU. ANATOLIA.** **Added/Corp** Ankara Universitesi. Eski Onasya-Akdeniz Medeniyetleri Arastrma Enstitusu. **VFOAT** Anatolia. (1965)-. Multiple languages (English, French and Turkish). **LC** DS155; .A59. ***Continues*** *Anatolia.*
**Ind/Abst** Leis. Recreat. Tour. Abstr.

US/0160-7383
**ANNALS OF TOURISM RESEARCH.** **See** Social Sciences.

SP
**ANNUAIRE DES STATISTIQUES DU TOURISME.** **Added/Corp** World Tourism Organization. **VFOAT** Yearbook of Tourism Statistics. (1986)-. English (French and Spanish). an. $125.00. World Tourism Organization / WTO, Calle Capitan Haya 42, E 28020 Madrid Spain. **Tel** 011 34 1 5710628, FAX 011 34 1 5713733, telex 42188 OMT-E. **LC** G149; .I73. **DD** 380.1/4591. ***Continues*** *World Travel and Tourism Statistics.*

US/0276-8968
**ANNUAL CONFERENCE / TRAVEL AND TOURISM RESEARCH ASSOCIATION.** **Main/Corp** Travel and Tourism Research Association (U.S.). **Added/Corp** University of Utah. Bureau of Economic and Business Research. **VFOAT** Annual Conference Proceedings. (1982)-. English. $75.00 (per year). Travel and Tourism Research Association, 10200 West 44th Avenue, Suite 304, Wheat Ridge CO 80033. **Tel** (801)581-3351. **LC** G149.5; .T73a. **DD** 380.1/4591. ***Continues*** *Annual Conference Proceedings.*

AT
**ANNUAL REPORT / ABORIGINAL HOSTELS LIMITED.** **Main/Corp** Aboriginal Hostels Limited. English. an. Aboriginal Hostels Ltd, PO Box 30, Woden Australian Capital Territory 2606 Australia. **LC** GN666; .A218A.

CN/0837-4171
**ANNUAL REPORT / DEPARTMENT OF TOURISM.** [Annu. rep. - Dep. Tour.]. **Main/Corp** Alberta. Alberta Tourism. (March 31, 1986)-. English. an. Communications Branch of Alberta Tourism, 10025 Jasper Avenue/18th Floor, Edmonton Alberta T5J 3Z3 Canada. **Tel** (403)427-5028. **LC** HC117.A6; A5163B. **DD** 354.71230082/6591712304/06. ctrl circ. ***Continues in part*** *Annual Report / Alberta. Alberta Tourism and Small Business, 0823-454X.*

UK
**ANNUAL REPORT - ENGLISH TOURIST BOARD.** **Main/Corp** English Tourist Board. (19??)-. Corporate Report. English. an. £10.00. English Tourist Board, Thames Tower, Blacks Road, Hammersmith, London W6 9EL United Kingdom. **Tel** FAX 011 44 81 563-0302. **LC** G155.G7; E47a. **DD** 354/.41/008243.

CN/0824-8915
**ANNUAL REPORT - MINISTRY OF TOURISM AND RECREATION (TORONTO).** (ANNUAL REPORT / MINISTRY OF TOURISM AND RECREATION.). [Annu. rep. - Minist. Tour. Recreat.]. **Main/Corp** Ontario. Ministry of Tourism and Recreation. 1982/83-. English. an. Ministry of Tourism and Recreation, Province of Ontario, Queen's Park, Toronto Ontario M7A 2E5 Canada. **LC** G155.C3; O48A. **DD** 354.7130082/7. ***Absorbed*** *Ontario. Ministry of Culture and Recreation. Annual Report.*

UK
**ANNUAL REPORT OF THE BRITISH TOURIST AUTHORITY.** **Main/Corp** British Tourist Authority. Vol. 1 (1967)-. Corporate Report. English. an. £10.00. British Tourist Authority, Thames Tower, Blacks Road, London W6 9EL England. **Tel** 011 44 81 8469000, FAX 011 44 156 30302. **LC** G155.G7; B67b. **DD** 354/.41/00826. Documents available from BLDSC.
**Desc:** A report on the Authority's activities during the year ending March 31, 1993, which looks at tourism in Britian today and the outlook for the future.

AT
**ANNUAL REPORT OF THE QUEENSLAND TOURIST & TRAVEL CORPORATION.** **Main/Corp** Queensland Tourist & Travel Corporation. (1980)-. English. Queensland Tourist & Travel Corporation, 307 Queen Street, Brisbane 4001 Australia. **LC** G155.A75; Q43a. **DD** 382/.45919430463.

UK
**ANNUAL REPORT ON ST. LUCIA, B.W.I.** ***Title Change.*** **Main/Corp** Great Britain. Colonial Office. (1946)-(19??). English. an. Her Majesty's Stationery Office, 51 Nine Elms Lane, London SW8 5DR England. **Tel** 011 44 71 873 8459, 011 44 71 873 8499, FAX 011 44 71 873 8499, 011 44 71 873 8456, telex 297138. **(Subscription address:** PO Box 276, Public Centre, London SW8 5DT England) **LC** F2100; .A55. **DD** 917.298. ***Continued by*** *St. Lucia (London, England).*

UK
**ANNUAL REPORT / THE HAKLUYT SOCIETY.** **Main/Corp** Hakluyt Society. (1984)-. Corporate Report. English. an. Free for members. Hakluyt Society, c/o The Map Library, British Library, Great Russell Street, London WCIB 3DG England. **Tel** 011 44 986 86359, FAX 011 44 986 868181. **Circ:** 2,300 (ctrl). ***Continues*** *Annual Report and Statement of Accounts for ... / The Hakluyt Society.*

IT
**ANNUARIO SEAT. VOL. G, P.TURISMO E TEMPO LIBERO.** **Added/Corp** SEAT (Firm). **VFOAT** Turismo e Tempo Libero; Annuario S.E.A.T. Vol. G, Turismo e Tempo Libero. (19??)-. Italian. an. L30,000.00. Seat, Via Aurelio Saffi 18, Turin 10138 Italy. **Tel** 011-33301-212248 I, FAX 4472953, telex 212248 I. **LC** G155.I8; A728. **DD** 914.5/04928/025. **Bk Rev.** **Circ:** 23,800.
**Desc:** Yearbook of Italian companies operations in sport, tourism, hobbies, photographic, filming, optical instruments, music, hotels, restaurants, classified by categories. Information on Italian market.

BL
**ANUARIO TURISTICO DE PERNAMBUCO.** V. 1- 1976-. Portuguese. Avenida Marques de Olinda 55, 50.000 Recife Brazil. **LC** G155.B7; A73.

US/0004-1521
**ARIZONA HIGHWAYS.** [Ariz. highw.]. **Added/Corp** Arizona. Highway Dept. Arizona. Dept. of Transportation. Vol. 1, No. 1 (April 1921)-. Periodical. English. mo (12 issues). $17.00 (one year), $29.00 (two year), $41.00 (three year) US & possessions. Arizona Highways, 2039 West Lewis Avenue, Phoenix AZ 85009. **Tel** (602)258-1000, (602)258-6641, FAX (602)254-4505. **ED** Robert J. Early. **LC** TE24.A6; A87. **DD** 917.91. **CODEN** AZHIAW. Index available (annual index $6.50). cum. index. **Bk Rev.** **Circ:** 410,000. Documents available from UMI Article Clearinghouse.
**Desc:** Features Arizona scenic photography and articles on Arizona travel, history, nature, contemporary events and arts and crafts.
**Ind/Abst** Acad. Abstr. Full Text Elite (Jan. 1984-); Acad. Abstr. (Jan. 1984-); Acad. Search (Jan. 1984-); Access (1975-?); GeoRef; Mag. Artic. Summar. Elite (Jan. 1984-); Mag. Artic. Summar. (Jan. 1984-); Mag. Artic. Summar. CD-ROM (Jan. 1984-); Mag. Search; Newsp. Period. Abstr. (1992-); Read. Guide Period. Lit.; West. Hist. Q.

US/0271-9827
**ARTHUR FROMMER'S DOLLARWISE GUIDE TO NEW ENGLAND.** ***Title Change.*** **VFOAT** Dollarwise Guide to New England. (19??)-(19??). English. be. Macmillan Publishing Co. / Indiana, 201 West 103rd Street, Indianapolis IN 46290. **Tel** (800)428-5331, (800)858-7674. **LC** F2.3; .B75. **DD** 917.4/0443. ***Continued by*** *Frommer's Guide to New England.*

US/0731-857X
**ARTHUR FROMMER'S DOLLARWISE GUIDE TO THE SOUTHEAST AND NEW ORLEANS.** ***Title Change.*** (ARTHUR FROMMER'S DOLLARWISE GUIDE TO THE SOUTHEAST AND NEW ORLEANS / BY SUSAN POOLE.). **VFOAT** Dollarwise Guide to the Southeast and New Orleans. (19??)-(19??). English. Macmillan Publishing Co. / Indiana, 201 West 103rd Street, Indianapolis IN 46290. **Tel** (800)428-5331, (800)858-7674. **LC** F207.3; .A78. **DD** 917.5/0443. ***Continued by*** *Frommer's Dollarwise Guide to the Southeast and New Orleans, 0731-8588.*
**Desc:** Includes guides to Virginia, North Carolina, South Carolina, Georgia, Florida, and the Mississippi and Alabama coasts.

US
**ARTHUR FROMMER'S GUIDE TO ATHENS.** ***Title Change.*** **VFOAT** Guide to Athens. (19??)-(19??). English. Macmillan Publishing Co. / Indiana, 201 West 103rd Street, Indianapolis IN 46290. **Tel** (800)428-5331, (800)858-7674. ***Continued by*** *Frommer's Guide to Athens, 0277-4534.*

US
**ARTHUR FROMMER'S GUIDE TO IRELAND : DUBLIN/SHANNON.** **VFOAT** Guide to Ireland : Dublin/Shannon. (1977/78)-. English. be (every two years). $10.00. Macmillan Publishing Co. / Indiana, 201 West 103rd Street, Indianapolis IN 46290. **Tel** (800)428-5331, (800)858-7674.

US/1060-2569
**ARTISTIC TRAVELER, THE.** [Artist. travel.]. Vol. 1, No. 1 (Nov./Dec. 1991)-. Periodical. English. mo. $29.00. Richard Hovey, 2221 NE Brookview Drive, Vancouver WA 98686-4142. **DD** 910.

US/1045-3881
**ASIA PACIFIC TRAVEL.** [Asia Pac. travel]. **VFOAT** AsiaPacific Travel. Vol. 1, No. 1 (1990)-. Periodical. English. Six times a year. $15.00. Health World, 1675 Rollins Road, Suite B 3, Burlingame CA 94010. **Tel** (415)697-8038, FAX (415)697-7937. **ED** Kumar Pati and Jeff Kravitz Kravitz. **LC** DS10; .A79. **DD** 910/.2/02. Index available. **Bk Rev.** **Ad Acc.** **Circ:** 125,000 (ctrl).
**Desc:** Aimed at the growing market of travelers to Asia and the Pacific Rim will "create a link between Westerners who would like to visit, tour or business in Asian countries, and their Asian counterparts visiting the United States."

# Travel and Tourism

SI
**ASIA-PACIFIC TRAVEL INDEX.** *Ceased.*
(1981)-(Jan. 1988). English. an. Asian Business Press Pte Ltd, PO Box 219, 9118 Singapore Singapore. **Tel** 011 65 2943366. **LC** G154; .T18. **DD** 915/.0428/025.
*Continues TTG Asia Yearbook.*

HK
**ASIA TRAVEL TRADE.** (19??)-. Periodical. English. mo. $40.00 (surface mail); $60.00 North America, Europe and Australia; $45.00 Asia. Interasia Publications, 190 Middle Road, 11 01 Fortune Ct, Singapore 0718 Singapore. **Tel** 011 852 5 7493170, FAX 011 852 5 3398521. **Bk Rev. Ad Acc. Circ:** 20,000 (ctrl).
**Desc:** Travel industry magazine for management. Concentrates on operational rather than travel product information. Has gained authoritative reputation.

NZ/1171-3631
**ASMAL AUSTRALIA TRAVEL.** [Asmal Aust. travel]. (1991)-. Periodical. English. Four times a year (Mar., June, Sept., Dec.). 171.00NZ$. Alasdair S. McIntyre & Associates, PO Box 38-201, Howick Auckland New Zealand. **Tel** 011 64 9 5343108, FAX 011 64 9 5343108. **DD** 338.47919405. *Continues Asmal Australia Update, 0114-3670.*
**Desc:** Record and describe trends present in the outbound travel markets of Australia.

NZ/1171-3690
**ASMAL NEW ZEALAND TRAVEL.** [Asmal N.Z. travel]. (1991)-. Periodical. English. qt. 171.00NZ$. Alasdair S. McIntyre & Associates, PO Box 38-201, Howick Auckland New Zealand. **Tel** 011 64 9 5343108, FAX 011 64 9 5343108. **DD** 338.47919305. *Continues Asmal New Zealand Update, 0113-8286.*
**Desc:** Record and describe trends present in the outbound travel markets of New Zealand.

US/0147-0043
**ASPEN VACATION GUIDE.** **Added/Corp** Aspen Reservations, inc. (19??)-. Periodical. English. sa. Advertising and Editorial Office, Box 10456, Aspen CO 81611.

US/0896-4114
**ASTA AGENCY MANAGEMENT.** (ASTA AGENCY MANAGEMENT : OFFICIAL PUBLICATION OF THE AMERICAN SOCIETY OF TRAVEL AGENTS.). [ASTA agency manage.]. **Added/Corp** American Society of Travel Agents. **VFOAT** Agency Management. **VAT** American Society of Travel Agents Agency Management. Vol. 56, No. 10 (Sept. 1987)-. Periodical. English. Twelve times a year. $36.00. American Society Travel Agents / Department of Accounting, 1101 King Street, Alexandria VA 22314. **Tel** (703)739-2782, FAX (703)684-8319. **LC** G149; .A57. **DD** 380.1/4591. *Continues ASTA Travel News, 0001-2637.*

HK
**ATT TRAVEL DIRECTORY.** (19??)-. Directory. $50.00. Interasia Publications, 190 Middle Road, 11 01 Fortune Ct, Singapore 0718 Singapore. **Tel** 011 852 5 7493170, FAX 011 852 5 3398521.

AT/1034-9006
**AUSTRALIAN GOURMET TRAVELLER 1989.** *See* Food and Food Industry.

UK
**AUSTRIA.** **Main/Corp** Michelin Tyre Company, Ltd. (19??)-. English. ir. $18.00. Michelin Travel Publications, Box 3305, Spartanburg SC 29304. **Tel** (800)423-0485, (803)599-0850, FAX (803)599-0852. **LC** DB16; .M5a. **DD** 914.36/0453. *Supersedes Austria and the Bavarian Alps.*

UK
**BAA AIRPORT TIMETABLE.** English. ir. £13.00 UK; £7.50 other. Reed Travel Group / England, World Timetable Center, Church Street, Dunstable, Bedfordshire LU5 4HB England. **Tel** 011 44 582 600111, FAX 011 44 582 695348.

BF/0067-2912
**BAHAMAS HANDBOOK AND BUSINESSMAN'S ANNUAL.** **VFOAT** Bahamas Handbook. (1960)-. English. an (published in Fall). $22.95. Etienne Dupuch Publications, PO Box N7513, Nassau Bahamas. **Tel** (809)323-5665, (809)323-5666, FAX (809)323-5728. **ED** S. P. Dupuch. **LC** F1650; .B3. Index available. **Ad Acc, Adv Mgr:** E. D. Hill.
**Desc:** Contains features, information on business, leisure, family island life, and government.

HU/0865-9222
**BALNEOLOGIA, GYOGYFURDOUGY, GYOGYIDEGENFORGALOM.** *See* Recreation, Leisure.

FR/0764-3578
**BANCS D'ESSAI DU TOURISME, LES.** (1986)-. Periodical. French. bm (6 issues). 160.00F France; 335.00F other. Bancs d'Essais due Tourisme, Bloc Pietri, 91037 Bondoufle Cedex France. **Tel** 011 33 1 60 868240. **UDC** 380.833.

US/1057-7718
**BANTAM'S AUSTRALIA.** [Bantam's Aust.]. **VFOAT** Australia. (1991)-. English. Bantam Books Inc, 666 Fifth Avenue, New York NY 10019. **Tel** (212)340-7500. **LC** DU95; .A735. **DD** 919.404/63. *Continues Australia (Bantam Books (Firm)), 1057-7726.*

US
**BANTAM'S BAHAMAS : A QUICK & EASY GUIDE.** (1991)-. English. Bantam Books Inc, 666 Fifth Avenue, New York NY 10019. **Tel** (212)340-7500. **LC** F1652; .B32. **DD** 917.29604. *Continues Bahamas (Bantam Books (Firm)).*

US/1056-0939
**BANTAM'S HAWAII.** [Bantam's Hawaii]. **VFOAT** Hawaii. (1991)-. English. $13.95 (U.S.), $16.95 (Can.). Bantam Books Inc, 666 Fifth Avenue, New York NY 10019. **Tel** (212)340-7500. **LC** DU622; .H3357. **DD** 919.69/04/4/05. *Continues Hawaii (Bantam Books (Firm)).*

US/1057-770X
**BANTAM'S SCOTLAND.** [Bantam's Scotl.]. **Added/Corp** Bantam Books (Firm). **VFOAT** Scotland. (1991)-. English. Bantam Books Inc, 666 Fifth Avenue, New York NY 10019. **Tel** (212)340-7500. **LC** DA870; .B26. **DD** 914.11/04859.

US/1057-7734
**BANTAM'S SOVIET UNION.** [Bantam's Sov. Union]. **Added/Corp** Bantam Books (Firm). **VFOAT** Soviet Union. (1991)-. English. Bantam Books Inc, 666 Fifth Avenue, New York NY 10019. **Tel** (212)340-7500. **LC** DK16; .B3. **DD** 914.704/854.

US/0145-8345
**BARRY BERNDES' ANNUAL EDITION OF SAN DIEGO GUIDE.** **VFOAT** San Diego Guide. 1st- 1969-. English. $1.95. San Diego Guide, PO Box 81544, San Diego CA 92138. **LC** F869.S22; B46. **DD** 917.94/98.

US/0146-8707
**BAXTER'S EURAILPASS TRAVEL GUIDE.** *See* Transportation-Railroads.

IS
**BAZAK GUIDE TO ISRAEL.** **VFOAT** Guide to Israel. (1974/1975)-. English. an. $22.00. Harper Collins Publishers, Keystone Industrial Park, Scranton PA 18512. **Tel** (800)242-7737, (800)233-4727, FAX (800)822-4090. **LC** DS103; .B34. **DD** 915.694/0454. *Continues Bazak Israel Guide.*

IS/0302-6221
**BAZAK GUIDE TO SPAIN.** (19??)-. English. $4.95. Harper Collins Publishers, Keystone Industrial Park, Scranton PA 18512. **Tel** (800)242-7737, (800)233-4727, FAX (800)822-4090. **LC** DP14; .L48. **DD** 914.6/04/82.

CN/0846-9962
**BC TOURISM ROOM REVENUES.** [BC tour. room revenues]. **Added/Corp** British Columbia. Ministry of Finance and Corporate Relations. Business Statistics. (Mar. 1991)-. Periodical. English. mo. Ministry of Finance, 1450 Government Street, Information Service, Victoria British Columbia V8W 3E7 Canada. **DD** 338.4.

US/1052-3723
**BEAM'S DIRECTORY OF INTERNATIONAL TOURIST EVENTS.** [Beam's dir. int. tour. events]. **VFOAT** Directory of International Tourist Events; Tourist Events. (1991)-. Directory. English. $19.95. TTA Press, PO Box 9930, Friendship Station, Washington DC 20016. **LC** GT3930; .B36. **DD** 910/.2/0205.

CN/0005-7460
**BEAUTIFUL BRITISH COLUMBIA.** **Added/Corp** British Columbia. Dept. of Travel Industry. Tourism British Columbia. British Columbia. Dept. of Recreation and Conservation. British Columbia. Ministry of the Provincial Secretary and Travel Industry. Vol. 1 (Summer 1959)-. Periodical. English. Four times a year (Seasonally). 14.91Can$ Can; 15.95Can$ others. Beautiful British Columbia, 929 Ellery Street, Victoria British Columbia, V9A 7B4 Canada. **Tel** (604)384-5456, (800)663-7611, FAX (604)384-2812. **ED** Bryan McGill. **DD** 917.11/044/05. Index available. cum. index. **Ad Acc, Adv Mgr:** Key Pacific, **Tel** (604)388-4324. **Circ:** 210,000. available on an online database from Federal Document Retrieval.
**Desc:** Reflects the pride British Columbia residents feel toward the natural beauty of their province. Dedicated to photography and featured articles on British Columbia's natural scenery, wilderness, parks, wildlife, outdoor attractions and travel adventures.
**Ind/Abst** Can. Index (?-?).

US/0893-1194
**BED & BREAKFAST AMERICAN STYLE.** *Suspended.* (BED & BREAKFAST AMERICAN STYLE / BY THE BERKSHIRE TRAVELLER, NORMAN T. SIMPSON). [Bed breakf. Am. style]. **VFOAT** Bed and Breakfast American Style. 1st Ed. (1981)-Suspended (1991). English. an. $10.95. Harper Collins Publishers, Keystone Industrial Park, Scranton PA 18512. **Tel** (800)242-7737, (800)233-4727, FAX (800)822-4090. **LC** TX907; .B394. **DD** 647.

US/0887-7505
**BED & BREAKFAST UPDATE.** *Ceased.* **VFOAT** Bed and Breakfast Update. Periodical. English. bm. Bed & Breakfast Update, 2516 Arizona Avenue/Suite 4, Santa Monica CA 90404.

US
**BED & BREAKFAST USA / TOURIST HOUSE ASSOCIATION OF AMERICA.** **Added/Corp** Tourist House Association of America. **VFOAT** Bed and Breakfast USA; Bed & Breakfast U.S.A. (19??)-. English. an. $14.45. E P Dutton, 2 Park Avenue, New York NY 10016. **LC** TX907; .B396. **DD** 647/.9473.

US
**BELIZE BUSINESS AND TRAVEL DIRECTORY.** **VFOAT** Belize. Directory. English. $4.00. Belize Tourist Board, PO Box 325, Belize City Belize C A, Belize City CA. **LC** F1443.5; .B44. **DD** 917.282/0453.

US/8750-9180
**BELLE FRANCE, LA.** (198?)-. Periodical. English. Twelve times a year. $87.00 North America; $105.00 other. Travel Guide Inc., PO Box 3485, Charlottesville VA 22903. **Tel** (804)295-1200. **ED** W. Carter Hoerr. Index available. cum. index. **Circ:** 10,000 (ctrl).
**Desc:** Newsletter on discriminating travel in France.

US/1054-5034
**BELL'S ALASKA, YUKON & BRITISH COLUMBIA TRAVEL GUIDE.** [Bell's Alsk. Yukon B. C. travel guide]. **VFOAT** Bell's Alaska, and British Columbia Travel Guide; Alaska, Yukon, and British Columbia Travel Guide; Alaska, Yukon & British Columbia Travel Guide. 28th. Edition (1988)-. English. an (Mar.). $9.95. Bells Alaska Travel Guide, 413 B 19th Street, Suite 170, Lynden WA 98264. **Tel** (604)769-3073, FAX (604)769-3073. **ED** Timothy J. Bell (editor's address: 418 Abel Place Kelowna British Columbia Canada, phone: (604)769-3073). **Bk Rev. Ad Acc, Adv Mgr:** Tim Bell, **Tel** (604)769-3073. **Circ:** 60,000 (ctrl). *Continues Alaska, Yukon & British Columbia Travel Guide.*
**Desc:** A travel guide that covers all of the ways to get to Alaska and the Yukon. Includes cruise ships, air carriers, buslines, and mile by mile description of all highways. Covers the accommdations, camping, and visitor facilities.

US/0749-436X
**BELTWAY NATURALIST, THE.** No. 1 (Mar. 1984)-. Periodical. English. Six times a year. Dominion House, 4616 Briar Parch Court, Fairfax VA 22032. **DD** 508.

●US/1057-4786
**BERLITZ TRAVELER'S GUIDE TO MEXICO, THE.** [Berlitz travel. guide Mex.]. **VFOAT** Mexico. (1992)-. English. $14.95. Berlitz Publishing Co., 257 Park Avenue South, New York NY 10010. **Tel** (212)598-2490, FAX (212)353-9706. **DD** 917. *Continues Penguin Guide to Mexico, 1043-4577.*

●US/1065-6294
**BERLITZ TRAVELLER'S GUIDE BERLIN, THE.** **VFOAT** Traveller's Guide to New England. (1993)-. English. $9.95. Berlitz Publishing Co., 257 Park Avenue South, New York NY 10010. **Tel** (212)598-2490, FAX (212)353-9706.

●US/1057-4689
**BERLITZ TRAVELLER'S GUIDE TO AUSTRALIA, THE.** (1992)-. Berlitz Publishing Co., 257 Park Avenue South, New York NY 10010. **Tel** (212)598-2490, FAX (212)353-9706.

●US
**BERLITZ TRAVELLER'S GUIDE TO CANADA, THE.** (1992)-. Berlitz Publishing Co., 257 Park Avenue South, New York NY 10010. **Tel** (212)598-2490, FAX (212)353-9706.

●US/1057-4735
**BERLITZ TRAVELLER'S GUIDE TO ENGLAND & WALES, THE.** [Berlitz travel. guide Engl. Wales]. **VFOAT** England and Wales, & Wales. (1992)-. English. $14.95. Berlitz Publishing Co., 257 Park Avenue South, New York NY 10010. **Tel** (212)598-2490, FAX (212)353-9706. **DD** 914. *Continues Penguin Guide to England & Wales, 0897-6864.*

●US/1057-476X
**BERLITZ TRAVELLER'S GUIDE TO FRANCE, THE.** **VFOAT** Travellers Guide to France; Berlitz Travellers France. (1992)-. English. an. $15.95. Berlitz Publishing Co., 257 Park Avenue South, New York NY 10010. **Tel** (212)598-2490, FAX (212)353-9706. **(Subscription address:** Macmillan Publishing, Front and Brown Street, Riverside NJ 08075.) **ED** Alan Tucker. **LC**

# Travel and Tourism

DC16; .P383. **DD** 914.404/838/05. *Continues* Penguin Guide to France, 0897-683X.
**Desc:** Provides travel information for touring France.

●US/1057-462X
**BERLITZ TRAVELLER'S GUIDE TO GERMANY, THE.** (1992)-. English. an. Berlitz Publishing Co., 257 Park Avenue South, New York NY 10010. **Tel** (212)598-2490, FAX (212)353-9706. **LC** DD258.25; .P46. **DD** 914.304/879.

●US
**BERLITZ TRAVELLER'S GUIDE TO GREECE, THE.** (1992)-. Berlitz Publishing Co., 257 Park Avenue South, New York NY 10010. **Tel** (212)598-2490, FAX (212)353-9706.

●US/1057-4700
**BERLITZ TRAVELLER'S GUIDE TO HAWAII, THE.** (1992)-. Berlitz Publishing Co., 257 Park Avenue South, New York NY 10010. **Tel** (212)598-2490, FAX (212)353-9706.

●US/1057-4719
**BERLITZ TRAVELLER'S GUIDE TO IRELAND, THE.** [Berlitz travel. guide Irel.]. **VFOAT** Ireland. (1992)-. English. $11.95. Berlitz Publishing Co., 257 Park Avenue South, New York NY 10010. **Tel** (212)598-2490, FAX (212)353-9706. **LC** DA980; .P46. **DD** 914.1504/824. *Continues* Penguin Guide to Ireland, 0897-6856.

●US/1057-4751
**BERLITZ TRAVELLER'S GUIDE TO LONDON, THE.** [Berlitz travel. guide Lond.]. **Added/Corp** Tucker, Alan, 1936-. **VFOAT** London; Berlitz Travellers Guide London. (1992)-. English. an. $12.95. Berlitz Publishing Co., 257 Park Avenue South, New York NY 10010. **Tel** (212)598-2490, FAX (212)353-9706. **(Subscription address:** Macmillan Publishing, Front and Brown Street, Riverside NJ 08075.) **ED** Alan Tucker. **LC** DA679; .P45. **DD** 914.2104/859. *Continues* Penguin Guide to London (New York, N.Y.), 1049-1457.
**Desc:** Provides travel information for touring London and the surrounding areas.

●US/1062-3655
**BERLITZ TRAVELLER'S GUIDE TO NEW ENGLAND, THE.** **VFOAT** Traveller's Guide to New England. (1993)-. English. $14.95. Berlitz Publishing Co., 257 Park Avenue South, New York NY 10010. **Tel** (212)598-2490, FAX (212)353-9706.

●US/1057-4743
**BERLITZ TRAVELLER'S GUIDE TO NEW YORK CITY, THE.** [Berlitz travel. guide N. Y. City]. **VFOAT** New York City. (1992)-. English. $13.95. Berlitz Publishing Co., 257 Park Avenue South, New York NY 10010. **Tel** (212)598-2490, FAX (212)353-9706. **DD** 917. *Continues* Penguin Guide to New York City, 0898-8072.

●US
**BERLITZ TRAVELLER'S GUIDE TO PORTUGAL, THE.** (1992)-. Berlitz Publishing Co., 257 Park Avenue South, New York NY 10010. **Tel** (212)598-2490, FAX (212)353-9706. **LC** DP516; .P4. **DD** 914.6904/44.

●US
**BERLITZ TRAVELLER'S GUIDE TO ROME AND NORTHERN ITALY, THE.** (1992)-. Berlitz Publishing Co., 257 Park Avenue South, New York NY 10010. **Tel** (212)598-2490, FAX (212)353-9706. **LC** DG416; .B366. **DD** 914.504/929. *Continues in part* Penguin Guide to Italy, 0897-6848.

●US
**BERLITZ TRAVELLER'S GUIDE TO ROME AND SOUTHERN ITALY, THE.** (1992)-. Berlitz Publishing Co., 257 Park Avenue South, New York NY 10010. **Tel** (212)598-2490, FAX (212)353-9706. **LC** DG416; .B367. **DD** 914.5/704929. *Continues in part* Penguin Guide to Italy, 0897-6848.

●US/1057-4727
**BERLITZ TRAVELLER'S GUIDE TO SAN FRANCISCO & NORTHERN CALIFORNIA, THE.** [Berlitz travel. guide San Franc. North. Calif.]. **VFOAT** San Francisco and Northern California; San Francisco & Northern California. (1992)-. English. $13.95. Berlitz Publishing Co., 257 Park Avenue South, New York NY 10010. **Tel** (212)598-2490, FAX (212)353-9706. **LC** F869.S33; .P46. **DD** 917.94/610453. *Continues* Penguin Guide to San Francisco & Northern California, 1049-1449.

●US
**BERLITZ TRAVELLER'S GUIDE TO SPAIN, THE.** (1992)-. Berlitz Publishing Co., 257 Park Avenue South, New York NY 10010. **Tel** (212)598-2490, FAX (212)353-9706.

●US/1057-4697
**BERLITZ TRAVELLER'S GUIDE TO THE CARIBBEAN, THE.** [Berlitz travel. guide Caribb.]. **VFOAT** Caribbean. (1992)-. English. $10.95. Berlitz Publishing Co., 257 Park Avenue South, New York NY 10010. **Tel** (212)598-2490, FAX (212)353-9706. **DD** 917. *Continues* Penguin Guide to the Caribbean, 0897-6821.

●US/1062-3663
**BERLITZ TRAVELLER'S GUIDE TO THE SOUTHWEST, THE.** **VFOAT** Traveller's Guide to the Southwest. (1993)-. English. $13.95. Berlitz Publishing Co., 257 Park Avenue South, New York NY 10010. **Tel** (212)598-2490, FAX (212)353-9706.

●UK/1054-4089
**BEST BED & BREAKFAST IN ENGLAND, SCOTLAND & WALES, THE.** *See* Hotels/Motels.

NE
**BEST GUIDE TO AMSTERDAM & BENELUX VENUES (FOR GAY MEN AND LESBIANS).** English (French and German). be. Fl19.95 Netherlands; $11.95 US; £7.95 Great Britain; DM24.95 German; 16.95Aus$ Australia. Best Guide, 66 N Z Voorburgwal Amsterdam The Netherlands. **Tel** (020)699 1583, FAX (020)6950907. **ED** B Crawford. **Ad Acc. Circ:** 8,500.
**Desc:** Travel and tourism guide to Amsterdam for gay men and lesbians. Contains detailed, objective, and up-to-date descriptions of venues in Amsterdam that cater to gay men, and also to lesbians.

NE
**BEST GUIDE TO GREAT BRITAIN (FOR GAY MEN).** English. te. Fl9.95 Netherlands; $11.95 US; 10.50Can$ Canada; 16.95Aus$ Australia; £7.95 Great Britain; 50.00F France; DM24.95 Germany; 13.50NZ$ New Zealand. Best Guide, 66 N Z Voorburgwal Amsterdam The Netherlands. **Tel** (020)699 1583, FAX (020)6950907. **Ad Acc. Circ:** 5,000.
**Desc:** Travel and tourism guide to Britain for male homosexuals. The most-used gay guide to the British gay scene. Over 1,000 establishments are listed (including hotels, bars, clubs, discos, restaurants and shops). Plus information on almost every service that a gay visitor to Britain might need.

●US/1045-3091
**BEST OF ANDALUCIA, THE.** (1992)-. English. te. $6.95. International Destinations Inc, 205 Arizona Avenue, Santa Monica CA 90401. **DD** 914.

US/0891-3722
**BEST OF ARIZONA, THE.** [Best Ariz.]. Vol. 1, No. 1 (Winter/Spring 1985-86)-. Periodical. English. sa. $6.00. The Best of Arizona, 5717 East Thomas Road, Suite 1, Scottsdale AZ 85251. **Tel** (602)946-0775. **DD** 917.

●US/1045-3083
**BEST OF CATALUNYA, THE.** [Best Catalunya]. **Added/Corp** International Destinations (Firm). (1992)-. English. te. $6.95. International Destinations Inc, 205 Arizona Avenue, Santa Monica CA 90401. **DD** 914.

US/1043-6553
**BEST OF CHINA WITH HONG KONG AND MACAU, THE.** [Best China Hong Kong Macau]. **VFOAT** Best of China. (1989/90)-. Periodical. English. an. $5.95. International Destinations Inc, 205 Arizona Avenue, Santa Monica CA 90401. **DD** 915.

US/1043-6545
**BEST OF HONG KONG, THE.** [Best Hong Kong]. (1989/90)-. English. an. $5.95. International Destinations Inc, 205 Arizona Avenue, Santa Monica CA 90401. **DD** 915.

US/1040-077X
**BEST OF INDIA, THE.** (THE BEST OF INDIA / INTERNATIONAL DESTINATIONS.). [Best of India]. **Added/Corp** International Destinations (Firm). (1990)-. English. an. Free to qualified recipients. International Destinations Inc, 205 Arizona Avenue, Santa Monica CA 90401. **LC** DS406; .B54. **DD** 915.404/52; 915.

US/1043-6537
**BEST OF MACAU, THE.** [Best Macau]. (1989/90)-. Periodical. English. an. $5.95. International Destinations Inc, 205 Arizona Avenue, Santa Monica CA 90401. **DD** 915.

●US/1045-3075
**BEST OF MADRID, THE.** [Best Madr.]. (1992)-. English. be. $6.95. International Destinations Inc, 205 Arizona Avenue, Santa Monica CA 90401. **DD** 914.

US/1040-0788
**BEST OF MOROCCO, THE.** (1989/90)-. English. an. Free to qualified recipients. International Destinations Inc, 205 Arizona Avenue, Santa Monica CA 90401. **LC** G155.M76; B49. **DD** 338.4/79164045.

●US/1045-3105
**BEST OF PORTUGAL, THE.** (THE BEST OF PORTUGAL: OFFICIAL RESOURCE GUIDE. INTERNATIONAL DESTINATIONS.). [Best Port.]. **Added/Corp** International Destinations (Firm). (1992)-. English. te. $6.95. International Destinations Inc, 205 Arizona Avenue, Santa Monica CA 90401.

●US/1045-3067
**BEST OF SPAIN, THE.** (THE BEST OF SPAIN. INTERNATIONAL DESTINATIONS.). [Best Spain]. **Added/Corp** International Destinations (Firm). (1992)-. English. te. $6.95. International Destinations, Inc, 205 Arizona Avenue, Santa Monica CA 90401. **LC** WMLC 90/0737. **DD** 914.

●US/1053-9484
**BEST OF THE REPUBLIC OF KOREA, THE.** [Best Repub. Korea]. **Added/Corp** Hanguk Kwangwang Kongsa. **VFOAT** Best of Korea. (1991-1993)-. English. $8.95. International Destinations Inc, 205 Arizona Avenue, Santa Monica CA 90401. **DD** 915.

US/1055-0879
**BEST PLACES TO STAY IN MEXICO.** [Best places stay Mex.]. **VFOAT** Mexico. 1st Ed. (1991)-. English. be. $13.95. Houghton Mifflin Company, Wayside Road, Burlington MA 01803. **Tel** (800)225-3362, (617)272-1500. **DD** 917.

●US/1060-7749
**BEST PLACES TO STAY IN THE MIDWEST.** (1992)-. English. be. $13.95. Houghton Mifflin Company, Wayside Road, Burlington MA 01803. **Tel** (800)225-3362, (617)272-1500.

●US/1060-7757
**BEST PLACES TO STAY IN THE SOUTH.** (1992)-. English. be. $13.95. Houghton Mifflin Company, Wayside Road, Burlington MA 01803. **Tel** (800)225-3362, (617)272-1500.

US/1054-9757
**BEST VACATION RENTALS. CARIBBEAN.** [Best vacat. rent. Caribb.]. **VFOAT** Caribbean. 1st Ed. (1991)-. English. be. $17.95. Macmillan Publishing Co. / Indiana, 201 West 103rd Street, Indianapolis IN 46290. **Tel** (800)428-5331, (800)858-7674. **DD** 643.

US/1054-9765
**BEST VACATION RENTALS, EUROPE : A TRAVELER'S GUIDE TO COTTAGES, CONDOS, AND CASTLES.** [Best vacation rent. Eur.]. **VFOAT** Europe. 1st Ed. (1991)-. English. be. $15.95. Macmillan Publishing Co. / Indiana, 201 West 103rd Street, Indianapolis IN 46290. **Tel** (800)428-5331, (800)858-7674. **LC** TX907.5.385; B47. **DD** 647.94401/05.

●US/1055-5633
**BIRNBAUM'S ACAPULCO.** **VFOAT** Acapulco. 1st Ed. (1992). English. $10.00 (U.S.), $13.50 (Can.). Harper Collins Publishers, Keystone Industrial Park, Scranton PA 18512. **Tel** (800)242-7737, (800)233-4727, FAX (800)822-4090. **DD** 917.

●US/1055-5625
**BIRNBAUM'S BAHAMAS, TURKS & CAICOS.** [Birnbaum's Bahamas Turks Caicos]. **VFOAT** Birnbaum's Bahamas, Turks, and Caicos; Bahamas, Turks & Caicos; Bahamas, Turks, and Caicos; Birnbaum's Bahamas and Turks & Caicos; Birnbaum's Bahamas and Turks & Caicos. 1st Ed. (1992). English. an. $10.00 (U.S.), $13.50 (Can.). Harper Collins Publishers, Keystone Industrial Park, Scranton PA 18512. **Tel** (800)242-7737, (800)233-4727, FAX (800)822-4090. **ED** Alex M. Birnbaum (phone: (212)207-7158). **LC** F1652; .B57. **DD** 917.29604. Index available. *Continues in part* Birnbaum's the Caribbean, Bermuda, and the Bahamas, 0883-248X.
**Desc:** Gives practical information for planning your trip, such as when and how to go, preparing for your trip, and practical information for when you get there. It also gives a cultural and historical survey of the islands, their people, food, music, religions, folk life, environment, and a comprehensive report on the islands' most compelling attractions. There is section on more than a dozen active and/or cerebral vacation themes and a section on walks and drives through the Bahamas and the Turks and Caicos.

●US/1056-4381
**BIRNBAUM'S BARCELONA.** **VFOAT** Barcelona. (1992). English. $9.95. Harper Collins Publishers, Keystone Industrial Park, Scranton PA 18512. **Tel** (800)242-7737, (800)233-4727, FAX (800)822-4090.

●US/1070-9746
**BIRNBAUM'S BERLIN.** (1994)-. English. an. $12.00. Harper Collins Publishers, Keystone Industrial Park, Scranton PA 18512. **Tel** (800)242-7737, (800)233-4727, FAX (800)822-4090.

Travel and Tourism

●US/1055-5684
**BIRNBAUM'S BERMUDA.** [Birnbaum's Bermuda]. **VFOAT** Bermuda. 1st Ed. (1992)-. English. an (Sep.). $10.00 US; $13.50 Canada. Harper Collins Publishers, Keystone Industrial Park, Scranton PA 18512. **Tel** (800)242-7737, (800)233-4727, FAX (800)822-4090. **ED** Alex Birnbaum (phone: (212)207-7158). **LC** F1632; .B57. **DD** 917.29904. Index available. ***Continues in part*** *Birnbaum's the Caribbean, Bermuda, and the Bahamas, 0883-248X.*
**Desc:** Gives practical information for planning your trip, such as when and how to go, preparing for your trip, and practical information for when you get there. Also gives a cultural and historical survey of the islands, their people, food, music, religions, folk life, environment, and a comprehensive report on the island's most compelling attractions and amenities. There is a section on more than a dozen active and/or cerebral vacation themes and a section on walks through Bermuda's nine parishes.

●US/1056-4357
**BIRNBAUM'S BOSTON.** **VFOAT** Boston. (1992)-. English. $9.95. Harper Collins Publishers, Keystone Industrial Park, Scranton PA 18512. **Tel** (800)242-7737, (800)233-4727, FAX (800)822-4090.

US/0884-1039
**BIRNBAUM'S CANADA.** [Birnbaum's Can.]. **VFOAT** Canada. 1985-. English. an. Harper Collins Publishers, Keystone Industrial Park, Scranton PA 18512. **Tel** (800)242-7737, (800)233-4727, FAX (800)822-4090. **LC** F1009; .C17. **DD** 917.1/04647. ***Continues*** *Canada (Boston, Mass.), 0193-7952.*

●US/1055-5641
**BIRNBAUM'S CANCUN, COZUMEL, AND ISLA MUJERES.** **VFOAT** Cancun, Cozumel, and Isla Mujeres. (1992)-. English. $9.95. Harper Collins Publishers, Keystone Industrial Park, Scranton PA 18512. **Tel** (800)242-7737, (800)233-4727, FAX (800)822-4090.

●US
**BIRNBAUM'S CARIBBEAN.** **VFOAT** Caribbean. (1992)-. English. $11.95. Harper Collins Publishers, Keystone Industrial Park, Scranton PA 18512. **Tel** (800)242-7737, (800)233-4727, FAX (800)822-4090. ***Continues in part*** *Birnbaum's the Caribbean, Bermuda, and the Bahamas, 0883-248X.*

●US/1056-4365
**BIRNBAUM'S CHICAGO.** [Birnbaum's Chic.]. **VFOAT** Chicago. (1992)-. English. $10.00 (U.S.), $13.50 (Can.). Harper Collins Publishers, Keystone Industrial Park, Scranton PA 18512. **Tel** (800)242-7737, (800)233-4727, FAX (800)822-4090. **DD** 977.

●US
**BIRNBAUM'S DISNEYLAND.** **VFOAT** Disneyland. (1992)-. English. Harper Collins Publishers, Keystone Industrial Park, Scranton PA 18512. **Tel** (800)242-7737, (800)233-4727, FAX (800)822-4090. **LC** GV1853.3.C22; D578. **DD** 917.94/96.

●US/1056-439X
**BIRNBAUM'S EASTERN EUROPE.** **VFOAT** Eastern Europe. (1992)-. English. $9.95. Harper Collins Publishers, Keystone Industrial Park, Scranton PA 18512. **Tel** (800)242-7737, (800)233-4727, FAX (800)822-4090.

US/0883-2498
**BIRNBAUM'S EUROPE.** [Birnbaum's Eur.]. 1985-. English. an. $13.95. Harper Collins Publishers, Keystone Industrial Park, Scranton PA 18512. **Tel** (800)242-7737, (800)233-4727, FAX (800)822-4090. **ED** Stephen Birnbaum. **LC** D909; .E82. **DD** 914/.04558. ***Continues*** *Europe, 0193-7936.*
**Ind/Abst** INIS Atomindex [Micro.].

US/0749-4815
**BIRNBAUM'S EUROPE FOR BUSINESS TRAVELERS.** [Birnbaum's Eur. bus. travel.]. **VFOAT** Europe for Business Travelers. 1985-. English. an. $8.95 per issue. Harper Collins Publishers, Keystone Industrial Park, Scranton PA 18512. **Tel** (800)242-7737, (800)233-4727, FAX (800)822-4090. **ED** Stephen Birnbaum. **LC** D909; .B57. **DD** 914/.04558.

●US/1056-4489
**BIRNBAUM'S FLORENCE.** **VFOAT** Florence. (1992)-. English. $9.95. Harper Collins Publishers, Keystone Industrial Park, Scranton PA 18512. **Tel** (800)242-7737, (800)233-4727, FAX (800)822-4090.

US/0749-2553
**BIRNBAUM'S FRANCE.** [Birnbaum's Fr.]. **VFOAT** France. (1985)-. English. an (Nov.). $18.00. Harper Collins Publishers, Keystone Industrial Park, Scranton PA 18512. **Tel** (800)242-7737, (800)233-4727, FAX (800)822-4090. **ED** Stephen Birnbaum. **LC** DC16; .B57. **DD** 914.4/04838.

●US/1068-7238
**BIRNBAUM'S GERMANY.** **VFOAT** Germany. (1994)-. English. $18.00. Harper Collins Publishers, Keystone Industrial Park, Scranton PA 18512. **Tel** (800)242-7737, (800)233-4727, FAX (800)822-4090.

US/0896-8683
**BIRNBAUM'S GREAT BRITAIN.** [Birnbaum's G. B.]. **VFOAT** Great Britain. English. an. $12.95. Harper Collins Publishers, Keystone Industrial Park, Scranton PA 18512. **Tel** (800)242-7737, (800)233-4727, FAX (800)822-4090. **LC** DA650; .B58. **DD** 914.104/858. ***Continues in part*** *Birnbaum's Great Britain and Ireland, 0884-1195.*

US/0883-2471
**BIRNBAUM'S HAWAII.** [Birnbaum's Hawaii]. **VFOAT** Hawaii. 1985-. English. an. $18.00. Harper Collins Publishers, Keystone Industrial Park, Scranton PA 18512. **Tel** (800)242-7737, (800)233-4727, FAX (800)822-4090. **ED** S Birnbaum. **LC** DU622; .H336. **DD** 919.69/044. ***Continues*** *Hawaii (Boston, Mass.), 0732-9024.*

●US/1060-3875
**BIRNBAUM'S HONOLULU.** **VFOAT** Honolulu. (1992)-. English. $10.00. Harper Collins Publishers, Keystone Industrial Park, Scranton PA 18512. **Tel** (800)242-7737, (800)233-4727, FAX (800)822-4090.

US/0896-8691
**BIRNBAUM'S IRELAND.** [Birnbaum's Irel.]. **VFOAT** Ireland. (1989)-. English. an. $18.00. Harper Collins Publishers, Keystone Industrial Park, Scranton PA 18512. **Tel** (800)242-7737, (800)233-4727, FAX (800)822-4090. **LC** DA980; .B57. **DD** 914.1504/824. ***Continues in part*** *Birnbaum's Great Britain and Ireland, 0884-1195.*

US/0890-1139
**BIRNBAUM'S ITALY.** [Birnbaum's Italy]. **VFOAT** Italy. 1987-. English. an. $12.95. Harper Collins Publishers, Keystone Industrial Park, Scranton PA 18512. **Tel** (800)242-7737, (800)233-4727, FAX (800)822-4090. **ED** Stephen Birnbaum. **LC** DG416; .B47. **DD** 914.5/04928/05.

●US/1055-5676
**BIRNBAUM'S IXTAPA & ZIHUATENEJO.** **VFOAT** Birnbaum's Ixtapa and Zihuatenejo; Ixtapa & Zihuatenejo; Ixtapa and Zihuatenejo. 1st Ed. (1992)-. English. an. $10.00 (U.S.), $13.50 (Can.). Harper Collins Publishers, Keystone Industrial Park, Scranton PA 18512. **Tel** (800)242-7737, (800)233-4727, FAX (800)822-4090. **ED** Alex Birnbaum, (212)207-7158. **DD** 917.
**Desc:** This gives practical information for planning your trip, such as how and when to go, preparing your trip, practical information once you get there and sources and resources. There is a section of Spanish words and phrases. There is also a section on three major driving routes from Mexico's Pacific beaches to nearby cities and ancient ruins.

●US/1061-5423
**BIRNBAUM'S LAS VEGAS.** **VFOAT** Las Vegas. (1993)-. English. $11.00. Harper Collins Publishers, Keystone Industrial Park, Scranton PA 18512. **Tel** (800)242-7737, (800)233-4727, FAX (800)822-4090.

●US/1056-4470
**BIRNBAUM'S LONDON.** [Birnbaum's Lond.]. **VFOAT** London. (1992)-. Periodical. English. an. $12.00. Harper Collins Publishers, Keystone Industrial Park, Scranton PA 18512. **Tel** (800)242-7737, (800)233-4727, FAX (800)822-4090. **LC** DA679; .B57. **DD** 914.

●US/1056-4462
**BIRNBAUM'S LOS ANGELES.** **VFOAT** Los Angeles. (1992)-. English. $9.95. Harper Collins Publishers, Keystone Industrial Park, Scranton PA 18512. **Tel** (800)242-7737, (800)233-4727, FAX (800)822-4090.

US/0884-1209
**BIRNBAUM'S MEXICO.** [Birnbaum's Mex.]. **VFOAT** Mexico. (1985)-. English. an (Nov.). $18.00. Harper Collins Publishers, Keystone Industrial Park, Scranton PA 18512. **Tel** (800)242-7737, (800)233-4727, FAX (800)822-4090. **ED** S. Birnbaum. **LC** F1209; .M486. **DD** 917.2/0483. ***Continues*** *Mexico, 0162-5500.*

●US/1056-4454
**BIRNBAUM'S MIAMI & FT. LAUDERDALE.** [Birnbaum's Miami & Ft. Lauderdale]. **VFOAT** Birnbaum's Miami and Ft. Lauderdale; Miami & Ft. Lauderdale; Miami and Ft. Lauderdale. (1992)-. English. $10.00 (U.S.), $13.50 (Can.). Harper Collins Publishers, Keystone Industrial Park, Scranton PA 18512. **Tel** (800)242-7737, (800)233-4727, FAX (800)822-4090. **DD** 975.

●US/1061-5415
**BIRNBAUM'S MONTREAL.** **VFOAT** Montreal. (1993)-. English. $11.00. Harper Collins Publishers, Keystone Industrial Park, Scranton PA 18512. **Tel** (800)242-7737, (800)233-4727, FAX (800)822-4090.

●US/1061-5431
**BIRNBAUM'S NEW ORLEANS.** **VFOAT** New Orleans. 1993-. English. $11.00. Harper Collins Publishers, Keystone Industrial Park, Scranton PA 18512. **Tel** (800)242-7737, (800)233-4727, FAX (800)822-4090.

●US/1056-4446
**BIRNBAUM'S NEW YORK.** [Birnbaum's N.Y.]. **VFOAT** New York. (1992)-. English. $10.00 (US), $13.50 (Canada). Harper Collins Publishers, Keystone Industrial Park, Scranton PA 18512. **Tel** (800)242-7737, (800)233-4727, FAX (800)822-4090. **DD** 974.

●US/1056-4438
**BIRNBAUM'S PARIS.** **VFOAT** Paris. (1992)-. English. $9.95. Harper Collins Publishers, Keystone Industrial Park, Scranton PA 18512. **Tel** (800)242-7737, (800)233-4727, FAX (800)822-4090.

●US/1055-5668
**BIRNBAUM'S PORTUGAL.** [Birnbaum's Port.]. **VFOAT** Portugal. (1992)-. English. $17.00. Harper Collins Publishers, Keystone Industrial Park, Scranton PA 18512. **Tel** (800)242-7737, (800)233-4727, FAX (800)822-4090. **DD** 914. ***Continues in part*** *Birnbaum's Spain/Portugal, 1042-6353.*

●US/1060-3883
**BIRNBAUM'S PUERTO VALLARTA.** **VFOAT** Puerto Vallarta. (1992)-. English. $10.00. Harper Collins Publishers, Keystone Industrial Park, Scranton PA 18512. **Tel** (800)242-7737, (800)233-4727, FAX (800)822-4090.

●US/1056-442X
**BIRNBAUM'S ROME.** **VFOAT** Rome. (1992)-. English. $9.95. Harper Collins Publishers, Keystone Industrial Park, Scranton PA 18512. **Tel** (800)242-7737, (800)233-4727, FAX (800)822-4090.

●US/1056-4403
**BIRNBAUM'S SAN FRANCISCO.** [Birnbaum's San Franc.]. **VFOAT** San Francisco. (1992)-. English. an (Dec.). $12.00. Harper Collins Publishers, Keystone Industrial Park, Scranton PA 18512. **Tel** (800)242-7737, (800)233-4727, FAX (800)822-4090. **LC** IN PROCESS. **DD** 919.

●US/1068-722X
**BIRNBAUM'S SANTA FE, TAOS, ALBUQUERQUE.** **VFOAT** Santa Fe, Taos, Albuquerque. (1994)-. English. $18.00. Harper Collins Publishers, Keystone Industrial Park, Scranton PA 18512. **Tel** (800)242-7737, (800)233-4727, FAX (800)822-4090.

US/0883-2463
**BIRNBAUM'S SOUTH AMERICA.** [Birnbaum's South Am.]. **VFOAT** South America. (1985)-. English. an (Nov.). $19.00. Harper Collins Publishers, Keystone Industrial Park, Scranton PA 18512. **Tel** (800)242-7737, (800)233-4727, FAX (800)822-4090. **ED** Stephen Birnbaum. **LC** F2211; .H68a. **DD** 918/.0438. ***Continues*** *Houghton Mifflin Company. South America, 0193-7944.*

●US/1055-565X
**BIRNBAUM'S SPAIN.** [Birnbaum's Spain]. **VFOAT** Spain. (1992)-. English. $17.00. Harper Collins Publishers, Keystone Industrial Park, Scranton PA 18512. **Tel** (800)242-7737, (800)233-4727, FAX (800)822-4090. **DD** 914. ***Continues in part*** *Birnbaum's Spain/Portugal, 1042-6353.*

●US/1061-5393
**BIRNBAUM'S TORONTO.** [Birnbaum's Tor.]. **VFOAT** Toronto. (1993)-. English. an. $11.00. Harper Collins Publishers, Keystone Industrial Park, Scranton PA 18512. **Tel** (800)242-7737, (800)233-4727, FAX (800)822-4090. **LC** F1059.5.T683; B56. **DD** 917.13/54104647.

US/0883-2501
**BIRNBAUM'S UNITED STATES.** [Birnbaum's U.S.]. **VFOAT** United States. (1985)-. English. an. $19.00. Harper Collins Publishers, Keystone Industrial Park, Scranton PA 18512. **Tel** (800)242-7737, (800)233-4727, FAX (800)822-4090. **ED** Stephen Birnbaum. **LC** E158; .U57. **DD** 917.3/04927. ***Continues*** *United States, 0162-2420.*

US/0883-251X
**BIRNBAUM'S USA FOR BUSINESS TRAVELERS.** [Birnbaum's USA bus. travel.]. **VFOAT** USA for Business Travelers. (1985)-. English. an (Dec.). $14.00. Harper Collins Publishers, Keystone Industrial Park, Scranton PA 18512. **Tel** (800)242-7737, (800)233-4727, FAX (800)822-4090. **ED** Stephen Birnbaum. **LC** E158; .U8. **DD** 917.3/04927. ***Continues*** *USA for Business Travelers, 0739-6384.*

●US/1061-5407
**BIRNBAUM'S VANCOUVER.** **VFOAT** Vancouver. 1993-. English. $11.00. Harper Collins Publishers, Keystone Industrial Park, Scranton PA 18512. **Tel** (800)242-7737, (800)233-4727, FAX (800)822-4090.

●US/1056-4411
**BIRNBAUM'S VENICE.** **VFOAT** Venice. (1992)-. English. $9.95. Harper Collins Publishers, Keystone Industrial Park, Scranton PA 18512. **Tel** (800)242-7737, (800)233-4727, FAX (800)822-4090.

# Travel and Tourism

●US/1061-544X
**BIRNBAUM'S WASHINGTON DC.** VFOAT Washington. (1993)-. English. $11.00. Harper Collins Publishers, Keystone Industrial Park, Scranton PA 18512. **Tel** (800)242-7737, (800)233-4727, FAX (800)822-4090.

●US/1056-4373
**BIRNBAUM'S WESTERN EUROPE.** VFOAT Western Europe. (1992)-. English. $9.95. Harper Collins Publishers, Keystone Industrial Park, Scranton PA 18512. **Tel** (800)242-7737, (800)233-4727, FAX (800)822-4090.

UK/0955-3010
**BITS. BSI INFORMATION TECHNOLOGY SERVICES.** (BITS.). [BITS, BSI Inf. Technol. Serv.]. VFOAT DISC BITS; Newsletter - BITS; Newsletter - BSI Information Technology Services; British Standards Institute Information Technology Services; Newsletter - British Standards Institute Information Technology Services; BITS Newsletter. (1987)-. Periodical. English. qt. 550F. Bits, Rue de la Loi 63, B-1040 Brussels Belgium. **Tel** 32 2 2307530, FAX 230 75 09. **Ind/Abst** Leis. Recreat. Tour. Abstr.

US/0164-5218
**BLACK ODYSSEY. Suspended.** (197?)-(1988). Periodical. English. mo. J F F Communications Inc, 114 East 28th Street, Room 700, New York NY 10016.

AT/0810-9567
**BLAIR'S GUIDE VICTORIA.** (BLAIRS GUIDE TO VICTORIA AND MELBOURNE.). [Blair guide Vic.]. (1983)-. English. ir. 17.95Aus$. Universal Press Pty Ltd, 64 Talavera Road, Macquarie Park, New South Wales, 2113 Australia. **Tel** 011 61 2 8881877, FAX 011 61 2 8889850. **ED** Bob McLeod. **DD** 919.45046305. Index available (Bound in next iss.). **Bk Rev. Ad Acc. Circ:** 20,000.

CK
**BOLETIN DE INVESTIGACIONES E INFORMACION TURISTICA. Main/Corp** Corporacion Nacional de Turismo de Colombia. (19??)-. Spanish. Apartado Aereo 8400, Bogota Colombia. **LC** G155.C6; C642a.

CN/0229-0898
**BONJOUR QUEBEC.** Vol. 1, No. 1 (July 1980)-. Periodical. English (French). qt. Free. Association Touristique De La Region De Quebec, 975 Place D'Youville, Palais Montcalm, Suite 300, Quebec, Quebec G1R 3P1. **DD** 917.14/47/005.

US
**BOSTON MAGAZINE.** VFOAT Boston. (19??)-. Periodical. English. mo. $15.00. Boston Magazine / Hort Hall, 300 Massachusetts Avenue, Boston MA 02115. **Tel** (617)262-9700. **(Subscription address:** CDS Agency Hard Copy, PO Box 4966, Des Moines IA 50340.**)** Circ: 127,194. available on microfilm from University Microfilms International (UMI). Documents available from UMI Article Clearinghouse. **Continues** Boston, 0006-4989. **Desc:** Typical features include "Boston Inc.," which spotlights different Boston companies; "RFD," which presents views of the staff writers on subjects of personal interest; and "Short Takes," which briefly describes fashionable shops, eateries, and merchandise in the Boston area. **Ind/Abst** Access (1975-); Can. Index (1975-?); Gen. Period. Index (1985-); Mag. Artic. Summar. Elite (Jan. 1984-June 1989); Mag. Artic. Summar. Select (Jan. 1984-June 1989); Mag. Artic. Summar. CD-ROM (Jan. 1984-June 1989); Mag. Index Plus (1989-); Mag. Search; Newsp. Period. Abstr. (1988-); Pop. Period. Index; Mag. Index (1977-).

FR
**BOTTIN MONDAIN; TOUT PARIS, TOUTE LA FRANCE.** French. an. 434.23F France; $75.00 US. Didot Bottin, 28 rue du Docteur Finlay, 75738 Paris Cedex 15 France. **Tel** (1)45 78 61 66, telex 204 286. **LC** DC704; .B67. **DD** 914.4/361/0025. **Ad Acc.** ctrl circ.

FR
**BRETAGNE (HACHETTE (FIRM)).** (BRETAGNE.). 1989-. French. an. 16.95F. Guide du Routard, 5 rue de l'Arrivee, 92190 Meudon France. **LC** DC611.B848; B68953. **DD** 914.4/104838/05.

US
**BRITAIN BY BRITRAIL. WRITTEN BY GEORGE WRIGHT FERGUSON.** VFOAT George Ferguson's Britain by Britrail; Ferguson's Britain by Britrail. (1980)-. English. an. $16.95. Globe Pequot Press, 6 Business Park Road, Old Saybrook CT 06475. **Tel** (800)243-0495, . **LC** DA650; .B834. **DD** 914.1/04858.

US/0095-1579
**BRITISH ISLES AND IRELAND TRAVEL GUIDE.** VFOAT AAA Travel Guide, British Isles and Ireland. (19??)-. an. $2.00. American Automobile Association, 1000 AAA Drive, Heathrow FL 32746. **Tel** (407)444-7000. **LC** GV1025.G7; B72. **DD** 914.1/04/857.

US/1041-4010
**BRITISH TRAVEL LETTER.** [Br. travel lett.]. (1988)-. Periodical. English. Ten times a year (monthly except Aug. and Jan.). $65.00 (one year), $99.00 (two year). British Publications Inc, 361-4 Post Road West, Suite 194, Westport CT 06880. **Tel** (203)221-7945, (203)221-0011. **ED** Neil Saunders (editor's address: 600 Worcester Road, Townson, MD 21204; Telephone: (410)494-9791). **LC** WMLC L 83/9260. **DD** 941. **Bk Rev** (Qty: 10). **Circ:** 5,000 (ctrl). **Desc:** Current information on Britain with emphasis on travelers visiting Britain.

US
**BUDGET TRAVEL IN CANADA (UNITED STATES EDITION).** (BUDGET TRAVEL IN CANADA.). 1981-. English. an. St. Martin's Press, 175 Fifth Avenue, New York NY 10010. **Tel** (800)221-7945, (212)982-3900, FAX (212)777-6359. **LC** F1009; .B83. **DD** 917.1/0646. **Ad Acc.**

BE
**BULLETIN D'INFORMATION DU BITS.** VFOAT BITS Information. Bulletin. French (English, German, Italian and Dutch). qt. 500F. Bits, Rue de la Loi 63, B-1040 Brussels Belgium. **Tel** 32 2 2307530, FAX 230 75 09. **ED** Raymond Stelandre. **Ad Acc. Circ:** 650. **Desc:** Information about worldwide social tourism.

FT
**BULLETIN SEMESTRIEL DE STATISTIQUE. See** Business-Commerce.

CN/0706-215X
**BULLETIN VOYAGES.** (1978)-. Bulletin. French. Fifty-one times per year. 47.56Can$ Canada; 59.20Can$ US; 70.86Can$ other. Editions Acra Ltee, CP 85 Succ "E", Montreal Quebec H2T 3A5 Canada. **Tel** (514)287-9773, FAX (514)842-6180. **ED** Etienne Ozan Groulse. **DD** 338.4/791/05. **Ad Acc, Adv Mgr:** Mrs. Honorat. **Circ:** 8,000 (ctrl). **Desc:** News briefs, events, news and editorials dealing with the world travel trade industry.

IT/0007-5795
**BULLETTINO STORICO EMPOLESE. See** History(General)-History of Europe.

US/0199-6096
**BUS TOURS MAGAZINE.** Periodical. English. bm. National Bus Trader Inc, 9698 West Judson Road, Polo IL 61064. **Tel** (815)946-2341, FAX (815)946-2347.

HU/0238-180X
**BUSINESS GUIDE HUNGARY. See** Business.

US/1045-3822
**BUSINESS GUIDE TO ATLANTA. See** Business.

US/1046-5057
**BUSINESS TRAVEL MANAGEMENT. See** Business.

US/8750-3670
**BUSINESS TRAVEL NEWS. See** Business.

US/0746-9497
**BUSINESS TRAVEL REVIEW. Ceased.** [Bus. travel rev.]. Periodical. English. mo. Maxco Publishing Company Inc, 151 Route 10E, Apt 204, Succasunna NJ 07876. **Tel** (201)584-2424. **DD** 380.

UK/0955-7288
**BUSINESS TRAVELER INTERNATIONAL.** [Bus. travel. int.]. VFOAT BTI; Business Traveler. (1988)-. Periodical. English. Eleven times a year. $29.97. Perry Publications Ltd, Compass House, 22 Redan Place, London W2 4SZ England. **Tel** 011 44 71 229 7799. **(Subscription address:** Business Traveller International / US, 51 East 42nd Street, Suite 1806, New York NY 10017.**) Continues** Business Traveler (British Ed.), 0309-9334.

US/0270-7969
**BUSINESS TRAVELER'S REPORT. Ceased.** [Bus. travel. rep.]. VFOAT BTR. Ceased (Jan. 1987). Periodical. English. mo. Business Travel Newsletter Associates, 210 East 52nd Street, New York NY 10022. **Tel** (305)483-2600.

CN/0834-0552
**BUSINESS TRAVELLER AND LEISURE TIME PLANNER.** [Bus. travel. leis. time plan.]. Vol. 2, No. 7 (Sept. 1985)-. Periodical. English. ir. Free to travel industry. $26.00 (one year) other. Business Traveller / Canada, c/o Druid Publishing Corporation, 24 Bellair Street, Toronto Ontario M5R 2C7 Canada. **DD** 380.1/459104/05. **Continues** Business Traveller, 0827-2948.

HK/0255-7312
**BUSINESS TRAVELLER ASIA-PACIFIC ED.** (1982)-. Periodical. English. Twelve times a year. HK$70.00 (one year); HK$104.00 (two years); HK$140.00 (three years) Australia; NZ$107.00 (one year); NZ$160.00 (two years); NZ$213.00 (three years) New Zealand; $80.00 (one year); $120.00 (two years); $160.00 (three years). Business Traveller / Hong Kong, 200 Lockhart Road, 13th Floor, Hong Kong Hong Kong. **Tel** 011 852 5 5119317, FAX 011 852 5 5196846, telex 62107. **UDC** 380.8 : 65.

FR/0068-5151
**CAHIERS DU TOURISME. SERIE A, LES.** [Cah. tour., Ser. A]. (19??)-. Monographic series. French. ir. Centre des Hautes Etudes Touristiques, Immeuble Euroff, 38 Avenue Europe, 13090 Aix-en-Provence France. **Tel** 011 33 42 200973. **UDC** 380.81 (44).

PE
**CALENDARIO TURISTICO.** VFOAT Calendario Turistico del Peru. (19??)-. Spanish. an. Ediciones Turisticas Peru, Av Tacna 543 - Of 62, Lima Peru. **LC** G155.P5; C34.

US/0164-8748
**CALIFORNIA EXPLORER.** Vol. 1 (Aug. 1978)-. Periodical. English. bm. $28.50 (one year), $46.00 (two years), $65.00 (three years). California Explorer, PO Box 6449, Tahoe City CA 96145. **Tel** (800)833-0159. **ED** Stuart Weiss (editor's phone: (916)581-3820). Index available. cum. index. **Ad Acc. Circ:** 10,000. **Desc:** A travel resource of the least traveled and well hidden places in California.

US/0737-884X
**CALIFORNIA ROAD ATLAS AND TRAVEL GUIDE. ZIP CODE EDITION. See** Geography.

CN/1186-947X
**CAMBRIDGE, ONTARIO, CANADA ... TOURIST GUIDEBOOK.** [Camb. Ont. Can. tour. guideb.]. **Added/Corp** Cambridge Visitor and Convention Bureau. VFOAT Cambridge Tourist Guide. (1991)-. English. Free. Cambridge Visitor and Convention Bureau, 531 King Street East, Cambridge Ontario N3H 3N4 Canada. **DD** 917.13/44. **Continues** Cambridge on the Grand., 1186-9461.

BL
**CAMINHOS DO TURISMO. Added/Corp** Rio Grande do Sul, Brazil (State). Secretaria de Turismo. Assessoria de Imprensa. Vol. 1 (April 1974)-. Portuguese. mo. Assessoria de Imprensa da Secretaria de Turismo, Porto Alegre Brazil. **LC** G155.B7; C34.

US/0736-1939
**CAMPING TRAILER & TRAVEL TRAILER TRADE-IN-GUIDE. Title Change. See** Transportation.

US
**CANADA JEWISH TRAVEL GUIDE.** (19??)-. Periodical. English. $11.95. Israelowitz Publishing, Box 228, Brooklyn NY 11229. **Tel** (718)951-7072, FAX (718)951-7072. **ED** Oscar Israelowitz.

CN/0829-0814
**CANADA JOURNAL (DEUTSCHE AUSG.). See** Business.

US/0883-2641
**CANADA (NEW YORK, N.Y. 1983).** (CANADA / ROBERT TURNBULL.). [Canada (N.Y. N.Y., 1983)]. (1983)-. English. an. New American Library, 120 Woodbine Street, Bergenfield NJ 07621. **Tel** (201)387-0600. **LC** F1009; .C18. **DD** 917.1/04647. **Circ:** 15,000. **Desc:** Annotated guidebook; awards stars to Canadian tourist sights, planned for the experienced traveler.

CN/1183-1987
**CANADA WEST TRAVEL NEWS.** [Can. West trav. news]. Vol. 3, No. 6 (Aug. 1990)-. Periodical. English. $30.00 Canada & US; $60.00 other. Host Resouces Inc, 1037 West Broadway/Suite 104, Vancouver British Columbia V6H 1E3 Canada. **Tel** (604)732-8870. **DD** 381./459171044. **Continues** British Columbia Travel Industry News, 0838-5467.

CN/0845-8987
**CANADIAN TOURIST TRAVEL GUIDE.** [Can. tour. travel guide]. Canadian Tourist Guide, 1212-31 Avenue NE, Calgary Alberta T2E 7S8 Canada.

CN/0008-5219
**CANADIAN TRAVEL COURIER. Title Change.** [Can. travel cour.]. (1965)-?. Periodical. English. bw. Maclean Hunter Canada / Montreal, 1001 bvd. de Maisonneuve W., Montreal Quebec H3A 3E1 Canada. **Tel** 514-845-5141, FAX 514-845-4302, telex 055-60604. **ED** Patrick Dineen and Kent Potter. **Ad Acc. Circ:** 18,500 (ctrl). available on microfilm and microfiche from University Microfilms International (UMI). Continued by Travel Courier. **Desc:** Serves the travel-trade industry, travel counsellors, airlines, cruise companies, railways, hotels, tourist boards, government travel offices, tour operators, and others allied to the field.

CN/0831-9138
**CANADIAN TRAVEL PRESS WEEKLY.** [Can. travel press wkly.]. VFOAT CTP. Vol. 18, No. 16 (March 13, 1986)-. Periodical. English. Forty-six times a

year (Thurs.). 53.50Can$ Canada; 65.00Can$ others. Baxter Publishing Company, 310 Dupont Street, Toronto Ontario M5R 1V9 Canada. **Tel** (416)968-7252, FAX (416)968-2377. **DD** 380.1/459104/05. **Ad Acc. Circ:** 13,000 (ctrl). ***Continues*** *Canadian Travel Press, 0045-5490.*
**Desc:** It deals with timely coverage of events of concern to the travel industry and carries in-depth destination reports from around the world. Issues will carry in-depth treatment of such topics as automation, business travel, tax and legal matters affecting the industry, and forcasting.

CN/0229-821X
**CANADIAN TRAVEL SURVEY. DOMESTIC TRAVEL.** (CANADIAN TRAVEL SURVEY / ENQUETE SUR LES VOYAGES DES CANADIENS.). [Can. travel surv., Domest. travel]. **Added/Corp** Canadian Government Office of Tourism. **VFOAT** Enquete sur les Voyages des Canadiens. (1978)-. Periodical. English (French). Six times a year. Free on request. Canadian Government Office of Tourism, 235 Queen Street, 4th Floor East, Ottawa Ontario K1A 0H5 Canada. **Tel** (613)954-3850. **DD** 338.4/7917104/05. ***Continues in part*** *Statistics Canada. Education, Science and Culture Division. Culture Statistics., 0706-263X.*

UK/0268-5558
**CARAVAN BUSINESS.** (1969)-. Trade Publication. English. mo. £15.00. A E Morgan Publications Ltd, Stanley House, 9 West Street, Epsom Surrey KT18 7RL England. **Tel** 011 44 3727 41411, FAX 0372 744493, telex 291561 VIA SOS G. **ED** G.D. Ritchie. **Bk Rev. Ad Acc.**
**Desc:** Includes special features and developments for park operators, caravan dealers and manufacturers.

US/0270-4803
**CARIBBEAN BARGAIN BOOK, THE.** [Caribb. bargain book]. English. $6.95. Simon & Schuster, 1230 Avenue of the Americas, New York NY 10020. **Tel** (212)698-7000. **ED** D Porter. **LC** F1609; .H28. **DD** 917.29/0452.

BB
**CARIBBEAN DIGEST. See** Economics-Economic History, Conditions.

US/1048-5171
**CARIBBEAN EVENTS MAGAZINE. See** General Interest-General Interest-North America.

US
**CARIBBEAN FLITE GUIDE. See** Aeronautics, Astronautics.

AQ
**CARIBBEAN HANDBOOK, THE.** (19??)-. English. an. $75.00. Ft Caribbean, 3A Sloane Avenue, London SW3 3JD England. **Tel** 011 44 71 581-8872, FAX 011 44 71 225 1588, telex 8954102 BBS. **ED** Lindsay Maxwell. **LC** HC151.A1; C373. **Bk Rev**, (Qty: 25). **Ad Acc. Circ:** 12,000 (ctrl).
**Desc:** Business, economic, and political reference for the Caribbean region, combining detailed information on each country and specialist features on key sectors.

UK
**CARIBBEAN ISLANDS HANDBOOK.** (1990)-. English. an (October). $21.95. National Textbook Company, 4255 West Touhy Avenue, Lincolnwood IL 60646. **Tel** (708)679-5500, (800)323-4900, FAX (708)679-2494, telex TWX 9102230736. **LC** F2171.3; .C365. **DD** 917.2904/52. Index available. **Ad Acc. Circ:** 10,000. ***Continues in part*** *South American Handbook, 0309-4529.*

US/1052-1011
**CARIBBEAN TRAVEL AND LIFE.** [Caribb. travel life]. (1987)-. Periodical. English. bm. $19.95 (one year), $34.95 (two years) US; $29.95 (one year), $54.95 (two years) other. Caribbean Travel and Life Inc, 8403 Colesville Road, Suite 830, Silver Spring MD 20910. **Tel** (301)588-2300, FAX (301)588-2256. **ED** V Gould Stoddcst. **DD** 917. **Bk Rev**, (Qty: Varies). **Ad Acc, Adv Mgr:** Joe DiMarino. **Circ:** 105,000. ***Continues*** *Caribbean Travel and Life Magazine, 0891-9496.*
**Desc:** Travel magazine for people who love the Caribbean.

UK
**CARIBBEAN TRAVEL NEWS EUROPE.** English. Four times a year. £15.40 UK and Northern Ireland; $25.00 other. Morgan Grampian, 40 Beresford Street Woolwich, London SE18 6BQ England. **Tel** 011 44 81 855 7777, FAX 011 44 81 855 5548, telex 896238.

US/0894-5446
**CAROLINA PIEDMONT.** ***Ceased.*** ( )-Ceased Vol. 11, No. 7 (July/Aug. 1988). Periodical. English. bm. Carolina Piedmont, PO Box 29541, Greensboro NC 27429. **DD** 917.

US
**CATSKILLS GUIDE.** (19??)-. Periodical. English. $4.95. Israelowitz Publishing, Box 228, Brooklyn NY 11229. **Tel** (718)951-7072, FAX (718)951-7072. **ED** Oscar Israelowitz.

CJ
**CAYMAN ISLANDS MAP & VISITORS GUIDE : OFFICIAL GUIDE OF THE CAYMAN ISLANDS, DEPARTMENT OF TOURISM. Added/Corp** Cayman Islands. Dept. of Tourism. **VFOAT** Cayman Islands Map and Visitors Guide. (19??)-. English. Cayman Free Press, POB 1365, Grand Cayman, British West Indies. **Tel** (809)949-5111. **LC** F1891.C5; C39. **DD** 917.292/104. ***Continues*** *Cayman Islands Holiday Guide.*

US/0890-9547
**CHARTERING MAGAZINE'S YACHT VACATIONS.** [Chart. mag. yacht vacat.]. **VFOAT** Yacht Vacations; Chartering; Chatering YV. (198?)-. Periodical. English. Twelve times a year. Yacht Vacations Magazine, 26011 Evergreen Road, Southfield MI 48078. **LC** WMLC L 83/2759. **DD** 794.

FR
**CHATEAUX DE LA LOIRE. Main/Corp** Pneu Michelin (Firm). (19??)-. French. ir. Manufacture Francaise des Pneumatiques Michelin, 46 avenue de Breteuil, 75431 Paris Cedex 07 France. **(Subscription address:** Michelin Travel Publications, PO Box 19008, Greenville SC 29602.) **LC** GV1025.F7; C5.

US/0192-8023
**CHILTON'S GOING PLACES. Added/Corp** Chilton Company. American Society of Travel Agents. **VFOAT** Going Places. Vol. 1 (Nov./Dec. 1976)-. Periodical. English. bm. $7.50 US; $9.00 other. Chilton Company, 201 King of Prussia Road, Radnor PA 19089. **Tel** (610)964-4122, (800)695-1214, FAX (610)964-4978, telex 6851035 CHILTON UW. **LC** G149; .C46. **DD** 910/.5.

HK
**CHINA TOURISM.** No. 43 (1984)-. Periodical. English (Chinese and French). bm (6 issues). $62.00. Hong Kong China Tourism Press, 17 F V Heun Building, 138 Queen's Road, Hong Kong. **Tel** 011 852 5 411331, FAX 011 852 5 8541721, telex 82225 HKCTPHX. **ED** Jenny Marsh, Megina Kwan, Tong Chi Kwong, Kuang Wen Dong. **LC** DS712; .C4816. **DD** 951.05/05. Index available. cum. index. **Bk Rev. Ad Acc. Circ:** 80,000 (ctrl). ***Continues*** *China Tourism Pictorial.*
**Desc:** Presents contents such as the latest travel attractions, minority peoples' customs and culture, ancient cities, scenic beauty and more.

US/1042-5918
**CHRIE COMMUNIQUE. See** Hotels/Motels.

US/0193-4244
**CICERONE (MIAMI).** (CICERONE.). Periodical. Spanish (Spanish). bm. 2759 SW 27th Avenue, Miami FL 33133. **LC** G149; .C52. **DD** 910/.5.

US/0746-8210
**CINCINNATI MAGAZINE. VFOAT** Cincinnati. (198?)-. Periodical. English. mo. $16.00 (1 year), $28.00 (2 year). Cincinnati Magazine, 409 Broadway, Cincinnati OH 45202. **Tel** (513)421-4300. **LC** F499.C5; C43. **DD** 977.1/78/005. ***Continues*** *Cincinnati, 0009-689X.*

CN/1183-7144
**CITE LIBRE (1991).** (CITE LIBRE.). Vol. 19, No 1 (Jul/Aug 1991)-. Periodical. French. bm (6 issues). 24.00Can$ Canada; 30.00Can$ other. Cite Libre Information, 1250 Rene Levesque Qt Bur 2500, Montreal Quebec H3B 4Y1 Canada. **Tel** (514)846-2317. **(Subscription address:** Periodica Inc., PO Box 444, 1155 Ducharme, Outrement Quebec H2V 4R6 Canada.) **DD** 971.4. ***Continues*** *Cahiers de Cite Libre., 0009-7489.*

US/0889-2741
**CITIES OF THE WORLD.** (CITIES OF THE WORLD : A COMPILATION OF CURRENT INFORMATION ON CULTURAL, GEOGRAPHICAL, AND POLITICAL CONDITIONS IN THE COUNTRIES AND CITIES OF SIX CONTINENTS, BASED ON THE DEPARTMENT OF STATE'S "POST REPORTS".). [Cities world]. **Added/Corp** United States. Dept. of State. Post Report. Vol. 1 (1982)-. English. ir. $280.00. Gale Research Inc., 835 Penobscot Building, Detroit MI 48226. **Tel** (800)877-GALE, (313)961-2242, FAX (313)961-6083, telex TWX 810-221-7086. **ED** Monica Hubbard, Beverly Baer. **LC** G153.4; .C56. **DD** 910/.2/02.
**Desc:** Covers more then 507 major cities and 2,900 smaller cities around the globe, providing up-to-date details on each city and the 177 countries in which they are located.

US/0045-6985
**CITY AND SUBURBAN TRAVEL.** ***Suspended.*** Vol. 1 (1957)-Suspended (1983). Periodical. English. mo. Transit Research Foundation, Box 3542 Terminal Annex, Los Angeles CA 90051.

US/1043-3937
**CITY GUIDE (NEW YORK, N.Y.).** ***Title Change.*** (CITY GUIDE.). [City guide]. Periodical. English. wk. City Guide Magazine, 853 7th Avenue, New York NY 10019. **Tel** (212)315-0800, FAX (212)397-9513. **ED** Peter Insalaco. **Ad Acc.** ctrl circ. ***Continues*** *City Guide, Broadway Magazine, 0892-2446.* ***Continued by*** *Official City Guide, 1055-1778.*
**Desc:** What to do, where to go, while visiting New York City.

UK
**CITY OF LONDON, THE.** (19??)-. English. Burrow Publishing Ltd, Publicity House, 106A Stafford Road, Wallington Surrey, SM6 9TD England. **Tel** 011 44 81 773 9944, 011 44 81 773 9955, FAX 011 44 81 773 8888. **LC** DA679; .C54. **DD** 914.21/2/048505.

TU
**CKS YAPAN YABANC ZIYARETCILER ANKETI. VFOAT** Departing Foreign Visitors Survey. (1986)-. English (Turkish). **LC** HA1911; .A3 subser; G155.T8.

US/1058-1065
**COASTAL NEWS (DESTIN, FLA.).** (COASTAL NEWS : THE EMERALD COAST'S NUMBER ONE INFORMATION & ENTERTAINMENT PUBLICATION.). [Coast. news]. (1991)-. Periodical. English. mo. $15.00. Coastal Publications, Inc., 114 Palmetto, Suite 6, Destin FL 32541. **DD** 917.

CN/0828-7651
**COLCHESTER COUNTY, NOVA SCOTIA, TRAVEL GUIDE.** (COLCHESTER COUNTY TRAVEL GUIDE.). [Colchester Cty N.S. travel guide]. Vol. 1, No. 1 (Summer 1984)-. English. an. Free. Colchester County Travel Guide, PO Box 697, Truto Novia Scotia B2N 5E7 Canada. **Tel** (902)895-7811. **ED** Maureen Smith and Eva Marks MacIsaac. **DD** 917.16/12. Index available. **Ad Acc.**

CK
**COLOMBIA A SU ALCANCE. VFOAT** Colombia at Your Finger Tips. Multiple languages (English and Spanish). Publicar Editores, Av de las Americas No 22-41 P 2, Apdo Aereo, 6625 Cali Colombia. **LC** F2264; .C6. **DD** 918.61/04/63.

US/0740-9109
**COLORADO FEVER. VFOAT** Colorado Fever Magazine. Vol. 1, No. 1 (1982)-. Periodical. English. bm. $10.95. Colorado Fever Magazine, PO Box 6758 Cherry Creek Station, Denver CO 80206.

MQ
**COMMENTAIRE DES PRINCIPAUX RESULTATS TOURISTIQUES POUR L'ANNEE ... / OFFICE DEPARTEMENTAL DU TOURISME DE LA MARTINIQUE.** French. an. **LC** G155.M37; R47. **DD** 338.4/7917298204/021. ***Continues*** *Resultats du Tourisme.*

SP
**COMPENDIUM OF TOURISM STATISTICS. Added/Corp** World Tourism Organization. 7th Ed. (1986)-. English (French and Spanish). an. $50.00. World Tourism Organization / WTO, Calle Capitan Haya 42, E 28020 Madrid Spain. **Tel** 011 34 1 5710628, FAX 011 34 1 5713733, telex 42188 OMT-E. **(Subscription address:** UNIPUB, 4611 F Assembly Drive, Lanham MD 20706.) **LC** G155.A1; T5896. **DD** 380.1/4591021. ***Continues*** *Tourism Compendium.*

US
**COMPLETE GUIDE TO AMERICA'S NATIONAL PARKS : THE OFFICIAL VISITOR'S GUIDE OF THE NATIONAL PARK FOUNDATION, THE. Added/Corp** National Park Foundation. (1979)-. English. be (every two years). $17.85. Random House Inc., 400 Hahn Road, Westminster MD 21157. **Tel** (800)726-0600, (800)733-3000, FAX (800)659-2436. **LC** E158; .C78. **DD** 917.304/928.

US
**COMPLETE UNITED STATES JEWISH TRAVEL GUIDE.** (19??)-. Periodical. English. $17.45. Israelowitz Publishing, Box 228, Brooklyn NY 11229. **Tel** (718)951-7072, FAX (718)951-7072. **ED** Oscar Israelowitz.

US/0893-9683
**CONDE NAST'S TRAVELER.** [Conde Nast's travel.]. **VFOAT** Traveler. Vol. 22, No. 9 (Sept. 1987)-. Periodical. English. mo. $15.00. Conde Nast Publications / New York, 350 Madison Avenue, New York NY 10017. **Tel** (212)880-8800, (800)777-0700. **(Subscription address:** Neodata / Colorado, PO Box 2606, Boulder Boulder CO 80322.) **ED** Harold Evans. **LC** AP2; .S542. **DD** 051. available on microfilm and microfiche from University Microfilms International (UMI). Documents available from UMI Article Clearinghouse. ***Continues*** *Signature, 0037-5039;* ***Absorbed*** *European Travel & Life, 0882-7737.*
**Desc:** Filled with the travel secrets of celebrated writers and professional travelers. Delivers the world to people who love to go and want to know.
**Ind/Abst** Acad. Search (Jan. 1994-); Access (1988-?); Mag. Artic. Summar. Elite (Jan. 1994-); Mag. Artic.

Summar. CD-ROM (Jan. 1994-); Newsp. Period. Abstr. (1991-); Pop. Period. Index; Read. Guide Abstr. Select Ed.; Read. Guide Period. Lit.

UK/0965-125X
**CONFERENCE & INCENTIVE TRAVEL.** [Conf. incent. travel]. **VFOAT** Conference and Incentive Travel. (1990)-. English. Ten times a year. £45.00 UK; £55.00 Eire & Europe; £87.00 America, Middle East, India & Africa; £92.00 Australia, New Zealand & Japan; £55.00 other. Haymarket Publishing Ltd., 12 14 Ansdell Street, London W8 5TR England. **Tel** 011 44 483 733800, FAX 011 44 483 776573. **(Subscription address:** Haymarket Publishing Ltd, PO Box 219, Subscriptions Department, Woking Surrey GU21 1ZW, United Kingdom.**)** **DD** 338.4791. ***Absorbed*** *Conference Britain, 0142-7474* ***and*** *Incentive Travel World, 0950-0758.*

UK/0260-2431
**CONFERENCE BLUE BOOK.** [Conf. blue book]. (1978)-. English. an. £50.00 UK; £70.00 other. Spectrum Communications Ltd, 16-18 Acton Park, Stanley Gardens, Vale London, W3 7QE England. **Tel** 011 44 081 740-4444. **ED** Julia Allen.
**Desc:** For all meeting organizers. Fully regionalized listing of over 4,000 UK venues indexed alphabetically detailing telephone numbers, meeting room capacity in theatre style and number of bedrooms. Concentrates on technical information.

UK
**CONFERENCE BLUE BOOK. See** Hotels/Motels.

UK
**CONFERENCE GREEN BOOK. See** Hotels/Motels.

CN/0713-3111
**CONNAISSONS NOS VOISINS.** **VFOAT** Let Us Know Our Neighbours. Vol. 1, No. 1 (Feb. 1981)-. Periodical. English (French). ir. $2.00 per no. Let Us Know Our Neighbours Communications, 75 5064 Avenue du Parc, Montreal Quebec H2V 4G1 Canada. **DD** 917.47/5304/05.

US/0746-8636
**CONNECTICUT TRAVELER.** Vol. 1, No. 1 (Dec. 1983)-. Periodical. English. mo. Free to members, $3.00 nonmembers. Connecticut Motor Club, 2276 Whitney Avenue, Hamden CT 06518. **Tel** (203)288-7441. **Circ:** 143,000.

US/1044-7652
**CONNECTIONS.** [Connections]. April/May 1989-. Periodical. English. bm. $14.95. Saga Charitable Foundation Inc MA 02116. **Tel** (617)451-6808. **ED** Rodica Iliescu-Stahl. **DD** 910. **Circ:** 300,000.
**Desc:** Includes healthy traveling, cruise connections, currency news and travel features.

●US/1060-1511
**CONSUMER REPORTS TRAVEL BUYING GUIDE.** [Consum. rep. trav. buy. guide]. **Added/Corp** Consumer Reports Books. **VFOAT** Travel Buying Guide. (1992)-. English. an. $11.49. Consumer Reports Books, 9180 Le Saint Drive, Fairfield OH 45014. **Tel** (800)272-0722. **LC** G149; .C65. **DD** 381.

US/0887-8439
**CONSUMER REPORTS TRAVEL LETTER. See** Consumer Interests.

US/0739-1587
**CORPORATE & INCENTIVE TRAVEL. See** Business.

US/0745-1636
**CORPORATE MEETINGS AND INCENTIVES.** [Corp. meet. incent.]. **VFOAT** Corporate Meetings and Incentives. Vol. 1, No. 1 (Sept./Oct. 1982)-. Periodical. English. mo. $60.00 US; $70.00 Canada; $116.00 other. Laux Company Inc, 63 Great Road, Maynard MA 01754. **Tel** (508)897-5552, FAX (508)897-6824. **ED** Connie Goldstein, (editor's phone: (212)951-6748). **LC** HD5260; .C67. **DD** 910/.2/02. **Bk Rev**. **Ad Acc, Adv Mgr:** B Ventro. **Circ:** 48,000 (ctrl). ***Continues*** *Worldwide Meetings & Incentives, 0273-8805.*
**Desc:** It provides focus on domestic worldwide meetings and incentive destinations. Reviews facilities and locations.

US/0882-8709
**CORPORATE TRAVEL.** [Corp. travel]. (1985)-. Periodical. English. mo. $65.00 US; $70.00 Canada & Mexico; $125.00 airmail other. Miller Freeman Inc., 600 Harrison Street, San Francisco CA 94107. **Tel** (415)905-2337, FAX (415)905-2240, telex 278273. **(Subscription address:** CMP Publications, Inc. / New York, PO Box 4037, Church Street Station, New York NY 10261-4037.**)** **DD** 338. **[CCC].**

FR
**CORSE.** **Main/Corp** Pneu Michelin (Firm). 1st Edition (1976)-. Trade Publication. French. ir. $16.00. Manufacture Francaise des Pneumatiques Michelin, 46 avenue de Breteuil, 75431 Paris Cedex 07 France. **(Subscription address:** Michelin Travel Publications, PO Box 19008, Greenville SC 29602.**)** **LC** DC611.C812; M245a. **DD** 914.4/945/0483.
**Desc:** Contains reports on Upper Corsica and Southern Corsica.

●US/1060-3786
**COUNTRY INNS AND BACK ROADS. CALIFORNIA.** **VFOAT** California. (1992)-. English. $10.00. Harper Collins Publishers, Keystone Industrial Park, Scranton PA 18512. **Tel** (800)242-7737, (800)233-4727, FAX (800)822-4090.

US/0893-1291
**COUNTRY INNS AND BACK ROADS (CONTINENTAL EUROPE ED.).** ***Ceased.*** **See** Hotels/Motels.

●US/1060-3778
**COUNTRY INNS AND BACK ROADS. NEW ENGLAND.** **VFOAT** New England. (1992)-. English. $10.00. Harper Collins Publishers, Keystone Industrial Park, Scranton PA 18512. **Tel** (800)242-7737, (800)233-4727, FAX (800)822-4090.

CN/0229-5229
**COUNTRY VACATIONS IN ALBERTA. See** Recreation, Leisure.

US/0279-4489
**COURIER (LEXINGTON, KY.).** (COURIER: OFFICIAL PUBLICATION OF THE NATIONAL TOUR BROKERS ASSOCIATION, INC.). [Courier]. **Added/Corp** National Tour Brokers Association. (19??)-. Periodical. English. Twelve times a year. $36.00. National Tour Association, PO Box 3071, Lexington KY 40596. **Tel** (606)253-1036.

FR/0249-9975
**COURRIER - O.C.C, LE.** **VFOAT** Courrier Nouvelles de Cluny; Courrier - Office Culturel de Cluny. (1978)-. Periodical. French. Four times a year (Mar., June, Sept., Dec.). 100.00F France; 120.00F others. Office Culturel de Cluny, Chateau de Machy, 69380 Chasse Lay France. **Tel** 011 33 1 78473432, FAX 011 33 1 78470822. **ED** Jean-Luc Grasset. **UDC** 792. Index available. cum. index. **Ad Acc, Adv Mgr:** Philippe Brame, **Tel** 78.91.39.32. **Circ:** 5,000. ***Continues*** *Nouvelles de Cluny, 0221-8046.*

US
**CRAIGHEAD'S COUNTRY REPORTS.** (19??)-. English. mo. $935.00 US; $955.00 Canada; $1045.00 Europe; $1095.00 other. Craighead Publications Inc, PO Box 1253, Darien CT 06820. **Tel** (203)655-1007, FAX (203)655-0018. ***Continues*** *Craighead's International Executive Travel and Relocation Service.*

●US/1058-3904
**CRAIGHEAD'S INTERNATIONAL BUSINESS, TRAVEL, AND RELOCATION GUIDE TO 71 COUNTRIES.** (CRAIGHEAD'S INTERNATIONAL BUSINESS, TRAVEL, AND RELOCATION GUIDE TO ... COUNTRIES.). [Craighead's int. bus. travel relocat. guide 71 ctries.]. **Added/Corp** Gale Research Inc. **VFOAT** International Business, Travel, and Relocation Guide to ... Countries. 6th Ed. (1992/1993)-. English. te. $460.00. Gale Research Inc., 835 Penobscot Building, Detroit MI 48226. **Tel** (800)877-GALE, (313)961-2242, FAX (313)961-6083, telex TWX 810-221-7086. **LC** HF5549.5.E45; D56. **DD** 910/.2/02. ***Continues*** *International Business Travel and Relocation Directory.*
**Desc:** Provides information on the business practices, economics, customs, communications, tours and attractions and other highlights of 71 different countries.

US
**CRAIGHEAD'S INTERNATIONAL EXECUTIVE TRAVEL AND RELOCATION SERVICE.** ***Title Change.*** (19??)-(19??). English. mo. Craighead Publications Inc, PO Box 1253, Darien CT 06820. **Tel** (203)655-1007, FAX (203)655-0018. ***Continues*** *Overseas Assignment Directory Service, 0735-231X.* ***Continued by*** *Craigheads Country Reports.*
**Desc:** For international oriented corporations, organizations, and government agencies whose personnel travel and relocate oversees. Information on over 70 countries.

CN/1187-2608
**"CRISS-CROSS" MONTREAL METROPOLITAIN.** ["Criss-cross" Montr. metrop.]. **VFOAT** "Criss-Cross" Directory, Metropolitan Montreal; "Criss-Cross" Metropolitan Montreal; Lovell ... "Criss-Cross" Montreal Metropolitain. (1991)-. English (French). Lovell Litho & Publications, 423 Rue St-Nicolas, Montreal Quebec H2Y 2P4 Canada. **DD** 917.14/28/0025. ***Continues*** *"Criss-cross", l'Annuaire rue-Adresse, Montreal Metropolitain., 0708-7152.*

CN/1187-2608
**"CRISS-CROSS" MONTREAL METROPOLITAIN.** ["Criss-cross" Montr. metrop.]. **VFOAT** "Criss-Cross" Metropolitan Montreal; Lovell ... "Criss-Cross" Montreal Metropolitain; Annuaire "Criss-Cross", Montreal Metropolitain; ross", Montreal Metropolitain. (1991)-. French (English). Lovell Litho & Publications, 423 Rue St-Nicolas, Montreal Quebec H2Y 2P4 Canada. **DD** 917.14/28/0025. ***Continues*** *"Criss-Cross", l'Annuaire Rue-Adresse, Montreal Metropolitain., 0708-7152.*

US/0886-5604
**CRUISE DIGEST.** ***Title Change.*** [Cruise dig.]. **Added/Corp** International Cruise Passengers' Association. (19??)-(199?). Periodical. English. bm. Cruise Digest Reports, 1521 Alton Road, Suite 350, Miami FL 33139. **Tel** (305)374-2224, FAX (305)374-2224. **DD** 910. **Ad Acc, Adv Mgr:** D Ward. **Circ:** 17,000. ***Continued by*** *Cruise Digest Reports.*

US/1047-3378
**CRUISE INDUSTRY NEWS (ANNUAL).** (CRUISE INDUSTRY NEWS.). [Cruise ind. news]. (1988)-. English. $450.00. Nissen-Lie Communications Inc, 441 Lexington Avenue, Suite 1209A, New York NY 10017. **Tel** (212)986-1025, FAX (212)986-1033. **DD** 380. **Ad Acc.**
**Desc:** The most authoritative and complete presentation of the cruise industry.

US/0893-1240
**CRUISE INDUSTRY NEWS (NEWSLETTER).** (CRUISE INDUSTRY NEWS.). [Cruise ind. news]. (1985)-. Trade Publication. English. Twenty-three times a year. $495.00. Nissen-Lie Communications Inc, 441 Lexington Avenue, Suite 1209A, New York NY 10017. **Tel** (212)986-1025, FAX (212)986-1033. **ED** Oivind Mathisen. **DD** 380. **Circ:** 1,000.
**Desc:** The industry's insider newsletter. Reports on cruise industry news and developments.

US/0893-1240
**CRUISE INDUSTRY NEWS QUARTERLY, THE.** Winter (1991)-. Periodical. English. Four times a year (Mar., June, Sept., Dec.). $26.00. Nissen-Lie Communications Inc., 441 Lexington Avenue, Suite 1209A, New York NY 10017. **Tel** (212)986-1025, FAX (212)986-1033. **ED** Oivind Mathisen. **Bk Rev**. **Ad Acc, Adv Mgr:** Angel A. Mathison. **Circ:** 10,000.
**Desc:** The editorial focus covers all aspects of cruise operations; shipbuilding; technical development; new ships; cruise companies; ship reviews; onboard services and passenger programs; food and beverage; ports and destinations; and personality profiles.

US/0897-5078
**CRUISE MAGAZINE.** [Cruise mag.]. Vol. 1, No. 1 (May 1987)-. Periodical. English. bm (6 issues). $17.88. Cruise Magazine, PO Box 1289, Gulf Breeze FL 32561. **DD** 910.
**Desc:** Up-to-date information on the ships, the schedules, itineraries, ports and pricing.

US/0199-5111
**CRUISE TRAVEL MAGAZINE.** (1979)-. Periodical. English. bm (6 issues). $18.00 US; $24.00 other. Century Publishing Company, 990 Grove Street, Evanston IL 60201-4370. **Tel** (708)491-6440, (800)321-3333, FAX (708)491-0459. **(Subscription address:** Kable Publishers Aide, 308 East Hitt Street, Subscriptions Department, Mt. Morris, IL 61054**)** **ED** Bob Meyers, Charles Dobertz. **Ad Acc. Circ:** 150,000. available on microfilm from University Microfilms International (UMI).
**Desc:** All about cruise ships, ports of call, schedules, and fortune.

●US/1060-0086
**CRUISES & TOURS.** [Cruises tours]. **VFOAT** Cruises and Tours. Began in 1992. Periodical. English. qt. $11.80. Vacation Publications Inc, 1502 Augusta Drive, Suite 415, Houston TX 77057. **Tel** (713)974-6903, FAX (713)974-0445. **DD** 910. ***Continues*** *Cruise Vacations, 1046-1388.*

US/0744-6004
**CRUISING AROUND THE WORLD.** [Cruis. world]. **VFOAT** Cruising. Vol. 1, No. 1 (Apr. 1982)-. Trade Publication. English (French and Spanish). mo. $17.00. Associated Publishers of South Florida, PO Box 738, Miami Beach FL 33139. **ED** Frank A Estrada. **Bk Rev**. **Ad Acc. Circ:** 23,000 (ctrl).
**Desc:** Travel trade magazine that contains information in general of the travel industry, cruise lines schedules, new hotels, destinations, tourist shopping, vacation planning, attractions and tours.

IT
**CUNEO PROVINCIA GRANDE.** **Added/Corp** Cuneo (Province) Camera di Commercio, Industria e Agricoltura. (1952)-. Periodical. Italian. Three times a year. L22000 Italy; L44000 other. Edizioni l'Archiere SRL, Via Roma 8, 12100 Cuneo Italy. **Tel** 011 39 171 693174.

SP
**CURRENT TRAVEL AND TOURISM INDICATORS.** ***Title Change.*** **Added/Corp** World Tourism Organization. **VFOAT** CTI. (19??)-(19??). Periodical. English (French). qt. World Tourism Organization / WTO, Calle Capitan Haya 42, E 28020 Madrid Spain. **Tel** 011 34 1 5710628, FAX 011 34 1

# Travel and Tourism

5713733, telex 42188 OMT-E. **LC** G155.A1; C87. **DD** 338.4/79105. *Continued by* Travel and Tourism Barometer, 1014-7306.

US/0091-9160
**DATAMEX. WESTERN HEMISPHERE.** (DATAMEX.). English. $150.00. American Express Company, PO Box 65 Wall Street Station, New York NY 10005. **LC** G153; .A45. **DD** 910/.202. *Continues* American Express International Index.

US
**DAY & NIGHT IN UPSTATE NEW YORK : THE TRAVEL AND ENTERTAINMENT MAGAZINE.** **VAT** Day and Night in Upstate New York. Periodical. English. mo. Day & Night Magazine, 419 Mandeville Street, Utica NY 13502.

CN/0229-2130
**DESTINATION (TORONTO, ONT.).** (DESTINATION.). [Destination]. Periodical. English. qt. Free. Destination, 2625 Yonge Street Canada. **DD** 910/.5. ctrl circ.

CN
**DESTINATIONS.** **VFOAT** Globe and Mail Destinations. Vol. 1, No. 1 (Spring 1986)-. Periodical. English. bm. The Globe and Mail Division, 444 Front Street West, Toronto Ontario M5V 2S9 Canada. **LC** IN PROCESS.
**Ind/Abst** Can. Period. Index (19??-).

US/0275-8024
**DESTINATIONS (KNOXVILLE, TENN.).** (DESTINATIONS.). **Main/Corp** Destinations (13-30 Corporation). Vol. 1, No. 1 (Fall 1980)-. Periodical. English. Three times a year. $9.00. Circulation Department / Knoxville, 13-30 Corporation, 505 Market Street, Knoxville TX 37902. **LC** G149; .D47a. **DD** 910.4/05.

US/0899-2398
**DIABETIC TRAVELER, THE.** (198?)-. Periodical. English. Four times a year (Jan., Apr., July, Oct.). $18.95. The Diabetic Traveler, PO Box 8223, Stamford CT 06905. **Tel** (203)327-5832, FAX (203)975-1748. **ED** Maury Rosenbaum. **DD** 910. **Bk Rev** (Qty: 4-6). **Ad Acc. Pr Rev.**
**Desc:** Contains ideas to help diabetics make an safe and economical travel arrangements. Furnishes hints on insulin adjustments over time zones, travel storage cases for diabetes supplies. Information on carrying medical history, foot care for the diabetic and coping with a common cold while traveling.

UK
**DIGEST OF TOURIST STATISTICS.** **Main/Corp** British Tourist Authority. (1972)-. English. ir. £40.00. British Tourist Authority, Thames Tower, Blacks Road, London W6 9EL England. **Tel** 011 44 81 8469000, FAX 011 44 156 30302. **LC** G155.G7; B67a. **DD** 338.4/7/914100212. Documents available from BLDSC.
**Desc:** A wealth of facts and figures relating to tourism to, within and from the United Kingdom; including data on international tourism, tourism and the economy, sightseeing, hotel numbers and occupancy rates.
**Ind/Abst** Leis. Recreat. Tour. Abstr.

ES
**DIRECTORIO DE LA INDUSTRIA TURISTICA DE EL SALVADOR.** English (Spanish). an. $1.00. Felicitaciones Centroamericanas, Apartado Postal 1642, San Salvador El Salvador. **LC** G155.E4; D57. **DD** 917.284/0452.

US
**DIRECTORIO TURISTICO / DEPARTAMENTO DE ASUNTOS ECONOMICOS, DIVISION DE COMERCIO INTERNACIONAL Y TURISMO.** *Ceased.* **Added/Corp** Organization of American States. International Trade and Tourism Division. **VFOAT** Tourism Directory. (19??)-Phrases complete. English (Spanish). ir. Organization of American States, 19th Street & Constitution Avenue NW, Suite 300, Washington DC 20006. **Tel** (202)458-6256. **LC** G155.L3; D57. **DD** 380.1/459104/091812. **Circ:** 1,000 (ctrl).
**Desc:** Provides information on key players in the Latin American and Caribbean tourism industry.

IO/0304-1484
**DIRECTORY HOTEL PARIWISATA & TRAVEL BUREAU.** See Hotels/Motels.

US/0732-6572
**DIRECTORY OF INCENTIVE TRAVEL INTERNATIONAL.** [Dir. incent. travel int.]. **VFOAT** DITI. Directory. English. an. $20.00 US; $23.00 (plus postage) other. Laux Company Inc, 63 Great Road, Maynard MA 01754. **Tel** (508)897-5552, FAX (508)897-6824. **ED** Connie Goldstein. **LC** HD5260; .D57. **DD** 910/.2/02. **Circ:** 40,061.

US/0277-5301
**DIRECTORY OF MEMBERS / SOCIETY OF AMERICAN TRAVEL WRITERS.** [Dir. memb. - Soc. Am. Travel Writers]. **Main/Corp** Society of American Travel Writers. (19??)-. Directory. English. an. $95.00. Society of American Travel Writers, 1155 Connecticut Ave. NW, Suite 500, Washington DC 20036. **Tel** (202)429-6639. **LC** G149.S65; A35. **DD** 910.4/02573. *Continues* Society of American Travel Writers. Roster of Members, 0091-4991.

US/0270-3815
**DIRECTORY OF NEW ENGLAND SKI TOURING CENTERS, A.** See Recreation, Leisure-Sports.

US
**DIRECTORY OF TRAVEL INFORMATION SOURCES FOR THE PACIFIC ISLANDS.** Dec. 1988-. Directory. English. ir. $4.95. Pilot Books, 103 Cooper Street, Babylon NY 11702-2319. **Tel** (516)422-2225, FAX (516)422-2227. **ED** Donald F Gould and Katherine Gould.
**Desc:** A comprehensive guide to books and informative sources for the South Seas traveller. Covers books; language guides; magazines and newsletters; travel book and map stores; travel book publishers; national tourist authorities; air access information; special interest travel services and consultants; health, safety and weather information, as well as other informative resources.

CN
**DIRECTORY OF U.S. TRAVEL AGENTS.** **Added/Corp** Passenger Network Services Corporation. **VFOAT** Directory of US Travel Agents. **VAT** Directory of United States Travel Agents. 11th Ed. (Aug. 1990)-. Directory. English. International Airlines Travel Agent Network, Suite 4060, 2000 Peel Street, Montreal, Quebec H3A 2W5 Canada. **LC** IN PROCESS. *Formed by the union of* Directory of U.S. Travel Agents (Airline Numeric Ed.) *and* Directory of U.S. Travel Agents (Airline Alpha-Geographic Ed.).

US/0898-6231
**DISCERNING TRAVELER, THE.** (198?)-. Periodical. English. bm (Jan., Mar., May, July, Sept., Nov.). $50.00 US; $60.00 Canada; $65.00 other. Discerning Traveler, 504 West Mermaid Lane, Philadelphia PA 19118. **Tel** (215)247-5578. **ED** Linda Glickstein. **DD** 973. cum. index. **Bk Rev** (Qty: 36). ctrl circ.
**Desc:** Destination oriented publication covering history of the area, lodging, restaurants, things to do, drives, walks, sports, museums, etc. Covers destinations from Quebec to Key West.

US/0419-4071
**DISCOVER AMERICA SALES GUIDE.** **VFOAT** Travel Trade, Discover America Sales Guide. Vol. 1 (1967)-. Periodical. English. ir. Travel Trade Publications, 15 West 44th Street, New York NY 10036. **Tel** (212)730-6600.

US
**DISCOVER COSTA RICA.** English (Spanish). an. North South Net Inc, 100 Almeria Avenue, Suite 202, Coral Gables FL 33134. **Tel** (305)441-9744, FAX (305)441-9739, telex 803029 VOYAGERMIA. **ED** Gloria Shanahan. **Ad Acc. Circ:** 10,000 (ctrl).
**Desc:** Magazine for hotel guests in the major hotels of Costa Rica. Provides information on where to go and what to do for tourists in Costa Rica.

US
**DISCOVER GUATEMALA.** English (Spanish). an. $14.95 US; $18.95 other. North South Net Inc, 100 Almeria Avenue, Suite 202, Coral Gables FL 33134. **Tel** (305)441-9744, FAX (305)441-9739, telex 803029 VOYAGERMIA. **ED** Gloria Shanahan. **Ad Acc. Circ:** 8,000 (ctrl).
**Desc:** Magazine for hotel guests in the major hotels of Guatemala. Provides information on where to go and what to do for the tourist in Guatemala.

HK
**DISCOVER INDIA.** English (French, German and Japanese). Twelve times a year $49.00 Hong Kong; $58.00 US & Canada. Media Transasia Thailand Ltd., 26 Chidlom Road, 14 Floor, Ploenchit, Bangkok 10500 Thailand. **Tel** 011 66 2 5199057, telex 84003. **Ad Acc. Adv Mgr:** Xavier Collaco.

US/0738-8071
**DISCOVER SOUTHWEST WISCONSIN'S HIDDEN VALLEYS.** **VFOAT** Hidden Valleys. (19??)-. English. an (Jan.). $2.00. Hidden Valleys Inc., Promoting Southwestern Wisconsin, PO Box 15/6711 Settlement Road, Cassville WI 53806-0015. **Tel** (608)725-5867. **Ad Acc.** ctrl circ.

US
**DISCOVER WILLIAMSBURG.** 1980-. English. an. Virginia Gazette, PO Box 419, Williamsburg VA 23185. **Tel** (804)220-1736.

CN/1186-7787
**DISCOVERING ALBERTA.** [Discov. Alta.]. **Added/Corp** Alberta Tourism. Tourism Industry Association of Alberta. (1991)-. English. **DD** 917.12304. *Continues* Alberta Vacation Planner., 0838-3200.

ET
**DISCOVERING ETHIOPIA.** V. 1- June/Aug. 1976-. Periodical. English. Ethiopian Tourist Office, PO Box 2183, Addis Ababa Ethiopia. **Tel** 447470. **LC** DT378.2; D55. **DD** 963/.005. **Ad Acc.** *Continues* Ethiopia Tourist News, 0376-9062.
**Desc:** General tourist information.

US/0012-3641
**DISCOVERY (SKOKIE, ILL.).** (DISCOVERY; THE ALLSTATE MOTOR CLUB MAGAZINE.). [Discovery]. **Added/Corp** Allstate Motor Club. Allstate Enterprises, inc. Vol. 1 (Summer 1961)-. Periodical. English. qt. $8.00 (one year), $15.50 (two year), $23.00 (three year). Allstate Motor Club, 1500 West Shure Drive, Arlington Heights IL 60004. **Tel** (708)632-8701. **ED** Claire McCrea. **LC** GV1024; .D6. **DD** 917. **Ad Acc. Circ:** 1,600,000 (ctrl). available on microfilm and microfiche from University Microfilms International (UMI). Documents available from UMI Article Clearinghouse.
**Desc:** Covers American travel; features vacation plans and geographic areas of interest.
**Ind/Abst** Newsp. Period. Abstr. (1988-).

US/0095-7178
**DISNEY NEWS.** *Title Change.* See Recreation, Leisure.

FR
**DOCUMENTATION TOURISTIQUE.** No. 1 (May 1969)-. Periodical. French. qt. 400.00F. Centre des Hautes Etudes Touristiques, Immeuble Euroff, 38 Avenue Europe, 13090 Aix-en-Provence France. **Tel** 011 33 42 200973. **ED** Baretje Rene. **Bk Rev. Circ:** 250.
**Desc:** International and pluridisciplinary approach of tourism, leisure and outdoor recreation. Analytical bibliography.

US
**DOLLAR WISE GUIDE TO ENGLAND.** (19??)-. English. Arthur Frommer / Pasmantier Publishers, 1230 Avenue of the Americas, New York NY 10020. **Tel** (212)373-8500.

US
**DOLLAR WISE GUIDE TO ENGLAND AND SCOTLAND / BY STANLEY HAGGART AND DARWIN PORTER.** (1979/80)-. Periodical. English. Arthur Frommer / Pasmantier Publishers, 1230 Avenue of the Americas, New York NY 10020. **Tel** (212)373-8500.

AT
**DOMESTIC TRAVEL IN VICTORIA.** **Added/Corp** Victorian Government Tourist Authority. (19??)-. English. an. 40.00Aus$. Victorian Tourism Commission, PO Box 279, World Trade Centre, Melbourne Victoria 3005 Australia. **Tel** (03)6199444, (03)6146226, telex AA38026. **LC** G155.A75; D65. **DD** 381/.45919450463. **Circ:** 150.
**Desc:** This report documents the domestic travel market to within Victoria over the three year period 1984/85-1986/87.

AT
**DOMESTIC TRAVEL IN WESTERN AUSTRALIA.** **Added/Corp** Western Australia. Western Australian Dept. of Tourism. Western Australian Tourism Commission. (19??)-. English. Western Australian Tourism Commission, 16 St George's Terrace, GPO Box X2261, Perth Western Australia 6001 Australia. **Tel** 011 09 220 1700, FAX 011 09 220 1702. **LC** G155.A75; D654. **DD** 381/.45919410463/021.

IT/1121-1792
**DOVE MILANO.** [Dove Milano]. (1991)-. Periodical. Italian. mo. $130.00. RCS Rizzoli Periodici, Via A Rizzoli 2, 20132 Milan Italy. **Tel** 011 39 2 27200720. **UDC** 379.85.

US/0012-5776
**DOWN EAST.** [Down East]. (Aug. 1954)-. Periodical. English. mo. $19.95 (one year), $35.00 (two year) US; $29.95 (one year), $55.00 (two year) other. Down East Enterprise Inc., PO Box 1357, Camden ME 04843. **Tel** (207)594-9544, FAX (207)594-5144. (Subscription address: CDS / SIFD Agency Control, 1901 Bell Avenue, Des Moines IA 50315.) **ED** Dale Kuhnert. **LC** F16; .D6. **DD** 974.1/005; 917.41. **Bk Rev. Ad Acc. Circ:** 65,000.
**Desc:** Covers Maine, its people, land and events.
**Ind/Abst** Access (1975-); Am. Hist. Life.

US/0273-9186
**DOWN HOME (BIRMINGHAM).** (DOWN HOME.). (19??)-. Periodical. English. qt. $7.50. Down Home / Birmingham, PO Box 1851, Birmingham AL 35201. **Tel** (205)322-2685.

US/0739-4780
**EASTERN TRAVEL SALES GUIDE.** Vol. 1, No. 1 (Spring/Summer 1983 Ed.)-. English. an. $40.00. Preferred Travel Publications, 47 Northam Avenue, Newbury Park CA 91320. **Tel** 800 847-3442 or, (805)498-8307. **ED** Julie A Jackson. **LC** G154; .E24. **DD** 380.1/45917304927/025. **Bk Rev. Ad Acc. Circ:** 2,000 (ctrl).
**Desc:** Geographical listings of retail travel agencies,

# Travel and Tourism

wholesale tour operators, airlines, cruise lines, car/motorhome rentals, state tourist offices and government tourist offices and other travel related companies.

CN/0228-667X
**ECHO DES VOYAGES, L'.** [Echo voyages]. No. 060 i.e. No. 1 (Feb. 4, 1980)-. Periodical. French. wk. $10.00. l'Echo des Voyages, CP 97 Snowdon, Montreal Quebec H3X 3T3 Canada. **DD** 910/.5.

US
**ECO TRAVELER.** (19??)-. English. Six times a year. $24.00. Skies America, 7730 Southwest Mohawk Street, Tualatin OR 97062. **Tel** (503)691-1955. **(Subscription address:** Eco Traveler, PO Box 469003, Escondido CA 92046.) **Continues** Just Go!.

US/0733-642X
**ECONOMIC REVIEW OF TRAVEL IN AMERICA, THE.** [Econ. Rev. Travel Am.]. **Added/Corp** United States Travel Data Center. (19??)-. English. Twice a year (Summer/Fall). $70.00. US Travel Data Center, 1100 New York Avenue, Suite 450, Washington DC 20005. **Tel** (202)408-1832. **LC** G155.U6; E32. **DD** 380.1/4591730492. **Circ:** 300 (ctrl).
**Desc:** This annual review is designed as a basic reference for consumer and industry travel trends, regional travel patterns, travel price inflation, travel and energy supply, and travel and employment. Use this report to prepare convincing presentations and analysis for government officials, legislators, and the public on the economic significance of tourism. It includes an executive summary, charts, tables, maps and extensive historic data.
**Ind/Abst** Stat. Ref. Index.

FR/0753-311X
**ECONOMIE DU TOURISME, L'.** French. qt. Free. Documentation Francaise, 29 Quai Voltaire, 75344 Paris Cedex 7 France. **Tel** 011 33 1 40157000, **FAX** 011 33 1 40157230, telex 204 826 DOCFRAN. **LC** G155.F8; E25. **DD** 380.1/45914404838.
**Desc:** Contains statistics and short comments on travel and tourism.

CN
**ECOTREKS.** Vol. 1, No. 1 (Oct. 1993)-. English. Six times a year. $25.00. Ecotreks, 38 Birch Hill Lane, Oakville, ONT L6K 2N9 Canada. **Tel** (905)845-4482, FAX (905)842-6458.
**Desc:** Newsletter of an adventure travel company specializing in exploring " the beaten track" by arranging mountain biking, scuba diving, sail/dive and surfing treks for small groups of people.

US/1052-0597
**EDUCATED TRAVELER, THE.** [Educ. travel.]. Vol. 1, No. 1 (Nov. 1990)-. Periodical. English. bm $45.00 (one year); $90.00 (two year). Educated Traveler, PO Box 220822, Chantilly VA 22022. **Tel** (703)471-1063, FAX (703)471-4807. **ED** Ann Waigand. **DD** 910. Index available (publish separately): $30). **Ad Acc. Circ:** 1500.
**Desc:** Newsletter focusing on international travel. It includes learning vacations, specialty classes and specialized tour guides.

US
**ELLIS ISLAND GUIDE.** (19??)-. Periodical. English. $9.45. Israelowitz Publishing, Box 228, Brooklyn NY 11229. **Tel** (718)951-7072, FAX (718)951-7072. **ED** Oscar Israelowitz.

US/0279-4853
**ENDLESS VACATION - RESORT CONDOMINIUMS INTERNATIONAL, THE.** (THE ENDLESS VACATION.). [Endless vacat. - Resort Condom. Int.]. **Added/Corp** Resort Condominiums International. (19??)-. Periodical. English. Ten times a year. $65.00. Endless Vacation Publications Inc., Robert Ancell, PO Box 80260, Indianapolis IN 46280-0260. **Tel** (317)871-9500 (800)338-7777. **ED** Helen A. Wernle. **LC** TX907; .E53. **DD** 910/.2/02. **Ad Acc. Circ:** 500,000. **Absorbed** Resort Condominiums International. Annual Directory Edition, 0276-9085; Endless Vacation (Vacation Horizons International), 0883-8852.
**Desc:** An upscale magazine for international travelers. Articles feature destinations around the globe. Columns offer sound, practical advice to vacationers.

CN/0703-0312
**ENROUTE.** See General Interest-General Interest-North America.

●CN/1189-4911
**ENTDECKEN SIE BRITISCH KOLUMBIEN, KANADA.** [Entdeck. Br. Kolumb. Kan.]. **VFOAT** Discover British Columbia, Canada. (1992)-. Periodical. English. Limited free distribution. Key Pacific Publishers, 3rd Floor, 1001 Wharf Street, Victoria, British Columbia V8W 1T6 Canada. **DD** 917.1104/05.

US/0745-6182
**ESCAPE (SALT LAKE CITY, UTAH).** (ESCAPE.). Vol. 2, No. 1 (Spring 1983)-. Periodical. English. qt. $8.00. Sunsets Unlimited Travel Club, PO Box 15100, Salt Lake City UT 84115.

FR/0336-1446
**ESPACES PARIS. 1970.** (ESPACES.). **VFOAT** Espaces, Tourisme, Loisirs, Environnement. (1970)-. Periodical. French. bm. 734.57F France; 780.00F other. Edns Touristiques Europeennes, 8 rue Cels, 75014 Paris France. **Tel** 011 33 1 43275590. **UDC** 379.8.
**Ind/Abst** Leis. Recreat. Tour. Abstr.

FR
**ESPANA, PORTUGAL. Main/Corp** Pneu Michelin (Firm). (1973)-. English (French, German, Italian, Portuguese and Spanish). an. $26.55. Manufacture Francaise des Pneumatiques Michelin, 46 avenue de Breteuil, 75431 Paris Cedex 07 France. **(Subscription address:** Michelin Travel Publications, PO Box 19008, Greenville SC 29602.) **LC** DP14; .M27a. **DD** 914.6/04/83.

SP/0423-5037
**ESTUDIOS TURISTICOS.** [Estud. tur.]. (1963)-. Periodical. Multiple languages. Four times a year. $40.00. Turespana, Almagro 36 3RO, 28010 Madrid Spain. **Tel** 011 34 1 3082349 or 3082108. **UDC** 380.8.
**Ind/Abst** Leis. Recreat. Tour. Abstr.

FR
**ETATS-UNIS. VFOAT** Etats Unis. 1989-. French. an. 56.00F. Guide du Routard, 5 rue de l'Arrivee, 92190 Meudon France. **LC** E158; .E885. **DD** 917.3/04927. **Continues in part** Etata-Unis, Canada.

FR/0078-9585
**ETUDES ET MEMOIRES. Main/Corp** Paris. Ecole Pratique des Hautes-Etudes. Centre d'Etudes Economiques. (1952)-. Monographic series. French. ir. Price varies per volume. Centre des Hautes Etudes Touristiques, Immeuble Euroff, 38 Avenue Europe, 13090 Aix-en-Provence France. **Tel** 011 33 42 200973. **ED** R. Baretje. **Bk Rev. Circ:** 300.
**Desc:** Tourism and outdoor recreation, multidisciplinary approach.

US/0085-0330
**EURAIL GUIDE.** See Transportation-Railroads.

US
**EUROPEAN GOURMET: THE GRAND DINING TOUR OF EUROPE, THE.** See Food and Food Industry.

US/0882-7737
**EUROPEAN TRAVEL & LIFE. Title Change.** [Eur. travel life]. **VFOAT** European Travel and Life. Vol. 1, No. 1 (May/June 1985)-Vol. 8, No. 4 (May 1992). Periodical. English. mo (except February and August). Murdoch Magazines, 200 Madison Avenue, 8th Floor, New York NY 10016. **Tel** (212)447-4700, (212)447-4732. **LC** D923; .E974. **DD** 940.55/05. available on microfilm and microfiche from University Microfilms International (UMI). **Absorbed by** Conde Nast's Traveler, 0893-9683.
**Desc:** This magazine offers the sense of elegance, style, glamour and romance that epitomizes Europe today with a wealth of uncommon knowledge of exciting places, personalities, and up-to-the moment information on cultural and political events.

CN/0381-8349
**EVASION.** [Evasion]. (1975)-. Periodical. French. mo. $1.25 le no; $10. par an,ee. $18. pour 2 ans. $24. pour 3 ans. **DD** 910/.5.
**Ind/Abst** Point Repere (1981).

UK/0956-0122
**EX LONDON.** See Aeronautics, Astronautics.

US/0890-9911
**EXCHANGE BOOK (YOUNGSTOWN, ARIZ.).** (EXCHANGE BOOK.). Periodical. English. sa. $16.00. Vacation Exchange Club, 12006 111th Avenue, Youngtown AZ 85363. **DD** 910.

CN/1187-3183
**EXCLUSIVE (OTTAWA).** (EXCLUSIVE.). [Exclusive]. **Added/Corp** Canadian Tourism Research Institute. Conference Board of Canada. (Feb. 1991)-. Periodical. English. mo. Free to members of the Institute. Canadian Tourism Research Institute, c/o Conference Board of Canada, 255 Smyth Road, Ottawa Ontario K1H 8M7 Canada. **DD** 388.4.

US/1055-4858
**EXECUTIVE FLIGHT PLANNER. AMERICAS. Ceased.** [Exec. flight plan., Am.]. **VFOAT** Americas. (19??)-(June 1994). Periodical. English. mo. Reed Travel Group / New Jersey, 500 Plaza Drive, Secaucus NJ 07096. **Tel** (201)902-2000, (800)360-0015, FAX (201)319-1628. **DD** 910. **Continues** ABC International's Executive Flight Planner.

US/0097-806X
**EXPLORATION (NORMAL, ILL.).** See Literature.

US/0884-1802
**EXXON TRAVEL CLUB TRAVEL GUIDE. CANADA.** [Exxon Travel Club travel guide, Can.]. **VFOAT** Canada; Canada Travel Guide. English. an. $5.95. Simon & Schuster, 1230 Avenue of the Americas, New York NY 10020. **Tel** (212)698-7000. **LC** F1009; .T72A. **DD** 917.14/04647. **Continues** Exxon Travel Club Canada Vacation Travel Guide, 0272-8311.

US/0743-6467
**EXXON TRAVEL CLUB TRAVEL GUIDE. CENTRAL USA. VFOAT** Central USA; Central U.S.A. 17th Ed. (1983)-. English. an. Simon & Schuster, 1230 Avenue of the Americas, New York NY 10020. **Tel** (212)698-7000. **LC** F787; .E95. **DD** 917.7. **Continues** Exxon Travel Club Central U.S.A. Vacation Travel Guide.

US/0429-9639
**FABULOUS MEXICO - WHERE EVERYTHING COSTS LESS.** (1960)-. English. Harian Publications, 1 Vernon Avenue, Floral Park NY 11001. **Tel** (516)352-9700. **DD** 917.2.

●US
**FAIRCHILD'S TRAVEL INDUSTRY PERSONNEL DIRECTORY. Added/Corp** Fairchild Publications. **VFOAT** Travel Industry Personnel Directory; Travel Directory; A.Personnel directory. (1993)-. English. an. $34.95. Fairchild Publications Inc, 7 West 34th Street, 4th Floor, New York NY 10001. **Tel** (212)630-4230. **ED** Marsheela Evans. **LC** G155.A1; T655. **DD** 910.58. **Ad Acc. Circ:** 9,000. **Continues** Travel Industry Personnel Directory, 0082-6146.
**Desc:** Complete lists of sales and executive personnel of domestic and regional airlines, shiplines, railroads, motorcoach and car rental companies and tour operators. Also includes U.S. and Canadian hotel representatives and names of domestic and international hotels that they handle.

US
**FAR EAST TRAVEL DIGEST.** (1976)-. English. an. $9.00. Travel Digest, 73 - 465 Ironwood Street, Palm Desert CA 92260. **Tel** (619)346-4792. **LC** DS504; .F36. **DD** 915/.04.

JA
**FAR EAST TRAVELLER.** English. ir. Price varies. **(Subscription address:** Japan Publications Trading Company, Ltd., PO Box 5030, Tokyo International, Tokyo 100-31 Japan.)

US/0195-8437
**FARM, RANCH & COUNTRY VACATIONS. VAT** Farm, Ranch and Country Vacations. (1979)-. English. be. $12.00. Adventure Guides, Inc., PO Box 698, Newfoundland NJ 07435. **LC** TX907; .F38a. **DD** 647/.9473. **Continues** Country Vacations U.S.A., 0147-3867.
**Desc:** A guide to hospitality of rural America.

US/0278-0941
**FEDERAL TRAVEL DIRECTORY (WASHINGTON, D.C. : 1981). Ceased.** (FEDERAL TRAVEL DIRECTORY.). **Added/Corp** United States. General Services Administration. Transportation and Public Utilities Service. United States. General Services Administration. United States. Military Traffic Management Command. Issue No. 6 (Oct. 1981)-(Jan. 1995). Directory. English. mo. Superintendent of Documents, US Government Printing Office, Washington DC 20402. **Tel** (202)275-3328, FAX (202)786-2377. **LC** Discard. **Continues** Federal Contract Air Service and Travel Directory, 0279-6010; **Absorbed** Federal Hotel/Motel Discount Directory, 0747-6442.
**Desc:** Contains schedules, fares, and telephone reservation numbers of airlines providing reduced rates for Federal employees traveling on official business. Also contains guidelines for using AMTRAK. Lists American lodging accommodations by State and city and foreign by country and city. Information should be verified when making specific reservations.

HK
**FENG KUANG HUA PAO. VFOAT** Scenery Pictorial. First published in Nov. 1975-. Periodical. Chinese. $3.00 single issue. Scenery Publishers, Room 408/10 Queen's Road C, Hong Kong Hong Kong. **LC** G149; .F44.

●US/1065-2701
**FESTIVAL MANAGEMENT & EVENT TOURISM. VFOAT** Festival Management and Event Tourism. (1993)-. Periodical. English. qt. $75.00 (institutions). Cognizant Communication Corporation, 3 Hartsdale Road, Elmsford NY 10523. **Tel** (914)592-7720. **[CCC]**.

●US/1064-0932
**FIELDING'S ALPINE EUROPE.** [Fielding's Alp. Eur.]. **VFOAT** Alpine Europe. (1992)-. English. $15.00. Fielding Worldwide, 308 South Catalina Avenue, Redondo Beach CA 90277. **Tel** (800)843-9389, (310)372-4474, FAX (212)261-6549. **LC** D909; .F445. **DD** 914.

●US/1061-4842
**FIELDING'S AUSTRALIA.** [Fielding's Aust.]. **VFOAT** Australia. 1st ed. (1992)-. English. Fielding Worldwide, 308 South Catalina Avenue, Redondo Beach CA 90277. **Tel** (800)843-9389, (310)372-4474, FAX (212)261-6549. **LC** DU95; .F53. **DD** 919.404/63.

●US/1064-0924
**FIELDING'S BENELUX.** [Fielding's Benelux]. **VFOAT** Benelux. (1992)-. English. Fielding Worldwide, 308 South Catalina Avenue, Redondo Beach CA 90277. **Tel** (800)843-9389, (310)372-4474, FAX (212)261-6549. **LC** DH16; .F54. **DD** 914.

US/0739-0769
**FIELDING'S BERMUDA AND THE BAHAMAS.** **VFOAT** Bermuda and the Bahamas. (1984)-. English. an. $16.95. Fielding Worldwide, 308 South Catalina Avenue, Redondo Beach CA 90277. **Tel** (800)843-9389, (310)372-4474, FAX (212)261-6549. **LC** F1632; .F53. **DD** 917.299/0452.

●US/1064-0940
**FIELDING'S BRITAIN.** [Fielding's Br.]. **VFOAT** Britain. (1992)-. English. $15.00. Fielding Worldwide, 308 South Catalina Avenue, Redondo Beach CA 90277. **Tel** (800)843-9389, (310)372-4474, FAX (212)261-6549. **DD** 914.

US/0736-2358
**FIELDING'S CARIBBEAN.** [Fielding's Caribb.]. (1981). English. an. $16.50. William Morrow & Company Inc, 1350 Avenue of the Americas, New York NY 10019. **ED** Randy Ladenheim-Gil. **LC** F1609; .F54. **DD** 917.29/0452. ***Continues*** *Fielding's Caribbean, Including Cuba, 0196-0105.*

US/0192-5326
**FIELDING'S EUROPE.** [Fielding's Eur.]. 32nd Ed. (1979)-. English. an. $15.00. Fielding Worldwide, 308 South Catalina Avenue, Redondo Beach CA 90277. **Tel** (800)843-9389, (310)372-4474, FAX (212)261-6549. **ED** Randy Ladenheim Gil. **LC** D909; .F45. **DD** 914/.0455. ***Continues*** *Fielding's Travel Guide to Europe, 0071-4801.*

US/0739-0777
**FIELDING'S FAR EAST.** [Fielding's Far East]. **VFOAT** Far East. 1984-. English. an. $14.95. William Morrow & Company Inc, 1350 Avenue of the Americas, New York NY 10019. **LC** DS504; .F53. **DD** 915/.0428.

US/1061-3366
**FIELDING'S HAWAII.** [Fielding's Hawaii]. **VFOAT** Hawaii. 1st Ed. (1991)-. English. ir. Fielding Worldwide, 308 South Catalina Avenue, Redondo Beach CA 90277. **Tel** (800)843-9389, (310)372-4474, FAX (212)261-6549. **LC** DU622; .F53. **DD** 919.6904/4.

US
**FIELDING'S ITALY.** **VFOAT** Italy. (1991)-. English. Fielding Worldwide, 308 South Catalina Avenue, Redondo Beach CA 90277. **Tel** (800)843-9389, (310)372-4474, FAX (212)261-6549. **LC** DG416; .F53. **DD** 914.504/929.

US/0739-0793
**FIELDING'S MEXICO.** (FIELDING'S MEXICO / LYNN V. FOSTER AND LAWRENCE FOSTER.). [Fielding's Mex.]. **VFOAT** Mexico. (19??)-. English. an. $16.95. Fielding Worldwide, 308 South Catalina Avenue, Redondo Beach CA 90277. **Tel** (800)843-9389, (310)372-4474, FAX (212)261-6549. **LC** F1209; .F527. **DD** 917.2/04834.

●US/1061-4834
**FIELDING'S SCANDINAVIA.** [Fielding's Scand.]. **VFOAT** Scandinavia. 1st ed. (1992)-. English. Fielding Worldwide, 308 South Catalina Avenue, Redondo Beach CA 90277. **Tel** (800)843-9389, (310)372-4474, FAX (212)261-6549. **LC** DL4; .F45. **DD** 914.804/88.

●US/1064-0991
**FIELDING'S SPAIN AND PORTUGAL.** [Fielding's Spain Port.]. **VFOAT** Spain and Portugal; Spain & Portugal; Fielding's Spain & Portugal. (1992)-. English. $17.00. Fielding Worldwide, 308 South Catalina Avenue, Redondo Beach CA 90277. **Tel** (800)843-9389, (310)372-4474, FAX (212)261-6549. **DD** 914.

FI/0355-5100
**FINLAND HANDBOOK.** [Finl. handb.]. English (German). an. Fmk98.00. Finnish Tourist Board, PO Box 53, SF 00521 Helsinki Finland. **Tel** 90-748 841, FAX 148 88 333, telex 12 26 90 MEK SF. **ED** Anja Riste and Tellervo Ahti. **LC** DK450.2; .F474. **DD** 914.71/04/3. Index available. **Circ:** 14,500.
**Desc:** Sales guide and reference book to travel covering all relevant information about travel to and within Finland.

US/0192-2289
**FIRSTCLASS (IRVING, TEX.).** (FIRSTCLASS.). [Firstclass]. **Added/Corp** Airline Passengers Association. **VAT** First Class. (19??)-. Periodical. English. bm (6 issues). Comes with membership to International Airline Passengers Association. International Airline Passengers Association, PO Box 660074, Dallas Service Center, Dallas TX 75266. **Tel** (214)520-1070. **LC** G149; .F56. **DD** 910.4/05.

US/0740-7653
**FLASHMAPS INSTANT GUIDE TO BOSTON.** Vol. 1-. English. an. Flashmaps Publications Inc, PO Box 13, Chappaqua NY 10514. **LC** F73.18. **DD** 917.44/6104/05.

US
**FLATBUSH GUIDE, THE.** (19??)-. Periodical. English. $6.45. Israelowitz Publishing, Box 228, Brooklyn NY 11229. **Tel** (718)951-7072, FAX (718)951-7072. **ED** Oscar Israelowitz. Index available. cum. index. **Bk Rev. Ad Acc.** ctrl circ.
**Desc:** Travel guide to an old Dutch settlement.

US/0194-9039
**FLIGHT REPORTS.** ***Ceased.*** **See** Aeronautics, Astronautics.

US/0516-9674
**FLORIDA TOUR BOOK.** **VFOAT** Tour Book, Florida. Fall 1965-. English. American Automobile Association, 1000 AAA Drive, Heathrow FL 32746. **Tel** (407)444-7000. **LC** GV1024; .F56. **DD** 917.59/04/6.
**Desc:** Vols. for 1967-69 include the Gulf Coast and New Orleans.

US/0743-0744
**FLORIDA TOURISM HOTLINE.** Periodical. English. mo. $125.00 US; $200.00 other. Florida Business Reports, 27501 South Federal Highway/Suite 209, Naranja FL 33032. **Tel** (305)247-4542. **ED** Blair Kelly. available on diskette (5 1/4 (IBM compatible computers)). ***Continues*** *Florida Letter on Tourism.*
**Desc:** Statistical trends, developments and opportunities in the sunshine state.

US/0889-0099
**FLORIDA TOURISM INDUSTRY REPORT.** ***Suspended.*** [Fla. tour. ind. rep.]. **VFOAT** Tourism Industry Report. Suspended with Vol. 10, No. 24, Aug. 17 (1992). Periodical. English. Eighteen times a year. $125.00. Southeastern Editorial Services Inc, PO Box 372390, Satellite Beach FL 32937. **Tel** (407)779-9815. **ED** Gary L Smith. **DD** 910. **Bk Rev. Circ:** 650.
**Desc:** An executive newsletter for travel industry professionals and those interested in new research, developments and topical issues related to tourism, especially in Florida.

US/0895-6154
**FLYFAIRE VACATIONS.** [Flyfaire Vacat.]. Periodical. English. sa. $5.95. Diamandis Communications Inc, 1499 Monrovia Avenue, New Port Beach CA 92663. **Tel** (714)720-5300. **DD** 910.

UK/0015-5160
**FOCUS ON JAMAICA.** **Added/Corp** Jamaica in Bond Merchants Association. Periodical. English. sa. Publishing & Distributing Company Ltd, Mitre House/177 Regent Street, London W1 England. **ED** Kenneth Jones.

PK/0046-4325
**FOCUS ON PAKISTAN.** V. 1- Feb 1971-. Periodical. English. qt. Pakistan Tourism Development Corporation, Hotel Metropole Club Road, Karachi 4 Pakistan. **DD** 915.49/005.

US
**FODOR'S ... ACAPULCO.** ***Title Change.*** **VFOAT** Acapulco. (1989)-(199?). English. ir. Random House Inc., 400 Hahn Road, Westminster MD 21157. **Tel** (800)726-0600, (800)733-3000, FAX (800)659-2436. **LC** F1391.A15; G66. **DD** 917.2/73. Each issue contains an index to its own contents (no volume index)--loose. ***Continues*** *Fodor's Fun in Acapulco.* ***Continued by*** *Fodor's Acapulco, Ixtapa, Zihuatanejo, 1070-8642.*

●US/1070-8642
**FODOR'S ACAPULCO, IXTAPA, ZIHUATANEJO.** [Fodor's Acapulco Ixtapa Zihuatanejo]. **VFOAT** Acapulco, Ixtapa, Zihuatanejo; Acapulco; Fodor's Acapulco. 5th Ed. (1992)-. English. ir. $10.00. Random House Inc., 400 Hahn Road, Westminster MD 21157. **Tel** (800)726-0600, (800)733-3000, FAX (800)659-2436. **LC** F1391.A15; G66. **DD** 917.2/73. Each issue contains an index to its own contents (no volume index)--loose. ***Continues*** *Fodor's ... Acapulco.*

●US/1068-3593
**FODOR'S ... AFFORDABLE FRANCE.** [Fodor's afford. Fr.]. **VFOAT** Affordable France. (1992)-. English. ir. $16.00; 21.00Can$ Canada. Random House Inc., 400 Hahn Road, Westminster MD 21157. **Tel** (800)726-0600, (800)733-3000, FAX (800)659-2436. **LC** DC16; .F59. **DD** 914.404/839.

US/0271-2776
**FODOR'S ALASKA.** **VFOAT** Alaska. (1980)-. English. an. $16.90. Random House Inc., 400 Hahn Road, Westminster MD 21157. **Tel** (800)726-0600, (800)733-3000, FAX (800)659-2436. **LC** F902.3; .F63. **DD** 917.98/045.
**Desc:** Features Alaskan people, history, climate, fishing and hunting, and touring in Alaska.

US/0883-6043
**FODOR'S AMSTERDAM.** [Fodor's Amst.]. (1984)-. English. ir. $10.90. Random House Inc., 400 Hahn Road, Westminster MD 21157. **Tel** (800)726-0600, (800)733-3000, FAX (800)659-2436. **LC** DJ411.A53; F58. **DD** 914.9/23.

US
**FODOR'S ARIZONA.** **VFOAT** Arizona. (1985)-. English. ir. $15.90. Random House Inc., 400 Hahn Road, Westminster MD 21157. **Tel** (800)726-0600, (800)733-3000, FAX (800)659-2436. **LC** F809.3; .F64. **DD** 917.91/0453.

US
**FODOR'S ... AUSTRALIA.** **VFOAT** Fodor's Australia, with Adventure Vacations in the Outback and the Great Barrier Reef; Australia. (1991)-. English. ir. $20.90. Random House Inc., 400 Hahn Road, Westminster MD 21157. **Tel** (800)726-0600, (800)733-3000, FAX (800)659-2436. **LC** DU95; .F682.

●US
**FODOR'S ... AUSTRALIA & NEW ZEALAND.** **VFOAT** Fodor's ... Australia and New Zealand; Australia & New Zealand; Australia and New Zealand. (1993)-. English. ir. $20.90. Random House Inc., 400 Hahn Road, Westminster MD 21157. **Tel** (800)726-0600, (800)733-3000, FAX (800)659-2436. **LC** DU95; .F63. **DD** 919. ***Continues*** *Fodor's Australia, New Zealand and the South Pacific, 0191-2321.*

US/0191-2321
**FODOR'S AUSTRALIA, NEW ZEALAND AND THE SOUTH PACIFIC.** ***Title Change.*** **VFOAT** Fodor's ... Australia, New Zealand, the South Pacific; Australia, New Zealand, the South Pacific; Australia, New Zealand and the South Pacific. (1978)-(199?). English. Random House Inc., 400 Hahn Road, Westminster MD 21157. **Tel** (800)726-0600, (800)733-3000, FAX (800)659-2436. **LC** DU95; .F63. **DD** 919. ***Continued by*** *Fodor's Australia & New Zealand.*
**Desc:** Contains an introduction to Australia: the land, history, politics, people, and art.

US/0071-6340
**FODOR'S AUSTRIA.** **VFOAT** Austria. (1969)-. English. ir. $19.90. Random House Inc., 400 Hahn Road, Westminster MD 21157. **Tel** (800)726-0600, (800)733-3000, FAX (800)659-2436. **LC** DB16; .A8. **DD** 914.36/04/5. ***Continues*** *Austria, 0567-1248.*

US
**FODOR'S BAHAMAS.** **Added/Corp** Fodor's Travel Guides (Firm). **VFOAT** Bahamas. (1986)-. English. ir. $14.90. Random House Inc., 400 Hahn Road, Westminster MD 21157. **Tel** (800)726-0600, (800)733-3000, FAX (800)659-2436. **LC** F1613; .F6. **DD** 917.296/04/05. ***Continues in part*** *Fodor's Caribbean and the Bahamas, 0271-4760.*

US/1050-737X
**FODOR'S BAJA & THE PACIFIC COAST RESORTS.** [Fodor's Baja Pac. Coast resorts]. **VFOAT** Baja & the Pacific Coast Resorts; Fodor's Baja and the Pacific Coast Resorts; Baja and the Pacific Coast Resorts; Fodor's Baja & the Pacific Coast Resorts, Puerto Vallarta, Mazatlan, Manzanillo; Fodor's Baja. (1990)-. English. ir. $13.90. Random House Inc., 400 Hahn Road, Westminster MD 21157. **Tel** (800)726-0600, (800)733-3000, FAX (800)659-2436. **LC** F1246; .F63. **DD** 917.2/204834/05. ***Continues*** *Fodor's Mexico's Baja, Puerto Vallarta, Mazatlan, Manzanillo, Copper Canyon.*

US/1050-9771
**FODOR'S ... BARBADOS.** [Fodor's Barbados]. **VFOAT** Barbados. 2nd ed., (1989)-. English. ir. Random House Inc., 400 Hahn Road, Westminster MD 21157. **Tel** (800)726-0600, (800)733-3000, FAX (800)659-2436. **LC** F2041; .F69. **DD** 917.298104. ***Continues*** *Fodor's Fun in Barbados.*

US
**FODOR'S BEIJING, GUANGZHOU, SHANGHAI.** **VFOAT** Beijing, Guangzhou, Shanghai; Fodor's ... Beijing, Guangzhou, Shanghai. (198?)-. English. ir. $12.85. Random House Inc., 400 Hahn Road, Westminster MD 21157. **Tel** (800)726-0600, (800)733-3000, FAX (800)659-2436. ***Continues*** *Fodor's Beijing (Peking), Guangzhou (Canton), and Shanghai.*

US
**FODOR'S BELGIUM AND LUXEMBOURG.** ***Title Change.*** **VFOAT** Belgium and Luxembourg. (1969)-(1993). English. Random House Inc., 400 Hahn Road, Westminster MD 21157. **Tel** (800)726-0600, (800)733-3000, FAX (800)659-2436. **DD** 914.93/04/4. ***Continues*** *Belgium and Luxembourg.* ***Merged with*** *Fodor's Holland, 0071-643X* ***to form*** *Fodor's The Netherlands, Belgium, Luxembourg, 1070-4590.*

●US/1065-4593
**FODOR'S ... BERLIN.** [Fodor's Berl.]. **VFOAT** Berlin; Fodor's ... Berlin, with Excursions to Dresden, Leipzig, and Potsdam. 1st Ed. (1992)-. English. ir. $14.90. Random House Inc., 400 Hahn Road, Westminster MD 21157. **Tel** (800)726-0600, (800)733-3000, FAX (800)659-2436. **LC** DD859; .F64. **DD** 914.3/1550487.

US/0192-3765
**FODOR'S BERMUDA.** **VFOAT** Bermuda. (19??)-. English. ir. $14.90. Random House Inc., 400 Hahn Road, Westminster MD 21157. **Tel** (800)726-0600, (800)733-3000, FAX (800)659-2436. **LC** F1632; .F6. **DD** 917.29/9/045. ***Supersedes in part*** *Fodor's Caribbean, Bahamas and Bermuda, 0098-2547.*
**Desc:** Features Bermuda past and present, exploring, sports, hotels, guest houses and cottages, dining and entertainment.

US/0882-0074
**FODOR'S BOSTON.** [Fodor's Boston]. (1984)-. English. ir. $14.90. Random House Inc., 400 Hahn Road, Westminster MD 21157. **Tel** (800)726-0600, (800)733-3000, FAX (800)659-2436. **LC** F73.18; .F63. **DD** 917.44/610443.
**Desc:** Essays on history, literature, architecture, food, and sightseeing.

US/0163-0628
**FODOR'S BRAZIL.** **VFOAT** Brazil. (19??)-. English. ir. $13.90. Random House Inc., 400 Hahn Road, Westminster MD 21157. **Tel** (800)726-0600, (800)733-3000, FAX (800)659-2436. **LC** F2509.5; .F62. **DD** 918.1/04/6.

●US/1065-4607
**FODOR'S BUDAPEST.** [Fodor's Bp.]. **VFOAT** Budapest; Fodor's Budapest, With Trips to the Lake Resorts and Medieval Towns Along the Danube. 1st Ed. (1992)-. English. ir. $13.90. Random House Inc., 400 Hahn Road, Westminster MD 21157. **Tel** (800)726-0600, (800)733-3000, FAX (800)659-2436. **LC** DB983.5; .F64. **DD** 914.39/120453.

US/0197-4998
**FODOR'S BUDGET EUROPE.** [Fodor's budg. Eur.]. **VFOAT** Budget Europe. (1980)-. English. ir. $19.90. Random House Inc., 400 Hahn Road, Westminster MD 21157. **Tel** (800)726-0600, (800)733-3000, FAX (800)659-2436. **LC** D909; .F632. **DD** 914/.04558. ***Continues*** *Fodor's Europe on a Budget, 0276-0738.*
**Desc:** Features trip planning, how much it will cost, tourist office information, and other traveling information.

US/0192-9925
**FODOR'S CALIFORNIA.** **VFOAT** California. (19??)-. English. ir. $18.90. Random House Inc., 400 Hahn Road, Westminster MD 21157. **Tel** (800)726-0600, (800)733-3000, FAX (800)659-2436. **LC** F859.3; .F63. **DD** 917.94/04/5.
**Desc:** Features tours of California, plus information on hotels, restaurants, resorts, museums, arts, parks, historic sites, shopping, nightlife, etc.

US/0160-3906
**FODOR'S CANADA.** [Fodor's Can.]. **VFOAT** Canada. (1978)-. English. ir. $20.90. Random House Inc., 400 Hahn Road, Westminster MD 21157. **Tel** (800)726-0600, (800)733-3000, FAX (800)659-2436. **LC** F1009; .F6. **DD** 917.1/04/644.

US/1051-6336
**FODOR'S ... CANCUN, COZUMEL, YUCATAN PENINSULA.** **Added/Corp** Fodor's Travel Publications, Inc. **VFOAT** Cancun, Cozumel, Yucatan Peninsula. (1990)-. English. an. $14.90. Random House Inc., 400 Hahn Road, Westminster MD 21157. **Tel** (800)726-0600, (800)733-3000, FAX (800)659-2436. **LC** F1376; .F63. **DD** 917.2/604834. ***Continues*** *Fodor's Cancun, Cozumel, Merida, and the Yucatan.*

US/1047-6768
**FODOR'S CAPE COD, MARTHA'S VINEYARD, NANTUCKET.** (FODOR'S ... CAPE COD.). [Fodor's Cape Cod]. **Added/Corp** Fodor's Travel Publications, Inc. **VFOAT** Fodor's ... Cape Cod Including Martha's Vineyard and Nantucket. (1989)-. English. an. $14.90. Random House Inc., 400 Hahn Road, Westminster MD 21157. **Tel** (800)726-0600, (800)733-3000, FAX (800)659-2436. **LC** F72.C3; F64. **DD** 917.44/920443. ***Continues*** *Fodor's Cape Cod and the Islands of Martha's Vineyard and Nantucket.*

US
**FODOR'S CARIBBEAN.** **VFOAT** Caribbean. (1986)-. English. ir. $19.90. Random House Inc., 400 Hahn Road, Westminster MD 21157. **Tel** (800)726-0600, (800)733-3000, FAX (800)659-2436. **LC** F1613; .F63. **DD** 917.29/0452. ***Continues in part*** *Fodor's Caribbean and the Bahamas, 0271-4760.*

US/0270-8183
**FODOR'S CENTRAL AMERICA.** [Fodor's Cent. Am.]. **VFOAT** Central America. (1980)-. English. ir. $17.90. Random House Inc., 400 Hahn Road, Westminster MD 21157. **Tel** (800)726-0600, (800)733-3000, FAX (800)659-2436. **LC** F1429; .F6. **DD** 917.28/0452.
**Desc:** A comprehensive guide to a tourists and amateur archaeologists.

US/0743-9326
**FODOR'S CHICAGO.** **VFOAT** Chicago. (1984)-. English. ir. $14.90. Random House Inc., 400 Hahn Road, Westminster MD 21157. **Tel** (800)726-0600, (800)733-3000, FAX (800)659-2436. **LC** F548.18; .F6. **DD** 917.73/110443. ***Continues*** *Fodor's Chicago and the Great Lakes Recreation Areas.*
**Desc:** An introduction to Chicago. Covers restaurants, hotels, entertainment, nightlife, and shopping.

US/1070-6895
**FODOR'S CHINA.** [Fodor's China]. **VFOAT** China. (199?)-. English. ir. $21.90. Random House Inc., 400 Hahn Road, Westminster MD 21157. **Tel** (800)726-0600, (800)733-3000, FAX (800)659-2436. **LC** DS705; .F63. **DD** 915.104/59. ***Continues*** *Fodor's People's Republic of China, 0192-2378.*

US/0195-7317
**FODOR'S CIVIL WAR SITES.** **VFOAT** Civil War Sites. (197?)-. English. an. $12.95. Random House Inc., 400 Hahn Road, Westminster MD 21157. **Tel** (800)726-0600, (800)733-3000, FAX (800)659-2436. **LC** E159; .F62. **DD** 917.3/04926.

US/0276-9018
**FODOR'S COLORADO.** [Fodor's Colo.]. **VFOAT** Colorado. (19??)-. English. ir. $14.90. Random House Inc., 400 Hahn Road, Westminster MD 21157. **Tel** (800)726-0600, (800)733-3000, FAX (800)659-2436. **LC** F774.3; .F63. **DD** 917.88/0433. Each issue contains an index to its own contents (no volume index)--loose.
**Desc:** An introduction to Colorado, its land and its people, history, exploring Denver, winter and summer resorts, Rocky Mountain National Park, Colorado Springs, and other information from the state.

US/1070-4477
**FODOR'S CRUISES AND PORTS OF CALL.** [Fodor's cruises ports call]. **Added/Corp** Fodor's Travel Publications, Inc. **VFOAT** Cruises and Ports of Call. (1991)-. English. an. $18.00. Random House Inc., 400 Hahn Road, Westminster MD 21157. **Tel** (800)726-0600, (800)733-3000, FAX (800)659-2436. **LC** G550; .F56. **DD** 910/.2/02. ***Continues*** *Fodor's Cruises Everywhere, 0160-3914.*

US
**FODOR'S DALLAS AND FORT WORTH.** **VFOAT** Dallas and Fort Worth; Fodor's Dallas, Fort Worth. (1983)-. English. ir. $10.85. Random House Inc., 400 Hahn Road, Westminster MD 21157. **Tel** (800)726-0600, (800)733-3000, FAX (800)659-2436. **LC** F394.D213; F64. **DD** 917.64/28120463.

US/1070-6402
**FODOR'S ... DISNEY WORLD & THE ORLANDO AREA.** [Fodor's Disney World Orlando area]. **VFOAT** Disney World & the Orlando Area; Fodor's Disney World and the Orlando Area; Disney World and the Orlando Area; Walt Disney World; Disney World; Fodor's Walt Disney World; Fodor's Disney World. (1989)-. English. ir. $14.90. Random House Inc., 400 Hahn Road, Westminster MD 21157. **Tel** (800)726-0600, (800)733-3000, FAX (800)659-2436. **LC** F319.O7; F63. **DD** 917.59/24. ***Continues*** *Fodor's Fun in Disney World and the Orlando Area.*

US/0734-8010
**FODOR'S EASTERN EUROPE.** [Fodor's East. Eur.]. **VFOAT** Eastern Europe. (1980)-. English. ir. $20.90. Random House Inc., 400 Hahn Road, Westminster MD 21157. **Tel** (800)726-0600, (800)733-3000, FAX (800)659-2436. **LC** DJK8; .F6. **DD** 914.7/04.

US/0147-8176
**FODOR'S EGYPT.** (19??)-. English. ir. $16.90. Random House Inc., 400 Hahn Road, Westminster MD 21157. **Tel** (800)726-0600, (800)733-3000, FAX (800)659-2436. **LC** DT45; .S56. **DD** 916.2/04/5.
**Desc:** Features Egypt's history, geography, people, taboos and customs.

US/0362-0204
**FODOR'S EUROPE.** (19??)-. English. ir. $22.40. Random House Inc., 400 Hahn Road, Westminster MD 21157. **Tel** (800)726-0600, (800)733-3000, FAX (800)659-2436. **LC** D909; .F63. **DD** 914/.04/55. ***Continues*** *Fodor's Guide to Europe, 0071-6375.*

US/1074-1216
**FODOR'S ... EUROPE'S GREAT CITIES.** [Fodor's Eur. great cities]. **Added/Corp** Fodor's Travel Publications, Inc. **VFOAT** Europe's Great Cities. (19??)-. English. an. $16.90. Random House Inc., 400 Hahn Road, Westminster MD 21157. **Tel** (800)726-0600, (800)733-3000, FAX (800)659-2436. **LC** D909; .F64. **DD** 914.04/559.

US/0192-3730
**FODOR'S FAR WEST.** **VFOAT** Far West. (1974)-. English. ir. $16.85. Random House Inc., 400 Hahn Road, Westminster MD 21157. **Tel** (800)726-0600, (800)733-3000, FAX (800)659-2436. **LC** F852.2; .F65. **DD** 917.9/04/926.

US/0193-9556
**FODOR'S FLORIDA.** **VFOAT** Florida. (19??)-. English. ir. $22.40. Random House Inc., 400 Hahn Road, Westminster MD 21157. **Tel** (800)726-0600, (800)733-3000, FAX (800)659-2436. **LC** F309.3; .F63. **DD** 917.59/04/6.
**Desc:** Gives basic information for planning a trip to Florida.

US/0532-5692
**FODOR'S FRANCE.** **VFOAT** France. (1969)-. English. ir. $19.90. Random House Inc., 400 Hahn Road, Westminster MD 21157. **Tel** (800)726-0600, (800)733-3000, FAX (800)659-2436. **LC** DC16; .F75. **DD** 914.4/04/83. ***Continues*** *France.*

US
**FODOR'S FUN IN PUERTO RICO. / J.P. MACBEAN.** **VFOAT** Fun in Puerto Rico. (1985)-. English. ir. $9.90. Random House Inc., 400 Hahn Road, Westminster MD 21157. **Tel** (800)726-0600, (800)733-3000, FAX (800)659-2436. **LC** F1959; .F63. **DD** 917.295/0453.

US
**FODOR'S FUN IN RIO DE JANEIRO.** (19??)-. English. ir. $12.90. Random House Inc., 400 Hahn Road, Westminster MD 21157. **Tel** (800)726-0600, (800)733-3000, FAX (800)659-2436.

US
**FODOR'S ... GERMANY.** **Added/Corp** Fodor's Travel Publications. **VFOAT** Fodor's Germany with Excursions to East Germany; Fodor's Germany with Expanded Coverage of Berlin and Eastern Germany. (1989)-. Periodical. English. ir. $20.90. Random House Inc., 400 Hahn Road, Westminster MD 21157. **Tel** (800)726-0600, (800)733-3000, FAX (800)659-2436. **LC** DD16; .F6. **DD** 914.3/04/87. ***Continues*** *Fodor's Germany : West and East.*

US/0071-6405
**FODOR'S GREAT BRITAIN.** (1969)-. English. ir. $19.90. Random House Inc., 400 Hahn Road, Westminster MD 21157. **Tel** (800)726-0600, (800)733-3000, FAX (800)659-2436. **LC** DA650; .G68. **DD** 914.2/04/85. ***Continues*** *Great Britain.*

US/0071-6413
**FODOR'S GREECE.** (1969)-. English. an. $19.90. Random House Inc., 400 Hahn Road, Westminster MD 21157. **Tel** (800)726-0600, (800)733-3000, FAX (800)659-2436. **LC** DF716; .G742. **DD** 914.95/04/7. ***Supersedes*** *Greece.*

US/0071-6421
**FODOR'S HAWAII.** (1969)-. English. ir. $18.90. Random House Inc., 400 Hahn Road, Westminster MD 21157. **Tel** (800)726-0600, (800)733-3000, FAX (800)659-2436. **LC** DU622; .H33. **DD** 919.69/04/4. ***Continues*** *Hawaii, 0361-4271.*

US/1057-8048
**FODOR'S HEALTHY ESCAPES.** [Fodor's healthy escapes]. **VFOAT** Healthy Escapes. 2nd Ed. (1991)-. English. ir. $17.90. Random House Inc., 400 Hahn Road, Westminster MD 21157. **Tel** (800)726-0600, (800)733-3000, FAX (800)659-2436. **LC** RA802; .F54. **DD** 613/.122/1257. ***Continues*** *Fodor's Health & Fitness Vacations., 1047-5052.*
**Desc:** Reports on everything from luxury pampering spas costing $4,000 a week to new-age spiritual retreats charging $25 a night. Reviews of 240 resorts in the United States, Canada, Mexico, and the Caribbean include comprehensive information on accomodations, dining facilities, and costs. Over 14 types of spa programs are covered, from weight loss to preventive medicine, holistic health to sports conditioning.

US/0071-643X
**FODOR'S HOLLAND.** ***Title Change.*** (1969)-(1993). English. an. Random House Inc., 400 Hahn Road, Westminster MD 21157. **Tel** (800)726-0600, (800)733-3000, FAX (800)659-2436. **LC** DJ16; .H56. **DD** 949/.2/049. ***Continues*** *Holland.* ***Merged with*** *Fodor's Belgium and Luxembourg* ***to form*** *Fodor's The Netherlands, Belgium, Luxembourg, 1070-4590.*

US/1070-6887
**FODOR'S ... HONG KONG.** [Fodor's Hong Kong]. **VFOAT** Hong Kong. (1989)-. English. ir. $15.90. Random House Inc., 400 Hahn Road, Westminster MD 21157. **Tel** (800)726-0600, (800)733-3000, FAX (800)659-2436. **LC** DS796.H74; F58. **DD** 915.1/25045. ***Continues*** *Fodor's Hong Kong and Macau, 0882-0066.*

US/0361-9761
**FODOR'S HUNGARY.** **VFOAT** Hungary. (19??)-. English. ir. $12.85. Random House Inc., 400 Hahn Road, Westminster MD 21157. **Tel** (800)726-0600, (800)733-3000, FAX (800)659-2436. **LC** DB905; .F63. **DD** 914.39/04/5.

Travel and Tourism

US/1045-2745
**FODOR'S I-75 MICHIGAN TO FLORIDA.** [Fodor's I-75 Mich. Fla.]. **Added/Corp** Fodor's Travel Publications, Inc. **VFOAT** Michigan to Florida; Fodor's I-75; I-75 Michigan to Florida. **VAT** Fodor's Interstate Seventy-five Michigan to Florida; Fodor's Interstate Seventy-five; Interstate Seventy-five Michigan to Florida. (1987)-. English. ir. $9.85. Random House Inc., 400 Hahn Road, Westminster MD 21157. **Tel** (800)726-0600, (800)733-3000, FAX (800)659-2436. **LC** GV1024; .F67. **DD** 917.3.

US
**FODOR'S INDIA, INCLUDING NEPAL.** **Added/Corp** Fodor's Travel Publications, Inc. **VFOAT** India, Including Nepal. (1988)-. English. ir. $21.90. Random House Inc., 400 Hahn Road, Westminster MD 21157. **Tel** (800)726-0600, (800)733-3000, FAX (800)659-2436. **LC** DS406; .F62. **DD** 915.4/0452. ***Continues*** *Fodor's India, Nepal and Sri Lanka, 0737-1039.*

US/0147-7919
**FODOR'S IRAN.** (19??)-. English. $12.50. Random House Inc., 400 Hahn Road, Westminster MD 21157. **Tel** (800)726-0600, (800)733-3000, FAX (800)659-2436. **LC** DS254; .F63. **DD** 915.5/04/5.

UK/0071-6464
**FODOR'S IRELAND.** (1968)-. English. ir. $18.90. Random House Inc., 400 Hahn Road, Westminster MD 21157. **Tel** (800)726-0600, (800)733-3000, FAX (800)659-2436. **LC** DA980; .F6. **DD** 914.15/04/9. ***Continues*** *Britain and Ireland.*

US/0090-0648
**FODOR'S IRELAND.** (1969)-. English. ir. $18.90. Random House Inc., 400 Hahn Road, Westminster MD 21157. **Tel** (800)726-0600, (800)733-3000, FAX (800)659-2436. **LC** DA978; .I7. **DD** 914.15/04/9. ***Continues*** *Ireland.*
**Desc:** Features Ireland's history, eating, drinking, and shopping.

US/0071-6588
**FODOR'S ISRAEL.** [Fodor's Isr.]. **VFOAT** Israel. (1969)-. English. an. $18.90. Random House Inc., 400 Hahn Road, Westminster MD 21157. **Tel** (800)726-0600, (800)733-3000, FAX (800)659-2436. **LC** DS103; .F62. **DD** 915.694/04/5. ***Continues*** *Israel.*

US/0361-977X
**FODOR'S ITALY.** **VFOAT** Italy. (19??)-. English. ir. $20.90. Random House Inc., 400 Hahn Road, Westminster MD 21157. **Tel** (800)726-0600, (800)733-3000, FAX (800)659-2436. **LC** DG416; .I817. **DD** 914.5/04/92. ***Continues*** *Fodor's Great Travel Values.*

US
**FODOR'S ... JAMAICA.** **VFOAT** Jamaica. (1990)-. English. ir. $10.85. Random House Inc., 400 Hahn Road, Westminster MD 21157. **Tel** (800)726-0600, (800)733-3000, FAX (800)659-2436. **LC** F1869; .F64. **DD** 917.29204/6. ***Continues*** *Fodor's Fun in Jamaica.*

US/0736-9956
**FODOR'S JAPAN.** [Fodor's Jpn.]. **VFOAT** Japan. (1983)-. English. an. $22.90. Random House Inc., 400 Hahn Road, Westminster MD 21157. **Tel** (800)726-0600, (800)733-3000, FAX (800)659-2436. **LC** DS811; .F6. **DD** 915.2/0448. ***Continues*** *Fodor's Japan and Korea, 0098-1613.*
**Desc:** Covers basic information on visas, entry, tours, etc. Also covers the Japanese way of life, history, fine arts, and crafts, performing arts, food and drink, and shopping.

US/0193-9114
**FODOR'S JORDAN AND THE HOLY LAND.** ***Ceased.*** **VFOAT** Jordan and the Holy Land. (1979)-(19??). English. Random House Inc., 400 Hahn Road, Westminster MD 21157. **Tel** (800)726-0600, (800)733-3000, FAX (800)659-2436. **LC** DS153.2; .S47. **DD** 915.695/04/4.

US
**FODOR'S KENYA & TANZANIA.** (FODOR'S KENYA.). (1985)-. English. ir. $18.90. Random House Inc., 400 Hahn Road, Westminster MD 21157. **Tel** (800)726-0600, (800)733-3000, FAX (800)659-2436. **LC** DT433.52; .F63. **DD** 916.76/2044.

US
**FODOR'S KOREA.** 1st Ed. (1983)-. English. ir. $17.90. Random House Inc., 400 Hahn Road, Westminster MD 21157. **Tel** (800)726-0600, (800)733-3000, FAX (800)659-2436. **LC** DS902.4; .F63. **DD** 915.19/50443.

●US/1070-6909
**FODOR'S ... LAS VEGAS, RENO, TAHOE.** [Fodor's Las Vegas Reno Tahoe]. **VFOAT** Las Vegas, Reno, Tahoe; Las Vegas; Fodor's Las Vegas. (1992)-. English. ir. $14.90. Random House Inc., 400 Hahn Road, Westminster MD 21157. **Tel** (800)726-0600, (800)733-3000, FAX (800)659-2436. **LC** F849.L35; F63. **DD** 917.93/1350433. ***Continues*** *Fodor's ... Las Vegas.*

US
**FODOR'S LISBON.** **Added/Corp** Fodor's Travel Guides (Firm). **VFOAT** Lisbon. (19??)-. English. ir. $10.85. Random House Inc., 400 Hahn Road, Westminster MD 21157. **Tel** (800)726-0600, (800)733-3000, FAX (800)659-2436. **LC** DP757; .F63. **DD** 914.69/42.

US
**FODOR'S LOIRE VALLEY.** **Added/Corp** Fodor's Travel Publications, Inc. **VFOAT** Loire Valley. (1987)-. English. ir. $11.85. Random House Inc., 400 Hahn Road, Westminster MD 21157. **Tel** (800)726-0600, (800)733-3000, FAX (800)659-2436. **LC** DC611.L81; F55. **DD** 914.4/504838.

US/0149-631X
**FODOR'S LONDON.** **VFOAT** London. (19??)-. English. ir. $14.90. Random House Inc., 400 Hahn Road, Westminster MD 21157. **Tel** (800)726-0600, (800)733-3000, FAX (800)659-2436. **LC** DA679; .F6. **DD** 914.21/04/857.

US
**FODOR'S LOS ANGELES.** **VFOAT** Los Angeles.; Fodor's ... Los Angeles, Including Orange County and Palm Springs. (19??)-. English. ir. $14.90. Random House Inc., 400 Hahn Road, Westminster MD 21157. **Tel** (800)726-0600, (800)733-3000, FAX (800)659-2436. **LC** F869.L8; F63. ***Continues*** *Fodor's Los Angeles and Nearby Attractions.*

US/0743-3336
**FODOR'S LOS ANGELES AND NEARBY ATTRACTIONS.** ***Title Change.*** **VFOAT** Los Angeles and Nearby Attractions. (1983)-(19??). Periodical. English. Random House Inc., 400 Hahn Road, Westminster MD 21157. **Tel** (800)726-0600, (800)733-3000, FAX (800)659-2436. **LC** F869.L83; F63. **DD** 917.94/930453. ***Continued by*** *Fodor's Los Angeles.*

US/0884-0393
**FODOR'S MADRID.** [Fodor's Madr.]. (1983)-. English. ir. $13.90. Random House Inc., 400 Hahn Road, Westminster MD 21157. **Tel** (800)726-0600, (800)733-3000, FAX (800)659-2436. **LC** DP355; .F55. **DD** 914.6/410483.

US
**FODOR'S MAUI.** (FODOR'S MAUI / GARY DIEDRICHS.). [Fodor's Mau.]. **VFOAT** Maui. (1988)-. English. ir. $11.90. Random House Inc., 400 Hahn Road, Westminster MD 21157. **Tel** (800)726-0600, (800)733-3000, FAX (800)659-2436. **LC** DU628.M3; F63. **DD** 919.69/2044. ***Continues*** *Fodor's Fun in Maui.*

US/0196-5999
**FODOR'S MEXICO.** [Fodor's Mex.]. **VFOAT** Mexico. (1972)-. English. ir. $20.90. Random House Inc., 400 Hahn Road, Westminster MD 21157. **Tel** (800)726-0600, (800)733-3000, FAX (800)659-2436. **LC** F1216; .F58. **DD** 917.2/04/82.
**Desc:** Features Mexico's climate, people, language, history, and Pre-Columbian heritage.

US/1045-277X
**FODOR'S MEXICO CITY AND ACAPULCO.** **VFOAT** Mexico City and Acapulco; Mexico City; Fodor's Mexico City. (1982)-. English. ir. $10.85. Random House Inc., 400 Hahn Road, Westminster MD 21157. **Tel** (800)726-0600, (800)733-3000, FAX (800)659-2436. **LC** F1386.A4; F63. **DD** 917.2/4.

US/1070-6399
**FODOR'S ... MIAMI & THE KEYS.** [Fodor's Miami Keys]. **VFOAT** Fodor's Miami and the Keys; Miami & the Keys; Miami and the Keys; Miami; Fodor's ... Miami. (1991)-. English. ir. $13.90. Random House Inc., 400 Hahn Road, Westminster MD 21157. **Tel** (800)726-0600, (800)733-3000, FAX (800)659-2436. **LC** F319.M6; F63. **DD** 917.59/3. ***Continues*** *Fodor's Miami, Fort Lauderdale, Palm Beach.*

US/0192-4540
**FODOR'S MID-ATLANTIC.** **VFOAT** Mid-Atlantic. (19??)-. English. an. $9.95, $6.95 paperbound. Random House Inc., 400 Hahn Road, Westminster MD 21157. **Tel** (800)726-0600, (800)733-3000, FAX (800)659-2436. **LC** F106; .M58. **DD** 917.5/04/4. ***Continues*** *Mid-Atlantic, 0192-3919.*

US
**FODOR'S ... MONTREAL & QUEBEC CITY.** **Added/Corp** Fodor's Travel Publications, Inc. **VFOAT** Montreal & Quebec City; Montreal and Quebec City; Quebec City. (1990)-. English. ir. $14.90. Random House Inc., 400 Hahn Road, Westminster MD 21157. **Tel** (800)726-0600, (800)733-3000, FAX (800)659-2436. ***Continues*** *Fodor's ... Montreal, 1046-8102.*

US
**FODOR'S MOROCCO.** **VFOAT** Morocco. (1991)-. English. ir. $19.85. Random House Inc., 400 Hahn Road, Westminster MD 21157. **Tel** (800)726-0600, (800)733-3000, FAX (800)659-2436. ***Continues*** *Fodor's North Africa, 0197-1271.*

●US
**FODOR'S MOSCOW, ST. PETERBURG, KIEV.** **VFOAT** Moscow, St. Petersburg, Kiev; Moscow, Saint Petersburg, Kiev; Fodor's Moscow, Saint Petersburg, Kiev. (1994)-. English. ir. $20.90. Random House Inc., 400 Hahn Road, Westminster MD 21157. **Tel** (800)726-0600, (800)733-3000, FAX (800)659-2436.

US
**FODOR'S MUNICH.** **VFOAT** Munich. (1984)-. English. ir. $13.90. Random House Inc., 400 Hahn Road, Westminster MD 21157. **Tel** (800)726-0600, (800)733-3000, FAX (800)659-2436. **LC** DD901.M76; F58. **DD** 914.3/36.

US/0192-3412
**FODOR'S NEW ENGLAND.** **VFOAT** New England. (19??)-. English. ir. $19.90. Random House Inc., 400 Hahn Road, Westminster MD 21157. **Tel** (800)726-0600, (800)733-3000, FAX (800)659-2436. **LC** F2.3; .F64. **DD** 917.4/04/4.
**Desc:** Features where to go in New England.

US
**FODOR'S NEW MEXICO.** **VFOAT** New Mexico; New Mexico--Santa Fe, Taos and Albuquerque. (1985)-. English. ir. $15.90. Random House Inc., 400 Hahn Road, Westminster MD 21157. **Tel** (800)726-0600, (800)733-3000, FAX (800)659-2436. **LC** F794.3; .F63. **DD** 917.89/0453.

US/0743-9385
**FODOR'S NEW ORLEANS.** **VFOAT** New Orleans. 1st Ed. (1984)-. English. ir. $14.90. Random House Inc., 400 Hahn Road, Westminster MD 21157. **Tel** (800)726-0600, (800)733-3000, FAX (800)659-2436. **LC** F379.N53; F63. **DD** 917.63/350463.
**Desc:** Features the way of life and history of New Orleans: music, food and drink, Mardi Gras and other festivals.

US
**FODOR'S NEW YORK CITY.** **Added/Corp** Fodor's Travel Publications, Inc. **VFOAT** New York City. (1988)-. English. ir. $16.90. Random House Inc., 400 Hahn Road, Westminster MD 21157. **Tel** (800)726-0600, (800)733-3000, FAX (800)659-2436. **LC** F128.18; .F6. **DD** 917.47/10443. ***Continues in part*** *Fodor's New York City, with Atlantic City, 0882-7338.*

US
**FODOR'S NEW ZEALAND.** **VFOAT** New Zealand. (1986)-. English. ir. $11.90. Random House Inc., 400 Hahn Road, Westminster MD 21157. **Tel** (800)726-0600, (800)733-3000, FAX (800)659-2436. **LC** DU405.5; .F63. **DD** 919.31/0437.

●US/1064-7643
**FODOR'S NOVA SCOTIA, PRINCE EDWARD ISLAND, AND NEW BRUNSWICK.** [Fodor's N.S. P.E.I. N.B.]. **Added/Corp** Fodor's Travel Publications, Inc. **VFOAT** Nova Scotia, Prince Edward Island, and New Brunswick; Fodor's Nova Scotia, Prince Edward Island, and New Brunswick with Newfoundland; Fodor's Nova Scotia. (1992)-. English. ir. $12.90. Random House Inc., 400 Hahn Road, Westminster MD 21157. **Tel** (800)726-0600, (800)733-3000, FAX (800)659-2436. **LC** F1035.8; .F56. **DD** 917.1504/04. ***Continues*** *Fodor's ... Canada's Atlantic Provinces, 1060-0191.*

US/1072-0391
**FODOR'S PACIFIC NORTH COAST.** [Fodor's Pac. north coast]. **Added/Corp** Fodor's Travel Guides (Firm). **VFOAT** Pacific North Coast. (1984)-. English. ir. $18.90. Random House Inc., 400 Hahn Road, Westminster MD 21157. **Tel** (800)726-0600, (800)733-3000, FAX (800)659-2436. **LC** F852.3; .F63. **DD** 917.9.

US/0149-1288
**FODOR'S PARIS.** **VFOAT** Paris. (1974)-. English. ir. $15.90. Random House Inc., 400 Hahn Road, Westminster MD 21157. **Tel** (800)726-0600, (800)733-3000, FAX (800)659-2436. **LC** DC708; .F6. **DD** 914.4/36/0483.
**Desc:** Features Parisian restaurants, fine art of cooking, entertainment, shopping in Paris, and history.

US
**FODOR'S PHILADELPHIA.** **Added/Corp** Fodor's Travel Guides (Firm). **VFOAT** Philadelphia. (1985)-. English. ir. $14.90. Random House Inc., 400 Hahn Road, Westminster MD 21157. **Tel** (800)726-0600, (800)733-3000, FAX (800)659-2436. **LC** F158.18; .F62. **DD** 917.48/110443.

US
**FODOR'S ... POCKET GUIDE TO LONDON.** [Fodor's poc. gui. to London]. **Added/Corp** Fodor's Travel Publications, Inc. **VFOAT** Pocket Guide to London. (1989)-. English. an. $11.90. Random House Inc., 400 Hahn Road, Westminster MD 21157. **Tel** (800)726-0600, (800)733-3000, FAX (800)659-2436. **LC** DA679; .F595. **DD** 914.2104/858. Each issue contains an index to its own contents (no volume index)--loose. ***Continues*** *Fodor's Fun in London.*

Travel and Tourism

US/1056-7712
**FODOR'S ... POCKET GUIDE TO NEW YORK CITY.** [Fodor's pocket guide N. Y. City]. **Added/Corp** Fodor's Travel Publications, Inc. **VFOAT** Pocket Guide to New York City. (1989)-. English. an. $11.90. Random House Inc., 400 Hahn Road, Westminster MD 21157. **Tel** (800)726-0600, (800)733-3000, FAX (800)659-2436. **LC** F128.18; .F53. **DD** 917.47/10443. ***Continues*** *Fodor's Fun in New York City.*

US
**FODOR'S ... POCKET GUIDE TO PARIS.** **Added/Corp** Fodor's Travel Publications, Inc. **VFOAT** Pocket Guide to Paris. (1989)-. Periodical. English. an. $11.90. Random House Inc., 400 Hahn Road, Westminster MD 21157. **Tel** (800)726-0600, (800)733-3000, FAX (800)659-2436. **LC** DC708; .F58. **DD** 914.4/3604838. ***Continues*** *Fodor's Fun in Paris.*

US/1046-8978
**FODOR'S ... POCKET GUIDE TO SAN FRANCISCO.** [Fodor's pocket guide San Fran.]. **Added/Corp** Fodor's Travel Publications, Inc. **VFOAT** Pocket Guide to San Francisco. (1989)-. Periodical. English. an. $10.90. Random House Inc., 400 Hahn Road, Westminster MD 21157. **Tel** (800)726-0600, (800)733-3000, FAX (800)659-2436. **LC** PAR. **DD** 917. ***Continues*** *Fodor's Fun in San Francisco.*

US/1041-9373
**FODOR'S ... POCKET GUIDE TO THE BAHAMAS.** [Fodor's pocket guide Bahamas]. **Added/Corp** Fodor's Travel Publications, Inc. **VFOAT** Pocket Guide to the Bahamas. (1989)-. English. an. $10.90. Random House Inc., 400 Hahn Road, Westminster MD 21157. **Tel** (800)726-0600, (800)733-3000, FAX (800)659-2436. **LC** F1652; .F64. **DD** 917.29604. ***Continues*** *Fodor's Fun in the Bahamas.*

US/0071-6510
**FODOR'S PORTUGAL.** **VFOAT** Portugal. (1969)-. English. an. $19.90. Random House Inc., 400 Hahn Road, Westminster MD 21157. **Tel** (800)726-0600, (800)733-3000, FAX (800)659-2436. **LC** DP516; .P57. **DD** 914.69/04/4. ***Continues*** *Portugal, 0196-1268.*

US/0276-2560
**FODOR'S ROME.** **VFOAT** Rome. (19??)-. English. ir. $15.90. Random House Inc., 400 Hahn Road, Westminster MD 21157. **Tel** (800)726-0600, (800)733-3000, FAX (800)659-2436. **LC** DG804; .F63. **DD** 914.5/63204928.
**Desc:** A brief look at history, wining and dining, entertainment, shopping, and the Vatican.

●US
**FODOR'S RUSSIA & THE BALTIC COUNTRIES.** **VFOAT** Fodor's Russia and the Baltic Countries; Russia & the Baltic Countries; Russia and the Baltic Countries; Fodor's Russia & the Baltics; Fodor's Russia and the Baltics. (1993)-. English. ir. $20.90. Random House Inc., 400 Hahn Road, Westminster MD 21157. **Tel** (800)726-0600, (800)733-3000, FAX (800)659-2436. **LC** DK16; .F6. ***Continues*** *Fodor's ... Russia, the Republics and the Baltics, 1062-6816.*

US/1062-6816
**FODOR'S ... RUSSIA, THE REPUBLICS AND THE BALTICS.** ***Title Change.*** [Fodor's Russ. Repub. Balt.]. **VFOAT** Russia, the Republics and the Baltics. (1992)-(1992). English. Random House Inc., 400 Hahn Road, Westminster MD 21157. **Tel** (800)726-0600, (800)733-3000, FAX (800)659-2436. **DD** 914. ***Continues*** *Fodor's Soviet Union, 0095-1358.* ***Continued by*** *Fodor's Russia & the Baltic Countries.*

US
**FODOR'S ... SAINT MARTIN, SINT MAARTEN.** **Added/Corp** Fodor's Travel Publications, Inc. **VFOAT** Fodor's St. Martin, Sint Maarten; Saint Martin, Sint Maarten; St. Martin, Sint Maarten. (1989)-. English. ir. $9.85. Random House Inc., 400 Hahn Road, Westminster MD 21157. **Tel** (800)726-0600, (800)733-3000, FAX (800)659-2436. **LC** F2103; .F63. **DD** 917.297/604. ***Continues*** *Fodor's Fun in St. Martin & Saint Maarten.*

US/1053-5950
**FODOR'S SAN DIEGO.** [Fodor's S. Diego]. **VFOAT** San Diego; Fodor's San Diego with Complete Restaurants Reviews. (1989)-. English. ir. $14.90. Random House Inc., 400 Hahn Road, Westminster MD 21157. **Tel** (800)726-0600, (800)733-3000, FAX (800)659-2436. **LC** F869.S22; F55. **DD** 917.94/980453. ***Continues*** *Fodor's San Diego and Nearby Attractions.*

US
**FODOR'S ... SAN FRANCISCO.** **Added/Corp** Fodor's Travel Publications, Inc. **VFOAT** San Francisco; San Francisco with Complete Restaurant Reviews; Fodor's ... San Francisco with Complete Restaurant Reviews. (1989)-. English. ir. $15.90. Random House Inc., 400 Hahn Road, Westminster MD 21157. **Tel** (800)726-0600, (800)733-3000, FAX (800)659-2436. **LC** F869.S33; F63. **DD** 917.94/61/0453. ***Continues*** *Fodor's San Francisco Plus Marin County and the Wine Country.*

US/0071-6529
**FODOR'S SCANDINAVIA.** **VFOAT** Scandinavia. (1969)-. English. an. $21.90. Random House Inc., 400 Hahn Road, Westminster MD 21157. **Tel** (800)726-0600, (800)733-3000, FAX (800)659-2436. **DD** 914.8/.04/8. ***Continues*** *Scandinavia (New York, N.Y.).*
**Desc:** Features Scandinavian history, arts, and food and drink.

US
**FODOR'S SCANDINAVIAN CITIES.** (19??)-. English. ir. $11.90. Random House Inc., 400 Hahn Road, Westminster MD 21157. **Tel** (800)726-0600, (800)733-3000, FAX (800)659-2436.

US/0743-0973
**FODOR'S SCOTLAND.** [Fodor's Scotl.]. **VFOAT** Scotland. (1983)-. Periodical. English. ir. $19.90. Random House Inc., 400 Hahn Road, Westminster MD 21157. **Tel** (800)726-0600, (800)733-3000, FAX (800)659-2436. **LC** DA870; .F64. **DD** 914.11/04858.
**Desc:** Features history, literature and the arts, food and drink, and sports.

US
**FODOR'S SELECTED RESORTS AND HOTELS OF THE U.S.** **See** Hotels/Motels.

US/1047-5680
**FODOR'S SHOPPING IN EUROPE.** [Fodor's shopp. Eur.]. **Added/Corp** Fodor's Travel Publications, Inc. **VFOAT** Shopping in Europe. (1989)-. English. ir. Random House Inc., 400 Hahn Road, Westminster MD 21157. **Tel** (800)726-0600, (800)733-3000, FAX (800)659-2436. **LC** TX907.5.I8; F64. **DD** 380.1/45/00254.

US
**FODOR'S SINGAPORE.** **Added/Corp** Fodor's Travel Guides (Firm) Fodor's Travel Publications, Inc. **VFOAT** Singapore. (1986)-. English. ir. $15.90. Random House Inc., 400 Hahn Road, Westminster MD 21157. **Tel** (800)726-0600, (800)733-3000, FAX (800)659-2436. **LC** DS598.S72; F63. **DD** 915.95/7045.

US/1050-5180
**FODOR'S SKIING IN NORTH AMERICA.** [Fodor's ski. North Am.]. **Added/Corp** Fodor's Travel Publications, Inc. **VFOAT** Skiing in North America. (1989)-. English. ir. $17.90. Random House Inc., 400 Hahn Road, Westminster MD 21157. **Tel** (800)726-0600, (800)733-3000, FAX (800)659-2436. **LC** GV854.4; .F63. **DD** 796.93025/73. ***Continues*** *Fodor's Ski Resorts of North America, 1042-4504.*

US/0147-8680
**FODOR'S SOUTH.** [Fodor's South]. **VFOAT** Fodor's ... the South. (197?)-. English. an. $18.90. Random House Inc., 400 Hahn Road, Westminster MD 21157. **Tel** (800)726-0600, (800)733-3000, FAX (800)659-2436. **LC** F207.3; .F62. **DD** 917.5/0443. ***Continues*** *Fodor's The South, 0147-8680.*
**Desc:** Features Southern states: Alabama, Florida, Georgia, Louisiana, Mississippi, North and South Carolina, Tennessee, and Virginia.

US/0362-0220
**FODOR'S SOUTH AMERICA.** (1970)-. English. ir. $21.90. Random House Inc., 400 Hahn Road, Westminster MD 21157. **Tel** (800)726-0600, (800)733-3000, FAX (800)659-2436. **LC** F2211; .F6. **DD** 918.04/3. ***Continues*** *Fodor's Guide to South America, 0071-6537.*

US/0160-8991
**FODOR'S SOUTH-EAST ASIA.** **VFOAT** South-East Asia; Fodor's Southeast Asia. (1975)-. English. ir. $20.90. Random House Inc., 400 Hahn Road, Westminster MD 21157. **Tel** (800)726-0600, (800)733-3000, FAX (800)659-2436. **LC** DS504; .F63. **DD** 915.9/04. ***Supersedes in part*** *Fodor's Japan and East Asia.*
**Desc:** Features the Asian way of life, Southeast Asian history, creative Southeast Asia, and religion.

US
**FODOR'S SOUTH PACIFIC.** **VFOAT** South Pacific. (1986)-. English. ir. $14.90. Random House Inc., 400 Hahn Road, Westminster MD 21157. **Tel** (800)726-0600, (800)733-3000, FAX (800)659-2436. **LC** DU15; .F64. **DD** 919/.04.

US/0361-9648
**FODOR'S SPAIN.** **VFOAT** Spain. (1969)-. English. ir. $19.90. Random House Inc., 400 Hahn Road, Westminster MD 21157. **Tel** (800)726-0600, (800)733-3000, FAX (800)659-2436. **LC** DP14; .S629. **DD** 914.6/04/82. ***Continues*** *Spain, 0361-9680; Fodor's Great Travel Values. Spain, 1041-8202.*

US/0196-1055
**FODOR'S SUNBELT LEISURE GUIDE.** **VFOAT** Sunbelt Leisure Guide. (19??)-. English. an. $12.95. Random House Inc., 400 Hahn Road, Westminster MD 21157. **Tel** (800)726-0600, (800)733-3000, FAX (800)659-2436. **LC** F207.3; .F618. **DD** 917.3.

US
**FODOR'S SWEDEN.** **Added/Corp** Fodor's Travel Publications, Inc. **VFOAT** Sweden. (1986)-. English. ir. $11.90. Random House Inc., 400 Hahn Road, Westminster MD 21157. **Tel** (800)726-0600, (800)733-3000, FAX (800)659-2436. **LC** DL607; .F6. **DD** 914.85/0458.

US/0071-6553
**FODOR'S SWITZERLAND.** [Fodor's Switz.]. **VFOAT** Switzerland. (19??)-. English. ir. $20.90. Random House Inc., 400 Hahn Road, Westminster MD 21157. **Tel** (800)726-0600, (800)733-3000, FAX (800)659-2436. **LC** DQ16; .S833. **DD** 914.94/04/7. ***Supersedes*** *Switzerland.*

US
**FODOR'S SYDNEY.** **Added/Corp** Fodor's Travel Guides (Firm). **VFOAT** Sydney. (1985)-. English. ir. $12.85. Random House Inc., 400 Hahn Road, Westminster MD 21157. **Tel** (800)726-0600, (800)733-3000, FAX (800)659-2436. **LC** DU178; .F63. **DD** 919.44/10463.

US/0743-3328
**FODOR'S TEXAS.** [Fodor's Tex.]. **VFOAT** Texas. (1983)-. Periodical. English. ir. $14.90. Random House Inc., 400 Hahn Road, Westminster MD 21157. **Tel** (800)726-0600, (800)733-3000, FAX (800)659-2436. **LC** F384.3; .F63. **DD** 917.64/0463.

US
**FODOR'S THE CAROLINAS AND THE GEORGIA COAST.** **Added/Corp** Fodor's Travel Publications, Inc. **VFOAT** Carolinas and the Georgia Coast. (1987)-. English. ir. $13.90. Random House Inc., 400 Hahn Road, Westminster MD 21157. **Tel** (800)726-0600, (800)733-3000, FAX (800)659-2436. **LC** F252.3; .F63. **DD** 917.5.

US/1073-6573
**FODOR'S THE HIMALAYAN COUNTRIES.** [Fodor's Himal. ctries.]. **Added/Corp** Fodor's Travel Publications, Inc. **VFOAT** Himalayan Countries; Fodor's Himalayan Countries. (1990)-. English. ir. $18.85. Random House Inc., 400 Hahn Road, Westminster MD 21157. **Tel** (800)726-0600, (800)733-3000, FAX (800)659-2436. **LC** IN PROCESS. **DD** 915.

●US/1070-4590
**FODOR'S THE NETHERLANDS, BELGIUM, LUXEMBOURG.** [Fodor's Neth. Belg. Luxembg.]. **Added/Corp** Fodor's Travel Publications, Inc. **VFOAT** Fodor's Netherlands, Belgium, Luxembourg; Netherlands, Belgium, Luxembourg. 1st Ed. (1993)-. English. ir. $18.90. Random House Inc., 400 Hahn Road, Westminster MD 21157. **Tel** (800)726-0600, (800)733-3000, FAX (800)659-2436. **LC** DH16; .F6. ***Formed by the union of*** *Fodor's Holland, 0071-643X* ***and*** *Fodor's Belgium and Luxembourg.*

US
**FODOR'S THE ROCKIES.** **Added/Corp** Fodor's Travel Publications, Inc. **VFOAT** Rockies; Fodor's the Rockies, U.S. and Canadian. (1987)-. English. ir. $19.90. Random House Inc., 400 Hahn Road, Westminster MD 21157. **Tel** (800)726-0600, (800)733-3000, FAX (800)659-2436. **LC** F721; .F64. **DD** 917.8/0433. ***Continues in part*** *Fodor's Rockies and Plains, 0191-0515.*

US/1070-6380
**FODOR'S ... THE U.S. & BRITISH VIRGIN ISLANDS.** [Fodor's U.S. Br. Virgin Isl.]. **Added/Corp** Fodor's Travel Publications, Inc. **VFOAT** U.S. & British Virgin Islands; U.S. and British Virgin Islands; United States & British Virgin Islands; US & British Virgin Islands; Fodor's ... the U.S. & British Virgin Islands Including St. Croix, St. John, St. Thomas, Tortola, Virgin Gorda; Fodor's ... Virgin Islands. (199?)-. English. ir. $15.90. Random House Inc., 400 Hahn Road, Westminster MD 21157. **Tel** (800)726-0600, (800)733-3000, FAX (800)659-2436. **LC** F2136.2; .F57. **DD** 917.297/204. ***Continues*** *Fodor's ... Virgin Islands.*

US/1070-4485
**FODOR'S THE UPPER GREAT LAKES REGION.** [Fodor's Up. Great Lakes reg.]. **Added/Corp** Fodor's Travel Publications, Inc. **VFOAT** Upper Great Lakes Region. 2nd Ed. (1991)-. English. ir. $16.90. Random House Inc., 400 Hahn Road, Westminster MD 21157. **Tel** (800)726-0600, (800)733-3000, FAX (800)659-2436. **LC** F551; .F7. **DD** 917.7. ***Continues*** *Fodor's Michigan, Wisconsin, Minnesota, 1047-5060.*

US
**FODOR'S TOKYO.** **VFOAT** Tokyo. (1985)-. English. ir. $14.90. Random House Inc., 400 Hahn Road, Westminster MD 21157. **Tel** (800)726-0600, (800)733-3000, FAX (800)659-2436. **LC** DS896.38; .F63. **DD** 915.2/1350448.

US/1044-6133
**FODOR'S ... TORONTO.** [Fodor's Tor.]. **VFOAT** Fodor's ... Toronto with Excursions to Stratford and Niagara Falls; Toronto. (1989)-. English. ir. $14.90. Random House Inc., 400 Hahn Road, Westminster MD

21157. **Tel** (800)726-0600, (800)733-3000, FAX (800)659-2436. **LC** F1059.5.T683; F64. **DD** 971.13/541044. ***Continues*** *Fodor's Toronto and Nearby Attractions, 1066-6141.*

US/0090-2349
**FODOR'S TUNISIA.** (1973)-. English. an. $8.75. Random House Inc., 400 Hahn Road, Westminster MD 21157. **Tel** (800)726-0600, (800)733-3000, FAX (800)659-2436. **LC** DT244; .F63. **DD** 916.1/1/04505.

US/0071-6618
**FODOR'S TURKEY. VFOAT** Turkey. (1969)-. English. ir. $20.90. Random House Inc., 400 Hahn Road, Westminster MD 21157. **Tel** (800)726-0600, (800)733-3000, FAX (800)659-2436. **LC** DR416; .F62. **DD** 915.61.

US
**FODOR'S ... USA.** (1990)-. English. an. $21.90. Random House Inc., 400 Hahn Road, Westminster MD 21157. **Tel** (800)726-0600, (800)733-3000, FAX (800)659-2436. ***Continues*** *Fodor's ... United States of America.*

US
**FODOR'S VACATIONS IN NEW YORK STATE.** (1990)-. English. ir. $17.85. Random House Inc., 400 Hahn Road, Westminster MD 21157. **Tel** (800)726-0600, (800)733-3000, FAX (800)659-2436. ***Continues*** *Fodor's New York State.*

US
**FODOR'S VIENNA. VFOAT** Vienna. (19??)-. English. ir. $13.90. Random House Inc., 400 Hahn Road, Westminster MD 21157. **Tel** (800)726-0600, (800)733-3000, FAX (800)659-2436. **LC** DB849; .F64. **DD** 914.36/130453.

US/1048-1060
**FODOR'S ... VIRGIN ISLANDS.** ***Title Change.*** [Fodor's Virg. Isl.]. **Added/Corp** Fodor's Travel Publications, Inc. **VFOAT** Virgin Islands. (1990)-(199?). English. Random House Inc., 400 Hahn Road, Westminster MD 21157. **Tel** (800)726-0600, (800)733-3000, FAX (800)659-2436. **LC** F2136.2; .F57. **DD** 917.297/204. ***Continues*** *Fodor's Virgin Islands, U.S. and British.* ***Continued by*** *Fodor's ... the U.S. & British Virgin Islands, 1070-6380.*

US/1075-0711
**FODOR'S VIRGINIA & MARYLAND.** [Fodor's Va. Md.]. **Added/Corp** Fodor's Travel Publications, Inc. **VFOAT** Virginia & Maryland; Virginia and Maryland; Fodor's Virginia and Maryland. 1st Ed. (1991)-. English. ir. $14.90. Random House Inc., 400 Hahn Road, Westminster MD 21157. **Tel** (800)726-0600, (800)733-3000, FAX (800)659-2436. **LC** F224.3; .F64. **DD** 917.5504/43. ***Continues*** *Fodor's Virginia.*

US/1044-923X
**FODOR'S WAIKIKI.** (FODOR'S ... WAIKIKI / RITA ARIYOSHI.). **VFOAT** Waikiki. (1989)-. English. ir. $11.90. Random House Inc., 400 Hahn Road, Westminster MD 21157. **Tel** (800)726-0600, (800)733-3000, FAX (800)659-2436. **LC** DU629.H7; F58. **DD** 919.69/3. ***Continues*** *Fodor's Fun in Waikiki.*

US/0743-9741
**FODOR'S WASHINGTON, D.C. VFOAT** Washington, D.C. (1984)-. English. ir. $15.90. Random House Inc., 400 Hahn Road, Westminster MD 21157. **Tel** (800)726-0600, (800)733-3000, FAX (800)659-2436. **LC** F192.3; .F57. **DD** 917.53/044. ***Continues*** *Fodor's Washington, D.C. and Vicinity, 0739-9383.*
**Desc:** Features the nation's capital, past and present, Washington's way of life, and how the federal government works.

US/1045-2737
**FODOR'S WILLIAMSBURG, JAMESTOWN & YORKTOWN.** [Fodor's Williamsbg. Jamest. Yorkt.]. **Added/Corp** Fodor's Travel Publications, Inc. **VFOAT** Fodor's Williamsburg, Jamestown, and Yorktown; Williamsburg, Jamestown & Yorktown; Historic Triangle, Williamsburg, Jamestown & Yorktown. (1987)-. English. ir. $10.85. Random House Inc., 400 Hahn Road, Westminster MD 21157. **Tel** (800)726-0600, (800)733-3000, FAX (800)659-2436. **LC** F234.W7; F63. **DD** 917.55/4204.

US/0071-657X
**FODOR'S YUGOSLAVIA.** (1969)-. English. ir. $18.90. Random House Inc., 400 Hahn Road, Westminster MD 21157. **Tel** (800)726-0600, (800)733-3000, FAX (800)659-2436. **LC** DR304.5; .Y58. **DD** 914.97/04/2. ***Continues*** *Yugoslavia, 0362-1227.*

US/0733-3196
**FOOTLOOSE LIBRARIAN, THE.** ***Ceased.*** (Sept. 1981)-Ceased (May 1991). Periodical. English. bm (except July/August). The Footloose Librarian, Box 972, Minneapolis MN 55401. **Tel** (612)874-8108. **ED** William J Cutts. Index available. **Bk Rev. Ad Acc. Circ:** 600 (ctrl).
**Desc:** A travel newsletter and network for librarians in the US and overseas. Members may swap services, e.g. Bed n' Breakfast, Housing Exchange.

US/0096-1353
**FORD'S DECK PLAN GUIDE. Main/Corp** Ford's Travel Guides. **VFOAT** Deck Plan Guide. (1974)-. English. an (July). $75.00 US; $81.00 other. Fords Travel Guides, 19448 Londelius Street, Northridge CA 91324. **Tel** (818)701-7414, FAX (818)701-7415. **ED** Judith A Howard. **LC** VM381; .F67a. **DD** 387.2/43. **Ad Acc. Circ:** 5,000 (ctrl).
**Desc:** Deck plans of over 130 cruise ships, all fold out pages, hard bound cover, post type construction permits, up-dating, updates are offered annually.

US
**FORD'S FREIGHTER TRAVEL GUIDE ... AND WATERWAYS OF THE WORLD. VFOAT** Freighter Travel Guide and Waterways of the World. 64th Ed. (Winter 1985)-. Periodical. English. sa (May, Nov.). $20.00 US; $25.00 other. Fords Travel Guides, 19448 Londelius Street, Northridge CA 91324. **Tel** (818)701-7414, FAX (818)701-7415. ***Continues*** *Ford's Freighter Travel Guide.*

US/0270-7985
**FOREIGN TOURIST ARRIVALS BY SELECTED STATES- AND PORTS-OF-ENTRY.** [Foreign tour. arriv. sel. states- and ports-of-entry]. 1978-. Government Publication. English. an. US Department of Commerce, 14th Street & Constitution Avenue NW, Washington DC 20230. **Tel** (202)482-2000, FAX (202)482-3772. **LC** G155.U6; F63. **DD** 338.4/7917304/0212. ***Continues*** *Foreign Visitor Arrivals by Selected Ports, 0192-6144.*

US
**FOREIGN TRAVEL & IMMUNIZATION GUIDE. VFOAT** Foreign Travel and Immunization Guide. 9th ed. (1980)-. English. Medical Economics Data, Five Paragon Drive, PO Box 27, Montvale NJ 07645. **Tel** (800)442-6657, (201)358-7200. **NLM** W1 FO561W. ***Continues*** *Foreign Travel Immunization Guide, 0193-0338.*

US/1055-8853
**FOUR DRAGONS GUIDEBOOK : A COMPREHENSIVE GUIDE TO HONG KONG, THAILAND, SINGAPORE, TAIWAN, THE.** [Four dragons guideb.]. 1st Ed. (1991)-. English. $18.95. Houghton Mifflin Company, Wayside Road, Burlington MA 01803. **Tel** (800)225-3362, (617)272-1500. **DD** 915.

US/0739-8158
**FRAM (BANGOR, ME.).** (FRAM.). [Fram]. **VFOAT** Journal of Polar Studies. Vol. 1, No. 1 (Winter Issue, 1984)-. Periodical. English. ir. price varies per volume. Polaris Publications, PO Box 8089, Bangor ME 04401. **DD** 910. **[CCC].**
**Ind/Abst** GeoRef.

US/0883-2617
**FRANCE (NEW YORK, N.Y. 1983).** (FRANCE.). [France]. 1983-. English. an. Fishers World Travel Guides, 100 Chestnut Street, Philadelphia PA 19106. **Tel** (800)327-5300. **ED** Georgia I Hesse. **LC** DC16; .F768. **DD** 914.4/04838.

●CN/1184-7530
**FREDERICTON, NEW BRUNSWICK, ATLANTIC CANADA TOUR PLANNING MANUAL.** [Frederict. N.B. Atl. Can. tour plan. man.]. **Added/Corp** Fredericton (N.B.). Visitors & Convention Bureau. **VFOAT** Fredericton Tour Planning Manual. (1992)-. English. Fredericton Visitor & Convention Bureau, PO Box 130, Fredericton, N.B. E3B 4X7. **DD** 917.15/515/044. ***Continues*** *Fredericton Tour Planning Manual., 0836-4664.*

GW
**FREMDENVERKEHR + I.E. UND DAS REISEBURO, DER. VAT** Fremdenverkehr und Das Reiseburo. Periodical. German. 5.00 single issue. Jaeger-Verlag GmbH, Postfach 11 04 52, W-6100 Darmstadt BRD Germany. **Tel** (06151)391-0, FAX (06151)391-200, telex 419548 DAV D. **LC** G155.A1; F674. **DD** 338.4/7/9105. ***Continues*** *Fremdenverkehr.*

SZ
**FREMDENVERKEHRSBILANZ DER SCHWEIZ / LA BALANCE TOURISTIQUE DE LA SUISSE, DIE. Added/Corp** Switzerland. Bundesamt fuer Statistik. **VFOAT** La Balance Touristique de la Suisse; Balance Touristique de la Suisse. (19??)-. Government Publication. French (German). an. 6.50F. Bundesamt fuer Statistik, Schwarztorstrasse 96, CH 3003 Bern Switzerland. **Tel** 031 3236011, FAX 031 3236061. **LC** G155.S8; F73. **DD** 380.1/45914940473.

US/1046-0330
**FREQUENT FLYER.** (OAG FREQUENT FLYER.). [Freq. flyer]. **Added/Corp** Official Airline Guides, Inc. Travel Magazines Division. (May 1989)-. Periodical. English. Twelve times a year. $24.00. Official Airline Guides, 2000 Clearwater Drive, Oak Brook IL 60521. **Tel** (800)323-3537. **LC** HE9803.A2; O17 Suppl. **DD** 387.7/42/097305. ***Continues*** *OAG/Frequent Flyer, 0277-2108.*

US/0279-6856
**FRIENDLY EXCHANGE.** (FRIENDLY EXCHANGE : THE MAGAZINE OF THE FARMERS INSURANCE GROUP.). **Added/Corp** Farmers Insurance Group. Vol. 1, No. 1 (1981)-. Periodical. English. qt. Meredith Corporation, Locust at 17th, Des Moines IA 50309. **Tel** (515)284-3000. **ED** Adele Malott. Index available. cum. index. **Ad Acc. Circ:** 4,000,000 (ctrl).

US/0884-9889
**FRIENDS (WARREN, MICH.).** ***Ceased.*** **See** Transportation-Automobiles.

NE/0165-313X
**FRIESLAND POST. See** Recreation, Leisure.

US/0734-1199
**FROM THE STATE CAPITALS. TOURIST BUSINESS PROMOTION (NEW HAVEN, CONN.).** (FROM THE STATE CAPITALS. TOURIST BUSINESS PROMOTION.). [From state cap., Tour. bus. promot.]. **VFOAT** Tourist Business Promotion. (1982)-. Periodical. English. mo. $211.50 library, $235.00 other. Wakeman Walworth Inc., 300 North Washington Street #204, Alexandria VA 22314. **Tel** (703)549-8606. **ED** Emily Novick. **[CCC].** ***Continues*** *From the State Capitals. Tourist Business Promotion Report.*
**Desc:** New plans and projects to lure vacationers, travellers and convention-goers. Developments on construction and renovation of convention centers and stadiums. Redevelopment of downtown and tourist attractions are also discussed.

US
**FROMMER'S ALASKA.** (1990)-. English. ir. $17.00. Macmillan Publishing Co. / Indiana, 201 West 103rd Street, Indianapolis IN 46290. **Tel** (800)428-5331, (800)858-7674. ***Continues*** *Frommer's Dollarwise Guide to Alaska / By John Gottberg, 1042-8283.*

US/0899-3181
**FROMMER'S AMSTERDAM AND HOLLAND.** [Frommer's Amst. Holl.]. **VFOAT** Amsterdam and Holland. (1990)-. English. be. $8.95. Macmillan Publishing Co. / Indiana, 201 West 103rd Street, Indianapolis IN 46290. **Tel** (800)428-5331, (800)858-7674. **ED** Linda Burnham. **LC** DJ16; .F76. **DD** 914.92/3520473. ***Continues*** *Frommer's Guide to Amsterdam & Holland, 0277-3546.*

●US/1053-2471
**FROMMER'S ARIZONA.** (1991)-. English. be. $12.95. Macmillan Publishing Co. / Indiana, 201 West 103rd Street, Indianapolis IN 46290. **Tel** (800)428-5331, (800)858-7674.

US/1044-2413
**FROMMER'S BELGIUM, HOLLAND & LUXEMBOURG.** ***Title Change.*** [Frommer's Belg. Holl. Luxemb.]. **VFOAT** Frommer's Belgium, Holland, and Luxembourg; Belgium, Holland & Luxembourg; Belgium, Holland, and Luxembourg. (1991)-(199?). English. be. Macmillan Publishing Co. / Indiana, 201 West 103rd Street, Indianapolis IN 46290. **Tel** (800)428-5331, (800)858-7674. **LC** DH16; .F74. **DD** 914.9204/73. ***Continues*** *Frommer's Dollarwise Guide to Belgium, Holland & Luxembourg, 1042-8291.* ***Continued by*** *Frommer's Comprehensive Travel Guide. Belgium, Holland & Luxembourg, 1040-9378.*

●US/1055-5366
**FROMMER'S BERLIN ON ... $ A DAY. VFOAT** Berlin on ... $ a Day. (1991)-. English. be. $10.95. Macmillan Publishing Co. / Indiana, 201 West 103rd Street, Indianapolis IN 46290. **Tel** (800)428-5331, (800)858-7674.

US/0899-322X
**FROMMER'S BOSTON.** [Frommer's Boston]. **VFOAT** Boston. (1989/1990)-. English. an. $13.00 (two years). Macmillan Publishing Co. / Indiana, 201 West 103rd Street, Indianapolis IN 46290. **Tel** (800)428-5331, (800)858-7674. **ED** Faye Hammel. **LC** F73.18; .F76. **DD** 917.44/610443. ***Continues*** *Frommer's Guide to Boston, 0277-4399.*

●US
**FROMMER'S BUDGET TRAVEL GUIDE. AUSTRALIA ... ON $ ... A DAY. VFOAT** Budget Travel Guide. Australia ... on $ ... a Day; Australia ... on $ ... a Day; Australia ... on ... Dollars a Day; Frommer's Australia on ... Dollars a Day; Frommer's Australia on $ ... a Day. (1991/1992)-. English. be. $13.95. Macmillan Publishing Co. / Indiana, 201 West 103rd Street, Indianapolis IN 46290. **Tel** (800)428-5331, (800)858-7674. **LC** DU95; .F76. **DD** 919.4/0463. ***Continues*** *Frommer's Australia on $ ... a Day, 8755-5425.*

●US
**FROMMER'S BUDGET TRAVEL GUIDE. EASTERN EUROPE ... ON $ ... A DAY. VFOAT** Frommer's Eastern Europe on ... Dollars a Day; Eastern Europe on ... Dollars a Day; Eastern Europe on $

Travel and Tourism

... a Day. (1991)-. English. be. $16.95. Macmillan Publishing Co. / Indiana, 201 West 103rd Street, Indianapolis IN 46290. **Tel** (800)428-5331, (800)858-7674. **LC** DJK8; .F76. ***Continues*** *Frommer's Eastern Europe & Yugoslavia on $ ... a Day, 1044-7792.*

US/1059-7603
**FROMMER'S BUDGET TRAVEL GUIDE. HAWAII ... ON $ ... A DAY.** [Frommer's budg. travel guide, Hawaii $ day]. **VFOAT** Budget Travel Guide. Hawaii ... on $ ... a Day; Hawaii ... on $ ... a Day; A.Frommer's Hawaii ... on $ ... a day. (1991)-. English. be. $14.95. Macmillan Publishing Co. / Indiana, 201 West 103rd Street, Indianapolis IN 46290. **Tel** (800)428-5331, (800)858-7674. **LC** DU622; .H32. **DD** 919.69/044. ***Continues*** *Frommer's Hawaii on $ ... a Day, 8755-9250.*

●US/1055-5331
**FROMMER'S BUDGET TRAVEL GUIDE. LONDON ... ON $ ... A DAY.** [Frommer's budg. travel guide, Lond. $ day]. **VFOAT** London ... on $ ... a Day; Frommer's London on $ ... a Day. (1993)-. English. be. $10.95. Macmillan Publishing Co. / Indiana, 201 West 103rd Street, Indianapolis IN 46290. **Tel** (800)428-5331, (800)858-7674. **DD** 914.

●US/1055-5323
**FROMMER'S BUDGET TRAVEL GUIDE. MADRID ... ON $ ... A DAY.** [Frommer's budg. travel guide, Madr. $ day]. **VFOAT** Madrid on ... $ a Day; Frommer's Madrid ... on $ ... a Day. (1992/1993)-. English. be. $10.95. Macmillan Publishing Co. / Indiana, 201 West 103rd Street, Indianapolis IN 46290. **Tel** (800)428-5331, (800)858-7674. **DD** 914.

US/1058-2541
**FROMMER'S BUDGET TRAVEL GUIDE. MEXICO ... ON $ ... A DAY.** [Frommer's budg. travel guide, Mex. $ day]. **VFOAT** Budget Travel Guide. Mexico ... on $ ... a Day; Mexico ... on $ ... a Day; Frommer's Mexico on $ ... a Day. (1991)-. English. $14.95. Macmillan Publishing Co. / Indiana, 201 West 103rd Street, Indianapolis IN 46290. **Tel** (800)428-5331, (800)858-7674. **LC** F1209; .F75. **DD** 917.204/835. ***Continues in part*** *Frommer's Mexico on $ ... a Day, Plus Belize and Guatemala, 1058-3165.*

●US/1053-2439
**FROMMER'S BUDGET TRAVEL GUIDE. SPAIN ... ON $ ... A DAY.** [Frommer's budg. travel guide, Spain $ day]. **VFOAT** Budget Travel Guide. Spain ... on $ ... a Day; Spain ... on $ ... a Day; Spain ... on ... Dollars a Day; Frommer's Spain on $ ... a Day. (1992)-. English. be. $15.95. Macmillan Publishing Co. / Indiana, 201 West 103rd Street, Indianapolis IN 46290. **Tel** (800)428-5331, (800)858-7674. **DD** 914. ***Continues in part*** *Frommer's Spain and Morocco Plus the Canary Islands on $ ... a Day, 0899-4099.*

●US/1065-4585
**FROMMER'S BUDGET TRAVEL GUIDE. WASHINGTON, D.C. ... ON $ ... A DAY.** [Frommer's budg. travel guide, Wash. D.C. $ day]. **VFOAT** Budget Travel Guide. Washington, D.C. ... on $ ... a Day.; Washington, D.C. ... on $ ... a Day; Washington, D.C. ... on ... Dollars a Day; Frommer's Washington, D.C. on ... Dollars a Day; Frommer's Washington, D.C. on $ ... a Day. (1992/93)-. English. be. Macmillan Publishing Co. / Indiana, 201 West 103rd Street, Indianapolis IN 46290. **Tel** (800)428-5331, (800)858-7674. **LC** F192.3; .W326. **DD** 917.53/004. ***Continues*** *Frommer's Washington, D.C. and Historic Virginia on $ ... a Day, 1042-8437.*

US/1040-9386
**FROMMER'S CALIFORNIA WITH KIDS.** [Frommer's Calif. kids]. **VFOAT** California With Kids. English. be. $14.95. Macmillan Publishing Co. / Indiana, 201 West 103rd Street, Indianapolis IN 46290. **Tel** (800)428-5331, (800)858-7674. **LC** F859.3; .F76. **DD** 917.940453.

US/1040-936X
**FROMMER'S CHICAGO.** [Frommer's Chic.]. **Added/Corp** Prentice-Hall, Inc. Trade Division. **VFOAT** Chicago. (1990)-. English. ir. $13.00. Macmillan Publishing Co. / Indiana, 201 West 103rd Street, Indianapolis IN 46290. **Tel** (800)428-5331, (800)858-7674. **LC** F548.18; .F76. **DD** 917.73/110443.

●US/1053-2463
**FROMMER'S COLORADO.** (1992)-. English. be. $12.95. Macmillan Publishing Co. / Indiana, 201 West 103rd Street, Indianapolis IN 46290. **Tel** (800)428-5331, (800)858-7674.

US
**FROMMER'S COMPREHENSINVE TRAVEL GUIDE.** English. Macmillan Publishing Co. / Indiana, 201 West 103rd Street, Indianapolis IN 46290. **Tel** (800)428-5331, (800)858-7674.

●US/1066-4939
**FROMMER'S COMPREHENSIVE TRAVEL GUIDE. ACAPULCO, IXTAPA & TAXCO.** **VFOAT** Acapulco, Ixtapa & Taxco; Acapulco, Ixtapa, and Taxco; Frommer's Acapulco, Ixtapa, and Taxco; Frommer's Acapulco, Ixtapa & Taxco. (1994)-. English. be. $15.00. Macmillan Publishing Co. / Indiana, 201 West 103rd Street, Indianapolis IN 46290. **Tel** (800)428-5331, (800)858-7674. ***Continues in part*** *Frommer's Comprehensive Travel Guide. Mexico City & Acapulco.*

●US/1064-3060
**FROMMER'S COMPREHENSIVE TRAVEL GUIDE. ATHENS.** [Frommer's compre. travel guide, Athens]. **VFOAT** Comprehensive Travel Guide. Athens; Athens; Frommer's Athens. (1991/1992)-. English. be. $8.95. Macmillan Publishing Co. / Indiana, 201 West 103rd Street, Indianapolis IN 46290. **Tel** (800)428-5331, (800)858-7674. **LC** DF916.5; .F76. **DD** 914.95/120476. ***Continues*** *Frommer's Athens, 0899-2924.*

●US/1047-7888
**FROMMER'S COMPREHENSIVE TRAVEL GUIDE. ATLANTA.** [Frommer's compr. travel guide, Atlanta]. **VFOAT** Atlanta; Frommer's Atlanta. (1992)-. English. be. $8.95. Macmillan Publishing Co. / Indiana, 201 West 103rd Street, Indianapolis IN 46290. **Tel** (800)428-5331, (800)858-7674. **ED** Editor: Rena Bulkin. **LC** F294A83; F76. **DD** 917.58/2310443.

●US/1064-525X
**FROMMER'S COMPREHENSIVE TRAVEL GUIDE. ATLANTIC CITY & CAPE MAY.** [Frommer's compr. travel guide, Atl. City Cape May]. **VFOAT** Comprehensive Travel Guide. Atlantic City & Cape May; Atlantic City & Cape May; Atlantic City and Cape May; Frommer's Atlantic City and Cape May; Frommer's Atlantic City & Cape May. (1991/1992)-. English. be. Macmillan Publishing Co. / Indiana, 201 West 103rd Street, Indianapolis IN 46290. **Tel** (800)428-5331, (800)858-7674. **LC** F144.A8; F76. **DD** 917.49/850443. ***Continues*** *Frommer's Atlantic City & Cape May, 0899-2916.*

●US/1064-3036
**FROMMER'S COMPREHENSIVE TRAVEL GUIDE. AUSTRALIA.** [Frommer's compre. travel guide, Aust.]. **VFOAT** Comprehensive Travel Guide. Australia; Australia; Frommer's Australia. (1992)-. English. be. $18.00. Macmillan Publishing Co. / Indiana, 201 West 103rd Street, Indianapolis IN 46290. **Tel** (800)428-5331, (800)858-7674. **DD** 919. ***Continues*** *Frommer's Australia, 1040-9408.*

US/1057-4018
**FROMMER'S COMPREHENSIVE TRAVEL GUIDE. AUSTRIA & HUNGARY.** [Frommer's compr. travel guide, Austria Hung.]. **VFOAT** Comprehensive Travel Guide. Austria & Hungary; Comprehensive Travel Guide. Austria and Hungary; Austria & Hungary; Austria and Hungary; Frommer's Austria and Hungary; Frommer's Austria & Hungary. (1991/1992)-. English. be. $14.95 (two years). Macmillan Publishing Co. / Indiana, 201 West 103rd Street, Indianapolis IN 46290. **Tel** (800)428-5331, (800)858-7674. **ED** Darwin Porter and Danforth Prince. **LC** DB16; .F76. **DD** 914.36/0453. ***Continues*** *Frommer's Dollarwise Guide to Austria & Hungary, 0899-3297.*

●US/1055-5374
**FROMMER'S COMPREHENSIVE TRAVEL GUIDE. BANGKOK.** [Frommer's compr. travel guide, Bangk.]. **VFOAT** Frommer's Bangkok. (1993)-. English. be. $10.95. Macmillan Publishing Co. / Indiana, 201 West 103rd Street, Indianapolis IN 46290. **Tel** (800)428-5331, (800)858-7674. **DD** 915.

●US/1064-3427
**FROMMER'S COMPREHENSIVE TRAVEL GUIDE. BARCELONA.** [Frommer's compre. travel guide, Barc.]. **VFOAT** Comprehensive Travel Guide. Barcelona; Barcelona; Frommer's Barcelona. (1992)-. English. be. $12.00. Macmillan Publishing Co. / Indiana, 201 West 103rd Street, Indianapolis IN 46290. **Tel** (800)428-5331, (800)858-7674. **LC** DP402.B24; F76. **DD** 914.6/720483. ***Continues*** *Frommer's Barcelona, Plus Majorca, Ibiza, and Minorca, 1045-9324.*

●US/1040-9378
**FROMMER'S COMPREHENSIVE TRAVEL GUIDE. BELGIUM, HOLLAND & LUXEMBOURG.** [Frommer's compr. travel guide, Belg. Holl. Luxembg.]. **VFOAT** Comprehensive Travel Guide. Belgium, Holland & Luxembourg; Belgium, Holland & Luxembourg; Frommer's Belgium, Holland and Luxembourg; Frommer's Belgium, Holland & Luxembourg. (1994)-. English. ir. $18.00. Macmillan Publishing Co. / Indiana, 201 West 103rd Street, Indianapolis IN 46290. **Tel** (800)428-5331, (800)858-7674. **LC** DH16; .F74. **DD** 914.9204/73. ***Continues*** *Frommer's Belgium, Holland & Luxembourg, 1044-2413.*

●US/1048-2660
**FROMMER'S COMPREHENSIVE TRAVEL GUIDE. BERLIN.** [Frommer's compr. travel guide, Berl.]. **VFOAT** Berlin; Frommer's Berlin. (1992)-. English. be. $8.95. Macmillan Publishing Co. / Indiana, 201 West 103rd Street, Indianapolis IN 46290. **Tel** (800)428-5331, (800)858-7674. **ED** Edited by: Beth Reiber. **DD** 914.

●US/1044-2383
**FROMMER'S COMPREHENSIVE TRAVEL GUIDE. BERMUDA & THE BAHAMAS.** **VFOAT** Bermuda & the Bahamas; Bermuda and the Bahamas; Frommer's Bermuda and the Bahamas; Frommer's Bermuda & the Bahamas. (1992-1993)-. English. be. Macmillan Publishing Co. / Indiana, 201 West 103rd Street, Indianapolis IN 46290. **Tel** (800)428-5331, (800)858-7674. **LC** F1632; .F76. **DD** 917.29604. ***Continues*** *Frommer's Bermuda and the Bahamas, Plus Turks and Caicos.*

●US/1064-3044
**FROMMER'S COMPREHENSIVE TRAVEL GUIDE. CALIFORNIA.** [Frommer's compre. travel guide, Calif.]. **VFOAT** Comprehensive Travel Guide. California; California; Frommer's California. (1992)-. English. be. $18.00. Macmillan Publishing Co. / Indiana, 201 West 103rd Street, Indianapolis IN 46290. **Tel** (800)428-5331, (800)858-7674. **DD** 917. ***Continues*** *Frommer's Comprehensive Travel Guide. California & Las Vegas.*

●US/1064-3443
**FROMMER'S COMPREHENSIVE TRAVEL GUIDE. CANADA.** [Frommer's compre. travel guide, Can.]. **VFOAT** Comprehensive Travel Guide. Canada; Canada; Frommer's Canada. (1992/1993)-. English. be. $18.00. Macmillan Publishing Co. / Indiana, 201 West 103rd Street, Indianapolis IN 46290. **Tel** (800)428-5331, (800)858-7674. **LC** F1009; .A77. **DD** 917.104/647. ***Continues*** *Frommer's Canada, 1044-2251.*

US/1058-2304
**FROMMER'S COMPREHENSIVE TRAVEL GUIDE. CARIBBEAN.** [Frommer's compr. travel guide, Caribb.]. **VFOAT** Comprehensive Travel Guide. Caribbean; Caribbean; A.Frommer's Caribbean. (1991)-. Periodical. English. be. $18.00. Macmillan Publishing Co. / Indiana, 201 West 103rd Street, Indianapolis IN 46290. **Tel** (800)428-5331, (800)858-7674. **(Subscription address:** Macmillian Publishing Company / Indiana, 201 West 103rd Street, Indianapolis IN 46290.**) ED** D. Porter and D. Prince. **LC** F1609; .F76. **DD** 917.2904/52/05. ***Continues*** *Frommer's Caribbean, 1044-2375.*

US/1057-6266
**FROMMER'S COMPREHENSIVE TRAVEL GUIDE. CRUISES.** [Frommer's compr. travel guide, Cruises]. **VFOAT** Cruises; Frommer's Cruises. (1990)-. English. $14.95. Macmillan Publishing Co. / Indiana, 201 West 103rd Street, Indianapolis IN 46290. **Tel** (800)428-5331, (800)858-7674. **LC** G550; .F78. **DD** 910. ***Continues*** *Frommer's Dollarwise Cruises, 0899-3343.*
**Desc:** Provides a guide to ocean travel and ocean liners as transportation.

●US/1055-5382
**FROMMER'S COMPREHENSIVE TRAVEL GUIDE. DELAWARE, MARYLAND, PENNSYLVANIA & THE NEW JERSEY SHORE.** [Frommer's compr. travel guide, Del. Md. Pa. N.J. shore]. **VFOAT** Comprehensive Travel Guide. Delaware, Maryland, Pennsylvania & the New Jersey Shore; Delaware, Maryland, Pennsylvannia & the New Jersey Shore; Delaware, Maryland, Pennsylvannia, and the New Jersey Shore; Frommer's Delaware, Maryland, Pennsylvannia, and the New Jersey Shore; Frommer's Delaware, Maryland, Pennsylvannia & the New Jersey Shore. (1993)-. English. be. $19.00. Macmillan Publishing Co. / Indiana, 201 West 103rd Street, Indianapolis IN 46290. **Tel** (800)428-5331, (800)858-7674. **DD** 917. ***Continues*** *Frommer's Mid-Atlantic States, 1050-2939.*

US/1057-2791
**FROMMER'S COMPREHENSIVE TRAVEL GUIDE. FLORIDA.** [Frommer's compr. travel guide, Fla.]. **VFOAT** Comprehensive Travel Guide. Florida; Frommer's Florida. (1991)-. English. an. $15.95. Macmillan Publishing Co. / Indiana, 201 West 103rd Street, Indianapolis IN 46290. **Tel** (800)428-5331, (800)858-7674. **LC** F309.3; .F76. **DD** 917.5904/63. ***Continues*** *Frommer's Florida, 1044-2391.*

US/1059-2830
**FROMMER'S COMPREHENSIVE TRAVEL GUIDE. FRANCE.** [Frommer's compr. travel guide, Fr.]. **VFOAT** Comprehensive Travel Guide. France; France; Frommer's France. (1991)-. English. Macmillan Publishing Co. / Indiana, 201 West 103rd

Travel and Tourism

Street, Indianapolis IN 46290. **Tel** (800)428-5331, (800)858-7674. **LC** DC29.3; .H33. **DD** 914.404/838. ***Continues** Frommer's Dollarwise France, 0899-3351.*

●US/1064-1238
**FROMMER'S COMPREHENSIVE TRAVEL GUIDE. HONOLULU & OAHU.** [Frommer's compre. travel guide, Honol. Oahu]. **VFOAT** Comprehensive Travel Guide. Honolulu & Oahu; Honolulu & Oahu; Honolulu and Oahu; Frommer's Honolulu and Oahu; Frommer's Honolulu & Oahu. (1993)-. English. an. $13.00. Macmillan Publishing Co. / Indiana, 201 West 103rd Street, Indianapolis IN 46290. **Tel** (800)428-5331, (800)858-7674. **(Subscription address:** Macmillian Publishing Company / Indiana, 201 West 103rd Street, Indianapolis IN 46290.**)** **LC** DU622; .F76. **DD** 919.6904/4. ***Continues** Frommer's Comprehensive Travel Guide. Hawaii, 1057-2058.*

US
**FROMMER'S COMPREHENSIVE TRAVEL GUIDE. ITALY.** **VFOAT** Frommer's Italy. (1991)-. English. $15.95. Macmillan Publishing Co. / Indiana, 201 West 103rd Street, Indianapolis IN 46290. **Tel** (800)428-5331, (800)858-7674. **LC** DG416; .F74. **DD** 914.5/04929/05. ***Continues** Frommer's Italy, 1044-2170.*

●US/1064-5233
**FROMMER'S COMPREHENSIVE TRAVEL GUIDE. JAPAN.** [Frommer's compr. travel guide, Jpn.]. **VFOAT** Comprehensive Travel Guide. Japan; Japan; Frommer's Japan. (1993)-. English. be. Macmillan Publishing Co. / Indiana, 201 West 103rd Street, Indianapolis IN 46290. **Tel** (800)428-5331, (800)858-7674. **LC** DS811; .F76. **DD** 915.2/0448. ***Continues** Frommer's Japan & Hong Kong, 1045-6899.*

●US/1064-5195
**FROMMER'S COMPREHENSIVE TRAVEL GUIDE. LAS VEGAS.** [Frommer's compr. travel guide, Las Vegas]. **VFOAT** Comprehensive Tavel Gide. Las Vegas; Las Vegas; Frommer's Las Vegas. (1991/1992)-. English. be. $13.95. Macmillan Publishing Co. / Indiana, 201 West 103rd Street, Indianapolis IN 46290. **Tel** (800)428-5331, (800)858-7674. **LC** F849.L35; F76. **DD** 917.93/1350433. ***Continues** Frommer's Las Vegas, 0899-3262.*

●US/1064-5225
**FROMMER'S COMPREHENSIVE TRAVEL GUIDE. LISBON, MADRID & THE COSTA DEL SOL.** [Frommer's compr. travel guide, Lisb. Madr. Costa Sol]. **VFOAT** Comprehensive Travel Guide. Lisbon, Madrid & the Costa del Sol; Lisbon, Madrid & the Costa del Sol; Lisbon, Madrid, and the Costa del Sol; Frommer's Lisbon, Madrid, and the Costa del Sol; Frommer's Lisbon, Madrid & the Costa del Sol. (1991/1992)-. English. be. $13.95. Macmillan Publishing Co. / Indiana, 201 West 103rd Street, Indianapolis IN 46290. **Tel** (800)428-5331, (800)858-7674. **LC** DP757; .F76. **DD** 914.6/410483. ***Continues** Frommer's Lisbon, Madrid & the Costa del Sol, 0899-2932.*

●US
**FROMMER'S COMPREHENSIVE TRAVEL GUIDE. LOS ANGELES.** **VFOAT** Comprehensive Travel Guide. Los Angeles; Los Angeles; Frommer's Los Angeles. (1992)-. English. be. $8.95. Macmillan Publishing Co. / Indiana, 201 West 103rd Street, Indianapolis IN 46290. **Tel** (800)428-5331, (800)858-7674. **ED** Mary Rakauskas. **LC** F869.L83; P76. **DD** 917.94/940453. ***Continues** Frommer's Los Angeles, 0899-3238.*

●US/1047-790X
**FROMMER'S COMPREHENSIVE TRAVEL GUIDE. MIAMI.** [Frommer's compr. travel guide, Miami]. **VFOAT** Comprehensive Travel Guide. Miami; Miami; Frommer's Miami. (1992)-. English. an. $13.00 (two years). Macmillan Publishing Co. / Indiana, 201 West 103rd Street, Indianapolis IN 46290. **Tel** (800)428-5331, (800)858-7674. **(Subscription address:** Macmillian Publishing Company / Indiana, 201 West 103rd Street, Indianapolis IN 46290.**)** **ED** Dan Levine. **LC** F319.M6; F76. **DD** 917.59/3810463.

●US/1051-6980
**FROMMER'S COMPREHENSIVE TRAVEL GUIDE. MINNEAPOLIS & ST. PAUL.** [Frommer's compr. travel guide, Minneap. St. Paul]. **Added/Corp** Stelling, Lucille Johnsen. **VFOAT** Comprehensive Travel Guide. Minneapolis & St. Paul; Minneapolis & St. Paul; Minneapolis and St. Paul; Frommer's Minneapolis and St. Paul; Frommer's Minneapolis & St. Paul. (1992)-. English. be. $8.95. Macmillan Publishing Co. / Indiana, 201 West 103rd Street, Indianapolis IN 46290. **Tel** (800)428-5331, (800)858-7674. **ED** Lucille Johnsen Stelling. **LC** F614.M6; F75. **DD** 917.76/5790453.

●US/1064-5284
**FROMMER'S COMPREHENSIVE TRAVEL GUIDE. MONTREAL & QUEBEC CITY.** [Frommer's compr. travel guide, Montr. Que. City]. **VFOAT** Comprehensive Travel Guide. Montreal & Quebec City; Montreal & Quebec City; Montreal and Quebec City; Frommer's Montreal and Quebec City; Frommer's Montreal & Quebec City. (1991/1992)-. English. be. $8.95 US. Macmillan Publishing Co. / Indiana, 201 West 103rd Street, Indianapolis IN 46290. **Tel** (800)428-5331, (800)858-7674. **LC** F1054.5.M83; F76. **DD** 917.14/28044. ***Continues** Frommer's Montreal & Quebec City, 0899-3165.*

●US/1055-5439
**FROMMER'S COMPREHENSIVE TRAVEL GUIDE. NEPAL.** [Frommer's compr. travel guide, Nepal]. **VFOAT** Comprehensive Travel Guide. Nepal; Nepal; Frommer's Nepal. (1992/1993)-. English. be. $18.00. Macmillan Publishing Co. / Indiana, 201 West 103rd Street, Indianapolis IN 46290. **Tel** (800)428-5331, (800)858-7674. **LC** DS493.3; .F76. **DD** 915.49604.

US/1056-5787
**FROMMER'S COMPREHENSIVE TRAVEL GUIDE. NEW ENGLAND.** [Frommer's compr. travel guide, N. Engl.]. **VFOAT** Comprehensive Travel Guide. New England; New England; Frommer's New England. (1991)-. English. Macmillan Publishing Co. / Indiana, 201 West 103rd Street, Indianapolis IN 46290. **Tel** (800)428-5331, (800)858-7674. **ED** T Brosnahan. **DD** 917. ***Continues** Frommer's New England, 1044-2286.*

●US/1053-2455
**FROMMER'S COMPREHENSIVE TRAVEL GUIDE. NEW MEXICO.** [Frommer's compr. travel guide, N. M.]. **VFOAT** Comprehensive Travel Guide. New Mexico; New Mexico; Frommer's New Mexico. (1992)-. English. be. $13.95. Macmillan Publishing Co. / Indiana, 201 West 103rd Street, Indianapolis IN 46290. **Tel** (800)428-5331, (800)858-7674. **DD** 978.

US/1057-7645
**FROMMER'S COMPREHENSIVE TRAVEL GUIDE. NEW ORLEANS.** [Frommer's compr. travel guide, New Orleans]. **VFOAT** Comprehensive Travel Guide. New Orleans; New Orleans; A.Frommer's New Orleans. (1991)-. English. be. $8.95. Macmillan Publishing Co. / Indiana, 201 West 103rd Street, Indianapolis IN 46290. **Tel** (800)428-5331, (800)858-7674. **LC** F379.N53; F76. **DD** 917.63/350463. ***Continues** Frommer's New Orleans, 0899-2908.*

●US/1064-5276
**FROMMER'S COMPREHENSIVE TRAVEL GUIDE. NEW YORK STATE.** [Frommer's compr. travel guide, N. Y. State]. **VFOAT** Comprehensive Travel Guide. New York State; New York State; Frommer's New York State. (1993)-. English. be. $19.00. Macmillan Publishing Co. / Indiana, 201 West 103rd Street, Indianapolis IN 46290. **Tel** (800)428-5331, (800)858-7674. **LC** F117.3; .F76. **DD** 917.47/0443/05. ***Continues** Frommer's New York State, 1044-2308.*

US
**FROMMER'S COMPREHENSIVE TRAVEL GUIDE. NORTHWEST.** **VFOAT** Frommer's Travel Guide. Northwest; Frommer's Northwest. (1991)-. English. be. $16.95. Macmillan Publishing Co. / Indiana, 201 West 103rd Street, Indianapolis IN 46290. **Tel** (800)428-5331, (800)858-7674.

●US
**FROMMER'S COMPREHENSIVE TRAVEL GUIDE. PARIS.** **VFOAT** Comprehensive Travel Guide. Paris; Paris; Frommer's Paris. (1991/1992)-. English. be. Macmillan Publishing Co. / Indiana, 201 West 103rd Street, Indianapolis IN 46290. **Tel** (800)428-5331, (800)858-7674. **LC** DC708; .F76. **DD** 914.4/3604838. ***Continues** Frommer's Paris, 0899-3203.*

●US/1064-5268
**FROMMER'S COMPREHENSIVE TRAVEL GUIDE. PORTUGAL.** [Frommer's compr. travel guide, Port.]. **VFOAT** Comprehensive Travel Guide. Portugal; Portugal; Frommer's Portugal. 12th Ed. (1992)-. English. be. $16.00. Macmillan Publishing Co. / Indiana, 201 West 103rd Street, Indianapolis IN 46290. **Tel** (800)428-5331, (800)858-7674. **LC** DP516; .A85. **DD** 914.69/0444. ***Continues** Frommer's Portugal, Madeira, and the Azores, 1044-2278.*

●US/1062-4775
**FROMMER'S COMPREHENSIVE TRAVEL GUIDE, PUERTO RICO.** **VFOAT** Puerto Rico; Frommer's Puerto Rico. (1992)-. English. be. $15.00. Macmillan Publishing Co. / Indiana, 201 West 103rd Street, Indianapolis IN 46290. **Tel** (800)428-5331, (800)858-7674.

●US/1060-3727
**FROMMER'S COMPREHENSIVE TRAVEL GUIDE. PUERTO VALLARTA, MANZANILLO & GUADALAJARA.** **VFOAT** Puerto Vallarta, Manzanillo & Guadalajara; Puerto Vallarta, Manzanillo, and Guadalajara. (1993)-. English. be. $14.00. Macmillan Publishing Co. / Indiana, 201 West 103rd Street, Indianapolis IN 46290. **Tel** (800)428-5331, (800)858-7674.

●US/1064-5241
**FROMMER'S COMPREHENSIVE TRAVEL GUIDE. RIO.** [Frommer's compr. travel guide, Rio]. **VFOAT** Comprehensive Travel Guide. Rio; Rio; Frommer's Rio. (1991/1992)-. English. be. Macmillan Publishing Co. / Indiana, 201 West 103rd Street, Indianapolis IN 46290. **Tel** (800)428-5331, (800)858-7674. **LC** F2646.A4; F68. **DD** 918.1/530463. ***Continues** Frommer's Rio, 0899-2762.*

US/1056-5795
**FROMMER'S COMPREHENSIVE TRAVEL GUIDE. ROME.** [Frommer's compr. travel guide, Rome]. **VFOAT** Comprehensive Travel Guide. Rome.; Rome; Frommer's Rome. (1991/92)-. English. be. Macmillan Publishing Co. / Indiana, 201 West 103rd Street, Indianapolis IN 46290. **Tel** (800)428-5331, (800)858-7674. **ED** D. Porter. **LC** DG804; .F79. **DD** 914.5/63204929. ***Continues** Frommer's Rome, 0899-319X.*

●US
**FROMMER'S COMPREHENSIVE TRAVEL GUIDE SALT LAKE CITY.** (1992)-. Macmillan Publishing Co. / Indiana, 201 West 103rd Street, Indianapolis IN 46290. **Tel** (800)428-5331, (800)858-7674.

●US/1047-787X
**FROMMER'S COMPREHENSIVE TRAVEL GUIDE, SAN DIEGO.** [Frommer's compr. travel guide, S. Diego]. **VFOAT** Comprehensive Travel Guide. San Diego; San Diego; Frommer's San Diego. (1992)-. English. be. $7.95. Macmillan Publishing Co. / Indiana, 201 West 103rd Street, Indianapolis IN 46290. **Tel** (800)428-5331, (800)858-7674. **DD** 917.

US
**FROMMER'S COMPREHENSIVE TRAVEL GUIDE. SAN FRANCISCO.** **VFOAT** Comprehensive Travel Guide. San Francisco; Frommer's San Francisco. (1991)-. English. $8.95. Macmillan Publishing Co. / Indiana, 201 West 103rd Street, Indianapolis IN 46290. **Tel** (800)428-5331, (800)858-7674. **LC** F869.S33; F76. **DD** 917.94/610453. ***Continues** Frommer's San Francisco.*

●US/1064-5209
**FROMMER'S COMPREHENSIVE TRAVEL GUIDE. SANTA FE, TAOS & ALBUQUERQUE.** [Frommer's compr. travel guide, Santa Fe Taos Albuq.]. **VFOAT** Comprehensive Ttravel Guide. Santa Fe, Taos & Albuquerque; Santa Fe, Taos & Albuquerque; Santa Fe, Taos, and Albuquerque; Frommer's Santa Fe, Taos, and Albuquerque; Frommer's Santa Fe, Taos & Albuquerque. (1991/1992)-. English. be. $8.95. Macmillan Publishing Co. / Indiana, 201 West 103rd Street, Indianapolis IN 46290. **Tel** (800)428-5331, (800)858-7674. **DD** 917. ***Continues** Frommer's Santa Fe, Taos and Albuquerque, 0899-2789.*

●US/1064-5187
**FROMMER'S COMPREHENSIVE TRAVEL GUIDE. SEATTLE & PORTLAND.** [Frommer's compr. travel guide, Seattle Portland]. **VFOAT** Comprehensive Ttravel Guide. Seattle & Portland; Seattle & Portland; Seattle and Portland; Frommer's Seattle and Portland; Frommer's Seattle & Portland. (1993)-. English. be. $12.00. Macmillan Publishing Co. / Indiana, 201 West 103rd Street, Indianapolis IN 46290. **Tel** (800)428-5331, (800)858-7674. **DD** 917. ***Continues** Frommer's Seattle & Portland, 1045-9308.*

●US
**FROMMER'S COMPREHENSIVE TRAVEL GUIDE. SOUTH PACIFIC.** [Frommer's compr. travel guide, South Pac.]. **VFOAT** Comprehensive Travel Guide. South Pacific; South Pacific; Frommer's South Pacific. (1993)-. English. be. Macmillan Publishing Co. / Indiana, 201 West 103rd Street, Indianapolis IN 46290. **Tel** (800)428-5331, (800)858-7674. **LC** DU15; .F76. **DD** 919.504. ***Continues** Frommer's South Pacific, 1044-2367.*

●US/1051-6840
**FROMMER'S COMPREHENSIVE TRAVEL GUIDE. ST. LOUIS & KANSAS CITY.** [Frommer's compr. travel guide, St. Louis Kans. City]. **VFOAT** Comprehensive Travel Guide. St. Louis & Kansas City; St. Louis & Kansas City; Saint Louis and Kansas City; Frommer's St. Louis & Kansas City. (1992)-. English. be. $8.95. Macmillan Publishing Co. / Indiana, 201 West 103rd Street, Indianapolis IN 46290. **Tel** (800)428-5331, (800)858-7674. **ED** Editor: Beth Reiber. **LC** F474.S23; F76. **DD** 917.78/4110443.

# Travel and Tourism

●US
**FROMMER'S COMPREHENSIVE TRAVEL GUIDE. SWITZERLAND & LIECHTENSTEIN.** VFOAT Comprehensive Travel Guide. Switzerland & Liechtenstein; Switzerland and Liechtenstein; Frommer's Switzerland & Liechtenstein; Frommer's Switzerland & Liechtenstein. (1993)-. English. be. Macmillan Publishing Co. / Indiana, 201 West 103rd Street, Indianapolis IN 46290. Tel (800)428-5331, (800)858-7674. LC DQ16; .F77. DD 914.9404/73. *Continues Frommer's Switzerland and Liechtenstein, 1044-2294.*

●US/1047-7896
**FROMMER'S COMPREHENSIVE TRAVEL GUIDE. TAMPA & ST. PETERSBURG.** (1992)-. English. be. $7.95. Macmillan Publishing Co. / Indiana, 201 West 103rd Street, Indianapolis IN 46290. Tel (800)428-5331, (800)858-7674.

●US/1058-4943
**FROMMER'S COMPREHENSIVE TRAVEL GUIDE. THE CAROLINAS & GEORGIA.** [Frommer's compr. travel guide, Carol. Ga.]. VFOAT Carolinas & Georgia; Carolinas and Georgia; Frommer's the Carolinas and Georgia; Frommer's the Carolinas & Georgia. (1993)-. English. be. $17.00. Macmillan Publishing Co. / Indiana, 201 West 103rd Street, Indianapolis IN 46290. Tel (800)428-5331, (800)858-7674. DD 917. *Continues in part Frommer's Southern Atlantic States, 1044-2316.*

●US/1055-5447
**FROMMER'S COMPREHENSIVE TRAVEL GUIDE. THE VIRGIN ISLANDS.** [Frommer's compr. travel guide. Virg. Isl.]. VFOAT Virgin Islands; Frommer's the Virgin Islands. (1992-1993)-. English. be. Macmillan Publishing Co. / Indiana, 201 West 103rd Street, Indianapolis IN 46290. Tel (800)428-5331, (800)858-7674. LC F2136.2; .F76. DD 917.

●US/1047-7853
**FROMMER'S COMPREHENSIVE TRAVEL GUIDE. TORONTO.** (1992). English. be. $7.95. Macmillan Publishing Co. / Indiana, 201 West 103rd Street, Indianapolis IN 46290. Tel (800)428-5331, (800)858-7674. LC F1059.5.T683; F76. DD 917.13/54104647.

●US
**FROMMER'S COMPREHENSIVE TRAVEL GUIDE, U.S.A.** VFOAT Frommer's Comprehensive Travel Guide. USA; Comprehensive Travel Guide. U.S.A.; Comprehensive Travel Guide. USA; Frommer's USA; Frommer's U.S.A. VAT Frommer's Comprehensive Travel Guide United States of America; Frommer's United States of America. (1992)-. English (translations available in French). be. $16.95. Macmillan Publishing Co. / Indiana, 201 West 103rd Street, Indianapolis IN 46290. Tel (800)428-5331, (800)858-7674. LC E158; .F74. DD 917.304/927/05. *Continues Frommer's Dollarwise USA, 0899-2797.*

●US/1058-4943
**FROMMER'S COMPREHENSIVE TRAVEL GUIDE. VIRGINIA.** [Frommer's compr. travel guide, Va.]. VFOAT Frommer's Virginia; Virginia. (1993)-. English. be. $14.00. Macmillan Publishing Co. / Indiana, 201 West 103rd Street, Indianapolis IN 46290. Tel (800)428-5331, (800)858-7674. DD 975. *Continues in part Frommer's Southern Atlantic States, 1044-2316.*

●US/1064-1416
**FROMMER'S COMPREHENSIVE TRAVEL GUIDE, YUCATAN.** VFOAT Yucatan. (1994)-. Periodical. English. be. $18.00. Macmillan Publishing Co. / Indiana, 201 West 103rd Street, Indianapolis IN 46290. Tel (800)428-5331, (800)858-7674.

●US/1055-5358
**FROMMER'S COPENHAGEN ON ... $ A DAY.** VFOAT Copenhagen on ... $ a Day. (1991)-. English. be. $10.95. Macmillan Publishing Co. / Indiana, 201 West 103rd Street, Indianapolis IN 46290. Tel (800)428-5331, (800)858-7674.

US/1051-6859
**FROMMER'S COSTA RICA, GUATEMALA & BELIZE ON $ ... A DAY.** VFOAT Frommer's Costa Rica, Guatemala, and Belize on $ ... a Day; Costa Rica, Guatemala, & Belize on $ ... a Day; Costa Rica, Guatemala, and Belize on $ ... a Day. (1991)-. English. be. $13.95. Macmillan Publishing Co. / Indiana, 201 West 103rd Street, Indianapolis IN 46290. Tel (800)428-5331, (800)858-7674.

US/0899-3327
**FROMMER'S DOLLARWISE SKIING EUROPE PLUS SUMMER SKIING IN ARGENTINA.** [Frommer's dollarw. ski. Eur. plus summer ski. Argent.]. VFOAT Dollarwise Skiing Europe Plus Summer Skiing in Argentina. (1989/90)-. English. be. $14.95. Macmillan Publishing Co. / Indiana, 201 West 103rd Street, Indianapolis IN 46290. Tel (800)858-7674. ED Catherine Foreht and Peter Foreht. LC GV854.88.E9; F76. DD 914. *Continues Frommer's Dollarwise Guide to Skiing Europe.*

US/1040-9394
**FROMMER'S DOLLARWISE SOUTHEAST ASIA.** [Frommer's dollarw. Southeast Asia]. VFOAT Dollarwise Southeast Asia. (1989/90)-. English. be. $14.95. Macmillan Publishing Co. / Indiana, 201 West 103rd Street, Indianapolis IN 46290. Tel (800)428-5331, (800)858-7674. ED John Levy and Kyle McCarthy. DD 915.

US/0899-3335
**FROMMER'S DOLLARWISE SOUTHWEST.** [Frommer's dollarw. Southwest incl. N. M. Ariz. Colo.]. VFOAT Dollarwise Southwest. (1990)-. English. be. $14.95. Macmillan Publishing Co. / Indiana, 201 West 103rd Street, Indianapolis IN 46290. Tel (800)428-5331, (800)858-7674. LC F787; .F76. DD 917.8804/33. *Continues Frommer's Dollarwise Guide to the Southwest.*

US/1044-226X
**FROMMER'S EGYPT.** [Frommer's Egypt]. VFOAT Egypt. 6th Ed. - (1990)-. English. be. $14.95 (two years). Macmillan Publishing Co. / Indiana, 201 West 103rd Street, Indianapolis IN 46290. Tel (800)428-5331, (800)858-7674. LC DT45; .F76. DD 916.204/55. *Continues Frommer's Dollarwise Guide to Egypt, 0731-4566.*

●US/1055-5404
**FROMMER'S ENGLAND.** VFOAT England. (1992)-. English. be. $16.95. Macmillan Publishing Co. / Indiana, 201 West 103rd Street, Indianapolis IN 46290. Tel (800)428-5331, (800)858-7674. *Continues in part Frommer's comprehensive Travel Guide. England & Scotland.*

●US/1058-496X
**FROMMER'S FAMILY TRAVEL GUIDE. LOS ANGELES WITH KIDS.** [Frommer's fam. travel guide, Los Angel. kids]. VFOAT Los Angeles With Kids; Frommer's Los Angeles With Kids. 1993-. English. be. $17.00. Macmillan Publishing Co. / Indiana, 201 West 103rd Street, Indianapolis IN 46290. Tel (800)428-5331, (800)858-7674. DD 979.

●US/1060-3719
**FROMMER'S FAMILY TRAVEL GUIDE. NEW YORK CITY WITH KIDS.** VFOAT New York City with Kids. (1992)-. English. be. $18.00. Macmillan Publishing Co. / Indiana, 201 West 103rd Street, Indianapolis IN 46290. Tel (800)428-5331, (800)858-7674. *Continues Candy Apple.*

●US/1058-4951
**FROMMER'S FAMILY TRAVEL GUIDE. SAN FRANCISCO WITH KIDS.** (1992)-. Macmillan Publishing Co. / Indiana, 201 West 103rd Street, Indianapolis IN 46290. Tel (800)428-5331, (800)858-7674.

●US/1058-4978
**FROMMER'S FAMILY TRAVEL GUIDE. WASHINGTON, D.C., WITH KIDS.** (1992)-. Macmillan Publishing Co. / Indiana, 201 West 103rd Street, Indianapolis IN 46290. Tel (800)428-5331, (800)858-7674.

US/0739-7143
**FROMMER'S ... GUIDE TO PHILADELPHIA & ATLANTIC CITY.** Title Change. [Frommer's guide Phila. Atlantic City]. VFOAT Frommer's ... Guide to Philadelphia and Atlantic City; Guide to Philadelphia & Atlantic City; Guide to Philadelphia and Atlantic City. (1981/82)-(1984). English. Macmillan Publishing Co. / Indiana, 201 West 103rd Street, Indianapolis IN 46290. Tel (800)428-5331, (800)858-7674. LC F158.18; .F76. DD 917.48/110443. *Continued by Frommer's ... Guide to Philadelphia, 0883-7759.*

US/8755-9250
**FROMMER'S HAWAII ON $ ... A DAY.** Title Change. [Frommer's Hawaii $ day]. VFOAT Hawaii on $ ... a day. VAT Frommer's Hawaii on ... Dollars a Day. (198?)-(19??). English. an. Macmillan Publishing Co. / Indiana, 201 West 103rd Street, Indianapolis IN 46290. Tel (800)428-5331, (800)858-7674. ED F Hammel and S Levey. LC DU622; .H32. DD 919.69/044. *Continues Hawaii on $ ... a Day, 0197-8527. Continued by Frommer's Budget Travel Guide. Hawaii ... on $ ... a Day, 1059-7603.*

US/1051-6816
**FROMMER'S INDIA ON $ ... A DAY.** Title Change. [Frommer's India $ day]. VFOAT India on $ ... a Day. (1988/1989 Ed.)-(19??). English. be. Macmillan Publishing Co. / Indiana, 201 West 103rd Street, Indianapolis IN 46290. Tel (800)428-5331, (800)858-7674. ED J Aaron. LC DS406; .F76. DD 915.4/0452. *Continues Frommer's India on $ ... & $ ... a Day, 0883-7422. Continued by Frommer's Budget Travel Guide. India on $ ... a Day, 1065-1608.*

US/8755-8440
**FROMMER'S ISRAEL ON $ ... & $ ... A DAY.** Title Change. [Frommer's Isr. $ $ day]. VFOAT Frommer's Israel On $ ... and $ ... A Day; Israel On $ ... and $ ... A Day; Israel On $ ... & $ ... A Day. VAT Frommer's Israel On ... Dollars and ... Dollars a Day. (1982/83)-(19??). English. be. Macmillan Publishing Co. / Indiana, 201 West 103rd Street, Indianapolis IN 46290. Tel (800)428-5331, (800)858-7674. ED T Brosnahan and S Brilliant. LC DS103; .I826. DD 915.694/0454. *Continues Israel On $ ... A Day. Continued by Frommer's Israel on $ ... a Day, 1068-6525.*

●US/1061-9429
**FROMMER'S JAMAICA, BARBARDOS.** (1992)-. English. be. Macmillan Publishing Co. / Indiana, 201 West 103rd Street, Indianapolis IN 46290. Tel (800)428-5331, (800)858-7674.

US/0899-2908
**FROMMER'S NEW ORLEANS.** Title Change. [Frommer's New Orleans]. VFOAT New Orleans. (1989/90)-(199?). English. be. Macmillan Publishing Co. / Indiana, 201 West 103rd Street, Indianapolis IN 46290. Tel (800)428-5331, (800)858-7674. ED Susan Poole. LC F379.N53; F76. DD 917.63/350463. *Continues Frommer's Guide to New Orleans, 0277-4410. Continued by Frommer's Comprehensive Travel Guide. New Orleans, 1057-7645.*

US/0899-7675
**FROMMER'S NEW YORK.** [Frommer's N. Y.]. VFOAT New York. 1989/90-. English. be. $5.95. Macmillan Publishing Co. / Indiana, 201 West 103rd Street, Indianapolis IN 46290. Tel (800)428-5331, (800)858-7674. LC F128.18; .F74. DD 917.47/10443. *Continues Frommer's Guide to New York, 0277-4380.*

US/8755-5433
**FROMMER'S NEW YORK ON $ ... A DAY.** [Frommer's N. Y. $ day]. VFOAT New York on $ ... a Day. (1982/1983)-. English. an. $16.00. Macmillan Publishing Co. / Indiana, 201 West 103rd Street, Indianapolis IN 46290. Tel (800)428-5331, (800)858-7674. ED J. Hamburg and N. Ketay. LC F128.18; .F4. DD 917.47/10443. *Continues New York on $ ... a Day, 0278-128X.*

●US/1051-6808
**FROMMER'S NORTHWEST.** (FROMMER'S COMPREHENSIVE TRAVEL GUIDE. NORTHWEST.). [Frommer's compr. travel guide, Northwest]. VFOAT Comprehensive Travel Guide. Northwest; Frommer's Northwest. (1992)-. English. be. $14.95. Macmillan Publishing Co. / Indiana, 201 West 103rd Street, Indianapolis IN 46290. Tel (800)428-5331, (800)858-7674. DD 917. *Continues Frommer's Dollarwise Northwest, Including Oregon, Washington, Vancouver/Victoria, Sun Valley, & Cruises to Alaska, 1044-7741.*

●US/1055-5315
**FROMMER'S PARIS ON ... $ A DAY.** VFOAT Paris on ... $ a Day. (1991)-. English. be. $10.95. Macmillan Publishing Co. / Indiana, 201 West 103rd Street, Indianapolis IN 46290. Tel (800)428-5331, (800)858-7674.

US/0899-3211
**FROMMER'S PHILADELPHIA.** [Frommer's Phila.]. VFOAT Philadelphia. (1990)-. English. an. $13.00 (two years). Macmillan Publishing Co. / Indiana, 201 West 103rd Street, Indianapolis IN 46290. Tel (800)428-5331, (800)858-7674. ED Jay Golan. LC F158.18; .F76. DD 917.48/110443. *Continues Frommer's ... Guide to Philadelphia, 0883-7759.*

●US/1047-7861
**FROMMER'S SALT LAKE CITY.** (FROMMER'S COMPREHENSIVE TRAVEL GUIDE. SALT LAKE CITY.). [Frommer's compr. travel guide, Salt Lake City]. VFOAT Frommer's Salt Lake City. (1992)-. English. be. $7.95. Macmillan Publishing Co. / Indiana, 201 West 103rd Street, Indianapolis IN 46290. Tel (800)428-5331, (800)858-7674. DD 917.

US/0278-1069
**FROMMER'S SCANDINAVIA ON $ ... A DAY.** [Frommer's Scand. $ day]. VFOAT Frommer's Scandinavia on ... Dollars a Day; Scandinavia on ... Dollars a Day; Frommer's Scandinavia on $ ... a Day, Including Denmark, Finland, Norway, Sweden, Iceland & Greenland; Scandinavia on $ ... a Day. (1982)-. English. be. $14.95. Macmillan Publishing Co. / Indiana, 201 West 103rd Street, Indianapolis IN 46290. Tel (800)428-5331, (800)858-7674. LC DL4; .F74. DD 914.8/0488. *Continues Scandinavia on $ ... a Day.*

●US/1055-5390
**FROMMER'S SCOTLAND.** VFOAT Scotland. (1993)-. English. be. $16.95. Macmillan Publishing Co. / Indiana, 201 West 103rd Street, Indianapolis IN 46290

# Travel and Tourism

**Tel** (800)428-5331, (800)858-7674. **LC** DA870; .F75. **DD** 914.1104/859/05. *Continues in part* Frommer's Comprehensive Travel Guide. England & Scotland.

US/0277-7827
**FROMMER'S SOUTH AMERICA ON $ ... A DAY.** [Frommer's South Am. $ day]. **VFOAT** Frommer's South America on ... Dollars a Day; South America on ... Dollars a Day; South America on $ ... a Day. **VAT** Frommer's South America on ... Dollars a Day. (19??)-. English. be. $19.00. Macmillan Publishing Co. / Indiana, 201 West 103rd Street, Indianapolis IN 46290. **Tel** (800)428-5331, (800)858-7674. **ED** A Greenberg. **LC** F2224; .F76. **DD** 918/.0438.

●US/1055-534X
**FROMMER'S STOCKHOLM ON ... $ A DAY.** **VFOAT** Stockholm on ... $ a Day. (1991)-. English. be. $10.95. Macmillan Publishing Co. / Indiana, 201 West 103rd Street, Indianapolis IN 46290. **Tel** (800)428-5331, (800)858-7674.

US/0899-2770
**FROMMER'S SYDNEY.** [Frommer's Syd.]. (1989/90)-. English. be. $5.95. Macmillan Publishing Co. / Indiana, 201 West 103rd Street, Indianapolis IN 46290. **Tel** (800)428-5331, (800)858-7674. **DD** 919.44/10463.

●US/1055-5412
**FROMMER'S THAILAND.** **VFOAT** Thailand. (1991)-. English. be. $16.95. Macmillan Publishing Co. / Indiana, 201 West 103rd Street, Indianapolis IN 46290. **Tel** (800)428-5331, (800)858-7674.

US/0899-2800
**FROMMER'S TOURING GUIDE TO BRAZIL.** [Frommer's tour. guides, Braz.]. **VFOAT** Brazil. (1990)-. English (translations available in French). be. $10.95. Macmillan Publishing Co. / Indiana, 201 West 103rd Street, Indianapolis IN 46290. **Tel** (800)428-5331, (800)858-7674. **DD** 981.

US/1044-078X
**FROMMER'S TOURING GUIDE TO LENINGRAD/MOSCOW.** **VFOAT** Frommer's Touring Guide to Leningrad Moscow; Touring Guide to Leningrad Moscow; Touring Guide to Leningrad/Moscow. (1991)-. Periodical. English. be. $10.95. Macmillan Publishing Co. / Indiana, 201 West 103rd Street, Indianapolis IN 46290. **Tel** (800)428-5331, (800)858-7674.

●US/1062-7367
**FYI EVERYWOMAN'S RESOURCE GUIDE TO L.I.** See Women's Interests.

US/1049-9431
**GARDENS & COUNTRYSIDES.** (GARDENS & COUNTRYSIDES : JOURNAL OF PICTURESQUE TRAVELS.). [Gard. countrys.]. **VFOAT** Gardens and Countrysides. Vol. 1, No. 1 (May/June 1990)-. Periodical. English. Twelve times a year. $67.00. Travel Publications Inc, 401 Austin Highway, Suite 209, San Antonio TX 78209. **DD** 712.

US
**GAY AIRLINES & TRAVEL CLUB NEWSLETTER, THE.** See Homosexuality.

SZ
**GEMEINDERVERZEICHNIS DER SCHWEIZ / BUNDESAMT FUR STATISTIK.** **VFOAT** Repertoire des Communes de la Suisse. French (German). 9.00F. Bundesamt fuer Statistik, Schwarztorstrasse 96, CH 3003 Bern Switzerland. **Tel** 031 3236011, FAX 031 3236061. **LC** DQ15; .G43. **DD** 914.94/01/4.

IT/0393-7895
**GENTE VIAGGI.** [Gente viaggi]. (1979)-. Periodical. Italian. mo. L67200 Italy; L118000 other. Rusconi Editore Spa, Servicio Abbonemento, V Le Sarca 235, 20126 Milan Italy. **Tel** 011 39 2 66192634. **UDC** 796.5.

GW
**GEO-KATALOG.** V. 1- 1973-. German (English and French). an. DM35.00. Geo Center, Postfach 800830, W 7000 Stuttgart 80 Germany. **Tel** 0711-7803053. **Ad Acc. Circ:** 2,000 (ctrl).
**Desc:** Maps, plans (city-maps), guides, atlases and other travel products.

UK/0954-0369
**GETTING ABOUT BRITAIN.** [Get. Br.]. (1988)-. English (German, French, Spanish and Italian). Three times a year. £7.00 UK; £10.00 other. Drumport Ltd, 21 Church Walk, Thames Ditton, Surrey KT7 ONP England /MW90. **Tel** 081-398 8332, +4481 398 8332. **ED** Clive Lewis. **DD** 380.590941. **Ad Acc. Circ:** 40,000.
*Continues* On the Move, 0269-3208.
**Desc:** Travel guide for overseas visitors journeying by train, plane, bus and ferry.

●SP
**GLOBAL TOURISM FORECASTS TO THE YEAR 2000 AND BEYOND : AFRICA.** (1994)-. English. ir. World Tourism Organization / WTO, Calle Capitan Haya 42, E 28020 Madrid Spain. **Tel** 011 34 1 5710628, FAX 011 34 1 5713733, telex 42188 OMT-E. **(Subscription address:** UNIPUB, 4611 F Assembly Drive, Lanham MD 20706.)

●SP
**GLOBAL TOURISM FORECASTS TO THE YEAR 2000 AND BEYOND : MIDDLE EAST.** (1994)-. English. ir. World Tourism Organization / WTO, Calle Capitan Haya 42, E 28020 Madrid Spain. **Tel** 011 34 1 5710628, FAX 011 34 1 5713733, telex 42188 OMT-E. **(Subscription address:** UNIPUB, 4611 F Assembly Drive, Lanham MD 20706.)

CN/0711-7108
**GLOBEHOPPER.** (THE GLOBEHOPPER.). [Globehopper]. **VFOAT** Globe Hopper. Vol. 1, No. 1 (Oct./Nov. 1981)-. Periodical. English. Six times a year. Interpress Inc., 136 Walton Street, Port Hope Ontario L1A 1N5 Canada. **Tel** (905)885-7948. **ED** Joanna Ebbutt. **DD** 910/.5. **Bk Rev. Ad Acc. Circ:** 100,000 (ctrl).
**Desc:** A consumer travel magazine written with the active (as opposed to "armchair") traveller in mind, covering all (safe) parts of the globe, and all modes of travel.

US/0893-0643
**GO.** (GO; THE AUTHENTIC GUIDE TO NEW ORLEANS.). [GO]. **VFOAT** Authentic Guide to New Orleans. 1972-. Periodical. English. mo. $15.00. Go Magazine Ltd, 541 Julia Street, New Orleans LA 70130. **DD** 917.

US/1047-3858
**GO!.** *Ceased.* [Travel life]. **VFOAT** Travellife. (1988)-Ceased with April (1992). Periodical. English. bm. Whittle Communications, 333 Main Avenue, Knoxville TN 37902. **Tel** (615)595-5000, FAX (615)595-5877. **LC** G154; .T696. **DD** 910/.23/73.

●CN/1189-4849
**GOLF VACATIONS (BURLINGTON).** See Recreation, Leisure-Sports.

US/0163-6227
**GOMER'S BUDGET TRAVEL DIRECTORY.** Directory. English. Gomer Guides, PO Box 310, Maplewood NJ 07040. **LC** E158; .L42. **DD** 917.3/04/926.

US/1059-6607
**GOULD'S PRIVATE SECURITY REPORTER : SERVING THE HOSPITALITY AND REAL ESTATE INDUSTRIES.** See Real Estate.

US/0706-7682
**GREAT EXPEDITIONS.** [Gt. exped.]. Vol. 1 (March/April 1978)-. Periodical. English. qt. $18.00 US; $26.00 (includes postage) other. Great Expeditions, PO Box 18036, Raleigh NC 27609. **Tel** (919)846-3600. **ED** George Kane. **DD** 910/.5. Index available. **Bk Rev. Ad Acc. Circ:** 25,000.
**Desc:** Honest, factual, first-hand travel reporting. New members receive a free copy of "Save on Travel," filled with proven methods to save hundreds, even thousands, of dollars. Provides valuable information not readily available through traditional channels such as guide books, travel agents and tourist boards.

US
**GREAT LAKES TOUR BOOK.** **VFOAT** Tour Book, Great Lakes. English. an. American Automobile Association, 1000 AAA Drive, Heathrow FL 32746. **Tel** (407)444-7000. **LC** F539.3; .G73. **DD** 917.7/04/3.
*Continues* Great Lakes States.

US/0887-6223
**GREAT LAKES TRAVEL & LIVING.** [Gt. Lakes travel living]. **VFOAT** Great Lakes Travel and Living; Great Lakes Travel & Living Magazine; GLT&L;. Vol. 1, Issue 1 (Aug. 1986)-. Periodical. English. Eight times a year. $15.00 US; $21.00 other. Great Lakes Travel & Living, PO Box 423, Mt. Morris IL 61054. **Tel** (312)654-0950. **DD** 977. **Ad Acc. Circ:** 50,000 (ctrl).
**Desc:** Covers regional travel and leisure subjects including calendar, events, history, food, outdoor recreation, inn and restaurant reviews. Coverage area is Illinois, Indiana, Ohio, Wisconsin, Minnesota, Michigan, Western Pennsylvania and New York, and Ontario.

●CN/1189-3311
**GREATER KINGSTON, ONTARIO CANADA, VISITOR'S GUIDE.** [Gt. Kingst. Ont. Can. visit. guide]. **Added/Corp** Kingston Area Economic Development Commission. **VFOAT** Your 1000 Islands Destination, Greater Kingston, Ontario Canada, Visitor's Guide. (1992). English. Free. Kingston Area Exonomic Development Commission, Suite 106, 275 Ontario Street, Kingston Ontario K7K 2X5. **DD** 917.13/72044.

CN/0847-3846
**GREATER QUEBEC AREA TOUR OPERATOR MANUAL.** [Gt. Que. area tour oper. man.]. **Added/Corp** Communaute Urbaine de Quebec (Quebec). Tourism and Convention Bureau. (1991)-. English. Communaute Urbaine de Quebec, Tourism and Convention Bureau, 60 D'Auteuil Rue, Quebec Quebec G1R 4C4 Canada. **DD** 917.14/471/044. *Continues* Quebec City Region, Group Tour Manual., 0835-6785.

US/0270-4358
**GREECE AND YUGOSLAVIA ON $15 & $20 A DAY.** [Greece Yuogosl. $15 $20 day.]. English. $4.95. Arthur Frommer / Pasmantier Publishers, 1230 Avenue of the Americas, New York NY 10020. **Tel** (212)373-8500. **LC** DF716; .W49. **DD** 914.95/0476.

GW
**GROSS- UND EINZELHANDEL, GASTGEWERBE, REISEVERKEHR. REIHE 8 : REISEVERKEHR. IV. GRENZUBERSCHREITENDER REISEVERKEHR.** **Main/Corp** Germany (West). Statistisches Bundesamt. **VFOAT** Fachserie F. **VAT** Gross- und Einzelhandel, Gastgewerbe, Reiseverkehr. Reihe Acht: Reiseverkehr. Vier. Grenzuberschreitender Reiseverkehr. German. DM3.20 single issue. W Kohlhammer Verlag GMBH, Postfach 800430, D70549 Stuttgart Germany. **Tel** 011 49 711 78631. **LC** G155.G3; G464B.

US/0017-4629
**GROSSE POINTER, THE.** Periodical. English. mo. $20.00 members, $30.00 nonmembers. Kelvin Publishing, 27421 Harper Avenue, St Clair Shores MI 48081. **Tel** (313)774-3530. **ED** Karen Adams. **Ad Acc. Circ:** 1,000 (ctrl).
**Desc:** Club magazine for the Grosse Pointe Yacht Club and its members.

UK/0962-8266
**GROUP TRAVEL ORGANISER.** [Group travel organ.]. (1989)-. Periodical. English. Ten times a year. £24.00 UK; £36.00 other. Landor Holdings Ltd, Quadrant House, 250 Kennington Lane, London SE11 5RD England. **Tel** 011 44 71 735 5058, FAX 011 44 71 587 0497.
**Desc:** Provides news and ideas for group trips and the supplier marketplace, plus information on destinations and attractions and the latest deals and discounts all directed at the group organizer.

CN/0710-3425
**GUELPH MAGAZINE.** [Guelph mag.]. Vol. 1, No. 1 (April 1980)-. Periodical. English. mo. $1.00 per no. Quintus Enterprises, 19 Prospect Avenue, Guelph Ontario N1E 4W7 Canada. **DD** 917.13/43/005.

MX
**GUIA COMPLETA DE LA CIUDAD DE MEXICO, DISTRITO FEDERAL Y SUS ALREDEDORES.** **VFOAT** Guia Roji, Mexico. Spanish. ir. Republica de Colombia, No 23, Mexico 1 DF Mexico. *Continues* Guia Roji (Guia Roja) : Informacion y Guia de la Ciudad de Mexico.

AG
**GUIA DE TURISMO : REPUBLICA ARGENTINA.** **Main/Corp** Ediciones Cicerone. **VFOAT** Guia de Turismo de la Republica Argentina. (1977)-. Spanish. Ediciones Cicerone, Peru 327, 2, Piso E, Buenos Aires Argentina. **LC** F2808.5; .E34a. **DD** 918.2/04/6.

AG
**GUIA TURISTICA Y DE CALLES DE LA CIUDAD DE MAR DEL PLATA.** **VFOAT** Guia Filcar Mar del Plata. (19??)-. Spanish. Filcar, Saavedra 138, Buenos Aires Argentina. **LC** F3011.M29; G78.

CN/0838-0015
**GUIDE DE LA ROUTE, FLORIDE.** [Guide route Fla.]. (1987)-. French (English). an. 7.00Can$. Canadian Automobile Association, 1775 Courtwood Crescent, Ottawa Ontario K2C 3J2 Canada. **Tel** (613)226-7631, FAX (613)225-7383, telex 053-4440. **ED** David Steventon. **DD** 917.59/0463. Index available. **Ad Acc. Circ:** 30,000 (ctrl).
**Desc:** A French language tourbook listing accommodations, sites to see, things to do, etc., in the state of Florida.

CN/0225-2600
**GUIDE DE LA ROUTE, PROVINCES DE L'ATLANTIQUE ET DU QUEBEC.** 1978-. French (English). an. 6.95Can$. Association Canadienne des Automobilistes / Ottawa, 1775 Courtwood Crescent, Ottawa Ontario K2C 3J2 Canada. **Tel** (613)226-7631, FAX (613)225-7383, telex 053-4440. **ED** Michael S McNeil. **DD** 917.15/044. Index available. **Ad Acc. Circ:** 15,000 (ctrl).
**Desc:** A French language tourbook listing accommodations, sites to see, things to do, etc., in the province of Quebec and the maritime provinces.

# Travel and Tourism

CN/0318-9414
**GUIDE DE ROUTE.** **Main/Corp** Club Automobile Quebec. **VFOAT** Road Book. First issue in 1925?. French. Quebec Automobile Club, PO Box 9600, 2600 Laurier Boulevard, Ste Foy Quebec G1V 4K8 Canada. **DD** 917.14/04/4.

IT
**GUIDE DELLE REGIONI D'ITALIA.** (1971/72)-. Italian. an. L240.000 Italy; L240.000 (add postage) other. Societa Italiana per Lo Studio dei Problemi Regionali, Via Della Scrofa 14, 00186 Rome Italy. **Tel** 011 39 6 6879852.
**Desc:** Regional directories of political administration, economical, cultural, tourist and public health information.

FR
**GUIDE DES MANIFESTATIONS DE PROMOTION TOURISTIQUE / MINISTERE DU TEMPS LIBRE, SECRETARIAT D'ETAT CHARGE DU TOURISME.** French. an. 17 rue de l'Ingenieur Keller, 75740 Paris Cedex 15 France. **LC** G155.F8; G85. **DD** 380.1/45914404/05.

CN/0825-6764
**GUIDE GRIMALDI DE MONTREAL, LE.** [Guide Grimaldi Montr.]. 1982/1983-. French. an. $9.95. Saint-Amor and Beauchamp, Bureau 103, 1155, Rue Nore-Dame, Lachine Quebec H8S 2C5. **DD** 912/.71427.

CN/1186-1886
**GUIDE PRATIQUE DE L'ORGANISATEUR DE CONGRES, RIMOUSKI LA PREFERENCE.** [Guide prat. organ. congr. Rimouski prefer.]. **Added/Corp** Rimouski (Quebec). Service de Developpement du Tourisme et des Congres. No 1 (1991)-. French. 50.00Can$ per volume. Service de Developpement du Tourisme et des Congres de Rimouski, 50 Ouest Rue Saint-Germain, Rimouski Quebec G5L 4B5 Canada. **DD** 060.

MG
**GUIDE ROUTIER ET TOURISTIQUE: MADAGASCAR, REUNION, MAURICE, COMORES ET SEYCHELLES.** **Added/Corp** Automobile Club de Madagascar. Service du Guide Routier. (19??)-. French. Automobile Club de Madagascar, Service du Guide Route, BP 571, Tananarive Malagasy Republic. **LC** GV1025.M3; G84. **DD** 916.9/1/045. **Continues** Automobile Club de Madagascar. Service du Guide Routier. Guide Routier, 0572-2330.

●US
**GUIDE TO COLLEGE PROGRAMS IN HOSPITALITY AND TOURISM : A DIRECTORY OF CHRIE MEMBER COLLEGES AND UNIVERSITIES, A.** **Added/Corp** Council on Hotel, Restaurant, and Institutional Education (U.S.). **VFOAT** Directory of CHRIE Member Colleges and Universities; College Programs in Hospitality and Tourism; Hospitality and Tourism; CHRIE Member Colleges and Universities. (1992)-. English. an. $19.45 (two years). CHRIE Council on Hotel Restaurant and Institutional Education, 1200 17th Street Northwest, Department A Adair, Washington DC 20036. **Tel** (202)331-5990. **LC** TX911.5; .G85. **DD** 647.94/071/173. **Continues** Guide to Hospitality and Tourism Education, 1050-933X.

US/0434-8877
**GUIDE TO GEORGIA.** (19??)-. Periodical. English. Twelve times a year. $8.00 one year; $15.00 two years; $21.00 three years. Guide to Georgia, 1655 Peachtree St., Atlanta GA 30309. **Tel** (404)892-0961, FAX (404)892-0961. **ED** Jim Crawford. **Bk Rev**, (Qty: 12/yr). **Ad Acc**, **Adv Mgr:** Jim Crawford. **Circ:** 20,000 (ctrl).
**Desc:** A monthly guide to attractions, events, and activities, plus feature articles, of interest to residents and visitors.

US
**GUIDE TO JEWISH EUROPE.** (19??)-. Periodical. English. an. $13.95. Israelowitz Publishing, Box 228, Brooklyn NY 11229. **Tel** (718)951-7072, FAX (718)951-7072. **ED** Oscar Israelowitz. Index available. **Bk Rev**. **Ad Acc**. **Circ:** 1,000 (ctrl).
**Desc:** Complete historic travel guide to Western Europe with maps, photos, restaurants and hotels.

US
**GUIDE TO JEWISH ITALY. Ceased.** (19??)-(19??)-. English. Israelowitz Publishing, Box 228, Brooklyn NY 11229. **Tel** (718)951-7072, FAX (718)951-7072. **ED** Annie Sacerdoti. Index available. **Bk Rev. Circ:** 2,000 (ctrl).
**Desc:** Historic Jewish sites in Italy.

US/1056-862X
**GUIDE TO MARTIN COUNTY.** [Guide Martin Cty.]. (1990)-. Periodical. English. $5.95. Mohr Graphics and Publishing, PO Box 410, Palm City FL 34990. **DD** 975.

IO/0377-7200
**GUIDE TO NORTH SUMATRA, INDONESIA.** (19??)-. English. Warren Publicity, PO Box 3062, Jakarta. **LC** DS646.15.S8; G85. **DD** 915.98/1.

US
**GUIDE TO THE JEWISH WEST.** (19??)-. Periodical. English. $13.95. Israelowitz Publishing, Box 228, Brooklyn NY 11229. **Tel** (718)951-7072, FAX (718)951-7072. **ED** Oscar Israelowitz.

US/0193-9130
**GUIDE TO TRAVEL AND RESIDENCE EXPENSES FOR THE MULTINATIONAL EXECUTIVE.** (19??)-. English. an. Travel and Living Costs Worldwide Inc, Harvard Square Box 92, Cambridge MA 02138. **LC** G153.4; .G84. **DD** 910/.202.

CN/0705-3711
**GUIDE TO U.S. CITIES.** 1977/78-. English. Maclean Hunter Canada / Montreal, 1001 bvd. de Maisonneuve W., Montreal, Quebec H3A 3E1 Canada. **Tel** 514-845-5141, FAX 514-845-4302, telex 055-60604. **DD** 917.3.

CN/0849-1992
**GUIDE TOURISTIQUE, CHAUDIERE-APPALACHES.** [Guide tour. Chaudiere-Appalach.]. **Added/Corp** Association Touristique Chaudiere-Appalaches. Quebec (Province). Ministere du Tourisme. (1990)-. French. Free. Association Touristique Chaudiere-Appalaches, 800 Autoroute Jean-Lesage, Bernieres, Quebec G7A 1C9 Canada. **DD** 917.14/7044. **Continues** Guide Touristique, Pays-de-l'Erable, 0835-2267.

BE
**GUIDE TOURISTIQUE EUROPEEN POUR ISRAELITES.** **VFOAT** European Travel Guide for Jews. Multiple languages (English and French). $1.20. **LC** DS102.9; .G84. **DD** 914/.04/5502403924.

CN/1180-0305
**GUIDE TOURISTIQUE, LANAUDIERE.** [Guide tour. Lanaudiere]. **Added/Corp** Tourisme Lanaudiere. Quebec (Province). Ministere du Tourisme. (1990/1991)-. French. Free. Tourisme Lanaudiere, PO Box 1210, Rawdon, Quebec J0K 1S0. **DD** 917.14/41044.

CN/1191-1670
**GULF ISLANDS GUARDIAN, THE.** [Gulf Isl. guard.]. **VFOAT** Guardian. Vol. 1, No. 1 (Summer 1991)-. Periodical. English. qt. $10.00 per year. Trust Islands Senior Writers, RR 1, Suite 10, C-1, Denman Island British Columbia V0R 1T0 Canada. **DD** 917.11/28/005.

US/0895-3767
**HACHETTE GUIDE TO GREAT BRITAIN, THE.** [Hachette guide G. B.]. 1st American Ed.-. Periodical. English. be. Pantheon Books, 201 East 50th Street, New York NY 10022. **LC** DA650; .H24. **DD** 914.104/858.

SZ/1013-5065
**HALLE SUD. Ceased.** [Halle sud]. (1984)-(1993). Periodical. French. qt.

CN/0227-6267
**HAMILTON GUIDEBOOK.** [Hamilton guideb.]. English. an. Free. Hamilton Guidebook, 110 George Street, Hamilton Quebec L8P 1E2 Canada. **DD** 917.13/52. ctrl circ.

US
**HAMMOND ROAD ATLAS & VACATION GUIDE.** See Geography-Cartography.

US
**HAMPTONS : THE MAGAZINE OF THE WORLD'S MOST SOPHISTICATED RESORT, THE.** (19??)-. Periodical. English. mo. The Hamptons, PO Drawer AR, Bridgehampton NY 11932.

US/0195-2080
**HAPPY WANDERER, THE.** Periodical. English. bm. Happy Wanderer, 7342 North Lincoln Avenue, Skokie IL 60077. **Tel** (312)676-1900. **ED** Mark Greenfield. **Ad Acc. Circ:** 250,000.

II/0440-4106
**HARYANA REVIEW. Added/Corp** Haryana. Public Relations Dept. Vol. 1 (April/June 1967)-. Periodical. English. qt. Haryana Public Relations Department, Chandigarh 160019 India. **LC** DS485.H34; A2. **DD** 915.4/55.

US/0744-5792
**HAWAII ISLAND GUIDE.** (1982)-. Periodical. English. mo. Hawaii Island Guide, 1314 South King Street/520, Honolulu HI 96814-2004. **Continues** Aloha Hawaii, 0279-4934.

US
**HAWAII MAGAZINE.** (19??)-. Periodical. English. bm. $17.97. Fancy Publications, PO Box 6050, Mission Viejo CA 92690. **Tel** (714)855-8822, (800)426-2516, FAX (714)855-3045. **(Subscription address:** Palm Coast Data, PO Box 420235, Agency Department, Palm Coast FL 32142.) **LC** WMLC 93/1311. **Continues** Hawaii (San Juan Capistrano, Calif.).

US
**HAWAII ON TEN AND FIFTEEN DOLLARS A DAY.** (19??)-. English. Arthur Frommer / Pasmantier Publishers, 1230 Avenue of the Americas, New York NY 10020. **Tel** (212)373-8500.

US/0892-0990
**HAWAII (SAN JUAN CAPISTRANO, CALIF.). Title Change.** (HAWAII.). **VFOAT** Hawaii Magazine. (1987)-(19??). Periodical. English. bm. Fancy Publications, PO Box 6050, Mission Viejo CA 92690. **Tel** (714)855-8822, (800)426-2516, FAX (714)855-3045. **LC** WMLC 93/1311. **DD** 917. **Continued by** Hawaii Magazine (Irvine, Calif.).

US/1042-8062
**HAWAII, THE BIG ISLAND.** [Hawaii Big Isl.]. **VFOAT** Hawaii. 1st Ed. (May 1989)-. English. be. $9.95 (add $2.00 shipping). Paradise Publications, 8110 SW Wareham, Portland OR 97233. **Tel** (503)246-1555. **ED** Gred Stilson and Christie Stilson. **DD** 919. Index available. cum. index. **Circ:** 10,000.
**Desc:** The only comprehensive travel publication for the Big Island of Hawaii. Detailed descriptions covering accommodations, restaurants, scenic points of interest, island history, beaches and general information such as travel safety tips, traveling with children, and travel for the physically impaired.

US/1042-8046
**HAWAII, THE BIG ISLAND UPDATE.** [Hawaii Big Isl. update]. (1989)-. Periodical. English. qt. $6.00. Paradise Publications, 8110 SW Wareham, Portland OR 97233. **Tel** (503)246-1555. **ED** Christie Stilson and John Penisten. **DD** 919. **Bk Rev. Ad Acc. Circ:** 2,000.
**Desc:** Features updated information on island restaurants, accommodations and other related material for the Hawaii bound traveler.

US/1074-4665
**HISTORIC TRAVELER, THE.** See History(General).

GW/0018-3113
**HOER ZU.** [Hor zu]. **VFOAT** Hoer Zu (Hamburg). (1947)-. Periodical. German. wk (52 issues). DM96.20 (basic rate). Axel Springer Verlag Ag, Brieffach 2460, D 20350 Hamburg Germany. **Tel** 011 49 40 34724503. **(Subscription address:** DSB ABO Betreuung GmbH, D 74168 Neckarsulm Germany; telephone: 011 49 7132 9590) **UDC** 654.19.

CN/0318-9104
**HOLIDAY NIAGARA.** Began with May 1972 issue. English. ir. 25.00Can$ per no. Holiday Niagara, PO Box 951, Niagara Falls Ontario L2E 6V8 Canada. **DD** 917.13/39/04.

TH/0439-3678
**HOLIDAY TIME IN THAILAND. Suspended.** Vol. 1 June 1960-Suspended Aug. 1988. Periodical. English. mo. Tourist Organ of Thailand, Ratchadammden Avenue, Bangkok Thailand. **LC** DS561; .H64. **DD** 915.93.0414.

US/8750-5649
**HOME & AWAY.** (HOME & AWAY : OFFICIAL PUBLICATION - HOOSIER MOTOR CLUB.). **VFOAT** Home and Away. Began in 1984. Periodical. English. bm. $2.50. PO Box 88505, Indianapolis IN 46208-0505. **Tel** (317)923-1500. **ED** Hugh Orr. **Ad Acc. Circ:** 180,000 (ctrl). **Continues** Hoosier Motorist Home & Away, 0199-6975.
**Desc:** Articles about different travel destinations for AAA Hoosier Motor Club members.

US/0744-1576
**HOME & AWAY. IOWA.** **VFOAT** Home and Away. Iowa. (19??)-. Periodical. English. bm. $6.00 (one year); $12.00 (two years); $15.00 (three year). Home & Away, Box 3535, 910 North 96th Street, Omaha NE 68103. **Tel** (402)390-1000. **Continues in part** Home & Away, 0199-7009.
**Desc:** Includes insert: Iowa motor news

US/0199-7009
**HOME & AWAY (OMAHA, NEB.). Title Change.** (HOME & AWAY.). **Added/Corp** Motor Club of Iowa. Cornhuskers Motor Club. North Dakota Automobile Club. South Dakota Automobile Club. **VAT** Home and Away. Vol. 1 (Jan./Feb. 1980)-(19??). Periodical. English. bm. Home & Away, Box 3535, 910 North 96th Street, Omaha NE 68103. **Tel** (402)390-1000. **ED** Barc Wade. **Ad Acc. Circ:** 1,750,000. **Continues** Nebraska Living. **Continued by** Home & Away. Iowa, 0744-1576.
**Desc:** Domestic and foreign travel, outdoor recreation, automotive safety and do-it-yourself auto repair, travel hints and how-to's.

UK/0072-6435
**HOME OFFICE RESEARCH STUDIES.** **Main/Corp** Great Britain. Home Dept. No. 1 (1969)-. Monographic series. English. ir. Price varies per volume.

# Travel and Tourism

Her Majesty's Stationery Office, 51 Nine Elms Lane, London SW8 5DR England. **Tel** 011 44 71 873 8459, 011 44 71 873 8499, FAX 011 44 71 873 8499, 011 44 71 873 8456, telex 297138. **(Subscription address:** Her Majesty's Stationery Office, PO Box 276, Publications Centre, London SW8 5DT England.**)**
**Ind/Abst** Leis. Recreat. Tour. Abstr.

US/0736-6736
**HONEYMOON HIDEAWAYS.** 1st Ed. (1983)-. English. an. $7.50. KB Associates, Inc., PO Box 53200, Atlanta GA 30355.

UK/0967-5698
**HORIZONS LONDON. 1991.** *Ceased.* [Horizons London. 1991.] (1991)-(March 1993). Periodical. English. bm. British Tourist Authority, Thames Tower, Blacks Road, London W6 9EL England. **Tel** 011 44 81 8469000, FAX 011 44 156 30302. **DD** 338.479141.
**Ind/Abst** Museum Abstr.

US
**HOSPITALITY & TOURISM EDUCATOR.** See Hotels/Motels.

US
**HOSPITALITY DIRECTIONS.** See Restaurants.

US
**HOSPITALITY INDEX, THE.** See Business-General Management.

US
**HOSTELLING NORTH AMERICA : A GUIDE TO HOSTELS IN CANADA AND THE UNITED STATES. Added/Corp** American Youth Hostels, Inc. Canadian Hostelling Association. **VFOAT** Guide to Hostels in Canada and the United States. (1991)-. English. an (Feb.). $5.00. American Youth Hostels, 733 15th Street Northwest, Suite 840, Washington DC 20005. **Tel** (202)783-6161, FAX (202)783-6171. **LC** TX907.2; H67. *Formed by the union of* Handbook (American Youth Hostels, Inc.) *and* Guide d'Auberges Canadiennes.

US/0162-9972
**HOTEL & TRAVEL INDEX.** See Hotels/Motels.

US/1056-4713
**HOTEL & TRAVEL INDEX (ABC INTERNATIONAL ED.).** See Aeronautics, Astronautics.

KE
**HOTLINE. Added/Corp** Kenya. Ministry of Tourism and Wildlife. (1974)-. Periodical. English. qt. Nairobi Ministry of Tourism and Wildlife, PO Box 30027, Nairobi Kenya Africa. **LC** G155.K4; H67. **DD** 916.76/2/04405.

MH
**HSIEN TAI AO-MEN. VFOAT** Macau Travelling Magazine. Chinese (Chinese). $1.00 single issue. H D & Macau Press, PO Box 174, Macau Macao. **LC** DS796.M2; H82.

HK
**HSING-TAO LU YU. VFOAT** Sing Tao Tour Magazine. Vol. 1 (Dec. 1975)-. Periodical. Chinese. mo. $6.50. Hsing-Tao Pao Yeh Yu Hsien Kung Su, News Building, 635 King's Road/8th Floor, Hsiang-Kang, People's Republic of China. **LC** G149; .H85.

US/0896-7296
**HUDSPETH REPORT, THE.** [Hudspeth rep.]. (1987)-. Periodical. English. mo. $18.00 (one year), $30.00 (two years). The Hudspeth Report, PO Box 76680, Atlanta GA 30358. **Tel** (404)255-3220. **DD** 917.

●CN/1189-3001
**HURONIA YEARLY VACATION PLANNER.** [Huronia yrly. vacat. plan.]. **Added/Corp** Huronia Tourist Association. (1991/92)-. English. Limited free distribution. Huronia Tourist Association, Box 91, Simcoe County Bldg., Midhurst, Ontario Loc 1X0. **DD** 917.13/17044/05.

●US
**I LOVE NY GROUP TRAVEL GUIDE FOR NEW YORK STATE. Added/Corp** New York (State). Division of Tourism. **VFOAT** I Love New York Group Travel Guide for New York State; I [Heart] NY Group Travel Guide for New York State; Group Travel Guide. (1992)-. English.

US/0094-3517
**ICTA ROSTER. Main/Corp** Institute of Certified Travel Agents. English. Institute of Certified Travel Agents, PO Box 9206, Arlington VA. **LC** G154; .I54A. **DD** 338.4/7/9106273.

●US/1055-8314
**IDEAL TRAVELER.** (1993)-. Periodical. English. qt. $29.99. Publishing & Business Consultants, PO Box 75392, Los Angeles CA 90075. **Tel** (213)732-3477, FAX (213)732-9123. **ED** Andeson Napoleon Atia. **Ad Acc.** Full Page (B&W) $5750.00. Half Page (B&W) $3575.00. Full Page (Color) $8750.00 (2 color). Half Page (Color)

$5500.00 (2 color). **Circ:** 161,000 total.
**Desc:** Of interest to the regional, national and international traveler. Features articles on travel safety, health, currencies and visas.

HU
**IDEGENFORGALMI. Main/Corp** Hungary. Kpzponti Statisztikai Hivatal. Idegenforgalmi Osztaly. Hungarian. mo. IPV, Budapest XIV, Angol U22, Budapest 1149 Hungary. **(Subscription address:** Kultura, PO Box 149, H-1389, Budapest 62 Hungary**) LC** G155.H9; H9C.

HU/0230-4414
**IDEGENFORGALMI EVKONYV / OSSZEALLITOTTA A KSH KERESKEDELMI ES KOZLEKEDESI STATISZTIKAI FOOSZTALY, IDEGENFORGALMI OSZTALY. VFOAT** Statisticheskii Ezhegodnik Turizma; Statistical Yearbook of Tourism. 1980-. Hungarian (summaries and/or abstracts in English and Russian). an. Statisztikai Kiado Vallalat, PO Box 99, H-1033 Budapest 3 Hungary. **Tel** 803-311, telex 22-6699-SKV-H. **LC** G155.H9; I338. **DD** 380.1/4591439. *Continues* Idegenforgalmi Statisztika.

HU
**IDEGENFORGALMI KOZLEMENYEK. Added/Corp** Orszagos Idegenforgalmi Tanacs (Hungary). (19??)-. Periodical. Hungarian. **LC** G155.A1; I29.
**Ind/Abst** Leis. Recreat. Tour. Abstr.

CN/0704-7428
**IMAGE DE LA MAURICIE.** (Sept. 1977)-. Periodical. French. mo. 15.00Can$. Publicite GM Inc, 564 rue des Prairies, Cap-de-la-Madeleine Quebec G8T 1K9 Canada. **Tel** (819)378-2176. **ED** Gilles Mercier. **DD** 917.14/465/005. **Ad Acc. Circ:** 10,000. *Continues* La Mauricie Touristique, 0700-3188.

US/0730-9813
**IMPACT OF TRAVEL ON STATE ECONOMIES, THE. Added/Corp** United States Travel Data Center. (1974)-. Periodical. an (Spring). $80.00. US Travel Data Center, 1100 New York Avenue, Suite 450, Washington DC 20005. **Tel** (202)408-1832. **LC** G155.U6; I48. **DD** 381/.45917304925.
**Desc:** This state-by-state travel impact study uses the Data Center's newly revised Travel Economic Impact Model and presents estimates of the travel-generated expenditures in each state for public transportation, auto transportation, lodging, food service, entertainment and recreation, and incidentals, along with business receipts, tax receipts, employment and payroll figures. This report also features the National Multiplier which measures the indirect effects of travel spending on the nation's economy.
**Ind/Abst** Stat. Ref. Index.

PL
**IMT; ILUSTROWANY MAGAZYN TURYSTYCZNY.** Mar. 1973-. Periodical. Polish. 80. RSW Prasa-Kriazka-Ruch, Centrala Kolportazu Prasy i Wydawnictw, Towarowa 28, 00-958 Warsaw Poland. **LC** G155.A1; S92. *Supersedes* Swiatowid.

UK/0019-3143
**IN BRITAIN.** [In Br.]. **Added/Corp** British Tourist Authority. British Travel Association. Vol. 22 (Dec. 1966)-. Periodical. English. mo. $39.95 (1 year), $71.95 (2 year), $101.95 (3 year) (surface mail) $55.45 (air mail) US; 45.95Can$ (1 year), 82.95Can$ (2 year), 116.95Can$ (3 year) (surface mail) 51.40 Can$ (air mail) Canada; £19.95 (1 year), £35.95 (2 year), £50.85 (3 year) other. Headway Home and Law Publ Ltd, Greater London House, Hampsted Road, London NW1 7QQ England. **Tel** 011 44 71 3883171, FAX 011 44 71 3879518, telex 269470. **LC** DA650; .C75. *Continues* Coming Events in Britain.

US/0743-1503
**IN JOPLIN METROPOLITAN. VFOAT** In Joplin. Vol. 1, No. 1 (July 1984)-. Periodical. English. Twelve times a year. $12.00. In Joplin Magazine, 517 South Main Street, Joplin MO 64801. **Tel** (417)782-4332. **ED** Judith Brock. **DD** 917. Index available. **Bk Rev. Ad Acc. Circ:** 10,000 (ctrl).
**Desc:** Features and informative departments on business, health, travel, reviews--all of particular interest to Midwestern living.
**Ind/Abst** Ozark Period. Index.

US/0090-8533
**INCENTIVE TRAVEL AND BUSINESS MEETINGS.** See Economics-Labor.

US/0737-8602
**INDIANA PRESERVATIONIST, THE.** (THE INDIANA PRESERVATIONIST / HISTORIC LANDMARKS FOUNDATION OF INDIANA.). **Added/Corp** Historic Landmarks Foundation of Indiana. (19??)-. English. bm. $25.00. Historic Landmarks Foundation of Indiana, 340 West Michigan, Indianapolis IN 46202. **Tel** (317)639-4534, FAX (317)639-6734. **ED** Liz Joss. **Ad Acc. Adv Mgr:** Stacey Gray. **Circ:** 5,000 (ctrl).

IO
**INDONESIA (INDONESIA. DIREKTORAT JENDERAL PARIWISATA).** (INDONESIA : TRAVEL INFORMATION MANUAL.). **VFOAT** Indonesia Travel Information Manual. English. an. Directorate General of Tourism, Jln Kramat Raya, PO Box 409, Jkt, Jakarta Indonesia. **LC** DS614; .I543A. **DD** 915.98/0438.

●US/1061-9852
**INDONESIA, MALAYSIA & SINGAPORE HANDBOOK.** (1993)-. English. Macmillan Publishing Co. / Indiana, 201 West 103rd Street, Indianapolis IN 46290. **Tel** (800)428-5331, (800)858-7674.

US/0019-7777
**INDUSTRIA TURISTICA (MIAMI).** (INDUSTRIA TURISTICA.). Periodical. Spanish. mo. $10.00. Charles Francis Publishing Inc, 7235 Northwest 19th Street, Suite G, Miami FL 33126.

US
**INDUSTRY AGENTS' HANDBOOK / AIRLINES REPORTING CORPORATION. Added/Corp** Airlines Reporting Corporation. **VFOAT** ARC Industry Agents' Handbook. (Dec. 31, 1984)-. English. Three times a year (Publishes one book and two supplements). $60.00. Airlines Reporting Corporation, 1530 Wilson Boulevard, Suite 800, Arlington VA 22209. **Tel** (703)816-8000, FAX (703)816-8104. **ED** Emelie Brown (phone: (703)816-8164). **LC** G154; .T69. **DD** 380.1/459104/06. *Continues* Travel Agents' Handbook (Washington, D.C.), 8755-8203.
**Desc:** Provides instruction to travel agents on how to write and process tickets as well as report and remit the proceedings of the tickets sales to carriers.

RU
**INFORMATION MOSCOW.** (19??)-. Periodical. English. sa. **LC** DK597; .I482.

US
**INSIDE CHICAGO.** Vol. 1, No. 1 (Jan./Feb. 1987)-. English. Eight times a year (every two months plus June and November issues). $15.00. Signature Publishing Inc, 2501 West Peterson Avenue, Chicago IL 60659. **Tel** (312)784-0800. **ED** Barbara Young and Shane Tritsch. **Bk Rev. Ad Acc. Circ:** 70,000 (ctrl).
**Desc:** Indepth look of what Chicago has to offer.

US/1057-9184
**INSIDER TRAVEL SECRETS.** (INSIDER TRAVEL SECRETS : THE TRAVEL NEWSLETTER OF CONSUMER CLUB INTERNATIONAL.). [Insid. travel secrets]. **Added/Corp** Consumer Club International. (1991)-. Newsletter. English. mo. $29.95. Consumer Club International, PO Box 64980, Department 267, Dallas TX 75206. **DD** 910.

AT/1034-148X
**INTERDATA LEISURE & TOURISM HANDBOOK, THE.** *Suspended.* [Interdata leis. tour. handb.]. (1989)-Suspended. English. an. IDP Interdata Pty Ltd, Suite 5 9 Natier Street, North Sydney New South Wales, 2060 Australia. **Tel** 11 61 2 957 2881. **DD** 382.45919. *Continues* Interdata Tourism Handbook, 0819-2499.

US/0148-2300
**INTERNATIONAL ADVENTURE TRAVELGUIDE. VFOAT** Adventure Travelguide. **VAT** International Adventure Travel Guide. 1978-. English. an. $9.95. Timber Press, 9999 Southwest Wilshire, Suite 124, Portland OR 97225. **Tel** (800)327-5680, (503)292-0745. **LC** GV191.35; .I57. **DD** 790/.025.

BF
**INTERNATIONAL BAHAMA LIFE.** Periodical. English. $16.00. O N Johnson/Johnson Publications, PO Box N-1505, Commonwealth of Bahamas, Nassau Bahamas. **LC** F1650; .I57. **DD** 917.29/6/005.

UK
**INTERNATIONAL CONFERENCES IN BRITAIN.** Trade Publication. English. an. £15.00. British Tourist Authority, Thames Tower, Blacks Road, London W6 9EL England. **Tel** 011 44 81 8469000, FAX 011 44 156 30302. Documents available from BLDSC.

US/0735-0112
**INTERNATIONAL DIRECTORY OF ACCESS GUIDES, THE.** See Physically Impaired.

NE
**INTERNATIONAL GAY HOTEL & RESORT GUIDE.** English. 10.50Aus$ Australia; 10.50Can$ Canada; 47.50F France; £4.25 Great Britain; Fl15.95 Netherlands; DM15.95 Germany; 15.25NZ$ New Zealand; $7.25 US. Best Guide, 66 N Z Voorburgwal Amsterdam The Netherlands. **Tel** (020)699 1583, FAX (020)6950907.
**Desc:** An inexpensive and popular pocket-sized guide

which lists gay hotels, resorts and guest houses throughout the USA and elsewhere. Nearly 500 listings given, for 32 countries spread across five continents.

CN/1182-3062
**INTERNATIONAL GUIDE, EDMONTON.** [Int. guide Edmont.]. **VFOAT** International Guide, Canada's West. (1991)-. English. International Guide, Suite 222, 999-8th Street SW, Calgary Alberta T2R 1J5 Canada. **DD** 917.123/3404/05. ***Continues in part*** *International Guide, Edmonton and Jasper., 0836-3951.*

US/0277-2442
**INTERNATIONAL LIVING (WASHINGTON, D.C.).** (INTERNATIONAL LIVING.). [Int. living]. (198?)-. Periodical. English. Twelve times a year. $36.00. International Living, 824 East Baltimore Street, Baltimore MD 21202. **Tel** (410)234-0515, (800)433-1528, FAX (410)837-3879. **ED** Kathleen Peddicord. **DD** 910. Index available. cum. index. **Bk Rev. Ad Acc. Circ:** 40,000.
**Desc:** Concise, detailed travel magazine for those interested in living, working, investing or studying abroad.

UK
**INTERNATIONAL RARE BOOK PRICES. VOYAGES, TRAVEL & EXPLORATION.** ***Title Change.*** **See** Publishing-Books and Bookmaking.

UK/0269-3747
**INTERNATIONAL TOURISM REPORTS.** **Added/Corp** Economist Intelligence Unit (Great Britain) Economist Publications (Firm). No. 1 (1986)-. Periodical. English. Four times a year. $401.25 (schools and educational libraries), $535.00 (other) North America. The Economist Intelligence Unit, 40 Duke Street, London W1A 1DW England. **Tel** 011 44 71 8301000. **(Subscription address:** Economist Intelligence Unit / North America Subscriptions, 111 West 57th Street, New York NY 10019.) **ED** Robyn Griffiths-Jones. **LC** G155.A1; I552. **DD** 338.4/791/05. Index available. cum. index. available on microfilm from World Microfilm Publications Ltd. ***Continues*** *International Tourism Quarterly.*
**Desc:** Examines and analyzes developments in individual tourism markets and comments on their medium-term prospect. Each report analysis trends in tourist arrivals and expenditure, accommodations and occupancy rates, transport, length of stay and purpose of visit. It also reports on national government policies toward tourism and the levels of public and private support, and includes a database on the world's eight largest destination countries.
**Ind/Abst** Leis. Recreat. Tour. Abstr.

CN/0705-5269
**INTERNATIONAL TRAVEL, ADVANCE INFORMATION.** [Int. travel, Adv. inf.]. **Added/Corp** Statistics Canada. International Travel Section. **VFOAT** Voyages Internationaux, Renseignements Preleminaires [sic]. Vol. 27, No. 1 (Jan. 1974)-. Periodical. English (French). mo. 70.00Can$ Canada; $84.00 US; $98.00 other. Statistics Canada, Publications Sales & Services, Main Building Room 1710, Ottawa Ontario K1A 0T6 Canada. **Tel** (613)951-5078, (800)267-6677, FAX (613)951-1584, telex 053-3585. **DD** 338.4/791710464/05. ***Continues*** *United States Vehicles Entering Canada.*

US/0191-8761
**INTERNATIONAL TRAVEL NEWS (SACRAMENTO, CALIF.).** (INTERNATIONAL TRAVEL NEWS.). [Int. travel news]. (1976)-. Periodical. English. mo. $16.00 (1 year); $31.00 (2 year); $45.00 (3 year). MHR Publishing Corporated, 2122 28th Street, Sacramento CA 95818. **Tel** (916)457-8990 (800)366-9192. **ED** David Tykol. **DD** 910. Index available. **Bk Rev. Ad Acc. Circ:** 40,000. available on an online database (file 648/Full-Text) from DIALOG.
**Desc:** For the high-frequency international traveler. Airlines cruises, trains, lodging, bargains, information, feature articles, tips from subscribers on where and how to go.
**Ind/Abst** Trade Ind. ASAP [Full Txt.]; Trade Ind. Index [Full Txt.].

US/1058-5575
**INTERNATIONAL VISITOR.** [Int. visit.]. **Added/Corp** United States Travel and Tourism Administration. Vol. 1, Issue 1 (Sept. 1991)-. Periodical. English. Ten times a year (July.Aug. and Nov/Dec. issues combined). $78.50 US; $83.50 Canada & Mexico; $88.50 other. Walter Mathews Associates, Inc., 28 West 38th Street, Suite 12W, New York NY 10018. **Tel** (212)921-8012. **ED** Walter Mathews. **DD** 338. **Bk Rev**, (Qty: 3). **Circ:** 10,000 (ctrl).

UK
**INTERNATIONAL YOUTH HOSTELS HANDBOOK.** ***Title Change.*** (19??)-(1992). English (French, German and Spanish). an. American Youth Hostels, 733 15th Street Northwest, Suite 840, Washington DC 20005. **Tel** (202)783-6161, FAX (202)783-6171. **Ad Acc. *Continued by*** *Hostelling North America A Guide to Hostels in Canada & United States.*
**Desc:** Listings of International Youth Hostels Federation hostels throughout the world.

●US/1064-3079
**INTERTEC RECREATIONAL VEHICLE TRADE-IN GUIDE.** [Intertec recreat. veh. trade-in guide]. **Added/Corp** Intertec Publishing Corporation. **VFOAT** Recreational Vehicle Trade-In Guide. **VAT** Intertec Recreational Vehicle Trade In Guide; Recreational Vehicle Trade In Guide. (1992)-. Periodical. English. an. $43.85. Intertec Publishing Corporation, 9800 Metcalf, Overland Park KS 66212. **Tel** (913)341-1300. **LC** HD9710.37.U6; I58. **DD** 629.226/029/473. ***Formed by the union of*** *Camping Trailer & Travel Trailer Trade-In-Guide, 0736-1939* ***and*** *Motor Home & Truck Camper Trade-In Guide.*

●UK
**IRELAND / MICHELIN.** **Added/Corp** Michelin Tyre Public Limited Company. **VFOAT** Michelin Ireland. 1st Ed. (1992)-. English. ir. Manufacture Francaise des Pneumatiques Michelin, 46 avenue de Breteuil, 75431 Paris Cedex 07 France. **(Subscription address:** Michelin Travel Publications, PO Box 19008, Greenville SC 29602.)

IE/0332-0103
**IRELAND TODAY.** ***Ceased.*** No. 856 (Nov. 18, 1974)-Ceased ?. English. mo. Ireland Department of Foreign Affairs, Information Section, Dublin 2 Ireland. **Tel** 011 353 1 780822, telex 93720 ESTR EL. **ED** Donald Denham. **LC** DA900; .E4. **DD** 941.5/005. Index available. **Bk Rev. Circ:** 20,000 (ctrl). ***Continues*** *Eire. Ireland.*
**Desc:** The bulletin of the Irish Department of Foreign Affairs. Aims to provide up-to-date information about Ireland while promoting a favorable image of the country internationally.

IE/0021-1419
**IRISH TRAVEL TRADE NEWS.** [Ir. travel trade news]. (1965)-. Trade Publication. English. mo (11 issues per year). 20p Ireland; 45p North America; 35p other. Intl Fairs & Exhibitions Ltd, Belgrave Hse 15 Belgrave Road, Rathmines Dublin 6 Ireland. **Tel** 01 965711, FAX 01 964142, telex 30840 ITTN EI. **ED** Michael Flood. **DD** 910. **Ad Acc.** ctrl circ.
**Desc:** Ireland's only travel and tourism trade magazine.

US/1056-392X
**ISLAND ESCAPES.** [Isl. escapes]. Vol. 1, No. 1 (June/July 1991)-. Periodical. English. bm. $90.00. Islands, 3886 State Street, Santa Barbara CA 93105. **Tel** (805)682-7177, (800)227-7585, FAX (805)569-0349. **DD** 917.

●US/1062-3396
**ISLANDS OF ALOHA, THE.** (THE ISLANDS OF ALOHA : THE OFFICIAL TRAVEL GUIDE OF THE HAWAII VISITORS BUREAU.). **Added/Corp** Hawaii Visitors Bureau. **VFOAT** Aloha. (1992)-. Periodical. English. $5.95. Davick Publications, 49 South Hotel Street, Honolulu HI 96813.

US/0745-7847
**ISLANDS (SANTA BARBARA, CALIF.).** (ISLANDS.). [Islands]. Vol. 1, No 1 (Oct./Nov. 1981)-. Periodical. English. bm. $19.95 (one year), $34.95 (two year). Islands, 3886 State Street, Santa Barbara CA 93105. **Tel** (805)682-7177, (800)227-7585, FAX (805)569-0349. **(Subscription address:** PO Box 2606, Boulder, CO 80322) **ED** Joan Tapper. **LC** G500; .I84. **DD** 909/.0942. **Bk Rev. Ad Acc. Circ:** 171,000.
**Desc:** For island travelers, focuses on islands throughout the world. Covers arts, sports, nature, food, books and people.

US
**ISRAEL ON $ ... A DAY.** ***Title Change.*** **VAT** Israel On Fifteen Dollars A Day. (19??)-(19??). English. ir. Arthur Frommer / Pasmantier Publishers, 1230 Avenue of the Americas, New York NY 10020. **Tel** (212)373-8500. **ED** Vols. for 1978-79 by A. Sherman and S. Brilliant. ***Continued by*** *Frommer's Israel On $ ... & $ ... A Day, 8755-8440.*

FR
**ITALIE.** **Main/Corp** Pneu Michelin (Firm). (19??)-. French. ir. Manufacture Francaise des Pneumatiques Michelin, 46 avenue de Breteuil, 75431 Paris Cedex 07 France. **(Subscription address:** Michelin Travel Publications, PO Box 19008, Greenville SC 29602.) **LC** DG416; .M3. **DD** 914.5/04/92.

IT/0393-3725
**ITALY ITALY.** (ITALY ITALY : A GUIDE TO ALL IT'S BEST.). [Italy Italy]. (1983?)-. Periodical. English (English). Five times a year. Societa Edit Italy Srl, Via Michele Mercati 51, 00197 Rome Italy. **Tel** 011 39 6 3221441.

US
**ITALY JEWISH TRAVEL GUIDE.** (19??)-. Periodical. English. $17.45. Israelowitz Publishing, Box 228, Brooklyn NY 11229. **Tel** (718)951-7072, FAX (718)951-7072. **ED** Annie Sacerdoti.

US/0883-2633
**ITALY (NEW YORK, N.Y. 1984).** (ITALY.). [Italy]. 83/84-. English. an. $14.95. Fishers World Travel Guides, 100 Chestnut Street, Philadelphia PA 19106. **Tel** (800)327-5300. **ED** Robert C Fisher. **LC** DG416; .I818. **DD** 914.5/04928. Index available. **Circ:** 20,000.
**Desc:** Annotated travel guide; awards stars to Italian hotels, restaurants and sights. First guidebook planned for the experienced traveler.

CN/0834-3950
**ITINERAIRE DE LA MONTEREGIE, L'.** [Itiner. Monteregie]. Vol. 1, No. 1 (March 1986)-. Periodical. French. bm. Association Touristique Regionale de la Monteregie, 1566 rue Bourgogne, Chambly Quebec J3L 1Y7 Canada. **DD** 381/.45917143044/06. ***Continues*** *Itineraire (Longueuil, Quebec), 0713-3197.*

US/0743-5223
**ITINERARY (BAYONNE, N.J.), THE.** ***Ceased.*** (THE ITINERARY.). [Itinerary]. (198?)-(19??). Periodical. English. bm. Whole Person Tours Inc, PO Box 1084, Bayonne NJ 07002-1084.

GW
**J + W TRAVEL INTERNATIONAL.** **Added/Corp** Telex Verlag Jaeger + Waldmann. **VFOAT** J and W Travel International; Jaeger + Waldmann Travel International. (198?)-. English (French and German). an. $80.00 US. Telex-Verlag Jaeger+Waldmann GmbH, PO Box 111454, D-64229 Darmstadt Germany. **Tel** 011 49 6151 33020, FAX 011 49 6151 330250, telex 419389 TLX D. **(Subscription address:** Universal Media Division / US Subscriptions, Division of Shamgar Inc., PO Box 45, Bethpage NY 11714.) **LC** G153; .T38. **DD** 380.1/459104/025. available on CD-ROM. ***Continues*** *Telex + Travel International.*

GW
**JAEGER'S INTERTRAVEL.** English (French, German, Italian and Spanish). an. DM115.00. Jaeger-Verlag GmbH, Postfach 11 04 52, W-6100 Darmstadt BRD Germany. **Tel** (06151)391-0, FAX (06151)391-200, telex 419548 DAV D. **ED** Gunter M Hulwa. **LC** G154; .J33. **DD** 910/.25. **Bk Rev. Ad Acc. Circ:** 5,100. available on labels; available on diskette; available on audiocassette; available on magnetic tape.
**Desc:** Lists more than 37,000 travel agencies and 8,000 tour operators - linked up in alphabetical order to continent and country.

GW/0075-2649
**JAHRBUCH FUER FREMDENVERKEHR.** (1952)-. German (Multiple languages). ir. DM45.00. DWIF, Herrmann Sack Str 2, W 8000 Munich 2 F R Germany. **Tel** 49 89 267091. **UDC** 338.48.
**Ind/Abst** Leis. Recreat. Tour. Abstr.

JA
**JAPAN TRAVEL BLUE BOOK.** an. ¥8840.00 US & Canada; ¥7300.00 Japan; ¥8540.00 Asia & Oceania; ¥9140.00 other. Travel Journal Inc, Izumiya 3-Chome Kojimachi, Chiyoda-ku Tokyo 102 Japan. **Tel** 011 81 3 3264 2091.

US/0279-7984
**JAX FAX TRAVEL MARKETING MAGAZINE.** [JAX FAX Travel Mark. Mag.]. **VFOAT** Jax Fax. **VAT** Jet Airtransport Exchange Facts Travel Marketing Magazine. (19??)-. Periodical. English. mo. $12.00 (one year), $20.00 (two year), $25.00 (three year). Jet Airtransport Exchange, 397 Post Road, Darien CT 06820. **Tel** (203)655-8746, FAX (203)655-6257. **ED** Julie Boston. **Ad Acc. Circ:** 28,000 (ctrl). ***Continues*** *JAX FAX, 0148-9542.*
**Desc:** Tour and airlines listings for travel agents and tour operators.

UK/0075-3750
**JEWISH TRAVEL GUIDE, THE.** (1951)-. English. an. $11.95. Sepher Hermon Press Inc., 1265 46th Street, Brooklyn NY 11219-2027. **Tel** (718)972-9010. **ED** Sidney Lightman. **LC** G153; .J4. **DD** 910.2. **Ad Acc. Circ:** 6,000.
**Desc:** Contains up-to-date information on Kosher restaurants, hotels, synagogues, places of historic interest and Jewish organizations the world over, including the Far East and countries behind the Iron Curtain. It also features a thoroughly revised section on New York City.

●US
**JIM CABELL'S WORLD TRAVEL COMMUNICATIONS PRESENTS THE '800' & FAX TRAVEL DIRECTORY.** **Added/Corp** Jim Cabell's World Travel Communications. **VFOAT** 800 & Fax Travel Directory; Eight Hundred and Fax Travel Directory. Vol. 1, No. 1 (1992)-. Directory. English. World Travel Communications, 1500 East Tropicana, Suite 100A, Las Vegas NV 89119.

UK/0966-9582
**JOURNAL OF SUSTAINABLE TOURISM.** (19??)-. English. qt. £79.00 UK;. Multilingual Matters Ltd., Frankfurt Lodge, Clevedon Hall, Clevedon Avon, BS21 7SJ England. **Tel** 011 44 275 876519, FAX 011 44 275 343096.

AT/1035-4662
**JOURNAL OF TOURISM STUDIES, THE.** **Added/Corp** James Cook University of North Queensland. National Centre for Studies in Travel & Tourism (Australia). Vol. 1, No. 1 (May 1990)-. Periodical. English. sa (Apr. & Sept.). 35.00Aus$ (one year), 70.00Aus$ (two years) Australia; 45.00Aus$ (one year), 90.00Aus$ (two years) other. Department of Tourism JCU, James Cook University, North QLD, Townsville QLD 4811 Australia. **Tel** 011 66 077 814111, FAX 011 66 77 796371. **ED** Philip Pearce (phone: (077)81 5133). **LC** G155.A1; J67. **DD** 338.4/791/05. **Ad Acc.**
**Ind/Abst** APAIS, Aust. Public Aff. Inf. Ser. (1992-); Leis. Recreat. Tour. Abstr.

●US/1054-8408
**JOURNAL OF TRAVEL AND TOURISM MARKETING.** [J. travel tour. mark.]. **VFOAT** Journal of Travel and Tourism Marketing; JTTM. Vol. 1, No. 1 (1992)-. Periodical. English. qt. $60.00 US; $84.00 other. The Haworth Press Inc, 10 Alice Street, Binghamton NY 13904-1580. **Tel** (607)722-5857, (800)3-HAWORTH, FAX (607)722-1424. **ED** Kaye Chon (editor's address: Associate Professor of Tourism, Department of Tourism and Convention Adm., William F Harrah College of Hotel Adm., University of Nevada-Las Vegas, 4505 Maryland Parkway, Las Vegas, NV 89154-6023). **LC** G155.A1; J673. **CODEN** JTTMET. **Bk Rev. Ad Acc. Pr Rev. Acid Free.** available on microfiche. Documents available from Haworth Document Delivery Service.
**Desc:** A managerially oriented and applied journal which will serve as a medium through which researchers and managers in the field of travel and tourism can exchange ideas and keep abreast with the latest developments in the field.

US/0047-2875
**JOURNAL OF TRAVEL RESEARCH.** (JOURNAL OF TRAVEL RESEARCH / THE TRAVEL RESEARCH ASSOCIATION.). [J. travel res.]. **Added/Corp** Travel Research Association. University of Colorado, Boulder. Business Research Division. Travel and Tourism Research Association (U.S.) University of Colorado (Boulder Campus). Business Research Division. (1972)-. Periodical. English. Four times a year (Feb., May, Aug., Nov.). $90.00 US; $95.00 Canada; $105.00 others. Business Research Division, Campus Box 420, University of Colorado at Boulder, Boulder CO 80309-0420. **Tel** (303)492-8227, FAX (303)492-3620. **ED** C. R. Goeldner. **LC** G155.A1; T6576. **DD** 910/.7/2. **Bk Rev. Ad Acc. Circ:** 1,900 (ctrl). available on microfilm and microfiche from University Microfilms International (UMI). Documents available from UMI Article Clearinghouse. ***Continues** Travel Research Bulletin, 0147-2399.*
**Desc:** Provides new information about travel research, new techniques, creative views, generalizations about travel; research, thought, practice and synthesis of travel research materials.
**Ind/Abst** ABI/INFORM Glob. Ed.; ABI Inform Ondisc (Summer 1983-); ABI/INFORM Ondisc: Expr. Ed.; Acad. Search (July 1993-); Bus. Period. Index; Gen. BusinessFile (1992-); Geogr. Abstr. Phys. Geogr.; Geogr. Abstr. Human Geogr.; INFO-SOUTH Abstr.; Int. Dev. Abstr. (?-?); Int. Labour Doc.; Leis. Recreat. Tour. Abstr.; Mag. Search; UMI ABI/Inform--Bus. Period. Ondisc (Spring 1987-) [Full Txt.]; Wilson Bus. Abstr.

BE
**JOURNALISTE DU TOURISME, LE.** French. Editions du Centre International Recherches de Georges Dopagne, 29 Avenue Brugmann, 1060 Brussels Belgium. **Tel** 011 32 2 538 7599.

RH
**JUMBO GUIDE TO RHODESIA.** English. 3.00Zin$. Wilrey Publications, PO Box 3430, Harare Zimbabwe. **LC** DT962.2; .J85. **DD** 916.89/1/044.

US/1050-639X
**JUST GO!.** ***Title Change.*** (JUST GO! : A MAGAZINE FOR ALTERNATIVE TRAVEL.). [Just go!]. Vol. 1, No 1 (Fall 1990)-(19??). Periodical. English. qt. Just Go, 544 Second Street, San Francisco CA 94107. **Tel** (415)546-7128. **(Subscription address:** Just Go, 284 Connecticut Street, San Francisco CA 94107.**)** **DD** 910. ***Continued by** Eco Traveler.*
**Desc:** Designed for those who want to travel for $100 per day or less, each issue provides news on family travel, singles travel, outdoor adventures, eco-tourism and practical travel tips.

NE
**K.V.S.A. GUIDE TO THE NORTH SEA CANAL, AMSTERDAM, YMIUDEN, VELSEN, BEVERWYK, ZAANSTAD, AND SCHIPOL AIRPORT.** **VFOAT** KVSA Guide to the North Sea Canal, Amsterdam, Ymuiden, Velsen, Beverwyk, Zaanstad, and Schiphol Airport. **VAT** K V S A Guide to the North Sea Canal, Amsterdam, Ymuiden, Veksen, Beverwyk, Zaanstad, and Schiphol Airport. 96th year (1988)-. English. an. WYT Uitgeefgrouep, Postbus 6438, 3000 AG Rotterdam Netherlands. **Tel** 011 31 10 4762566, 4255944. **LC** VK825; .K2. ***Continues** Guide ... to the North Sea Canal, Ymuiden, Velsen, Beverwyk, Zaanstad, Amsterdam, and Schiphol Airport.*

US/1056-3385
**KAMAAINA'S GUIDE TO HAWAII'S DIVE SHOPS & TOUR OPERATIONS.** [Kamaaina's guide Hawaii's dive shops tour oper.]. **VFOAT** Kamaaina Gaido Bukku, Daibingu Shoppu & TsuÅa Kaisha in Hawai. (1991)-. Periodical. English (Creoles and Pidgins, English-based). $20.00. Kamaaina Press, PO Box 4467, Honolulu HI 96812. **DD** 796.

CN/1191-0135
**KAMLOOPS LIVING.** [Kamloops living]. (Winter/Spring 1991)-. Periodical. English. sa. $3.75 (single issue). Kamloops Living, 360 West St. Paul Street, Kamloops, British Columbia V2C 1G4 Canada. **DD** 917.11.

CN/1183-5877
**KANADA EXPLORER.** [Kan. explor.]. Vol. 1 (Summer 1991)-. Periodical. German. qt. $4.00 per issue. Kanada Explorer Inc., PO Box 1054, Winnipeg Manitoba R3C 2X8 Canada. **DD** 917.104/64.

US/0895-9382
**KAUAI.** [Kauai]. (1987)-. English. be. $9.95 (add $2.00 for postage). Paradise Publications, 8110 SW Wareham, Portland OR 97233. **Tel** (503)246-1555. **ED** Greg and Christie Stilson. **DD** 919. Index available. cum. index. **Circ:** 10,000.
**Desc:** The only comprehensive travel publication for Hawaii's Garden Isle of Kaua'i. Detailed descriptions covering accommodations, restaurants, scenic points of interest, island history, beaches and general information such as travel safety tips, traveling with children, and travel for the physically impaired.

US/0898-1418
**KAUAI UPDATE, THE.** [Kauai update]. Vol. 2, No. 3 (Summer 1988)-. Periodical. English. qt. $6.00. Paradise Publications, 8110 SW Wareham, Portland OR 97233. **Tel** (503)246-1555. **ED** Christie and Greg Stilson. **DD** 910. **Bk Rev. Ad Acc. Circ:** 2,000.
**Desc:** Features updated information on the Hawaiian Island of Maui. Includes restaurants, accommodations and other related material for the Hawaii bound traveler or island resident.

US/0453-5812
**KENTUCKY TRAVEL GUIDE.** Vol. 3, No. 1 (Winter/Spring 1969)-. English. an. $2.00. Editorial Services Company Inc, 3924 Dupont Square South, Louisville KY 40207. ***Continues** Welcome to Kentucky.*

US/0192-3536
**KEY. THIS WEEK IN MIAMI BEACH.** **VFOAT** Key. (19??)-. Periodical. English (summaries and/or abstracts in Spanish, German and French). Fifty-two times a year. $55.00. McCaskill Publishers Company Inc, PO Box 530565, Miami FL 33138. **Tel** (305)754-5534. **ED** Clark McAskill Jr. **Circ:** 10,000. ***Continues** This Week in Miami Beach.*

CN/0711-4680
**KOSOY'S TRAVEL GUIDE TO EUROPE.** [Kosoy's travel guide Eur.]. **VFOAT** Travel Guide to Europe; Kosoy Travel Guide to Europe. **VAT** Travel Guide to Europe (Toronto). English. ir. $5.95 per vol. Kosoy Travel Guides, 40 Shallmar Boulevard, Toronto Ontario M6C 2J9 Canada. **DD** 914.0455.

CN/0711-4702
**KOSOY'S TRAVEL GUIDE TO FLORIDA AND THE SOUTH.** [Kosoy's travel guide Fla. South]. **VFOAT** Travel Guide to Florida and the South; Kosy Travel Guide to Florida & the South. **VAT** Kosoy Travel Guide to Florida and the South. 2nd Ed.-. English. ir. $5.95 per vol. Kosoy Travel Guides, 40 Shallmar Boulevard, Toronto Ontario M6C 2J9 Canada. **DD** 917.5. ***Continues** Kosoy's Budget-Travel Guide to Florida, 0711-4907.*

CH
**KUAN KUANG TUNG CHI NIEN PAO.** **VFOAT** Annual Report on Tourism Statistics, Republic of China. 1972-. Chinese. Ministry of Communications, PO Box 1490, Taipei Taiwan. **LC** G155.T25; K78.

CH
**KUAN KUANG TZU LIAO.** ***Title Change.*** **VFOAT** Monthly Report on Tourism, Republic of China. Periodical. Multiple languages (English and Chinese). mo. Ministry of Communications, PO Box 1490, Taipei Taiwan. **LC** G155.F6; K8. ***Continues** Kuan Kuang Yueh Pao.* ***Continued by** Monthly Report on Tourism, Republic of China.*

KO
**KWANGWANG CHONGBO.** Periodical. Korean. ir. Kukche Kwangwang Kongsa, 60 Chungmu-ro 3-ka Chung-ku, Seoul Korea. **LC** G155.A1; K9.

JA
**KYOTO-SHI KANKO CHOSA NEMPO.** Japanese. an. Kyoto-shi Bunka Kankokyoku, Okazaki Saishojicho, Sakayo-ku 606, Kyoto-shi Japan. **LC** G155.J27; K94.

US/0075-8159
**LATIN AMERICAN TRAVEL & PAN AMERICAN HIGHWAY GUIDE.** (1966)-. English. ir. $9.95. Compsco Publ Co, 663 5th Avenue, New York NY 10022. **ED** E.A. Jahn. **LC** F1409.2; .L35. **DD** 918/.04/3. **Bk Rev. Ad Acc. Circ:** 125,000.

US
**LEARNING VACATIONS.** ***Ceased.*** (1977)-(19??). English. Peterson's Guides, 202 Carnegie Center, Department 2342, Princeton NJ 08543. **Tel** (800)338-3282, FAX (609)452-0966. **ED** Gerson G Eisenberg.
**Desc:** The bestselling travel guide covers 400 programs for every interest, age, and budget. Perfect for anyone who is tired of a routine vacation and looking for something new.

UK/0261-1392
**LEISURE, RECREATION, AND TOURISM ABSTRACTS.** **See** Recreation, Leisure-Abstracting, Bibliographies and Statistics.

CN/1184-146X
**LEISURE WORLD.** [Leis. world]. Vol. 1, No. 1 (Dec. 1989)-. Periodical. English. bm. 15.00Can$ North America; 20.00Can$ other. Ontario Motorist Publishing Company, PO Box 580, Windsor Ontario N9A 6N3 Canada. **Tel** (519)971-3207, FAX (519)255-7379. **ED** Doug L. O'Neil and Kate McGrindle. **DD** 910/.5. **Ad Acc. Circ:** 280,000 (ctrl). ***Continues** Leisure Ontario., 0838-2913.*
**Desc:** Contains travel and lifestyle features as well as automotive information.

CN/0712-5747
**LEISUREWAYS.** **See** Recreation, Leisure.

US
**LET'S GO. BUDGET GUIDE TO ISRAEL AND EGYPT.** **Added/Corp** Harvard Student Agencies. **VFOAT** Budget Guide to Israel and Egypt (Including Jordan); Israel and Egypt, Including Jordan; Let's Go. Israel and Egypt, Including Jordan; Israel & Egypt; Israel and Egypt; Let's Go. Israel & Egypt, Including Jordan. (198?)-. English. an. St. Martin's Press, 175 Fifth Avenue, New York NY 10010. **Tel** (800)221-7945, (212)982-3900, FAX (212)777-6359. **LC** DS103; .L44. ***Continues** Let's Go. Budget Guide to Israel and Egypt, 0882-9535.*

●US
**LET'S GO. BUDGET GUIDE TO USA & CANADA.** (1993)-. English. an. St. Martin's Press, 175 Fifth Avenue, New York NY 10010. **Tel** (800)221-7945, (212)982-3900, FAX (212)777-6359. ***Continues** Let's Go. The Budget Guide to the USA, 0275-9837.*

US
**LET'S GO: THE BUDGET GUIDE TO BRITAIN AND IRELAND.** **Main/Corp** Harvard Student Agencies. **VFOAT** Let's Go: Britain and Ireland; Budget Guide to Britain and Ireland; Britain and Ireland. (19??)-. English. an (Dec.). $16.95. St. Martin's Press, 175 Fifth Avenue, New York NY 10010. **Tel** (800)221-7945, (212)982-3900, FAX (212)777-6359. **LC** DA650; .H34a. **DD** 914.1/04857.

US/0898-8366
**LET'S GO. THE BUDGET GUIDE TO CALIFORNIA AND HAWAII INCLUDING RENO, LAS VEGAS, GRAND CANYON, AND BAJA CALIFORNIA.** (LET'S GO. BUDGET GUIDE TO CALIFORNIA AND HAWAII.). [Let's go, budg. guide Calif. Hawaii incl. Reno Las Vegas Gd. Canyon Baja Calif.]. **Added/Corp** Harvard Student Agencies. **VFOAT** California and Hawaii; Budget Guide to California and Hawaii (including Reno, Las Vegas, Grand Canyon, and Baja California); Let's Go, California and Hawaii; Let's Go, California & Hawaii. (1988)-. English. an (Nov.). $14.95. St. Martin's Press, 175 Fifth Avenue, New York NY 10010. **Tel** (800)221-7945, (212)982-3900, FAX (212)777-6359. **LC** F859.3; .L49. **DD** 917.94/0453. ***Continues in part** Let's Go. Budget Guide to California & the Pacific Northwest, 0749-3320.*

US/0163-4585
**LET'S GO: THE BUDGET GUIDE TO EUROPE.** (LET'S GO. THE BUDGET GUIDE TO EUROPE / WRITTEN BY HARVARD STUDENT AGENCIES, INC.). **Added/Corp** Harvard Student Agencies. **VFOAT** Budget Guide to Europe; Let's Go. Europe; Let's Go. Budget Guide to Europe Including Egypt, Israel, Morocco, Tunisia, Turkey and the USSR; Let's Go. Budget Guide to Europe Including United Germany, Morocco, and Turkey. (1976)-. English. an (Dec.). $17.95. St. Martin's Press, 175 Fifth Avenue, New York NY 10010. **Tel** (800)221-7945, (212)982-3900, FAX (212)777-6359. **LC** D909; .H38. **DD** 914.04/558. ***Continues** Let's Go. Student Guide to Europe., 0075-8868.*

US
**LET'S GO: THE BUDGET GUIDE TO FRANCE.** **Main/Corp** Harvard Student Agencies. **VFOAT** Let's Go: France; Budget Guide to France. (1978)-. English. an. $16.99. St. Martin's Press, 175 Fifth Avenue, New York NY 10010. **Tel** (800)221-7945, (212)982-3900, FAX (212)777-6359. **ED** Ralph E. Hall and James B. Witkin. **LC** DC16; .H37a. **DD** 914.4/04837.

●US/1064-1009
**LET'S GO. THE BUDGET GUIDE TO GREECE & TURKEY.** (LET'S GO. THE BUDGET GUIDE TO GREECE & TURKEY / WRITTEN BY HARVARD STUDENT AGENCIES, INC.). [Let's go, budg. guide Greece Turk.]. **Added/Corp** Harvard Student Agencies. **VFOAT** Budget Guide to Greece & Turkey; Budget Guide to Greece and Turkey; Greece & Turkey; Greece and Turkey; Let's Go. Greece & Turkey. 1st Ed. (1992)-. English. St. Martin's Press, 175 Fifth Avenue, New York NY 10010. **Tel** (800)221-7945, (212)982-3900, FAX (212)777-6359. **DD** 914. ***Continues*** *Let's Go. Budget Guide to Greece, 0749-0569.*

US/1043-4690
**LET'S GO. THE BUDGET GUIDE TO ITALY (INCLUDING TUNISIA).** (LET'S GO. THE BUDGET GUIDE TO ITALY (INCLUDING TUNISIA) / WRITTEN BY HARVARD STUDENT AGENCIES, INC.). **Added/Corp** Harvard Student Agencies. **VFOAT** Budget Guide to Italy (Including Tunisia); Let's Go. Budget Guide to Italy, Including Tunisia and Malta; Let's Go. Italy (Including Tunisia). (1988)-. English. an. $16.99. St. Martin's Press, 175 Fifth Avenue, New York NY 10010. **Tel** (800)221-7945, (212)982-3900, FAX (212)777-6359. **LC** DG416; .C7465. **DD** 914.504/928. ***Continues*** *Harvard Student Agencies. Let's Go. Budget Guide to Italy, 0192-2920.*

US/1057-6274
**LET'S GO. THE BUDGET GUIDE TO LONDON.** (LET'S GO. THE BUDGET GUIDE TO LONDON / WRITTEN BY HARVARD STUDENT AGENCIES, INC.). [Let's go, budget guide Lond.]. **Added/Corp** Harvard Student Agencies. **VFOAT** Budget Guide to London; Let's Go. London. (1991)-. English. $10.95. St. Martin's Press, 175 Fifth Avenue, New York NY 10010. **Tel** (800)221-7945, (212)982-3900, FAX (212)777-6359. **LC** DA679; .L56. **DD** 914.2104/859/05.

US
**LET'S GO. THE BUDGET GUIDE TO LONDON / WRITTEN BY HARVARD STUDENT AGENCIES, INC.** **Added/Corp** Harvard Student Agencies. **VFOAT** Let's Go. London; Budget Guide to London. (1991)-. English. $10.95. St. Martin's Press, 175 Fifth Avenue, New York NY 10010. **Tel** (800)221-7945, (212)982-3900, FAX (212)777-6359.

US
**LET'S GO. THE BUDGET GUIDE TO MEXICO.** **VFOAT** Budget Guide to Mexico. Began in 1969?. English. an. $9.95. St. Martin's Press, 175 Fifth Avenue, New York NY 10010. **Tel** (800)221-7945, (212)982-3900, FAX (212)777-6359. **LC** PAR.
**Desc:** Now in its third year, this terrifically popular guide has been greatly expanded to include more of what readers asked for.

US/1059-0412
**LET'S GO. THE BUDGET GUIDE TO NEW YORK CITY.** (LET'S GO. THE BUDGET GUIDE TO NEW YORK CITY / WRITTEN BY HARVARD STUDENT AGENCIES, INC.). [Let's go, budg. guide N. Y. City]. **Added/Corp** Harvard Student Agencies. **VFOAT** Budget Guide to New York City; Let's Go. New York City. (1991)-. English. $10.95. St. Martin's Press, 175 Fifth Avenue, New York NY 10010. **Tel** (800)221-7945, (212)982-3900, FAX (212)777-6359. **DD** 917.

US/0898-6215
**LET'S GO. THE BUDGET GUIDE TO PACIFIC NORTHWEST, WESTERN CANADA, AND ALASKA INCLUDING ALBERTA AND BRITISH COLUMBIA--VANCOUVER, BANFF AND LAKE LOUISE, CALGARY, GLACIER/WATERTON NATIONAL PARKS.** (LET'S GO. BUDGET GUIDE TO PACIFIC NORTHWEST, WESTERN CANADA, AND ALASKA.). [Let's go, budg. guide Pac. Northwest West. Can. Alsk. incl. Alta. B. C.--Vanc. Banff Lake Louise Calg. Glacier/Watert. Natl. Parks]. **Added/Corp** Harvard Student Agencies. **VFOAT** Let's Go. Pacific Northwest, Western Canada, and Alaska; Budget Guide to Pacific Northwest, Western Canada, and Alaska (including Alberta and British Columbia--Vancouver, Banff and Lake Louise, Calgary, Glacier/Waterton National Parks); Pacific Northwest, Western Canada, and Alaska; Let's Go. Pacific Northwest, Western Canada, and Alaska. (1988)-. English. an (Nov.). $14.95. St. Martin's Press, 175 Fifth Avenue, New York NY 10010. **Tel** (800)221-7945, (212)982-3900, FAX (212)777-6359. **LC** F852.3; .L48. **DD** 917.95/04. ***Continues in part*** *Let's Go. Budget Guide to California & the Pacific Northwest, 0749-3320.*

●US
**LET'S GO. THE BUDGET GUIDE TO SPAIN & PORTUGAL.** **Added/Corp** Harvard Student Agencies. **VFOAT** Budget Guide to Spain & Portugal; Budget Guide to Spain and Portugal; Let's Go. Budget Guide to Spain and Portugal. (1992)-. English. an. St. Martin's Press, 175 Fifth Avenue, New York NY 10010. **Tel** (800)221-7945, (212)982-3900, FAX (212)777-6359. ***Continues*** *Let's Go. Budget Guide to Spain, Portugal & Morocco, 0885-3541.*

US/0275-9837
**LET'S GO. THE BUDGET GUIDE TO THE USA.** ***Title Change.*** (LET'S GO. THE BUDGET GUIDE TO THE USA / WRITTEN BY HARVARD STUDENT AGENCIES.). [Let's go, Budg. guide USA]. **Added/Corp** Harvard Student Agencies. **VFOAT** Let's Go. USA. **VAT** Let's Go. The Budget Guide to the United States of America. (1981)-(1993). English. an. St. Martin's Press, 175 Fifth Avenue, New York NY 10010. **Tel** (800)221-7945, (212)982-3900, FAX (212)777-6359. **ED** K. W. Warren. **LC** E158; .L39. **DD** 917.3/04927. ***Continued by*** *Let's Go. Budget Guide to USA & Canada.*

US/0090-788X
**LET'S GO : THE STUDENT GUIDE TO THE UNITED STATES AND CANADA.** **VFOAT** Student Guide to the United States and Canada. 1972/73-. English. be. $3.95. Harvard Student Agencies Inc, E P Dutton & Company, 2 Trowbridge Street, New York NY 02138. **LC** E169.02; .L36. **DD** 917/.04/5305.

UK
**LET'S HALT AWHILE IN GREAT BRITAIN.** **See** Hotels/Motels.

UK
**LET'S HALT AWHILE IN IRELAND.** (1981)-. English. Schley Courtenay Ltd, London England. **LC** TX910.I7; C6. ***Continues in part*** *Let's Halt Awhile in Great Britain and Ireland.*

FR/1146-1918
**LETTRE TOURISTIQUE PARIS, LA.** (19??)-. Periodical. French. Twenty-two times a year (18 issues + 4 special issues). 400.00F France; 440.00F others. API Publications, 400 rue Saint Honore, 75001 Paris France. **Tel** 011 33 1 42974660, FAX 011 33 1 42868756. **UDC** 379.83/.85. cum. index. **Bk Rev**, (Qty: 4). **Ad Acc**, **Adv Mgr:** Maria Porcher, **Tel** 42610916. **Circ:** 3,000. ***Continues*** *L'Agent de Voyages, 1146-190X.*

XR/0024-2896
**LIDE A ZEME.** Vol. 1, (1952)-. Czech. Twelve times a year. kcs91.00. Editorial Board of Lide a Zeme, Mlada Fronta Radlicka 61, 150 02 Prague, 5 Czech Republic. **Tel** 011 42 2 544941. **ED** Miluse Zakova. **Bk Rev**. **Circ:** 45,000.
**Desc:** Dedicated to the popularization of geographical sciences and travel. Every issue includes a number of black and white photos, small maps and plans of interesting areas from all over the world.

US/0894-5128
**LODGING AND RESTAURANT INDEX.** (LODGING AND RESTAURANT INDEX / JUDITH M. NIXON, IN COOPERATION WITH THE RESTAURANT, HOTEL, AND INSTITUTIONAL MANAGEMENT INSTITUTE, PURDUE UNIVERSITY [AND THE] HOSPITALITY, LODGING AND TRAVEL RESEARCH FOUNDATION, AN AFFILIATE OF THE AMERICAN HOTEL AND MOTEL ASSOCIATION.). [Lodg. restaur. index]. **Added/Corp** Purdue University. Restaurant, Hotel, and Institutional Management Institute. Hospitality, Lodging, and Travel Research Foundation. Consortium of Hospitality Research Information Services. (1985)-. English. Four times a year. $150.00 US & Canada; $195.00 others. Purdue University RHIMI, 1586 Stewart Center, Room 116, West Lafayette IN 47907. **Tel** (317)494-2749. **LC** TX911.3.M27; L6. **DD** 647/.95/068. ***Continues*** *RHI Index.*

US
**LODGING OUTLOOK.** **Added/Corp** Smith Travel Research (Firm). **VFOAT** STR Lodging Outlook. (198?)-. Periodical. English. Twelve times a year. $200.00 US; $225.00 others. Smith Travel Research, PO Box 659, Gallatin TN 37066. **Tel** (615)452-2790, FAX (615)451-1757. **Circ:** 800.
**Desc:** News and information on lodging.

●US/1064-2900
**LOIRE VALLEY INSIGHT GUIDES.** English. Appleton Century Crofts, Prentice Hall, 200 Old Tappan Road, Old Tappan NJ 07675. **Tel** (201)767-5188, (800)922-0579.

UK
**LONDON LOG.** English. bm. £16.00 UK; £20.00 other. London Tourist Board, 26 Grosvenor Gardens / Dist. Department, London SW1W 0DU England. **Tel** 011 44 71 730 3450. **Bk Rev**. **Pr Rev. Circ:** 5,000 (ctrl).
**Desc:** Contains information on new developments in London tourism, with regular features and listings of forthcoming major events.

UK
**LONDON THEATRE GUIDE.** **See** Theater.

US/0882-1895
**LONG ISLAND RECREATION & VISITORS GUIDE.** **VFOAT** Long Island Recreation and Visitors Guide; LI Recreation and Visitors Guide; LI Recreation & Visitors Guide. (1975)-. English. an. $4.75. Long Island Business News, 2150 Smithtown Avenue, Ronkonkoma, Long Island NY 11779-7327. **Tel** (516)737-1700. **LC** F127.L8; L924. **DD** 917.47/210443. ***Continues*** *Long Island U.S.A.*

CN/0227-8499
**LOOK AT LONDON.** V. 1- Jan. 78-. Periodical. English. qt. Free. Visitors & Convention Services 5035, London Ontario N6A 4L9 Canada. **DD** 917.13/26/005. ctrl circ.

TH
**LOOKEAST.** (19??)-. Periodical. English. mo. $18.03. Gemini International Services, 116/340 Mooban Pricha Soi 1, Bangkok 10110 Thailand. **Tel** 2519016.

CC
**LU YU TIEN TI (SHANGHAI, CHINA).** (LU YU TIEN TI / LUYOU TIANDI.). **VFOAT** Luyou Tiandi. (19??)-. Periodical. Chinese. bm. RMBY0.38. Shanghai Wenhua Chubanshe, 74 Shaoxing Lu, Shanghai 200020, People's Republic of China. **Tel** 011 86 4372608. **(Subscription address:** China Books & Periodicals Inc., 2929 24th Street, San Francisco CA 94110.) **LC** DS712; .L82. **DD** 915.1/0457.

AT
**M-SERIES MONOGRAPHS.** (19??)-. Monographic series. English. ir. Price varies per volume. Committee for Economic Development of Australia, 123 Lonsdale Street, GPO Box 2117T, Melbourne Victoria 3000 Australia. **Tel** 011 61 03 6623544, FAX 011 61 03 6637271. Index available. cum. index. **Pr Rev. Circ:** 2000 (ctrl).
**Desc:** Economic analysis of macro and micro subjects.

US/1057-0381
**MAIN STREET MESSAGE.** [Main Str. message]. **Added/Corp** Main Street Sioux City (Organization). No. 1 (Aug. 1991)-. Periodical. English. mo. Main Street Message, 417 4th Street, Suite 290, Sioux City IA 51101. **DD** 910.

CN/1184-0498
**MAJOR EVENTS.** (MAJOR EVENTS FOR ..). [Major events]. **Added/Corp** Alberta. Alberta Tourism. (Sept. 14, 1990)-. English. **DD** 790/.097123/05. ***Continues*** *Alberta Events Calendar., 0825-768X.*

CN/0703-6248
**MANITOBA VACATION GUIDE.** ***Title Change.*** [Manit. vacat. guide]. **Added/Corp** Manitoba. Dept. of Tourism, Recreation and Cultural Affairs. Manitoba. Dept. of Economic Development and Tourism. Travel Manitoba. (19??)-(19??). English. Department of Business Development and Tourism, Department 7257, Winnipeg Manitoba R3C 3H8 Canada. **LC** F1062; .M3. **DD** 917.12/7/043. ***Continues*** *Manitoba Canada Vacation Handbook, 0703-6256.* ***Continued by*** *Manitoba Vacation Planner, 1185-4391.*

CN/0227-8138
**MARCHE BYWARD.** [Marche Byward]. **VFOAT** Byward Market. Began publication in July 1979?. Periodical. English (French). mo. Free. Market Association, 41 York Street, Ottawa K1N 5S2 Canada. **DD** 917.13/84/05.

US/0735-827X
**MARMAC GUIDE TO ATLANTA, A.** (A MARMAC GUIDE TO ATLANTA / BY SUSAN HUNTER SMITH.). **VFOAT** Atlanta. 2nd Ed. (1983)-. English. an. $9.95. Marmac Publishing Company Inc., 6303 Barfield Road, Suite 208, Atlanta GA 30328. **Tel** (404)257-1481. **LC** F294.A83; H68. **DD** 917.58/2310443. Each issue contains an index to its own contents (no volume index)--loose. **Circ:** 75,000. ***Continues*** *How, When, & Where in Atlanta, 0275-2212.*

US/0735-8261
**MARMAC GUIDE TO HOUSTON AND GALVESTON, A.** **VFOAT** Marmack Guide to Houston. 1st-. English. an. $6.95. Marmac Publishing Company Inc., 6303 Barfield Road, Suite 208, Atlanta GA 30328. **Tel** (404)257-1481. **LC** F394.H83; M37. **DD** 917.64/14110463.

US/0736-8135
**MARMAC GUIDE TO NEW ORLEANS, A.** (1984)-. English. an (May). $9.95. Marmac Publishing Company Inc., 6303 Barfield Road, Suite 208, Atlanta GA 30328. **Tel** (404)257-1481. **LC** F379.N53; M37. **DD** 917.63/350463. ***Continues*** *How, When & Where in New Orleans.*

US/0736-8127
**MARMAC GUIDE TO PHILADELPHIA, A.** [Marmac guide Phila.]. (1984)-. English. an (Aug.). $9.95. Marmac Publishing Company Inc., 6303 Barfield Road, Suite 208, Atlanta GA 30328. **Tel** (404)257-1481. **LC**

F158.18; .M375. **DD** 917.48/110443. Index available (Bound in all issues). **Bk Rev. Ad Acc.** ctrl circ. ***Continues** How, When & Where in Philadelphia.*

FR
**MAROC. Main/Corp** Pneu Michelin (Firm). (1974)-. French. ir. Manufacture Francaise des Pneumatiques Michelin, 46 avenue de Breteuil, 75431 Paris Cedex 07 France. **(Subscription address:** Michelin Travel Publications, PO Box 19008, Greenville SC 29602.**) LC** DT304; .M26a. **DD** 916.4/04/5.
**Desc:** Travel in Morocco.

US/0300-7502
**MARYLAND TRAVEL SCENE. Added/Corp** Maryland. Division of Tourism. (1961)-. Periodical. English. Twelve times a year. Free. Office of Tourist Development, 45 Calvert Street, Annapolis MD 21401. **Tel** (410)269-2686.

US/1062-2772
**MATURE GROUP TRAVELER.** [Mature group travel.]. Began in June (1991)-. Periodical. English. qt. $12.00. **DD** 910.

US/1043-2280
**MATURE TRAVELER.** [Matur. travel.]. (198?)-. Periodical. English. mo. $29.95. Gem Publishing Group, PO Box 50820, Reno NV 89513. **Tel** (702)786-7419. **ED** Gene Malott. **DD** 910. cum. index. **Bk Rev**, (Qty: 5-6). **Ad Acc. Circ:** 2,200.
**Desc:** News of discounts and special trips only for 49ers and older seniors - travel tips and senior travel advocacy.

US/0895-9609
**MAUI.** [Maui]. 4th Ed. (Spring 1990)-. English. be. $9.95 (add $2.00 shipping). Paradise Publications, 8110 SW Wareham, Portland OR 97233. **Tel** (503)246-1555. **ED** Greg and Christie Stilson. **LC** DU628.M3; M36. **DD** 919.69/21044. Index available. cum. index. **Circ:** 10,000.
**Desc:** The only comprehensive travel publication for Hawaii's Valley Isle of Maui. Detailed descriptions covering accommodations, restaurants, scenic points of interests, island history, beaches and general information such as travel safety tips, traveling children, and travel for the physically impaired.

US/0895-9390
**MAUI UPDATE, THE.** [Maui update]. Vol. 1, No. 4 (Fall 1987)-. Periodical. English. qt. $6.00. Paradise Publications, 8110 SW Wareham, Portland OR 97233. **Tel** (503)246-1555. **ED** Christie Stilson and John Peinsten. **DD** 919. **Bk Rev. Ad Acc. Circ:** 2,000.
**Desc:** Features updated information on the Hawaiian Island of Maui. Includes restaurants, accommodations and other related material for the Hawaii bound traveler or island resident.

US/0730-0018
**MAVERICK GUIDE TO AUSTRALIA, THE.** (THE MAVERICK GUIDE TO AUSTRALIA / ROBERT W. BONE.). [Maverick guide Aust.]. (1979)-. English. an. $14.70 (two years). Pelican Publishing Company, PO Box 3110, Gretna LA 70054. **Tel** (504)368-1175, (800)843-1724, FAX (504)368-1195. **ED** Robert Bone. **LC** DU95; .M25. **DD** 919.4/0463.
**Desc:** Offers hundreds of valuable inside tips on what to do and and see in Australia as well as what to avoid.

US/0278-6613
**MAVERICK GUIDE TO HAWAII, THE.** [Maverick guide Hawaii]. Began with 1977 Vol. English. an. Pelican Publishing Company, PO Box 3110, Gretna LA 70054. **Tel** (504)368-1175, (800)843-1724, FAX (504)368-1195. **LC** DU622; .M35. **DD** 919.69/044.
**Desc:** Updated regularly, there is no better guide to Hawaii. A consumer-oriented book that is as fun to read as it is reliable to use. "You can do no better than to take along The Maverick Guide to Hawaii". UPI.

●US
**MAVERICK GUIDE TO MALAYSIA AND SINGAPORE / LEN RUTLEDGE. VFOAT** Malaysia and Singapore. (1992)-. English. $14.95. Pelican Publishing Company, PO Box 3110, Gretna LA 70054. **Tel** (504)368-1175, (800)843-1724, FAX (504)368-1195.

US/0278-5501
**MAVERICK GUIDE TO NEW ZEALAND, THE.** (THE MAVERICK GUIDE TO NEW ZEALAND / ROBERT W. BONE.). (19??)-. English. an. $15.70. Pelican Publishing Company, PO Box 3110, Gretna LA 70054. **Tel** (504)368-1175, (800)843-1724, FAX (504)368-1195. **ED** Bob Bone. **LC** DU405.5; .M38. **DD** 919.31/0437. Index available. cum. index. **Bk Rev.**
**Desc:** Information on all the islands and the many things to see and do while visiting.

US
**MAVERICK GUIDE TO THAILAND. VFOAT** Thailand. (1991)-. English. Pelican Publishing Company, PO Box 3110, Gretna LA 70054. **Tel** (504)368-1175, (800)843-1724, FAX (504)368-1195. **LC** DS563; .M38. **DD** 915.9304/44.

US/1058-000X
**MAXIMUM TRAVEL PER DIEM ALLOWANCES FOR FOREIGN AREAS.** [Maximum trav. allow. foreign areas]. **Main/Corp** United States. Dept. of State. Allowances Staff. **Added/Corp** United States. Dept. of State. Allowances Staff. United States. Dept. of State. Office of Allowances. (198?)-. Government Publication. English. mo. $24.00 domestic; $30.00 other. Superintendent of Documents, US Government Printing Office, Washington DC 20402. **Tel** (202)275-3328, FAX (202)786-2377. **DD** 353.
**Desc:** Provides information on maximum rates of per diem allowances established for travel areas, with effective date for each rate.

CN/0225-8285
**MEETINGS & INCENTIVE TRAVEL.** [Meet. incent. travel]. **VFOAT** Portfolio of Canadian Resorts. **VAT** Meetings and Incentive Travel; M&I.T. Meetings and Incentive Travel. Vol. 9 (Jan./Feb. 1980)-. Periodical. English. Seven times a year. 40.00Can$ Canada; 86.00Can$ other. MacLean Hunter Ltd. Business Publishers / Canada, Box 9100, Station A, Toronto ONT M5W 1A5 Canada. **Tel** (416)946-8420, (800)567-0444. **(Subscription address:** Indas, 35 Riviera Drive, Building 17, Markham Ontario L3R 8N4 Canada.**) DD** 658.8/106. available on microfilm and microfiche from University Microfilms International (UMI). ***Continues** Canadian Sales Meetings & Conventions, 0318-1049.*
**Ind/Abst** Can. Bus. Index.

CN/0841-9663
**MEETINGS MONTHLY, NEWS BULLETIN.** [Meet. mon. news bull.]. **VFOAT** Meetings Monthly. (March 14, 1988)-. Bulletin. English. mo. $20.00 North America; $40.00 other. Publicom Inc, 1055 Beaver Hall Hill/Suite 17, Montreal Quebec H2Z 1S5 Canada. **Tel** (514)874-0874, FAX (514)866-3839, telex 055-61866. **ED** Guy J Jonkman. **DD** 060/.68. **Bk Rev. Ad Acc. Circ:** 12,561 (ctrl). ***Continues** Meetings Monthly, 0841-9655.*
**Desc:** Travel trade news and sellers guide for meeting planners and travel trade industry.

US/0360-6597
**MEMBERSHIP ROSTER - AMERICAN SOCIETY OF TRAVEL AGENTS INC.** [Memb. roster - Am. Soc. Travel Agents]. **Main/Corp** American Society of Travel Agents. (19??)-. English. an. $125.00. American Society of Travel Agents Inc., Accounting Department, 1101 King Street, Alexandria VA 22314. **Tel** (703)739-2782. **LC** G154; .A46. **DD** 910. ***Continues** American Society of Travel Agents. Lists of Members.*

IT
**MERIDIANI.** Vol. 1, No. 1 (1988)-. Periodical. Italian. Six times a year. L60000.00 Italy; L131000.00 other. Editoriale Domus, Via Achille Grandi 5-7, 20089 Rozzano Milan Italy. **Tel** 011 39 2 82472276, FAX 011 39 2 8255033. **LC** WMLC 93/435.

CN/0836-4443
**METROPOLITAN TORONTO ... ANNUAL VISITORS GUIDE.** [Metrop. Tor. annu. visit. guide]. **VFOAT** Metropolitan Toronto Annual Visitors Guide. (1987)-. English. an. Free. Toronto Convention & Visitors Association, Queen's Quay Terminal at Harbour Front, PO Box 126, 207 Queen's Quay West, Toronto Ontario M5J 1A7 Canada. **Tel** (416)368-9990. **ED** Leanne Rogers. **DD** 917.13/541044/05. **Ad Acc. Circ:** 725,000 (ctrl). ***Continues** Discovery Guide (Toronto, Ont.), 0821-7920.*
**Desc:** The only guide a visitor can use to plan a comprehensive visit to the Metropolitan Toronto area. It is a complete ongoing source of information about Toronto.

UK
**MEXICO & CENTRAL AMERICAN HANDBOOK. VFOAT** Mexico and Central American Handbook. (1991)-. English. an (Published in October). $21.95. National Textbook Company, 4255 West Touhy Avenue, Lincolnwood IL 60646. **Tel** (708)679-5500, (800)323-4900, FAX (708)679-2494, telex TWX 9102230736. **LC** F1209; .M4863. **DD** 917.204. Index available. **Ad Acc. Circ:** 10,000. ***Continues in part** South American Handbook, 0309-4529.*

MX
**MEXICO DESCONOCIDO.** (19??)-. Periodical. Spanish. mo. $50.00. Editorial Jilguero SA, Monte Pelvoux 110 Primer Piso, Chapultepec Mexico DFCP 11000. **Tel** 011 52 5404040, 011 52 2026585. **LC** F1216; .M387. **DD** 972/.005. Index available. cum. index. **Bk Rev**, (Qty: 2). **Ad Acc, Adv Mgr:** Alejandro Guerrero Molina. **Circ:** 76000 (ctrl). available on microfilm; available on an online database.
**Desc:** About folklore, customs, ceremonies, and religion.
**Ind/Abst** Ethnoarts Index.

US/0883-2625
**MEXICO (NEW YORK, N.Y. 1983).** (MEXICO.). [Mexico]. 1983-. English. an. Fishers World Travel Guides, 100 Chestnut Street, Philadelphia PA 19106. **Tel** (800)327-5300. **ED** F Lemkowitz. **LC** F1209; .M4865. **DD** 917.2/04834.

MX
**MEXICO NOW : A MONTHLY REPORT FROM SOUTH OF THE BORDER.** (197?)-. Periodical. English. Twelve times a year. $25.00. Mexico Now, Apartado Postal 1192, Mazatlan Sinaloa Mexico. **ED** Dixie Davis. Index available. cum. index. **Bk Rev.**
**Desc:** Each issue contains current events update, travel notes, a article on traveling, customs, the arts and politics.

US/1048-5147
**MEXICO TOURISM NEWS MAGAZINE. VFOAT** Mexico Tourism News; Mexico Tourism; Tourism Mexico. (1991)-. Periodical. English. qt. $10.00. American International Hispanic Media, 1219 Palo Verde, Carson City NV 89701.

US/8756-1395
**MEXICO TRAV'LER, THE.** Periodical. English. mo. $25.00. Mexico Trav'Ler, 121 North. College, Suite 301, Ft. Collins CO 80524. **DD** 917.

US/0273-9372
**MIAMI MENSUAL. See** General Interest-General Interest-North America.

US/0735-1798
**MICHIGAN LIVING. Added/Corp** Automobile Club of Michigan. **VFOAT** Michigan Living A.A.A. Motor News; Michigan Living AAA Motor News. Vol. 63, No. 9 (March 1981)-. Periodical. English. mo. $9.00 (one year), $15.00 (two year) US; $13.50 (one year) $24.00 (two year) Canada; $24.00 other. Automobile Club of Michigan, Auto Club Drive, Dearborn MI 48126. **Tel** (313)336-1521. **ED** Ronald Garbinski. **LC** TL1; .D4. **DD** 917.74. Index available. **Bk Rev. Ad Acc, Adv Mgr:** Kerry Rende. **Circ:** 1,010,956. ***Continues** Michigan Living Motor News, 0161-2859.*
**Desc:** Coverage of one-day, weekend or extended vacation travel in Michigan, USA and worldwide. Michigan events, entertainment, dining and the outdoors. Autos and auto industry news.

UK/0140-8321
**MIDDLE EAST TRAVEL.** ***Suspended.*** Periodical. English. mo. $60.00 US. IC Publications Ltd., 7 Coldbath Square, London EC1R 4LQ England. **Tel** 011 44 71 713-7711, FAX 011 44 71 713-7898, telex 8811757.

US/0569-2865
**MIDEASTERN TOUR BOOK.** (MIDEASTERN TOUR BOOK; INCLUDING CHICAGO, IL, AND NEW YORK CITY, N.Y.). **Added/Corp** American Automobile Association. **VFOAT** Tour Book: Mideastern. Periodical. English. American Automobile Association, 1000 AAA Drive, Heathrow FL 32746. **Tel** (407)444-7000. **LC** E106; .A5. **DD** 917.3; 917.4.

US/0026-3435
**MIDWEST MOTORIST, THE. Added/Corp** Auto Club of Missouri. (19??)-. Periodical. English. Six times a year (Jan., Mar., May, July, Sept., Nov.). $3.00. Auto Club of Missouri, 12901 North Forty Drive, St Louis MO 63141. **Tel** (314)576-7350, FAX (314)523-7427. **ED** Michael J. Right. **Ad Acc, Adv Mgr:** Deborah Klein. **Circ:** 391,000 (ctrl).
**Desc:** Features articles on travel, area history, auto safety, highway and transportation news, automotive news, and consumer issues.
**Ind/Abst** Ozark Period. Index.

US
**MINNESOTA CALENDAR OF EVENTS.** 1977-. English. an. Minnesota Office of Tourism, 375 Jackson Street #250, St Paul MN 55101. ***Continues** Calendar of Events (Minneapolis, MN.).*

UK
**MINTEL LEISURE INTELLIGENCE. See** Recreation, Leisure.

CN/1185-216X
**MLD CANADIAN TRAVELLER.** [MLD Can. trav.]. Vol. 6, No. 1 (Jan. 1991)-. Periodical. English. MLD Canadian Traveller, 210-1015 Burrard Street, Vancouver British Columbia V6Z 1Y5 Canada. **DD** 338.4791/05. ***Continues** TravelTrade Canada., 0841-9191.*

US/0899-6806
**MOBIL ROAD ATLAS AND TRIP PLANNING GUIDE, UNITED STATES, CANADA, AND MEXICO. See** Geography.

US/0076-9827
**MOBIL TRAVEL GUIDE : CALIFORNIA AND THE WEST.** [Mobil travel guide, Calif. West]. **VFOAT** California and the West. (1969)-. English. an. $13.95. Random House Inc., 400 Hahn Road, Westminster MD 21157. **Tel** (800)726-0600, (800)733-3000, FAX (800)659-2436. **(Subscription address:** Mobil Travel Guides, PO Box 493, Mt. Morris IL 61054.**) LC** F859.3; .M6. **DD** 917.94/04/5. ***Continues** Mobil Travel Guide : Good Food, Lodging and Sightseeing, California and the West, 0076-9827.*

US/1075-5926
**MOBIL TRAVEL GUIDE. FREQUENT TRAVELERS' GUIDE TO MAJOR CITIES.** [Mobil travel guide, Freq. travel. guide major cities]. **Added/Corp** Mobil Oil Corporation. **VFOAT** Cities; Mobil Travel Guide. Major Cities; Frequent Traveler's Guide to Major Cities; Major Cities. (1991)-. English. an. $14.95. Random House Inc., 400 Hahn Road, Westminster MD 21157. **Tel** (800)726-0600, (800)733-3000, FAX (800)659-2436. **(Subscription address:** Mobil Travel Guides, PO Box 493, Mt. Morris IL 61054.**) LC** E158; .R28a; E158; .R28. **DD** 647/.9473/005. ***Continues*** *Mobil Travel Guide. Major Cities, 0737-9153.*
**Desc:** Coverage of 46 major cities, plus airport and street maps.

US/0076-9789
**MOBIL TRAVEL GUIDE. GREAT LAKES AREA.** [Mobil travel guide, Great Lakes area]. **Added/Corp** Mobil Oil Corporation. **VFOAT** Great Lakes Area. (1961)-. English. an. $13.95. Random House Inc., 400 Hahn Road, Westminster MD 21157. **Tel** (800)726-0600, (800)733-3000, FAX (800)659-2436. **(Subscription address:** Mobil Travel Guides, PO Box 493, Mt. Morris IL 61054.**) LC** F551; .M64.

US/0076-9797
**MOBIL TRAVEL GUIDE : MIDDLE ATLANTIC STATES.** [Mobil travel guide, Middle Atl. States]. **Added/Corp** Mobil Oil Corporation. **VFOAT** Middle Atlantic States; Middle Atlantic. (1962/63)-. English. an. $13.95. Random House Inc., 400 Hahn Road, Westminster MD 21157. **Tel** (800)726-0600, (800)733-3000, FAX (800)659-2436. **(Subscription address:** Mobil Travel Guides, PO Box 493, Mt. Morris IL 61054.**) LC** F106; .M67. **DD** 917.4.

US/1040-1075
**MOBIL TRAVEL GUIDE. NORTHEAST.** [Mobil travel guide, Northeast]. **Added/Corp** Mobil Oil Corporation. **VFOAT** Northeast. (1989)-. English. an. $13.95. Random House Inc., 400 Hahn Road, Westminster MD 21157. **Tel** (800)726-0600, (800)733-3000, FAX (800)659-2436. **(Subscription address:** Mobil Travel Guides, PO Box 493, Mt. Morris IL 61054.**) LC** F2.3; .M59. **DD** 917.404/43. ***Continues*** *Mobil Travel Guide. Northeastern States, 0076-9800.*

US/0076-9819
**MOBIL TRAVEL GUIDE. NORTHWEST AND GREAT PLAINS STATES.** [Mobil travel guide, Northwest Great Plains States]. **Added/Corp** Mobil Oil Corporation. **VFOAT** Northwest and Great Plains States; Northwest and Great Plains. (1962/63)-. English. an. $13.95. Random House Inc., 400 Hahn Road, Westminster MD 21157. **Tel** (800)726-0600, (800)733-3000, FAX (800)659-2436. **(Subscription address:** Mobil Travel Guides, PO Box 493, Mt. Morris IL 61054.**) LC** F597; .M7. **DD** 917.8.

US/1040-1067
**MOBIL TRAVEL GUIDE. SOUTHEAST.** [Mobil travel guide, Southeast]. **Added/Corp** Mobil Oil Corporation. **VFOAT** Southeast. (1989)-. English. an. $13.95. Random House Inc., 400 Hahn Road, Westminster MD 21157. **Tel** (800)726-0600, (800)733-3000, FAX (800)659-2436. **(Subscription address:** Mobil Travel Guides, PO Box 493, Mt. Morris IL 61054.**) LC** F207.3; .M59. **DD** 917.5. ***Continues*** *Mobil Travel Guide : Southeastern States, 0076-9835.*

US/0076-9843
**MOBIL TRAVEL GUIDE. SOUTHWEST AND SOUTH CENTRAL AREA. Added/Corp** Mobil Oil Corporation. **VFOAT** Southwest and South Central Area; Southwest and South Central. (1962/1963)-. English. an. $13.95. Random House Inc., 400 Hahn Road, Westminster MD 21157. **Tel** (800)726-0600, (800)733-3000, FAX (800)659-2436. **(Subscription address:** Mobil Travel Guides, PO Box 493, Mt. Morris IL 61054.**) LC** F207.3; .M6. **DD** 917.6/0443. ***Continues*** *Mobil Travel Guide. South Central and Southwestern States.*

US/1040-3507
**MOBIL TRAVEL GUIDE. WASHINGTON, D.C.** [Mobil travel guide, Wash. D. C.]. **VFOAT** Washington, D.C. (1989)-. English. an. Random House Inc., 400 Hahn Road, Westminster MD 21157. **Tel** (800)726-0600, (800)733-3000, FAX (800)659-2436. **LC** F192.3; .M57. **DD** 917.5304/4.

CH
**MONTHLY REPORT ON TOURISM, REPUBLIC OF CHINA.** Chinese (English). mo. free. Ministry of Communications, PO Box 1490, Taipei Taiwan. **ED** Jason Chung. **Circ:** 2,500 (ctrl). ***Continues*** *Kuan Kuang Tzu Liao.*

JM
**MONTHLY STATISTICAL REPORT / JAMAICA TOURIST BOARD. Added/Corp** Jamaica. Tourist Board. Vol. 1, No. 1 (Jan. 1991)-. Statistical Publication. English. mo. ***Continues*** *Visitor Statistics.*

CN/1183-2142
**MONTREAL PASSIONS.** [Montr. passions]. Vol. 1, No 1 (Jan. 1991)-. Periodical. English (French). bm. $39.50 Canada; $59.90 other. Editions M. P., Inc., Suite 100, 203 Place D'Youville, Montreal Quebec H2Y 2B3 Canada. **DD** 971.4/28/005.

US/1041-5734
**MOTORCYCLE TOURING.** [Motorcycle tour.]. (1990)-. English. sa. $19.95 North America; $32.00 other. Whitehorse Press, 154 Brookline Street, Boston MA 02118. **Tel** (617)482-3350, (800)842-7077, FAX (617)482-6621. **ED** Daniel Kennedy. **LC** GV1059.5; .M674. **DD** 796.7/5025. Index available. **Bk Rev. Circ:** 4,000.
**Desc:** Includes 33 listings for motorcycle tour operators, 145 guided tours, plus listings for motorcycle rental agencies, shipping facilities.

●US/1062-7103
**MOUNTAIN BIKE ACTION TRAVEL GUIDE.** (1992)-. English. $3.50 (single issue). Daisy/Hi-Torque Publishing Company, 10600 Sepulveda Blvd., Mission Hills CA 91345.

US/0162-6523
**MOUNTAIN VACATION & TRAVEL GUIDE COVERING WESTERN NORTH CAROLINA. Main/Corp** Carolina Life, Inc. **VAT** Mountain Vacation and Travel Guide Covering Western North Carolina. English. an. $3.50. Carolina Life, Inc., PO Box 548, Hendersonville NC 28739. **LC** F252.3; .C37A. **DD** 917.56/04/4.

US/0161-9551
**MTM, MOTORCOACH TOUR MART.** 1978-. English. an. $70.00. Talmage, PO Box 1237, East Orleans MA 02643. **LC** G153.4; .M18. **DD** 917.3/04/92.

US/0093-7487
**MULTINATIONAL EXECUTIVE TRAVEL COMPANION.** (19??)-. English. ir (Apr. or May). $60.00. Strand Publishing Company Inc., 207 Atlantic Street, Stamford CT 06901. **Tel** (203)324-3007, FAX (203)967-8404. **ED** Dale W. Strand. **LC** G153; .M84. **DD** 910/.202. Index available. cum. index. **Bk Rev**, (Qty: 4-8). **Ad Acc.** ctrl circ.
**Desc:** The only business-travel guide covering over 145 major cities worldwide with hard to find information on travel, hotels/motels, restaurants, and entertainment.

US/0196-0024
**MYRA WALDO'S TRAVEL GUIDE TO SOUTH AMERICA. *Ceased.* VFOAT** Travel Guide to South America. Periodical. English. ir. Macmillan Publishing Company, 866 3rd Avenue, New York NY 10022. **Tel** (212)702-2000, (800)257-5755. **(Subscription address:** Front and Brown Street, Riverside, NJ 08370**) LC** F2211; .W34. **DD** 918/.0438.

US/0196-3651
**MYRA WALDO'S TRAVEL GUIDE TO SOUTHERN EUROPE.** [Myra Waldo's travel guide South. Eur.]. **VFOAT** Travel Guide to Southern Europe. (1980)-. Periodical. English. ir. $9.95. Macmillan Publishing Company, 100 Front Street, Box 500, Riverside NJ 08075-7500. **Tel** (800)257-5755, (609)461-6500, FAX (609)461-7070. **LC** D974; .W23. **DD** 914/.04558. ***Supersedes in part*** *Myra Waldo's Travel and Motoring Guide to Europe.*

US/0195-7759
**MYRA WALDO'S TRAVEL GUIDE TO THE ORIENT AND ASIA.** English. ir. $10.95. Macmillan Publishing Company, 866 3rd Avenue, New York NY 10022. **Tel** (212)702-2000, (800)257-5755. **(Subscription address:** Front and Brown Street, Riverside, NJ 08370**) LC** DS4; .W28. **DD** 915/.04428. ***Supersedes in part*** *Myra Waldo's Travel Guide to the Orient and the Pacific.*

US/0195-7767
**MYRA WALDO'S TRAVEL GUIDE TO THE SOUTH PACIFIC. *Ceased.*** [Myra Waldo's travel guide South Pac.]. (1980)-?. English. ir. Macmillan Publishing Company, 866 3rd Avenue, New York NY 10022. **Tel** (212)702-2000, (800)257-5755. **(Subscription address:** Front and Brown Street, Riverside, NJ 08370**)** ***Continues in part*** *Myra Waldo's Travel Guide to the Orient and the Pacific.*

US
**NATIONAL DIRECTORY OF FREE TOURIST ATTRACTIONS.** (1977)-. Directory. English. be. $5.95 (US); $7.95 (other). Pilot Books, 103 Cooper Street, Babylon NY 11702-2319. **Tel** (516)422-2225, FAX (516)422-2227. **ED** Raymond Carlson. **LC** E158; .N252.
**Desc:** Lists free gardens, restored villages, ships, museums and other interesting presentations of history, science and fine art throughout the United States.

US/0747-0932
**NATIONAL GEOGRAPHIC TRAVELER.** [Natl. Geogr. travel.]. **Added/Corp** National Geographic Society (U.S.). **VFOAT** Traveler. Vol. 1, No. 1 (Spring 1984)-. Periodical. English. Six times a year. $17.95 US; $22.75 Canada; $25.50 other. National Geographic Society, 11555 Darnestown, Gaithersburg MD 20878. **Tel** (202)857-7000, (800)638-4077, FAX (202)429-5727, telex 64194 NATGEO. **(Subscription address:** National Geographic Society, Attention: Agent Desk, PO Box 98035, Washington DC 20090-8035.**) ED** Richard Busch and Paul Martin. **LC** G1; .N278. **DD** 910/.5. **Circ:** 700,000. available on microfilm and microfiche from University Microfilms International (UMI). Documents available from UMI Article Clearinghouse.
**Ind/Abst** Acad. Abstr. Full Text Elite (Jan. 1987-); Acad. Abstr. (Jan. 1987-); Acad. Search (Jan. 1987-); Access (1983-); Gen. Period. Index (1992-); INFO-SOUTH Abstr.; Mag. Artic. Summar. Elite (Jan. 1987-); Mag. Artic. Summar. Select (Jan. 1987-); Mag. Artic. Summar. CD-ROM (Jan. 1987-); Mag. Index Plus (1992-); Mag. Search; Newsp. Period. Abstr. (1992-); Pop. Period. Index.

US/0279-3083
**NATIONAL MOTORIST.** (NATIONAL MOTORIST / NATIONAL AUTOMOBILE CLUB.). [Natl. mot.]. **Added/Corp** National Automobile Club. (19??)-. Periodical. English. bm. $3.00. National Motorist, 188 Embarcadero, Suite 300, San Francisco CA 94105. **Tel** (415)777-4000, FAX (415)882-2141. **ED** Jane M. Offers. **DD** 629. **Bk Rev**, (Qty: 10). **Ad Acc. Circ:** 125,000.
**Desc:** Travel publication for National Automobile Club members. Club is in California only. Covers Western travel, also international travel automotive/legislative news for California motorists.

US/0362-7829
**NATIONAL TRAVEL EXPENDITURE STUDY. Main/Corp** United States Travel Data Center. (19??)-. English. ir. $35.00. US Travel Data Center, 1100 New York Avenue, Suite 450, Washington DC 20005. **Tel** (202)408-1832. **LC** G155.U6; U58b. **DD** 338.4/7/91730492. **Circ:** 400 (ctrl).
**Desc:** Total travel spending and averages for various categories and trip and traveler characteristics.

●US
**NATIONAL TRAVEL SURVEY SEASONAL REPORTS.** (1993)-. English. Four times a year (Fall). $400.00. US Travel Data Center, 1100 New York Avenue, Suite 450, Washington DC 20005. **Tel** (202)408-1832.
**Desc:** Individual seasonal reports covering Winter, Spring, Summer, and Autumn include U.S. travel characteristics and trends, analysis of conditions influencing travel and regional perspectives from the Data Center's monthly National Travel Survey.

US/1058-398X
**NEW "DIVERS SPEAK OUT" ... DIVE TRAVEL DIRECTORY, THE.** [New "divers speak out" dive travel dir.]. **VFOAT** "Divers Speak Out"; Dive Travel Directory "Divers Speak Out"; All New ... Dive Travel Directory "Divers Speak Out"; All New "Divers Speak Out". Directory. English. ATCOM Inc., 2315 Broadway, New York NY 10024-4397. **Tel** (800)521-7004, (212)873-5900, FAX (212)799-1728. **DD** 910.

US/0553-0601
**NEW HORIZONS WORLD GUIDE. Added/Corp** Pan American World Airways, inc. **VFOAT** Pan Am's Travel Facts about 138 Countries. (1951)-. English. ir. Pan American Airways, Pan Am Building/48th Floor, New York NY 10017.

US/0195-3605
**NEW ORLEANS MARDI GRAS GUIDE.** 1977-. English. an. Arthur Hardy, PO Box 8058, New Orleans LA 70182.

US/0893-1895
**NEW WORLD OF TRAVEL, THE.** (THE NEW WORLD OF TRAVEL / BY ARTHUR FROMMER.). [New world travel]. **VFOAT** Arthur Frommer's New World of Travel. (1988)-. English. an. $16.95. Macmillan Publishing Co. / Indiana, 201 West 103rd Street, Indianapolis IN 46290. **Tel** (800)428-5331, (800)858-7674. **(Subscription address:** Macmillian Publishing Company / Indiana, 201 West 103rd Street, Indianapolis IN 46290.**) LC** PAR. **DD** 910.

US
**NEW YORK CITY JEWISH TRAVEL GUIDE.** (19??)-. Periodical. English. $13.95. Israelowitz Publishing, Box 228, Brooklyn NY 11229. **Tel** (718)951-7072, FAX (718)951-7072. **ED** Oscar Israelowitz.

US
**NEW YORK CITY SUBWAY GUIDE.** (19??)-. Periodical. English. $9.45. Israelowitz Publishing, Box 228, Brooklyn NY 11229. **Tel** (718)951-7072, FAX (718)951-7072. **ED** Oscar Israelowitz. Index available. **Bk Rev.** ctrl circ.
**Desc:** Complete travel guide to the New York City subway system with a listing of museums and historic sights.

NZ
**NEW ZEALAND HISTORIC PLACES.** See History(General)-History of Australia and Oceania.

SP/1012-8042
**NEWSLETTER OF THE INTERNATIONAL ACADEMY FOR THE STUDY OF TOURISM.** [Newsl. Int. Acad. Study Tour.]. **Main/Corp** International Academy for the Study of Tourism. Vol. 1, No. 2 (1988)-. Newsletter. English. qt. Free. International Academy for the Study of Tourism, c/o R W Butler/Dept of Geography, University of Western Ontario, London Ontario N6A 5C2 Canada. **DD** 380.1/459104/072. ***Continues*** *International Academy for the Study of Tourism.*

US/0749-985X
**NEWSLINE - TRAVEL INDUSTRY ASSOCIATION OF AMERICA.** (NEWSLINE.). [Newsline - Travel Ind. Assoc. Am.]. Periodical. English. mo. Travel Industry Association of America, 1899 L Street NW, Washington DC 20036. **Tel** (212)293-1433, telex 248799. **ED** Robin Longman. **DD** 910. **Bk Rev. Circ:** 3,200 (ctrl).
**Desc:** Informs travel industry leaders, government officials and leading industry analysts on marketing, promotional and governmental initiatives of Travel Industry Association of America, Umbrell Association for U.S. travel industry.

CN/0714-4202
**NIAGARA'S SEASONS.** (NIAGARA'S SEASONS / REGION NIAGARA TOURIST COUNCIL.). [Niagara's seas.]. **Added/Corp** Niagara (Ont. :Regional Municipality). Tourist Council. (1981)-. English. an. Free. Niagara's Seasons, c/o Region Niagara Tourist Council, PO Box 1042, Thorold Ontario L2R 4T7 Canada. **Tel** (416)685-1571. **DD** 917.13/38/04405. **Circ:** 200,000.

CN/0705-3940
**NOMAD (WILLOWDALE).** (NOMAD.). V. 1-Aug. 1977-. Periodical. English. bm. $3.00 per issue. Nomad, 251 Consumer Road/Suite 817, Willowdale Ontario M2J 4R3 Canada. **DD** 910/.5.

US
**NORTH AMERICAN GUIDE TO NUDE RECREATION.** **Added/Corp** American Sunbathing Association. (19??)-. Periodical. English. an. $29.95. American Sunbathing Association, 1703 North Main Street Suite E, Kissimmee FL 34744. **Tel** (407)933-2064, FAX (407)933-7577. **LC** GV451; .N825. **DD** 613/.194/0257. ***Continues*** *Nudist Park Guide.*

US/0468-6853
**NORTHEASTERN TOUR BOOK.** **VFOAT** Tour Book Northeastern, Connecticut, Maine, Massachusetts, New Hampshire, New York, Rhode Island, Vermont. English. an. American Automobile Association, 1000 AAA Drive, Heathrow FL 32746. **Tel** (407)444-7000. **LC** GV1024; .N84. **DD** 917.4/04/4. ***Continues*** *Northeastern States.*

CN/0707-3364
**NORTHLAND TODAY MAGAZINE.** **VAT** Northland Today. V. 1- Apr. 1978-. Periodical. English. mo. $4.50 Canada; $7.00 other. Rosebrugh Publishing, 265 2D Avenue West, North Bay Ontario P1B 4A1. **DD** 917.13/14/044.

US/0192-1169
**NORTHWEST BOAT TRAVEL.** See Boats and Boating.

●US/1062-1415
**NORTHWEST COLORADO OFFICIAL TRAVEL GUIDE.** **VFOAT** Colorado. (1992)-. English. Free.

US/1059-9681
**NORTHWEST TRAVEL.** [Northwest travel]. Vol. 1, No. 1 (Feb./Mar. 1991)-. Periodical. English. Six times a year (Feb., April, June, Aug., Oct., Dec.). $14.95 US; $21.95 other. Oregon Coast Magazine, PO Box 18000, Florence OR 97439. **Tel** (503)997-8401, FAX (503)997-1124. **ED** Dave Peden and Judy Fleagle. **DD** 917. **Ad Acc. Circ:** 50,000.
**Desc:** Travel, history, art, and recreation information in the Pacific Northwest; includes many full-page, full-color photographs.

US/0094-078X
**NORTHWESTERN TOUR BOOK.** **VFOAT** Tour Book, Northwestern: Idaho, Montana, Oregon, Washington, Wyoming. English. an. American Automobile Association, 1000 AAA Drive, Heathrow FL 32746. **Tel** (407)444-7000. **LC** GV1024; .N87. **DD** 917.9. ***Continues*** *Northwestern States.*

SP/0213-3105
**NOSA TERRA, A.** See Sociology-Manners and Customs.

CN/0229-2718
**NOTES DU CENTRE D'ETUDES DU TOURISME, LES.** [Notes Cent. etud. tour.]. Vol. 1, (June, 15, 1977)-. Periodical. French. mo. Free. Centre d'Etudes du Tourisme, CP 8000 Succursale A, Montreal Quebec H3C 3L4 Canada. **Tel** (514)875-9180. **ED** Jean Pelletier and Daniel Dumas. **DD** 016.3384/791714. **Bk Rev. Circ:** 1,500.
**Desc:** Newsletter on travel and tourism related research: short thematic listing of books, reports and periodical articles; book reviews; library recent acquisitions.

CN/1185-202X
**NOUVELLES DU BUREAU NATIONAL.** [Nouv. Bur. natl.]. **Added/Corp** Alliance Canadienne des Associations Touristiques. Vol. 1, No. 1 (Apr. 1990)-. Periodical. French. bm. Limited free distribution. Alliance Canadienne des Associations Touristiques, 1106-75 Rue Albert, Ottawa, Ontario K1P 5E7 Canada. **DD** 338.4.

CN/0707-087X
**NOVA SCOTIA HOSTELLER.** See Hotels/Motels.

US/1053-0746
**NUDE PACIFIC TRAVEL GUIDE.** [Nude Pac. travel guide]. Ed. 91E (May 1991)-. English. Free (libraries). Tahanga Research Association, PO Box 8714, La Jolla CA 92038-8714. **LC** WMLC 91/976. **DD** 911. ***Continues in part*** *Nude Asia-Pacific-Africa, 0816-8741.*

NZ/1170-5469
**NZTD DOMESTIC RESEARCH SERIES.** [NZTD domest. res. ser.]. **VFOAT** New Zealand Tourist Department Domestic Research Series. (1991)-. Monographic series. English. ir. **DD** _a338.47919305. ***Continues*** *NZTP Domestic Research Series, 0112-9767.*
**Ind/Abst** Leis. Recreat. Tour. Abstr.

NZ
**NZTD ECONOMIC RESEARCH SERIES.** **Added/Corp** New Zealand. Tourism Dept. Research Services. **VFOAT** ER. (1990)-. Monographic series. English. ***Continues*** *NZTP Economic Research Series, 0112-9864.*
**Ind/Abst** Leis. Recreat. Tour. Abstr.

NZ/1170-831X
**NZTD REGIONAL RESEARCH SERIES.** [NZTD reg. res. ser.]. **VFOAT** New Zealand Tourist Department Regional Research Series. (1991)-. Monographic series. English. New Zealand Tourism Department, Research Section, PO Box 95, Wellington New Zealand. **Tel** 728860, FAX 781736. **DD** _a338.47919305. ***Continues*** *NZTP Regional Research Series, 0112-9783.*

NZ/0112-9724
**NZTP OVERSEAS MARKET RESEARCH SERIES.** [NZTP overseas mark. res. ser.]. **VFOAT** New Zealand Tourist and Publicity Overseas Market Research Series. (1986)-. Monographic series. English. ir. **DD** 338.4791931.
**Ind/Abst** Leis. Recreat. Tour. Abstr.

US/1057-0918
**OAG DESKTOP FLIGHT GUIDE (NORTH AMERICAN ED.).** (OAG DESKTOP FLIGHT GUIDE.). [OAG deskt. flight guide]. **Added/Corp** Official Airline Guides, Inc. **VFOAT** Official Airline Guides Desktop Flight Guide; Desktop Flight Guide. Vol. 17, No. 15 (May 1, 1991)-. Periodical. English (Spanish). Twenty-four times a year. $330.00. Official Airline Guides, 2000 Clearwater Drive, Oak Brook IL 60521. **Tel** (800)323-3537. **(Subscription address:** Neodata / Colorado, PO Box 2606, Boulder Boulder CO 80322.) **LC** HE9802.A2; O322. **DD** 387. **CODEN** ODFEEE. ***Continues*** *Official Airline Guide (North American Ed.), 0191-1619.*
**Desc:** Contains comprehensive airline schedule information for the United States, Canada, Mexico and the Caribbean. Direct flights, connections, departure time, arrivals, ground transportation information are included.

US/1057-0454
**OAG DESKTOP FLIGHT GUIDE (WORLDWIDE ED.).** (OAG DESKTOP FLIGHT GUIDE.). [OAG deskt. flight guide]. **Added/Corp** Official Airline Guides, Inc. **VFOAT** Official Airline Guides Desktop Flight Guide; Desktop Flight Guide. Vol. 16, No. 3 (May 1991)-. Periodical. English (French, German, Japanese and Spanish). Twelve times a year. $397.00 with Fares; $299.00 without Fares. Official Airline Guides, 2000 Clearwater Drive, Oak Brook IL 60521. **Tel** (800)323-3537. **(Subscription address:** Neodata / Colorado, PO Box 2606, Boulder Boulder CO 80322.) **LC** HE9768; .O33. **DD** 387.7/42/0212. **CODEN** ODGEEJ. ***Continues*** *Official Airline Guide (Worldwide Ed. : 1976), 0364-3875.*
**Desc:** Provides flight schedules and selected fares to and within Europe, the Middle East, the Far East, Australia, Africa, the Pacific Basin, South America, Central America and Greenland as well as between these areas and North America.

UK
**OAG FLIGHT PLANNER EUROPE, MIDDLE EAST & AFRICA.** (19??)-. English. mo. $98.00. Reed Travel Group / England, World Timetable Center, Church Street, Dunstable, Bedfordshire LU5 4HB England. **Tel** 011 44 582 600111, FAX 011 44 582 695348. ***Continues*** *ABC Executive Flight Planner Europe, Middle East & Africa.*

US
**OAG FLIGHTDISK (EUROPEAN ED.).** (OAG FLIGHTDISK.). (19??)-. English. Twelve times a year. $214.00. Official Airline Guides, 2000 Clearwater Drive, Oak Brook IL 60521. **Tel** (800)323-3537.

US
**OAG FLIGHTDISK (NORTH AMERICAN ED.).** (OAG FLIGHTDISK.). (19??)-. English. Twelve times a year. $232.50. Official Airline Guides, 2000 Clearwater Drive, Oak Brook IL 60521. **Tel** (800)323-3537. **(Subscription address:** Neodata / Colorado, PO Box 2606, Boulder Boulder CO 80322.)
**Desc:** Provides flight schedules for the most frequently-traveled city pairs in North America.

UK
**OAG FLIGHTDISK PREMIUM WORLDWIDE EDITION.** (19??)-. English. mo. £350.00 Europe; £420.00 other. Reed Travel Group / England, World Timetable Center, Church Street, Dunstable, Bedfordshire LU5 4HB England. **Tel** 011 44 582 600111, FAX 011 44 582 695348.

US
**OAG FLIGHTDISK (WORLDWIDE ED.).** (OAG FLIGHTDISK.). (19??)-. English. Twelve times a year. $269.00. Official Airline Guides, 2000 Clearwater Drive, Oak Brook IL 60521. **Tel** (800)323-3537.

US
**OAG OFFICIAL TRAVELER FLIGHT GUIDE.** (19??)-. Periodical. English. Twelve times a year. $39.95. Official Airline Guides, 2000 Clearwater Drive, Oak Brook IL 60521. **Tel** (800)323-3537.

●US/1073-0338
**OAG OFFICIAL TRAVELER. TRAVEL GUIDE.** See Hotels/Motels.

US/0745-5275
**OAG PACIFIC AREA POCKET FLIGHT GUIDE.** [OAG Pac. area pocket flight guide]. **Added/Corp** Official Airline Guides. **VFOAT** Pocket Flight Guide; Official Airline Guide; O.A.G. Pacific Area Pocket Flight Guide. **VAT** Official Airline Guide Pacific Area Pocket Flight Guide. (198?)-. English (Japanese). Twelve times a year. $86.00. Official Airline Guides, 2000 Clearwater Drive, Oak Brook IL 60521. **Tel** (800)323-3537.
**Desc:** Handy, pocket-sized guides designed for the traveler to carry along during travel. Contains a summary of direct flights for all airlines, and major connections, for the most popular departure and destination cities.

US/8750-0310
**OAG POCKET FLIGHT GUIDE (EUROPE & MIDDLE EAST ED.).** (OAG POCKET FLIGHT GUIDE.). [OAG pocket flight guide]. **VFOAT** O.A.G. Pocket Flight Guide; Pocket Flight Guide. **VAT** Official Airline Guides Pocket Flight Guide (Europe & Middle East Ed.). (19??)-. Periodical. English. Twelve times a year. $86.00. Official Airline Guides, 2000 Clearwater Drive, Oak Brook IL 60521. **Tel** (800)323-3537. **(Subscription address:** Neodata / Colorado, PO Box 2606, Boulder Boulder CO 80322.) ***Continues*** *OAG Europe & Middle East Pocket Flight Guide, 0191-1546.*
**Desc:** Contains quick reference airline schedules designed for frequent flyers to take along when they travel. Lists most frequently travelled routes throughout the US and Canada, plus the Caribbean and Mexico. Included are arrival times, airline names, flight numbers, etc.

US
**OAG POCKET FLIGHT GUIDE (LATIN AMERICAN/CARIBBEAN ED.).** (OAG POCKET FLIGHT GUIDE.). (19??)-. English. Twelve times a year. $86.00. Official Airline Guides, 2000 Clearwater Drive, Oak Brook IL 60521. **Tel** (800)323-3537. **(Subscription address:** Neodata / Colorado, PO Box 2606, Boulder Boulder CO 80322.)
**Desc:** Contains a summary of direct flights for all airlines and major connections for the most popular departure and destination cities.

US/0743-8249
**OAG POCKET FLIGHT GUIDE (NORTH AMERICAN EDITION).** (OAG POCKET FLIGHT GUIDE.). [OAG pocket flight guide]. **Added/Corp** Official Airline Guides, Inc. **VFOAT** O.A.G. Pocket Flight Guide; Pocket Flight Guide. **VAT** Official Airline Guides Pocket Flight Guide (North American Ed.). (19??)-. Periodical. English. Twelve times a year. $86.00. Official Airline Guides, 2000 Clearwater Drive, Oak Brook IL 60521. **Tel** (800)323-3537. **(Subscription address:** Neodata / Colorado, PO Box 2606, Boulder Boulder CO 80322.) **LC** HE9803.A2; O17. **DD** 387.7/42/0973. **CODEN** ONAGDU. ***Continues*** *Official Airline Guides, Inc. OAG North American Pocket Flight Guide, 0191-1538.*
**Desc:** Contains a summary of direct flights for all airlines

and major connections for the most popular departure and destination cities.
**Ind/Abst** Int. Aerosp. Abstr.

US/1067-8158
**OAG POCKET FLIGHT GUIDE (WORLDWIDE ED.).** (OAG POCKET FLIGHT GUIDE / OFFICIAL AIRLINE GUIDES.). [OAG pocket flight guide]. **Added/Corp** Official Airline Guides, Inc. **VFOAT** Pocket Flight Guide; OAG Worldwide Pocket Flight Guide. **VAT** Official Airline Guides Pocket Flight Guide. (19??)-. English. Twelve times a year. £84.00. Official Airline Guides, 2000 Clearwater Drive, Oak Brook IL 60521. **Tel** (800)323-3537. **LC** HE9768; .O15.

UK
**OAG TRAVEL DISC [CD ROM].** (19??)-. English. mo. £430.00 Europe; £498.00 other. Reed Travel Group / England, World Timetable Center, Church Street, Dunstable, Bedfordshire LU5 4HB England. **Tel** 011 44 582 600111, FAX 011 44 582 695348.

US/0894-1718
**OAG TRAVEL PLANNER. (EUROPEAN EDITION).** (19??)-. English. Four times a year. $142.00 North America; $151.00 Europe; $172.00 Middle East and Africa; $191.00 other. Official Airline Guides, 2000 Clearwater Drive, Oak Brook IL 60521. **Tel** (800)323-3537. **(Subscription address:** Neodata / Colorado, PO Box 2606, Boulder Boulder CO 80322.)

●US/1069-2150
**OAG TRAVEL PLANNER (PACIFIC ASIA ED.).** (OAG TRAVEL PLANNER.). [OAG travel plan.]. **Added/Corp** Official Airline Guides, Inc. American Hotel & Motel Association. **VFOAT** Travel Planner. **VAT** Official Airline Guides Travel Planner. Vol. 9, No. 6 (Jan./Mar. 1992)-. Directory. English. Four times a year. $142.00. Official Airline Guides, 2000 Clearwater Drive, Oak Brook IL 60521. **Tel** (800)323-3537. **(Subscription address:** Neodata / Colorado, PO Box 2606, Boulder Boulder CO 80322.) **DD** 647. ***Continues** OAG Travel Planner, Hotel & Motel Redbook (Pacific Asia Ed.), 0894-1734.*
**Desc:** Contains information on how to reach over 2,500 Pacific Asia destinations, over 3,700 hotel listings, airport diagrams, city center and country maps, travel related directory sections and country basics.

UK
**OAG WAG FARES SUPPLEMENT.** (19??)-. English. mo. £60.00 Europe; £70.00 other. Reed Travel Group / England, World Timetable Center, Church Street, Dunstable, Bedfordshire LU5 4HB England. **Tel** 011 44 582 600111, FAX 011 44 582 695348.

UK
**OAG WORLD AIRWAYS GUIDE.** (19??)-. English. ir. £430.00 Europe; £498.00 other. Reed Travel Group / England, World Timetable Center, Church Street, Dunstable, Bedfordshire LU5 4HB England. **Tel** 011 44 582 600111, FAX 011 44 582 695348.

US/0097-8779
**OAG WORLDWIDE CRUISE & SHIPLINE GUIDE.** ***Title Change.*** **Added/Corp** Reuben H. Donnelley Corporation. Official Airline Guides, Inc. **VFOAT** Worldwide Cruise & Shipline Guide. **VAT** Official Airline Guide Worldwide Cruise and Shipline Guide. Vol. 1 (Jan./Feb. 1975)-(19??). English. bm. OAG Worldwide Cruise & Shipline Guide, Official Airline Guides, 2000 Clearwater Drive, OakBrook IL 60521. **Tel** (312)574-6000, FAX TELEX 210144312-574-6091. **LC** HE568; .O23. **DD** 387.5/2/025. **Ad Acc. Circ:** 10,000. ***Continued by** OAG Cruise and Shipline Guide, 1061-799X.*
**Desc:** Contains directory of cruise and ferry operators, worldwide cruise listings, port-to-port ferry schedules, ship profiles, port diagrams, passenger freighter services and more.

US/1042-8054
**OAHU.** [Oahu]. 1st Ed. (June 1989)-. English. be. $11.95 (add $2.00 shipping). Paradise Publications, 8110 SW Wareham, Portland OR 97233. **Tel** (503)246-1555. **ED** Greg and Christie Stilson. **DD** 919. Index available. cum. index. **Circ:** 10,000.
**Desc:** The only comprehensive travel publication for Hawaii's Capitol Isle of Oahu. Detailed descriptions covering accommodations, restaurants, scenic points of interest, island history, beaches and general information such as travel safety tips, traveling with children, and travel for the physically impaired.

US/1042-8038
**OAHU UPDATE, THE.** [Oahu update]. (1989)-. Periodical. English. qt. $6.00. Paradise Publications, 8110 SW Wareham, Portland OR 97233. **Tel** (503)246-1555. **ED** Christie Stilson and Ken Bierly. **DD** 919. **Bk Rev. Ad Acc. Circ:** 2,000.
**Desc:** Features updated information on island restaurants, accommodations and other related material for the Hawaii bound traveler or island resident.

US/0883-3664
**ODYSSEUS (FLUSHING, N.Y.).** (ODYSSEUS.). 1st Ed.-. English (French). an. $16.95 US; $24.95 other. Odysseus Enterprises, PO Box 7605, Flushing NY 11352. **Tel** (718)445-2471, telex 6719473. **ED** Joseph H Bain. **LC** E158; .O28. **DD** 917.3/04927/0880664. Index available. **Bk Rev. Ad Acc. Circ:** 300,000 (ctrl).
**Desc:** Accommodations and travel guide for the gay community (USA/International).

CN/0316-8077
**OFFICIAL ARROW STREET GUIDE OF OTTAWA AND DISTRICT.** ***Suspended.*** **VFOAT** Ottawa & District Including Hull. -Suspended March 1975. Periodical. English. an. Might Directories, 220 Bartley Drive, Toronto Ontario M4A 2H4 Canada. **Tel** (416)751-2751. **DD** 917.13/84.

US/1055-1778
**OFFICIAL CITY GUIDE.** **VFOAT** City Guide. (19??)-. Periodical. English (Japanese). wk. $29.00 US; $36.00 other. City Guide Magazine, 853 7th Avenue, New York NY 10019. **Tel** (212)315-0800, FAX (212)397-9513. **ED** Peter Insalaco. **Ad Acc, Adv Mgr:** Paul Insalaco, **Tel** (212)315-0800. **Circ:** 216,667. ***Continues** City Guide (New York, N.Y.), 1043-3937.*
**Desc:** Magazine for visitors to New York City.

●US/1065-2450
**OFFICIAL CRUISE GUIDE.** [Off. cruise guide]. (1993)-. English. an. $49.00. Reed Travel Group / New Jersey, 500 Plaza Drive, Secaucus NJ 07096. **Tel** (201)902-2000, (800)360-0015, FAX (201)319-1628. **LC** IN PROCESS. **DD** 387. ***Continues** Official Hotel & Resort Guide's Cruise Guide.*
**Desc:** Information on cruise lines and ships for travel agents.

US/1043-1195
**OFFICIAL GUIDE TO AMERICAN HISTORIC INNS, THE.** **See** Hotels/Motels.

US/8755-0458
**OFFICIAL GUIDE TO TRAVEL AGENT & TRAVEL CAREERS, THE.** **See** Occupations and Careers.

US/0030-0381
**OFFICIAL STEAMSHIP GUIDE INTERNATIONAL.** (OFFICIAL STEAMSHIP GUIDE.). **VFOAT** Official Steamship Guide. Vol. 64, No. 2 (Aug. 1963)-. English. mo. $70.00. Transportation Guide Inc, 111 Cherry Street, New Canaan CT 06840. **Tel** (203)966-9784. **ED** Marlene Dobrin. **LC** HE568; .O4. **Ad Acc. Circ:** 10,000. ***Continues** Official Steamship & Airways Guide International.*
**Desc:** A magazine listing all cruises in the world.

CN/1186-7949
**OFFICIAL TRAVELLER'S GUIDE TO CANADA, THE.** [Off. travel. guide Can.]. **Added/Corp** Tourism Industry Association of Canada. **VFOAT** Canada, The World Next Door. (1991)-. English. Limited free distribution. **DD** 917.104.

CN/0822-5729
**ON TARGET WEEKLY.** [On target wkly.]. **Added/Corp** Canadian Travel Press. **VAT** On Target (Toronto). No. 1 (Feb. 11, 1982)-. Periodical. English. wk. Canadian Travel Press, Suite 3000, 100 Adelaide Street, West Toronto Ontario M5H 1S3. **DD** 338.4/7917104/05.

●US
**ON THE LOOSE IN EASTERN EUROPE / WRITTEN BY BERKELEY STUDENTS IN COOPERATION WITH THE ASSOCIATED STUDENTS OF THE UNIVERSITY OF CALIFORNIA.** **Added/Corp** University of California, Berkeley. Associated Students. **VFOAT** Eastern Europe. (1992)-. English. an. $15.50 (U.S.), $19.50 (Canada). Random House Inc., 400 Hahn Road, Westminster MD 21157. **Tel** (800)726-0600, (800)733-3000, FAX (800)659-2436. **ED** Katie Clark. **LC** DJK8; .O5. **DD** 914.704.

●US
**ON THE LOOSE IN MEXICO / WRITTEN BY BERKELEY STUDENTS IN COOPERATION WITH THE ASSOCIATED STUDENTS OF THE UNIVERSITY OF CALIFORNIA.** **Added/Corp** University of California, Berkeley. Associated Students. **VFOAT** Mexico. (1992)-. English. an. Random House Inc., 400 Hahn Road, Westminster MD 21157. **Tel** (800)726-0600, (800)733-3000, FAX (800)659-2436. **ED** Deborah Meacham. **LC** F1209; .O6. **DD** 917.204/835.

●US
**ON THE LOOSE IN THE PACIFIC NORTHWEST & ALASKA / WRITTEN BY BERKELEY STUDENTS IN COOPERATION WITH THE ASSOCIATED STUDENTS OF THE UNIVERSITY OF CALIFORNIA.** **Added/Corp** University of California, Berkeley. Associated Students. (1993)-. Monographic series. English. an. Proce varies per volume. Random House Inc., 400 Hahn Road, Westminster MD 21157. **Tel** (800)726-0600, (800)733-3000, FAX (800)659-2436. **LC** IN PROCESS.

US/0162-5950
**ON-YOUR-OWN GUIDE TO ASIA, THE.** English. ir. $8.45 each volume. Volunteers in Asia Inc, Box 4543, Stanford CA 94309. **Tel** (415)723-3228. **ED** Terry George. **LC** DS504; .O5. **DD** 915/.04/42.
**Desc:** A travel guidebook emphasizing economical accommodations, unusual places of interest and local customs and culture.

CN/1184-969X
**ONTARIO BLUEWATER VISITOR GUIDE.** [Ont. bluewater visit. guide]. (1991)-. English. Ontario Bluewater Visitor Guide, Box 99, Wellesley Ontario N0B 2T0 Canada. **DD** 917.13/204/05. ***Continues** Ontario Bluewater Vacation Guide., 0831-0076.*

CN
**ONTARIO/CANADA CAMPING.** **Main/Corp** Ontario. Ministry of Industry and Tourism. English. Ministry of Industry and Tourism, 900 Bay Street, Queen's Park, Toronto Ontario M7A 2E4 Canada. **LC** GV191.46.O6; O57A. **DD** 917.13/04/4.

CN/0712-1636
**ONTARIO VACATION FARMS.** [Ont. vacat. farms]. **Main/Corp** Ontario Vacation Farm Association. English. an. Free. Ontario Vacation Farm Association, Rural Route #2, Alma Ontario N0B 1A0 Canada. **Tel** (519)846-9788, FAX 519-846-9378. **ED** Sharon Grose. **DD** 917.13/044. **Bk Rev. Circ:** 30,000 (ctrl).
**Desc:** An introduction to vacation farm hosting in Ontario, plus rates, locations and descriptions of more than 90 farms which welcome guests to their homes year round.

NE/0168-3845
**OP PAD (DEN HAAG).** (OP PAD.). [Op pad Den Haag]. (1983)-. Periodical. Dutch. Nine times a year. Fl64.80 (nonmember) Netherlands; Fl92.60 (nonmember) other; Fl51.30 (ANWB member). ANWB Koninklijke Nederlandse Toeristenbond, POB 93200, 2509 BA s'Gravenhage, Netherlands. **Tel** 011 31 70 3146231. **UDC** 796.54.

US/0744-8317
**OREGON COAST.** (June/July 1982)-. Periodical. English. Six times a year (Jan., Mar., May, July, Sep., Nov.). $14.95 US; $21.95 other. Oregon Coast Magazine, PO Box 18000, Florence OR 97439. **Tel** (503)997-8401, FAX (503)997-1124. **ED** Dave Peden and Judy Fleagle. **Ad Acc. Circ:** 80,000.
**Desc:** Travel, history, and recreation information on the Oregon coast; has several full-page, full-color scenic photographs in each issue.

●US/1061-4265
**ORIGINAL GREAT SMOKY MOUNTAIN SAMPLER, THE.** (1992)-. Periodical. English. bm. $1.95 (single issue). Phelps Publications, PO Box 5316, Sevierville TN 37864.

US/0734-4066
**ORIGINAL NEW ENGLAND GUIDE, THE.** **VFOAT** New England Guide. (198?)-. English. an. Jolicoeurs Business, 177 East Industrial Drive, Manchester NH 03103. **Tel** (603)668-7330 HTTI UR. **ED** Kathie Kull. **LC** F1.3; .N4. **DD** 917.4/0443. **Ad Acc. Circ:** 175,000. ***Continues** New England Guide.*
**Desc:** Offers the traveler general features and specific facts about the seacoast, the urban centers, and the rural villages of this six-state region.

CN/0849-2093
**OTTAWA-HULL, CANADA'S CAPITAL.** (OTTAWA-HULL, CANADA'S CAPITAL : VISITOR GUIDE / OTTAWA-HULL, LA CAPITALE DU CANADA : GUIDE TOURISTIQUE.). [Ott.-Hull Can. cap.]. **Added/Corp** Canada's Capital Visitors and Convention Bureau. Canada. National Capital Commission. **VFOAT** Ottawa-Hull, la Capitale du Canada. (1989/1990)-. English (French). Free. Canada's Capital Visitors and Convention Bureau, 7th Floor, 222 Queen Street, Ottawa, Ontario K1P 5V9 Canada. **DD** 917.13/83044/05. ***Continues** Ottawa and Canada's Capital Region., 0849-2085.*

●CN/1191-2650
**OTTAWA VALLEY OFFICIAL TRAVEL GUIDE.** [Ott. Val. off. travel guide]. **Added/Corp** Ottawa Valley Tourist Association. **VFOAT** Ottawa Valley Travel Guide. (1992)-. English. Ottawa Valley Tourist Association, 169 William Street, Pembroke Ontario K8A 1N7 Canada. **DD** 917.13/8104/05. ***Continues** Ottawa Valley ... Travel Guide., 1182-3089.*

US/1044-6699
**OUR WORLD (DAYTONA BEACH, FLA.).** (OUR WORLD : THE INTERNATIONAL GAY TRAVEL MAGAZINE.). [Our world]. Vol. 1, No. 1 Feb. (1989)-. Periodical. English. mo (except Feb. and Aug.). $35.00. Our World Publishing, 1104 North Nova Road, Suite 251, Daytona Beach FL 32117. **Tel** (904)441-5367, FAX (904)441-5604. **ED** Wayne Whiston. **LC** G149; .O9. **DD**

910/.8664. **Bk Rev. Ad Acc. Circ:** 50,000.
**Desc:** A travel magazine for gay men and women, featuring hotels, resorts, trips, and tours.

US/0899-1413
**OUT WEST (SACRAMENTO, CALIF.).** (OUT WEST.). [Out West]. **VFOAT** Newspaper That Roams Out West. (Winter 1987/1988)-. Periodical. English. Four times a year. $11.95. Out West Publishing, 408 Broad Street, Suite 11, Nevada City CA 95959. **Tel** (916)478-9080. **ED** Chuck Woodbury. **DD** 917. **Bk Rev. Circ:** 13,500 (ctrl).
**Desc:** Contains reports about people and places along the back roads of the West.

US/0748-0830
**OUTLOOK FOR SUMMER TRAVEL.** (OUTLOOK FOR SUMMER TRAVEL / U.S. TRAVEL DATA CENTER.). [Outlook summer travel]. **Added/Corp** United States Travel Data Center. (1982)-. English. an. $35.00. US Travel Data Center, 1100 New York Avenue, Suite 450, Washington DC 20005. **Tel** (202)408-1832. **LC** G155.U6; O93. **DD** 380.1/45917304927. **Circ:** 400.
**Desc:** Forecasts the level of vacation travel activity for the upcoming summer in various key market segments.

US/0737-8815
**OUTLOOK FOR TRAVEL AND TOURISM.** (OUTLOOK FOR TRAVEL AND TOURISM: PROCEEDINGS OF THE ... TRAVEL OUTLOOK FORUM.). [Outlook Travel Tour.]. **Main/Conf** Travel Outlook Forum. **Added/Corp** United States Travel Data Center. Travel and Tourism Research Association (U.S.) Travel Industry Association of America. **VFOAT** Outlook for Travel & Tourism. (1982)-. Proceedings. English. an (December). $130.00. US Travel Data Center, 1100 New York Avenue, Suite 450, Washington DC 20005. **Tel** (202)408-1832. **LC** G155.U6; T69a. **DD** 380.1/45917304927. **Circ:** 1,400. ***Continues*** *Proceedings - Travel Outlook Forum, 0160-4651.*
**Desc:** This report is a must for writing and updating marketing plans. Experts forecast trends for industry sectors and popular market segment such as domestic and international visitors, business and leisure travel air and auto travel and accommodations in this highly rated report. Essential to understanding the shape of travel markets in the coming year.

US/0735-231X
**OVERSEAS ASSIGNMENT DIRECTORY SERVICE.** ***Title Change.*** [Overseas assign. dir. serv.]. (1977)-(19??). English. mo. Craighead Publications Inc, PO Box 1253, Darien CT 06820. **Tel** (203)655-1007, FAX (203)655-0018. **ED** Terry S. Mollo. **Circ:** 200. ***Continued by*** *Craigheads International Executive Travel and Relocation Service.*
**Desc:** Provides a single convenient resource for information on currency rates, hotels, schools, medical facilities, housing, holidays, economic conditions and much more.

CN/1184-8944
**OVTA NEWS.** [OVTA news]. **Added/Corp** Ottawa Valley Tourist Association. **VFOAT** Ottawa Valley Tourist Association News. (Feb. 1991)-. Periodical. English. bm. Ottawa Valley Tourist Association, 169 William Street, Pembroke Ontario K8A 1N7 Canada. **DD** 381. ***Continues*** *The Travel Professional., 0827-7958.*

US/0363-4817
**PACIFIC AREA DESTINATION HANDBOOK.** **Main/Corp** Pacific Area Travel Association. (1976/77)-. English. an. $75.00. Pacific Asia Travel Association, 1 Montgomery Street, Telesis Tower/Suite 1000, San Francisco CA 94104. **Tel** (415)986-4646, FAX (415)986-3458, telex 170685. **LC** DS4; .P33a. **DD** 919/.04.

US/0742-4981
**PAGES (NORTHEAST ED.).** (PAGES : PILOTS' AIRPORT GUIDE TO ENTERTAINMENT AND SERVICES.). **VFOAT** P.A.G.E.S.; P.A.G.E.S. N.E.; Pilots' Airport Guide to Entertainment and Services; P.A.G.E.S. Northeastern States; PAGES Northeastern States; PAGES NE. English. an. $15.95. Osage Aero Company, PO Box 809, Fair Lawn NJ 07410. **ED** A Martin. **LC** TX907; .P24. **DD** 917.4/0443. **Bk Rev. Ad Acc. Circ:** 5,000 (ctrl).
**Desc:** Guide to airports in the Northeast. Describes hotels, motels and car rentals near airports that are used by private pilots.

PK
**PAKISTAN HOTEL AND TRAVEL REVIEW.** **See** Hotels/Motels.

PK
**PAKISTAN HOTELS & TOURISM.** **See** Hotels/Motels.

US
**PAN AMERICAN YEARBOOK, THE.** 1945-. English. ir. Pan American Associates, 1150 Avenue of the Americas, New York NY 10036. **LC** E11. **DD** 917.

NE/0031-0867
**PANORAMA.** (1913)-. Periodical. English. Fifty-two times a year. F387.40. Medianet BV, Postbus 6298, 2001 LN Haarlem Netherlands. **Tel** 011 31 23 173311. **LC** AP15; .P25.

SP/0214-8021
**PAPERS DE TURISME.** [Pap. tur.]. (1989)-. Periodical. Spanish. tq. **UDC** 338.48.
**Ind/Abst** Leis. Recreat. Tour. Abstr.

SI
**PAPINEAU'S GUIDE TO BALI.** **VFOAT** Guide to Bali. English (French and German). MPH Magazines, National Stadium, Zone 4 Kallang, Singapore 1439 Singapore. **LC** DS647.B2; P35. **DD** 915.98/6. ***Continues*** *Papineau's Guide to Bali, Island Paradise.*

SI/0377-2659
**PAPINEAU'S GUIDE TO JAKARTA.** (PAPINEAU'S GUIDE TO JAKARTA, INDONESIA'S CONVENTION CITY.). 1973-. English. Andre Publications, Tanglin PO Box 7, Singapore 10 Singapore. **LC** DS646.29.D5; P35. **DD** 915.98/2.

SI/0129-8682
**PAPINEAU'S GUIDE TO SINGAPORE.** **VFOAT** Guide to Singapore. 31st Ed. (1980)-. English. an. 5 Stadium Walk, Suite 5/Third Floor, Singapore 1439 Singapore. **LC** DS598.S7; G8. **DD** 915.95/7045. ***Continues*** *Papineau's Guide to Singapore and Spotlight on Malaysia.*

SI/0129-9743
**PAPINEAU'S GUIDE TO SRI LANKA.** **VFOAT** Guide to Sri Lanka. 1st Ed.-. English. $5.00 U.S. MPH Magazines, National Stadium, Zone 4 Kallang, Singapore 1439 Singapore. **LC** DS489; .P34. **DD** 915.49/3043.

SI/0129-8534
**PAPINEAU'S GUIDE TO THAILAND.** **VFOAT** Guide to Thailand. English. MPH Magazines, National Stadium, Zone 4 Kallang, Singapore 1439 Singapore. **LC** DS566.2; .P36. **DD** 915.93/0444.

FR
**PARIS / MICHELIN.** **Added/Corp** Pneu Michelin (Firm). (19??)-. French. ir. Manufacture Francaise des Pneumatiques Michelin, 46 avenue de Breteuil, 75431 Paris Cedex 07 France. **(Subscription address:** Michelin Travel Publications, PO Box 19008, Greenville SC 29602.**)**

UK/0031-224X
**PARKS & SPORTS GROUNDS.** [Parks sports grounds]. **VFOAT** Parks, Golf Courses & Sports Grounds (1935); Parks and Sports Grounds. (1935)-. Periodical. English. mo. £25.00 UK; £27.00 other. Clarke & Hunter Ltd., 61 London Road, Staines, Middlesex TW18 4BN England. **Tel** 011 44 0784 61326, 011 44 0784 61327, FAX 011 44 0784 462073. **ED** Alan Guthrie. **DD** 635.9642. **Bk Rev**, (Qty: 12). **Ad Acc, Adv Mgr:** Jennifer Archer. **Circ:** 5,800. ***Continues*** *Leisure and Amenity Management.*

NP
**PARYATANA : PARYATANA SAMBANDHI PATRIKA.** **Added/Corp** Nepal. Dept. of Tourism. **VFOAT** Paryatana Sambandhi Patrika; Nepalese Journal of Tourism; Tourism. (Jan. 1991)-. Nepali (English). sa.

CN/0228-2631
**PASSEPORT.** [Passeport]. V. 1- March 1980-. Periodical. French. $6.00. Gourmet Passport, 2401 De La Province, Longueuil Quebec J4G 1G3. **DD** 910/.2/02.

US/0031-272X
**PASSPORT (CHICAGO).** (PASSPORT.). [Passport]. (1966)-. Periodical. English. mo. $65.00 (1 year), $115.00 (2 year), $160.00 (3 year) US, Canada, and Mexico; $85.00 (1 year), $155.00 (2 year), $220.00 (3 year) other. Remy Publishing Company, 350 Hubbard Street, Suite 440, Chicago IL 60610. **Tel** (312)464-0300, FAX (312)464-0166. **DD** 910.

US
**PATA ANNUAL STATISTICAL REPORT.** **Main/Corp** Pacific Area Travel Association. (1974)-. Statistical Publication. English. an. $500.00 nonmembers, $250.00 members. Pacific Asia Travel Association, 1 Montgomery Street, Telesis Tower/Suite 1000, San Francisco CA 94104. **Tel** (415)986-4646, FAX (415)986-3458, telex 170685. **ED** Jordan Yee. available on diskette. ***Continues*** *PATA Statistical Report.*
**Desc:** Contains information on travel in the pacific asia area.

US/1056-0025
**PAUL EDWARDS' TRAVEL CONFIDENTIAL.** [Paul Edwards' travel confid.]. **VFOAT** Travel Confidential. (1991)-. Periodical. English. mo. $195.00. Lowell Communications, 88 Bleecker Street, New York NY 10012. **DD** 910. ***Continues*** *Travel Smarter, 1055-0488.*

CN/1186-6101
**PEACE RIVER, ALASKA HIGHWAY TOUR AND VACATION GUIDE.** ***Title Change.*** [Peace River Alsk. Highw. tour vacat. guide]. **Added/Corp** Peace River, Alaska Highway Tourist Association. (1991)-(1992). English. Peace River, Alaska Highway Tourist Association, Fort St. John, British Columbia V1J 4J3 Canada. **DD** 917.11/8704/05. ***Continues*** *Super, Natural Peace River, Alaska Highway Tour and Vacation Guide., 1186-6098.* ***Continued by*** *Northeastern British Columbia Tour & Vacation Guide, 1197-5059.*

US/0740-5529
**PELICAN GUIDE TO THE BAHAMAS.** (PELICAN GUIDE TO THE BAHAMAS / JAMES E. MOORE.). [Pelican guide Bahamas]. (1984)-. English. ir. Pelican Publishing Company, PO Box 3110, Gretna LA 70054. **Tel** (504)368-1175, (800)843-1724, FAX (504)368-1195. **LC** F1652; .P44. **DD** 917.296/0452.
**Desc:** An in-depth look at the 700 islands that comprise the Bahamas. First-hand information, from low-cost to luxury.

AT
**PENGUIN ACCOMMODATION GUIDE.** (19??)-. English. an. 29.95Aus$ Australia; 38.45Aus$ New Zealand & Papua New Guinea; 42.75Aus$ Fiji, Indonesia, Malaysia; 46.45Aus$ India & Japan; 53.35Aus$ US & Israel. Peter Isaacson Publications, 46-50 Porter Street, Prahran Victoria, 3181 Australia. **Tel** 011 61 3 2457777, FAX 011 61 3 2457605.

US/1043-4607
**PENGUIN GUIDE TO GREECE, THE.** [Penguin guide Greece]. (1990)-. English. an. $13.95. Viking Penguin Inc, 40 West 23rd Street, New York NY 10010. **LC** DF716; .P46. **DD** 914.9504/76.

US/0898-8072
**PENGUIN GUIDE TO NEW YORK CITY, THE.** ***Title Change.*** [Penguin guide N. Y. City]. **VFOAT** New York City. (1989)-(19??). English. an. Viking Penguin Inc, 40 West 23rd Street, New York NY 10010. **LC** F128.18; .P36. **DD** 917.47/10443/05. ***Continued by*** *Berlitz Travellers Guide to New York City, 1057-4743.*

US/1043-4585
**PENGUIN GUIDE TO PORTUGAL, THE.** ***Title Change.*** [Penguin guide Port.]. **VFOAT** Guide to Portugal; Penguin Portugal. (1990)-. English. an. Viking Penguin Inc, 40 West 23rd Street, New York NY 10010. **LC** DP516; .P4. **DD** 914.6904/44. ***Continued by*** *Berlitz Travellers Guide to Portugal, 1057-4646.*

US/1043-4593
**PENGUIN GUIDE TO SPAIN, THE.** [Penguin guide Spain]. **VFOAT** Guide to Spain; Penguin Spain. (1990)-. English. an. $13.95. Viking Penguin Inc, 40 West 23rd Street, New York NY 10010. **LC** DP14; .P43. **DD** 914.604/83.

●US/1049-1465
**PENGUIN GUIDE TO TURKEY.** (THE BERLITZ TRAVELLER'S GUIDE TO TURKEY.). (1992)-. English. $14.95. Berlitz Publishing Co., 257 Park Avenue South, New York NY 10010. **Tel** (212)598-2490, FAX (212)353-9706.

US/0744-4230
**PENNSYLVANIA MAGAZINE (CAMP HILL, PA.).** (PENNSYLVANIA MAGAZINE.). [Pa. mag.]. Vol. 1, No. 1 (Fall 1981)-. Periodical. English. bm. $18.97 (US); $33.92 (other). Pennsylvania Magazine, PO Box 576, Camp Hill PA 17011. **Tel** (717)761-6620. **ED** Albert E. Holliday. **LC** F146; .P64. **DD** 974.8/005. Index available ($5.00). cum. index. **Bk Rev**, (Qty: 30). **Ad Acc, Adv Mgr:** Susan Getter. **Circ:** 50,000.
**Desc:** A statewide feature magazine focusing on history, travel, people, events, organizations and lifestyles.

CN/0048-3451
**PERSONNEL GUIDE TO CANADA'S TRAVEL INDUSTRY.** [Pers. guide Can. travel ind.]. (19??)-. Periodical. English. Twice a year (Spring & Fall). 45.00Can$ US; 50.00Can$ others. Baxter Publishing Company, 310 Dupont Street, Toronto Ontario M5R 1V9 Canada. **Tel** (416)968-7252, FAX (416)968-2377. **DD** 338.47917104. **Ad Acc, Adv Mgr:** Celyne Benitah & Robin Catto.
**Desc:** Provides complete listings of all travel agencies, tour operators, wholesalers, airlines, car rentals, hotel representatives, tourist boards, travel insurance firms and cruise lines operating in Canada, as well as tour destinations together with the companies who serve them.

CN/1188-1771
**PHYSICIAN'S GUIDE FOR TRAVEL & MEDICAL CONVENTION PLANNING.** **See** Medical Science and Technology-Hospital Administration and Medical Centers.

US/0745-4554
**PHYSICIANS' TRAVEL & MEETING GUIDE.** [Phys. travel meet. guide]. **VFOAT** Physicians' Travel and Meeting Guide. Vol. 1, No. 1 (Winter/Spring

# Travel and Tourism

1983)-. Periodical. English. mo. $95.00 (institutions), $60.00 (physicians). Excerpta Medica / US, PO Box 3085, Princeton NJ 08543-3085. **Tel** (908)874-8550, FAX (908)874-5611. **(Subscription address:** Physicians' Travel & Meeting Guide, PO Box 3095, Denville NJ 07834.) **DD** 910. available on microfilm from University Microfilms International (UMI).
**Desc:** A broad interest travel magazine that places special emphasis on the needs of physicians and their families. An international calendar of medical conferences, seminars and meetings is included in each issue.

**IT**
**PIEMONTE TUTTOVACANZA.** Italian. bm. Editurist Srl, Strada Santanna 9, 10131 Turin Italy. **Tel** 011 39 11 8191360.

**US**
**PINKERTON EYE ON TRAVEL.** English. mo. $199.00 (monthly edition), $99.00 (quarterly edition), $30.00 (personalized trip package). Pinkerton Risk Assessment Services, 1600 Wilson Boulevard, Suite 901, Arlington VA 22209-2507. **Tel** (703)525-6111, FAX (703)525-2454. **Continues** International Travel Briefings.

●**US**
**PINKERTON WORLD STATUS MAP.** **Added/Corp** Pinkerton Risk Assessment Services. **VFOAT** World Status Map; Official Advisories for International Travelers. Vol. 10, No. 2 (Mar.-Apr. 1992)-. Periodical. English. bm. Pinkerton Risk Assessment Services, 1600 Wilson Boulevard, Suite 901, Arlington VA 22209-2507. **Tel** (703)525-6111, FAX (703)525-2454. **LC** G153.4; .W67. **Continues** World Status Map, 0887-9559.

US/0194-8431
**PITTSBURGH.** **Added/Corp** Metropolitan Pittsburgh Public Broadcasting, Inc. QED Communications, Inc. **VFOAT** Pittsburgh Magazine. Vol. 6, No. 7 (July/Aug. 1975)-. Periodical. English. mo. $15.00 (1 year), $26.00 (2 year), $36.00 (3 year). Metropolitan Pittsburgh Public Broadcasting Inc, 4802 Fifth Avenue, Pittsburgh PA 15213. **Tel** (412)622-1360. **ED** Bruce VanWyngarden, Jeanne Marie Laskas, Mark Shelton, and John Altdorfer. **LC** F159.P6; P59. **DD** 974.8/86. **CODEN** PIMAEF. **Ad Acc. Circ:** 60,000. **Continues** Pittsburgh Renaissance.
**Desc:** Evaluates, analyzes, criticizes and takes readers behind the scenes to understand the people, places, and the flavor of Pittsburgh.
**Ind/Abst** Access (1986-).

US/0094-3452
**PLACE (INDIANA).** (PLACES.). V. 1- Mar. 1974-. Periodical. English. qt. $7.00. Edited Places, 432 Locust Street, Indiana IN 15701. **LC** G149; .P55. **DD** 910.
**Ind/Abst** Archit. Period. Index; J. Plan. Lit.

US/0191-7366
**PLEASURE BOATING.** **Title Change.** See Boats and Boating.

US/0883-2382
**PLEASURE HUNT MAGAZINE.** **Title Change.** **VFOAT** Pleasure Hunt. (198?)-(19??). Periodical. English. bm. Delaware Valley Magazine, 2260 Cabot Boulevard West, Langhorne PA 19047. **DD** 917. **Continued by** Delaware Valley, 1052-4592.

**US**
**PLEASURE TRAVEL MARKETS: THE HIGHLIGHTS REPORTS.** English. $25.00. US Travel Data Center, 1100 New York Avenue, Suite 450, Washington DC 20005. **Tel** (202)408-1832.
**Desc:** These reports offer quick summaries of the annual findings from the Pleasure Travel Market reports.

**IT**
**POLITICA DEL TURISMO.** Maggioli Editore, Casella Postale 290, 47037 Rimini, Italy. **Tel** 011 39 541 628666, FAX 011 39 541 742217.

●US/1070-9479
**PORTHOLE (DEERFIELD BEACH, FLA.).** (PORTHOLE : THE INTELLIGENT CRUISE MAGAZINE.). [Porthole]. **Added/Corp** International Cruise Passengers Association. (1993)-. Periodical. English. Six times a year. $35.00 US and Canada; $45.00 other. Porthole Magazine, 10 Fairway Drive, Suite 200, Deerfield Beach FL 33441. **Tel** (305)374-2224. **ED** Douglas Ward (Editor's Phone: (305)426-0046). **DD** 910. **Ad Acc, Adv Mgr:** Bill Panoff, **Tel** (305)426-0046. **Circ:** 5,000. **Continues** Cruise Digest Reports.
**Desc:** Provides in-depth cruise ship feature reports, product evaluations, general cruise industry news, destinations and special features.

US/0893-4746
**PREFERRED TRAVELLER.** [Prefer. travel.]. **VFOAT** Encore Preferred Traveller. Vol. 10, No. 1 (Spring 1987)-. Periodical. English. bm. **LC** G149; .P74. **DD** 910/.5. **Continues** Touring & Travel (U.S. Edition), 0747-2730.

FR/0247-2406
**PREVENIR MARSEILLE.** (PREVENIR.). (1980)-. Periodical. French. Twice a year. 200.00F (one year), 390.00F (two years). Prevenir /CVM, 3-5 Rue de Vincennes, 93100 Montreuil France. **Tel** 33 1 49885330, FAX 33 1 48707676. **UDC** 360.

US/0887-4131
**PRIVILEGED TRAVELER, THE.** **Ceased.** [Privil. travel.]. (1986)-Vol. 2, No. 1 (Aug. 1987). Periodical. English. bm. The Privileged Traveler Inc, 42 Usonia Road, Pleasantville NY 10570. **Tel** (914)769-3833. **ED** Ann McGovern. **DD** 910. Index available. **Bk Rev. Circ:** 12,000.
**Desc:** Contains unique information for the upscale, discerning traveler.

PL/0138-0478
**PROBLEMY TURYSTYKI.** [Probl. Tur.]. **VFOAT** Problems of Tourism. (1978)-. Periodical. Polish. qt. **UDC** 796.5.
**Ind/Abst** For. Abstr.; Leis. Recreat. Tour. Abstr.

**GW**
**PROFITRAVEL.** See Business.

**US**
**PROGRAM REPORT OF THE UNITED STATES TRAVEL AND TOURISM ADMINISTRATION.** **Main/Corp** United States Travel and Tourism Administration. 1st (1982)-. English. an. US Travel and Tourism Administration, Department of Commerce, Washington DC 20230. **LC** G155.U6; U57I. **DD** 382/.45917304. **Continues** Program Report of the United States Travel Service, 0502-5397.

UK/0952-5424
**PROGRESS IN TOURISM, RECREATION, AND HOSPITALITY MANAGEMENT.** Vol. 1 (1989)-. English. sa. $95.00. John Wiley & Sons Ltd., Baffins Lane, Chichester West Sussex PO19 1UD England. **Tel** 0243 779777, FAX 0243 776128 BTG:JWP001, telex 86290 WIBOOKG. **(Subscription address:** John Wiley / Philadelphia, PO Box 7247, Philadelphia PA 19170.) **LC** G155.A1; P76. **DD** 338.4/791.
**Desc:** Review of leading-edge research in tourism, recreation, and hospitality management.

**FR**
**PROMET TURISTA U PRIMORSKIM OPCINAMA / SOCIJALISTICKA REPUBLIKA HRVATSKA, REPUBLICKI ZAVOD ZA STATISTIKU.** Began with Vol. for 1975. Serbo-Croatian (Roman). 200.00. Republicki Zavod za Statistiku, Central Bureau of Statistics of the Republic of Croatia, Ilica 3, Zagreb Croatia. **Tel** 011 385 41 45 44 22, FAX 011 385 41 42 94 13, 011 385 41 42 37 11, telex 21130 DZSTAT RH. **Continues** Republicki Zavod Za Statistiku. Promet Turista u Primorskim Mjestima.

**GW**
**PROMOBIL.** See Transportation-Automobiles.

**GW**
**PROMOBIL SPEZIAL.** (19??)-. German. an. Vereinigte Motor Verlag GmbH, Motor Presse, POB 106036, D 70049 Stuttgart Germany. **Tel** 011 49 711 1821506, 011 49 711 1821545. **Ad Acc.**

**FR**
**PROVENCE.** **Main/Corp** Pneu Michelin (Firm). (1978)-. English (French). Michelin Travel Publications, Box 3305, Spartanburg SC 29304. **Tel** (800)423-0485, (803)599-0850, FAX (803)599-0852. **DD** DC611.P958; M26a. **DD** 914.4/904837. **Supersedes** Provence, Avec Carte Touristique.

**FR**
**PROVENCE-COTE D'AZUR (HACHETTE (FIRM)).** See Geography.

**UK**
**PROVENCE / MICHELIN.** **Added/Corp** Michelin Tyre Public Limited Company. Michelin Tyre Company, Ltd. (1980)-. English. ir. Manufacture Francaise des Pneumatiques Michelin, 46 avenue de Breteuil, 75431 Paris Cedex 07 France. **(Subscription address:** Michelin Travel Publications, PO Box 19008, Greenville SC 29602.) **LC** DC611.P958; P73. **DD** 914.4/904838.
**Desc:** Tourist guide to Provence region of France. Sightseeing tours, history of region, description of sights.

US/1053-3842
**PUNCH IN INTERNATIONAL TRAVEL & ENTERTAINMENT MAGAZINE.** (PUNCH IN INTERNATIONAL TRAVEL & ENTERTAINMENT MAGAZINE [COMPUTER FILE].). [Punch int. trav. entertain. mag.]. **VFOAT** Punch In. Vol. 1, issue 1- (1990)-. Periodical. English. mo. $35.00. J P Walman, Box 31, F.D.R. Station, New York NY 10150.

**RU**
**PUTESHESTVIE V SSSR.** Russian. bm. $38.00 airmail. **(Subscription address:** Victor Kamkin, 4956 Boiling Brook Parkway, Rockville MD 20852.)

**IT**
**Q T DIRECTORY.** (19??)-. Directory. Italian (English and German). an. $50.00 Italy; $100.00 other. AP1 SRL, Via Pezzotti 4, 20141 Milan Italy. **Tel** 39-2-8321087, FAX 39-2-8323710, telex 8375628. **ED** Cladia Levizzani. **Circ:** 10,000.
**Desc:** Directory of convention centers, hotels with function rooms covering Italy, Europe, and overseas.

**IT**
**QUALITY TRAVEL.** (19??)-. Italian. Ten times a year. L100000.00 Italy; L150000.00 other. Promos Srl, C So Porta Romana 122, 20122 Milan Italy. **Tel** 011 39 2 58314981.

**RH**
**QUARTERLY INTERNATIONAL MIGRATION AND TOURIST STATISTICS / ZIMBABWE.** **Title Change.** See Travel and Tourism-Abstracting, Bibliographies and Statistics.

**TR**
**QUARTERLY TRAVEL REPORT / REPUBLIC OF TRINIDAD AND TOBAGO, CENTRAL STATISTICAL OFFICE.** See Travel and Tourism-Abstracting, Bibliographies and Statistics.

**US**
**QUE PASA SAN ANTONIO.** $12.00 North America; $20.00 Mexico. Posada Publishing Co, POB 1684, Austin TX 78767. **Tel** (512)443-8936, FAX (512)733-9974. **ED** June Hayes. Index available. **Bk Rev. Ad Acc. Circ:** 30,000 (ctrl).
**Desc:** Bilingual city guide for tourists and locals. Includes shopping, food and attractions.

CN/0225-0454
**QUEBEC VOYAGES.** [Que. voyages]. **VFOAT** Marketing Voyages. No. 1- Summer 1979-. Periodical. English (French and German). sa. $1.50 each number. Systemes Marketing Voyages Ltee, Suite 502, 1121 St. Catherine Street West, Montreal Quebec H3B 1J5. **DD** 338.4/79171404.

**AT**
**QUEENSLAND ACCOMMODATION AND CARAVANNING DIRECTORY.** **Main/Corp** Royal Automobile Club of Queensland. (19??)-. Directory. English. Twice a year. $8.00. Royal Automobile Club of Queensland, 2649 Logan road, Eight Mile Plains, Queensland 4113 Australia. **Tel** 361-2435, FAX 849-0610. **LC** GV198.67.A8; R69a. **DD** 649/.94943. **Ad Acc, Adv Mgr:** Kayleen Dunsford. **Circ:** 125,000 (ctrl).
**Desc:** Details of hotels, motels, private hotels, guest houses, serviced apartments, holiday units, flats, resorts, cottages, holiday farms and caravan parks throughout Queensland.

IT/0042-546X
**QUI TOURING.** [Qui touring]. (1971)-. Periodical. Italian. bw. Free to members; L84500 membership Italy; L105000 membership other. Touring Club Italiano, Corso Italia 10, Milan 20122 Italy. **Tel** 011 39 2 85261, FAX 011 39 2 8526299. **UDC** 910.

●US/1064-0339
**QUICK TRIPS TRAVEL LETTER.** [Quick trips travel lett.]. (1992)-. Periodical. English. Twelve times a year. $45.00. Quicktrips Travel Letter, PO Box 3308, Crofton MD 21114. **Tel** (301)262-0177. **ED** Judy Colbert. **DD** 910. cum. index. **Bk Rev, (Qty: 36+). Circ:** 2,000 (ctrl).
**Desc:** Features information for 3, 4, and 5 day getaways. Also includes special packages and travel tips.

**AT**
**R A C V S OUT AND ABOUT.** **Title Change.** (19??)-(19??). English. m. R A C V, 550 Princess Highway, Noble Park, Victoria 3174 Australia. **Tel** (03)7902646, FAX (03)7902844, telex AA154309. **Ad Acc. Circ:** 100,000 (ctrl). **Continued by** R A C V's Attractions Australia.
**Desc:** Contains a list of tourist attractions for Victoria, South Australia; Tasmania, Western Australia; ACT.

**AT**
**R A C V'S ATTRACTIONS AUSTRALIA.** (19??)-. English. be. 5.00Aus$. R A C V, 550 Princess Highway, Noble Park, Victoria 3174 Australia. **Tel** (03)7902646, FAX (03)7902844, telex AA154309. **ED** Alan Bowes. Index available. **Ad Acc. Circ:** 100,000 (ctrl). **Continues** R A C V S Out and About.

**UK**
**RAC CAMPING & CARAVANNING GUIDE - EUROPE.** English. RAC Motoring Services Ltd, RAC House, PO Box 100, South Croydon Surrey CR2 6XW England. **ED** Mrs Jo Perry. **Ad Acc.**

US/0164-8780
**RANCH & COAST.** **Ceased.** **VFOAT** Ranch & Coast Magazine. **VAT** Ranch and Coast. (19??)-(1992). Periodical. English. mo. LA West Media Mag. Inc., 462 Stevens Avenue Suite 204, Solana CA 92075. **Tel** (619)481-7659. **(Subscription address:** Kable Publ.,308 E. Hitt St., Subs. Dept., Mt. Morris IL 61054) **ED** Mary Shepardson. **Circ:** 20,000.

# Travel and Tourism

**US**
### RAND MCNALLY BUSINESS TRAVELER'S ROAD ATLAS. (19??)-.
English. an. $9.95. Rand McNally & Company, PO Box 32, Skokie IL 60076. **Tel** (708)673-0813, (800)444-4062.
**Desc:** Provides information on convention centers, cellular phone roaming numbers, and tax information. Also includes lodging, airport and city maps, and travel information for over 75 cities in the US and Canada.

US/1075-1688
### RAND MCNALLY ROAD ATLAS & TRIP PLANNER. (RAND MCNALLY ROAD ATLAS & TRIP PLANNER : UNITED STATES, CANADA, MEXICO.).
[Rand McNally road atlas trip plan.]. **Main/Corp** Rand McNally and Company. **VFOAT** Road Atlas & Trip Planner; Road Atlas and Trip Planner; Rand McNally Road Atlas and Trip Planner. (1991)-. English. an. $4.95. Rand McNally & Company, PO Box 32, Skokie IL 60076. **Tel** (708)673-0813, (800)444-4062. **DD** 912. *Continues Rand McNally Interstate Road Atlas.*
**Desc:** Full-color road maps focusing on the interstate and US highway systems; also travel planning charts.

**US**
### RAND MCNALLY ROAD ATLAS & VACATION GUIDE. (19??)-. English. an. $18.95.
Rand McNally & Company, PO Box 32, Skokie IL 60076. **Tel** (708)673-0813, (800)444-4062. Index available.
**Desc:** Includes extensive vacation planning information in a regional and state-by-state format along with maps and mileage charts.

**US**
### RAND MCNALLY ROAD ATLAS OF EUROPE. (19??)-. English. an. $11.95.
Rand McNally & Company, PO Box 32, Skokie IL 60076. **Tel** (708)673-0813, (800)444-4062.
**Desc:** Updated road maps for all 42 European countries, including the Czech and Slovak Republics; also maps of major cities, international road signs, and travel-planning information and tips.

IT/0392-7164
### RASSEGNA DI STUDI TURISTICI.
**Suspended.** [Rass. studi tur.]. (1966)-(Dec. 1993). Periodical. Italian. qt. Casa Editrice Agnesotti, Via Luigi Rizzo 18, 00136 Rome Italy. **Tel** 011 39 6 39732058. **UDC** 380.81.
**Ind/Abst** Leis. Recreat. Tour. Abstr.

US/0034-1452
### RECOMMEND FLORIDA. VFOAT Recommend.
Periodical. English. mo. Recommend Travel Publications, 19501 NE 10th Avenue/Suite 200, North Miami Beach FL 33179. **Tel** (305)653-0123. **ED** Laurel Herman. Index available. **Ad Acc.** **Circ:** 48,000 (ctrl).
**Desc:** Destination information for the travel agent industry.

●SP
### RECOMMENDATIONS ON TOURISM STATISTICS. See Travel and Tourism-Abstracting, Bibliographies and Statistics.

NE/0165-4179
### RECREATIE EN TOERISME. (1983)-.
Periodical. Dutch. Eleven times a year. Price varies. Arko Uitgeverij, Postbus 616, 3430 AP Nieuwegein Netherlands. **Tel** 011 31 3402 51090. **UDC** 379.4. *Continues Recreatie, 0486-1825.*
**Ind/Abst** Leis. Recreat. Tour. Abstr.

US/1040-0265
### REFLEXIONES (SANTA FE, N.M.).
(REFLEXIONES.). [Reflexiones]. (1987)-. Periodical. English. mo. $12.00. Reflexiones, PO Box 1961, Santa Fe NM 87504. **Tel** (505)984-2057. **ED** Gayle Spencer and David J. Donaldson. **DD** 305. **Ad Acc.**
**Desc:** Current happenings in San Antonio of interest to the tourist population.

CN/0704-6685
### REGINA MAGAZINE. 1- 1977-. English. an.
Regina Chamber of Commerce, 2145 Albert Street, Regina Saskatchewan S4P 2V1 Canada. **Tel** (306)757-4658. **DD** 917.124/4. *Supersedes Regina, 0315-212X.*

AT
### REGIONAL TOURISM MONITOR.
**Added/Corp** Western Australian Tourism Commission. **VFOAT** Western Australian Regional Tourism Research Monitor. (1985)-. Government Publication. English. an. 20.00Aus$ each, 65.00Aus$ full set. Western Australian Tourism Commission, 16 St George's Terrace, GPO Box X2261, Perth Western Australia 6001 Australia. **Tel** 011 09 220 1700, FAX 011 09 220 1702. **ED** Mark Sparrow and Elizabeth Smith. **LC** G155.A75; R44. **DD** 380.1/45919419463. **Pr Rev. Circ:** 200 (ctrl).
**Desc:** A Western Australia based survey which provides information on visitor numbers, characteristics, activities and expenditure.

BL
### RELATORIO - EMPRESA DE TURISMO DA BAHIA. Main/Corp Empresa de Turismo da Bahia.
Portuguese. Empresa de Turismo du Bahia, rua Marechal Floriano 1-Canela, Salvador Brazil. **LC** G155.B7; E48A.

US/1058-4811
### RELAX (BANNOCKBURN, ILL.). (RELAX.).
[Relax]. Vol. 1, No. 1 (Mar. 1985)-. Periodical. English. mo. $65.00 US and possessions; $80.00 Canada; $120.00 other. Advanstar Communications Inc., 131 West First Street, Duluth MN 55802. **Tel** (218)723-9477, (800)346-0085. **ED** David Walker. **DD** 910. **Circ:** 112,727.
**Desc:** Focuses on travel and leisure ideas for the practicing physician. Feature stories focus on domestic and foreign locations, with stories relating to the sites of major medical meetings.

CN/1183-7489
### REPERTOIRE TOURISTIQUE (MONTREAL). Title Change. (REPERTOIRE TURISTIQUE.). [Repert. tour.]. (1991)-(1993). French. ir.
Les Editions Hemisphere, CP 645 Tour de la Bourse, Montreal Quebec H4U 1J9 Canada. **DD** 338.4/791714/0025. *Continued by Le Sextant, Repertoire, 1200-2240.*

AT
### REPORT FOR THE YEAR ... / DEPARTMENT OF TOURISM. Main/Corp Tasmania. Dept. of Tourism. English. an. T J Hughes, Government Printer, Hobart Tasmania Australia. LC G155.A75; T37B. DD 380.1/4591946046. *Continues Tasmania. Tourism Development Authority. Report for Year ... .*

SZ/0251-3102
### REVUE DE TOURISME. (REVUE DE TOURISME. ZEITSCHRIFT FUER FREMDENVERKEHR.). [Rev. tour.]. Added/Corp
Association Internationale d'Experts Scientifiques du Tourisme. **VFOAT** Tourist Review; Zeitschrift fur Fremdenverkehr. (Jan. 1946)-. Periodical. French (English, French and German). qt (March, June, Sept., Dec.). 57.00F Switzerland; 64.00F other. AIEST, Varnebueelstrasse 19, CH 9000 St. Gallen Switzerland. **Tel** 011 41 71 302547, FAX 011 41 71 302536. Index available. **Bk Rev. Ad Acc. Adv Mgr:** Evelyn Moeckli. ctrl circ.
**Ind/Abst** Leis. Recreat. Tour. Abstr.

FR
### REVUE GENERALE DE HOTELLERIE.
French. mo. $10.00 France; $14.00 other. Presse Perodique Professionnel, 14 BD Montmartre, 75 Paris France.

CN/0824-1309
### REVUE VOYAGEUR, LA. Ceased. [Rev. Voyageur]. VFOAT Voyageur Magazine. Vol. 1, No. 1 (July/August 1984)-(199?). Periodical. French (English). qt. La Revue Voyageur Magazine, c/o Publications de Vacances Quebec, 575 Arago Street West, Quebec Quebec G1N 2M4 Canada. **Tel** (418)687-3443. **ED** Curtis J Sommerville. **DD** 910/.5. **Ad Acc. Circ:** 100,000 (ctrl).
**Desc:** An on-board bus publication distributed through the Voyageur and Voyageur Colonial bus system in the Province of Quebec and the Province of Ontario.

US/1041-1380
### RHODE ISLAND MONTHLY. [R. I. mon.]. Vol. 1, No. 1 (May 1988)-. Periodical. English. Twelve times a year. $14.95. Rhode Island Monthly, 18 Imperial Place, Providence RI 02903. **Tel** (401)421-2552, (800)274-4549, FAX (401)831-5624. **ED** Viki Saunders (phone: (401)421-2552). **DD** 917. **Ad Acc, Adv Mgr:** K. Schultz, **Tel** (401)421-2552. **Circ:** 35,000.
**Desc:** Lifestyle magazine for the people of Rhode Island and the surrounding areas.

US/0198-0386
### ROAD & TRACK ROAD ATLAS & TRAVEL GUIDE. [Road track road atlas travel guide]. **VFOAT** Road & Track's Road Atlas & Travel Guide; Road Atlas & Travel Guide. **VAT** Road and Track Road Atlas and Travel Guide. Periodical. English. qt. Diamandis Communications Inc, 1499 Monrovia Avenue, New Port Beach CA 92663. **Tel** (714)720-5300. **LC** G1201.P2; R57. **DD** 912/.73.

US/0731-1737
### ROCKY MOUNTAIN MAGAZINE ... MEETING AND CONVENTION GUIDE TO THE ROCKY MOUNTAIN REGION. VFOAT Meeting and Convention Guide to the Rocky Mountain Region; Meeting and Convention Guide; Rocky Mountain Magazine's Meeting and Convention Guide. Vol. 1 (1982)-. English. an. Rocky Mountain Country Ltd Partnership, 1741 High Street, Denver CO 80218.

XV/0557-2282
### RODNA GRUDA SLOVENIJA. See Ethnic Interests.

CN/0703-8674
### ROLLIN' HOMES. V. 1- Apr. 1976-. Periodical. English. qt. 0.50Can$ per no. Rollin' Homes Publications, R.R. #4, Brampton Ontario L6T 3S1 Canada. **DD** 796.7/9/05.

FR
### ROME. Main/Corp Pneu Michelin (Firm). 1.- Ed. English (French). $9.95. Michelin Guides and Maps, PO Box 3305, Spartanburg SC 29304. **Tel** (803)599-0850. **LC** DG804; .M33A. **DD** 914.5/632/0492.

UK
### ROME (PARIS, FRANCE). (ROME / MICHELIN.). **Added/Corp** Michelin Tyre Public Limited Company. (1985)-. English. ir. Manufacture Francaise des Pneumatiques Michelin, 46 avenue de Breteuil, 75431 Paris Cedex 07 France. (**Subscription address:** Michelin Travel Publications, PO Box 19008, Greenville SC 29602.) **LC** DG804; .R68293. **DD** 914.5/63204927.

US
### RUNZHEIMER MEAL LODGING COST INDEX. See Consumer Interests.

US/0730-8663
### RUNZHEIMER REPORTS ON TRAVEL MANAGEMENT. (198?)-. Periodical. English. Twelve times a year. $295.00. Runzheimer International / Wisconsin, Runzheimer Park, Rochester WI 53167. **Tel** (414)767-2200, FAX (414)767-2254, (800)558-1702. **ED** Jean T. Dalber. **LC** Discard. [CCC]. Index available. cum. index. *Absorbed Travel Business Manager, 0886-6147 and Travel Smart for Business, 0741-5818.*
**Desc:** Covers all aspects of corporate travel management.

AT/1321-2923
### RUSSIA, SIBERIA, MONGOLIA, AND NORTH KOREA TRAVEL NEWS. English. qt. $15.00. Red Bear Tours, 320B Glenferrie Road, Malvern, Victoria, 3144 Australia. **Tel** 011 61 3 824-7183, 008 337-031 (toll free), FAX 011 61 3 823 3956. **ED** Athol Yates. **Circ:** 1,800. *Continues Russian Travel News, 1320-1670.*
**Desc:** Travel news, tips and options for independent travellers, students and special interest groups to Russia, Mongolia, and North Korea.

SP
### RUTAS GUIA TURISTICA DE BARCELONA. VFOAT Rutas de Barcelona.
Multiple languages (English, French, German and Spanish). Ger/Publi, Sants 340-344 Entlo 3, Barcelona Spain. **LC** DP302.B36; R87.

US
### RV: THE FAMILY CAMPING VEHICLES YEAR END REPORT. English. $16.00.
Recreation Vehicle Industry Association, PO Box 2999, 1896 Preston WH Dr., Reston VA 22090-0999. **Tel** (703)620-6003.

CN/0827-2956
### SASKATOON THE BEAUTIFUL. [Saskat. beautiful]. Began publication in 1967. English. an. Free. Dominion Heritage Publishing, 508-606 Victoria Avenue, Saskatoon Sask S7N 0Z1. **DD** 917.124/2.

US
### SAVVY BUSINESS TRAVELER. See Business.

US/1057-3275
### SAVVY SHOPPER, THE. (1990)-. English. mo. $57.00 (1 year), $99.00 (2 year), $119.00 (3 year). Hammar Publications, 12 Rambling Road, Northport NY 11768. **Tel** (516)757-7290. **ED** Diane Marshall. Index available. cum. index. **Bk Rev. Ad Acc. Circ:** 1,400 (ctrl). available on diskette.
**Desc:** Advises readers of what to buy and where to shop when they travel, with focus on products that are particular to a destination and the best buys.

US
### SCANDINAVIA ON $ ... A DAY: DENMARK, SWEDEN, FINLAND, NORWAY AND ICELAND. Title Change.
(19??)-(19??). English. Arthur Frommer / Pasmantier Publishers, 1230 Avenue of the Americas, New York NY 10020. **Tel** (212)373-8500. **ED** 1979/80- S.M. Haggart and D. Porter. *Continued by Frommer's Scandinavia On $ ... A Day, 0278-1069.*

SZ/0036-7230
### SCHWEIZ; LA SUISSE; LA SVIZZERA; SWITZERLAND, DIE. Added/Corp Switzerland.
Schweizerische Bundesbahnen. Generaldirektion. Schweizerische Zentrale fuer Verkehrsforderung, Zurich. **VFOAT** Suisse; Svizzera; Switzerland. (July 15, 1927)-. Periodical. German. mo. Swiss National Tourist Office, 608 Fifth Avenue, New York NY 10029. **LC** DQ1; .S26.
**Ind/Abst** Archit. Period. Index (1978-1980).

US/0746-3944
**SEE THE TREASURE COAST.** Periodical. English. mo. Brownell Associates, 3675 Clark Road, Sarasota FL 33583. ***Continues*** *See Vero Beach, Ft. Pierce, Stuart Resort Area, 0273-5644.*

●US/1070-5856
**SF UNIQUE VACATION SELECTIONS.** [SF unique vacat. sel.]. **VFOAT** Unique Vacation Selections. Vol. 1, No. 1 (Summer 1993)-. Periodical. English. qt. Market Communications, 1945 Privet Drive, Burlingame CA 94010. **DD** 910. ***Continues*** *SF (Los Angeles, Calif.), 1044-1360.*

●AT
**SIBERIAN BAM RAILWAY GUIDE : A HANDBOOK TO THE SECOND TRANS-SIBERIAN RAILWAY FOR RAIL ENTHUSIASTS AND TRAVELLERS, THE.** (June 1994)-. English. ir (Published every 18 months). 28.00Aus$. Red Bear Tours, 320B Glenferrie Road, Malvern, Victoria, 3144 Australia. **Tel** 011 61 3 824-7183, 008 337-031 (toll free), FAX 011 61 3 822 3956. **ED** Athol Yates, Tatyana Pozar-Burgar & Rashit Yahin.

US/0741-7624
**SIDE STREETS OF THE WORLD.** ***Ceased.*** **VFOAT** Side Streets. Jan. 1984-Ceased Dec. 1989. Periodical. English. mo. T McBrian Communications Inc, 155 Spring Street/4th Floor, New York NY 10012-3812. **Tel** (212)431-1652. **ED** Sheila F Buckmaster. **LC** G149; .S49. **DD** 910/.5. **Bk Rev**. **Ad Acc**. **Circ:** 200,000 (ctrl).
**Desc:** A newsletter that concentrates on different destinations.

US/0886-6503
**SIERRA HERITAGE.** (19??)-. Periodical. English. bm. $20.00 (1 year), $35.00 (2 year) US; $26.00 (1 year), $47.00 (2 year) other. Sierra Heritage, PO Box 9148, Auburn CA 95604. **Tel** (916)823-3986, FAX (916)83-3986. **ED** Caetlin O'Riordan. **Bk Rev**, (Qty: 6-10 per year). **Ad Acc**, **Adv Mgr:** Donna Lewis, **Tel** (916)823-3986. **Circ:** 8,750.
**Desc:** Covering the history of the Gold Rush, the Sierra has outstanding and mixed recreation; skiing, fishing, hiking, boating, etc., making the region on of the most interesting and desireable for tourism in the West.

SI
**SINGAPORE (SINGAPORE).** (SINGAPORE.). (1969)-. English. an. Singapore National Printers, 303 Upper Serangoon Road, Singapore 1334 Singapore. **Tel** 011 65 2820611. **LC** DS598.S7; S6. **DD** 915.95/2/035. ***Continues*** *Singapore Year Book.*

US/0091-6323
**SOUL JOURNEY.** Feb. 1973-. Periodical. English. mo. Communicators, Ltd., 1014 National Press Building, Washington DC 20004. **LC** G149; .S67. **DD** 910/.5.

US/0278-4386
**SOURCE II, THE.** **VAT** Source Two. Vol. 1, No. 1 (Aug./Sept. 1981)-. Periodical. English. bm. $60.00. Armin D Lehmann, 19300 Rinaldi Street, Box 7985, Northridge CA 91327-7985.

US/0584-3103
**SOUTH AMERICA TRAVEL DIGEST.** **Added/Corp** South American Travel Organization. (1965)-. English. ir (approximately every 18 to 24 months). Travel Digest, 73 - 465 Ironwood Street, Palm Desert CA 92260. **Tel** (619)346-4792. **LC** F2201; .S68.

UK/0309-4529
**SOUTH AMERICAN HANDBOOK.** (THE SOUTH AMERICAN HANDBOOK.). [South Am. handb.]. 1st. Ed. (1924)-. English. an. National Textbook Company, 4255 West Touhy Avenue, Lincolnwood IL 60646. **Tel** (708)679-5500, (800)323-4900, FAX (708)679-2494, telex TWX 9102230736. **LC** F1401; .S71. ***Continues*** *Anglo-South American Handbook.* ***Continued in part by*** *Caribbean Islands Handbook* ***and*** *Mexico & Central American Handbook.*

US/1061-9836
**SOUTH ASIAN HANDBOOK (NEW YORK, N.Y.).** (SOUTH ASIAN HANDBOOK.). 1993-. English. Macmillan Publishing Co. / Indiana, 201 West 103rd Street, Indianapolis IN 46290. **Tel** (800)428-5331, (800)858-7674.

CN/0708-9821
**SOUTH WEST NOVA.** Vol. 2, (Summer/Autumn 1978)-. Periodical. English. Free. Lescarbot Print, Box 402, 4 Alma Street, Yarmouth Nova Scotia B5A 4B3 Canada. **Tel** (902)742-9119. **DD** 917.16/3. ***Continues*** *In Town, 0702-8156.*

SA
**SOUTHERN AFRICAN AND INDIAN OCEAN ISLANDS TRAVEL INDUSTRY'S YEARBOOK, DIRECTORY AND WHO'S WHO, THE.** **VFOAT** Southern Africa's Travel Industry. 1976/77-. Directory. English. 10.00. World Freight & Markets Pty Ltd, PO Box 6202, 200 Johannesburg South Africa. **LC** G155.S57; S73. **DD** 338.4/7/916804025.

US/1043-6375
**SOUTHERN LINKS (HILTON HEAD ISLAND, S.C.).** ***Title Change.*** **See** Recreation, Leisure-Sports.

UK
**SPAIN.** **Main/Corp** Michelin Tyre Company, Ltd. Tourist Service. 1st- Ed.; 1974-. English. Michelin Tyre Company Ltd, 81 Fulham Road, London SW3 6RD England. **Tel** (01)861-2121. **LC** DP43; .M44A. **DD** 914.6/04/82.

US
**SPAIN AND MOROCCO ON $10 AND $15 A DAY.** (197?)-. English. $4.50. Appleton Century Crofts, Prentice Hall, 200 Old Tappan Road, Old Tappan NJ 07675. **Tel** (201)767-5188, (800)922-0579. **ED** S. Haggart and D. Porter. ***Continues*** *Spain and Morocco on $5 and $10 a day.*

US/0889-7085
**SPECIALTY TRAVEL INDEX: THE DIRECTORY TO SPECIAL INTEREST TRAVEL.** [Spec. travel index]. (19??)-. Directory. English. sa. $10.00 US; $13.00 Canada and Mexico; $12.00, $20.00 (airmail) other; $30.00 Australia and New Zealand. Specialty Travel Index, 305 San Anselmo Avenue, Suite 217, San Anselmo CA 94960. **Tel** (415)459-4900, FAX (415)459-4974. **ED** C. Steen Hansen. **DD** 910. **Bk Rev**. **Ad Acc**.
**Desc:** Directory and magazine of special interest travel.

CN/0824-6572
**ST. CATHARINES.** (ST. CATHARINES : YOUR OFFICIAL GUIDE TO THE GARDEN CITY.). [St. Catharines]. 1983-. English. an. Free. St Catharines & District Chamber of Commerce, 60 James Street Box 940, St Catharines Ontario L2R 6Z4 Canada. **DD** 917.13/38.

US/0882-8741
**ST. GEORGE MAGAZINE.** [St. George mag.]. **VFOAT** St. George; Saint George Magazine. (1984)-. Periodical. English. bm (6 issues). $14.00. St. George Magazine, 165 North 100 East, Suite #2, St. George UT 84770. **Tel** (801)673-6333. **ED** Lyman Hafen. **DD** 917. **Bk Rev**. **Ad Acc**. **Circ:** 10,000.

UK
**STANDARD GUIDEBOOK TO THE ISLES OF SCILLY, THE.** (1936)-. English. be. £2.25. Bowley Publications, PO Box 1, St Mary's, Isles of Scilly TR21 0PR United Kingdom. **Tel** 0736-67450. **ED** R L Bowley. **LC** DA670.S2; B75. **DD** 914.23/7. **Bk Rev**. **Ad Acc**. **Circ:** 250,000. ***Continues*** *Bowley, R. L. Isles of Scilly.*
**Desc:** Includes a large-scale map of the Isles of Scilly, a plan of Hugh Town, color photographs, detailed maps of each of the inhabited islands, travel details, natural history and more.

US
**STANDARD HIGHWAY MILEAGE GUIDE.** **See** Encyclopedias and General Reference Books.

BB
**STATISTICAL NEWS.** **Added/Corp** Caribbean Tourism Research and Development Centre. **VFOAT** CTRC Statistical News. (19??)-. Statistical Publication. English. Four times a year. $75.00. Caribbean Tourism Research and Development Centre, 25 F Walcott Building Culloden Far, St. Michael Barbados. **Tel** (809)427-5242, FAX (809)429-3065, telex 2488 WB. **LC** G155.C35; S7. **DD** 380.1/45917290452.
**Desc:** Covers regional tourism trends and reviews current marketplace and destination developments.

AT
**STATISTICAL REVIEW - AUSTRALIAN TOURIST COMMISSION.** **Main/Corp** Australian Tourist Commission. Statistical Publication. English. an. Free. GPO Box 73B, Melbourne Victoria 3001 Australia. **LC** G155.A75; A88A. **DD** 338.4/7/9194046. **Ad Acc**. **Circ:** 2,500 (ctrl).
**Desc:** Presents a detailed statistical summary of overseas visitors arriving in, and departing from, Australia during the calendar year.

IT
**STATISTICHE DEL TURISMO.** **Added/Corp** Istituto Centrale di Statistica (Italy). Vol. 1 (1985-1986)-. Italian. ir. L13000. Istituto Nazionale Statistica, GBP SEZ4 Via Cesare Balbo 16, 00184 Rome Italy. **Tel** 011 39 6 46735118. **LC** G155.I8; S7. **DD** 338.4/7914504/05. ***Continues in part*** *Annuario Statistico del Commercio Interno e del Turismo.*

US/0749-2561
**STEPHEN BIRNBAUM TRAVEL GUIDE, A.** **VFOAT** Stephen Birnbaum Travel Guides. Monographic series. English. ir. Price varies per volume. Houghton Mifflin Company, Wayside Road, Burlington MA 01803. **Tel** (800)225-3362, (617)272-1500. **DD** 910. ***Continues*** *Get Em and Go Travel Guide, 0162-5497.*

US
**STRATEGIC INFORMATION ON US AIR TRAVEL.** English. bm. $350.00 (full service); $95.00 (travel alert bulletin). Nationwide Intelligence, Box 1922, Saginaw MI 48605. **Tel** (517)752-6123, (800)333-4130, FAX (517)752-1605. **ED** David W Oppermann. Index available. cum. index. **Circ:** 300 (ctrl). available on an online database.
**Desc:** Briefings on airlines, airports and cities.

US/1051-3868
**STUDENT TRAVELER (KNOXVILLE, TENN.).** (STUDENT TRAVELER.). [Stud. travel.]. (Fall/Winter 1990)-. Periodical. English. sa. Free. Whittle Communications, 333 Main Avenue, Knoxville TN 37902. **Tel** (615)595-5000, FAX (615)595-5877. **DD** 917. ***Continues*** *America, 1047-3904.*

US
**STUDENT TRAVELS MAGAZINE.** English. Twice a year (published Sept., and Jan.). $1.00. CIEE, 205 East 42nd Street, New York NY 10017. **Tel** (212)661-1414, FAX (212)972-3231. **ED** Tony Bogar & Robin Honig Marblehead Communications 376 Boyleston Street Boston, MA 02116 (617)424-7700. **Ad Acc**. **Circ:** 900,000 (ctrl).
**Desc:** Provides valuable on transportation, accommodations, International Student Identity Cards, insurance, and travel documents. Also, contains feature articles on a wide range of topics such as studying abroad, travelling on a low budget, and working abroad.

●CN/1193-1175
**SUBURBAN TORONTO CRISS-CROSS DIRECTORY.** [Suburb. Tor. criss-cross dir.]. **VFOAT** Might's Suburban Metro Toronto Criss Cross Directory. (1992)-. Directory. English. $140.00. Might Directories, 220 Bartley Drive, Toronto Ontario M4A 2H4 Canada. **Tel** (416)751-2751. **DD** 917.13/5. ***Continues*** *Suburban Metro Toronto Criss-Cross Directory., 0710-0728.*

US/0095-3482
**SUMMARY AND ANALYSIS OF INTERNATIONAL TRAVEL TO THE U.S.** **Added/Corp** United States Travel Service. **VAT** Summary and Analysis of International Travel to the United States. (197?)-. Periodical. English. Four times a year (Mar., June, Sept., Dec.). $125.00. US Travel Data Center, 1100 New York Avenue, Suite 450, Washington DC 20005. **Tel** (202)408-1832. **LC** G155.U6; U57b. **DD** 338.4/7917304926. ***Continues*** *United States Travel Service. Office of Policy and Research. Summary and Analysis of International Travel to the U.S., 0095-3482.*
**Desc:** These reports define the size of inbound travel markets to the U.S. Information is provided on non-resident arrivals for 90 countries of residence by region, type of visa, mode of transportation, age, port of entry, and first intended address in the U.S.

US
**SUNBOUND.** (19??)-. Periodical. English. qt. $4.00. Auto-Train Corporation, 1801 K Street NW, Washington DC 20006. **LC** F309.3; .S95. **DD** 917.59/04/6.

CN/1186-7914
**SUNSHINE CIRCLE TOUR MAGAZINE : SUNSHINE COAST AND VANCOUVER ISLAND, THE.** [Sunshine circ. tour mag.]. (1991)-. English. Free. Paramount Communications Inc., 207-1110 Government Street, Victoria British Columbia V8W 1Y2 Canada. **DD** 917.11/1044/05.

FI/0359-0607
**SUOMEN MATKAILU.** **See** General Interest-General Interest-Europe.

US/0735-0376
**SURVEY AND ANALYSIS OF BUSINESS TRAVEL POLICIES & COSTS.** [Surv. anal. bus. travel policies costs]. **Added/Corp** Runzheimer and Company. Transportation Division. **VAT** Survey and Analysis of Business Travel Policies and Costs. (1983)-. English. be. $345.00. Runzheimer International / Wisconsin, Runzheimer Park, Rochester WI 53167. **Tel** (414)767-2200, FAX (414)767-2254, (800)558-1702. **ED** Judith Godshalk. **LC** HD28; .S87. **DD** 658.3/83.
**Desc:** A statistical survey of corporate business travel practices.

US/0361-8307
**SURVEY OF STATE TRAVEL OFFICES.** [Surv. State travel off.]. **Main/Corp** United States Travel Data Center. **VFOAT** State Travel Offices. (19??)-. English. an (Spring). $75.00. US Travel Data Center, 1100 New York Avenue, Suite 450, Washington DC 20005. **Tel** (202)408-1832. **LC** G155.U6; U58a. **DD** 353.9/3/82.
**Desc:** This annual survey provides extensive information on tourism developement budgets and operations of all 50 states, the District of Columbia, American Samoa, Puerto Rico, Guam and the Northern Mariana Islands. Refer to the Summary & Analysis section or compare state-by-state budgeting and program details on general

administration, and advertising and promotion, packages tours, press and public relations, welcome centers, and other activities of the agencies responsible for travel development across the U.S.

US/0146-4698
**SURVEY OF TRAVEL IN KENTUCKY.** English. an. Department of Public Information / Frankfort, Commonwealth of Kentucky, 1923 Capitol Plaza Trail, Frankfort KY 40601. **LC** G155.U6; C623. **DD** 338.4/7/91769044.

JA
**TABI.** (19??)-. Periodical. Japanese. mo. $142.00 California; $148.00 other US. **(Subscription address:** Kinokuniya Company Ltd., 38-1 Sakuragaoka 5, chome Setagaya-ku, Tokyo 156 Japan.**)**

US
**TASTE FULL.** **See** Food and Food Industry.

AT
**TECHNICAL AND FURTHER EDUCATION. HOSPITALITY AND TOURISM.** **Main/Corp** Western Australia. Technical Education Division. **VFOAT** Hospitality and Tourism. (19??)-. English. ir. Nelson Wadsworth, PO Box 4725, Melbourne Victoria, 3001 Australia. **Tel** 03 329-5199. **LC** WMLC L 83/1797.

CN/0823-5708
**TEMPS LIBRE (MONTREAL).** (AEMPS LIBRE : LE MAGAZINE DE L'ORGANISATION POUR LE TUDIENTE AU QUEBEC (OTEQ).). [Temps libre]. **Added/Corp** Organisation pour le Tourisme Etudiant au Quebec. Vol. 1, No 1 (Autumn 1983)-. Periodical. French. qt. 10.00Can$ (1 year), 20.00Can$ (2 year), 30.00Can$ (3 year). Temps Libre--Tourisme Jeunesse, CP 1000 Succ. M/4545P Coubertin, Montreal Quebec H1V 3R2 Canada. **Tel** (514)252-3117, FAX (514)252-3119. **DD** 910/88375. Index available. cum. index. **Bk Rev**, (Qty: 4). **Ad Acc**. **Circ:** 50,000.
**Desc:** Low budget travel, transportation, accommodation, specialized services for youth and student youth exchange programs; description of books and guides. Outdoor activities.

CN/0712-8657
**TEOROS.** [Teoros]. **Added/Corp** Universite du Quebec a Montreal. **VFOAT** Cahiers de Recherche Teoros. Vol. 1 No. 1 (Feb. 1982)-. Periodical. French. Three times a year. $5.42. Universite Quebec, CP 888, Succursale A, Montreal Quebec H3C 3P8 Canada. **Tel** (514)282-3650. **DD** 338.4/791714044/05.
**Ind/Abst** Leis. Recreat. Tour. Abstr.; Point Repere (1991-).

IT
**TEST : TERZIARIO SERVIZI E TURISMO.** ***Ceased.*** (19??)-(1992). Italian. mo. FILCAMS/CGIL, Corso di Porta Vittoria 43, 20122 Milan Italy. **Tel** 2/55025333, FAX 2/5453423.

US/0040-4349
**TEXAS HIGHWAYS (AUSTIN, TEX.).** (TEXAS HIGHWAYS.). [Tex. highw.]. **Added/Corp** Texas. Travel and Information Division. Texas. Highway Dept. Division of Information and Statistics. (1954)-. Periodical. English. mo. $12.50. Texas Highways Magazine, PO Box 5016, Austin TX 78763. **Tel** (512)483-3689. **ED** Frank Lively. **LC** TE24.T4; T38. **DD** 917.64/0463/05. Index available (bound in issue). **Bk Rev**. **Circ:** 400,000. ***Continues*** *Construction & Maintenance Bulletin.*
**Desc:** Interprets scenic, recreational, historical, cultural, and ethnic treasures of the state of Texas. Goal is to educate and to entertain, to encourage recreational travel to and within the state and to tell the Texas story to readers around the world.

US/1055-8861
**THAILAND GUIDEBOOK, THE.** (1991)-. English. $18.95. Houghton Mifflin Company, Wayside Road, Burlington MA 01803. **Tel** (800)225-3362, (617)272-1500.

●US/1061-9844
**THAILAND, INDOCHINA & BURMA HANDBOOK.** (1993)-. English. Macmillan Publishing Co. / Indiana, 201 West 103rd Street, Indianapolis IN 46290. **Tel** (800)428-5331, (800)858-7674.

TH
**THAILAND TRAVEL TRADE YEARBOOK.** **VFOAT** Travel Trade Yearbook. English. Media Transasia Thailand Ltd, 26 Chidlom Road, 14th Floor, Ploenchit, Bangkok 10500 Thailand. **Tel** 011 66 2 5199057. **LC** DS566.2; .T465. **DD** 915.93/0444/05.

US/8756-4920
**THIS IS ALASKA.** [This Alsk.]. English. qt. $5.95. Alaska Technical Publishing Company, 1041 East 76th Street/Suite C, Anchorage AK 99518. **Tel** (907)349-7506. **ED** Frank Martone. **LC** F902.3; .T47. **DD** 917.98/045. **Circ:** 8,000.

US/1058-3378
**THIS IS LAGUNA.** [This Laguna]. (July 1991)-. Periodical. English. bm. $10.00. This is Laguna, PO Box 1568, Laguna Beach CA 92652. **DD** 917.

US/0896-4599
**THIS MONTH ON LONG ISLAND.** [This mon. Long Isl.]. **VFOAT** On Long Island. (198?)-. Periodical. English. Twelve times a year. $23.00. This Month on Long Island, One Dupont Street, Plainview NY 11803. **Tel** (516)349-8282, FAX (516)349-1801. **ED** Robert Lipper. **DD** 917. Index available. **Ad Acc**. ctrl circ.
**Desc:** Tourist publication serving the Long Island region. Reference information on events, attractions and entertainment, as well as local history, facts and figures.

US/0731-728X
**THOMAS COOK BUSINESS TRAVELER.** **VFOAT** Business Traveler. Vol. 1, No. 1 (Spring 1982)-. Periodical. English. qt. Norback & Company, 621 Alexander Road, Princeton NJ 08540.

UK/0144-7475
**THOMAS COOK OVERSEAS TIMETABLE.** **Added/Corp** Thomas Cook Ltd. (Winter 1980)-. English (French, Italian, German, Spanish and Portuguese). Six times a year (Jan., Mar., May, July, Sept., Nov.). $121.80. Thomas Cook Ltd., PO Box 227, Peterborough PE3 6SB England. **Tel** 011 44 733 268943, FAX 011 44 733 505792, telex 32581. **ED** P. I. Tremlett. **LC** HE1805; .T48. **DD** 385/.2042/05. **CODEN** TCOTDF. Index available. **Ad Acc**. **Circ:** 13,000. ***Continues in part*** *Thomas Cook International Timetable, 0141-2701.*
**Desc:** Detailed surface transportation schedule for worldwide rail ferry and intercity bus services. Covers world except Europe and Britain. Widely used within travel industry as a reference.

UK
**THOMAS COOK RAILPASS GUIDE.** ***Ceased.*** (19??)-(19??). English. an. Thomas Cook Ltd., PO Box 227, Peterborough PE3 6SB England. **Tel** 011 44 733 268943, FAX 011 44 733 505792, telex 32581. **ED** B R Baker. **Ad Acc**. **Circ:** 7,500.
**Desc:** Guide to rail, city transit, and national bus passes worldwide.

GW/0723-6875
**TI. GESCHAFTSREISE.** **VFOAT** Touristik-Information. Geschaftsreise; Geschaftsreise; DVZ-Ti. Geschaftsreise. (1980)-. Periodical. German. sm. **UDC** 910.4::339.1.
**Ind/Abst** Leis. Recreat. Tour. Abstr.

CN/0701-1741
**TIAC NEWSLETTER.** (INFORMATION AITC.). **Main/Corp** Travel Industry Association of Canada. **VFOAT** TIAC Newsletter. (May 1981)-. Periodical. French (English). bm. Association de l'Industrie Touristique du Canada, Bureau 1016/130 rue Albert, Ottawa Ontario K1P 5G4 Canada. **DD** 338.4/7917104/05. ***Continues*** *Association de l'Industrie Touristique du Canada. T I A C Newsletter., 0701-1741.*

NE
**TIM : TRAVEL INFORMATION MANUAL.** **VFOAT** Travel Information Manual. Periodical. English. mo. F267.00. TIM Travel Information Manual, PO Box 902, 2130 EA Hoofddorp Netherlands. **Tel** 011 31 2503 73525, FAX 011 31 2503 73515. **LC** PAR.
**Desc:** Monthly informatin about passenger travel documentation and regulations, vaccinations, airport taxes, currencies and customs.

AU
**TIROLER VERKEHRSWIRTSCHAFTLICHE ZAHLEN.** **Added/Corp** Institut fuer Verkehr und Tourismus. (1972)-. German. an. S100.00. Institut fur Verkehr und Tourismus, Wilhelm-Greil-Str, 14, A-6010, Innsbruck, Austria. **ED** Dr. Helmut Lamprecht and Klaus Wergles. **LC** G155.A8; T57. **Circ:** 300.

SA
**TOERISME EN MIGRASIE.** **Main/Corp** South Africa. Dept. of Statistics. **VFOAT** Tourism and Migration. Afrikaans (English). ir (annual report and monthly statistical news releases). R2.50 per issue; new releases are free. Central Statistical Service, The Government Printer, Private Bag X85, Pretoria 0001 South Africa. **Tel** 012-3228622, FAX 012-3226325, telex 320450. **LC** G155.S57; S68B. **DD** 338.4/7/9168046. **Circ:** 350.
**Desc:** Shows the number of immigrants and emigrants and the net gain/loss to the population of South Africa. Contains information regarding certain characteristics of these classes of migrants, such as age distribution, occupations, mode of travel, country of permanent residence (immigrants), or intended permanent residence (emigrants) and country of birth and citizenship.

US/0739-1420
**TOLL-FREE TRAVEL/VACATION PHONE DIRECTORY.** **VFOAT** Travel/Vacation Phone Directory; Travel and Vacation Toll-Free Directory. Directory. English. an. $6.95. Celebrity Publishing Inc, PO Box 98, Suffern NY 10901. **LC** G155.U6; T64. **DD** 381/.459173/0402573.

US/0889-3349
**TOUR & TRAVEL NEWS.** [Tour travel news]. **VFOAT** Tour and Travel News. (198?)-. Periodical. English. Fifty times a year. $95.00 US. CMP Publications Inc., c/o B. Werner, One Jericho Plaza, Wing A, 2nd Floor, Jericho NY 11753. **Tel** (516)733-6700. **[CCC]**. available on an online database (files 16,570/Full-Text) from DIALOG.
**Ind/Abst** F&S Index Plus Text, Int. [Full Txt.] [Select. Cov.]; Mark. Advert. Ref. Serv. [Full Txt.]; PROMT [Full Txt.].

US/0361-4948
**TOUR BOOK : ALABAMA, LOUISIANA, MISSISSIPPI.** **VFOAT** Alabama, Louisiana, Mississippi Tour Book. English. an. American Automobile Association, 1000 AAA Drive, Heathrow FL 32746. **Tel** (407)444-7000. **LC** F324.3; .T68. **DD** 917.6.

US/0362-3599
**TOUR BOOK : ARIZONA, NEW MEXICO.** **VFOAT** Arizona, New Mexico Tour Book. English. an. American Automobile Association, 1000 AAA Drive, Heathrow FL 32746. **Tel** (407)444-7000. **LC** F809.3; .T68. **DD** 917.89/04/505.

US/0363-1486
**TOUR BOOK : ARKANSAS, KANSAS, MISSOURI, OKLAHOMA.** **Main/Corp** American Automobile Association. **VFOAT** Arkansas, Kansas, Missouri, Oklahoma. English. an. American Automobile Association, 1000 AAA Drive, Heathrow FL 32746. **Tel** (407)444-7000. **LC** F409.3; .A46A. **DD** 917.6.

US/0363-1788
**TOUR BOOK: ATLANTIC PROVINCES AND QUEBEC.** **Main/Corp** American Automobile Association. **Added/Corp** American Automobile Association. Canadian Automobile Association. American Automobile Association. Atlantic Provinces and Quebec; New Brunswick, Newfoundland, Nova Scotia, Prince Edward Island, Quebec Tour Book. **VFOAT** American Automobile Association, Canadian Automobile Association. **VAT** Atlantic Provinces and Quebec, New Brunswick, Newfoundland, Nova Scotia, Prince Edward Island, Quebec. Tour Book. (19??)-. English. an. American Automobile Association, 1000 AAA Drive, Heathrow FL 32746. **Tel** (407)444-7000. **LC** F1035.8; .A46a. **DD** 917.15'044. ***Supersedes in part*** *Eastern Canada Tour Book, 0569-2857.*

US/0363-1494
**TOUR BOOK: CONNECTICUT, MASSACHUSETTS, RHODE ISLAND.** **Main/Corp** American Automobile Association. **Added/Corp** American Automobile Association. Connecticut, Massachusetts, Rhode Island Tour Book. **VFOAT** Connecticut, Massachusetts, Rhode Island Tour Book. (19??)-. English. an. American Automobile Association, 1000 AAA Drive, Heathrow FL 32746. **Tel** (407)444-7000. **LC** F92.3; .A46a. **DD** 917.4.

US/0361-4956
**TOUR BOOK : GEORGIA, NORTH CAROLINA, SOUTH CAROLINA.** **VFOAT** Georgia, North Carolina, South Carolina Tour Book. English. an. American Automobile Association, 1000 AAA Drive, Heathrow FL 32746. **Tel** (407)444-7000. **LC** F284.3; .T68. **DD** 917.5.

US/0160-6921
**TOUR BOOK : HAWAII.** **VFOAT** Hawaii, Tour Book. English. an. American Automobile Association, 1000 AAA Drive, Heathrow FL 32746. **Tel** (407)444-7000. **LC** DU622; .T62. **DD** 919.69/04/4.

US/0363-2695
**TOUR BOOK: IDAHO, MONTANA, WYOMING.** **Added/Corp** American Automobile Association. **VFOAT** Idaho, Montana, Wyoming Tour Book. (1976/77)-. English. an. American Automobile Association, 1000 AAA Drive, Heathrow FL 32746. **Tel** (407)444-7000. **LC** F744.3; .T68. **DD** 917.8.

US/0363-1508
**TOUR BOOK: ILLINOIS, INDIANA, OHIO.** **Main/Corp** American Automobile Association. **VFOAT** Illinois, Indiana, Ohio Tour Book. (19??)-. English. an. American Automobile Association, 1000 AAA Drive, Heathrow FL 32746. **Tel** (407)444-7000. **LC** F539.3; .A46A. **DD** 917.7.

US/0361-4964
**TOUR BOOK: KENTUCKY-TENNESSEE.** **Added/Corp** American Automobile Association. **VFOAT** Kentucky-Tennessee Tour Book. (19??)-. English. an. American Automobile Association, 1000 AAA Drive, Heathrow FL 32746. **Tel** (407)444-7000. **LC** F449.3; .T68. **DD** 351.892.

US/0363-1516
**TOUR BOOK: MAINE, NEW HAMPSHIRE, VERMONT.** **Main/Corp** American Automobile Association. **Added/Corp** American Automobile Association. Maine, New Hampshire, Vermont Tour Book. **VFOAT** Maine, New

# Travel and Tourism

Hampshire, Vermont Tour Book. (19??)-. English. an. American Automobile Association, 1000 AAA Drive, Heathrow FL 32746. **Tel** (407)444-7000. **LC** F17.3; .A46a. **DD** 917.4.

US/0363-1524
**TOUR BOOK: MICHIGAN, WISCONSIN.** **Main/Corp** American Automobile Association. **Added/Corp** American Automobile Association. Michigan, Wisconsin Tour Book. **VFOAT** Michigan, Wisconsin Tour Book. (19??)-. English. an. American Automobile Association, 1000 AAA Drive, Heathrow FL 32746. **Tel** (407)444-7000. **LC** F564.3; .A46a. **DD** 917.74/04/4.

US/0363-1532
**TOUR BOOK: NEW JERSEY, PENNSYLVANIA.** **Main/Corp** American Automobile Association. **Added/Corp** American Automobile Association. New Jersey, Pennsylvania Tour Book. **VFOAT** New Jersey, Pennsylvania Tour Book. (19??)-. English. an. American Automobile Association, 1000 AAA Drive, Heathrow FL 32746. **Tel** (407)444-7000. **LC** F132.3; .A65a. **DD** 917.48/04/4.

US/0363-1540
**TOUR BOOK: NEW YORK.** **Main/Corp** American Automobile Association. **Added/Corp** American Automobile Association. New York Tour Book. **VFOAT** New York Tour Book. (19??)-. English. an. American Automobile Association, 1000 AAA Drive, Heathrow FL 32746. **Tel** (407)444-7000. **LC** F117.3; .A46a. **DD** 917.47/04/4.

US/0363-1567
**TOUR BOOK: OREGON, WASHINGTON.** **VFOAT** Oregon, Washington Tour Book. (19??)-. English. an. American Automobile Association, 1000 AAA Drive, Heathrow FL 32746. **Tel** (407)444-7000. **LC** F874.3; .T67. **DD** 917.95/04/4.

US/0363-1575
**TOUR BOOK: TEXAS.** **Main/Corp** American Automobile Association. **Added/Corp** American Automobile Association. Texas Tour Book. **VFOAT** Texas Tour Book. (19??)-. English. an. American Automobile Association, 1000 AAA Drive, Heathrow FL 32746. **Tel** (407)444-7000. **LC** F384.3; .A46a. **DD** 917.64/04/6.

US/0362-3602
**TOUR BOOK : WESTERN CANADA AND ALASKA.** **VFOAT** Western Canada and Alaska, Alberta, British Columbia, Manitoba, Saskatchewan, Northwest Territories, Yukon Territory and Alaska Tour Book. English. an. American Automobile Association, 1000 AAA Drive, Heathrow FL 32746. **Tel** (407)444-7000. **LC** F1060.4; .T68. **DD** 917.12/04/305.

CN/0226-3513
**TOUR BRITISH COLUMBIA.** [Tour B.C.]. **VAT** Tour B.C. Monographic series. English. Price varies per volume. Public Information Office / British Columbia, Tourism British Columbia, 1117 Wharf Street, Victoria British Columbia V8W 2Z2 Canada. **DD** 917.11/044. **Supersedes** Discover British Columbia.

US/0362-9821
**TOURBOOK: COLORADO, UTAH.** **Main/Corp** American Automobile Association. **VFOAT** Colorado, Utah: Tourbook. (19??)-. English. an. American Automobile Association, 1000 AAA Drive, Heathrow FL 32746. **Tel** (407)444-7000. **LC** F774.3; .A44a. **DD** 917.88/04/3.

US/0364-0086
**TOURBOOK : MID-ATLANTIC.** **Main/Corp** American Automobile Association. **VFOAT** Mid-Atlantic: Delaware. District of Columbia, Maryland, Virginia West Virginia, Tourbook. English. an. American Automobile Association, 1000 AAA Drive, Heathrow FL 32746. **Tel** (407)444-7000. **LC** F106; .A5112A. **DD** 917.5/04/4.

US/0733-8368
**TOURBOOK. NORTH CENTRAL.** [TourB., North Cent.]. **VFOAT** Tour Book. North Central; North Central, Iowa, Minnesota, Nebraska, North Dakota, South Dakota Tourbook. English. an. American Automobile Association, 1000 AAA Drive, Heathrow FL 32746. **Tel** (407)444-7000. **LC** GV1024; .N82. **DD** 917.7. **Continues** North Central Tour Book, 0733-835X.

FR
**TOURING.** **Added/Corp** Touring-Club de France. (19??)-. Periodical. English (French). mo. 50.00F. **LC** G149; .T64. **DD** 910/.5.

US/1055-6850
**TOURING AMERICA.** [Tour. Am.]. Vol. 1, No. 1 (July 1991)-. Periodical. English. bm. $17.97. Fancy Publications, PO Box 6050, Mission Viejo CA 92690. **Tel** (714)855-8822, (800)800-2516, FAX (714)855-3045. **(Subscription address:** Palm Coast Data, PO Box 420235, Agency Department, Palm Coast FL 32142.**) ED** Gene Booth. **LC** E158; .T69. **DD** 917.04/539. **Circ:** 95,000.

CN/0838-6846
**TOURING (MONTREAL. ED. FRANCAISE).** (TOURING.). [Touring]. **Added/Corp** Touring Club Montreal. Vol. 62, No 1 (1984)-. Periodical. French. ir. Touring Club Montreal, 1425 de la Montagne Street, Montreal Quebec H3G 2R7 Canada. **DD** 796.7/06/0714281. **Continues in part** Touring (Touring Club Montreal)., 0229-5466.

CN
**TOURING (TOURING CLUB MONTREAL). ENGLISH.** Touring Club Montreal, 1425 de la Montagne Street, Montreal Quebec H3G 2R7 Canada.

IS
**TOURISM AND HOTEL SERVICES STATISTICS QUARTERLY.** **See** Travel and Tourism-Abstracting, Bibliographies and Statistics.

IE/0791-3443
**TOURISM AND TRAVEL DUBLIN.** (TOURISM AND TRAVEL RELEASE.). [Tour. travel Dublin]. (1987)-. Periodical. English. an. 1.50p. Central Statistics Office / Ireland, Ardee Road, Dublin 6 Ireland. **Tel** 977144, FAX 972300. **DD** 314.17 382.09417. **Circ:** 500. available on diskette.
**Desc:** This release provides estimates of the number of visits made and the expenditure by visitors to Ireland and by Irish visitors abroad.

SI
**TOURISM ASIA.** English. Six times a year. 48.00Sing$ Singapore; 95.00Sing$ other. Venture Publishing Pte. Ltd., 38 Kim Tian Rd., 02-05 Kim Tian Plaza, Singapore 0316 Singapore. **Tel** 011 65 2788700, FAX 011 65 2786881, telex RS20549.

●UK/1354-8166
**TOURISM ECONOMICS. See** Economics.

CN/0838-3863
**TOURISM IN CANADA.** (TOURISM IN CANADA / STATISTICS CANADA, EDUCATION, CULTURE AND TOURISM DIVISION, TRAVEL, TOURISM AND RECREATION SECTION.). [Tour. Can.]. **Added/Corp** Statistics Canada. Travel, Tourism and Recreation Section. **VFOAT** Tourisme au Canada. (1988)-. English (French). be. 42.00Can$ Canada. Statistics Canada, Publications Sales & Services, Main Building Room 1710, Ottawa Ontario K1A 0T6 Canada. **Tel** (613)951-5078, (800)267-6677, FAX (613)951-1584, telex 053-3585. **LC** G155.C3; T73. **DD** 338.4/7917104/05. **Continues** Tourism and Recreation, a Statistical Digest., 0824-9032.
**Desc:** Consists of analytical texts, charts, and tables drawn from numerous sources, grouped together in nine chapters covering topics such as visitors to Canada, Canadian travellers, industries comprising the tourism sector, employment and the economic significance of tourism.

UK
**TOURISM IN ENGLISH.** **Added/Corp** English Tourist Board. (19??)-. English. English Tourist Board, Thames Tower, Blacks Road, Hammersmith, London W6 9EL United Kingdom. **Tel** FAX 011 44 81 563-0302. **LC** G155.G7; T67. **DD** 338.4/7/914204857.

JA
**TOURISM IN JAPAN.** English. Department of Tourism and Ministry of Transport, 1-3 Kasumigaseki 2-chome Chiyoda-ku, Tokyo Japan. **LC** G155.J27; T68. **DD** 380.1/4591520448.

UK/0309-8958
**TOURISM INTELLIGENCE QUARTERLY.** (19??)-. English. Four times a year. £78.00 UK; £85.00 Europe; £90.00 other. British Tourist Authority, Thames Tower, Blacks Road, London W6 9EL England. **Tel** 011 44 81 8469000, FAX 011 44 156 30302.

UK/0261-3700
**TOURISM LONDON. 1978.** [Tourism Lond. 1978]. (1978)-. English. bm. John Offord Publications, 12 The Avenue, Eastbourne East Sussex BN21 3YA England. **Tel** 0323 645871. **DD** 338.479141005.
**Ind/Abst** Museum Abstr.

UK/0261-5177
**TOURISM MANAGEMENT (1982). See** Business-General Management.

SP
**TOURISM MARKET TRENDS.** (19??)-. English (French). ir. $50.00. World Tourism Organization / WTO, Calle Capitan Haya 42, E 28020 Madrid Spain. **Tel** 011 34 1 5710628, FAX 011 34 1 5713733, telex 42188 OMT-E. **(Subscription address:** UNIPUB, 4611 F Assembly Drive, Lanham MD 20706.**)**

UK
**TOURISM MARKETPLACE. Ceased.** (19??)-(19??). English. mo. AMS Marketing, 37 St. Barnabas Street, B Anderson, London SW1 W8QB England. **Tel** 011 44 71 730 8253.

FR
**TOURISM POLICY AND INTERNATIONAL TOURISM IN OECD MEMBER COUNTRIES.** **Main/Corp** Organisation for Economic Co-operation and Development. Committee on Tourism. (1974)-. English. an. Price varies per volume. OECD Publications and Information Center, 2 rue Andre-Pascal, 75775 Paris Cedex 16 France. **Tel** 011 33 1 45248167, US:(202)785-6323, FAX 011 33 1 45248500 OR 45248176, telex 620 160 OCDE. **(Subscription address:** OECD Publications Center, 2001 L Street, Suite 700, Washington DC 20036.**) LC** G155.A1; O66. **DD** 382/.45/91. **Continues** Organisation for Economic Co-operation and Development. Committee on Tourism. International Tourism and Tourism Policy in OECD Member Countries.

II
**TOURISM RECREATION RESEARCH.** **Added/Corp** Centre for Tourism Research (India). Vol. 2, No. 2 (Dec. 1977)-. English. sa. $100.00. Centre for Tourism Research, Lucknow, India. **(Subscription address:** Prints India, 11 Darya Ganj, New Delhi 110002 India.**) LC** G155.I4; T64. **DD** 338.4/79154045. **Continues** Tourism Research.
**Ind/Abst** Int. Dev. Abstr. (?-?); Leis. Recreat. Tour. Abstr.; Rural Dev. Abstr.; SPORT Discus; SportSearch (May 1987-).

SP
**TOURISM TO THE YEAR 2000 AND BEYOND; QUALITATIVE ASPECTS.** (19??)-. Monographic series. English (French and Spanish). ir. $35.00. World Tourism Organization / WTO, Calle Capitan Haya 42, E 28020 Madrid Spain. **Tel** 011 34 1 5710628, FAX 011 34 1 5713733, telex 42188 OMT-E. **(Subscription address:** UNIPUB, 4611 F Assembly Drive, Lanham MD 20706.**)**

SP
**TOURISM TO THE YEAR 2000 AND BEYOND; REGIONAL FORECAST STUDIES.** (19??)-. Monographic series. English (French and Spanish). ir. $125.00. World Tourism Organization / WTO, Calle Capitan Haya 42, E 28020 Madrid Spain. **Tel** 011 34 1 5710628, FAX 011 34 1 5713733, telex 42188 OMT-E. **(Subscription address:** UNIPUB, 4611 F Assembly Drive, Lanham MD 20706.**)**

CN/1191-789X
**TOURISM TODAY OTTAWA.** (TOURISM TODAY.). [Tour. today Ott.]. **VFOAT** Tourisme d'Aujourd'Hui. (1992). Periodical. Multiple languages. ir. Tourism Industry Association of Canada, Suite 1016, 130 Albert Street, Ottawa, Ontario K1P 5G4 Canada. **DD** 338.4. **Continues** Newsletter - Tourism Industry Association of Canada (1990), 1184-7255.

FR
**TOURISME.** French. qt. 180.00F France; 210.00F other. Le Tourisme, 7 rue Cesar Franck, 75015 Paris France. **Tel** 567 75 25.

SZ
**TOURISME DANS LE CANTON DU VALAIS. TOURISMUS IM KANTON WALLIS.** **Main/Corp** Switzerland. Statistisches Amt. **VFOAT** Tourismus im Kanton Wallis. French (German). 6.00F. Bureau Federal de Statistique, Hallwylstr 15, CH 3003 Berne Switzerland. **LC** G155.S8; S93J. **DD** 338.4/7/914947.

BE
**TOURISME EN BELGIQUE, LE.** French (Dutch). an. Tourist Office for Flanders, Grasmarkt 61, 1000 Brussels Belgium. **Tel** 02/513.90.90, FAX 02/513.88.03. **LC** G155.B37; T68. **DD** 380.1/45914930443.

FR
**TOURISME EN FRANCE, LE.** Began with 1976 Vol. French. ir (every 3 years). 100.00F France; $14.00 US. 19 rue de Calais, 75009 Paris France. **Tel** (1)42 81 91 33. **LC** G155.F8; T68. **DD** 380.1/45914404/05. **Circ:** 1,500.
**Desc:** A general review of tourism industry in France : organization, equipments, domestic and foreign touristic traffic, the place of tourisme in the French economy, touristic markets, bibliography, etc.

CN/0836-205X
**TOURISME+, LE JOURNAL DES VOYAGES.** [Tour. + j. voyag.]. Vol. 8, No. 137 (Sept. 25, 1986)-. Periodical. French. Forty-six times a year. Free to trade; 41.53Can$ (nontrade) Canada; 94.86Can$ (other). Publications Transcontinental Inc, 1100 Rene-Levesque, 24Fl Boulevard West, Montreal Quebec H3B 4X9 Canada. **Tel** (514)392-9000, FAX (514)392-4724. **ED** Michel Villeneuve. **DD** 381/.4591/05. **Ad Acc.** ctrl circ. **Formed by the union of** Le Journal des Voyages, 0226-6601 **and** Tourisme, 0225-0462.

CN/0848-9815
**TOURISME OUTAOUAIS BONJOUR.** [Tour. Outaouais bonjour]. **Added/Corp** Outaouais Tourist Association. **VFOAT** Tourisme Outaouais

# Travel and Tourism

**Bonjour!.** Vol. 1, No. 1 (Oct. 1988)-. Periodical. English (French). Tourisme Outaouais, 768 Boulevard, St Joseph Hull Quebec J8Y 4B8 Canada. **DD** 338.4/7917142204/06. *Continues* Tourisme Outaouais., 0712-6832.

US/1050-6152
**TOURISM'S TOP TWENTY.** [Tour. top twenty]. **Added/Corp** University of Colorado (Boulder Campus). Business Research Division. United States Travel Data Center. (1980)-. English. Four times a year. $50.00. US Travel Data Center, 1100 New York Avenue, Suite 450, Washington DC 20005. **Tel** (202)408-1832. **LC** G155.A1; T5928. **DD** 338.
 **Desc:** Compiled every four years by the Business Research Division of the University of Colorado at Boulder, this publication provides fast facts on travel and tourism in the areas of advertising, air travel, airlines, airports, automobile travel, boating, bus travel, cities/ports, countries, economics indicators, employment, hotels/motels, outdoor recreation, resorts, restaurants, sports states, theme parks travel destinations/origination, travel expenditures, receipts, water travel, and world tourism.

SZ
**TOURISMUS IM KANTON GRAUBUNDEN.** **Main/Corp** Switzerland. Eidgenossisches Statistisches Amt. **VFOAT** Tourisme dans le Canton des Grisons. Multiple languages (French and German). 75.00. Eidgenossisches Statistisches Amt, Hallwylstrasse 15, CH-3003 Bern Switzerland. **LC** G155.S8; S93A. **DD** 338.4/7/914947047.

SZ
**TOURISMUS IN DER SCHWEIZ IN DER HOTELLERIE UND DEN UBRIGEN BEHERBERGUNGSFORMEN.** See Hotels/Motels.

SZ
**TOURISMUS IN FREMDENORTEN UND STADTEN. TOURISME DANS QUELQUES CENTRES TOURISTIQUES ET VILLES.** *Title Change.* **Main/Corp** Switzerland. Eidgenossisches Statistisches Amt. **Added/Corp** Switzerland. Eidgenossisches Statistisches Amt. Tourism dans Quelques Centres Touristiques et Villes. **VFOAT** Tourisme dans Quelques Centres Touristiques et Villes. (197?)-(198?). French (German). Hallwylstrasse 15, CH-3003 Bern Switzerland. **LC** G155.S8; S93d. *Continued by* Tourismus in Fremdenverkehrsorten und Stadten.

SZ
**TOURISMUS IN FREMDENVERKEHRSORTEN UND STADTEN.** **Added/Corp** Switzerland. Bundesamt fur Statistik. **VFOAT** Tourisme dans Quelques Centres Touristiques et Villes. (1987)-. French (German). **LC** G155.S8; S93d. *Continues* Switzerland. EidgenEossisches Statistisches Amt. Tourismus in Fremdenorten und Stadten.

LE
**TOURIST & HOTEL GUIDE FOR LEBANON.** English. Librairie Orientale, Place de l'Etoile, BP 1986, Beirut Lebanon. **LC** DS80.A5; T68. **DD** 915.69/2/044.

US/0194-4894
**TOURIST ATTRACTIONS & PARKS.** See Recreation, Leisure.

BU
**TOURIST BULGARIA.** **Added/Corp** Balkanturist. (19??)-. English. mo. **(Subscription address:** Hemus Foreign Trade Organization, 6 Tzar Osvoboditel Boulevard, 1000 Sofia Bulgaria.) **LC** G155.B8; T68. **DD** 380.1/4591497704.

CN/0824-6114
**TOURIST COUNCIL NEWS.** (TOURIST COUNCIL NEWS / REGIONAL NIAGARA.). [Tour. Counc. news]. Vol. No. 1, Issue No. 1 (June 83)-. Periodical. English. qt. Free. Region Niagara Tourist Council, 2201 St. David's Road, PO Box 1042, Thorold Ontario L2V 4T7 Canada. **Tel** (416)685-1571. **DD** 381/.45917133804/05. **Circ:** 300.

UA
**TOURIST GUIDE BOOK.** **Main/Corp** Nadi Al-Sayyarat Wal-Al-Rihlat Al-Misri. 1973-. English. 10 Kasr E-Nil Street, Cairo UAR Egypt. **LC** DT45; .N33A. **DD** 916.2/04/5.

CN/0319-0439
**TOURIST GUIDE BOOK OF ONTARIO.** Began publication in 1921. Periodical. English. an. Free. Tourist Guide Book of Ontario, 1215 Ouellette Avenue, PO Box 580, Windsor Ontario N9A 6N3 Canada. **Tel** (519)255-1212, FAX (519)255-7379. **ED** M Lancaster. **DD** 917.13/04/4. **Ad Acc. Circ:** 150,000 (ctrl).
 **Desc:** A tourist publication on Ontario and surrounding border areas listing cities, towns, places to stay, dine and shop. Helpful in vacation planning.

CN/1180-0186
**TOURIST GUIDE, GREATER QUEBEC AREA.** [Tour. guide gt. Que. area]. **Added/Corp** Communaute Urbaine de Quebec (Quebec). Tourism and Convention Bureau. Quebec (Province). Ministere du Tourisme. 7th Ed. (1990/1991)-. English. Free. Communaute Urbaine de Quebec, Tourism and Convention Bureau, 60 D'Auteuil Street, Quebec Quebec G1R 4C4 Canada. **DD** 917.14/47044. *Continues* Tourist Guide, Quebec City Region., 0831-2788.

CN/1180-0313
**TOURIST GUIDE, LANAUDIERE.** [Tour. guide Lanaudiere]. **Added/Corp** Tourisme Lanaudiere. Quebec (Province). Ministere du Tourisme. (1990/1991 ed)-. English. Free. Tourisme Lanaudiere, PO Box 1210, Rawdon, Quebec J0K 1S0. **DD** 917.14/41044.

CN/0846-9717
**TOURIST RECEPTION CENTRE SURVEY.** [Tour. recept. cent. surv.]. English. Economic Development and Tourism, 1919 Saskatchewan Drive, Regina Saskatchewan S4P 3V7 Canada. **LC** G155.C3; T64. **DD** 380.1/45917127/043.

MW
**TOURIST REPORT - MALAWI. NATIONAL STATISTICAL OFFICE.** **Main/Corp** Malawi. National Statistical Office. Statistical Publication. English. National Statistical Office, PO Wards Strip NCO, Papua New Guinea. **Tel** 011 675 27182 271172, FAX 011 657 255057, telex FINANCE NE 22312. **LC** G155.M32; A3. **DD** 338.4/7/91689704405.

II
**TOURIST TRADE OF INDIA.** Periodical. English. A 3 Delisle Road, Byculla 27 Bombay India. **LC** G155.I5; T68. **DD** 338.4/7/9154045.

FR
**TOURISTIC ANALYSIS REVIEW.** *Ceased.* **Added/Corp** Universite de Droit, d'Economie et des Sciences d'Aix-Marseille. Centre des Hautes Eetudes Touristiques. No. 1 (1973)-(19??). Periodical. English. Four times a year. Centre des Hautes Etudes Touristiques, Immeuble Euroff, 38 Avenue Europe, 13090 Aix-en-Provence France. **Tel** 011 33 42 200973. **ED** Baretje Rene. **Bk Rev. Circ:** 250.
 **Desc:** International approach of tourism and outdoor recreation.

AT/0815-1318
**TOURISTICS.** **Added/Corp** Western Australian Tourism Commission. Research and Planning Division. (198?)-. Periodical. English. Three times a year (Jan., May, Sept.). $10.00. Western Australian Tourism Commission, 16 St George's Terrace, GPO Box X2261, Perth Western Australia 6001 Australia. **Tel** 011 09 220 1700, FAX 011 09 220 1702. **LC** G155.A75; T69. **DD** 380.1/45919410463/021. **Circ:** 300.

SZ
**TOURISTISCHE NACHFRAGE DER BUNDESDEUTSCHEN IN DER SCHWEIZ, DIE.** **Added/Corp** Switzerland. Bundesamt fur Statistik. **VFOAT** La Demande Touristique des Allemands de l'Ouest en Suisse; Demande Touristique des Allemands de l'Ouest en Suisse. (19??)-. French (German). Bundesamt fuer Statistik, Schwarztorstrasse 96, CH 3003 Bern Switzerland. **Tel** 031 3236011, FAX 031 3236061. **LC** G155.S8; T684.

US/0890-2852
**TOURS & RESORTS.** *Title Change.* [Tours resorts]. **VFOAT** Tours and Resorts; Tours & Resorts; Tours & Resorts Magazine. (198?)-(June/July 1993). Periodical. English. bm. Century Publishing Company, 990 Grove Street, Evanston IL 60201-4370. **Tel** (708)491-6440, (800)321-3333, FAX (708)491-0459. **ED** Robert Meyers and Ray Gudas. **DD** 910. **Ad Acc. Circ:** 250,000. available on microfiche; available on microfilm. *Continued by* Travelamerica, 1068-2554.
 **Desc:** Information on tours by land, air and sea all over the world.

US/0278-467X
**TOURS AND VISITS DIRECTORY.** [Tours visits dir.]. 2nd Ed.-. Directory. English. ir. $98.00. Gale Research Inc., 835 Penobscot Building, Detroit MI 48226. **Tel** (800)877-GALE, (313)961-2242, FAX (313)961-6083, telex TWX 810-221-7086. **LC** T49.5; .T67. **DD** 917.3/04927. *Continues* Behind the Scenes, 0270-3416.
 **Desc:** Over 2,500 entries describe free and low-cost tours available on-site from business, industry, and government.

CN/0847-9348
**TOURS ON MOTORCOACH.** [Tours motorcoach]. Vol. No. 1 (1989)-. Periodical. English. mo. $20.00 Canada and US; $40.00 other. Publicom Inc, 1055 Beaver Hall Hill/Suite 17, Montreal Quebec H2Z 1S5 Canada. **Tel** (514)874-0874, FAX (514)866-3839, telex 055-61866. **ED** John Stephenson. **DD** 338.4/7917104/05. **Bk Rev. Ad Acc. Circ:** 12,127 (ctrl).
 **Desc:** Travel destinations and motorcoach tour descriptions for group tour organizers.

FR/0150-7540
**TOUTES LES NOUVELLES DE L'HOTELLERIE ET DU TOURISME.** See Hotels/Motels.

CN/0823-8502
**TOWN & COUNTRY BED & BREAKFAST IN B.C., CANADA.** *Ceased.* [Town ctry. bed breakf. B.C. Can.]. 4th Ed. (1984)-(199?). English. sa. Town & Country Bed & Breakfast in British Columbia Canada, PO Box 46544 Station G, Vancouver British Columbia V6R 4G6 Canada. **Tel** (604)731-5942. **ED** Pauline Scoten and Helen Burich. **DD** 647./94711. **Circ:** 4,000. *Continues* Town & Country Bed & Breakfast in B.C., 0714-8062.
 **Desc:** Home accommodation guide listing homes in most areas of British Columbia, Canada.

US/0360-7534
**TRA DIGEST.** [TRA dig.]. **Main/Corp** Travel Research Associates. **VAT** Travel Research Associates Digest. V. 1- Summer/Fall 1975-. English. sa. $30.00. Travel Research Associates, 203 Middlesex Turnpike, Burlington MA 01803. **LC** G153; .T745A. **DD** 910/.202.

US
**TRADEMARK INFORMATION FOR TRAVELERS / U.S. CUSTOMS SERVICE.** Began with Apr. 1, 1977. English. Department of the Treasury US Customs Service, Fifteenth Street and Pennsylvania Avenue Northwest, Washington DC 20220. *Continues* Trademark Information.

US/1061-2343
**TRANSITIONS ABROAD.** See Education.

II
**TRANSPORT & TOURISM JOURNAL.** See Transportation.

BE/0041-1442
**TRANSPORT ET TOURISME.** [Transp. tour.]. (1965)-. Periodical. French. mo. **UDC** 656.13. *Continues* Transport par Route, 0773-6398.
 **Ind/Abst** Leis. Recreat. Tour. Abstr.

US/0197-3320
**TRANSPORTATION AND TRAVEL : OFFICIAL TABLE OF DISTANCES, FOREIGN TRAVEL.** [Transp. travel, Off. table distances, foreign travel]. **Main/Corp** United States. Dept. of the Army. English. **LC** UG633; .A3763 subser; G109. **DD** 358.4 S; 910.4/0287.

INT/0255-5506
**TRAVAIL DANS LE MONDE, LE.** [Trav. monde]. (1984)-. Monographic series. French. an. L20250. Bureau Internationale du Travail, Via Panisperna 28, 00184 Rome Italy. **Tel** 011 39 6 6784334. **UDC** 341.12: 331. **CODEN** NU051.

US/1049-6211
**TRAVEL 50 & BEYOND.** [Travel 50 beyond]. **VFOAT** Travel Fifty and Beyond; Travel Fifty & Beyond; Travel 50 and Beyond. (1990)-. Periodical. English. qt. $11.80 North America; (add $4.00 postage) other. Vacation Publications Inc, 1502 Augusta Drive, Suite 415, Houston TX 77057. **Tel** (713)974-6903, FAX (713)974-0445. **ED** R. Alan Fox and Mary Lu Abbott. **DD** 910. **Ad Acc. Circ:** 40,000.
 **Desc:** Covers travel tips and new vacation ideas for travelers age 50 and over.

US/0192-155X
**TRAVEL 800.** **VAT** Travel Eight Hundred. (1972)-. Periodical. English. sa. $36.00. Preferred Travel Publications, 47 Northam Avenue, Newbury Park CA 91320. **Tel** 800 847-3442 or, (805)498-8307. **ED** Julie Jackson. **Bk Rev. Circ:** 8,500 (ctrl).
 **Desc:** A reservation directory of tour operators, airlines, cruise lines, car rentals, railroads, government tourist offices and lodging accommodations worldwide.

CN/0836-7353
**TRAVEL A LA CARTE.** [Travel carte]. Vol. 13, No. 4 (Fall 1987)-. Periodical. English. Six times a year. 12.00Can$ Canada; 20.00Can$ others. Interpress Inc., 136 Walton Street, Port Hope Ontario L1A 1N5 Canada. **Tel** (905)885-7948. **ED** Heather Kerrigan. **DD** 910/.5. **Ad Acc. Circ:** 150,000 (ctrl). *Formed by the union of* Canada a la Carte, 0831-3512 *and* Touring & Travel, 0318-4390.
 **Ind/Abst** Can. Index (?-?).

UK/0041-1981
**TRAVEL AGENCY.** [Travel agency]. (1963)-. Periodical. English. mo. £60.00. Maclean Hunter Ltd. / UK, Chalk Lane Cockfosters Road, Barnet Herts EN4 0BU England. **Tel** 011 44 81 2423000, FAX 011 44 81 9759753, telex 299072. **DD** 910.2. **Ad Acc. Circ:** 11,310 (ctrl). *Continues* Travel Topics.
 **Desc:** News and destination reports for the UK travel agent.
 **Ind/Abst** Leis. Recreat. Tour. Abstr.

US/1053-9360
**TRAVEL AGENT.** [Travel agent]. (1990)-. Periodical. English. wk. Free to qualified travel agents;

$250.00 US; $350.00 other. Travel Agent, 801 2nd Avenue, 12th Floor, New York NY 10017. **Tel** (212)370-5050. **(Subscription address:** Travel Agent, PO Box 1456, Riverton NJ 08077.**)** **DD** 917. ***Continues*** *Travel Agent Magazine, 1041-0783.*
**Ind/Abst** Trade Ind. Index.

US/0194-620X
**TRAVEL AGENT INTERNACIONAL, EL.** Apr. 1979-. Periodical. Spanish. mo. Travel Agent Y American Traveler Inc., 2 West 46th Street, New York NY 10036.

US/8755-7738
**TRAVEL AGENTS' ANNUAL PRODUCTION, UNITED STATES ONLY.** (TRAVEL AGENTS' ANNUAL PRODUCTION, UNITED STATES ONLY / AIR TRAFFIC CONFERENCE OF AMERICA.). [Travel agents' annu. prod. U. S. only]. **Added/Corp** Air Traffic Conference of America. Publications Services. **VFOAT** T.C. Agency List; Travel Agents' Annual Production, US Only; ATC Agency List; Travel Agents' Annual Production, U.S. Only. (19??)-. English. Air Traffic Conference of America, 1709 New York Avenue NW, Washington DC 20006-5206. **LC** G155.U6; T678. **DD** 380.1/45910/02573.

US/1068-7416
**TRAVEL ALERT BULLETIN.** (TRAVEL ALERT BULLETIN. / NATIONWIDE INTELLIGENCE.). [Travel alert bull.]. (19??)-. Academic Scholarly Publication. English. sm. $95.00. Nationwide Intelligence, PO Box 1922, Saginaw WI 48605. **Tel** 800 333-4130, (517)752-6123, FAX (517)752-1605. **DD** 910. **CODEN** TALBEZ. Documents available from CASDDS.
**Desc:** Provides strategic information for intelligent travel decisions.
**Ind/Abst** Chem. Abstr.

US/0748-7398
**TRAVEL & LEARNING ABROAD.** [Travel learn. abroad]. **VFOAT** Travel and Learning Abroad. Vol. 1, No. 1 (July/Aug. 1984)-. Periodical. English. bm. $10.50 (individual), $16.00 (library). Raico Publishing Company, 67 Main Street, Brattleboro VT 05301. **DD** 370.

US/0041-2007
**TRAVEL & LEISURE.** [Travel leis.]. **VAT** Travel and Leisure. Vol. 1, (Feb./Mar. 1971)-. Periodical. English. mo. $32.00. American Express Publishing Company, 1120 Avenue of the Americas, New York NY 10036. **Tel** (212)382-5642. **(Subscription address:** CDS Agency Hard Copy, PO Box 4966, Des Moines IA 50340.**)** **ED** Pamela Fiori. **LC** G149; .T7572. **DD** 910/.5. **Ad Acc. Circ:** 925,000 (ctrl). available on microfilm and microfiche from University Microfilms International (UMI). Documents available from UMI Article Clearinghouse. ***Continues*** *Travel & Camera, 0049-4542.*
**Desc:** The how-to book of travel. Covers where to stay, eat, see and do. Regular columns include travel and health, travel and money and traveling photographer.
**Ind/Abst** Access (1975-); Gen. Period. Index (1992-); Mag. Index Plus (1992-); Mag. Search; Newsp. Period. Abstr. (1986-).

US/0895-2698
**TRAVEL & LEISURE'S WORLD TRAVEL OVERVIEW.** ***Ceased.*** (TRAVEL & LEISURE'S WORLD TRAVEL OVERVIEW : THE ANNUAL REVIEW OF THE TRAVEL INDUSTRY WORLDWIDE.). [Travel leis. world travel overv.]. **VFOAT** Travel and Leisure's World Travel Overview; World Travel Overview. Ceased with (1988/89). English. an. American Express Publishing Corporation, 1120 Avenue of the Americas, New York NY 10036. **LC** G155.A1; T64. **DD** 380.1/4591021.

UK/0269-3755
**TRAVEL & TOURISM ANALYST.** **Added/Corp** Economist Intelligence Unit (Great Britain). **VFOAT** Travel and Tourism Analyst. (19??)-. Periodical. English. bm. $708.75 (schools and educational libraries), $945.00 (other)°North America. The Economist Intelligence Unit, 40 Duke Street, London W1A 1DW England. **Tel** 011 44 71 8301000. **(Subscription address:** Economist Intelligence Unit / North America Subscriptions, 111 West 57th Street, New York NY 10019.**)** **LC** G155.A1; T65. **[CCC].**
**Desc:** A business information publication for the international travel and tourism industry containing reports and forecasts. Covers all markets and sectors.
**Ind/Abst** Leis. Recreat. Tour. Abstr.

SP/1014-7306
**TRAVEL AND TOURISM BAROMETER : TTB.** **Added/Corp** World Tourism Organization. **VFOAT** TTB. (May 1991)-. Periodical. English (French and Spanish). Four times a year. $300.00. World Tourism Organization / WTO, Calle Capitan Haya 42, E 28020 Madrid Spain. **Tel** 011 34 1 5710628, FAX 011 34 1 5713733, telex 42188 OMT-E. **(Subscription address:** UNIPUB, 4611 F Assembly Drive, Lanham MD 20706.**)** **LC** G155.A1; C87. **DD** 338.4/79105. ***Continues*** *Current Travel and Tourism Indicators.*

US/1070-8855
**TRAVEL & TOURISM EXECUTIVE REPORT.** [Travel tour. exec. rep.]. **Added/Corp** Association of Travel Marketing Executives (U.S.). **VFOAT** Travel and Tourism Executive Report. Vol. 7, No. 1 (Jan. 1987)-. Periodical. English. Ten times a year. $65.00 (one year), $110.00 (two year), $150.00 (three year). Leisure Industry / Recreation News, PO Box 43563, Washington DC 20010. **Tel** (202)232-7107, FAX (202)462-6021. **ED** Marj Jensen. **DD** 338. **Ad Acc. Circ:** 1,000 (ctrl). ***Continues*** *Travel & Tourism Executive Newsletter.*
**Desc:** Reports and trends on the travel marketing issues and "how to" articles.

US/1040-8142
**TRAVEL AND TOURISM INDEX, THE.** ***Suspended.*** [Travel tour. index]. **Added/Corp** Brigham Young University--Hawaii Campus. Business Division. **VFOAT** Travel & Tourism Index. (1984)-Suspended (1993). Periodical. English. qt. $40.00. Travel and Tourism Index, Box 1773, BYU Hawaii Campus, Laie HI 96762. **Tel** (808)293-5647, FAX (808)293-3645. **LC** Z6004.T6; T7; G155.A1. **DD** 016.3384/79105.

AT/0817-2935
**TRAVEL AUSTRALIA SYDNEY.** [Travel Aust.Syd.]. **VFOAT** Australian Tourism Magazine. (1986)-. Periodical. English. Eleven times a year. 55.00Aus$. Australian Tourism Ptd Ltd., GPO Box 7039, Sydney NSW 2001 Ausralia. **Tel** 011 61 2 264 5900, FAX 011 61 2 231 5559. **ED** Shamoli Dutt. **DD** 381.4591940463. **Bk Rev. Ad Acc, Adv Mgr:** I. Burgess. **Circ:** 7,000.
**Desc:** Quick and easy reading on travel.

US/1058-7098
**TRAVEL BOOKS WORLDWIDE.** [Travel books worldw.]. (May 1991)-. Periodical. English. Ten times a year. $36.00. Travel Books Worldwide, 2510 South Street, PO Box 162266, Sacremento CA 95816-2266. **Tel** (916)452-5200, FAX (916)452-5200. **ED** Peter Manston. **DD** 910. **Bk Rev,** (Qty: 180). **Circ:** 1,800.
**Desc:** Review and bibliography of travel guides and travel related titles including coffee table books, cookbooks, armchair travel, special interest travel, etc.

HK/1011-7768
**TRAVEL BUSINESS ANALYST ASIA ED.** [Travel bus. anal. Asia ed.]. (1988)-. Periodical. English. mo. $350.00. Travel Business Analyst, GPO Box 12761, Hong Kong Hong Kong. **Tel** 011 852 5 072310, FAX 011 852 5 074620, telex 62107. **ED** Murray Bailey. **UDC** 38. cum. index. **Bk Rev,** (Qty: 4). **Ad Acc.**
**Desc:** Travel business information, statistics and analysis for senior management in the travel industry and investors in the travel business.

HK/0256-419X
**TRAVEL BUSINESS ANALYST EUROPE ED.** [Travel bus. anal. Eur. ed.]. (1981)-. Periodical. English. mo (July-Aug. and Dec.-Jan. combined). $350.00. Travel Business Analyst, GPO Box 12761, Hong Kong Hong Kong. **Tel** 011 852 5 072310, FAX 011 852 5 074620, telex 62107. **ED** Nancy Cockerell. **UDC** 38. cum. index. **Bk Rev,** (Qty: 3). **Ad Acc.** ***Continues*** *Travel Business Analyst (UK ed.), 0255-8866.*
**Desc:** Travel business information, statistics, and analysis for senior management in the travel industry and investors in the travel business.

US/0886-6147
**TRAVEL BUSINESS MANAGER, THE.** ***Title Change.*** [Travel bus. manager]. (198?)-(19??). Periodical. English. sm. Sontag / Annis & Associates Inc., 51 Monroe Street Suite 1501, Rockville MD 20850. **Tel** (301)294-9404. **DD** 658. ***Merged into*** *Runzheimer Reports on Travel Management, 0730-8663.*

US/0884-0687
**TRAVEL BUSINESS REPORT.** ***Ceased.*** [Travel bus. rep.]. -?. Periodical. English. mo. Travel Business Report, PO Box 889 Midtown Station, New York NY 10018. **DD** 338. ***Continues*** *Travel Business.*

CN/0834-258X
**TRAVEL CHINA NEWSLETTER.** [Trav. China newsl.]. Vol. 1, No. 1 (Autumn 1986)-. Newsletter. English. mo. $67.00. Blendon Information Services, 126 Willowdale Avenue, Suite 1, Willowdale ONT M2N 442 Canada. **Tel** (416)223-5397, FAX (416)225-9297. **ED** Ruth Lor Malloy. **DD** 915.1/0458. **Bk Rev.**

UK
**TRAVEL CLUB.** English. Four times a year. £10.00 UK and Northern Ireland; $24.00 other. Morgan Grampian, 40 Beresford Street Woolwich, London SE18 6BQ England. **Tel** 011 44 81 855 7777, FAX 011 44 81 855 5548, telex 896238.

US/1040-0001
**TRAVEL COLLECTOR.** ***Ceased.*** **See** Hobbies.

US/1053-721X
**TRAVEL CONSULTANTS DIRECTORY, THE.** [Travel consult. dir.]. (1991)-. Directory. English. $29.95. The Balboa Group, 1559 East Pacific Coast Highway, Suite 243, Hermosa Beach CA 90254. **DD** 910.

CN/1182-9699
**TRAVEL COURIER (TORONTO).** (TRAVEL COURIER.). [Travel cour.]. **VFOAT** Travel Courier East. Vol. 24, No. 23 (Nov. 9, 1989)-. Periodical. English. Fifty times a year (Thurs.). 42.80Can$ Canada; 80.00Can$ US; 95.00Can$ others. Baxter Publishing Company, 310 Dupont Street, Toronto Ontario M5R 1V9 Canada. **Tel** (416)968-7252, FAX (416)968-2377. **DD** 338.4/7917104/05. **Ad Acc, Adv Mgr:** Celyne Benitah / Robin Catto. **Circ:** 7,000. available on microfilm and microfiche from University Microfilms International (UMI). ***Continues*** *Canadian Travel Courier, 0008-5219;* ***Absorbed*** *On Target Weekly, 0822-5729.*
**Desc:** Provides concise, easy-to-read articles designed for immediate reading. Includes current national trade news and destination reports as well as other regular editorial features.

US/0272-569X
**TRAVEL EXPENSE MANAGEMENT.** [Travel expense manage.]. **Added/Corp** Management Alternatives. **VFOAT** Travel Expense Management Digest. (19??)-. Periodical. English. Eight times a year. $397.00 (one year), $715.00 (two years), $998.00 (three years). Health Resources Publishing, 3100 Highway 138, Wall Township NJ 07719-1442. **Tel** (908)681-1133, FAX (908)681-0490. **DD** 658. **[CCC].**
**Desc:** Digest of up-to-the-minute developments in the important field of travel and expense cost control.

US/0277-4097
**TRAVEL GUIDE FLORIDA.** Vol. 1, No. 1-. English. $2.50. Traveler Publications, 1731 NW 6th Street, Suite 24, Box 1284, Gainesville FL 32601. **LC** G1316.E63; T7. **DD** 917.59/0463.

US/0732-2313
**TRAVEL GUIDE, MEXICO.** [Travel guide, Mex.]. **VFOAT** Travel Guide to Mexico. English. an. American Automobile Association, 1000 AAA Drive, Heathrow FL 32746. **Tel** (407)444-7000. **LC** F1209; .T716. **DD** 917.2/0433.

US/0732-0434
**TRAVEL GUIDE, MEXICO AND CENTRAL AMERICA.** [Travel guide, Mex. Cent. Am.]. **VFOAT** Travel Guide to Mexico and Central America. English. an. American Automobile Association, 1000 AAA Drive, Heathrow FL 32746. **Tel** (407)444-7000. **LC** F1209; .T717. **DD** 917.2/04833.

CN/0711-4710
**TRAVEL GUIDE TO MEXICO, CENTRAL AMERICA AND SOUTH AMERICA, A.** [Travel guide Mex., Cent. Am. South Am.]. **VFOAT** Kosoy Travel Guide to Mexico, Central America and South America. English. ir. $6.95 each volume. Kosoy Travel Guides, 40 Shallmar Boulevard, Toronto Ontario M6C 2J9 Canada. **DD** 918/.043.

US
**TRAVEL HANDBOOK.** **VFOAT** Travel. Government Publication. English. US Department of Housing and Urban Development, 451 Seventh Street SW, Washington DC 20401. **Tel** (202)708-0980, FAX (202)708-0299.

US/0199-025X
**TRAVEL HOLIDAY.** [Travel holiday]. **VFOAT** Travel-Holiday. Vol. 151, No. 2 (Feb. 1979)-. Periodical. English. Ten times a year. $13.97 (surface mail). R D Publications, 28 West 23rd Street, New York NY 10010. **Tel** (800)365-5005, (212)366-8630. **(Subscription address:** CDS / SIFD Agency Control, 1901 Bell Avenue, Des Moines IA 50315.**)** **LC** G149; .T78. **DD** 910.4/05. Index available. cum. index. **Bk Rev. Ad Acc. Circ:** 850. available on microfilm and microfiche from University Microfilms International (UMI). Documents available from UMI Article Clearinghouse, Magazine Collection. ***Continues*** *Travel, Incorporating Holiday, 0161-7184.*
**Desc:** Expert advice on vacation planning from a weekend get-away to a grand tour; tips on finding deals on airfare, cruises, hotels and car rentals; local cuisine and customs; staying healthy away from home; plus color photos of enchanting destinations and travel essays from reowned authors.
**Ind/Abst** Acad. Abstr. Full Text Elite (Jan. 1989-); Acad. Abstr. (Jan. 1989-); Acad. Ind. [Computer File] (1986-1988); Acad. Search (Jan. 1989-); Book Rev. Index; Expand. Acad. Index (1984-1988); Gen. Period. Index (1985-); Mag. Artic. Summar. Elite (Jan. 1989-); Mag. Artic. Summar. Select (Jan. 1989-); Mag. Artic. Summar. CD-ROM (Jan. 1989-); Mag. Index Plus (1989-); Mag. Index Sel. Microfiche (1986-) [Full Txt.]; Mag. Index. Sel. (1986-); Mag. Search; Newsp. Period. Abstr. (1988-); Read. Guide Abstr. Select Ed.; Read. Guide Period. Lit.; Resource/One Ondisc (1988-); Mag. Index (Feb. 1979-); TOM Gen. Index (1985-) [Full Txt.].

US/0085-7351
**TRAVEL IDEAS.** (1971)-. English. an. Available on newsstand only. Meredith Corporation, Locust at 17th, Des Moines IA 50309. **Tel** (515)284-3000. **LC** GV1024; .B48. **DD** 917/.04/9205. ***Continues*** *Better Homes and Gardens Travel Ideas.*

US
**TRAVEL IN VIRGINIA.** Began with 1975 vol. English. an. Virginia State Travel Service, 6 Nort 6th Street, Richmond VA 23219. **LC** G155.U6; T684. **DD** 380.1/45917550443. ***Continues*** *Economic Analysis of Travel in Virginia.*

US/8756-8799
**TRAVEL INDUSTRY INDICATORS.** [Travel ind. indic.]. (198?)-. Periodical. English. Twelve times a year (Nov./Dec. issue combined). $95.00. Travel Industry Indicators, PO Box 6627, Surfside FL 33154. **Tel** (305)868-3818, FAX (305)868-1670, telex 220883. **ED** James V. Cammisa Jr. **DD** 330.
**Desc:** Provides a report and analysis of U.S. domestic and international travel activity for tourism destinations, airlines, hotels, cruise lines and ground transport operators. Includes 12 statistical indicators, forecasts, and interpretation of factors, trends, and emerging developments influencing both business and pleasure travel demand.

UK/0959-6186
**TRAVEL INDUSTRY MONITOR.**
**Added/Corp** Economist Intelligence Unit (Great Britain). (Apr. 1990)-. Periodical. English. mo. $446.25 (schools and educational libraries), $595.00 (other) North America. The Economist Intelligence Unit, 40 Duke Street, London W1A 1DW England. **Tel** 011 44 71 8301000. **(Subscription address:** Economist Intelligence Unit / North America Subscriptions, 111 West 57th Street, New York NY 10019.**)** **LC** G155.A1; T72.

US/0082-6146
**TRAVEL INDUSTRY PERSONNEL DIRECTORY.** ***Title Change.*** [Travel ind. pers. dir.]. **Added/Corp** Fairchild Publications. **VFOAT** Fairchild's ... Travel Industry Personnel Directory. (1954)-(1992). Directory. English. an. Fairchild Publications Inc, 7 West 34th Street, 4th Floor, New York NY 10001. **Tel** (212)630-4230. **ED** Marsheela Evans. **LC** G155.A1; T655. **DD** 910.58. **Ad Acc. Circ:** 9,000. ***Continues*** *Travel Agent. Personnel Directory.* ***Continued by*** *Fairchild's Travel Industry Personnel Directory.*
**Desc:** Provides contact information covering the entire industry's services. There are complete lists of: sales and executive personnel of domestic and regional airlines, shiplines, railroads, motorcoach and car rental companies and tour operators; U.S. and Canadian hotel representatives and names of domestic and international hotels that they handle.

US/0738-9515
**TRAVEL INDUSTRY WORLD YEARBOOK.** [Travel ind. world yearb.]. **VFOAT** Big Picture. Vol. 27 (1983)-. English. an (Oct.). $82.00. Child & Waters, 516 5th Avenue, Rye NY 10580. **Tel** (914)921-0988. **ED** Somerset R. Waters. **LC** G155.A1; B54. **DD** 380.1/459104. Index available. ***Continues*** *The Big Picture (New York, N.Y.), 0895-4763.*
**Desc:** Report of worlwide travel trends and future prospects. Contains travel marketing, economic, statistical, and political information with comments as to effect on U.S. and international travel. Index locates travel information from 312 cities, states and countries.
**Ind/Abst** Stat. Ref. Index.

JA
**TRAVEL JOURNAL.** Japanese. wk (50 issues). ¥71000.00 Noth & Central America; ¥61000.00 Asia & Oceania; ¥28000.00 Japan; ¥81000.00 other. Travel Journal Inc, Izumiya 3-Chome Kojimachi, Chiyoda-ku Tokyo 102 Japan. **Tel** 011 81 3 3264 2091.

JA
**TRAVEL JOURNAL INTERNATIONAL: TJI.** English. sm (24 issues). ¥53000.00 North America; ¥53500.00 Europe; ¥50000.00 Southeast Asia; ¥47000.00 Japan. Travel Journal Inc, Izumiya 3-Chome Kojimachi, Chiyoda-ku Tokyo 102 Japan. **Tel** 011 81 3 3264 2091.

BE/0772-0033
**TRAVEL JOURNALIST, THE.** (1982)-. Periodical. English. qt. **UDC** 380.81.
**Ind/Abst** Leis. Recreat. Tour. Abstr.

US/1041-5203
**TRAVEL LEISURE & ENTERTAINMENT NEWS MEDIA.** [Guide travel leis. entertain. news media]. **VFOAT** Travel, Leisure, and Entertainment News Media. English. $99.00 (guide), $159.00 (disk), $199.00 (combination). Larriston Communications, PO Box 20229, New York NY 10025. **Tel** (212)864-0150. **LC** P88.8; .G83. **DD** 001.51/02573. Index available. available on diskette.
**Desc:** Lists specialized contacts in travel, leisure and entertainment fields at major newspapers, magazines, TV shows and radio.

CN/0713-2840
**TRAVEL-LOG.** (TRAVEL-LOG / TRAVEL, TOURISM AND RECREATION SECTION, EDUCATION, SCIENCE AND CULTURE DIVISION.). [Travel-log]. **Added/Corp** Statistics Canada. Travel, Tourism and Recreation Section. Statistics Canada. **VFOAT** Info-Voyages. Vol. 1, No. 1, (1982)-. Periodical. English (French). qt. 40.00Can$ Canada; $48.00 US; $56.00 other. Statistics Canada, Publications Sales & Services, Main Building Room 1710, Ottawa Ontario K1A 0T6 Canada. **Tel** (613)951-5078, (800)267-6677, FAX (613)951-1584, telex 053-3585. **DD** 381/.45917104/00212.
**Desc:** Presents a diverse range of tourism topics in an easy-to-read and attractive format drawing together the latest data from several tourism-related surveys conducted by Statistics Canada.

US
**TRAVEL MANAGEMENT DAILY.** (19??)-. English. da (312 per year). $705.00 US, Canada and Caribbean (fax service); $625.00 other (mail service). Official Airline Guides, 2000 Clearwater Drive, Oak Brook IL 60521. **Tel** (800)323-3537. available via fax.

US
**TRAVEL MANAGEMENT NEWSLETTER.** (19??)-. English. sw (104 per year). $370.00. Official Airline Guides, 2000 Clearwater Drive, Oak Brook IL 60521. **Tel** (800)323-3537. available via fax.

US
**TRAVEL MARKET REPORT : FULL-YEAR RESULTS FROM THE NATIONAL TRAVEL SURVEY.** **Added/Corp** United States Travel Data Center. (1990)-. English. an (Summer). $165.00. US Travel Data Center, 1100 New York Avenue, Suite 450, Washington DC 20005. **Tel** (202)408-1832. **LC** G155.U6; T87. ***Formed by the union of*** *Travel Executive Briefing (Annual), 1044-9396* ***and*** *Travel Market Close-Up (Annual), 1044-9388.*
**Desc:** This annual report contains an executive briefing summarizing the overall trends and events affecting the domestic travel industry along with details for the complete calendar year. Includes analysis of tourism conditions by region, transportation mode, trip distance and duration, purpose of trip, types of lodging used, income, age and other demographics, use of rental car, package tour and travel agent. Full-year travel statistics are compiled from the National Travel Survey interviewing 1,500 U.S. adults each month to monitor the volume and characteristics of travel by U.S. residents.

US/0737-2620
**TRAVEL MARKET REPORT : NATIONAL TRAVEL SURVEY TABULATIONS AND ANALYSIS.** **Added/Corp** United States Travel Data Center. **VFOAT** National Travel Survey Tabulations and Analysis. (1989/1990)-. Periodical. English. qt. US Travel Data Center, 1100 New York Avenue, Suite 450, Washington DC 20005. **Tel** (202)408-1832. **LC** G155.U6; T74. ***Formed by the union of*** *Travel Executive Briefing (Quarterly), 0737-2620* ***and*** *Travel Market Close-Up, National Travel Survey Tabulations.*
**Ind/Abst** Stat. Ref. Index.

US/0275-3545
**TRAVEL MARKETING AND AGENCY MANAGEMENT GUIDELINES.** (19??)-. Periodical. English. bm. $35.00 (one year), $60.00 (two years), $85.00 (three years). RKS Marketing, Inc., 19300 Rinaldi Street, PO Box 7985, Northridge CA 91327. **Tel** (818)886-7940. **ED** Ronald Silver and Mark Silver. **Bk Rev**, (Qty: 3). **Circ:** 350.
**Desc:** Concise, practical, legal management and marketing articles in an eight page advice letter for travel agencies.

US/0145-7810
**TRAVEL MASTER.** **See** Hotels/Motels.

UK/0267-3606
**TRAVEL MEDICINE INTERNATIONAL.**
**See** Medical Science and Technology.

●US/1048-5139
**TRAVEL MEXICO EVENTS.** [Travel Mex. events]. **VFOAT** Mexico Events. Vol. 1, No. 1 (Winter 1992/1993)-. Periodical. English. bm (6 issues). $11.00. Travel Mexico Magazine Group, 5838 Edison Place, Suite 100, Carlsbad CA 92009. **Tel** (619)929-0707. **(Subscription address:** Kable Publishers Aide, 308 East Hitt Street, Subscription Department, Mt. Morris IL 61054-1473.**)** **DD** 917.

●US/1048-5163
**TRAVEL MEXICO MAGAZINE.** **VFOAT** Travel Mexico; Mexico Travel. (1994)-. Periodical. English. bm. $2.50 (single issue). American International Hispanic Media, 1219 Palo Verde, Carson City NV 89701.

●US/1048-5155
**TRAVEL MEXICO UPDATE.** **VFOAT** Mexico Update. (1991)-. Periodical. English. qt. Free. American International Hispanic Media, 1219 Palo Verde, Carson City NV 89701.

●US/1069-286X
**TRAVEL NEWS AMERICAS.** (TRAVEL NEWS AMERICAS / PATA.). [Travel news Am.]. **Added/Corp** Pacific Asia Travel Association. **VFOAT** PATA Travel News Americas. **VAT** Pacific Asia Travel Association Travel News Americas. Vol. 1, No. 1 (Mar./Apr. 1993)-. Periodical. English. mo. PATA / Pacific Asia Travel Association, Telesis Tower, Suite 1750, 1 Montgomery Street, San Francisco CA 94104. **Tel** (415)986-4646, FAX (415)986-3458. **DD** 381. ***Continues*** *PATA Travel News, 0838-9772.*

HK
**TRAVEL NEWS ASIA.** English. bw. 156.00HK$; $20.00 airmail Asia; $30.00 airmail other. Far East Trade Press Ltd, BL C 10 F Seaview E, 2 8 Watson, North Point Hong Kong. **Tel** 011 852 5 5668381. **ED** Mike Sullivan. **Ad Acc, Adv Mgr:** Sue Dyer. **Circ:** 17,000 (ctrl).

US/0147-1422
**TRAVEL NORTH AMERICA.** V. 1- Fall 1973-. Periodical. English. qt. $12.00. Travel North America, One Park Avenue, New York NY 10016. **Tel** (212)206-8900, FAX (212)645-2459, telex 236735 GOPUB UR. **LC** G155.N58; T73. **DD** 338.4/7/9170453.

US/0898-0055
**TRAVEL PREVIEW.** [Travel preview]. Vol. 1, No. 1 (Summer 1988)-. Periodical. English. qt. $5.00 US; $10.00 Canada. Travel News Bureau, 1501 East Chapman Avenue, Suite 365, Fullerton CA 92631. **Tel** (714)870-1977. **ED** Richard S Calhoun. **DD** 910. **Ad Acc. Circ:** 100,000 (ctrl).
**Desc:** Designed to help travelers find information on destinations, attractions, accommodations and more. Contains information on more than 100 different destinations, 50 attractions, and 200 lodgings.

US/0744-6233
**TRAVEL PRINTOUT.** **Added/Corp** United States Travel Data Center. (1972)-. Periodical. English. mo. $75.00 (US); $80.00 (Canada and Mexico); $85.00 (other). US Travel Data Center, 1100 New York Avenue, Suite 450, Washington DC 20005. **Tel** (202)408-1832. **ED** Ida Simmons. **Circ:** 2,000.
**Desc:** A newsletter reporting results of research on travel by Americans, the cost of travel, and the level of travel activity in the US.

US/1043-6138
**TRAVEL PUBLISHING NEWS.** ***Ceased.*** [Trav. publ. news]. Vol. 1, No. 1, Spring (1989)-Ceased with Vol 3. Periodical. English. qt. Winterbourne Press, 2015 17th Avenue, San Francisco CA 94116. **Tel** (415)731-8239. **DD** 910. **Bk Rev. Circ:** 300.
**Desc:** Reviews travel books; lists topics of upcoming travel articles, reviews travel magazines.

US/1053-1998
**TRAVEL REVIEW, THE.** ***Ceased.*** [Travel rev.]. Premier Issue (1990)-?. Periodical. English. bm. Travel Review, PO Box 414, Glen Echo MD 20812. **LC** WMLC 90/0851. **DD** 910.
**Desc:** Provides information on where to stay and what to do and also how much it costs. This publication lists something here for every energy level, and every type of traveler.

CN/0822-9228
**TRAVEL SCOOP.** [Travel scoop]. Vol. 12 (Jan. 1983)-. Periodical. English. Ten times a year (Feb/Mar. and July/Aug. issues combined). $39.00 (one year); $69.00 (two years). Travel Scoop, 1110 Yonge Street, Suite 200, Toronto Ontario M4W 2L6 Canada. **Tel** (416)926-0111, FAX (416)926-0222. **ED** Ann Wallace. **DD** 910/.5. Index Bound in First Issue (Dec.). cum. index. **Bk Rev**, (Qty: 20-30). **Circ:** 7,000.
**Desc:** A consumer newsletter for travelers.

US/0741-5826
**TRAVEL SMART.** (1976)-. Periodical. English. mo. $44.00. Communications House, 40 Beechdale Road, Dobbs Ferry NY 10522. **Tel** (914)693-8300, (800)327-3633. **ED** H J Teison. Index available. **Bk Rev. Circ:** 10,000. ***Absorbed*** *Joy of Travel, 0277-7738.*
**Desc:** 12 page monthly newsletter that tells how to travel better for less. "Most up-to-date guidance available. N.Y. Times; "Pulls No Punches" - Newsweek; "Subscribers Don't Move Lips When They Read" - Boston Globe; "Library Patrons Look Forward To It."

US/0741-5818
**TRAVEL SMART FOR BUSINESS.** ***Title Change.*** (19??)-(19??). Periodical. English. Twelve times a year. Communications House, 40 Beechdale Road, Dobbs Ferry NY 10522. **Tel** (914)693-8300, (800)327-3633. **ED** Herbert J. Teisen , Deborah Gaines, and Lea Lane. ***Merged into*** *Runzheimer Reports on Travel Management, 0730-8663.*
**Desc:** Provides information for travelers. Covers steps of the trip from air travel, hotel accommodations, and restaurants and night clubs.

US/1055-0488
**TRAVEL SMARTER.** [Travel smarter]. Vol. 1, No. 1 (Mar. 1991)-. Periodical. English. mo. $195.00 US; $225.00 Canada. Lowell Communications, 88 Bleecker Street, New York NY 10012. **DD** 910.

US/0895-4135
**TRAVEL TIDINGS.** [Travel tidings]. (1984)-. Periodical. English. mo. $15.00 US; $25.00 Canada& Mexico. Travel News Bureau, 1501 East Chapman Avenue, Suite 365, Fullerton CA 92631. **Tel** (714)870-1977. **ED** Richard S. Calhoun. **DD** 910. **Bk Rev. Ad Acc. Circ:** 5,000 (ctrl).
**Desc:** Listing of unknown and little traveled destinations, attractions, accommodations, etc.

RU/0320-0167
**TRAVEL TO THE USSR.** **VAT** Travel to the Union of Soviet Socialist Republics. (1973)-. Periodical. English (French, German and Russian). bm. $29.00. **(Subscription address:** Victor Kamkin, 4956 Boiling Brook Parkway, Rockville MD 20852.) **ED** V. Chernov. **LC** DK29; .T72. **Ad Acc. Circ:** 200,000 (ctrl). ***Continues*** *Travel to the Soviet Union.*
**Desc:** Acquaints the reader with the Soviet Union's tourist centers and sights, important cultural and sports events, and diversified and attractive national scenery. Illustrated.

UK
**TRAVEL TRADE DIRECTORY.** ***Title Change.*** (1982)-(199?). English. an. Morgan Grampian, 40 Beresford Street Woolwich, London SE18 6BQ England. **Tel** 011 44 81 855 7777, FAX 011 44 81 855 5548, telex 896238. **ED** I. C. Laurie. **LC** G155.G7; U64. **DD** 380.1/459104/02541. **Ad Acc. Circ:** 5,500. ***Continues*** *United Kingdom & Ireland Travel Trade Directory.* ***Continued by*** *Travel Trade Gazette Directory.*
**Desc:** A complete single-volume guide to the travel trade.

●UK
**TRAVEL TRADE GAZETTE DIRECTORY.** **VFOAT** TTG Directory. (Apr. 1992)-. English. Twice a year. £69.50. Benn Business Information Service Ltd, Riverbank House, Angel Lane, Tonbridge Kent TN9 1SE England. **Tel** 011 44 732 362666, FAX 011 44 732 770483, telex 95454 BBIS. **LC** G155.G7; U64. **DD** 380.1/459104/02541. ***Continues*** *Travel Trade Directory.*

US/0041-2066
**TRAVEL TRADE (NEW YORK, N.Y.).** (TRAVEL TRADE; THE BUSINESS PAPER OF THE TRAVEL INDUSTRY.). [Travel trade]. Vol. 1 (July 1929)-. Periodical. English. Fifty-two times a year. $10.00 US, $25.00 others (industry); $75.00 US, $90.00 others (non-industry). Travel Trade Publications, 15 West 44th Street, New York NY 10036. **Tel** (212)730-6600. **DD** 338.

US
**TRAVEL TRENDS IN THE UNITED STATES AND CANADA.** **Added/Corp** Travel Research Association. University of Colorado, Boulder. Business Research Division. (1969)-. English. ir. $45.00 (latest edition). Business Research Division, Campus Box 420, University of Colorado at Boulder, Boulder CO 80309-0420. **Tel** (303)492-8227, FAX (303)492-3620. **ED** C. R. Goeldner. **Bk Rev. Ad Acc. Circ:** 500 (ctrl).
**Desc:** Statistics on US and Canada on visits to recreation areas, number of tourists, tourist expenditures, length of stay, economic impact of tourism and mode of transportation.

US/0041-2082
**TRAVEL WEEKLY.** [Travel wkly.]. (19??)-. Periodical. English. sw (104 per year). Price varies per location. Reed Travel Group / New Jersey, 500 Plaza Drive, Secaucus NJ 07096. **Tel** (201)902-2000, (800)360-0015, FAX (201)319-1628. **LC** G155.A1; T67. **DD** 380.1/459105. available on microfilm and microfiche from University Microfilms International (UMI); available on an online database (file 648/Full-Text) from DIALOG; and NEXIS. ***Continues*** *Travel Items and Courier Weekly.*
**Desc:** National newspaper of the travel industry. Latest news, insights, trends and forecasts.
**Ind/Abst** Bus. Index (1985-); Gen. BusinessFile (1985-); Gen. Period. Index (1985-); INFO-SOUTH Abstr.; Infobank (1979-); Mag. Search; Mark. Advert. Ref. Serv.; Trade Ind. ASAP [Full Txt.]; Trade Ind. Index (1981-) [Full Txt.].

US/0739-5698
**TRAVEL WEEKLY'S WORLD TRAVEL DIRECTORY.** ***Ceased.*** [Travel wkly. World travel dir.]. **VFOAT** World Travel Directory. (1978)-(19??). Directory. English. an. Reed Travel Group / New Jersey, 500 Plaza Drive, Secaucus NJ 07096. **Tel** (201)902-2000, (800)360-0015, FAX (201)319-1628. **LC** G154; .W64. **DD** 380.1/4591025. ***Continues*** *World Travel Directory.*
**Desc:** Names, addresses, and complete company profiles of 72,000 travel agencies worldwide.

US/0041-2104
**TRAVELAGE EAST.** [TravelAge East]. **VFOAT** TravelAge East Incorporating TravelAge SouthEast. **VAT** Travel Age East. (1967)-. Periodical. English. Fifty-one times per year. $63.00 US; $92.00 Canada; $85.50 Mexico; $108.00 (surface mail) other. Cahners Publishing Company, 249 West 17th Street, New York NY 10011. **Tel** (212)645-0067, FAX (212)242-6987. **(Subscription address:** Cahners Publishing Company / Colorado, Paid Subscription Service Center, PO Box 7610, Highlands Ranch CO 80126-7610.) **ED** Martin Deutsch. **DD** 910. ***Absorbed*** *TravelAge SouthEast, 0744-1592.*
**Desc:** In-depth regional news presented in each issue includes a weekly bulletin of late breaking stories, the latest word on family trip news and a schedule of upcoming local industry events.

US/0744-1606
**TRAVELAGE MIDAMERICA.** **VFOAT** Travel Age Mid America. (19??)-. Periodical. English. Fifty-one times per year. $63.00 US; $92.00 Canada; $85.50 Mexico; $108.00 (surface mail) other. Cahners Publishing Company, 249 West 17th Street, New York NY 10011. **Tel** (212)645-0067, FAX (212)242-6987. **(Subscription address:** Cahners Publishing Company / Colorado, Paid Subscription Service Center, PO Box 7610, Highlands Ranch CO 80126-7610.) **DD** 910.
**Desc:** In-depth regional news presented in each issue includes a weekly bulletin of late breaking stories, the latest word on family trip news and a schedule of upcoming local industry events.

US/0041-1973
**TRAVELAGE WEST.** **VFOAT** Travel Age West. **VAT** Travel Age West. (1969)-. Periodical. English. Fifty-one times per year. $63.00 US; $92.00 Canada; $85.50 Mexico; $108.00 (surface mail) other. Cahners Publishing Company, 249 West 17th Street, New York NY 10011. **Tel** (212)645-0067, FAX (212)242-6987. **(Subscription address:** Cahners Publishing Company / Colorado, Paid Subscription Service Center, PO Box 7610, Highlands Ranch CO 80126-7610.) **ED** Robert Carlsen. **Ad Acc. Circ:** 34,000.
**Desc:** In-depth regional news presented in each issue includes a weekly bulletin of late breaking stories, the latest word on family trip news and a schedule of upcoming local industry events.

●US/1068-2554
**TRAVELAMERICA (EVANSTON, ILL.).** (TRAVELAMERICA.). [Travelamerica]. **VFOAT** Travel America; Travel America Magazine. Vol. 8, No. 6 (July 1993)-. Periodical. English. bm (6 issues). $22.00 US; $30.00 other. Century Publishing Company, 990 Grove Street, Evanston IL 60201-4370. **Tel** (708)491-6440, (800)321-3333, FAX (708)491-0459. **(Subscription address:** Kable Publishers Aide, 308 East Hitt Street, Subscriptions Department, Mt. Morris, IL 61054) **DD** 917. ***Continues*** *Tours & Resorts, 0890-2852.*
**Desc:** The U.S. vacation magazine.

US/0363-1796
**TRAVELCADE MAGAZINE.** (19??)-. Periodical. English. mo. $9.00. Travelcade Publications Inc, Box 58 Germantown Pike, Lafayette Hill PA 19444. **LC** G149; .T843. **DD** 910/.5.

US/0161-8075
**TRAVELER'S ALMANAC.** 2nd Ed. (1976)-. English. an. B Muster, 6900 Santa Monica Boulevard, Los Angeles CA 90038. **LC** G153.4; .T73. **DD** 910/.202. ***Continues*** *World Traveler's Almanac, 0161-8083.*

US/0146-5988
**TRAVELER'S TOLL-FREE TELEPHONE DIRECTORY.** **VAT** Traveler's Toll Free Telephone Directory. Directory. English. $2.25. Landmark Publishers, Box 3287, Burlington VT 05401. **LC** TX907; .T826. **DD** 647/.9473.

CN/0228-5916
**TRAVELIFE.** [Travelife]. Periodical. English. ir. $1.25 each number. Travelife Publications Ltd, 12th Floor/797 Don Mills Road Canada. **DD** 910/.5.

US/1051-9335
**TRAVELIN' (EUGENE, OR.).** (TRAVELIN' : EXPLORING BACKROADS AND BYWAYS OF THE WEST.). **VFOAT** Travelin' Magazine. Vol. 1, No. 1 (May/June 1990)-. Periodical. English. bm (6 issues). $14.95 (one year), $24.95 (two year) US; $17.95 (one year), $27.95 (two year) Canada; $20.95 (one year), $30.995 (two year) other. Travelin, PO Box 23005, Eugene OR 97402. **Tel** (503)485-8533. **DD** 917.

US/1052-1615
**TRAVELIN TALK NEWSLETTER, THE.** [Travel. talk newsl.]. (Spring 1989)-. Newsletter. English. qt (June, Sept., Dec., March). $25.00 (libraries and institutions), $15.00 (individuals). Travelin Talk, c/o Rick Crowder, PO Box 3534, Clarksville TN 37043. **Tel** (615)552-6670, FAX (615)552-1182. **ED** Rick Crowder. **DD** 362. **Bk Rev**, (Qty: 4). **Pr Rev. Circ:** 2,000 (ctrl). available on audiocassette; available in large print.
**Desc:** Update of the Travelin' Talk Network providing assistance to travelers with disabilities, resources, tips, news, and features.

US/0899-2169
**TRAVELING HEALTHY NEWSLETTER.** [Travel. heal. newsl.]. Vol. 1, No. 1 (July/Aug. 1988)-. Newsletter. English. bm. $32.00 (one year), $60.00 (two year) US; $38.00 (one year), $63.00 (two year) other. Traveling Healthy, 108-48 70th Road, Forest Hills NY 11375. **Tel** (718)263-2072. **ED** Karl Neumann. **DD** 613. cum. index.

US
**TRAVELLER MAGAZINE.** English. sa (Winter & Summer). $18.00. Dialogue Diaspora, 2101 S Street Northwest, Washington DC 20008. **Tel** (202)462-1779, (800)998-0864. **(Subscription address:** American Visions, PO Box 37049, Washington, DC 20013; Telephone (202)462-1779)

US/1045-5841
**TRAVELLERS AGENDA.** (TRAVELLERS AGENDA : NATIONAL CALENDAR OF THE PERFORMING ARTS.). [Travel. agenda]. Vol. 1, No. 1 (July 1989)-. Periodical. English. qt. $110.00. Travellers Resource Clearinghouse, PO Box 13346, Tucson AZ 85732. **LC** PN2000; .T85. **DD** 791/.0973/05.

UK
**TRAVELLER'S GUIDE TO THE MIDDLE EAST.** 1st Ed. (1978)-. Periodical. English. an. $19.95. IC Publications Ltd., 7 Coldbath Square, London EC1R 4LQ England. **Tel** 011 44 71 713-7711, FAX 011 44 71 713-7898, telex 8811757. **ED** John Seekings. **LC** DS43; .T68. **DD** 915.6/044/05. **Bk Rev. Ad Acc. Circ:** 6,810 (ctrl).

HK/0252-9629
**TRAVELNEWS ASIA.** (1975)-. Periodical. English. bw. $50.00 Asia; $60.00 other. Far East Trade Press Ltd, BL C 10 F Seaview E, 2 8 Watson, North Point Hong Kong. **Tel** 011 852 5 5668381. **UDC** 380.8. **[CCC]. Circ:** 16.

US
**TRAVELOGUE MAGAZINE.** (19??)-. English. Twice a year. $7.00 US; $9.00 Canada & Mexico; $13.00 other. Travelogue Magazine, 6518 Whitman Avenue, Van Nuys CA 91406. **Tel** (818)785-1963. ***Continues*** *Performer / Program Magazine.*

US/0270-2398
**TRAVELORE REPORT, THE.** (19??)-. Newsletter. English. mo. $30.00 US and Canada; $48.00 other. Travelore Report, 1512 Spruce Street, Philadelphia PA 19102-4520. **Tel** (215)735-3838. **ED** Ted Barkus. **[CCC].** Index available. cum. index. **Bk Rev.** ctrl circ.
**Desc:** Reporting on exceptional travel values, rating resorts, hotels, plus alerts to international disturbances.

AT
**TRAVELTRADE.** English. ir. 48.00Aus$ Australia; 180.00Aus$ other. Reed Business Publishing Pty Ltd. / Australia, 1 5 Railway Street, Level 12 North Tower, Chatswood W 2067 NSW Australia. **Tel** 011 61 2 3725222, FAX 011 61 2 4197533.

CN/0225-6207
**TRAVELWEEK BULLETIN.** **Added/Corp** Concepts Travel Media. **VFOAT** C T M Travelweek Bulletin. **VAT** CTM Travelweek Bulletin; Concepts Travel Media Travelweek Bulletin. Vol. 5, Issue 40 (Sept. 29, 1977)-. Bulletin. English. ir (weekly May 1 - Sep. 14, twice weekly Sep. 14 - April 30). 45.00Can$ Canada; 85.00Can$ US; 100.00Can$ other. Travelweek Bulletin, 553 Church Street, Toronto Ontario M4Y 2E2 Canada. **Tel** (416)924-0963, FAX (416)924-7657, telex 06-219621. **ED** Pat Dineen. **DD** 338.4/791/05. **Ad Acc, Adv Mgr:** Tina Cancilla. **Circ:** 7,400. ***Continues*** *C T M Weekly Bulletin, 0380-2019.*
**Desc:** Canada's national travel trade publication.

US/0162-9816
**TRAVLTIPS.** **Added/Corp** TravLtips Cruise and Freighter Travel Association. **VFOAT** TravLtips Freighter Bulletin. (19??)-. Periodical. English. bm (6 issues). $15.00. Cruise & Freighter Travel Association, 163-09 Depot Road, Flushing NY 11358. **Tel** (718)939-2400. **ED** Edmund M. Kirk. **Ad Acc. Circ:** 25,000.
**Desc:** Gives first hand accounts of cruises taken by members of our association.

●CN/1188-9918
**TREASURE TRAILS.** [Treasure trails]. **Added/Corp** New Brunswick. Dept. of Economic Development and Tourism. (Summer 1992)-. English. **DD** 917.15.

US/1056-8298
**TREKWEST (SACRAMENTO, CALIF.).** (TREKWEST.). [TrekWest]. **VFOAT** Trek West. Vol. 1, No. 1 (July 1991)-. Periodical. English. qt. $16.00. Trekwest, PO Box 41289, Sacramento CA 95841. **DD** 917.

SP
**TTC : REVISTA DEL MINISTERIO DE TRANSPORTES, TURISMO Y COMUNICACIONES.** ***Title Change.*** **Added/Corp** Spain. Ministerio de Transportes, Turismo y Comunicaciones. **VAT** Transportes, Turismo y Comunicaciones. (198?)-No. 56 (1992). Periodical. Spanish. Seven times a year. Centro Publicaciones del MTTC, Almagro 36 3, 28010 Madrid Spain. **LC** HE261.A15; B64. **DD** 380.5/068. ***Continues*** *Boletin de Informacion (Madrid, Spain), 0212-1506.* ***Continued by*** *Estudios de Transportes.*

IT
**TTG ITALIA : TRAVEL TRADE GAZETTE.** TTG Italia, Via A Nota 6, 10122 Turin Italy.

UK/0262-5709
**TTG. TRAVEL TRADE GAZETTE. EUROPA.** [TTG. Travel trade gaz. Eur.]. (1974)-. English. Twenty-six times a year. £60.00 UK and Ireland; $140.00 other. Morgan Grampian, 40 Beresford Street Woolwich, London SE18 6BQ England. **Tel** 011 44 81 855 7777, FAX 011 44 81 855 5548, telex 896238. **DD** 914. available on microfilm and microfiche from University

Microfilms International (UMI). ***Continues*** *TTG International, 0039-8500.*
**Ind/Abst** PROMT [Full Txt.].

UK/0262-4397
**TTG. TRAVEL TRADE GAZETTE. U.K. AND IRELAND.** [TTG. Travel trade gazette. U.K. Irel.]. (1972)-. English. wk. £75.00 UK and Northern Ireland; $175.00 other. Morgan Grampian, 40 Beresford Street Woolwich, London SE18 6BQ England. **Tel** 011 44 81 855 7777, FAX 011 44 81 855 5548, telex 896238. **DD** 914. available on microfilm and microfiche from University Microfilms International (UMI).
**Ind/Abst** PROMT [Full Txt.].

IT
**TURISMO DOMANI.** Turismo Domani, Loc Baia S Barbara, 71012 Rodi Garganico FG Italy.

IT
**TURISMO ED AMBIENTE.** Urbafor Sas, Via Peyron 33, 10143 Turin Italy.

NQ
**TURISMO, ENCUESTA. Main/Corp** Nicaragua. Oficina Ejecutiva de Encuestas y Censos. Spanish. Oficina Ejecutiva de Encuestas y Censas, Apartado 4031, Managua Nicaragua. **LC** G155.N53; N52A.

SZ
**TURISMO NEL CANTONE TICINO, IL. VFOAT** Tourismus Im Kanton Tessin. German (Italian). an. 6.00F. Ufficio Federale di Statistica, Hallwylstrasse 15, Bern 3003 Switzerland. **LC** G155.S8; T86.

YU
**TURIZAM. Main/Corp** Savezni Zavod Za Statistiku (Yugoslavia). Serbo-Croatian (Roman). Kneza Milosa 20, Belgrad Yugoslavia. **LC** HA1631; .A33 subser; G155.Y8.

IT/0392-8020
**TUTTOTURISMO.** [Tuttoturismo]. (1977)-. Periodical. Italian. mo. $102.00. Editoriale Domus, Via Achille Grandi 5-7, 20089 Rozzano Milan Italy. **Tel** 011 39 2 82472276, FAX 011 39 2 8255033. **UDC** 796.5.

UA
**U.A.R. TOURISM IN THE FOREIGN PRESS. Added/Corp** United Arab Republic. Maslahat al-Siyahah. (1???)-. Periodical. English. qt. **LC** G155.E3; A35.

US/0898-4247
**U.S. AND WORLD WIDE TRAVEL ACCOMMODATIONS GUIDE.** [U. S. world wide travel accommod. guide]. **Added/Corp** Teachers Tax Service. Teachers Tax and Travel Services. Campus Travel Service. **VFOAT** US and World Wide Travel Accommodations Guide. **VAT** United States and World Wide Travel Accommodations Guide. (1980)-. English. be. $13.00 US; $14.78 (includes postage) Canada; $16.67 (includes postage) other. Campus Travel Service, PO Box 8355, Newport Beach CA 92660. **Tel** (714)720-3729. **DD** 910.

US/1058-4722
**U.S./CANADA PROFILES.** (U.S./CANADA PROFILES / WEISSMANN TRAVEL REPORTS.). [U. S./Can. profiles]. **Added/Corp** Weissmann Travel Reports (Firm). **VFOAT** US/Canada Profiles. **VAT** United States Canada Profiles. (1991)-. English. Four times a year. $290.52 Texas; $269.00 others in US; $289.00 Canada Puerto Rico & US Virgin Islands; $319.00 others. Weissmann Travel Reports, PO Box 49279, Austin TX 78765. **Tel** (800)776-0720, (512)320-8700. **LC** E158; .U473. **DD** 917.304/928.

UK
**UK INTERNATIONAL TRAVEL MONITOR.** (19??)-. English. Four times a year. £375.00. Intermarket Research Publishers, Tower House Southampton, c/o J Fuller, London WC2E 7HN England. **Tel** 011 44 71 379 6017. **ED** Joan Pullen.
**Desc:** Data and commentary on travel to and from the UK by destination and origin.

US
**UNITED STATES HOLOCAUST MEMORIAL MUSEUM GUIDE.** (19??)-. Periodical. English. $9.95. Israelowitz Publishing, Box 228, Brooklyn NY 11229. **Tel** (718)951-7072, FAX (718)951-7072. **ED** Oscar Israelowitz.

●US/1064-5640
**UNOFFICIAL GUIDE TO LAS VEGAS, THE.** (1993)-. Periodical. English. $13.00. Macmillan Publishing Co. / Indiana, 201 West 103rd Street, Indianapolis IN 46290. **Tel** (800)428-5331, (800)858-7674.

●US
**UPDATES AND INFORMATION ALERTS USTTA.** (1993)-. English. Four times a year. $50.00. US Travel Data Center, 1100 New York Avenue, Suite 450, Washington DC 20005. **Tel** (202)408-1832.
**Desc:** Keep up to date on the latest information available over the course of the year, receiving quarterly mailings that include a current bibliography of selected USTTA research publications and marketing manuals.

US/0739-2311
**UTAH HOLIDAY.** ***Ceased.*** **VFOAT** Utah Holiday Magazine. (Oct. 1971)-(1993). Periodical. English. mo. Tuesday Publishing Inc., PO Box 985, Salt Lake City UT 84110. **Tel** (801)532-3737, FAX (801)532-3742.

CN/0831-3067
**VACANCES POUR TOUS.** [Vacanc. tous]. **Added/Corp** Societe Vacances-familles. Vol. 13, No. 1 (Spring 1985)-. Periodical. French. Eight times a year (Jan., Feb., Mar., May, June, July, Sept., Nov.). 20.00Can$ (one year), 35.00Can$ (two year). Les Editions EJS, 95 Chanoine-Cote, Vanier Quebec, G1M 1T8 Canada. **Tel** (418)686-1940, FAX (418)686-1942. **ED** Eric Sohier. **DD** 910/.5. **Ad Acc, Adv Mgr:** Eric Chasse, **Tel** (418)682-5464. **Circ:** 55,000 (ctrl). ***Continues*** *Le Journal Vacances-Familles, 0831-3059.*

US/0193-9831
**VACATION & TRAVEL GUIDE. Main/Corp** Rand McNally and Company. **VAT** Vacation and Travel Guide. (19??)-. English. an. $7.95. Rand McNally & Company, PO Box 32, Skokie IL 60076. **Tel** (708)673-0813, (800)444-4062. **LC** E158; .R28b. **DD** 917.3/04/926.

US/1059-5996
**VACATION AND TRAVEL TOUR GUIDEBOOK, THE.** [Vacat. travel tour guideb.]. **VFOAT** Vacation & Travel Tour Guidebook. (1991)-. English. Tudor Publishers, PO Box 3443, Greensboro NC 27402. **LC** G155.A1; V33. **DD** 910/.2/02.

US/1059-3845
**VACATION RENTAL MAGAZINE.** (1991)-. Periodical. English. mo. $24.00. American Publishing Group, PO Box 10189, Salinas CA 93912-7189.

US/1046-2104
**VACATION STUDY ABROAD (NEW YORK, N.Y.).** (VACATION STUDY ABROAD.). [Vacat. study abroad]. **Added/Corp** Institute of International Education (New York, N.Y.). 38th Ed. (1988)-. English. an. $40.95. Institute of International Education / New York, 809 United Nations Plaza, New York NY 10017. **Tel** (212)984-5412, FAX (212)984-5452. **ED** Marguerite Howard. **LC** LB2375; .S8. **DD** 370.19/6/025. Index available. **Ad Acc. Circ:** 5,000. ***Continues*** *Learning Traveler. Vol. 2, Vacation Study Abroad, 0271-1702.*
**Desc:** Reference directory to over 1,500 summer study abroad programs.

CN/0316-991X
**VACATION (TORONTO).** (VACATION.). Fall/Winter 1974-. Periodical. English. qt. Free to travel agents in Canada and Eastern United States, $2.00 others. Vacation Magazine Inc, 111 Pears Avenue, Toronto Ontario M5R 1S9 Canada. **DD** 910/.5.

US/0362-6040
**VACATION TRAVEL BY CANADIANS IN THE UNITED STATES.** (VACATION TRAVEL BY CANADIANS IN THE UNITED STATES / CONDUCTED BY TRAVELDATA INTERNATIONAL.). [Vacat. travel Can. U.S.]. **Added/Corp** United States Travel Service. United States Travel Service. Office of Policy and Research. United States Travel Service. Office of Research and Analysis. Traveldata International. **VFOAT** Canadian Vacation Travel. (197?)-. English. an. US Travel and Tourism Administration, Department of Commerce, Washington DC 20230. **LC** G155.U6; V24. **DD** 381/.45917304926. available on microfiche (Vols. for (1977-) distributed to depository libraries).

US/0894-9093
**VACATIONS (HOUSTON, TEX.).** (VACATIONS.). [Vacations]. (1987)-. Periodical. English. Four times a year (Jan., Apr., July, Oct.). Vacation Publications Inc, 1502 Augusta Drive, Suite 415, Houston TX 77057. **Tel** (713)974-6903, FAX (713)974-0445. **ED** R. Alan Fox and Mary Lu Abbott. **DD** 910. **Ad Acc. Circ:** 300,000.
**Desc:** Provides a wealth of new travel ideas along with educational articles and dollars and cents information.

US/0896-6559
**VACATIONS UNLIMITED.** [Coast Coast Travel Inc.]. **VFOAT** Consumer Travel. 1989-. Periodical. English. qt. $9.00. Vacation Media Agency, Drawer 1916, Longwood FL 32750. **DD** 647.

CN/0711-7906
**VALLEE DES FORTS.** (LA VALLEE DES FORTS.). [Val. forts]. **VFOAT** Valley of the Forts. (1982)-. English (French). an. $1.15 Each Number. Valley of the Forts, c/o Cartaffiche, 23 rue des Oblats, Lasalle Quebec H8R 3K9 Canada. **DD** 917.14/3/005.

US/1046-0454
**VALLEY MAGAZINE (SELINSGROVE, PA.).** (VALLEY MAGAZINE.). **VFOAT** Valley. Vol. 1, No. 1 (Spring 1989)-. Periodical. English. qt. $12.00. Meadowood Publications Inc, PO Box 219, Port Trevorton PA 17864-0219. **Tel** (717)374-7795, FAX (717)374-6474. **ED** Stephen A. Newton. **DD** 974. **Bk Rev. Ad Acc. Circ:** 30,000.
**Desc:** Designed to be the one all-inclusive source of information for people who travel throughout this area, (Lock Haven, PA to the West Branch of the Susquehanna River to Berwick, PA on river's North branch and south to Havre de Grace, MD). Feature articles, photography, and illustrations covering this region and the people.

BE
**VALUATION COMPENDIUM. See** Business-Commerce.

BE
**VALUATION EXPLANATION NOTES. See** Business-Commerce.

CN/1185-3093
**VANCOUVER SUBURBAN DIRECTORY.** ***Title Change.*** [Vanc. suburb. dir.]. **Added/Corp** B.C. Directories. (1991)-(1992). Directory. English. Vancouver Suburban Directory, 100 East 4th Avenue, Vancouver British Columbia V5T 1G3 Canada. **DD** 917.11/33/0025. ***Continues*** *Vancouver Suburban City Directory., 0842-960X.* ***Split into*** *Vancouver Suburban South Directory, 1189-928X* ***and*** *Vancouver Suburban Northeast Directory, 1196-4065.*

CN/0380-9552
**VANCOUVER (VANCOUVER, 1975).** (VANCOUVER.). [Vancouver]. Vol. 8, No. 7 (July 1975)-. Periodical. English. mo (10 issues). 18.00Can$ (one year), 35.00Can$ (two year) Canada; 32.00Can$ (one year), 58.00Can$ (two year) US; 34.00Can$ (one year), 60.00Can$ (two year) other. Telemedia Publishing, Suite 300 E, Tower 555 West 12th Avenue, Vancouver, British Columbia V5Z 4G4, Canada. **Tel** (604)877-7732, FAX (604)877-4848, (604)877-4849. **ED** Jim Sutherland. **DD** 971.1/33. **Ad Acc, Adv Mgr:** Janet MacDonald. **Circ:** 70,000 (ctrl). available on microfilm and microfiche from Micromedia Limited. ***Continues*** *Vancouver Magazine., 0828-5519.*
**Ind/Abst** Can. Index.

VE/0042-2932
**VE VENEZUELA.** (1965)-. Periodical. Multiple languages (Spanish and English). ir. $6.00 US & Canada; $4.00 Venezuela; $7.00 other. VE Venezuela, Surface Mail, Apartado del Este 60182, Caracas Venezuela. **Tel** 011 2 283 523327. **ED** Lynn Grossberg. **DD** 918.7. **Ad Acc. Circ:** 10,000 (ctrl).
**Desc:** Tourist attractions of Venezuela and the Caribbean.

US/0883-7821
**VENTURE ROAD.** (VENTURE ROAD : THE OFFICIAL PUBLICATION OF THE VENTURE TOURING SOCIETY.). [Venture road]. Began in 1985?. Periodical. English. mo. $24.00. The Venture Touring Society, 1615 South Eastern Avenue, Las Vegas NV 89104. **ED** Joe Schaerer. **DD** 796. **Ad Acc. Circ:** 4,000 (ctrl). ***Continues*** *Adventure Road (Las Vegas, Nev.), 8750-4510.*

US/0198-9626
**VICTORIAN TRAVELER'S COMPANION. Main/Corp** Victorian Society in America. 1980-. English. an. Victorian Society in America, East Washington Square, 219 South 6th Street, Philadelphia PA 19106. **Tel** (215)627-4252. **LC** E159; .V53A. **DD** 917.3/04926.

CN/0828-4849
**VIKING TOURIST GUIDE. VAT** Viking (Yarmouth. 1978). Periodical. English. ir. Free. Viking Tourist Guide, PO Box 128, Yarmouth Nova Scotia B5A 4B1 Canada. **DD** 917.15/044. **Ad Acc.** ctrl circ. ***Continues*** *Viking, 0049-6448.*

CN/0826-7731
**VILLE (MONTREAL), EN.** (EN VILLE.). [En ville]. **Added/Corp** Association des Hotels du Grand Montreal. Vol. 1, No. 1 (Jan. 1985)-. Periodical. French (French). Twelve times a year. 25.00Can$ Canada; $25.00 US. En Ville Publications, 8270 Mountain Sights, Suite 201, Montreal Quebec H4P 2B7 Canada. **Tel** (514)731-9471, FAX (514)731-9471. **ED** Linda Armitage. **DD** 790/.09714/281. **Ad Acc. Circ:** 42,000 (ctrl). ***Continues*** *Bonjour (Association des Hotels du Grand Montreal), 0710-006X.*
**Desc:** Stories on the city of Montreal, maps, shopping, dining, and other activities taking place in the city. Exclusive guest publication of the Hotel Association of Greater Montreal.

US
**VISITOR ACCOMMODATIONS, FACILITIES, AND SERVICES FURNISHED BY CONCESSIONERS IN THE NATIONAL PARK SYSTEM. Main/Corp** United States. National Park Service. 1976-77-. English. be. US Department of the Interior / National Park Service, 1849 C Street NW, Room 3104, Washington DC 20240. **Tel** (202)208-4621, FAX (202)208-7520.

IE/0790-6056
**VISITOR DUBLIN.** [Visitor Dublin]. (1985)-. Periodical. English. Three times a year. $30.00. Mac Publishing Ltd., 44 Leinster Road, Rathmines, Dublin 6 Ireland. **Tel** 011 353 1 966000. **DD** 914.1504.

# Travel and Tourism

**CN/0823-6615**
**VISITOR GUIDE TO FRONTIER VISTA TRAVEL REGION.** [Visit. guide Front. Vista travel reg.]. English. an. Free. Frontier Vista Travel Association, 960 James Street, Moose Jaw Saskatchewan S6H 3H6 Canada. **DD** 917.124/3. ctrl circ.

**CN/0839-6607**
**VISITOR GUIDE TO PRAIRIE VALLEYS TRAVEL REGION.** [Visit. guide Prairie Valleys travel reg.]. **Added/Corp** Prairie Valleys Travel Association. (1980)-. English. an. Free. Prairie Valleys Travel Association, PO Box 576, Fort Quappelle Saskatchewan S0G 1S0 Canada. **DD** 917.124/4. ctrl circ.

**CN/0823-6593**
**VISITOR GUIDE TO WOODLAND PARK TRAVEL REGION.** [Visit. guide Woodl. Park travel reg.]. English. an. Free. Woodland Park Travel Association, PO Box 821, Foam Lake, Sask S0A 1A0 Canada. **DD** 917.129/2. ctrl circ.

**CN/0711-1335**
**VISITOR (KITCHENER, ONT.).** (VISITOR.). [Visitor]. Vol. 10, No. 2 (Spring 1988)-. Periodical. English. qt. 5.00Can$. Fairway Press, 225 Fairway Road, Kitchener Ontario N2G 4E5 Canada. Tel (519)894-1630. **ED** Katherine Brenner and Janne Dean. **DD** 917.13/44044/05. **Ad Acc. Circ:** 45,000 (ctrl). **Continues** Waterloo Region Magazine, 0826-7529.
**Desc:** A complete tourist guide to Kitchener, Waterloo, Cambridge, and Stratford and surrounding towns and villages; accommodations, attractions, entertainment, shopping and dining, tours and events are also covered.

**CN/0713-7613**
**VISITORS & CONVENTION SERVICES NEWSLETTER.** [Visit. Conv. Serv. newsl.]. **VAT** Visitors and Convention Services Newsletter. English. mo. Visitors & Convention Services, London Ontario N6A 4L9 Canada. **DD** 338.4/7917132604/05.

**US/0895-6464**
**VISTA DE MEXICO, LA.** [Vista Mex.]. Vol. 1, No. 1 (1988)-. Periodical. English. bm. $24.00 US; $30.00 other. Deyo Communications, 5289 Aurora Court, Lilburn GA 30247. Tel (404)923-1926. **ED** Steve Deyo. **DD** 917. Index available. cum. index. **Ad Acc. Circ:** 1,500.

**US/0507-1577**
**VISTA/U.S.A.** **Added/Corp** Exxon Travel Club. Humble Travel Club. **VAT** Vista United States of America. (1965)-. Periodical. English. qt (4 issues). $3.00. Exxon Travel Club Inc., PO Box 3633, Houston TX 77253. Tel (201)538-7600. **ED** Kathleen M. Caccavale. **LC** G149; .V58. **Ad Acc. Circ:** 900,000 (ctrl).
**Desc:** Travel-related and general interest articles.
**Ind/Abst** Acad. Abstr. (July 1993-); Acad. Search (July 1993-); Mag. Artic. Summar. Elite (July 1993-); Mag. Artic. Summar. CD-ROM (July 1993-).

**NE/0772-8425**
**VLAAMSE TOERISTISCHE BIBLIOTHEEK.** Dutch. qt. Uitgeverij de Nederlandse, Boekhandel NV, Kapelsestraat 222, B-2080 Kapellen Netherlands.

**CN/0228-698X**
**VOILA QUEBEC.** (VOILA QUEBEC : LE GUIDE TOURISTIQUE DE QUEBEC : THE TOURIST GUIDE TO QUEBEC.). [Voila Que.]. Vol. 1, No. 1 (Summer 1979)-. Periodical. English (French). qt. $2.00. Voila Quebec, 3765 Blvd., Hammel Quebec, Quebec G2E 2H1. **DD** 917.14/471/005.

**CN/0711-6136**
**VOYAGE EN GROUPE.** [Voyage groupe]. **VFOAT** Group Travelling. Vol. 1, No. 1 (Jan./Feb. 1982)-. Periodical. English (French). bm. 8.00Can$ Canada; $6.35 other. Voyage en Groupe, 425 rue Harris, St-Laurent Quebec H4N 2G8 Canada. Tel (514)744-3867. **ED** Andre Quesnel. **DD** 917.14/04/05. Index available. cum. index. **Bk Rev. Ad Acc. Circ:** 12,500 (ctrl).
**Desc:** Magazine which gives ideas to people in charge of groups on where to go and how to reach the different resources and tourist attractions that can receive groups.

**CN/0822-9678**
**WARDAIR WORLD (1983).** (WARDAIR WORLD.). [Wardair world]. Autumn/Winter 1983-. Periodical. English (French). qt. Ireland Publishing, Suite 601, 211 Yonge Street, Toronto Ontario M5B 1M4 Canada. **DD** 910/.5. **Continues** Monde de Wardair, 0821-7963.

**US/0161-0260**
**WASHINGTON CALENDAR MAGAZINE.** 1st- Year; Oct. 1976-. Periodical. English. mo. $10.00. Washington Calender Magazine, Inc., 7900 Westpark Drive, McLean VA 22101. **LC** F192.3; .W32. **DD** 917.53/04/4.

**US**
**WASHINGTON, D.C. ON $ ... AND $ ... A DAY.** **Title Change.** (1968/69) Ed – (19??). English. ir. Arthur Frommer / Pasmantier Publishers, 1230 Avenue of the Americas, New York NY 10020. Tel (212)373-8500. **LC** F192.3; .W326. **Continued by** Washington, D.C. On $ ... A Day, 8755-545X.

**US/0897-8328**
**WASHINGTON EXECUTIVE TRAVEL REPORT. Ceased.** [Wash. exec. travel rep.]. Periodical. English. mo. Washington Executive Travel Report, PO Box 53160, Washington DC 20009. **DD** 910.

**US/1046-3089**
**WASHINGTON FLYER MAGAZINE.** [Wash. flyer mag.]. **VFOAT** Washington Flyer. Vol. 1, No. 1 (Sept./Oct. 1989)-. Consumer Publication. English. Six times a year. $15.00. Ackerly Airport Advertising, 11 Canal Center Plaza / Suite 111, Alexandria VA 22314. Tel (703)739-9292. **DD** 051.

**US**
**WEEKENDS.** (19??)-. Periodical. English. bm (6 issues). $10.00. Weekends, 481 Bronson Road, Southport CT 06490. Tel (203)255-4281. **ED** Patricia Morgan. **Bk Rev**, (Qty: 6). **Ad Acc.** ctrl circ.
**Desc:** Complete guide to planning getaway weekends.

**CS/0043-2210**
**WELCOME TO CZECHOSLOVAKIA. Ceased.** (1966)-(1992). English. qt. Orbis, 120 41 Prague 2, Vinohradska 46 Czech Republic.
**Desc:** Tourist review.

●**US/1059-0021**
**WELCOME TO THE USA.** (WELCOME TO THE USA: GENERAL AMERICAN-RUSSIAN GUIDE & RUSSIAN YELLOW PAGES.). [Welcome USA]. **VFOAT** Russian Yellow Pages; Dobro Pozhalovat V SSHA. (1992)-. Russian (English). Russian Yellow Pages, Inc., 519 8th Avenue, 5th Floor, New York NY 10018. **LC** E184.R9; W44. **DD** 338.

**CN/1185-9369**
**WELLAND TOURISM NEWS / TOURISM OF WELLAND NIAGARA.** [Welland tour. news]. **Added/Corp** Tourism of Welland Niagara. Vol. 1, No. 1 (Spring 1991)-. Periodical. English. qt. Limited free distribution. Tourism of Welland Niagara, 32 East Main Street, Welland Ontario L3B 3W3 Canada. **DD** 338.4/79171338044/05.

**US**
**WEST AFRICA (SOUTH YARRA, VIC.).** (WEST AFRICA : A TRAVEL SURVIVAL KIT.). 1st Ed. (1988)-. English. ir. Lonely Planet Publications, 155 Filbert Street 251, Oakland CA 94607. Tel (510)893-8555.

**US/1058-8493**
**WESTERN AMERICA VACATION TRAVELER.** [West. Am. vacat. travel.]. **VFOAT** Vacation Traveler. Vol. 1, No. 1 (May/June 1991)-. Periodical. English. bm. $67.00. Western America Vacation Traveler, 35 East 68th Street, New York NY 10021. **DD** 917.

**US/1052-3219**
**WESTERN LINKS (HILTON HEAD ISLAND, S.C.).** See Recreation, Leisure-Sports.

**UK**
**WHAT'S ON IN LONDON.** (19??)-. English. Fifty-two times a year. £49.95 UK; £80.08 Europe; £160.16 Arab, & Middle East; £193.96 US, Canada, South Africa, & South America; £206.44 Australia & New Zealand. Where to Go Limited, 182 Pentonville Road, London N1 9LB England. Tel 01 2784393. **ED** Michael Darvell. cum. index. **Circ:** 32,000 (ctrl).
**Desc:** A guide to London's theatre, ballet, operas, music, art, museums, jazz, restaurants, etc.

**US/0739-9693**
**WHERE TO GO IN MINNEAPOLIS & ST. PAUL.** [Where to go in Minneapolis St. Paul]. Where To Go in Minneapolis and Saint Paul. 1st Ed. -. English. be. $14.95. Where To Go, PO Box 204, Excelsior MN 55331. Tel (612)546-1318. **ED** Jeffrey Kaufman. **LC** F614.M6; W47. **DD** 917.76/5790453. **Ad Acc. Circ:** 20,000.
**Desc:** A delectable menu of what's grand, elegant, charming, cosmopolitan, and distinctively Minnesota about the Minneapolis and St. Paul area.

**UK**
**WHERE TO STAY IN SCOTLAND, BED AND BREAKFAST. Title Change.** See Hotels/Motels.

**CN/1180-9671**
**WHERE VANCOUVER.** [Where Vanc.]. (Apr. 1990)-. Periodical. English. mo. 19.26Can$. Where Vancouver Inc, 6th Estate, 2208 Spruce Street, Vancouver, British Columbia V6H 2P3 Canada. Tel (604)736-5586. **DD** 917.11/33. **Continues** Key to Vancouver., 0829-0601.

**UK**
**WHO GOES WHERE.** English. £2.40. **LC** G153; .W59. **DD** 910/.202.

**US**
**WINGS OF ALOHA.** See Aeronautics, Astronautics.

**US/0897-7313**
**WINSTON'S TRAVEL DELUXE. Ceased.** [Winston's travel deluxe]. **VFOAT** Travel Deluxe. Vol. 3, No. 1 (Jan./Feb. 1988)-(1993). Periodical. English. bm. Winston's Travel Deluxe, PO Box 9, Sausalito CA 94966. Tel (415)332-9612. **DD** 910. **Continues** Winston's Travel Discoveries.

**US/0273-9755**
**WISCONSIN ESCAPE.** **VFOAT** Escape. Periodical. English. mo. $9.00. Heidel Publ Inc, PO Box 1009, Green Lake WI 54941. Tel (414)294-3704. **Continues** Wisconsin Holiday News, 0191-8982.

**GW**
**WOHNMOBIL & CARAVAN.** (19??)-. German. mo (11 issues). DM54.00. J. Hoffmann GmbH & Co., An der Stadtgrenze, PO Box 1360, W 3070 Nienburg Germany. Tel 011 49 5021 8020.

**US/0090-080X**
**WOMAN'S GUIDE TO WASHINGTON, D.C, A.** English. Montag Associates, 1120 Connecticut Avenue NW, Washington DC 20036. **LC** F191; .W65. **DD** 917.53/04/4.

**US/0882-8458**
**WOMEN'S TRAVEL CONNECTIONS.** [Women's travel connect.]. **VFOAT** Connections. Vol. 3, No. 2 (Feb. 1985)-. Periodical. English. an. $24.00. Women's Travel Connection, PO Box 6117, New York NY 10150. Tel (212)751-6758. **ED** Jeanine Moss. **DD** 910. **Bk Rev. Circ:** 2,000. **Continues** Connections (New York, N.Y.: 1983).
**Desc:** A newsletter for the woman traveler, covering lodging, dining, transport, culture, security, shopping and publications.

**US**
**WOMEN'S TRAVELLER.** English. an. $10.00. Damron Company Inc, Box 11270, San Francisco CA 94101. Tel (415)255-0404, FAX (415)255-9428. **ED** Ginal M. Gatta. **Bk Rev. Ad Acc. Circ:** 12,000 (ctrl).
**Desc:** Travel guidebook for the women's and lesbian community in the US and Canada.

**US/0198-1110**
**WOODALL'S FLORIDA (GERMAN ED.).** (WOODALL'S FLORIDA.). German. an. Woodall Publishing Company, 28167 North Keith Drive, Lake Forest IL 60015. Tel (708)362-6700. **Ad Acc.**
**Desc:** Contains expanded listings for all campgrounds listed in each state or group of states.

**US/0742-3950**
**WOODALL'S ... TENT CAMPING GUIDE. WESTERN REGION.** **VFOAT** Western Region; Tent Camping Guide. Western Region; Woodall's ... Tent Camping Guide. Western Ed. 1988-. English. an. $4.95 US; $6.95 Canada. Woodall Publishing Company, 28167 North Keith Drive, Lake Forest IL 60015. Tel (708)362-6700. **LC** GV191.42.W47; W66. **Continues** Woodall's The Tenting Directory. Western Region, 0742-3950.

**US/0362-3823**
**WOODALL'S TRAILERING PARKS & CAMPGROUNDS. CANADIAN EDITION.** (WOODALL'S TRAILERING PARKS & CAMPGROUNDS.). **VFOAT** Trailering Parks & Campgrounds. **VAT** Woodall's Trailering Parks and Campgrounds. Canadian Edition. English. Woodall Publishing Company, 28167 North Keith Drive, Lake Forest IL 60015. Tel (708)362-6700. **LC** TX907; .W68. **DD** 647/.407.

**US/0095-9243**
**WOODALL'S TRAILERING PARKS & CAMPGROUNDS. WESTERN EDITION.** See Recreation, Leisure-Outdoor Life.

**UK**
**WORKING HOLIDAYS (LONDON, ENGLAND).** See Education.

**CN/0887-8070**
**WORKING HOLIDAYS. SUPPLEMENT FOR NORTH AMERICAN READERS.** [Work. holidays, Suppl. North Am. read.]. (1981)-. English. an. Canadian Bureau for International Education, 220 Laurier Avenue West, Suite 1100, Ottawa Ontario K1P 6A4 Canada. Tel (613)237-4820, FAX (613)237-1073. **DD** 914.0455.

**US/0146-4248**
**WORLD BOOK & TRAVEL REPORT.** **VAT** World Book and Travel. V. 1- Winter 1976-. English. $5.95. 2000-B Governor's Circle, Houston TX 77092. **LC** Z1035.A1; N6. **DD** 028.1.

**US/0887-9559**
**WORLD STATUS MAP. Title Change.** [World status map]. **VFOAT** War Zones and Danger Areas for Travelers; Official Advisories for International Travelers.

# Travel and Tourism

(1983)-Vol. 10, No.1 (Jan.-Feb. 1992). Periodical. English. mo. Pinkerton Risk Assessment Services, 1600 Wilson Boulevard, Suite 901, Arlington VA 22209-2507. **Tel** (703)525-6111, FAX (703)525-2454. **ED** Eugene Mastrangelo. **LC** G153.4; .W67. **DD** 910. **Bk Rev**, (Qty: 6/yr). *Continued by Pinkerton World Status Map.*

UK
## WORLD TRAVEL AND TOURISM REVIEW. Added/Corp C.A.B. International. VFOAT
WTTR. Vol. 1 (1991)-. English. **LC** G155.A1; W67. **Ind/Abst** Leis. Recreat. Tour. Abstr.

US/0163-1780
## WORLD TRAVELING. Vol. 1 (Sept. 1978)-.
Periodical. English. Four times a year. $12.00. Upscale Publishing Inc, 25882 Orchard Lake Road, Suite L 7, Farmington Hills MI 48018. **Tel** (313)423-1120. **ED** Terri Mitan. **Bk Rev**. **Ad Acc**. **Circ**: 70,000.
**Desc:** The only travel magazine with a travel guide enclosed (international go getter's guide to ...).

US/1053-9158
## WORLDWIDE BROCHURES (PRINT ED.). (WORLDWIDE BROCHURES : THE OFFICIAL TRAVEL BROCHURE DIRECTORY.). [Worldw. broch.].
**VFOAT** Worldwide Travel Brochures. (1989)-. Directory. English. qt. $39.00. Travel Companions International, Inc., 1227 Kenneth Street, Detroit Lakes MN 56501. **Tel** (218)847-1694, (800)852-6752, FAX (218)847-7090. **ED** Janet Mohr, Kevin Sohl and Jefferey Mohr. **DD** 910. Index available. cum. index. **Bk Rev**. **Ad Acc**. ctrl circ. available on diskette; available on an online database.
**Desc:** Lists more than 10,000 full-color travel brochures from all corners of the globe. Contains more than 500,000 references complete with the names, addresses, fax and telephone numbers of the companies offering brochures.

●US/1051-6247
## WORLDWIDE TRAVEL INFORMATION CONTACT BOOK. [Worldw. trav. inf. contact book]. Added/Corp Gale Research Inc. VFOAT World
Wide Travel Information Contact Book. (1992)-. English. be. $175.00. Gale Research Inc., 835 Penobscot Building, Detroit MI 48226. **Tel** (800)877-GALE, (313)961-2242, FAX (313)961-6083, telex TWX 810-221-7086. **ED** Burkhard Herbote. **LC** G149; .W67. **DD** 338.4/791025.
**Desc:** More than 25,000 entries provide key contact data on sources of detailed and usually free information related to international travel. Lists national and international ministries, departments, and boards of tourism, hotel, travel, and transportation associations, clubs and much more. Organized within 300 country, state/province, and other geographic sub- sections, entries span the globe, including hard-to-find information sources in third world countries. Each entry list the agency's name, address, telephone, and fax and telex numbers when available.

US/0890-4766
## WORLDWIDE TRAVEL PLANNER.
*Ceased.* [Worldw. travel plan.]. **VFOAT** World Wide Travel Planner. (19??)-(19??). English. bm. Worldwide Travel Planner, 7842 North Lincoln Avenue, Skokie IL 60077. **Tel** (312)676-1900, FAX (312)676-0063. **ED** Mark Greenfield. **DD** 910. **Bk Rev**. **Ad Acc**. **Circ**: 250,000 (ctrl).
**Desc:** Information on hotels, resorts, etc., worldwide.

SP/1014-7276
## WTO NEWS. Added/Corp World Tourism
Organization. **VFOAT** WTO. (19??)-. Periodical. English (French and Spanish). Six times a year (also Calendar of Events). $55.00. World Tourism Organization / WTO, Calle Capitan Haya 42, E 28020 Madrid Spain. **Tel** 011 34 1 5710628, FAX 011 34 1 5715198, telex 42188 OMT-E. (**Subscription address:** UNIPUB, 4611 F Assembly Drive, Lanham MD 20706.)

US/0162-7635
## YACHTSMAN'S GUIDE TO THE GREATER ANTILLES. Title Change. Main/Corp
Tropic Isle Publishers. English. an. PO Box 340866, Coral Gables FL 33134. **LC** GV776.29.A57; T76A. **DD** 917.29/14/5. *Continued by Yachtsman's Guide to the Virgin Islands & Puerto Rico, 0735-9020.*

US/0735-9020
## YACHTSMAN'S GUIDE TO THE VIRGIN ISLANDS & PUERTO RICO. [Yachtsman's
guide Virg.-Isl. P.R.]. **VFOAT** Yachtsman's Guide to the Virgin Islands and Puerto Rico. Ed. No. 1 (1983-'84)-. English. an. $11.95 US; $13.95 other. Tropic Isle Publishers Inc, PO Box 611141, North Miami FL 33161. **LC** GV817.V5; Y34. *Continues in part Yachtsman's Guide to the Greater Antilles, 0162-7635.*

US
## YANKEE MAGAZINE'S TRAVEL GUIDE TO NEW ENGLAND. VFOAT Travel Guide to
New England. (Summer/Fall 1991)-. Periodical. English. Yankee Travel Guides, PO Box 10778, Des Moines IA 50340-0778. **LC** F2.3; .Y35. **DD** 917.404/42. *Continues Yankee Magazine's Travel Guide to New England, New York and Eastern Canada, 1055-226X.*

US/1061-4699
## YANKEE TRAVELER (DUBLIN, N.H.), THE. (THE YANKEE TRAVELER.). [Yank. trav.].
(199?)-. Periodical. English. Nine times a year. $36.00. Yankee Publishing Inc., Main Street, Dublin NH 03444. **Tel** (603)563-8111, (800)736-1100. (**Subscription address:** CDS / SIFD Agency Control, 1901 Bell Avenue, Des Moines IA 50315.) **DD** 917.

CN
## YORK RIVER UPLANDS COUNTRY ROADS. (19??)-. Directory. English. Pine Publishing,
Box 100, Boulter Ontario K0L 1G0. *Continues York River Uplands Directory, 1186-8686.*

YU
## YUGOSLAV TOURIST NEWS AND COMMERCIAL INFORMATION. Vol. 1, No. 1,
(July 1959)-. Periodical. English. mo. Yugoslav Tourist Association, Mose Pijade 8/11, Belgrade Yugoslavia. **LC** G155.Y8.

YU
## YUGOSLAVIA TRAVEL AGENTS' MANUAL / ASSOCIATION OF YUGOSLAV. VFOAT Yugoslavia. English. Poslovna
Zajednica Turistickih Organizacija Udruzenog Rada Jugoslavije, Majke Jevrosime 51/V, 11000 Belgrad Yugoslavia. **LC** G154; .Y84. **DD** 914.97/0424/025.

US/1060-720X
## ZAGAT UNITED STATES TRAVEL SURVEY. CENTRAL STATES. See
Hotels/Motels.

---

## ABSTRACTING, BIBLIOGRAPHIES AND STATISTICS

UK
## AA GUIDE TO CAMPING AND CARAVANNING. Main/Corp Automobile
Association (Great Britain). **VFOAT** Guide to Camping and Caravanning. (1973)-. English. an. £7.99. Exel Logistics, 3 Sheldon Way Larkfield, Aylesford Kent ME206SF England. **Tel** 011 44 622 882000. (**Subscription address:** Automobile Association, PO Box 51, Fanum House, Basingstoke RG21 2E2 England; telephone: 011 44 256 20123) **ED** Barbara Littlewood. **Circ**: 21,000.
**Desc:** Covers about 4,000 selected sites in 19 countries with descriptions of facilities and five-language specimen site booking letters, plus practical advice and location maps.

US/0149-8770
## ANNUAL REPORT - OKLAHOMA TOURISM AND RECREATION DEPARTMENT. Main/Corp Oklahoma. Tourism
and Recreation Dept. (19??)-. Periodical. English. an. 500 Will Rogers Building, Oklahoma City OK 73105. **Tel** (405)521-2406. **ED** Eugene Dilbeck. **LC** G155.U6; O547a. **DD** 353.9/766/00826. **Circ**: 1,000.
**Desc:** Gives statistical and operational information for the department's 1986 fiscal year.

BF
## BAHAMAS TOURISM STATISTICS.
**VFOAT** Bahamas Tourism Statistical Review. 1983-. English. an. Ministry of Tourism, Research and Statistics, PO Box N-3701, Nassau Bahamas. **LC** G155.B25; T69. *Continues Tourism Statistical Review.*

SA
## BRABY'S CAPE PROVINCE DIRECTORY. Main/Corp A.C. Braby (Pty) Ltd.
**VFOAT** Cape Province Directory. (19??)-. Directory. Afrikaans (English). an. R55.00. AC Braby Pty Ltd, PO Box 1426, Pinetown 3600 South Africa. **Tel** 011 27 31 7017021, FAX 011 27 31 7017036, telex 624529. **ED** A. Stagg. **LC** DT821; .B69a. **DD** 916.8/7/0025. **Bk Rev**. **Ad Acc**.
**Desc:** Commercial directory with alphabetical and classified sections; also contains maps of the area.

BB
## CARIBBEAN TOURISM STATISTICAL REPORT. Statistical Publication. English. an. $95.00
US; $100.00 Europe; $85.00 Carribbean/Venezuela. Caribbean Tourism Research and Development Centre, 25 F Walcott Building Culloden Far, St. Michael Barbados. **Tel** (809)427-5242, FAX (809)429-3065, telex 2488 WB. **ED** Aorley Sobers, Vickon Curtin and Sherman Williams. **LC** G155.C35; C37. **DD** 380.1/459125/0452012. **Ad Acc**. *Continues Caribbean Tourism Statistics.*

BB
## DIGEST OF TOURISM STATISTICS / BARBADOS STATISTICAL SERVICE.
**Added/Corp** Barbados Statistical Service. (1980)-. Statistical Publication. English. an. 1.00Bar$ Barbados; 0.50Bar$ US. Barbados Statistical Service, National Insurance Building, Fairchild Street, Bridgetown Barbados. **Tel** 427-7841. **LC** G155.B27; D53. **DD** 380.1/45917298104/0212. **Circ**: 300. *Continues Digest of Tourist Statistics.*

AT/1036-2606
## DIRECTORY OF TOURISM STATISTICS.
[Dir. tour. stat.]. **Added/Corp** Australian Bureau of Statistics. (1991)-. English. an. 49.50Aus$. Australian Bureau of Statistics, PO Box 10, Belconnen Australian Capital Territory, 2616 Australia. **Tel** 011 61 6 2527911, FAX 011 61 6 2516009. **DD** 338.479194.
**Desc:** Contains comprehensive information on public sector sources of tourism statistics together with brief articles showing how each source may be used in relation to tourism.

PO/0377-2306
## ESTATISTICAS DO TURISMO.
(STATISTIQUES DU TOURISME.). 1969-. French (Portuguese). qt. Documentation Francaise, 29 Quai Voltaire, 75344 Paris Cedex 7 France. **Tel** 011 33 1 40157000, FAX 011 33 1 40157230, telex 204 826 DOCFRAN. **LC** G155.P75; A25.

KE/0377-1385
## MIGRATION AND TOURISM STATISTICS. Main/Corp Kenya. Central Bureau of
Statistics. (1971)-. English. Sh10.00. Government Printer / Kenya, PO Box 30128, Nairobi Kenya. **Tel** 334075. **LC** G155.K4; K45a. **DD** 338.4/7/916762044.

RH
## MONTHLY MIGRATION AND TOURIST STATISTICS FOR ... . Title Change.
**Added/Corp** Zimbabwe. Central Statistical Office. (1980)-(19??). Periodical. English. mo. *Continues Monthly Migration and Tourist Statistics. Continued by Quarterly International Migration and Tourist Statistics.*

RH
## QUARTERLY INTERNATIONAL MIGRATION AND TOURIST STATISTICS / ZIMBABWE. Title Change.
**Added/Corp** Zimbabwe. Central Statistical Office. (1990)-(Sept. 1992). Statistical Publication. English. qt. **LC** JV9025.Z55; Q23. **DD** 338.4/7916891045/021. *Continues Monthly Migration and Tourist Statistics for ... . Continued by Quaterly Migration and Tourist Statistics.*

TR
## QUARTERLY TRAVEL REPORT / REPUBLIC OF TRINIDAD AND TOBAGO, CENTRAL STATISTICAL OFFICE. Added/Corp Trinidad and Tobago. Central
Statistical Office. (Jan./Mar. 1979)-. Statistical Publication. English. Four times a year. Ackerman & Palumbo, 1666 Kennedy Causeway, Miami Beach FL 33141. **Tel** (305)865-0072. **LC** G155.T7; Q37. **DD** 380.1/45917298304.

●SP
## RECOMMENDATIONS ON TOURISM STATISTICS. (1994)-. English. ir. World Tourism
Organization / WTO, Calle Capitan Haya 42, E 28020 Madrid Spain. **Tel** 011 34 1 5710628, FAX 011 34 1 5713739, telex 42188 OMT-E. (**Subscription address:** UNIPUB, 4611 F Assembly Drive, Lanham MD 20706.)

HK
## STATISTICAL REVIEW OF TOURISM, HONG KONG, A. Statistical Publication. English.
an. HK$80.00 Hong Kong; $16.00 other. Hong Kong Tourist Association, 35/F Jardine House, Connaught Road C, Hong Kong Hong Kong. **Tel** 5-244191, FAX 852-5-8104877, telex 74720 HX. **LC** G155.H63; H65B. **DD** 380.1/4591525/045021. **Circ**: 6,000 (ctrl). *Continues Digest of Annual Statistics - Hong Kong Tourist Association. Research Dept.*
**Desc:** A pictorial and statistical review of tourism in Hong Kong.

IT/0075-1782
## STATISTICHE DEL COMMERCIO INTERNO. Vol. 26 Ed. (1986)-. Italian. an. Istituto
Nazionale Statistica, GBP SEZ4 Via Cesare Balbo 16, 00184 Rome Italy. **Tel** 011 39 6 46735118. **LC** HF199; .A6884. *Continues in part Annuario Statistico del Commercio Interno e del Turismo, 0075-1782.*

NE/0168-5538
## STATISTIEK VREEMDELINGENVERKEER / CENTRAAL BUREAU VOOR DE STATISTIEK, HOOFDAFDELING SOCIAAL-CULTURELE STATISTIEKEN.
**VFOAT** Tourism Statistics. Dutch. an. Fl25.00. Centraal Bureau voor de Statistiek, AFD ALG Zaken, Postbus 959, 2270 AZ Voorburg Netherlands. **Tel** 011 31 70 3373800, FAX 011 31 038 7429, telex 32692 CBS NL. **LC** G155.N2; A32. *Continues Statistiek van het Vreemdelingenverkeer.*

IO
**STATISTIK PERJALANAN WISATAWAN DOMESTIK JAWA TENGAH.** Indonesian. Biro Pusat Statistik, JLN Dr Sutomo 8 Kotak, Pos 1003, Jakarta 10710 Indonesia. **Tel** 3728007, 374908. **LC** G155.I5; S785 .

FR
**STATISTIQUES DU TOURISME. Main/Corp** France. Ministere de la Jeunesse, des Sports et des Loisirs. French. 100F. Documentation Francaise, 29 Quai Voltaire, 75344 Paris Cedex 7 France. **Tel** 011 33 1 40157000, FAX 011 33 1 40157230, telex 204 826 DOCFRAN. **LC** G155.F8; F75A. **DD** 338.4/7/9144048305. ***Continues*** *Statistiques du Tourisme.*

IS
**TOURISM AND HOTEL SERVICES STATISTICS QUARTERLY. Main/Corp** Israel. Lishkah Ha-Merkazit Li-Statistikah. **Added/Corp** Israel. Misrad Ha-Taasiyah, Ha-Mishar Veha-Tayarut. Israel. Lishkah Ha-Merkazit Li-Statistikah. Monthly Statistics of Tourism and Hotel Services. **VFOAT** Rivon Statisti Le-Tayarut Ule-Sherute Haarahah. (19??)-. English (Hebrew). IL65.00. Government Publishing House, Street B/No 29 Hakirya, Tel-Aviv Israel. **Tel** (00-972)2-211400. **LC** TX910.I75; I73a. **DD** 338.4/7647945694. ***Continues*** *Yarhon Statisti Le-Tayarut Ule-Serute Harahah, 0302-8224.*

US/0897-389X
**TRAVEL & TOURISM LAW BIBLIOGRAPHY. See** Law-Abstracting, Bibliographies and Statistics.

JO
**TRAVEL STATISTICS. Main/Corp** Jordan. Wizarat Al-Siyahah Wa-Al-Athar. English. Ministry of Tourism & Antiques, PO Box 88, Amman Jordan. **LC** G155.J6; J67A. **DD** 338.4/7/915695044.

JM
**TRAVEL STATISTICS, JAMAICA. *Title Change.*** English. an. **LC** G155.J25; T7. **DD** 380.1/4591729046. ***Continued by*** *Annual travel Statistics.*

CN/0380-5956
**TRAVELLER ACCOMMODATION STATISTICS.** (TRAVELLER ACCOMMODATION STATISTICS / STATISTICS CANADA, MERCHANDISING AND SERVICES DIVISION.). [Travel. accommod. stat.]. **Main/Corp** Statistics Canada. Merchandising and Services Division. **Added/Corp** Statistics Canada. Merchandising and Services Division. Statistics Canada. Service Trades Section. Statistics Canada. Accomodation and Food Services Section. Statistics Canada. Services, Science and Technology Division. **VFOAT** Statistique de l'Hebergement des Voyageurs. (1969)-. English (French). an. 24.00Can$ Canada; $29.00 US; $34.00 other. Statistics Canada, Publications Sales & Services, Main Building Room 1710, Ottawa Ontario K1A 0T6 Canada. **Tel** (613)951-5078, (800)267-6677, FAX (613)951-1584, telex 053-3585. **LC** TX910.C2; A27. **DD** 338.4/76479471. ***Continues*** *Hotels (Ottawa, Ont.).*
**Desc:** Statistics on hotels, motels, tourist camping grounds and other types of traveller accommodations (e.g. receipts, employment, expenses, occupancy).

# VETERINARY SCIENCES

US
**AAEP REPORT. Added/Corp** American Association of Equine Practitioners. **VAT** American Association of Equine Practitioners Report. Vol. 1, No. 1 (July 1987)-. Periodical. English. Ten times a year. $20.00 Comes with American Association of Equine Practitioners membership. American Association of Equine Practitioners, 4075 Iron Works Pike, Lexington KY 40511. **Tel** (606)233-0147, FAX (606)233-1968.
**Ind/Abst** Index Vet.

US/0198-9863
**ABSTRACTS - AMERICAN SOCIETY OF ANIMAL SCIENCE.** [Abstr. - Am. Soc. Anim. Sci.]. **Added/Corp** American Society of Animal Science. (1977)-. English. an. Comes with Journal of Animal Science. American Society of Animal Science, 309 West Clark Street, Champaign IL 61820-4690. **Tel** (217)356-3182, FAX (217)398-4119. **DD** 636. **NLM** W1 JO536H v.49 etc. suppl.
**Desc:** Consists of abstracts of papers presented at the national and sectional meetings of the Amercan Society of Animal Science.

US
**ABSTRACTS OF PAPERS PRESENTED AT THE ... ANNUAL MEETING OF THE CONFERENCE OF RESEARCH WORKERS IN ANIMAL DISEASE. Main/Conf** Conference of Research Workers in Animal Disease. English. an. Ohio Agricultural Research and Development Center, Wooster OH 44691.

AT/1032-3945
**ACCART NEWS.** (ACCART NEWS / AUSTRALIAN COUNCIL FOR THE CARE OF ANIMALS IN RESEARCH AND TEACHING.). [ACCART news]. **Added/Corp** Australian Council for the Care of Animals in Research and Teaching. **VAT** Australian Council for the Care of Animals in Research and Teaching News. Vol. 1, No. 1 (Spring 1988)-. Periodical. English. qt.
**Ind/Abst** Index Vet.

US/1068-8021
**ACJ (PLATTE CITY, MO.). See** Agriculture-Livestock and Poultry.

PL/0860-2840
**ACTA ACADEMIAE AGRICULTURAE AC TECHNICAE OLSTENENSIS. VETERINARIA.** (VETERINARIA.). [Acta Acad. Agric. Tech. Olst., Vet.]. (1986)-. Periodical. Polish. Akademia Rolniczo-Techniczna, Biblioteka Glowna, Kortowo bl.41 10-957 Olsztyn, Poland. **CODEN** AAAVEZ. ***Continues*** *Zeszyty Naukowe Akademii Rolniczo-Technicznej w Olsztynie. Weterynaria.*
**Ind/Abst** Agric. Eng. Abstr.; For. Prod. Abstr. (1991-); Helminthol. Abstr. (1991-); Index Vet.; Nutr. Abstr. Rev., Ser. B, Live Feeds and Feed.; Poult. Abstr.; Vet. Bull.

●DK/0906-4702
**ACTA AGRICULTUR SCANDINAVICA. SECTION A, ANIMAL SCIENCE. See** Agriculture.

IT/0001-6136
**ACTA MEDICA VETERINARIA.** [Acta med. vet. (Naples)]. **Added/Corp** Naples. Universita. Facolta di Medicina Veterinaria. Vol. 1 (Jan./April 1955)-. Periodical. Italian (English, French, German, Portuguese and Spanish). Four times a year. L100000 Italy; L200000 others. Editoriale Scientifica SRL, Via Generale Orsini 42, 80132 Naples Italy. **Tel** 011 39 81 7646084. **NLM** W1 AC856M. **CODEN** AMVEAX. Documents available from BIOSIS Document Express, CASDDS.
**Ind/Abst** Anim. Breed. Abstr.; Biol. Abstr.; Chem. Abstr. (1955-1977); Dairy Sci. Abstr.; Helminthol. Abstr. (19??-19??); Index Vet.; Nutr. Abstr. Rev., Ser. B, Live Feeds and Feed.; Pig News Inf.; Poult. Abstr.; Protozoolog. Abstr.; Rev. Med. Vet. Entomol.; Small Anim. Abstr. Bibliogr.; Vet. Bull.

YU/0567-8315
**ACTA VETERINARIA (BEOGRAD).** (ACTA VETERINARIA (BELGRADE).). [Acta vet.]. **Added/Corp** Belgrad. Univerzitet. Veterinarski Fakultet. **VFOAT** Acta Veterinaria. Vol. 1 (1951)-. Periodical. Serbo-Croatian (Cyrillic) (summaries and/or abstracts in English, French and German). Six times a year. $64.00. Acta Veterinaria Veterinarski, Univerzitet u Beogradu, 11000 Belgrade JNA 18 Yugoslavia. **Tel** 011 38 11 684351. **ED** Milovan Tovanovic. **NLM** W1 AC9553. **CODEN** ACVTA8. **Pr Rev. Circ:** 1,000. Documents available from The Genuine Article, BIOSIS Document Express, CASDDS.
**Desc:** Animal physiology along with pathology, endocrinology, immunology, animal nutrition, parasitology, radiology, surgery, toxicology, etc.
**Ind/Abst** Biodeter. Abstr.; Biol. Abstr.; Chem. Abstr.; Ecol. Abstr. (?-?); Food Sci. Technol. Abstr.; Helminthol. Abstr.; Index Vet.; Maize Abstr.; Nutr. Abstr. Rev., Ser. A, Hum. Exp.; Life Sci. Collect.; Poult. Abstr.; Protozoolog. Abstr.; Res. Alert [Select. Cov.]; Rev. Med. Vet. Mycology; SCISEARCH; Small Anim. Abstr. Bibliogr.; Soils Fert.; Vet. Bull.

HU/0236-6290
**ACTA VETERINARIA HUNGARICA (BUDAPEST. 1983).** (ACTA VETERINARIA HUNGARICA.). [Acta vet. Hung.]. **Added/Corp** Magyar Tudomanyos Akademia. **VFOAT** Acta Veterinaria. Vol. 31, No. 1-3 (1983)-. Academic Scholarly Publication. English. qt. $96.00. Akademiai Kiado, Publishing House of the Hungarian Academy of Sciences, Prielle Kornelia u. 19-35, H-1117 Budapest Hungary. **Tel** 011 36 1 1811991, FAX 011 36 1 1811991, telex 22-6228 AKNYO H. **ED** Janos Meszaros and Andras Szekely (editor's address: Acta Veterinaria, Veterinary Medical Research Institute of the Hungarian Academy of Sciences, PO Box 18, H-1581 Budapest Hungary). **NLM** W1; AC955R. **CODEN** AVHUEA. **[CCC]. Pr Rev.** Documents available from The Genuine Article, CASDDS. ***Continues*** *Acta Veterinaria Academiae Scientiarum Hungaricae.*
**Desc:** Publishes studies concerned with research on morphology, physiology, biochemistry, microbiology, immunology, reproduction biology and clinical veterinary medicine, etiology, pathogenesis, diagnostics and control of infectious, parasitic and metabolic diseases. It also contains reports and reviews on the economic aspects and the security of intensive livestock breeding.
**Ind/Abst** AgBiotech News Inf.; Anim. Breed. Abstr.; Chem. Abstr. (1983-); Curr. Contents, Agric. Biol. Environ. Sci.; Dairy Sci. Abstr.; Helminthol. Abstr. (1991-); Index Med.; Index Vet.; Nutr. Abstr. Rev., Ser. B, Live Feeds and Feed.; PESTDOC; Pig News Inf.; Poult. Abstr.; Protozoolog. Abstr.; Res. Alert [Select. Cov.]; Rev. Agric. Entomol.; Rev. Med. Vet. Mycology; SCISEARCH; Vet. Bull.

JA/0001-7221
**ACTA VETERINARIA JAPONICA.** [Acta vet. Jpn.]. **Added/Corp** Nihon Daigaku. Juigaku Kenkyujo. Vol. 1 (1956)-. Periodical. English (Japanese). ir. Research Institute of Veterinary Science, Nihon University, Shimo Uma, Setagayaku Tokyo 154 Japan. **NLM** ZSF 615 A188.
**Ind/Abst** AGRICOLA.

DK/0044-605X
**ACTA VETERINARIA SCANDINAVICA.** [Acta vet. scand.]. Vol.1, Issue 1 (1959)-. Periodical. English (French and German; summaries and/or abstracts in German). qt. Kr1070.00. Den Danske Dyraegeforening, Rosenlunds Alle 8, DK-2720 Vanlose Denmark. **Tel** 45 31 710888, FAX 45 31 710322. **NLM** W1 AC956E. **CODEN** AVSCA7. **Pr Rev.** Documents available from The Genuine Article, BIOSIS Document Express, CASDDS.
**Ind/Abst** AgBiotech News Inf.; Anim. Breed. Abstr.; Biocont. News Inf. (1991-); Biol. Abstr.; Chem. Abstr.; CSA Neuro. Abstr. (?-?); Curr. Contents, Agric. Biol. Environ. Sci.; Dairy Sci. Abstr.; EMBASE; Energy Res. Abstr.; Food Sci. Technol. Abstr.; Grasslands For. Abstr.; Helminthol. Abstr. (19??-19??); Immunol. Abstr.; Index Med.; Index Vet.; INIS Atomindex [Micro.]; Microbiol. Abstr. Sect. B (19??-19??); Nutr. Abstr. Rev., Ser. B, Live Feeds and Feed.; Nutr. Abstr. Rev., Ser. A, Hum. Exp.; Life Sci. Collect.; PESTDOC; Pig News Inf.; Poult. Abstr.; Protozoolog. Abstr.; Res. Alert [Full Cov.]; Rev. Med. Vet. Entomol.; Rev. Med. Vet. Mycology; Rev. Plant Pathol.; Sci. Cit. Index; SCISEARCH; Small Anim. Abstr. Bibliogr.; Soils Fert.; Vet. Bull.; Virol. AIDS Abstr.; Wheat Barley Trit. Abstr.; Wildl. Rev.

DK/0065-1699
**ACTA VETERINARIA SCANDINAVICA. SUPPLEMENTUM.** [Acta vet. Scand. Suppl.]. No. 1 (1961)-. Monographic series. English (French, German and Danish). ir. Price varies per volume. Den Danske Dyraegeforening, Rosenlunds Alle 8, DK-2720 Vanlose Denmark. **Tel** 45 31 710888, FAX 45 31 710322. **LC** SF604; .A25. **NLM** W1 AC956F. **CODEN** AVSPAC. Documents available from BIOSIS Document Express, CASDDS.
**Ind/Abst** Biol. Abstr.; Chem. Abstr.; Energy Res. Abstr.; Food Sci. Technol. Abstr.; Index Med.; Life Sci. Collect.

MR/0851-0466
**ACTES DE L'INSTITUT AGRONOMIQUE ET VETERINAIRE HASSAN II. See** Agriculture.

FR/0001-7523
**ACTION VETERINAIRE, L'.** [Action vet.]. (1946)-. Periodical. French. Forty-Four times a year. 430.00F France; 550.00F others. Compagnie Gen Developpement, 11 rue Godefroy Cavaignac, 75541 Paris Cedex 11 France. **Tel** 011 33 1 43790630, FAX 011 33 1 43791775, telex 211351. **Bk Rev. Ad Acc. Circ:** 5,000.
**Ind/Abst** Helminthol. Abstr. (1991-); Index Vet.; Pig News Inf.; Protozoolog. Abstr.; Small Anim. Abstr. Bibliogr.; Vet. Bull.

US/1041-7826
**ADVANCES IN SMALL ANIMAL MEDICINE AND SURGERY.** [Adv. small anim. med. surg.]. (1988)-. Periodical. English. mo. $60.00 (individual), $80.00 (institution) US; $80.00 (individual), $98.00 (institution) other. W.B. Saunders Company, A Subsidiary of Harcourt Brace Jovanovich, Inc., The Curtis Center/Suite 300, Independence Square West, Philadelphia PA 19106-3399. **Tel** (215)238-7800 or, 5587, FAX (215)238-7883, telex 173146. **(Subscription address:** W. B. Saunders Company / North America Subscriptions, c/o Periodicals, 6277 Sea Harbour Drive, 4th Floor, Orlando FL 32887.**) ED** Rhea V. Morgan. **DD** 636. **[CCC].** Index available. cum. index.
**Desc:** Commentary on developments in veterinary medicine.

UK
**ADVANCES IN SMALL ANIMAL PRACTICE (OXFORD, ENGLAND : 1988).** (ADVANCES IN SMALL ANIMAL PRACTICE.). Vol. 1 (1988)-. Academic Scholarly Publication. English. an. Blackwell Scientific Publications Ltd, Marston Book Services, PO Box 87, Oxford OX2 ODT UK. **Tel** 011 44 865 791155, FAX 011 44 865 791927, telex 837 515 MARDIS G. **NLM** W1; AD858B.
**Ind/Abst** AGRICOLA [Full Cov.]; Index Vet.

US/0065-3519
**ADVANCES IN VETERINARY SCIENCE AND COMPARATIVE MEDICINE.** [Adv. vet. sci. comp. med.]. Vol. 13 (1969)-. Academic Scholarly Publication. English. an. $99.00 (Vol. 37). Academic Press, Inc., 6277 Sea Harbor Drive, Orlando FL 32887. **Tel** (800)543-9534, (407)345-4100, FAX (407)363-9661. **ED** C. E. Cornelius. **LC** SF745; .A39. **DD** 636.089/05.

**NLM** W1 AD885. **CODEN** AVSCB8. **[CCC]. Pr Rev.** Documents available from The Genuine Article, BIOSIS Document Express, CASDDS. ***Continues*** *Advances in Veterinary Science, 0096-7653.*
**Ind/Abst** AgBiotech News Inf.; AGRICOLA [Select. Cov.]; Anim. Breed. Abstr.; Biol. Abstr.; Chem. Abstr.; Dairy Sci. Abstr.; EMBASE; Index Med. (1969-1987); Index Sci. Rev. [Full Cov.]; Index Vet.; Nutr. Abstr. Rev., Ser. B, Live Feeds and Feed.; Nutr. Abstr. Rev., Ser. A, Hum. Exp.; Life Sci. Collect.; PESTDOC; Pig News Inf.; Poult. Abstr.; Protozoolog. Abstr.; Res. Alert [Full Cov.]; Sci. Cit. Index (19??-19??); SCISEARCH; Vet. Bull.

US/0199-543X
**AFA WATCHBIRD, THE.** **See** Pets.

UK/0567-431X
**AGRICULTURAL AND VETERINARY CHEMICALS.** **See** Chemistry.

GW/0233-2809
**AGROSELEKT. REIHE 4, VETERINARMEDIZIN.** ***Ceased.*** **Added/Corp** Institut fur Landwirtschaftliche Information und Dokumentation (Akademie der Landwirtschaftswissenschaften der DDR). **VFOAT** Veterinarmedizin. Vol. 30, No. 1 (1985)-Ceased (Dec. 1990). Periodical. German. mo. Akademie-Verlag GmbH, Muehlenstrasse 33 34, D 13162 Berlin Germany. **Tel** 011 49 30 47889300, FAX 011 49 30 47889357. **(Subscription address:** VCH Publishers Inc., 303 Northwest 12th Avenue, Journals Department, Deerfield FL 33442.**)** **NLM** ZSF 615; L264. ***Continues*** *Landwirtschaftliches Zentralblatt. Abteilung IV, Veterinarmedizine, 0023-821X.*

US
**AHI QUARTERLY.** **Added/Corp** Animal Health Institute. **VAT** Animal Health Institute Quarterly. Vol. 12, No. 1 (Jan./Mar. 1991)-. Periodical. English. qt. **NLM** W1; AH298. ***Continues*** *Animal Health Letter.*

US/1044-0100
**ALTERNATIVES REPORT, THE.** [Altern. rep.]. **Added/Corp** Tufts University. Center for Animals and Public Policy. Vol. 1, No. 1 (May/June l989)-. Periodical. English. Six times a year. $48.00 North America; $65.00 other. Tufts University / Center for Animals, 200 Westbord Road, Center for Animals, North Grafton MA 01536. **Tel** (508)839-7991, FAX (508)839-2953. **ED** Andrew N. Rowan. **DD** 619. **NLM** W1; AL987KG.
**Desc:** Replacement, reduction and refinement in animal research, teaching, and testing.

●US
**ALUMNI DIRECTORY / UNIVERSITY OF ILLINOIS, COLLEGE OF VETERINARY MEDICINE.** **See** College and School Publications-Alumni.

US/0002-9645
**AMERICAN JOURNAL OF VETERINARY RESEARCH.** [Am. j. vet. res.]. **Added/Corp** American Veterinary Medical Association. Vol. 1, No. 1 (1940)-. Academic Scholarly Publication. English. mo. $165.00 US and Possessions; $175.00 other. American Veterinary Medical Association, 1931 North Meacham Road, Suite 100, Schaumburg IL 60173-4360. **Tel** (708)925-8070, FAX (708)925-1329. **LC** SF601; .A3. **DD** 619.05. **NLM** W1 AM53. **CODEN** AJVRAH. **Ad Acc. Pr Rev.** available on microfilm and microfiche from University Microfilms International (UMI). Documents available from The Genuine Article, BIOSIS Document Express, CASDDS.
**Desc:** Provides reports of basic research in veterinary medicine and associated biological sciences.
**Ind/Abst** AgBiotech News Inf.; AGRICOLA [Full Cov.]; Agrofor. Abstr. (1991-); Anim. Breed. Abstr.; Biol. Agric. Index; Biol. Abstr.; Calcium Calcif. Tissue Abstr.; Chem. Abstr.; CSA Neuro. Abstr.; Curr. Contents, Agric. Biol. Environ. Sci.; Dairy Sci. Abstr.; EMBASE [Select. Cov.]; Energy Res. Abstr.; Fish Rev.; Health Plan. Adminis.; Helminthol. Abstr. (19??-19??); Immunol. Abstr.; Index Med.; Index Vet.; INIS Atomindex [Micro.]; Microbiol. Abstr. Sect. B; Microbiol. Abstr. Sect. A; Microbiol. Abstr. Sect. C; NAPRALERT; Nutr. Abstr. Rev., Ser. B, Live Feeds and Feed.; Nutr. Abstr. Rev., Ser. A, Hum. Exp.; Life Sci. Collect.; PESTDOC; Pig News Inf.; Poult. Abstr.; Protozoolog. Abstr.; Ref. Upd. Basic Ed.; Ref. Upd. Deluxe Ed.; Res. Alert [Full Cov.]; Rev. Med. Vet. Entomol.; Rev. Med. Vet. Mycology; Rev. Plant Pathol.; Risk Abstr.; Sci. Cit. Index; SCISEARCH; Small Anim. Abstr. Bibliogr.; Soc. Sci. Cit. Index [Select. Cov.]; Soyabean Abstr.; Stat. Theory Method Abstr. (1959-1963); Vet. Bull.; Virol. AIDS Abstr.; Weed Abstr.; Wheat Barley Trit. Abstr.; Wildl. Rev.

US/0162-2013
**AMERICAN KENNEL CLUB STUD BOOK REGISTER.** **See** Pets.

US/0003-0686
**AMERICAN RACING PIGEON NEWS, THE.** **See** Agriculture.

PO
**ANAIS DA FACULDADE DE MEDICINA VETERINARIA / UNIVERSIDADE TECNICA DE LISBOA.** **Added/Corp** Faculdade de Medicina Veterinaria (Lisbon, Portugal). Vols. 25/26 (1988-1989)-. Portuguese (summaries and/or abstracts in English and French). an. **NLM** W1; AN1093D. ***Continues*** *Escola Superior de Medicina Veterinaria (Lisbon, Portugal). Anais da Escola Superior de Medicine Veterinaria.*
**Ind/Abst** Helminthol. Abstr. (1991-); Index Vet.; Small Anim. Abstr. Bibliogr.

BL
**ANAIS DAS ESCOLAS DE AGRONOMIA E DE VETERINARIA : ORGAO OFICIAL DAS ESCOLAS DE AGRONOMIA E VETERINARIA, UNIVERSIDADE FEDERAL DE GOIAS.** **See** Agriculture.

AG/0365-5148
**ANALECTA VETERINARIA.** [Analecta Vet.]. Vol. 1 (1969)-. Periodical. Spanish. Universidad Nacional, Facultad de Ciencias Veterinarias Revista, La Plata Argentina. **CODEN** ANVTAH. Documents available from CASDDS. ***Supersedes*** *Revista / La Plata. Universidad Nacional. Facultad de Ciencias Veterinarias.*
**Ind/Abst** Chem. Abstr. (1969-1978).

RM
**ANALELE INSTITUTULUI DE BIOLOGIE SI NUTRITIE ANIMALA BALOTESTI.** **Added/Corp** Institutul de Biologie si Nutritie Animala Balotesti. **VFOAT** Analele I.B.N.A.; Analele IBNA. Vol. 13 (1988)-. Romanian (summaries and/or abstracts in English, German and Russian). an. ***Continues*** *Lucrarile Stiintifice ale Institutului de Cercetari pentru Nutritia Animalelor.*
**Ind/Abst** Grasslands For. Abstr.; Nutr. Abstr. Rev., Ser. B, Live Feeds and Feed.

SP/0373-1170
**ANALES DE LA FACULTAD DE VETERINARIA DE LEON.** [An. fac. vet. Leon]. Vol. 1 (1955)-. Periodical. Castilian (English and French). an. 1000ptas. Servicio de Publicaciones / Leon, Universidad de Leon, Leon Spain. **Tel** 987 240451, FAX 987 24 61 51. **ED** Teresa Teran Somaza. **NLM** W1 AN148. **CODEN** AFVLA5. Index available. **Ad Acc. Circ:** 800 (ctrl). Documents available from CASDDS.
**Ind/Abst** Anim. Breed. Abstr.; Chem. Abstr.; Dairy Sci. Abstr.; Food Sci. Technol. Abstr.; Index Vet.; Poult. Abstr.; Protozoolog. Abstr.; Vet. Bull.

SP/0213-5434
**ANALES DE VETERINARIA DE MURCIA.** [An. vet. Murcia]. Vol. 1 (1985)-. Spanish (summaries and/or abstracts in English). an. 1500ptas. Universidad de Murcia / Servicio de Publicaciones, Calle Santo Cristo 1, 30001 Murcia Spain. **Tel** 011 34 68 363013. **ED** D Jose Serrano Marino. **CODEN** AVMAE9. Index available. cum. index. **Bk Rev.** ctrl circ. Documents available from BIOSIS Document Express.
**Desc:** Publishes original articles from the field of veterinary science, usually in the form of experimental studies.
**Ind/Abst** Anim. Breed. Abstr.; Biol. Abstr. (1986-); Dairy Sci. Abstr.; Index Vet.; Nutr. Abstr. Rev., Ser. B, Live Feeds and Feed.; Poult. Abstr.

MX/0185-2590
**ANALES DEL INSTITUTO DE BIOLOGIA. SERIE ZOOLOGIA.** [An. Inst. Biol., Ser. zool.]. (1930)-. Monographic series. Spanish. an. **DD** 591.
**Ind/Abst** Helminthol. Abstr. (1991-); Index Vet.; Pig News Inf.; Protozoolog. Abstr.; Rev. Agric. Entomol.

SP/0365-3536
**ANALES DEL INSTITUTO DE INVESTIGACIONES VETERINARIAS.** **Main/Corp** Instituto de Investigaciones Veterinarias. Vol. 5 (1953)-. Spanish. ir. Consejo Superior Investigacion Cientificas (CSIC), Vitruvio 8, 28006 Madrid Spain. **Tel** 011 34 1 5612833, FAX 011 34 1 4113077, telex 42182. **NLM** W1 AN171N. **CODEN** AIVMAT. Documents available from BIOSIS Document Express, CASDDS. ***Continues*** *Madrid. Universidad. Facultad de Veterinaria. Anales de la Facultad de Veterinaria de la Universidad de Madrid y del Instituto de Investigaciones Veterinarias.*
**Ind/Abst** Biol. Abstr.; Chem. Abstr.

GW/0340-2096
**ANATOMIA, HISTOLOGIA, EMBRYOLOGIA.** (ZENTRALBLATT FUER VETERINARMEDIZIN. REIHE C, ANATOMIA, HISTOLOGIA, EMBRYOLOGIA : JOURNAL DE WELTVEREINIGUNG DER VETERINARANATOMEN.). [Anat., hist., embryol.]. **Added/Corp** World Association of Veterinary Anatomists. **VFOAT** Journal of Veterinary Medicine. Series C, Anatomia, Histologia, Embryologia. Vol. 2, No. 1 (March 1973)-. Periodical. English (French, German and Spanish). Four times a year (Mar., June, Sep., Dec.). DM782.00 Europe; DM778.00 other. Blackwell Wissenschafts-Verlag, Kurfuerstendamm 57, D 10707 Berlin Germany. **Tel** 011 49 30 32790623, 011 49 30 32790624, FAX 011 49 30 327 90610. **ED** James E. Breazile, Fred Sinowatz. **NLM** W1 AN192F. **CODEN** AHEMA5. **[CCC].** Index available. cum. index. **Bk Rev. Ad Acc. Circ:** 500. Documents available from The Genuine Article, BIOSIS Document Express. ***Continues*** *Zentralblatt fuer Veterinarmedizin. Reihe C, Anatomie, Histologie, Embryologie, 0300-8649.*
**Desc:** Official journal of the World Association of Veterinary Anatomists.
**Ind/Abst** Biol. Abstr.; Curr. Contents, Agric. Biol. Environ. Sci.; Curr. Contents Life Sci.; EMBASE; Energy Res. Abstr. (Dec. 1980-); Health Plan. Adminis.; Index Med.; Index Vet.; Life Sci. Collect.; PESTDOC; Poult. Abstr.; Res. Alert [Select. Cov.]; Vet. Bull.

●IT/1121-1431
**ANIMAL BIOLOGY.** **Added/Corp** "Halocynthia" Association. Vol. 1, No. 1 (1992)-. Periodical. English. Three times a year. L130000.00. Halocynthia, Via Archirafi 18, I 90123 Palermo Italy. **Tel** 011 39 91 6161603. **NLM** W1; AN228EF. ***Continues*** *Acta Embryologiae et Morphologiae Experimentalis ("Halocynthia" Association), 0391-9706.*

US/1049-5398
**ANIMAL BIOTECHNOLOGY.** [Anim. biotechnol.]. Vol. 1, No. 1 (1990)-. Academic Scholarly Publication. English. sa. $295.00 US; $302.00 other. Marcel Dekker Inc., 270 Madison Avenue, New York NY 10016. **Tel** (212)696-9000, (800)228-1160, FAX (212)685-4540, telex 421419. **(Subscription address:** Marcel Dekker Inc, PO Box 5017, Monticello NY 12701.**)** **ED** Lawrence B. Schook, Peter H. Bick, Harris A. Lewin, Keith W. Kelley and Bryan A. White. **LC** SF140.B54; A55. **DD** 636. **NLM** W1; AN228EJ. **CODEN** ANBTEN. **[CCC].** Documents available from Article Express International, The Genuine Article, CASDDS.
**Desc:** Covers the identification and manipulation of genes and their products, stressing applications in domesticated animals. Publishes full-length, short research communications, as well as appropriate reviews. Provides a forum for regulatory or scientific issues related to cell and molecular biology, immunogenetics, transgenic animals, and microbiology.
**Ind/Abst** Anim. Breed. Abstr.; Chem. Abstr.; Curr. Aware. Biol. Sci., CABS; Dairy Sci. Abstr.; Eng. Index Annu. [Select. Cov.]; Environ. Period. Bibliogr.; Food Sci. Technol. Abstr.; Index Vet.; Pig News Inf.; Poult. Abstr.; Ref. Upd. Deluxe Ed.; Res. Alert [Full Cov.]; Vet. Bull.

UK
**ANIMAL HEALTH & NUTRITION SERVICE.** English. ir. £3050.00. Wood Mackenzie Consultants Ltd., Kintore House, 74 77 Queen Street, Edinburgh EH2 4NS Scotland. **Tel** 011 44 031 225 8525, FAX 011 44 031 243 4435, telex 72555.

US/0884-092X
**ANIMAL HEALTH NEWSLETTER.** (ANIMAL HEALTH NEWSLETTER / CORNELL UNIVERSITY COLLEGE OF VETERINARY MEDICINE.). [Anim. health newsl.]. **Added/Corp** New York State College of Veterinary Medicine. **VFOAT** Cornell Animal Health Newsletter. Vol. 1, No. 1 (March 1983)-. Periodical. English. mo. $32.00 (one year), $56.00 (two year), $80.00 (three year). W. H. White Publications, Inc., 53 Park Place, 8th Floor, New York NY 10007. **Tel** (212)608-6515. **(Subscription address:** Neodata / Colorado, PO Box 2606, Boulder Boulder CO 80322.**)** **DD** 636. Index available (bound in Jan. issue).

IT
**ANIMAL HEALTH YEARBOOK.** **Added/Corp** Food and Agriculture Organization of the United Nations. World Health Organization. International Office of Epizootics. **VFOAT** Annuaire de la Sante Animale; Anuario de Sanidad Animal. (1959)-. Monographic series. English (French). ir. Price varies per volume. Food and Agriculture Organization (FAO) / Italy, GIPC166 via Terme di Caracalla, 00100 Rome Italy. **Tel** 011 39 6 522 52925, FAX 011 39 6 522 55784. **(Subscription address:** UNIPUB, 4611 F Assembly Drive, Lanham MD 20706.**)** **LC** SF600; .F2. **DD** 636.089/44. **NLM** W2 MU5 F2. ***Continues*** *FAO/OIE Animal Health Yearbook.*
**Desc:** Covers communicable diseases in animals, animal health and veterinary medicine.
**Ind/Abst** Protozoolog. Abstr.

CC
**ANIMAL HUSBANDRY & VETERINARY MEDICINE.** (1984)-. Periodical. Chinese. Southwest Agricultural University, Beibei, China.
**Ind/Abst** Nutr. Abstr. Rev., Ser. B, Live Feeds and Feed.

US
**ANIMAL MORBIDITY REPORT (ANNUAL).** (ANIMAL MORBIDITY REPORT.). **Added/Corp** United States. Animal and Plant Health Inspection Service. Veterinary Services. (19??)-. English. an. US Department of Agriculture / Animal & Plant Health Inspection Service, 741 Federal Building 1, 6505 Belcres Road, Hyattsville MD 20782. **Tel** (301)436-7817. **LC** SF623; .U53a. **DD** 636.089/44273.

UK/0262-2238
**ANIMAL PHARM.** [Anim. pharm]. Periodical. English. £330.00 UK and Europe; $650.00 US & Canada; ¥95,000 Japan; £330.00 N. Africa/Mid East; £355.00 other. PJB Publications, 18-20 Hill Rise, Richmond

Surrey TW10 6UA England. **Tel** 011 44 81 948 3262. **CODEN** ANPHEN. **[CCC].** Documents available from UMI Article Clearinghouse.
**Ind/Abst** Curr. Biotechnol.; Index Vet.; Pharm. News Index (Nov. 1984-); Pig News Inf.; Trade Ind. Index.

NE/0378-4320
**ANIMAL REPRODUCTION SCIENCE.** [Anim. reprod. sci.]. Vol. 1 (May 1978)-. Academic Scholarly Publication. English. Sixteen times a year (4 volumes). Fl1488.00. Elsevier Science Publishers BV, PO Box 211, 1000 AE Amsterdam Netherlands. **Tel** 011 31 20 5803642, FAX 011 31 20 5862696, telex 15682. **ED** H A Robertson. **NLM** W1 AN228V. **CODEN** ANRSDV. **[CCC]. Pr Rev.** available on microfilm and microfiche from University Microfilms International (UMI). Documents available from The Genuine Article, BIOSIS Document Express, CASDDS.
**Desc:** Publishes scientific papers dealing with the study of reproduction in all animals which could be regarded as being useful to man. It aims to bridge the gap between fundamental research and management aspects.
**Ind/Abst** AgBiotech News Inf.; Anim. Breed. Abstr.; Biol. Abstr.; Chem. Abstr.; Curr. Aware. Biol. Sci., CABS; Curr. Contents, Agric. Biol. Environ. Sci.; Dairy Sci. Abstr.; EMBASE; Index Vet.; Nutr. Abstr. Rev., Ser. B, Live Feeds and Feed.; Life Sci. Collect.; PESTDOC; Pig News Inf.; Poult. Abstr.; Protozoolog. Abstr.; Res. Alert [Full Cov.]; Sci. Cit. Index; SCISEARCH; Vet. Bull.; Wildl. Rev.

PL/0860-4037
**ANIMAL SCIENCE PAPERS AND REPORTS / POLISH ACADEMY OF SCIENCES INSTITUTE OF GENETICS AND ANIMAL BREEDING, JASTRZEBIEC. See** Agriculture.

US
**ANIMAL SCIENCE RESEARCH REPORT. Added/Corp** Oklahoma Agricultural Experiment Station. (1977)-. English. an. Oklahoma State University / Animal Science Research Report, 206 Animal Science Building, Stillwater OK 74078. **Tel** (405)744-5000. ***Continues*** *Oklahoma Agricultural Experiment Station. Animal Sciences and Industry Research Report.*
**Ind/Abst** Nutr. Abstr. Rev., Ser. A, Hum. Exp.; Pig News Inf.; Soyabean Abstr.

UK/0264-4754
**ANIMAL TECHNOLOGY.** (ANIMAL TECHNOLOGY : JOURNAL OF THE INSTITUTE OF ANIMAL TECHNICIANS.). [Anim. technol.]. **Added/Corp** Institute of Animal Technicians (Great Britain). Vol. 34, No. 1 (May 1983)-. Periodical. English. tq (3 issues). £40.00 US. Institute of Animal Technology Ltd., c/o J. Wills, 2 Millstrea Cot, Little Mill East, Kent TN12 5JU England. **Tel** 011 44 622 71194. **ED** G. E. Ward. **NLM** W1; AN228W. **Bk Rev. Ad Acc. Circ:** 1,500. ***Continues*** *Institute of Animal Technicians (Great Britain). Journal, 0020-2711.*
**Ind/Abst** AGRICOLA [Select. Cov.]; Agric. Eng. Abstr. (1991-); Anim. Breed. Abstr.; Helminthol. Abstr. (1991-); Index Vet.; Nutr. Abstr. Rev., Ser. B, Live Feeds and Feed.; Nutr. Abstr. Rev., Ser. A, Hum. Exp.; Pig News Inf.; Poult. Abstr.; Protozoolog. Abstr.; Rev. Med. Vet. Entomol.; Vet. Bull.

BE/0775-6992
**ANIMALIS FAMILIARIS BRUSSEL.** [Anim. fam.Bruss.]. (1986)-. Periodical. Dutch. qt. **UDC** 619.
**Ind/Abst** Index Vet.

US/0547-8626
**ANIMALS FOR RESEARCH.** ***Ceased.*** **Added/Corp** National Research Council (U.S.). Institute of Laboratory Animal Resources. 7th (July 1968)-?. Periodical. English. National Academy Press, 2101 Constitution Avenue NW, Lockbox 285, Washington DC 20055. **Tel** (800)624-6242, (202)334-3313, FAX (202)334-2451. **(Subscription address:** National Academy of Sciences, Box 285, Washington DC 20055) **NLM** QY 26 A598. ***Continues*** *Laboratory Animals. Part II. Animals for Research, 0195-9506.*

UK/0254-3923
**ANIMALS INTERNATIONAL.** (ANIMALS INTERNATIONAL / WORLD SOCIETY FOR THE PROTECTION OF ANIMALS.). [Anim. int.]. **Added/Corp** World Society for the Protection of Animals. Vol. 1, No. 1 (Jan.-March 1981)-. Periodical. English. qt. World Society for the Protection of Animals, 106 Jermyn Street, London SW1Y 6EE England. **LC** PAR. **DD** 636. ***Formed by the union of*** *Animalia* ***and*** *ISPA News.*
**Ind/Abst** AGRICOLA [Select. Cov.].

BE/0003-4118
**ANNALES DE MEDECINE VETERINAIRE.** [Ann. med. vet.]. **Added/Corp** Liege. Universite. Faculte de Medecine Veterinaire. Vol. 1 (1852)-. Periodical. French (summaries and/or abstracts in English). Eight times a year. 1800.00F Belgium; 2500.00F other. Annales Medecine Veterinaire, Univ. Liege / Sart Tillman/ BT 43, 4000 Liege Belgium. **Tel** 011 32 41 564124, FAX 011 32 41 564122. **NLM** W1 AN373. **CODEN** AMVRA4. **Pr Rev.** Documents available from The Genuine Article, BIOSIS Document Express, CASDDS. ***Supersedes*** *Repertoire de Medecine.*
**Ind/Abst** AgBiotech News Inf.; Anim. Breed. Abstr.; Biol. Abstr.; Chem. Abstr.; Curr. Abstr.; Curr. Contents; Curr. Contents, Agric. Biol. Environ. Sci.; Dairy Sci. Abstr.; Helminthol. Abstr. (1991-); Index Vet.; Key Word Index Wildl. Res.; Nutr. Abstr. Rev., Ser. B, Live Feeds and Feed.; Life Sci. Collect.; PESTDOC; Pig News Inf.; Poult. Abstr.; Protozoolog. Abstr.; Res. Alert [Full Cov.]; Rev. Med. Vet. Entomol.; Rev. Med. Vet. Mycology; Rev. Plant Pathol.; Sci. Cit. Index; SCISEARCH; Small Anim. Abstr. Bibliogr.; Vet. Bull.; Virol. AIDS Abstr.

FR/0003-4193
**ANNALES DE RECHERCHES VETERINAIRES.** ***Title Change.*** [Ann. rech. vet.]. **VFOAT** Annals of Veterinary Research. Vol. 1 (1970)-(19??). Academic Scholarly Publication. French (English). qt (1 volume). Editions Scientifique Elsevier, 141 rue de Javel, 75747 Paris Cedex 15 France. **Tel** 011 33 1 47 07 11 22, FAX 011 33 1 43 36 80 93. **NLM** W1; AN381. **CODEN** ARCVBP. **[CCC].** Index available. **Bk Rev. Pr Rev. Circ:** 1,000. available on microfilm and microfiche from University Microfilms International (UMI). Documents available from The Genuine Article, BIOSIS Document Express, CASDDS. ***Supersedes*** *Recherches Veterinaires.* ***Continued by*** *Veterinary Research.*
**Desc:** Scientific aspects in the field of veterinary and comparative medicine and related subjects.
**Ind/Abst** AgBiotech News Inf.; Anim. Breed. Abstr.; Biol. Abstr.; Chem. Abstr.; Curr. Contents, Agric. Biol. Environ. Sci.; Dairy Sci. Abstr.; EMBASE; Field Crop Abstr.; Grasslands For. Abstr.; Health Plan. Adminis.; Helminthol. Abstr. (19??-19??); Immunol. Abstr.; Index Med.; Index Vet.; Microbiol. Abstr. Sect. B (19??-19??); Nutr. Abstr. Rev., Ser. B, Live Feeds and Feed.; Nutr. Abstr. Rev., Ser. A, Hum. Exp.; Life Sci. Collect.; PESTDOC; Pig News Inf.; Poult. Abstr.; Protozoolog. Abstr.; Res. Alert [Full Cov.]; Rev. Med. Vet. Entomol.; Rev. Med. Vet. Mycology; Rev. Plant Pathol.; Sci. Cit. Index (19??-19??); SCISEARCH; Small Anim. Abstr. Bibliogr.; Vet. Bull.; Virol. AIDS Abstr.; Wildl. Rev.

PL/0301-7737
**ANNALES UNIVERSITATIS MARIAE CURIE-SKODOWSKA. SECTIO DD, MEDICINA VETERINARIA.** [Ann. Univ. Mariae Curie-Skodowska, Sect. DD]. **Added/Corp** Uniwersytet Marii Curie-Skodowskiej. Akademia Rolnicza (Lublin, Poland). **VFOAT** Medicina Veterinaria. Vol. 27 (1972)-. Polish (summaries and/or abstracts in English and Russian). an. Uniwersytet Marii Curie-Sklodowskiej, Pl Marii Curie-Sklodowskiej 5, 20-031 Lublin Poland. **Tel** 37-53-04, telex 0643223. **NLM** W1 AN47MB. **CODEN** ACDDA6. Documents available from BIOSIS Document Express. ***Continues*** *Annales Universitatis Mariae Curie-Skodowska. Sectio DD, Weterynaria, 0301-7737.*
**Ind/Abst** Biol. Abstr. (-1984); Dairy Sci. Abstr.; Fish Rev. (Jan. 1989-July 1992); Index Vet.; Nutr. Abstr. Rev., Ser. B, Live Feeds and Feed.; Small Anim. Abstr. Bibliogr.; Wildl. Rev. (Jan. 1989-July 1992).

IT/0365-4729
**ANNALI DELLA FACOLTA DI MEDICINA VETERINARIA DI PISA.** [Ann. Fac. med. vet.]. **Main/Corp** Universita di Pisa. Facolta di Medicina Veterinaria. (1948)-. Italian (summaries and/or abstracts in English). an. Universita di Pisa, Facolta di Medicina Veterinaria, Pisa Italy. **LC** SF604; .P5. **DD** 636.089/05. **NLM** W1 AN483K. **CODEN** AMVPAW. Documents available from CASDDS.
**Ind/Abst** Anim. Breed. Abstr.; Chem. Abstr.; Dairy Sci. Abstr.; Fish Rev. (Jan. 1989-July 1992); Food Sci. Technol. Abstr.; Grasslands For. Abstr.; Helminthol. Abstr.; Index Vet.; Maize Abstr.; Plant Breed. Abstr.; Poult. Abstr.; Rev. Med. Vet. Entomol.; Small Anim. Abstr. Bibliogr.; Vet. Bull.; Wildl. Rev. (Jan. 1989-July 1992); World Agric. Econ.

IT/0496-4748
**ANNALI DELLA FACOLTA DI MEDICINA VETERINARIA DI TORINO.** [Ann. Fac. med. vet. Torino]. **Added/Corp** Facolta di Medicina Veterinaria di Torino. (1950)-. Italian (summaries and/or abstracts in English, French and German). **NLM** W1 AN483M. **CODEN** AMVTAA. Documents available from BIOSIS Document Express.
**Ind/Abst** Biol. Abstr.; Index Vet.; Protozoolog. Abstr.; Small Anim. Abstr. Bibliogr.

IT/0393-4802
**ANNALI DELLA FACOLTA DI MEDICINA VETERINARIA. UNIVERSITA DI PARMA.** (ANNALI DELLA FACOLTA DI MEDICINA VETERINARIA.). [Ann. fac. med. vet., Univ. Parma]. (1981)-. Periodical. Italian. an.
**Ind/Abst** Index Vet.; Nutr. Abstr. Rev., Ser. B, Live Feeds and Feed.

PL/0208-5763
**ANNALS OF WARSAW AGRICULTURAL UNIVERSITY, SGGW-AR. VETERINARY MEDICINE.** [Am. Wars. Agric. Univ., SGGW-AR, Vet. med.]. **VFOAT** Veterinary Medicine. No. 10 (1980)-. Academic Scholarly Publication. English. ir. Warsaw Agricultural University Press, Ul Nowoursynowska 166, 02-766 Warsaw Poland. **CODEN** AWAMDP. Documents available from BIOSIS Document Express, CASDDS. ***Continues*** *Zeszyty Naukowe Szkoy Gownej Gospodarstwa Wiejskiego--Akademii Rolniczej w Warszawie. Weterynaria, 0324-9085.*
**Ind/Abst** Biol. Abstr. (1986-); Chem. Abstr. (1980); Food Sci. Technol. Abstr.; Index Vet.; Poult. Abstr.; Protozoolog. Abstr.; Vet. Bull.

US
**ANNUAL FINANCIAL REPORT / TEXAS ANIMAL HEALTH COMMISSION. See** Public Administration-Public Finance and Taxation.

US
**ANNUAL PHI ZETA RESEARCH DAY OF THE ZETA CHAPTER. Main/Corp** Phi Zeta. Zeta Chapter. **Added/Corp** Michigan State University. College of Veterinary Medicine. (Apr. 11, 1990)-. English.

AT
**ANNUAL REPORT / AGRICULTURAL & VETERINARY CHEMICALS ASSOCIATION OF AUSTRALIA. Added/Corp** Agricultural & Veterinary Chemicals Association of Australia Ltd. **VFOAT** Annual Report. Periodical. English.

KE
**ANNUAL REPORT / KENYA AGRICULTURAL RESEARCH INSTITUTE, VETERINARY RESEARCH DEPARTMENT. Main/Corp** Kenya Agricultural Research Institute. Veterinary Research Dept. (1980)-. English. an. Kenya Agricultural Research Institute Library, PO Box 30148, Nairobi Kenya. **Tel** 0154-32880-1-6, telex KARI NAIROBI. **LC** SF756.37.K42; K44A. **DD** 354.676/20082/336.

NZ/0110-9901
**ANNUAL REPORT - NATIONAL HYDATIDS COUNCIL.** (ANNUAL REPORT YEAR ENDED 31 MARCH ... / NATIONAL HYDATIDS COUNCIL.). [Annu. rep. - Natl. Hydatids Counc.]. **Main/Corp** National Hydatids Council (N.Z.). Began with 16th (1975/76). English. an. Free. Ministry of Agriculture and Fisheries, PO Box 2526, Wellington New Zealand. **Tel** (64)(04)720-367, telex MAFWN N231532. **LC** SF810.H8; N37A. **DD** 636.7/0894554. **NLM** W1 NA485PB. **Circ:** 5,000 (ctrl). ***Continues*** *National Hydatids Council (N.Z.). Annual Report & Statement of Accounts Year Ended 31 March ..., 0300-0591.*
**Desc:** National Hydatids Council's annual report to the Minister of Agriculture.

US/0735-1992
**ANNUAL REPORT - NATIONAL INSTITUTE OF HEALTH (U.S.). DIVISION OF RESEARCH SERVICES.** ***Title Change.*** **See** Medical Science and Technology.

UK/0142-6591
**ANNUAL REPORT OF THE ANIMAL HEALTH TRUST. Main/Corp** Animal Health Trust. (1978)-. English. an (June). £4.50. Animal Health Trust, PO Box 5 Balaton LGE, Snailwell Road, Newmarket Suffolk CB8 7DW England. **Tel** 011 44 638 661111, FAX 011 44 638 665789, telex 818418. **NLM** W1 AN228W. **Circ:** 10,000. ***Continues*** *Animal Health.*
**Desc:** Aims to be pre-eminent in the understanding of diseases in animals through scientific endeavor and its application to their welfare; approach is to develop new technology and knowledge, to promote post-graduate education and to communicate findings to others.

II
**ANNUAL REPORT OF THE DEPARTMENT OF ANIMAL HUSBANDRY AND VETERINARY SERVICES IN KARNATAKA, INDO-DANISH PROJECT HESSARGHATTA AND BANGALORE DAIRY, BANGALORE.** ***Ceased.*** **Main/Corp** Karnataka, India. Dept. of Animal Husbandry and Veterinary Services. (19??)-?. English. Department of Animal Husbandry & Veterinary Services, Krishi Bhavan, New Delhi India. **LC** SF15.I42; M9a. **DD** 354/.54/87008233. ***Continues*** *Mysore. Dept. of Animal Husbandry and Veterinary Science. Annual Report.*

UK/0952-7222
**ANNUAL REPORT / THE ROWETT RESEARCH INSTITUTE. Main/Corp** Rowett Research Institute. (1988)-. English. an. £12.00. Rowett Research Institute, Greenburn Road Bucksburn, Aberdeen AB2 9SB Scotland. **Tel** 011 44 224 712751, FAX 0224 715349, telex 739988 ROWETT G. **ED** I Brenner and C Cook. **NLM** W1; RO50R. **Circ:** 1,500 (ctrl). ***Continues*** *Report / Rowett Research Institute, 0952-7222.*
**Desc:** Reports on science carried out during the previous year.

GW
**ANNUAL REPORT / ZENTRALINSTITUT FUER VERSUCHSTIERZUCHT.** **Main/Corp** Zentralinstitut fur Versuchstierzucht. **VFOAT** Jahresbericht. 1982-. English. an. ***Continues*** *Annual Report / Zentralinstitut fur Versuchstiere.*

II
**ANNUAL SCIENTIFIC REPORT OF THE I.V.R.I. CAMPUS, BANGALORE, FOR THE YEAR ... .** **Main/Corp** I.V.R.I. Campus, Bangalore. **VAT** Annual Scientific Report of the Indian Veterinary Research Institute Campus, Bangalore, for the Year ... . English. an.

US
**APHIS 82.** **Main/Corp** United States. Animal and Plant Health Inspection Service. English. US Department of Agriculture / Animal & Plant Health Inspection Service, 741 Federal Building 1, 6505 Belcres Road, Hyattsville MD 20782. **Tel** (301)436-7817. **LC** SB981; .A334. **DD** 353/.008/233.

NE/0168-1591
**APPLIED ANIMAL BEHAVIOUR SCIENCE.** [Appl. anim. behav. sci]. Vol. 12, No. 1-2 (Mar. 1984)-. Academic Scholarly Publication. English. Sixteen times a year (4 volumes). Fl1680.00. Elsevier Science Publishers BV, PO Box 211, 1000 AE Amsterdam Netherlands. **Tel** 011 31 20 5803642, FAX 011 31 20 5862696, telex 15682. **ED** A F Fraser. **NLM** W1; AP516. **CODEN** AABSEV. **[CCC].** available on microfilm and microfiche from University Microfilms International (UMI). Documents available from The Genuine Article, BIOSIS Document Express. ***Continues*** *Applied Animal Ethology, 0304-3762.*
**Desc:** Deals with studies of the behaviour of all animals domesticated in any fashion.
**Ind/Abst** AgBiotech News Inf.; AGRICOLA [Select. Cov.]; Agric. Eng. Abstr. (19??-19??); Agrofor. Abstr. (1991-); Anim. Behav. Abstr.; Anim. Breed. Abstr.; Biol. Abstr. (1986-); Curr. Aware. Biol. Sci., CABS; Curr. Contents, Agric. Biol. Environ. Sci.; Dairy Sci. Abstr.; Ecol. Abstr.; Fish Rev.; Geogr. Abstr. Phys. Geogr.; Grasslands For. Abstr.; Index Vet.; Key Word Index Wildl. Res.; Nutr. Abstr. Rev., Ser. B, Live Feeds and Feed.; Life Sci. Collect.; Pig News Inf.; Poult. Abstr.; Psychol. Abstr. (1974-); PsycINFO; PsycLit; Res. Alert [Full Cov.]; Sci. Cit. Index; SCISEARCH; Small Anim. Abstr. Bibliogr.; Soc. Sci. Cit. Index [Select. Cov.]; Vet. Bull.; Weed Abstr.; Wildl. Rev.

AT/1033-9280
**AQIS BULLETIN.** **See** Food and Food Industry.

UK/0167-5427
**AQUATIC MAMMALS.** **See** Zoology.

GW/0233-0652
**ARBEITEN ZUR MECHANISIERUNG DER PFLANZEN- UND TIERPRODUKTION.** **See** Food and Food Industry.

GW/0003-9055
**ARCHIV FUER EXPERIMENTELLE VETERINAERMEDIZIN.** ***Ceased.*** [Arch. exp. Veterinarmed.]. Vol. 6 (1953)- Vol. 45, No. 1 (199?). Academic Scholarly Publication. German (English, French and Russian). bm. Deutscher Judo Verband, Redaktion Ippon Segewaldweg 40, D 12557 Berlin Germany. **Tel** 011 49 711 210770, telex 051 678. **NLM** W1 AR192. **CODEN** AXVMAW. **Pr Rev.** Documents available from The Genuine Article, BIOSIS Document Express, CASDDS. ***Continues*** *Experimentelle Veterinarmedizin.*
**Ind/Abst** AgBiotech News Inf.; Anim. Breed. Abstr.; Biol. Abstr. (-1975); Chem. Abstr.; Curr. Biotechnol.; EMBASE; Food Sci. Technol. Abstr.; Health Plan. Adminis.; Helminthol. Abstr. (19??-19??); Index Med.; Index Vet.; Maize Abstr.; Nutr. Abstr. Rev., Ser. B, Live Feeds and Feed.; Life Sci. Collect.; PESTDOC; Pig News Inf.; Poult. Abstr.; Res. Alert [Full Cov.]; Rev. Med. Vet. Entomol.; Sci. Cit. Index (19??-19??); SCISEARCH; Small Anim. Abstr. Bibliogr.; Vet. Bull.; Virol. AIDS Abstr.; Wildl. Rev.

GW/0720-1893
**ARCHIV FUER TIERARZTLICHE FORTBILDUNG.** [Arch. Tierarztl. Fortbild.]. Academic Scholarly Publication. German. ir. Schluetersche Verlag Druckerei, Postfach 5440, D-30054 Hannover Germany. **Tel** 011 49 511 85500, FAX 011 49 511 1236400, telex 923978. **CODEN** ATFODZ. Documents available from CASDDS.
**Ind/Abst** Chem. Abstr.

GW/0003-942X
**ARCHIV FUER TIERERNAHRUNG.** [Arch. Tierernahr.]. **VFOAT** Archives of Animal Nutrition. Vol. 1 (July/Aug. 1950)-. Periodical. German (summaries and/or abstracts in English and Russian; table of contents in Russian and English). mo. $226.00 (academic institutions), $352.00 (corporate institutions). Harwood Academic Publishers, PO Box 90, Reading RG1 8JL England. **Tel** 011 44 734 560080. **(Subscription address:** International Publishers Distributor at one of the following addresses: 820 Town Center Drive, Langhorne, PA 19047; or PO Box 90, Reading Berkshire RG1 8JL UK; or Kent Ridge PO Box 1180, Singapore 9111, Republic of Singapore) **NLM** W1 AR266J. **CODEN** ARTIA2. **[CCC].** **Pr Rev.** Documents available from The Genuine Article, BIOSIS Document Express, CASDDS.
**Ind/Abst** BioBusiness; Biodeter. Abstr. (1991-); Biol. Abstr.; Chem. Abstr. (1950-1985)(19??-); Curr. Contents, Agric. Biol. Environ. Sci.; Dairy Sci. Abstr. (1950-1985); EMBASE; Field Crop Abstr.; Food Sci. Technol. Abstr.; Grasslands For. Abstr.; Index Med.; Index Vet.; INIS Atomindex [Micro.]; Maize Abstr.; Nutr. Abstr. Rev., Ser. B, Live Feeds and Feed.; Nutr. Abstr. Rev., Ser. A, Hum. Exp.; Life Sci. Collect.; PESTDOC; Pig News Inf.; Plant Breed. Abstr.; Postharvest News Inf.; Potato Abstr.; Poult. Abstr.; Protozoolog. Abstr.; Res. Alert [Full Cov.]; Rev. Med. Vet. Mycology; Rice Abstr.; Sci. Cit. Index (19??-19??); SCISEARCH; Soils Fert.; Soyabean Abstr.; Vet. Bull.; Wheat Barley Trit. Abstr.

IR
**ARCHIVES DE L'INSTITUTE RAZI.** **Main/Corp** Institut Razi. Periodical. English (French). an. Free. Razi Institute, Hessarak - Karaj, PO Box 11365-1558, Tehran Iran. **Tel** 02221 22005-8, telex 214295 IADC-IR. **LC** SF602; .I48A. **DD** 636.089/05. **NLM** W1 HE989. ***Continues*** *Archives de l'Institut d'Hessarek.*
**Desc:** Contains articles of scientific subjects on: research, production of human and veterinary biologics, identification of animal and poultry diseases and zoonoses.
**Ind/Abst** Rev. Med. Vet. Entomol.; Trop. Dis. Bull.

IT/0004-0479
**ARCHIVIO VETERINARIO ITALIANO.** [Arch. vet. ital.]. Vol. 1 (1950)-. Periodical. Italian (summaries and/or abstracts in English, French, German and Spanish). bm (6 issues). L50000 Italy; L70000 other. Cittastudi Scrl, Piazza L da Vinci 7, 20133 Milan Italy. **Tel** 011 39 2 70634844. **NLM** W1 AR604M. **CODEN** AVEIAN. Documents available from BIOSIS Document Express, CASDDS.
**Ind/Abst** AgBiotech News Inf.; Anim. Breed. Abstr.; Biodeter. Abstr.; Biol. Abstr.; Chem. Abstr.; Dairy Sci. Abstr.; Fish Rev.; Food Sci. Technol. Abstr.; Index Vet.; Nutr. Abstr. Rev., Ser. B, Live Feeds and Feed.; Nutr. Abstr. Rev., Ser. A, Hum. Exp.; Life Sci. Collect.; PESTDOC; Protozoolog. Abstr.; SCISEARCH; Vet. Bull.; Wildl. Rev.

CL/0301-732X
**ARCHIVOS DE MEDICINA VETERINARIA.** [Arch. med. vet.]. Vol. 1;(1969)-. Academic Scholarly Publication. Spanish (summaries and/or abstracts in English). sa. $45.00. Universidad Austral de Chile, Facultad Med Veterinar de Chile, Casilla 567, Valdivia Chile. **Tel** 011 56 213911, FAX 011 56 212953, telex 271035 UNAUS CL. **ED** Pedro J Saelzer. **NLM** W1 AR694N. **CODEN** AMVED2. **Circ:** 1,000 (ctrl). Documents available from The Genuine Article, BIOSIS Document Express, CASDDS.
**Desc:** Review articles, original articles, short communications in animal diseases, animal nutrition, pharmacology, parasitology, laboratory technical diagnosis in animals.
**Ind/Abst** Anim. Breed. Abstr.; Biol. Abstr.; Chem. Abstr.; Curr. Contents, Agric. Biol. Environ. Sci.; Dairy Sci. Abstr.; Fish Rev.; Helminthol. Abstr. (1991-); Index Vet.; Nutr. Abstr. Rev., Ser. B, Live Feeds and Feed.; Pig News Inf.; Poult. Abstr.; Protozoolog. Abstr.; Res. Alert [Select. Cov.]; Rev. Med. Vet. Entomol.; SCISEARCH; Vet. Bull.; Wildl. Rev.

●PL
**ARCHIVUM VETERINARIUM POLONICUM / POLISH ACADEMY OF SCIENCES, COMMITTEE OF VETERINARY SCIENCES.** **Added/Corp** Polska Akademia Nauk. Komitet Nauk Weterynaryjnych. **VFOAT** Archivum Veterinarium Polonicum. Vol. 32, No. 1-2 (1992)-. Periodical. English (Russian; summaries and/or abstracts in Polish; table of contents in English). ir. Price varies. **(Subscription address:** ARS Polona, PO Box 1001, 00068 Warsaw Poland.) **NLM** W1; AR755RM. **CODEN** AVPOEW. ***Continues*** *Polskie Archiwum Weterynaryjne, 0079-3647.*
**Ind/Abst** AGRICOLA; Anim. Breed. Abstr. (1992-); Biol. Abstr.; Chem. Abstr.; EMBASE; Index Med.; Index Vet.; Nutr. Abstr. Rev., Ser. B, Live Feeds and Feed.; Pig News Inf.; Poult. Abstr.; Rev. Med. Vet. Mycology; Small Anim. Abstr. Bibliogr.; Vet. Bull.; Chem. Abstr.; Index Med.

US/0093-142X
**ARKANSAS ANIMAL MORBIDITY REPORT.** [Arkansas animal morb. rep.]. **Added/Corp** Arkansas. Dept. of Health. Arkansas. Dept. of Health. Epizootic Disease. Arkansas. Division of Communicable Disease Control. Section of Veterinary Medicine. Arkansas. Division of Veterinary Public Health. (1956)-. Periodical. English. Four times a year. Free. Arkansas Health Services Agency, 4815 West Markham Street, Little Rock AR 72205. **Tel** (501)661-2509, FAX (501)661-2399. **ED** Thomas D. McChesney. **Circ:** 500.
**Desc:** Statistical information on diseases in animals in Arkansas; updated veterinary medical narratives.
**Ind/Abst** Bibliogr. Agric.

BL/0102-0935
**ARQUIVO BRASILEIRO DE MEDICINA VETERINARIA E ZOOTECNIA.** [Arq. bras. med. vet. zootec.]. **Added/Corp** Universidade Federal de Minas Gerais. Escola de Veterinaria. Vol. 35, No. 1 (Feb. 1983)-. Periodical. Portuguese (summaries and/or abstracts in English). bm. $100.00. Escola de Veterinaria, PO Box 567, Belo Horizonte Brazil. **Tel** 011 55 31 4481536. **NLM** W1; AR856. **CODEN** ABMZDB. ***Continues*** *Minas Gerais, Brazil. Universidade Federal. Escola de Veterinaria. Arquivos da Escola de Veterinaria da Universidade Federal de Minas Gerais.*
**Ind/Abst** Agrindex; Anim. Breed. Abstr.; BioBusiness; Biocont. News Inf.; Biodeter. Abstr. (1991-); Dairy Sci. Abstr.; Fish Rev.; Food Sci. Technol. Abstr.; Helminthol. Abstr. (1991-); Index Vet.; Nutr. Abstr. Rev., Ser. B, Live Feeds and Feed.; Life Sci. Collect.; Pig News Inf.; Poult. Abstr.; Protozoolog. Abstr.; Rev. Med. Vet. Entomol.; Rev. Med. Vet. Mycology; Small Anim. Abstr. Bibliogr.; Vet. Bull.; Trop. Dis. Bull.; Wildl. Rev.

BL/0100-2597
**ARQUIVOS DA ESCOLA DE MEDICINA VETERINARIA DA UNIVERSIDADE FEDERAL DA BAHIA.** **Added/Corp** Universidade Federal da Bahia. Escola de Medicina Veterinaria. **VFOAT** ARQ. EMV; A.R.Q. E.M.V. Vol. 1, No. 1 (1976)-. Periodical. Portuguese (summaries and/or abstracts in English). an.
**Ind/Abst** Dairy Sci. Abstr.; Helminthol. Abstr. (1991-); Index Vet.; Protozoolog. Abstr.; Rev. Med. Vet. Entomol.; Vet. Bull.

BL
**ARQUIVOS - FACULDADE DE VETERINARIA, UFRGS.** **Main/Corp** Universidade Federal do Rio Grande do Sul. Faculdade de Veterinaria. **VFOAT** Arquivos da Faculdade de Veterinaria, UFRGS. (197?)-. Periodical. Portuguese (summaries and/or abstracts in English).
**Ind/Abst** Fish Rev. (Jan. 1989-July 1992); Nutr. Abstr. Rev., Ser. B, Live Feeds and Feed.; Protozoolog. Abstr.; Rev. Med. Vet. Entomol.; Wildl. Rev. (Jan. 1989-July 1992).

BL/0102-7794
**ARQUIVOS FLUMINENSES DE MEDICINA VETERINARIA.** [Arq. flumin. med. vet.]. **VFOAT** Medicina Veterinaria. (Jan./June 1986)-. Periodical. Portuguese (summaries and/or abstracts in English). qt.
**Ind/Abst** Poult. Abstr.; Protozoolog. Abstr.

BL/0102-6380
**ARS VETERINARIA.** [Ars vet.]. **Added/Corp** Universidade Estadual Paulista. Faculdade de Ciencias Agrarias e Veterinarias. Vol. 1, No. 1 (Nov. 1985)-. Periodical. Portuguese (English). sa. $30.00. Prof Alvimar Jose da Costa, Unesp Rodovia Carlos Tonanni, KM 5 14870 Jaboticab SP Brazil. **Tel** 011 55 163 224000. **NLM** W1; AR945K. **CODEN** ARSVE6. Documents available from BIOSIS Document Express.
**Ind/Abst** Anim. Breed. Abstr.; Biocont. News Inf.; Biol. Abstr.; Dairy Sci. Abstr.; Food Sci. Technol. Abstr.; Index Vet.; Poult. Abstr.; Protozoolog. Abstr.; Soyabean Abstr.

NO/0801-9533
**ARSMELDING - NORGES VETERINRHGSKOLE.** (ARSMELDING.). [Arsmeld. - Nor. vet.hgsk.]. **Main/Corp** Norges Veterinrhgskole. 1985-. Norwegian. an. ***Continues*** *Arsberetning - Norges Veterinrhgskole, 0377-8789.*

AT
**ARTICLE SUMMARIES.** English. Eight times a year. 145.00Aus$ (non-members Postgraduate Committee in Veterinary Science); 118.00Aus$ (members). Postgraduate Committee in Veterinary Science, Post Office Box A561, Sydney S NSW 2000 Australia. **Tel** 11 61 02 264 1274, FAX 11 61 02 261 4620.

KO/1011-2367
**ASIAN-AUSTRALASIAN JOURNAL OF ANIMAL SCIENCES.** [Asian-australas. j. anim. sci.]. **Added/Corp** Asian-Australasian Association of Animal Production Societies. **VFOAT** Asian Australasian Journal of Animal Sciences; AJAS. Vol. 1, No. 1 (Mar. 1988)-. Periodical. English. Four times a year (Mar., June, Sept., Dec.). $20.00 (members); $25.00 (non-members); $35.00 (institutions & libraries). Seoul National University Department of Animal Sciences, College of Agriculture, Suweon 170 00 Korea. **Tel** 011 82 2 2920890, FAX 011 82 2 2923801. **ED** I. L. Han. **CODEN** AJASEL. Index available. **Ad Acc, Adv Mgr:** Jong K. Ha. **Circ:** 600 (ctrl). Documents available from BIOSIS Document Express.
**Ind/Abst** AGRICOLA [Full Cov.]; Biol. Abstr. (1988-); Soc. Sci. Cit. Index [Select. Cov.].

TH
**ASIAN LIVESTOCK : MONTHLY PUBLICATION OF THE ANIMAL PRODUCTION AND HEALTH COMMISSION FOR ASIA, THE FAR EAST AND THE SOUTH-WEST PACIFIC.** **See** Agriculture-Livestock and Poultry.

UA/1012-5973
**ASSIUT VETERINARY MEDICAL JOURNAL.** Vol. 1 , No. 1 & 2 (May 1974)-. Academic Scholarly Publication. English (Egyptian). ir.
**Ind/Abst** Anim. Breed. Abstr.; Biodeter. Abstr.; Dairy Sci. Abstr.; EMBASE; Helminthol. Abstr. (19??-19??); Index Vet.; Nutr. Abstr. Rev., Ser. B, Live Feeds and Feed.; Poult. Abstr.; Protozoolog. Abstr.; Rev. Med. Vet. Entomol.; Rev. Med. Vet. Mycology; Small Anim. Abstr. Bibliogr.; Vet. Bull.

IT/0392-0674
**ATTI DEL CONVEGNO NAZIONALE - SOCIETA ITALIANA DELLE SCIENZE VETERINARIE.** [Atti conv. naz. - Soc. ital. sci. vet.]. **Added/Corp** Societa Italiana delle Scienze Veterinarie. Vol. 30 (1976)-. Italian (summaries and/or abstracts in English and French). Faculta di Medicina Veterinarie, Via Nizza 52, Turin, Italy. **NLM** W1 AT759I. **CODEN** ASISAI. Documents available from BIOSIS Document Express. ***Continues*** *Societa Italiana delle Scienze Veterinarie. Atti della Societa Italiana delle Scienze Veterinarie.*
**Ind/Abst** Biol. Abstr.

AT
**AUSTRALIAN STANDARD DIAGNOSTIC TECHNIQUES FOR ANIMAL DISEASES.** **Added/Corp** Australian Agricultural Council. Standing Committee on Agriculture. (1975)-. Monographic series. English. Price varies per volume. CSIRO Publications, PO Box 89, 314 Albert Street, East Melborne Victoria 3002 Australia. **Tel** 011 61 3 4187333, 4187217, FAX 011 61 3 4190459, telex AA 30236. **NLM** W1; AU696S.
**Ind/Abst** Anal. Abstr.

AT/0005-0423
**AUSTRALIAN VETERINARY JOURNAL.** [Aust. vet. j.]. **Added/Corp** Australian Veterinary Association. Vol. 3 (1927)-. Academic Scholarly Publication. English. mo. 270.00Aus$. Australian Veterinary Association, PO Box 371, 134 136 Hampden Road, Artarmon New South Wales 2064 Australia. **Tel** 011 61 2 4112733. **ED** K L Hughes. **NLM** W1 AU698. **CODEN** AUVJA2. Index available. cum. index. **Bk Rev. Ad Acc. Pr Rev. Circ:** 4,000 (ctrl). Documents available from The Genuine Article, BIOSIS Document Express, CASDDS. ***Continues*** *Journal of the Australian Veterinary Association.*
**Desc:** Clinical findings and research on health of agricultural and companion animals and wildlife.
**Ind/Abst** AgBiotech News Inf.; AGRICOLA [Full Cov.]; Agrofor. Abstr. (19??-19??); Anim. Breed. Abstr.; Biodeter. Abstr. (1991-); Biol. Abstr.; Chem. Abstr.; Curr. Biotechnol.; Curr. Contents, Agric. Biol. Environ. Sci.; Dairy Sci. Abstr.; EMBASE; Entomol. Abstr.; Field Crop Abstr.; Food Sci. Technol. Abstr.; Grasslands For. Abstr.; Health Plan. Adminis.; Helminthol. Abstr. (19??-19??); Index Med.; Index Vet.; Leadscan; Maize Abstr.; Microbiol. Abstr. Sect. B; Microbiol. Abstr. Sect. C; Nutr. Abstr. Rev., Ser. B, Live Feeds and Feed.; Nutr. Abstr. Rev., Ser. A, Hum. Exp.; Life Sci. Collect.; PESTDOC; Pig News Inf.; Poult. Abstr.; Protozoolog. Abstr.; Res. Alert [Full Cov.]; Rev. Med. Vet. Entomol.; Rev. Med. Vet. Mycology; Rev. Plant Pathol.; Sci. Cit. Index; SCISEARCH; Small Anim. Abstr. Bibliogr.; Soils Fert.; Vet. Bull.; Trop. Dis. Bull.; Virol. AIDS Abstr.; Weed Abstr.; Wildl. Rev.

AT/0310-138X
**AUSTRALIAN VETERINARY PRACTITIONER.** [Aust. vet. pract.]. (1971)-. Periodical. English. qt. 150.00Aus$ (institution), 130.00Aus$ (individual) Australia; 145.00Aus$ (other). Australian Small Animal Veterian, PO Box 243, Bondi New South Wales, 2026 Australia. **Tel** 11 61 2 3607189, FAX (02)360-7184. **ED** R B Atwell and Jenny Wade. **Bk Rev. Ad Acc. Pr Rev. Circ:** 1,000. Documents available from The Genuine Article.
**Desc:** Applicable to practising small animal veterinarians.
**Ind/Abst** Anim. Breed. Abstr.; Curr. Contents, Agric. Biol. Environ. Sci.; Helminthol. Abstr. (1991-); Index Vet.; Life Sci. Collect.; Protozoolog. Abstr.; Res. Alert [Select. Cov.]; SCISEARCH; Small Anim. Abstr. Bibliogr.; Vet. Bull.

AT/0811-6997
**AVA NEWS.** [AVA news]. **Added/Corp** Australian Veterinary Association. **VAT** Australian Veterinary Association News. (1982)-. English. Twelve times a year. 160.00Aus$. Australian Veterinary Association, PO Box 371, 134 136 Hampden Road, Artarmon New South Wales 2064 Australia. **Tel** 011 61 2 4112733. ***Continues*** *A.V.A. Newsletter, 0155-7173.*
**Ind/Abst** Index Vet.; Small Anim. Abstr. Bibliogr.

CL/0716-260X
**AVANCES EN CIENCIAS VETERINARIAS.** **Added/Corp** Universidad de Chile. Facultad de Ciencias Veterinarias y Pecuarias. (1986)-. Periodical. Spanish (summaries and/or abstracts in English). sa. $25.00. Facultad de Ciencias Veterinarias, Universidad de Chile, Casilla 2 Correo 15, Santa Rosa 11735, Santiago Chile. **Tel** FAX 5416840. **ED** Patricio Berrios-Etchegaray. Index available. cum. index. **Ad Acc. Circ:** 300 (ctrl).
**Ind/Abst** Anim. Breed. Abstr.; BHA : Biblio. Hist. Art; Index Vet.; Pig News Inf.; Protozoolog. Abstr.; Small Anim. Abstr. Bibliogr.; Vet. Bull.

CL/0378-4509
**AVANCES EN PRODUCCION ANIMAL.** [Adv. prod. anim.]. (June 1976)-. Periodical. Spanish (summaries and/or abstracts in English). sa. **CODEN** APANDD.
**Ind/Abst** Nutr. Abstr. Rev., Ser. B, Live Feeds and Feed.

US/0005-2086
**AVIAN DISEASES.** [Avian dis.]. **Added/Corp** American Association of Avian Pathologists. Vol. 1 (May 1957)-. Periodical. English (summaries and/or abstracts in Spanish). Four times a year (Feb., May, Aug., Nov.). $100.00 US, $110.00 others (surface mail); $135.00 (airmail). American Association of Avian Pathologists, University of Pennsylvania, New Bolton Center, 382 West Street Road, Kennett Square PA 19348-1692. **Tel** (215)444-5800, ext 2257, FAX (215)444-5387. **ED** D. P. Anderson. **NLM** W1 AV401. **CODEN** AVDIAI. Index available. **Bk Rev. Ad Acc. Pr Rev. Circ:** 1,800. available on microfilm and microfiche from University Microfilms International (UMI). Documents available from The Genuine Article, BIOSIS Document Express, CASDDS.
**Ind/Abst** AgBiotech News Inf.; AGRICOLA [Full Cov.]; Anim. Breed. Abstr.; AQUAREF; Biocont. News Inf. (1991-); Biol. Abstr.; Chem. Abstr.; Curr. Aware. Biol. Sci., CABS; Curr. Contents, Agric. Biol. Environ. Sci.; Dairy Sci. Abstr.; Health Plan. Adminis.; Helminthol. Abstr.; Immunol. Abstr.; Index Med.; Index Vet.; Microbiol. Abstr. Sect. B; Microbiol. Abstr. Sect. A; Microbiol. Abstr. Sect. C; Nutr. Abstr. Rev., Ser. B, Live Feeds and Feed.; Life Sci. Collect.; PESTDOC; Poult. Abstr.; Protozoolog. Abstr.; Res. Alert [Full Cov.]; Rev. Med. Vet. Entomol.; Rev. Med. Vet. Mycology; Rev. Plant Pathol.; Sci. Cit. Index; SCISEARCH; Small Anim. Abstr. Bibliogr.; Vet. Bull.; Virol. AIDS Abstr.; Wildl. Rev.

UK/0307-9457
**AVIAN PATHOLOGY.** (AVIAN PATHOLOGY : JOURNAL OF THE W.V.P.A.). [Avian pathol.]. **Added/Corp** World Veterinary Poultry Association. Vol. 1, No. 1 (1972)-. Academic Scholarly Publication. English (French and German). qt (Mar., Jun., Sep., Dec). £118.00. Carfax Publishing Company, PO Box 25 Abingdon, Oxfordshire OX14 3UE England. **Tel** 011 44 235 555335, FAX (0279)31067, telex 817484. **(Subscription address:** US and Canada/ PO Box 2025, Dunnellon, FL 34430-2025; telephone:(904)489-6996) **ED** L. N. Payne, J. M. Bradbury, D. Cavanagh and J. K. A. Cook. **NLM** W1 AV414. **CODEN** AVPADN. **[CCC]. Bk Rev. Ad Acc. Pr Rev. Circ:** 700 (ctrl). available on microfiche. Documents available from The Genuine Article, BIOSIS Document Express, CASDDS.
**Desc:** Concerned with diseases of domestic poultry and other birds, original papers on all disciplines associated with the study of disease including bacteriology, epizootiology, genetics, immunology, toxicology, and virology.
**Ind/Abst** AgBiotech News Inf.; AGRICOLA [Full Cov.]; Anim. Breed. Abstr.; Biol. Abstr.; Chem. Abstr.; Curr. Aware. Biol. Sci., CABS; Curr. Contents, Agric. Biol. Environ. Sci.; Index Vet.; Life Sci. Collect.; PESTDOC; Poult. Abstr.; Protozoolog. Abstr.; Res. Alert [Full Cov.]; Rev. Med. Vet. Entomol.; Rev. Med. Vet. Mycology; Sci. Cit. Index; SCISEARCH; Small Anim. Abstr. Bibliogr.; Vet. Bull.; Wildl. Rev. (19??-199?).

US/0898-6657
**AVMA DIRECTORY.** [AVMA dir.]. **Main/Corp** American Veterinary Medical Association. Division of Membership and Field Services. **VFOAT** AVMA ... Directory, Caring for Animals. **VAT** American Veterinary Medical Association Directory. (1984)-. Directory. English. an. $90.00 US and Posessions; $105.00 other. American Veterinary Medical Association, 1931 North Meacham Road, Suite 100, Schaumburg IL 60173-4360. **Tel** (708)925-8070, FAX (708)925-1329. **LC** SF611; .A53. **DD** 636.089/06073. **NLM** SF 611; A512. ***Continues*** *Directory - American Veterinary Medical Association, 0066-1147.*
**Desc:** Provides historic and current guidance information about the profession, alphabetic and geographic listings of all AVMA members and many nonmembers, and listings for many governmental agencies, allied veterinary groups and other organizations concerned with animal health and welfare.

AT/0816-1623
**AVPI. AGRICULTURAL AND VETERINARY PRODUCT INDEX.** **See** Agriculture.

JA/0389-1836
**AZABU DAIGAKU JUI GAKUBU KENKYU HOKOKU.** [Azabu Daigaku Jui Gakubu kenkyu hokoku]. **VFOAT** Azabu Daigaku Juigakubu Kenkyu Hokoku; Bulletin of Azabu University. Veterinary Medicine. (1980)-. Academic Scholarly Publication. Japanese (English). sa. Azabu Daigaku Juigakubu, (Faculty of Veterinary Medicine, Azabu University), 17-71, Fuchinobe, 1 Chome, Sagamiharashi, Kanagawaken 229 Japan. **CODEN** ADJHDO. Documents available from BIOSIS Document Express, CASDDS. ***Continues*** *Azabu Juika Daigaku Kenkyu Hokoku.*
**Ind/Abst** Biol. Abstr.; Chem. Abstr.

UK
**BABRAHAM.** Corporate Report. English. an. Babraham Institute, Babraham Hall, Babraham, Cambridge CB2 4AT, United Kingdom. **Tel** 0223 832312, FAX 0223 836122. **ED** Caroline Edmonds. ctrl circ. ***Continues*** *Report / Agricultural Research Council. Institute of Animal Physiology.*
**Desc:** Reviews the current science undertaken by the Institute, and highlights notable past and future events; describes the support and external liaison functions of the Babraham Institute.

BG/0003-3588
**BANGLADESH JOURNAL OF ANIMAL SCIENCE.** **Added/Corp** Bangladesh Animal Science Association. Pakistan Animal Science Association. Pakistan Animal Science Association. Animal Science Journal of Pakistan. Vol. 1 (July 1968)-. Periodical. English.
**Ind/Abst** Agric. Eng. Abstr.; Grasslands For. Abstr.; Maize Abstr.; Postharvest News Inf.

BG/1012-5949
**BANGLADESH VETERINARIAN, THE.** [Bangladesh vet.]. (1984)-. Periodical. English. sa.
**Ind/Abst** Index Vet.; Nutr. Abstr. Rev., Ser. B, Live Feeds and Feed.; Poult. Abstr.; Protozoolog. Abstr.; Rev. Med. Vet. Mycology; Small Anim. Abstr. Bibliogr.; Vet. Bull.

BG/0378-8113
**BANGLADESH VETERINARY JOURNAL.** [Bangladesh vet. j.]. **Added/Corp** Bangladesh Veterinary Association. Began with: Vol. 4 in Jan./Oct. (1970)-. Academic Scholarly Publication. English. qt. Bangladesh Veterinary Association, Bangladesh Agricultural University, Mymensingh, Bangladesh. **NLM** W1 BA646. **CODEN** BVJODC. Documents available from CASDDS. ***Continues*** *Pakistan Journal of Veterinary Science.*
**Ind/Abst** Anim. Breed. Abstr.; Chem. Abstr.; Dairy Sci. Abstr.; Helminthol. Abstr. (1991-); Index Vet.; Nutr. Abstr. Rev., Ser. B, Live Feeds and Feed.; Protozoolog. Abstr.; Rev. Agric. Entomol.; Rev. Med. Vet. Mycology.

US/1043-0849
**BARKER, THE.** (THE BARKER : THE OFFICIAL PUBLICATION OF THE CHINESE SHAR-PEI CLUB OF AMERICA, INC.). [Barker]. (1989)-. Periodical. English. bm. $35.00 US; $45.00 Canada; $55.00 other. Chinese Shar-Pei Club of America, PO Box 11510, Kansas City MO 64138. **Tel** (816)737-1697. **ED** Marge B Calltharp. **DD** 636. Index available. **Bk Rev. Ad Acc. Pr Rev. Circ:** 7,000.

NZ
**BEHAVIOURAL & POLITICAL ANIMAL STUDIES.** **Added/Corp** Animal Archives. **VFOAT** Behavioural and Political Animal Studies. Vol. 1, No. 1 (July 1988)-. Periodical. English. sa.

GW/0005-9366
**BERLINER UND MUNCHENER TIERARZTLICHE WOCHENSCHRIFT.** [Berl. Muench. tieraerztl. Wochenschr.]. Vol. 54, No. 26/27 (July 1938)-. Academic Scholarly Publication. German. mo. DM534.00 Europe; DM535.00 other. Blackwell Wissenschafts-Verlag, Kurfuerstendamm 57, D 10707 Berlin Germany. **Tel** 011 49 30 32790623, 011 49 30 32790624, FAX 011 49 30 327 90610. **ED** H.O. Schmidtke. **NLM** W1 BE882F. **CODEN** BEMTAM. **[CCC].** Index available. cum. index. **Bk Rev. Ad Acc. Circ:** 2,500. Documents available from The Genuine Article, CASDDS. ***Continues*** *Berliner Tierarztliche Wochenschrift.*
**Desc:** The oldest veterinary medical journal for the practitioner.
**Ind/Abst** AgBiotech News Inf.; Anim. Breed. Abstr.; Biodeter. Abstr.; Chem. Abstr.; Dairy Sci. Abstr.; Energy Res. Abstr.; Food Sci. Technol. Abstr.; Helminthol. Abstr. (19??-19??); Hortic. Abstr.; Index Med.; Index Vet.; Nutr. Abstr. Rev., Ser. B, Live Feeds and Feed.; Nutr. Abstr. Rev., Ser. A, Hum. Exp.; Life Sci. Collect.; PESTDOC; Pig News Inf.; Poult. Abstr.; Protozoolog. Abstr.; Res. Alert [Full Cov.]; Rev. Med. Vet. Entomol.; Rev. Med. Vet. Mycology; Rev. Plant Pathol.; Sci. Cit. Index; SCISEARCH; Small Anim. Abstr. Bibliogr.; Soils Fert.; Vet. Bull.

BT/0259-0859
**BHUTAN JOURNAL OF ANIMAL HUSBANDRY.** [Bhutan j. anim. husb.]. (1983)-. Periodical. English. an. ***Continues*** *The Journal of Animal Husbandry Bhutan, 0259-0840.*
**Ind/Abst** Poult. Abstr.

AT/1034-9219
**BIENNIAL REPORT / CSIRO AUSTRALIAN ANIMAL HEALTH LABORATORY.** **Added/Corp** Australian Animal Health Laboratory. (1987/1989)-. English. be. CSIRO Publications, PO Box 89, 314 Albert Street, East Melborne Victoria 3002 Australia. **Tel** 011 61 3 4187333, 4187217, FAX 011 61 3 4190459, telex AA 30236. ***Continues*** *Australian Animal Health Laboratory. Annual Report, 0818-643X.*

US/0570-1244
**BIENNIAL SYMPOSIUM ON ANIMAL REPRODUCTION; [PROCEEDINGS].** (1953)-. English. be. American Society of Animal Science, 309 West Clark Street, Champaign IL 61820-4690. **Tel** (217)356-3182, FAX (217)398-4119. **ED** C. O. Woody. **Circ:** 800.

XR
**BIOPHARM.** (1991)-. Periodical. Czech (Slovak and English; summaries and/or abstracts in Russian). bm. Documents available from The Genuine Article. ***Continues*** *Biologizace a Chemizace Zivocisne Vyroby - Veterinaria, 0139-8571.*
**Ind/Abst** Index Vet.; Res. Alert [Full Cov.].

UK
**BIOTRANSFORMATIONS : A SURVEY OF THE BIOTRANSFORMATIONS OF DRUGS AND CHEMICALS IN ANIMALS.** **See** Medical Science and Technology.

RU/0366-4899
**BIULLETEN. Added/Corp** Vsesoiuznyi Institut Eksperimentaloi Veterinarii. Vol. 1 (1967)-. Academic Scholarly Publication. Russian. Price varies per volume. **NLM** W1 BI99LR. **CODEN** BVEVA5. Documents available from CASDDS.
**Ind/Abst** Chem. Abstr. (1967-1979).

RU
**BIULLETIN VSESOIUZNOGO NAUCHNO-ISSLEDOVATELSKOGO INSTITUTA FIZIOLOGII, BIOKHIMII I PITANIIA SELSKOKHOZIAISTVENNYKH ZHIVOTNYKH.** [Bjull. Vses. naucno-issled. inst. fiziol., biohim. pitanija sel'skohoz. zivotn.]. **Main/Corp** Vsesoiuznyi Nauchno-Issledovatelsloi Institut Fiziologii, Biokhimii i Pitaniia Selskokhoziaistvennykh Zhivotnykh (Soviet Union). **VFOAT** Biulleten Vnii Fiziologii, Biokhimii i Pitaniia S.-KH. Zhivotnykh. (1972)-. Academic Scholarly Publication. Russian (summaries and/or abstracts in English). qt. **CODEN** BFBPAU. Documents available from CASDDS. ***Continues*** *Biulletin Vsesoiuznogo Nuachno-Issledovatelskogo Instituta Fiziologii i Biokhimii Selskokhoziaistvnnykh Zhivotnykh.*
**Ind/Abst** AGRICOLA; Chem. Abstr.; For. Prod. Abstr. (1991-); Nutr. Abstr. Rev., Ser. B, Live Feeds and Feed.; Postharvest News Inf.; Poult. Abstr.

BL/0067-9615
**BOLETIM DE INDUSTRIA ANIMAL. See** Agriculture-Livestock and Poultry.

BL
**BOLETIM DO INSTITUTO DE PESQUISAS VETERINARIAS DESIDERIO FINAMOR. Added/Corp** Instituto de Pesquisas Veterinarias "Desiderio Finamor" (Rio Grande do Sul, Brazil). (1972)-. Bulletin. Portuguese (summaries and/or abstracts in English). Instituto Pesquisas Veterinarias Desiderio Finamor Biblioteca, Caixa Postal 2076, 90.001-970 Porto Alegre, Rio Grande Do Sul Brasil. **Tel** FAX 011 051 481 3337. **Ad Acc.** ctrl circ. ***Continues*** *Arquivos do Instituto de Pesquisas Veterinarias Desiderio Finamor.*
**Ind/Abst** Poult. Abstr.

CL/0716-114X
**BOLETIN MICOLOGICO. Added/Corp** Universidad de Valparaiaso. Catedra de Micologia. **VFOAT** Mycologycal Bulletin. Vol. 1, No. 1 (1982)-. Periodical. Spanish (summaries and/or abstracts in English). sa. Universidad de Valparaiso / Facultad de Medicina, Catedra de Micologia, Casilla 92-V, Valparaiso Chile. **NLM** W1; BO4294.
**Ind/Abst** Biocont. News Inf.; Maize Abstr.; Rev. Med. Vet. Mycology; Rev. Plant Pathol.; Wheat Barley Trit. Abstr.

IT/0004-5977
**BOLLETTINO - ASSOCIAZIONE ITALIANA VETERINARI PER PICCOLI ANIMALI.** [Boll. - Assoc. ital. vet. piccoli anim.]. (1962)-. Periodical. Multiple languages. qt. Associazione Italiana Veterinari per Piccoli Animali, Secretario, Dott G. Vincenzi, Via Quadri 160 36100, Vicenza, Italy. **UDC** 619.
**Ind/Abst** Helminthol. Abstr. (1991-); Index Vet.; Nutr. Abstr. Rev., Ser. B, Live Feeds and Feed.; Small Anim. Abstr. Bibliogr.; Vet. Bull.

IT
**BOLLETTINO SCIENTIFICO DELLA FACOLTA DI ZOOTECNIA & VETERINARIA / UNIVERSITE NAZIONALE SOMALA, FACOLTA ZOOTECNIA E VETERINARIA. Added/Corp** Universita Nazionale della Somalia. Facolta di Zootecnia e Veterinaria. (1980)-. Italian (English; summaries and/or abstracts in French). an.
**Ind/Abst** Anim. Breed. Abstr.; Helminthol. Abstr. (1991-); Index Vet.; Poult. Abstr.; Small Anim. Abstr. Bibliogr.

US/0524-1685
**BOVINE PRACTITIONER, THE.** ***Suspended.*** [Bov. pract.]. No. 1 (Jan. 1967)-Suspended. English. an. $20.00 US; $25.00 (overseas) other. Dr Eric I Williams, 1226 North Lincoln, Stillwater OK 74075. **Tel** (405)372-3693, FAX (405)372-0939. **ED** Eric I Williams. **CODEN** BOVPBO. Index available. cum. index. **Bk Rev. Ad Acc. Circ:** 6,000 (ctrl). Documents available from BIOSIS Document Express.
**Desc:** A journal for veterinarians and others interested in cattle diseases and presentation.
**Ind/Abst** AGRICOLA [Full Cov.]; Biol. Abstr.; Index Vet.; Life Sci. Collect.; Vet. Bull.

BL/0303-7525
**BRAZILIAN JOURNAL OF VETERINARY RESEARCH AND ANIMAL SCIENCE : REVISTA DA FACULDADE DE MEDICINA VETERINARIA E ZOOTECNIA DA UNIVERSIDADE DE SAO PAULO. Added/Corp** Universidade de Sao Paulo. Faculdade de Medicina Veterinaria e Zootecnia. **VFOAT** BJVRAS. Vol. 27, No. 1 (1990)-. Periodical. English (Portuguese). sa. ***Continues*** *Revista da Faculdade de Medicina Veterinaria e Zootecnia da Universidade de Sao Paulo, 0303-7525.*

UK
**BRITISH CATTLE VETERINARY ASSOCIATION PROCEEDINGS FOR ... . Main/Corp** British Cattle Veterinary Association. (19??)-. Proceedings. English. an.

UK
**BRITISH PHARMACOPOEIA (VETERINARY). Added/Corp** Great Britain. Medicines Commission. **VFOAT** British Pharmacopoeia. (1977)-. English. ir. £70.00. Her Majesty's Stationery Office, 51 Nine Elms Lane, London SW8 5DR England. **Tel** 011 44 71 873 8459, 011 44 71 873 8499, FAX 011 44 71 873 8499, 011 44 71 873 8456, telex 297138. **(Subscription address:** Her Majesty's Stationery Office, PO Box 276, Publications Centre, London SW8 5DT England.)

UK/0007-1935
**BRITISH VETERINARY JOURNAL, THE.** [Br. vet. j.]. Vol. 105 (1949)-. Periodical. English. bm (6 issues). £136.00 UK and Europe; $245.00 other (institution). Harcourt Brace & Company Ltd., Foots Cray, High Street, Sidcup Kent DA14 5HP England. **Tel** 011 44 81 300 3322, FAX 011 44 81 309 0807. **(Subscription address:** W. B. Saunders Company / North America Subscriptions, c/o Periodicals, 6277 Sea Harbour Drive, 4th Floor, Orlando FL 32887.) **ED** A. J. Higgins. **NLM** W1 BR771. **CODEN** BVJOA9. **[CCC]. Bk Rev. Ad Acc. Pr Rev. Circ:** 1,100. available on microfilm and microfiche from University Microfilms International (UMI). Documents available from The Genuine Article, BIOSIS Document Express, CASDDS. ***Continues*** *Veterinary Journal.*
**Desc:** Scientific papers of world wide interest in the field of veterinary surgery and medicine.
**Ind/Abst** AgBiotech News Inf.; AGRICOLA [Full Cov.]; Agric. Eng. Abstr. (1991-); Anim. Breed. Abstr.; Biol. Abstr.; Chem. Abstr.; Curr. Contents, Agric. Biol. Environ. Sci.; Dairy Sci. Abstr.; EMBASE; Food Sci. Technol. Abstr.; Grasslands For. Abstr.; Health Plan. Adminis.; Helminthol. Abstr. (1991-); Index Med.; Index Vet.; Microbiol. Abstr. Sect. B; Nutr. Abstr. Rev., Ser. B, Live Feeds and Feed.; Nutr. Abstr. Rev., Ser. A, Hum. Exp.; Life Sci. Collect.; PESTDOC; Pig News Inf.; Poult. Abstr.; Protozoolog. Abstr.; Res. Alert [Full Cov.]; Rev. Agric. Entomol.; Rev. Med. Vet. Entomol.; Rev. Med. Vet. Mycology; Rev. Plant Pathol.; Saf. Health Work; Sci. Cit. Index; SCISEARCH; Small Anim. Abstr. Bibliogr.; Soyabean Abstr.; Vet. Bull.; Wildl. Rev.

UK/0263-967X
**BSAP OCCASIONAL PUBLICATION.** (BSAP OCCASIONAL PUBLICATION : [AN OCCASIONAL PUBLICATION OF THE BRITISH SOCIETY OF ANIMAL PRODUCTION].). [BSAP occas. publ.]. **Added/Corp** British Society of Animal Production. **VFOAT** B.S.A.P. Occasional Publication. **VAT** British Society of Animal Production Occasional Publication. No. 1 (1978)-. Monographic series. English. **LC** UNC. **DD** 636. **CODEN** BOPUDB.
**Ind/Abst** Soyabean Abstr.

US
**BULLETIN - AMERICAN ANIMAL HOSPITAL ASSOCIATION. Main/Corp** American Animal Hospital Association. **VFOAT** Bulletin of the American Animal Hospital Association; AAHA Bulletin. (19??)-. Periodical. English. 1746 Cole Boulevard, Golden CO 80401.

FR/0001-4192
**BULLETIN DE L'ACADEMIE VETERINAIRE DE FRANCE.** [Bull. Acad. vet. Fr.]. **Added/Corp** Academie Veterinaire de France. Recueil de Medecine Veterinaire. Vol. 81 (1928)-. Bulletin. French. qt (Jan., Mar., June, Nov.). 570.00F France; 660.00F other. Academie Veterinaire de France, 60 Blvd de Latour Maubourg, 75007 Paris France. **Tel** 011 33 1 47001259. **ED** Marc Catsaras. **NLM** W1 BU527. **CODEN** BAVFAV. **Bk Rev. Circ:** 500. Documents available from BIOSIS Document Express, CASDDS. ***Continues*** *Societe Centrale de Medecine Veterinaire. Bulletin - Societe Centrale de Medecine Veterinaire.*
**Desc:** Publishes transactions of the Veterinary Academy of France as gathered from its sessions. Also publishes scientific information presented before the Academy.
**Ind/Abst** AgBiotech News Inf.; Anim. Breed. Abstr.; Biol. Abstr.; Chem. Abstr. (1928-1982); Dairy Sci. Abstr.; Food Sci. Technol. Abstr.; Index Vet.; Nutr. Abstr. Rev., Ser. B, Live Feeds and Feed.; Nutr. Abstr. Rev., Ser. A, Hum. Exp.; Life Sci. Collect.; PESTDOC; Pig News Inf.; Poult. Abstr.; Protozoolog. Abstr.; Small Anim. Abstr. Bibliogr.; Vet. Bull.

FR/0399-2519
**BULLETIN DES G.T.V.** (BULLETIN DES G.T.V. DOSSIERS TECHNIQUES VETERINAIRES.). [Bull. GTV]. **Main/Corp** Groupement Techniques Veterinaires. **VFOAT** Dossiers Techniques Veterinaires. (1973)-. Academic Scholarly Publication. French (English; summaries and/or abstracts in Spanish). bm. 600.00F France; 820.00F other. Section Nationale des Groupements Techniques Veterinaires de Syndicat National des Veterinaires Practiciens Francais, 10 Place Leon-Blum, 75011 Paris France. **Tel** 33 1 43791152, FAX 33 1 43720700. **ED** Dr. Georges Gauthey (editor's phone: 33 1 43792054). **CODEN** BGTVDC. cum. index. **Ad Acc, Adv Mgr:** same as editor. **Circ:** 2,800 (ctrl). Documents available from CASDDS.
**Ind/Abst** Agric. Eng. Abstr. (1991-); Agrofor. Abstr. (1991-); Chem. Abstr.; Helminthol. Abstr. (1991-); Index Vet.; Nutr. Abstr. Rev., Ser. B, Live Feeds and Feed.; Poult. Abstr.; Protozoolog. Abstr.; Rev. Med. Vet. Entomol.; Soyabean Abstr.; Vet. Bull.

FR/0243-7880
**BULLETIN D'INFORMATION DES LABORATOIRES DES SERVICES VETERINAIRES.** ***Suspended.*** Bulletin. French. Four times a year. 350.00F. Centre National D'Etudes Veterinaires et Alimentaires, 7 Avenue du General de Gaulle, 94704 Maisons-Alfort Cedex France. **Tel** 43 68 15 91, FAX 43 68 97 62. **ED** F Moutou. **Circ:** 400.
**Ind/Abst** Index Vet.; Poult. Abstr.

FR/0395-7500
**BULLETIN MENSUEL DE LA SOCIETE VETERINAIRE PRATIQUE DE FRANCE. Main/Corp** Societe Veterinaire Pratique de France. Vol. 1, (1917)-. Bulletin. French. mo.
**Ind/Abst** Anim. Breed. Abstr.; Index Vet.; Pig News Inf.; Poult. Abstr.; Protozoolog. Abstr.; Rev. Med. Vet. Entomol.; Small Anim. Abstr. Bibliogr.; Vet. Bull.

KE/0378-9721
**BULLETIN OF ANIMAL HEALTH AND PRODUCTION IN AFRICA. See** Agriculture-Livestock and Poultry.

PL/0042-4870
**BULLETIN OF THE VETERINARY INSTITUTE IN PUAWY.** [Bull. Vet. Inst. Puawy]. **VFOAT** Biuletyn Instytutu Weterynarii w Puawach. Vol. 6, No. 3/4 (July/Dec. 1962)-. Academic Scholarly Publication. English. qt. **CODEN** BVIPA7. Documents available from CASDDS. ***Continues*** *Biuletyn Instytutu Weterynarii w Puawach, 0079-791X.*
**Ind/Abst** Chem. Abstr.; Food Sci. Technol. Abstr.; Microbiol. Abstr. Sect. B (19??-19??); Life Sci. Collect.; Pig News Inf.

FR/0300-9823
**BULLETIN - OFFICE INTERNATIONAL DES EPIZOOTIES (PARIS).** [Bull. - Off. int. epizoot.]. **Main/Corp** International Office of Epizootics, Paris. (May/June 1931)-. Bulletin. English (French and Spanish). mo. $160.00. OIE - Office International des Epizooties, 12 rue de Prony, 75017 Paris France. **Tel** 011 33 1 4415 1888, FAX 011 33 1 42 67 09 87, telex EPIZOTI 642 285F. **ED** L. Blajan. **LC** SF781; .I59a. **DD** 636.089/69. **NLM** W1 BU901D. **CODEN** OTEBA6. **Bk Rev. Circ:** 600 (ctrl). Documents available from BIOSIS Document Express. ***Continues*** *Mensuel - Office International des Epizooties.*
**Desc:** The 117 member countries of the OIE report on changes in their animal health status to this international organization. The data, reflecting the worldwide situation for the most serious animal diseases, are condensed each month in the OIE Bulletin. Published in English, French and Spanish, with international veterinary news appended.
**Ind/Abst** Biol. Abstr.; Dairy Sci. Abstr.; EMBASE; Index Vet.; Vet. Bull.

FR/0153-6281
**BULLETIN TECHNIQUE DE L INSEMINATION ARTIFICIELLE. VFOAT** BTIA. Bulletin Technique de l'Insemination Artificielle. (1976)-. Bulletin. French. Four times a year (Mar., June, Sept., Dec.). 159.00F France; 215.00F other. Sodipa B.T.I.A., BP 47 le Suquet, 63370 Lempes France. **Tel** 011 33 73421717, FAX 011 33 73913560. **ED** Pulvery Pascal. **UDC** 63. **Ad Acc. Circ:** 3,000 (ctrl).
**Desc:** For the veterinarians, owners and specialists in the reproduction and insemination of cattle.

US/0512-1345
**BULLETIN - WISCONSIN VETERINARY MEDICAL ASSOCIATION. Main/Corp** Wisconsin Veterinary Medical Association. Bulletin. English. mo. Wisconsin Veterinary Medical Association, 301 North Broom Street, Madison WI 53703. **Tel** (608)257-3665, FAX (608)251-5572.

SP
**BULLETIN / WORLD VETERINARY ASSOCIATION. Added/Corp** World Veterinary Association. Vol. 4, No. 2 (June 1987)-. Bulletin. English (summaries and/or abstracts in German, Spanish and French). Secretariat of the World Veterinary Association, Isabel La Catolica 12, 28013 Madrid Spain. ***Continues*** *Informative Bulletin (World Veterinary Association).*

UK
**BVDA JOURNAL : BRITISH VETERINARY DENTAL ASSOCIATION.** (19??)-. Periodical. English. Four times a year. £20.00. Simon Guyton, 18 Hanley Road, Upper Shirley, Southampton SO1 5AN England. **Tel** 011 44 703 512211. **ED** Helen Bebbington. **Bk Rev. Ad Acc. Pr Rev. Circ:** 130 (ctrl).
**Desc:** Articles about veterinary dentistry.

BL
**CADASTRO DAS INSTITUICOES DE PESQUISA, PESQUISADORES E SUAS ATIVIDADES NO RIO GRANDE DO SUL : I. MEDICINA VETERINARIA.** 1975-. Portuguese. Caixa Postal 1646 90.000, Porto Alegre Brazil. **LC** SF611; .C3.

GW/0526-765X
**CAHIERS BLEUS VETERINAIRES, LES.** [Cah. bleus vet.]. 1-. Monographic series. French. ir. Price varies per volume. Behringwerke, Emil Von Behring STR 76, D 35041 Marburg Germany. **Tel** 011 49 6421 392793.
**Ind/Abst** AGRICOLA.

US/0008-1612
**CALIFORNIA VETERINARIAN, THE.** [Calif. vet.]. Vol. 1, No. 1 (Sept./Oct. 1947)-. Periodical. English. mo. $35.00. California Veterinary Medical Association, 5231 Madison Avenue, Sacramento CA 95841. **Tel** (916)344-4985. **ED** Kathleen M Edwards. **DD** 636. **NLM** W1 CA443F. Index available. **Ad Acc. Circ:** 6,670. available on microfilm and microfiche from University Microfilms International (UMI).
**Desc:** Veterinary medicine articles, advertising, classifieds, association news, calendar.
**Ind/Abst** AGRICOLA; Anim. Breed. Abstr.; Index Vet.; PESTDOC; Small Anim. Abstr. Bibliogr.; Vet. Bull.; Wildl. Rev.

SO/0281-7985
**CAMEL FORUM.** (CAMEL FORUM. WORKING PAPER.). **Added/Corp** Akademiyada Cilmiga Fanka iyo Suugaanta (Somalia) Somali Camel Research Project. **VFOAT** Working Paper. No. 1 (Mar. 1983)-. Monographic series. English (summaries and/or abstracts in Somali). **LC** SF401.C2; C25. **DD** 636.2/95/096773.
**Ind/Abst** World Agric. Econ.

SY
**CAMEL NEWSLETTER. Added/Corp** Arab Center for the Studies of Arid Zones and Dry Lands. Vol. 1, No. 1 (Apr. 1984)-. Newsletter. English. sa.
**Ind/Abst** Index Vet.; Nutr. Abstr. Rev., Ser. B, Live Feeds and Feed.

CN/0823-2504
**CANADA CHINCHILLA.** (CANADA CHINCHILLA / NATIONAL CHINCHILLA BREEDERS OF CANADA.). **Added/Corp** National Chinchilla Breeders of Canada. (March 1983)-. Periodical. English (French; summaries and/or abstracts in French). Ten times a year. 30.00Can$. National Chinchilla Breeders of Canada, RR 10, Brampton Ontario L6V 3N2 Canada. **Tel** (416)451-8736. **ED** Thomas A. Riedstra. **DD** 636/.93234. **Ad Acc. Circ:** 400 (ctrl). ***Continues*** *National Chinchilla Breeders of Canada. Monthly Bulletin, 0027-8963.*
**Desc:** Covers the chinchilla; illness, disease, animal husbandry, ranch management, show results, pelt marketing.

CN/0830-9000
**CANADIAN JOURNAL OF VETERINARY RESEARCH.** [Can. j. vet. res.]. **Added/Corp** Canadian Veterinary Medical Association. **VFOAT** Revue Canadienne de Recherche Veterinaire; Can J Vet Res; C.J.V.R.-R.C.R.V. Vol. 50, No. 1 (Jan. 1986)-. Academic Scholarly Publication. English (summaries and/or abstracts in French). qt. 75.00Can$ Canada; 90.00Can$ other. Canadian Veterinary Medical Association, 339 Booth Street, Ottawa Ontario K1R 7K1 Canada. **Tel** (613)236-1162, FAX (613)236-9681. **ED** J. B. Derbyshire. **DD** 636.089/05. **CODEN** CJVRE9. **[CCC].** Index available. **Bk Rev. Ad Acc. Pr Rev.** ctrl circ. available on microfilm and microfiche from University Microfilms International (UMI). Documents available from The Genuine Article, BIOSIS Document Express, CASDDS. ***Continues*** *Canadian Journal of Comparative Medicine, 0008-4050.*
**Desc:** This journal has a wide international readership through the publishing of high quality scientific papers in the field of veterinary and comparative medicine including anatomy, physiology, biochemistry, pharmacology, microbiology, immunology, pathology, epidemiology, and clinical sciences.
**Ind/Abst** AgBiotech News Inf.; AGRICOLA [Full Cov.]; Anim. Breed. Abstr.; Biol. Abstr. (1986-); Chem. Abstr. (1986-); CSA Neuro. Abstr. (?-?); Curr. Contents, Agric. Biol. Environ. Sci.; Dairy Sci. Abstr.; Fish Rev.; Food Sci. Technol. Abstr.; Helminthol. Abstr. (19??-19??); Index Med.; Index Vet.; Microbiol. Abstr. Sect. B (19??-19??); Microbiol. Abstr. Sect. A; Microbiol. Abstr. Sect. C; Nutr. Abstr. Rev., Ser. B, Live Feeds and Feed.; PESTDOC; Pig News Inf.; Poult. Abstr.; Protozoolog. Abstr.; Ref. Upd. Deluxe Ed.; Res. Alert [Full Cov.]; Rev. Med. Vet. Entomol.; Sci. Cit. Index; SCISEARCH; Small Anim. Abstr. Bibliogr.; Vet. Bull.; Virol. AIDS Abstr.; Wildl. Rev.

CN/0318-1839
**CANADIAN SOCIETY OF ANIMAL SCIENCE. PROCEEDINGS OF THE ANNUAL MEETING OF THE GENERAL SOCIETY AND THE WESTERN BRANCH.** (PROCEEDINGS OF THE ANNUAL MEETING OF THE GENERAL SOCIETY AND THE ... BRANCH.). **Main/Corp** Canadian society of Animal Science. 21st- 1971-. Proceedings. English. an. Canadian Society of Animal Science, Suite 907/151 Slater Street, Ottawa Ontario K1P 5H4 Canada. ***Supersedes*** *Canadian Society of Animal Production. Proceedings of the Annual Meeting of the General Society and the ... Branch.*

CN/0825-754X
**CANADIAN VET SUPPLIES.** ***Ceased.*** [Can. vet supplies]. **VFOAT** Vet Supplies. Vol. 1, No. 1 (Summer 1984)-(Oct. 1993). Periodical. English. qt. SELC Publishing Inc., 2100 Guy Suite 200, Montreal Quebec H3H 2M8 Canada. **Tel** (514)248-3356, FAX (514)248-2195. **ED** Mario Martel. **DD** 636.089/028. **Bk Rev. Ad Acc. Circ:** 4,540.
**Desc:** Deals exclusively with the tools used in the practice of veterinary medicine, including special features on new products, university news and new appointments within the industry.

CN/0008-5286
**CANADIAN VETERINARY JOURNAL.** (THE CANADIAN VETERINARY JOURNAL / LA REVUE VETERINAIRE CANADIENNE.). [Can. vet. j.]. **Added/Corp** Canadian Veterinary Medical Association. **VFOAT** Revue Veterinaire Canadienne. Vol. 19, No. 1 (Jan. 1978)-. English (summaries and/or abstracts in French). mo. 95.00Can$ Canada; $105.00 other. Canadian Veterinary Medical Association, 339 Booth Street, Ottawa Ontario K1R 7K1 Canada. **Tel** (613)236-1162, FAX (613)236-9681. **DD** 636.089/0971. **[CCC].** available in microform from University Microfilms International (UMI). ***Continues*** *Revue Veterinaire Canadienne., 0008-5286.*
**Ind/Abst** Agric. Eng. Abstr.; Health Plan. Adminis.; Helminthol. Abstr. (19??-19??); INIS Atomindex [Micro.]; Sci. Cit. Index; Small Anim. Abstr. Bibliogr.

US/0740-0586
**CANADIAN VETERINARY PHARMACEUTICALS & BIOLOGICALS.** [Can. vet. pharm. biol.]. **VFOAT** Canadian Veterinary Pharmaceuticals and Biologicals; C.V.P.B.; CVPB. (1985)-. English. ir. Harwal Publishing Company, 601 West State Street, PO Box 96, Media PA 19063-2620. **NLM** SF 917; C212.

CN
**CANFAX.** (19??)-. English. Fifty-one times per year (weekly except week of Christmas). 200.00Can$ trade / cattle breeders and feeders; Free, other. Canfax, 6715-8 Street Northeast, Suite 215, Calgary, Alberta, T2E 7H7 Canada. **Tel** (403)275-5110, FAX (403)275-6943. **ED** Anne Dunford. **Circ:** 650.

US/1057-6622
**CANINE PRACTICE (1990).** (CANINE PRACTICE.). [Canine pract.]. Vol. 15, No. 1 (May/June 1990)-. Periodical. English. Six times a year. $28.00 US; $15.00 (veterinary students), $35.00 Canada and Mexico; $45.00 other. Veterinary Practice Publishing Company, PO Box 4457, Santa Barbara CA 93140-4457. **Tel** (805)965-1028, FAX (805)965-0722. **LC** SF991; .C274. **DD** 636. **NLM** W1; CA704Q. **CODEN** CPRAEE. available on microfilm and microfiche from University Microfilms International (UMI). Documents available from BIOSIS Document Express, The Genuine Article. ***Continues in part*** *Companion Animal Practice, 0894-9794.*
**Desc:** The journal of canine medicine and surgery for the practitioner.
**Ind/Abst** AGRICOLA [Full Cov.]; Biol. Abstr.; Curr. Contents, Agric. Biol. Environ. Sci.; Helminthol. Abstr. (1991-); Index Vet.; Nutr. Abstr. Rev., Ser. B, Live Feeds and Feed.; Life Sci. Collect.; Protozoolog. Abstr.; Res. Alert [Select. Cov.]; Rev. Med. Vet. Entomol.; Rev. Med. Vet. Mycology; Rev. Plant Pathol.; SCISEARCH; Small Anim. Abstr. Bibliogr.; Vet. Bull.

CR/1018-1210
**CARAPHIN NEWS. See** Biology-Botany.

US/0889-3152
**CAT MEWS FOR A HEALTHIER CAT.** [Cat mews heal. cat]. **VFOAT** Cat Mews. Jan./Feb. (1987)-. Periodical. English. bm (6 issues). $18.00 US; $32.00 other. Cat Mews for a Healthier Cat, 57 Whitehall Boulevard/Suite 7, Garden City NY 11530. **Tel** (516)294-8275. **ED** Susan Behn. **DD** 636. Index available. cum. index. **Circ:** 1,500. available on audiocassette.
**Desc:** The journal is dedicated to improved feline health through practical information and prevention. Includes semi-technical information on feline health and disease. Issues provide in-depth information on single topic.

UK/0952-2875
**CAT WORLD BRIGHTON.** [Cat world Brighton]. (1982)-. Periodical. English. Twelve times a year. £27.80. TG Scott Subscriber Services, 6 Bourne Enterprise Center, Wrotham Road, Borough Green, Kent TN15 8DG England. **Tel** 011 44 01 732 884023, FAX 011 44 01 732 884034. **DD** 636.8005. ***Continues*** *Cat World Weekly.*
**Desc:** The informative breed features, in depth veterinary articles, consumer guides, articles by some of the British top writers, and cats experts.

II
**CENTAUR : HOUSE JOURNAL OF THE INDIAN ASSOCIATION OF EQUINE INTERESTS. See** Horses and Horsemanship.

CE/0009-0891
**CEYLON VETERINARY JOURNAL.** ***Title Change.*** (19??)-(19??). English. an. Sri Lanka Veterinary Association, Veterinary Research Institute, Gannoruwa, Peradeniya, Sri Lanka. **Tel** KANDY 88311. **ED** S. T. Fernando. **Ad Acc. Circ:** 500. ***Continued by*** *Sri Lanka Veterinary Journal.*
**Desc:** Original articles, short communications, and reviews pertaining to research in veterinary medicine and animal husbandry.
**Ind/Abst** Anim. Breed. Abstr.; Dairy Sci. Abstr.; Field Crop Abstr.; Grasslands For. Abstr.; Index Vet.; Nutr. Abstr. Rev., Ser. B, Live Feeds and Feed.; Nutr. Abstr. Rev., Ser. A, Hum. Exp.; Protozoolog. Abstr.; Soils Fert.; Vet. Bull.

II/0379-542X
**CHEIRON.** [Cheiron]. **Added/Corp** Madras Veterinary College. Research Council. Vol. 1 (Oct. 1972)-. Periodical. English. bm. $20.00. Madras Veterinary College Association, Vepery Drive M, Ranganathan Madras 7 India. **(Subscription address:** Prints India, 11 Darya Ganj, New Delhi 110002 India.**) NLM** W1 CH154E. **CODEN** CHRNAR. Documents available from CASDDS.
**Ind/Abst** Biocont. News Inf.; Biodeter. Abstr.; Chem. Abstr.; Helminthol. Abstr. (1991-); Index Vet.; Microbiol. Abstr. Sect. B (19??-19??); Nutr. Abstr. Rev., Ser. B, Live Feeds and Feed.; Nutr. Abstr. Rev., Ser. A, Hum. Exp.; Life Sci. Collect. (?-1990); Pig News Inf.; Poult. Abstr.; Protozoolog. Abstr.; Rev. Med. Vet. Entomol.; Rev. Med. Vet. Mycology; Vet. Bull.

JA
**CHIKUSAN NO KENKYU. ANIMAL HUSBANDRY. VFOAT** Animal Husbandry. Vol. 1 (Jan. 1947)-. Academic Scholarly Publication. Japanese. mo. $188.00. Yokendo, 5-30-15 Hongo, Bunkyo-ku Tokyo Japan. **Tel** 814-0911. **(Subscription address:** Kyowa Book Company Inc., 1 38 Kanda Jinbocho Chiyoda-ku, Tokyo 101 Japan.**) ED** Akira Suzuki. **CODEN** CKNKAJ. **Bk Rev. Ad Acc. Circ:** 20,000. Documents available from CASDDS.
**Desc:** Features articles covering the scientific technologies of animal breeding, nutrition, feeds, management, and veterinary medicine concerning dairy, beef, pork, poultry, sheep and laboratory animals.
**Ind/Abst** Chem. Abstr.; Curr. Biotechnol.; Food Sci. Technol. Abstr.

BL/0103-006X
**CIENCIA VETERINARIA JABOTICABAL.** [Cienc. vet. Jaboticabal]. (1987)-. Periodical. Portuguese. **UDC** 63.
**Ind/Abst** Index Vet.; Poult. Abstr.; Rev. Med. Vet. Mycology; Small Anim. Abstr. Bibliogr.; Vet. Bull.

CU/0253-5750
**CIENCIA Y TECHNICA EN LA AGRICULTURA. VETERINARIA.** [Cienc. tec. agric., Vet.]. **VFOAT** Veterinaria. 1979-. Academic Scholarly Publication. Spanish. **CODEN** CASVDA. Documents available from BIOSIS Document Express, CASDDS.
**Ind/Abst** Biodeter. Abstr.; Biol. Abstr. (1985-); Chem. Abstr. (1979-1980); Helminthol. Abstr.; Index Vet.; Pig News Inf.; Protozoolog. Abstr.; Small Anim. Abstr. Bibliogr.; Vet. Bull.

CR/0250-5649
**CIENCIAS VETERINARIAS (HEREDIA).** (CIENCIAS VETERINARIAS.). [Cienc. vet.]. Vol. 1, No. 1 (Sept./Dec. 1979)-. Periodical. Spanish (summaries and/or abstracts in English). Three times a year. **NLM** W1 CI266F.
**Ind/Abst** Dairy Sci. Abstr.; Fish Rev.; Helminthol. Abstr. (19??-19??); Index Vet.; Pig News Inf.; Poult. Abstr.; Protozoolog. Abstr.; Rev. Med. Vet. Entomol.; Rev. Med. Vet. Mycology; Vet. Bull.; Wildl. Rev.

BL/0100-0039
**CIENTIFICA (JABOTICABAL).**
(CIENTIFICA.). [Cientifica]. **Added/Corp** Faculdade de Medicina Veterinaria e Agronomie "Prof. Antonio Ruete." Universidade Estadual Paulista. Faculdade de Ciencias Agrarias e Veterinarias. Vol. 1 (1974)-. Periodical. Portuguese (English; summaries and/or abstracts in English). sa. $60.00. Fundacao Desenvolvimento Unesp, Av Rio Branco 1210, 01206 Sao Paulo SP Brazil. **Tel** 011 55 11 2237088. **CODEN** CNTFBM. Index available. **Bk Rev. Ad Acc. Circ:** 1,000 (ctrl). Documents available from BIOSIS Document Express, CASDDS.
**Ind/Abst** Abstr. Trop. Agric.; Agric. Eng. Abstr. (1991-); Agrindex; Biol. Abstr.; Chem. Abstr. (-1988); Food Sci. Technol. Abstr.; For. Abstr.; Hortic. Abstr.; Irr. Drain. Abstr.; Life Sci. Collect.; Plant Breed. Abstr.; Plant Grow. Reg. Abstr.; Postharvest News Inf.; Seed Abstr.; Soils Fert.; Soyabean Abstr.; Weed Abstr.; Wheat Barley Trit. Abstr.

IT/0009-9082
**CLINICA VETERINARIA; RASSEGNA DI POLIZIA SANITARIA E DI IGIENE.**
***Suspended.*** [Clin. vet.]. (1878)-(1988). Periodical. Italian. mo. $11.88. Instituto Sierotera Pico, Milanese S Belfanti, Via Darwin, Milan Italy. **NLM** W1 CL61. **CODEN** CLVEAE. Documents available from CASDDS.
**Ind/Abst** Chem. Abstr.; Dairy Sci. Abstr.; EMBASE; Food Sci. Technol. Abstr.; Helminthol. Abstr.; Index Vet.; Nutr. Abstr. Rev., Ser. B, Live Feeds and Feed.; PESTDOC; Pig News Inf.; Poult. Abstr.; Protozoolog. Abstr.; Soyabean Abstr.; Vet. Bull.

UK/0147-9571
**COMPARATIVE IMMUNOLOGY, MICROBIOLOGY AND INFECTIOUS DISEASES.** **See** Biology-Microbiology.

US/1058-2401
**COMPARTIVE MEDICINE.** ***Ceased.***
(COMPARATIVE MEDICINE: ANIMAL MODELS FOR BIOMEDICAL RESEARCH.). **VFOAT** Comparative Medicine. (1992)-(1992). Academic Scholarly Publication. English. qt. Academic Press, Inc., 6277 Sea Harbor Drive, Orlando FL 32887. **Tel** (800)543-9534, (407)345-4100, FAX (407)363-9661. **ED** Henry Baker. **[CCC].**
**Desc:** Focuses on topics relevant to the use of animal models in biomedical science, particularly human and animal health research. The journal features research articles as well as critical reviews of timely topics written by recognized leaders in the field.

US
**COMPENDIUM OF VETERINARY PRODUCTS.** **VFOAT** CVP. 1st Ed. (1991)-. English. an. $82.50. North American Compendiums Inc., 942 Military Street, Port Huron MI 48060. **Tel** (313)985-5028.

US/0193-1903
**COMPENDIUM ON CONTINUING EDUCATION FOR THE PRACTICING VETERINARIAN, THE.** (THE COMPENDIUM ON CONTINUING EDUCATION FOR THE PRACTICING VETERINARIAN.). [Compend. contin. educ. pract. vet.]. Vol. 1, No. 8 (Aug. 1979)-. Periodical. English. mo. $75.00 US; $140.00 Canada; $192.00 other. Veterinary Learning Systems, 425 Phillips Boulevard 100, Trneton NJ 08618. **Tel** (609)882-5600, (800)426-9119. **ED** Dudley Johnston. **DD** 636. Index available. cum. index. **Ad Acc. Pr Rev. Circ:** 27,000. available on microfilm and microfiche from University Microfilms International (UMI). Documents available from The Genuine Article. ***Continues*** *Compendium on Continuing Education for the Small Animal Practitioner, 0164-5455.*
**Desc:** Publishes over 100 pages of peer review articles and case reports in each issue, educating the practicing veterinarian by bringing forth the latest information as it affects the practice of veterinary medicine and surgery. Testing based on the content of Compendium articles qualifies veterinarians for continuing education credits.
**Ind/Abst** AgBiotech News Inf.; AGRICOLA [Full Cov.]; Agric. Eng. Abstr. (1991-); Anim. Breed. Abstr.; Curr. Contents, Agric. Biol. Environ. Sci.; Dairy Sci. Abstr.; Helminthol. Abstr. (1991-); Index Vet.; Nutr. Abstr. Rev., Ser. B, Live Feeds and Feed.; Pig News Inf.; Poult. Abstr.; Protozoolog. Abstr.; Res. Alert [Select. Cov.]; Rev. Med. Vet. Entomol.; Rev. Med. Vet. Mycology; SCISEARCH; Small Anim. Abstr. Bibliogr.; Vet. Bull.; World Agric. Econ.

CN/0822-868X
**COMPENDIUM PHARMACO-THERAPEUTIQUE VETERINAIRE.** [Compend. pharm.-ther. vet.]. **VFOAT** CDMV Compendium; CDMV Compendium (Ed. Francaise). 1st Ed. (1983)-. French (English). ir (every two years). 55.00Can$. Compendium Pharmaco-Therapeutique Veterinaire, CP 608, Saint-Hyacinthe Quebec J2S 6H5 Canada. **Tel** (514)773-6073, telex 05-830515. **DD** 636.089/51/05. **Circ:** 1,500.
**Desc:** Lists and describes the veterinary products available at CDMV. It aims to give the veterinary practitioner brief but essential pharmacological data on different therapeutic classes.

US/0362-5532
**COMPILATION OF LAW RELATING TO THE PRACTICE OF VETERINARY MEDICINE AND SURGERY.** ***Title Change.*** **See** Law.

US
**COMPILATION OF LAWS RELATING TO THE PRACTICE OF VETERINARY MEDICINE, SURGERY AND ANIMAL HEALTH TECHNOLOGY WITH RULES AND REGULATIONS, GENERAL PROVISIONS OF THE BUSINESS AND PROFESSIONS CODE, INCLUDING THE CONSUMER AFFAIRS.** **Main/Corp** California. **Added/Corp** California. Dept. of Consumer Affairs. California. Board of Examiners in Veterinary Medicine. California. Animal Health Technician Examining Committee. **VFOAT** Veterinary Medicine, Surgery and Animal Health Technology. English. Consumer Affairs Building, 1020 N Street, Sacramento CA 95814. **LC** KFC547.V3; A294. **DD** 344.794/049; 347.940449. ***Continues*** *Compilation of Laws Relating to the Practice of Veterinary Medicine and Surgery, with Rules and Regulations, General Provisions of the Business and Professions Code, including the Consumer Affairs Act, and Excerpts from the Government Code, 0362-5532.*

BL/0100-3313
**COMUNICACOES CIENTIFICAS DA FACULDADE DE MEDICINA VETERINARIA E ZOOTECNIA DA UNIVERSIDADE DE SAO PAULO.** [Comun. cient. Fac. Med. Vet. Zootec. Univ. Sao Paulo]. Vol. 1 (1977)-. Academic Scholarly Publication. Portuguese. **NLM** W1 CO427VF. **CODEN** CCFPD9. Documents available from BIOSIS Document Express, CASDDS.
**Ind/Abst** Agrofor. Abstr.; Anim. Breed. Abstr.; Biol. Abstr. (1988-); Chem. Abstr.; Dairy Sci. Abstr.; Helminthol. Abstr. (1991-); Index Vet.; Pig News Inf.; Rev. Med. Vet. Entomol.

US/0891-9747
**CONTEMPORARY ISSUES IN SMALL ANIMAL PRACTICE.** [Contemp. issues small anim. pract.]. Vol. 1 (1985)-. Monographic series. English. ir. Price varies per volume. Churchill Livingstone, 1-3 Baxter's Place, Leith Walk, Edinburgh EH1 3AF Scotland. **Tel** 011 44 31 556 2424, FAX 011 44 31 558 1278, telex 727511. **(Subscription address:** US and Canada/ Churchill Livingstone Inc., 5 South 250 Frontenac Road, Naperville, IL 60563; (telephone: (800)553-5426 or (708)416-3939)) **ED** Michael Schaer. **DD** 636. **NLM** W1; CO769MRW.
**Desc:** Features writings of today's foremost experts in this highly authoritative book series providing invaluable, clinically-oriented reviews of selected topics currently of great importance to small animal veterinary practitioners.
**Ind/Abst** AGRICOLA [Full Cov.].

●US/1060-0558
**CONTEMPORARY TOPICS IN LABORATORY ANIMAL SCIENCE.** (CONTEMPORARY TOPICS IN LABORATORY ANIMAL SCIENCE / AMERICAN ASSOCIATION FOR LABORATORY ANIMAL SCIENCE.). [Contem. top. lab. anim. sci.]. **Added/Corp** American Association for Laboratory Animal Science. **VFOAT** Contemporary Topics. Vol. 31, No. 1 (Jan. 1992)-. Periodical. English. bm (6 issues). $80.00 US; $95.00 Canada and Mexico; $120.00 other. American Association for Laboratory Animal Science, 70 Timber Creek Drive, Suite 5, Cordova TN 38018. **Tel** (901)754-8620, FAX (901)753-0043. **DD** 619. **NLM** W1; CO77GP. **Ad Acc. Pr Rev. Acid Free.** ***Continues*** *AALAS Bulletin, 1056-1471.*
**Desc:** Features a refereed section with a wide variety of manuscripts on laboratory animal management, surgical and technical techniques, philosophical issues, nutrition, husbandry, and clinical matters.

US/0010-8901
**CORNELL VETERINARIAN, THE.** ***Ceased.*** [Cornell vet.]. **Added/Corp** New York State Veterinary College. New York State College of Veterinary Medicine. Vol. 1 (June 1911)-(Jan. 1994). Periodical. English. Four times a year. Cornell Veterinarian, College of Veterinary Medicine, Cornell University, Ithaca NY 14853. **Tel** (607)253-3715. **ED** Maurice E. White. **NLM** W1 CO881. **CODEN** COVEAZ. Index available. cum. index. **Bk Rev. Ad Acc. Pr Rev. Circ:** 1,000. Documents available from The Genuine Article, BIOSIS Document Express, CASDDS.
**Desc:** Covers current veterinary medicine research and current diseases of animals.
**Ind/Abst** AgBiotech News Inf.; AGRICOLA [Full Cov.]; Anim. Breed. Abstr.; Biol. Agric. Index; Biol. Abstr.; Chem. Abstr.; Coal Abstr.; CSA Neuro. Abstr. (?-?); Curr. Contents, Agric. Biol. Environ. Sci.; Dairy Sci. Abstr.; EMBASE; Fish Rev.; Food Sci. Technol. Abstr.; Grasslands For. Abstr.; Health Plan. Adminis.; Helminthol. Abstr.; Index Med.; Index Vet.; Leadscan; Nutr. Abstr. Rev., Ser. B, Live Feeds and Feed.; Nutr. Abstr. Rev., Ser. A, Hum. Exp.; Life Sci. Collect.; PESTDOC; Pig News Inf.; Poult. Abstr.; Protozoolog. Abstr.; Res. Alert [Full Cov.]; Rev. Med. Vet. Entomol.; Rev. Med. Vet. Mycology; Rev. Plant Pathol.; Sci. Cit. Index; SCISEARCH; Small Anim. Abstr. Bibliogr.; Stat. Theory Method Abstr. (1959-1963); Vet. Bull.; Wildl. Rev.

US/0589-7432
**CORNELL VETERINARIAN. SUPPLEMENT.** ***Ceased.*** (1966)-(Jan. 1994). English. qt. Cornell Veterinarian, College of Veterinary Medicine, Cornell University, Ithaca NY 14853. **Tel** (607)253-3715. **ED** Lennart Krook. **DD** 636. Index available. cum. index. **Bk Rev. Ad Acc. Circ:** 1,000.
**Desc:** The journal publishes papers of veterinary medicine research and current diseases of animals.

AT
**CSIRO RANGELANDS RESEARCH.** **See** Environmental Issues-Conservation and Natural Resources.

US
**CURRENT TECHNIQUES IN SMALL ANIMAL SURGERY.** Vol. 1 (1975)-. Monographic series. English. Price varies per volume.
**Ind/Abst** AGRICOLA.

US/0070-2218
**CURRENT VETERINARY THERAPY.** [Curr. vet. ther.]. (1965)-. English. ir. Holt Rinehart and Winston, 6277 Sea Harbor Drive, Orlando FL 32887. **Tel** (407)345-2500, 800 545-2522. **LC** SF745; .C8. **DD** 636.0896; 636. **NLM** W1 CU823. **CODEN** CVTHDI. Documents available from CASDDS.
**Ind/Abst** Chem. Abstr. (1964/1965-1983).

CN/0849-2395
**CVO UPDATE.** [CVO update]. **Added/Corp** College of Veterinarians of Ontario. **VAT** College of Veterinarians of Ontario Update. Vol. 6, No. 6 (March/April 1990)-. Periodical. English. bw. Ontario Veterinary Association, Suite 24/25 340 Woodlawn Road West, Guelph Ontario N1H 2X1 Canada. **Tel** (519)824-5600, FAX (519)824-6497. **DD** 636.089/06/0713. ***Continues*** *Update (Ontario Veterinary Association)., 0821-6320.*

DK/0106-6854
**DANSK VETERINAERTIDSSKRIFT.** [Dan. vet.tidsskr.]. **Added/Corp** Dansk Dyrlaegerforening. Vol. 58 (Jan. 1975)-. Periodical. Danish. Twenty-four times a year. kr730.00. Den Danske Dyrlaegeforening, Rosenlunds Alle 8, DK 2720 Vanlose Denmark. **Tel** 011 45 31 710888, FAX 011 45 31 710322. **ED** Bent Christensen. **DD** 636. **NLM** W1 DA693. ***Continues*** *Medlemsblad for den Dansk Dyrlaegeforening, 0011-6564.*
**Ind/Abst** AgBiotech News Inf.; AGRICOLA; Anim. Breed. Abstr.; Biodeter. Abstr.; Dairy Sci. Abstr.; Food Sci. Technol. Abstr.; Helminthol. Abstr. (19??-19??); Index Vet.; Nutr. Abstr. Rev., Ser. B, Live Feeds and Feed.; Nutr. Abstr. Rev., Ser. A, Hum. Exp.; Pig News Inf.; Protozoolog. Abstr.; Rev. Med. Vet. Entomol.; Rev. Med. Vet. Mycology; Small Anim. Abstr. Bibliogr.; Vet. Bull.

US/0418-5978
**DELTA PRIMATE REPORT.** **Added/Corp** Tulane University. Delta Regional Primate Research Center. Vol. 1 (1966)-. Periodical. English. Tulane University / Delta Primate, Delta Regional Primate Research Center, New Orleans LA 70118. **DD** 591.

GR/0437-2085
**DELTION TES HELLENIKES KTENIATRIKES HETAIREIAS. PERIODOS B.** (DELTION TES HELLENIKES KTENIATRIKES HETAIREIAS.). **VFOAT** Bulletin of the Hellenic Veterinary Medical Society. (1951)-. Periodical. Greek, Modern (English). qt. **NLM** W1 DE132H.
**Ind/Abst** AGRICOLA; Index Vet.; Poult. Abstr.; Protozoolog. Abstr.

GW/0179-714X
**DEUTSCHE ZEITSCHRIFT FUER BIOLOGISCHE VETERINAR-MEDIZIN.** [Dtsch. Z. biol. Vet.-Med.]. **VFOAT** Biologische Veterinar-Medizin; DZBVM. Vol. 1, No. 1 (March 1986)-. Periodical. German. qt. Karl F Haug Verlag GmbH and Company, Postfach 102840, D 69018 Heidelberg Germany. **Tel** 011 49 6221 40620. **NLM** W1; DE895L.

GW/0340-1898
**DEUTSCHES TIERARZTEBLATT.** [Dtsch. Tierarztebl.]. V. 22- ; Jan. 1974-. Periodical. German. mo. DM144.00. Schlueterscher Verlag Druckerei, Postfach 5440, D-30054 Hannover Germany. **Tel** 011 49 511 85500, FAX 011 49 511 1236400, telex 923978. **ED** Dr Schlegel. **NLM** W1 DE997C. **[CCC]. Bk Rev. Ad Acc. Circ:** 17,700 (ctrl). ***Continues*** *Deutsches Tierarzteblatt und Mitteilungsblatt der Tierarztekammern der l'Ander, 0301-0465.*
**Desc:** Bulletin of the veterinary committees of the West German states, official publication of the German Veterinary Society.
**Ind/Abst** AGRICOLA; Index Vet.; Pig News Inf.; Vet. Bull.

US/0361-9745
**DEVELOPMENTAL STUDIES AND LABORATORY INVESTIGATIONS CONDUCTED BY VETERINARY SERVICES DIAGNOSTIC LABORATORIES.** **Main/Corp** United States. Animal and Plant Health Inspection Service. English. US Department of Agriculture / Animal & Plant Health Inspection Service, 741 Federal Building 1, 6505 Belcres Road, Hyattsville MD 20782. **Tel** (301)436-7817. **LC** SF771; .U53A. **DD** 636.089/607/5.

NE/0167-5168
**DEVELOPMENTS IN ANIMAL AND VETERINARY SCIENCES.** [Dev. anim. vet. sci.]. Academic Scholarly Publication. English. Price varies per volume. Elsevier Science Publishing Company Inc, Madison Square Station, PO Box 882, New York NY 10159-0882. **Tel** (212)633-3950, FAX (212)633-3990. **CODEN** DAVSDR. Documents available from BIOSIS Document Express, CASDDS.
**Ind/Abst** AGRICOLA [Select. Cov.]; Biol. Abstr.; Chem. Abstr. (1976-1980); Life Sci. Collect.

US/0924-5359
**DEVELOPMENTS IN VETERINARY VIROLOGY.** ***Ceased.*** [Dev. vet. virol.]. (1985)-(19??). Monographic series. English. ir. Kluwer Academic Publishers / Massachusetts, PO Box 358, Accord Station, Hingham MA 02018. **Tel** (617)871-6600. **LC** UNC. **NLM** W1; DE998V. **CODEN** DVVIE9.
**Ind/Abst** AGRICOLA [Full Cov.].

CN/1193-7998
**DIRECTORY - COLLEGE OF VETERINARIANS OF ONTARIO.** (DIRECTORY / THE COLLEGE OF VETERINARIANS OF ONTARIO.). [Dir. - Coll. Vet. Ont.]. **Main/Corp** College of Veterinarians of Ontario. (199?)-. English. be. Free to members. College of Veterinarians of Ontario, 2106 Gordon Street, RR 3, Guelph Ontario N1H 6Y7 Canada. **Tel** FAX (519)824-6497. **DD** 636.089/025/713. ***Continues*** *Ontario Veterinary Association. Directory., 0822-8248.*

US/0146-1621
**DIRECTORY OF ANIMAL DISEASE DIAGNOSTIC LABORATORIES.** (DIRECTORY OF ANIMAL DISEASE DIAGNOSTIC LABORATORIES / UNITED STATES DEPARTMENT OF AGRICULTURE, ANIMAL AND PLANT HEALTH INSPECTION SERVICE, VETERINARY SERVICES.). **Added/Corp** United States. Animal and Plant Health Inspection Service. Veterinary Services. American Association of Veterinary Laboratory Diagnosticians. (19??)-. Directory. English. US Department of Agriculture / Animal & Plant Health Inspection Service, 741 Federal Building 1, 6505 Belcres Road, Hyattsville MD 20782. **Tel** (301)436-7817. **LC** SF769; .D57. **DD** 636.089/6/0072073. **Circ:** 1,000 (ctrl).
**Desc:** Information on laboratories performing diagnostic tests for diseases of domestic and wild animals, as well as diseases of animals that affect man.

US
**DIRECTORY OF INTERNSHIP AND RESIDENCIES MATCHING PROGRAM FOR ... / PREPARED BY THE AMERICAN ASSOCIATION OF VETERINARY CLINICIANS.** **Added/Corp** American Association of Veterinary Clinicians. Ralston Purina Company. **VFOAT** Veterinary Internship and Residency Matching Program. (19??)-. Directory. English. an. $20.00. American Association Veterinary Clinician, 1024 Dublin Road, Columbus OH 43215. **Tel** (614)488-0617.

US
**DIRECTORY OF MEMBERSHIP OF THE AMERICAN ANIMAL HOSPITAL ASSOCIATION.** **Main/Corp** American Animal Hospital Association. **VFOAT** Membership Directory. (1980-81)-. Directory. English. ***Continues*** *AAHA Membership, 0272-0078.*

FR/1012-5329
**DISEASE INFORMATION.** **Added/Corp** International Office of Epizootics. Vol. 1, No. 1 (July 2-8, 1988). Periodical. English. wk. 530.00F. OIE - Office International des Epizooties, 12 rue de Prony, 75017 Paris France. **Tel** 011 33 1 4415 1888, FAX 011 33 1 42 67 09 87, telex EPIZOTI 642 285F. Index available. cum. index. **Bk Rev. Ad Acc. Circ:** 250 (ctrl).
**Desc:** Notification of occurrence of new disease outbreaks worldwide.

CN/1180-338X
**DISKUSSIONS (GUELPH).** **See** Computers.

JA/0388-7421
**DOBUTSU IYAKUHIN KENSAJO NEMPO.** (ANNUAL REPORT OF THE NATIONAL VETERINARY ASSAY LABORATORY.). [Dobutsu Iyakuhin Kensajo nenpo]. **Main/Corp** Norin Suisansho Dobutsu Iyakuhin Kensajo (Japan). **VFOAT** Norin Suisansho Dobutsu Iyakuhin Kensajo Nempo; Dobutsu Iyakuhin Kensajo Nempo. Academic Scholarly Publication. Japanese (summaries and/or abstracts in English). an. Norin Suisansho Dobutsu Iyakuhin Kensajo, 15-1 Tokura 1 Kokubunji, Tokyo 185 Japan. **Tel** 0423 21 1841. **ED** Ichiro Kaizuka. **LC** SF917. **CODEN** DIKNAA. **Circ:** 630 (ctrl). Documents available from CASDDS. ***Continues*** *Norinsho Dobutsu Iyakuhin Kensajo Nempo, 0388-7421.*
**Ind/Abst** Chem. Abstr.; Index Vet.; Pig News Inf.; Poult. Abstr.; Vet. Bull.

●US/1057-9605
**DOCTOR VETERINARIAN BOARD REVIEW.** [Dr. vet. board rev.]. 1st ed. (1991-1992)-. English. $75.00. Infoconnect Ltd, PO Box 1882, Davis CA 95617-1882. **DD** 636.

●US/1057-9591
**DOCTOR VETERINARIAN QUICK REVIEW.** [Dr. vet. quick rev.]. 1st Ed. (1991-1992)-. English. $75.00. Infoconnect Ltd, PO Box 1882, Davis CA 95617-1882. **DD** 636.

TU/1011-0925
**DOGA BILIM DERGISI. SERI D1, VETERINERLIK VE HAYVANCILIK.** ***Title Change.*** [Doga bilim derg., Seri D1, Vet. hayvanc.]. Vol. 7 (1983)-(1985). Periodical. Turkish. Scientific and Technical Research Council of Turkey, Ataturk Bulvari 221, Kavaklidere Ankara Turkey. **Tel** 3420845, FAX 1175902, telex BTAK TR 43186. ***Continues in part*** *Doga Bilim Dergisi. Seri D.* ***Continued by*** *Doga. Turkish Journal of Veterinary and Animal Sciences, 1010-7649.*
**Ind/Abst** Anim. Breed. Abstr.; Dairy Sci. Abstr.; Index Vet.; Nutr. Abstr. Rev., Ser. B, Live Feeds and Feed.; Protozoolog. Abstr.; Vet. Bull.

TU/1010-7592
**DOGA. TURK VETERINERLIK VE HAYVANCILIK.** [Doga, Turk vet. hayvanc.]. **VFOAT** Turk Veterinerlik ve Hayvancilik; Doga. Turkish Journal of Veterinary Sciences; Turkish Journal of Veterinary Sciences. (1986)-. Periodical. Multiple languages. tq. ***Continues*** *Doga Bilim Dergisi. Seri D1. Veterinerlik ve Hayvancilik, 1011-0925.*
**Ind/Abst** Nutr. Abstr. Rev., Ser. A, Hum. Exp.; Wheat Barley Trit. Abstr.

TU/1010-7649
**DOGA. TURKISH JOURNAL OF VETERINARY AND ANIMAL SCIENCES.** [Doga. Turk. vet hayvanc.]. **VFOAT** Turkish Journal of Veterinary Sciences and Animal Sciences; Doga. Turk Veterinerlik Ve Hayvanclk Dergisi; Turk Veterinerlik Ve Hayvanclk Dergisi. (1986)-. Periodical. Turkish (Turkish and English). Three times a year. Scientific and Technical Research Council of Turkey, Ataturk Bulvari 221, Kavaklidere Ankara Turkey. **Tel** 3420845, FAX 1175902, telex BTAK TR 43186. **ED** Prof Halil Akcapinar. **Circ:** 700. Documents available from CASDDS. ***Continues*** *Doga Bilim Dergisi. Seri D1, Veterinerlik Ve Hayvanclk.*
**Ind/Abst** Chem. Abstr.; Index Vet.; Protozoolog. Abstr.; Rev. Med. Vet. Mycology; Small Anim. Abstr. Bibliogr.; Vet. Bull.

US/0739-7240
**DOMESTIC ANIMAL ENDOCRINOLOGY.** **See** Medical Science and Technology-Endocrinology.

FR/0150-0112
**DOSSIERS DE L'ELEVAGE, LES.** ***Suspended.*** **VFOAT** Dossiers Veterinaires des Elevages Rationnels. Periodical. French. ir. Point Veterinaire, 9 rue Alexandre, 94702 Maisons Alfort France. **Tel** 011 33 1 45170225.
**Ind/Abst** Index Vet.; Vet. Bull.

GW/0341-6593
**DTW. DEUTSCHE TIERAERZTLICHE WOCHENSCHRIFT.** [DTW. Dtsch. Tieraerztl. Wochenschr.]. **VFOAT** Deutsche Tieraerztliche Wochenschrift. (1971)-. Academic Scholarly Publication. German (summaries and/or abstracts in English). Twelve times a year. DM328.00 Germany; DM346.00 other. Verlag M & H Schaper GmbH & Co, Postfach 16 42, D 31046 Alfeld Leine Germany. **Tel** 011 49 5181 80090. **ED** Hapke. **NLM** W1 D17. **CODEN** DDTWDG. **[CCC]. Bk Rev. Ad Acc. Pr Rev. Circ:** 1,000. Documents available from BIOSIS Document Express, CASDDS. ***Continues*** *Deutsche Tieraerztliche Wochenschrift, 0012-0847.*
**Desc:** Animal production health diagnosis, treatment, prophylaxis vaccination residues in food, laboratory medicine, hygiene, and environment.
**Ind/Abst** AGRICOLA; Anim. Breed. Abstr.; Biodeter. Abstr.; Biol. Abstr. (1988-); Chem. Abstr.; Curr. Contents, Agric. Biol. Environ. Sci.; Dairy Sci. Abstr.; Energy Res. Abstr.; Field Crop Abstr.; Food Sci. Technol. Abstr.; Grasslands For. Abstr.; Health Plan. Adminis.; Helminthol. Abstr.; Index Med.; Index Vet.; Nutr. Abstr. Rev., Ser. B, Live Feeds and Feed.; Nutr. Abstr. Rev., Ser. A, Hum. Exp.; Life Sci. Collect.; PESTDOC; Pig News Inf.; Potato Abstr.; Poult. Abstr.; Protozoolog. Abstr.; Rev. Med. Vet. Mycology; Rev. Plant Pathol.; Small Anim. Abstr. Bibliogr.; Vet. Bull.

US/0012-7337
**DVM.** [DVM]. **VAT** Doctor of Veterinary Medicine. Vol. 1 (1969)-. Periodical. English. mo. $39.00 US and possessions; $60.00 Canada; $125.00 other. Advanstar Communications Inc., 131 West First Street, Duluth MN 55802. **Tel** (218)723-9477, (800)346-0085. **[CCC].**
**Ind/Abst** AGRICOLA.

US
**DVM MANAGEMENT CONSULTANTS' REPORTS.** **VFOAT** DVM Management Consultants' Reports. Tech Talk; DVM Management Consultants' Reports. Keys to Reception Skills. Vol. 18, No. 3 (March 1987)-. Periodical. English. Ten times a year. $92.00 US; $102.00 other. American Veterinary Publishing Company, 5782 Thornwood Drive, Goleta CA 93117. **Tel** (805)967-5988. ***Formed by the union of*** *DVM Management* ***and*** *Practice Productivity Consultants' Report.*

UA/0301-8199
**EGYPTIAN JOURNAL OF VETERINARY SCIENCE.** [Egypt. j. vet. sci.]. **Added/Corp** Jamiyah al-Tibbiyah al Baytariyah al-Arabiyah. Markaz al-Qawmi lil-Ilam wa-al-Tawthiq. Vol. 9 (1972)-. Academic Scholarly Publication. English (summaries and/or abstracts in Arabic). sa. National Information & Documentation Center, A1-Tahrir St Dokki AGWAF, Cairo Egypt. **Tel** 011 20 2 701696, telex 93069. **NLM** W1 EG916. **CODEN** EJVSAU. Documents available from CASDDS. ***Continues*** *United Arab Republic Journal of Veterinary Science.*
**Ind/Abst** Chem. Abstr.; Dairy Sci. Abstr.; EMBASE; Helminthol. Abstr. (1991-); Hortic. Abstr.; Index Vet.; Rev. Med. Vet. Entomol.; Vet. Bull.

JA/0424-7086
**EISEI DOBUTSU.** **See** Zoology-Entomology.

GR/0018-0068
**ELLENIKE KTENIATRIKE.** ***Ceased.*** (HELLENIKE KTENIATRIKE.). [Ell. kteniatr.]. **VFOAT** Medecine Veterinaire Hellenique; Hellenic Veterinary Medicine. Vol. 1 (1958)-(1986). Periodical. Greek, Modern (summaries and/or abstracts in English, French and German). qt. Medecine Veterianaire, Mongenthou 1 E Kteniatrike, Thessalonki Greece. **Tel** 30 031 271 229. **ED** Nicolas Aspiotis Morgentour. **NLM** W1 HE788M. **CODEN** EKTEAJ. **Bk Rev. Ad Acc.** Documents available from BIOSIS Document Express, CASDDS.
**Ind/Abst** AGRICOLA; Biol. Abstr.; Chem. Abstr.; Index Vet.; Vet. Bull.

US/1062-6034
**EMU TODAY & TOMORROW.** **See** Zoology.

FR
**EPIDEMIOLOGIE ET SANTE ANIMALE : BULLETIN DE L'ASSOCIATION POUR L'ETUDE DE L'EPIDEMIOLOGIE DES MALADIES ANIMALES.** **See** Public Health and Safety.

US/0739-9065
**EQUINE VETERINARY DATA.** **See** Horses and Horsemanship.

UK/0425-1644
**EQUINE VETERINARY JOURNAL.** [Equine vet. j.]. **Added/Corp** British Equine Veterinary Association. Vol. 1, (July 1968)-. Periodical. English. Six times a year. £60.00 UK; $108.00 US; £72.00 other. TG Scott Subscriber Services, 6 Bourne Enterprise Center, Wrotham Road, Borough Green, Kent TN15 8DG England. **Tel** 011 44 01 732 884023, FAX 011 44 01 732 884034. **ED** Peter Rossdale. **NLM** W1 EQ967. **CODEN** EQVJAI. **Bk Rev. Ad Acc. Pr Rev. Circ:** 2,400. Documents available from The Genuine Article, BIOSIS Document Express.
**Desc:** Original scientific papers covering all aspects of research, clinical articles and specific specialised issues such as physiology, ophthalmology and perinatology.
**Ind/Abst** AgBiotech News Inf.; AGRICOLA [Full Cov.]; Anim. Breed. Abstr.; Biol. Abstr.; Curr. Contents, Agric. Biol. Environ. Sci.; Dairy Sci. Abstr.; Helminthol. Abstr. (19??-19??); Index Med.; Index Vet.; Nutr. Abstr. Rev., Ser. B, Live Feeds and Feed.; Nutr. Abstr. Rev., Ser. A, Hum. Exp.; Life Sci. Collect.; PESTDOC; Pig News Inf.; Protozoolog. Abstr.; Res. Alert [Full Cov.]; Rev. Med. Vet. Entomol.; Sci. Cit. Index; SCISEARCH; Vet. Bull.; Wheat Barley Trit. Abstr.

GW/0863-2332
**ERKRANKUNGEN DER ZOOTIERE : VERHANDLUNGSBERICHT DES INTERNATIONALEN SYMPOSIUMS UEBER DIE ERKRANKUNGEN DER ZOOTIERE.** ***Ceased.*** **Added/Corp** Deutsche Akademie der Wissenschaften zu Berlin. Institut fuer Vergleichende Pathologie. Forschungsstelle fuer Wirbeltierforschung im Tierpark Berlin. Abteilung fuer Zoo- und Wildtiererkrankungen. Institut fuer Wild- und Zootierforschung im Forschungsverbund Berlin. **VFOAT** Internationales Symposium. (19??)-(1992). German (English, French and Russian). an. Akademie-Verlag GmbH, Muehlenstrasse 33 34, D 13162 Berlin Germany. **Tel** 011 49 30 47889300, FAX 011 49 30 47889357.

**(Subscription address:** VCH Publishers Inc., 303 Northwest 12th Avenue, Journals Department, Deerfield FL 33442.**)** **NLM** W3 ER67. cum. index. ***Continues*** *Proceedings / International Symposium on Diseases in Zoo Animals.*

TU/1016-3573
**ETLIK VETERINER MIKROBIYOLOJI DERGISI.** [Etlik vet. mikrobiyol. derg.]. **VFOAT** Journal of Etlik Veterinary Microbiology. (1987)-. Periodical. Turkish (summaries and/or abstracts in English). **CODEN** EVMDES. ***Continues*** *Etlik Veteriner Mikrobiyoloji Enstitusu Dergisi, 0259-272X.*
**Ind/Abst** Dairy Sci. Abstr.; Helminthol. Abstr.; Index Vet.; Protozoolog. Abstr.; Rev. Med. Vet. Entomol.; Rev. Med. Vet. Mycology; Small Anim. Abstr. Bibliogr.; Vet. Bull.

TU/0259-272X
**ETLIK VETERINER MIKROBIYOLOJI ENSITITUSU DERGISI.** ***Title Change.*** **Added/Corp** Etlik Veteriner Mikrobiyoloji Enstitusu. **VFOAT** Journal of the Etlik Veterinary Microbiological Institute, Ankara, Turkey. Vol. 4, No. 11/12 (1977)-(19??). Periodical. Turkish (summaries and/or abstracts in English). ir. **CODEN** EVMEEV. ***Continues*** *Etlik Veteriner Bakteriyoloji Enstitusu. Dergisi.* ***Continued by*** *Etlik Veteriner Mikrobiyoloji Dergisi, 1016-3573.*
**Ind/Abst** Anim. Breed. Abstr.; Food Sci. Technol. Abstr.; Nutr. Abstr. Rev., Ser. B, Live Feeds and Feed.; Rev. Med. Vet. Entomol.

FR/0297-4444
**ETUDES ET SYNTHESES DE L'I.E.M.V.T.** **VFOAT** Etudes et Syntheses de l'IEMVT; Etudes et Syntheses de l'Institut d'Elevage et de Medecine Veterinaire des Pays Tropicaux. (1984)-. Monographic series. French. ir. Price varies per volume. Expansion Scientifique Francaise, 31 Boulevard de la Tour-Maubourg, 75007 Paris France. **Tel** 011 33 1 40 62 64 00, 011 33 1 40626439. **UDC** 619:614.23(213).
**Ind/Abst** Anim. Breed. Abstr.; Grasslands For. Abstr.; Helminthol. Abstr. (1991-); Index Vet.; Protozoolog. Abstr.

FR
**EUROPEAN JOURNAL OF COMPANION ANIMAL PRACTICE, THE.** **Added/Corp** Federation of European Companion Animal Veterinary Associations. **VFOAT** EJCAP. Vol. 1 (Sept. 1990)-. Periodical. English. an. $20.00 per issue. Fecava, 82 Avenue de Villiers, F 75017 Paris France. **Tel** 011 33 1 42677296.
**Ind/Abst** Index Vet.; Small Anim. Abstr. Bibliogr.; Vet. Bull.

US/1057-6223
**FDA VETERINARIAN.** [FDA vet.]. **Added/Corp** Center for Veterinary Medicine (U.S.). **VAT** Food and Drug Administration veterinarian. Vol. 1, No. 1 (Sept./Oct. 1986)-. Government Publication. English. bm. $8.00 US; $10.00 other. Superintendent of Documents, US Government Printing Office, Washington DC 20402. **Tel** (202)275-3328, FAX (202)786-2377. **NLM** W1; FD333. ***Continues*** *FDA Veterinarian, 1057-6223.*

US/0164-6257
**FEDERAL VETERINARIAN, THE.** [Fed. vet.]. **Added/Corp** National Association of Federal Veterinarians. (1922)-. Periodical. English. Twelve times a year. $30.00. National Association of Federal Veterinarians, 1101 Vermont Avenue Northwest, Suite 710, Washington DC 20005. **Tel** (202)289-6334. **ED** Edward L. Menning, DVM, MPH. **DD** 362. **NLM** W1 FE243. **Bk Rev**, (Qty: 10/yr). **Ad Acc. Circ:** 1,800 (ctrl). ***Supersedes*** *Bureau Veterinarian.*
**Desc:** News and feature articles about medical and management issues involving public health, preventive medicine, regulatory veterinary medicine, foodborne disease, epidemiology, meat hygiene, inspection, and zoonoses.

US
**FELINE HEALTH TOPICS.** **Added/Corp** Cornell Feline Health Center. **VFOAT** Feline Health Topics for Veterinarians. Vol. 1, No. 1 (1986)-. Periodical. English. Four times a year. Comes with membership to the Cornell Feline Health Center. Cornell Feline Health Center, Cornell University, 618 Veterinary Research Tower, Ithaca NY 14853. **Tel** (607)255-2000, (607)253-3414, FAX (607)253-3419. ***Continues*** *Veterinary News (Ithaca, N.Y.).*
**Ind/Abst** Index Vet.; Rev. Med. Vet. Entomol.; Small Anim. Abstr. Bibliogr.

US/1057-6614
**FELINE PRACTICE (1990).** (FELINE PRACTICE.). [Feline pract.]. Vol. 18, No. 1 (May/June 1990)-. Periodical. English. Six times a year. $28.00 US; $15.00 (veterinary students), $35.00 Canada and Mexico; $45.00 other. Veterinary Practice Publishing Company, PO Box 4457, Santa Barbara CA 93140-4457. **Tel** (805)965-1028, FAX (805)965-0722. **LC** SF985; .F42. **DD** 636. **NLM** W1; FE455. **CODEN** FELPEJ. Documents available from BIOSIS Document Express. ***Continues in part*** *Companion Animal Practice, 0894-9794.*
**Desc:** The journal of feline medicine and surgery for practitioners.
**Ind/Abst** AGRICOLA [Full Cov.]; Biol. Abstr.; Curr. Contents, Agric. Biol. Environ. Sci.; Dairy Sci. Abstr.; Helminthol. Abstr. (1991-); Nutr. Abstr. Rev., Ser. B, Live Feeds and Feed.; Nutr. Abstr. Rev., Ser. A, Hum. Exp.; Life Sci. Collect.; Protozoolog. Abstr.; Res. Alert; Rev. Med. Vet. Mycology; Rev. Plant Pathol.; SCISEARCH; Small Anim. Abstr. Bibliogr.

GW/0015-363X
**FLEISCHWIRTSCHAFT, DIE.** **See** Agriculture-Livestock and Poultry.

●US/1067-8964
**FOCUS ON VETERINARY SCIENCE & MEDICINE.** **Added/Corp** Institute for Scientific Information. **VFOAT** Focus on Veterinary Science and Medicine. (1993)-. Academic Scholarly Publication. English. mo. $247.00. Institute for Scientific Information, 3501 Market Street, Philadelphia PA 19104. **Tel** (215)386-0100, (800)523-1850, FAX (215)386-6362, telex 84-5305. **(Subscription address:** Institute for Scientific Information, PO Box 71416, Chicago IL 60694.**)**

CN/1182-8781
**FOCUS - ONTARIO VETERINARY MEDICAL ASSOCIATION.** (FOCUS : THE MAGAZINE OF THE ONTARIO VETERINARY MEDICAL ASSOCIATION.). [Focus - Ont. Vet. Med. Assoc.]. **Added/Corp** Ontario Veterinary Medical Association. Vol. 9, No. 3 (May/June)-. Periodical. English. bm. Ontario Veterinary Medical Association, PO Box 934, Guelph, Ontario N1H 6J6 Canada. **DD** 636.089/09713/05. ***Continues*** *Focus (Society of Ontario Veterinarians)., 0848-1784.*

XO/0015-5748
**FOLIA VETERINARIA.** [Folia vet.]. Vol. 1 (1956)-. Academic Scholarly Publication. English. sa. Price varies per volume. College of Veterinary Medicine, Czechoslovakia. **Tel** 095 321 11/77322. **NLM** W1 FO298K. **CODEN** FVMCAW. **Bk Rev**. Documents available from CASDDS.
**Ind/Abst** Chem. Abstr.; Helminthol. Abstr.; Index Vet.; Nutr. Abstr. Rev., Ser. B, Live Feeds and Feed.; Pig News Inf.; Rev. Med. Vet. Entomol.; Vet. Bull.

IT/0301-0724
**FOLIA VETERINARIA LATINA.** [Folia vet. lat.]. Vol. 1 (1971)-. Academic Scholarly Publication. English (French, Italian and Spanish). qt. **NLM** W1 FO298P. **CODEN** FVTLAQ. Documents available from BIOSIS Document Express, CASDDS.
**Ind/Abst** Biol. Abstr.; Chem. Abstr.; Curr. Contents, Agric. Biol. Environ. Sci.; Dairy Sci. Abstr.; EMBASE; Food Sci. Technol. Abstr.; Health Plan. Adminis.; Index Med.; Vet. Bull.

UK/0950-1878
**FOOT AND MOUTH DISEASE BULLETIN.** [Foot mouth dis. bull.]. **Added/Corp** Wellcome Research Laboratories (Great Britain). Group Veterinary Biologicals. Wellcome Research Laboratories (Great Britain). F.M.D. Technical Division. Wellcome Foot and Mouth Disease Vaccine Laboratory (Great Britain). F.M.D. Technical Division. Coopers Animal Health Ltd. Foot and Mouth Disease Vaccine Laboratory. (19??)-. Bulletin. English.
**Ind/Abst** Index Vet.

US/0091-8199
**FOREIGN ANIMAL DISEASE REPORT.** [Foreign anim. dis. rep.]. Periodical. English. qt. USDA Emergency Programs, 6505 Belcrest Road, Hyattsville MD 20782. available on microfiche (Vols. for 1986- distributed to depository libraries). Documents available from Documents on Demand.
**Ind/Abst** AGRICOLA [Full Cov.]; Am. Stat. Index; Index Vet.; Pig News Inf.; Poult. Abstr.; Protozoolog. Abstr.; Rev. Med. Vet. Entomol.; Small Anim. Abstr. Bibliogr.

GW/0939-7701
**FORSCHUNGSVORHABEN / ZENTRALSTELLE FUER AGRARDOKUMENTATION UND -INFORMATION.** **See** Agriculture.

GW
**FORTSCHRITTE DER VERHALTENSFORSCHUNG.** **VFOAT** Advances in Ethology. No. 8 (1972)-. Monographic series. English. ir. Free to subscribers of Ethology : Zeitschrift fuer Tierpsychologie. Blackwell Wissenschafts-Verlag, Kurfuerstendamm 57, D 10707 Berlin Germany. **Tel** 011 49 30 32790623, 011 49 30 32790624, FAX 011 49 30 327 90610. ***Continues*** *Zeitschrift fuer Tierpsychologie. Beiheft.*
**Ind/Abst** Psychol. Abstr. (1972-); PsycINFO; PsycLit.

GW/0301-2794
**FORTSCHRITTE DER VETERINARMEDIZIN.** (FORTSCHRITTE DER VETERINARMEDIZIN / ADVANCES IN VETERINARY MEDICINE.). [Fortschr. Veterinarmed.]. **VFOAT** Advances in Veterinary Medicine. Vol. 15 (1971)-. Monographic series. German (summaries and/or abstracts in English, French and Spanish). ir. Price varies per volume. Blackwell Wissenschafts-Verlag, Kurfuerstendamm 57, D 10707 Berlin Germany. **Tel** 011 49 30 32790623, 011 49 30 32790624, FAX 011 49 30 327 90610. **(Subscription address:** Blackwell Wissenschafts VLG, Postfach 800620, Koch Neff Oetinger, D 70506 Stuttgart Germany.**)** **ED** Stanley Terlecki, Valerie Barnard. **LC** UNC. **NLM** W1 FO893. **CODEN** AVYMAX. Documents available from BIOSIS Document Express, CASDDS. ***Continues*** *Zentralblatt fuer Veterinarmedizin. Beiheft, 0514-714X.*
**Ind/Abst** Biol. Abstr.; Chem. Abstr.; EMBASE; Index Vet.; Vet. Bull.

NE
**GEITEHOUDER, DE.** **See** Agriculture-Livestock and Poultry.

US/0886-5760
**GEORGIA VETERINARIAN, THE.** (GEORGIA VETERINARIAN.). [Ga. vet.]. **Added/Corp** Georgia Veterinary Medical Association. Vol. 1 (Sept. 1948)-. Periodical. English. Six times a year. $25.00. Georgia Veterinarian Medical Association, PO Box 5426 Campus Station, Athens GA 30604. **Tel** (404)542-5718. **ED** J.T. Mercer. **DD** 636. **NLM** W1 GE451K. **Bk Rev**. **Ad Acc. Circ:** 2,000 (ctrl).
**Desc:** Association business, case reports and scientific articles.
**Ind/Abst** AGRICOLA [Full Cov.]; Fish Rev.; Wildl. Rev.

UK
**GOAT VETERINARY SOCIETY JOURNAL.** **Added/Corp** Goat Veterinary Society. (1979)-. Periodical. English. sa. £15.00 England; £17.50 other. Ministry of Agriculture Fisheries & Food, Kendal Road, Harlescott Shrewsbury, Shropshire SY1 4HD England. **Tel** 011 44 743 367621, FAX (0902)743602, telex 337559.
**Ind/Abst** Anim. Breed. Abstr.; Dairy Sci. Abstr.; Index Vet.; Nutr. Abstr. Rev., Ser. B, Live Feeds and Feed.; Protozoolog. Abstr.; Rev. Med. Vet. Mycology; Vet. Bull.

IT
**GUIDA DI VETERINARIA E ZOOTECNIA.** (1989)-. Periodical. Italian. be. L110000.00 Italy; L126000.00 Europe; L142000.00 other. Org Edit Medico Farmaceutica, CP 10434, 20110 Milan Italy. **Tel** 011 39 2 675051.

US
**GUIDE FOR ACCREDITED VETERINARIANS, A.** **Main/Corp** United States. Animal and Plant Health Inspection Service. Veterinary Services. (19??)-. English. US Department of Agriculture / Animal & Plant Health Inspection Service, 741 Federal Building 1, 6505 Belcres Road, Hyattsville MD 20782. **Tel** (301)436-7817. **LC** SF740; .U54a. **DD** 636.089/44/0973. ***Continues*** *United States. Animal and Plant Health Service. A Guide for Accredited Veterinarians.*

US
**GUIDE FOR THE CARE AND USE OF LABORATORY ANIMALS / PREPARED BY THE COMMITTEE ON CARE AND USE OF LABORATORY ANIMALS OF THE INSTITUTE OF LABORATORY ANIMAL RESOURCES, COMMISSION OF LIFE SCIENCES, NATIONAL RESEARCH COUNCIL.** **Added/Corp** Institute of Laboratory Animal Resources (U.S.). Committee on Care and Use of Laboratory Animals. (1972)-. English. ir. Free on request. Science and Health Reports, National Institutes of Health, Bethesda MD 20205. **LC** SF406; .G8. **DD** 636.08/85/05. ***Continues*** *Guide for Laboratory Animal Facilities and Care.*

US
**HAMPSHIRE HERDSMAN.** ***Title Change.*** (19??)-(19??). Periodical. English. Eleven times a year. Hampshire Swine Registry, 6748 North Frostwood Parkway, PO Box 9518, Peoria IL 61612. **Tel** (309)692-1571. ***Merged into*** *Seedstock Edge.*

US/0739-4276
**HAMSTER INFORMATION SERVICE.** Periodical. English. qt. $12.00 US; $15.00 other. F Homburger for the Hamster Society, Bio-Research Institute, 380 Green Street, Cambridge MA 02139. **NLM** W1; HA498D.

KO/0367-5807
**HAN'GUK CHUKSAN HAKHOE CHI.** [Han'guk Chuksan Hakhoe chi]. **Main/Corp** Han'Guk Chuksan Hakhoe. **VFOAT** Korean Journal of Animal Sciences. (1958)-. Academic Scholarly Publication. Korean (English; summaries and/or abstracts in English). bm (6 issues). $40.00. Korean Society of Animal Sciences, Seoul National University, Department of Animal Sciences, Suweon 170 Korea. **Tel** 011 331 43 1240. **ED** Chung Soo Chung. **LC** SF1; .H36a. **CODEN** HGCHAG. **[CCC]**. Index available. **Ad Acc. Pr Rev. Circ:** 1,500. Documents available from BIOSIS Document Express, CASDDS. ***Continues*** *Han'guk Ch'uksan Hakhoe. Chi. The Research Bulletin.*
**Desc:** Publishes research papers related to animal science.
**Ind/Abst** Biol. Abstr.; Chem. Abstr.; Curr. Biotechnol.; Food Sci. Technol. Abstr.; Index Vet.; Irr. Drain. Abstr.; Maize Abstr.; Nutr. Abstr. Rev., Ser. B, Live Feeds and Feed.; Nutr. Abstr. Rev., Ser. A, Hum. Exp.; Plant Breed.

Abstr.; Postharvest News Inf.; Poult. Abstr.; Rev. Med. Vet. Mycology; Rice Abstr.; Seed Abstr.; Soils Fert.; Sorghum Mill. Abstr.; Soyabean Abstr.; Vet. Bull.; Weed Abstr.

KO
**HANGUK CHUKSAN KWAHAK YONGU POGO.** **VFOAT** Annual Research Reports of the Korea Institute of Animal Sciences. V. 1- Series (1981)-. Periodical. English (Korean). an. Hanguk Chuksan Kwahak Yonguso, 129 Ami-ri Pubal-Myon Ich On-gun, Kyonggi-do Korea 172-18. **LC** SF1; .H37.

KO
**HANGUK SUUI KONGJUNG POGON HAKHOE CHI.** **VFOAT** Korean Journal of Veterinary Public Health. Periodical. Korean (English). Hanguk Suui Kongjung Pogon Hakhoe 50, 3-ka Chungmu-ro, Chung-ku, Seoul South Korea. **LC** SF740; .H36. **CODEN** HKPHEB.
**Ind/Abst** Protozoolog. Abstr.

II/0367-5610
**HARYANA AGRICULTURAL UNIVERSITY JOURNAL OF RESEARCH.** **See** Agriculture.

II
**HARYANA VETERINARIAN, THE.** **Added/Corp** Haryana Agricultural University. College of Veterinary Sciences. Haryana Agricultural University. College of Veterinary Medicine. Vol. 9, No. 2, (Dec. 1970)-. Periodical. English. sa. $25.00. College of Veterinary Sciences University, Hissar India. **(Subscription address:** Prints India, 11 Darya Ganj, New Delhi, 110002 India, (Phone: 011 91 11 3268645)) ***Continues*** *Punjab Veterinarian.*
**Ind/Abst** Anim. Breed. Abstr.; Dairy Sci. Abstr.; Helminthol. Abstr.; Index Vet.; Poult. Abstr.; Small Anim. Abstr. Bibliogr.

CN/0846-4782
**HEALTH OF ANIMALS.** [Health anim.]. **Added/Corp** Canada. Agriculture Canada. Canada. Health of Animals Directorate. **VFOAT** Hygiene Veterinaire. (1987)-. Government Publication. English (French). Free on request. Agriculture Canada, Communications Branch, Ottawa Ontario K1A 0C7 Canada. **DD** 354.710082/336. ***Continues*** *National Animal Health Program (Canada) Annual Review., 0839-8143.*

UK
**HENSTON VETERINARY BOVINE VADE MECUM.** (19??)-. English. an. £30.00 UK; £33.00 others. Henston, 2 Church Street, High Wycombe HP11 2DE England. **Tel** 011 44 494 474433, FAX 011 44 494 464353. ***Separated from*** *Henston Veterinary Vade Mecum. Large Animals.*

UK/0969-2681
**HENSTON VETERINARY EQUINE VADE MECUM.** (19??)-. English. an. £27.00 UK; £30.00. Henston, 2 Church Street, High Wycombe HP11 2DE England. **Tel** 011 44 494 474433, FAX 011 44 494 464353. ***Separated from*** *Henston Veterinary Vade Mecum. Large Animals.*

UK/0268-4276
**HENSTON VETERINARY VADE MECUM. LARGE ANIMALS, THE.** ***Title Change.*** **VFOAT** Veterinary Vade Mecum; Large Animals; Henston Large Animal Veterinary Vade Mecum. (1985)-(19??). English. an. Henston, 2 Church Street, High Wycombe HP11 2DE England. **Tel** 011 44 494 474433, FAX 011 44 494 464353. **ED** J. M. Evans. **NLM** SF 915; H5261. Index available. **Ad Acc. Circ:** 4,000 (ctrl). ***Continues in part*** *Henston Veterinary Vade Mecum.* ***Split into*** *Henston Veterinary Bovine Vade Mecum* ***and*** *Henston Veterinary Equine Vade Mecum.*
**Desc:** Initial source of information on diseases and conditions affecting large animals and the range of products available for treatment prevention.

UK/0268-4268
**HENSTON VETERINARY VADE MECUM. SMALL ANIMALS, THE.** **VFOAT** Veterinary Vade Mecum. Small Animals. (1983/84)-. English. an (April). £33.50. Henston Ltd, The Cheques, 2 Church Street, High Wycombe, Bucks, HP11 2DE England. **Tel** (0)494-474433, FAX (0)494-464353. **ED** Allan J. Henderson. **NLM** SF 915; H526. **Ad Acc, Adv Mgr:** John O'Hara. **Circ:** 4,000 (ctrl). ***Continues in part*** *Henston Veterinary Vade Mecum.*
**Desc:** List of all known diseases relevant to dogs and cats and lists all licensed products available for their treatment in the UK.

DK/0105-1423
**HISTORIA MEDICINAE VETERINARIAE.** **Added/Corp** Amici Historiae Medicinae Veterinariae. (1976)-. Periodical. Dutch (English, French and German; summaries and/or abstracts in German and French). qt. kr333.00, $53.00. Historia Medicinae Veterinaria, Sondergade 39, DK-4130 Viby Sjoelland Denmark. **ED** Ivan Katic, Vibeke Dantzer and Sigrid T. Jorgensen. **LC** SF615; .H57. **DD** 636.089/09. **NLM** W1 HI781. Index available. cum. index. **Bk Rev. Ad Acc. Circ:** 350 (ctrl).
**Desc:** Designed to satisfy the curiosity of persons interested in the history of veterinary medicine as a science and as a profession. It is the only international multilingual journal devoted to this subject.
**Ind/Abst** AGRICOLA (19??-); Biol. Abstr. 919??-); Index Vet. (19??-); Protozoolog. Abstr. (19??-); Rev. Med. Vet. Entomol. (19??-); Small Anim. Abstr. Bibliogr. (19??-); Vet. Bull. (19??-).

CC/0529-5127
**HSU MU SHOU I HSUEH PAO / CHUNG-KUO HSU MU SHOU I HSUEH HUI.** **VFOAT** Acta Veterinaria et Zootechnica Sinica; Xumu Shouyi Xuebao. (1956)-. Periodical. Chinese (summaries and/or abstracts in English). qt. RMBY0.70. Chinese Academy of Agriculture, Institute of Animal Husbandry, Ma Lian Wa, Haidian Qu, Beijing 100094, People's Republic of China. **Tel** 2581177. **ED** Dong Wei. **LC** SF604; .H75. **DD** 636.089/05.
**Ind/Abst** Helminthol. Abstr.; Index Vet.; Pig News Inf.; Poult. Abstr.; Protozoolog. Abstr.; Rev. Med. Vet. Entomol.; Rev. Med. Vet. Mycology; Vet. Bull.; World Agric. Econ.

CH/0253-9128
**HUIBAO - TAIWAN UMU SHOUYI XUEHUI.** (TAI-WAN HSU MU SHOU I HSUEH HUI HUI PAO.). [Huibao - Taiwan umu shouyi xuehui]. **Main/Corp** Tai-wan Sheng hsu mu shou i Hsueh hui. **Added/Corp** Tai-wan Sheng hsu mu shou i Hsueh hui. Journal of the Taiwan Association of Animal Husbandry and Veterinary Medicine. **VFOAT** Journal of the Taiwan Association of Animal Husbandry and Veterinary Medicine; Taiwan Journal of Veterinary Medicine and Animal Husbandry. (195?)-. Chinese (summaries and/or abstracts in English). Taiwan Association of Veterinary Medicine and Animal Husbandry, 376 Chung Cheng Road, Tamsui 251, Taipei, Taiwan. **LC** SF55.T28; T3a. ***Continues*** *Tai-wan Sheng hsu mu Shou i Hsueh hui. Tai-wan hsu mu shou i Hsueh hui chi kan, 0494-5603.*
**Ind/Abst** AGRICOLA; Helminthol. Abstr. (1991-); Nutr. Abstr. Rev., Ser. B, Live Feeds and Feed.

JA
**IBARAKI-KEN EISEI KENKYUJO NEMPO.** **See** Public Health and Safety.

FI/1018-4635
**ICLAS NEWS.** (19??)-. English. Twice a year. Free. ICLAS - International Council for Laboratory Animal Science, PO Box 6, SF 702, Dept. of Physiology, 11 Kuopio, Finland. **Tel** 011 358 9 71163080, 011 358 9 71163110, FAX 011 358 9 71163410, 011 358 9 71163112, telex 4221KUYSF. **ED** Osmo Hanninen. **Ad Acc. Circ:** 200 (ctrl). ***Continues*** *ICLAS Bulletin.*
**Desc:** News and reports of members, courses and meetings. Annual reports of ICLA's plan of action and information on new publications.

US/0018-9960
**ILAR NEWS.** **See** Medical Science and Technology.

FI
**ILMOITUS TARTTUVISTA ELAINTAUDEISTA / SUOMI.** **VFOAT** Rapport Om Smittsamma Djursjunkdomar; Bulletin des Epizooties. Periodical. Finnish (French and Swedish). mo. ***Continues*** *Ilmoitus Tarttuvista Kotielaintaudeista Suomessa.*

KE/0255-4585
**ILRAD REPORTS.** [ILRAD rep.]. **VFOAT** I.L.R.A.D. Reports; Reports. **VAT** International Laboratory for Research on Animal Diseases Reports. Vol. 1, No. 1 (July 1983)-. Periodical. English. qt. **NLM** W1; IL946F.
**Ind/Abst** AgBiotech News Inf.; Anim. Breed. Abstr.; Index Vet.; Protozoolog. Abstr.; Rev. Med. Vet. Entomol.; Trop. Dis. Bull.

AT/0813-1643
**IMVS NEWSLETTER / PREPARED BY THE STAFF OF THE INSTITUTE OF MEDICAL AND VETERINARY SCIENCE.** **Added/Corp** Institute of Medical and Veterinary Science (S. Aust.). **VFOAT** I.M.V.S. Newsletter. **VAT** Institute of Medical and Veterinary Science Newsletter. (19??)-. Periodical. English. Institute of Medical and Veterinary Science / South Australia, Adelaide SA Australia. ***Continues*** *Newsletter (Institute of Medical and Veterinary Science (S. Aust.). Laboratory Animal Center).*

UK/0263-841X
**IN PRACTICE (LONDON 1979).** (IN PRACTICE.). [In pract.]. **Added/Corp** British Veterinary Association. Vol. 1, No. 1 (Jan. 1979)-. Periodical. English. Six times a year. £37.00 UK; £42.00 Africa; £47.50 other. TG Scott Subscriber Services, 6 Bourne Enterprise Center, Wrotham Road, Borough Green, Kent TN15 8DG England. **Tel** 011 44 01 732 884023, FAX 011 44 01 732 884034. **ED** Edward Boden. **NLM** W1 IN102M. **CODEN** IPRCDH. **[CCC].** cum. index. **Ad Acc. Circ:** 11,000. Documents available from BIOSIS Document Express.
**Desc:** State of the art clinical reviews and updates on farm and companion animals, all specially commissioned from leading authorities. Covers all aspects of the practising veterinarian's work.
**Ind/Abst** AGRICOLA [Full Cov.]; Anim. Breed. Abstr.; Biol. Agric. Index; Biol. Abstr.; Dairy Sci. Abstr.; EMBASE [Select. Cov.]; Helminthol. Abstr.; Index Med.; Index Vet.; Nutr. Abstr. Rev., Ser. B, Live Feeds and Feed.; Nutr. Abstr. Rev., Ser. A, Hum. Exp.; PESTDOC; Pig News Inf.; Poult. Abstr.; Protozoolog. Abstr.; Small Anim. Abstr. Bibliogr.; Soc. Sci. Cit. Index [Select. Cov.]; Vet. Bull.

UK/0019-3941
**INDEX OF VETERINARY SPECIALITIES.** (19??)-. Abstracting/Indexing Service. English. bm. £18.50. A E Morgan Publications Ltd, Stanley House, 9 West Street, Epsom Surrey KT18 7RL England. **Tel** 011 44 3727 41411, FAX 0372 744493, telex 291561 VIA SOS G. **ED** C. Cattrall. **Ad Acc. Circ:** 3,700. available in microform from University Microfilms International (UMI).
**Desc:** Ethical veterinary pharmaceutical products; prescribing guide for veterinarians (UK).

UK/0019-4123
**INDEX VETERINARIUS.** **See** Veterinary Sciences-Abstracting, Bibliographies and Statistics.

II/0019-5057
**INDIAN JOURNAL OF ANIMAL HEALTH.** [Indian j. anim. health]. **Added/Corp** West Bengal Veterinary Association. (1962)-. Periodical. English. sa. $35.00. Indian Journal of Animal Health, 61-4 Belgachia Road, Calcutta India 700037. **Tel** 56-5520. **(Subscription address:** Prints India, 11 Darya Ganj, New Delhi, 110002 India, (Phone: 011 91 11 3268645)) **ED** A. Chatterjee. **NLM** W1 IN206NJ. **CODEN** IJAHA4. **Bk Rev. Ad Acc. Circ:** 2,500 (ctrl). Documents available from BIOSIS Document Express, CASDDS.
**Desc:** Covers all aspects of veterinary science including its relation to public health.
**Ind/Abst** AGRICOLA; Anim. Breed. Abstr.; Biol. Abstr.; Chem. Abstr.; Dairy Sci. Abstr.; Food Sci. Technol. Abstr.; Helminthol. Abstr. (1991-); Nutr. Abstr. Rev., Ser. B, Live Feeds and Feed.; Nutr. Abstr. Rev., Ser. A, Hum. Exp.; Life Sci. Collect.; Pig News Inf.; Poult. Abstr.; Protozoolog. Abstr.; Rev. Agric. Entomol.; Rev. Med. Vet. Entomol.; Rev. Med. Vet. Mycology; Rev. Plant Pathol.; Rice Abstr.; Small Anim. Abstr. Bibliogr.

II/0970-3209
**INDIAN JOURNAL OF ANIMAL NUTRITION.** **See** Agriculture-Livestock and Poultry.

II
**INDIAN JOURNAL OF ANIMAL REPRODUCTION : JOURNAL OF THE INDIAN SOCIETY FOR THE STUDY OF ANIMAL REPRODUCTION, THE.** **Added/Corp** Indian Society for the Study of Animal Reproduction. (198?)-. Periodical. English. sa. $50.00. **(Subscription address:** Prints India, 11 Darya Ganj, New Delhi, 110002 India, (Phone: 011 91 11 3268645))
**Ind/Abst** AgBiotech News Inf.; Anim. Breed. Abstr.; Dairy Sci. Abstr.; Index Vet.; Nutr. Abstr. Rev., Ser. B, Live Feeds and Feed.; Pig News Inf.; Small Anim. Abstr. Bibliogr.; Vet. Bull.

II/0367-6722
**INDIAN JOURNAL OF ANIMAL RESEARCH.** **See** Agriculture-Livestock and Poultry.

II/0367-8318
**INDIAN JOURNAL OF ANIMAL SCIENCES, THE.** [Indian j. anim. sci.]. Vol. 39, No. 1 (Feb. 1969)-. Academic Scholarly Publication. English. mo. $80.00. Indian Council of Agricultural Research, Mgr Krishi Anusandham Bhavan, New Delhi 110 012 India. **Tel** 011 91 11 5713657, telex 031-62249 ICAR IN. **(Subscription address:** Prints India, 11 Darya Ganj, New Delhi, 110002 India, (Phone: 011 91 11 3268645)) **NLM** W1 IN206NR. **CODEN** IJLAA4. **Pr Rev.** available on microfilm and microfiche from University Microfilms International (UMI). Documents available from The Genuine Article, BIOSIS Document Express, CASDDS. ***Continues*** *Indian Journal of Veterinary Science and Animal Husbandry.*
**Ind/Abst** AgBiotech News Inf.; AGRICOLA; Agric. Eng. Abstr. (1991-); Agrindex; Agrofor. Abstr. (1991-); Anim. Breed. Abstr.; BioBusiness; Biodeter. Abstr. (1991-); Biol. Abstr.; Chem. Abstr.; CSA Neuro. Abstr. (?-?); Curr. Contents, Agric. Biol. Environ. Sci.; Dairy Sci. Abstr.; Ecol. Abstr. (?-?); EMBASE; Field Crop Abstr.; Fish Rev.; Food Sci. Technol. Abstr.; For. Prod. Abstr.; For. Abstr.; Genet. Abstr.; Grasslands For. Abstr.; Helminthol. Abstr. (19??-19??); Hortic. Abstr.; Immunol. Abstr.; Index Vet.; Leis. Recreat. Tour. Abstr.; Maize Abstr.; Microbiol. Abstr. Sect. B; Microbiol. Abstr. Sect. C; Nutr. Abstr. Rev., Ser. B, Live Feeds and Feed.; Nutr. Abstr. Rev., Ser. A, Hum. Exp.; Life Sci. Collect.; PESTDOC; Pig News Inf.; Poult. Abstr.; Protozoolog. Abstr.; Res. Alert [Select. Cov.]; Rev. Med. Vet. Entomol.; Rev. Med. Vet. Mycology; Rice Abstr.; Rural Dev. Abstr.; SCISEARCH; SEA Abstr.; Small Anim. Abstr. Bibliogr.; Sorghum Mill. Abstr.; Soyabean Abstr.; Sug. Indus. Abstr.; Vet. Bull.; Virol. AIDS Abstr.; Weed Abstr.; Wheat Barley Trit. Abstr.; Wildl. Rev.; World Agric. Econ.

II
**INDIAN JOURNAL OF COMPARATIVE MICROBIOLOGY, IMMUNOLOGY, AND INFECTIOUS DISEASES.** **Added/Corp** Indian Association of Veterinary Microbiologists, Immunologists,

and Specialists in Infectious Diseases. (19??)-. Periodical. English. qt. $100.00. Indian Association of Veterinary Microbiologists, Izatnagar, India. **(Subscription address:** Prints India, 11 Darya Ganj, New Delhi 110002 India.**)** **NLM** W1; IN207CT.
**Ind/Abst** Biodeter. Abstr.; Food Sci. Technol. Abstr.; Helminthol. Abstr. (1991-); Index Vet.; Pig News Inf.; Poult. Abstr.; Protozoolog. Abstr.; Small Anim. Abstr. Bibliogr.; Vet. Bull.

II/0971-1937
**INDIAN JOURNAL OF VETERINARY ANATOMY.** [Indian J. Vet. Anat.]. (1989)-. Periodical. English. sa. **UDC** 636.089.
**Ind/Abst** Index Vet.; Poult. Abstr.

II/0970-051X
**INDIAN JOURNAL OF VETERINARY MEDICINE.** [Indian j. vet. med.]. **Added/Corp** Indian Society for Veterinary Medicine. Punjab Agricultural University. Dept. of Veterinary Medicine. Vol. 1, No. 1 (Dec. 1981)-. Periodical. English. Twice a year (June and December). $40.00. Indian Veterinary Res Institute, Division Experimental Medicine Sur, Izatnagar 243122 India. **Tel** 11 91 581 71232. **(Subscription address:** Prints India, 11 Darya Ganj, New Delhi, 110002 India, (Phone: 011 91 11 3268645)**)** **ED** Dr. S. K. Dwivedi. **NLM** W1; IN241D. **Bk Rev**, (Qty: 1). **Ad Acc. Circ:** 400 (ctrl).
**Ind/Abst** Agrofor. Abstr. (1991-); Dairy Sci. Abstr.; Fish Rev. (Jan. 1989-July 1992);; Grasslands For. Abstr.; Index Vet.; Nutr. Abstr. Rev., Ser. B, Live Feeds and Feed.; Poult. Abstr.; Protozoolog. Abstr.; Rev. Med. Vet. Entomol.; Rev. Med. Vet. Mycology; Vet. Bull.; Wheat Barley Trit. Abstr.; Wildl. Rev. (Jan. 1989-July 1992).

II/0250-4758
**INDIAN JOURNAL OF VETERINARY PATHOLOGY.** [Indian j. vet. pathol.]. **Added/Corp** Indian Association of Veterinary Pathologists. Vol. 1 (1976)-. Periodical. English. an. $125.00. Indian Association of Veterinary Pathologists, Izatnagar, India. **(Subscription address:** Prints India, 11 Darya Ganj, New Delhi, 110002 India, (Phone: 011 91 11 3268645)**)** **NLM** W1 IN24TF. **CODEN** IJVPDY.
**Ind/Abst** Index Vet.

II/0254-4105
**INDIAN JOURNAL OF VETERINARY SURGERY.** (INDIAN JOURNAL OF VETERINARY SURGERY : JOURNAL OF THE INDIAN SOCIETY FOR VETERINARY SURGERY.). [Ind. j. vet. surg.]. **Added/Corp** Indian Society for Veterinary Surgery. Vol. 1, No. 1 (Jan. 1980)-. Periodical. English. sa. $45.00 (one year), $85.00 (two year). Indian Society for Veterinary Surgery, College of Veterinary Sciences, H.A.U Hisar, 125 004 (Haryana) India. **(Subscription address:** Prints India, 11 Darya Ganj, New Delhi 110002 India.**)** **ED** Gaj Raj Singh. **NLM** W1 IN241I. **CODEN** IJVSD9. Documents available from BIOSIS Document Express.
**Ind/Abst** Anim. Breed. Abstr.; Biol. Abstr.; Fish Rev.; Index Vet.; Poult. Abstr.; Small Anim. Abstr. Bibliogr.; Vet. Bull.; Wildl. Rev.

II/0019-6479
**INDIAN VETERINARY JOURNAL, THE.** [Indian vet. j.]. **Added/Corp** Indian Veterinary Association. (1924)-. Periodical. English. mo. $35.00. Indian Veterinary Journal, 7 Chamiers Road, Nandanam Madras 600 035 India. **Tel** 011-91-451006. **(Subscription address:** Prints India, 11 Darya Ganj, New Delhi, 110002 India, (Phone: 011 91 11 3268645)**)** **ED** V S Alwar. **LC** SF604. **NLM** W1 IN278. **CODEN** IVEJAC. **Bk Rev. Ad Acc. Pr Rev. Circ:** 4,500. Documents available from The Genuine Article, BIOSIS Document Express, CASDDS.
**Desc:** A monthly record of veterinary medicine, surgery, animal husbandry and other allied subjects useful to the veterinary, dairy, livestock and poultry development professions all over the world.
**Ind/Abst** AgBiotech News Inf.; AGRICOLA; Agrofor. Abstr. (1991-); Anim. Breed. Abstr.; Biodeter. Abstr.; Biol. Abstr. (1987-); Chem. Abstr.; CSA Neuro. Abstr.; Curr. Contents, Agric. Biol. Environ. Sci.; Dairy Sci. Abstr.; Field Crop Abstr.; Food Sci. Technol. Abstr.; Grasslands For. Abstr.; Helminthol. Abstr. (19??-19??); Hortic. Abstr.; Microbiol. Abstr. Sect. C; Nutr. Abstr. Rev., Ser. B, Live Feeds and Feed.; Nutr. Abstr. Rev., Ser. A, Hum. Exp.; Life Sci. Collect.; PESTDOC; Pig News Inf.; Poult. Abstr.; Protozoolog. Abstr.; Res. Alert [Select. Cov.]; Rev. Agric. Entomol.; Rev. Med. Vet. Entomol.; Rev. Med. Vet. Mycology; Rev. Plant Pathol.; Rice Abstr.; SCISEARCH; Small Anim. Abstr. Bibliogr.; Soc. Sci. Cit. Index [Select. Cov.]; Sug. Indus. Abstr.; Wildl. Rev.

II/0250-5266
**INDIAN VETERINARY MEDICAL JOURNAL.** [Indian vet. med. j.]. **Added/Corp** U.P. Veterinary Association. Vol. 1, No. 1 (Mar. 1977)-. Academic Scholarly Publication. English. qt. $54.00. U.P. Veterinary Asscoiation, Lucknow, India. **(Subscription address:** Prints India, 11 Darya Ganj, New Delhi, 110002 India, (Phone: 011 91 11 3268645)**)** **NLM** W1 IN278D. **CODEN** IVMJDL. Documents available from BIOSIS Document Express, CASDDS. ***Continues** U.P. Veterinary Journal.*
**Ind/Abst** AGRICOLA; Anim. Breed. Abstr.; Biodeter. Abstr. (1991-); Biol. Abstr. (?-1987); Chem. Abstr.; Dairy Sci. Abstr.; Fish Rev.; Helminthol. Abstr. (19??-19??); Hortic. Abstr.; Index Vet.; Nutr. Abstr. Rev., Ser. B, Live Feeds and Feed.; Pig News Inf.; Poult. Abstr.; Protozoolog. Abstr.; Rev. Med. Vet. Mycology; Rice Abstr.; Small Anim. Abstr. Bibliogr.; Wheat Barley Trit. Abstr.; Wildl. Rev.

US
**INFORMATION BULLETIN / CORNELL FELINE HEALTH CENTER. Added/Corp** Cornell Feline Health Center. No. 5 (Sept. 1983)-. Bulletin. English. Cornell Feline Health Center, Cornell University, 618 Veterinary Research Tower, Ithaca NY 14853. **Tel** (607)255-2000, (607)253-3414, FAX (607)253-3419. ***Continues** Feline Information Bulletin.*
**Ind/Abst** Index Vet.; Small Anim. Abstr. Bibliogr.

FR
**INFORMATIONS - AEC, DEPARTEMENT ALIMENTATION ANIMALE. Main/Corp** Societe de Chimie Organique et Biologique. Departement Alimentation Animale. Mar. 1973-. Academic Scholarly Publication. English. **CODEN** AEINDA. Documents available from CASDDS.
**Ind/Abst** Chem. Abstr. (1973-1979).

FR
**INFORMATIONS TECHNIQUES DE SERVICES VETERINAIRES. Added/Corp** France. Direction des Services Veterinaires. (197?)-. Periodical. French. Price varies per volume. Informations Techniques des Services Veterinaires, 175 rue du Chevaleret, 75646 Paris Cedex 13 France. **Tel** 011 33 1 49558124. **Ad Acc. *Continues** France. Direction des Services Veterinaires. Informations Techniques des Directions des Services Veterinaires.*

NE
**INTERNATIONAL JOURNAL FOR VETERINARY HOMOEOPATHY. *Title Change.*** Vol. 1, No. 1 (April 1986)-(19??). Periodical. English. sa. International Association for Veterinary Homoeopathy, J Van der Heul, Beststraat 7, 9501 HV Stadskanaal Netherlands. ***Continued by** Dynamis.*

US/0099-5851
**IOWA STATE UNIVERSITY VETERINARIAN.** [Iowa State Univ. vet.]. **Added/Corp** American Veterinary Medical Association. Iowa State University Student Chapter. Vol. 22 (1959)-. Periodical. English. sa (May and December). $12.00. Iowa State University College of Veterinary Medicine, 200 Vet Administration ISUV, Ames IA 50011. **Tel** (515)294-0867. **ED** John H. Greve. **DD** 636. **NLM** W1 IO537. **Bk Rev. Ad Acc. Circ:** 2,200. ***Continues** Iowa State College Veterinarian.*
**Ind/Abst** AGRICOLA [Full Cov.]; Anim. Breed. Abstr.; Nutr. Abstr. Rev., Ser. B, Live Feeds and Feed.; Life Sci. Collect.; Small Anim. Abstr. Bibliogr.

KE
**IPR ... REPORT / INSTITUTE OF PRIMATE RESEARCH. Main/Corp** Institute of Primate Research (Kenya). **Added/Corp** Institute of Primate Research (Kenya). **VFOAT** Report. (1983)-. English. **LC** QL737.P9; I47a. **DD** 599.8/072676/2. ***Continues** Institute of Primate Research (Kenya). IPR Annual Report.*

IE/0368-0762
**IRISH VETERINARY JOURNAL.** [Ir. vet. j.]. **Added/Corp** Irish Veterinary Association. (1946)-. Periodical. English (Gaelic (Scots)). Four times a year (Jan., Apr., July, Oct.). 60.00p. Irish Veterinary Association, 53 Lansdowne Road, Ballsbridge, Dublin 4 Ireland. **Tel** 011 353 1 7021226, FAX 011 353 1 6604345. **ED** Patrick O'Mahony. **NLM** W1 IR459. **CODEN** IVTJAJ. Index available. cum. index. **Bk Rev. Ad Acc. Pr Rev. Circ:** 1,200. Documents available from The Genuine Article, CASDDS.
**Desc:** Science articles and papers describing cases encountered during general practice and studies of cases met within the laboratory. General news and items of interest to practitioners are also included.
**Ind/Abst** AgBiotech News Inf.; AGRICOLA; Anim. Breed. Abstr.; Chem. Abstr. (1946-1981); Curr. Contents, Agric. Biol. Environ. Sci.; Dairy Sci. Abstr.; EMBASE; Helminthol. Abstr. (19??-19??); Index Vet.; Nutr. Abstr. Rev., Ser. B, Live Feeds and Feed.; Life Sci. Collect.; Pig News Inf.; Protozoolog. Abstr.; Res. Alert [Full Cov.]; Rev. Med. Vet. Entomol.; Rev. Med. Vet. Mycology; Rev. Plant Pathol.; Sci. Cit. Index; SCISEARCH; Small Anim. Abstr. Bibliogr.; Vet. Bull.; Wildl. Rev.

IE
**IRISH VETERINARY NEWS.** English. mo. £20.00, £35.00 North America. Jude Publications, 2-6 Tara Street, Dublin 4 Ireland. **Tel** 01-713500, 713596, FAX 01-713074. **ED** Austin Shinnors, Bertie Gibson. **Bk Rev. Ad Acc. Circ:** 1,700 (ctrl).
**Desc:** Veterinary scientific and clinical material, news and views of profession, practice management and current topics.
**Ind/Abst** AgBiotech News Inf.; Anim. Breed. Abstr.; Biodeter. Abstr. (1991-); Helminthol. Abstr. (1991-); Index Vet.; Nutr. Abstr. Rev., Ser. B, Live Feeds and Feed.; Pig News Inf.; Protozoolog. Abstr.; Small Anim. Abstr. Bibliogr.; Vet. Bull.

IS/0334-9152
**ISRAEL JOURNAL OF VETERINARY MEDICINE. Added/Corp** Israel Veterinary Medical Association. (19??)-. Periodical. English (Hebrew). qt (Mar., June, Sept., Dec.). $75.00. Israel Veterinary Medical Association, PO Box 3076, Rishon, Le Zion 75130 Israel. **Tel** 11 972 8 476977. **ED** Prof. Arieh Hadani. **Bk Rev**, (Qty: 4-6). **Ad Acc. Circ:** 1,200. ***Continues** Refuah Veterinarith.*
**Desc:** This publication includes clinical and research articles in veterinary science.
**Ind/Abst** Dairy Sci. Abstr.; Helminthol. Abstr. (1991-); Index Vet.; PESTDOC; Poult. Abstr.; Protozoolog. Abstr.; Rev. Med. Vet. Entomol.; Small Anim. Abstr. Bibliogr.; Vet. Bull.

TU/0378-2352
**ISTANBUL UNIVERSITESI VETERINER FAKULTESI DERGISI.** [Istanb. Univ. vet. fak. derg.]. **Main/Corp** Istanbul Universitesi. Veteriner Fakultesi. **VFOAT** Journal of the Faculty of Veterinary Medicine, University of Istanbul. Vol. 1, No. 1- 1975-. Academic Scholarly Publication. Turkish. **CODEN** IUVDD7. Documents available from CASDDS.
**Ind/Abst** AGRICOLA; Chem. Abstr. (1975-1982); Life Sci. Collect.; Rev. Med. Vet. Mycology.

RU/0134-2681
**ITOGI NAUKI I TEHNIKI - VSESOUZNYJ INSTITUT NAUCNOJ I TEHNICESKOJ INFORMACII. SERIA ZIVOTNOVODSTVO I VETERINARIJA.** (ITOGI NAUKI I TEKHNIKI. ZHIVOTNOVODSTVO I VETERINARIIA.). [Itogi nauki teh. - Vses. inst. naucn. teh. inf., Ser. Zivotn. vet.]. **Added/Corp** Vsesoiuznyi Institut Nauchnoi i Tekhnicheskoi Informatsii (Soviet Union). **VFOAT** Zhivotnovodstvo i Veterinariia. (1969)-. Monographic series. Russian. Price varies per volume. VINITI - Vsesoyuznyi Institut Nauchno-Tekhnicheskoi Informatsii, All-Union Scientific and Technical Information Institute, Baltiiskaia Ulitsa 14, 125219 Moscow Russia. **Tel** 238-46-00, FAX 9430060, telex 411160. **NLM** W1 ZH323. **CODEN** INTVD2. Documents available from CASDDS. ***Continues** Gelmintozy Selsko-khoziaistvennykh Zhivotnykh.*
**Desc:** Information on veterinary medicine and stock-breeding.
**Ind/Abst** Chem. Abstr. (1972-1980).

SZ
**IUCN RED LIST OF THREATENED ANIMALS. VFOAT** Red List of Threatened Animals. English. ir. International Union for Conservation of Nature and Natural Resources, rue Mauverney 28, CH1196 Gland Switzerland. **Tel** 011 41 22 647181, FAX 011 41 22 642926, telex 419605.

AT/1033-2863
**IVS ANNUAL CROWS NEST.** (IVS ANNUAL). [IVS annu. Crows Nest]. **VFOAT** Index of Veterinary Specialties Annual. (1989)-. English. an. 68.00Aus$ Australia; 72.00Aus$ other. Mims Australia, 98 Albany Street, Crows Nest NSW 2065 Australia. **Tel** 011 61 2 9067966, FAX 011 61 2 9063955. **ED** Katheryn Tuckwell; Linda Badewitz-Dodd. **DD** 016.636089. Index available. **Ad Acc, Adv Mgr:** G Hand. **Circ:** 3,000. ***Continues** IVS (Crows Nest), 1033-2855.*
**Desc:** Full disclosure prescribing information of veterinary pharmaceuticals. Therapeutically classified.

SA/0019-0918
**IVS. INDEX OF VETERINARY SPECIALITIES.** [IVS, Index Vet. Spec.]. **VFOAT** Index of Veterinary Specialities; Indeks van Veeartseny-Spesialiteite. (1963)-. Periodical. English. qt. R49.12 South Africa; R110.00 other. MIMS Pty Ltd., PO Box 2059, Pretoria 0001 South Africa. **Tel** 011 27 12 348-5010, FAX 011 27 12 477716. **ED** Dr A Immelman. **DD** 636.089016. **Ad Acc. Circ:** 2,044 (ctrl).
**Desc:** Veterinary medicines listed in pharmacological order and alphabetically.

JA/0047-1917
**JAPANESE JOURNAL OF VETERINARY RESEARCH, THE.** [Jpn. j. vet. res.]. **Added/Corp** Hokkaido, Daigaku, Sapporo, Japan. Faculty of Veterinary Medicine. Vol. 2 (1954)-. Periodical. English. ir. Hokkaido Daigaku Juigakubu, (Faculty of Veterinay Medicine, Hokkaido University), Nishi 9 Chome, Kita 18 Jo, Kitaku, Sapporoshi, Hokkaido 060 Japan. **(Subscription address:** Japan Publications Trading Company, Ltd., PO Box 5030, Tokyo International, Tokyo 100-31 Japan.**)** **NLM** W1 JA976J. **CODEN** JJVRAE. **Pr Rev.** Documents available from The Genuine Article, BIOSIS Document Express. ***Continues** Juigaku Kenkyu.*
**Ind/Abst** AgBiotech News Inf.; AGRICOLA; Anim. Breed. Abstr.; Biol. Abstr.; Curr. Contents, Agric. Biol. Environ. Sci.; EMBASE [Select. Cov.]; Helminthol. Abstr. (1991-); Index Med.; Index Vet.; Microbiol. Abstr. Sect. B; Nematol. Abstr.; Nutr. Abstr. Rev., Ser. B, Live Feeds and Feed.; Life Sci. Collect.; Pig News Inf.; Poult. Abstr.; Protozoolog. Abstr.; Res. Alert [Full Cov.]; Rev. Med. Vet. Entomol.; Sci. Cit. Index; SCISEARCH; Small Anim. Abstr. Bibliogr.; Vet. Bull.

IE/0332-0588
**JOURNAL - IRISH GRASSLAND AND ANIMAL PRODUCTION.** [J. - Ir. grassl. anim. prod.]. (1962)-. Periodical. English. an. **DD** 630.
**Ind/Abst** Nutr. Abstr. Rev., Ser. B, Live Feeds and Feed.

II/0021-8804
**JOURNAL OF ANIMAL MORPHOLOGY AND PHYSIOLOGY, THE.** See Zoology.

GW/0931-2439
**JOURNAL OF ANIMAL PHYSIOLOGY AND ANIMAL NUTRITION (1986). VFOAT** Zeitschrift fuer Tierphysiologie, Tierernahrung und Futtermittelkunde (1986). (1986)-. Periodical. Multiple languages. Ten times a year. DM908.00. Blackwell Wissenschafts-Verlag, Kurfuerstendamm 57, D 10707 Berlin Germany. **Tel** 011 49 30 32790623, 011 49 30 32790624, FAX 011 49 30 327 90610. **ED** K.D. Guenther, M. Kirchgessner. **UDC** 619 :612. **CODEN** 636.085. Documents available from The Genuine Article.
**Desc:** Publishes original papers on research in the fields of animal physiology, physiology and biochemistry of nutrition, animal feeding, feed technology and food preservation.
**Ind/Abst** Res. Alert [Full Cov.]; Sci. Cit. Index; SCISEARCH.

US/0021-8812
**JOURNAL OF ANIMAL SCIENCE.** [J. anim. sci.]. **Added/Corp** American Society of Animal Science. American Society of Animal Production. American Society of Animal Science. Abstracts. American Dairy Science Association. Combined annual meeting. American Society of Animal Science. ASAS section abstracts. Vol. 1 (Feb. 1942)-. Academic Scholarly Publication. English. mo. $160.00 US Canada and Mexico; $185.00 other (includes supplement). American Society of Animal Science, 309 West Clark Street, Champaign IL 61820-4690. **Tel** (217)356-3182, FAX (217)398-4119. **ED** Austin J. Lewis. **LC** SF1; .J6. **DD** 636.05. **NLM** W1 JO536H. **CODEN** JANSAG. Index available. cum. index. **Pr Rev. Circ:** 7,500. available on microfilm and microfiche from University Microfilms International (UMI). Documents available from The Genuine Article, BIOSIS Document Express, UMI Article Clearinghouse, CASDDS. ***Supersedes*** *Record of Proceedings of the Annual Meeting - American Society of Animal Production, 0096-0837.*
**Desc:** Increases knowledge and understanding of animals, especially farm animals, and to improve care and productivity of animals, both commercially and in research. Back issues are available.
**Ind/Abst** AgBiotech News Inf.; AGRICOLA [Full Cov.]; Agric. Eng. Abstr. (1991-); Agrofor. Abstr. (1991-); Anim. Behav. Abstr.; Anim. Breed. Abstr.; BioBusiness; Biol. Agric. Index; Biol. Abstr.; Chem. Abstr.; Chemorecept. Abstr.; Cot. Trop. Fibr. Abstr. Bibliogr.; CSA Neuro. Abstr.; Curr. Biotechnol.; Curr. Contents, Agric. Biol. Environ. Sci.; Dairy Sci. Abstr.; EMBASE; Energy Res. Abstr.; Environ. Period. Bibliogr. (?-?); Expand. Acad. Index (1992-); Fish Rev. (Jan. 1989-July 1992); Food Sci. Technol. Abstr.; For. Abstr.; Genet. Abstr.; Grasslands For. Abstr.; Helminthol. Abstr.; Index Med.; INIS Atomindex [Micro.]; Int. Aerosp. Abstr.; Maize Abstr.; Microbiol. Abstr. Sect. B (19??-19??); Newsp. Period. Abstr. (1992-); Nutr. Abstr. Rev., Ser. B, Live Feeds and Feed.; Nutr. Abstr. Rev., Ser. A, Hum. Exp.; Life Sci. Collect.; PESTDOC; Pig News Inf.; Plant Breed. Abstr.; Poult. Abstr.; Protozoolog. Abstr.; Ref. Upd. Basic Ed.; Ref. Upd. Deluxe Ed.; Res. Alert [Full Cov.]; Rev. Med. Vet. Entomol.; Rev. Med. Vet. Mycology; Rice Abstr.; Sci. Cit. Index; SCISEARCH; Small Anim. Abstr. Bibliogr.; Soc. Sci. Cit. Index [Select. Cov.]; Soils Fert.; Sorghum Mill. Abstr.; Soyabean Abstr.; Stat. Theory Method Abstr. (1959-1963); Sug. Indus. Abstr.; Wildl. Rev. (Jan. 1989-July 1992); World Agric. Econ.

II/0971-2119
**JOURNAL OF APPLIED ANIMAL RESEARCH.** [J. Appl. Anim. Res.]. (1992)-. Periodical. English. qt. $100.00. Izatnagar Garuda Scientific Publications. **(Subscription address:** Prints India, 11 Darya Ganj, New Delhi 110002 India.**)** **UDC** 636.

II/0971-1643
**JOURNAL OF BOMBAY VETERINARY COLLEGE, THE.** [J. Bombay Vet. Coll.]. (1989)-. Periodical. English. sa. **UDC** 636.
**Ind/Abst** Helminthol. Abstr. (1991-); Index Vet.; Poult. Abstr.; Protozoolog. Abstr.; Rev. Med. Vet. Mycology; Small Anim. Abstr. Bibliogr.; Vet. Bull.

UK/0021-9975
**JOURNAL OF COMPARATIVE PATHOLOGY.** See Medical Science and Technology-Pathology.

US/0147-0833
**JOURNAL OF EQUINE MEDICINE AND SURGERY, THE.** See Horses and Horsemanship.

US/0737-0806
**JOURNAL OF EQUINE VETERINARY SCIENCE.** See Horses and Horsemanship.

GW/0939-8600
**JOURNAL OF EXPERIMENTAL ANIMAL SCIENCE (1991).** (JOURNAL OF EXPERIMENTAL ANIMAL SCIENCE.). [J. exp. anim. sci.]. Vol. 34, No. 1 (1991)-. Academic Scholarly Publication. English (German). Four times a year. DM266.00 Germany; DM274.00 other. Gustav Fischer Verlag Jena, Postfach 100537, D 07705 Jena Germany. **Tel** 011 49 3641 27332, FAX 011 49 3641 626500. **(Subscription address:** VCH Publishers Inc., 303 Northwest 12th Avenue, Journals Department, Deerfield FL 33442.**)** **NLM** W1; JO644GM. **CODEN** JEXSEU. Documents available from The Genuine Article, BIOSIS Document Express, CASDDS. ***Continues*** *Zeitschrift fur Versuchstierkunde, 0044-3697.*
**Ind/Abst** Biol. Abstr. (1991-); Chem. Abstr.; Curr. Aware. Biol. Sci., CABS; Curr. Contents, Agric. Biol. Environ. Sci.; Curr. Contents Life Sci.; Dairy Sci. Abstr.; EMBASE [Select. Cov.]; Index Med. (1991-); Index Vet.; Life Sci. Collect.; PESTDOC; Pig News Inf.; Res. Alert [Full Cov.]; Sci. Cit. Index; SCISEARCH; Small Anim. Abstr. Bibliogr.; Vet. Bull.

US/0022-2585
**JOURNAL OF MEDICAL ENTOMOLOGY.** See Zoology-Entomology.

SZ/0047-2565
**JOURNAL OF MEDICAL PRIMATOLOGY.** [J. med. primatol.]. (1972)-. Periodical. English. Eight times a year. kr2400.00 US and Canada; kr2430.00 other. Munksgaard International Publishers Ltd, PO Box 2148, DK-1016 Copenhagen K Denmark. **Tel** 011 45 33 12 70 30, FAX 011 45 33 12 93 87, telex 19431 MUNKS DK. **ED** E I Goldsmith and J Moor-Jankowski. **LC** QL737.P9. **DD** 599/.8/04205. **UDC** 599.8:61. **NLM** W1 JO754. **CODEN** JMPMAO. **[CCC]. Bk Rev. Pr Rev.** available on microfilm from University Microfilms International (UMI). Documents available from The Genuine Article, BIOSIS Document Express, CASDDS.
**Ind/Abst** Biol. Abstr.; Chem. Abstr.; Curr. Contents, Agric. Biol. Environ. Sci.; Curr. Contents Life Sci.; Curr. Primate Ref.; Dairy Sci. Abstr.; EMBASE; Index Med.; Nutr. Abstr. Rev., Ser. B, Live Feeds and Feed.; Nutr. Abstr. Rev., Ser. A, Hum. Exp.; Life Sci. Collect.; Protozoolog. Abstr.; Res. Alert [Full Cov.]; Sci. Cit. Index; SCISEARCH.

UK/0022-4510
**JOURNAL OF SMALL ANIMAL PRACTICE, THE.** [J. small anim. pract.]. **Added/Corp** British Small Animal Veterinary Association. World Small Animal Veterinary Association. Vol. 1 (Apr. 1960)-. Academic Scholarly Publication. English. Twelve times a year. £119.00 UK; £136.00 other. TG Scott Subscriber Services, 6 Bourne Enterprise Center, Wrotham Road, Borough Green, Kent TN15 8DG England. **Tel** 011 44 01 732 884023, FAX 011 44 01 732 884034. **ED** W. D. Tavernor. **NLM** W1 JO877L. **CODEN** JAPRAN. **[CCC].** Index available. cum. index. **Bk Rev. Ad Acc. Pr Rev. Circ:** 3,800. Documents available from The Genuine Article, BIOSIS Document Express, CASDDS.
**Desc:** Clinical research articles, authoritative reviews and symposium proceedings covering all aspects of medicine and surgery relating to dogs, cats and other small animals.
**Ind/Abst** AGRICOLA [Full Cov.]; Anim. Breed. Abstr.; Biol. Abstr.; Chem. Abstr.; Curr. Contents, Agric. Biol. Environ. Sci.; Dairy Sci. Abstr.; EMBASE; Fish Rev.; Helminthol. Abstr. (19??-19??); Index Med.; Nutr. Abstr. Rev., Ser. B, Live Feeds and Feed.; Life Sci. Collect.; PESTDOC; Protozoolog. Abstr.; Res. Alert [Full Cov.]; Rev. Med. Vet. Entomol.; Rev. Med. Vet. Mycology; Sci. Cit. Index; SCISEARCH; Small Anim. Abstr. Bibliogr.

US
**JOURNAL OF SMALL EXOTIC ANIMAL MEDICINE.** Vol. 1, No. 1 (July/Sept. 1991)-. Periodical. English. qt. $50.00 North America; $55.00 other. Gray Publishing, PO Box 618686, Orlando FL 32861. **Tel** (407)521-6111, FAX (407)521-6611. **CODEN** JSEMEF.

US/0587-2871
**JOURNAL OF THE AMERICAN ANIMAL HOSPITAL ASSOCIATION, THE.** [J. Am. Anim. Hosp. Assoc.]. **Main/Corp** American Animal Hospital Association. Vol. 4 (Feb. 1968)-. Academic Scholarly Publication. English. bm (6 issues). $97.00. American Animal Hospital Association - Colorado, PO Box 150899, Denver CO 80215. **Tel** (303)279-2500, FAX (303)279-1816. **ED** Jill Ellen Frucci. **LC** SF601; .A63. **DD** 636.089/05. **NLM** W1 JO908A. **CODEN** JAAHBL. Index available (bound in last issue). cum. index. **Ad Acc. Pr Rev. Circ:** 12,700. available on microfilm and microfiche from University Microfilms International (UMI). Documents available from The Genuine Article, BIOSIS Document Express, CASDDS. ***Continues*** *Animal Hospital, 0570-1198.*
**Desc:** Scientific refereed articles on small animal medicine and surgery.
**Ind/Abst** AGRICOLA [Full Cov.]; Biol. Agric. Index; Biol. Abstr.; Chem. Abstr.; Curr. Contents, Agric. Biol. Environ. Sci.; EMBASE [Select. Cov.]; Helminthol. Abstr. (19??-19??); Index Vet.; Nutr. Abstr. Rev., Ser. B, Live Feeds and Feed.; Life Sci. Collect.; PESTDOC; Poult. Abstr.; Protozoolog. Abstr.; Res. Alert [Full Cov.]; Rev. Med. Vet. Entomol.; Rev. Med. Vet. Mycology; Rev. Plant Pathol.; Risk Abstr.; Sci. Cit. Index; SCISEARCH; Small Anim. Abstr. Bibliogr.; Vet. Bull.

US
**JOURNAL OF THE AMERICAN HOLISTIC VETERINARY MEDICAL ASSOCIATION.** **Added/Corp** American Holistic Veterinary Medical Association. **VFOAT** Journal of the American Holistic Veterinary Medical Association. Vol. 8, No. 2 (May-July 1989)-. Periodical. English. qt. **NLM** W1; JO22DJ. ***Continues*** *Newsletter of the American Holistic Veterinary Medical Assn.*

US/0003-1488
**JOURNAL OF THE AMERICAN VETERINARY MEDICAL ASSOCIATION.** [J. Am. Vet. Med. Assoc.]. **Main/Corp** American Veterinary Medical Association. Vol. 48 (Oct. 1915)-. Academic Scholarly Publication. English. sm (24 issues). $120.00 US and Possessions; $140.00 other. American Veterinary Medical Association, 1931 North Meacham Road, Suite 100, Schaumburg IL 60173-4360. **Tel** (708)925-8070, FAX (708)925-1329. **LC** SF601; .A5. **NLM** W1 JO911J. **CODEN** JAVMA4. Index available. **Bk Rev. Ad Acc. Circ:** 48,000 (ctrl). available on microfilm and microfiche from University Microfilms International (UMI). Documents available from The Genuine Article, BIOSIS Document Express, CASDDS. ***Continues*** *American Veterinary Review;* ***Absorbed*** *Scientific Proceedings of the American Veterinary Medical Association, 0097-661X; Proceedings of the American Veterinary Medical Association, 0160-4805.* ***Continued in part by*** *Proceedings. Annual Meeting of the American Veterinary Medical Association, 0097-0565.*
**Desc:** Provides news of the profession, reports of scientific research and opportunities for member dialogue through letters and special commentaries.
**Ind/Abst** AgBiotech News Inf.; AGRICOLA [Full Cov.]; Anim. Breed. Abstr.; Biol. Agric. Index; Biol. Abstr.; Calcium Calcif. Tissue Abstr.; Chem. Abstr.; Chemorecept. Abstr.; Curr. Contents, Agric. Biol. Environ. Sci.; Dairy Sci. Abstr.; EMBASE [Select. Cov.]; Energy Res. Abstr.; Food Sci. Technol. Abstr.; Grasslands For. Abstr.; Helminthol. Abstr. (19??-19??); Immunol. Abstr.; Index Med.; Index Vet.; INIS Atomindex [Micro.]; Int. Aerosp. Abstr.; Key Word Index Wildl. Res.; Maize Abstr.; Microbiol. Abstr. Sect. B; Microbiol. Abstr. Sect. A; Microbiol. Abstr. Sect. C; NAPRALERT; Nutr. Abstr. Rev., Ser. B, Live Feeds and Feed.; Nutr. Abstr. Rev., Ser. A, Hum. Exp.; Life Sci. Collect.; PESTDOC; Pig News Inf.; Poult. Abstr.; Protozoolog. Abstr.; Ref. Upd. Basic Ed.; Ref. Upd. Deluxe Ed.; Res. Alert [Full Cov.]; Rev. Med. Vet. Entomol.; Rev. Med. Vet. Mycology; Rev. Plant Pathol.; Sci. Cit. Index; SCISEARCH; Small Anim. Abstr. Bibliogr.; Soc. Sci. Cit. Index [Select. Cov.]; Soils Fert.; Soyabean Abstr.; Vet. Bull.; Virol. AIDS Abstr.; Weed Abstr.; Wheat Barley Trit. Abstr.; Wildl. Rev.; World Agric. Econ.

US/1044-8314
**JOURNAL OF THE ASSOCIATION OF AVIAN VETERINARIANS.** [J. Assoc. Avian Vet.]. **Added/Corp** Association of Avian Veterinarians. **VFOAT** JAAV. Vol. 1, No. 1 (Spring 1989)-. Periodical. English. Four times a year. $70.00 US; $75.00 Canada & Mexico; $80.00 other; Including annual proceedings: $110.00 US; $115.00 Canada; $120.00 other. Association of Avian Veterinarians, PO Box 811720, Boca Raton FL 33481. **Tel** (407)393-8901, FAX (407)393-8902. **ED** Linda Hamson. **DD** 636. **NLM** W1; JO912EP. **CODEN** JAAVEW. Index available. cum. index. **Ad Acc. Pr Rev. Circ:** 3,600. ***Continues*** *AAV Today, 0892-9904.*
**Ind/Abst** Fish Rev.; Wildl. Rev.

UA/0379-3044
**JOURNAL OF THE EGYPTIAN VETERINARY MEDICAL ASSOCIATION.** [J. Egypt. Vet. Med. Assoc.]. **Main/Corp** Egyptian Veterinary Medical Association. Vol. 27 (Jan./June 1967)-. Academic Scholarly Publication. English (summaries and/or abstracts in Arabic). qt. **NLM** W1 JO92FG. **CODEN** EVMJB9. Documents available from CASDDS. ***Continues*** *Journal of the Arab Veterinary Medical Association.*
**Ind/Abst** Chem. Abstr.; Food Sci. Technol. Abstr.; Helminthol. Abstr.; Protozoolog. Abstr.; Rev. Med. Vet. Entomol.; Rev. Med. Vet. Mycology.

TU
**JOURNAL OF THE FACULTY OF VETERINARY MEDICINE UNIVERSITY ANKARA.** Turkish. qt. $10.00. Ankara Universitesi, Veteriner Fakultesi Dekanligi, Ankara Turkey.

SA/0301-0732
**JOURNAL OF THE SOUTH AFRICAN VETERINARY ASSOCIATION.** [J. S. Afr. Vet. Assoc.]. **Added/Corp** South African Veterinary Association. **VFOAT** Tydskrif van die Suid-Afrikaanse Veterinere Vereniging. Vol. 43 (March 1972)-. Academic Scholarly Publication. English (Afrikaans; summaries and/or abstracts in English). Four times a year (Mar., June, Sept., Dec.). $250.00. South African Veterinary Association, PO Box 25033, Monument Park, Pretoria 0105 South Africa. **Tel** 011 27 12 34611501, FAX 011 27 12 3462929. **ED** Professor J. Van Heerden. **NLM** W1

JO955Q. **CODEN** JAVTAP. Index available. **Bk Rev. Ad Acc. Pr Rev. Circ:** 1,700. Documents available from The Genuine Article, BIOSIS Document Express, CASDDS. ***Continues*** *Journal of the South African Veterinary Medical Association, 0038-2809.*
**Desc:** Scientific veterinary medical journal.
**Ind/Abst** AgBiotech News Inf.; AGRICOLA [Full Cov.]; Anim. Breed. Abstr.; Biol. Abstr.; Chem. Abstr.; Curr. Contents, Agric. Biol. Environ. Sci.; EMBASE [Select. Cov.]; Grasslands For. Abstr.; Helminthol. Abstr. (19??-19??); Hortic. Abstr.; Index Med.; Index Vet.; Nutr. Abstr. Rev., Ser. B, Live Feeds and Feed.; Life Sci. Collect.; PESTDOC; Pig News Inf.; Protozoolog. Abstr.; Res. Alert [Select. Cov.]; Rev. Med. Vet. Entomol.; Rev. Med. Vet. Mycology; SCISEARCH; Small Anim. Abstr. Bibliogr.; Vet. Bull.; Wildl. Rev. (19??-199?).

UK
**JOURNAL OF VETERINARY ANAESTHESIA. Added/Corp** Association of Veterinary Anaesthetists of Great Britain and Ireland. Vol. 18 (1991)-. Academic Scholarly Publication. English. sa. £32.00 (institutions), £20.00 (individuals). University of Newcastle upon Tyne, Biology Centre, Medical School, Newcastle upon Tyne NE2 4HH England. **Tel** 011 44 91 222 6715. **ED** L.W. Hall. **LC** SF914; .J68. **NLM** W1; JO97K. **CODEN** JVANEJ. Documents available from CASDDS. ***Continues*** *Journal of the Association of Veterinary Anaesthetists.*
**Ind/Abst** Chem. Abstr.

II/0971-0701
**JOURNAL OF VETERINARY AND ANIMAL SCIENCES. Added/Corp** Kerala Agricultural University. Vol. 21, No. 1 (June 1990)-. Periodical. English. sa. $30.00. Kerala Agricultural University, Kerala, India. **(Subscription address:** Prints India, 11 Darya Ganj, New Delhi, 110002 India, (Phone: 011 91 11 3268645)) ***Continues*** *Kerala Journal of Veterinary Science, 0374-8774.*

US/0898-7564
**JOURNAL OF VETERINARY DENTISTRY.** [J. vet. dent.]. **Added/Corp** American Veterinary Dental Society. Academy of Veterinary Dentistry (U.S.) American Veterinary Dental College. **VFOAT** JVD. (198?)-. Periodical. English. Four times a year. $60.00. American Veterinary Dental Society, 708 Southe Owyhee, Boise ID 83705. **Tel** (208)344-0194, FAX (208)344-7333. **DD** 636. ***Continues*** *Veterinary Dentistry.*
**Desc:** Provides and organized and regulated, continuing education forum which can serve as a reference source in the veterinary office. Also provides practice suggestions for veterinarians and veterinary technicians, exposure to new equipment and dental products, abstracts and clinical articles, and news features.
**Ind/Abst** Index Vet.

US/1040-6387
**JOURNAL OF VETERINARY DIAGNOSTIC INVESTIGATION.** (JOURNAL OF VETERINARY DIAGNOSTIC INVESTIGATION : OFFICIAL PUBLICATION OF THE AMERICAN ASSOCIATION OF VETERINARY LABORATORY DIAGNOSTICIANS, INC.). [J. vet. diagn. invest.]. **Added/Corp** American Association of Veterinary Laboratory Diagnosticians. Vol. 1, No. 1 (Jan. 1989)-. Periodical. English. qt. $50.00 North America; $60.00 other. American Association of Veterinary Laboratory Diagnosticians, PO Box 6023, Columbia MO 65205. **Tel** (314)882-6811, FAX (314)882-1411. **DD** 636. **NLM** W1; JO97N. Documents available from The Genuine Article.
**Ind/Abst** AGRICOLA [Full Cov.]; Curr. Contents, Agric. Biol. Environ. Sci.; Index Vet.; Pig News Inf.; Res. Alert [Select. Cov.]; Rev. Med. Vet. Mycology; SCISEARCH; Small Anim. Abstr. Bibliogr.; Vet. Bull.

US/1056-6392
**JOURNAL OF VETERINARY EMERGENCY & CRITICAL CARE. *Title Change.*** [J. vet. emerg. crit. care]. **Added/Corp** Veterinary Emergency & Critical Care Society. **VFOAT** Journal of Veterinary Emergency and Critical Care; Journal of the Veterinary Emergency & Critical Care Society. Vol. 1, No. 1 (Fall 1985)-(19??). Periodical. English. sa. Veterinary Emergency and Critical Care Society, 12583 Northwinds Drive, St Louis MO 63146. **DD** 636. ***Continues*** *Journal of Veterinary Critical Care.* ***Merged with*** *Journal of Veterinary Emergency and Critical Care (Santa Barbara, Calif.), 1056-6392* ***to form*** *Lifeline (Fort Sam Houston, Tex.).*
**Ind/Abst** Poult. Abstr.

US/1056-6392
**JOURNAL OF VETERINARY EMERGENCY AND CRITICAL CARE (SANTA BARBARA, CALIF.).** (JOURNAL OF VETERINARY EMERGENCY AND CRITICAL CARE : OFFICIAL JOURNAL OF THE SOCIETY OF VETERINARY EMERGENCY AND CRITICAL CARE.). [J. vet. emerg. crit. care]. **Added/Corp** Veterinary Emergency & Critical Care Society. American College of Veterinary Emergency and Critical Care. **VFOAT** Veterinary Emergency and Critical Care. Vol. 1, No. 1 (Jan./June 1991)-. Periodical. English. sa. $25.00 (individuals), $35.00 (institutions). VECCS, 15729 San Pedro Avenue, San Antonio TX 78232. **Tel** (210)826-1488. **DD** 636. **NLM** W1; JO97NR. ***Formed by the union of*** *Journal of Veterinary Emergency & Critical Care, 1056-6392* ***and*** *Lifeline (Fort Sam Houston, Tex.).*
**Desc:** Covers veterinary emergencies and critical care.
**Ind/Abst** Bibliogr. Agric.

US/0891-6640
**JOURNAL OF VETERINARY INTERNAL MEDICINE.** [J. vet. intern. med.]. **Added/Corp** American College of Veterinary Internal Medicine. Vol. 1, No. 1 (Jan./March 1987)-. Academic Scholarly Publication. English. Six times a year. $69.00 (US), $84.00 (other)institution; $49.00 (US), $64.00 (other) individual. W.B. Saunders Company, A Subsidiary of Harcourt Brace Jovanovich, Inc., The Curtis Center/Suite 300, Independence Square West, Philadelphia PA 19106-3399. **Tel** (215)238-7800 or, 5587, FAX (215)238-7883, telex 173146. **(Subscription address:** W. B. Saunders Company / North America Subscriptions, c/o Periodicals, 6277 Sea Harbour Drive, 4th Floor, Orlando FL 32887.) **DD** 636. **NLM** W1; JO97PC. **CODEN** JVIMEM. **[CCC]. Pr Rev.** available on microfilm from University Microfilms International (UMI). Documents available from The Genuine Article, CASDDS.
**Ind/Abst** AGRICOLA [Full Cov.]; Anim. Breed. Abstr.; Chem. Abstr. (1987-); Curr. Contents, Agric. Biol. Environ. Sci.; Dairy Sci. Abstr.; Helminthol. Abstr. (1991-); Index Med.; Index Vet.; Nutr. Abstr. Rev., Ser. B, Live Feeds and Feed.; PESTDOC; Protozoolog. Abstr.; Res. Alert [Select. Cov.]; Rev. Med. Vet. Entomol.; Rev. Med. Vet. Mycology; SCISEARCH; Small Anim. Abstr. Bibliogr.; Vet. Bull.

US/0748-321X
**JOURNAL OF VETERINARY MEDICAL EDUCATION.** [J. vet. med. educ.]. **Added/Corp** Association of American Veterinary Medical Colleges. **VFOAT** JVME. Vol. 1 (Spring 1974)-. Periodical. English. sa. $20.00 (individuals), $30.00 (institutions) nonmembers US and Canada; $30.00 other. Journal of Veterinary Medical Education, c/o Dr Talbot, 1309 Hillcrest Drive, Blacksburg VA 24061. **Tel** (703)231-4669, FAX (703)552-8143. **ED** Dr. Richard B. Talbot. **LC** NOT IN LC. **DD** 636. **NLM** W1 JO97P. available on microfilm and microfiche from University Microfilms International (UMI).
**Ind/Abst** AGRICOLA [Full Cov.]; Agric. Eng. Abstr. (1991-); Contents Pages Educ.; Curr. Index J. Educ.; Dairy Sci. Abstr.; Index Vet.; Pig News Inf.; Soc. Sci. Cit. Index [Select. Cov.]; Vet. Bull.

JA/0916-7250
**JOURNAL OF VETERINARY MEDICAL SCIENCE.** (THE JOURNAL OF VETERINARY MEDICAL SCIENCE / THE JAPANESE SOCIETY OF VETERINARY SCIENCE.). [J. vet. med. sci.]. **Added/Corp** Nihon Jui Gakkai. Vol. 53, No. 1 (February 1991)-. Academic Scholarly Publication. English. bm (6 issues). $250.00. Nihon Juigakkai (Japan Society of Veterinary Science), c/o Department of Veterinary Pharmacology, Faculty of Agriculture, University of Tokyo, 1-1-1 Yayoi, Bunkyo-ku Tokyo 113 Japan. **(Subscription address:** Kyowa Book Company Inc., 1-38 Kanda Jinbo-Cho, Chiyoda-Ku Tokyo 101, Japan) **NLM** W1; JO97PB. **CODEN** JVMSEQ. **[CCC].** Documents available from The Genuine Article, BIOSIS Document Express, CASDDS. ***Continues*** *Japanese Journal of Veterinary Science, 0021-5295.*
**Ind/Abst** AgBiotech News Inf.; Anim. Breed. Abstr.; Biodeter. Abstr. (1991-); Biol. Abstr.; Chem. Abstr.; Curr. Contents, Agric. Biol. Environ. Sci.; Dairy Sci. Abstr.; Fish Rev. (Jan. 1989-July 1992); Helminthol. Abstr. (19??-19??); Immunol. Abstr.; Index Med. (1991-); Index Vet.; Microbiol. Abstr. Sect. B (19??-19??); PESTDOC; Poult. Abstr.; Protozoolog. Abstr.; Res. Alert [Full Cov.]; Rev. Med. Vet. Entomol.; Rev. Med. Vet. Mycology; Sci. Cit. Index; SCISEARCH; Small Anim. Abstr. Bibliogr.; Vet. Bull.; Wildl. Rev. (Jan. 1989-July 1992).

GW/0931-184X
**JOURNAL OF VETERINARY MEDICINE. SERIES A.** [J. vet. med., Ser. A]. **VFOAT** Zentralblatt fuer Veterinarmedizin. Reihe A; Journal of Veterinary Medicine / A. (1986)-. Periodical. Multiple languages. Ten times a year. DM1331.00 Europe; DM1328.00 other. Blackwell Wissenschafts-Verlag, Kurfuerstendamm 57, D 10707 Berlin Germany. **Tel** 011 49 30 32790623, 011 49 30 32790624, FAX 011 49 30 327 90610. **ED** Oskar-Rueger Kaaden, Anton Mayr, Erwin Scharrer, H. Bruno Schiefer, Heinrich Sporri. **UDC** 619. **[CCC].** Documents available from The Genuine Article. ***Continues*** *Zentralblatt fuer Veterinarmedizin. Reihe A, Animal Physiology, Pathology and Clinical Veterinary Medicine, 0177-0543.*
**Desc:** Fields of interest include physiology, endocrinology, biochemistry, pharmacology, internal medicine, surgery, genetics, and others.
**Ind/Abst** Nutr. Abstr. Rev., Ser. B, Live Feeds and Feed.; Poult. Abstr.; Protozoolog. Abstr.; Res. Alert [Full Cov.]; Sci. Cit. Index; SCISEARCH.

GW/0931-1793
**JOURNAL OF VETERINARY MEDICINE. SERIES B.** [J. vet. med., Ser. B]. **VFOAT** Zentralblatt fuer Veterinarmedizin. Reihe B. (1986)-. Periodical. Multiple languages. Ten times a year. DM1331.00 Europe; DM1328.00 other. Blackwell Wissenschafts-Verlag, Kurfuerstendamm 57, D 10707 Berlin Germany. **Tel** 011 49 30 32790623, 011 49 30 32790624, FAX 011 49 30 327 90610. **ED** Oskar-Rueger Kaaden, Anton Mayr, Erwin Scharrer, H. Bruno Schiefer, Heinrich Sporri. **UDC** 619. **[CCC].** Documents available from The Genuine Article. ***Continues*** *Zentralblatt fuer Veterinarmedizin. Reihe B, Infectious Diseases, Immunology, Food Hygiene, Veterinary Public Health, 0931-2021.*
**Desc:** Includes reports on topics in epidemiology, pathogenesis, diagnostic techniques, laboratory methods, application of chemotherapy, and vaccines to infectious and parasitic diseases.
**Ind/Abst** AgBiotech News Inf.; Dairy Sci. Abstr.; Helminthol. Abstr. (1991-); Microbiol. Abstr. Sect. B (19??-19??); PESTDOC; Poult. Abstr.; Protozoolog. Abstr.; Res. Alert [Full Cov.]; Rev. Med. Vet. Entomol.; Rev. Med. Vet. Mycology; Sci. Cit. Index; SCISEARCH; Virol. AIDS Abstr.; Wheat Barley Trit. Abstr.

II/0971-1031
**JOURNAL OF VETERINARY PARASITOLOGY.** (JOURNAL OF VETERINARY PARASITOLOGY / INDIAN ASSOCIATION FOR THE ADVANCEMENT OF VETERINARY PARASITOLOGY.). [J. vet. parasitol.]. **Added/Corp** Indian Association for the Advancement of Veterinary Parasitology. Vol. 1, No. 1/2 (June/Dec. 1987)-. Periodical. English. sa. $100.00 (general), Free (members). **(Subscription address:** Prints India, 11 Darya Ganj, New Delhi, 110002 India, (Phone: 011 91 11 3268645)) **NLM** W1; JO97PL. **CODEN** JVPAEL.
**Ind/Abst** Index Vet.; Poult. Abstr.; Protozoolog. Abstr.; Rev. Med. Vet. Entomol.; Vet. Bull.

UK/0140-7783
**JOURNAL OF VETERINARY PHARMACOLOGY AND THERAPEUTICS.** **See** Pharmacy and Pharmacology.

II
**JOURNAL OF VETERINARY PHYSIOLOGY AND ALLIED SCIENCES. Added/Corp** Society of Veterinary Physiologists, Pharmacologists and Biochemists of India. Indian Veterinary Research Institute. Vol. 1, No. 1 (Dec. 1982)-. Periodical. English. sa. $30.00 (institutions), $25.00 (non-members). Society of Veterinary Physiologists & Pharmacologists, Izatnagar, Bareilly, U.P., India. **(Subscription address:** Prints India, 11 Darya Ganj, New Delhi, 110002 India, (Phone: 011 91 11 3268645))
**Ind/Abst** Grasslands For. Abstr.; Index Vet.; Nutr. Abstr. Rev., Ser. B, Live Feeds and Feed.

US/0090-3558
**JOURNAL OF WILDLIFE DISEASES.** [J. wildl. dis.]. **Added/Corp** Wildlife Disease Association. Vol. 6 (Jan. 1970)-. Periodical. English. Four times a year. $87.50. Wildlife Disease Association. **(Subscription address:** Journal of Wildlife Diseases, PO Box 1897, Lawrence KS 66044-8897.) **ED** Danny Pence. **NLM** W1 JO972D. **CODEN** JWIDAW. **Bk Rev. Pr Rev.** ctrl circ. Documents available from The Genuine Article, BIOSIS Document Express, CASDDS. ***Continues*** *Bulletin of the Wildlife Disease Association, 0098-373X.*
**Desc:** An official publication of the Wildlife Disease Association. It is international in scope and publishes the results of original research and observations on the disease of wild animals.
**Ind/Abst** ASTIS Curr. Aware. Bull. (1978-); AGRICOLA [Select. Cov.]; Anim. Breed. Abstr.; AQUAREF; ASTIS Bibliogr. (1978-); Biol. Agric. Index; Biol. Abstr.; Biol. Dig.; Chem. Abstr.; CSA Neuro. Abstr. (?-?); Curr. Contents, Agric. Biol. Environ. Sci.; Curr. Ref. Fish Res.; Ecology Abstr.; EMBASE; Energy Res. Abstr. (April 1974-); Entomol. Abstr.; Environ. Period. Bibliogr. (?-?); Fish Rev.; Helminthol. Abstr. (19??-19??); Index Med.; Index Vet.; Key Word Index Wildl. Res.; Microbiol. Abstr. Sect. B (1978-); Microbiol. Abstr. Sect. C; Ocean. Abstr.; Life Sci. Collect.; Pig News Inf.; Pollut. Abstr. Indexes; Poult. Abstr.; Protozoolog. Abstr.; Ref. Upd. Deluxe Ed.; Res. Alert [Full Cov.]; Rev. Agric. Entomol.; Rev. Med. Vet. Entomol.; Rev. Med. Vet. Mycology; Sci. Cit. Index; SCISEARCH; Vet. Bull.; Virol. AIDS Abstr.; Wildl. Rev. (1978-).

US/1042-7260
**JOURNAL OF ZOO AND WILDLIFE MEDICINE : OFFICIAL PUBLICATION OF THE AMERICAN ASSOCIATION OF ZOO VETERINARIANS.** [J. zoo wildl. med.]. Vol. 20, No. 1 (March 1989)-. Periodical. English. qt. $125.00 North America; $140.00 other. Journal of Zoo and Wildlife Medicine. **(Subscription address:** Journal of Zoo and Wildlife Medicine, PO Box 1897, Lawrence KS 66044-8897.) **ED** James Carpenter. **DD** 590. **NLM** W1; JO974I. **CODEN** JZWMEI. Index available. cum. index. **Bk Rev. Ad Acc, Adv Mgr Tel** (215)387-9094. **Pr Rev. Acid Free. Circ:** 800 (ctrl). Documents available from The Genuine Article, Documents on Demand. ***Continues*** *Journal of Zoo Animal Medicine, 0093-4526.*
**Desc:** The journal publishes peer-reviewed papers on original reserach finding and clinical observations as well as case reports in the field of veterinary medicine dealing with captive and free-ranging wild animals.
**Ind/Abst** AGRICOLA [Select. Cov.]; Curr. Aware. Biol.

Sci., CABS; Curr. Contents, Agric. Biol. Environ. Sci.; Environ. Abstr.; Fish Rev.; Helminthol. Abstr. (1991-); Index Vet.; PESTDOC; Protozoolog. Abstr.; Res. Alert [Full Cov.]; Rev. Med. Vet. Entomol.; Rev. Med. Vet. Mycology; Sci. Cit. Index; SCISEARCH; Small Anim. Abstr. Bibliogr.; Vet. Bull.; Wildl. Rev.

FR/0767-9874
**JOURNEES DE LA RECHERCHE PORCINE EN FRANCE.** [Journ. rech. porc. Fr.]. **Main/Corp** Institut National de la Recherche Agronomique. **Added/Corp** Institut Technique du Porc. (19??)-. Periodical. French. **CODEN** JRPRD9.
**Ind/Abst** Dairy Sci. Abstr.; Nutr. Abstr. Rev., Ser. B, Live Feeds and Feed.; Pig News Inf.; Soyabean Abstr.; Wheat Barley Trit. Abstr.

MY
**JURNAL VETERINAR MALAYSIA.** **Added/Corp** Veterinary Association Malaysia. Vol. 1, No. 1 (June 1989)-. Periodical. English (summaries and/or abstracts in Malay). sa (June & Dec.). $24.00. Faculty of Veterinary Medicine and Animal Science, University of Pertanian Malaysia, 43400 Serdang Malaysia. **Tel** 011 60 3 9486101 ext. 1851, FAX 011 60 3 9486317, telex UNIPER MA 37454. **ED** Dr. M.K. Vidyadaran. **CODEN** JVEME2. Documents available from BIOSIS Document Express. ***Formed by the union of*** *Kajian Veterinar Malaysia* ***and*** *Malaysian Veterinary Journal.*
**Ind/Abst** Biol. Abstr.; Index Vet.; Vet. Bull.

JA/0911-4319
**KACHIKU KOKINZAI KENKYUKAIHO.** [Kachiku Kokinzai Kenkyukaiho]. **VFOAT** Proceedings of the Japanese Society of Antimicrobials for Animals. (1984)-. Periodical. Japanese. an. Kachiku Kokinzai Kenkyukai, (Japanese Soc. of Antimicrobials for Animals), Nihon Jui Chikusan Daigaku Jui, Biseibutsugaku Kyoshitsu, 7-1, Kyonancho 1 Chome, Musashinoshi, Tokyoto 180 Japan. **DD** 636. Documents available from CASDDS. ***Continues*** *Kachiku no Taiseikin Kenkyukaiho, 0911-3789.*
**Ind/Abst** Chem. Abstr.

US
**KAL KAN VIDEO FORUM.** English. Four times a year. $79.00. Video Forum / New Jersey, 425 Phillips Blvd, #100, Trenton NJ 08618. **Tel** (800)426-9119. **Circ:** 2,500.
**Desc:** Emphasis on small animal veterinary topics.

US
**KANSAS VETERINARIAN.** Periodical. English. bm. $10.00. Kansas Veterinary Medical Association, 227 South Wind Place, Manhattan KS 66502. **Tel** (913)539-4273.

US/1061-9976
**KENNEL HEALTHLINE.** ***Ceased.*** **VFOAT** Kennel Health Line. Vol. 5, No. 8, (Aug. 1988)-(Sept. 1992). Periodical. English. mo. MacLean Hunter Publishing Corporation / Chicago, IL, 29 North Wacker Drive, Chicago IL 60606-3298. **Tel** (312)726-2802, FAX (312)726-3091. **DD** 636. ***Continues*** *Kennel Doctor, 0886-7917.*

GW/0023-2076
**KLEINTIER-PRAXIS.** [Kleintier-Praxis]. Vol. 1 (April 1956)-. Periodical. German (summaries and/or abstracts in English, French and Italian; table of contents in English). Twelve times a year. DM210.40 Germany; DM228.00 other. Verlag M & H Schaper GmbH & Co, Postfach 16 42, D 31046 Alfeld Leine Germany. **Tel** 011 49 5181 80090. **NLM** W1 KL183. **[CCC]. Pr Rev.**
**Ind/Abst** AGRICOLA; CSA Neuro. Abstr. (?-?); Energy Res. Abstr.; Helminthol. Abstr. (1991-); Nutr. Abstr. Rev., Ser. B, Live Feeds and Feed.; Life Sci. Collect.; PESTDOC; Protozoolog. Abstr.; Rev. Med. Vet. Mycology; Soc. Sci. Cit. Index [Select. Cov.].

US/0093-7355
**LAB ANIMAL.** [Lab anim.]. Vol. 1 (Jan. 1972)-. Periodical. English. Ten times a year. $70.00. Nature Publishing Company, 65 Bleecker Street, 12th Floor, New York NY 10012. **Tel** (212)477-9600, (800)524-0328, FAX (212)477-8020. **(Subscription address:** Lab Animal Order Department, PO Box 1710, Riverton NJ 08077-7310.**)** **DD** 619. **NLM** W1 LA125. available on microfilm and microfiche from University Microfilms International (UMI).
**Ind/Abst** AGRICOLA [Select. Cov.].

US/0190-2474
**LABCHOWS DIGEST.** **VAT** Lab Chows Digest. V. 1- Nov. 1977-. Periodical. English. Ralston Purina Company, Checkerboard Square, St Louis MO 63188. **NLM** W1 LA139. ***Continues*** *Laboratory Animal Digest, 0458-5925.*

US/0023-6764
**LABORATORY ANIMAL SCIENCE (CHICAGO).** (LABORATORY ANIMAL SCIENCE.). [Lab. anim. sci.]. **Added/Corp** American Association for Laboratory Animal Science. Vol. 21 (Feb. 1971)-. Academic Scholarly Publication. English. bm (6 issues). $80.00 US; $95.00 Canada and Mexico; $120.00 other. American Association for Laboratory Animal Science, 70 Timber Creek Drive, Suite 5, Cordova TN 38018. **Tel** (901)754-8620, FAX (901)753-0043. **NLM** W1 LA206J. **CODEN** LBASAE. **Pr Rev. Acid Free.** Documents available from The Genuine Article, BIOSIS Document Express, CASDDS. ***Continues*** *Laboratory Animal Care, 0094-5331.*
**Desc:** The official journal of the American Association for Laboratory Animal Science. It is the only scientific journal published in the U.S.A. that is devoted exclusively to the care, use and production of animals used in biomedical research.
**Ind/Abst** AGRICOLA [Full Cov.]; Anim. Breed. Abstr.; Biol. Abstr.; Chem. Abstr.; CSA Neuro. Abstr. (?-?); Curr. Aware. Biol. Sci., CABS; Curr. Contents, Agric. Biol. Environ. Sci.; Curr. Contents Life Sci.; Curr. Primate Ref.; Dairy Sci. Abstr.; EMBASE; Energy Res. Abstr. (1973-); Fish Rev.; Helminthol. Abstr. (19??-19??); Index Med.; INIS Atomindex [Micro.]; Int. Aerosp. Abstr.; Nutr. Abstr. Rev., Ser. B, Live Feeds and Feed.; Nutr. Abstr. Rev., Ser. A, Hum. Exp.; Life Sci. Collect.; PESTDOC; Pig News Inf.; Poult. Abstr.; Protozoolog. Abstr.; Ref. Upd. Basic Ed.; Ref. Upd. Deluxe Ed.; Res. Alert [Full Cov.]; Rev. Med. Vet. Entomol.; Sci. Cit. Index; SCISEARCH; Small Anim. Abstr. Bibliogr.; Virol. AIDS Abstr.; Wildl. Rev.

UK/0023-6772
**LABORATORY ANIMALS (LONDON).** (LABORATORY ANIMALS.). [Lab. anim.]. V. 1- Apr. 1967-. Academic Scholarly Publication. English. qt. £85.00 UK and Europe; $160.00 US; £89.00 other. Royal Society of Medicine Press, 1 Wimpole Street, London W1M 8AE England. **Tel** 011 44 71 2902928. **ED** J Seamer. **LC** SF405.5; .L33. **NLM** W1 LA206K. **CODEN** LBANAX. **[CCC].** Index available. cum. index. **Bk Rev. Ad Acc. Pr Rev. Circ:** 1,750. Documents available from The Genuine Article, BIOSIS Document Express, CASDDS.
**Desc:** All aspects of laboratory animal science, technology and education.
**Ind/Abst** AGRICOLA [Select. Cov.]; Anim. Breed. Abstr.; Biol. Abstr.; Chem. Abstr.; Curr. Aware. Biol. Sci., CABS; Curr. Contents, Agric. Biol. Environ. Sci.; Curr. Contents Life Sci.; EMBASE; Fish Rev.; Helminthol. Abstr. (19??-19??); Index Med.; Index Vet.; Microbiol. Abstr. Sect. B; Nutr. Abstr. Rev., Ser. B, Live Feeds and Feed.; Nutr. Abstr. Rev., Ser. A, Hum. Exp.; Life Sci. Collect.; Pig News Inf.; Poult. Abstr.; Protozoolog. Abstr.; Ref. Upd. Deluxe Ed.; Res. Alert [Full Cov.]; Rev. Med. Vet. Entomol.; Rev. Med. Vet. Mycology; Sci. Cit. Index; SCISEARCH; Small Anim. Abstr. Bibliogr.; Soils Fert.; Vet. Bull.

US/0023-6861
**LABORATORY PRIMATE NEWSLETTER.** V. 1- Jan. 1962-. Newsletter. English. qt. Free to qualified subscribers, $2.00 (back issues) US, add $5.00 (surface mail), $10.00 (airmail) other. Judith E Schrier, Psychology Department, Brown University, Providence RI 02912. **Tel** (401)863-2511. **ED** Judith E Schrier. **LC** SF407.P7; L3. **DD** 636/.98. **NLM** W1 LA231H. **Bk Rev. Circ:** 1,200 (ctrl).
**Desc:** A central source of information about nonhuman primates and related matters, which will be of use both to the community of scientists who use these animals in their research and to those persons whose work supports such research.

UK/0144-0314
**LAC MANUAL SERIES.** [LAC man. ser.]. **VFOAT** Manual Series - Laboratory Animals Centre. **VAT** Laboratory Animals Centre Manual Series. No. 1- 1974-. Monographic series. English. Price varies per volume. **NLM** W1 L1M.

UK/0308-9568
**LAC NEWS.** **Main/Corp** Medical Research Council (Gt. Brit.). Laboratory Animals Centre. No. 51, (Jan. 1977)-. Periodical. English. sa. ***Continues*** *Medical Research Council (Gt. Brit.). Laboratory Animals Centre. LAC News Letter.*

SZ/0023-821X
**LANDWIRTSCHAFTLICHES ZENTRALBLATT. ABTEILUNG IV. VETERINARMEDIZIN.** V. 1- Jan. 1956-. Periodical. German. mo. Deutscher Judo Verband, Redaktion Ippon Segewaldweg 40, D 12557 Berlin Germany. **Tel** 011 49 711 210770, telex 051 678.

●CN/1188-8717
**LAPIN MAGAZINE.** [Lapin mag.]. **Added/Corp** Syndicat des Producteurs de Lapins du Quebec. (Spring 1992)-. Periodical. French. qt. Free for members. Syndicat des Producteurs de Lapins du Quebec, 555 Boulevard Rolland-Therrien, Longueuil Quebec J4H 3Y9 Canada. **DD** 636.

US/1043-7533
**LARGE ANIMAL VETERINARIAN COVERING HEALTH & NUTRITION.** [Large anim. vet. cover. health nutr.]. **VFOAT** Large Animal Veterinarian Animal Veterinarian Nutrition; Large. Vol. 43, No. 5 (Sept./Oct. 1988)-. Periodical. English. bm. $36.00. Watt Publishing Company, 122 South Wesley Avenue, Mount Morris IL 61054. **Tel** (815)734-4171, FAX (815)734-7021, telex TWX 910-642-2891. **ED** Tim Phillips. **DD** 636. **[CCC]. Ad Acc, Adv Mgr:** Clay Schreiber. **Pr Rev. Circ:** 21,000 (ctrl). available on microfilm and microfiche from University Microfilms International (UMI). ***Continues*** *Animal Health & Nutrition for Large Animal Veterinarians, 0896-4807.*
**Desc:** Aimed at the large animal practitioner and nutrition of food animals.
**Ind/Abst** Biol. Agric. Index; Index Vet.; Poult. Abstr.

US/1069-1774
**LARGE ANIMAL VETERINARY REPORT.** **VFOAT** Veterinary Report. (1990)-. Periodical. English. mo. $50.00 US; $60.00 Canada and Mexico; $75.00 other. Equine Veterinary Data, Box 1209, Wildomar CA 92595. **Tel** (714)678-1889, FAX (714)678-1885. **ED** William E Jones. Index available. cum. index. **Bk Rev. Ad Acc. Circ:** 750 (ctrl).
**Desc:** Covers livestock veterinary information.

US
**LAW AND ETHICS OF THE VETERINARY PROFESSION.** **See** Law.

CC
**LIAO-NING HSU MU SHOU I.** **VFOAT** Liao Ning Xu Mu Shou Yi. Periodical. Chinese. bm. RMBY0.32. Post Office, Liao-Yang Shih, People's Republic of China. **LC** SF604; .L45. **DD** 636/.089/05.

RU/0202-3334
**LIETUVOS VETERINARIJOS AKADEMIJOS MOKSLO DARBAI.** [Liet. vet. Akad. Mokslo Darb.]. **VFOAT** Naucnye Trudy Litovskoj Veterinarioj Akademii. (19??)-. Periodical. Multiple languages.
**Ind/Abst** Index Vet.; Pig News Inf.; Poult. Abstr.

CN/0705-4718
**LITHIUM AND ANIMAL BEHAVIOR.** ***Ceased.*** [Lithium anim. behav.]. Vol. 1 (1977)-Ceased (19??). English. ir. Human Sciences Press, PO Box 735, 233 Spring Street, New York NY 10013. **Tel** (212)620-8000, FAX (212)807-1047, telex 23421139. **ED** D F Smith. **DD** 615/.2/381. **NLM** W1 LI821N.
**Ind/Abst** Life Sci. Collect.; Psychol. Abstr. (1977-).

II/0970-3004
**LIVESTOCK ADVISER.** [Livest. advis.]. Vol. 1 (Jan. 1976)-. Periodical. English. mo. $30.00. Livestock Adviser, Bangalore, India. **(Subscription address:** Prints India, 11 Darya Ganj, New Delhi, 110002 India, (Phone: 011 91 11 3268645)**)**
**Ind/Abst** Agrofor. Abstr. (1991-); Anim. Breed. Abstr.; Dairy Sci. Abstr.; Food Sci. Technol. Abstr.; For. Prod. Abstr. (1991-); For. Abstr.; Grasslands For. Abstr.; Helminthol. Abstr. (1991-); Maize Abstr.; Nutr. Abstr. Rev., Ser. B, Live Feeds and Feed.; Life Sci. Collect. (1985-); Pig News Inf.; Rev. Med. Vet. Entomol.; Soils Fert.; Sug. Indus. Abstr.; Wheat Barley Trit. Abstr.; World Agric. Econ.

US/0899-6202
**LLAMA BANNER.** **See** Agriculture.

RM/0563-5586
**LUCRARI STIINTIFICE. INSTITUTUI AGRONOMIC TIMISOARA, SERIA MEDICINA VETERINARA.** (LUCRARI STIINTIFICE. SERIA MEDICINA VETERINARA.). [Lucr. stiint., Inst. Agron. Timisoara, Ser. med. vet.]. **Added/Corp** Institutul Agronomic, Timisoara. **VFOAT** Lucrari Stiintifice ale Institutului Agronomic Timisoara; Seria Medicina Veterinara. Vol. 8 (1965)-. Periodical. Romanian (summaries and/or abstracts in English and Russian). an. DM164.00. **(Subscription address:** Kubon & Sagner, ABT Zeitschriftenimport, D 80328 Munich Germany.**)** **NLM** W1 LU315M. ***Continues in part*** *Lucrari Stiintifice ale Institutului Agronomic Timisoara.*
**Ind/Abst** Life Sci. Collect.; Poult. Abstr.

RM/0368-7732
**LUCRARILE INSTITUTULUI DE CERCETARI VETERINARE SI BIOPREPARATE "PASTEUR".** (LUCRARILE INSTITUTULUI DE CERCETARI VETERINARE SI BIOPREPARATE "PASTEUR." / MINISTERUL AGRICULTURII, INDUSTRIEI ALIMENTARE SI APELOR, ACADEMIA DE STIINTE AGRICOLE SI SILVICE, INSTITUTUL DE CERCETARI VETERINARE SI BIOPREPARATE "PASTEUR" BUCURESTI.). [Lucr. inst. cercet. vet. bioprep. Pasteur]. **Added/Corp** Institutul de Cercetari Veterinare si Biopreparate "Pasteur" (Romania). Vol. 1 (1962)-. Romanian (summaries and/or abstracts in English, French, German and Russian; table of contents in English, French, German and Russian). **LC** WMLC L 83/4197. **NLM** W1 LU315T. **CODEN** LICVAE. Documents available from CASDDS. ***Formed by the union of*** *Lucrarile Institutului de Seruri si Vaccinuri "Pasteur"* ***and*** *Lucrarile Institutului de Patologie si Igiena Anamala.*
**Ind/Abst** Anim. Breed. Abstr.; Chem. Abstr.; Index Vet.; Protozoolog. Abstr.; Rev. Med. Vet. Mycology; Vet. Bull.

RM/0254-0509
**LUCRAERI STIINTIFICE - INSTITUTUL AGRONOMIC "NICOLAE BALCESCU," BUCURESTI, SERIA C, MEDICINA VETERINARA.** (LUCRARI STIINTIFICE. SERIA C, MEDICINA VETERINARA / MINISTERUL EDUCATIEI SI INVATAMINTULUI, INSTITUTUL AGRONOMIC

"NICOLAE BALCESCU."). [Lucr. stiint. - Inst. Agron. "Nicolae Balcescu," Bucur. Ser. C Med. vet.]. **Added/Corp** Institutul Agronomic "N. Balcescu.". **VFOAT** Medicina Veterinara; Lucrari Stiintifice. Medicina Veterinara. Vol. 13 (1970)-. Periodical. Romanian. ir. Institutul Agronomic N Balcescu, B-Dul Marasti, NR 59, Bucuresti Sectorul 1 Romania. **LC** SF604; . L83. ***Continues in part*** *Lucrari Stiintifice. Seria C, Zootehnie si Medicina Veterinara, 0524-8108.*
**Ind/Abst** AGRICOLA; Index Vet.; Nutr. Abstr. Rev., Ser. B, Live Feeds and Feed.; Pig News Inf.; Poult. Abstr.

II/0379-0517
**MADRAS VETERINARY COLLEGE ANNUAL, THE.** [Madras Vet. Coll. annu.]. **Main/Corp** Madras Veterinary College. **Added/Corp** Madras Veterinary College. Annual. (19??)-. English. an. Free. Madras Veterinary College Association, Vepery Drive M, Ranganathan Madras 7 India. **ED** Dr. M. Ranganathan. **NLM** W1 MA204. **CODEN** MVCADM. Documents available from CASDDS.
**Ind/Abst** Chem. Abstr.

HU/0025-004X
**MAGYAR ALLATORVOSOK LAPJA.** [M. allatorv. l.]. **VFOAT** Vengerskii Veterinarnyi Zhurnal; Hungarian Veterinary Journal; Ungarische Tierarztliche Monatschrift. V. 1- ; 1946-. Academic Scholarly Publication. Hungarian (summaries and/or abstracts in Russian and German). mo. 840.00ft. Agroinform, Kitaibel Pal 4, 1024 Budapest Hungary. **Tel** 135-1927, FAX 135-0344, telex 224439. **(Subscription address:** Kultura, PO Box 149, H-1309, Budapest 62 Hungary**) ED** Ferenc Hollo. **NLM** W1 MA388. **CODEN** MGALA5. Index available. cum. index. **Bk Rev. Ad Acc. Circ:** 3,500 (ctrl). Documents available from The Genuine Article, CASDDS. ***Supersedes*** *Allatorvosi Lapok.*
**Desc:** Features scientific and practical papers with broad English abstracts.
**Ind/Abst** AgBiotech News Inf.; Agric. Eng. Abstr. (1991-); Anim. Breed. Abstr.; Biodeter. Abstr.; Chem. Abstr.; CSA Neuro. Abstr. (?-?); Curr. Contents, Agric. Biol. Environ. Sci.; Dairy Sci. Abstr.; Food Sci. Technol. Abstr.; Helminthol. Abstr. (1991-); Index Vet.; Maize Abstr.; Nutr. Abstr. Rev., Ser. B, Live Feeds and Feed.; Nutr. Abstr. Rev., Ser. A, Hum. Exp.; Life Sci. Collect.; PESTDOC; Pig News Inf.; Poult. Abstr.; Protozoolog. Abstr.; Res. Alert [Select. Cov.]; Rev. Agric. Entomol.; Rev. Med. Vet. Entomol.; Rev. Med. Vet. Mycology; SCISEARCH; Small Anim. Abstr. Bibliogr.; Soc. Sci. Cit. Index [Select. Cov.]; Vet. Bull.; Virol. AIDS Abstr.; Weed Abstr.; Wheat Barley Trit. Abstr.

US/0741-5575
**MAJOR PROBLEMS IN VETERINARY MEDICINE.** ***Ceased.*** [Major probl. vet. med.]. Vol. 1-Ceased (1986). Monographic series. English. ir. W.B. Saunders Company, A Subsidiary of Harcourt Brace Jovanovich, Inc., The Curtis Center/Suite 300, Independence Square West, Philadelphia PA 19106-3399. **Tel** (215)238-7800 or, 5587, FAX (215)238-7883, telex 173146. **(Subscription address:** W. B. Saunders Company / North America Subscriptions, c/o Periodicals, 6277 Sea Harbour Drive, 4th Floor, Orlando FL 32887.**) NLM** W1 MA492Y.

MY/0126-5652
**MALAYSIAN VETERINARY JOURNAL, THE.** ***Ceased.*** [Malays. vet. j.]. Ceased Vol. 8, No. 3/4 (Dec. 1986). Periodical. English. an. University of Malaya Central Animal Facility, Kuala Lumpur Malaysia. **NLM** W1 MA5247SF. **CODEN** MVEJDP. Documents available from BIOSIS Document Express. ***Continues*** *Journal of the Malaysian Veterinary Medical Association.*
**Ind/Abst** Biol. Abstr.; Life Sci. Collect.

CN/0225-9591
**MEDECIN VETERINAIRE DU QUEBEC, LE.** [Med. vet. Que.]. **Added/Corp** Ordre des Medecins Veterinaires du Quebec. Vol. 10 No. 1 (Jan. 1980)-. Periodical. French. qt. 35.00Can$ Canada; 45.00Can$ other. Order of Veterinaire Surgeon, 795 Avenue du Palais, Saint-Hyacinthe Quebec J2S5C6 Canada. **Tel** (514)774-1427, FAX (514)774-7635. **DD** 636.089/05. **CODEN** MVEQDC. **Circ:** 2,300 (ctrl). Documents available from BIOSIS Document Express. ***Continues*** *M V-Quebec, 0704-6995.*
**Ind/Abst** AgBiotech News Inf.; Anim. Breed. Abstr.; Biol. Abstr.; Dairy Sci. Abstr.; Helminthol. Abstr. (1991-); Index Vet.; Pig News Inf.; Point Repere (1983-); Poult. Abstr.; Protozoolog. Abstr.; Rev. Med. Vet. Entomol.; Rev. Med. Vet. Mycology; Small Anim. Abstr. Bibliogr.; Vet. Bull.; Wildl. Rev. (19??-199?).

UK/0269-283X
**MEDICAL AND VETERINARY ENTOMOLOGY.** **See** Zoology-Entomology.

●RM
**MEDICINA VETERINARA SI CRESTEREA ANIMALELOR.** **Added/Corp** Romania. Ministerul Agriculturii si Alimentatiei. Vol. 42, No. 1 (1992)-. Periodical. Romanian (summaries and/or abstracts in English; table of contents in English, French and German). mo. DM206.00. **(Subscription address:** Kubon & Sagner, ABT Zeitschriftenimport, D 80328 Munich Germany.**)** ***Continues*** *Zootehnie si Medicina Veterinara.*

SP/0212-8292
**MEDICINA VETERINARIA (BARCELONA, SPAIN).** (MEDICINA VETERINARIA.). **VFOAT** MV. Vol. 1, No. 1 (Jan. 1984)-. Periodical. Spanish (summaries and/or abstracts in English; table of contents in English). mo (11 issues). 9000ptas Spain; 13000ptas other. Pulso Ediciones SA, Sant Elies 21 4-Art, 08006 Barcelona Spain. **Tel** 011 34 3 2000877, FAX 011 34 3 2022117. **LC** SF604; .M42. **NLM** W1; ME6306. **CODEN** MEVEEB.
**Ind/Abst** AgBiotech News Inf.; Anim. Breed. Abstr.; Dairy Sci. Abstr.; Fish Rev.; Helminthol. Abstr. (19??-19??); Index Vet.; Nutr. Abstr. Rev., Ser. B, Live Feeds and Feed.; Pig News Inf.; Poult. Abstr.; Protozoolog. Abstr.; Rev. Agric. Entomol.; Rev. Med. Vet. Entomol.; Rev. Med. Vet. Mycology; Small Anim. Abstr. Bibliogr.; Vet. Bull.; Wheat Barley Trit. Abstr.; Wildl. Rev.

PL/0025-8628
**MEDYCYNA WETERYNARYJNA.** [Med. wet.]. **Added/Corp** Poland. Ministerstwo Rolnictwa i Reform Rolnych. Polskie Towarzystwo Nauk Weterynaryjnych. Panstwowe Wydawnictwo Rolnicze i Lesne. Vol. 1 (May/June 1945)-. Academic Scholarly Publication. Polish. mo. Price on Request. **(Subscription address:** ARS Polona, PO Box 1001, 00068 Warsaw Poland.**) NLM** W1 ME8718. **CODEN** MDWTAG. Documents available from BIOSIS Document Express, CASDDS.
**Ind/Abst** AGRICOLA; Agric. Eng. Abstr. (1991-); Anim. Breed. Abstr.; Biodeter. Abstr. (1991-); Biol. Abstr.; Chem. Abstr.; Dairy Sci. Abstr.; EMBASE; Food Sci. Technol. Abstr.; Helminthol. Abstr. (19??-19??); Hortic. Abstr.; Index Vet.; Maize Abstr.; Microbiol. Abstr. Sect. B (19??-19??); Nutr. Abstr. Rev., Ser. B, Live Feeds and Feed.; PESTDOC; Pig News Inf.; Poult. Abstr.; Protozoolog. Abstr.; Rev. Agric. Entomol.; Rev. Med. Vet. Entomol.; Rev. Med. Vet. Mycology; Sug. Indus. Abstr.; Vet. Bull.

US/1068-0810
**MEMBERSHIP DIRECTORY - AMERICAN ASSOCIATION OF EQUINE PRACTITIONERS.** (MEMBERSHIP DIRECTORY.). [Membersh. dir. - Am. Assoc. Equine Pract.]. **Main/Corp** American Association of Equine Practitioners. **VFOAT** Member Directory; A.A.E.P. Membership Directory. **VAT** American Association of Equine Practitioners Membership Directory. (1988)-. Directory. English. an. $20.00 (members); $40.00 (non-members) Comes with American Association of Equine Practictioners membership. American Association of Equine Practitioners, 4075 Iron Works Pike, Lexington KY 40511. **Tel** (606)233-0147, FAX (606)233-1968. **DD** 636. ***Continues*** *American Association of Equine Practitioners. A.A.E.P. Directory.*

CN/1185-9334
**MEMBERSHIP DIRECTORY / THE CANADIAN SOCIETY OF ANIMAL SCIENCE.** [Membsh. dir. - Can. Soc. Anim. Sci.]. **Main/Corp** Canadian Society of Animal Science. (1991)-. Directory. English. Canadian Society of Animal Science, Suite 907/151 Slater Street, Ottawa Ontario K1P 5H4 Canada. **DD** 636.

US/0076-6542
**MERCK VETERINARY MANUAL, THE.** **Added/Corp** Merck & Co. 1st Edition (1955)-. Monographic series. English. ir (Published every five years). Price varies per volume. Merck & Company, PO Box 2000, Rahway NJ 07065. **Tel** (908)594-4600. **LC** SF748; .M47.

US
**MINNESOTA. LIVESTOCK SANITARY BOARD. ANNUAL REPORT.** (ANNUAL REPORT / STATE OF MINNESOTA. BOARD OF ANIMAL HEALTH.). **Main/Corp** Minnesota. Board of Animal Health. English. an. **LC** SF624.M6; M52A. **DD** 353.97760082/336. ***Continues*** *Annual Report / Minnesota. Livestock Sanitary Board.*

US/0271-1893
**MINNESOTA NUTRITION CONFERENCE.** (MINNESOTA NUTRITION CONFERENCE : PROCEEDINGS / MINNESOTA AGRICULTURAL EXTENSION SERVICE.). [Minn. Nutr. Conf.]. **Main/Conf** Minnesota Nutrition Conference. **Added/Corp** University of Minnesota. Agricultural Extension Service. **VFOAT** Minnesota Nutrition Conference Proceedings. (19??)-. Academic Scholarly Publication. English. an. $15.00. University of Minnesota Office of Special Programs, 405 Coffey Hall, 1429 Echles, St Paul MN 55108. **Tel** (612)625-1978, FAX (612)625-2207. **ED** Gerald Wagner. **LC** SF95; .M658a. **DD** 630. **CODEN** MNCPDB. Index available. **Circ:** 500. Documents available from CASDDS.
**Desc:** Scientific papers and research findings on animal nutrition.
**Ind/Abst** Chem. Abstr. (-1982).

US
**MINNESOTA VETERINARIAN, THE.** **Added/Corp** Minnesota. University. College of Veterinary Medicine. Vol. 1 (1961)-. Periodical. English. sa. ***Supersedes*** *Veterinary Grad.*

US/0362-8140
**MODERN VETERINARY PRACTICE (1973).** (MODERN VETERINARY PRACTICE.). [Mod. vet. pract.]. **VFOAT** MVP. V. 54- Jan. 1973-. Academic Scholarly Publication. English. mo. $42.00 (one year), $67.00 (two year) US; $49.00 (one year), $79.00 (two year) Canada; $66.00 (one year), $109.00 (two year) other. American Veterinary Publishing Company, 5782 Thornwood Drive, Goleta CA 93117. **Tel** (805)967-5988. **NLM** W1 MO177. **CODEN** MVPRAX. **[CCC].** available on microfilm and microfiche from University Microfilms International (UMI). Documents available from BIOSIS Document Express, CASDDS. ***Continues*** *MVP, Modern Veterinary Practice.*
**Ind/Abst** AGRICOLA; Anim. Breed. Abstr.; Biol. Abstr.; Chem. Abstr.; Dairy Sci. Abstr.; Energy Res. Abstr. (Aug. 1982-); Helminthol. Abstr.; Index Med.; Index Vet.; Life Sci. Collect.; PESTDOC (?-?); Pig News Inf.; Rev. Med. Vet. Entomol.; Vet. Bull.

GW/0026-9263
**MONATSHEFTE FUER VETERINAERMEDIZIN.** (MONATSHEFTE FUER VETERINAERMEDIZIN : ZEITSCHRIFT DER WISSENSCHAFTLICHEN GESELLSCHAFT FUER VETERINAERMEDIZIN IN DER DEUTSCHEN DEMOKRATISCHEN REPUBLIK.). [Monatsh. veterinÉarmed.]. **Added/Corp** Wissenschaftliche Gesellschaft fuer Veterinaermedizin in der Deutschen Demokratischen Republik. Wissenschaftliche Gesellschaft fuer Veterinaermedizin der Deutschen Demokratischen Republik. Vol. 1 (July 1946)-. Periodical. German (English; summaries and/or abstracts in English and Russian; table of contents in English and Russian). mo. Terra Verlag, Postfach 102144, D-78421 Konstanz Germany. **Tel** 011 49 7531 812244, telex 733271. **LC** SF603; .M63. **NLM** W1 MO359. **CODEN** MVMZA8. **[CCC].** Index available. **Bk Rev. Ad Acc. Pr Rev. Circ:** 4,600. Documents available from The Genuine Article, BIOSIS Document Express, CASDDS.
**Desc:** Contains important original articles from all fields of veterinary medicine, of agriculture and food production, and a number of subjects related to veterinary medicine. A comprehensive section is devoted to extracts of outstanding research findings and practical experience at home and abroad. Publishes further on informations and book reviews.
**Ind/Abst** AgBiotech News Inf.; AGRICOLA; Agric. Eng. Abstr. (1991-); Anim. Breed. Abstr.; Biodeter. Abstr.; Biol. Abstr.; Chem. Abstr.; Curr. Biotechnol.; Curr. Contents, Agric. Biol. Environ. Sci.; Dairy Sci. Abstr.; EMBASE; Fish Rev.; Food Sci. Technol. Abstr.; Helminthol. Abstr. (19??-19??); Index Vet.; Maize Abstr.; Microbiol. Abstr. Sect. B; Nutr. Abstr. Rev., Ser. B, Live Feeds and Feed.; Nutr. Abstr. Rev., Ser. A, Hum. Exp.; Ornamental Hort.; Life Sci. Collect.; PESTDOC; Poult. Abstr.; Protozoolog. Abstr.; Res. Alert [Full Cov.]; Rev. Agric. Entomol.; Rev. Med. Vet. Entomol.; Rev. Med. Vet. Mycology; Sci. Cit. Index; SCISEARCH; Small Anim. Abstr. Bibliogr.; Vet. Bull.; Wildl. Rev.

IR/0042-0123
**NAMAH-I DANISHKADAH-I DAMPIZISHKI.** (JOURNAL OF VETERINARY FACULTY, UNIVERSITY OF TEHRAN.). [Namah-i Danishkadah-i dampizishki]. **Main/Corp** Teheran. University. Veterinary Faculty. **VFOAT** Revue de la Faculte Veterinaire, Universite de Teheran. 1937-. Academic Scholarly Publication. Persian (English and French). qt. $11.00. University of Iran, Veterinary Faculty, Tehran Iran. **ED** R Naghshineh. **CODEN** JVFTDR. Index available. **Bk Rev.** Documents available from CASDDS.
**Ind/Abst** AGRICOLA; Anim. Breed. Abstr.; Chem. Abstr. (1937-1981); Dairy Sci. Abstr.; Food Sci. Technol. Abstr.; Helminthol. Abstr. (1991-); Index Vet.; Maize Abstr.; Nutr. Abstr. Rev., Ser. A, Hum. Exp.; Poult. Abstr.; Small Anim. Abstr. Bibliogr.; Sug. Indus. Abstr.; Vet. Bull.

AT/0728-8727
**NATIONAL DOG.** [Natl. dog]. (1982)-. Periodical. English. mo. 48.00Aus$ (Australia); 93.00Aus$ (other). Sterling Media, PO Box 392, Baulkham Hills, 2153 Australia. **Tel** 11 61 2 6862033, FAX 11 61 2 6861939. **DD** 636.7005. ***Continues*** *National Dog Newspaper, 0811-4021.*

US/0503-5090
**NATIONAL TICK SURVEILLANCE PROGRAM.** (NATIONAL TICK SURVEILLANCE PROGRAM / UNITED STATES DEPARTMENT OF AGRICULTURE, ANIMAL AND PLANT HEALTH INSPECTION SERVICE, VETERINARY SERVICES.). English. US Department of Agriculture / Animal & Plant Health Inspection Service, 741 Federal Building 1, 6505 Belcres Road, Hyattsville MD 20782. **Tel** (301)436-7817. **LC** SF810.T5; U53A. **DD** 636.089/4/433. **NLM** W2 A A5N. available on microfiche (Vols. for (1983) distributed to depository libraries).

RU/0203-6827
**NAUCNYE TRUDY - VSESOJUZNYJ NAUCNO-ISSLEDOVATELSKIJ INSTITUT FIZIOLOGII BIOHIMII I PITANIJA SELSKO-HOZJAJSTEVENNYH ZIVOTNYH.** (NAUCHNYE TRUDY - VSESOIUZNYI NAUCHNO-ISSLEDOVATELSKII INSTITUT

FIZIOLOGII, BIOKHIMII I PITANIIA SELSKOKHOZIAISTVENNYKH ZHIVOTNYKH.). [Naucn. tr. - Vses. naucno-issled. inst. fiziol. biohim. pitan. s-h zivotn.]. **Main/Corp** Vsesoiuznyi Nauchno-Issledovatelskii Institut Fiziologii, Biokhimii i Pitaniia Selskokhoziaistvennykh Zhivotnykh (Soviet Union). **Added/Corp** Vsesoiuznaia Akademiia Selskokhoziaistvennykh Nauk. No. 12 (1973)-. Academic Scholarly Publication. Russian (summaries and/or abstracts in English). VINITI - Vsesoyuznyi Institut Nauchno-Tekhnicheskoi Informatsii, All-Union Scientific and Technical Information Institute, Baltiiskaia Ulitsa 14, 125219 Moscow Russia. **Tel** 238-46-00, FAX 9430060, telex 411160. **CODEN** TFBPAO. Documents available from CASDDS. ***Continues*** *Vsesoiuznyi Nauchno-Issledovatelskii Institut Fiziologii i Biokhimii Selskokhoziaistvennykh Zhivotnykh. Trudy - Vsesoiuznyi Nauchno-Issledovatelskogo Instituta Fiziologii Biokhimii i Pitaniia Selskokhoziaistvennykh Zhivotnykh.*
**Ind/Abst** Chem. Abstr.

US/0277-3015
**NEW METHODS (SAN FRANCISCO, CALIF.).** (NEW METHODS.). [New methods]. Vol. 4, No. 1 (May 1981)-. Periodical. English. mo. $29.00. New Methods, PO Box 22605, San Francisco CA 94122. **Tel** (415)664-3469. **ED** Ronald S Lippert. **DD** 636. **[CCC].** Index available. cum. index. **Bk Rev. Ad Acc. Circ:** 5,600. ***Continues*** *Methods.*
**Desc:** National network service in the animal and veterinary fields. Resource bank for information.

NZ/0048-0169
**NEW ZEALAND VETERINARY JOURNAL.** [N. Z. vet. j.]. **Added/Corp** New Zealand Veterinary Association. Vol. 1 (1952)-. Academic Scholarly Publication. English. Six times a year. 170.00Aus$ (institution), 85.00Aus$ (individual), Australia; 140.00Aus$ (institution), 70.00Aus$ (individual), North and South America 160.00Aus$ (institution), 80.00Aus$ (individual), Africa, Asia and Europe. New Zealand Veterinary Association, PO Box 27499, Wellington New Zealand. **Tel** 011 64 4 843632. **ED** Andrew W. Keber. **NLM** W1 NE986. **CODEN** NEZTAF. **[CCC].** Index available. **Bk Rev. Pr Rev. Circ:** 1,800 (ctrl). Documents available from The Genuine Article, BIOSIS Document Express, CASDDS.
**Desc:** Refereed scientific articles covering a wide range of veterinary and agricultural subjects.
**Ind/Abst** AgBiotech News Inf.; AGRICOLA; Anim. Behav. Abstr.; Anim. Breed. Abstr.; Biol. Abstr. (1962-1984); Chem. Abstr.; CSA Neuro. Abstr. (?-?); Curr. Contents, Agric. Biol. Environ. Sci.; Dairy Sci. Abstr.; EMBASE; Helminthol. Abstr. (19??-19??); Index Med.; Index Vet.; Leadscan; Nutr. Abstr. Rev., Ser. B, Live Feeds and Feed.; Life Sci. Collect.; PESTDOC; Pig News Inf.; Poult. Abstr.; Protozoolog. Abstr.; Res. Alert [Full Cov.]; Rev. Med. Vet. Mycology; Sci. Cit. Index; SCISEARCH; Small Anim. Abstr. Bibliogr.; Vet. Bull.; Wildl. Rev.

US
**NEWSLETTER / CORNELL UNIVERSITY LIBRARIES, FLOWER VETERINARY LIBRARY.** **See** Library and Information Sciences.

US
**NEWSLETTER OF THE NEBRASKA VETERINARY TECHNICIAN ASSOCIATION.** (19??)-. Newsletter. English. $15.00 (membership) comes with Nebraska Veterinary Technician Association membership. Nebraska Veterinary Technician Association, Box 212, Curtis NE 69025.

AT
**NEWSLETTER / THE AUSTRALIAN FEDERATION FOR THE WELFARE OF ANIMALS.** **Added/Corp** Australian Federation for the Welfare of Animals. (19??)-. Newsletter. English. qt. 24.00Aus$. Australian Federation for the Welfare of Animals, PO Box 114, Walkerville SA 5081 Australia. **Tel** 011 61 8 3446337, FAX 011 61 8 3449227. **ED** Dr. A. Blackshaw. **Circ:** 200 (ctrl).
**Desc:** Newsletter for AFWA, an independent national body of people who wish to put common sense into animal welfare.

JA/0078-0839
**NIHON DAIGAKU NOJUIGAKUBU GAKUJUTSU KENKYU HOKOKU.** **See** Agriculture.

JA/0373-8361
**NIHON JUI CHIKUSAN DAIGAKU KENKYU HOKOKU.** [Bull. Nippon vet. zootech. coll.]. **VFOAT** Bulletin of the Nippon Veterinary and Zootechnical College. Academic Scholarly Publication. Japanese (summaries and/or abstracts in English; table of contents in English). an. **NLM** W1; NI916F. Documents available from CASDDS. ***Continues*** *Nihon Jui Chikusan Daigaku Kiyo.*
**Ind/Abst** AGRICOLA; Chem. Abstr.; Index Vet.; Nutr. Abstr. Rev., Ser. B, Live Feeds and Feed.; Pig News Inf.; Poult. Abstr.; Rev. Med. Vet. Mycology; Vet. Bull.; World Agric. Econ.

JA/0446-6454
**NIPPON JUISHIKAI ZASSHI.** (JOURNAL OF THE JAPAN VETERINARY MEDICAL ASSOCIATION.). [Nippon Juishikai zasshi]. **Main/Corp** Nippon Juishi Kai. **Added/Corp** Japan Veterinary Medical Association. Journal. **VFOAT** Zasshi. Vol. 1 (1948)-. Periodical. Japanese (English; table of contents in English). mo. $214.00. Nihon Juishi Gakkai, (Japan Veterinary Medical Assoc.), 1-1, Minamiaoyama 1 Chome, Minatoku, Tokyoto 107 Japan. **(Subscription address:** Maruzen Company Ltd., PO Box 5050, Import & Export Department, Tokyo 100 31 Japan.**)** **NLM** W1 NI916N. **CODEN** NIPJAV. Documents available from BIOSIS Document Express, CASDDS.
**Ind/Abst** AgBiotech News Inf.; AGRICOLA; Anim. Breed. Abstr.; Biol. Abstr. (-1987); Chem. Abstr.; Helminthol. Abstr. (1991-); Index Vet.; Nutr. Abstr. Rev., Ser. B, Live Feeds and Feed.; Pig News Inf.; Poult. Abstr.; Protozoolog. Abstr.; Rev. Med. Vet. Entomol.; Small Anim. Abstr. Bibliogr.; Vet. Bull.

KO/1013-9400
**NONGSA SIHOM YON'GU NONMUNJIP. CH'UKSAN P'YON.** **VFOAT** Research Reports of the Rural Development Administration. Livestock; Research Reports of R.D.A., L. (1988)-. Periodical. Multiple languages. ir. Rural Development Administration, Plant Environment Mycology and Farm Products Utilization, Suweon 170 Korea.
**Ind/Abst** Agric. Eng. Abstr.; Crop Physiol. Abstr.; Field Crop Abstr.; Pig News Inf.; Poult. Abstr.; Rice Abstr.; Seed Abstr.; Sorghum Mill. Abstr.; Weed Abstr.

KO/1013-9419
**NONGSA SIHOM YON'GU NONMUNJIP. KACH'UK UISAENG P'YON.** **VFOAT** Research Reports of the Rural Development Administration. Veterinary; Research reports of R.D.A., V. (1988)-. Periodical. Multiple languages. ir.
**Ind/Abst** Index Vet.; Pig News Inf.; Protozoolog. Abstr.; Vet. Bull.

US/0890-3727
**NORDEN NEWS.** ***Title Change.*** [Norden news]. **Added/Corp** Norden Laboratories (Lincoln, Neb.). (19??)-(19??). Periodical. English. Norden Laboratories, 601 West Cornhusker Highway Box 80809, Lincoln NE 68502. **DD** 636. ***Continued by*** *Topics in Veterinary Medicine, 1064-5101.*

JA/0388-2403
**NORIN SUISANSHO KACHIKU EISEI SHIKENJO KENKYU HOKOKU.** [Norin Suisansho Kachiku Eisei Shikenjo kenkyu hokoku]. **Added/Corp** Norin Suisansho Kachiku Eisei Shikenjo (Japan). **VFOAT** Bulletin of the National Institute of Animal Health; Kachiku Eishi Kenkyu Hokoku. (1978)-. Academic Scholarly Publication. Japanese. sa. Norin Suisansho Kachiku Eisei Shikenjo, (National Inst. of Animal Health, Ministry of Agriculture, Forestry & Fisheries), 1-1, Kannondai 3 Chome, Tsukubashi, Ibarakiken 305, Japan. **NLM** W1; NO254F. **CODEN** NSKHD5. Documents available from BIOSIS Document Express, CASDDS. ***Continues*** *Norinsho Kachiku Eisei Shikenjo Kenkyu Hokoku;* ***Absorbed*** *Norinsho Kachiku Eisei Shikenjo (Japan). National Institute of Animal Health Quarterly.*
**Ind/Abst** Biol. Abstr. (1985-); Chem. Abstr.

JA
**NORIN SUISANSHO KACHIKU EISEI SHIKENJO NEMPO.** **Main/Corp** Norin Suisansho Kachiku Eisei Shikenjo. 1977-. Japanese. an. Buneido, 27-18 Hongo 2-chome Bunkyo-ku 113, Tokyo Japan. **LC** SF705; .K32A. ***Continues*** *Norinsho Kachiku Eisei Shikenjo Nempo.*

JA
**NORINSHO KACHIKU EISEI SHIKENJO NEMPO.** **Main/Corp** Norinsho Kachiku Eisei Shikenjo (Japan). Began with the Report for 1958. Japanese. ¥1900. Buneido, 27-18 Hongo 2-chome Bunkyo-ku 113, Tokyo Japan. **LC** SF705; .K32A.

NO
**NORSK VETERINARTIDSSKRIFT.** (1988)-. Periodical. Norwegian. mo. Kr500.00 Norway & Nordic countries; Kr600.00 Europe; Kr650.00 other. Norsk Veterinarforening, Sognsv 4, N-0451 Oslo 4 Norway. **Tel** 47 22 567650, FAX 47 22 690450. **ED** Ulf Erik Gustavsen. **Ad Acc. Circ:** 4,230.
**Ind/Abst** Anim. Breed. Abstr.; Dairy Sci. Abstr.; Food Sci. Technol. Abstr.; Helminthol. Abstr. (1991-).

NO/0332-5741
**NORSK VETERINRTIDSSKIRFT 1970.** [Nor. vet.-tidsskr. 1970]. (1970)-. Periodical. Norwegian. mo. Norsk Veterinaerforening, Sekretariat, Sognsveien 4, Oslo 4, Norway. **DD** 636.089. ***Continues*** *Medlemsblad den Norske Veterinrforening, 0369-6545.*
**Ind/Abst** Biodeter. Abstr.; Index Vet.; PESTDOC; Poult. Abstr.; Protozoolog. Abstr.; Small Anim. Abstr. Bibliogr.; Vet. Bull.

IT
**NUOVO PROGRESSO VETERINARIO : ORGANO DELL' ASSOCIAZIONE NAZ. VETERINARI ITALIANI, IL.** ***Title Change.*** **Added/Corp** Associazione Nazionale Veterinari Italiani. Federazione Nazionale Sindicati Veterinari Italiani. **VFOAT** Progresso Veterinario. (1960)-Vol 47, 24 (1992). Periodical. Italian. sm. Il Progresso Veterinario, Corso Vittorio Emanuele N 73, 10128 Turin Italy. **Tel** 011 39 11 5628352. **NLM** W1 NU372N. ***Continues*** *Progresso Veterinario (Turin, Italy : 1945).* ***Continued by*** *Progresso Veterinario (Turin, Italy : 1993).*
**Ind/Abst** Helminthol. Abstr. (1991-); Index Vet.; Rev. Med. Vet. Entomol.

US/0160-6948
**NUTRIENT REQUIREMENTS OF DOMESTIC ANIMALS.** Academic Scholarly Publication. English. ir. Price varies per volume. National Research Council, 2101 Constitution Avenue, Washington DC 20418. **CODEN** NRDAA7. Documents available from CASDDS.
**Ind/Abst** AGRICOLA; Chem. Abstr.

IT/0392-1913
**OBIETTIVI E DOCUMENTI VETERINARI.** [Obiettivi doc. vet.]. (1980)-. Periodical. Italian. Ten times a year. L58000 (Italy); L80000 (other). Edagricole, PO Box 2157, 40100 Bologna Italy. **Tel** 011 39 51 492211 Ext. 22, FAX 011 39 51 493660, telex 510336 EDAGRI.
**Ind/Abst** Anim. Breed. Abstr.; Biodeter. Abstr.; Helminthol. Abstr.; Nutr. Abstr. Rev., Ser. B, Live Feeds and Feed.; Nutr. Abstr. Rev., Ser. A, Hum. Exp.; Pig News Inf. (1991-); Poult. Abstr.; Protozoolog. Abstr. (1991-); Rev. Med. Vet. Entomol.; Rev. Med. Vet. Mycology; Small Anim. Abstr. Bibliogr.; Weed Abstr.

JA/0470-925X
**OBIHIRO CHIKUSAN DAIGAKU GAKUJUTSU KENKYU HOKOKU DAI-1-BU.** **See** Agriculture.

UK/0572-7022
**OCCASIONAL SYMPOSIUM.** [Br. Grassl. Soc. Occas. Symp.]. **Main/Corp** British Grassland Society. (1964)-. Periodical. English. British Grassland Society, Animal Grass Research Institute, Hurley Maidenhead BKS SL6 5LR England.
**Ind/Abst** AGRICOLA [Full Cov.]; Rev. Med. Vet. Entomol.

KO
**OEGUK KWAHAK KISUL TONGBO. SUUI CHUKSAN.** **VFOAT** Zhivotnovodstvo I Veterinariia. Periodical. Korean. **LC** SF1; .O37.

US/0474-0785
**OKLAHOMA VETERINARIAN, THE.** ***Ceased.*** [Okla. veterin.]. **Added/Corp** Oklahoma Veterinary Medical Association. Vol. 1 (1954)-(June 1993). Periodical. English. an. Oklahoma Veterinarian, 1547 South Lewis, Tulsa OK 74104.
**Ind/Abst** Fish Rev.; Wildl. Rev.

SA/0030-2465
**ONDERSTEPOORT JOURNAL OF VETERINARY RESEARCH, THE.** [Onderstepoort j. vet. res.]. Vol. 25 (1951)-. Periodical. English. qt. R50.00 South Africa; R66.00 other. The Director Division of Agriculture Information, Private Bag X144, Pretoria 0001 South Africa. **LC** SF601; .O58. **NLM** W1 ON108. **CODEN** OJVRAZ. cum. index. **Pr Rev.** available on microfilm from University Microfilms International (UMI). Documents available from The Genuine Article, BIOSIS Document Express, CASDDS. ***Continues*** *Onderstepoort Journal of Veterinary Science and Animal Industry.*
**Ind/Abst** AgBiotech News Inf.; AGRICOLA [Full Cov.]; Biocont. News Inf. (1991-); Biol. Abstr.; Chem. Abstr.; CSA Neuro. Abstr. (?-?); Curr. Contents, Agric. Biol. Environ. Sci.; Dairy Sci. Abstr.; Entomol. Abstr.; Fish Rev.; Food Sci. Technol. Abstr.; Helminthol. Abstr. (19??-19??); Index Med.; Microbiol. Abstr. Sect. B (19??-19??); Nutr. Abstr. Rev., Ser. B, Live Feeds and Feed.; Life Sci. Collect.; PESTDOC; Pig News Inf.; Poult. Abstr.; Protozoolog. Abstr.; Res. Alert [Full Cov.]; Rev. Med. Vet. Entomol.; Rev. Med. Vet. Mycology; Sci. Cit. Index; SCISEARCH; Trop. Dis. Bull.; Virol. AIDS Abstr.; Wildl. Rev.

CN/0844-5303
**ONT. SHEEP NEWS.** **See** Agriculture-Livestock and Poultry.

●US/1068-5774
**OSTRICH NEWS RATITE DIRECTORY, THE.** **VFOAT** Ratite Directory. (1992)-. Directory. English. **LC** SF511; .N384. **DD** 636.6. ***Continues*** *National Ostrich/Ratite Directory, 1050-981X.*
**Desc:** Information on ostrich farms and farming.

PK/1015-3055
**PAKISTAN JOURNAL OF AGRICULTURE, AGRICULTURAL ENGINEERING & VETERINARY SCIENCES.** **See** Agriculture.

PK
**PAKISTAN VETERINARIAN : A PUBLICATION OF PAKISTAN VETERINARY MEDICAL ASSOCIATION, THE.** **Added/Corp** Pakistan Veterinary Medical Association. (19??)-. Periodical. English. mo.
**Ind/Abst** Index Vet.; Nutr. Abstr. Rev., Ser. B, Live Feeds and Feed.; Poult. Abstr.

PK/0253-8318
**PAKISTAN VETERINARY JOURNAL.** [Pak. vet. j.]. **Added/Corp** University of Agriculture, Faisalabad. Faculty of Veterinary Science. **VFOAT** PVC. Vol. 1, No. 1 (Jan. 1981)-. Academic Scholarly Publication. English. Four times a year. University of Agriculture / Pakistan, Faculty of Veterinary Science, Faisalabad Pakistan. **Tel** 25911-19/322, 424. **ED** M. Nawaz. **CODEN** PVJODU. cum. index. **Bk Rev. Ad Acc. Circ:** 500. Documents available from BIOSIS Document Express, CASDDS.
**Desc:** Covers veterinary medicine, anatomy, physiology, pharmacology, parasitology, microbiology, pathology, surgery, animal reproduction, livestock management, nutrition, breeding, poultry, and biology.
**Ind/Abst** Anim. Breed. Abstr.; Biol. Abstr.; Chem. Abstr.; Dairy Sci. Abstr.; Helminthol. Abstr. (19??-19??); Index Vet.; Nutr. Abstr. Rev., Ser. B, Live Feeds and Feed.; Poult. Abstr.; Rev. Med. Vet. Mycology; Small Anim. Abstr. Bibliogr.; Vet. Bull.; Wheat Barley Trit. Abstr.; Wildl. Rev.

II
**PERFORMANCE BUDGET ON ANIMAL HUSBANDRY & VETERINARY.** **Main/Corp** Assam (India). Veterinary Dept. English. an. Veterinary Department, Gauhati Assam India. **LC** SF604; .A77A. **DD** 354.54/1620082336.

US/0738-4394
**PERSPECTIVES IN ETHOLOGY.** [Perspect. ethol.]. Vol. 1 (1973)-. Monographic series. English. ir. Price varies per volume. Plenum Press, 233 Spring Street, New York NY 10013-1578. **Tel** (212)620-8000, (800)221-9369, FAX (212)463-0742, (212)807-1047, telex 23/421139. **ED** P.P.G. Bateson and Peter H. Klopfer. **LC** QL750; .P47. **DD** 591.5/1. **NLM** W1 PE871AN.
**Ind/Abst** AGRICOLA [Select. Cov.].

US
**PERSPECTIVES ON CATS.** **Added/Corp** Cornell Feline Health Center. (1983)-. Periodical. English. qt. $15.00, $25.00 (Cornell Feline Health Center membership) US; $35.00, $30.00 (Cornell Feline Health Center membership) other. Cornell Feline Health Center, Cornell University, 618 Veterinary Research Tower, Ithaca NY 14853. **Tel** (607)255-2000, (607)253-3414, FAX (607)253-3419. **ED** June E. Tuttle. Index available. cum. index. **Circ:** 5,900 (ctrl). ***Continues** Feline Health Perspectives.*
**Desc:** Cat health topics of interest to cat owners and breeders.
**Ind/Abst** Nutr. Abstr. Rev., Ser. B, Live Feeds and Feed.; Rev. Med. Vet. Entomol.; Small Anim. Abstr. Bibliogr.

MY/0126-6128
**PERTANIKA.** ***Title Change.*** **See** Agriculture.

BL/0100-736X
**PESQUISA VETERINARIA BRASILEIRA.** (PESQUISA VETERINARIA BRASILEIRA : REVISTA DO COLEGIO BRASILEIRO DE PATOLOGIA ANIMAL.). [Pesqui. vet. bras.]. **Added/Corp** Colegio Brasileiro de Patologia Animal. **VFOAT** Brazilian Journal of Veterinary Research. Vol. 1, No. 1 (Jan./Mar. 1981)-. Periodical. English (Portuguese). Four times a year. $50.00. Rev Pesquisa Vet Brasileira, Embrapa Seropedica 23851-970, Rio de Janeiro Brazil. **Tel** 011 55 21 6821082, FAX 011 55 21 6821230, telex 21-32723. **ED** Jurgen Dobereiner. **NLM** W1; PE923H. **CODEN** PVBRDX. Index available (4th iss.). cum. index. **Ad Acc, Adv Mgr:** Luis Carlos de Oleveira, **Tel** (021)263-7561. **Circ:** 1,000. Documents available from The Genuine Article, BIOSIS Document Express.
**Ind/Abst** Anim. Breed. Abstr.; Biol. Abstr.; Curr. Contents, Agric. Biol. Environ. Sci.; Fish Rev. (Jan. 1989-July 1992); Grasslands For. Abstr.; Helminthol. Abstr. (1991-); Index Vet.; Nutr. Abstr. Rev., Ser. B, Live Feeds and Feed.; Pig News Inf.; Poult. Abstr.; Protozoolog. Abstr.; Res. Alert [Select. Cov.]; Rev. Med. Vet. Entomol.; SCISEARCH; Small Anim. Abstr. Bibliogr.; Vet. Bull.; Wildl. Rev. (Jan. 1989-July 1992).

US/0731-468X
**PET ANIMAL HEALTH LETTER, THE.** [Pet anim. health lett.]. Vol. 1, No. 1 (Feb. 1982)-. Periodical. English. mo. $24.00. Veterinary Letter Publications, PO Box 450521, Atlanta GA 30345.

US/1050-7418
**PET VETERINARIAN.** ***Ceased.*** [Pet vet.]. Vol. 1, No. 1 (July/Aug. 1989)-(1992). Periodical. English. bm. Watt Publishing Company, 122 South Wesley Avenue, Mount Morris IL 61054. **Tel** (815)734-4171, FAX (815)734-7021, telex TWX 910-642-2891. **DD** 636.
**Ind/Abst** Anim. Breed. Abstr.; Index Vet.; Pig News Inf.; Small Anim. Abstr. Bibliogr.

GW/0177-7726
**PFERDEHEILKUNDE.** Vol. 1, No. 1 (March 1985)-. Periodical. German. Six times a year. DM242.99 Germany; DM272.00 other. Hippiatrika Verlagsgesellschaf, Postfach 1211, D 75352 Calw Germany. **Tel** 011 49 7053 6218.
**Ind/Abst** Helminthol. Abstr. (19??-19??); Index Vet.; Nutr. Abstr. Rev., Ser. B, Live Feeds and Feed.; Vet. Bull.

PH/0115-2173
**PHILIPPINE JOURNAL OF VETERINARY AND ANIMAL SCIENCES.** [Philipp. j. vet. anim. sci.]. **Added/Corp** Philippine Society of Animal Science. Philippine Veterinary Medical Association. Philippine Council for Agricultural Research. Vol. 1 (Jan./Mar. 1975)-. Periodical. English. Four times a year (Mar., June, Sep., Dec.). $80.00. Philippin Society of Animal Science, c/o Institute of Animal Science, University of the Philippines, Los Banos College, Laguna 4301 Philippines. **Tel** 63 94 2730. **ED** Dr. Salcedo L Eduardo. **CODEN** PJVSDI. **Ad Acc, Adv Mgr:** Manny, **Tel** 63 94 2728. **Pr Rev. Circ:** 500. Documents available from CASDDS.
**Ind/Abst** Anim. Breed. Abstr.; Chem. Abstr.; Dairy Sci. Abstr.; Grasslands For. Abstr.; Nutr. Abstr. Rev., Ser. B, Live Feeds and Feed.; Pig News Inf.; Postharvest News Inf.; Poult. Abstr.; Sug. Indus. Abstr.

PH/0031-7705
**PHILIPPINE JOURNAL OF VETERINARY MEDICINE.** [Philipp. j. vet. med.]. **Added/Corp** University of the Philippines. College of Veterinary Medicine. Vol. 1 (June 1962)-. Periodical. English. Four times a year (Mar., June, Sept., Dec.). $30.00 Philippines; $40.00 US, Canada, Pan America, & Europe; $35.00 others. University of Philippines / Los Banos, College of Veterinary Medicine, Laguna 4031 Philippines. **Tel** 011 63 94 2727, 011 63 94 2730. **ED** Dr. Salcedo L. Edurdo. **NLM** W1 PH576P. **CODEN** PJVMAV. **Bk Rev**, (Qty: 1). **Ad Acc. Circ:** 300. Documents available from BIOSIS Document Express, CASDDS.
**Desc:** Contains results of researches related to animal science and veterinary medicine.
**Ind/Abst** AGRICOLA; Biol. Abstr.; Chem. Abstr.; Helminthol. Abstr. (1991-); Life Sci. Collect.; Philip. Sci. Technol. Abstr.; Pig News Inf.; Protozoolog. Abstr.; Rev. Med. Vet. Entomol.; Small Anim. Abstr. Bibliogr.

●UK/1352-9749
**PIG JOURNAL, THE.** (1994)-. Periodical. English. sa. £20.00 UK; £22.00 other. Pig Veterinary Society, c/o T W Heard, Grove House, Corston Malmesbury Wilts SN16 0HL, England. **Tel** 011 44 666 822967, FAX 011 44 666 822009, telex 46624. **ED** Donald Basinger, Dr. Stan Done, Professor Richard Penny and Dr. Annop Kunavongkrit. ***Continues** Pig Veterinary Journal, 0956-0939.*
**Desc:** Dedicated to the pig, pig health and pig production.

UK/0956-0939
**PIG VETERINARY JOURNAL.** ***Title Change.*** **Added/Corp** Pig Veterinary Society. **VFOAT** Pig Veterinary Journal of the Pig Veterinary Society. (1989)-(1994). English. Twice a year (Apr., Nov.). Pig Veterinary Society, c/o T W Heard, Grove House, Corston Malmesbury Wilts SN16 0HL, England. **Tel** 011 44 666 822967, FAX 011 44 666 822009, telex 46624. **ED** Professor R.H.C. Perry, Dr. S. Done, D. Basinger MRCVS. Index available. cum. index. **Ad Acc, Adv Mgr:** J. Heard. **Circ:** 800 (ctrl). ***Continues** Pig Veterinary Society. Pig Veterinary Society Proceedings, 0141-3074.* ***Continued by** The Pig Journal, 1352-9749.*
**Ind/Abst** Index Vet. (?-?); Nutr. Abstr. Rev., Ser. B, Live Feeds and Feed. (?-?); Pig News Inf. (?-?); Vet. Bull. (?-?).

FR/0335-4997
**POINT VETERINAIRE, LE.** [Point vet.]. V. 1- (No. 1- ); Nov. 1973-. Periodical. French (English). ir (eight no. a year). 450F. Le Point Veterinaire, 25 rue Bourgelat, 94700 Maison Alfort France. **Tel** 43.53.20.01, telex 231616. **[CCC].** Index available. cum. index. **Bk Rev. Ad Acc. Circ:** 6,000 (ctrl).
**Desc:** Technical information for veterinary practitioners on pathology, surgery, therapeutics, epidemiology, etc. of large and small animals (dogs, cats, horses, cows, goats, sheep, poultry, etc.).
**Ind/Abst** AGRICOLA; Anim. Breed. Abstr.; Dairy Sci. Abstr.; Helminthol. Abstr. (19??-19??); Index Vet.; Nutr. Abstr. Rev., Ser. B, Live Feeds and Feed.; Pig News Inf.; Poult. Abstr.; Protozoolog. Abstr.; Rev. Med. Vet. Entomol.; Rev. Med. Vet. Mycology; Small Anim. Abstr. Bibliogr.; Soyabean Abstr.; Vet. Bull.

GW/0032-681X
**PRAKTISCHE TIERARZT.** (DER PRAKTISCHE TIERARZT.). [Prakt. tierarzt]. **Added/Corp** Bundesverband Praktischer Tierarzte. Vol. 1, (1951)-. Periodical. German. Thirteen times a year. DM184.00 Germany; DM214.00 other. Schluetersche Verlag Druckerei, Postfach 5440, D-30054 Hannover Germany. **Tel** 011 49 511 85500, FAX 011 49 511 1236400, telex 923978. **NLM** W1 PR283. **CODEN** PRTIAV. **[CCC]. Bk Rev. Ad Acc. Pr Rev. Circ:** 6,800 (ctrl). Documents available from The Genuine Article, CASDDS.
**Ind/Abst** AgBiotech News Inf.; AGRICOLA; Agric. Eng. Abstr.; Anim. Breed. Abstr.; Chem. Abstr.; Curr. Contents, Agric. Biol. Environ. Sci.; Dairy Sci. Abstr.; Energy Res. Abstr. (Sept. 1980-); Helminthol. Abstr.; Key Word Index Wildl. Res.; Maize Abstr.; Nutr. Abstr. Rev., Ser. B, Live Feeds and Feed.; Life Sci. Collect.; PESTDOC; Pig News Inf.; Poult. Abstr.; Protozoolog. Abstr.; Res. Alert [Select. Cov.]; Rev. Med. Vet. Entomol.; Rev. Med. Vet. Mycology; SCISEARCH; Small Anim. Abstr. Bibliogr.; Soc. Sci. Cit. Index [Select. Cov.]; Soyabean Abstr.; World Agric. Econ.

FR/0758-1882
**PRATIQUE MEDICALE & CHIRURGICALE DE L'ANIMAL DE COMPAGNIE.** [Prat. med. chir. anim. cie.]. **VFOAT** Pratique Medicale et Chirurgicale de L'Animal de Compagnie. Began with: V. 18, No. 1 (Jan./Feb. 1983). Periodical. French (summaries and/or abstracts in English, German, Italian and Spanish). bm. 1,050F France; 1,028.40F other. Conference Nationale des Veterinaires Specialises en Petits Animaux, 82 Avenue de Villiers, F-75017 Paris France. **Tel** 011 33 1 42677296. ***Continues** Animal de Compagnie.*
**Ind/Abst** AGRICOLA; Anim. Breed. Abstr.; Dairy Sci. Abstr.; Helminthol. Abstr. (19??-19??); Index Vet.; Nutr. Abstr. Rev., Ser. B, Live Feeds and Feed.; PESTDOC; Protozoolog. Abstr.; Rev. Med. Vet. Entomol.; Rev. Med. Vet. Mycology; Small Anim. Abstr. Bibliogr.; Vet. Bull.

FR/0395-8639
**PRATIQUE VETERINAIRE EQUINE.** [Prat. v,et. ,equine]. **Added/Corp** Association Veterinaire Equine Francaise. Vol 10 No 1 (19??)-. Periodical. French. qt. 528.99F (schools and universities), 587.66 other, European Union; 617.04F (schools and universities), 587.66F (other), non-union. Ecole Nationale Veterinaire, Administration & Redaction, 31076 Toulouse Cedex France. **Tel** 011 33 61 193835. **NLM** W1 PR303.
**Ind/Abst** AGRICOLA; Helminthol. Abstr. (1991-); Index Vet.; Protozoolog. Abstr.; Rev. Med. Vet. Entomol.

CI/0350-4441
**PRAXIS VETERINARIA.** [Prax. vet.]. Academic Scholarly Publication. Serbo-Croatian (Roman) (English). sa. Free. PLIVA, I L Ribara 89, 41000 Zagreb Croatia. **Tel** 417 462, FAX 576 690, telex 21 246. **ED** Zdenko Radman. **CODEN** PRVEDW. Index available. cum. index. **Bk Rev. Circ:** 5,000 (ctrl). Documents available from CASDDS.
**Desc:** We publish scientific and technical works of veterinary medicine as well as genetic engineering related to the development of veterinary medicine and cattle feeding.
**Ind/Abst** AgBiotech News Inf.; Anim. Breed. Abstr.; Chem. Abstr.; Helminthol. Abstr.; Index Vet.; Nutr. Abstr. Rev., Ser. B, Live Feeds and Feed.; Pig News Inf.; Poult. Abstr.; Small Anim. Abstr. Bibliogr.; Vet. Bull.

NE/0167-5877
**PREVENTIVE VETERINARY MEDICINE.** [Prev. vet. med.]. Vol. 1 No. 1 (Aug. 1982)-. Academic Scholarly Publication. English. Sixteen times a year (4 volumes). Fl1492.00. Elsevier Science Publishers BV, PO Box 211, 1000 AE Amsterdam Netherlands. **Tel** 011 31 20 5803642, FAX 011 31 20 5862696, telex 15682. **ED** H P Riemann. **NLM** W1 PR507Z. **[CCC]. Pr Rev.** available on microfilm and microfiche from University Microfilms International (UMI). Documents available from The Genuine Article, BIOSIS Document Express.
**Desc:** A journal which disseminates information and reports of significance in the field of animal (mammalian, aquatic and avian) health programs and preventive veterinary medicine.
**Ind/Abst** Agric. Eng. Abstr. (1991-); Anim. Breed. Abstr.; Biol. Abstr.; Curr. Contents, Agric. Biol. Environ. Sci.; Dairy Sci. Abstr.; Helminthol. Abstr. (1991-); Index Vet.; Nutr. Abstr. Rev., Ser. B, Live Feeds and Feed.; Life Sci. Collect.; PESTDOC; Pig News Inf.; Poult. Abstr.; Protozoolog. Abstr.; Res. Alert [Full Cov.]; Rev. Med. Vet. Entomol.; Sci. Cit. Index; SCISEARCH; Small Anim. Abstr. Bibliogr.; Soc. Sci. Cit. Index [Select. Cov.]; Vet. Bull.; World Agric. Econ.

US/0032-8324
**PRIMATE NEWS.** [Primate news]. Began in 1963. Periodical. English. an. Free. Oregon Regional Primate, 505 NW 185th Avenue, Beaverton OR 97006. **Tel** (503)645-1141. **ED** James Parker and Joel Ito. **NLM** W1 PR522D. **CODEN** PRNWBA. ctrl circ. Documents available from CASDDS.
**Desc:** Published for employees and friends of the Oregon Regional Primate Research Center to provide information on recent research and events at the center.
**Ind/Abst** Chem. Abstr.

BE/0777-8309
**PRO VETERINARIO ENGLISH ED.** [Pro vet.Engl. ed.]. (19??)-. Periodical. English. tq. Upjohn Co, 7000 Portage Road, Kalamazoo MI 48008. **Tel** (616)323-4000. **UDC** 619.
**Ind/Abst** Helminthol. Abstr. (1991-).

US/1041-0228
**PROBLEMS IN VETERINARY MEDICINE.** ***Ceased.*** [Probl. vet. med.]. Vol. 1, No. 1 (Jan.-March 1989)-(199?). Periodical. English. qt. J.B. Lippincott Company, 227 East Washington Square, Philadelphia PA 19106-3780. **Tel** (215)238-4200 or 4454, FAX (215)238-4227. **(Subscription address:** Journal Fulfillment Department, Lippincott/Harper, Downsville Pike, Route 3, Box 20-B, Hagerstown, MD 21740;

telephone: (800)638-3030) **ED** William J Kay and Nancy O Brown. **DD** 636. **NLM** W1; PR573P. **[CCC].** available on microfilm from University Microfilms International (UMI).
**Desc:** Focuses on clinical problems encountered by the veterinarian in everyday practice: diagnostic questions, complications, unexpected occurrences, high-risk challenges, management of treatment difficulties.
**Ind/Abst** AGRICOLA [Full Cov.]; Index Vet.; Small Anim. Abstr. Bibliogr.; Vet. Bull.

US/0082-8750
**PROCEEDINGS, ANNUAL MEETING OF THE UNITED STATES ANIMAL HEALTH ASSOCIATION.** [Proc. annu. meet. U.S. Anim. Health Assoc.]. **Main/Corp** United States Animal Health Association. 73rd (Oct. 12-17, 1969)-. Proceedings. English. an. $20.00. US Animal Health Association, PO Box 28176, Richmond VA 23228. **Tel** (804)266-3275. **LC** SF601; .U4. **DD** 636. **NLM** W1 PR583M. **Circ:** 1,300. ***Continues*** *Proceedings, ... Annual Meeting of the United States Live Stock Sanitary Association.*
**Desc:** Study of animal health science, milk and meat hygiene and information relating to the unification of laws, regulations, policies and methods pertaining to milk and meat hygiene.
**Ind/Abst** Anim. Breed. Abstr.; Biodeter. Abstr.; Curr. Law Index; Dairy Sci. Abstr.; Helminthol. Abstr. (1991-); Index Med.; Index Leg. Period.; Index Vet.; Leg. Resour. Index (?-?); Nutr. Abstr. Rev., Ser. B, Live Feeds and Feed.; Pig News Inf.; Poult. Abstr.; Protozoolog. Abstr.; Rev. Med. Vet. Mycology; Soyabean Abstr.; Vet. Bull.

US/0098-3543
**PROCEEDINGS OF ... ANNUAL MEETING - AMERICAN ASSOCIATION OF VETERINARY LABORATORY DIAGNOSTICIANS.** ***Ceased.*** [Proc. annu. meet. - Am. Assoc. Vet. Lab. Diagn.]. **Main/Corp** American Association of Veterinary Laboratory Diagnosticians. Meeting. 12th (1969)-?. Academic Scholarly Publication. English. an. American Association of Veterinary Laboratory Diagnosticians, PO Box 6023, Columbia MO 65205. **Tel** (314)882-6811, FAX (314)882-1411. **ED** M W Vorhies. **LC** SF771. **DD** 636.089/607/5. **NLM** W1 PR584RV. **CODEN** PAMDDZ. **Circ:** 800. Documents available from CASDDS.
**Ind/Abst** Chem. Abstr.

US/0743-0450
**PROCEEDINGS OF THE ANNUAL CONVENTION - AMERICAN ASSOCIATION OF BOVINE PRACTITIONERS. CONVENTION.** ***Title Change.*** (PROCEEDINGS OF THE ... ANNUAL CONVENTION / AMERICAN ASSOCIATION OF BOVINE PRACTITIONERS.). [Proc. annu. conv. - Am. Assoc. Bovine Pract., Conv.]. **Main/Corp** American Association of Bovine Practitioners. Convention. **VFOAT** Bovine Proceedings. (1971)-(1992). English. an. American Association of Bovine Practitioners, PO Box 2319, West Lafayette IN 47906. **Tel** (317)494-8560. **ED** Eric I. Williams. **LC** SF961; .A54a. **DD** 636.2/089/06073. Index available. cum. index. **Bk Rev. Ad Acc. Circ:** 6,000 (ctrl). ***Continued by*** *American Association of Bovine Practitioners. Conference. American Association of Bovine Practitioners Conference : [proceedings], 0743-0450.*
**Desc:** A journal for veterinarians and others in allied fields that are interested in cattle diseases and prevention. A report of our annual meeting.
**Ind/Abst** AGRICOLA (?-?) [Full Cov.].

US/0065-7182
**PROCEEDINGS OF THE ANNUAL CONVENTION OF THE AMERICAN ASSOCIATION OF EQUINE PRACTITIONERS.** **See** Horses and Horsemanship.

US/0894-7708
**PROCEEDINGS OF THE ANNUAL VETERINARY MEDICAL FORUM.** (PROCEEDINGS OF THE ... ANNUAL VETERINARY MEDICAL FORUM / AMERICAN COLLEGE OF VETERINARY INTERNAL MEDICINE.). [Proc. annu. Vet. Med. Forum]. **Added/Corp** American College of Veterinary Internal Medicine. **VFOAT** ACVIM Proceedings. (1986)-. English. an. $45.00. ACVIM, 62 No Main Street, Suite C 1A, Blacksburg VA 24060. **Tel** (800)245-9081. **DD** 636. **NLM** W1; VE932F. **CODEN** PAVME6. ***Continues*** *American College of Veterinary Internal Medicine. Medical Forum. Proceedings of the ... Annual Medical Forum, 0897-2311.*
**Ind/Abst** Helminthol. Abstr. (1991-); Index Vet.; Small Anim. Abstr. Bibliogr.

CN/0708-7624
**PROCEEDINGS OF THE CANADIAN ASSOCIATION FOR LABORATORY ANIMAL SCIENCE.** [Proc. Can. Assoc. Lab. Anim. Sci.]. **Main/Corp** Canadian Association for Laboratory Animal Science. Convention. Academic Scholarly Publication. English. an. Canadian Association for Laboratory Animal Science, 2627 Morley Trail North West, Calgary Alberta T2M 4G6 Canada. **DD** 636.08/85. **CODEN** PCASDY. Documents available from CASDDS.
**Ind/Abst** Chem. Abstr.

NE
**PROCEEDINGS OF THE INTERNATIONAL CONGRESS ON ANIMAL REPRODUCTION & ARTIFICIAL INSEMINATION.** (19??)-. Proceedings. English. ir. FI295.00. International Congress on Animal Reproduction & Artificial Insemination, Schoonoord PO Box 501, 3700 Am Zeist Netherlands. **Tel** 011 31 30531243.

NE/0510-8004
**PROCEEDINGS--SYMPOSIUM OF THE WORLD ASSOCIATION OF VETERINARY HYGIENISTS.** **Main/Corp** World Association of Veterinary Food Hygienists. 3rd (1962)-. English (French and German). ir. Price varies per volume. World Association of Veterinary Food Hygienists, Postfach 330013, D 1000 Berlin 33 Germany. ***Continues*** *Proceedings - Symposium of the International Association of Veterinary Food Hygienists.*

US
**PROCEEDINGS / WESTERN SECTION, AMERICAN SOCIETY OF ANIMAL SCIENCE AND WESTERN BRANCH, CANADIAN SOCIETY OF ANIMAL SCIENCE.** Proceedings. English. an.
**Ind/Abst** Grasslands For. Abstr.; Nutr. Abstr. Rev., Ser. B, Live Feeds and Feed.; Wheat Barley Trit. Abstr.

LU
**PRODUCCION ANIMAL. GLOSSARIUM.** **VFOAT** Glossarium, Animal Production; Glossariu, Produccion Animal; Animal Production. Glossarium. Multiple languages (Danish, Dutch, English, French, German, Greek, Modern, Italian and Portuguese, Spanish).

FR/0990-0632
**PRODUCTIONS ANIMALES (PARIS, 1988).** (PRODUCTIONS ANIMALES / INSTITUT NATIONAL DE LA RECHERCHE AGRONOMIQUE.). [Prod. anim.]. **Added/Corp** Institut National de la Recherche Agronomique (France). Vol. 1, No. 1 (Feb. 1988)-. Periodical. French (summaries and/or abstracts in English). ir (5 issues). 375.00F France; 390.00F other. Institut National de la Recherche Agronomique, Route de Staint Cyr, 78026 Versailles Cedex France. **Tel** 011 33 1 30833406, FAX 011 33 1 30833449, telex INRAPUB 699 368 F. **ED** C. Demarquilly, D. Micol & B. Sauveur. **CODEN** PROAEK. **Circ:** 1,300 (ctrl). ***Continues*** *Centre de Recherches Zootechniques et Veterinaires de Theix. Bulletin Technique, 0395-7519.*
**Desc:** Deals with all species of zootechnical interest covering feed and nutrition, physiology, pathology, genetics, production techniques, product quality and production economics.
**Ind/Abst** AgBiotech News Inf.; Anim. Breed. Abstr.; Dairy Sci. Abstr.; Grasslands For. Abstr.; Index Vet.; Maize Abstr.; Nutr. Abstr. Rev., Ser. B, Live Feeds and Feed.; Pig News Inf.; Poult. Abstr.; Soc. Sci. Cit. Index [Select. Cov.]; Soyabean Abstr.; Sug. Indus. Abstr.; Wheat Barley Trit. Abstr.; World Agric. Econ.

IT/0033-0000
**PRODUZIONE ANIMALE.** Vol. 1 (1962)-. Periodical. Italian (summaries and/or abstracts in English). qt. Istituto di Produzione Animale, Facolta di Agraria, Naples Italy.
**Ind/Abst** Anim. Breed. Abstr.; Index Vet.; Poult. Abstr.; Vet. Bull.

US/1061-5768
**PROGRESS IN VETERINARY & COMPARATIVE OPHTHALMOLOGY.** ***Title Change.*** [Prog. vet. comp. ophthalmol.]. **Added/Corp** Fidia Research Foundation. **VFOAT** Progress in Veterinary and Comparative Ophthalmology; Veterinary & Comparative Ophthalmology; PVCO. Vol. 1, No. 1 (Spring 1991)-(199?). Periodical. English. qt. Fidia Research Foundation, 1640 Wisconsin Ave. NW, Suite 3, Washington DC 20007. **LC** SF891; .P76. **DD** 636. **NLM** W1; PR685V. ***Continued by*** *Veterinary & Comparative Ophtalmology, 1076-4607.*

US/1061-575X
**PROGRESS IN VETERINARY NEUROLOGY.** [Prog. vet. neurol.]. **Added/Corp** Fidia Information Network for Veterinary Science and Medicine. Fidia Research Foundation. **VFOAT** PVN. Vol. 1, No. 1 (Spring 1990)-. Periodical. English. qt. $50.00 US; $60.00 Canada & Mexico; $75.00 other. Veterinary Practice Publishing Company, PO Box 4457, Santa Barbara CA 93140-4457. **Tel** (805)965-1028, FAX (805)965-0722. **DD** 636. **CODEN** PVNEEL. Documents available from The Genuine Article.
**Desc:** International journal of veterinary neurology and neurosurgery.
**Ind/Abst** Index Vet.; Res. Alert [Full Cov.]; Small Anim. Abstr. Bibliogr.; Vet. Bull.

●IT
**PROGRESSO VETERINARIO : ORGANO UFFICIALE DELLA FEDERAZIONE NAZIONALE ORDINI VETERINARI ITALIANI.** **Added/Corp** Federazione Nazionale Ordini Veterinari Italiani. Anno 48, 1 (1993)-. Periodical. Italian (French). sm. L50000. Il Progresso Veterinario, Corso Vittorio Emanuele N 73, 10128 Turin Italy. **Tel** 011 39 11 5628352. ***Continues*** *Nuovo Progresso Veterinario.*

US/1045-2044
**PROJECT BREED DIRECTORY.** **See** Ethics.

NZ/0112-9643
**PUBLICATION - VETERINARY CONTINUING EDUCATION, MASSEY UNIVERSITY.** (PUBLICATION.). [Publ. - Vet. Contin. Educ. Massey Univ.]. **Added/Corp** Massey University. Veterinary Continuing Education. New Zealand Veterinary Association. Foundation for Continuing Education. (1983)-. Monographic series. English.
**Ind/Abst** Index Vet.; Small Anim. Abstr. Bibliogr.

US/0555-6953
**PULSE (PICO RIVERA).** (PULSE.). **Added/Corp** Southern California Veterinary Medical Association. (1959)-. Periodical. English. mo. $30.00. Southern California Veterinary Medical Association, 8338 Rosemead Boulevard, Pico Rivera CA 90660-5197. **Tel** (310)948-4979. **ED** Don Mahan. **Ad Acc. Circ:** 1,054 (ctrl).

IT/0394-5898
**QUATTRO ZAMPE.** [Quattro zampe]. **VFOAT** Quattrozampe. (1987)-. Periodical. Italian. Twelve times a year. L48000.00 Italy. RCS Rizzoli Periodici, Via A Rizzoli 2, 20132 Milan Italy. **Tel** 011 39 2 27200720. **UDC** 636.08.

FR/0483-786X
**R.T.V.A.** (REVUE TECHNIQUE VETERINAIRE DE L'ALIMENTATION : RTVA.). [R.T.V.A.]. **Added/Corp** Association Veterinaire d'Hygiene Alimentaire (France). **VFOAT** RTVA. (19??)-. Academic Scholarly Publication. French. mo. Editions Meteore, 42 rue de Louvre, 75001 Paris France. **CODEN** RRTADW. Documents available from CASDDS.
**Ind/Abst** Chem. Abstr.

NO/0333-256X
**RANGIFER.** **See** Zoology.

SW/0347-9838
**RAPPORT - SVERIGES LANTBRUKSUNIVERSITET, INSTITUTIONEN FOR HUSDJURS UTFODRING OCH VARD.** (RAPPORT / INSTITUTIONEN FOR HUSDJURENS UTFODRING OCH VARD.). [Rapp. - Sver. lantbruksuniv. Inst. husdjurens utfodr. vard.]. (1978)-. Monographic series. Swedish (English). Price varies per volume. Swedish University of Agricultural Sciences / Animal Husbandry, Department of Animal Husbandry, Uppsala Sweden. ***Continues*** *Rapport (Lantbrukshogskolan. Institutionen for Husdjurens Utfodring Och Vard), 0346-766X.*
**Ind/Abst** Dairy Sci. Abstr.; Nutr. Abstr. Rev., Ser. B, Live Feeds and Feed.; Poult. Abstr.; Rice Abstr.

SW/0283-0698
**RAPPORT (SVERIGES LANTBRUKSUNIVERSITET. INSTITUTIONEN FOR HUSDJURSHYGIEN).** (RAPPORT / SVERIGES LANTBRUKSUNIVERSITET, VETERINARMEDICINSKA FAKULTETEN, INSTITUTIONEN FOR HUSDJURSHYGIEN.). [Rapp. - Sver. lantbr. univ., Vet. med. fak., Inst. husdjurshyg.]. **Added/Corp** Sveriges Lantbruksuniversitet. Institutionen for Husdjurshygien. **VFOAT** Report. (1985)-. Monographic series. Swedish (English). ir. Price varies per volume. Sveriges Lantbruksuniversitet, Veterinarmedicinska Fakulteten, Institutionen for Husdjurshygien, Box 345, S-532 00 Skara Sweden. ***Continues*** *Rapport (Sveriges Lantbruksuniversitet. Institutionen for Husdjurshygien Med Hovslagarskolan), 0348-7016.*
**Ind/Abst** Agric. Eng. Abstr.; Index Vet.

IT/0300-3485
**RASSEGNA DI DIRITTO LEGISLAZIONE E MEDICINA LEGALE VETERINARIA.** **Added/Corp** Universita Degli Studi di Milano. Istituto di Medicina Legale Veterinaria. (1967)-. Periodical. Italian. Four times a year. L50000 Italy; L70000 other. Cittastudi Scrl, Piazza L da Vinci 7, 20133 Milan Italy. **Tel** 011 39 2 70634844.

US/0309-1848
**RAT NEWS LETTER.** [Rat news letter]. No.1 (Apr. 1977)-. Periodical. English. sa. $24.00 (institutions), $16.00 (individuals). Rat News Letter University of Pittsburgh, 2542 Harlo Drive, Allison Park PA 15101. **Tel** (412)647-6190. **ED** Dr Viktor STOLC. **DD** 619. **NLM** W1 RA9475. **CODEN** RNLEDA. Index available. **Bk Rev. Ad Acc.** Documents available from BIOSIS Document

Express.
**Ind/Abst** AgBiotech News Inf.; Anim. Breed. Abstr.; Biol. Abstr.

UK/0269-5642
**RECENT ADVANCES IN ANIMAL NUTRITION.** [Recent adv. anim. nutr.]. (1977)-. Academic Scholarly Publication. English. an. Price varies per volume. University of New England / Department of Biochemical and Nutrition, c/o D. J. Farrell, Armidale NSW 2351 Australia. **Tel** 011 61 67 732510, FAX 011 61 67 728235. **NLM** W1; RE105RN. **CODEN** RAANES. Documents available from CASDDS.
**Ind/Abst** AGRICOLA [Full Cov.]; Chem. Abstr.

FR/0034-1843
**RECUEIL DE MEDECINE VETERINAIRE.** [Recl. med. vet.]. (19??)-. Academic Scholarly Publication. French (summaries and/or abstracts in Spanish and English). Ten times a year (4 serial issues and 3 special double issues). 950.00F France. Ecole Nationale Veterinaire, 7 Avenue du General de Gaulle, 94704 Maisons-Alfort France. **Tel** 011 33 16 43967176, FAX 011 33 16 43751210. **NLM** W1 RE114. **CODEN** RMVEAG. Index available (bound in last issue). **Bk Rev. Ad Acc. Pr Rev. Circ:** 3,500 (ctrl). Documents available from The Genuine Article, BIOSIS Document Express, CASDDS.
**Desc:** Dealing with veterinary medicine, each issue is concerned with research, post-graduate education and reviews.
**Ind/Abst** AgBiotech News Inf.; AGRICOLA; Agric. Eng. Abstr. (1991-); Anim. Breed. Abstr.; Biodeter. Abstr.; Biol. Abstr.; Chem. Abstr.; Curr. Contents, Agric. Biol. Environ. Sci.; Dairy Sci. Abstr.; EMBASE; Fish Rev. (Jan. 1989-July 1992); Food Sci. Technol. Abstr.; Grasslands For. Abstr.; Helminthol. Abstr. (19??-19??); Index Vet.; Key Word Index Wildl. Res.; Microbiol. Abstr. Sect. B; Nutr. Abstr. Rev., Ser. B, Live Feeds and Feed.; Nutr. Abstr. Rev., Ser. A, Hum. Exp.; Life Sci. Collect.; PESTDOC; Pig News Inf.; Poult. Abstr.; Protozoolog. Abstr.; Res. Alert [Select. Cov.]; Rev. Agric. Entomol.; Rev. Med. Vet. Entomol.; Small Anim. Abstr. Bibliogr.; Soc. Sci. Cit. Index [Select. Cov.]; Vet. Bull.; Virol. AIDS Abstr.; Wildl. Rev. (Jan. 1989-July 1992).

UK/0305-6643
**REGISTERS AND DIRECTORY - ROYAL COLLEGE OF VETERINARY SURGEONS.** [Regist. dir. - R. Coll. Vet. Surg.]. **Main/Corp** Royal College of Veterinary Surgeons. Directory. English. an. Royal College of Veterinary Surgeons, 32 Belgrave Square, London SW1 England. **Tel** 011 44 71 2354971. **NLM** SF 611 R888R. ***Continues*** *Register of Veterinary Surgeons.*

UK
**REPORT / AGRICULTURAL RESEARCH COUNCIL, INSTITUTE OF ANIMAL PHYSIOLOGY.** ***Title Change.*** **Main/Corp** Institute of Animal Physiology (Great Britain). **VFOAT** Report for ... . (1960/61)-(1994). English. be. Babraham Institute, Babraham Hall, Babraham, Cambridge CB2 4AT, United Kingdom. **Tel** 0223 832312, FAX 0223 836122. **LC** SF768; .A33a. **DD** 636.089/2/005. ***Continued by*** *Babraham.*

AT/1031-1580
**REPORT / CSIRO, DIVISION OF ANIMAL HEALTH.** [Rep. - CSIRO Div. anim. Health]. **Added/Corp** Commonwealth Scientific and Industrial Research Organization (Australia). Division of Animal Health. 1987-. English. ***Continues*** *Research Report (Commonwealth Scientific and Industrial Research Organization (Australia). Division of Animal Health), 0812-7336.*

FR
**REPORT ON THE DISEASE STATUS WORLDWIDE IN ... / OFFICE INTERNATIONAL DES EPIZOOTIES.** (1986)-. French (English). an. OIE - Office International des Epizooties, 12 rue de Prony, 75017 Paris France. **Tel** 011 33 1 4415 1888, FAX 011 33 1 42 67 09 87, telex EPIZOTI 642 285F. **NLM** W1; RE212HK.

US
**REPORTED ARTHROPOD-BORNE ENCEPHALITIDES IN HORSES AND OTHER EQUIDAE.** **Main/Corp** United States. Animal and Plant Health Inspection Service. English. an. $3.00. US Department of Agriculture / Animal & Plant Health Inspection Service, 741 Federal Building 1, 6505 Belcres Road, Hyattsville MD 20782. **Tel** (301)436-7817. **LC** SF959.E5; U54A. **DD** 636.1/08/945983200973. ***Continues*** *Reported Arthropod-Borne Encephalitides in Horses and Other Equidae.*

PO/0870-1067
**REPOSITORIO DE TRABALHOS DO L.N.I.V.** [Repos. trab. L.N.I.V.]. **Main/Corp** Laboratorio Nacional de Investigacao Veterinaria. **VAT** Repositorio de Trabalhos do Laboratorio Nacional de Investigacao Veterinaria. Portuguese (summaries and/or abstracts in English and French). an. Free. Laboratorio Nacional de Investigacao Veterinaria, Estrada de Benfica 701, Lisbon Portugal. **Tel** 70 20 75/6/7, telex 18248 VETERI P. **ED** J L Nunes Petisca. **LC** SF604; .L23A. **Circ:** 1,000.
**Desc:** Selection of research works effectuated in this laboratory by several departments.
**Ind/Abst** AGRICOLA; Biodeter. Abstr.; Helminthol. Abstr. (19??-19??); Index Vet.; Maize Abstr.; Nutr. Abstr. Rev., Ser. B, Live Feeds and Feed.; Pig News Inf.; Poult. Abstr.; Protozoolog. Abstr.; Rev. Med. Vet. Entomol.; Rev. Med. Vet. Mycology; Rice Abstr.; Small Anim. Abstr. Bibliogr.; Soyabean Abstr.; Vet. Bull.

GW/0936-6768
**REPRODUCTION IN DOMESTIC ANIMALS 1990.** (REPRODUCTION IN DOMESTIC ANIMALS.). [Reprod. domest. anim.]. **VFOAT** Zuchthygiene. Vol. 25 (Jan. 1990)-. Periodical. English (German; summaries and/or abstracts in English and German). Eight times a year. DM598.00. Blackwell Wissenschafts-Verlag, Kurfuerstendamm 57, D 10707 Berlin Germany. **Tel** 011 49 30 32790623, 011 49 30 32790624, FAX 011 49 30 327 90610. **ED** D. Rath. **LC** S494; .Z8; SF871; .Z8. **DD** 631/.53/05. **NLM** W1; RE213KL. **CODEN** RDANEF. Documents available from The Genuine Article, BIOSIS Document Express, CASDDS. ***Continues*** *Zuchthygiene, 0044-5371.*
**Desc:** Offers comprehensive information concerning physiology, pathology, and biotechnology of reproduction.
**Ind/Abst** Anim. Breed. Abstr.; Biol. Abstr. (1990-); Chem. Abstr.; Curr. Contents, Agric. Biol. Environ. Sci.; Dairy Sci. Abstr.; Index Vet.; PESTDOC; Pig News Inf.; Res. Alert [Full Cov.]; Sci. Cit. Index; SCISEARCH; Vet. Bull.

UK/0034-5288
**RESEARCH IN VETERINARY SCIENCE.** [Res. vet. sci.]. **Added/Corp** British Veterinary Association. Vol. 1 (Jan. 1960)-. Academic Scholarly Publication. English. Six times a year. £114.00 UK; £119.00 Africa; £160.00 other. TG Scott Subscriber Services, 6 Bourne Enterprise Center, Wrotham Road, Borough Green, Kent TN15 8DG England. **Tel** 011 44 01 732 884023, FAX 011 44 01 732 884034. **ED** Dr. Alex Livingstone. **LC** SF601; .R38. **DD** 636.089/05. **NLM** W1 RE231. **CODEN** RVTSA9. **[CCC]. Ad Acc. Pr Rev.** available on microfilm and microfiche from University Microfilms International (UMI). Documents available from The Genuine Article, BIOSIS Document Express, CASDDS.
**Desc:** Its international cadre of contributors covers the whole spectrum of veterinary research and comparative medicine.
**Ind/Abst** AgBiotech News Inf.; AGRICOLA [Full Cov.]; Anim. Breed. Abstr.; Biol. Abstr.; Chem. Abstr.; CSA Neuro. Abstr. (?-?); Curr. Contents, Agric. Biol. Environ. Sci.; Dairy Sci. Abstr.; EMBASE [Select. Cov.]; Fish Rev.; Food Sci. Technol. Abstr.; Helminthol. Abstr. (19??-19??); Immunol. Abstr.; Index Med.; Index Vet.; Microbiol. Abstr. Sect. B; Microbiol. Abstr. Sect. A; Microbiol. Abstr. Sect. C; Nutr. Abstr. Rev., Ser. B, Live Feeds and Feed.; Life Sci. Collect.; PESTDOC; Pig News Inf.; Poult. Abstr.; Protozoolog. Abstr.; Ref. Upd. Deluxe Ed.; Res. Alert [Full Cov.]; Rev. Agric. Entomol.; Rev. Med. Vet. Entomol.; Rev. Med. Vet. Mycology; Sci. Cit. Index; SCISEARCH; Small Anim. Abstr. Bibliogr.; Soc. Sci. Cit. Index [Select. Cov.]; Soyabean Abstr.; Vet. Bull.; Virol. AIDS Abstr.; Wheat Barley Trit. Abstr.; Wildl. Rev.

UK/0034-6624
**REVIEW OF MEDICAL AND VETERINARY MYCOLOGY.** **See** Veterinary Sciences-Abstracting, Bibliographies and Statistics.

PE
**REVIEW - VETERINARY INSTITUTE FOR TROPICAL AND HIGH ALTITUDE RESEARCH, SAN MARCOS UNIVERSITY INVESTIGATION CENTRE.** **Main/Corp** Universidad Nacional Mayor de San Marcos. Instituto Veterinario de Investigaciones Tropicales y de Altura. Centro de Investigacion. **Added/Corp** Food and Agriculture Organization of the United Nations. **VFOAT** Informe - Instituto Veterinario de Investigaciones Tropicales y de Altura. U.N.M.S.M. Centro de Investigacion. No. 21 (July/Dec. 1971)-. Periodical. Spanish.

AG/0326-0550
**REVISTA ARGENTINA DE PRODUCCION ANIMAL.** [Rev. argent. prod. anim.]. (1980)-. Periodical. Spanish. bm. Asociacion Argentina de Produccion Animal, Casilla de Correo 276 Balcarie, Buenos Aires Argentina. **UDC** 636.082.4.001.5.
**Ind/Abst** Field Crop Abstr.; Index Vet.; Nutr. Abstr. Rev., Ser. B, Live Feeds and Feed.; Pig News Inf.; Plant Breed. Abstr.; Poult. Abstr.; Seed Abstr.; Soils Fert.; Sorghum Mill. Abstr.; Soyabean Abstr.; Vet. Bull.; World Agric. Econ.

BL/0102-0803
**REVISTA BRASILEIRA DE REPRODUCAO ANIMAL.** [Rev. bras. reprod. anim.]. **Added/Corp** Colegio Brasileiro de Reproducao Animal. (1977)-. Periodical. Portuguese (summaries and/or abstracts in English). qt. **CODEN** RBRAED. Documents available from BIOSIS Document Express.
**Ind/Abst** Biol. Abstr.; Index Vet.; Pig News Inf.; Vet. Bull.

CU/0048-7678
**REVISTA CUBANA DE CIENCIAS VETERINARIAS.** ***Suspended.*** [Rev. cub. cienc. vet.]. Vol. 1 (1970)-Suspended as of 12/93. Periodical. Spanish (summaries and/or abstracts in English; table of contents in English). tq. Ediciones Cubanas, Obispo 527, Altos ESQ Bernaza, CP 10100 Havana Cuba. **Tel** 011 632980, 631942, FAX 011 631011, telex 512337, 6540. **NLM** W1 RE359E.
**Ind/Abst** AGRICOLA; Anim. Breed. Abstr.; Biocont. News Inf. (1991-); Helminthol. Abstr. (1991-); Index Vet.; Nutr. Abstr. Rev., Ser. B, Live Feeds and Feed.; Nutr. Abstr. Rev., Ser. A, Hum. Exp.; Pig News Inf.; Poult. Abstr.; Protozoolog. Abstr.; Rev. Med. Vet. Entomol.; Vet. Bull.

VE
**REVISTA DE LA FACULTAD DE CIENCIAS VETERINARIAS : ORGANO DE LA FACULTAD DE CIENCIAS VETERINARIAS.** Vol. 27, No. 1/8 (1978)-. Periodical. Spanish (summaries and/or abstracts in English). ir. **NLM** W1; RE408RF. ***Continues*** *Revista de Medicina Veterinaria y Parasitologia.*
**Ind/Abst** Biodeter. Abstr.; Helminthol. Abstr. (1991-); Protozoolog. Abstr.; Rev. Med. Vet. Mycology.

AG/0325-6391
**REVISTA DE MEDICINA VETERINARIA.** [Rev. med. vet.]. **Added/Corp** Sociedad de Medicina Veterinaria. Vol. 1 (Aug. 1915)-. Periodical. Spanish (English; summaries and/or abstracts in English). bm. $100.00. Sociedad de Medicina Veterinar, Chile 1856, Buenos Aires Argentina. **Tel** 011 54 1 3838786, or 3817415, FAX 011 54 1 3838760. **NLM** W1 RE436V. **CODEN** RMEVAG. Index available. cum. index. **Ad Acc. Circ:** 10,500 (ctrl). Documents available from CASDDS. ***Supersedes*** *Revista - Sociedad de Medicina Veterinaria.*
**Desc:** Original scientific articles and summaries of other publications of veterinary science.
**Ind/Abst** AGRICOLA; Chem. Abstr.; Food Sci. Technol. Abstr.; Helminthol. Abstr. (19??-19??); Index Vet.; Nutr. Abstr. Rev., Ser. B, Live Feeds and Feed.; Pig News Inf.; Poult. Abstr.; Protozoolog. Abstr.; Rev. Med. Vet. Entomol.; Small Anim. Abstr. Bibliogr.; Vet. Bull.

PO/0035-0389
**REVISTA PORTUGUESA DE CIENCIAS VETERINARIAS.** [Rev. Port. cienc. vet.]. **Added/Corp** Sociedade Portuguesa de Ciencias Veterinarias. Vol. 60 (1966)-. Periodical. Portuguese (summaries and/or abstracts in English, French and Spanish). qt. Sociedade Portuguesa de Ciencias Veterinarias, Rua D Dinis 2 A RC, 1200 Lisbon Portugal. **Tel** 011 351 1 2880188. **ED** Prof. Dr. Luis Manuel Morgado Tavares. **NLM** W1 RE716QM. Index available (bound in 4th issue). **Bk Rev. Ad Acc. Circ:** 1200 (ctrl). ***Continues*** *Revista de Ciencias Veterinarias.*
**Desc:** Scientific papers on veterinary medicine and animal production; bibliographic indexes and abstracts; technical books reviews, and short news about veterinary life in Portugal and the world.
**Ind/Abst** AGRICOLA; Anim. Breed. Abstr.; Food Sci. Technol. Abstr.; Grasslands For. Abstr.; Helminthol. Abstr. (19??-19??); Index Vet.; Maize Abstr.; Nutr. Abstr. Rev., Ser. B, Live Feeds and Feed.; Pig News Inf.; Poult. Abstr.; Rev. Med. Vet. Mycology; Small Anim. Abstr. Bibliogr.; Vet. Bull.; Wheat Barley Trit. Abstr.

FR/1151-3551
**REVUE DE BIOTHERAPIE VETERINAIRE.** (1990)-. Periodical. French. **UDC** 619(44).
**Ind/Abst** Index Vet.

FR/0035-1555
**REVUE DE MEDECINE VETERINAIRE.** [Rev. med. vet.]. (1937)-. Academic Scholarly Publication. French. mo (11 issues). 714.99F France; 850.00F other. Ecole Nationale Veterinaire, Administration & Redaction, 31076 Toulouse Cedex France. **Tel** 011 33 61 193835. **ED** Alain Milon. **NLM** W1 RE796P. **CODEN** RVMVAH. Index available. cum. index. **Bk Rev. Ad Acc. Pr Rev. Circ:** 3,000. Documents available from The Genuine Article, BIOSIS Document Express, CASDDS. ***Continues*** *Revue Veterinaire et Journal de Medecine Veterinaire et de Zootechnie Reunis.*
**Desc:** Covers all subjects related to veterinary science above farm animals or pets. Each issue contains a book review, review papers and original papers.
**Ind/Abst** AgBiotech News Inf.; AGRICOLA; Anim. Breed. Abstr.; Biol. Abstr.; Chem. Abstr.; Curr. Contents, Agric. Biol. Environ. Sci.; Dairy Sci. Abstr.; EMBASE; Fish Rev.; Helminthol. Abstr. (1991-); Index Vet.; Microbiol. Abstr. Sect. B (19??-19??); Nutr. Abstr. Rev., Ser. B, Live Feeds and Feed.; Life Sci. Collect.; PESTDOC; Pig News Inf.; Poult. Abstr.; Protozoolog. Abstr.; Res. Alert [Full Cov.]; Rev. Med. Vet. Entomol.; Sci. Cit. Index; SCISEARCH; Small Anim. Abstr. Bibliogr.; Vet. Bull.; Wildl. Rev.; World Agric. Econ.

NL/0767-7189
**REVUE D'ELEVAGE ET DE MEDECINE VETERINAIRE DE NOUVELLE CALEDONIE.** (1982)-. Periodical. Multiple languages. sa. Institut d'Elevage et de Medecine Veterinaire des Pays Tropicaux, 10 rue Pierre Curie,

94704 Maisons-Alfort, Cedex, France. **UDC** 636(213).
**Ind/Abst** Agrofor. Abstr. (1991-); For. Abstr.; Helminthol. Abstr. (1991-); Index Vet.; Protozoolog. Abstr.

FR/0035-1865
**REVUE D'ELEVAGE ET DE MEDECINE VETERINAIRE DES PAYS TROPICAUX.** [Rev. elev. med. vet. pays trop.]. (Jan./ March 1947)-. Periodical. French (summaries and/or abstracts in English and Spanish). qt. 310.00F France; 510.00F other. Cirad Emvt, 10 rue Pierre Curie, 94704 Maisons Alfort France. **Tel** 011 33 1 43688873. **(Subscription address:** Expansion Scientifique Francaise, 31 Blvd. de la Tour Maubourg, 75007 Paris France.**)** **NLM** W1 RE8088. ***Supersedes*** *Recueil de Medecine Veterinaire Exotique.*
**Ind/Abst** AGRICOLA; Anim. Breed. Abstr.; Curr. Contents, Agric. Biol. Environ. Sci.; Dairy Sci. Abstr.; EMBASE; Food Sci. Technol. Abstr.; Grasslands For. Abstr.; Helminthol. Abstr. (19??-19??); Index Med.; Index Vet.; Nutr. Abstr. Rev., Ser. B, Live Feeds and Feed.; Life Sci. Collect.; PESTDOC; Pig News Inf.; Poult. Abstr.; Protozoolog. Abstr.; Rev. Med. Vet. Entomol.; Rev. Med. Vet. Mycology; Vet. Bull.; World Agric. Econ.

FR/0253-1933
**REVUE - OFFICE INTERNATIONAL DES EPIZOOTIES.** (REVUE SCIENTIFIQUE ET TECHNIQUE / OFFICE INTERNATIONAL DES EPIZOOTIES, INTERNATIONAL OFFICE OF EPIZOOTICS, OFICINA INTERNACIONAL DE EPIZOOTIAS.). [Rev. - Off. Int. epizoot.]. **Added/Corp** International Office of Epizootics. **VFOAT** Revue Scientifique et Technique de l'OIE; Revue Scientifique et Technique de l'O.I.E. Vol. 1, No. 1 (March 1982)-. Periodical. English (French and Spanish). qt (4 issues). 700.00F. OIE - Office International des Epizooties, 12 rue de Prony, 75017 Paris France. **Tel** 011 33 1 4415 1888, FAX 011 33 1 42 67 09 87, telex EPIZOTI 642 285F. **(Subscription address:** Sci. Med. Publishers of France, 100 East 42nd Street, Suite 1002, New York, NY 10017**)** **ED** L. Blajan. **LC** SF781; .R48. **DD** 636.089/69/05. **NLM** W1; RE967Q. **CODEN** RTOEDX. Index available. **Circ:** 800 (ctrl). Documents available from BIOSIS Document Express.
**Desc:** The scientific and technical review of this international animal health organization presents the latest findings in a variety of fields such as the epidemiology of the most serious diseases in many animal species, control methods, laboratory research, technical advances and information systems.
**Ind/Abst** AgBiotech News Inf.; Agrindex; Anim. Breed. Abstr.; Biol. Abstr. (?-1985, 199?-); Dairy Sci. Abstr.; Helminthol. Abstr. (19??-); Index Med.; Index Vet.; PESTDOC; Pig News Inf.; Poult. Abstr.; Protozoolog. Abstr.; Rev. Agric. Entomol.; Rev. Med. Vet. Entomol.; Vet. Bull.; Zool. Rec.

GW/0178-2010
**RFL. RUNDSCHAU FUER FLEISCHUNTERSUCHUNG UND LEBENSMITTELUBERWACHUNG.** [RFL, Rundsch. Fleischunters. Lebensm.uberwach.]. **VFOAT** Rundschau fur Fleischuntersuchung und Lebensmitteluberwachung (1985). (1985)-. Periodical. German. Eleven times a year. DM105.40 (Germany); DM128.40 (other). Verlag M & H Schaper GmbH & Co, Postfach 16 42, D 31046 Alfeld Leine Germany. **Tel** 011 49 5181 80090. **UDC** 351.773. ***Continues*** *Rundschau fur Fleischuntersuchung und Lebensmitteluberwachung, 0341-0668.*
**Ind/Abst** AgBiotech News Inf.; Agric. Eng. Abstr.; Dairy Sci. Abstr.; Helminthol. Abstr. (1991-); Index Vet.; Poult. Abstr.; Small Anim. Abstr. Bibliogr.; Vet. Bull.

IT/0304-0607
**RIVISTA DI ZOOTECNIA E VETERINARIA.** [Riv. zootec. vet.]. (1973)-. Periodical. Italian. bm. Centraluet, Via Colleoni 15, 20041 Agrate BR MI Italy. **CODEN** RZOVBM. Documents available from BIOSIS Document Express, CASDDS. ***Formed by the union of*** *Rivista de Zootecnia; Rassegna Mensile di Scienza e Practice Zootechnia* ***and*** *Veterinaria.*
**Ind/Abst** AGRICOLA; Biol. Abstr. (-1982); Chem. Abstr. (-1988); Fish Rev. (Jan. 1989-July 1992); Food Sci. Technol. Abstr.; Life Sci. Collect.; PESTDOC; Wildl. Rev. (Jan. 1989-July 1992).

PL/0137-1657
**ROCZNIKI NAUKOWE ZOOTECHNIKI.** [Rocz. nauk. zootech.]. **VFOAT** Polish Journal of Animal Science and Technology; Pol'Skii Zhurnal Zootekhniki i Tekhnologii. Vol. 1 (1974)-. Academic Scholarly Publication. Polish (summaries and/or abstracts in English, Russian and Russian; table of contents in English and Russian). Panstwowe Wydawn Naukowe, Miodowa 10, PO Box 391, 00251 Warsaw Poland. **CODEN** RNZOD8. Documents available from CASDDS.
**Ind/Abst** AGRICOLA; Chem. Abstr.; Fish Rev. (Jan. 1989-July 1992); Food Sci. Technol. Abstr.; Wildl. Rev. (Jan. 1989-July 1992).

PL/0137-1665
**ROCZNIKI NAUKOWE ZOOTECHNIKI. MONOGRAFIE I ROZPRAWY.** [Rocz. naukowe zootech., monogr. rozpr.]. **VFOAT** Roczniki Naukowe Zootechniki. (1975)-. Periodical. Polish (summaries and/or abstracts in English and Russian). Panstwowe Wydawn Naukowe, Miodowa 10, PO Box 391, 00251 Warsaw Poland. ***Supersedes*** *Zeszyty Naukowe. Seria A.*
**Ind/Abst** AGRICOLA; Food Sci. Technol. Abstr.; Grasslands For. Abstr.; Nutr. Abstr. Rev., Ser. B, Live Feeds and Feed.; Pig News Inf.; Postharvest News Inf.; Potato Abstr.; Poult. Abstr.

FR/0339-722X
**S.T.A.L.** (SCIENCES ET TECHNIQUES DE L'ANIMAL DE LABORATOIRE. STAL.). [S.T.A.L.]. **VFOAT** STAL. Vol. 1 (1976)-. Periodical. French (summaries and/or abstracts in English). qt. $25.28. Mons J Maillard, Inra-Centre de Tours B P 1, 37380 Monnaie La France. **NLM** W1 S645. **CODEN** STALDT. **Pr Rev.** Documents available from The Genuine Article, BIOSIS Document Express.
**Ind/Abst** Anim. Breed. Abstr.; Biol. Abstr.; Curr. Aware. Biol. Sci., CABS; Curr. Contents, Agric. Biol. Environ. Sci.; Index Vet.; Nutr. Abstr. Rev., Ser. A, Hum. Exp.; Life Sci. Collect.; Res. Alert [Select. Cov.]; Small Anim. Abstr. Bibliogr.; Soc. Sci. Cit. Index [Select. Cov.]; Vet. Bull.

CN/0711-2467
**SASKATCHEWAN VETERINARY MEDICAL ASSOCIATION NEWSLETTER.** (NEWSLETTER / SASKATCHEWAN VETERINARY MEDICAL ASSOCIATION.). [Sask. Vet. Med. Assoc. newsl.]. **Added/Corp** Saskatchewan Veterinary Medical Association. **VAT** Newsletter - Saskatchewan Veterinary Medical Association. Vol. 1, No. 1 (May 1968)-. Newsletter. English. bm. Free. Saskatchewan Veterinary Medical Association, 1025 Boychuk Drive/Suite 11, Saskatoon Saskatchewan S7H 5B2 Canada. **Tel** (306)955-7862. **ED** G Roy Kelly. **DD** 636.089/097124. **Circ:** 450 (ctrl).

RU
**SBORNIK NAUCHNYKH RABOT SIBNIVI.** **Main/Corp** Sibirskii Nauchno-Issledovatelskii Veterinarnyi Institut. No. 22 (1975)-. Periodical. Russian. ***Continues*** *Sibirskii Zonalnyi Nauchno-Issledovatelskii Veterinarnyi Institut, Omsk. Sbornik Nauchnykh Rabot.*

RU/0136-3751
**SBORNIK NAUCHNYKH TRUDOV (VSESOIUZNYI NAUCHNO-ISSLEDOVATELSKII INSTITUT FIZIOLOGII, BIOKHIMII I PITANIIA).** **See** Agriculture-Livestock and Poultry.

RU/0130-8734
**SBORNIK NAUCHNYKH (VETERINARNAIA AKADEMIIA).** (SBORNIK NAUCHNYKH TRUDOV / VETERINARNAIA IMENI K.I. SKRIABINA.). [Sb. nauchn. trud. - Vet. Akad. im. K.I. Skrjabina.]. **Added/Corp** Moskovskaia Veterinarnaia Akademiia. (1973)-. Academic Scholarly Publication. Russian. ir. Price varies per volume. **CODEN** SMVSD4. Documents available from CASDDS.
**Ind/Abst** Chem. Abstr.; Poult. Abstr.

RU/0371-0955
**SBORNIK RABOT / MINISTERSTVO SLSKOGO KHOZIAISTVA SSSR, LENINGRADSKII VETERINARNYI INSTITUT.** [Sb. rab. - Leningr. vet. inst.]. **Added/Corp** Leningradskii Veterinarnyi Institut. Vol. 11 (1950)-. Monographic series. Russian. Price varies per volume. **CODEN** SLVIAW. Documents available from CASDDS. ***Continues*** *Leningradskii Veterinarnyi Institut. Sbornik Nauchnykh Trudov.*
**Ind/Abst** Chem. Abstr.; Helminthol. Abstr. (1991-).

XR/0139-5297
**SBORNIK VEDECKYCH PRACI USTREDNIHO STATNIHO VETERINARNIHO USTAVU.** [Sb. ved. pr. Ustred. statniho vet. ustavu]. (1967)-. Multiple languages. tw. **UDC** 619.
**Ind/Abst** Index Vet.; Rev. Med. Vet. Mycology; Vet. Bull.

DK/0901-3393
**SCANDINAVIAN JOURNAL OF LABORATORY ANIMAL SCIENCE.** (SCANDINAVIAN JOURNAL OF LABORATORY ANIMAL SCIENCE : OFFICIAL QUARTERLY JOURNAL OF THE SCANDINAVIAN FEDERATION FOR LABORATORY ANIMAL SCIENCE.). [Scand. j. lab. anim. sci.]. **Added/Corp** Scandinavian Federation for Laboratory Animal Science. (1985)-. Periodical. English (Danish, Norwegian and Swedish; summaries and/or abstracts in Finnish). Four times a year. kr500.00. Royal Veterinary & Agricultural University, Dep Vet Pathology Bulowsvej 13, 1870 Frederiksberg C Denmark. **Tel** 011 46 45 1 351788. **NLM** W1; SC15Q. **CODEN** SJLSE2. ***Continues*** *Scand LAS Nyt.*
**Ind/Abst** Index Vet.; Pig News Inf.; Rev. Med. Vet. Entomol.; Small Anim. Abstr. Bibliogr.; Vet. Bull.

US/1052-7559
**SCAW NEWSLETTER.** **See** Animal Welfare.

SZ/0036-7281
**SCHWEIZER ARCHIV FUER TIERHEILKUNDE.** [Schweiz. arch. tierheilkd.]. **Added/Corp** Gesellschaft Schweizerischer Tierarzte. Vol. 1 (1859)-. Academic Scholarly Publication. German. mo. 199.00F. Verlag Hans Huber Ag Bern, Laenggass Strasse 76, CH 3000 Bern 9 Switzerland. **Tel** 011 41 31 3004500. **ED** M. Wanner. **NLM** W1 SC394. **CODEN** SATHAA. **[CCC].** cum. index. **Pr Rev. Circ:** 2,500. Documents available from The Genuine Article, CASDDS.
**Ind/Abst** AGRICOLA; Anim. Breed. Abstr.; Chem. Abstr.; CSA Neuro. Abstr. (?-?); Curr. Contents, Agric. Biol. Environ. Sci.; Dairy Sci. Abstr.; EMBASE; Food Sci. Technol. Abstr.; Helminthol. Abstr. (19??-19??); Index Med.; Key Word Index Wildl. Res.; Nutr. Abstr. Rev., Ser. B, Live Feeds and Feed.; Life Sci. Collect.; PESTDOC; Pig News Inf.; Poult. Abstr.; Protozoolog. Abstr.; Res. Alert [Full Cov.]; Rev. Med. Vet. Entomol.; Rev. Med. Vet. Mycology; Sci. Cit. Index; SCISEARCH; Small Anim. Abstr. Bibliogr.; Soc. Sci. Cit. Index [Select. Cov.].

FR/0750-7682
**SCIENCES VETERINAIRES, MEDECINE COMPAREE.** [Sci. vet. med. comp.]. **Added/Corp** Societe des Sciences Veterinaires et de Medecine Comparee de Lyon (France). (1982)-. Academic Scholarly Publication. French. an. 380.00F France; 475.00F other. Societe Sciences Veterinaires, BP 83, Ecole National Veterinaire, F-69280 Marcy l'Etoile France. **Tel** 011 33 78 870084. **NLM** W1; SC79T. **CODEN** SVMCD8. Documents available from CASDDS. ***Continues*** *Bulletin de la Societe des Sciences Veterinaires et de Medecine Comparee de Lyon, 0301-1194.*
**Ind/Abst** AgBiotech News Inf.; Anim. Breed. Abstr.; Chem. Abstr.; Helminthol. Abstr. (19??-19??); Index Vet.; Nutr. Abstr. Rev., Ser. B, Live Feeds and Feed.; Nutr. Abstr. Rev., Ser. A, Hum. Exp.; Protozoolog. Abstr.; Rev. Med. Vet. Entomol.; Small Anim. Abstr. Bibliogr.; Vet. Bull.

US/0164-1999
**SCIENTIFIC PRESENTATIONS OF THE ANNUAL MEETING - AMERICAN ANIMAL HOSPITAL ASSOCIATION.** (SCIENTIFIC PRESENTATIONS OF THE ... ANNUAL MEETING - AMERICAN ANIMAL HOSPITAL ASSOCIATION.). [Sci. presentations annu. meet. - Am. Anim. Hosp. Assoc.]. **Main/Corp** American Animal Hospital Association. **VFOAT** Scientific Proceedings, Annual Meeting; AAHA Proceedings. 42nd (1975)-. Academic Scholarly Publication. English. an. $42.00. American Animal Hospital Association - Colorado, PO Box 150899, Denver CO 80215. **Tel** (303)279-2500, FAX (303)279-1816. **LC** SF605; .A44a. **DD** 636.089. **NLM** W1 SC862BP. **CODEN** SPAHDN. **Ad Acc.** Documents available from CASDDS. ***Continues*** *Scientific Presentations and Seminar Synopses of the Annual Meeting, 0364-1961.*
**Desc:** Includes manuscripts representing the majority of the scientific sessions held at AAHA annual meetings.
**Ind/Abst** Chem. Abstr. (1975-1982).

CN
**SCIENTIFIC PROCEEDINGS / AMERICAN COLLEGE OF VETERINARY INTERNAL MEDICINE.** **Main/Corp** American College of Veterinary Internal Medicine. (1979)-. English. ir. University of Guelph / Virginia, c/o Dr. Pyle Secretary of Treasure, 805 Horseshoe Lane, Blacksburg VA 24060. **Tel** (800)245-9081, (703)951-8543, FAX (703)951-4268. **Circ:** 1,400. ***Continues*** *Proceedings of the Annual Scientific Meeting of the American College of Veterinary Internal Medicine.*
**Desc:** Deals with veterinary articles in internal medicine, cardiology, neurology and oncology.

US
**SEEDSTOCK EDGE.** (19??)-. English. Ten times a year. $15.00. Seedstock Edge, PO Box 2339, La Fayette IN 47906. **Tel** (317)463-3593. ***Absorbed*** *Yorkshire Journal, 0044-0612; Duroc News, 0012-7299; Hampshire Herdsman.*

IT/0037-1521
**SELEZIONE VETERINARIA.** [Sel. vet.]. **Main/Corp** Istituto Zooprofilattico Sperimentale della Lombardia e dell 'Emilia. (1960)-. Academic Scholarly Publication. Italian. Eleven times a year. L80000. Istituto Zooprofilattico Sperimentale della Lombardia e dell Emila, Selz Veterinaria / Via Bianchi 7, 25125 Brescia Italy. **Tel** 011 39 30 2290330, FAX 011 39 30 225613, telex 305381. **CODEN** SVETDJ. Index available. **Bk Rev. Ad Acc. Circ:** 2,900. Documents available from CASDDS.
**Desc:** Publications on veterinary sciences including biology, microbiology, fish culture and fisheries, sanitation, and environmental technology.
**Ind/Abst** AgBiotech News Inf.; AGRICOLA; Anim. Breed. Abstr.; Chem. Abstr. (1960-1983); Dairy Sci. Abstr.; Helminthol. Abstr.; Index Vet.; Key Word Index Wildl. Res.; Nutr. Abstr. Rev., Ser. B, Live Feeds and Feed.; Pig News Inf.; Protozoolog. Abstr.; Rev. Med. Vet. Mycology; Small Anim. Abstr. Bibliogr.; Soils Fert.; Soyabean Abstr.; Vet. Bull.

FR/0396-5015
**SEMAINE VETERINAIRE, LA.** (SEMAINE VETERINAIRE : HEBDOMADAIRE DE L'ACTUALITE VETERINAIRE.). [Sem. vet.]. (1976)-. Periodical. French. Forty times a year. 695.40F France; 905.00F other. Point Veterinaire, 9 rue Alexandre, 94702 Maisons Alfort France. **Tel** 011 33 1 45170225. **UDC** 61. **[CCC].** Index available. cum. index. **Bk Rev. Ad Acc. Circ:** 6,000 (ctrl).

●US/1055-937X
**SEMINARS IN AVIAN AND EXOTIC PET MEDICINE.** (1992)-. Periodical. English. qt. $76.00 (individual), $100.00 (institution), $46.00 (student) US; $99.00 (individual), $124.00 (institution), $63.00 (student) other. W.B. Saunders Company, A Subsidiary of Harcourt Brace Jovanovich, Inc., The Curtis Center/Suite 300, Independence Square West, Philadelphia PA 19106-3399. **Tel** (215)238-7800 or, 5587, FAX (215)238-7883, telex 173146. **(Subscription address:** W. B. Saunders Company / North America Subscriptions, c/o Periodicals, 6277 Sea Harbour Drive, 4th Floor, Orlando FL 32887.**) [CCC].**

US/0882-0511
**SEMINARS IN VETERINARY MEDICINE AND SURGERY (SMALL ANIMALS).** [Sem. vet. med. surg. (small anim.)]. Vol. 1, No. 1 (Feb. 1986)-. Periodical. English. qt. $69.00 (individual), $105.00 (institution) US; $115.00 (individual), $126.00 (institution) other. W.B. Saunders Company, A Subsidiary of Harcourt Brace Jovanovich, Inc., The Curtis Center/Suite 300, Independence Square West, Philadelphia PA 19106-3399. **Tel** (215)238-7800 or, 5587, FAX (215)238-7883, telex 173146. **(Subscription address:** W. B. Saunders Company / North America Subscriptions, c/o Periodicals, 6277 Sea Harbour Drive, 4th Floor, Orlando FL 32887.**) ED** Steven P. Arnoczky, Philip R. Fox, Mark E. Peterson, and Larry Patrick Tilley. **DD** 636. **NLM** W1; SE489RH. **CODEN** SVMSEN. **[CCC]. Pr Rev.** Documents available from The Genuine Article.
**Desc:** Dedicated to the dissemination of up-to-date information on topics of current interest to small animal veterinarians.
**Ind/Abst** AGRICOLA [Full Cov.]; Curr. Contents, Agric. Biol. Environ. Sci.; Dairy Sci. Abstr.; Helminthol. Abstr. (19??-19??); Index Med. (1986-); Index Vet.; Nutr. Abstr. Rev., Ser. B, Live Feeds and Feed.; Protozoolog. Abstr.; Res. Alert [Select. Cov.]; Small Anim. Abstr. Bibliogr.; Vet. Bull.

SI/0129-3826
**SINGAPORE VETERINARY JOURNAL.** [Singap. vet. j.]. **Added/Corp** Singapore Veterinary Association. Vol. 1 (Oct. 1977)-. English. an. Singapore Veterinary Association, City Veterinary Center, 40 Kampong, Singapore Republic of Singapore. **NLM** W1 SI527.
**Ind/Abst** Index Vet.; Nutr. Abstr. Rev., Ser. B, Live Feeds and Feed.; Pig News Inf.; Poult. Abstr.; Small Anim. Abstr. Bibliogr.

UK
**SMALL ANIMAL ABSTRACTS BIBLIOGRAPHY.** **See** Veterinary Sciences-Abstracting, Bibliographies and Statistics.

●US
**SMALL ANIMAL MEDICINE.** (Jan. 1995)-. Periodical. English. qt. $89.95 (institutions), $59.95 (individuals) US; $93.95 (institutions), $63.95 (individuals) Canada; $103.95 (institutions), $73.95 (individuals) other. Mosby Year Book Inc., 11830 Westline Industrial Drive, St Louis MO 63146. **Tel** (800)325-4177, (314)872-8370, FAX (314)432-1380, telex 44-2402.

US/0894-3710
**SMALL ANIMAL PRACTICE.** ***Ceased.*** [Small anim. pract.]. Vol. 1, No. 1 Jan.(1988)-Ceased with Vol. 2 Dec. (1989). Periodical. English. mo. Williams & Wilkins Company, 428 East Preston Street, Baltimore MD 21202-3993. **Tel** (410)528-4000, (800)638-6423, FAX (410)528-8596, telex 87669. **(Subscription address:** US/ PO Box 64380, Baltimore, MD 21264-4380; Japan/ Igaku- Shoin MYW Ltd, 1-28-36 Hongo, Bunkyo-Ku Tokyo 113 Japan; European/ The Broadway House, 2-6 Fulham Broadway, London SW6 1AA England; telephone: (800)638-6423**) DD** 636. **[CCC].** Documents available from Quick Copies.

UK/0961-3501
**SMALL ANIMALS.** **Added/Corp** C.A.B. International. Information Services. C.A.B. International. Division of Animal Health and Medical Parasitology. (1990)-. English. an. $90.00 US. CAB International Centre, Wallingford, Oxon OX10 8DE United Kingdom. **Tel** 44 491 832111, FAX 44 491 833508, telex 847964 (COMAGG G). **NLM** ZSF 615; S635. ***Continues*** *Small Animal Abstracts, 0306-7580.*

US/0739-3806
**SPECULUM (COLUMBUS, OHIO), THE.** (THE SPECULUM.). [Speculum]. **Added/Corp** Ohio State University. College of Veterinary Medicine. Vol. 1-2, (Winter 1946)-(Spring 1947); New Series., Vol. 1 (Winter 1948)-. Periodical. English. Twice a year (July & Dec.). Free. Ohio State University, College of Veterinary Medicine, 190 Coffey Road, Columbus OH 43210. **Tel** (614)292-1171. **ED** Bonnie Christopher Bates. **Ad Acc. Circ:** 6,300.

CE
**SRI LANKA VETERINARY JOURNAL : THE OFFICIAL JOURNAL OF THE SRI LANKA VETERINARY ASSOCIATION, THE.** **Added/Corp** Sri Lanka Veterinary Association. Veterinary Research Institute (Peradeniya, Sri Lanka). Vol. 30, No. 1 (Jan./June 1982)-. Periodical. English (summaries and/or abstracts in Sinhalese and Tamil). an. $20.00. Sri Lanka Veterinary Association, Veterinary Research Institute, Gannoruwa, Peradeniya, Sri Lanka. **Tel** 08 88312. **ED** Dr. R. Sivakanesa. **Bk Rev. Ad Acc. Pr Rev. Circ:** 500. ***Continues*** *Ceylon Veterinary Journal, 0009-0891.*
**Desc:** The original works and reviews of veterinary and allied sciences. Articles of clinical interest and research notes are also included.
**Ind/Abst** Dairy Sci. Abstr.; Index Vet.; Life Sci. Collect.; Pig News Inf.; Poult. Abstr.; Protozoolog. Abstr.

PL/0239-5096
**STAN HODOWLI I WYNIKI OCENY SWIN W ROKU.** **Added/Corp** Instytut Zootechniki (Poland) Centralna Stacja Hodowli Zwierzat (Poland). **VFOAT** Report on Pig Breeding in Poland in .... (1982)-. Polish (summaries and/or abstracts in English). an. ***Continues*** *Wyniki Oceny Swin na Podstawie Badan Przeprowadzonych w Stacjach Kontroli Uzytkowosci Rzeznej Trzody Chlewnej Instytutu Zootechniki za rok ....*
**Ind/Abst** Pig News Inf.

US
**STOCK-FINDER, THE.** **VFOAT** Stockfinder. Vol. 1, (1983)-. English. Veterinary Information Company Inc, 2084 W Danby Road, Newfield NY 14867. **Tel** (607)257-4303, FAX (607)257-2445, telex 4900001852V1C U1. **ED** Lawrence S. Rivkin. ctrl circ.
**Desc:** An online database of products (drugs and supplies) used in the animal health field. World-wide access by computer and electronic ordering are featured.

SJ/1016-5711
**SUDAN JOURNAL OF ANIMAL PRODUCTION, THE.** [Sudan j. anim. prod.]. (1988)-. Periodical. English. sa. Veterinary Research Administration, PO Box 8067 El Amarat, Khartoum Sudan. **UDC** 637.
**Ind/Abst** Index Vet.; Nutr. Abstr. Rev., Ser. B, Live Feeds and Feed.; Poult. Abstr.; Sorghum Mill. Abstr.; Sug. Indus. Abstr.; Wheat Barley Trit. Abstr.

SJ/0562-5084
**SUDAN JOURNAL OF VETERINARY SCIENCE AND ANIMAL HUSBANDRY, THE.** [Sudan j. vet. sci. anim. husb.]. **Added/Corp** Sudan Veterinary Association. Vol. 1 (March 1960)-. Periodical. English. ir. Sudan Veterinary Association, PO Box 2382, Khartoum Sudan. **NLM** W1 SU161. **CODEN** SJVSAE. Documents available from BIOSIS Document Express.
**Ind/Abst** Biol. Abstr. (-1980); Index Vet.

FI/0039-5501
**SUOMEN ELAINLAAKARILEHTI.** [Suom. elainlaakaril.]. **VFOAT** Finsk Veterinartidskrift. 1895-. Periodical. Finnish (Swedish and English). mo.
**Ind/Abst** AGRICOLA; Anim. Breed. Abstr.; Dairy Sci. Abstr.; Food Sci. Technol. Abstr.; Helminthol. Abstr.; Index Vet.; Nutr. Abstr. Rev., Ser. B, Live Feeds and Feed.; Nutr. Abstr. Rev., Ser. A, Hum. Exp.; Pig News Inf.; Poult. Abstr.; Protozoolog. Abstr.; Rev. Med. Vet. Entomol.; Vet. Bull.

NZ/0112-4927
**SURVEILLANCE (WELLINGTON).** (SURVEILLANCE.). [Surveillance]. **Added/Corp** New Zealand. Animal Health Division. New Zealand. MAF Quality Management. New Zealand. MAF Policy. New Zealand. MAF Regulatory Authority. (1974)-. Periodical. English. Four times a year (Apr., Aug., Oct., Dec.). New Zealand Ministry Agriculture & Fisheries, PO Box 2526, Wellington New Zealand. **Tel** 6404 720367 Ext. 8528.

SW/0346-2250
**SVENSK VETERINARTIDNING.** [Sven. veterinartidn.]. **Added/Corp** Sveriges Veterinarforbund. Sveriges Veterinarforbund. Medlemsblad Sveriges Veterinarforbund. (1958)-. Periodical. Swedish (summaries and/or abstracts in English). Sixteen times a year. Kr700.00 Sweden; Kr735.00 Scandinavian; Kr1,000.00 other. Svensk Veterinaertidning, Box 12709, S 112 94 Stockholm Sweden. **Tel** 46 08 6542480, FAX 011 46 8 6517082. **ED** Johan Beck-Friis. **NLM** W1 SV258. **Ad Acc.** ctrl circ.
**Ind/Abst** AgBiotech News Inf.; AGRICOLA; Anim. Breed. Abstr.; Dairy Sci. Abstr.; Food Sci. Technol. Abstr.; Helminthol. Abstr. (19??-19??); Index Vet.; Nutr. Abstr. Rev., Ser. B, Live Feeds and Feed.; Nutr. Abstr. Rev., Ser. A, Hum. Exp.; Pig News Inf.; Poult. Abstr.; Protozoolog. Abstr.; Rev. Med. Vet. Entomol.; Small Anim. Abstr. Bibliogr.; Vet. Bull.

SZ/0254-6337
**SWISS VET.** [Swiss vet]. (1984)-. Periodical. German. Twelve times a year. 100.00F Switzerland; 120.00F Europe; 200.00F other. Verlag Dr Felix Wuest AG, Seestrasse 5/Postfach, CH-8700 Kuesnacht Switzerland. **Tel** 011 41 1 9110055, FAX (01)9106080, telex 825705. **UDC** 619.
**Ind/Abst** Dairy Sci. Abstr.; Food Sci. Technol. Abstr.; Helminthol. Abstr. (1991-); Index Vet.; Nutr. Abstr. Rev., Ser. B, Live Feeds and Feed.; Pig News Inf.; Small Anim. Abstr. Bibliogr.; Vet. Bull.

KO
**TAEHAN SUUI HAKHOE CHI.** **Main/Corp** Taehan Suui Hakhoe. **VFOAT** Korean Journal of Veterinary Research. Periodical. English (Korean). Institute of Veterinary Research, Office of Rural Development, Anyang Korea. **LC** SF604; .T33.

CH/0258-526X
**TAIWAN HSU MU SHOU I HSUEH HUI HUI PAO.** [Taiwan xumu shouyi xuehui huibao]. **Main/Corp** T'ai-wan Hsu Mu Shou i Hsueh Hui. **VFOAT** Taiwan Journal of Veterinary Medicine and Animal Husbandry. No. 17 (Dec. 1970)-. Periodical. Chinese (table of contents in English). sa. ***Continues*** *T'ai-wan Hsu Mu Shou i Hsueh Hui. Hui Pao. Journal of the Taiwan Association of Animal Husbandry and Veterinary Medicine 0494-5603.*
**Ind/Abst** AGRICOLA; Index Vet.; Pig News Inf.; Poult. Abstr.; Protozoolog. Abstr.; Vet. Bull.

TZ
**TANZANIAN VETERINARY BULLETIN : THE TROPICAL VETERINARIAN / TANZANIA VETERINARY ASSOCIATION.** Vol. 1, No. 1 (Jan. 1979)-. Bulletin. English. Tanzanian Veterinary Bulletin, PO Box 3050, Morogoro Tanzania. **Tel** 05 3511. **ED** B M Kessy. **Ad Acc.**
**Ind/Abst** Index Vet.

US/0898-0268
**TENDER LOVING CARE PRACTICE PROMOTIONS.** **VFOAT** Practice Promotions; TLC's Practice Promotions. 1989-. Periodical. English. qt. Free to veterinary practices, $25.00 non-veterinarians. TLC Publications, 3623 Torre Drive, Amarillo TX 79109-4347.

●US/1071-0566
**TEXAS VETERINARIAN.** [Tex. vet.]. **Added/Corp** Texas Veterinary Medical Association. Vol. 53, No. 2 (Apr. 1993)-. Periodical. English. Six times a year. $50.00 (individuals), $40.00 (institutions-US), $55.00 (institutions outside US) nonmembers; $30.00 (US), $40.00 (Canada), $55.00 (other) member institutions; Free to individual members. Texas Veterinary Medical Association, 6633 Highway 290 East #201, Austin TX 78723-1134. **Tel** (512)452-4224, FAX (512)452-6633. **ED** Don Ward. **DD** 636. Index available in last issue of volume--attached. **Bk Rev. Ad Acc, Adv Mgr:** Ellen Smith. **Circ:** 3,000. ***Continues*** *Texas Veterinary Medical Journal, 0040-4756.*
**Desc:** Contains news of veterinary science, state and regional veterinary concerns, practice management, organized veterinary medicine and individual veterinarians.

US/0040-4756
**TEXAS VETERINARY MEDICAL JOURNAL.** ***Title Change.*** **Added/Corp** Texas Veterinary Medical Association. (19??)-(19??). Periodical. English. bm. Texas Veterinary Medical Association, 6633 Highway 290 East #201, Austin TX 78723-1134. **Tel** (512)452-4224, FAX (512)452-6633. **ED** David Lancaster. Index available. **Bk Rev. Ad Acc. Circ:** 3,000 (ctrl). ***Continues*** *Texas Veterinary Bulletin.* ***Continued by*** *Texas Veterinarian, 1071-0566.*
**Desc:** Contains news of veterinary science, state and regional veterinary concerns, practice management, organized veterinary medicine and individual veterinarians.

US/0093-691X
**THERIOGENOLOGY.** [Theriogenology]. Vol. 1 (Jan. 1974)-. Academic Scholarly Publication. English. Sixteen times a year. $515.00 US; $600.00 other. Butterworth Heinemann / Woburn, MA, 225 Wildwood Avenue, Unit B, Woburn MA 01801. **Tel** (800)366-2665, FAX (617)928-2620, telex 880052. **NLM** W1 TH677K. **CODEN** THGNBO. **[CCC].** Index available. **Bk Rev. Ad Acc. Pr Rev. Circ:** 1,000 (ctrl). available on microfilm and microfiche from University Microfilms International (UMI). Documents available from The Genuine Article, BIOSIS Document Express, CASDDS.
**Desc:** An international journal of rapid communication about reproduction in domestic and wild animals. Current and concise research is published as original papers or clinical articles. Other information published in the journal includes review articles, economic and ecological evaluations, together with notices of forthcoming meetings.
**Ind/Abst** AgBiotech News Inf.; AGRICOLA [Full Cov.]; Anim. Breed. Abstr.; Biol. Abstr.; Chem. Abstr.; CSA Neuro. Abstr. (?-?); Curr. Aware. Biol. Sci., CABS; Curr. Contents, Agric. Biol. Environ. Sci.; Curr. Contents Life

Sci.; Dairy Sci. Abstr.; Energy Res. Abstr. (Aug. 1982-); Index Vet.; Nutr. Abstr. Rev., Ser. B, Live Feeds and Feed.; Life Sci. Collect.; PESTDOC; Pig News Inf.; Poult. Abstr.; Protozoolog. Abstr.; Ref. Upd. Deluxe Ed.; Res. Alert [Full Cov.]; Rev. Med. Vet. Mycology; Sci. Cit. Index; SCISEARCH; Small Anim. Abstr. Bibliogr.; Sug. Indus. Abstr.; Vet. Bull.

AG
**THERIOS : REVISTA DE MEDICINA VETERINARIA Y PRODUCCION ANIMAL.** VFOAT Revista Therios. Vol. 1, No. 1 (March 1983)-. Periodical. Spanish. mo. $60.00. Ciencia Veterinaria Edit. s.r.l., Loyola 1114, 1414 Buenos Aires Argentina. **Tel** 011 54 1 8554220, FAX 011 54 1 8559434. **ED** Paula Rodriquez. Index available. cum. index. **Bk Rev**, (Qty: 20 per year). **Ad Acc, Adv Mgr:** Juan Jose Ruiz. **Pr Rev. Acid Free. Circ:** 5,000 (ctrl). Documents available from CASDDS.
**Desc:** Publishes either original papers or adaptation of articles published in internationally-recognized journals.
**Ind/Abst** Helminthol. Abstr. (1991-); Plant Breed. Abstr.; Poult. Abstr.; Protozoolog. Abstr.

GW/0303-6286
**TIERARZTLICHE PRAXIS.** [Tierarztl. Prax.]. Vol. 1 (1973)-. Periodical. German. Six times a year. DM392.00 (institutions), DM298.00 (individuals) Europe; $243.50 (institutions), $191.50 (individuals) other. F K Schattauer Verlagsgesellschaft mbH, Postfach 10 45 45, D 70040 Stuttgart Germany. **Tel** 011 49 711 2298726. **ED** H. Bostedt, W. Kraft, U. Matis and B. Mayr. **NLM** W1 TI349. **CODEN** TAZPB8. **[CCC].** Index available. **Bk Rev. Ad Acc.** ctrl circ.
**Ind/Abst** AgBiotech News Inf.; Anim. Breed. Abstr.; Helminthol. Abstr. (1991-); Index Med.; Index Vet.; Nutr. Abstr. Rev., Ser. B, Live Feeds and Feed.; PESTDOC; Pig News Inf.; Protozoolog. Abstr.; Rev. Agric. Entomol.; Rev. Med. Vet. Entomol.; Rev. Med. Vet. Mycology; Small Anim. Abstr. Bibliogr.; SportSearch; Vet. Bull.; Weed Abstr.

GW/0930-6447
**TIERARZTLICHE PRAXIS. SUPPLEMENT.** [Tierarztl. Prax. Suppl.]. **VFOAT** Tierarztliche Praxis. Sonderheft. Vol. 1 (1985)-. Periodical. German (English; summaries and/or abstracts in German and English; table of contents in German and English). Available only to subscribers of Tieraerztliche Praxis. F K Schattauer Verlagsgesellschaft mbH, Postfach 10 45 45, D 70040 Stuttgart Germany. **Tel** 011 49 711 2298726. **NLM** W1; TI349a.
**Ind/Abst** Index Med. (1985-).

GW/0049-3864
**TIERARZTLICHE UMSCHAU.** Vol. 1 (1946)-. Periodical. German (summaries and/or abstracts in English). mo. DM156.00 Germany; DM172.00 other. Terra Verlag, Postfach 102144, D-78421 Konstanz Germany. **Tel** 011 49 7531 812244, telex 733271. **ED** Eberhard Heizmann and O Straub. **NLM** W1 TI352. **[CCC].** Index available. **Bk Rev. Ad Acc. Pr Rev. Circ:** 7,200. Documents available from The Genuine Article.
**Desc:** All aspects of veterinary medicine.
**Ind/Abst** AgBiotech News Inf.; AGRICOLA; Anim. Breed. Abstr.; Biodeter. Abstr. (1991-); Curr. Contents, Agric. Biol. Environ. Sci.; Dairy Sci. Abstr.; Energy Res. Abstr. (Jan. 1979-); Food Sci. Technol. Abstr.; Helminthol. Abstr. (19??-19??); Index Vet.; Key Word Index Wildl. Res.; Nutr. Abstr. Rev., Ser. B, Live Feeds and Feed.; Life Sci. Collect.; PESTDOC; Pig News Inf.; Poult. Abstr.; Protozoolog. Abstr.; Res. Alert [Full Cov.]; Rev. Agric. Entomol.; Rev. Med. Vet. Entomol.; Rev. Med. Vet. Mycology; Sci. Cit. Index; SCISEARCH; Small Anim. Abstr. Bibliogr.; Vet. Bull.

GW
**TIERLABORATORIUM / HERAUSGEGEBEN VON DEN ZENTRALEN TIERLABORATORIEN UND DEM INSTITUT FUER VERSUCHSTIERKUNDE DER FREIEN UNIVERSITAT BERLIN.** **Added/Corp** Freie Universitat Berlin. Fachrichtung Versuchstierkunde und Versuchstierkrankheiten. Freie Universitat Berlin. Zentrale Tierlaboratorien. Freie Universitat Berlin. Institut fur Versuchstierkunde. (1974)-. German (summaries and/or abstracts in English). an. **NLM** W1; TI378.
**Ind/Abst** Index Vet.; Nutr. Abstr. Rev., Ser. B, Live Feeds and Feed.; Rev. Med. Vet. Mycology; Vet. Bull.

●US/1065-6650
**TIGER TRIBE.** (TIGER TRIBE : HOLISTIC HEALTH & MORE FOR CATS.). [Tiger tribe]. (July/Aug. 1992)-. Periodical. English. bm. $18.00. Tiger Tribe Publications, 1407 East College Street, Iowa City IA 52245-4410. **DD** 636.

NE/0040-7453
**TIJDSCHRIFT VOOR DIERGENEESKUNDE.** (TIJDSCHRIFT VOOR DIERGENEESKUNDE. NETHERLANDS JOURNAL OF VETERINARY SCIENCE.). [Tijdschr. diergeneeskd.]. **Added/Corp** Koninklijke Nederlandse Maatschappij voor Diergeneeskunde. **VFOAT** Netherlands Journal of Veterinary Sciences. Vol. 43 (1916)-. Periodical. Dutch (English). Twenty-four times a year. Fl275.00 Netherlands; Fl295.00 other. Koninklijke Nederlandse M Dier, PO Box 14031, 3508 SB Utrecht, Netherlands. **Tel** 011 31 30 510111, FAX 011 31 30 511787. **NLM** W1 TI652. **CODEN** TIDIAY. Index available. **Bk Rev. Ad Acc.** Full Page (B&W) Fl1775.00. Half Page (B&W) Fl1125.00. **Circ:** 4,500. Documents available from The Genuine Article, BIOSIS Document Express, CASDDS. ***Continues*** *Tijdschrift voor Veeartsenijkunde.* ***Superseded in part by*** *Veterinary Quarterly, 0165-2176.*
**Desc:** Issued by the Royal Netherlands Veterinary Association.
**Ind/Abst** AgBiotech News Inf.; AGRICOLA; Anim. Breed. Abstr.; Biol. Abstr.; Chem. Abstr.; CSA Neuro. Abstr. (?-?); Curr. Contents, Agric. Biol. Environ. Sci.; Dairy Sci. Abstr.; Fish Rev.; Helminthol. Abstr. (19??-19??); Index Med.; Microbiol. Abstr. Sect. B (19??-19??); Microbiol. Abstr. Sect. C; Nutr. Abstr. Rev., Ser. B, Live Feeds and Feed.; Life Sci. Collect.; PESTDOC; Pig News Inf.; Poult. Abstr.; Protozoolog. Abstr.; Res. Alert [Select. Cov.]; Rev. Med. Vet. Entomol.; Rev. Med. Vet. Mycology; Small Anim. Abstr. Bibliogr.; Soc. Sci. Cit. Index [Select. Cov.]; SportSearch; Trop. Dis. Bull.; Virol. AIDS Abstr.; Wildl. Rev.

US/1064-5101
**TOPICS IN VETERINARY MEDICINE.** [Top. vet. med.]. **Added/Corp** Smithkline Beecham Animal Health (Firm). Vol. 1, No. 1 (Summer 1990)-. Periodical. English. Three times a year (Mar., July, Nov.). Free. Smithkline Beecham Animal Health, 812 Springdale Drive, Exton PA 19341. **Tel** (215)363-3777, FAX (215)363-3284. **ED** Kathleen Etchison. **DD** 636. **Circ:** 45,000 (ctrl). ***Continues*** *Norden News, 0890-3727.*

US
**TRANSACTIONS OF THE ... ANNUAL SCIENTIFIC PROGRAM OF THE AMERICAN COLLEGE OF VETERINARY OPHTHALMOLOGISTS.** English.

US/1062-8266
**TRENDS MAGAZINE.** (TRENDS MAGAZINE / AMERICAN ANIMAL HOSPITAL ASSOCIATION.). [Trends mag.]. **Added/Corp** American Animal Hospital Association. **VFOAT** Trends. Vol. 4, No. 4 (Aug. 1988)-. Periodical. English. bm. $60.00 (non-members); Also comes with American Animal Hospital Association membership. American Animal Hospital Association - Colorado, PO Box 150899, Denver CO 80215. **Tel** (303)279-2500, FAX (303)279-1816. **DD** 362. ***Continues*** *Trends (Mishawaka, Ind.), 0883-1696.*
**Desc:** Published as a practice management publication of the American Animal Hospital Association.

UK/0049-4747
**TROPICAL ANIMAL HEALTH AND PRODUCTION.** [Trop. anim. health prod.]. **Added/Corp** University of Edinburgh. Centre for Tropical Veterinary Medicine. Vol. 1 (Aug. 1969)-. Academic Scholarly Publication. English (summaries and/or abstracts in French and Spanish). qt. £69.50 UK & Europe; $136.00 US; £77.00 other. Edinburgh University Press, 22 George Square, Edinburgh EH8 9LF Scotland. **Tel** 011 44 31 650 6207, FAX 011 44 31 662 0053. **ED** A.G. Hunter. **LC** SF601; .T74. **DD** 636.089/69/88305. **NLM** W1 TR88. **CODEN** TAHPAJ. **Ad Acc, Adv Mgr:** Kathryn MacLean. **Pr Rev. Circ:** 500. Documents available from The Genuine Article, BIOSIS Document Express, CASDDS.
**Desc:** Publishes the results of original research, investigation and observation in the fields of animal disease and animal production.
**Ind/Abst** AgBiotech News Inf.; AGRICOLA [Full Cov.]; Agrofor. Abstr. (1991-); Anim. Breed. Abstr.; BioBusiness; Biol. Abstr.; Chem. Abstr.; Curr. Contents, Agric. Biol. Environ. Sci.; Dairy Sci. Abstr.; EMBASE; Grasslands For. Abstr.; Helminthol. Abstr. (19??-19??); Index Med.; Nutr. Abstr. Rev., Ser. B, Live Feeds and Feed.; Life Sci. Collect.; PESTDOC; Pig News Inf.; Poult. Abstr.; Protozoolog. Abstr.; Res. Alert [Full Cov.]; Rev. Med. Vet Entomol.; Sci. Cit. Index; SCISEARCH; Small Anim. Abstr. Bibliogr.; Trop. Dis. Bull.

RU/0203-6703
**TRUDY VIEV.** (TRUDY VIEV / VSESOIUZNYI ORDENA LENINA INSTITUT EKSPERIMENTALNOI VETERINARII, VSESOIUZNOI ORDENA LENINA AKADEMII SELSKOKHOZIAISTVENNYKH NAUK IMENI V.I. LENINA.). [Tr. VIEV]. **Added/Corp** Vsesoiuznyi Institut Eksperimentalnoi Veterinarii, (Soviet Union) Vsesoiuznyi Nauchno-Issledovatelskii Institut Eksperimentalnoi Veterinarii Im. Ia.R. Kobalenko. **VAT** Trudy Vsesoiuznogo Ordena Lenina Instituta Eksperimentalnoi. (1977)-. Academic Scholarly Publication. Russian (table of contents in English). Price varies per volume. **CODEN** TRVIDK. Documents available from CASDDS. ***Continues*** *Trudy Vsesoiuznogo Ordena Lenina Instituta Eksperimentalnoi Veterinarii, 0371-6511.*
**Ind/Abst** Chem. Abstr. (?-1981); Poult. Abstr.

UK/0142-193X
**TSETSE AND TRYPANOSOMIASIS INFORMATION QUARTERLY.** **See** Zoology.

GW/0376-1185
**TU.** [TU]. **Added/Corp** Vereinigung der Technischer Uberwachungs-Vereine. **VFOAT** TU, Technische Uberwachung; T. U. Vol. 11, No. 1 (Jan. 1970)-. Academic Scholarly Publication. German. Nine times a year. DM296.00 Germany; DM329.00 other. VDI Verlag GmbH, Postfach 101054, D 40001 Dusseldorf Germany. **Tel** 011 49 211 6188313, FAX 011 49 211 6188133. **CODEN** TUSZA6. **[CCC].** Documents available from CASDDS. ***Continues*** *Technische Uberwachung, 0372-2457.*
**Ind/Abst** Alum. Ind. Abstr.; Chem. Abstr.; Coal Abstr.; EMBASE; Energy Res. Abstr. (May 1980-); Met. Abstr.; Saf. Health Work.

GW/0303-6340
**UEBERSICHTEN ZUR TIERERNAHRUNG.** (Jan 1973)-. Periodical. German (summaries and/or abstracts in English). ir (2-4 times per year). DM8.60. Deutsche Landwirtschafts Gesellschaft, Verlags GmbH, Eschborner Landstr 122, D 60489 Frankfurt Germany. **Tel** 011 49 69 247880, FAX 011 49 69 24788580. **NLM** W1 UE22. **CODEN** UETIDW.
**Ind/Abst** Index Vet.; Nutr. Abstr. Rev., Ser. B, Live Feeds and Feed.; Pig News Inf.

SW/0042-2703
**VARA PALSDJUR.** [Vara palsdjur]. **Added/Corp** Sveriges Palsdjursuppfodares Riksforbund. (1930)-. Periodical. Swedish. mo.
**Ind/Abst** Index Vet.; Nutr. Abstr. Rev., Ser. B, Live Feeds and Feed.

XO/0375-4928
**VEDECKE PRACE VYSKUMNEHO USTAVU LUK A PASIENKOV V BANSKEJ BYSTRICI.** [Ved. pr. vysk. ust. luk pasienkov Banskej Bystrici]. **Added/Corp** Ustav luk a Pasienkov v Banskej Bystrici. Vyskumny Ustav luk a Pasienkov v Banskej Bystrici. (1965)-. Periodical. Czech (summaries and/or abstracts in Russian, English and German). **CODEN** VPVLAY.
**Ind/Abst** Agric. Eng. Abstr.; Agrofor. Abstr.; For. Abstr.; Grasslands For. Abstr.; Hortic. Abstr.; Postharvest News Inf.; Soils Fert.

II/0970-7573
**VET MHOW.** [VetMhow]. (1987)-. Periodical. English. qt. **UDC** 636.
**Ind/Abst** Index Vet.

UK
**VETDOC.** **See** Veterinary Sciences-Abstracting, Bibliographies and Statistics.

AG/0326-4629
**VETERINARIA ARGENTINA.** [Vet. argent.]. Vol. 1, No. 1 (Jan./Feb. 1984)-. Periodical. Spanish (summaries and/or abstracts in English; table of contents in English). mo (10 per year). $110.00 the Americas; $120.00 Europe; $70.00 Argentina, Chile, Bolivia, Paraguay and Uruguay; $160.00 other. Veterinaria Argentina, Viamonte 494 / 2 Piso 6, 1053 Buenos Aires Argentina. **Tel** 011 54 1 3119997, FAX 011 54 1 3128720. Index available. **Bk Rev**, (Qty: 20 per year). **Ad Acc, Adv Mgr:** Sr Speroni. **Pr Rev. Circ:** 4,500. ***Continues in part*** *Gaceta Veterinaria.*
**Ind/Abst** Anim. Breed. Abstr.; Dairy Sci. Abstr.; Helminthol. Abstr. (19??-19??); Index Vet.; Nutr. Abstr. Rev., Ser. B, Live Feeds and Feed.; Pig News Inf.; Poult. Abstr.; Protozoolog. Abstr.; Rev. Med. Vet. Entomol.; Rev. Med. Vet. Mycology; Small Anim. Abstr. Bibliogr.; Vet. Bull.

IT/0394-3151
**VETERINARIA CREMONA.** (VETERINARIA.). [Veterinaria Cremona]. (1987)-. Periodical. Italian. qt. L80000 Italy; L100000 other. Scivac Soc Cult It Veterinaria, Animal Compag V Pallavicino 26, 26100 Cremona Italy. **Tel** 39 372 460440. **UDC** 619.
**Ind/Abst** Helminthol. Abstr. (1991-); Small Anim. Abstr. Bibliogr. (19??-).

BL/0102-5716
**VETERINARIA E ZOOTECNIA.** **Added/Corp** Universidade Estadual Paulista. Vol. 1 (1985)-. Portuguese (summaries and/or abstracts in English; table of contents in English). **NLM** W1; VE898U.
**Ind/Abst** Index Vet.; Protozoolog. Abstr.; Small Anim. Abstr. Bibliogr.

MX/0301-5092
**VETERINARIA (MEXICO).** (VETERINARIA MEXICO / FACULTAD DE MEDICINA VETERINARIA Y ZOOTECNIA.). [Veterinaria]. **Added/Corp** Universidad Nacional Autonoma de Mexico. Facultad de Medicina Veterinaria y Zootecnia. Vol. 7, No. 1 (Jan./March 1976)-. Academic Scholarly Publication. Spanish (summaries and/or abstracts in English). Four times a year. $50.00. UNAM - Universidad Nacional Autonoma de Mexico / Medica, Revista de la Facultad de Medicina, Veterinaria y Zootecnica, Ciudad Universitaria, 04510 Mexico DF Mexico. **Tel** 11 52 5 6225875, FAX 11 52 5 5508697,

5500057. **ED** Raymundo Martinez Pena. Index available (in the last issue of each volume). **Bk Rev. Ad Acc, Adv Mgr:** Renate Thumule. **Pr Rev. Circ:** 2,000 (ctrl). Documents available from BIOSIS Document Express, CASDDS. ***Continues*** *Veterinaria (Universidad Nacional Automona de Mexico. Facultad de Medicina Veterinaria y Zootecnia).*
**Desc:** Contains information on veterinary medicine and zoo techniques. Also unpublished articles, short communication and review articles.
**Ind/Abst** AgBiotech News Inf.; Anim. Breed. Abstr.; Biol. Abstr.; Chem. Abstr.; Dairy Sci. Abstr.; Fish Rev. (Jan. 1989-July 1992); Grasslands For. Abstr.; Helminthol. Abstr. (19??-19??); Index Vet.; Microbiol. Abstr. Sect. B (19??-19??); Nutr. Abstr. Rev., Ser. B, Live Feeds and Feed.; Life Sci. Collect.; Pig News Inf.; Plant Grow. Reg. Abstr.; Poult. Abstr.; Protozoolog. Abstr.; Rev. Med. Vet. Entomol.; Small Anim. Abstr. Bibliogr.; Soc. Sci. Cit. Index [Select. Cov.]; Vet. Bull.; Wildl. Rev. (Jan. 1989-July 1992); World Agric. Econ.

BN/0372-6827
**VETERINARIA (SARAJEVO).**
(VETERINARIA.). [Veterinaria]. Vol. 1 (1952)-. Periodical. Serbo-Croatian (Cyrillic) (Serbian; summaries and/or abstracts in English). qt. **NLM** W1 VE898R. **CODEN** VTRNAE. Documents available from CASDDS.
**Ind/Abst** AGRICOLA; Biodeter. Abstr.; Chem. Abstr.; Dairy Sci. Abstr.; Fish Rev.; Food Sci. Technol. Abstr.; Index Vet.; Maize Abstr.; Nutr. Abstr. Rev., Ser. B, Live Feeds and Feed.; Pig News Inf.; Poult. Abstr.; Protozoolog. Abstr.; Rev. Med. Vet. Mycology; Small Anim. Abstr. Bibliogr.; Soils Fert.; Vet. Bull.; Wildl. Rev.

VE/0379-8275
**VETERINARIA TROPICAL.** Vol. 1 (Jan./Dec. 1976)-. Periodical. Spanish (summaries and/or abstracts in English and Spanish). an. Bs50.00 or $5.00. Fondo Nacional de Investigaciones Agropecuarios, Avenida Universidad via 62 Limon, Apartado 2103, Maracay Venezuela. **ED** Aydee Cabrera de Green. **NLM** W1 VE899T. **CODEN** VETRE3. **Circ:** 800. ***Supersedes*** *Boletin del Instituto de Investigaciones Veterinarias.*
**Ind/Abst** Helminthol. Abstr.; Index Vet.; Pig News Inf.; Poult. Abstr.; Protozoolog. Abstr.; Vet. Bull.

CN/0849-5009
**VETERINARIAN MAGAZINE.** ***Ceased.*** [Vet. mag.]. Vol. 1, No. 1 (April 1989)-(19??). Periodical. English. Six times a year (Feb., Apr., June, Aug., Oct., Dec.). H G K Communications Inc, 248 Mary Street, Rockwood Ontario N0B 2K0 Canada. **Tel** (519)856-4050, FAX (519)856-4146. **ED** Maggie Clark. **DD** 636.089/05. **Ad Acc, Adv Mgr:** L. Hewitt. **Circ:** 4,600 (ctrl).
**Desc:** Communicates professional information to veterinarians across Canada about companion animals, food animals, research, nutrition, new procedures and clinic management as well as providing product and service news. VM strives towards complete communication in all fields of interest to Canada's veterinarians.

US
**VETERINARIANS' PRODUCT & THERAPEUTIC REFERENCE. VFOAT** Veterinarians' P & TR. 1972-. English. Therapeutic Communications, 435 Bloomfield Avenue, Caldwell NJ 07006. **LC** SF917. **DD** 636.089/5/1016.

UN/0321-0502
**VETERINARIIA (UKRAINE. MINISTERSTVO SILSKOHO HOSPODARSTVA).** (VETERINARIIA / MINISTERSTVO SILSKOHO HOSPODARSTVA UKRAINSKOI RSR.). [Veterinariia]. **Added/Corp** Ukraine. Ministerstvo Silskoho Hospodarstva. (1964)-. Academic Scholarly Publication. Russian. Twelve times a year. $89.75 US & Canada; $99.95 Europe; $114.95 other. **(Subscription address:** East View Publications Inc., 3020 Harbor Lane North, Suite 110, Minneapolis MN 55447.**) NLM** W1 VE938G. **CODEN** VMSKAT. Documents available from CASDDS.
**Ind/Abst** AGRICOLA (19??-); Chem. Abstr. (19??-); Helminthol. Abstr. (1991-); Index Vet. (19??-); PESTDOC (?-?); Poult. Abstr. (19??-); Rev. Med. Vet. Entomol. (19??-); Vet. Bull. (19??-).

RU/0042-4846
**VETERINARIJA (MOSKVA).**
(VETERINARIIA.). [Vet.]. **Added/Corp** Soviet Union. Ministerstvo Selskogo Khoziaistva. (1941)-. Academic Scholarly Publication. Russian (summaries and/or abstracts in English and German). mo. $89.95. Izdatelstvo Kolos, Sadovaia-Spasskaia 18, 107807 GSP Moscow B-53 Russia. **(Subscription address:** East View Publications Inc., 3020 Harbor Lane North, Suite 110, Minneapolis MN 55447.**) CODEN** VETNAL. Documents available from BIOSIS Document Express, CASDDS. ***Continues*** *Sovetskaia Veterinariia, 0302-6388.*
**Ind/Abst** AGRICOLA; Agric. Eng. Abstr.; Biol. Abstr. (?-1990); Chem. Abstr.; Food Sci. Technol. Abstr.; Helminthol. Abstr.; Index Vet.; PESTDOC; Poult. Abstr.; Protozoolog. Abstr.; Rev. Med. Vet. Entomol.; Rev. Med. Vet. Mycology; Small Anim. Abstr. Bibliogr.; Sug. Indus. Abstr.; Vet. Bull.

TU
**VETERINARIUM. Added/Corp** Konya Animal Diseases Research Institute. **VFOAT** Journal of Konya Animal Diseases Research Institute. (19??)-. Periodical. English.
**Ind/Abst** Biodeter. Abstr.; Index Vet.; Nutr. Abstr. Rev., Ser. B, Live Feeds and Feed.; Protozoolog. Abstr.; Rev. Med. Vet. Mycology; Small Anim. Abstr. Bibliogr.; Vet. Bull.

BU/0205-3829
**VETERINARNA SBIRKA.** [Vet. sb.].
**Added/Corp** Bulgaria. Ministerstvo na Zemedelieto i Khranitelnata Promishlenost. Selskostopanska Akademiia Georgi Dimitrov. Natsionalen Agrarno-Promishlen Suiuz (Bulgaria). (1891)-. Academic Scholarly Publication. Bulgarian (summaries and/or abstracts in English and Russian; table of contents in English and Russian). Ten times a year. DM223.00. **(Subscription address:** Kubon & Sagner, ABT Zeitschriftenimport, D 80328 Munich Germany.**) NLM** W1 VE916H. **CODEN** VESBAE. Documents available from BIOSIS Document Express, CASDDS.
**Ind/Abst** AGRICOLA; Anim. Breed. Abstr.; Biodeter. Abstr. (1991-); Biol. Abstr.; Chem. Abstr.; Dairy Sci. Abstr.; Food Sci. Technol. Abstr.; Helminthol. Abstr. (19??-19??); Index Vet.; Maize Abstr.; Nutr. Abstr. Rev., Ser. B, Live Feeds and Feed.; Nutr. Abstr. Rev., Ser. A, Hum. Exp.; Pig News Inf.; Poult. Abstr.; Protozoolog. Abstr.; Rev. Agric. Entomol.; Rev. Med. Vet. Entomol.; Rev. Med. Vet. Mycology; Vet. Bull.; Wheat Barley Trit. Abstr.

BW
**VETERINARNAIA NAUKA-PROIZVODSTVU. VFOAT** Trudy - Nauchno-Issledovatelskii Veterinarnyi Institut. Vol. 11 (1973)-. Periodical. Russian. an. ***Continues*** *Nauchnye Trudy / Nauchno-Issledovatel'skii Veterinarnyi Institut.*
**Ind/Abst** Poult. Abstr.

XR/0375-8427
**VETERINARNI MEDICINA.** (May 1962)-. Academic Scholarly Publication. Czech (summaries and/or abstracts in Russian, English and German; table of contents in Russian, English and German). mo. $121.70. Artia Pegas Press Ltd., Palac Metro Narodni TR 25, 11000 Prague 1 Czech Republic. **Tel** 011 42 2 24196265 or 24196266, 24196266. **CODEN** VTMDAR. Documents available from The Genuine Article, CASDDS.
**Ind/Abst** AgBiotech News Inf. (19??-); AGRICOLA (19??-); Agric. Eng. Abstr. (1991-); Anim. Breed. Abstr. (19??-); Biodeter. Abstr. (1991-); Chem. Abstr. (19??-); Curr. Contents, Agric. Biol. Environ. Sci. (19??-); Dairy Sci. Abstr. (19??-); EMBASE (19??-); Food Sci. Technol. Abstr. (19??-); Grasslands For. Abstr. (19??-); Helminthol. Abstr. (19??-19??); Index Med. (19??-); Index Vet. (19??-); Maize Abstr. (19??-); Nutr. Abstr. Rev., Ser. B, Live Feeds and Feed. (19??-); Life Sci. Collect. (19??-); Pig News Inf. (19??-); Poult. Abstr. (19??-); Protozoolog. Abstr. (19??-); Res. Alert (19??-) [Full Cov.]; Rev. Agric. Entomol. (19??-); Rev. Med. Vet. Entomol. (19??-); Rev. Med. Vet. Mycology (19??-); Sci. Cit. Index; SCISEARCH (19??-); Small Anim. Abstr. Bibliogr. (19??-); Vet. Bull. (19??-); Wheat Barley Trit. Abstr. (19??-).

BU/0324-1068
**VETERINARNO-MEDICINSKI NAUKI.**
[Vet.-med. nauki]. **VFOAT** Veterinary Science. (1964)-. Academic Scholarly Publication. Bulgarian. qt. 1.30lv per issue. Bulgarska Akademiia na Naukite, 7 Noemvri 1, Sofia Bulgaria. **UDC** 619.
**Ind/Abst** Agric. Eng. Abstr.

YU/0350-7149
**VETERINARSKA STANICA.** [Vet. stn.]. (1971)-. Periodical. Serbo-Croatian (Roman). bm. **UDC** 619.
**Ind/Abst** Agric. Eng. Abstr.; Index Vet.; Nutr. Abstr. Rev., Ser. B, Live Feeds and Feed.; Pig News Inf.; Poult. Abstr.; Rev. Agric. Entomol.; Rev. Med. Vet. Mycology; Vet. Bull.

CI/0372-5480
**VETERINARSKI ARHIV.** [Vet. arh.]. Vol. 1 (April 30, 1931)-. Academic Scholarly Publication. Serbo-Croatian (Roman) (English). mo. **NLM** W1 VE918. **CODEN** VEARA6. Documents available from BIOSIS Document Express, CASDDS.
**Ind/Abst** AGRICOLA; Anim. Breed. Abstr.; Biodeter. Abstr. (1991-); Biol. Abstr.; Chem. Abstr.; Helminthol. Abstr. (1991-); Nutr. Abstr. Rev., Ser. B, Live Feeds and Feed.; Life Sci. Collect.; PESTDOC; Pig News Inf.; Poult. Abstr.; Protozoolog. Abstr.; Rev. Agric. Entomol.; Rev. Med. Vet. Entomol.; Rev. Med. Vet. Mycology; Small Anim. Abstr. Bibliogr.

YU/0350-2457
**VETERINARSKI GLASNIK.** [Vet. glas.]. (1947)-. Periodical. Serbo-Croatian (Cyrillic) (table of contents in Serbo-Croatian (Roman), English and Russian). mo. $83.65. Fam Book Service, 69 Fifth Avenue/Suite 8F, New York NY 10003. **NLM** W1 VE919.
**Ind/Abst** AGRICOLA (19??-); Agric. Eng. Abstr. (1991-); Anim. Breed. Abstr. (19??-); Biodeter. Abstr. (1991-); Dairy Sci. Abstr. (19??-); Helminthol. Abstr. (19??-19??); Index Vet. (19??-); Maize Abstr. (19??-); Nutr. Abstr. Rev., Ser. B, Live Feeds and Feed. (19??-); Nutr. Abstr. Rev., Ser. A, Hum. Exp. (19??-); Pig News Inf. (19??-); Poult. Abstr. (19??-); Protozoolog. Abstr. (19??-); Rev. Agric. Entomol. (19??-); Rev. Med. Vet. Entomol. (19??-); Rev. Med. Vet. Mycology (19??-); Small Anim. Abstr. Bibliogr. (19??-); Soyabean Abstr. (19??-); Vet. Bull. (19??-).

XR/0506-8231
**VETERINARSTVI.** [Veterinarstvi]. (1951)-. Academic Scholarly Publication. Czech (table of contents in English, German and Russian). mo. $111.10. Artia Pegas Press Ltd., Palac Metro Narodni TR 25, 11000 Prague 1 Czech Republic. **Tel** 011 42 2 24196265 or 24196266, 24196266. **NLM** W1 VE92. **CODEN** VTERAT. Documents available from CASDDS.
**Ind/Abst** AgBiotech News Inf. (19??-); AGRICOLA (19??-); Agric. Eng. Abstr. (19??-); Biodeter. Abstr. (1991-); Chem. Abstr. (19??-); Dairy Sci. Abstr. (19??-); Helminthol. Abstr. (19??-19??); Index Vet. (19??-); Nutr. Abstr. Rev., Ser. B, Live Feeds and Feed. (19??-); Nutr. Abstr. Rev., Ser. A, Hum. Exp. (19??-); PESTDOC (19??-); Pig News Inf. (19??-); Poult. Abstr. (19??-); Protozoolog. Abstr. (19??-); Rev. Med. Vet. Entomol. (19??-); Rev. Med. Vet. Mycology (19??-); Small Anim. Abstr. Bibliogr. (19??-); Vet. Bull. (19??-).

US
**VETERINARY ACUPUNCTURE NEWSLETTER. Added/Corp** International Veterinary Acupuncture Society. Vol. 9, No. 2 (Apr.-June 1983)-. Periodical. English. qt. Only available with International Veterinary Acupuncture Society membership. International Veterinary Acupuncture Society, 1750 1 30th St. Box 142, Boulder CO 80301. **Tel** (303)449-7936. ***Continues*** *I.V.A.S. Newsletter (International Veterinary Acupuncture Society).*

●US/1076-4607
**VETERINARY & COMPARATIVE OPHTHALMOLOGY.** [Vet. comp. ophtalmol.].
**Added/Corp** International Society of Veterinary Ophthalmology. **VFOAT** Veterinary and Comparative Ophthalmology. Vol. 4, No. 1 (Spring 1994)-. Periodical. English. qt. $50.00 US; $60.00 Canada & Mexico; $75.00 other. Veterinary Practice Publishing Company, PO Box 4457, Santa Barbara CA 93140-4457. **Tel** (805)965-1028, FAX (805)965-0722. **DD** 636. ***Continues*** *Progress in Veterinary & Comparative Ophthalmology, 1061-5768.*
**Desc:** International journal of veterinary neurology and neurosurgery.

GW/0932-0814
**VETERINARY AND COMPARATIVE ORTHOPAEDICS AND TRAUMATOLOGY.** (VETERINARY AND COMPARATIVE ORTHOPAEDICS AND TRAUMATOLOGY / VCOT.). [Vet. comp. orthop. traumatol.]. **VFOAT** V.C.O.T.; VCOT. Vol. 1, No. 1 (Jan. 25, 1988)-. Periodical. English. qt. DM310.00 (institutions), DM248.00 (individuals) Europe; $195.70 (institutions), $152.70 (individuals) other. F K Schattauer Verlagsgesellschaft mbH, Postfach 10 45 45, D 70040 Stuttgart Germany. **Tel** 011 49 711 2298726. **ED** G. Sumner-Smith (editor's address: Ontario Veterinary College, University of Guelph, Guelph Ontario N1G 2W1 Canada). **LC** SF910.5; .V47. **NLM** W1; VE922. **[CCC].** Index available. **Bk Rev. Ad Acc.** ctrl circ.
**Desc:** Deals with the increasing number of orthopaedic and traumatological conditions and diseases in both man and animals, which have many orthopaedic problems and disorders in common; individual traumatological features also have many similarities.
**Ind/Abst** AGRICOLA [Full Cov.]; Index Vet.; Vet. Bull.

US/0145-6296
**VETERINARY AND HUMAN TOXICOLOGY.** [Vet. hum. toxicol.]. Vol. 19 (Feb. 1977)-. Academic Scholarly Publication. English. bm. $60.00 US; $70.00 Canada; $80.00 (surface mail), $100.00 (air mail) other. Comparative Toxicology Laboratories, VCS-Kansas State University, Manhattan KS 66506-5606. **Tel** (913)532-4334, FAX (913)532-4481, telex 821034. **ED** F.W. Oehme. **LC** SF757.5; .V48. **DD** 636.089/59/005. **NLM** W1 VE923. **CODEN** VHTODE. **Bk Rev**, (Qty: 50-60). **Ad Acc. Pr Rev. Circ:** 1,800 (ctrl). Documents available from The Genuine Article, BIOSIS Document Express, CASDDS, Documents on Demand. ***Continues*** *Veterinary Toxicology, 0091-5300.*
**Desc:** Publishes toxicology contributions that relate to the broad field of toxicology, including news items and announcements, manuscripts of original research, scientific reviews, and field observations in domestic and wild animals or man. Papers presented at meetings and those of general educational value to toxicologists and related scientists are also considered for publication.
**Ind/Abst** AGRICOLA [Select. Cov.]; Biodeter. Abstr. (1991-); Biol. Abstr.; Chem. Abstr.; CSA Neuro. Abstr. (?-?); Cumul. Index Nurs. Allied Health Lit.; Curr. Contents, Agric. Biol. Environ. Sci.; Dairy Sci. Abstr.; EMBASE; Energy Inf. Abstr.; Environ. Abstr.; Fish Rev.; Grasslands For. Abstr.; Health Saf. Sci. Abstr.; Helminthol. Abstr. (1991-); Index Med.; Index Vet.; Int. Pharm. Abstr.; Microbiol. Abstr. Sect. B; Microbiol. Abstr. Sect. C; Nutr. Abstr. Rev., Ser. B, Live Feeds and Feed.; Nutr. Abstr. Rev., Ser. A, Hum. Exp.; Ornamental Hort.; Life Sci. Collect.; Pig News Inf.; Pollut. Abstr. Indexes; Protozoolog. Abstr.; Res. Alert [Full Cov.]; Rev. Agric. Entomol.; Rev. Med. Vet. Entomol.; Rev. Med. Vet. Mycology; Sci. Cit. Index; SCISEARCH; Small Anim.

Abstr. Bibliogr.; Soc. Sci. Cit. Index [Select. Cov.]; Vet. Bull.; Toxicol. Abstr.; Weed Abstr.; Wheat Barley Trit. Abstr.; Wildl. Rev.

UK/0083-5870
**VETERINARY ANNUAL, THE.** [Vet. annu.]. Vol. 1 (1959)-. English. an. $125.00. Blackwell Scientific Publishers, 238 Main Street, Cambridge MA 02142. **Tel** (617)547-7110, (800)835-6770, FAX (617)547-0789. **LC** SF601; .V518. **NLM** W1 VE924.
**Ind/Abst** AgBiotech News Inf.; AGRICOLA [Full Cov.]; Anim. Breed. Abstr.; Helminthol. Abstr. (1991-); Index Vet.; Pig News Inf.; Protozoolog. Abstr.; Rev. Med. Vet. Mycology; Small Anim. Abstr. Bibliogr.

US
**VETERINARY BIOLOGICAL PRODUCTS. LICENSEES. VFOAT** Veterinary Biological Products. Licensees and Permittees. Periodical. English. sa. Free. US Department of Agriculture / Animal & Plant Health Inspection Service, 741 Federal Building 1, 6505 Belcres Road, Hyattsville MD 20782. **Tel** (301)436-7817. **Circ:** 700 (ctrl). ***Continues*** *Establishments Holding U.S. Veterinary Licenses to Produce Biological Products.*
**Desc:** Lists of all USDA licensed establishments, licenses, permittees as well as the biological products they are authorized to produce or import.

FR/1018-533X
**VETERINARY BIOTECHNOLOGY NEWSLETTER / OFFICE INTERNATIONAL DES EPIZOOTIES. Added/Corp** International Office of Epizootics. **VFOAT** Lettre d'Information sur la Biotechnologie Veterinaire. Vol. 1 (1991)-. Newsletter. English (French and Spanish). an. 40.00F. OIE - Office International des Epizooties, 12 rue de Prony, 75017 Paris France. **Tel** 011 33 1 4415 1888, FAX 011 33 1 42 67 09 87, telex EPIZOTI 642 285F. **NLM** W1; VE925.
**Desc:** Covers animal diseases and biological products.

UK/0042-4854
**VETERINARY BULLETIN (LONDON). See** Veterinary Sciences-Abstracting, Bibliographies and Statistics.

US
**VETERINARY CANCER SOCIETY, ... ANNUAL CONFERENCE. Main/Corp** Veterinary Cancer Society. Conference. Oct. 27-29 (1991)-. English. **NLM** W1; VE929C. ***Continues*** *Program & Abstracts.*

●US/1076-3872
**VETERINARY CLINICAL NUTRITION.** [Veterinary clin. nutr.]. Vol. 1, No. 1 (1994)-. Periodical. English. qt. $50.00 US; $60.00 Canada & Mexico; $75.00 other. Veterinary Practice Publishing Company, PO Box 4457, Santa Barbara CA 93140-4457. **Tel** (805)965-1028, FAX (805)965-0722. **DD** 636.
**Desc:** Practical and original editorial in all aspects of nutrition.

US/0275-6382
**VETERINARY CLINICAL PATHOLOGY.** (VETERINARY CLINICAL PATHOLOGY / AMERICAN SOCIETY FOR VETERINARY CLINICAL PATHOLOGY.). [Vet. clin. pathol.]. **Added/Corp** American Society for Veterinary Clinical Pathology. Vol. 6, No. 3 (Nov./Dec. 1977)-. Academic Scholarly Publication. English. qt. $50.00 US; $60.00 Canada & Mexico; $75.00 other. Veterinary Practice Publishing Company, PO Box 4457, Santa Barbara CA 93140-4457. **Tel** (805)965-1028, FAX (805)965-0722. **ED** A.H. Rebar. **DD** 636. **CODEN** VCPADJ. **Bk Rev. Ad Acc. Circ:** 1,500. Documents available from CASDDS. ***Continues*** *American Society of Veterinary Clinical Pathologists. Bulletin of the American Society of Veterinary Clinical Pathologists, 0147-0701.*
**Desc:** Official journal of the American Society for Veterinary Clinical Pathology.
**Ind/Abst** AGRICOLA [Full Cov.]; Chem. Abstr.; Dairy Sci. Abstr.; Index Vet.; Nutr. Abstr. Rev., Ser. B, Live Feeds and Feed.; Pig News Inf.; Protozoolog. Abstr.; Small Anim. Abstr. Bibliogr.; Vet. Bull.

US/0749-0739
**VETERINARY CLINICS OF NORTH AMERICA. EQUINE PRACTICE, THE.** [Vet. clin. North Am., Equine pract.]. **VFOAT** Equine Practice; Veterinary Clinics. Vol. 1, No. 1 (April 1985)-. Monographic series. English. tq. $79.00 (individual), $96.00 (institution) US; $110.00 (individual), $116.00 (institution) other. W.B. Saunders Company, A Subsidiary of Harcourt Brace Jovanovich, Inc., The Curtis Center/Suite 300, Independence Square West, Philadelphia PA 19106-3399. **Tel** (215)238-7800 or, 5587, FAX (215)238-7883, telex 173146. **(Subscription address:** W. B. Saunders Company / North America Subscriptions, c/o Periodicals, 6277 Sea Harbour Drive, 4th Floor, Orlando FL 32887.**) ED** Diane W. Zuckerman. **DD** 636. **NLM** W1; VE929F. **[CCC].** Index available. **Pr Rev. Circ:** 2,500. available on microfilm from University Microfilms International (UMI). Documents available from The Genuine Article. ***Continues in part*** *Veterinary Clinics of North America. Large Animal Practice, 0196-9846.*
**Ind/Abst** AgBiotech News Inf.; AGRICOLA [Full Cov.]; Anim. Breed. Abstr.; Curr. Contents, Agric. Biol. Environ. Sci.; Index Med. (1985-); Index Vet.; Res. Alert [Select. Cov.]; Rev. Med. Vet. Mycology; Vet. Bull.

US/0749-0720
**VETERINARY CLINICS OF NORTH AMERICA. FOOD ANIMAL PRACTICE, THE.** [Vet. clin. North Am., Food anim. pract.]. **VFOAT** Food Animal Practice; Veterinary Clinics. Vol. 1, No. 1 (March 1985)-. Monographic series. English. tq. $64.00 (individual), $77.00 (institution) US; $89.00 (individual), $94.00 (institution) other. W.B. Saunders Company, A Subsidiary of Harcourt Brace Jovanovich, Inc., The Curtis Center/Suite 300, Independence Square West, Philadelphia PA 19106-3399. **Tel** (215)238-7800 or, 5587, FAX (215)238-7883, telex 173146. **(Subscription address:** W. B. Saunders Company / North America Subscriptions, c/o Periodicals, 6277 Sea Harbour Drive, 4th Floor, Orlando FL 32887.**) ED** Diane Zuckerman. **DD** 636. **NLM** W1; VI929G. **[CCC].** Index available. **Pr Rev. Circ:** 2,000. available on microfilm from University Microfilms International (UMI). Documents available from The Genuine Article. ***Continues in part*** *Veterinary Clinics of North America. Large Animal Practice, 0196-9846.*
**Ind/Abst** AGRICOLA [Full Cov.]; Anim. Breed. Abstr.; Curr. Contents, Agric. Biol. Environ. Sci.; Dairy Sci. Abstr.; Grasslands For. Abstr.; Helminthol. Abstr. (1991-); Index Med. (1985-); Index Vet.; Nutr. Abstr. Rev., Ser. B, Live Feeds and Feed.; Pig News Inf.; Protozoolog. Abstr.; Res. Alert [Select. Cov.]; Rev. Agric. Entomol.; Rev. Med. Vet. Entomol.; Rev. Med. Vet. Mycology; Vet. Bull.

US/0195-5616
**VETERINARY CLINICS OF NORTH AMERICA. SMALL ANIMAL PRACTICE, THE.** [Vet. clin. North Am., Small anim. pract.]. **VFOAT** Small Animal Practice. Vol. 9, No. 1 (Feb. 1979)-. Monographic series. English. bm. $93.00 (individual), $111.00 (institution) US; $127.00 (individual), $135.00 (institution) other. W.B. Saunders Company, A Subsidiary of Harcourt Brace Jovanovich, Inc., The Curtis Center/Suite 300, Independence Square West, Philadelphia PA 19106-3399. **Tel** (215)238-7800 or, 5587, FAX (215)238-7883, telex 173146. **(Subscription address:** W. B. Saunders Company / North America Subscriptions, c/o Periodicals, 6277 Sea Harbour Drive, 4th Floor, Orlando FL 32887.**) NLM** W1 VE929S. **CODEN** VNAPDW. **[CCC]. Circ:** 6,000. available in hardback; available on microfilm and microfiche from University Microfilms International (UMI). Documents available from The Genuine Article, BIOSIS Document Express. ***Continues in part*** *Veterinary Clinics of North America, 0091-0279.*
**Desc:** Practical updates for the clinician on the latest advances plus topics of current interest. Illustrated.
**Ind/Abst** AGRICOLA [Full Cov.]; Anim. Breed. Abstr.; Biol. Abstr.; Curr. Contents, Agric. Biol. Environ. Sci.; EMBASE [Select. Cov.]; Energy Res. Abstr.; Helminthol. Abstr. (19??-19??); Index Med.; Index Vet.; Nutr. Abstr. Rev., Ser. B, Live Feeds and Feed.; Life Sci. Collect.; Protozoolog. Abstr.; Res. Alert [Full Cov.]; Rev. Agric. Entomol.; Rev. Med. Vet. Entomol.; Rev. Med. Vet. Mycology; Sci. Cit. Index; SCISEARCH; Small Anim. Abstr. Bibliogr.; Soc. Sci. Cit. Index [Select. Cov.]; Vet. Bull.

UK/0959-4493
**VETERINARY DERMATOLOGY.** [Vet. dermatol.]. **Added/Corp** European Society of Veterinary Dermatology. Vol. 1, No. 1 (Autumn 1989)-. Periodical. English. qt. $209.00 The Americas; £140.00 other. Pergamon Press, An Imprint of Elsevier Science Ltd., The Boulevard, Langford Lane, Kidlington, Oxford OX5 1GB United Kingdom. **Tel** 011 44 865 843000, 011 44 865 843699, FAX 011 44 865 843010. **(Subscription address:** Elsevier Science Ltd. Oxford Fulfillment Centre, PO Box 800, Kidlington, Oxford OX5 1DX United Kingdom.**) ED** David Lloyd and Carol Foil. **CODEN** VEDEEK. **[CCC]. Pr Rev.** available on microfilm and microfiche from University Microfilms International (UMI).
**Desc:** The study of dermatology over a wide variety of species serves as a unifying discipline for veterinarians and research scientists. The unique accessibility of the skin allows the ready demonstration of both gross and histological features, and makes an effective visual format essential.
**Ind/Abst** AGRICOLA [Full Cov.]; Helminthol. Abstr. (1991-); Index Vet.; Nutr. Abstr. Rev., Ser. B, Live Feeds and Feed.; Pig News Inf.; Rev. Med. Vet. Mycology; Small Anim. Abstr. Bibliogr.; Vet. Bull.

FR/1010-3538
**VETERINARY DRUG REGISTRATION NEWSLETTER.** (1988)-. Newsletter. English (French and Spanish). sa. 350.00F. OIE - Office International des Epizooties, 12 rue de Prony, 75017 Paris France. **Tel** 011 33 1 4415 1888, FAX 011 33 1 42 67 09 87, telex EPIZOTI 642 285F. **ED** J. Boisseau. **Circ:** 300.
**Desc:** Covers and latest developments in veterinary drugs.

US/0042-4862
**VETERINARY ECONOMICS.** [Vet. econ.]. (Oct. 1960)-. Periodical. English. Twelve times a year. $35.00 US; $50.00 Canada and Mexico; $70.00 other. Veterinary Medicine Publishing Co., 9073 Lenexa Drive, Lenexa KS 66215. **Tel** (913)492-4300, (800)255-6864, FAX (913)492-4157. **ED** Rebecca R. Turner. **DD** 636. **NLM** W1 VE93R. Index available. **Ad Acc. Circ:** 38,000 (ctrl). available on microfilm and microfiche from University Microfilms International (UMI).
**Desc:** Articles on management, finance, economics targeted to the veterinarian.
**Ind/Abst** Account. Tax Datab. (1974-) [Full Txt.]; AGRICOLA; Index Vet.; Rev. Med. Vet. Entomol.; Small Anim. Abstr. Bibliogr.

US/1047-6326
**VETERINARY FORUM.** [Vet. forum]. (198?)-. Periodical. English. mo. $35.00. Forum Publications, 1610-A Frederica Road, St Simons Island GA 31522-2509. **Tel** (912)638-4848. **DD** 636.
**Desc:** Ideas and services for practitioners by practitioners.

US
**VETERINARY HERITAGE: BULLETIN OF THE AMERICAN VETERINARY HISTORY SOCIETY. Added/Corp** American Veterinary History Society. Vol. 6, No. 1 (Nov. 1982)-. Bulletin. English. sa. $10.00 (libraries), $15.00 (individuals). Washington State University College of Veterinary Medicine, Pullman WA 99164-7010. **NLM** W1; VE931G. ***Continues*** *Newsletter (American Veterinary Historical Society).*

UK/0301-6943
**VETERINARY HISTORY. Added/Corp** Veterinary History Society (Great Britain). No. 1 (Summer 1973)-No. 12 (Winter 1978/79); New Series, Vol. 1 (Summer 1979)-. Periodical. English. sa (Published in Jan. & July). £4.00 (individuals), £6.00 (institutions) UK; £6.00 (individuals), £8.00 (institutions) other. Veterinary History Society, 32 Belgrave Square, London SW1X 8QP England. **ED** A. W. Johnson. **NLM** W1 VE931H. Index available. cum. index. **Bk Rev. Ad Acc. Circ:** 165.
**Desc:** All matters connected with history of veterinary art and science, livestock farming and related subjects.
**Ind/Abst** Index Vet.

NE/0165-2427
**VETERINARY IMMUNOLOGY AND IMMUNOPATHOLOGY.** [Vet. immunol. immunopathol.]. Vol. 1 (Nov. 1979)-. Academic Scholarly Publication. English. Twenty-four times a year (6 volumes). Fl2076.00. Elsevier Science Publishers BV, PO Box 211, 1000 AE Amsterdam Netherlands. **Tel** 011 31 20 5803642, FAX 011 31 20 5862696, telex 15682. **ED** J Goudswaard and R E W Halliwell. **NLM** W1 VE931HJ. **CODEN** VIIMDS. **[CCC]. Pr Rev.** available on microfilm and microfiche from University Microfilms International (UMI). Documents available from The Genuine Article, BIOSIS Document Express, CASDDS.
**Desc:** A scientific journal dealing with the study of veterinary immunology and immunopathology applied to domestic animals, laboratory animals and other species that are useful to man.
**Ind/Abst** AgBiotech News Inf.; AGRICOLA; Anim. Breed. Abstr.; Biol. Abstr.; Chem. Abstr.; Curr. Aware. Biol. Sci., CABS; Curr. Contents, Agric. Biol. Environ. Sci.; Curr. Contents Life Sci.; Dairy Sci. Abstr.; EMBASE; Fish Rev.; Genet. Abstr.; Helminthol. Abstr. (19??-19??); Immunol. Abstr.; Index Med.; Index Vet.; Microbiol. Abstr. Sect. B (19??-19??); Nutr. Abstr. Rev., Ser. B, Live Feeds and Feed.; Life Sci. Collect.; PESTDOC; Pig News Inf.; Poult. Abstr.; Protozoolog. Abstr.; Ref. Upd. Deluxe Ed.; Res. Alert [Full Cov.]; Rev. Med. Vet. Entomol.; Rev. Med. Vet. Mycology; Sci. Cit. Index; SCISEARCH; Small Anim. Abstr. Bibliogr.; Vet. Bull.; Virol. AIDS Abstr.

US/1042-1696
**VETERINARY MANAGEMENT UPDATE.** ***Title Change.*** [Vet. manage. update]. **Added/Corp** American Health Consultants. (1988)-(19??). Periodical. English. mo. American Health Consultants, 3525 Piedmont Road, Suite 400, Atlanta GA 30305. **Tel** (800)688-2421, (404)262-7436. **DD** 658. ***Continues*** *Procom Practice Marketing & Management, 0740-6983.* ***Continued by*** *Snyder Management Advisory.*

US/1059-0994
**VETERINARY MEDICAL REVIEW (COLUMBIA, MO.).** (VETERINARY MEDICAL REVIEW.). [Vet. med. rev.]. **Added/Corp** University of Missouri-Columbia. College of Veterinary Medicine. University of Missouri--Columbia. Cooperative Extension Service. **VFOAT** VMR; Missouri Veterinarian. No. 116, Jan./Feb. (1980). Periodical. English. sa. Free on request. Veterinary Medical Library, West 218 Veterinary Medicine, Columbia MO 65211. **Tel** (314)882-2461. **DD** 636. ***Continues*** *University of Missouri- Columbia. School of Veterinary Medicine. Faculty Newsletter.*; ***Absorbed*** *Missouri Veterinarian.*
**Ind/Abst** Index Vet. (19??-); Vet. Bull. (19??-).

US
**VETERINARY MEDICAL SCHOOL ADMISSION REQUIREMENTS IN THE UNITED STATES AND CANADA. / SPONSORED BY THE ASSOCIATION OF AMERICAN VETERINARY MEDICAL COLLEGES. Added/Corp** Association of American Veterinary Medical Colleges. (19??)-. English. an. $16.00. Betz Publishing Company Incorporated, PO Box 1745, Rockville MD 20849. **Tel** (800)634-4365, FAX

(301)340-0030. **ED** Eugenia Kelman, Ph.D. **LC** S533; .V47. **DD** 630/.7/1173.
**Desc:** Extensive information about each veterinary school to assist students in selecting the school or schools to which they want to apply. Physical description of school and application information, including enrollment and tuition rates.

US/8750-7943
**VETERINARY MEDICINE (1985).** (VETERINARY MEDICINE.). [Vet. med.]. Vol. 80, No. 1 (Jan. 1985)-. Periodical. English. Twelve times a year. $49.00 US; $57.95 Canada and Mexico; $78.95 other. Veterinary Medicine Publishing Co., 9073 Lenexa Drive, Lenexa KS 66215. **Tel** (913)492-4300, (800)255-6864, FAX (913)492-4157. **ED** Tracy Reulor. **DD** 636. **NLM** W1; VE933. **[CCC].** Index available. cum. index. **Bk Rev. Ad Acc. Pr Rev. Acid Free. Circ:** 24,000. available on microfilm and microfiche from University Microfilms International (UMI). Documents available from The Genuine Article. ***Continues*** *Veterinary Medicine, Small Animal Clinician, 0042-4889.*
**Desc:** Addresses troublesome diagnostic and therapeutic problems by providing clinical information. Each issue has symposia, photo essays, and case workups.
**Ind/Abst** AgBiotech News Inf.; AGRICOLA [Full Cov.]; Anim. Breed. Abstr.; Biol. Agric. Index; Curr. Contents, Agric. Biol. Environ. Sci.; Dairy Sci. Abstr.; Helminthol. Abstr. (19??-19??); Index Vet.; Maize Abstr.; Microbiol. Abstr. Sect. B (19??-19??); Nutr. Abstr. Rev., Ser. B, Live Feeds and Feed.; Life Sci. Collect.; PESTDOC (1985-); Pig News Inf.; Protozoolog. Abstr.; Res. Alert [Select. Cov.]; Rev. Med. Vet. Entomol.; Rev. Med. Vet. Mycology; Small Anim. Abstr. Bibliogr.; Vet. Bull.; Wildl. Rev.

US/0895-7703
**VETERINARY MEDICINE REPORT.** ***Ceased.*** [Vet. med. rep.]. (1988)-Ceased Vol. 2, No. 4. Periodical. English. qt. Mosby Year Book Inc., 11830 Westline Industrial Drive, St Louis MO 63146. **Tel** (800)325-4177, (314)872-8370, FAX (314)432-1380, telex 44-2402. **ED** John E Oliver. **NLM** W1; VE933D. **[CCC].** Index available.
**Desc:** Combines the depth of texts with the timeliness of journals in one convenient clinical resource. Provides a comprehensive analysis of three to four main topics drawn from the subspecialties of small animal medicine. Subspecialties covered include internal medicine, dermatology, surgery, ophthalmology, and dentistry.
**Ind/Abst** AGRICOLA [Full Cov.]; Index Vet.; Small Anim. Abstr. Bibliogr.

NE/0378-1135
**VETERINARY MICROBIOLOGY.** [Vet. microbiol.]. Vol. 1 (July 1976)-. Academic Scholarly Publication. English. Twenty times a year (5 vols.). Fl1805.00. Elsevier Science Publishers BV, PO Box 211, 1000 AE Amsterdam Netherlands. **Tel** 011 31 20 5803642, FAX 011 31 20 5862696, telex 15682. **ED** P B Spradbrow and A J Frost. **NLM** W1 VE933F. **CODEN** VMICDQ. **[CCC]. Pr Rev.** available on microfilm and microfiche from University Microfilms International (UMI). Documents available from The Genuine Article, BIOSIS Document Express, CASDDS, ADONIS.
**Desc:** Concerned with microbiological diseases of all animals that are useful to man. This includes animals that supply food or other products to mankind (livestock, poultry, game, fish, fur-bearing animals), animals living in captivity (in zoos or safari parks) and wild animals when these are of interest in the study of interrelationships of diseases in domesticated and wild animals.
**Ind/Abst** ADONIS; AgBiotech News Inf.; AGRICOLA; Biol. Abstr.; Chem. Abstr.; Curr. Contents, Agric. Biol. Environ. Sci.; Curr. Contents Life Sci.; Dairy Sci. Abstr.; EMBASE; Immunol. Abstr.; Index Med.; Index Vet.; Microbiol. Abstr. Sect. A; Life Sci. Collect.; PESTDOC; Pig News Inf.; Ref. Upd. Deluxe Ed.; Res. Alert [Full Cov.]; Rev. Agric. Entomol.; Rev. Med. Vet. Entomol.; Rev. Med. Vet. Mycology; Sci. Cit. Index; SCISEARCH; Small Anim. Abstr. Bibliogr.; Vet. Bull.; Virol. AIDS Abstr.; Wildl. Rev.

US/0360-1730
**VETERINARY NEWS (ALBANY).** ***Title Change.*** (VETERINARY NEWS.). **Added/Corp** New York State Veterinary Medical Society. Vol. 1 (1939)-. Periodical. English. sm. A E Morgan Publications Ltd, Stanley House, 9 West Street, Epsom Surrey KT18 7RL England. **Tel** 011 44 3727 41411, FAX 0372 744493, telex 291561 VIA SOS G. **NLM** W1 VE933Q. ***Continued by*** *Veterinary Practice, 0042-4897.*

UK
**VETERINARY NURSING JOURNAL.** **See** Medical Science and Technology-Nursing.

NE/0304-4017
**VETERINARY PARASITOLOGY.** [Vet. parasitol.]. Vol. 1 (June 1975)-. Academic Scholarly Publication. English. Twenty times a year (5 vols.). Fl1860.00. Elsevier Science Publishers BV, PO Box 211, 1000 AE Amsterdam Netherlands. **Tel** 011 31 20 5803642, FAX 011 31 20 5862696, telex 15682. **ED** S M Gaafar. **NLM** W1 VE933U. **CODEN** VPARDI. **[CCC]. Pr Rev.** available on microfilm and microfiche from University Microfilms International (UMI). Documents available from The Genuine Article, BIOSIS Document Express, CASDDS, ADONIS.
**Desc:** Concerned with those aspects of helminthology, protozoology and entomology which are of interest to animal health practitioners and others with a special interest in parasitology.
**Ind/Abst** ADONIS; AgBiotech News Inf.; Biocont. News Inf. (1991-); Biol. Abstr.; Chem. Abstr.; Curr. Contents, Agric. Biol. Environ. Sci.; Dairy Sci. Abstr.; EMBASE; Entomol. Abstr.; Helminthol. Abstr. (1991-); Immunol. Abstr.; Index Med.; Microbiol. Abstr. Sect. C; Nutr. Abstr. Rev., Ser. B, Live Feeds and Feed.; Life Sci. Collect.; PESTDOC; Pig News Inf.; Protozoolog. Abstr.; Res. Alert [Full Cov.]; Rev. Med. Vet. Entomol.; Sci. Cit. Index; SCISEARCH; Small Anim. Abstr. Bibliogr.; Trop. Dis. Bull.; Wildl. Rev.

US/0300-9858
**VETERINARY PATHOLOGY.** [Vet. pathol.]. **Added/Corp** American College of Veterinary Pathologists. Arbeitsgemeinschaft der Veterinarpathologen. Vol. 8 (1971)-. Academic Scholarly Publication. English (German). Six times a year. $107.00 US; $116.00 Canada and Mexico; $128.00 other. American College of Veterinary Pathology. **(Subscription address:** Veterinary Pathology, PO Box 1897, Lawrence KS 66044-8897.**) LC** SF769; .P34. **DD** 636.089/607/05. **NLM** W1 VE933V. **CODEN** VTPHAK. **Ad Acc. Pr Rev. Acid Free.** available on microfilm from University Microfilms International (UMI). Documents available from The Genuine Article, CASDDS. ***Continues*** *Pathologia Veterinaria, 0031-2975.*
**Desc:** Reports the latest scientific advances in veterinary pathology. It is the official publication of the American College of Veterinary Pathologists.
**Ind/Abst** AgBiotech News Inf.; AGRICOLA [Select. Cov.]; Anim. Breed. Abstr.; Calcium Calcif. Tissue Abstr.; Chem. Abstr.; CSA Neuro. Abstr. (?-?); Curr. Contents, Agric. Biol. Environ. Sci.; Curr. Contents Life Sci.; Dairy Sci. Abstr.; EMBASE [Select. Cov.]; Fish Rev.; Helminthol. Abstr. (1991-); Immunol. Abstr.; Index Med.; Index Vet.; Microbiol. Abstr. Sect. B (19??-19??); Microbiol. Abstr. Sect. C; Nutr. Abstr. Rev., Ser. B, Live Feeds and Feed.; Nutr. Abstr. Rev., Ser. A, Hum. Exp.; Life Sci. Collect.; PESTDOC; Pig News Inf.; Poult. Abstr.; Protozoolog. Abstr.; Ref. Upd. Basic Ed.; Ref. Upd. Deluxe Ed.; Res. Alert [Full Cov.]; Rev. Med. Vet. Entomol.; Rev. Med. Vet. Mycology; Sci. Cit. Index; SCISEARCH; Small Anim. Abstr. Bibliogr.; Vet. Bull.; Virol. AIDS Abstr.; Wildl. Rev.

US/0272-4669
**VETERINARY PHARMACEUTICALS & BIOLOGICALS.** (VETERINARY PHARMACEUTICALS & BIOLOGICALS : VPB.). [Vet. pharm. biol.]. **VFOAT** Veterinary Pharmaceuticals and Biologicals; VPB. (1981)-. English. be. $64.00 (two-year). Veterinary Medicine Publishing Co., 9073 Lenexa Drive, Lenexa KS 66215. **Tel** (913)492-4300, (800)255-6864, FAX (913)492-4157. **ED** Carl E. Aronson. **LC** SF917; .V49. **DD** 636.089/51. **NLM** SF 917 C737. ***Continues*** *Complete Desk Reference of Veterinary Pharmaceuticals & Biologicals (Media, Pa.).*

UK/0042-4897
**VETERINARY PRACTICE.** **VFOAT** VP, Veterinary Practice. Vol. 1 (Sept. 1969)-. Trade Publication. English. sm. £24.00. A E Morgan Publications Ltd, Stanley House, 9 West Street, Epsom Surrey KT18 7RL England. **Tel** 011 44 3727 41411, FAX 0372 744493, telex 291561 VIA SOS G. **ED** C. Cattrall. **Bk Rev. Ad Acc. Pub. Size:** Tabloid. **Circ:** 6,500 (ctrl). available on microfilm from University Microfilms International (UMI); available with charts; available with illustrations. ***Supersedes*** *Veterinary News, 0506-8282.*
**Ind/Abst** Dairy Sci. Abstr.; Index Vet.; Rev. Agric. Entomol.; Rev. Med. Vet. Entomol.; Small Anim. Abstr. Bibliogr.

UK/0268-9189
**VETERINARY PRACTICE MANAGEMENT (EPSOM AND EWELL, SURREY).** (VETERINARY PRACTICE MANAGEMENT.). (19??)-. Periodical. English. ir. A E Morgan Publications Ltd, Stanley House, 9 West Street, Epsom Surrey KT18 7RL England. **Tel** 011 44 3727 41411, FAX 0372 744493, telex 291561 VIA SOS G.

UK
**VETERINARY PRACTICE NURSE.** English. qt. £20.00. Targeted Bus Programmes Limited, 14 16 Peterbourough Road, London SW6 3BN England. **Tel** 011 44 71 7311335.

US/1047-8639
**VETERINARY PRACTICE STAFF.** [Vet. pract. staff]. Vol. 1, No. 1 (Sept. 1989)-. Periodical. English. bm. $28.00 US; $35.00 Canada and Mexico; $45.00 other. Veterinary Practice Publishing Company, PO Box 4457, Santa Barbara CA 93140-4457. **Tel** (805)965-1028, FAX (805)965-0722. **DD** 636.
**Desc:** Current ideas and new information for the employees of the veterinary clinic.
**Ind/Abst** Soc. Sci. Cit. Index [Select. Cov.].

NE/0165-2176
**VETERINARY QUARTERLY, THE.** [Vet. q.]. **Added/Corp** Koninklijke Nederlandse Maatschappij voor Diergeneeskunde. Vol. 1 (Jan. 1979)-. Academic Scholarly Publication. English. qt. $221.00. Kluwer Academic Publishers, Postbus 322, 3300 AH Dordrecht, The Netherlands. **Tel** 011 (31) 78 524400, FAX 011 31 78 183273, telex 20083. **ED** W.B. Sybesma. **NLM** W1 VE9332F. **CODEN** VEQUDU. **[CCC]. Ad Acc. Pr Rev. Acid Free. Circ:** 1,000. available on microfilm and microfiche from University Microfilms International (UMI). Documents available from The Genuine Article, BIOSIS Document Express, CASDDS. ***Supersedes in part*** *Tijdschrift Voor Diergeneeskunde.*
**Desc:** Publishes papers on all aspects of veterinary science. Also bridges the ever-widening gap between veterinary practice and the specializations by publishing the results of applied veterinary research.
**Ind/Abst** AgBiotech News Inf.; AGRICOLA; Anim. Breed. Abstr.; Biol. Abstr.; Chem. Abstr.; Curr. Contents, Agric. Biol. Environ. Sci.; Dairy Sci. Abstr.; EMBASE [Select. Cov.]; Fish Rev.; Food Sci. Technol. Abstr.; Helminthol. Abstr. (19??-19??); Index Med.; Index Vet.; Nutr. Abstr. Rev., Ser. B, Live Feeds and Feed.; Life Sci. Collect.; PESTDOC; Pig News Inf.; Poult. Abstr.; Protozoolog. Abstr.; Ref. Upd. Deluxe Ed.; Res. Alert [Full Cov.]; Rev. Med. Vet. Entomol.; Sci. Cit. Index; SCISEARCH; Small Anim. Abstr. Bibliogr.; Soc. Sci. Cit. Index [Select. Cov.]; Vet. Bull.; Wildl. Rev.

●US/1058-8183
**VETERINARY RADIOLOGY & ULTRASOUND.** (VETERINARY RADIOLOGY & ULTRASOUND: THE OFFICIAL JOURNAL OF THE AMERICAN COLLEGE OF VETERINARY RADIOLOGY AND THE INTERNATIONAL VETERINARY RADIOLOGY ASSOCIATION.). [Vet. radiol. ultrasound]. **Added/Corp** American College of Veterinary Radiology. International Veterinary Radiology Association. **VFOAT** Veterinary Radiology and Ultrasound. Vol. 33, No. 1 (Jan./Feb. 1992)-. Periodical. English. bm. $72.00 (individual), $92.00 (institution) US; $82.00 (individual), $102.00 (institution) other. Veterinary Radiology, 2520 Beechridge Road, North Carolina State Univeraity, Raleigh NC 27608. **Tel** (919)881-4165, FAX (919)821-9578. **ED** Donald E. Thrall. **LC** SF757.8; .A4; SF757.8; .A4. **DD** 636.089/60757/05; 636. **NLM** W1; VE9332JF. **CODEN** VRULED. **Ad Acc, Adv Mgr:** L. Ayres. **Pr Rev. Circ:** 1,000 (ctrl). Documents available from The Genuine Article, BIOSIS Document Express. ***Continues*** *Veterinary Radiology, 0196-3627.*
**Desc:** The most cost effective way to stay abreast of the ever advancing radiographic technologies. Devoted to veterinary imaging and radiotherapeutic technologies.
**Ind/Abst** AGRICOLA; Biol. Abstr.; Curr. Contents, Agric. Biol. Environ. Sci.; Life Sci. Collect.; Res. Alert [Full Cov.]; Sci. Cit. Index; SCISEARCH.

UK/0042-4900
**VETERINARY RECORD.** (THE VETERINARY RECORD : JOURNAL OF THE BRITISH VETERINARY ASSOCIATION.). [Vet. rec.]. **Added/Corp** British Veterinary Association. Vol. 1 (1888/89)-. Academic Scholarly Publication. English (Spanish). Fifty-one times per year. £111.00 UK; £130.00 Africa; £154.00 other. TG Scott Subscriber Services, 6 Bourne Enterprise Center, Wrotham Road, Borough Green, Kent TN15 8DG England. **Tel** 011 44 01 732 884023, FAX 011 44 01 732 884034. **ED** Martin Alder. **NLM** W1 VE934. **CODEN** VETRAX. **[CCC].** Index available. **Bk Rev. Ad Acc. Pr Rev. Circ:** 10,500. available on microfilm and microfiche from University Microfilms International (UMI). Documents available from The Genuine Article, CASDDS. ***Supersedes*** *Veterinary Record and Transactions of the Veterinary Medical Association.*
**Desc:** Contains comprehensive coverage of clinical, professional and political topics. Includes lively news, comments and letters sections.
**Ind/Abst** AgBiotech News Inf.; AGRICOLA [Full Cov.]; Agric. Eng. Abstr. (1991-); Anim. Breed. Abstr.; Biol. Agric. Index; Chem. Abstr.; CSA Neuro. Abstr. (?-?); Curr. Contents, Agric. Biol. Environ. Sci.; Dairy Sci. Abstr.; EMBASE [Select. Cov.]; Fish Rev.; Grasslands For. Abstr.; Helminthol. Abstr. (19??-19??); Hortic. Abstr.; Index Med.; Microbiol. Abstr. Sect. B (19??-19??); Microbiol. Abstr. Sect. A; Microbiol. Abstr. Sect. C; Nutr. Abstr. Rev., Ser. B, Live Feeds and Feed.; Ornamental Hort. (1991-); Life Sci. Collect.; PESTDOC; Pig News Inf.; Poult. Abstr.; Protozoolog. Abstr.; Ref. Upd. Basic Ed.; Ref. Upd. Deluxe Ed.; Res. Alert [Full Cov.]; Rev. Agric. Entomol.; Rev. Med. Vet. Entomol.; Rev. Med. Vet. Mycology; Sci. Cit. Index; SCISEARCH; Small Anim. Abstr. Bibliogr.; Soc. Sci. Cit. Index [Select. Cov.]; Virol. AIDS Abstr.; Wildl. Rev.

US
**VETERINARY REGISTER.** **Added/Corp** Indiana. State Board of Veterinary Medical Examiners. (1973)-. English. be. Indiana State Board of Veterinary Medical Examiners, 700 North High School Road, Suite 200, Indianapolis IN 46224. **LC** SF624.I64; A35. **DD** 636.089/025/772. ***Continues*** *Indiana. State Board of Veterinary Medical Examiners. List of Graduate Licensed Veterinarians Registered in Indiana.*

US
**VETERINARY REPORTS.** **Added/Corp** Solvay Veterinary. Vol. 1, No. 1 (1988)-. Periodical. English. Veterinary Learning Systems, 425 Phillips Boulevard 100, Trneton NJ 08618. **Tel** (609)882-5600, (800)426-9119. ***Continues*** *Dermatology Reports.*
**Ind/Abst** Index Vet.; Pig News Inf.

●FR/0928-4249
**VETERINARY RESEARCH.** **Added/Corp** Institut National de la Recherche Agronomique (France).

Vol. 24, No. 1 (1993)-. Academic Scholarly Publication. English (French). bm. 1235.00F France; 1505.00F other. Editions Scientifique Elsevier, 141 rue de Javel, 75747 Paris Cedex 15 France. **Tel** 011 33 1 47 07 11 22, FAX 011 33 1 43 36 80 93. **(Subscription address:** Editions Scientifiques Elsevier / for North America, PO Box 7247-7576, Philadelphia PA 19170-7576.**)** **ED** J. Charley-Poulain & J. Laporte. **NLM** W1; VE934J. **CODEN** VEREEM. ***Continues*** *Annales de Recherches Veterinaires, 0003-4193.*
**Desc:** Covers all aspects of veterinary and comparative medicine and related subjects.
**Ind/Abst** Sci. Cit. Index.

NE/0165-7380
**VETERINARY RESEARCH COMMUNICATIONS.** [Vet. res. commun.]. Vol. 4, No. 2 (Aug. 1980)-. Academic Scholarly Publication. English. bm. $436.00. Kluwer Academic Publishers, Postbus 322, 3300 AH Dordrecht, The Netherlands. **Tel** 011 (31) 78 524400, FAX 011 31 78 183273, telex 20083. **ED** M M H Sewell. **NLM** W1 VE934M. **CODEN** VRCODX. **[CCC]. Pr Rev. Acid Free.** available on microfilm and microfiche from University Microfilms International (UMI). Documents available from The Genuine Article, BIOSIS Document Express, CASDDS. ***Continues*** *Veterinary Science Communications, 0378-4312.*
**Desc:** Publishes research articles and topical reviews on all aspects of the veterinary sciences which are meant for an international audience.
**Ind/Abst** AgBiotech News Inf.; Agric. Eng. Abstr. (1991-); Biol. Abstr.; Chem. Abstr.; Curr. Contents, Agric. Biol. Environ. Sci.; Dairy Sci. Abstr.; EMBASE [Select. Cov.]; Fish Rev.; Helminthol. Abstr. (19??-19??); Index Med.; Index Vet.; Nutr. Abstr. Rev., Ser. B, Live Feeds and Feed.; Life Sci. Collect.; PESTDOC; Pig News Inf.; Poult. Abstr.; Protozoolog. Abstr.; Res. Alert [Full Cov.]; Rev. Med. Vet. Entomol.; Rev. Med. Vet. Mycology; Sci. Cit. Index; SCISEARCH; Small Anim. Abstr. Bibliogr.; Vet. Bull.; Virol. AIDS Abstr.; Wildl. Rev.; World Agric. Econ.

AT
**VETERINARY REVIEW (SYDNEY, N.S.W.).** (VETERINARY REVIEW.). **Added/Corp** University of Sydney. Post-Graduate Foundation in Veterinary Science. **VFOAT** A.Review. (19??)-. Proceedings. English. ir. Price varies per volume. University of Sydney / Veterinary Science, Post-Graduate Foundation in Veterinary Science, Suite 93/Lincoln House, 280 Pitt Street, Sydney 2000 New South Wales Australia. **Tel** 02 264 2122, FAX 61 2 261 4620. **NLM** W1; VE934P. **Bk Rev**, (Qty: 2).
**Ind/Abst** Index Vet.

US
**VETERINARY SCOPE.** Vol. 1 (1954)-. Periodical. English. ir. Free. Upjohn Co, 7000 Portage Road, Kalamazoo MI 48008. **Tel** (616)323-4000. **ED** Ronald A Miller. **Circ:** 35,000 (ctrl).
**Desc:** Newsletter concerning practical veterinary medicine topics, veterinary pharmaceutical research and development; issued twice annually; readers include practicing veterinarians, veterinary educators and students.

US/0161-3499
**VETERINARY SURGERY.** [Vet. surg.]. **VFOAT** VS. Vol. 7 (Jan./March 1978)-. Periodical. English. bm. $91.00 (US), $106.00 (other) individual; $125.00 (US), $153.00 (other) institution. W.B. Saunders Company, A Subsidiary of Harcourt Brace Jovanovich, Inc., The Curtis Center/Suite 300, Independence Square West, Philadelphia PA 19106-3399. **Tel** (215)238-7800 or, 5587, FAX (215)238-7883, telex 173146. **(Subscription address:** W. B. Saunders Company / North America Subscriptions, c/o Periodicals, 6277 Sea Harbour Drive, 4th Floor, Orlando FL 32887.**)** **ED** Colin E. Harvey. **LC** SF911. **DD** 636.089/7/005. **NLM** W1 VE938C. **CODEN** VESUD6. **[CCC]. Bk Rev. Ad Acc. Pr Rev. Circ:** 2,023. available on microfilm from University Microfilms International (UMI). Documents available from The Genuine Article, BIOSIS Document Express. ***Continues*** *Journal of Veterinary Surgery;* ***Absorbed*** *Veterinary Anesthesia, 0149-3949.*
**Desc:** Publishes up-to-the-minute reports on clinical and research topics of special interest to veterinary surgeons and anesthesiologists.
**Ind/Abst** AGRICOLA [Full Cov.]; Biol. Abstr.; Curr. Contents, Agric. Biol. Environ. Sci.; Index Med.; Index Vet.; Pig News Inf.; Poult. Abstr.; Res. Alert [Full Cov.]; Sci. Cit. Index; SCISEARCH; Small Anim. Abstr. Bibliogr.; Vet. Bull.; Wildl. Rev.

US/8750-8990
**VETERINARY TECHNICIAN.** [Vet. tech.]. Vol. 5, No. 1 (Jan./Feb. 1984)-. Periodical. English. mo (except Jan./Feb. and Nov./Dec. combined). $48.00 (institution), $35.00 (individual) US; $58.00 (institution), $42.00 (individual) Canada & Mexico; $63.00 (institution), $49.00 (individual) other. Veterinary Learning Systems, 425 Phillips Boulevard 100, Trenton NJ 08618. **Tel** (609)882-5600, (800)426-9119. **ED** Richard B. Ford. **DD** 636. Index available (Bound in last issue). **Bk Rev. Ad Acc. Circ:** 8,000. ***Continues*** *Animal Health Technician, 0733-6004.*
**Desc:** Reviewed articles and features covering various aspects of veterinary medicine as it applies to veterinary staff.
**Ind/Abst** Acad. Search (Jan. 1993-); Anim. Breed. Abstr. (19??-); Helminthol. Abstr. (19??-19??); Index Vet. (19??-); INFO-SOUTH Abstr. (19??-); Mag. Search (19??-); Nutr. Abstr. Rev., Ser. B, Live Feeds and Feed. (19??-); Protozoolog. Abstr. (19??-); Rev. Med. Vet. Entomol. (19??-); Rev. Med. Vet. Mycology (19??-); Small Anim. Abstr. Bibliogr. (19??-); Vet. Bull. (19??-); Vocat. Search (Jan. 1993-).

UK/1352-9374
**VETERINARY TIMES.** Vol. 14, No. 9 (Sept. 1984)-. Periodical. English. mo. £45.00 UK; £59.00 other. Veterinary Business Development Ltd., Olympus House, Werrington Centre, Peterborough PE4 6NA England. **Tel** 011 44 733 325522, FAX 011 44 733 325512. **ED** David Ritchie. **Bk Rev**, (Qty: varies). **Ad Acc, Adv Mgr:** Trisha Anderson, **Tel** same as publisher. **Acid Free. Circ:** 9,300 (ctrl). ***Continues*** *Veterinary Drug.*
**Desc:** For veterinary surgeons in practice.
**Ind/Abst** Index Vet.; Small Anim. Abstr. Bibliogr.

US
**VETERINARY UPDATE.** English. qt. $112.00 US; $138.00 other (small animal and large animal); $189.00 US; $232.00 other (mixed practice). American Veterinary Publishing Company, 5782 Thornwood Drive, Goleta CA 93117. **Tel** (805)967-5988.

●US/1059-8456
**VETERINARY UPDATE (LARGE ANIMALS).** (VETERINARY UPDATE : CLINICAL ABSTRACT SERVICE.). [Vet. update]. Vol. 33, No. 1 (Jan./Feb./Mar. 1992)-. Periodical. English. qt. American Veterinary Publications, 5782 Thronwood Drive, Goleta CA 93117. **DD** 636. ***Formed by the union of*** *Veterinary Update (Large Animals (Food))* ***and*** *Veterinary Update (Large Animals (Equine)).*

TU/0003-3685
**VETERINER FAKULTESI DERGISI.** Vol. 1 (1954)-. Periodical. Turkish (English, French and German). qt. Ankara Universitesi, Veteriner Fakultesi Dekanligi, Ankara Turkey. **NLM** W1 VE938E. **CODEN** VTFDAQ.
**Ind/Abst** Anim. Breed. Abstr.; Biodeter. Abstr. (1991-); Dairy Sci. Abstr.; Helminthol. Abstr. (1991-); Index Vet.; Nutr. Abstr. Rev., Ser. B, Live Feeds and Feed.; Poult. Abstr.; Protozoolog. Abstr.; Rev. Med. Vet. Entomol.; Rev. Med. Vet. Mycology; Small Anim. Abstr. Bibliogr.; Vet. Bull.

TU/1011-2057
**VETERINER FAKULTESI DERGISI. SELCUK UNIVERSITESI.** [Vet. Fakult. derg., Selcuk Univ.]. **VFOAT** Journal of the Faculty of Veterinary Medicine. University of Selcuk. (1985)-. Periodical. Turkish. ir.
**Ind/Abst** Biodeter. Abstr.; Index Vet.; Nutr. Abstr. Rev., Ser. B, Live Feeds and Feed.; Protozoolog. Abstr.; Rev. Med. Vet. Mycology; Small Anim. Abstr. Bibliogr.; Vet. Bull.

TU/0377-6395
**VETERINER HEKIMLER DERNEGI DERGISI. VFOAT** Acta Veterinaria Turcica. 1974-. Periodical. Turkish. **NLM** W1 VE938F. ***Continues*** *Turk Veteriner Hekimleri Dernegi Dergisi, 0376-8104.*
**Ind/Abst** Index Vet.

BE/0303-9021
**VLAAMS DIERGENEESKUNDIG TIJDSCHRIFT.** [Vlaams diergeneeskd. tijdschr.]. **VFOAT** Flemish Veterinary Journal. Vol. 1 (July 1931)-. Academic Scholarly Publication. Dutch (Flemish; summaries and/or abstracts in English). bm. 700F (individuals), 400F (students) Belgium; 1000F other. Vlaams Diergeneeskundig Tijds, Casinoplein 24, B-9000 Gent Belgium. **Tel** 091/23 37 65, FAX 091/33 22 34. **ED** P Simoens. **NLM** W1 VL21. **CODEN** VDTIAX. Index available. **Bk Rev. Ad Acc. Pr Rev. Circ:** 1,500 (ctrl). Documents available from The Genuine Article, CASDDS.
**Desc:** The journal publishes original and review articles on different aspects of veterinary medicine, meat inspection included. All animal species are treated.
**Ind/Abst** AgBiotech News Inf.; AGRICOLA; Anim. Breed. Abstr.; Chem. Abstr.; Curr. Contents, Agric. Biol. Environ. Sci.; Dairy Sci. Abstr.; Grasslands For. Abstr.; Helminthol. Abstr. (19??-19??); Nutr. Abstr. Rev., Ser. B, Live Feeds and Feed.; Life Sci. Collect.; PESTDOC; Pig News Inf.; Poult. Abstr.; Protozoolog. Abstr.; Res. Alert [Select. Cov.]; Rev. Med. Vet. Entomol.; Rev. Med. Vet. Mycology; Small Anim. Abstr. Bibliogr.

GW/0341-9851
**VMR; VETERINARY MEDICAL REVIEW.** [VMR, vet. med. rev.]. **VFOAT** Veterinary Medical Review. Vol. 1 (1976)-. Academic Scholarly Publication. English. sa. N G Elwert Verlag, Postfach 1128, Reitgasse 7+9, W-3550 Marburg Germany. **Tel** 06421 25023, FAX 06421 15487. **CODEN** VVMRDI. Documents available from CASDDS. ***Continues*** *Veterinary Medical Review, 0506-8274.*
**Ind/Abst** AGRICOLA [Full Cov.]; Chem. Abstr.; Helminthol. Abstr. (1991-); Index Vet.; Life Sci. Collect.; PESTDOC; Poult. Abstr.; Protozoolog. Abstr.; Small Anim. Abstr. Bibliogr.

UK/0964-7082
**WALTHAM INTERNATIONAL FOCUS.** [Walth. int. focus]. **Added/Corp** Waltham Centre for Pet Nutrition. **VFOAT** Focus; Waltham Focus. Vol. 1, No. 1 (1991)-. Periodical. English. qt.

TH/0125-6491
**WETCHASAN SATTAWAPHAET. Added/Corp** Chulalongkonmahawitthayalai. Khana SattawaphAaetsat. **VFOAT** Thai Journal of Veterinary Medicine. (19??)-. Periodical. Thai. qt. **CODEN** TJVMDA. Documents available from CASDDS.
**Ind/Abst** Chem. Abstr.; Helminthol. Abstr. (1991-); Hortic. Abstr.; Index Vet.; Pig News Inf.; Poult. Abstr.; Protozoolog. Abstr.; Small Anim. Abstr. Bibliogr.; Vet. Bull.

AU/0043-535X
**WIENER TIERARZTLICHE MONATSSCHRIFT.** ***Title Change.*** [Wien. Tierarztl. Monatsschr.]. Vol. 1 (1914)-. Periodical. German. mo. Ostag/Oesterr Anzeigengesellschaft, Postfach 16, Wickenburggasse, 1011 Vienna Austria. **Tel** (02082)2317-0. **UDC** 619. **NLM** W1 WI41. **CODEN** WTMOA3. **Bk Rev. Ad Acc.** Documents available from The Genuine Article, CASDDS. ***Continues*** *Tierarztliche Zeitschrift, 0371-7569.* ***Merged with*** *Deutsche Tierarztliche Wochenschrift; Berliner und Munchener Tierarztlicher Wochenschrift* ***and*** *Tierarztliche Rundschau* ***to form*** *Tierarztliche Zeitschrift.*
**Ind/Abst** AgBiotech News Inf.; AGRICOLA; Anim. Breed. Abstr.; Chem. Abstr.; Curr. Contents, Agric. Biol. Environ. Sci.; Dairy Sci. Abstr.; Food Sci. Technol. Abstr.; Helminthol. Abstr.; Key Word Index Wildl. Res.; Nutr. Abstr. Rev., Ser. B, Live Feeds and Feed.; Nutr. Abstr. Rev., Ser. A, Hum. Exp.; Life Sci. Collect.; PESTDOC; Pig News Inf.; Postharvest News Inf.; Poult. Abstr.; Protozoolog. Abstr.; Res. Alert [Full Cov.]; Rev. Med. Vet. Entomol.; Rev. Med. Vet. Mycology; Sci. Cit. Index; SCISEARCH; Small Anim. Abstr. Bibliogr.

US
**WILDLIFE DISEASE NEWSLETTER. Added/Corp** Wildlife Disease Association. (19??)-. Periodical. English. $70.00 (includes Journal of Wildlife Diseases). Wildlife Disease Association, PO Box 886, Ames IA 50010. **Tel** (515)233-1931.
**Ind/Abst** Helminthol. Abstr.

US/0736-6094
**WILDLIFE DISEASE REVIEW.** ***Suspended.*** [Wildl. dis. rev.]. Vol. 1, No. 1 (1983)-. Periodical. English. mo. $195.00. Wildlife Disease Review, PO Box 8938, Fort Collins CO 80525. **LC** Z6674; .W55; SF996.4.

US
**WISCONSIN REGISTERED LICENSED VETERINARIANS. BULLETIN.** Bulletin. English. sa. $2.00. Department of Regulation and Licensing / Wisconsin, 1400 East Washington Avenue, Madison WI 53702. **LC** SF611; .W5. **DD** 636/.089/025775. **NLM** SF 25 W811. ***Continues*** *Wisconsin Registered Licensed Veterinarians. Bulletin.*

NE
**WORLD ANIMAL SCIENCE. B, DISCIPLINARY APPROACH. VFOAT** Disciplinary Approach. 1-. Monographic series. English. Price varies per volume.

CH/0257-5574
**XUMU SHOUYI XUEBAO.** [Xumu shouyi xuebao]. **VFOAT** Journal of the Animal Husbandry Veterinary Medical Association. (1969)-. Periodical. Multiple languages. ir.
**Ind/Abst** NAPRALERT.

JA/0388-9335
**YAMAGUCHI JUIGAKU ZASSHI. VFOAT** Yamaguchi Journal of Veterinary Medicine. No. 1 (Jan. 1974)-. Periodical. Japanese (English and German; summaries and/or abstracts in English). Yamaguchiken Jui Gakkai, 1080-3 Higashi Kurashiki 3 chome, Ogorimachi, Yoshikigun, Yamaguchiken 754 Japan.
**Ind/Abst** Helminthol. Abstr. (1991-); Index Vet.

US/0192-5210
**YANKEE HORSETRADER.** ***Ceased.*** **See** Horses and Horsemanship.

US/0044-0612
**YORKSHIRE JOURNAL.** ***Title Change.*** **Added/Corp** American Yorkshire Club. (1???)-(19??). Periodical. English. mo. American Yorkshire Club Inc, 1769 US 52 North Box 2417, West Lafayette IN 47906. **Tel** (317)463-3593. **ED** Darrell D. Anderson. Index available. **Ad Acc. Circ:** 3,000 (ctrl). ***Merged into*** *Seedstock Edge.*
**Desc:** Provides information for Yorkshire breeders to help breed and improve the Yorkshire breed.

●US/1078-0343
**YOUR DOG.** (YOUR DOG / TUFTS UNIVERSITY SCHOOL OF MEDICINE.). [Your dog]. **Added/Corp** Tufts University School of Medicine. July (1994)-. Periodical. English. mo (12 issues). $16.00. Tufts University / School of Veterinary Medicine, North Grafton MA 01536. **Tel** (508)839-5302, (800)829-0926. **DD** 636.

XV/0353-8044
**ZBORNIK VETERINARSKE FAKULTETE, UNIVERZA LJUBLJANA.** [Zb. Vet. fak. Univ. Ljublj.]. **Added/Corp** Univerza v Ljubljani. Veterinarska Fakulteta. **VFOAT** Research Reports, Veterinary Faculty, University Ljubljana. (1990)-. Periodical. Slovenian (summaries and/or abstracts in English; table of contents in English). sm. ***Continues*** *Zbornik Biotehniske Fakultete Univerze Edvarda Kardelja v Ljubljani. Veterinarstvo, 0300-0362.*
**Ind/Abst** Fish Rev. (Jan. 1989-July 1992); Index Vet.; Pig News Inf.; Poult. Abstr.; Small Anim. Abstr. Bibliogr.; Vet. Bull.; Wildl. Rev. (Jan. 1989-July 1992).

GW/0514-7158
**ZENTRALBLATT FUER VETERINARMEDIZIN. REIHE A.** ***Title Change.*** [Zentralbl. veterinarmed., Reihe A]. **VFOAT** Journal of Veterinary Medicine. Series A. Vol. 10 (Jan. 1963)-(19??). Academic Scholarly Publication. English (German, French and Spanish). Ten times a year. Blackwell Wissenschafts-Verlag, Kurfuerstendamm 57, D 10707 Berlin Germany. **Tel** 011 49 30 32790623, 011 49 30 32790624, FAX 011 49 30 327 90610. **ED** A Mayr, E Scharrer H Spoerri and E G White. **NLM** W1 ZE799B. **CODEN** ZVRAAX. Index available. cum. index. **Bk Rev. Ad Acc. Circ:** 2,500. Documents available from BIOSIS Document Express, CASDDS. ***Supersedes in part*** *Zentralblatt fur Veterinarmedizin, 0044-4294.* ***Continued by*** *Journal of Veterinary Medicine. Series A, 0931-184X.*
**Desc:** Animal physiology, pathology and clinical veterinary medicine.
**Ind/Abst** AGRICOLA; Agric. Eng. Abstr.; Biol. Abstr.; Chem. Abstr. (1963-1985)(19??-); Curr. Contents, Agric. Biol. Environ. Sci.; Curr. Contents Life Sci.; EMBASE [Select. Cov.]; Energy Res. Abstr.; Fish Rev. (19??-199?); Helminthol. Abstr. (1991-); Index Med.; Life Sci. Collect.; PESTDOC; Pig News Inf.; Poult. Abstr.; Small Anim. Abstr. Bibliogr.; Wildl. Rev. (19??-199?).

PL/0137-1975
**ZESZYTY NAUKOWE. WETERYNARIA.** [Zesz. nauk. Akad. roln. Wroc., Wet.]. **Main/Corp** Akademia Rolnicza We Wrocawiu. **VFOAT** Weterynaria. Vol. 34 (1976)-. Periodical. Polish (summaries and/or abstracts in English and Russian). Panstwowe Wydawn Naukowe, Miodowa 10, PO Box 391, 00251 Warsaw Poland. ***Continues*** *Zeszyty Naukowe. Weterynaria.*
**Ind/Abst** AGRICOLA; Poult. Abstr.; Protozoolog. Abstr.

BU/0514-7441
**ZHIVOTNOVUDNI NAUKI.** [Zhivotn. nauki]. **Added/Corp** Akademiia na Selskostopanskite Nauki. **VFOAT** Animal Science. (1964)-. Bulgarian (summaries and/or abstracts in English, German and Russian). Eight times a year. DM200.00. **(Subscription address:** Kubon & Sagner, ABT Zeitschriftenimport, D 80328 Munich Germany.**) LC** SF1; .Z46. **CODEN** ZHVNAS. Documents available from BIOSIS Document Express, CASDDS.
**Ind/Abst** AGRICOLA; Biol. Abstr.; Chem. Abstr.; EMBASE; Index Vet.; Nutr. Abstr. Rev., Ser. B, Live Feeds and Feed.; Nutr. Abstr. Rev., Ser. A, Hum. Exp.; Rice Abstr.; Sorghum Mill. Abstr.; Vet. Bull.

CH/1000-6419
**ZHONGGUO SHOUYI KE-JI.** **VFOAT** Chinese Journal of Veterinary Science and Technology. (1971)-. Periodical. Chinese. mo. **DD** 636.089.
**Ind/Abst** Index Vet.; Poult. Abstr.; Protozoolog. Abstr.; Rev. Med. Vet. Mycology; Vet. Bull.

CC/0529-6005
**ZHONGGUO SHOUYI ZAZHI.** (CHUNG-KUO SHOU I TSA CHIH.). [Zhongguo shouyi zazhi]. **Added/Corp** Chung-kuo hsu mu shou i Hsueh hui. **VFOAT** Chinese Journal of Veterinary Medicine. (19??)-. Periodical. Chinese. mo. $16.21. **(Subscription address:** China International Book Trading Corporation, PO Box 399, Library Service Department, Beijing 100044 People's Republic of China.**) LC** SF604; .C48. **DD** 636.089/05. **CODEN** ZSZAEM. Documents available from CASDDS.
**Ind/Abst** Biodeter. Abstr.; Chem. Abstr. (1986-); Helminthol. Abstr.; Index Vet.; Nutr. Abstr. Rev., Ser. B, Live Feeds and Feed.; Pig News Inf.; Poult. Abstr.; Protozoolog. Abstr.; Rev. Med. Vet. Entomol.; Rev. Med. Vet. Mycology; Vet. Bull.

CC/0258-7033
**ZHONGGUO XUMU ZAZHI.** (CHUNG-KUO HSU MU TSA CHIH.). [Zhongguo xumu zazhi]. **VFOAT** Chinese Journal of Animal Science; Zhongguo Xumu Zazhi. (1963)-. Academic Scholarly Publication. Chinese (summaries and/or abstracts in English). bm. **(Subscription address:** China International Book Trading Corporation, PO Box 399, Library Service Department, Beijing 100044 People's Republic of China.**) CODEN** ZXZADM. Documents available from CASDDS.
**Ind/Abst** Chem. Abstr.; Index Vet.; Poult. Abstr.; Soyabean Abstr.

CH/0253-9179
**ZHONGHUA MINGUO SHOUYI XUEHUI ZAZHI.** (CHUNG-HUA MIN KUO SHOU I HSUEH HUI TSA CHIH.). [Zhonghua minguo shouyi xuehui zazhi]. **Main/Corp** Chung-Hua Min Kuo Shou i Hsueh Hui. **Added/Corp** Chung-hua min kuo shou i Hsueh hui. Journal of the Chinese Society of Veterinary Science. **VFOAT** Journal of the Chinese Society of Veterinary Science. Vol. 1 (April 1975)-. Academic Scholarly Publication. Chinese (English). qt. $40.00. Chinese Society of Veterinary Science, 142 Chou San Road, Taipei, 107 Taiwan. **(Subscription address:** China International Book Trading Corporation, PO Box 399, Library Service Department, Beijing 100044 People's Republic of China.**) CODEN** CKSCDN. Documents available from BIOSIS Document Express, CASDDS.
**Ind/Abst** Biol. Abstr. (1985-); Chem. Abstr.; Helminthol. Abstr. (1991-); Index Vet.; Nutr. Abstr. Rev., Ser. B, Live Feeds and Feed.; Pig News Inf.; Poult. Abstr.; Protozoolog. Abstr.; Rev. Med. Vet. Mycology; Vet. Bull.

RH/1016-1511
**ZIMBABWE VETERINARY JOURNAL.** [Zimb. vet. j.]. **Added/Corp** Zimbabwe Veterinary Association. Vol. 11, No. 1/2 (June 1980)-. Periodical. English. qt (Mar., June, Sept., Dec.). $50.00. Zimbabwe Veterinary Journal, PO Box A195, Avondale Harare Zimbabwe. **Tel** (011-263-4)445859. **ED** F W G Hill, C M Foggin and K P Lander. Index available. **Bk Rev. Ad Acc. Circ:** 350 (ctrl). ***Continues*** *Rhodesian Veterinary Journal, 0253-3278.*
**Desc:** Original and review papers on diseases of domestic and wild animals in Southern Africa.
**Ind/Abst** AGRICOLA [Full Cov.]; Anim. Breed. Abstr.; Biocont. News Inf.; Grasslands For. Abstr.; Helminthol. Abstr. (19??-19??); Index Vet.; Nutr. Abstr. Rev., Ser. B, Live Feeds and Feed.; Pig News Inf.; Poult. Abstr.; Protozoolog. Abstr.; Rev. Med. Vet. Entomol.; Small Anim. Abstr. Bibliogr.; Vet. Bull.; Weed Abstr.; Wildl. Rev.

FR
**ZOO-SANITARY SITUATION IN MEMBER COUNTRIES IN ... / OFFICE INTERNATIONAL DES EPIZOOTIES.** **VFOAT** Zoo Sanitary Situation in Member Countries in ... . 1981-. English (French and Spanish). **LC** SF740; .Z66. **DD** 636.089/44/021. ***Separated from*** *Bulletin - Office International des Epizooties.*

PL/0084-5825
**ZWIERZETA LABORATORYJNE.** **See** Zoology.

PL/0137-6810
**ZYCIE WETERYNARYJNE.** **Added/Corp** Zrzeszenie Lekarzy i Technikow Weterynarii. (19??)-. Periodical. Polish (table of contents in English). mo. Price on Request. **(Subscription address:** ARS Polona, PO Box 1001, 00068 Warsaw Poland.**)**
**Ind/Abst** Index Vet.; Protozoolog. Abstr.

## ABSTRACTING, BIBLIOGRAPHIES AND STATISTICS

UK
**ANNOTATED BIBLIOGRAPHY / THE COMMONWEALTH BUREAU OF ANIMAL HEALTH.** Bibliography. English.
**Ind/Abst** Nutr. Abstr. Rev., Ser. B, Live Feeds and Feed.; Nutr. Abstr. Rev., Ser. A, Hum. Exp.; Rev. Med. Vet. Mycology; Rev. Plant Pathol.

UK/0019-4123
**INDEX VETERINARIUS.** **Added/Corp** Commonwealth Agricultural Bureaux. Imperial Bureau of Animal Health. Commonwealth Bureau of Animal Health. Vol. 1 (Apr. 1933)-. Abstracting/Indexing Service. English. mo. $969.00 US. CAB International Centre, Wallingford, Oxon OX10 8DE United Kingdom. **Tel** 44 491 832111, FAX 44 491 833508, telex 847964 (COMAGG G). **ED** J. R. Metcalfe. **LC** Z6674; .I5; SF745. **DD** 016.636089. **NLM** ZSF 615 I38. cum. index. **Ad Acc. Circ:** 800. available on magnetic tape and CD-ROM; available on an online database from Tsukuba Daigaku; CAN/OLE; STN International; JICST; DATA-STAR; DIMDI; ESA-IRS; BRS; and DIALOG.
**Desc:** A subject and author index to world veterinary literature, including conference papers, chapters in books, items of minor or local interest, and items from the borderline fields of veterinary medicine.
**Ind/Abst** Dairy Sci. Abstr.; Protozoolog. Abstr.

UK/0034-6624
**REVIEW OF MEDICAL AND VETERINARY MYCOLOGY.** [Rev. med. vet. mycol.]. **Added/Corp** Commonwealth Mycological Institute (Great Britain). (1951)-. Abstracting/Indexing Service. English. qt. $277.00 US. CAB International Centre, Wallingford, Oxon OX10 8DE United Kingdom. **Tel** 44 491 832111, FAX 44 491 833508, telex 847964 (COMAGG G). **ED** J. L. Halsall MSc. Index available. **Circ:** 700. available on magnetic tape and CD-ROM; available on an online database from Tsukuba Daigaku; CAN/OLE; STN International; JICST; DATA-STAR; DIMDI; ESA-IRS; BRS; and DIALOG. ***Continues*** *Annotated Bibliography of Medical Mycology.*
**Desc:** Surveys the whole field of medical and veterinary mycology. Includes mycoses, allergic disorders associated with fungi, mycotoxins and appropriate fungicidal antibiotic treatment.
**Ind/Abst** Trop. Dis. Bull.

UK
**SMALL ANIMAL ABSTRACTS BIBLIOGRAPHY.** (19??)-. Abstracting/Indexing Service. English. an. £47.00 UK; £51.00 other. CAB International Centre, Wallingford, Oxon OX10 8DE United Kingdom. **Tel** 44 491 832111, FAX 44 491 833508, telex 847964 (COMAGG G). ***Continues*** *Small Animal Abstracts.*

UK
**VETDOC.** Abstracting/Indexing Service. English. wk. $11660.00. Derwent Publications Ltd., Derwent House 14, Great Queen Street, London WC2B 5DF England. **Tel** 011 44 71 3442800. **(Subscription address:** Derwent Inc., 1313 Dolley Madison Blvd., Suite 303, McLean VA 22101**)** Index available. cum. index. ctrl circ. available on an online database.
**Desc:** Covers all aspects of veterinary drug development, evaluation and use in animals, animal disease incidence and diagnosis, toxicology and nutrition. All articles giving significant information on one or more veterinary drugs (including pesticides in a veterinary context and vaccines) are selected whether the subject of the paper is analysis, chemistry, pharmaceutics, pharmacology, metabolism, toxicology, legislation, disease treatment, prophylaxis. etc. Papers on anatomy, surgery and general pathology; general animal husbandry and rearing; routine feedstuffs; preservation of animal products such as meat, milk and eggs; diseases at slaughter; poisoning with plants and natural substances or pesticides found in the environment are not included. Items of interest only to Ringdoc (human), Pestdoc (agrochemical and related subjects) or biotechnology are not included.

UK/0042-4854
**VETERINARY BULLETIN (LONDON).** (THE VETERINARY BULLETIN.). [Vet. bull.]. **Added/Corp** Commonwealth Agricultural Bureaux. Imperial Bureau of Animal Health. Commonwealth Bureau of Animal Health. Vol. 1 (Apr. 1931)-. Abstracting/Indexing Service. English. mo. $781.00 US. CAB International Centre, Wallingford, Oxon OX10 8DE United Kingdom. **Tel** 44 491 832111, FAX 44 491 833508, telex 847964 (COMAGG G). **ED** M. R. Hails BSc. **LC** SF601; .V52. **DD** 636.089; 619.05. **NLM** ZSF 615 V587. **Ad Acc. Circ:** 1,900. available on magnetic tape and CD-ROM; available on an online database from Tsukuba Daigaku; CAN/OLE; STN International; JICST; DATA-STAR; DIMDI; ESA-IRS; BRS; and DIALOG. ***Supersedes*** *Tropical Veterinary Bulletin, 0372-2635;* ***Absorbed*** *Veterinary Reviews.*
**Desc:** Covers the field of animal health. Special emphasis on prevention, control and treatment of diseases; effects of disease on production of food, skins, wool and health aspects of animal husbandry.
**Ind/Abst** AGRICOLA; Anim. Breed. Abstr.; Index Vet.; PESTDOC; Pig News Inf.; Protozoolog. Abstr.; Trop. Dis. Bull.; Wildl. Rev. (19??-199?).

## WATER RESOURCES

US/0740-9923
**305(B) TECHNICAL REPORT FOR OKLAHOMA.** **See** Environmental Issues-Pollution and Waste Management.

IT
**ACQUE SOTTERRANEE; RICERCHE, SFRUTTAMENTO, CONSERVAZIONE.** Italian. Geo Graph, Via Turati 9, 20090 Segrate Milan Italy.

US
**ADVANCE PROGRAM.** **See** Engineering-Electricity, Electrical Engineering, Electronics.

UK/0309-1708
**ADVANCES IN WATER RESOURCES.** [Adv. water resour.]. **VFOAT** Adv. Water Resource. (Sep. 1977)-. Academic Scholarly Publication. English. Six times a year. $366.00 The Americas; £245.00 other. Elsevier Applied Science, An Imprint of Elsevier Science Ltd., The Boulevard, Langford Lane, Kidlington, Oxford OX5 1GB United Kingdom. **Tel** 011 44 865 843000, 011 44 865 843699, FAX 011 44 865 843010. **ED** M. A. Celia and C. A. Brebbia. **LC** TC1; .A27. **DD** 627/.05. **CODEN** AWREDI. **[CCC].** Index available. **Bk Rev. Pr Rev. Circ:** 500. Documents available from Article Express International, The Genuine Article, Ask*IEEE, Documents on Demand. ***Absorbed*** *Hydrosoft (Southampton, England), 0268-6856.*
**Desc:** Publishes papers in most areas of water resources but editorial policy is to encourage papers on basic developments, simulation techniques and papers that emphasize practical applications.
**Ind/Abst** AGRICOLA [Select. Cov.]; Appl. Mech. Rev.; AQUAREF; Aquat. Sci. Fish. Abstr. (Computer File); Coal Abstr.; Curr. Contents Eng. Tech. Appl. Sci.; EMBASE; Energy Res. Abstr. (July 1980-); Eng. Index Annu.; Environ. Abstr.; Environ. Eng. Abstr.; Environ. Period. Bibliogr.; Fish Rev.; Fluid Abstr., Civil Eng.; Fluid Abstr.

# Water Resources

Proc. Eng.; FLUIDEX (1977-); GeoRef; INSPEC (1985-); Int. Aerosp. Abstr.; Int. Civil Eng. Abstr.; Irr. Drain. Abstr.; Mech. Eng. Abstr.; Life Sci. Collect.; Pollut. Abstr. Indexes; Res. Alert [Select. Cov.]; SCISEARCH; Soils Fert.

AG
**AGUA - TECNOLOGIA Y TRATAMIENTO.** Vol. 1, No. 1 (Jan./March 1975)-. Periodical. Spanish. qt. 150.000Arg$ Argentina. BAC Producciones s.r.l., Emilio Mitre 130, Piso 1F, 1424 Buenos Aires Argentina. **Tel** 011 54 1 4325273, FAX 011 54 1 4325273. cum. index. **Ad Acc, Adv Mgr:** Carlos Gonzalez Acha. **Circ:** 5,000.
**Desc:** Technically-specialized magazine on water resources.

LE
**ALAM AL-MIYAH AL-ARABI.** **VFOAT** Arab Water World. (Jan. 1977)-. Periodical. Arabic (English). bm. **LC** TD314; .A4.
**Ind/Abst** Bibliogr. Mission. (1977-); Fluid Abstr., Civil Eng.; Fluid Abstr. Proc. Eng.; FLUIDEX.

US
**ALASKA BASIN OUTLOOK REPORT.** (19??)-. Government Publication. English. ir. US Department of Agriculture / Soil Conservation Service / Anchorage, 201 East 9th Avenue 300, Anchorage AK 99501-3687. **Tel** (907)271-2424. available with charts.
**Desc:** Gives statistics on rainfall in Alaska.

US
**ALASKA FEDERAL-STATE-PRIVATE COOPERATIVE SNOW SURVEYS BASIN OUTLOOK REPORTS.** **Title Change.**
**Added/Corp** United States. Soil Conservation Service. **VFOAT** Basin Outlook Reports. (1990)-(199?). English. mo. US Department of Agriculture / Soil Conservation Service / Anchorage, 201 East 9th Avenue 300, Anchorage AK 99501-3687. **Tel** (907)271-2424. available on microfiche (Vols. for April 1990 distributed to depository libraries). **Continues** Alaska Snow Surveys and Federal-State-Private Cooperative Snow Surveys. **Continued by** Alaska Snow Survey Report.

US
**ALASKA SNOW SURVEY REPORT / UNITED STATES DEPARTMENT OF AGRICULTURE, SOIL CONSERVATION SERVICE.** **Title Change.** **Added/Corp** United States. Soil Conservation Service. **VFOAT** Alaska Basin Outlook Report. (1993)-(199?). Periodical. English. mo. US Department of Agriculture / Soil Conservation Service / Anchorage, 201 East 9th Avenue 300, Anchorage AK 99501-3687. **LC** GB2625.A4; U5a. **DD** 551.57/9/798. **Continues** Alaska Federal-State-Private Cooperative Snow Surveys Basin Outlook Reports. **Continued by** Alaska Basin Outlook Report.

US
**ALASKA SNOW SURVEYS AND FEDERAL-STATE-PRIVATE COOPERATIVE SNOW SURVEYS.** **Title Change.** **VFOAT** Alaska Snow Surveys and Federal State Private; Cooperative Snow Surveys; Alaska Snow Surveys. English. mo. US Department of Agriculture / Soil Conservation Service / Anchorage, 201 East 9th Avenue 300, Anchorage AK 99501-3687. **Tel** (907)271-2424. **LC** GB2625.A4; U5A. **DD** 551.57/9/798. **Circ:** 600. available on microfiche (Vols. for 1986- distributed to depository libraries). **Continues** Federal-State-Private Snow Surveys and Water Supply Outlook for Alaska (Anchorage, Alaska : 1983), 8755-4445. **Continued by** Alaska Federal-State-Private Cooperative Snow Surveys Basin Outlook Reports; Outlook Reports.

US/0094-6362
**ALGAE ABSTRACTS.** **Added/Corp** Water Resources Scientific Information Center. Vol. 1 (1969)-. English. ir. Plenum Press, 233 Spring Street, New York NY 10013-1578. **Tel** (212)620-8000, (800)221-9369, FAX (212)463-0742, (212)807-1047, telex 23/421139. **NLM** Z 5356.A6 A394. Each issue contains an index to its own contents (no volume index)--loose.

BL
**ANAIS HIDROGRAFICOS.** **Main/Corp** Brazil. Diretoria de Hidrografia e Navegacao. (1933)-. Portuguese. Diretoria de Hidrografia E Navegacao, Ministerio da Marinha, ILHA Fiscal, Rio de Janeiro Brazil. **LC** VK597.B8; A32. **Circ:** 1,300 (ctrl). available with charts; available with illustrations. **Continues** Brazil. Directoria de Navegacao. Divisao de Hidrografia. Anais Hidrograficos.

CN/0388-557X
**ANNUAIRE. QUALITE DES EAUX.** (ANNUAIRE QUALITE DES EAUX (QUEBEC).). **Main/Corp** Quebec (Province). Service Qualite des Eaux. Periodical. French. an. **LC** TD227.Q42; A55. **DD** 553/.7/09714.

US/0731-874X
**ANNUAL PROCEEDINGS. WATER SYMPOSIUM / ARIZONA WATER SYMPOSIUM.** [Annu. proc. - Ariz. Water Symp.]. **Main/Conf** Arizona Water Symposium. **VAT** Arizona Water Symposium Annual Proceedings. 22nd-. Proceedings. English. an. **LC** TD224.A7; A92. **Continues** Arizona Watershed Symposium. Proceedings, 0571-0162.

US/0198-1994
**ANNUAL PROGRESS REPORT - WATER MANAGEMENT RESEARCH PROJECT.** (ANNUAL PROGRESS REPORT, WATER MANAGEMENT RESEARCH PROJECT / SUBMITTED TO THE U. S. AGENCY FOR INTERNATIONAL DEVELOPMENT.). **Main/Corp** Colorado. State University, Fort Collins. Water Management Research Project. **VFOAT** Water Management Research in Arid and Sub-Humid Lands of Less Developed Countries. 1974/75-. English. an. Colorado State University, Fort Collins CO 80521. **Tel** (303)491-8652. **LC** TC401; .C64A. **DD** 333.91/009172/4.

UK
**ANNUAL REPORT AND ACCOUNTS - NATIONAL WATER COUNCIL.** **Main/Corp** Great Britain. National Water Council. (1974/1975)-. English. an. £1.75. National Water Council, 1 Queen Anne's Gate, London SW1 9BT England. **LC** TD257; .G75a. **DD** 354/.41/008232.

UK/0144-9370
**ANNUAL REPORT AND ACCOUNTS - WATER RESEARCH CENTRE.** **Title Change.** See Environmental Issues-Pollution and Waste Management.

US/0743-5134
**ANNUAL REPORT / ARIZONA DEPARTMENT OF WATER RESOURCES.** [Annu. rep. - Ariz., Dep. Water Resour.]. **Main/Corp** Arizona. Dept. of Water Resources. 1980-1981-. English. an. Arizona Department of Water Resources, 99 East Virginia Avenue, Phoenix AZ 85004. **LC** HD1694.A7; A32. **DD** 353.97910082/325/06. **Continues** Arizona Water Commission. Annual Report, 0091-6366.

US/0276-0177
**ANNUAL REPORT - CENTER FOR RESEARCH IN WATER RESOURCES, THE UNIVERSITY OF TEXAS AT AUSTIN.** [Annu. rep. - Univ. Tex. Austin, Cent. Res. Water Resour.]. **Main/Corp** Texas. University at Austin. Center for Research in Water Resources. **Added/Corp** University of Texas at Austin. Center for Research in Water Resources. CRWR Annual Report. **VFOAT** CRWR Annual Report; Center for Research in Water Resources Annual Report. (19??)-. Monographic series. English. ir. Price varies per volume. Center for Research in Water Resources, UTA Balcones Research Center 119, Austin TX 78758. **Tel** (512)471-3131. Bk Rev.
**Desc:** Reports of water related research.

US
**ANNUAL REPORT / D.C. WATER RESOURCES RESEARCH CENTER.** **Main/Corp** University of the District of Columbia. Water Resources Research Center. English. an. University of the District of Columbia Water Resources Research, VNC, Washington DC 20008. **Continues** Annual Report (Washington Technical Institute. Water Resources Research Center), 0272-3263.

US/0418-5455
**ANNUAL REPORT / DELAWARE RIVER BASIN COMMISSION.** [Annu. rep. - Del. River Basin Comm.]. **Main/Corp** Delaware River Basin Commission. (1963)-. English. an. Free with membership. Water Resources Association of the Delaware River Basin, Box 867, David Road, Valley Forge PA 19481. **Tel** (215)783-0634. **ED** Bruce E Stewart. **DD** 333.9. Bk Rev. **Ad Acc. Circ:** 800 (ctrl).
**Desc:** Update on association accomplishments and activities, committee reports, financial information, and a look at the future.
**Ind/Abst** GeoRef.

AT
**ANNUAL REPORT / DEPARTMENT OF WATER RESOURCES.** **Main/Corp** New South Wales. Dept. of Water Resources. **VFOAT** New South Wales. Dept of Water Resources, 10 Valentine Avenue, Parramatta New South Wales 2150 Australia. **Tel** TC922; .N43. **DD** 354.9440082/325. **Continues** Annual Report / New South Wales. Water Resources Commission, 0155-9834.

US
**ANNUAL REPORT FOR THE FISCAL YEAR JULY 1 ... TO JUNE 30 ... / THE METROPOLITAN WATER DISTRICT OF SOUTHERN CALIFORNIA.** **Main/Corp** Metropolitan Water District of Southern California. **VFOAT** Annual Report. 1980-1981-. English. an. **LC** TD224.C3; M36. **DD** 352.6/1/0979493. **Continues** Metropolitan Water District of Southern California. Annual Report Appendix for the Fiscal Year July 1 ... to June 30 ... .

MY
**ANNUAL REPORT - KUCHING WATER BOARD.** See Public Administration-Public Utilities.

AT
**ANNUAL REPORT - METROPOLITAN WATER BOARD.** **Main/Corp** Metropolitan Water Board. English. Government Printer / Metropolitan Water Board, GPO Box 307C, Hobart Tasmania 7000 Australia. **LC** TD322.T38; M48A. **DD** 354/.946/00871.

US
**ANNUAL REPORT / NEW JERSEY WATER SUPPLY AUTHORITY.** **Main/Corp** New Jersey Water Supply Authority. (1982)-. English. an. **LC** TC424.N5; N53a. **DD** 363.6/1/09749.

US
**ANNUAL REPORT OF THE DEPARTMENT OF WATER AND NATURAL RESOURCES ON THE WATER RESOURCES MANAGEMENT SYSTEM (SOUTH DAKOTA).** **Main/Corp** South Dakota. Dept. of Water and Natural Resources. English. an. **LC** TC424.S8; S68A. **DD** 353.97830082/325/06. **Continues** South Dakota. Dept. of Natural Resource Development. Annual Report of the Department of Natural Resource Development on the Water Resources Management System.

US/0362-3289
**ANNUAL REPORT OF THE IDAHO DEPARTMENT OF WATER RESOURCES.** **Main/Corp** Idaho. Dept. of Water Resources. (19??)-. English. an. Idaho Department of Water Resources, Statehouse, Boise ID 83720. **LC** GB705.I2; I23a. **DD** 353.9/796/008232.

CN/0318-3912
**ANNUAL REPORT OF THE MANITOBA WATER SERVICES BOARD.** **Main/Corp** Manitoba Water Services Board. 1st (1972/73)-. English. an. Manitoba Water Services Board, 693 Taylor Avenue, Winnipeg Manitoba R3M 2K2, Canada. **LC** TD227.M3; M29A. **DD** 354/.7127/00871. **Supersedes** Manitoba Water Supply Board. Annual Report, 0542-5646.

US
**ANNUAL REPORT OF THE VIRGINIA WATER COMMISSION TO THE GOVERNOR AND THE GENERAL ASSEMBLY OF VIRGINIA.** **Main/Corp** Virginia. Water Commission. (1991)-. English. **Continues** Report of the State Water Commission to the Governor and the General Assembly of Virginia.

US/0099-1635
**ANNUAL REPORT - OKLAHOMA WATER RESOURCES BOARD.** **Main/Corp** Oklahoma Water Resources Board. (19??)-. English. an. Oklahoma Water Resources Board, 2241 NW 40th Street, Oklahoma City OK 73112. **LC** TD224.O5; O368a; TD224.O5; A3 subser. **DD** 353.97660082/325/06.

US/0095-4659
**ANNUAL REPORT ON THE COMPREHENSIVE WATER RESOURCES PLAN.** (ANNUAL REPORT ON THE COMPREHENSIVE WATER RESOURCES PLAN (WEST VIRGINIA).). **Main/Corp** West Virginia. Dept. of Natural Resources. English. an. Department of Natural Resources / West Virginia, State Capitol, Charleston WV 25305. **Tel** (304)558-9152. **LC** TC424.W4; W45A. **DD** 333.9/1/009754.

US/0276-4539
**ANNUAL REPORT, PUBLIC WATER SUPPLIES FOR THE STATE OF OKLAHOMA, SOUTH CENTRAL DISTRICT.** [Annu. rep., public water supplies State Okla., South Cent. Dist.]. **VFOAT** Public Water Supplies for the State of Oklahoma, South Central District; Public Water Supply Report ..., South Central District. English. an. State Water Quality Laboratory, 1000 NE 10th, Oklahoma City OK 73152. **LC** TD224.O5; A7. **DD** 363.6/1.

US
**ANNUAL REPORT / SAVANNAH VALLEY AUTHORITY.** **Main/Corp** Savannah Valley Authority (S.C.). (1987/88)-. English. PO Drawer K, McCormick SC 29835. **LC** HD1695.C57; C57a. **DD** 353.97570082/325/097579. **Continues** Annual Report of the Clarks Hill-Russell Authority to the Governor and General Assembly.

US
**ANNUAL REPORT/SOUTHWEST FLORIDA WATER MANAGEMENT DISTRICT.** **Main/Corp** Southwest Florida Water Management District. (1986)-. English. **LC** HD1694.F6; S66a. **DD** 333.91/00975905.

US
**ANNUAL REPORT / STATE WATER QUALITY ADVISORY COMMITTEE.** **Main/Corp** Maryland. State Water Quality Advisory Committee. (19??)-. English. an. Maryland Department of Health and Mental Hygiene, 201 West Preston Street, Baltimore MD 21201. **Tel** (410)225-6500. **LC** TD224.M3; M29a. **DD** 353.97520082/325.

AT/0311-2101
**ANNUAL REPORT - THE WATER QUALITY COUNCIL OF QUEENSLAND.** **Main/Corp** Water Quality Council of Queensland. 1st-1972/73-. English. an. Water Quality Council of Queensland Commission, GPO Box 2454, Brisbane Queensland 4001 Australia. **LC** TD321.Q8; Q45A. **DD** 354/.943/00871.

US/0191-4049
**ANNUAL REPORT - VIRGINIA ENVIRONMENTAL ENDOWMENT.** **See** Environmental Issues.

US/0736-3923
**ANNUAL REPORT - VIRGINIA WATER RESOURCES RESEARCH CENTER.** ***Ceased.*** (ANNUAL REPORT / VIRGINIA WATER RESOURCES RESEARCH CENTER, VIRGINIA POLYTECHNIC INSTITUTE AND STATE UNIVERSITY.). **Main/Corp** Virginia Water Resources Research Center. (1973)-(19??). English. an. Virginia Water Resources Research Center, 617 North Main Street, Blacksburg VA 24060. **Tel** (703)961-5624, FAX (703)231-6673. **LC** TC424.V8; V6a. **DD** 333.91/09755. ***Continues*** *Virginia Polytechnic Institute and State University. Water Resources Research Center. Water Resources Research in Virginia, Annual Report, 0095-1250.*

AT/1031-5225
**ANNUAL REPORT / WATER AUTHORITY OF WESTERN AUSTRALIA.** **Main/Corp** Water Authority of Western Australia. English. an. Water Authority of Western Australia, PO Box 100, Leederville Western Australia 6007 Australia. **Tel** (09)620-2620, FAX (09)620-3200, telex AA95160. **LC** HD1700.W4; W38A. **DD** 354.9410087/1/006. **Circ:** 1,500 (ctrl).
**Desc:** Satisfies requirements of financial administration and Audit Act and promotes public understanding of the activities of the Water Authority.

US
**ANNUAL REPORT / WATER WORKS AND SEWER BOARD OF THE CITY OF BIRMINGHAM.** **Main/Corp** Water Works and Sewer Board of the City of Birmingham. (1986)-. English. The Water Works Board of Birmingham, 3600 1st Avenue North, Birmingham AL 35212. **LC** TD225.B62; W3. ***Continues*** *Annual Report - Water Works Board of the City of Birmingham.*

US/0511-8182
**ANNUAL REPORT - WESTERN STATES WATER COUNCIL.** **Main/Corp** Western States Water Council. 1st (1966)-. Monographic series. English. Price varies per volume. Western States Water Council, Creekview Plaza/Suite A201, 942 East 7145 South, Midvale UT 84047. **Tel** (801)561-5300. **LC** HD1695.W4; W44. **DD** 333.9; 353.9/3/87100978.

US/0731-5120
**ANNUAL WATER-RESOURCES REVIEW, WHITE SANDS MISSILE RANGE.** [Annu. water-resor. rev., White Sands Missile Range]. English. an. Open-File Services Section, Western Distribution Branch, Geological Survey, Box 25425, Federal Building, Denver CO 80225. **LC** GB705.N6; A65. **DD** 553.7/09789/6.

US/0253-4525
**APPROPRIATE TECHNOLOGY FOR WATER SUPPLY AND SANITATION.** **See** Environmental Issues-Pollution and Waste Management.

UK/0003-7214
**AQUA (LONDON).** ***Title Change.*** (AQUA.). [Aqua]. No. 1 (June 1952)-?. Academic Scholarly Publication. Multiple languages (English and French). bm. Blackwell Scientific Publications Ltd, Marston Book Services, PO Box 87, Oxford OX2 ODT UK. **Tel** 011 44 865 791155, FAX 011 44 865 791927, telex 837 515 MARDIS G. **ED** (editor's address: IWSA, 1 Queen Anne's Gate, London SW1H 9BT United Kingdom). **LC** TD201. **DD** 363/6/1/05. **CODEN** AQUAAA. **[CCC]. Bk Rev. Ad Acc.** available on microfilm and microfiche from University Microfilms International (UMI). Documents available from Article Express International, BIOSIS Document Express, CASDDS, Documents on Demand. ***Continued by*** *Journal of Water Supply Research & Technology : Aqua.*
**Desc:** The primary aim of this journal is to offer a scientific, technical and managerial forum for those concerned with any part of the field whether research, consultancy, operations or management.
**Ind/Abst** Biol. Abstr.; Chem. Abstr.; Ecol. Abstr.; Eng. Index Annu. [Select. Cov.]; Environ. Abstr.; Environ. Period. Bibliogr.; Fluid Abstr., Civil Eng.; Fluid Abstr. Proc. Eng.; FLUIDEX (1973-); Food Sci. Technol. Abstr.; Geol. Abstr.; GeoRef; Int. Civil Eng. Abstr.; Soft. Abstr. Eng.

US/1048-8111
**AQUA TERRA (EUREKA SPRINGS, ARK.).** (AQUA TERRA : WATER CONCEPTS FOR THE ECOLOGICAL SOCIETY.). **Added/Corp** Water Center (U.S.). Vol. 1, Issue 1 (Spring 1991)-. Periodical. English. sa. $5.95. The Water Center, PO Box 264, Eureka Springs AR 72632. **DD** 333.

US/1042-6221
**AQUACULTURE SITUATION AND OUTLOOK REPORT.** (AQUACULTURE SITUATION AND OUTLOOK REPORT / UNITED STATES DEPARTMENT OF AGRICULTURE, ECONOMIC RESEARCH SERVICE.). [Aquac. situat. outlook rep.]. **Added/Corp** United States. Dept. of Agriculture. Economic Research Service. (Oct. 1988)-. Periodical. English. sa. $16.00 (1 year), $30.00 (2 year), $44.00 (3 year). Economic Research Service USDA, 341 Victory Drive, Herndon VA 22070. **Tel** (800) 999-6779. **LC** SH34; .A84. **DD** 338.3/71/097305. ***Continues*** *Aquaculture Outlook & Situation, 0278-131X.*
**Ind/Abst** World Agric. Econ.

UK
**AQUALERT.** English. mo. £195.00. Water Research Centre, WRC PLC Frankland Road, Blagrove Swindon SN5 8YF England. **Tel** 011 44 793 511711, FAX 011 44 793 511712, telex 449541.
**Desc:** An SDI service for the water industry - providing a personalized selection of abstracts from databases relevant to a particular interest. Experts at the Water Research centre in London, generate the lists once a month from the most up to date information in the Aqualine database.

CN
**AQUAREF.** **See** Water Resources-Abstracting, Bibliographies and Statistics.

US/0587-341X
**AQUARIUS (LOGAN).** (AQUARIUS.). [Aquarius]. No. 1 (1977)-. English. sa. Utah Water Research Laboratory, Utah State University, Logan UT 84322-8200. **Tel** (801)750-3200, FAX (801)750-3663, telex 3729283. **ED** Leaunda Hemphill. **Circ:** 800.
**Desc:** A newsletter for the Utah Center for Water Resources, Utah State University.
**Ind/Abst** GeoRef.

SZ/1015-1621
**AQUATIC SCIENCES.** **See** Earth Sciences-Hydrology.

US/0092-0622
**AQUEDUCT (LOS ANGELES).** (AQUEDUCT.). **Added/Corp** Metropolitan Water District of Southern California. Vol. 40 No. 5 (May 1973)-. Periodical. English. Four times a year. Free. Metropolitan Water District Southern California, PO Box 54153, Los Angeles CA 90054. **Tel** (310)250-6487. **ED** Penny Lawbaugh. **Circ:** 40,000 (ctrl). ***Continues*** *Aqueduct News.*
**Desc:** Features stories on California water issues.
**Ind/Abst** Urban Aff. Abstr.

GW/0003-9136
**ARCHIV FUER HYDROBIOLOGIE.** [Arch. Hydrobiol.]. **Added/Corp** International Association of Theoretical and Applied Limnology. Vol. 12 (1918)-. Academic Scholarly Publication. English (German). Twelve times a year. $75.00. E. Schweizerbartsche Verlagsbuchhandlung, Johannesstrasse 3A, D-70176 Stuttgart Germany. **Tel** 011 49 711 625001, FAX 011 49 711 625005, telex 723363 SCHB D. **ED** H J Elster and H C W Ohle. **LC** QH301; .A493. **DD** 574.92/05. **CODEN** AHYBA4. **[CCC]. Bk Rev. Ad Acc. Pr Rev.** Documents available from The Genuine Article, BIOSIS Document Express, CASDDS, Documents on Demand. ***Continues*** *Archiv fuer Hydrobiologie und Planktonkunde.*
**Desc:** Limnology, ecology, fisheries, water supply, water hygiene, water chemistry.
**Ind/Abst** AGRICOLA; Anim. Behav. Abstr.; Aquat. Sci. Fish. Abstr. (Computer File); Biodeter. Abstr. (19??-19??); Biol. Abstr.; Chem. Abstr.; Curr. Contents, Agric. Biol. Environ. Sci.; Curr. Ref. Fish Res.; Ecol. Abstr. (?-?); EMBASE; Energy Inf. Abstr.; Energy Res. Abstr. (June 1974-); Entomol. Abstr.; Environ. Abstr.; Fish Rev.; Food Sci. Technol. Abstr.; Fresh. Aqua. Contents Tables; GeoRef; Irr. Drain. Abstr.; Microbiol. Abstr. Sect. C; Nutr. Abstr. Rev., Ser. B, Live Feeds and Feed.; Life Sci. Collect.; Pollut. Abstr. Indexes; Protozoolog. Abstr.; Res. Alert [Full Cov.]; Rev. Med. Vet. Entomol.; Sci. Cit. Index; SCISEARCH; Sel. Water Resour. Abstr.; Soc. Sci. Cit. Index [Select. Cov.]; Soils Fert.; Weed Abstr.; Wildl. Rev.

US/1045-8727
**ARCHIVES REPORT / CALIFORNIA WATER RESOURCES CENTER, UNIVERSITY OF CALIFORNIA.** [Arch. rep. - Calif. Water Resour. Cent.]. **Main/Corp** California Water Resources Center. Archives. **Added/Corp** California Water Resources Center. Water Resources Center Archives (Calif.). No. 24 (1978)-. Monographic series. English. Price varies per volume. University of California Davis Water Resources Center, Davis CA 95616. **LC** TD224; .C3. **DD** 016.33391/009794; 333. ***Continues*** *Archives Series Report, 0575-4976.*
**Ind/Abst** GeoRef.

US/0749-1735
**ARIZONA DEPARTMENT OF WATER RESOURCES BULLETIN.** [Ariz. Dep. Water Resour. bull.]. 1 (Jan. 1983)-. Bulletin. English. ir. Price varies per volume. Arizona Department of Water Resources, 99 East Virginia Avenue, Phoenix AZ 85004.
**Ind/Abst** GeoRef.

US/1058-1383
**ARROYO (TUCSON, ARIZ.).** (ARROYO.). [Arroyo]. **Added/Corp** University of Arizona. Water Resources Research Center. Vol. 1, No. 1 (Spring, 1987)-. Periodical. English. qt. free. Water Resources Research Center / Arizona, 350 North Campbell, University of Arizona, Tucson AZ 85721. **Tel** (602)792-9591, FAX (602)792-8518. **ED** Joseph Gelt. **DD** 551. **Circ:** 2,400. Documents available from Documents on Demand. ***Formed by the union of*** *Arizona Water Resources News Bulletin* ***and*** *Arizona Water Resources Project : Information.*
**Desc:** Intended to transfer information about the questions and concerns of water users, manager, regulators and others from the research arena to the community of water research users in Arizona.
**Ind/Abst** Environ. Abstr.; GeoRef.

AT/1032-2426
**AUSTRALIAN JOURNAL OF SOIL AND WATER CONSERVATION.** [Aust. j. soil water conserv.]. (1988)-. Periodical. English. Four times a year (Feb., May, Aug., Nov.). 30.00Aus$ Australia; 50.00Aus$ other. Soil & Water Conservation Australia, PO Box W21, West Pennant Hills, New South Wales, 2125 Australia. **Tel** 011 61 2 4843703, FAX 011 61 2 9806728. **ED** Peter Charman, (editor's address: P. O. Box 5423, West Chatswood, NSW 2057 Australia (02) 411 6810). **DD** 631.70994. **Bk Rev**, (Qty: 6). **Ad Acc. Pr Rev. Circ:** 3,000 (ctrl).
**Desc:** Articles of technical, research, and reviews on the effect of native and feral animals on the land and its economics viability.
**Ind/Abst** Grasslands For. Abstr.; Irr. Drain. Abstr.; Potato Abstr.; Soils Fert.; Weed Abstr.; Wheat Barley Trit. Abstr.; World Agric. Econ.

AT/0314-2523
**AUSTRALIAN REPRESENTATIVE BASINS PROGRAM REPORT SERIES.** [Aust. represent. basins program rep. ser.]. **Added/Corp** Australian Water Resources Council. No. 1 (1976)-. English. Australian Bureau of Statistics, PO Box 10, Belconnen Australian Capital Territory, 2616 Australia. **Tel** 011 61 6 2527911, FAX 011 61 6 2516009.
**Ind/Abst** AESIS Q.

AT
**AUSTRALIAN WATER RESOURCES COUNCIL OCCASIONAL PAPERS SERIES.** **Added/Corp** Australian Water Resources Council. Australia. Dept. of National Development and Energy. **VFOAT** Occasional Papers Series; AWRC Occasional Papers Series; A.W.R.C. Occasional Papers Series. (19??)-. Monographic series. English. Price varies per volume. Australian Bureau of Statistics, PO Box 10, Belconnen Australian Capital Territory, 2616 Australia. **Tel** 011 61 6 2527911, FAX 011 61 6 2516009.
**Ind/Abst** AESIS Q.

AT/0155-2643
**AUSTRALIAN WATER RESOURCES COUNCIL - TECHNICAL PAPER.** (TECHNICAL PAPER - AUSTRALIAN WATER RESOURCES COUNCIL.). [Aust. Water Resour. Counc. - Tech. Pap.]. **Main/Corp** Australian Water Resources Council. **VFOAT** Australian Water Resources Council Technical Paper; AWRC Technical Paper; A.W.R.C. Technical Paper. No. 1 (1971)-. Monographic series. English. Price varies per volume. Australian Bureau of Statistics, PO Box 10, Belconnen Australian Capital Territory, 2616 Australia. **Tel** 011 61 6 2527911, FAX 011 61 6 2516009. **CODEN** AWRTAQ. Documents available from BIOSIS Document Express, CASDDS.
**Ind/Abst** AESIS Q.; Bioeng. Abstr.; Biol. Abstr.; Chem. Abstr. (1971-1982); Ei Page One; GeoRef; Life Sci. Collect.

AT/0728-9502
**AUSTRALIAN WATER RESOURCES COUNCIL WATER MANAGEMENT SERIES.** (WATER MANAGEMENT SERIES.). [Aust. Water Resour. Counc. water manage. ser.]. **Added/Corp** Australian Water Resources Council. **VFOAT** Australian

# Water Resources

Water Resources Council Water Management Series. No. 1 (1982)-. Monographic series. English. Price varies per volume. Australian Water Resources, PO Box 5, Natl Dev & Energy, Canberra Act 2600 Australia. **Tel** 011 61 2 458222. **Continues** Hydrological Series (Australian Water Resources Council).
**Ind/Abst** AESIS Q.

AT
## AUSTRALIAN WATER RESOURCES COUNCIL WATER RESOURCES SERIES. **Added/Corp** Australian Water Resources Council. **VFOAT** Water Resources Series. No. 1 (1982)-. Monographic series. English. Price varies per volume. Australian Water Resources, PO Box 5, Natl Dev & Energy, Canberra Act 2600 Australia. **Tel** 011 61 2 458222.
**Ind/Abst** AESIS Q.

US/0894-847X
## AWRA MONOGRAPH SERIES. [AWRA monogr. ser.]. **Added/Corp** American Water Resources Association. **VFOAT** A.W.R.A. Monograph Series. **VAT** American Water Resources Association Monograph Series. (19??)-. Monographic series. English. ir. Price varies per volume. AWRA - American Water Resources Association, 950 Herndon Parkway, Suite 300, Herndon VA 22070-5528. **Tel** (703)904-1225, **FAX** (703)904-1228. **DD** 333. cum. index.
**Ind/Abst** AGRICOLA [Select. Cov.]; GeoRef.

US/0273-3218
## AWWA MAINSTREAM. [AWWA mainstream]. **Added/Corp** American Water Works Association. **VFOAT** Mainstream. **VAT** American Water Works Association Mainstream. Vol. 25, No. 3 (Mar. 1981)-. Periodical. English. mo. $13.00; Comes also with membership. American Water Works Association / Colorado, 6666 West Quincy Avenue, Denver CO 80235. **Tel** (303)794-7711, (303)794-7310 (editorial), **FAX** (303)794-7310 (editorial), (303)795-1989 (marketing). **ED** Mary A. Parmelee. **Circ:** 40,000. **Continues** Willing Water 0149-8037, 0149-8037.
**Desc:** News and feature items about the drinking water industry, including coverage of governmental actions, water utility experiences, technological advances, and association activities.

US/0160-9548
## BASIC DATA SERIES. GROUND-WATER RELEASE. [Basic data ser., Ground-water release]. **Added/Corp** Kansas Geological Survey. **VFOAT** Ground-Water Release; Ground Water Release. No. 1, (1969)-. Monographic series. English. ir. Prices varies per volume. Kansas Geological Survey, 1930 Constant Avenue, University of Kansas, Lawrence KS 66046. **Tel** (913)864-3965. **LC** UNC. **DD** 553.79/097814. **CODEN** GSKSDT.
**Ind/Abst** GeoRef.

GW/0937-3756
## BBR : WASSER UND ROHRBAU. **Added/Corp** Hauptverband der Deutschen Bauindustrie. Bundesfachabteilung Wasserwerks-, Rohr- und Spezialgrundbau. Hauptverband der Deutschen Bauindustrie. Bundesfachabteilung Spezialtiefbau-, Brunnen- und Rohrleitungsbau. Hauptverband der Deutschen Bauindustrie. Bundesfachabteilung Brunnen-, Kanal- und Rohrleitungsbau. (Mar. 1989)-. Periodical. German. mo. **LC** TN860; .B58. Documents available from CASDDS. **Continues** Brunnenbau, Bau von Wasserwerken, Rohrleitungsbau, 0340-3874.
**Ind/Abst** Chem. Abstr.

PL/0239-622X
## BIBLIOGRAFIA GOSPODARKI I INZYNIERII WODNEJ. **VFOAT** Bibliografiia Po Vodnomu Khoziaistvu i Vodokhozia-Istvennomu Stroitelstvu; Bibliography of Water Economy and Engineering. (1971)-. Periodical. Polish. ir. $75.00. Instytut Meteorologii i Gospodarki Wodnej, Ul Podlesna 61, 01-673 Warszawa Poland. **Tel** 34-16-51 W 307, telex 814331. **ED** Krystyna Storozynska. **LC** Z7935; .B49; TD215. Index available. cum. index. **Ad Acc**. **Circ:** 220 (ctrl).

US/0090-2055
## BIBLIOGRAPHY OF WATER QUALITY RESEARCH REPORTS. Bibliography. English. Environmental Protection Agency / Publications Distribution Section, Waterside Mall, 401 M Street SW, Washington DC 20460. **Tel** (703)487-4650. **LC** Z5862.2.W3; B53. **DD** 016.3339/1.

US
## BIENNIAL REPORT - NORTH DAKOTA. STATE WATER CONSERVATION COMMISSION. **Main/Corp** North Dakota. State Water Conservation Commission. 1st- 1937/38-. English. be. **LC** TC824.N9; A32.
**Desc:** Reports for 1938/40-1944/46 include the Biennial report of the State Engineer.

US/0466-6992
## BIENNIAL REPORT OF THE DEPARTMENT OF WATER RESOURCES. **Main/Corp** Nebraska. Dept. of Water Resources. 32d- 1957/58-. English. be. Free. Nebraska Department of Water Resources, PO Box 94676, Lincoln NE 68509-4676. **Tel** (402)471-2363. **ED** Susan France. **LC** HD1694.N2; A26. **DD** 333.9109782. **Circ:** 350. **Supersedes in part** Nebraska. Dept. of Roads and Irrigation. Report.
**Desc:** Current listing of Nebraska's water rights and an overview of events concerning water in Nebraska.

US/0736-8410
## BIENNIAL REPORT UNDER THE GREAT LAKES WATER QUALITY AGREEMENT OF 1978. (BIENNIAL REPORT UNDER THE GREAT LAKES WATER QUALITY AGREEMENT OF 1978 / INTERNATIONAL JOINT COMMISSION.). [Bienn. rep. Great Lakes Water Qual. Agreem. 1978]. **Main/Corp** International Joint Commission. 1st (June 1982)-. English (French). be. Free. International Joint Commission, 100 Oellette Avenue, Windsor Ont N9A 6T3 Canada. **Tel** (313)226-2170. **LC** TD223.3; .I44A. **DD** 354.1/871/0977. **Circ:** 5,000. **Continues** Annual Report ... Great Lakes Water Quality.

UK
## BRITISH WATER SUPPLY YEAR BOOK, THE. **Added/Corp** British Waterworks Association. (19??)-. English. Turret Group, 177 Hagden Lane, Watford Herts WD1 8LN United Kingdom. **Tel** 011 44 923 228577, **FAX** 011 44 923 221346. **LC** TD257.A1; B7. **DD** 3636/.1/0942. **Continues** British Waterworks Year Book and Directory with Statistical Tables.
**Ind/Abst** Int. Civil Eng. Abstr.

US/0084-8263
## BULLETIN - CALIFORNIA. DEPT. OF WATER RESOURCES. (BULLETIN / STATE OF CALIFORNIA, DEPARTMENT OF WATER RESOURCES.). [Bull. - Calif., Dep. Water Resour.]. **VFOAT** State Water Resources Board Bulletin. (1956)-. Bulletin. English. ir. Price varies per volume. Department of Water Resources / California, PO Box 942836, Sacramento CA 94236-0001. **Tel** (916)445-3553. **LC** GB705.C2. **DD** 333.9. **CODEN** CAWRAF. Documents available from Article Express International. **Continues** California. State Water Resources Board. Bulletin.
**Ind/Abst** Bioeng. Abstr.; Ei Page One; Eng. Index Annu.; GeoRef.

CN/0836-0278
## BULLETIN / CANADIAN WATER AND WASTEWATER ASSOCIATION. [Bull. - Can. Water Wastewater Assoc.]. **Added/Corp** Canadian Water and Wastewater Association. **VFOAT** Bulletin. **VAT** Bulletin - Association Canadienne des eaux Potables et Usees. Vol. 1, No. 1 (Fall 1987)-. Bulletin. English (French). qt. Canadian Water and Wastewater Association, 3rd Floor, 24 Clarence Street, Ottawa Ontario K1N 5P3 Canada. **DD** 363.6/1/0971. **Bk Rev**. **Circ:** 8,000 (ctrl).
**Desc:** Serves as the newsletter of the Canadian Water and Wastewater Association.

US
## BULLETIN - DEPARTMENT OF NORTHERN AFFAIRS AND NATIONAL RESOURCES, WATER RESOURCES BRANCH. **Main/Corp** Canada. Department of Northern Affairs and National Resources. Water Resources Branch. Bulletin. English. Price varies per volume.

US/0360-9804
## BULLETIN - ILLINOIS STATE WATER SURVEY. [Bull. Ill. State Water Surv.]. **Main/Corp** Illinois State Water Survey. **Added/Corp** Illinois. Dept. of Registration and Education. No. 15 (1917)-. Monographic series. English. ir. Price varies per volume. Illinois State Water Survey, 2204 Griffith Drive, Champaign IL 61820-7495. **Tel** (217)333-2210. **CODEN** ISWSA6. Index available. cum. index. Documents available from CASDDS. **Continues** University of Illinois. Water Survey Series.
**Ind/Abst** Chem. Abstr. (1917-1981); GeoRef.

CN/0836-0987
## BULLETIN - INSTITUT NATIONAL DE RECHERCHE SUR LES EAUX. (BULLETIN). [Bull. - Inst. natl. rech. eaux]. **VFOAT** Bulletin INRE. (1988)-. Bulletin. French. qt. Free. National Water Research Institute, 867 Lakeshore Road, PO Box 5050, Burlington Ontario L7R 4A6 Canada. **Tel** (416)336-4884, **FAX** (416)336-4989, telex 0618296. **DD** 354.71008232505.

US/0462-8128
## BULLETIN - MISSISSIPPI BOARD OF WATER COMMISSIONERS. (BULLETIN). [Bull. - Miss. Board Water Comm.]. **Main/Corp** Mississippi Board of Water Commissioners. Bulletin. English. Price varies per volume. **LC** TD224.M65; A3. **DD** 628. **CODEN** MBWBAG.
**Ind/Abst** GeoRef.

AT/0157-308X
## BULLETIN OF THE AUSTRALIAN LITTORAL SOCIETY. **See** Environmental Issues-Conservation and Natural Resources.

US/0097-2576
## BULLETIN (OHIO. DIVISION OF WATER). (BULLETIN / STATE OF OHIO, DEPARTMENT OF NATURAL RESOURCES, DIVISION OF WATER). [Bull. - State Ohio Dep. Nat. Resour. Div. Water]. No. 13 (Dec. 1950)-. Bulletin. English. ir. Price varies per volume. Department of Natural Resources / Ohio, Fountain Square, Columbus OH 43224. **Tel** (614)265-6590. **LC** TD224.O3; A35. **CODEN** ODWBAI. **Continues** Bulletin (Ohio. Water Resources Board).
**Ind/Abst** GeoRef.

US/0512-4727
## BULLETIN - WATER RESEARCH INSTITUTE (MORGANTOWN). (BULLETIN - WATER RESEARCH INSTITUTE.). **Main/Corp** West Virginia University. Water Research Institute. No. 1- 1969-. Bulletin. English. Price varies per volume. West Virginia University Water Research Institute, Morgantown WV 26506.

US/0548-4901
## BULLETIN - WATER RESOURCES RESEARCH CENTER (DURHAM). (BULLETIN - WATER RESOURCES RESEARCH CENTER.). **Main/Corp** University of New Hampshire. Water Resources Research Center. **VFOAT** WRRC Bulletin. Vol. 1 (1967)-. Bulletin. English. Price varies per volume. University of New Hampshire Water Resource Research Center, Durham NH 03824. **Tel** (603)862-2144. **DD** 628.

US
## CALIFORNIA STATE AGENCIES' WATER QUALITY RELATED ACTIVITIES. **Main/Corp** California. State Water Resources Control Board. English. an. California State Water Resources Control Board, Division of Planning and Research, PO Box 100, Sacramento CA 95801. **LC** TD224.C3; C28D. **DD** 353.97940082/325/06.

US/0195-8658
## CALIFORNIA WATER. 1978-. Periodical. English. an. Department of Water Resources / California, PO Box 942836, Sacramento CA 94236-0001. **Tel** (916)445-3553. **LC** TC424.C2; C34. **DD** 333.91/009794.

US/0147-9164
## CALIFORNIA WATER PLAN OUTLOOK, THE. **Main/Corp** California. Dept. of Water Resources. 1974-. English. $5.00. Department of Water Resources / California, PO Box 942836, Sacramento CA 94236-0001. **Tel** (916)445-3553. **LC** HD1694.C2; A27. **DD** 333.9/1/009794. **Circ:** 1,000 (ctrl). **Continues** Water for California-Outlook.
**Desc:** Shows current water situation in California including weather, reservoir storage, stream flows, runoff forecasts and snow and tide data.

US/0147-9806
## CALIFORNIA WATER PLAN OUTLOOK, SUMMARY REPORT, THE. **Main/Corp** California. Dept. of Water Resources. 1974-. English. Department of Water Resources / California, PO Box 942836, Sacramento CA 94236-0001. **Tel** (916)445-3553. **LC** TC424.C2; C28A. **DD** 333.9/1/009794.

CN/0227-4787
## CANADA WATER ACT : ANNUAL REPORT, THE. [Can. water act, Annu. rep.]. **Main/Corp** Canada. Environment Canada. **Added/Corp** Canada. Environment Canada. Loi sur les Ressources Eneau du Canada: Rapport Annuel. **VFOAT** Loi Sur les Ressources en Fau du Canada: Rapport Annuel. (1978/1979)-. English (French). an. Free. Editorial and Publications Division, Inland Waters Directorate, Environment Canada, Ottawa Ontario K1A 0H3 Canada. **Tel** (819)997-2601. **LC** TC426; .C35a. **DD** 333.91/00971. **Continues** Canada. Fisheries and Environment Canada. Canada Water Act: Annual Report, 0227-4787.
**Ind/Abst** GeoRef.

CN/0708-4285
## CANADA WATER YEAR BOOK. **Added/Corp** Canada. Environment Canada. (1975)-. English (French). an. 9.95Can$. Canada Communication Group Publishers, Order Processing, Ottawa Ontario K1A 0S9 Canada. **Tel** (819)956-4800, (819)956-4802. **LC** GB707; .C354. **DD** 333.9/1/00971.

CN/0701-1784
## CANADIAN WATER RESOURCES JOURNAL. (CANADIAN WATER RESOURCES JOURNAL. REVUE CANADIENNE DES RESSOURCES EN EAU.). [Can. water resour. j.]. **Added/Corp** Canadian Water Resources Association. **VFOAT** Revue Canadienne des Ressources en Eau. Vol. 1 (Oct. 1976)-.

Periodical. English (French). Four times a year. 90.95Can$ Canada; 105.00Can$ US; 115.00Can$ other Comes with Canadian Water Resources Association membership. Canadian Water Resources Association / Ontario, PO Box 1329, Membership Service Office, Cambridge Ontario N1R 7G6 Canada. **Tel** (519)622-4764. **DD** 333.9/1/00971. **Bk Rev**. **Ad Acc**. ctrl circ. ***Supersedes*** *Reclamation, 0380-7509.*
**Ind/Abst** ASTIS Curr. Aware. Bull. (1978-); AQUAREF; ASTIS Bibliogr. (1978-); Ei Page One; GeoRef; Environ.

CN/1180-050X
**CANADIAN WATER WELL.** [Can. water well]. Vol. 4, No. 10 (June 1978)-. Periodical. English (summaries and/or abstracts in French). Four times a year (Jan., Apr., June, Sept.). 22.00Can$ Canada; 33.00Can$ US; 55.00Can$ others. AIS Communications Limited, 145 Thames Road West, Exeter Ontario N0M 1S3 Canada. **Tel** (519)235-2400, FAX (519)235-0798. **ED** Scott Hill. **DD** 628.1. **Ad Acc**. ctrl circ.

US
**CATALOG OF INFORMATION ON WATER DATA. INDEX TO WATER-DATA ACQUISITION.** **Added/Corp** Geological Survey (U.S.). Office of Water Data Coordination. (197?)-. Catalog. English. ir. National Technical Information Service - NTIS, Room 2027S, 5285 Port Royal Road, Springfield VA 22161. **Tel** (703)487-4630, (703)487-4660, (703)487-4650, FAX (703)321-8547, telex 89-9405. **LC** TD223; .U535a. **DD** 363.73/942/0975. ***Continues*** *Catalog of Information on Water Data.*

US/0748-0075
**CHEMICAL AND PHYSICAL CHARACTERISTICS OF WATER IN ESTUARIES OF TEXAS.** [Chem. phys. charact. water estuar. Tex.]. Began with Sept. 1967/Sept. 1968. English. an. Texas Department of Water Resources, PO Box 13087, Austin TX 78711. **LC** TD224.T4; A333 subser. **DD** 333.91/009764; 363.7/394.

CC
**CHUNG-KUO SHUI LI.** **Added/Corp** China. Shui Li Tien Li Pu. **VFOAT** China Water Conservancy. (19??)-. Periodical. Chinese. mo. $16.21. **(Subscription address:** China International Book Trading Corporation, PO Box 399, Library Service Department, Beijing 100044 People's Republic of China.**)** **LC** HD1698.C52; C49. **DD** 333.91/00951.
**Desc:** Contains information on water resources development.

US
**CIVIL WORKS WATER RESOURCES DEVELOPMENT PROGRAM.** **Main/Corp** North Carolina. Dept. of Natural Resources and Community Development. English. Department of Natural Resources and Community Development / North Carolina, PO Box 27687, Raleigh NC 27611. **LC** TC424.N8; N57A. **DD** 363.6/1/09756. ***Continues*** *Civil Works Water Resources Development Program, 0145-9619.*

US/0277-8467
**CLEAN WATER ACTION NEWS.** [Clean water action news]. Periodical. English. qt. Clean Water Action Project, 317 Pennsylvania Avenue SE, Washington DC 20003. **CODEN** CWANEH.
**Ind/Abst** BioBusiness.

US/0009-8620
**CLEAN WATER REPORT.** Vol. 1 (Jan. 1964)-. Periodical. English. bw (26 issues). $257.50 US. Business Publishers Inc., 951 Pershing Drive, Silver Spring MD 20910-4464. **Tel** (301)587-6300, (800)274-0122, FAX (301)585-9075. **(Subscription address:** CJE Associates, 237 Gretna Greene Court, Alexandria VA 22304.**)** **ED** Jaime Steve. **NLM** W1 CL123H. **[CCC]**. ***Absorbed*** *Water Reporter.*
**Desc:** Covers clean water act, drinking water, ground water, wetlands, oceans, great lakes, legislation and litigation, Federal Register Notices, upcoming events, business and technology, states news and publications.

US/0092-9433
**CLEAN WATER (WASHINGTON).** (CLEAN WATER: REPORT TO CONGRESS.). [Clean water]. **Main/Corp** United States. Environmental Protection Agency. (1973)-. English. ir. $23.00 (nonmembers), $17.00 (members). Environmental Protection Agency / Washington, 401 M Street SW, Washington DC 20460. **Tel** (202)382-2090. **LC** TD223; .U52a. **DD** 363.6/1. **NLM** W1 A E4C.
**Ind/Abst** GeoRef.

US/0164-2030
**CLEARWATERS.** [Clearwaters]. **Added/Corp** New York Water Pollution Control Association. (19??)-. Periodical. English. qt. $6.00. New York Water Pollution Control Association, 90 Presidential Avenue, Suite 122, Syracuse NY 13202. **Tel** (315)422-7811. **DD** 628. **CODEN** CLEADM.
**Ind/Abst** Sel. Water Resour. Abstr.

US
**COLLECTED REPRINTS - WATER RESOURCES RESEARCH CENTER, UNIVERSITY OF HAWAII.** ***Ceased.*** **Main/Corp** University of Hawaii. Water Resources Research Center. **VFOAT** WRRC Contribution; Contribution. Vol. 1 (1968)-(March 1993). English. ir. University of Hawaii at Manoa, 2540 Dole Street, Holmes Hall 283, Honolulu HI 96822. **Tel** (808)956-7847. **ED** Faith N. Fujimura. cum. index. **Circ:** 300 (ctrl).
**Desc:** Hawaii water resources: rainfall, wastewater reuse, solar radiation, water rights, groundwater, storm runoff, seawater indicator bacteria, floods, conservation economics, runoff impoundment.

US/0092-2684
**COLORADO WATER RESOURCES CIRCULAR.** [Colo. water resour. circ.]. **Added/Corp** Colorado Water Conservation Board. No. 15 (1972)-. English. Colorado Water Conservation Board, 1845 Sherman Street, Denver CO 80203. **LC** GB1025.C7; A32. **DD** 553/.7/09788. **CODEN** CLWCBE. ***Continues*** *Ground Water Series. Circular, 0160-0974.*
**Ind/Abst** GeoRef.

AT/0725-4695
**CONFERENCE SERIES / AUSTRALIAN WATER RESOURCES COUNCIL.** [Aust. Water Resour. Counc. conf. ser.]. **Added/Corp** Australian Water Resources Council. No. 1 (1981)-. Monographic series. English. ir. Free on request. Australian Water Resources, PO Box 5, Natl Dev & Energy, Canberra Act 2600 Australia. **Tel** 011 61 2 458222. **CODEN** AWRSDQ. Documents available from Article Express International, BIOSIS Document Express, CASDDS.
**Ind/Abst** AESIS Q.; Bioeng. Abstr.; Biol. Abstr. (?-1988); Chem. Abstr.; Ei Page One; Eng. Index Annu.; Fish Rev. (Jan. 1989-July 1992); GeoRef; Wildl. Rev. (Jan. 1989-July 1992).

US/0589-400X
**CONNECTICUT WATER RESOURCES BULLETIN.** [Conn. water resour. bull.]. **Added/Corp** Geological Survey (U.S.) Connecticut. Dept. of Environmental Protection. No. 1 (19??)-. Bulletin. English. ir. Price varies per volume. Connecticut Department of Environmental Protection, 165 Capitol Avenue, Room 115, Hartford CT 06106. **Tel** (203)566-2110, FAX (203)566-7932. **LC** TD201; .C65. **DD** 553/.7/09746. **CODEN** CWCBAL. Documents available from BIOSIS Document Express. ***Continues*** *Connecticut. Water Resources Commission. Connecticut Water Resources Bulletin.*
**Ind/Abst** Biol. Abstr.; GeoRef.

US/0575-4941
**CONTRIBUTION (CALIFORNIA WATER RESOURCES CENTER).** **See** Earth Sciences-Hydrology.

US/0890-9172
**CONTRIBUTIONS OF THE GREAT BASIN FOUNDATION.** ***Ceased.*** [Contrib. Gt. Basin Found.]. No. 1 (1985)-(19??). Monographic series. English. sa. Great Basin Foundation, 1236 Concord Street, San Diego CA 92106. **DD** 333.
**Desc:** Contributions consist of shorter papers deriving chiefly from research conducted by The Great Basin Foundation.

FR/1146-5786
**COURANTS PARIS. 1990.** (COURANTS.). (1990)-. Periodical. French. Seven times a year. 455.44F France; 560.00F other. PYC Edition, 5 Avenue de Verdun, BP 105, 94208 Ivry S Seine Cedex France. **Tel** 011 33 1 49608636. **ED** Dominique Bornstein. **UDC** 502(44). Index available. **Bk Rev**. **Ad Acc**. **Circ:** 5,000.
**Desc:** Technical and economical problems about water.

AT/1032-1403
**CSIRO WATER RESOURCES SERIES.** **Added/Corp** Commonwealth Scientific and Industrial Research Organization (Australia). Division of Water Resources. **VFOAT** Water Resources Series. (1989)-. Monographic series. English. Price varies per volume. CSIRO Publications, PO Box 89, 314 Albert Street, East Melborne Victoria 3002 Australia. **Tel** 011 61 3 4187333, 4187217, FAX 011 61 3 4190459, telex AA 30236.
**Ind/Abst** Geogr. Abstr. Phys. Geogr.; GeoRef; Soils Fert.

US
**DENVER WATER NEWS.** (19??)-. Periodical. English. mo. $2.40. Department of Natural Resources / Colorado, 1313 Sherman Street, Room 818, Denver CO 80203. **Tel** (303)839-3581.

US/0360-3946
**DEPARTMENT PUBLICATIONS - STATE OF CALIFORNIA, RESOURCES AGENCY, DEPARTMENT OF WATER RESOURCES.** (DEPARTMENT PUBLICATIONS - STATE OF CALIFORNIA, DEPT. OF WATER RESOURCES.). **Main/Corp** California. Dept. of Water Resources. July/Dec. 1972-. English. an. Department of Water Resources / California, PO Box 942836, Sacramento CA 94236-0001. **Tel** (916)445-3553. **LC** GB705.C2; C22A. **DD** 016.5514/8/09794. ***Continues*** *Abstracts of DWR Publications.*

NE/0011-9164
**DESALINATION.** [Desalination]. Vol. 1 (April 1966)-. Academic Scholarly Publication. English. Fifteen times a year (5 volumes). Fl2475.00. Elsevier Science Publishers BV, PO Box 211, 1000 AE Amsterdam Netherlands. **Tel** 011 31 20 5803642, FAX 011 31 20 5862696, telex 15682. **ED** M. Balaban. **LC** TD478; .D4. **CODEN** DSLNAH. **[CCC]**. **Bk Rev**. **Ad Acc**. **Pr Rev**. available on microfilm and microfiche from University Microfilms International (UMI). Documents available from Article Express International, The Genuine Article, BIOSIS Document Express, Ask*IEEE, CASDDS, Documents on Demand.
**Desc:** Dedicated to keeping pace with the water desalting and purification field in all its aspects. Covers theoretical and applied research, technological and industrial development, and the experience of operators and users.
**Ind/Abst** AGRICOLA [Select. Cov.]; AQUAREF; Aquat. Sci. Fish. Abstr. (Computer File); Bioeng. Abstr.; Biol. Abstr.; Chem. Abstr.; Chem. Titles; Curr. Biotechnol.; Curr. Contents Eng. Tech. Appl. Sci.; Ei Page One; EMBASE; Energy Inf. Abstr.; Energy Res. Abstr.; Eng. Index Annu.; Environ. Abstr.; Environ. Period. Bibliogr.; Fluid Abstr., Civil Eng.; Fluid Abstr. Proc. Eng.; FLUIDEX (1973-); Food Sci. Technol. Abstr.; Health Saf. Sci. Abstr.; HTFS Dig.; INSPEC (Oct. 1970-); Int. Civil Eng. Abstr.; Ocean. Abstr.; Life Sci. Collect.; Pollut. Abstr. Indexes; Proc. Chem. Eng.; Res. Alert [Full Cov.]; Sci. Cit. Index; SCISEARCH; Soft. Abstr. Eng.; Soyabean Abstr.; Theoret. Chem. Eng.

CN
**DETAILED SURFACE WATER QUALITY DATA. ALBERTA, MANITOBA, NORTHWEST TERRITORIES, AND SASKATCHEWAN.** **Added/Corp** Canada. Inland Waters Directorate. Western and Northern Region. Water Quality Branch. Canada. Environment Canada. **VFOAT** Donnees Detaillees sur la Qualite des Eaux de Surface. Alberta, Manitoba, Territoires du Nord-Ouest et Saskatchewan. (1982)-. English (French). **LC** TD226; .D48. **DD** 363.7/3942/0971. ***Formed by the union of*** *Detailed Surface Water Quality Data. Northwest Territories, 0823-4833;* ***Detailed Surface Water Quality*** *Data. Manitoba, 0715-6014; Detailed Surface Water Quality Data. Alberta* ***and*** *Detailed Surface Water Quality Data. Saskatchewan, 0823-3551.*

GW/0012-0235
**DEUTSCHE GEWAESSERKUNDLICHE MITTEILUNGEN.** [Dtsch. Gewasserkd. Mitt.]. **Added/Corp** Bundesanstalt fur Gewasserkunde (Germany). Vol. 1 (April 1957)-. Periodical. German (summaries and/or abstracts in English). Six times a year. DM50.00. Bundesanstalt fuer Gewaesserkunde, Kaiserin Augusta Anlagen 15, West 5400 Koblenz F R Germany. **Tel** 011 49 261 13061 ext 319, FAX 011 49 261 1306302, telex 862499. **ED** H Liebscher. **LC** GB651; .D4. **DD** 551.4; 627. **CODEN** DGMTAO. **Bk Rev**. **Circ:** 1,600. Documents available from CASDDS. ***Supersedes*** *Bundesanstalt fur Gewasserkunde. Mitteilungen.*
**Desc:** Covers quantitative and qualitative hydrology, water pollution control, water protection (from basic research to practical use in water resource management).
**Ind/Abst** Chem. Abstr.; Electron. Commun. Abstr. J.; EMBASE; Energy Res. Abstr. (June 1971-); GeoRef; ISMEC Bull.; Life Sci. Collect.; Pollut. Abstr. Indexes; Saf. Sci. Abstr. J.

GW/0170-9976
**DEUTSCHES GEWASSERKUNDLICHES JAHRBUCH. RHEINGEBIET. TEIL III, MITTEL- UND NIEDERRHEIN MIT IJSSELGEBIET.** **VFOAT** Rheingebiet; Mittel- und Niederrhein Mit Ijsselgebiet. German. an. **LC** WMLC L 83/460. ***Continues in part*** *Deutsches Gewasserkundliches Jahrbuch. Rheingebiet.*

UK/0263-3736
**DEVELOPMENTS IN WATER TREATMENT.** [Dev. water treat.]. (1980)-. Academic Scholarly Publication. English. ir (numbered series). Price varies. Routledge Chapman & Hall Inc, 29 West 35th Street, New York NY 10001. **Tel** (212)244-3336, (212)244-6412. **CODEN** DWTRDW. Documents available from CASDDS.
**Ind/Abst** Chem. Abstr.

CN/0704-7878
**DIRECTORY - AMERICAN WATER WORKS ASSOCIATION, ONTARIO SECTION.** **Main/Corp** American Water Works Association. Ontario Section. 1977-. Directory. English. an. American Water Works Association / Canada, Ontario Section, 45-23rd Street, Toronto Ontario M8V 3M6 Canada. **Tel** (416)252-7060. **DD** 628.1/06/2713. ctrl circ.
**Desc:** List of committees membership listing.

US/0364-9296
**DIRECTORY OF WATER RESOURCES EXPERTISE.** 1st Ed., (1974)-. Directory. English. California Water Resources Center, University of California, Riverside CA. **LC** TC424.C2; D57. **DD** 333.9/1/0025794.

GW
**DOKUMENTATION WASSER ABFALL.** (19??)-. Periodical. German. Nine times a year.

DM268.20. Erich Schmidt Verlag GmbH, Postfach 304240, D 10724 Berlin Germany. **Tel** 011 49 30 25008525. ***Continues*** *Dokumentation Wasser.*

US/1055-2782
**DRINKING WATER & BACKFLOW PREVENTION.** [Drink. water backflow prev.]. (1990)-. Periodical. English. Twelve times a year. $32.50 (U.S.), $46.50 (Canada), $50.00 (overseas). SFA Enterprises Inc, PO Box 33209, Northglenn CO 80233. **Tel** (303)451-0978, (303)451-0980, FAX (303)452-9776, telex 3762848. **ED** Stuart F Asay. **DD** 696. cum. index. **Bk Rev**. **Ad Acc**. **Circ:** 3,000 (ctrl). ***Continues*** *Backflow Prevention, 8755-3457.*
**Desc:** Dedicated to water system safety. DWBP keeps you informed of all the current industry news and upcoming events from manufacturers and organizations. We have legal experts who write on water industry topics. Other information includes code changes, legislation and standard development.

US/1055-9140
**DRINKING WATER RESEARCH : AN UPDATE FROM THE AWWA RESEARCH FOUNDATION.** [Drink. water res.]. **Added/Corp** AWWA Research Foundation. Vol. 1, No. 1 (Jan./Feb. 1991)-. Periodical. English. bm. $40.00. AWWA, 6666 West Quincy Avenue, Denver CO 80235. **LC** TD353; .D74. **DD** 628.1.

GW/0724-7605
**DVGW-NACHRICHTEN. See** Petroleum and Natural Gas.

GW/0012-5156
**DW DOKUMENTATION WASSER. *Title Change.*** (DOKUMENTATION WASSER.). [DW Dok. Wasser]. **Added/Corp** Deutscher Arbeitskreis Wasserforschung. (1960)-(19??). Periodical. German. mo. Erich Schmidt Verlag GmbH, Postfach 304240, D 10724 Berlin Germany. **Tel** 011 49 30 25008525. **LC** Z7935; .D6. **NLM** ZWA 675 D658. **[CCC]. Bk Rev. Ad Acc. *Continued by*** *Dokumentation Wasser Abfall / DWA, 0945-6937.*
**Desc:** Water documentation.
**Ind/Abst** Energy Res. Abstr. (March 1982-); GeoRef.

FR/0755-5016
**EAU, L'INDUSTRIE, LES NUISANCES, L'. See** Environmental Issues-Pollution and Waste Management.

FI/0786-0021
**ENERGIAN TUOTANTO JA VESIHUOLTO. See** Energy.

TH/0125-5088
**ENVIRONMENTAL SANITATION REVIEWS. Added/Corp** Environmental Sanitation Information Center (Bangkok, Thailand). No. 1 (Aug. 1980)-. Periodical. English. tq. Asian Institute of Technology / Regional Energy Resources Information Center / RERIC, PO Box 2754, 10501 Bangkok, Thailand. **Tel** 011 66 2 516-0110-29, 011 66 2 516-0130-44, FAX 011 66 2 516-2126. **CODEN** ENSRD9.
**Ind/Abst** Abstr. AIT Rep. Publ. Energy.

UY
**ESTADISTICA - OSE. Main/Corp** Uruguay. Administracion de Las Obras Sanitarias del Estado. Statistical Publication. Spanish. **LC** TD53; .O3A.

NE/0925-5060
**EUROPEAN WATER POLLUTION CONTROL : OFFICIAL PUBLICATION OF THE EUROPEAN WATER POLLUTION CONTROL ASSOCIATION (EWPCA). Added/Corp** European Water Pollution Control Association. Vol. 1, No. 1 (Jan. 1991)-. Academic Scholarly Publication. English (French and German). bm (1 volume). Fl325.00. Elsevier Science Publishers BV, PO Box 211, 1000 AE Amsterdam Netherlands. **Tel** 011 31 20 5803642, FAX 011 31 20 5862696, telex 15682. **ED** J de Jong. **LC** TD255; .E96. **DD** 363.73/9456/094. **CODEN** EWPCED. **[CCC]. Bk Rev. Ad Acc. Pr Rev. Circ:** 4,000. available on microfilm and microfiche from University Microfilms International (UMI). Documents available from Article Express International.
**Desc:** A focal point for communication between all European technologists and researchers concerned with water quality. Official publication of the European Water Pollution Control Association.
**Ind/Abst** Biodeter. Abstr. (1991-); Curr. Aware. Biol. Sci., CABS; Ei Page One; Eng. Index Annu.; Fluid Abstr., Civil Eng.; Fluid Abstr. Proc. Eng.; FLUIDEX; Geogr. Abstr. Phys. Geogr.; Geogr. Abstr. Human Geogr.

US
**FACETS OF FRESHWATER. Added/Corp** Freshwater Foundation. Freshwater Biological Research Foundation. Freshwater Society. (1976)-. Periodical. English. qt. $35.00. Freshwater Foundation, Spring Hill Center, 725 County Road 6, Wayzata MN 55391. **Tel** (612)449-0092. **ED** Gretchen Kehler.

US/1048-3063
**FEDERATION HIGHLIGHTS.** (FEDERATION HIGHLIGHTS / WATER POLLUTION CONTROL FEDERATION.). [Fed. highlights]. **Added/Corp** Water Pollution Control Federation. Vol. 25, No. 9 (Sept. 1988)-. Periodical. English. mo. $19.00 US; $29.00 other. Water Environment Federation, 601 Wythe Street, Alexandria VA 22314-1994. **Tel** (703)684-2400, FAX (703)684-2492. **DD** 363. available on microfilm and microfiche from University Microfilms International (UMI). ***Continues*** *Highlights, 0049-6987.*

US/0430-4845
**FINANCIAL STATISTICS OF PUBLIC UTILITIES. See** Public Administration-Public Utilities.

US
**FISCAL YEAR PROGRAM REPORT / WATER RESOURCES RESEARCH CENTER, PURDUE UNIVERSITY. Main/Corp** Purdue University. Water Resources Research Center. 20th (Fiscal Year 1984)-. English. an. Free. Purdue Water Resources Research Center, Lilly Hall, Purdue University, West Lafayette IN 47907. **Tel** (317)494-8041, FAX (317)494-0395, telex 4930593. **ED** J R Wright. **Circ:** 300. ***Continues*** *Annual Report of the Purdue University Water Resources Research Center.*

US/0896-1794
**FLORIDA WATER RESOURCES JOURNAL.** [Fla. water resour. j.]. **Added/Corp** Florida Water & Pollution Control Operators Association. American Water Works Association. Florida Section. Florida Pollution Control Association. (198?)-. Periodical. English. mo. $24.00. Florida Water Resources Journal, PO Box 1702518, Gainesville FL 32605. **Tel** (904)374-4946. **LC** TD485; .F58. **DD** 628/.09759. **Bk Rev. Ad Acc. Pr Rev. Circ:** 8,000 (ctrl). ***Continues*** *Overflow Magazine.*
**Desc:** Concentrates on water treatment and distribution, and wastewater collection and treatment in Florida.

US
**FLUORIDATED DRINKING WATER, PROFICIENCY TESTING.** English. mo. Centers for Disease Control, 1600 Clifton Road NE, Atlanta GA 30333. **Tel** (404)639-3311, FAX (404)639-3296.

RU/0130-5824
**FORMIROVANIE I KONTROL KACESTVA POVERHNOSTNYH VOD. See** Biology.

GW/0071-7983
**FORTSCHRITTE DER WASSERCHEMIE UND IHRER GRENZGEBIETE. *Title Change.*** [Fortschr. Wasserchem. Grenzgeb.]. **Added/Corp** Chemische Gesellschaft in der Deutschen Demokratischen Republik. Vol. 1 (1964)-(19??). German. ir. Akademie-Verlag GmbH, Muehlenstrasse 33 34, D 13162 Berlin Germany. **Tel** 011 49 30 47889300, FAX 011 49 30 47889357. **(Subscription address:** VCH Publishers Inc., 303 Northwest 12th Avenue, Journals Department, Deerfield FL 33442.**) LC** TD430; .F6. **NLM** W1 FO895. cum. index. ***Continued by*** *Acta Hydrochimica et Hydrobiologica, 0071-7983.*

RU/0869-8902
**GARMONIIA. See** Public Health and Safety.

GW/0016-3651
**GAS- UND WASSERFACH. WASSER, ABWASSER : GWF, DAS. Added/Corp** Deutscher Verein von Gas- und Wasserfachmannern. Deutscher Verein des Gas- und Wasserfaches. **VFOAT** Wasser, Abwasser; GWF; GWF-Wasser/Abwasser. Vol. 111 (1970)-. Academic Scholarly Publication. German (table of contents in English and French). mo. DM350.00. R Oldenbourg Verlag, Postfach 801360, D 81613 Munich Germany. **Tel** 011 49 89 450190, FAX 011 49 89 45019305. **CODEN** GWWAAQ. **[CCC].** Documents available from Article Express International, CASDDS. ***Continues in part*** *GWF, Das Gas- und Wasserfach.*
**Desc:** Journal for water resource management, development and application. Special attention is devoted to waste water handling and purification. Also covers hydrogeological and microbiological aspects of water technology.
**Ind/Abst** Bioeng. Abstr.; Chem. Abstr.; Coal Abstr.; Ei Page One; EMBASE; Energy Res. Abstr. (Jan. 1971-); Eng. Index Annu.; Fluid Abstr., Civil Eng.; Fluid Abstr. Proc. Eng.; FLUIDEX (1973-1989); Gas Abstr.; GeoRef.

US/0888-5168
**GENERAL SERIES - UTAH WATER RESEARCH LABORATORY.** (GENERAL SERIES / UTAH WATER RESEARCH LABORATORY, CENTER FOR WATER RESOURCES RESEARCH AND AGRICULTURAL AND IRRIGATION ENGINEERING.). [Gen. ser. - Utah Water Res. Lab.]. English. ir. Utah Water Research Laboratory, Utah State University, Logan UT 84322-8200. **Tel** (801)750-3200, FAX (801)750-3663, telex 3729283. **ED** Colleen Riley. **DD** 353. **Circ:** 300.
**Desc:** Annual and summary of annual reports including: landslide, flash floods, and debris flow proceedings.
**Ind/Abst** GeoRef.

GW/0342-6068
**GEWASSERSCHUTZ, WASSER, ABWASSER.** (GEWASSERSCHUTZ, WASSER, ABWASSER : GWA.). [Gewasserschutz, Wasser, Abwasser]. **VFOAT** GWA; G.W.A. (1968)-. Academic Scholarly Publication. German. ir. Price varies per volume. Gesellschft Forderung Siedlung, Rwth Aachen Templergraben 55, D 52062 Aachen Germany. **Tel** 011 49 241 805216. **CODEN** GWABDO. Documents available from CASDDS.
**Ind/Abst** Chem. Abstr.; GeoRef; Soils Fert.

RU/0367-4665
**GIDROKHIMICHESKIE MATERIALY. See** Chemistry.

RU/0016-9714
**GIDROTEHNICESKOE STROITELSTVO (MOSKVA).** (GIDROTEKHNICHESKOE STROITELSTVO.). [Gidroteh. stroit.]. **Added/Corp** Soviet Union. Narodnyi Komissariat Elektrostantsii. Soviet Union. Ministerstvo Elektrostantsii. Soviet Union. Ministerstvo Elektrostantsii i Elektropromyshlennosti. Soviet Union. Ministerstvo Stroitelstva Elektrostantsii. Soviet Union. Ministerstvo Energetiki i Elektrifikatsii. Nauchno-Tekhnicheskoe Obshchestvo Energetiki i Elektrotekhnicheskoi Promyshlennosti (Soviet Union) Nauchno-Tekhnicheskoe Obshchestvo Energetiki i Elektrotekhnicheskoi Promyshlennosti Imeni Akademika G.M. Krzhizhanovskogo. TSentralnoe Pravlenie. (1930)-. Academic Scholarly Publication. Russian. mo. $199.95. Ministerstvo Goryuchego i Energetiki Rossii, Bolshoi Cherkasskii Per. 2-10, 103012 Moscow Russia. **(Subscription address:** East View Publications Inc., 3020 Harbor Lane North, Suite 110, Minneapolis MN 55447.**) CODEN** GTSTA8. Documents available from Article Express International, Ask*IEEE, CASDDS. ***Continues*** *Biulleten Gidrotekhstroia.*
**Ind/Abst** Chem. Abstr. (-1981); Ei Page One; Eng. Index Annu.; Fluid Abstr., Civil Eng.; Fluid Abstr. Proc. Eng.; FLUIDEX (1973-); INSPEC (1968-).

PL/0017-2448
**GOSPODARKA WODNA.** [Gosp. wod.]. (1935)-. Academic Scholarly Publication. Polish (summaries and/or abstracts in Russian, French and English). mo. $84.00. **(Subscription address:** ARS Polona, PO Box 1001, 00068 Warsaw Poland.**) CODEN** GOWOAC. Documents available from CASDDS.
**Ind/Abst** Chem. Abstr.; Energy Res. Abstr. (Oct. 1975-).

US/0072-7326
**GREAT LAKES RESEARCH CHECKLIST. See** Water Resources-Abstracting, Bibliographies and Statistics.

US
**GREAT LAKES RESEARCH VESSELS SUPPLEMENT; PRELIMINARY SCHEDULES.** 1979-. English. an. ***Supersedes in part*** *Great Lakes Research Vessels : Capabilities and Preliminary Schedules.*

US
**GREAT LAKES UNITED, THE. See** Environmental Issues.

US/0046-645X
**GROUND WATER AGE.** [Ground water age]. **VFOAT** GWA. Vol. 1 (Sept. 1966)-. Periodical. English. Twelve times a year. $39.00 US & Canada; $90.00 others. National Trade Publications, 13 Century Hill Drive, Latham NY 12110. **Tel** (518)783-1281, FAX (518)783-1386. **ED** Tom Williams. **LC** TD403; .G7. **DD** 333.9/104/05. **CODEN** GWAGD5. **[CCC]. Bk Rev. Ad Acc. Pr Rev. Circ:** 22,000 (ctrl). available on microfilm from Xerox; available on microfilm and microfiche from University Microfilms International (UMI).
**Desc:** Provides technical, sales and marketing information to the water well industry. Reports industry developments affecting the industry's growth.
**Ind/Abst** BioBusiness; Coal Abstr.; EMBASE; GeoRef.

US/0098-3691
**GROUND-WATER DATA FOR MICHIGAN.** [Ground-water data Mich.]. **VFOAT** Ground Water Data for Michigan. Began in 1973. English. an. Michigan Department of the Interior, Box 30028, R Thomas Segall, Lansing MI 48909. **LC** GB1025.M5; A27. **DD** 553.7/9/09774. available on microfiche (Vols. for (1980-) distributed to depository libraries). ***Continues*** *Summary of Ground-Water Hydrologic Data in Michigan, 0085-6924.*

US
**GROUND-WATER LEVELS IN ARKANSAS. Added/Corp** Arkansas Geological Commission. Geological Survey (U.S.). **VFOAT** Ground Water Levels in Arkansas. English. **LC** GB1025.A8; G46a. **DD** 553.7/9/09767. ***Continues*** *Ground-Water Levels in Observation Wells in Arkansas, 0736-2757.*

US/0548-6165
**GROUND-WATER LEVELS IN NEW MEXICO. BASIC DATA REPORT.** [Ground-water levels N.M., Basic data rep.]. **VFOAT** Basic Data Report. (1961)-. English. an. Office of the

State Engineer, Santa Fe NM 87503. **Tel** (505)827-6110. **LC** GB1025.N6; A35. **DD** 551.49/2/09789. **CODEN** NMEBA. **Circ:** 500. ***Continues in part*** *Ground-Water Levels in New Mexico.*
**Desc:** Water resource data and investigations agency report.
**Ind/Abst** GeoRef.

US/0499-5198
**GROUND-WATER LEVELS IN THE UNITED STATES. NORTH-CENTRAL STATES.** **Main/Corp** United States. Geological Survey. English. US Geological Survey / Denver, PO Box 25286, Denver CO 80225. **Tel** (303)493-8401. ***Supersedes in part*** *Water Levels and Artesian Pressure in Observation Wells in the United States.*

US/0502-1464
**GROUND-WATER LEVELS IN THE UNITED STATES. SOUTH-CENTRAL STATES.** **Main/Corp** United States. Geological Survey. 1956-59-. English. US Geological Survey / Denver, PO Box 25286, Denver CO 80225. **Tel** (303)493-8401. ***Supersedes in part*** *Water Levels and Artesian Pressure in Observation Wells in the United States.*

US
**GROUND-WATER LEVELS IN THE UNITED STATES. SOUTHWESTERN STATES.** **Main/Corp** United States. Geological Survey. 1956/60-. English. US Geological Survey / Denver, PO Box 25286, Denver CO 80225. **Tel** (303)493-8401. ***Supersedes in part*** *Water Levels and Artesian Pressure in Observation Wells in the United States.*

US/0741-8507
**GROUND WATER MODELING NEWSLETTER.** (GROUND WATER MODELING NEWSLETTER / HOLCOMB RESEARCH INSTITUTE.). [Ground water model. newsl.]. **Added/Corp** Holcomb Research Institute. International Ground Water Modeling Center. **VFOAT** G.W.M. Newsletter; GWM Newsletter; IGWMC Ground Water Modeling Newsletter. (198?)-. Periodical. English. Four times a year. Holcomb Research Institute, IGWMC, Butler University, 4600 Sunset Avenue, Indianapolis IN 46208. **Tel** (317)283-9421. **ED** Paul van der Heijde.
**Desc:** The latest information and news about in ground water modeling.

US/0090-5070
**GROUND WATER NEWSLETTER / WATER INFORMATION CENTER, WIC, THE.** [Ground water newsl.]. **Added/Corp** Water Information Center, Inc. **VFOAT** Groundwater Newsletter. Vol. 1, No. 1, May 8 (1972)-. Newsletter. English. sm. $247.00 US and Canada; $267.00 other (one year); $420.00 US and Canada; $357.00 other (two year). Water Information Center Inc, 1099 18th Street, Suite 2150, Denver CO 80202. **Tel** (303)391-8799. **ED** Judith M Schoeck. **DD** 628. **CODEN** GWNEDU. **[CCC].**
**Desc:** Provides comprehensive coverage of the latest information on groundwater matters, hazardous wastes, new technology, studies and legislation.
**Ind/Abst** GeoRef.

US/0738-1204
**GROUNDWATER QUALITY MONITORING PROGRAM.** (GROUND WATER QUALITY MONITORING PROGRAM / BY DALE TRIPPLER AND THOMAS P. CLARK.). **Added/Corp** Minnesota Pollution Control Agency. Program Development and Facility Review Section. Vol. 3 (1980)-. English. an. Minnesota Pollution Control Agency, Division of Solid and Hazardous Waste, Program Development and Facility MN. **LC** TD224.M6; G76. **DD** 363.7/394. ***Continues*** *Groundwater Quality Monitoring Program, 0738-1204.*

AT/0810-8404
**GROUNDWATER RESEARCH / CSIRO, [DIVISION OF GROUNDWATER RESEARCH].** **Main/Corp** Commonwealth Scientific and Industrial Research Organization (Australia). Division of Groundwater Research. (198?)-. English. CSIRO Publications, PO Box 89, 314 Albert Street, East Melborne Victoria 3002 Australia. **Tel** 011 61 3 4187333, 4187217, FAX 011 61 3 4190459, telex AA 30236. **LC** GB1175; .C65a. **DD** 553.7/9/07209411.

FR
**GUIDE DE L'EAU.** French. an. 920.00F France; 782.77F other. Pierre Johanet et Ses Fils, 7 Avenue Franklin Roosevelt, 75008 Paris France. **Tel** 1 43 59 08 89, FAX 1 42 25 59 47, telex 649712.

NE/0166-8439
**H2O.** [H2O]. **VFOAT** H Twee O. (1968)-. Periodical. Dutch. bw (26 issues). Fl145.00. Secretaris Stiching H2O, Postbus 70, 2280 AB Rijswijk Netherlands. **Tel** 011 31 70 953525 26. **UDC** 628.1.

NE
**H2O TIJDSCHRIFT VOOR DRINKWATERVOORZIENING EN AFVALWATERBEHANDELING.** (19??)-. Periodical. Dutch. Twenty-six times a year. Fl120.00 Netherlands; Fl160.00 other. Stichting H2O, Postbus 70, 2280 AB Rijswijk, Netherlands. **Tel** 011 31 70 3953535. **ED** G. B. Vinke. Index available. **Ad Acc. Circ:** 4,500.
**Desc:** Covers drinking water supply, waste water management, ground water catchment, aquatic ecology and surface water management.

UN/0204-3556
**HIMIJA I TEHNOLOGIJA VODY.** (KHIMIIA I TEKHNOLOGIIA VODY.). [Him. tehnol. vody]. **Added/Corp** Akademiia Nauk SSSR. Otdelenie Obshchei i Tekhnicheskoi Khimii. Akademiia Nauk Ukrainskoi RSR. Viddil Khimii ta Khimichnoi Tekhnolohii. (1979)-. Academic Scholarly Publication. Russian (summaries and/or abstracts in English). mo. $299.95. Izdatelstvo Naukova Dumka / Ukrainian Academy of Sciences, Vladimirskaia Ulitsa 54, 252601 Kiev Ukraine. **Tel** 225-63-66, telex 131376. **(Subscription address:** East View Publications Inc., 3020 Harbor Lane North, Suite 110, Minneapolis MN 55447.) **LC** TD204; .K45. **CODEN** KTVODL. Documents available from Article Express International, CASDDS.
**Ind/Abst** Chem. Abstr.; Coal Abstr.; Curr. Biotechnol.; Ei Page One; Eng. Index Annu.; Pollut. Abstr. Indexes; Sug. Indus. Abstr.

US
**HYDATA NEWS AND VIEWS.** **Added/Corp** American Water Resources Association. (19??)-. Periodical. English. bm (6 issues). $23.00 US; $29.00 other. AWRA - American Water Resources Association, 950 Herndon Parkway, Suite 300, Herndon VA 22070-5528. **Tel** (703)904-1225, FAX (703)904-1228. Index available (bound in all issues). **Ad Acc. Circ:** 4,200 (ctrl). available on microfilm.

US/0731-6445
**HYDRO-ABSTRACTS.** [Hydro-abstr.]. **Added/Corp** Environmental Hydrology Corporation. Vol. 1, No. 1 (Jan. 1980)-. English. mo. $135.00. International Scientific Press, 2145 Draper Avenue, St. Paul MN 55113. **Tel** (612)636-4082. ***Continues*** *Water Resources Abstracts, 0043-1362.*

US
**HYDROLOGIC DATA.** **See** Earth Sciences-Hydrology.

US/0147-3697
**HYDROLOGIC REPORT (LOS ANGELES).** (HYDROLOGIC REPORT - LOS ANGELES COUNTY FLOOD CONTROL DISTRICT.). [Hydrol. rep.]. **Main/Corp** Los Angeles County Flood Control District. (19??)-. English. ir. $25.00. Los Angeles County Department of Public Works, 900 South Fremont Avenue, Alhambra CA 91803. **Tel** (818)458-6109. **LC** TC425.L65; L66a. **DD** 551.4/8/0979493. ctrl circ.
**Desc:** Hydraulic data for Los Angeles County: precipitation, runoff, evaporation, dam operation, conservation and groundwater.
**Ind/Abst** GeoRef.

US/0272-6106
**HYDROLOGY AND WATER RESOURCES IN ARIZONA AND THE SOUTHWEST.** **See** Earth Sciences-Hydrology.

NP
**ICIMOD OCCASIONAL PAPER.** **See** Economics.

II/0019-5537
**INDIAN JOURNAL OF POWER AND RIVER VALLEY DEVELOPMENT.** [Indian j. power river val. dev.]. **VFOAT** Indian Journal of Power & River Valley Development. (December 1950)-. Periodical. English. Twelve times a year. $48.00. Books & Journals Private Ltd, 6-2 Madan Street, Calcutta 72 India. **Tel** 011 91 33 271711, 011 91 33 275867, FAX 011 91 33 24829737, telex 021-4427 ITOP IN, 021-4513 ITO IN. **(Subscription address:** Prints India, 11 Darya Ganj, New Delhi 110002 India.) **ED** P. K. Menon and P. K. Chanda. **LC** TC1; .I55. **CODEN** IJPRA7. **Ad Acc. Circ:** 2,000 (ctrl). available on microfilm and microfiche from University Microfilms International (UMI). Documents available from Article Express International, Ask*IEEE.
**Desc:** Devoted to all aspects of thermal and hydropower systems engineering and technology, irrigation and river valley projects, the most important and basic sector in the country's plans for economic development.
**Ind/Abst** AGRICOLA; Coal Abstr.; Ei Page One; Energy Res. Abstr.; Eng. Index Annu.; Fish Rev.; Fluid Abstr., Civil Eng.; Fluid Abstr. Proc. Eng.; FLUIDEX (1973-); GeoRef; Indian Geosci. Abstr.; INSPEC (Jan. 1969-); Irr. Drain. Abstr.; Leis. Recreat. Tour. Abstr.; Rural Dev. Abstr.; Soils Fert.; Stat. Theory Method Abstr. (1959-1963); Wildl. Rev.; World Agric. Econ.

●US/1067-5337
**INDUSTRIAL WASTEWATER.** [Ind. wastewater]. **Added/Corp** Water Environment Federation. Vol. 1, No. 1 (Apr. 1993)-. Periodical. English. bm. $144.00 US; $187.00 other. Water Environment Federation, 601 Wythe Street, Alexandria VA 22314-1994. **Tel** (703)684-2400, FAX (703)684-2492. **DD** 363.
**Desc:** Covers industrial wastewater management issues including, regulations, treatment technologies, and pollution prevention strategies.

US/1058-3645
**INDUSTRIAL WATER TREATMENT.** [Ind. water treat.]. (19??)-. Periodical. English. Six times a year. $18.00 US; $63.00 others. Tall Oaks Publishing Inc, PO Box 621669, 60 Golden Eagle Lane, Littleton CO 80127. **Tel** (303)973-6600, (800)662-1660, FAX (303)973-5327. **(Subscription address:** Tall Oaks Publishing Company, PO Box 621669, Littleton CO 80162.) **DD** 628. ***Continues*** *Industrial Water Engineering, 0019-8862.*

US/0884-8246
**INFORMATION CIRCULAR - MISSOURI. DIVISION OF GEOLOGICAL SURVEY AND WATER RESOURCES.** **See** Earth Sciences-Geology.

US/0471-265x
**INFORMATION CIRCULAR - STATE OF OHIO, DEPARTMENT OF NATURAL RESOURCES, DIVISION OF WATER.** **Main/Corp** Ohio. Department of Natural Resources. Division of Water. No. 1 (1953)-. Monographic series. English. ir. Price varies per volume. Department of Natural Resources / Ohio, Fountain Square, Columbus OH 43224. **Tel** (614)265-6590. **ED** Merrianne Hackathorn.

FR/0012-9003
**INFORMATION EAUX.** [Inf. eaux]. **Added/Corp** Association Francaise pour l'Etude des Eaux. Vol. 20, No. 193 (Jan. 1971)-. Periodical. French. Thirty-one times a year. 5000.00F. Office International De l Eau, Rue Edouard Chamberland, 87065 Limoges Cedex France. **Tel** 011 33 55 114780. **NLM** W1 IN4203. cum. index. **Bk Rev.** ***Continues*** *Eaux et Industries.*
**Desc:** Covers water, hydrology, hydrogeology, water quality, drinking water, water and wastewater treatment, seawater, sludge treatment, corrosion, irrigation and drainage, sanitation, and developing countries.
**Ind/Abst** GeoRef.

US/0198-8735
**INFORMATION SERIES - COLORADO WATER RESOURCES RESEARCH INSTITUTE.** **See** Environmental Issues-Conservation and Natural Resources.

US
**INLAND SEAS INDEX.** English. an. $9.00. Great Lakes Historical Society, 480 Main Street, Vermilion OH 44089. **Tel** (216)967-3467, FAX (216)967-1519.

UK/0962-0311
**INSTITUTION OF WATER OFFICERS JOURNAL.** (1965)-. English. qt.
**Ind/Abst** Fluid Abstr., Civil Eng.; Fluid Abstr. Proc. Eng.; FLUIDEX (19??-).

MC/0020-6938
**INTERNATIONAL HYDROGRAPHIC BULLETIN. BULLETIN HYDROGRAPHIQUE INTERNATIONAL.** **Added/Corp** International Hydrography Bureau. **VFOAT** Bulletin Hydrographique International. (1928)-. Periodical. English (French). Twelve times a year. 350.00F EEC countries; 400.00F others. International Hydrographic Bureau, BP 445, 7 Avenue President J. F. Kennedy, MC 98011 Cedex Monaco. **Tel** 011 33 93506587, FAX 011 33 93 25 2003, telex 479164 MC. **LC** VK588; .I45.
**Ind/Abst** Aquat. Sci. Fish. Abstr. (Computer File); Ocean. Abstr.

UK/0790-0627
**INTERNATIONAL JOURNAL OF WATER RESOURCES DEVELOPMENT.** [Int. j. water resour. dev.]. **VFOAT** Water Resources Development. Vol. 1, No. 1 (Apr. 1983)-. Periodical. English. qt (Mar., Jun., Sep. and Dec.). £158.00. Carfax Publishing Company, PO Box 25 Abingdon, Oxfordshire OX14 3UE England. **Tel** 011 44 235 555335, FAX (0279)31067, telex 817484. **(Subscription address:** US and Canada/ PO Box 2025, Dunnellon, FL 34430-2025; telephone:(904)489-6996) **ED** Asit K. Biswas. **[CCC].** Index available. **Bk Rev. Ad Acc.** available on microfilm and microfiche from University Microfilms International (UMI). Documents available from Article Express International, Documents on Demand.
**Desc:** Covers all aspects of water development and management in both industrialized and Third World countries. Content focuses on the practical implementation of policies for water resources development, monitoring and evaluation of technical projects, and, to a lesser extent, water resources research.
**Ind/Abst** AGRICOLA [Select. Cov.]; Ei Page One; Eng. Index Annu.; Environ. Abstr.; Environ. Period. Bibliogr.;

Fish Rev.; For. Abstr.; Irr. Drain. Abstr.; Rev. Med. Vet. Entomol.; Rural Dev. Abstr.; Soils Fert.; Wheat Barley Trit. Abstr.; World Agric. Econ.

●IS
**INTERNATIONAL WATER & IRRIGATION REVIEW.** **See** Agriculture-Crop Production and Soil.

US/0893-8776
**INTERNATIONAL WATER REPORT.** **See** Environmental Issues-Pollution and Waste Management.

US/0094-0569
**INVENTORY OF INTERSTATE CARRIER WATER SUPPLY SYSTEMS BY STATES AND ENVIRONMENTAL PROTECTION AGENCY REGIONS.** **Main/Corp** United States. Environmental Protection Agency. Water Supply Division. **VFOAT** Inventory of Interstate Carrier Water Supply Systems. English. Environmental Protection Agency / Water Supply Division, 401 M Street SW, Washington DC 20460. **LC** TD223; .U52C. **DD** 363.6/1.

US/0092-9158
**INVENTORY OF WASTE WATER PRODUCTION AND WASTE WATER RECLAMATION PRACTICES IN CALIFORNIA.** **See** Environmental Issues-Pollution and Waste Management.

US
**IRC BULLETIN / UNITED STATES ENVIRONMENT PROTECTION AGENCY, NATIONAL TRAINING AND OPERATIONAL TECHNOLOGY CENTER.** ***Ceased.*** **VFOAT** EPA IRC Bulletin. **VAT** Instructional Resources Center Bulletin. Bulletin. English. an. EPA Instructional Resources Center, Ohio State University 1200 Chambers, Columbus OH 43212. **Tel** (614)292-6717. **ED** Robert W Howe. **Circ:** 15,000 (ctrl).
**Desc:** Provides information on water quality education and training with an emphasis on publications, audio-visual aids, and training opportunities. Also includes selected information on recent events.

GW/0537-796X
**IWL-FORUM.** [IWL-Forum]. **Added/Corp** Institut fur Gewerbliche Wasserwirtschaft und Luftreinhaltung (North Rhine-Westphalia, Germany). **VFOAT** IWL Forum; Forum. **VAT** Institut fur Gewerbliche Wasserwirtschaft und Luftreinhaltung-Forum; Institut fur Gewerbliche Wasserwirtschaft und Luftreinhaltung Forum. (19??)-. Monographic series. German. Institut fur Gewerbliche Wasserwirtschaft und Luftreinhaltung, Koln Germany. **LC** TD273.7; .I9. **DD** 363.7/3/094355. Documents available from CASDDS.
**Ind/Abst** Chem. Abstr.

UK
**IWSA YEAR BOOK : AN OFFICIAL PUBLICATION OF THE INTERNATIONAL WATER SUPPLY ASSOCIATION.** **Main/Corp** International Water Supply Association. **VFOAT** IWSA Yearbook; I.SW.S.A. Yearbook; Annuaire de d'A.I.D.E.; Annuaire de l'AIDE; Year Book; Annuaire. (19??)-. Periodical. English (Multiple languages). an. £25.00 (members); £35.00 (non-members) Comes with International Water Supply Association membership. International Water Supply Association, 1 Queen Anne's Gate, London SW1H 9BT England. **Tel** 011 44 71 222 8111, telex 918518. **ED** L. R. Bays. **LC** TD201; .I688a. **DD** 363.6/1/025. **Ad Acc.** **Circ:** 3,000 (ctrl).
**Desc:** List of members of Association and addresses of water supply organisations in the world. Directory of manufacturers and consultants.

BU/0525-0811
**IZVESTIIA.** **Main/Corp** Bulgarska Akademiia Na Naukite Naukite, Sofia. Institut Po Vodni Problemi. (1963)-. Academic Scholarly Publication. Bulgarian (summaries and/or abstracts in English, French and Russian). Bulgarska Akademiia na Naukite, 7 Noemvri 1, Sofia Bulgaria. **DD** 627.

GW
**JAHRESBERICHT.** **Main/Corp** Erftverband (Germany). (1985)-. German. an. Erftverband, Paffendorfer Weg 42, Postfach 1320, W-5010 Bergheim Germany. **LC** TD273.7; .G76A. ***Continues*** *Jahresbericht.*

JA
**JAPAN'S WATERWORKS YEARBOOK.** (19??)-. English. ir. $6.00. Journal of Waterworks Industry Taiyuji-cho Kita-ku, Osaka Japan. **LC** TD305.A1; J3. **DD** 363.6/1/0952.

YU
**JAVNI VODOVOD I KANALIZACIJA U NASELJIMA SR SRBIJE.** **Main/Corp** Republicki Zavod za Statistiku sr Srbije. 1970-. Serbo-Croatian (Roman). **LC** HA1651; .A334 subser; TD295.S5.

US/0003-150X
**JOURNAL / AMERICAN WATER WORKS ASSOCIATION.** [J. - Am. Water Works Assoc.]. **Added/Corp** American Water Works Association. **VFOAT** Journal AWWA. Vol. 40, No. 1 (Jan. 1948)-. Academic Scholarly Publication. English (Spanish). mo. $93.50 US, Canada, Mexico and Puerto Rico; $121.00 other. American Water Works Association / Colorado, 6666 West Quincy Avenue, Denver CO 80235. **Tel** (303)794-7711, (303)794-7310 (editorial), FAX (303)794-7310 (editorial), (303)795-1989 (marketing). **ED** Nancy M. Zeilig. **LC** TD201; .A512. **DD** 628.1/05. **CODEN** JAWWA5. **[CCC].** Index available in last issue of volume--attached. cum. index. **Ad Acc.** **Pr Rev.** **Circ:** 38,500. available on microfilm and microfiche from University Microfilms International (UMI). Documents available from Article Express International, The Genuine Article, BIOSIS Document Express, CASDDS, Documents on Demand. ***Continues*** *Journal of the American Water Works Association, 0003-150X.*
**Desc:** Technical articles and news for managers, engineers, chemists, academics and regulatory-agency personnel involved in the water supply industry.
**Ind/Abst** Abstr. Bull. Inst. Pap. Sci. Tech.; Appl. Sci. Technol. Index; AQUAREF; BioBusiness; Biol. Abstr.; Chem. Abstr.; Coal Abstr.; Corros. Abstr. (-199?); Ei Page One; EMBASE; Energy Res. Abstr.; Eng. Index Annu.; Environ. Abstr.; Environ. Period. Bibliogr.; Fluid Abstr., Civil Eng.; Fluid Abstr. Proc. Eng.; FLUIDEX (1974-); Food Sci. Technol. Abstr.; GeoRef; INIS Atomindex [Micro.]; Int. Aerosp. Abstr.; Int. Civil Eng. Abstr.; Life Sci. Collect.; Res. Alert [Full Cov.]; Sci. Cit. Index; SCISEARCH; Soc. Sci. Cit. Index [Select. Cov.]; Soft. Abstr. Eng.

US/0025-0805
**JOURNAL - MAINE WATER UTILITIES ASSOCIATION.** **See** Public Administration-Public Utilities.

II
**JOURNAL OF INDIAN WATER RESOURCES SOCIETY / IWRS.** **Added/Corp** Indian Water Resources Society. (19??)-. Periodical. English. $15.00. Indian Water Resources Society, Roorkee, India. **(Subscription address:** Prints India, 11 Darya Ganj, New Delhi, 110002 India, (Phone: 011 91 11 3268645)**)** **LC** TC503; .J68. **DD** 333.91/00954.

II/0970-275X
**JOURNAL OF INDIAN WATER WORKS ASSOCIATION.** **Added/Corp** Indian Water Works Association. (19??)-. Periodical. English. qt. $40.00. Indian Water Works Association, Bombay, India. **(Subscription address:** Prints India, 11 Darya Ganj, New Delhi 110002 India.**)** **LC** TD303.A1; J68. **DD** 628.1/0954.

US/0096-4255
**JOURNAL OF THE MISSOURI WATER AND SEWERAGE CONFERENCE.** ***Title Change.*** **See** Environmental Issues-Pollution and Waste Management.

US/0028-4939
**JOURNAL OF THE NEW ENGLAND WATER WORKS ASSOCIATION.** **See** Public Administration-Public Utilities.

●US/1063-455X
**JOURNAL OF WATER CHEMISTRY AND TECHNOLOGY.** **See** Environmental Issues-Pollution and Waste Management.

IQ/0255-0148
**JOURNAL OF WATER RESOURCES.** (AL-MAJALLAH AL-ILMIYAH LIL-MAWARID AL-MAIYAH.). [J. water resour.]. **Added/Corp** IHP-Iraqi National Committee. **VFOAT** Journal of Water Resources. No. 1 (1982)-. Periodical. Arabic (English). sa. $30.00. S B 26054, Waziriyah Baghdad Iraq. **Tel** 7185100, telex 212290. **ED** N Al-Ansar. **LC** GB651; .M27. **CODEN** JWREEG. **Bk Rev.** **Ad Acc.** ctrl circ. Documents available from BIOSIS Document Express.
**Ind/Abst** Biol. Abstr. (?-1983).

US/0733-9496
**JOURNAL OF WATER RESOURCES PLANNING AND MANAGEMENT.** [J. water resour. plan. manage.]. **Added/Corp** American Society of Civil Engineers. Water Resources Planning and Management Division. **VFOAT** A.S.C.E. Water Resources Planning and Management; ASCE Water Resources Planning and Management. **VAT** American Society of Civil Engineers Water Resources Planning and Management. Vol. 109, No. 1 (Jan. 1983)-. Academic Scholarly Publication. English. bm. $140.00 (nonmember) US; $152.00 (nonmember) other. American Society of Civil Engineers / ASCE, 345 East 47th Street, New York NY 10017-2398. **Tel** (212)705-7179, FAX (212)705-7300, telex 422847 ASCE UI. **(Subscription address:** American Society of Civil Engineers, Publisher Fulfillment Agency, Box 828, Somerset NJ 08875.**)** **LC** TC401; .A552b. **DD** 333.91/005. **CODEN** JWRMD5. **[CCC].** Index available. cum. index. **Bk Rev.** **Ad Acc.** **Pr Rev.** **Circ:** 4,800 (ctrl). available on microfilm and microfiche from University Microfilms International (UMI); available on CD-ROM from American Society of Civil Engineers. Documents available from Article Express International, The Genuine Article, Documents on Demand. ***Continues*** *Journal of the Water Resources Planning and Management Division, 0145-0743.*
**Desc:** Examines social, economic, environmental and administrative concerns relating to the utilization and conservation of water.
**Ind/Abst** Appl. Sci. Technol. Index; AQUAREF; ASCE Annu. Comb. Index (1983-); ASCE Publ. Inf. (1983-); Coal Abstr.; Curr. Contents, Agric. Biol. Environ. Sci.; Curr. Contents Eng. Tech. Appl. Sci.; Ecol. Abstr. (?-?); Ei Page One; EMBASE; Energy Inf. Abstr.; Eng. Index Annu.; Environ. Abstr.; Expand. Acad. Index (1992-); Field Crop Abstr.; Fluid Abstr., Civil Eng.; Fluid Abstr. Proc. Eng.; FLUIDEX (1983-); Geogr. Abstr. Phys. Geogr. (?-?); Geogr. Abstr. Human Geogr. (?-?); GeoRef; Int. Abstr. Oper. Res. [Select. Cov.]; Int. Civil Eng. Abstr.; J. Plan. Lit.; Leis. Recreat. Tour. Abstr.; Res. Alert [Full Cov.]; Rev. Agric. Entomol.; Sci. Cit. Index; SCISEARCH; Soc. Sci. Cit. Index [Select. Cov.]; Soils Fert.; Trans. Am. Soc. Civ. Eng. (1983-).

UK/0003-7214
**JOURNAL OF WATER SUPPLY RESEARCH AND TECHNOLOGY - AQUA.** (19??)-. Academic Scholarly Publication. English. bm (6 issues). $209.00 US & Canada; £135.00 other. Blackwell Scientific Publications Ltd, Marston Book Services, PO Box 87, Oxford OX2 ODT UK. **Tel** 011 44 865 791155, FAX 011 44 865 791927, telex 837 515 MARDIS G. **[CCC].** ***Continues*** *Aqua, 0003-7214.*
**Ind/Abst** Curr. Aware. Biol. Sci., CABS; Fluid Abstr., Civil Eng.; Fluid Abstr. Proc. Eng.; FLUIDEX (19??-); Geogr. Abstr. Human Geogr. (?-?); GeoRef; Int. Dev. Abstr. (?-?).

US
**KANSAS WATER PLAN / KANSAS WATER OFFICE.** **Added/Corp** Kansas Water Office. (19??)-. English. an. Kansas Water Office / Topeka, 109 Southwest Ninth Street, Suite 200, Topeka KS 66612. **Tel** (913)296-3185. **LC** TC424.K2; K37. **DD** 333.91/15/09781.

●US/1069-0212
**KEYSTONE WATER QUALITY MANAGER.** [Keyst. water qual. manage.]. **Added/Corp** Water Pollution Control Association of Pennsylvania. (1993)-. Periodical. English. bm. $25.00. Pennsylvania Water Environment Association, 251 Baltimore Street, 2nd Floor, Gettysburg PA 17325. **Tel** (717)337-1972, FAX (717)337-3826. **ED** Lynn L. Hill. **DD** 628. **Ad Acc.** **Circ:** 4,300 (ctrl). ***Continues*** *Water Pollution Control Association of Pennsylvania magazine, 0890-4553.*

US/0734-1679
**KHIMIIA I TEKHNOLOGIIA VODY.** ***Title Change.*** **See** Environmental Issues-Pollution and Waste Management.

JA/0454-1545
**KOGYO YOSUI.** **Added/Corp** Kogyo Yosui Kenkyukai (Japan). Vol. 1, No. 1 (1955)-. Periodical. Japanese. mo. Nihon Kogyo Yosui Kyokai, 4-3 Hirakawacho 2, Chiyoda-ku 102 Tokyo Japan. **CODEN** KOYOAW. Documents available from CASDDS.
**Ind/Abst** Chem. Abstr.

JA
**KOKUDO RIYO HAKUSHO / KOKUDOCHO HEN.** **See** Real Estate.

JA
**KOWAN GIJUTSU KENKYUJO HOKOKU.** **Main/Corp** Unyusho Kowan Gijutsu Kenkyujo (Japan). **VFOAT** Report of the Port and Harbour Research Institute; Report of the P.H.R.I. Vol. 7, No. 1 (Mar. 1968)-. Periodical. Japanese (English; summaries and/or abstracts in English and Japanese). qt. Japan Minsitry of Transport, 1-1 3-chome, Nagase, Yokosuka, Japan. ***Formed by the union of*** *Kowan Gijutsu Kenkyujo. Kowan Gijutsu Kenkyujo Hokoku* ***and*** *Kowan Gijutsu Kenkyujo. Report of the Port and Harbour Technical Research Institute, 0554-7121.*
**Ind/Abst** Abstr. J. Earthq. Eng.

US/1040-2381
**LAKE AND RESERVOIR MANAGEMENT.** **See** Environmental Issues-Pollution and Waste Management.

US/0361-8188
**LAKE MICHIGAN WATER QUALITY REPORT.** [Lake Mich. water qual. rep.]. **Main/Corp** Illinois. Environmental Protection Agency. Academic Scholarly Publication. English. be. Illinois Environmental Protection Agency, 2200 Churchill Road, Springfield IL 62706. **LC** TD223.3; .I36B. **DD** 551.4/82/09774. **CODEN** LMWRDV. **Circ:** 300. Documents available from CASDDS.
**Desc:** Agency report on water quality in Lake Michigan (southwestern portion).
**Ind/Abst** Chem. Abstr.

# Water Resources

**AT/1320-5331**
**LAKES AND RESERVOIRS.** (19??)-. Academic Scholarly Publication. English. Twice a year. 171.00Aus$ (institutions), 86.00Aus$ (individuals) Australia; ¥12000 (institutions), ¥6000 (individuals) Japan; $120.00 (institutions), $60.00 (individuals) other. Blackwell Scientific Publications Australia, 54 University Street, PO Box 378, Carlton Victoria 3053 Australia. **Tel** 011 61 3 3470300, FAX 011 61 3 3475001, telex 10716421.

**US/0192-9453**
**LAND AND WATER (FORT DODGE).** See Environmental Issues-Conservation and Natural Resources.

**AT/1033-1360**
**LAND AND WATER RESEARCH NEWS.** See Earth Sciences.

**IT/0254-6280**
**LAND AND WATER ROME.** (19??)-. Periodical. English. UDC 341.16: 63. **Ind/Abst** Soils Fert.

**US/0148-7876**
**LIBRARY BULLETIN - TEXAS DEPARTMENT OF WATER RESOURCES.** **Main/Corp** Texas. Dept. of Water Resources. Vol. 9, No. 9 (Sept. 1977)-. Bulletin. English. Twelve times a year. Free. Department of Water Resources / Texas, PO Box 13807, Capitol Station, Austin TX 78701. **Tel** (512)475-3781. **Continues** Library Bulletin - Texas Water Development Board, 0146-1761.

**US**
**LLANO ESTACADO PLAYA LAKE WATER RESOURCES STUDY.** (LLANO ESTACADO PLAYA LAKE WATER RESOURCES STUDY : A SPECIAL INVESTIGATION : STATUS REPORT.). Fiscal Year 1978-. English. Southwest Heritage Magazine Inc, College of Southwest, 6610 Lovington Highway, Hobbs NM 88240. **Tel** (505)392-6561. **Continues** Llano Estacado Total Water Management Study.

**IQ/1012-3466**
**MAGALLAT AL-BUHUT AL-ZIRA'IYYAT WA-AL-MAWARID AL-MA'IYYAT. AL-INTAG AL-HAYAWANI.** See Agriculture.

**IQ/1012-3474**
**MAGALLAT AL-BUHUT AL-ZIRA'IYYAT WA-AL-MAWARID AL-MA'IYYAT. AL-INTAG AL-NABATI.** See Agriculture.

**IQ/1012-3482**
**MAGALLAT AL-BUHUT AL-ZIRA'IYYAT WA-AL-MAWARID AL-MA'IYYAT. AL-TURBAT WA-MASADIR AL-MIYAH.** See Agriculture.

**US/0147-4596**
**MAINE WATER QUALITY STATUS.** English. an. Maine Department of Environmental Protection, State House Station 17, Augusta ME 04333. **Tel** (207)289-2811, FAX (207)289-7826. **LC** TD224.M2; M34A. **DD** 363.7/39456/09741.

**PL**
**MATERIALY BADAWCZE. SERIA: GOSPODARKA WODNA I OCHRONA WOD.** No. 1 (1974)-. Periodical. Polish (summaries and/or abstracts in English and Russian). ir. $30.00. Instytut Meteorologii i Gospodarki Wodnej, Ul Podlesna 61, 01-673 Warszawa Poland. **Tel** 34-16-51 W 307, telex 814331. **ED** Stefan Reichhart. **Ad Acc. Circ:** 250 (ctrl). **Ind/Abst** GeoRef.

**NE/0074-0411**
**MEDEDELING - INSTITUUT VOOR CULTUURTECHNIEK EN WATERHUISHOUDING.** See Agriculture-Crop Production and Soil.

**UK/0140-5098**
**MIDDLE EAST WATER & SEWAGE.** Title Change. [Middle East water & sewage]. **VFOAT** Wutar and Suwij Al-Sharq Al-Awsat; Ab va Fazilab-I Khavarmiyanah. Vol. 1 (July/Aug. 1977)-(19??). Periodical. Arabic (English). qt. Industrial & Marine Publishing Ltd, Queensway House, 2 Queensway, Redhill Surrey RH1 1QS England. **Tel** 0737 68611. **LC** TD311.A1; M53. **DD** 628/.05. **Merged with** African Water & Sewage; Asian Water & Sewage, 1011-5870; European Water & Sewage and Far East Water & Sewage **to form** Water & Sewage International, 0956-0157. **Ind/Abst** Fluid Abstr., Civil Eng.; Fluid Abstr. Proc. Eng.; FLUIDEX (1977-); Pollut. Abstr. Indexes.

**US/0403-1911**
**MINUTES OF THE MEETING - ARKANSAS-WHITE-RED BASINS INTER-AGENCY COMMITTEE.** **Main/Corp** Arkansas-White-Red Basins Inter-Agency Committee. 1st-. Periodical. English. Southwestern Division, Corps of Engineers, Dallas TX 75235. **Tel** (501)378-5551. **LC** HD1695.A8; A69. **DD** 333.9. cum. index.

**US**
**MISSOURI RIVER BASIN REGION, WATER RESOURCES RESEARCH INSTITUTES.** **VFOAT** Water Resources Budget Projection. English. **LC** HD1695.M45; M6. **DD** 333.9/1.

**US**
**MISSOURI WATER AND WASTEWATER CONFERENCE.** English. an. $7.00. Missouri Water and Wastewater Conference, PO Box 774, Jefferson City MO 65102. **Tel** (314)635-3365. **Continues** Missouri Water and Sewerage Conference, 0096-4255.

**GW/0933-2022**
**MITTEILUNG (DEUTSCHE FORSCHUNGSGEMEINSCHAFT. KOMMISSION FUR WASSERFORSCHUNG).** (MITTEILUNG ... DER SENATSKOMMISSION FUER WASSERFORSCHUNG.). [Mitt. Senatskomm. Wasserforsch.]. **Added/Corp** Deutsche Forschungsgemeinschaft. Kommission fur Wasserforschung. 1986-. Academic Scholarly Publication. German. VCH Verlagsgesellschaft MBH, W-6940 Weinheim Germany. **CODEN** MSWAEY. Documents available from CASDDS. **Continues** Mitteilung der Kommission fur Wasserforschung in Verbindung mit der Kommission zur Prufung von Lebensmittelizusatz- und Inhaltstoffen, 0341-8758. **Ind/Abst** Chem. Abstr. (1986-); GeoRef.

**JA/0026-7015**
**MIZU SHORI GIJUTSU.** [Mizu shori gijutsu]. **Added/Corp** Nihon Mizu Shori Gijutsu Kenkyukai. **VFOAT** Water Purification and Liquid Wastes Treatment. (1960)-. Academic Scholarly Publication. Japanese. mo. $245.00. **(Subscription address:** Maruzen Company Ltd., PO Box 5050, Import & Export Department, Tokyo 100 31 Japan.**)** **LC** TD430; .M574. **CODEN** MSYGAO. Documents available from CASDDS. **Ind/Abst** Chem. Abstr.; Sug. Indus. Abstr.

**IT**
**MONDO SOMMERSO.** (19??)-. Italian. Ten times a year. L60000 Italy; L90000 other. Media Sea Communications, Via G A Amadeo 41, 20133 Milan Italy. **Tel** 011 39 2 70100020.

**US/0149-8509**
**MONTANA WATER POLLUTION CONTROL PROGRAM PLAN.** **Main/Corp** Montana. Water Quality Bureau. English. an. **LC** TD224.M9; M67A. **DD** 363.6/1/09786.

**CL**
**MUJER/FEMPRESS / UNIDAD DE COMMUNICACION ALTERNATIVA DE LA MUJER, ILET.** **Added/Corp** Instituto Latinoamericano de Estudios Transnacionales. Unidad de Communicacion Alternativa de la Mujer. **VFOAT** Mujer Fempress; Fempress. No. 61 (Aug. 1986)-. Periodical. Spanish. mo. **Continues** Mujer (Santiago, Chile). **Ind/Abst** LABORDOC.

**US/0279-7739**
**NATIONAL DRILLERS BUYERS GUIDE.** (19??)-. Consumer Publication. English. mo. free. National Drillers Buyers Guide, PO Box 400, Bontifay FL 32425. **Tel** (904)547-4244, FAX (904)547-5277. **ED** W. C. Faison. **Ad Acc. Circ:** 34,000 (ctrl).

**US/0736-2609**
**NATIONAL WATER CONDITIONS.** (NATIONAL WATER CONDITIONS / UNITED STATES, DEPARTMENT OF THE INTERIOR, GEOLOGICAL SURVEY [AND] CANADA, DEPARTMENT OF THE ENVIRONMENT, WATER RESOURCES BRANCH.). [Natl. water cond.]. **Added/Corp** Geological Survey (U.S.) Canada. Water Resources Branch. (July 1982)-. Periodical. English. mo. Free on request. US Geological Survey, 419 National Center, Reston VA 22092. **Tel** (703)648-6817. **LC** GB701; .N35. **DD** 553.7/0973. available on microfilm and microfiche from University Microfilms International (UMI). Documents available from Ask*IEEE, Documents on Demand. **Continues** Water Resources Review (1982). **Ind/Abst** Energy Res. Abstr. (June 1978-); Environ. Abstr.; INSPEC (Jan. 1985-).

**US/0271-0692**
**NATIONAL WATER LINE.** **Added/Corp** National Water Resources Association. (19??)-. Periodical. English. Ten times a year. $150.00. National Water Resources Association, 3800 North Fairfax Drive Suite 4, Arlington VA 22203. **Tel** (703)524-1544.

**US**
**NATIONAL WATER QUALITY INVENTORY : REPORT TO CONGRESS / UNITED STATES ENVIRONMENTAL PROTECTION AGENCY, OFFICE OF WATER REGULATIONS AND STANDARDS.** Began with 1974. English. be. US Environmental Protection Agency / Office of Water Regulations and Standards, Office of Water Regulations and Standards, 401 M Street SW, Washington DC 20460. **LC** TD223; .U52D. **DD** 363.6/1. **Circ:** 2,000. **Desc:** A summary of state-reported information on the quality of rivers, lakes, estuaries and ground water.

**US/0470-3480**
**NATIONAL WATERSHED CONGRESS; PROCEEDINGS.** [Natl. Watershed Congr.]. No. 1 (1954)-. Proceedings. English. an. NACD, Box 855, League City TX 77573. **Tel** (713)332-3402. **LC** HD1694; .A15. **DD** 333.91. **Ind/Abst** GeoRef.

**US/0730-6369**
**NEW JERSEY/USEPA REGION II WATER RESOURCES MANAGEMENT AGREEMENT.** (NEW JERSEY/USEPA REGION II WATER RESOURCES MANAGEMENT AGREEMENT / PREPARED BY NEW JERSEY DEPARTMENT OF ENVIRONMENTAL PROTECTION, DIVISION OF WATER RESOURCES [AND] U.S. ENVIRONMENTAL PROTECTION AGENCY, REGION II.). **Main/Corp** New Jersey. Division of Water Resources. **Added/Corp** United States. Environmental Protection Agency. Region II. **VFOAT** Water Resources Management Agreement; New Jersey State EPA Agreement. **VAT** New Jersey, United States Environmental Protection Agency Region Two Water Resources Management Agreement. (1980)-. Government Publication. English. an. United States Environmental Protection Agency / New York, Region II, 26 Federal Plaza, New York NY 10007. **LC** TD224.N5; N36a. **DD** 363.7/39456/09749.

**US/0897-5094**
**NEW WAVES.** (NEW WAVES : THE RESEARCH NEWSLETTER OF THE TEXAS WATER RESOURCES INSTITUTE.). [New waves]. **Added/Corp** Texas Water Resources Institute. Vol. 1, No. 1 (Jan. 1988)-. Newsletter. English. qt. Free. Texas Water Resources Institute, 301 Scoates Hall, Texas A & M University, College Station TX 77843-2118. **Tel** (409)845-8571, FAX (409)845-8554. **ED** Ric Jensen. **DD** 333. Documents available from Documents on Demand. **Desc:** Deals with university researchers doing water research in Texas. **Ind/Abst** Environ. Abstr.

**US/0549-799X**
**NEWS - WATER RESOURCES RESEARCH INSTITUTE OF THE UNIVERSITY OF NORTH CAROLINA.** [News - Water Resour. Res. Inst. Univ. N. C.]. **Main/Corp** Water Resources Research Institute of the University of North Carolina. **VFOAT** WRRI News. **VAT** Water Resources Research Institute News. No. 1 (Feb. 1966)-. Periodical. English. bm. Water Resources Research Institute of the University of North Carolina, 219 Oberlin Road, Box 7912, NC State University, Raleigh NC 27695-7912. **DD** 333. Documents available from Documents on Demand. **Ind/Abst** Environ. Abstr.

**US**
**NEWSLETTER (UNIVERSITY OF MASSACHUSETTS AT AMHERST. WATER RESOURCES RESEARCH CENTER).** (NEWSLETTER / WATER RESOURCES RESEARCH CENTER, UNIVERSITY OF MASSACHUSETTS.). Newsletter. English. Water Resources Research Center / Massachusetts, University of Massachusetts, Blaisdell House, Amherst MA 01003. **Tel** (413)545-2842.

**JA/0369-4550**
**NIPPON KAISUI GAKKAI-SHI.** [Nippon Kaisui Gakkai-Shi]. **VFOAT** Bulletin of the Society of Sea Water Science, Japan. (1965)-. Academic Scholarly Publication. Japanese. ir. $169.50. **(Subscription address:** Japan Publications Trading Company, Ltd., PO Box 5030, Tokyo International, Tokyo 100-31 Japan.**)** **CODEN** NKAGBU. Documents available from CASDDS. **Continues** Nippon Shio Gakkai-Shi, 0369-5646. **Ind/Abst** Chem. Abstr.

**NO/0333-3280**
**NORSK INSTITUTT FOR VANNFORSKNING.** [Nor. inst. vannforsk.]. 1958/67-. Academic Scholarly Publication. Norwegian. an. Norwegian Institut for Water Research Library, PO Box 69, Korsvoll, N-0808 Oslo 8 Norway. **Tel** 472 235280, FAX 472 394189, telex 74190 NIVAN. **ED** Anne Grete Bangsund. **LC** TD281.A1; N67A. **CODEN** NIVAD3. **Circ:** 2,500 (ctrl). Documents available from CASDDS. **Ind/Abst** Chem. Abstr.

**US/0739-4977**
**OFFICIAL PROCEEDINGS - INTERNATIONAL WATER CONFERENCE.** (OFFICIAL PROCEEDINGS / THE INTERNATIONAL WATER CONFERENCE ANNUAL MEETING.). [Off. proc. - Int. Water Conf.]. **Main/Conf** International Water Conference. **VFOAT** Proceedings, International Water Conference. 41st (1980)-. Proceedings. English. an. $30.00. Pennsylvania Sheraton Hotel, Pittsburgh PA 15219. **LC** TD201; .I682A. **DD**

# Water Resources

628.1/05. Documents available from Article Express International. **Continues** International Water Conference Annual Meeting, 0074-9575.
**Ind/Abst** Bioeng. Abstr.; Ei Page One; Eng. Index Annu.

RU
**OKHRANA PRIRODNYKH VOD URALA.**
**Added/Corp** Uralskii Nauchno-Issledovatelskii Institut Kompleksnogo Ispolzovaniia i Okhrany Vodnykh Resursov. (19??)-. Academic Scholarly Publication. Russian. Sredne-Uralskoe Knizhnoe Izdatelstvo, Malysheva 24, Sverdlovsk Russia. **LC** TD286.U7; O33. **CODEN** OPVUAI. Documents available from CASDDS.
**Ind/Abst** Chem. Abstr. (?-1982).

US
**ON-SITE INSIGHTS.** English. qt. Free. Texas Water Resources Institute, 301 Scoates Hall, Texas A & M University, College Station TX 77843-2118. **Tel** (409)845-8571, **FAX** (409)845-8554.
**Desc:** Information about on-site wastewater treatment systems in Texas.

●US/1061-9291
**ON TAP (MORGANTOWN, W.VA.). See** Sociology-Social Services and Welfare.

CN/0380-1624
**ONTARIO PIPELINE. Added/Corp** American Water Works Association. Ontario Section. Ontario Municipal Water Association. (Mar. 1971)-. Periodical. English. Three times a year. Free. The American Water Works Association, 6666 West Quincy Avenue, Denver CO 80235. **Tel** (303)794-7711. **Bk Rev**. **Circ:** 2,000 (ctrl).

US/0149-8029
**OPFLOW. Added/Corp** American Water Works Association. Vol. 1 (Jan. 1975)-. Periodical. English. mo. $10.50; Comes also with membership. American Water Works Association / Colorado, 6666 West Quincy Avenue, Denver CO 80235. **Tel** (303)794-7711, (303)794-7310 (editorial), FAX (303)794-7310 (editorial), (303)795-1989 (marketing). **[CCC]**.

CN/0083-8799
**PAPERS PRESENTED AT THE ANNUAL CONVENTION. See** Environmental Issues-Pollution and Waste Management.

PH
**PHILIPPINES WATER RESOURCES ABSTRACTS. Added/Corp** National Water Resources Council (Philippines). Vol. 1 (Jan. 1976)-. Periodical. English. qt. National Water Resources Council, Quezon City Philippines.
**Ind/Abst** Fluid Abstr., Civil Eng.; Fluid Abstr. Proc. Eng.; FLUIDEX (1976-).

LV/0130-8246
**POLIMERY V MELIORACII I VODNOM HOZJAJSTVE. See** Engineering-Hydraulic Engineering.

US/0092-0320
**POLLUTING INCIDENTS IN AND AROUND U.S. WATERS. See** Environmental Issues-Pollution and Waste Management.

US
**POTOMAC BASIN REPORTER. Added/Corp** Interstate Commission on the Potomac River Basin. Vol. 27, No. 7 (July 1971)-. Periodical. English. Ten times a year. (Free upon request). Instate Com Potomac River Basin, 6110 Executive Bldg, Suite 300, Rockville MD 20852. **Tel** (301)984-1908. **ED** Curtis M Dalpra. **LC** HD1695.P56; I54. **DD** 333.9/1/009752. **Bk Rev**, (Qty: 2-10). **Continues** Newsletter - Interstate Commission on the Potomac River Basin.

US/0565-0631
**PREAUTHORIZATION OF PLANNING ACTIVITIES OF THE BUREAU OF RECLAMATION, THE CORPS OF ENGINEERS, AND THE SOIL CONSERVATION SERVICE. Main/Corp** Arkansas-White-Red Basins Inter-Agency Committee. Standing Committee on Exchange of Program Information. (19??)-. English. **LC** TC423.6; .A74a. **DD** 333.9/102/0976.

US/0360-814X
**PROCEEDINGS AWWA ANNUAL CONFERENCE. See** Public Administration-Public Utilities.

US/0164-0755
**PROCEEDINGS - AWWA WATER QUALITY TECHNOLOGY CONFERENCE.** [Proc. - AWWA Water Qual. Technol. Conf.]. **Main/Conf** AWWA Water Quality Technology Conference. **Added/Corp** American Water Works Association. AWWA Research Foundation. American Water Works Association. Water Quality Division. **VFOAT** Technology Conference Proceedings. **VAT** Proceedings - American Water Works Association Water Quality Technology Conference. (1973)-. Academic Scholarly Publication. English. an (Feb./March). $91.50 (non-members), $72.50 (members) US Canada and Mexico; $128.10 (non-members), $101.50 (members) other. American Water Works Association / Colorado, 6666 West Quincy Avenue, Denver CO 80235. **Tel** (303)794-7711, (303)794-7310 (editorial), FAX (303)794-7310 (editorial), (303)795-1989 (marketing). **LC** TD370; .A9a. **DD** 628.1/61. **CODEN** PWQCD2. Documents available from CASDDS.
**Desc:** Information about latest advances in water analysis and treatment.
**Ind/Abst** Chem. Abstr.

US/0495-2340
**PROCEEDINGS OF THE ANNUAL CONFERENCE ON WATER FOR TEXAS. Main/Conf** Conference on Water for Texas. **Added/Corp** Texas A & M University. Water Resources Institute. Texas Agricultural and Mechanical College System. Water Research and Information Center. Agricultural and Mechanical College of Texas. **VFOAT** Water for Texas. 2nd (1956)-. Proceedings. English. Free copies will be sent to those who paid to be on the conference register, $25.00 others. Texas Water Resources Institute, 301 Scoates Hall, Texas A & M University, College Station TX 77843-2118. **Tel** (409)845-8571, FAX (409)845-8554. **LC** TD201; .T37. **DD** 333.9; 628.1. **Circ:** 250. **Continues** Water for Texas.

CN/0833-5192
**PROCEEDINGS OF THE ... ANNUAL CONVENTION, INCLUDING THE ... ANNUAL CONVENTION OF THE WESTERN CANADA SECTION, AMERICAN WATER WORKS ASSOCIATION, AND THE ... ANNUAL CONVENTION OF THE WESTERN CANADA POLLUTION CONTROL ASSOCIATION, WATER POLLUTION CONTROL FEDERATION.** (PROCEEDINGS OF THE ANNUAL CONVENTION / WESTERN CANADA WATER AND SEWAGE CONFERENCE.). [Proc. annu. conv. incl. annu. conv. West. Can. Sect. Am. Water Works Assoc. annu. conv. West. Can. Pollut. Control. Assoc. Water Pollut. Control Fed.]. **Added/Corp** Western Canada Water and Sewage Conference. (1983)-. Academic Scholarly Publication. English. an. $10.00. Western Canada Water & Sewage Conference, PO Box 6168 Station A, Calgary, Alberta, T2H2L4, Canada. **CODEN** PAWCEF. Documents available from CASDDS.
**Ind/Abst** Chem. Abstr. (1983).

US/0160-5518
**PROCEEDINGS OF THE ANNUAL MISSOURI RIVER BASIN GOVERNORS' CONFERENCE. Main/Conf** Missouri River Basin Governors' Conference on Water. First conference held in 1976. Proceedings. English. Missouri River Basin Commission, 10050 Regency Circle/Suite 403, Omaha NE 68114. **LC** HD1695.M45; M58A. **DD** 333.9/1.

US/0161-4924
**PROCEEDINGS OF THE ANNUAL NEW MEXICO WATER CONFERENCE.** [Proc. annu. N. M. Water Conf.]. **Main/Conf** New Mexico Water Conference. 1972-. Proceedings. English. an. $5.00. New Mexico Water Resources Research Institute, New Mexico State University, Box 3167, Las Cruces NM 88003. **Tel** (505)646-1813. **ED** Cathy Ortega-Klett. **LC** GB705.N6; N64 subser; TD224.N6. **DD** 333.9/1/009789 S 333.9/1/009789. **Continues** New Mexico Water Conference, New Mexico State University. Proceedings - Annual Water Conference.
**Ind/Abst** GeoRef.

●UK/0965-0946
**PROCEEDINGS OF THE INSTITUTION OF CIVIL ENGINEERS. WATER, MARITIME AND ENERGY. See** Engineering-Hydraulic Engineering.

US
**PROCEEDINGS OF THE NATIONAL CONFERENCE ON COMPLETE WATER REUSE. Added/Corp** American Institute of Chemical Engineers. United States. Environmental Protection Agency. Office of Technology Transfer. (197?)-. Academic Scholarly Publication. English. ir. Price varies per volume. American Institute of Chemical Engineers, 345 East 47th Street, New York NY 10017. **Tel** (212)705-7663, (212)705-7703, FAX (212)705-8400. Documents available from CASDDS.
**Ind/Abst** Chem. Abstr.

US/0886-9235
**PROCEEDINGS OF THE NATIONAL GROUND WATER QUALITY SYMPOSIUM. Ceased.** [Proc. Natl. Ground Water Qual. Symp.]. **Main/Conf** National Ground Water Quality Symposium. **Added/Corp** United States. Environmental Protection Agency. National Water Well Association. Robert S. Kerr Environmental Research Laboratory. 1st (Aug. 1971)-?. Proceedings. English. ir. National Water Well Association, 6375 Riverside Drive, Dublin OH 43017. **Tel** (614)761-1711. **LC** TD223; .N36a. **DD** 363.7/3942/0973.
**Ind/Abst** GeoRef.

US
**PROCEEDINGS OF THE ... NATIONAL OUTDOOR ACTION CONFERENCE ON AQUIFER RESTORATION, GROUND WATER MONITORING, AND GEOPHYSICAL METHODS / SPONSORS, THE ASSOCIATION OF GROUND WATER SCIENTISTS AND ENGINEERS (DIVISION OF NWWA) & U.S. EPA-EMSL. Added/Corp** Association of Ground Water Scientists and Engineers (U.S.) United States. Environmental Protection Agency. Electromagnetic Sciences Laboratory (SRI International). (May 18-21, 1987)-. Proceedings. English. an. National Water Well Association, 6375 Riverside Drive, Dublin OH 43017. **Tel** (614)761-1711. **LC** GB1001.2; .N382. **Continues** National Symposium and Exposition on Aquifer Restoration and Ground Water Monitoring. Proceedings of the ... National Symposium on Aquifer Restoration and Ground Water Monitoring.
**Ind/Abst** Biodeter. Abstr.

UK
**PROCEEDINGS OF THE ... WORLD CONGRESS OF THE INTERNATIONAL WATER SUPPLY ASSOCIATION. Main/Corp** International Water Supply Association. World Congress. 14th (1982)-. Proceedings. English. Pergamon Press, An Imprint of Elsevier Science Ltd., The Boulevard, Langford Lane, Kidlington, Oxford OX5 1GB United Kingdom. **Tel** 011 44 865 843000, 011 44 865 843699, FAX 011 44 865 843010. **(Subscription address:** US/ 395 Saw Mill River Road, Elmsford, NY 10523; Can/ 150 Consumers Road/Suite 104, Willowdale Ontario M2J 1P9; Aus-NZ/ POB 544, Potts Point NSW 2011) **Continues** International Water Supply Association, 0074-9583.

CN/0849-3650
**PROGRAM OVERVIEW - WASTEWATER TECHNOLOGY CENTRE, CANADA. See** Environmental Issues-Pollution and Waste Management.

US
**PROGRAM REQUIREMENTS MEMORANDA FOR FISCAL YEAR ... : MUNICIPAL WASTEWATER TREATMENT WORKS CONSTRUCTION GRANTS PROGRAM / UNITED STATES ENVIRONMENTAL PROTECTION AGENCY, OFFICE OF WATER PROGRAMS OPERATIONS. See** Environmental Issues-Pollution and Waste Management.

CN/0713-4916
**PROGRESS REPORT - SOCIETE D'ENERGIE DE LA BAIE JAMES. See** Business.

US/0565-0682
**PROJECT SKYWATER BIENNIAL REPORT.** 1967-. English. be. Bureau of Reclamation, PO Box 25007, Denver CO 80225. **Tel** (303)234-3000. **DD** 333.9.

US
**PUBLIC WATER SUPPLY REPORT. Added/Corp** Oklahoma. State Environmental Laboratory. (1982)-. English. Three times a year. Oklahoma State Department of Health, 1000 Northeast 10th Street, Oklahoma City OK 73117. **Tel** (405)271-4200, (405)271-5600, FAX (405)271-7339. **LC** TD224.O5; P8. **DD** 363.6/1.

SP
**PUBLICACIONES. See** Earth Sciences-Hydrology.

US/0889-6224
**PUBLICATION / ARKANSAS WATER RESOURCES RESEARCH CENTER.** [Publ. - Ark. Water Resour. Res. Cent.]. **Main/Corp** Arkansas Water Resources Research Center. **Added/Corp** Arkansas Water Resources Research Center. (197?)-. Monographic series. English. Free. Water Resources Research Center / Arizona, 350 North Campbell, University of Arizona, Tucson AZ 85721. **Tel** (602)792-9591, FAX (602)792-8518. **LC** GB705.A8; A26. **DD** 333.9; 628.1/09767. **CODEN** PAWCDE. **Continues** Publication (University of Arkansas (Fayetteville Campus). Water Resources Research Center).
**Ind/Abst** GeoRef.

US/0096-1728
**PUBLICATION - CALIFORNIA STATE WATER RESOURCES CONTROL BOARD.** [Publ. - Calif. State Water Resour. Control Board]. **Main/Corp** California. State Water Resources Control Board. Monographic series. English. Price varies

# Water Resources

per volume. California State Water Resources Control Board, Division of Planning and Research, PO Box 100, Sacramento CA 95801. **CODEN** CWQPAV. **Continues** Publication - State Water Quality Control Board.
**Ind/Abst** GeoRef.

US
**PUBLICATION - CORNELL UNIVERSITY WATER RESOURCES AND MARINE SCIENCES CENTER.** **Main/Corp** Cornell University. Water Resources and Marine Sciences Center. **Added/Corp** United States. Office of Water Resources Research. No. 22 (1969)-. Monographic series. English. ir. Price varies per volume. Water Resources State Engineers, 1313 Sherman, Room 818, Denver CO 80203. **Tel** (303)866-3581. **LC** TD224.N7; C65. **DD** 333.9/1/008S. **Continues** Cornell University. Water Resources Center. Publication -Cornell University Water Resources Center,, 0590-6881.

US/0071-6200
**PUBLICATION - FLORIDA WATER RESOURCES RESEARCH CENTER.** (PUBLICATION - FLORIDA. UNIVERSITY, GAINESVILLE. WATER RESOURCES RESEARCH CENTER.). [Publ. - Fla. Water Resour. Res. Cent.]. **Main/Corp** University of Florida. Water Resources Research Center. No. 1 (1966)-. Monographic series. English. Price varies per volume. University of Florida Water Resources Research Center, Gainesville FL 32611. **CODEN** FWRRA7.
**Ind/Abst** GeoRef.

US
**PUBLICATION IWR.** **Main/Corp** University of Alaska. Institute of Water Resources. Monographic series. English. Price varies per volume. University of Alaska / Water Research, Fairbanks Water Research Center, Institution of Northern Engineering, Fairbanks AK 99775.

US/0542-9315
**PUBLICATION - WATER RESOURCES RESEARCH CENTER, UNIVERSITY OF MASSACHUSETTS AT AMHERST.** [Publ. - Water Resour. Res. Cent., Univ. Mass. Amherst]. **Main/Corp** University of Massachusetts at Amherst. Water Resources Research Center. Monographic series. English. Nine times a year. Price varies per volume. Water Resources Research Center / Massachusetts, University of Massachusetts, Blaisdell House, Amherst MA 01003. **Tel** (413)545-2842. **ED** John R Cole. **LC** TD224.M4; M37. **DD** 333.9/1/009744 S. **CODEN** MUWPAL. **Bk Rev. Circ:** 1,100. Documents available from CASDDS. **Continues** Publication - Water Resources Research Center, University of Massachusetts, Amherst.
**Desc:** A newsletter for water researchers in Massachusetts and New England, with research results and news, publications, funding sources, conference announcements, calls for papers, etc. partially funded by USGS.
**Ind/Abst** Chem. Abstr.; GeoRef.

US/0360-1625
**PUBLICATIONS OF THE WEST VIRGINIA GEOLOGICAL SURVEY.** See Earth Sciences-Geology.

US
**PUGET SOUND UPDATE : ... ANNUAL REPORT OF THE PUGET SOUND AMBIENT MONITORING PROGRAM.** **Added/Corp** Puget Sound Ambient Monitoring Program. Washington (State). Puget Sound Water Quality Authority. (1990)-. English. Puget Sound Water Quality Authority, 217 Pine Street, Suite 1100, Seattle WA 98101. **LC** TD225.P78; P64.

IT/0390-6329
**QUADERNI - ISTITUTO DI RICERCA SULLE ACQUE.** [Quad. - Ist. ric. acque]. **Main/Corp** Istituto di Ricerca Sulle Acque (Italy). Began in 1970. Academic Scholarly Publication. Italian. Three times a year. **CODEN** QIRADG. Documents available from CASDDS.
**Ind/Abst** Chem. Abstr.; GeoRef.

CN/0706-6589
**RAPPORT MANUSCRIT CANADIEN DES SCIENCES HALIETIQUES ET AQUATIQUES.** [Rapp. manuscr. can. sci. halieut. aquat.]. **Added/Corp** Canada. Dept. of Fisheries and Oceans. (1979)-. French (summaries and/or abstracts in English). an. Gouvernement du Quebec, 600 St Amable 4E Etage, Quebec Quebec G1R 4Z1 Canada. **DD** 333.91/00971.

IT
**RAPPORTO DI ATTIVITA / ISTITUTO DI RICERCA SULLE ACQUE.** **Main/Corp** Istituto di Ricerca Sulle Acque (Italy). Italian. Via Reno 1, 00198 Rome Italy. **LC** TC479; .I78A. **DD** 333.91/00945.

US/0575-4968
**REPORT - CALIFORNIA WATER RESOURCES CENTER.** [Rep. - Calif. Water Resour. Cent.]. **Main/Corp** University of California. Water Resources Center. No. 34-. Academic Scholarly Publication. English. Price varies per volume. University of California Davis Water Resources Center, Davis CA 95616. **LC** TD224.C3; C3. **CODEN** RUCCD8. Documents available from Article Express International, CASDDS. **Continues** Report - University of California, Water Resources Center, Universitywide, 0375-5975.
**Ind/Abst** AGRICOLA [Select. Cov.]; Bioeng. Abstr.; Chem. Abstr.; Ei Page One; Eng. Index Annu.; GeoRef.

CN/0845-1214
**REPORT / GREAT LAKES SCIENCE ADVISORY BOARD.** [Rep. - Gt. Lakes Sci. Advis. Board]. **Main/Corp** Great Lakes Science Advisory Board. **Added/Corp** International Joint Commission. (1987)-. English. be. International Joint Commission, 100 Oellette Avenue, Windsor Ont N9A 6T3 Canada. **Tel** (313)226-2170. **DD** 363.7/394/0977. **Continues** Annual Report (Great Lakes Science Advisory Board), 0710-8702.

NE
**REPORT / INSTITUTE FOR LAND AND WATER MANAGEMENT RESEARCH (ICW).** **Added/Corp** Instituut voor Cultuurtechniek en Waterhuishouding. (1982)-. Monographic series. English (summaries and/or abstracts in Dutch). Price varies per volume.
**Ind/Abst** Geogr. Abstr. Phys. Geogr.; Int. Dev. Abstr.

US
**REPORT - NEW ENGLAND INTERSTATE WATER POLLUTION CONTROL COMMISSION.** See Environmental Issues-Pollution and Waste Management.

US/0097-5672
**REPORT OF INVESTIGATION (ILLINOIS STATE WATER SURVEY).** **Title Change.** [Rep. invest. - Ill. State Water Surv.]. **Added/Corp** Illinois State Water Survey. (1948)-(19??). Monographic series. English. Illinois State Water Survey, 2204 Griffith Drive, Champaign IL 61820-7495. **Tel** (217)333-2210. **LC** GB705.I3; A3. **DD** 628.1. **CODEN** ILWIAT. Documents available from Article Express International, BIOSIS Document Express, CASDDS. **Continued by** Research Report (Illinois State Water Survey), 1059-826X.
**Ind/Abst** Bioeng. Abstr.; Biol. Abstr. (-1982); Chem. Abstr.; Ei Page One; Eng. Index Annu.; GeoRef.

RH
**REPORT OF THE SECRETARY FOR WATER DEVELOPMENT (RHODESIA).** **Main/Corp** Rhodesia. Ministry of Water Development. Periodical. English. **Continues** Rhodesia. Ministry of water Development. Report of the Director.

CN/0845-0919
**REPORT ON GREAT LAKES WATER QUALITY : REPORT TO THE INTERNATIONAL JOINT COMMISSION / GREAT LAKES WATER QUALITY BOARD.** [Rep. Gt. Lakes water qual.]. **Main/Corp** Great Lakes Water Quality Board. 1980-. English. an. International Joint Commission, 100 Oellette Avenue, Windsor Ont N9A 6T3 Canada. **Tel** (313)226-2170. **LC** TD223.3; .G74A. **DD** 363.7/394/0977. available on microfiche (Vols. for (1981-) distributed to depository libraries). **Continues** Great Lakes Water Quality ... Annual Report to the International Joint Commission, 0706-1013.

CN/0318-5869
**REPORT SERIES (CANADA. INLAND WATERS DIRECTORATE).** (REPORT SERIES - INLAND WATERS DIRECTORATE.). [Rep. ser. - Inland Waters Dir.]. No. 24- 1973-. Monographic series. English (summaries and/or abstracts in French). Price varies per volume. Inland Waters Directorate, Place Vincent Massey, Ottawa Ontario K1A 0H3 Canada. **DD** 551.4. **CODEN** CIDRBB. Documents available from Article Express International. **Continues** Canada. Inland Waters Branch. Report Series, 0375-6009.
**Ind/Abst** ASTIS Curr. Aware. Bull. (1978-); Bioeng. Abstr.; Ei Page One; Eng. Index Annu.; GeoRef.

US/0145-2215
**REPORT - SPECIAL STUDIES SECTION, FIELD OPERATIONS DIVISION, TEXAS WATER QUALITY BOARD.** See Public Administration-Public Utilities.

US/0160-8851
**REPORT - STATE ENGINEER'S OFFICE, WYOMING WATER PLANNING PROGRAM.** [Rep. - State Eng. Off. Wyo. Water Plan. Program]. **Main/Corp** Wyoming. Water Planning Program. Monographic series. English. Price varies per volume. US Geological Survey, 2617 East Lincolnway/#B, Cheyenne WY 82001. **CODEN** WWPPB9.
**Ind/Abst** GeoRef.

US/0163-1160
**REPORT - TEXAS TECH UNIVERSITY, WATER RESOURCES CENTER.** **Main/Corp** Texas Tech University. Water Resources Center. (19??)-. Monographic series. English. ir. Price varies per volume. Texas Tech University / Water Resources Center, PO Box 4630, Lubbock TX 79409. **LC** TD224.T4; T422 subser. **DD** 333.91/009764S; 333.91/009764.

US/0733-3633
**REPORT TO THE COLORADO WATER QUALITY CONTROL COMMISSION.** (REPORT TO THE COLORADO WATER QUALITY CONTROL COMMISSION / BY WATER QUALITY CONTROL DIVISION, COLORADO DEPARTMENT OF HEALTH.). **Main/Corp** Colorado. Dept. of Health. Water Quality Control Division. **VFOAT** Water Quality Control Division's ... Annual Report to the Colorado Water Quality Control Commission. English. an. Water Quality Control Division, Denver CO 80220. **Tel** (303)320-8333. **LC** TD224.C7; C63A. **DD** 353.97880082/325.

US/0069-9063
**REPORT - UNIVERSITY OF CONNECTICUT. INSTITUTE OF WATER RESOURCES.** (REPORT - INSTITUTE OF WATER RESOURCES, UNIVERSITY OF CONNECTICUT.). [Rep. - Univ. Conn., Inst. Water Resour.]. **Main/Corp** University of Connecticut. Institute of Water Resources. **Added/Corp** United States. Office of Water Resources Research. **VFOAT** Report - Institute of Water Resources of The University of Connecticut. No. 1 (1967)-. Monographic series. English. an. Price varies per volume. University of Connecticut Institute of Water Resources, Storrs CT 06268. **Tel** (203)486-4523. **DD** 333.9. **CODEN** CUWRAJ.
**Desc:** Water resources reports based on research supported under the U.S. geological survey.
**Ind/Abst** GeoRef.

AT/0548-6882
**REPORT (UNIVERSITY OF NEW SOUTH WALES. WATER RESEARCH LABORATORY).** See Earth Sciences-Hydrology.

SA
**REPORT - WATER RESEARCH COMMISSION.** **Main/Corp** Water Research Commission. 1971/73-. English (Afrikaans). an. Free. Water Research Commission, 705 van der Ste; Box 824, 179 Pretorius Street, Pretoria 0001 South Africa. **Tel** 11 27 12 3300340, **FAX** 27 12 70 5925, telex 320464 WATKO SA. **ED** M J Pieterse. **LC** HD1699.S58; W3A. **DD** 333.9/1/00968. **Circ:** 3,000 (ctrl).
**Desc:** Contains reports and financial statements for the Water Research Commission

US/0069-4657
**REPORT - WATER RESOURCES RESEARCH INSTITUTE, CLEMSON UNIVERSITY.** (REPORT - WATER RESOURCES RESEARCH INSTITUTE.). [Rep. - Water Resour. Res. Inst., Clemson Univ.]. **Main/Corp** Clemson University. Water Resources Research Institute. **VFOAT** Technical Report - Water Resources Research Institute; WRRI Report. No. 1 (1967)-. Monographic series. English. an. Price varies per volume. Clemson University / Water Resources, Water Resources Research Institute, Clemson SC 29634-2900. **Tel** (803)656-3271. **ED** Paul B Zielinski. **LC** HD1694.S6; C55. **CODEN** CUWRBK. **Circ:** 300 (ctrl). Documents available from CASDDS.
**Ind/Abst** Chem. Abstr. (1967-1983); GeoRef.

US/0078-1525
**REPORT / WATER RESOURCES RESEARCH INSTITUTE OF THE UNIVERSITY OF NORTH CAROLINA.** [Rep. - Water Resour. Res. Inst. Univ. N. C.]. No. 1 (1967)-. Monographic series. English. ir. Price varies per volume. Water Resources Research Institute / North Carolina, 124 Riddich Building, NC Street, University, Raleigh NC 27650. **Tel** (919)937-2815. **LC** HD1694.N8; N6. **DD** 333.9. **CODEN** RWRCDT. Documents available from Article Express International, CASDDS.
**Ind/Abst** Bioeng. Abstr.; Chem. Abstr.; Ei Page One; Eng. Index Annu.; GeoRef; Soils Fert.

US/0486-476X
**RESEARCH AND DEVELOPMENT NEWS.** [Res. dev. news]. **Main/Corp** Water Information Center, inc. Vol. 1 (Aug. 1960)-. Periodical. English. ir. $219.00 US & Canada; $249.00 others Comes with Water Newsletter. Water Information Center Inc, 1099 18th Street, Suite 2150, Denver CO 80202. **Tel** (303)391-8799. **ED** Judith Schoeck and Mary Schwarz. **DD** 628. **[CCC]**. **Bk Rev**.

US/1059-826X
**RESEARCH REPORT - ILLINOIS STATE WATER SURVEY.** (RESEARCH REPORT.). [Res. rep. - Ill. State Water Surv.]. **Added/Corp** Illinois State

Water Survey. (1991)-. Monographic series. English. Illinois State Water Survey, 2204 Griffith Drive, Champaign IL 61820-7495. **Tel** (217)333-2210. **DD** 628. ***Continues*** *Report of Investigation (Illinois State Water Survey), 0097-5672.*

US/0453-5669
**RESEARCH REPORT / UNIVERSITY OF KENTUCKY, WATER RESOURCES INSTITUTE.** [Res. rep., Univ. Ky. Water Resour. Inst.]. **Added/Corp** University of Kentucky. Water Resources Institute. United States. Office of Water Resources Research. United States. Office of Water Research and Technology. No. 1 (1966)-. Monographic series. English. Price varies per volume. University of Kentucky Water Resources Research Institute, Lexington KY. **DD** 668. **CODEN** RRUIDR. Documents available from CASDDS.
**Ind/Abst** Chem. Abstr. (1973-1982); GeoRef.

US
**RESEARCH REPORT - WATER RESOURCES RESEARCH CENTER.** **Main/Corp** University of New Hampshire. Water Resources Research Center. No. 1- June 1969-. Monographic series. English. Price varies per volume. University of New Hampshire Water Resource Research Center, Durham NH 03824. **Tel** (603)862-2144. **DD** 628.

US
**RESEARCH REPORT WI.** **Main/Corp** North Dakota State University. Water Resources Research Institute. Monographic series. English. Price varies per volume. NDSU WRRI, 202 Ceres Hall, Fargo ND 58102. ***Continues*** *WI. Water Resources Research Institute.*

US
**RESOURCE NOTES.** English. Free. University of Nebraska - Lincoln, 901 North 17th Street, 113 Nebraska Hall, Lincoln NE 80517. **Tel** (402)472-3471. **ED** Charles Flowerday.
**Desc:** Report of the Conservation and Survey Division. Lists information of past, present, and future research.

TI/0330-0005
**RESSOURCES EN EAU DE TUNISIE.** [Ressour. eau Tunis.]. French. **LC** TD319.T85; R47. **DD** 551.5/781/09611.
**Ind/Abst** GeoRef.

FR/0992-7158
**REVUE DES SCIENCES DE L'EAU (PARIS).** (REVUE DES SCIENCES DE L'EAU.). [Rev. sci. eau]. **Added/Corp** Groupement d'Interet Scientifique Pour Les Sciences de L'eau. INRS-Eau. **VFOAT** Journal of Water Science. Vol. 1, No. 1/2 (1988)-. Periodical. French (English). qt. $142.00. Lavoisier Abonnements, 14 rue de Provigny, F 94236 Cachan Cedex France. **Tel** 011 33 1 47406700. **(Subscription address:** VCH Publishers Inc., 303 Northwest 12th Avenue, Journals Department, Deerfield FL 33442.) **CODEN** RSEAEX. Documents available from Article Express International, BIOSIS Document Express, CASDDS. ***Formed by the union of*** *Revue Internationale des Sciences de l'Eau, 0830-9590* ***and*** *Revue des Sciences de l'Eau, 0298-6663.*
**Ind/Abst** AQUAREF (199?-); Aquat. Sci. Fish. Abstr. (Computer File); Biol. Abstr. (1989-); Chem. Abstr.; Ecol. Abstr. (?-?); Energy Inf. Abstr.; Eng. Index Annu.; Environ. Period. Bibliogr.; Geogr. Abstr. Phys. Geogr.; Pollut. Abstr. Indexes.

AT
**RIVERLANDER.** **Added/Corp** Murray Valley Development League. Vol. 1 (Jan./Feb. 1946)-. Newsletter. English. ir. 25.00Aus$ Comes with Murray Valley League for Development and Conservation membership. Murray Valley League, Rundle Mall, PO Box 89, Adelaide South Australia, 5000 Australia. **Tel** 011 61 08 2267781, FAX 011 61 08 2235062. **Bk Rev. Ad Acc. Circ:** 7,000.
**Desc:** Concerned with multiple uses of the River Murray and the research and management required.

US/0898-8048
**RIVERS (FORT COLLINS, COLO.).** (RIVERS.). (1990)-. Periodical. English. qt. $115.00 US; $130.00 other. Sel & Associates, 3024 Phoenix Drive, Fort Collins CO 80525. **Tel** (303)226-6225, (303)224-1220, FAX (303)482-0251. **ED** Susan E. Lamb. **LC** GB1201; .R52. **DD** 551.48/3. **CODEN** RIVREV. Index available. cum. index. **Bk Rev**, (Qty: 12). **Pr Rev. Circ:** 600. Documents available from The Genuine Article, BIOSIS Document Express, Documents on Demand.
**Desc:** Address issues relevant to North American, European, and Australian instream flow; covers multiagency actions, water resource planning, fisheries biology, water law, riparian corridor management, and regulations involved with flow usage.
**Ind/Abst** Biol. Abstr. (1991-); Ecol. Abstr.; Environ. Abstr.; Fish Rev.; Geogr. Abstr. Human Geogr.; GeoRef; Res. Alert [Select. Cov.]; Soc. Sci. Cit. Index [Select. Cov.].

SA/0258-2244
**SA WATER BULLETIN.** [SA Waterbull.]. **VFOAT** South African Waterbulletin. (1975)-. Periodical. Multiple languages. qt. Free on request. Water Resource Commission, 705 Van der Ste, Box 824 179 Pretorius Street, Pretoria 0001 South Africa. **Tel** 011 27 12 3300340, FAX 011 27 12 3312565. **UDC** 551.49.
**Desc:** Covers water and water research in South Africa.
**Ind/Abst** Sci. Cit. Index; SCISEARCH.

US
**SACRAMENTO-SAN JOAQUIN DELTA WATER QUALITY SURVEILLANCE PROGRAM : MONITORING RESULTS PURSUANT TO CONDITIONS SET FORTH IN DELTA WATER RIGHTS DECISION ... / STATE OF CALIFORNIA, THE RESOURCES AGENCY, DEPARTMENT OF WATER RESOURCES.** **Added/Corp** California. Dept. of Water Resources. **VFOAT** Water Quality Surveillance Program. (1975)-. English. an. **LC** TD224.C3; S26. **DD** 363.7/342/097945.

CN/0822-7551
**SASKATCHEWAN WATER NEWS.** (SASKATCHEWAN WATER NEWS : NEWSLETTER OF THE CANADIAN WATER RESOURCES ASSOCIATION, SASKATCHEWAN SECTION.). [Sask. water news]. **VFOAT** Water News. Vol. 1, No. 1 (Winter 1982)-. Newsletter. English. qt. $2.00. Saskatchewan Water News, c/o L Martz Kelsey Institute, PO Box 1520, Saskatoon Saskatchewan S7K 3R5 Canada. **DD** 333.91/00971.

GW/0172-665X
**SCHRIFTENREIHE DES BAYERISCHEN LANDESAMTES FUER WASSERWIRTSCHAFT.** **See** Earth Sciences-Hydrology.

GW/0170-8147
**SCHRIFTENREIHE DES DEUTSCHEN VERBANDES FUER WASSERWIRTSCHAFT UND KULTURBAU.** (SCHRIFTENREIHE DES DEUTSCHEN VERBANDES FUER WASSERWIRTSCHAFT UND KULTURBAU / DVWK.). [Schriftenr. Dtsch. Verb. Wasserwirtsch. Kult.bau.]. **Added/Corp** Deutscher Verband fur Wasserwirtschaft und Kulturbau. **VFOAT** DVWK Schriften. **VAT** Deutscher Verband fur Wasserwirtschaft und Kulturbau Schriften. (1979)-. Monographic series. German. Price varies per volume. Paul Parey (Berlin), Seelbuschring 9-17, 1000 Berlin 42 Germany. **Tel** 030-70784-00. **CODEN** SDVKDJ. Documents available from CASDDS. ***Continues*** *Schriftenreihe des Kuratoriums fur Wasser und Kulturbauwesen.*
**Ind/Abst** Chem. Abstr.

GW
**SCHRIFTENREIHE DES ISWW KARLSRUHE.** **Added/Corp** Universitat Karlsruhe. Institut fur Siedlungswasserwirtschaft. **VFOAT** ISWW-Karlsruhe; ISWW Karlsruhe. **VAT** Schriftenreihe des Institut fur Siedlungswasserwirtschaft Karlsruhe. (1982)-. Monographic series. German. Institut fur Siedlungswasserwirtschaft, Karlsruhe Germany. Documents available from CASDDS. ***Continues*** *Institut fur Siedlungswasserwirtschaft, Universitat Karlsruhe : [Schriftenreihe], 0722-7698.*
**Ind/Abst** Chem. Abstr.

US
**SELECTED URBAN STORM WATER RUNOFF ABSTRACTS.** **Added/Corp** United States. Federal Water Pollution Control Administration. Franklin Institute (Philadelphia, Pa.). Science Information Service. United States. Environmental Protection Agency. Office of Research and Monitoring. (19??)-. Government Publication. English. ir. Superintendent of Documents, US Government Printing Office, Washington DC 20402. **Tel** (202)275-3328, FAX (202)786-2377. **LC** TD653; .S45. **DD** 628/.2.

HU
**SERIES OF MANUALS.** **See** Earth Sciences-Hydrology.

CN/0045-303X
**SNOW SURVEY BULLETIN.** (SNOW SURVEY BULLETIN / WATER RIGHTS BRANCH, WATER RESOURCES INVESTIGATION.). **Added/Corp** British Columbia. Surface Water Section. British Columbia. Water Rights Branch. British Columbia. Water Investigations Branch. British Columbia. Hydrology Division. British Columbia. Hydrology Section. **VFOAT** British Columbia Snow Survey Bulletin. (April 1, 1949)-. English. mo. free. Ministry of the Environment, Parliament Building, Water Investigation, Victoria British Columbia V8V 1X5 Canada. **Tel** (604)387-1111. **LC** QC929.S7; B8. **DD** 551.57/842711. ***Continues*** *Snow Survey Report.*

US/0196-0717
**SOUTHWEST & TEXAS WATER WORKS JOURNAL.** ***Ceased.*** [Southwest Tex. water works j.]. **VFOAT** Southwest and Texas Water Works Journal; Water. Vol. 61, No. 7 Oct. (1979)-Ceased with March (1990). Academic Scholarly Publication. English. mo. American Water Works Association / Texas, PO Box 769, 306-E Adams Drive, Temple TX 76501. **Tel** (817)778-1313. **ED** Lawrence W Ingram. **LC** TD201. **DD** 628.1/0976. **CODEN** STWJDV. **Ad Acc. Circ:** 9,660. Documents available from CASDDS. ***Continues*** *Water (Temple, Tex.), 0099-8729.*
**Desc:** Deals with areas of water in regards to sewerage, purification, wastewater, engineering, and related fields.
**Ind/Abst** Chem. Abstr.

US/0571-026X
**SPECIAL GROUND-WATER REPORT (LITTLE ROCK).** (SPECIAL GROUND-WATER REPORT / STATE OF ARKANSAS, ARKANSAS GEOLOGICAL AND CONSERVATION COMMISSION.). **Added/Corp** Geological Survey (U.S.) Arkansas Geological and Conservation Commission. **VFOAT** Special Ground Water Report. No. 1 (1960)-. Monographic series. English. Price varies per volume. Arkansas Geological Commission, 3815 West Roosevelt Road, Little Rock AR 72204. **Tel** (501)371-1646. **LC** WMLC L 83/9509. **DD** 551.4.

PR
**SPECIAL REPORT - WATER RESOURCES AUTHORITY, A.** **Main/Corp** Puerto Rico. Water Resources Authority. English. Government Development Bank for Puerto Rico, PO Box 42001, San Juan PR 00940. **Tel** (809)722-2525, FAX (809)268-5496. **LC** HD9685.P92; P85A. **DD** 354/.7295/00871.

GW
**STAATSBURGERKUNDLICHE ARBEITSMAPPE.** ***Title Change.*** German. Erich Schmidt Verlag GmbH, Postfach 304240, D 10724 Berlin Germany. **Tel** 011 49 30 25008525. ***Continued by*** *Arbeitsmappe Sozial- und Wirtschaftskunde.*

US/0741-3386
**STATE OF TEXAS WATER QUALITY MANAGEMENT, ANNUAL WORK PROGRAM, THE.** **Main/Corp** Texas. Dept. of Water Resources. English. an. Texas Department of Water Resources, PO Box 13087, Austin TX 78711. **LC** TD224.T4; T4216C. **DD** 353.97640082/325/06. ***Continues*** *State of Texas Water Quality Management Program, 0160-6905.*

US/0160-6905
**STATE OF TEXAS WATER QUALITY MANAGEMENT PROGRAM.** ***Title Change.*** **Main/Corp** Texas. Dept. of Water Resources. English. an. Texas Department of Water Resources, PO Box 13087, Austin TX 78711. **LC** TD224.T4; T4216C. **DD** 614.7/72/09764. ***Continues*** *State of Texas Water Quality Management Program, 0160-6905.* ***Continued by*** *State of Texas Water Quality Management, Annual Work Program, 0741-3386.*

US/0092-6442
**STATE WATER PLAN PUBLICATION (LINCOLN).** (STATE WATER PLAN PUBLICATION.). **Main/Corp** Nebraska. Natural Resources Commission. English. Natural Resources Commission, PO Box 94876, Lincoln NE 68509. **LC** TC424.N2; N4A. **DD** 333.9/1/009782.

US
**STATE WATER PROGRAM; BIENNIAL REPORT (WASHINGTON (STATE)).** **Main/Corp** Washington (State). Dept. of Ecology. Planning and Development Division. 1st- 1971/73-. English. be. Washington State Department of Ecology, Olympia WA 98504. **LC** HD1694.W2; A26. **DD** 333.9/1/009797.

US/0730-9864
**STATE WATER PROJECT ANNUAL REPORT OF OPERATIONS.** (STATE WATER PROJECT ANNUAL REPORT OF OPERATIONS / STATE OF CALIFORNIA, THE RESOURCES AGENCY, DEPARTMENT OF WATER RESOURCES, DIVISION OF OPERATIONS AND MAINTENANCE.). **Main/Corp** California. Dept. of Water Resources. Division of Operations and Maintenance. (1976)-. English. an. California State Water Project, Sacramento CA 95819. **LC** TC424.C2; A385. **DD** 333.91/0099794. ***Continues*** *California State Water Project Annual Report, 0090-5968.*

US/0731-8936
**STATUS OF WATER QUALITY IN COLORADO.** **Added/Corp** Colorado. Dept. of Health. Water Quality Control Division. (19??). English. be. Water Quality Control Division, Denver CO 80220. **Tel** (303)320-8333. **LC** TD224.C7; S72. **DD** 363.7/3942/09788.
**Desc:** An assessment of water quality in the state of Colorado.

US
**STORAGE IN RESERVOIRS, DAILY DISCHARGE RECORDS OF MISCELLANEOUS STREAMS AND CANAL DIVERSIONS / STATE OF NEBRASKA, DEPARTMENT OF WATER RESOURCES.** **Added/Corp** Nebraska. Dept. of Water Resources. **VFOAT** Daily Discharge Records of

# Water Resources

Miscellaneous Streams and Canal Diversions; Hydrographic Report. (1969/70)-. English. an. Nebraska Department of Water Resources, PO Box 94676, Lincoln NE 68509-4676. **Tel** (402)471-2363. **LC** TD224.N18; A3. **DD** 333.91/0213/09782. *Continues Canal Diversions and Miscellaneous Stream Discharge Records.*

NZ/0111-977X
**STREAMLAND.** See Agriculture-Crop Production and Soil.

AT/0812-7735
**STREAMLINE UPDATE / DEPARTMENT OF RESOURCES AND ENERGY.**
**Added/Corp** Australia. Dept. of Resources and Energy. Australia. Dept. of Primary Industries and Energy. Land and Water Resources Research and Development Corporation (Australia). Issue 1 (Sept. 1983)-. Periodical. English. Five times a year. 120.00Aus$ Australia; 170.00Aus$ others. Infoscan Pty Ltd., PO Box 155, Canberra ACT 2601 Australia. **Tel** 011 61 6 2366267. **LC** IN PROCESS.
**Ind/Abst** AESIS Q.

RM/0521-3479
**STUDI ALIMENTARI CU APA.** [Stud. Aliment. Apa]. **Main/Corp** Institutul de Studii, Cercetari Si Proiectari Pentru Gospodarirea Apelor. (19??)-. Academic Scholarly Publication. Multiple languages (English, French and Romanian). Institutul de Studii / Cercetari Si Proiectari, Splaiul Independentei 294, Bucurest 17 Romania. **LC** TD204; .B78. **CODEN** SDAABI. Documents available from BIOSIS Document Express, CASDDS. *Continues Bucharest. Institutul de Studii si Cercetari Hidrotehnice. Studii de Alimentari cu Apa.*
**Ind/Abst** Biol. Abstr. (-1979); Chem. Abstr.

FR/0081-7449
**STUDIES AND REPORTS IN HYDROLOGY.** [Stud. rep. hydrol.]. **VFOAT** Etudes et Rapports d'Hydrologie; Estudios e Informes de Hidrologia; Issledovaniia I Doklady po Gidrologii. No. 1 (1969)-. Monographic series. English (French, Russian and Spanish). ir. Price varies per volume. UNIPUB, 4611-F Assembly Drive, Lanham MD 20706-4391. **Tel** (800)274-4888, FAX (301)459-0056, telex 28787 GATT CH. **ED** John S Gladwell. **DD** 551.4. **CODEN** IHSRB9. ctrl circ.
**Desc:** Individual reports on aspects of scientific hydrology, water resources planning and management, education and training -- available for purchase.
**Ind/Abst** GeoRef.

RM
**STUDII DE ECONOMIA APELOR.**
**Main/Corp** Institutul de Studii, Cercetari Si Proiectari Pentru Gospodarirea Apelor. 2 (1972)-. Periodical. Romanian (summaries and/or abstracts in English, French and Russian). Institutul de Studii / Cercetari Si Proiectari, Splaiul Independentei 294, Bucurest 17 Romania. **LC** TC401; .I58a. *Continues Studii de Economia Apelor.*

GW/0585-7953
**STUTTGARTER BERICHTE ZUR SIEDLUNGSWASSERWIRTSCHAFT.**
[Stuttg. Ber. Siedlungswasserwirtsch.]. **Added/Corp** Forschungs- und Entwicklungsinstitut fuer Industrie- und Siedlungswasserwirtschaft sowie Abfallwirtschaft. (1958)-. Academic Scholarly Publication. German. Price varies per volume. R Oldenburg Verlag, Postfach 801360, D 81613 Munich Germany. **Tel** 011 49 89 450190, FAX 011 49 89 45019305. **CODEN** SBSWBO. Documents available from CASDDS.
**Ind/Abst** Chem. Abstr.

JA
**SUIDO JITSUMU ROPPO / KOSEISHO KANKYO EISEIKYOKU SUIDO KANKYOBU SUIDO SEIBIKA HENSHU.**
**Main/Corp** Japan. 1977-. Japanese. ¥4050. Gyosei Corporation Ltd., 4-2 Nishi Goken-cho, Shinjuku-Ku Tokyo 162 Japan. **Tel** 33269-4145, FAX 33268-2315.

JA/0039-4858
**SUIRI KAGAKU. WATER SCIENCE.**
**Added/Corp** Suiri Kagaku Kenkyujo. **VFOAT** Water Science. No. 103 (June 1975)-. Periodical. Japanese. bm. $100.00. Suiri Kagaku Kenkyusho, 1-7-22 Koraku, Bunkyo-ku Tokyo Japan. (**Subscription address:** Kyowa Book Company Inc., 1 38 Kanda Jinbocho Chiyoda-ku, Tokyo 101 Japan.) **ED** Masao Yosimura. **Circ:** 1,900.
**Desc:** Deals with water science.
**Ind/Abst** Life Sci. Collect.

US/0093-0539
**SUMMARY OF GROUND WATER DATA FOR TENNESSEE.** [Summ. ground water data Tenn.]. **Main/Corp** Tennessee. Division of Water Resources. (19??)-. English. an. Tennessee Department of Conservation, Division of Geology, 401 Church Street, Nashville TN 27243-0445. **Tel** (615)532-1516, (615)532-1500. **LC** GB1025.T2; T45a. **DD** 553/.79/09768.

US
**SUMMARY OF WATER QUALITY.**
**Main/Corp** Massachusetts. Water Quality and Research Section. **Added/Corp** Massachusetts. Water Quality and Research Section. Massachusetts. Division of Water Pollution Control. Technical Services Branch. (19??)-. English. an. **LC** TD224.M4; M39a. **DD** 363.7/3942/09744.

FI/0039-5471
**SUO.** See Agriculture.

CN/0576-2367
**SURFACE WATER DATA. BRITISH COLUMBIA.** (SURFACE WATER DATA.). [Surf. water data, B.C.]. **Main/Corp** Water Survey of Canada. **VFOAT** Donnees sur les Eaux de Surface. **VAT** Donnees sur les Eaux de Surface. Colombie-Britannique. 1965-. English. an. Water Survey of Canada, Water Resources Branch, 521 Federal Building, 269 Main Street, Winnipeg Manitoba R3C 1B2 Canada. **LC** GB1230.B7; C38A. **DD** 553.7/8/09711.
**Ind/Abst** GeoRef.

RU/0371-4268
**SVJAZANNAJA VODA V DISPERSNYH SISTEMAH.** (SVIAZANNAIA VODA V DISPERSNYKH SISTEMAKH.). [Svjazannaja voda dispersnyh sist.]. **Added/Corp** Moskovskii Gosudarstvennyi Universitet Im. M.V. Lomonosova. (1970)-. Academic Scholarly Publication. Russian. ir. Izdatelstvo Moskovskogo Universiteta, K-9 Ulitsa Gertsena 5/7, 103009 Moscow Russia. **Tel** (301)881-5973. **CODEN** SVDSA8. Documents available from CASDDS.
**Ind/Abst** Chem. Abstr. (1970-).

CH
**TAI-PEI TZU LAI SHUI SHIH YEH TUNG CHI NIEN PAO.** **Added/Corp** Tai-pei Tzu Lai Shui Shih Yeh Chu. **VFOAT** Tung Chi Nien Pao. (19??)-. Chinese. **LC** TD302.6.T3; T33a. *Continues Tai-pei Tzu Lai Shui Chang. Chu Chi Shih. Tung Chi Nien Pao.*
**Desc:** Information concerning water and water-supply.

CN/0822-8043
**TALK OF THE THAMES.** [Talk Thames]. **Added/Corp** Thames River Implementation Committee. Upper Thames River Conservation Authority. (Spring 1981)-. Periodical. English. sa. Upper Thames River Conservation Authority, PO Box 6278 Station D, London Ontario N5W 5S1 Canada. **DD** 363.7/3946/0971325.

GW
**TASCHENBUCH FUER DAS GAS-UND WASSERFACH.** **Added/Corp** Deutscher Verein von Gas-und Wasserfachmannern. Verband der Deutschen Gas-und Wasserwerke. (1954)-. German. R Oldenbourg Verlag, Postfach 801360, D 81613 Munich Germany. **Tel** 011 49 89 450190, FAX 011 49 89 45019305. *Continues Jahrbuch fur das Gas und Wasserfach.*

NE/0074-042X
**TECHNICAL BULLETIN - INSTITUTE FOR LAND AND WATER MANAGEMENT RESEARCH.** See Agriculture-Crop Production and Soil.

NE
**TECHNICAL BULLETINS (INSTITUUT VOOR CULTUURTECHNIEK EN WATERHUISHOUDING : 1981).**
(TECHNICAL BULLETINS / ICW.). Monographic series. English. Price varies per volume. Institute for Land and Water Management Research (ICW), PO Box 35, 6700 AA Wageningen The Netherlands. **Tel** 011 31 8370 19100, FAX 011 31 8370 11524, telex 75230 VISI N. *Continues Technical Bulletin (Instituut voor Cultuurtechniek en Waterhuishouding : 1958-81), 0074-042X;* **Absorbed in part** *Verspreide Overdrukken, 0074-0438.*

AT
**TECHNICAL MEMORANDUM.** See Agriculture.

US/0278-6206
**TECHNICAL PROCEEDINGS / ANNUAL CONFERENCE AND INTERNATIONAL TRADE FAIR OF THE NATIONAL WATER SUPPLY IMPROVEMENT ASSOCIATION.** [Tech. proc., Annu. conf. int. trade fair Natl. Water Supply Improv. Assoc.]. **Main/Corp** National Water Supply Improvement Association. Conference and International Trade Fair. Academic Scholarly Publication. English. an. $100.00. IDA, PO Box 387, Topsfield MA 01983. **Tel** (714)963-5661. **CODEN** TPASDX. Documents available from CASDDS.
**Ind/Abst** Chem. Abstr.

US/0197-0526
**TECHNICAL REPORT - CORNELL UNIVERSITY WATER RESOURCES AND MARINE SCIENCES CENTER.** [Tech. rep. - Cornell Univ. Water Resour. Mar. Sci. Cent.]. **Main/Corp** Cornell University. Water Resources and Marine Sciences Center. **Added/Corp** United States. Office of Water Resources Research. (1967)-. Monographic series. English. ir. Price varies per volume. National Technical Information Service - NTIS, Room 2027S, 5285 Port Royal Road, Springfield VA 22161. **Tel** (703)487-4630, (703)487-4660, (703)487-4650, FAX (703)321-8547, telex 89-9405. **LC** UNC. *Continues Technical Report - Cornell University, Water Resources Center.*
**Ind/Abst** GeoRef.

US/0580-9746
**TECHNICAL REPORT - INSTITUTE OF WATER RESEARCH (EAST LANSING).**
(TECHNICAL REPORT - INSTITUTE OF WATER RESEARCH, MICHIGAN STATE UNIVERSITY.). [Tech. rep. - Inst. Water Res. (East Lansing)]. **Main/Corp** Michigan State University. Institute of Water Research. No. 1 (1968)-. Monographic series. English. Price varies per volume. **CODEN** TRMWDH.
**Ind/Abst** GeoRef.

US/0459-8768
**TECHNICAL REPORT - LOUISIANA WATER RESOURCES RESEARCH INSTITUTE.** (TECHNICAL REPORT.). [Tech. rep. - La. Water Resour. Res. Inst.]. No. 1 (1967)-. Monographic series. English. ir. Price varies per volume. Louisiana State University, Baton Rouge LA 70803. **Tel** (504)388-2855. **LC** TC424.L8; A29.
**Ind/Abst** GeoRef.

US/0555-8026
**TECHNICAL REPORT - PURDUE UNIVERSITY, WATER RESOURCES RESEARCH CENTER.** (TECHNICAL REPORT.). [Tech. rep. - Purdue Univ. Water Resour. Res. Cent.]. No. 1 (1966)-. Monographic series. English. ir. Price varies per volume. Purdue Water Resources Research Center, Lilly Hall, Purdue University, West Lafayette IN 47907. **Tel** (317)494-8041, FAX (317)494-0395, telex 4930593. **ED** J R Wright. **LC** TD201; .P9. **DD** 333.91/009772. **CODEN** PWRTBM. cum. index. **Circ:** 300. Documents available from CASDDS.
**Ind/Abst** Chem. Abstr. (1966-1983); GeoRef; Soils Fert.; Weed Abstr.

US/0275-5483
**TECHNICAL REPORT - TEXAS WATER RESOURCES INSTITUTE.** (TECHNICAL REPORT.). [Tech. rep. - Tex. Water Resour. Inst.]. No. 37; June 1971-. Monographic series. English. Price varies per volume. Texas A & M University / TWRI, Texas Water Resources Institute, College Station TX 77843. **LC** TD224.T4; T38. **DD** 553/.7/09764. **CODEN** TRTIDA. *Continues Technical Report - Water Resources Institute, Texas A & M University.*
**Ind/Abst** GeoRef.

GU/0272-9555
**TECHNICAL REPORT - WATER AND ENERGY RESEARCH INSTITUTE, UNIVERSITY OF GUAM.** [Tech. rep. - Water Resour. Res. Cent., Univ. Guam]. **Main/Corp** University of Guam. Water Resources Research Center. No. 1 (1976)-. Monographic series. English. ir. Price varies per volume. Water & Energy Research Institute, University of Guam, UOG Station, Mangilao 96923 Guam. **Tel** (671)734-1382, FAX (671)734-3118. **ED** Dr. Shahram Khosrowpanah. Index available. cum. index. **Circ:** 100.
**Ind/Abst** GeoRef.

US/0272-8729
**TECHNICAL REPORT - WATER RESOURCES RESEARCH CENTER, UNIVERSITY OF HAWAII.** (TECHNICAL REPORT.). [Tech. rep. - Water Resour. Res. Cent., Univ. Hawaii]. **Added/Corp** University of Hawaii at Manoa. Water Resources Research Center. (1972)-. Monographic series. English. University of Hawaii at Manoa, 2540 Dole Street, Holmes Hall 283, Honolulu HI 96822. **Tel** (808)956-7847. **LC** TC1; .H36. **DD** 553.7/09969. *Continues Technical Report (University of Hawaii (Honolulu). Water Resources Research Center), 0073-1307.*
**Ind/Abst** AGRICOLA.

BE/0040-120X
**TECHNIQUE DE L'EAU ET DE L'ASSAINISSEMENT, LA.** Vol. 1 No. 1 (Feb. 1947)-. Periodical. French. Ten times a year. Technique Eau and Assainissement, rue Tenbosch 43, 1050 Bruxelles Belgium. **Tel** 011 32 2 6470073.

US/0565-596X
**TECHNIQUES OF WATER-RESOURCES INVESTIGATIONS OF THE UNITED STATES GEOLOGICAL SURVEY.** [Tech. wat.-resources investig. U.S. Geol. Surv.]. **Added/Corp**

Geological Survey (U.S.) U.S. Atomic Energy Commission. **VFOAT** Model for Simulation of Flow in Singular and Interconnected Channels. (196?)-. Monographic series. English. ir. Price varies per volume. US Geological Survey / Denver, PO Box 25286, Denver CO 80225. **Tel** (303)493-8401. **LC** TC177; .U57a. **CODEN** XTWRA.
**Ind/Abst** Geogr. Abstr. Phys. Geogr.

SP/0211-8173
**TECNOLOGIA DEL AGUA.** [Tecnol. agua]. (1981)-. Periodical. Spanish (summaries and/or abstracts in English). Fourteen times a year. $215.00. Elsevier Prensa SA, Avenida Paral Lel 180, 08015 Barcelona Spain. **Tel** 011 34 3 3255350, FAX 011 34 3 4252880. **CODEN** TEAGEN. **Ad Acc.** Full Page (B&W) 145000ptas. Half Page (B&W) 120000ptas. Full Page (Color) 175000ptas. Half Page (Color) 135000ptas. **Circ:** 7,000.
**Desc:** Technical magazine exclusively dedicated to water and hydrology and all associated issues.

US/0564-7495
**TEXAS WATER DEVELOPMENT BOARD PUBLICATIONS CATALOG.** **Main/Corp** Texas Water Development Board. **VFOAT** Publications Catalog - Texas Water Development Board. Catalog. English. Water Development Board, PO Box 13087, Austin TX 78711.

US/0492-9829
**TEXAS WATER REPORT.** (TEXAS WATER REPORT; A FACTUAL WEEKLY PUBLICATION ON TEXAS WATER AND SOIL CONSERVATION.). [Tex. water rep.]. (195?)-. Periodical. English. Fifty-one times per year. Texas Water Report, Box 12368, Austin TX 78711. **Tel** (512)478-5663.

US/0744-1320
**TEXAS WATER RESOURCES.** [Texas water resour.]. **Added/Corp** Texas Water Resources Institute. Vol. 1 (Nov. 1974)-. Periodical. English. Four times a year (Mar., June, Sept., Dec.). Free. Texas Water Resources Institute, 301 Scoates Hall, Texas A & M University, College Station TX 77843-2118. **Tel** (409)845-8571, FAX (409)845-8554. **ED** Ric Jensen. **DD** 333. **CODEN** TWREDN. **Circ:** 10,500 (ctrl). Documents available from Documents on Demand.
**Desc:** Provides training for water resources professionals.
**Ind/Abst** Environ. Abstr.; GeoRef.

BE
**TRIBUNE DE L'EAU / MINISTERE DE LA REGION WALLONNE, UNION WALLONNE DES ENTREPRISES, [ET] CEBEDEAU.** **See** Environmental Issues-Pollution and Waste Management.

US/0091-1593
**TRIENNIAL REPORT ON WATER RESOURCES DEVELOPMENT.** **Main/Corp** United Nations. Dept. of Economic and Social Affairs. (19??)-. Government Publication. English. te. United Nations Publications, 2 United Nations Plaza, Room DC2 0853, Department 007C, New York NY 10017. **Tel** (212)963-8303, (800)253-9646. **LC** JX1977; .A2 subser. **DD** 333.9/1.

CH
**TUNG CHI NIEN PAO - TAI-PEI TZU LAI SHUI CHANG CHU CHI SHIH.** ***Title Change.*** **Main/Corp** Tai-Pei Tzu Lai Shui Chang. Chu Chi Shih. **VFOAT** Tai-Pei Tzu Lai Shui Chang Tung Chi Nien Pao. (19??)-(19??). Chinese. **LC** TD302.6.T3; T33a. ***Continued by*** *Tai-Pei Tzu Lai Shui Shih Yeh Tung Chi Nien Pao.*

US/0749-1980
**U.S. WATER NEWS.** [U. S. water news]. **VFOAT** U. S. Water News. **VAT** United States Water News. Vol. 1, No. 1 (July 1984)-. Periodical. English. mo. $44.00 (one year), $79.00 (two years) US; $54.00 (one year), $99.00 (two years) Canada; $89.00 (one year), $169.00 (two years) other. US Water News, 230 Main Street, Halstead KS 67056. **Tel** (316)835-2222, (800)251-0046, FAX (316)835-2223. **ED** Steve Seibel. **DD** 363. **CODEN** USWNEP. **Bk Rev. Ad Acc, Adv Mgr:** Phil Friedman, **Tel** (201)461-5422. **Circ:** 25,000. Documents available from Documents on Demand.
**Desc:** Reports news of current events in water from across the nation; reports on problems in the water community; reveals political, legislative, and court decisions affecting water and the water industry. Adresses the issues of federal, state, and local water policy; water rights; water quality and pollution; lawsuits; financial news in the water industry; innovative conservation practices; public water supply; and industrial water use.
**Ind/Abst** BioBusiness (1990-); Environ. Abstr.

US/0747-8291
**ULTRAPURE WATER.** [Ultrapure water]. Vol. 1, No. 1 (July/Aug. 1984)-. Academic Scholarly Publication. English. Nine times a year. $18.00 US, Canada & Mexico; $63.00 others. Tall Oaks Publishing Inc, PO Box 621669, 60 Golden Eagle Lane, Littleton CO 80127. **Tel** (303)973-6600, (800)662-1660, FAX (303)973-5327. **DD** 628. **CODEN** ULWAE5. Index available. cum. index. **Bk Rev. Ad Acc. Circ:** 13,000 (ctrl). available on microfilm from University Microfilms International (UMI). Documents available from CASDDS. ***Absorbed*** *Industrial Water Engineering, 0019-8862.*
**Ind/Abst** BioBusiness; Chem. Abstr. (1984-); Fluid Abstr., Civil Eng.; Fluid Abstr. Proc. Eng.; FLUIDEX.

US/0041-6592
**UNDERWATER LETTER, THE.** **See** Earth Sciences-Oceanography.

JA/0917-7221
**USUI GIJUTSU SHIRYO.** (1991)-. Periodical. Japanese. qt. Usui Choryu Shinto Gijutsu Kyokai, Association for Rainwater Storage and Infiltration Technology, 3-28 Kioi-cho, Chiyoda-ku, Tokyo 102 Japan.

SW/0042-2886
**VATTEN.** [Vatten]. **Added/Corp** Foreningen for Vattenhygien (Sweden). **VFOAT** Journal of Water Management and Research. (1967)-. Academic Scholarly Publication. Swedish (English). qt. Free, members; Kr660.00 non-members. Swedish Association for Water Hygiene, c/o B. Oster, S-106 36 Stockholm Sweden. **Tel** 011 46 8 7280100, FAX 011 46 8 328645. **CODEN** VTTNAO. Index available. cum. index. **Ad Acc.** ctrl circ. Documents available from BIOSIS Document Express, CASDDS. ***Continues*** *Vattenhygien.*
**Ind/Abst** Aquat. Sci. Fish. Abstr. (Computer File); Biodeter. Abstr. (1991-); Biol. Abstr.; Chem. Abstr.; Coal Abstr.; Curr. Biotechnol.; EMBASE; Energy Res. Abstr. (Nov. 1978-); Environ. Period. Bibliogr.; GeoRef; Ocean. Abstr.; Life Sci. Collect.; Soils Fert.

XR
**VEDECKE PRACE / NAUCHNYE TRUDY / SCIENTIFIC STUDIES.** **See** Agriculture-Crop Production and Soil.

GW/0342-474X
**VEROFFENTLICHUNGEN DES INSTITUTS FUER WASSERFORSCHUNG GMBH DORTMUND UND DER HYDROLOGISCHEN ABTEILUNG DER DORTMUNDER STADTWERKE AG.** **Main/Corp** Dortmund. Institut fur Wasserforschung. (19??)-. Academic Scholarly Publication. German. **CODEN** VIWSDE. Documents available from CASDDS.
**Ind/Abst** Chem. Abstr. (1958-1986)(19??-).

NE
**VERSLAG ONDERZOEK KWALITEIT OPPERVLAKTEWATER IN ZEELAND.** **See** Environmental Issues-Pollution and Waste Management.

HU
**VIZGAZDALKODAS ES KORNYEZETVEDELEM.** **VFOAT** Vizgazdalkodas. Hungarian. Orszagos Vizugyi Foigazgatosag, Budapest Hungary. **LC** TD265.5; .V58.

PN/0322-8231
**VODNI HOSPODARSTVI.** **Added/Corp** Czech Socialist Republic (Czechoslovakia). Ministerstvo Lesniho a Vodniho Hospodarstvi a Drevozpracujiciho Prumyslu. Slovak Socialist Republic (Czechoslovakia). Ministerstvo Lesneho a Vodneho Hospodarstva a Drevospracujuceho Priemyslu. Czech Republic (Czechoslovakia). Ministerstvo Zivotniho Prostredi. Slovak Republic (Czechoslovakia). Ministerstvo Lesneho a Vodneho Hospodarstva a Drevospracujuceho Priemyslu. **VFOAT** Water Management; Vodnoe Khoziaistvo. (1990)-. Academic Scholarly Publication. Czech (summaries and/or abstracts in English and Russian). mo. Kcs144.00. **CODEN** VOHSEG. Documents available from CASDDS. ***Formed by the union of*** *Vodni Hospodarstvi. A, 0322-8282* ***and*** *Vodni Hospodarstvi. B, 0322-8231.*
**Ind/Abst** Agric. Eng. Abstr.; Chem. Abstr.; Soils Fert.

RU/0321-0596
**VODNYE RESURSY.** [Vod. resur.]. **Added/Corp** Akademiia Nauk SSSR. (1972)-. Academic Scholarly Publication. Russian. bm. $196.00. Izdatelstvo Nauka / Akademiia Nauk, Publishing House of the Russian Academy of Sciences, Leninskii Porspekt 14, 117901 Moscow Russia. **Tel** 011 95 954-21-53, FAX 011 95 938-21-44, telex 411964. **(Subscription address:** Victor Kamkin, 4956 Boiling Brook Parkway, Rockville, MD 20852) **CODEN** VDRSBK. **[CCC].** Documents available from CASDDS.
**Desc:** Information on hydrology and water resources development.
**Ind/Abst** AGRICOLA; Chem. Abstr.; Energy Res. Abstr. (July 1976-); GeoRef.

GW/0083-6915
**VOM WASSER.** [Vom Wasser]. **Added/Corp** Verein Deutscher Chemiker. Fachgruppe fur Wasserchemie. Verein Deutscher Chemiker. Fachgruppe fur Wasserchemie, Einschliesslich Abfallstoff- und Korrosionsfragen. Verein Deutscher Chemiker. Arbeitsgruppe Wasserchemie, Einschliesslich Abfallstoff- und Korrosionsfragen. Verein Deutscher Chemiker. Arbeitsgruppe Wasser. Gesellschaft Deutscher Chemiker. Fachgruppe Wasserchemie. (1927)-. Academic Scholarly Publication. German. ir. $107.50 North America. VCH Gesellschaft GmbH, Postfach 101161, D 69451 Weinheim Germany. **Tel** 011 49 6201 606459, FAX 011 49 6201 606184. **(Subscription address:** VCH Publishers Inc., 303 Northwest 12th Avenue, Journals Department, Deerfield FL 33442.**) LC** TD203; .V4. **DD** 628.1/05. **NLM** W1 VO604. **CODEN** VJWWAU. **[CCC].** cum. index. Documents available from Article Express International, BIOSIS Document Express, CASDDS.
**Ind/Abst** Aquat. Sci. Fish. Abstr. (Computer File) (19??-); Biol. Abstr. (19??-); Chem. Abstr. (19??-); Ei Page One (19??-); EMBASE (19??-); Energy Res. Abstr. (19??-); Eng. Index Annu. (19??-); GeoRef (19??-).

US/0161-5912
**WASHINGTON STATE'S WATER.** (WASHINGTON STATE'S WATER : A REPORT.). **Main/Corp** State of Washington Water Research Center. 7th- 1971-. English. an. Washington State Water Research Center, Washington State University, Pullman WA 99164-3002. **Tel** (509)335-5531. **ED** David C Flaherty. **LC** TD224.W2; S82A. **DD** 333.9/1/009797. **Circ:** 3,000 (ctrl). ***Continues*** *Washington's Water, 0161-5904.*
**Desc:** Executive summary of research projects and final reports completed during the past or previous year. Descriptions of conferences and other activities carried out during the year.

GW/0511-3520
**WASSER-KALENDER (BERLIN).** (WASSER-KALENDER.). [Wasser-Kal.]. (1967)-. Academic Scholarly Publication. German. an. Erich Schmidt Verlag GmbH, Postfach 304240, D 10724 Berlin Germany. **Tel** 011 49 30 25008525. **ED** Rudolf Wagner. **LC** TD203; .W3. **DD** 628.1/05. **CODEN** WAKADP. **Bk Rev. Ad Acc.** ctrl circ. Documents available from CASDDS.
**Desc:** Water research calendar.
**Ind/Abst** Chem. Abstr. (1967-1983).

GW/0512-5030
**WASSER UND ABWASSER IN FORSCHUNG UND PRAXIS.** [Wasser Abwasser Forsch. Prax.]. Academic Scholarly Publication. German. ir. Price varies per volume. Erich Schmidt Verlag GmbH, Postfach 304240, D 10724 Berlin Germany. **Tel** 011 49 30 25008525. **CODEN** WAFPDB. Documents available from CASDDS.
**Desc:** Water and waste water studies.
**Ind/Abst** Chem. Abstr. (1969-1982).

GW
**WASSERVERSORGUNG UND ABWASSERBESEITIGUNG IN DER WIRTSCHAFT.** German. ir (every four years). DM9.90. Niedersachsisches Landesverwaltungsamt, Postfach 107, 3000 Hannover Germany. **Tel** (0511)108-9466. **LC** TD273; .W38. **Bk Rev. Circ:** 170.
**Desc:** Supply with water and removal of sewage in different branches of trade.

GW/0043-0978
**WASSERWIRTSCHAFT.** [Wasserwirtschaft]. (1911)-. Academic Scholarly Publication. German. mo. DM207.25, $150.00 Germany; DM214.75, $155.43 other. Franckhsche Verlagshandlung Kosmos Verlag, Postfach 106011, D-70049 Stuttgart Germany. **Tel** 011 49 711 2191332. **ED** Fry Gunter Marotz. **CODEN** WSWTAR. **[CCC]. Ad Acc. Circ:** 3,000. available in microform. Documents available from Article Express International, CASDDS. ***Continues*** *Deutsche Wasserwirtschaft.*
**Ind/Abst** Bioeng. Abstr. (19??-); Chem. Abstr. (19??-); Coal Abstr. (19??-); Ei Page One (19??-); EMBASE (19??-); Energy Res. Abstr. (19??-); Eng. Index Annu. (19??-); Fluid Abstr., Civil Eng. (19??-); Fluid Abstr. Proc. Eng. (19??-); FLUIDEX (19??-); GeoRef (19??-); Int. Civil Eng. Abstr. (19??-); Soft. Abstr. Eng. (19??-).

AT/0311-3558
**WASTE DISPOSAL AND WATER MANAGEMENT IN AUSTRALIA.** **See** Environmental Issues-Pollution and Waste Management.

CN/0820-0211
**WATDOC NEWSLETTER.** [WATDOC newsl.]. **Main/Corp** Canada. Water Resources Document Reference Centre. **VFOAT** WATDOC Nouvelles. No. 1 (Dec. 1974)-. Newsletter. English (French). WATDOC, Client Services, Interpretation and Access Division, Surveys and Information Systems Branch, Ecosystem Sciences and Evaluation Directorate, Environment Canada, Ottawa, Ontario K1A 0H3 Canada. **Tel** (819)953-1529, .
**Desc:** Describing various reference sources available from Environment Canada.

US
**WATER ACTIVITIES TRADE REPORT.** **See** Engineering-Hydraulic Engineering.

UK/0956-0157
**WATER & ENVIRONMENT INTERNATIONAL.** **VFOAT** Water and Environment International; Water and Environment; Water & Environment. (19??)-. Periodical. English. bm.

£75.00 UK; £77.00, $143.00 other. Argus Press Group, Queensway House, 2 Queensway Redhill, Surrey RH1 1QS England. **Tel** 011 44 737 768611, 011 44 737 761685, FAX 011 44 737 760510, telex 948669 TOPJNL G. **LC** TD365; .W34. **DD** 333.91/005.
**Desc:** Covers the worldwide water and sewage industries.
**Ind/Abst** Fluid Abstr., Civil Eng.; Fluid Abstr. Proc. Eng.; FLUIDEX; Pollut. Abstr. Indexes.

●UK/0968-3321
**WATER & ENVIRONMENT MANAGEMENT.** (1993)-. English. £36.00 UK; £76.00 others. Thomas Telford Ltd, Thomas Telford House, 1 Heron Quay, London E14 9XF England. **Tel** 011 44 71 987 6999, FAX 011 44 71 538 4101, telex 298105.

UK/0951-7359
**WATER AND ENVIRONMENTAL MANAGEMENT : JOURNAL OF THE INSTITUTION OF WATER AND ENVIRONMENTAL MANAGEMENT.** **See** Environmental Issues-Pollution and Waste Management.

US/0271-8049
**WATER AND LAND RESOURCE ACCOMPLISHMENTS. FEDERAL RECLAMATION PROJECTS, SUMMARY REPORT.** **See** Environmental Issues-Conservation and Natural Resources.

UK/0956-0157
**WATER & SEWAGE INTERNATIONAL.** ***Title Change.*** [Water sew. int.]. **VFOAT** Water & Sewage; Water and Sewage International. (1989)-(19??). Periodical. English. bm. **CODEN** WSINEB. ***Formed by the union of*** *African Water & Sewage; Asian Water & Sewage, 1011-5870; European Water & Sewage; Far East Water & Sewage* **and** *Middle East Water & Sewage, 0140-5098.* ***Continued by*** *Water & Environment International.*

US/0148-2785
**WATER AND SEWER PROGRAMS FOR OHIO.** **Main/Corp** Ohio. Dept. of Economic and Community Development. 1974-. English. an. Ohio Department of Economic and Community Development, PO Box 1001, Columbus OH 43266. **Tel** (614)466-2285. **LC** TD224.O3; O24A. **DD** 363.6/1.

UK/0950-6551
**WATER & WASTE TREATMENT (1985).** **See** Environmental Issues-Pollution and Waste Management.

US/0043-1141
**WATER AND WASTES DIGEST.** [Water wastes dig.]. Vol. 1 (1961)-. Periodical. English. Six times a year. $35.00 (one year), $55.00 (two year), $75.00 (three year) US and possessions; $55.00 (one year), $75.00 (two year), $95.00 (three year) other. Scranton Gillette Communications Inc., 380 East Northwest Highway, Des Plaines IL 60016-2282. **Tel** (708)298-6622, FAX (708)390-0408. **ED** Ian Lisk. **[CCC]. Ad Acc. Circ:** 100,703 (ctrl). available on microfilm and microfiche from University Microfilms International (UMI).
**Ind/Abst** Abstr. Bull. Inst. Pap. Sci. Tech.; Pollut. Abstr. Indexes; Text. Technol. Dig.

US/0748-2612
**WATER & WASTEWATER DIGEST.** **See** Environmental Issues-Pollution and Waste Management.

US/0891-5385
**WATER & WASTEWATER INTERNATIONAL.** [Water wastewater int.]. **VFOAT** Water and Wastewater International. (1986)-. Periodical. English. Seven times a year. $125.00. MacDonald Communications / Texas, 3300 South Gessner, Suite 118, Houston TX 77063. **Tel** (713)266-0610, FAX (713)266-6657. **ED** Pam Wolfe. **DD** 333. Index available. **Bk Rev. Ad Acc. Circ:** 16,000 (ctrl).
**Ind/Abst** Fluid Abstr., Civil Eng.; Fluid Abstr. Proc. Eng.; FLUIDEX; GeoRef.

BE/0770-7193
**WATER (BRUSSEL).** (WATER.). [Water]. (1981)-. Academic Scholarly Publication. Dutch. Six times a year. Water Energie Leefmilieu VZW, Kipdorp 11, 2000 Antwerp Belgium. **Tel** 03/237 64 48, FAX 03/488 23 11. **CODEN** WATREK. Documents available from CASDDS.
**Ind/Abst** AESIS Q.; Chem. Abstr.

UK/0950-8686
**WATER CHEMISTRY OF NUCLEAR REACTOR SYSTEMS.** [Water chem. nucl. react. syst.]. **Added/Corp** British Nuclear Energy Society. Institution of Chemical Engineers (Great Britain) Royal Society of Chemistry (Great Britain). (Oct. 24-27 1977)-. Academic Scholarly Publication. English. te. British Nuclear Reactor Society, London England. **CODEN** WCNSD6. Documents available from CASDDS.
**Ind/Abst** Chem. Abstr.

US/0272-9210
**WATER CHLORINATION.** (WATER CHLORINATION : ENVIRONMENTAL IMPACT AND HEALTH EFFECTS : PROCEEDINGS OF THE ... CONFERENCE ON WATER CHLORINATION: ENVIRONMENTAL IMPACT AND HEALTH EFFECTS.). Vol. 3 (Oct. 28-Nov. 2, 1979)-. Academic Scholarly Publication. English. ir. Butterworth & Company Ltd. / Canada, 75 Clegg Road, Markham Ontario L6G 1A1 Canada. **Tel** (905)479-2665, (800)668-6481. **LC** TD196.C5; C66a. **DD** 628.1/662. **CODEN** WEIEDL. Documents available from BIOSIS Document Express, CASDDS. ***Continues*** *Conference on the Environmental Impact of Water Chlorination. Water Chlorination, 0272-9210.*
**Ind/Abst** Biol. Abstr. (1985-); Chem. Abstr.

US/0502-8450
**WATER CIRCULAR.** **VFOAT** Utah State Engineer Water Circular. No. 1- 1965-. Monographic series. English. Price varies per volume. Utah Department of Natural Resources, Salt Lake City UT 84114. **LC** WMLC L 82/102. **DD** 551.4.

US/0746-4029
**WATER CONDITIONING & PURIFICATION.** [Water cond. purif.]. **VFOAT** Water Conditioning and Purification. Vol. 25, No. 1 (Feb. 1983)-. Periodical. English. Twelve times a year. $34.00 US & Canada; $85.00 other. Water Conditioning & Purification, 4651 North First Avenue, Suite 101, Tucson AZ 85718. **Tel** (602)293-5446, FAX (602)887-2383. **ED** Darlene J. Scheel. **DD** 338. **CODEN** WCPUEN. Index Bound in First Issue (Published in December). cum. index. **Ad Acc. Circ:** 17,500 (ctrl). Documents available from Documents on Demand. ***Continues*** *Water Conditioning, 0043-1184.*
**Desc:** Covers all aspects of the water treatment industry. A comprehensive publication designed to assist the water professional, our magazine furnishes information on technologies, products, regulartory actions and marketing trends for residential, commercial and industrial applications.
**Ind/Abst** BioBusiness (1990-); Environ. Abstr.

US
**WATER CONNECTION : THE NEW ENGLAND INTERSTATE WATER POLLUTION CONTROL COMMISSION NEWSLETTER.** **Added/Corp** New England Interstate Water Pollution Control Commission. Vol. 1, No. 1 (June 1984)-. Newsletter. English. qt. Documents available from Documents on Demand. ***Continues*** *Aqua News.*
**Ind/Abst** Environ. Abstr.

UK
**WATER DATA - GREAT BRITAIN. DEPT. OF THE ENVIRONMENT. WATER DATA UNIT.** **Main/Corp** Great Britain. Dept. of the Environment. Water Data Unit. English. an. **LC** TD257; .G73A. **DD** 363.6/1/0941.

US
**WATER DESALINATION REPORT.** English. wk. $300.00 US; $325.00 other. Water Desalination Report, PO Box 10, Traceys Landing MD 20779. **Tel** (301)261-5010, FAX (301)261-5010. **ED** Mike Smith. **Bk Rev.**
**Desc:** Weekly newsletter for desalting company management.

●US/1074-2972
**WATER ENVIRONMENT LABORATORY SOLUTIONS.** **See** Environmental Issues-Pollution and Waste Management.

US
**WATER ENVIRONMENT REGULATION WATCH.** English. mo. $79.00 US; $99.00 other. Water Environment Federation, 601 Wythe Street, Alexandria VA 22314-1994. **Tel** (703)684-2400, FAX (703)684-2492.

●US/1061-4303
**WATER ENVIRONMENT RESEARCH.** (WATER ENVIRONMENT RESEARCH : A RESEARCH PUBLICATION OF THE WATER ENVIRONMENT FEDERATION.). [Water environ. res.]. **Added/Corp** Water Environment Federation. **VFOAT** JWPCA; Water Environment Research (JWPCA). Vol. 64, No. 1 (Jan./Feb. 1992)-. Academic Scholarly Publication. English. Seven times a year (published bi-monthly with one extra issue in June). $158.00 US; $205.00 other (also comes with Water Environment & Technology). Water Environment Federation, 601 Wythe Street, Alexandria VA 22314-1994. **Tel** (703)684-2400, FAX (703)684-2492. **LC** TD365; .R48. **DD** 628.1/68. **CODEN** WAERED. **[CCC]. Ad Acc. Pr Rev.** available on microfilm and microfiche from University Microfilms International (UMI). Documents available from Article Express International, The Genuine Article, BIOSIS Document Express, Ask*IEEE, CASDDS, Documents on Demand. ***Continues*** *Research Journal of the Water Pollution Control Federation, 1047-7624.*
**Desc:** Serves the needs of engineers, scientists, researcher, academics, and other professionals interested in new assessment methods, water and waste-water treatment processes, and water quality problems and solutions.
**Ind/Abst** Abstr. Bull. Inst. Pap. Sci. Tech.; AGRICOLA; Appl. Sci. Technol. Index (1992-); AQUAREF; BioBusiness (1992-); Biol. Abstr. (1992-); Chem. Abstr.; Curr. Aware. Biol. Sci., CABS; Curr. Contents, Agric. Biol. Environ. Sci.; Curr. Contents Eng. Tech. Appl. Sci.; Ei Page One; Energy Res. Abstr. (1992-); Eng. Index Annu.; Environ. Abstr.; Environ. Period. Bibliogr.; GeoRef (1992-); INSPEC; Int. Aerosp. Abstr. (1992-); Leadscan; Lit. Pat. Abstr., Oilfield Chem. (1992-); Lit. Abstr., Catal. Catal.; Lit. Abstr., Health Environ.; Lit. Abstr., Pet. Refin. Petrochem.; Lit. Abstr., Pet. Substit.; Lit. Abstr., Transp. Storage; Res. Alert [Full Cov.]; Sci. Cit. Index; SCISEARCH.

●US
**WATER ENVIRONMENT RESEARCH MICROFORM: A RESEARCH PUBLICATION OF THE WATER ENVIRONMENT FEDERATION.** **Added/Corp** Water Environment Federation. **VFOAT** JWPCA; Water Environment Research (JWPCA). Vol. 64, No. 1 (Jan./Feb. 1992)-. Academic Scholarly Publication. English. bm. Water Environment Federation, 601 Wythe Street, Alexandria VA 22314-1994. **Tel** (703)684-2400, FAX (703)684-2492. Documents available from BIOSIS Document Express, Ask*IEEE, CASDDS. ***Continues*** *Research Journal of the Water Pollution Control Federation, 1047-7624.*
**Ind/Abst** Abstr. Bull. Inst. Pap. Sci. Tech.; AGRICOLA; Biol. Abstr.; Chem. Abstr.; Energy Res. Abstr.; GeoRef; INSPEC; Int. Aerosp. Abstr.

US/0194-1194
**WATER EQUIPMENT NEWS.** [Water equip. news]. (19??)-. Periodical. English. Twelve times a year. Free to water well industries in the US and Canada; $35.00 individuals US Canada, and Mexico; $40.00 central Caribbean and Central America; $60.00 South America, Europe and Iceland; $80.00 other. Mut and Jef Enterprises Inc., PO Box 597, Champaign IL 61820. **Tel** (217)344-7443. **ED** Jeffrey Farlow-Cornell. **DD** 628. **Bk Rev. Ad Acc. Circ:** 23,400 (ctrl).
**Desc:** A digest of new and used equipment for water suppliers and a summary of news in the industry throughout all of North America.

US
**WATER IMPACTS.** English. mo. Free. Michigan State University / 334 Natural Resources Building, East Lansing MI 48824. **Tel** (517)353-3742. Documents available from Documents on Demand.
**Ind/Abst** Environ. Abstr.

UK
**WATER INDUSTRY. UNITED KINGDOM SERVICE AND COSTS ... AND CHARGES FOR SERVICE ... .** **Added/Corp** Chartered Institute of Public Finance and Accountancy. **VFOAT** United Kingdom Service and Costs ... and Charges for Service ...; Service and Costs ... and Charges for Service ... . English. Chartered Institute of Public Finance and Accountancy, 2 3 Robert Street, London WC2N 6BH England. **Tel** 011 44 1 895 8823. **LC** HD4465.G7; W38. **DD** 338.4/336361/0941021. ***Continues*** *Water Industry. Book 2, United Kingdom Charges for Service in ... .*

US/0511-3598
**WATER INFORMATION BULLETIN (BOISE).** (WATER INFORMATION BULLETIN.). [Water inf. bull.]. **Added/Corp** Idaho. Dept. of Water Resources. Idaho. Dept. of Reclamation. Idaho. Dept. of Water Administration. Geological Survey (U.S.). No. 1 (1966)-. Bulletin. English. Price varies per volume. Idaho Department of Water Resources, Statehouse, Boise ID 83720. **LC** TD224.I2; W3. **DD** 333.9/1/009796; 628. **CODEN** WBIRD5. Documents available from CASDDS.
**Ind/Abst** Chem. Abstr.; GeoRef.

US/0250-8060
**WATER INTERNATIONAL.** [Water int.]. **Added/Corp** International Water Resources Association. Vol. 1 (July 1975)-. English. qt. $75.00 (one year), $140.00 (two year) US, Canada, and Mexico; $90.00 (one year), $170.00 (two year) other. International Water Resources Association, 1101 West Peabody Drive, Urbana IL 61801. **Tel** (217)244-4459, FAX (217)244-6633, telex 5101011969. **ED** W. H. C. Maxwell. **LC** GB651; .W313. **DD** 553/.7/05. Index available. **Bk Rev. Pr Rev. Circ:** 1,500. Documents available from The Genuine Article.
**Desc:** Official magazine of the International Water Resources Association. Serves as a vehicle to bring its readers current news about IWRA, activities of IWRA and its committees and members and other important and interesting events in the international water resources field.
**Ind/Abst** AESIS Q.; Agrofor. Abstr. (1991-); Ecol. Abstr. (?-?); Environ. Period. Bibliogr.; Fluid Abstr., Civil Eng.; Fluid Abstr. Proc. Eng.; FLUIDEX (19??-); For. Abstr.; Geogr. Abstr. Phys. Geogr. (?-?); Geogr. Abstr. Human Geogr.; Geol. Abstr.; GeoRef; Health Saf. Sci. Abstr.; Int. Dev. Abstr.; Irr. Drain. Abstr.; Life Sci. Collect.; Pollut.

# Water Resources

Abstr. Indexes; Res. Alert [Select. Cov.]; Rice Abstr.; Rural Dev. Abstr.; Soc. Sci. Cit. Index [Select. Cov.]; Soils Fert.; Trop. Dis. Bull.; World Agric. Econ.

US
**WATER INTERNATIONAL : OFFICIAL JOURNAL OF THE INTERNATIONAL WATER RESOURCES ASSOCIATION.**
*Ceased.* English. International Water Resources Assn., 205 North Mathews Ave/ Univ. IL, (217)333-0536. **Tel** (217)333-0536, FAX (217)333-08046. Documents available from Documents on Demand.
**Ind/Abst** Aquat. Sci. Fish. Abstr. (Computer File); Environ. Abstr.; Geogr. Abstr. Phys. Geogr.

US
**WATER INVENTORY REPORT. Added/Corp** Ohio. Division of Water. **VFOAT** Ohio Water Inventory Report. No. 24 (1977)-. Periodical. English. $2.50. Ohio Division of Water, Fountain Square, Columbus OH 43224. **LC** TD224.O3; A356. *Continues* Ohio Water Plan Inventory: Report.

US/0892-9548
**WATER JOURNAL.** [Water j.]. (1916)-. Periodical. English. Three times a year. Free. BTR, Bailey & Gallatin Avenue, Union Town PA 15401. **Tel** (412)439-7700. **ED** Jack F. Pektas. **DD** 333. **Circ:** 15,000 (ctrl).
**Desc:** Information for water utility directors, meter shop managers, distribution directors and others involved in managing municipal or privately owned water utilities.
**Ind/Abst** Pollut. Abstr. Indexes (19??-); Urban Aff. Abstr. (19??-).

UK/0959-9754
**WATER LAW.** [Water law]. (1990)-. Periodical. English. Four times a year. $255.00. John Wiley & Sons Ltd., Baffins Lane, Chichester West Sussex PO19 1UD England. **Tel** 0243 779777, FAX 0243 776128 BTG:JWP001, telex 86290 WIBOOKG. **(Subscription address:** North, South and Central America/ John Wiley & Sons, Inc., Subscription Department, 605 Third Avenue, New York, NY 10158-0012, USA; telephone: (212)850-6645; FAX: (212)850-6021) **ED** William Howarth, BA, LLB. **DD** 346.04691. Index available. **Bk Rev. Ad Acc. Pr Rev. Circ:** 200 (ctrl).
**Desc:** Monitors and comments on UK and EC legislation relating to the water industry and aquatic environment.

●CN
**WATER LEVELS. GREAT LAKES AND MONTREAL HARBOUR. Added/Corp** Canadian Hydrographic Service. **VFOAT** Bulletin Mensuel des Niveaux de l'Eau des Grands Lacs et du Port de Montreal. (1992)-. Periodical. English. mo. *Continues* Monthly Water Level Bulletin.

US/0196-075X
**WATER LINE NEWSLETTER.** V. 1- Jan. 1977-. Newsletter. English. mo. Water Resources Planning, Department of Natural Resources, 3rd Floor/Centennial Building, St Paul MN 55155.

US
**WATER MANAGEMENT TECHNICAL REPORT. Main/Corp** Colorado State University. No. 1- 1969-. Monographic series. English. Price varies per volume. **CODEN** CSWDAV.
**Ind/Abst** GeoRef.

AT/0310-0367
**WATER (MELBOURNE).** See Environmental Issues-Pollution and Waste Management.

US
**WATER NEWS.** *Ceased.* **Added/Corp** Virginia Polytechnic Institute and State University. Water Resources Research Center. Vol. 6, No. 7 (Oct. 1975)-(June 1994). Periodical. English. Twelve times a year. Virginia Water Resources Research Center, 617 North Main Street, Blacksburg VA 24060. **Tel** (703)961-5624, FAX (703)231-6673. **ED** Elizabeth Crumbley, (703)231-8038. **Bk Rev. Circ:** 13,000. Documents available from Documents on Demand.
*Continues* News - Virginia Water Resources Research Center, 0091-0228.
**Desc:** Devoted to water (and land-related) resource issues, primarily in Virginia.
**Ind/Abst** Environ. Abstr.

CN/0821-0233
**WATER NEWS (CAMBRIDGE).** (WATER NEWS / CANADIAN WATER RESOURCES ASSOCIATION.). [Water news]. **Added/Corp** Canadian Water Resources Association. Vol. 1, No. 1 (March 1982)-. Periodical. English. qt. Canadian Water Resources Association / Alberta, PO Box 1329, Membership Services, Cambridge, Ontario, N1R 7G6 Canada. **Tel** (519)622-4764. **ED** J. A. Ross. **DD** 333.91/1/0971. **Bk Rev. Ad Acc. Circ:** 1,400.
**Desc:** Canadian or related water resources news items. Collected by and for water resources professionals and other interested persons.

US/0043-1273
**WATER NEWSLETTER.** [Water newsl.].
**Added/Corp** Water Information Center, Inc. Vol. 1, Feb. 17 (1959)-. Periodical. English. sm. $372.00 US and Canada; $402.00 other. Water Information Center Inc, 1099 18th Street, Suite 2150, Denver CO 80202. **Tel** (303)391-8799. **ED** Judith Schoeck. **DD** 627; 628. **[CCC].**
**Bk Rev.**
**Desc:** Provides comprehensive water-oriented information--legislation, treatment techniques, research and products. Its supplement, research and development news, covers upcoming meetings and new publications. The quarterly international water report offers a wide range of information on global water matters. Professional technical advisors assist in this solid coverage of the water field.

US/0544-3482
**WATER NEWSLETTER. Main/Corp** University of Minnesota. Water Resources Research Center. **VFOAT** Water; Water Resources Research Newsletter. Newsletter. English. ir. Water Resources Research Center University of Minnesota Center, 1445 Gortner Avenue, St Paul MN 55108.

US/0145-2800
**WATER OPERATION AND MAINTENANCE BULLETIN.** [Water oper. maint. bull.]. Began with No. 75, March 1971. Bulletin. English. ir. varies. Bureau of Reclamation, PO Box 25007, Denver CO 80225. **Tel** (303)234-3000. **LC** TC801; .U15. **DD** 627/.52/05. Index available. cum. index. **Pr Rev.** ctrl circ. *Continues* Irrigation Operation and Maintenance Bulletin.
**Desc:** Technical and other general aspects on the use of water and its maintenance.

US
**WATER POLLUTION CONTROL NEWS.** See Environmental Issues-Pollution and Waste Management.

US/0091-4541
**WATER POLLUTION CONTROL PLAN (SPRINGFIELD).** (WATER POLLUTION CONTROL PLAN.). **Main/Corp** Illinois. Environmental Protection Agency. English. Illinois Environmental Protection Agency, 2200 Churchill Road, Springfield IL 62706. **LC** TD224.I3; I58A. **DD** 363.6.

VI
**WATER POLLUTION REPORT.** English. Virgin Island of the US, Division of Environmental Health, St Thomas Virgin Islands. **LC** TD233.V5; W3. **DD** 628.1/68/08 S.

CN/0197-9140
**WATER POLLUTION RESEARCH JOURNAL OF CANADA.** See Environmental Issues-Pollution and Waste Management.

US/0502-0395
**WATER POLLUTION SURVEILLANCE SYSTEM : ANNUAL COMPILATION OF DATA.** See Environmental Issues-Pollution and Waste Management.

US/1057-2163
**WATER PROTECTION, CONSERVATION, MANAGEMENT.** (WATER PROTECTION, CONSERVATION, MANAGEMENT / AGRICULTURAL EXTENSION SERVICE, THE UNIVERSITY OF TENNESSEE, INSTITUTE OF AGRICULTURE.). [Water prot. conserv. manage.]. **Added/Corp** University of Tennessee, Knoxville. Agricultural Extension Service. United States. Dept. of Agriculture. Vol. 1, No. 1 (Jan. 1988)-. English. qt. **DD** 333.
**Ind/Abst** AGRICOLA [Select. Cov.].

US
**WATER QUALITY AND POLLUTION CONTROL IN MICHIGAN.** See Environmental Issues-Pollution and Waste Management.

US/0745-1512
**WATER QUALITY ASSOCIATION NEWSLETTER.** See Environmental Issues-Pollution and Waste Management.

US/0043-1346
**WATER QUALITY CONTROL DIGEST.**
*Ceased.* Vol. 1 (1969)-Ceased Vol. 19, No. 6 (Nov. 1988). English. bm. University Digest, 5844 Little Pine Lane, Rochester MI 48064. **Tel** (313)651-2528. **ED** Arthur D Even. **LC** Z7173.W3; W3. **DD** 016.6281/68.
**Desc:** Includes four sections: (1) ground and surface water; (2) sources and effects of pollution; (3) treatment/avoidance of pollution; (4) general sections subdivided as applicable.

US/0096-6304
**WATER QUALITY INSTRUMENTATION.**
Vol. 1 (1972)-. English. Instrument Society of America, 67 Alexander Drive, Research Triangle NC 27709. **Tel** (919)549-8411, FAX (919)549-8288, telex 802 540. **ED** J Scales. **LC** TD423; .W28. **DD** 628.1/61/08.

US/0148-1797
**WATER QUALITY MANAGEMENT DIRECTORY.** Directory. English. an. US Environmental Protection Agency, 401 M Street SW, Washington DC 20460. **Tel** (202)755-9163. **LC** TD223; .W294. **DD** 363.6/1.

US/0097-7519
**WATER QUALITY MONITORING DATA FOR GEORGIA STREAMS.** [Water qual. monit. data Ga. streams]. **Main/Corp** Georgia. Environmental Protection Division. English. an. Environmental Protection Protection, Department of Natural Resources, 47 Trinity Avenue SW, Atlanta GA 30334. **LC** TD224.G4; G34A. **DD** 363.6/1/09758.
**Ind/Abst** GeoRef.

US/0270-9503
**WATER QUALITY SERIES (LOGAN).**
(WATER QUALITY SERIES.). [Water qual. ser.]. **VFOAT** Report Q; UWRL/Q; Water Quality Series UWRL/Q. Monographic series. English. ir. Price varies per volume. Utah Water Research Laboratory, Utah State University, Logan UT 84322-8200. **Tel** (801)750-3200, FAX (801)750-3663, telex 3729283.
**Desc:** Research completion reports.
**Ind/Abst** GeoRef.

US/0275-7249
**WATER-RELATED DISEASE OUTBREAKS SURVEILLANCE. ANNUAL SUMMARY.** See Environmental Issues-Pollution and Waste Management.

US
**WATER REPORTER, THE.** *Title Change.*
**Added/Corp** Information News Service, Inc. Vol. 10, No. 17 (March 14, 1986)-(Aug. 1992). Periodical. English. mo. CJE Associates, 237 Gretna Green Court, Alexandria VA 22304-5602. **Tel** (703)823-0662. **ED** Lawrence Mosher. Index available. **Bk Rev.** *Continues* Water Newsletter. *Absorbed by* Clean Water Report, 0009-8620.

UK/0043-1354
**WATER RESEARCH (OXFORD).** (WATER RESEARCH.). [Water res.]. **Added/Corp** International Association on Water Pollution Research. Vol. 1 (Jan. 1967)-. Academic Scholarly Publication. English. Twelve times a year. $1841.00 (regular subscription); $3845.00 (combination subscription with Water Science and Technology) The Americas; £1235.00 (regular subscription); £2580.00 (combination subscription with Water Science and Technology) other. Pergamon Press, An Imprint of Elsevier Science Ltd., The Boulevard, Langford Lane, Kidlington, Oxford OX5 1GB United Kingdom. **Tel** 011 44 865 843000, 011 44 865 843699, FAX 011 44 865 843010. **(Subscription address:** Elsevier Science Ltd. Oxford Fulfillment Centre, PO Box 800, Kidlington, Oxford OX5 1DX United Kingdom.) **ED** K. Ives. **LC** TD420; .W37. **DD** 628/.168/05. **NLM** W1 WA692A. **CODEN** WATRAG. **[CCC].** cum. index. **Pr Rev.** available on microfilm and microfiche from University Microfilms International (UMI); available on microfiche from the publisher. Documents available from Article Express International, The Genuine Article, BIOSIS Document Express, Ask*IEEE, Petroleum Abstracts Document Delivery Service, CASDDS, Documents on Demand. *Supersedes in part* Air and Water Pollution.
**Ind/Abst** Abstr. Bull. Inst. Pap. Sci. Tech.; AGRICOLA; Appl. Sci. Technol. Index; Aqualine Abstr.; AQUAREF; Aquat. Sci. Fish. Abstr. (Computer File); BioBusiness; Biocont. News Inf.; Biodeter. Abstr.; Bioeng. Abstr.; Biol. Abstr.; Chem. Abstr.; Chem. Titles; Coal Abstr.; Curr. Aware. Biol. Sci.; CABS; Curr. Biotechnol.; Curr. Contents, Agric. Biol. Environ. Sci.; Curr. Ref. Fish Res.; Ecol. Abstr.; Ecology Abstr.; Ei Page One; EMBASE; Energy Res. Abstr.; Eng. Index Annu.; Environ. Abstr.; Environ. Period. Bibliogr.; Fish Rev.; Food Sci. Technol. Abstr.; For. Abstr.; Geogr. Abstr. Phys. Geogr. (?-?); Geogr. Abstr. Human Geogr.; Geol. Abstr.; GeoRef; Health Saf. Sci. Abstr.; HTFS Dig.; INSPEC (1978-); Int. Civil Eng. Abstr.; Int. Dev. Abstr. (?-?); J. Plan. Lit.; Environ.; Metals Abstr. Rev., Ser. B, Live Feeds and Feed.; Life Sci. Collect.; PESTDOC; Pet. Abstr.; Pollut. Abstr. Indexes; Potato Abstr.; Protozoolog. Abstr.; Ref. Upd. Deluxe Ed.; Res. Alert [Full Cov.]; Rev. Agric. Entomol.; Rice Abstr.; Rural Dev. Abstr.; Sci. Cit. Index; SCISEARCH; Soc. Sci. Cit. Index [Select. Cov.]; Soft. Abstr. Eng.; Soils Fert.; Sug. Indus. Abstr.; Weed Abstr.; Wildl. Rev.

UK/0730-9619
**WATER RESEARCH TOPICS.** [Water res. top.]. V. 1-. Academic Scholarly Publication. English. Halsted Press, 605 Third Avenue, New York NY 10016. **Tel** (718)658-0888. **LC** TD201; .W342. **DD** 628.1. **CODEN** WRTODR. Documents available from CASDDS.
**Ind/Abst** Chem. Abstr.

US/0364-4340
**WATER RESOURCE DATA FOR INDIANA.** (WATER RESOURCES DATA. INDIANA.). [Water resour. data Indiana]. **VFOAT** USGS Water Resources Data. Indiana; U.S.G.S. Water Resources Data. Indiana; Indiana. Water Year 1981-. English. an. US Department of the Interior / US Geological Survey, Virginia, National Technical Information Service, 5285 Port Royal Road, Springfield VA 22161. **Tel** (800)553-6847, (703)487-4812. **LC** GB1225.I3; A412. **DD** 553.7/09772. available on microfiche (Vols. for (1982-) distributed to depository libraries). ***Continues*** *Water Resources Data for Indiana, 0364-4340.*

US/1040-9009
**WATER RESOURCES ABSTRACTS (COLLEGE PARK, MD.).** ***Title Change.*** (WATER RESOURCES ABSTRACTS [COMPUTER FILE].). [Water resour. abstr.]. **Added/Corp** National Information Services Corporation. Water Resources Scientific Information Center. (1989)-(19??). English. qt. National Information Services Corp, 3100 St Paul Street, Wyman Towers, Suite 6, Baltimore MD 21218. **Tel** (410)243-0797, FAX (410)243-0982. **(Subscription telephone:** (410)243-0797**) DD** 627. ***Continues*** *Selected Water Resources Abstracts (College Park, MD.).* ***Continued by*** *Water Resources Abstracts. Volume 1, 1053-5624.*
**Desc:** System requirements: IBM PC, XT, AT, PS/2 Model 30 or other compatible with MS-DOS 3.1 or higher, MS-DOS CD-ROM extensions, CD-ROM drive, 512K RAM. IBM AT 80286 or 80386 microprocessor is recommended.

US/1053-5624
**WATER RESOURCES ABSTRACTS. VOLUME 1.** (WATER RESOURCES ABSTRACTS. VOLUME 1 [COMPUTER FILE].). [Water resour. abstr., Vol. 1]. **Added/Corp** National Information Services Corporation. Water Resources Scientific Information Center. (1990)-. English. qt. $701.00 US; $715.00 other. National Information Services Corp, 3100 St Paul Street, Wyman Towers, Suite 6, Baltimore MD 21218. **Tel** (410)243-0797, FAX (410)243-0982. **LC** Z6004.H9. **DD** 627. Index available. cum. index. ***Continues*** *Water Resources Abstracts (College Park, MD.), 1040-9009.*
**Desc:** System requirements: IBM PC, XT, AT, PS/2 Model 30 or other compatible with DOS 3.1 or higher, 512K RAM, CD-ROM drive with MS-DOS CD-ROM extensions. IBM AT 80286 or 80386 class microprocessor is recommended.

US
**WATER RESOURCES ABSTRACTS [COMPUTER FILE].** **Added/Corp** SilverPlatter Information, Inc. Water Resources Scientific Information Center. **VFOAT** WRA. (1991)-. English. qt. $750.00. OCLC Asia Pacific Services, 6565 Frantz Road, Dublin OH 43017. **Tel** (800)848-5878, (614)764-6394 or 6000, FAX (614)764-6096. ***Continues*** *Selected Water Resources Abstracts (Dublin, Ohio), 1049-7390.*

US
**WATER RESOURCES ACTIVITIES IN FLORIDA / U.S. GEOLOGICAL SURVEY.** **Added/Corp** Geological Survey (U.S.). (1985)-. English. US Geological Survey District Office, 227 North Bronough Street/Suite 3015, Tallahassee FL 32301. **LC** TC424.F6; U54a. **DD** 553.7/09759. available on microfiche (Vols. for (1985/86-) distributed to depository libraries). ***Continues*** *Water Resources Investigations in Florida, 0195-3885.*

US
**WATER-RESOURCES ACTIVITIES OF THE U.S. GEOLOGICAL SURVEY IN ILLINOIS.** ***Title Change.*** **Main/Corp** Geological Survey (U.S.). **Added/Corp** Geological Survey (U.S.). Water Resources Division. **VFOAT** Water Resources Activities of the U.S. Geological Survey in Illinois. **VAT** Water Resources Activities of the U.S. Geological Survey in Illinois. (1988)-(198?). English. District Chief / Illinois, US Geological Survey WRD, 102 East Main Street/4th Floor, Urbana IL 61801. **LC** TC424.I3; U54a. **DD** 353.97730082/325. ***Continues*** *Geological Survey (U.S.). Water Resources Division. Water Resources Activities in Illinois, 0276-6477.* ***Continued by*** *Geological Survey (U.S.). Water Resources Division. Illinois District. Water Resources Activities in Illinois.*

US
**WATER-RESOURCES ACTIVITIES OF THE U.S. GEOLOGICAL SURVEY IN NEW MEXICO.** **Main/Corp** Geological Survey (U.S.). **VFOAT** Water Resources Activities of the U.S. Geological Survey in New Mexico. (198?)-. English. **LC** GB658.7; .G46b. **DD** 553.7/09789. ***Continues*** *Geological Survey (U.S.). Water Resources Division. New Mexico District. Water-Resources Investigations of the U.S. Geological Survey New Mexico District.*
**Desc:** Concerned with the water supply and hydrology.

US/0731-7638
**WATER RESOURCES BASIC RECORDS REPORT.** [Water resour. basic rec. rep.]. No. 7-. Academic Scholarly Publication. English. Price varies per volume. US Geological Survey / Louisiana, PO Box 66492, Baton Rouge LA 70806. **LC** TA24.L7; A23. **CODEN** LDBRAU. Documents available from CASDDS. ***Continues*** *Basic Records Reports.*
**Ind/Abst** Chem. Abstr. (-1983); GeoRef.

CN/0383-5456
**WATER RESOURCES BULLETIN : GROUND WATER SERIES.** [Water resour. bull., Ground water ser.]. Bulletin. English. Price varies per volume. **LC** TD227.O5; W37. **DD** 553.7/9/09713. **CODEN** OWRBAO.
**Ind/Abst** GeoRef.

US/0094-7636
**WATER-RESOURCES BULLETIN (SALT LAKE CITY).** (WATER-RESOURCES BULLETIN.). [Water-resour. bull.]. **Added/Corp** Utah Geological and Mineralogical Survey. Utah Geological and Mineral Survey. **VFOAT** Water Resources Bulletin. (1962)-. Bulletin. English. ir. Utah Geological & Mineral Survey, 2363 South Foothill Drive, Salt Lake City UT 84109. **Tel** (801)467-7970. **LC** TD224.U8; A3. **DD** 553/.7/09792 S. **CODEN** UGWBA3. **Circ:** 1,000 (ctrl). ***Continues*** *Water-Resources Bulletin.*
**Desc:** Water resource research by Utah Geological and Mineral Survey.
**Ind/Abst** Agric. Eng. Abstr.; Environ. Period. Bibliogr.; GeoRef.

US/0043-1370
**WATER RESOURCES BULLETIN (URBANA).** (WATER RESOURCES BULLETIN.). [Water resour. bull.]. **Added/Corp** American Water Resources Association. Vol. 1 (1965)-. Periodical. English. bm (6 issues). $115.00 US. AWRA - American Water Resources Association, 950 Herndon Parkway, Suite 300, Herndon VA 22070-5528. **Tel** (703)904-1225, FAX (703)904-1228. **ED** Dale Meridith. **LC** GB651; .W315. **DD** 333.9/1. **NLM** W1 WA692AE. **CODEN** WARBAQ. Index available (bound in Dec. issue). **Bk Rev. Ad Acc. Pr Rev. Circ:** 3,972 (ctrl). available on microfilm and microfiche from University Microfilms International (UMI). Documents available from Article Express International, The Genuine Article, CASDDS, Documents on Demand.
**Desc:** Interdisciplinary journal containing original and technical articles on all aspects of water resource research and management.
**Ind/Abst** AGRICOLA [Select. Cov.]; AQUAREF; Aquat. Sci. Fish. Abstr. (Computer File); Bioeng. Abstr.; Chem. Abstr.; Coal Abstr.; Curr. Aware. Biol. Sci., CABS; Curr. Contents, Agric. Biol. Environ. Sci.; Curr. Ref. Fish Res.; Ecology Abstr.; Ei Page One; EMBASE; Energy Inf. Abstr.; Energy Res. Abstr. (April 1974-); Eng. Index Annu.; Environ. Abstr.; Environ. Period. Bibliogr.; Fish Rev.; For. Prod. Abstr.; For. Abstr.; GeoRef; Health Saf. Sci. Abstr.; Int. Aerosp. Abstr.; Int. Civil Eng. Abstr.; J. Plan. Lit.; Leis. Recreat. Tour. Abstr.; Maize Abstr.; Nematol. Abstr.; Plant Grow. Reg. Abstr.; Pollut. Abstr. Indexes; Res. Alert [Full Cov.]; Rev. Agric. Entomol.; Risk Abstr.; Sci. Cit. Index; SCISEARCH; Soc. Sci. Cit. Index [Select. Cov.]; Soft. Abstr. Eng.; Soils Fert.; Wildl. Rev.; World Agric. Econ.

US/0270-0034
**WATER RESOURCES COORDINATION DIRECTORY.** **Added/Corp** Water Resources Council (U.S.). (19??)-. English. ir. US Water Resources Council, 2120 L Street NW, Washington DC 20037. **LC** TC423; .W35. **DD** 333.91/0025/73.

US/0741-0689
**WATER RESOURCES DATA. ALASKA.** [Water resour. data, Alsk.]. **VFOAT** Alaska; USGS Water Resources Data. Alaska; U.S.G.S. Water Resources Data. Alaska. English. an. US Department of the Interior Geological Survey, 4230 University Drive 201, Anchorage AK 99508-4626. **Tel** (907)271-4138. **ED** P J Still and R D Lamke. **LC** GB1225.A4; W377. **DD** 553.7/09798. **Circ:** 350. available on microfiche (Vols. for (1982-) distributed to depository libraries). ***Continues*** *Water Resources Data for Alaska.*

US
**WATER RESOURCES DATA. ARIZONA.** **VFOAT** Arizona. (1981)-. English. an. National Technical Information Service - NTIS, Room 2027S, 5285 Port Royal Road, Springfield VA 22161. **Tel** (703)487-4630, (703)487-4660, (703)487-4650, FAX (703)321-8547, telex 89-9405. **LC** GB1225.A6; A412. **DD** 553.78/09771. available on microfiche (Vols. for 1983- distributed to depository libraries). ***Continues*** *Water Resources Data for Arizona, 0565-6109.*

US
**WATER RESOURCES DATA. CALIFORNIA.** **VFOAT** California. (1981)-. English. an. National Technical Information Service - NTIS, Room 2027S, 5285 Port Royal Road, Springfield VA 22161. **Tel** (703)487-4630, (703)487-4660, (703)487-4650, FAX (703)321-8547, telex 89-9405. **LC** GB1225.C3; A412. **DD** 553.7/8/09794. available on microfiche (Vols. for 1984- distributed to depository libraries). ***Continues*** *Water Resources Data for California, 0364-4057.*

US/0741-0697
**WATER RESOURCES DATA. COLORADO.** **VFOAT** Colorado; USGS Water Resources Data. Colorado; U.S.G.S. Water Resources Data. Colorado. English. an. US Department of the Interior / US Geological Survey, Virginia, National Technical Information Service, 5285 Port Royal Road, Springfield VA 22161. **Tel** (800)553-6847, (703)487-4812. **LC** GB1225.C6; A412. **DD** 553.7/09788. available on microfiche (Vols. for (1981-) distributed to depository libraries). ***Continues*** *Water Resources Data for Colorado.*

US/0275-2689
**WATER RESOURCES DATA FOR FLORIDA.** (WATER RESOURCES DATA. FLORIDA.). [Water resour. data Fla.]. **Added/Corp** Geological Survey (U.S.). Water Resources Division. **VFOAT** Florida; USGS Water Resources Data. Florida; U.S.G.S. Water Resources Data. Florida. (1981)-. English. an. US Department of the Interior / US Geological Survey, Virginia, National Technical Information Service, 5285 Port Royal Road, Springfield VA 22161. **Tel** (800)553-6847, (703)487-4812. **LC** GB1225.F6; A42. **DD** 553.7/09759. available on microfiche (Vols. for (1982-) distributed to depository libraries). ***Continues*** *Water Resources Data for Florida, 0275-2689.*

US/0364-4332
**WATER RESOURCES DATA FOR ILLINOIS.** (WATER RESOURCES DATA. ILLINOIS.). [Water resour. data Ill.]. **VFOAT** Illinois; USGS Water Resources Data. Illinois; U.S.G.S. Water Resources Data. Illinois. Water Year 1981-. English. an. US Department of the Interior / US Geological Survey, Virginia, National Technical Information Service, 5285 Port Royal Road, Springfield VA 22161. **Tel** (800)553-6847, (703)487-4812. **LC** GB1225.I27; A412. **DD** 553.7/09773. available on microfiche (Vols. for (1981-) distributed to depository libraries). ***Continues*** *Water Resources Data for Illinois, 0364-4332.*

US/0364-4375
**WATER RESOURCES DATA FOR MICHIGAN.** (WATER RESOURCES DATA. MICHIGAN.). [Water resour. data Mich.]. **VFOAT** USGS Water Resources Data. Michigan; U.S.G.S. Water Resources Data. Michigan. Water Year 1981-. English. an. US Department of the Interior / US Geological Survey, Virginia, National Technical Information Service, 5285 Port Royal Road, Springfield VA 22161. **Tel** (800)553-6847, (703)487-4812. **LC** GB1225.M5; A412. **DD** 553.7/09744. available on microfiche (Vols. for (1981-) distributed to depository libraries). ***Continues*** *Water Resources Data for Michigan, 0364-4375.*

US/0364-4383
**WATER RESOURCES DATA FOR MINNESOTA.** (WATER RESOURCES DATA. MINNESOTA.). [Water resour. data Minn.]. **VFOAT** Minnesota; USGS Water Resources Data. Minnesota; U.S.G.S. Water Resources Data. Minnesota. Water Year 1981-. English. an. District Chief / Minnesota, Water Resources Division, US Geological Survey, 702 PO Building, St Paul MN 55101. **LC** GB1225.M6; W37. **DD** 553.7/09776. Index available. **Ad Acc. Circ:** 500. available on microfiche (Vols. for (1981-) distributed to depository libraries). ***Continues*** *Water Resources Data for Minnesota, 0364-4383.*

US/0364-510X
**WATER RESOURCES DATA FOR MISSISSIPPI.** [Water resour. data Miss.]. **Added/Corp** Geological Survey (U.S.) Geological Survey (U.S.). Water Resources Division. Mississippi. Dept. of Natural Resources. Mississippi. Dept. of Environmental Quality. **VFOAT** Water Resources Data. Mississippi; USGS Water Resources Data for Mississippi; U.S.G.S. Water Resources Data for Mississippi. (1965)-. English. an. National Technical Information Service - NTIS, Room 2027S, 5285 Port Royal Road, Springfield VA 22161. **Tel** (703)487-4630, (703)487-4660, (703)487-4650, FAX (703)321-8547, telex 89-9405. **LC** GB1225.M63; W37. **DD** 551.48/3/09762. ***Continues*** *Surface Water Records of Mississippi.*

US/0364-4065
**WATER RESOURCES DATA FOR NEW MEXICO.** (WATER RESOURCES DATA. NEW MEXICO.). [Water resour. data N.M.]. **Added/Corp** Geological Survey (U.S.). Water Resources Division. **VFOAT** USGS Water Resources Data. New Mexico; New Mexico; U.S.G.S. Water Resources Data. New Mexico. (1981)-. English. ir. US Department of the Interior / US Geological Survey, Virginia, National Technical Information Service, 5285 Port Royal Road, Springfield VA 22161. **Tel** (800)553-6847, (703)487-4812. **LC** GB1225.N6; A412. **DD** 553.7/09789. available on microfiche (Vols. for (1983-) distributed to depository libraries). ***Continues*** *Water Resources Data for New Mexico, 0364-4065.*

US/0197-0755
**WATER RESOURCES DATA FOR PENNSYLVANIA.** (WATER RESOURCES DATA. PENNSYLVANIA.). [Water resour. data Pa.]. **VFOAT**

Pennsylvania; USGS Water Resources Data. Pennsylvania; U.S.G.S. Water Resources Data. Pennsylvania. Water Year 1981-. English. an. US Department of the Interior / US Geological Survey, Virginia, National Technical Information Service, 5285 Port Royal Road, Springfield VA 22161. **Tel** (800)553-6847, (703)487-4812. **LC** GB1225.P4; A4. **DD** 553.7/09748. available on microfiche (Vols. for (1981)- distributed to depository libraries). ***Continues*** *Water Resources Data for Pennsylvania, 0197-0755.*

US/0364-4421
**WATER RESOURCES DATA FOR WEST VIRGINIA.** (WATER RESOURCES DATA. WEST VIRGINIA.). [Water resour. data W. Va.]. **VFOAT** West Virginia; USGS Water Resources Data. West Virginia; U.S.G.S. Water Resources Data. West Virginia. Water Year 1981-. English. an. US Department of the Interior / US Geological Survey, Virginia, National Technical Information Service, 5285 Port Royal Road, Springfield VA 22161. **Tel** (800)553-6847, (703)487-4812. **LC** TD224.W4; A37. **DD** 553.7/09754. available on microfiche (Vols. for (1981-) distributed to depository libraries). ***Continues*** *Water Resources Data for West Virginia, 0364-4421.*

US/0364-4324
**WATER RESOURCES DATA. IDAHO.** [Water resourc. data Ida.]. **VFOAT** Idaho; USGS Water Resources Data, Idaho; U.S.G.S. Water Resources Data, Idaho. English. an. US Department of the Interior / Geological Survey, Idaho, Box 036, Federal Building, 550 West Fort Street, Boise ID 83724. **LC** GB1225.I2; A412. **DD** 553.7/09796. available on microfiche (Vols. for (1982)- distributed to depository libraries). ***Continues*** *Water Resources Data for Idaho, 0364-4324.*

US/0364-4359
**WATER RESOURCES DATA. IOWA.** [Water resour. data Iowa]. **VFOAT** Iowa; USGS Water Resources. Iowa; U.S.G.S. Water Resources. Iowa. English. an. US Department of the Interior / US Geological Survey, Virginia, National Technical Information Service, 5285 Port Royal Road, Springfield VA 22161. **Tel** (800)553-6847, (703)487-4812. **LC** GB1225.I8; A412. **DD** 553.7/09777. available on microfiche (Vols. for (1981-) distributed to depository libraries). ***Continues*** *Water Resources Data for Iowa, 0364-4359.*

US/0741-4803
**WATER RESOURCES DATA. KANSAS.** [Water resour. data, Kans.]. **VFOAT** USGS Water Resources Data. Kansas; U.S.G.S. Water Resources Data. Kansas. Water Year 1981-. English. an. US Department of the Interior / US Geological Survey, Virginia, National Technical Information Service, 5285 Port Royal Road, Springfield VA 22161. **Tel** (800)553-6847, (703)487-4812. **LC** GB1225.K2; A42. **DD** 553.7/09781. available on microfiche (Vols. for (1981-) distributed to depository libraries). ***Continues*** *Water Resources Data for Kansas, 0741-4803.*

US/0364-4081
**WATER RESOURCES DATA. KENTUCKY.** [Water resour. data Ky.]. **VFOAT** USGS Water Resources Data. Kentucky; U.S.G.S Water Resources Data. Kentucky. Water Year 1981-. English. an. US Department of the Interior / US Geological Survey, Virginia, National Technical Information Service, 5285 Port Royal Road, Springfield VA 22161. **Tel** (800)553-6847, (703)487-4812. **LC** GB1225.K4; A42. **DD** 553.7/09769. available on microfiche (Vols. for (1981-) distributed to depository libraries). ***Continues*** *Water Resources Data for Kentucky, 0364-4081.*

US
**WATER RESOURCES DATA. LOUISIANA.** **VFOAT** Water Resources Data, Louisiana; U.S.G.S. Water Resources Data. Louisiana; USGS Water Resources Data. Louisiana. Water Year 1981-. English. an. US Department of the Interior / US Geological Survey, Virginia, National Technical Information Service, 5285 Port Royal Road, Springfield VA 22161. **Tel** (800)553-6847, (703)487-4812. **LC** GB1225.L6; W37. **DD** 553.7/09763. available on microfiche (Vols. for (1981-) distributed to depository libraries). ***Continues*** *Water Resources Data for Louisiana, 0276-1297.*

US/0364-4367
**WATER RESOURCES DATA. MARYLAND AND DELAWARE.** [Water resour. data Md. Del.]. **VFOAT** Maryland and Delaware; USGS Water Resources Data. Maryland and Delaware; U.S.G.S. Water Resources Data. Maryland and Delaware. Water Year 1981-. English. an. US Department of the Interior / US Geological Survey, Virginia, National Technical Information Service, 5285 Port Royal Road, Springfield VA 22161. **Tel** (800)553-6847, (703)487-4812. **LC** GB1225.M3; A4. **DD** 553.7/09752. available on microfiche (Vols. for (1981-) distributed to depository libraries). ***Continues*** *Water Resources Data for Maryland and Delaware, 0364-4367.*

US
**WATER RESOURCES DATA. MASSACHUSETTS AND RHODE ISLAND.** **VFOAT** USGS Water Resources Data; Water Resources Data Massachusetts and Rhode Island; U.S.G.S. Water Resources Data; U.S.G.S. Water Resources Data. Massachusetts and Rhode Island. **VAT** United States Geological Survay Water Resources Data. English. an. National Technical Information Service - NTIS, Room 2027S, 5285 Port Royal Road, Springfield VA 22161. **Tel** (703)487-4630, (703)487-4660, (703)487-4650, FAX (703)321-8547, telex 89-9405. **LC** GB1225.M4; W38. **DD** 553.7/09744. ***Continues*** *Water Resources Data for Massachusetts and Rhode Island.*

US/0741-6296
**WATER RESOURCES DATA. MISSOURI.** [Water resour. data, Mo.]. **VFOAT** Missouri. 1981-. English. an. US Department of the Interior / US Geological Survey, Virginia, National Technical Information Service, 5285 Port Royal Road, Springfield VA 22161. **Tel** (800)553-6847, (703)487-4812. **LC** GB1225.M65; A42. **DD** 553.7/09778. available on microfiche (Vols. for (1981-) distributed to depository libraries). ***Continues*** *Water Resources Data for Missouri, 0741-6296.*

US/0364-4073
**WATER RESOURCES DATA. MONTANA.** [Water resour. data Mont.]. **VFOAT** USGS Water Resources Data. Montana; U.S.G.S. Water Resources Data. Montana. Water Year 1981-. English. an. US Department of the Interior / US Geological Survey, Virginia, National Technical Information Service, 5285 Port Royal Road, Springfield VA 22161. **Tel** (800)553-6847, (703)487-4812. **LC** GB1225.M9; A42. **DD** 553.7/09786. available on microfiche (Vols. for (1985-) distributed to depository libraries). ***Continues*** *Water Resources Data for Montana, 0364-4073.*

US/0363-1974
**WATER RESOURCES DATA. NEBRASKA.** [Water resour. data Neb.]. **VFOAT** USGS Water Resources Data. Nebraska; U.S.G.S. Water Resources Data. Nebraska. Water Year 1981-. English. an. US Department of the Interior / US Geological Survey, Virginia, National Technical Information Service, 5285 Port Royal Road, Springfield VA 22161. **Tel** (800)553-6847, (703)487-4812. **LC** GB705.N2; U53A. **DD** 553.7/09782. available on microfiche (Vols. for (1981-) distributed to depository libraries). ***Continues*** *Water Resources Data for Nebraska, 0363-1974.*

US
**WATER RESOURCES DATA. NEVADA.** **VFOAT** Water Resources Data, Nevada. English. an. US Department of the Interior / US Geological Survey, Virginia, National Technical Information Service, 5285 Port Royal Road, Springfield VA 22161. **Tel** (800)553-6847, (703)487-4812. **LC** GB1225.N3; A4. **DD** 553.7/09793. available on microfiche (Vols. for (1982-) distributed to depository libraries). ***Continues*** *Water Resources Data for Nevada, 0364-4391.*

US
**WATER RESOURCES DATA. NEW HAMPSHIRE AND VERMONT.** **VFOAT** Water Resources Data, New Hampshire and Vermont. Water Year 1981-. English. an. $18.50. US Geological Survey / Boston, Water Resources Division, 150 Causeway Street, Boston MA 02114. **LC** GB1225.N4; W37. **DD** 553.78/09742. Index available. **Circ:** 300 (ctrl). available on microfiche (Vols. for (1981-) distributed to depository libraries). ***Continues*** *Water Resources Data. New Hampshire and Vermont, 0735-8903.*
**Desc:** Tables and lists of water resources data collected by the United States Geological Survey during October to September of the water year.

US
**WATER RESOURCES DATA. NEW JERSEY.** **VFOAT** New Jersey. English. an. National Technical Information Service - NTIS, Room 2027S, 5285 Port Royal Road, Springfield VA 22161. **Tel** (703)487-4630, (703)487-4660, (703)487-4650, FAX (703)321-8547, telex 89-9405. available on microfiche (Vols. for 1981 distributed to depository libraries). ***Continues*** *Water Resources Data for New Jersey, 0095-4187.*

US
**WATER RESOURCES DATA. NEW YORK.** **VFOAT** USGS Water Resources Data; U.S.G.S. Water Resources Data. New York. **VAT** United States Geological Survey Water Resources Data. New York. English. an. National Technical Information Service - NTIS, Room 2027S, 5285 Port Royal Road, Springfield VA 22161. **Tel** (703)487-4630, (703)487-4660, (703)487-4650, FAX (703)321-8547, telex 89-9405. **LC** GB1225.N7; A4. **DD** 553.78/09747. available on microfiche (Vols. for 1984- distributed to depository libraries). ***Continues*** *Water Resources Data for New York, 0147-2283.*

US/0734-5747
**WATER RESOURCES DATA. NORTH CAROLINA.** [Water resour. data, N.C.]. **VFOAT** USGS Water Resources Data, North Carolina; U.S.G.S. Water Resources Data, North Carolina. English. an. $45.00. US Department of the Interior / US Geological Survey, Virginia, National Technical Information Service, 5285 Port Royal Road, Springfield VA 22161. **Tel** (800)553-6847, (703)487-4812. **LC** GB1225.N8; W37. **DD** 553.7/09756. available on microfiche (Vols. for (1981-) distributed to depository libraries). ***Continues*** *Water Resources Data for North Carolina, 0734-5747.*

US
**WATER RESOURCES DATA. NORTH DAKOTA.** **VFOAT** North Dakota. Water Year (1981)-. English. an. National Technical Information Service - NTIS, Room 2027S, 5285 Port Royal Road, Springfield VA 22161. **Tel** (703)487-4630, (703)487-4660, (703)487-4650, FAX (703)321-8547, telex 89-9405. available on microfiche (Vols. for 1981- distributed to depository libraries). ***Continues*** *Water Resources Data for North Dakota, 0364-4405.*

US
**WATER RESOURCES DATA. OHIO.** **VFOAT** USGS Water Resources Data; U.S.G.S. Water Resources Data. Ohio. (Water Year 1981)-. English. an. National Technical Information Service - NTIS, Room 2027S, 5285 Port Royal Road, Springfield VA 22161. **Tel** (703)487-4630, (703)487-4660, (703)487-4650, FAX (703)321-8547, telex 89-9405. **LC** GB1225.O3; A412. **DD** 553.78/09771. available on microfiche (Vols. for 1984- distributed to depository libraries). ***Continues*** *Water Resources Data for Ohio, 0364-4413.*

US
**WATER RESOURCES DATA. OKLAHOMA.** **VFOAT** Oklahoma. (1981)-. English. an. National Technical Information Service - NTIS, Room 2027S, 5285 Port Royal Road, Springfield VA 22161. **Tel** (703)487-4630, (703)487-4660, (703)487-4650, FAX (703)321-8547, telex 89-9405. **LC** GB1225.O5; A4. **DD** 553.78/.09766. available on microfiche (Vols. for 1981- distributed to depository libraries). ***Continues*** *Water Resources Data for Oklahoma, 0095-5671.*

US
**WATER RESOURCES DATA. OREGON.** **VFOAT** USGS Water Resources Data; U.S.G.S. Water Resources Data. Oregon. Water Year (1981)-. English. an. National Technical Information Service - NTIS, Room 2027S, 5285 Port Royal Road, Springfield VA 22161. **Tel** (703)487-4630, (703)487-4660, (703)487-4650, FAX (703)321-8547, telex 89-9405. **LC** GB705.O7; A32. **DD** 553.78/09795. available on microfiche (Vols. for 1983- distributed to depository libraries). ***Continues*** *Water Resources Data for Oregon (Portland, Or.).*

US/8756-9809
**WATER RESOURCES DATA. PUERTO RICO AND THE U.S. VIRGIN ISLANDS.** [Water resour. data, P.R. U.S. Virg. Isl.]. **VFOAT** U.S.G.S. Water Resources Data. Puerto Rico and the U.S. Virgin Islands. Water Year 1983-. English. an. US Department of the Interior / US Geological Survey, Virginia, National Technical Information Service, 5285 Port Royal Road, Springfield VA 22161. **Tel** (800)553-6847, (703)487-4812. **LC** GB717; .U53A. **DD** 551.48/097295. available on microfiche (Vols. for Water Year 1983- distributed to depository libraries). ***Continues*** *Water Resources Data. Puerto Rico, 8756-9795.*

US/0732-9997
**WATER RESOURCES DATA. SOUTH CAROLINA.** [Water resour. data S.C.]. **VFOAT** South Carolina; USGS Water Resources Data; U.S.G.S. Water Resources Data. Water Year 1981-. English. an. US Department of the Interior / US Geological Survey, Virginia, National Technical Information Service, 5285 Port Royal Road, Springfield VA 22161. **Tel** (800)553-6847, (703)487-4812. **LC** GB1225.S6; A35. **DD** 553.7/09757. available on microfiche (Vols. for (1983-) distributed to depository libraries). ***Continues*** *Water Resources Data for South Carolina, 0732-9997.*

US/0741-451X
**WATER RESOURCES DATA. SOUTH DAKOTA.** [Water resour. data, S.D.]. **Added/Corp** Geological Survey (U.S.). Water Resources Division. **VFOAT** South Dakota. (1981)-. English. an. US Department of the Interior / US Geological Survey, Virginia, National Technical Information Service, 5285 Port Royal Road, Springfield VA 22161. **Tel** (800)553-6847, (703)487-4812. **LC** GB1225.S8; A412. **DD** 553.7/09783. available on microfiche (Vols. for 1981- distributed to depository libraries). ***Continues*** *Water Resources Data for South Dakota.*

US
**WATER RESOURCES DATA SUMMARY.** (WATER RESOURCES DATA SUMMARY / BUREAU OF LAND MANAGEMENT, IDAHO STATE OFFICE.). **VFOAT** Idaho Water Resources Data Summary. English. an. US Department of the Interior / Idaho, Federal Building Box 042, 550 West Fort Street, Boise ID 83724.

# Water Resources

US/0163-9447
**WATER RESOURCES DATA. TENNESSEE.** [Water resour. data Tenn.]. **Added/Corp** Geological Survey (U.S.). Water Resources Division. Tennessee. Division of Water Resources. Tennessee Valley Authority. Tennessee. Division of Water Management. Tennessee. Dept. of Health and Environment. Tennessee. Office of Water Management. **VFOAT** USGS Water Resources Data. Tennessee; U.S.G.S. Water Resources Data. Tennessee. (1982)-. English. an. National Technical Information Service - NTIS, Room 2027S, 5285 Port Royal Road, Springfield VA 22161. **Tel** (703)487-4630, (703)487-4660, (703)487-4650, FAX (703)321-8547, telex 89-9405. **LC** GB1225.T4; W38. **DD** 553.7/09768. **Continues** *Water Resources Data for Tennessee, 0163-9447.*

US/0742-1575
**WATER RESOURCES DATA. TEXAS.** [Water resour. data., Tex.]. **VFOAT** Texas. English. an. US Department of the Interior / US Geological Survey, Virginia, National Technical Information Service, 5285 Port Royal Road, Springfield VA 22161. **Tel** (800)553-6847, (703)487-4812. **LC** GB1025.T4; A44. **DD** 553.7/09764. available on microfiche (Vols. for 1981- distributed to depository libraries). **Continues** *Water Resources Data for Texas, 0742-1575.*

US/0276-1319
**WATER RESOURCES DATA. VIRGINIA.** [Water resour. data Va.]. **VFOAT** Water Resources Data, Virginia U.S.G.S. Water Resources Data. Virginia. English. an. US Department of the Interior / US Geological Survey, Virginia, National Technical Information Service, 5285 Port Royal Road, Springfield VA 22161. **Tel** (800)553-6847, (703)487-4812. **LC** GB1225.V8; W37. **DD** 553.7/09755. available on microfiche (Vols. for (1981, 1985-) distributed to depository libraries). **Continues** *Water Resources Data for Virginia, 0276-1319.*

US/0364-3557
**WATER RESOURCES DATA. WASHINGTON.** [Water resour. data Wash.]. **VFOAT** Washington; USGS Water Resources Data. Washington; U.S.G.S. Water Resources Data. Washington. (1981)-. English. an. US Department of the Interior / US Geological Survey, Virginia, National Technical Information Service, 5285 Port Royal Road, Springfield VA 22161. **Tel** (800)553-6847, (703)487-4812. **LC** GB1225.W3; A412. **DD** 553.7/09797. available on microfiche (Vols. for (1981-) distributed to depository libraries). **Continues** *Water Resources Data for Washington, 0364-3557.*

US/0740-8803
**WATER RESOURCES DATA. WISCONSIN.** [Water resour. data, Wis.]. **VFOAT** Wisconsin; Water Resources Data, Wisconsin; USGS Water Resources Data. Wisconsin; U.S.G.S. Water Resources Data. Wisconsin. Water Year 1981-. English. an. US Department of the Interior / US Geological Survey, Virginia, National Technical Information Service, 5285 Port Royal Road, Springfield VA 22161. **Tel** (800)553-6847, (703)487-4812. **LC** GB1225.W6; A412. **DD** 553.7/09775. available on microfiche (Vols. for (1981-) distributed to depository libraries). **Continues** *Water Resources Data for Wisconsin, 0740-8803.*

US/0364-3565
**WATER RESOURCES DATA. WYOMING.** [Water resour. data Wyo.]. **VFOAT** Wyoming; USGS Water Resources Data. Wyoming; U.S.G.S. Water Resources Data. Wyoming. Water Year 1981-. English. an. US Department of the Interior / US Geological Survey, Virginia, National Technical Information Service, 5285 Port Royal Road, Springfield VA 22161. **Tel** (800)553-6847, (703)487-4812. **LC** GB1225.W8; A412. **DD** 553.7/09787. available on microfiche (Vols. for (1981-) distributed to depository libraries). **Continues** *Water Resources Data for Wyoming, 0364-3565.*

US
**WATER RESOURCES DEVELOPMENT BY THE U.S. ARMY CORPS OF ENGINEERS IN ARKANSAS (1979).** (WATER RESOURCES DEVELOPMENT BY THE U.S. ARMY CORPS OF ENGINEERS IN ARKANSAS.). **VFOAT** Water Resources Development, Arkansas. Began with 1979. English. be. Southwestern Division, Corps of Engineers, Dallas TX 75235. **Tel** (501)378-5551. **LC** TC424.A8; W36. Index available. ctrl circ. **Continues** *Water Resources Development in Arkansas.* **Desc:** Covers operation and maintenance of completed Army Corps of Engineers projects in Arkansas and scope and progress of studies underway. Information also is provided on current flood plain management studies, authorized surveys underway and special studies on flood-related problems in urban areas.

US
**WATER RESOURCES DEVELOPMENT BY THE U.S. ARMY CORPS OF ENGINEERS IN IDAHO (1979).** (WATER RESOURCES DEVELOPMENT BY THE U. S. ARMY CORPS OF ENGINEERS IN IDAHO / NORTH PACIFIC DIVISION.). **VFOAT** Water Resources Development, Idaho. **VAT** Water Resources Development by the United States Army Corps of Engineers in Idaho. Jan. 1979-. English. be. The Division, PO Box 2870, Portland OR 97208. **LC** TC424.I2; W39. **Continues** *Water Resources Development in Idaho by the U.S. Army Corps of Engineers.*

US
**WATER RESOURCES DEVELOPMENT BY THE U.S. ARMY CORPS OF ENGINEERS IN ILLINOIS. Added/Corp** United States. Army. Corps of Engineers. North Central Division. United States. Army. Corps of Engineers. Chicago District. **VFOAT** Water Resources Development in Illinois. (19??)-. English. be. Division Engineer / Illinois, US Army Division North Central, 536 South Clark Street, Chicago IL 60605. **LC** TC424.I3; W38. **DD** 333.91/15/09773.

US
**WATER RESOURCES DEVELOPMENT BY THE U.S. ARMY CORPS OF ENGINEERS IN NORTH CAROLINA.** **VFOAT** Water Resources Development in North Carolina. English. be. Free. US Army Engineer Division, South Atlantic Corps of Engineers, 510 Title Building, 30 Pryor Street SW, Atlanta GA 30303. **Tel** (404)331-6641. **LC** TC424.N8; W37. **DD** 627./09756. **Circ:** 2,500 (ctrl). **Desc:** Status report on existing water resources studies and projects completed or underway by U.S. Army Corps of Engineers in the state of North Carolina.

US
**WATER RESOURCES DEVELOPMENT BY THE U.S. ARMY CORPS OF ENGINEERS IN TEXAS.** **VFOAT** Water Resources Development in Texas. English. ir. Division Engineer / Texas, US Army Engineer Division Southwestern, 1114 Commerce Street, Dallas TX 75242. **Tel** (918)581-7829. ctrl circ.

US
**WATER RESOURCES DEVELOPMENT BY THE US ARMY CORPS OF ENGINEERS IN KANSAS / US ARMY CORPS OF ENGINEERS, SOUTHWESTERN DIVISION.** **VFOAT** Water Resources Development in Kansas. English. Division Engineer / Texas, US Army Engineer Division Southwestern, 1114 Commerce Street, Dallas TX 75242. **Tel** (918)581-7829. **LC** TC424.K2; W35. **DD** 333.91/15/09781. **Circ:** 1,000 (ctrl). **Desc:** A reference document provided to keep the public and other interested parties informed of local Corps of Engineers water resources activities.

US/0744-0480
**WATER RESOURCES DEVELOPMENT BY THE US ARMY CORPS OF ENGINEERS IN OKLAHOMA.** [Water resour. dev. US Army Corps of Eng. Okla.]. **VFOAT** Water Resources Development in Oklahoma. English. be. Division Engineer / Texas, US Army Engineer Division Southwestern, 1114 Commerce Street, Dallas TX 75242. **Tel** (918)581-7829. **LC** TC424.O5; W34. **DD** 333.91/15/09766. **Circ:** 1,000 (ctrl). **Desc:** A reference document provided to keep the public and other interested parties informed of local Corps of Engineers water resources activities.

US/0732-6408
**WATER RESOURCES DEVELOPMENT IN IOWA.** (WATER RESOURCES DEVELOPMENT IN IOWA ... BY THE US ARMY CORPS OF ENGINEERS.). [Water resour. dev. Iowa]. (1981)-. English. be. Free. US Army Engineer Division North Central, 536 South Clark Street, Chicago IL 60605. **Tel** (312)353-6319. **LC** TC424.I8; W37. **DD** 353.0082/325. **Circ:** 2,000 (ctrl). **Continues** *Water Resources Development by the U. S. Army Corps of Engineers in Iowa (Chicago, Ill. : 1979).*

US
**WATER RESOURCES DEVELOPMENT IN LOUISIANA (UNITED STATES. ARMY. CORPS OF ENGINEERS. LOWER MISSISSIPPI VALLEY DIVISION : 1981).** (WATER RESOURCES DEVELOPMENT IN LOUISIANA.). 1981-. English. be. Division of Engineer, US Army Engineer Division, Lower Mississippi Valley, PO Box 80, Vicksburg MS 39180. **LC** TC4424.L8; W37. **DD** 333.91/15/09763. **Continues** *Water Resources Development by the U.S. Army Corps Engineers in Louisiana (1979).*

US/0278-5781
**WATER RESOURCES DEVELOPMENT IN MICHIGAN (1981).** (WATER RESOURCES DEVELOPMENT IN MICHIGAN / BY THE U S ARMY CORPS OF ENGINEERS.). [Water resour. dev. Mich.]. **Added/Corp** United States. Army. Corps of Engineers. United States. Army. Corps of Engineers. North Central Division. (1981)-. English. be. Free. US Army Engineer Division North Central, 536 South Clark Street, Chicago IL 60605. **Tel** (312)353-6319. **LC** TC424.M5; W37. **DD** 333.91/15/09776. **Circ:** 2,000 (ctrl). available on diskette. **Continues** *Water Resources Development by the U.S. Army Corps of Engineers in Michigan.*

US/0278-5447
**WATER RESOURCES DEVELOPMENT IN MINNESOTA.** [Water resour. dev. Minn.]. 1981-. English. be. Free. US Army Engineer Division North Central / Illinois, 536 South Clark Street, Chicago IL 60605. **Tel** (612)220-0201. **(Subscription address:** Public Affairs Office, 1421 US Post Office, St Paul, MN 55101-1479) **LC** TC424.M6; W37. **DD** 333.91/15/09776. **Circ:** 1,000. **Continues** *Water Resources Development by the U.S. Army Corps of Engineers in Minnesota.* **Desc:** Contains descriptions of water resources projects in Minnesota undertaken by the US Army Corps of Engineers.

US
**WATER RESOURCES DEVELOPMENT IN WISCONSIN (UNITED STATES. ARMY. CORPS OF ENGINEERS. NORTH CENTRAL DIVISION : 1981).** (WATER RESOURCES DEVELOPMENT IN WISCONSIN.). (1981)-. English. be. US Army Corps of Engineers / North Central Division, Public Affairs Office, 536 South Clark Street, Chicago IL 60605-1592. **Tel** (312)353-6319. **Circ:** 2,000 (ctrl). **Continues** *Water Resources Development by the U.S. Army Corps of Engineers in Wisconsin (1979).*

US
**WATER RESOURCES DIVISION TRAINING BULLETIN. Main/Corp** Geological Survey (U.S.). Water Resources Division. Bulletin. English. an. US Geological Survey / Denver, PO Box 25286, Denver CO 80225. **Tel** (303)493-8401.

US/0548-3557
**WATER RESOURCES. INFORMATION SERIES. REPORT - NEVADA.** [Water resour. inf. ser. rep.]. Monographic series. English. Price varies per volume. Nevada Division of Water Resources, Carson City NV 89701. **DD** 333.9. **CODEN** NCGRAZ. Documents available from CASDDS. **Continues** *Ground-Water Resources. Information Series. Report.* **Ind/Abst** Chem. Abstr.; GeoRef.

US
**WATER-RESOURCES INVESTIGATIONS IN ARIZONA / UNITED STATES GEOLOGICAL SURVEY, WATER RESOURCES DIVISION, IN COOPERATION WITH THE ARIZONA WATER COMMISSION AND OTHER STATE, MUNICIPAL, AND FEDERAL AGENCIES.** English. Chief Hydrologist, US Geological Survey, 420 National Center, Reston VA 22092.

US
**WATER-RESOURCES INVESTIGATIONS IN MISSOURI / DEPARTMENT OF THE INTERIOR, UNITED STATES GEOLOGICAL SURVEY IN COOPERATION WITH THE MISSOURI DIVISION OF GEOLOGY AND LAND SURVEY, AND OTHER STATE, MUNICIPAL, AND FEDERAL AGENCIES.** English. Chief Hydrologist, US Geological Survey, 420 National Center, Reston VA 22092.

US/0277-9293
**WATER-RESOURCES INVESTIGATIONS IN NEVADA.** (WATER-RESOURCES INVESTIGATIONS IN NEVADA / DEPARTMENT OF THE INTERIOR, UNITED STATES GEOLOGICAL SURVEY IN COOPERATION WITH THE NEVADA DEPARTMENT OF CONSERVATION AND NATURAL RESOURCES AND OTHER STATE, MUNICIPAL, AND FEDERAL AGENCIES.). [Water-resour. invest. Nev.]. English. Free. District Chief / Nevada, Water Resources Division, US Geological Survey, Room 227/Federal Building, 705 North Plaza Street, Carson City NV 89710. **LC** TC424.N3; W37. **DD** 333.91/009793.

US
**WATER-RESOURCES INVESTIGATIONS IN NORTH CAROLINA / DEPARTMENT OF THE INTERIOR, UNITED STATES GEOLOGICAL SURVEY, IN COOPERATION WITH NORTH CAROLINA DEPARTMENT OF NATURAL AND ECONOMIC RESOURCES AND OTHER STATE, MUNICIPAL, AND FEDERAL AGENCIES.** English. Chief Hydrologist, US Geological Survey, 420 National Center, Reston VA 22092. **Continues** *Water Resources Investigations in North Carolina.*

US
**WATER-RESOURCES INVESTIGATIONS IN OREGON / DEPARTMENT OF THE INTERIOR, UNITED STATES GEOLOGICAL SURVEY IN COOPERATION WITH THE OREGON WATER RESOURCES DEPARTMENT AND OTHER STATE, MUNICIPAL, AND FEDERAL AGENCIES.** English. Chief Hydrologist, US Geological Survey, 420 National Center, Reston VA 22092.

US
**WATER-RESOURCES INVESTIGATIONS IN SOUTH CAROLINA / DEPARTMENT OF THE INTERIOR, UNITED STATES GEOLOGICAL SURVEY IN COOPERATION WITH THE SOUTH CAROLINA WATER RESOURCES COMMISSION AND OTHER STATE, MUNICIPAL, AND FEDERAL AGENCIES.** English. Chief Hydrologist, US Geological Survey, 420 National Center, Reston VA 22092.

US
**WATER-RESOURCES INVESTIGATIONS IN TEXAS.** **Main/Corp** Geological Survey (U.S.). Water Resources Division. Texas District. (1972)-. English. an. US Geological Survey / Texas, 8011 Cameron Road/Suite B-1, Austin TX 78753-6700. **Tel** (512)832-5791. available on microfiche. ***Continues*** *Geological Survey (U.S.). Water Resources Division. Texas District. Program of the Water Resources Division, Texas District for the Fiscal Year and Summary of District Activities during Fiscal Year, 0565-6060.*

US
**WATER-RESOURCES INVESTIGATIONS OF THE U.S. GEOLOGICAL SURVEY IN MISSOURI.** Fiscal Year 1980-. English. an. US Geological Survey and Water Resources Division, 1400 Independence Road, Mail Stop 200, Rolla MO 65401. ***Continues*** *Programs and Activities of the Missouri District, Water Resources Division, U.S. Geological Survey.*

US/0196-1357
**WATER-RESOURCES INVESTIGATIONS OF THE U.S. GEOLOGICAL SURVEY NEW MEXICO DISTRICT.** ***Title Change.*** **Main/Corp** Geological Survey (U.S.). Water Resources Division. New Mexico District. **VFOAT** Water-Resources Investigations of the U.S. Geological Survey in New Mexico. **VAT** Water Resources Investigations of the United States Geological Survey New Mexico District. (1977/78)-(198?). English. an. US Geological Survey / New Mexico, Water Resources Division, PO Box 26659, Albuquerque NM 87125. **LC** GB658.7; .U53a. **DD** 553.7/09789. ***Continued by*** *Geological Survey (U.S.). Water-Resources Activities of the U.S. Geological Survey in New Mexico.*

US
**WATER-RESOURCES INVESTIGATIONS REPORT / U.S. GEOLOGICAL SURVEY.** **Added/Corp** Geological Survey (U.S.). **VFOAT** Water-Resources Investigations; U.S. Geological Survey Water-Resources Investigations Report; US Geological Survey Water-Resources Investigations Report. **VAT** Water Resources Investigations Report; Water Resources Investigations. (1982)-. Monographic series. English. ir. Price varies per volume. U S Geological Survey / Virginia, National Center, 12201 Sunrise Valley Drive, Reston VA 22092. **LC** GB701; .W375. **DD** 553.7/0973. ***Continues*** *Water-Resources Investigations.*
**Ind/Abst** AGRICOLA; Aquat. Sci. Fish. Abstr. (Computer File).

US/0377-8053
**WATER RESOURCES JOURNAL.** [Water resour. j.]. **Added/Corp** United Nations. Economic and Social Commission for Asia and the Pacific. United Nations. Economic Commission for Asia and the Far East. (Dec. 1962)-. Government Publication. English. qt. United Nations Publications, 2 United Nations Plaza, Room DC2 0853, Department 007C, New York NY 10017. **Tel** (212)963-8303, (800)253-9646. **LC** JX1977; .A2 subser; GB773. **DD** 300/.8; 553/.7/095. **NLM** W1 WA692AG. ***Supersedes*** *Flood Control Journal.*
**Ind/Abst** AGRICOLA (19??-); Aquat. Sci. Fish. Abstr. (Computer File) (19??-); Food Sci. Technol. Abstr. (19??-); GeoRef (19??-); Indian Geosci. Abstr. (19??-).

NE/0920-4741
**WATER RESOURCES MANAGEMENT (DORDRECHT, NETHERLANDS).** (WATER RESOURCES MANAGEMENT.). [Water resour. manag.]. **VFOAT** WARM. Vol. 1, No. 1 (1987)-. Periodical. English. qt. $362.00. Kluwer Academic Publishers, Postbus 322, 3300 AH Dordrecht, The Netherlands. **Tel** 011 (31) 78 524400, FAX 011 31 78 183273, telex 20083. **ED** G Tsakiris. **LC** TC401; .W3657. **DD** 333.91/005. **CODEN** WRMAEJ. **[CCC]. Ad Acc. Pr Rev. Circ:** 150. available on microfilm and microfiche from University Microfilms International (UMI). Documents available from Documents on Demand.
**Desc:** An international, multidisciplinary forum for the presentation of original contributions and the exchange of knowledge and experience on the management of water resources. The journal publishes contributions on: water resources assesment, assessment, conservation and control (with an emphasis on policies and strategies); planning and design of water rsource systems; resource operaton, maintenance and operation of water resource systems. Also covered in the journal are water demand and consumption; applied surface and groundwater hydrology; water management techniques; simulation and modelling of water resource systems; forecasting and control of quantity and quality of water; economic and social aspects of water use; legislation and water resources protection.
**Ind/Abst** AGRICOLA [Full Cov.]; Environ. Abstr.; Environ. Period. Bibliogr.; Geogr. Abstr. Phys. Geogr.; Geogr. Abstr. Human Geogr.; GeoRef; Meteorol. Geoastrophys. Abstr. (199?-).

US/0270-9600
**WATER RESOURCES MONOGRAPH.** [Water resour. monogr.]. **Added/Corp** American Geophysical Union. **VFOAT** Water Resources Monograph Series. (1971)-. Monographic series. English. ir. Price varies per volume. American Geophysical Union, 2000 Florida Avenue Northwest, Washington DC 20009. **Tel** (202)462-6903, (800)966-2481, FAX (202)328-0566. **CODEN** WRMSE5. **[CCC]. Bk Rev. Ad Acc.** Documents available from BIOSIS Document Express, Ask*IEEE.
**Desc:** This book series brings information from the research community to the practitioner. Each book describes a specific technique or approach to water resources planning.
**Ind/Abst** Biol. Abstr.; GeoRef; INSPEC.

US/0270-9481
**WATER RESOURCES PLANNING SERIES.** [Water resour. plann. ser.]. Report P-78-001-. Monographic series. English. ir. Price varies per volume. Utah Water Research Laboratory, Utah State University, Logan UT 84322-8200. **Tel** (801)750-3200, FAX (801)750-3663, telex 3729283.
**Ind/Abst** GeoRef.

US/0076-9614
**WATER RESOURCES REPORT (ROLLA).** (WATER RESOURCES REPORT / MISSOURI DEPARTMENT OF NATURAL RESOURCES, DIVISION OF GEOLOGY AND LAND SURVEY.). [Water resour. rep.]. No. 31 (1976)-. Monographic series. English. ir. Price varies per volume. Missouri Department of Natural Research, PO Box 250, Rolla MO 65401. **CODEN** MGWAAE. ***Continues*** *Water Resources Report, 0076-9614.*
**Ind/Abst** GeoRef.

US/0043-1397
**WATER RESOURCES RESEARCH.** [Water resour. res.]. **Added/Corp** American Geophysical Union. Vol. 1 (1965)-. Periodical. English. mo. $675.00. American Geophysical Union, 2000 Florida Avenue Northwest, Washington DC 20009. **Tel** (202)462-6903, (800)966-2481, FAX (202)328-0566. **ED** Ronald Cummings and Donald Nielsen. **LC** GB651; .W32. **DD** 553/.7/0973. **NLM** W1 WA692AH. **CODEN** WRERAQ. **[CCC]. Bk Rev. Ad Acc. Pr Rev. Acid Free.** ctrl circ. available on microfilm. Documents available from Article Express International, The Genuine Article, Ask*IEEE, Petroleum Abstracts Document Delivery Service, CASDDS, Documents on Demand.
**Desc:** Interdisciplinary in nature, this journal provides a comprehensive source for students, scientists, and engineers to obtain the latest ideas concerning hydrologic processes in the environment.
**Ind/Abst** Abstr. Bull. Inst. Pap. Sci. Tech.; AESIS Q.; AGRICOLA [Select. Cov.]; Agric. Eng. Abstr.; AQUAREF; Aquat. Sci. Fish. Abstr. (Computer File); Bioeng. Abstr.; Chem. Abstr.; Coal Abstr.; Crop Physiol. Abstr.; Curr. Aware. Biol. Sci., CABS; Curr. Contents, Agric. Biol. Environ. Sci.; Curr. Contents Eng. Tech. Appl. Sci.; Curr. Ref. Fish Res.; Ecol. Abstr. (?-?); Econ. Lit. Index; Ei Page One; EMBASE; Energy Res. Abstr.; Eng. Index Annu.; Environ. Abstr.; Fish Rev. (Jan. 1989-July 1992); Fluid Abstr., Civil Eng.; Fluid Abstr. Proc. Eng.; FLUIDEX (1973-); For. Abstr.; Geogr. Abstr. Phys. Geogr.; Geogr. Abstr. Human Geogr.; Geol. Abstr.; GeoRef; Grasslands For. Abstr.; HTFS Dig.; INSPEC (April 1972-); Int. Abstr. Oper. Res. [Select. Cov.]; Int. Aerosp. Abstr.; Int. Civil Eng. Abstr.; Int. Dev. Abstr.; J. Econ. Lit.; J. Plan. Lit.; Leis. Recreat. Tour. Abstr.; Maize Abstr.; Meteorol. Geoastrophys. Abstr.; Nematol. Abstr.; Pet. Abstr.; Res. Alert [Full Cov.]; Rural Dev. Abstr.; Sci. Cit. Index; SCISEARCH; Soc. Sci. Cit. Index [Select. Cov.]; Soft. Abstr. Eng.; Soils Fert.; Wheat Barley Trit. Abstr.; Wildl. Rev. (Jan. 1989-July 1992); World Agric. Econ.

US/0092-3699
**WATER RESOURCES RESEARCH SERIES (NASHVILLE).** (WATER RESOURCES RESEARCH SERIES.). [Water resour. res. ser.]. No. 1 (1969)-. Monographic series. English. Price varies per volume. Tennessee Department of Conservation, Division of Water Resources, 2611 West End, Nashville TN 37203. **CODEN** TWRSAS.
**Ind/Abst** GeoRef.

US/0501-2953
**WATER RESOURCES SERIES.** (WATER RESOURCES SERIES / ECONOMIC COMMISSION FOR ASIA AND THE FAR EAST.). **Added/Corp** United Nations. Economic Commission for Asia and the Far East. United Nations. Economic and Social Commission for Asia and the Pacific. United Nations. Office of Technical Co-operation. (1963)-. Government Publication. English. ir. Price varies per volume. United Nations Publications, 2 United Nations Plaza, Room DC2 0853, Department 007C, New York NY 10017. **Tel** (212)963-8303, (800)253-9646. **LC** JX1977; .A2. ***Continues*** *Flood Control Series.*
**Ind/Abst** GeoRef; Life Sci. Collect.

US/0084-3210
**WATER RESOURCES SERIES (LARAMIE).** (WATER RESOURCES SERIES.). [Water resour. ser.]. No. 1- May 1966-. Monographic series. English. Price varies per volume. University of Wyoming Water Resources Research Institute, PO Box 3008, Laramie WY 82070. **DD** 628. **CODEN** WUWWAG.
**Ind/Abst** GeoRef; Soils Fert.; World Agric. Econ.

US/0495-1026
**WATER RESOURCES SERIES (NASHVILLE, TENN.).** (WATER RESOURCES SERIES.). [Water resour. ser.]. **Added/Corp** Tennessee. Division of Water Resources. (19??)-. Monographic series. English. ir. Price varies per volume. Tennessee Department of Conservation, Division of Geology, 401 Church Street, Nashville TN 27243-0445. **Tel** (615)532-1516, (615)532-1500. **LC** GB651; .T44a. **DD** 553.7/0968. **CODEN** TWWRAG. Documents available from CASDDS.
**Ind/Abst** Chem. Abstr.

US/0161-2867
**WATER RESOURCES SPECIAL REPORT.** [Water resour. spec. rep.]. No. 1-. Academic Scholarly Publication. English. Price varies per volume. **CODEN** LWSRBB. Documents available from CASDDS.
**Ind/Abst** Chem. Abstr.; GeoRef.

US/0518-6374
**WATER RESOURCES SUMMARY (LITTLE ROCK).** (WATER RESOURCES SUMMARY.). **Added/Corp** United States. Geological Survey. Arkansas Geological Commission Arkansas Geological and Conservation Commission. Monographic series. English. Price varies per volume. Arkansas Geological Commission, 3815 West Roosevelt Road, Little Rock AR 72204. **Tel** (501)371-1646. **LC** TC424.A8; W38a. **DD** 551.4.

US/0083-7709
**WATER RESOURCES SYMPOSIUM.** [Water resour. symp.]. **Added/Corp** University of Texas at Austin. Center for Research in Water Resources. (1968)-. Academic Scholarly Publication. English. ir. Price varies per volume. Center for Research in Water Resources, UTA Balcones Research Center 119, Austin TX 78758. **Tel** (512)471-3131. **DD** 333. **NLM** W3 WA34. **CODEN** WARSA9. Index available (Free on request). Documents available from Article Express International, CASDDS.
**Desc:** Conference proceedings related to water use.
**Ind/Abst** Chem. Abstr. (19??-); Ei Page One (19??-); Energy Res. Abstr. (June 1978-); Eng. Index Annu. (19??-); GeoRef (19??-).

US
**WATER REUSE.** **VFOAT** OWRT/RU; RU. 79/1-. Monographic series. English. Price varies per volume. OWRT, Room 1310/18th & C Streets NW, Washington DC 20240.

US
**WATER RIGHTS RESUME. DIVISION 6.** English. Twelve times a year. $12.00. Clerk of the Water Court, Division 6, District Court, Steamboat Springs CO 80477. **Tel** (303)879-5020, FAX (303)879-3531. **ED** Janice M. Johner. **Circ:** 75 (ctrl).

SA/0378-4738
**WATER S. A.** [Water SA]. **VAT** Water South Africa. Vol. 1 (Apr. 1975)-. Academic Scholarly Publication. English (Afrikaans). qt. Free on request. Water Research Commission, 705 van der Ste; Box 824, 179 Pretorius Street, Pretoria 0001 South Africa. **Tel** 11 27 12 3300340, FAX 27 12 70 5925, telex 320464 WATKO SA. **(Subscription address:** PO Box 824, Pretoria 0001 South Africa**) ED** I. G. Buchan. **LC** TD201; .W345. **DD** 628.1. **CODEN** WASADV. Index available. cum. index. **Bk Rev. Ad Acc. Pr Rev. Circ:** 2,500 (ctrl). Documents available from Article Express International, The Genuine Article, BIOSIS Document Express, CASDDS, Documents on Demand.
**Desc:** The journal publishes refereed original work in all branches of water science, technology and engineering.
**Ind/Abst** Abstr. Bull. Inst. Pap. Sci. Tech.; Aqualine

Abstr.; BioBusiness; Biodeter. Abstr.; Bioeng. Abstr.; Biol. Abstr.; Chem. Abstr.; Coal Abstr.; Curr. Aware. Biol. Sci., CABS; Curr. Contents, Agric. Biol. Environ. Sci.; Curr. Ref. Fish Res.; Ei Page One; EMBASE; Eng. Index Annu. [Select. Cov.]; Environ. Abstr.; Fish Rev.; Food Sci. Technol. Abstr.; GeoRef; Health Saf. Sci. Abstr.; Helminthol. Abstr. (1991-); Irr. Drain. Abstr.; J. Ferrocement; Nutr. Abstr. Rev., Ser. A, Hum. Exp.; Life Sci. Collect.; Pollut. Abstr. Indexes; Res. Alert [Full Cov.]; Risk Abstr.; Soils Fert.; Weed Abstr.; Wheat Barley Trit. Abstr.

UK/0273-1223
**WATER SCIENCE AND TECHNOLOGY.** (WATER SCIENCE AND TECHNOLOGY : A JOURNAL OF THE INTERNATIONAL ASSOCIATION ON WATER POLLUTION RESEARCH.). [Water sci. technol.]. **Added/Corp** International Association on Water Pollution Research. International Association on Water Quality. **VFOAT** Water Science & Technology. Vol. 13, No. 1 (1981)-. Academic Scholarly Publication. English. Twenty-four times a year. $2370.00 (regular subscription), $3845.00 (combination subscription with Water Research) The Americas; £1590.00 (regular subscription), £2580.00 (combination subscription with Water Research) other. Pergamon Press, An Imprint of Elsevier Science Ltd., The Boulevard, Langford Lane, Kidlington, Oxford OX5 1GB United Kingdom. **Tel** 011 44 865 843000, 011 44 865 843699, FAX 011 44 865 843010. **(Subscription address:** Elsevier Science Ltd. Oxford Fulfillment Centre, PO Box 800, Kidlington, Oxford OX5 1DX United Kingdom.**) ED** Elizabeth Izod. **LC** TD419; .W38. **DD** 628.1/68/05. **CODEN** WSTED4. **[CCC]. Pr Rev.** available on microfilm and microfiche from University Microfilms International (UMI). Documents available from Article Express International, The Genuine Article, BIOSIS Document Express, CASDDS, Documents on Demand. ***Continues** Progress in Water Technology, 0306-6746.*
**Ind/Abst** Abstr. Bull. Inst. Pap. Sci. Tech.; AgBiotech News Inf.; AGRICOLA [Select. Cov.]; Agric. Eng. Abstr. (1991-); Aqualine Abstr.; AQUAREF; Aquat. Sci. Fish. Abstr. (Computer File); BioBusiness; Biocont. News Inf. (1991-); Biodeter. Abstr. (1991-); Biol. Abstr.; Chem. Abstr.; Coal Abstr.; Curr. Aware. Biol. Sci., CABS; Curr. Biotechnol.; Curr. Contents, Agric. Biol. Environ. Sci.; Curr. Ref. Fish Res.; Dairy Sci. Abstr.; Ecol. Abstr.; Ecology Abstr.; Ei Page One; EMBASE; Energy Inf. Abstr.; Eng. Index Annu.; Environ. Abstr.; Environ. Period. Bibliogr.; Fish Rev.; Fluid Abstr., Civil Eng.; Fluid Abstr. Proc. Eng.; FLUIDEX (1981-); Food Sci. Technol. Abstr.; For. Prod. Abstr.; Geogr. Abstr. Phys. Geogr.; Geogr. Abstr. Human Geogr.; Geol. Abstr.; GeoRef; Helminthol. Abstr. (19??-19??); Index Sci. Rev.; Index Vet.; Int. Dev. Abstr.; J. Ferrocement; J. Plan. Lit.; Microbiol. Abstr. Sect. B (19??-19??); Microbiol. Abstr. Sect. A; Microbiol. Abstr. Sect. C; Nematol. Abstr.; Nutr. Abstr. Rev., Ser. B, Live Feeds and Feed.; Life Sci. Collect.; PESTDOC; Pig News Inf.; Pollut. Abstr. Indexes; Potato Abstr.; Poult. Abstr.; Protozoolog. Abstr.; Res. Alert [Full Cov.]; Rev. Agric. Entomol.; Risk Abstr.; Sci. Cit. Index; SCISEARCH; Soc. Sci. Cit. Index [Select. Cov.]; Soils Fert.; Sorghum Mill. Abstr.; Sug. Indus. Abstr.; Vet. Bull.; Virol. AIDS Abstr.; Weed Abstr.; Wildl. Rev.

UK/0266-4615
**WATER SCIENCE REVIEWS.** ***Ceased.*** **See** Chemistry-Inorganic Chemistry.

UK/0307-1782
**WATER SERVICES YEARBOOK.** (1978)-. Periodical. English. an. £70.00 UK; £81.00, $162.00 other. Argus Press Group, Queensway House, 2 Queensway Redhill, Surrey RH1 1QS England. **Tel** 011 44 737 768611, 011 44 737 761685, FAX 011 44 737 760510, telex 948669 TOPJNL G. ***Continues** Water Services Handbook.*

SA/0257-8700
**WATER SEWAGE & EFFLUENT.** [Water sew. effl.]. **VFOAT** Water Sewage and Effluent. (1980)-. Periodical. English. qt. R30.70 South Africa; R44.00 other Africa; R84.00 other. Brooke Pattrick Publishing Limited, PO Box 422, Bedfordview 2008 South Africa. **Tel** 011 27 11 6224666, FAX 011 27 11 6167196. **UDC** 626.

UK/0306-2775
**WATER SPACE.** (1974)-. English. qt.
**Ind/Abst** Archit. Period. Index (Autumn 1977-1979).

UK/0735-1917
**WATER SUPPLY.** (WATER SUPPLY : THE REVIEW JOURNAL OF THE INTERNATIONAL WATER SUPPLY ASSOCIATION.). [Water supply]. **Added/Corp** International Water Supply Association. Vol. 1, No. 1 (March 1983)-. Academic Scholarly Publication. English (French). qt (4 issues). $594.00 US & Canada; £383.50 other. Blackwell Scientific Publications Ltd, Marston Book Services, PO Box 87, Oxford OX2 ODT UK. **Tel** 011 44 865 791155, FAX 011 44 865 791927, telex 837 515 MARDIS G. **LC** TD201; .W348. **DD** 628.1/05. **CODEN** WASUDN. **[CCC]. Ad Acc. Circ:** 300. available on microfilm and microfiche from University Microfilms International (UMI). Documents available from Article Express International, CASDDS.
**Desc:** A research journal publishing papers submitted at IWSA conferences. These conferences include the biennial IWSA congresses, specialized conferences and workshops and some regional conferences.
**Ind/Abst** Chem. Abstr. (1983-); Ecol. Abstr. (?-?); Ei Page One; EMBASE; Eng. Index Annu.; Environ. Period. Bibliogr.; Fluid Abstr., Civil Eng.; Fluid Abstr. Proc. Eng.; FLUIDEX (1983-); Geogr. Abstr. Phys. Geogr.; Geogr. Abstr. Human Geogr.; GeoRef; Int. Dev. Abstr.

UK/0364-7714
**WATER SUPPLY & MANAGEMENT.** ***Ceased.*** [Water supply manage.]. **VFOAT** Water Supply and Management. Vol. 1, No. 3-?. Academic Scholarly Publication. English. bm. A B Morse Company, 200 James Street, Barrington IL 60010. **LC** TD201; .W3468. **DD** 333.91/15. **CODEN** WSMADP. available on microfilm and microfiche from University Microfilms International (UMI). Documents available from Article Express International, CASDDS. ***Continues** Aqua (Oxford, Oxfordshire), 0147-3298.*
**Ind/Abst** AGRICOLA; AQUAREF; Bioeng. Abstr.; Chem. Abstr.; Coal Abstr.; Ei Page One; EMBASE; Eng. Index Annu.; Fluid Abstr., Civil Eng.; Fluid Abstr. Proc. Eng.; FLUIDEX (1977-); GeoRef.

US/0732-5312
**WATER SUPPLY OUTLOOK ... FOR THE NORTHEASTERN UNITED STATES. See** Earth Sciences-Hydrology.

US
**WATER SUPPLY OUTLOOK FOR THE WESTERN UNITED STATES. See** Earth Sciences-Hydrology.

UK
**WATER SUPPLY PAPERS OF THE INSTITUTE OF GEOLOGICAL SCIENCES. RESEARCH REPORT.** No. 4-. Monographic series. English (summaries and/or abstracts in French and German). Price varies per volume. Her Majesty's Stationery Office, 51 Nine Elms Lane, London SW8 5DR England. **Tel** 011 44 71 873 8459, 011 44 71 873 8499, FAX 011 44 71 873 8499, 011 44 71 873 8456, telex 297138. **(Subscription address:** PO Box 276, Public Centre, London SW8 5DT England**) CODEN** GWRRAI. ***Continues** Water Supply Papers of the Geological Survey of Great Britain.*
**Ind/Abst** GeoRef.

US
**WATER SYSTEMS NEWS AND HOME WATER REPORT.** (19??)-. Periodical. English. Twenty-five times a year. $435.00 US; $478.00 other. Water Systems News, 4282 Main Street, Chincoteague Island VA 23336. **Tel** (804)336-6782, FAX (804)336-1409. **ED** Annette Keen (editor's phone: (518)382-0565). Index available. cum. index.

US/0192-3633
**WATER TECHNOLOGY.** [Water technol.]. (197?)-. Periodical. English. Twelve times a year. $40.00 US & Canada; $90.00 others. National Trade Publications, 13 Century Hill Drive, Latham NY 12110. **Tel** (518)783-1281, FAX (518)783-1386. **ED** Susan Mayer. **DD** 628. **CODEN** WATTEQ. **[CCC]. Ad Acc. Circ:** 16,000 (ctrl).
**Desc:** Provides technical sales and marketing information to water treatment dealers, bottled water dealers, professional and specifying engineers and water treatment consultants.
**Ind/Abst** BioBusiness.

CC/0921-2639
**WATER TREATMENT.** [Water treat.]. **Added/Corp** Desalination and Water Re-Use Society, China. (1989)-. Academic Scholarly Publication. English. qt. $152.00. Development Center of Water Treatment Technology, PO Box 1207 Hangzhou, Zhejiang 310012 China, People's Republic of China. **Tel** 011 86 886924 ext. 403, FAX 011 86 0571 8054199, telex 35035. **ED** Gao Zhixiong. **LC** TD430; .W373. **DD** 628.1/62. **CODEN** WTREE2. **[CCC].** Index available. **Ad Acc. Circ:** 500. Documents available from CASDDS.
**Desc:** Serving those engaged in water treatment.
**Ind/Abst** Chem. Abstr.; Curr. Biotechnol.; EMBASE.

US/0276-7481
**WATER UTILITY OPERATING DATA. Added/Corp** American Water Works Association. (197?)-. English. be. $15.00 members, $30.00 others. AWWA, 6666 West Quincy Avenue, Denver CO 80235. **LC** HD4461; .A65a. **DD** 363.6/1/0973. ***Continues** AWWA Operating Data for Water Utilities, 0194-1828.*

US/0192-3374
**WATER, WASTEWATER-CHEMICAL AND RADIOLOGICAL ANALYSES : TABULATION.** English. an. Department of Social Services / Utah, Division of Family Services, 333 South 2nd East, Salt Lake City UT 84111. **LC** TD224.U8; W37. **DD** 553/.7/09792.

US/0043-1443
**WATER WELL JOURNAL.** [Water well j.]. **Added/Corp** National Water Well Association. **VFOAT** WWJ. (Summer 1947)-. Academic Scholarly Publication. English. mo. $24.00 North America; $48.00 other. Ground Water Publishing, 6375 Riverside Drive, Dublin OH 43017. **Tel** (614)761-3222, (800)332-2104, FAX (614)761-3446. **ED** Anita Bacco Stanley. **LC** TD405; .W3. **DD** 622/.37/905. **CODEN** WWJOA9. **[CCC]. Bk Rev. Ad Acc. Circ:** 37,000 (ctrl). Documents available from Documents on Demand. ***Supersedes** Illinois Well Driller.*
**Desc:** The voice of the ground-water industry for more than 30 years. Covers topics of importance to drillers, suppliers, manufacturers and scientists alike.
**Ind/Abst** Ei Page One; EMBASE; Environ. Abstr.; Fluid Abstr., Civil Eng.; Fluid Abstr. Proc. Eng.; FLUIDEX; GeoRef; Sel. Water Resour. Abstr.

CN/0226-4552
**WATER WELL RECORDS FOR ONTARIO.** [Water well rec. Ont.]. **Main/Corp** Ontario. Water Resources Branch. Began publication in 1975. Periodical. English. Hydrology and Monitoring Section, Water Resources Branch, Ministry of the Environment, 135 St Clair Avenue West, Toronto Ontario M4V 1P5 Canada. **DD** 628.1/14/09713. ***Supersedes** Water Well Records for Ontario, 0226-4552.*

UK/0262-9909
**WATERBULLETIN.** [Water bull.]. **VFOAT** Water Bulletin. No. 1 (April 2, 1982)-. Academic Scholarly Publication. English. Fifty-two times a year (Fri.). £50.00 UK; £70.00 EEC Countries; £75.00 others. Water Authorities Association, St. Peter's House Hardshead, Sheffield S11 EU5 England. **Tel** 011 42 742737331. **ED** Les Freeman. **LC** TD257; .W4. **DD** 363.6/1/0941. **Bk Rev. Ad Acc. Circ:** 5,744 (ctrl). ***Formed by the union of** Water (London, England), 0305-3105 **and** Bulletin (National Water Council (Great Britain)).*
**Desc:** Reports on the water industry in the United Kingdom; news and in-depth features plus information and advisory section.
**Ind/Abst** Coal Abstr.; EMBASE; Fluid Abstr., Civil Eng.; Fluid Abstr. Proc. Eng.; FLUIDEX (1982-).

UK/0262-8104
**WATERLINES.** [Waterlines]. **VFOAT** Water Lines. **VAT** Water Lines. (198?)-. Periodical. English. qt. $37.00 (institutions), $28.00 (individuals). Intermediate Technology Publishing Ltd., 103-104 Southampton Row, London WC1B 4HH England. **Tel** 011 44 71 436 9761, FAX 011 44 71 436 2013, telex 268312. **ED** Corwen McCutcheon, Neal Burton. **Bk Rev. Ad Acc. Circ:** 3,500.
**Desc:** Contains illustrated, practical articles by specialists and fieldworkers on appropriate technology for water supply and sanitation in the 3rd world.
**Ind/Abst** Fluid Abstr., Civil Eng.; Fluid Abstr. Proc. Eng.; FLUIDEX; Geogr. Abstr. Human Geogr.; Int. Dev. Abstr.; Rural Dev. Abstr.; Trop. Dis. Bull.; World Agric. Econ.

US
**WATERMASTER SERVICE IN THE WEST COAST BASIN, LOS ANGELES COUNTY. Main/Corp** California. Dept. of Water Resources. Southern District. English. an. Department of Water Resources / California, PO Box 942836, Sacramento CA 94236-0001. **Tel** (916)445-3553. **LC** TD224.C3; C24A. **DD** 333.91/0417/0979493.

NE/0043-1486
**WATERSCHAPSBELANGEN.** ***Title Change.*** [Waterschapsbelangen]. (19??)-(19??). Academic Scholarly Publication. Dutch. sm. Unie Van Waterschappen, J V Oldenbarneveltlaan 5, Postbus 80200, 2582 Gravenhage Netherlands. **Tel** 070-519751. **LC** HD1683.N2; W3. Index available. **Bk Rev. Ad Acc.** ***Continued by** Het Waterschap.*
**Desc:** Water-management, water-resources, press-releases, studies about water-problems, new land-reclamation, dikes, etc. juridical articles.
**Ind/Abst** EMBASE.

US/0747-9735
**WATERWORLD NEWS.** ***Title Change.*** **See** Environmental Issues-Pollution and Waste Management.

●US/1068-5839
**WATERWORLD REVIEW.** [Waterworld rev.]. **VFOAT** Water World Review. Vol. 9, No. 1 (Jan./Feb. 1993)-. Trade Publication. English. Six times a year. $25.00 US; $32.00 Canada and Mexico; $38.00 other. PennWell Publishing Company, 1421 South Sheridan, PO Box 1260, Tulsa OK 74101. **Tel** (918)835-3161, (800)331-4463, FAX (918)831-9497. **(Subscription address:** WaterWorld Review, Publishing Services, PO Box 2847, Tulsa OK 74101.**) LC** TD430; .W396. **DD** 628.1/05. ***Continues** Waterworld News, 0747-9735.*
**Desc:** Provides comprehensive coverage of public and private clean water and wastewater systems, as well as industrial wastewater systems.

US/0735-5424
**WESTERN WATER.** [West. water]. (Sept./Oct. 1975)-. Periodical. English. bm. $22.00 (US); $27.00 (Canada); $34.00 (other). Western Water Education Foundation, 717 K Street #517, Sacramento CA 95814-3406. **Tel** (916)444-6240, FAX (916)448-7699. **ED** Rita Schmidt Sudman. **Circ:** 16,000 (ctrl). ***Continues** Western Water News.*
**Desc:** Educational non-partisan material on California water issues.
**Ind/Abst** Environ. Period. Bibliogr.; GeoRef; PAIS Int. Print.

# Water Resources — Abstracting, Bibliographies and Statistics

**UK**
**WHO'S WHO IN THE WATER INDUSTRY. YEARBOOK.** (19??)-. Directory. English. an. £30.00. Turret Group, 177 Hagden Lane, Watford Herts WD1 8LN United Kingdom. **Tel** 011 44 923 228577, FAX 011 44 923 221346.

AU/0379-5349
**WIENER MITTEILUNGEN, WASSER, ABWASSER, GEWASSER.** [Wien. Mitt., Wasser-Abwasser-Gewasser]. (1968)-. Academic Scholarly Publication. German. **LC** TD203; .W27. **CODEN** WMWAAU. Documents available from CASDDS.
**Ind/Abst** Chem. Abstr.; Maize Abstr.; Wheat Barley Trit. Abstr.

US/0740-4700
**WISCONSIN WATER QUALITY ... REPORT TO CONGRESS.** [Wisc. water qual., rep. Cong.]. **Main/Corp** Wisconsin. Dept. of Natural Resources. **VFOAT** Wisconsin Water Quality. 1982-. English. be. Free in single copies. Department of Natural Resources / Wisconsin, Bureau of Research, PO Box 7921, Madison WI 53707. **Tel** (608)266-2121. **LC** TD224.W6; W56A. **DD** 363.7/3942/09775. **Circ:** 500 (ctrl). **Continues** Wisconsin ... Water Quality Inventory Report to Congress, 0191-3190.

NZ/0110-0815
**WISPAS.** [Wispas]. **VFOAT** Water in the Soil-Plant-Atmosphere System. (1975)-. Periodical. English. ir.
**Ind/Abst** Agric. Eng. Abstr.; Field Crop Abstr.; Potato Abstr.

**US**
**WMS REPORT. Added/Corp** Water Management Synthesis Project. Water Management Synthesis II Project. **VAT** Water Management Synthesis Report. (1981)-. Monographic series. English.
**Ind/Abst** Helminthol. Abstr. (1991-); Protozoolog. Abstr.

**UK**
**WORLD BANK STUDIES IN WATER SUPPLY AND SANITATION. VFOAT** Studies in Water Supply and Sanitation. Began publication in 1982. Monographic series. English. Price varies per volume.

**US**
**WORLD RIVERS REVIEW.** Periodical. English. qt. $100.00 institutions; $50.00 non-profit organizations; $30.00 individuals. International Rivers Network, 1847 Berkeley Way, Berkeley CA 94703. **Tel** (510)848-1155, FAX (510)848-1008, telex 6503532706. **ED** Juliette Majot. **Bk Rev.** ctrl circ.

**UK**
**WORLD WATER AND ENVIRONMENTAL ENGINEER.** Vol. 13, No. 2 (June 1990)-. Periodical. English. mo. £73.00 UK; £82.00 other. Faversham House Group Ltd, Faversham House, 111 Saint James Road, Croydon Surrey CR9 2TH England. **Tel** 011 44 81 684 4082. **(Subscription address:** Computer Action, Gerrard House, 2/6 Homesdale Road, Bromley BR2 9WL England.) **LC** TD201; .W73. **Continues** World Water, 0140-9050.
**Ind/Abst** Environ. Period. Bibliogr.; Fluid Abstr., Civil Eng.; Fluid Abstr. Proc. Eng.; FLUIDEX (19??-); Soils Fert.

US/0073-5442
**WRC RESEARCH REPORT.** [W.R.C. res. rep.]. **Main/Corp** Illinois. University at Urbana-Champaign. Water Resources Center. **Added/Corp** University of Illinois at Urbana-Champaign. Water Resources Center. **VFOAT** Research Report. **VAT** Water Resources Center Research Report. No. 1 (1966)-. Monographic series. English. ir. Free. WRC Research Report, University of Illinois, 2535 Hydrosystems Lab, 205 North Mathews, Urbana IS 61801-2397. **Tel** (217)333-0536, FAX (217)333-8046, telex 5101011969. **ED** Holly B Korab. **LC** HD1694; .A136. **DD** 333.9/1/008. **CODEN** IUWRAH. **Circ:** 350. Documents available from Article Express International, BIOSIS Document Express. **Continues** WRC Research Report, 0073-5442.
**Desc:** Project summary reports of projects funded by the Water Resources Center.
**Ind/Abst** Bioeng. Abstr.; Biol. Abstr.; Ei Page One; Eng. Index Annu.; GeoRef.

**US**
**WRD INFORMATION GUIDE.** See Earth Sciences-Hydrology.

US/0544-3466
**WRRC BULLETIN.** (BULLETIN / WATER RESOURCES RESEARCH CENTER, UNIVERSITY OF MINNESOTA.). [WRRC bull.]. **Added/Corp** University of Minnesota. Water Resesouces Research Center. United States. Department of the Interior. **VFOAT** W.R.R.C. Bulletin. **VAT** Water Resources Research Center Bulletin. (1965)-. Monographic series. English. ir. Price varies per volume. University of Minnesota Biological Sciences Center, 866 Biological Sciences Center, St. Paul MN 55108. **CODEN** MWCBAT. Documents available from Article Express International.
**Ind/Abst** Bioeng. Abstr.; Ei Page One; Eng. Index Annu.; GeoRef.

US/0163-9765
**WRRI.** (WRRI / WATER RESOURCES RESEARCH INSTITUTE, OREGON STATE UNIVERSITY.). [WRRI]. **Added/Corp** Oregon State University. Water Resources Research Institute. United States. Office of Water Resources Research. **VAT** Water Resources Research Institute. (1970)-. English. ir. Free. Water Resources Research Institute, Oregon State University, Corvallis OR 97331. **Tel** (503)754-4022. **LC** HD1694.O7; A13. **DD** 333.91/00795/05. **CODEN** OSUWD9. Documents available from CASDDS.
**Ind/Abst** Chem. Abstr.; GeoRef.

US/0097-5729
**WRRI BULLETIN.** [WRRI bull.]. **Main/Corp** Auburn University. Water Resources Research Institute. **VAT** Water Resources Research Institute Bulletin. (19??)-. Monographic series. English. ir. Price varies per volume. Auburn University / WRRI, 202 Hargis Hall, Auburn AL 36849. **LC** TC1; .A85. **CODEN** WRRBA9. Documents available from BIOSIS Document Express, CASDDS.
**Ind/Abst** Biol. Abstr.; Chem. Abstr.; GeoRef.

US/0731-7557
**WRRI REPORT.** [WRRI rep.]. **Main/Corp** New Mexico Water Resources Research Institute. **VAT** Water Resources Research Institute Report. No. 3-. Monographic series. English. ir. Price varies per volume. New Mexico Water Resources Research Institute, New Mexico State University, Box 3167, Las Cruces NM 88003. **Tel** (505)646-1813. **CODEN** NMWRAG. cum. index. **Continues** W.R.R.I. Publication.
**Desc:** Five-ten technical reports on water-related topics.
**Ind/Abst** GeoRef.

**US**
**WSTB NEWSLETTER. Added/Corp** National Research Council Water Science and Technology Board. **VFOAT** Water Science and Technology Board Newsletter. (19??)-. Newsletter. English. Four times a year. Free on request. National Academy Press, 2101 Constitution Avenue NW, Lockbox 285, Washington DC 20055. **Tel** (800)624-6242, (202)334-3313, FAX (202)334-2451.
**Desc:** Information on current studies and feature articles related to water resources.

US/0098-0846
**WYOMING STATE PLAN. Main/Corp** Wyoming. Water Quality Division. English. Wyoming Department of Environmental Quality Water Division, Cheyenne WY 82002. **LC** HC107.W93; E59A. **DD** 333.9/1/009787.

US/0147-4197
**WYOMING WATER POLLUTION CONTROL PROGRAM PLAN. Main/Corp** Wyoming. Water Quality Division. English. an. Water Quality Division, Hathaway Building, Cheyenne WY 82002. **LC** TD224.W8; W96A. **DD** 363.6/1/09787.

US/0092-2676
**YEAR REPORT - TEMPORARY STATE COMMISSION ON THE WATER SUPPLY NEEDS OF SOUTHEASTERN NEW YORK.** (YEAR REPORT.). [Year rep. - Tempor. State Comm. Water Supply Needs Southeast. N. Y.]. **Main/Corp** New York (State). Temporary State Commission on the Water Supply Needs of Southeastern New York. (1972)-. English. an. Department of State / New York, 162 Washington Avenue, Albany NY 12231. **Tel** (518)474-6957. **LC** TD224.N7; N47a. **DD** 333.9/1/009.747.

JA/0385-1001
**ZOSUI GIJUTSU.** (ZOSUI GIJUTSU / ZOSUI SOKUSHIN SENTA.). [Zosui gijutsu]. **Added/Corp** Zosui Sokushin Senta (Tokyo, Japan). **VFOAT** Journal of Water Re-use Technology; Journal of Water Reuse Technology. (1975)-. Academic Scholarly Publication. Japanese. qt. Agune, (Agne Publishing Inc.), 31-9, Nishiwaseda 3 Chome, Shinjukuku, Tokyo 160, Japan. **CODEN** ZGIJDF. Documents available from CASDDS.
**Ind/Abst** Chem. Abstr.; Coal Abstr.

## ABSTRACTING, BIBLIOGRAPHIES AND STATISTICS

**CN**
**AQUAREF.** Abstracting/Indexing Service. English (French). bm. 40.00Can$ per connect hour (available in Canada only). WATDOC, Client Services, Interpretation and Access Division, Surveys and Information Systems Branch, Ecosystem Sciences and Evaluation Directorate, Environment Canada, Ottawa, Ontario K1A 0H3 Canada. **Tel** (819)953-1529, . **(Subscription address:** CAN/OLE CAN/SDI, CISTI, Client Services, National Research Council Canada, Ottawa Ontario K1A 0S2 Canada; Telex: 053-3115) available on CD-ROM from OPTIM Corporation; and National Information Service Corporation (NISC). **Continues** Canadian Environment; Environnement.
**Desc:** Bibliographic database providing references to scientific and technical literature published by Canadian Environment and other federal, provincial, territorial and municipal government departments and agencies, universities and research establishments. Includes Canadian and some international journals. The file is updated every two months.

US/0092-0355
**BASIN BIBLIOGRAPHY (OLYMPIA).** (BASIN BIBLIOGRAPHY.). Bibliography. English. Water Resources Information System, Olympia WA 98504. **LC** Z7935; .B37. **DD** 016.3339/1/009797.

**II**
**BIBLIOGRAPHY OF IRRIGATION, DRAINAGE, RIVER TRAINING AND FLOOD CONTROL. BIBLIOGRAPHIE RELATIVE AUX IRRIGATIONS, AU DRAINAGE, A LA REGULARISATION DES COURS D'EAU ET LA MAITRISE DES CRUES. Added/Corp** International Commission on Irrigation and Drainage. **VFOAT** Bibliographie Relative aux Irrigations, au Drainage, a la Regularisation des Cours d'Eau et la Maitrise des Crues. (19??)-. Bibliography. English (French). an. $25.00. International Commission on Irrigation and Drainage, 48 Nyaya Marg Chanakyapuri, New Delhi 110021 India. **Tel** 011 91 11 3016837, telex 031-65920 ICID IN. **(Subscription address:** Prints India, 11 Darya Ganj, New Delhi, 110002 India, (Phone: 011 91 11 3268645)) **Continues** Bibliography on Irrigation, Drainage, River Training and Flood Control.

US/0072-7326
**GREAT LAKES RESEARCH CHECKLIST. Added/Corp** Great Lakes Commission. University of Michigan. Great Lakes Research Division. No. 1 (Dec. 1959)-. English. sa. Free. Great Lakes Commission, 400 Fourth St., Ann Arbor MI 48103. **Tel** (313)665-9135, FAX (313)665-4370. **ED** Albert G. Ballert. **DD** 016.977. **Circ:** 800 (ctrl). available on microfilm from University Microfilms International (UMI).
**Desc:** Bibliography of Great Lakes; articles and books.

**US**
**PCB IN WATER : A BIBLIOGRAPHY.** Began with V. 1 (Oct. 1968). Government Publication. English. US Department of the Interior / Water Resources Scientific Information Center, Washington DC 20240.

**US**
**SELECTED ANNOTATED BIBLIOGRAPHY ON THE ANALYSIS OF WATER RESOURCE SYSTEMS, A.** V. 6- Sept. 1975-. Bibliography. English. an. **ED** D P Loucks. **NLM** ZWA 675 S46. **Continues** Selected Annotated Bibliography on the Analysis of Water Resource Systems.

**IO**
**STATISTIK AIR MINUM = WATER SUPPLY STATISTICS. Added/Corp** Indonesia. Biro Pusat Statistik. Indonesia. Bagian Statistik Pertambangan, Energi, dan Konstruksi. **VFOAT** Water Supply Statistics. (19??)-. English (Indonesian). Biro Pusat Statistik, JLN Dr Sutomo 8 Kotak, Pos 1003, Jakarta 10710 Indonesia. **Tel** 3728007, 374908. **LC** HD4465.I55; S73. **DD** 333.91/009598. **Bk Rev. Ad Acc.** ctrl circ.

**UK**
**THAMES WATER STATISTICS. Main/Corp** Thames Water Authority. Planning Directorate. Central Information Unit. English. an. Thames Water Authority / Reading England, Reading Bridge House, Reading England. **LC** TC464.T4; T43A. **DD** 363.6/1/09422.

US/1064-6418
**TWINE LINE : OHIO SEA GRANT PROGRAM NEWSLETTER.** See Fish and Fisheries.

US/0149-029X
**WATER INDUSTRY STATISTICAL PROFILE, A. Main/Corp** Missouri Public Service Commission. Office of Economic Research. Statistical Publication. English. an. $4.50. Public Service Commission / Missouri, c/o Economic Research, PO Box 360, Jefferson City MO 65101. **LC** HD4464.M8; M57A. **DD** 338.4/3.

# Women's Interests

# WOMEN'S INTERESTS

FR
**20 ANS.** mo. 200.00F Europe; 255.00F US & Canada; 285.00F other. Excelsior Publications, 1 rue du Colonel Pierre Avia, 75503 Paris Cedex 15 France. **Tel** 011 33 1 46484848, FAX 011 33 1 46484793.

US/0567-5111
**ABOGADA INTERNACIONAL. THE INTERNATIONAL WOMAN LAWYER, LA.** See Law-International Law.

US/1061-768X
**ABOUT WOMEN ON CAMPUS.** See Education.

US/1053-4083
**ACTION ALERT (WASHINGTON, D.C. 1980).** (ACTION ALERT. AAUW.). [Action alert]. **Added/Corp** American Association of University Women. **VFOAT** AAUW Action Alert; AA. (1980)-. Periodical. English. mo. $25.00 (nonmembers); $20.00 (members). American Association of University Women, 1111 16th Street Northwest, Membership Department, Washington DC 20037. **Tel** (202) 785-7759. **DD** 346.

CN/0820-5728
**ACTION - NATIONAL ACTION COMMITTEE ON THE STATUS OF WOMEN.** *Title Change.* (ACTION : A BULLETIN FROM THE NATIONAL ACTION COMMITTEE ON THE STATUS OF WOMEN.). [Action - Natl. Action Comm. Status Women]. **Added/Corp** National Action Committee on the Status of Women. **VFOAT** Action. (1986)-(199?). Bulletin. English (French). Eight times a year. Action Bulletin, 344 Bloor Street West/Suite 505, Toronto Ontario M5S 1W9 Canada. **Tel** (416)922-3246. **ED** Pat Daley. **DD** 305.4/2/06071. **Circ:** 300. *Continues* Action Bulletin (National Action Committee on the Status of Women), 0832-1418. *Continued by* Action Now (Toronto, Ont.), 0820-5728.

CN/0701-1547
**ACTION (WINNIPEG).** (ACTION.). **Added/Corp** Manitoba Action Committee on the Status of Women. (May 1973)-. Periodical. English. Nine times a year. 50.00Can$ (institutions); 25.00Can$ (individuals). Manitoba Action Committee on the Status of Women, 702 70 Arthur Street, Winnipeg Manitoba R3B 1G7 Canada. **Tel** (204)946-5049. **DD** 301.41/2/097127. **Bk Rev. Ad Acc. Circ:** 500 (ctrl).
**Desc:** A voluntary non-profit organization working through political action, public education and personal growth to improve attitudes, raise issues and remove inequalities affecting women today.

AT/1031-282X
**ACTIVE (BELCONNEN).** See Recreation, Leisure-Sports.

US/0883-0029
**AEGIS (WASHINGTON, D.C.).** *Suspended.* See Political Science-Civil Rights.

US/0886-1099
**AFFILIA.** See Sociology-Social Services and Welfare.

US/0162-8038
**AFFIRMATIONS.** See Religion and Theology.

CN/0849-987X
**AFFIRMATIVE ACTION/STATUS OF WOMEN.** See Political Science-Civil Rights.

UK/0953-9816
**AFRICAN WOMAN. Added/Corp** Akina Mama wa Afrika (Organization). No. 1 (March 1988)-. Periodical. English. Four times a year (June, July, Dec., Jan.). £20.00 (institutions), £8.00 (individuals) Africa & UK; £25.00 (institutions), £10.00 (individuals) other. African Woman, London Women Center, Wesley House, 4 Wild Court, London WC2B 5AU England. **Tel** 011 44 71 4301044, FAX 011 44 71 8313947. **ED** Bisi Adeleye-Fayemi (editor's phone: 44 71 4050678). **LC** DA125.N4; A38. **DD** 305.48/896041/05. **Bk Rev. Pr Rev. Circ:** 5,000 (ctrl).
**Desc:** Economics, politics, culture and development issues are all discussed with and African women's perspective, in an accessible style. Features interviews, news, reviews, and listings from across the continent and the diaspora and fills a gaping hole in both the African print media and development publishing.

US/0091-3812
**AGENCY ACCOUNTABILITY SURVEY.** See Economics-Labor.

US
**AGENDA.** See Journalism.

JA
**AGORA (TOKYO JAPAN : 1972).** (AGORA.). (1972)-. Periodical. Japanese. mo. $165.00. Boc Shuppanbu, 9-6 Shinjuku 1, Shinjuku-ku Tokyo-to 160 Japan. **Tel** (03)354-3941. **(Subscription address:** Japan Publications Trading Company, Ltd., PO Box 5030, Tokyo International, Tokyo 100-31 Japan.) **ED** Chiyo Saito. **LC** HQ1761; .A35 . **Bk Rev. Ad Acc. Circ:** 900.
**Desc:** Books on feminism.

SJ/0255-4070
**AHFAD JOURNAL, THE. Added/Corp** KullÂiyat al-Ahfad al-Jamiiyah lil-Banat. **VFOAT** Majallat Al-Ahfad. Vol. 1 (1984)-. Academic Scholarly Publication. English (Arabic). Twice a year (June & Dec.). $40.00 (institutions), $25.00 (individuals). Ahfad University College for Women, 4141 North Henderson Road, Suite 1216, Arlington VA 22203. **Tel** (703)525-9045, FAX (703)351-0782. **ED** Amna ElSadile Bodri. **LC** HQ1793.5; .A13. **DD** 305.4/09624/05. **Bk Rev.** (Qty: 8-10). **Pr Rev. Circ:** 200. available on microfilm and microfiche from University Microfilms International (UMI). Documents available.
**Desc:** Research and scholarly articles on the roles of women in developing countries and women in development.
**Ind/Abst** Index Islam. Lit.; Int. Bibliogr. Sociol.; Int. Labour Doc.; LABORDOC; Multicult. Educ. Abstr.; Sociol. Educ. Abstr.; Stud. Women Abstr.; Middle East J.; Women Stud. Abstr.

QA
**AL-JAWHARAH.** Periodical. Arabic. 15.00. Muassasat Al-Ahd Lil-Sihafah Wa-Al-Tibaah Wa-Al-Nashr, PO Box 2531, Al-Dawhah Qatar. **Tel** 414575. **ED** Abdullah Al-Aussaini. **LC** AP95.A6; J38. **Bk Rev. Ad Acc. Circ:** 16,000 (ctrl).
**Desc:** This is the only women's magazine here, so we cover all that concerns women. Home, fashions, child care, cosmetics, etc.

AE
**AL-JAZAIRIYAH. Added/Corp** Ittihad al-Watani lil-Nisa al-Jazairiyat. **VFOAT** Djazairia; Jazairia. (1970)-. Periodical. Arabic. mo. **LC** HQ1791.5; .J38.

SJ
**AL-MARAH AL-JADIDAH.** V. 1 (March 1975)-. Periodical. Arabic. £s0.05. PO Box 363, Al-Khartum Sudan. **LC** HQ1104; .M37.

LE
**AL-RAIDAH. Added/Corp** Beirut University College. Institute for Women's Studies in the Arab World. No. 1 (May 1976)-. Periodical. Arabic. qt. £5.00. Beirut University College Institute for Women's Studies, PO Box 11-4080, Beirut Lebanon. **LC** HQ1784; .A27.

FR
**AL-SHARQIYAH. VFOAT** Elle; Women's Saudi Arabian Magazine; Arab Woman's Magazine; Sharikah-Elle. Periodical. Arabic. mo. 185.00. Al-Sharikah Al-Sharqiyah Al-Alamiyah, 6 R Ancelle, 92521 Neuilly Y-Sue-Seine Cedex Paris France. **LC** AP95.A6; S43.

US/1055-2227
**ALASKAMEN USA.** [AlaskaMen USA]. **VFOAT** Alaska Men USA. Vol. 3, Issue 1 (Jan. 1990)-. Periodical. English. qt (4 issues). $34.95. AlaskaMen Magazine, 1013 East Dimond Boulevard #522, Anchorage AK 99515. **Tel** (907)522-1492, FAX (907)344-1493. **ED** Susie Carter. **DD** 920. **Ad Acc. Circ:** 100,000. *Continues* AlaskaMen, 1041-4002.
**Desc:** A magazine targeted to the unmarried female audience of career-oriented, educated, self-sufficient professionals. Contains profiles and photos of the most elegible bachelors in Alaska and the USA. Also included are articles on health, beauty, single parenting, travel, sports and entertainment.

CN/1182-7718
**ALBERTA ADVISORY COUNCIL ON WOMEN'S ISSUES.** (ALBERTA ADVISORY COUNCIL ON WOMEN'S ISSUES : [NEWSLETTER].). [Alta. Advis. Counc. Women's Issues]. **Added/Corp** Alberta Advisory Council on Women's Issues. **VFOAT** AACWI; AACWI Newsletter. Vol. 3, No. 2 (May 1990)-. Periodical. English. **DD** 354.71230081/3. *Continues* Alberta Advisory Council on Women's Issues. Council Communique, 0844-6415.

US/1058-5826
**ALBERTSEN'S SINGLES DIRECTORY.** See Men's Interests.

US
**ALF NEWS / ASSOCIATION OF LIBERTARIAN FEMINISTS. Added/Corp** Association of Libertarian Feminists. **VAT** Association of Libertarian Feminists News. No. 33 (Winter 1990)-. Periodical. English. Association of Libertarian Feminists, 515 Revere Beach Boulevard #808, Revere MA 02151. **Tel** (617)574-1004, (617)286-1719. *Continues* Association of Libertarian Feminists News.

NO
**ALLE KVINNER; MAGAZINE FOR WOMEN.** Periodical. Norwegian. wk. Bladcentraalen, Postboks 5162, Majorstuen Oslo 3 Norway.

CN/0710-0884
**ALMANACH DE LA FEMME.** [Alm. femme]. 81-. French. an. $4.95 per volume. Messageries Dynamiques Inc, 775 Boulevard Lebeau, Saint-Laurent Quebec H4N 1S5 Canada. **Tel** (800)463-4645, (514)332-0680. **DD** 305.4/09714.

US/0191-0183
**AMERICAN BAPTIST WOMAN, THE.** See Religion and Theology-Protestantism.

US/1059-4701
**AMERICAN SINGLES MAGAZINE.** See Men's Interests.

US/1042-5985
**AMERICAN UNIVERSITY STUDIES. SERIES XXVII, FEMINIST STUDIES.** [Am. univ. stud. Ser. XXVII, Fem. stud.]. **VFOAT** Feminist Studies. (1990)-. English. ir. Peter Lang Publishing, 62 West 45th Street, 4th Floor, New York NY 10036. **Tel** (212)764-1471, (800)770-5264, telex 6973364 PLNY. **DD** 305.

US
**AMERICAN WOMAN (NEW YORK, N.Y.: 1987).** (THE AMERICAN WOMAN.). **Added/Corp** Congressional Caucus for Women's Issues. Women's Research and Education Institute. Women's Research & Education Institute. (1988)-. Periodical. English. an. $10.95 paper edition; $24.95 hardcover edition. W W Norton & Company Inc, 500 Fifth Avenue, New York NY 10110. **Tel** (800)233-4830. **ED** Sara E Rix. **LC** HQ1402; .A52. **DD** 305.4/0973.

US/1054-9595
**AMERICAN WOMAN (NEW YORK, N.Y. 1991).** (AMERICAN WOMAN.). [Am. woman]. Vol. 1, No. 1 (March/April 1991)-. Periodical. English. bm (6 issues). GCR Publishing Group, 1700 Broadway, 34th Floor, New York NY 10019. **Tel** (212)541-7100, (800)435-0715, FAX (212)245-1241. **(Subscription address:** Kable Publishers Aide, 308 East Hitt Street, Subscription Department, Mt. Morris IL 61054-1473.) **ED** Lynn Varacalli. **DD** 051. **Bk Rev.**
**Desc:** Magazine for the woman who wants to reach her potential, both personally and professionally. A national lifestyle that speaks directly to the evolving woman of today.

IT/1120-432X
**AMICA.** (1962)-. Periodical. Italian. wk. $240.00 US. RCS Rizzoli Periodici, Via A Rizzoli 2, 20132 Milan Italy. **Tel** 011 39 2 27200720. **UDC** 64.

FR
**AMINA.** (19??)-. Periodical. French. mo. 145.00F France; 220.00F French speaking Africa and Europe; 350.00F other. Societe SAPEF, 11 rue de Teheran, 75008 Paris France. **Tel** 011 33 1 45627476, FAX 011 33 1 45632248, telex 641916F. **ED** Assiatou Diallo. **LC** HQ1101; .A45. **Bk Rev. Ad Acc. Circ:** 92,000.
**Desc:** Magazine of female information for African and West Indies women.

UK
**ANNABEL.** No. 1, (Mar. 1966)-. Periodical. English. Twelve times a year. $18.96 UK; $23.01 other. D C Thomson and Company Ltd, 80 Kingsway East, Dundee DD1 8SL Scotland. **Tel** 011 44 382 23131. **LC** HQ1101; .A55.

US/0741-9899
**ANNOTATED GUIDE TO WOMEN'S PERIODICALS IN THE U.S. & CANADA, THE.** [Annot. guide women's period. U.S. Can.]. **VFOAT** Annotated Guide to Women's Periodicals in the United States and Canada. Vol. 2, No. 1 (April 1983)-. Periodical. English. sa. $20.00. The Women's Programs Office, Earlham College, c/o NSIWS, Box E-94, Earlham College, Richmond IN 47374. **Tel** (317)962-6561. **ED** Terry Mehlman. **LC** Z7962; .A56; HQ1101. **DD** 016.3054/05. **Ad Acc. Circ:** 200 (ctrl). *Continues* Annotated Guide to Women's Periodicals in the U.S.
**Desc:** Provides up-to-date information on over 250 feminist and alternative women's periodicals. Arranged by subject. Title and geographical indices.

CN/0823-0188
**ANNUAIRE DES FEMMES DE MONTREAL, L'.** See Sociology-Social Services and Welfare.

TZ
**ANNUAL REPORT AND REPORT OF ... TRAINING PROGRAMME - EASTERN AND SOUTHERN AFRICAN MANAGEMENT INSTITUTE. Main/Corp** Eastern and Southern African Management Institute. **VFOAT** Training for Development Planning and Women: An African Perspective. 16 Sept. 1980-15 Sept. 1981)-. English. an. Eastern and Southern African Management Institute, PO Box 3030, Arusha Tanzania. **LC** HN780.Z9; C647A. **DD** 307./14/088042.

# Women's Interests

**US/0362-9252**
**ANNUAL REPORT - COMMISSION ON THE STATUS OF WOMEN OF SOUTH DAKOTA.** **Main/Corp** South Dakota. Commission on the Status of Women. (19??)-. English. Commission on the Status of Women / South Dakota, Capitol Lake Plaza Building No 300, 711 Wells, Pierre SD 57501. **LC** HQ1438.S6; S68A. **DD** 353.9/783/008.

**CN/0823-5864**
**ANNUAL REPORT INCLUDING ... OBJECTIVES AND ACTION PLANS - EQUAL OPPORTUNITIES FOR WOMEN.** (ANNUAL REPORT INCLUDING ... OBJECTIVES AND ACTION PLANS.). [Annu. rep. incl. obj. action plans - Equal Oppor. Women]. **Main/Corp** Canada. Health and Welfare Canada. Equal Opportunity for Women. English (French). an. Health and Welfare Canada Equal Opportunities for Women, Ottawa Ontario. **LC** RA184; .D46B. **DD** 354.710084.

**AT**
**ANNUAL REPORT OF THE NATIONAL WOMEN'S ADVISORY COUNCIL ... .** **Main/Corp** National Women's Advisory Council (Australia). 1st (1979)-. English. an. **LC** HQ1821; .N37A. **DD** 354.940081/3.

**US/0093-7118**
**ANNUAL REPORT. THE STATUS OF WOMEN IN FLORIDA.** (THE STATUS OF WOMEN IN FLORIDA.). **Main/Corp** Florida. Governor's Commission on the Status of Women. 1973-. English. an. Governor's Commission on the Status of Women, The Capitol, Tallahassee FL 32304. **LC** HQ1438.F6; F58A. **DD** 301.41/2/09259.

**US/1056-4578**
**ANNUAL REVIEW OF WOMEN IN WORLD RELIGIONS, THE.** See Religion and Theology.

**CN/0715-9900**
**APOSTROPHE (SILLERY).** (APOSTROPHE.). [Apostrophe]. (1983)-. Periodical. French. qt. $4.95 per no. Apostrophe, App 1/1337 Av Maguire, Sillery Quebec G1T 1Z2 Canada. **LC** UNC. **DD** 305.4/2/05.

**CN/0843-7920**
**AQUELARRE (VANCOUVER).** (AQUELARRE.). [Aquelarre]. **Added/Corp** Aquelarre Latin American Women's Cultural Society. (July/Aug./Sept. 1989)-. Periodical. Spanish (English and Spanish). Four times a year (Mar., June, Sept., Dec.). 22.00Can$ (individuals), 29.00Can$ (institutions). Aquelarre Publications, PO Box 21508, Vancouver British Columbia, V5N 4A0 Canada. **Tel** (604)251-6678, FAX (604)253-3073. **DD** 305.4/098. **Bk Rev. Ad Acc, Adv Mgr:** Miriam, **Tel** (604)251-6678. Full Page (B&W) 250.00Can$. Half Page (B&W) 120.00Can$. Full Page (Color) 400.00Can$.

**US/1058-9511**
**ARAB WOMEN YEAR 2000.** (1991)-. Periodical. English. bm. $35.00. Arab Women Year 2000, 2201 Plaza Drive, Woodbridge NJ 07095.

**DK**
**ARBOG FOR KVINDESTUDIER VED AUC.** **VFOAT** Arbog for Kvindestudier Ved A.U.C. Danish. an. Aalborg Universitetsforlag, Postbox 159, 9100 Aalborg Denmark. **LC** HQ1672; .A72.

**IT**
**ARREDARE LA TAVOLA.** (19??)-. Italian. sa. Free on request. Bitossi Diffusione, Via Pietra Marina 19, 50053 Sovigliana Vinc FI Italy. **Tel** 011 39 571 509955.

**IT**
**ASIAN WOMAN / OFFICIAL PUBLICATION OF THE ASIAN WOMEN'S INSTITUTE.** **Added/Corp** Asian Women's Institute. (19??)-. English. qt. $25.00. Asian Women's Institute, 475 Riverside Drive/Room 439, New York NY 10115.
**Ind/Abst** Hum. Rights Intern. Rep.

**US**
**AT THE CROSSROADS : FEMINISM, SPIRITUALITY AND NEW PARADIGM SCIENCE EXPLORING EARTHLY AND UNEARTHLY REALITY.** (199?)-. English. Twice a year (June & December). $24.00 (two year) US; $36.00 (two year). Spirited Women Book Co., PO Box 112, St. Paul AR 72760. **Tel** (501)677-2235. **ED** Jeanne Neath.
**Desc:** Brings feminism, spirituality and new paradigm science together to explore reality, especially the spiritual reality that Western cultures so often deny. Brings a feminist perspective to a wide variety of topics including shamanism, parapsychology, alternative healing, traditional and new paradigm science.

**CN/0702-7818**
**ATLANTIS (WOLFVILLE).** (ATLANTIS.). [Atlantis]. **Added/Corp** Institute for the Study of Women. (Fall 1975)-. Periodical. English (French). sa. 20.00Can$ (individuals), 35.00Can$ (institutions) Canada; 30.00Can$ (individuals), 40.00Can$ (institutions) US; 35.00Can$ (individuals), 45.00Can$ (institutions) other. Mount Saint Vincent University / Atlantis, Halifax Nova Scotia B3M 2J6 Canada. **Tel** (902)457-6569, FAX (902)445-3960. **ED** Susan M. Clark and Deborah C. Poff. **LC** HQ1180; .A85. **DD** 305.4/05. Index available. **Bk Rev. Ad Acc. Pr Rev. Circ:** 800 (ctrl). available on microfilm from Micromedia Limited.
**Desc:** Devoted to women's studies. Critical and research manuscripts are blind refereed, and published along with creative and artistic selections.
**Ind/Abst** Altern. Press Index; Am. Hist. Life (1976-); Can. Index; Can. Period. Index (19??-); MLA Int. Bibl. Books Artic. Mod. Lang. Lit.; SportSearch; Women Stud. Abstr.

**US**
**AUNT EDNA'S READING LIST.** Periodical. English. mo. Aunt Edna's Reading List, 2002 H Hunnewell Street, Honolulu HI 96822. **Tel** (808)942-2739. **Bk Rev. Ad Acc. Circ:** 300 (ctrl).
**Desc:** Brief, down-to-earth book reviews of feminist books. Emphasis on women's small presses.

**AT/0816-4649**
**AUSTRALIAN FEMINIST STUDIES.** [Aust. fem. stud.]. **Added/Corp** University of Adelaide. Research Centre for Women's Studies. No. 1 (Summer 1985)-. Periodical. English. Twice a year (May & Nov.). 38.00Aus$ (individuals), 60.00Aus$ (institutions), surface mail, 53.00Aus$ (individuals), 75.00 (institutions) airmail Australia; 30.00Aus$ (individuals), 60.00Aus$ (institutions), surface mail, 43.00Aus$ (individuals), 75.75Aus$ (institutions) airmail others. University of Adelaide / Women's Studies, Research Center of Women's Studies, Box 498, Adelaide South Australia 5005 Australia. **Tel** 011 61 8 303 5267, FAX 011 61 8 224 0464, telex UNIVAD AA89141. **ED** Susan Maganey. **LC** HQ1101; .A95. **DD** 305.42/05. **Bk Rev. Ad Acc. Circ:** 600.
**Desc:** Publishes transdisciplinary scholarship and discussion in the fields of feminist research and women's studies courses.
**Ind/Abst** Altern. Press Index (199?-); APAIS, Aust. Public Aff. Inf. Ser.; Aust. Educ. Index; Women Stud. Abstr.

**AT/1033-9434**
**AUSTRALIAN WOMEN'S BOOK REVIEW.** **VFOAT** AWBR. Vol. 1 (Sept. 1989)-. Periodical. English. Four times a year (Mar., June, Sept., Dec.). 24.00Aus$ (individuals), 40.00Aus$ (institutions). Australian Women's Book Review, PO Box 14428 MMC, Melbourne Victoria 3000 Australia. **Tel** 011 61 3 3652656, 011 61 3 3652148, FAX 011 61 3 3652242. **ED** Michele Grossman and Barbara Brook. **Bk Rev**, (Qty: 70). **Ad Acc, Adv Mgr:** M. Grossman, **Tel** 03 365-2247. **Circ:** 1,200 (ctrl).
**Desc:** Reviews a wide range of writing by women, including fiction, poetry, history, biography, women's health, children's literature and teenage fiction. Each issue contains a feature article and several reviews, all written by women.

**AT/0005-0458**
**AUSTRALIAN WOMEN'S WEEKLY, THE.** (1933)-. Periodical. English. mo. 42.00Aus$ Australia; 137.40Aus$ other. Australian Consolidated Press Ltd, GPO Box 5252, Sydney New South Wales 2001 Australia. **Tel** 011 61 2 2600000.

**CN/0228-4146**
**AUTRE PAROLE, L'.** See Religion and Theology.

**NE/0926-910X**
**AVANTGARDE (NEDERLANDSE ED.).** (AVANTGARDE.). [Avantgarde Ned. ed.]. (1980)-. Periodical. Dutch. ir. (8 issues). Fl57.00. PVO Abonnementenservices, Postbus 77, 5126 ZH Gilze Netherlands. **Tel** 011 31 1615 7450. **UDC** (054). **Ad Acc.**
**Desc:** Lifestyles for women.

**NE**
**AVENUE MAGAZINE.** Medianet BV, Postbus 6298, 2001 LN Haarlem Netherlands. **Tel** 011 31 23 173311.

**SG**
**AWA.** Periodical. French. 4000. B P 2578, Dakar Senegal. **LC** HQ1102; .A9. **DD** 301.41/2/09663.

**US/1057-5839**
**AWIS MAGAZINE.** See Science and Technology.

**IV**
**AWOURA.** No. 1- Feb. 1972?-. Periodical. French. BP 2273, Abidjan Ivory Coast. **LC** AP27; .A93. **DD** 054/.1.

**NE/0927-1368**
**BABY & PEUTER.** [Baby & peuter]. **VFOAT** Baby en Peuter. **Added/Corp** Ariadne Baby & Peuter; Ariadne Extra. (1991)-. Periodical. Dutch. sa (April & Oct.). Fl15.00. Medianet BV, Postbus 6298, 2001 LN Haarlem Netherlands. **Tel** 011 31 23 173311. **UDC** 646-053.3 + 646-053.4.

**II**
**BANHI.** **Added/Corp** Jt. Women's Programme (India) Uliyama Keri Stadi Eyanda Risarca Sentara. (1981)-. English. CISRS, 16, Pandit Pant Marg,, New Delhi, 110001, India. **LC** HQ1741; .B36. **DD** 305.4/2/0954.
**Ind/Abst** Hum. Rights Intern. Rep.

**US**
**BARNARD OCCASIONAL PAPERS ON WOMEN'S ISSUES. BARNARD COLLEGE WOMEN'S CENTER, THE.** Ceased. **Added/Corp** Barnard College. Women's Center. Barnard Center for Research on Women. (198?)-(19??). English. Twice a year. Barnard College Womens Center, 3009 Broadway, New York NY 10027. **Tel** (212)280-2067. cum. index.

**CN/0836-4796**
**BC WOMAN TO WOMAN MAGAZINE.** [B.C. woman woman mag.]. **VFOAT** Woman to Woman Magazine; Woman to Woman. **VAT** British Columbia Woman to Woman Magazine. Vol. 1, No. 11 (Dec. 1986)-. Periodical. English. mo. 17.00Can$ (one year), 38.00Can$ (two year), Canada; 31.00Can$ (one year), 48.00Can$ (two year) other. Woman to Woman Magazine, 704 Clarkson Street, Westminister, British Columbia, V3M 1E2 Canada. **Tel** (604)540-8448, FAX (604)524-0041. **ED** Anne Brennan. **DD** 051. **Circ:** 33,000. **Continues** British Columbia's Woman to Woman Magazine., 0830-9256.

**GW/0722-0189**
**BEITRAEGE ZUR FEMINISTISCHEN THEORIE UND PRAXIS.** [Beitr. fem. Theor. Praxis]. **Added/Corp** Sozialwissenschaftliche Forschung und Praxis fuer Frauen e. V. (1978)-. Monographic series. German. tq. Price varies per volume. Sozialwissenschaftliche Forschung und Praxis fuer Frauen e.V., Herwarthstr. 22, 5000 Cologne 1, Germany.
**Ind/Abst** PAIS Int. Print.

**US/0884-2957**
**BELLES LETTRES (ARLINGTON, VA.).** See Literature.

**SP/0005-8629**
**BELLEZA Y MODA.** [Belleza moda]. (1969)-. Periodical. Spanish. Eleven times a year. 21620ptas US; 3600ptas Spain; 18220ptas Europe; 28450ptas other. Belleza y Moda, Apartado de Correos 93032, 08080 Barcelona Spain. **Tel** 011 34 3 2020613. **UDC** 646.

**IO**
**BERITA KOWANI.** **Main/Corp** Kongres Wanita Indonesia. (1979)-. Indonesian (English). Three times a year. Free. Bidang Kpid Kowani, Jl Imam Bonjol 58, Jakarta Pusat Indonesia. **Tel** 364921-364679. **ED** Herman Mudjirun, Kartini Radjasa. **LC** HQ2004.A1; W3613. **Circ:** 1,000. **Continues** Berita Kongres Wanita Indonesia, Kowani.

**GW**
**BERUHMTE FRAUEN.** (1988)-. German. an. Springer-Verlag GmbH & Company KG, Heidelberger Platz 3, D 14197 Berlin Germany. **Tel** 011 49 30 8207223, FAX 011 49 30 8214091, telex 183 319 SPBLN D. (Subscription address: Springer Verlag New York Inc. / for North America, 44 Hartz Way, Secaucus NJ 07096.)

**CG/0376-6624**
**BIBI.** Began with Apr. 1972 issue. Multiple languages (French and Lingala). Lutayi-Kanza, 33 Av Victoire Com Kasa-Vubu, B P 6507 Kin/Mdolo, Kinshasa Congo. **LC** HQ1810; .B52. **DD** 301.41/2/091751.

**US/0277-7533**
**BIG MAMA RAG.** Suspended. [Big Mama rag]. (1973)-(April 1984). Periodical. English. mo. $22.00 (institutions), $9.00 (individuals) surface mail US; $24.00 (institutions), $15.00 (individuals) surface mail Canada and Mexico; $21.00 (institutions), $18.00 (individuals) airmail; $26.00 (institutions), $18.00 (individuals) surface mail other. Big Mama Rag, 1724 Gaylord, Denver CO 80206. **Tel** (303)322-2010. **DD** 396.
**Ind/Abst** Altern. Press Index (-199?).

**US/0045-222X**
**BLACK MARIA.** Ceased. See Literature.

**US/1041-3936**
**BLUE SWAN REVIEW : GUIDE TO WOMEN'S FASHION CATALOGS, THE.** See Clothing Industry and Fashion.

**US/0749-1018**
**BODY TALK.** Vol. 1, No. 1 (Fall 1984)-. Periodical. English. sa. The Women's Center of Cincinnati and Dayton Ohio, PO Box 43100, Cincinnati OH 45243. **Tel** (513)621-1698. **Circ:** 2,000.
**Desc:** Health care newsletter primarily women's health issues.

# Women's Interests

**MX**
**BOLETIN DOCUMENTAL SOBRE LAS MUJERES.** (19??)-. Periodical. Spanish. qt. Cidal AC, Apartado Postal No 42-A, Cuernavaca Morelos Mexico. **LC** HQ1104; .B63.

**CL**
**BOLETIN / ISIS INTERNACIONAL, RED DE SALUD DE LAS MUJERES LATINOAMERICANAS Y DEL CARIBE.** **Added/Corp** Latin American and Caribbean Women's Health Network. (July-Aug. 1985)-. Periodical. Spanish. bm. **LC** RA564.85; .B65. **DD** 613/.0424/09805. **Ind/Abst** Hum. Rights Intern. Rep.

**IT**
**BOOK SERIES (ISIS INTERNATIONAL).** (BOOK SERIES.). **Added/Corp** Isis International. **VFOAT** Isis International Book Series. (1987)-. Monographic series. English. ir. Price varies per volume. Isis International, PO Box 1837, Quezon City 1100 Philippines. **Tel** 011 63 2 997512. **Continues** Isis International Women's Journal.

**US/0893-5572**
**BOSTON WOMAN.** [Boston woman]. (198?)-. Periodical. English. Four times a year. $18.00. Boston Woman, Box 1260, Brookline MA 02146. **Tel** (617)783-8000. **DD** 051.

**CN**
**BOUGE.** French. ir. 20.00Can$. Ciaft, 1265 rue Berri, Suite 930, Mantreal, Quebec, H2L 4X4 Canada. **Tel** (514)844-0760.

**CN/0713-4266**
**BREAKING THE SILENCE (OTTAWA, ONT.).** **Ceased.** (BREAKING THE SILENCE.). Vol. 1, No. 1 (Spring 1982)-Ceased (Nov. 1989). Periodical. English (French). qt. Breaking the Silence, PO Box 4857 Station E, Ottawa Ontario K1S 5J1 Canada. **Tel** (613)722-3052. **DD** 362.8/3/0971384. **Bk Rev. Ad Acc. Circ:** 1,500.
**Desc:** Committed to providing a voice for women and covers a wide range of social, political and cultural topics written by and for women.

**CN/0228-7293**
**BREAKTHROUGH FOR WOMEN.** [Breakthrough women]. **VAT** Breakthrough (Toronto). No. 1 (June 1980)-. Periodical. English. qt. Breakthrough Publications, PO Box 506, Station A, Toronto Ontario M5W 1E6. **DD** 305.4/2/0971.

**UK/0006-9787**
**BRIDES AND SETTING UP HOME.** See Family and Marriage.

**UK/0957-3933**
**BRIDES OF BERKSHIRE.** (1988)-. Periodical. English. sa. Kingsclere Publications Ltd, Highfield House, 2 Highfield Avenue, Newbury Berkshire RG14 5DS England.

**UK/0957-7432**
**BRIDES OF BRISTOL BATH & AVON.** (198?)-. English. sa. Kingsclere Publications Ltd, Highfield House, 2 Highfield Avenue, Newbury Berkshire RG14 5DS England.

**UK/0957-3941**
**BRIDES OF DEVON & CORNWALL.** (1989)-. Periodical. English. sa. Kingsclere Publications Ltd, Highfield House, 2 Highfield Avenue, Newbury Berkshire RG14 5DS England.

**UK/0957-7270**
**BRIDES OF EAST ANGLIA.** (1989)-. English. sa. Kingsclere Publications Ltd, Highfield House, 2 Highfield Avenue, Newbury Berkshire RG14 5DS England.

**UK/0957-395X**
**BRIDES OF HERTS, BUCKS & BEDS.** (1989)-. Periodical. English. sa. Kingsclere Publications Ltd, Highfield House, 2 Highfield Avenue, Newbury Berkshire RG14 5DS England.

**UK/0957-7440**
**BRIDES OF NORTH EAST ENGLAND.** (198?)-. English. sa. Kingsclere Publications Ltd, Highfield House, 2 Highfield Avenue, Newbury Berkshire RG14 5DS England.

**UK/0957-7289**
**BRIDES OF SCOTLAND.** (198?)-. English. sa. Kingsclere Publications Ltd, Highfield House, 2 Highfield Avenue, Newbury Berkshire RG14 5DS England.

**UK/0957-3968**
**BRIDES OF SOMERSET.** (1989)-. Periodical. English. sa. Kingsclere Publications Ltd, Highfield House, 2 Highfield Avenue, Newbury Berkshire RG14 5DS England.

**UK/0957-3976**
**BRIDES OF SURREY.** (1988)-. Periodical. English. sa. Kingsclere Publications Ltd, Highfield House, 2 Highfield Avenue, Newbury Berkshire RG14 5DS England.

**UK/0958-7039**
**BRIDES OF THE NORTH WEST.** (1990)-. English. an. Kingsclere Publications Ltd, Highfield House, 2 Highfield Avenue, Newbury Berkshire RG14 5DS England.

**UK/0957-3984**
**BRIDES OF YORKSHIRE & HUMBERSIDE.** (1989)-. Periodical. English. sa. Kingsclere Publications Ltd, Highfield House, 2 Highfield Avenue, Newbury Berkshire RG14 5DS England.

**US/1046-8358**
**BRIDGES (SEATTLE, WASH.).** (BRIDGES.). [Bridges]. **VFOAT** Bridges: A Journal for Jewish Feminists and Our Friends. (1990)- Vol. 4 (1993)-. Periodical. English. Twice a year (April and October). $25.00 (libraries and institutions), $15.00 (individual),. Bridges, PO Box 18437, Seattle WA 98118. **Tel** (206)721-5008. **ED** Clare Kinbers. **LC** WMLC 91/933; HQ1172; .B74. **DD** 305. **Bk Rev,** (Qty: (6-8)). **Circ:** 3,000 (ctrl). available on audiocassette.
**Desc:** Combines traditional Jewish values of justice and repair of the world with insights hones by the feminist and lesbian/gay community movements. Interviews, poetry, fiction, essays, book reviews, and artwork, which all recognize and honor difference.

**US/0883-9611**
**BROOMSTICK.** **Ceased.** [Broomstick]. Vol. 1, No 1 (Nov. 1978)-Vol. 15. Periodical. English. bm. Options for Women over 40, 3543 18th Street/#3, San Francisco CA 94110. **Tel** (415)552-7460. **ED** Polly Taylor and Mickey Spencer. **LC** HQ1059.5.U5; B76. **DD** 305.4. Index available. **Bk Rev. Ad Acc. Circ:** 5,000. available in microform.
**Desc:** A national feminist magazine by, for, and about women over 40.
**Ind/Abst** Altern. Press Index.

**US**
**BUENHOGAR (HEARST CORPORATION).** See Home Economics.

**CN/0827-0139**
**BULLETIN AEF.** (LE BULLETIN AEF, ACTION EDUCATION FEMMES.). [Bull. AEF]. **Added/Corp** Action Education Femmes. **VAT** Bulletin Action Education Femmes. (Oct. 1986)-. Periodical. French. qt. 60.00Can$ institutions; 10.00Can$ individuals. Action Education des Femmes, 435 Boulevard St. Laurent Bureau 208, Ottawa Ontario K1K 2Z8 Canada. **Tel** (613)741-9978. **DD** 305.4/0971. **Continues** Magazine AEF, Action Education Femmes, 0834-1745.

**US/1058-9988**
**BULLETIN / AMERICAN ASSOCIATION OF UNIVERSITY WOMEN.** See Education-Higher Education.

**FR**
**BULLETIN (CENTRE DE RECHERCHES DE REFLEXION ET D'INFORMATION FEMINISTES (PARIS, FRANCE)).** (BULLETIN - CENTRE DE RECHERCHES DE REFLEXION ET D'INFORMATION FEMINISTES.). **VFOAT** CRIF. No. 1 (Autumn 1982)-. Bulletin. French (summaries and/or abstracts in English). sa. CRIF, 1 rue des Fosses-Saint-Jacques, 75005 Paris France.

**CN/0840-4011**
**BULLETIN - INSTITUT SIMONE DE BEAUVOIR.** (LE BULLETIN / UNIVERSITE CONCORDIA, INSTITUT SIMONE DE BEAUVOIR.). [Bull. - Inst. Simone de Beauvoir]. **Added/Corp** Simone de Beauvoir Institute (Montreal, Quebec). **VFOAT** Newsletter. **VAT** Newsletter - Simone de Beauvoir Institute. (198?)-. Bulletin. English (summaries and/or abstracts in French). an. $12.00 (institutions), $6.00 (students), $10.00 (general public). Simone de Beauvoir Institute, 1455 de Maisonneuve Boulevard West, Montreal Quebec H3G 1M8 Canada. **Tel** (514)848-2370. **DD** 305.4/05.

**UK**
**BULLETIN / LABOUR HERITAGE WOMEN'S RESEARCH COMMITTEE.** **Added/Corp** Labour Heritage (Group). Women's Research Council. **VFOAT** Women's Research Committee Bulletin; Labour Heritage Women's Research Committee Bulletin. No. 2 (Spring 1988)-. Bulletin. English. **Continues** L.H. Worc Bulletin.

**CN/0229-5814**
**BULLETIN MATCH.** [Match newsl.]. **VFOAT** Match Newsletter. Vol. 4, No. 1 (Jan. 1980)-. Bulletin. English (Spanish and French). Five times a year. $15.00 (individuals), $25.00 (institutions), $25.00 (groups), Free (Third World women's groups). Match International Centre, 202-200 Elgin Street / Suite 1102, Ottawa Ontario K2P 1L5 Canada. **Tel** (613)238-1312. **DD** 362.8/3/091724. **Bk Rev.** ctrl circ. *Formed by the union of* Match Bulletin, 0229-5822 and Match Newsletter. Anglais, 0229-5814.
**Desc:** A nonprofit, nongovernmental development agency that concentrates its support on women through overseas project funding and education in Canada. Is committed to a feminist vision of development. Such a vision requires the eradication of all forms of injustice, particularly the exploitation and marginalization of women.

**US/0083-3606**
**BULLETIN - U.S. DEPT. OF LABOR, EMPLOYMENT STANDARDS ADMINISTRATION, WOMEN'S BUREAU.** See Economics-Labor.

**US/0748-4240**
**BURRELLE'S WOMEN'S MEDIA DIRECTORY.** See Communication.

**CN/0045-3587**
**BUSINESS & PROFESSIONAL WOMAN (OTTAWA).** (THE BUSINESS & PROFESSIONAL WOMAN.). **Added/Corp** Canadian Federation of Business and Professional Women's Clubs. Canadian Federation of Business and Professional Women. (1934)-. Periodical. English (French). Four times a year (Feb., May, July, Nov.). 3.00Can$. Canadian Federation of Business and Professional Women, 56 Sparks Street / Room 308, Ottawa Ontario K10 5A9 Canada. **Tel** (613)234-7619. **ED** Val Dunn. **Ad Acc. Adv Mgr Tel** (416)424-1393. **Circ:** 4,000. *Absorbed* Ontario Messenger (Toronto, Ont.), 0831-6848.
**Desc:** This newspaper features articles on the professionals and business women of Canada.

**CN/0708-5842**
**BUSINESS (TORONTO).** (BUSINESS.). **Added/Corp** Women's Conference Institute. Vol. 1 (June 1979)-. Periodical. English. mo. $8.00 Canada; $10.00 US and UK. Women's Conference Institute, Suite 30, 43 Victoria Street, Toronto Ontario M5C 2A2. **DD** 331.4/81/658.

● **US/1076-7363**
**BUSINESS WOMEN'S NETWORK DIRECTORY, THE.** See Business.

**CN/0824-5355**
**BY APPOINTMENT ONLY.** (BY APPOINTMENT ONLY : REGINA WOMEN'S NETWORK ENGAGEMENT CALENDAR.). [By appointm. only]. **VFOAT** Regina Women's Network Engagement Calendar. 1984-. English. an. $7.95 per volume. Regina Women's Network, PO Box 3422, Regina Saskatchewan S4P 3N8 Canada. **DD** 920.72/097124.

**CN/0702-9241**
**CALGARY WOMEN'S NEWSPAPER.** Began with Feb. 1975 issue. Periodical. English. mo. $4.00. Calgary Status of Women Action Committee, 320 5th Avenue SE, Calgary Alberta T2G 0E5 Canada. **Tel** (403)262-1873. **DD** 301.41/2/0971233.

**US/0008-1663**
**CALIFORNIA WOMAN, THE.** **Added/Corp** California Federation of Business and Professional Women's Clubs. (19??)-. Periodical. English. Five times a year. $6.00. California Federation of Business & Professional Women's Clubs, 3420 South Half Moon Drive, Bakersfield CA 93309. **Tel** (805)837-8291. **ED** Laurie Anderson. **Bk Rev. Ad Acc. Circ:** 12,000 (ctrl).
**Desc:** Magazine for working women.

**US/0147-1627**
**CALYX (CORVALLIS).** See Literature.

**CN/0832-8781**
**CANADIAN JOURNAL OF WOMEN AND THE LAW.** See Law.

**CN/0382-4624**
**CANADIAN LIVING.** [Can. living]. Vol. 1 (Dec. 1975)-. Periodical. English. Thirteen times a year. 27.98Can$ Canada; 37.00Can$ US; 59.00Can$ other. Telemedia Publishing Inc., 555 West 12th Avenue, Suite 300, North York Ontario V5Z 4L4 Canada. **Tel** (604)877-7732. (Subscription address: Indas, 35 Riviera Drive, Building 17, Markham Ontario L3R 8N4 Canada.) **ED** Bonnie Cowan. **DD** 051. **Ad Acc. Circ:** 500,000. *Absorbed* Expression (Toronto, Ont. : 1988), 0835-345X.
**Desc:** Home-service magazine designed to give Canadian women a helping hand whether they are working full-time, part-time or at home with their families; offers practical, positive and realistic editorial to help Canadian women better cope with today's changing world as it relates to themselves and their families. Places a strong emphasis on living in Canada.
**Ind/Abst** Acad. Abstr. (Jan. 1994-); Acad. Search (Jan. 1994-); Can. Index (?-?); Can. Period. Index; Index Inf. (March 1990-); Mag. Artic. Summar. Elite (Jan. 1994-); Mag. Artic. Summar. CD-ROM (Jan. 1994-).

CN/0847-2882
**CANADIAN WOMEN'S PERIODICALS INDEX.** (CANADIAN WOMEN'S PERIODICALS INDEX.). [Can. women's period. index]. **Added/Corp** Canadian Research Institute for the Advancement of Women. University of Alberta. Women's Program and Resource Centre. University of Alberta. Women's Research Centre. **VFOAT** Index des Periodiques pour Femmes Canadiennes. Vol. 5, No. 1 (May/Aug, 1989)-. Periodical. English (French). Three times a year (Feb., June, Oct.). 30.00Can$ (members); 40.00Can$ (non-members). CDN Womens Periodicals Index, 11019 90 Avenue, University of Alberta, Edmonton ALTA T6G 2E1 Canada. **Tel** (403)492-3093, FAX (403)492-1186. **DD** 016.3054/05. ***Continues*** *Canadian Women's Periodicals, Title Word Index, 0829-9552.*

CN/0713-3235
**CANADIAN WOMEN'S STUDIES.** [Can. women's stud.]. **Added/Corp** York University (Toronto, Ont.) Centennial College of Applied Arts and Technology. **VFOAT** Canadian Woman Studies; Cahiers de la Femme; CWS/CF. Vol. 1, No. 1 (Fall 1978)-. Periodical. English (French). Four times a year (Mar., June, Sept., Dec.). 40.00Can$ (institutions), 30.00Can$ (individuals) Canada; 46.00Can$ (institutions), 36.00Can$ (individuals) other. York University / Ontario, Canada, 212 Founders College, 4700 Keele Street, North York Ontario M3J 1P3 Canada. **Tel** (416)736-5356. **ED** Luciana Ricciotelli. **LC** HQ1451; .C63. **DD** 305.4/0971/05. **[CCC]. Bk Rev**, (Qty: varies). **Ad Acc. Circ:** 5,000 (ctrl). ***Continues*** *Canadian Women's Studies, 0706-8204.*
**Desc:** Feminist magazine founded with the goal of making current writing and research on a wide variety of feminist topics accessible to the largest possible community of women. Publishes experiential articles and essays; book, art and film reviews; and creative work. Each issue on specific theme.
**Ind/Abst** Can. Index; Can. Period. Index; Multicult. Educ. Abstr.; Stud. Women Abstr.

US/1051-1075
**CAREER WOMAN.** [Career woman]. Vol. 17, No. 1 (Fall 1989)-. Periodical. English. Three times a year. $13.00 (one year), $25.00 (two year), $36.00 (three year). Equal Opportunity Publications Inc, 150 Motor Parkway Suite 420, Hauppage NY 11788. **Tel** (516)273-0066, FAX (516)273-8936. **LC** HD6093; .C75. **DD** 331.4/0973/05. ***Continues*** *Collegiate Career Woman, 8755-9218.*
**Desc:** A recruitment magazine for college-graduating women. Covers all career disciplines, including business, computers, and management.

US/1060-3670
**CAWP NEWS & NOTES.** (CAWP NEWS & NOTES / CENTER FOR THE AMERICAN WOMAN AND POLITICS.). [CAWP News Notes]. **Added/Corp** Center for the American Woman and Politics (Eagleton Institute of Politics). **VFOAT** CAWP News & Notes; CAWP News and Notes. Vol. 7, No. 1 (spring 1989)-. Periodical. English. tq. $25.00. Eagleton Institute of Politics / CAWP, Rutgers University, New Brunswick NJ 08901. **Tel** (201)932-9384. **ED** Luey Baruch. **DD** 353. ***Continues*** *News & Notes About Women Public Officials, 1041-5661.*

CN/0827-0732
**CAYENNE.** (CAYENNE : A SOCIALIST FEMINIST BULLETIN.). [Cayenne]. Nov./Dec. 1984-. Bulletin. English. qt. 12.00Can$ (individuals), 19.00Can$ (institutions) Canada; 16.80Can$ (individuals), 26.60Can$ (institutions) other. Cayenne, 229 College Street/#309, Toronto Ontario M5T 1R4 Canada. **DD** 305.4/2/0971.
**Desc:** A socialist feminist quarterly of news, features and debate, with special emphasis on the women's movement in Canada and internationally.

US
**CDRR NEWS.** 1992. English. qt. $25.00. CMRW, 2845 24th Street, San Francisco CA 94110. **Tel** (415)826)4401. **Circ:** 1400. ***Continues*** *Second Opinion.*
**Desc:** Analyzes the wide range of reproductive rights issues to educate and inspire activism among its readers. Past issues have covered the struggle for abortion access and family planning with articles on Title X "gag rule," the misuses of Norplant and Utah's restrictive abortion law. It addresses such topics as women and AIDS and midwives in California.

CN/1183-7675
**CELIBATAIRES MAGAZINE. See** Men's Interests.

US
**CHALLENGE. Added/Corp** National Federation of Republican Women. (1978)-. Periodical. English. Twelve times a year. $15.00. National Federation of Republican Women, 310 First Street Southeast, Washington DC 20003. **Tel** (703)548-9688. **ED** Kathy Hunter. **Bk Rev. Circ:** 145,000 (ctrl). ***Continues*** *Winning Spirit.*
**Desc:** Official publication of the largest women's political organization in the U.S. Provides information and news on Republican Party policy, initiatives and programs, as well as legislative updates and NFRW news.

IT
**CHARME MODA.** Italian (English, French and German). mo. L60000.00 Italy; L100000.00 Europe; L150000.00 other. CP Erre Editori, Vial Eupili 4, 20145 Milan Italy. **Tel** (02)33101738, FAX (02)3450677. **ED** Charme Moda. **Ad Acc, Adv Mgr:** Paola Riboldi. **Pr Rev. Circ:** 25,000.

CN/0317-2635
**CHATELAINE (EDITION FRANCAISE).** (CHATELAINE.). [Chatelaine]. Vol. 1 (Oct. 1960)-. Periodical. French. mo. Maclean Hunter Canada / Montreal, 1001 bvd. de Maisonneuve W., Montreal, Quebec H3A 3E1 Canada. **Tel** 514-845-5141, FAX 514-845-4302, telex 055-60604. **Bk Rev. Ad Acc. Circ:** 178,592. available on microfilm and microfiche from University Microfilms International (UMI). ***Supersedes*** *Revue Moderne, 0700-6012.*
**Ind/Abst** Can. Period. Index (19??-); Point Repere (1983-).

CN/0009-1995
**CHATELAINE (TORONTO, ONT.: 1928).** (CHATELAINE.). [Chatelaine]. Vol. 1 No. 1 (Mar. 1928)-. Periodical. English. Twelve times a year. 18.67Can$ Canada; 40.00Can$ US; 44.00Can$ others. MacLean Hunter Publ. Limited / Toronto, 777 Bay Street, 8th Floor Agency Control, Toronto Ontario M5W 1A7 Canada. **Tel** (416)596-5000, (800)268-6811, FAX (416)596-5526. **ED** Mildred Istona. **LC** AP5; .C5. **DD** 051. **[CCC]. Bk Rev. Ad Acc.** available on microfilm and microfiche from University Microfilms International (UMI). Documents available from UMI Article Clearinghouse, Magazine Collection. ***Absorbed*** *Canadian Home Journal, 0382-7690.*
**Desc:** A magazine for Canadian women featuring solution-oriented articles on subjects of special interest to women and their dynamic roles in today's changing society.
**Ind/Abst** Acad. Search (July 1993-); Can. Index; Can. Period. Index; Gen. Period. Index (1985-); INFO-SOUTH Abstr.; Mag. Index Plus (1989-); Mag. Search; Newsp. Period. Abstr. (1988-); Point Repere; Mag. Index (1983-).

US/0009-5702
**CHRISTIAN WOMAN. See** Religion and Theology.

CN/0316-330X
**CHRONICLE - CANADIAN FEDERATION OF UNIVERSITY WOMEN.** (THE CHRONICLE.). [Chron. - Can. Fed. Univ. Women]. **Added/Corp** Canadian Federation of University Women. **VFOAT** Chronique; University Women's Federation Chronicle. **VAT** Chronique - Federation Canadienne des Femmes Diplomees des Universites. (1920)-. English (French). tq. $12.00; $1.25 (single issue) US; $15.00; $1.56 (single issue) other. Canadian Federation of University / Women Maliposa College, Wakesiah Campus, 900 5th Street, Nanimo British Columbia V9R 5S5 Canada. **DD** 301.41/2/06271.

BE
**CHRONIQUE FEMINISTE. Added/Corp** Universite des Femmes (Brussels, Belgium). **VFOAT** Chronique. No. 15 (Sept./Oct. 1985)-. Periodical. French. Five times a year. 500F Belgium; 700F other. University des Femmes, 1A Place Quetulut, B 1030 Brussels Belgium. **Tel** 011 32 02 2196107. **ED** Fanny Filosof. **Bk Rev. Circ:** 2,000 (ctrl). ***Continues*** *Chronique (Brussels, Belgium).*

CC/0529-603X
**CHUNG-KUO FU NU / ZHONGGUO FUNU. VFOAT** Zhongguo Funu; Women of China. Jan. (1956)-. Periodical. Chinese. sm. RMBY13.20. Zhongguo Funu Zazhishe, A24 Shijia Hutong, Beijing 100010, People's Republic of China. **Tel** 5126988. **(Subscription address:** China International Book Trading Corporation, PO Box 399, Library Service Department, Beijing 100044 People's Republic of China.**) ED** Shao Yan. **LC** HQ1766; .H75. **DD** 305.4/0951. **Ad Acc.** available with illustrations. ***Continues*** *Hsin Chung-kuo fu Nu.*

US/0009-6598
**CHURCH WOMAN, THE. See** Religion and Theology.

CN/0713-052X
**CLASS / CANADIAN LADIES ASSOCIATION OF SHOOTING SPORTS. See** Recreation, Leisure-Sports.

AT/0310-1797
**CLEO.** [Cleo]. (1972)-. Periodical. English. mo. 54.00Aus$ Australia; 60.00Aus$ New Zealand; 93.60Aus$ other. Australian Consolidated Press Ltd, GPO Box 5252, Sydney New South Wales 2001 Australia. **Tel** 011 61 2 2600000. **DD** _a052.

IT
**CLIO NOTIZIE. *Ceased.* Added/Corp** Clio (Association). **VFOAT** Notizie. (1988)-(Dec. 1992). Periodical. Italian. qttq. Franco Angeli Riviste SRL, Viale Monza 106, 20127 Milan Italy. **Tel** 011 39 2 2827651, 011 39 2 2895762. **LC** WMLC 93/1716.

US/0199-8919
**CLUW NEWS. See** Economics-Labor.

US/0275-8091
**COLLECTIONS (PHILADELPHIA, PA.). See** Medical Science and Technology.

US/0885-937X
**COLLEGE WOMAN (BURBANK, CALIF.).** ***Suspended.* See** Education-Higher Education.

US/1042-9549
**COLORADO WOMAN.** [Colo. woman]. **VFOAT** Colorado Woman News. Vol. 2, No. 4 (Spring 1988)-. Periodical. English. mo. $25.00. Front Range Woman Inc, PO Box 22274, Denver CO 80222. **Tel** (303)355-9229, FAX (303)355-9332. **ED** Judith Spitzer. **DD** 051. **Bk Rev**, (Qty: 25). **Ad Acc, Adv Mgr:** Sharon Silvas. **Circ:** 50,000. ***Continues*** *Front Range Woman Newsletter.*
**Desc:** Features Colorado women and news for this target market.

●US/1071-1880
**COLORADO WOMEN'S YELLOW PAGES.** (1994)-. English.

US/1062-6220
**COLUMBIA JOURNAL OF GENDER AND LAW. See** Law.

CN/0715-478X
**COMMON GROUND (CHARLOTTETOWN).** (COMMON GROUND.). [Common ground]. **Added/Corp** Women's Network Project Committee. Vol. 1, No. 1 (Mar./Apr. 1982)-. Periodical. English. Six times a year (Jan., Mar., May, July, Sept., Nov.). 12.50Can$ Canada; 17.50Can$ other. Womens Network Inc., Box 233, Charlottetown C1A 7K4 Canada. **Tel** (902)368-5040. **ED** Anne McCallum. **DD** 305.4/09717. **Bk Rev**, (Qty: 2-6). **Ad Acc. Circ:** 1,000. available on microfilm.
**Desc:** This magazine discusses issues important to women in a changing society. It strives to present positive and varied images of womens and to support the network of Islanders promoting women's equality.

CN/0821-2589
**COMMUNIQUE / THE INSTITUTE FOR THE STUDY OF WOMEN.** [Commun. - Inst. Study Women]. **Main/Corp** Institute for the Study of Women. (Spring 1982)-. Periodical. English. Twice a year. Free on request. Institute for the Study of Women, Mount Saint Vincent University, 166 Bedford Highway, Halifax Nova Scotia B3M 2J6 Canada. **Tel** (902)443-4450. **DD** 305.4/05.

IT
**COMPAGNA.** Vol. 1- Jan. 1972-. Periodical. Italian. 4,500. Edizioni Dedalo Spa, Casella Postale 362, Bari 70100 Italy. **Tel** 011 39 080 5311400, FAX 011 39 080 5311414. **LC** HQ1104.; C65.

UK/0141-1144
**COMPANY.** [Company]. **VFOAT** Company Magazine. (1978)-. Periodical. English. mo (12 issues). $49.50 US; $54.00 Canada. National Magazine Company Ltd., Perrymount Road, Haywards Heath, West Sussex RH16 3DH England. **Tel** 011 44 444 440421.

IT/0393-4888
**CONFEZIONE.** [Confezione]. (1985)-. Periodical. Italian. Nine times a year. L70000 Italy; L135000 Europe; L180000 other. Tecniche Nuove SPA, Via Ciro Menotti 14, 20129 Milan Italy. **Tel** 011 39 2 75701, FAX 011 39 2 7610351, telex 334647 TECHS I. **UDC** 687.

IT
**CONFIDENZE.** (19??)-. Italian. L87600 Italy; L130000 others. Arnoldo Mondadori Editore, UFF Cont Abbonamenti, 20090 Segrate MI Italy. **Tel** 011 39 2 75422015, telex 320457 MONDMI I.

US/0886-7062
**CONNEXIONS (OAKLAND, CALIF.).** (CONNEXIONS.). [Connexions]. **Added/Corp** Peoples Translation Service. No. 1 (Summer 1981)-. Periodical. English. qt. $30.00 (institutions), $17.00 (individuals). Peoples Translation Service, PO Box 14431, Oakland CA 94712. **Tel** (510)549-3505. **ED** Donna Scism. **LC** HQ1101; .C63. **DD** 305.4/05. **Ad Acc. Circ:** 5,000. available on microfiche. Documents available from UMI Article Clearinghouse.
**Desc:** Translations or reprints from international press by and about the concerns of women in other countries. Issues are thematic.
**Ind/Abst** Altern. Press Index; Hum. Rights Intern. Rep.; Left Index; Newsp. Period. Abstr. (1992-).

US/0147-104X
**CONTRIBUTIONS IN WOMEN'S STUDIES.** No. 1 (1978)-. Monographic series. English. ir. Price varies per volume. Greenwood Press Inc., PO Box 5007, Westport CT 06881-5007. **Tel** (203)226-3571, FAX (203)222-1502.
**Desc:** These texts and monographs are concerned with the historical aspects of women's studies and the progress and problems of today's woman.

●US/1061-4117
**COPING NEWSLETTER.** (COPING NEWSLETTER: FOR WOMEN PROFESSIONALS BALANCING CAREER AND FAMILY.). [Coping newsl.].

# Women's Interests

**Added/Corp** CAE Consultants, Inc. (Mar. 1992)-. Periodical. English. bm. $35.00. Cae Consultants, Inc., 41 Tavers Avenue, Yonkers NY 10705. **DD** 305.

NE
**COSMOPOLITAN.** Medianet BV, Postbus 6298, 2001 LN Haarlem Netherlands. **Tel** 011 31 23 173311.

US/0010-9541
**COSMOPOLITAN (1952).** (COSMOPOLITAN.). [Cosmopolitan]. Vol. 132, No. 4 (April 1952)-. Periodical. English. Twelve times a year. $24.97. The Hearst Corporation, 250 West 55th Street, New York NY 10019. **Tel** (212)649-4014. **(Subscription address:** CDS Agency Hard Copy, PO Box 4966, Des Moines IA 50340.**)** **LC** AP2; .H4. **DD** 051. **Bk Rev. Ad Acc.** available on microfilm from University Microfilms International (UMI); available on an online database (file 647/Full-Text) from DIALOG. Documents available from UMI Article Clearinghouse, Magazine Collection. **Continues** Hearst's International Combined with Cosmopolitan, 0740-6436.
 **Desc:** Features articles relating to female sexuality, staying healthy, beauty care, and fashion; also contains other regular departments.
 **Ind/Abst** Acad. Abstr. Full Text Elite (July 1989-); Acad. Abstr. (July 1989-); Access (1975-1987); Consum. Health Nutr. Index (?-?); Health Ref. Cent. (1987-) [Full Txt.] [Select. Cov.]; Mag. Artic. Summar. Elite (July 1989-); Mag. Artic. Summar. Select (July 1989-); Mag. Artic. Summar. CD-ROM (July 1989-); Mag. ASAP Plus [Full Txt.]; Mag. ASAP Sel. [Full Txt.]; Mag. Index Plus (1989-); Mag. Index. Sel. (1986-); Mag. Search; Med. Rev. Dig.; Newsp. Period. Abstr. (1988-); Mag. Index (1977-); TOM Gen. Index (1992-) [Full Txt.].

AT/0310-2076
**COSMOPOLITAN AUSTRALIAN EDITION.** [Cosmopolitan Aust. ed.]. (1973)-. Periodical. English. mo. 54.00Aus$ Australia; 60.00Aus$ New Zealand; 93.60Aus$ other. Australian Consolidated Press Ltd, GPO Box 5252, Sydney New South Wales 2001 Australia. **Tel** 011 61 2 2600000. **DD** _a052.

UK
**COSMOPOLITAN. (ENGLAND EDITION).** English. mo. $45.00 US; $48.00 Canada. National Magazine Company Ltd., Perrymount Road, Haywards Heath, West Sussex RH16 3DH England. **Tel** 011 44 444 440421.

FR/1161-2258
**COSMOPOLITAN (PARIS).** (COSMOPOLITAN.). [Cosmopolitan]. (1973)-. Periodical. French. Twelve times a year. $75.00. **(Subscription address:** International Subscription Inc., 30 Montgomery Street, 7th Floor, Jersey City, NJ 07302; Phone: (800)544-6748 or (201)451-9420**)**

US/0892-8525
**COUNTRY WOMAN.** [Ctry. woman]. Vol. 17, No. 3 (March/April 1987)-. Periodical. English. Six times a year. $16.98 US; $25.98 other. Reiman Publications, 5400 South 60th Street, Greenvale WI 53129. **Tel** (414)423-0100 Ext. 421, FAX (414)423-1143. **ED** Ann Kaiser. **DD** 640. **Circ:** 600,000. available on microfilm from University Microfilms International (UMI). **Continues** Farm Woman, 0888-1472.
 **Desc:** Exclusively for women who love the country way of life. Decorating ideas, crafts, homemaking hints, humor, recipes, etc.

UK
**COUNTRYWOMAN, THE.** Began publication with Mar. 1934 issue. Periodical. English. Assn Country Women, Vincent House, Vincent Square, London SW1P 2NB England. **Tel** 01 834 8635. **LC** HD6073.A38.

CN/0822-3033
**COUP DE POUCE (MONTREAL).** (COUP DE POUCE.). [Coup pouce]. No. 1 (Feb. 1984)-. Periodical. French. Thirteen times a year. 27.48Can$ Canada; 50.86Can$ other. Les Editions Telemedia, 2001 rue University Bureau 900, Montreal Quebec H3A 2A6 Canada. **Tel** (514)875-1974. **(Subscription address:** Abonnement Quebec, 25 Boulevard Taschereau, Bureau 201, Greenfield PK Quebec J4V 3P1 Canada.**) DD** 054/.1.
 **Desc:** Offers recipes, decorating advice, needlecraft, health and beauty care, gift ideas, fashion and a thousand and one other useful and interesting tips. Feature articles cover a wide range of topics from the importance of laughter to the return of ballroom dancing.
 **Ind/Abst** Can. Period. Index; Point Repere (1991-).

GW
**COURAGE.** Periodical. German (German). 3.00 single issue. Postfach 309, 1 Berlin 62 Germany. **LC** HQ1103; .C68.

US/0736-4733
**CREATIVE WOMAN (PARK FOREST SOUTH, ILL.), THE.** (THE CREATIVE WOMAN.). [Creat. woman]. **Added/Corp** Governors State University. Vol. 1, No. 1 (Summer 1977)-. Periodical. English. qt. $16.00. Tapp Group, 1212 South Naper Boulevard #119, c/o M. Choudhury, Naperville IL 60540. **Tel** (708)255-1232, FAX (708)255-1243. **ED** Margaret Choudhury. **DD** 305. **Bk Rev. Ad Acc, Adv Mgr:** Kristine Rynne, **Tel** (708)355-7693. **Circ:** 500 (ctrl).

 **Desc:** Special topic each issue, presented from a feminist perspective; publishes fiction, poetry, articles, and photography.

BE/0772-8867
**CREW REPORTS.** [CREW Reports]. (1981)-. Periodical. French. Eleven times a year. $211.00. Centre for Research on European Women, 21 rue de la Tourelle, B 1040 Brussels Belgium. **Tel** (32 2)230 51 58, 2305837, FAX (32 2)230 62 30.

US/1066-288X
**CRITICAL MATRIX.** [Crit. matrix]. **Added/Corp** Princeton University. Program in Women's Studies. Vol.1, No.1 (1985)-. Monographic series. English. Twice a year. $28.00 (institutions), $15.00 (individuals) US; $32.50 (institutions), $19.50 (individuals) Canada & Mexico; $35.50 (institutions), $22.50 (individuals) other. Critical Matrix, Princeton University, 113 Dickinson Hall, Princeton NJ 08544. **Tel** (609)258-5430, FAX (609)258-1833. **ED** Cynthia Cupples and Heather Hadlock. **LC** HQ1101; .C75. **DD** 305.4. Index available. cum. index. **Bk Rev,** (Qty: 2). **Ad Acc. Circ:** 500 (ctrl).
 **Desc:** Forum for research, criticism, theory, and creative work in feminism and gender studies.
 **Ind/Abst** MLA Int. Bibl. Books Artic. Mod. Lang. Lit.

IT
**CUCINA BELLA E BUONA.** Di Baio Editore, Via Settembrini 11, 20124 Milan Italy.

US/0739-1749
**DAUGHTERS OF SARAH. See** Religion and Theology.

CN/0828-654X
**DEMOCRATIC WOMEN.** (DEMOCRATIC WOMEN : ORGAN OF THE DEMOCRATIC WOMEN'S UNION OF CANADA.). [Democr. women]. Periodical. English. mo. $0.50 per issue. Democratic Women's Union of Canada, PO Box 382 Station U, Toronto Ontario M8Z 5P7 Canada. **DD** 335/.0088042.

US/1040-7391
**DIFFERENCES (BLOOMINGTON, IND.).** (DIFFERENCES.). [Differences]. Vol. 1, No. 1 (Winter 1989)-. Periodical. English. Three times a year. $60.00. Indiana University Press, 601 North Morton Street, Bloomington IN 47404. **Tel** (812)855-3830, (800)842-6796. **LC** HQ1101; .D54. **DD** 305.42/05. **CODEN** DIFFEX. Documents available from UMI Article Clearinghouse.
 **Ind/Abst** Expand. Acad. Index (1992-); Film Lit. Index (19??-); Left Index; Linguist. Lang. Behav. Abstr.; Newsp. Period. Abstr. (1989-); Soc. Plann. Policy Dev. Abstr.; Sociol. Abstr.; Women Stud. Abstr.

US/1058-4188
**DIRECTIONS FOR PENNSYLVANIA SINGLES!.** [Dir. Pa. singles!]. **VFOAT** Directions. Vol. 1, No. 1 July/August (1991)-. Periodical. English. bm. $12.00. Triangle Publishing, Inc., 1350 Indian Springss Road, Indiana PA 15701. **DD** 646.

US
**DIRECTORY OF ORGANIZATIONS PROMOTING EQUAL EMPLOYMENT OPPORTUNITIES FOR WOMEN, CALIFORNIA. See** Economics-Labor.

US/0272-1864
**DIRECTORY OF ORGANIZATIONS WORKING FOR WOMEN'S EDUCATIONAL EQUITY. See** Education.

US/1052-7737
**DIRECTORY OF SELECTED RESEARCH & POLICY CENTERS WORKING ON WOMEN'S ISSUES, A. Ceased.** [Dir. sel. res. policy centers work. women's issues]. **Added/Corp** Women's Research & Education Institute. **VFOAT** Directory of Selected Research and Policy Centers Working on Women's Issues. 4th Ed., (1987)-5th Ed. Directory. English. an. Women's Research Education Institute, 1700 18th Street Northwest, Suite 400, Washington DC 20009. **Tel** (202)328-7070, FAX (202)328-3514. **LC** HQ1181.U5; D55. **DD** 305.4/072973. **Continues** Directory of Selected Women's Research & Policy Centers.

US/1042-2420
**DIRECTORY OF WOMEN ENTREPRENEURS, THE. Ceased. See** Business.

US/1048-4418
**DIRECTORY OF WOMEN HISTORIANS. See** History(General).

AT
**DIRECTORY OF WOMEN IN BUSINESS PROFESSIONS & MANAGEMENT.** (19??)-. Directory. English. be. 25.00Aus$ Australia. Directory of Women in Business Professions & Management, 56 Rose Str, Melbourne Victoria 3143 Australia. **Tel** (03)822 4396. **ED** A. Stressac. **Ad Acc. Circ:** 9,000.

US
**DIRECTORY OF WOMEN IN SPORTS BUSINESS, THE. See** Recreation, Leisure-Sports.

US/0732-5967
**DIRECTORY OF WOMEN IN THE MATHEMATICAL SCIENCES. See** Mathematics.

US/1040-1156
**DIRECTORY OF WOMEN'S MEDIA.** [Dir. women's media]. **Added/Corp** Women's Institute for Freedom of the Press. (1988)-. Directory. English. an. $30.00, $24.00 (up to three copies), $18.00 (three or more). National Council for Research on Women, 530 Broadway, 10th Floor, New York NY 10012-3920. **Tel** (212)274-0730, FAX (212)274-0821. **ED** Susan A. Hallgarth. **LC** Z7962; .I52; HQ1101. **DD** 305.4/025/73. **Continues** Index Directory of Women's Media, 0197-3401.
 **Desc:** Originally published by the Women's Institute for Freedom of the Press including brief descriptions of over 1,300 print and electronic media, publishers, bookstores, libraries, archives, distributors, and other media sources by, for, and about women.

CN/0836-4192
**DIRECTORY / WESTCOASTS WOMEN'S NETWORK. Ceased.** [Dir. - Westcoast Women's Netw.]. **Main/Corp** Westcoast Women's Network. **VFOAT** Westcoast Women's Network Directory. (1984/85)-(199?). Directory. English. Vancouver Women's Network, c/o University of British Columbia Education, Vancouver British Columbia V6T 2A4 Canada. **DD** 305.4/3/02571133. **Continues** Women's Network Directory, 0824-2755.

CN/0225-4786
**DONNA (DOWNSVIEW).** (DONNA.). [Donna]. Yearly V. 1- July 15, 1979-. Periodical. Italian (English). mo (except Jan. and Aug.). 0.50Can$ per no. Donna, Unit 13/101 Toro Road, Downsview Ontario M3J 2Z1 Canada. **DD** 051.

IT
**DONNA. INTERNATIONAL EDITION.** Rusconi Editore Spa, Servicio Abbonements, V Le Sarca 235, 20126 Milan Italy. **Tel** 011 39 2 66192634.

IT
**DONNA MODERNA.** (19??)-. Italian. L74400 Italy; L186200 other. Arnoldo Mondadori Editore, UFF Cont Abbonamenti, 20090 Segrate MI Italy. **Tel** 011 39 2 75422015, telex 320457 MONDMI I.

1018-1342
**DOSSIER - WOMEN LIVING UNDER MUSLIM LAWS.** [Doss. - Women Liv. Under Muslim Laws]. **VFOAT** Dossier - Femmes sous lois Musulmanes; Dossier - Nisa fi Zill al-Tasriat al-Islamiyyat. (1990)-. Periodical. Multiple languages.
 **Ind/Abst** Hum. Rights Intern. Rep.

IT
**DWF. VFOAT** D.W.F.; Donnawomanfemme; Donna, Woman, Femme. No. 1 (Spring 1986)-. Periodical. Italian (summaries and/or abstracts in English and French). qt. L50000.00 Italy; L80000.00 other. Cooperativa Utopia Srl, Via S Benedetto in Arenula 6, 00186 Rome Italy. **Tel** 011 39 6 6864171. **Bk Rev,** (Qty: 15-20). **Ad Acc.** ctrl circ. **Continues** Nuova Dwf.
 **Desc:** Covers politics and feminine culture.

CN/1186-0189
**ECHANGE DU YWCA QUEBEC, L'.** [Echange YWCA Que.]. **Added/Corp** YWCA de Quebec. **VFOAT** Echange du YWCA de Quebec. Vol. 1 (Dec. 12, 1990)-. Periodical. French. Free. YWCA de Quebec, 855 Avenue Holland, Quebec, Quebec G1S 3S5 Canada. **DD** 267.

NE
**ELEGANCE.** (19??)-. Dutch. mo (12 issues). Fl99.50 Netherlands; Fl183.50 other. BV Uitgeversmaatschappij Bonaventura, PO Box 2158, 1000 CD Amsterdam Netherlands. **Tel** 011 31 20 6914111, 011 31 20 5674911.

IT
**ELEGANTISSIMA.** L39.400 (surface mail) US; (add L3.600 airmail) Europe; (add L10.800 airmail) Asia, Africa and America; (add L17.100 airmail) Oceania; (add L9.600 registered mail). A Pieroni SRL, Viale Vittorio Veneto 28, 20124 Milan Italy. **Tel** 39 2 29000282, 29002876.

IT
**ELITE : IL MENSILE DELLA DONNA CHE SCEGLIE. Ceased.** (19??)-(June 1993). Italian. mo. Newton Periodici, Via Germanico 197, 00192 Rome Italy. **Tel** 011 39 6 3242966.

NE
**ELLE.** Dutch. mo. Fl7.50 (per number), Fl85.00 (per year). PVO ABO Services, Postbus 77, Burg Krollaan 14 A, 5126 ZH Gilze Netherlands. **Tel** (020)6244961, FAX

# Women's Interests

(020)6238538. **ED** Mrs. L Hendrikse. **Bk Rev. Ad Acc.**
**Desc:** Interviews, feature articles, fashion, cooking, travel and interior decorating and design information.

AT
**ELLE (AUSTRALIAN EDITION).** (ELLE.). (19??)-. Periodical. English. mo. 59.40Aus$ Australia; 82.60Aus$ New Zealand; 96.00Aus$ other. Australian Consolidated Press Ltd, GPO Box 5252, Sydney New South Wales 2001 Australia. **Tel** 011 61 2 2600000.

IT/1120-4397
**ELLE ED. ITALIANA.** [Elle Ed. ital.]. (1987)-. Periodical. Italian. mo. $102.00 US. RCS Rizzoli Periodici, Via A Rizzoli 2, 20132 Milan Italy. **Tel** 011 39 2 27200720. **(Subscription address:** Express Magazine, 4011 Boulevard Robert, Montreal, Quebec H1Z 4H6 Canada**) UDC** 391 & B79.

GW/0935-462X
**ELLE (MUNICH, GERMANY).** (ELLE.). [Elle]. (1988)-. Periodical. German. mo. Elle, 90 rue de Flandre, 75943 Paris Cedex 19 France. **Tel** 011 33 1 44894489.

FR/0013-6298
**ELLE (NEUILLY-SUR-SEINE, FRANCE).** (ELLE.). No. 1 (1945)-. Periodical. French. wk. $170.00. Elle, 90 rue de Flandre, 75943 Paris Cedex 19 France. **Tel** 011 33 1 44894489.

US/0888-0808
**ELLE (NEW YORK, N.Y.).** (ELLE.). [Elle] Vol. 1, No. 1 (Sept. 1985)-. Periodical. English. mo. $26.00. Hachette Magazines Inc., 1633 Broadway, New York NY 10019. **Tel** (212)767-6000. **(Subscription address:** Neodata / Colorado, PO Box 2606, Boulder Boulder CO 80322.**) LC** TT500; .E44. **DD** 391/.2/05. **Bk Rev. Ad Acc.**
**Desc:** Covers fashion, beauty, entertainment, food, travel and personalities. Strives to reach a contemporary and fashion-forward female audience.
**Ind/Abst** Access (1986-).

CN/0843-6363
**ELLE QUEBEC. See** Beauty and Cosmetics.

SP
**ELLE (SPANISH EDITION).** (ELLE.). (19??)-. Periodical. Spanish. mo. 8750ptas. Hachette Publicaciones, Calle Santa Engracia 6, 28010 Madrid, Spain. **Tel** 011 34 1 3198583. **Ad Acc.**

GW
**EMMA.** (19??)-. Periodical. German. bm. DM88.80 US and Canada; DM70.80 Germany; DM79.80 Europe; DM96.00 other. Emma-Frauenverlagsgesellschaft, Kolpingplatz 1A, W 5000 Cologne 1 Germany. **Tel** 011 49 221 210282. **(Subscription address:** Zenit Pressevertrieb GmbH, Postfach 810640, W 7000 Stuttgart 80 Germany**) LC** HQ1103; .E47. **DD** 301.41/2/0943. Index available. **Bk Rev. Ad Acc. Circ:** 45,000 (ctrl). available on microfiche.

CN/0823-8693
**ENGANCE NEWSLETTER. VAT** Enhance. Vol. 1, No 1 (1984)-. Newsletter. English. Enhance Newsletter, PO Box 16042 Station F, Ottawa Ontario K2C 3S9 Canada. **DD** 305.4/05.

CN/0225-5545
**ENTRELLES, L'.** [Entrelles]. **Main/Corp** Entrelles (Organisation). V. 1, No. 2- Mar. 1979-. Periodical. French. bm. Free. Entrelles, 1398, Succursale B, Hull Quebec J8X 3Y1 Canada. **DD** 305.4/09714/2. Continues Femme d'ICI, 0225-5537.

US/1051-2624
**ENTREPRENEURIAL WOMAN.** [Entrep. woman]. Vol. 1, No. 1 (March/April 1990)-. Periodical. English. sa. Entrepreneurial Magazine, PO Box 19787, 2392 Morse Avenue, Irvine CA 92714. **Tel** (714)261-2325. **LC** HD6054.4.U6; E58. **DD** 658.4/21/082. **Ad Acc.**
**Desc:** Places emphasis on the personalities behind successful, woman-owned businesses.

US/0749-9574
**EPISCOPAL WOMEN'S HISTORY PROJECT, THE. See** Religion and Theology-Protestantism.

US/1059-164X
**EQUAL MEANS.** (1991)-. English. Three times a year. $40.00. MS Foundation for Women, 141 Fifth Avenue 6S, New York NY 10010. **Tel** (510)549-9931, FAX (510)549-9995. **ED** Kalima Rose. **Bk Rev. Ad Acc. Circ:** 3500 (ctrl).
**Desc:** The only national publication committed to presenting women's community development models and women's economic analyses. Provides an important new tool for educators, policy makers and the general public.

US/0740-2201
**EQUAL PLAY. Suspended.** [Equal play]. **Added/Corp** Women's Action Alliance. Non-Sexist Child Development Project. Vol. 1, No. 1 (Winter 1980)-(1992). Periodical. English. qt. $10.00 (individuals), $20.00 (institutions) US; $12.50 (individuals), $22.50 (institutions) other. Women's Actions Alliance, 370 Lexington Avenue, New York NY 10017. **Tel** (212)532-8330.

●US/1063-0589
**EQUAL TIME (MENTOR, OHIO).** (EQUAL TIME.). **Added/Corp** Femality House, Inc. (1992)-. Periodical. English. mo ((10 issues)). $19.00 (1 year), $36.00 (2 year) US; $24.00 (1 year), $41.00 (2 year) Canada. Femality House, Inc., 6571 Wilson Mills Road, Cleveland OH 44143-3404. **Tel** 473-1020, FAX 473-0878. **ED** Donna McKee. **Bk Rev,** (Qty: 10). **Ad Acc, Adv Mgr Tel** 473-1020. **Acid Free. Circ:** 15,000.
**Desc:** Provides information that impowers women, increases awareness of issues that affect women, including ecological awareness, and encourages cooperation and greater unity among women.

MX
**ERES MAGAZINE.** (19??)-. Spanish. sm. $36.50 (one year), $73.00 (two year), $109.50 (three year). Editorial Eres Inc, PO Box 371104, San Diego CA 92037. **Tel** (619)276-8709, FAX (619)276-1364. **ED** Laura D.B. de Laviada 011 525 280 4036 Andres Bello 45 Piso 14 Polanco CP 11560 Mexico. **Ad Acc, Adv Mgr:** A. Schoutton, **Tel** (619)276-8709. **Circ:** 500,000 Mexico, 22,500 US.
**Desc:** Focuses on personal growth, health, relationships and entertainment. Contains interviews with celebrities plus coverage in fashion, music, TV and cinema.

US/0014-0880
**ESSENCE.** [Essence]. Vol. 1, (May 1970)-. Periodical. English. mo. $18.00. Essence, 1500 Broadway, New York NY 10036. **Tel** (212)642-0613. **(Subscription address:** Neodata / Colorado, PO Box 2606, Boulder Boulder CO 80322.**) ED** Susan L. Taylor. **LC** E185.86; .E7. **DD** 051. available on microfilm and microfiche from University Microfilms International (UMI). Documents available from UMI Article Clearinghouse, Magazine Collection.
**Desc:** A service magazine for black women. Features general editorials, women's fashion, beauty tips, health care, advice on interpersonal relationships, fiction and poetry.
**Ind/Abst** Acad. Abstr. Full Text Elite (Sept. 1984-); Acad. Abstr. (Sept. 1984-); Acad. Search (Sept. 1984-); Book Rev. Index (1984-); Curr. Lit. Fam. Plan.; Gen. Period. Index (1985-); Health Ref. Cent. (1987-) [Select. Cov.]; INFO-SOUTH Abstr.; Mag. Artic. Summar. Elite (Sept. 1984-); Mag. Artic. Summar. Select (Sept. 1984-); Mag. Artic. Summar. CD-ROM (Sept. 1984-); Mag. ASAP Plus [Full Txt.]; Mag. ASAP Sel. [Full Txt.]; Mag. Express (1988-) [Full Txt.]; Mag. Index Plus (1989-); Mag. Index Sel. Microfiche (1990-) [Full Txt.]; Mag. Index. Sel. (1986-); Mag. Search; Med. Rev. Dig.; Newsp. Period. Abstr. (1988-); Read. Guide Abstr. Select Ed.; Read. Guide Period. Lit.; Resource/One Ondisc; Mag. Index (1977-); TOM Gen. Index (1985-) [Full Txt.]; Vocat. Search (Sept. 1984-).

CN/0842-4624
**ESSENTIEL (SAINT-LAURENT).** (L'ESSENTIEL.). [Essentiel]. Vol. 1, No 1 (Oct. 1988)-. Periodical. French. mo. 44.00Can$ Canada; 88.00Can$ other. Publications Quebecor le Nordais, 5800 rue St. Denis, Bar 605, Montreal Quebec H2S 3L5 Canada. **Tel** (514)272-6330. **DD** 054/.1.

CN
**ESTIMATES. PART III, CANADIAN ADVISORY COUNCIL ON THE STATUS OF WOMEN. Main/Corp** Canada. **VFOAT** Budget des Depenses. Partie III, Conseil Consultatif Canadien de la Situation de la Femme. (19??)-. Periodical. English (French). $3.00 Canada; $3.60 other. Canada Communication Group Publishers, Order Processing, Ottawa Ontario K1A 0S9 Canada. **Tel** (819)956-4800, (819)956-4802. **LC** HQ1457; .C33a. **DD** 305.4/0971.

CN
**ESTIMATES. PART III, STATUS OF WOMEN CANADA. Main/Corp** Canada. **VFOAT** Budget des Depenses. Partie III, Condition Feminine Canada. English (French). $3.00 Canada; $3.60 other. Canadian Government Publishing Center, Supply and Services Canada, Hull Quebec K1A 0S9 Canada. **Tel** (613)990-8116, telex 053-4296. **LC** HQ1457; .C34A. **DD** 354.7100813.

BL/0104-026X
**ESTUDOS FEMINISTAS. Added/Corp** Universidade Federal do Rio de Janeiro. Centro Interdisciplinar de Estudos Contemporaneos. **VFOAT** Revista Estudos Feministas. (199?)-. Periodical. Portuguese (English; summaries and/or abstracts in French; translations available in French). sa. Universidade Federal de Rio de Janeiro / Brazil, Escuela de Comunicacao, Av. Pasteur 250, fundos, 22290 Rio de Janeiro RJ Brazil. **Tel** 021-275-1647. **ED** Lena Lavinas. **LC** HQ1180; .E88. **CODEN** ESFEE9.

US/0897-4683
**ETHNIC WOMAN, THE. See** Ethnic Interests.

●US/1350-5068
**EUROPEAN JOURNAL OF WOMEN'S STUDIES, THE.** Vol. 1, Issue 1 (Spring 1994)-. Periodical. English (French and German). qt. £79.00. Sage Publications Ltd., 6 Bonhill Street, London EC2A 4PU, UK. **Tel** 071 374 0645, FAX 071 374 8741, telex 296207 SAGE G.

XO/0139-8717
**EVA BRATISLAVA. See** Clothing Industry and Fashion.

IT
**EVA (MILAN, ITALY).** (EVA.). Vol. 1, No. 1 (1987)-. Periodical. Italian. wk.

CN/0319-7530
**EVERYWOMAN'S ALMANAC. VFOAT** Every Woman's Almanac. 1976-. English. an. Women's Educational Press, Suite 305, 280 Bloor Street West, Toronto Ontario M5S 1W1 Canada. **DD** 301.41/2/05.

II
**EVE'S WEEKLY. Suspended. VFOAT** Eve's. (1947)-(1991). Periodical. English. Fifty-two times a year. Eve's Weekly Ltd, JK Somani Building, Bombay 400 023 India. **Tel** 27144.

US/0199-2880
**EXECUTIVE FEMALE, THE. See** Business-General Management.

UK
**FAMILY CIRCLE. BRITISH EDITION.** English. mo. $58.40 US; $46.70 Canada. IPC Magazines Ltd., Perrymount Road, Haywards Heath, West Sussex RH16 3DH England. **Tel** 011 44 444 440441.

US
**FAMILY VOICE / CONCERNED WOMEN FOR AMERICA. See** Political Science.

GW/0942-8151
**FASHION GUIDE DUSSELDORF. See** Clothing Industry and Fashion.

US
**FEDERATION NEWSLETTER (UNITARIAN UNIVERSALIST WOMEN'S FEDERATION).** (FEDERATION NEWSLETTER : A JOURNAL OF THE UNITARIAN UNIVERSALIST WOMEN'S FEDERATION). **VFOAT** UUWF Federation Newsletter. V. 1, No. 1 (Oct. 15, 1976)-. Newsletter. English. qt. Unitarian Universalist Women's Federation, 25 Beacon Street, Boston MA 02108.

MX/0185-4666
**FEM.** [Fem]. **Added/Corp** Nueva Cultura Feminista (Mexico City, Mexico). (Oct./Dec. 1976)-. Periodical. Spanish. mo. $60.00 The Americas; $72.00 Europe; $84.00 other. Difusion Cultural Feminista Ac, AP 90 013 Deleg Gustavo Madero, 07501 Mexico DF Mexico. **Tel** 011 52 5 5507306. **ED** Esperanea Brito de Marti. **LC** HQ1104; .F39. **DD** 305.4/2/05. **Ad Acc, Adv Mgr:** Patricia Gonzalez, **Tel** 011 52 5 536 9261. **Circ:** 16,000 (ctrl).
**Desc:** Covers women and feminism.
**Ind/Abst** Chicano Index; HAPI Hisp. Am. Period. Index.

US/0888-4102
**FEMALE BODYBUILDING AND WEIGHT TRAINING. See** Health and Personal Fitness.

MY
**FEMINA.** Periodical. Malayalam. Avenida Armando Lombardi, 800 Sala 233 Barra da Tijuca, CEP 22 600 Rio de Janeiro RJ Brazil. **Tel** (021)399-4705.

AG
**FEMINARIA.** Vol. 1, No. 1 (June 1988)-. Periodical. Spanish. Three times a year. Andres Avellaneda, University of Florida, Department of Romance Languages and Literature, Gainesville FL 33611. **Tel** (904)375-5906. **Ind/Abst** HAPI Hisp. Am. Period. Index.

CN
**FEMINIE.** (1990)-. English. mo. Free at local newsstands; 39.00Can$ by mail. Feminie Publications Inc, 615 Yonge Street, Suite 601, Toronto Ontario, M4Y 1Z5 Canada. **Tel** (416)921-8145, FAX (416)921-5941. **ED** Alice Hawke. **Bk Rev,** (Qty: 24). **Ad Acc, Adv Mgr:** Sharon Barlow, **Tel** (416)921-3682. **Acid Free. Circ:** 12,000.
**Desc:** Focuses on personal empowerment and based on a wholistic philosophy which advocates the equal support of the mind, body, spirit, and emotions. Provides an open forum for women to publish their views and opinions.

CN/0707-9036
**FEMININ PLURIEL.** V. 1, No. 1 (Sept. 1981)-. Periodical. French. mo. $2.00 each no.; $16.00 yearly. Parallele 4 Communications, Audio-Scripto-Visuelles, 4936 Coolbrook, Montreal Quebec H3X 2K9 Canada. **DD** 054/.1.

UK/0959-3535
**FEMINISM & PSYCHOLOGY. VFOAT** Feminism and Psychology. (Spring 1991)-. Periodical.

English. qt. £85.00. Sage Publications Ltd., 6 Bonhill Street, London EC2A 4PU, UK. **Tel** 071 374 0645, FAX 071 374 8741, telex 296207 SAGE G. **ED** Sue Wilkinson. **LC** HQ1206; .F446. **DD** 150/.82. Index available. **Bk Rev. Ad Acc. Acid Free.** Documents available from The Genuine Article.
**Desc:** Fosters the development of feminist theory and practice in psychology and represents the concerns of women in a wide range of contexts across the academic-applied 'divide'.
**Ind/Abst** Curr. Contents Soc. Behav. Sci.; Res. Alert [Full Cov.]; Soc. Sci. Cit. Index [Full Cov.].

●US/1070-549X
**FEMINISM AND THE SOCIAL SCIENCES.** **See** Social Sciences.

CN/0832-5340
**FEMINISME EN REVUE, LE.** [Fem. rev.]. Vol. 1, No. 1 (Nov. 1987)-. Periodical. French. ir. Free to members. Federation des Femmes du Quebec, 5225 rue Berri, Bureau 100, Montreal Quebec H2J 2S4 Canada. **Tel** (514)948-3262. **DD** 305.4/09714. ***Continues*** *FFQ Petite Presse, 0228-8478.*

US/1041-1801
**FEMINISMS (COLUMBUS, OHIO).** ***Ceased.*** (FEMINISMS / THE OHIO STATE UNIVERSITY CENTER FOR WOMEN'S STUDIES.). [Feminisms]. **Added/Corp** Ohio State University. Center for Women's Studies. Vol. 1, No. 1 (Winter 1988)-Vol. 5, No. 3 (May/June 1992). Periodical. English. bm. Ohio State University / Center for Womens Studies, 207 Dulles Hall, 230 W 17th Avenue, Columbus OH 43210. **Tel** (614)292-1021. **ED** Kim Davies. **LC** HQ1101; .F444. **DD** 305. Index available. cum. index. **Bk Rev. Circ:** 400. ***Formed by the union of*** *Sojourner (Columbus, Ohio), 0889-4981* ***and*** *Women's Studies Review, 0195-6604.*
**Desc:** Our goal is varieties of feminist expression and to continue the condition of connecting the center for women's studies to the women's community through our publication.

GW/0179-8367
**FEMINIST, DER.** (1976)-. Academic Scholarly Publication. German (translations available in English). an. DM9.50. Der Feminist, Christrosenweg 5, 81377 Munich Germany. **Tel** 011 089 7149 187. **ED** Hannelore Mabry. **LC** HQ1103; .F38. **DD** 305.4/2/05. Index available. cum. index. **Bk Rev. Ad Acc. Circ:** 4,000.
**Desc:** Covers political and economical aspects of feminism: analysis of the history of the first and second women's movements, the theory of patriarchy, disputes with Marxism, radical feminism and pacifism, criticism of the bible and theology.

CN/0831-3377
**FEMINIST ACTION.** ***Ceased.*** (FEMINIST ACTION : NEWS FROM THE NATIONAL ACTION COMMITTEE ON THE STATUS OF WOMEN.). [Fem. action]. **VFOAT** Action Feministe. Vol. 1, No. 1 (July 1985)-Vol. 6, No. 2. Periodical. English (French). Eight times a year. Feminist Action, 344 Bloor Street West, Suite 505, Toronto Ontario M5S 1W9 Canada. **Tel** (416)922-3246. **ED** Pat Daley. **DD** 305.4/2/06071. **Circ:** 300. ***Formed by the union of*** *Memo (National Action Committee on the Status of Women), 0830-0712* ***and*** *Status of Women News, 0381-9418.* ***Continued in part by*** *Action Feministe.*

UK
**FEMINIST ACTION (LONDON).** (FEMINIST ACTION.). 1984-. English. **ED** J Holland.

US/0741-6555
**FEMINIST BOOKSTORE NEWS.** [Fem. bookst. news]. **VFOAT** FBN. (19??)-. Trade Publication. English. bm. $75.00 (one year), $140.00 (two year). Feminist Bookstore News, PO Box 882554, San Francisco CA 94188. **Tel** (415)626-1556. **ED** Carol Seajay. **DD** 362. cum. index. **Bk Rev. Ad Acc, Adv Mgr:** Sandy. **Circ:** 500 (ctrl). ***Continues*** *Feminist Bookstore Newsletter.*
**Desc:** The trade magazine of the Women-in-Print movement. Reviews 200 books of feminist interest per issue with complete ordering information for small presses.

US/0742-7441
**FEMINIST COLLECTIONS (MADISON, WIS.).** (FEMINIST COLLECTIONS : A QUARTERLY OF WOMEN'S STUDIES RESOURCES / WOMEN'S STUDIES LIBRARIAN, THE UNIVERSITY OF WISCONSIN SYSTEM.). [Fem. collect.]. **Added/Corp** University of Wisconsin System. Women's Studies Librarian. Vol. 1 (Feb. 1980)-. Periodical. English. qt. $7.00 University of Wisconsin affiliated individual; $12.60 University of Wisconsin affiliated organization; $13.25 Wisconsin individual and Wisconsin women's program; $25.00 (individuals), $46.00 (institutions) other. University of Wisconsin Women's Studies Librarian, 728 State Street, 430 Memorial Library, Madison WI 53706. **Tel** (608)263-5754, FAX (608)265-2754. **ED** Phyllis Holman Weisbard, Carolyn Wilson, Linda Shult, Ingrid Markhardt. **LC** Z688.W65; F46. **DD** 305. Index available. **Bk Rev. Circ:** 1,400.
**Desc:** Reviews women studies resources in print, film and video. Focus on reference works.
**Ind/Abst** Stud. Women Abstr.

●UK/1354-5701
**FEMINIST ECONOMICS.** **See** Economics.

UK/0732-6378
**FEMINIST FORUM.** [Fem. forum]. 5th issue (1982)-. Periodical. English. $235.00. Pergamon Press, An Imprint of Elsevier Science Ltd., The Boulevard, Langford Lane, Kidlington, Oxford OX5 1GB United Kingdom. **Tel** 011 44 865 843000, 011 44 865 843699, FAX 011 44 865 843010. **(Subscription address:** Elsevier Science Ltd. Oxford Fulfillment Centre, PO Box 800, Kidlington, Oxford OX5 1DX United Kingdom.**) LC** HQ1101; .W776. **DD** 305.4/05. ***Continues*** *Women's Studies International Quarterly Forum, 0733-0065.*
**Desc:** Supplement to Women's Studies International Forum.

US/0270-6679
**FEMINIST ISSUES.** [Fem. issues]. **Added/Corp** Feminist Forum, Inc. Vol. 1, No. 1 (Summer 1980)-. Periodical. English. Twice a year. Fl116.00 (individual), Fl199.00 (institution). Transaction Publishers / Rutgers State University, New Brunswick NJ 08903. **Tel** (908)932-2280 Ext. 105, FAX (908)932-3138. **ED** Mary Jo Lakeland and Susan Ellis Wolf. **LC** HQ1101; .F45. **DD** 305.4/2/05. **[CCC]. Bk Rev. Ad Acc. Circ:** 600. available on labels; available on microfilm and microfiche from University Microfilms International (UMI). Documents available from UMI Article Clearinghouse.
**Desc:** Devoted to feminist social and political analysis, with emphasis on an international exchange of ideas. Explores central feminist questions in ways relevant to the daily lives of women everywhere.
**Ind/Abst** Altern. Press Index; Expand. Acad. Index (1992-); Left Index; Middle East Abstr. Index; Newsp. Period. Abstr. (1992-); Romant. Move.; Sage Fam. Stud. Abstr. (?-?); Stud. Women Abstr.; Middle East J.; Women Stud. Abstr.

US/0742-7433
**FEMINIST PERIODICALS (MADISON, WIS.).** (FEMINIST PERIODICALS : A CURRENT LISTING OF CONTENTS.). [Fem. period.]. **Added/Corp** University of Wisconsin System. Women's Studies Librarian. Vol. 1, No. 1 (1980)-. Periodical. English. qt. $7.00 University of Wisconsin affiliated individual; $12.60 University of Wisconsin affiliated organization; $13.25 Wisconsin individual and Wisconsin women's program; $25.00 (individuals), $46.00 (institutions) other. University of Wisconsin Women's Studies Librarian, 728 State Street, 430 Memorial Library, Madison WI 53706. **Tel** (608)263-5754, FAX (608)265-2754. **ED** Phyllis Holman Weisbard, Carolyn Wilson, Linda Shult, Ingrid Markhardt. **LC** Z7963.F44; F45; HQ1101. **DD** 016.30542/05. **Circ:** 1,400.
**Desc:** A reproduction of table of contents pages of over 90 major feminist periodicals.

UK
**FEMINIST PRAXIS.** **Added/Corp** University of Manchester. Sociology Dept. Monograph No. 31 (1990)-. Monographic series. English. Price varies per volume. University of Manchester / Department of Sociology, Manchester M13 9PL England. ***Continues*** *Studies in Sexual Politics.*
**Ind/Abst** Soc. Plann. Policy Dev. Abstr.

UK/0141-7789
**FEMINIST REVIEW.** [Fem. rev.]. (1979)-. Periodical. English. Three times a year. $110.00 (US & Canada); £68.00 (UK); £74.00 (other). Routledge, 11 New Fetter Lane, London EC4P 4EE England. **Tel** 071 583 9855, FAX 071 842 2298. **(Subscription address:** Kinokuniya Company Ltd., 38-1 Sakuragaoka 5, chome Setagaya-ku, Tokyo 156 Japan.**) LC** HQ1154; .F4465. **DD** 305.4/2/05. **[CCC]. Bk Rev. Ad Acc. Circ:** 3,500. Documents available from The Genuine Article, UMI Article Clearinghouse.
**Desc:** Explores the diverse, theoretical and strategic issues and the differing experiences of women, in the struggle for a socialist feminist future.
**Ind/Abst** Acad. Abstr. Full Text Elite (Jan. 1992-); Acad. Abstr. (Jan. 1992-); Acad. Search (Jan. 1992-); Altern. Press Index; Appl. Soc. Sci. Index Abstr.; Arts Humanit. Citation Index [Select. Cov.]; Curr. Contents Soc. Behav. Sci.; Expand. Acad. Index (1989-); INFO-SOUTH Abstr.; Int. Bibliogr. Sociol.; Int. Labour Doc.; Left Index; Mag. Search; Middle East Abstr. Index; Newsp. Period. Abstr. (1991-); Res. Alert [Full Cov.]; Res. High. Educ. Abstr.; Sage Race Relat. Abstr.; Soc. Plann. Policy Dev. Abstr.; Soc. Sci. Source (Jan. 1992-); Soc. Sci. Cit. Index [Full Cov.]; Soc. Sci. Index; Soc. Sci. Index Fulltext (Autumn 1988-) [Full Txt.]; Sociol. Abstr.; Stud. Women Abstr.

US/0046-3663
**FEMINIST STUDIES.** (FEMINIST STUDIES: FS.). [Fem. stud.]. **VFOAT** FS. (Summer 1972)-. Periodical. English. Three times a year. $30.00 (1 year), $57.00 (2 year), $80.00 (3 year) individual; $65.00 (1 year), $125.00 (2 year), $180.00 (3 year) institution. Feminist Studies, %Women's Studies Program, University of Maryland, College Park MD 20742. **Tel** (301)405-7415, FAX (301)314-9190. **ED** Claire G. Moses. **LC** HQ1101; .F46. **DD** 305.4/2/05. **CODEN** FMSDA2. Index available. cum. index. **Bk Rev. Ad Acc. Pr Rev.** available on microfilm and microfiche from University Microfilms International (UMI). Documents available from The Genuine Article, UMI Article Clearinghouse.
**Desc:** Founded to encourage analytic responses to feminist issues and to open new areas of research, criticism, and speculation. The editors are committed to providing a forum for feminist analysis, debate and exchange.
**Ind/Abst** Acad. Abstr. Full Text Elite (July 1990-); Acad. Abstr. (July 1990-); Acad. Ind. [Computer File] (1987-); Acad. Search (July 1990-); Altern. Press Index; Am. Hist. Life (1972-); Appl. Soc. Sci. Index Abstr.; ARTbibliogr. Mod. (1984-); Arts Humanit. Citation Index [Select. Cov.]; BHA : Biblio. Hist. Art; Child. Lit. Abstr. (19??-); Expand. Acad. Index (1987-); INFO-SOUTH Abstr.; Lit. Crit. Regist. (1972-); Mag. Search; Middle East Abstr. Index; MLA Int. Bibl. Books Artic. Mod. Lang. Lit.; Multicult. Educ. Abstr. (1972-); Newsp. Period. Abstr. (1990-); Philos. Index; Psychol. Abstr. (1978-); Res. Alert [Full Cov.]; Romant. Move. (1978-); Sage Fam. Stud. Abstr. (?-?); Sage Race Relat. Abstr.; Soc. Plann. Policy Dev. Abstr.; Soc. Sci. Source (Jul. 1990-); Soc. Sci. Cit. Index (1972-) [Full Cov.]; Soc. Sci. Index; Soc. Sci. Index Fulltext (Fall 1988-) [Full Txt.]; Sociol. Abstr.; Stud. Women Abstr. (1984-); West. Hist. Q.; Women Stud. Abstr.

US/0882-4843
**FEMINIST TEACHER.** **See** Education-Teaching and Curriculum.

CN/0318-2452
**FEMME.** V. 1- Feb. 1975-. French. mo. $1.00 each no., $10.00 yearly. Editions Lizon, 385 Boul Lebeau Ville Saint-Laurent, Montreal Quebec H4N 1S3 Canada. **DD** 054/.1.

FR/0764-0021
**FEMME ACTUELLE.** (1984)-. Periodical. French. wk. 282.08 France; 500.00F other. Prisma Presse, 6 rue Daru, 75379 Paris Cedex 08, France. **Tel** 011 33 1 44153000, FAX 011 33 1 47641042. **(Subscription address:** Ca M Interesse, Service Abbonements B 110, 60732 Ste Geneva Cedex 9 France.**) UDC** 087.6.

CN/0847-5261
**FEMME ET LA LOI, LA.** **See** Law.

FR/0764-4523
**FEMME PARIS, 1984.** [Femme Paris, 1984]. (1984)-. Periodical. French. bm. 107.74F France; 186.00F other. EDI 7, 6 rue Ancelle, 92525 Neuilly Sur Seine, Cedex France. **Tel** 011 33 1 40886000. **(Subscription address:** EDI 7, 90 rue de Flandre SVC Abonmnts, 75947 Paris Cedex 19 France.**) UDC** 087.2-055.2. ***Continues*** *F (Paris), 0754-0612.*

CN/0838-9446
**FEMME PLUS (MONTREAL).** (FEMME PLUS.). [Femme plus]. **VFOAT** Homme Plus. Vol. 1 No 1 (Feb. 1988)-. Periodical. French. mo. 44.00Can$ Canada; 88.00Can$ other. Publications Quebecor le Nordais, 5800 rue St. Denis, Bar 605, Montreal Quebec H2S 3L5 Canada. **Tel** (514)272-6330. **DD** 305.4/09714.
**Ind/Abst** Point Repere (Feb. 1991-).

FR/0014-9926
**FEMME PRATIQUE.** [Femme prat.]. (1958)-. Periodical. French. mo (11 issues). 109.70F (one year), 205.68F (two year) France; 299.00F other. Editions Maredage, Zac de Fregy, 77610 Fontenay Presigny France. **Tel** 011 33 1 64252193, FAX 011 33 1 64252101. **(Subscription address:** Femme Pratique Service Abonnement, BP 26, F 77932 Perthes Cedex France**) UDC** 087-055.2.

CN/0226-9902
**FEMMES D'ACTION.** [Femmes action]. **Added/Corp** Federation des Femmes Canadiennes-Francaises. Vol. 10 No. 1 (Spring/Summer 1980)-. Periodical. French. qt (five issues per year). 12.00Can$, 23.00Can$ (institutions) Canada; 20.00Can$, 26.00Can$ (airmail) other. Femmes d'action, 525-325 rue Dalhousie, Ottawa Ontario K1N 7G2 Canada. **Tel** (613)232-5791. **ED** Micheline Piche. **DD** 305.4/06/071. **Bk Rev. Ad Acc. Circ:** 3,000. ***Continues*** *Femme d'Action, 0226-9899.*
**Desc:** The only national magazine in French covering exclusively the sociological, economic, political and cultural status of the life of women in their minority situation in Canada.
**Ind/Abst** Can. Period. Index.

CN/0705-3851
**FEMMES D'ICI.** **Added/Corp** Association Feminine D'Education et D'Action Sociale. Vol. 12, (Sept. 1977)-. Periodical. French. Five times a year (Jan., Mar., May, Sept., Nov.). 14.02Can$. Association Feminine d'Education et d'Action Sociale, 5999 de Marseilles, Montreal QUE H1N 1K6 Canada. **Tel** (514)251-1636. **DD** 301.41/2/05. ***Continues*** *Association Feminine D'Education et D'Action Sociale. A F E A S., 0381-7598.*

US/0361-4581
**FILMS BY AND/OR ABOUT WOMEN.** ***Ceased.*** **See** Motion Picture.

US/1059-3950
**FINANCIAL WOMAN TODAY.** **See** Business-Banking and Finance.

CN/0706-3857
**FIREWEED.** (Autumn 1978)-. Periodical. English. qt. 27.00Can$ (institutions), 18.00Can$ (individuals)

Canada; 36.00Can$ (institutions), 24.00Can$ (individuals) other. Fireweed Collective, PO Box 279 Station B, Toronto Ontario M5T 2W2 Canada. **Tel** (416)504-1339. **DD** C810/.8/09287. **[CCC]. Bk Rev**, (Qty: infrequently). **Ad Acc, Adv Mgr:** Z. Dhanam. **Circ:** 2,000.
**Desc:** Idea-oriented journal of politics and the creative arts, combining analytical articles, fiction, poetry, photos and drawings. Its editorial policy of diversity is reflected in thematic issues. The bound book format provides for in-depth articles and debate on current issues relevant to feminists.
**Ind/Abst** Soc. Plann. Policy Dev. Abstr.

CN/0383-7912
**FIREWEED : A FEMINIST QUARTERLY.** V. 1- May/June 1976-. English. qt. $21.00 Canada; $34.00 other. Fireweed, PO Box 279 Station B Canada. **Tel** (416)323-9512. **DD** 917.19/1/043. **Bk Rev. Circ:** 1,500.
**Desc:** Feminist culture and literature, poetry, fiction, visual performance, art and theory.

US/1040-9467
**FIRST FOR WOMEN.** [First women]. **VFOAT** First. Vol. 1; (1989)-. Periodical. English. Seventeen times a year. $24.00 US; $37.00 other. Heinrich Bauer North America, PO Box 1649, 270 Sylvan Avenue, Englewood NJ 07631. **Tel** (201)569-0006. **ED** Dena Vane (editor's phone: (201)569-6699). **DD** 646. **Ad Acc. Circ:** 1.2 million.

US
**FLAME (SEATTLE, WASH.).** (THE FLAME: NEWSLETTER OF THE COALITION ON WOMEN AND RELIGION.). **Added/Corp** Coalition on Women and Religion (Seattle, Wash.). No. 1 (Jan. 7, 1975)-. Newsletter. English. qt. $12.00 (comes with membership for Coalition on Women and Religion). Coalition on Women & Religion, 4759 15th Avenue NE, Seattle WA 98105. **Tel** (206)324-8963. **ED** Nancy G. Weinstein. **Bk Rev**, (Qty: 4). **Circ:** 225.
**Desc:** Newsletter with feminist and religious information, book reviews, articles, spiritually affirming messages and reports from sisters all over the world.

CN/0708-4927
**FLARE (TORONTO).** (FLARE.). [Flare]. Vol. 1 (Sept. 1979)-. Periodical. English. Twelve times a year. 15.00Can$ Canada, 37.00Can$ others (surface mail); 60.00Can$ US, 105.00Can$ others (airmail). MacLean Hunter Publ. Limited / Toronto, 777 Bay Street, 8th Floor Agency Control, Toronto Ontario M5W 1A7 Canada. **Tel** (416)596-5000, (800)268-6811, FAX (416)596-5526. **ED** Bonnie Hurowitz. **DD** 051. **Bk Rev. Ad Acc.** available on microfilm and microfiche from University Microfilms International (UMI). ***Supersedes** Miss Chatelaine, 0026-5918.*
**Desc:** Canada's national fashion, beauty and lifestyle magazine for young working women.
**Ind/Abst** Can. Index; Can. Period. Index (19??-).

US
**FLYER (EVANSTON, ILL.).** (THE FLYER.). **Added/Corp** United Methodist Church (United States). Commission on the Status and Role of Women. Vol. 1, No. 1 (June 1978)-. Periodical. English. Four times a year. $5.00. Commission on the Status & Role of Women, 1200 Davis, United Methodist Church, Evanston IL 60201. **Tel** (312)869-7330. **Circ:** 16,000 (ctrl).

●UK/0968-2864
**FOCUS ON GENDER.** (March 1993)-. English. Three times a year. £20.00. Oxfam Publications, 274 Banbury Road, Oxford OX2 7DZ England. **Tel** 011 41 865 313196, FAX 011 41 865 313117. **(Subscription address:** Carfax Publishing Co., PO Box 25, Abingdon, Oxfordshire OX14 3UE United Kingdom.**) ED** Bridget Walker. Index available. **Bk Rev. Circ:** 100.
**Desc:** Focuses specifically on gender and women's issues internationally and aims to explore the links between gender and development initiatives around the world.

US/1056-3199
**FOCUS (WASHINGTON, D.C. 1990). See** Education-Higher Education.

CN/0713-8547
**FOCUS WOMEN.** (FOCUS WOMEN : STATUS OF WOMEN/UVIC ACTION GROUP ... ANNUAL CONFERENCE REPORT.). [Focus women]. **Main/Corp** Victoria Status of Women Action Group. Conference. English. Victoria Status of Women, PO Box 8484, Victoria British Columbia V8W 3S1 Canada. **Tel** (604)381-1012. **DD** 305.4/2/06071134.

US/0160-9831
**FOLKLORE WOMEN'S COMMUNICATION. See** Folklore.

●US/1064-7996
**FOR THE BRIDE BY DEMETRIOS (UNITED KINGDOM ED.). See** Family and Marriage.

US/0745-3086
**FORWARD (MADISON, WIS.).** (FORWARD / LEAGUE OF WOMEN VOTERS OF WISCONSIN.). **Added/Corp** League of Women Voters of Wisconsin. (19??)-. Periodical. English. Five times a year. $3.00. Wisconsin League of Women Voters, 625 West Washington Avenue, Madison WI 53703. **Tel** (608)256-0827. **Circ:** 2,800.

GW
**FRAUEN UND FILM. See** Motion Picture.

CN/0821-5294
**FREE SPACE.** [Free space]. Periodical. English. mo. Free Space, 1 19 St Francis Street, Ottawa Ontario K1Y 1W6 Canada. **DD** 305.4/09713/84.

US/0272-4367
**FREEDOM SOCIALIST, THE. See** Political Science-Socialism, Communism, Anarchism, Utopianism.

CN/0824-1961
**FRIEND INDEED.** (A FRIEND INDEED : FOR WOMEN IN THE PRIME OF LIFE.). [Friend indeed]. Vol. 1, No. 1 (Apr. 1984)-. Periodical. English (French). mo (except July and August). 30.00Can$. A Friend Indeed, Box 515, Place du Parc Station, Montreal Quebec H2W 2P1 Canada. **Tel** (514)843-5730, FAX (514)843-5681. **(Subscription address:** Friend Indeed Publications, PO Box 1710, Champlain NY 12919.**) ED** Janine O'Leary Cobb. **DD** 618.1/75/005. **[CCC].** Index available. cum. index. **Bk Rev**, (Qty: 1). **Circ:** 6,000 (ctrl).
**Desc:** Newsletter of information, support and exchange for women during menopause and/or midlife. Features monthly topic plus extensive letters section.

US/0740-5618
**FRIENDLY WOMAN, THE. Added/Corp** Society of Friends. Vol. 1, No. 1 (Nov. 1974)-. Periodical. English. qt. $12.00 (one year), $20.00 (two year). Friendly Woman, PO Box 100830, Denver CO 80050. **LC** BX7748.W64; F75. **DD** 289.6/088042. Index available. **Bk Rev. Circ:** 1,000.
**Desc:** A journal for the exchange of ideas, feelings, hopes, and experiences by and among Quaker women.

US/0160-9009
**FRONTIERS (BOULDER).** (FRONTIERS.). [Frontiers]. **Added/Corp** University of Colorado, Boulder. Women Studies Program. Vol. 1 (Fall 1975)-. Periodical. English. Three times a year. $20.00 (individuals); $33.00 (institutions). University Press of Colorado, PO Box 849, Niwot CO 80544. **Tel** (303)530-5337, FAX (303)530-5306. **ED** Charlotta C. Hensley. **LC** HQ1101; .F76. Index available. cum. index. **Bk Rev. Ad Acc. Pr Rev. Circ:** 1,000 (ctrl). available on microfilm and microfiche from University Microfilms International (UMI). Documents available from The Genuine Article, UMI Article Clearinghouse.
**Desc:** Appeals to academic and community feminists by publishing articles and creative work that are substantive and accessible to all readers interested in women's issues.
**Ind/Abst** Acad. Ind. [Computer File] (1992-); Am. Hist. Life (1977-); Am. Humanit. Index (199?-); Arts Humanit. Citation Index [Select. Cov.]; Expand. Acad. Index (1992-); Hum. Resour. Abstr. (?-?); Lit. Crit. Regist.; MLA Int. Bibl. Books Artic. Mod. Lang. Lit.; Multicult. Educ. Abstr.; Newsp. Period. Abstr. (1992-); Res. Alert [Full Cov.]; Soc. Plann. Policy Dev. Abstr.; Soc. Sci. Cit. Index [Full Cov.]; Sociol. Abstr.; Stud. Women Abstr. (1977-); Women Stud. Abstr.

CC
**FU NU SHENG HUO.** (19??)-. Periodical. Chinese. mo. RMBY0.25. Fu Nu Sheng Huo, Post Office, Cheng-Tu Shih, People's Republic of China. **LC** HQ1766; .F8. **DD** 305.4/0951.

JA
**FUJIN KORON.** (1916)-. Periodical. Japanese. mo. $171.00. **(Subscription address:** Japan Publications Trading Company, Ltd., PO Box 5030, Tokyo International, Tokyo 100-31 Japan.**) LC** HQ1104; .F825.

JA/0388-1709
**FUJIN KYOIKU JOHO. See** Education.

JA
**FUJIN RODO NO JITSUJO.** ***Title Change.*** **See** Economics-Labor.

UK
**FWZ REVIEW.** ***Title Change.*** **Main/Corp** Federation of Women Zionists of Great Britain and Ireland. (Sept. 1974)-(19??). Periodical. English. Three times a year. Federation of Women Zionists, 107 Gloucester Place, London W1H 4BY England. **LC** DS149.A1; J49. **DD** 956.94/001/0941. ***Continues** Jewish Woman's Review.* ***Continued by** Vision.*

●US/1062-7367
**FYI EVERYWOMAN'S RESOURCE GUIDE TO L.I. VFOAT** Everywoman's Resource Guide to L.I.; FYI. **VAT** FYI Everywoman's Resource Guide to Long Island. (1993)-. English. $7.95. Jag Publishers Ltd., PO Box 271, Greenvale NY 11548. **Tel** (516)625-3033, FAX (516)625-3411.

CN/0704-4550
**GAZETTE DES FEMMES, LA.** [Gaz. femmes]. **Added/Corp** Quebec (Province). Conseil du Statut de la Femme. Vol. 1 (Oct. 1979)-. Periodical. French. bm. Free. Conseil du Statut de la Femme du Quebec, 8 Rue Cook, 3E Etage/Bureau 300, Quebec G1R 5J7 Canada. **Tel** (418)643-4326. **ED** Therese Mailloux and Francine Gagnon. **DD** 305.4/09714. **Bk Rev. Circ:** 48,000. ***Supersedes** Quebec (Province) Conseil du Statut de la Femme. Le Bulletin du C S F, 0708-3378.*
**Desc:** General information on women's movement and feminism issues; new rights, research reports, book reviews.
**Ind/Abst** Point Repere (1983-).

JA
**GENDAI NI IKIRU JOSEI JITEN. VFOAT** Josei Jiten. 1981-. Japanese. an. ¥3800. Nichigai Asoshietsu, c/o Dai 3 Shimokawa Building, 23-8 Omori Kita 1-chome, Ota-ku 143, Tokyo-to Japan. **Tel** 03-763-7581 OR 03-764-0845. **LC** HQ1762; .G453.

UK/0953-5233
**GENDER & HISTORY. VFOAT** Gender and History. (Spring 1989)-. Academic Scholarly Publication. English. Three times a year. £81.00 UK and Europe; $128.00 North America; £98.00 other. Basil Blackwell Publishers Ltd, 108 Cowley Road, Oxford 0X4 1JF England. **Tel** 011 44 865 791100, FAX 011 44 865 791347, telex 837022 OXBOOK G. **(Subscription address:** Blackwell Publishers / UK, Marston Book Services, PO Box 87, Oxford OX2 0DT England.**) ED** Leonore Davidoff and Nancy Hewitt. **LC** HQ1101; .G46. **DD** 305.3/05. **[CCC].** Index available. **Bk Rev. Ad Acc.** available on microfilm and microfiche from University Microfilms International (UMI).
**Desc:** Only specialist journal discussing historical questions of gender and the roles of women and men in the past.
**Ind/Abst** Am. Hist. Life (1989-); Int. Bibliogr. Sociol.; Women Stud. Abstr.

●UK/0966-369X
**GENDER, PLACE AND CULTURE: A JOURNAL OF FEMINIST GEOGRAPHY. See** Sociology-Manners and Customs.

US/0745-2209
**GFWC CLUBWOMAN. Added/Corp** General Federation of Women's Clubs. **VFOAT** G.F.W.C. Clubwoman. **VAT** General Federation of Women's Clubs Clubwoman. (19??)-. Periodical. English. qt. $6.00 (one year), $11.00 (two years), $16.50 (three years). General Federation of Women's Club, 1734 North Street NW, Washington DC 20036. **Tel** (202)347-3168. **ED** E Deborah Koehle. **LC** HQ1871; .G46. **DD** 367/.088042. **Ad Acc. Circ:** 24,000 (ctrl).

IT/0017-0062
**GIOIA.** [Gioia]. (1937)-. Periodical. Italian. wk. L124800 Italy; L290000 other. Rusconi Editore Spa, Servicio Abbonements, V Le Sarca 235, 20126 Milan Italy. **Tel** 011 39 2 66192634. **UDC** (05).

US/0017-0747
**GLAMOUR.** [Glamour]. (1941)-. Periodical. English. mo. $15.00 (one year), $28.00 (two year). Conde Nast Publications / New York, 350 Madison Avenue, New York NY 10017. **Tel** (212)880-8800, (800)777-0700. **(Subscription address:** Neodata / Colorado, PO Box 2606, Boulder Boulder CO 80322.**) ED** Ruth Whitney. **LC** TT500; .G46. **Ad Acc.** available on microfilm and microfiche from University Microfilms International (UMI). Documents available from UMI Article Clearinghouse, Magazine Collection. ***Continues** Glamour of Hollywood;* ***Absorbed** Charm.*
**Desc:** A fashion/beauty monthly; how to use new fashion, look great, keep fit, give parties, travel stylishly, advance careers, enjoy life.
**Ind/Abst** Acad. Abstr. Full Text Elite (Jan. 1989-); Acad. Abstr. (Jan. 1989-); Consum. Health Nutr. Index (?-?); Consum. Index Prod. Eval. Inf. Source; Gen. Period. Index (1985-); Health Ref. Cent. (1987-) [Select. Cov.]; Mag. Artic. Summar. Elite (Jan. 1989-); Mag. Artic. Summar. Select (Jan. 1989-); Mag. Artic. Summar. CD-ROM (Jan. 1989-); Mag. Index Plus (1989-); Mag. Index Sel. Microfiche (1990-) [Full Txt.]; Mag. Index. Sel. (1986-); Mag. Search; Med. Rev. Dig.; Newsp. Period. Abstr. (1988-); Read. Guide Abstr. Select Ed.; Read. Guide Period. Lit.; Mag. Index (1977-); TOM Gen. Index (1985-) [Full Txt.]; Vocat. Search (Jan. 1989-).

●IT
**GLAMOUR MILANO.** (GLAMOUR.). (1992)-. Periodical. Italian. mo. L28800 Italy; L79800 other. Edizioni Conde Nast Spa, Piazza Castello 27, 20121 Milan Italy. **Tel** 011 39 2 85611. **(Subscription address:** Arnoldo Mondadori Editore, Uff Cont Abbonamenti, 20090 Segrate Mi Italy**) *Continues*** *Lei (Milano. 1976), 1120-7736.*

FR/0990-6479
**GLAMOUR PARIS.** (GLAMOUR.). (1988)-. Periodical. French. Ten times a year. $65.00 US; 137.12F France; 180.00F Belgium; 280.00F others. Les Editions Conde Nast, Service Abonnements B620, 60732 S Genevieve Cedex 9 France. **Tel** 011 33 45 673505, 44 034400. **UDC** 087.2-055.2.

US/0898-4719
**GOLF FOR WOMEN : GFW. See** Recreation, Leisure-Sports.

US/0017-209X
**GOOD HOUSEKEEPING (U.S. ED.).** **See** Home Economics.

PL/0137-4249
**GOSPODYNI WARSZAWA.** (GOSPODYNI.). [Gospodyni Warsz.]. (1966)-. Periodical. Polish. wk. $78.00. **(Subscription address:** ARS Polona, PO Box 1001, 00068 Warsaw Poland.**)** **UDC** 631(438). ***Continues*** *Gospodyni Wiejska, 0867-437X.*

US/1064-4377
**GRANTS FOR WOMEN AND GIRLS.** **See** Philanthropy.

IT
**GRAZIA.** (19??)-. L78000 Italy; L226800 other. Arnoldo Mondadori Editore, UFF Cont Abbonamenti, 20090 Segrate MI Italy. **Tel** 011 39 2 75422015, telex 320457 MONDMI I.

IT
**GUIDA CUCINA.** (19??)-. Italian. L50700 Italy; L113100 other. Arnoldo Mondadori Editore, UFF Cont Abbonamenti, 20090 Segrate MI Italy. **Tel** 011 39 2 75422015, telex 320457 MONDMI I.

GR
**GYNAIKA.** Greek, Modern. bw. E. Terzopolos Publishing Enterprises S.A., 7 Odos Fragoklisias, GR-151 25, Marousi, Greece. **Tel** 011 30 1 6899160, FAX 011 30 1 6899162.

KO
**HANGUK YWCA.** **VFOAT** Korea YWCA; Hanguk Y.W.C.A.; Korea Y.W.C.A. Periodical. Korean. mo. Taehan YWCA Yonghaphoe, 1-3 1-ka Myong-dong Chung-ku, Seoul Korea. **LC** BV1360.K8; H35.

UK
**HARPERS & QUEEN.** **VFOAT** Harpers Bazaar & Queen; Harpers Bazaar and Queen; Harpers and Queen. (1970)-. English. Twelve times a year. £73.50 US; £93.00 others. National Magazine Company Ltd., 72 Broadwick Street, London W1V 2BP England. **Tel** 011 44 71 5395214, FAX 011 44 071 4376886, telex 263 879 NATMAG G. available on microfilm and microfiche from University Microfilms International (UMI). ***Continues*** *Queen.*

IT/1121-7375
**HARPER'S BAZAAR ITALIA.** **See** Clothing Industry and Fashion.

●UK/0966-2995
**HARPIES & QUINES.** [Harpies quines]. **VFOAT** Harpies and Quines. (1992)-. Periodical. English. bm (6 issues). £14.00 UK. Harpies and Quines, PO Box 543, Glasgow G49 LY Scotland. **Tel** 011 44 41 3531550, FAX 011 44 41 3320175. **ED** Charlotte Ross. **DD** 305.4209411. **Bk Rev**, (Qty: 30). **Ad Acc**, **Adv Mgr:** Helen Chambers. **Circ:** 6,000.
**Desc:** Feminist magazine covering women's issues.

●US/1070-910X
**HARVARD WOMEN'S HEALTH WATCH.** **See** Medical Science and Technology-Gynecology and Obstetrics.

US/0270-1456
**HARVARD WOMEN'S LAW JOURNAL.** **See** Law.

●US/1061-4109
**HAWAII'S VOICES.** **Added/Corp** Women of Hawaii in the Arts Project. (1992)-. Periodical. English. qt. Free (members), $12.00 (non-members). WOHA, 94-535 Anania Court, #103, Miliani HI 96789.

US/1040-7359
**HAWORTH SERIES ON WOMEN.** ***Title Change.*** [Haworth ser. women]. (1989)-(19??). Monographic series. English. ir. The Haworth Press Inc, 10 Alice Street, Binghamton NY 13904-1580. **Tel** (607)722-5857, (800)3-HAWORTH, FAX (607)722-1424. **DD** 305. Documents available from Haworth Document Delivery Service. ***Continued by*** *Haworth Women's Studies, 1062-7847.*

US/0739-9332
**HEALTH CARE FOR WOMEN INTERNATIONAL.** **See** Medical Science and Technology-Gynecology and Obstetrics.

CN/0226-1510
**HEALTHSHARING.** ***Ceased.*** **See** Public Health and Safety.

AT/0311-4198
**HECATE.** [Hecate]. Vol. 1 (Jan. 1975)-. Periodical. English. Twice a year. 40.00Aus$ (institutions), 15.00Aus$ (individuals). Hecate, PO Box 99, St Lucia Queensland 4067 Australia. **Tel** 011-61-7-3653146, FAX 011-61-7-3652799. **ED** Carole Ferrier. Index available. cum. index. **Bk Rev**, (Qty: 2-10). **Ad Acc.** **Pr Rev. Circ:** 2,000. Documents available from UMI Article Clearinghouse.
**Desc:** Interdisciplinary writing from women's liberation socialist perspectives about Australia and elsewhere, plus creative writing.
**Ind/Abst** Altern. Press Index; Annu. Bibliogr. Engl. Lang. Lit.; APAIS, Aust. Public Aff. Inf. Ser. (1977-); Expand. Acad. Index (1992-); Left Index; Multicult. Educ. Abstr. (1977-); Newsp. Period. Abstr. (1992-); Stud. Women Abstr.; Women Stud. Abstr.

SI
**HER WORLD ANNUAL.** English. an. 7.00Sing$ Singapore; $3.39 US. Times Periodicals Pte Ltd, 422 Thomson Road, Singapore 1129 Singapore. **Tel** 011 65 2550011. **ED** Betty Khoo. **Bk Rev.** **Ad Acc. Circ:** 34,000 (ctrl).
**Desc:** Fashion, beauty, personalities, cookery, decor and handicraft.

US/0146-3411
**HERESIES.** (HERESIES : A FEMINIST PUBLICATION ON ART & POLITICS.). [Heresies]. **Added/Corp** Heresies Collective, inc. No. 1 (Jan. 1977)-. Periodical. English. sa. $38.00 (institutions), $27.00 (individuals) (four issues),. Heresies, PO Box 1306 Canal Street Station, New York NY 10013. **Tel** (212)227-2108. **ED** Avis Lang. **LC** HQ1101; .H43. **DD** 305.4/05. **Circ:** 5,000.
**Desc:** A feminist journal of art and politics. Each issue focuses on a particular theme, and is developed by a different editorial collective.
**Ind/Abst** Acad. Search (July 1993-); Altern. Press Index; Am. Humanit. Index; Art Index; ARTbibliogr. Mod.; Avery Index Archit. Period. Suppl. Colum. Univ.; BHA : Biblio. Hist. Art; Humanit. Source (Jul. 1993-); INFO-SOUTH Abstr.; Mag. Search; Middle East Abstr. Index; Multicult. Educ. Abstr.; Women Stud. Abstr.

CN/0711-7485
**HERIZONS.** (HERIZONS : THE MANITOBA WOMEN'S NEWSPAPER.). [Herizons]. Vol. 2 (Sept. 1981)-. Periodical. English. Four times a year. 21.03Can$ Canada; 30.00Can$ other. Herizons, PO Box 128, Winnipeg Manitoba R3C 2G1 Canada. **Tel** (024)774-6225. **DD** 305.4/2/0971. **Bk Rev**, (Qty: 20). **Ad Acc. Circ:** 5,000. ***Continues*** *Manitoba Women's Newspaper, 0228-7285.*
**Desc:** To inspire hope and foster a state of wellness that enriches women's lives and to build awareness of issues as they affect women.
**Ind/Abst** Altern. Press Index (?-?).

FR
**HEURES CLAIRES DES FEMMES.** New Ser. No. 1- Mar. 1957-. Periodical. French. Union des Femmes Francaises, 15 rue Martel, Paris 75480 France. ***Formed by the union of*** *Heures Claires* ***and*** *Femmes Francaises.*

US
**HIGHER EDUCATION OPPORTUNITIES FOR MINORITIES AND WOMEN ANNOTATED SELECTIONS.** **See** Education-Higher Education.

UK
**HOME AND COUNTRY : THE MAGAZINE OF THE NATIONAL FEDERATION OF WOMEN'S INSTITUTES.** **Added/Corp** National Federation of Women's Institutes. **VFOAT** Home & Country. (19??)-. Periodical. English. Twelve times a year. $6.99. Adprint, 69 Thorpe Road, Norwich NR1 1UA England. **Tel** 0603 619421 619424. available on microfilm from University Microfilms International (UMI).

US/0146-9487
**HOMEMAKER OF THE NATIONAL EXTENSION HOMEMAKERS COUNCIL, THE.** **See** Home Economics.

CN/0318-7802
**HOMEMAKER'S MAGAZINE.** [Homemak. mag.]. Vol. 8 (Jan./Feb. 1973)-. Periodical. English. Eight times a year. 16.50Can$ Canada; 17.95Can$ US; 20.00Can$ other. Telemedia Publishing Inc., 555 West 12th Avenue, Suite 300, North York Ontario V5Z 4L4 Canada. **Tel** (604)877-7732. **(Subscription address:** Indas, 35 Riviera Drive, Building 17, Markham Ontario L3R 8N4 Canada.**)** **ED** Jane Gale. **Ad Acc. Circ:** 1,400,000 (ctrl). ***Continues*** *Homemaker's Digest, 0318-7810;* ***Absorbed*** *Recipes Only Magazine, 0823-7409.*
**Desc:** Canada's authoritative women's magazine, reflects the goals and concerns of today's woman, from the traditional areas (food, fashion, beauty and home decor) to politics, career aspirations and community responsibilities, with particular emphasis on personal relationships. Seeks to make women aware of their potential and encourage them to fulfill it in whatever field of endeavour they choose.
**Ind/Abst** Can. Index; Can. Period. Index.

US/0194-5319
**HOOSIER BUSINESS WOMAN, THE.** **Added/Corp** Indiana Federation of Business and Professional Women's Clubs. Indiana Federation of Business and Professional Women. (19??)-. Periodical. English. Four times a year (Mar., May, Aug., Nov.). $2.20. Indiana Federation of Business and Professional Women, PO Box 272, Shelbyville IN 46176. **Tel** (317)398-3260. **ED** Bette Lux (editor's address: RR1 Box 216, Waldron, IN 46182, telephone: (317)392-2982). **Circ:** 5,000 (ctrl).
**Desc:** News and information concerning working women and activities of the organization and it's members.

US
**HOT FLASH: A NEWSLETTER FOR MIDLIFE AND OLDER WOMEN.** (198?)-. Newsletter. English. qt. $25.00 individuals; $35.00 women's health or consumer groups; $50.00 institutional; $75.00 corporations. Hot Flash, Newsletter for Midlife & Older Women, PO Box 816 c/o Dr. Porcino, Stony Brook NY 11790-0609. **Tel** (516)246-3305. **ED** Jane Porcino. Index available. cum. index. **Bk Rev. Circ:** 7,000.
**Desc:** A newsletter which addresses the myriad of health issues which affect all women in the second half of their lives.

US/0747-8887
**HOT WIRE.** ***Ceased.*** [Hot wire]. Vol. 1, No. 1 (Nov. 1984)-Vol. 10 (Sept. 1994). Periodical. English. Three times a year. Hot Wire, 5210 North Wayne, Chicago IL 60640. **Tel** (312)769-9009, FAX (312)728-7002. **ED** Toni Armstrong Jr. **LC** ML82; .H69. **DD** 780/.88042. **Ad Acc. Circ:** 14,000.
**Desc:** Specializes in women-identified music and culture (primarily the performing arts, writing/publishing and film/video) by, for and about women.
**Ind/Abst** Music Artic. Guide (?-?); Music Index.

US/0882-7907
**HURRICANE ALICE.** [Hurric. Alice]. **Added/Corp** Women's Learning Institute (Minneapolis, Minn.) Hurricane Alice Foundation (Minneapolis, Minn.). Vol. 1, No. 1 (Spring 1983)-. Periodical. English. Four times a year. $20.00 US; $25.00 Canada; $29.00 other. Hurricane Alice, 207 Lind Hall/207 Church Street SE, Minneapolis MN 55455. **Tel** (612)625-1834. **ED** Martha Roth and Carolyn Law. **LC** HQ1101; .H87. **DD** 305.4/2/05. **Bk Rev**, (Qty: 10-12/year). **Ad Acc, Adv Mgr:** Jayne Paynek. **Circ:** 1,000. available on audiocassette (with Braille labels).
**Desc:** A feminist cultural review, committed to reviewing all the works of culture with a feminist eye.
**Ind/Abst** Am. Humanit. Index.

SW/0018-8026
**HUSMODERN.** Periodical. Swedish. Swedish Torsgaten 21, 10544 Stockholm Sweden.

US/0887-5367
**HYPATIA (EDWARDSVILLE, ILL.).** (HYPATIA.). Vol. 1, No. 1 (Spring 1986)-. Academic Scholarly Publication. English. Four times a year. $60.00. Indiana University Press, 601 North Morton Street, Bloomington IN 47404. **Tel** (812)855-3830, (800)842-6796. **ED** Linda Lopez McAlister. **LC** HQ1101; .H96. **DD** 305.4/2/01. **Ad Acc. Pr Rev. Circ:** 1,200. available on microfilm; available on CD-ROM. Documents available from UMI Article Clearinghouse. ***Continues in part*** *Women's Studies International Forum, 0277-5395.*
**Desc:** Publishes scholarly research in feminist philosophy and theory.
**Ind/Abst** Acad. Abstr. Full Text Elite (July 1990-); Acad. Abstr. (July 1990-); Acad. Ind. [Computer File] (1989-); Acad. Search (July 1990-); Altern. Press Index; BHA : Biblio. Hist. Art; Expand. Acad. Index (1989-); Humanit. Source (Jul. 1990-); INFO-SOUTH Abstr.; Mag. Search; Newsp. Period. Abstr. (1988-); Philos. Index; Sage Fam. Stud. Abstr.; Soc. Plann. Policy Dev. Abstr.; Sociol. Abstr.; Stud. Women Abstr.; Women Stud. Abstr.

●US/1064-1955
**HYPERTENSION IN PREGNANCY.** **See** Medical Science and Technology-Gynecology and Obstetrics.

CN/0229-5385
**HYSTERIA (KITCHENER).** (HYSTERIA.). **Added/Corp** Hysteria Magazine Collective. Vol. 1, No. 1 (Spring 1980)-. Periodical. English. qt. 10.00Can$, 18.00Can$ (institutions) Canada; 12.00Can$, 20.00Can$ (institutions) US. Hysteria, Box 2481 Station B, Kitchener Ontario N2H 6M3 Canada. **Tel** (519)576-8094. **ED** Catherine Edwards. **DD** 305.4/2/05. **Bk Rev. Ad Acc. Circ:** 1,200.
**Desc:** Attractive and lively forum for Canadian feminism; offers news, opinion, theory, creative writing, graphics, reviews of books and films and information on new resources and upcoming events. Special features on pressing issues like sexuality and media violence.

US/0019-137X
**IDEALS.** [Ideals]. (1944)-. Periodical. English. Eight times a year. $19.95 (one year), $35.95 (two year) US; $25.95 (one year), $47.95 (two year) other. Ideals Publications Inc., PO Box 140300, Nashville TN 37214. **Tel** (615)885-8270, (800)558-4343, FAX (615)885-9570. **ED** Nancy Skarmeas. **DD** 051. **Circ:** 250,000. available on microfilm and microfiche from University Microfilms International (UMI). Documents available from UMI Article Clearinghouse.
**Desc:** A pictorial magazine featuring poetry, articles, recipes and crafts of inspirational and nostalgic nature targetted to the mature woman.
**Ind/Abst** Mag. Artic. Summar. Elite (July 1989-); Mag. Artic. Summar. Select (July 1989-); Mag. Artic. Summar. CD-ROM (July 1989-); Mag. Search; Mid. Search (Jul. 1989-); Newsp. Period. Abstr. (1992-); Prim. Search (Jul. 1989-).

CN/0384-5990
**IMAGES (NELSON).** ***Ceased.*** (IMAGES.). **Added/Corp** Kootenay Women's Council. (1972)-(19??). Periodical. English. qt. Images Collective, PO Box 736, Nelson British Columbia V1L 5R4 Canada. **Tel** (604)352-9916. **DD** 301.41/2/05. **Bk Rev. Ad Acc. Circ:** 750.
**Desc:** A rural Canadian feminist paper with articles, news, fiction, poetry and graphics on issues which concern women in rural British Columbia and the world.

US/1047-3777
**IN VIEW. See** Education-Higher Education.

UK
**INDEPENDENT SCHOOLS YEARBOOK. GIRLS' SCHOOLS : THE OFFICIAL BOOK OF REFERENCE OF THE GIRLS' SCHOOLS ASSOCIATION.** ***Title Change.*** **See** Education.

CN/0843-798X
**INFO-AEF : FEUILLET D'INFORMATION DU RESEAU D'ACTION-EDUCATION-FEMMES.** [Info-AEF]. **VFOAT** Info-Action-Education-Femmes. Vol. 1, No. 1 (April 1989)-. Periodical. French. Three times a year. Free (members). Reseau National d'Action-Education-Femmes, 50 rue Vaoughan, Ottawa Ontario K1M 1X1 Canada. **DD** 305.4/06/071.

US/1042-413X
**INITIATIVES (WASHINGTON, D.C.). See** Education-School Organization and Administration.

US/1049-9709
**INNER WOMAN.** [Inn. woman]. Vol. 4, No. 1 (Spring 1990)-. Periodical. English. qt. $7.50 US; $11.50 Canada. Silver Owl Publications Inc, Box 51186, Seattle WA 98115-1186. **Tel** (206)524-9071. **ED** Krysta Gibson. **DD** 305. **Bk Rev. Ad Acc. Circ:** 30,000 (ctrl). ***Continues*** *Spiritual Women's Times, 1044-2774.*
**Desc:** Deals with women's spirituality, healing and evolution.

US
**INTER-AMERICAN COMMISSION OF WOMEN : NEWSLETTER. Main/Corp** Inter-American Commission of Women. Vol. No. 34 (Sept. 1981)-. Newsletter. English. General Secretariat of the Organization of American States, 1889 F Street NW, Washington DC 20006. **Tel** (202)789-6284. **LC** HQ1239; .I4815. **DD** 305.4/06/01. ***Continues*** *Inter-American Commission of Women. News Bulletin.*

US
**INTERCAMBIOS (LOS ANGELES, CALIF.).** (INTERCAMBIOS : A PUBLICATION OF THE NATIONAL NETWORK OF HISPANIC WOMEN.). **Added/Corp** National Network of Hispanic Women (U.S.). (1989)-. Periodical. English. sa (2 issues). $25.00. Intercambios, PO Box 390543, Mountain View CA 94039. **Tel** (415)962-8324. ***Continues*** *Intercambios Femeniles.*

US
**INTERCOM : WOMEN IN COMMUNICATIONS. See** Communication.

US/0746-9292
**INTERCONNECTION JOURNAL, THE.** (THE INTERCONNECTION JOURNAL / WESA.). **Added/Corp** Women's Educational Service Association (U.S.). (198?)-. Periodical. English. bm. WESA, 363 West Drake, Ft Collins CO 80526. ***Continues*** *Her Street Journal, 0745-0303.*

US/0892-6719
**INTERFAITH WOMEN'S NEWS & NETWORK. VFOAT** Interfaith Women's News and Network. (198?)-. Newsletter. English. qt. $4.00 individuals; $5.00 institutions. Interfaith Women's News & Network, 790 11th Avenue, 32H, New York NY 10019-3514. **Tel** (212)581-5010. **ED** Diana Trebbi. **DD** 305. **Bk Rev. Circ:** 200 (ctrl). ***Continues*** *Ecumenical Women's News & Network.*
**Desc:** For Jewish, Protestant and Catholic women seeking to improve their status in western denominations.

US/0742-9436
**INTERFEM.** [InterFem]. Vol. 1, No. 1 (Nov. 1983)-. English. mo. $48.00. Interfem Inc., PO Box 17379, Milwaukee WI 53217. **LC** HQ1101; .I46. **DD** 305.4/2/0973.

●UK/0965-3775
**INTERNATIONAL WHO'S WHO OF WOMEN, THE.** (1992)-. English. an. $350.00. Europa Publications Ltd, 18 Bedford Square, London WC1B 3JN England. **Tel** 011 44 71 5808236, telex 21540 EUROPA G. **(Subscription address:** Gale Research Co., 835 Penobscot Building, Detroit MI 48226.) **LC** CT3202; .I58.
**Desc:** Provides detailed information on the lives and achievements of over 4,000 of the most eminent and successful women in the world today.

UK/0020-9120
**INTERNATIONAL WOMEN'S NEWS JOURNAL OF THE INTERNATIONAL ALLIANCE OF WOMEN, INCORPORATING LE DROIT DES FEMMES. Added/Corp** International Alliance of Women. **VFOAT** Journal of the International Alliance of Women; Droit des Femmes. Vol. 73, (Feb. 1978)-. Periodical. English (French). Four times a year (Mar., June, Sept., Dec.). £10.00. International Alliance of Women, Kerklaan 43 N M Peters, 1251 JS Laren Netherslands. **Tel** 31 2153-82193, FAX 31 2153-02193. **ED** Jan Marsh. **Circ:** 1,100 (ctrl). ***Continues*** *International Women's News; Nouvelles Feministes Internationales.*
**Desc:** Equal rights and equal responsibilities between men and women; status of women throughout the world.

IT
**INTIMITA.** (19??)-. Italian. wk. 300000L Italy; 13900000L other. Ind Grafiche Cino Del Duca, Via Borgogna 5, 20122 Milan Italy. **Tel** 011 39 2 781051.

US/0271-8227
**IOWA WOMAN. VFOAT** Between Mountain and Sea. (Jan/Feb 1980)-. Periodical. English. qt. $18.00. Iowa Woman Endeavors, Inc., PO Box 680, Iowa City IA 52244. **Tel** (319)987-2879. **ED** Marianne Abel. **LC** HQ1438.I7; I69. **DD** 305.4/09777. Index available. cum. index (published each volume). **Bk Rev**, (Qty: 20). **Ad Acc. Circ:** 2,000. available in microform from University Microfilms International (UMI).
**Desc:** Features fiction, essays, poetry, reviews and visual art by women everywhere.
**Ind/Abst** Altern. Press Index; Am. Humanit. Index (Fall 1977-); MLA Int. Bibl. Books Artic. Mod. Lang. Lit.

CN
**IRANIAN WOMEN QUARTERLY.** (19??)-. Persian. Four times a year. $16.82 (institutions), $12.00 (individuals). Iranian Women Publishing of Canada, PO Box 964, Station F, Toronto Ontario M4Y 2N9 Canada. **Tel** (416)920-5228. **ED** Shahin Assayesh. **Bk Rev. Ad Acc. Circ:** 1,000-2,000 (ctrl).
**Desc:** Cultural/social magazine on women's issues published in Toronto for Iranian women in Canada.

US/0197-4610
**JERSEY WOMAN.** ***Title Change.*** Vol. 1 (Feb./Mar. 1979)-(19??). Periodical. English. Eleven times a year. Jersey Women Magazine, 27 McDermott Place, Bergenfield NJ 07261. **Tel** (201)384-0201. **ED** Louise B Hafesh. **Bk Rev. Ad Acc. Circ:** 15,000. ***Continued by*** *New Jersey Woman Magazine.*
**Desc:** Only magazine in New Jersey written for and by New Jersey women, promotes the talents and accomplishments of state females. Also provides forum for exchange of ideas, news information, career updates and fashion.

JA
**JOSEI MONDAI TOSHO SOMOKUROKU (MICROFORM).** 1984-. Japanese. ¥540. Josei Mondai Tosho Somokuroku Kankokai, c/o Tohan 6-ban, 24-go Higashigoken-cho Shinjuku-ku, Tokyo-to Japan. **LC** Z7961; .J69; HQ1.

CN/0705-3843
**JOURNAL - CANADIAN FEDERATION OF UNIVERSITY WOMEN. Main/Corp** Canadian Federation of University Women. V. 21, No. 3-Fall 1977-. Periodical. English (French). Free. E Conway, 16111-78A Avenue, Edmonton Alberta T5R 3G2 Canada. **DD** 301.41/2/06271. ctrl circ. ***Continues*** *Canadian Federation of University Women. Bulletin, 0319-7417.*

GW/0178-7284
**JOURNAL FUER DIE FRAU.** [J. Frau]. (1980)-. Periodical. German. bw. DM97.20. Axel Springer Verlag Ag, Brieffach 2460, D 20350 Hamburg Germany. **Tel** 011 49 40 34724503. **ED** G. Siebel. **UDC** 087-055.2. **Ad Acc, Adv Mgr:** D. Koring. ***Continues*** *Journal fuer Haushalt & Familie, 0172-3251.*

US/0895-2833
**JOURNAL OF FEMINIST FAMILY THERAPY. See** Family and Marriage.

US/8755-4178
**JOURNAL OF FEMINIST STUDIES IN RELIGION. See** Religion and Theology.

UK/0958-9236
**JOURNAL OF GENDER STUDIES. Added/Corp** Hull Centre for Gender Studies. Vol. 1, No. 1 (May 1991)-. Periodical. English. Three times a year. £72.00. Carfax Publishing Company, PO Box 25 Abingdon, Oxfordshire OX14 3UE England. **Tel** 011 44 235 555335, FAX (0279)31067, telex 817484. **(Subscription address:** US and Canada/ PO Box 2025, Dunnellon, FL 34430-2025; telephone:(904)489-6996) **ED** Judith Bryce, Jenny Hockey & Jenny Wolmark. **CODEN** JGESEH. Index available. available on microfiche.

US/1062-6751
**JOURNAL OF GENDER STUDIES (SOUTH PORTLAND, ME.). See** Men's Interests.

US/0362-062X
**JOURNAL OF REPRINTS OF DOCUMENTS AFFECTING WOMEN. See** Law.

US
**JOURNAL OF THE ... CONVENTION - NATIONAL WOMAN'S RELIEF CORP. Main/Corp** National Woman's Relief Corps. English. an. National Woman's Relief Corps, 2916 Broadway, Toledo OH 43614. Index available in last issue of volume--attached. ***Continues*** *Woman's Relief Corps. Journal of the ... National Convention.*

US/0895-2841
**JOURNAL OF WOMEN & AGING.** [J. women aging]. **VFOAT** Journal of Women and Aging; Women & Aging; Women and Aging. Vol. 1 (1989)-. Periodical. English. qt. $120.00 US; $168.00 other. The Haworth Press Inc, 10 Alice Street, Binghamton NY 13904-1580. **Tel** (607)722-5857, (800)3-HAWORTH, FAX (607)722-1424. **ED** J. Dianne Garner (editor's address: Department of Social Work, Washburn University, Topeka, KS 66621). **LC** HV1457; .J685. **DD** 155.67/082. **NLM** W1; JO972H. **CODEN** JWAGE5. **Bk Rev. Ad Acc. Pr Rev. Acid Free. Circ:** 383. available on microfilm and microfiche from University Microfilms International (UMI). Documents available from UMI Article Clearinghouse, Haworth Document Delivery Service.
**Desc:** Enhances the knowledge of a wide variety of professionals who are concerned with the health and well-being of women as they age in order to deliver quality care and services to older women, practitioners, researchers and educators need access to the most current information that they can find.
**Ind/Abst** Abstr. Anthropol. (19??-); Abstr. Soc. Gerontol.; Expand. Acad. Index (1992-); Newsp. Period. Abstr. (1992-); Sage Fam. Stud. Abstr.; Soc. Plann. Policy Dev. Abstr.; Soc. Work Abstr. [Select. Cov.]; Women Stud. Abstr.

●US/1059-7115
**JOURNAL OF WOMEN'S HEALTH. See** Medical Science and Technology.

US/1042-7961
**JOURNAL OF WOMEN'S HISTORY.** [J. women's hist.]. Vol. 1 No. 1 (Spring 1989)-. Periodical. English. Four times a year. $60.00. Indiana University Press, 601 North Morton Street, Bloomington IN 47404. **Tel** (812)855-3830, (800)842-6796. **ED** Christie Farnham and Joan Hoff-Wilson. **LC** HQ1101; .J68. **DD** 305.4/09/05. **Bk Rev. Ad Acc. Pr Rev. Circ:** 1,200. Documents available from UMI Article Clearinghouse.
**Desc:** Publishes narrative and synthetic examples of historical work by women.
**Ind/Abst** Acad. Ind. [Computer File] (1992-); Altern. Press Index (199?-); Am. Hist. Life (1989-); Expand. Acad. Index (1992-); Film Lit. Index (19??-); Newsp. Period. Abstr. (1992-); Middle East J.; U.S. Polit. Sci. Doc. (199?-); Women Stud. Abstr.

US/1064-1084
**JOURNAL OF WOMEN'S MINISTRIES. See** Religion and Theology.

US/0885-8004
**JOYFUL WOMAN MAGAZINE, THE. VFOAT** Joyful Woman. (198?)-. Periodical. English. bm (6 issues). $15.00. The Joyful Woman Magazine, PO Box 90028, Chattanooga TN 37412. **Tel** (615)894-4500, FAX (615)894-0907. **ED** Joy Rice Martin. **DD** 248. cum. index. **Bk Rev**, (Qty: 6). **Ad Acc. Circ:** 12,000 (ctrl). ***Continues*** *Joyful Woman, 0164-4882.*

KO
**JU BU SAENG HWAL.** (19??)-. Korean. mo. $99.00. Hak Won Publishing Co Ltd, 44-37 Yeoido-Dong, Young Deung Po-Ku Seoul Korea. **Tel** 011 82 2 782 4711, FAX 011 82 2 784 5436. **ED** Dong Hwi Lee (editor's address: 2605 West Olympic Boulevard, Los Angeles, CA 90006; phone: (213)487-4702). **Ad Acc, Adv Mgr:** Doug Park, **Tel** (213)487-4702. **Circ:** 20,000.
**Desc:** Magazine containing information about homemaking, family and marriage, and fashion. Includes recipes and some short stories.

JA
**JUGOSHI NOTO / ONNATACHI NO IMA O TOU KAI.** No. 1-. Periodical. Japanese. ir. 1500. JCA, Shuppan 1-42, Kanda Jinbo-Cho, Chiyoda-ku Japan. **LC** HQ1761; .J84.

US/0274-8584
**JUNIOR LEAGUE REVIEW.** ***Ceased.*** **Added/Corp** Association of Junior Leagues. (19??)-(Fall 1994). Periodical. English. an. Association of Junior Leagues Inc, 660 First Avenue, New York NY 10016. **Tel** (212)683-1515, FAX (212)481-7196. **ED** Betsey B. Steeger. **LC** HQ1903; .A814. **DD** 369.5. **Circ:** 191,000.
**Desc:** Contains news of the volunteer sector, reaching out to women of all races, religions, and national origins who demonstrate an interest in and commitment to voluntarism.

CN/0835-0892
**JURISFEMME (OTTAWA). See** Law.

# Women's Interests

**US/1062-6255**
**JUST PEACE (WASHINGTON, D.C.).**
(JUST PEACE / WOMEN FOR MEANINGFUL SUMMITS, WMS/USA.). [Just peace]. **Added/Corp** Women for Meaningful Summits. No. 1 (Winter 1991)-. Periodical. English. qt. Women for Meaningful Summits, 1819 H Street NW, Suite 640, Washington DC 20006. **DD** 305.

JA
**KAIHATSU TO KENSHU. See** Occupations and Careers.

**US/0735-7885**
**KALLIOPE. See** The Arts.

IO
**KARTINI.** No. 1 (Nov. 1974)-. Periodical. Indonesian. bw. $84.00 US. Jalan Gajah Mada 104-110A, Jakarta 11140 Indonesia. **Tel** (21)6297809, telex 41216.
**Desc:** Women's interest magazine.

●**US/1058-6652**
**KEEN ON NEW YORK SURVEY OF TOP-RATED SERVICES, THE. See** Men's Interests.

US
**KENA.** Periodical. Spanish. Twelve times a year. $48.00. Ruiz Spanish Language Magazines, PO Box 2389, El Paso TX 79952. **Tel** (915)544-6282.

MX
**KENA.** (1???)-. Spanish. mo. $40.00 Mexico; $44.00 other. Hispanic Books Distributors Inc, 1665 West Grant Road, Tucson AZ 85745. **Tel** (602)882-9484, (800)634-2124, FAX (602)882-7696.
**Desc:** Each issue covers a specific topic: arts and crafts, cooking, parties, health and beauty or needlecrafts.

**CN/0317-9095**
**KINESIS (VANCOUVER).** (KINESIS.).
**Added/Corp** Vancouver Status of Women. Vol. 4 No. 29 (Jan. 1974)-. Periodical. English. Ten times a year. 45.00Can$ (institution), 20.00Can$ (individual) Canada; 53.00Can$ (institution), 28.00Can$ (individual) Other;. Vancouver Status of Women, 1720 Grant Street, Suite 301, Vancouver BC V5L 2Y6 Canada. **Tel** (604)255-5499. **ED** Esther Shannon. **Bk Rev. Ad Acc. Circ:** 2,000. **Continues** Vancouver Status of Women. Newsletter, 0317-9109.
**Desc:** Canada's oldest feminist newspaper. Provides news, background, features, analysis, theory, commentary and extensive arts coverage.
**Ind/Abst** Altern. Press Index (199?-).

**CN/0383-9915**
**KINGSTON WOMEN'S CENTRE NEWSLETTER. Main/Corp** Kingston Women's Centre. Began publication in 197-. Newsletter. English. ir. Kingston Women's Centre, 200 Montreal Street, Kingston Ontario K7K 3G4 Canada. **DD** 301.41/2/05.

**PL/0023-2548**
**KOBIETY I ZYCIE.** [Kobiety .Zycie]. (1945)-. Periodical. Polish. wk. $91.00. **(Subscription address:** ARS Polona, PO Box 1001, 00068 Warsaw Poland.**)**

CC
**KUANG-TUNG FU NU. VFOAT** Guangdongfunu. (1982)-. Periodical. Chinese. mo. NT$0.23. Kuang-Chou Shih Yu Chu Canton, China. **LC** AP95.C4; K8435. **DD** 305.4/2/095127.

US
**LA WOMAN / LOS ANGELES CITY COMMISSION ON THE STATUS OF WOMEN. Added/Corp** Los Angeles City Commission on the Status of Women. (1990)-. English. qt. **Continues** Los Angeles Woman.

**US/0023-7124**
**LADIES' HOME JOURNAL.** [Ladies' home j.]. Vol. 1 (Dec. 1889)-. Periodical. English. mo. $19.97. Meredith Corporation, Locust at 17th, Des Moines IA 50309. **Tel** (515)284-3000. **(Subscription address:** Neodata / Colorado, PO Box 2606, Boulder Boulder CO 80322.**) ED** Myrna Blyth. **LC** AP2; .L135. **DD** 640. **Ad Acc. Circ:** over 16 million. available on microfilm and microfiche from University Microfilms International (UMI); available on an online database (file 647/Full-Text) from DIALOG. Documents available from UMI Article Clearinghouse. **Continues** Ladies Home Journal and Practical Housekeeper, 0364-2380.
**Desc:** Presents advice, information and entertainment. Every issue contains dozens of recipes, celebrity profiles, articles on relationships, and tips on health, beauty and fashion, real-life stories and fiction, as well as expert advice on money and career management, and more.
**Ind/Abst** Acad. Abstr. Full Text Elite (Jan. 1989-); Acad. Abstr. (Jan. 1989-); Consum. Health Nutr. Index; Cumul. Index Nurs. Allied Health Lit.; Foods Adlibra; Gen. Period. Index (1985-); Health Ref. Cent. (1987-) [Select. Cov.]; Mag. Artic. Summar. Elite (Jan. 1989-); Mag. Artic. Summar. Select (Jan. 1989-); Mag. Artic. Summar. CD-ROM (Jan. 1989-); Mag. ASAP Plus [Full Txt.]; Mag. Index Plus (1989-); Mag. Index Sel. Microfiche (1986-) [Full Txt.]; Mag. Index. Sel. (1986-); Mag. Search; Newsp.

Period. Abstr. (1988-); Peace Res. Abstr. J. (1968-1969); Read. Guide Abstr. Select Ed.; Read. Guide Period. Lit.; Resource/One Ondisc (1988-); Mag. Index (1977-); TOM Gen. Index (1985-) [Full Txt.]; Vocat. Search (Jan. 1989-).

**US/0092-8909**
**LADY GOLFER (SCOTTSDALE). See** Recreation, Leisure-Sports.

**US/0023-7191**
**LADY'S CIRCLE.** (19??)-. Periodical. English. bm. $11.97, (one year), $23.94, (two year) U.S.; $19.97 (one year) $39.94 (two year) Canada. Lopez Publications Inc., 152 Madison Avenue, Suite 905 & 906, New York NY 10016. **Tel** (212)689-3933. **ED** Mary Jane Cahill. **Bk Rev. Ad Acc. Circ:** 60,963.
**Desc:** Articles on personalities, gallant survivors, compassionate do-gooders, diet, fashion/beauty, needlework, knitting and crochet, medicine, psychology, how to save money, how-to crafts, children.

IT
**LAPIS (MILAN, ITALY).** (LAPIS.). No. 1 (Nov. 1987)-. Periodical. Italian. qt. L40000 Italy; L60000 other. La Tartaruga, Via Turati 38, 20121 Milan Italy. **Tel** 011 39 2 6555036. **LC** WMLC 93/4156.

US
**LEAGUE OF ACTION SERVICE.** (19??)-. Periodical. English. ir (monthly while Congress is in session). $10.00. League of Women Voters of the United States, 1730 M Street Northwest, 10th Floor, Washington DC 20036. **Tel** (202)429-1965, FAX (202)429-0854.

**US/0897-0149**
**LEAR'S (NEW YORK, N.Y.). Ceased.**
(LEAR'S.). [Lear's]. Vol. 1 (March/April 1988)-(April 1994). Periodical. English. bm. Lears, 655 Madison Avenue, New York NY 10021. **Tel** (212)888-0007. **LC** HQ1059.4; .L43. **DD** 305.4.
**Desc:** Covers your health and well-being, your fitness, your family, your relationships, like they've never been covered before.
**Ind/Abst** Acad. Abstr. (Jan. 1994-); Acad. Search (Jan. 1994-April 1994); Mag. Artic. Summar. Elite (Jan. 1994-Apr. 1994); Mag. Artic. Summar. CD-ROM (Jan. 1994-).

**US/0748-4321**
**LEGACY (AMHERST, MASS.). See** Literature.

IT
**LEGGERE DONNA. Added/Corp** Centro Documentazione Donna (Ferrara, Italy). (198?)-. Periodical. Italian. bm. L35000 (individuals), L40000 (institutions) Italy; L60000 other. Luciana Tufani, Via Ticchioni 38-1, 44100 Ferrara Italy. **Tel** 011 39 532-53186, FAX 011 39 532 902206. Index available (L15000). **Bk Rev. Ad Acc.** ctrl circ.

**IT/1120-7736**
**LEI MILANO. 1976. Title Change.** (1976)-(1992). Periodical. Multiple languages. mo. Edizioni Conde Nast Spa, Piazza Castello 27, 20121 Milan Italy. **Tel** 011 39 2 85611. **UDC** 391. **Continued by** Glamour (Milano), 1121-5348.

**US/0739-1803**
**LESBIAN NEWS (CANOGA PARK, CALIF.), THE. See** Homosexuality.

**US/0277-4356**
**LETRAS FEMENINAS. See** Literature.

**CN/0225-6975**
**LIFELINES (SHERWOOD PARK. 1979).
See** Birth Control.

**US/1061-8732**
**LIGHTHOUSE (CAMBRIDGE, MASS.).**
(LIGHTHOUSE.). [Lighthouse]. Vol. 1, No. 1 (Nov. 1990)-. Periodical. English. Lighthouse Magazine, c/o Dean of Students Office, 4 University Hall, Harvard University, Cambridge MA 02138. **DD** 305.
**Desc:** A Harvard-Radcliffe student publication that addresses women's issues.

**AT/0813-8990**
**LILITH (FITZROY, VIC.).** (LILITH.). **Added/Corp** Lilith Collective. No. 1 (Winter 1984)-. English. an.
**Ind/Abst** Am. Hist. Life (1984-).

**US/0146-2334**
**LILITH (NEW YORK). See** Religion and Theology-Judaism.

**US/0893-8083**
**LISTEN REAL LOUD. Suspended.** (LISTEN REAL LOUD / NATIONWIDE WOMEN'S PROGRAM, AMERICAN FRIENDS SERVICE COMMITTEE.). [Listen real loud]. **Added/Corp** American Friends Service Committee. Nationwide Women's Program. Vol. 6, No. 2 (1985)-Suspended. Periodical. English. Four times a year. American Friends Service Committee /

Pennsylvania, 1501 Cherry Street, Philadelphia PA 19102. **Tel** (215)241-7275. **DD** 305. **Continues** AFSC Women's Newsletter.

**CN/0704-7886**
**LUNDI, LE.** Vol. 1 (Feb. 19, 1977)-. Periodical. French. wk. 104.00Can$ Canada; 204.00Can$ other. Publications Quebecor le Nordais, 5800 rue St. Denis, Bar 605, Montreal Quebec H2S 3L5 Canada. **Tel** (514)272-6330. **DD** 054/.1.

**CN/0318-1480**
**LYSISTRATA (VICTORIA). Title Change.**
(LYSISTRATA.). May 1975-. Periodical. English. Women's Centre, 552 Pandora Avenue, Victoria British Columbia Canada. **DD** 301.41/2/06271134. **Supersedes** Women's Centre (Victoria, B.C.). Newsletter, 0318-1472. **Continued by** SWAG (Victoria Status of Women Action Group), 0229-4982.

**CN/0541-6620**
**MADAME AU FOYER.** [Madame foyer]. Vol. 1 (Oct. 1966)-. Periodical. French. Ten times a year. 16.50Can$ Canada; 17.95Can$ US; 20.00Can$ other. Telemedia Publishing Inc., 555 West 12th Avenue, Suite 300, North York Ontario V5Z 4L4 Canada. **Tel** (604)877-7732. **(Subscription address:** Telemedia ProCom, PO Box 715, Station K, Toronto Ontario M4P 3CP Canada.**) ED** Pierrette Laberge-Ferth. **Ad Acc. Circ:** 330,600 (ctrl).
**Desc:** Reflection of goals and concerns of today's woman, from traditional areas- food, fashion, decor and beauty-to politics, career aspirations, and community responsibilities, with particular emphasis on personal relationships.
**Ind/Abst** Can. Period. Index.

**US/0024-9394**
**MADEMOISELLE (NEW YORK, N.Y. 1935).** (MADEMOISELLE.). [Mademoiselle]. Vol. 1 (Feb. 1935)-. Periodical. English. mo. $15.00. Conde Nast Publications / New York, 350 Madison Avenue, New York NY 10017. **Tel** (212)880-8800, (800)777-0700.
**(Subscription address:** Neodata / Colorado, PO Box 2606, Boulder Boulder CO 80322.**) ED** Amy Levin. **LC** AP2; .M2334. **DD** 051. **Bk Rev. Ad Acc. Circ:** 1,100,000 (ctrl). available on microfilm and microfiche from University Microfilms International (UMI). Documents available from UMI Article Clearinghouse, Magazine Collection.
**Desc:** Magazine for the young sophisticate. Covers trend-setting looks, lifestyle, travel and to-the-point counsel on fitness, careers, fashions, decoration, cars and loving relationships.
**Ind/Abst** Acad. Abstr. Full Text Elite (Jan. 1989-); Acad. Abstr. (Jan. 1989-); Biogr. Index; Consum. Health Nutr. Index (?-?); Consum. Index Prod. Eval. Inf. Source; Gen. Period. Index (1985-); Mag. Artic. Summar. Elite (Jan. 1989-); Mag. Artic. Summar. Select (Jan. 1989-); Mag. Artic. Summar. CD-ROM (Jan. 1989-); Mag. Index Plus (1989-); Mag. Index Sel. Microfiche (1990-) [Full Txt.]; Mag. Index. Sel. (1986-); Mag. Search; Med. Rev. Dig.; Newsp. Period. Abstr. (1988-); Read. Guide Abstr. Select Ed.; Read. Guide Period. Lit.; Mag. Index (1977-); TOM Gen. Index (1985-) [Full Txt.].

TZ
**MAELEXO BINAFSI YA WAGOMBEA UBUNGE WA TAIFA VITI MAALUM VYA WANAWAKE. See** Political Science.

**US/0275-5629**
**MAENAD.** [Maenad]. Vol. 1, No. 1 (Fall 1980)-. Periodical. English. qt. $24.00 institutions, $19.00 international. P. Estey, PO Box 738, Gloucester MA 01930. **LC** HQ1101; .M33. **DD** 305.4/0973.

CN
**MAGISTRA. See** Religion and Theology-Catholicism.

IR
**MAHJUBAH. See** Religion and Theology-Islam, Bahaism, Theosophy.

IT
**MANI DI FATA.** Casa Edit Mani di Fata Srl, Via Vettabbia #7, 20122 Milan Italy.

**II/0257-7305**
**MANUSHI.** [Manushi]. **Added/Corp** Samta (Association). (19??)-. Periodical. English. bm (6 issues). $36.00. Manushi, C1/202 Lajpat Nagar 1, New Delhi 110024 India. **Tel** 011 91 11 6833022, 6839158. **(Subscription address:** Prints India, 11 Darya Ganj, New Delhi 110002 India.**) ED** Madhu Kishwar (Editor's Phone: 6839158 or 6833022). **LC** HQ1104; .M35. **DD** 305.4/0954. Index available. cum. index. **Bk Rev. Circ:** 10,000.
**Desc:** Life conditions, struggles, achievements of Indian women, past and present; civil rights and other movements for change; women oriented fiction, poetry, and film reviews.
**Ind/Abst** Altern. Press Index (?-199?); Hum. Rights Intern. Rep.; Stud. Women Abstr.; Women Stud. Abstr.

NE/0921-3848
**MARA (KAMPEN).** See Religion and Theology.

IT
**MARIE CLAIRE (ITALIAN EDITION).**
L43200 Italy; L87000 other. Arnoldo Mondadori Editore, UFF Cont Abbonamenti, 20090 Segrate MI Italy. **Tel** 011 39 2 75422015, telex 320457 MONDMI I. ***Continues*** *Donna Piu.*

FR
**MARIE FRANCE.** ***Ceased.*** (19??)-(19??). French. mo. Societe Bauer, c/o Mme Rosenbauer, 37 rue Bergere, 75009 Paris France. **Tel** 011 33 1 45235509, 05345486.

CN/0823-6356
**MARIE-PIER.** [Marie-pier]. Periodical. French. wk. $59.00. Marie-Pier, CP 216, Succursale Longueuil, Longueuil Quebec J4K 4Y3 Canada. **DD** 054/.1.

US/1047-1677
**MARKETING TO WOMEN (1989).**
(MARKETING TO WOMEN : MW.). [Mark. women]. **VFOAT** MW. Vol. 2, No. 8 (May 1989)-. Periodical. English. Twelve times a year. $265.00 (one year), $530.00 (two years) US and Canada; $315.00 (one year), $630.00 (two years) other. About Women Inc. Publications, 33 Broad Street, Boston MA 02109. **Tel** (617)723-4337, FAX (617)723-7107. **ED** E. Janice Leeming. **DD** 658. Index available. cum. index. **Circ:** 2,500 (ctrl). available on an online database from Predicasts, Inc. ***Continues*** *WomenScope, 1040-5240.*
**Desc:** Provides news and information for the women's interest and marketing.
**Ind/Abst** Mark. Advert. Ref. Serv. [Full Txt.]; PROMT [Full Txt.]; PTS Newsl. Database [Full Txt.].

US/0279-3490
**MARYLAND CLUB WOMAN, THE.**
Periodical. English. qt. Mrs J N May, Circulation Manager, 717 Cabin Branch Lane, Linthicum MD 21090. **LC** HQ1905.M3; M3. **DD** 396.062752.

CN/1182-6169
**MATRIART (TORONTO).** See The Arts-Art.

US/0024-8908
**MCCALL'S.** [McCall's]. Vol. 48, No. 12, (Sept. 1921)-. Periodical. English. mo. $13.94. McCall Publishing Company, 110 5th Avenue, New York NY 10011. **Tel** (212)463-1000. **(Subscription address:** CDS Agency Hard Copy, PO Box 4966, Des Moines IA 50340.) **LC** TT500; .M2. **DD** 051. **CODEN** MCCAEQ. **Ad Acc.** available on microfilm and microfiche from University Microfilms International (UMI). Documents available from UMI Article Clearinghouse, Magazine Collection. ***Continues*** *McCall's Magazine, 0197-1255.*
**Desc:** A reliable source of contemporary information for today's woman. Quality features on self, family, children, career, money, and the law. Provides insight into modern situations. Special emphasis on food, beauty, fashion, and health. Also features home management, decorating, crafts, pets, fiction and more.
**Ind/Abst** Acad. Abstr. Full Text Elite (Feb. 1989-); Acad. Abstr. (Feb. 1989-); Consum. Health Nutr. Index; Consum. Index Prod. Eval. Inf. Source; Cumul. Index Nurs. Allied Health Lit.; Foods Adlibra; Gen. Period. Index (1985-); Health Ref. Cent. (1987-) [Select. Cov.]; Infobank (Jan. 1969-); Mag. Artic. Summar. Elite (Jan. 1989-); Mag. Artic. Summar. Select (Jan. 1989-); Mag. Artic. Summar. CD-ROM (Feb. 1989-); Mag. Index Plus (1989-); Mag. Index Sel. Microfiche (1990-) [Full Txt.]; Mag. Index. Sel. (1986-); Mag. Search; Med. Rev. Dig.; Newsp. Period. Abstr. (1988-); Read. Guide Abstr. Select Ed.; Read. Guide Period. Lit.; Mag. Index (1977-); TOM Gen. Index (1985-) [Full Txt.]; Vocat. Search (Feb. 1989-).

FI/0025-6277
**ME NAISET.** (19??)-. Finnish. Fifty-two times a year. Fmk636.00. Sanoma Corporation, PO Box 240, SF-00101 Helsinki 10 Finland. **Tel** 011 358 0 901201, FAX 011 358 0 205599, telex 125848. **ED** Ulla-Maija Paavilainen and Veijo Kayhty. **LC** AP80; .M4. **Ad Acc. Circ:** 100,000 (ctrl).

US/0145-9651
**MEDIA REPORT TO WOMEN.** See Communication.

US/0090-9408
**MEH LADY.** See Education-Higher Education.

US/1043-8734
**MELPOMENE (MINNEAPOLIS, MINN.).**
(MELPOMENE.). [Melpomene]. **Added/Corp** Melpomene Institute for Women's Health Research. **VFOAT** Melpomene Journal. (1982)-. Periodical. English. Three times a year. $50.00 (one year), $90.00 (two years) libraries and schools; $32.00 (one year), $55.00 (two years) individuals. Melpomene Institute, 1010 University Avenue, St Paul MN 55104. **Tel** (612)642-1951. **ED** Judy Remington. **LC** RA564.85; .M44. **DD** 613. Index available. cum. index. **Bk Rev. Circ:** 2,500 (ctrl).
**Ind/Abst** SPORT Discus.

IT/0392-4564
**MEMORIA (TURIN, ITALY).** ***Ceased.*** See History(General).

●US/1062-7332
**MENOPAUSE MANAGEMENT.** (1992)-. Periodical. English. bm. $25.00. Conwood Group, 9 Mount Pleasant Turnpike, Denville NJ 07834.

US/1055-856X
**MICHIGAN FEMINIST STUDIES.** (MICHIGAN FEMINIST STUDIES : MFS.). [Mich. fem. stud.]. **Added/Corp** University of Michigan. Women's Studies Program. **VFOAT** MFS. No. 4 (Fall 1989)-. Monographic series. English. ir. Price varies per volume. University of Michigan Women's Studies, 230 A West Engineering, Ann Arbor MI 48109. **Tel** (313)763-2047. **DD** 305. ***Continues*** *New Occasional Papers in Women's Studies, 1050-4893.*
**Ind/Abst** Annu. Bibliogr. Engl. Lang. Lit.

●US/1061-348X
**MIDLIFE WOMAN.** [Midlife woman]. **Added/Corp** MidLife Women's Network. Vol. 1, No. 1 (1992)- Vol. 2 (Jan. 1993)-. Periodical. English. Six times a year (Feb., Apr., June, Aug., Oct., Dec.). $25.00 (individual), $50.00 (insitution) US; $30.00 (individual), $55.00 (institution) Canada & Mexico; $35.00 (individual), $60.00 (institution), other. Midlife Women's Network, 5129 Logan Avenue South, Minneapolis MN 55419-1019. **Tel** (612)925-0020, FAX (612)925-5430. **ED** Carole Moore. **DD** 613. **Bk Rev**, (Qty: 24).
**Desc:** Designed to inform and empower women who want to improve their health and their lives during the important midlife years; menopause, social roles, relationships, etc.

US/0736-718X
**MINERVA (ARLINGTON, VA.).** See Military and Defense.

US
**MINNESOTA VOTER, THE.** See Public Administration.

US/0198-9898
**MINNESOTA WOMAN'S YEARBOOK.** See Sociology-Social Services and Welfare.

US/1053-2749
**MINORITIES & WOMEN IN BUSINESS.**
***Ceased.*** [Minor. women bus.]. **VFOAT** Minorities and Women in Business. Vol. 1, No. 2 (Dec./Jan. 1985)-(Mar./April 1994). Periodical. English. bm. Minorities and Women in Business, PO Drawer 210, 441 South Springs St, Burlington NC 27216. **Tel** (919)229-1462, FAX (919)222-7455. **ED** Karin C Bassler. **LC** HD2346.U5; M544; HD2346.U5; M54. **DD** 658.02/2/08. **Bk Rev**, (Qty: 1-4). **Ad Acc, Adv Mgr:** John Enoch. **Circ:** 60,000. ***Continues*** *Minorities in Business.*
**Desc:** A bi-monthly business publication operated by, and serving, minority and women entrepreneurs. Each issue presents practical information to help small business owners run their enterprises more effectively so they may participate more fully in the economy. Male and female role models set strong examples; article topics include marketing, contract opportunities, financial management and current business trends with small business ramifications.

US
**MINORITIES AND WOMEN IN HIGHER EDUCATION.** See Political Science-Civil Rights.

CN/1184-1451
**MINUTES OF PROCEEDINGS AND EVIDENCE OF THE SUB-COMMITTEE ON THE STATUS OF WOMEN OF THE STANDING COMMITTEE ON HEALTH AND WELFARE, SOCIAL AFFAIRS, SENIORS AND ON THE STATUS OF WOMEN.** [Minutes proc. evid. Sub-Comm. Status Women Stand. Comm. Health Welf. Soc. Aff. Sr. Status Women]. **Main/Corp** Canada. Parlement. Chambre des Communes. Sous-Comite sur la Condition Feminine. **VFOAT** Proces-Verbaux et Temoignages du Sous-Comite sur la Condition Feminine du Comite Permanent de la Sante et du Bien-Etre Social, des Affaires Sociales, du Troisieme Age et de la Condition Feminine. 34th Parliament, 2nd Session, Issue No. 1 (Nov. 20/Nov. 27/Dec. 4, 1990)-. Proceedings. French (English). **DD** 362.83/0971.

●RU/0869-494X
**MIR ZHENSHCHINY.** (Jan. 1992)-. Periodical. Russian. mo. $89.95. **(Subscription address:** East View Publications Inc., 3020 Harbor Lane North, Suite 110, Minneapolis MN 55447.) **LC** AP50; .S6. ***Continues*** *Sovetskaia Zhenshchina.*

US/1044-5153
**MIRABELLA (NEW YORK, N.Y.).**
(MIRABELLA.). [Mirabella]. Vol. 1, No. 1 (June 1989)-. Periodical. English. mo. $24.00. News America Publishing Inc., PO Box 500, Radnor PA 19088. **Tel** (215)293-8500. **(Subscription address:** Neodata / Colorado, PO Box 2606, Boulder Boulder CO 80322.) **ED** Amy Gross. **LC** TT500; .M37. **DD** 391/.2/05. **Circ:** 225,000. available on microfilm and microfiche from University Microfilms International (UMI).
**Desc:** A lifestyle resource available to 30-50 year old women. Editorial content includes fashion, art, artists, book and film reviews and travel.
**Ind/Abst** Access (1990-).

UK
**MIZZ.** English. IPC Magazines Ltd., Perrymount Road, Haywards Heath, West Sussex RH16 3DH England. **Tel** 011 44 444 440421.

US
**MLD, A WOMEN'S MAILING LIST DIRECTORY.** **Added/Corp** National Council for Research on Women (U.S.). **VFOAT** Women's Mailing List Directory. (1990)-. Directory. English. National Council for Research on Women, 530 Broadway, 10th Floor, New York NY 10012-3920. **Tel** (212)274-0730, FAX (212)274-0821. **LC** HQ1883; .M542.

IT
**MODA.** See Clothing Industry and Fashion.

AT/0155-4611
**MODE AUSTRALIA.** See Clothing Industry and Fashion.

AT/0729-5081
**MODE FOR BRIDES.** See Family and Marriage.

CN/1181-6074
**MOTHER OF THYME.** [Mother thyme]. Vol. 1, No. 1 (Fall 1990)-. Periodical. English. qt. $2.50. Artemis Enterprises, Rural Route 2, Box 54, Dundas, Ontario L9H 5E2 Canada. **DD** 305.42/05.

US
**MOVING OUT.** See Literature.

US/0047-8318
**MS.** [Ms.]. **VFOAT** Ms. Magazine. Vol. 1, No. 1 (July/Aug. 1990)-. Periodical. English. bm (6 issues). $45.00. Lang Communications, 230 Park Avenue, New York NY 10169. **Tel** (212)551-9500, FAX (212)599-4597. **(Subscription address:** Neodata / Colorado, PO Box 2606, Boulder Boulder CO 80322.) **ED** Robin Morgan. **LC** HQ1101; .M5514. **DD** 305.42/05. **Ad Acc.** available on microfilm and microfiche from University Microfilms International (UMI). Documents available from, UMI Article Clearinghouse. ***Continues*** *Ms., 0047-8318.*
**Desc:** Contains no advertising, and 100 pages of editorial in every bimonthly issue. Presents breakthrough investigative journalism, national and international news, interviews and profiles, fiction, poetry, prizewinning photojournalism, and feminist voices of the world.
**Ind/Abst** Abr. Read. Guide Period. Lit.; Acad. Abstr. Full Text Elite (Jan. 1984-); Acad. Abstr. (Jan. 1984-1989); Acad. Search (Jan. 1984-); Book Rev. Digest; Book Rev. Index; Child. Lit. Abstr. (19??-); Consum. Index Prod. Eval. Inf. Source; Film Lit. Index; INFO-SOUTH Abstr.; Mag. Artic. Summar. Elite (Jan. 1984-); Mag. Artic. Summar. Select (Jan. 1984-); Mag. Artic. Summar. CD-ROM (Jan. 1984-); Mag. Express (1986-) [Full Txt.]; Mag. Search; Med. Rev. Dig.; Newsp. Period. Abstr. (1986-1989); Read. Guide Abstr. Select Ed.; Read. Guide Period. Lit.; Resource/One Ondisc; Mag. Index (1990-); Women Stud. Abstr.

CU/0864-0327
**MUCHACHA.** ***Suspended.*** (March 1980)-Suspended (1990). Periodical. Spanish. Twelve times a year. Ediciones Cubanas, Obispo 527, Altos ESQ Bernaza, CP 10100 Havana Cuba. **Tel** 011 632980, 631942, FAX 011 631011, telex 512337, 6540. **LC** HQ1104; .M76. **DD** 305.4/097291/05. **Circ:** 300,000 (ctrl).
**Desc:** A magazine for girls between the ages of 14 and 28 that publishes articles and features on such topics as sex education, vocational guidance, work education and human relations in the home, at school and at work.

CU
**MUJERES.** Began in 1959?. Periodical. Spanish. mo. 0.40Cub$ Cuba; $18.20 North America; $21.20 South America; $26.20 Western Europe; $28.20 other. Ediciones Cubanas, Obispo 527, Altos ESQ Bernaza, CP 10100 Havana Cuba. **Tel** 011 632980, 631942, FAX 011 631011, telex 512337, 6540. **LC** AP63; .M73. **Circ:** 250,000.
**Desc:** Contributes to women's development in cultural, ideological and political orders; endorses their struggle for equality.

SP
**MUJERES (MADRID, SPAIN).** (MUJERES.). Periodical. Spanish. 125ptas (single issue). Instituto de la Mujer, Ministerio de Cultura, Almagro 36 2A Planta, 28019 Madrid Spain. **LC** HQ1691; .M84. **DD** 305.4/0946.

US/0737-0032
**MUSICAL WOMAN, THE.** See Music.

UK
**MY WEEKLY.** English. £42.90. D C Thomson & Co Ltd, 7 Bank Street, Dundee DD1 9HU Scotland. **Tel** 011 44 382 23131.

# Women's Interests

**US**
**N W S ACTION.** English. National Women's Studies Association, University of Maryland, College Park MD 20742-1325.
**Ind/Abst** Women Stud. Abstr.

**IS**
**NAAMAT.** 1- October 1976-. Periodical. Hebrew. mo (ten issues per year). IL30.00. Te-Nuat Nashim Ovdot U-Mitnadvot, Ha-Histdrut Ha-Kelalit Shel, Ha-Ovdim Bo-erota Yisrael, 93 Arlozorov Street. **Tel** 03-269747. **ED** Zivia Cohen. **LC** HQ1728.5; .A3. Index available. **Bk Rev. Ad Acc. Circ:** 15,000 (ctrl).
**Desc:** Published by NAAMAT, the largest women's organization in Israel; covers issues concerning women's status.

**US/0740-0225**
**NASE ZITTJA.** (OUR LIFE.). **Added/Corp** Ukrainian National Women's League of America. **VFOAT** Nashe Zhyttia. (1944-). Periodical. English (Ukrainian). Eleven times a year (July and August issue combined). $30.00. Ukrain National Women League of America, 108 Second Avenue, New York NY 10003. **Tel** (212)674-5508, FAX (212)254-2672. **ED** Irena Chaban. **LC** HQ1104; .O8. **Circ:** 4,100 (ctrl).
**Desc:** The official publication of Ukrainian National Women's League of America. Printed monthly in Ukrainian with approximately seven pages in English.

**US**
**NATIONAL ASSOCIATION FOR GIRLS & WOMEN IN SPORT.** See Recreation, Leisure-Sports.

**US/0027-8831**
**NATIONAL BUSINESS WOMAN.** (NATIONAL BUSINESS WOMAN : THE MAGAZINE OF THE NATIONAL FEDERATION OF BUSINESS AND PROFESSIONAL WOMEN'S CLUBS.). [Natl. bus. woman]. **Added/Corp** National Federation of Business and Professional Women's Clubs. Vol. 35, No. 11 (Nov. 1956)-. Periodical. English. qt. $10.00. National Federation of Business & Professional Women, 2012 Massachusetts Avenue NW, Washington DC 20036. **Tel** (202)293-1100. **ED** Maryanne Sugarman Costa. **LC** HD6050; .N3. **DD** 331. **Ad Acc. Circ:** 75,000 (ctrl). **Continues** Independent Woman.
**Desc:** Important to working women with an emphasis on policy, legislative affairs and workplace activity.
**Ind/Abst** Work Relat. Abstr.

**US/0740-2813**
**NATIONAL DIRECTORY OF WOMEN ELECTED OFFICIALS.** See Political Science.

**US/0886-389X**
**NATIONAL DIRECTORY OF WOMEN-OWNED BUSINESS FIRMS.** See Business.

**US/0360-3296**
**NATIONAL MEMBERSHIP DIRECTORY - WOMEN IN COMMUNICATIONS, INC.** See Communication.

**US/0730-6334**
**NATIONAL MINORITY BUSINESS INFORMATION SYSTEM.** See Business.

**US/0149-4740**
**NATIONAL NOW TIMES.** (NATIONAL NOW TIMES : OFFICIAL TIMES OF THE NATIONAL ORGANIZATION FOR WOMEN (NOW).). [Natl. NOW times]. **Main/Corp** National Organization for Women. **Added/Corp** National Organization for Women. **VFOAT** National Times. Vol. 10 No. 12 (Dec. 1977)-. Periodical. English. mo (10 issues). $35.00. National Now Times, 1000 16th Street NW, Suite 700, Washington DC 20036. **Tel** (202)331-0066. **ED** Sheri O'Dell and Maria K. Bachman. **DD** 305. **Bk Rev. Ad Acc. Circ:** 161,000. available on microfilm and microfiche from University Microfilms International (UMI). Documents available from UMI Article Clearinghouse. **Continues** Do It NOW.
**Ind/Abst** Altern. Press Index; Expand. Acad. Index (1992-); Newsp. Period. Abstr. (1992-).

**US/0741-9147**
**NATIONAL WOMEN'S HEALTH REPORT.** See Public Health and Safety.

**CN/0827-3944**
**NATIVE WOMEN'S NEWS.** See Ethnic Interests.

**US/0161-2115**
**NCJW JOURNAL.** See Ethnic Interests.

**US/8755-867X**
**NETWORK NEWS - NATIONAL WOMEN'S HEALTH NETWORK (U.S.).** See Public Health and Safety.

**CN/0826-4929**
**NETWORK OF SASKATCHEWAN WOMEN (1983).** (NETWORK OF SASKATCHEWAN WOMEN.). [Netw. Sask. women]. **Added/Corp** Saskatchewan Action Committee, Status of Women. (Sept. 1983)-. Periodical. English. Four times a year (Mar., June, Sept., Dec.). 25.00Can$ (organization); 10.00Can$ (individual). Saskatchewan Action Committee, 2343 Cornwall Street, Regina Saskatchewan S4P 2L4 Canada. **Tel** (306)525-8329, FAX (306)757-4548. **ED** Kripa Sekhar. **DD** 305.4/2/097124. **Ad Acc. Circ:** 550 (ctrl). **Continues** Network (Saskatoon, Sask.), 0712-5925.
**Desc:** Covers social, political and economic issues as they relate to women, from a feminist perspective.

**US/0890-3530**
**NETWORK (SALT LAKE CITY, UTAH).** (NETWORK.). [Network]. (197?)- Vol.16 (Apr. 1993)-. Periodical. English. Twelve times a year. $12.00 (one year), $19.00 (two years), $26.00 (three years). Network, PO Box 57187, Salt Lake City UT 84157. **Tel** (801)262-6682. **ED** Lynne A. Tempest, (801)262-8091. **DD** 305. **Bk Rev,** (Qty: 10-12). **Ad Acc, Adv Mgr:** Kate Olson, **Tel** (801)262-8091. **Circ:** 40,000.

**US/8756-9981**
**NEW BEGINNINGS (FRANKLIN PARK, ILL.).** (NEW BEGINNINGS.). [New begin.]. **Added/Corp** La Leche League International. Vol. 1, No. 1 (Jan./Feb. 1985)-. Periodical. English. bm $18.00 one year; $30.00 membership; $50.00 professionals. La Leche League International, 9616 Minneapolis Avenue, Franklin Park IL 60131. **Tel** (708)455-7730. **DD** 392. **Continues** La Leche League News.

**US/0742-7123**
**NEW BOOKS ON WOMEN AND FEMINISM.** **Added/Corp** University of Wisconsin System. Women's Studies Librarian. **VFOAT** New Books on Women & Feminism; Women and Feminism; Women & Feminism. No. 1 (June 1979)-. Periodical. English. sa. $7.00 University of Wisconsin affiliated individual; $12.60 University of Wisconsin affiliated organization; $13.25 Wisconsin individual and Wisconsin women's program; $25.00 (individuals), $46.00 (institutions) other. University of Wisconsin Women's Studies Librarian, 728 State Street, 430 Memorial Library, Madison WI 53706. **Tel** (608)263-5754, FAX (608)265-2754. **ED** Phyllis Holman Weisbard, Carolyn Wilson, Linda Shult, Ingrid Markhardt. **LC** Z7963.F44; N49; Z7961; .N41. **DD** 305. **Circ:** 1,400.
**Desc:** An inclusive bibliography of new titles published on women and feminism.

**US/0160-1075**
**NEW DIRECTIONS FOR WOMEN.** **Ceased.** [New dir. women]. (1975)-(Oct. 1993). Periodical. English. bm. New Directions for Women, 108 West Palisade Avenue, Englewood NJ 07631. **Tel** (201)568-0226, FAX (201)568-6532. **ED** Phyllis Kriegel and Lynn Wenzel. **[CCC]. Bk Rev. Ad Acc. Adv Mgr:** Susan Valentine. **Circ:** 65,000. available on microfilm from University Microfilms International (UMI). **Continues** New Directions for Women in New Jersey, 0748-2981.
**Desc:** National feminist newspaper. News coverage extends to virtually all political, economic, medical, cultural and social issues addressed by the movement.
**Ind/Abst** Altern. Press Index; Am. Humanit. Index (-199?); Book Rev. Index (1984-); Hum. Rights Intern. Rep.; Stud. Women Abstr.; Women Stud. Abstr.

**US**
**NEW JERSEY WOMAN MAGAZINE.** (19??)-. Periodical. English. Six times a year. $15.00. New Jersey Woman, 27 McDermott Place, Bergenfield NJ 07621. **Tel** (201)384-0201. **ED** Louise B. Hafesh. **Ad Acc, Adv Mgr:** Leslie Malon. **Continues** Jersey Woman.

**US/1053-1351**
**NEW MATURE WOMAN.** [New mature woman]. (1990)-. Periodical. English. bm. $7.95. New Mature Woman, 6901 West Stockman Road, Glendale AZ 85308. **DD** 306.

**US/0028-6974**
**NEW WOMAN.** [New woman]. Vol. 1 (June 1971)-. Periodical. English. mo $17.00. K 3 Magazine Corporation, 200 Madison Avenue 8th Floor, New York NY 10016. **Tel** (212)447-4700, (212)447-4732. **(Subscription address:** Neodata / Colorado, PO Box 2606, Boulder Boulder CO 80322.) **LC** HQ1101; .N48. **DD** 301.41/2/05. **Bk Rev. Ad Acc.** available on microfilm and microfiche from University Microfilms International (UMI). Documents available from UMI Article Clearinghouse.
**Desc:** Magazine for women interested in self-discovery and personal growth. Topics range from psychology, relationships, careers and self-assertion to health, fashion, and beauty.
**Ind/Abst** Newsp. Period. Abstr. (1988-).

**US/1043-2221**
**NEW WOMEN/NEW CHURCH.** See Religion and Theology.

**US**
**NEW YORK WOMAN.** **Ceased.** Vol. 1 (1970)-(1992). English. American Express Publishing Company, 1120 Avenue of the Americas, New York NY 10036. **Tel** (212)382-5642.
**Ind/Abst** Access (1988-1992).

**US/0028-8969**
**NEWS & LETTERS.** See Economics.

**CN/0226-1944**
**NEWS - FEMINIST PARTY OF CANADA.** [News - Fem. Party Can.]. **Main/Corp** Feminist Party of Canada. **VFOAT** Nouvelles - Parti Feministe du Canada. V. 1- July 1979-. Periodical. English (French). qt. Feminist Party of Canada, PO Box 5117, Station A, Toronto Ontario M5W 1N8 Canada. **DD** 305.4/2.

●**US/1064-6973**
**NEWS FOR ENTREPRENEURIAL MOTHERS.** See Business.

**US**
**NEWSLETTER - ASSOCIATION FOR WOMEN IN MATHEMATICS.** See Mathematics.

**US/0732-2771**
**NEWSLETTER - ASSOCIATION OF AMERICAN LAW SCHOOLS. SECTION ON WOMEN IN LEGAL EDUCATION.** See Law.

**US/0276-9565**
**NEWSLETTER - CAMPUS MINISTRY WOMEN (ORGANIZATION).** **Ceased.** (CAMPUS MINISTRY WOMEN NEWSLETTER.). [Newsl. - Campus Minist. Women (Organ.)]. **Main/Corp** Campus Ministry Women (Organization). **Added/Corp** Campus Ministry Women (Organization). Newsletter. (Nov./Dec. 1976)-(19??). Newsletter. English. Five times a year. Campus Ministry Women, 802 Monroe, Ann Arbor MI 48104. **Tel** (313)662-5189. **ED** Ann Marie Coleman. **Circ:** 200. **Continues** Interim, 0276-9557.
**Desc:** Offers support and exchange of ideas, and raises women's issues within the wider state and national campus ministry circle of organizations.

**CN/0229-7256**
**NEWSLETTER - CANADIAN RESEARCH INSTITUTE FOR THE ADVANCEMENT OF WOMEN.** (NEWSLETTER.). [Newsl. - Can. Res. Inst. Adv. Women]. **Added/Corp** Canadian Research Institute for the Advancement of Women. **VFOAT** Bulletin de Nouvelles. **VAT** Bulletin de Nouvelles - Institut Canadien de Recherches pour l'Avancement de la Femme. (Mar. 1979)-. Periodical. English (French). qt. 100.00Can$ institutions; 25.00Can$ individuals. Canadian Research Institute for the Advancement of Women, Suite 408 / 151 Slater Street, Ottawa Ontario K1P 5H3 Canada. **Tel** (613)563-0681, FAX (613)563-7739. **ED** Linda O'Neil. **DD** 362.8/3/06071. **Bk Rev. Ad Acc. Circ:** 1,200.
**Desc:** Includes CRIAW news, listings of research projects and requests, books, periodicals, reports, grants available, conferences, news of organizations, etc., related to feminist research.

**US**
**NEWSLETTER / HARVARD WOMEN'S LAW ASSOCIATION.** See Law.

**CN/0712-3035**
**NEWSLETTER (NATIONAL COUNCIL OF WOMEN OF CANADA).** (NEWSLETTER / THE NATIONAL COUNCIL OF WOMEN OF CANADA.). [Newsl. - Natl. Counc. Women Can.]. **Added/Corp** National Council of Women of Canada. (19??)-. Newsletter. English. ir (3 or 4 per year). $6.00. National Council of Women, 270 MacLaren Street, Ottawa Ontario K2P 0M3 Canada. **Tel** (613)233-4953. **DD** 305.4/06/071.

**CN/0227-6879**
**NEWSLETTER / ONTARIO COMMITTEE ON THE STATUS OF WOMEN.** **Suspended.** [Newsl. - Ont. Comm. Status Women]. **VAT** Ontario Committee on the Status of Women Newsletter; Ontario Committee on the Status of Women News. (1972)-Suspended. Newsletter. English. Three times a year. Free to members, 15.00Can$ (nonmembers) Canada; $10.00 (nonmembers) other. Ontario Committee on the Status of Women, PO Box 188, Station Q, Toronto Ontario M4T 2M1 Canada. **DD** 305.4/2/09713.

**CN/0382-8271**
**NEWSLETTER - OTTAWA WOMEN'S CENTRE.** **Main/Corp** Ottawa Women's Centre. **VFOAT** Ottawa Women's Centre Newsletter. Began with June 1972 issue. Newsletter. English. ir. $3.00. Ottawa Women's Centre, 821 Somerset Street West, Ottawa K1R 6R4. **DD** 301.41/2/06271384.

**CN/0707-0195**
**NEWSLETTER - PROVINCIAL COUNCIL OF WOMEN OF BRITISH COLUMBIA.** **Main/Corp** Provincial Council of Women of British Columbia. Sept. 1977-. Newsletter. English. ir. Free to members. Provincial Council of Women of British

Columbia, Apartment 101/1315-7th Avenue, New Westminster British Columbia V3M 2J9 Canada. **DD** 301.41/2/062711.

CN/0715-4283
**NEWSLETTER - TASK FORCE ON WOMEN'S ISSUES.** (NEWSLETTER / TASK FORCE ON WOMEN'S ISSUES, CANADIAN PSYCHIATRIC ASSOCIATION.). [Newsl. - Task Force Women's Issues]. Newsletter. English. qt. Free. Task Force / Women's Issues, c/o P. Stephenson, Task Force on Women's Issues, 717 West 10th Avenue, Vancouver BC V5Z 1L6 Canada. **DD** 155.6/33/05.

CN/0711-4478
**NEWSLETTER - WOMEN'S EQUAL RIGHTS ASSOCIATION.** (WOMEN'S EQUAL RIGHTS ASSOCIATION : NEWSLETTER.). [Newsl. - Women's Equal Rights Assoc.]. **Added/Corp** Women's Equal Rights Association. **VAT** W.E.R.A. Women's Equal Rights Association; Women's Equal Rights Association. (1978)-. Newsletter. English. Women's Equal Rights Association, 1306 17th Avenue, Prince Georce BC V2L 3P1. **DD** 305.4/2/0607112. ***Continues*** *Women's Collective Newsletter, 0711-446X.*

CN/0316-5094
**NEWSMAGAZINE - CENTRE FOR WOMEN. HUMBER COLLEGE OF APPLIED ARTS AND TECHNOLOGY. CENTRE FOR CONTINUOUS LEARNING. See** Education-Higher Education.

US/0888-9775
**NEWYORK WOMAN.** ***Ceased.*** [N. Y. woman]. **VFOAT** New York Woman. Vol. 1, No. 1 (Sept./Oct. 1986)-Vol. 6, No. 4 (Jan. 1992). Periodical. English. Ten times a year. Esquire Magazine Group, 2 Park Avenue, New York NY 10016. **LC** HQ1439.N6; N49. **DD** 305.4/09747/1.
**Desc:** A magazine with all the verve and vitality, enthusiasm and excitement of New York from a woman's point of view.

CN/0838-6498
**NEXUS II.** [Nexus II]. **VFOAT** Nexus Two. Vol. 1, No. 1 (October 1987)-. Periodical. English. Free. Nexus II, 50 Yates Street, St. Catharines Ontario L2R 5R5. **DD** 305.4/09713/38. ***Continues*** *Nexus (St. Catharines, Ont.)., 0821-6401.*

US/0898-8900
**NICHI-BEI JOSEI JANARU.** (NICHI-BEI JOSEI JANARU / U.S.-JAPAN WOMEN'S JOURNAL.). [Nichi-Bei josei janaru]. **Added/Corp** U.S.-Japan Center for Information on Women. **VFOAT** U.S.-Japan Women's Journal. No. 1 (Spring 1988)-. Periodical. Japanese (translations available in English). Twice a year. $30.00 (individuals); $55.00 (institutions). US-Japan Women's Center, 926 Bautista Ct., Palo Alto CA 94303. **Tel** (415)857-9049, FAX (415)494-8160. **ED** Yoko Kawashima. **LC** HQ1104; .N5. **DD** 305. cum. index. **Ad Acc.**
**Desc:** The purpose of this journal is to disseminate information on Japanese women to the U.S., to enlarge the basis of information available in Japan on feminist theory and on the status of American women as well as women in other countries, and to stimulate the comparative study of womens issues.

HU
**NOK LAPJA. Added/Corp** Magyar Nok Demokratikus Szovetsege. Magyar Nok Orszagos Tanacsa. (1948)-. Periodical. Hungarian. wk. 99.00Can$. Pannonia Books, PO Box 1017 Postal Station B, Toronto Ontario M5T 2T8 Canada. **Tel** (416)966-5156, FAX (416)966-5156. **ED** Iren Nemeti. **LC** HQ1104; .N58. **Bk Rev. Ad Acc. Circ:** 800,000.
**Desc:** Magazine for women including short stories, fashion, cooking, embroidery, health childcare and miscellaneous news for women.

NO/0803-8740
**NORA: NORDIC JOURNAL OF WOMEN'S STUDIES. VFOAT** Nordic Journal of Women's Studies. (1993)-. Periodical. English. sa. Kr315.00, $55.00. Scandinavian University Press, PO Box 2959 Toeyen, N 0608 Oslo 6 Norway. **Tel** 011 47 2 2575400, FAX 011 47 2 2575353, telex 71896 UROR N. **(Subscription address:** Scandinavian University Press, 200 Meacham Ave., Elmont NY 11003.**) ED** Harriet B. Nielsen and Torill Steinfeld. **LC** HQ1101; .N67.
**Desc:** Shows a Nordic profile in women's research, with regard to content and theoretical and methodological approaches. The Nordic welfare states are usually considered models of the successful application of policies of gender and social equality. The journal aims to discuss and examine the realities and myths of women's lives in the Nordic countries, historically and today.

US
**NORTH CAROLINA COUNCIL OF WOMEN'S ORGANIZATIONS ANNUAL DIRECTORY. See** Societies and Clubs.

US
**NORTH CENTRAL WOMEN'S STUDIES NEWSLETTER.** Vol. 3, No. 3 (Nov. 1980)-. Newsletter. English. ir. North Central Womens Studies Association, Coll Mount St Joseph, c/o V Forde, Mount Saint Joseph OH 45051. ***Continues*** *Northcentral Newsletter of the National Women's Studies Association.*

CN/0824-4081
**NORTHERN WOMAN JOURNAL.** [North. woman j.]. **Added/Corp** Northern Women's Centre (Ont.). (1976)-. Periodical. English. Four times a year. 8.00Can$ (individuals), 16.00Can$ (institutions). Northern Woman Journal, PO Box 144, Thunder Bay Ontario P7C 4V5 Canada. **Tel** (807)345-8803. **ED** Jane Saunders. **DD** 305.4/09713/1. **Bk Rev. Ad Acc. Circ:** 250 (ctrl). ***Continues*** *Northern Woman, 0319-1966.*
**Desc:** A feminist newspaper providing information and analysis on issues of concern to women, including health, violence, employment, law reform, day care and isolation; includes a news update on regional (Northwest Ontario), national and international women's issues.

CN/1181-7496
**NORTHERNHER (YELLOWKNIFE).** (NORTHERNHER.). [Northernher]. **VFOAT** Northern Her. Vol. 1, No. 1 (Mar./Apr. 1991)-. Periodical. English. bm. $3.75 per issue, $22.00 per year. Northerner, PO Box 2641, Yellowknife NWT X1A 2P9 Canada. **DD** 305.4/09719.

US
**NORTHWEST WOMEN.** Vol. 4, No. 3 (Holiday 1988)-. Periodical. English. bm. Northwest Women, 7904 Southwest 14th Avenue, Portland OR 97219. ***Continues*** *Northwest Women in Business.*

NQ
**NOSOTRAS. Added/Corp** AMNLAE (Organization). (199?)-. Periodical. Spanish. ir. AMNLAE, Del Reparto San Juan, 2c. al sur Casa 598, Apdo. Postal 278, Managua Nicaragua. **Tel** 71661. **ED** Christian Santos.

CN/0824-0671
**NOUVELLE FEMME (MONTREAL, QUEBEC).** (NOUVELLE FEMME.). [Nouv. femme]. No. 1, (Dec. 1983)-. Periodical. French. bm. $12,00. Nouvelle Femme, C P 51 Succursale D, Montreal Quebec H3K 3B9 Canada. **DD** 054/.1.

FR/0248-4951
**NOUVELLES QUESTIONS FEMINISTES.** No. 1 (March 1981)-. Periodical. French (summaries and/or abstracts in English). Three times a year. 500.00F. Association Nouvelles Questions Feministes, C. Delphy, 59-61 Rue Pouchet, 75017 Paris Cedex 17 France. **Tel** 011 33 140251191. **ED** Andree Michel and Christine Delphy. **LC** HQ1102; .Q47. **DD** 305.4/2/05. **Bk Rev. Ad Acc. Circ:** 1,000. ***Continues*** *Questions Feministes, 0154-9960.*

US/0741-9627
**NOW L.A. / OFFICIAL PUBLICATION OF THE LOS ANGELES CHAPTER, NATIONAL ORGANIZATION FOR WOMEN (NOW). VFOAT** N.O.W. LA. **VAT** National Organization for Women Los Angeles. Vol. 1, No 1-2 (Feb./Mar. 1983)-. Periodical. English. ir. $10.00. Los Angeles Chapter of the National Organization for Women, 8909 West Olympic Boulevard, Room 112, Beverly Hills CA 90211. **Tel** (310)652-5572. **ED** Jean Stapleton. **Bk Rev. Ad Acc. Circ:** 2,500 (ctrl).
**Desc:** Covers news of activities, legislation and events related to women's rights as well as features and reviews of topics relating to equality of the sexes.

US/8750-7005
**NOW-NYS ACTION REPORT.** (NOW-NYS ACTION REPORT / NOW, NATIONAL ORGANIZATION FOR WOMEN.). **Added/Corp** National Organization for Women. New York Chapter. **VFOAT** NOW NYS Action Report. **VAT** National Organization for Women New York State Action Report. Vol. 1, No. 1 (Fall 1984)-. Periodical. English. ir (4 issues). comes with National Organization of Women New York State Chapter membership. National Organization for Women - NOW, PO Box 287, West Seneca NY 14224. **Tel** (716)675-1433.

US/1056-120X
**NWFN NEWSJOURNAL : A WOMEN'S FITNESS RESOURCE. See** Health and Personal Fitness.

US
**NWSA DIRECTORY OF WOMEN'S STUDIES PROGRAMS, WOMEN'S CENTERS, AND WOMEN'S RESEARCH CENTERS : A PUBLICATION OF THE NATIONAL WOMEN'S STUDIES ASSOCIATION. Added/Corp** National Women's Studies Association. **VFOAT** Directory of Women's Studies Programs, Women's Centers, and Women's Research Centers. **VAT** National Women's Studies Association Directory of Women's Studies Programs, Women's Centers, and Women's Research Centers. (1990)-. Directory. English. ***Continues*** *Directory of Women's Studies Programs.*

US/1040-0656
**NWSA JOURNAL.** (NWSA JOURNAL : A PUBLICATION OF THE NATIONAL WOMEN'S STUDIES ASSOCIATION.). [NWSA j.]. **Added/Corp** National Women's Studies Association. **VAT** National Women's Studies Association Journal. Vol. 1, No. 1 (Autumn 1988)-. Periodical. English. Three times a year. $115.00 US; $125.00 other. Indiana University Press, 601 North Morton Street, Bloomington IN 47404. **Tel** (812)855-3830, (800)842-6796. **LC** HQ1186.U6; N87; HQ1101; .N3. **DD** 305. **CODEN** NWJOEG. **[CCC].**
**Desc:** Interdisciplinary, multicultural, feminist journal publishing scholarly articles of interest to women's studies teachers, researchers, and others who are concerned with feminist issues.
**Ind/Abst** Am. Hist. Life (1988-); Am. Humanit. Index (199?-); Left Index; Lit. Crit. Regist.; PAIS Int. Print (1991-); Soc. Plann. Policy Dev. Abstr.; Women Stud. Abstr.

US/0892-5984
**OF A LIKE MIND. See** New Age Publications.

US/0030-0071
**OFF OUR BACKS.** [Off our backs]. Vol. 1, (Feb. 1970)-. Periodical. English. Eleven times a year (Combined Aug./Sept. issues). $33.00 (institution), $21.00 (individual). Off Our Backs, 2423 18th Street Northwest, Washington DC 20009. **Tel** (202)234-8072. Index available. **Bk Rev**, (Qty: 25-30). **Ad Acc. Circ:** 20,000. available on microfilm and microfiche from Historical Society of Wisconsin. Documents available from UMI Article Clearinghouse.
**Desc:** Feminist news journal specializes in conference coverage, in depth reviews, interviews as well as the news.
**Ind/Abst** Altern. Press Index; Chicano Index; Expand. Acad. Index (1992-); Newsp. Period. Abstr. (1992-); Stud. Women Abstr.; Women Stud. Abstr.

US/1071-1643
**OKLAHOMA WOMEN'S FRONT PAGE NEWS.** (OKLAHOMA WOMEN'S FRONT PAGE NEWS : OKLAHOMA'S STATEWIDE NEWSPAPER FOR WOMEN.). [Okla. women's front page news]. **VFOAT** Front Page News. Vol. 1, No. 1 (Aug. 1991)-. Periodical. English. mo. $15.00. Oklahoma Women's Front Page News, Box A 0235, Oklahoma City OK 73162. **Tel** (405)720-9500, FAX (722)4339. **ED** Candace St.Clare. **DD** 305. **Bk Rev**, (Qty: 12). **Ad Acc. Circ:** 20,000.

US/0734-0141
**ON CAMPUS WITH WOMEN.** [On campus women]. **Added/Corp** Project on the Status and Education of Women (Association of American Colleges). (1971)-. Periodical. English. Four times a year. $28.00 one year; $50.00 two years. Association of American Colleges, 1818 R Street Northwest, Washington DC 20009. **Tel** (202)387-3760, FAX (202)265-9532. **ED** Bernice R. Sandler. **Bk Rev. Circ:** 4,500. available on microfilm and microfiche from University Microfilms International (UMI).
**Desc:** Provides information on women in higher education. Some articles are included in the women's studies, sexual harassment, athletics, employment, traditionally male fields, campus violence and minority women.
**Ind/Abst** Women Stud. Abstr.

US/0895-6014
**ON THE ISSUES.** (ON THE ISSUES / CHOICES.). [On issues]. **Added/Corp** Choices (Organization). Vol. 1, (Fall 1983)-. Periodical. English. Four times a year (Feb., May, Aug., Nov.). $24.75 (institutions); $30.75 (individual). On the Issues, PO Box 3000, Department OT1, Denvelle NJ 07834. **Tel** (201)627-2427, FAX (201)672-5872. **ED** Ronni Sandroff (phone: (718)275-6020). **LC** RA564.85; .O5. **DD** 362.1/98/05. **Bk Rev. Ad Acc. Circ:** 25,000.
**Ind/Abst** Access (1992-); Altern. Press Index (199?-).

CN/0827-8717
**ON YOUR OWN, A DIRECTORY FOR WOMEN. See** Sociology-Social Services and Welfare.

US/0739-6708
**ONE WOMAN.** [One woman]. **VFOAT** 1 Woman. Winter 1983-. Periodical. English. qt. $10.00. One Woman Publishing, 36 East 12th Street, New York NY 10003.

●US/1066-2960
**ONE WOMAN'S OPINION.** (1993)-. Periodical. English. mo. $24.00. M M Van Baaren, PO Box 366, Newton Center MA 02159.

CN/0384-5230
**OPTIMST, THE. Added/Corp** Victoria Faulkner Women's Centre. **VFOAT** Newsletter. (197?)-. Periodical. English. Four times a year. 12.00Can$ (institutions), 7.00Can$ (individuals). OptiMST, Box 31011, Main Street PO, 211 Main Street, Whitehorse Yukon Y1A 5P7 Canada. **Tel** (403)668-3549. **DD** 301.41/2/097191. **Bk Rev**, (Qty: 2-4). **Ad Acc. Circ:** 800.
**Desc:** News, articles, features of interest to women. Written by Yukon women.

# Women's Interests

NE
**OPZIJ.** Weekbladpers, Postbus 1050, 1000 BB Amsterdam, Netherlands. **Tel** 011 31 20 5518711. **Ind/Abst** Child. Lit. Abstr. (19??-).

US/1048-8871
**OUTDOOR WOMAN. See** Recreation, Leisure-Outdoor Life.

US/1044-5706
**OUTLOOK (WASHINGTON, D.C. 1989).** (OUTLOOK / AMERICAN ASSOCIATION OF UNIVERSITY WOMEN.). [Outlook]. **Main/Corp** American Association of University Women. **VFOAT** American Association of University Women Outlook; AAUW Outlook. Vol. 83, No. 1 (Jan./Feb. 1989)-. Periodical. English. Four times a year. $15.00. American Association of University Women, 1111 16th Street Northwest, Membership Department, Washington DC 20037. **Tel** (202) 785-7759. **ED** Karen A Johnson. **LC** LC1756.A2; A5. **DD** 378/.0082. cum. index. **Bk Rev. Ad Acc. Circ:** 140,000. available in microform. **Continues** Graduate Woman, 0161-5661.
**Desc:** Provides information to AAUW membership on issues of concern to women, including current legislative action, innovative educational and community activities and programs, and profiles outstanding members, former grant recipients, and branch advocacy efforts. Occasionally reviews books on social, political or educational issues.
**Ind/Abst** Work Relat. Abstr.

●US/1063-1798
**OUTREACH (WASHINGTON, D.C. 1992). See** Business.

US
**OUTSTANDING YOUNG WOMEN OF AMERICA. Added/Corp** Montgomery (Ala.). Junior Chamber of Commerce. (1965)-. English. an. $59.95. Outstanding Americans, 316 Morgans Turn, Peachtree GA 30269. **Tel** (404)441-0439, (404)631-9691. **LC** CT3260; .O75.
**Desc:** A biographical directory of the 30,000 women chosen from more than 150,000 nominees each year to the outstanding young women of America program.

CN/1185-2542
**OWITT NEWS.** (THE OWITT NEWS / OTTAWA WOMEN IN TECHNOLOGY & TRADES.). [OWITT news]. **Added/Corp** Ottawa Women in Technology & Trades. **VFOAT** Ottawa Women in Technology & Trades News; Ottawa Women in Technology and Trades News. Vol. 1, No. 1 (Jan. 1990)-. Periodical. English. mo. Ottawa Women in Technology and Trades, PO Box 5666, Merivale Depot, Nepean, Ontario K2C 3M1 Canada. **DD** 331.4/8/097138405.

IT
**PAESE DELLE DONNE, IL.** (19??)-. English. wk. L40.000. Assoc Il Paese delle Donne, Via Farini 62, 00185 Rome Italy.
**Desc:** Information on women's activities.

CN/0711-4222
**PAKIZAH INTIRNASHINAL.** [Pakizah intirnashinal]. **VFOAT** Pakeezah; Pakeeza International. V. 2, No. 9 (Sept. 1980)-. Periodical. English (Urdu). sm. 12.00Can$ Canada; $16.00 US. Pakeeza International, 21 Lexington Avenue, Rexdale Ontario M9V 2G4 Canada. **Tel** (416)924-7444, FAX (416)924-7469. **ED** Shahtaj Fatima. **DD** 059/.91439. **Bk Rev. Ad Acc. Circ:** 2,000 (ctrl). **Continues** Pakizah, 0711-4214.
**Desc:** Current topics on North American and Indo Pak and Islamic issues.

US/0500-490X
**PAMPHLET - U.S. DEPARTMENT OF LABOR, EMPLOYMENT STANDARDS ADMINISTRATION, WOMEN'S BUREAU. See** Economics-Labor.

US/0733-1207
**PANDORA.** [Pandora]. Fall 1982-. Periodical. English. qt. $5.00. Yuma Daily Sun, PO Box 271, Caldwell NJ 07006. **Tel** (602)783-3333.
**Desc:** Feminist periodical committed to working with women to help them express their experience in a non-oppressive way.

US/0278-0224
**PARITY. See** Economics-Labor.

CN/0841-7997
**PARTENAIRE (SAINT-HUBERT).** (PARTENAIRE.). [Partenaire]. **Added/Corp** Association des Femmes Collaboratrices. **VFOAT** Partenaire. Vol. 9, No 1 (1988)-. Periodical. French. qt. Free (members). ADFC, 3925 Grande Allee/Suite 101, St Hubert Quebec J4T 2V8 Canada. **Tel** (514)462-7101. **DD** 331.4/3. **Continues** A.D.F.C. Informe., 0825-0502.

US/0015-9093
**PEACE AND FREEDOM. Added/Corp** Women's International League for Peace and Freedom.

United States Section. (1941)-. Periodical. English. Six times a year (Jan., Mar., May, July, Sept., Nov.). $12.00. Women's International League for Peace and Freedom, 1213 Race Street, Philadelphia PA 19107-1691. **Tel** (215)563-7110, FAX (215)864-2022. **ED** Wendy Rosenfield. Index available (January issue). **Bk Rev. Circ:** 12,000. available on microfilm and microfiche from University Microfilms International (UMI).
**Desc:** Journal of an international women's organization devoted to issues of peace, freedom, justice, the environment, and activities of over 100 branches in the U.S.
**Ind/Abst** Altern. Press Index; Peace Res. Abstr. J. (1966-1970, 1972-1977).

US/0031-4242
**PEN WOMAN (1944), THE.** (THE PEN WOMAN.). **Added/Corp** National League of American Pen Women. National League of American Pen Women. (1924)-. Periodical. English. Six times a year. $7.00. National League of American Penwomen, 1300 17th Street Northwest, Washington DC 20036. **Tel** (202)785-1997. **Supersedes** Penwoman.

US/0191-1554
**PERFORMING WOMAN, THE. See** Music.

US/1062-1083
**PERSPECTIVES - AMERICAN BAR ASSOCIATION. COMMISSION ON WOMEN IN THE PROFESSION. See** Law.

GW/0031-630X
**PETRA.** (PETRA : DIE MODERNE FRAU.). [Petra]. (1964)-. Periodical. German. mo. DM72.30. Jahreszeiten Verlag GmbH, Postfach 60 12 20, D 22212 Hamburg Germany. **Tel** 011 49 40 27173529. **UDC** 088.

US
**PHELONS WOMENS APPAREL & ACCESSORY SHOPS.** English. te. $130.00 (plus s&h). Phelon Sheldon & Marsar Inc, 15 Industrial Avenue, PO Box 517, Fairview NJ 07022. **Tel** (201)941-8804, (800)234-8804, FAX (201)941-5515. **ED** Kenneth W Phelon Jr. ctrl circ. **Continues** Phelons Womens Apparel Shops.

US/1045-0904
**PHOEBE (ONEONTA, N.Y.).** (PHOEBE: AN INTERDISCIPLINARY JOURNAL OF FEMINIST SCHOLARSHIP, THEORY, AND AESTHETICS.). [Phoebe]. **Added/Corp** State University of New York College at Oneonta. Women's Studies Program. Vol. 1, No. 1 (Feb. 1989)-. Periodical. English. Twice a year (Spring and Fall). $25.00 (institution), $15.00 (individual). Women's Studies / New York, State University of New York, Oneonta NY 13820. **Tel** (607)431-2014, FAX (607)431-2107. **ED** Kathleen O'Mara and Marilyn Wesley (poetry editor). **LC** HQ1101; .P45. **DD** 305. **Bk Rev**, (Qty: 15-20). **Ad Acc. Adv Mgr:** D. Simons. **Circ:** 400.
**Desc:** Feminist scholarship and women's fiction and poetry.
**Ind/Abst** Women Stud. Abstr.

VM
**PHU NU DIEN DAN.** (19??)-. Vietnamese. Twelve times a year. $80.00 US; $90.00 Canada; $110.00 Europe; $120.00 other. **(Subscription address:** Phu Nu Dien Dan, PO Box 2498, Garden Grove, CA 92642 USA) **ED** Hanh Ngoc. **LC** AP95.V5; P54. **Ad Acc. Circ:** 3,000 (ctrl).
**Desc:** Women's magazine. Helpful articles on various aspects of practical life (family, marriage, health, beauty care, etc.). Also literary contributions by contemporary Vietnamese authors.

CN/1185-9504
**PINK & BLUE DIRECTORY, THE.** [Pink blue dir.]. **VFOAT** Pink and Blue Directory. Premier Ed. (1991)-. Directory. English. sa. The Pink & Blue Directory, PO Box 159, 887 Queens Street E, Toronto, Ont M4M 1J2. **DD** 362.83/9.

IT/1120-4451
**PIU BELLA.** (1988)-. Periodical. Italian. wk. $265.00. RCS Rizzoli Periodici, Via A Rizzoli 2, 20132 Milan Italy. **Tel** 011 39 2 27200720. **UDC** 391. **Continues** Bella.

US/0148-902X
**PLAINSWOMAN. Suspended.** Vol. 1 (Oct. 1977)-Suspended with Vol. 11, No. 9-10. Periodical. English. mo (except Feb. and August). $15.00 US; $20.00, $23.00 (airmail) other. Plainswoman, Box 8027, Grand Forks ND 58202. **Tel** (701)777-8043. **ED** Elizabeth Hampsten. Index available. **Bk Rev. Circ:** 600. available on audiocassette.
**Desc:** A regional magazine featuring reminiscences, interviews, essays, poetry and fiction which reflects political and social issues of women, and their historical development.
**Ind/Abst** Am. Humanit. Index.

US/0032-1494
**PLAYGIRL.** Periodical. English. mo. $18.50. Playgirl Inc, 801 Second Avenue, New York NY 10017-4706. **Tel** (212)986-5100. **ED** Nancie S Martin. **Bk Rev. Ad Acc. Circ:** 745,467. available on microfilm from University Microfilms International (UMI).
**Desc:** Published for the spirited woman of today. Featuring exclusive interviews, fiction, beauty, health, and of course our men.
**Ind/Abst** Index Period. Artic. Relat. Law.

CU
**PLENARIA NACIONAL. Main/Corp** Federacion de Mujeres Cubanas. Periodical. Spanish.

US/0274-5526
**PLEXUS (OAKLAND, CALIF.).** (PLEXUS.). [Plexus]. (197?)-. Periodical. English. Twelve times a year. Plexus, 584 Castro Street/#344, San Francisco CA 94114-2512. **Tel** (415)451-2585. **ED** Karen Schiller. **DD** 305. **Bk Rev. Ad Acc. Circ:** 12,000.
**Desc:** News and articles by, for, and about women. Includes reviews, news, sports and a monthly calendar of events.

US
**PMS ACCESS.** English. bm. $18.00. PMS Access, 429 Gammon Place, PO Box 9326, Madisoon WI 57315. **Tel** (608)833-4PMS, 800-222-4PMS, (608)833-4PMS, FAX (608)833-7412.
**Desc:** Provides information on pertinent PMS issues along with other women's health concerns.

●US/1069-6652
**POLITICAL WOMAN (WHITE PLAINS, N.Y.). See** Political Science.

CN/0229-5059
**PRAIRIE WOMAN.** [Prairie woman]. Periodical. English. bm. $4.00. Prairie Woman, PO Box 4021, Saskatoon Saskatchewan Canada. **DD** 305.4/2/05. **Continues** Saskatoon Women's Liberation Newsletter, 0381-8764.

US/0032-7824
**PRESS WOMAN, THE. Title Change. See** Journalism.

CN/0700-6543
**PRIORITIES (VANCOUVER).** (PRIORITITES.). **Added/Corp** B.C. NDP Women's Rights Committee. (1???)-. English. Four times a year (within the seasons). 10.00Can$ (individual); 15.00 (institution). Priorities, 3110 Boundary Road, Burnaby BC V5M 4A2 Canada. **Tel** (604)430-8600. **ED** Diane E. Dupuis. **Bk Rev**, (Qty: varies). **Ad Acc. Circ:** 1,000 (ctrl).
**Desc:** This magazine is for the womens, who's interest is on the women's rights.

US/0093-8858
**PRO SE. See** Law.

US
**PROBE (CHICAGO, ILL.). See** Religion and Theology.

US/0891-1207
**PROFESSIONAL COMMUNICATOR, THE. See** Communication.

US/0190-1796
**PROFESSIONAL WOMEN AND MINORITIES. Added/Corp** Commission on Professionals in Science and Technology. Scientific Manpower Commission. 1st Ed. (1975)-. Periodical. English. ir. $125.00 (nonmember), $100.00 (member). Commission on Professionals in Science and Technology, 1500 Massachusetts Avenue Northwest, Suite 831, Washington DC 20005. **Tel** (202)223-6995. **ED** Betty M. Vetter and Eleanor L. Babco. **LC** HD6278.U5; P76. **DD** 331.11/43/0973. **[CCC].** Index available. **Circ:** 1,000. available in microform.
**Desc:** Participation of women and minorities in education and in the work force.
**Ind/Abst** Stat. Ref. Index.

US
**PROGRAM & LEGISLATIVE ACTION BULLETIN. See** Political Science.

US/0033-0833
**PROGRESSIVE WOMAN. Ceased.** (19??)-Vol. 5, No. 8 (1993). Periodical. English. mo. Progressive Woman, Box 510, Middleburg IN 46540. **LC** HQ1101. **DD** 335.43/05.

XN
**PROSVETENA ZENA.** Periodical. Serbo-Croatian (Cyrillic). mo. **LC** HQ1104; .P7.

PL
**PRZYJACIOKA.** (Mar. 21, 1948)-. Periodical. Polish. wk. $52.00. **(Subscription address:** ARS Polona, PO Box 1001, 00068 Warsaw Poland.) **LC** AP54; .P86.

●US
**PSICOLOGIA, PSICOPATOLOGIA & PSICOSOMATICA DELLA DONNA.** **See** Psychology.

UK/0361-6843
**PSYCHOLOGY OF WOMEN QUARTERLY.** [Psychol. women q.]. **Added/Corp** American Psychological Association. Division of the Psychology of Women. Vol. 1 (Fall 1976)-. Academic Scholarly Publication. English. qt. $113.00 US, Canada and Mexico; £77.00 other. Cambridge University Press, The Edinburgh Building, Shaftesbury Road, Cambridge CB2 2RU United Kingdom. **Tel** 011 44 223 312393, FAX 011 44 223 325959. **(Subscription address:** Cambridge University Press / North America, 110 Midland Avenue, Port Chester NY 10573.) **ED** Judith Worell. **LC** HQ1206; .P76. **DD** 155.6/33/05. **NLM** W1 PS746UN. **CODEN** PWOQDY. **Pr Rev.** available on microfilm and microfiche from University Microfilms International (UMI). Documents available from The Genuine Article, UMI Article Clearinghouse.
**Desc:** Publishes empirical studies, article reviews, and theoretical articles aimed at establishing a greater understanding of women's issues and sex roles in society. Articles deal with problems in social psychology, career development, gender, and counselling processes. Each year a special issue is published.
**Ind/Abst** Acad. Abstr. Full Text Elite (Jan. 1992-); Acad. Abstr. (Jan. 1992-); Acad. Search (Jan. 1992-); Appl. Soc. Sci. Index Abstr.; Chicano Index; Commun. Abstr.; Crim. Justice Abstr.; Curr. Contents Soc. Behav. Sci.; Curr. Index J. Educ.; Expand. Acad. Index (1989-); High. Educ. Abstr. (1979-); INFO-SOUTH Abstr.; Mag. Search; Multicult. Educ. Abstr.; Newsp. Period. Abstr. (1991-); Psychol. Abstr. (1976-); PsycINFO; PsycLit; Res. Alert [Full Cov.]; Res. High. Educ. Abstr.; Sage Fam. Stud. Abstr.; Soc. Plann. Policy Dev. Abstr.; Soc. Sci. Source (Jan. 1992-); Soc. Sci. Cit. Index [Full Cov.]; Soc. Sci. Index; Soc. Sci. Index Fulltext (Dec. 1988-) [Full Txt.]; Sociol. Abstr.; Spec. Educ. Needs Abstr.; Stud. Women Abstr.; Women Stud. Abstr.

CN/0380-8297
**PUBLICATION - SASKATCHEWAN ADVISORY COUNCIL ON THE STATUS OF WOMEN.** **Main/Corp** Saskatchewan. Advisory Council on the Status of Women. No. 1- 1974-. Monographic series. English. Price varies per volume. Saskatchewan Advisory Council on the Status of Women, 214-230 22nd Street East, Saskatoon Sask S7K 0E9. **DD** 301.4/2/0971.

US/1056-3008
**PULSE (SALT LAKE CITY, UTAH).** (PULSE / EXECUTIVE WOMEN INTERNATIONAL.). [Pulse]. **Added/Corp** Executive Women International. Vol. 1, No. 1 (Winter 1991)-. Periodical. English. qt. $2.00 (single issue). Executive Women International, East 4800 Street, Suite 1, Salt Lake City UT 84117. **DD** 658.

IT
**PUNTO, IL.** Italian. ir. L35000 Italy; 39000 other (one year), L65000 Italy; L67600 other (two year). Fratelli Pini Editori Srl, Via Vitt Emanuele 99, 22100 Como Italy. **Tel** 011 39 31 264584.

US/1062-6565
**QUARTERLY NEWSLETTER - WOMEN'S THEOLOGICAL CENTER (BOSTON, MASS.).** **See** Religion and Theology.

CN/0705-3762
**R A I F. RESEAU D'ACTION ET D'INFORMATION POUR LES FEMMES.** (R A I F.). [RAIF, Reseau action inf. femmes]. **Main/Corp** Reseau d'Action et d'Information pour les Femmes. **Added/Corp** Reseau d'action et d'information pour les femmes. **VAT** Reseau d'Action et d'Information pour les Femmes. (Dec. 1973)-. Periodical. French. Five times a year. 22.00Can$ (individuals), 30.00Can$ (institutions). Rese d'Act Information Femmes, C.P. 36088, Place Ste Foy, Ste Foy, Quebec G1V 1CO Canada. **Tel** (418)658-1973. **DD** 305.4/2/09714. **Bk Rev. Circ:** 700.
**Desc:** Deals with all matters concerning women especially legislation, rights, and news with a feminist analysis. Proactive lobbyist offer many solutions to legislative and social problems. It is not funded to be independent, but rather interested in changing values. It features book and film reviews and service advertising to inform women where to find help and information in other provinces and countries.

LE
**RAIDA / INSTITUTE FOR WOMEN'S STUDIES IN THE ARAB WORLD, BEIRUT UNIVERSITY COLLEGE.** **Added/Corp** Beirut University College. Institute for Women's Studies in the Arab World. No. 1 (May 1976)-. Periodical. English (French). Four times a year. $25.00. Institute for Women's Studies in the Arab World, PO Box 11-4080, Beirut University College, Beirut Lebanon. **Tel** 811 968. **(Subscription address:** Institutes of Womens Studies in the Arab World, 475 Riverside Drive, Room 1846, New York NY 10115.) **ED** Rose Ghurayyib. **LC** HQ1726.5; .R34. **DD** 305.4/09174927. **Bk Rev. Circ:** 1,000 (ctrl).
**Desc:** Covers the news of Arab women and all conferences and projects relating to improving the conditions of Arab women and that world, and enhancing their integration in economic development.
**Ind/Abst** Hum. Rights Intern. Rep.

IT/0033-9113
**RAKAM.** [Rakam]. (1930)-. Periodical. Italian. mo. L48000.00 Italy; L85000.00 other. Rusconi Editore Spa, Servicio Abbonements, V Le Sarca 235, 20126 Milan Italy. **Tel** 011 39 2 66192634. **UDC** 746.

US
**RAZON MESTIZA, LA.** **Added/Corp** Concilio Mujeres. (1974)-. Periodical. Spanish. mo. Concilio Mujeres, 725 Rhode Island Street, San Francisco CA 94107.

CN/0838-4479
**RECHERCHES FEMINISTES.** [Rech. fem.]. **Added/Corp** Universite Laval. Groupe de Recherche et d'Echange Multidisciplinaires Feministes. Vol. 1, No. 1, (1988)-. Periodical. French (summaries and/or abstracts in English). sa. 24.50Can$ (individuals), 38.00Can$ (institutions) Canada; 30.00Can$ (individuals), 43.00Can$ (institutions) other;. GREMF, Jean Durand 3E ET/ University Laval, Quebec, Quebec G1K 7P4 Canada. **Tel** (418)656-5418, FAX (418)656-3266. **ED** Huguette Dagenais. **DD** 305.4/2/09714. **Bk Rev. Circ:** 700 (ctrl).
**Desc:** Deals with social science, social problems with housing, and deviations and delinquency in Canada.
**Ind/Abst** PAIS Int. Print; Point Repere (Vol. 3, No 1 1990-); Women Stud. Abstr.

US/0034-2106
**REDBOOK.** (REDBOOK : THE MAGAZINE FOR YOUNG ADULTS.). [Redbook]. **VFOAT** Redbook Magazine Incorporating American Home; Redbook Magazine. (19??)-. Periodical. English. mo. $14.97. The Hearst Corporation, 250 West 55th Street, New York NY 10019. **Tel** (212)649-4014. **(Subscription address:** CDS Agency Hard Copy, PO Box 4966, Des Moines IA 50340.) **LC** AP2; .R2829. **DD** 051. **Bk Rev. Ad Acc.** available on microfilm and microfiche from University Microfilms International (UMI); available on an online database (file 635/Full-Text) from DIALOG. Documents available from UMI Article Clearinghouse. ***Continues*** *Redbook Magazine;* ***Absorbed*** *American Home, 0002-8789.*
**Desc:** Magazine containing short news notes and in-depth articles on a variety of health topics such as surviving cancer, nutrition, stress control, exercise, and skin care.
**Ind/Abst** Acad. Abstr. Full Text Elite (Jan. 1989-); Acad. Abstr. (Jan. 1989-); AGRICOLA; Consum. Health Nutr. Index; Consum. Index Prod. Eval. Inf. Source; Curr. Lit. Fam. Plan.; Health Ref. Cent. (1987-) [Full Txt.] [Select. Cov.]; Mag. Artic. Summar. Elite (Jan. 1989-); Mag. Artic. Summar. Select (Jan. 1989-); Mag. Artic. Summar. CD-ROM (Jan. 1989-); Mag. ASAP Plus [Full Txt.]; Mag. Index Plus (1989-); Mag. Index Sel. Microfiche (1990-) [Full Txt.]; Mag. Index. Sel. (1986-); Mag. Search; Newsp. Period. Abstr. (1988-); Read. Guide Abstr. Select Ed.; Read. Guide Period. Lit.; Mag. Index (1977-); TOM Gen. Index (1985-) [Full Txt.].

●BL
**REDE NACIONAL FEMINISTA DE SAUDE E DIREITOS REPRODUTIVOS : BOLETIM.** **See** Birth Control.

AT/0310-4168
**REFRACTORY GIRL.** [Refract. girl]. **Added/Corp** Refractory Girl Collective. No. 1 (Summer 1973)-. English. qt. 25.00Aus$ (individuals), 35.00Aus$ (institutions). Refractory Girl, PO Box 248, Glebe NSW, 2037 Australia. **Tel** 11 61 2 5571955. **ED** Angela Matheson. **Bk Rev. Ad Acc. Circ:** 2,000 (ctrl).
**Desc:** A feminist studies journal covering the whole womens area. Includes some creative writing, artwork.
**Ind/Abst** APAIS, Aust. Public Aff. Inf. Ser. (1973-).

US/0886-3946
**REGIONAL DIRECTORY OF MINORITY & WOMEN-OWNED BUSINESS FIRMS. WESTERN EDITION.** **See** Business.

US/0887-8331
**REGISTRY OF WOMEN IN RELIGIOUS STUDIES, A.** ***Suspended.*** **See** Religion and Theology.

US
**REPORT AND RECOMMENDATIONS TO THE GOVERNOR AND THE GENERAL ASSEMBLY - ILLINOIS. COMMISSION ON THE STATUS OF WOMEN.** **Main/Corp** Illinois. Commission on the Status of Women. English. an. Commission on the Status of Women / Illinois, 1166 Debbie Lane, Macomb IL 61455. **LC** HQ1438.I3; I44A. **DD** 301.41/2/09773. ***Continues*** *Women - Agents of Change.*

●US
**REPORT OF ACTIVITIES / WOMEN'S EDUCATIONAL EQUITY ACT PROGRAM.** **See** Education.

CN/0707-8412
**RESOURCES FOR FEMINIST RESEARCH : RFR.** [Resour. fem. res.]. **VFOAT** RFR; R.F.R.; DFR; D.R.F.; Documentation sur la Recherche Feministe. (March 1979)-. Periodical. English (French). qt. 25.00Can$ (individuals), 40.00Can$ (institutions) Canada; 40.00Can$ (individuals), 65.00Can$ (institutions) other. Resources for Feminist Research, 252 Bloor Street West, Toronto Ontario M5S 1V6 Canada. **Tel** (416)923-6641, FAX (416)926-4725. **ED** Mary Louis Adams, Philinda Masters and Melanie Randall. **LC** HQ1101; .R47. **DD** 305.4/05. **[CCC].** Index available. **Bk Rev. Ad Acc. Circ:** 2,000. available in microform. ***Continues*** *Canadian Newsletter of Research on Women, 0319-4477.*
**Desc:** Internationally acclaimed interdisciplinary journal of feminist scholarship. Founded in 1972 it is one of Canada's oldest feminist publications. Each issue contains articles, reviews, abstracts of published and unpublished works, reports of work in progress and bibliographies.
**Ind/Abst** Am. Hist. Life (1977-); Can. Index; Can. Period. Index; Int. Labour Doc.; Multicult. Educ. Abstr.; Soc. Plann. Policy Dev. Abstr.; Sociol. Abstr.; Stud. Women Abstr.; Women Stud. Abstr.

US/0894-7597
**RESPONSE TO THE VICTIMIZATION OF WOMEN AND CHILDREN.** ***Title Change.*** **See** Sociology-Social Services and Welfare.

IT
**RETI.** ***Ceased.*** Vol. 1, No. 1 (Sept./Oct. 1987)-(1992). Periodical. Italian. bm. Tritone Edizioni, Via Fontantella Borghese 77, 00187 Rome Italy. **Tel** 011 39 6 6874252. ***Continues*** *Donne e Politica.*

US
**REVISTA TU.** Periodical. Spanish. Twelve times a year. $57.00. Ruiz Spanish Language Magazines, PO Box 2389, El Paso TX 79952. **Tel** (915)544-6282.

US/0162-9328
**RIGHT WOMAN, THE.** Periodical. English. mo. $15.00. The Right Woman, 919 18th Street NW, Washington DC 20006.

●US/0732-2666
**RISK MANAGEMENT FOR EXECUTIVE WOMEN.** **See** Insurance.

US/1061-124X
**ROMANCE OF LIFE.** (ROMANCE OF LIFE / THE FLAVIA CLUB.). [Roman. life]. **Added/Corp** Flavia Club. (1991)-. Periodical. English. qt. $30.00 (members). The Flavia Club, 925 De La Vina, 3rd Floor, Santa Barbara CA 93101. **DD** 646.

CN/0316-1609
**ROOM OF ONE'S OWN.** **See** Literature.

US/0272-0515
**ROUNDTABLE REPORT.** ***Ceased.*** **See** Public Health and Safety.

US/1062-6298
**SACRED RIVER.** [Sacred river]. Vol. 1, Issue 1 (April 1991)-. Periodical. English. mo. Sacred River, PO Box 5131, Berkeley CA 94705. **DD** 305.

US/0741-8639
**SAGE (ATLANTA, GA.).** ***Ceased.*** (SAGE.). Vol. 1, No. 1 (Spring 1984)-Vol. 9. Periodical. English. Twice a year. Sage, PO Box 42741, Atlanta GA 30311. **Tel** (404)681-3643 ext. 2161. **ED** Beverly Guy (editor's phone: (404)223-7528). **LC** E185.86; .S24. **DD** 975.8/231. Index available. **Bk Rev. Circ:** 1,200. Documents available from UMI Article Clearinghouse.
**Desc:** Provides interdisciplinary forum for critical discussion of issues relating to black women; promotes feminist scholarship. Thematic in focus. Publishes essays, interviews, book and film review, resource listings, and announcements.
**Ind/Abst** Altern. Press Index; Am. Hist. Life (1984-); Am. Humanit. Index; Curr. Index J. Educ.; Expand. Acad. Index (1992-); MLA Int. Bibl. Books Artic. Mod. Lang. Lit.; Multicult. Educ. Abstr.; Newsp. Period. Abstr. (1990-); Psychol. Abstr. (1984-); PsycINFO; PsycLit; Soc. Plann. Policy Dev. Abstr.; Stud. Women Abstr.; Women Stud. Abstr.

US/0275-5300
**SAGE YEARBOOKS IN WOMEN'S POLICY STUDIES.** [Sage yearb. women's policy stud.]. Vol. 1 (1976)-. Monographic series. English. an. Price varies per volume. SAGE Periodical Press, 2455 Teller Road, Thousand Oaks CA 91320. **Tel** (805)499-0721, FAX (805)499-0871, telex 100799. **Acid Free.**

IT
**SALE & PEPE.** (19??)-. Italian. L31200 Italy; L55980 other. Arnoldo Mondadori Editore, UFF Cont Abbonamenti, 20090 Segrate MI Italy. **Tel** 011 39 2 75422015, telex 320457 MONDMI I.

II/0970-5880
**SAMYA SHAKTI : A JOURNAL OF WOMEN'S STUDIES. Added/Corp** Centre for Women's Development Studies (New Delhi, India). Vol. 1, No. 1 (July 1983)-. Periodical. English. an. $28.75. Centre for Women's Development Studies, B 43 Panchsheel Enclave, New Delhi 110017 India. **Tel** 011 91 11 6438428. **ED** Vina Mazumdar. **LC** HQ1180; .S27. **Bk Rev.**
**Ind/Abst** Hum. Rights Intern. Rep.

CN/0832-6770
**SANTE.** No. 1 (Oct. 1984)-. Periodical. French. Ten times a year. 19.94Can$ Canada; 29.95Can$ other. Publications Transcontinental Inc, 1100 Rene-Levesque, 24Fl Boulevard West, Montreal Quebec H3B 4X9 Canada. **Tel** (514)392-9000, FAX (514)392-4724. **DD** 613/.04244/05.
**Ind/Abst** Point Repere (1989-); SPORT Discus.

UK/0265-5780
**SAYYIDATI. See** Health and Personal Fitness.

US/1046-5790
**SAZZ (NEW YORK, N.Y.).** (SAZZ : FOR THE INTERNATIONAL WOMAN OF STYLE.). [Sazz]. Premiere Issue (Spring 1990)-. Periodical. English. bm. $15.97. SAZZ Magazine, 1501 Broadway, Suite 411, New York NY 10036. **Tel** (212)764-0561. **ED** Mary Anne Holley. **DD** 052. **Circ:** 150,000.
**Desc:** The only fashion and lifestyle magazine for career-minded black women who are enjoying their success. Positioned at the top of the black consumer market, the magazine will target urban professional women between the ages of 25 and 54 who are college educated and earn incomes of $25,000 and up.

AT/0313-4423
**SCARLET WOMAN.** [Scarlet woman]. No. 1 (April 1975)-. Periodical. English. Twice a year. 6.00Aus$. Scarlet Woman, 62 Regent Street, Chippendale New South Wales 2008 Australia. **Tel** (02) 633 6577.
**Ind/Abst** APAIS, Aust. Public Aff. Inf. Ser. (1983-).

●US
**SEATTLE BRANCH NEWSLETTER / AMERICAN ASSOCIATION OF UNIVERSITY WOMEN. See** Education-Higher Education.

BB/1043-6359
**SELECTED BIBLIOGRAPHY OF MATERIALS AND RESOURCES ON WOMEN, A.** (SELECTED BIBLIOGRAPHY OF MATERIALS AND RESOURCES ON WOMEN IN THE CARIBBEAN AVAILABLE AT WAND'S RESEARCH AND DOCUMENTATION CENTRE.). [Sel. bibliogr. mater. resour. women]. **Added/Corp** University of the West Indies (Cave Hill, Barbados). Women and Development Unit. Research and Documentation Centre. (198?)-. English. an. Women and Development Unit, School of Continuing Studies, Pinelands St Michael Barbados. **Tel** 809 436 6312, FAX 809 426 3006. **LC** Z7964.C38; S44; HQ1501. **DD** 016.3054/09729.

US/0149-0699
**SELF (NEW YORK).** (SELF.). [Self]. Vol. 1, (Jan. 1979)-. Periodical. English. mo. $15.00 (one year), $28.00 (two year). Conde Nast Publications / New York, 350 Madison Avenue, New York NY 10017. **Tel** (212)880-8800, (800)777-0700. **(Subscription address:** Neodata / Colorado, PO Box 2606, Boulder Boulder CO 80322.) **ED** Anthea Disney. **LC** RA778.A1; S44. **DD** 613/.04244. **Ad Acc.** available on microfilm and microfiche from University Microfilms International (UMI). Documents available from UMI Article Clearinghouse.
**Desc:** The latest in matters of body, mind and spirit for the self- aware woman. Guidance on sex, beauty, exercise and diet, fitness, and emotional well being, money, careers, and coping skills.
**Ind/Abst** Acad. Abstr. Full Text Elite (Jan. 1992-); Acad. Abstr. (Jan. 1992-); Consum. Health Nutr. Index (?-?); Health Source (Jan. 1992-); Mag. Artic. Summar. Elite (Jan. 1992-); Mag. Artic. Summar. CD-ROM (Jan. 1992-); Mag. Search; Newsp. Period. Abstr. (1988-).

US/0884-4372
**SEXUAL COERCION & ASSAULT. See** Sociology.

PL/0137-8694
**SEZAM.** (1978)-. Periodical. Polish. qt. $6.00. **(Subscription address:** ARS Polona, PO Box 1001, 00068 Warsaw Poland.) **UDC** 391. **CODEN** 64.

US/0744-5121
**SHAPE (WOODLAND HILLS, CALIF.). See** Health and Personal Fitness.

UK
**SHE. Added/Corp** Yale University. Coeducation Office. (1971/72)-. English. Twelve times a year. £16.80 UK, US and Canada; £38.00 other. National Magazine Company Ltd., 72 Broadwick Street, London W1V 2BP England. **Tel** 011 44 71 5395214. **(Subscription address:** Tower Publishing, Tower House, Sovereign Park Market Harborough, Leicester LE16 9EF England.)

AT
**SHE (AUSTRALIAN EDITION).** (SHE.). (19??)-. Periodical. English. mo. 47.40Aus$ Australia; 54.90Aus$ New Zealand; 83.90Aus$ other. Australian Consolidated Press Ltd, GPO Box 5252, Sydney New South Wales 2001 Australia. **Tel** 011 61 2 2600000.

AA
**SHQIPTARJA E RE.** ***Ceased.*** **VFOAT** The New Albanian Woman. (19??)-(19??). English. bm. Book Distribution Entreprise, Rruga Konference e Pezes, Tirana Albania.

JA
**SHUFU NO TOMO. VFOAT** Friend of Housewives. (19??)-. Periodical. Japanese. Twelve times a year. $162.00. **(Subscription address:** Japan Books & Records, 3450 West Peterson Avenue, Chicago IL 60659.)

WJ
**SHUUN AL-MARAH. Added/Corp** Jamiyat Shuun Al-Marah (Nablus). (May 1991)-. Periodical. Arabic. **LC** HQ1728.5; .S58.

US/0097-9740
**SIGNS (CHICAGO, ILL.).** (SIGNS.). [Signs]. **Added/Corp** University of Chicago. Press. Vol. 1 (Autumn 1975)-. Periodical. English. qt (4 issues). $88.00 institution, $36.00 individual, $29.00 NWSA individual member, $25.00 student US; $100.16 institutions, $44.52 individuals, $37.03 NWSA individual members, $32.75 students Canada; $94.00 institutions, $42.00 individuals, $35.00 NWSA individual members, $31.00 students other. University of Chicago Press / Journals Division, PO Box 37005, 5720 South Woodlawn, Chicago IL 60637. **Tel** (312)753-3347, FAX (312)753-0811. **(Subscription telephone:** (312)753-8083) **ED** Ruth-Ellen Boetcher Joeres and Barbara Laslett. **LC** HQ1101; .S5. **DD** 301.41/2/05. **[CCC]. Ad Acc. Pr Rev. Acid Free.** available on microfilm and microfiche from University Microfilms International (UMI). Documents available from The Genuine Article, UMI Article Clearinghouse.
**Desc:** International journal of women's studies. The essays appearing cut across disciplines, across various feminist perspectives, and across the divisions between academic thought and daily life.
**Ind/Abst** ABC POL SCI; Abstr. Anthropol.; Acad. Abstr. Full Text Elite (July 1990-); Acad. Abstr. (July 1990-); Acad. Ind. [Computer File] (1987-); Acad. Search (July 1990-); Am. Hist. Life (1975-); Am. Bibliogr. Slavic East Europ. Stud.; Am. Humanit. Index; Appl. Soc. Sci. Index Abstr.; Arts Humanit. Citation Index [Select. Cov.]; Book Rev. Index (1984-); Commun. Abstr. (?-?); Crim. Penol. Police Sci. Abstr.; Curr. Contents Soc. Behav. Sci.; Curr. Index J. Educ.; Expand. Acad. Index (1987-); Index Period. Artic. Relat. Law; INFO-SOUTH Abstr.; Int. Bibliogr. Sociol.; Int. Labour Doc.; Lit. Crit. Regist.; Mag. Search; Middle East Abstr. Index; MLA Int. Bibl. Books Artic. Mod. Lang. Lit.; Multicult. Educ. Abstr.; Newsp. Period. Abstr. (1988-); Psychol. Abstr. (1975-); PsycINFO; PsycLit; Res. Alert [Full Cov.]; Res. High. Educ. Abstr.; Sage Fam. Stud. Abstr.; Soc. Plann. Policy Dev. Abstr.; Soc. Sci. Source (Jul. 1990-); Soc. Sci. Cit. Index [Full Cov.]; Soc. Sci. Index; Soc. Sci. Index Fulltext (Winter 1989-) [Full Txt.]; Sociol. Abstr.; Stud. Women Abstr.; Women Stud. Abstr.

US/0198-9855
**SING HEAVENLY MUSE!. See** Literature.

US
**SINGLE GENTLEMEN & WOMEN. See** Men's Interests.

US/1058-0638
**SINGLES CHOICE. See** Men's Interests.

US/1057-2015
**SINGLES SOLUTIONS. See** Men's Interests.

HK
**SISTERS PICTORIAL.** Chinese. Twenty-six times a year. $88.00. Sisters Press Ltd, Room 903 8 9F, Kodak House II, 321 Java Road, North Point Hong Kong. **Tel** 011 852 5908738. **Circ:** 75,911.

JM
**SISTREN. VFOAT** Sistren Magazine. Periodical. English. Sistren Magazine, 20 Kensington Cres, Kingston 5 Jamaica West Indes.

AT
**SMART WOMAN & PORTFOLIO.** (19??)-. Periodical. English. bm (6 issues). 22.00Aus$ Australia. Federal Publishing Co Pty Ltd, PO Box 199, 180 Bourke Road, Alexandria New South Wales, 2015 Australia. **Tel** 011 61 2 693 6666, FAX 011 61 2 693 9935. **(Subscription address:** Federal Publishing Co. Pty Ltd., PO Box 199, Alexandria NSW 2015 Australia.)

US/0191-8699
**SOJOURNER (CAMBRIDGE).** (SOJOURNER / MASSACHUSETTS INSTITUTES OF TECHNOLOGY.). Vol. 1, No. 1 (Sept. 1, 1975)-. Periodical. English. mo. $19.00 (individuals), $29.00 (institutions). Sojourner, 42 Seaverns Avenue, Boston MA 02130. **Tel** (617)524-0415. **ED** Shane Snowdon. **LC** HQ1402; .S64. **Bk Rev. Ad Acc. Circ:** 25,000. available on microfilm and microfiche from University Microfilms International (UMI).
**Desc:** National forum for news, interviews, essays, and reviews of books, films, and music; of particular interest to women.
**Ind/Abst** Hum. Rights Intern. Rep.

US/0097-9562
**SOROPTIMIST OF THE AMERICAS, THE.** V. 48- Aug./Sept. 1974-. English. bm. Soroptimist International of the Americas, 1616 Walnut Street, Philadelphia PA 19103. **Tel** (215)732-0512. **LC** HD6050; .A653. **DD** 369.5. ***Continues** American Soroptimist.*

US/0749-5528
**SOUTHERN CALIFORNIA WOMEN'S CAUCUS FOR ART. See** The Arts-Art.

US/0744-5938
**SOUTHWEST WOMAN.** Vol. 2, No. 93 (May 1982)-. Periodical. English. mo. Southwest Woman, 11824 Radium, San Antonio TX 78216. ***Continues** Southwest Secretary, 0274-8967.*

RU
**SOVETSKAIA JENSCINA.** Russian. mo. **(Subscription address:** East View Publications Inc., 3020 Harbor Lane North, Suite 110, Minneapolis MN 55447.)

RU/0201-6982
**SOVETSKAIA ZHENSHCHINA.** ***Ceased.*** (SOVIET WOMAN.). [Sov. woman]. **Added/Corp** Vsesoiuznyi Tsentralnyi Sovet Professionalnykh Soiuzov. Antifashistskii Komitet Sovetskikh Zhenshchin. (1945)-(199?). Periodical. English (French, German, Spanish, Portuguese, Chinese, Korean, Hindi, Bengali, Japanese, Arabic, Vietnamese, Hungarian and Russian). mo. **(Subscription address:** Victor Kamkin, 4956 Boiling Brook Parkway, Rockville MD 20852.) **DD** 396.
**Desc:** Well-illustrated magazine with vast textual material covering the lives of Soviet women, showing them at work and at rest.

UK/0306-7971
**SPARE RIB.** ***Ceased.*** [Spare rib]. No. 1 (July 1972)-(Jan. 1993). Periodical. English. mo. Spare Rib, 27 Clerkenwell Close, London EC1R 0AT England. **Tel** 01 253 9792/3, FAX 01 251 1773. **Bk Rev. Ad Acc. Circ:** 30,000 (ctrl). available on audiocassette (for the blind).
**Desc:** A magazine on women's ideas and struggles worldwide, asserting the vital role of women in the shaping of a new social and economic order for the globe.
**Ind/Abst** Altern. Press Index; Stud. Women Abstr.

RH
**SPEAK OUT.** (1983)-. qt. $15.00 Africa; $20.00 Europe; $22.00 Asia; $25.00 other. Women's Action Group, PO Box 135, Harare Zimbabwe.

US/0099-0388
**SPORTSWOMAN, THE. See** Recreation, Leisure-Sports.

IT
**SPOSA.** Agenzia Italiana di Esportazione, Via Manzoni 12, 20089 Rozzano Milan, Italy. **Tel** 011 39 2 57512575.

US/0272-202X
**SPRINGER SERIES, FOCUS ON WOMEN.** [Springer ser., Focus women]. **VFOAT** Focus on Women. Vol. 1 (1980)-. Monographic series. English. ir. Price varies per volume. Springer-Verlag New York Inc., 175 5th Avenue, New York NY 10010. **Tel** (212)460-1500, telex 232 235 SPB UR. **(Subscription address:** Springer Verlag New York Inc. / for North America, 44 Hartz Way, Secaucus NJ 07096.) **ED** V. Franks. **LC** UNC. **NLM** W1 SP685KD.

US/0739-9146
**STATUS NEWS. See** Journalism.

CN/0383-6940
**STRENGTH.** Began with V. 3, No. 1 (Sept. 1975). Periodical. English. ir. Free to members. The Women's Place, 42-B King Street South Waterloo, Ontario N2J 1N8 Canada. **DD** 301.41/2/06271344. ***Continues** Woman's Place, 0383-6932.*

US
**STUDIES IN WOMEN AND RELIGION.** Vol. 1 (1979)-. Monographic series. English. ir. Price varies per volume. Edwin Mellen Press, PO Box 450, Lewiston NY 14092. **Tel** (716)754-2788. Index available (bound in all issues).

UK/0262-5644
**STUDIES ON WOMEN ABSTRACTS. See** Women's Interests-Abstracting, Bibliographies and Statistics.

# Women's Interests

MY
**SUARA AISYIYAH. Main/Corp** Aisyiyah (Association). Periodical. Indonesian. 100 each issue. P P Aisyiyah Yogyakarta, Jalan Kha Dahlan 99, Yogyakarta Indonesia. **LC** HQ1170; .A546A.

US/0886-1498
**SUCCESSFUL SALESWOMAN.** See Business.

YU
**SUN, THE. VFOAT** Spouse's Underground Newsletter. Vol. 1, No. 1 (1991)-. Periodical. English. Three times a year.

BE
**SUPPLEMENT ... TO WOMEN OF EUROPE. Added/Corp** Commission of the European Communities. Information for Women's Organisations and Press. (1978)-. Monographic series. English. ir. Price varies per volume. Office for Official Publications of the European Communities, 2 Rue Mercier, 2985 Luxembourg Luxembourg. **Tel** 011 352 499281, **FAX** 011 352 488573.

US
**SYMPHONY OF VOICES : AN ASIAN AMERICAN WOMEN'S JOURNAL, A.** *Title Change.* (Spring 1991)-(1992). English. *Continued by Unbinding the Foot.*

US
**TEEN VOICES MAGAZINE.** *Title Change.* See Children and Youth Interests.

●US/1058-5427
**TEXAS JOURNAL OF WOMEN AND THE LAW.** (1992)-. English. $25.00. University of Texas School of Law, 727 East 26th Street 2101, Austin TX 78705. **Tel** (512)471-1106.

US/0279-2443
**TEXAS WOMAN (FORT WORTH, TEX.).** (TEXAS WOMAN.). **Added/Corp** Texas Federation of Business and Professional Women's Clubs. (1934)-. Periodical. English. Six times a year. $3.00. Texas Federation of Business and Professional Women's Clubs Arlington TX 76015-2332, 3019 Medlin Drive, Suite 200, Arlington TX 76015. **Tel** (817)467-0712. **ED** Gilda Murray. **Bk Rev. Ad Acc.**
**Desc:** Articles of appeal to working Texas women, update on new laws, economic trends, political issues, high tech growth affecting women.

NE
**TIJDSCHRIFT VOOR VROUWENSTUDIES.** Vol. 1, No. 1-. Periodical. Dutch. ir. 30.00. Uitgeverij Sun, PO Box 1609, 6501 BP Nijmegen Netherlands. **Tel** 011 31 80 221700. **LC** HQ1657; .T54.

CN/1184-0455
**TIMES FEMNIST.** [Times fem.]. **Added/Corp** Victoria Status of Women Action Group. Vol. 17, No. 1 (June 1990)-. Periodical. English. bm. Victoria Status of Women, PO Box 8484, Victoria British Columbia V8W 3S1 Canada. **Tel** (604)381-1012. **DD** 305.4/2/0971105. *Continues News (Victoria Status of Women Action Group).*, 0820-5191.

US/1071-3786
**TODAY'S CHICAGO WOMAN.** [Today's Chic. woman]. **VFOAT** Today's Woman; Chicago Woman. (Oct. 1982)-. Periodical. English. mo. $12.00 Illinois; $18.00 US; $50.00 Canada; $160.00 other. Leigh Communications Incorporated, 233 East Ontario, Suite 1300, Chicago IL 60611. **Tel** (312)951-7600. **ED** Sherren Leigh. **DD** 305. **Bk Rev. Ad Acc, Adv Mgr:** Karen Iglar. **Circ:** 160,000.
**Desc:** Forum for discussion of issues relating to women.

US/0163-1799
**TODAY'S CHRISTIAN WOMAN.** See Religion and Theology.

US/0748-7355
**TODAY'S SINGLE. Added/Corp** National Association of Christian Singles (U.S.). Vol. 1, No 1 (Winter 1980)-. Periodical. English. Four times a year (Jan., Apr., July, Oct.). $10.00 Comes with National Association of Christian Singles Membership. National Association of Christian Singles, NACS, 1933 West Wisconsin Avenue, Milwaukee WI 53233. **Tel** (414)344-7300.

US/1054-9587
**TODAY'S WOMAN.** [Today's woman]. Vol. 1, No. 1 (Mar./Apr. 1991)-. Periodical. English. bm. $14.00 (foreign). Today's Woman, PO Box 463, Mt. Morris IL 61054-7753. **DD** 051.

JA
**TOMIN FUJIN NO GONJO.** Japanese. Tokyo-to Minseikyoku, 8-1 Marunouchi-3 Chome, Chiyoda-ku, Tokyo Japan. **LC** HQ1765.T64; T64.

JA
**TOMIN FUJIN NO ISHIKI TO JITTAI CHOSA HOKOKUSHO. Added/Corp** Tokyo (Japan). Minseikyoku. Fujinbu. (19??)-. Periodical. Japanese. Tokyo-To Minseikyoku Fujinbu, 8-1 Marunouchi 3 Chiyoda-ku, Tokyo 100 Japan. **LC** HQ1765.T64; T643.

US/0739-344X
**TRADESWOMEN.** [Tradeswomen]. **VFOAT** Trades Women; Tradeswomen Magazine. (Spring 1981)-. Periodical. English. qt. $10.00 (individuals), $25.00 (institutions), $15.00 (individual, Canada). Tradeswomen Inc., PO Box 40664, San Francisco CA 94140. **Tel** (415)821-7334.
**Ind/Abst** Altern. Press Index (199?-).

US/0738-9779
**TRIBUNE - INTERNATIONAL WOMEN'S TRIBUNE CENTRE, THE.** (THE TRIBUNE : A WOMEN AND DEVELOPMENT QUARTERLY.). [Trib. - Int. Women's Trib. Cent.]. **Added/Corp** International Women's Tribune Centre. (1982)-. Periodical. English (Spanish and French). qt. $12.00 North America; $16.00 other. International Women's Tribune Centre, 777 United Nation Plaza, 3rd Floor, New york NY 10017. **Tel** (212)687-8633, **FAX** (212)661-2704. **DD** 305. **Circ:** 16,000 (ctrl). *Continues Newsletter (International Women's Tribune Centre).*
**Desc:** This magazine is on women and environmentally-friendly enterprises, with an option to also "catch you up" on some of the issues and events of the past year in the overall area of women, environment and development.
**Ind/Abst** Hum. Rights Intern. Rep.

US/0748-4593
**TRIBUNE - INTERNATIONAL WOMEN'S TRIBUNE CENTRE (FEB. FRANCAISE), LA.** (LA TRIBUNE / CENTRE DE LA TRIBUNE INTERNATIONAL DE LA FEMME.). [Trib. - Int. Women's Trib. Cent.]. Began with No. 1 June 1983. Periodical. French. sa. $8.00 US; $12.00 Australia, New Zealand, Europe, Japan; free to people in Third World countries. International Women's Tribune Centre, 777 United Nation Plaza, 3rd Floor, New york NY 10017. **Tel** (212)687-8633, **FAX** (212)661-2704. **Circ:** 3,000 (ctrl).
**Desc:** A highly visual, low-cost media journal for women and women's groups involved in development activities in the French speaking Third World. Includes issues, projects, resources and publications available on selected issues of relevance to women.

US/0736-928X
**TRIVIA.** See Literary and Political Reviews.

UK
**TROUBLE AND STRIFE. VFOAT** Trouble & Strife. No. 1 (Winter 1983)-. Periodical. English. Three times a year. £25.00 UK; £40.00 other (institution). Trouble and Strife, PO Box 8, Diss, Norfolk 1P22 EXG England. **LC** HQ1101; .T74. **DD** 305.4/2/05. Index available (published in 3rd issue). **Bk Rev. Ad Acc. Circ:** 2,000.
**Desc:** Radical feminist magazine.
**Ind/Abst** Stud. Women Abstr.

UK/0262-4125
**TRUE STORY LONDON.** See General Interest.

US/0732-7730
**TULSA STUDIES IN WOMEN'S LITERATURE.** See Literature.

CN/0711-7426
**TW (TORONTO, ONT.).** (TW : TODAY'S WOMAN.). [TW, Today's woman]. **VFOAT** Today's Woman; TW : Today's Woman; Today's Woman Magazine; TW Magazine. Vol. 1, No 1 (Winter 1980)-. Periodical. English. ir. Free. TW Magazine, 401 Richmond Street West, Toronto Ontario M5V 1X3 Canada. **DD** 051. ctrl circ.

US
**TWR'S INSIDER REPORT.** (19??)-. English. Six times a year. $20.00. Jag Publishers Ltd., PO Box 271, Greenvale NY 11548. **Tel** (516)625-3033, **FAX** (516)625-3411. **ED** Jane S. Gitlin. **Bk Rev. (Qty: 50). Ad Acc. Circ:** 2,500. *Continues Women's Record.*
**Desc:** Business, finance, leadership, entrepreneurship issues for high level professional women in the metro New York region.

CN/0228-9024
**U OF T WOMAN'S NEWSMAGAZINE.** [U of T women's newsmagazine]. **VAT** University of Toronto Woman's Newsmagazine. No. 1-. English. Free on University of Toronto Campus. U of T Woman's Newsmagazine, 132 Medland Street, Toronto Ontario M6P 2N5 Canada. **DD** 305.4/2/05.

US/1059-9770
**U.S.-JAPAN WOMEN'S JOURNAL. ENGLISH SUPPLEMENT.** (U.S.-JAPAN WOMEN'S JOURNAL. ENGLISH SUPPLEMENT = NICHI-BEI JOSEI JANARU. ENGLISH SUPPLEMENT.). [U.S.-Japan women's j., Engl. suppl.]. **Added/Corp** U.S.-Japan Women's Center. **VFOAT** Nichi-Bei Josei Janaru. English Supplement. No. 1 (1991)-. Periodical. English. Twice a year. $30.00 (individuals); $55.00 (institutions). US-Japan Women's Center, 926 Bautista Ct., Palo Alto CA 94303. **Tel** (415)857-9049, **FAX** (415)494-8160. **ED** Yoko Kawashima. **LC** HQ1101; .U538. cum. index. **Ad Acc.**
**Desc:** The purpose of this journal is to disseminate information on Japanese women to the U.S., to enlarge the basis of information available in Japan on feminist theory and on the status of American women as well as women in other countries, and to stimulate the comparative study of womens issues.

US
**UCLA WOMEN'S LAW JOURNAL.** See Law.

●US
**UNBINDING THE FOOT : THE ASIAN/PACIFIC AMERICAN WOMEN'S JOURNAL.** See Ethnic Interests.

●US
**UNIDOS.** See Business.

CN/0707-0063
**UNION WOMAN. Suspended.** See Economics-Labor.

CN/0848-144X
**UNIVERSELLES (QUEBEC).** (UNIVERSELLES.). [Universelles]. **Added/Corp** Collectif le 5e monde. Vol. 1, No 1 (Jan. 1988)- Vol. 5 (1993)-. Periodical. French. Three times a year. $10.00 non-supporting, $20.00 supporting. Cimquieme Monde, 454 Rue Caron, Quebec G1K 8K8 Canada. **Tel** (418)647-5855, **FAX** (418)647-5719. **DD** 305.42. **Circ:** 500.
**Desc:** Women's condition in third world countries, women and development issues. International solidarity and feminism.

US
**UPDATE / CONGRESSIONAL CAUCUS FOR WOMEN'S ISSUES.** See Public Administration.

US/0893-3308
**UPDATE - WOMEN IN COMMUNICATIONS, INC. BOSTON PROFESSIONAL CHAPTER.** *Title Change.* See Communication.

PL/0500-7194
**URODA WYD. POLSKIE.** (URODA.). [Uroda wyd. pol.]. (1957)-. Periodical. Polish (German). mo. Price on Request. **(Subscription address:** ARS Polona, PO Box 1001, 00068 Warsaw Poland.**) UDC** 646.7.
**Desc:** Magazine for Polish women.

PN/0505-0146
**VANIDADES CONTINENTAL.** See Home Economics.

IT
**VERA.** (19??)-. Italian. L33800 Italy; L59400 other. Arnoldo Mondadori Editore, UFF Cont Abbonamenti, 20090 Segrate MI Italy. **Tel** 011 39 2 75422015, telex 320457 MONDMI I.

CN/0831-0866
**VERITABLE AMIE.** (UNE VERITABLE AMIE POUR LES FEMMES DANS LA FORCE DE L'AGE.). [Verit. amie.]. **VFOAT** Une Veritable Amie. Vol. 1, No 1 (Feb. 1985)-. Periodical. French. mo (except Jul. and Aug.). $30.00Can$. Friend Indeed Publications Inc, PO Box 515/ Sta Place du Parc, Montreal Que H2W 2P1 Canada. **Tel** (514)843-5730. **ED** Janine O'Leary Cobb and Lucette Proulx-Sammut. **DD** 618.1/75/005. **[CCC].** Index available ($3.50). cum. index. **Bk Rev. Circ:** 3,500 (ctrl).
**Desc:** Newsletter of information, support and exchange for women during menopause and/or midlife. Features monthly topic plus extensive letters section.

US/1040-6883
**VICTORIA (NEW YORK, N.Y.).** (VICTORIA.). [Victoria]. (1988)-. Periodical. English. mo. $17.97. The Hearst Corporation, 250 West 55th Street, New York NY 10019. **Tel** (212)649-4014. **(Subscription address:** CDS Agency Hard Copy, PO Box 4966, Des Moines IA 50340.**) LC IN PROCESS. DD** 051. available on microfilm from University Microfilms International (UMI). *Continues Good Housekeeping's Victoria.*
**Desc:** Publication for women with a timeless point of view. Includes features on home, garden, fashion, beauty, crafts and collectibles, and the special world of children.

CN/0703-9875
**VIE DE FEMME.** Vol. 1, No 1 (22 Oct. 1977)-. Periodical. French. wk. $.50 each number. Vie de Femme, 4270 rue Papineau, Montreal Quebec H2H 1S9 Canada. **DD** 305.4/09714.

CN/0228-5479
**VIE EN ROSE, LA. Ceased.** [Vie rose]. Vol. 1, No. 1 (March/April/May 1980)-?. Periodical. French. mo. La

## Women's Interests

Vie en Rose, 15 Prince Arthur, St Lambert Quebec J4P 1X1 Canada. **DD** 305.4/09714.
**Ind/Abst** Point Repere (1983-).

US/0194-5289
**VIEWPOINT (MARLOW HEIGHTS).** (VIEWPOINT.). Periodical. English. qt. $2.00 US; $3.50 Canada. Viewpoint, 5211 Auth Road, Camp Springs MD 20748. **Continues** Women's Viewpoint, 0164-8020.

US/0742-1494
**VINTAGE '45. Ceased.** Ceased (March 1989). Periodical. English. qt. Vintage 45, PO Box 26G, Orinda CA 94563.

US/0164-7288
**VIRTUE. See** Religion and Theology.

UK
**VISION.** (19??)-. English. Twice a year. Free to members. Federation of Women Zionists, 107 Gloucester Place, London W1H 4BY England. **ED** Diana Wolfin. **Bk Rev.** (Qty: 6). **Ad Acc, Adv Mgr:** Michele Pollock. **Circ:** 15,000 (ctrl). Documents available. **Continues** FWZ Review.

CN/0829-6014
**VITALITY. Ceased. See** Health and Personal Fitness.

KE
**VIVA.** Vol. 1, No. 1 (Dec. 1974)-. Periodical. English. mo. $14.00 Kenya; $200.00 North America; $230.00 other. Viva Publishers, PO Box 51951, Nairobi Kenya. **Tel** 334101. **ED** Horace Awori and Barbara Kimenye. **LC** HQ1101; .V58. **DD** 301.41/2/096762. **Bk Rev. Ad Acc. Circ:** 25,000.
**Desc:** Features on women and social issues that affect women in general.

US/0148-4230
**VOCAL MAJORITY, THE. Added/Corp** National Organization for Women. Washington, D.C. Chapter. National Organization for Women. National Capital Area Chapter. (1970)-. Periodical. English. Twelve times a year. $15.00. National Organization for Women, 425 13th Street Northwest, Suite 1001, Washington DC 20004. **Tel** (202)387-6895. **LC** HQ1; .V6. **DD** 301.41/2/05.

IT/0042-8027
**VOGUE.** (VOGUE ITALIA.). **VFOAT** Vogue. (1950)-. Periodical. Italian. Fourteen times a year. L79200, $55.00 Italy; L145800, $101.24 other. Edizioni Conde Nast Spa, Piazza Castello 27, 20121 Milan Italy. **Tel** 011 39 2 85611. **(Subscription address:** Arnoldo Mondadori Editore, UFF Cont Abbonamenti, 20090 Segrate Mi Italy.) **LC** TT500; .V714. **DD** 646/.34/05.

UK
**VOGUE. (BRITISH EDITION).** English. mo. $94.50. Vogue, Perrymount Road, Haywards Heath, West Sussex RH16 3DH England.

US/0890-9237
**VOGUE KNITTING INTERNATIONAL. See** Sewing and Needlework.

GW/0176-6104
**VOGUE MUNCHEN.** [Vogue Munch.]. **VFOAT** Vogue (Deutsche Ausg.); Vogue Deutsch. (1979)-. Periodical. German. mo. DM71.64 (plus postage). Conde Nast Verlag, Leopoldstr 44, D 80802 Munich Germany. **Tel** 011 49 89 381040, **FAX** 011 49 89 38104230, telex 528188. **(Subscription address:** Deutscher Pressevertriev Buch, POB 101602 Hansa GmbH, D 20010 Hamburg Germany) **ED** Angelica Blechschnidt. **UDC** 391:687. **Ad Acc, Adv Mgr:** Dagmar Huber.

US/0042-8000
**VOGUE (NEW YORK).** (VOGUE.). [Vogue]. Vol. 1, (Dec. 17, 1892)-. Periodical. English. mo. $28.00. Conde Nast Publications / New York, 350 Madison Avenue, New York NY 10017. **Tel** (212)880-8800, (800)777-0700. **(Subscription address:** Neodata / Colorado, PO Box 2606, Boulder Boulder CO 80322.) **ED** Grace Mirabella. **LC** TT500; .V7. **DD** 646/.34/05. **Bk Rev. Ad Acc. Circ:** 1,000,000 (ctrl). available on microfilm and microfiche from University Microfilms International (UMI). Documents available from UMI Article Clearinghouse, Magazine Collection. **Absorbed** Vanity Fair (New York, N.Y.), 0733-8899.
**Desc:** Covers the world's of fashion including beauty, clothes, accessories, jewels, health, fitness, travel, residences, art, entertaining, plus fascinating people, exciting entertainment, and more.
**Ind/Abst** Acad. Abstr. Full Text Elite (Jan. 1984-); Acad. Abstr. (Jan. 1984-); Acad. Ind. [Computer File] (1984-); Biogr. Index; Consum. Index Prod. Eval. Inf. Source; Expand. Acad. Index (1984-); Gen. Period. Index (1985-); Infobank (Jan. 1969-); Mag. Artic. Summar. Elite (Jan. 1984-); Mag. Artic. Summar. Select (Jan. 1984-); Mag. Artic. Summar. CD-ROM (Jan. 1984-); Mag. Index Plus (1989-); Mag. Index Sel. (1986-); Mag. Search; Med. Rev. Dig.; Newsp. Period. Abstr. (1988-); Read. Guide Abstr. Select Ed.; Read. Guide Period. Lit.; Resource/One Ondisc (1988-); Mag. Index (1977-); TOM Gen. Index (1985-).

FR
**VOGUE PARIS. VFOAT** Vogue. (19??)-. Periodical. French. Ten times a year. $165.00. Les Editions Conde Nast, Service Abonnements B620, 60732 S Genevieve Cedex 9 France. **Tel** 011 33 45 673505, 44 034400. **(Subscription address:** International Subscriptions, 30 Montgomery Street, 7th Floor, Jersey City NJ 07302.) **LC** TT500; .V716. **DD** 391/.2/05. **Continues** Vogue.

UK/0142-338X
**VOGUE PATTERNS (BRITISH EDITION). See** Sewing and Needlework.

IT
**VOGUE SPOSA.** Four times a year. $55.00. Edizioni Conde Nast Spa, Piazza Castello 27, 20121 Milan Italy. **Tel** 011 39 2 85611.

II
**VOICE OF THE WORKING WOMAN, THE. See** Economics-Labor.

US/1062-628X
**VOICES FROM THE ATTIC.** (VOICES FROM THE ATTIC: NEWSLETTER OF THE WOMEN'S STUDIES RESEARCH CENTER, UNIVERSITY OF WISCONSIN, MADISON.). [Voices attic]. **Added/Corp** University of Wisconsin--Madison. Women's Studies Research Center. Vol. 12, No. 1 (Dec. 1991)-. Newsletter. English. sa. Women's Studies Research Center, 209 North Brooks Street, Madison WI 53715. **DD** 305. **Continues** Women's Studies Research Center Newsletter.

FR/0986-7481
**VOICI PARIS.** (VOICI). (1987)-. Periodical. French. wk. 376.10F France; 596.00F other. Prisma Presse, 6 rue Daru, 75379 Paris Cedex 08, France. **Tel** 011 33 1 44153000, **FAX** 011 33 1 47641042. **(Subscription address:** Ca M Interesse, Service Abbonements B 110, 60732 Ste Geneva Cedex 9 France.) **UDC** 087.2 - 055.2.

CN/0715-8726
**VOX BENEDICTINA. Title Change. See** Religion and Theology-Catholicism.

NE/0925-482X
**VROUWENBELANGEN LEIDEN.** (VROUWENBELANGEN.). [Vrouwenbelangen Leiden]. (1982)-. Periodical. Dutch. qt. $17.78. Penn Ned Ver Vrouwenbelangen, Janskerhof 1, 3512 BK Utrecht Netherlands. **Tel** 011 31 30 367415. **UDC** 396. **Continues** Vrouwen en Hum Belangen, 0166-5812.

US/0887-2627
**WASHINGTON WOMAN (ARLINGTON, VA.).** (THE WASHINGTON WOMAN.). Vol. 1, No. 1 (March 1984)-. Periodical. English. mo. $18.00 MD., VA., D.C., $21.00 other states. Washington Woman News, PO Box 1458, Tacoma WA 98401. **Tel** (206)383-4252. **LC** HQ1439.W3; W37. **DD** 305.4/2/09753.

US/1055-4912
**WASHINGTON WOMAN NEWS.** [Wash. woman news]. (Dec./Jan. 1991)-. Periodical. English. mo. $25.00 (institution); $15.00 (individual). Washington Woman News, PO Box 1458, Tacoma WA 98401. **Tel** (206)383-4252. **DD** 305. **Continues** Puget Sound Women's Digest.

US
**WCA NATIONAL UPDATE. See** The Arts.

US/1059-6712
**WCOE (CARMICHAEL, CALIF.). See** Building and Construction.

US/0896-4696
**WEIGHT WATCHERS WOMEN'S HEALTH AND FITNESS NEWS. Ceased. See** Public Health and Safety.

US/1071-1767
**WFS QUARTERLY. See** Fire Prevention.

US/0083-9841
**WHO'S WHO OF AMERICAN WOMEN. See** Biographies.

UK/0049-7614
**WIDENING HORIZONS.** Periodical. English (English, French and Spanish). qt. £2.50 UK; $5.00 US. International Federation of Business & Professional Women, 24-30 Holborn, London EC1N 2HS England. **Tel** (441)242 1601, telex 265119 WINTER G. **ED** Tuulikki Juusela and Debbi Scholes. **LC** HD6050; .W5. **Circ:** 7,000. **Continues in part** Independent Woman.
**Desc:** Contains news, views, features, profiles, meeting dates, etc., from members, the United Nations and other organizations concerning the status of women worldwide.

●US/1065-9080
**WILLA / WOMEN IN LITERATURE AND LIFE ASSEMBLY. See** Literature.

US/0145-7985
**WIN NEWS.** (NEWS - WOMEN'S INTERNATIONAL NETWORK.). [WIN news]. **Main/Corp** Women's International Network. **VFOAT** Women's International Network News. **VAT** Women's International Network News. Vol. 1 (Jan. 1975)-. Periodical. English. qt. $40.00 (1 year), $75.00 (2 year) US; $44.00 (1 year), $83.00 (2 year) (surface mail), $54.00 (1 year), $93.00 (2 year) (air mail) other. Womens International Network News, 187 Grant Street, Lexington MA 02173. **Tel** (617)862-9431, **FAX** (617)862-9431. **ED** Fran P Hosken. **LC** HQ1101; .W763A. **DD** 301.41/2/05. Index available. **Bk Rev. Ad Acc. Circ:** 1,100. Documents available from UMI Article Clearinghouse.
**Desc:** Ongoing columns on women and health, women and development, women and media. International career opportunities are listed; an investigation on genital/sexual mutilations is regularly recorded; direct reports from around the world: Africa, the Middle East, Asia and Pacific, Europe and the Americas are featured in every issue.
**Ind/Abst** Expand. Acad. Index (1992-); Hum. Rights Intern. Rep.; Newsp. Period. Abstr. (1992-); Stud. Women Abstr.

CN/1186-8872
**WINGS : WOMEN IN NEWS GATHERING. See** Journalism.

CN/0709-6844
**WINNEPEG WOMAN.** [Winn. woman]. Vol. 1 (July/Aug. 1979)-. Periodical. English. ir. $13.99. Pennex Ltd, 107 Paramount Road, Winnipeg Manitoba R2X 2W6 Canada. **DD** 301.41/2/097127.

US/0508-9921
**WISCONSIN BUSINESS WOMAN, THE. See** Business.

US/1052-3421
**WISCONSIN WOMEN'S LAW JOURNAL. See** Law.

US/0883-119X
**WISE WOMAN, THE.** [Wise woman]. (19??)-. Periodical. English. qt. $15.00 (one year), $27.00 (two year), $38.00 (three year). The Wise Woman, 2441 Cordova Street, Oakland CA 94602. **Tel** (510)536-3174. **ED** Ann Forfreedom. **DD** 305. **Bk Rev. Ad Acc.**
**Desc:** Journal of feminist issues, feminist spirituality, Goddess lore, and feminist witchcraft. Includes articles, poetry, photos, cartoons, exclusive interviews, news and more.

AT/0815-0753
**WISENET.** (1985)-. English. Three times a year (Mar., July, Nov.). 30.00Aus$ (institutions), 25.00Aus$ (individuals) Australia; 40.00Aus$ (institutions), 35.00Aus$ (individuals) other. Wisenet, PO Box 647, Glebe New South Wales 2037 Australia. **Tel** 011 61 062494726, **FAX** 011 61 062498377. **ED** Anne Skates (editor's address: Australian Museum, College Street Sydney NSW 2000 Australia. **Bk Rev.** (Qty: 3-4 per year). **Ad Acc. Circ:** 500 (ctrl).
**Desc:** Journal of the Women in Science Inquiry Network.

US/0272-1996
**WLW JOURNAL. Ceased. See** Library and Information Sciences.

CH
**WOMAN.** Chinese. mo. $99.00. Epoch Publicity Agency, PO Box 3782, Taipei Taiwan. **Tel** 011 886 2 7524425.

US/1042-4849
**WOMAN. Ceased.** [Woman]. **VFOAT** Woman Magazine. (1979)-(Sept. 1990). Periodical. English. mo. Conde Nast Publications / New York, 350 Madison Avenue, New York NY 10017. **Tel** (212)880-8800, (800)777-0700. **DD** 305. available on microfilm and microfiche from University Microfilms International (UMI).
**Desc:** Creates a bond with its readers, helping them make the choices that will enhance their lifestyles. The magazine women trust and turn to.

US/0049-7770
**WOMAN ACTIVIST, THE. See** Political Science.

UK/0962-2152
**WOMAN ALIVE.** [Woman alive]. (1991)-. Consumer Publication. English. mo. £17.80 (one year), £35.00 (two year) UK; £24.00 (one year) Europe, surface mail; £36.00 air mail (one year) other. Herald House Publishing, 96 Dominion Road, Worthing West Sussex, BN14 8JP England. **Tel** 011 44 903 821082, **FAX** 011 44 903 821081. **ED** Elizabeth Round. **DD** 248.8943. **Bk Rev,** (Qty: 80). **Ad Acc, Adv Mgr:** Steven Bayes. **Circ:** 15,000. **Continues** Christian Woman (Worthing), 0269-0616.
**Desc:** Women's Bible-based magazine. Includes fashions, crafts, cookery, interviews, and social topics.

UK
**WOMAN & HOME.** English. Twelve times a year. $63.20 US; $47.55 Canada. IPC Magazines Ltd., Perrymount Road, Haywards Heath, West Sussex RH16 3DH England. **Tel** 011 44 444 440421.

US/0043-728X
**WOMAN CONSTITUTIONALIST.** [Woman constit.]. **Added/Corp** Women for Constitutional Government. Vol. 1, No. 1 (Sept. 5, 1964)-. Periodical.

# Women's Interests

English. mo. Woman Constitutionalist, 310 West Robb Street, PO Box 220, Summit MS 39666. available on microfilm and microfiche from University Microfilms International (UMI).

**US/1054-8580**
**WOMAN DIVER.** See Recreation, Leisure-Sports.

**UK**
**WOMAN ENGINEER, THE.** See Engineering.

**US/0887-2120**
**WOMAN ENGINEER. (GREENLAWN, N.Y.), THE.** See Engineering.

**US/0195-9743**
**WOMAN IN HISTORY.** [Woman hist.]. Vol. 1-. Monographic series. English. mo. Price varies per volume. Monument Press Etc., 513 S. Rosemont Press, Dallas TX 75208. **DD** 306.

**US/0163-3244**
**WOMAN LOCALLY.** [Woman local.]. **VFOAT** Capitaland Woman. V. 1- Oct. 1978-. Periodical. English. mo. $15.00. Capitaland Woman Publishers, 97 Columbia Street, Albany NY 12210. **Tel** (518)449-8292. **ED** Chris Apostle. **DD** 301. **Bk Rev**. **Ad Acc**. **Circ**: 25,000.
**Desc**: Women's issues, thoughts, experiences in one geographical location, and how worldly issues affect their lives.

**US/0743-2356**
**WOMAN OF POWER.** [Woman power]. (Spring 1984-). Periodical. English. qt. $30.00 (1 year), $54.00 (2 year) US; $40.00 (1 year), $70.00 (2 year) Canada; $50.00 (1 year), $84.00 (3 year) other. Woman of Power Inc, PO Box 2785827, Orleans MA 02653. **Tel** (508)240-7877. **ED** Char McKee. **LC** HQ1101; .W386. **DD** 305.42/05. **Ad Acc**. **Circ**: 15,000.
**Desc**: Magazine of feminism, spirituality and politics. Prints the highest quality women's literary and artistic works with a special theme for each issue.

**US**
**WOMANEWS.** (1979)-. Periodical. English. Ten times a year. Womanews, PO Box 220 Village Station, New York NY 10014.

**CN/0849-4975**
**WOMANIST (OTTAWA). (THE WOMANIST.).** [Womanist]. (Sept./Oct. 1988)-. Periodical. English. qt. 30.00Can$ (institutions), 20.00Can$ (individuals). Womanist, 41 York Street 3rd Floor, Ottawa K1N 5S7 Canada. **Tel** (613)233-2621. **ED** Joan Riggs. **DD** 305.42/05. **Bk Rev**, (Qty: 10). **Ad Acc**.

**US/0270-7993**
**WOMAN'S ART JOURNAL.** See The Arts-Art.

**US/0043-7336**
**WOMAN'S DAY.** [Woman's day]. Vol. 1, No. 1 (Oct. 7, 1937)-. Periodical. English. Seventeen times a year. $16.00. Hachette Magazines Inc., 1633 Broadway, New York NY 10019. **Tel** (212)767-6000. **(Subscription address:** Neodata / Colorado, PO Box 2606, Boulder Boulder CO 80322.**)** **LC** AP2; .W7135. **DD** 051. **Ad Acc**. available on microfilm and microfiche from University Microfilms International (UMI); available on an online database (files 647,648/Full-Text) from DIALOG. Documents available from UMI Article Clearinghouse.
**Desc**: Written and edited for the contemporary woman. Covers issues important to women today: food and nutrition, health and fitness, family and children, beauty and fashion as well as careers and money management.
**Ind/Abst** Acad. Abstr. Full Text Elite (July 1989-); Acad. Abstr. (July 1989-); Access (1975-); AGRICOLA; Consum. Health Nutr. Index (?-?); Consum. Index Prod. Eval. Inf. Source; Foods Adlibra; Gen. Period. Index (1985-); Health Ref. Cent. (1987-) [Full Txt.]; [Select. Cov.]; Index Inf.; Mag. Artic. Summar. Elite (July 1989-); Mag. Artic. Summar. Select (July 1989-) [Full Txt.]; Mag. Artic. Summar. CD-ROM (July 1989-); Mag. ASAP Plus [Full Txt.]; Mag. Index Plus (1989-); Mag. Search; Newsp. Period. Abstr. (1988-); Mag. Index (1977-); Vocat. Search (July 1989-).

**AT**
**WOMAN'S DAY (AUSTRALIA).** (WOMAN'S DAY.). (19??)-. Periodical. English. wk. 119.60Aus$ Australia; 145.00Aus$ New Zealand; 275.20Aus$ other. Australian Consolidated Press Ltd, GPO Box 5252, Sydney New South Wales 2001 Australia. **Tel** 011 61 2 2600000.

**US/0898-6126**
**WOMAN'S ENTERPRI$E.** [Woman's enterp.]. **VFOAT** Woman's Enterprise; WE. (1987)-. Periodical. English. bm. $6.99 US; $12.99 other. Woman's Enterpri$e, PO Box 3100, Agoura Hills CA 91301. **Tel** (810)889-8740, FAX (818)889-4726. **ED** Caryne Brown. **DD** 338. **Bk Rev**. **Ad Acc**. **Circ**: 125,000.
**Desc**: A small business magazine for women who are or want to be in business for themselves.

**US/0164-9515**
**WOMAN'S EXECUTIVE BULLETIN.** Ceased. See Business.

**PH**
**WOMAN'S HOME COMPANION.** Periodical. English. wk. $40.00. Woman's Home Companion, 70 18th Avenue Murphy, Quezon City Philippines. available on microfilm from University Microfilms International (UMI).
**Ind/Abst** Index Philip. Period.

**UK/0043-7344**
**WOMAN'S JOURNAL.** English. mo. £22.00 UK; $49.60 US and Canada; £31.00 other. IPC Magazines Ltd., Perrymount Road, Haywards Heath, West Sussex RH16 3DH England. **Tel** 011 44 444 440421. **[CCC]**.

●**US/1065-0733**
**WOMAN'S LIFE (NEW YORK, N.Y. 1993).** (WOMAN'S LIFE). (1992)-. Periodical. English. Eight times a year. $11.97 US; $14.16 Canada; $23.94 other. Harris Publications, 1115 Broadway/8th Floor, New York NY 10010. **Tel** (212)807-7100.

**UK**
**WOMAN'S OWN.** English. wk. $156.00. European Publishers Rep Inc, 11-03 46th Avenue, Long Island NY 11101. **Tel** (800)627-6060, (718)937-4606.

**US/0043-7379**
**WOMAN'S PULPIT, THE.** See Religion and Theology.

**US/0190-4620**
**WOMAN'S TOUCH.** Added/Corp Assemblies of God. Women's Ministries Dept. **VFOAT** Woman's Touch. Leader Edition. (19??)-. Periodical. English (Spanish). bm. $7.50 (leader edition), $6.00 (regular edition) US; $9.25 (leader edition), $7.00 (regular edition)other. Gospel Publishing House, 1445 Boonville Avenue, Springfield MO 65802. **Tel** (417)862-2781, FAX (417)866-1146. **ED** Sandra Goodwin Clopine and Aleda Swartzendruber. **Bk Rev**. **Circ**: 20,000. Continues Slant.

**KE**
**WOMAN'S VOICE (NAIROBI, KENYA).** (WOMAN'S VOICE : OFFICIAL JOURNAL OF MAENDELEO YA WANAWAKE.). Vol. 1, No. 1 (Apr.-June 1979)-. Periodical. English (English). qt. 7.50 each issue. Peter Moll Africa Ltd, Richmond House, Mfangano Street, Box 40106, Nairobi Kenya. **LC** HQ1101; .W724. **DD** 305.4/09676/2. Continues Sauti Ya Mabibi.

**UK/0043-7417**
**WOMAN'S WEEKLY LONDON. (1961).** [Woman's wkly. Lond. 1961]. (1961)-. Periodical. English. wk. £44.21 UK. World Wide Subscription Services, Unit 4, Gibbs Reed Farm, East Sussex TN5 7HE England. **Tel** (0580)200657, FAX (0580)200616. **DD** 640. Continues Woman's Weekly and Woman's Companion.

**US/0272-961X**
**WOMAN'S WORLD (ENGLEWOOD, N.J.).** (WOMAN'S WORLD.). (Oct. 14, 1980)-. Periodical. English. wk. $78.00. Heinrich Bauer North America, PO Box 1649, 270 Sylvan Avenue, Englewood NJ 07631. **Tel** (201)569-0006. **(Subscription address:** German Language Publications, 153 South Deanstreet, Englewood, NJ 07631; phone (201)871-1010**)** **ED** Stephanie Saible (editor's phone: (201)569-6699. **Ad Acc**. **Circ**: 1.2 million.

**AT/0311-8479**
**WOMANSPEAK.** Vol. 1 (1974)-. Periodical. English. Five times a year. 16.00Aus$ (institutions), 12.00Aus$ (individuals). Womanspeak, PO Box 103, Spit Junction News South Wales 2088 Australia. **Tel** 011 61 9698984. Index available. **Bk Rev**. **Ad Acc**. **Circ**: 1,500.
**Desc**: Feminist publication, non-profit making, published by a small collective in New South Wales and circulation in all states.
**Ind/Abst** Hum. Rights Intern. Rep.

**UK/0957-4042**
**WOMEN.** Vol. 1, No. 1 (Apr. 1990)-. Periodical. English. Three times a year. £48.00 UK and Europe; $90.00 other. Oxford University Press, Walton Street, Oxford OX2 6DP England. **Tel** 011 44 865 56767, FAX 011 44 865 267773, telex 837330 OXPRES G. **(Subscription address:** Oxford University Press / USA, Journals Marketing Department, Oxford University Press, 2001 Evans Road, Cary NC 27513.**)** **ED** Helen Carr and Isobel Armstrong. **LC** HQ1591; .W64. **[CCC]**. Index available. **Bk Rev**. **Ad Acc**. available on microfilm and microfiche from University Microfilms International (UMI).
**Desc**: Explores the past and present role and representation of women in the arts and culture.
**Ind/Abst** Br. Humanit. Index.

●**US/1068-2449**
**WOMEN AGAINST SEXUAL HARASSMENT RAG, THE.** **VFOAT** Wash Rag. Vol. 1, Issue 1 (1992)-. Periodical. English. ir (Every two to four months). $10.00. Tesseract Publications, Rural Route 1 Box 27, Fairview SD 57027. **Tel** (605)987-5070, FAX (605)987-5071. **ED** Janet Leitz (editor's address: PO Box 505, Hudson, SD 57034-0505 phone: (605)987-5070). **DD** 305. **Circ**: 100.

**US/0890-3395**
**WOMEN ALIVE.** See Religion and Theology.

**US/0897-4454**
**WOMEN & CRIMINAL JUSTICE.** See Law-Law Enforcement and Criminology.

**CN/0229-480X**
**WOMEN AND ENVIRONMENTS.** [Women environ.]. Added/Corp WEED Foundation. **VFOAT** Women & Environments. Vol. 4, No. 1 (June 1980)-. Periodical. English. Four times a yearTri-quarterly. 31.97Can$ (institutions), 21.97Can$ (individuals) US and Canada; 36.97Can$ (institutions), 26.97Can$ (individuals) other. WEED Foundation, 736 Bathurst Street, Toronto Ontario M55 2R4 Canada. **Tel** (416)516-2379, FAX (416)531-6214. **LC** HQ1233; .W58. **DD** 305.4/05. **Bk Rev**, (Qty: 10). **Ad Acc**, **Adv Mgr**: Kim Pearson. **Circ**: 1,400 (ctrl). Documents available from UMI Article Clearinghouse. Continues Women and Environments International Newsletter, 0229-4796.
**Desc**: Feminist magazine that explores women's relationships with their various environments. Includes articles, reviews and notes on women's work, organizations, events and publications that keep the reader in touch with the specific needs of women in housing, the work place, urban centers, neighborhoods and other natural and built environments.
**Ind/Abst** Acad. Search (July 1993-); Altern. Press Index (1997-); Avery Index Archit. Period. Suppl. Colum. Univ. (Fall 1989-Spring 1990); Can. Period. (?-?); Can. Period. Index; Expand. Acad. Index (1992-); INFO-SOUTH Abstr.; Newsp. Period. Abstr. (1991-); Sage Fam. Stud. Abstr.; Soc. Sci. Source (Jul. 1993-); Soc. Sci. Index; Soc. Sci. Index Fulltext (Fall 1988-) [Full Txt.]; Stud. Women Abstr.; Women Stud. Abstr.

**US/1045-7704**
**WOMEN & GUNS.** [Women guns]. **VFOAT** Women and Guns. (1989)-. Periodical. English. mo. $24.00 US; $42.00 Canada. Second Amendment Foundation, PO Box 488, Station C, Buffalo NY 14209. **Tel** (716)885-6408, FAX (716)884-4471. **ED** Sunny James. **DD** 799. **Ad Acc**. **Circ**: 3,000.
**Desc**: Targeted to female gun owners who want to learn more about pleasure shooting and self-defense. Offers information on competition shooting, legislative issues and differences between types of guns.

**US/0363-0242**
**WOMEN & HEALTH.** See Medical Science and Technology-Gynecology and Obstetrics.

**US/1045-893X**
**WOMEN AND INTERNATIONAL DEVELOPMENT ANNUAL, THE.** [Women int. dev. annu.]. Added/Corp Michigan State University. Office of Women in International Development. Vol. 1 (1989)-. English. Westview Press Inc, 5500 Central Avenue, Boulder CO 80301. **Tel** (303)444-3541, FAX (303)449-3356. **LC** HQ1240; .W655. **DD** 305.42/05.

**US/0147-1759**
**WOMEN & LITERATURE.** Ceased. See Literature.

**US/0739-666X**
**WOMEN AND MINORITIES IN SCIENCE AND ENGINEERING.** See Science and Technology.

**US/0195-7732**
**WOMEN & POLITICS.** See Political Science.

**US**
**WOMEN AND REVOLUTION.** (1972)-. Periodical. English. qt. $2.00. Spartacist Publishing Company, Box 1377 General Post Office, New York NY 10016. **Tel** (212)732-7862.
**Ind/Abst** Altern. Press Index; Left Index.

**US**
**WOMEN AND THE LABOR FORCE : STATE OF ILLINOIS.** See Economics-Labor.

**CN/0847-5253**
**WOMEN AND THE LAW (FREDERICTON).** See Law.

**US/0270-3149**
**WOMEN & THERAPY.** See Psychology.

**US/0196-8394**
**WOMEN & WORK.** Ceased. See Economics-Labor.

**US/0882-0910**
**WOMEN AND WORK (BEVERLY HILLS, CALIF.).** See Economics-Labor.

**US/0149-7081**
**WOMEN ARTISTS NEWS.** See The Arts.

**US**
**WOMEN AS MANAGERS.** (19??)-. English. Twenty-six times a year. $58.50. Economics Press Inc, 12 Daniel Road, Fairfield NJ 07004. **Tel** (201)227-1224, (800)526-2554, FAX (201)227-9742.

# Women's Interests

**Desc:** Newsletter for women in management positions. Provides information that shows a better picture of what it takes to be successful in management - and what it will take to climb the ladder of success.

US/0273-0014
**WOMEN (BOCA RATON).** (WOMEN.). [Women]. Vol. 1, Article 1-. English. ir (approximately 20 articles each year). Social Issues Resources Series Inc, PO Box 2348, Boca Raton FL 33427. **Tel** (800)327-0513, (407)994-0079. **ED** Eleanor C Goldstein. **LC** HQ1101; .W748. **DD** 305.4/05.
**Desc:** Interdisciplinary resource material consisting of reprinted articles from popular and professional journals, newspapers, magazines, and government documents.

IT
**WOMEN IN ACTION. Added/Corp** Isis International. **VFOAT** Women's Journal Supplement. No. 1 (1984)-. Periodical. English. Four times a year. $20.00 (individuals), $40.00 (institutions). Isis International, PO Box 1837, Quezon City 1100 Philippines. **Tel** 011 63 2 997512. **LC** IN PROCESS. *Continues in part Women's International Bulletin.*
**Ind/Abst** Fish Rev. (Jan. 1989-July 1992); Wildl. Rev. (Jan. 1989-July 1992); Women Stud. Abstr.

CN/0714-6795
**WOMEN IN BUSINESS. See** Business.

US/0043-7441
**WOMEN IN BUSINESS (KANSAS CITY, MO.). See** Business.

US/0735-3421
**WOMEN IN DESIGN INTERNATIONAL COMPENDIUM. See** The Arts-Crafts and Decorative Arts.

US
**WOMEN IN EDUCATION (VENTURA, CALIF.). See** Education.

●US/1060-8303
**WOMEN IN HIGHER EDUCATION. See** Education-Higher Education.

●UK/0964-9425
**WOMEN IN MANAGEMENT REVIEW. See** Business-Abstracting, Bibliographies and Statistics.

US/0162-6892
**WOMEN IN MEDICAL ACADEMIA. See** Medical Science and Technology.

US
**WOMEN IN NATURAL RESOURCES. Added/Corp** Alfred W. Bowers Laboratory of Anthropology. **VFOAT** WiNR. Vol. 9, No. 1 (1987)-. Periodical. English. Four times a year (Mar., June, Sept., Dec.). $19.00 (individuals), $35.00 (Institutions). University of Idaho / Department of Anthropology, Bowers Lab, Moscow ID 83843. **Tel** (208)885-6754. **ED** Dixie L. Ehrenreich. **LC** SD387.F6; W65. Index available. cum. index. **Bk Rev. Ad Acc. Circ:** 1,000 (ctrl). *Continues Women in Forestry.*
**Desc:** A journal for professional women in forestry, range, wildlife, fisheries and related social sciences.

US
**WOMEN IN NEBRASKA; A LABOR FORCE ANALYSIS. See** Economics-Labor.

US
**WOMEN IN PUBLIC SERVICE : A QUARTERLY OF THE CENTER FOR WOMEN IN GOVERNMENT. Added/Corp** State University of New York at Albany. Center for Women in Government. Vol. 1, No. 1 (Summer 1991)-. Periodical. English. qt. *Continues News on Women in Government.*

US
**WOMEN IN THE ARTS BULLETIN. See** The Arts-Art.

US/1058-7217
**WOMEN IN THE ARTS / THE NATIONAL MUSEUM OF WOMEN IN THE ARTS. See** The Arts-Art.

US
**WOMEN IN THE COAST GUARD. Added/Corp** United States. Coast Guard. Office of Personnel and Training. **VFOAT** Women in the Coast Guard Newsletter. (1991)-. Periodical. English. qt. Cardiology Times, 95 Madison Avenue, Suite 1407, New York NY 10016.

CN
**WOMEN IN THE LABOUR FORCE. Main/Corp** Ontario. Women's Bureau. No. 1 (1975)-. Monographic series. English. Price varies per volume. Labour Canada / Women's Bureau, Ottawa Ontario K1A 0J2 Canada. **Tel** (819)997-1550.

CN/0382-2192
**WOMEN IN THE LABOUR FORCE. FACTS AND FIGURES. See** Economics-Labor.

CN/0713-3332
**WOMEN IN THE UNIVERSITY GRADUATING POPULATION. See** Education-Higher Education.

US/0145-7802
**WOMEN IN THE WORKING WORLD. See** Economics-Labor.

US/0095-1188
**WOMEN LAW REPORTER. See** Law.

US/0043-7468
**WOMEN LAWYERS' JOURNAL. See** Law.

CN/0821-4794
**WOMEN LIKE ME. See** Business.

CC
**WOMEN OF CHINA. Added/Corp** Chung-Hua Chuan Kuo Fu Nu Lien Ho Hui. Chung-Hua Chuan Kuo Min Chu Fu Nu Lien Ho Hui. Kuo Chi Kung Tso Pu. Chung-Hua Chuan Kuo Min Chu Fu Nu Lien Ho Hui. **VFOAT** Zhongguofunu; Chung-Kuo Fu Nu; Zhong Guo Fu Nu. (1953)-. Periodical. English. Twelve times a year. $40.50. Zhongguo Funu Zazhishe, A24 Shijia Hutong, Beijing 100010, People's Republic of China. **Tel** 5126988. (**Subscription address:** China International Book Trading Corporation, PO Box 399, Library Service Department, Beijing 100044 People's Republic of China.) **LC** HQ1736; .A433. **DD** 396.05.
**Desc:** Focuses on the women's movement in China. Describes women's role in socialist construction, their rights and status, marriage, family life, family planning and children's education.

BE/0258-6169
**WOMEN OF EUROPE. Added/Corp** Commission of the European Communities. (19??)-. Periodical. English (English, German, Italian, Spanish, Dutch, Danish, Greek and Modern, Portuguese). mo. Free on request. Office for Official Publications of the European Communities, 2 Rue Mercier, 2985 Luxembourg Luxembourg. **Tel** 011 352 499281, **FAX** 011 352 488573. **LC** HQ1101; .W754. **DD** 305.4/094. ctrl circ.
**Desc:** Provides information on: aspects of community policy principally affecting women; the development of equal opportunity in the twelve European Community countries; and the activities of European women's associations.

KO/0512-1817
**WOMEN OF KOREA.** Periodical. English. qt. Korea Publications Export, Pyongyang DPRK Korea. **LC** HQ1765.6; .A45. **DD** 305.4/09519/3.

US/1068-8501
**WOMEN OF THE EAST, INC. Title Change.** (WOMEN OF THE EAST, INC. : OF AND ABOUT WOMEN ON THE EAST COAST -IN CHRIST- GIVING TO NEED OF THE FIRE VICTIMS, THE ELDERLY, AND THE GIFTED CHILDREN OF SINGLE PARENTS.). [Women East Inc.]. Vol. 1, No. 1 (Winter 1992-1993)-(1993). Periodical. English. qt. DPK Publications, 118 47th Street Northeast, Washington DC 20019. **DD** 305. *Continued by Women of the East News,* 1068-851X.

US/0732-992X
**WOMEN ORGANIZING. Ceased.** [Women organ.]. **Added/Corp** New American Movement (Organization). Socialist Feminist Commission. (1977)-(19??). Periodical. English. sa. New American Research Institute, 3244 North Clark, Chicago IL 60657. **LC** HQ1402; .W64. **DD** 305.4/0973.

US/0049-7835
**WOMEN STUDIES ABSTRACTS. See** Women's Interests-Abstracting, Bibliographies and Statistics.

US/0043-7492
**WOMEN TO BY OF FOR AND ABOUT. Ceased.** Vol. 1 (1970)-(19??). Periodical. English. New Moon Publishing Inc., PO Box 90, Corvallis OR 97339. **Tel** (503)757-8477, **FAX** (503)757-0028. **LC** HQ1101; .W7555. **DD** 301.41/2/0973.

CN/0711-4435
**WOMEN TODAY (BEETON).** (WOMEN TODAY.). [Women today]. Vol. 1, No. 1 (June 2, 1980)-. Periodical. English. mo. $3.00. Women Today, PO Box 104, Beeton Ontario L0G 1A0. **DD** 051.

US
**WOMEN TODAY (WASHINGTON, D.C. : 1982).** (WOMEN TODAY.). Vol. 12, Issue #15 (Nov. 19, 1982)-. Periodical. English. bw. Triangle News Service Inc, National Press Building/Suite 801, Washington DC 20045. **Tel** (301)622-5677. cum. index. *Continues Frontline News for Women.*

US
**WOMEN UNLIMITED.** Vol. 1, No. 1 (Jan./Feb. 1989)-. English. Eleven times a year. $21.00. Women Unlimited, PO Box 60756, Longmeadow MA 01116. **Tel** (413)733-1231, (800)427-1231, **FAX** (413)737-1008. **ED** Alice Stelzer. Index available. cum. index. **Bk Rev. Ad Acc. Circ:** 15,000.
**Desc:** Published especially for women in Hamden and Hampshire counties, Massachusetts. It covers a full range of issues of importance to women.

US/0095-1536
**WOMEN (WASHINGTON).** (WOMEN.). **Main/Corp** United States. Citizens' Advisory Council on the Status of Women. (1970)-. Government Publication. English. an. Superintendent of Documents, US Government Printing Office, Washington DC 20402. **Tel** (202)275-3328, **FAX** (202)786-2377. **LC** HD6093; .C57A. **DD** 301.41/2/0973.

US/1043-979X
**WOMEN WITH WHEELS. See** Transportation-Automobiles.

SZ/0253-2042
**WOMEN, WORK AND DEVELOPMENT. Added/Corp** International Labour Office. (1982)-. Monographic series. English. ir. Price varies per volume. International Labour Office - ILO, Publications Sales Service, CH-1211 Geneva 22 Switzerland. **Tel** 011 41 22 7996111.

●US/1056-4535
**WOMEN WRITERS OF ITALY. See** Literature.

US
**WOMENEWS / PENNSYLVANIA COMMISSION FOR WOMEN. Added/Corp** Pennsylvania Commission for Women. **VAT** Women News. Vol. 1, No. 1 (May, 1977)-. Periodical. English. qt. Free. PA Commission for Women, Room 209, Finance Building, Harrisburg PA 17120. **Tel** (717)787-8128, **FAX** (717)772-0653. **ED** Kelly Toth McCall. **Circ:** 15,000. *Continues Pennsylvania Commission for Women. News.*
**Desc:** News and information concerning the women of Pennsylvania and the Pennsylvania Commission for Women.

US/0164-7911
**WOMEN'S AD REVIEW.** [Women's ad rev.]. (1978)-. Periodical. English. Twelve times a year. $234.00. Retail Reporting Corporation, 302 Fifth Avenue, New York NY 10001. **Tel** (212)279-7000, (800)251-4545, **FAX** (221)279-7014. **DD** 659. *Absorbed Sportswear on Parade.*
**Desc:** A report on the advertising and sales promotion of department and specialty stores to show merchandise trends and marketing ideas as well as ideas in copy and graphics.

UK
**WOMEN'S ART MAGAZINE. See** The Arts-Art.

US/0509-089X
**WOMEN'S CIRCLE. See** Sewing and Needlework.

US/0146-1133
**WOMEN'S COACHING CLINIC. Title Change. See** Recreation, Leisure-Sports.

CN/0827-2263
**WOMEN'S CONCERNS. See** Religion and Theology.

US/0736-4784
**WOMEN'S DIRECTORY FOR THE CEDAR RAPIDS AND IOWA CITY AREA, A. VFOAT** Women's Directory. 1st Ed. (1982)-. Directory. English. an. PRN Corporation, PO Box 10058, Berkeley CA 94709. **LC** HQ1439.C4; W65. **DD** 061/.7762.

CN/0714-9786
**WOMEN'S EDUCATION. See** Education.

NE
**WOMENS GLOBAL NETWORK FOR REPRODUCTIVE RIGHTS NEWSLETTER.** Newsletter. English (Spanish and French). qt. Fl60.00 members; Fl70.00 non-members. Womens Global Network for Reproductive Rights, Nieuwe Zijds, Voorburgwal32, 1012 RZ Amsterdam Netherlands. **Tel** 20 6209672, **FAX** 20 6222450. Index available. **Bk Rev. Circ:** 1,295 (ctrl).
**Desc:** Covers population policy; lesbianism; norplant; maternal, mortality and morbidity; reproductive rights; women and aids; abortion around the world.

US
**WOMEN'S GUIDE TO BOOKS, THE.** No. 1-1974-. English. MSS Information Corporation, 133 East 58th Street, New York NY 10022. **ED** S Strausberg.

UK
**WOMEN'S HEALTH. See** Health and Personal Fitness.

US/1047-2800
**WOMEN'S HEALTH ADVISER POSTER.** [Women's health advis.]. (1985)-. Periodical. English. mo. Whittle Communications, 333 Main Avenue, Knoxville TN 37902. **Tel** (615)595-5000, FAX (615)595-5877. **DD** 613.

US/1049-3867
**WOMEN'S HEALTH ISSUES.** (WOMEN'S HEALTH ISSUES : OFFICIAL PUBLICATION OF THE JACOBS INSTITUTE OF WOMEN'S HEALTH.). [Women's health issues]. **Added/Corp** Jacobs Institute of Women's Health. **VFOAT** WHI. Vol. 1, No. 1 (Fall 1990)-. Academic Scholarly Publication. English. qt (1 volume). $100.00 US; $130.00 other. Elsevier Science Publishing Company Inc, Madison Square Station, PO Box 882, New York NY 10159-0882. **Tel** (212)633-3950, FAX (212)633-3990. **LC** RG1; .W65. **DD** 362.1/98. **NLM** W1; WO465L. **[CCC].**
**Desc:** Devoted exclusively to women's health issues covering such crucial topics as maternal/fetal rights, access to mammography, nutritional needs in pregnancy, spouse abuse, health care of the older woman, and drug and alcohol abuse.
**Ind/Abst** Index Med. (Fall 1990-).

●US
**WOMEN'S HEALTH JOURNAL.** **See** Medical Science and Technology.

●US/1062-4163
**WOMEN'S HEALTH LETTER.** **See** Medical Science and Technology.

US/8756-7849
**WOMEN'S HEALTH UPDATE.** ***Ceased.*** **See** Medical Science and Technology-Gynecology and Obstetrics.

●UK/0961-2025
**WOMEN'S HISTORY REVIEW.** (1992)-. Periodical. English. qt. $98.00. Triangle Journals Ltd., PO Box 65, Wallingford, Oxfordshire OX10 0YG United Kingdom. **Tel** 011 44 491 838013, FAX 011 44 491 834968. **CODEN** WOHIEV.
**Ind/Abst** Am. Hist. Life (1992-).

US/0510-7385
**WOMEN'S HOUSEHOLD.** ***Title Change.*** (19??)-(9??)-. Periodical. English. mo. House of White Birches, 306 East Parr Road, Berne IN 46711. **Tel** (219)589-8741, FAX (219)589-8093. **ED** Nena Cady. **Ad Acc. Circ:** 62,000. ***Merged into** Womens Circle, 0509-089X.*
**Desc:** Discusses and offers help and gossip on all homemaking subjects such as sewing, recipes, hobbies, handicrafts and pen pals.

●US/1063-0554
**WOMEN'S INFORMATION DIRECTORY.** (1992)-. Directory. English. be. $75.00. Gale Research Inc., 835 Penobscot Building, Detroit MI 48226. **Tel** (800)877-GALE, (313)961-2242, FAX (313)961-6083, telex TWX 810-221-7086.

CN/0821-5596
**WOMEN'S INVESTMENT NETWORK NEWSLETTER.** **See** Business-Investments.

US/0043-7557
**WOMEN'S LEAGUE OUTLOOK.** **See** Religion and Theology-Judaism.

US/0736-9433
**WOMEN'S LEGAL DEFENSE FUND NEWSLETTER, THE.** **See** Law.

US/0889-549X
**WOMEN'S LETTER, THE.** [Women's lett.]. Vol. 1, No. 1 (Sept. 1986)-. Periodical. English. mo. $45.00. Women's Letter, 25 Larchmont Avenue, Larchmont NY 10538. **DD** 305.
**Ind/Abst** Health Index (1989-); Health Ref. Cent. (Jan. 1990-) [Full Cov.].

US
**WOMEN'S MUSIC PLUS.** **Added/Corp** Empty Closet Enterprises. Not Just a Stage (Organization : Chicago, Ill.). (1984)-. Directory. English. an. $15.00. Women's Music Plus, 5210 North Wayne, Chicago IL 60640. **Tel** (312)769-9009, FAX (312)728-7002. **LC** NX180.F4; W6585. **DD** 700/.1/03. ***Continues** We Shall Go Forth Directory.*
**Desc:** More than 4,000 addresses, phone numbers, descriptions and contact information for feminist and/or lesbian performers, festivals, producers, bookstores, publications, writers, publishers, etc. Includes CD sampler of women's music.

US/0092-6639
**WOMEN'S ORGANIZATIONS & LEADERS DIRECTORY.** **VAT** Women's Organizations and Leaders Directory. (1973)-. English. be. Today News Service Inc., National Press Building, Washington DC 20045. **Tel** (202)347-7777. **LC** HQ1883; .W64. **DD** 301.41/2/06273. **NLM** HQ 1883 W872.

CN/0823-9142
**WOMEN'S ORGANIZATIONS IN HAMILTON-WENTWORTH.** [Women's organ. Hamilt.-Wentworth]. English. an. Community Information Service Hamilton-Wentworth, Public Library, 55 York Boulevard, Hamilton Ontario L8N 4E4 Canada. **Tel** (416)528-0104. **DD** 305.4/025/71352. ***Continues** Women's Organizations in Hamilton and District, 0700-5547.*

US/0735-6927
**WOMEN'S POLITICAL REPORTER / GEORGIA WOMEN'S POLITICAL CAUCUS.** **See** Political Science.

US/0195-1688
**WOMEN'S POLITICAL TIMES.** **See** Political Science.

US/0360-4780
**WOMEN'S PROGRAM.** **Main/Corp** Michigan. Women's Commission. English. Women's Commission, 230 North Washington Avenue, Lansing MI 48933. **LC** HQ1438.M5; M58A. **DD** 353.9/774/00996.

US/0882-1135
**WOMEN'S QUARTERLY REVIEW.** [Women's q. rev.]. **VFOAT** WQ Review. Issue #1 (Fall 1984)-. Periodical. English. qt (4 issues). $10.00 individuals, $25.00 institutions. Women's Quarterly Review, PO Box 708, New York NY 10150. **Tel** (212)749-3389. **ED** Camille Errante. **DD** 305. **Bk Rev. Ad Acc. Circ:** 5,000.
**Desc:** Feminist magazine concerning women's changing roles in society and the arts.
**Ind/Abst** Am. Humanit. Index.

US/0888-4609
**WOMEN'S RECORD, THE.** ***Title Change.*** **VFOAT** TWR. (198?)-(19??). Periodical. English. mo. The Women's Record, 55 Northern Boulevard, Greenvale NY 11548. **Tel** (516)625-3033, FAX (516)625-3411. **ED** Marcia Byalick. **Bk Rev**, (Qty: 12). **Ad Acc. Circ:** 30,000 (ctrl). ***Continued by** TWR's Insider Report.*

US/1052-1763
**WOMEN'S RECOVERY NETWORK.** [Women's recovery netw.]. (1991)-. Periodical. English. bm. $45.00 (institution), $27.00 (individuals). Webwords Press, PO Box 141554, Columbus OH 43214. **DD** 362. available on audiocassette.

UK/0306-1426
**WOMEN'S REPORT.** **Added/Corp** Women's Lobby. Fawcett Society. (19??)-. Periodical. English. Fawcett House, 46 Harleyford Road, London SE11 5AY England. **LC** HQ1101; .W757. **DD** 301.41/2/05.

US
**WOMEN'S RESEARCH NETWORK NEWS : A NEWSLETTER OF THE NATIONAL COUNCIL FOR RESEARCH ON WOMEN.** **Added/Corp** National Council for Research on Women (U.S.). **VFOAT** Newsletter of the National Council for Research on Women; WRNN. Vol. 1, No. 1 (Fall 1988)-. Newsletter. English. qt. $35.00 US (individuals); $100.00 (institutions). National Council for Research on Women, 530 Broadway, 10th Floor, New York NY 10012-3920. **Tel** (212)274-0730, FAX (212)274-0821. **ED** Debra Schultz. **Circ:** 1,500 (ctrl).
**Desc:** The National Council for Research on Women's quarterly newsletter including news from the council and member centers, news from international centers, caucuses, publications and resources, upcoming events, job opportunities, opportunities for research, study and affiliation as well as other news of interest to the women's research, action, policy and funding communities.

US/0738-1433
**WOMEN'S REVIEW OF BOOKS, THE.** **See** Literary and Political Reviews.

CN/0711-463X
**WOMEN'S RIGHTS BULLETIN.** [Women's rights bull.]. No. 1-. Bulletin. English. Free. Women's Rights Bulletin, c/o OFL, 15 Gervais Drive, Don Mills Ontario M3C 1Y8 Canada. **DD** 331.4/09713.

US/0085-8269
**WOMEN'S RIGHTS LAW REPORTER.** **See** Law.

US/8750-653X
**WOMEN'S SPORTS AND FITNESS.** **See** Recreation, Leisure-Sports.

●US/1061-1568
**WOMEN'S SPORTS EXPERIENCE, THE.** **See** Recreation, Leisure-Sports.

US/0049-7878
**WOMEN'S STUDIES.** [Women's stud.]. Vol. 1 (1972)-. Periodical. English. Four times a year. $255.00 (academic institutions), $397.00 (corporate institutions). Gordon & Breach Science Publishers, Inc., PO Box 786, Cooper Station, New York NY 10276. **Tel** (212)206-8900, FAX (212)645-2459. **(Subscription address:** International Publishers Distributor at one of the following addresses: 820 Town Center Drive, Langhorne, PA 19047; or PO Box 90, Reading Berkshire RG1 8JL UK; or Kent Ridge PO Box 1180, Singapore 9111, Republic of Singapore**)** **ED** Wendy Martin. **LC** HQ1101; .W77. **DD** 301.41/2/05. **[CCC].** Index available. **Bk Rev. Ad Acc.** Documents available from The Genuine Article, UMI Article Clearinghouse.
**Desc:** Articles about the effect of women on art, literature, history, sociology, law, political science, economics, anthropology, and the physical and life sciences.
**Ind/Abst** Abstr. Engl. Stud.; Acad. Abstr. Full Text Elite (Jan. 1992-); Acad. Abstr. (Jan. 1992-); Acad. Ind. [Computer File] (1986-); Acad. Search (Jan. 1992-); Am. Hist. Life (1972-); Annu. Bibliogr. Engl. Lang. Lit.; Appl. Soc. Sci. Index Abstr.; Arts Humanit. Citation Index [Full Cov.]; Expand. Acad. Index (1986-); Humanit. Index; INFO-SOUTH Abstr.; Int. Bibliogr. Sociol.; Mag. Search; Middle East Abstr. Index; MLA Int. Bibl. Books Artic. Mod. Lang. Lit.; Newsp. Period. Abstr. (1991-); Res. Alert [Full Cov.]; Romant. Move.; Women Stud. Abstr.

US/0749-1409
**WOMEN'S STUDIES IN COMMUNICATION.** **See** Communication.

US/1058-6369
**WOMEN'S STUDIES INDEX.** [Women's stud. index]. (1989)-. English. an. GK Hall & Co, 100 Front Street, Riverside NJ 08075. **Tel** (800)257-5755 ext. 2223. **LC** Z7962; .W66. **DD** 305.
**Desc:** Access is provided to 78 important American and international journals and magazines - feminist and mainstream women's periodicals plus titles in related fields.

UK/0277-5395
**WOMEN'S STUDIES INTERNATIONAL FORUM.** [Women's stud. int. forum]. Vol. 5, No. 1, (1982)-. Periodical. English. bm. $254.00 The Americas; £170.00 other. Pergamon Press, An Imprint of Elsevier Science Ltd., The Boulevard, Langford Lane, Kidlington, Oxford OX5 1GB United Kingdom. **Tel** 011 44 865 843000, 011 44 865 843699, FAX 011 44 865 843010. **(Subscription address:** Elsevier Science Ltd. Oxford Fulfillment Centre, PO Box 800, Kidlington, Oxford OX5 1DX United Kingdom.**)** **ED** Christine Zmroczek. **LC** HQ1101; .W775. **DD** 305.4/05. **CODEN** WSINDA. **[CCC]. Bk Rev. Ad Acc.** available on microfilm and microfiche from University Microfilms International (UMI). Documents available from The Genuine Article, UMI Article Clearinghouse. ***Continues** Women's Studies International Quarterly, 0148-0685. **Continued in part by** Hypatia, 0887-5480.*
**Desc:** Designed to aid the distribution and exchange of women's studies research from many disciplines and from around the world. The policy of the journal is to establish a feminist forum for discussion and debate and to account for and value cultural and political differences.
**Ind/Abst** Altern. Press Index; Am. Hist. Life (1981-)(1982-); Appl. Soc. Sci. Index Abstr.; Arts Humanit. Citation Index [Select. Cov.]; Br. Humanit. Index; Curr. Contents Soc. Behav. Sci.; Expand. Acad. Index (1992-); Geogr. Abstr. Human Geogr. (?-?); Int. Bibliogr. Sociol.; Int. Labour Doc.; Middle East Abstr. Index; Multicult. Educ. Abstr.; Newsp. Period. Abstr. (1992-); Psychol. Abstr. (1982-); PsycINFO (?-?); Res. Alert [Full Cov.]; Res. High. Educ. Abstr.; Soc. Plann. Policy Dev. Abstr.; Soc. Sci. Cit. Index [Full Cov.]; Sociol. Abstr.; Stud. Women Abstr.; Women Stud. Abstr.

NZ
**WOMEN'S STUDIES JOURNAL.** **Added/Corp** Women's Studies Association New Zealand. **VFOAT** NZ Women's Studies Journal. Vol. 1, No. 1 (Aug. 1984)-. Periodical. English. sa (2 issues). 36.00NZ$ (institutions), 27.00NZ$ (individuals) New Zealand; 52.00NZ$ (institutions), 42.00NZ$ (individuals) other. New Zealand Women Studies Journal, Box 5067, Auckland New Zealand. **Tel** 011 64 3 4791100. **ED** Maud Cahill and Annabel Cooper. **Bk Rev**, (Qty: 15-20). **Ad Acc. Pr Rev. Circ:** 300.
**Desc:** Publishes recent academic work in women's studies in New Zealand - across all disciplines, not exclusively, but particularly with a New Zealand and Pacific emphasis.
**Ind/Abst** Annu. Bibliogr. Engl. Lang. Lit.

US/0732-1562
**WOMEN'S STUDIES QUARTERLY.** [Women's stud. q.]. Vol. 9, No. 1 (Spring 1981)-. Periodical. English. sa. $35.00 (institution), $25.00 (individual) US; $43.00 (institution). $33.00 (individual) other. The Feminist Press at The City University of New York, 311 East 94th Street, New York NY 10128. **Tel** (212)360-5791. **ED** Amy Swerdlow. **LC** HQ1181.U5; W657. **DD** 305.4/2/0973. **Bk Rev. Ad Acc, Adv Mgr:** S. Cozzi, **Tel** (212) 360-5790. **Circ:** 1,000. available on microfilm and microfiche from University Microfilms International (UMI). Documents available from UMI Article Clearinghouse. ***Continues** Women's Studies Newsletter, 0363-1133.*
**Desc:** Focuses on the transformation of teaching WSQ offers vital material for scholars and writers-as well as teachers-who need to be informed about the new scholarship on women and gender. All issues are multicultural in focus and international in breadth.
**Ind/Abst** Altern. Press Index; Am. Hist. Life (1989-);

## Women's Interests

Educ. Index; Expand. Acad. Index (1992-); Newsp. Period. Abstr. (1990-); Romant. Move.; Sage Race Relat. Abstr.

US
**WOMEN'S STUDIES QUARTERLY INDEX.** English. ir (once every 5 years in Nov.). $35.00. The Feminist Press at The City University of New York, 311 East 94th Street, New York NY 10128. **Tel** (212)360-5791.

US/0882-8458
**WOMEN'S TRAVEL CONNECTIONS.** See Travel and Tourism.

US/1058-4870
**WOMEN'S WORK.** See Economics-Labor.

US/0360-1986
**WOMEN'S WORK (WASHINGTON).** See Economics-Labor.

SZ
**WOMEN'S WORLD / ISIS-WICCE.** Added/Corp Isis-WICCE (Organization). (Mar. 1984)-. Periodical. English. qt. **LC** HQ1101; .W758. **DD** 305.4/05. Continues in part Women's International Bulletin. **Ind/Abst** Hum. Rights Intern. Rep.

US/0043-759X
**WOMEN'S WORLD (WASHINGTON, D.C.).** (WOMEN'S WORLD.). [Women's world]. Periodical. English. qt. Membership only. Womens World, 1640 Rhode Island Avenue NW, Washington DC 20036. **Tel** (202)857-1320. **ED** Susan Tomchin. **DD** 296. **Bk Rev.** Circ. 120,000.
**Desc:** Publishes articles of interest to Jewish women on Jewish life and culture, the status of women, and health and social issues.
**Ind/Abst** Int. Labour Doc.

US
**WOMEN'S YELLOW PAGES, THE.** VFOAT New York Women's Yellow Pages. 1978/79-. English. St. Martin's Press, 175 Fifth Avenue, New York NY 10010. **Tel** (800)221-7945, (212)982-3900, FAX (212)777-6359.

US/0890-9695
**WOMENWISE.** See Public Health and Safety.

US/0733-4826
**WORKING TOGETHER FOR YESTERDAY, TODAY, AND TOMORROW (LINCOLN, NEB.).** (WORKING TOGETHER FOR YESTERDAY, TODAY, AND TOMORROW.). English. an. Nebraska Commission on the Status of Women, PO Box 94985, 301 Centennial Mall South, Lincoln NE 68509. **LC** HQ1905.N2; W67. **DD** 305.4/06/0782.

US/0145-5761
**WORKING WOMAN.** [Work. woman]. Vol. 1 (Nov. 1976)-. Periodical. English. mo. $11.97 (one year), $23.95 (two year), $35.95 (three year). Lang Communications, 230 Park Avenue, New York NY 10169. **Tel** (212)551-9500, FAX (212)599-4597. **(Subscription address:** CDS Agency Hard Copy, PO Box 4966, Des Moines IA 50340.**)** **LC** HQ1101; .W78. **DD** 301.41/2/0973. **[CCC].** **Ad Acc.** available on microfilm and microfiche from University Microfilms International (UMI); available on an online database (files 647,648/Full-Text) from DIALOG. Documents available from UMI Article Clearinghouse.
**Desc:** A sophisticated and contemporary magazine aimed at the business woman.
**Ind/Abst** ABI/INFORM Glob. Ed.; ABI Inform Ondisc (Jan. 1985-); Acad. Abstr. Full Text Elite (Jan. 1984-); Acad. Abstr. (Jan. 1984-); Acad. Ind. [Computer File] (1984-); Acad. Search (Jan. 1984-); Bus. ASAP (1990-) [Full Txt.]; Bus. Index (1985-); Expand. Acad. Index (1984-); Gen. BusinessFile (1985-); Gen. Period. Index (1985-); Health Ref. Cent. (1987-) [Full Txt.] [Select. Cov.]; INFO-SOUTH Abstr.; Mag. Artic. Summar. Elite (Jan. 1984-); Mag. Artic. Summar. Select (Jan. 1984-); Mag. Artic. Summar. CD-ROM (Jan. 1984-); Mag. ASAP Plus (1986-) [Full Txt.]; Mag. ASAP Sel. [Full Txt.]; Mag. Express (1986-) [Full Txt.]; Mag. Index Plus (1989-); Mag. Index. Sel. (1986-); Mag. Search; Newsp. Period. Abstr. (1986-); Read. Guide Abstr. Select Ed.; Read. Guide Period. Lit.; Resource/One Ondisc; Mag. Index (1978-); TOM Gen. Index (1993-) [Full Txt.]; UMI ABI/Inform--Bus. Period. Ondisc (Dec. 1987-) [Full Txt.]; Vocat. Search (Jan. 1984-); Work Relat. Abstr.

CN/0384-0654
**WORKING WOMEN IN CANADA.** Added/Corp Metropolitan Toronto Central Library. Business Library. (March 1973)-. Periodical. English. Metropolitan Toronto Library Board / Business Library, 229 College Street, Toronto Ontario M5T 1R4 Canada. **DD** 016.3314/0971.

UK
**WORLD WHO'S WHO OF WOMEN, THE.** See Biographies.

US/0892-3116
**WREE-VIEW OF WOMEN FOR RACIAL AND ECONOMIC EQUALITY, THE.** See Political Science-Civil Rights.

US/1043-9366
**YALE JOURNAL OF LAW AND FEMINISM.** See Law.

CN
**YEARBOOK - NATIONAL COUNCIL OF WOMEN OF CANADA (MICROFICHE).** (YEARBOOK - NATIONAL COUNCIL OF WOMEN OF CANADA.). **Main/Corp** National Council of Women of Canada. 1- 1894-. English. an. National Council of Women, 270 MacLaren Street, Ottawa Ontario K2P 0M3 Canada. **Tel** (613)233-4953. **DD** 301.41/2/06271.

●US/1048-8626
**YEARBOOK OF WOMEN STUDIES, A.** (1992)-. English. $19.95 (softbound), $29.95 (casebound). Edwin Mellen Press, PO Box 450, Lewiston NY 14092. **Tel** (716)754-2788.

KO
**YEO WON.** Korean. mo. $204.00. **(Subscription address:** Koryo Books, 35 West 32nd Street, New York, NY 10001)
**Desc:** Contains articles on fashion, current events, health tips and much more for women.

KO
**YODAESAENG.** See Education-Higher Education.

KO
**YOSONG.** Periodical. Korean. mo. Hanguk Yosong Tanche Hyobuihoe Yongsan-ku, Seoul Korea. **LC** HQ1104; .Y68. ctrl circ.

CN/1189-4695
**YOU TORONTO. 1990.** See Clothing Industry and Fashion.

US/0278-3932
**YOUNG WOMAN.** 1981-. Periodical. English. 13-30 Corporation, 505 Market Street, Knoxville TN 37902. **Tel** (615)521-0600. **LC** HQ1229; .Y83. **DD** 305.2/3.

SZ
**ZEITSPIEGEL FRAU.** (Sept. 1989)-. Periodical. German. Zeitspiegel Frau, Gasser AG, Druck und Verlag, Kasernenstrasse 1, CH-7007 Chur Switzerland. **LC** HQ1701; .Z45. Continues Schweizer Frauenblatt.

UK
**ZERO.** Ceased. No. 1 (June 1977)-(1992). English. mo. Dennis Publishing Ltd, 19 Bolsover Street, London W1P 7HJ England. **Tel** 011 44 71 6311433.
**Desc:** Anarchist/anarca-feminist monthly.

RU/0044-4456
**ZHENSHCHINY MIRA.** Added/Corp Women's International Democratic Federation. (1958)-. Periodical. Russian. bm $49.95. **(Subscription address:** East View Publications Inc., 3020 Harbor Lane North, Suite 110, Minneapolis MN 55447.**)**

UN
**ZHINKA.** VFOAT Woman. (193?)-. Periodical. Ukrainian (English). mo. $109.95. **(Subscription address:** East View Publications Inc., 3020 Harbor Lane North, Suite 110, Minneapolis MN 55447.**)**

CN/0513-9856
**ZINOCYY SVIT.** (ZHINOCHYI SVIT.). [Zin. svit]. VFOAT Woman's World. 1- Vol. 1- Jan. 1950-. Periodical. Ukrainian (English). mo. 15.00Can$. Woman's World, 937 Main Street Canada. **Tel** (204)943-8230. **ED** Anne Wach. **LC** HQ1104; .Z46. **Bk Rev**.

US/0279-3229
**ZONTIAN.** [Zontian]. Added/Corp Zonta International. (19??)-. Periodical. English. Four times a year. $7.00. Zonta International Publishing, 557 West Randolph Street, Chicago IL 60661. **Tel** (312)930-5848. **ED** Lorelei Marshall. **DD** 305. **Circ:** 24,000 (ctrl).
**Desc:** Program coverage of this women's service organization.

PL/0514-0994
**ZWIERCIADO.** [Zwierciado]. (1957)-. Periodical. Polish. mo. Price on Request. **(Subscription address:** ARS Polona, PO Box 1001, 00068 Warsaw Poland.**)** UDC 301.

## ABSTRACTING, BIBLIOGRAPHIES AND STATISTICS

SW/0348-7962
**NY LITTERATUR OM KVINNOR : EN BIBLIOGRAFI / GOTEBORGS UNIVERSTIETSBIBLIOTEK, KVINNOHISTORISKA SAMLINGARNA.** VFOAT New Literature on Women. Began 1980: 1. English (Swedish). qt. Kr60.00. Box 5069, S-402 22 Goteborg Sweden. **LC** HQ1686; .K9. **DD** 016.3054/09485. Continues Kvinnohistoriskt Arkiv, 0454-7209.

UK/0262-5644
**STUDIES ON WOMEN ABSTRACTS.** Vol. 1, No. 1 (1983)-. Abstracting/Indexing Service. English. bm (6 issues). £199.00. Carfax Publishing Company, PO Box 25 Abingdon, Oxfordshire OX14 3UE England. **Tel** 011 44 235 555335, FAX (0279)31067, telex 817484. **(Subscription address:** US and Canada/ PO Box 2025, Dunnellon, FL 34430-2025; telephone:(904)489-6996**)** **ED** June Purvis. **LC** HQ1180; .S78. **DD** 305.4. **[CCC].** Index available in last issue of volume--attached. **Bk Rev. Ad Acc.** available on microfiche.
**Desc:** The major focus is on education, employment, women in the family and the community, medicine and health, female sex and gender role socialisation, social policy, the social psychology of women, female culture, media treatment of women, and historical studies. Both theoretical and empirical materials are abstracted.

US/0049-7835
**WOMEN STUDIES ABSTRACTS.** [Women stud. abstr.]. Vol. 1 (Winter 1972)-. Abstracting/Indexing Service. English. Four times a year. $135.00 US; $168.00 (surface mail), $188.00 (airmail) other. Rush Publishing Co. Inc., PO Box 1, Rush NY 14543. **Tel** (716)533-1376, (716)533-4418. **(Subscription address:** Swets Publishing Service, PO Box 825, 2160 SZ Lisse, the Netherlands.**)** **ED** Sara Stauffer Whaley. **LC** Z7962; .W65. **DD** 016.30141/2/05. **NLM** Z 7962 W872. **[CCC].** Index available. cum. index. **Circ:** 1,000. available on microfilm and microfiche from University Microfilms International (UMI).
**Desc:** Abstracts and listings of scholarly articles on women, from education and sex roles to the women's movement.

## ZOOLOGY

FR/0984-4708
**30 MILLIONS D'AMIS PARIS. 1987.** (30 MILLIONS D'AMIS.). VFOAT Trente Millions d'Amis (Paris. 1987). (1987)-. Periodical. French. mo. 250.00F. 30 Millions d'Amis, 78 rue Jules Guesde, 92300 Levallois-Perret France. **Tel** 011 33 1 40874000, FAX 011 33 1 4087407. **ED** Loic Michel. **UDC** 636. available with illustrations. Continues in part 30 Millions d'Amis, la Vie des Betes, 0246-2591.
**Ind/Abst** Point Repere (1979-1986,1987-).

US/0731-0390
**AAZPA ... ANNUAL CONFERENCE PROCEEDINGS.** [AAZPA annu. conf. proc.]. **Main/Corp** American Association of Zoological Parks and Aquariums. **Added/Corp** American Association of Zoological Parks and Aquariums. Annual Conference Proceedings. VFOAT A.A.Z.P.A. ... Annual Conference Proceedings; AAZPA Annual Conference. **VAT** American Association of Zoological Parks and Aquariums Annual Conference Proceedings. (19??)-. Proceedings. English. an. $12.00. American Association of Zoological Parks and Aquariums, Oglebay Park, Wheeling WV 26003. **Tel** (304)242-2160, FAX (304)242-2283. **LC** QL76.5.U6; A47b. **DD** 636.08/899/05.

US/0731-0439
**AAZPA REGIONAL CONFERENCE PROCEEDINGS.** [AAZPA reg. conf. proc.]. **Main/Corp** American Association of Zoological Parks and Aquariums. VFOAT A.A.Z.P.A. Regional Conference Proceedings; AAZPA Regional Proceedings. **VAT** American Association of Zoological Parks and Aquariums Regional Conference Proceedings. Proceedings. English. an. $40.00 (nonmembers); $30.00 (schools and libraries). American Association of Zoological Parks and Aquariums, Oglebay Park, Wheeling WV 26003. **Tel** (304)242-2160, FAX (304)242-2283. **LC** QL76.5.U6; A47A. **DD** 636.08/899/05. **Ad Acc. Circ:** 375. Continues AAZPA Regional Workshop Proceedings, 0731-0420.

CN/0821-5111
**ABEILLE.** (L'ABEILLE : ORGANE DE LA FEDERATION DES ASSOCIATIONS APICOLES DU QUEBEC.). [Abeille]. Added/Corp Federation des Associations Apicoles du Quebec. Federation des Producteurs de Miel du Quebec. Federation des

Apiculteurs du Quebec. Vol. 1, No. 1 (July. 1980)-. Periodical. French. tq. 23.11Can$ Canada; 25.00Can$ other. Federation Apicutluers du Quebec, 3005 Sicott, St-Hyacinthe Quebec J2S 2I7 Canada. **Tel** (514)773-4795. **ED** Jean-Pierre Chapleau. **DD** 638/.1/09714. **Ad Acc.** ctrl circ. ***Continues*** *Bulletin Apicole (Saint-Hyacinthe, Quebec), 0821-5103.*
**Desc:** A publication that gives information about beekeeping in Quebec (Canada) and all subjects that are linked with with it.

FR/0373-4625
**ABEILLE DE FRANCE ET L'APICULTEUR, L'.** No. 1 (1920)-. Periodical. French. mo. Abeille de France, 5 rue Copenhague, F 75008 Paris France. **Tel** 011 33 1 45224842, FAX 011 33 1 42937785. ***Absorbed*** *Apiculteur.*

NE
**ABSTRACTS OF PAPERS READ AT THE ... INTERNATIONAL SYMPOSIUM OF ODONATOLOGY.** **Main/Conf** International Symposium of Odonatology. **Added/Corp** Societas Internationalis Odonatologica. (Sept. 20-23, 1973)-. English (French and German). be. Societas Internationalis Odonatologica, PO Box 256, 3720 AG Bilthoven, The Netherlands. **Tel** 011 31 30285904. ***Continues*** *European Symposium on Odonatology. Abstracts of Papers Read at the ... European Symposium on Odonatology.*

FR/0044-586X
**ACAROLOGIA.** [Acarologia]. Vol. 1 (Jan. 1959)-. Periodical. French (English and German). Four times a year. 480.00F (individuals), 700.00F (institutions),. Dawson France SA, BP 40, 91121 Palaiseau Cedex France. **Tel** 011 33 1 69104700, telex 220064F. **ED** Yues Coimeau. **LC** QL458.A2; A2. **NLM** W1 AC585. **CODEN** ACRLAW. Index available. cum. index. **Bk Rev. Pr Rev.** Documents available from The Genuine Article, BIOSIS Document Express, CASDDS.
**Ind/Abst** AGRICOLA [Full Cov.]; Biocont. News Inf. (19??-19??); Biodeter. Abstr.; Biol. Abstr.; Chem. Abstr. (1959-1986); Curr. Aware. Biol. Sci., CABS; Curr. Contents, Agric. Biol. Environ. Sci.; Entomol. Abstr.; Fish Rev.; Index Med.; Index Vet.; PESTDOC; Poult. Abstr.; Protozoolog. Abstr.; Res. Alert [Select. Cov.]; Rev. Agric. Entomol.; Rev. Med. Vet. Entomol.; Rice Abstr.; SCISEARCH; Soils Fert.; Vet. Bull.; Wildl. Rev.

PL/0860-2603
**ACTA ACADEMIAE AGRICULTURAE AC TECHNICAE OLSTENENSIS. ZOOTECHNICA.** (ZOOTECHNICA.). [Acta Acad. Agric. Tech. Olst., Zootech.]. (1985)-. Academic Scholarly Publication. Polish. Akademia Rolniczo-Techniczna, Biblioteka Glowna, Kortowo bl.41 10-957 Olsztyn, Poland. **CODEN** AATZE6. Documents available from CASDDS. ***Continues*** *Zeszyty Naukowe Akademii Rolniczo-Technicznej w Olsztynie. Zootechnika, 0324-9239.*
**Ind/Abst** AGRICOLA; Agric. Eng. Abstr.; Chem. Abstr. (1985-); Field Crop Abstr.; Nutr. Abstr. Rev., Ser. B, Live Feeds and Feed.; Postharvest News Inf.; Potato Abstr.; Poult. Abstr.; Soils Fert.

JA/0001-5202
**ACTA ARACHNOLOGICA.** [Acta arachnol.]. **Added/Corp** Toa Kumo Gakkai. Vol. 1 (1936)-. Periodical. Japanese (English). an. $1.10. Sunset Shoin Post 113, 22-19 2-chome Hishikata, Sunkyoku Tokyo Japan. **(Subscription address:** Japan Publications Trading Company, Ltd., PO Box 5030, Tokyo International, Tokyo 100-31 Japan.) **LC** WMLC L 83/445. **CODEN** AACHBY. Documents available from BIOSIS Document Express. ***Absorbed in part by*** *Atypus, 0287-4075.*
**Ind/Abst** AGRICOLA [Full Cov.]; Biol. Abstr.

GW/0177-9214
**ACTA BIOLOGICA BENRODIS.** **See** Natural History.

PL/0001-530X
**ACTA BIOLOGICA CRACOVIENSIA. SERIES: ZOOLOGIA.** [Acta biol. crac., ser. zool.]. **Added/Corp** Polska Akademia Nauk. Komisja Biologiczna. Vol. 1 (Jan./May 1958)-. English (French, German and Russian). sa. Panstwowe Wydawn Naukowe, Miodowa 10, PO Box 391, 00251 Warsaw Poland. **LC** QL1; .A27. **CODEN** ABCZAQ. Documents available from The Genuine Article, BIOSIS Document Express, CASDDS.
**Ind/Abst** AGRICOLA; Biol. Abstr.; Chem. Abstr.; EMBASE; Res. Alert [Select. Cov.]; SCISEARCH.

CI/0350-5510
**ACTA ENTOMOLOGICA JUGOSLAVICA.** [Acta entomol. Jugosl.]. Vol. 7 (1971)-. Periodical. English (French, German and Serbo-Croatian (Roman)). sa. **LC** QL462; .A34. **CODEN** AEJGAP. Documents available from BIOSIS Document Express. ***Continues*** *Jugoslavensko Entomolosko Drustvo, Belgrade. Glasnik 1926-31.*
**Ind/Abst** Biocont. News Inf.; Biol. Abstr.; CSA Neuro. Abstr. (?-?); For. Abstr.; Life Sci. Collect.; Rev. Med. Vet. Entomol.

LI
**ACTA ENTOMOLOGICA LITUANICA.** **Added/Corp** Zoologijos ir Parazitologijos Institutas (Lietuvos TSR Mokslu Akademija) Lietuvos Entomologu Draugija. Vol. 1 (1970)-. Lithuanian (Russian; summaries and/or abstracts in English). Documents available from CASDDS.
**Ind/Abst** Biocont. News Inf. (1991-); Chem. Abstr.; Nematol. Abstr.; Potato Abstr.; Rev. Agric. Entomol.; Rev. Med. Vet. Entomol.

XO/0524-2363
**ACTA FACULTATIS RERUM NATURALIUM UNIVERSITATIS COMENIANAE. ZOOLOGIA.** [Acta Fac. rerum nat. Univ. Comen., Zool.]. **Main/Corp** Univerzita Komenskeho v Bratislave. Prirodovedecka Fakulta. **VFOAT** Zoologia. (1956)-. Academic Scholarly Publication. Slovak. Slovenske Pedagogicke Nakladetelstvo, Sasinkova 5, 891 12 Bratislava, Slovakia. **CODEN** AFNZA7. Documents available from CASDDS.
**Ind/Abst** Biocont. News Inf. (1991-); Chem. Abstr. (1956-1982); Crop Physiol. Abstr.; Ecol. Abstr.; For. Abstr.; Index Vet.; Life Sci. Collect.; Poult. Abstr.; Rev. Agric. Entomol.; Rev. Med. Vet. Entomol.

LV
**ACTA HYDROENTOMOLOGICA LATVICA / SOCIETAS ENTOMOLOGICA LATVICA, SOCIETAS INTERNATIONALIS ODONATOLOGICA.** **Added/Corp** Latvijas Entomologijas Biedriba. Societas Internationalis Odonatologica. (1991)-. Latvian (English and Russian). Zinatne / Science Publishing House, Turgeneva Iela 19, Riga Latvia 1530. **Tel** 3712 212 797.

LI/0567-7939
**ACTA PARASITOLOGICA LITUANICA.** (ACTA PARASITOLOGICA LITUANICA / AKADEMIIA NAUK LITOVSKOI SSR, INSTITUT ZOOLOGII I PARAZITOLOGII. OBSHCHESTVO GELMINTOLOGOV LITVY.). [Acta parasitol. Litu.]. **Added/Corp** Zoologijos ir Parazitologijos Institutas (Lietuvos TSR Mokslu Akademija) Lietuvos Helmintologu Draugija. Vsesoiuznoe Obshchestvo Protozoologov. Litovskoe Otdelenie. **VFOAT** APL, Acta Parasitologica Lituanica. Vol. 5 (1965)-. Russian (summaries and/or abstracts in English and Lithuanian; table of contents in English and Lithuanian). ir. Mintis / Idea, Z Sierakausko 15, Vilnius 2600 Lithuania. **Tel** 3702 632 943. Documents available from CASDDS. ***Continues*** *Acta Parasitologica Lithuanica.*
**Ind/Abst** Chem. Abstr.; Helminthol. Abstr.; Nematol. Abstr.; Life Sci. Collect.; Poult. Abstr.; Protozoolog. Abstr.; Rev. Med. Vet. Mycology.

PL/0065-1583
**ACTA PROTOZOOLOGICA.** [Acta protozool.]. **Added/Corp** Polska Akademia Nauk. Instytut Biologii Doswiadczalnej. Vol. 1 (1963)-. Periodical. English (French, German and Russian; summaries and/or abstracts in Polish). qt. $90.00. **(Subscription address:** ARS Polona, PO Box 1001, 00068 Warsaw Poland.) **NLM** W1 AC929D. **CODEN** ACPZAU. **Pr Rev.** Documents available from The Genuine Article, BIOSIS Document Express, CASDDS.
**Ind/Abst** Biocont. News Inf. (19??-19??); Biodeter. Abstr.; Biol. Abstr.; Chem. Abstr.; Curr. Aware. Biol. Sci., CABS; Curr. Contents, Agric. Biol. Environ. Sci.; Curr. Ref. Fish Res.; EMBASE; Entomol. Abstr.; GeoRef; Helminthol. Abstr. (1991-); Index Vet.; Microbiol. Abstr. Sect. C; Nutr. Abstr. Rev., Ser. B, Live Feeds and Feed.; Life Sci. Collect.; Protozoolog. Abstr.; Res. Alert [Full Cov.]; Rev. Agric. Entomol.; Rev. Med. Vet. Entomol.; Sci. Cit. Index; SCISEARCH.

XR/0862-5247
**ACTA SOCIETATIS ZOOLOGICAE BOHEMOSLOVACAE.** **Added/Corp** Ceskoslovenska Spolecnost Zoologicka. Vol. 54, No. 1 (Feb. 1990)-. Periodical. English (German). qt. DM124.00. Academia, Publishing House of the Czechoslovak Academy of Sciences, Czech AC SCI, Vodickova 40, PO Box 896, 112 29 Prague 1, Czech Republic. **Tel** 011 42 2 245117. **(Subscription address:** Kubon & Sagner, ABT Zeitschriftenimport, D 80328 Munich Germany.) **ED** Karel Hurka. **LC** QL1; .C4. **CODEN** ASZBEM. Index available. **Bk Rev.** Documents available from BLDSC, CASDDS. ***Continues*** *Vestnik Ceskoslovenske Spolecnosti Zoologicke, 0042-4595.*
**Ind/Abst** Helminthol. Abstr. (1991-); Rev. Agric. Entomol.; Rev. Med. Vet. Entomol.

BU/0324-0770
**ACTA ZOOLOGICA BULGARICA.** [Acta zool. bulg.]. **Added/Corp** Bulgarska Akademiia na Naukite. (1975)-. Multiple languages (Bulgarian; summaries and/or abstracts in English, French, German and Russian). ir. 1.60lv per issue. Izdatelstvo na Bulgarskata Akademiia Na Naukite, 6 Rouski Boulevard, Sofia Bulgaria. **Tel** FAX 80 13 41, telex 22267 HEMKIK. **LC** QL298.B8; A36. **CODEN** AZBUD7. **Circ:** 520. Documents available from BIOSIS Document Express, CASDDS. ***Supersedes*** *Izvestiia na Zoologicheskiia Institut S Muzei, 0068-3981.*
**Ind/Abst** Biocont. News Inf. (19??-19??); Biol. Abstr.; Chem. Abstr.; Fish Rev. (19??-199?); Nematol. Abstr.; Life Sci. Collect.; Protozoolog. Abstr.; Rev. Agric. Entomol.; Soils Fert.

PL/0065-1710
**ACTA ZOOLOGICA CRACOVIENSIA.** (ACTA ZOOLOGICA CRACOVIENSIA / POLSKA AKADEMIA NAUK, INSTYTUT ZOOLOGICZNY, ODDZIA W KRAKOWIE.). [Acta zool. Cracoviensia]. **Added/Corp** Polska Akademia Nauk. Instytut Zoologiczny. Oddzia w Krakowie. Zakad Zoologii Systematycznej w Krakowie (Polska Akademia Nauk) Zakad Zoologii Systematycznej i Doswiadczalnej (Polska Akademia Nauk). Vol. 1, No. 1 (Sept. 15, 1956)-. Monographic series. Multiple languages (English, French, German and Polish; summaries and/or abstracts in Russian). ir. Price varies per volume. **(Subscription address:** ARS Polona, PO Box 1001, 00068 Warsaw Poland.) **LC** QL1; .A32. **DD** 590. **CODEN** AZCRAY. Documents available from BIOSIS Document Express.
**Ind/Abst** Biol. Abstr.; GeoRef; Life Sci. Collect.

BE/0001-7280
**ACTA ZOOLOGICA ET PATHOLOGICA ANTVERPIENSIA.** ***Ceased.*** [Acta zool. pathol. Antverp.]. **Added/Corp** Societe Royale de Zoologie d'Anvers. No. 39 (1966)-(19??). Periodical. Multiple languages (Dutch, English, French and German). ir. Societe Royale de Zoologie, 26 Koningin Astridplein, Antwerp 1 Belgium. **Tel** 011 32 323 116 40. **ED** F J Daman. **NLM** W1 AC957E. **CODEN** AZPAAE. Index available. **Circ:** 1,200 (ctrl). available on microfilm from University Microfilms International (UMI). Documents available from BIOSIS Document Express, CASDDS. ***Supersedes*** *Bulletins de la Societe Royale de Zoologie d'Anvers.*
**Ind/Abst** Anim. Breed. Abstr.; Biol. Abstr.; Chem. Abstr.; Fish Rev. (Jan. 1989-July 1992); Health Plan. Adminis.; Helminthol. Abstr.; Index Med.; Index Vet.; Life Sci. Collect.; Protozoolog. Abstr.; Rev. Med. Vet. Entomol.; Rev. Med. Vet. Mycology; Rev. Plant Pathol.; Vet. Bull.; Trop. Dis. Bull.; Wildl. Rev. (Jan. 1989-July 1992).

FI/0001-7299
**ACTA ZOOLOGICA FENNICA.** [Acta zool. Fenn.]. **Added/Corp** Societas pro Fauna et Flora Fennica. Vol. 1 (1926)-. English (German). ir. Fmk99.00. Academic Bookstore Akateeminen, Postilokero 23, FIN-00371 Helsinki Finland. **Tel** 011 358 0 12141. **LC** QH7; .S78. **DD** 591.94897. **NLM** W1 AC957J. **CODEN** AZFEAA. cum. index. Documents available from BIOSIS Document Express.
**Ind/Abst** Biol. Abstr.; Ecol. Abstr.; Ecology Abstr.; Entomol. Abstr.; Fish Rev.; For. Abstr.; Geogr. Abstr. Phys. Geogr.; Geol. Abstr.; GeoRef; Key Word Index Wildl. Res.; Life Sci. Collect.; Wildl. Rev.

HU/0236-7130
**ACTA ZOOLOGICA HUNGARICA.** ***Suspended.*** [Acta zool. Hung.]. **Added/Corp** Magyar Tudomanyos Akademia. Vol. 30, No. 1-2 (1984)-Suspended (199?). Academic Scholarly Publication. English (French, German and Russian). qt. Akademiai Kiado, Publishing House of the Hungarian Academy of Sciences, Prielle Kornelia u. 19-35, H-1117 Budapest Hungary. **Tel** 011 36 1 1811991, FAX 011 36 1 1811991, telex 22-6228 AKNYO H. **ED** Janos Balogh (editor's address: Zoosystemical and Ecological Institute, Eotvos Lorand University, Puskin u 3, H-1088 Budapest Hungary). **LC** QL1; .A28. **[CCC].** Documents available from The Genuine Article. ***Continues*** *Acta Zoologica Academiae Scientiarum Hungaricae, 0001-7264.*
**Desc:** Publishes original papers in the field of zoological taxonomy, faunistics, zoocoenology, and production biology.
**Ind/Abst** AGRICOLA (Sept. 27, 1990); Biocont. News Inf. (1991-); Curr. Aware. Biol. Sci., CABS; Curr. Contents, Agric. Biol. Environ. Sci.; Curr. Ref. Fish Res.; Entomol. Abstr.; Helminthol. Abstr. (1991-); Nematol. Abstr.; Res. Alert [Select. Cov.]; Rev. Agric. Entomol.; Rev. Med. Vet. Entomol.; SCISEARCH.

AG/0065-1729
**ACTA ZOOLOGICA LILLOANA.** [Acta zool. Lilloana]. Vol. 1 (1943)-. Monographic series. Multiple languages (English and Spanish; summaries and/or abstracts in French and German). Price varies per volume. Centro Info Geobiologica Noa, Miguel Lillo 251, 4000 San Miguel Argentina. **Tel** 011 54 81 330868. **LC** QL1. **DD** 591/.05. **UDC** 59. **CODEN** AZOLA8. Documents available from BIOSIS Document Express, CASDDS.
**Ind/Abst** Biol. Abstr.; Chem. Abstr. (1943-1980); Life Sci. Collect.

MX/0065-1737
**ACTA ZOOLOGICA MEXICANA.** [Acta zool. mex.]. **Added/Corp** Museo de Historia Natural de la Ciudad de Mexico. Instituto de Ecologia (Mexico). Vol. 1, No. 1 (July 1955)-. Spanish (English, French and Portuguese). Six times a year. $10.00 Mexico; $15.00 others. Instituto de Ecologia AC, Apartado Postal 18 845, 11800 Mexico DF Mexico. **Tel** 011 52 5 271-0350, 011 52 5 277-1150. **ED** Eugenia Maury. **CODEN** AZMEEF. **Bk Rev. Ad Acc. Pr Rev.** Documents available from BIOSIS Document Express.
**Desc:** Topics include behavior, zoogeography, ecology and systematic of terrestrial fauna.

**Ind/Abst** Biol. Abstr. (1984-); Fish Rev.; Nutr. Abstr. Rev., Ser. B, Live Feeds and Feed.; Life Sci. Collect.; Rev. Med. Vet. Entomol.; Wildl. Rev.

SW/0001-7272
**ACTA ZOOLOGICA (STOCKHOLM).** (ACTA ZOOLOGICA.). [Acta zool.]. **Added/Corp** International Union of Biological Sciences. Svenska Sektionen for Zoologi. Kungl. Svenska Vetenskapsakademien. Statens Naturvetenskapliga Forskningsrad (Sweden). Vol. 1 (1920)-. Periodical. English. qt. $306.00 The Americas; £205.00 other. Pergamon Press, An Imprint of Elsevier Science Ltd., The Boulevard, Langford Lane, Kidlington, Oxford OX5 1GB United Kingdom. **Tel** 011 44 865 843000, 011 44 865 843699, FAX 011 44 865 843010. **(Subscription address:** Elsevier Science Ltd. Oxford Fulfillment Centre, PO Box 800, Kidlington, Oxford OX5 1DX United Kingdom.**)** **ED** Claus Nielsen and Ase Jaspersen. **LC** QL1; .A3. **DD** 591/.05. **NLM** W1 AC957. **CODEN** AZOSAT. **[CCC]**. cum. index. **Bk Rev. Ad Acc. Pr Rev.** available on microfilm from University Microfilms International (UMI). Documents available from The Genuine Article, BIOSIS Document Express, CASDDS. ***Absorbed*** *Zoon.*
**Desc:** An international journal for zoology, publishing original contributions in the fields of animal organisation, structure and function.
**Ind/Abst** AGRICOLA; Biol. Abstr.; Chem. Abstr.; CSA Neuro. Abstr. (?-?); Curr. Aware. Biol. Sci., CABS; Curr. Contents, Agric. Biol. Environ. Sci.; Curr. Ref. Fish Res.; EMBASE; Fish Rev.; GeoRef; Helminthol. Abstr. (1991-); Index Vet.; Life Sci. Collect.; Protozoolog. Abstr.; Res. Alert [Full Cov.]; Rev. Agric. Entomol.; Rev. Med. Vet. Entomol.; Sci. Cit. Index; SCISEARCH; Vet. Bull.; Wildl. Rev.

XO/0567-8331
**ACTA ZOOTECHNICA.** [Acta zootech.]. **Added/Corp** Vysoka Skola Polnohospodarska v Nitre. Agronomicka Faculta. Vol. 13 (1966)-. Periodical. Czech (summaries and/or abstracts in Russian, English and German; table of contents in Russian, English and German). **CODEN** ACZOAD. Documents available from CASDDS. ***Supersedes in part*** *Sbornik Vysokej Skoly Polnohospodarskej v Nitre, Agronomicka Faculta.*
**Ind/Abst** Chem. Abstr.; Poult. Abstr.

VE
**ACTAS Y TRABAJOS DEL ... ENCUENTRO VENEZOLANO DE ENTOMOLOGIA. Main/Corp** Encuentro Venezolano de Entomologia. **Added/Corp** Sociedad Venezolana de Entomologia. Universidad Central de Venezuela. Facultad de Agronomia. (1976)-. Spanish. an. Apartado 4579, Maracay Venezuela.

NE
**ADVANCES IN INVERTEBRATE REPRODUCTION : PROCEEDINGS OF THE ... INTERNATIONAL CONGRESS OF INVERTEBRATE REPRODUCTION.** ***Ceased.*** (July 23-28, 1989)-Completed Series Vol. 5 (19??). English. te. Elsevier Science Publishers BV, PO Box 211, 1000 AE Amsterdam Netherlands. **Tel** 011 31 20 5803642, FAX 011 31 20 5862696, telex 15682. **LC** QL364.15; .I58a. **DD** 592/.016. Documents available from CASDDS. ***Continues*** *International Society of Invertebrate Reproduction. International Symposium. Advances in Invertebrate Reproduction.*
**Ind/Abst** Chem. Abstr.

NE
**ADVANCES IN ODONATOLOGY : PROCEEDINGS OF THE ... INTERNATIONAL SYMPOSIUM OF ODONATOLOGY. Added/Corp** Societas Internationalis Odonatologica. Nederlandse Entomologische Vereniging. **VFOAT** Proceedings of the Sixth International Symposium of Odonatology. Vol. 1 (1982)-. Monographic series. English (French and German). ir. Price varies per volume. Societas Internationalis Odonatologica, PO Box 256, 3720 AG Bilthoven, The Netherlands. **Tel** 011 31 30285904. **ED** Jean Legrand. Index available. cum. index. **Bk Rev. Circ:** 400. Documents available from BIOSIS Document Express. ***Continues in part*** *Odonatologica, 0375-0183.*
**Ind/Abst** Biol. Abstr.; Entomol. Abstr.; Genet. Abstr.; Ref. Z.; Zool. Rec.

US
**ADVANCES IN PRIMATOLOGY.** (1970)-. Monographic series. English. ir. Price varies per volume. Plenum Press, 233 Spring Street, New York NY 10013-1578. **Tel** (212)620-8000, (800)221-9369, FAX (212)463-0742, (212)807-1047, telex 23/421139. **ED** John G. Fleagle adn Ross D. MacPhee. **LC** QL737.P9; A4. **DD** 599.8. **NLM** W1 AD785. **Pr Rev.**

RH
**AFRICA CALLS.** No. 162 (Sept./Oct. 1987)-. Periodical. English. bm (6 issues). 22.00Zin$. Modus Publications Pvt Ltd., PO Box 66070, Kopje Harare Zimbabwe. **Tel** 011 263 4 738722. **LC** DT962.A2; R38. **DD** 916.89104/5. ***Continues*** *Africa Calls From Zimbabwe.*

UK/0141-6707
**AFRICAN JOURNAL OF ECOLOGY. See** Environmental Issues-Ecology.

BE/0763-6776
**AFRICAN SMALL MAMMAL NEWSLETTER.** No. 1 (Feb. 1978)-. Periodical. English (French and German). an (Dec.). Free on request. African Small Mammal Newsletter, Transvaal Museum, PO Box 413, Pretoria 0001 South Africa. **ED** E. Van der Straeten.
**Ind/Abst** Fish Rev. (Jan. 1989-July 1992); Wildl. Rev. (Jan. 1989-July 1992).

KE/0002-0281
**AFRICANA.** ***Suspended.*** **Added/Corp** East African Wild Life Society. Quarterly Review. World Wildlife Fund--Kenya. Quarterly Notes. Vol. 1 (Mar. 1962)-(1991). Periodical. English. qt. Nation Newspapers Limited, PO Box 49010, Nairobi Kenya East Africa. **Tel** 011 254 2 228831. **LC** QL337.E25; A4. **DD** 591.9676/05.
**Ind/Abst** Hum. Rights Intern. Rep.

UK/0963-6420
**AFRO-ASIAN JOURNAL OF NEMATOLOGY.** [Afro-Asian j. nematol.]. **Added/Corp** Afro-Asian Society of Nematologists. (1991)-. Periodical. English (French). sa (June and Dec.). $120.00. International Institute of Parasitology, 395A Hatfield Road, St. Albans Herts AL40XU England. **Tel** 011 44 727 833151, FAX 011 44 727 868721. **ED** Dr. M.R. Siddiqi. **Bk Rev**, (Qty: 1). **Ad Acc. Pr Rev. Circ:** 50.

UK/0269-0543
**AGRICULTURAL ZOOLOGY REVIEWS. See** Agriculture.

FR/0002-5208
**ALEXANOR.** [Alexanor]. Vol. 1 (1959)-. Periodical. French. qt. 205.68F France; 220.00F France. Alexanor, 45 rue de Buffon, 75005 Paris France. **Tel** 011 33 1 40793340 ext. 3412. **ED** Gerard Chr Luquet. **CODEN** ALEXBX. Index available. **Bk Rev. Ad Acc. Circ:** 1,250 (ctrl). Documents available from BIOSIS Document Express.
**Desc:** General lepidopterology; systematics, nomenclature, biology, ecology, ethology, biogeography, capture and preservation methods, rearing.
**Ind/Abst** Biol. Abstr.; Entomol. Abstr.; Life Sci. Collect.; Zool. Rec.

HU/0002-5658
**ALLATTANI KOEZLEMENYEK.** [Allatt. koezl.]. **Added/Corp** Magyar Biologiai Tarsasag. Allattani Szakosztaly. Vol. 63 (1976)-. Periodical. Hungarian (summaries and/or abstracts in English, German and Russian). qt. $30.00. Magyar Biologiai Tarsasag, Fo u. 68, 1027 Budapest, Hungary. **(Subscription address:** Kultura, PO Box 149, H 1389 Budapest 62 Hungary.**)** **ED** I. Andrassy. **CODEN** ALLKAS. **Bk Rev. Circ:** 400. Documents available from BIOSIS Document Express.
**Desc:** Contains different articles of the zoological sciences, neurologies, memorials and proceedings of the Hungarian Zoological Society.
**Ind/Abst** Biol. Abstr.

FR/0753-4973
**ALYTES.** [Alytes]. **Added/Corp** Societe Batrachologique de France. Vol. 1 No. 1 (Feb. 1982)-. Periodical. French (French and Spanish; summaries and/or abstracts in English). Four times a year. 500.00F (institution), 250.00F (individual). ISSCA, Lab des Reptiles and Amphibiens, Museum National D'Histoire Naturelle, 25 rue Cuvier, 75005 Paris France. **Tel** 011 33 1 40793485, FAX 011 33 1 40793484. **ED** Alain Dubois. **CODEN** ALTSES. Index available. **Bk Rev. Ad Acc. Pr Rev. Circ:** 200. Documents available from BIOSIS Document Express.
**Desc:** Original papers dealing with all aspects of study and conservation of amphibians.
**Ind/Abst** Biol. Abstr.; Curr. Aware. Biol. Sci., CABS; Ecology Abstr.

US/0364-9504
**AMERICAN ARACHNOLOGY.** Began in 1973. English. American Arachnology Society, 940 Poly Drive, Billings MT 59102. **LC** QL453.1.U6; A43. **DD** 595/.4/05. **UDC** 595.4. **CODEN** AMARD4.

US/1072-2440
**AMERICAN CONCHOLOGIST.** (AMERICAN CONCHOLOGIST : QUARTERLY BULLETIN OF THE CONCHOLOGISTS OF AMERICA, INC.). [Am. conchol.]. **Added/Corp** Conchologists of America. (1987)-. Periodical. English. qt. $15.00 (organizational membership), $12.50 (individual membership) North America; $20.00 Caribbean, Central & South America; $25.00 other. Conchologists of America Inc, 2644 Kings Highway, Louisville KY 40205-2649. **Tel** (502)458-5719. **ED** Lynn Scheu (editor's address: 1222 Holsworth Lane, Louisville KY 40222-6616, phone (502)423-0469). **DD** 594. Index available. cum. index. **Bk Rev**, (Qty: 12). **Ad Acc, Adv Mgr:** W. Sage. **Circ:** 1,400. ***Continues*** *Conchologists of America Bulletin, 0747-105X.*
**Desc:** Devoted to the interest of shell collectors - the beauty of shells, their scientific aspects and the collecting and preservation of mollusks.

US/0275-2565
**AMERICAN JOURNAL OF PRIMATOLOGY.** [Am. j. primatol.]. **VFOAT** Primatology. (1981)-. Academic Scholarly Publication. English. mo. $1,032.00 US; $1,152.00 Canada and Mexico; $1,197.00 other. John Wiley & Sons, Inc., 605 Third Avenue, New York NY 10158-0012. **Tel** (212)850-6000, (212)850-6645, FAX (212)850-6088, telex 12-7063. **(Subscription address:** John Wiley & Sons / England, Baffins Lane, Chichester, West Sussex PO19 1UD England.**)** **ED** Michael J. Raleigh. **LC** QL737.P9; A566. **NLM** W1 AM51F. **CODEN** AJPTDU. **[CCC]. Bk Rev. Pr Rev.** Documents available from The Genuine Article, BIOSIS Document Express, CASDDS.
**Desc:** Publishes original research reports, scholarly reviews, brief reports, and book reviews on all topics relevant to the study of primates, including all aspects of their anatomy, behavior, development, ecology, evolution, genetics, nutrition, physiology, reproduction, systematics, conservation, husbandry, and use in biomedical research.
**Ind/Abst** Anim. Behav. Abstr.; Anthropol. Lit.; Biol. Abstr.; Chem. Abstr.; CSA Neuro. Abstr. (?-?); Curr. Aware. Biol. Sci., CABS; Curr. Contents, Agric. Biol. Environ. Sci.; Curr. Contents Life Sci.; Curr. Primate Ref.; Dairy Sci. Abstr.; Ecology Abstr.; EMBASE; Index Vet.; Nutr. Abstr. Rev., Ser. B, Live Feeds and Feed.; Life Sci. Collect.; Psychol. Abstr. (1981-); PsycINFO; Ref. Upd. Deluxe Ed.; Res. Alert [Full Cov.]; Sci. Cit. Index; SCISEARCH; Soc. Sci. Cit. Index [Select. Cov.]; Wildl. Rev.

US/0740-2783
**AMERICAN MALACOLOGICAL BULLETIN.** [Am. malacol. bull.]. **Added/Corp** American Malacological Union. Vol. 1 (July 1983)-. Periodical. English. Twice a year (Feb. & July). $32.00. American Malacological Union, PO Box 1106, University of Maryland, Princess Anne MD 21853. **(Subscription address:** Harbour Branch Oceangraphic Institute, 5600 US 1 N, Fort Pierce FL 34946.**)** **ED** Robert S. Prezant. **LC** QL401; .A54. **DD** 594/.005. Index available. cum. index. **Ad Acc. Pr Rev. Circ:** 800. Documents available from The Genuine Article. ***Continues*** *Bulletin of the American Malacological Union, Inc., 0096-5537.*
**Desc:** Original research, detailed reviews, and symposia dealing with mollusks.
**Ind/Abst** Aquat. Sci. Fish. Abstr. (Computer File); Curr. Aware. Biol. Sci., CABS; Curr. Contents, Agric. Biol. Environ. Sci.; Ecol. Abstr.; Ecology Abstr.; Ocean. Abstr.; Res. Alert [Select. Cov.]; SCISEARCH.

US/0003-0082
**AMERICAN MUSEUM NOVITATES.** [Am. Mus. novit.]. **Added/Corp** American Museum of Natural History. (1921)-. Monographic series. English. ir. Price varies per volume. American Museum of Natural History, Central Park West at 79th Street, New York NY 10024. **Tel** (212)769-5500, (800)234-5252, telex 910 240 8933 MICRO PRESS VQ. **ED** Brenda Jones. **LC** QL1; .A436. **DD** 505. **CODEN** AMUNAL. Index Available, published separately, free-automatically sent. **Bk Rev. Circ:** 1,500 (ctrl). available on microfilm and microfiche from University Microfilms International (UMI). Documents available from BIOSIS Document Express.
**Desc:** Contains descriptions of new forms and reports in zoology, paleontology, geology and mineralogy.
**Ind/Abst** AGRICOLA [Select. Cov.]; Biol. Abstr.; GeoRef; Int. Aerosp. Abstr.

US/0003-0511
**AMERICAN PIGEON JOURNAL.** Vol. 1 (1912)-. Periodical. English. mo. $18.00 (one year), $34.00 (two year), $48.00 (three year) US; $21.00 (one year), $40.00 (two year), $57.00 (three year) other. American Pigeon Journal, PO Box 278, Warrenton MO 63383. **Tel** (314)456-2122. **ED** William L. "Mike" Worley. **Bk Rev. Ad Acc. Circ:** 7,600. ***Absorbed*** *American Pigeon Keeper; Pigeon Loft.*
**Desc:** Devoted to the raising of pigeons for pleasure and profit.

US/0003-1569
**AMERICAN ZOOLOGIST.** [Am. zool.]. **Added/Corp** American Society of Zoologists. Vol. 1 (Feb. 1961)-. Periodical. English. ir (6 issues). $400.00 (institutions), $200.00 (individuals) US. American Society of Zoologists, 401 North Michigan Avenue, Chicago IL 60611. **Tel** (312)527-6697, FAX (312)527-6640. **ED** Milton Fingerman. **LC** QL1; .A448. **DD** 590/.5. **NLM** W1 AM874. **CODEN** AMZOAF. Index available (bound in Nov. issue). **Bk Rev. Ad Acc. Pr Rev. Acid Free. Circ:** 6,300 (ctrl). Documents available from The Genuine Article, BIOSIS Document Express, UMI Article Clearinghouse, CASDDS.
**Desc:** Contains papers from symposia dealing with a wide variety of zoological disciplines.
**Ind/Abst** Acad. Ind. [Computer File] (1992-); AGRICOLA [Select. Cov.]; Anim. Behav. Abstr.; Anim. Breed. Abstr.; Biol. Agric. Index; Biol. Abstr.; Biol. Dig.; Chem. Abstr.; CSA Neuro. Abstr.; Curr. Aware. Biol. Sci., CABS; Curr. Contents, Agric. Biol. Environ. Sci.; Curr. Contents Life Sci.; Curr. Ref. Fish Res.; Dairy Sci. Abstr.; Ecol. Abstr.; Ecology Abstr.; Entomol. Abstr.; Environ. Period. Bibliogr.; Expand. Acad. Index (1989-); Fish Rev.; Gen. Sci. Index; GeoRef; Helminthol. Abstr. (19??-19??); Index Vet.; Key Word Index Wildl. Res.; Newsp. Period. Abstr. (1991-); Nutr. Abstr. Rev., Ser. B, Live Feeds and Feed.; Nutr. Abstr. Rev., Ser. A, Hum. Exp.; Life Sci. Collect.;

Plant Breed. Abstr.; Poult. Abstr.; Protozoolog. Abstr.; Ref. Upd. Basic Ed.; Ref. Upd. Deluxe Ed.; Res. Alert [Full Cov.]; Rev. Agric. Entomol.; Rev. Med. Vet. Entomol.; Sci. Cit. Index; SCISEARCH; Soc. Plann. Policy Dev. Abstr.; Sociol. Abstr. (?-?); Vet. Bull.; Wildl. Rev.

GW/0173-5373
**AMPHIBIA-REPTILIA.** (AMPHIBIA-REPTILIA : PUBLICATION OF THE SOCIETAS EUROPAEA HERPETOLOGICA.). [Amphib.-reptil.]. **Added/Corp** Societas Europaea Herpetologica. **VFOAT** Amphibia Reptilia. Vol. 1, No. 1 (Aug. 1980)-. Periodical. English (French, German and Spanish; summaries and/or abstracts in German). qt. Fl173.00 Netherlands; $99.00 other. E. J. Brill, Postbus 9000, 2300 PA Leiden Netherlands. **Tel** 011 31 71 312624, FAX 011 31 71 317532, telex 39296 BRILL NL. **ED** R. A. Avery and Ch. Klaver. **LC** QL640; .A5. **DD** 597.6/05. **CODEN** AMREEH. **[CCC]. Bk Rev. Ad Acc.** ctrl circ. Documents available from BIOSIS Document Express.
**Desc:** A multi-disciplinary journal devoted to all aspects of herpetology, to disseminate knowledge and ideas between specialists on such subjects as biochemical technology in herpetological research to electron microscopy.
**Ind/Abst** Biol. Abstr.; Ecol. Abstr.; Fish Rev.; Geogr. Abstr. Phys. Geogr.; Geol. Abstr.; Life Sci. Collect.; Wildl. Rev.

MX/0368-8720
**ANALES DEL INSTITUTO DE BIOLOGIA, UNIVERSIDAD NACIONAL AUTONOMA DE MEXICO. SERIE ZOOLOGIA.** [An. Inst. Biol., Univ. Nac. Auton. Mex., Ser. zool.]. **Main/Corp** Universidad Nacional Autonoma de Mexico. Instituto de Biologia. Vol. 38 (1967)-. Monographic series. Spanish (English and Multiple languages; summaries and/or abstracts in English). ir. Price varies per volume. Instituto de Biologia Universidad Nacional, Apartado Post 70-233, Mexico 20 DF Mexico. **ED** Roberto Johansen Naime. Index available. **Bk Rev. Pr Rev. Circ:** 600 (ctrl). available on photocopies. ***Continues in part*** *Anales del Instituto de Biologia, 0076-7174.*
**Desc:** Dedicated to zoological subjects.
**Ind/Abst** Ecology Abstr.; Entomol. Abstr.; Helminthol. Abstr.; Life Sci. Collect.

GW/0003-3162
**ANGEWANDTE PARASITOLOGIE.** ***Title Change.*** [Angew. parasitol.]. **Added/Corp** Parasitologische Gesellschaft der DDR. Vol. 1 (June 1960)-(1992). Periodical. German (German; summaries and/or abstracts in English and Russian). qt. Gustav Fischer Verlag Jena, Postfach 100537, D 07705 Jena Germany. **Tel** 011 49 3641 27332, FAX 011 49 3641 626500. **(Subscription address:** 303 NW 12th Avenue, Deerfield Beach FL 33442; telephone: (305)428-5566) **ED** Klaus Odening. **LC** QL757; .A7. **DD** 591.5/249/05. **NLM** W1; AN223M. **CODEN** AWPAAR. **[CCC].** Index available. **Bk Rev. Ad Acc. Circ:** 680. Documents available from BIOSIS Document Express. ***Continued by*** *Applied Parasitology.*
**Desc:** Publishes short original papers and reviews from all fields of parasitology with concentration on articles in applied parasitology: zooparasites of man, domestic animals, animals at the zoo, wild and anoxious animals as well; diagnostics, methods of investigation, control-procedures and their effects, harmfulness, bionomy of parasites, environmental parasitology, clinical picture, etc.
**Ind/Abst** Biol. Abstr.; EMBASE; Health Plan. Adminis.; Helminthol. Abstr. (19??-19??); Index Med.; Index Vet.; Life Sci. Collect.; Protozoolog. Abstr.; Rev. Med. Vet. Entomol.; Small Anim. Abstr. Bibliogr.; Soils Fert.; Vet. Bull.; Trop. Dis. Bull.

US/0301-8695
**ANIMAL BEHAVIOR ABSTRACTS. See** Zoology-Abstracting, Bibliographies and Statistics.

UK/0003-3472
**ANIMAL BEHAVIOUR.** [Anim. behav.]. Vol. 6 (Jan./April 1958)-. Academic Scholarly Publication. English. mo. $595.00. Academic Press Ltd., A Division of Harcourt Brace & Company Ltd., 24-28 Oval Road, London NW1 7DX England. **Tel** 071 267 4466, FAX 071 482 2293, 071 485 4752, telex 25775 ACPRES G. **(Subscription address:** Harcourt Brace & Company, Ltd., Foots Cray, High Street, Sidcup Kent DA14 5HP England.) **ED** T. J. Roper and M. West. **LC** QL750. **DD** 591.51. **UDC** 591.5. **NLM** W1 AN228E. **CODEN** ANBEA8. **[CCC]. Bk Rev. Ad Acc. Pr Rev.** available on microfilm and microfiche from University Microfilms International (UMI). Documents available from The Genuine Article, BIOSIS Document Express, UMI Article Clearinghouse, CASDDS. ***Continues*** *British Journal of Animal Behaviour, 0950-5601.*
**Desc:** An international publication with wide appeal, containing critical reviews, original papers, and research articles on all aspects of animal behavior. Book reviews and books received sections are also included. A short communications section allows for the rapid publication of brief, but important topical research results.
**Ind/Abst** Acad. Abstr. Full Text Elite (July 1990-); Acad. Abstr. (July 1990-); Acad. Ind. [Computer File] (1987-); Acad. Search (July 1990-); AGRICOLA [Select. Cov.]; Anim. Behav. Abstr.; Anim. Breed. Abstr.; Biocont. News Inf. (19??-19??); Biol. Agric. Index; Biol. Abstr.; Chem. Abstr.; Chemorecept. Abstr.; CSA Neuro. Abstr. (?-?); Curr. Aware. Biol. Sci., CABS; Curr. Contents, Agric. Biol. Environ. Sci.; Curr. Contents Life Sci.; Curr. Ref. Fish Res.; Dairy Sci. Abstr.; Ecol. Abstr.; Ecology Abstr.; Entomol. Abstr.; Expand. Acad. Index (1987-); Fish Rev.; Gen. Sci. Index; Gen. Sci. Source (Jul. 1990-); Geogr. Abstr. Phys. Geogr.; Helminthol. Abstr.; Immunol. Abstr.; Index Vet.; INFO-SOUTH Abstr.; Key Word Index Wildl. Res.; Mag. Search; Newsp. Period. Abstr. (1989-); Nutr. Abstr. Rev., Ser. B, Live Feeds and Feed.; Nutr. Abstr. Rev., Ser. A, Hum. Exp.; Life Sci. Collect.; PESTDOC; Postharvest News Inf.; Poult. Abstr.; Protozoolog. Abstr.; Psychol. Abstr. (1958-); PsycINFO (1990-); PsycLit; Ref. Upd. Deluxe Ed.; Res. Alert [Full Cov.]; Rev. Agric. Entomol.; Rev. Med. Vet. Entomol.; Sci. Cit. Index; SCISEARCH; Soc. Sci. Cit. Index [Select. Cov.]; Vet. Bull.; Weed Abstr.; Wildl. Rev.

US/0164-9531
**ANIMAL KEEPERS' FORUM. Added/Corp** American Association of Zoo Keepers. Vol. 1 (Nov. 1974)-. Periodical. English. Twelve times a year. $25.00 (affiliate & associate); $30.00 (professional); $50.00 (institutional) Comes with American Association of Zoo Keepers membership. American Association of Zoo Keepers, Inc., 635 Gage Boulevard, National Headquarters, Topeka KS 66606-2066. **Tel** (800)242-4519, FAX (913)273-1980. **ED** Susan D. Chan, (phone: (913)272-5821 Ext. 31). Index available (Jan.). cum. index. **Bk Rev**, (Qty: 15-20). **Ad Acc, Adv Mgr:** Susan D. Chan, **Tel** (913)272-5821, Ext. 31. **Pr Rev. Circ:** 2,650 (ctrl).
**Desc:** Written for those in the zookeeping profession and other individuals who have an interest in captive exotic animal care. It contains articles on exotic animal husbandry, exhibit design, veterinary information, environmental and behavioral enrichment column, monthly listing of jobs available nationwide. Also contains news about the association, its conferences and symposia.
**Ind/Abst** Key Word Index Wildl. Res.; Wildl. Rev.

US/0090-4996
**ANIMAL LEARNING & BEHAVIOR.** [Anim. Learn. Behav.]. **Added/Corp** Psychonomic Society. **VAT** Animal Learning and Behavior. Vol. 1 (Feb. 1973)-. Periodical. English. qt (Feb., May, Aug., Nov.). $87.00 US; $93.00 other. Psychonomic Society Publications, 1710 Fortview Road, Austin TX 78704. **Tel** (512)462-2442, FAX (512)462-1101. **ED** Vincent Lolordo. **LC** QL785; .A725. **DD** 591.5. **NLM** W1 AN228TE. **CODEN** ALBVAB. **[CCC].** Index available. **Ad Acc. Pr Rev. Circ:** 1,400. available on microfilm and microfiche from University Microfilms International (UMI). Documents available from The Genuine Article, BIOSIS Document Express, UMI Article Clearinghouse. ***Supersedes in part*** *Psychonomic Science, 0033-3131.*
**Desc:** Covers broad categories of animal learning, motivation, emotion, and comparative behavior.
**Ind/Abst** Acad. Search (July 1993-); AGRICOLA [Select. Cov.]; Biol. Abstr.; Curr. Contents Life Sci.; Curr. Contents Soc. Behav. Sci.; EMBASE; Expand. Acad. Index (1989-); Fish Rev.; Gen. Sci. Index; Gen. Sci. Source (Jul. 1993-); INFO-SOUTH Abstr.; Mag. Search; Newsp. Period. Abstr. (1991-); Nutr. Abstr. Rev., Ser. B, Live Feeds and Feed.; Nutr. Abstr. Rev., Ser. A, Hum. Exp.; Life Sci. Collect.; Psychol. Abstr. (1973-); PsycINFO; PsycLit; Ref. Upd. Deluxe Ed.; Res. Alert [Full Cov.]; Sci. Cit. Index; SCISEARCH; Soc. Sci. Cit. Index [Full Cov.]; Wildl. Rev.

GW/0340-3165
**ANIMAL RESEARCH AND DEVELOPMENT.** [Anim. res. dev.]. **Added/Corp** Institut fuer Wissenschaftliche Zusammenarbeit mit Hochschulen der Entwicklungslaander (Taubingen, Germany). Vol. 1 (1975)-. English. Twice a year. Institut fuer Wissenschaftliche Zusammenarbeit, A Wirt Recht Street, Landhausstr 18, D 72074 Tuebingen Germany. **Tel** 011 49 7071 21882, FAX 011 49 711 26753. **LC** QL1; .A473. **DD** 591/.05.
**Ind/Abst** EMBASE.

US
**ANIMAL SCIENCE AND TECHNOLOGY.** (19??)-. Periodical. English. mo. $280.00. **(Subscription address:** Maruzen Company Ltd., PO Box 5050, Import & Export Department, Tokyo 100 31 Japan.)

US/0019-3127
**ANIMALAND. Added/Corp** Staten Island Zoological Society. Vol. 36, No. 4 (Winter 1969)-. Periodical. English. ir. Staten Island Zoological Society, 614 Broadway, Staten Island NY 10310. **LC** QL1; .S883. **DD** 590/.5. ***Continues*** *Staten Island Zoological Society. In Animaland with the Staten Island Zoological Society, Inc.*

AU/0255-0105
**ANNALEN DES NATURHISTORISCHEN MUSEUMS IN WIEN. SERIE B, FUER BOTANIK UND ZOOLOGIE. See** Biology-Botany.

FR/0037-9271
**ANNALES DE LA SOCIETE ENTOMOLOGIQUE DE FRANCE.** [Ann. Soc. entomol. Fr.]. **Main/Corp** Societe Entomologique de France. Vol. 1-11 (1832-1842)-. Periodical. French (English). Four times a year (Mar., June, Sept., Dec.). 750.00F France & French Possessions; 850.00F others. Societe Entomologique de France, 45 rue de Buffon, 75005 Paris France. **Tel** 011 33 1 40793391. **ED** J. Bitsch. **UDC** 595.7. **NLM** W1 AN342. **CODEN** ASEQAQ. Index available. cum. index. **Ad Acc, Adv Mgr:** J. Y. Raspius. **Pr Rev. Circ:** 550. Documents available from The Genuine Article, BIOSIS Document Express. ***Absorbed*** *Revue de Pathologie Vegetale et d'Entomologie Agricole de France.* ***Continued in part by*** *Bulletin de la Societe Entomologique de France.*
**Desc:** Deals with entomology: systematics, taxonomy, phylogeny, comparative morphology, evolution, biogeography, and ecology.
**Ind/Abst** Biocont. News Inf. (19??-19??); Biol. Abstr.; Curr. Contents, Agric. Biol. Environ. Sci.; For. Abstr.; Helminthol. Abstr. (1991-); Hortic. Abstr.; Maize Abstr.; Life Sci. Collect.; Postharvest News Inf.; Potato Abstr.; Res. Alert [Select. Cov.]; Rev. Agric. Entomol.; Rev. Med. Vet. Entomol.; SCISEARCH; Seed Abstr.; Soils Fert.

FR/0003-4150
**ANNALES DE PARASITOLOGIE HUMAINE ET COMPAREE.** ***Title Change.*** **See** Biology.

FR/0003-424X
**ANNALES DE ZOOTECHNIE. Added/Corp** Paris. Institut National de la Recherche Agronomique. Vol. 10 (1961)-. Academic Scholarly Publication. French (English). qt (4 issues). 940.00F France; 1125.00F other. Editions Scientifique Elsevier, 141 rue de Javel, 75747 Paris Cedex 15 France. **Tel** 011 33 1 47 07 11 22, FAX 011 33 1 43 36 80 93. **(Subscription address:** Editions Scientifiques Elsevier / for North America, PO Box 7247-7576, Philadelphia PA 19170-7576.) **ED** A. Rerat. **CODEN** AZOOAH. **[CCC]. Pr Rev.** available on microfilm and microfiche from University Microfilms International (UMI). Documents available from The Genuine Article, BIOSIS Document Express, CASDDS. ***Continues*** *Paris. Institut National de la Recherche Agronomique. Annales. Serie D. Annales de Zootechnie.*
**Desc:** Contains scientific articles on general or comparative zootechny.
**Ind/Abst** Anim. Breed. Abstr.; Biol. Abstr.; Chem. Abstr.; Curr. Contents, Agric. Biol. Environ. Sci.; Dairy Sci. Abstr.; Ecol. Abstr. (?-?); Fish Rev. (Jan. 1989-July 1992); Food Sci. Technol. Abstr.; Grasslands For. Abstr.; Index Vet.; Maize Abstr.; Nutr. Abstr. Rev., Ser. B, Live Feeds and Feed.; Life Sci. Collect.; Pig News Inf.; Poult. Abstr.; Res. Alert [Full Cov.]; Sci. Cit. Index; SCISEARCH; Soyabean Abstr.; Vet. Bull.; Wheat Barley Trit. Abstr.; Wildl. Rev. (Jan. 1989-July 1992).

FR/0003-4339
**ANNALES DES SCIENCES NATURELLES. ZOOLOGIE ET BIOLOGIE ANIMALE.** [Ann. sci. nat., Zool. biol. anim.]. **VFOAT** Zoologie et Biologie Animale. 2nd Ed. Ser. V. Vol. 1-20, (1834/43)-. Periodical. French (English; summaries and/or abstracts in English). qt. $279.00. Masson Editeur, Box Postale 22, 41353 Vineuil 16 France. **Tel** 011 33 54 438994. **ED** Leroy de Puytozac. **LC** QH3; .A62. **DD** 574/.05. **CODEN** ASNBAQ. **[CCC].** Index available. cum. index. **Bk Rev. Ad Acc. Pr Rev. Circ:** 1,500. available on microfilm and microfiche from University Microfilms International (UMI). Documents available from The Genuine Article, BIOSIS Document Express. ***Supersedes in part*** *Annales des Sciences Naturelles;* ***Absorbed*** *Annales des Sciences Geologiques.*
**Desc:** Covers experimental and general zoology, anatomy, endocrinology, animal etiology and sociology, and animal biology.
**Ind/Abst** Biol. Abstr.; Curr. Aware. Biol. Sci., CABS; Curr. Contents, Agric. Biol. Environ. Sci.; Curr. Ref. Fish Res.; Fish Rev.; GeoRef; Helminthol. Abstr. (1991-); Index Vet.; Life Sci. Collect.; Protozoolog. Abstr.; Res. Alert [Full Cov.]; Rev. Med. Vet. Entomol.; Sci. Cit. Index; SCISEARCH; Wildl. Rev.

PL/0239-4243
**ANNALES UNIVERSITATIS MARIAE CURIE-SKODOWSKA. SECTIO EE, ZOOTECHNICA.** [Ann. Univ. Mariae Curie-Skodowska, Sect. EE Zootech.]. **Added/Corp** Uniwersytet Marii Curie-Skodowskiej. **VFOAT** Zootechnica. Vol. 1 (1983)-. Periodical. Polish (summaries and/or abstracts in English and Russian). an. z300.00. Uniwersytet Marii Curie-Skodowskiej / Pologne, Biuro Wydawnictw Plac, Marii Curie-Skodowskiej 5, 20-031 Lublin, Pologne. **LC** SF84; .A56. **DD** 591/6/09438. **CODEN** AUEZE3. Documents available from BIOSIS Document Express.
**Ind/Abst** Agric. Eng. Abstr.; Biol. Abstr.

PL/0003-4541
**ANNALES ZOOLOGICI.** (ANNALES ZOOLOGICI / POLSKA AKADEMIA NAUK, INSTYTUT ZOOLOGICZNY.). [Ann. zool.]. **Added/Corp** Polska Akademia Nauk. Instytut Zoologiczny. Vol. 16, No. 1 (May 29, 1954)-. Periodical. English (French and German; summaries and/or abstracts in Polish and Russian). mo. **(Subscription address:** ARS Polona, PO Box 1001, 00068 Warsaw Poland.) **CODEN** AZOGAR. Index available in last issue of volume--attached. Documents available from BIOSIS Document Express. ***Continues*** *Annales Musei Zoologici Polonici.*
**Ind/Abst** Biocont. News Inf.; Biol. Abstr.; GeoRef; Soils Fert.

IT/0365-3498
**ANNALI DELL'ISTITUTO SPERIMENTALE PER LA ZOOTECNIA.** [Ann. ist. sper. zootec.]. **Main/Corp** Istituto Sperimentale per la Zootecnia (Rome, Italy). Vol. 1 (1968)-. Periodical. Italian (summaries and/or abstracts in English and French). sa. **CODEN** AISZAJ. Documents available from CASDDS. ***Supersedes*** *Rome (City). Istituto Sperimentale Zootecnico. Annali dell'Istituto Sperimentale Zootecnia di Roma.*
**Ind/Abst** Chem. Abstr.

IT
**ANNALI, NUOVA SERIE : SEZIONE 3, BIOLOGIA ANIMALE. SUPPLEMENTO.** **Main/Corp** Universita di Ferrara. **VAT** Annali, Nuova Serie : Sezione Tre, Biologia Animale. Supplemento. French (French). an. Via Festa del Perdono 7, Milan 20122 Italy. **LC** QL368.A22; C65 subser. **DD** 591/.05.

II
**ANNALS OF ENTOMOLOGY.** (July 1983)-. Periodical. English. sa. $200.00. Jugal Kishore and Co, 4-B Neshville Road, Dehra Dun 248 001 India. **Tel** 011 91 135 23622. **(Subscription address:** Prints India, 11 Darya Ganj, New Delhi 110002 India.**)** **LC** QL461; .A56. **DD** 595.7/005.
**Desc:** An international research journal.
**Ind/Abst** Agrofor. Abstr. (1991-); For. Abstr.; Protozoolog. Abstr.; Rev. Agric. Entomol.; Rev. Med. Vet. Entomol.; Rev. Plant Pathol.

XO/0570-202X
**ANNOTATIONES ZOOLOGICAE ET BOTANICAE.** [Annot. zool. bot.]. (1964)-. Monographic series. Czech. Price varies per volume. **LC** QL1; .A49. **CODEN** AZBTAZ. Documents available from BIOSIS Document Express.
**Ind/Abst** Biol. Abstr.; GeoRef; Rev. Agric. Entomol.; Rev. Med. Vet. Entomol.

US/8755-4690
**ANNUAL PROGRESS REPORT, CHILKAT RIVER COOPERATIVE BALD EAGLE STUDY.** [Annu. prog. rep. Chilkat River coop. bald eagle study]. English. an. National Audubon Society, 700 Broadway, New York NY 10003. **Tel** (212)979-3117. **DD** 598. **UDC** 598.9(047)(73).

US/1046-3143
**ANNUAL REPORT - HARVARD UNIVERSITY. MUSEUM OF COMPARATIVE ZOOLOGY.** (ANNUAL REPORT / MUSEUM OF COMPARATIVE ZOOLOGY.). [Annu. rep. - Harv. Univ., Mus. Comp. Zool.]. **Main/Corp** Harvard University. Museum of Comparative Zoology. 1962-. English. Harvard University Museum of Comparative Zoology, 26 Oxford Street, Cambridge MA 02138. **Tel** (617)495-2466. **DD** 591. ***Continues*** *Annual Report of the Director of the Museum of Comparative Zoology at Harvard College, 0735-1003.*

US/0445-1953
**ANNUAL UPLAND GAME BIRD REPORT (BOISE).** (ANNUAL UPLAND GAME BIRD REPORT (IDAHO).). **Main/Corp** Idaho. Fish and Game Department. English. an. Idaho Department of Fish and Game, PO Box 25, Boise ID 83707. **Tel** (208)334-3748, FAX (208)334-2114. **LC** SK387; .A25. **UDC** 598.6(047)(796).

UK/0140-1890
**ANTENNA.** V. 1- July 1977-. Periodical. English. qt. £33.00 (airfreight); £17.00 (nonmembers UK); £18.00 (nonmembers all except UK); Free on request (members). Royal Entomological Society, 41 Queens Gate, London SW7 5HR England. **Tel** 011 41 71 5848361. **ED** J A BUllock, B B Angus. **LC** QL461; .A62. **DD** 595.7/005. **UDC** 595.7. **Bk Rev. Ad Acc. Circ:** 2,250 (ctrl). ***Continues*** *Proceedings of the Royal Entomological Society of London. Journal of Meetings.*
**Desc:** Contains reports of all Society meetings, workshops, symposia and other activities. Also contains scientific articles, readers' correspondence, an important diary section, and other items of interest to all entomologists.
**Ind/Abst** Biocont. News Inf. (19??-19??); Rev. Agric. Entomol.; Rev. Med. Vet. Entomol.; Rice Abstr.

FR/0761-3032
**ANTHROPOZOOLOGICA PARIS.** [Anthropozoologica Paris]. (1984)-. Periodical. French (English). an. 220.00F Europe; 240.00F other. Soc. Recher. Interdisciplinaire, Lab Anatomie Comp, 55 rue Buffon, 75005 Paris France. **Tel** 011 33 1 40793312, FAX 4073 34 84, telex MUSNAHN 202641F. **ED** J.D. Viene. **UDC** 636.08. **Bk Rev. Ad Acc. Pr Rev. Circ:** 350 (ctrl).
**Desc:** Interdisciplinary forum for papers concerning the history and evolution of the relationships between man and animals.

US/0892-7936
**ANTHROZOOS.** [Anthrozoos]. **Added/Corp** Delta Society. Vol. 1, No. 1 (Summer 1987)-. Periodical. English. Four times a year. $40.00 US; $50.00. Delta Society, 321 Burnett Avenue South, Suite 303, Renton WA 98055-2569. **Tel** (206)226-7357, FAX (206)235-1076. **ED** Andrew Rowan. **LC** QL85; .A57. **DD** 591. **[CCC].** Index available. cum. index. **Bk Rev. Ad Acc. Pr Rev. Circ:** 1,000. Documents available from The Genuine Article. ***Continues*** *Journal of the Delta Society, 8755-5883.*
**Desc:** Research results of studies on the effects of animals on human health and well being and the meaning of animals and the natural world in human life.
**Ind/Abst** AGRICOLA [Select. Cov.]; Curr. Contents Soc. Behav. Sci.; Ecol. Abstr.; Environ. Period. Bibliogr.; Fish Rev. (Jan. 1989-July 1992); Index Vet.; Linguist. Lang. Behav. Abstr.; Psychol. Abstr. (1987-); PsycINFO (1990-); PsycLit; Res. Alert [Full Cov.]; Soc. Plann. Policy Dev. Abstr.; Soc. Sci. Cit. Index [Full Cov.]; Sociol. Abstr.; Wildl. Rev. (Jan. 1989-July 1992).

GW
**ANTHUS.** Periodical. German. ir. 14.00. Kilda-Verlag, Munsterstrasse 71, W-4402 Greven Germany. **LC** QL671; .A55.

BE/0773-5251
**APEX (BRUSSELS).** (APEX / SOCIETE BELGE DE MALACOLOGIE.). [Apex]. **Added/Corp** Societe Belge de Malacologie. Vol. 1, No. 1 (1986)-. Periodical. English (French). Three times a year. 700F Belgium; 1100F other. Societe Belge de Malacologie, Av M Maeterlinck 56 Bte 8, B 1030 Brussels Belgium. **Tel** 011 32 2 3441547. **(Subscription address:** J Buyle, Avenue Marice Maeterlinck 56/Suite 8, B-1030 Bruxelles Belgium**)** **ED** R Duchamps. **CODEN** APEXAQ. **Ad Acc.** Documents available from BIOSIS Document Express. ***Continues*** *Informations (Societe Malacologie de Belgique), 0379-1904.*
**Ind/Abst** Biol. Abstr. (1986-).

RM/0378-2425
**APICULTURA IN ROMANIA.** ***Title Change.*** [Apic. Rom.]. **Added/Corp** Asociatia Crescatorilor de Albine din R.S. Romania. Asociatia Crescatorilor de Albine din Romania. Vol. 50, No. 12 (Dec. 1975)-(19??). Academic Scholarly Publication. Romanian (table of contents in English, French, German and Russian). mo. **(Subscription address:** Ilexim Press Department, PO Box 1, 136-1-137, Bucharest, Romania.**)** **CODEN** APRODX. Documents available from BIOSIS Document Express, CASDDS. ***Continues*** *Apicultura, 0518-1305.* ***Continued by*** *Romania Apicola.*
**Desc:** Review of science and practice in beekeeping.
**Ind/Abst** Biol. Abstr.; Chem. Abstr.

UK/0003-648X
**APICULTURAL ABSTRACTS.** **See** Zoology-Abstracting, Bibliographies and Statistics.

FR/0044-8435
**APIDOLOGIE.** [Apidologie]. **Added/Corp** Institut National de la Recherche Agronomique (France) Arbeitsgemeinschaft der Institute fuer Bienenforschung (Celle, Germany). Vol. 1, No. 1 (1970)-. Academic Scholarly Publication. French (German and English; summaries and/or abstracts in English and German). bm (1 volume). 1260.00F France; 1535.00F other. Editions Scientifique Elsevier, 141 rue de Javel, 75747 Paris Cedex 15 France. **Tel** 011 33 1 47 07 11 22, FAX 011 33 1 43 36 80 93. **(Subscription address:** Editions Scientifiques Elsevier / for North America, PO Box 7247-7576, Philadelphia PA 19170-7576.**)** **ED** G. Arnold, G. Koeniger, & W.S. Sheppard. **CODEN** APDGB5. **[CCC].** Index available. **Bk Rev. Pr Rev. Circ:** 800. available on microfilm and microfiche from University Microfilms International (UMI). Documents available from The Genuine Article, BIOSIS Document Express, CASDDS. ***Formed by the union of*** *Annales de l'Abeille* ***and*** *Zeitschrift fur Bienenforschung.*
**Desc:** Concerned with all subjects related to bees and beekeeping.
**Ind/Abst** Anim. Behav. Abstr.; Apic. Abstr.; Biol. Abstr.; Chem. Abstr.; Curr. Aware. Biol. Sci., CABS; Curr. Contents, Agric. Biol. Environ. Sci.; Ecol. Abstr.; Entomol. Abstr.; GeoRef; Hortic. Abstr.; Index Vet.; Life Sci. Collect.; Protozoolog. Abstr.; Res. Alert [Full Cov.]; Rev. Agric. Entomol.; Sci. Cit. Index; SCISEARCH.

IT/0392-2863
**AQUARIUM MILANO.** [AquariumMilano]. (1973)-. Periodical. Italian. mo (11 issues per year). L60000 Italy; L90000 other. Primaris, Via Prandina 33, 20128 Milan Italy. **Tel** 011 39 2 26300237. **UDC** 57/59. ***Continues*** *Acquari e Natura.*

UK/0167-5427
**AQUATIC MAMMALS.** [Aquat. mamm.]. **Added/Corp** Dolfinarium Harderwijk. Netherlands Foundation for Aquatic Mammal Research. European Association for Aquatic Mammals. Vol. 1 (Jan. 1972)-. Periodical. English (French and German). Three times a year. £95.00. Aquatic Mammals, c/o Paul Nachtigall, PO Box 1106, Kailua HI 96734. **Tel** (808)257-5256, FAX (808)257-5236. **ED** Paul Nachtigall. Index available. cum. index. **Bk Rev**, (Qty: 6). **Pr Rev. Circ:** 200.
**Desc:** Papers dealing with all aspects of the care, conservation, medicine, and science of aquatic mammals.
**Ind/Abst** Anim. Behav. Abstr.; Dairy Sci. Abstr.; Fish Rev.; Index Vet.; Key Word Index Wildl. Res.; Ocean. Abstr.; Life Sci. Collect.; Vet. Bull.; Zool. Rec.; Wildl. Rev.

FI/0570-5177
**AQUILO SER ZOOLOGICA.** [Aquilo. Ser. zool.]. **Added/Corp** Oulun Luonnoystavain Yhdistys. Vol. 1 (1963)-. Finnish (English and German). Societas Amicorum Naturae Oulensis, Oulun Luonnonystaevaein Yhdistys ry, c/o Department of Zoology, University of Oulu, Linnnanmaa Oula Finland. **Tel** 358 81 353133. **ED** Eino Erleinaro. **CODEN** AQZOA9. Index available. **Circ:** 200. Documents available from BIOSIS Document Express.
**Ind/Abst** ASTIS Curr. Aware. Bull. (1978-); Aquat. Sci. Fish. Abstr. (Computer File); ASTIS Bibliogr. (1978-); Biol. Abstr.; Fish Rev. (19??-199?); Key Word Index Wildl. Res.; Life Sci. Collect.; Wildl. Rev. (19??-199?).

FR/0763-1901
**ARACHNOLOGIA : BULLETIN D'INFORMATION ET DE LIAISON DU CENTRE INTERNATIONAL DE DOCUMENTATION ARACHNOLOGIQUE.** **Added/Corp** International Arachnologic Documentation Center. (1984)-. Bulletin. French (English). Twice a year (May, June). 40.00F. Cida Lab Zoologie Arthropode, 61 Rue De Buffon, Paris 75005 France. **Tel** 011 33 1 43322864. cum. index. **Ad Acc. Circ:** 600.

GW/0003-9284
**ARCHIV FUER MOLLUSKENKUNDE DER SENCKENBERGISCHE NATURFORSCHENDE GESELLSCHAFT.** (ARCHIV FUER MOLLUSKENKUNDE.). [Arch. Molluskenkd. Senckenberg. Naturforsch. Ges.]. **Added/Corp** Senckenbergische Naturforschende Gesellschaft. Vol. 52 (1920)-. Periodical. German (English, French and Spanish). Three times a year. DM85.00 (latest volume). Verlag Dr. Waldemar Kramer, Postfach 600445, D-60334 Frankfurt Germany. **Tel** 011 49 69 449045. **ED** R. Janssen. **CODEN** AMKUAQ. Index available (free). cum. index. **Circ:** 750 (ctrl). Documents available from BIOSIS Document Express. ***Continues*** *Nachrichtsblatt der Deutschen Malakozooligischen Gesellschaft.*
**Desc:** Scientific serial publication devoted mainly to the systematics and taxonomy of mollusks (both living and fossil).
**Ind/Abst** Aquat. Sci. Fish. Abstr. (Computer File); Biol. Abstr.; GeoRef; Life Sci. Collect.

GW/0003-9365
**ARCHIV FUER PROTISTENKUNDE.** [Arch. protistenkd.]. (1902)-. Periodical. German (English and French). Four times a year. DM1059.00 Germany; DM1068.00 other. Gustav Fischer Verlag Jena, Postfach 100537, D 07705 Jena Germany. **Tel** 011 49 3641 27332, FAX 011 49 3641 626500. **(Subscription address:** VCH Publishers Inc., 303 Northwest 12th Avenue, Journals Department, Deerfield FL 33442.**)** **ED** S Jost Casper. **LC** QL366; .A7. **NLM** W1 AR254. **CODEN** APRKAI. **[CCC].** Index available. **Bk Rev. Ad Acc. Pr Rev. Circ:** 480. Documents available from The Genuine Article, BIOSIS Document Express.
**Desc:** Reflects the development of protistology. The scope of protistology covered includes enclosed protozoology, protophytology (phycology including blue-green algae), and mycology. Preference is given to papers dealing with results in the fields of morphology, taxonomy, physiology, biochemistry, cytology, genetics, parasitology, toxicology, biogeography and ecology.
**Ind/Abst** Biocont. News Inf.; Biol. Abstr.; Curr. Aware. Biol. Sci., CABS; Curr. Contents, Agric. Biol. Environ. Sci.; Ecology Abstr.; EMBASE; GeoRef; Helminthol. Abstr.; Index Vet.; Maize Abstr.; Microbiol. Abstr. Sect. C; Life Sci. Collect.; Protozoolog. Abstr.; Res. Alert [Full Cov.]; Rev. Agric. Entomol.; Rev. Med. Vet. Entomol.; Sci. Cit. Index; SCISEARCH; Soils Fert.; Vet. Bull.

RM/1016-4855
**ARCHIVA ZOOTECHNICA.** [Arch. zootech.]. (1989)-. Periodical. English. an. **UDC** 636.08.
**Ind/Abst** Soyabean Abstr.

BL/0066-7870
**ARQUIVOS DE ZOOLOGIA.** [Arq. zool.]. **Added/Corp** Universidade de Sao Paulo. Museu de Zoologia. Vol. 15 (1967)-. Periodical. Portuguese (English). ir. $25.00. Universidade de Sao Paulo / Museu Zoologia, Museu de Zoologia, Caixa Post 7172, 01000 Sao Paulo SP Brazil. **Tel** 011 55 11 274-3455. **CODEN** ARQZA4. Index available. **Circ:** 684 (ctrl). Documents available from BIOSIS Document Express. ***Continues*** *Arquivos de Zoologia do Estado de Sao Paulo, 0066-7870.*
**Ind/Abst** Biol. Abstr.; Life Sci. Collect.

PO/0871-4843
**ARQUIVOS DO MUSEU BOCAGE. NOVA SERIE.** **See** Natural History.

US/0066-8036
**ARTHROPODS OF FLORIDA AND NEIGHBORING LAND AREAS.** **Added/Corp** Florida. Division of Plant Industry. Vol. 1 (1965)-. Monographic series. English. ir. Price varies per volume. Florida Department of Agriculture & Consumer Services, State Capitol, 10th Floor, Tallahassee FL 32399. **Tel** (904)488-6971, FAX (904)488-8087. **LC** QL434; .A75. **DD** 595/.2/09759.

**Desc:** Deals with arthropods of Florida and neighboring land areas. It is largely of interest to taxonomic entomologists.

US/1051-3825
**ASIATIC HERPETOLOGICAL RESEARCH.** [Asiat. herpetol. res.]. **Added/Corp** Asiatic Herpetological Research Society. Chung-Kuo Liang Chi Pa Hsing Tung Wu Hsueh Hui. Vol. 3 (1990)-Vol. 5 (1993)-. Periodical. English. an. $20.00 (individual); $40.00 (institution). CCSSAR Museum Vertebrate Zoolog, University of California, Berkeley CA 94720. **Tel** (510)642-3567. **LC** QL661.A1; A85. **DD** 597.6/095/05. **CODEN** AHEREO. ***Continues*** *Chinese Herpetological Research.*

FR/0769-6027
**ATOUT CHAT.** (1985)-. Periodical. French. mo. 160.00F France; 215.00F other. Atour Chat, BP 205, 78003 Versailles, Cedex France. **Tel** 3950 7216. **UDC** 636.8.

AT/0004-959X
**AUSTRALIAN JOURNAL OF ZOOLOGY.** [Aust. j. zool.]. **Added/Corp** Commonwealth Scientific and Industrial Research Organization (Australia) Australian National Research Council. Australian Academy of Science. Vol. 1 (Jan. 1953)-. Periodical. English. bm. 220.00Aus$ Australia & New Zealand; $220.00 other. CSIRO Publications, PO Box 89, 314 Albert Street, East Melborne Victoria 3002 Australia. **Tel** 011 61 3 4187333, 4187217, FAX 011 61 3 4190459, telex AA 30236. **ED** D. W. Morton. **LC** QL1; .A865. **DD** 591/.05. **NLM** W1 AU626. **CODEN** AJZOAS. **[CCC].** Index available. **Ad Acc. Pr Rev. Acid Free. Circ:** 1,400 (ctrl). available on microfilm from University Microfilms International (UMI). Documents available from The Genuine Article, BIOSIS Document Express, CASDDS, Documents on Demand.
**Desc:** Publishes original contributions to any branch of zoology, except the taxonomy of invertebrates.
**Ind/Abst** AGRICOLA [Select. Cov.]; Anim. Breed. Abstr.; Biocont. News Inf. (19??-19??); Biol. Abstr.; Chem. Abstr.; CSA Neuro. Abstr. (?-?); Curr. Aware. Biol. Sci., CABS; Curr. Contents, Agric. Biol. Environ. Sci.; Curr. Ref. Fish Res.; Dairy Sci. Abstr.; Ecol. Abstr.; Ecology Abstr.; Entomol. Abstr.; Environ. Abstr.; Fish Rev.; For. Prod. Abstr.; For. Abstr.; GeoRef; Helminthol. Abstr. (19??-19??); Hortic. Abstr.; Index Vet.; Nutr. Abstr. Rev., Ser. B, Live Feeds and Feed.; Nutr. Abstr. Rev., Ser. A, Hum. Exp.; Ocean. Abstr.; Life Sci. Collect.; Protozoolog. Abstr.; Res. Alert [Full Cov.]; Rev. Agric. Entomol.; Rev. Med. Vet. Entomol.; Sci. Cit. Index; SCISEARCH; Soils Fert.; Vet. Bull.; Weed Abstr.; Wildl. Rev.

AT/0310-0049
**AUSTRALIAN MAMMALOGY.** [Aust. mammal.]. **Added/Corp** Australian Mammal Society. Vol. 1 (Dec. 1972)-. Periodical. English. an. $35.00. Australian Mammal Society, GPO Box 2200, Canberra ACT 2601 Australia. **Tel** 011 61 6 2573299, FAX 011 61 08-317594. **(Subscription address:** CSIRO Wildlife and Ecology, PO Box 84, Lyneham Australian Capital Territory 2602 Australia**) ED** P. Copley. **CODEN** AUMACY. Index available. **Bk Rev. Pr Rev. Circ:** 700. Documents available from BIOSIS Document Express.
**Desc:** Research articles and notes on all aspects of Australasian mammals. A notes section provides opportunity for publication of observations about Australian mammals.
**Ind/Abst** Biol. Abstr.; GeoRef; Key Word Index Wildl. Res.; Wildl. Rev.

AT/0817-9573
**AUSTRALIAN PRIMATOLOGY.** [Aust. Primatol.]. **Added/Corp** stralian Primate Society. (1986)-. English. qt. 25.00Aus$. CSIRO / Australian Primate Society, Division Human Nutrition, Majors Road, Ohalloran Hill 5158 Australia. **Tel** 011 61 8 3980336. **(Subscription address:** Australian National University / Department of Psychology, GPO Box 4, Canberra ACT 2601 Australia.)

AT/0310-1304
**AUSTRALIAN SHELL NEWS.** [Aust. shell news]. **Added/Corp** Malacological Society of Australia. No. 14 (April 1976)-. Periodical. English. qt. 30.00Aus$. Malacological Society of Australia, Australian Museum, 6 8 College Street, Sydney South NSW 2000 Australia. **Tel** 011 61 3 6699880. **Bk Rev. Ad Acc. Pr Rev. Circ:** 400. ***Continues*** *Australian Newsletter.*
**Ind/Abst** Aquat. Sci. Fish. Abstr. (Computer File); Life Sci. Collect.

AT
**AUSTRALIAN ZOOLOGICAL REVIEWS.** **Added/Corp** Royal Zoological Society of New South Wales. No. 1 (1989)-. Periodical. English. ir. Royal Zoological Society of New South Wales, PO Box 20, Mosman, New South Wales 2088 Australia. **Tel** 011 61 2 9697336. **LC** QL51.2.A8; A9. **DD** 591.994/05.
**Ind/Abst** Fish Rev. (Jan. 1989-July 1992); Wildl. Rev. (Jan. 1989-July 1992).

AT/0067-2238
**AUSTRALIAN ZOOLOGIST, THE.** [Aust. zool.]. **Added/Corp** Royal Zoological Society of New South Wales. Royal Zoological Society of New South Wales. Proceedings. Vol. 1 (June 13, 1914)-. Periodical. English. Four times a year. 50.00Aus$ (includes Australian Zoological Reviews). Royal Zoological Society of New South Wales, PO Box 20, Mosman, New South Wales 2088 Australia. **Tel** 011 61 2 9697336. **LC** QL1; .A87. **DD** 591.994. **CODEN** AUZOA3. **Bk Rev. Ad Acc. Circ:** 1,500 (ctrl). Documents available from BIOSIS Document Express. ***Absorbed*** *Koolewong, 0310-9682.* ***Superseded in part by*** *Proceedings of the Royal Zoological Society of New South Wales.*
**Desc:** A magazine presenting a blend of scientific reports of interest to general zoologists and naturalists with news and feature articles.
**Ind/Abst** AGRICOLA; Biol. Abstr.; Ecol. Abstr.; Environ. Period. Bibliogr.; Fish Rev.; Geogr. Abstr. Phys. Geogr.; Geogr. Abstr. Human Geogr.; Geol. Abstr.; Life Sci. Collect.; Wildl. Rev.

FR/0150-939X
**AVICULTEUR, L'.** [Aviculteur]. (1962)-. Periodical. French. Eleven times a year. 428.99F France; 538.00F other. Editions du Boisbaudry, BP 6359, 35036 Rennes Cedex France. **Tel** 011 33 99 322121.
**Ind/Abst** AGRICOLA.

US/0408-1749
**BADGER BIRDER, THE.** **Added/Corp** Wisconsin Society for Ornithology. No. 1 (Sept. 1962)-. Periodical. English. Ten times a year. $4.00. Wisconsin Society for Ornithology Inc., W330 N8275 West Shore Drive, Hartland WI 53029. **Tel** (414)966-1072.

BG/0304-9027
**BANGLADESH JOURNAL OF ZOOLOGY.** [Bangladesh j. zool.]. **Added/Corp** Zoological Society of Bangladesh. Vol. 1 (Dec. 1973)-. Academic Scholarly Publication. English. sa. TK400.00 Bangladesh; $20.00 (per issue) other. Zoological Society of Bangladesh, c/o Department of Zoology, University of Dhaka, Dhaka 1000 Bangladesh. **Tel** 505505, FAX 880 2 865583. **ED** SMH Kabir. **LC** QL334.B34; B35. **DD** 591/.05. **CODEN** BJZOA5. Index available. **Circ:** 300. available in bound issues. Documents available from BIOSIS Document Express.
**Desc:** Presents research papers on zoology, applied zoology, entomology, fisheries, wildlife biology, parasitology and other branches of zoology.
**Ind/Abst** Biocont. News Inf. (19??-19??); Biodeter. Abstr. (19??-19??); Biol. Abstr.; Cot. Trop. Fibr. Abstr. Bibliogr.; Helminthol. Abstr. (1991-); Index Vet.; Nutr. Abstr. Rev., Ser. B, Live Feeds and Feed.; Life Sci. Collect.; Plant Breed. Abstr.; Postharvest News Inf.; Potato Abstr.; Protozoolog. Abstr.; Rev. Agric. Entomol.; Rice Abstr.; Seed Abstr.

NE/0005-6219
**BASTERIA.** [Basteria]. **Added/Corp** Nederlandse Malacologische Vereniging. Vol. 1 (Feb. 1936)-. Periodical. Dutch (English, German, French and Multiple languages). Six times a year. F82.50 Netherlands. Nederlandse Malacologische ver Watertoren 28, c/o Hon Hoeksema, 4366 KC Middelburg Netherlands. **Tel** 11 31 1180 16532. **ED** Dr. A.C. van Brussen. **LC** QL401; .B3. **DD** 594.05. **CODEN** BSTRAD. Index available in last issue of volume--attached. cum. index. **Bk Rev**, (Qty: 5). **Circ:** 600. Documents available from BIOSIS Document Express.
**Desc:** The science of malacology, dealing with shells and the mollusks.
**Ind/Abst** Biol. Abstr.; GeoRef.

US/0005-6227
**BAT RESEARCH NEWS.** [Bat res. news]. (Jan. 1964)-. Periodical. English. qt. $15.00. State University College at Potsdam, Department of Biology, Potsdam NY 13676. **Tel** (315)267-2259. **ED** G. Horst. **DD** 599. Index available. **Bk Rev. Ad Acc. Pr Rev.** ctrl circ. ***Continues*** *Bat Banding News.*
**Desc:** Issued primarily for biologists interested in bats.
**Ind/Abst** Fish Rev.; Wildl. Rev.

NE/0067-4745
**BEAUFORTIA.** [Beaufortia]. Vol. 1, No. 1 (March 1951)-. Periodical. English (French and German). an (the parts appear irregularly). Fl130.00. Zoological Museum Universitei, Plantage Middenlaan 53, Amsterdam Netherlands. **UDC** 59. **CODEN** BUFOAG. Index available. **Circ:** 650 (ctrl). Documents available from BIOSIS Document Express. ***Supersedes*** *Amsterdam Naturalist.*
**Desc:** A series of miscellaneous publications in the field of zoology.
**Ind/Abst** AQUAREF; Biol. Abstr.; GeoRef; Life Sci. Collect.

UK/0005-7703
**BEE CRAFT.** **Added/Corp** British Beekeepers' Association. Vol. 1 (1919)-. Periodical. English. Twelve times a year. £7.74 UK, £10.60 others (surface mail); £8.56 (airmail). Bee Craft, 15 Westway, South White Copthrn Bk, Crawley West Sussex RH103QS England. **Tel** 0342 712119. **ED** Robert C. Young and David A. Ribbans. Index available. **Bk Rev. Ad Acc. Circ:** 7,500.
**Desc:** Information for bee keepers, articles of general interest, advertisements and legislation.

UK/0005-772X
**BEE WORLD.** [Bee world]. **Added/Corp** International Bee Research Association. Bee Research Association. Apis Club. Vol. 1 (June 1919)-. Academic Scholarly Publication. English. qt. £35.00 UK; $65.00 other. International Bee Research Association, 18 North Road, Cardiff CF1 3DY United Kingdom. **Tel** 011 44 1 372409, FAX 011 44 1 665522, telex 23152. **ED** P. A. Munn. **CODEN** BEWOAN. cum. index. **Bk Rev. Ad Acc. Pr Rev. Circ:** 2,000. Documents available from The Genuine Article, CASDDS.
**Desc:** Provides the international beekeeping community with news and articles on recent developments in practical and scientific work.
**Ind/Abst** AGRICOLA [Full Cov.]; Agrofor. Abstr. (1991-); Chem. Abstr. (1919-1983); Curr. Aware. Biol. Sci., CABS; Curr. Contents, Agric. Biol. Environ. Sci.; Entomol. Abstr.; For. Abstr.; Life Sci. Collect.; Protozoolog. Abstr.; Res. Alert [Full Cov.]; Rev. Agric. Entomol.; Sci. Cit. Index; SCISEARCH.

US/0163-1047
**BEHAVIORAL AND NEURAL BIOLOGY.** ***Title Change.*** [Behav. neural biol.]. Vol. 25 (Jan. 1979)-(1994). Academic Scholarly Publication. English. bm. Academic Press, Inc., 6277 Sea Harbor Drive, Orlando FL 32887. **Tel** (800)543-9534, (407)345-4100, FAX (407)363-9661. **ED** James L. McGaugh and William T. Greenough. **LC** QL750; .B53. **DD** 591.5. **NLM** W1 BE129N. **CODEN** BNBIDY. **[CCC]. Pr Rev.** Documents available from The Genuine Article, BIOSIS Document Express, CASDDS. ***Continues*** *Behavioral Biology, 0091-6773.* ***Continued by*** *Neurobiology of Learning and Memory, 1074-7427.*
**Desc:** Publishes papers in all areas of neural-oriented behavioral research and in the areas of neural plasticity and the mechanisms of learning and memory. Contains theoretical research or review papers, research reports, brief reports, rapid communications, mini-reviews and commentaries.
**Ind/Abst** Anim. Breed. Abstr.; Biol. Agric. Index; Biol. Abstr.; Chem. Abstr.; Chemorecept. Abstr.; CSA Neuro. Abstr. (?-?); Curr. Aware. Biol. Sci., CABS; Curr. Contents Life Sci.; Curr. Ref. Fish Res.; Dairy Sci. Abstr.; EMBASE; Energy Res. Abstr. (April 1981-); Fish Rev.; Index Med. (1979-); Index Vet.; Nutr. Abstr. Rev., Ser. A, Hum. Exp.; Life Sci. Collect.; Psychol. Abstr. (1979-); PsycINFO; PsycLit; Ref. Upd. Deluxe Ed.; Res. Alert [Full Cov.]; Sci. Cit. Index; SCISEARCH; Soc. Sci. Cit. Index [Select. Cov.]; Vet. Bull.; Wildl. Rev.

US/0148-3781
**BEHAVIORAL PRIMATOLOGY.** ***Ceased.*** Vol. 1 (1977)-(1994). Periodical. English. ir. Lawrence Erlbaum Associates, 365 Broadway, Suite 102, Hillsdale NJ 07642. **Tel** (201)666-4110, (800)926-6579, FAX (201)666-2394. **LC** QL737.P9; B387. **DD** 599/.8/045. **NLM** W1 BE13P.

NE/0376-6357
**BEHAVIOURAL PROCESSES.** [Behav. processes]. Vol. 1 (July 1976)-. Academic Scholarly Publication. English (summaries and/or abstracts in French and German). Six times a year (2 volumes). Fl916.00. Elsevier Science Publishers BV, PO Box 211, 1000 AE Amsterdam Netherlands. **Tel** 011 31 20 5803642, FAX 011 31 20 5862696, telex 15682. **ED** G Thines and J E R Staddon. **LC** QL750; .B56. **DD** 591.5. **NLM** W1 BE135F. **CODEN** BPRODA. **[CCC].** available on microfilm and microfiche from University Microfilms International (UMI). Documents available from The Genuine Article, BIOSIS Document Express, CASDDS. ***Absorbed*** *Behaviour Analysis Letters, 0166-47794.*
**Desc:** Provides rapid publication of complete research papers which are relevant to the understanding of fundamental behavioural processes. The journal is interdisciplinary and deals with organisms ranging from single-celled bodies right through to primates, including man.
**Ind/Abst** Anim. Behav. Abstr.; Biol. Abstr.; Chem. Abstr (1976-1982); CSA Neuro. Abstr. (?-?); Curr. Contents, Agric. Biol. Environ. Sci.; Curr. Contents Life Sci.; Curr. Ref. Fish Res.; Dairy Sci. Abstr.; EMBASE; Entomol. Abstr.; Index Vet.; Key Word Index Wildl. Res.; Life Sci. Collect.; Pig News Inf.; Psychol. Abstr. (1976-); PsycINFO; PsycLit; Ref. Upd. Deluxe Ed.; Res. Alert [Full Cov.]; Rev. Med. Vet. Entomol.; Sci. Cit. Index; SCISEARCH; Soc. Sci. Cit. Index [Select. Cov.]; Vet. Bull.

CH/0254-671X
**BEILEI XUEHUI HUIZHI.** (PEI LEI HSUEH HUI HUI CHIH.). [Beilei xuehui huizhi]. **Main/Corp** Chung-Hua Min Kuo Pei Lei Hsueh Hui. **Added/Corp** Chung-hua Min Kuo Pei Lei Hsueh Hui. Bulletin of the Malacological Society of China. **VFOAT** Bulletin of the Malacological Society of China. (1974)-. Bulletin. Multiple languages (Chinese and English). $5.00. Malacological Society of China, c/o Taiwan Museum, No 2 Siang Yang Road, Taipei Taiwan. **Tel** (02)361-3963. **LC** QL401; .C45a.
**Ind/Abst** Life Sci. Collect.

BE/0777-6276
**BELGIAN JOURNAL OF ZOOLOGY.** [Belg. j. zool.]. Vol. 120 (June 1990)-. Periodical. English (French). sa. 1,500.00F. Soc Royale Zoologique Belgique, Rue Vautier 29, B1040 Brussels Belgium. **Tel** 011 32 2 6480475. **ED** W Veraes. **LC** QL401; .S6. **DD** 591/.05. Index available. cum. index. **Bk Rev. Ad Acc.** ctrl circ. Documents available from The Genuine Article,

BIOSIS Document Express. **Continues** *Annales de la Societe Royale Zoologique de Belgique, 0049-1136.* **Ind/Abst** Biol. Abstr.; Curr. Aware. Biol. Sci., CABS; Curr. Contents, Agric. Biol. Environ. Sci.; Ecol. Abstr.; Res. Alert [Full Cov.]; Rev. Agric. Entomol.; Sci. Cit. Index; SCISEARCH.

LH
**BERICHTE DER BOTANISCH-ZOOLOGISCHE GESELLSCHAFT.** **See** Biology-Botany.

BL/0067-6691
**BIBLIOGRAFIA BRASILEIRA DE ZOOLOGIA.** V. 1, (1955). Portuguese. ir. Instituto Brasileira de Informacao em Ciencia e Tecnologia, Ave General Justo 171-3, Rio de Janeiro Brazil. **Tel** 242-2915. **LC** WMLC L 83/479. **UDC** 59(01)(81).

II/0409-4093
**BIBLIOGRAPHY OF INDIAN ZOOLOGY.** Vol. 1/3; 1958/60-. Bibliography. English. an. Rs15.00. Indian Books & Periodicals Syndicate, B-5/62 Dev Nagar P L Road Karol Bagh, New Delhi 110005 India. **Tel** 660110/243. **LC** Z7993; .B5; QL309. **UDC** 59(01)(540).

AT/1033-2731
**BIENNIAL REPORT / DIVISION OF WILDLIFE AND ECOLOGY.** [Bienn. rep. - Div. Wildl. Ecol.]. **Main/Corp** Commonwealth Scientific and Industrial Research Organization (Australia). Division of Wildlife and Ecology. (1986/1988)-. English. be. CSIRO Publications, PO Box 89, 314 Albert Street, East Melborne Victoria 3002 Australia. **Tel** 011 61 3 4187333, 4187217, FAX 011 61 3 4190459, telex AA 30236. **LC** QL338; .C65a. **DD** 591.994. **Continues** *Report / Commonwealth Scientific and Industrial Research Organization (Australia), 1034-0599.*

NE/0067-8546
**BIJDRAGEN TOT DE DIERKUNDE.** [Bijdr. dierkd.]. **Added/Corp** Genootschap Natura Artis Magistra, te Amsterdam. Koninklijk Zoologisch Genootschap Natura Artis Magistra, te Amsterdam. Universiteit van Amsterdam. Commissie van Toezicht op het Beheer van de Artis-Bibliotheek. Universiteit van Amsterdam. Commissie voor de Artis-Bibliotheek. **VFOAT** Contributions to Zoology; Contributions to Zoology, Amsterdam. No. 1 (1848)-. Periodical. English (English, French and German). Four times a year. F225.00. SPB Academic Publishing, PO Box 97747, 2509 GC The Hague Netherlands. **Tel** 011 31 70 3280616, 011 31 70 3250616. **ED** J. H. Stock, B. M. Lensink and F. F. Pieters. **LC** QL1; .Z753. **CODEN** BJDIAD. Index available. **Bk Rev. Pr Rev. Circ:** 600. Documents available from The Genuine Article, BIOSIS Document Express.
**Desc:** Articles in the field of any branch of zoology. Preferred language is English but French and German are also permitted. Topics include ecology, ethology, morphology, physiology and taxonomy.
**Ind/Abst** Biol. Abstr.; Curr. Aware. Biol. Sci., CABS; Curr. Contents, Agric. Biol. Environ. Sci.; Ecol. Abstr. (?-?); Fish Rev.; GeoRef; Life Sci. Collect.; Protozoolog. Abstr.; Res. Alert [Full Cov.]; Sci. Cit. Index; SCISEARCH; Soc. Sci. Cit. Index [Select. Cov.]; Wildl. Rev.

UK/0952-4622
**BIOACOUSTICS (BERKHAMSTED).** (BIOACOUSTICS.). [Bioacoustics]. **Added/Corp** British Library. National Sound Archive. Vol. 1, No. 1 (1988)-. Periodical. English. Four times a year. $89.00. AB Academic Publishers, PO Box 42 Bicester, OXON OX6 7NW England. **Tel** 011 44 869 320949. **ED** Brian Lewis. **CODEN** BIOAE7. **Bk Rev. Ad Acc. Pr Rev.** Documents available from BIOSIS Document Express.
**Desc:** All aspects of wildlife sound recording and research.
**Ind/Abst** Biol. Abstr.; Ecol. Abstr.; Fish Rev.; Psychoanal. Abstr.; Psychol. Abstr. (1988-); PsycINFO; PsycScan: Appl. Exp. Eng. Psych.; PsycScan: LD/MR; PsycScan: Neuropsych.; Wildl. Rev.

US
**BIOLOGY OF THE REPTILIA.** English. ir. John Wiley & Sons, Inc., 605 Third Avenue, New York NY 10158-0012. **Tel** (212)850-6000, (212)850-6645, FAX (212)850-6088, telex 12-7063. **(Subscription address:** John Wiley & Sons / England, Baffins Lane, Chichester, West Sussex PO19 1UD England.**)**

US/0741-5699
**BIOSCIENCE RESEARCH REPORTS. RESEARCH NOTES IN ANIMAL BEHAVIOUR.** [Biosci. res. rep., Res. notes anim. behav.]. **VFOAT** Research Notes in Animal Behaviour. 1-. Monographic series. English. ir. Price varies per volume. Longman Group Ltd., Fourth Avenue, Longman House, Harlow Essex CM19 5SR England. **Tel** 011 44 279 429655, FAX 011 44 279 431059, telex 81259. **(Subscription address:** PO Box 1584, Birmingham, AL 35201**) DD** 591.5/05. **UDC** 591.5(047). **NLM** W1 BI91W.

US/0161-1836
**BIRDING.** [Birding]. **Added/Corp** American Birding Association. (Jan./Feb. 1969)-. Periodical. English. Six times a year. $36.00 (individual); $41.00 (institutions); $43.00 (family) Comes with American Birding Association membership. American Birding Association, PO Box 6599, Colorado Springs CO 80934-6599. **Tel** (719)634-7736. **ED** Paul Lehman (editor's address: PO Box 1273, Goleta, CA 93116, phone: (805)967-2450). **LC** QL677.5; .B483. **DD** 598.2/073. **CODEN** BIRDEV. Index available. **Bk Rev. Ad Acc. Adv Mgr:** Susanna Lawson, **Tel** (804)983-3021. **Circ:** 13,000 (ctrl).
**Desc:** Gives active field birders information on identifying and locating wild birds.
**Ind/Abst** AQUAREF; Wildl. Rev.

US/0162-0738
**BIRDING NEWS SURVEY.** Vol. 1 (Fall 1978)-. Periodical. English. qt. Avian Publications Inc, PO Box 310, Elizabethtown KY 42701.

US/0893-312X
**BISHOP MUSEUM BULLETIN IN ZOOLOGY.** [Bish. Mus. bull. zool.]. **Added/Corp** Bernice Pauahi Bishop Museum. **VFOAT** Bishop Museum Bulletins in Zoology. Vol. 1 (1988)-. Bulletin. English. ir. Price varies per volume. Bishop Museum Press, PO Box 19000-A, Honolulu HI 96817. **Tel** (808)847-3511. **DD** 591. **CODEN** BMBZEB. Documents available from BIOSIS Document Express. **Continues in part** *Bernice Pauahi Bishop Museum. Bernice P. Bishop Museum Bulletin, 0005-9439.*
**Ind/Abst** Biol. Abstr. (1988-).

BL/0101-3580
**BOLETIM DE ZOOLOGIA.** [Bol. zool.]. 1-. Bulletin. Portuguese (English). Free. Instituto de Biociencias, Departamento de Zoologia-USP, Caixa Postal 20 520, 01498 Sao Paulo Brasil. **Tel** 55 (011) 210 21 22 RAMAL. **ED** Walter Narchi. **LC** QL242; .B64. **UDC** 59. Index available. **Ad Acc. Circ:** 500 (ctrl). Documents available from BIOSIS Document Express. **Supersedes** *Boletim de Zoologia e Biologia Marinha.*
**Ind/Abst** Biol. Abstr.; Ecol. Abstr.; Life Sci. Collect.

BL/0080-312X
**BOLETIM DO MUSEU NACIONAL. NOVA SERIE, ZOOLOGIA.** [Bol. Mus. Nac., Nova ser., Zool.]. **Main/Corp** Brazil. Museu Nacional. **VFOAT** Zoologia. Began with: No. 1 (Jan. 30, 1942). Bulletin. Portuguese (summaries and/or abstracts in English, French and German). ir. Museu Nacional Boletin NS Zoo, Rio de Janeiro ZC-08 Brazil. **Tel** 264-8262. **(Subscription address:** Biblioteca, Museu Nacional - UFRJ, Av Gal Herculano Gomes, Horto Botanico, Quinta da Boa Vista, Sao Cristovao, 20941 Rio de Janeiro Brasil**) LC** QL1; .R562. **UDC** 59. **CODEN** BMJZAD. **Circ:** 1,000 (ctrl). Documents available from BIOSIS Document Express. **Continues in part** *Boletim do Museu Nacional.*
**Desc:** It contains works due to research developed by the researchers of the Museu Nacional.
**Ind/Abst** Biol. Abstr.; Life Sci. Collect.; Rev. Med. Vet. Entomol.

IT
**BOLLETTINO DEL LABORATORIO DI ENTOMOLOGIA AGRARIA FILIPPO SILVESTRI PORTICI.** **Main/Corp** Istituto Superiore Agrario. Laboratorio di Entomologia Agraria Filippo Silvestri. Vol. 9 (1949)-. Periodical. Italian. an. Universita degli Studi Istituto di Entomologia Agraria, 80055 Portici, Naples Italy. **CODEN** BLESAS. Documents available from BIOSIS Document Express. **Continues** *Bollettino del Laboratorio di Entomologia Agraria di Portici.*
**Ind/Abst** Biocont. News Inf. (19??-19??); Biol. Abstr.; Entomol. Abstr.; Life Sci. Collect.; Potato Abstr.

IT/0373-5176
**BOLLETTINO DELL'INSTITUTO DI ENTOMOLOGIA DELL'UNIVERSITA DEGLI STUDI DI BOLOGNA.** [Boll. Ist. entomol. Universita studi Bologna]. **Main/Corp** Universita di Bologna. Istituto di Entomologia. Vol. 8 (1935-36)-. Italian (English and German; summaries and/or abstracts in English and Italian). Tipografia Compositori, Viale XII Giugno 1, 40124 Bologna Italy. **CODEN** BIEUAD. **Continues** *Bollettino del Laboratorio di Entomologia del R. Istituto Superiore Agrario di Bologna.*
**Ind/Abst** Biocont. News Inf.; CSA Neuro. Abstr. (?-?); Dairy Sci. Abstr.; Ecology Abstr.; Life Sci. Collect. (?-1985); Potato Abstr.

IT/0373-4137
**BOLLETTINO DI ZOOLOGIA.** [Boll. zool.]. **Added/Corp** Unione Zoologica Italiana. Vol. 1 (Feb. 1930)-. Periodical. Italian. qt. L110000 (Italy); L120000 (other). Enrico Mucchi Editore SRL, Via Emilia Est 1527, 41100 Modena Italy. **Tel** 011 39 59 374094, FAX 059/374096. **LC** QL1; .B55. **DD** 590.5. **CODEN** BZOOAS. Index available. cum. index. **Bk Rev. Ad Acc. Pr Rev. Circ:** 1,500 (ctrl). Documents available from The Genuine Article, BIOSIS Document Express.
**Ind/Abst** Biocont. News Inf. (1991-); Biol. Abstr.; CSA Neuro. Abstr. (?-?); Curr. Contents, Agric. Biol. Environ. Sci.; Curr. Ref. Fish Res.; Ecology Abstr.; Entomol. Abstr.; GeoRef; Life Sci. Collect.; Res. Alert [Select. Cov.]; Rev. Agric. Entomol.; Rev. Med. Vet. Entomol.; SCISEARCH; Soils Fert.; Weed Abstr.

IT/0366-2403
**BOLLETTINO DI ZOOLOGIA AGRARIA E DI BACHICOLTURA.** **See** Agriculture.

IT/0394-7149
**BOLLETTINO MALACOLOGICO.** (BOLLETTINO MALACOLOGICO : PUBBLICAZIONE MENSILE EDITA DELLA UNIONE MALACOLOGICA ITALIANA.). [Boll. malacol.]. **Added/Corp** Unione Malacologica Italiana. Societa Italiana di Malacologia. (198?)-. Periodical. Italian (English and Spanish). Three times a year. L76000.00 (institutions), L55000.00 (individuals) Italy; L96000.00 (institutions), L61000.00 (individuals) other. Naturama, Societa Italiana di Malacologia, Cas Postale 28 Succ. 26, 90146 PALERMO 26 Italy. **Tel** 11 39 91 6713521. **LC** QL401; .B65. **DD** 594/.005. Index available. cum. index. **Bk Rev. Ad Acc. Pr Rev. Circ:** 1,000. **Continues** *Bollettino Malacologico della Unione Malacologica Italiana, 0394-7130.*
**Ind/Abst** Rev. Agric. Entomol.

GW/0006-7172
**BONNER ZOOLOGISCHE BEITRAGE.** (BONNER ZOOLOGISCHE BEITRAGE : HERAUSGEBER: ZOOLOGISCHES FORSCHUNGSINSTITUT UND MUSEUM ALEXANDER KOENIG, BONN.). [Bonn. zool. Beitr.]. **Added/Corp** Zoologisches Forschungsinstitut und Museum Alexander Koenig. Vol. 1 (1950)-. Periodical. German (English and Spanish; summaries and/or abstracts in French). qt. $33.85. Zoologisches Forschungsinstitut und Museum Alexander Koenig, Adenauerallee 150, D 53113 Bonn Germany. **Tel** 011 49 228 9122216. **ED** R. Hutterer. **LC** QL1; .B65. **CODEN** BZOBAN. Index available. **Bk Rev. Circ:** 500 (ctrl). Documents available from BIOSIS Document Express.
**Desc:** Scientific periodical for zoology. Coveres anatomy, animal geography, ecology, ethology, morphology and systematics. It mainly contains papers on vertebrates and insects.
**Ind/Abst** Biol. Abstr.; Fish Rev.; GeoRef; Key Word Index Wildl. Res.; Life Sci. Collect.; Wildl. Rev.

US/0006-9698
**BREVIORA.** [Breviora]. **Added/Corp** Harvard University. Museum of Comparative Zoology. No. 1 (Feb. 8, 1952)-. Monographic series. English. ir. Price varies per volume. Harvard University Museum of Comparative Zoology, 26 Oxford Street, Cambridge MA 02138. **Tel** (617)495-2466. **ED** K. J. Boss. **LC** QL1; .B74. **DD** 590/.5. **CODEN** BRVRAG. Index Available, published separately, free-automatically sent. cum. index. **Circ:** 900 (ctrl). Documents available from BIOSIS Document Express.
**Desc:** Covers systematics and evolution.
**Ind/Abst** Biol. Abstr.; GeoRef; Life Sci. Collect.

US/0193-4406
**BRIMLEYANA.** [Brimleyana]. **Added/Corp** North Carolina State Museum of Natural History. No. 1 March (1979)-. English. ir. $15.00 (individuals) $20.00 (institutions) US; $20.00 (individuals), $25.00 (institutions) other. North Carolina State Museum of Natural Sciences, PO Box 27647, Raleigh NC 27611. **Tel** (919)733-7450. **ED** Frank J Radovsky. **LC** QL155; .B75. **DD** 591.975/05. **CODEN** BRIMD7. Index available. **Pr Rev. Circ:** 300. Documents available from The Genuine Article, BIOSIS Document Express.
**Desc:** Systematics, ecology, zoogeography, evolution, behavior and paleozoology of vertebrate and invertebrate animals of the Southeast.
**Ind/Abst** Biol. Abstr.; Biol. Dig.; Curr. Aware. Biol. Sci., CABS; Curr. Contents, Agric. Biol. Environ. Sci.; Ecol. Abstr. (?-?); Fish Rev.; Helminthol. Abstr. (1991-); Res. Alert [Select. Cov.]; Rev. Med. Vet. Entomol.; SCISEARCH; Wildl. Rev.

UK/0007-0327
**BRITISH BEE JOURNAL.** [Br. bee j.]. V. 80- (Whole No. 3652- ); July 5, 1952-. Periodical. English. mo. £7.45 UK; £9.40 other. British Bee Publishing Ltd, 46 Queen Street Geddington, Kettering Northamptonshire NN14 1AZ England. **Tel** (0536)742250. **ED** C C Tonsley. **UDC** 638.1(410). **Bk Rev. Ad Acc. Circ:** 3,500. **Continues** *British Bee Journal & Bee-Keepers Advisor.*

UK
**BRITISH HERPETOLOGICAL SOCIETY BULLETIN, THE.** No. 1 (June 1980)-. Bulletin. English. British Herpetological Society / Zoology Society of London, Regents Park, London WC1 4RY England. **Continues** *British Herpetological Society Newsletter.*

UK/0952-7583
**BRITISH JOURNAL OF ENTOMOLOGY AND NATURAL HISTORY.** **See** Natural History.

US/8756-3479
**BROOKFIELD ZOO BISON.** [Brookfield Zoo bison]. **Added/Corp** Brookfield Zoo (Ill.) Chicago Zoological Society (Ill.). **VFOAT** Bison. Vol. 1, No. 1 (Nov./Dec. 1983)-. Periodical. English. ir. $7.50 (zoo members), $10.00 others. Chicago Zoological Society, c/o Library, Brookfield Zoo, Brookfield IL 60513. **Tel** (312)485-0263. **ED** Karin Nelson. **DD** 590. **Circ:** 30,000 (ctrl). **Continues** *Brookfield Bison.*
**Desc:** A membership magazine for the Chicago Zoological Society (Brookfield Zoo) covering animals,

exhibits, and events at Brookfield Zoo, and research around the world supported by the Society.
**Ind/Abst** Biol. Dig.

CN/1184-2709
**BROWSE (WEST HILL. 1991).** (BROWSE : METRO TORONTO ZOO NEWSLETTER.). [Browse]. **Added/Corp** Metropolitan Toronto Zoo. **VFOAT** Metro Toronto Zoo Newsletter; New Browse. (Jan. 1991)-. Newsletter. English. mo. Metropolitan Toronto Zoo, PO Box 280, West Hill Ontario M1E 4R5 Canada. **DD** 590/.74/471354105. ***Continues*** *The New Browse., 0834-2903.*

TH/0125-6726
**BUFFALO BULLETIN.** [Buffalo Bull.]. (1982)-. Periodical. English. mo. **DD** 636.293.
**Ind/Abst** Index Vet.; Vet. Bull.

AA/0259-2843
**BULETINI I SHKENCAVE ZOOTEKNIKE E VETERINARE.** [Bul. shk. zootek. vet.]. (1983)-. Periodical. Albanian.
**Ind/Abst** Index Vet.; Pig News Inf.; Postharvest News Inf.; Protozoolog. Abstr.; Rev. Med. Vet. Entomol.; Weed Abstr.; Wheat Barley Trit. Abstr.; World Agric. Econ.

BE/0374-6038
**BULLETIN & I.E. ET ANNALES DE LA SOCIETE ROYALE BELGE D'ENTOMOLOGIE. Main/Corp** Societe Royale Belge d'Entomologie. **VFOAT** Bulletin et Annales de la Societe Royale Belge d'Entomologie. Vol. 108; June 30 (1972)-. Bulletin. Dutch (French). qt. 1400F. Societe Royale Belge D'Entomologie, rue Vautier 31, 1040 Bruxelles Belgium. **LC** QL461; .S4. **DD** 595.7/005. **CODEN** BASEBE. Index available. cum. index. **Bk Rev. Ad Acc.** Documents available from BIOSIS Document Express. ***Continues*** *Bulletin & I.E. et Annales de la Societe Royale d'Entomologie de Belgique.*
**Ind/Abst** Biocont. News Inf.; Biol. Abstr.; Entomol. Abstr.; Fish Rev. (19??-199?); Life Sci. Collect.; Rev. Agric. Entomol.; Zool. Rec.; Wildl. Rev. (19??-199?).

FR/0521-6761
**BULLETIN APICOLE DE DOCUMENTATION SCIENTIFIQUE ET TECHNIQUE ET D'INFORMATION.** **Added/Corp** Laboratoire de Recherches Apicoles. (19??)-. Bulletin. French. **DD** 638.

UK/0524-4994
**BULLETIN / BRITISH ARACHNOLOGICAL SOCIETY.** [Bull. - Br. Arachnol. Soc.]. **Added/Corp** British Arachnological Society. **VFOAT** Bulletin of the British Arachnological Society. Vol. 1, (Jan. 1969)-. Periodical. English. Three times a year (Mar., July, Nov.). £20.00 UK, £24.00 others; £65.00 others. British Arachnological Society, 71 Havant Road, London E17 3JE England. **Tel** 011 44 81 5212952. **ED** Dr. Merrett. **LC** QL451; .B75. **DD** 595/.4/05. Index available (published separately). **Pr Rev. Circ:** 700. ***Continues*** *Bulletin of the British Spider Study Group.*
**Desc:** Papers, reviews and notes concerned with the study of arachnology.
**Ind/Abst** AGRICOLA [Full Cov.]; Entomol. Abstr.; Life Sci. Collect.

CN/0319-6674
**BULLETIN - CANADIAN SOCIETY OF ZOOLOGISTS. Main/Corp** Canadian Society of Zoologists. (1974)-. Periodical. English (French). qt. comes with Canadian Society of Zoologists Membership. Editor CSZ Bulletin, MN or HP Arai, Department of Biological Sciences, University of Calgary, 2500 University Drive NW, Calgary Alberta T2N 1N4 Canada. **Tel** (514)457-2000. **ED** Mary N. Arai, Hisao P. Arai, and Jean Marc Renaud. **Bk Rev. Ad Acc. Circ:** 1,000 (ctrl). ***Continues*** *Canadian Society of Zoologists. Newsletter, 0319-6666.*
**Desc:** Activities of the Society, articles on institutions, policies and topical issues in Canadian zoology.

FR/0037-962X
**BULLETIN DE LA SOCIETE ZOOLOGIQUE DE FRANCE.** [Bull. soc. zool. Fr.]. **Main/Corp** Societe Zoologique de France. **Added/Corp** Societe Zoologique de France. Vol. 1 (1876)-. Academic Scholarly Publication. French (summaries and/or abstracts in English). Four times a year. 490.00F. Societe Zoologique de France, 195 rue Saint-Jacques, 75005 Paris France. **Tel** 011 33 1 43256310. **ED** Jean Lonj d'Hondt. **LC** QL1; .S852. **CODEN** BZOFAZ. cum. index. **Bk Rev. Pr Rev.** Documents available from The Genuine Article, BIOSIS Document Express, CASDDS.
**Ind/Abst** Biol. Abstr.; Chem. Abstr.; Curr. Ref. Fish Res.; Dairy Sci. Abstr.; EMBASE; Fish Rev.; GeoRef; Helminthol. Abstr. (1991-); Life Sci. Collect.; Poult. Abstr.; Protozoolog. Abstr.; Res. Alert [Full Cov.]; Rev. Agric. Entomol.; Rev. Med. Vet. Entomol.; Sci. Cit. Index; SCISEARCH; Wildl. Rev.

BD
**BULLETIN D'INFORMATION IRAZ / INSTITUT DE RECHERCHE AGRONOMIQUE ET ZOOTECHNIQUE.** **See** Agriculture.

FR/0181-0626
**BULLETIN DU MUSEUM NATIONAL D'HISTOIRE NATURELLE. SECTION A : ZOOLOGIE, BIOLOGIE ET ECOLOGIE ANIMALES.** [Bull. mus. natl. hist. nat., Sect. A: zool., biol. ecol. anim.]. **Added/Corp** Museum National d'Histoire Naturelle (France). **VFOAT** Zoologie, Biologie et Ecologie Animales. Vol. 1 (March 1979)-. Periodical. French (summaries and/or abstracts in English and French). Four times a year. 800.00F. Editions du Museum, 57 rue Cuvier, 75005 Paris Cedex 05 France. **Tel** 011 33 1 40793700. **LC** QL1; .B746. **CODEN** BMNADT. Index Available, published separately, free-automatically sent. Documents available from BIOSIS Document Express. ***Continues*** *Bulletin du Museum National d'Histoire Naturelle. Zoologie;* ***Absorbed in part*** *Bulletin du Museum National d'Histoire Naturelle. Ecologie Gener.*
**Ind/Abst** Aquat. Sci. Fish. Abstr. (Computer File); Biol. Abstr.; Ecol. Abstr.; Fish Rev. (Jan. 1989-July 1992); GeoRef; Helminthol. Abstr. (1991-); Life Sci. Collect.; Rev. Agric. Entomol.; Wildl. Rev. (Jan. 1989-July 1992).

CN/0071-0741
**BULLETIN - ENTOMOLOGICAL SOCIETY OF CANADA.** [Bull. - Entomol. Soc. Can.]. **Main/Corp** Entomological Society of Canada (1951-). Vol. 1, (March 1969)-. Bulletin. English (French). Entomological Society of Canada, 393 Winston Avenue, Ottawa Ontario K2A 1Y8 Canada. **Tel** (613)725-2619, FAX (613)725-9349. **ED** R. B. Aiken. **LC** QL461; .E567. **DD** 595.7/0062/71. **NLM** W1 BU651U. **Bk Rev. Ad Acc. Circ:** 1,800 (ctrl).
**Ind/Abst** Biocont. News Inf.; Hortic. Abstr.; Maize Abstr.; Life Sci. Collect.; Plant Breed. Abstr.; Rev. Agric. Entomol.

NZ/0110-4527
**BULLETIN - ENTOMOLOGICAL SOCIETY OF NEW ZEALAND.** [Bull. - Entomol. Soc. N.Z.]. **Main/Corp** Entomological Society of New Zealand. **Added/Corp** Entomological Society of New Zealand. **VFOAT** Bulletin of the Entomological Society of New Zealand. (1972)-. Monographic series. English. ir. Price varies per volume. Entomological Society of New Zealand, Private Bag 92169, Auckland New Zealand. **Tel** 011 64 9 8493660, FAX 011 64 9 8463330. **ED** A. C. G. Heath. **LC** UNC. **CODEN** BESZD5. **Ad Acc. Circ:** 700. Documents available from BIOSIS Document Express.
**Desc:** Comprises occasional publications on the Entomology of New Zealand, the offshore sub-antarctic islands.
**Ind/Abst** Biol. Abstr.; Rev. Med. Vet. Entomol.

BE/0303-9129
**BULLETIN - INSTITUT ROYAL DES SCIENCES NATURELLES DE BELGIQUE. ENTOMOLOGIE.** [Bull. - Inst. r. sci. nat. Belg., Entomol.]. **Main/Corp** Institut Royal des Sciences Naturelles de Belgique. **Added/Corp** Institut Royal des Sciences Naturelles de Belgique. **VFOAT** Bulletin. Entomologie; Entomologie. Vol. 48 (1972)-. Monographic series. French (English). an. 40.00F. Institut Royal des Sciences Naturelles de Belgique, rue Vautier 29, 1040 Brussels Belgium. **Tel** 011 32 2 6482123, FAX 011 32 2 6464433. **LC** QL461; .B84. **DD** 595.7. **CODEN** BIETBB. **Circ:** 750. Documents available from BIOSIS Document Express. ***Continues in part*** *Bulletin - Institut Royal des Sciences Naturelles de Belgique.*
**Desc:** Scientific papers on entomology and arachnology, ecology and systematics.
**Ind/Abst** Biol. Abstr.; GeoRef; Rev. Agric. Entomol.; Rev. Med. Vet. Entomol.

●US/1061-3781
**BULLETIN OF AMERICAN ODONATOLOGY.** (BULLETIN OF AMERICAN ODONA[T]OLOGY: JOURNAL OF THE DRAGONFLY SOCIETY OF AMERICA.). [Bull. Am. odonatol.]. **Added/Corp** Dragonfly Society of America. **VFOAT** Bulletin of American Odonatology. Vol. 1, No. 1 (Mar. 1992)-. Bulletin. English. qt. $15.00 (members), $18.75 (non-members). DSA, 469 Crailhope Road, Center KY 42214. **DD** 595.

II/0970-0765
**BULLETIN OF PURE & APPLIED SCIENCES. SECTION A, ANIMAL SCIENCE.** [Bull. pure appl. sci., A Animal sci.]. **VFOAT** Bulletin of Pure and Applied Sciences. Animal Science. Vol. 2, No. 1 & 2 (1983)-. Academic Scholarly Publication. English. an. $24.00. Dr Ajay Kumar Sharma, PO Box 38, Modinagar 201204 India. **(Subscription address:** Prints India, 11 Darya Ganj, New Delhi 110002 India.**) ED** A K Sharma. **LC** QL1; .B94. **DD** 590/.5. **CODEN** BPAAEK. **Bk Rev. Ad Acc. Circ:** 50 (ctrl). available on microfiche; available on microfilm. Documents available from CASDDS. ***Continues in part*** *Bulletin of Pure & Applied Sciences.*
**Ind/Abst** Chem. Abstr. (1983-).

US/0097-3211
**BULLETIN OF THE ALLYN MUSEUM.** **See** Museums and Galleries.

UK/0007-1498
**BULLETIN OF THE BRITISH MUSEUM (NATURAL HISTORY). ZOOLOGY SERIES.** ***Title Change.*** **Added/Corp** British Museum (Natural History). **VFOAT** Zoology Series; Bulletin of the British Museum (Natural History). Miscellanea; Miscellanea; Bulletin British Museum (Natural History). Zoology Series. Vol. 32, No. 1 (1977)-Vol. 58, No. 2 (Nov. 26, 1992). Periodical. English. ir. Intercept Ltd., PO Box 716, Andover Hampshire SP10 1YG England. **Tel** 011 44 264 334748, FAX 011 44 264 334058, telex 41103 PEPSOS G. **LC** QL1; .B75. **DD** 591. ***Continues*** *Bulletin of the British Museum (Natural History). Zoology.* ***Continued by*** *Bulletin of the Natural History Museum. Zoology Series, 0968-0470.*
**Ind/Abst** Fish Rev.; Helminthol. Abstr.; Life Sci. Collect.; Wildl. Rev.

UA/0081-0991
**BULLETIN OF THE ENTOMOLOGICAL SOCIETY OF EGYPT. ECONOMIC SERIES.** [Bull. Entomol. Soc. Egypt., Econ. ser.]. **Main/Corp** Jamiyah Al-Misriyah Li-Ilm Al-Hasharat. Academic Scholarly Publication. English. an. $5.65. Entomological Society of Egypt, PO Box 430, Cairo Egypt. **UDC** 595.7(620). **CODEN** BEGEBG. Documents available from BIOSIS Document Express, CASDDS.
**Ind/Abst** Biol. Abstr.; Chem. Abstr.; Soyabean Abstr.

US/0363-2172
**BULLETIN OF THE GEORGIA HERPETOLOGICAL SOCIETY. Main/Corp** Georgia Herpetological Society. Vol. 2, No. 2 (June 1976)-. Bulletin. English. $8.00. John C Zegel, 5341 Smoke Rise Drive, Stone Mountain GA 30083. **LC** QL640; .S6813. **DD** 598.1/05. **UDC** 598.1(758). ***Continues*** *Bulletin of the Southeastern Herpetological Society.*

US/0025-4231
**BULLETIN OF THE MARYLAND HERPETOLOGICAL SOCIETY.** [Bull. Md. Herpetol. Soc.]. **Main/Corp** Maryland Herpetological Society. **VFOAT** Bulletin of the MDHS. Vol. 1 (Nov. 1965)-. Bulletin. English. qt (Mar., June, Sept., Dec.). $20.00 US; $30.00 other. Natural Historical Society of Maryland, 2643 North Charles Street, Baltimore MD 21218. **Tel** (410)235-6116. **ED** Herbert S. Harris, Jr. (editor's telephone: (410)969-1431). **LC** QL653.M3; M35a. **CODEN** MHSBB5. Index available. **Bk Rev**, (Qty: 1-6). **Ad Acc. Circ:** 500. Documents available from BIOSIS Document Express.
**Desc:** Original articles on biology, taxonomy, distribution, etc., of amphibians and reptiles.
**Ind/Abst** Biol. Abstr.; Fish Rev.; Zool. Rec.; Wildl. Rev.

US/0027-4100
**BULLETIN OF THE MUSEUM OF COMPARATIVE ZOOLOGY.** [Bull. Mus. Comp. Zool.]. April 1863-. Bulletin. English. ir. Price varies per volume. Harvard University Museum of Comparative Zoology, 26 Oxford Street, Cambridge MA 02138. **Tel** (617)495-2466. **ED** K J Boss. **LC** QL1; .H3. **DD** 590. **UDC** 59. **CODEN** MCZBA4. Index available. cum. index. Documents available from BIOSIS Document Express.
**Ind/Abst** Biol. Abstr.; Fish Rev.; GeoRef; Life Sci. Collect.; Wildl. Rev.

JA/0385-2423
**BULLETIN OF THE NATIONAL SCIENCE MUSEUM. SERIES A, ZOOLOGY.** **Added/Corp** Kokuritsu Kagaku Hakubutsukan (Japan). **VFOAT** Zoology. Vol. 1 (March 1975)-. Bulletin. English. National Science Museum, Ueno Park, Tokyo 110 Japan. **LC** QL325; .B84. **DD** 591/.05. Documents available from BIOSIS Document Express.
**Ind/Abst** AGRICOLA [Select. Cov.]; Biol. Abstr.; Entomol. Abstr.; Helminthol. Abstr.

●UK/0968-0470
**BULLETIN OF THE NATURAL HISTORY MUSEUM. ZOOLOGY SERIES. Added/Corp** British Museum (Natural History). **VFOAT** Zoology Series; Bulletin of the National History Museum Zoology. Vol. 59, No. 1 (June 24, 1993)-. Periodical. English. Twice a year. £78.75. Intercept Ltd., PO Box 716, Andover Hampshire SP10 1YG England. **Tel** 011 44 264 334748, FAX 011 44 264 334058, telex 41103 PEPSOS G. **LC** QL1; .B75. **DD** 591. ***Continues*** *Bulletin of the British Museum (Natural History). Zoology Series, 0007-1498.*

US/0553-9587
**BULLETIN OF THE PHILADELPHIA HERPETOLOGICAL SOCIETY.** ***Suspended.*** [Bull. Phila. Herpetol. Soc.]. Vol. 1- 1953-?. Bulletin. English. an. $6.00. Philadelphia Herpetological Society, 2103 Solly Avenue, Philadelphia PA 19152. **Tel** (215)353-1223. **ED** Robert C Feuer. **LC** QL640; .P5. **DD**

597.6/05. **UDC** 598.1. **Bk Rev. Ad Acc. Circ:** 300. ***Continues** Philadelphia Herpetological Society Bulletin, 0884-0113.*
**Desc:** Concerns any phase of herpetology (amphibians and reptiles).

II/0255-9587
**BULLETIN OF THE ZOOLOGICAL SURVEY OF INDIA.** [Bull. Zool. Surv. India]. **Main/Corp** Zoological Survey of India. V. 1- 1978-. Bulletin. English. $10.00. Controller of Publications / Civil Lines, Government of India, Civil Lines, New Delhi 110054 India. **Tel** 3015984, telex 3166415. **LC** QL309; I58B. **DD** 591/.05. **UDC** 59(540).
**Ind/Abst** Trop. Dis. Bull.

UK/0007-5167
**BULLETIN OF ZOOLOGICAL NOMENCLATURE, THE.** [Bull. zool. nomencl.]. **Main/Corp** International Commission on Zoological Nomenclature. Vol. 1 (May 1943)-. Bulletin. English (French). qt. £85.00 or $165.00. International Trust for Zoological Nomenclature, Cromwell Road, British Museum of Natural History, London SW7 5BD England. **Tel** 11 44 71 9389387. **ED** P K Tubbs. **NLM** W1 BU899K. **CODEN** BZONAP. Index available. **Circ:** 380 (ctrl). Documents available from BIOSIS Document Express. ***Absorbed** Opinions and Declarations Rendered by the International Commission on Zoological Nomenclature.*
**Desc:** Contains applications to the international commission in zoological nomenclature on particular problems in nomenclature, and comments on them by zoologists. Also contains the commission's rulings on these problems.
**Ind/Abst** AGRICOLA; Biol. Abstr.; Fish Rev.; Life Sci. Collect.; Wildl. Rev.

CN
**BULLETIN - OFFICE DES RECHERCHES SUR LES PECHERIES DU CANADA.** **Main/Corp** Canada. Office des Recherches sur les Pecheries. Bulletin. French (English). Price varies per volume. Technical Services BR Environment Canada, Ottawa Ontario K1A 0H3 Canada. **DD** 591. **UDC** 639.2(71). ***Continues** Bulletin - Office de Biologie.*

FR/0181-0006
**BULLETIN SIGNALETIQUE. 364, PROTOZOAIRES ET INVERTEBRES, ZOOLOGIE GENERALE ET APPLIQUEE.** **Added/Corp** Centre National de la Recherche Scientifique (France). Centre de Documentation. Institut National de la Recherche Agronomique (France). Service de Documentation. **VFOAT** Protozoaires et Invertebres, Zoologie Generale et Appliquee. Vol. 40 (1979)-. Bulletin. French. mo. Centre National de la Recherche Scientifique, Informascience, 26 rue Boyer, 75971 Paris France. **Tel** 61.41.11.05, telex CNRSDOC 220880 F. **LC** Z7993; .B84; QL1. **DD** 016.592. **NLM** ZQ 1 B936. ***Continues in part** Bulletin Signaletique. 360, Biologie Animale, Physiologie et Pathologie des Invertebres, Ecologie.*

FR
**BULLETIN SIGNALETIQUE SCIENCES AGRONOMIQUES ZOOLOGIE DES INVERTEBRES SECTION 980.** Bulletin. French. ir. 1345.97F France; 1490.00F other. CNRS / Institut d'Information Scientifique et Technique, (Centre National de la Recherche Scientifique), 15 Quai Anatole France, Paris 75700 France. **Tel** 011 33 1 47531515, telex 299 356 F. **(Subscription address:** Institut de l'Information Science et Technique Diffusion, 2 Alee du Parc de Brabois, 54514 Vandoeuvre Nancy France**)**

FR/1164-5431
**BULLETIN SIGNALETIQUE UCD DE JOUY-EN-JOSAS.** **VFOAT** Bulletin Signaletique - INRA-CRJ, UCD de Jouy-en-Josas; Bulletin Signaletique Unite Centrale de Documentation de Jouy-en-Josas. (1991)-. Periodical. French. wk. Inst Natl Rech Agronomique, Domaine Vilvert, 18350 Jouy en Josas France. **Tel** 011 33 1 34652453. **UDC** 011/016. **CODEN** 663/664(44). ***Continues** Bulletin Signaletique des Productions Animales, 0242-1968.*

FR/0335-3710
**BULLETIN TECHNIQUE APICOLE.** [Bull. tech. apic.]. Vol. 1 (1974)-. Academic Scholarly Publication. French. qt. **CODEN** BTAPDO. Documents available from CASDDS. ***Supersedes** Bulletin Technique Apicole A.N.D.I.A., 0335-3729.*
**Ind/Abst** Chem. Abstr. (1974-1981).

NE/0165-9464
**BULLETIN ZOOLOGISCH MUSEUM, UNIVERSITEIT VAN AMSTERDAM.** [Bull. - Zool. Mus., Univ. Amst.]. **Added/Corp** Universiteit van Amsterdam. Zoologisch Museum. Vol. 1, No. 1 (Aug. 31, 1966)-. Monographic series. English. ir. Price varies per volume. Bibliotheek Institute Tax Zoologisch, Plantage Middenlaan 53, 1018 DK Amsterdam Netherlands. **LC** QL1; .A46. **CODEN** BZMAAA. Documents available from BIOSIS Document Express.
**Ind/Abst** Biol. Abstr.; GeoRef; Life Sci. Collect.

AU/1018-6107
**BURGENLANDISCHE HEIMATBLATTER.** (19??)-. Periodical. German. qt. **UDC** 59.
**Ind/Abst** Am. Hist. Life (1963-1986).

GW
**BUTTERFLIES OF EUROPE.** Monographic series. English. ir (intervals of 18 months to 24 months). DM248.00. Aula Verlag GmbH, Luisenplatz 2, D 65185 Wiesbaden Germany. **Tel** 011 49 611 373060. **ED** Otakar Kudrna.
**Desc:** Deals in 8 volumes with systematics, taxonomy, distribution and biology of all European butterflies.

BE/0770-3767
**CAHIER D'ETHOLOGIE APPLIQUEE.** [Cah. ethol. appl.]. (1981)-. Periodical. French. Four times a year. 2500F (Belgium); 2750F (other). Institut de Zoologie, Univ Liege Quai Van Beneden 22, B-4020 Liege Belgium. **Tel** 011 32 41 665081. **UDC** 591.5.
**Ind/Abst** Anim. Behav. Abstr.

SW/0346-9395
**CALIDRIS.** [Calidris]. (1972)-. Periodical. Swedish. qt. **UDC** 598.2.08.
**Ind/Abst** Ecol. Abstr.; Geogr. Abstr. Phys. Geogr.

CN/0008-4301
**CANADIAN JOURNAL OF ZOOLOGY.** [Can. j. zool.]. **Added/Corp** National Research Council of Canada. **VFOAT** Journal Canadien de Zoologie. Vol. 29, No. 1 (Feb. 1951)-. Academic Scholarly Publication. English (French). mo. 449.00Can$ (institutions), 166.00Can$ (individuals) Canada; $449.00 (institutions), $175.00 (individuals) other. National Research Council of Canada, Receiver General for Canada, Ottawa Ontario K1A 0R6 Canada. **Tel** (613)993-0362, FAX (613)952-7656. **ED** J. G. Eales. **LC** QL1; .N1532. **DD** 590.5. **NLM** W1 CA624. **CODEN** CJZOAG. **[CCC]**. Index available. **Ad Acc. Pr Rev. Circ:** 1,700. available on microfilm and microfiche from University Microfilms International (UMI). Documents available from The Genuine Article, BIOSIS Document Express, CASDDS, Documents on Demand. ***Continues** Canadian Journal of Research. Section D, Zoological Sciences.*
**Desc:** Papers are published in the fields of animal ecology, biochemistry and physiology, developmental biology, genetics, parasitology, systematics and evolution, animal behaviour, and morphology.
**Ind/Abst** Abstr. Bull. Inst. Pap. Sci. Tech.; AGRICOLA [Select. Cov.]; Anim. Behav. Abstr.; Aquat. Sci. Fish. Abstr. (Computer File); Biocont. News Inf. (19??-19??); Biol. Agric. Index; Biol. Abstr.; Chem. Abstr.; CSA Neuro. Abstr.; Curr. Contents, Agric. Biol. Environ. Sci.; Curr. Ref. Fish Res.; Dairy Sci. Abstr.; Ecol. Abstr.; Ecology Abstr.; EMBASE; Entomol. Abstr.; Environ. Abstr.; Environ. Period. Bibliogr.; Field Crop Abstr.; Fish Rev.; For. Prod. Abstr.; For. Abstr.; Genet. Abstr.; Geol. Abstr.; GeoRef; Grasslands For. Abstr.; Helminthol. Abstr. (19??-19??); Hortic. Abstr.; Index Med. (July 1965-1980); Index Vet.; INIS Atomindex [Micro.]; Int. Dev. Abstr. (?-?); Key Word Index Wildl. Res.; Microbiol. Abstr. Sect. C; Nematol. Abstr.; Nutr. Abstr. Rev., Ser. B, Live Feeds and Feed.; Nutr. Abstr. Rev., Ser. A, Hum. Exp.; Ocean. Abstr.; Plant Breed. Abstr.; Protozoolog. Abstr.; Ref. Upd. Deluxe Ed.; Res. Alert [Full Cov.]; Rev. Agric. Entomol.; Rev. Med. Vet. Entomol.; Rice Abstr.; Sci. Cit. Index; SCISEARCH; Soils Fert.; Vet. Bull.; Weed Abstr.; Wheat Barley Trit. Abstr.; Wildl. Rev.

US
**CARDINAL NEWS, THE.** V. 21, No. 1 (March 1982)-. Periodical. English. bm. $18.00. Illinois Audubon Society, PO Box 608, Wayne IL 60184. **Tel** (312)584-6290. **UDC** 598.2. **Bk Rev. Ad Acc. Circ:** 5,000. ***Continues** Audubon Newsletter.*

US
**CATALOGUE OF AMERICAN AMPHIBIANS AND REPTILES.** **Added/Corp** American Society of Ichthyologists and Herpetologists. Herpetological Catalogue Committee. (1963)-. Periodical. English. Twenty-five times a year. $20.00 (institutions), $15.00 (individuals). Society for the Study Amphibians & Reptiles, PO Box 626, Hays KS 67601. **Tel** (913)628-1437. **LC** QL651; .A55. **DD** 598.10973.
**Desc:** Consists of loose-leaf accounts, written by specialists, of the species of amphibians and reptiles inhabiting the Americas.

II/0970-5112
**CECIDOLOGIA INTERNATIONALE.** [Cecidol. int.]. **Added/Corp** Cecidological Society of India. Vol. 1, No. 1, 2, 3 (1980)-. Periodical. English. Three times a year (Mar., July, Dec.). $103.00 US; $110.00 Canada. Cecidological Society of India, 14 Park Road, Allahabad 211002 India. **CODEN** CEINEX. Documents available from BIOSIS Document Express. ***Formed by the union of** Cecidologia Indica, 0008-8676 **and** Marcellia, 0025-2794.*
**Ind/Abst** Biocont. News Inf.; Biol. Abstr.; Life Sci. Collect.

MX
**CENTZONTLE : REVISTA DE LA SOCIEDAD MEXICANA DE ORNITOLOGIA.** **Added/Corp** Sociedad Mexicana de Ornitologia. (Sept. 1979)-. Periodical. Spanish (English). an. $12,000 Mexico; $40.00 US. Sociedad Mexicana Ornitologia, Apartado Postale 70-581, Mexico 20 DF Mexico. **Tel** 550-59-14. **ED** Salvador Avila Beltran. **Bk Rev. Ad Acc. Circ:** 1,000.
**Desc:** Original works of research in ornithology as well as of all aspects related to this specialty.

US/0097-031X
**CETOLOGY.** ***Ceased.*** [Cetology]. Monographic series. English. ir. Biological Systems Inc, PO Box 26, St Augustine FL 32085. **Tel** (904)797-5057. **ED** David K Caldwell. **LC** QL737.C4; C38. **DD** 599.5/05. **UDC** 599.5. **CODEN** CTGYAL. Documents available from BIOSIS Document Express.
**Desc:** Biology of marine mammals.
**Ind/Abst** Aquat. Sci. Fish. Abstr. (Computer File); Biol. Abstr.; Ocean. Abstr.; Life Sci. Collect.

US/0747-9840
**CHAMP CHANNELS.** [Champ channels]. Vol. 1, No. 1 (April 1983)-. Periodical. English. qt. $9.00 US; $10.00 other. Lake Champlain Phenomena Investigation, PO Box 2134, Wilton NY 12866. **Tel** (518)587-7638. **ED** Joseph W Zarzynski. **DD** 001. **UDC** 591.9(285). **Bk Rev. Circ:** 200.
**Desc:** Focuses on cryptozoology, specifically the Loch Ness and Lake Champlain monsters.

US/0009-1987
**CHAT (TRYON), THE.** (THE CHAT.). [Chat]. **Added/Corp** Carolina Bird Club. Vol. 1, (March 1937)-. Periodical. English. Four times a year (Jan., Mar., June, Sept.). $12.00 (individuals), $15.00 (institutions) (comes with membership). Carolina Bird Club, PO Box 27647, Raleigh NC 27611. **Tel** (919)733-7450. **ED** H.T. Hendrickson. **LC** QL671; .C45. Index available. cum. index. **Bk Rev. Pr Rev. Circ:** 1,060.
**Ind/Abst** Fish Rev. (Jan. 1989-July 1992); Wildl. Rev. (Jan. 1989-July 1992).

CH/0001-3943
**CHUNG YANG YEN CHIU YUAN TUNG WU YEN CHUI SO CHI KAN.** ***Title Change.*** [Bull. inst. zool., Acad. sin.]. **Added/Corp** Chung-Kuo Ko Hsueh Yuan. Tung Wu Yen Chiu So. **VFOAT** Tung Wu Yen Chiu So Chi Kan; Chung Yang Yen Chiu Yuan, Tung Wu Yen Chiu So Chi Kan. Vol. 1 (1962)-(199?). Academic Scholarly Publication. English (summaries and/or abstracts in Chinese). Four times a year. Institute of Zoology, Academia Sinica, Nankang, Taipei Taiwan 115. **ED** Jen-Leih Wu. **LC** QL307.2; .C54. Index available. cum. index. **Pr Rev.** ctrl circ. Documents available from The Genuine Article, BIOSIS Document Express, CASDDS. ***Continues** Sinensia. **Continued by** Zoological Studies.*
**Desc:** Welcomes original articles and researches of experimental, descriptive, or analytical nature, including investigations of all levels of zoological organization from the molecular to the population.
**Ind/Abst** Biocont. News Inf.; Biol. Abstr.; Chem. Abstr.; Curr. Aware. Biol. Sci., CABS; Curr. Ref. Fish Res.; Entomol. Abstr.; Fish Rev. (199?-); Hortic. Abstr.; Protozoolog. Abstr.; Res. Alert [Full Cov.]; Rev. Agric. Entomol.; Sci. Cit. Index (19??-19??); Zool. Rec.; Wildl. Rev.

US/0590-6334
**CICINDELA.** [Cicindela]. (March 1969)-. Periodical. English. qt. $7.00. R L Huber, 4637 West 69th Terrace, Prairie Village KS 66208. **Tel** (913)236-4043. **ED** Ronald L. Huber. **LC** QL596.C56; C5. **DD** 595.7. **Bk Rev. Circ:** 150.
**Desc:** Studies on tiger beetles.
**Ind/Abst** AGRICOLA [Full Cov.]; Life Sci. Collect.

FR
**CIDA / CENTRE INTERNATIONAL DE DOCUMENTATION ARACHNOLOGIQUE.** French. CIDA, Lab Zoologie Arthropode, 61 rue de Buffon, Paris 75005 France.

CU/0259-2932
**CIENCIA Y TECNICA EN LA AGRICULTURA. GANADO PORCINO.**
**See** Science and Technology.

US/0010-065X
**COLEOPTERISTS' BULLETIN, THE.** [Coleopt. bull.]. **Added/Corp** Coleopterists' Society. Vol. 1 (April 1947)-. Bulletin. English. qt. $50.00 institutions; $30.00 (Society membership). Coleopterists Society, PO Box 767, Natchez MS 39121. **Tel** (601)442-2824, FAX (601)442-2866. **ED** Floyd Werner. **DD** 595. **CODEN** COBLAO. Index available. **Pr Rev. Circ:** 850. Documents available from The Genuine Article, BIOSIS Document Express.
**Desc:** Objective is the advancement of the science of coleopterology in all its aspects of theory, principles, methodology and practice, for living and fossil beetles.
**Ind/Abst** AGRICOLA [Full Cov.]; Biocont. News Inf.; Biodeter. Abstr.; Biol. Abstr.; CSA Neuro. Abstr. (?-?); Curr. Aware. Biol. Sci., CABS; Curr. Contents, Agric. Biol. Environ. Sci.; Ecol. Abstr.; Ecology Abstr.; Entomol. Abstr.; For. Abstr.; Geogr. Abstr. Phys. Geogr.; Life Sci. Collect.; Postharvest News Inf.; Res. Alert [Select. Cov.]; Rev. Agric. Entomol.; Rev. Med. Vet. Entomol.; Zool. Rec.

SP
**COMPTES-RENDUS / COLLOQUE D'ARACHNOLOGIE D'EXPRESSION FRANCAISE.** **Main/Corp** Colloque d'Arachnologie d'Expression Francaise. French (summaries and/or abstracts in English and Spanish). Eunibar SA, Diputacion 216, Barcelona-11 Spain. **LC** QL451; .C64A. **DD** 595.4/05.

UY/0027-0113
**COMUNICACIONES ZOOLOGICAS DEL MUSEO DE HISTORIA NATURAL DE MONTEVIDEO.** [Comun. Zool. Mus. Hist. Nat. Montevideo]. **Added/Corp** Museo de Historia Natural de Montevideo. Vol. 1, No. 1 (1943)-. Spanish (English and French). an. Free on request. Museo de Historia Natural, Casilla de Correo 399, 11000 Montevideo Uruguay. **Tel** 011 598 2 960908. **LC** QL71.M7; A5. **DD** 590/.5. **CODEN** CZMMAN. Documents available from BIOSIS Document Express.
**Ind/Abst** Biol. Abstr.

CN
**CONTRIBUTIONS DE L'INSTITUT DE BIOLOGIE DE L'UNIVERSITE DE MONTREAL (1948).** (CONTRIBUTIONS DE L'INSTITUT DE BIOLOGIE DE L'UNIVERSITE DE MONTREAL.). **Main/Corp** Universite de Montreal. Institut de Biologie. No. 21 (1948)-. Monographic series. Multiple languages (French and English). Price varies per volume. Institut de Biologie de Universite de Montreal, CP 6128, Montreal Quebec H3C 3J7 Canada. **LC** QL1; .M65. **DD** 590.82. ***Continues*** *Contributions de l'Institut de Biologie Generale et de Zoologie de l'Universite de Montreal.*

SZ/0092-4016
**CONTRIBUTIONS TO PRIMATOLOGY.** [Contrib. primatol.]. Vol. 1 (1974)-. Monographic series. English. an. 120.00F (approx. per volume). S. Karger AG, Allschwilerstrasse 10, PO Box - Postfach - Case Postale, CH-4009 Basel Switzerland. **Tel** 011 41 61 306-1111, FAX 011 41 61 306-1234, telex CH 962 652. **ED** F. S. Szalay. **LC** UNC. **DD** 591. **NLM** W1 CO778UP. **CODEN** CPMYAN. Documents available from BIOSIS Document Express. ***Continues*** *Bibliotheca Primatologica, 0067-8139.*
**Desc:** Offers in-depth studies of primatologic research from an evolutionary perspective. Revealing the broad significance of primate evolutionary biology, individual monographs draw their focus from systematic, behavioral, phylogenetic, and morphologic studies of primate evolution. In its years of publication, the series has demonstrated the gains in knowledge made possible when various subdisciplines are united through a shared concern with the primates.
**Ind/Abst** Biol. Abstr.; Curr. Primate Ref.; GeoRef; Life Sci. Collect.; Ref. Upd. Deluxe Ed.

SZ/0376-4230
**CONTRIBUTIONS TO VERTEBRATE EVOLUTION.** ***Ceased.*** [Contrib. vertebr. evol.]. V. 1-(1977)-Vol 7?. Monographic series. English. ir. S. Karger AG, Allschwilerstrasse 10, PO Box - Postfach - Case Postale, CH-4009 Basel Switzerland. **Tel** 011 41 61 306-1111, FAX 011 41 61 306-1234, telex CH 962 652. **ED** M K Hecht and F S Szalay. **UDC** 596. **NLM** W1 CO778XE. **CODEN** CVEVDJ. **[CCC].** Documents available from BIOSIS Document Express.
**Desc:** Studies covering the phylogeny, taxonomy, adaptions and biogeography of vertebrate groups.
**Ind/Abst** Biol. Abstr.; GeoRef.

US/0045-8511
**COPEIA.** [Copeia]. **Added/Corp** American Society of Ichthyologists and Herpetologists. (April 1913)-. Periodical. English. qt. $90.00 institution. ASIH Copeia, Department of Zoology, Southern Illinois University, Carbondale IL 62901. **Tel** (618)453-4113. **ED** Michael E. Douglas. **LC** QL1; .C65. **DD** 579/.005. **NLM** W1 CO826. **CODEN** COPAAR. **[CCC].** Index available (bound in last issue). **Bk Rev. Pr Rev. Acid Free. Circ:** 3,600 (ctrl). available on microfilm and microfiche from University Microfilms International (UMI). Documents available from The Genuine Article, BIOSIS Document Express.
**Desc:** Primarily serves as a publications outlet for scientific publications in ichthyology and herpetology. In addition, it includes news of members and their activities, a summary of the annual meetings, and notices of new publications of interest to members.
**Ind/Abst** Anim. Behav. Abstr.; Anim. Breed. Abstr.; Aquat. Sci. Fish. Abstr. (Computer File); Biocont. News Inf. (1991-); Biol. Agric. Index; Biol. Abstr.; Chemorecept. Abstr.; CSA Neuro. Abstr. (?-?); Curr. Aware. Biol. Sci., CABS; Curr. Contents, Agric. Biol. Environ. Sci.; Curr. Ref. Fish Res.; Ecology Abstr.; Fish Rev.; Genet. Abstr.; GeoRef; Mar. Sci. Contents Tables; Nutr. Abstr. Rev., Ser. B, Live Feeds and Feed.; Nutr. Abstr. Rev., Ser. A, Hum. Exp.; Ocean. Abstr.; Life Sci. Collect.; Protozoolog. Abstr.; Res. Alert [Full Cov.]; Rev. Med. Vet. Entomol.; Sci. Cit. Index; SCISEARCH; Wildl. Rev.

CN/0700-4966
**CORDULIA.** ***Suspended.*** (Jan. 1975)-Suspended. Periodical. French (English). Four times a year. Cordulia, College Bourget, CP 1000, Rigaud Quebec J0P 1P0 Canada. **DD** 591'.9'714.

NE/0011-216X
**CRUSTACEANA.** [Crustaceana]. Vol. 1 (Jan. 1960)-. Periodical. English (French and German; summaries and/or abstracts in French and German). ir (6 issues). Fl360.00 Netherlands; $205.75 other. E. J. Brill, Postbus 9000, 2300 PA Leiden Netherlands. **Tel** 011 31 71 312624, FAX 011 31 71 317532, telex 39296 BRILL NL. **ED** J.H. Stock. **LC** QL435.A1; C75. **CODEN** CRUSAP. **[CCC]. Pr Rev. Circ:** 656. Documents available from The Genuine Article, BIOSIS Document Express, CASDDS.
**Desc:** Features papers on crustacean research in all its aspects, including taxonomy, ecology, physiology, anatomy, genetics, palaeontology and biometry. All groups of crustacea are included.
**Ind/Abst** Aquat. Sci. Fish. Abstr. (Computer File); Biol. Abstr.; Chem. Abstr.; CSA Neuro. Abstr. (?-?); Curr. Aware. Biol. Sci., CABS; Curr. Contents, Agric. Biol. Environ. Sci.; Ecol. Abstr.; Ecology Abstr.; Fish Rev. (Jan. 1989-July 1992); GeoRef; Mar. Sci. Contents Tables; Ocean. Abstr.; Life Sci. Collect.; Plant Breed. Abstr.; Pollut. Abstr. Indexes; Res. Alert [Full Cov.]; Rev. Med. Vet. Entomol.; Sci. Cit. Index; SCISEARCH; Wildl. Rev. (Jan. 1989-July 1992).

NE/0167-6563
**CRUSTACEANA. SUPPLEMENT.** ***Ceased.*** (CRUSTACEANA. SUPPLEMENT.). [Crustaceana, Suppl.]. (1968)-Vol. 16 (19??). Monographic series. English (French and German). ir. E. J. Brill, Postbus 9000, 2300 PA Leiden Netherlands. **Tel** 011 31 71 312624, FAX 011 31 71 317532, telex 39296 BRILL NL. **LC** QL435.A1; C752. **DD** 591. **CODEN** CRUSBQ. **Pr Rev.** Documents available from BIOSIS Document Express.
**Ind/Abst** Biol. Abstr.; Life Sci. Collect.; Rev. Med. Vet. Entomol.

US/0736-7023
**CRYPTOZOOLOGY.** (CRYPTOZOOLOGY: INTERDISCIPLINARY JOURNAL OF THE INTERNATIONAL SOCIETY OF CRYPTOZOOLOGY.). [Cryptozoology]. **Added/Corp** International Society of Cryptozoology. Vol. 1 (Winter 1982)-. Academic Scholarly Publication. English. an. $45.00. International Society of Cryptozoology, PO Box 43070, Tucson AZ 85733. **Tel** (602)884-8369. **ED** J. Richard Greenwell. **LC** QL89; .C79. **DD** 591. **Bk Rev. Ad Acc. Pr Rev. Acid Free. Circ:** 900 (ctrl).
**Desc:** Publishes scholarly, refereed articles on the reported presence or recent occurrence of 'unexpected' animals not generally recognized by contemporary zoology, but which are or were known, or hinted at, through both native and Western accounts, historical manuscripts, oral traditions, works of art, etc.

AT/0726-6588
**CSIRO DIVISION OF ENTOMOLOGY REPORT.** (CSIRO DIVISION OF ENTOMOLOGY REPORT / DIVISION OF ENTOMOLOGY, COMMONWEALTH SCIENTIFIC AND INDUSTRIAL RESEARCH ORGANIZATION, AUSTRALIA.). [CSIRO Div. Entomol. rep.]. **Added/Corp** Commonwealth Scientific and Industrial Research Organization (Australia). Division of Entomology. **VFOAT** Division of Entomology Report. **VAT** Commonwealth Scientific and Industrial Research Organization, Division of Entomology Report. (1978)-. Monographic series. English. ir. Price varies per volume. CSIRO / Division of Entomology, GPO Box 1700, Canberra ACT 2601 Australia. **Tel** 011 61 62464911, FAX 011 61 62470218.
**Ind/Abst** Maize Abstr.

DK/0374-7344
**DANISH REVIEW OF GAME BIOLOGY.** [Dan. rev. game biol.]. **Added/Corp** Vildtbiologiske Station (Kal, Denmark) Jagtfondets Vildtbiologiske Undersgelser (Denmark) Jagtraadets Vildtbiologiske Undersgelser (Denmark). Vol. 1, Pt. 1 (1945)-. Monographic series. English (summaries and/or abstracts in Danish and Russian). ir. Free on request. Game Biology Station, Kalo Grenevej 12, DK 8410 Ronde Denmark. **Tel** 011 45 86 372500, FAX 011 45 86 372435. **ED** Jan Bertelsen. **LC** QL1; .D3. **DD** 599. **CODEN** DRGBAH. Index available. Documents available from BIOSIS Document Express.
**Desc:** Includes the transactions for the 3rd Congress of the International Union of Game Biologists, Aarhus.
**Ind/Abst** Biol. Abstr.; Key Word Index Wildl. Res.; Nutr. Abstr. Rev., Ser. B, Live Feeds and Feed.; Nutr. Abstr. Rev., Ser. A, Hum. Exp.; Stat. Theory Method Abstr. (1973); Zool. Rec.; Wildl. Rev.

UK/0957-0276
**DEER FARMING INVERNESS.** (DEER FARMING.). [Deer farmingInverness]. (1983)-. Periodical. English. qt.
**Ind/Abst** Index Vet.

GW/0012-0553
**DEUTSCHE PELZTIERZUCHTER, DER.** ***Ceased.*** [Dtsch. pelztierzucht.]. **Added/Corp** Reichsfachgruppe Pelztierzuchter. Vol. 1 (1926)-(19??). Periodical. German. mo. Animal Verlag Gmbh, Peiner Weg 84, W 3167 Burgdoff Germany. **Tel** 49 51363135.
**Ind/Abst** Anim. Breed. Abstr.; Index Vet.; Nutr. Abstr. Rev., Ser. B, Live Feeds and Feed.; Rev. Med. Vet. Mycology.

CN/0046-029X
**DINNY'S CALGARY DIGEST.** **Added/Corp** Calgary Zoological Society. **VFOAT** Dinny's Digest. Vol. 1 (Oct. 1969)-. Periodical. English. Four times a year (Jan., Apr., July, Oct.). 12.00Can$ (one year), 22.00Can$ (two years), 30.00Can$ (three years). Calgary Zoological Society, PO Box 3036, Postal Station B, Calgary Alberta T2M 4R8 Canada. **Tel** (403)265-9310. **ED** David Banks. **Circ:** 11,000 (ctrl).
**Desc:** Includes articles concerning vertebrate zoology and horticultural interest at the Calgary Zoo as well as current events at the zoo.

CN/1187-7286
**DIRECTORY / CANADIAN SOCIETY OF ZOOLOGISTS.** [Dir. - Can. Soc. Zoolog.]. **Main/Corp** Canadian Society of Zoologists. **VFOAT** Repertoire. **VAT** Repertoire - Societe Canadienne de Zoologie; Canadienne de Zoologie. (1991)-. Directory. English. ir. Canadian Society of Zoologists, c/o Dr. Fenwick, University of Ottawa, Box 450-A, Ottawa Ontario K1H GN5 Canada. **Tel** (613)564-2436. **DD** 591/.025/71.

US/0085-0039
**DIRECTORY OF THE PUBLIC AQUARIA OF THE WORLD.** 1st - Ed.; 1962-. Directory. English. Waikiki Aquarium, 2777 Kalakaua Avenue, Honolulu HI 96815. **Tel** (808)923-9741. **ED** Charles DeLuca. **LC** QL78; .D57. **DD** 590/.74. **UDC** 591.082(100). **Ad Acc. Circ:** 200.
**Desc:** A directory of aquariums of the world, covering address, attendance, specimens, directory, and educational facilities.

JA/0287-0223
**DOBUTSU BUNRUI GAKKAI SHI.** **Added/Corp** Dobutsu Bunrui Gakkai (Japan). **VFOAT** Proceedings of the Japanese Society of Systematic Zoology. (19??)-. Periodical. English (Japanese). sa. Japan Soceity of Systematic Zoology, 3 23 1 Hyakunin-cho Shinjuku-ku, Tokyo 160 Japan. **Tel** 011 81 3 33642311. **LC** QL352; .D62.

JA
**DOBUTSU TO DOBUTSUEN. ANIMALS AND ZOOS.** **Added/Corp** Tokyo Dobutsuen Kyokai. **VFOAT** Animals and Zoos. (19??)-. Periodical. Japanese (English). Twelve times a year. $54.00. Tokyo Zoological Park Society, C O Ueno 8009 83 Ueno Park, Taito Ku Tokyo 110 Japan. **Tel** 011 81 3 3828 8235.
**Ind/Abst** Fish Rev. (Jan. 1989-July 1992); Wildl. Rev. (Jan. 1989-July 1992).

UK/0265-5640
**DODO (TRINITY).** (THE DODO; JOURNAL OF THE JERSEY WILDLIFE PRESERVATION TRUST.). [Dodo]. **Added/Corp** Jersey Wildlife Preservation Trust. No. 14 (1977)-. English. an. $15.00. Jersey Wildlife Preservation Trust, Les Augres Manor, Trinity Jersey Channel Islands. **ED** Jeremy J C Mallinson. **LC** QL76.5.C55; T744. **DD** 636.08/99. **Circ:** 3,000 (ctrl). ***Continues*** *Jersey Wildlife Preservation Trust. Annual Report.*
**Desc:** Field studies concerning the captive breeding of endangered species as an aid to their conservation.
**Ind/Abst** Index Vet.; Key Word Index Wildl. Res.; Life Sci. Collect.; Psychol. Abstr. (1979-); PsycINFO (?-1985); PsycLit; Vet. Bull.; Wildl. Rev.

TU
**DOGA. TURK ZOOLOJI DERGISI.** **VFOAT** Turkish Journal of Zoology. (19??)-. Periodical. Turkish. **CODEN** DTZDEY. Documents available from BIOSIS Document Express, CASDDS.
**Ind/Abst** Biol. Abstr. (1987-); Chem. Abstr.; Postharvest News Inf.; Rev. Agric. Entomol.; Rev. Med. Vet. Entomol.

RU
**DOKLADY NA EZHEGODNOM CHTENII PAMIATI N. A. KHOLODKOVSKOGO.** **Added/Corp** Vsesoiuznoe Entomologicheskoe Obshchestvo. **VFOAT** Chteniia Pamiati Nikolaia Aleksandrovicha Kholodkovskogo. (1948)-. Monographic series. Russian. Price varies per volume. Izdatelstvo Nauka St. Petersburg, Mendeleevskaia Liniia 1, 199034 St. Petersburg, B-34 Russia. **Tel** 218-26-12. **LC** QL461; .V824.

CC/1000-0739
**DONGWU FENLEI XUEBAO.** (TUNG WU FEN LEI HSUEH PAO. ACTA ZOOTAXONOMICA SINICA.). [Dongwu fenlei xuebao]. **Added/Corp** Chung-kuo Tung wu Hsueh Hui. Chung-kuo kun Chung Hsueh Hui. **VFOAT** Acta Zootaxonomica Sinica. (1976)-. Academic Scholarly Publication. Chinese (summaries and/or abstracts in English). qt. $89.00. Science Press, 16 Donghuangchenggen North Street, Beijing 100707, People's Republic of China. **Tel** 011 86 1 4019821, 011 86 1 4010642, FAX 011 86 1 4012180, 011 86 1 4019810, telex 210147. **LC** QL35l; .T84. **DD** 590/.12. **CODEN** DFXUEB. Index available in last issue of volume--attached. Documents available from BIOSIS Document Express.
**Ind/Abst** Biocont. News Inf.; Biol. Abstr. (1985-); Helminthol. Abstr. (1991-); Nematol. Abstr.; Protozoolog. Abstr.; Rev. Agric. Entomol.

CC/1000-1786
**DONGWUXUE JIKAN.** (TUNG WU HSUEH CHI KAN.). [Dongwuxue jikan]. **Added/Corp** Chung-kuo ko Hsueh Yuan. Tung wu yen Chiu so. **VFOAT** Sinozoologia. Vol. 1 (May 1981)-. Periodical. Chinese (summaries and/or abstracts in English). Hsin Hua Shu Tien / Beijing, Pei-Ching Fa Hsing So, Beijing, People's Republic of China. **Tel** 657331-565. **ED** T H Dan. **LC** QL1; .T942. **DD** 591. **CODEN** DOJIE2. **Ad Acc. Circ:** 2,000. Documents available from BIOSIS Document Express.
**Desc:** Comprehensive journal on zoology. It publishes original research manuscripts and provides a forum for new methods, techniques and findings in this field.
**Ind/Abst** Biol. Abstr. (1987-).

CC/0254-5853
**DONGWUXUE YANJIU.** (TUNG WU HSUEH YEN CHIU.). [Dongwuxue yanjiu]. **Added/Corp** "Tung Wu Hsueh Yen Chiu" Pien Chi Wei Yuan Hui. **VFOAT** Zoological Research; Dongwuxue Yanjiu. (1980)-. Periodical. Chinese (summaries and/or abstracts in English; table of contents in English). qt. $2.50. **(Subscription address:** China International Book Trading Corporation, PO Box 399, Library Service Department, Beijing 100044 People's Republic of China.**)** **LC** QL1; .T945. **DD** 591/.05. **CODEN** DOYADI. Documents available from BIOSIS Document Express.
**Ind/Abst** Biol. Abstr. (?-1988); Fish Rev. (Jan. 1989-July 1992); NAPRALERT; Wildl. Rev. (Jan. 1989-July 1992).

CC/0250-3263
**DONGWUXUE ZAZHI.** (TUNG WU HSUEH TSA CHIH. DONGWUXUE ZAZHI.). [Dongwuxue zazhi]. **Added/Corp** Chung-kuo Tung wu Hsueh Hui. **VFOAT** Dongwuxue Zazhi; Chinese Journal of Zoology. (1976)-. Academic Scholarly Publication. English. bm. $60.00. Science Press, 16 Donghuangchenggen North Street, Beijing 100707, People's Republic of China. **Tel** 011 86 1 4019821, 011 86 1 4010642, FAX 011 86 1 4012180, 011 86 1 4019810, telex 210147. **(Subscription address:** China International Book Trading Corporation, PO Box 399, Library Service Department, Beijing 100044 People's Republic of China.**)** **LC** QL1; .T943. **CODEN** TWHCDZ. Documents available from CASDDS.
**Ind/Abst** AGRICOLA; Chem. Abstr.; Helminthol. Abstr. (1991-); Index Vet.; Protozoolog. Abstr.

AT/1031-6280
**DONKEY DIGEST.** English. 16.00Aus$ Australia; 20.00Aus$ other. Donkey Society of Australia, Booloumba Creek, MS 16, Maleny QLD-4552 Australia. **ED** Jenifer Simpson. **Bk Rev. Ad Acc. Circ:** 500 (ctrl).
**Desc:** Covers all aspects of donkeys.

US/1065-8408
**DREISSENA POLYMORPHA INFORMATION REVIEW.** [Dreissena polymorpha inf. rev.]. **Added/Corp** New York Sea Grant Extension Program. New York Zebra Mussel Information Clearinghouse. Vol. 1, No. 1 (Sept./Oct. 1990). Periodical. English. bm. $60.00. Cornell University / Brockport, 250 Hartwell Hall, Brockport NY 14420. **Tel** (716) 395-2516, FAX (716) 395-2729. **DD** 591.

NE
**DUTCH BIRDING.** Periodical. Dutch (English). qt. Dutch Birding Association, Postbus 75611, 1070 AP Amsterdam Netherlands.
**Ind/Abst** Ecol. Abstr.

NE
**ECHINODERM STUDIES.** Vol. 1 (1983)-. English. be. F84.93 (2 year). AA Balkema, Box 1675, 3000 BR Rotterdam Netherlands. **Tel** 011 31 10 4145822, FAX 011 31 10 4135947, telex 41605. **ED** Michel Jangoux and John M Lawrence. **LC** QL381; .E32. **DD** 593.9/05.

US/0735-7494
**ECHINODERMS NEWSLETTER, THE.** **Added/Corp** National Museum of Natural History (U.S.). Dept. of Invertebrate Zoology (Echinoderms). (19??)-. Newsletter. English. ir. Smithsonian Institution National Museum of Natural History, Mail Stop 106, Washington DC 20560. **Tel** (202)357-1930. ***Continues*** *Echinoderm Newsletter.*

CN/1184-1877
**ECOZOO.** **Added/Corp** Societe Zoologique de Quebec. **VFOAT** Eco Zoo. (1990)-. Periodical. French. qt. La Societe Zoologique de Quebec, 9141 Avenue du Zoo, Charlesbourg Quebec G1G 4G4 Canada. **Tel** (418)627-3072. **LC** QL221.Q4; C3. **DD** 591/.05. **CODEN** ECOZE5. ***Continues*** *Carnets de Zoologie, 0008-669X.*
**Ind/Abst** Point Repere (1990-).

RU/0136-9121
**EKOLOGICHESKAIA I EKSPERIMENTALNAIA PARAZITOLOGIIA.** **Added/Corp** Leningradskii Gosudarstvennyi Universitet Imeni A.A. Zhdanova. Russian S.F.S.R. Golovnoi Sovet po Biologii. Russian S.F.S.R. Ministerstvo Vysshego i Srednego Setsialnogo Obrazovzania. Vol. 1 (1975)-. Periodical. Russian (summaries and/or abstracts in English). 1.29rub (single issue). St Petersburg State University / Izdatelstvo Leningradskogo Universiteta, Universitetskaia Nab 7/9, 199034 St Petersburg Russia. **Tel** 011 95 218-97-88, FAX 011 95 218-51-52, telex 121481. **LC** QL757; .E46.

US/0737-108X
**ELEPHANT (DETROIT, MICH.).** (ELEPHANT : THE PUBLICATION OF THE ELEPHANT INTEREST GROUP.). [Elephant]. **Added/Corp** Elephant Interest Group. (19??)-. Periodical. English. ir. $12.00. The Elephant Interest Group, H Shoshani, 106 E Hickory Grove Road, Bloomfield Hills MI 48013. **Tel** (313)540-3947. **ED** Jeheskel Shoshani, Sandra L. Shoshani. **LC** QL737.P98; E42. **DD** 599.6/1/05. Index available. cum. index. **Bk Rev. Pr Rev. Circ:** 500 (ctrl). available on microfilm from University Microfilms International (UMI). ***Continues*** *Elephant Newsletter.*
**Desc:** Covers mostly living species of elephants, occasionally also extinct ones. Includes categorized and annotated elephant bibliography with special section for junior readers.

SP/0214-1353
**ELYTRON.** (ELYTRON : BULLETIN OF THE EUROPEAN ASSOCIATION OF COLEOPTEROLOGY.). [Elytron]. **Added/Corp** European Association of Coleopterology. Vol. 1 (1987)-. English (Italian and Spanish). an. comes with membership. Asociacion Europea de Coleopterologia, Universidad de Barcelona, C Diagonal 645, 08028 Barcelona Spain. **Tel** 011 34 3 330 8851 ext. 165. **CODEN** ELTREZ. Documents available from BIOSIS Document Express.
**Ind/Abst** Biocont. News Inf. (1991-); Biodeter. Abstr.; Biol. Abstr. (1989-); Entomol. Abstr.; Rev. Agric. Entomol.; Rev. Med. Vet. Entomol.

US/1062-6034
**EMU TODAY & TOMORROW.** [Emu Today Tomorrow]. **VFOAT** Emu Today and Tomorrow. (19??)-. Periodical. English. mo. $20.00. Emu Today & Tommorrow, PO Box 7, Nardin OK 74646. **Tel** (405)628-2933, FAX (405)628-2011. **ED** Sherrie Lewis. **DD** 636. **Ad Acc, Adv Mgr:** Denise Whitehead.
**Desc:** Publication devoted primarily to emu ranchers, but also publishes articles and advertisements on other exotic animals.

FR/0301-4282
**ENCYCLOPEDIE ENTOMOLOGIQUE PARIS.** (ENCYCLOPEDIE ENTOMOLOGIQUE.). [Encycl. entomol.Paris]. (1924)-. Monographic series. French. ir. CCLS, BP 22, 41353 Vineuil France. **Tel** 011 33 54 787741. **UDC** 595.70.

US
**ENGELHARDTIA.** V. 1- 1968-. Periodical. English. qt. $20.00. Northeastern Field Naturalist Society, PO Box 6, Central Islip Long Island NY 11722. ***Supersedes*** *Lon Island Herpetological Society. Bulletin - Long Island Herpetological Society; Long Island Herpetological Society. Journal - Long Island Herpetological Society.*

US
**ENGLISH TRANSLATIONS OF SELECTED TAXONOMIC PAPERS IN NEMATOLOGY.** **Added/Corp** California. Dept. of Food and Agriculture. Vol. 1 (1983)-. Periodical. English (translations available in French).

AU/0250-4413
**ENTOMOFAUNA.** [Entomofauna]. Vol. 1, No. 1 (Jan. 1, 1980)-. Monographic series. German. ir. S350.00. Maximilian Schwarz, Eibenweg 6, A 4052 Ansfelden Austria. **Tel** 011 43 732 307824. Index Available, published separately, free-automatically sent.
**Ind/Abst** Biocont. News Inf. (1991-); Life Sci. Collect.; Rev. Agric. Entomol.; Rev. Med. Vet. Entomol.

GR/0254-5381
**ENTOMOLOGIA HELLENICA.** [Entomol. hell.]. Vol. 1, No. 1 (June 1983)-. Periodical. English (French; summaries and/or abstracts in French and Greek, Modern). sa.
**Ind/Abst** AGRICOLA [Full Cov.]; Biocont. News Inf.; Life Sci. Collect. (1985-); Potato Abstr.

JA
**ENTOMOLOGICAL REVIEW OF JAPAN, THE.** **Added/Corp** Kinki Coleopterological Society. Transactions - Kinki Coleopterological Society. Vol. 1 (Jan. 1946)-. Periodical. Multiple languages (English and Japanese). sa. $98.50. Nihon Kochu Gakkai, (Japan Coleopterological Soc.), c/o Mr. Masao Hayashi, 2-8-199, Takaai 3 Chome, Higashisumiyoshiku, Osakashi, Osakafu 546, Japan. **(Subscription address:** Japan Publications Trading Company, Ltd., PO Box 5030, Tokyo International, Tokyo 100-31 Japan.**)** cum. index. ***Absorbed*** *Entomological Review of Japan.*
**Ind/Abst** Biodeter. Abstr.; Rev. Med. Vet. Entomol.

RU/0367-1445
**ENTOMOLOGICESKOE OBOZRENIE.** (ENTOMOLOGICHESKOE OBOZRENIE / VSESOKILUZNOE ENTOMOLOGICHESKOE OBSHCHESTVO.). [Entomol. obozr.]. **Added/Corp** Vsesoiuznoe Entomologicheskoe Obshchestvo. **VFOAT** Revue d'Entomologie de l'URSS. Vol. 25, No. 1/2, (1933)-. Periodical. Russian (French, German and English). qt. $178.00. **(Subscription address:** East View Publications Inc., 3020 Harbor Lane North, Suite 110, Minneapolis MN 55447.**)** **CODEN** ETOBAE. Documents available from BIOSIS Document Express. ***Continues*** *Russkoe Entomologicheskoe Obozrenie.*
**Desc:** Information on insects.
**Ind/Abst** AGRICOLA; Biocont. News Inf.; Biol. Abstr.; Cot. Trop. Fibr. Abstr. Bibliogr.; For. Prod. Abstr.; For. Abstr.; Life Sci. Collect.; PESTDOC; Rev. Med. Vet. Entomol.

RU
**ENTOMOLOGICHESKIE ISSLEVDOVANIIA NA DALNEM VOSTOKE.** **Added/Corp** Biologo-Pochvennyi Institut (Akademiia Nauk SSSR). **VFOAT** Entomological Researches in the Far East. (1970)-. Russian (table of contents in English). ir.

IR
**ENTOMOLOGIE ET PHYTOPATHOLOGIE APPLIQUEES.** (1946)-. Persian (French; summaries and/or abstracts in English and French). Kunst und Wissen Erich Bieber, Dufourstrasse 51, CH-8008 Zurich Switzerland. **Tel** (011)411694420.
**Ind/Abst** Biocont. News Inf.; Biodeter. Abstr.; Cot. Trop. Fibr. Abstr. Bibliogr.; Maize Abstr.; Nematol. Abstr.; Plant Breed. Abstr.; Wheat Barley Trit. Abstr.

NE/0013-8827
**ENTOMOLOGISCHE BERICHTEN.** [Entomol. ber.]. Vol, 1 No. 1 (Sept. 1, 1901)-. Periodical. Multiple languages (Dutch, English, French and German). mo. Fl190.00. Nederlandse Entomologische, Plantage Middenlaan 64, Amsterdam 1018 DH Netherlands. **NLM** W1; EN931CF. **CODEN** ETBRAV. Documents available from BIOSIS Document Express.
**Ind/Abst** AGRICOLA; Biocont. News Inf.; Biodeter. Abstr.; Biol. Abstr.; Ecol. Abstr.; Entomol. Abstr.; For. Abstr.; Geogr. Abstr. Phys. Geogr.; Life Sci. Collect.; Rev. Agric. Entomol.; Rev. Med. Vet. Entomol.

GW/0013-8835
**ENTOMOLOGISCHE BLATTER FUER BIOLOGIE UND SYSTEMATIK DER KAFER.** [Entomol. Bl. Biol. Syst. Kafer]. (1945)-. Periodical. German (summaries and/or abstracts in English). ir. Verlag Geecke & Evers, Durerstrasse 13, W-4150 Krefeld Germany. **CODEN** EBBSAA. **[CCC].** Documents available from BIOSIS Document Express. ***Continues*** *Entomologische Blatter, 0342-412X.*
**Ind/Abst** AGRICOLA; Biocont. News Inf.; Biodeter. Abstr.; Biol. Abstr.; Life Sci. Collect.

GW/0044-5223
**ENTOMOLOGISCHE MITTEILUNGEN AUS DEM ZOOLOGISCHEN MUSEUM HAMBURG.** [Entomol. Mitt. Zool. Mus. Hamb.]. (1969)-. Monographic series. German (English). ir. Price varies per volume. Zoologisches Museum und Institut, Martin L. King Platz 3, W-2000 Hamburg 13 Germany. **LC** QL461; .H28. **CODEN** EMZMAJ. Documents available from BIOSIS Document Express. ***Continues*** *Entomologische Mitteilungen aud dem Zoologischen Staatsinstitut U. Zoologischen Museum Hamburg.*
**Ind/Abst** AGRICOLA; Biocont. News Inf. (1991-); Biodeter. Abstr.; Biol. Abstr.; For. Prod. Abstr. (1991-); For. Abstr.; Nematol. Abstr.; Life Sci. Collect.; Postharvest News Inf.; Rev. Agric. Entomol.; Rev. Med. Vet. Entomol.; Soils Fert.; Weed Abstr.; Wheat Barley Trit. Abstr.

GW/0232-5535
**ENTOMOLOGISCHE NACHRICHTEN UND BERICHTE.** [Entomol. Nachr. Ber.]. Vol. 26, No. 1 (1982)-. Periodical. German (summaries and/or abstracts in English and Russian). bm. **CODEN** ENBEDL. Documents available from BIOSIS Document Express. ***Formed by the union of*** *Entomologische Nachrichten (Dresden, Germany), 0425-1083* ***and*** *Entomologische Berichte (Berlin, DDR), 0425-1075.*
**Ind/Abst** Biocont. News Inf. (1991-); Biodeter. Abstr.; Biol. Abstr.; For. Prod. Abstr.; Rev. Agric. Entomol.; Rev. Med. Vet. Entomol.

GW/0020-1839
**ENTOMOLOGISCHE ZEITSCHRIFT MIT INSEKTENBOERSE.** Vol. 91, No. 1/2 (Jan. 1981)-. Periodical. German. Twenty-four times a year. DM74.40 Germany; DM84.00 others. Alfred Kernen Verlag, Postfach 103244, D 45032 Essen Germany. **Tel** 011 49 201 3202430. **(Subscription address:** Zenit Pressvertrieb GmbH, Postfach 810640, D 70523 Stuttgart Germany.**)** **LC** QL461; .E7995. **DD** 595.7/005. ***Formed by the union of*** *Entomologische Zeitschrift, 0013-8843* ***and*** *Insektenboerse, 0020-1839.*

UK/0013-8916
**ENTOMOLOGIST'S RECORD AND JOURNAL OF VARIATION, THE.** [Entomol. rec. j. var.]. Vol.1 (Apr. 1890)-. Periodical. English. bm (Jan., Mar., May, July, Sept., Nov.). £25.00 institutions; £20.00 individuals. Entomologist's Record and Journal of Variation, 31 Oakdene Road, Brockham Betchworth Surrey RH3 7JV England. **Tel** 011 44 737 843151. **ED** P. A. Sokoloff. **NLM** W1 EN933. **CODEN** ERJVAZ. Index available. **Bk Rev,** (Qty: 6). **Ad Acc. Circ:** 700.

Documents available from BIOSIS Document Express.
**Desc:** General entomology emphasizing British and European Lepidoptera.
**Ind/Abst** AGRICOLA; Biol. Abstr.; Ecology Abstr.; Life Sci. Collect.

US/0013-8932
**ENTOMOLOGY CIRCULAR.** [Entomol. circ.]. English. Florida Department of Agriculture & Consumer Services, State Capitol, 10th Floor, Tallahassee FL 32399. **Tel** (904)488-6971, FAX (904)488-8087. **CODEN** FPECAI. Documents available from BIOSIS Document Express.
**Ind/Abst** Biocont. News Inf. (19??-19??); Biol. Abstr. (-1979); For. Prod. Abstr. (1991-); For. Abstr.; Rev. Agric. Entomol.; Rev. Med. Vet. Entomol.

UK/0269-4565
**EPITHELIA.** ***Ceased.*** Vol. 1, No. 1 (1987)-Vol. 1, No. 4 (?). Periodical. English. qt. Oxford University Press, Walton Street, Oxford OX2 6DP England. **Tel** 011 44 865 56767, FAX 011 44 865 267773, telex 837330 OXPRES G. **NLM** W1; EP462D. **[CCC].**

GR/1105-2651
**EPITHEORESE ZOOTEHNIKES EPISTEMES.** [Epitheor. Zooteh. Epistem.]. **VFOAT** Animal Science Review; Revue de Zootechnie. (1984)-. Periodical. Multiple languages. sa. **UDC** 591.
**Ind/Abst** Index Vet.; Nutr. Abstr. Rev., Ser. B, Live Feeds and Feed.; Pig News Inf.; Poult. Abstr.; Soyabean Abstr.; World Agric. Econ.

FR
**ETHNOZOOTECHNIE.** Monographic series. French. Price varies per volume.
**Ind/Abst** Anim. Breed. Abstr.

GW/0179-1613
**ETHOLOGY.** [Ethology]. Vol. 71, 1 (Jan. 1986)-. Periodical. English (German). Twelve times a year. DM1163.00 Europe; DM1154.00 other. Blackwell Wissenschafts-Verlag, Kurfuerstendamm 57, D 10707 Berlin Germany. **Tel** 011 49 30 32790623, 011 49 30 32790624, FAX 011 49 30 327 90610. **ED** Jane Brockmann, Kate Lessels, Walter Pflumm, Wolfgang Wickler. **LC** QL750; .Z43. **DD** 591.51/05. **NLM** W1; ET447R. Index available. cum. index. **Bk Rev. Ad Acc. Pr Rev. Circ:** 2,500. Documents available from The Genuine Article. ***Continues** Zeitschrift fuer Tierpsychologie, 0044-3573.*
**Desc:** Descriptions of behavior of animals. Basis of discussions concerns their adaptability and onto- and phylogenesis function and interplay of their sense organs, neural and hormone systems.
**Ind/Abst** AGRICOLA [Select. Cov.]; Anim. Behav. Abstr.; Anim. Breed. Abstr.; Chemorecept. Abstr.; Curr. Aware. Biol. Sci., CABS; Curr. Contents, Agric. Biol. Environ. Sci.; Curr. Contents Life Sci.; Dairy Sci. Abstr.; Ecology Abstr.; Entomol. Abstr.; Fish Rev.; Key Word Index Wildl. Res.; Psychol. Abstr.; PsycINFO (1990-); PsycLit; Res. Alert [Full Cov.]; Rev. Agric. Entomol.; Rev. Med. Vet. Entomol.; Sci. Cit. Index; SCISEARCH; Soc. Sci. Cit. Index [Select. Cov.]; Wildl. Rev.

IT/0394-9370
**ETHOLOGY, ECOLOGY & EVOLUTION.** [Ethol. ecol. evol.]. **Added/Corp** Universita di Firenze. Dipartimento di Biologia Animale e Genetica. **VFOAT** Ethology, Ecology and Evolution; EEE. Vol. 1, No. 1 (May 1989)-. Academic Scholarly Publication. English. Four times a year. $150.00. Monitore Zoologico Italiano, Via Romana 17, 50125 Firenze Italy. **Tel** 011 39 55 220507. **LC** QL750; .E89. **DD** 591.5/1. **NLM** W1; ET448G. **CODEN** EEEVEP. **Pr Rev.** Documents available from The Genuine Article, BIOSIS Document Express, CASDDS. ***Continues** Monitore Zoologico Italiano, 0026-9786.*
**Desc:** Behavior evolution and animal ecology.
**Ind/Abst** Anim. Behav. Abstr.; Biol. Abstr.; Chem. Abstr.; Curr. Aware. Biol. Sci., CABS; Curr. Contents, Agric. Biol. Environ. Sci.; Ecology Abstr.; Entomol. Abstr.; Fish Rev. (Jan. 1989-July 1992); Res. Alert [Select. Cov.]; SCISEARCH; Soc. Sci. Cit. Index [Select. Cov.]; Wildl. Rev. (Jan. 1989-July 1992).

SP/1130-3204
**ETOLOGIA.** **Added/Corp** Sociedad Espanola de Etologia. No. 1 (1989)-. English (Spanish). Etologia, Departamento de Psicologia, Universidad de Oviedo, 33005 Oviedo Spain. **LC** QL750; .E895. **DD** 591.51/05. **CODEN** ETOLEE.
**Ind/Abst** Ecol. Abstr.

NE/0924-3860
**EUROPEAN JOURNAL OF MORPHOLOGY.** See Medical Science and Technology-Anatomy.

NE/0168-8162
**EXPERIMENTAL & APPLIED ACAROLOGY.** [Exp. appl. acarol.]. **VFOAT** Experimental and Applied Acarology. Vol. 1, No. 1 (March 1985)-. Academic Scholarly Publication. English. Twelve times a year. £368.00 (institution), £158.00 (individual) UK; $538.00 (institution), $315.80 (individual) US. Chapman & Hall, 2-6 Boundary Row, London SE1 8HN England. **Tel** 011 44 71 865 0066, FAX 011 44 71 522 9623, telex 290164 Chapmag. **(Subscription address:** International Thomson Publishing Svcs. Ltd., Subscription Department North Way Andover, Hampshire SP10 5BE England.**)** **ED** W. Helle and L. P. S. van der Geest. **NLM** W1; EX641. **CODEN** EAACEM. **[CCC].** available on microfilm and microfiche from University Microfilms International (UMI). Documents available from The Genuine Article, BIOSIS Document Express, CASDDS.
**Desc:** Publishes original scientific papers in the field of experimental and applied acarology.
**Ind/Abst** AgBiotech News Inf.; AGRICOLA; Biocont. News Inf. (19??-19??); Biodeter. Abstr.; Biol. Abstr. (1985-); Chem. Abstr. (1985-?); CSA Neuro. Abstr. (?-?); Curr. Aware. Biol. Sci., CABS; Curr. Contents, Agric. Biol. Environ. Sci.; Ecol. Abstr.; Ecology Abstr.; EMBASE; Entomol. Abstr.; Environ. Period. Bibliogr.; Fish Rev. (1989-19??); Geogr. Abstr. Phys. Geogr.; Hortic. Abstr.; Index Med. (1985-); Index Vet.; Int. Dev. Abstr. (?-?); Maize Abstr.; Nematol. Abstr.; PESTDOC; Plant Breed. Abstr.; Postharvest News Inf.; Res. Alert [Select. Cov.]; Rev. Agric. Entomol.; Rev. Med. Vet. Entomol.; SCISEARCH; Small Anim. Abstr. Bibliogr.; Sorghum Mill. Abstr.; Vet. Bull.; Weed Abstr.; Wildl. Rev. (1989-19??).

GW
**FALKE, DER.** Vol. 1 (Feb. 1954)-. Periodical. German. bm. Deutscher Judo Verband, Redaktion Ippon Segewaldweg 40, D 12557 Berlin Germany. **Tel** 011 49 711 210770, telex 051 678.
**Ind/Abst** Key Word Index Wildl. Res.

IT/0430-1226
**FAUNA D'ITALIA.** [Fauna Ital.]. Vol. 1 (1956)-. Monographic series. Italian. ir. Price varies per volume. Edizioni Calderini, Casella Postale 2202, 40139 Bologna Italy. **Tel** 39-51-492211, FAX 39-51-493660, telex 1-510336 EDAGRI. **CODEN** FIITA6. Index available. **Bk Rev. Ad Acc. Circ:** 2,000. Documents available from BIOSIS Document Express.
**Desc:** Classifies, locates, and describes all animals forms living in Italy. Topics covered are morphology, ecology, behavior and distributions.
**Ind/Abst** Biol. Abstr. (-1972).

BU/0428-0636
**FAUNA NA BULGARIIA / BULGARSKA AKADEMIIA NA NAUKITE, INSTITUT PO ZOOLOGIIA.** **Added/Corp** Institut po Zoologiia (Bulgarska Akademiia na Naukite). **VFOAT** Fauna Bulgarica; Fauna Bolgarii. Vol. 1 (1950)-. Monographic series. Bulgarian. ir. Price varies per volume. Izdatelstvo na Bulgarskata Akademiia Na Naukite, 6 Rouski Boulevard, Sofia Bulgaria. **Tel** FAX 80 13 41, telex 22267 HEMKIK. **LC** QL298.B8; B823.

NO/0332-768X
**FAUNA NORVEGICA. SER. A., NORWEGIAN FAUNA EXCEPT ENTOMOLOGY AND ORNITHOLOGY.** [Fauna norv., Ser. A]. **Added/Corp** Norsk Zoologisk Tidsskriftsentral. **VFOAT** Ser. A., Norwegian Fauna Except Entomology and Ornithology; Norwegian Fauna Except Entomology and Ornithology. Vol. 1, No. 1 (1980)-. Periodical. English (German and Norwegian). Kr15 (members), Kr25 (non-members). Fauna Norvegica, Zoologisk Museum, Sarsgt 1 0562, Oslo Norway. **Tel** 001 47 2 686960. **LC** QL289; .F39. **DD** 591.9481/05. **CODEN** FNSAD3. Documents available from BIOSIS Document Express.
**Ind/Abst** Biol. Abstr.; Ecol. Abstr.; Ecology Abstr.; Life Sci. Collect.

NO/0332-7701
**FAUNA NORVEGICA. SER. C., CINCLUS.** [Fauna norv., Ser. C]. **Added/Corp** Norsk Zoologisk Tidsskriftsentral. Norsk Ornitologisk Forening. **VFOAT** Cinclus; Cinclus, Norwegian Journal of Ornithology; Norwegian Journal of Ornithology. (1979)-. Periodical. English (Norwegian and German; summaries and/or abstracts in Norwegian and English). Twice a year (June & Dec.). Kr105.00. Fauna Norvegica, Zoologisk Museum, Sarsgt 1 0562, Oslo Norway. **Tel** 001 47 2 686960. **LC** QL690.N8; F38. **DD** 598.29481. **CODEN** FNSCD9. **[CCC].** Documents available from BIOSIS Document Express.
**Ind/Abst** Anim. Behav. Abstr.; Biol. Abstr.; Ecol. Abstr.; Ecology Abstr.; Fish Rev. (Jan. 1989-July 1992); Life Sci. Collect.; Wildl. Rev. (Jan. 1989-July 1992).

US
**FAUNA OF THE NATIONAL PARKS OF THE UNITED STATES : FAUNA SERIES.** **VFOAT** Fauna Series. No. 1 (May 1932)-. Monographic series. English. ir. Price varies per volume. **LC** QL155; .A45.

NO/0014-8881
**FAUNA (OSLO).** (FAUNA.). [Fauna]. **Added/Corp** Norsk zoologisk forening. Vol. 1, No. 1 (Feb. 1948)-. Periodical. Norwegian (summaries and/or abstracts in English). qt. Kr250.00 Nordic countries (Denmardk, the Faroes, Finland, Greenland, Iceland and Sweden); Kr300.00 other. Norsk Zoologisk Forening, Po Box 102 Blindern, N-0314 Oslo Norway. **Tel** 47 56 79367. **ED** Roard Solheim (editor's address: N-5843 Slinde, Norway; editor's phone: 47 5767 9367). **LC** QL289; .F38. **CODEN** FUNAAO. **[CCC]. Bk Rev. Ad Acc. Circ:** 1,500. Documents available from BIOSIS Document Express.
**Desc:** Review articles and original papers in all fields of zoology with emphasis on Norwegian fauna.
**Ind/Abst** AGRICOLA; Biol. Abstr.; Ecology Abstr.; Energy Res. Abstr. (Jan. 1974-); Key Word Index Wildl. Res.; Life Sci. Collect.

PL/0303-4909
**FAUNA POLSKI.** (FAUNA POLSKI. FAUNA POLONIAE.). **Added/Corp** Polska Akademia Nauk. Instytut Zoologiczny. **VFOAT** Fauna Poloniae. (1973)-. Monographic series. Polish. **LC** UNC.
**Ind/Abst** Biodeter. Abstr.; Postharvest News Inf.; Rev. Agric. Entomol.

UN
**FAUNA UKRAINY.** **Added/Corp** Akademia nauk URSR. Instytut Zoologii. (1956)-. Monographic series. Ukrainian. **LC** QL281; .F35.
**Ind/Abst** Helminthol. Abstr. (1991-); Poult. Abstr.; Protozoolog. Abstr.

FR
**FAUNE DE L'EUROPE ET DU BASSIN MEDITERRANEEN.** Vol. 1 (1965)-. Monographic series. French. ir. Price varies per volume. Scientific & Medical Publishers of France, 100 East 42nd Street, Suite 1002, New York NY 10017-5613. **Tel** (212)983-6278. **LC** QL253; .F3.

FR/0428-0709
**FAUNE DE MADAGASCAR.** **Added/Corp** Tananarive, Malagasy Republic. Institut de Recherches Scientifiques de la Republique Malgache. (1956)-. Monographic series. French. ir. Price varies per volume. Librairie du Museum, BP 429, 75233 Paris Cedex 05 France. **Tel** 011 33 1 47073805. **(Subscription address:** Librairie Thomas, 28 rue Fosses, St. Bernard, 75005 Paris France.**)**
**Desc:** Describes forms and species, including newly-discovered items, of Madagascaran fauna, with illustrations and keys. Also offers characteristics for comparison with near species and discusses ecological significance.

US/0196-2140
**FERNALD CLUB YEARBOOK.** **Main/Corp** Massachusetts. University. Fernald Entomological Club. **Added/Corp** Massachusetts. University. Fernald Entomological Club. Yearbook. Vol. 1 (1932)-. English. an. Department of Entomology, Fernald Hall, University of Massachusetts, Amherst MA 01002.

DK/0109-2529
**FICHES D'IDENTIFICATION DU PLANCTON.** [Fiches d'identif. planct.]. **Added/Corp** International Council for the Exploration of the Sea. No. 172 (1986)-. Monographic series. English (French). ir. Price varies per volume. CA Reitzels Forlag AS, Norregade 20, DK-1165 Copenhagen K Denmark. **Tel** 011 45 3 3122400. **LC** QL639.25; .F53. **DD** 597/.03. **CODEN** FIPLEL. **Circ:** 600. Documents available from BIOSIS Document Express. ***Continues** Fiches d'Identification du Zooplancton.*
**Desc:** Keys for the identification of the major plankton species in the North Atlantic. Line drawings with taxonomic and and physical descriptions, followed by bibliographic references.
**Ind/Abst** Biol. Abstr. (1987-).

US/0015-0754
**FIELDIANA : ZOOLOGY.** **Added/Corp** Field Museum of Natural History Field Columbian Museum Zoological Series. Vol. 1 (1895)-. Periodical. English. ir. price varies per volume. Field Museum of Natural History, Roosevelt Road at Lake Shore Drive, Chicago IL 60605-2496. **Tel** (312)922-9410 ext. 402, FAX (312)922-0671. **ED** Timothy Plowman. **LC** QL1; .F4. **Bk Rev. Ad Acc. Circ:** 550 (ctrl). Documents available from BIOSIS Document Express, CASDDS.
**Desc:** Taxonomy, morphology, evolutionary, and zoogeography studies.
**Ind/Abst** Biol. Abstr.; Chem. Abstr.; Ecol. Abstr.; Ecology Abstr.; Fish Rev.; Geogr. Abstr. Phys. Geogr.; Rev. Med. Vet. Entomol.; Wildl. Rev.

US/0741-3866
**FINS AND FEATHERS (CONNECTICUT ED.).** ***Title Change.*** (FINS AND FEATHERS.). [Fins feathers]. **VFOAT** Connecticut Fins and Feathers. Periodical. English. mo. Fins and Feathers, 318 West Franklin Avenue, Minneapolis MN 55040-9989. **DD** 799. ***Merged with** Fins and Feathers (... Ed.) **to form** Fins and Featehrs (Mount Morris, Ill.), 1053-6965.*

US/0741-3874
**FINS AND FEATHERS (KANSAS, ED.).** ***Title Change.*** (FINS AND FEATHERS.). [Fins feathers]. **VFOAT** Kansas Fins and Feathers. Periodical. English. mo. Fins and Feathers, 318 West Franklin Avenue, Minneapolis MN 55040-9989. **DD** 799. ***Merged with** Fins and Feathers (... Ed.) **to form** Fins and Feathers (Mount Morris, Ill.), 1053-6965.*

US/0741-4005
**FINS AND FEATHERS (SOUTH DAKOTA ED.).** ***Title Change.*** (FINS AND FEATHERS.). [Fins feathers]. **VFOAT** South Dakota Fins and Feathers. Periodical. English. mo. Fins and Feathers, 318 West

Franklin Avenue, Minneapolis MN 55040-9989. **DD** 799. ***Merged with*** *Fins and Feathers (... Ed.)* ***to form*** *Fins and Feathers (Mount Morris, Ill.), 1053-6965.*

US/0741-7101
**FINS AND FEATHERS (VIRGINIA, ED.).** ***Title Change.*** (FINS AND FEATHERS.). [Fins feathers]. **VFOAT** Virginia Fins and Feathers. Periodical. English. mo. Fins and Feathers, 318 West Franklin Avenue, Minneapolis MN 55040-9989. **DD** 799. ***Merged with*** *Fins and Feathers (... Ed.)* ***to form*** *Fins and Feathers (Mount Morris, Ill.), 1053-6965.*

UK/1050-4648
**FISH AND SHELLFISH IMMUNOLOGY.** [Fish shellfish immunol.]. (1991)-. Academic Scholarly Publication. English. Eight times a year. $290.00. Academic Press Ltd., A Division of Harcourt Brace & Company Ltd., 24-28 Oval Road, London NW1 7DX England. **Tel** 071 267 4466, FAX 071 482 2293, 071 485 4752, telex 25775 ACPRES G. **(Subscription address:** Harcourt Brace & Company, Ltd., Foots Cray, High Street, Sidcup Kent DA14 5HP England.**) ED** A. E. Ellis and M. F. Tatner. **LC** QL638.97; .F55. **DD** 597/.029/05. **Pr Rev.**
**Desc:** Aims to rapidly publish high-quality, peer-reviewed contributions in the expanding fields of fish and shellfish immunology. It will present studies on the basic mechanisms of both the specific and nonspecific defense systems, the cells, tissues, and humoral factors involved, their dependence on environmental and intrinsic factors, response to pathogens, response to vaccination, and applied studies on the development of specific vaccines for use in the aquaculture industry.

UK
**FLEA NEWS.** No. 1 (II. 1974)-. Periodical. English. ir. Iowa State University Department of Entomology, Ames IA 50011-3222.

GW
**FLIES OF THE NEARCTIC REGION.** Vol. 1 (1980)-. Monographic series. English. ir (three to five issues per year). Price varies per volume. E. Schweizerbartsche Verlagsbuchhandlung, Johannesstrasse 3A, D-70176 Stuttgart Germany. **Tel** 011 49 711 625001, FAX 011 49 711 625005, telex 723363 SCHB D. **ED** Graham C D Griffiths.
**Ind/Abst** AGRICOLA.

DK/0015-3818
**FLORA OG FAUNA.** [Flora fauna]. **Added/Corp** Naturhistorisk Forening for Jylland. Naturhistorisk Forening for Sjaelland. Naturhistorisk Forening for Lolland-Falster. Naturhistorisk Forening for Fyn. Bornholms Naturhistoriske Forening. (1899)-. Periodical. Danish (summaries and/or abstracts in English). qt. kr170.00. Palle Jorum Flora OG Fauna, c/o Natural History Museum, Universitetsparken Building 210, 8000 Aarhus C Denmark. **Tel** 011 45 6 129777. **ED** Thomas Secher Jensen. **CODEN** FLFAAN. Index available. cum. index. **Bk Rev. Circ:** 700 (ctrl). Documents available from BIOSIS Document Express.
**Desc:** Presents original contributions to Danish faunistic and floristic knowledge and to the study of biology, ecology and systematics of Danish animal and plant species.
**Ind/Abst** AGRICOLA; Biol. Abstr.; Ecol. Abstr.; Energy Res. Abstr. (Aug. 1977-); Life Sci. Collect.

US/0738-999X
**FLORIDA FIELD NATURALIST.** [Fla. field nat.]. Vol. 1; Spring 1973-. Periodical. English. qt. $20.00. Florida Ornithological Society History, Florida Museum of Natural History, University of Florida, Gainesville FL 32611. **Tel** (904)336-2230. **(Subscription address:** 330 E Swoope Street, Lake Alfred, FL 33143**) ED** James A Rodgers. **LC** QL684.F6; F56. **CODEN** FFNADO. Index available. cum. index. **Bk Rev. Ad Acc. Pr Rev. Circ:** 675 (ctrl). Documents available from BIOSIS Document Express.
**Desc:** Biology and natural history of vertebrate animals in and near Florida and Caribbean.
**Ind/Abst** Biol. Abstr.; Key Word Index Wildl. Res.; Wildl. Rev.

PL/0015-5497
**FOLIA BIOLOGICA (WARSZAWA).** (FOLIA BIOLOGICA.). [Folia biol. (Warsz.)]. **Added/Corp** Zakad Zoologii Doswiadczalnej (Polska Akademia Nauk) Zakad Zoologii Systematycznej i Do,swiadczalnej (Polska Akademia Nauk). Dept. of Experimental Zoology. Vol. 1, Part 1 (1953)-. Academic Scholarly Publication. English (Polish; summaries and/or abstracts in Russian; table of contents in Russian). qt. Price on Request. **(Subscription address:** ARS Polona, PO Box 1001, 00068 Warsaw Poland.**) NLM** W1 FO128R. **CODEN** FOBGA8. **Pr Rev.** Documents available from The Genuine Article, BIOSIS Document Express, CASDDS.
**Ind/Abst** AGRICOLA; Biol. Abstr.; Chem. Abstr.; Curr. Contents Life Sci.; Curr. Ref. Fish Res.; EMBASE; Helminthol. Abstr. (19??-19??); Immunol. Abstr.; Index Med.; Index Vet.; Life Sci. Collect.; Pig News Inf.; Poult. Abstr.; Res. Alert [Select. Cov.]; Rev. Agric. Entomol.; Rev. Med. Vet. Entomol.

PL/0015-5659
**FOLIA MORPHOLOGICA.** [Folia morphol.]. **Added/Corp** Polskie Towarzystwo Anatomiczne. (1929)-. Academic Scholarly Publication. Polish (French and German; summaries and/or abstracts in English and Russian; table of contents in English and Russian). qt. Price on Request. **(Subscription address:** ARS Polona, PO Box 1001, 00068 Warsaw Poland.**) LC** QL799; .F6. **NLM** W1 FO255. **CODEN** FOMOAJ. available in microform. Documents available from BIOSIS Document Express, CASDDS.
**Ind/Abst** Biol. Abstr. (-1987); Chem. Abstr.; EMBASE; Index Med.; Index Vet.; Vet. Bull.

XR/0015-5683
**FOLIA PARASITOLOGICA / CZECHOSLOVAK ACADEMY OF SCIENCE.** [Folia parasitologica]. **Added/Corp** Parasitologicky Ustav (Ceskoslovenska Akademie Ved). Vol.13 (1966)-. Academic Scholarly Publication. English (Multiple languages; summaries and/or abstracts in Russian). qt. $160.00 (1 year), $300.00 (2 year). Czech Academy of Sciences, Branisovska 31, 37005 Ceske Budejovice, Czech Republic. **Tel** 011 42 38 817 ext. 213, 214. **ED** Jan Prokopic. **NLM** W1 FO277R. **CODEN** FPARA9. **[CCC].** cum. index. **Bk Rev. Pr Rev.** Documents available from The Genuine Article, BIOSIS Document Express, CASDDS. ***Continues*** *Ceskoslovenska Parasitologie.*
**Desc:** Publishes original papers from all branches of general medical and veterinary parasitology.
**Ind/Abst** AGRICOLA; Biol. Abstr.; Chem. Abstr.; Curr. Aware. Biol. Sci., CABS; Curr. Contents, Agric. Biol. Environ. Sci.; Curr. Ref. Fish Res.; For. Abstr.; Health Plan. Adminis.; Helminthol. Abstr. (19??-19??); Index Med.; Index Vet.; Microbiol. Abstr. Sect. C; Life Sci. Collect.; Pig News Inf.; Poult. Abstr.; Protozoolog. Abstr.; Ref. Z.; Res. Alert [Full Cov.]; Rev. Med. Vet. Entomol.; Sci. Cit. Index; SCISEARCH; Trop. Dis. Bull.; Virol. AIDS Abstr.

SZ/0015-5713
**FOLIA PRIMATOLOGICA.** [Folia primatol.]. Vol. 1 (1963)-. Periodical. English (French and German). Eight times a year. $302.00. S. Karger AG, Allschwilerstrasse 10, PO Box - Postfach - Case Postale, CH-4009 Basel Switzerland. **Tel** 011 41 61 306-1111, FAX 011 41 61 306-1234, telex CH 962 652. **ED** R.H. Crompton. **LC** QL737.P9; F6. **NLM** W1 FO282J. **CODEN** FPRMAB. **[CCC]. Ad Acc. Pr Rev.** available on microfilm from University Microfilms International (UMI). Documents available from The Genuine Article, BIOSIS Document Express, CASDDS.
**Desc:** Gives a wide range of natural scientists access to key investigations of non-human primates. Topics range from physiology, biochemistry and pathology, through taxonomy, phylogeny and paleontology, to behavior, psychology and ecology. Questions concerning reproduction and immunology, as well as comparative and functional morphology, are also regularly featured. In-depth articles on all these subjects are contributed by the world's leading primatologists who value the rapid publication of their latest work.
**Ind/Abst** Abstr. Anthropol.; Anim. Behav. Abstr.; Anthropol. Index; Anthropol. Lit.; Biol. Abstr.; Chem. Abstr. (1963-1986); CSA Neuro. Abstr. (?-?); Curr. Contents, Agric. Biol. Environ. Sci.; Curr. Contents Life Sci.; Curr. Primate Ref.; Dairy Sci. Abstr.; Ecology Abstr.; GeoRef; Index Med.; Index Vet.; Int. Aerosp. Abstr.; Nutr. Abstr. Rev., Ser. B, Live Feeds and Feed.; Nutr. Abstr. Rev., Ser. A, Hum. Exp.; Life Sci. Collect.; Psychol. Abstr. (1963-); PsycINFO; PsycLit; Ref. Upd. Deluxe Ed.; Res. Alert [Full Cov.]; Sci. Cit. Index; SCISEARCH; Soc. Sci. Cit. Index [Select. Cov.]; Vet. Bull.; Wildl. Rev.

XR/0139-7893
**FOLIA ZOOLOGICA (BRNO).** (FOLIA ZOOLOGICA.). [Folia zool.]. **Added/Corp** Ceskoslovenska Akademie Ved. Vol. 26 (1977)-. Periodical. English (German; summaries and/or abstracts in German and Russian). Four times a year. f170.00. Institute Systematic Ecological, Biology, CSAV Kvetna 8, 60365 Brno Czech Republic. **ED** Josef Kratochvil. **LC** QL1; .Z748. **CODEN** FOZODJ. **[CCC].** Index available. **Bk Rev. Pr Rev. Circ:** 1,000. Documents available from The Genuine Article, BIOSIS Document Express. ***Continues*** *Zoologicke Listy.*
**Desc:** Brings together comprehensive articles on the results of original research in vertebrate zoology, e.g. mammalogy, ornithology, ichthyology and morphology.
**Ind/Abst** AGRICOLA; Biocont. News Inf.; Biodeter. Abstr.; Biol. Abstr.; Curr. Aware. Biol. Sci., CABS; Curr. Contents, Agric. Biol. Environ. Sci.; Curr. Ref. Fish Res.; Ecol. Abstr.; Ecology Abstr.; Fish Rev.; For. Prod. Abstr.; For. Abstr.; Index Vet.; Key Word Index Wildl. Res.; Nutr. Abstr. Rev., Ser. B, Live Feeds and Feed.; Life Sci. Collect.; Protozoolog. Abstr.; Ref. Z.; Res. Alert [Full Cov.]; Rev. Med. Vet. Entomol.; Sci. Cit. Index; SCISEARCH; Wildl. Rev.

GW/0071-7991
**FORTSCHRITTE DER ZOOLOGIE (STUTTGART).** (FORTSCHRITTE DER ZOOLOGIE.). [Fortschr. Zool.]. **Added/Corp** Deutsche Zoologische Gesellschaft. **VFOAT** Progress in Zoology. Vol. 1 (1935)-. Monographic series. English (German). ir. Price varies per volume. Forschungsanst Holzwirtschaft, Alfred Moeller Str, D 16225 Eberswalde Germany. **Tel** 011 49 3334 65343. **ED** M. Lindner. **LC** QL1; .F6. **DD** 590.5. **NLM** W1 FO941. **CODEN** FOZOAG. **[CCC].** Documents available from BIOSIS Document Express, CASDDS. ***Supersedes in part*** *Ergebnisse und Fortschritte der Zoologie.*
**Ind/Abst** AGRICOLA; Biol. Abstr.; Calcium Calcif. Tissue Abstr.; Chem. Abstr.; CSA Neuro. Abstr. (?-?); Index Med.; Life Sci. Collect.; Vitis Vitic. Enol. Abstr.

IT/0429-288X
**FRAGMENTA ENTOMOLOGICA.** [Fragm. entomol.]. Vol. 1 (1951)-. Monographic series. Italian (English and French; summaries and/or abstracts in French and English). Price varies per volume.
**Ind/Abst** AGRICOLA; Life Sci. Collect.; Rev. Agric. Entomol.; Rev. Med. Vet. Entomol.; Vitis Vitic. Enol. Abstr.

PL/0015-9301
**FRAGMENTA FAUNISTICA.** [Fragm. faun.]. **Added/Corp** Polska Akademia Nauk. Instytut Zoologiczny. Instytut Zoologii (Polska Akademia Nauk). Vol. 7, No. 1 (Oct. 25, 1954)-. Periodical. Polish (English, French and German; summaries and/or abstracts in Russian). ir. **(Subscription address:** ARS Polona, PO Box 1001, 00068 Warsaw Poland.**) LC** QL1; .F7. **CODEN** FRGFAH. Documents available from BIOSIS Document Express. ***Continues*** *Fragmenta Faunistica Musei Zoologici Polonici.*
**Ind/Abst** AGRICOLA; Biocont. News Inf.; Biol. Abstr.; For. Abstr.; Nematol. Abstr.; Life Sci. Collect.; Soils Fert.

IT/0532-7679
**FRUSTULA ENTOMOLOGICA.** [Frustula entomol.]. Vol. 1 (1958)-. Monographic series. Italian (summaries and/or abstracts in English and French). Price varies per volume.
**Ind/Abst** AGRICOLA; Biocont. News Inf. (1991-); Biodeter. Abstr. (1991-); Maize Abstr.; Life Sci. Collect.; Rev. Agric. Entomol.; Rev. Med. Vet. Entomol.; Weed Abstr.

PO/0253-0597
**GARCIA DE ORTA : SERIE DE ZOOLOGIA.** [Garcia de Orta. Ser. de zool.]. **VFOAT** Serie de Zoologia. Vol. 1; 1972-. Academic Scholarly Publication. Portuguese (English, French, Spanish, Italian and German). sa. 1800$00. Instituto de Investigacao Cientifica Tropical, Centro de Documentacao e Informacao, rua Jau 47, 1 300 Lisbon Portugal. **Tel** 645321. **LC** QL1; .G37. **CODEN** GOZOAR. Index available. **Circ:** 1,000 (ctrl). Documents available from CASDDS. ***Supersedes in part*** *Garcia de Orta.*
**Desc:** Publishes articles from all fields included in zoological studies, such as mammalogy, ornithology, herpetology, ichthyology, entomology, and helminthology.
**Ind/Abst** Chem. Abstr. (1972-1979); Helminthol. Abstr. (1991-); Life Sci. Collect.; Protozoolog. Abstr.; Rev. Agric. Entomol.; Rev. Med. Vet. Entomol.

US/0435-1363
**GASTROPODIA.** [Gastropodia]. V. 1- (No. 1- ); 1952-. Periodical. English. ir. $9.35 (four issues). Glenn R Webb, 14 Henry Road, Fleetwood PA 19522. **Tel** (215)682-7291. **ED** Glenn R Webb. **CODEN** GSTPAS. **Bk Rev. Ad Acc. Circ:** 53 (ctrl). Documents available from BIOSIS Document Express.
**Desc:** A journal for the publication of original papers on mollusks.
**Ind/Abst** Biol. Abstr.

CL/0016-531X
**GAYANA : ZOOLOGIA.** [Gayana, Zool.]. **Added/Corp** Universidad de Concepcion. Facultad de Ciencias Biologicas y de Recursos Naturales. Universidad de Concepcion. Instituto de Biologia. Universidad de Concepcion. Instituto Central de Biologia. **VFOAT** Zoologia. No. 1 (1961)-. Monographic series. Spanish. ir. Price varies per volume. Universidad de Concepcion / Chile, Casilla 1557, Apartado 19, Concepcion Chile. **Tel** 011 56 41 234985 ext. 2591. **LC** QL1; .G38. **DD** 591.983/05. **CODEN** GBCZAO. ctrl circ. Documents available from BIOSIS Document Express.
**Ind/Abst** Biol. Abstr.; GeoRef; Life Sci. Collect.

GW/0016-5816
**GEFIEDERTE WELT, DIE.** Vol. 1 (1872)-. Periodical. German. mo (12 issues). DM104.40 Germany; DM117.60 other. Verlag Eugen Ulmer, Postfach 700561, D 70574 Stuttgart Germany. **Tel** 011 49 711 4507108, FAX 011 49 711 4507120, telex 7-23634. **[CCC].** Index available. ***Absorbed*** *Vogel-Kosmos.*
**Ind/Abst** Fish Rev.; Wildl. Rev.

GW/0016-5840
**GEGENBAURS MORPHOLOGISCHES JAHRBUCH.** ***Ceased.*** [Jahrb. Morphol. mikrosk. anat., 1 Abt. Gegenbaurs morphol. Jahrb.]. (1954)-(19??). Periodical. German. Deutscher Judo Verband, Redaktion Ippon Segewaldweg 40, D 12557 Berlin Germany. **Tel** 011 49 711 210770, telex 051 678. **LC** QL801; .G25. **NLM** W1 GE107. ***Continues*** *Gegenbaurs Morphologisches Jahrbuch und Beitrage zur Anatomie Funktioneller Systeme.*
**Ind/Abst** AGRICOLA; Anim. Breed. Abstr.; CSA Neuro. Abstr. (?-?); GeoRef; Health Plan. Adminis.; Index Med.; Index Vet.; Life Sci. Collect.; Pig News Inf.; Vet. Bull.

US
**GLADYS PORTER ZOO NEWS.** **Main/Corp** Gladys Porter Zoo. **Added/Corp** Valley Zoological Society. **VFOAT** Zoo News. (19??)-. Periodical. English. qt. Free with Valley Zoological Society membership.

Gladys Porter Zoo, 500 Ringgold Street, Brownsville TX 78520. **Tel** (512)546-7187. **ED** David G Barker. **Circ:** 3,000 (ctrl).
**Desc:** Information on animals in zoo's collection, new arrivals, happenings at the Gladys Porter Zoo.

US/0017-114X
**GLEANINGS IN BEE CULTURE.** ***Title Change.*** [Glean. bee cult.]. **VFOAT** Bee Culture. Vol. 2-120 (Jan. 1, 1874)-(Dec. 1992). Academic Scholarly Publication. English. mo. A I Root Company, 623 West Liberty Street, PO Box 706, Medina OH 44258. **Tel** (216)725-6677, FAX (216)725-5624, telex 753856. **ED** Kim Flottum. **LC** SF521; .G5. **CODEN** GLBCAK. Index available. cum. index. **Bk Rev. Ad Acc. Circ:** 13,000. available on microfilm from University Microfilms International (UMI). Documents available from BIOSIS Document Express, CASDDS. ***Continues** Novices' Gleanings in Bee Culture. **Continued by** Bee Culture.*
**Desc:** Geared for the hobbyist beekeeper. Contains articles on honey production, nectar and pollen, and how-to information on beekeeping.
**Ind/Abst** AGRICOLA; Biol. Agric. Index; Biol. Abstr.; Chem. Abstr.

SP/0367-5041
**GRAELLSIA.** (GRAELLSIA / EDITADA POR EL INSTITUTO ESPANOL DE ENTOMOLOGIA DEL CONSEJO SUPERIOR DE INVESTIGACIONES CIENTIFICAS.). [Graellsia]. **Added/Corp** Consejo Superior de Investigaciones Cientificas (Spain). Instituto Espanol de Entomologia. (1943)-. Periodical. Spanish (Portuguese and English). an. 3750ptas Spain; 2500ptas other (Vol. 48- 1992). Consejo Superior Investigacion Cientificas (CSIC), Vitruvio 8, 28006 Madrid Spain. **Tel** 011 34 1 5612833, FAX 011 34 1 4113077, telex 42182. **LC** QL461; .G7. **DD** 595.7/005. **CODEN** GRAEAT. Documents available from BIOSIS Document Express.
**Desc:** Publishes research from Spanish and Portuguese entomologists on morphology, physiology and ecology of Iberian arthropods.
**Ind/Abst** Biocont. News Inf. (19??-19??); Biol. Abstr.; Ecology Abstr.; Entomol. Abstr.; Maize Abstr.; Life Sci. Collect.; Rev. Agric. Entomol.; Rev. Med. Vet. Entomol.

CN/0714-8283
**GUILLEMOT, LE.** [Guillemot]. Vol. 1, No. (Winter 1981)-. Periodical. French. qt. $2.50 Per No. Guillemot, c/o Club des Ornithologues de la Gaspesie, C P 245, Perce Quebec G0C 2L0 Canada. **DD** 598.29714/77. **UDC** 598.2(714).

JA/0285-3191
**HACHU RYOSEIRUIGAKU ZASSHI.** [Hachu ryoseiruigaku zasshi]. **Added/Corp** Nihon Hachu Ryoseirui Gakkai. **VFOAT** Acta Herpetologica Japonica; Japanese Journal of Herpetology. Vol. 1 (1964)-. Monographic series. Japanese (English; summaries and/or abstracts in English). qt. $176.00. Herpetological Society of Japan, c/o Department of Zoology, Faculty of Science, Kyoto University, Kitashirakawa-Oiwakecho Sakyo, Kyoto, 606 Japan. **CODEN** HRYZAJ. Documents available from BIOSIS Document Express.
**Ind/Abst** Biol. Abstr.

FR/0397-765X
**HALIOTIS. Added/Corp** Societe Francaise de Malacologie. Vol. 1, No. 1 (1971)-. French (English). an. 280.00F (institutions), 200.00F (individuals). Societe Francaise Malacologie, 55 rue de Buffon, 75005 Paris France. **Tel** 33 1 40793096. **Circ:** 500. ***Continues** Haliotis, 0397-765X.*
**Desc:** Scientific papers on molluscs.

II
**HANDBOOK SERIES / ZOOLOGICAL SURVEY OF INDIA. Added/Corp** Zoological Survey of India. No. 1 (1980)-. Monographic series. English. Price varies per volume.

GW
**HANDBUCH DER PALAOHERPETOLOGIE. VFOAT** Encyclopedia of Paleoherpetology. Periodical. English (German). ir. VCH Publishers Inc, 220 East 23rd Street, New York NY 10010. **Tel** (212)683-8333, , FAX (212)481-0897. **(Subscription address:** VCH Publishers Inc., 303 Northwest 12th Avenue, Journals Department, Deerfield FL 33442.**) UDC** 569.812.

GW
**HANDBUCH DER ZOOLOGIE.** Vol. 1 (1923)-. Monographic series. German. ir. Price varies per volume. Walter de Gruyter Inc., PO Box 303421, D 10728 Berlin Germany. **Tel** 011 49 30 260050, FAX 011 49 30 26005251. **(Subscription address:** US and Canada/ 200 Saw Mill River Road, Hawthorne, NY 10532**)**
**Ind/Abst** AGRICOLA.

KO/0440-2332
**HANGUG JAMSA HAGNOI JI.** (HANGUK CHAMSA HAKHOE CHI.). [Hangug jamsa haghoi ji]. **VFOAT** Sericultural Journal of Korea. Academic Scholarly Publication. Korean (summaries and/or abstracts in English). sa. $15.00. Hunkuk Chamsa Hakhoe, 61 Sodun-dong, Suwon 441-100 South Korea. **Tel** 0331 292 6183, FAX 0331 292 4622. **ED** Chung Hee Nam (editor's address: Department of Natural Fiber Science, Suwon, South Korea). **LC** SF553.K6. **UDC** 638.1(519). **CODEN** HCHCAW. Documents available from CASDDS.
**Ind/Abst** Chem. Abstr.

KO/1011-2014
**HANGUK KOMI YONGUSO YONGU POGOSO.** [Kor. arachnol.]. **VFOAT** Korean Arachnology; Korean Arachnol.; Bulletin of Arachnological Institute of Korea. Periodical. Korean (English). sa. W10000 Korea; ¥5000 Japan; $25.00 other. Arachnology Institute of Korea, 42 Dosun Dong Songdong GU, Seoul 133-040 Korea. **Tel** (02)294-8900, FAX (02)296-0562. **ED** Joo-Pil Kim. **LC** PAR. **UDC** 595.4(519). **CODEN** KOARER. Index available. cum. index. **Circ:** 600 (ctrl). Documents available from BIOSIS Document Express.
**Desc:** Articles, notes and miscellaneous relating to Korean arachnology.
**Ind/Abst** Biol. Abstr. (1985-).

GW/0176-2621
**HELDIA.** (HELDIA : MUNCHNER MALAKOLOGISCHE MITTEILUNGEN.). [Heldia]. Vol. 1, Vol. 1 (1984)-. Periodical. German. Twice a year. DM70.00. Heldia, Raiffeisenstrasse 5, W 8059 Woerth Germany. **Tel** 011 49 8122 7132.

XO/0440-6605
**HELMINTHOLOGIA.** [Helminthologia]. **Added/Corp** Ceskoslovenska Akademie Ved. Slovenska Akadamia Vied. Vol. 1 (1959)-. Academic Scholarly Publication. English (French, German and Russian). Four times a year. $160.00 US; $235.00 others. Slovenska Akademia Vied / Slovak Academy of Sciences, PO Box 57, 81005 Bratislava Slovakia. **Tel** 011 42 7 3782715, 011 42 7 3782925, FAX 011 42 7 496849, telex 93261. **LC** QL392; .H38. **NLM** W1 HE796B. **CODEN** HMTGA4. Documents available from BIOSIS Document Express, CASDDS.
**Ind/Abst** AGRICOLA; Biol. Abstr.; Chem. Abstr.; EMBASE; Fish Rev. (Jan. 1989-July 1992); Helminthol. Abstr. (1991-); Nematol. Abstr.; Poult. Abstr.; Rev. Agric. Entomol.; Rev. Med. Vet. Entomol.; Small Anim. Abstr. Bibliogr.; Vet. Bull.; Trop. Dis. Bull.; Wheat Barley Trit. Abstr.; Wildl. Rev. (Jan. 1989-July 1992).

UK/0957-6789
**HELMINTHOLOGICAL ABSTRACTS.** **See** Zoology-Abstracting, Bibliographies and Statistics.

BU/0324-1947
**HELMINTOLOGIJA (SOFIJA).** (KHELMINTOLOGIIA.). [Helmintologija]. **Added/Corp** Bulgarska Akademiia na Naukite. **VFOAT** Helminthology. (1976)-. Academic Scholarly Publication. Bulgarian (summaries and/or abstracts in English and Russian; table of contents in English and Russian). sa. Izdatelstvo na Bulgarskata Akademiia Na Naukite, 6 Rouski Boulevard, Sofia Bulgaria. **Tel** FAX 80 13 41, telex 22267 HEMKIK. **LC** QL392.A1; B814. **NLM** W1 KH38. **CODEN** KHELDD. Documents available from BIOSIS Document Express, CASDDS. ***Supersedes** Bulgarska Akademiia na Naukite. Tsentralna Khelmintologichna Laboratoriia. Izestiia.*
**Ind/Abst** Biol. Abstr.; Chem. Abstr.; EMBASE; Helminthol. Abstr. (1991-); Index Vet.; Nematol. Abstr.; Vet. Bull.

US/0440-7296
**HERP. VFOAT** N.Y.H.S. Bulletin. Periodical. English. sa. New York Herpetological Society, Central Park West at 79th Street, New York NY 10024. **LC** QL640. **DD** 598.1'05. **UDC** 597.6+598.1.

AT
**HERPETOFAUNA. Added/Corp** Australian Affiliation of Herpetological Societies. (19??)-. Periodical. English. Twice a year (June, Dec.). $15.00. Australian Affiliation of Herpetological Societies, PO Box R307 Royal Exchange, New South Wales 2000 Australia. **Tel** 011 61 2 4494606. **Bk Rev. Pr Rev. Circ:** 900. ***Formed by the union of** South Australian Herpetologist **and** Bulletin of Herpetology.*
**Ind/Abst** Ecol. Abstr.

UK/0269-8498
**HERPETOFAUNA NEWS.** [Herpetof. news]. (1985)-. Periodical. English. tq. £6.00. Herpetofauna Conservation International, PO Box 1, Halesworth, Suffolk 1P19 9AW England. **Tel** 011 44 98 684518. **ED** Tom Langton. **DD** 597.605. **Bk Rev. Ad Acc. Circ:** 1,000 (ctrl).
**Desc:** Reports on news, views, features and meetings concerning reptiles and amphibians and their conservation.

US/0018-0831
**HERPETOLOGICA.** [Herpetological]. Vol. 1; (July 1936)-. Periodical. English. qt. $70.00 (membership). Herpetologist's League / Department of Biological Sciences, PO Box 70726 East TSU, Johnson City TN 37614. **Tel** (615)929-6929. **ED** Robert Jaeger. **LC** QL640; .H4. **DD** 598.105. **UDC** 597.6+598.1. **CODEN** HPTGAP. Index available. cum. index. **Bk Rev. Pr Rev. Acid Free. Circ:** 1,500 (ctrl). available on microfilm and microfiche from University Microfilms International (UMI). Documents available from The Genuine Article, BIOSIS Document Express, CASDDS.
**Desc:** Publishes original papers dealing largely or exclusively with the biology of amphibians and reptiles. Theoretically and primarily quantitative manuscripts are particularly encouraged.
**Ind/Abst** Anim. Behav. Abstr.; Biol. Abstr.; Chem. Abstr.; Curr. Aware. Biol. Sci., CABS; Curr. Contents, Agric. Biol. Environ. Sci.; Ecol. Abstr.; Ecology Abstr.; GeoRef; Life Sci. Collect.; Protozoolog. Abstr.; Res. Alert [Full Cov.]; Sci. Cit. Index; SCISEARCH; Soc. Sci. Cit. Index [Select. Cov.]; Wildl. Rev.

US/0161-147X
**HERPETOLOGICAL CIRCULAR.** [Herpetol. circ.]. **Added/Corp** Society for the Study of Amphibians and Reptiles. No. 1 (1973)-. Periodical. English. ir. Price varies. SSAR Publications, St.Louis University, Department of Biology, St.Louis MO 63103. **Tel** (513)529-4901. **(Subscription address:** Dr. Robert Aldridge / SSAR Publications, 3507 Laclede Street, Department of Biology, St. Louis MO 63103.**) CODEN** HCSRDX.

UK/0268-0130
**HERPETOLOGICAL JOURNAL, THE. Added/Corp** British Herpetological Society. Vol. 1, No. 1 (Dec. 1985)-. Periodical. English. Four times a year. $80.00 US; £40.00 UK. British Herpetological Society / Zoology Society of London, Regents Park, London WC1 4RY England. **ED** T. J. C. BeeBee. Index available. cum. index. **Bk Rev. Ad Acc. Pr Rev. Circ:** 850. Documents available from The Genuine Article. ***Continues** British Journal of Herpetology, 0007-1056.*
**Desc:** The journal publishes papers describing original research in all areas of herpetology.
**Ind/Abst** Anim. Behav. Abstr.; CSA Neuro. Abstr. (?-?); Curr. Aware. Biol. Sci., CABS; Ecol. Abstr. (?-?); Ecology Abstr.; Res. Alert [Select. Cov.]; SCISEARCH; Wildl. Rev.

US/0733-1347
**HERPETOLOGICAL MONOGRAPH.** [Herpetol. monogr.]. **Added/Corp** Herpetologists League. **VFOAT** Herpetological Monographs. (1982)-. English. ir. Comes with a Herpetologists League membership. Herpetologist's League / Department of Biological Sciences, PO Box 70726 East TSU, Johnson City TN 37614. **Tel** (615)929-6929. **ED** George R. Zug. **LC** QL640; .H423. **DD** 597.6. **Circ:** 750.
**Desc:** Serves as a publication outlet for larger manuscripts dealing with the systematics and biology of amphibians and reptiles.

US/0018-084X
**HERPETOLOGICAL REVIEW.** [Herpetol. rev.]. **Added/Corp** Society for the Study of Amphibians and Reptiles. Herpetologists League. Herpetological Information Search Systems. Vol. 1 (Sept. 1967)-. Periodical. English. Four times a year (Mar., June, Sept., Dec.). $20.00 Comes with the Journal of Herpetology. Society for the Study Amphibians & Reptiles, PO Box 626, Hays KS 67601. **Tel** (913)628-1437. **ED** Martin Rosenberg. **LC** QL640; .H425. **DD** 597. **CODEN** HEPRB. **Bk Rev. Ad Acc. Circ:** 2,400. Documents available from BIOSIS Document Express. ***Absorbed** Newsletter of the Ohio Herpetological Society. **Superseded in part by** HISS News-Journal, 0090-9203; HISS Titles and Reviews **and** Recent Herpetological Literature.*
**Desc:** A unique means of communication among persons interested in amphibians and reptiles. Semi-technical and non-technical articles, society news, letters from readers, research requests and illustrations.
**Ind/Abst** Biol. Abstr.; Wildl. Rev.

US/0441-666X
**HERPETOLOGY (PASADENA).** (HERPETOLOGY.). [Herpetalogy]. Began With V. 1, No. 1, Apr. 1967?. Periodical. English. Three times a year. $15.00. Southwestern Herpetologists Society, PO Box 7469, Van Nuys CA 91409. **Tel** (805)684-7716. **ED** P Brown. **DD** 597. **UDC** 597.6+598.1. **Bk Rev. Circ:** 300 (ctrl).
**Desc:** General interest topic in natural history of reptiles and amphibians.

US/0440-7326
**HERPETON. Added/Corp** Southwestern Herpetologists Society. Vol. 1 (Aug. 1966)-. Periodical. English. ir. Southwestern Herpetologists Society, PO Box 7469, Van Nuys CA 91409. **Tel** (805)684-7716. **ED** P Brown. **LC** QL640; .H45. **DD** 598/.1/05. **CODEN** HERPBY. **Circ:** 450 (ctrl). Documents available from BIOSIS Document Express.
**Desc:** Original research in herpetology.
**Ind/Abst** Biol. Abstr.

US/0090-5410
**HERPETON (GLENDORA, CALIF.).** (HERPETON.). [Herpeton]. Periodical. English. qt. South Western Herpetologists Society, Box 2054 D, Pasadena CA 91105. **LC** QL640; .H44. **DD** 597. **UDC** 597.6+598.1.

II/0970-2903
**HIMALAYAN JOURNAL OF ENVIRONMENT AND ZOOLOGY.** **See** Environmental Issues-Ecology.

PL
**HODOWCA GOEBI POCZTOWYCH. Added/Corp** Polski Zwiazek Hodowcow Goebi Pocztowych. Vol. 50, No. 1 (Jan. 1976)-. Periodical. Polish. mo. Price on Request. **(Subscription address:** ARS Polona, PO Box 1001, 00068 Warsaw Poland.**)**

JA/0385-437X
**HONYURUI KAGAKU.** [Honyurui kagaku]. **Added/Corp** Nihon Honyurui Gakkai. **VFOAT** Mammalian Science. Vol. 1 (1961/62)-. Periodical. Japanese. sa. Honyurui Kenkyu Gurupu, (Mammalian Research Assoc.), Aichi Gakuin Daigaku Shigakubu, Dai 2 Kaibogaku, Kyoshitsu, 1-100, Kusumotocho, Chikusaku, Nagoyashi, Aichiken 464 Japan. **(Subscription address:** Japan Publications Trading Company, Ltd., PO Box 5030, Tokyo International, Tokyo 100-31 Japan.**)** **LC** QL700; .H665. **CODEN** HONKE4. cum. index. Documents available from BIOSIS Document Express. ***Absorbed*** *Honyu Dobutsugaku Zasshi, 0546-0670.*
**Ind/Abst** Biol. Abstr. (1991-).

AG/0073-3407
**HORNERO, EL.** [Hornero]. Vol. 1 (1919)-. Spanish (English; summaries and/or abstracts in English). ir. $10.00 (members), $15.00 (non-members) Argentina; $15.00 others. Asociacion Ornitologica del Plata, 1002 25 de Mayo 749, 1002 Buerno Aires Argentina. **Tel** 011 54 1 3128958. **ED** Manuel Nores. **UDC** 598.2(82). **CODEN** HRNOAX. Index available. **Bk Rev. Ad Acc. Pr Rev. Circ:** 1,000. Documents available from BIOSIS Document Express.
**Desc:** Publishes articles dealing with various ornithological topics on a scientific basis.
**Ind/Abst** Biol. Abstr.; Key Word Index Wildl. Res.; Zool. Rec.; Wildl. Rev.

AT/1032-1314
**ICHTHYOLITH ISSUES.** [Ichthyolith issues]. (1988)-. English. ir. 20.00Aus$. Microvertebrate Qld Museum, PO Box 300S, Brisbane 4101, Australia. **Tel** 11 66 7 840 7677. **DD** 567.05.

YU/0579-7152
**ICHTHYOLOGIA.** **VFOAT** Acta Biologica Iugoslavica. Ichthyologia. Vol. 1 (1969)-. Serbo-Croatian (Roman). Unija Bioloskih Nauchih, Drustava Jugoslavie Beograd ZM, 1108 Nemanjina 6 Yugoslavia. **LC** QL614. Documents available from BIOSIS Document Express.
**Ind/Abst** Aquat. Sci. Fish. Abstr. (Computer File); Biol. Abstr.

SA/0251-1258
**ICHTHYOLOGICAL BULLETIN OF THE J.L.B. SMITH INSTITUTE OF ICHTHYOLOGY.** (ICHTHYOLOGICAL BULLETIN OF THE J L B SMITH INSTITUTE OF ICHTHYOLOGY, RHODES UNIVERSITY, GRAHAMSTOWN.). [Ichthyol. bull. J.L.B. Smith Inst. Ichthyol.]. **Added/Corp** J.L.B. Smith Institute of Ichthyology. No. 34 (1972)-. Bulletin. English. ir. Price varies per volume. J L B Smith Institute of Ichthyology, Rhodes University South Africa. **LC** QL614; .I28. **CODEN** ICHBB7. Documents available from BIOSIS Document Express. ***Continues*** *Ichthyological Bulletin (Rhodes University. Dept. of Ichthyology), 0073-4381.*
**Ind/Abst** Aquat. Sci. Fish. Abstr. (Computer File); Biol. Abstr.; Fish Rev. (Jan. 1989-July 1992); Ocean. Abstr.; Life Sci. Collect.; Wildl. Rev. (Jan. 1989-July 1992).

BL/0073-4721
**IHERINGIA. SERIE ZOOLOGIA.** [Iheringia. Ser. zool.]. No. 35 (Sept. 6, 1967)- 1967. Periodical. Portuguese (German, Spanish, Italian, French and English). ir. Fundacao Zoobotanica do Rio Grande do Sul Biblioteca, Caixa Postal 1188, 90.001 Porto Alegre RS Brazil. **Tel** (0512)36-15-11. **ED** Arno Antonio Lise. **LC** QL1; .I25. **DD** 590/.5. **UDC** 59(81). **CODEN** IHZOAY. Index available. cum. index. **Circ:** 600 (ctrl). Documents available from BIOSIS Document Express. ***Continues*** *Iheringia. Zoologia, 0100-0535.*
**Desc:** Zoology, systematics of invertebrates and vertebrates, Rio Grande of Brazil and neotropical region.
**Ind/Abst** AGRICOLA; Biol. Abstr.; GeoRef; Life Sci. Collect.; Wildl. Rev.

MM
**IL-MERILL.** **VFOAT** Il Merill. Periodical. English. Malta Ornithological Society, PO Box 498, Valletta Malta.

FR
**INDEX OF ENTOMOPHAGOUS INSECTS.** (19??)-. English. ir. Librairie le Francois, 91 Boulevard Saint-German, 75006 Paris France. **Tel** 011 33 1 43263952, 011 33 1 43268808.

II/0255-7150
**INDIAN JOURNAL OF COMPARATIVE ANIMAL PHYSIOLOGY.** [Indian j. comp. anim. physiol.]. **Added/Corp** Indian Society for Comparative Animal Physiologists. **VFOAT** Journal of Comparative Animal Physiology. Vol. 1, No. 1 (Jan. 1983)-. Academic Scholarly Publication. English. sa. $75.00. S V University, Department of Zoology, c/o Professor K S Swami, Tirupati-517502 AP India. **(Subscription address:** Prints India, 11 Darya Ganj, New Delhi, 110002 India, (Phone: 011 91 11 3268645)**)** **NLM** W1; IN207CL. **CODEN** ICAPDG. Documents available from CASDDS.
**Ind/Abst** Chem. Abstr. (1983-); Fish Rev. (Jan. 1989-July 1992); Wildl. Rev. (Jan. 1989-July 1992).

II/0019-5227
**INDIAN JOURNAL OF HELMINTHOLOGY / HELMINTHOLOGICAL SOCIETY OF INDIA.** **Added/Corp** Helminthlogical Society of India. Vol. 1, No. 1 (Oct. 1948)-. Periodical. English. sa. $40.00. Helminthological Society of India, Lucknow, India. **(Subscription address:** Prints India, 11 Darya Ganj, New Delhi 110002 India.**)** **LC** OL386; .I5. **NLM** W1 IN209.
**Ind/Abst** Field Crop Abstr.; Helminthol. Abstr. (19??-19??); Index Vet.; Nematol. Abstr.; Pig News Inf.; Poult. Abstr.; Protozoolog. Abstr.; Rice Abstr.; Vet. Bull.

II/0303-6960
**INDIAN JOURNAL OF NEMATOLOGY : OFFICIAL PUBLICATION OF THE NEMATOLOGICAL SOCIETY OF INDIA.** [Indian j. nematol.]. **Added/Corp** Nematological Society of India. Vol. 1 (Mar. 1971)-. Periodical. English. sa. $35.00. Nematological Society of India, New Delhi, India. **(Subscription address:** Prints India, 11 Darya Ganj, New Delhi 110002 India.**)** **LC** QL391.N4; I48. **CODEN** IJNEDT. Documents available from BIOSIS Document Express, CASDDS.
**Ind/Abst** AGRICOLA; Agrofor. Abstr. (1991-); Biocont. News Inf. (1991-); Biol. Abstr.; Chem. Abstr.; Cot. Trop. Fibr. Abstr. Bibliogr.; Crop Physiol. Abstr.; For. Prod. Abstr. (1991-); For. Abstr.; Helminthol. Abstr.; Hortic. Abstr.; Irr. Drain. Abstr.; Maize Abstr.; Nematol. Abstr.; Plant Breed. Abstr.; Plant Grow. Reg. Abstr.; Potato Abstr.; Protozoolog. Abstr.; Rev. Agric. Entomol.; Rev. Plant Pathol.; Rice Abstr.; Seed Abstr.; Soils Fert.; Sorghum Mill. Abstr.; Soyabean Abstr.; Vitis Vitic. Enol. Abstr.; Weed Abstr.; Wheat Barley Trit. Abstr.

II/0445-7722
**INDIAN JOURNAL OF SERICULTURE.** **Added/Corp** India. Central Silk Board. Vol. 1 (July 1962)-. Academic Scholarly Publication. English. Twice a year (June, Dec.). Rs25.00. Central Sericulture Research & Training Institute, Central Silk Board, Manandavadi Road, Mysore 570 008 India. **Tel** 0821 21406 24408. **LC** [SF541]. **DD** 638/.2/0954. **CODEN** IJSEAH. Documents available from BIOSIS Document Express, CASDDS.
**Ind/Abst** Biol. Abstr.; Chem. Abstr.; Plant Breed. Abstr.; Rev. Agric. Entomol.

II/0971-104X
**INDIAN JOURNAL OF ZOOLOGICAL SPECTRUM.** [Indian J. Zool. Spectr.]. (1990)-. Periodical. English. sa. $75.00. **(Subscription address:** Prints India, 11 Darya Ganj, New Delhi 110002 India.**)** **UDC** 59.

II/0302-7562
**INDIAN JOURNAL OF ZOOLOGY.** [Indian j. zool.]. V. 1- 1973-. English. sa. $48.00. Department of Zoology, Saifia College, Bhopal India. **LC** QL1; .I28. **DD** 591/.05. **UDC** 59. **CODEN** IJZLA5. Documents available from BIOSIS Document Express, CASDDS.
**Ind/Abst** Biol. Abstr.; Chem. Abstr.; Life Sci. Collect.; Protozoolog. Abstr.

II/0368-0983
**INDIAN ZOOLOGIST.** [Indian Zool.]. (1970)-. English. sa. $20.00. **(Subscription address:** Prints India, 11 Darya Ganj, New Delhi 110002 India.**)** **CODEN** IZOOB4.

US/0736-0460
**INDO-PACIFIC FISHES.** [Indo-Pac. fishes]. **Added/Corp** Bernice Pauahi Bishop Museum. Division of Ichthyology. No. 1 (Nov. 1982)-. Monographic series. English. ir. Price varies per volume. Bishop Museum Press, PO Box 19000-A, Honolulu HI 96817. **Tel** (808)847-3511. **DD** 567.
**Desc:** This series treats revisions of general or higher categories of fishes within the Indo-West Pacific region.

MX
**INFORMADOR APICOLA, EL.** Vol. 3, No. 31 (Oct. 1972)-. Periodical. Spanish. mo.

●US/1064-3826
**INTERNATIONAL DIRECTORY OF PRIMATOLOGY.** [Int. dir. primatol.]. **Added/Corp** Wisconsin Regional Primate Research Center. 1st (1992)-. English. be. $10.00. Wisonsin Regional Primate Research Center, 1220 Capitol Court, Madison WI 53706. **Tel** (608)263-3512. **LC** QL737.P9; I513. **DD** 599.8/0601. **NLM** QL 737.P9; I6102i.

US/0164-7954
**INTERNATIONAL JOURNAL OF ACAROLOGY.** Vol. 1 (June 1975)-. Periodical. English. qt. $290.00. Indira Publishing House, PO Box 250456, West Bloomfield MI 48325. **Tel** (313)661-2529, FAX (313)661-4066. **ED** V. Prasad. **CODEN** IJOADM. Index available. **Ad Acc. Pr Rev.** Documents available from BIOSIS Document Express.
**Desc:** A journal of mites and ticks, agriculture, general, medical, veterinary and aquatic, biology, ecology, control, morphology, histology, genetics and taxonomy.
**Ind/Abst** Biocont. News Inf. (19??-19??); Biodeter. Abstr.; Biol. Abstr.; Ecology Abstr.; Entomol. Abstr.; Hortic. Abstr.; Index Vet.; Maize Abstr.; Rev. Agric. Entomol.; Rev. Med. Vet. Entomol.; Vitis Vitic. Enol. Abstr.; Wildl. Rev.

US/0164-0291
**INTERNATIONAL JOURNAL OF PRIMATOLOGY.** [Int. j. primatol.]. **Added/Corp** International Primatological Society. Vol. 1 (March 1980)-. Academic Scholarly Publication. English. Six times a year. $325.00 institutions, $56.00 individuals US; $380.00 institutions, $66.00 individuals other. Plenum Press, 233 Spring Street, New York NY 10013-1578. **Tel** (212)620-8000, (800)221-9369, FAX (212)463-0742, (212)807-1047, telex 23/421139. **ED** Russell H. Tuttle. **LC** QL737.P9; I517. **DD** 599.8/05. **NLM** W1 IN775K. **CODEN** IJPRDA. **[CCC].** Index available. **Pr Rev.** available on microfilm and microfiche from University Microfilms International (UMI). Documents available from The Genuine Article, CASDDS.
**Desc:** This is a multi-disciplinary journal devoted to basic primatology, i.e., studies in which the primate is featured. Brings together field and lab studies, also publishes articles in fundamental primatology.
**Ind/Abst** Acad. Search (July 1993-); Anim. Behav. Abstr.; Anthropol. Lit.; Chem. Abstr.; Curr. Aware. Biol. Sci., CABS; Curr. Contents, Agric. Biol. Environ. Sci.; Curr. Primate Ref.; Ecology Abstr.; Life Sci. Collect.; Psychol. Abstr. (1981-); PsycINFO; PsycLit; Ref. Z.; Res. Alert [Full Cov.]; Sci. Cit. Index; SCISEARCH; Soc. Sci. Cit. Index [Select. Cov.]; Wildl. Rev.

US/1052-5408
**INTERNATIONAL NEMATOLOGY NETWORK NEWSLETTER.** [Int. nematol. netw. newsl.]. Newsletter. English. qt. **DD** 632.
**Ind/Abst** AGRICOLA [Full Cov.]; Agrofor. Abstr. (1991-); Biocont. News Inf.; Field Crop Abstr.; For. Prod. Abstr. (1991-); Hortic. Abstr.; Maize Abstr.; Nematol. Abstr.; Plant Breed. Abstr.; Potato Abstr.; Rev. Plant Pathol.; Rice Abstr.; Weed Abstr.; Wheat Barley Trit. Abstr.

UK
**INTERNATIONAL SERIES IN PURE AND APPLIED BIOLOGY. ZOOLOGY DIVISION.** **VFOAT** Zoology Division; International Series in Pure and Applied Biology. Division, Zoology. (1976)-. Monographic series. English. ir. Price varies per volume. Pergamon Press, An Imprint of Elsevier Science Ltd., The Boulevard, Langford Lane, Kidlington, Oxford OX5 1GB United Kingdom. **Tel** 011 44 865 843000, 011 44 865 843699, FAX 011 44 865 843010. **LC** UNC. ***Continues*** *International Series of Monographs on Pure and Applied Biology. Division, Zoology.*

UK/0020-9155
**INTERNATIONAL ZOO-NEWS.** **Added/Corp** Zoo-Centrum. (195?)-. Periodical. English. Eight times a year. $75.00. Zoo Centrum, 80 Cleveland Road, Chichester, West Sussex PO19 2HF United Kingdom. **Tel** 011 44 243 782803. **ED** Nicholas Gould. **Bk Rev. Ad Acc. Circ:** 500 (ctrl).
**Desc:** A magazine providing news from and about the zoos of the world.

UK/0074-9664
**INTERNATIONAL ZOO YEARBOOK.** [Int. zoo yearb.]. **Added/Corp** Zoological Society of London. Vol. 1 (1959)-. English. an. £56.00. Zoological Society of London, Regents Park, London NW1 4RY England. **Tel** 011 44 71 7223333, FAX (01)483-4436, telex 265247 LONZOO. **ED** P. J. S. Olney. **LC** QL76; .I55. **DD** 591. **NLM** QL 76 I61. **CODEN** IZYBAE. cum. index. **Circ:** 2,000. Documents available from BIOSIS Document Express, CASDDS.
**Desc:** Two-thirds comprises scientific papers on animal breeding, management, conservation; one-third lists world's zoos (including addresses), vertebrates bred in captivity, and rare animal census.
**Ind/Abst** Biol. Abstr.; Chem. Abstr.; Curr. Primate Ref.; Dairy Sci. Abstr.; Fish Rev.; Index Vet.; Key Word Index Wildl. Res.; Vet. Bull.; Wildl. Rev.

IS/0792-4259
**INVERTEBRATE REPRODUCTION & DEVELOPMENT.** [Invertebr. reprod. dev.]. **Added/Corp** International Society of Invertebrate Reproduction. **VFOAT** Invertebrate Reproduction and Development. Vol. 15, No. 1 (Feb. 1989)-. Periodical. English (French). Six times a year. $590.00. Balaban Publishers, PO Box 2039, 76120 Rehovot Israel. **Tel** 011 972 8 476216, FAX 011 972 8 467632. **ED** D.W. Golding, J.R. Collier and J. Hoffmann. **NLM** W1; IN993VD. **CODEN** IRDEE2. Index available. cum. index. **Bk Rev. Ad Acc. Circ:** 400. available on diskette; available on microfilm and microfiche from University Microfilms International (UMI). Documents available from The Genuine Article, BIOSIS Document Express, CASDDS. ***Continues*** *International Journal of Invertebrate Reproduction and Development, 0168-8170.*
**Desc:** Scientific journal publishing original research in the fields of sexual, reproductive and developmental (embryonic and postembryonic) biology of the Invertebrata.
**Ind/Abst** AgBiotech News Inf.; Aquat. Sci. Fish. Abstr. (Computer File); Biocont. News Inf. (1991-); Biol. Abstr.; Chem. Abstr.; Curr. Aware. Biol. Sci., CABS; Curr. Contents, Agric. Biol. Environ. Sci.; Curr. Contents Life Sci.; Ecology Abstr.; Entomol. Abstr.; Postharvest News

Inf.; Res. Alert [Full Cov.]; Rev. Agric. Entomol.; Rev. Med. Vet. Entomol.; Sci. Cit. Index; SCISEARCH; Soc. Sci. Cit. Index [Select. Cov.].

AT/0818-0164
**INVERTEBRATE TAXONOMY.** [Invertebr. taxon.]. **Added/Corp** Australian Academy of Science. Commonwealth Scientific and Industrial Research Organization (Australia). Vol. 1, No. 1 (1987)-. Periodical. English. bm. 280.00Aus$ Australia; $280.00 other. CSIRO Publications, PO Box 89, 314 Albert Street, East Melborne Victoria 3002 Australia. **Tel** 011 61 3 4187333, 4187217, FAX 011 61 3 4190459, telex AA 30236. **ED** D. W. Morton. **LC** QL362.5; .I58. **DD** 592/.0012. **CODEN** ITAXEO. **Ad Acc. Acid Free. Circ:** 450. available in microform from University Microfilms International (UMI). Documents available from BIOSIS Document Express. ***Continues*** *Australian Journal of Zoology. Supplementary Series, 0310-9089.*
**Desc:** Original contributions to the taxonomy and systematics of invertebrates, with special relevance to the Indo-Pacific Region. Papers include comprehensive treatments of groups of animals delimited on taxonomic, geographic, ecological or other biologically meaningful criteria. General papers on methodology, pertinent to the study of invertebrate systematics, are also published.
**Ind/Abst** AGRICOLA [Full Cov.]; Biocont. News Inf. (1991-); Biol. Abstr. (1987-); Ecol. Abstr.; Entomol. Abstr.; Helminthol. Abstr. (1991-); Rev. Agric. Entomol.; Rev. Med. Vet. Entomol.; Weed Abstr.

SZ/1010-3635
**INVESTIGATIONS ON CETACEA.** [Investig. cetacea]. **Added/Corp** Universitat Bern. Hirnanatomisches Institut. (1969)-. Periodical. English (German). ir. 240.00F. Investigations on Cetacea, Chrottegaessli 23, CH 3065 Bolligen Switzerland. **Tel** 011 41 31 581240. **ED** Professor G. Pilleri. **CODEN** INVCDN. ctrl circ. Documents available from BIOSIS Document Express.
**Ind/Abst** Biol. Abstr.; Ocean. Abstr.

IS/0021-2210
**ISRAEL JOURNAL OF ZOOLOGY.** [Isr. j. zool.]. **Added/Corp** Moatsah ha-Leumit le-Mehkar ule-Fituah (Israel). Vol. 1 No. 1/4 (Dec. 1963)-. Academic Scholarly Publication. Multiple languages (English, French and German). qt. $70.00 individual, $140.00 institution. Laser Pages Publishing Ltd., PO Box 50257, Jerusalem 91502 Israel. **Tel** 011 972 2 829770, FAX 011 972 2 818782. **ED** Y. L. Werner. **NLM** W1 IS63V. **CODEN** IJZOAE. Index available in last issue of volume--attached. cum. index. **Bk Rev. Ad Acc. Pr Rev. Circ:** 350. Documents available from The Genuine Article, BIOSIS Document Express. ***Continues*** *Bulletin of the Research Council of Israel. Section B, Zoology, 0375-9156.*
**Desc:** Zoology as reflected in the rich terrestrial and marine environments of Israel and the Mediterranean, a crossroad linking three continents.
**Ind/Abst** AGRICOLA; Biocont. News Inf.; Biol. Abstr.; Curr. Aware. Biol. Sci., CABS; Curr. Contents, Agric. Biol. Environ. Sci.; Ecol. Abstr.; Ecology Abstr.; EMBASE; Field Crop Abstr.; GeoRef; Grasslands For. Abstr.; Helminthol. Abstr. (1991-); Index Vet.; Key Word Index Wildl. Res.; Life Sci. Collect.; Protozoolog. Abstr.; Res. Alert [Full Cov.]; Rev. Agric. Entomol.; Rev. Med. Vet. Entomol.; Rice Abstr.; Sci. Cit. Index; SCISEARCH; Vet. Bull.; Vitis Vitic. Enol. Abstr.; Wildl. Rev.

RU/0202-702X
**ITOGI NAUKI I TEKHNIKI. SERIIA ZOOLOGIIA POZVONOCHNYKH.**
**Added/Corp** Vsesoiuznyi Institut Nauchnoi i Tekhnicheskoi Informatsii (Soviet Union). **VFOAT** Zoologiia Pozvonochnykh; Seriia Zoologiia Pozvonochnykh; Itogi Nauki i Tekhniki. Zoologiia Pozvonochnykh. (198?)-. Monographic series. Russian. ir. Price varies per volume. VINITI - Vsesoiuznyi Institut Nauchno-Tekhnicheskoi Informatsii, All-Union Scientific and Technical Information Institute, Baltiiskaia Ulitsa 14, 125219 Moscow Russia. **Tel** 238-46-00, FAX 9430060, telex 411160. **LC** QL673; .I8. ***Continues*** *Itogi Nauki i Tekhniki. Zoologiia Pozvonochnykh.*

US/0075-3920
**JOHNSONIA.** ***Ceased.*** [Johnsonia]. Ceased Vol. 5. Monographic series. English. ir. Harvard University Department of Mollusks, Cambridge MA 02138. **Tel** (617)495-2468. **ED** Kenneth J Boss. **UDC** 594.1. **CODEN** JHNSAV. cum. index. Documents available from BIOSIS Document Express.
**Ind/Abst** Biol. Abstr.; Life Sci. Collect.

II/0253-7214
**JOURNAL OF ADVANCED ZOOLOGY.** [J. adv. zool.]. (1980)-. Academic Scholarly Publication. English. Twice a year. $50.00. Association for the Advancement of Zoology, 2 Zahid Building Golghar, Gorakhpur-273 001 India. **Tel** 336925. **(Subscription address:** Prints India, 11 Darya Ganj, New Delhi, 110002 India, (Phone: 011 91 11 3268645)) **ED** S. P. Tripathi. **LC** QL1; .J82. **DD** 591/.05. **UDC** 59. **CODEN** JAZODX. Index available. **Bk Rev. Ad Acc. Circ:** 1,000 (ctrl). available on microfilm; available in microform; available on CD-ROM; available on diskette; available on videocassette. Documents available from The Genuine Article, BIOSIS Document Express, CASDDS.
**Desc:** This is a research journal which high quality scientific papers on different aspects of zoology from foreign and Indian workers.
**Ind/Abst** Agrofor. Abstr.; Biocont. News Inf. (1991-); Biodeter. Abstr.; Biol. Abstr.; Chem. Abstr.; CSA Neuro. Abstr. (?-?); Curr. Aware. Biol. Sci., CABS; Curr. Contents, Agric. Biol. Environ. Sci.; Curr. Ref. Fish Res.; For. Prod. Abstr.; Helminthol. Abstr. (19??-19??); Index Vet.; Nematol. Abstr.; Poult. Abstr.; Res. Alert [Select. Cov.]; Rev. Agric. Entomol.; Rev. Med. Vet. Entomol.; Rice Abstr.; SCISEARCH.

BE/0776-7943
**JOURNAL OF AFRICAN ZOOLOGY.**
**VFOAT** Revue de Zoologie Africaine. **VAT** J. Afr. Zool. Vol. 104, 1 (28. II. 1990)-. Periodical. English (French). bm. 5200.00F Europe; 5600.00F other. Editions Agar Publishers, 39 Venelle du Bois de Saras, B-1300 Wavre Belgium. **LC** QL336; .A3. **DD** 591.96/05. **CODEN** JAZOEY. **Bk Rev. Ad Acc. Pr Rev.** Documents available from BIOSIS Document Express. ***Continues*** *Revue de Zoologie Africaine, 0771-0488.*
**Ind/Abst** Biol. Abstr.; Ecol. Abstr.; Geogr. Abstr. Phys. Geogr.; Helminthol. Abstr. (1991-); Rev. Agric. Entomol.; Rev. Med. Vet. Entomol.; Zool. Rec.

UK/0021-8790
**JOURNAL OF ANIMAL ECOLOGY, THE.** [J. anim. ecol.]. **Added/Corp** British Ecological Society. Vol. 1 (May 1932)-. Academic Scholarly Publication. English. Six times a year. $335.00 US & Canada; £197.00 Europe; £216.00 other. Blackwell Scientific Publications Ltd, Marston Book Services, PO Box 87, Oxford OX2 ODT UK. **Tel** 011 44 865 791155, FAX 011 44 865 791927, telex 837 515 MARDIS G. **ED** L. C. Taylor and J. M. Elliot. **LC** QL750; .J65. **DD** 591.505. **NLM** W1 JO536E. **CODEN** JAECAP. **[CCC].** Index available. **Bk Rev. Ad Acc. Pr Rev. Circ:** 3,700. available on microfilm and microfiche from University Microfilms International (UMI). Documents available from The Genuine Article, BIOSIS Document Express, CASDDS.
**Desc:** Publishes original research papers on any aspect of experimental, analytical or theoretical approach to real data.
**Ind/Abst** Abstr. Anthropol.; AGRICOLA; AQUAREF; Biocont. News Inf. (1991-); Biol. Agric. Index; Biol. Abstr.; Biostatistica (19??-19??); Chem. Abstr.; Curr. Aware. Biol. Sci., CABS; Curr. Contents, Agric. Biol. Environ. Sci.; Curr. Ref. Fish Res.; Ecol. Abstr. (?-?); Ecology Abstr.; Entomol. Abstr.; Environ. Period. Bibliogr.; Field Crop Abstr.; Fish Rev.; For. Prod. Abstr.; For. Abstr.; Fresh. Aqua. Contents Tables; Grasslands For. Abstr.; Helminthol. Abstr. (19??-19??); Key Word Index Wildl. Res.; Math. Rev.; Nutr. Abstr. Rev., Ser. B, Live Feeds and Feed.; Nutr. Abstr. Rev., Ser. A, Hum. Exp.; Life Sci. Collect.; Poult. Abstr.; Protozoolog. Abstr.; Res. Alert [Full Cov.]; Rev. Agric. Entomol.; Rev. Med. Vet. Entomol.; Sci. Cit. Index; SCISEARCH; Soils Fert.; Stat. Theory Method Abstr. (1967-); Trop. Dis. Bull.; Wildl. Rev.

II/0021-8804
**JOURNAL OF ANIMAL MORPHOLOGY AND PHYSIOLOGY, THE.** [J. anim. morphol. physiol.]. **Added/Corp** Society of Animal Morphologists and Physiologists. Vol. 1 (June 1954)-. Academic Scholarly Publication. English. sa. $35.00. Society Animal Morphology and Physiology, University of Baroda, c/o Department of Zoology, Baroda 390 002 India. **(Subscription address:** Prints India, 11 Darya Ganj, New Delhi, 110002 India, (Phone: 011 91 11 3268645)) **ED** J. C. George, R. V. Shah, Bonny Pilo. **LC** QL801; .J75. **NLM** W1 JO536F. **CODEN** JAMPA2. **Bk Rev. Ad Acc. Circ:** 300 (ctrl). Documents available from BIOSIS Document Express, CASDDS.
**Desc:** Morphology and physiology of animals.
**Ind/Abst** AGRICOLA; Anim. Breed. Abstr.; Biol. Abstr.; Chem. Abstr.; CSA Neuro. Abstr. (?-?); EMBASE; Entomol. Abstr.; Life Sci. Collect.

UK/0021-8839
**JOURNAL OF APICULTURAL RESEARCH.** [J. apic. res.]. **Added/Corp** International Bee Research Association. Bee Research Association. Vol. 1 (1962)-. Periodical. English. qt. £80.00 UK; $145.00 other. International Bee Research Association, 18 North Road, Cardiff CF1 3DY United Kingdom. **Tel** 011 44 1 372409, FAX 011 44 1 665522, telex 23152. **ED** R. Pickard. **CODEN** JACRAQ. **Ad Acc. Pr Rev. Circ:** 585. Documents available from The Genuine Article, BIOSIS Document Express, CASDDS.
**Desc:** Publishes original research papers on beekeeping subjects.
**Ind/Abst** AGRICOLA [Full Cov.]; BioBusiness; Biol. Abstr.; Chem. Abstr.; Chemorecept. Abstr.; Curr. Aware. Biol. Sci., CABS; Curr. Contents, Agric. Biol. Environ. Sci.; Dairy Sci. Abstr.; Entomol. Abstr.; Food Sci. Technol. Abstr.; Maize Abstr.; Life Sci. Collect.; Protozoolog. Abstr.; Res. Alert [Full Cov.]; Rev. Agric. Entomol.; Rev. Med. Vet. Entomol.; Sci. Cit. Index; SCISEARCH.

US/0161-8202
**JOURNAL OF ARACHNOLOGY, THE.** [J. archnol.]. **Added/Corp** American Arachnological Society. Texas Tech University. Graduate School. Vol. 1, (Jan. 1973)-. Periodical. English (Spanish). Three times a year (Spring, Summer and Fall). $80.00. American Arachnological Society, Department of Entomology, American Museum of National History, Central Park West at 79th, New York NY 10024-5192. **Tel** (212)769-5612, FAX (212)769-5277. **ED** J. E. Carico. **LC** QL451; .J68. **DD** 595/.4/05. **CODEN** JARCDP. Index available. **Bk Rev. Ad Acc. Pr Rev. Circ:** 600. Documents available from The Genuine Article, BIOSIS Document Express.
**Desc:** Systematics, phylogenetics, biogeography, morphology, physiology, behavior and ecology of arachnids (spiders, scorpions, etc.).
**Ind/Abst** AGRICOLA [Full Cov.]; Biocont. News Inf. (1991-); Biol. Abstr.; Cot. Trop. Fibr. Abstr. Bibliogr.; Curr. Aware. Biol. Sci., CABS; Curr. Contents, Agric. Biol. Environ. Sci.; Ecol. Abstr. (?-?); Ecology Abstr.; Entomol. Abstr.; For. Abstr.; Life Sci. Collect.; Res. Alert [Select. Cov.]; Rev. Agric. Entomol.; Rev. Med. Vet. Entomol.; SCISEARCH.

UK/0022-0019
**JOURNAL OF CONCHOLOGY.** [J. conchol.]. **Added/Corp** Conchological Society of Great Britain and Ireland. (1879)-. Periodical. English. sa (May, Nov.). £35.00. Conchological Society of Great Britain and Ireland, 16 Edward Street, Dunoon Rosehill, Argyll PA23 7JF, England. **Tel** 11 44 369 3608. **ED** Brian F Coles. Index available in last issue of volume--attached. cum. index. **Bk Rev. Ad Acc. Pr Rev. Circ:** 1,000 (ctrl). Documents available from The Genuine Article. ***Continues*** *Quarterly Journal of Conchology.*
**Desc:** Scientific journal related to mollusks.
**Ind/Abst** Curr. Contents, Agric. Biol. Environ. Sci.; Ecol. Abstr. (?-?); Life Sci. Collect.; Res. Alert [Full Cov.]; Sci. Cit. Index; SCISEARCH.

II/0378-9519
**JOURNAL OF ENTOMOLOGICAL RESEARCH.** [J. entomol. res.]. Vol. 1, (June 1977)-. Academic Scholarly Publication. English. Four times a year (Mar., June, Sept., Dec.). Rs 500.00 India; $50.00 other. Malhotra Publishing House, A38/3 Mayapuri Industrial Area, New Delhi 110064 India. **Tel** 011 91 11 31591928, FAX 011 91-11-5724135, telex 31-63206 MEER IN. **(Subscription address:** Prints India, 11 Darya Ganj, New Delhi, 110002 India, (Phone: 011 91 11 3268645)) **ED** Dr. Prakash Sarup. **CODEN** JEREDP. **Bk Rev. Ad Acc. Pr Rev. Circ:** 600 (ctrl). Documents available from CASDDS.
**Ind/Abst** AGRICOLA; Agrofor. Abstr. (1991-); Biocont. News Inf. (19??-19??); Biodeter. Abstr.; Chem. Abstr.; Cot. Trop. Fibr. Abstr. Bibliogr.; Curr. Aware. Biol. Sci., CABS; Entomol. Abstr.; Field Crop Abstr.; For. Abstr.; Maize Abstr.; Nematol. Abstr.; Life Sci. Collect.; Plant Breed. Abstr.; Postharvest News Inf.; Potato Abstr.; Rev. Plant Pathol.; Rice Abstr.; Seed Abstr.; Soils Fert.; Sorghum Mill. Abstr.; Soyabean Abstr.; Wheat Barley Trit. Abstr.

●US/1066-5234
**JOURNAL OF EUKARYOTIC MICROBIOLOGY, THE.** [J. eukaryot. microbiol.]. **Added/Corp** Society of Protozoologists. Vol. 40, Issue 1 (Jan.-Feb. 1993)-. Academic Scholarly Publication. English. bm. $141.00 North America; $153.00 other. Society of Protozoologists. **(Subscription address:** Journal of Eukaryotic Microbiology, PO Box 1897, Lawrence KS 66044-8897.) **LC** QL366; .J6. **DD** 593.1/05. **CODEN** JEMIED. Documents available from BIOSIS Document Express, CASDDS. ***Continues*** *Journal of Protozoology, 0022-3921.*
**Ind/Abst** Biol. Agric. Index; Biol. Abstr.; Chem. Abstr.; Energy Res. Abstr.; GeoRef; Index Med.; Int. Aerosp. Abstr.; Life Sci. Collect.; PESTDOC; Sci. Cit. Index.

US/0022-104X
**JOURNAL OF EXPERIMENTAL ZOOLOGY, THE.** [J. exp. zool.]. **Added/Corp** Wistar Institute of Anatomy and Biology. American Society of Zoologists. Vol. 1 (May 1904)-. Academic Scholarly Publication. English. Eighteen times a year. $2,153.00 US; $2,333.00 Canada and Mexico; $2,400.50 other. John Wiley & Sons, Inc., 605 Third Avenue, New York NY 10158-0012. **Tel** (212)850-6000, (212)850-6645, FAX (212)850-6088, telex 12-7063. **(Subscription address:** John Wiley & Sons / England, Baffins Lane, Chichester, West Sussex PO19 1UD England.) **ED** Francis H. Ruddle. **LC** QL1; .J85. **DD** 591/.07/24. **NLM** W1 JO644Y. **CODEN** JEZOAO. **[CCC]. Pr Rev.** Documents available from The Genuine Article, BIOSIS Document Express, CASDDS.
**Desc:** Reports the results of original research of an experimental or analytical nature in zoology, including investigations of all levels of biological organization, from the molecular to the organismal.
**Ind/Abst** AgBiotech News Inf.; AGRICOLA; Anim. Breed. Abstr.; Biocont. News Inf.; Biol. Agric. Index; Biol. Abstr.; Chem. Abstr.; CSA Neuro. Abstr.; Curr. Aware. Biol. Sci., CABS; Curr. Contents, Agric. Biol. Environ. Sci.; Curr. Contents Life Sci.; Curr. Ref. Fish Res.; Dairy Sci. Abstr.; Ecol. Abstr. (?-?); EMBASE; Energy Res. Abstr.; Fish Rev.; Genet. Abstr.; Helminthol. Abstr. (1991-); Index Med.; INIS Atomindex [Micro.]; Key Word Index Wildl. Res.; Maize Abstr.; Nematol. Abstr.; Nutr. Abstr. Rev., Ser. B, Live Feeds and Feed.; Nutr. Abstr. Rev., Ser. A, Hum. Exp.; Life Sci. Collect.; Pig News Inf.; Poult. Abstr.; Protozoolog. Abstr.; Ref. Upd. Deluxe Ed.; Res. Alert [Full Cov.]; Rev. Agric. Entomol.; Rev. Med. Vet. Entomol.; Sci. Cit. Index; SCISEARCH; Wildl. Rev.

US/1059-8324
**JOURNAL OF EXPERIMENTAL ZOOLOGY. SUPPLEMENT.** [J. exp. zool., Suppl.]. **Added/Corp** American Society of Zoologists. Division of Comparative Physiology and Biochemistry.

(1987)-. Monographic series. English. ir. Price varies per volume. Wiley Liss, 605 3rd Avenue, New York NY 10158. **Tel** (212)850-8800, (212)850-6645. **(Subscription address:** John Wiley / Philadelphia, PO Box 7247, Philadelphia PA 19170.**)** **DD** 591.

US/0096-1191
**JOURNAL OF FORAMINIFERAL RESEARCH.** [J. foraminiferal res.]. Vol. 1, Jan. (1971)-. Periodical. English. qt. $80.00 (institutions), $35.00 (individuals) surface mail. Harvard University Museum of Comparative Zoology, 26 Oxford Street, Cambridge MA 02138. **Tel** (617)495-2466. **ED** Johanna Resig (editor's address: Dept. of Geology and Geophysics, University of Hawaii, Honolulu, HI 96822). **LC** QL368.F6; J74. **DD** 593/.12/05. **UDC** 593.12. **CODEN** JFARAH. Index available. **Bk Rev. Ad Acc. Pr Rev. Circ:** 800 (ctrl). Documents available from The Genuine Article, BIOSIS Document Express, Petroleum Abstracts Document Delivery Service. ***Supersedes*** *Contributions from the Cushman Foundation for Foraminiferal Research, 0011-409X.*
**Desc:** Publishes results of research on fossil and living foraminifera and allied organisms.
**Ind/Abst** AESIS Q.; Biol. Abstr.; Curr. Contents Phys. Chem. Earth Sci.; Ecol. Abstr.; Geogr. Abstr. Phys. Geogr.; Geol. Abstr.; GeoRef; Pet. Abstr.; Res. Alert [Full Cov.]; Sci. Cit. Index; SCISEARCH.

UK/0022-149X
**JOURNAL OF HELMINTHOLOGY.** [J. helminthol.]. **Added/Corp** London School of Hygiene and Tropical Medicine. Vol. 1 (1923)-. Academic Scholarly Publication. English (French). Four times a year. $202.00. CAB International Centre, Wallingford, Oxon OX10 8DE United Kingdom. **Tel** 44 491 832111, FAX 44 491 833508, telex 847964 (COMAGG G). **ED** R. Muller and L. F. Khalil. **NLM** W1 JO67C. **CODEN** JOHLAT. Index available. **Bk Rev. Ad Acc. Pr Rev. Circ:** 700. Documents available from The Genuine Article, BIOSIS Document Express, CASDDS.
**Desc:** The journal publishes papers on all aspects of animal parasitic helminths, particularly those of medical and veterinary importance, but only in exceptional circumstances.
**Ind/Abst** AgBiotech News Inf.; AGRICOLA [Select. Cov.]; Biocont. News Inf.; Biol. Abstr.; Chem. Abstr.; Curr. Aware. Biol. Sci., CABS; Curr. Contents, Agric. Biol. Environ. Sci.; Curr. Ref. Fish Res.; Ecol. Abstr.; EMBASE; Fish Rev.; Helminthol. Abstr. (19??-19??); Index Med.; Int. Dev. Abstr.; Nutr. Abstr. Rev., Ser. B, Live Feeds and Feed.; Nutr. Abstr. Rev., Ser. A, Hum. Exp.; Life Sci. Collect.; PESTDOC; Pig News Inf.; Poult. Abstr.; Protozoolog. Abstr.; Res. Alert [Full Cov.]; Rev. Med. Vet. Entomol.; Sci. Cit. Index; SCISEARCH; Trop. Dis. Bull.; Wildl. Rev.

US/0022-1511
**JOURNAL OF HERPETOLOGY.** [J. herpetol.]. **Added/Corp** Society for the Study of Amphibians and Reptiles. Vol. 1, (March 1968)-. Periodical. English. Four times a year (Mar., Jun., Sep., Dec.). $35.00 (individual), $60.00 (institutions). Society for the Study Amphibians & Reptiles, PO Box 626, Hays KS 67601. **Tel** (913)628-1437. **ED** Samuel Sweet. **LC** QL640; .J6. **DD** 598.1. **CODEN** JHERAH. Index available. cum. index. **Pr Rev. Acid Free. Circ:** 2,400 (ctrl). Documents available from The Genuine Article, BIOSIS Document Express, CASDDS. ***Supersedes*** *Journal of the Ohio Herpetological Society, 0473-9868 .*
**Desc:** Scientific articles dealing with any aspect of reptiles and amphibians including behavior ecology, biosystematics, evolution, genetics, physiology, and natural history.
**Ind/Abst** Anim. Behav. Abstr.; Biol. Abstr.; Chem. Abstr.; Curr. Aware. Biol. Sci., CABS; Curr. Contents, Agric. Biol. Environ. Sci.; Ecol. Abstr.; Ecology Abstr.; Geol. Abstr.; Life Sci. Collect.; Protozoolog. Abstr.; Res. Alert [Full Cov.]; Sci. Cit. Index; SCISEARCH; Wildl. Rev.

US/0022-2372
**JOURNAL OF MAMMALOGY.** ***Title Change.*** [J. mammal.]. **Added/Corp** American Society of Mammalogists. Vol. 1 (Nov. 1919)-. Periodical. English. qt. American Society of Mammalogists, c/o H.D. Smith, Zoology Department, Brigham Young University, Provo UT 84602. **Tel** (801)378-2492. **ED** Clyde Jones. **LC** QL700; .J6. **DD** 599.05. **NLM** W1 JO748G. **CODEN** JOMAAL. Index available. cum. index. **Bk Rev. Ad Acc. Acid Free. Circ:** 4,500. available on microfilm and microfiche from University Microfilms International (UMI). Documents available from The Genuine Article, BIOSIS Document Express, UMI Article Clearinghouse, CASDDS. ***Continued by*** *Recent Literature on Mammalogy, 0193-6077.*
**Desc:** Publishes results of original research on terrestrial and marine mammals. All aspects of biology of mammals are covered in the worldwide scope of this journal.
**Ind/Abst** Abstr. Anthropol.; Acad. Ind. [Computer File] (1992-); Acad. Search (July 1993-); AGRICOLA [Select. Cov.]; Anim. Behav. Abstr.; Anim. Breed. Abstr.; AQUAREF; Biol. Agric. Index; Biol. Abstr.; Chem. Abstr.; Chemorecept. Abstr.; CSA Neuro. Abstr. (?-?); Curr. Aware. Biol. Sci., CABS; Curr. Contents, Agric. Biol. Environ. Sci.; Dairy Sci. Abstr.; Ecol. Abstr.; Ecology Abstr.; Energy Res. Abstr. (Sept. 1971-); Expand. Acad. Index (1989-); For. Prod. Abstr.; For. Abstr.; Gen. Sci. Index; Gen. Sci. Source (Jul. 1993-); Geol. Abstr.; Index Med. (Nov. 1965-1981); INFO-SOUTH Abstr.; INIS Atomindex [Micro.]; Key Word Index Wildl. Res.; Newsp. Period. Abstr. (1991-); Nutr. Abstr. Rev., Ser. B, Live Feeds and Feed.; Nutr. Abstr. Rev., Ser. A, Hum. Exp.; Life Sci. Collect.; Res. Alert [Full Cov.]; Rev. Med. Vet. Entomol.; Sci. Cit. Index; SCISEARCH; Soc. Sci. Cit. Index [Select. Cov.]; Stat. Theory Method Abstr. (1959-1963); Wildl. Rev.

UK/0260-1230
**JOURNAL OF MOLLUSCAN STUDIES.** (THE JOURNAL OF MOLLUSCAN STUDIES.). [J. molluscan stud.]. **Added/Corp** Malacological Society of London. Vol. 42 (April 1976)-. Periodical. English (French). qt. £95.00 UK and Europe; $170.00 other. Oxford University Press, Walton Street, Oxford OX2 6DP England. **Tel** 011 44 865 56767, FAX 011 44 865 267773, telex 837330 OXPRES G. **(Subscription address:** Oxford University Press / USA, Journals Marketing Department, Oxford University Press, 2001 Evans Road, Cary NC 27513.**)** **ED** J. D. Taylor. **LC** QL401; .M18. **DD** 594/.005. **CODEN** JMSTDT. **[CCC].** Index available. **Bk Rev. Ad Acc. Pr Rev. Circ:** 600. available on microfilm and microfiche from University Microfilms International (UMI). Documents available from The Genuine Article, BIOSIS Document Express. ***Continues*** *Malacological Society of London. Proceedings of the Malacological Society of London, 0025-1194.*
**Desc:** Extended and rapidly growing use of mollusks in various fields. Papers on aspects of research into classical neurophysiological and behavioural research using mollusks as experimental material.
**Ind/Abst** Biocont. News Inf.; Biol. Abstr.; Chemorecept. Abstr.; Curr. Aware. Biol. Sci., CABS; Curr. Contents, Agric. Biol. Environ. Sci.; Ecol. Abstr.; Ecology Abstr.; GeoRef; Helminthol. Abstr. (1991-); Life Sci. Collect.; Potato Abstr.; Protozoolog. Abstr.; Res. Alert [Full Cov.]; Rev. Agric. Entomol.; Sci. Cit. Index; SCISEARCH.

UK
**JOURNAL OF MOLLUSCAN STUDIES. SUPPLEMENT, THE.** ***Ceased.*** **Added/Corp** Malacological Society of London. (1976)-(19??). Monographic series. English. British Museum of Natural History, Cromwell Road, London SW7 5BD England. **Tel** 011 44 71 9389123. **CODEN** JMSSDQ. Documents available from BIOSIS Document Express.
**Ind/Abst** Biol. Abstr. (1976-1978).

US/0022-300X
**JOURNAL OF NEMATOLOGY.** [J. nematol.]. Vol. 1- (Jan. 1969)-. Periodical. English. qt. $70.00 US; $80.00 other. Society of Nematologists, 700 Experiment Station Road, University of Florida, Lake Alfred Fl 33850. **Tel** (813)956-1151. **ED** Robert D Riggs. **LC** QL386.A1; J66. **DD** 595/.1/05. **UDC** 595.13. **CODEN** JONEB5. **Pr Rev. Acid Free. Circ:** 1,350 (ctrl). available on microfilm from University Microfilms International (UMI). Documents available from The Genuine Article, BIOSIS Document Express, CASDDS.
**Desc:** The official organ of the Society of Nematologists. Papers deal with pathogenicity, ecology, physiology, taxonomy, and biology of nematodes.
**Ind/Abst** AgBiotech News Inf.; AGRICOLA [Full Cov.]; Agrofor. Abstr.; BioBusiness; Biocont. News Inf. (19??-19??); Biol. Agric. Index; Biol. Abstr.; Chem. Abstr.; Cot. Trop. Fibr. Abstr. Bibliogr.; Crop Physiol. Abstr.; Curr. Contents, Agric. Biol. Environ. Sci.; Ecol. Abstr. (?-?); Ecology Abstr.; EMBASE; Entomol. Abstr.; For. Prod. Abstr. (19??-19??); For. Abstr.; Geogr. Abstr. Human Geogr. (?-?); Helminthol. Abstr.; Hortic. Abstr.; Int. Dev. Abstr. (?-?); Irr. Drain. Abstr.; Microbiol. Abstr. Sect. A; Microbiol. Abstr. Sect. C; Nematol. Abstr.; Life Sci. Collect.; PESTDOC; Plant Breed. Abstr.; Plant Grow. Reg. Abstr.; Potato Abstr.; Protozoolog. Abstr.; Res. Alert [Full Cov.]; Rev. Agric. Entomol.; Rev. Med. Vet. Entomol.; Rev. Plant Pathol.; Rice Abstr.; Sci. Cit. Index; SCISEARCH; Seed Abstr.; Soils Fert.; Soyabean Abstr.; Vitis Vitic. Enol. Abstr.; Weed Abstr.

US/0022-3395
**JOURNAL OF PARASITOLOGY, THE.** [J. parasitol.]. **Added/Corp** American Society of Parasitologists. Helminthological Society of Washington. Proceedings of the Helminthological Society of Washington. Vol. 1, (Sept. 1914)-. Academic Scholarly Publication. English. Six times a year (Feb., Apr., June, Aug., Oct., Dec.). $110.00 US; $115.00 other. American Society of Parasitologists. **(Subscription address:** Journal of Parasitology, PO Box 1897, Lawrence KS 66044-8897.**)** **LC** QL757; .J68. **NLM** W1 JO827H. **CODEN** JOPAA2. **Pr Rev. Acid Free.** available on microfilm from University Microfilms International (UMI). Documents available from The Genuine Article, BIOSIS Document Express, CASDDS.
**Desc:** This magazine contain sections called Second International Congress of Parasitology.
**Ind/Abst** AgBiotech News Inf.; AGRICOLA [Select. Cov.]; Aquat. Sci. Fish. Abstr. (Computer File); Biocont. News Inf.; Biol. Agric. Index; Biol. Abstr.; Chem. Abstr.; CSA Neuro. Abstr. (?-?); Curr. Aware. Biol. Sci., CABS; Curr. Contents, Agric. Biol. Environ. Sci.; Curr. Contents Life Sci.; Curr. Ref. Fish Res.; Ecol. Abstr.; Ecology Abstr.; EMBASE; Energy Res. Abstr.; Entomol. Abstr.; Fish Rev.; Helminthol. Abstr. (19??-19??)(1991-); Immunol. Abstr.; Index Med.; Index Vet.; INIS Atomindex [Micro.]; Microbiol. Abstr. Sect. C; Nematol. Abstr.; Life Sci. Collect.; PESTDOC; Pig News Inf.; Poult. Abstr.; Protozoolog. Abstr.; Ref. Upd. Deluxe Ed.; Res. Alert [Full Cov.]; Rev. Agric. Entomol.; Rev. Med. Vet. Entomol.; Sci. Cit. Index; SCISEARCH; Small Anim. Abstr. Bibliogr.; Soc. Sci. Cit. Index [Select. Cov.]; Vet. Bull.; Trop. Dis. Bull.

US/0142-7873
**JOURNAL OF PLANKTON RESEARCH.** [J. plankton res.]. Vol. 1 (April 1979)-. Academic Scholarly Publication. English. mo. £210.00 UK and Europe; $355.00 other. Oxford University Press, Walton Street, Oxford OX2 6DP England. **Tel** 011 44 865 56767, FAX 011 44 865 267773, telex 837330 OXPRES G. **(Subscription address:** Oxford University Press / USA, Journals Marketing Department, Oxford University Press, 2001 Evans Road, Cary NC 27513.**)** **ED** D. H. Cushing. **LC** QH90.8.P5; J68. **DD** 574.92. **CODEN** JPLRD9. **[CCC]. Ad Acc. Pr Rev. Circ:** 600. available on microfilm from University Microfilms International (UMI). Documents available from The Genuine Article, BIOSIS Document Express, CASDDS.
**Desc:** Covers zoo- and phytoplankton in all environments, publishing original papers on ecology (larval and juvenile stages), physiology and distribution (life history and taxonomy).
**Ind/Abst** AQUAREF; Aquat. Sci. Fish. Abstr. (Computer File); Biol. Abstr.; Chem. Abstr.; Curr. Aware. Biol. Sci., CABS; Curr. Contents, Agric. Biol. Environ. Sci.; Ecol. Abstr.; Ecology Abstr.; EMBASE; Fresh. Aqua. Contents Tables; Geogr. Abstr. Phys. Geogr.; GeoRef; Mar. Sci. Contents Tables; Microbiol. Abstr. Sect. C; Ocean. Abstr.; Life Sci. Collect.; Res. Alert [Full Cov.]; Sci. Cit. Index; SCISEARCH.

US/0022-3921
**JOURNAL OF PROTOZOOLOGY, THE.** ***Title Change.*** [J. protozool.]. **Added/Corp** Society of Protozoologists. Society of Protozoologists. Program and Abstracts of the Annual Meeting of the Society of Protozoologists. Vol. 1-39 (Feb. 1954)-(Nov./Dec. 1992). Academic Scholarly Publication. English (French and German). bm. Journal of Protozoology, PO Box 1897, Lawrence KS 66044-8897. **Tel** (913)843-1221, FAX (913)843-1274. **ED** Edna Kaneshiro. **LC** QL366; .J6. **DD** 593. **NLM** W1 JO853. **CODEN** JPROAR. **Bk Rev. Ad Acc. Pr Rev. Acid Free. Circ:** 2,000 (ctrl). Documents available from The Genuine Article, BIOSIS Document Express, CASDDS. ***Continued by*** *Journal of Eukaryotic Microbiology, 1066-5234.*
**Desc:** Publishes original work, descriptive or experimental, protozoology sinsu lato. A common medium for the cell biologist, taxonomist, physiologist, biochemist, ecologist, parasitologist, geneticist, immunologist, morphogeneticist and phylogeneticist working with protozoan material.
**Ind/Abst** AgBiotech News Inf.; AGRICOLA [Select. Cov.]; Biocont. News Inf. (1991-); Biol. Agric. Index; Biol. Abstr.; Biol. Dig.; Chem. Abstr.; Curr. Aware. Biol. Sci., CABS; Curr. Contents, Agric. Biol. Environ. Sci.; Curr. Contents Life Sci.; Curr. Ref. Fish Res.; Ecol. Abstr.; Ecology Abstr.; EMBASE; Energy Res. Abstr.; Fish Rev.; Genet. Abstr.; Geogr. Abstr. Phys. Geogr.; GeoRef; Helminthol. Abstr.; Immunol. Abstr.; Index Med.; Int. Aerosp. Abstr.; Microbiol. Abstr. Sect. C; Nutr. Abstr. Rev., Ser. B, Live Feeds and Feed.; Ocean. Abstr.; Life Sci. Collect.; PESTDOC; Postharvest News Inf.; Poult. Abstr.; Protozoolog. Abstr.; Ref. Upd. Deluxe Ed.; Res. Alert [Full Cov.]; Rev. Agric. Entomol.; Rev. Med. Vet. Entomol.; Sci. Cit. Index (19??-19??); SCISEARCH; Trop. Dis. Bull.; Virol. AIDS Abstr.

US/0892-1016
**JOURNAL OF RAPTOR RESEARCH, THE.** [J. raptor res.]. **Added/Corp** Raptor Research Foundation. (1987)-. Periodical. English. qt (Mar., June, Sept., Dec.). $24.00 (individuals), $30.00 (institutions) US; $27.00 (individuals), $33.00 (institutions) other. Raptor Research Foundation, 12805 St Croix Trail, Hastings MN 55033. **Tel** (612)437-4359, FAX (612)438-2908. **ED** Joseph Schmutz (editor's address: University of Saskatchewan, Department of Biology, Saskatoon Saskatchewan S7N 0W0 Canada). **DD** 598. **CODEN** JRREEF. Index available. cum. index. **Bk Rev. Pr Rev. Acid Free. Circ:** 1,200 (ctrl). Documents available from The Genuine Article, BIOSIS Document Express. ***Continues*** *Raptor Research, 0099-9059.*
**Desc:** The purpose of the journal is to stimulate the dissemination of information concerning raptorial birds among interested persons worldwide and to promote a better public understanding and appreciation of the value of birds of prey.
**Ind/Abst** Biol. Abstr. (1987-); Curr. Contents, Agric. Biol. Environ. Sci.; Ecol. Abstr.; Fish Rev.; Key Word Index Wildl. Res.; Res. Alert [Full Cov.]; SCISEARCH; Wildl. Rev.

JA/0368-4113
**JOURNAL OF SCIENCE OF THE HIROSHIMA UNIVERSITY. SERIES B. DIVISION 1. ZOOLOGY.** [J. sci. Hiroshima Univ., Ser. B, Div. 1]. **Main/Corp** Hiroshima Daigaku. Vol. 1 (Dec. 1930)-. Periodical. English (Japanese). an. Free on request. Hiroshima University Faculty of Science, 1 89 Higashisenda Machi 1Chome, Naka Ku Hiroshima 730 Japan. **Tel** 81 82 241 1221. **NLM** W1 HI584. **CODEN** JSHBAR. Documents available from BIOSIS Document Express.
**Ind/Abst** Biol. Abstr.; CSA Neuro. Abstr. (?-?); Life Sci. Collect.; Trop. Dis. Bull.; Vitis Vitic. Enol. Abstr.

AT/0004-9050
**JOURNAL OF THE AUSTRALIAN ENTOMOLOGICAL SOCIETY.** [J. Aust. entomol. soc.]. **Added/Corp** Australian Entomological Society. Vol. 6, No. 1 (June 1967)-. Periodical. English. qt. 90.00Aus$ Australia; 105.00Aus$ other. Australian Entomology Branch, Department of Prim Ind, Meiers Road, Indooroopilly Queensland 4068 Australia. **ED** N W Heather. **LC** QL487; .E5. **DD** 595.7/005. **CODEN** AESJBC. Index available. **Bk Rev. Circ:** 900 (ctrl). Documents available from The Genuine Article, BIOSIS Document Express, CASDDS. ***Continues*** *Journal of the Entomological Society of Queensland.*
**Desc:** General entomology especially in an Australian setting or to the fauna of the Australian region.
**Ind/Abst** AGRICOLA [Full Cov.]; Agrofor. Abstr. (19??-19??); Biocont. News Inf. (19??-19??); Biodeter. Abstr. (19??-19??); Biol. Abstr.; Chem. Abstr. (-1988); Curr. Aware. Biol. Sci., CABS; Curr. Contents, Agric. Biol. Environ. Sci.; Ecology Abstr.; Entomol. Abstr.; For. Prod. Abstr.; For. Abstr.; Hortic. Abstr.; Index Vet.; Maize Abstr.; Life Sci. Collect.; PESTDOC; Plant Breed. Abstr.; Postharvest News Inf.; Poult. Abstr.; Protozoolog. Abstr.; Res. Alert [Full Cov.]; Rev. Agric. Entomol.; Rev. Med. Vet. Entomol.; Rev. Plant Pathol.; Sci. Cit. Index; SCISEARCH; Seed Abstr.; Sorghum Mill. Abstr.; Vet. Bull.; Weed Abstr.; Wheat Barley Trit. Abstr.

SA/0013-8789
**JOURNAL OF THE ENTOMOLOGICAL SOCIETY OF SOUTHERN AFRICA.** ***Title Change.*** [J. Entomol. Soc. South. Afr.]. Vol.1 (Mar. 30, 1939)-(1992). Periodical. English (Afrikaans). sa. Entomological Society of Southern Africa, PO Box 103, Pretoria 0001 South Africa. **Tel** 21 12 2062623, FAX 21 12 3235275. **ED** P.E. Hulley. **LC** QL461; .E688. **NLM** W1 JO92P. **CODEN** JESAAF. Index available. **Bk Rev**, (Qty: 4/yr). **Pr Rev. Circ:** 700. Documents available from The Genuine Article, BIOSIS Document Express. ***Continued by*** *African Entomology, 1021-3589.*
**Desc:** Publication by members of original research on academic and applied entomology and arachnology, with emphasis on the Southern African Fauna, at nominal page charges.
**Ind/Abst** AGRICOLA [Full Cov.]; Agrofor. Abstr. (1991-); Biocont. News Inf. (19??-19??); Biol. Abstr.; Curr. Aware. Biol. Sci., CABS; Curr. Contents, Agric. Biol. Environ. Sci.; Ecology Abstr.; Entomol. Abstr.; Field Crop Abstr.; For. Abstr.; Grasslands For. Abstr.; Index Vet.; Maize Abstr.; Life Sci. Collect.; Plant Breed. Abstr.; Res. Alert [Select. Cov.]; Rev. Agric. Entomol.; Rev. Med. Vet. Entomol.; SCISEARCH; Small Anim. Abstr. Bibliogr.; Soils Fert.; Sorghum Mill. Abstr.; Zool. Rec.; Weed Abstr.

US/1049-233X
**JOURNAL OF THE HELMINTHOLOGICAL SOCIETY OF WASHINGTON.** [J. Helminthol. Soc. Wash.]. **Added/Corp** Helminthological Society of Washington. Vol. 57, No. 1 (Jan. 1990)-. Periodical. English. Twice a year. $37.00 US; $39.00 Canada and Mexico; $42.00 other. Helminthological Society of Washington. **(Subscription address:** Journal of the Helminthological Society of Washington, PO Box 1897, Lawrence KS 66044-8897.**) ED** Ralph P. Eckerlin. **LC** IN PROCESS. **DD** 595. **NLM** W1; JO928G. **CODEN** JHSWE4. Index available. **Acid Free.** Documents available from The Genuine Article, BIOSIS Document Express. ***Continues*** *Proceedings of the Helminthological Society of Washington, 0018-0130.*
**Desc:** Publishes original research papers on the biology, immunology, ecology, biochemistry, and systematics of all groups of parasites, particularly the protozoa, helminths, and anthropods.
**Ind/Abst** AGRICOLA [Select. Cov.]; Biol. Abstr.; Curr. Aware. Biol. Sci., CABS; Curr. Contents, Agric. Biol. Environ. Sci.; Helminthol. Abstr. (1991-); Index Vet.; PESTDOC; Protozoolog. Abstr.; Res. Alert [Full Cov.]; Rev. Agric. Entomol.; Rev. Med. Vet. Entomol.; Sci. Cit. Index; SCISEARCH; Small Anim. Abstr. Bibliogr.; Vet. Bull.; Trop. Dis. Bull.

SA/0441-6651
**JOURNAL OF THE HERPETOLOGICAL ASSOCIATION OF AFRICA.** [J. Herpetol. Assoc. Afr.]. **Main/Corp** Herpetological Association of Africa. **VFOAT** H.A.A; H.A.A. Journal. No. 1 (1965)-. Periodical. English. ir. $20.00 (one year), $56.00 (three years). Herpetological Association of Africa, PO Box 20142, Durban North 4016 South Africa. **Tel** 051 479609. **ED** W. Branch. **CODEN** HAAJA4. **Bk Rev. Pr Rev. Circ:** 450 (ctrl). Documents available from BIOSIS Document Express. ***Supersedes*** *Journal of the Herpetological Association of Rhodesia.*
**Desc:** Covers all aspects of herpetology, primarily African herpetology, but also overseas. Regularly lists new literature on African herpetology.
**Ind/Abst** Biol. Abstr.; Fish Rev. (Jan. 1989-July 1992); Wildl. Rev. (Jan. 1989-July 1992).

AT/1040-5208
**JOURNAL OF THE INTERNATIONAL ASSOCIATION OF ZOO EDUCATORS.** (JOURNAL, INTERNATIONAL ASSOCIATION OF ZOO EDUCATORS.). [J. Int. Assoc. Zoo Educ.]. **Added/Corp** International Association of Zoo Educators. **VFOAT** Journal of the International Association of Zoo Educators; IZE Journal. No. 15 (1986)-. Periodical. English. sa. $60.00 (full membership). Jersey Wildlife Preservation Trust, Les Augres Manor, Trinity Jersey Channel Islands. **ED** Steve Mcauley. **DD** 590. **Circ:** 250. ***Continues*** *International Association of Zoo Educators. Newsletter.*

US/0024-0966
**JOURNAL OF THE LEPIDOPTERISTS' SOCIETY.** [J. Lepid. Soc.]. **Added/Corp** Lepidopterists' Society. Vol. 13, No. 1 (1959)-. Periodical. English. Four times a year. $50.00. The Lepidopterists Society, Robert J. Borth, 6926 North Belmont Lane, Fox Point WI 53217. **Tel** (414)351-3816. **ED** Stephanie McKown (editor's address: 650 Cotterell Drive, Boise, ID 83709). **LC** QL541; .L45. **DD** 595. **CODEN** JLPSAZ. cum. index. **Bk Rev. Ad Acc. Circ:** 1,660 (ctrl). Documents available from BIOSIS Document Express. ***Continues in part*** *Lepidopterists' News, 0457-5628.*
**Desc:** Technical and semi-technical articles on all aspects of the study of moths and butterflies of the world (taxonomy, biology, ecology, life history, etc.).
**Ind/Abst** AGRICOLA [Full Cov.]; Agrofor. Abstr.; Biocont. News Inf. (19??-19??); Biol. Abstr.; Ecol. Abstr.; Entomol. Abstr.; For. Abstr.; Life Sci. Collect.

AT/0085-2988
**JOURNAL OF THE MALACOLOGICAL SOCIETY OF AUSTRALIA.** ***Title Change.*** [J. Malacol. Soc. Aust.]. **Main/Corp** Malacological Society of Australia. Vol. 1 (1957)-(19??). English. an. Malacological Society of Australia, Australian Museum, 6 8 College Street, Sydney South NSW 2000 Australia. **Tel** 011 61 3 6699880. **ED** F. E. Wells. **LC** QL401; .M16. **DD** 594/.0994. **CODEN** JMLAA2. cum. index. **Bk Rev. Ad Acc. Pr Rev. Circ:** 1,000. Documents available from BIOSIS Document Express. ***Continued by*** *Molluscan Research.*
**Desc:** Scientific papers on malacology: molluscan taxonomy, biology, ecology, and biogeography.
**Ind/Abst** Biol. Abstr.; Geol. Abstr.; GeoRef; Life Sci. Collect.

JA/0914-1855
**JOURNAL OF THE MAMMALOGICAL SOCIETY OF JAPAN.** **Added/Corp** Nihon Honyu Dobutsu Gakkai. Vol. 12, Nos. 1-2 (Sept. 1987)-. Periodical. English. sa. $88.40 US, Canada, Central America & West Indies; $89.20 Europe, Africa, South America, former USSR, Middle & Near East; $87.50 Asia, Australia, New Zealand. **(Subscription address:** Japan Publications Trading Company, Ltd., PO Box 5030, Tokyo International, Tokyo 100-31 Japan.**) LC** QL700; .J63. **DD** 599/.005. ***Continues in part*** *Honyu Dobutsugaku Zasshi, 0546-0670.*

US/0028-7199
**JOURNAL OF THE NEW YORK ENTOMOLOGICAL SOCIETY.** [J. N. Y. Entomol. Soc.]. **Added/Corp** New York Entomological Society. Vol. 1 (March 1893)-. Periodical. English. Four times a year. $65.00 US, Canada & Mexico; $75.00 other. New York Entomological Society Natural History, Central Park, West 79th Street, New York NY 10024. **Tel** (212)769-5613, FAX (212)769-5233. **DD** 595. **NLM** W1 JO942V. **CODEN** JNYEAI. cum. index. **Bk Rev. Pr Rev.** Documents available from The Genuine Article, BIOSIS Document Express, CASDDS.
**Ind/Abst** AGRICOLA [Full Cov.]; Biocont. News Inf. (19??-19??); Biol. Abstr.; Chem. Abstr.; CSA Neuro. Abstr. (?-?); Curr. Aware. Biol. Sci., CABS; Curr. Contents, Agric. Biol. Environ. Sci.; Ecology Abstr.; Entomol. Abstr.; For. Abstr.; Life Sci. Collect.; Res. Alert [Select. Cov.]; Rev. Agric. Entomol.; Rev. Med. Vet. Entomol.; SCISEARCH; Soyabean Abstr.; Weed Abstr.; Wildl. Rev.

US/0740-0152
**JOURNAL OF THE NORTH AMERICAN WOLF SOCIETY.** [J. - North Am. Wolf Soc.]. **Main/Corp** North American Wolf Society. Periodical. English. Three times a year. $15.00. North American Wolf Society, Route 2 Troy Pike, Windhover Farm, Versailles KY 40383.

II/0049-8769
**JOURNAL OF THE ZOOLOGICAL SOCIETY OF INDIA.** [J. Zool. Soc. India]. **Main/Corp** Zoological Society of India. Vol. 1 (Jan. 1949)-. Periodical. English. sa. $25.00. Zoological Society of India, Utkal University, P G Department of Zoology, Bhubaneswar 4 Orissa India. **(Subscription address:** Prints India, 11 Darya Ganj, New Delhi, 110002 India, (Phone: 011 91 11 3268645)**) ED** B K Behura. **LC** QL1; .Z6952. **DD** 590.6254. **CODEN** JZSIAG. Index available. **Bk Rev. Ad Acc. Circ:** 500. Documents available from BIOSIS Document Express.
**Ind/Abst** Biol. Abstr.; GeoRef; Life Sci. Collect.

UK/0952-8369
**JOURNAL OF ZOOLOGY (1987).** (JOURNAL OF ZOOLOGY : PROCEEDINGS OF THE ZOOLOGICAL SOCIETY OF LONDON.). [J. zool.]. **Added/Corp** Zoological Society of London. **VFOAT** Proceedings of the Zoological Society of London. Vol. 211, Pt. 1 (Jan. 1987)-. Academic Scholarly Publication. English. mo. £410.00 UK and Europe; $825.00 other. Oxford University Press, Walton Street, Oxford OX2 6DP England. **Tel** 011 44 865 56767, FAX 011 44 865 267773, telex 837330 OXPRES G. **(Subscription address:** Oxford University Press / USA, Journals Marketing Department, Oxford University Press, 2001 Evans Road, Cary NC 27513.**) ED** M. A. Edwards. **LC** QL1; .J879. **DD** 590/.5. **NLM** W1; JO974ZD. **CODEN** JOZOEU. **[CCC].** Index available. **Ad Acc. Pr Rev. Circ:** 1,500. available on microfilm and microfiche from University Microfilms International (UMI). Documents available from The Genuine Article, BIOSIS Document Express, CASDDS. ***Formed by the union of*** *Journal of Zoology. Series A, 0269-364X* ***and*** *Journal of Zoology. Series B, 0268-196X.*
**Desc:** Original papers within the general field of experimental and descriptive zoology. Includes comparative and functional morphology and paleontology, biometrics, comparative cytology and immunology, reproductive biology and embryology, genetics, ecology, neurobiology and behaviour, general animal physiology, and related topics.
**Ind/Abst** AGRICOLA [Select. Cov.]; Anim. Behav. Abstr.; Biol. Agric. Index (1987-); Biol. Abstr. (1987-); Chem. Abstr. (1987-); Chemorecept. Abstr.; CSA Neuro. Abstr. (?-?); Curr. Aware. Biol. Sci., CABS; Curr. Ref. Fish Res.; Ecol. Abstr.; Ecology Abstr.; EMBASE (1987-); Entomol. Abstr.; Fish Rev.; Geogr. Abstr. Phys. Geogr.; GeoRef (1987-); Helminthol. Abstr. (1991-); Index Vet.; Ocean. Abstr.; Life Sci. Collect. (1987-); Postharvest News Inf.; Ref. Upd. Deluxe Ed.; Res. Alert [Full Cov.]; Rev. Agric. Entomol.; Rev. Med. Vet. Entomol.; Sci. Cit. Index; SCISEARCH; Soc. Sci. Cit. Index [Select. Cov.]; Vet. Bull.

US/0276-5195
**K.C. ZOO BOOMERANG.** **VFOAT** Zoo Boomerang; Boomerang. **VAT** Kansas City Zoo Boomerang. Periodical. English. Kansas City Zoo, Swope Park, Kansas City MO 64132. **UDC** 59.006(781).

JA/0385-9932
**KACHIKU HANSHOKUGAKU ZASSHI (TOKYO. 1977).** (KACHIKU HANSHOKUGAKU ZASSHI.). [Kachiku hanshokugaku zasshi]. **Added/Corp** Kanchiku Hanshoku Kenkyukai. **VFOAT** Japanese Journal of Animal Reproduction. (1977)-. Academic Scholarly Publication. Japanese (English). Five times a year. ¥5000.00. Azabu University, Sagamihara Shi, Japanese Society of Animal Reproduction, Kanagawa 229 Japan. **CODEN** KHZADH. Documents available from BIOSIS Document Express, CASDDS.
**Ind/Abst** Biol. Abstr.; Chem. Abstr.; Index Vet.; Pig News Inf.; Poult. Abstr.; Small Anim. Abstr. Bibliogr.; Vet. Bull.

JA
**KANAGAWA-KEN SANGYO SENTA SHIKEN KENKYU KOKOKU.** **Main/Corp** Kanagawa-ken Sangyo Senta. Vol. 1- Issue 47- 1972-. Japanese. Kanagawa-ken Sangyo Senta, 2010 Nakashinden, Ebina Japan. **LC** SF541; .K36A. ***Supersedes*** *Shiken Chosa Seiseki Gaiyo.*

PL
**KATALOG FAUNY POLSKI.** [Kat. fauny Pol.]. **Main/Corp** Instytyt Zoologii. **VFOAT** Catalogus Faunae Poloniae. No. 1 (1960)-. Polish. Panstwowe Wydawn Naukowe, Miodowa 10, PO Box 391, 00251 Warsaw Poland.
**Ind/Abst** Rev. Med. Vet. Entomol.

HU/0133-4565
**KISTENYESZTOK LAPJA.** [Kisteny. l.]. V. 20, No. 8- (Aug. 1976)-. Periodical. Hungarian. mo. Hirlapkiado Vallalat, Blaha Luiza Ter 3, 1959 Budapest VII Hungary. **Tel** 135-816.
**Ind/Abst** AGRICOLA.

PL/0075-6342
**KLUCZE DO OZNAZCZANIA KREGOWCOW POLSKI.** Vol. 1 1962-. Monographic series. Polish (English and Russian). Price varies per volume. Panstwowe Wydawn Naukowe, Miodowa 10, PO Box 391, 00251 Warsaw Poland. **LC** QL1; .K57.
**Ind/Abst** Rev. Med. Vet. Entomol.

SA/0075-6458
**KOEDOE.** [Koedoe]. **Added/Corp** South Africa. National Parks Board of Trustees. No. 1 (1958)-. English (summaries and/or abstracts in Afrikaans). sa. (June and Dec.). R45.60 South Africa; R60.00 other. National Parks Board of Trustees, PO Box 787, Pretoria 0001 South Africa. **Tel** 011 27 012 3439770, FAX 011 27 012 3430907, telex 321324 SA. **ED** G. de Graaff and J. C. Rautenbach. **LC** QL337.S65; A35. **DD** 574. **CODEN** KOEDB2. Index available (free on request). cum. index. **Bk Rev. Pr Rev. Circ:** 1,000 (ctrl). Documents available from BIOSIS Document Express.
**Desc:** Covers aspects of scientific research undertaken by and on behalf of the National Parks Board of South Africa with emphasis on zoology, botany and veterinary problems.
**Ind/Abst** Biocont. News Inf.; Biol. Abstr.; Ecol. Abstr.; Ecology Abstr.; Field Crop Abstr.; Fish Rev.; For. Abstr.; Geogr. Abstr. Phys. Geogr.; Geogr. Abstr. Human Geogr. (?-?); Grasslands For. Abstr.; Index Vet.; Key Word Index Wildl. Res.; Plant Genet. Resour. Abstr.; Rev. Med. Vet. Entomol.; Soils Fert.; Vet. Bull.; Zool. Rec.

AU/0075-6547
**KOLEOPTEROLOGISCHE RUNDSCHAU.** (KOLEOPTEROLOGISCHE RUNDSCHAU / HERAUSGEGEBEN VON DER ZOOLOGISCH-BOTANISCHEN GESELLSCHAFT GEMEINSAM MIT DER FORSTLICHEN BUNDESVERSUCHSANST ALT.). [Koleopterol. Rundsch.]. **Added/Corp** Zoologisch-Botanische Gesellschaft in Wien. Forstliche Bundes-Versuchsanstalt Wien. Vol. 7 (1919)-. German (summaries and/or abstracts in English). an. S300.00. Zoologisch Botanische Gesellschaft in Oesterreich, Althanstrasse 14, Postfach 287, A-1019 Vienna Austria. **Tel** 0222 313361465, FAX 0222 31336700. **LC** QL571; .K64. **DD** 595.76/05. **CODEN** KLRUAS. Documents available from BIOSIS Document Express. ***Continues*** *Coleopterologische Rundschau;* ***Absorbed*** *Wiener Entomologische Zeitung.*
**Ind/Abst** Biol. Abstr.; Life Sci. Collect.

KE
**KOMBA.** Periodical. English. Wildlife Clubs of Kenya Association, PO Box 40658, Nairobi Kenya. **Tel** 742564. **ED** Nathaniel Arap-Chumo. **LC** QL84.6.K4; K65. **DD** 333.95/416/096762. **UDC** 59(676.2). **Bk Rev. Ad Acc. Circ:** 6,000 (ctrl).
**Desc:** A magazine for wildlife club members.

CC
**KUN CHUNG HSUEH YEN CHIU CHI KAN / CHUNG-KUO KO HSUEH YUAN SHANG-HAI KUN CHUNG YEN CHIU SO PIEN.** V. 1 (1980)-. Chinese (summaries and/or abstracts in English). RMBY1.95. Hsin Hua Shu Tien / Shang-Hai Fa Hsing So, Shanghai, People's Republic of China. **LC** QL461; .K87. **DD** 595.7.

NE/0023-7051
**LACERTA.** [Lacerta]. **Added/Corp** Nederlandse Vereniging voor Herpetologie en Terrariumkunde "Lacerta.". (19??)-. Periodical. Dutch (summaries and/or abstracts in English). Six times a year. F52.00 Belgium, Netherlands and Luxemburg; $38.00 US and Europe; F75.00 other. N. V. H. T. Lacerta, Meubelmaker 13, 3335 VG Zwijndrecht, Netherlands. **Tel** 011 31 78 10 35 77. cum. index. **Bk Rev. Ad Acc. Circ:** 2,000 (ctrl). available on microfilm and microfiche from University Microfilms International (UMI). Documents available from BIOSIS Document Express. ***Continues*** *Lacertanieuws.*
**Desc:** Publication for the Dutch Society for Herpetology. Articles on amphibians and reptiles (ecology, ethology, reproduction).
**Ind/Abst** Biol. Abstr.

DK/0075-8787
**LEPIDOPTERA.** [Lepidoptera]. **Added/Corp** Lepidopterologisk Forening. Vol. 1 (June 1967)-. Periodical. Danish (summaries and/or abstracts in English). sa. kr220.00 Europe and Mediterranean Basin; kr230.00 other. Lepidopterologisk Forening, Sondervigveg 29 Fle Vilhelmsen, 2720 Vanlose Denmark. **Tel** 011 45 2 800745. **CODEN** LEPDAV. Index available. Documents available from BIOSIS Document Express.
**Desc:** About Danish butterflies.
**Ind/Abst** AGRICOLA; Biol. Abstr.

GW
**LERCHE, DIE.** (1988)-. Periodical. German. qt. Verlag Plane, Postfach 827, 4600 Dortmund 1 Germany. **Tel** 0211-359188. **LC** ML5; E542. ***Continues*** *Eiserne Lerche.*

CN/0384-8159
**LIFE SCIENCES CONTRIBUTIONS / ROYAL ONTARIO MUSEUM.** **See** Museums and Galleries.

CN/0082-5093
**LIFE SCIENCES MISCELLANEOUS PUBLICATION.** [Life sci. misc. publ.]. **Added/Corp** Royal Ontario Museum. **VFOAT** Life Sciences Miscellaneous Publications. (1???)-. Monographic series. English. ir. Price varies per volume. Royal Ontario Museum Publications Service, 100 Queens Park, Toronto Ontario M5S 2C6 Canada. **Tel** (416)586-5581. **DD** 591/.05. **CODEN** ROLMB5.
**Ind/Abst** GeoRef.

CN/0082-5107
**LIFE SCIENCES OCCASIONAL PAPERS.** ***Ceased.*** (LIFE SCIENCES OCCASIONAL PAPERS / ROM, ROYAL ONTARIO MUSEUM.). [Life sci. occas. pap.]. **Added/Corp** Royal Ontario Museum. **VFOAT** Life Sciences Occasional Paper. No. 11 (July 22, 1968)-(1992). Monographic series. English. ir. Royal Ontario Museum Publications Service, 100 Queens Park, Toronto Ontario M5S 2C6 Canada. **Tel** (416)586-5581. **LC** QL1.; T654. **DD** 590. **CODEN** ROLOAA. ***Continues*** *Occasional Papers of the Royal Ontario Museum of Zoology.*
**Ind/Abst** Fish Rev. (199?-); GeoRef; Wildl. Rev. (199?-).

FR
**LISTE DES TRAVAUX ARACHNOLOGIQUES PARUS EN ... OU ACTUELLEMENT SOUS PRESSE.** **Added/Corp** International Arachnologic Documentation Center. (19??)-. French (English and Spanish). an. Centre International de Documentation Arachnologique, 61 rue de Buffon, 75005 Paris France. **Tel** 40 79 3574. **ED** J Heurtault. **LC** Z7996.A6; L57; QL451. **DD** 016.5954. **Bk Rev.** ***Continues*** *Liste des Travaux Arachnologiques Mondiaux.*

US/0887-9923
**LLAMAS.** [Llamas]. **VFOAT** Llamas Magazine. No. 29 (Sept./Oct. 1985)-. Periodical. English. Six times a year. Clay Press Inc., 46 Main Street, Jackson CA 95642. **Tel** (209)223-0469. **DD** 636. ***Continues*** *3L Llama, 0739-1064.*

UK
**LONDON BIRD REPORT.** No. 1 (1936)-. English. an. London Natural History Society, 3 Chatsworth Edwards, West Harrow, Middlesex HA2 0RS England. **Tel** 011 44 0273 654714.

CK/0085-2899
**LOZANIA.** [Lozania]. **Added/Corp** Universidad Nacional de Colombia. Instituto de Ciencias Naturales. **VFOAT** Acta Zoologica Colombiana. No. 1 (1952)-. Monographic series. Spanish (summaries and/or abstracts in English, French, Dutch and Latin). ir. Price varies per volume. Inst de Ciencias Naturales, Apartado 7495, Museo Historia, Bogota Colombia. **Tel** 011 57 1 2684336. **ED** Santiago Diaz and Pedro Miguel Ruiz. **LC** QL244; .L68. **CODEN** LZNAAN. **Ad Acc. Circ:** 1,000. Documents available from BIOSIS Document Express.
**Desc:** Deals with zoology, systematics, taxonomy, Colombian fauna, natural sciences and new species.
**Ind/Abst** Biol. Abstr.; Fish Rev. (19??-199?).

RM/0374-8898
**LUCRARI STIINTIFICE, INSTITUL AGRONOMIC "N. BALCESCU," BUCURESTI, SERIA D, ZOOTEHNIE.** (LUCRARI STIINTIFICE. SERIA D: ZOOTEHNIE.). **Added/Corp** Institutul Agronomic "N. Balcescu.". **VFOAT** Zootehnie; Lucrari Stiintifice. Zootehnie. Vol. 13 (1970)-. Romanian (summaries and/or abstracts in English, French and Russian). an. DM164.00. Institutul Agronomic N Balcescu, B-Dul Marasti, NR 59, Bucuresti Sectorul 1 Romania. **(Subscription address:** Kubon & Sagner, ABT Zeitschriftenimport, D 80328 Munich Germany.**)** Index available. cum. index. **Bk Rev. Ad Acc.** ctrl circ. Documents available from BIOSIS Document Express. ***Continues in part*** *Lucrari Stiintifice. Seria C, Zootehnie si Medicina Veterinara, 0524-8108.*
**Ind/Abst** Biol. Abstr.

RM
**LUCRARI STIINTIFICE. ZOOTEHNIE.** **Main/Corp** Institutul Agronomic N. Balcescu. **VFOAT** Zootehnie. Vol. 16 (1976)-. Periodical. Romanian (summaries and/or abstracts in English, French and Russian). an. ***Continues*** *Institutul Agronomic "N. Balcescu". Lucrari Stiintifice. Seria D: Zootehnie.*
**Ind/Abst** Poult. Abstr.

NE/0024-7634
**LUTRA.** [Lutra]. **Added/Corp** Vereniging voor Zoogdierkunde en Zoogdierbescherming. No. 19-20, (1958/1959)-Vol. 2 (May 1960)-. Periodical. Dutch (English, French and German; summaries and/or abstracts in English, French and German). Twice a year (Sept. & Dec.). Fl56.60 Netherlands; Fl75.47 others. Vereniging Voor Zoogdieren, Emmalaan 41, 3581 HP Utrecht Netherlands. **Tel** 011 31 30 544642. **ED** C. Smeenk. **CODEN** LUTAAI. **Bk Rev. Ad Acc. Pr Rev. Circ:** 800 (ctrl). Documents available from BIOSIS Document Express. ***Continues*** *Vereniging voor Zoogdierkunde en Zoogdierbescherming. Mededelingenblad.*
**Desc:** Journal of the Netherlands/Belgian Mammal Society. Papers on the biology of wild-living mammals, mainly of the Benelux-countries; also of other European countries.
**Ind/Abst** Biol. Abstr.; Fish Rev.; GeoRef; Key Word Index Wildl. Res.; Wildl. Rev.

US/8756-9620
**MAINE BIRDLIFE.** **See** Natural History.

JA
**MAKUNAGI.** **Added/Corp** Soshi Gakkai (Japan). **VFOAT** Makunagi. Vol. 31, No. 1 (1966)-. Periodical. Japanese. ir. Entomological Laboratory, University of Osaka Prefecture, Sakai Japan. **LC** QL531; .M35.

US/0076-2997
**MALACOLOGIA.** [Malacologia]. **Added/Corp** Institute of Malacology. University of Michigan. Museum of Zoology. Mollusk Division. Vol. 1 (1962)-. Monographic series. English (French, German, Russian and Spanish; summaries and/or abstracts in German, Russian and Spanish). ir. $21.00 (individuals), $35.00 (institutions). Academy of Natural Sciences, 1900 Benjamin Franklin Parkway, Philadelphia PA 19103. **Tel** (215)299-1130, FAX (215)299-1028. **ED** G.M. Davis. **LC** QL401; .M15. **DD** 594/.005. **NLM** W1 MA495. **CODEN** MALAAJ. Index available. cum. index. **Circ:** 700. Documents available from The Genuine Article, BIOSIS Document Express, CASDDS.
**Desc:** An international journal of malacology which publishes papers on the morphology, ecology, evolution, fossil record, classification, distribution, physiology, biochemistry, cytology, genetics and parasitism of mollusks.
**Ind/Abst** AgBiotech News Inf.; Aquat. Sci. Fish. Abstr. (Computer File); Biol. Abstr.; Chem. Abstr.; Curr. Aware. Biol. Sci., CABS; Curr. Contents, Agric. Biol. Environ. Sci.; Energy Res. Abstr.; GeoRef; Helminthol. Abstr.; Index Med.; INIS Atomindex [Micro.]; Life Sci. Collect.; Res. Alert [Full Cov.]; Rev. Agric. Entomol.; Sci. Cit. Index; SCISEARCH; Soc. Sci. Cit. Index [Select. Cov.].

US/0076-3004
**MALACOLOGICAL REVIEW.** [Malacol. rev.]. **Added/Corp** University of Michigan. Museum of Zoology. (1968)-. English (French, Spanish and German). an. $33.00 US; $36.00 other. Malacological Review, Campus Box 315, Hunter Building, University of Colorado, Boulder CO 80309. **Tel** (303)492-7359, FAX (303)492-5105. **ED** Shi-Kui Wu. **LC** QL401; .M155. **DD** 594/.6/05. **NLM** W1 MA496. **CODEN** MLGRBL. **Bk Rev. Pr Rev. Circ:** 500. available on microfilm and microfiche from University Microfilms International (UMI). Documents available from BIOSIS Document Express.
**Desc:** Original or review articles on various aspects of Malacology, information on current publications.
**Ind/Abst** Biocont. News Inf. (1991-); Biol. Abstr.; GeoRef; Helminthol. Abstr. (19??-19??); Life Sci. Collect.; Rev. Agric. Entomol.

US/0892-6506
**MALACOLOGY DATA NET.** [Malacol. data net]. **Added/Corp** Ecosearch, Inc. **VFOAT** Ecosearch Series. No. 1 (Apr. 11, 1986)-. Periodical. English. ir. $16.00 US and Canada; $20.00 other. Ecosearch Inc., 325 East Bayview, Portland TX 78374. **Tel** (512)643-1689. **LC** QL401; .M185. **DD** 594/.005. Index available. **Bk Rev. Ad Acc. Circ:** 150 (ctrl).
**Desc:** Devoted to publication of original research papers pertaining to the systematics, distributions, ecology, and biology of mollusks.

HU/0230-0648
**MALAKOLOGIAI TAJEKOZTATO.** **VFOAT** Malacological Informing; Malacological Newsletters. Vol. 1 (1980)-. Hungarian (Hungarian). an. **LC** QL401; .M187.

GW/0070-7260
**MALAKOLOGISCHE ABHANDLUNGEN.** Vol. 1 (1964)-. Monographic series. German (English and French). ir. Price varies per volume. Staatliches Museum fuer Tierkunde Dresden, Augustusstrasse 2, D 01067 Dresden Germany. **LC** QL401; .M19. **CODEN** SMTMB8. **Bk Rev. Circ:** 250 (ctrl). Documents available from BIOSIS Document Express. ***Supersedes in part*** *Abhandlungen und Berichte aus dem Staatlichen Museum fur Tierkunde in Dresden.*
**Desc:** Taxonomy, systematics, morphology, biology, ecology, zoogeography, faunistics of the invertebrate group mollusca in global range.
**Ind/Abst** Biol. Abstr.

UK/0305-1838
**MAMMAL REVIEW.** [Mammal rev.]. **Added/Corp** Mammal Society. Vol. 1 (Feb. 1970)-. Academic Scholarly Publication. English. qt (4 issues). $157.00 US & Canada; £91.50 Europe; £101.00 other. Blackwell Scientific Publications Ltd, Marston Book Services, PO Box 87, Oxford OX2 ODT UK. **Tel** 011 44 865 791155, FAX 011 44 865 791927, telex 837 515 MARDIS G. **ED** D. W. Yalden and G. R. Hosey. **LC** QL700; .M24. **DD** 599/.005. **NLM** W1 MA534. **CODEN** MMLRAI. **[CCC]. Bk Rev. Ad Acc. Pr Rev. Circ:** 1,550. available on microfilm and microfiche from University Microfilms International (UMI). Documents available from The Genuine Article, BIOSIS Document Express. ***Supersedes in part*** *Mammal Society. Bulletin.*
**Desc:** Reviews and reports on any aspect of mammalogy (not the results of original research), reports on status and distribution of mammalian species.
**Ind/Abst** Anim. Breed. Abstr.; Art Archaeol. Tech. Abstr.; Biol. Abstr.; Curr. Aware. Biol. Sci., CABS; Curr. Contents, Agric. Biol. Environ. Sci.; Ecol. Abstr.; Ecology Abstr.; Key Word Index Wildl. Res.; Nutr. Abstr. Rev., Ser. B, Live Feeds and Feed.; Life Sci. Collect.; Res. Alert [Full Cov.]; Rev. Agric. Entomol.; Rev. Med. Vet. Entomol.; Sci. Cit. Index; SCISEARCH; Wildl. Rev.

GW/0301-2778
**MAMMALIA DEPICTA.** [Mamm. depicta]. (1966)-. Monographic series. English (French and German). ir. Price varies per volume. Blackwell Wissenschafts-Verlag, Kurfuerstendamm 57, D 10707 Berlin Germany. **Tel** 011 49 30 32790623, 011 49 30 32790624, FAX 011 49 30 327 90610.

FR/0025-1461
**MAMMALIA (PARIS).** (MAMMALIA.). [Mammalia]. **Added/Corp** Paris. Museum National d'Histoire Naturelle. Laboratoire de Zoologie des Mammiferes. France. Centre National de la Recherche Scientifique. Vol. 1 (Sept. 1936)-. Periodical. French (English; table of contents in English). qt. 685.60F France; 700.00F other. Dawson France SA, BP 40, 91121 Palaiseau Cedex France. **Tel** 011 33 1 69104700, telex 220064F. **ED** Jean Dorst. **LC** QL700; .M25. **DD** 599/.005. **NLM** W1 MA534L. **CODEN** MAMLAN. cum. index. **Pr Rev. Circ:** 550. Documents available from The Genuine Article, BIOSIS Document Express.
**Desc:** Covers morphology, biology (ecology, behavior physiology) systematics, and biogeography of mammals.
**Ind/Abst** AGRICOLA; Anim. Behav. Abstr.; Biol. Abstr.; CSA Neuro. Abstr. (?-?); Curr. Aware. Biol. Sci., CABS;

Curr. Contents Phys. Chem. Earth Sci.; Ecol. Abstr.; Ecology Abstr.; Geogr. Abstr. Phys. Geogr.; GeoRef; Index Vet.; Key Word Index Wildl. Res.; Life Sci. Collect.; Res. Alert [Full Cov.]; Rev. Med. Vet. Entomol.; Sci. Cit. Index; SCISEARCH; Soils Fert.; Vet. Bull.; Virol. AIDS Abstr.; Wildl. Rev.

US
**MAMMALS : A MULTIMEDIA ENCYCLOPEDIA.** (19??)-. English. $79.95. National Geographic Society, 11555 Darnestown, Gaithersburg MD 20878. **Tel** (202)857-7000, (800)638-4077, FAX (202)429-5727, telex 64194 NATGEO. **(Subscription address:** National Geographic Society / CD-ROM Products, 1145 17th Street NW, Educational Media Division, Washington DC 20036.**)**

CC
**MAO PI TUNG WU SSU YANG. Added/Corp** Chung-kuo tu Chan hsu Chan Chin chu kou Tsung Kung ssu. Chi-lin Nung yeh ta Hsueh. **VFOAT** Maopi Dongwu Siyang; Fur Animal Farming. (19??)-. Periodical. Chinese. qt. **LC** SF403; .M36.
**Ind/Abst** Index Vet.; Nutr. Abstr. Rev., Ser. B, Live Feeds and Feed.; Nutr. Abstr. Rev., Ser. A, Hum. Exp.

US
**MARINE MAMMAL NEWS.** (19??)-. English. Twelve times a year. $67.50. Nautilus Press Inc, 1201 National Press Building, Washington DC 20045. **Tel** (202)347-6643. **ED** John R. Botzum. **Bk Rev**. ctrl circ.
**Desc:** Newsletter containing reports on government actions impacting whales, dolphins, seals, and other marine animals.

US/0275-8652
**MARYLAND ENTOMOLOGIST.** [Md. entomol.]. V. 1- Feb. 1977-. Periodical. English. ir. $6.00. Todd, 10174 Green Clover Drive, Ellicott City MD 21043-1641. **Tel** (410)944-4630. **ED** C L Staines, R H Arnett, E J Gerberg, A P Platt, T E Wallermaier. **Bk Rev**. **Circ:** 140.
**Desc:** Articles accepted on any aspect of entomology.
**Ind/Abst** AGRICOLA [Full Cov.].

SP
**MEDITERRANEA.** No. 1- Sept. 1976-. Periodical. Spanish (summaries and/or abstracts in English). sa. 200 each issue. Departamento de Ciencias Ambientales Y Recursos Naturales, Facultad de Ciencias, Universidad de Alicante, Apartado 99, 03080 Alicante Spain. **Tel** (965)66511. **LC** QL254; .M4.
**Desc:** Mediterranean terrestrial ecology.
**Ind/Abst** Fish Rev.; Wildl. Rev.

CN/0380-9633
**MEGADRILOGICA.** [Megadrilogica]. Vol. 1 Sept. (1968)-. Periodical. English (French and German; summaries and/or abstracts in German, Spanish, Chinese, Japanese, Gaelic (Scots) and French). ir. Price varies. Oligahetology Lab Sir Sanford, Fleming College, PO Box 8000, Lindsay Ontario K9V 5E6 Canada. **Tel** (705)324-9144. **DD** 595/.146/05. **CODEN** MGDLAK. **Circ:** 1,000 (ctrl). Documents available from BIOSIS Document Express.
**Desc:** Journal is devoted to the publication of research on all aspects of terrestrial earthworms (Oligochaeta).
**Ind/Abst** Biol. Abstr. (1968-); For. Abstr. (1973-); Zool. Rec. (1968-).

HU/0465-6016
**MEHESZET.** [Meheszet]. (1955)-. Periodical. Hungarian. mo. $26.50. **(Subscription address:** Kultura, PO Box 149, H 1389 Budapest 62 Hungary.**)**
**Ind/Abst** AGRICOLA.

US/0076-6321
**MELSHEIMER ENTOMOLOGICAL SERIES.** [Melsheimer entomol. ser.]. No. 1 (Sept. 1967)-. English. sa. $10.00 non-students, $6.00 students. Entomological Society of Pennsylvania, 106 Patterson Building, University Park PA 16802. **Tel** (814)863-4640. **ED** Mike Blumenthal. **CODEN** MLESBE. **Circ:** 110. Documents available from BIOSIS Document Express.
**Ind/Abst** AGRICOLA; Biol. Abstr.

FR/0184-0266
**MEMOIRES DE BIOSPEOLOGIE. See** Biology.

CN/0071-0784
**MEMOIRES DE LA SOCIETE ENTOMOLOGIQUE DU QUEBEC.** ***Ceased.*** [Mem. de la Soc. entomol.]. **Main/Corp** Societe Entomologique du Quebec. **VFOAT** Memoirs of the Entomological Society of Quebec. (197?)-(19??). Periodical. French (summaries and/or abstracts in English). Societe Entomologique du Quebec, c/o M Michele Letendre, Complex Scientifique D-1-59, 2700 rue Einstein, Ste Foy Quebec G1A 1E6 Canada. **LC** QL461; .E6874. **DD** 595.7. **CODEN** SEQMA4. Documents available from BIOSIS Document Express. ***Continues*** *Memoires de la Societe Entomologique du Quebec, 0071-0784.*
**Ind/Abst** Biol. Abstr.

FR/0078-9747
**MEMOIRES DU MUSEUM NATIONAL D'HISTOIRE NATURELLE. SERIE A, ZOOLOGIE.** ***Title Change.*** [Mem. Mus. natl. hist. nat. Ser. A]. **Added/Corp** Museum National d'Histoire Naturelle (France). **VFOAT** Zoologie. (1950)-(1992). Monographic series. French. ir. E. J. Brill, Postbus 9000, 2300 PA Leiden Netherlands. **Tel** 011 31 71 312624, FAX 011 31 71 317532, telex 39296 BRILL NL. **LC** QL1.P34; A25. **CODEN** MMNZAI. Documents available from BIOSIS Document Express. ***Continues in part*** *Memoires du Museum National d'Histoire Naturelle (1936).* ***Merged with*** *Memoires du Museum National d'Histoire Naturelle. Serie B, Botanique, 0078-9755; Memoires du Museum National d'Histoire Naturelle. Serie C, Sciences de la Terre, 0078-9863* ***to form*** *Memoires du Museum National d'Histoire Naturelle (1993), 1243-4442.*
**Ind/Abst** Biol. Abstr.; GeoRef.

CN/0071-075X
**MEMOIRS OF THE ENTOMOLOGICAL SOCIETY OF CANADA.** (MEMOIRES DE LA SOCIETE ENTOMOLOGIQUE DU CANADA.). [Mem. Entomol. Soc. Can.]. No. 43 (1965)-. Monographic series. English (French). ir. Price varies per volume. Entomological Society of Canada, 393 Winston Avenue, Ottawa Ontario K2A 1Y8 Canada. **Tel** (613)725-2619, FAX (613)725-9349. **DD** 595.7/005. **[CCC].** Index available. cum. index. **Pr Rev. Circ:** 1,100 (ctrl). available in microform.
**Ind/Abst** Biocont. News Inf.; Curr. Aware. Biol. Sci., CABS; Ecology Abstr.

US/0475-3208
**MEMOIRS OF THE PACIFIC COAST ENTOMOLOGICAL SOCIETY.** [Mem. Pac. Coast Entomolo. Soc.]. **Main/Corp** Pacific Coast Entomological Society. Monographic series. English. ir. Price varies per volume. California Academy of Science, Golden Gate Park, San Francisco CA 94118. **Tel** (415)750-7344. **ED** J A Chemsak. **CODEN** PCEMBY. ctrl circ. Documents available from BIOSIS Document Express.
**Desc:** Monographic works on entomology.
**Ind/Abst** Biol. Abstr.

II
**MEMOIRS OF THE ZOOLOGICAL SURVEY OF INDIA. Main/Corp** Zoological Survey of India. Vol. 15 (Dec. 1970)-. Monographic series. English. ir. Price varies per volume. Indian Books and Periodicals, 2429 Tilak Street, Pahar Ganj, New Delhi 110005 India. **Bk Rev**. ***Continues*** *Memoirs of the Indian Museum.*
**Ind/Abst** Life Sci. Collect.

PL/0076-6372
**MEMORABILIA ZOOLOGICA.** [Memorabilia zool.]. **Added/Corp** Instytut Zoologii (Polska Akademia Nauk) Polska Akademia Nauk. Instytut Zoologiczny. Vol. 1 (1958)-. Monographic series. Polish (summaries and/or abstracts in English, French, German and Russian). ir. Price varies per volume. Zaklad Narodowy Im Ossolinskch, Ul Szewska 37, Wroclaw Poland. **CODEN** MEZOAN. Documents available from BIOSIS Document Express.
**Ind/Abst** AGRICOLA; Biocont. News Inf.; Biol. Abstr.; Rev. Agric. Entomol.

BL/0073-9901
**MEMORIAS DO INSTITUTO BUTANTAN (SAO PAULO). See** Medical Science and Technology-Allergy and Immunology.

US/0093-9560
**MHS REVIEW. Main/Corp** Massachusetts Herpetological Society. **VAT** Massachusetts Herpetological Society Review. Periodical. English. sa. David Taylor, Massachusetts Herpetological Society, PO Box 263, Byfield MA 01922. **LC** QL640; .M37A. **DD** 598.1/05.

HU/0230-9017
**MISCELLANEA ZOOLOGICA HUNGARICA.** ***Suspended.*** [Misc. zool. Hung.]. Vol. 1 (1982)-?. Periodical. English (French, German, Hungarian and Russian). Termeszettudomanyi Muzeum Konyvtara, Baross U 13, 1088 Budapest Hungary.

US/0076-8405
**MISCELLANEOUS PUBLICATIONS - MUSEUM OF ZOOLOGY, UNIVERSITY OF MICHIGAN.** (MISCELLANEOUS PUBLICATIONS / UNIVERSITY OF MICHIGAN, MUSEUM OF ZOOLOGY.). [Misc. publ. - Mus. Zool., Univ. Mich.]. **Added/Corp** University of Michigan. Museum of Zoology. No. 1 (1916)-. Monographic series. English. ir. Price varies per volume. University of Michigan Museum of Zoology, 1109 Geddes Road, Room 1080, Ann Arbor MI 48109-1079. **Tel** (313)764-0476. **ED** S.V. Fink. **LC** QL1; .M63. **DD** 591. **CODEN** MPMZA2. **Pr Rev. Circ:** 400. Documents available from BIOSIS Document Express.
**Desc:** Comprehensive original or review articles on systematics, taxonomy, and evolution.
**Ind/Abst** Biol. Abstr.; Life Sci. Collect.

SP/0211-6529
**MISCELLANIA ZOOLOGICA.** (MISCELLANIA ZOOLOGICA / MUSEU DE ZOOLOGIA.). [Misc. zool.]. **Added/Corp** Museu de Zoologia (Barcelona, Spain). Vol. 5 (1979)-. Periodical. Catalan (English, Italian and Spanish). an. 1500ptas. Museu de Zoologia, Ap de Correus 593, Barcelona 08003 Spain. **Tel** 93/3196912. **ED** Anna Omedes. **LC** QL1; .M87a. **DD** 590/.5. **CODEN** MZOODG. Index available. **Ad Acc. Pr Rev. Circ:** 1,000 (ctrl). Documents available from BIOSIS Document Express. ***Continues*** *Museu de Zoologia (Barcelona, Spain). Miscelanea Zoologica, 0540-3278.*
**Ind/Abst** Acoust. Abstr.; Agrindex; Anim. Behav. Abstr.; Biol. Abstr.; Curr. Primate Ref. (-1990); Ecol. Abstr.; Ecology Abstr.; Entomol. Abstr.; Environ. Period. Bibliogr. (?-?); Genet. Abstr.; Geogr. Abstr. Phys. Geogr.; Key Word Index Wildl. Res.; Mar. Sci. Contents Tables; Ocean. Abstr.; Life Sci. Collect.; Ref. Z.; Zool. Rec.

US/0737-0393
**MISSISSIPPI KITE, THE.** ***Suspended.*** [Miss. kite]. -Suspended June 1989. Periodical. English. sa. $10.00 (members). Mississippi Ornithological Society, 1 Glad Acres, Pass Christian MS 39571.

GW/0072-9612
**MITTEILUNGEN AUS DEM HAMBURGISCHEN ZOOLOGISCHEN MUSEUM UND INSTITUT. Main/Corp** Hamburg. Zoologisches Museum und Institut. **Added/Corp** Hamburg. Zoologisches Museum and Institut. Mitteilungen. V. 1-32. Hamburg. Zoologisches Museum and Institut. Mitteilungen. V. 33-37. Hamburg. Zoologisches Museum and Institut. Mitteilungen. V. 38-46. Vol. 1 (1884)-. German (summaries and/or abstracts in English). ir. Price varies per volume. Zoologisches Museum und Institut, Martin L. King Platz 3, W-2000 Hamburg 13 Germany. **LC** QL1; .H23. cum. index.
**Ind/Abst** Fish Rev.; Rev. Agric. Entomol.; Wildl. Rev.

GW/0373-8493
**MITTEILUNGEN AUS DEM ZOOLOGISCHEN MUSEUM IN BERLIN.** [Mitt. Zool. Mus. Berl.]. **Main/Corp** Zoologisches Museum in Berlin. **Added/Corp** Zoologisches Museum in Berlin. (1901)-. Periodical. German (German and French). Three times a year. $175.00. Akademie-Verlag GmbH, Muehlenstrasse 33 34, D 13162 Berlin Germany. **Tel** 011 49 30 47889300, FAX 011 49 30 47889357. **(Subscription address:** VCH Publishers Inc., 303 Northwest 12th Avenue, Journals Department, Deerfield FL 33442.**) LC** QL1; .B38. **DD** 590/.5. **CODEN** MTZMAK. cum. index. Documents available from BIOSIS Document Express. ***Continues*** *Mitteilungen aus der Zoologischen Sammlung des Museums fur Naturkunde in Berlin.*
**Ind/Abst** AGRICOLA; Biocont. News Inf. (1991-); Biol. Abstr.; Life Sci. Collect.; Plant Breed. Abstr.; Rev. Agric. Entomol.; Rev. Med. Vet. Entomol.

GW/0340-4943
**MITTEILUNGEN DER MUNCHNER ENTOMOLOGISCHEN GESELLSCHAFT.** [Mitt. Munch. Entomol. Ges.]. **Main/Corp** Munchner Entomologische Gesellschaft. (1910)-. German (English). an. Comes with membership. Munchner Entomologische Gesellschaft, EV Munchhausenstrasse 21, D-81247 Munich Germany. **Tel** 011 49 89 87070. **LC** QL461; .M8. **DD** 595.706243. ***Absorbed*** *Entomologisches Nachrichtenblatt.*
**Ind/Abst** AGRICOLA; Life Sci. Collect.

AT
**MOLLUSCAN RESEARCH.** (19??)-. English. an (Jan.). 45.00Aus$. Malacological Society of Australia, Australian Museum, 6 8 College Street, Sydney South NSW 2000 Australia. **Tel** 011 61 3 6699880. ***Continues*** *Journal of the Malacological Society of Australia.*

IT/0391-1632
**MONITORE ZOOLOGICO ITALIANO. MONOGRAFIA.** [Monogr., Monit. zool. ital.]. **VFOAT** Italian Journal of Zoology. (1975)-. Monographic series. Italian. ir. L65000 Vol. 1, L102000 Vol. 2. Monitore Zoologico Italiano, Via Romana 17, 50125 Firenze Italy. **Tel** 011 39 55 220507. **[CCC]. Circ:** 500.
**Desc:** Monograph subjects on zoology and/or biology.
**Ind/Abst** Biocont. News Inf. (1991-); CSA Neuro. Abstr. (?-?); Curr. Ref. Fish Res.; Fish Rev. (Jan. 1989-July 1992); Rev. Agric. Entomol.; Wildl. Rev. (Jan. 1989-July 1992).

US/0740-9729
**MONOGRAPHS IN PRIMATOLOGY.** [Monogr. primatol.]. (1983)-. Monographic series. English. ir. Price varies per volume. John Wiley & Sons, Inc., 605 Third Avenue, New York NY 10158-0012. **Tel** (212)850-6000, (212)850-6645, FAX (212)850-6088, telex 12-7063. **(Subscription address:** John Wiley & Sons / England, Baffins Lane, Chichester, West Sussex PO19 1UD England.**) LC** UNC. **DD** 599.8. **NLM** W1 MO568N. **CODEN** MONPD5. **[CCC].** Documents available from BIOSIS Document Express.
**Desc:** A scholarly book series covering areas of primatology - human and non-human.
**Ind/Abst** Biol. Abstr.

US/0162-8321
**MONOGRAPHS OF MARINE MOLLUSCA.** [Monogr. mar. mollusca]. **Added/Corp** American Malacologists Inc. No. 1 (Dec. 15, 1978)-. Monographic series. English. ir. Price varies per volume. Trophon Corporation, PO Box 7279, Silver Spring MD 20901-0340. **Tel** (202)786-2073, FAX 202357-2343. **ED** R. Bieler and M.G. Harasewych. **CODEN** MMMOEI. **Pr Rev. Circ:** 1,200 (ctrl). Documents available from BIOSIS Document Express.
**Desc:** Illustrated monographs of marine mollusks of the world and fossil shells.
**Ind/Abst** Biol. Abstr. (1985-); GeoRef.

US/0097-0387
**MONOGRAPHS OF THE WESTERN FOUNDATION OF VERTEBRATE ZOOLOGY.** [Monogr. West. Found. Vertebr. Zool.]. **Main/Corp** Western Foundation of Vertebrate Zoology. No. 1-. Monographic series. English. ir. Price varies per volume. Western Foundation of Vertebrate Zoology, 439 Calle San Pablo, Camarillo CA 93012. **Tel** (310)208-8003, FAX (310)208-5804. **ED** Jack C Von Bloeker Jr, Michael L Morrison and Kimberly A With. **DD** 596. **CODEN** WFVMAC. **Circ:** 1,000. Documents available from BIOSIS Document Express.
**Desc:** Papers of intermediate length reporting original research in vertebrate zoology with emphasis on ornithology.
**Ind/Abst** Biol. Abstr. (-1980).

US
**MOS NEWSLETTER.** **Main/Corp** Mississippi Ornithological Society. **Added/Corp** Mississippi Ornithological Society. Newsletter. (1???)-. Newsletter. English. Mississippi Ornithological Society, 1 Glad Acres, Pass Christian MS 39571. **LC** UNC.

●CN/1188-4584
**MOULES ZEBREES, ALERTE.** [Zebra mussel watch]. **Added/Corp** Ontario. Ministere des Richesses Naturelles. **VFOAT** Alerte aux Moules Zebrees; Zebra Mussel Watch. No 1 (Jan. 1992)-. French (English). **DD** 594/.11.

GW/0580-3896
**MYOTIS.** [Myotis]. **Added/Corp** Zoologisches Forschungsinstitut und Museum Alexander Koenig. (19??)-. Monographic series. German (English and French). an. price varies per volume. Zoologisches Forschungsinstitut und Museum Alexander Koenig, Adenauerallee 150, D 53113 Bonn Germany. **Tel** 011 49 228 9122216. **ED** Hubert Roer. **LC** QL737.C5; M9. **DD** 599.4/005. **Bk Rev**. **Ad Acc**. **Circ:** 200.
**Desc:** Scientific journal for the study of bats.

DK/0077-6033
**NATURA JUTLANDICA.** [Nat. Jutl.]. **Added/Corp** Naturhistorisk museum (Aarhus, Denmark). (1948)-. Periodical. English (English). ir. $20.00. Natural History Museum / Denmark, Universitetsparken Building 210, 8000 Aarhus C Denmark. **Tel** 011 45 86 129777, FAX 011 45 86 130882. **ED** Anders Holm Joensen. **LC** QH7; .N13. **DD** 574/.05. **CODEN** NAJUAC. Index available. **Circ:** 700 (ctrl). Documents available from BIOSIS Document Express.
**Desc:** Scientific publication in zoology (systematics, biology, ecology).
**Ind/Abst** Biol. Abstr.; Ecol. Abstr.; Fish Rev.; Geogr. Abstr. Phys. Geogr.; GeoRef; Life Sci. Collect.; Wildl. Rev.

JA/0915-9444
**NATURAL HISTORY RESEARCH.** **See** Environmental Issues-Ecology.

US/0890-3735
**NATURE SOCIETY NEWS.** [Nat. Soc. news]. **Added/Corp** Nature Society (Griggsville, Ill.). (197?)-. Periodical. English. mo. $12.00. Nature Society, Purple Martin Junction, Griggsville IL 62340. **Tel** (217)833-2323, FAX (217)833-2123. **ED** Harry Wright. **DD** 598. **Bk Rev**, (Qty: 12-24). ***Continues*** *Purple Martin News.*

BL
**NATUREZA EM REVISTA.** No. 1- Dec. 1976-. Periodical. Portuguese. sa. Cr$40.00. Fundacao Zoobotanica do Rio Grande do Sul Biblioteca, Caixa Postal 1188, 90.001 Porto Alegre RS Brazil. **Tel** (0512)36-15-11. **LC** QL242; .N37.

US/0028-1344
**NAUTILUS (PHILADELPHIA), THE.** (THE NAUTILUS.). [Nautilus]. **Added/Corp** American Malacologists, Inc. Delaware Museum of Natural History. Vol. 3, (1889)-. Periodical. English. Four times a year (Jan., Apr., July, Oct.). $25.00 (individuals); $40.00 (institutions). Trophon Corporation, PO Box 7279, Silver Spring MD 20901-0340. **Tel** (202)786-2073, FAX 202357-2343. **ED** M. G. Harasewych. **LC** QL401; .N25. **DD** 594. **CODEN** NUTLA5. Index available (No. 4 each vol.). cum. index. **Pr Rev. Circ:** 600 (ctrl). Documents available from The Genuine Article, BIOSIS Document Express. ***Continues*** *Conchologists' Exchange.*
**Desc:** Original scientific contributions on biology and evolution of mollusks.
**Ind/Abst** Aquat. Sci. Fish. Abstr. (Computer File); Biol. Abstr.; Curr. Aware. Biol. Sci., CABS; Curr. Contents, Agric. Biol. Environ. Sci.; GeoRef; Helminthol. Abstr. (1991-); Ocean. Abstr.; Life Sci. Collect.; Res. Alert [Select. Cov.]; SCISEARCH.

US/0028-1816
**NEBRASKA BIRD REVIEW, THE.** [Nebr. bird rev.]. **Added/Corp** Nebraska Ornithologists' Union. Vol. 1, (Jan. 1933)-. Periodical. English. Four times a year (Mar., June, Sept., Dec.). $12.50 US; $15.00 Canada and Mexico; $17.50 other. Nebraska Ornithologist's Union, 3018 O Street, Lincoln NE 68510. **Tel** (402)435-3832. **ED** Rosalind Morris (phone: (402)435-3382). **CODEN** NBBRA4. Index available (Bound in 4th iss. in Dec.). **Bk Rev**, (Qty: 1-2). **Pr Rev. Circ:** 310. Documents available from BIOSIS Document Express.
**Desc:** Articles, records, and notes relating to ornithology of the Nebraska region.
**Ind/Abst** Biol. Abstr.; Wildl. Rev.

BL/0102-2997
**NEMATOLOGIA BRASILEIRA.** [Nematol. bras.]. Vol. 8, No. 1 (1984)-. Portuguese (summaries and/or abstracts in English). **LC** QL391.N4. **CODEN** NEBRET. Documents available from BIOSIS Document Express. ***Continues*** *Sociedade Brasileira de Nematologia. Publicacao, 0101-7020.*
**Ind/Abst** Agrofor. Abstr. (1991-); Biol. Abstr. (1985-); Maize Abstr.; Nematol. Abstr.; Potato Abstr.; Rice Abstr.

US/0199-817X
**NEMATOLOGY NEWSLETTER.** [Nematol. newsl.]. **Added/Corp** Society of Nematologists. (19??)-. Newsletter. English. qt. comes with Journal of Nematology. Society of Nematologists, 700 Experiment Station Road, University of Florida, Lake Alfred Fl 33850. **Tel** (813)956-1151. **DD** 595.
**Ind/Abst** Nematol. Abstr.

US/0099-5444
**NEMATROPICA.** [Nematropica]. **Added/Corp** Organization of Tropical American Nematologists. Vol. 1 (May 1971)-. Periodical. English (Spanish). sa. $25.00 (institutions), $10.00 (individuals) (includes OTAN Newsletter). Organization of Tropical American Nematologists, Auburn University, Department of Plant Pathology, c/o P.S. King, Auburn AL 36849. **Tel** (205)844-4714. **ED** Gregory R. Noel. **LC** QL391.N4; N4. **DD** 595. **CODEN** NMTPAT. **Bk Rev**. **Ad Acc**. **Circ:** 450 (ctrl). Documents available from The Genuine Article, BIOSIS Document Express.
**Desc:** Research articles, notes, and reviews of the biology, ecology, taxonomy, physiology, and management of nematodes, especially plant-parasitic species.
**Ind/Abst** AGRICOLA [Full Cov.]; Biocont. News Inf. (1991-); Biol. Abstr.; Curr. Aware. Biol. Sci., CABS; Curr. Contents, Agric. Biol. Environ. Sci.; For. Prod. Abstr.; Helminthol. Abstr.; Hortic. Abstr.; Maize Abstr.; Nematol. Abstr.; Plant Breed. Abstr.; Potato Abstr.; Res. Alert [Select. Cov.]; Rev. Agric. Entomol.; SCISEARCH; Sorghum Mill. Abstr.; Soyabean Abstr.; Wheat Barley Trit. Abstr.

AG/0548-1686
**NEOTROPICA.** [Neotropica]. **Added/Corp** Sociedad Zoologica del Plata. Vol. 1, No. 1 (April 1954)-. Periodical. Spanish (English; summaries and/or abstracts in English). Twice a year. $41.00. Mercedes Azpelicueta, Sociedad Zoologica del Plata, 1900 La Plata Argentina. **Tel** 011 54 21 218805, FAX 5421530189, telex 31216 CESLA AR. **ED** Mercedes Azpelicueta and Cristina Claps. **LC** QL235; .N4. **DD** 591.98. **CODEN** NTRPAY. Index available. **Pr Rev. Circ:** 500 (ctrl).
**Ind/Abst** GeoRef; Helminthol. Abstr. (19??-19??); Life Sci. Collect.; Rev. Med. Vet. Entomol.

NE/0028-2960
**NETHERLANDS JOURNAL OF ZOOLOGY.** ***Ceased.*** [Neth. j. zool.]. Vol. 18 (May 1968)-(1992). Periodical. English. qt. E. J. Brill, Postbus 9000, 2300 PA Leiden Netherlands. **Tel** 011 31 71 312624, FAX 011 31 71 317532, telex 39296 BRILL NL. **ED** A Veerman. **CODEN** NEJZAL. **Bk Rev**. **Ad Acc**. **Pr Rev. Circ:** 1,300 (ctrl). Documents available from The Genuine Article, BIOSIS Document Express, CASDDS. ***Continues*** *Archives Neerlandaises de Zoologie.*
**Desc:** Covers the entire field of zoology and is open for publications of scientific papers on zoology in its widest sense.
**Ind/Abst** AGRICOLA; Anim. Behav. Abstr.; Biocont. News Inf.; Biol. Abstr.; Chem. Abstr.; CSA Neuro. Abstr. (?-?); Curr. Aware. Biol. Sci., CABS; Curr. Contents, Agric. Biol. Environ. Sci.; Curr. Ref. Fish Res.; Ecol. Abstr.; Ecology Abstr.; Entomol. Abstr.; Fish Rev.; Geol. Abstr.; Helminthol. Abstr.; Life Sci. Collect.; Res. Alert [Full Cov.]; Rev. Med. Vet. Entomol.; Sci. Cit. Index; SCISEARCH; Wildl. Rev.

GW/0722-3773
**NEUE ENTOMOLOGISCHE NACHRICHTEN.** [Neue entomol. Nachr.]. (1982)-. Periodical. German (summaries and/or abstracts in English). ir. Price varies. Entomologisches Museum, c/o Dr. Ulf Eitschberger, Humboldtstrabe 13A, D-95168 Marktleuthen Germany. **Tel** 0049 9285 480, FAX 0049 9285 8238. **LC** QL461; .N429. **DD** 595.7/005. **CODEN** NENAD3. **Ad Acc**. ctrl circ. Documents available from BIOSIS Document Express.
**Ind/Abst** Biol. Abstr.; Rev. Med. Vet. Entomol.

FR
**NEUROPTERA INTERNATIONAL. SUPPLEMENTAL SERIES.** Monographic series. English (summaries and/or abstracts in French). Price varies per volume.
**Ind/Abst** Entomol. Abstr.

NZ/0077-9962
**NEW ZEALAND ENTOMOLOGIST, THE.** [N. Z. entomol.]. **Added/Corp** Entomological Society of New Zealand. Vol. 1 (Dec. 1951)-. Periodical. English. an. $38.00. Entomological Society of New Zealand, Private Bag 92169, Auckland New Zealand. **Tel** 011 64 9 8493660, FAX 011 64 9 8463330. **ED** A C G Heath (editor's address: Wallaceville Research Centre, PO Box 40-063, Upperhutt New Zealand). **LC** QL487.5; .N48. **CODEN** NEZEA4. Index available. cum. index. **Bk Rev**. **Ad Acc**, **Adv Mgr:** same as editor. **Pr Rev. Circ:** 500. Documents available from BIOSIS Document Express, CASDDS.
**Desc:** Papers covering all aspects of New Zealand entomology, from taxonomy to chemical control; occasionally includes material on the Southwest Pacific region.
**Ind/Abst** AGRICOLA; Biol. Abstr.; Chem. Abstr.; Curr. Aware. Biol. Sci., CABS; Ecology Abstr.; Entomol. Abstr.; For. Abstr.; Life Sci. Collect.; Rev. Agric. Entomol.; Weed Abstr.; Wildl. Rev. (19??-199?).

NZ/0301-4223
**NEW ZEALAND JOURNAL OF ZOOLOGY.** [N. Z. j. zool.]. **Added/Corp** New Zealand. Dept. of Scientific and Industrial Research. Vol. 1 (Feb. 1974)-. Academic Scholarly Publication. English. qt (Mar., June, Sep., Dec.). £110.00 (institution), £30.00 (individual). SIR Publishing, PO Box 399, Wellington, New Zealand. **Tel** 011 64 4 472 7421, FAX 011 64 4 473 1841. **ED** Craig W. Matthews. **LC** QL340; .N46. **DD** 591/.05. **NLM** W1 NE975. **CODEN** NZJZAW. **[CCC]. Bk Rev**. **Ad Acc**. **Pr Rev. Circ:** 800 (ctrl). Documents available from The Genuine Article, BIOSIS Document Express, CASDDS, Documents on Demand.
**Desc:** Publishes papers on original research in all branches of zoology pertinent to New Zealand and associated territories.
**Ind/Abst** AGRICOLA; Anim. Behav. Abstr.; Anim. Breed. Abstr.; Biocont. News Inf. (19??-19??); Biol. Abstr.; Chem. Abstr. (1974-1983); Curr. Aware. Biol. Sci., CABS; Curr. Contents, Agric. Biol. Environ. Sci.; Curr. Ref. Fish Res.; Ecol. Abstr.; Ecology Abstr.; Entomol. Abstr.; Environ. Abstr.; Fish Rev. (19??-199?); For. Abstr.; Geol. Abstr.; Helminthol. Abstr.; Key Word Index Wildl. Res.; Maize Abstr.; Nematol. Abstr.; Life Sci. Collect.; Protozoolog. Abstr.; Res. Alert [Select. Cov.]; Rev. Agric. Entomol.; Rev. Med. Vet. Entomol.; SCISEARCH; Wildl. Rev. (19??-199?).

US
**NEWS FROM THE PHILADELPHIA ZOO.** Periodical. English. 34th Street and Girard Avenue, Philadelphia PA 19104.

US/0091-1348
**NEWS OF THE LEPIDOPTERISTS' SOCIETY.** [News Lepid. Soc.]. **Main/Corp** Lepidopterists' Society. No. 1 (Jan. 1973)-. Periodical. English. bm. comes with Journal of the Lepidopterists Society. The Lepidopterists Society, Robert J. Borth, 6926 North Belmont Lane, Fox Point WI 53217. **Tel** (414)351-3816. **ED** William Miller. **DD** 595. Index available. cum. index. **Bk Rev**. **Circ:** 1,500. ***Continues in part*** *Lepidopterists' News, 0457-5628.*
**Ind/Abst** AGRICOLA.

UK
**NEWSLETTER (BRITISH ARACHNOLOGICAL SOCIETY).** (THE NEWSLETTER / BRITISH ARACHNOLOGICAL SOCIETY.). **Added/Corp** British Arachnological Society. **VFOAT** B.A.S. Newsletter; BAS Newsletter. No. 40 (July 1984)-. Newsletter. English. £14.00 (general), £12.50 (members) outside UK. J R Parker, c/o M J Roberts, 200 Abbey Lane, Sheffield S8 0BU England. ***Continues*** *Secretary's News Letter (British Arachnological Society).*

CN/0383-9567
**NEWSLETTER - NOVA SCOTIA BIRD SOCIETY.** **Main/Corp** Nova Scotia Bird Society. V. 1- (March 1959)-. Newsletter. English. $12.00 (single issues), $15.00 (family), $20.00 (institutions. Nova Scotia Museum, 1747 Summer Street, Halifax Nova Scotia B3H 3A6 Canada. **Tel** (902)429-4610, FAX (902)424-0560. **ED** J Shirley Cohrs. **Bk Rev**. **Circ:** 800 (ctrl).

US/0278-7806
**NEWSLETTER OF THE HAWK MIGRATION ASSOCIATION OF NORTH AMERICA, THE.** [Newsl. Hawk Migr. Assoc. North Am.]. **Main/Corp** Hawk Migration Association of North America. Vol. 1, (Spring 1975)-. Newsletter. English. Twice a year (Feb., Aug.). $10.00 (individuals); $25.00 (institutions) Comes with Hawk Migration Association of North American Membership. Hawk Migration Association of North America, 337 Loomis Street, Southwick MA 01077.

AT
**NEWSLETTER / THE AUSTRALIAN FEDERATION FOR THE WELFARE OF ANIMALS.** See Veterinary Sciences.

KE
**NEWSLETTER - THE WILDLIFE CLUBS OF KENYA ASSOCIATION.** ***Ceased.*** **Main/Corp** Wildlife Clubs of Kenya Association. (19??)-?. Newsletter. English. Three times a year. Wildlife Clubs of Kenya Association, PO Box 40658, Nairobi Kenya. **Tel** 742564. **LC** QL337.K4; W54a. **DD** 591.9/6/05.

NR/0331-0094
**NIGERIAN JOURNAL OF ENTOMOLOGY.** [Niger. j. entomol.]. V. 1- Dec. 1974-. Academic Scholarly Publication. English. sa. Dr Anthony Youdeowei, Department of Agricultural Biology, University of Ibadan Nigeria. **LC** QL461; .E66515. **DD** 595.7/005. **CODEN** NJENDW. Documents available from BIOSIS Document Express, CASDDS. ***Supersedes*** *Bulletin of the Entomological Society of Nigeria, 0425-1067.*
**Ind/Abst** AGRICOLA; Biocont. News Inf.; Biol. Abstr.; Chem. Abstr. (1974-1978); Cot. Trop. Fibr. Abstr. Bibliogr.; Helminthol. Abstr.; Poult. Abstr.; Protozoolog. Abstr.; Rev. Med. Vet. Entomol.; Rice Abstr.; Sorghum Mill. Abstr.

JA
**NIHON DOBUTSUEN SUIZOKUKAN NENPO.** Japanese. an. Nihon Dobutsuen Suizokukan Kyokai, (Japanese Assoc. of Zoological Gardens & Aquariums), Ueno Dobutsuen, 9, Ueno Koen, Taitoku, Tokyoto 110, Japan. **LC** QL76.5.J3; N54.

JA
**NIHON SENCHU KENKYUKAI SHI.** **Main/Corp** Nihon Senchu Kenkyukai. **VFOAT** Japanese Journal of Nematology. V. 1 (June 1972)-. Periodical. Japanese (summaries and/or abstracts in English). an. Nihon Senchu Kenkyukai, (Japanese Nematological Soc.), Norin Suisansho Nogyo Gijutsu, Kenkyujo, 1-1, Kannondai 3 Chome, Tsukubashi, Ibarakiken 305, Japan.
**Ind/Abst** AGRICOLA; Nematol. Abstr.; Rev. Agric. Entomol.

JA/0913-882X
**NIHON YOTON GAKKAISHI.** [Nihon Yoton Gakkaishi]. **VFOAT** Japanese Journal of Swine Science (1987). (1987)-. Periodical. Multiple languages. qt. Nihon Yoton Gakkai, (Japanese Soc. of Swine Science), 37-20, Yoyogi 1 Chome, Shibuyaku, Tokyoto 151, Japan. **DD** 636.4. ***Continues*** *Nihon Yoton Kenkyukaishi, 0388-8460.*
**Ind/Abst** Agric. Eng. Abstr.; Index Vet.; Nutr. Abstr. Rev., Ser. B, Live Feeds and Feed.; Vet. Bull.; World Agric. Econ.

JA/0037-2455
**NIPPON SANSHI-GAKU ZASSHI.** [Nippon sanshi-gaku zasshi]. **VFOAT** Journal of Sericultural Science of Japan. (Feb. 1930)-. Academic Scholarly Publication. Japanese (Japanese; summaries and/or abstracts in English). bm. $130.00. Sericulture Society of Japan, National Institute of Sericulture and Entomological Science, 1-2 Ohashi, Tsukuba-shi, Ibaraki 305 Japan. **(Subscription address:** Maruzen Company Ltd., PO Box 5050, Import & Export Department, Tokyo 100 31 Japan.**)** **CODEN** NISZAQ. Documents available from CASDDS.
**Ind/Abst** AGRICOLA; Art Archaeol. Tech. Abstr.; BioBusiness; Chem. Abstr.; Life Sci. Collect.

UK/0078-0952
**NOMENCLATOR ZOOLOGICUS.** (1939)-. Academic Scholarly Publication. English. ir. Price varies. Zoological Society of London, Regents Park, London NW1 4RY England. **Tel** 011 44 71 7223333, FAX (01)483-4436, telex 265247 LONZOO. **ED** M. Edwards and Mary Tobias.
**Desc:** Lists names of genera and subgenera in zoology with bibliographical reference for the original description of each.

US/0078-1304
**NORTH AMERICAN FAUNA.** [North Am. fauna]. **Added/Corp** United States. Bureau of Biological Survey. United States. Bureau of Sport Fisheries and Wildlife. U.S. Fish and Wildlife Service. No. 1 (1889)-. Monographic series. English. Price varies per volume. U S Fish and Wildlife Service / District of Columbia, Research and Development, Department of the Interior, Washington DC 20240. **LC** QL155; .A4. **CODEN** XIWFAS. Documents available from BIOSIS Document Express.
**Ind/Abst** Biol. Abstr.

CN
**NOVA SCOTIA BIRDS.** Vol. 23, No. 1 (Jan. 1981)-. Periodical. English. Three times a year. Nova Scotia Museum, 1747 Summer Street, Halifax Nova Scotia B3H 3A6 Canada. **Tel** (902)429-4610, FAX (902)424-0560. ***Continues*** *Newsletter / Nova Scotia Bird Society.*
**Ind/Abst** Fish Rev.; Wildl. Rev.

US/0278-3274
**NOVITATES ARTHROPODAE.** V. 1- Jan. 1979-. Monographic series. English. ir. Price varies per volume. J.B. Publishing Company, 430 Ivy Avenue, Crete NE 68333. **Tel** (402)826-3356. **ED** William F Rapp. **CODEN** NOARDP. **Circ:** 100. Documents available from BIOSIS Document Express.
**Desc:** Comprehensive treatment of the American species of Dacnusinae. The Dacnusinae are parasites of diptera, mainly stem boring and leaf mining maggots.
**Ind/Abst** Biol. Abstr.

US/1050-4842
**OCCASIONAL PAPERS OF THE MUSEUM OF NATURAL SCIENCE.** [Occas. pap. Mus. Nat. Sci.]. No. 64 (Aug. 9, 1989)-. Monographic series. English. ir. Price varies per volume. Lousiana State University, Museum of Natural Science, Baton Rouge LA 70803. **LC** QL3; .L37. **DD** 591. Documents available from BIOSIS Document Express. ***Continues*** *Occasional Papers of the Museum of Zoology, 0097-0425.*
**Ind/Abst** Biol. Abstr.

US/0076-8413
**OCCASIONAL PAPERS OF THE MUSEUM OF ZOOLOGY, UNIVERSITY OF MICHIGAN.** [Occas. pap. Mus. Zool. Univ. Mich.]. **Added/Corp** University of Michigan. Museum of Zoology. No. 1 (1913)-. Monographic series. English. ir. Price varies per volume. University of Michigan Museum of Zoology, 1109 Geddes Road, Room 1080, Ann Arbor MI 48109-1079. **Tel** (313)764-0476. **ED** S. V. Fink. **LC** QL1; .M5. **DD** 591. **CODEN** MUZOAX. Index available. **Pr Rev. Circ:** 400. Documents available from BIOSIS Document Express.
**Desc:** Brief, original or review articles on systematics, taxonomy and evolution.
**Ind/Abst** AGRICOLA; Biol. Abstr.; Life Sci. Collect.

US/0511-7542
**OCCASIONAL PAPERS OF THE WESTERN FOUNDATION OF VERTEBRATE ZOOLOGY.** [Occas. pap. West. Found. Vertebr. Zool.]. **Main/Corp** Western Foundation of Vertebrate Zoology. No. 1- June 1968-. Monographic series. English. ir. Price varies per volume. Western Foundation of Vertebrate Zoology, 439 Calle San Pablo, Camarillo CA 93012. **Tel** (310)208-8003, FAX (310)208-5804. **ED** Jack C von Bloeker Jr, Michael L Morrison and Kimberly A With. **LC** QL1; .W4. **DD** 596/.008. **Circ:** 1,000.
**Desc:** Papers of short length reporting original research in vertebrate zoology.

US/0073-0807
**OCCASIONAL PAPERS ON MOLLUSKS.** [Occas. pap. mollusks]. **Main/Corp** Harvard University. Museum of Comparative Zoology. Dept. of Mollusks. **Added/Corp** Harvard University. Museum of Comparative Zoology. Dept. of Mollusks. Vol. 1 No. 1 (Feb. 27, 1945)-. Monographic series. English. ir. Price varies per volume. The Department of Mollusks, Harvard University, Museum of Comparative Zoology, Cambridge MA 02138. **Tel** (617)495-2468. **ED** Kenneth J. Boss. **LC** QL401; .H3. **CODEN** OPMOAN. Index available. cum. index. **Bk Rev.** Documents available from BIOSIS Document Express.
**Ind/Abst** Biol. Abstr.

US/0749-2421
**OCCASIONAL PAPERS (UNIVERSITY OF NEW MEXICO. MUSEUM OF SOUTHWESTERN BIOLOGY).** See Environmental Issues-Ecology.

US/0030-0055
**OF SEA AND SHORE.** [Of sea shore]. Periodical. English. qt. Of Sea & Shore, Box 219, Port Gambles WA 98364. **CODEN** OSSHDM. available in microform from Xerox; available on microfilm and microfiche from University Microfilms International (UMI).

US/0884-5956
**OHIO LEPIDOPTERIST.** [Ohio lepid.]. **Added/Corp** Ohio Lepidopterists. (19??)-. Periodical. English. Four times a year (Mar., June, Sept., Dec.). $7.50. Ohio Lepidopterist, 1241 Kidale Sq N, Columbus OH 43229. **Tel** (614)265-6774. **DD** 595.
**Desc:** Papers and articles of general interest to persons interested in the study of butterflies moths.

FR/0751-6002
**OKAPI.** [Okapi]. (1971)-. Periodical. French. sm (22 issues). 102.51Can$. Bayard Presse, Svc Client, 3 rue Bayard/Dept 2, 75393 Paris Cedex 08 France. **Tel** 011 33 1 44356060, 011 33 1 44356262. **UDC** 087.5.

GW/0173-0711
**OKOLOGIE DER VOGEL.** [Okol. Vogel]. **VFOAT** Ecology of Birds. (1979)-. Periodical. German (summaries and/or abstracts in English). Ludwigstr 5, DR J Hdzinger, W-7000 Stuttgart 1 Germany.

CN/0228-0787
**ONTARIO NEST RECORDS SCHEME.** [Ont. nest rec. scheme]. **VFOAT** ONRS. Began publication in 1961?. English. an. Free. Department of Ornithology, Royal Ontario Museum, 100 Queen's Park Crescent, Toronto Ontario M5S 2C6 Canada. **Tel** (416)586-5519. **ED** G K Peck. **DD** 598/.07/20713. **Circ:** 400 (ctrl).
**Desc:** Small, stapled, mimeographed report of nest records received in preceding year or two with totals from all years.

HU/0473-1034
**OPUSCULA ZOOLOGICA - INSTITUTUM ZOOSYSTEMATICUM UNIVERSITATIS BUDAPESTINENSIS.** (OPUSCULA ZOOLOGICA.). [Opusc. zool. - Inst. Zoosyst. Univ. Budap.]. **Added/Corp** Eoetvoes Lorand Tudomanyegyetem. Elet- es Foeltdudomanyi Kar. Eoetvoes Lorand Tudomanyegyetem. Allatrendszertani Intezet. Eoetvoes Lorand Tudomanyegyetem. Termeszettudomanyi Kar. Eoetvoes Lorand Tudomanyegyetem. Allatrendszertani es Oekologiai Tanszek. Vol. 1 (1956)-. Periodical. German (English). sa. $12.00. Universitas Budapestinensis, Institutum Zoosystematicum et Oecologicum, Puskin u. 3, 1088 Budapest, 8 Hungary. **(Subscription address:** Kultura, PO Box 149, H 1389 Budapest 62 Hungary.**)** **ED** I. Andrassy, A. Berczik. **LC** QL1; .O65. **CODEN** OPUZAS. **Ad Acc. Circ:** 800 (ctrl). available with illustrations. Documents available from BIOSIS Document Express.
**Ind/Abst** Biol. Abstr.; Rev. Agric. Entomol.

US/0890-2313
**OREGON BIRDS.** [Or. birds]. Periodical. English. qt. $7.00 (individuals), $11.00 (family memberships). Oregon Field Ornithologists, PO Box 10373, Eugene OR 97440. **DD** 598.

US/0030-5553
**ORIOLE (ATLANTA), THE.** (THE ORIOLE.). [Oriole]. **Added/Corp** Georgia Ornithological Society. Vol. 1 (Jan. 1936)-. Periodical. English. Four times a year. $16.00 (regular membership), $25.00 (sustaining membership), $50.00 (patron membership) Comes with Georgia Ornithologcial Society membership. Georgia Ornithological Society, PO Box 1684, Cartersville GA 30120. **Tel** (404)387-3642. **LC** QL671; .O45. **DD** 598.29758. **CODEN** OROLA4. Index available (index published every 5 years). **Circ:** y. Documents available from BIOSIS Document Express.
**Ind/Abst** Biol. Abstr.; Fish Rev. (Jan. 1989-July 1992); Wildl. Rev. (Jan. 1989-July 1992).

RU/0474-7313
**ORNITOLOGIIA.** Vol. 2 (1959)-. Russian. ir. Izdatelstvo Moskovskogo Universiteta, K-9 Ulitsa Gertsena 5/7, 103009 Moscow Russia. **Tel** (301)881-5973. **LC** QL671; .O86. ***Continues in part*** *Moskovskii Gosudarstvennyi Universitet. Uchenye Zapiski.*
**Desc:** Information on ornithology.

SA
**OSTRICH. SUPPLEMENT, THE.** **Added/Corp** South African Ornithological Society. No. 1 (1941)-. Monographic series. English. ir. Price varies per volume. South African Ornithological Society, PO Box 87234, Johannesburg 2041 South Africa. **Tel** 011 782.1547. **ED** A Craig. **Bk Rev. Circ:** 4,500.
**Ind/Abst** Fish Rev. (Jan. 1989-July 1992); Wildl. Rev. (Jan. 1989-July 1992).

US/0886-6864
**OTAN NEWSLETTER.** (OTAN NEWSLETTER. CARTA INFORMATIVA ONTA.). [OTAN newsl.]. **Main/Corp** Organization of Tropical American Nematologists. **VFOAT** Carta Informativa ONTA. **VAT** Organization of Tropical American Nematologists Newsletter. (19??)-. Periodical. English (Spanish). an. $10.00 (individuals); $25.00 (institutions) Comes with Nematropica. Organization of Tropical American Nematologists, Auburn University, Department of Plant Pathology, c/o P.S. King, Auburn AL 36849. **Tel** (205)844-4714. **LC** QL1; .O742. **DD** 595.
**Ind/Abst** AGRICOLA.

US/0740-6940
**PACIFIC FLYWAY WATERFOWL REPORT.** Began with No. 79 (May 1978) issue. Periodical. English. sa. USFWS, 500 NE Multnomah Street, Portland OR 97232. **LC** QL696.A52; P33. **DD** 598.4/10978. ***Continues*** *Pacific Waterfowl Flyway Report.*

PK
**PAKISTAN JOURNAL OF NEMATOLOGY : AN OFFICIAL PUBLICATION OF PAKISTAN SOCIETY OF NEMATOLOGISTS.** **Added/Corp** Pakistan Society of Nematologists. Vol. 1, No. 1 (Jan. 1983)-. Periodical. English. sa (Jan., July). $41.00. Pakistan Society of Nematologists, National Nematology Research Center, University of Karachi, Karachi 32 Pakistan. **Tel** 011 92 21 4963373, 011 92 21 4963124, FAX 011 92 21 4963373, 011 92 21 4963124. **ED** Dr. A. Shaffar. **LC** QL391.N4; P34. **DD** 595.1/82. **Circ:** 500.
**Ind/Abst** Biocont. News Inf. (1991-); Irr. Drain. Abstr.; Nematol. Abstr.; Potato Abstr.; SCISEARCH.

PK/0030-9923
**PAKISTAN JOURNAL OF ZOOLOGY.** [Pak. j. zool.]. V. 1 (Jan. 1969)-. Academic Scholarly Publication. English. qt. Rs500.00 Pakistan; $65.00 US.

University of the Punjab, Zoology Society of Pakistan, c/o Department of Zoology, Lahore 20 Pakistan. **Tel** 864933. **ED** Muzaffer Ahmad and A R Shakoori. **LC** QL1. **DD** 591/.05. **NLM** W1 PA358T. **CODEN** PJZOAN. Index available. cum. index. **Ad Acc. Circ:** 600 (ctrl). available on diskette; available on microfilm. Documents available from BIOSIS Document Express, CASDDS.
**Desc:** Publishes research papers in the fields of biochemistry, cell biology, entomology, toxicology, endocrinology, fisheries, genetics, morphology, molecular biology, physiology, taxonomy, vertebrate, invertebrate zoology, ecology, pathology, paleontology and pest control.
**Ind/Abst** Agrofor. Abstr. (1991-); Anim. Breed. Abstr.; Biocont. News Inf.; Biodeter. Abstr. (1991-); Biol. Abstr.; Chem. Abstr.; Cot. Trop. Fibr. Abstr. Bibliogr.; CSA Neuro. Abstr. (?-?); Curr. Contents, Agric. Biol. Environ. Sci.; Ecology Abstr.; EMBASE; Entomol. Abstr.; Food Sci. Technol. Abstr.; For. Abstr.; Helminthol. Abstr.; Key Word Index Wildl. Res.; Nematol. Abstr.; Nutr. Abstr. Rev., Ser. B, Live Feeds and Feed.; Ocean. Abstr.; Life Sci. Collect.; Plant Breed. Abstr.; Postharvest News Inf.; Rev. Agric. Entomol.; Rev. Med. Vet. Mycology; Zool. Rec.

BL/0031-1049
**PAPEIS AVULSOS DE ZOOLOGIA (SAO PAULO).** (PAPEIS AVULSOS DE ZOOLOGIA.). [Pap. avulsos zool.]. **Added/Corp** Sao Paulo (Brazil : State). Departamento de Zoologia. Universidade de Sao Paulo. Museu de Zoologia. Vol. 20 (1967)-. English (Portuguese and French; summaries and/or abstracts in Portuguese). ir. $25.00. Universidade de Sao Paulo / Museu Zoologia, Museu de Zoologia, Caixa Post 7172, 01000 Sao Paulo SP Brazil. **Tel** 011 55 11 274-3455. **LC** QL1; .S35. **DD** 591/.8. **CODEN** PAZOAS. Index available. **Circ:** 684 (ctrl). Documents available from BIOSIS Document Express. ***Continues** Papeis Avulsos do Departamento de Zoologia.*
**Desc:** Zoological papers.
**Ind/Abst** AGRICOLA; Biol. Abstr.; Life Sci. Collect.; Zool. Rec.

AT/0079-8916
**PAPERS - QUEENSLAND. UNIVERSITY, BRISBANE. DEPT. OF ENTOMOLOGY.**
**Main/Corp** Queensland. University, Brisbane. Dept. of Entomology. Vol. 1 (1955)-. English. ir. University of Brisbane, Department of Entomology, Queensland Australia. **DD** 595.7.

FR/1146-5476
**PASCAL. E 57, BIOLOGIE MARINE.**
***Ceased.* See** Biology.

FR/1146-5271
**PASCAL. F 54, REPRODUCTION DES VERTEBRES, EMBRYOLOGIE DES VERTEBRES ET DES INVERTEBRES.**
**VFOAT** PASCAL. F 54, Reproduction in Vertebrates, Embryologie in Vertebrates and Invertebrates; PASCAL. F Cinquante Quatre, Reproduction des Vertebres, Embryologie des Vertebres et des Invertebres. (1990)-. Periodical. Multiple languages. Ten times a year. 865.00F France; 915.00F other. CNRS / Institut d'Information Scientifique et Technique, (Centre National de la Recherche Scientifique), 15 Quai Anatole France, Paris 75700 France. **Tel** 011 33 1 47531515, telex 299 356 F. **(Subscription address:** Institut d'Information Scientifique et Technique, 2 Allee du Parc de Brabois, 54514 Vandoeuvre Nancy France**) UDC** 011. ***Continues** Pascal Folio. F54: Reproduction des Vertebres Embroyologie des Vertebres et des Invertebres.*

FR/1146-5077
**PASCAL. T 260, ZOOLOGIE FONDAMENTALE ET APPLIQUEE DES INVERTEBRES.** **VFOAT** PASCAL. T 260, Fundamental and Applied Zoology of Invertebrates; PASCAL. T Deux-Cent-Soixante, Zoologie Fondamentale et Appliquee des Invertebres. (1990)-. Periodical. Multiple languages. Ten times a year. 1520.00F France; 1615.00F other. CNRS / Institut d'Information Scientifique et Technique, (Centre National de la Recherche Scientifique), 15 Quai Anatole France, Paris 75700 France. **Tel** 011 33 1 47531515, telex 299 356 F. **(Subscription address:** Institute d'Information Scientifique et Technique Diffusion, 2 Allee du Parc de Brabois, 54514 Vandoeuvre Nancy France**) UDC** 011/016. ***Continues** Pascal Thema. T260: Zoologie Fondamentale et Appliquee des Invertebres.*

CH
**PEI LEI HSUEH PAO.** **VFOAT** Bulletin of Malacology, Republic of China; Bulletin of Malacology. Vol. 1 (1978)-. Chinese (English). an. $10.00. Malacological Society of China, c/o Taiwan Museum, No 2 Siang Yang Road, Taipei Taiwan. **Tel** (02)361-3963. **ED** 353903539135392. cum. index (every ten years). **Circ:** 800 (ctrl). ***Continues** Pei Lei Hsueh Hui Hui Chih.*
**Ind/Abst** Life Sci. Collect.

MY
**PERHILITAN.** Began with issue for Jan. 1981. Periodical. Malay. sa. Ketua Pengarah, Jabatan Perlindungan Hidupan Liar Dan Taman Negara K20 Jl Duta, Kuala Lumpur Malaysia. **LC** QL322; .P47. **DD** 508.595.

PH/0369-9536
**PHILIPPINE ENTOMOLOGIST.** (PHILIPPINE ENTOMOLOGIST.). [Philipp. Entomol.]. **Added/Corp** Philippine Association of Entomologists. Vol. 1 (April 1968)-. Periodical. English. sa (April and Oct.). P600.00 (institutions), P300.00 (individuals) Philippines; $50.00 other. Philippine Association Entomologists, Inc., University of Philippines at Los Banos, Department of Entomology, Laguna 4031 Philippines. **Tel** 63 2 2893, 63 2 2351, FAX 63 2 81170598, telex 40904 SEARCA PM. **ED** Venus J Calilung. **CODEN** PHETBM. Index available. cum. index. **Bk Rev. Ad Acc. Acid Free. Circ:** 400 (ctrl). Documents available from CASDDS.
**Desc:** This journal publishes papers dealing with all aspects of basic and applied entomology and related disciplines (acarology, vertebrate pests).
**Ind/Abst** Agrofor. Abstr. (1991-); Biocont. News Inf. (19??-19??); Chem. Abstr.; Cot. Trop. Fibr. Abstr. Bibliogr.; Food Sci. Technol. Abstr.; For. Abstr.; Hortic. Abstr.; Maize Abstr.; Nematol. Abstr.; Life Sci. Collect.; Philip. Sci. Technol. Abstr.; Plant Breed. Abstr.; Postharvest News Inf.; Poult. Abstr.; Rev. Agric. Entomol.; Rev. Med. Vet. Entomol.; Rice Abstr.; Soyabean Abstr.

PH/0079-1466
**PHILIPPINE SCIENTIST, THE. See**
Biology-Marine Biology.

US/0031-935X
**PHYSIOLOGICAL ZOOLOGY.** [Physiol. zool.]. Vol. 1 (Jan. 1928)-. Periodical. English. bm. $220.00 institution, $63.00 individual, $50.00 ASZ individual member, $38.00 student US; $245.40 institution, $77.41 individual, $63.50 ASZ inidividual member, $50.66 students, Canada; $230.00 institutions, $73.00 individual, $60.00 ASZ individual member, $48.00 students other. University of Chicago Press / Journals Division, PO Box 37005, 5720 South Woodlawn, Chicago IL 60637. **Tel** (312)753-3347, FAX (312)753-0811. **(Subscription telephone:** (312)753-8083**) ED** C. Ladd Prosser and James E. Heath. **LC** QL1; .P5. **DD** 591.05. **NLM** W1 PH932. **CODEN** PHZOA9. **[CCC]. Pr Rev. Acid Free.** available on microfilm and microfiche from University Microfilms International (UMI). Documents available from The Genuine Article, BIOSIS Document Express, CASDDS.
**Desc:** Serves the scientific community as an outlet for research in environmental and adaptational physiology and biochemistry. From cellular mechanisms to organ systems and whole animal adaptations, from protozoa to mammals, from developmental stages to adult organisms, its scope comprehends all aspects of physiological ecology as well as comparative physiology and biochemistry.
**Ind/Abst** AgBiotech News Inf.; AGRICOLA; Anim. Breed. Abstr.; Biocont. News Inf.; Biol. Agric. Index; Biol. Abstr.; Chem. Abstr.; CSA Neuro. Abstr. (?-?); Curr. Aware. Biol. Sci., CABS; Curr. Contents, Agric. Biol. Environ. Sci.; Curr. Contents Life Sci.; Curr. Ref. Fish Res.; Dairy Sci. Abstr.; Ecol. Abstr.; Ecology Abstr.; Entomol. Abstr.; Fish Rev.; Index Vet.; Key Word Index Wildl. Res.; Nutr. Abstr. Rev., Ser. B, Live Feeds and Feed.; Ocean. Abstr.; Life Sci. Collect.; Ref. Upd. Deluxe Ed.; Res. Alert [Full Cov.]; Rev. Agric. Entomol.; Sci. Cit. Index; SCISEARCH; Wildl. Rev.

AG/0326-1441
**PHYSIS. SECCIONES A, B Y C.** (PHYSIS.). [Physis, Secc. A B y C]. **Added/Corp** Asociacion Argentina de Ciencias Naturales. Vol. 36 No. 92 (June 1977)-. Periodical. Spanish (summaries and/or abstracts in English). Twice a year. $100.00. Association of Argentina Cienc Naturales, Ciudad University Nunez, Department of Biologia, 1428 Buenos Aires Argentina. **ED** Dr. Juan Carlos Giacchi. Index available. cum. index. **Bk Rev. Circ:** 500. ***Formed by the union of** Physis. Seccion A. Los Oceanos y Sus Organismos, 0325-0342; Physis. Seccion B. Los Aguas Continentales y Sus Organismos, 0325-0350 **and** Physis. Seccion C. Los Continentes y Los Organismos Terrestres, 0325-0369.*
**Desc:** Devoted to zoology and botany (systematics, physiology, distribution, ecology, histology, embryology, anatomy, etc.), mainly of South America.
**Ind/Abst** Aquat. Sci. Fish. Abstr. (Computer File); Mar. Sci. Contents Tables; Life Sci. Collect.; Zentralbl. Math. Ihre Grenzgeb.

GW/0722-4060
**POLAR BIOLOGY.** [Polar biol.]. Vol. 1, No. 1 (July 1982)-. Academic Scholarly Publication. English. Eight times a year. DM1120.00. Springer-Verlag GmbH & Company KG, Heidelberger Platz 3, D 14197 Berlin Germany. **Tel** 011 49 30 8207223, FAX 011 49 30 8214091, telex 183 319 SPBLN D. **(Subscription address:** Springer Verlag New York Inc. / for North America, 44 Hartz Way, Secaucus NJ 07096.**) ED** G Hempel and W R Siegfried. **LC** QL104; .P64. **DD** 574.909/1. **CODEN** POBIDP. **[CCC]. Pr Rev. Circ:** 160. available on microfilm and microfiche from University Microfilms International (UMI). Documents available from The Genuine Article, CASDDS.
**Desc:** Presents articles on topics that include life history, ecology, distribution, abundance, biogeography, the physiology of growth and reproduction, biochemistry and metabolism, behaviour and sensory physiology, genetics, embryology and morphology, dynamics of populations, taxonomy and systematics.
**Ind/Abst** AGRICOLA ( -1987); Aquat. Sci. Fish. Abstr. (Computer File); Biodeter. Abstr. (1991-); Chem. Abstr.; Curr. Aware. Biol. Sci., CABS; Curr. Contents, Agric. Biol. Environ. Sci.; Curr. Ref. Fish Res.; Ecol. Abstr. (?-?); GeoRef; Index Vet.; Key Word Index Wildl. Res.; Nutr. Abstr. Rev., Ser. B, Live Feeds and Feed.; Ocean. Abstr.; Life Sci. Collect.; Res. Alert [Full Cov.]; Rev. Med. Vet. Entomol.; Sci. Cit. Index; SCISEARCH; Soils Fert.

PL
**POLSKA BIBLIOGRAFIA PARAZYTOLOGICZNA.** (1965)-. Multiple languages. an. **(Subscription address:** ARS Polona, PO Box 1001, 00068 Warsaw Poland.**) LC** Z6900; .P64; QL757. **NLM** ZQX 4 P778. ***Supersedes in part** Wiadomosci Parazytologiczne.*

PL/0137-1649
**PRACE I MATERIAY ZOOTECHNICZNE / INSTYTUT GENETYKE I HODOWLI ZWIERZAT POLSKIEJ AKADEMII NAUK.**
***Title Change.*** **VFOAT** Polskii Nauchnyi Zhurnal Po Zootekhnii; Polish Journal of Animal Science. (1972)-. Periodical. Polish (English). Panstwowe Wydawn Naukowe, Miodowa 10, PO Box 391, 00251 Warsaw Poland. ***Continued by** Animal Science Papers and Reports, 0860-4037.*
**Ind/Abst** Food Sci. Technol. Abstr.; Nutr. Abstr. Rev., Ser. B, Live Feeds and Feed.

PL
**PRACE ZOOLOGICZNE.** **Main/Corp** Wyzsza Szkoa Pedagogiczna W Krakowie. Began in 1967. Polish (summaries and/or abstracts in English and Russian). Z12.00 each issue. Naukowe Szkoy Pedagogicznej, Ksiegarnia Naukowa Komu Ksiazki, 31-118 Ul Pod Wale 6, Krakow Poland. **LC** AS142.K66; A2 subser; QL1.

II
**PRANIKEE : JOURNAL OF ZOOLOGICAL SOCIETY OF ORISSA.**
**Added/Corp** Zoological Society of Orissa. **VFOAT** Journal of Zoological Society of Orissa. (19??)-. English. an. $15.00. Utkal University / Zoology, Post-Graduate Department of Zoology, Bhubaneswar, India. **(Subscription address:** Prints India, 11 Darya Ganj, New Delhi 110002 India.**)**

UK/0305-8417
**PRIMATE EYE.** [Primate eye]. (1974)-. Periodical. English. Three times a year (Feb., June, Oct.). £11.00 (individual), £15.00 (institution), surface mail; £14.00 (individual), £18.00 (institution), airmail. Primate Society of Great Britain, University of Liverpool, Department Human Anatomy, Liverpool L69 3BX England. **Tel** 011 44 51 794 5498 5500, FAX 011 44 51 794 5517. **ED** Dr. D. Brandon-Jones. **Bk Rev**, (Qty: 3). **Ad Acc. Circ:** 500.
**Desc:** News, research reports, book reviews and other items concerning the fossil.

GW/0343-3528
**PRIMATE REPORT.** [Primate rep.]. **Added/Corp** Commission of the European Communities. Committee on Medical and Public Health Research. No. 1 (Aug. 1977)-. Monographic series. English. Price varies per volume. Verlag Erich Goltze KG, Stresemannstrasse 28, D 37079 Goettingen Germany. **Tel** 011 49 551 63078. **NLM** W1; PR522DT.
**Ind/Abst** Curr. Primate Ref.

JA/0032-8332
**PRIMATES.** [Primates]. **Added/Corp** Nihon Monki Senta. Vol. 1 (Sept. 1957)-. Periodical. English (French and German). qt. $324.00. Japan Monkey Centre, 26 Kanrin, Inuyama Aichi Japan. **(Subscription address:** Maruzen Company Ltd., PO Box 5050, Import & Export Department, Tokyo 100 31 Japan.**) ED** Dr. Masao Kawai. **LC** QL737.P9; P68. **NLM** W1 PR522F. **CODEN** PRMTBU. cum. index. **Pr Rev.** Documents available from The Genuine Article, BIOSIS Document Express, CASDDS.
**Desc:** An international journal of primatology, whose general objective is to provide for the elucidation of the entire aspect of primates in connection with man.
**Ind/Abst** Abstr. Anthropol.; Anim. Behav. Abstr.; Anthropol. Lit.; Biol. Abstr.; Chem. Abstr.; Curr. Contents, Agric. Biol. Environ. Sci.; Curr. Primate Ref.; Ecology Abstr.; Helminthol. Abstr. (1991-); Nutr. Abstr. Rev., Ser. B, Live Feeds and Feed.; Life Sci. Collect.; Psychol. Abstr. (1966-); PsycINFO; PsycLit; Res. Alert [Full Cov.]; Sci. Cit. Index; SCISEARCH; Soc. Sci. Cit. Index [Select. Cov.]; Wildl. Rev.

RU
**PRIRODNYE RESURSY VOLZHSKO-KAMSKOGO KRAIA: ZHIVOTNYI MIR.** **Added/Corp** Kazanskii Institut Biologii. **VFOAT** Zhivotnyi Mir. (1964)-. Periodical. Russian. **LC** QL281; .P774.

XR
**PRIRODOVEDNE PRACE USTAVU AKADEMIE VED CESKE REPUBLIKY V BRNE. See** Natural History.

XR/0032-8758
**PRIRODOVEDNE PRACE USTAVU CESKOSLOVENSKE AKADEMIE VED V BRNE.** ***Title Change.*** [Prirodoved. pr. Ustavu Cesk. akad. ved Brne]. **Added/Corp** Ceskoslovenska Akademie Ved v Brne. **VFOAT** Acta Scientiarum Naturalium Academiae Scientiarum Bohemoslovacae Brno. (1967)-(1992). Monographic series. Czech (English and German; summaries and/or abstracts in Russian and English). mo. Academia, Publishing House of the Czechoslovak Academy of Sciences, Czech AC SCI, Vodickova 40, PO Box 896, 112 29 Prague 1, Czech Republic. **Tel** 011 42 2 245117. **(Subscription address:** Artia Pegas Press Ltd., Palac Metro Narodni Trida 25, 11210 Prague 1 Czech Republic.**)** **LC** QH1; .P943. **DD** 570. **CODEN** PPUCA4. **Circ:** 700 (ctrl). Documents available from BIOSIS Document Express. ***Continues*** *Prace Brnenske Zakladny Ceskoslovenske Akademie Ved.* ***Continued by*** *Prirodovedne Prace Ustavu Akademie Ved Ceske Republiky v Brne.*
**Desc:** Brings articles on research in zoology, archaeology, botany, and geography.
**Ind/Abst** Biol. Abstr.; Ecol. Abstr.; Fish Rev.; For. Abstr.; Geogr. Abstr. Phys. Geogr.; GeoRef; Grasslands For. Abstr.; Helminthol. Abstr. (19??-19??); Index Vet.; Life Sci. Collect.; Plant Grow. Reg. Abstr.; Poult. Abstr.; Rev. Agric. Entomol.; Wildl. Rev.

RU
**PROBLEMY ZOOLOGII.** **Added/Corp** Zoologicheskii Institut (Akademiia Nauk SSSR). (19??)-. Periodical. Russian. 0.38rub. Izdatelstvo Nauka St. Petersburg, Mendeleevskaia Liniia 1, 199034 St. Petersburg, B-34 Russia. **Tel** 218-26-12. **LC** QL281; .P78.

US/0090-4473
**PROCEEDINGS; ANNUAL AAZPA CONFERENCE.** **Main/Corp** American Association of Zoological Parks and Aquariums. **VAT** Proceedings. Annual American Association of Zoological Parks and Aquariums Conference. (19??)-. English. an. $30.00 (schools and libraries), $40.00 (nonmember). American Association of Zoological Parks and Aquariums, Oglebay Park, Wheeling WV 26003. **Tel** (304)242-2160, FAX (304)242-2283. **LC** QL77.5; .A44. **DD** 590/.744/05. **Ad Acc. Circ:** 375.
**Ind/Abst** Fish Rev. (19??-199?); Wildl. Rev. (19??-199?).

PK
**PROCEEDINGS OF ... PAKISTAN CONGRESS OF ZOOLOGY.** **Main/Conf** Pakistan Congress of Zoology. 1st (April 30-May 1, 1980)-. Proceedings. English. qt. $58.50. Zoological Society of Pakistan New Campus, Lahore 20 Pakistan. **Tel** 864028. **ED** Mufaffer Ahmad and A R Shakoon. **LC** QL1; .P268A. **Bk Rev.** **Ad Acc. Circ:** 500 (ctrl).
**Ind/Abst** Helminthol. Abstr. (1991-); Index Vet.

US/0191-3875
**PROCEEDINGS OF SYMPOSIUM - DESERT TORTOISE COUNCIL.** **Main/Corp** Desert Tortoise Council. (1976)-. English. an. $12.00 (latest edition). Desert Tortoise Council, 5319 Cirritos Avenue, Long Beach CA 90805. **Tel** (213)590-5113. **ED** Mary Trotter and K. S. Hashagen. **LC** QL666.C584; D47a. **DD** 598.1/3. Index available (free).
**Desc:** Scientific papers on desert tortoise studies.

II/0569-0242
**PROCEEDINGS OF THE ALL-INDIA CONGRESS OF ZOOLOGY.** **Main/Conf** I-India Congress of Zoology. **Added/Corp** Zoological Society of India. (1959)-. Proceedings. English. ir. Zoological Society of India, Utkal University, P G Department of Zoology, Bhubaneswar 4 Orissa India. **DD** 591.

CN/0822-5915
**PROCEEDINGS OF THE ... ANNUAL MEETING / ACADIAN ENTOMOLOGICAL SOCIETY.** [Proc. annu. meet. Acadian Entomol. Soc.]. **Main/Corp** Acadian Entomological Society. Meeting. **VAT** Proceedings of the ... Annual Meeting - Acadian Entomological Society. Proceedings. English. an. Free to Members. G Boiteau, Agriculture Canada Research Station, PO Box 20280, Fredericton New Brunswick E3B 4Z7 Canada. **DD** 595.7/006/0715. ***Continues*** *Proceedings of the Acadian Entomological Society, 0701-2101.*

CN/0071-0768
**PROCEEDINGS OF THE ENTOMOLOGICAL SOCIETY OF ONTARIO.** [Proc. Entomol. Soc. Ont.]. **Main/Corp** Entomological Society of Ontario. V. 90- 1959-. Academic Scholarly Publication. English. an. 20.00Can$. Entomological Society of Ontario, University of Guelph, Guelph Ontario N1G 2W1 Canada. **Tel** (519)824-4120. **ED** P Kevan. **DD** 595.7/005. **CODEN** PESOAL. **Pr Rev.** Documents available from The Genuine Article, BIOSIS Document Express, CASDDS. ***Continues*** *Entomological Society of Ontario. Annual Report, 0317-1914.*
**Ind/Abst** AGRICOLA; Biocont. News Inf. (1991-); Biol. Abstr.; Chem. Abstr.; Curr. Contents, Agric. Biol. Environ. Sci.; For. Abstr.; Life Sci. Collect.; Res. Alert [Select. Cov.]; Rev. Agric. Entomol.; Rev. Med. Vet. Entomol.; SCISEARCH.

US/0013-8797
**PROCEEDINGS OF THE ENTOMOLOGICAL SOCIETY OF WASHINGTON.** [Proc. Entomol. Soc. Wash.]. **Main/Corp** Entomological Society of Washington. Vol. 1, (Feb. 1884)-. Proceedings. English. qt. $60.00 US; $70.00 other. Entomological Society of Washington, Smithsonian Institution, NB 168, Washington DC 20560. **Tel** (202)382-1802. **ED** Thomas J. Henry. **LC** QL461; .E69. **DD** 595.7/005. **NLM** W1 PR585HN. **CODEN** PESWAB. **Bk Rev**, (Qty: 6-10/yr). **Pr Rev. Circ:** 750. Documents available from The Genuine Article, BIOSIS Document Express, CASDDS.
**Desc:** A refereed, entomological journal that publishes results of original research in all subdisciplines on entomology (except chemical control), book reviews, minutes of the monthly meetings of the Society, and other occasional items.
**Ind/Abst** AgBiotech News Inf.; AGRICOLA [Full Cov.]; Agrofor. Abstr. (1991-); Biocont. News Inf. (19??-19??); Biol. Abstr.; Chem. Abstr.; Cot. Trop. Fibr. Abstr. Bibliogr.; CSA Neuro. Abstr. (?-?); Curr. Aware. Biol. Sci., CABS; Curr. Contents, Agric. Biol. Environ. Sci.; Ecology Abstr.; Entomol. Abstr.; For. Prod. Abstr. (1991-); For. Abstr.; Hortic. Abstr.; Maize Abstr.; Nematol. Abstr.; Ornamental Hort.; Life Sci. Collect.; Pig News Inf.; Potato Abstr.; Res. Alert [Select. Cov.]; Rev. Agric. Entomol.; Rev. Med. Vet. Entomol.; SCISEARCH; Sorghum Mill. Abstr.; Weed Abstr.; Wheat Barley Trit. Abstr.; Wildl. Rev.

II/0253-4118
**PROCEEDINGS OF THE INDIAN ACADEMY OF SCIENCES. ANIMAL SCIENCES.** ***Title Change.*** (PROCEEDINGS. ANIMAL SCIENCES / INDIAN ACADEMY OF SCIENCES.). [Proc. Indian Acad. Sci., Anim. sci.]. **Added/Corp** Indian Academy of Sciences. **VFOAT** Animal Sciences; Proceedings of the Indian Academy of Sciences. Animal Sciences. Vol. 89, No. 1 (Feb. 1980)-(19??). Academic Scholarly Publication. English. bm. Indian Academy of Sciences Circulation, PO Box 8005, Department of Sadashivanagar, Bangalore 560 080 India. **Tel** 011 91 812 342546, 342310, telex 0845-2178 ACAD IN. **ED** T N Ananthakrishnan. **LC** QL1; .P69. **DD** 590/.5. **CODEN** PIANDR. Index available. **Circ:** 750. available on microfilm and microfiche from University Microfilms International (UMI). Documents available from BIOSIS Document Express, CASDDS. ***Continues*** *Proceedings. B, Animal Sciences.* ***Absorbed by*** *Journal of Biosciences, 0250-5991.*
**Desc:** Covers such principal areas as physiology, biochemistry, bioecology, parasitology, aquatic biology, ethology, taxonomy, morphology and toxicology.
**Ind/Abst** AGRICOLA; Agrofor. Abstr. (1991-); Biocont. News Inf.; Biodeter. Abstr. (1991-); Biol. Abstr.; Chem. Abstr.; CSA Neuro. Abstr. (?-?); Ecol. Abstr.; Ecology Abstr.; Energy Res. Abstr. (June 1981-19??); For. Abstr.; Geogr. Abstr. Phys. Geogr.; GeoRef; Helminthol. Abstr. (1991-); Nematol. Abstr.; Nutr. Abstr. Rev., Ser. B, Live Feeds and Feed.; Life Sci. Collect.; Plant Breed. Abstr.; Plant Grow. Reg. Abstr. (-19??); Postharvest News Inf.; Ref. Z.; Rev. Agric. Entomol.; Rev. Med. Vet. Entomol.; Rice Abstr.; SCISEARCH; Soils Fert.

AT/0074-7211
**PROCEEDINGS OF THE INTERNATIONAL ORNITHOLOGICAL CONGRESS.** **Main/Corp** International Ornithological Congress. (1984)-. Proceedings. English (French, German and Italian). 62.50Aus$. Australian Academy of Science, GPO Box 783, Canberra ACT 2601 Australia. **Tel** 011 61 6 2475777, FAX 011 61 6 2574620, telex ACSI AA 62406. **LC** QL671; .I7. **DD** 598.2082. **CODEN** PIORA4. Documents available from BIOSIS Document Express, CASDDS.
**Desc:** This free interchange of views enables scientists to keep abreast with the latest developments in their field.
**Ind/Abst** Biol. Abstr. (-1976); Chem. Abstr. (1884-1974); Fish Rev.; Key Word Index Wildl. Res.; Wildl. Rev.

US/0511-7550
**PROCEEDINGS OF THE WESTERN FOUNDATION OF VERTEBRATE ZOOLOGY.** [Proc. West. Found. Vertebr. Zool.]. **Added/Corp** Western Foundation of Vertebrate Zoology (U.S.). Vol. 1, No. 1 (April 1963)-. Monographic series. English. ir. $9.00. Western Foundation of Vertebrate Zoology, 439 Calle San Pablo, Camarillo CA 93012. **Tel** (310)208-8003, FAX (310)208-5804. **ED** Jack C. von Bloeker Jr., Michael L. Morrison and Kiberly A. With. **LC** QL605; .W44. **DD** 596/.005. **CODEN** PWFVA2. **Pr Rev. Circ:** 1,000. Documents available from BIOSIS Document Express.
**Desc:** Papers reporting original research in vertebrate zoology with emphasis on ornithology.
**Ind/Abst** Biol. Abstr.; Zool. Rec.

II/0373-5893
**PROCEEDINGS OF THE ZOOLOGICAL SOCIETY.** [Proc. Zool. Soc.]. **Main/Corp** Zoological Society (Calcutta, India). Vol. 7, No. 1 (March 1954)-. Proceedings. English. Twice a year (Apr., Oct.). The Zoological Society, 35 Ballygunge Circular Road, Calcutta 700019 India. **Tel** 75-3681. **(Subscription address:** Prints India, 11 Darya Ganj, New Delhi 110002 India.**)** **ED** A. S. Mukherjee. **CODEN** PZSIAE. Index available. **Ad Acc. Circ:** 400 (ctrl). Documents available from BIOSIS Document Express. ***Continues*** *Zoological Society of Bengal. Proceedings of the Zoological Society of Bengal.*
**Ind/Abst** Biol. Abstr.

UY
**PRODUCCION OVINA / SECRETARIADO URUGUAYO DE LA LANA.** **Added/Corp** Uruguay. Depto de Investigacion de la Produccion Ovina. Vol. 1, No. 1 (1988)-. Periodical. Spanish (summaries and/or abstracts in English).
**Ind/Abst** Grasslands For. Abstr.; Nutr. Abstr. Rev., Ser. B, Live Feeds and Feed.

AU/0934-8727
**PROTOPLASMA. SUPPLEMENTUM.** [Protoplasma, Suppl.]. (1988)-. Monographic series. English. Price varies per volume. Springer-Verlag, Sachsenplatz 4-6, PO Box 89, A-1201 Vienna Austria. **Tel** 43 222 3302415, FAX 43 222 3302426. **CODEN** PRSUEW. Documents available from BIOSIS Document Express.
**Ind/Abst** AGRICOLA [Select. Cov.]; Biol. Abstr. (1989-).

UK/0309-1287
**PROTOZOOLOGICAL ABSTRACTS.** **See** Zoology-Abstracting, Bibliographies and Statistics.

PL/0033-247X
**PRZEGLAD ZOOLOGICZNY.** [Prz. zool.]. **Added/Corp** Polskie Towarzystwo Zoologiczne. Vol. 1 (1957)-. Academic Scholarly Publication. Polish (summaries and/or abstracts in English; table of contents in English). qt. Price on Request. **(Subscription address:** ARS Polona, PO Box 1001, 00068 Warsaw Poland.**)** **LC** QL1; .P7. **DD** 591/.05. **NLM** W1 PR94. **CODEN** PZOOAC. Documents available from BIOSIS Document Express, CASDDS.
**Ind/Abst** Biol. Abstr.; Chem. Abstr.; GeoRef; Key Word Index Wildl. Res.; Life Sci. Collect.; Rev. Med. Vet. Entomol.

US/0033-2615
**PSYCHE (CAMBRIDGE, MASS.).** (PSYCHE.). [Psyche]. **Added/Corp** Cambridge Entomological Club. Vol. 1 (May 1874)-. Academic Scholarly Publication. English. Four times a year. $30.00. Cambridge Entomological Club, 26 Oxford Street, Cambridge MA 02138. **Tel** (617) 495-2464, (617) 495-2316. **ED** Frank M. Carpenter. **LC** QL461; .P9. **DD** 595. **NLM** W1 PS229. **CODEN** PYCHAQ. Index available. **Pr Rev. Circ:** 750. Documents available from BIOSIS Document Express, CASDDS.
**Ind/Abst** AGRICOLA; Anim. Behav. Abstr.; Biocont. News Inf.; Biol. Abstr.; Chem. Abstr.; Ecology Abstr.; EMBASE; Entomol. Abstr.; GeoRef; Index Med.; Life Sci. Collect.; Psychol. Abstr.

PL/0478-7080
**PSZCZELARSTWO.** [Pszczelarstwo]. **Added/Corp** Polski Zwiazek Pszczelarski. (19??)-. Periodical. Polish. mo. Price on Request. **(Subscription address:** ARS Polona, PO Box 1001, 00068 Warsaw Poland.**)** **CODEN** PZCZAJ. Documents available from CASDDS.
**Ind/Abst** AGRICOLA; Chem. Abstr.

US/0161-5009
**PUBL HERPETOL.** [Publ. herpetol.]. **VFOAT** Publications in Herpetology. 1-. Monographic series. English. Price varies per volume. Herpetological Information Search Systems of the American Museum of Natural History, Central Park West at 79th Street, New York NY 10024. **CODEN** PUHEDH.

US/0272-2658
**PUBLIC EDUCATION SERIES.** [Pub. educ. ser.]. **Added/Corp** University of Kansas. Museum of Natural History. No 1 (1974)-. Monographic series. English. Price varies per volume. Publications Museum of Natural History, University of Kansas, Lawrence KS 66045. **Tel** (913)864-4154. **(Subscription address:** University Press of Kansas, 329 Carruth, Lawrence, KS 66045**)** **ED** Joseph T Collins. **Circ:** 1,500 (ctrl).
**Desc:** Each number is on a different zoological subject, ichthyology, herpetology, mammalogy and archeology.

CL/0577-8298
**PUBLICACIONES.** **Main/Corp** Chile. Universidad, Santiago. Centro de Estudios Entomolgicos. No. 1- 1960-. Periodical. Spanish. Av Bernardo O Higgins 1058, Casilla 10 D Santiago Chile.

US
**PUBLICATION E.** **Main/Corp** Purdue University. Cooperative Extension Service. 1950-. English.
**Ind/Abst** AGRICOLA.

SP/0210-4814
**PUBLICATIONES DEL DEPARTAMENTO DE ZOOLOGIA / UNIVERSIDAD DE BARCELONA, FACULTAD DE BIOLOGIA.** **Added/Corp** Universidad de Barcelona. Departamento de Zoologia. Vol. 1 (1976)-. Spanish (Spanish; summaries and/or abstracts in English, French

and German). Departmento del Zoologia, Facultad de Biologia, Universidad de Barcelona, Barcelona 7 Spain. **Ind/Abst** Fish Rev. (19??-199?); Wildl. Rev. (19??-199?).

PK/1016-1597
**PUNJAB UNIVERSITY JOURNAL OF ZOOLOGY.** [Punjab Univ. j. zool.]. **VFOAT** Journal of Zoology. (1986)-. Periodical. English. University of Punjab Department of Zoology, Lahore 20 Pakistan. **CODEN** PUJZEN. Documents available from BIOSIS Document Express. ***Continues** Bulletin of the Department of Zoology, University of the Punjab, 0375-0620.*
**Ind/Abst** Biol. Abstr. (1988-).

US/0090-323X
**QUARTERLY - MIAMI MALACOLOGICAL SOCIETY.** (QUARTERLY.). **Main/Corp** Miami Malacological Society. V. 1- April/June 1967-. Periodical. English. qt. $1.50. Mrs M Ellen Crovo Corresponding Secretary, 2915 SW 102nd Avenue, Miami FL 33165. **LC** QL401; .M5. **DD** 594/.005.

NE
**RABBIT BRAIN RESEARCH.** Academic Scholarly Publication. English. ir. Elsevier Science Publishing Company Inc, Madison Square Station, PO Box 882, New York NY 10159-0882. **Tel** (212)633-3950, FAX (212)633-3990.

US
**RANGER RICK'S NATURESCOPE. See** Natural History.

NO/0333-256X
**RANGIFER.** [Rangifer]. (1981)-. Periodical. Norwegian. qt. Kr150.00 Nordic countries; Kr175.00 other Europe; Kr200.00 other. Rangifer, P.O.Box 378, N 9401 Harstad Norway. **Tel** 011 47 82 64172. **DD** 599.73.
**Ind/Abst** Index Vet.; Vet. Bull.

NE
**RAPID COMMUNICATIONS. Added/Corp** Societas Internationalis Odonatologica. No. 1 (1980)-. Monographic series. German. ir. Price varies per volume. Societas Internationalis Odonatologica, PO Box 256, 3720 AG Bilthoven, The Netherlands. **Tel** 011 31 30285904.

NE
**RAPID COMMUNICATIONS (SUPPLEMENTS).** No. 1 (1983)-. Monographic series. Multiple languages. ir. Price varies per volume. Societas Internationalis Odonatologica, PO Box 256, 3720 AG Bilthoven, The Netherlands. **Tel** 011 31 30285904. **ED** B Kiauta. **Pr Rev. Circ:** 300. Documents available from BIOSIS Document Express.
**Desc:** Contains extensive faunistic and other information on dragonflies and damselflies, with discussion papers, etc.
**Ind/Abst** Biol. Abstr.; Entomol. Abstr.; Genet. Abstr.; Ref. Z.; Zool. Rec.

CN
**RAPPORT DES INVENTAIRES AERIENS DU GROS GIBIER. Main/Corp** Quebec (Province). Comite des Inventaires Aeriens du Gros Gibier. French. Gouvernement du Quebec, 600 St Amable 4E Etage, Quebec Quebec G1R 4Z1 Canada. **LC** QL721.5.Q4; Q42A. **DD** 333.95/9/09714. **Circ:** 100 (ctrl).

UK/0305-1218
**RATEL.** (RATEL : JOURNAL OF THE ASSOCIATION OF BRITISH WILD ANIMAL KEEPERS.). [Ratel]. **Added/Corp** Association of British Wild Animal Keepers. (1974)-. Periodical. English. Six times a year (Feb., Apr., June, Aug., Oct., Dec.). £14.00 UK; £19.00 other. Association of British Wild Animal Keepers, 12 Tackley Road, Eastville, Bristol BS5 6UQ England. **Tel** 011 44 272 515950. **ED** David Field. **LC** QL77.5; .R37. **DD** 636.08/899/05. **Bk Rev. Ad Acc. Circ:** 350 (ctrl).
**Ind/Abst** Life Sci. Collect.; Wildl. Rev.

US/0034-0146
**RAVEN, THE.** V. 1- 1930-. Periodical. English. qt. $4.00 (nonmembers). Virginia Society of Ornithology, 520 Rainbow Forest Drive, Lynchburg VA 24502.

AT/0067-1975
**RECORDS OF THE AUSTRALIAN MUSEUM.** [Rec. Aust. Mus.]. **Main/Corp** Australian Museum. **Added/Corp** Australian Museum. Vol. 1 (March 1890)-. Monographic series. English. Three times a year. 100.00Aus$ Australia; $70.00 US. Australian Museum, 6 College Street, P.O. Box A285, Sydney South 2000 Australia. **Tel** 011 61 2 3398200, FAX 61-2-3398313. **ED** Jim Lowry. **LC** QH1; .A985. **CODEN** RAUMAJ. Index available. cum. index. **Circ:** 800 (ctrl). Documents available from BIOSIS Document Express.
**Desc:** Original research in the fields of anthropology, geology and zoology relevant to Australia, the Southwest Pacific and the Indian Ocean.
**Ind/Abst** Biol. Abstr.; Fish Rev.; GeoRef; Life Sci. Collect.; Wildl. Rev.

AT/0812-7387
**RECORDS OF THE AUSTRALIAN MUSEUM. SUPPLEMENT.** [Rec. Aust. Mus., Suppl.]. **Added/Corp** Australian Museum. Vol. 1 (Sept. 19, 1983)-. Monographic series. English. ir. Price varies per volume. Australian Museum, 6 College Street, P.O. Box A285, Sydney South 2000 Australia. **Tel** 011 61 2 3398200, FAX 61-2-3398313. **ED** Jim Lowry. **LC** UNC. **CODEN** RAMSEZ. Index available. cum. index. **Circ:** 800 (ctrl). Documents available from BIOSIS Document Express. ***Continues** Australian Museum Memoir.*
**Desc:** Monographic papers of original research in the fields of taxonomy and other museum-related zoological studies.
**Ind/Abst** Biol. Abstr. (1985-); Fish Rev.; GeoRef; Life Sci. Collect.; Wildl. Rev.

II/0375-1511
**RECORDS OF THE ZOOLOGICAL SURVEY OF INDIA.** [Rec. Zool. Surv. India]. **Main/Corp** India (Republic). Zoological Survey. **Added/Corp** Zoological Survey of India. **VFOAT** India Records. (June 1963)-. English. qt. Price varies. Controller of Publications / Civil Lines, Government of India, Civil Lines, New Delhi 110054 India. **Tel** 3015984, telex 3166415. **(Subscription address:** Prints India, 11 Darya Ganj, New Delhi 110002 India.**) LC** QL1; .I3. **DD** 591/.05. **CODEN** RZSIA2. ***Continues** Records of the Indian Museum.*
**Ind/Abst** GeoRef.

II/0970-0714
**RECORDS OF THE ZOOLOGICAL SURVEY OF INDIA. MISCELLANEOUS PUBLICATION. OCCASIONAL PAPER.** [Rec. Zool. Surv. India, Misc. publ., Occas. pap.]. **Main/Corp** Zoological Survey of India. **VFOAT** Miscellaneous Publication; Occasional Paper; Records of the Zoological Survey of India Occasional Paper. (1976)-. Monographic series. English. an. Price varies per volume. Controller of Publications / Civil Lines, Government of India, Civil Lines, New Delhi 110054 India. **Tel** 3015984, telex 3166415. **(Subscription address:** Prints India, 11 Darya Ganj, New Delhi 110002 India.**) UDC** 59.

US/0034-2165
**REDSTART, THE.** [Redstart]. **Added/Corp** Brooks Bird Club. (19??)-. Periodical. English. Four times a year (Jan., Apr., July, Oct.). $14.00. Brooks Bird Club Inc, 707 Warwood Avenue, Wheeling WV 26003. **Tel** (304)547-5253. **ED** Albert R. Buckelew (editor's address: Bethany College, Biology Department, Bethany, WV 26032). **CODEN** RDSTAH. Index available. **Bk Rev.** Documents available from BIOSIS Document Express.
**Desc:** Contains field and banding notes, reports on the foray, sortie, Christmas count and other events.
**Ind/Abst** Biol. Abstr.; Wildl. Rev.

UK/0143-8700
**REPORT OF THE INTERNATIONAL WHALING COMMISSION.** (REPORT OF THE COMMISSION / INTERNATIONAL WHALING COMMISSION.). [Rep. Int. Whal. Comm.]. **Main/Corp** International Whaling Commission. **VFOAT** Report of the International Whaling Commission. (1976)-. English. an (May or June). International Whaling Commission, The Red House, Station Road Histon, Cambridge CB4 4NP England. **Tel** 011 44 223 233971, FAX 011 44 223 232876, telex 817960. **ED** G. P. Donovan. **LC** SH381; .I484. **Pr Rev. Circ:** 500. ***Continues** International Commission on Whaling. Report of the Commission, 0074-9591.*
**Desc:** Covers management actions taken by the IWC, the report of its scientific committee and more than 50 scientific papers on cetacean biology and management.
**Ind/Abst** Aquat. Sci. Fish. Abstr. (Computer File); Ecol. Abstr.; Fish Rev. (Jan. 1989-July 1992); Geogr. Abstr. Human Geogr.; Ocean. Abstr.; Life Sci. Collect.; Wildl. Rev. (Jan. 1989-July 1992).

US
**REPORT TO FARMERS ... ANNUAL SWINE FIELD DAY. Main/Corp** Florida. University, Gainesville. Agricultural Extension Service. (1960)-. Periodical. English. an.
**Ind/Abst** Nutr. Abstr. Rev., Ser. B, Live Feeds and Feed.; Pig News Inf.

NE
**REPORTS OF THE ODONATA SPECIALIST GROUP, SPECIES SURVIVAL COMMISSION, INTERNATIONAL UNION FOR THE CONSERVATION OF NATURE AND NATURAL RESOURCES (I.U.C.N.).** **Added/Corp** International Union for Conservation of Nature and Natural Resources. Odonata Specialist Group. Societas Internationalis Odonatologica. (1982)-. Monographic series. English. ir. Price varies per volume. Societas Internationalis Odonatologica, PO Box 256, 3720 AG Bilthoven, The Netherlands. **Tel** 011 31 30285904.

US/1059-0668
**REPTILE & AMPHIBIAN MAGAZINE.** [Reptile amphib. mag.]. **VFOAT** Reptile and Amphibian Magazine. (Nov./Dec. 1989)-. Periodical. English. bm. $16.00 (1 year), $28.00 (2 year) US; $19.00 (1 year), $34.00 (2 year) Canada; $26.00 (1 year), $48.00 (2 year) other. Reptile & Amphibian Magazine, RD 3 Box 3709-A, Pottsville PA 17901. **Tel** (717)622-6050, FAX (717)622-5858. **ED** Norman Frank, DVM. **DD** 597. Index available. cum. index. **Bk Rev. Ad Acc. Circ:** 11,500.
**Desc:** Journal for amateur herpetologists; contains features on natural history, life cycles, captive care and breeding, and ecology of reptiles and amphibians.

BL/0101-8175
**REVISTA BRASILEIRA DE ZOOLOGIA.** Vol. 1, No. 1 (1982)-. Periodical. Portuguese (English). qt. $50.00. Sociedade Brasileira de Zoologia, Caixa Postal 19020, 81531-970 Curitiba PR Brazil. **Tel** 011 55 41 2665433. **LC** QL242; .R48. **DD** 591/.05. **Bk Rev. Circ:** 1,200 (ctrl).
**Ind/Abst** Ecology Abstr.; For. Prod. Abstr. (1991-); For. Abstr.; Nematol. Abstr.; Protozoolog. Abstr.; Rev. Agric. Entomol.; Rev. Med. Vet. Entomol.

BL/0100-4859
**REVISTA DA SOCIEDADE BRASILEIRA DE ZOOTECNIA.** [Rev. Soc. Bras. Zootec.]. **Added/Corp** Sociedade Brasileira de Zootecnia. Vol. 1 (1972)-. Academic Scholarly Publication. Portuguese (summaries and/or abstracts in English). qt. **CODEN** RSBZBM. Documents available from CASDDS.
**Ind/Abst** Agrofor. Abstr. (1991-); Chem. Abstr.; Dairy Sci. Abstr.; Field Crop Abstr.; Fish Rev. (Jan. 1989-July 1992); For. Abstr.; Grasslands For. Abstr.; Index Vet.; Maize Abstr.; Nutr. Abstr. Rev., Ser. B, Live Feeds and Feed.; Pig News Inf.; Plant Genet. Resour. Abstr.; Postharvest News Inf.; Poult. Abstr.; Rev. Agric. Entomol.; Rice Abstr.; Seed Abstr.; Soils Fert.; Sorghum Mill. Abstr.; Soyabean Abstr.; Sug. Indus. Abstr.; Vet. Bull.; Weed Abstr.; Wheat Barley Trit. Abstr.; Wildl. Rev. (Jan. 1989-July 1992).

AG/0373-5680
**REVISTA DE LA SOCIEDAD ENTOMOLOGICA ARGENTINA.** [Rev. Soc. entomol. Argent.]. **Main/Corp** Sociedad Entomologica Argentina. Vol. 1 (1926)-. Spanish. an. Librart SRL, Corrientes 127, Buenos Aires Argentina. cum. index.
**Ind/Abst** Biocont. News Inf. (1991-); Maize Abstr.; Life Sci. Collect.; Rev. Agric. Entomol.; Rev. Med. Vet. Entomol.; Rev. Plant Pathol.

MX
**REVISTA DE LA SOCIEDAD MEXICANA DE LEPIDOPTEROLOGIA. Main/Corp** Sociedad Mexicana de Lepidopterologia. V. 1, No. 1- June 1975-. Periodical. Spanish (summaries and/or abstracts in English). sa. Sociedad Mexicana de Lepidopterologia, Apdo Postal 70-153, Mexico DF Mexico. **LC** QL553.M4; S6A. **CODEN** RSMLD3. Documents available from BIOSIS Document Express.
**Ind/Abst** AGRICOLA; Biol. Abstr.

AG/0372-4638
**REVISTA DEL MUSEO DE LA PLATA. SECCION ZOOLOGIA. See** Museums and Galleries.

CM/0257-3385
**REVUE SCIENCE ET TECHNIQUE. SERIE SCIENCES AGRONOMIQUES ET ZOOTECHNIQUES. See** Agriculture-Crop Production and Soil.

SZ/0035-418X
**REVUE SUISSE DE ZOOLOGIE.** [Rev. suisse zool.]. **Added/Corp** Schweizerische Zoologische Gesellschaft. Museum d'Histoire Naturelle de Geneve. (1893)-. Periodical. French (German and English). Four times a year. 230.00F. Museum d'Histoire Naturelle de Geneve, CP 434, CH 1211 Geneva 6 Switzerland. **Tel** FAX 011 41 22 7353445. **LC** QL1; .R4. **DD** 590/.5. **NLM** W1 RE969. **CODEN** RSZOA6. Index available in last issue of volume--attached. **Pr Rev.** Documents available from The Genuine Article, BIOSIS Document Express, CASDDS. ***Supersedes** Recueil Zoologique Suisse.*
**Desc:** Publication of research articles by members of the Swiss Zoological Society, based on material in the Museum of Natural History in Geneva.
**Ind/Abst** Biocont. News Inf. (1991-); Biol. Abstr.; Chem. Abstr.; CSA Neuro. Abstr. (?-?); Curr. Aware. Biol. Sci., CABS; Curr. Contents, Agric. Biol. Environ. Sci.; Curr. Ref. Fish Res.; Fish Rev.; Helminthol. Abstr. (19??-19??); Index Med. (May 1965-June 1979); Index Vet.; Key Word Index Wildl. Res.; Life Sci. Collect.; Protozoolog. Abstr.; Res. Alert [Full Cov.]; Rev. Agric. Entomol.; Rev. Med. Vet. Entomol.; Sci. Cit. Index; SCISEARCH; Soils Fert.; Wildl. Rev.

IT/0375-0736
**RICERCHE DI BIOLOGIA DELLA SELVAGGINA.** [Ric. biol. selvaggina]. **Added/Corp** Universita di Bologna. Labotatorio di Zoologia Applicata alla Caccia. No. 51 (1971)-. Monographic series. Italian (summaries and/or abstracts in English, French and German). Price varies per volume. Istituto Nazionale di Biologia della Selvaggina, A Ghigi, Via Fornacetta 9, 40064 Bologna Italy. **DD** 591. **CODEN** RBSVA9. Documents available from BIOSIS Document Express.

*Continues* *Ricerche di Zoologia Applicata alla Caccia.* **Ind/Abst** Biol. Abstr.; Fish Rev. (Jan. 1989-July 1992); Wildl. Rev. (Jan. 1989-July 1992).

UK
**ROYAL ENTOMOLOGICAL SOCIETY SYMPOSIUM.** English. Royal Entomological Society, 41 Queens Gate, London SW7 5HR England. **Tel** 011 41 71 5848361.

GW/0036-3375
**SALAMANDRA (FRANKFURT-AM-MAIN).** (SALAMANDRA.). [Salamandra]. **Added/Corp** Deutsche Gesellschaft fuer Herpetologie und Terrarienkunde. Vol. 1 (Sept. 1965)-. Periodical. German (summaries and/or abstracts in English). Four times a year. DM80.00. Deutsche ges Herpetologie DGHT, PO Box 1421, D 53351 Rheinbach Germany. **Tel** 011 49 2255 6086. **LC** QL640; .S24. **CODEN** SALAAH. **Bk Rev. Circ:** 4,000. Documents available from BIOSIS Document Express.
**Desc:** Reports and scientific news regarding herpetology (natural history of reptiles and amphibians).
**Ind/Abst** Biol. Abstr.; Life Sci. Collect.

II
**SANCTUARY ASIA. See** Environmental Issues-Conservation and Natural Resources.

JA
**SANSHI SHIKENJO NEMPO. Main/Corp** Norinsho Sanshi Shikenjo (Japan). 1960-. Japanese. Norin Suisansho Sanshi Shikenjo, (Sericultural Experiment Station, Ministry of Agriculture, Forestry & Fisheries), 1-2, Owashi, Tsukubashi, Ibarakiken 305 Japan. **LC** SF553.J3; S36.

GW/0036-2344
**SAUGETIERKUNDLICHE MITTEILUNGEN.** ***Suspended.*** **See** Biology.

RU
**SBORNIK TRUDOV ZOOLOGICHESKOGO MUZEIA.** [Sb. tr. Zool. muz.]. **Main/Corp** Moskovskii Universitet. Zoologicheskii Muzei. **Added/Corp** Moskovskii Gosudarstvennyi Universitet Mm. M.V. Lomonosova. Zoologicheskii Muzei. **VFOAT** Sbornik Trudov Zoologicheskogo Muzeia MGU; Archives du Musee Zoologique de l'Universite de Moscou; A.Archives of Zoological Museum Moscow State University. Vol. 8, (1961)-. Academic Scholarly Publication. Russian. Price varies per volume. Izdatelstvo Moskovskogo Universiteta, K-9 Ulitsa Gertsena 5/7, 103009 Moscow Russia. **Tel** (301)881-5973. **CODEN** SZMMAT. Documents available from CASDDS. ***Continues*** *Sbornik Trudov Gosudarstvennogo Zoologicheskogo Muzeia.*
**Ind/Abst** Chem. Abstr. (1961-1978).

SZ/0036-7540
**SCHWEIZERISCHE BIENEN-ZEITUNG.** [Schweiz. bienen-ztg.]. **Added/Corp** Verein Deutsch-Schweizerischer Bienenfreunde. Vol. 1-9, (1869-77)- Vol. 1, (1878)-. Periodical. German. Twelve times a year. $35.00. Sauerlaender AG, Laurenzenvorstadt 89, CH 5001 Aarau Switzerland. **Tel** 011 41 64 268626. **[CCC].**
**Ind/Abst** AGRICOLA.

JA/0917-0537
**SCIENTIFIC REPORTS OF CETACEAN RESEARCH. Added/Corp** Nihon Kujirarui Kenkyujo. No. 1 (Sept. 1990)-. English. Institute of Cetacean Research, Tokyo Suisan Building, 4-18 Toyomi-Cho, Chuo-ku, Tokyo 104 Japan. **LC** QL737.C4; S38. **DD** 599.5/05. **CODEN** SRCTEG. ***Continues*** *Scientific Reports of the Whales Research Institute, 0083-9086.*

JA/0370-9531
**SEITAI NO KAGAKU. See** Biology.

US/0747-6078
**SHELLS AND SEA LIFE.** ***Ceased.*** [Shells sea life]. **VFOAT** S and SL; Shells & Sea Sea Life; S & SL. (1984)-(1991). Periodical. English. mo. Shells and Sea Life, 1701 Hyland, Bayside CA 95524-9302. **Tel** (707)822-1024. **ED** Steven J Long and M Sally Long. **DD** 594. Index available. **Bk Rev. Ad Acc. Circ:** 2,000 (ctrl). available on microfiche. ***Continues*** *Opisthobranch Newsletter.*
**Desc:** A semi-technical magazine on marine life and mollusks for all levels of interest from beach walker to professional scientist.

CC
**SHOU LEI HSUEH-PAO. VFOAT** Acta Theriologica Sinica. Vol. 1, No. 1 (June 1981)-. Chinese. sa. RMBY1.30. Science Press, 16 Donghuangchenggen North Street, Beijing 100707, People's Republic of China. **Tel** 011 86 1 4019821, 011 86 1 4010642, FAX 011 86 1 4012180, 011 86 1 4019810, telex 210147. **LC** QL700; .S46. **DD** 599.
**Ind/Abst** Ecol. Abstr.

US/0890-7021
**SIALIA.** [Sialia]. **Added/Corp** North American Bluebird Society. Vol. 1, No. 1 (Winter 1979)-. Periodical. English. qt. $15.00 US; $20.00 Canada; $17.00 other. North America Bluebird Society, 2 Countryside Court, Silver Spring MD 20904. **Tel** (301)384-2798. **(Subscription address:** Box 6295, Silver Spring, MD 20916-6295**) ED** Joanne Solem. **DD** 598. Index available. cum. index. **Bk Rev. Circ:** 5,000.
**Desc:** Conservation education and opinion.
**Ind/Abst** Fish Rev.; Wildl. Rev.

NE/0921-4488
**SMALL RUMINANT RESEARCH.** (SMALL RUMINANT RESEARCH : THE JOURNAL OF THE INTERNATIONAL GOAT ASSOCIATION.). [Small rumin. res.]. **Added/Corp** International Goat Association. Vol. 1, No. 1 (March 1988)-. Academic Scholarly Publication. English. Twelve times a year (4 volumes). Fl1512.00. Elsevier Science Publishers BV, PO Box 211, 1000 AE Amsterdam Netherlands. **Tel** 011 31 20 5803642, FAX 011 31 20 5862696, telex 15682. **CODEN** SRUREW. **[CCC].** available on microfilm and microfiche from University Microfilms International (UMI). Documents available from The Genuine Article, BIOSIS Document Express. ***Continues in part*** *International Goat and Sheep Research, 0197-7393.*
**Ind/Abst** AgBiotech News Inf.; AGRICOLA [Full Cov.]; Agrofor. Abstr. (1991-); Anim. Breed. Abstr.; Biol. Abstr.; Curr. Contents, Agric. Biol. Environ. Sci.; Dairy Sci. Abstr.; For. Abstr.; Grasslands For. Abstr.; Helminthol. Abstr. (1991-); Index Vet. (1988-); Maize Abstr.; Nutr. Abstr. Rev., Ser. B, Live Feeds and Feed.; Protozoolog. Abstr.; Res. Alert [Select. Cov.]; Rev. Med. Vet. Entomol.; Sorghum Mill. Abstr.; Soyabean Abstr.; Vet. Bull.; Wheat Barley Trit. Abstr.

US/0081-0282
**SMITHSONIAN CONTRIBUTIONS TO ZOOLOGY.** [Smithson. contrib. zool.]. **Added/Corp** Smithsonian Institution. No. 1 (1969)-. Monographic series. English. ir. Price varies per volume. Superintendent of Documents, US Government Printing Office, Washington DC 20402. **Tel** (202)275-3328, FAX (202)786-2377. **ED** Barbara Spann. **LC** QL1; .S54. **DD** 591/.08 S. **NLM** W1 SM454N. **CODEN** SMCZBU. **Circ:** 1,700 (ctrl). Documents available from BIOSIS Document Express.
**Desc:** Monographs that report the research of Smithsonian staff in zoology (ornithology, ichthyology, entomology, mammalogy, herpetology, mollusks, and marine invertebrates).
**Ind/Abst** AGRICOLA; Aquat. Sci. Fish. Abstr. (Computer File); Biocont. News Inf. (1991-); Biol. Abstr.; Curr. Aware. Biol. Sci., CABS; Fish Rev.; Geol. Abstr.; GeoRef; Key Word Index Wildl. Res.; Life Sci. Collect.; Rev. Agric. Entomol.; Rev. Med. Vet. Entomol.; Trop. Dis. Bull.; Wildl. Rev.

JA/0386-3425
**SNAKE.** (THE SNAKE.). [Snake]. **Added/Corp** Nihon Hebizoku Gakujutsu Kenkyujo. Vol. 1 (Aug. 1969)-. Academic Scholarly Publication. English (Japanese). sa (Published in June & December). $34.00. Japan Snake Institute, Yabuzuka-Honmachi, Nittagun Gunma Prefecture, 379-23 Japan. **Tel** 011 81 277 785193, FAX 011 81 277 785520. **ED** Y. Sawai. **LC** QL640; .S6. **DD** 615.9/42. **NLM** W1 SN105. **CODEN** NJGKBV. **[CCC].** Index available. cum. index. **Bk Rev**, (Qty: 1-3). **Ad Acc. Circ:** 500. Documents available from BIOSIS Document Express, CASDDS.
**Desc:** The journal of the Japan Snake Institute publishes general papers on the biology of snakes, snake venom and snake bites.
**Ind/Abst** Biol. Abstr.; Chem. Abstr.; Wildl. Rev.

US/0361-6525
**SOCIOBIOLOGY.** [Sociobiology]. **Added/Corp** California State University, Chico. Dept. of Biological Sciences. Vol. 1 (1975)-. English (French, Spanish and German). ir. $45.00. California State University - Chico / Department of Biological Sciences, c/o Dr. David Kistner, Chico CA 95929. **Tel** (916)898-5116. **ED** Dr. D.H. Kistner. **LC** QH301; .S762. **DD** 591/.05. **CODEN** SOCIDT. **[CCC].** Index available in last issue of volume--attached. **Bk Rev. Pr Rev. Circ:** 500 (ctrl). Documents available from The Genuine Article, BIOSIS Document Express.
**Desc:** Interested in papers dealing with the social biology of animals, particularly social insects.
**Ind/Abst** AGRICOLA [Select. Cov.]; Agrofor. Abstr. (1991-); Anim. Behav. Abstr.; Biocont. News Inf. (1991-); Biodeter. Abstr. (1991-); Biol. Abstr. (1985); Curr. Aware. Biol. Sci., CABS; Curr. Contents, Agric. Biol. Environ. Sci.; Dairy Sci. Abstr.; Ecol. Abstr. (?-?); Ecology Abstr.; Entomol. Abstr.; Fish Rev. (Jan. 1989-July 1992); For. Abstr.; Maize Abstr.; Nutr. Abstr. Rev., Ser. A, Hum. Exp.; Life Sci. Collect.; Res. Alert [Select. Cov.]; Rev. Agric. Entomol.; Rev. Med. Vet. Entomol.; Rural Dev. Abstr.; Sci. Cit. Index; Zool. Rec.; Wildl. Rev. (Jan. 1989-July 1992).

US/0899-0220
**SOMATOSENSORY & MOTOR RESEARCH.** [Somatosens. motor res.]. **VFOAT** Somatosensory and Motor Research. Vol. 6, No. 1 (1988)-. Academic Scholarly Publication. English. Four times a year. $185.00 (institutions); $205.00 others. Guilford Publications Inc., 72 Spring Street, New York NY 10012. **Tel** (212)431-9800, (800)365-7006, FAX (212)966-6708. **(Subscription address:** Turpin Distribution Services Limited, Blackhorse Road, Letchworth, Hertfordshire SG6 1HN, United Kingdom.**) ED** Thomas Woolsey. **DD** 599. **NLM** W1; SO887LE. **CODEN** SMOREZ. **[CCC].** Index available. **Ad Acc.** available on microfilm from University Microfilms International (UMI). Documents available from The Genuine Article, CASDDS. ***Continues*** *Somatosensory Research, 0736-7244.*
**Desc:** Contains original papers that encompass the entire range of investigations relating to somatic sensation, its neural basis, and the neural mechanisms of somatic motor function.
**Ind/Abst** Anim. Behav. Abstr.; Chem. Abstr. (1988-); CSA Neuro. Abstr.; Curr. Aware. Biol. Sci., CABS; Curr. Contents Life Sci.; EMBASE; Index Med. (1988-); Life Sci. Collect. (1988-); Psychol. Abstr. (1983-); PsycINFO (1990-); PsycLit; Ref. Upd. Deluxe Ed.; Res. Alert [Full Cov.]; Sci. Cit. Index; SCISEARCH; Soc. Sci. Cit. Index [Select. Cov.].

SW
**SOUTH AFRICAN ANIMAL LIFE.**
**Added/Corp** Lunds Universitet. Sydafrika-Expeditionen, 1950-1951. Vol. 1 (1955)-. Periodical. English (English, French and German). Swedish Natural Science Research Council, Editorial Service, PO Box 2316, S104 35 Stockholm Sweden. **ED** Bertil Hamstrom, Per Brinck and Gustaf Rudebeck. **LC** QL337.S65; H3. **DD** 591.968.

SA/0038-2019
**SOUTH AFRICAN BEE JOURNAL.**
**Added/Corp** South African Federation of Beekeepers Associations. South African Association of Beekeepers. **VFOAT** Suid Afrikaanse Byetydskrif. Vol. 1 (April 1921)-. Periodical. Afrikaans (English). bm. $4.96. South African Federation of Beekeepers, Editor, 34 Sea View Road, Somerset West 7130 South Africa. ***Supersedes in part*** *African Beekeeping.*
**Ind/Abst** Rev. Agric. Entomol.; Sug. Indus. Abstr.

SA/0254-1858
**SOUTH AFRICAN JOURNAL OF ZOOLOGY.** [S. Afr. j. zool.]. **Added/Corp** Foundation for Education, Science, and Technology (South Africa). Bureau for Scientific Publications. Zoological Society of Southern Africa. **VFOAT** Suid-Afrikaanse Tydskrif vir Dierkunde. Vol. 14 (1979)-. Academic Scholarly Publication. English (Afrikaans and English). qt. R87.00 South Africa; R90.00 other. Foundation for Education Science & Technology, PO Box 1758, Pretoria 0001 South Africa. **Tel** 011 27 12 3226404, FAX 011 27 12 3207803. **ED** H. R. Hepburn. **LC** QL337.S65; Z64. **NLM** W1 SO9058. **CODEN** SAJZDH. **[CCC].** Index available. **Bk Rev. Circ:** 800 (ctrl). Documents available from The Genuine Article, BIOSIS Document Express, CASDDS. ***Continues*** *Zoologica Africana, 0044-5096.*
**Desc:** Original research articles on any aspect of zoology in Africa, especially ecology, ethology, physiology and taxonomy.
**Ind/Abst** AGRICOLA [Select. Cov.]; Aquat. Sci. Fish. Abstr. (Computer File); Biol. Abstr.; Chem. Abstr.; Curr. Aware. Biol. Sci., CABS; Curr. Contents, Agric. Biol. Environ. Sci.; Curr. Ref. Fish Res.; Ecol. Abstr.; Ecology Abstr.; Entomol. Abstr.; Fish Rev.; Index Vet.; Key Word Index Wildl. Res.; Maize Abstr.; Nematol. Abstr.; Nutr. Abstr. Rev., Ser. B, Live Feeds and Feed.; Ocean. Abstr.; Life Sci. Collect.; Res. Alert [Full Cov.]; Rev. Agric. Entomol.; Rev. Med. Vet. Entomol.; Sci. Cit. Index; SCISEARCH; Wildl. Rev.

US/0748-0539
**SPECIAL PUBLICATION (AMERICAN SOCIETY OF ICHTHYOLOGISTS AND HERPETOLOGISTS).** (SPECIAL PUBLICATION / AMERICAN SOCIETY OF ICHTHYOLOGISTS AND HERPATOLOGISTS.). [Spec. publ. - Am. Soc. Ichthyol. Herpetol.]. **Added/Corp** American Society of Ichthyologists and Herpetologists. (1984)-. Monographic series. English. ir. Price varies per volume. ASIH Copeia, Department of Zoology, Southern Illinois University, Carbondale IL 62901. **Tel** (618)453-4113. **ED** Robert Karl Johnson. **DD** 597. ctrl circ.
**Desc:** A publications outlet for scientific publications in ichthyology and herpetology.

US/0569-8219
**SPECIAL PUBLICATION / AMERICAN SOCIETY OF MAMMALOGISTS.** [Spec. publ. Am. Soc. Mammal.]. **Added/Corp** American Society of Mammalogists. No. 1 (1967)-. Monographic series. English. ir. Price varies per volume. American Society of Mammalogists, c/o H.D. Smith, Zoology Department, Brigham Young University, Provo UT 84602. **Tel** (801)378-2492. **ED** Timothy E. Lawlor. **CODEN** AMAMBL. Index available (bound in all issues). Documents available from BIOSIS Document Express.
**Desc:** Monographs which deal with selected topics in mammalogy.
**Ind/Abst** Biol. Abstr.

US/0070-2242
**SPECIAL PUBLICATION - CUSHMAN FOUNDATION FOR FORAMINIFERAL RESEARCH.** [Spec. pub. - Cushman Found. Foraminifer. Res.]. **Main/Corp** Cushman Foundation for Foraminiferal Research. No. 1 (1952)-. Monographic series. English. ir. Price varies per volume. Cushman Foundation, Harvard University, Museum of Comparative Zoology, Cambridge MA 02138. **Tel** (617)496-5406. **ED** S. J. Culver. **CODEN** SPCFAO. **Bk Rev. Ad Acc. Circ:** 800 (ctrl). ***Continues*** *Cushman Laboratory for Foraminiferal Research Special Publication, 0197-548X.*

**Desc:** Results of research on fossil and living foraminifera and related organisms.
**Ind/Abst** GeoRef.

SA/0075-2088
**SPECIAL PUBLICATION / J. L. B. SMITH INSTITUTE OF ICHTHYOLOGY.** [Spec. publ. - J.L.B. Smith Inst. Ichthyol.]. Monographic series. English. ir. Price varies per volume. J L B Smith Institute of Ichthyology, Rhodes University South Africa. **LC** QL614; .S55. **CODEN** SPSIEF. Documents available from BIOSIS Document Express. ***Continues*** *Special Publication (Rhodes University. Dept. of Ichthyology).*
**Ind/Abst** Aquat. Sci. Fish. Abstr. (Computer File); Biol. Abstr. (1985-); Ocean. Abstr.

SW
**SPECIAL REPORT - OTTENBY BIRD OBSERVATORY.** English. ir. $3.00. Ottenby Bird Observatory, PL 1500, S-380 65 Degerhamn Sweden.

US/0190-6798
**SPEEDY BEE.** V. 1- Feb. 1972-. Periodical. English. mo. $15.75 US; $18.75 Canada and Mexico; $28.25 Central America, Columbia and Venezuela; $33.25 Western Europe; $38.25 other. The Speedy Bee, PO Box 998, Jesup GA 31545. **Tel** (912)427-4018. **ED** Troy Fore. **DD** 338. **Bk Rev. Ad Acc. Circ:** 4,000.
**Desc:** Tabloid newspaper for beekeepers and honey industry. News, how-to's, features, advertising.

US/1045-0076
**SPHENISCID PENGUIN NEWSLETTER : SPN. VFOAT** SPN. (1988)-. Newsletter. English. sa. Free to zoos, aquaria, researchers, and others. SPN, Washington Park Zoo, 4001 SW Canyon Road, Portland OR 97221. **Tel** (503)226-1561. **ED** Cynthia Cheney. **DD** 598.
**Desc:** Covers all aspects of spheniscid penguins (the four species Spheniscus demersus, S. humboldti, S. magellanicus, and S. mendiculus) including captive husbandry, field research, research in zoological institutions, and conservation programs.
**Ind/Abst** Fish Rev.; Wildl. Rev.

GW/0341-8391
**SPIXIANA.** [Spixiana]. Vol. 1, No. 1; Aug. 1, 1977-. Periodical. English (French and German). Three times a year. DM120.00, $60.00. Zoologische Staatssammlung, Munchhausenstrasse 21, D 81247 Muenchen 60 Germany. **Tel** 011 49 89 8107123. **ED** E J Fittkau and M Baehr. **LC** QL1; .S878. **DD** 590/.5. **CODEN** SPIXD9. Index available. **Bk Rev. Circ:** 540 (ctrl). Documents available from BIOSIS Document Express. ***Formed by the union of*** *Opuscula Zoologica, 0030-4158* ***and*** *Veroffentlichungen der Zoologischen Staatssammlung Munchen, 0077-2135.*
**Desc:** Covers zoological systematics with emphasis in morphology, phylogeny, zoogeography and ecology.
**Ind/Abst** AGRICOLA; Biol. Abstr.; Entomol. Abstr.; Fish Rev.; Key Word Index Wildl. Res.; Life Sci. Collect.; Wildl. Rev.

GW/0177-7424
**SPIXIANA. SUPPLEMENT.** [Spixiana, Suppl.]. Vol. 1 (March 31, 1978)-. German (English and French). ir. DM80.00. Verlag Dr Friedrich Pfeil, PO Box 65 00 86, W-8000 Munich 65 Germany. **Tel** (0043)89-8888196, FAX (0043)89-8341873. **ED** E J Fittkau and M Baehr. **LC** QL1; .S8782. **DD** 590/.5. **CODEN** SPSUDG. Index available. cum. index. **Circ:** 400 (ctrl). Documents available from BIOSIS Document Express.
**Desc:** Covers zoological systematics, with emphasis in morphology, phylogeny, zoogeography, and ecology.
**Ind/Abst** Biol. Abstr.; Life Sci. Collect.

DK/0375-2909
**STEENSTRUPIA.** [Steenstrupia]. Vol. 1, No. 1 (Nov. 2, 1970)-. Monographic series. English. an. Price varies per volume. Steenstrupia, Universitetsparken 15, DK-2100 Copenhagen Denmark. **Tel** 31 35 41 11. **ED** Henrik Enghoff. **LC** QL1; .S8834. **DD** 591/.05. **CODEN** STRUB3. Index available. **Circ:** 500 (ctrl). Documents available from BIOSIS Document Express.
**Desc:** Journal of systematic zoology. Accepts papers by staff members of Zoologisk Museum, Copenhagen, and/or mainly based on Zoologisk Museum's collections.
**Ind/Abst** Biol. Abstr.; Life Sci. Collect.

RU
**STROITELSTVO GELMINTOLOGICHESKOI NAUKI I PRAKTIKI V SSSR. Added/Corp** Akademiia Nauk SSSR. Gelmintologicheskaia Laboratoriia. Vol. 1 (1962)-. Academic Scholarly Publication. Russian. Izdatelstvo Nauka / Akademiia Nauk, Publishing House of the Russian Academy of Sciences, Leninskii Porspekt 14, 117901 Moscow Russia. **Tel** 011 95 954-21-53, FAX 011 95 938-21-44, telex 411964.

NE/0165-0521
**STUDIES ON NEOTROPICAL FAUNA AND ENVIRONMENT.** [Stud. neotrop. environ.]. Vol. 11 (June 1976)-. Periodical. English (French, German, Portuguese and Spanish; summaries and/or abstracts in French, Spanish, Portuguese, German and English). qt. Fl454.00. Swets & Zeitlinger BV, Heereweg 347B PO Box 825, 2160 SZ Lisse Holland. **Tel** 011 31 2521 35111, FAX 02521-15888, telex 41325. **(Subscription address:** Swets Publishing Service, PO Box 825, 2160 SZ Lisse The Netherlands**) ED** E J Fittkau. **LC** QL235; .S85. **DD** 591.9/8. **CODEN** SNFEDP. **[CCC]. Bk Rev. Ad Acc. Circ:** 600. Documents available from The Genuine Article, BIOSIS Document Express. ***Continues*** *Studies on the Neotropical Fauna.*
**Desc:** International journal dealing with the ecology, systematics and distribution of the neotropical fauna. The Journal publishes original contributions showing such integrated approach, to the advantage of our knowledge of the neotropical fauna.
**Ind/Abst** AGRICOLA; Biol. Abstr.; Curr. Aware. Biol. Sci., CABS; Curr. Contents, Agric. Biol. Environ. Sci.; Ecol. Abstr.; Ecology Abstr.; Entomol. Abstr.; Fish Rev.; Geol. Abstr.; Helminthol. Abstr. (19??-19??); Life Sci. Collect.; Res. Alert [Select. Cov.]; Rev. Med. Vet. Entomol.; Soils Fert.; Wildl. Rev.

NE/0166-5189
**STUDIES ON THE FAUNA OF CURACAO AND OTHER ISLANDS.** (STUDIES ON THE FAUNA OF CURACAO AND OTHER CARIBBEAN ISLANDS.). [Stud. fauna Curacao other isl.]. Vol. 1 (June 1953)-. Periodical. English. Foundation for Scientific Research in Surinam and the Netherlands, c/o Zoological Lab, Plompetorengrachi 9-11, 3512 CA Utrecht Netherlands. **Tel** 030-392478. **ED** L J Westermann-Van der Steen and P Wagenaar Hummelinck. **LC** QH7; .N2842 subser. **DD** 591.9/428. **Circ:** 500. ***Continues*** *Studies of the Fauna of Curacao, Aruba, Bonaire and the Venezuelan Islands.*
**Desc:** Zoological research on the Caribbean Islands, emphasis on the Netherlands Antilles, but also includes tropical American mainland. The articles deals with species occurring also on the islands.
**Ind/Abst** AGRICOLA; Fish Rev.; Wildl. Rev.

US
**SUPPLEMENT TO ... JOURNAL OF NEMATOLOGY. Added/Corp** Society of Nematologists. **VFOAT** Supplement to the Journal of Nematology; Annals of Applied Nematology. Vol. 21, No. 4S (Oct. 1989)-. English. Society of Nematologists, 700 Experiment Station Road, University of Florida, Lake Alfred Fl 33850. **Tel** (813)956-1151. ***Continues*** *Annals of Applied Nematology.*

IT
**SUPPLEMENTO ALLE RICERCHE DI BIOLOGIA DELLA SELVAGGINA / LABORATORIO DI ZOOLOGIA APPLICATA ALLA CACCIA. Added/Corp** Laboratorio di Zoologia Applicata alla Caccia (Bologna, Italy) Istituto Nazionale di Biologia della Selvaggina (Italy) Istituto Nazionale di Biologia della Selvaggina "Alessandro Ghigi.". Vol. 7 (1976)-. Monographic series. Italian (English, French and German). Institute Nazionale per la Fauna Selvatica, Via Fornacetta 9, 40064 Bologna Italy. **Tel** 051 798746, FAX 051 796628. **ED** Mario Spagnesi. **LC** QL1; .B6 Suppl. Index available. cum. index. ctrl circ. ***Continues*** *Supplemento alle Ricerche di Zoologia Applicata alla Caccia, 0375-149X.*

KE
**SWARA / EAST AFRICAN WILD LIFE SOCIETY.** Vol. 1, No. 1 (July-Aug. 1978)-. Periodical. English. bm. Sh190.00 Kenya; $22.00 US. East African Wildlife Society, Keith Tucker Chief American Representative, PO Box 82002, San Diego CA 92138. **Tel** (619)225-1233, FAX (619)226-4003, telex 4950610. **ED** Shereen Karmali. **LC** QL337.E25; S94. **DD** 333.95/416/0968. **Bk Rev. Ad Acc. Circ:** 15,000 (ctrl).

UK/0084-5612
**SYMPOSIA OF THE ZOOLOGICAL SOCIETY OF LONDON.** [Symp. Zool. Soc. London]. **Added/Corp** Zoological Society of London. **VFOAT** Zoological Society of London Symposia. No. 1 (1960)-. Monographic series. English. ir. Price varies per volume. Oxford University Press, Walton Street, Oxford OX2 6DP England. **Tel** 011 44 865 56767, FAX 011 44 865 267773, telex 837330 OXPRES G. **(Subscription address:** Oxford University Press / USA, Journals Marketing Department, Oxford University Press, 2001 Evans Road, Cary NC 27513.**) LC** QL1; .Z733. **DD** 591. **NLM** W1 SY432Q. **CODEN** SZSLAM. Documents available from BIOSIS Document Express, CASDDS.
**Ind/Abst** Biol. Abstr.; Chem. Abstr.; GeoRef; Index Vet.; Key Word Index Wildl. Res.; Life Sci. Collect.; Wildl. Rev.

UK/0082-1101
**SYNOPSES OF THE BRITISH FAUNA.** [Synop. Br. fauna]. **Added/Corp** Linnean Society of London. No. 1 (1944)-. Monographic series. English. ir. Price varies per volume. Universal Book Services, Warmonderweg 80, 2341 KZ Oegstgeest Netherlands. **Tel** 011 31 71 170208. **DD** 591. **CODEN** SBFSDH. Index available. **Bk Rev. Ad Acc.** ctrl circ. Documents available from BIOSIS Document Express.
**Ind/Abst** Biol. Abstr.; GeoRef.

US
**SYNOPSIS OF THE HERPETOFAUNA OF MEXICO.** V. 1- 1971-. Monographic series. English. ir. Price varies per volume. John Johnson Books, Rural Free Delivery, #1 Box 513, North Bennington VT 05257. **Tel** (802)442-6738. **ED** Hobart M Smith and Rozella B Smith. **Circ:** 5,000.
**Desc:** A series of books intended for the serious herpetologist.

US
**SYSTEMA HELMINTHUM.** (1958)-. English. Interscience Publishers, 605 3rd Avenue, New York NY 10016. **LC** QL386; .Y3. **DD** 595.1.

NE/0165-5752
**SYSTEMATIC PARASITOLOGY.** [Syst. parisitol.]. **Added/Corp** Junk (W.) (FIRM). Vol. 1 (Sept. 1979)-. Periodical. English. Nine times a year. $1,047.00. Kluwer Academic Publishers, Postbus 322, 3300 AH Dordrecht, The Netherlands. **Tel** 011 (31) 78 524400, FAX 011 31 78 183273, telex 20083. **ED** D I Gibson. **LC** QL757; .S94. **DD** 591.5/249. **NLM** W1 SY696. **CODEN** SYPAD4. **[CCC]. Ad Acc. Pr Rev. Acid Free. Circ:** 350. available on microfilm and microfiche from University Microfilms International (UMI). Documents available from The Genuine Article, BIOSIS Document Express.
**Desc:** Publishes papers on the systematics, taxonomy and nomenclature of the following groups: nematoda (including plant-parasitic), monogenea, digenea, cestoda, acanthocephala, aspidogastrea, cestodaria, arthropoda (parasitic copepods, hymenopterans, mites, ticks, etc.), protozoa (parasitic groups) and parasitic genera in other groups (mollusca, turbellaria, etc.)
**Ind/Abst** AGRICOLA [Select. Cov.]; Biol. Abstr.; Curr. Aware. Biol. Sci., CABS; Curr. Contents, Agric. Biol. Environ. Sci.; Helminthol. Abstr. (19??-19??); Index Vet.; Microbiol. Abstr. Sect. B; Microbiol. Abstr. Sect. C; Nematol. Abstr.; Protozoolog. Abstr.; Ref. Upd. Deluxe Ed.; Res. Alert [Full Cov.]; Rev. Agric. Entomol.; Rev. Med. Vet. Entomol.; Sci. Cit. Index; SCISEARCH; Trop. Dis. Bull.

US/0892-6476
**TALON (AURORA, COLO.).** (TALON.). [Talon]. **Added/Corp** Raptor Education Foundation (Aurora, Colo.). (Spring 1985)-. Periodical. English. Three times a year. $20.00 Comes with Raptor Education Foundation Active membership. Raptor Education Foundation, 21901 East Hampden Avenue, Aurora CO 80013. **Tel** (303)680-8500, FAX (303)680-8500. **ED** Sherrie York and Peter Reshetniail. **DD** 598. **Bk Rev.** (Qty: 4-6). **Circ:** 1,000 (ctrl).
**Desc:** Membership newsletter containing information about raptors and environmental concerns.

US/0098-6860
**TECHNICAL NOTE (UNITED STATES. BUREAU OF LAND MANAGEMENT).** (TECHNICAL NOTE / U.S. DEPARTMENT OF THE INTERIOR, BUREAU OF LAND MANAGEMENT.). **VAT** Technical Note - Bureau of Land Management, United States Department of the Interior. Monographic series. English. Price varies per volume. Denver Service Center, Federal Center Building 50, Denver CO 80225. **LC** QL84.2; .U54A. **DD** 639/.9/0973.

JA
**TENNEN KINENBUTSU NARA NO SHIKA CHOSA HOKOKU. Added/Corp** Kasuga Kenshokai. **VFOAT** Nara No Shika Chosa Hokoku. (1974)-. Japanese. Kasuga Kenshokai, 160 Kasugano, Nara 630 Japan. **LC** QL737.U55; T46.

CI/0495-4025
**THALASSIA JUGOSLAVICA.** [Thalassia Jugosl.]. **Added/Corp** Centar za Istrazivange Mora. Jugoslavenska Akademija Znanosti i Umjetnosti. Bioloski Institut. Vol. 1 (1956)-. Academic Scholarly Publication. Serbo-Croatian (Roman) (English and German). Four times a year. $80.00. Ruder Boskovic Institute, Zagreb Labs, PO Box 1016, Zagreb Croatia. **LC** QL1; .T45. **CODEN** THJUAP. Documents available from BIOSIS Document Express, CASDDS.
**Ind/Abst** Aquat. Sci. Fish. Abstr. (Computer File); Biol. Abstr.; Chem. Abstr.; Energy Res. Abstr. (July 1976-); Life Sci. Collect.

GW
**THESES ZOOLOGICAE.** (1981)-. Monographic series. English (German). ir (one volume per year). Price varies per volume. Koeltz Scientific Books, PO Box 1360, D 61453 Koenigstein Germany. **Tel** 011 49 6174 4492, 3189, FAX 011 49 6174 1634. **ED** Ronald Fricke. Index available. **Bk Rev. Circ:** 300.
**Desc:** Series of zoological monographs (taxonomic and systematic).
**Ind/Abst** Rev. Med. Vet. Entomol.

GW/0342-3018
**TIERFREUND NURNBERG. See** Children and Youth Interests.

FR
**TRAITE DE ZOOLOGIE.** Vol. 1 (1948)-. Monographic series. French. ir. Price varies per volume. Scientific & Medical Publishers of France, 100 East 42nd Street, Suite 1002, New York NY 10017-5613. **Tel** (212)983-6278. **ED** Pierre P. Grasse.

US/0418-7598
**TRANSACTIONS - DESERT BIGHORN COUNCIL. See** Environmental Issues-Conservation and Natural Resources.

JA/0037-3680
**TRANSACTIONS OF THE SHIKOKU ENTOMOLOGICAL SOCIETY.** [Trans. Shikoku Entomol. Soc.]. **VFOAT** Shikoku Konchu Gakkai Kaiho. Began with issue for Jan. 1950. English. sa. Shikoku Konchu Gakkai, (Shikoku Entomological Society), Ehime Daigaku Nogakubu, Konchugaku Kyoshitsu, 5-7, Tarumi 3 Chome, Matsuyamashi, Ehimeken 790, Japan. **(Subscription address:** Japan Publications Trading Company, Ltd., PO Box 5030, Tokyo International, Tokyo 100-31 Japan.**)** **LC** QL461; .T73. **CODEN** TSHEAA. Documents available from BIOSIS Document Express.
**Ind/Abst** AGRICOLA; Biocont. News Inf. (1991-); Biol. Abstr.; Entomol. Abstr.; For. Abstr.; Life Sci. Collect.; Rev. Agric. Entomol.

FR
**TRAVAUX DE LA STATION MARINE DE VILLEFRANCHE-SUR-MER. Main/Corp** Station Marine de Villefranche-Sur-Mer. No. 40- 1975-. French (English). an. C E R O B, Bibliotheque, Station Zoologique, BP 28, 06230 Villefranche-Sur-Mer France. **Tel** 93 76 37 82. ***Continues** Travaux de la Station Zoologique de Villefranche-sur-Mer.*

IT/0394-6975
**TROPICAL ZOOLOGY. Added/Corp** Centro di Studio Per la Faunistica ed Ecologia Tropicali (Italy). Vol. 1, No. 1 (June 1988)-. Periodical. English. sa. L100000. Mozzon Giuntina SPA, Via Mannelli 29R, 50136 Florence, Italy. **Tel** 011 39 55 2476781, FAX 055/2478568. **LC** QL109; .T76. **DD** 591.909/3/05. **CODEN** TRZOEP. Documents available from BIOSIS Document Express. ***Continues** Monitore Zoologico Italiano. Supplemento, 0374-9444.*
**Ind/Abst** Biol. Abstr. (1989-); Entomol. Abstr.; Fish Rev.; Wildl. Rev.

AI/0371-6562
**TRUDY EREVANSKOGO ZOOVETERINARNOGO INSTITUTA.** (TRUDY EREVANSKOGO ZOOVETERINARNOGO INSTITUTA / MINISTERSTVO SELSKOKHOZIAISTVA SSSR : ARNIANSKII SELSKOKHOZIAISTVENNYI INSTITUT.). [Tr. Erevan. zoovet. inst.]. **Added/Corp** Erevanskii Zooveterinarnyi Institut. Armianskii Selkokhoziaistvennyi Institut. (1934)-. Russian. ir. **CODEN** TEZVAJ. Documents available from CASDDS.
**Ind/Abst** Chem. Abstr.; Poult. Abstr.

RU/0568-5524
**TRUDY GELMINTOLOGICHESKOI LABORATORII.** [Tr. Gelmintol. lab.]. **Main/Corp** Akademiia Nauk SSSR. Gelmintologicheskaia Laboratoriia. (1948)-. Academic Scholarly Publication. Russian. Izdatelstvo Nauka / Akademiia Nauk, Publishing House of the Russian Academy of Sciences, Leninskii Porspekt 14, 117901 Moscow Russia. **Tel** 011 95 954-21-53, FAX 011 95 938-21-44, telex 411964. **LC** QL392.
**Desc:** Information on worms and intestinal parasites.
**Ind/Abst** Helminthol. Abstr. (1991-); Index Vet.; Nematol. Abstr.; Plant Breed. Abstr.; Poult. Abstr.; Rev. Med. Vet. Entomol.; Rev. Plant Pathol.; Soils Fert.; Trop. Dis. Bull.; Wheat Barley Trit. Abstr.

RU/0135-5813
**TRUDY KOMI NAUCHNOGO TSENTRA URO AN SSSR / AKADEMIIA NAUK SSSR, URALSKOE OTDELENIE, KOMI NAUCHNYI TSENTR. Added/Corp** Akademiia Nauk SSSR. Komi Nauchnyi Tsentr. **VFOAT** Trudy Komi Nauchnogo Tsentra UrO Akademii Nauk SSSR. No. 89 (1987)-. Monographic series. Russian. Price varies per volume. ***Continues** Trudy Komi Filiala, 0568-6148.*
**Ind/Abst** Helminthol. Abstr. (1991-).

RU/0373-1278
**TRUDY VSESOIUZNOGO ENTOMOLOGICHESKOGO OBSHCHESTVA. Main/Corp** Vsesoiuznoe Entomologicheskoe Obshchestvo. Vol. 43 (1951)-. Academic Scholarly Publication. Russian. Izdatelstvo Nauka / Akademiia Nauk, Publishing House of the Russian Academy of Sciences, Leninskii Porspekt 14, 117901 Moscow Russia. **Tel** 011 95 954-21-53, FAX 011 95 938-21-44, telex 411964. Documents available from CASDDS. ***Continues** Trudy Russkago Entomologicheskogo Obshchesrva.*
**Ind/Abst** Chem. Abstr.; Cot. Trop. Fibr. Abstr. Bibliogr.; Rev. Med. Vet. Entomol.

RU/0206-0477
**TRUDY ZOOLOGICHESKOGO INSTITUTA.** [Tr. Zool. Inst.]. **Added/Corp** Zoologicheskii Institut (Akademiia Nauk SSSR). **VFOAT** Travaux de l'Institut Zoologique de l'Academie des Sciences de l'Urss. Vol. 1 (1932)-. Monographic series. Russian (English, German and Russian; summaries and/or abstracts in English, French, German and Russian). Price varies per volume. Izdatelstvo Nauka / Akademiia Nauk, Publishing House of the Russian Academy of Sciences, Leninskii Porspekt 14, 117901 Moscow Russia. **Tel** 011 95 954-21-53, FAX 011 95 938-21-44, telex 411964. **LC** QL1; .A4253. **NLM** W1 TR966. **CODEN** TZOIA4. Documents available from CASDDS. ***Continues** Zoologicheskii Muzei (Akademiia Nauk SSSR). Ezhegodnik Zoologicheskii Muzei.*
**Ind/Abst** Chem. Abstr. (?-1983); GeoRef; Helminthol. Abstr. (1991-); Potato Abstr.; Rev. Med. Vet. Entomol.; Soils Fert.

UK/0142-193X
**TSETSE AND TRYPANOSOMIASIS INFORMATION QUARTERLY.** [Tsetse trypanosomiasis inf. q.]. **Added/Corp** Tsetse and Trypanosomiasis Information and News Service. Centre for Overseas Pest Research. (1978)-. Periodical. English (French). Four times a year. £27.50. Natural Resources Institute, Central Avenue, Chatham Maritime, Chatham Kent ME4 4TB England. **Tel** 011 44 634 880088, FAX 0634 880066 77, telex 203907 8 LONG. **ED** J.M. Child. **NLM** ZWC 705 T879. Index available (published separately). **Circ:** 1,100 (ctrl).
**Desc:** Abstracts, bibliographic references and news items on all aspects of tsetse flies and human and animal trypanosomiasis in Africa.

US/0082-6782
**TULANE STUDIES IN ZOOLOGY AND BOTANY.** [Tulanne stud. zool. bot.]. **Added/Corp** Tulane University. Dept. of Biology. Vol. 15, No. 1 (Oct. 16, 1968)-. Periodical. English. Twice a year. $8.00. Tulane University / Department of Biology, New Orleans LA 70118. **Tel** (504)865-5191. **ED** Steven P. Darwin. **LC** QL1; .T94. **DD** 574/.05. **CODEN** TSZBAN. Index available. **Pr Rev. Circ:** 600. Documents available from BIOSIS Document Express. ***Continues** Tulane Studies in Zoology, 0090-9246.*
**Desc:** Ecology and taxonomy of plants and animals.
**Ind/Abst** Biol. Abstr.; Fish Rev.; Life Sci. Collect.; Wildl. Rev.

CC/0001-7302
**TUNG WU HSUEH PAO.** [Tung wu hsueh pao]. **Added/Corp** Chung-kuo Tung Wu Hsueh Hui. **VFOAT** Acta Zoologica Sinica. (19??)-. Academic Scholarly Publication. Chinese (summaries and/or abstracts in English, French and Russian). Four times a year. $89.00. Science Press, 16 Donghuangchenggen North Street, Beijing 100707, People's Republic of China. **Tel** 011 86 1 4019821, 011 86 1 4010642, FAX 011 86 1 4012180, 011 86 1 4019810, telex 210147. **(Subscription address:** China International Book Trading Corporation, PO Box 399, Library Service Department, Beijing 100044 People's Republic of China.**)** **LC** QL1; .T9426. **DD** 591/.05. **NLM** W1 TU724H. **CODEN** TWHPA3. available on microfilm from University Microfilms International (UMI). Documents available from BIOSIS Document Express, CASDDS.
**Ind/Abst** AGRICOLA; Aquat. Sci. Fish. Abstr. (Computer File); Biocont. News Inf.; Biol. Abstr.; Chem. Abstr.; Curr. Ref. Fish Res.; Ecol. Abstr.; Fish Rev. (Jan. 1989-July 1992); GeoRef; Helminthol. Abstr.; Life Sci. Collect.; Poult. Abstr.; Rev. Agric. Entomol.; Rev. Med. Vet. Entomol.; Soils Fert.; Wildl. Rev. (Jan. 1989-July 1992).

●US/1061-5776
**UNDERCURRENTS: MYSTIC MARINELIFE AQUARIUM QUARTERLY.** [Undercurrents]. **Added/Corp** Mystic Marinelife Aquarium. Vol. 1, No. 1 (Winter 1992)-. Periodical. English. qt. Mystic Marinelife Aquarium, Coogan Boulevard, Mystic CT 06355-1997. **DD** 597. ***Formed by the union of** Seaword, 0273-4168; **Seawatch and** Schoolword.*

US/0068-6506
**UNIVERSITY OF CALIFORNIA PUBLICATIONS IN ZOOLOGY.** [Univ. Calif. publ. zool.]. **Added/Corp** University of California, Berkeley. Vol. 3, No. 1 (1906)-. Academic Scholarly Publication. English. ir. Price varies per volume. University of California Press, 2120 Berkeley Way, Berkeley CA 94720. **Tel** (510)642-4191, (510)642-3907, FAX (510)642-9917. **DD** 591. **NLM** W1 UN937N. **Circ:** 1,250 (ctrl). Documents available from BIOSIS Document Express, CASDDS. ***Continues** University of California Publications. Zoology, 0068-6506.*
**Ind/Abst** Biol. Abstr.; Chem. Abstr.; GeoRef; Life Sci. Collect.; Trop. Dis. Bull.; Wildl. Rev.

II
**UTTAR PRADESH JOURNAL OF ZOOLOGY. Added/Corp** Uttar Pradesh Zoological Society. (19??)-. Periodical. English. sa. $40.00. Uttar Pradesh Zoological Society, Muzaffarnagar, India. **(Subscription address:** Prints India, 11 Darya Ganj, New Delhi 110002 India.**)** **LC** QL1; .U87. **DD** 590/.5.
**Ind/Abst** Biocont. News Inf. (1991-); For. Prod. Abstr. (1991-); For. Abstr.; Helminthol. Abstr. (1991-); Nematol. Abstr.; Rev. Agric. Entomol.; Rev. Med. Vet. Entomol.

US/0042-3211
**VELIGER, THE.** [Veliger]. **Added/Corp** California Malacozoological Society. Northern California Malacozoological Club. Vol. 1 (June 1958)-. Periodical. English. qt. $60.00 (institution), $32.00 (individual) US; $66.00 (institutions), $38.00 (individual) Canada and Mexico; $72.00 (institutions), $44.00 (individual) other. California Malacozoological Society, 2559 Puesta Del Sol Road, Santa Barbara CA 93105. **Tel** (805)682-4711. **ED** D. W. Phillips. **LC** QL401; .V4. **DD** 594/.09164. **NLM** W1 VE15K. **CODEN** VLGHAL. Index available (bound in issue). cum. index. **Bk Rev. Pr Rev. Circ:** 1,000. Documents available from The Genuine Article, BIOSIS Document Express.
**Desc:** Papers dealing with various aspects of mollusks, such as the ecology, reproduction, distribution, taxonomy, paleontology, microbiology, conchology, etc.
**Ind/Abst** Aquat. Sci. Fish. Abstr. (Computer File); Biol. Abstr.; Curr. Contents, Agric. Biol. Environ. Sci.; Ecology Abstr.; Ocean. Abstr.; Life Sci. Collect.; Res. Alert [Full Cov.]; Rev. Agric. Entomol.; Sci. Cit. Index; SCISEARCH; Soc. Sci. Cit. Index [Select. Cov.].

JA/0042-3580
**VENUS; JAPANESE JOURNAL OF MALACOLOGY. Added/Corp** Malacological Society of Japan. **VFOAT** Japanese Journal of Malacology; Kairuigaku Zasshi. (1948)-. Periodical. Japanese (English). qt (Mar., June, Sept., Dec.). $95.00. Nihon Kairui Gakkai, (Malacological Society. of Japan), Kokuritsu Kagaku, Hakubutsukan Bunkan, 23-1, Hyakunincho 3 Chome, Shinjukuku, Tokyoto 160, Japan. **(Subscription address:** Maruzen Company Ltd., PO Box 5050, Import & Export Department, Tokyo 100 31 Japan.**)** **ED** T. Okutani and S. Nishiwaki. **CODEN** KRZSA2. **Bk Rev. Circ:** 1,000 (ctrl). Documents available from BIOSIS Document Express. ***Continues** Japanese Journal of Malacology.*
**Desc:** Devoted to publishing original research papers, short notes, and relation to any field of sciences on the mollusc.
**Ind/Abst** Biol. Abstr.; Life Sci. Collect.

GW/0070-4342
**VERHANGLUNGEN DER DEUTSCHEN ZOOLOGISCHEN GESELLSCHAFT.** [Verh. Dtsch. Zool. Ges.]. **Main/Corp** Deutsche Zoologische Gesellschaft. **VFOAT** Verhandlungen der Zoologischen Gesellschaft; Zoologischer Anzeiger. Supplementband; Proceedings of the German Zoological Society. (1950)-. Academic Scholarly Publication. German (English). ir. Price varies per volume. Gustav Fischer Verlag Stuttgart, Postfach 720143, Wollgrasweg 49, D 70577 Stuttgart Germany. **Tel** 011 49 711 458030, FAX 0711-4580334, telex 2627-7111488. **(Subscription address:** VCH Publishers Inc., 303 Northwest 12th Avenue, Journals Department, Deerfield FL 33442.**)** **ED** H.-D. Phannenstiel. **CODEN** VDZGAN. **[CCC].** Documents available from CASDDS. ***Continues** Deutsche Zoologische Gesellschaft. Verhandlungen der Deutschen Zoologen, 0070-4342.*
**Ind/Abst** AGRICOLA (19??-); Agrofor. Abstr. (19??-); Chem. Abstr. (19??-); GeoRef (19??-); Helminthol. Abstr. (1991-); Index Vet. (19??-); Life Sci. Collect. (19??-); Protozoolog. Abstr. (19??-); Rev. Agric. Entomol. (19??-); Rev. Med. Vet. Entomol. (19??-).

UN/0084-5604
**VESTNIK ZOOLOGII.** (VESTNIK ZOOLOGII / AKADEMIIA NAUK UKRAINSKOI SSR, INSTITUT ZOOLOGII.). [Vestn. zool.]. **Added/Corp** Instytut Zoolohii (Akademiia Nauk Ukrainskoi RSR). **VFOAT** Zoological Record. (1967)-. Academic Scholarly Publication. Russian (summaries and/or abstracts in English; table of contents in English). bm. $89.95. Izdatelstvo Naukova Dumka / Ukrainian Academy of Sciences, Vladimirskaia Ulitsa 54, 252601 Kiev Ukraine. **Tel** 225-63-66, telex 131376. **(Subscription address:** East View Publications Inc., 3020 Harbor Lane North, Suite 110, Minneapolis MN 55447.**)** **NLM** W1 VE845B. **CODEN** VEZOAK. available on microfilm and microfiche from University Microfilms International (UMI). Documents available from BIOSIS Document Express, CASDDS.
**Ind/Abst** AGRICOLA; Biocont. News Inf. (1991-); Biol. Abstr.; Chem. Abstr.; Dairy Sci. Abstr.; Helminthol. Abstr.; Nematol. Abstr.; Life Sci. Collect.; Rev. Agric. Entomol.; Rev. Med. Vet. Entomol.; Weed Abstr.

BL/0102-5716
**VETERINARIA E ZOOTECNIA. See** Veterinary Sciences.

US/1047-2665
**VIVARIUM (LAKESIDE, CALIF.), THE.** (THE VIVARIUM.). [Vivarium]. **Added/Corp** American Federation of Herpetoculturists. Vol. 1, No. 1 (Winter 1988)-. Periodical. English. Six times a year. $26.00 (individuals members); $32.00 (foreign members); $46.00 (institutions members); $60.00 (sustaining members). American Federation of Herpetoculturists, PO Box 300067, Escondido CA 92030-0067. **Tel** (619)561-4948, FAX (619)747-5224. **LC** SF515; .V58. **DD** 639.3/9. **CODEN** VVRMET. **Ad Acc, Adv Mgr Tel** (619)747-4948. **Circ:** 8,000.
**Desc:** A national herpetocultural journal to document the accomplishments of herpetoculturists and to promote a general philosophy of herpetoculture whereby captive progagation can contribute to the conservation of biological diversity.

NE
**VOGELJAAR, HET.** Vol. 5 (1957)-. Academic Scholarly Publication. Dutch. Six times a year. Fl22.50. W A Werkman, Boterbloemstraat 20, 5321 BR Hedel Netherlands. **Tel** 011 31 4199 1967. ***Continues** Wiek en Sneb.*
**Ind/Abst** EMBASE; Fish Rev. (Jan. 1989-July 1992); Wildl. Rev. (Jan. 1989-July 1992).

GW/0049-6650
**VOGELWARTE, DIE.** [Vogelwarte]. **Added/Corp** Vogelwarte Helgoland. Vogelwarte Radolfzell. Deutsche Ornithologische Gesellschaft. Vol. 15 (Dec. 1948)-. Periodical. German. sa. $137.60. Verlagsdruckerei Schmidt GmbH, Nuernberger Strasse 27 31, D 91413 Neustadt Aisch Germany. **Tel** 011 49 9161 2028. ***Continues** Vogelzug.*
**Ind/Abst** Ecol. Abstr.; Fish Rev.; Geogr. Abstr. Phys. Geogr.; Key Word Index Wildl. Res.; Wildl. Rev.

GW
**VOGELWELT. BEIHEFT.** No. 1 (1968)-. Periodical. German. ir. Duncker und Humblot Verlag, Postfach 410329, D-12113 Berlin Germany. **Tel** 011 49 30 79000612, 011 49 30 79000613.

US/0199-221X
**WAS, WESTERN APICULTURAL SOCIETY JOURNAL.** [WAS., West. Apic. Soc. j.]. **Main/Corp** Western Apicultural Society of North America. **VFOAT** Western Apicultural Society Journal. V. 1- Apr. 1978-. Periodical. English. bm. $15.00 members, $5.00 nonmembers. WAS, 115 Court Street, Woodland CA 95695.

GW
**WELT DER TIERE, DIE.** Periodical. German. 23.40. Kilda-Verlag, Munsterstrasse 71, W-4402 Greven Germany. **LC** QL81.5; .W44.
**Ind/Abst** Life Sci. Collect.

US/0273-4419
**WHALEWATCHER.** (WHALEWATCHER : JOURNAL OF THE AMERICAN CETACEAN SOCIETY.). [Whalewatcher]. **Added/Corp** American Cetacean Society. American Cetacean Society. Los Angeles Chapter. (1967)-. Periodical. English. qt. $25.00 US; $35.00 other. American Cetacean Society, National Headquarters, PO Box 2639, San Pedro CA 90731. **Tel** (310)548-6279, FAX (213)548-6950. **ED** Beth Kneeland. **LC** QL737.C4; W45. **DD** 599.5/05. Index available. **Bk Rev. Ad Acc. Pr Rev. Circ:** 5,000 (ctrl).
**Desc:** A journal that reports on research and conservation of marine mammals, especially whales and dolphins.

GW
**WILDHALTUNG. Added/Corp** Bundesverband fur Landwirtschaftliche Wildhaltung. Deutscher Wildgehege-Verband. Osterreichischer Wildgehege-Verband. (1991)-. Periodical. German. bm. Verlag Eugen Ulmer, Postfach 700561, D 70574 Stuttgart Germany. **Tel** 011 49 711 4507108, FAX 011 49 711 4507120, telex 7-23634. ***Formed by the union of** Wildtiere in Gehegen, 0930-0856 **and** Landwirtschaftliche Wildhaltung, 0930-3006.*

US/1048-4949
**WILDLIFE CONSERVATION. See** Environmental Issues-Conservation and Natural Resources.

US/0084-0173
**WILDLIFE MONOGRAPHS.** [Wildl. monogr.]. **Added/Corp** Wildlife Society. (March 1958)-. Monographic series. English. ir. Price varies per volume. Wildlife Society, 5410 Grosvenor Lane, Bethesda MD 20814. **Tel** (301)897-9770, FAX (301)530-2471. **LC** QL1; .W54. **DD** 690/.05. **CODEN** WLMOAF. Documents available from The Genuine Article, BIOSIS Document Express, UMI Article Clearinghouse.
**Ind/Abst** Acad. Abstr. Full Text Elite (July 1990-); Acad. Abstr. (July 1990-); Acad. Search (July 1990-); AQUAREF; Biol. Abstr.; Curr. Aware. Biol. Sci., CABS; Curr. Contents, Agric. Biol. Environ. Sci.; Curr. Ref. Fish Res.; Ecol. Abstr.; Environ. Period. Bibliogr.; For. Abstr.; Gen. Sci. Source (Jul. 1990-); INFO-SOUTH Abstr.; Leis. Recreat. Tour. Abstr.; Mag. Artic. Summar. Elite (July 1990-); Mag. Artic. Summar. Select (July 1990-); Mag. Artic. Summar. CD-ROM (July 1990-); Mag. Search; Newsp. Period. Abstr. (1992-); Life Sci. Collect.; Res. Alert [Full Cov.]; Sci. Cit. Index; SCISEARCH; Stat. Theory Method Abstr. (1980-1981); Wildl. Rev.

AT/1035-3712
**WILDLIFE RESEARCH. Added/Corp** Commonwealth Scientific and Industrial Research Organization (Australia). Australian Academy of Science. Vol. 18, No. 1 (1991)-. Periodical. English. bm. 220.00Aus$ Australia & New Zealand; $220.00 other. CSIRO Publications, PO Box 89, 314 Albert Street, East Melborne Victoria 3002 Australia. **Tel** 011 61 3 4187333, 4187217, FAX 011 61 3 4190459, telex AA 30236. **ED** D.W. Morton. **LC** QL338; .A83. **DD** 599/.05/05. **CODEN** WRESEX. Index available (Bound into last issue of the current volume). **Ad Acc. Acid Free. Circ:** 900. available on microfilm and microfiche from University Microfilms International (UMI). Documents available from The Genuine Article, Documents on Demand. ***Continues** Australian Wildlife Research, 0310-7833.*
**Desc:** International journal for publication of original contributions on the biology and management of wild vertebrates (excluding fish). Papers include studies of animal habitats, biodiversity, ecology, ecophysiology, nutrition, reproductive biology, behavioural ecology, population dynamics, modelling, reviews, descriptions and assessments of field and laboratory techniques, and technical notes. Technical notes describe techniques or instrumentation, with detailed assessment.
**Ind/Abst** Curr. Aware. Biol. Sci., CABS; Environ. Abstr.; Index Vet.; Pig News Inf.; Res. Alert [Full Cov.]; Sci. Cit. Index; SCISEARCH; Zool. Rec.; Wildl. Rev. (199?-).

US/1042-511X
**WINGING IT.** (WINGING IT : NEWSLETTER OF THE AMERICAN BIRDING ASSOCIATION, INC.). [Winging it]. **Added/Corp** American Birding Association. Vol. 1, No. 1 (Jan. 1989)-. Periodical. English. Twelve times a year. $36.00 (individuals); $41.00 (institution); $43.00 (family) Comes with American Birding Association membership. American Birding Association, PO Box 6599, Colorado Springs CO 80934. **Tel** (719)578-1614, FAX (719)578-1480. **ED** Paul Lehman (editor's address: PO Box 1273, Goleta, CA 93116, phone: (805)967-2450). **DD** 598. **Ad Acc, Adv Mgr:** Susanna Lawson, **Tel** (804)983-3021. **Circ:** 13,000 (ctrl).
**Ind/Abst** Fish Rev. (Jan. 1989-July 1992); Wildl. Rev. (Jan. 1989-July 1992).

US/8756-4505
**WINGTIPS (LANSING, N.Y.).** ***Ceased.*** (WINGTIPS.). [Wingtips]. (1984)-Vol. 2, No. 3 ?. Periodical. English. qt. Bluestone Publishing, Box 226, Lansing NY 14882. **Tel** (607)533-7642. **ED** Helen S Lapham and Linda A Elligott. **LC** QL671; .W73. **DD** 598/.05. Index available. cum. index. **Bk Rev. Ad Acc. Circ:** 1,000.
**Desc:** Bridges the gap between amateur and professional ornithologists. Articles, announcements of grants/internships and meetings world-wide, recent research and endangered species updates.

US
**WOLF PARK NEWS. Added/Corp** North American Wildlife Park Foundation. (198?)-. Periodical. English. sa. North American Wildlife Park, Foundation Wolf Park, Battle Ground IN 47920. **Tel** (317)567-2265. ***Continues** Predator.*
**Ind/Abst** Biol. Dig.

US/0899-9317
**WOLVES AND RELATED CANIDS.** (March 1988)-. Periodical. English. qt. $25.00 US; $27.00 Canada; $30.00 other. Wolves and Related Canids, P.O.Box 1026, Agoura CA 91301. **Tel** (818)348-9451. **ED** Deborah Warrick. **DD** 599. **Bk Rev**, (Qty: 4-6). **Ad Acc. Circ:** 1,000 (ctrl).

US
**WORLD OF ANIMALS.** (19??)-. English. $99.95. National Geographic Society, 11555 Darnestown, Gaithersburg MD 20878. **Tel** (202)857-7000, (800)638-4077, FAX (202)429-5727, telex 64194 NATGEO. **(Subscription address:** National Geographic Society / CD-ROM Products, 1145 17th Street NW, Educational Media Division, Washington DC 20036.**)**

US/0884-6677
**Y.E.S. QUARTERLY.** [Y.E.S. q.]. **Added/Corp** Young Entomologists' Society. **VAT** Young Entomologists' Society Quarterly. Vol. 1, No. 1 (Winter 1984)-. Periodical. English. qt. $12.00, member Young Entomologist Society, $25.00 non-member US; $16.00, member Young Entomologist Society, $29.00 non-member Canada; $17.00 member Young Entomologis Society, $30.00 non-member other. Young Entomologists Society Inc, 1915 Peggy Place, Lansing MI 48910. **Tel** (517)887-0499. **ED** Gary A Dunn. **DD** 595. **CODEN** YESQES. Index available. cum. index. **Bk Rev**, (Qty: 8-12). **Ad Acc. Circ:** 300. ***Continues** TIEG, 0272-3077.*
**Desc:** Journal of amateur entomology intended for older youth (junior and senior high school) and adult amateur entomologists. Articles include insect collecting, outdoor projects, experiments, insect identification, and care of collections.

JA/0513-417X
**YADORIGA. VFOAT** Yadoriga. Japanese. Nihon Rinshi Gakkai, (Lepidopterological Soc. of Japan), c/o Ogata Byoin, 3-18, Imabashi, Higashiku, Osakashi, Osakafu 541, Japan. **LC** QL541; .Y33.

KO
**YANGBONGGYE. VFOAT** The Korean Bee Journal; Korean Bee Journal. Periodical. Korean (Korean). mo. 2.500. Yangbonggye SA, 29 Pongsan-dong, Taegu Korea 630. **LC** SF521; .Y33.

US/0098-2644
**YEARBOOK OF HERPETOLOGY. Added/Corp** Herpetological Information Search Systems. Herpetological Information Search Systems. HISS Yearbook of Herpetology. **VFOAT** HISS Yearbook of Herpetology. Vol. 1 (1974)-. English. an. DR Dowling, 26 Washington Place, New York University, New York NY 10003. **Tel** (212)598-3096. **LC** QL640; .Y42. **DD** 598.1/05.

US/0192-8031
**YELLOWSTONE GRIZZLY BEAR INVESTIGATIONS.** (YELLOWSTONE GRIZZLY BEAR INVESTIGATIONS : REPORT OF THE INTERAGENCY STUDY TEAM.). **Main/Corp** Interagency Grizzly Bear Study Team. English. an. US Department of the Interior / National Park Service, 1849 C Street NW, Room 3104, Washington DC 20240. **Tel** (202)208-4621, FAX (202)208-7520. **LC** QL737.C27; I54A. **DD** 599/.74446. available on microfiche (Vols. for (1985-) distributed to depository libraries).

●CN/1188-4584
**ZEBRA MUSSEL WATCH.** [Zebra mussel watch]. **Added/Corp** Ontario. Ministry of Natural Resources. **VFOAT** Moules Zebrees, Alerte. No. 1 (Jan. 1992)-. English (French). **DD** 594/.11.

GW
**ZEITSCHRIFT DER ARBEITSGEMEINSCHAFT OSTERRICHISCHER ENTOMOLOGEN.** Vol. 1 (1949)-. German. qt. $6.08. Lange and Springer GmbH and Company, Follerstr 2, POB 101610, W-5000 Cologne 1 Germany. **Tel** 011/49/221/20830, FAX 011/49/221/208323. **(Subscription address:** North America/ Journal Fulfillment Services, 44 Hartz Way, Secaucus, NJ 07094**)**

GW/0044-2291
**ZEITSCHRIFT FUER ANGEWANDTE ZOOLOGIE.** [Z. angew. Zool.]. (1954)-. Periodical. Multiple languages (English and German). qt. DM520.00. Duncker und Humblot Verlag, Postfach 410329, D-12113 Berlin Germany. **Tel** 011 49 30 79000612, 011 49 30 79000613. **NLM** W1 ZE232. **CODEN** ZANZA9. **[CCC].** Documents available from BIOSIS Document Express, CASDDS. ***Supersedes** Zeitschrift fur Hygienische Zoologie und Schadlingsbekampfung.*
**Ind/Abst** Biol. Abstr.; Chem. Abstr.; For. Abstr.; Index Vet.; Nutr. Abstr. Rev., Ser. B, Live Feeds and Feed.; PESTDOC; Postharvest News Inf.; Protozoolog. Abstr.; Rev. Agric. Entomol.; Rev. Med. Vet. Entomol.; Vet. Bull.

GW/0514-2563
**ZEITSCHRIFT FUER ANGEWANDTE ZOOLOGIE. BEIHEFTE.** No. 1-. Monographic series. German. Price varies per volume. Duncker und Humblot Verlag, Postfach 410329, D-12113 Berlin Germany. **Tel** 011 49 30 79000612, 011 49 30 79000613. **ED** H Kemper.
**Ind/Abst** Biocont. News Inf. (19??-19??); Helminthol. Abstr. (19??-19??); Key Word Index Wildl. Res.; Maize Abstr.; Poult. Abstr.; Rev. Med. Vet. Entomol.; Sorghum Mill. Abstr.

GW/0044-3468
**ZEITSCHRIFT FUER SAUGETIERKUNDE. See** Biology.

GW/0044-3565
**ZEITSCHRIFT FUER TIERPHYSIOLOGIE, TIERERNAHRUNG UND FUTTERMITTELKUNDE.** [Z. Tierphysiol., Tierernahr. Futtermittelkd.]. **VFOAT** Journal of Animal Physiology and Animal Nutrition. (Jan. 1958)-. Academic Scholarly Publication. English (German). Ten times a year. DM939.00 Europe; DM938.00 other. Blackwell Wissenschafts-Verlag, Kurfuerstendamm 57, D 10707 Berlin Germany. **Tel** 011 49 30 32790623, 011 49 30 32790624, FAX 011 49 30 327 90610. **ED** K.D. Guenther and M. Kirchgessner. **LC** SF95; .Z4. **DD** 636.08/5. **NLM** W1 ZE625K. **CODEN** ZTTFAA. Index Available in last issue of each volume--loose separately paged. cum. index. **Bk Rev. Ad Acc. Circ:** 2,500. Documents available from BIOSIS Document Express, CASDDS. ***Continues** Zeitschrift fuer Tierernahrung und Futtermittelkunde.*
**Ind/Abst** AGRICOLA; Biol. Abstr.; Chem. Abstr. (1958-1985)(19??-); Curr. Contents, Agric. Biol. Environ. Sci.; EMBASE; Energy Res. Abstr. (Jan. 1971-); Index Med.; Index Vet.; Nutr. Abstr. Rev., Ser. B, Live Feeds and Feed.; Nutr. Abstr. Rev., Ser. A, Hum. Exp.; Life Sci. Collect.; PESTDOC; Pig News Inf.; Potato Abstr.; Sug. Indus. Abstr.; Vet. Bull.; Wheat Barley Trit. Abstr.

GW/0044-3808
**ZEITSCHRIFT FUER ZOOLOGISCHE SYSTEMATIK UND EVOLUTIONSFORSCHUNG.** [Z. Zool. Syst. Evolutionsforsch.]. Vol. 1, No. 1/2 (May 1963)-. Periodical. German (English, French and German; summaries and/or abstracts in English and French). Four times a year. DM564.00 Europe; DM560.00 other. Blackwell Wissenschafts-Verlag, Kurfuerstendamm 57, D 10707 Berlin Germany. **Tel** 011 49 30 32790623, 011 49 30 32790624, FAX 011 49 30 327 90610. **ED** Heinrik Enghoff, Wolf Herre, Gunther Osche, Diether Sperlich. **LC** QL351; .Z4. **DD** 590/.12. **CODEN** ZZSEAA. **[CCC].** Index available. cum. index. **Bk Rev. Ad Acc. Pr Rev. Circ:** 2,500. Documents available from The Genuine Article, BIOSIS Document Express.
**Desc:** Publishes original articles on systematic zoology interlined with research on evolution. The aim is to synthesize the results from research in anatomy, morphology, animal geography, ecology, physiology, and genetics.
**Ind/Abst** Biol. Abstr.; CSA Neuro. Abstr. (?-?); Curr. Contents, Agric. Biol. Environ. Sci.; Curr. Ref. Fish Res.; Fish Rev.; GeoRef; Life Sci. Collect.; Res. Alert [Full Cov.]; Sci. Cit. Index; SCISEARCH; Wildl. Rev.

CH/0258-462X
**ZHONGHVA KUNCHONG.** (CHUNG-HUA KUN CHUNG.). [Zhonghua kunchong]. **VFOAT** Chinese

Journal of Entomology. (1981)-. Periodical. Chinese (English). qt. **LC** QL461. **DD** 595.7. **CODEN** CKUCEY. Documents available from BIOSIS Document Express.
**Ind/Abst** Biocont. News Inf.; Biol. Abstr. (1988-); Cot. Trop. Fibr. Abstr. Bibliogr.; Entomol. Abstr.; Hortic. Abstr.; Postharvest News Inf.; Rev. Agric. Entomol.; Soyabean Abstr.

BE/0044-5029
**ZOO ANVERS.** [Zoo Anvers]. **Added/Corp** Societe Royale de Zoologie d'Anvers. Oct. (1971)-. Periodical. French (French). qt. 420F. Societe Royale de Zoologie, 26 Koningin Astridplein, Antwerp 1 Belgium. **Tel** 011 32 323 116 40. **ED** F. J. Daman. **LC** QL77.A6; Z6. **Bk Rev. Ad Acc. Circ:** 21,000 (ctrl). Documents available from BIOSIS Document Express. ***Continues*** *Zoo d'Anvers, 0044-5029.*
**Ind/Abst** AGRICOLA; Biol. Abstr.; Wildl. Rev.

US/0733-3188
**ZOO BIOLOGY.** [Zoo biol.]. Vol. 1 (1982)-. Academic Scholarly Publication. English. Six times a year. $558.00 US; $618.00 Canada and Mexico; $640.50 other. John Wiley & Sons, Inc., 605 Third Avenue, New York NY 10158-0012. **Tel** (212)850-6000, (212)850-6645, FAX (212)850-6088, telex 12-7063. **(Subscription address:** John Wiley & Sons / England, Baffins Lane, Chichester, West Sussex PO19 1UD England.**) ED** Donald G. Lindburg. **LC** QL77.5; .Z66. **DD** 591. **NLM** W1; ZO57F. **CODEN** ZOBIDX. **[CCC]. Bk Rev. Pr Rev.** Documents available from The Genuine Article, CASDDS.
**Desc:** Concerned with reproduction, demographics, behavior, medicine, husbandry, management, conservation, and all empirical aspects of the exhibition and maintenance of wild animals in captive settings.
**Ind/Abst** AgBiotech News Inf.; Agric. Eng. Abstr. (1991-); Anim. Behav. Abstr.; Chem. Abstr.; Curr. Contents, Agric. Biol. Environ. Sci.; Curr. Primate Ref.; Curr. Ref. Fish Res.; Ecology Abstr.; Fish Rev.; Grasslands For. Abstr.; Helminthol. Abstr. (1991-); Index Vet.; Key Word Index Wildl. Res.; Nutr. Abstr. Rev., Ser. B, Live Feeds and Feed.; Life Sci. Collect.; Psychol. Abstr. (1982-); PsycINFO; PsycLit; Res. Alert [Select. Cov.]; SCISEARCH; Soyabean Abstr.; Vet. Bull.; Wildl. Rev.

US/0163-416X
**ZOO GOER, THE.** (THE ZOOGOER.). **Added/Corp** Friends of the National Zoo. (19??)-. Periodical. English. Six times a year (Jan., Mar., May, July, Sept., Nov.). $12.00. National Zoo, Fonz Membership Division, Washington DC 20008. **Tel** (202)673-4960, FAX (202)673-4738. **ED** Susan Lumpkin (phone: (202)673-4628). **Bk Rev**, (Qty: 5). **Ad Acc. Circ:** 27,000.
**Desc:** A color magazine that highlights the animals and people of the National Zoological Park in Washington DC.

US/1046-4565
**ZOO LIFE (LOS ANGELES, CALIF.).** ***Suspended.*** (ZOO LIFE.). [Zoo life]. Vol. 1, No. 1 (1989)-(Apr. 1993). Periodical. English. qt. Ingle Publishing Company, 11661 San Vicente Boulevard, Los Angeles CA 90049. **Tel** (310)820-8841. **DD** 590.
**Desc:** The only national, full-color periodical dedicated to zoos, aquariums and wildlife parks and their animals, conservation, aquatic innovations and dynamic wildlife exhibits coast to coast.

US/0276-3303
**ZOO VIEW.** [Zoo view]. Periodical. English. qt. $7.00 North America; $15.00 other. Greater Los Angeles Zoo Association, 5333 Zoo Drive, Los Angeles CA 90027. **Tel** (310)664-1100, FAX (310)662-6879. **ED** Leslie Croyder. **DD** 590. **Circ:** 50,000 (ctrl).
**Desc:** The purpose is to educate readers about exotic animals and to promote interest in the LA Zoo. Overall, the magazine aspires to encourage members to value and protect the wildlife of the world.

US/0737-9005
**ZOOBOOKS (SAN DIEGO, CALIF.).** (ZOOBOOKS.). [Zoobooks]. **VFOAT** Zoo Books. Vol. 1, No. 1 (Nov. 1983)-. Monographic series. English. mo. $16.95 (10 months), $29.90 (20 months). Wildlife Education Ltd, 9820 Willow Creek Road, Suite 300, San Diego CA 92131. **Tel** (619)578-2440, 800 992-5034, FAX (619)578-9658. **ED** John Bonnett Wexo. **DD** 591.
**Ind/Abst** Child. Mag. Guide; Mag. Artic. Summar. Elite (July 1989-); Mag. Artic. Summar. Select (July 1989-); Mag. Artic. Summar. CD-ROM (July 1989-); Mag. Search; Mid. Search (Jul. 1989-); Prim. Search (Jul. 1989-).

GW/0044-5088
**ZOOLOGICA.** [Zoologica (Stuttgart)]. Vol. 1 No. 1 (1887)-. Monographic series. German (English). Twice a year. $51.00-$150.00. E. Schweizerbartsche Verlagsbuchhandlung, Johannesstrasse 3A, D-70176 Stuttgart Germany. **Tel** 011 49 711 625001, FAX 011 49 711 625005, telex 723363 SCHB D. **ED** F Schaller. **CODEN** ZLGAAA. **[CCC]. Bk Rev.**
**Desc:** Provides a forum for original zoological contributions.

SA/0044-5096
**ZOOLOGICA AFRICANA.** ***Title Change.*** [Zool. afr.]. **Added/Corp** Zoological Society of Southern Africa. South Africa. Dept. of Education, Arts, and Science. Vol. 1 (Mar. 1965)-Vol. 13, No. 2 (19??). Periodical. English. sa. **NLM** W1 ZO605A. **CODEN** ZOOAA3. Documents available from CASDDS. ***Continued by*** *South African Journal of Zoology, 0254-1858.*
**Ind/Abst** Chem. Abstr.

PL/0044-510X
**ZOOLOGICA POLONIAE; ARCHIVUM SOCIETATIS ZOOLOGORUM POLONIAE.** [Zool. Pol.]. Vol. 1 (1935)-. Monographic series. Multiple languages (English, French, Polish, German and Italian; summaries and/or abstracts in Russian). Price varies per volume. **(Subscription address:** ARS Polona, PO Box 1001, 00068 Warsaw Poland.**) ED** Benedykt Fulinski, Jan Hirschler, and Gustaw Poluszynski. **LC** QL1; .Z63. **DD** 590.5. **CODEN** ZOPOAG. Documents available from CASDDS.
**Ind/Abst** AGRICOLA; Chem. Abstr.

US
**ZOOLOGICA RECORD / SECTION 13. INSECTA. SECTION A, GENERAL INSECTA AND SMALLER ORDERS.** (19??)-. English. ir. $163.00 (Vol. 130), $174.00 (Vol. 131). BioSciences Information Service, Biological Abstracts / BIOSIS, 2100 Arch Street, Philadelphia PA 19103-1399. **Tel** (800)523-4806 US, (215)587-4800 Pennsylvania and worldwide, FAX (215)587-2016, telex 831739.

UK/0300-3256
**ZOOLOGICA SCRIPTA.** [Zool. scr.]. **Added/Corp** Kungl. Svenska Vetenskapsakademien. Norske Videnskaps-Akademi i Oslo. Vol. 1 (1971)-. Periodical. English (French and German). qt. $418.00 The Americas; £280.00 other. Pergamon Press, An Imprint of Elsevier Science Ltd., The Boulevard, Langford Lane, Kidlington, Oxford OX5 1GB United Kingdom. **Tel** 011 44 865 843000, 011 44 865 843699, FAX 011 44 865 843010. **(Subscription address:** Elsevier Science Ltd. Oxford Fulfillment Centre, PO Box 800, Kidlington, Oxford OX5 1DX United Kingdom.**) ED** Marit Christiansen. **LC** QL1; .A552. **DD** 574/.05. **NLM** W1 ZO606BJ. **CODEN** ZLSCA8. **[CCC]. Bk Rev. Ad Acc. Pr Rev.** available on microfilm and microfiche from University Microfilms International (UMI). Documents available from The Genuine Article. ***Supersedes*** *Arkiv for Zoologi;* ***Absorbed*** *Norwegian Journal of Zoology, 0029-6864.*
**Ind/Abst** Biocont. News Inf.; Curr. Aware. Biol. Sci., CABS; Curr. Contents, Agric. Biol. Environ. Sci.; Curr. Ref. Fish Res.; Ecol. Abstr.; GeoRef; Helminthol. Abstr. (19??-19??); Nematol. Abstr.; Life Sci. Collect.; Res. Alert [Full Cov.]; Rev. Agric. Entomol.; Rev. Med. Vet. Entomol.; Sci. Cit. Index; SCISEARCH.

UK/0024-4082
**ZOOLOGICAL JOURNAL OF THE LINNEAN SOCIETY.** [Zool. j. Linn. Soc.]. **Main/Corp** Linnean Society of London. Vol. 48 (Feb. 1969)-. Academic Scholarly Publication. English. mo. $665.00. Academic Press Ltd., A Division of Harcourt Brace & Company Ltd., 24-28 Oval Road, London NW1 7DX England. **Tel** 071 267 4466, FAX 071 482 2293, 071 485 4752, telex 25775 ACPRES G. **(Subscription address:** Harcourt Brace & Company, Ltd., Foots Cray, High Street, Sidcup Kent DA14 5HP England.**) ED** D. B. Norman. **LC** QH1; .L54. **DD** 591/.05. **NLM** W1 ZO607. **CODEN** ZJLSA7. **[CCC]. Pr Rev.** Documents available from The Genuine Article, BIOSIS Document Express. ***Continues*** *Journal of the Linnean Society of London. Zoology.*
**Desc:** Publishes original papers on zoology with an emphasis on the diversity, systematics, interrelationships, and habits of animals both living and extinct. However, papers often impinge closely on related disciplines in agriculture, fisheries, forestry, parasitology, medicine, and veterinary science. This important, long-established, and respected forum has a wide circulation among zoologists, and while narrowly specialized papers are not automatically excluded, the editor fosters submissions that bear this broad readership in mind.
**Ind/Abst** AGRICOLA; Biol. Abstr.; Curr. Contents, Agric. Biol. Environ. Sci.; Curr. Ref. Fish Res.; Ecol. Abstr. (?-?); Ecology Abstr.; EMBASE; Fish Rev.; Key Word Index Wildl. Res.; Life Sci. Collect.; Res. Alert [Full Cov.]; Rev. Agric. Entomol.; Sci. Cit. Index; SCISEARCH; Wildl. Rev.

US/0740-7610
**ZOOLOGICAL PARKS AND AQUARIUMS IN THE AMERICAS.** Began with 1978-79. English. be. $30.00 (schools and libraries), $50.00 (nonmembers). American Association of Zoological Parks and Aquariums, Oglebay Park, Wheeling WV 26003. **Tel** (304)242-2160, FAX (304)242-2283. **ED** Linda Boyd. **LC** QL76; .Z74. **DD** 590/.74/47. **Ad Acc. Circ:** 2,500. ***Continues*** *Zoos & Aquariums in the Americas.*

CH
**ZOOLOGICAL RECORD.** (199?)-. Academic Scholarly Publication. Chinese (summaries and/or abstracts in English). Four times a year. $120.00. Institute of Zoology, Academia Sinica, Nankang, Taipei Taiwan 115. **(Subscription address:** Wei-Ming Book Co. Ltd., 10/F-2, No. 149 Roosevelt Road, Sec. 3, PO Box 592, Taipei Taiwan 10770.**) ED** Jen-Leih Wu (Chief Editor). **LC** QL307.2. **UDC** 59(529.1). **CODEN** BIZYAS. Index available. cum. index. **Pr Rev.** ctrl circ. Documents available from The Genuine Article, CASDDS. ***Continues*** *Bulletin of the Institute of Zoology, Academia Sinica, 0001-3943.*
**Desc:** Welcomes original articles and researches of experimental, descriptive, or analytical nature, including investigations of all levels of zoological organization from the molecular to the population.
**Ind/Abst** Biocont. News Inf.; Biol. Abstr.; Chem. Abstr.; Curr. Aware. Biol. Sci., CABS; Curr. Ref. Fish Res.; Entomol. Abstr.; Fish Rev. (199?-); Hortic. Abstr.; Protozoolog. Abstr.; Res. Alert [Full Cov.]; Rev. Agric. Entomol.; Zool. Rec.; Wildl. Rev.

UK
**ZOOLOGICAL RECORD : BEING RECORDS OF ZOOLOGICAL LITERATURE, SECTION 7. BRACHIOPODA.** (19??)-. Periodical. English. an. $64.00 (Vol. 130), $69.00 (Vol. 131). BioSciences Information Service, Biological Abstracts / BIOSIS, 2100 Arch Street, Philadelphia PA 19103-1399. **Tel** (800)523-4806 US, (215)587-4800 Pennsylvania and worldwide, FAX (215)587-2016, telex 831739. available in microform.
**Desc:** Index of brachiopoda literature.

UK
**ZOOLOGICAL RECORD: BEING RECORDS OF ZOOLOGICAL LITERATURE, SECTION 10. CRUSTACEA.** (19??)-. Periodical. English. ir. $152.00 (Vol. 130), $162.00 (Vol. 131). BioSciences Information Service, Biological Abstracts / BIOSIS, 2100 Arch Street, Philadelphia PA 19103-1399. **Tel** (800)523-4806 US, (215)587-4800 Pennsylvania and worldwide, FAX (215)587-2016, telex 831739.
**Desc:** Index of crustacea literature.

UK/0144-3607
**ZOOLOGICAL RECORD (LONDON). See** Zoology-Abstracting, Bibliographies and Statistics.

●US/1072-1983
**ZOOLOGICAL RECORD ON CD. See** Zoology-Abstracting, Bibliographies and Statistics.

US/1053-802X
**ZOOLOGICAL RECORD SEARCH GUIDE, THE.** [Zool. rec. search guide]. **Added/Corp** BioSciences Information Service of Biological Abstracts. **VFOAT** Search Guide. (1985)-. English. ir. $75.00. BioSciences Information Service, Biological Abstracts / BIOSIS, 2100 Arch Street, Philadelphia PA 19103-1399. **Tel** (800)523-4806 US, (215)587-4800 Pennsylvania and worldwide, FAX (215)587-2016, telex 831739. **LC** Z699.5.Z66; Z66. **DD** 025.06591.
**Desc:** Reference tool to support users of Zoological Record and its online version.

US
**ZOOLOGICAL RECORD / SECTION 1. COMPREHENSIVE ZOOLOGY.** (19??)-. English. ir. $88.00 (Vol. 130), $95.00 (Vol. 131). BioSciences Information Service, Biological Abstracts / BIOSIS, 2100 Arch Street, Philadelphia PA 19103-1399. **Tel** (800)523-4806 US, (215)587-4800 Pennsylvania and worldwide, FAX (215)587-2016, telex 831739.

US
**ZOOLOGICAL RECORD / SECTION 2. PROTOZOA.** (19??)-. English. ir. $192.00 (Vol. 130), $205.00 (Vol. 131). BioSciences Information Service, Biological Abstracts / BIOSIS, 2100 Arch Street, Philadelphia PA 19103-1399. **Tel** (800)523-4806 US, (215)587-4800 Pennsylvania and worldwide, FAX (215)587-2016, telex 831739.

US
**ZOOLOGICAL RECORD / SECTION 3. PORIFERA & ARCHAEOCYATHA.** (19??)-. English. ir. $64.00 (Vol. 130), $69.00 (Vol. 131). BioSciences Information Service, Biological Abstracts / BIOSIS, 2100 Arch Street, Philadelphia PA 19103-1399. **Tel** (800)523-4806 US, (215)587-4800 Pennsylvania and worldwide, FAX (215)587-2016, telex 831739.

US
**ZOOLOGICAL RECORD / SECTION 4. COELENTERATA & CTENOPHORA.** (19??)-. English. ir. $70.00 (Vol. 130), $75.00 (Vol. 131). BioSciences Information Service, Biological Abstracts / BIOSIS, 2100 Arch Street, Philadelphia PA 19103-1399. **Tel** (800)523-4806 US, (215)587-4800 Pennsylvania and worldwide, FAX (215)587-2016, telex 831739.

US
**ZOOLOGICAL RECORD / SECTION 5. ECHINODERMATA.** (19??)-. English. ir. $64.00 (Vol. 130), $69.00 (Vol. 131). BioSciences Information Service, Biological Abstracts / BIOSIS, 2100 Arch Street, Philadelphia PA 19103-1399. **Tel** (800)523-4806 US, (215)587-4800 Pennsylvania and worldwide, FAX (215)587-2016, telex 831739.

# Zoology

**US**
**ZOOLOGICAL RECORD / SECTION 6. WORMS AND FOSSIL MISCELLANEA, SECTION A. PLATYHELMINTHES AND NEMATODA TOGETHER WITH NEMERTINEA, MESOZOA, NEMATOMORPHA, ACANTHOCEPHALA AND PLACOZOA.** (19??)-. English. ir. $192.00 (Vol. 130), $205.00 (Vol. 131). BioSciences Information Service, Biological Abstracts / BIOSIS, 2100 Arch Street, Philadelphia PA 19103-1399. **Tel** (800)523-4806 US, (215)587-4800 Pennsylvania and worldwide, FAX (215)587-2016, telex 831739.

**US**
**ZOOLOGICAL RECORD / SECTION 6. WORMS AND FOSSIL MISCELLANEA, SECTION B. ANNELIDA TOGETHER WITH ROTIFERA, CHAETOGNATHA, ECHIURA, SIPUNCULA, GASTROTRICHA, KINORHYNCHA, PRIAPULIDA, GNATHOSTOMULIDA AND POGONOPHORA.** (19??)-. English. ir. $110.00 (Vol. 130), $117.00 (Vol. 131). BioSciences Information Service, Biological Abstracts / BIOSIS, 2100 Arch Street, Philadelphia PA 19103-1399. **Tel** (800)523-4806 US, (215)587-4800 Pennsylvania and worldwide, FAX (215)587-2016, telex 831739.

**US**
**ZOOLOGICAL RECORD / SECTION 6. WORMS AND FOSSIL MISCELLANEA, SECTION C. CONODONTA AND FOSSIL MISCELLANEA.** (19??)-. English. ir. $64.00 (Vol. 130), $69.00 (Vol. 131). BioSciences Information Service, Biological Abstracts / BIOSIS, 2100 Arch Street, Philadelphia PA 19103-1399. **Tel** (800)523-4806 US, (215)587-4800 Pennsylvania and worldwide, FAX (215)587-2016, telex 831739.

**US**
**ZOOLOGICAL RECORD / SECTION 8. BRYOZOA (POLYZOA) AND ENTROPROCTA.** (19??)-. English. ir. $64.00 (Vol. 130), $69.00 (Vol. 131). BioSciences Information Service, Biological Abstracts / BIOSIS, 2100 Arch Street, Philadelphia PA 19103-1399. **Tel** (800)523-4806 US, (215)587-4800 Pennsylvania and worldwide, FAX (215)587-2016, telex 831739.

**US**
**ZOOLOGICAL RECORD / SECTION 9. MOLLUSCA.** (19??)-. English. ir. $192.00 (Vol. 130), $205.00 (Vol. 131). BioSciences Information Service, Biological Abstracts / BIOSIS, 2100 Arch Street, Philadelphia PA 19103-1399. **Tel** (800)523-4806 US, (215)587-4800 Pennsylvania and worldwide, FAX (215)587-2016, telex 831739.

**US**
**ZOOLOGICAL RECORD / SECTION 11. TRILOBITOMORPHA.** (19??)-. English. $64.00 (Vol. 130), $69.00 (Vol. 131). BioSciences Information Service, Biological Abstracts / BIOSIS, 2100 Arch Street, Philadelphia PA 19103-1399. **Tel** (800)523-4806 US, (215)587-4800 Pennsylvania and worldwide, FAX (215)587-2016, telex 831739.

**US**
**ZOOLOGICAL RECORD / SECTION 12. ARACHNIDA TOGETHER WITH MYRIAPODA, MEROSTOMATA, PANTOPODA, TARDIGRADA, SYMPHYLIDA, PAUROPODA, ONYCHOPHORA, ARTHROPLEURIDA AND PENTASTOMIDA.** (19??)-. English. ir. $128.00 (Vol. 130), $136.00 (Vol. 131). BioSciences Information Service, Biological Abstracts / BIOSIS, 2100 Arch Street, Philadelphia PA 19103-1399. **Tel** (800)523-4806 US, (215)587-4800 Pennsylvania and worldwide, FAX (215)587-2016, telex 831739.

**US**
**ZOOLOGICAL RECORD / SECTION 13. INSECTA. SECTION B, COLEOPTERA.** (19??)-. English. ir. $192.00 (Vol. 130), $205.00 (Vol. 131). BioSciences Information Service, Biological Abstracts / BIOSIS, 2100 Arch Street, Philadelphia PA 19103-1399. **Tel** (800)523-4806 US, (215)587-4800 Pennsylvania and worldwide, FAX (215)587-2016, telex 831739.

**US**
**ZOOLOGICAL RECORD / SECTION 13. INSECTA. SECTION C, DIPTERA.** (19??)-. English. ir. $163.00 (Vol. 130), $174.00 (Vol. 131). BioSciences Information Service, Biological Abstracts / BIOSIS, 2100 Arch Street, Philadelphia PA 19103-1399. **Tel** (800)523-4806 US, (215)587-4800 Pennsylvania and worldwide, FAX (215)587-2016, telex 831739.

**US**
**ZOOLOGICAL RECORD / SECTION 13. INSECTA. SECTION D, LEPIDOPTERA.** (19??)-. English. ir. $163.00 (Vol. 130), $174.00 (Vol. 131). BioSciences Information Service, Biological Abstracts / BIOSIS, 2100 Arch Street, Philadelphia PA 19103-1399. **Tel** (800)523-4806 US, (215)587-4800 Pennsylvania and worldwide, FAX (215)587-2016, telex 831739.

**US**
**ZOOLOGICAL RECORD / SECTION 13. INSECTA. SECTION E, HYMENOPTERA.** (19??)-. English. ir. $135.00 (Vol. 130), $144.00 (Vol. 131). BioSciences Information Service, Biological Abstracts / BIOSIS, 2100 Arch Street, Philadelphia PA 19103-1399. **Tel** (800)523-4806 US, (215)587-4800 Pennsylvania and worldwide, FAX (215)587-2016, telex 831739.

**US**
**ZOOLOGICAL RECORD / SECTION 13. INSECTA. SECTION F, HEMIPTERA.** (19??)-. English. ir. $140.00 (Vol. 130), $150.00 (Vol. 131). BioSciences Information Service, Biological Abstracts / BIOSIS, 2100 Arch Street, Philadelphia PA 19103-1399. **Tel** (800)523-4806 US, (215)587-4800 Pennsylvania and worldwide, FAX (215)587-2016, telex 831739.

**US**
**ZOOLOGICAL RECORD / SECTION 14. PROTOCHORDATA.** (19??)-. English. ir. $64.00 (Vol. 130), $69.00 (Vol. 131). BioSciences Information Service, Biological Abstracts / BIOSIS, 2100 Arch Street, Philadelphia PA 19103-1399. **Tel** (800)523-4806 US, (215)587-4800 Pennsylvania and worldwide, FAX (215)587-2016, telex 831739.

**US**
**ZOOLOGICAL RECORD / SECTION 15. PISCES.** (19??)-. English. ir. $262.00 (Vol. 130), $280.00 (Vol. 131). BioSciences Information Service, Biological Abstracts / BIOSIS, 2100 Arch Street, Philadelphia PA 19103-1399. **Tel** (800)523-4806 US, (215)587-4800 Pennsylvania and worldwide, FAX (215)587-2016, telex 831739.

**US**
**ZOOLOGICAL RECORD / SECTION 16. AMPHIBIA.** (19??)-. English. ir. $105.00 (Vol. 130), $112.00 (Vol. 131). BioSciences Information Service, Biological Abstracts / BIOSIS, 2100 Arch Street, Philadelphia PA 19103-1399. **Tel** (800)523-4806 US, (215)587-4800 Pennsylvania and worldwide, FAX (215)587-2016, telex 831739.

**US**
**ZOOLOGICAL RECORD / SECTION 17. REPTILIA.** (19??)-. English. ir. $155.00 (Vol. 130), $165.00 (Vol. 131). BioSciences Information Service, Biological Abstracts / BIOSIS, 2100 Arch Street, Philadelphia PA 19103-1399. **Tel** (800)523-4806 US, (215)587-4800 Pennsylvania and worldwide, FAX (215)587-2016, telex 831739.

**US**
**ZOOLOGICAL RECORD / SECTION 18. AVES.** (19??)-. English. ir. $240.00 (Vol. 130), $255.00 (Vol. 131). BioSciences Information Service, Biological Abstracts / BIOSIS, 2100 Arch Street, Philadelphia PA 19103-1399. **Tel** (800)523-4806 US, (215)587-4800 Pennsylvania and worldwide, FAX (215)587-2016, telex 831739.

**US**
**ZOOLOGICAL RECORD / SECTION 19. MAMMALIA.** (19??)-. English. ir. $262.00 (Vol. 130), $280.00 (Vol. 131). BioSciences Information Service, Biological Abstracts / BIOSIS, 2100 Arch Street, Philadelphia PA 19103-1399. **Tel** (800)523-4806 US, (215)587-4800 Pennsylvania and worldwide, FAX (215)587-2016, telex 831739.

**US**
**ZOOLOGICAL RECORD / SECTION 20. LIST OF NEW GENERIC AND SUBGENERIC NAMES.** (19??)-. English. ir. $41.00 (Vol. 130), $44.00 (Vol. 131). BioSciences Information Service, Biological Abstracts / BIOSIS, 2100 Arch Street, Philadelphia PA 19103-1399. **Tel** (800)523-4806 US, (215)587-4800 Pennsylvania and worldwide, FAX (215)587-2016, telex 831739.

**US/1041-4657**
**ZOOLOGICAL RECORD SERIAL SOURCES.** [Zool. rec. ser. sources]. **Added/Corp** BioSciences Information Service of Biological Abstracts. (1987/88)-. English. an. $50.00. BioSciences Information Service, Biological Abstracts / BIOSIS, 2100 Arch Street, Philadelphia PA 19103-1399. **Tel** (800)523-4806 US, (215)587-4800 Pennsylvania and worldwide, FAX (215)587-2016, telex 831739. **LC** Z7991; .Z88; QL1. **DD** 016.591/05. **NLM** Z 7991; Z87. **CODEN** ZRSSEY.

**JA/0289-0003**
**ZOOLOGICAL SCIENCE.** [Zoo. sci.]. **Added/Corp** Nihon Dobutsu Gakkai. Vol. 1, No. 1 (Feb. 1984)-. Academic Scholarly Publication. English. bm. DM420.00. VSP International Science Publishers, Godfried van Seystlaan 47, 3703 BR Zeist Netherlands. **Tel** 011 31 3404 25790, FAX 011 31 3404 32081, telex 40217 USP NL. **(Subscription address:** VSP International Science Publishers, PO Box 346, 3700 AH Zeist Netherlands.) **ED** S. Kawashima and H. Kobayashi. **LC** QL1; .Z675. **DD** 591/.05. **NLM** W1; ZO607E. **CODEN** ZOSCEX. **[CCC]. Bk Rev. Ad Acc. Pr Rev. Circ:** 1,500. Documents available from The Genuine Article, CASDDS. *Formed by the union of* Dobutsugaku Zasshi, 0044-5118 and Annotationes Zoologicae Japonenses, 0003-5092.
**Desc:** The official journal of the Zoological Society of Japan. Publishes articles from the many subspecialties within zoology: biochemistry, physiology, endocrinology, and cell biology.
**Ind/Abst** AgBiotech News Inf.; Anim. Behav. Abstr.; Anim. Breed. Abstr.; Chem. Abstr. (1984-); Chemorecept. Abstr.; CSA Neuro. Abstr.; Curr. Aware. Biol. Sci.; CABS; Curr. Contents, Agric. Biol. Environ. Sci.; Curr. Contents Life Sci.; Curr. Ref. Fish Res.; Dairy Sci. Abstr.; Ecology Abstr.; Entomol. Abstr.; Genet. Abstr.; Helminthol. Abstr. (19??-19??); Index Vet.; Nematol. Abstr.; Nutr. Abstr. Rev., Ser. B, Live Feeds and Feed.; Life Sci. Collect.; Protozoolog. Abstr.; Res. Alert [Full Cov.]; Rev. Agric. Entomol.; Rev. Med. Vet. Entomol.; Sci. Cit. Index; SCISEARCH; SEA Abstr.

**CH/1021-5506**
**ZOOLOGICAL STUDIES.** (19??)-. Chinese. Four times a year. $120.00. Institute of Zoology, Academia Sinica, Nankang, Taipei Taiwan 115. **ED** Jen-Leih Wu. *Continues* Bulletin of the Institute of Zoology, Academia Sinica.

**RU/0044-5134**
**ZOOLOGICESKIJ ZURNAL.** (ZOOLOGICHESKII ZHURNAL.). [Zool. z.]. **Added/Corp** Russian S.F.S.R. Narodnyi Komissariat Prosveshcheniia. Sektor Nauki. Vol. 11, No. 1, (1932)-. Periodical. Russian (summaries and/or abstracts in English and German). mo. $259.00. Izdatelstvo Meditsina / Russian Academy of Medical Sciences, Ulitsa Solyanka 14, 109801 Moscow Russia. **Tel** 011 95 297-05-04. **(Subscription address:** East View Publications Inc., 3020 Harbor Lane North, Suite 110, Minneapolis MN 55447.) **CODEN** ZOLZAT. **[CCC]. Pr Rev.** Documents available from The Genuine Article, BIOSIS Document Express. *Continues* Russkii Zoologicheskii Zhurnal.
**Ind/Abst** AGRICOLA; Biocont. News Inf. (19??-19??); Biol. Abstr.; Curr. Ref. Fish Res.; Ecol. Abstr. (?-?); Ecology Abstr.; Fish Rev.; GeoRef; Helminthol. Abstr. (19??-19??); Maize Abstr.; Nematol. Abstr.; Ocean. Abstr.; Life Sci. Collect.; Protozoolog. Abstr.; Res. Alert [Full Cov.]; Rev. Agric. Entomol.; Rev. Med. Vet. Entomol.; Sci. Cit. Index; SCISEARCH; Soils Fert.; Wheat Barley Trit. Abstr.; Wildl. Rev.

**GW/0375-5231**
**ZOOLOGISCHE ABHANDLUNGEN / STAATLICHES MUSEUM FUER TIERKUNDE IN DRESDEN.** [Zool. Abh.]. **Main/Corp** Dresden. Staatliches Museum fur Tierkunde. Vol. 26, No. 1; March 24, 1961-. German (summaries and/or abstracts in English). ir. Staatliches Museum fuer Tierkunde Dresden, Augustusstrasse 2, D 01067 Dresden Germany. **CODEN** ZASMAT. **Bk Rev. Circ:** 750 (ctrl). Documents available from BIOSIS Document Express. *Continues in part* Abhandlungen und Berichte aus dem Staatlichen museum fur Tierkunde in Dresden, 0138-4147.
**Desc:** Taxonomy, systematics, morphology, anatomy, bionomics, ecology, zoogeography of the vertebrate groups in global range.
**Ind/Abst** Biol. Abstr.; Fish Rev.; Key Word Index Wildl. Res.; Life Sci. Collect.; Wildl. Rev.

**GW/0044-5150**
**ZOOLOGISCHE BEITRAEGE.** [Zool. Beitr.]. (1950)-. Periodical. German (summaries and/or abstracts in English). ir (3 issues). DM610.20. Duncker und Humblot Verlag, Postfach 410329, D-12113 Berlin Germany. **Tel** 011 49 30 79000612, 011 49 30 79000613. **ED** W. Dohle, G. Weigmann and I. Zerbst-Boroffka. **LC** QL1; .Z7593. **CODEN** ZOBEAI. **[CCC]. Circ:** 300. Documents available from BIOSIS Document Express. *Continues* Zoologische Beitrage.
**Desc:** Study of zoology.
**Ind/Abst** Biol. Abstr.; Life Sci. Collect.

**NE/0459-1801**
**ZOOLOGISCHE BIJDRAGEN.** **Suspended.** (ZOOLOGISCHE BIJDRAGEN / UITGEGEVEN DOOR HET RIJKSMUSEUM VAN NATUURLIJKE HISTORIE TE LEIDEN.). [Zool. bijdr.]. **Added/Corp** Rijksmuseum van Natuurlijke Historie te Leiden. Netherlands. Ministerie van Onderwijs, Kunsten en Wetenschappen. Nationaal Natuurhistorisch Museum (Netherlands). (1955)-Suspended. Monographic series. Dutch (English). ir. Price varies per volume. Museum Natuurlijk Historie, PO Box 321, AH 2300 Leiden Netherlands. **Tel** 011 31 71 143844. **(Subscription address:** Universal Book Services, Warmonderweg 80, 2341 KZ Oegstgeest

Netherlands.)
**Ind/Abst** Fish Rev. (Jan. 1989-July 1992); Life Sci. Collect.; Wildl. Rev. (Jan. 1989-July 1992).

BE/0563-1750
**ZOOLOGISCHE DOCUMENTATIE.** (DOCUMENTATION ZOOLOGIQUE / MUSEE ROYAL DE L'AFRIQUE CENTRALE / ZOOLOGISCHE DOCUMENTATIE / KONINKLIJK MUSEUM VOOR MIDDEN-AFRIKA.). [Zool. doc.]. **Added/Corp** Musee Royal de l'Afrique Centrale. **VFOAT** Zoologische Docementatie. No. 1 (1961)-. Monographic series. French (English and French). ir. Price varies per volume. Musee Royal de l'Afrique Centrale, Stenweg OP Leuven 13, 1980 Tervuren Belgium. **Tel** 011 32 2 7675401. **LC** QH71.T4; A32. **DD** 591. **Bk Rev. Circ:** 500 (ctrl).
**Ind/Abst** Life Sci. Collect.

GW/0044-5169
**ZOOLOGISCHE GARTEN; ZEITSCHRIFT FUER DIE GESAMTE TIERGARTNEREI.** [Zool. Gart.]. **Added/Corp** Kommission fuer Tiergarten der Deutschen Demokratischen Republik. Internationale Verband von Direktoren Zoologischer Garten. Verband Deutscher Zoodirektoren. Zoologische Garten Mitteleuropas. Zoologische Garten Deutschlands. Vol. 1.-Vol. 63, (1860)-(1922); New Ser. Vol. 1 (1929)-. Periodical. German (German and French). Six times a year. DM194.00 Germany; DM210.00 other. Gustav Fischer Verlag Jena, Postfach 100537, D 07705 Jena Germany. **Tel** 011 49 3641 27332, FAX 011 49 3641 626500. **(Subscription address:** VCH Publishers Inc., 303 Northwest 12th Avenue, Journals Department, Deerfield FL 33442.) **ED** H Dathe. **[CCC].** Index available. cum. index. **Bk Rev. Ad Acc. Circ:** 1,420.
**Desc:** Accepts all papers concerning the keeping of animals in zoological gardens (in the widest sense).
**Ind/Abst** Dairy Sci. Abstr.; Fish Rev.; Helminthol. Abstr.; Index Vet.; Key Word Index Wildl. Res.; Nutr. Abstr. Rev., Ser. B, Live Feeds and Feed.; Protozoolog. Abstr.; Vet. Bull.; Wildl. Rev.

GW/0044-5185
**ZOOLOGISCHE JAHRBUCHER. ABTEILUNG FUER ALLGEMEINE ZOOLOGIE UND PHYSIOLOGIE DER TIERE.** ***Title Change.*** [Zool. Jahrb., Abt. allg. Zool. Physiol. Tiere]. (1910)-(19??). Periodical. English (French and German). Four times a year. Gustav Fischer Verlag Jena, Postfach 100537, D 07705 Jena Germany. **Tel** 011 49 3641 27332, FAX 011 49 3641 626500. **ED** H Penzlin. **LC** QL1; .Z768. **DD** 590.5. **NLM** W1 ZO612E. **CODEN** ZJZPAY. **[CCC].** Index available. **Bk Rev. Ad Acc. Pr Rev. Circ:** 390. Documents available from The Genuine Article, CASDDS. ***Continues in part*** *Zoologische Jahrbuecher.* ***Merged into*** *Zoology, 0944-2006.*
**Desc:** Presents important original on subjects of general zoology and the physiology of animals including reproductive, developmental and behavioural biology. Experimental studies considering comparative and phylogenetic aspects, thus contributing to deeper insights into the causal relationship of events in the animal organism, are preferred in publication.
**Ind/Abst** AGRICOLA; Chem. Abstr.; CSA Neuro. Abstr. (?-?); Curr. Contents, Agric. Biol. Environ. Sci.; Helminthol. Abstr. (1991-); Nutr. Abstr. Rev., Ser. B, Live Feeds and Feed.; Nutr. Abstr. Rev., Ser. A, Hum. Exp.; Life Sci. Collect.; Res. Alert [Full Cov.]; Rev. Agric. Entomol.; Rev. Med. Vet. Entomol.; Sci. Cit. Index; SCISEARCH; Soc. Sci. Cit. Index [Select. Cov.]; Vitis Vitic. Enol. Abstr.

GW/0044-5177
**ZOOLOGISCHE JAHRBUCHER. ABTEILUNG FUER ANATOMIE UND ONTOGENIE DER TIERE.** ***Title Change.*** [Zool. Jahrb. Abt. Anat. Ontog. Tiere]. **VFOAT** International Journal for Zoological Sciences. (1888)-(199?). Academic Scholarly Publication. English (French and German). ir (4 times per year). Gustav Fischer Verlag Jena, Postfach 100537, D 07705 Jena Germany. **Tel** 011 49 3641 27332, FAX 011 49 3641 626500. **(Subscription address:** 303 NW 12th Avenue, Deerfield Beach FL 33442; telephone: (305)428-5566) **ED** J H Scharf. **LC** QL1; .Z769. **DD** 590.5. **NLM** W1 ZO612G. **CODEN** ZJAOA8. **[CCC].** Index available. **Bk Rev. Ad Acc. Circ:** 380. ***Continues in part*** *Zoologische Jahrbucher.* ***Merged with*** *Zoologische Jahrbuecher - Abteilung fuer Allgemeine Zoologie und Physiologie* ***to form*** *Zoology.*
**Desc:** The scope of this series on the anatomy and ontogeny of animals comprises short communications on most recent findings as well as survey articles on the morphology, ontogeny and phylogeny of greater taxonomic units. The up-to-date level is reflected by the publication of histochemical and histophysical investigations (mainly on invertebrates) and by electron microscopic and morphometric studies.
**Ind/Abst** AGRICOLA; CSA Neuro. Abstr. (?-?); EMBASE; Life Sci. Collect.; Rev. Med. Vet. Entomol.

GW/0044-5193
**ZOOLOGISCHE JAHRBUCHER. ABTEILUNG FUER SYSTEMATIK, OKOLOGIE UND GEOGRAPHIE DER TIERE.** ***Title Change.*** [Zool. Jahrb., Abt. Syst. Okol. Geogr. Tiere]. **VFOAT** Abteilung fuer Systematik, Okologie und Geographie der Tiere. Vol. 1 (1926)-(1994). Periodical. German (English and French). Four times a year. Gustav Fischer Verlag Jena, Postfach 100537, D 07705 Jena Germany. **Tel** 011 49 3641 27332, FAX 011 49 3641 626500. **ED** Gerhard Schaller. **LC** QL1; .Z7692. **DD** 590.5. **CODEN** ZJOGAK. **[CCC].** Index available. **Bk Rev. Ad Acc. Circ:** 430. Documents available from BIOSIS Document Express. ***Continues*** *Zoologische Jahrbucher. Abteilung fur Systematik, Geographie und Biologie der Tiere, 0323-7087.* ***Merged into*** *Zoology, 0944-2006.*
**Desc:** This series on the systematization, oecology and geography of animals is open to studies overlapping several disciplines and likewise to monographic work, which is indispensable in this field of science. Adequate publications can scarcely be found in the scientific literature because of the common journal publication schedules generally restricting to short, more or less casuistic case reports.
**Ind/Abst** AGRICOLA; Biol. Abstr.; Ecol. Abstr.; GeoRef; Life Sci. Collect.; Rev. Agric. Entomol.; Rev. Med. Vet. Entomol.; Soils Fert.; Weed Abstr.

NE/0024-0672
**ZOOLOGISCHE MEDEDELINGEN.** (ZOOLOGISCHE MEDEDEELINGEN / UITGEGEVEN VANWEGE 'S RIJKSMUSEUM VAN NATUURLIJKE HISTORIE TE LEIDEN.). [Zool. meded.]. **Main/Corp** Rijksmuseum van Natuurlijke Historie Te Leiden. **Added/Corp** Rijksmuseum van Natuurlijke Historie te Leiden. Nationaal Natuurhistorisch Museum (Netherlands). Vol. 1 (July 1915)-. Periodical. English (Dutch and French). Twice a year. Price varies. Museum Natuurlijk Historie, PO Box 321, AH 2300 Leiden Netherlands. **Tel** 011 31 71 143844. **LC** QL1; .L7. **CODEN** ZMRHAP. Index available. cum. index. **Bk Rev. Pr Rev. Circ:** 730 (ctrl). Documents available from BIOSIS Document Express. ***Formed by the union of*** *Revue Methodique et Critique des Collections Deposees dans Cet Etablissement* ***and*** *Notes From the Leyden Museum.*
**Ind/Abst** AGRICOLA; Biocont. News Inf. (1991-); Biol. Abstr.; GeoRef; Life Sci. Collect.; Rev. Agric. Entomol.; Rev. Med. Vet. Entomol.

NE/0024-1652
**ZOOLOGISCHE VERHANDELINGEN.** (ZOOLOGISCHE VERHANDELINGEN / UITGEGEVEN DOOR HET RIJKSMUSEUM VAN NATUURLIJKE HISTORIE TE LEIDEN (MINISTERIE VAN CULTUUR, RECREATIE EN MAATSCHAPPELIJK WERK)). [Zool. verh.]. **Added/Corp** Rijksmuseum van Natuurlijke Historie te Leiden. Nationaal Natuurhistorisch Museum (Netherlands) Netherlands. Ministerie van Cultuur, Recreatie en Maatschappelijk Werk. Netherlands. Ministerie van Onderwijs, Kunsten en Wetenschappen. No. 1 (Oct. 27, 1948)-. Monographic series. English (Dutch and French). ir. Price varies per volume. Museum Natuurlijk Historie, PO Box 321, AH 2300 Leiden Netherlands. **Tel** 011 31 71 143844. **(Subscription address:** Universal Book Services, Warmonderweg 80, 2341 KZ Oegstgeest Netherlands.) **LC** QL1; .L72. **DD** 591. **CODEN** ZVRHAK. Documents available from BIOSIS Document Express.
**Ind/Abst** Biocont. News Inf. (1991-); Biol. Abstr.; Fish Rev. (Jan. 1989-July 1992); GeoRef; Life Sci. Collect.; Rev. Agric. Entomol.; Wildl. Rev. (Jan. 1989-July 1992).

BE
**ZOOLOGISCHE WETENSCHAPPEN / KONINKLIJK MUSEUM VOOR MIDDEN-AFRIKA / SCIENCES ZOOLOGIQUES / MUSEE ROYAL DE L'AFRIQUE CENTRALE.** **Added/Corp** Musee Royal de l'Afrique Centrale. **VFOAT** Sciences Zoologiques. Vol. 244 (1984)-. Monographic series. English (French, German and Italian). ir. Price varies per volume. Musee Royal de l'Afrique Centrale, Stenweg OP Leuven 13, 1980 Tervuren Belgium. **Tel** 011 32 2 7675401. ***Continues*** *Annalen. Reeks in 8p0s. Zoologische Wetenschappen, 0379-1785.*

GW/0044-5231
**ZOOLOGISCHER ANZEIGER.** **Added/Corp** Deutsche Zoologische Gesellschaft. **VFOAT** Zoological Advertiser. Vol. 1 (1878)-. Periodical. German (English, French and Italian). Four times a year. DM466.00 Germany; DM474.00 other. Gustav Fischer Verlag Jena, Postfach 100537, D 07705 Jena Germany. **Tel** 011 49 3641 27332, FAX 011 49 3641 626500. **(Subscription address:** VCH Publishers Inc., 303 Northwest 12th Avenue, Journals Department, Deerfield FL 33442.) **ED** H E Gruner. **LC** QL1; .Z77. **NLM** W1 ZO614. **CODEN** ZOANA6. **[CCC].** Index available. **Ad Acc. Pr Rev. Circ:** 520. Documents available from The Genuine Article, BIOSIS Document Express, CASDDS.
**Desc:** Accepts contributions concerning any topical branches of zoology. Preference is given to papers dealing with morphological and functional problems in the field of the various systems covered by zoological science, including the submicroscopic, cellular systems, tissues, organs and individual organisms as well as populations and ecosystems.
**Ind/Abst** Biocont. News Inf.; Biol. Abstr.; Chem. Abstr.; CSA Neuro. Abstr. (?-?); Curr. Aware. Biol. Sci., CABS; Curr. Contents, Agric. Biol. Environ. Sci.; Curr. Ref. Fish Res.; Ecol. Abstr.; Fish Rev.; For. Abstr.; Geogr. Abstr. Phys. Geogr.; GeoRef; Helminthol. Abstr. (19??-19??); Key Word Index Wildl. Res.; Nutr. Abstr. Rev., Ser. B, Live Feeds and Feed.; Life Sci. Collect.; Protozoolog. Abstr.; Res. Alert [Full Cov.]; Rev. Agric. Entomol.; Sci. Cit. Index; SCISEARCH; Soils Fert.; Wildl. Rev.

●GW/0944-2006
**ZOOLOGY : ANALYSIS OF COMPLEX SYSTEMS, ZACS.** **VFOAT** ZACS. (1994)-. English. Four times a year. DM456.00 Germany; DM464.00 other. Gustav Fischer Verlag Jena, Postfach 100537, D 07705 Jena Germany. **Tel** 011 49 3641 27332, FAX 011 49 3641 626500. **(Subscription address:** VCH Publishers Inc., 303 Northwest 12th Avenue, Journals Department, Deerfield FL 33442.) ***Formed by the union of*** *Zoologische Jahrbuecher - Abteilung fuer Anatomie und Ontogenie der Tiere, 0044-5177* ***and*** *Zoologische Jahrbuecher - Abteilung fuer Allgemeine Zoologie und Physiologie, 0044-5185.*

US
**ZOOMIN'.** (1990)-. Periodical. English. qt. $12.00. Friends of the Zoo, 3515 Broadway, Suite 103, Kansas City MO 64111. **Tel** (816)756-3560.

GW/0720-213X
**ZOOMORPHOLOGY.** [Zoomorphology]. Vol. 96, No. 1/2 (Oct. 1980)-. Periodical. English. Four times a year. DM996.00. Springer-Verlag GmbH & Company KG, Heidelberger Platz 3, D 14197 Berlin Germany. **Tel** 011 49 30 8207223, FAX 011 49 30 8214091, telex 183 319 SPBLN D. **(Subscription address:** Springer Verlag New York Inc. / for North America, 44 Hartz Way, Secaucus NJ 07096.) **ED** O Kraus. **LC** QL1; .Z28. **DD** 591.4/05. **NLM** W1; ZO641P. **CODEN** ZMPHDI. **[CCC].** Documents available from The Genuine Article, BIOSIS Document Express. ***Continues*** *Zoomorphologie.*
**Desc:** Publishes original papers based on morphological investigation of invertebrates and vertebrates at the macroscopic, microscopic and and ultrastructural levels, including embryological studies.
**Ind/Abst** Biol. Abstr.; CSA Neuro. Abstr. (?-?); Curr. Aware. Biol. Sci., CABS; Curr. Contents, Agric. Biol. Environ. Sci.; Curr. Ref. Fish Res.; Fish Rev.; Helminthol. Abstr. (19??-19??); Life Sci. Collect.; Res. Alert [Full Cov.]; Rev. Med. Vet. Entomol.; Sci. Cit. Index; SCISEARCH; Wildl. Rev.

SA/0044-5274
**ZOON.** [Zoon]. (1963)-. Periodical. Afrikaans (English). qt (4 issues). Free on request. National Zoological Gardens of South Africa, PO Box 754, Pretoria 0001 South Africa. **Tel** 011 27 12 283265, 011 27 12 286020. **ED** Carika Oschman. **DD** _a590.744. **Ad Acc.**

US
**ZOONOOZ.** **Added/Corp** Zoological Society of San Diego. Vol. 1 (Jan./Feb. 1926)-. Periodical. English. mo. $15.00 (1 year), $40.00 (3 year). Zoological Society of San Diego, PO Box 271, San Diego CA 92112. **Tel** (619)231-1515, (619)231-0251. **ED** Marjorie Betts Shaw. **LC** QL1; .Z8. **DD** 590.74. Index available. **Bk Rev. Circ:** 130,000.
**Desc:** Focuses on the natural history, care and management, current world status and future of animals and plants in zoological gardens and in nature.

GW/0720-1842
**ZOOPHYSIOLOGY.** [Zoophysiology]. Vol. 11 (1979)-. Monographic series. English. ir. Price varies per volume. Springer-Verlag GmbH & Company KG, Heidelberger Platz 3, D 14197 Berlin Germany. **Tel** 011 49 30 8207223, FAX 011 49 30 8214091, telex 183 319 SPBLN D. **(Subscription address:** Springer Verlag New York Inc. / for North America, 44 Hartz Way, Secaucus NJ 07096.) **NLM** W1 ZO615M. **CODEN** ZOOPDH. Documents available from BIOSIS Document Express. ***Continues*** *Zoophysiology and Ecology, 0084-5663.*
**Desc:** Numbered series on zoophysiology.
**Ind/Abst** Biol. Abstr.; Life Sci. Collect.

US/1060-3859
**ZOOSCAPE (LOS ANGELES, CALIF.).** (ZOOSCAPE / GREATER LOS ANGELES ZOO ASSOCIATION.). **Added/Corp** Greater Los Angeles Zoo Association. **VFOAT** Zoo Scape. Vol. 15, No. 6 (Dec./Jan. 1991)-. Periodical. English. mo. $5.00. Greater Los Angeles Zoo Association, 5333 Zoo Drive, Los Angeles CA 90027. **Tel** (213)664-1100. ***Continues*** *GLAZAnews, 0897-8263.*

US/0276-329X
**ZOOSOUNDS.** [Zoosounds]. **Added/Corp** Oklahoma Zoological Society. **VFOAT** Zoo Sounds. **VAT** Zoo sounds. (19??)-. Periodical. English. bm. Oklahoma Zoological Society, PO Box 18424, Oklahoma City OK 73154.
**Ind/Abst** Fish Rev. (Jan. 1989-July 1992); Wildl. Rev. (Jan. 1989-July 1992).

IT/0392-0593
**ZOOTECNIA INTERNATIONAL.** (ZOOTECNIA AND INTERNATIONAL.). [Zootec. int.]. (1979)-. Periodical. Multiple languages. mo.
**Ind/Abst** Index Vet.; Nutr. Abstr. Rev., Ser. B, Live Feeds and Feed.

GW/0044-5401
**ZUCHTUNGSKUNDE.** See Biology.

PL/0084-5825
**ZWIERZETA LABORATORYJNE.** [Zwier. lab.]. Vol. 1- 1963-. Academic Scholarly Publication. Polish (English). an. Price varies per volume. Panstwowe Wydawn Naukowe, Miodowa 10, PO Box 391, 00251 Warsaw Poland. **(Subscription address:** ARS Polona, Krakowskie Przedmiescie 7, 00-068 Warszawa, Poland) **ED** Czeslaw Radzikowski. **LC** QL55. **NLM** W1 ZW201. **CODEN** ZWLAAA. **Ad Acc. Circ:** 300 (ctrl). Documents available from CASDDS.
**Desc:** Original papers and short articles concerning laboratory animal science: breeding, immunogenetics, biology, genetics, nutrition, care, environmental and health control.
**Ind/Abst** Anim. Breed. Abstr.; Chem. Abstr.; Index Vet.; Life Sci. Collect.; Poult. Abstr.; Vet. Bull.

## ABSTRACTING, BIBLIOGRAPHIES AND STATISTICS

US/0001-3579
**ABSTRACTS OF ENTOMOLOGY.** **Added/Corp** BioSciences Information Service of Biological Abstracts. Vol. 1 (April 1970)-. Abstracting/Indexing Service. English. mo. $245.00. BioSciences Information Service, Biological Abstracts / BIOSIS, 2100 Arch Street, Philadelphia PA 19103-1399. **Tel** (800)523-4806 US, (215)587-4800 Pennsylvania and worldwide, FAX (215)587-2016, telex 831739. **LC** Z5856; .A35. **DD** 595.7/008. **NLM** ZQX 500 A164. **CODEN** AEMYA. cum. index.
**Desc:** Contains abstracts and content summaries, including U.S. patents, of pure and applied research studies involving insects, arachnids and insecticides including chemical, physical and biological controls, economic entomology, physiology, pathology, systematics, medical entomology and ecology.
**Ind/Abst** Plant Breed. Abstr.

US/0301-8695
**ANIMAL BEHAVIOR ABSTRACTS.** [Anim. behav. abstr.]. Vol. 10, No. 1 (March 1982)-. Abstracting/Indexing Service. English. qt (plus annual index). $545.00 US; $585.00 other. Cambridge Scientific Abstracts, 7200 Wisconsin Avenue, #601, Bethesda MD 20814-4823. **Tel** (301)961-6750, (800)843-7751, FAX (301)961-6720. **ED** Robert Hilton. **DD** 591. **UDC** 591.5(048.3). Index available. cum. index. **Bk Rev.** available on magnetic tape; available on an online database; available on CD-ROM; available via Internet (to the current year's abstracts and five-year backfiles) from Cambridge Scientific Abstracts. ***Continues** Animal Behaviour Abstracts, 0301-8695.*
**Desc:** Covers animal behavior including communication, aggression, biochemistry, anatomy, behavioral ecology, navigation, rhythms and memory.

UK/0003-648X
**APICULTURAL ABSTRACTS.** [Apic. abstr.]. **Added/Corp** International Bee Research Association. Bee Research Association. Vol. 13 (Spring 1962)-. Abstracting/Indexing Service. English. qt. £140.00 UK; $245.00 other. International Bee Research Association, 18 North Road, Cardiff CF1 3DY United Kingdom. **Tel** 011 44 1 372409, FAX 011 44 1 665522, telex 23152. **ED** D. G. Lowe. **CODEN** APIBAE. Index available. cum. index. **Bk Rev. Ad Acc. Circ:** 1,000 (ctrl). available on an online database from CAB Abstracts Database. Documents available from CASDDS.
**Desc:** Abstract journal for apiculture.
**Ind/Abst** Chem. Abstr.; For. Prod. Abstr.; For. Abstr.; Plant Breed. Abstr.

US/0013-8924
**ENTOMOLOGY ABSTRACTS.** [Entomol. abstr.]. (1969)-. Abstracting/Indexing Service. English. mo (includes annual index). $895.00 US; $995.00 other. Cambridge Scientific Abstracts, 7200 Wisconsin Avenue, #601, Bethesda MD 20814-4823. **Tel** (301)961-6750, (800)843-7751, FAX (301)961-6720. **ED** Robert Hilton. **LC** QL461; .E9853. **DD** 016.5957. **NLM** ZQX 500 E61. Index available. cum. index. available on magnetic tape; available on an online database from STN International; and DIALOG; available on CD-ROM from SilverPlatter (US); available via Internet (to the current year's abstracts and five-year backfiles) from Cambridge Scientific Abstracts.
**Desc:** All aspects of entomology, including the biology, behavior, ecology, and biogeography of insects, arachnids, myriapods, onychophorans and terrestrial isopods. Applied entomology and methodology.

UK/0957-6789
**HELMINTHOLOGICAL ABSTRACTS.** **Added/Corp** C.A.B. International. Information Services. C.A.B. International. Bureau of Animal Health. C.A.B. International. Institute of Parasitology. Vol. 59, No. 1 (Jan. 1990)-. Abstracting/Indexing Service. English. mo. $491.00 US. CAB International Centre, Wallingford, Oxon OX10 8DE United Kingdom. **Tel** 44 491 832111, FAX 44 491 833508, telex 847964 (COMAGG G). **ED** C. W. Gordon, BA MlInfSc. **LC** QL392.A1; H42. **NLM** ZQX 200; H479A. **CODEN** HEABEC. **Circ:** 1,200. available on magnetic tape and CD-ROM; available on an online database from Tsukuba Daigaku; CAN/OLE; STN International; JICST; DATA-STAR; DIMDI; ESA-IRS; BRS; and DIALOG. ***Continues** Helminthological Abstracts. Series A, Animal and Human Helminthology, 0300-8339.*
**Desc:** Covers the literature on parasitic helminths such as gastrointestinal nematodes, liver flukes, hydatid, trichinella, schistosomes, filariids, and taenia.
**Ind/Abst** Helminthol. Abstr. (1991-); Trop. Dis. Bull.

UK/0309-1287
**PROTOZOOLOGICAL ABSTRACTS.** **Added/Corp** Commonwealth Institute of Helminthology. Commonwealth Agricultural Bureaux. Vol. 1 (Jan. 1977)-. Abstracting/Indexing Service. English. mo. $508.00 US. CAB International Centre, Wallingford, Oxon OX10 8DE United Kingdom. **Tel** 44 491 832111, FAX 44 491 833508, telex 847964 (COMAGG G). **ED** P. M. Neenan. **NLM** ZWC 700; P967. **Ad Acc. Circ:** 500. available on magnetic tape and CD-ROM; available on an online database from Tsukuba Daigaku; CAN/OLE; STN International; JICST; DATA-STAR; DIMDI; ESA-IRS; BRS; and DIALOG.
**Desc:** Valuable to those concerned with medical, veterinary and zoological parasitology as well as immunologists, biochemists, zoologists and taxonomists. Covers all aspects of parasitic protozoa.
**Ind/Abst** Fish Rev.; Protozoolog. Abstr.; Trop. Dis. Bull.; Wildl. Rev.

UK/0957-6762
**REVIEW OF AGRICULTURAL ENTOMOLOGY.** [Rev. agric. entomol.]. **Added/Corp** C.A.B. International. Bureau of Crop Protection. C.A.B. International. Institute of Entomology. C.A.B. International. Information Services. **VFOAT** CAB Abstracts. Vol. 78, No. 1 (Jan. 1990)-. Abstracting/Indexing Service. English. mo. $685.00 US. CAB International Centre, Wallingford, Oxon OX10 8DE United Kingdom. **Tel** 44 491 832111, FAX 44 491 833508, telex 847964 (COMAGG G). **Circ:** 1,850. available on magnetic tape and CD-ROM; available on an online database from Tsukuba Daigaku; CAN/OLE; STN International; JICST; DATA-STAR; DIMDI; ESA-IRS; BRS; and DIALOG. ***Continues** Review of Applied Entomology. Series A, Agricultural, 0305-0076.*
**Desc:** Covers the literature on insects and other pests of cultivated plants, forest trees and stored products, beneficial anthropods such as parasites and predators.
**Ind/Abst** Postharvest News Inf.; Trop. Dis. Bull.

UK/0957-6770
**REVIEW OF MEDICAL AND VETERINARY ENTOMOLOGY.** **Added/Corp** C.A.B. International. Bureau of Animal Health. C.A.B. International. Institute of Entomology. C.A.B. International. Information Services. Vol. 78, No. 1 (Jan. 1990)-. Abstracting/Indexing Service. English. mo. $366.00 US. CAB International Centre, Wallingford, Oxon OX10 8DE United Kingdom. **Tel** 44 491 832111, FAX 44 491 833508, telex 847964 (COMAGG G). **NLM** Z 5858.E2; R454. **Circ:** 1,250. available on magnetic tape and CD-ROM; available on an online database from Tsukuba Daigaku; CAN/OLE; STN International; JICST; DATA-STAR; DIMDI; ESA-IRS; BRS; and DIALOG. ***Continues** Review of Applied Entomology. Series B, Medical and Veterinary, 0305-0084.*
**Desc:** Deals with insects and other anthropods which transmit diseases or are otherwise injurious to man and to animals of significance to man.
**Ind/Abst** Trop. Dis. Bull.

US/0082-6391
**TRIBOLIUM INFORMATION BULLETIN.** 1958. Bulletin. English. an. $29.00. Tribolium Information Bulletin, c/o A Sokoloff, Biology Department, California State University, 5500 University Parkway, San Bernardino CA 92407. **Tel** (909)887-7394. **ED** Alexander Sokoloff. **LC** QL596.T2; T73. Index available. **Pr Rev. Circ:** 100. available on microfilm.
**Desc:** Research, teaching and technical notes on Tribolium and other beetles. Lists labs using beetles in research. Yearly compilation of bibliography. Includes personal and geographical directory.

UK/0144-3607
**ZOOLOGICAL RECORD (LONDON).** (THE ZOOLOGICAL RECORD.). [Zool. rec.]. **Added/Corp** Zoological Society of London. Zoological Record Association (London, England). Vol. 7 (1870)-. Abstracting/Indexing Service. English. ir. $2550.00 (Vol. 130), $2710.00 (Vol. 131). BioSciences Information Service, Biological Abstracts / BIOSIS, 2100 Arch Street, Philadelphia PA 19103-1399. **Tel** (800)523-4806 US, (215)587-4800 Pennsylvania and worldwide, FAX (215)587-2016, telex 831739. **LC** Z7991; .Z87; QL1. **DD** 016.59. **NLM** ZQL 15 Z88. **CODEN** ZOREAU. Index available. available on an online database; available in microform. ***Continues** Record of Zoological Literature.*
**Desc:** Provides coverage of virtually every aspect of zoology, including biochemistry, behavior, ecology, evolution, genetics, immunology, nomenclature, physiology, taxonomy and zoogeography.
**Ind/Abst** GeoRef; Nematol. Abstr.; Rev. Agric. Entomol.

•US/1072-1983
**ZOOLOGICAL RECORD ON CD.** (ZOOLOGICAL RECORD ON CD [COMPUTER FILE].). (1993)-. English. qt. $3080.00 US & Canada; $3380.00 other. BioSciences Information Service, Biological Abstracts / BIOSIS, 2100 Arch Street, Philadelphia PA 19103-1399. **Tel** (800)523-4806 US, (215)587-4800 Pennsylvania and worldwide, FAX (215)587-2016, telex 831739. available in print (Zoological Record) from BIOSIS; available on an online database.
**Desc:** Supplies a comprehensive collection of references to zoological research articles worldwide.

## ENTOMOLOGY

US/0001-3579
**ABSTRACTS OF ENTOMOLOGY.** See Zoology-Abstracting, Bibliographies and Statistics.

CS/0001-5601
**ACTA ENTOMOLOGICA BOHEMOSLOVACA.** ***Title Change.*** (ACTA ENTOMOLOGICA BOHEMOSLOVACA / CZECHOSLOVAK ACADEMY OF SCIENCES.). [Acta entomol. Bohemoslov.]. **Added/Corp** Entomologicky Ustav (Ceskoslovenska Akademie Ved) Ceskoslovenska Spolecnost Entomologicka. Vol. 62 No. 1 (1965)-(1992). Academic Scholarly Publication. English (German and French). bm. Czech Academy of Sciences, Branisovska 31, 37005 Ceske Budejovice, Czech Republic. **Tel** 011 42 38 817 ext. 213, 214. **(Subscription address:** Kluwer Academic Publishers Group, Journals Department, Distribution Centre, PO Box 322, 3300 AH Dordrecht, The Netherlands (Phone: 31-78-524400, FAX: 31-78-524474)) **ED** I Hodek and T Soldan. **LC** QL461; .C4. **NLM** W1 AC8013. **CODEN** AEBOA9. Index available. **Bk Rev. Pr Rev. Circ:** 1,200. Documents available from The Genuine Article, BIOSIS Document Express, CASDDS. ***Continues** Casopis Ceskoslovenske Spolecnosti Entomologicke.* ***Continued by** European Journal of Entomology, 1210-5759.*
**Desc:** Covers the whole field of general and experimental entomology and also publishes taxonomical studies such as revision and papers concerning descriptive taxonomy, especially those related to the fauna of the Palearctic region.
**Ind/Abst** AGRICOLA; Biocont. News Inf. (19??-19??); Biol. Abstr.; Chem. Abstr.; CSA Neuro. Abstr. (?-?); Curr. Contents, Agric. Biol. Environ. Sci.; Ecol. Abstr.; Ecology Abstr.; Entomol. Abstr.; For. Prod. Abstr.; For. Abstr.; Hortic. Abstr.; Maize Abstr.; Nematol. Abstr.; Life Sci. Collect.; Protozoolog. Abstr.; Res. Alert [Select. Cov.]; Rev. Agric. Entomol.; Rev. Med. Vet. Entomol.; SCISEARCH; Wheat Barley Trit. Abstr.

CL/0716-5072
**ACTA ENTOMOLOGICA CHILENA.** (ACTA ENTOMOLOGICA CHILENA / INSTITUTO DE ENTOMOLOGIA, UNIVERSIDAD METROPOLITANA DE CIENCIAS DE LA EDUCACION.). [Acta entomol. chil.]. **Added/Corp** Universidad Metropolitana de Ciencias de la Educacion (Santiago, Chile). Instituto de Entomologia. Vol. 13 (June 1986)-. Spanish (summaries and/or abstracts in English). an. $25.00. Instituto de Entomologia, Universidad Metropolitana de Ciencias de la Educacion, Ave Jose Pedro Alessandri 774, Casilla 147, Santiago Chile. **Tel** 2392522, FAX 2392067. **ED** Jaime Solervicens. **LC** WMLC 93/1477. **CODEN** AECHEV. **Bk Rev. Ad Acc. Pr Rev. Circ:** 350. Documents available from BIOSIS Document Express. ***Continues** Publicaciones Entomologicas.*
**Desc:** Covers taxonomy, biology, distribution, hosts, morphology and physiology of insects in Chile.
**Ind/Abst** Biol. Abstr. (1988-); Entomol. Abstr.; For. Abstr.; Rev. Med. Vet. Entomol.

HU/0238-1249
**ACTA PHYTOPATHOLOGICA ET ENTOMOLOGICA HUNGARICA.** See Biology-Botany.

US/0934-6112
**ADVANCES IN DISEASE VECTOR RESEARCH.** [Adv. dis. vector res.]. Vol. 5 (1988)-. Monographic series. English. ir. Price varies per volume. Springer-Verlag New York Inc., 175 5th Avenue, New York NY 10010. **Tel** (212)460-1500, telex 232 235 SPB UR. **(Subscription address:** Springer Verlag New York Inc. / for North America, 44 Hartz Way, Secaucus NJ 07096.) **ED** K.F. Harris. **NLM** W1; AD548M. **CODEN** ADVRED. Documents available from BIOSIS Document Express. ***Continues** Current Topics in Vector Research, 0737-8491.*
**Desc:** Provides information on animals as carriers of disease and vector-pathogen relationships.
**Ind/Abst** AgBiotech News Inf.; Biol. Abstr. (1988-); Index Vet.; Maize Abstr.; Nematol. Abstr.; Protozoolog. Abstr.; Rev. Agric. Entomol.; Rev. Med. Vet. Entomol.; Rev. Plant Pathol.; Rice Abstr.

UK/0065-2806
**ADVANCES IN INSECT PHYSIOLOGY.** [Adv. insect physiol.]. Vol. 1 (1963)-. Academic Scholarly Publication. English. ir. $82.50 (Vol. 25). Academic Press, Inc., 6277 Sea Harbor Drive, Orlando FL 32887. **Tel**

(800)543-9534, (407)345-4100, FAX (407)363-9661. **ED** J. W. L. Beament, J. E. Treherne and V. B. Wigglesworth. **LC** QL495; .A23. **DD** 595.7. **UDC** 595.7. **NLM** W1 AD651. **CODEN** AIPYAZ. Documents available from The Genuine Article, BIOSIS Document Express, CASDDS.
**Ind/Abst** AGRICOLA [Full Cov.]; Biol. Agric. Index; Biol. Abstr.; Chem. Abstr.; Curr. Aware. Biol. Sci., CABS; Index Sci. Rev. [Full Cov.]; Life Sci. Collect.; Res. Alert [Full Cov.]; Rev. Med. Vet. Entomol.; Sci. Cit. Index; SCISEARCH; Trop. Dis. Bull.; Vitis Vitic. Enol. Abstr.

●SA/1021-3589
**AFRICAN ENTOMOLOGY.** (AFRICAN ENTOMOLOGY : JOURNAL OF THE ENTOMOLOGICAL SOCIETY OF SOUTHERN AFRICA.). [Afr. entomol.]. **Added/Corp** Entomological Society of Southern Africa. Vol. 1, No. 1 (Mar. 1993)-. Periodical. English. Twice a year (Mar., Sep.). $80.00. Entomological Society of Southern Africa, PO Box 103, Pretoria 0001 South Africa. **Tel** 21 12 2062623, FAX 21 12 3235275. **LC** QL461; .E688. **DD** 595.7096. **CODEN** AFREE2. **Bk Rev**, (Qty: 10). **Pr Rev. Circ:** 650. ***Continues*** *Entomological Society of Southern Africa. Journal of the Entomological Society of Southern Africa, 0013-8789.*
**Ind/Abst** AGRICOLA.

UK
**AMATEUR ENTOMOLOGIST : THE JOURNAL OF THE AMATEUR ENTOMOLOGISTS' SOCIETY, THE.** Began with Vol. 4, No. 32 in Jan. 1939. Periodical. English. £8.00 UK; £10.00 other. Amateur Entomologists Society, 5 Oakfield Plaistow, West Sussex RH14 0QD England. **ED** B O C Gardiner and P W Cribb. Index available. **Bk Rev. Ad Acc. Circ:** 2,000 (ctrl). ***Continues in part*** *Entomologists' Bulletin.*

US/1046-2821
**AMERICAN ENTOMOLOGIST (LANHAM, MD.).** (AMERICAN ENTOMOLOGIST.). [Am. entomol.]. **Added/Corp** Entomological Society of America. Vol. 36, No. 1 (Spring 1990)-. Periodical. English. qt. $30.00 (individuals), $55.00 (institutions) US; $42.00 (individuals), $67.00 (institutions) other. Entomological Society of America, 9301 Annapolis Road, Suite 300, Lanham MD 20706. **Tel** (301)731-4535, FAX (301)731-4538. **(Subscription address:** Entomological Society of America / ESA, PO Box 177, Hyattsville MD 20781-0177.) **ED** J. E. McPherson. **LC** QL461; .E56. **DD** 595.7/005. **CODEN** AENUEN. **Bk Rev.** available on microfilm and microfiche from University Microfilms International (UMI). Documents available from BIOSIS Document Express, Documents on Demand. ***Continues*** *Bulletin of the Entomological Society of America, 0013-8754.*
**Desc:** A magazine of general entomological interest. The magazine contains feature articles, scientific reports, commentaries, and book reviews. Articles include historical, synthetic, or speculative material as well as primary research.
**Ind/Abst** AGRICOLA [Full Cov.]; Biol. Abstr.; Energy Inf. Abstr.; Environ. Abstr.; Life Sci. Collect.

BL/0301-8059
**ANAIS DA SOCIEDADE ENTOMOLOGICA DO BRASIL.** (ANAIS.). [An. Soc. Entomol. Bras.]. **Main/Corp** Sociedade Entomologica do Brasil. Vol. 1 (1972)-. Portuguese (summaries and/or abstracts in English). Twice a year. $45.00 Comes with Sociedade Entomologica do Brasil membership. Sociedade Entomologica do Brasil, Rua Marcelo Gama 896, 90450 Porto Allegre RS Brasil. **LC** SB935.B7; S63a. **DD** 595.7/0981. **CODEN** ASENBI. Documents available from BIOSIS Document Express, CASDDS.
**Ind/Abst** Biocont. News Inf.; Biodeter. Abstr.; Biol. Abstr.; Chem. Abstr.; For. Abstr.; Hortic. Abstr.; Life Sci. Collect.; Postharvest News Inf.; Potato Abstr.; Poult. Abstr.; Rev. Agric. Entomol.; Rev. Med. Vet. Entomol.; Seed Abstr.; Soils Fert.; Soyabean Abstr.

US/0013-8746
**ANNALS OF THE ENTOMOLOGICAL SOCIETY OF AMERICA.** [Ann. Entomol. Soc. Am.]. **Main/Corp** Entomological Society of America. Vol. 1 (March 1908)-. Periodical. English. bm. $75.00 (individual), $150.00 (institution) US; $95.00 (individual), $170.00 (institution) other. Entomological Society of America, 9301 Annapolis Road, Suite 300, Lanham MD 20706. **Tel** (301)731-4535, FAX (301)731-4538. **(Subscription address:** Entomological Society of America / ESA, PO Box 177, Hyattsville MD 20781-0177.) **ED** Carl W. Schaefer and Leo Lachance. **LC** QL461; .E62. **DD** 595.7/005. **NLM** W1 AN626S. **CODEN** AESAAI. **[CCC]. Ad Acc. Pr Rev. Circ:** 2,000 (ctrl). available on microfilm and microfiche from University Microfilms International (UMI). Documents available from The Genuine Article, BIOSIS Document Express, CASDDS, Documents on Demand.
**Desc:** Reports on basic aspects of the biology of insects, including taxonomy, systematics, techniques, morphology, behavior, karyology, and reproduction.
**Ind/Abst** AGRICOLA [Full Cov.]; Biocont. News Inf. (19??-19??); Biodeter. Abstr.; Biol. Agric. Index; Biol. Abstr.; Chem. Abstr.; Chemorecept. Abstr.; Cot. Trop. Fibr. Abstr. Bibliogr.; CSA Neuro. Abstr. (?-?); Curr. Aware. Biol. Sci., CABS; Curr. Contents, Agric. Biol. Environ. Sci.; Ecol. Abstr. (?-?); Ecology Abstr.; Energy Inf. Abstr.; Entomol. Abstr.; Environ. Abstr.; For. Prod. Abstr.; For. Abstr.; Hortic. Abstr.; Immunol. Abstr.; Index Vet.; INIS Atomindex [Micro.]; Maize Abstr.; Life Sci. Collect.; PESTDOC; Plant Breed. Abstr.; Postharvest News Inf.; Potato Abstr.; Protozoolog. Abstr.; Res. Alert [Full Cov.]; Rev. Agric. Entomol.; Rev. Med. Vet. Entomol.; Sci. Cit. Index; SCISEARCH; Soyabean Abstr.; Vet. Bull.; Trop. Dis. Bull.; Vitis Vitic. Enol. Abstr.; Weed Abstr.; Wheat Barley Trit. Abstr.; Wildl. Rev.

US/0066-4170
**ANNUAL REVIEW OF ENTOMOLOGY.** [Annu. rev. entomol.]. **Added/Corp** Entomological Society of America. Vol. 1 (1956)-. English. an (January). $47.00 US; $52.00 other. Annual Reviews Inc., 4139 El Camino Way, PO Box 10139, Palo Alto CA 94303-0139. **Tel** (415)493-4400, (800)523-8635, FAX (415)855-9815. **ED** Thomas E. Mittler, Frank J. Radovsky, and Vincent H. Resh. **LC** QL461; .A6. **DD** 595.7. **NLM** W1 AN771. **CODEN** ARENAA. **[CCC].** Index available. cum. index. **Pr Rev.** ctrl circ. available on microfilm and microfiche from University Microfilms International (UMI). Documents available from The Genuine Article, BIOSIS Document Express, CASDDS, Documents on Demand.
**Desc:** Comprehensive, thorough coverage of latest advances in entomology, written by acknowledged experts in the field. Extensive literature citations included.
**Ind/Abst** AgBiotech News Inf.; AGRICOLA [Full Cov.]; Agrofor. Abstr. (1991-); Biocont. News Inf. (19??-19??); Biodeter. Abstr.; Biol. Agric. Index; Biol. Abstr.; Chem. Abstr.; Curr. Aware. Biol. Sci., CABS; Curr. Contents, Agric. Biol. Environ. Sci.; Ecology Abstr.; EMBASE; Energy Inf. Abstr.; Entomol. Abstr.; Environ. Abstr.; For. Prod. Abstr. (19??-19??); For. Abstr.; Health Plan. Adminis.; Helminthol. Abstr.; Hortic. Abstr.; Index Med.; Index Sci. Rev. [Full Cov.]; Index Vet.; Nematol. Abstr.; Life Sci. Collect.; PESTDOC; Plant Breed. Abstr.; Poult. Abstr.; Ref. Upd. Deluxe Ed.; Res. Alert [Full Cov.]; Rev. Med. Vet. Entomol.; Rev. Med. Vet. Mycology; Rev. Plant Pathol.; Sci. Cit. Index; SCISEARCH; Soils Fert.; Trop. Dis. Bull.; Vitis Vitic. Enol. Abstr.; Weed Abstr.

IT/0518-1259
**APICOLTORE MODERNO, L'.** [Apic. mod.]. **Added/Corp** Turin. Universita. Istituto di Apicoltura. Vol. 1 (Jan. 1909)-. Academic Scholarly Publication. Italian (summaries and/or abstracts in English and French). bm (6 issues). L25000 Italy; L30000 other. Apicoltore Moderno, via l'da Vinci 44, 10095 Grugliasco TO Italy. **Tel** 011 39 11 4033893. **ED** C. Vidano. **CODEN** APMOD8. Index available. **Bk Rev. Ad Acc. Pr Rev. Circ:** 2,500. Documents available from BIOSIS Document Express, CASDDS.
**Ind/Abst** AGRICOLA; Biocont. News Inf.; Biol. Abstr.; Chem. Abstr.; For. Abstr.; Rev. Agric. Entomol.; Weed Abstr.

JA/0003-6862
**APPLIED ENTOMOLOGY AND ZOOLOGY.** [Appl. entomol. zool.]. **Added/Corp** Nihon Oyo Dobutsu Konchu Gakkai. (June 1966)-. Periodical. English (French and German). qt. $118.00. Nihon Oyo Dobutsu Konchu Gakkai, (Japanese Society of Applied Entomology and Zoology), Nihon Shokubutsu Boeki Kyokai, 43-11, Komagome, 1 Chome, Toshimaku, Tokyoto 170 Japan. **(Subscription address:** Japan Publications Trading Company, Ltd., PO Box 5030, Tokyo International, Tokyo 100-31 Japan.) **LC** QL461; .A63. **CODEN** APEZAW. **[CCC]. Pr Rev.** Documents available from The Genuine Article, BIOSIS Document Express, CASDDS.
**Ind/Abst** Anim. Behav. Abstr.; Art Archaeol. Tech. Abstr.; Biocont. News Inf. (19??-19??); Biodeter. Abstr. (19??-19??); Biol. Abstr.; Chem. Abstr.; CSA Neuro. Abstr. (?-?); Curr. Aware. Biol. Sci., CABS; Curr. Contents, Agric. Biol. Environ. Sci.; Ecology Abstr.; Entomol. Abstr.; Field Crop Abstr.; For. Prod. Abstr.; For. Abstr.; Hortic. Abstr.; Maize Abstr.; Microbiol. Abstr. Sect. A; Microbiol. Abstr. Sect. C; Nematol. Abstr.; Life Sci. Collect.; PESTDOC; Plant Breed. Abstr.; Postharvest News Inf.; Protozoolog. Abstr.; Res. Alert [Full Cov.]; Rev. Agric. Entomol.; Rev. Med. Vet. Entomol.; Rice Abstr.; Sci. Cit. Index; SCISEARCH; SEA Abstr.; Seed Abstr.; Soyabean Abstr.; Wheat Barley Trit. Abstr.

NE/0165-0424
**AQUATIC INSECTS.** [Aquat. insects]. Vol. 1, No. 1 (Jan. 1979)-. Periodical. English. qt. Fl398.00 (Institutions). Swets & Zeitlinger BV, Heereweg 347B PO Box 825, 2160 SZ Lisse Holland. **Tel** 011 31 2521 35111, FAX 02521-15888, telex 41325. **(Subscription address:** Swets Publishing Service, PO Box 825, 2160 SZ Lisse The Netherlands) **ED** Peter Zwich. **CODEN** AQINDQ. **[CCC].** Index available. **Bk Rev. Ad Acc. Pr Rev. Circ:** 800. Documents available from The Genuine Article, BIOSIS Document Express.
**Desc:** Aquatic Insects is an international journal publishing original research on both the taxonomy and the ecology of aquatic insects. The journal is of prime interest for amateur and professional entomologists specialising in a wide spectrum of different insect groups.
**Ind/Abst** Abstr. Bull. Inst. Pap. Sci. Tech.; Aquat. Sci. Fish. Abstr. (Computer File); Biocont. News Inf. (1991-); Biol. Abstr.; Curr. Aware. Biol. Sci., CABS; Curr. Contents, Agric. Biol. Environ. Sci.; Ecol. Abstr.; Ecology Abstr.; Entomol. Abstr.; For. Abstr.; Geogr. Abstr. Phys. Geogr.; Ocean. Abstr.; Life Sci. Collect.; Res. Alert [Full Cov.]; Rev. Med. Vet. Entomol.; Sci. Cit. Index; SCISEARCH.

US/0739-4462
**ARCHIVES OF INSECT BIOCHEMISTRY AND PHYSIOLOGY.** [Arch. insect biochem. physiol.]. **Added/Corp** Entomological Society of America. Vol. 1, No. 1 (1983)-. Academic Scholarly Publication. English. mo. $880.00 US; $1,008.00 Canada and Mexico; $1,053.00 other. John Wiley & Sons, Inc., 605 Third Avenue, New York NY 10158-0012. **Tel** (212)850-6000, (212)850-6645, FAX (212)850-6088, telex 12-7063. **(Subscription address:** John Wiley & Sons / England, Baffins Lane, Chichester, West Sussex PO19 1UD England.) **ED** Richard T. Mayer and Jeffrey P. Shapiro. **LC** QL495; .A7. **DD** 595.7/01. **NLM** W1; AR455BF. **CODEN** AIBPEA. **[CCC]. Pr Rev.** Documents available from The Genuine Article, CASDDS.
**Desc:** An international forum for scientists interested in the field of insect biochemistry and physiology. The journal publishes original research articles, announcements of meetings, and brief review articles relating to significant advances in the field.
**Ind/Abst** AgBiotech News Inf.; AGRICOLA [Full Cov.]; Biocont. News Inf.; Chem. Abstr. (1983-); Chem. Titles; Curr. Contents, Agric. Biol. Environ. Sci.; Curr. Contents Life Sci.; EMBASE; Entomol. Abstr.; Index Med.; Life Sci. Collect.; Postharvest News Inf.; Potato Abstr.; Ref. Upd. Deluxe Ed.; Res. Alert [Full Cov.]; Rev. Agric. Entomol.; Rev. Med. Vet. Entomol.; Sci. Cit. Index; SCISEARCH.

US/0160-5674
**ATALA.** [Atala]. V. 1- April 1973-. Periodical. English (Spanish). sa. $25.00 (institutions), $15.00 (regular) US. The Xerces Society, 10 Southwest Ash Street, Portland OR 97204. **Tel** (503)222-2788. **ED** Lawrence F Gall. **LC** QL541; .A82. **DD** 595.7/005. **UDC** 595.7. **Bk Rev. Circ:** 1,000.
**Desc:** International journal of invertebrate conservation, accepting papers, book reviews, opinions of authors, subjects related to aspects of conservation.
**Ind/Abst** Ecology Abstr.; Entomol. Abstr.

GW/0171-0079
**ATALANTA (MUNCHEN).** (ATALANTA.). [Atalanta]. **Added/Corp** Gesellschaft zur Forderung der Erforschung von Insektenwanderungen (Munich, Germany). Vol. 1 (March 1964)-. Periodical. German (English and French). Four times a year. DM40.00. Deutsche Forschung fur Schmett, Humboldstrasse 13, D95168 Markleuthen F R Germany. **Tel** 11 49 9285480, FAX 11 49 92858238. **ED** Ulf Eitschberger. **LC** WMLC 93/1569. **CODEN** ATLNDS. Index available in last issue of volume--attached. **Bk Rev. Ad Acc. Circ:** 1,200 (ctrl). Documents available from BIOSIS Document Express.
**Desc:** Insect migration, lepidoptera, description of new species, faunistics, ecology, etc.
**Ind/Abst** Biol. Abstr.; Life Sci. Collect.; Surf. Treat. Technol. Abstr.

AT/0311-1881
**AUSTRALIAN ENTOMOLOGICAL MAGAZINE.** ***Title Change.*** [Aust. entomol. mag.]. **Added/Corp** Entomological Society of Queensland. Vol. 1 (July 1972)-(19??). Periodical. English. Four times a year. Australian Entomological Magazine, PO Box 537, Indooroopilly Queensland, 4068 Australia. **Tel** 011 61 7 864-1447, FAX 011 61 7 864-1640. **ED** G Daniels. **CODEN** AEMZAT. Index available. cum. index. **Bk Rev. Ad Acc, Adv Mgr:** M. Schneider. **Pr Rev. Circ:** 420 (ctrl). Documents available from BIOSIS Document Express. ***Continued by*** *Australian Entomologist.*
**Desc:** Original research papers in entomology with emphasis on the Australia-South Pacific region.
**Ind/Abst** AGRICOLA; Biocont. News Inf. (19??-19??); Biol. Abstr.; Ecology Abstr.; Entomol. Abstr.; For. Abstr.; Life Sci. Collect.; Rev. Agric. Entomol.; Rev. Med. Vet. Entomol.; Weed Abstr.

●AT
**AUSTRALIAN ENTOMOLOGIST.** (1993)-. English. Four times a year (Mar., June, Sept., Nov.). 20.00Aus$ (institutions), 16.00Aus$ (individuals) Australia; 22.00Aus$ (institutions), 20.00Aus$ (individuals) other. Australian Entomological Magazine, PO Box 537, Indooroopilly Queensland, 4068 Australia. **Tel** 011 61 7 864-1447, FAX 011 61 7 864-1640. **ED** Dr. K.J. Lambkin. **Bk Rev**, (Qty: 4-8). **Ad Acc, Adv Mgr:** A.P. Mackey. **Pr Rev. Circ:** 400. ***Continues*** *AUstralian Entomological Magazine.*

GW/0005-805X
**BEITRAEGE ZUR ENTOMOLOGIE.** (BEITRAEGE ZUR ENTOMOLOGIE / DEUTSCHES ENTOMOLOGISCHES INSTITUT.). [Beitr. Entomol.]. **Added/Corp** Deutsches Entomologisches Institut. Vol. 1, No. 1 (Oct. 1951)-. Periodical. German. Twice a year. $160.00. Akademie-Verlag GmbH, Muehlenstrasse 33 34, D 13162 Berlin Germany. **Tel** 011 49 30 47889300, FAX 011 49 30 47889357. **(Subscription address:** VCH Publishers Inc., 303 Northwest 12th Avenue, Journals Department, Deerfield FL 33442.) **LC** QL461; .B33. **DD** 595.7/005. **CODEN** BEIEAP. Documents available from BIOSIS Document Express.
**Ind/Abst** Biocont. News Inf. (19??-19??); Biol. Abstr.; CSA Neuro. Abstr. (?-?); Entomol. Abstr.; Hortic. Abstr.; Life Sci. Collect.; Potato Abstr.; Rev. Agric. Entomol.; Rev. Med. Vet. Entomol.; Soils Fert.; Wheat Barley Trit. Abstr.

AU
**BERICHTE DER ARBEITSGEMEINSCHAFT FUER OKOLOGISCHE ENTOMOLOGIE IN GRAZ.** **Main/Corp** Arbeitsgemeinschaft fur Okologische Entomologie In Graz. No. 1 (1973)-. Periodical. German. ir. Arbeitsgemeinschaft fur Okologische Entomologie in Graz, Heinrichstr 5/III, Graz Austria. **LC** QL482.A9; A72a.

GW
**BIBLIOGRAPHY OF PALAEARCTIC LEPIDOPTERA / SOCIETAS EUROPAEA LEPIDOPTEROLOGICA.** **VFOAT** Bibliographia Europaea Lepidopterologica. Bibliography. English. **LC** Z5858.L5; B52; QL554. **DD** 016.59578/094.
**Ind/Abst** Biocont. News Inf.

AU/0006-2146
**BIENENVATER.** **See** Agriculture.

AT/1037-3500
**BIENNIAL REPORT / DIVISION OF ENTOMOLOGY, CSIRO.** **Main/Corp** Commonwealth Scientific and Industrial Research Organization (Australia). Division of Entomology. (1983)-. English. be. ***Continues*** *Annual Report - Commonwealth Scientific & Industrial Research Organization, Division of Entomology.*

UK/0958-3157
**BIOCONTROL SCIENCE & TECHNOLOGY.** **See** Agriculture-Crop Production and Soil.

US/0893-3146
**BISHOP MUSEUM BULLETIN IN ENTOMOLOGY.** [Bishop Mus. bull. entomol.]. **Added/Corp** Bernice Pauahi Bishop Museum. **VFOAT** Bishop Museum Bulletins in Entomology. (1988)-. Bulletin. English. ir. Free. Bishop Museum Press, PO Box 19000-A, Honolulu HI 96817. **Tel** (808)847-3511. **DD** 595. ***Continues in part*** *Bernice Pauahi Bishop Museum. Bernice P. Bishop Museum Bulletin, 0005-9439.*
**Ind/Abst** AGRICOLA [Full Cov.]; Rev. Agric. Entomol.

PO/0870-7227
**BOLETIM DA SOCIEDADE PORTUGUESA DE ENTOMOLOGIA.** [Bol. Soc. Port. Entomol.]. (1979)-. Periodical. Multiple languages. ir.
**Ind/Abst** Biocont. News Inf.; Entomol. Abstr.; Rev. Agric. Entomol.

SP/0210-8984
**BOLETIN DE LA ASOCIACION ESPANOLA DE ENTOMOLOGIA.** [Bol. Asoc. Esp. Entomol.]. **Main/Corp** Asociacion Espanola de Entomologia. Vol. 1 (1977)-. Spanish. **CODEN** BAEEDE. Documents available from BIOSIS Document Express.
**Ind/Abst** Biocont. News Inf.; Biol. Abstr.; Rev. Agric. Entomol.; Rev. Med. Vet. Entomol.

IT/0373-3491
**BOLLETTINO DELLA SOCIETA ENTOMOLOGICA ITALIANA.** [Boll. Soc. entomol. ital.]. **Main/Corp** Societa Entomologica Italiana. **Added/Corp** Societa Entomologica Italiana. Atti della Societa Entomologica Italiana. Vol. 1 (1869)-. Monographic series. Italian (English, French and Spanish). Three times a year. L40000 Italy; L80000 European Union; L60000 other. Societa Entomologica Italiana, Via Brigata Liguria 9, 16121 Genova Italy. **Tel** 011 39 10 261862, 011 39 10 564567. **LC** QL461; .S3. **DD** 595.7/005. **CODEN** BENIAS. Index available. cum. index. **Bk Rev. Ad Acc. Circ:** 1,500 (ctrl). Documents available from BIOSIS Document Express. ***Absorbed*** *Informatore del Giovane Entomologo, 0390-0045.*
**Desc:** Covers works on entomology.
**Ind/Abst** Biocont. News Inf. (1991-); Biol. Abstr.; Entomol. Abstr.; Life Sci. Collect.; Rev. Agric. Entomol.; Rev. Med. Vet. Entomol.

FR/0037-928X
**BULLETIN DE LA SOCIETE ENTOMOLOGIQUE DE FRANCE.** [Bull. Soc. entomol. Fr.]. **Main/Corp** Societe Entomologique de France. (1896)-. Bulletin. French. Five times a year (Feb., Apr., June, Sept., Nov.). 400.00F France; 450.00F other. Societe Entomologique de France, 45 rue de Buffon, 75005 Paris France. **Tel** 011 33 1 40793391. **LC** QL461; .S61. **NLM** W1 BU516M. cum. index. **Bk Rev. Ad Acc. Circ:** 1,200. ***Supersedes in part*** *Annales de la Societe Entomologique de France.*
**Desc:** Covers taxonomy and biology of insects.
**Ind/Abst** Biocont. News Inf. (1991-); Entomol. Abstr.; For. Abstr.; Life Sci. Collect.; Rev. Agric. Entomol.; Rev. Med. Vet. Entomol.; Seed Abstr.

UA
**BULLETIN DE LA SOCIETE ENTOMOLOGIQUE D'EGYPTE.** **Added/Corp** Jamiyah Al-Misriyah Li-Ilm Al-Hasharat. **VFOAT** Majalat Al-Jamiyah Al-Misriyah Li-Ilm Al-Hasharat. No. 61 (1977)-. Bulletin. French (English and French; summaries and/or abstracts in Arabic and English). Entomological Society of Egypt, PO Box 430, Cairo Egypt. **CODEN** BSEEAZ. Documents available from BIOSIS Document Express. ***Continues*** *Bulletin of the Entomological Society of Egypt, 0251-4214.*
**Ind/Abst** Biol. Abstr.; Soyabean Abstr.

CN/0704-4666
**BULLETIN D'INVENTAIRE DES INSECTES DU QUEBEC.** ***Suspended.*** **Added/Corp** Societe d'Inventaire des Insectes du Quebec. **VFOAT** Quebec Insect Survey Bulletin. Vol. 1 (Mar. 1979)-(19??). Periodical. French (English; summaries and/or abstracts in English). Four times a year. $4.00. Societe d'Inventaire des Insectes du Quebec, College Bourget CP 1000, Rigaud Quebec J0P 1P0 Canada. **DD** 595.709714.

UK/0007-4853
**BULLETIN OF ENTOMOLOGICAL RESEARCH.** [Bull. entomol. res.]. **Main/Corp** Commonwealth Institute of Entomology. **Added/Corp** Great Britain. Colonial Office. Entomological Research Committee. Imperial Bureau of Entomology. Commonwealth Agricultural Bureaux. Imperial Institute of Entomology. Commonwealth Institute of Entomology. C.A.B. International. Institute of Entomology. Vol. 1 (Apr. 1910)-. Periodical. English. qt. $327.00 US. CAB International Centre, Wallingford, Oxon OX10 8DE United Kingdom. **Tel** 44 491 832111, FAX 44 491 833508, telex 847964 (COMAGG G). **ED** J. R. Metcalfe. **LC** QL461; .B9. **NLM** W1 BU76. **CODEN** BEREA2. **Ad Acc. Pr Rev.** Documents available from The Genuine Article, BIOSIS Document Express, CASDDS, Documents on Demand.
**Desc:** Contains papers dealing with original research concerning insects, mites or ticks of economic importance in the agricultural, medical or veterinary fields in any part of the world.
**Ind/Abst** AgBiotech News Inf.; AGRICOLA [Full Cov.]; Agrofor. Abstr. (19??-19??); Anim. Behav. Abstr.; Biocont. News Inf. (19??-19??); Biodeter. Abstr. (1991-); Biol. Agric. Index; Biol. Abstr.; Biotechnol. Res. Abstr.; Chem. Abstr.; Curr. Aware. Biol. Sci., CABS; Curr. Contents, Agric. Biol. Environ. Sci.; Ecol. Abstr.; Ecology Abstr.; Energy Inf. Abstr.; Entomol. Abstr.; Environ. Abstr.; Field Crop Abstr.; For. Prod. Abstr.; For. Abstr.; Geogr. Abstr. Phys. Geogr.; Grasslands For. Abstr.; Hortic. Abstr.; Index Vet.; Int. Dev. Abstr.; Irr. Drain. Abstr.; Maize Abstr.; Ornamental Hort.; Life Sci. Collect.; PESTDOC; Plant Breed. Abstr.; Postharvest News Inf.; Potato Abstr.; Protozoolog. Abstr.; Res. Alert [Full Cov.]; Rev. Agric. Entomol.; Rev. Med. Vet. Entomol.; Rice Abstr.; Sci. Cit. Index; SCISEARCH; Seed Abstr.; Soils Fert.; Vet. Bull.; Trop. Dis. Bull.; Weed Abstr.; Wheat Barley Trit. Abstr.

II/0013-8762
**BULLETIN OF ENTOMOLOGY.** [Bull. entomol.]. **Added/Corp** Entomological Society of India. Vol. 1 (1960)-. Bulletin. English. sa. $30.00. Entomological Society of India Institute, New Delhi 110012 India. **(Subscription address:** Prints India, 11 Darya Ganj, New Delhi 110002 India.**) CODEN** BENTAR. Documents available from BIOSIS Document Express.
**Ind/Abst** Agrofor. Abstr. (1991-); Biocont. News Inf. (19??-19??); Biodeter. Abstr. (1991-); Biol. Abstr.; Maize Abstr.; Nematol. Abstr.; Plant Breed. Abstr.; Potato Abstr.; Protozoolog. Abstr.; Rev. Agric. Entomol.; Rev. Med. Vet. Entomol.; Seed Abstr.

UK/0266-836X
**BULLETIN OF THE AMATEUR ENTOMOLOGISTS' SOCIETY, THE.** **Main/Corp** Amateur Entomologists' Society (Great Britain). Vol. 4, No. 32 (Jan. 1939)-. Periodical. English. Six times a year (Feb., Apr., June, Aug., Oct., Dec.). £11.00 UK; £14.00 other. Amateur Entomologists Society, 5 Oakfield Plaistow, West Sussex RH14 0QD England. **ED** B. O. C. Gardiner. Index available. **Bk Rev. Ad Acc, Adv Mgr:** R. Dyke. **Circ:** 2,000 (ctrl). ***Continues in part*** *Amateur Entomologists' Bulletin.*

UK/0524-6431
**BULLETIN OF THE BRITISH MUSEUM (NATURAL HISTORY). ENTOMOLOGY SERIES.** ***Title Change.*** [Bull. Br. Mus. Nat. Hist., Entomol. ser.]. **Added/Corp** British Museum (Natural History). **VFOAT** Entomology Series; Bulletin British Museum (Natural History). Entomology Series. Vol. 36, No. 1 (Sept. 1977)-Vol. 61, No. 2 (Nov. 1992). Periodical. English. ir. British Museum of Natural History, Cromwell Road, London SW7 5BD England. **Tel** 011 44 71 9389123. **LC** QL461; .B56. **DD** 595.7/005. ***Continues*** *Bulletin of the British Museum (Natural History). Entomology, 0524-6431.* ***Continued by*** *Bulletin of the Natural History Museum. Entomology Series, 0968-0454.*
**Ind/Abst** Biocont. News Inf.; Life Sci. Collect.; Rev. Agric. Entomol.; Rev. Med. Vet. Entomol.

US/0068-5631
**BULLETIN OF THE CALIFORNIA INSECT SURVEY.** [Bull. Calif. Insect Surv.]. **Added/Corp** California Insect Survey. University of California, Berkeley. Division of Entomology and Parasitology. Vol. 1, No. 1 (June 30, 1950)-. Bulletin. English. ir. Price varies per volume. University of California Press, 2120 Berkeley Way, Berkeley CA 94720. **Tel** (510)642-4191, (510)642-3907, FAX (510)642-9917. **(Subscription address:** California Princeton Fulfillment Services, 1445 Lower Ferry Road, Ewing, NJ 08618; telephone: (800)777-4726 or (609)883-1759**) LC** QL475.C3; C3. **DD** 595.7097494. **CODEN** BCINA4. **Pr Rev. Circ:** 800 (ctrl). Documents available from BIOSIS Document Express.
**Desc:** Contributions from the Division of Entomology and Parasitology, College of Agriculture, University of California.
**Ind/Abst** Biol. Abstr.; Trop. Dis. Bull.

●UK/0968-0454
**BULLETIN OF THE NATURAL HISTORY MUSEUM. ENTOMOLOGY SERIES.** **Added/Corp** British Museum (Natural History). **VFOAT** Entomology Series; Bulletin of the Natural History Museum Entomology. Vol. 62, No. 1 (June 1993)-. Periodical. English. Twice a year. £78.75. Intercept Ltd., PO Box 716, Andover Hampshire SP10 1YG England. **Tel** 011 44 264 334748, FAX 011 44 264 334058, telex 41103 PEPSOS G. **LC** IN PROCESS; QL461; .B56. **DD** 595.7/005. ***Continues*** *Bulletin of the British Museum (Natural History). Entomology Series, 0524-6431.*

FR/0029-7224
**CAHIERS O.R.S.T.O.M. SERIE ENTOMOLOGIE MEDICALE ET PARASITOLOGIE.** ***Ceased.*** [Cah. - O.R.S.T.O.M., Entomol. med. parasitol.]. **VFOAT** Serie Entomologie Medicale et Parasitologie. Ceased Vol. 25, No. 4. Periodical. French (summaries and/or abstracts in English). qt. Editions de l'ORSTOM, 72 Route d'Aulnay, 93143 Bondy Cedex France. **Tel** 011 33 1 48025500. **UDC** 576.8 + 595.7. **CODEN** CAOEA4. Documents available from BIOSIS Document Express. ***Continues*** *Cahiers O.R.S.T.O.M. Serie Entomologie Medicale.*
**Desc:** First hand works on systematics and biology of arthropods of medical and veterinary interest, parasitology of great tropical endemics, methods for struggling against vectors and harmful insects.
**Ind/Abst** Biocont. News Inf. (19??-19??); Biol. Abstr.; Helminthol. Abstr. (1991-); Life Sci. Collect.; Protozoolog. Abstr.; Rev. Med. Vet. Entomol.

CN/0008-347X
**CANADIAN ENTOMOLOGIST, THE.** [Can. entomol.]. **Added/Corp** Entomological Society of Canada (1863-1871) Entomological Society of Canada (1951- ) Entomological Society of Ontario. Vol. 1 (Aug. 1868)-. Periodical. English (French). bm. 187.25Can$ Canada; $180.00 other. Entomological Society of Canada, 393 Winston Avenue, Ottawa Ontario K2A 1Y8 Canada. **Tel** (613)725-2619, FAX (613)725-9349. **ED** A B Ewen. **LC** QL461; .C2. **NLM** W1 CA553. **CODEN** CAENAF. **[CCC].** Index available. **Bk Rev. Ad Acc. Pr Rev. Circ:** 1,500. available on microfilm and microfiche from University Microfilms International (UMI). Documents available from The Genuine Article, BIOSIS Document Express, CASDDS, Documents on Demand.
**Ind/Abst** ASTIS Curr. Aware. Bull. (1978-); AGRICOLA [Full Cov.]; Anim. Behav. Abstr.; AQUAREF; ASTIS Bibliogr. (1978-); Biocont. News Inf. (19??-19??); Biodeter. Abstr.; Biol. Agric. Index; Biol. Abstr.; Can. Environ.; Chem. Abstr.; Chemorecept. Abstr.; Curr. Aware. Biol. Sci., CABS; Curr. Contents, Agric. Biol. Environ. Sci.; Ecol. Abstr.; Ecology Abstr.; EMBASE; Entomol. Abstr.; Environ. Abstr.; Field Crop Abstr.; For. Prod. Abstr. (19??-19??); For. Abstr.; Geogr. Abstr. Phys. Geogr.; Grasslands For. Abstr.; Hortic. Abstr.; Index Vet.; Environ.; Maize Abstr.; Microbiol. Abstr. Sect. A; Nematol. Abstr.; Life Sci. Collect.; PESTDOC; Plant Breed. Abstr.; Postharvest News Inf.; Potato Abstr.; Poult. Abstr.; Protozoolog. Abstr.; Res. Alert [Full Cov.]; Rev. Agric. Entomol.; Rev. Med. Vet. Entomol.; Rev. Plant Pathol.; Sci. Cit. Index; SCISEARCH; Sel. Water Resour. Abstr.; Soils Fert.; Soyabean Abstr.; Weed Abstr.; Wheat Barley Trit. Abstr.

CC/0257-4799
**CANYE KEXUE.** (TSAN YEH KO HSUEH.). [Canye kexue]. **Added/Corp** Chung-kuo Tsan Hsueh hui. **VFOAT** Canye Kexue; Acta Sericologica Sinica. (1963)-. Periodical. Chinese (summaries and/or abstracts in English). qt. Documents available from CASDDS.
**Ind/Abst** Chem. Abstr.; Plant Breed. Abstr.; Rev. Agric. Entomol.; Rev. Plant Pathol.

JA
**CHO TO GA. TYO TO GA.** **Added/Corp** Nihon Rinshi Gakkai. Nihon Rinsi Gakkai Kaiho. Nihon Rinshi Gakkai. Transactions of the Lepidopterological Society of Japan. **VFOAT** Nihon Rinshi Gakkai Kaiho: Transactions of the Lepidopterological Society of Japan; Tyo to Ga; Butterflies and Moths. Vol. 1 (1945)-. English (Japanese). qt. ¥10000. Nihon Rinshi Gakkai, (Lepidopterological Soc. of Japan), c/o Ogata Byoin, 3-18, Imabashi, Higashiku, Osakashi, Osakafu 541, Japan. **ED** Toshiro Yasuda. **LC** QL541; .C47. **DD** 595.7/8/05. Index available. **Ad Acc. Circ:** 1,500 (ctrl).
**Ind/Abst** Life Sci. Collect. (1985-).

AG/0326-3789
**CIRPON, REVISTA DE INVESTIGACION.** **Added/Corp** Centro de Investigaciones para la Regulacion de Poblaciones de Organismos Nocivos (Argentina). **VFOAT** Revista de Investigacion. Vol. 1, No.

1 (1983)-. Periodical. Spanish. qt. **LC** SB935.A7; C57. **DD** 628.9/657/0982.
**Ind/Abst** Biocont. News Inf.

II/0970-3292
**COLEMANIA (BANGALORE).**
(COLEMANIA.). [Colemania]. Vol. 1, No. 1 (Summer 1981)-. Periodical. English. $60.00. **(Subscription address:** Prints India, 11 Darya Ganj, New Delhi, 110002 India, (Phone: 011 91 11 3268645)) **LC** IN PROCESS. **CODEN** CLMNDX.

●US
**CONTEMPORARY TOPICS IN ENTOMOLOGY.** (1992)-. Monographic series. English. ir. Price varies per volume. Routledge Chapman & Hall Inc, 29 West 35th Street, New York NY 10001. **Tel** (212)244-3336, (212)244-6412.

US/0569-4450
**CONTRIBUTIONS OF THE AMERICAN ENTOMOLOGICAL INSTITUTE.** [Contrib. Am. Entomol. Inst.]. **Main/Corp** American Entomological Institute. Vol. 1 (1964)-. Monographic series. English (Spanish). ir. Price varies per volume. Associated Publishers / Florida, PO Box 140103, Gainesville FL 32614. **Tel** (904)371-4071, FAX (904)371-4071. **ED** V. K. Gupta. **LC** QL461; .A36. **DD** 595. **Circ:** 140.
**Desc:** Taxonomy of insects.
**Ind/Abst** AGRICOLA [Full Cov.]; Entomol. Abstr.; Life Sci. Collect.; Rev. Med. Vet. Entomol.

GW/0012-0073
**DEUTSCHE ENTOMOLOGISCHE ZEITSCHRIFT.** (DEUTSCHE ENTOMOLOGISCHE ZEITSCHRIFT / HERAUSGEGEBEN VON DER DEUTSCHEN ENTOMOLOGISCHEN GESELLSCHAFT.). [Dtsch. entomol. Z.]. **Added/Corp** Deutsche Entomologische Gesellschaft. Deutsches Entomologisches National-Museum (Germany) Zoologisches Museum (Berlin, Germany). Vol. 25, Nos. 1 & 2 (May and Oct. 1881)-. Periodical. German. Twice a year. $210.00. Akademie-Verlag GmbH, Muehlenstrasse 33 34, D 13162 Berlin Germany. **Tel** 011 49 30 47889300, FAX 011 49 30 47889357. **(Subscription address:** VCH Publishers Inc., 303 Northwest 12th Avenue, Journals Department, Deerfield FL 33442.) **LC** QL461; .D5. **DD** 595.7/005. **NLM** W1 DE627. **CODEN** DENZAX. cum. index. **Pr Rev.** Documents available from The Genuine Article, BIOSIS Document Express. ***Absorbed*** *Zeitschrift fur Sustematische Hymenopterologie und Dipterologie; Berliner Entomologische Zeitschrift.*
**Ind/Abst** AGRICOLA; Biocont. News Inf. (19??-19??); Biol. Abstr. (?-1978); Curr. Aware. Biol. Sci., CABS; Curr. Contents, Agric. Biol. Environ. Sci.; Life Sci. Collect.; Res. Alert [Select. Cov.]; SCISEARCH.

UK/0307-6946
**ECOLOGICAL ENTOMOLOGY.** [Ecol. entomol.]. **Added/Corp** Royal Entomological Society of London. Vol. 1 (Feb. 1976)-. Academic Scholarly Publication. English. qt (4 issues). $240.00 (institutions), $71.00 (individuals) US & Canada; £141.00 (institutions), £41.50 (individuals) Europe; £155.00 (institutions), £45.50 (individuals) other. Blackwell Scientific Publications Ltd, Marston Book Services, PO Box 87, Oxford OX2 ODT UK. **Tel** 011 44 865 791155, FAX 011 44 865 791927, telex 837 515 MARDIS G. **ED** J. H. Lawton. **LC** QL461; .R65. **DD** 595.7/05. **NLM** W1 EC911G. **CODEN** EENTDT. **[CCC].** Index available. **Bk Rev. Ad Acc. Pr Rev.** available on microfilm and microfiche from University Microfilms International (UMI). Documents available from The Genuine Article, BIOSIS Document Express. ***Supersedes*** *Transactions of the Royal Entomological Society of London.*
**Desc:** Covers field biology and natural history of terrestrial and aquatic insects.
**Ind/Abst** AGRICOLA [Full Cov.]; Agrofor. Abstr.; Anim. Behav. Abstr.; Biocont. News Inf. (19??-19??); Biol. Agric. Index; Biol. Abstr.; Chemorecept. Abstr.; Curr. Aware. Biol. Sci., CABS; Curr. Contents, Agric. Biol. Environ. Sci.; Ecol. Abstr.; Ecology Abstr.; Entomol. Abstr.; For. Prod. Abstr.; For. Abstr.; Index Vet.; Maize Abstr.; Life Sci. Collect.; PESTDOC; Postharvest News Inf.; Potato Abstr.; Protozoolog. Abstr.; Res. Alert [Full Cov.]; Rev. Agric. Entomol.; Rev. Med. Vet. Entomol.; Rev. Plant Pathol.; Rice Abstr.; Sci. Cit. Index; SCISEARCH; Seed Abstr.; Soils Fert.; Vet. Bull.; Weed Abstr.; Wheat Barley Trit. Abstr.

JA/0424-7086
**EISEI DOBUTSU.** (EISEI DOBUTSU / JAPANESE JOURNAL OF SANITARY ZOOLOGY.). [Eisei dobutsu]. **Added/Corp** Nihon Eisei Dobutsu Gakkai. Nihon Eisei Konchu Gakkai. **VFOAT** Japanese Journal of Sanitary Zoology. (Apr. 1950)-. Academic Scholarly Publication. Japanese (English). qt. $144.00. Business Center for Academic Societies Japan, Hon-Komagome 5-16-9, Bunkyo-ku, Tokyo 113 Japan. **Tel** 011 81 3 3817 5811. **(Subscription address:** Kyowa Book Company Inc., 1 38 Kanda Jinbocho Chiyoda-ku, Tokyo 101 Japan.) **ED** Nobuo Kumado. **NLM** W1 EI555. **CODEN** ESDBAK. cum. index. **Bk Rev. Ad Acc. Circ:** 1,100 (ctrl). Documents available from BIOSIS Document Express, CASDDS.
**Ind/Abst** AGRICOLA; Biocont. News Inf. (1991-); Biol. Abstr.; Chem. Abstr.; Ecology Abstr.; Entomol. Abstr.; Helminthol. Abstr.; Index Vet.; Nematol. Abstr.; Nutr. Abstr. Rev., Ser. A, Hum. Exp.; Life Sci. Collect.; PESTDOC; Protozoolog. Abstr.; Rev. Med. Vet. Entomol.; Rice Abstr.; Vet. Bull.; Trop. Dis. Bull.

NE/0013-8703
**ENTOMOLOGIA EXPERIMENTALIS ET APPLICATA.** [Entomol. exp. appl.]. **Added/Corp** Nederlandse Entomologische Vereniging. Vol. 1, No. 1 (Feb. 1958)-. Periodical. English (French and German). mo. $1,420.00. Kluwer Academic Publishers, Postbus 322, 3300 AH Dordrecht, The Netherlands. **Tel** 011 (31) 78 524400, FAX 011 31 78 183273, telex 20083. **ED** A K Minks, L M Schoonhoven and S B Menken. **NLM** W1 EN923H. **CODEN** ETEAAT. **[CCC]. Bk Rev. Ad Acc. Pr Rev. Acid Free. Circ:** 200. available on microfilm and microfiche from University Microfilms International (UMI). Documents available from The Genuine Article, BIOSIS Document Express, CASDDS.
**Desc:** Covers the fields of experimental biology and ecology, both pure and applied, of insects and other land arthropods.
**Ind/Abst** AgBiotech News Inf.; AGRICOLA [Full Cov.]; Agrindex; Agrofor. Abstr. (1991-); Anim. Behav. Abstr.; Biocont. News Inf. (19??-19??); Biodeter. Abstr. (19??-19??); Biol. Abstr.; Chem. Abstr.; Chemorecept. Abstr.; Cot. Trop. Fibr. Abstr. Bibliogr.; CSA Neuro. Abstr. (?-?); Curr. Aware. Biol. Sci., CABS; Curr. Contents, Agric. Biol. Environ. Sci.; Ecol. Abstr.; Ecology Abstr.; Entomol. Abstr.; Field Crop Abstr.; For. Prod. Abstr. (19??-19??); For. Abstr.; Geogr. Abstr. Phys. Geogr.; Hortic. Abstr.; Index Vet.; Maize Abstr.; Life Sci. Collect.; PESTDOC; Plant Breed. Abstr.; Plant Genet. Resour. Abstr.; Postharvest News Inf.; Potato Abstr.; Protozoolog. Abstr.; Ref. Upd. Deluxe Ed.; Res. Alert [Full Cov.]; Rev. Agric. Entomol.; Rev. Med. Vet. Entomol.; Rev. Plant Pathol.; Rice Abstr.; Sci. Cit. Index; SCISEARCH; Seed Abstr.; Soils Fert.; Sorghum Mill. Abstr.; Soyabean Abstr.; Sug. Indus. Abstr.; Vet. Bull.; Trop. Dis. Bull.; Virol. AIDS Abstr.; Vitis Vitic. Enol. Abstr.; Wheat Barley Trit. Abstr.

GW/0171-8177
**ENTOMOLOGIA GENERALIS.** [Entomol. gen.]. **VFOAT** Journal for Scientific Entomology; Zeitschrift fur Wissenschaftliche Entomologie. Vol. 5 (March 1978)-. Periodical. German (summaries and/or abstracts in English). Four times a year. $251.00. E. Schweizerbartsche Verlagsbuchhandlung, Johannesstrasse 3A, D-70176 Stuttgart Germany. **Tel** 011 49 711 625001, FAX 011 49 711 625005, telex 723363 SCHB D. **LC** QL461; .E53. **CODEN** ENGND5. **[CCC].** Index available in last issue of volume--attached. **Pr Rev.** Documents available from The Genuine Article, BIOSIS Document Express. ***Continues*** *Entomologica Germanica, 0340-2266.*
**Ind/Abst** AGRICOLA [Full Cov.]; Biocont. News Inf. (19??-19??); Biol. Abstr.; Curr. Aware. Biol. Sci., CABS; Curr. Contents, Agric. Biol. Environ. Sci.; Ecology Abstr.; Entomol. Abstr.; Life Sci. Collect.; Res. Alert [Select. Cov.]; Rev. Agric. Entomol.; Rev. Med. Vet. Entomol.; SCISEARCH; Vitis Vitic. Enol. Abstr.; Weed Abstr.

IT/0425-1016
**ENTOMOLOGICA.** (ENTOMOLOGICA; ANNALI DI ENTOMOLOGIA GENERALE E APPLICATA.). [Entomologica]. Vol. 1 (1965)-. Italian (summaries and/or abstracts in English). an. Istituto Entomologia Agraria dell'Universita, Via Celoria 2, 20133 Milan Italy. **Tel** 011 39 2 236 3439. **CODEN** ENUBA2. Documents available from BIOSIS Document Express.
**Ind/Abst** Biocont. News Inf. (19??-19??); Biol. Abstr.; Life Sci. Collect.

SZ/0253-2484
**ENTOMOLOGICA BASILIENSIA.** (ENTOMOLOGICA BASILIENSIA / NATURHISTORICSHES MUSEUM BASEL, ENTOMOLOGISCHE ABTEILUNG.). [Entomol. basil.]. **Added/Corp** Naturhistorisches Museum Basel. Entomologische Abteilung. Vol. 1 (1975)-. German (English and French; summaries and/or abstracts in English and German). ir. 75.00F. **(Subscription address:** Karger Libri AG, Petersgraben 31, CH 4009 Basel 11 Switzerland.) **ED** M. Brancucci, W. Wittmer. Index available.
**Desc:** Covers taxonomy, systematics and faunistic of insects and other arthropods.
**Ind/Abst** Life Sci. Collect.; Rev. Med. Vet. Entomol.

FI/0785-8760
**ENTOMOLOGICA FENNICA.** (1990)-. Periodical. English. qt. Academic Bookstore Akateeminen, Postilokero 23, FIN-00371 Helsinki Finland. **Tel** 011 358 0 12141. **(Subscription address:** Bookstore Tiedekirja, Kirkkokatu 14, SF 00170 Helsinki Finland.) **LC** QL482.F5; E58. **Bk Rev. Circ:** 700 (ctrl). Documents available from The Genuine Article, BIOSIS Document Express. ***Formed by the union of*** *Acta Entomologica Fennica, 0001-561X; Annales Entomologici Fennici, 0003-4428* ***and*** *Notulae Entomologicae, 0029-4594.*
**Desc:** Concerns entomology-Finland, taxonomic entomology, insect biogeography, insect ecology, insect physiology, acarology, arachnology, and applied entomology.
**Ind/Abst** AGRICOLA [Full Cov.]; Biol. Abstr.; Curr. Aware. Biol. Sci., CABS; Curr. Contents, Agric. Biol. Environ. Sci.; Entomol. Abstr.; Res. Alert [Select. Cov.]; SCISEARCH.

DK/0013-8711
**ENTOMOLOGICA SCANDINAVICA.** [Entomol. scand.]. **Added/Corp** Societas Entomologica Scandinavica. Vol. 1 (Feb. 1970)-. Periodical. English (French and German). Four times a year. kr1238.00. Apollo Books, Kirkeby Sand 19, DK 5771 Stenstrup Denmark. **Tel** 011 45 62 263737, telex 39296 BRILL NL. **ED** N. Moller Andersen and Verner Michelsen. **LC** QL461; .E564. **DD** 595.7/05. **CODEN** ENTSBF. **Bk Rev. Ad Acc. Pr Rev. Circ:** 550. Documents available from The Genuine Article, BIOSIS Document Express.
**Desc:** Covers systematic entomology.
**Ind/Abst** AGRICOLA; Biocont. News Inf. (19??-19??); Biol. Abstr.; Curr. Aware. Biol. Sci., CABS; Curr. Contents, Agric. Biol. Environ. Sci.; Entomol. Abstr.; For. Abstr.; GeoRef; Life Sci. Collect.; Protozoolog. Abstr.; Res. Alert [Select. Cov.]; Rev. Agric. Entomol.; Rev. Med. Vet. Entomol.; SCISEARCH; Soils Fert.

US/0013-872X
**ENTOMOLOGICAL NEWS.** [Entomol. news]. **Added/Corp** American Entomological Society. Academy of Natural Sciences of Philadelphia. Entomological Section. Vol. 36 (1925)-. Periodical. English. Five times a year. $18.00 US; $20.00 other. American Entomological Society, Academy of Natural Sciences of Philadelphia, 1900 Race Street, Philadelphia PA 19103. **Tel** (215)561-3978, FAX (215)299-1028. **NLM** W1 EN923R. **CODEN** ETMNA6. **Bk Rev. Ad Acc. Pr Rev. Circ:** 700. available on microfilm and microfiche from University Microfilms International (UMI). Documents available from The Genuine Article, BIOSIS Document Express, CASDDS. ***Continues*** *Entomological News and Proceedings of the Entomological Section of the Academy of Natural Sciences of Philadelphia.*
**Desc:** Classification, taxonomy, systematics, and ecology of insects.
**Ind/Abst** AGRICOLA [Full Cov.]; Biocont. News Inf. (19??-19??); Biodeter. Abstr.; Biol. Abstr.; Chem. Abstr.; Coal Abstr.; Cot. Trop. Fibr. Abstr. Bibliogr.; Curr. Aware. Biol. Sci., CABS; Curr. Contents, Agric. Biol. Environ. Sci.; Ecology Abstr.; Entomol. Abstr.; For. Abstr.; Index Med.; Life Sci. Collect.; Res. Alert [Select. Cov.]; Rev. Agric. Entomol.; Rev. Med. Vet. Entomol.; SCISEARCH; Soils Fert.; Wildl. Rev.

KO
**ENTOMOLOGICAL RESEARCH BULLETIN.** **Added/Corp** Koryo Taehakkyo. Pusol Hanguk Konchung Yonguso. **VFOAT** Konchung Yonguji. Vol. 11 (Dec. 1985)-. Bulletin. English (summaries and/or abstracts in Korean). an. Free on request (Korea); $50.00 (library and institute); $30.00 (individual). Korean Entomological Institute, Korea University, 126-1 5 Anam-dong Sungbuk-ku, Seoul 136-701 Korea. **Tel** (02)920 1793, FAX (02)924-6094. **ED** Tae-Young Moon. **LC** QL461; .Y65. Index available. **Ad Acc. Pr Rev. Circ:** 1000 (ctrl).

US/0013-8738
**ENTOMOLOGICAL REVIEW.** [Entomol. rev.]. **Added/Corp** Entomological Society of America. Consultants Bureau Enterprises. Scripta Technica, inc. Vol. 37 (1958)-. Periodical. English (translations available in Russian). Nine times a year. $1,395.00 US; $1,485.00 Canada and Mexico; $1,518.75 other. Scripta Technica, A Subsidiary of John Wiley & Sons, Inc., 7961 Eastern Avenue, Silver Spring MD 20910. **Tel** (301)588-0484, FAX (301)588-5278. **(Subscription address:** John Wiley / Philadelphia, PO Box 7247, Philadelphia PA 19170.) **ED** George C. Steyskal. **DD** 595. **NLM** W1 EN923V. **CODEN** ENREBV. **[CCC]. Ad Acc. Circ:** 425. available on microfilm and microfiche from University Microfilms International (UMI). Documents available from BIOSIS Document Express, CASDDS.
**Desc:** Translation of the basic Russian journal in entomology which deals with all aspects of the science, including systematics, faunistics, ecology, morphology, physiology and biochemistry of insects, as well as biological and chemical control of pests.
**Ind/Abst** AGRICOLA [Full Cov.]; Biol. Abstr.; Chem. Abstr.; Ecology Abstr.; Entomol. Abstr.; Life Sci. Collect.; Soils Fert.

GW/0373-8981
**ENTOMOLOGISCHE ABHANDLUNGEN.** [Entomol. Abh.]. **Added/Corp** Staatliches Museum fuer Tierkunde in Dresden (Germany). **VFOAT** Abhandlungen und Berichte aus der Staatlichen Museum fuer Tierkunde in Dresden. Entmologische Abhandlungen. No. 26 (1962)-. Multiple languages (English, French and German). Staatliches Museum fuer Tierkunde Dresden, Augustusstrasse 2, D 01067 Dresden Germany. **LC** QL461; .E728. **DD** 595.7. **CODEN** SMTEBI. **Bk Rev. Circ:** 550 (ctrl). Documents available from BIOSIS Document Express. ***Supersedes in part*** *Abhandlungen und Berichte aus dem Staatliches Museum fuer Tierkundein Dresden, 0138-4147.*
**Desc:** Taxonomy, systematics, zoogeography of the invertebrate groups insecta and arachnida in global range.
**Ind/Abst** Biol. Abstr.; Life Sci. Collect.

SZ
**ENTOMOLOGISCHE BERICHTE LUZERN : MITTEILUNGEN DER ENTOMOLOGISCHEN GESELLSCHAFT LUZERN.** **Added/Corp** Entomologische Gesellschaft Luzern. **VFOAT** Mitteilungen der Entomologischen Gesellschaft Luzern. No. 1 (Jan. 1979)-. German.
**Ind/Abst** Entomol. Abstr.

SW/0013-886X
**ENTOMOLOGISK TIDSKRIFT / ENTOMOLOGISKA FORENINGEN I STOCKHOLM.** [Entomol. tidskr.]. **Added/Corp** Entomologiska Foreningen i Stockholm. **VFOAT** Journal Entomologique. (1880)-. Periodical. Swedish (English, French and German). Three times a year. Kr180.00, Kr120.00 (members). Sveriges Entomologiska Forenin Naturhistoriska / Swedish Museum of Natural History, Box 50007, 104 05 Stockholm Sweden. **Tel** 011 46 8 6664089. **NLM** W1 EN931GH. **CODEN** ETTIAQ. cum. index. Documents available from BIOSIS Document Express.
**Ind/Abst** AGRICOLA; Biocont. News Inf.; Biodeter. Abstr.; Biol. Abstr.; Entomol. Abstr.; For. Abstr.; Life Sci. Collect.; Rev. Agric. Entomol.; Rev. Med. Vet. Entomol.

DK/0013-8851
**ENTOMOLOGISKE MEDDELELSER.** [Entomol. medd.]. **Added/Corp** Entomologisk Forening, Copenhagen. Vol. 1 (1887)-. Periodical. Multiple languages (Danish, English and German). ir. kr255.00. Entomologisk Forening, Universitetsparken 15, Zoologisk Museum, DK-2100 Copenhagen Denmark. **Tel** 011 45 35 321000. **ED** L Lyneborg. **CODEN** ETMDAA. Index available. **Bk Rev. Circ:** 700. Documents available from BIOSIS Document Express.
**Ind/Abst** Biocont. News Inf.; Biodeter. Abstr.; Biol. Abstr.; Ecol. Abstr. (?-?); Ecology Abstr.; Entomol. Abstr.; Life Sci. Collect.; Rev. Agric. Entomol.; Rev. Med. Vet. Entomol.

UK/0013-8878
**ENTOMOLOGIST, THE.** [Entomologist]. **Added/Corp** British Trust for Entomology. Royal Entomological Society of London. Vol. 10, No. 164 (Jan. 1877)-. Periodical. English. Four times a year. $47.50. Royal Entomological Society, 41 Queens Gate, London SW7 5HR England. **Tel** 011 41 71 5848361. ***Continues*** *Newman's Entomologist;* ***Absorbed*** *Journal of the Society for British Entomology; Transcations of the Society for British Entomology.*
**Ind/Abst** AGRICOLA [Full Cov.]; Curr. Aware. Biol. Sci., CABS; Plant Breed. Abstr.; Rev. Agric. Entomol.; Rev. Med. Vet. Entomol.; Wheat Barley Trit. Abstr.

FR/0013-8886
**ENTOMOLOGISTE, L'.** [Entomologiste]. Vol. 1 (1944)-. Periodical. French. bm. 186.09F France; 190.00F other EEC; 220.00F non-EEC Europe; 250.00F other. L'Entomologiste, 45 Bis rue de Buffon, F 75005 Paris France. **NLM** W1 EN931J. **CODEN** ETMGAJ. cum. index. **Bk Rev.** Documents available from BIOSIS Document Express.
**Ind/Abst** Biol. Abstr.; Entomol. Abstr.; Life Sci. Collect.

UK/0013-8894
**ENTOMOLOGIST'S GAZETTE.** [Entomol. gaz.]. Vol. 1 (Jan. 1950)-. Periodical. English. qt. $50.00. GEM Publishing Company, Brightwood Bell Lane/Brightwell, Wallingford Oxon 0X10 OQD England. **Tel** 011 44 491 33882, FAX 011 44 491 25161. **ED** W G Tremewan. **LC** WMLC 93/1940. **NLM** W1 EN931K. **CODEN** ETGAA5. **Bk Rev. Ad Acc, Adv Mgr:** G. Morton, **Tel** 44-491-33882. **Circ:** 500. Documents available from BIOSIS Document Express.
**Desc:** A periodical of Palearctic entomology.
**Ind/Abst** AGRICOLA; Biocont. News Inf. (19??-19??); Biol. Abstr.; Entomol. Abstr.; Fish Rev.; For. Abstr.; Index Vet.; Life Sci. Collect.; Rev. Agric. Entomol.; Rev. Med. Vet. Entomol.; Vet. Bull.; Wildl. Rev.

UK/0013-8908
**ENTOMOLOGIST'S MONTHLY MAGAZINE, THE.** [Entomol. mon. mag.]. Vol. 1 (June 1864)-. Periodical. English. Three times a year. $55.00 US and Canada; £28.00 (air mail) Mexico; £29.00 (air mail), £25.00 (surface mail) other. GEM Publishing Company, Brightwood Bell Lane/Brightwell, Wallingford Oxon 0X10 OQD England. **Tel** 011 44 491 33882, FAX 011 44 491 25161. **ED** K.G.V. Smith. **LC** QL461; .E98. **DD** 595.7/005. **CODEN** ENMMAT. Index available. cum. index. **Bk Rev. Ad Acc, Adv Mgr:** G. Morton, **Tel** 44-491-33882. **Circ:** 525. Documents available from BIOSIS Document Express.
**Desc:** Articles on all orders of insects and terrestrial arthropods, specializing in the British fauna and groups other than Lepidoptera.
**Ind/Abst** Biocont. News Inf.; Biodeter. Abstr. (1991-); Biol. Abstr.; Ecology Abstr.; Entomol. Abstr.; For. Prod. Abstr.; For. Abstr.; Hortic. Abstr.; Life Sci. Collect.; Postharvest News Inf.; Rev. Agric. Entomol.; Rev. Med. Vet. Entomol.; Soils Fert.

US/0013-8924
**ENTOMOLOGY ABSTRACTS.** **See** Zoology-Abstracting, Bibliographies and Statistics.

II/0377-9335
**ENTOMON.** [Entomon]. **Added/Corp** Association for Advancement of Entomology (India). (1976)-. Academic Scholarly Publication. English. Four times a year. $50.00. University of Kerala Department of Zoology, Association for the Advancement of Entomology, Trivandrum 695581 India. **(Subscription address:** Prints India, 11 Darya Ganj, New Delhi, 110002 India, (Phone: 011 91 11 3268645)) **ED** V.K.K. Prabhu. **LC** QL461; .E98576. **DD** 595.7/005. **CODEN** ENTOD5. Index available. **Bk Rev,** (Qty: 500). **Pr Rev. Circ:** 500. Documents available from The Genuine Article, BIOSIS Document Express, CASDDS.
**Desc:** Covers entomology.
**Ind/Abst** Agrofor. Abstr.; Biocont. News Inf. (19??-19??); Biodeter. Abstr.; Biol. Abstr.; Chem. Abstr.; Cot. Trop. Fibr. Abstr. Bibliogr.; Curr. Aware. Biol. Sci., CABS; Curr. Contents, Agric. Biol. Environ. Sci.; Ecology Abstr.; Entomol. Abstr.; For. Prod. Abstr.; For. Abstr.; Hortic. Abstr.; Maize Abstr.; Nematol. Abstr.; Life Sci. Collect.; Plant Breed. Abstr.; Postharvest News Inf.; Protozoolog. Abstr.; Res. Alert [Select. Cov.]; Rev. Agric. Entomol.; Rev. Med. Vet. Entomol.; Rev. Plant Pathol.; Rice Abstr.; SCISEARCH; Soils Fert.; Sorghum Mill. Abstr.; Soyabean Abstr.; Wheat Barley Trit. Abstr.

US/0046-225X
**ENVIRONMENTAL ENTOMOLOGY.** [Environ. entomol.]. **Added/Corp** Entomological Society of America. Vol. 1 (Feb. 1972)-. Periodical. English. bm. $75.00 (individual), $150.00 (institution) US; $95.00 (individual), $170.00 (institution) other. Entomological Society of America, 9301 Annapolis Road, Suite 300, Lanham MD 20706. **Tel** (301)731-4535, FAX (301)731-4538. **(Subscription address:** ESA, PO Box 177, Hyattsville, MD 20781-0177) **ED** Ronald E. Stinner and William P. Kemp. **LC** SB599; .E44. **DD** 632/.7/05. **NLM** W1 EN981Q. **CODEN** EVETBX. **[CCC]. Ad Acc. Pr Rev. Circ:** 2,000. available on microfilm and microfiche from University Microfilms International (UMI). Documents available from The Genuine Article, BIOSIS Document Express, CASDDS, Documents on Demand.
**Desc:** Devoted to research on the interaction of insects with the biological, chemical, and physical aspects of their environments.
**Ind/Abst** AGRICOLA [Full Cov.]; Anim. Behav. Abstr.; BioBusiness; Biocont. News Inf. (19??-19??); Biodeter. Abstr. (19??-19??); Biol. Agric. Index; Biol. Abstr.; Biotechnol. Res. Abstr.; Chem. Abstr.; Chemorecept. Abstr.; Coal Abstr.; Cot. Trop. Fibr. Abstr. Bibliogr.; Curr. Aware. Biol. Sci., CABS; Curr. Contents, Agric. Biol. Environ. Sci.; Ecol. Abstr. (?-?); Ecology Abstr.; EMBASE; Energy Inf. Abstr.; Energy Res. Abstr. (May 1973-); Entomol. Abstr.; Environ. Abstr.; Environ. Period. Bibliogr.; Field Crop Abstr.; Fish Rev.; For. Prod. Abstr.; For. Abstr.; Geogr. Abstr. Human Geogr. (?-?); Grasslands For. Abstr.; Hortic. Abstr.; Index Vet.; INIS Atomindex [Micro.]; Irr. Drain. Abstr.; Maize Abstr.; Microbiol. Abstr. Sect. A; Microbiol. Abstr. Sect. C; Nematol. Abstr.; Ornamental Hort. (19??-19??); Life Sci. Collect.; PESTDOC; Plant Breed. Abstr.; Plant Grow. Reg. Abstr.; Pollut. Abstr. Indexes; Postharvest News Inf.; Potato Abstr.; Poult. Abstr.; Protozoolog. Abstr.; Res. Alert [Full Cov.]; Rev. Agric. Entomol.; Rev. Med. Vet. Entomol.; Rev. Plant Pathol.; Rice Abstr.; Sci. Cit. Index; SCISEARCH; Seed Abstr.; Soils Fert.; Sorghum Mill. Abstr.; Soyabean Abstr.; Vet. Bull.; Virol. AIDS Abstr.; Vitis Vitic. Enol. Abstr.; Weed Abstr.; Wheat Barley Trit. Abstr.; Wildl. Rev.

SP/0013-9440
**EOS (MADRID).** (EOS.). [EOS]. **Added/Corp** Museo Nacional de Ciencias Naturales (Spain). Seccion de Entomologia. Consejo Superior de Investigaciones Cientificas (Spain). Instituto Espanol de Entomologia. Instituto "Jose de Acosta.". Vol. 1 (March 30, 1925)-. Periodical. Spanish. qt. 2000ptas Spain; 3000ptas others. Museo Nacional de Ciencias Naturales, Jose Abascal 2, D Luis Arguero, 28006 Madrid Spain. **Tel** 011 34 1 411328. **CODEN** EOSMAW. Documents available from BIOSIS Document Express.
**Ind/Abst** Biol. Abstr.; For. Abstr.; Rev. Agric. Entomol.; Rev. Med. Vet. Entomol.

US/0273-7353
**ESA NEWSLETTER - ENTOMOLOGICAL SOCIETY OF AMERICA.** (ESA NEWSLETTER.). [ESA newsletter - Entomol. Soc. Am.]. **Added/Corp** Entomological Society of America. **VAT** Entomological Society of America Newsletter. Vol. 1 (Feb. 1978)-. Newsletter. English. mo. $18.00 (individual), $35.00 (institution) US; $24.00 (individual), $41.00 (institution) other. Entomological Society of America, 9301 Annapolis Road, Suite 300, Lanham MD 20706. **Tel** (301)731-4535, FAX (301)731-4538. **ED** Richard V. Carr. **Circ:** 9,500 (ctrl).
**Desc:** Provides information on insects, insect management and persons studying insects. Contains news of the activities of registered professional entomologists.

JA/0071-1268
**ESAKIA.** **Added/Corp** Hikosan Seibutsugaku Kenkyujo. No. 1 (Jan. 20, 1960)-. Monographic series. English. Price varies per volume. Kyushu Daigaku Nogakubu Fuzoku Hikosan Seibutsugaku Jikkenjo, (Hikosan Biological Lab., Fac. of Agriculture, Kyushu University), Hikosan, Soedacho, Tagawagun, Fukuokaken 824-07 Japan.
**Ind/Abst** Entomol. Abstr.; Life Sci. Collect.; SEA Abstr.

●XR/1210-5759
**EUROPEAN JOURNAL OF ENTOMOLOGY.** **Added/Corp** Institute of Entomology (Czech Academy of Sciences) Czech Entomological Society. **VFOAT** Eur. J. Entomol. Vol. 90, No. 1 (1993)-. Academic Scholarly Publication. English. qt. $140.00 (institutions), $50.00 (individuals) Europe; $160.00 (institutions), $70.00 (individuals) other. Czech Academy of Sciences, Branisovska 31, 37005 Ceske Budejovice, Czech Republic. **Tel** 011 42 38 817 ext. 213, 214. **LC** QL461; .E9884. **DD** 595.7/005. **CODEN** EJENE2. Documents available from CASDDS. ***Continues*** *Acta entomologica Bohemoslovaca, 0001-5601.*
**Ind/Abst** Chem. Abstr.

CN/0318-6725
**FABRERIES.** **Added/Corp** Association des Entomologistes Amateurs du Quebec. Vol. 1 (Jan. 1975)-. Periodical. French. Four times a year. 30.00Can$. Association des Entomologistes Amateurs du Quebec, INS de MTL, 4581 Sherbrooke Estate, Montreal Quebec, H1X 2B2 Canada. **Tel** (514)291-4312. **ED** Bernard Landry (phone: (613)996-1665). **DD** 595.7/005. Index available. cum. index. **Bk Rev.**
**Ind/Abst** Life Sci. Collect. (1985-); Rev. Agric. Entomol.

DK/0106-8377
**FAUNA ENTOMOLOGICA SCANDINAVICA.** [Fauna entomol. scand.]. **Added/Corp** Societas Entomologica Scandinavica. Vol. 1 (1973)-. Monographic series. English. ir. Price varies per volume. E. J. Brill, Postbus 9000, 2300 PA Leiden Netherlands. **Tel** 011 31 71 312624, FAX 011 31 71 317532, telex 39296 BRILL NL. **CODEN** FESCDE. Documents available from BIOSIS Document Express.
**Ind/Abst** Biol. Abstr.; Life Sci. Collect.; Rev. Agric. Entomol.

NO/0332-7698
**FAUNA NORVEGICA. SER. B.** [Fauna Nor. ser. B.]. **Added/Corp** Norsk Zoologisk Tidsskriftsentral. Norsk Entomologisk Forening. **VFOAT** Norwegian Journal of Entomology. Vol. 26 (1979)-. Periodical. English (English). sa. Kr85.00. Fauna Norvegica, Zoologisk Museum, Sarsgt 1 0562, Oslo Norway. **Tel** 001 47 2 686960. **LC** QL461; .N67. **CODEN** FNSBD6. **[CCC].** Documents available from BIOSIS Document Express. ***Continues*** *Norwegian Journal of Entomology.*
**Ind/Abst** AGRICOLA; Biocont. News Inf.; Biol. Abstr.; Ecol. Abstr.; Ecology Abstr.; Entomol. Abstr.; For. Abstr.; Geogr. Abstr. Phys. Geogr.; Geol. Abstr.; Life Sci. Collect.; Rev. Med. Vet. Entomol.; Weed Abstr.; Wildl. Rev.

NZ/0111-5383
**FAUNA OF NEW ZEALAND.** [Fauna N.Z.]. **Added/Corp** New Zealand. Dept. of Scientific and Industrial Research. Science Information Division. No. 1 (1982)-. Monographic series. English. ir. Price varies per volume. Science Information Publishing Center, Box 9741, Wellington New Zealand. **Tel** 011 64 4 858939, FAX 011 64 4 850631, telex NZ 32076 RESERCH. **ED** C.T. Duval. **Ad Acc. Circ:** 300 (ctrl).
**Desc:** Series on taxonomy of New Zealand's insects or other terrestrial invertebrates, with text keys and illustrations.
**Ind/Abst** Entomol. Abstr.; Life Sci. Collect.; Rev. Agric. Entomol.; Rev. Med. Vet. Entomol.

GW/0375-2135
**FAUNISTISCHE ABHANDLUNGEN (LEIPZIG).** (FAUNISTISCHE ABHANDLUNGEN / STAATLICHES MUSEUM FUER TIERKUNDE IN DRESDEN.). [Faun. Abh.]. **Added/Corp** Staatliches Museum fuer Tierkunde in Dresden (Germany). (1963)-. Monographic series. German (English and French). ir. Price varies per volume. Staatliches Museum fuer Tierkunde Dresden, Augustusstrasse 2, D 01067 Dresden Germany. **CODEN** SMTFBL. Documents available from BIOSIS Document Express. ***Continues in part*** *Abhandlungen und Berichte aus dem Staatlichen Museum fur Tierkunde in Dresden, 0138-4147.*
**Ind/Abst** AGRICOLA; Biol. Abstr.; Fish Rev. (Jan. 1989-July 1992); Life Sci. Collect.; Wildl. Rev. (Jan. 1989-July 1992).

US/0015-4040
**FLORIDA ENTOMOLOGIST, THE.** (THE FLORIDA ENTOMOLOGIST : OFFICIAL ORGAN OF THE FLORIDA ENTOMOLOGICAL SOCIETY.). [Fla. entomol.]. **Added/Corp** Florida Entomological Society. Vol. 4, No. 1 (July 1920)-. Periodical. English (Spanish). qt (Mar., June, Sept., Dec.). $25.00 (individuals), $30.00 (institutions). Florida Entomological Society, PO Box 7326, Winter Haven FL 33883. **Tel** (813)324-5502. **ED** John McLaughlin. **LC** QL461; .F6. **CODEN** FETMAC. **Bk Rev. Pr Rev. Circ:** 1,000. Documents available from The Genuine Article, BIOSIS Document Express, CASDDS. ***Continues*** *Florida Buggist.*
**Desc:** General entomological and related sciences relating to subtropical US, Caribbean Islands, Central and South America.
**Ind/Abst** AGRICOLA [Full Cov.]; Agrofor. Abstr. (1991-);

Anim. Behav. Abstr.; Biocont. News Inf. (1991-); Biodeter. Abstr.; Biol. Abstr.; Chem. Abstr.; Cot. Trop. Fibr. Abstr. Bibliogr.; Curr. Aware. Biol. Sci., CABS; Curr. Contents, Agric. Biol. Environ. Sci.; Ecology Abstr.; EMBASE; Entomol. Abstr.; Field Crop Abstr.; For. Prod. Abstr. (1991-); For. Abstr.; Hortic. Abstr.; Index Vet.; Irr. Drain. Abstr.; Maize Abstr.; Nematol. Abstr.; Ornamental Hort. (19??-19??); Life Sci. Collect.; PESTDOC; Plant Breed. Abstr.; Postharvest News Inf.; Potato Abstr.; Res. Alert [Full Cov.]; Rev. Agric. Entomol.; Rev. Med. Vet. Entomol.; Rice Abstr.; Sci. Cit. Index; SCISEARCH; Soc. Sci. Cit. Index [Select. Cov.]; Sorghum Mill. Abstr.; Soyabean Abstr.; Vitis Vitic. Enol. Abstr.; Weed Abstr.; Wildl. Rev.

HU/0373-9465
**FOLIA ENTOMOLOGICA HUNGARICA.** [Folia entomol. Hung.]. **VFOAT** Rovartani Kozlemenyek. Vol. 23, No. 1-12 (1970)-. Periodical. Hungarian. sa. **CODEN** ROKOA5. Documents available from BIOSIS Document Express. ***Continues*** *Rovartani Kozlemenyek.*
**Ind/Abst** AGRICOLA; Biocont. News Inf. (19??-19??); Biol. Abstr.; Life Sci. Collect.; Rev. Agric. Entomol.; Rev. Med. Vet. Entomol.; Weed Abstr.

MX/0430-8603
**FOLIA ENTOMOLOGICA MEXICANA.** [Folia entomol. Mex.]. **Added/Corp** Sociedad Mexicana de Entomologia. (1961)-. Spanish (English and French). Three times a year. $35.00. Sociedad Mexicana de Entomologia, Apartado 63, 91000 Xalapa Veracruz Mexico. **Tel** 011 52 281 86000, FAX 011 52 281 86910. **ED** R. Novelo. **LC** QL477; .F64. **CODEN** FEMXAA. Index available. cum. index. **Bk Rev. Pr Rev. Circ:** 1,000 (ctrl). Documents available from BIOSIS Document Express.
**Desc:** Covers the subject of entomology.
**Ind/Abst** AGRICOLA; Biocont. News Inf.; Biodeter. Abstr. (19??-19??); Biol. Abstr.; Ecology Abstr.; Maize Abstr.; Life Sci. Collect.; Potato Abstr.; Rev. Agric. Entomol.; Rev. Med. Vet. Entomol.; Soils Fert.

●US/1062-9718
**FORUM OF THE AMERICAN TARANTULA SOCIETY.** **Added/Corp** American Tarantula Society. Vol. 1, No. 1 (1992)-. Periodical. English. $15.00. American Tarantula Society, PO Box 3594, South Padre Island TX 78597. **DD** 595.

AT/0158-0760
**GENERAL AND APPLIED ENTOMOLOGY.** [Gen. appl. entomol.]. **Added/Corp** Entomological Society of Australia (N.S.W.). Vol. 10 (July 1978)-. Academic Scholarly Publication. English. an. Entomological Society of Australia, PO Box 22, Five Dock New South Wales 2046 Australia. **LC** QL487; .E49. **DD** 595.7/005. **CODEN** GAENDS. Documents available from BIOSIS Document Express, CASDDS. ***Continues*** *Journal of the Entomological Society of Australia (N.S.W.), 0071-0725.*
**Ind/Abst** Biocont. News Inf.; Biodeter. Abstr.; Biol. Abstr.; Chem. Abstr.; Hortic. Abstr.; Index Vet.; Life Sci. Collect.; Rev. Med. Vet. Entomol.; Rev. Med. Vet. Mycology; Vet. Bull.

IT/0392-7296
**GIORNALE ITALIANO DI ENTOMOLOGIA.** [G. ital. entomol.]. Vol. 1, No. 1 (1982)-. Periodical. Italian (English and French). Three times a year. L61000.00 (institutions), L51000.00 (individuals) Italy; L89000.00 (institutions), L74000.00 (individuals) other. Marco Berra, CP 188, 26100 Cremona Italy. **Tel** 11 39 372 436909. **ED** Marco Berra. **LC** QL482.I8; G56. **DD** 595.7/005. **CODEN** GIENDG. Index available. **Ad Acc. Pr Rev. Circ:** 250. Documents available from BIOSIS Document Express.
**Desc:** Covers everything on entomology.
**Ind/Abst** Biocont. News Inf. (19??-19??); Biol. Abstr.; Entomol. Abstr.; Ornamental Hort.; Life Sci. Collect.; Rev. Agric. Entomol.

US/0090-0222
**GREAT LAKES ENTOMOLOGIST, THE.** [Great Lakes entomol.]. Vol. 5; Spring 1972-. Periodical. English. qt (Jan., Apr., Jul., Oct.). $20.00. Michigan Entomology Society, Michigan State University, East Lansing MI 48824. **Tel** (517)355-1803. **ED** Mark F. O'Brien, Museum of Zoology, University of Michigan, Ann Arbor, MI 48109. **LC** QL461; .M47. **DD** 595.7/09/77. **UDC** 595.7(77). **CODEN** GRLEAG. **[CCC].** Index available. cum. index (index published separately). **Ad Acc. Pr Rev. Circ:** 650 (ctrl). available on microfilm and microfiche from University Microfilms International (UMI). Documents available from The Genuine Article, BIOSIS Document Express. ***Continues*** *Michigan Entomologist, 0026-2145.*
**Desc:** Papers dealing with any aspect of entomology; appropriate subjects are those of interest to professional and amateur entomologists in the North Central states and Canada, as well as general papers and revisions directed to a larger audience while retaining an interest to readers in our geographic area. Also includes book reviews.
**Ind/Abst** AGRICOLA [Full Cov.]; Biocont. News Inf.; Biodeter. Abstr. (1991-); Biol. Abstr.; Curr. Aware. Biol. Sci., CABS; Curr. Contents, Agric. Biol. Environ. Sci.; Ecology Abstr.; Entomol. Abstr.; For. Prod. Abstr.; For. Abstr.; Maize Abstr.; Life Sci. Collect.; Plant Breed. Abstr.; Postharvest News Inf.; Potato Abstr.; Protozoolog. Abstr.; Res. Alert [Select. Cov.]; Rev. Agric. Entomol.; Rev. Med. Vet. Entomol.; SCISEARCH; Seed Abstr.; Weed Abstr.; Wildl. Rev.

UK
**HANDBOOKS FOR THE IDENTIFICATION OF BRITISH INSECTS.** Vol. 1, 1949-. Monographic series. English. ir. Price varies per volume. Gem Publishing Company, Brightwell Cum Sotw, Wallingford OX10 0QD UK. **Tel** 44-491-33882, FAX 44-491-25161. **LC** QL482.G8; R58. **UDC** 575.7(035)(410).
**Ind/Abst** Biocont. News Inf.; For. Prod. Abstr.; For. Abstr.; Rev. Med. Vet. Entomol.

KO/1011-9493
**HANGUK KONCHUNG HAKHOE CHI.** [Hanguk Konchung hakhoe chi]. **Main/Corp** Hanguk Konchung Hakkoe. **VFOAT** Korean Journal of Entomology. (1971)-. Periodical. English (Korean). sa. **LC** QL461; .H284a. **CODEN** KJETAE. Documents available from BIOSIS Document Express.
**Ind/Abst** Biocont. News Inf.; Biol. Abstr.

KO
**HANGUK UNGYONG KONCHUNG HAKHOE CHI.** **Added/Corp** Hanguk Ungyong Konchung Hakhoe. **VFOAT** Korean Journal of Applied Entomology. (1986)-. Periodical. Korean (English). qt. W10,000 Korea; $25.00 other. The Korean Society of Applied Entomology, Department of Agricultural Biology, College of Agriculture, Seoul National University, Suwon 441-707 Korea. **Tel** (331)291-3681. **ED** Kui Moon Choi. **LC** SB599; .H36a. **CODEN** HUKHEM. **Circ:** 600 (ctrl). Documents available from BIOSIS Document Express. ***Continues*** *Hanguk Singmul Poho Hakhoe Chi, 0367-6285.*
**Ind/Abst** Biocont. News Inf.; Biodeter. Abstr.; Biol. Abstr. (1988-); Entomol. Abstr.; For. Abstr.; Nematol. Abstr.; Postharvest News Inf.; Rev. Agric. Entomol.; Rev. Med. Vet. Entomol.; Rice Abstr.; Seed Abstr.; Soils Fert.; Soyabean Abstr.; Sug. Indus. Abstr.

HK
**HONG KONG CHENG FU YU NUNG CHU KAN WU.** **See** Agriculture.

II/0367-8288
**INDIAN JOURNAL OF ENTOMOLOGY, THE.** [Indian j. entomol.]. **Added/Corp** Entomological Society of India. Vol. 1 (June 1939)-. Periodical. English. qt. $100.00. Entomological Society of India Institute, New Delhi 110012 India. **(Subscription address:** Prints India, 11 Darya Ganj, New Delhi 110002 India.**)** **LC** QL461; .I48. **DD** 595.7/005. **NLM** W1 IN208L. **CODEN** IJENA8. Documents available from BIOSIS Document Express, CASDDS.
**Ind/Abst** AGRICOLA; Agrofor. Abstr. (1991-); Biocont. News Inf.; Biodeter. Abstr. (19??-19??); Biol. Abstr.; Chem. Abstr.; Cot. Trop. Fibr. Abstr. Bibliogr.; Crop Physiol. Abstr.; EMBASE; Entomol. Abstr.; Field Crop Abstr.; For. Prod. Abstr. (19??-19??); For. Abstr.; Hortic. Abstr.; Irr. Drain. Abstr.; Maize Abstr.; Nematol. Abstr.; Nutr. Abstr. Rev., Ser. B, Live Feeds and Feed.; Ornamental Hort. (1991-); Life Sci. Collect.; Plant Breed. Abstr.; Plant Grow. Reg. Abstr.; Postharvest News Inf.; Potato Abstr.; Poult. Abstr.; Protozoolog. Abstr.; Rev. Agric. Entomol.; Rev. Med. Vet. Entomol.; Rice Abstr.; Seed Abstr.; Soils Fert.; Sorghum Mill. Abstr.; Soyabean Abstr.; Wheat Barley Trit. Abstr.

II
**INDIAN ODONATOLOGY.** **Added/Corp** Societas Internationalis Odonatologia. South Asian Regional Office. Vol. 1 (Dec. 1, 1988)-. English. an. $30.00. Societas Internationalis Odonatologia, South Asia Regional Office, Jodhpur, India. **(Subscription address:** Prints India, 11 Darya Ganj, New Delhi, 110002 India, (Phone: 011 91 11 3268645)**)**

●UK/0965-1748
**INSECT BIOCHEMISTRY AND MOLECULAR BIOLOGY.** Vol. 22, No. 1 (Jan. 1992)-. Academic Scholarly Publication. English. Ten times a year. $857.00 (regular subscription), $1744.00 (combination subscription with Journal of Insect Physiology) The Americas; £575.00 (regular subscription), £1170.00 (combination subscription with Journal of Insect Physiology) other. Pergamon Press, An Imprint of Elsevier Science Ltd., The Boulevard, Langford Lane, Kidlington, Oxford OX5 1GB United Kingdom. **Tel** 011 44 865 843000, 011 44 865 843699, FAX 011 44 865 843010. **(Subscription address:** Elsevier Science Ltd. Oxford Fulfillment Centre, PO Box 800, Kidlington, Oxford OX5 1DX United Kingdom.**)** **LC** QL495; .I49. **NLM** W1; IN456VD. **CODEN** IBMBES. **[CCC].** available on microfilm and microfiche from University Microfilms International (UMI). Documents available from The Genuine Article, BIOSIS Document Express, CASDDS. ***Continues*** *Insect Biochemistry, 0020-1790.*
**Ind/Abst** Biol. Abstr.; Chem. Abstr.; Curr. Aware. Biol. Sci., CABS; Curr. Contents, Agric. Biol. Environ. Sci.; Curr. Contents Life Sci.; Ref. Upd. Deluxe Ed.; Res. Alert [Full Cov.]; Sci. Cit. Index; SCISEARCH.

CN/0590-7748
**INSECT LIBERATIONS IN CANADA.** (INSECT LIBERATIONS IN CANADA; PARASITES AND PREDATORS. LACHERS D'INSECTES AU CANADA; PRASITES ET PREDATEURS.). [Insect liber. Can.]. **Main/Corp** Canada. Dept. of Agriculture. Research Program Services Section. **Added/Corp** Canada. Agriculture Canada. Research Program Services Section. **VFOAT** Lachers d'Insectes au Canada; Parasites et Predateurs. (1967)-. Periodical. English. an. Free. ***Continues*** *Research Institute, Belleville, Ont. Insect Liberations in Canada; Parasites and Predators.; Summary of Parasite and Predator Liberation in Canada and of Insect Shipments from Canada in 1966., 0711-964X.*
**Ind/Abst** Biocont. News Inf.

●UK
**INSECT MOLECULAR BIOLOGY.** **Added/Corp** Royal Entomological Society of London. Vol. 1, No. 1 (1992)-. Academic Scholarly Publication. English. qt (4 issues). $221.00 (institutions), $102.00 (individuals) US & Canada; £129.50 (institutions), £60.00 (individuals) Europe; £142.50 (institutions), £66.00 (individuals) other. Blackwell Scientific Publications Ltd, Marston Book Services, PO Box 87, Oxford OX2 ODT UK. **Tel** 011 44 865 791155, FAX 011 44 865 791927, telex 837 515 MARDIS G. **LC** QL493.5; .I57. **DD** 595.7/087322/05. **NLM** W1; IN456VL. **CODEN** IMBIE3.
**Ind/Abst** Curr. Aware. Biol. Sci., CABS.

KE/0191-9040
**INSECT SCIENCE AND ITS APPLICATION.** (INSECT SCIENCE AND ITS APPLICATION / SPONSORED BY THE INTERNATIONAL CENTRE OF INSECT PHYSIOLOGY AND ECOLOGY (ICIPE) AND THE AFRICAN ASSOCIATION OF INSECT SCIENTISTS (AAIS).). [Insect sci. appl.]. **Added/Corp** International Centre of Insect Physiology and Ecology. African Association of Insect Scientists. Vol. 1, No. 1 (1980)-. Academic Scholarly Publication. English (French). bm. $255.00 (institution). International Centre for Insect Physiology and Ecology (ICIPE), PO Box 30772, Nairobi Kenya. **Tel** 011 254 2802501. **ED** Thomas R. Odhiambo. **LC** SB818; .I57. **NLM** W1 IN456W. **CODEN** ISIADL. **[CCC]. Pr Rev. Circ:** 139. available on microfilm and microfiche from University Microfilms International (UMI). Documents available from The Genuine Article, BIOSIS Document Express, CASDDS.
**Desc:** Deals with scientific research on tropical insects, crop pest and vector management, and the use of insects for human welfare.
**Ind/Abst** AGRICOLA [Full Cov.]; Agrofor. Abstr. (19??-19??); Biocont. News Inf. (19??-19??); Biodeter. Abstr. (19??-19??); Biol. Abstr.; Biotechnol. Res. Abstr.; Chem. Abstr.; Cot. Trop. Fibr. Abstr. Bibliogr.; Curr. Aware. Biol. Sci., CABS; Curr. Contents, Agric. Biol. Environ. Sci.; Ecology Abstr.; Entomol. Abstr.; Field Crop Abstr.; Food Sci. Technol. Abstr.; For. Prod. Abstr. (19??-19??); Helminthol. Abstr. (19??-19??); Hortic. Abstr.; Index Vet.; Maize Abstr.; Microbiol. Abstr. Sect. A; Nematol. Abstr.; Life Sci. Collect.; PESTDOC; Plant Breed. Abstr.; Plant Genet. Resour. Abstr.; Postharvest News Inf.; Potato Abstr.; Protozoolog. Abstr.; Res. Alert [Select. Cov.]; Rev. Agric. Entomol.; Rev. Med. Vet. Entomol.; Rev. Plant Pathol.; Rice Abstr.; Rural Dev. Abstr.; SCISEARCH; Seed Abstr.; Soils Fert.; Sorghum Mill. Abstr.; Soyabean Abstr.; Trop. Dis. Bull.; Virol. AIDS Abstr.; Weed Abstr.; Wheat Barley Trit. Abstr.; World Agric. Econ.

US/1043-6057
**INSECT WORLD (LANSING, MICH.).** **See** Children and Youth Interests.

SZ
**INSECTA HELVETICA. CATALOGUS.** Vol. 1- 1966-. Monographic series. German (French). ir. Price varies per volume. Insecta Helvetica, Entomol Inst Eth-Zentrum, CH-8092 Zurich Switzerland. **Tel** 01-256 39 22. **UDC** 595.7(494). **Circ:** 600.
**Desc:** List and distribution of insect species in Switzerland.

JA/0020-1804
**INSECTA MATSUMURANA.** [Insecta matsumurana]. **Added/Corp** Hokkaido Teikoku Daigaku. Konchugaku Kyoshitsu. Hokkaido Daigaku. Konchugaku Kyoshitsu. Hokkaido Daigaku. Nogakubu. (1927)-. Periodical. English (German; summaries and/or abstracts in Japanese). ir. Entomological Institute Faculty of Agriculture, Hokkaido University, Sapporo Japan. **LC** QL461; .I56. **CODEN** IMATAR. Documents available from BIOSIS Document Express.
**Ind/Abst** Biol. Abstr.; Entomol. Abstr.; Life Sci. Collect.

US/0749-6737
**INSECTA MUNDI.** [Insecta mundi]. Vol. 1, No. 1 (Jan. 1985)-. Periodical. English (French, German, Italian, Portuguese and Spanish). Four times a year. $53.00 US; $59.00 Canada; $63.00 other. Center for Systematic Entomology, PO Box 140429, Gainesville FL 32614. **Tel** (904)377-3299, FAX (904)377-3299. **ED** Michael Thomas. **DD** 595. **CODEN** INMUEX. **Bk Rev**, (Qty: 8-10). **Ad Acc. Pr Rev. Circ:** 500. Documents available from BIOSIS Document Express.
**Desc:** Prompt publication of papers on the systematics of the insects of the world, including descriptions of new taxa, informal taxonomic notes, bibliographies, checklists, catalogs, and reviews.
**Ind/Abst** Biol. Abstr. (1985-)(1985-1989).

FR/0020-1812
**INSECTES SOCIAUX.** (INSECTES SOCIAUX / UNION INTERNATIONALE POUR L'ETUDE DES INSECTES SOCIAUX.). [Insectes sociaux]. **Added/Corp** International Union for the Study of Social Insects. **VFOAT** Social Insects. Vol. 1, No. 1 (Jan. 1954)-. Periodical. French (English, French and German). qt. 365.50F Switzerland; 378.40F other. Birkhaeuser Verlag Ag, Klosterberg 23, PO Box 133, CH-4010 Basel Switzerland. **Tel** 011 41 61 2717400, FAX 011 41 0 61 2717666, telex 963475 birk ch. **(Subscription address:** Birkhauser Verlag AG, PO Box 151, CH 4106 Therwil Switzerland; Phone: 011 41 61 7217740**) ED** J. Billen, R. L. Jeanne and L. Passera. **NLM** W1 IN456X. **CODEN** INSOA7. **[CCC]. Pr Rev.** available on microfilm and microfiche from University Microfilms International (UMI). Documents available from The Genuine Article, BIOSIS Document Express, CASDDS. ***Continues*** *International Union for the Study of Social Insects. Section Francaise. Bulletin Edite por la Section Francaise de l'Union Internationale pour l'Etude des Insectes Sociaux.*
**Desc:** Covers the various aspects of the biology and evolution of social insects and other presocial arthropods. Publishes original research papers and reviews, as well as short communications.
**Ind/Abst** AGRICOLA; Anim. Behav. Abstr.; Biocont. News Inf.; Biol. Abstr.; Chem. Abstr.; Chemorecept. Abstr.; Curr. Aware. Biol. Sci., CABS; Ecology Abstr.; Entomol. Abstr.; Life Sci. Collect.; Protozoolog. Abstr.; Res. Alert [Full Cov.]; Rev. Agric. Entomol.; Rev. Med. Vet. Entomol.; Sci. Cit. Index; SCISEARCH; Soils Fert.

US/0098-1222
**INSECTS OF VIRGINIA, THE. Added/Corp** Virginia Polytechnic Institute and State University. Research Division. No. 1 (Sept. 1969)-. English. ir. Virginia Polytechnic Institute and State University, 617 North Main Street, Blacksburg VA 24060. **Tel** (313)764-4392. **LC** AS36; .V512 subser; QL475.V5. **DD** 081 S; 595.7/09/755.

UK/0020-7322
**INTERNATIONAL JOURNAL OF INSECT MORPHOLOGY & EMBRYOLOGY.** [Int. j. insect morphol. embryol.]. **VFOAT** Insect Morphology & Embryology. **VAT** International Journal of Insect Morphology and Embryology. Vol. 1 (Sept. 1971)-. Periodical. English. Four times a year. $522.00 The Americas; £350.00 other. Pergamon Press, An Imprint of Elsevier Science Ltd., The Boulevard, Langford Lane, Kidlington, Oxford OX5 1GB United Kingdom. **Tel** 011 44 865 843000, 011 44 865 843699, FAX 011 44 865 843010. **(Subscription address:** Elsevier Science Ltd. Oxford Fulfillment Centre, PO Box 800, Kidlington, Oxford OX5 1DX United Kingdom.**) ED** Ayodhya P. Gupta. **LC** QL494; .I5. **DD** 595.7/04/05. **NLM** W1 IN769E. **CODEN** IJIMBQ. **[CCC]. Pr Rev.** available on microfilm and microfiche from University Microfilms International (UMI). Documents available from The Genuine Article, BIOSIS Document Express, CASDDS.
**Ind/Abst** AGRICOLA [Full Cov.]; Biocont. News Inf. (1991-); Biol. Abstr.; Chem. Abstr.; Chemorecept. Abstr.; CSA Neuro. Abstr. (?-?); Curr. Aware. Biol. Sci., CABS; Curr. Contents, Agric. Biol. Environ. Sci.; Entomol. Abstr.; Life Sci. Collect.; Postharvest News Inf.; Res. Alert [Full Cov.]; Rev. Agric. Entomol.; Rev. Med. Vet. Entomol.; Sci. Cit. Index; SCISEARCH.

TU/0256-6672
**INTERNATIONAL QUARTERLY OF ENTOMOLOGY.** [Int. q. entomol.]. Vol. 1, No. 1 (Jan. 1985)-. Periodical. English (French and German). qt. 70.00TL. Genel Basin Ltd, PO Box 100 Konak, Izmir Turkey. **ED** Tahsin Yazicioglu. **UDC** 595.7. **CODEN** IQENER. **[CCC]. Bk Rev. Ad Acc.** Documents available from BIOSIS Document Express.
**Desc:** Covers entomology, arthropods, insects, systematic zoology, ecology, zoogeography, paleontology, agricultural and medical entomology.
**Ind/Abst** Biol. Abstr. (-1985).

IS/0075-1243
**ISRAEL JOURNAL OF ENTOMOLOGY.** [Isr. j. entomol.]. **Added/Corp** Hevrah ha-Entomologit be-Yisrael. Vol. 1 (1966)-. English. an (April). $35.00. Entomological Society of Israel, PO Box 6, Bet Dagan 50200 Israel. **Tel** 011 972 3 9604180. **LC** QL461; .I8. **DD** 595.7'005. **CODEN** IJENB9. **Pr Rev. Circ:** 250. Documents available from BIOSIS Document Express, CASDDS.
**Desc:** Original contributions on all aspects of entomology.
**Ind/Abst** AGRICOLA; Biol. Abstr.; Chem. Abstr.; Entomol. Abstr.; Life Sci. Collect.; PESTDOC.

JA/0915-5805
**JAPANESE JOURNAL OF ENTOMOLOGY TOKYO. 1989.** [Jpn. j. entomol. Tokyo, 1989]. **VFOAT** Konchu (Tokyo. 1989); Kontyu (Tokyo. 1989). (1989)-. Periodical. Multiple languages. qt. **DD** 595.7. ***Continues*** *Kontyu (Tokyo. 1926), 0013-8770.*
**Ind/Abst** Rev. Agric. Entomol.; Rice Abstr.

US/0735-939X
**JOURNAL OF AGRICULTURAL ENTOMOLOGY.** [J. agric. entomol.]. **Added/Corp** South Carolina Entomological Society. **VFOAT** Agricultural Entomology. Vol. 1, No. 1 (Jan. 1983)-. Academic Scholarly Publication. English. Four times a year (Jan., Apr., July. Oct.). $28.00 US; $35.00 Canada & Mexico; $42.00 others. South Carolina Entomological Society, 630 College Street, c/o Dr. Bob Nash, Central SC 29630. **Tel** (803)639-2453 Ext 351. **ED** Catherine A. Walgenbach (phone: (704)697-6815). **LC** SB818; .J68. **DD** 630/.2/957. **CODEN** JAENES. Index available. cum. index. **Ad Acc, Adv Mgr:** Howard W. Fescemyer, **Tel** (803)656-5050. **Pr Rev. Circ:** 450 (ctrl). Documents available from The Genuine Article, CASDDS.
**Desc:** Publishes results of research on insects and other anthropods of agricultural importance (livestock and poultry included) and articles in entomology.
**Ind/Abst** AGRICOLA [Full Cov.]; Agrofor. Abstr. (1991-); Biocont. News Inf. (19??-19??); Biodeter. Abstr.; Chem. Abstr. (1984-); Cot. Trop. Fibr. Abstr. Bibliogr.; Curr. Aware. Biol. Sci., CABS; Curr. Contents, Agric. Biol. Environ. Sci.; Dairy Sci. Abstr.; Entomol. Abstr.; Field Crop Abstr.; For. Prod. Abstr. (1991-); Hortic. Abstr.; Index Med.; Index Vet.; Maize Abstr.; Nematol. Abstr.; Nutr. Abstr. Rev., Ser. B, Live Feeds and Feed.; Pig News Inf.; Plant Breed. Abstr.; Plant Grow. Reg. Abstr.; Postharvest News Inf.; Potato Abstr.; Poult. Abstr.; Res. Alert [Full Cov.]; Rev. Agric. Entomol.; Rev. Med. Vet. Entomol.; Rev. Plant Pathol.; Rice Abstr.; Sci. Cit. Index; Seed Abstr.; Sorghum Mill. Abstr.; Soyabean Abstr.; Vet. Bull.; Wheat Barley Trit. Abstr.; World Agric. Econ.

II/0970-3810
**JOURNAL OF APHIDOLOGY.** [J. Aphidol.]. (1987)-. Periodical. English. an. Rs200.00 India; $40.00 other other. The Aphidological Society of India, Dr S P Kurl, Aphid Research Laboratory, Department of Zoology, M M Postgraduate College, Modinagar 201 204 India. **Tel** 2492 PP. **ED** K. D. Verma, D. R. C. Bakhetia, S. P. Kurl and S. M. Paul Khurana. **UDC** 595.75. **Bk Rev. Ad Acc. Circ:** 300 (ctrl).
**Ind/Abst** For. Abstr.

GW/0931-2048
**JOURNAL OF APPLIED ENTOMOLOGY 1986.** [J. appl. entomol. 1986]. **VFOAT** Zeitschrift fuer Angewandte Entomologie (1986). (1986)-. Periodical. Multiple languages. Ten times a year. DM1298.00. Blackwell Wissenschafts-Verlag, Kurfuerstendamm 57, D 10707 Berlin Germany. **Tel** 011 49 30 32790623, 011 49 30 32790624, FAX 011 49 30 327 90610. **ED** Wolfgang Schwenke. **UDC** 595.70. **[CCC]. *Continues*** *Zeitschrift fuer Angewandte Entomologie, 0044-2240.*
**Desc:** Presents original articles on current research in entomology applied to agriculture, forestry, biomedical areas, food, and feed storage.
**Ind/Abst** Anim. Behav. Abstr.; Chemorecept. Abstr.; Entomol. Abstr.; Postharvest News Inf.; Potato Abstr.; Rev. Agric. Entomol.

US/0022-0493
**JOURNAL OF ECONOMIC ENTOMOLOGY.** [J. econ. entomol.]. **Added/Corp** Entomological Society of America. American Association of Economic Entomologists. Vol. 1 (Feb. 1908)-. Academic Scholarly Publication. English. bm. $95.00 (individual), $190.00 (institution) US; $115.00 (individual), $210.00 (institution) other. Entomological Society of America, 9301 Annapolis Road, Suite 300, Lanham MD 20706. **Tel** (301)731-4535, FAX (301)731-4538. **(Subscription address:** ESA, PO Box 177, Hyattsville, MD 20781-0177**) ED** Jacqueline A. Robertson, Gerald M. Ghidiu, Lloyd T. Wilson, and Emmett Lampert. **LC** SB599; .J5. **DD** 632.705. **NLM** W1 JO627. **CODEN** JEENAI. **[CCC]. Ad Acc. Pr Rev. Circ:** 3,400 (ctrl). available on microfilm and microfiche from University Microfilms International (UMI). Documents available from The Genuine Article, BIOSIS Document Express, CASDDS, Documents on Demand.
**Desc:** Provides vital information for all libraries serving the agricultural community. Each volume contains over 200 original and significant research reports on the economic effects of insects.
**Ind/Abst** AgBiotech News Inf.; AGRICOLA [Full Cov.]; Agrofor. Abstr. (1991-); Anim. Behav. Abstr.; BioBusiness; Biocont. News Inf. (19??-19??); Biodeter. Abstr. (19??-19??); Biol. Agric. Index; Biol. Abstr.; Biol. Dig.; Biotechnol. Res. Abstr.; Chem. Abstr.; Chemorecept. Abstr.; Cot. Trop. Fibr. Abstr. Bibliogr.; Curr. Aware. Biol. Sci., CABS; Curr. Contents, Agric. Biol. Environ. Sci.; Dairy Sci. Abstr.; Ecol. Abstr.; Ecology Abstr.; EMBASE; Energy Inf. Abstr.; Energy Res. Abstr.; Entomol. Abstr.; Environ. Abstr.; Environ. Period. Bibliogr.; Field Crop Abstr.; Fish Rev. (Jan. 1989-July 1992); Food Sci. Technol. Abstr.; For. Prod. Abstr. (19??-19??); For. Abstr.; Geogr. Abstr. Phys. Geogr.; Geogr. Abstr. Human Geogr.; Grasslands For. Abstr.; Helminthol. Abstr. (1991-); Hortic. Abstr.; Index Med.; INIS Atomindex [Micro.]; Irr. Drain. Abstr.; Leis. Recreat. Tour. Abstr.; Maize Abstr.; Microbiol. Abstr. Sect. A; Nematol. Abstr.; Ornamental Hort. (19??-19??); Life Sci. Collect.; PESTDOC; Pig News Inf.; Plant Breed. Abstr.; Plant Genet. Resour. Abstr.; Plant Grow. Reg. Abstr.; Postharvest News Inf.; Potato Abstr.; Poult. Abstr.; Protozoolog. Abstr.; Res. Alert [Full Cov.]; Rev. Med. Vet. Entomol.; Rev. Med. Vet. Mycology; Rev. Plant Pathol.; Rice Abstr.; Rural Dev. Abstr.; Sci. Cit. Index; SCISEARCH; Seed Abstr.; Soc. Sci. Cit. Index [Select. Cov.]; Soils Fert.; Sorghum Mill. Abstr.; Soyabean Abstr.; Stat. Theory Method Abstr. (1959-1963); Trop. Dis. Bull.; Virol. AIDS Abstr.; Vitis Vitic. Enol. Abstr.; Weed Abstr.; Wildl. Rev. (Jan. 1989-July 1992); World Agric. Econ.

II/0378-9519
**JOURNAL OF ENTOMOLOGICAL RESEARCH. See** Zoology.

US/0749-8004
**JOURNAL OF ENTOMOLOGICAL SCIENCE.** [J. entomol. sci.]. **Added/Corp** Georgia Entomological Society. Vol. 20, No. 1 (Jan. 1985)-. Academic Scholarly Publication. English. qt. $30.00 US; $35.00 other. Georgia Entomological Society, Georgia Experiment Station, Griffin GA 30223. **Tel** (404)228-7288, FAX (404)228-7270. **ED** Wayne Gardner. **LC** SB818; .G4615. **DD** 595.7/005. **CODEN** JESCEP. Index available. cum. index. **Pr Rev. Circ:** 800. Documents available from The Genuine Article, BIOSIS Document Express, CASDDS. ***Continues*** *Journal of the Georgia Entomological Society, 0016-8238.*
**Desc:** Publishes original research articles in entomology and acarology.
**Ind/Abst** AGRICOLA [Full Cov.]; Anim. Behav. Abstr.; Biocont. News Inf. (19??-19??); Biodeter. Abstr. (19??-19??); Biol. Abstr. (1985-); Chem. Abstr. (1985-); Chemorecept. Abstr.; Cot. Trop. Fibr. Abstr. Bibliogr.; CSA Neuro. Abstr. (?-?); Curr. Aware. Biol. Sci., CABS; Curr. Contents, Agric. Biol. Environ. Sci.; Ecology Abstr.; Entomol. Abstr.; Food Sci. Technol. Abstr.; For. Abstr.; Grasslands For. Abstr.; Hortic. Abstr.; Index Vet.; Maize Abstr.; Microbiol. Abstr. Sect. A; Life Sci. Collect.; Plant Breed. Abstr.; Plant Genet. Resour. Abstr.; Postharvest News Inf.; Res. Alert [Full Cov.]; Rev. Med. Vet. Entomol.; Rev. Med. Vet. Mycology; Rev. Plant Pathol.; Rice Abstr.; Sci. Cit. Index; SCISEARCH; Seed Abstr.; Soils Fert.; Soyabean Abstr.; Vet. Bull.; Virol. AIDS Abstr.; Weed Abstr.; Wheat Barley Trit. Abstr.

●US/1070-9428
**JOURNAL OF HYMENOPTERA RESEARCH. Added/Corp** International Society of Hymenopterists. **VFOAT** JHR. Vol. 1, No. 1 (Aug. 1992)-. English. an (Aug.). $50.00. International Society of Hymenopterists, National Museum of Natural History, NHB 168, Washington DC 20560. **Tel** (202)382-1782, FAX (202)786-9422. **ED** Paul M. Marsh. **DD** 595. **Pr Rev. Circ:** 300 (ctrl).
**Desc:** Scientific papers reporting research on all aspects of hymenoptera- bees, wasps, ants, and sawflies.

US/0892-7553
**JOURNAL OF INSECT BEHAVIOR.** [J. insect behav.]. Vol. 1, No. 1 (Jan. 1988)-. Periodical. English. Six times a year. $245.00 institutions, $55.00 individuals US; $285.00 institutions, $64.00 individuals other. Plenum Press, 233 Spring Street, New York NY 10013-1578. **Tel** (212)620-8000, (800)221-9369, FAX (212)463-0742, (212)807-1047, telex 23/421139. **ED** William J. Bell and Thomas L. Payne. **LC** QL496; .J65. **DD** 595.7/051/05. **NLM** W1; JO71L. **CODEN** JIBEE8. **[CCC].** available on microfilm and microfiche from University Microfilms International (UMI). Documents available from The Genuine Article, BIOSIS Document Express.
**Desc:** Extends to all aspects of insect and terrestrial arthropod behavior. Topics include motor patterns and orientation, quantitative ethology, social behavior, pharmacological probes into behavior, and genetic and developmental determinants.
**Ind/Abst** AGRICOLA [Full Cov.]; Biocont. News Inf. (19??-19??); Biol. Abstr. (1988-); Curr. Aware. Biol. Sci., CABS; Curr. Contents, Agric. Biol. Environ. Sci.; For. Abstr.; Postharvest News Inf.; Potato Abstr.; Res. Alert [Select. Cov.]; Rev. Med. Vet. Entomol.; SCISEARCH; Soyabean Abstr.

UK/0022-1910
**JOURNAL OF INSECT PHYSIOLOGY.** [J. insect physiol.]. Vol. 1 (March 1957)-. English (French and German; summaries and/or abstracts in English). mo. $1081.00 (regular subscription), $1744.00 (combination subscription with Insect Biochemistry and Molecular Biology) The Americas; £725.00 (regular subscription), £1170.00 (combination subscription with Insect Biochemistry and Molecular Biology) other. Pergamon Press, An Imprint of Elsevier Science Ltd., The Boulevard, Langford Lane, Kidlington, Oxford OX5 1GB United Kingdom. **Tel** 011 44 865 843000, 011 44 865 843699, FAX 011 44 865 843010. **(Subscription address:** Elsevier Science Ltd. Oxford Fulfillment Centre, PO Box 800, Kidlington, Oxford OX5 1DX United Kingdom.**) ED** L. Strong. **LC** QL461; .J87. **DD** 595.705. **NLM** W1 JO714. **CODEN** JIPHAF. **[CCC]. Pr Rev.** available on microfilm and microfiche from University Microfilms International (UMI); available on microfiche from the publisher. Documents available from The Genuine Article, BIOSIS Document Express, CASDDS.
**Desc:** Publishes original papers, short reviews and proceedings of selected symposia covering a wide variety of aspects of the physiological mechanisms in insects, although closely related topics in other groups of arthropods will be accepted if they are of general interest. Main interests are in the fields of endocrinology, phermones, neurobiology, physiological pharmacology, behaviour, nutrition, homeostasis and reproductive processes of insects.
**Ind/Abst** AgBiotech News Inf.; AGRICOLA [Full Cov.]; Agrofor. Abstr. (1991-); Anim. Behav. Abstr.; Biocont. News Inf. (19??-19??); Biol. Agric. Index; Biol. Abstr.; Chem. Abstr.; Chemorecept. Abstr.; CSA Neuro. Abstr.; Curr. Aware. Biol. Sci., CABS; Curr. Contents, Agric. Biol.

Environ. Sci.; Curr. Contents Life Sci.; Ecol. Abstr.; Entomol. Abstr.; For. Prod. Abstr. (1991-); Helminthol. Abstr. (1991-); Index Med.; Nutr. Abstr. Rev., Ser. B, Live Feeds and Feed.; Nutr. Abstr. Rev., Ser. A, Hum. Exp.; Life Sci. Collect.; PESTDOC; Plant Breed. Abstr.; Postharvest News Inf.; Ref. Upd. Deluxe Ed.; Res. Alert [Full Cov.]; Rev. Med. Vet. Entomol.; Rev. Med. Vet. Mycology; Sci. Cit. Index; SCISEARCH; Seed Abstr.; Soils Fert.; Soyabean Abstr.; Trop. Dis. Bull.; Weed Abstr.

II/0970-3837
**JOURNAL OF INSECT SCIENCE.** (JOURNAL OF INSECT SCIENCE : A BIANNUAL JOURNAL DEVOTED TO BASIC AND APPLIED ASPECTS OF ENTOMOLOGY.). [J. insect sci.]. **Added/Corp** Indian Society for the Advancement of Insect Science. (1988)-. Periodical. English. sa. $50.00. Indian Society for the Advancement of Insect Science, Ludhiana, India. **(Subscription address:** Prints India, 11 Darya Ganj, New Delhi, 110002 India, (Phone: 011 91 11 3268645)) **CODEN** JINSE8. Documents available from BIOSIS Document Express.
**Ind/Abst** Agrofor. Abstr. (1991-); Biocont. News Inf. (1991-); Biodeter. Abstr. (1991-); Biol. Abstr. (1991-); Cot. Trop. Fibr. Abstr. Bibliogr.; Entomol. Abstr.; Field Crop Abstr.; For. Abstr.; Hortic. Abstr.; Maize Abstr.; Postharvest News Inf.; Rev. Agric. Entomol.; Rice Abstr.; Seed Abstr.; Sorghum Mill. Abstr.; Soyabean Abstr.; Wheat Barley Trit. Abstr.

US/0022-2011
**JOURNAL OF INVERTEBRATE PATHOLOGY.** [J. invertebr. pathol.]. **Added/Corp** Society for Invertebrate Pathology. Vol. 7, No. 1 (Mar. 1965)-. Academic Scholarly Publication. English. bm (6 issues). $450.00 US and Canada; $550.00 other. Academic Press, Inc., 6277 Sea Harbor Drive, Orlando FL 32887. **Tel** (800)543-9534, (407)345-4100, FAX (407)363-9661. **ED** Carol Reinisch. **LC** SB942; .J6. **DD** 592. **NLM** W1; JO727. **CODEN** JIVPAZ. **[CCC]. Pr Rev.** Documents available from The Genuine Article, BIOSIS Document Express, CASDDS. ***Continues** Journal of Insect Pathology, 0095-9049.*
**Desc:** Articles and notes on all aspects of original research concerned with the causations and manifestations (including immunologic responses) of infectious and noninfectious diseases of invertebrates.
**Ind/Abst** AgBiotech News Inf.; AGRICOLA [Full Cov.]; Aquat. Sci. Fish. Abstr. (Computer File); BioBusiness (?-1990); Biocont. News Inf. (19??-19??); Biol. Abstr.; Chem. Abstr.; CSA Neuro. Abstr. (?-?); Curr. Aware. Biol. Sci., CABS; Curr. Contents, Agric. Biol. Environ. Sci.; Curr. Contents Life Sci.; EMBASE; Energy Res. Abstr.; Entomol. Abstr.; For. Prod. Abstr.; For. Abstr.; Helminthol. Abstr. (1991-); Hortic. Abstr.; Immunol. Abstr.; Index Med.; INIS Atomindex [Micro.]; Int. Aerosp. Abstr.; Irr. Drain. Abstr.; Maize Abstr.; Microbiol. Abstr. Sect. B; Microbiol. Abstr. Sect. A; Microbiol. Abstr. Sect. C; Nematol. Abstr.; Life Sci. Collect.; PESTDOC; Postharvest News Inf.; Potato Abstr.; Protozoolog. Abstr.; Res. Alert [Full Cov.]; Rev. Med. Vet. Entomol.; Rev. Med. Vet. Mycology; Rev. Plant Pathol.; Sci. Cit. Index; SCISEARCH; Soils Fert.; Sug. Indus. Abstr.; Trop. Dis. Bull.; Virol. AIDS Abstr.; Weed Abstr.

US/0022-2585
**JOURNAL OF MEDICAL ENTOMOLOGY.** [J. med. entomol.]. **Added/Corp** Bernice Pauahi Bishop Museum. Dept. of Entomology. Vol. 1 (April 1964)-. Periodical. English. bm. $75.00 (individual), $150.00 (institution) US; $95.00 (individual), $170.00 (institution) other. Entomological Society of America, 9301 Annapolis Road, Suite 300, Lanham MD 20706. **Tel** (301)731-4535, FAX (301)731-4538. **(Subscription address:** ESA, PO Box 177, Hyattsville, MD 20781-0177) **ED** William K. Reisen and C. Dayton Steelman. **LC** RA639.5; .J6. **NLM** W1 JO75E. **CODEN** JMENA6. **[CCC].** Index available. cum. index. **Bk Rev. Ad Acc. Pr Rev. Circ:** 1,500. available on microfilm and microfiche from University Microfilms International (UMI); available on CD-ROM; available in microform. Documents available from The Genuine Article, BIOSIS Document Express, CASDDS.
**Desc:** Devoted exclusively to medical and veterinary entomology and acarology. Papers are fully refereed and include systematics, bionomics, genetics, immunology, arbovirology, epidemiology, computer modeling, and biological and chemical control.
**Ind/Abst** AgBiotech News Inf.; AGRICOLA [Full Cov.]; Anim. Behav. Abstr.; Biocont. News Inf. (19??-19??); Biol. Abstr.; Biol. Dig.; Chem. Abstr.; Chemorecept. Abstr.; Curr. Contents, Agric. Biol. Environ. Sci.; Dairy Sci. Abstr.; Ecology Abstr.; EMBASE; Energy Res. Abstr.; Entomol. Abstr.; Helminthol. Abstr. (19??-19??); Index Med.; INIS Atomindex [Micro.]; Irr. Drain. Abstr.; Microbiol. Abstr. Sect. B; Microbiol. Abstr. Sect. C; Life Sci. Collect.; PESTDOC; Pig News Inf.; Protozoolog. Abstr.; Res. Alert [Full Cov.]; Rev. Agric. Entomol.; Rev. Med. Vet. Entomol.; Rice Abstr.; Sci. Cit. Index; SCISEARCH; Small Anim. Abstr. Bibliogr.; Trop. Dis. Bull.; Virol. AIDS Abstr.; Wildl. Rev.

US/0022-4324
**JOURNAL OF RESEARCH ON THE LEPIDOPTERA, THE.** [J. res. lepid.]. **Added/Corp** Lepidoptera Research Foundation. Vol. 1 (Aug. 1962)-. Periodical. English. ir. $28.00. Lepidoptera Research Foundation, 9620 Heather Road, Beverly Hills CA 90210. **Tel** (310)274-1052, FAX (310)275-3290. **ED** Rudolf Mattoni. **CODEN** JRLPAE. cum. index. **Bk Rev. Pr Rev. Circ:** 600 (ctrl). Documents available from BIOSIS Document Express, CASDDS.
**Desc:** Purpose is to combine the work in the Lepidoptera field for the aid of students who study this group of insects in a way not presently available. Publishes primarily critical papers.
**Ind/Abst** AGRICOLA [Full Cov.]; Biol. Abstr.; Chem. Abstr.; Ecology Abstr.; Entomol. Abstr.; For. Abstr.; Life Sci. Collect.; Rev. Agric. Entomol.; Rev. Med. Vet. Entomol.

CN/0071-0733
**JOURNAL OF THE ENTOMOLOGICAL SOCIETY OF BRITISH COLUMBIA.** [J. Entomol. Soc. B.C.]. **Main/Corp** Entomological Society of British Columbia. Vol. 63, (Dec. 1, 1966)-. Academic Scholarly Publication. English. an (Dec.). 20.00Can$ Canada & US; 24.00Can$ other. Entomological Society of British Columbia, 6600 Northwest Marine Drive, AGRI Can Res, Vancouver BE V6T 1X2 Canada. **Tel** (604)494-7711. **ED** R. Ring. **DD** 595.7/09711. **CODEN** JEBCA4. **Circ:** 400. available on microfiche from University Microfilms International (UMI). Documents available from BIOSIS Document Express, CASDDS. ***Continues** Entomological Society of British Columbia. Proceedings, 0316-9049.*
**Desc:** Papers on entomological research.
**Ind/Abst** AGRICOLA [Full Cov.]; Biocont. News Inf. (19??-19??); Biodeter. Abstr.; Biol. Abstr.; Chem. Abstr.; Ecology Abstr.; Entomol. Abstr.; For. Abstr.; Life Sci. Collect.; Rev. Agric. Entomol.; Rev. Med. Vet. Entomol.; Weed Abstr.

US/0022-8567
**JOURNAL OF THE KANSAS ENTOMOLOGICAL SOCIETY.** [J. Kans. Entomol. Soc.]. **Main/Corp** Kansas Entomological Society. Vol. 1 (Jan. 1928)-. Periodical. English. qt. $75.00 US; $78.00 Canada and Mexico; $90.00 other. Kansas Entomological Society. **(Subscription address:** Journal of the Kansas Entomological Society, PO Box 1897, Lawrence KS 66044-8897.) **ED** Leonard C. Ferrington, Jr. **LC** QL461. **UDC** 595.7(781). **CODEN** JKESA7. **Pr Rev. Acid Free. Circ:** 800 (ctrl). available on microfilm and microfiche from University Microfilms International (UMI). Documents available from The Genuine Article, BIOSIS Document Express, CASDDS.
**Ind/Abst** AGRICOLA [Full Cov.]; Biocont. News Inf. (19??-19??); Biodeter. Abstr. (19??-19??); Biol. Abstr.; Chem. Abstr.; CSA Neuro. Abstr. (?-?); Curr. Aware. Biol. Sci., CABS; Curr. Contents, Agric. Biol. Environ. Sci.; Ecology Abstr.; Entomol. Abstr.; For. Abstr.; Maize Abstr.; Nematol. Abstr.; Life Sci. Collect.; Plant Breed. Abstr.; Postharvest News Inf.; Potato Abstr.; Protozoolog. Abstr.; Res. Alert [Full Cov.]; Rev. Agric. Entomol.; Rev. Med. Vet. Entomol.; Sci. Cit. Index; SCISEARCH; Seed Abstr.; Sorghum Mill. Abstr.; Soyabean Abstr.; Wildl. Rev.

JA/0013-8770
**KONCHU.** [Konchu]. **Added/Corp** Tokyo Konchu Gakkai. Nihon Konchu Gakkai. **VFOAT** Kontyu; Japanese Journal of Entomology. (1926)-. Periodical. Japanese (English; summaries and/or abstracts in English). qt. $100.00. Nihon Konchu Gakkai, (Engtomological Society of Japan), Kokuritsu Kagaku Hakubutsukan, Dobutsu Kenkyubu, 23-1, Hyakunincho, 3 Chome, Shinjukuku, Tokyoty 160, Japan. **(Subscription address:** Kyowa Book Company Inc., 1-38 Kanda Jinbo-Cho, Chiyoda-Ku Tokyo 101, Japan) **LC** QL461; .K66. **CODEN** KONTAQ.
**Ind/Abst** AGRICOLA; Biocont. News Inf.; Ecology Abstr.; Entomol. Abstr.; For. Abstr.; Rev. Agric. Entomol.; Rev. Med. Vet. Entomol.; SEA Abstr.

CC/0452-8255
**KUN CHUNG CHIH SHIH.** **Added/Corp** Chung-Kuo Kun Chung Hsueh Hui. **VFOAT** Kunchong Zhishi. (19??)-. Academic Scholarly Publication. Chinese. bm. $23.04. **(Subscription address:** China International Book Trading Corporation, PO Box 399, Library Service Department, Beijing 100044 People's Republic of China.) **LC** QL461; .K86. **DD** 595.7/005. **CODEN** KCCSAK. Documents available from CASDDS.
**Ind/Abst** Chem. Abstr.; Rev. Med. Vet. Entomol.

CC
**KUN CHUNG FEN LEI HSUEH PAO.** **Added/Corp** Hsi Pei Nung Hsueh Yuan (China). **VFOAT** Entomotaxonomia. Vol. 1 (Oct. 1979)-. Academic Scholarly Publication. Chinese (summaries and/or abstracts in English). Four times a year. RMBY5.00. Entomotaxonomia, c/o Northwest College of Agriculture, Yanlging. Shaanxi 712100, People's Republic of China. **Tel** 0086 910 712222 ext. 2509, FAX 0086 910-712559. **ED** Yuan Feng. **LC** QL468; .K86. **DD** 595.7/0012. **CODEN** KFXUDJ. Index Bound in First Issue. **Circ:** 1,000. Documents available from BIOSIS Document Express.
**Desc:** Devoted to the publication of papers and briefs on insect taxonomy and to discussions including principles, systems and techniques of systematics, new ideas related to methods, up-to-date achievements, descriptions and records of new species, generate and other taxonomy from China and East Asia, as well as other parts.
**Ind/Abst** Biocont. News Inf.; Biol. Abstr.; Entomol. Abstr.; Rev. Agric. Entomol.; Rev. Med. Vet. Entomol.

CC/0454-6296
**K'UN CH'UNG HSUEH PAO.** (KUN CHUNG HSUEH PAO.). [K'un ch'ung hsueh pao]. **Added/Corp** Chung-Kuo Kun Chung Hsueh Hui. **VFOAT** Acta Entomologica Sinica. (1950)-. Academic Scholarly Publication. Chinese (summaries and/or abstracts in English). qt. $96.00. Chinese Academy of Sciences / Institute of Zoology, Science Press, 16 Donghuangchenggen North Street, Beijing 100707, People's Republic of China. **Tel** 011 86 1 4019821, FAX 011 86 4012180, telex 210147. **ED** Qin Junde. **LC** QL461; .K865. **DD** 595.7/005. **NLM** W1 KU701J. **CODEN** KCHPA2. Index available. **Ad Acc. Circ:** 11,000. Documents available from BIOSIS Document Express, CASDDS.
**Ind/Abst** AGRICOLA; Biocont. News Inf.; Biol. Abstr.; Chem. Abstr.; Ecol. Abstr.; GeoRef; Hortic. Abstr.; NAPRALERT; Rev. Agric. Entomol.; Rev. Med. Vet. Entomol.; Rice Abstr.; SCISEARCH.

CC
**KUN CHUNG TIEN TI.** **Added/Corp** Kuang-Tung Sheng Kun Chung Hsueh Hui. **VFOAT** Natural Enemies of Insects. (1979)-. Periodical. Chinese (summaries and/or abstracts in English). qt. $20.00. Guangdong Entomological Society, 105 Xingand Road West, Liang, Guangzhou 510260, People's Republic of China. **Tel** 011 86 448651. **LC** SB933.25; .K86. **DD** 632/.96/05.
**Ind/Abst** Biocont. News Inf.; Biodeter. Abstr.; For. Abstr.; Nematol. Abstr.; Protozoolog. Abstr.; Rev. Agric. Entomol.; Rev. Med. Vet. Entomol.; Wheat Barley Trit. Abstr.

CH/1002-0926
**KUNCHONGXUE YANJIU JIKAN.** **VFOAT** Contributions from Shanghai Institute of Entomology. (1980)-. Periodical. Chinese. an. **DD** 595.7. Documents available from CASDDS.
**Ind/Abst** Biocont. News Inf.; Chem. Abstr.

CN/0318-6784
**LYMAN ENTOMOLOGICAL MUSEUM AND RESEARCH LABORATORY MEMOIR.** **See** Museums and Galleries.

UK/0269-283X
**MEDICAL AND VETERINARY ENTOMOLOGY.** [Med. vet. entomol.]. **Added/Corp** Royal Entomological Society of London. Vol. 1, No. 1 (Jan. 1987)-. Academic Scholarly Publication. English. qt (4 issues). $254.00 (institutions), $71.00 (individuals) US & Canada; £149.00 (institutions), £41.50 (individuals) Europe; £164.00 (institutions), £45.50 (individuals) other. Blackwell Scientific Publications Ltd, Marston Book Services, PO Box 87, Oxford OX2 0DT UK. **Tel** 011 44 865 791155, FAX 011 44 865 791927, telex 837 515 MARDIS G. **NLM** W1; ME186T. **CODEN** MVENE4. **[CCC]. Pr Rev.** available on microfilm and microfiche from University Microfilms International (UMI). Documents available from The Genuine Article, BIOSIS Document Express.
**Ind/Abst** AgBiotech News Inf.; AGRICOLA [Full Cov.]; Biocont. News Inf. (19??-19??); Biol. Abstr. (1987-); Curr. Aware. Biol. Sci., CABS; Curr. Contents, Agric. Biol. Environ. Sci.; Dairy Sci. Abstr.; Ecology Abstr.; Entomol. Abstr.; Fish Rev. (Jan. 1989-July 1992); Helminthol. Abstr. (19??-19??); Index Vet.; Int. Dev. Abstr.; Irr. Drain. Abstr.; Nutr. Abstr. Rev., Ser. A, Hum. Exp.; PESTDOC; Poult. Abstr.; Protozoolog. Abstr.; Res. Alert [Select. Cov.]; Rev. Agric. Entomol.; Rev. Med. Vet. Entomol.; Rice Abstr.; Sci. Cit. Index; SCISEARCH; Vet. Bull.; Trop. Dis. Bull.; Wildl. Rev. (Jan. 1989-July 1992).

US/0076-6224
**MELANDERIA (PULLMAN, WASH.).** (MELANDERIA.). [Melanderia]. **Added/Corp** Washington State Entomological Society. Vol. 1 (1969)-. Periodical. English. ir. $25.00. Washington State Entomological Society, Washington State University, Department of Entomology, Pullman WA 99164. **Tel** (509)335-3681. **DD** 595. **CODEN** MLDABN. Documents available from BIOSIS Document Express.
**Ind/Abst** AGRICOLA; Biol. Abstr.; Life Sci. Collect.

US/0065-8162
**MEMOIRS OF THE AMERICAN ENTOMOLOGICAL INSTITUTE.** [Mem. Am. Entomol. Inst.]. **Main/Corp** American Entomological Institute. No. 1 (1961)-. Monographic series. English. ir. Price varies per volume. Associated Publishers / Florida, PO Box 140103, Gainesville FL 32614. **Tel** (904)371-4071, FAX (904)371-4071. **CODEN** MAEIA8. **Circ:** 180. Documents available from BIOSIS Document Express.
**Desc:** Taxonomy of insects.
**Ind/Abst** Biol. Abstr.; Entomol. Abstr.; Life Sci. Collect.

US/0065-8170
**MEMOIRS OF THE AMERICAN ENTOMOLOGICAL SOCIETY.** [Mem. Am. Entomol. Soc.]. **Main/Corp** American Entomological Society. **Added/Corp** American Entomological Society. No. 1 (1916)-. Monographic series. English. ir. Price varies per volume. American Entomological Society, Academy of Natural Sciences of Philadelphia, 1900 Race Street, Philadelphia PA 19103. **Tel** (215)561-3978, FAX (215)299-1028. **ED** Paul M. Marsh. **LC** QL461; .A373. **DD** 595.7082. **CODEN** AESMAK. Index available. **Circ:** 400

(ctrl). Documents available from BIOSIS Document Express.
**Desc:** Classification, taxonomy, systematics, and ecology of insects.
**Ind/Abst** Biol. Abstr.; Life Sci. Collect.

CN/0071-075X
**MEMOIRS OF THE ENTOMOLOGICAL SOCIETY OF CANADA.** [Mem. Entomol. Soc. Can.]. **Added/Corp** Entomological Society of Canada (1951- ). No. 31 (1963)-. Monographic series. English. ir. Prices varies per volume. Entomological Society of Canada, 393 Winston Avenue, Ottawa Ontario K2A 1Y8 Canada. **Tel** (613)725-2619, FAX (613)725-9349. **NLM** W1 ME895S. **CODEN** MESCAK. **[CCC].** Documents available from The Genuine Article, BIOSIS Document Express. ***Continues*** *Canadian Entomologist. Supplement., 0700-5415.*
**Ind/Abst** Biol. Abstr.; Curr. Contents, Agric. Biol. Environ. Sci.; Entomol. Abstr.; For. Abstr.; Life Sci. Collect.; Plant Genet. Resour. Abstr.; Res. Alert [Select. Cov.]; Rev. Agric. Entomol.; SCISEARCH.

IT/0037-8747
**MEMORIE DELLA SOCIETA ENTOMOLOGICA ITALIANA.** [Mem. Soc. entomol. ital.]. **Main/Corp** Societa Entomologica Italiana. Vol. 1 (1922)-. Periodical. Italian. an. Societa Entomologica Italiana, Via Brigata Liguria 9, 16121 Genova Italy. **Tel** 011 39 10 261862, 011 39 10 564567. **LC** WMLC L 83/1131. cum. index. **Bk Rev. Ad Acc. Circ:** 1,500 (ctrl).
**Desc:** Works on entomology.
**Ind/Abst** AGRICOLA; Entomol. Abstr.; For. Abstr.; Life Sci. Collect.; Rev. Agric. Entomol.

GW/0344-9084
**MITTEILUNGEN DER DEUTSCHEN GESELLSCHAFT FUER ALLGEMEINE UND ANGEWANDTE ENTOMOLOGIE.**
**Added/Corp** Deutsche Gesellschaft fuer Allgemeine und Angewandte Entomologie. Vol. 1, No. 1 (Feb. 1978)-. Periodical. German (summaries and/or abstracts in English). ir. Paul Parey (Berlin), Seelbuschring 9-17, 1000 Berlin 42 Germany. **Tel** 030-70784-00. **LC** QL461; .M62. **DD** 595.7.
**Ind/Abst** Agrofor. Abstr.; Biocont. News Inf. (1991-); Cot. Trop. Fibr. Abstr. Bibliogr.; For. Abstr.; Nematol. Abstr.; Pig News Inf.; Plant Breed. Abstr.; Potato Abstr.; Protozoolog. Abstr.; Rev. Med. Vet. Entomol.; Wheat Barley Trit. Abstr.

SW
**MITTEILUNGEN DER ENTOMOLOGISCHEN GESELLSCHAFT BASEL.** **Main/Corp** Entomologische Gesellschaft Basel. (1951)-. Periodical. German. qt.
**Ind/Abst** Rev. Agric. Entomol.; Soyabean Abstr.

SZ/0036-7575
**MITTEILUNGEN DER SCHWEIZERISCHEN ENTOMOLOGISCHEN GESELLSCHAFT.** [Mitt. Schweiz. entomol. Ges.]. **Main/Corp** Schweizerische Entomologische Gesellschaft. **Added/Corp** Schweizerische Naturforschende Gesellschaft. **VFOAT** Bulletin de la Societe Entomologique Suisse; Mitteilungen der Schweizer. Entomologischen Gesellschaft. (Feb. 1862)-. Periodical. German (French and English). sa (two double issues per year). 119.50F Switzerland; 132.00F other Europe; 136.00F other. Schweizerische Entomologische Gesellschaft, CSCF Terreaux 14, CH 2000 Neuchatel Switzerland. **ED** Georg Benz and Michel Sartori. **NLM** W1 SC46. **CODEN** MSEGAQ. **Bk Rev. Circ:** 650. Documents available from BIOSIS Document Express.
**Desc:** Covers systematic, ecologic, and applied entomology.
**Ind/Abst** AGRICOLA; Biocont. News Inf.; Biol. Abstr.; Ecology Abstr.; Entomol. Abstr.; For. Abstr.; Maize Abstr.; Nematol. Abstr.; Life Sci. Collect.; Rev. Agric. Entomol.; Rev. Med. Vet. Entomol.; Vitis Vitic. Enol. Abstr.

GW/0027-7452
**NACHRICHTENBLATT DER BAYERISCHEN ENTOMOLOGEN.**
[Nachrichtenbl. Bayer. Entomol.]. **Added/Corp** Munchner Entomologische Gesellschaft. Vol. 1 (Jan. 1952)-. Periodical. German. Four times a year. Free to members; DM60.00 membership. Muenchner Entomologische Gesellschaft, Muenchhausenstrasse 21, D 81247 Munich Germany. **Tel** 011 49 89 81070.
**Ind/Abst** Life Sci. Collect.

JA/0028-4955
**NEW ENTOMOLOGIST.** [New entomol.]. **Added/Corp** Shinshu Konchu Gakkai. **VFOAT** Nyu Entomorojisuto. Vol. 1, No. 1 (Apr. 1, 1951)-. Periodical. Japanese. qt. $60.00. Shinshu Konchu Gakkai, (Entomological Soc. of Shinshu), Shinshu Daigaku Nogakubu Oyo, Konchugaku Kyoshitsu, 8304, Minamiminowamura, Kamiinagun, Naganoken 399-45 Japan. **(Subscription address:** Maruzen Company Ltd., PO Box 5050, Import & Export Department, Tokyo 100 31 Japan.**)** **CODEN** NENTAN. Documents available from BIOSIS Document Express.
**Ind/Abst** AGRICOLA; Biol. Abstr. (-1984).

JA/0021-4914
**NIHON OYO DOBUTSU KONCHU GAKKAISHI.** [Jpn. j. appl. entomol. zool.]. **Added/Corp** Nihon Oyo Dobutsu Konchugakkai. **VFOAT** Japanese Journal of Applied Entomology and Zoology. Vol. 1, No. 1 (March 1957)-. Academic Scholarly Publication. Japanese (summaries and/or abstracts in English; table of contents in English). qt. $86.00. Nihon Oyo Dobutsu Konchu Gakkai, (Japanese Society of Applied Entomology and Zoology), Nihon Shokubutsu Boeki Kyokai, 43-11, Komagome, 1 Chome, Toshimaku, Tokyoto 170 Japan. **(Subscription address:** Japan Publications Trading Company, Ltd., PO Box 5030, Tokyo International, Tokyo 100-31 Japan.**)** **ED** Toshiaki Ikeshoji. **CODEN** NIPTAR. **Ad Acc. Pr Rev. Circ:** 2,300 (ctrl). Documents available from The Genuine Article, BIOSIS Document Express, CASDDS. ***Formed by the union of*** *Oyo Dobutsu Zasshi* ***and*** *Oyo Konchu.*
**Desc:** An organ paper of the Japanese Society of Applied Entomology and Zoology.
**Ind/Abst** AGRICOLA; BioBusiness; Biocont. News Inf.; Biodeter. Abstr.; Biol. Abstr.; Chem. Abstr.; Curr. Aware. Biol. Sci., CABS; Curr. Contents, Agric. Biol. Environ. Sci.; Ecology Abstr.; EMBASE; Entomol. Abstr.; Fish Rev. (19??-199?); For. Abstr.; Hortic. Abstr.; Maize Abstr.; Life Sci. Collect.; PESTDOC; Postharvest News Inf.; Potato Abstr.; Res. Alert [Select. Cov.]; Rev. Agric. Entomol.; Rice Abstr.; SCISEARCH; Seed Abstr.; Soyabean Abstr.; Wheat Barley Trit. Abstr.; Wildl. Rev. (19??-199?).

US
**NORTH DAKOTA INSECTS PUBLICATION.** **Added/Corp** North Dakota. State University of Agriculture and Applied Science, Fargo. Dept. of Entomology. North Dakota. State University of Agriculture and Applied Science, Fargo. Dept. of Agricultural Entomology. **VFOAT** North Dakota Insects. No. 1 (1960)-. Monographic series. English. ir. Price varies per volume. Schafer Post Series, Entomology Department, North Dakota State University, Fargo ND 58105. **Tel** (701)237-7582.

FR/0374-9797
**NOUVELLE REVUE D'ENTOMOLOGIE.**
[Nouv. rev. entomol.]. (1971)-. Periodical. French (English, German, Italian and Spanish). qt. 290.00F France; 390.00F other. Laboratoire de Etres Organises, BP 96, F-94123 Fontenay-Sous-Bois Cedex France. **CODEN** NRETAZ. Index available. **Bk Rev. Circ:** 400. Documents available from BIOSIS Document Express.
**Desc:** Contains papers of subscribers which are required on systematic and biogeography of the insects. Also includes reviews of books, scientific informations and an important literature notice.
**Ind/Abst** Biocont. News Inf.; Biol. Abstr.; Entomol. Abstr.; Life Sci. Collect.; Rev. Agric. Entomol.; Rev. Med. Vet. Entomol.

US/0362-2622
**OCCASIONAL PAPERS IN ENTOMOLOGY.** No. 21- 1975-. Monographic series. English. Price varies per volume. California Department of Food and Agriculture, 1220 N Street, Sacramento CA 95814. **Tel** (916)654-0433, FAX (916)324-1681. **ED** Fred G Andrews. **LC** QL461; .C15. **DD** 595.7/001/2. **Circ:** 1,000 (ctrl). ***Continues*** *Occasional Papers - Bureau of Entomology. Department of Agriculture. Sacramento, California, 0575-2213.*
**Desc:** Insect systematics.

US/0884-5956
**OHIO LEPIDOPTERIST.** **See** Zoology.

SZ/1010-5220
**OPUSCULA ZOOLOGICA FLUMINENSIA.** [Opusc. zool. Fluminensia]. (1984)-. Monographic series. German (English, French and Italian). Casa d'Uors, Postfach 324 CH-8896, Flumsberg-Grossberg, Switzerland. **LC** QL461; .O64. **CODEN** OZFLEJ.
**Ind/Abst** Entomol. Abstr.

US/0030-5316
**ORIENTAL INSECTS.** [Orient. insects]. **Added/Corp** Association for the Study of Oriental Insects. Vol. 1 (Sept. 1967)-. Periodical. English. an (Apr. or May). $60.00. Associated Publishers / Florida, PO Box 140103, Gainesville FL 32614. **Tel** (904)371-4071, FAX (904)371-4071. **ED** V. K. Gupta (phone: (904)392-1901 Ext. 145). **LC** QL461; .O72. **DD** 595.7/09/5. **CODEN** ORINAE. Index available (bound in issue). **Bk Rev**, (Qty: 3-4). **Ad Acc. Pr Rev. Circ:** 250. Documents available from The Genuine Article, BIOSIS Document Express.
**Desc:** An international journal of taxonomic entomology of insects and other land anthropods of the Old World tropics. Faunistics and ecological works also published. Both original and review articles are accepted for publication.
**Ind/Abst** AGRICOLA; Biocont. News Inf. (1991-); Biol. Abstr.; Curr. Aware. Biol. Sci., CABS; Entomol. Abstr.; Life Sci. Collect.; Res. Alert [Select. Cov.]; Rev. Agric. Entomol.; Rev. Med. Vet. Entomol.; SCISEARCH; Zool. Rec.

US
**ORIENTAL INSECTS MONOGRAPH.**
**Added/Corp** Association for the Study of Oriental Insects. English. ir. $55.00 (add $2.50 for postage) US, (add $5.00 for postage) other. Associated Publishers / Florida, PO Box 140103, Gainesville FL 32614. **Tel** (904)371-4071, FAX (904)371-4071. **ED** V K Gupta. **Pr Rev. Circ:** 100 (ctrl). Documents available from BIOSIS Document Express.
**Desc:** Monographic works on insects and other land arthropods of old world tropics.
**Ind/Abst** AGRICOLA; Biol. Abstr.; Zool. Rec.

US/0031-0603
**PAN-PACIFIC ENTOMOLOGIST, THE.**
[Pan-Pac. entomol.]. **Added/Corp** Pacific Coast Entomological Society. California Academy of Sciences, San Francisco. Pacific Coast Entomological Society. Proceedings. Vol. 1 (July 1924)-. Periodical. English. qt (Jan., Apr., July, Oct.). $40.00. Pacific Coast Entomological Society, California Academy of Sciences, Golden Gate Park, San Francisco CA 94118-4599. **Tel** (415)750-7230, FAX (415)750-7228. **ED** John T. Sorensen (editor's address: California Dept of Food and Agriculture, 1220 North St, Room 340, Sacramento CA 95814; editor's phone: (916)654-1391). **LC** QL461; .P3. **DD** 595.705. **CODEN** PPETA9. Index available (bound in fourth issue). **Bk Rev**, (Qty: 2-4 per year). **Pr Rev. Circ:** 850. Documents available from The Genuine Article, BIOSIS Document Express, CASDDS.
**Desc:** Systematic and biological aspects of entomology. Technical articles on biology and taxonomy of insects and their relatives (spiders, centipedes, millipedes).
**Ind/Abst** AGRICOLA [Full Cov.]; Biocont. News Inf. (19??-19??); Biol. Abstr.; Chem. Abstr.; Curr. Aware. Biol. Sci., CABS; Curr. Contents, Agric. Biol. Environ. Sci.; Ecology Abstr.; Entomol. Abstr.; Fish Rev.; For. Prod. Abstr. (1991-); For. Abstr.; Life Sci. Collect.; Poult. Abstr.; Res. Alert [Select. Cov.]; Rev. Agric. Entomol.; Rev. Med. Vet. Entomol.; SCISEARCH; Seed Abstr.; Wildl. Rev.

UK/0307-6962
**PHYSIOLOGICAL ENTOMOLOGY.**
[Physiol. entomol.]. **Added/Corp** Royal Entomological Society of London. Vol. 1 (March 1976)-. Academic Scholarly Publication. English. qt (4 issues). $260.00 (institutions), $76.00 (individuals) US & Canada; £153.00 (institutions), £45.00 (individuals) Europe; £168.00 (institutions), £49.00 (individuals) other. Blackwell Scientific Publications Ltd, Marston Book Services, PO Box 87, Oxford OX2 ODT UK. **Tel** 011 44 865 791155, FAX 011 44 865 791927, telex 837 515 MARDIS G. **ED** G. J. Goldsworthy. **LC** QL495; .P55. **DD** 595.7/01/05. **CODEN** PENTDE. **[CCC].** Index available (bound in last issue). **Bk Rev. Ad Acc. Pr Rev.** available on microfilm and microfiche from University Microfilms International (UMI). Documents available from The Genuine Article, BIOSIS Document Express, CASDDS. ***Supersedes*** *Journal of Entomology. Series A. Physiology & Behaviour, 0308-5007.*
**Desc:** Covers the physiology of insects.
**Ind/Abst** AGRICOLA [Full Cov.]; Anim. Behav. Abstr.; Biocont. News Inf. (19??-19??); Biol. Abstr.; Chem. Abstr.; Chemorecept. Abstr.; CSA Neuro. Abstr. (?-?); Curr. Aware. Biol. Sci., CABS; Curr. Contents, Agric. Biol. Environ. Sci.; Ecol. Abstr. (?-?); Mass Spect. Bull.; Life Sci. Collect.; Potato Abstr.; Res. Alert [Full Cov.]; Rev. Agric. Entomol.; Rev. Med. Vet. Entomol.; Sci. Cit. Index; SCISEARCH; Seed Abstr.; Wheat Barley Trit. Abstr.

II
**PHYTOPHAGA.** Vol. 1, No. 1 (Jan. 1987)-. Periodical. English. sa. $60.00. **(Subscription address:** Prints India, 11 Darya Ganj, New Delhi 110002 India.**)** **CODEN** PHYTEN.
**Ind/Abst** Plant Breed. Abstr.; Rev. Agric. Entomol.

IT/0393-8131
**PHYTOPHAGA.** [Phytophaga]. (1983)-. Periodical. Multiple languages. an. ***Continues*** *Bollettino dell' Istituto di Entomologia Agraria e dell' Osservatorio di Fitopatologia di Palermo, 0078-8619.*
**Ind/Abst** Biocont. News Inf.

PL/0032-3780
**POLSKIE PISMO ENTOMOLOGICZNE.**
(POLSKIE PISMO ENTOMOLOGICZNE. BULLETIN ENTOMOLOGIQUE DE POLOGNE.). [Pol. pis. entomol.]. **Added/Corp** Polskie Towarzystwo Entomologiczne. Polski Zwiazek Entomologiczny. Polskie Towarzystwo Przyrodnikow Imienia Kopernika. Sekcja Entomologiczna. **VFOAT** Bulletin Entomologique de Pologne. Vol. 1 (1922)-. Bulletin. English (French, German and Polish). qt. $60.00. **(Subscription address:** ARS Polona, PO Box 1001, 00068 Warsaw Poland.**)** **LC** QL461; .P6. **DD** 595.7/005. **CODEN** PEBEA8. Documents available from BIOSIS Document Express, CASDDS. ***Absorbed*** *Polskie Pismo Entomologiczne. Seria B: Entomologia Stosowana.*
**Ind/Abst** Biodeter. Abstr.; Biol. Abstr.; Chem. Abstr.; Entomol. Abstr.; For. Abstr.; Nematol. Abstr.; Life Sci. Collect.; Rev. Med. Vet. Entomol.

CN/0071-0709
**PROCEEDINGS OF THE ANNUAL MEETING OF THE ENTOMOLOGICAL SOCIETY OF ALBERTA.** **Main/Corp** Entomological Society of Alberta. Vol. 1 (1953)-. English. an. Free to members of the Entomological Society of Alberta. Entomological Society of Alberta, Alberta University, Department of Entomology, Edmonton Alberta T6G 2E3 Canada. **Tel** (403)492-4652. **DD** 595.7/005. **Bk Rev. Ad Acc. Circ:** 120.

**Desc:** Abstracts of scientific papers presented at annual meetings, plus general information about the Entomological Society.

SA/1010-2566
**PROCEEDINGS OF THE ... ENTOMOLOGICAL CONGRESS - ENTOMOLOGICAL SOCIETY OF SOUTHERN AFRICA.** [Proc. Entomol. Congr.]. **Main/Conf** Entomological Congress. Proceedings. English (Afrikaans). ir (every 2-3 years). R65.00, R35.00 membership. Entomological Society of Southern Africa, PO Box 103, Pretoria 0001 South Africa. **Tel** 21 12 2062623, FAX 21 12 3235275. **ED** C H Scholtz. **CODEN** PCEAEZ. **Circ:** 600 (ctrl). Documents available from BIOSIS Document Express. ***Continues*** *Proceedings of the ... Congress of the Entomological Society of Southern Africa.*
**Desc:** Covers entomology both pure and applied aspects.
**Ind/Abst** Biol. Abstr. (1987-); Entomol. Abstr.; Zool. Rec.

CN/0315-2146
**PROCEEDINGS OF THE ENTOMOLOGICAL SOCIETY OF MANITOBA. Main/Corp** Entomological Society of Manitoba. (1945)-. Proceedings. English. an. 8.00Can$. Entomological Society of Manitoba, Research Stat. 195, Dafoe Road, Winnipeg MANI R3T 2M9 Canada. **Tel** (204)269-2100. **ED** Dr. A.R. Westwood. **[CCC]. Ad Acc. Pr Rev. Circ:** 375 (ctrl). ***Absorbed*** *Manitoba Entomologist., 0076-3810.* ***Continued in part by*** *Manitoba Entomologist., 0076-3810.*
**Desc:** Fosters the advancement, exchange, and dissemination of entomological knowledge.
**Ind/Abst** Seed Abstr.

US/0073-134X
**PROCEEDINGS OF THE HAWAIIAN ENTOMOLOGICAL SOCIETY.** [Proc. Hawaii. Entomol. Soc.]. **Main/Corp** Hawaiian Entomological Society. V. 1- 1905/07-. Proceedings. English. an. $10.00. Hawaiian Entomological Society, c/o Department of Entomology, University of Hawaii, 3050 Maile Way, Honolulu HI 96822. **Tel** (808)948-7076. **ED** Jack W Beardsley. **CODEN** PHESAI. Index available. **Circ:** 450. available on microfilm from University Microfilms International (UMI). Documents available from BIOSIS Document Express, CASDDS.
**Desc:** General entomology with special interest in Hawaiian and Pacific insects.
**Ind/Abst** AGRICOLA [Full Cov.]; Biocont. News Inf.; Biol. Abstr.; Chem. Abstr.; For. Abstr.; Life Sci. Collect.; Protozoolog. Abstr.; Rev. Med. Vet. Entomol.

US/1049-0221
**PROCEEDINGS OF THE ILLINOIS MOSQUITO AND VECTOR CONTROL ASSOCIATION.** [Proc. Ill. Mosq. Vector Control Assoc.]. **Main/Corp** Illinois Mosquito and Vector Control Association. Meeting. Vol. 1 (Nov. 3-4, 1990)-. Proceedings. English. an. $7.00 (individuals), $12.00 (libraries). South Cook County Mosquito Abatement District, PO Box 1030, Harvey IL 60426. **DD** 614.
**Ind/Abst** Biocont. News Inf.; Rev. Med. Vet. Entomol.

US/0043-0773
**PROCEEDINGS OF THE WASHINGTON STATE ENTOMOLOGICAL SOCIETY.** [Proc. Wash. State Entomol. Soc.]. **Main/Corp** Washington State Entomological Society. **Added/Corp** Oregon Entomological Society. **VFOAT** Bulletin of the Oregon Entomological Society. No. 1 (Sept. 1954)-. English. sa. $15.00. Washingotn State Entomological Soc., Washington State Univ., Dept. of Entomology, Pullman WA 99164. **Tel** (509)335-3681. **LC** QL461; .W37a. **DD** 595.7/005.

IT/0370-4327
**REDIA.** [Redia]. **Added/Corp** Istituto Sperimentale per la Zoologia Agraria. R. Stazione de Entomologia Agraria in Firenze. Vol. 1 (1903)-. Italian. an. IST Sperim Zoologia Agaria, Via Della Lanciola Cascine RIC, Florence Italy 50125. **Tel** 011 39 55 209182. **CODEN** REDIAI. cum. index. Documents available from BIOSIS Document Express.
**Ind/Abst** AGRICOLA; Biocont. News Inf. (19??-19??); Biol. Abstr.; For. Abstr.; Hortic. Abstr.; Maize Abstr.; Nematol. Abstr.; Ornamental Hort. (1991-); Life Sci. Collect.; Rev. Agric. Entomol.; Rev. Med. Vet. Entomol.; Rev. Plant Pathol.; Vitis Vitic. Enol. Abstr.

GW/0070-7279
**REICHENBACHIA / STAATLICHES MUSEUM FUER TIERKUNDE IN DRESDEN.** [Reichenbachia]. Vol. 1, No. 1 (Aug. 22, 1962)-. Periodical. German. ir. DM27.00. Staatliches Museum fuer Tierkunde Dresden, Augustusstrasse 2, D 01067 Dresden Germany. **LC** QL461. **CODEN** RCHBA3. **Bk Rev. Circ:** 350 (ctrl). Documents available from BIOSIS Document Express. ***Continues in part*** *Abhandlungen und Berichte Aus dem Staatlichen Museum fur Tierkunde in Dresden.*

**Desc:** Taxonomy and systematics of the invertebrate groups insecta and archnida in global range.
**Ind/Abst** Biol. Abstr.; Life Sci. Collect.

UK/0957-6762
**REVIEW OF AGRICULTURAL ENTOMOLOGY. See** Zoology-Abstracting, Bibliographies and Statistics.

UK/0957-6770
**REVIEW OF MEDICAL AND VETERINARY ENTOMOLOGY. See** Zoology-Abstracting, Bibliographies and Statistics.

BL/0085-5626
**REVISTA BRASILEIRA DE ENTOMOLOGIA.** [Rev. bras. entomol.]. Vol. 1, (1954)-. Monographic series. Multiple languages (Portuguese, English and Spanish). Four times a year (Mar., June, Sept., Dec.). $60.00. Soc Brasileira de Entomologia, Caixa Postal 9063, 01051 Sao Paulo SP Brazil. **Tel** 00550112743455 Ext. 60. **ED** Ubirajara R. Martins de Souta. **LC** WMLC L 83/1539. **CODEN** RBREAL. Index available (Bound in 4th iss.). **Bk Rev**, (Qty: varies). **Ad Acc. Circ:** 600 (ctrl). Documents available from BIOSIS Document Express.
**Desc:** Original papers on entomology systematic, ecology, morphology, agricultural entomology and medical entomology.
**Ind/Abst** Biocont. News Inf.; Biol. Abstr.; Entomol. Abstr.; For. Abstr.; Life Sci. Collect.; Ref. Z.; Rev. Agric. Entomol.; Rev. Med. Vet. Entomol.; Zool. Rec.

CL/0034-740X
**REVISTA CHILENA DE ENTOMOLOGIA.** (REVISTA CHILENA DE ENTOMOLOGIA : PUBLICACION DE LA FACULDAD DE FILOSOFIA Y EDUCACION, UNIVERSIDAD DE CHILE, Y DE LA SOCIEDAD CHILENA DE ENTOMOLOGIA.). [Rev. chil. entomol.]. **Added/Corp** Sociedad Chilena de Entomologia. Universidad de Chile. Facultad de Filosofia y Educacion. Vol. 1 (1951)-. Periodical. Spanish (English). an. Price varies per volume. Mario Elgueta D, Casilla 21132, Santiago Chile. **Tel** 56 2 90011. **ED** Mario Elgueta D. **LC** QL461; .R43. Index available (in each volume). **Bk Rev. Ad Acc. Circ:** 400. Documents available from BIOSIS Document Express.
**Desc:** Taxonomy and applied entomology, population biology of insects and insect etology.
**Ind/Abst** Biocont. News Inf.; Biodeter. Abstr.; Biol. Abstr.; Entomol. Abstr.; Maize Abstr.; Life Sci. Collect.

CK
**REVISTA COLOMBIANA DE ENTOMOLOGIA. Added/Corp** Sociedad Colombiana de Entomologia. Vol. 2, No. 3 (Sept. 1976)-. Periodical. Spanish (summaries and/or abstracts in English).

NQ/1021-0296
**REVISTA NICARAGUENSE DE ENTOMOLOGIA.** [Rev. nicar. entomol.]. (1987)-. Periodical. Spanish. qt.
**Ind/Abst** Biocont. News Inf.; Cot. Trop. Fibr. Abstr. Bibliogr.; Entomol. Abstr.; Rev. Agric. Entomol.

PE/0080-2425
**REVISTA PERUANA DE ENTOMOLOGIA.** V. 1- June 1958-. Spanish (English). an. $10.00, $12.00 airmail. Sociedad Entomologica del Peru, Apartado 4796 Local Fermin Tanguis, Av Arequipa 8Va Cuadra, Lima Peru. **ED** Pedro G Aguilar. Index available. cum. index. **Bk Rev. Circ:** 1,000.
**Desc:** Pure and applied entomology (medical, agricultural and veterinary aspects of insects and related arthropods).

FR/0375-0868
**REVUE FRANCAISE D'ENTOMOLOGIE.** [Rev. fr. entomol.]. **Added/Corp** Laboratoire d'Entromologie (Museum National d'Histoire Naturelle). Laboratoire d'Entromologie (Museum National d'Histoire Naturelle). Association des Amis. (1934)-. Periodical. French (English). qt. 422.00F France; 490.00F other. AALEM, 45 rue de Buffon, F-75005 Paris France. **Tel** 011 33 1 40793600. **LC** QL461; .R5. **DD** 595.7/005. **CODEN** RFENDE. Index available. cum. index. **Bk Rev. Ad Acc. Circ:** 300 (ctrl). Documents available from BIOSIS Document Express.
**Desc:** Entomology, taxonomy, biogeography.
**Ind/Abst** AGRICOLA; Biol. Abstr.; Rev. Agric. Entomol.; Rev. Med. Vet. Entomol.; Zool. Rec.

PL/0867-1966
**ROCZNIK MUZEUM GORNOSLASKIEGO W BYTOMIU. ENTOMOLOGIA. Added/Corp** Muzeum Gornoslaskie w Bytomiu. **VFOAT** Annals of the Upper Silesian Museum in Bytomiu. Entomology; Entomologia. No. 1 (1990)-. Periodical. Polish.

NE/0924-4611
**SERIES ENTOMOLOGICA.** [Ser. entomol.]. **VFOAT** SENT. Vol. 1 (1966)-. Monographic series. English. ir. Price varies per volume. Kluwer Academic Publishers, Postbus 322, 3300 AH Dordrecht, The Netherlands. **Tel** 011 (31) 78 524400, FAX 011 31 78 183273, telex 20083. **(Subscription address:** Kluwer Academic Publishers / US Subscriptions, PO Box 253, Accord Station, Hingham MA 02018.) **CODEN** SEENAF. Documents available from BIOSIS Document Express.
**Ind/Abst** Biol. Abstr.; CSA Neuro. Abstr. (?-?).

SP/0300-5267
**SHILAP. SOCIEDAD HISPANO-LUSO-AMERICANA DE LEPIDOPTEROLOGIA.** [SHILAP, Soc. Hispano-Luso-Am. Lepid.]. **VFOAT** Sociedad Hispano-Luso-Americana de Lepidopterologia; Revista de Lepidopterologia. (1973)-. Periodical. Multiple languages. qt.
**Ind/Abst** Entomol. Abstr.; For. Abstr.; Rev. Agric. Entomol.

US
**SOUTHEASTERN AREA SOUTHERN PINE BEETLE OUTBREAK STATUS. Added/Corp** United States Forest Service- Southeastern Area. United States-Forest Service-Forest Pest Management. United States Forest Service-Division of State and Private Forestry. Southeastern Area. (Jan. 1974)-. Periodical. English. sa.

US/0147-1724
**SOUTHWESTERN ENTOMOLOGIST, THE.** [Southwest. entomol.]. **Added/Corp** Southwestern Entomological Society. Vol. 1 (Mar. 1976)-. Academic Scholarly Publication. English (Spanish). qt. $20.00 (institutions), $10.00 (individuals). Southwestern Entomological Society, 17360 Coit Road, Allen Knutson, Dallas TX 75252. **Tel** (214)231-5362, FAX (214)231-5600. **ED** Jeff Slosser. **LC** QL475.S68; S68. **DD** 595.70979/05. **CODEN** SENTDD. Index available. **Pr Rev. Circ:** 500. Documents available from The Genuine Article, BIOSIS Document Express, CASDDS.
**Desc:** Research reports on insects impacting on agricultural production.
**Ind/Abst** AGRICOLA [Full Cov.]; Agric. Eng. Abstr. (1991-); Biocont. News Inf. (19??-19??); Biol. Abstr.; Chem. Abstr.; Chemorecept. Abstr.; Cot. Trop. Fibr. Abstr. Bibliogr.; Curr. Aware. Biol. Sci., CABS; Curr. Contents, Agric. Biol. Environ. Sci.; Ecology Abstr.; Entomol. Abstr.; Field Crop Abstr.; For. Abstr.; Hortic. Abstr.; Index Vet.; Maize Abstr.; Ornamental Hort. (1991-); Life Sci. Collect.; PESTDOC; Plant Breed. Abstr.; Plant Grow. Reg. Abstr.; Potato Abstr.; Res. Alert [Full Cov.]; Rev. Agric. Entomol.; Rev. Med. Vet. Entomol.; Rice Abstr.; Sci. Cit. Index; SCISEARCH; Seed Abstr.; Soils Fert.; Sorghum Mill. Abstr.; Soyabean Abstr.; Sug. Indus. Abstr.; Vet. Bull.; Weed Abstr.; Wheat Barley Trit. Abstr.

US/1055-8799
**SOUTHWESTERN ENTOMOLOGIST. SUPPLEMENT (WESLACO, TEX.).** (SOUTHWESTERN ENTOMOLOGIST. SUPPLEMENT.). **Added/Corp** Southwestern Entomological Society. No. 13 (June 1989)-. Periodical. English (Spanish). Southwestern Entomological Society, 17360 Coit Road, Allen Knutson, Dallas TX 75252. **Tel** (214)231-5362, FAX (214)231-5600. **LC** QL475.S68; S69. **DD** 595.70979. ***Continues*** *Supplement to the Southwestern Entomologist, 0277-7878.*

US/0172-6188
**SPRINGER SERIES IN EXPERIMENTAL ENTOMOLOGY.** (1979)-. Monographic series. English. ir. Price varies per volume. Springer-Verlag New York Inc., 175 5th Avenue, New York NY 10010. **Tel** (212)460-1500, telex 232 235 SPB UR. **(Subscription address:** Springer Verlag New York Inc. / for North America, 44 Hartz Way, Secaucus NJ 07096.)
**Desc:** Topics include techniques in pheromone research, and neurochemical techniques in insects.

US/0271-6348
**STUDIES ON THE MORPHOLOGY AND SYSTEMATICS OF SCALE INSECTS.** [Stud. morphol. syst. scale insects]. **Added/Corp** Virginia Polytechnic Institute. Dept. of Entomology. Virginia Polytechnic Institute and State University. Dept. of Entomology. **VFOAT** Morphology and Systematics of Scale Insects. No. 1 (March 1969)-. Monographic series. English. ir. Price varies per volume. Virginia Polytechnic Institute and State University, 617 North Main Street, Blacksburg VA 24060. **Tel** (313)764-4392. **LC** AS36; .V512 subser. **DD** 081 S.

UK/0080-4363
**SYMPOSIA OF THE ROYAL ENTOMOLOGICAL SOCIETY OF LONDON.** [Symp. R. Entomol. Soc. Lond.]. **Added/Corp** Royal Entomological Society of London. No. 1 (1961)-. English. ir. £36.00. Royal Entomological Society, 41 Queens Gate, London SW7 5HR England. **Tel** 011 41 71 5848361. **CODEN** RESSBM. Documents available from BIOSIS Document Express, CASDDS.
**Ind/Abst** AGRICOLA [Full Cov.]; Biol. Abstr.; Chem. Abstr. (1961-1976).

UK/0307-6970
**SYSTEMATIC ENTOMOLOGY.** [Syst. entom.]. **Added/Corp** Royal Entomological Society of London. Vol. 1 (Jan. 1976)-. Academic Scholarly

Publication. English. qt (4 issues). $240.00 (institutions), $71.00 (individuals) US & Canada; £141.00 (institutions), £41.50 (individuals) Europe; £155.00 (institutions), £45.50 (individuals) other. Blackwell Scientific Publications Ltd, Marston Book Services, PO Box 87, Oxford OX2 ODT UK. **Tel** 011 44 865 791155, FAX 011 44 865 791927, telex 837 515 MARDIS G. **ED** I. Gauld and J. Cox. **LC** QL461; .S94. **DD** 595.7/001/2. **CODEN** SYENDM. **[CCC].** Index available (bound in last issue). **Bk Rev. Ad Acc. Pr Rev.** available on microfilm and microfiche from University Microfilms International (UMI). Documents available from The Genuine Article, BIOSIS Document Express. ***Supersedes** Journal of Entomology. Series B: Taxonomy & Systematics.*
**Desc:** Covers taxonomy and systematics of insects.
**Ind/Abst** AgBiotech News Inf.; AGRICOLA [Full Cov.]; Biocont. News Inf. (19??-19??); Biol. Abstr.; Curr. Aware. Biol. Sci., CABS; Curr. Contents, Agric. Biol. Environ. Sci.; Entomol. Abstr.; GeoRef; Maize Abstr.; Life Sci. Collect.; Res. Alert [Full Cov.]; Rev. Agric. Entomol.; Rev. Med. Vet. Entomol.; Sci. Cit. Index; SCISEARCH; Weed Abstr.

NE/0040-7496
**TIJDSCHRIFT VOOR ENTOMOLOGIE.** Vol. 1- ; 1857-. Periodical. Multiple languages. ir. Nederlandse Entomologische, Plantage Middenlaan 64, Amsterdam 1018 DH Netherlands. **LC** QL461; .N3. ***Supersedes** Nederlandse Entomologische Vereniging. Handelingen.*
**Ind/Abst** Biocont. News Inf.; For. Abstr.; Rev. Agric. Entomol.; Rev. Med. Vet. Entomol.; Rice Abstr.

US/0002-8320
**TRANSACTIONS OF THE AMERICAN ENTOMOLOGICAL SOCIETY (1890).** (TRANSACTIONS OF THE AMERICAN ENTOMOLOGICAL SOCIETY.). [Trans. Am. Entomol. Soc.]. **Main/Corp** American Entomological Society. **Added/Corp** American Entomological Society. Vol. 17, No. 1 (1890)-. Periodical. English. qt. $18.00 US; $20.00 other. American Entomological Society, Academy of Natural Sciences of Philadelphia, 1900 Race Street, Philadelphia PA 19103. **Tel** (215)561-3978, FAX (215)299-1028. **ED** Daniel Otte. **LC** QL461; .A39. **DD** 595. **Pr Rev. Circ:** 500 (ctrl). available on microfilm from University Microfilms International (UMI). Documents available from The Genuine Article. ***Continues** Transactions of the American Entomological Society and Proceedings of the Entomological Section of the Academy of Natural Sciences.*
**Desc:** Classification, taxonomy, systematics and ecology of insects.
**Ind/Abst** AGRICOLA [Full Cov.]; Curr. Aware. Biol. Sci., CABS; Curr. Contents, Agric. Biol. Environ. Sci.; Entomol. Abstr.; Life Sci. Collect.; Postharvest News Inf.; Res. Alert [Select. Cov.]; Rev. Agric. Entomol.; Rev. Med. Vet. Entomol.

US/1048-8138
**TROPICAL LEPIDOPTERA.** [Trop. lepid.]. **Added/Corp** Association for Tropical Lepidoptera. Vol. 1, No. 1 (May 1990)-. Periodical. English. Twice a year (May & November). $35.00 (basic), $50.00 (sustaining), $100.00 (patron) Comes with Association of Tropical and Lepidoptera membership. Association Tropical Lepidoptera, PO Box 141210, Gainesville FL 32614-1210. **Tel** (904)372-3505 Ext. 139. **ED** Dr. J. B. Heppner, (editor's address: PO Box 147100, Gainesville, FL 32614, phone: (904)372-3505 Ext. 139). **LC** QL560.6; .T76. **DD** 595.78/0913/05. **CODEN** TRLEER. Index available (Bound in Nov. issue). cum. index. **Bk Rev**, (Qty: 10). **Ad Acc. Pr Rev. Circ:** 1,100 (ctrl).

TU/1010-6960
**TURKIYE ENTOMOLOJI DERGISI.** [Turk. entomol. derg.]. **VFOAT** Turkish Journal of Entomology. (1987)-. Periodical. Turkish. qt. ***Continues** Turkiye Bitki Koruma Dergisi, 0254-5454.*
**Ind/Abst** Agrofor. Abstr.; Biocont. News Inf.; Maize Abstr.; Nematol. Abstr.; Postharvest News Inf.; Potato Abstr.; Rev. Agric. Entomol.; Rev. Plant Pathol.; Weed Abstr.

UK
**TYMBAL / AUCHENORRHYNCHA NEWSLETTER.** (19??)-. Newsletter. English. sa (July and Nov.). £4.00 UK; £6.00 US; £5.00 other. CAB International Institute of Entomology, 56 Queens Gate, c/o Mike Wilson, London SW7 5JR England. **Tel** 011 44 1 5840067.

US/0068-6417
**UNIVERSITY OF CALIFORNIA PUBLICATIONS IN ENTOMOLOGY.** [Univ. Calif. publ. entomol.]. **Added/Corp** University of California, Berkeley. Vol. 4, No. 1 (Aug. 1926)-. Academic Scholarly Publication. English. ir. Price varies per volume. University of California Press, 2120 Berkeley Way, Berkeley CA 94720. **Tel** (510)642-4191, (510)642-3907, FAX (510)642-9917. **LC** QL461; .C17. **DD** 595.7082. **CODEN** UCPEAH. **Circ:** 900 (ctrl). Documents available from BIOSIS Document Express, CASDDS. ***Continues** University of California Publications. Technical Bulletins. Entomology.*
**Ind/Abst** Biol. Abstr.; Chem. Abstr.; GeoRef; Life Sci. Collect.; Trop. Dis. Bull.

YU
**ZBORNIK RADOVA O ENTOMOFAUNI SR SRBIJE.** **VFOAT** Recueil des Travaux sur la Faune d'Insectes de la Serbie. Vol. 1-. Periodical. Serbo-Croatian (Cyrillic) (summaries and/or abstracts in English, French and German). **LC** QL482.Y8; Z37.

GW/0044-2240
**ZEITSCHRIFT FUER ANGEWANDTE ENTOMOLOGIE.** [Z. angew. Entomol.]. **Added/Corp** Deutsche Gesellschaft fur Angewandte Entomologie. **VFOAT** Journal of Applied Entomology. Vol. 1 (1914)-. Periodical. English (German). Ten times a year. DM1339.00 Europe; DM1328.00. Blackwell Wissenschafts-Verlag, Kurfuerstendamm 57, D 10707 Berlin Germany. **Tel** 011 49 30 32790623, 011 49 30 32790624, FAX 011 49 30 327 90610. **ED** Wolfgang Schwenke. **LC** SB599; .Z37. **DD** 632.705. **NLM** W1 ZE231N. **CODEN** ZANEAE. Index available. cum. index. **Bk Rev. Ad Acc. Circ:** 2,500. Documents available from The Genuine Article, BIOSIS Document Express, CASDDS.
**Desc:** Presents original articles on current research in entomology applied to agriculture, forestry, biomedical areas, food and feed storage.
**Ind/Abst** AgBiotech News Inf.; AGRICOLA; Agrofor. Abstr.; Biocont. News Inf.; Biodeter. Abstr.; Biol. Abstr. (1986-); Chem. Abstr.; Chemorecept. Abstr.; Curr. Aware. Biol. Sci., CABS; Curr. Contents, Agric. Biol. Environ. Sci.; Ecology Abstr.; Energy Res. Abstr.; Environ. Period. Bibliogr. (?-?); For. Prod. Abstr.; For. Abstr.; Helminthol. Abstr. (1991-); Maize Abstr.; Microbiol. Abstr. Sect. A; Nematol. Abstr.; Nutr. Abstr. Rev., Ser. B, Live Feeds and Feed.; Life Sci. Collect.; PESTDOC; Plant Breed. Abstr.; Poult. Abstr.; Res. Alert [Full Cov.]; Rev. Med. Vet. Entomol.; Rev. Plant Pathol.; Rice Abstr.; Sci. Cit. Index; SCISEARCH; Seed Abstr.; Soyabean Abstr.; Virol. AIDS Abstr.; Weed Abstr.

## ORNITHOLOGY

PL/0001-6454
**ACTA ORNITHOLOGICA.** [Acta ornithol.]. **Added/Corp** Polska Akademia Nauk. Instytut Zoologiczny. Vol. 5 (1960)-. Polish (English and German; summaries and/or abstracts in French and Russian). ir. **(Subscription address:** ARS Polona, PO Box 1001, 00068 Warsaw Poland.) **LC** QL671; .A22. **CODEN** AORNAK. Documents available from BIOSIS Document Express. ***Continues** Acta Ornithologica Musei Zoologici Polonici.*
**Ind/Abst** Biol. Abstr.; Fish Rev. (Jan. 1989-July 1992); Life Sci. Collect.; Ref. Z.; Zool. Rec.; Wildl. Rev. (Jan. 1989-July 1992).

LI/0135-3861
**ACTA ORNITHOLOGICA LITUANICA / AKADEMIIA NAUK LITOVSKOI SSR, INSTITUT ZOOLOGII I PARAZITOLOGII [AND] LITOVSKOE ORNITOLOGICHESKOE OBSHCHESTVO--OTDELENIE VSESOIUZNOGO ORNITOLOGICHESKOGO OBSHCHESTVA.** **Added/Corp** Zoologijos ir Parazitologijos Institutas (Lietuvos TSR Mokslu Akademija) Lietuvos Ornitologu Draugija.a. Volume 1 (1989)-. Monographic series. Russian (English; summaries and/or abstracts in Lithuanian; table of contents in Lithuanian).
**Ind/Abst** Fish Rev. (Jan. 1989-July 1992); Wildl. Rev. (Jan. 1989-July 1992).

US/0516-3870
**ALABAMA BIRDLIFE.** (ALABAMA BIRDLIFE : JOURNAL OF THE ALABAMA ORNITHOLOGICAL SOCIETY.). [Ala. birdlife]. **Added/Corp** Alabama Ornithological Society. **VFOAT** Alabama Bird-Life. Vol. 1, No. 1/2 (1953)-. Periodical. English. Twice a year (Aug., & Dec.). $10.00 Comes with Alabama Ornithological Society membership. Alabama Ornithological Society, Eufaula NWR, Route 2 Box 97 B, Eufaula AL 26027. **Tel** (205)687-4065, FAX (205)687-5906. **ED** Daniel Drennen (editor's address: 323 Cherry Street, Eufaula, AL 36027). **LC** WMLC 93/3925. **DD** 598. **Pr Rev. Circ:** 500.
**Desc:** To record and further the study of birds in Alabama and Northwest Florida. Covers any facts of bird ecology, natural history, behavior, management or related topics of birds.
**Ind/Abst** Fish Rev. (Jan. 1989-July 1992); Wildl. Rev. (Jan. 1989-July 1992).

FR/0002-4619
**ALAUDA.** Vol. 1, No. 1 (April 25, 1929)-. Periodical. French (summaries and/or abstracts in English, German and Spanish). qt. 260.00F France; 300.00F other. Soc d'Etudes Ornithologiques, 4 Avenue du Petit Chateau, Mnhnle F-91800 Brunoy France. **Tel** 33 1 60464851. **ED** Dejonghe, J Francois (eidtor's phone: 33 1 47302448). **CODEN** ALUDAI. **Bk Rev**, (Qty: 4). **Ad Acc, Adv Mgr:** Brichambaut. Documents available from BIOSIS Document Express.
**Desc:** Ornithology and ecology.
**Ind/Abst** Biol. Abstr.; Ecol. Abstr.; Ecology Abstr.; Geogr. Abstr. Phys. Geogr.; Key Word Index Wildl. Res.; Life Sci. Collect.; Wildl. Rev.

US/0004-7686
**AMERICAN BIRDS.** ***Title Change.*** [Am. birds]. **Added/Corp** National Audubon Society. U.S. Fish and Wildlife Service. Vol. 25, No. 1 (Feb. 1971)-Vol. 48, No. 1 (Spring 1994). Periodical. English. Five times a year. National Audubon Society, 700 Broadway, New York NY 10003. **Tel** (212)979-3117. **ED** Susan Roney Drennan. **LC** QL671; .A78. **DD** 598.2/97. **CODEN** ABRDAZ. **Bk Rev**, (Qty: 2 per year). **Ad Acc, Adv Mgr:** John Gourlay, **Tel** (212)546-9127. **Circ:** 19,500. available on microfilm and microfiche from University Microfilms International (UMI). Documents available from BIOSIS Document Express. ***Continues** Audubon Field Notes, 0097-7144. **Continued by** National Audubon Field Notes.*
**Desc:** A seasonal journal devoted to the birds of Americas, their changing distribution, population, migration, rare occurrence, ecology and behavior. Includes field identification, site guides and centers of learning.
**Ind/Abst** AQUAREF; Biol. Agric. Index; Biol. Abstr.; Biol. Dig.; Key Word Index Wildl. Res.; Wildl. Rev.

US/0002-7782
**AMERICAN CAGE-BIRD MAGAZINE.** ***Title Change.*** **See** Pets.

US/0748-8319
**AMERICAN HAWKWATCHER.** No. 1 (Aug. 1982)-. Monographic series. English. ir. Price varies per volume. American Hawkwatcher, 629 Green Street, Allentown PA 18102. **ED** Donald S Heintzelman. **LC** QL696.F3; A46. **DD** 598.916. **UDC** 598.2(7/8).
**Desc:** A serial devoted to presenting results of original hawk migration and other research dealing with birds of prey in the Americas.

US/0003-0686
**AMERICAN RACING PIGEON NEWS, THE.** **See** Animal Welfare.

UK
**ANNUAL REPORT AND ACCOUNTS - BRITISH TRUST FOR ORNITHOLOGY.** **Main/Corp** British Trust for Ornithology. (19??)-. English. an. £29.00. British Trust for Ornithology, The Nunnery, Thetford Norfolk 1P24 2PU England. **Tel** 011 44 842 750050, FAX 011 44 842 750030. **ED** Andy Elvin. **LC** QL671; .B8322. **DD** 598/.06/041. **Acid Free. Circ:** 10,000 (ctrl). available in print.
**Desc:** Covers reports and accounts for British Trust for ornithology.

CY/0590-4935
**ANNUAL REPORT - CYPRUS ORNITHOLOGICAL SOCIETY.** **Main/Corp** Cyprus Ornithological Society. Periodical. English. an. $6.00 Cyprus; $8.00 other. Cyprus Ornithological Society, 4 Kararis Street, Strovolos 154 Cyprus. **ED** C Charalambides and M Charalambides. **Circ:** 500 (ctrl).
**Desc:** Yearly report of the activities of the society.

NZ/0549-0162
**ANNUAL REPORT OF THE NEW ZEALAND BIRD BANDING SCHEME.** **Main/Corp** New Zealand Bird Banding Scheme. 13th (1962/63)-. Periodical. English. **LC** QL693; .O73. **DD** 598.2. ***Continues** Annual Report of the Banding Committee, 0474-7305.*

UK
**ANNUAL REVIEW FOR ... / THE GAME CONSERVANCY.** **See** Environmental Issues-Conservation and Natural Resources.

GW/0030-5715
**ANZEIGER DER ORNITHOLOGISCHE GESELLSCHAFT IN BAYERN.** [Anz. Ornithol. Ges. Bayern]. **Main/Corp** Ornithologische Gesellschaft in Bayern, Munich. Vol. 1 (1919)-. Periodical. German (English). Three times a year. DM150.00 Germany; $30.00 US. Ornithologische Gesellschaft in Bayern, Muenchhausenstr 21, W-8000 Muenchen 60 Germany. **Tel** 89-8107-123. **ED** Josef Reichholf. **LC** QL671; .O63. **UDC** 598.2. **CODEN** AOGBAV. Index available. **Bk Rev. Ad Acc. Circ:** 1,200 (ctrl). Documents available from BIOSIS Document Express.
**Desc:** Ornithology and ecology.
**Ind/Abst** Biol. Abstr.; Fish Rev. (Jan. 1989-July 1992); Key Word Index Wildl. Res.; Life Sci. Collect.; Wildl. Rev. (Jan. 1989-July 1992).

HU/0374-5708
**AQUILA.** (AQUILA : A MAGYAR ORNITHOLOGIAI KOZPONT FOLYOIRATA.). [Aquila]. **Added/Corp** Magyar Madartani Intezet. Magyar Ornithologiai Kozpont. Magyar Kir,alyi Madartani Intezet. (1894)-. Hungarian (English, French, German and Italian). an. KTM Orszagos Tormeszeivedelmi, Hivatal Madartani Intezet, 1121 Budapest Kol U 21 Hungary. **LC** QL671; .A6.
**Ind/Abst** Fish Rev. (Jan. 1989-July 1992); GeoRef; Wildl. Rev. (Jan. 1989-July 1992).

NE/0373-2266
**ARDEA.** [Ardea]. **Added/Corp** Nederlandse Ornithologische Unie. Nederlandsche Ornithologische Vereeniging. Vol. 1 (April 1912)-. Periodical. English (French and German; summaries and/or abstracts in Dutch). sa. Fl112.00 (institution), Fl77.00 (individual). Nederlandse Ornithologische UN, Sportlaan 13, 2225 JN Katwijk The Netherlands. **Tel** 011/31/1718/13296. **LC** QL671; .A67. **DD** 598.29492/05. **CODEN** ADEAA9. Index Available, published separately, free-automatically sent. **Pr Rev.** Documents available from The Genuine Article, BIOSIS Document Express. ***Continues*** *Jaarboekje (Nederlandsche Ornithologische Vereeniging).*
**Ind/Abst** Biol. Abstr.; Curr. Aware. Biol. Sci., CABS; Curr. Contents, Agric. Biol. Environ. Sci.; Ecol. Abstr.; Geogr. Abstr. Phys. Geogr.; GeoRef; Key Word Index Wildl. Res.; Life Sci. Collect.; Protozoolog. Abstr.; Res. Alert [Full Cov.]; Sci. Cit. Index; SCISEARCH; Wildl. Rev.

SP/0570-7358
**ARDEOLA.** [Ardeola]. **Added/Corp** Sociedad Espanola de Ornitologia. Vol. 1 (1954)-. Spanish (summaries and/or abstracts in English). sa (2 issues). 5000ptas Spain; 7500ptas other. Sociedad Espanola Ornithologia, U Complutense Fac Biologia, 28040 Madrid Spain. **Tel** 011 34 1 5493554. **CODEN** ARDEDF.
**Ind/Abst** Ecol. Abstr.; Fish Rev.; Key Word Index Wildl. Res.; Wildl. Rev.

US/0004-6809
**ATLANTIC NATURALIST. See** Environmental Issues-Conservation and Natural Resources.

US/0097-7136
**AUDUBON. See** Environmental Issues-Conservation and Natural Resources.

US/0004-8038
**AUK, THE.** [Auk]. **Added/Corp** American Ornithologists' Union. Vol. 1 (1884)-. Periodical. English. qt. $70.00 US, Mexico and Canada; $85.00 other. Ornithological Society of North America, PO Box 1897, Lawrence KS 66044-8897. **Tel** (913)843-1221, FAX ((913)843-1274. **(Subscription address:** The Auk, PO Box 1897, Lawrence KS 66044-8897.**) ED** Alan H. Brush. **LC** QL671; .N9. **DD** 598. **CODEN** AUKJAF. cum. index. **Ad Acc. Pr Rev. Acid Free. Circ:** 6,000. available on microfilm and microfiche from University Microfilms International (UMI). Documents available from The Genuine Article, BIOSIS Document Express, UMI Article Clearinghouse, CASDDS. ***Supersedes*** *Bulletin of the Nuttall Ornithological Club.*
**Desc:** Reports the results of recent research on the ecology, systematics, physiology, behavior, and anatomy of birds, and includes a worldwide review of current ornithological literature.
**Ind/Abst** AGRICOLA; Anim. Behav. Abstr.; AQUAREF; Biol. Agric. Index; Biol. Abstr.; Chem. Abstr.; Curr. Aware. Biol. Sci., CABS; Curr. Contents, Agric. Biol. Environ. Sci.; Ecol. Abstr. (?-?); Ecology Abstr.; Environ. Period. Bibliogr.; Expand. Acad. Index (1992-); Genet. Abstr.; GeoRef; Helminthol. Abstr. (1991-); Index Vet.; Key Word Index Wildl. Res.; Newsp. Period. Abstr. (1992-); Ocean. Abstr.; Life Sci. Collect.; Protozoolog. Abstr.; Psychol. Abstr. (1952-); PsycINFO; PsycLit; Res. Alert [Full Cov.]; Sci. Cit. Index; SCISEARCH; Vet. Bull.; Wildl. Rev.

AT/0045-0316
**AUSTRALIAN BIRD WATCHER.** (THE AUSTRALIAN BIRDWATCHER.). [Aust. bird watch.]. **Added/Corp** Bird Observers Club (Melbourne, Vic.). Vol. 1, No. 1 (March 1959)-. Periodical. English. qt. 20.00Aus$ Australia; 28.00Aus$ other. Bird Observers Club, PO Box 185, Nunawading Victoria 3131 Australia. **Tel** 03-8775342. Index available. cum. index. **Bk Rev. Circ:** 1,200.
**Desc:** Encourages the study and conservation of birds and their habitat; welcomes original papers and short notes on Australian ornithology, particularly those reporting data derived from watching birds in the field.
**Ind/Abst** Fish Rev.; Wildl. Rev.

AT/1030-8954
**AUSTRALIAN BIRDKEEPER.** [Aust. birdkeep.]. (1987)-. Periodical. English. Six times a year (Feb., Apr., June, Aug., Oct., Dec.). 42.00Aus$ Australia; 58.50Aus$ New Zealand; 62.50Aus$ others. Australian Birdkeeper, PO Box 6288, South Tweed Heads, New South Wales, 2486 Australia. **Tel** 011 61 75 907777, FAX 011 61 907130. **ED** Nigel Steele-Boyce. **DD** 598.05. Index available. cum. index. **Bk Rev**, (Qty: 12). **Ad Acc. Circ:** 16,000.
**Desc:** The keeping, breeding, and husbandary all cage & aviary birds and associated products and services.

AT/0311-8150
**AUSTRALIAN BIRDS : JOURNAL OF THE N. S. W. FIELD ORNITHOLOGISTS CLUB. Added/Corp** New South Wales Field Ornithologists Club. (1974)-. Periodical. English. qt (Mar., June, Sept., Dec.). 25.00Aus$. New South Wales Field Ornithologists Club, PO Box C436, Clarence Street, Sydney New South Wales, 2000 Australia. **Tel** 011 61 43 244911, FAX 011 61 43 247747. **ED** Pete Roberts, (editor's address: 33 Carlyle Road, Lindfield, 416 5605). **LC** WMLC L 83/9368. **Bk Rev. Circ:** 700. ***Continues*** *Birds (Gold League Birdwatchers).*
**Ind/Abst** Fish Rev. (Jan. 1989-July 1992); Wildl. Rev. (Jan. 1989-July 1992).

BE/0005-1993
**AVES.** [Aves]. Vol. 1; Feb. 1964-. Periodical. French (summaries and/or abstracts in Dutch, English and German). qt. 290F. Soc d'Etudes Ornithologiques, 4 Avenue du Petit Chateau, Mnhnle F-91800 Brunoy France. **Tel** 33 1 60464851. **UDC** 598.2. **CODEN** AVESAJ. **Bk Rev. Ad Acc. Circ:** 1,000 (ctrl). Documents available from BIOSIS Document Express.
**Desc:** Ornithology and zoology, bird population dynamics, acoustics, biogeography, biology, and ethology.
**Ind/Abst** Biol. Abstr.; Key Word Index Wildl. Res.; Life Sci. Collect.; Wildl. Rev.

US
**AVIAN BIOLOGY.** Vol. 1 (1971)-. Academic Scholarly Publication. English. ir. $94.00 (Vol. 9). Academic Press, Inc., 6277 Sea Harbor Drive, Orlando FL 32887. **Tel** (800)543-9534, (407)345-4100, FAX (407)363-9661. **DD** 598.2; 598.2.

US/0005-2086
**AVIAN DISEASES. See** Veterinary Sciences.

UK/0307-9457
**AVIAN PATHOLOGY. See** Veterinary Sciences.

US/0567-2856
**AVICULTURAL BULLETIN.** [Avic. bull.]. **VFOAT** Avicultural Magazine. Bulletin. English. mo. $15.00 US; $20.00 other. Avicultural Society of America, PO Box 5516, Riverside CA 92517. **Tel** (310)645-5842, (909)780-4102. **ED** Jean Hessler. **DD** 636. **UDC** 636.5/.6(73). **Bk Rev. Ad Acc. Circ:** 1,000.
**Desc:** Dissemination of information for the care, breeding, and feeding of birds in captivity, the perpetuation of species threatened with extinction. Publication of matter pertaining to aviculture.

CN/0317-5650
**AVICULTURAL JOURNAL, THE.** ***Ceased.*** (May 1975)-(1992). English. Avicultural Advancement Council of Canada, PO Box 5126 Station B, Victoria British Columbia V8R 6N3 Canada. **Tel** (604)592-0230. **ED** Mark S Curtis and Doreen E Albion. **DD** 636.6/86/06271. **UDC** 636.5/.6. **Bk Rev. Ad Acc. Circ:** 310 (ctrl).
**Desc:** Contains articles on all types of birds, their genetics and health of birds. Articles by knowledgeable veterinarians for our readers. Many writers from all over the world.

UK/0005-2256
**AVICULTURAL MAGAZINE, THE. Added/Corp** Avicultural Society. Vol. 1-8, (Nov. 1894)-(Oct. 1902); New Series., Vol. 1-7, (Nov. 1902)-(Oct. 1909); 3rd Series, Vol. 1-13, (Nov. 1909)-(Dec. 1922); 4th Series, Vol. 1-13, (1923)-(1935); 5th Series, Vol. 1-10, (1936)-(1946); Vol. 52 (1947)-. Periodical. English. qt. £18.00 UK; £21.00 others. Avicultural Society, Bristol Clifton, W England Zoological Society, Bristol BS8 3HA United Kingdom. **Tel** 011 44 272 738951. **ED** Mary Harvey. **LC** QL671; .A93. **DD** 636.606242. cum. index. **Bk Rev. Ad Acc. Circ:** 800 (ctrl). available on microfilm and microfiche from University Microfilms International (UMI).
**Ind/Abst** Fish Rev.; Key Word Index Wildl. Res.; Wildl. Rev.

UK/0005-3392
**B.T.O. NEWS. Main/Corp** British Trust for Ornithology. **VAT** British Trust for Ornithology News. No. 1 (Jan. 1964)-. Periodical. English. Six times a year (Jan., Mar., May, July, Sept., Nov.). £17.00 Comes with British Trust for Ornithology Membership. British Trust for Ornithology, The Nunnery, Thetford Norfolk 1P24 2PU England. **Tel** 011 44 842 750050, FAX 011 44 842 750030. **ED** Paul Green. **LC** QL690.G7; B84a. **DD** 598.2/073/0941. **Bk Rev. Ad Acc. Circ:** 8,000 (ctrl).
**Desc:** Contains news, reviews, letters, and up-to-the-minute information on trends in British bird populations.

GW/0005-8211
**BEITRAEGE ZUR VOGELKUNDE.** [Beitr. Vogelkd.]. (1949)-. Periodical. German (German and French). Four times a year. Aula Verlag GmbH, Luisenplatz 2, D 65185 Wiesbaden Germany. **Tel** 011 49 611 373060. **CODEN** BEVOAI. **[CCC].** Index available. **Ad Acc. Circ:** 1,150. Documents available from BIOSIS Document Express.
**Desc:** Scope includes publications on all topics of ornithology, mainly on the distribution, habitats, habits and breeding behaviour of birds. In addition to comprehensive treatise, information on most recent results of observation.
**Ind/Abst** Biol. Abstr.; Key Word Index Wildl. Res.; Life Sci. Collect.; Wildl. Rev.

SI/0156-1383
**BIRD BEHAVIOUR.** [Bird behav.]. Vol. 1, No. 2 (Nov. 1977)-. Periodical. English. Twice a year. $75.00 North America; $100.00 other. Cognizant Communication Corporation, 3 Hartsdale Road, Elmsford NY 10523. **Tel** (914)592-7720. **CODEN** BBEHDU. **[CCC].** Documents available from BIOSIS Document Express. ***Continues*** *Babbler, 0314-5921.*
**Desc:** An interdisciplinary journal that publishes original research on behavioral ecology, experimental psychology and behavioral physiology in birds.
**Ind/Abst** Anim. Behav. Abstr. (?-?); Biol. Abstr.; Ecol. Abstr. (?-?); Environ. Period. Bibliogr. (?-?); Fish Rev. (Jan. 1989-1992); Life Sci. Collect. (?-?); Psychol. Abstr. (1980-?); PsycINFO (?-?); PsycLit (?-?); SCISEARCH (?-?); Wildl. Rev. (Jan. 1989-1992).

●US/1073-5186
**BIRD BREEDER. See** Pets.

UK/0959-2709
**BIRD CONSERVATION INTERNATIONAL. Added/Corp** International Council for Bird Preservation. Vol. 1, No. 1 (Mar. 1991)-. Academic Scholarly Publication. English (summaries and/or abstracts in French, Portuguese and Spanish). qt (Mar., Jun., Sep., Dec.). $116.00 US, Canada & Mexico; £68.00 other. Cambridge University Press, The Edinburgh Building, Shaftesbury Road, Cambridge CB2 2RU United Kingdom. **Tel** 011 44 223 312393, FAX 011 44 223 325959. **(Subscription address:** Cambridge University Press / North America, 110 Midland Avenue, Port Chester NY 10573.**) ED** N. J. Collar and R. W. Rands. **LC** QL676.5; .B48. **DD** 639.9/78/05. **CODEN** BCOIEN. Documents available from Documents on Demand.
**Desc:** Focuses on the major conservation issues affecting birds, especially globally threatened species and their habitats. Through original papers and reviews the journal provides international up-to-date coverage of bird conservation topics.
**Ind/Abst** Curr. Aware. Biol. Sci., CABS; Ecol. Abstr.; Environ. Abstr.; Environ. Period. Bibliogr.

UK/0955-4238
**BIRD KEEPER.** [Bird keep.]. (1988)-. Periodical. English. bm. £19.60 UK; £21.65 other. IPC Magazines Ltd., Perrymount Road, Haywards Heath, West Sussex RH16 3DH England. **Tel** 011 44 444 440421. **DD** 636.6.

US/0893-4630
**BIRD OBSERVER (BELMONT, MASS.).** (BIRD OBSERVER.). [Bird obs.]. **Added/Corp** Bird Observer of Eastern Massachusetts. Vol. 15, No. 1 (Feb. 1987)-. Periodical. English. Six times a year. $16.00 (one year), $30.00 (two years). Bird Observer, PO Box 236, Arlington MA 02174. **Tel** (617)495-2375. **DD** 598. Index available. **Bk Rev. Ad Acc. Circ:** 750. ***Continues*** *Bird Observer of Eastern Massachusetts.*
**Desc:** Publishes articles on where to go birding, field indentification, bird sightings, reviews and the field sighting reports for eastern Massachusetts.
**Ind/Abst** Fish Rev. (Jan. 1989-July 1992); Wildl. Rev. (Jan. 1989-July 1992).

UK/0006-3657
**BIRD STUDY.** (BIRD STUDY : THE JOURNAL OF THE BRITISH TRUST FOR ORNITHOLOGY.). [Bird study]. **Added/Corp** British Trust for Ornithology. Vol. 1, No. 1 (Mar. 1954)-. Academic Scholarly Publication. English. Three times a year (Mar., July, Nov.). $122.00 US & Canada; £72.00 Europe; £79.00 other. Blackwell Scientific Publications Ltd, Marston Book Services, PO Box 87, Oxford OX2 ODT UK. **Tel** 011 44 865 791155, FAX 011 44 865 791927, telex 837 515 MARDIS G. **ED** A. G. Gosler. **LC** QL671; .B828. **DD** 598.205. **CODEN** BISTAC. **[CCC]. Bk Rev. Pr Rev. Circ:** 3,000 (ctrl). available on microfilm and microfiche from University Microfilms International (UMI). Documents available from The Genuine Article, BIOSIS Document Express, Documents on Demand. ***Absorbed*** *Bird Migration, 0523-6894.*
**Desc:** Original papers on all aspects of field ornithology, especially distribution, status, censusing, migration, population, habitat and breeding ecology.
**Ind/Abst** Anim. Behav. Abstr.; Biol. Abstr.; Curr. Aware. Biol. Sci., CABS; Curr. Contents, Agric. Biol. Environ. Sci.; Ecol. Abstr.; Ecology Abstr.; Environ. Abstr.; Environ. Period. Bibliogr.; For. Prod. Abstr.; For. Abstr.; Helminthol. Abstr. (1991-); Key Word Index Wildl. Res.; Nutr. Abstr. Rev., Ser. B, Live Feeds and Feed.; Life Sci. Collect.; Res. Alert [Full Cov.]; Sci. Cit. Index; SCISEARCH; Wildl. Rev.

CN/1185-5967
**BIRD TRENDS.** [Bird trends]. **Added/Corp** Canadian Wildlife Service. No. 1 (Summer 1991)-. English. Canadian Wildlife Services, Ottawa Canada. **DD** 598.2971.

US/0164-3037
**BIRD WATCHER'S DIGEST.** Vol. 1 (Sept. 1978)-. Periodical. English. bm. $17.95 (one year), $29.95 (two year), $39.95 (three year) US; $22.95 (one year), $39.95 (two year), $54.95 (three year) Canada; $27.95 (one year), $49.95 (two year), $69.95 (three year). Pardson Inc., PO Box 110, Marietta OH 45750. **Tel** (614)373-5285. **ED** Mary Bowers. **LC** QL677.5; .B482. **DD** 598/.07/234705. Index available. cum. index. **Bk Rev**, (Qty: 50). **Ad Acc, Adv Mgr:** A. Thompson, **Tel** 800-879-2473. **Circ:** 81,000.
**Desc:** Articles on attracting and feeding birds, identification, bird behavior, and unusual birding adventures; also humor, art, poetry, birding tips, and column by Roger Troy Peterson.
**Ind/Abst** Biol. Dig.

US/0199-5979
**BIRD WORLD (NORTH HOLLYWOOD).** (BIRD WORLD.). (April/May 1978)-. Periodical. English. bm. $15.00. Bird World, PO Box 70, Hollywood CA 91603. **Tel** (818)769-6111. **ED** Kathy Lyon. **LC** SF460; .B57. **DD** 636.6/86. Index available. **Bk Rev. Ad Acc. Circ:** 15,000 (ctrl).
**Desc:** Columns regarding nutrition and veterinary care. Professional, legal, and business aspects covered. Conservation biology highlighted, technical articles about many aspects of bird care, studies, research and breeding.
**Ind/Abst** Fish Rev.; Wildl. Rev.

CN/1188-2549
**BIRDERS JOURNAL.** [Birders j.]. (Oct. 1991)-. Periodical. English. bm. $45.00 institutions; $38.00 individuals. Birder Journal Publishing, Suite 289, 8 Midtown Drive, Oshawa Ontario L1J 8L2 Canada. **Tel** (905)427-6097. **DD** 598/.07234713/05.

US/0895-495X
**BIRDER'S WORLD.** [Bird. world]. Vol. 1, No. 1 (Jan./Feb. 1987)-. Periodical. English. bm. $25.00 (one year), 44.00 (two year). Birder's World, 44 East 8th Street, Suite 410, Holland MI 49423. **Tel** (800)424-2473, (616)396-5618. **(Subscription address:** Neodata / Colorado, PO Box 2606, Boulder Boulder CO 80322.) **DD** 598.
**Desc:** Focuses on bird life and birding experiences around the country. Articles highlighted with full-color photography.
**Ind/Abst** Fish Rev.; Wildl. Rev.

SA/0006-5838
**BIRDING IN SOUTHERN AFRICA. Added/Corp** Southern African Ornithological Society. **VFOAT** Birding; Birding in SA. Vol. 41, No. 3 (Sept. 1989)-. Periodical. English (Afrikaans). qt. Free to members of the South African Ornithological Society; $40.00 individual membership fee. Southern African Ornithological Society, PO Box 87234, Greenside Trans 2034 South Africa. **Tel** 011 27 11 8884147, FAX 011 27 11 7827013. **ED** G Bennett. **LC** QL692.S6; B64. **DD** 598.2968. **CODEN** BSAFEM. Index available. cum. index. **Bk Rev. Ad Acc. Circ:** 5,000 (ctrl). ***Continues*** *Bokmakierie, 0006-5838.*
**Desc:** Popular magazine for all bird lovers.
**Ind/Abst** Fish Rev. (Jan. 1989-July 1992); Wildl. Rev. (Jan. 1989-July 1992).

UK/0006-3665
**BIRDS : MAGAZINE FOR MEMBERS OF THE ROYAL SOCIETY FOR THE PROTECTION OF BIRDS. Added/Corp** Royal Society for the Protection of Birds. Vol. 1 (Jan./Feb. 1966)-. Periodical. English. Four times a year. £20.00 Comes with Royal Society for the Protection of Birds membership. Royal Society Protection Birds, The Lodge Sandy, Bedsfordshire SG19 2DL England. **Tel** 011 44 767 680551. **LC** WMLC 93/4146. ***Continues*** *Bird Notes (London, England), 0406-3392.*
**Ind/Abst** Child. Lit. Abstr. (19??-); Ecol. Abstr.; Key Word Index Wildl. Res.

US
**BIRDS OF DISTINCTION.** Vol. 3, No. 4 (4th Quarter 1990)-. Periodical. English. qt. $16.00 US; $19.00 Canada. The Canary and Finch Journal, 19235 SW Pilkington Road, Lake Oswego OR 97035. **LC** SF461; .C36. ***Continues*** *Canary & Finch Journal, 1048-4566.*

●US/1061-5466
**BIRDS OF NORTH AMERICA, THE.** [Birds N. Am.]. **Added/Corp** American Ornithologists' Union. Academy of Natural Sciences of Philadelphia. (1992)-. Monographic series. English. sa. $195.00. Academy of Natural Sciences, 1900 Benjamin Franklin Parkway, Philadelphia PA 19103. **Tel** (215)299-1130, FAX (215)299-1028. **ED** Alan Poole & Frank Gill. **LC** QL681; .B625. **DD** 598/.05. **CODEN** BNOAE8. Index available. cum. index. **Pr Rev. Acid Free. Circ:** 925.
**Desc:** Covers all breeding birds of Canada and the United States. Scientific reference source suitable for graduate and undergraduate research and teaching in ornithology, conservation, environmental studies, wildlife management and realted disciplines.

IC
**BLIKI : TIMARIT UN FUGLA. See** Natural History.

US
**BOOKS ABOUT BIRDS.** Vol. 1, (Sept. 1974)-. Periodical. English. Five times a year. $8.00. Books About Birds, PO Box 106, 9502 Kew Gardens, Jamaica NY 11415. **Tel** (718)544-3279. **ED** Jessie Kitching. **DD** 016; 598.2. **Bk Rev.**
**Desc:** News of bird books, books just published, auction news, reviews, dealers' prices and collectors' items.

UK/0007-0335
**BRITISH BIRDS.** (BRITISH BIRDS; AN ILLUSTRATED MAGAZINE DEVOTED TO THE BIRDS ON THE BRITISH LIST.). [Br. birds]. Vol. 1 (June 1907)-. Periodical. English. Twelve times a year. £91.70 (institutions), £74.60 (individuals) US & Canada; £39.60 (individuals), £48.70 (institutions) others. British Birds Ltd, Fountains Park Lane, Blunham Bedford MK44 3NJ England. **Tel** 011 44 767 40467, FAX 011 44 767 40025. **ED** J. T. R. Sharrock (phone: 011 44 767 640025). **CODEN** BRBIAP. **[CCC].** Index available (bound in Dec. issue). cum. index. **Bk Rev. Ad Acc, Adv Mgr:** S. Barnes, **Tel** 44 621 815085. **Circ:** 11,000. available on microfilm from University Microfilms International (UMI). Documents available from BIOSIS Document Express, Documents on Demand. ***Absorbed*** *Zoologist.*
**Desc:** Feature notes on every aspect of birdwatching, from ecology, biology and behavior to identification and rare bird occurrences. Covers Europe, North Africa and the Middle East.
**Ind/Abst** Anim. Behav. Abstr.; AQUAREF; Biol. Abstr.; Ecol. Abstr.; Ecology Abstr.; Energy Inf. Abstr.; Environ. Abstr.; Key Word Index Wildl. Res.; Life Sci. Collect.; Protozoolog. Abstr.; Wildl. Rev.

CN/1183-3521
**BRITISH COLUMBIA BIRDS.** (BRITISH COLUMBIA BIRDS : JOURNAL OF BRITISH COLUMBIA FIELD ORNITHOLOGISTS.). (1991)-. English. sa. Comes with membership. British Columbia Field Ornithologists, PO Box 8059, Victoria, British Columbia, V8W 3R7 Canada.

UK
**BRITISH HOMING WORLD.** V. 1- (No. ); 1933-. Periodical. English. wk. £23.84. British Homing World, Severn Farm Industrial Estate, Severn Road, Welshpool Powys SY21 7DF England. **Tel** 0938 2360. **ED** J R Thomas. **UDC** 798.9: 636.596(410). **Ad Acc.**
**Desc:** Articles on the management and conditioning of pigeons for racing. Up-to-date news and race results. Particulars of winning birds are regularly featured.

JM
**BROADSHEET / GOSSE BIRD CLUB. Main/Corp** Gosse Bird Club (Jamaica). **VFOAT** Gosse Bird Club Broadsheet. (1963)-. Periodical. English. sa. $8.00. Gosse Bird Club, PO Box 1002, Kingston 8 Jamaica. **(Subscription address:** The Press - University of the West Indies, 1A Aqueduct Flats, Mona Campus, Kingston 7, Jamaica) **LC** QL688; .G6.
**Desc:** Publishes available information on Jamaica's birds.

US
**BULLETIN / COLONIAL WATERBIRD SOCIETY. Added/Corp** Colonial Waterbird Society. **VFOAT** Colonial Waterbird Society Bulletin. Vol. 15, No. 2 (Dec. 1991)-. Bulletin. English. sa. $45.00 institutional membership; $25.00 individual membership. Colonial Waterbird Society, 8096 River Bay Drive West, Indianapolis IN 46240. **Tel** (317)849-5789. **LC** QL671; .N44. **Bk Rev. Pr Rev. Circ:** 500-600. ***Continues*** *Newsletter (Colonial Waterbird Society), 1053-9956.*

UK
**BULLETIN / DIPLOMATIC SERVICE ORNITHOLOGICAL SOCIETY.** No. 1 (Oct. 1977)-. Bulletin. English. an. ***Continues*** *Newsletter / Diplomatic Service Ornithological Society.*

US/0022-8729
**BULLETIN - KANSAS ORNITHOLOGICAL SOCIETY. Main/Corp** Kansas Ornithological Society. Vol.1 (Apr. 1950). Bulletin. English. qt. $10.00 US; $12.00 other. Kansas Ornithological Bulletin, 1816 Cypress Lane, Newton KS 67114. **Tel** (913)532-6659. **(Subscription address:** Division of Biological Sciences, Kansas State University, Manhattan KS 66506) **ED** Max Thompson. **UDC** 598.2(781). Index available. cum. index. **Bk Rev. Pr Rev. Circ:** 400 (ctrl).
**Desc:** The study of birds with emphasis on their occurrence, nesting and population dynamics applied to Kansas.
**Ind/Abst** Fish Rev.; Wildl. Rev.

UK/0007-1595
**BULLETIN OF THE BRITISH ORNITHOLOGIST'S CLUB.** [Bull. Br. Ornithol. Club]. **Main/Corp** British Ornithologists' Club. Vol. 1 (1892/1893)-. Periodical. English. Four times a year (Mar., June, Sept., Dec.). $40.00 (one year), $74.00 (two years), $108.00 (three years) US; £20.00 others. British Ornithologist's Club, Hammerkop Frogmill Hurley, Maidenhead Berkshire SL6 5NL, England. **Tel** 011 44 628 824214. **ED** Dr. D. W. Snow. **CODEN** BBOCAS. Index available. cum. index. **Bk Rev. Circ:** 800. Documents available from BIOSIS Document Express.
**Desc:** Short papers on taxonomy including descriptions of new forms, nests and eggs, papers on field studies, anatomy, ethology, food, moult, nomenclature parasitology and voice worldwide coverage.
**Ind/Abst** Biol. Abstr.; Wildl. Rev.

UK
**BULLETIN OF THE INTERNATIONAL COUNCIL FOR BIRD PRESERVATION. See** Environmental Issues-Conservation and Natural Resources.

US/0040-4543
**BULLETIN OF THE TEXAS ORNITHOLOGICAL SOCIETY. Main/Corp** Texas Ornithological Society. **Added/Corp** Texas Ornithological Society. TOS bulletin. **VFOAT** TOS Bulletin. **VAT** Texas Ornithological Society Bulletin. Vol. 1 (Apr. 1967)-. Bulletin. English. sa. $15.00. Texas Ornithological Society, 326 Liveoak, Ingram TX 78025. **(Subscription address:** 326 Live Oak, Ingram, TX 78025) **ED** Karen L P Benson. **Bk Rev. Pr Rev. Circ:** 600 (ctrl). ***Supersedes*** *Texas Ornithological Society. Newsletter.*
**Desc:** Natural history, conservation and history of the study of Texas birds.
**Ind/Abst** Zool. Rec.

UK
**BULLETIN - ORNITHOLOGICAL SOCIETY OF THE MIDDLE EAST. Main/Corp** Ornithological Society of the Middle East. No. 1 (Autumn 1978)-. Periodical. English. Twice a year. £10.00 Comes with Ornithological Society of the Middle East membership. Ornithological Society of the Middle East, c/o The Lodge, Sandy Bedfordshire SG19 2DL England. **ED** Mark Boyd. **Bk Rev. Ad Acc. Circ:** 850 (ctrl). ***Continues in part*** *Bulletin - Ornithological Society of Turkey.*
**Desc:** Short papers, book reviews, details of meetings and expeditions and lists of current literature concerning ornithology in the Middle East.
**Ind/Abst** Fish Rev.; Ref. Z.; Zool. Rec.; Wildl. Rev.

CN/0007-5256
**BULLETIN ORNITHOLOGIQUE (ORSAINVILLE).** (BULLETIN ORNITHOLOGIQUE.). [Bull. ornithol.]. **Added/Corp** Club des Ornithologues de Quebec. (1956)-. Bulletin. French. Four times a year (Mar., July, Sept., Dec.). $20.00 (individuals); $22.30 (institutions). Club des Ornithologues du Quebec Inc, 1000 de la Verendrye, Quebec QUE G1J 4V7 Canada. **Tel** (418)667-6373. ***Absorbed*** *Feuille de Contact (Club des Ornithologues du Quebec), 0710-2356.*

US/0740-3771
**BULLETIN / PACIFIC SEABIRD GROUP. Main/Corp** Pacific Seabird Group. **VFOAT** P.S.B. Bulletin; PSB Bulletin. Vol. 1, No. 1 (Jan. 1974)-. Bulletin. English. sa. $20.00 (institutions), $15.00 (individuals) US; $25.00 other. Pacific Seabird Group, PO Box 178, Tenino WA 98589. **Tel** (206)264-5886. **ED** Martha Springer. **LC** QL683.P37; P32a. **DD** 598.4/0979. **Bk Rev. Circ:** 475.
**Desc:** Informs select international readership about current research on seabirds, conservation issues, legislation and policy decisions.
**Ind/Abst** Fish Rev.; Wildl. Rev.

ZA/0378-4525
**BULLETIN - ZAMBIAN ORNITHOLOGICAL SOCIETY.** (THE BULLETIN OF THE ZAMBIAN ORNITHOLOGICAL SOCIETY.). [Bull. - Zambian Ornithol. Soc.]. **Main/Corp** Zambian Ornithological Society. Vol. 1 (June 1969)-. Bulletin. English. sa. **LC** QL692.Z3; Z34a. **DD** 598.1/9689/4.
**Ind/Abst** Fish Rev. (Jan. 1989-July 1992); Wildl. Rev. (Jan. 1989-July 1992).

US/0362-9902
**C.F.O. JOURNAL. *Title Change.*** [C.F.O. j.]. **Main/Corp** Colorado Field Ornithologists. **VAT** Colorado Field Ornithologists Journal. No. 23 (Spring 1975)-(19??). Periodical. English. qt. Colorado Field Ornithologists, 1782 Locust Street, Denver CO 08022-1632. **Tel** (303)333-8352. **ED** Mark Janos. **LC** QL684.C6; C64. **DD** 598.2/9788/05. **CODEN** CFOJDN. Index available. **Bk Rev. Ad Acc. Circ:** 500. available on microfilm and microfiche from University Microfilms International (UMI). ***Continues*** *Colorado Field Ornithologist, 0010-1591.* ***Continued by*** *Colorado Field Ornithologists' Journal, 1066-7342.*
**Desc:** A journal of Colorado field ornithology containing articles on distribution, behavior, and occurrence of birds. Also book reviews, seasonal Colorado reports and records committee decisions.

●US/1062-7383
**CAGED BIRD HOBBYIST.** [Caged bird hobbyist]. **VFOAT** Caged Bird Hobbyist Magazine. (1992)-. Periodical. English. Seven times a year. $11.97. Pet Business Inc, 5400 Northwest 84th Avenue, Miami FL 33166. **Tel** (305)592-9890. **DD** 598.
**Desc:** Provides information on birds typically kept indoors or in aviaries. Written for new and prospective bird owners, and more advanced hobbyists. Offers taming, training, breeding and veterinary advice. Typical issues include four-color photographs of birds.

AT/0314-8211
**CANBERRA BIRD NOTES.** [Canb. bird notes]. (1968)-. Periodical. English. Four times a year. 25.00Aus$. Canberra Ornithologists Group, PO Box 301 Civic Square, Canberra Act, 2608 Australia. **Tel** 11 61 62 467401. **DD** 598.2073.

US
**CHECK-LIST OF BIRDS OF THE WORLD. Added/Corp** Museum of Comparative Zoology (Cambridge, Mass.). **VFOAT** Birds of the World. Vol. 1 (1931)-. Monographic series. English. ir. Price varies per volume. Museum of Comparative Zoology, Harvard University, Bird Department, 26 Oxford Street, Cambridge MA 02158. **Tel** (617)495-2471. **ED** J. L.

Peters, E. Mayr and R. A. Paynter. cum. index. **Circ:** 2,000.
**Desc:** Scientific compilation of bird names and distribution of species and subspecies.

US
**CIRCULAR / NATIONAL AUDUBON SOCIETY.** **Added/Corp** National Audubon Society. No. 1, (1919)-. Monographic series. English. Six times a year. $20.00. National Audubon Society, 700 Broadway, New York NY 10003. **Tel** (212)979-3117. **ED** Micheal Robbins, (212)546-9245. **Ad Acc**, **Adv Mgr Tel** (212)546-9127. **Circ:** 485,000.

US/0738-6028
**COLONIAL WATERBIRDS.** (COLONIAL WATERBIRDS : JOURNAL OF THE COLONIAL WATERBIRD GROUP.). [Colon. waterbirds]. **Added/Corp** Colonial Waterbird Group (U.S.) Colonial Waterbird Society. Vol. 4 (1981)-. English (French and Spanish). Twice a year (May & Dec.). $25.00 (individuals), $45.00 (institutions) Comes with Colonial Waterbird Society membership. Colonial Waterbird Society, 8096 River Bay Drive West, Indianapolis IN 46240. **Tel** (317)849-5789. **ED** Ralph Morris. **LC** QL671; .C65. **DD** 598.29/24/0973. **CODEN** COWAEW. Index available. cum. index. **Bk Rev. Ad Acc. Pr Rev. Circ:** 525. Documents available from The Genuine Article, BIOSIS Document Express. ***Continues** Colonial Waterbird Group (U.S.). Conference. Proceedings.*
**Desc:** Articles on biology, management and conservation of colonial nesting waterbirds; Research papers and other related items, such as, heron, stork, ibis, cormorant, gull and tern seabird.
**Ind/Abst** Anim. Behav. Abstr.; Aquat. Sci. Fish. Abstr. (Computer File); Biol. Abstr. (1985-); Curr. Aware. Biol. Sci., CABS; Curr. Contents, Agric. Biol. Environ. Sci.; Ecology Abstr.; Helminthol. Abstr. (1991-); Key Word Index Wildl. Res.; Ocean. Abstr.; Res. Alert [Select. Cov.]; SCISEARCH; Wildl. Rev.

US/1066-7342
**COLORADO FIELD ORNITHOLOGISTS' JOURNAL.** [Colo. Field Ornithol. j.]. **Added/Corp** Colorado Field Ornithologists. **VFOAT** C.F.O. Journal. Vol. 25, No. 4 (Fall 1991)-. Periodical. English. qt. $12.00. Colorado Field Ornithologists, 1782 Locust Street, Denver CO 08022-1632. **Tel** (303)333-8352. **DD** 598. **Bk Rev. Circ:** 400. ***Continues** C.F.O. Journal, 0362-9902.*

US/0010-5422
**CONDOR (LOS ANGELES, CALIF.), THE.** (THE CONDOR.). [Condor]. **Added/Corp** Cooper Ornithological Club. Cooper Ornithological Society. Vol. 2, No. 1 (Jan./Feb. 1900)-. Periodical. English. qt. $60.00. Ornithological Society of North America, PO Box 1897, Lawrence KS 66044-8897. **Tel** (913)843-1221, FAX ((913)843-1274. **ED** Martin L. Morton. **LC** QL671; .C7. **CODEN** CNDRAB. **Bk Rev. Ad Acc. Pr Rev. Acid Free. Circ:** 3,500. available on microfilm and microfiche from University Microfilms International (UMI). Documents available from The Genuine Article, BIOSIS Document Express, UMI Article Clearinghouse. ***Continues** Bulletin of the Cooper Ornithological Club.*
**Desc:** Articles deal with all aspects of ornithology, including ecology, behavior, natural history, physiology, anatomy, taxonomy and biogeography.
**Ind/Abst** Anim. Behav. Abstr.; AQUAREF; Biol. Agric. Index; Biol. Abstr.; Curr. Aware. Biol. Sci., CABS; Curr. Contents, Agric. Biol. Environ. Sci.; Ecol. Abstr. (?-?); Ecology Abstr.; Environ. Period. Bibliogr.; Expand. Acad. Index (1992-); For. Abstr.; GeoRef; Index Vet.; Key Word Index Wildl. Res.; Newsp. Period. Abstr. (1992-); Ocean. Abstr.; Life Sci. Collect.; Res. Alert [Full Cov.]; Sci. Cit. Index; SCISEARCH; Vet. Bull.; Wildl. Rev.

US
**CONNECTICUT WARBLER, THE. See** Natural History.

US/0270-2894
**CONTINENTAL BIRDLIFE.** [Cont. birdlife]. Vol. 1, No. 1 (Feb. 1979)-. Periodical. English. bm (6 issues). $12.00. Continental Birdlife, 2416 East Adams, Tucson AZ 85719. **Tel** (602)795-4924. **LC** QL681; .C594. **DD** 598.297.

GW
**CORAX.** Periodical. German (German). ir. Schleswig-Holstein und Hamburg, Germany. **LC** QL690.G3; C67. ***Supersedes** Faunistische Arbeitsgemeinschaft fur Schleswig-Holstein, Hamburg und Lubeck. Mitteilungen.*
**Ind/Abst** Fish Rev.; Key Word Index Wildl. Res.; Wildl. Rev.

AT/0155-0438
**CORELLA.** **Added/Corp** Australian Bird Study Association. Vol. 1, (Mar. 1977). Periodical. English. Five times a year (Mar., May, July, Sept., Dec.). 40.00Aus$ Australia; 45.00Aus$ New Zealand & Papua New Guineau; 50.00Aus$ other. Australian Bird Study Association, PO Box A313, Sydney New South Wales, 2000 Australia. **Tel** 011 61 2 237 6695. **ED** M. D. Murray (phone: (02)445414). Index available. **Bk Rev**, (Qty: 4). **Pr Rev. Circ:** 600. ***Supersedes** Australian Bird Bander, 0004-8747.*
**Desc:** The results of the research into Australia birds with a strong emphasis on seabirds. Many of the papers are based on studies involving banding.
**Ind/Abst** Fish Rev.; Key Word Index Wildl. Res.; Wildl. Rev.

US/0742-390X
**CURRENT ORNITHOLOGY.** [Curr. ornithol.]. Vol. 1 (1983)-. Monographic series. English. ir. Price varies per volume. Plenum Press, 233 Spring Street, New York NY 10013-1578. **Tel** (212)620-8000, (800)221-9369, FAX (212)463-0742, (212)807-1047, telex 23/421139. **ED** Dennis M. Power. **LC** QL671; .C87. **DD** 598/.05.
**Ind/Abst** Fish Rev.; Key Word Index Wildl. Res.; Wildl. Rev.

DK/0011-6394
**DANSK ORNITHOLOGISK FORENINGS TIDSSKRIFT.** [Dan. ornithol. foren. tidsskr.]. **Added/Corp** Dansk Ornitologisk Forening. **VFOAT** Dansk Ornitologisk Forenings Tidsskrift. Vol. 1, (1907)-. Periodical. Danish (summaries and/or abstracts in English). Four times a year. Kr150.00. Dansk Ornithologisk Forening, Vesterbrogade 140, DK 1620 Copenhagen Denmark. **Tel** 011 45 33 314404, FAX 011 45 33 312435. **ED** Kaj Kampp. **LC** QL671; .D3. **CODEN** DOFTAB. Index Available, published separately, free-automatically sent. cum. index. **Bk Rev. Circ:** 8,500 (ctrl). Documents available from BIOSIS Document Express.
**Desc:** Covers 1) ornithology in Denmark, Europe, Greenland, Faeroes, Scandinavia, and Arctic: 2) breeding-biology migration, ecology, avifaunistics, phenology distribution, conservation, hunting, bird-banding, populations, pollution, bird protection.
**Ind/Abst** ASTIS Curr. Aware. Bull. (1978-); ASTIS Bibliogr. (1978-); Biol. Abstr.; Fish Rev.; Life Sci. Collect.; Wildl. Rev.

US
**DELMARVA ORNITHOLOGIST.** **Main/Corp** Delmarva Ornithological Society. Vol. 2 (Feb. 1965)-. Periodical. English. sa. 2.00 (single issue). Delmarva Ornithological Society, PO Box 4247, Greenville DE 19807. ***Continues** Delaware Ornithologists.*

AT/0158-4197
**EMU.** (THE EMU : OFFICIAL ORGAN OF THE AUSTRALASIAN ORNITHOLOGISTS' UNION.). [Emu]. **Added/Corp** Australasian Ornithologists' Union. Royal Australasian Ornithologists' Union. Vol. 1 (Oct. 1901)-. Periodical. English. qt. 115.00Aus$ Australia; 130.00Aus$ other. Royal Australasian Ornithologists Union, 407 415 Riversdale Road, Hawthorn East Victoria 3123 Australia. **Tel** 011 61 3 8822622, FAX 011 61 3 370 9194. **LC** QL671; .E5. **CODEN** EMUUAI. **[CCC].** cum. index. **Pr Rev.** Documents available from The Genuine Article, BIOSIS Document Express.
**Ind/Abst** Anim. Behav. Abstr.; Biol. Abstr.; Curr. Aware. Biol. Sci., CABS; Curr. Contents, Agric. Biol. Environ. Sci.; Ecol. Abstr.; Ecology Abstr.; Geogr. Abstr. Phys. Geogr.; GeoRef; Key Word Index Wildl. Res.; Life Sci. Collect.; Res. Alert [Full Cov.]; Sci. Cit. Index; SCISEARCH; Wildl. Rev.

CN/0707-7165
**ENVOL (MONTREAL. 1978).** (ENVOL.). **VFOAT** Flight. **VAT** Flight (Montreal). April 1978-. Periodical. French (English). Free to members. Club d'Amateurs d'Oiseaud de Montreal, 228 de la Salle, Mont St-Hilaire Quebec J3H 3C2 Canada. **DD** 598.2/05.

GW
**ERGEBNIS DER WASSER- UND WATVOGELZAHLUNGEN ... IN NIEDERSACHSEN UND AN DER WESTKUSTE VON SCHLESWIG-HOLSTEIN.** (1980/81)-. German. 8.00. Niedersachsisches Landesverwaltungsamt, Postfach 107, 3000 Hannover Germany. **Tel** (0511)108-9466. **LC** QL690.G3; E73. **DD** 912/.15984/094359.

UK/0950-1746
**FORKTAIL.** [Forktail]. No. 1 (Oct. 1986)-. Periodical. English. an. $20.00 individual membership; $33.00 corporate membership. Oriental Bird Club, The Lodge, Sandy Bedford SG19 2DL England. **Tel** 011 44 509 231655. **(Subscription address:** Oriental Bird Club Kukila, 1720 Gilbert Avenue, c/o Dr. R. Kennedy, Cincinnati OH 45202.) **ED** N.J. Collar and T.P. Inskipp. **DD** 598.295. **Circ:** 800 (ctrl).
**Desc:** Publishes information on oriental birds.

US
**GAME BIRD BULLETIN. See** Environmental Issues-Conservation and Natural Resources.

SP/0212-923X
**GARCILLA. See** Natural History.

DK
**GASEUNDERSGELSER I JAMESON LAND / GRNLANDS FISKERI- OG MILJUNDERSGELSER.** **VFOAT** Undersgelser AF GS I Jameson Land. Danish (summaries and/or abstracts in English). Zoologisk Museum, Universitetsparken 15, DK2100 Kbenhavn Denmark. **LC** QL696.A52; G39. **DD** 598.4/1.

BE/0251-1193
**GERFAUT, LE.** (LE GERFAUT. DE GIERVALK.). [Gerfaut]. **Added/Corp** Institut Royal des Sciences Naturelles de Belgique. **VFOAT** Giervalk. (May 15, 1911)-. Periodical. Dutch (English, French and German; summaries and/or abstracts in English and French). qt. Institut Royal de Sciences Naturelles de Belgique, 29 rue Vautier, 1040 Brussels Belguim. **Tel** 011 32 2 6482123. **ED** P. Devillers and V. Damme. **LC** QL671; .G4. **CODEN** GRFTAV. Index available. **Bk Rev. Circ:** 700 (ctrl). Documents available from BIOSIS Document Express.
**Desc:** Publishes original articles that contain new information or new interpretations of existing knowledge on any subject relative to wild birds.
**Ind/Abst** Biol. Abstr.; Ecol. Abstr.; GeoRef; Key Word Index Wildl. Res.

UK/0019-1019
**IBIS (LONDON, ENGLAND).** (THE IBIS.). [Ibis]. **Added/Corp** British Ornithologists' Union. Vol. 1 (Jan. 1859)-. Periodical. English. qt. $180.00. British Ornithologist Society. **(Subscription address:** Ibis / North America Subscriptions, PO Box 1897, Lawrence KS 66044-8897.) **LC** QL671; .I12. **DD** 598. **CODEN** IBISAL. **[CCC].** cum. index. **Ad Acc. Pr Rev.** available on microfilm and microfiche from University Microfilms International (UMI). Documents available from The Genuine Article, BIOSIS Document Express, Documents on Demand.
**Desc:** Provides original research reports on the systematics, ecology, physiology, behavior, and anatomy of birds.
**Ind/Abst** Anim. Behav. Abstr.; Anim. Breed. Abstr.; AQUAREF; Biol. Agric. Index; Biol. Abstr.; Curr. Contents, Agric. Biol. Environ. Sci.; Ecol. Abstr.; Ecology Abstr.; Environ. Abstr.; Environ. Period. Bibliogr.; Field Crop Abstr.; Fish Rev.; For. Abstr.; GeoRef; Index Vet.; Key Word Index Wildl. Res.; Maize Abstr.; Life Sci. Collect.; Protozoolog. Abstr.; Res. Alert [Full Cov.]; Rev. Agric. Entomol.; Rev. Med. Vet. Entomol.; Sci. Cit. Index; SCISEARCH; Seed Abstr.; Vet. Bull.; Wildl. Rev.

US/1061-9801
**ILLINOIS AUDUBON. See** Natural History.

US/0019-6525
**INDIANA AUDUBON QUARTERLY.** **Added/Corp** Indiana Audubon Society. Vol. 28 (1950)-. English. qt (Feb., May, Aug., Nov.). $17.00. The Indiana Audubon Quarterly, 901 Maplewood Drive, New Castle IN 47362. **Tel** (317)529-5225, . **ED** Charles E. Keller; (editor's address: 2505 East Maynard Street, Indianapolis, IN 46227-4962; Phone: (317)786-5822). Index available (bound in issue). cum. index. **Bk Rev**, (Qty: 100-200). **Circ:** 600 (ctrl). ***Continues** Yearbook (Indiana Audubon Society).*
**Desc:** Ornithological information - studies, field notes, migration data, census information, etc.
**Ind/Abst** Fish Rev.; Wildl. Rev.

US/0021-0455
**IOWA BIRD LIFE.** [Iowa bird life]. **Added/Corp** Iowa Ornithologists' Union. Vol. 1, (Mar. 1931)-. Periodical. English. Four times a year (Feb., May, Aug., Nov.). $15.00. Iowa Ornithologists Union, c/o Pam Allen, 1601 Pleasant Street, West Des Moines IA 50265. **ED** James Dinsmore, (editor's address: 4024 Arkansas Drive, Ames, IA 50010; Phone: (515)292-3152). **CODEN** IOBLAM. **Bk Rev**, (Qty: varies). **Circ:** 600. Documents available from BIOSIS Document Express. ***Continues** Iowa Ornithologists' Union. Bulletin.*
**Desc:** Materials and articles relating to birds and bird findings in Iowa. Publication encourages interest in identification, study, and protection.
**Ind/Abst** Biol. Abstr.; Fish Rev. (Jan. 1989-July 1992-); Wildl. Rev. (Jan. 1989-July 1992).

IE/0332-0111
**IRISH BIRDS.** [Ir. birds]. **Added/Corp** Irish Wildbird Conservancy. Vol. 1 (1977)-. English. an. £10.00 UK & Ireland; £12.00 other. Irish Wildbird Conservancy, Ruttledge House, 8 Longford Place, Monkstown County, Dublin Ireland. **Tel** (01)804322, FAX (01)844407. **ED** Hugh Brazier. **LC** QL690.I7; I75. **DD** 598.2/9418/35. **CODEN** IBIRDL. **Bk Rev**, (Qty: 2-10). **Ad Acc**, **Adv Mgr:** O. O'sullivan. **Pr Rev. Circ:** 1,200. Documents available from BIOSIS Document Express. ***Supersedes** Irish Bird Report.*
**Desc:** Scientific papers, short notes and articles on all aspects of birds and ornithology in Ireland.
**Ind/Abst** Biol. Abstr.; Ecology Abstr.; Key Word Index Wildl. Res.; Life Sci. Collect.; Zool. Rec.

US
**JACK-PINE WARBLER.** **Added/Corp** Michigan Audubon Society. **VFOAT** Jack Pine Warbler; JPW. Vol. 1, No. 1 (Jan./Feb. 1991)-. Periodical. English. bm. $15.00 US; $20.00 other (non-members); Free (members). Michigan Audubon Society, PO Box 80527, Lansing MI 48908. **Tel** (517)886-9144, FAX (517)886-9466. **ED** Rick Campbell (editor's address: 1051 Avon Manor, Rochester Hills MI 48367; editor's telephone: (313)852-1969). **CODEN** JWARE4. **Bk Rev**, (Qty: 6). **Ad Acc**, **Adv Mgr:** Rick Campbell, **Tel** (313)852-1969. **Circ:** 8,000. ***Formed by the union of** Jack-Pine Warbler (1927), 0021-3845 **and** Michigan Audubon News (1984), 0897-2745.*

**Desc:** Contains Michigan Audubon Society News, natural history/outdoor education articles, and bird population surveys and bird watching reports.

GW/0021-8375
**JOURNAL FUER ORNITHOLOGIE.** [J. Ornithol.]. Vol. 1 (Jan. 1853)-. Periodical. German (English and French). Four times a year (Jan., Apr., July, Oct.). DM260.00 Germany; DM286.40 others. R Friedlander and Sohn, Schlesische STR 26 AUFG A 3 ST, D 1000 Berlin 36 F R Germany. **Tel** 011 49 30 6124034. **ED** Deutsche Ornithologen- Gesellschaft. **LC** QL671; .J8. **UDC** 598.2. **CODEN** JORNAH. **Bk Rev. Ad Acc. Pr Rev.** Documents available from The Genuine Article, BIOSIS Document Express, CASDDS. ***Absorbed*** *Naumannia.*
**Desc:** Articles on scientific ornithology.
**Ind/Abst** Biol. Abstr.; Chem. Abstr.; Curr. Aware. Biol. Sci., CABS; Curr. Contents, Agric. Biol. Environ. Sci.; Ecol. Abstr.; Geogr. Abstr. Phys. Geogr.; GeoRef; Key Word Index Wildl. Res.; Life Sci. Collect.; Res. Alert [Full Cov.]; Rev. Med. Vet. Entomol.; Sci. Cit. Index; SCISEARCH; Wildl. Rev.

●DK/0908-8857
**JOURNAL OF AVIAN BIOLOGY.** **Added/Corp** Scandinavian Ornithologists' Union. Vol. 25, No. 1 (Mar. 1994)-. Periodical. English. qt. Kr725.00 US & Canada; Kr705.00 other. Munksgaard International Publishers Ltd, PO Box 2148, DK-1016 Copenhagen K Denmark. **Tel** 011 45 33 12 70 30, FAX 011 45 33 12 93 87, telex 19431 MUNKS DK. **ED** Sven-Axel Bengtson. **LC** QL671; .O56. **CODEN** JAVBE9. Index available. **Bk Rev. Ad Acc. Pr Rev. Circ:** 750 (ctrl). Documents available from The Genuine Article, BIOSIS Document Express. ***Continues*** *Ornis Scandinavica, 0030-5693.*
**Desc:** Original work in all aspects of ornithology.
**Ind/Abst** Anim. Behav. Abstr.; AQUAREF; Biol. Abstr.; Curr. Aware. Biol. Sci., CABS; Curr. Contents, Agric. Biol. Environ. Sci.; Ecol. Abstr.; Ecology Abstr.; Geogr. Abstr. Phys. Geogr.; Key Word Index Wildl. Res.; Life Sci. Collect.; Res. Alert; Sci. Cit. Index; SCISEARCH; Wildl. Rev.

US/0273-8570
**JOURNAL OF FIELD ORNITHOLOGY.** [J. field ornithol.]. **Added/Corp** Northeastern Bird-Banding Association (U.S.). Vol. 51, No. 1 (Winter 1980)-. Periodical. English. Four times a year (Jan., Apr., July, Oct.). $45.00 US & Canada & Mexico; $51.00 other. Association of Field Ornithologists, PO Box 2057, Lake Placid FL 33852. **Tel** (813)465-2571. **(Subscription address:** Journal of Field Ornithology, PO Box 1897, Lawrence KS 66044-8897.) **CODEN** JFORDM. **Ad Acc. Pr Rev. Acid Free. Circ:** 1,000 (ctrl). available on microfilm and microfiche from University Microfilms International (UMI). Documents available from The Genuine Article, BIOSIS Document Express. ***Continues*** *Bird-Banding, 0006-3630.*
**Desc:** Features an extensive review of current ornithological literature.
**Ind/Abst** AQUAREF; Biol. Abstr.; Curr. Contents, Agric. Biol. Environ. Sci.; Ecology Abstr.; Index Vet.; Key Word Index Wildl. Res.; Life Sci. Collect.; Protozoolog. Abstr.; Res. Alert [Full Cov.]; Rev. Med. Vet. Entomol.; Sci. Cit. Index; SCISEARCH; Wildl. Rev.

US/1044-8314
**JOURNAL OF THE ASSOCIATION OF AVIAN VETERINARIANS.** **See** Veterinary Sciences.

US/0160-5070
**KENTUCKY WARBLER, THE.** [Ky. warbler]. **Added/Corp** Kentucky Ornithological Society. Vol. 1 (1925)-. Periodical. English. qt. $8.00 US; $10.00 Canada; $12.00 other. Kentucky Ornithological Society, 9101 Spokane Way, c/o Mrs. Stamm, Louisville KY 40241. **Tel** (502)425-1635. **ED** Blaine Ferrell. **CODEN** KEWAA. **Bk Rev. Circ:** 500 (ctrl).
**Desc:** Subjects deal primarily with studies on birds of Kentucky, Christmas counts, annual eagle censuses reports of spring, and fall meetings, review of ornithology books.
**Ind/Abst** Fish Rev.; Wildl. Rev.

US/0023-1606
**KINGBIRD, THE.** [Kingbird]. **Added/Corp** Federation of New York State Bird Clubs. (Nov./Dec. 1950)-. Periodical. English. qt (Mar., June, Sept., Dec.). $18.00. Federation of New York State Bird, PO Box 296, Attn: B. Lincoln, Somers NY 10589. **Tel** (914)277-8264. **ED** Paul de Benedictis (editors address: 306 Kensington Place, Syracuse, NY 13210; (314)464-5719). **LC** QL671; .K5. **DD** 598.205. **CODEN** KNGBAW. Index available (published separately). cum. index. **Circ:** 850 (ctrl). Documents available from BIOSIS Document Express.
**Desc:** Organized to further the study of bird life and to disseminate knowledge thereof; to educate the public in the need of conserving natural resources and to encourage the establishment and maintenance of sanctuaries.
**Ind/Abst** Biol. Abstr.; Fish Rev.; Wildl. Rev.

IO/0126-9223
**KUKILA.** **Added/Corp** Indonesian Ornithological Society. Vol. 1, No. 1 (Oct. 1975)-. Periodical. English. Twice a year. $15.00 surface mail; $20.00 air mail. Ornithological Society Indonesia, c/o Birdlife International, PO Box 310, Bogor 16003 Indonesia. **Tel** 0251-325862, FAX 0251-325862. **ED** D.A. Holmes. **Bk Rev. Circ:** 300.
**Desc:** Includes scientific papers and other communications on Indonesian ornithology.

NE/0024-3620
**LIMOSA.** [Limosa]. Vol. 1 (Oct. 1928)-. Periodical. Dutch. qt. F77.00. Nederlandse Ornithologische UN, Sportlaan 13, 2225 JN Katwijk The Netherlands. **Tel** 011/31/1718/13296. **CODEN** LIMOA9. cum. index. Documents available from BIOSIS Document Express. ***Supersedes*** *Jaarbericht - Club Van Nederlandsche Vogelkundigen.*
**Ind/Abst** Biol. Abstr.; Ecol. Abstr.; Fish Rev.; Geogr. Abstr. Phys. Geogr.; Key Word Index Wildl. Res.; Wildl. Rev.

FI/0357-3524
**LINTUMIES / SUOMEN LINTUTIETEELLINEN YHDISTYS.** **Added/Corp** Suomen Lintutieteellinen Yhdistys. Lintutieteellisten Yhdistysten Liitto (Finland). (1965)-. Periodical. Finnish (summaries and/or abstracts in English). Six times a year. Fmk100.00 Finland; Fmk110.00 other. Lintumies Lehti, LYL, Box 17, SF-18101 Heinola Finland. **Tel** 358 10 52579, FAX 358 0 17342279. **ED** Kari Degerstedt. **LC** QL690.F6; L56. **DD** 598.294897. **CODEN** LNTME9. Index available. **Bk Rev. Ad Acc. Circ:** 3,000.

CN/0228-2151
**LISTE DES MEMBRES DU CLUB DES ORNITHOLOGUES DE SIC QUEBEC.** [Liste memb. Club ornithol. Que.]. **Main/Corp** Club des Ornithologues du Quebec. French. an. Free to members. Club des Ornithologues du Quebec Inc, 1000 de la Verendrye, Quebec QUE G1J 4V7 Canada. **Tel** (418)667-6373. **DD** 598/.025/714.

US/1059-521X
**LIVING BIRD (1991).** (LIVING BIRD.). [Living bird]. **Added/Corp** Cornell University. Laboratory of Ornithology. Vol. 10, No. 4 (Autumn 1991)-. Periodical. English. qt. Free to members of the Cornell University Laboratory of Ornithology. Cornell University Laboratory of Ornithology, 159 Sapsucker Woods Road, Ithaca NY 14850. **Tel** (607)254-2473, (607)254-2421. **DD** 598. **CODEN** LIBIE8. ***Continues*** *Living Bird Quarterly, 0732-9210.*

FR/0297-5785
**L'OISEAU MAGAZINE : REVUE DE LA LIGUE FRANCAISE POUR LA PROTECTION DES OISEAUX.** **Added/Corp** Ligue Francaise pour la Protection des Oiseaux. (1985)-. French. Four times a year. 110.00F France; 140.00F other. L'Oiseau Magazine, La Corderie Royale, BP 263, 17305 Rochefort Cedex France. **Tel** 46 82 12 34, FAX 46 83 95 86, telex 791040F. **ED** Yann Hermieu. **LC** QL690.F8; O36. **DD** 598.2944/05. **Bk Rev**, (Qty: 50). **Ad Acc.** Full Page (Color) 100000F. Half Page (Color) 6000F. **Circ:** 13,000 (ctrl).

US/0024-645X
**LOON, THE.** [Loon]. (1964)-. Periodical. English. Four times a year. $20.00 Comes with Minnesota Ornithologists Union membership. Minnesota Ornithological Union, Bell Museum of Natural History, 10 Church Street SE, Minneapolis MN 55455. **Tel** (612)624-7083. **ED** Robert B. Janssen. **CODEN** LOONAO. Index available. **Bk Rev. Circ:** 1,200. Documents available from BIOSIS Document Express. ***Continues*** *Flicker, 0199-9672.*
**Desc:** Keeps an accurate record of the occurrence of birds in Minnesota.
**Ind/Abst** Biol. Abstr.; Fish Rev.; Wildl. Rev.

CN/0225-0721
**MAGAZINE - CANADIAN ORNAMENTAL PHEASANT AND GAME BIRD ASSOCIATION.** **See** Hobbies.

SA
**MARINE ORNITHOLOGY.** **Added/Corp** African Seabird Group. Vol. 18, no. 1/2 (Dec. 1990)-. Periodical. English. sa. $40.00. African Seabird Group, Fitzpatrick Institute, University of Capetown, Rondebosch 7700 South Africa. **Tel** 011 27 21 6503294, FAX 27 21 650 3295. **ED** J. Cooper. **LC** QL671; .C67. **CODEN** MAOREL. cum. index. **Bk Rev. Ad Acc. Pr Rev. Circ:** 400 (ctrl). ***Continues*** *Cormorant, 0250-0213.*
**Desc:** Covers scientific studies of seabirds of the world.

US/0147-9725
**MARYLAND BIRDLIFE.** **Added/Corp** Maryland Ornithological Society. (1945)-. Periodical. English. qt (Mar., June, Sept., Dec.). $10.00. C. S. Robbins, 7902 Brooklyn Br Road, Laurel MD 20707. **Tel** (301)498-0281, FAX (301)498-0438. **ED** Chandler S. Robbins. **CODEN** MBIREW. Index available. cum. index. **Bk Rev**, (Qty: 5-10). **Circ:** 2,000 (ctrl).
**Desc:** Documenting distribution, migration, and ecology of birds in Maryland.

●US/1065-2043
**MEADOWLARK (EVANSTON, ILL.).** (MEADOWLARK : A JOURNAL OF ILLINOIS BIRDS.). [Meadowlark]. **Added/Corp** Illinois Ornithological Society. **VFOAT** Journal of Illinois Birds. Vol. 1, No. 1 (Summer 1992)-. Periodical. English. qt. $30.00. Illinois Ornithological Society, Box 1971, Evanston IL 60204-1971. **LC** QL684.I3; M43. **DD** 598.29773/05.

US/0026-3575
**MIGRANT, THE.** [Migrant]. **Added/Corp** Tennessee Ornithological Society. (June 1930)-. Periodical. English. Four times a year (Mar., June, Sept., Dec.). $15.00 (library); $10.00 (individual) Comes with Tennessee Ornithological Society membership. Tennessee Ornithological Society, PO Box 171381, Memphis TN 38187-1381. **Tel** (901)382-4767. **ED** J. Wallace Coffey, (editor's address: 100 Bellebrook Drive, Bristol, TN 37620). **CODEN** MGNTAQ. Index available. **Bk Rev. Circ:** 1,000. Documents available from BIOSIS Document Express.
**Desc:** Records and encourages the study of ornithology in Tennessee with focus on field observations and records of birdlife in the state.
**Ind/Abst** Biol. Abstr.; GeoRef; Wildl. Rev.

CN
**MIGRATORY BIRDS CONVENTION ACT AND MIGRATORY BIRD REGULATIONS.** **See** Environmental Issues-Conservation and Natural Resources.

US
**MOUTHPIECE.** **Added/Corp** Minnesota Ornithologists' Union. Bell Museum of Natural History. Vol. 27, No. 3 (Aug. 1990)-. Newsletter. English. qt. comes with membership. Minnesota Ornithological Union, Bell Museum of Natural History, 10 Church Street SE, Minneapolis MN 55455. **Tel** (612)624-7083. ***Continues*** *Newsletter (Minnesota Ornithologists' Union).*

US
**MULTI MEDIA BIRDS OF AMERICA. CD-ROM.** ***Title Change.*** (19??)-(19??). English. Creative Multimedia Corporation, 513 Northwest Avenue, Suite 400, Portland OR 97209. **Tel** (503)241-4351. Index available. **Bk Rev.** ***Continued by*** *Multimedia Audubons Birds.*

●US
**MULTIMEDIA AUDUBONS BIRDS.** (1992)-. English. ir. $54.49 US. Creative Multimedia Corporation, 513 Northwest Avenue, Suite 400, Portland OR 97209. **Tel** (503)241-4351. ***Continues*** *Multi Media Birds of America.*

US/0271-7948
**NATIONAL POULTRY IMPROVEMENT PLAN. DIRECTORY OF PARTICIPANTS HANDLING WATERFOWL, EXHIBITION POULTRY, AND GAME BIRDS.** **See** Agriculture-Livestock and Poultry.

CN/0317-9575
**NEWSLETTER - LONG POINT BIRD OBSERVATORY.** **Main/Corp** Long Point Bird Observatory. **VFOAT** L P B O Newsletter. (Spring 1969)-. Newsletter. English. Three times a year. $15.88. Long Point Bird Observatory, PO Box 160, Port Rowan Ontario N0E 1M0 Canada. **Tel** (519)586-2909. **ED** Martin K. McNicholl. **DD** 598.1/07/230971336. **Bk Rev. Ad Acc. Circ:** 800 (ctrl).
**Desc:** Observatory activities and people, locally and provincially. Articles on birds and other nature, biographies of naturalists, profiles of related organizations.

JA
**NIHON CHOGAKKAI SHI.** **VFOAT** Japanese Journal of Ornithology. (1986)-. Periodical. Japanese (English). Three times a year. Ornithological Society of Japan, Hyakunin Cho 3 23 1 Dep Zoolog, Shinjuku Tokyo 160 Japan. **LC** QL691.J4; .T67. **CODEN** JJOREH. Documents available from BIOSIS Document Express. ***Continues*** *Tori (Nihon Chogakkai).*
**Ind/Abst** Biol. Abstr. (1988-).

US/0363-8979
**NORTH AMERICAN BIRD BANDER.** Vol. 1 (Jan./March 1976)-. Periodical. English. Four times a year (Jan., Mar., Sept., Dec.). $15.00 (comes with Western, Eastern and Inland Bird Banding Association membership). Western Bird Banding Association, PO Box 848, Pt. Reyes CA 94956. **Tel** (415)663-1436. **LC** QL677.5; .N66. **DD** 598.2/0723. available on microfilm and microfiche from University Microfilms International (UMI). ***Formed by the union of*** *Western Bird Bander and EBBA News;* ***Absorbed*** *Inland Bird Banding.*
**Ind/Abst** Fish Rev.; Key Word Index Wildl. Res.; Wildl. Rev.

US/1051-1733
**NORTHWESTERN NATURALIST : A JOURNAL OF VERTEBRATE BIOLOGY.** **See** Natural History.

PL/0550-0842
**NOTATKI ORNITOLOGICZNE.** [Not. ornitol.]. **Added/Corp** Polskie Towarzystwo Zoologiczne. Sekcja Ornitologiczna. Uniwersytet Warszawski. Koo Naukowe Biologow. Vol. 1 (1960)-. Polish (summaries and/or

abstracts in English). qt. Price on request. **(Subscription address:** ARS Polona, PO Box 1001, 00068 Warsaw Poland.**)** **LC** WMLC L 83/2374. **DD** 598.2. **CODEN** NOORAO. Documents available from BIOSIS Document Express.
**Ind/Abst** Biol. Abstr.; Fish Rev.; Wildl. Rev.

NZ/0029-4470
**NOTORNIS.** [Notornis]. **Added/Corp** Ornithological Society of New Zealand. Vol. 4 (July 1950)-. Periodical. English. qt. 120.00Aus$ Australia; 130.00Aus$ other (institutions). Ornithological Society of New Zealand, PO Box 316, Drury South Auckland New Zealand. **LC** QL671; .N65. **DD** 598/.05. **CODEN** NTNSAN. **[CCC].** Documents available from BIOSIS Document Express. ***Supersedes*** *New Zealand Bird Notes.*
**Ind/Abst** Biol. Abstr.; Ecol. Abstr. (?-?); GeoRef; Wildl. Rev.

NZ
**NOTORNIS / ORNITHOLOGICAL SOCIETY OF NEW ZEALAND. Added/Corp** Ornithological Society of New Zealand. (19??)-. Periodical. English. 40.00NZ$ (ordinary membership), 20.00NZ$ (junior membership), 60.00NZ$ (husband and wife membership), 800.00NZ$ (life membership), 80.00NZ$ (institutions), 80.00NZ$ (supporting), 200.00NZ$ (corporate). Ornithological Society of New Zealand, PO Box 316, Drury South Auckland New Zealand.

US
**OBSERVER : PRBO IN PRINT : QUARTERLY JOURNAL OF THE POINT REYES BIRD OBSERVATORY. Added/Corp** Point Reyes Bird Observatory. No. 87 (Winter 1989-1990)-. Periodical. English. qt. $35.00. Point Reyes Bird Observatory, 4990 Shore Highway, Stinson Beach CA 94970-9701. **Tel** (415)868-1221, FAX (415)868-1946. ***Continues*** *Newsletter (Point Reyes Bird Observatory).*

FR/0030-1531
**OISEAU ET LA REVUE FRANCAISE D'ORNITHOLOGIE.** ***Ceased.*** (L'OISEAU ET LA REVUE FRANCAISE D'ORNITHOLOGIE.). [Oiseau rev. fr. ornithol.]. **Added/Corp** Societe Ornithologie de France. Vol. 1 (Jan./Feb. 1931)-Vol. 63. Periodical. French (English). qt. Societe Ornithologique France, 55 rue Buffon, 75005 Paris France. **Tel** 43 31 02 49. **ED** Jean Louis Mougin. Index available. **Bk Rev. Circ:** 1,000 (ctrl). ***Supersedes*** *Revue d'Histoire Naturelle. Deuxieme Partie: l'Oiseau et la Revue Francaise d'Ornithologie.*
**Desc:** Studies on wild birds.
**Ind/Abst** Ecol. Abstr.; Key Word Index Wildl. Res.; Life Sci. Collect.

CN/0475-025X
**ONTARIO BIRD BANDING.** [Ont. bird band.]. **Added/Corp** Ontario Bird Banding Association. Vol. 1 (June 1965)-. Periodical. English. an. 15.00Can$. Ontario Bird Banding Association, 10 Paulson Court, St Thomas Ontario N5R 1M9 Canada. **Tel** (519)631-2631. **ED** William McIlveen. **CODEN** ONBBAH. **Bk Rev. Circ:** 250 (ctrl). Documents available from BIOSIS Document Express.
**Desc:** Articles promote understanding of native bird species as well as techniques in capturing and banding these birds.
**Ind/Abst** AQUAREF; Biol. Abstr.; Wildl. Rev.

CN/0822-3890
**ONTARIO BIRDS.** (ONTARIO BIRDS : THE JOURNAL OF THE ONTARIO FIELD ORNITHOLOGISTS.). [Ont. birds]. **Added/Corp** Ontario Field Ornithologists. Vol. 1, No. 1 (April 1983)-. Periodical. English. Three times a year (Apr., Aug., Dec.). 22.00Can$ US, 33.00Can$ others Comes with Ontario Field Ornithologists membership. Ontario Field Ornithologists, PO Box 62014, Burlington Ontario L3R 4K2 Canada. **ED** Donald M. Fraser. **DD** 598/.07/234713. **CODEN** ONBIE8. **Bk Rev. Circ:** 650 (ctrl). Documents available from BIOSIS Document Express.
**Desc:** Contains articles or short notes on the status and distribution of birds in Ontario, tips on bird identification, behavioral observations, location guides to significant birdwatching areas in Ontario, reviews and other material of interest on Ontario birds.
**Ind/Abst** Biol. Abstr. (1986-).

NE
**ONZE VOGELS. Added/Corp** Nederlandse Bond van Vogelliefhebbers. (19??)-. Bulletin. Dutch. mo. Fl33.50 Netherlands; Fl65.00 other. Nederlandse Bond van Vogelliefhebbers, Postbox 74, 4600 AB Bergen, Op Zoom, Netherlands. **Tel** 31-1640-35007, FAX 31-1640-39020. **ED** Board. **LC** SF461.A1; O5. Index available. cum. index. **Bk Rev. Ad Acc. Circ:** 50,000 (ctrl). available on an online database.

FI/0030-5685
**ORNIS FENNICA.** [Ornis fenn.]. Vol. 1 (1924)-. Periodical. English (Finnish and Swedish). qt. $32.50. Finnish Ornithological Society, P Rautatiekatu 13, SF 00100 Helsinki, 10 Finland. **Tel** 11 358 0 1917388. **ED** Olli Jarvinen, Samuel Panelius, Kari Senius. **LC** QL671; .O55. **CODEN** ORFEA6. Index available. **Bk Rev. Ad Acc. Pr Rev. Circ:** 1,250. Documents available from The Genuine Article, BIOSIS Document Express, CASDDS.
**Desc:** Covers ornithology.
**Ind/Abst** Biol. Abstr.; Chem. Abstr.; Curr. Aware. Biol. Sci., CABS; Curr. Contents, Agric. Biol. Environ. Sci.; Ecol. Abstr. (?-?); Ecology Abstr.; Key Word Index Wildl. Res.; Life Sci. Collect.; Res. Alert [Select. Cov.]; SCISEARCH; Wildl. Rev.

NO/0030-5693
**ORNIS SCANDINAVICA.** ***Title Change.*** (ORNIS SCANDINAVICA : SCANDINAVIAN JOURNAL OF ORNITHOLOGY.). [Ornis Scand.]. **Added/Corp** Scandinavian Ornithologists' Union. Vol. 1 (1970)-(1993). Periodical. English (French and German). Four times a year. Munksgaard International Publishers Ltd, PO Box 2148, DK-1016 Copenhagen K Denmark. **Tel** 011 45 33 12 70 30, FAX 011 45 33 12 93 87, telex 19431 MUNKS DK. **ED** Sven-Axel Bengtson. **LC** QL671; .O56. **DD** 598.2/05. **CODEN** ORSCAV. **[CCC].** Index available. **Bk Rev. Ad Acc. Pr Rev. Circ:** 750 (ctrl). Documents available from The Genuine Article, BIOSIS Document Express. ***Continued by*** *Journal of Avian Biology, 0908-8857.*
**Desc:** Original work in all aspects of ornithology.
**Ind/Abst** Anim. Behav. Abstr.; AQUAREF; Biol. Abstr.; Curr. Aware. Biol. Sci., CABS; Curr. Contents, Agric. Biol. Environ. Sci.; Ecol. Abstr.; Ecology Abstr.; Geogr. Abstr. Phys. Geogr.; Key Word Index Wildl. Res.; Life Sci. Collect.; Res. Alert [Full Cov.]; Sci. Cit. Index; SCISEARCH; Wildl. Rev.

SW
**ORNIS SVECICA. Added/Corp** Sveriges Ornitologiska Forening. Vol. 1, No. 1 (1991)-. Periodical. English (Swedish). sa. Free (members of the association). Sveriges Ornitologiska Forening, Box 14219, S-10440 Stockholm Sweden. **Tel** 08/662 64 34.

US/0078-6594
**ORNITHOLOGICAL MONOGRAPHS.** [Ornithol. monogr.]. **Added/Corp** American Ornithologists' Union. No. 1 (1964)-. Monographic series. English. ir (2-3 times a year). Price varies per volume. American Ornithologists Union, Southeastern College, 100 College Street, Winfield KS 67156. **Tel** (316)221-8304. **ED** David Johnston. **LC** QL671; .O58. **DD** 598./05. **CODEN** ORMNBZ. **Circ:** 600.
**Ind/Abst** Fish Rev.; Key Word Index Wildl. Res.; Wildl. Rev.

US/0274-564X
**ORNITHOLOGICAL NEWSLETTER.** [Ornithol. newsl.]. **Added/Corp** American Ornithologists' Union. Cooper Ornithological Society. Wilson Ornithological Society. Association of Field Ornithologists. (1976)-. Newsletter. English. bm. $10.00 US, Canada and Mexico; $15.00 other. Ornithological Society of North America, PO Box 1897, Lawrence KS 66044-8897. **Tel** (913)843-1221, FAX ((913)843-1274. **ED** Richard Banks. **DD** 598. **Circ:** 7,000.
**Desc:** News and information about meetings, people and events in the American Ornithologists Union, Cooper Ornithological Society and Wilson Ornithological Society.

UK
**ORNITHOLOGICAL REPORT FOR - YORKSHIRE NATURALISTS' UNION.** English. an. £12.00. Yorkshire Naturalists Union, D. Bramley, c/o Doncaster Museum, Doncaster DN1 2AE United Kingdom. **Tel** 011 44 302 535246. **LC** QL690.G7; O76. **DD** 598.29428/1. **Circ:** 750.

SZ/0030-5707
**ORNITHOLOGISCHE BEOBACHTER.** (DER ORNITHOLOGISCHE BEOBACHTER.). [Ornithol. Beob.]. **Added/Corp** Ala, Societe Suisse pour l'Etude des Oiseaux et leur Protection. Vol. 1 (1902)-. Periodical. German (summaries and/or abstracts in English and French). Four times a year (Mar., June, Sept., Dec.). 45.00F Switzerland; 55.00F others. Ala Geschaeftsstelle, Frau K Kunz, Kraehenbergstrasse 53, CH-2543 Lengnau Switzerland. **Tel** 011 41 65 525895. **CODEN** ORBEAK. **Bk Rev. Ad Acc. Circ:** 1,500. Documents available from BIOSIS Document Express.
**Desc:** Study of birds.
**Ind/Abst** Biol. Abstr.; Ecol. Abstr.; Geogr. Abstr. Phys. Geogr.; Key Word Index Wildl. Res.; Wildl. Rev.

GW/0030-5723
**ORNITHOLOGISCHE MITTEILUNGEN.** [Ornithol. Mitt.]. **Added/Corp** Vereinigung fur Vogelforschung und Vogelschutz Gottingen. Bund fur Vogelschutz. Institut fur Biologie um Welt und Lebenschutz (Wiesbaden, Germany). (1948)-. Periodical. German. mo. DM58.00. Biologie Verlag, Postfach 1449, D-65004 Wiesbaden Germany. **Tel** 011 49 6129 8117. **ED** Herbert Bruns. **LC** QL671; .B85. **DD** 598. **CODEN** ORMIAJ. Index available. **Bk Rev.** Documents available from BIOSIS Document Express.
**Ind/Abst** Biol. Abstr.; Key Word Index Wildl. Res.

GW
**ORNITHOLOGISCHE VERHANDLUNGEN / HERAUSGEGEBEN VON DER ORNITHOLOGISCHEN GESELLSCHAFT IN BAYERN V. Added/Corp** Ornithologische Gesellschaft in Bayern. Vol. 1 (1991)-. German (English). ***Continues*** *Verhandlungen der Ornithologischen Gesellschaft in Bayern, 0177-1671.*

GW/0940-3256
**ORNITHOLOGISCHER ANZEIGER / HERAUSGEGEBEN VON DER ORNITHOLOGISCHEN GESELLSCHAFT IN BAYERN E.V. Added/Corp** Ornithologische Gesellschaft in Bayern. Vol. 30, Issue 1/2 (Sept. 1991)-. German. sa. **CODEN** ORANEC. Documents available from BIOSIS Document Express. ***Continues*** *Anzeiger der Ornithologischen Gesellschaft in Bayern.*
**Ind/Abst** Biol. Abstr.

SA/0030-6525
**OSTRICH, THE.** [Ostrich]. **Added/Corp** South African Ornithological Society. Vol. 1 (Mar. 1930)-. Periodical. English. qt. Free to members of the South African Ornithological Society; $40.00 individual membership fee. Southern African Ornithological Society, PO Box 87234, Greenside Trans 2034 South Africa. **Tel** 011 27 11 8884147, FAX 011 27 11 7827013. **ED** A. Craig. **LC** QL671; .O88. **DD** 598/.05. **CODEN** OSTHAO. Index available. cum. index. **Pr Rev. Circ:** 4,000 (ctrl). Documents available from The Genuine Article, BIOSIS Document Express.
**Desc:** Scientific journal providing a medium for scientists to publish results of their research on African ornithology.
**Ind/Abst** Biol. Abstr.; Curr. Aware. Biol. Sci., CABS; Curr. Contents, Agric. Biol. Environ. Sci.; Ecol. Abstr. (?-?); Helminthol. Abstr. (1991-); Index Vet.; Key Word Index Wildl. Res.; Life Sci. Collect.; Protozoolog. Abstr.; Res. Alert [Select. Cov.]; SCISEARCH; Wildl. Rev.

CN/0827-2298
**OTTAWA BANDING GROUP.** (THE OTTAWA BANDING GROUP : NEWSLETTER.). [Ottawa Band. Group]. Vol. 1, No. 1 (1983)-. Newsletter. English. Three times a year. $10.00. Ottawa Banding Group, PO Box 3633 Station C, Ottawa Ontario K1Y 4J7 Canada. **Tel** (613)231-7285. **ED** Janette Dean. **DD** 598/.07/23206071384. **Bk Rev. Ad Acc. Circ:** 50 (ctrl).
**Desc:** Informative articles on birds caught during bird-banding activities in the Ottawa area; mainly small passerine birds, but also larger owls, ducks and hawks.

US/0031-2703
**PASSENGER PIGEON, THE.** [Passenger pigeon]. **Added/Corp** Wisconsin Society for Ornithology. Vol. 1 (Jan. 1939)-. Periodical. English. Four times a year (Mar., June, Sept., Dec.). $18.00 one year; $34.00 two years; $50.00 three years. Wisconsin Society for Ornithology Inc., W330 N8275 West Shore Drive, Hartland WI 53029. **Tel** (414)966-1072. **ED** Becky Isenring (editor's address: 6829 Taylor Road, Sauk City, WI 53583; telephone: (608)643-6906). **LC** QL671; .P3. **DD** 598.29775. **CODEN** PPGNAZ. Index available in last issue of volume--attached. **Bk Rev,** (Qty: infrequent). **Ad Acc. Circ:** 1,475. Documents available from BIOSIS Document Express.
**Desc:** Study of Wisconsin birds including preservation of species and habitats.
**Ind/Abst** Biol. Abstr.; Wildl. Rev.

II/0031-3297
**PAVO.** [Pavo]. **Added/Corp** Society of Animal Morphologists & Physiologists (India) Maharaja Sayajirao University of Baroda. Dept. of Zoology. Vol. 1 (Mar. 1963)-. Periodical. English. sa. $30.00. Society of Animal Morphologists & Physiologists, Baroda, India. **(Subscription address:** Prints India, 11 Darya Ganj, New Delhi 110002 India.**)** **LC** QL671; .P35. **DD** 598/.05. **CODEN** PAVOA8.

US/1043-0083
**PJG (MIAMI, FLA.). See** Gardening and Horticulture.

US/0067-8945
**PROCEEDINGS - BIRD CONTROL SEMINAR.** ***Suspended.*** [Proc. Bird Control Semin.]. **Main/Conf** Bird Control Seminar. 1st (1962)-Suspended. Proceedings. English. an. $25.00 (per issue). BGS University, Department of Biology, Bowling Green OH 43403. **Tel** (419)372-8375. **CODEN** PBCNBK. Documents available from BIOSIS Document Express, CASDDS.
**Ind/Abst** Biol. Abstr.; Chem. Abstr.

US/0550-4082
**PUBLICATIONS OF THE NUTTALL ORNITHOLOGICAL CLUB.** [Publ. Nuttall Ornithol. Club.]. **Added/Corp** Nuttall Ornithological Club. No. 1 (1957)-. Monographic series. English. ir. Price varies per volume. Nuttall Ornithological Club, Harvard University, Cambridge MA 02138. **Tel** (617)495-2471. **ED** R.A. Paynter Jr. **CODEN** NUOPAQ. **Bk Rev. Circ:** 1,000.
**Desc:** Scientific studies of birds.
**Ind/Abst** Key Word Index Wildl. Res.

US/0746-2638
**QUAIL UNLIMITED MAGAZINE.** (QUAIL UNLIMITED MAGAZINE / QUAIL UNLIMITED.). [Quail unltd. mag.]. **Added/Corp** Quail Unlimited. (19??)-. Periodical. English. qt. $20.00 (includes membership). Quail Unlimited, PO Box 10041, Augusta GA 30903. **Tel** (803)637-5731. **ED** Diana Kogone. **Bk Rev. Ad Acc. Circ:** 100,000.
**Desc:** A magazine dedicated to the research of the quail species.

CN/0843-9656
**QUEBECOISEAUX (MONTREAL).** (QUEBECOISEAUX.). [QuebecOiseaux]. **Added/Corp** Association Quebecoise des Groupes d'Ornithologues. **VFOAT** Quebec-Oiseaux. Vol. 1, No 1 (Aug./Sept./Oct. 1989)-. Periodical. French. qt. 16.00Can$ (one year), 32.00Can$ (two years). QuebecOiseaux, CP 514, Drummondville Quebec J2B 6W4 Canada. **Tel** (819)477-7834. **DD** 598/.09714. **Ad Acc.**

US/1048-8030
**RAPTOR REPORT.** [Raptor rep.]. **Added/Corp** Society for the Preservation of Birds of Prey. (1973)-. Periodical. English. sa. $10.00 (1 year). Society for the Preservation of Birds of Prey, PO Box 66070 Mar Vista Station, Los Angeles CA 90066. **Tel** (310) 397-8216. **DD** 598. ***Supersedes*** *California condor.*

US
**RECORDS OF NEW JERSEY BIRDS.** (19??)-. English. Four times a year. $25.00. New Jersey Audubon Society, 790 Ewing Avenue, PO Box 125, Franklin Lakes NJ 07417. **Tel** (201)891-1211. **ED** Richard Kane. **Ad Acc. Circ:** 3,500 (ctrl).
**Desc:** Reports of bird sightings throughtout New Jersey. Also includes research and reports.

US
**RECORDS OF NEW JERSEY BIRDS / NEW JERSEY AUDUBON SOCIETY.** **Added/Corp** New Jersey Audubon Society. Vol. 8, No. 4 (Winter 1982)-. English. qt. ***Continues*** *NJ Audubon : Records of New Jersey Birds.*
**Ind/Abst** Fish Rev. (19??-199?); Wildl. Rev. (19??-199?).

US/0197-3169
**RECORDS OF VERMONT BIRDS.** **Added/Corp** Vermont Institute of Natural Science. (19??)-. Periodical. English. Four times a year. Vermont Institute of Natural Sciences, Church Hill Road, Woodstock VT 05091. **Tel** (802)457-2779. **ED** Sarah B. Laughlin. **Circ:** 1,200 (ctrl).
**Desc:** Newsletter on the distribution, abundance, and migration pattern of Vermont birds.

US/0274-502X
**REPORT - AUDUBON SOCIETY OF RHODE ISLAND.** **See** Environmental Issues-Conservation and Natural Resources.

US/0190-2245
**REPORT OF THE MIGRATORY BIRD CONSERVATION COMMISSION.** **Main/Corp** United States. Migratory Bird Conservation Commission. 1929/30-. English. an. Migratory Bird Commission, Interior Department Building, Washington DC 20240. **LC** SK361; .A34. **DD** 353.008/232.

UK
**REPORT ON THE BIRDS OF THE DONCASTER DISTRICT.** **Main/Corp** Doncaster and District Ornithological Society. **VFOAT** Doncaster Bird Report. 1951-. English. an. **LC** N1219.5.
**Desc:** Vols. for 1956 include the society's annual report. 1st.

PL
**RING. SERIES B, THE.** **Added/Corp** Polskie Towarzystvo Zodogiczne. **VFOAT** International Ornithological Information Service IOIS Ring/IOIS. (1963)-. Periodical. English. Twice a year. Price on Request. **(Subscription address:** ARS Polona, PO Box 1001, 00068 Warsaw Poland.**)**

UK/0307-8698
**RINGING & MIGRATION.** [Ring. migr.]. **Added/Corp** British Trust for Ornithology. Ringing and Migration Committee. **VAT** Ringing and Migration. Vol. 1 (1975)-. Periodical. English. Three times a year (June, October and December). £22.50. British Trust for Ornithology, The Nunnery, Thetford Norfolk 1P24 2PU England. **Tel** 011 44 842 750050, FAX 011 44 842 750030. **ED** Robert W Furness. **LC** QL671; .R55. **DD** 598.2/07/23. **CODEN** RIMIDQ. Index available. **Circ:** 3,000 (ctrl). Documents available from BIOSIS Document Express.
**Desc:** Scientific papers and reports on the ringing and migration of birds. Includes annual ringing reports.
**Ind/Abst** Biol. Abstr.; Curr. Aware. Biol. Sci., CABS; Ecol. Abstr.; Key Word Index Wildl. Res.; Life Sci. Collect.; Wildl. Rev.

NO
**RINGMERKING AV FORSKJELLIGE FUGLEARTER.** **Main/Corp** Statens Viltunderskelser (Norway). **Added/Corp** Statens Viltundersketser (Norway). Bird-Banding. **VFOAT** Bird-Banding. Norwegian (summaries and/or abstracts in English). **LC** SK529; .A25; QL690.N8.

US/1062-5232
**ROGER TORY PETERSON INSTITUTE'S BIRDS, BATS & BUTTERFLIES.** [Roger Tory Peterson Inst. birds bats butterflies]. **Added/Corp** Roger Tory Peterson Institute. **VFOAT** Birds, Bats & Butterflies; Birds, Bats, and Butterflies. No. 1 (1991)-. Periodical. English. qt. Free (members). Roger Tory Peterson Institute of Natural History, 110 Marvin Parkway, Jamestown NY 14701. **DD** 508.

UK
**RSPB BIRD LIFE.** **Main/Corp** Royal Society for the Protection of Birds. **VAT** Royal Society for the Protection of Birds Bird Life. English. an. £1.50. **LC** QL690.G7; R68A. **DD** 598.2/941/05.

UK
**RSPB CONSERVATION REVIEW.** **See** Environmental Issues-Conservation and Natural Resources.

UK/0260-4736
**SANDGROUSE.** **Added/Corp** Ornithological Society of the Middle East. No. 1 (1980)-. English. an. £10.00 (airmail), £13.00 (airmail) other. Ornithological Society of the Middle East, c/o The Lodge, Sandy Bedfordshire SG19 2DL England. **ED** D. Brooks. Index available. **Circ:** 1,000 (ctrl).
**Desc:** Papers on all aspects of ornithology in the Middle East.
**Ind/Abst** Ref. Z.; Zool. Rec.; Wildl. Rev.

UK/0036-9144
**SCOTTISH BIRDS.** [Scott. birds]. Vol. 1 (Autumn 1958)-. Periodical. English. Four times a year (Mar., Jun., Sep., Dec.). £30.00 (includes Scottish Bird News and Scottish Bird Report). Scottish Ornithologists Club, 21 Regent Terrace, Edinburgh EH7 5BT Scotland. **Tel** 11 44 31 5566042. **ED** Nick Picozzi. **LC** QL690.S4; S35. **CODEN** SCTBB7. Index available. cum. index. **Bk Rev. Ad Acc. Circ:** 3,000. available on diskette. Documents available from BIOSIS Document Express. ***Supersedes in part*** *Scottish Naturalist.*
**Ind/Abst** Biol. Abstr.; Key Word Index Wildl. Res.; Life Sci. Collect.; Wildl. Rev.

UK
**SEA SWALLOW, THE.** **Added/Corp** Royal Naval Bird Watching Society. (19??)-. English. an (Oct.). £6.00. Sea Swallow, 19 Downlands Way Winchester, Hants SO21 3HS England. **Tel** 011 44 962 885258. **ED** Dr. M. B. Casement. Index available. **Bk Rev**, (Qty: 2-3). **Ad Acc, Adv Mgr:** same as editor. **Pr Rev. Circ:** 450.
**Desc:** General articles on seabirds; summary of seabirds and landbirds reported from sea.

DK
**SKAGEN FUGELSTATION.** **Main/Corp** Dansk Ornithologisk Forening. Danish. Dansk Ornithologisk Forening, Vesterbrogade 140, DK 1620 Copenhagen Denmark. **Tel** 011 45 33 314404, FAX 011 45 33 312435. **LC** QL690.D3; D36A.

AT/0038-2973
**SOUTH AUSTRALIAN ORNITHOLOGIST.** [South Aust. ornithol.]. Vol.1 (1914). Periodical. English. sa. 20.00Aus$. South Australian Ornithological Association, c/o South Australian Museum, North Terrace, Adelaide South Australia 5000 Australia. **ED** John Cox. **CODEN** SAORAF. Index available. cum. index. **Bk Rev**, (Qty: 2-3/yr). **Pr Rev. Circ:** 650 (ctrl).
**Desc:** General ornithology (Australian). Mostly South Australian.
**Ind/Abst** Life Sci. Collect.; Wildl. Rev.

US/0038-3252
**SOUTH DAKOTA BIRD NOTES.** [S.D. bird notes]. **Added/Corp** South Dakota Ornithologists' Union. Vol. 1, No. 1 (July 1949)-. Periodical. English. qt (Mar., June, Sept., Dec.). $9.00 US; $11.00 other. South Dakota Ornithologists Union, 1620 Elmwood Drive, Brookings SD 57006. **Tel** (605)693-4572. **ED** Dan Tallman (editor's telephone: (605)622-7707). **CODEN** SDBNAR. Index available (published separately). cum. index. **Bk Rev**, (Qty: 10). **Circ:** 300. available on microfiche. Documents available from BIOSIS Document Express.
**Desc:** Publication devoted to biology and ecology of South Dakota birds. A seasonal report is included.
**Ind/Abst** Biol. Abstr.; Wildl. Rev.

SA
**SOUTHERN BIRDS.** 1-(1975)-. Monographic series. English. Price varies per volume. Witwatersrand Bird Club, Box 650284, Benmore, Transvaal 2010 South Africa. ***Supersedes*** *South African Avifauna Series, 0081-2358.*

US
**STATUS OF WATERFOWL AND FALL FLIGHT FORECASTS / C.U.S. FISH AND WILDLIFE SERVICE AND CANADIAN WILDLIFE SERVICE.** ***Title Change.*** **Added/Corp** U.S. Fish and Wildlife Service. Canadian Wildlife Service. U.S. Fish and Wildlife Service. Office of Migratory Bird Management. **VFOAT** Status of Waterfowl & Fall Flight Forecasts. (19??)-(1993). English. ir. Migratory Bird Management, Patuxent Wildlife Research Center, Laurel MD 20708. **LC** SK361; .S73. **DD** 333.95/8. ***Continued by*** *Waterfowl Population Status.*

UK
**STUDY REPORT / INTERNATIONAL COUNCIL FOR BIRD PRESERVATION.** **Added/Corp** International Council for Bird Preservation. (19??)-. Monographic series. English. ir. Price varies per volume. International Council for Bird Preservation, 32 Cambridge Road, Girton Cambridge CB3 0PJ England. **Tel** 011 44 223 277318, FAX 011 44 223 277200.

CN/1185-5959
**TENDANCES CHEZ LES OISEAUX.** [Tend. oiseaux]. **Added/Corp** Service Canadien de la Faune. No 1 (1991)-. French. **DD** 598.2971.

US
**TENNESSEE WARBLER : NEWSLETTER OF THE TENNESSEE ORNITHOLOGICAL SOCIETY, THE.** **Added/Corp** Tennessee Ornithological Society. Vol. 1, No. 1 (Mar. 1979)-. Periodical. English. Twice a year. $15.00 Comes with Tennessee Onithological Society membership. Tennessee Ornithological Society, PO Box 171381, Memphis TN 38187-1381. **Tel** (901)382-4767.

US
**UTAH BIRDS : JOURNAL OF THE UTAH ORNITHOLOGICAL SOCIETY.** **Added/Corp** Utah Ornithological Society. Vol. 1, No. 1 (1985)-. Periodical. English. qt. $15.00 institutional, $12.00 individual. Utah Ornithological Society, PO Box 1042, Cedar City UT 84721. **Tel** (801)586-2401. **ED** Steven Hedges. Index available. **Bk Rev. Pr Rev. Circ:** 200 (ctrl).

SW/0042-2649
**VAR FAGELVARLD.** **Added/Corp** Sveriges Ornitologiska FËorening. (1942)-. Periodical. Swedish. ir (eight issues per year). $60.25. Sveriges Ornitologiska Forening, Box 14219, S-10440 Stockholm Sweden. **Tel** 08/662 64 34. **LC** QL671; .V2. **DD** 598/.05. Index available (Free). **Bk Rev. Ad Acc.**
**Ind/Abst** Fish Rev. (19??-); Key Word Index Wildl. Res. (19??-); Wildl. Rev. (19??-).

GW
**VERHANDLUNGEN DER ORNITHOLOGISCHE GESELLSCHAFT IN BAYERN.** **Main/Corp** Ornithologische Gesellschaft in Bayern, Munich. Vol. 1 (1898)-. Periodical. German (English). an. $40.00 US. Ornithologische Gesellschaft in Bayern, Muenchhausenstr 21, W-8000 Muenchen 60 Germany. **Tel** 89-8107-123. **ED** Josef Reichholf. Index available in last issue of volume--attached. **Bk Rev. Ad Acc. Circ:** 1,200 (ctrl). Documents available from BIOSIS Document Express.
**Desc:** Studies on birds.
**Ind/Abst** Biol. Abstr.; Key Word Index Wildl. Res.; Life Sci. Collect.; Wildl. Rev. (19??-199?).

US/0505-7043
**VIRGINIA AVIFAUNA.** **Added/Corp** Virginia Society of Ornithology. No. 1 (Dec. 1957)-. Monographic series. English. Price varies per volume. Virginia Society of Ornithology, 520 Rainbow Forest Drive, Lynchburg VA 24502. **DD** 598.2.

GW/0042-7993
**VOGELWELT, DIE.** [Vogelwelt]. **Added/Corp** Deutscher Verein zum Schutze der Vogelwelt. (1949)-. Periodical. German. bm. DM66.20 Germany; DM67.70 other. Aula Verlag GmbH, Luisenplatz 2, D 65185 Wiesbaden Germany. **Tel** 011 49 611 373060. **ED** R. Berndt, E. Bezzel, K. Haarmann and C. Koinig MA. **CODEN** VGLWAM. **[CCC]. Ad Acc. Circ:** 1,300. Documents available from BIOSIS Document Express. ***Continues*** *Deutsche Vogelwelt.*
**Desc:** The study of birds and protection of birds.
**Ind/Abst** Biol. Abstr.; Fish Rev.; Key Word Index Wildl. Res.; Life Sci. Collect.; Wildl. Rev.

US
**VSO NEWSLETTER.** **Main/Corp** Virginia Society of Ornithology. **Added/Corp** Virginia Society of Ornithology. Newsletter - Virginia Society of Ornithology. **VFOAT** Newsletter - Virginia Society of Ornithology. (1956)-. Newsletter. English. $10.00. Virginia Society Ornithology, 520 Rainbow Forest Drive, Lynchburg VA 24502. **Tel** (703)961-6165.

US/1056-6759
**WACKY WORLD OF PEAFOWL REPORT, THE.** [Wacky world peafowl rep.]. Vol. 1, No. 1 (May/June 1991)-. Periodical. English. bm. $20.00. The Wacky World of Peafowl Report, RR 1-MB, Minden IA 51553. **DD** 636.

JA
**WATASHITACHI NO SHIZEN. NATURE.** **See** Environmental Issues-Conservation and Natural Resources.

US/0160-1121
**WESTERN BIRDS.** [West. birds]. **Added/Corp** California Field Ornithologists. (1973)-. Periodical. English. Four times a year (Jan., Apr., Aug., Oct.). $18.00 (includes Western Field Ornithologists membership). Western Field Ornithologists, c/o Dorothy Myers, 6011

Saddletree Lane, Yorba Linda CA 92686. **Tel** (714)779-2201. **ED** Philip Unitt (editor's address: 3411 Felton Street, San Diego CA 92104). **CODEN** WSBDAA. **Ad Acc, Adv Mgr:** Dorothy S. Myers. **Pr Rev. Circ:** 1,000. Documents available from BIOSIS Document Express. *Continues California Birds, 0045-3897.*
  **Desc:** Solicits papers for amateur field ornithologists and that also contribute to scientific literature.
  **Ind/Abst** Biol. Abstr.; Fish Rev.; Wildl. Rev.

US/0892-5534
**WILDBIRD.** [WildBird]. **VFOAT** Wild Bird. Vol. 1, No. 1 (May/June 1987)-. Periodical. English. mo. $23.97. Fancy Publications, PO Box 6050, Mission Viejo CA 92690. **Tel** (714)855-8822, (800)426-2516, FAX (714)855-3045. **(Subscription address:** Neodata / Colorado, PO Box 2606, Boulder Boulder CO 80322.**)** **LC** QL677.5; .W54. **DD** 598/.07234.
  **Desc:** Illustrated with full color photos and art, this journal takes you on a guided tour of the American birding scene. You'll find out about top birdwatching locales, take an in-depth look at the natural history and behavior of fascinating bird species, and keep abreast of all the news and developments in the field of bird watching.
  **Ind/Abst** Biol. Dig.; Fish Rev.; Wildl. Rev.

UK/0954-6324
**WILDFOWL (SLIMBRIDGE).** (WILDFOWL.). [Wildfowl]. **Main/Corp** Wildfowl Trust. **Added/Corp** Wildfowl & Wetlands Trust. 19th (1968)-. English. an. £18.00. Wildfowl Trust, Slimbridge, Gloucester GL2 7BT England. **Tel** 11 44 453 890333, FAX 11 44 453 890827. **ED** Janet Kear. **LC** SK351; .W575. **DD** 639/.97/82924. Index available. **Circ:** 2,000 (ctrl). *Continues Wildfowl Trust. Annual Report of the Wildfowl Trust.*
  **Desc:** Scientific papers on waterfowl, etc.
  **Ind/Abst** Curr. Aware. Biol. Sci., CABS; Ecol. Abstr.; Fish Rev. (Jan. 1989-July 1992); Key Word Index Wildl. Res.; Life Sci. Collect.; Wildl. Rev. (Jan. 1989-July 1992).

US/0043-5643
**WILSON BULLETIN (WILSON ORNITHOLOGICAL SOCIETY), THE.** (THE WILSON BULLETIN.). [Wilson bull.]. **Added/Corp** Wilson Ornithological Society. Wilson Ornithological Club. Nebraska Ornithologists' Union. Vol. 6 (1894)-. Bulletin. English. qt (4 issues). $40.00 North America; $45.00 other. Ornithological Society of North America, PO Box 1897, Lawrence KS 66044-8897. **Tel** (913)843-1221, FAX (913)843-1274. **ED** Keith L. Bildstein. **DD** 598. **CODEN** WILBAI. **Bk Rev. Pr Rev. Acid Free. Circ:** 3,500. available on microfilm and microfiche from University Microfilms International (UMI). Documents available from The Genuine Article, BIOSIS Document Express, UMI Article Clearinghouse. *Continues Journal of the Wilson Ornithological Chapter of the Agassiz Association.*
  **Desc:** Articles are based on original studies of birds and general notes that describe observations of particular interest. Contributions are of interest both to professional and advanced amateurs.
  **Ind/Abst** Anim. Behav. Abstr.; AQUAREF; Biocont. News Inf. (19??-19??); Biol. Abstr.; Curr. Aware. Biol. Sci., CABS; Curr. Contents, Agric. Biol. Environ. Sci.; Ecol. Abstr. (?-?); Ecology Abstr.; Expand. Acad. Index (1992-); For. Abstr.; Gen. Sci. Index; GeoRef; Index Vet.; Key Word Index Wildl. Res.; Newsp. Period. Abstr. (1991-); Ocean. Abstr.; Life Sci. Collect.; Pop. Period. Index; Poult. Abstr.; Protozoolog. Abstr.; Res. Alert [Full Cov.]; Rev. Med. Vet. Entomol.; Sci. Cit. Index; SCISEARCH; Soils Fert.; Wildl. Rev.

AT/1036-7810
**WING SPAN (MOONEE PONDS).** (WING SPAN / ROYAL AUSTRALASIAN ORNITHOLOGISTS UNION.). [Wing span]. **Added/Corp** Royal Australasian Ornithologists' Union. **VFOAT** Wingspan. (Mar. 1991)-. Periodical. English. Four times a year. 40.00Aus$ membership with subscription to EMU, 70.00Aus$ membership without subscription to EMU, (individuals); 115.00Aus$ Australia, 130.00Aus$ others (institutions) Comes with Royal Australasian Ornithologists Union membership or publications subscription. Royal Australasian Ornithologists Union, 407 415 Riversdale Road, Hawthorn East Victoria 3123 Australia. **Tel** 011 61 3 8822622, FAX 011 61 3 370 9194. **CODEN** WINSEF. *Continues Royal Australasian Ornithologists' Union. RAOU Newsletter, 0817-5748.*

US
**WOODCOCK STATUS REPORT. Main/Corp** United States. Fish and Wildlife Service. English. an. US Department of the Interior / Fish and Wildlife Service, Virginia, Office of Training and Education, 4401 North Fairfax Drive, Room 741, Arlington VA 22203. **LC** SK361; .A256 subser; QL696.C48. **DD** 639/.9/90973 S; 333.9/5. *Continues Woodcock Status Report.*

UK
**WORLD BIRDWATCH : THE NEWSLETTER OF THE INTERNATIONAL COUNCIL FOR BIRD PRESERVATION.** See *Environmental Issues-Conservation and Natural Resources.*

JA/0044-0183
**YAMASHINA CHORUI KENKYUJO, KENKYU HOKOKU. Main/Corp** Yamashina Chorui Kenkyujo, Tokyo. **Added/Corp** Yamashina Chorui Kenkyujo, Tokyo. Miscellaneous Reports of the Yamashina Institute for Ornithology. Yamashina Chorui Kenkyujo, Tokyo. Journal of the Yamashina Institute for Ornithology. **VFOAT** Miscellaneous Reports of the Yamashina Institute for Ornithology; Journal of the Yamashina Institute for Ornithology. No. 1 (1952)-. Periodical. Multiple languages (English and Japanese). sa. $131.50. Yamashina Chorui Kenkyujo, (Yamashina Inst. for Ornithology), 115, Tsutsumine, Konoyama, Abikoshi, Chibaken 270-11, Japan. **(Subscription address:** Japan Publications Trading Company, Ltd., PO Box 5030, Tokyo International, Tokyo 100-31 Japan.**)**

ZA/0378-4533
**ZAMBIAN ORNITHOLOGICAL SOCIETY NEWSLETTER.** [Newsl. - Zambian Ornithol. Soc.]. (1972)-. Newsletter. English. Twelve times a year. $30.00. Zambian Ornithological Society, PO Box 33944, Lusaka 10101 Zambia. **ED** Carl Beel. cum. index. **Bk Rev**, (Qty: 1-2). **Circ:** 250 (ctrl).
  **Desc:** A newsletter, including records of bird sightings througout Zambia.